King James Version

Bible Commentary for Today

The Most Up-to-Date Commentary on the
Time-Honored Text of the King James Version

Edward E. Hindson
Daniel R. Mitchell

GENERAL EDITORS

THOMAS NELSON
Since 1798

THOMAS NELSON

King James Version Bible Commentary for Today
Copyright © 2010 by Zondervan

Originally published as *Zondervan King James Version Commentary — Old Testament* and *Zondervan King James Version Commentary — New Testament*.

Published in Nashville, Tennessee, by Thomas Nelson. Thomas Nelson is a registered trademark of HarperCollins Christian Publishing, Inc.

Thomas Nelson titles may be purchased in bulk for educational, business, fundraising, or sales promotional use. For information, please e-mail SpecialMarkets@ThomasNelson.com.

ISBN 978-0-310-15354-2 (hardcover)

ISBN 978-0-310-15357-3 (ebook)

Maps by International Mapping. Copyright © 2010 by Zondervan. All rights reserved.

Cover design: LUCAS Art & Design, Jenison, MI
Cover art: © Cienpies Design / Alamy; Tashat / Shutterstock

Printed in the United States of America

23 24 25 26 27 28 29 30 31 32 33 34 /TRM/ 15 14 13 12 11 10 9 8 7 6 5 4 3 2 1

CONTENTS

GENERAL EDITORS

Edward Hindson, MA, ThM, ThD, DPhil • Assistant Chancellor, Dean of the Institute of Biblical Studies and Distinguished Professor of Religion at Liberty University, Lynchburg, Virginia. Author or editor of forty books, including the Gold Medallion–winning *Knowing Jesus Study Bible* (Zondervan) and the *Zondervan KJV Study Bible*. He has also served as a visiting lecturer at Oxford University and the Harvard Divinity School and is a Life Fellow of the International Biographical Association, Cambridge, England.

Daniel Mitchell, ThM, STM, ThD • Dean and Professor of Theological Studies at Liberty Theological Seminary, Lynchburg, Virginia. Author of commentaries on First and Second Corinthians (AMG Publishers). He was a general editor of the *King James Study Bible* (Thomas Nelson) and consulting editor of the *Zondervan KJV Study Bible*. He has also taught at Western Seminary (Portland, Oregon), Tyndale Theological Seminary (Amsterdam, Holland), and ABECAR Institute in Sao Paulo, Brazil.

AUTHORS AND CONTRIBUTORS

Barth Campbell, MA, PhD • Late Professor of New Testament Studies, Simpson University, Redding, California

Mal Couch, MA, ThM, PhD • Founder and former President, Tyndale Theological Seminary, Fort Worth, Texas

Steven Ger, ThM, PhD • President, Sojourner Ministries, Garland, Texas

Harvey Hartman, ThM, ThD • Professor of Biblical Studies, Liberty University, Lynchburg, Virginia

Ronald Hawkins, MDiv, DMin, EdD • Vice Provost and Professor of Counseling and Practical Theology, Liberty University, Lynchburg, Virginia

Fred Smith, MDiv, PhD • Associate Professor of Biblical Studies and Theology, Liberty Theological Seminary, Lynchburg, Virginia

Jon Venema, MDiv, PhD • Associate Professor of New Testament Literature and Languages, Western Theological Seminary, Portland, Oregon

Gary Yates, ThM, PhD • Associate Professor of Biblical Studies, Liberty Theological Seminary, Lynchburg, Virginia

ACKNOWLEDGMENTS

The two-volume *King James Version Bible Commentary for Today* is based upon the original study notes in the *Zondervan KJV Study Bible*.

PREFACE

The message of the Bible represents the timeless truth of God. As each generation seeks to apply that truth to its specific context, an up-to-date commentary needs to be created for them. The editors and authors of the *King James Version Bible Commentary for Today* have endeavored to do just that. This team of scholars represents conservative evangelical scholarship at its best. We have approached the time-honored text of the King James Version with humility and respect as we explore its meaning and message for our generation.

The King James text used in this commentary follows that of the *Zondervan KJV Study Bible* (2002), which is based upon the final revision of fifteen different printings of the King James Version from 1611 to 1769 by F. H. A. Scrivener in 1873. The Scrivener edition of the King James Version sought to standardize the marginal notes, explanatory comments, italicized type, punctuation, spelling, and capitalization of the various editions of the King James Version, resulting in the most highly regarded edition of the Authorized Version, known as the *Cambridge Paragraph Bible*, edited by Dr. Scrivener in 1873.

Understanding the meaning of the Bible is a challenge that faces every reader of the biblical text. Explaining the meaning of that text to the average reader is then the challenge of every expository commentator. In the biblical story of Philip and the Ethiopian eunuch, who was reading the book of Isaiah, Philip asked him if he understood what he was reading. The eunuch replied, "How can I except some man should guide me?" (Acts 8:31). That is exactly what the editors and authors of this unique two-volume commentary have endeavored to do.

We have assembled a team of biblical scholars from a variety of backgrounds to comment on the sixty-six books of the biblical canon. Their comments are intended to provide the reader with clear explanations of both antiquated English terms of the King James text (e.g., "letteh" in 2 Thess. 2:7) and Hebrew, Aramaic, and Greek words from the original languages of the Bible (e.g., Greek, *harpazo* in 1 Thess. 4:17). They have also focused their comments on the intended meaning of the original authors, providing linguistic, historical, and archaeological insights that illuminate our understanding of the biblical text (e.g., the kinsman-redeemer in Ruth 2:20; 4:4).

We acknowledge that we are fallible humans attempting to explain the infallible truths of God's Word. Therefore, we have approached this challenge with sincere respect for the Scriptures and personal devotion to God, who is the ultimate author of its inspired message both to our generation and to every generation that has been blessed by its life-changing truths. The psalmist reminds us, "His truth endureth to all generations" (Ps. 117:2). Jesus said, "And ye shall know the truth and the truth shall make you free" (John 8:32). Thus, our comments are intended both to explain the meaning of the biblical text and to apply its truths to our lives. Therefore, the *King James Version Bible Commentary for Today* is both expository and practical, designed for use by pastors and lay readers alike.

The Old Testament comprises thirty-nine books of the Hebrew canon following the arrangement of the Septuagint. In Jesus' time it was divided into three main sections: Law, Prophets, and Writings (cf. Luke 24:44). Altogether the books of the Old Testament present the story of God's intervention into the human race from a diverse collection of materials written over a millennium by at least two dozen authors. They take the reader on a journey with patriarchs, judges, kings, prophets, and priests as God traces the history of His people, Israel. In these fascinating pages we meet some of the most incredible people who have ever lived and share their spiritual journey from tragedy to triumph.

Ultimately the Old Testament is incomplete without the New Testament. It ends with the expectation of the coming King, which is fulfilled in the New Testament. Thus, the approach of this commentary involves a Christological perspective which views both testaments as a whole. We believe that one cannot fully understand the message of the New Testament without a proper understanding of its Old Testament foundation. The history, tradition, and ceremonies of the Hebrew Bible are the basis of numerous examples quoted in the pages of the New Testament. References to the sacrifices (John 1:29), the priesthood (Heb. 7:14–28), the exodus and the wilderness journey (1 Cor. 10:1–11), Noah (1 Peter 3:20–21), Jonah (Matthew 12:39–40), Melchizedek (Heb. 7:1–3), Hagar and Sarah (Gal. 4:22–26), and Elijah (Matt. 11:14) all presume that the New Testament reader is familiar with these Old Testament references.

The story of the Old Testament is God's story. It is a revelation of His promise in which the end is anticipated from the beginning. It is the story of God's love for humanity which centers on the promise of a coming king and a righteous kingdom. The Hebrew Scriptures are filled with promises, pictures, and predictions of Christ. God appeared to the patriarchs, called Moses, anointed David, and established Israel's laws and institutions to point the way to the coming of the Promised One. The apostle Peter declared "to him give all the prophets witness" (Acts 10:43).

The New Testament has guided the Christian church for over two thousand years. This one testament is composed of twenty-seven books, penned by godly men through the inspiration of the Holy Spirit. It tells of the life of Jesus Christ, His atoning death for our sins, His miraculous resurrection, His ascension to heaven, and the promise of His second coming. It also tells the story of the birth and growth of the church and the people and principles that shaped its early history. The New Testament concludes with the book of Revelation pointing ahead to the glorious return of Christ.

Without the New Testament, the message of the Bible would be incomplete. The Old Testament points ahead to the coming Messiah, the King of Israel and the Savior of the world. In commenting on the Hebrew Scriptures, Jesus said, "All things must be fulfilled which were written in the Law of Moses, and in the prophets, and in the psalms, concerning me" (Luke 24:44). But the Old Testament ends without His arrival. All of its ceremonies, pictures, types, and prophecies are left awaiting the coming of the "Lamb of God, which taketh away the sin of the world" (John 1:29).

Jesus Christ is the greatest person who has ever lived. There have been great men and women whose lives have made an impact while they were here on earth. But the greatest of them does not hold a candle to the blazing brilliance of His life. His person, character wisdom, love, and grace leap off the pages of the New Testament into the hearts of all who believe in Him. It is our sincere hope that you will come to know Him better and live for Him more effectively as our comments enlighten your mind and challenge your soul.

Edward Hindson
Daniel Mitchell

KING JAMES VERSION

BIBLE COMMENTARY

for

TODAY

OLD TESTAMENT

THE FIRST BOOK OF MOSES, CALLED GENESIS

INTRODUCTION

Title

The first phrase in the Hebrew text of 1:1 is *bereshith* ("In [the] beginning"), which is also the Hebrew title of this book (books in ancient times customarily were named after their first word or two). The English title, Genesis, is Greek in origin and comes from the word *geneseos*, which appears in the Greek translation (Septuagint) of 2:4 and 5:1. Depending on its context, the word can mean "birth," "genealogy," or "history of origin." In both its Hebrew and Greek forms, then, the title of Genesis appropriately describes its contents, since it is primarily a book of beginnings.

Author

Historically, Jews and Christians alike have held that Moses was the author/compiler of the first five books of the Old Testament. These books, known also as the Pentateuch (meaning "five-volumed book"), were referred to in Jewish tradition as the five-fifths of the law (of Moses). The Bible itself suggests Mosaic authorship of Genesis, since Acts 15:1 refers to circumcision as "the manner of Moses," an allusion to Genesis 17. A certain amount of later editorial updating does appear to be indicated, however (see, e.g., discussions on 14:14; 36:31; 47:11).

Date

The historical period during which Moses lived seems to be fixed with a fair degree of accuracy by 1 Kings, which states that "the fourth year of Solomon's reign over Israel" was the same as "the four hundred and eightieth year after the children of Israel were come out of the land of Egypt" (1 Kings 6:1). Since the former was roughly 966 BC, the latter—and thus the date of the exodus—was roughly 1446 BC (assuming that the 480 years in 1 Kings 6:1 is to be taken literally; see Judges, Introduction: "Background"). The forty-year period of Israel's wanderings in the wilderness, which lasted approximately from 1446 to 1406 BC, is the most likely time in which Moses could have written the bulk of what is today known as the Pentateuch.

During the last three centuries, many scholars have claimed to find in the Pentateuch four underlying sources. The presumed documents, allegedly dating from the tenth to the fifth centuries BC, are called J (for Jahweh/Yahweh, the personal name for God in the Old Testament), E (for Elohim, a generic name for God), D (for Deuteronomic), and P (for Priestly). Each of these documents is claimed to have its own characteristics and theology, which often contradict that of the other documents. The Pentateuch is thus depicted as a patchwork of stories, poems, and laws. This view is not supported by conclusive evidence, however, and intensive archaeological and literary research has tended to undercut many of the arguments used to challenge Mosaic authorship.

Background

Chapters 1–38 reflect a great deal of what is known from other sources about ancient Mesopotamian life and culture. Creation, genealogies, destructive floods, geography and mapmaking, construction techniques, migrations of peoples, sale and purchase of land, legal customs and procedures, sheepherding and cattle-raising—all these subjects and many others were matters of vital concern to the peoples of Mesopotamia during this time. They were also of interest to the individuals, families, and tribes whose stories are in the first thirty-eight chapters of Genesis. The author appears to locate Eden, man's first home, in or near Mesopotamia: the Tower of Babel was built there, Abram was born there, Isaac took a wife from there, and Jacob lived there for twenty years. Although these patriarchs settled in Canaan, their original homeland was Mesopotamia.

The closest ancient literary parallels to Genesis 1–38 also come from Mesopotamia. *Enuma elish*, the story of the god Marduk's rise to supremacy in the Babylonian pantheon, is slightly similar in some respects (though thoroughly mythical and polytheistic) to the Genesis 1 creation account. Some of the features of certain king lists from Sumer bear striking resemblance to the genealogy in Genesis 5. The eleventh tablet of the *Gilgamesh* epic is quite similar in outline to the flood narrative in Genesis 6–8. Several of the major events of Genesis 1–8 are narrated in the same order as similar events in the *Atrahasis* epic. In fact, the latter features the same motif—creation, rebellion, flood—found in the biblical account. Clay tablets found recently at the ancient (ca. 2500–2300 BC) site of Ebla (modern Tell Mardikh) in northern Syria may also contain some intriguing parallels (see chart, *Zondervan KJV Study Bible*, p. xix).

Two other important sets of documents demonstrate the reflection of Mesopotamia in the first thirty-eight chapters of Genesis. The Mari letters (see chart, *KJV Study Bible*, p. xix), dating from the patriarchal period, reveal that the names of the patriarchs (including especially Abram, Jacob, and Job) were typical of that time. The letters also clearly illustrate the freedom of travel that was possible between various parts of the Amorite world in which the patriarchs lived. The Nuzi tablets (see chart, *KJV Study Bible*, p. xix), though dating from a few centuries after the patriarchal period, shed light on patriarchal customs, which tended to survive virtually intact for many centuries. The inheritance right of an adopted household member or slave (15:1–4), the obligation of a barren wife to furnish her husband with sons through a servant girl (16:2–4), strictures against expelling such a servant girl and her son (21:10–11), the authority of oral statements in ancient Near Eastern law, such as the deathbed bequest (27:1–4, 22–23, 33)—these and other legal customs, social contracts, and provisions are graphically illustrated in Mesopotamian documents.

As chapters 1–38 are Mesopotamian in character and background, so chapters 39–50 reflect Egyptian influence, though not quite as directly. Examples of such influence are: Egyptian grape cultivation (40:9–11), the riverside scene (chap. 41), Egypt as Canaan's breadbasket (chap. 42), Canaan as the source of numerous products for Egyptian consumption (chap. 43), Egyptian religious and social customs (the end of chaps. 43 and 46), Egyptian administrative procedures (chap. 47), Egyptian funerary practices (chap. 50), and several Egyptian words and names used throughout these chapters. The closest specific literary parallel from Egypt is *Tale of Two Brothers*, which bears some resemblance to the story of Joseph and Potiphar's wife (chap. 39). Egyptian autobiographical narratives (such as the *Story of Sinuhe* and the *Report of Wenamun*) and certain historical legends offer more general literary parallels.

Theme and Theological Message

Genesis speaks of beginnings—of the heavens and the earth, of light and darkness, of seas and skies, of land and vegetation, of sun and moon and stars, of sea and air and land animals, of human beings (made in God's own image, the climax of His creative activity), of sin and redemption, of blessing and cursing, of society and civilization, of marriage and family, of art and craft and industry. A key word in Genesis is the Hebrew word for "generations," which also serves to divide the book into its ten major parts (see "Literary Features" and "Literary Outline," below) and which includes such concepts as birth, genealogy, and history.

The book of Genesis is foundational to understanding the rest of the Bible. Its message is rich and complex, and listing its main elements gives a succinct outline of the biblical message as a whole. It is supremely a book of relationships, highlighting those between God and nature, God and man, and man and man. It is thoroughly monotheistic, taking for granted that there is only one God worthy of the name and opposing the ideas that there are many gods (polytheism), that there is no god at all (atheism), and that everything is divine (pantheism). It clearly teaches that the one true God is sovereign over all that exists (His entire creation) and that, through divine election, He often exercises His unlimited freedom to overturn human customs, traditions, and plans. It introduces the way in which God initiates and makes covenants with His chosen people, pledging His love and faithfulness to them and calling them to promise theirs to Him. It establishes sacrifice as the substitution of life for life (chap. 22). It gives the first hint of God's provision for redemption from the forces of evil (compare 3:15 with Rom. 16:17–20) and contains the oldest and most profound definition of faith (15:6). More than half of Hebrews 11—the New Testament roll of the faithful—refers to characters in Genesis.

Literary Features

The message of a book is often enhanced by its literary structure and characteristics. Genesis is divided into ten main sections, which begin with the Hebrew word translated "generation[s]" (see 2:4; 5:1; 6:9; 10:1; 11:10; 11:27; 25:12; 25:19; 36:1 [repeated for emphasis at 36:9]; and 37:2). The first five sections can be grouped together and, along with the introduction to the book as a whole (1:1–2:3), can be appropriately called "primeval history" (1:1–11:26), sketching the period from Adam to Abraham. The last five sections constitute a much longer but equally unified account, relating the story of God's dealings with Abraham, Isaac, Jacob, and Joseph and their families, and is often called "patriarchal history" (11:27–50:26). This latter group of sections is in turn composed of three narrative cycles (Abraham-Isaac, 11:27–25:11; Isaac-Jacob, 25:19–35:29; 37:1; and Jacob-Joseph, 37:2–50:26), interspersed by the genealogies of Ishmael (25:12–18) and Esau (chap. 36).

The narrative frequently concentrates on the life of a later son in preference to the firstborn: Seth over Cain, Isaac over Ishmael, Jacob over Esau, Judah and Joseph over their brothers, and Ephraim over Manasseh. Such emphasis on divinely chosen men and their families is perhaps the most obvious literary and theological characteristic of the book of Genesis as a whole. It strikingly underscores the fact that the people of God are not the product of natural human developments but are the result of God's sovereign and gracious intrusion in human history. He brings out of the fallen human race a new humanity consecrated to Himself, called and destined to be the people of His kingdom and the channel of His blessing to the whole earth.

Numbers with symbolic significance figure prominently in Genesis. The number ten, in addition to being the number of sections into which Genesis is divided, is also the number of names appearing in the genealogies of chapters 5 and 11 (see discussion on 5:5). The number seven (and its multiples) also occurs frequently. The Hebrew text of 1:1 consists of exactly seven words, and that of 1:2 of exactly fourteen (twice seven). There are seven days of creation, seven names in the genealogy of chapter 4 (see discussion on 4:17–18; see also 4:15, 24; 5:31), various sevens in the flood story, seventy descendants of Noah's sons (chap. 10), a sevenfold promise to Abram (12:2–3), seven years of abundance and then seven years of famine in Egypt (chap. 41), and seventy descendants of Jacob (chap. 46). Other significant numbers, such as twelve and forty, are used with similar frequency.

The book of Genesis is basically prose narrative, punctuated here and there by brief poems (the longest is the so-called Blessing of Jacob, 49:2–27). Much of the prose has a lyrical quality and uses the full range of figures of speech and other devices that characterize the world's finest epic literature: the vertical and horizontal parallelism between the two sets of three days in the creation account (see discussion on 1:11); the ebb and flow of sin and judgment in chapter 3 (the serpent and woman and man sin successively, God questions them in reverse order, then He judges them in the original order); the powerful monotony of "and he died" in the genealogies in chapter 5; the climactic hinge effect of the phrase "And God remembered Noah" (8:1) at the midpoint of the flood story; the hourglass structure of the account of the Tower of Babel in 11:1–9 (narrative in vv. 1–2, 8–9, discourse in vv. 3–4, 6–7, with v. 5 acting as transition); the macabre pun in 40:19 (see also 40:13); the alternation between brief accounts about firstborn sons and lengthy accounts about younger sons. These and numerous other literary devices add interest to the narrative and provide interpretive signals to which the reader should pay close attention.

It is no coincidence that many of the subjects and themes of the first three chapters of Genesis are reflected in the last three chapters of Revelation. One can only marvel at the superintending influence of the Lord Himself, who assures that "all scripture is given by inspiration of God" (2 Tim. 3:16) and that "holy men of God spake as they were moved by the Holy Ghost" (2 Peter 1:21).

Outlines

Literary Outline

I. Introduction (1:1–2:3)

II. Body (2:4–50:26)
  A. "The generations of the heavens and of the earth" (2:4–4:26)
  B. "The book of the generations of Adam" (5:1–6:8)
  C. "The generations of Noah" (6:9–9:29)
  D. "The generations of the sons of Noah, Shem, Ham, and Japheth" (10:1–11:9)
  E. "The generations of Shem" (11:10–26)
  F. "The generations of Terah" (11:27–25:11)
  G. "The generations of Ishmael, Abraham's son" (25:12–18)
  H. "The generations of Isaac, Abraham's son" (25:19–35:29)
  I. "The generations of Esau" (36:1–37:1)
  J. "The generations of Jacob" (37:2–50:26)

Thematic Outline

I. Primeval History (1:1–11:26)
  A. Creation (1:1–2:3)
    1. Introduction (1:1–2)
    2. Body (1:3–31)
    3. Conclusion (2:1–3)
  B. Adam and Eve in Eden (2:4–25)
  C. The Fall and Its Consequences (chap. 3)
  D. The Rapid "Progress" of Sin (4:1–16)
  E. Two Genealogies (4:17–5:32)
    1. The Genealogy of Pride (4:17–24)
    2. The Genealogy of Death (4:25–5:32)
  F. The Extent of Sin before the Flood (6:1–8)
  G. The Great Flood (6:9–9:29)
    1. Preparing for the Flood (6:9–7:10)
    2. Judgment and Redemption (7:11–8:19)
      a. The Rising of the Waters (7:11–24)
      b. The Receding of the Waters (8:1–19)
    3. The Flood's Aftermath (8:20–9:29)
      a. A New Promise (8:20–22)
      b. New Ordinances (9:1–7)
      c. A New Relationship (9:8–17)
      d. A New Temptation (9:18–23)
      e. A Final Word (9:24–29)

Bibliography

Davis, John J. *Paradise to Prison: Studies in Genesis*. Reprinted. Salem, WI: Sheffield, 1998.

Hamilton, Victor. *The Book of Genesis: Chapters 1–17*. The New International Commentary on the Old Testament. Grand Rapids, MI: Eerdmans, 1990.

———. *The Book of Genesis: Chapters 18–50*. The New International Commentary on the Old Testament. Grand Rapids, MI: Eerdmans 1995.

Kidner, Derek. *Genesis: An Introduction and Commentary*. Tyndale Old Testament Commentaries 1. Downers Grove, IL: InterVarsity, 1967.

Morris, Henry M. *The Genesis Record: A Scientific and Devotional Commentary on the Book of Beginnings*. Grand Rapids, MI: Baker, 1976.

Ross, Allen P. *Creation and Blessing: A Guide to the Study and Exposition of the Book of Genesis*. Grand Rapids, MI: Baker, 1988.

Sailhamer, John H. "Genesis." In *The Expositor's Bible Commentary*, edited by Frank E. Gaebelein, vol. 2. Grand Rapids, MI: Zondervan, 1990.

Stigers, Harold G. *A Commentary on Genesis*. Grand Rapids, MI: Zondervan, 1976.

Waltke, Bruce K. *Genesis: A Commentary*. With the assistance of Cathi J. Fredricks. Grand Rapids, MI: Zondervan, 2001.

Wenham, Gordon, J. *Genesis 1–15*. Word Biblical Commentary 1. Waco, TX: Word, 1987.

———. *Genesis 16–50*. Word Biblical Commentary 2. Dallas: Word, 1994.

Youngblood, Ronald. *The Book of Genesis: An Introductory Commentary*. Grand Rapids, MI: Baker, 1992.

EXPOSITION

I. Primeval History (1:1–11:26)

A. Creation (1:1–2:3)

1. Introduction (1:1–2)

1:1. The Bible begins with an affirmation of God's existence and His creative activity. The opening verse, although part of God's creative activity on day one, introduces the six days of creation (see also Exod. 20:11). The truth of this majestic verse was joyfully affirmed by poet (Ps. 102:25) and prophet (Isa. 40:21). The Bible always assumes and never argues God's existence, as is seen in its opening phrase, **In the beginning God**. Although everything else had a beginning, God has always been (Ps. 90:2). John 1:1–10—which stresses the work of Christ, the Word, in creation—opens with the same phrase, "In the beginning." Contrary to evolutionary science, Scripture clearly states that **God created**. The Hebrew noun *Elohim* is plural, but the verb is singular—a normal usage in the Old Testament when reference is to the one true God. Though this use of the plural may express intensification rather than number and be called the plural of majesty, or of potentiality, it also allows for introducing the Creator as the triune God (for plural pronoun "us," see 1:26; 3:22; 11:7). In the Old Testament, the Hebrew verb for "create" is used only of divine, never of human, activity. God created **the heaven and the earth**, but on day two, He formed the dry land and sea. In six days (Exod. 20:11), He filled the heaven, earth, and sea with "all things" (Isa. 44:24). That God created everything is also taught in Ecclesiastes 11:5; Jeremiah 10:16; John 1:3; Colossians 1:16; and Hebrews 1:2. The positive, life-oriented teaching of verse 1 is beautifully summarized in Isaiah 45:18.

1:2. The focus of this creation account is **the earth**. As created on day one, it was **without form, and void**. This descriptive phrase, which appears elsewhere only in Jeremiah 4:23, gives structure to the rest of the chapter (see discussion on 1:11). God's "dividing" and "gathering" on days one to three gave form, and His "making" and "filling" on days four to six removed the void. The descriptive words **darkness … the deep … the waters** complete the picture of a world awaiting God's light-giving, order-making, and life-creating word. However, the awesome (and for ancient man, fearful) picture of the original state of the visible creation is relieved by the conjunction **And**, or "but." What follows is a majestic announcement that the mighty **Spirit of God** hovers over creation. The announcement anticipates God's creative words that follow. The Spirit of God was active in creation, and His creative power continues today (see Job 33:4; Ps. 104:30). Like a bird that provides for and protects its young (see Deut. 32:11; Isa. 31:5), the Spirit **moved upon the face of the waters** that covered an earth awaiting its forming and filling.

2. Body (1:3–31)

1:3. The completion of God's work on day one is introduced with **And God said**. Merely by speaking, God brought all things into being (Pss. 33:6, 9; 148:5; Heb. 11:3). God's first recorded creative word, **Let there be light**, called forth light in the midst of the primeval darkness. This light is not to be confused with the "lights in the firmament of heaven" that God created on day four (1:14) but rather was a light source that divided day and night and delineated time for the first three days of creation. Light is necessary for making God's creative works visible and life possible. In the Old Testament, light is also symbolic of life and blessing (see 2 Sam. 22:29; Job 3:20; 30:26; 33:30; Pss. 49:19; 56:13; 97:11; 112:4; Isa. 53:11; 58:8, 10; 59:9; 60:1, 3). In the New Testament, Paul uses the word "light" to illustrate God's re-creating work in sin-darkened hearts (2 Cor. 4:6).

1:4. Everything God created is **good** (see 1:10, 12, 18, 21, 25); in fact, the conclusion of chapter 1 declares everything that God made to be "very good" (1:31). The creation, as fashioned and ordered by God, had no lingering traces of disorder and no dark and threatening forces arrayed against God or man. Even darkness and the deep were given benevolent functions in a world fashioned to bless and sustain life (see Pss. 104:19–26; 127:2).

1:5. And God called the light Day. The newly created light was "called" day (see also 1:8, 10). In ancient times, to name something or someone implied having dominion or ownership (see 17:5, 15; 41:45; 2 Kings 23:34; 24:17; Dan. 1:7). Both day and night belong to the Lord (Ps. 74:16). With this creative act, **the first day** was ended. Some say that the creation days were literal twenty-four-hour days, others that they were indefinite periods. Several factors, however, support the first interpretation: (1) though the Hebrew word for "day" (*yom*) has multiple possible meanings, one might expect a primary (literal) meaning in its first reference to time in the Old Testament (i.e., a literal day) rather than a secondary (nonliteral or metaphorical) meaning; (2) the normal and usual interpretation of *yom* accompanied by a numerical adjective ("first," "second," etc.) in the Old Testament is a literal day; (3) the qualifying phrase **And the evening and the morning were the first day** suggests a twenty-four-hour day-night cycle; and (4) a creative week of seven indefinite periods of time would hardly serve as a meaningful pattern for man's cycle of work and rest (Exod. 20:11). Moreover, Moses had at his disposal words in the Hebrew language that represent long periods of time; thus he was capable of providing necessary clarification if something other than a twenty-four-hour day had been intended.

1:6–8. On day two, God created the **firmament** (i.e., the "expanse") to **divide the waters from the waters** (v. 6). This refers to the atmosphere, or **Heaven** (v. 8), as seen from the earth. "Strong, and as a molten looking glass" (Job 37:18) and "as a curtain" (Isa. 40:22) are among the many pictorial phrases used to describe it. The only possible outcome, whether stated or implied, to God's **Let there be** is **and it was so** (v. 7; see also 1:9, 11, 15, 24, 30).

1:9–10. Having the created waters gathered to **one place** (v. 9) is a picturesque way of referring to the **Seas** (v. 10) that surround the dry ground on all sides and into which the waters of the lakes and rivers flow. The earth was "standing out of the water" (2 Peter 3:5) and was "founded … upon the seas" (Ps. 24:2), and the waters are not to cross the boundaries set for them (Ps. 104:7–9; Jer. 5:22).

1:11–13. The phrase **God said** is used twice on the third day (1:9, 11) and three times (1:24, 26, 29) on the sixth day. These two days are climactic, as the following chart of the structure of chapter 1 reveals (see discussion on 1:2 regarding "without form, and void").

Days of Forming	Days of Filling
1. "light" (1:3)	4. "lights" (1:14)
2. "waters … under the firmament … waters … above the firmament" (1:7)	5. "every living creature that moveth, which the waters brought forth abundantly … every winged fowl" (1:21)
3a. "dry land" (1:9) 3b. "grass" (1:11)	6a₁. "cattle, and creeping thing, and beast of the earth" (1:24) 6a₂. "man" (1:26) 6b. "every green herb for meat" (1:30)

Both the horizontal and vertical relationships between the days demonstrate the literary beauty of the chapter and stress the orderliness and symmetry of God's creative activity. Having made three locales—heaven, earth, and sea—God engages in filling His creation and preparing a place that will support life. He begins with plants, which will provide both food and oxygen for living creatures. Both the creation and the reproduction of plants (and animals) are orderly. Each reproduces **after his kind** (vv. 11, 12; see also 1:12, 21, 24–25).

1:14–19. On day four, God made two lights to **be for signs** (v. 14) in the ways mentioned in this verse, not in any astrological or other such sense. God simply created **two great lights** (v. 16). Though clearly understood to be the sun and moon, the words "sun" and "moon" seem to be deliberately avoided here, since both were used as proper names for the pagan deities associated with these heavenly bodies. They are light-givers to be appreciated, not powers to be feared, because the one true God made them (see Isa. 40:26). Perhaps because of the emphasis on the **greater light** and the **lesser light**, the **stars** seem to be mentioned almost as an afterthought (v. 16). Psalm 136:9 indicates that the stars help the moon "rule by night." The great Creator-King assigns subordinate regulating roles to certain of His creatures (see Gen. 1:26, 28).

The three main functions of the heavenly bodies are: (1) to give light on earth, (2) to rule the day and night, and (3) to divide light from darkness (vv. 17–18). The fact that the sun clearly is newly created on day four, after the creation of vegetation on day three, argues for a literal twenty-four-hour creative day.

1:21. On day five, God created marine life and flying creatures. As on day three when the newly exposed dry land was devoid of any plant life, so the sea contained no marine creatures. With one statement, God created the smallest to the largest creatures. The Hebrew word underlying the phrase **great whales** (lit., "sea monsters") was used in Canaanite mythology to name a dreaded sea monster. He is often referred to figuratively in Old Testament poetry as one of God's most powerful opponents. He is pictured as national (Babylon in Jer. 51:34; Egypt in Isa. 51:9; Ezek. 29:3; 32:2) or cosmic (Job 7:12; Ps. 74:13; Isa. 27:7, though some take the latter as a reference to Egypt). In Genesis, however, the creatures of the sea are portrayed not as enemies to be feared but as part of God's good creation to be appreciated.

On the same creative day, God created flying creatures. The term **winged fowl** denotes anything that flies, including insects (see Deut. 14:19–20).

1:22–23. God pronounced His benediction, **Be fruitful, and multiply** (v. 22), on living things that inhabit the water and that fly in the air. By His blessing, they flourish and fill both realms with life

(see discussion on 1:28). God's rule over His created realm promotes and blesses life.

1:24–25. On day six, God created creatures to live and move on land. Though the three categories of creatures are not clearly defined, **beast of the earth** included the wild beasts, **cattle** included animals to be domesticated, and **every creeping thing** would have included the reptiles. Each creature reproduced within its kind.

1:26. In this verse, the language changes noticeably. Instead of the impersonal fiat "Let there be," the language now reflects a more personal involvement of the Creator. **Let us make man in our image, after our likeness**. The personal pronouns reveal the triune God conferring and, perhaps speaking as the Creator-King, announcing His crowning work to the members of His heavenly court (see 3:22; 11:7; Isa. 6:8; see also 1 Kings 22:19–23; Job 15:8; Jer. 23:18). No distinction should be made between "image" and "likeness," which are synonyms in both the Old Testament (Gen. 5:1; 9:6) and the New Testament (1 Cor. 11:7; Col. 3:10; James 3:9). Since man is made in God's image, every human being is worthy of honor and respect; he is to be neither murdered (Gen. 9:6) nor cursed (James 3:9). "Image" includes such characteristics as "righteousness and true holiness" (Eph. 4:24) and "knowledge" (Col. 3:10). Believers are to be "conformed to the image" of Christ (Rom. 8:29) and will someday be "like him" (1 John 3:2). Man is the climax of God's creative activity and was created to **have dominion**. God has crowned him "with glory and honour" and made him "to have dominion" over the rest of His creation (Ps. 8:5–8). Since man was created in the image of the Divine King, delegated sovereignty (kingship) was bestowed on him. (For redeemed man's ultimate kingship, see discussions on Heb. 2:5–9.)

1:27. This verse is highly significant as the first occurrence of poetry in the Old Testament (which is about 40 percent poetry). The word **created** is used here three times to describe the central divine act of the sixth day (see discussion on 1:1). Mankind was created **male and female**. Alike they bear the image of God, and together they share in the divine benediction that follows.

1:28. God blessed them, and God said ... re-plenish ... subdue ... have dominion. Mankind goes forth under this divine benediction—flourishing, filling the earth with his kind, and exercising domin-ion over the other earthly creatures (see 1:26; 2:15; Ps. 8:6–8). Human culture, accordingly, is not anti-God (though fallen man often has turned his efforts into proud rebellion against God). Rather, it is the expression of man's bearing the image of his Creator and sharing, as God's servant, in God's kingly rule. As God's representative in the creaturely realm, man is steward of God's creatures. He is not to exploit, waste, or despoil them but to care for them and use them in the service of God and man.

1:29–30. People and animals are portrayed as being vegetarian prior to man's sin (chap. 3). A new dietary permission is given after the flood (9:3).

1:31. God's approval of all that He created is noted with **very good** (see discussion on 1:4). Per-haps to stress the finality and importance of **the sixth day**, in the Hebrew text, the definite article is first used here in regard to the creation days.

3. Conclusion (2:1–3)

2:1–3. God **ended his work** and **rested** (v. 2). He ceased His labor on the seventh day, not because He was weary but because nothing formless or empty remained. His creative work was completed, and it was totally effective, absolutely perfect, "very good" (1:31). It did not have to be repeated, repaired, or revised, and the Creator "rested" to commemorate it (see also Exod. 31:17).

God blessed the seventh day, and sanctified it: because ... he had rested (v. 3). Although the word "sabbath" is not used here, the Hebrew verb trans-lated "rested" (v. 2) is the origin of the noun "sab-bath." Exodus 20:11 quotes the first half of verse 3 but substitutes "sabbath" for "seventh," clearly equat-ing the two. The first record of obligatory Sabbath observance is found in the account of Israel on her way from Egypt to Sinai (Exodus 16), and according to Nehemiah 9:13–14, keeping the Sabbath was not an official covenant obligation until the giving of the law at Mount Sinai.

B. Adam and Eve in Eden (2:4–25)

2:4. The Hebrew word for "generations" occurs ten times in Genesis—at the beginning of each main section (see Introduction: "Literary Features"). The phrase **the generations** (i.e., "account") **of the heav-ens and of the earth** introduces the record of what happened to God's creation. The blight of sin and rebellion brought a threefold curse that darkens the story of Adam and Eve in God's good and beauti-ful garden: (1) on Satan (3:14), (2) on the ground, because of man (3:17), and (3) on Cain (4:11). A general account of creation is given in 1:1–2:3, while 2:4–4:26 focuses on the beginning of human history. The Creator is once again identified, this time as **the LORD God**. "LORD" (Hebrew, *YHWH*; "Yahweh") is the personal and covenant name of God (see *KJV Study Bible* note on Exod. 3:14–15), emphasizing His role as Israel's Redeemer and covenant Lord (see *KJV Study Bible* note on Exod. 6:6), while "God" (Hebrew, *Elohim*) is a general term. Both names occur thousands of times in the Old Testament, and often, as here, they appear together—clearly indi-cating that they refer to the same, one and only, God.

2:5–6. The **plants** and **herbs** mentioned in verse 5 may refer to vegetation that required special cultivation and did not appear until man was created to care for it. Though the Hebrew for **mist** (v. 6) may be uncertain, it is clear that the earth was watered or irrigated by some source other than rain.

2:7. The creation of the male from **dust** shows the personal touch of God. The Hebrew for the verb **formed** commonly referred to the work of a potter (see Isa. 45:9; Jer. 18:6), who fashions vessels from clay (see Job 33:6). The verbs "make" (Gen. 1:26), "created" (1:27), and "formed" are used to describe God's creation of both man and animals (2:19; 1:21, 25). The Hebrew for **man** (*adam*) sounds like, and may be related to, the Hebrew for "ground" (*ada-mah*); it is also the name Adam (see 2:20). Humans and animals alike have the breath of life in them (1:30; Job 33:4). After God breathed the **breath of life** into this object that He had just formed, **man be-came a living soul**. The Hebrew phrase here trans-lated "living soul" is translated "creature that hath life" in 1:20 and "living creature" in 1:24. The words of 2:7 therefore imply that people, at least physically, have affinity with the animals. The great difference is that man is made "in the image of God" (1:27) and has an absolutely unique relation both to God as His servant and to the other creatures as their divinely appointed steward (Ps. 8:5–8).

2:8. From the standpoint of the author of Genesis, the garden was **eastward**, perhaps near where the Tigris and Euphrates rivers (see 2:14) meet, in what is today southern Iraq. **Eden** is a name synonymous with "paradise" and is related to either (1) a Hebrew word meaning "bliss" or "delight" or (2) a Mesopotamian word meaning "a plain." Perhaps the author subtly suggests both.

2:9. Characteristic of the garden was its trees, with particular emphasis on two. First was the **tree of life**, signifying and giving life, without death, to those who eat its fruit (3:22; Rev. 2:7; 22:2, 14). Second was the **tree of knowledge of good and evil**, signifying and giving knowledge of good and evil, leading ultimately to death, to those who eat its fruit (2:17; 3:3). "Knowledge of good and evil" refers to moral knowledge or ethical discernment (Deut. 1:39; Isa. 7:15–16). Adam and Eve possessed both life and moral discernment as they came from the hand of God. Their access to the fruit of the Tree of Life showed that God's will and intention for them was life. Ancient pagans believed that the gods intended for man always to be mortal. In eating the fruit of the Tree of Knowledge of Good and Evil, Adam and Eve sought a creaturely source of discernment in order to be morally independent of God.

2:10–14. Four rivers emerge from Eden. The location of **Pison** (v. 11) is unknown. The Hebrew word may be a common noun meaning "gusher." Also unknown is the location of **Havilah**, which is perhaps mentioned again in 10:29. It is probably to be distinguished from the Havilah of 10:7, which was in Egypt.

The location of **Gihon** (v. 13) is unknown. The Hebrew word may be a common noun meaning "spurter." Both the Pison and the Gihon may have been streams in Lower Mesopotamia near

the Persian Gulf. These names may have been current when Moses wrote, or he may have learned of them through oral or written records. The **Hiddekel** (v. 14) is the Tigris River. **Assyria** is literally "Asshur," an ancient capital city of Assyria (thus, "Assyria" and "Asshur" are related words). The **Euphrates** is often called simply "the river" (1 Kings 4:21, 24) because of its size and importance. However, since these rivers are part of a pre-flood description of the earth's topography, the landscape was likely altered by the flood of Noah's day, and there is no certainty that the rivers named here were the same as those known today. Thus, it is impossible to determine with any confidence the location of the garden of Eden.

2:15–17. Prior to man's sin and the stated consequences of sin as related to his labors (3:17–19), man is charged to govern the earth responsibly under God's sovereignty. He is to **dress** and **keep** the garden (v. 15). This instruction precedes the command and benediction of 1:28, which is directed to both man and woman after the woman's creation.

Every tree (v. 16), including the Tree of Life (2:9), was given for food. The exception, the Tree of Knowledge of Good and Evil (see discussion on 2:9) carried with it the first prohibition in Scripture. It is most emphatic. If man ate from the forbidden tree, he would **surely die** (v. 17). Despite the serpent's denial (3:4), disobeying God ultimately results in death.

2:18–25. Unlike the other so-called creation accounts in ancient Near Eastern literature, Genesis contains the only full account of the creation of woman.

Prior to God's evaluation that all He created was very good (1:31), He stated, **It is not good that the man should be alone** (v. 18). Without female companionship and a partner in reproduction, the man could not fully realize his humanity. Therefore, God determined to make a **help** that corresponded to him and was suitable for him.

Man (Adam), however, was unaware of his uniqueness and all-aloneness, so he was instructed to observe and name the animals that God had created before creating Adam. Whatever Adam **called**

every living creature (v. 19), that was its name. This was his first act of dominion over the creatures around him (see discussion on 1:5).

Again the personal touch of God is noted (see discussions on 1:26; 2:7) as He put man to sleep and carefully fashioned his counterpart, woman, from his side. Having just examined the animals he had named, Adam now recognized this new creation as one of his kind, having been "built" from his own flesh, and he called her **Woman** (v. 23).

The divine commentary for the new, model relationship follows. Instead of remaining under the protective custody of his parents, a man leaves them and establishes a new family unit with his wife. He will **cleave** to her, **and they shall be one flesh** (v. 24). The divine intention for husband and wife was monogamy. Together they were to form an inseparable union, of which "one flesh" is both a sign and an expression. Freedom from shame (**naked ... not ashamed**; v. 25), signifying moral innocence, would soon be lost as a result of sin (3:7).

C. The Fall and Its Consequences (chap. 3)

3:1. The Great Deceiver clothed himself as a **serpent**, one of God's good creatures. He insinuated a falsehood and portrayed rebellion as clever but essentially innocent self-interest. Therefore, the Devil, or Satan, is later referred to as "that old serpent" (Rev. 12:9; 20:2). The Hebrew word for **subtil** is almost identical to that for "naked." Though naked, the man and his wife felt no shame (2:25). The craftiness of the serpent led them to sin, and they then became ashamed of their nakedness (see 3:7). **Yea, hath God said ...?** The question and the response changed the course of human history. Throughout history, Satan has consistently caused people to doubt the goodness of God and His Word. By causing the woman to doubt God's goodness and His Word, Satan brought evil into the world. Here the Deceiver undertook to alienate man from God. In Job 1–2, Satan, as the accuser, acted to alienate God from man (see also Zech. 3:1).

3:2–3. Hooked by Satan's dialogue, the woman rehearsed the prohibition. She added to God's word, however, **Ye shall not ... touch it** (v. 3), distorting His

directive and demonstrating that the serpent's subtle challenge was working its poison.

3:4–5. Ye shall not surely die ... God doth know (v. 4–5). Satan first blatantly denies a specific divine pronouncement (see 2:17) and then accuses God of having unworthy motives. In Job 1:9–11; 2:4–5, Satan accuses the righteous man of the same. Supposedly the truth was this: **your eyes shall be opened, and ye shall be as gods** (the Hebrew word *Elohim* would be better rendered "God" here; v. 5). The statement is only half true. Their eyes were opened, to be sure (see 3:7), but the result was quite different from what the serpent had promised. They would know **good and evil** (see discussion on 2:8–9), but as "knowledgeable" sinners, they would be separated from God.

3:6–7. All the trees that God created were "pleasant to the sight, and good for food" (2:9), but now the one prohibited tree seemed especially **good for food ... pleasant to the eyes ... to be desired to make one wise** (v. 6). Compare this list with the three aspects of temptation seen in 1 John 2:16 and Luke 4:3, 5, 9. When the woman yielded and ate of the forbidden fruit, she did not instantaneously die; but when the man, the head of the race, also participated, the results of their sin were felt. They did not experience immediate physical death, but a spiritual separation from God was immediately realized. **They knew that they were naked** (v. 7). No longer innocent like children, they had a new awareness of themselves and of each other in their nakedness and shame, especially as they stood before God. Their own feeble and futile attempt to hide their shame, which only God could cover (see discussion on 3:21), was to make for themselves **aprons** of leaves.

3:8–10. The garden (v. 8), which was once a place of joy and fellowship with God, became a place of fear and of hiding from God. **Where art thou?** is a rhetorical question (v. 9; see 4:9). The omniscient God knew where Adam was, but Adam needed to know that he was no longer with God but separated and hiding from Him.

3:11–13. Confronted with his disobedience, the man blamed God and the woman—anyone but himself—for his sin: **The woman whom thou gavest ... gave me** (v. 12). Likewise, when the woman was addressed, she blamed the serpent rather than herself.

3:14 – 15. The serpent, which was the most cunning of the wild animals (3:1), was then **cursed** (v. 14) and brought low. The serpent, the woman, and the man were all judged, but only the serpent and the ground were cursed—the latter because of Adam (3:17). The symbol of death itself, **dust** (see 3:19), would be the serpent's food.

It shall bruise thy head, and thou shalt bruise his heel (v. 15). The antagonism between people and snakes is used to symbolize the outcome of the titanic struggle between God and the Evil One, a struggle played out in the hearts and history of mankind. The offspring of the woman would eventually crush the serpent's head, a promise fulfilled in Christ's victory over Satan—a victory in which all believers will share (see Rom. 16:20).

3:16. The woman's judgment, **I will greatly multiply thy sorrow and thy conception**, fell on what was most uniquely hers as a woman and as a "help meet" (2:20) for her husband. Similarly, the man's "sorrow" (3:17) was a judgment on him as worker of the soil. Some believe that the Hebrew root underlying "sorrow" should here be understood in the sense of burdensome labor (see Prov. 5:10, "labours"; 14:23, "labour"). As a sign of grace in the midst of judgment, she would **bring forth children**, and the human race would continue. The terms **desire** and **rule** have produced varying interpretations. (1) Her sexual attraction for the man, and his headship over her, would become intimate aspects of her life, in which she would experience trouble and anguish rather than unalloyed joy and blessing. (2) Due to sin, the God-ordained marriage relationship would no longer be naturally harmonious. The woman would turn against her husband, and he in turn would rule over her. Thus, the New Testament instructions for the woman to submit to her husband and for the husband to love sacrificially his wife are necessary.

3:17 – 20. Prior to his fall, man was assigned work to do, but unaffected by sin, it would have been pleasurable. Now he would have to work hard and long (judgment), but he would still be able to produce food that would sustain life (grace).

Man's labor would not be able to stave off death. He would **return unto the ground ... unto dust** (v. 19). The origin of his body (see 2:7) and the source of his food (3:17) became a symbol of his eventual death.

Adam understood God's grace to him and his wife, that they would not immediately die physically and that she would have children. Thus, in faith he named his wife **Eve** ("living"), for she would become **the mother of all living** (v. 20).

3:21. God graciously provided Adam and Eve with more effective clothing (see 3:7) to cover their shame (see 3:10). God's act of clothing them with skins, which required the death of innocent animals, is symbolic of the merits of Christ's future sacrifice for sin on the cross, whereby the unrighteous sinner can be clothed in Christ's righteousness (2 Cor. 5:21). Possibly God instructed Adam and Eve at this point concerning the need of animal sacrifice as a part of worship.

3:22 – 24. In a terribly perverted way, Satan's prediction (3:5) came true. Now, lest the couple **live for ever**, they must be cut off from the **tree of life** (v. 22). Sin, which always results in death (Rom. 6:23; James 1:14 – 15), cuts the sinner off from God's gift of eternal life.

Before he sinned, man had worked in a beautiful and pleasant garden (2:15). Now he was **sent ... forth from the garden ... to till the ground** (v. 23). He would have to work hard on the ground, which had been cursed with thorns and thistles (3:18).

Perhaps appearing similar to the statues of winged figures that stood guard at the entrances to palaces and temples in ancient Mesopotamia (see *KJV Study Bible* note on Exod. 25:18), **Cherubims** guarded the garden entrance to prevent man from entering (v. 24). Man, who had been placed in the garden **to keep** it, was now kept (same Hebrew word) from it. The **flaming sword** of God's judgment stood between fallen man and God's garden. The reason is given in verse 22. Only through God's redemption in Christ does man have access again to the Tree of Life (Rev. 2:7; 22:2, 14, 19).

D. The Rapid "Progress" of Sin (4:1–16)

4:1–2. Two things are quickly evident from this chapter. First, Eve is indeed the "mother of all living" (3:20), and second, her children are born in the image of their fallen father (see 5:3). When Cain was born, Eve acknowledged that God is the ultimate source of life (see Acts 17:25) and her son was **from the Lord** (v. 1).

The name **Abel** (v. 2) means "breath" or "temporary" or "meaningless" (the translation of the same basic Hebrew word that is in Eccl. 1:2; 12:8) and hints at the shortness of Abel's life.

4:3–4. Cain brought of the fruit … Abel … brought of the firstlings of his flock and of the fat thereof. The contrast is not between an offering of plant life and an offering of animal life but between a careless, thoughtless offering and a choice, generous offering (see Lev. 3:16). Motivation and heart attitude are all-important, and God looked with favor on Abel and his offering because of Abel's faith (Heb. 11:4). Abel's offering of the firstlings is indicative of his recognition that the productivity of the flock is from the Lord and it all belongs to Him.

4:5–6. God did not look with favor on Cain and his offering, and Cain (whose motivation and attitude were bad from the outset) reacted predictably. **Why art thou wroth …?** (v. 6) is a question meant to probe Cain's conscience concerning his sinful attitude and to bring repentance.

4:7. The Hebrew word for **lieth** is the same as an ancient Babylonian word referring to an evil demon crouching at the door of a building to threaten the people inside. Sin may thus be pictured here as just such a demon, waiting to pounce on Cain; it desires to have him. He may already have been plotting his brother's murder. In Hebrew, **unto thee shall be his desire** is the same expression used in "thy desire shall be to thy husband" in 3:16 (see also Song 7:10). Cain must in turn rule over sin's intent.

4:8. The Samaritan Pentateuch and the Greek Septuagint include Cain's invitation: "Let us go out to the field." There Cain **rose up against Abel his brother, and slew him**. The first murder was especially monstrous because it was committed against a brother (see 3:9–11; 1 John 3:12) and against a good man (Matt. 23:35; Heb. 11:4)—a striking illustration of the awful consequences of the fall.

4:9–10. Where is Abel thy brother? is another rhetorical question (v. 9; see discussion on 3:9). **I know not** is an outright lie. Cain's response, **Am I my brother's keeper?** is a statement of callous indifference—all too common throughout the course of human history.

Thy brother's blood crieth unto me (v. 10). Abel, in one sense a prophet (Luke 11:50–51), still speaks, though dead (Heb. 11:4), for his spilled blood continues to cry out to God against all those who do violence to their human brothers. But the blood of Christ "speaketh better things than that of Abel" (Heb. 12:24).

4:11–12. The ground had been cursed because of human sin (3:17), and now Cain himself is **cursed** (v. 11). Formerly he had worked the ground, and it had produced life for him (3:2–3). Now the ground, soaked with his brother's blood, would symbolize death and would no longer yield for him its produce (4:12). And estranged from his fellow man and finding even the ground inhospitable, he became a **vagabond** (v. 12) in the land of wandering (see discussion on 3:16).

4:13. My punishment is greater than I can bear. Confronted with his crime and its resulting curse, Cain responded not with remorse but with self-pity. His sin was virtually uninterrupted: impiety (4:3), anger (4:5), jealousy, deception, and murder (4:8), falsehood (4:9) and self-seeking (4:13). The final result was alienation from God Himself (4:14, 16).

4:14–16. The words **every one … whosoever … any** (vv. 14–15) seem to imply the presence of substantial numbers of people outside Cain's immediate family (see 5:4), but perhaps they only anticipate the future rapid growth of the race.

God gave Cain a **mark** (v. 15), a warning sign to protect him, or to assure him of protection, from an avenger. For the time being, the life of the murderer was spared (but see 6:7; 9:6).

Though the location of **Nod** (v. 16) is unknown, the name is from the same Hebrew word translated "vagabond" in 4:12, 14.

E. Two Genealogies (4:17–5:32)

1. The Genealogy of Pride (4:17–24)

4:17–18. The age-old question "Where did Cain get his wife?" can only be answered with "his sister" (see 5:4). Though she is unnamed, she gave him a son, **Enoch** (v. 17). The Hebrew for **city** can refer to any permanent settlement, however small. Cain tried to redeem himself from his wandering state by the activity of his own hands; in the land of wandering, he built a city.

Together with that of Adam, the names listed in verses 17–18, **Cain, Enoch, Irad, Mehujael, Methusael,** and **Lamech,** add up to a total of seven, a number often signifying completeness (see 4:15). Each of the six names listed here is paralleled by a similar or identical name in the genealogy of Seth in chapter 5: Cainan (5:12), Enoch (5:21), Jared (5:18), Mahalaleel (5:15), Methuselah (5:25), and Lamech (5:28). The similarity between the two sets of names is striking and may suggest the selective nature of such genealogies (see discussion on 5:5; see also 1 Chronicles, Introduction: "Genealogies").

4:19. Polygamy entered history with Lamech, who **took unto him two wives.** Haughty Lamech, the seventh from Adam in the line of Cain, perhaps sought to attain the benefits of God's primeval blessing (see 1:28 and discussion) by his own device — multiplying his wives. Monogamy, however, was the original divine intention (see 2:23–24).

4:20–22. Lamech's three sons, **Jabal, Jubal,** and **Tubal-cain,** had similar names, each derived from a Hebrew verb meaning "to bring, carry, lead" and emphasizing activity. These sons were creative. Jubal made simple musical instruments, and Tubal-cain, whose name was especially appropriate since "cain" means "metalsmith," made implements for agriculture and construction and probably also made weapons. These inventions were intended to relieve somewhat the hardships of life in a cursed world.

4:23–24. I have slain a man to my wounding (v. 23). Here is an example of violent and wanton destruction of human life by one who proclaimed his complete independence from God by taking vengeance with his own hands (see Deut. 32:35). Lamech proudly claimed to be master of his own destiny, thinking that he and his sons, by their own achievements, would redeem themselves from the curse on the line of Cain. This titanic claim climaxes the catalog of sins that began with Cain's prideful selfishness at the beginning of the chapter.

Lamech's vicious announcement of personal revenge of **seventy and sevenfold** (v. 24) found its counterpoint in Jesus' response to Peter's question about forgiveness in Matthew 18:21–22.

2. The Genealogy of Death (4:25–5:32)

4:25–26. With Abel dead and Cain alienated, Adam and Eve were provided with **another seed** (v. 25), a third son, Seth, to replace the deceased son. The name is possibly related to the Hebrew word for "appoint" (the Hebrew verb is *shat*; the name is *Sheth*). Other possible sons (see 5:4) are not named. Seth's son was named **Enos** (v. 26), which means "man" (as does Adam; see discussion on 2:7). Lamech's proud self-reliance, so characteristic of the line of Cain, is contrasted with the dependence on God found in the line of Seth, who **began ... to call upon the name of the Lord.**

5:1–2. Though the story of Adam ends here, the **book of the generations** (v. 1; see discussion on 2:4) begins the account of his descendants. This is the race that was created **in the likeness of God** (see 1:26), both **male and female** (v. 2; see 1:27), and was **blessed** by Him (see 1:28). **Adam,** though the name given to the first man, is the Hebrew word for "man," which often refers to both sexes (mankind) in the early chapters of Genesis (e.g., 3:22–24).

5:3–4. The age of Adam and Eve at the birth of Cain and Abel is not given. However, Adam was 130 years old when Seth was born to replace the deceased Abel. As God created man in His own perfect image (see discussion on 1:26), so now sinful Adam had a son in **his own likeness, after his image** (v. 3), an imperfect image marred by sin.

Only three of Adam's sons are named, but the fact that Adam had other **sons and daughters** (v. 4) allows for his children to intermarry (see discussion on 4:17) and for a potentially very large family and many descendants when he died.

5:5 – 17. Beginning here, the chapter reads like an obituary, for in spite of Adam's longevity of life, **nine hundred and thirty years** (v. 5), he died, as did all his descendants. **And he died** is repeated as a sad refrain throughout the chapter, the only exception being Enoch (see discussion on 5:24). The phrase is a stark reminder of God's warning, "Thou shalt surely die" (2:17), and his judgment on sin resulting from Adam's fall.

Whether the large numbers describing human longevity in the early chapters of Genesis are literal or have a conventional literary function, or both, has been debated. Some scholars believe that several of the numbers have symbolic significance, such as Enoch's 365 (5:23) years (365 being the number of days in a year, thus a full life) and Lamech's 777 (5:31) years (777 being an expansion and multiple of seven, the number of completeness; compare the "seventy and sevenfold" of Lamech's namesake in 4:24). That there are exactly ten names in the Genesis 5 list (as in the genealogy of 11:10 – 26) suggests that it (or the Genesis 11 list) may be stylized and may possibly include gaps (see Matt. 1:1 – 17, which lists three sets of fourteen generations, with names known in the Old Testament omitted to make fourteen). In the Old Testament, "father" and "son" sometimes mean "ancestor" and "descendant," not necessarily an immediate father-son relationship. While the pre-flood life spans are long, they are consistently long. Beginning with Noah and Shem, life spans after the flood, though still lengthy, begin to decrease and continue to do so in the patriarchal period. There is no hint of transitioning from literary or symbolic numbers to real or literal numbers at any point. Therefore, it seems best to accept the ages as literal and very long.

Other ancient genealogies outside the Bible exhibit similarly large figures. For example, three kings in a Sumerian list (which also contains exactly ten names) are said to have reigned 72,000 years each. These are seemingly exaggerated time spans, but it is possible that a different numbering system was in use (e.g., a sexagesimal system instead of a decimal system, used in the Old Testament), thus making the lengthy life spans somewhat comparable.

5:18 – 24. For the summary on Enoch, the phrase **walked with God** (v. 22) replaces the word "lived" in the other genealogies of the chapter and highlights that there is a difference between walking with God and merely living. Only of Enoch was it said, **and he was not; for God took him** (v. 24). The phrase replaces the "and he died" of the other genealogies of the chapter. Like Elijah, who was "taken" (2 Kings 2:10) to heaven, Enoch was taken away (see Pss. 49:15; 73:24) to the presence of God without experiencing death (Heb. 11:5). Lamech, the seventh from Adam in the genealogy of Cain, was evil personified. But "Enoch also, the seventh from Adam" (Jude 14) in the genealogy of Seth, "had this testimony, that he pleased God" (Heb. 11:5).

5:25 – 27. Methuselah's life span of **nine hundred sixty and nine years** (v. 27) is the longest recorded in Scripture. Only Noah and his family survived the flood. If the figures concerning life spans are literal and the list is free of gaps, Methuselah died in the year of the flood (the figures in 5:25, 28; and 7:6 add up to exactly 969).

5:28 – 32. With the birth of **Noah** (v. 29; the Hebrew root of this name is "rest, relief"), a prophetic hope is given. Somehow this son will someday bring relief from the curse God placed upon the earth. Instead of listing only one son, Noah's three sons, who will survive the coming flood with him, **Shem, Ham, and Japheth** (v. 32), are all listed.

F. The Extent of Sin before the Flood (6:1 – 8)

6:1. God had instructed the first male and female of mankind, "Be fruitful, and multiply" (1:28). Here it is noted that **men** (Hebrew, *adam;* "man" or "mankind"; see discussion on 5:1 – 2) had indeed begun to **multiply**.

6:2. The sons of God and **the daughters of men** have posed problems of identification and interpretation. The phrase "the sons of God" here has been interpreted to refer either to angels or to human beings. In such places as Job 1:6 and 2:1, it refers to angels, and perhaps also in Psalm 29:1 (where "O ye mighty" can be literally rendered "sons of God"). Some interpreters also appeal to Jude 6–7 (as well as to Jewish literature) in referring the phrase to angels here. Supporting this view is the distinction that is made between "the sons of God" and "the daughters of men [Hebrew, *adam*, as in 6:1]." That there are two different kinds of beings cohabiting is implied.

Others, however, maintain that intermarriage and cohabitation between angels and human beings, though commonly mentioned in ancient mythologies, are surely excluded by the very nature of the created order (chap. 1; Mark 12:25). Elsewhere, expressions equivalent to "the sons of God" often refer to human beings, though in contexts quite different from the present one (Deut. 14:1; 32:5; Ps. 73:15; Isa. 43:6; Hos. 1:10; 11:1; Luke 3:38; 1 John 3:1–2, 10). "The sons of God" (Gen. 6:2, 4) possibly refers to godly men, and "the daughters of men" to sinful women (significantly, they are not called "the daughters of God"), probably from the wicked line of Cain. If so, the context suggests that verses 1–2 describe the intermarriage of the Sethites ("the sons of God") of chapter 5 with the Cainites ("the daughters of men") of chapter 4, indicating a breakdown in the separation of the two groups. This viewpoint, however, does not consider the other "sons and daughters" (5:4) of Adam.

Another plausible suggestion is that "the sons of God" refers to royal figures (kings were closely associated with gods in the ancient Near East) who proudly perpetuated the corrupt lifestyle of Lamech, from the line of Cain (virtually a royal figure), and established for themselves royal harems.

6:3. In the Hebrew, two key phrases in this verse are obscure: **strive with** (which could be translated "remain in") and **is flesh** (which could be translated "is corrupt"). The verse seems to announce that the period of grace between God's declaration of judg-

ment and its arrival would be 120 years (see 1 Peter 3:20). If "remain in" is accepted, the verse announces that man's life span would henceforth be limited to 120 years. This interpretation is contradicted, however, by the lengthy life spans recorded in 11:10–26.

6:4. Living at that time were **giants**, people of great size and strength (see Num. 13:31–33). The Hebrew word is *nephilim*, which means "fallen ones." In men's eyes, they were **the mighty men ... of old, men of renown**, but in God's eyes, they were sinners ("fallen ones") ripe for judgment.

6:5–6. God saw what He had created, and it was "very good" (1:31), but what man had done and become was **only evil continually** (v. 5). This is one of the Bible's most vivid descriptions of total depravity. And because man's nature remained unchanged, things were no better after the flood (8:21).

Only the creature created in God's image sinned against Him. That **it repented the LORD** (v. 6) does not indicate that God had second thoughts about having created but rather a necessary change in dealing with sinful man. God was **grieved ... at his heart**. Man's sin is indeed God's sorrow (see Eph. 4:30).

6:7–8. I will destroy man ... from the face of the earth (v. 7). The period of grace (see 6:3 and discussion) was coming to an end. Though morally innocent, the animal world, **beast ... creeping thing ... fowls**, as creatures under man's corrupted rule, shared in his judgment. The only exception to God's resolved destruction was Noah (and his family) because **he found grace in the eyes of the LORD** (v. 8).

G. The Great Flood (6:9 – 9:29)

1. Preparing for the Flood (6:9 – 7:10)

6:9–12. The generations of Noah (v. 9) begins the account of Noah and the flood (see discussion on 2:4). Noah's godly life was a powerful contrast to the wicked lives of his contemporaries (see 6:5, 12). This description of Noah, **just ... perfect**, does not imply sinless perfection but that he was righteous and blameless before God and his contemporaries. Like Enoch, he **walked with God** (see discussion on 5:22). The description of the earth, **corrupt ... filled with violence** (v. 11), is a sad elaboration of 6:5.

6:13–16. Noah, God's choice for survival, was instructed to build an **ark** (v. 14). The Hebrew for this word is used elsewhere only in reference to the basket that saved the baby Moses (Exod. 2:3, 5). Just as Moses' mother made his basket watertight, Noah was to waterproof his ark **with pitch** (see Exod. 2:3). Though the dimensions and number of floors are given, nothing is said of a rudder or sails, usually associated with a boat. This is clearly a barge-like structure built for the purpose of floating over the waters of the flood to preserve alive its precious cargo.

6:17. The purpose of **the flood of waters upon the earth** was **to destroy all flesh ... under heaven**. The Bible describes the deluge as worldwide, indicated by the universal terms of the text, both here and elsewhere (6:7, 12–13; 7:4, 19, 21–23; 8:21; 9:11, 15). Some argue that nothing in the narrative of chapters 6–9 prevents the flood from being understood as regional—destroying everything in its wake but of relatively limited scope and universal only from the standpoint of Moses' geographic knowledge. The universal language used to describe the drought and famine in the time of Joseph (41:54, 57) is cited. The purpose of the flood, however, was to destroy all land-living, air-breathing creatures (including sinful mankind). Except for Noah and his family, nothing living on earth was exempt from the destruction of the flood. Present knowledge of the spread of the ancient human population would seem to necessitate a worldwide flood in light of the extent of the destruction. Other factors supporting a global deluge include the size of the ark, the extent of the flood, and the duration of the flood (over one year). The promise of God not to send such a flood in the future was signified by the rainbow as a divine commitment to future generations (9:8–17). The apostle Peter, likewise, seems to assume that the flood and its devastation were universal and total, except for Noah and his family (2 Peter 3:6).

6:18. Noah would understand the full implications of God's **covenant** with him only after the floodwaters had dried up (see 9:8–17). **Thou shalt come into the ark.** The story of Noah's salvation

from the flood illustrates God's redemption of His children (see Heb. 11:7; 2 Peter 2:5) and typifies baptism (see 1 Peter 3:20–21). God extended His loving concern to the whole family, **thy sons, and thy wife, and thy sons' wives with thee,** of righteous Noah — a consistent pattern in God's dealings with His people, underscoring the moral and responsible relationship of parents to their children (see 17:7–27; 18:19; Deut. 30:19; Pss. 78:1–7; 102:28; 103:17–18; 112:1–2; Acts 2:38–39; 16:31; 1 Cor. 7:14).

6:19–21. Most animals were doomed to die in the flood (see discussion on 6:7), but at least one pair of each kind, **two of every sort** (v. 19), was preserved to restock the earth after the waters subsided.

6:22. Hebrews 11:7 stresses Noah's faith and fear. The Genesis account stresses Noah's obedience. **According to all that God commanded him, so did he** (see 7:5, 9, 16).

7:1. The beginning of God's final word to Noah before the flood is **Come ... into the ark**. God's first word to Noah after the flood begins similarly: "Go forth of the ark" (8:16). Not only was Noah a **righteous** exception in his generation (see 6:8–9), but as a "preacher of righteousness" (2 Peter 2:5), he warned his contemporaries of coming judgment and testified to the vitality of his own faith (see Heb. 11:7).

7:2–5. God gave Noah an additional instruction regarding the animals to be preserved (6:19–20). Whereas all the animals would reproduce after the flood, more of the ceremonially clean animals would be needed, for the burnt offerings that Noah would sacrifice (see 8:20) and for food (see 9:3). Therefore, of **every clean beast**, Noah was to take **by sevens,** (i.e., seven pairs) **the male and his female** (lit., "the man and his wife"; v. 2). Not until Leviticus 11 does God delineate the clean and unclean animals for Israel's dietary restrictions.

Noah was forewarned of rainfall that would continue **forty days and forty nights** (v. 4). This is a literal period of time but also a length of time that often characterizes a critical period in redemptive history (see 7:12; Deut. 9:11; Matt. 4:1–11).

7:6–10. Noah went in ... into the ark, because of the waters that were about to come upon the earth (v. 7). Once more Noah is noted for his obedience (see 6:22; 7:9, 16). Noah and his family were saved, but life continued as usual for everyone else until it was too late (see Matt. 24:37–39). The faith of Noah was immediately tried, for the rains did not begin for seven days.

2. Judgment and Redemption (7:11–8:19)

a. The Rising of the Waters (7:11–24)

7:11–16. Over the next forty days, the earth was inundated by torrential waters (**the fountains of the great deep broken up**, v. 11) and in the heavens (**the windows of heaven were opened**). Only **Noah, and ... the sons of Noah, and Noah's wife, and the three wives of his sons** (v. 13), who had boarded the ark, were saved. Of the earth's population, "a few, that is, eight souls" (1 Peter 3:20; see 2 Peter 2:5), survived the flood.

Four of the five categories of animate life mentioned in 1:21–25 were preserved in the ark, representatives of **every beast ... all the cattle ... every creeping thing that creepeth upon the earth ... every fowl** (v. 14). The fifth category—sea creatures—could remain alive outside the ark.

After Noah did as **God had commanded him: and the LORD shut him in** (v. 16). "God" gave the command, but in His role as redeeming "LORD" (see discussion on 2:4; *KJV Study Bible* note on Exod. 6:6), He closed the door of the ark behind Noah and his family. Neither divine name is mentioned in the rest of chapter 7, as the full fury of the flood was unleashed on sinful mankind.

7:17–24. The waters rose until all the **high hills** and **mountains** (the same Hebrew word) **under the whole heaven** were covered (v. 19–20). The terms are descriptive of a global flood, for certainly water that seeks its level would not cover the highest mountains locally and not impact the rest of the earth's surface. The water rose **fifteen cubits upward** above the highest mountain (v. 20). The ark was thirty cubits high (6:15), so the water was deep enough to keep it from running aground.

The purpose of the flood was accomplished (see 6:17), for all land-living, air-breathing creatures (human and animal) **died** (v. 22). God's gift at creation, the **breath of life** (see 1:30; 2:7), was taken away because of sin. Obedient Noah and his family, on board the ark, were the notable exceptions.

b. The Receding of the Waters (8:1–19)

8:1–2. Thus far the flood narrative has been an account of judgment; hereafter it is a story of redemption. **God remembered Noah** (v. 1). Though He had not been mentioned since 7:16 or heard from for 150 days (see 7:24), God had not forgotten Noah and his family. In the Bible, to "remember" is not merely to recall to mind; it is to express concern for someone, to act with loving care for him. When God remembers His people (see 30:22; Exod. 2:24; 6:5; 1 Sam. 1:11), He does so "for good" (Neh. 5:19; 13:31).

The Hebrew word translated "Spirit" in Genesis 1:2 is here rendered **wind** and introduces a series of parallels between the events of chapters 8–9 and those of chapter 1: compare 8:2 with 1:7; 8:5 with 1:9; 8:7 with 1:20; 8:17 with 1:25; 9:1 with 1:28a; 9:2 with 1:28b; 9:3 with 1:30. Chapter 1 describes the original beginning, while chapters 8–9 describe a new beginning after the flood.

8:3–5. After 150 days, the floodwaters began to recede, and the **mountains** (the word is plural and refers to a range of mountains) **of Ararat** provided a place of grounding for the ark (v. 4). The name Ararat is related to Assyrian Urartu, which became an extensive and mountainous kingdom (see Jer. 51:27; Isa. 37:38) including much of the territory north of Mesopotamia and east of modern Turkey. The ark's landfall was probably in southern Urartu.

It seems too much to assume that the earth was cleared of water simply by evaporation. Psalm 104:6–9 describes waters that "stood above the mountains." An alternate reading for Psalm 104:8 (see *KJV Study Bible* marginal note) states, "The mountains ascend, the valleys descend." God apparently changed the earth's topography, elevating the mountains while lowering the valleys and oceans to accommodate the excess of water and provide dry ground for the ark's occupants.

8:6 – 12. Forty days later, Noah opened the window and began to test the earth's readiness for occupancy by sending out birds. The raven, a large and strong bird of prey, was able to soar and look for carrion until the waters receded enough for it to find a place to light and never returned the ark. A dove, after being sent from the ark a second time, returned **to him … and lo, in her mouth was an olive leaf pluckt off** (v. 11). Olives do not grow at high elevations, and the fresh leaf was a sign to Noah that the water had receded from the earth. The modern symbol of peace represented by a dove carrying an olive branch in its beak has its origin in this story.

8:13 – 14. The date formula **the six hundredth and first year, in the first month, the first day of the month** (v. 13), signals mankind's new beginning after the flood. Noah saw for himself that the surface of the ground was drying. **In the second month, on the seven and twentieth day of the month** (v. 14), more than a year after the flood began (see 7:11), the earth is described as **dried**.

8:16 – 17. Not until God issued the command, **Go forth of the ark** (v. 16; see discussion on 7:1), did Noah disembark. There is no indication that the animals reproduced on board the ark. They were released to **breed abundantly … be fruitful … and multiply** (v. 17). The animals and birds could now find new habitats and reproduce.

3. The Flood's Aftermath (8:20 – 9:29)

a. A New Promise (8:20 – 22)

8:20 – 22. Since worship is a very personal matter, it is to God as **the LORD** (v. 20; see discussion on 2:4) that Noah brought his sacrifice (see 4:4). Of a representative of every clean animal and bird, Noah offered **burnt offerings**.

The Lord's smelling **a sweet savour** (v. 21) is a figurative way of saying that the Lord takes delight in His children's worship of Him (see Eph. 5:2; Phil. 4:18). He promised not to **curse the ground**. The reference appears to be to the curse of Genesis 3:17, although a different Hebrew word for "curse" is used. It may be that the Lord pledged never to add curse upon curse as He had in regard to Cain (4:12). The

phrase **for the imagination of man's heart is evil** is almost identical to that in 6:5. Because of man's extreme wickedness, God had destroyed him (6:7) by means of a flood (6:17). Although righteous Noah and his family had been saved, he and his offspring were descendants of Adam and carried in their hearts the inheritance of sin. God graciously promises never again to deal with sin by sending such a devastating deluge (see 9:11, 15). Human history is held open for God's dealing with sin in a new and redemptive way — the way that was prepared for by God's action at Babel (see discussions on 11:6, 8) and that begins to unfold with the call of Abram (12:1). The phrase **from his youth** replaces the "continually" of 6:5 and emphasizes the truth that sin infects a person's life from his conception and birth (Pss. 51:5; 58:3).

Times and seasons, created by God in the beginning (see 1:14) but perhaps more pronounced after the flood, will never cease till the end of history (v. 22).

b. New Ordinances (9:1 – 7)

9:1 – 7. At this new beginning, God renewed His original benediction (1:28) and His provision for man's food (v. 3; 1:29 – 30). Because sin had brought violence into man's world and because God now appointed meat as a part of man's food (9:3), further divine provisions and stipulations are added (9:4 – 6). Yet God's benediction dominates and encloses the whole (9:7).

9:1 – 2. As the first couple had been instructed, so Noah (through his family) was to reproduce and fill the earth. God reaffirmed that mankind would rule over all creation, including the animals: **into your hand are they delivered** (v. 2; see discussion on 1:26).

9:3 – 4. Man's diet was originally vegetarian (1:29 – 30). Now God added a new provision. Meat, without any restrictions regarding the kind of animal, could be used to supplement mankind's diet. **Every moving thing that liveth shall be meat for you** (v. 3). This provision would later be limited to only clean animals (Leviticus 11).

One restriction regarding eating meat was in effect: the **flesh with the life thereof, which is the blood thereof, shall ye not eat** (v. 4). Leviticus 17:14 stresses the intimate relationship between blood and life by twice declaring that "the life of all flesh is the blood thereof." Life is the precious and mysterious gift of God, and man is not to seek to preserve it or increase the life force within him by eating "life" that is "in the blood" (Lev. 17:11)—as many pagan peoples throughout history have thought they could do.

9:5–7. An exception to the killing of creatures (for food) was human life. **Your blood of your lives will I require; at the hand of every beast will I require it** (v. 5). God Himself is the great defender of human life (see 4:9–12), which is precious to Him because man was created in His image (v. 6) and because man is the earthly representative and focal point of God's kingdom. In the theocracy (kingdom of God) established at Sinai, a domestic animal that had taken human life was to be stoned to death (Exod. 21:28–32).

Whoso sheddeth man's blood, by man shall his blood be shed (v. 6). In the later theocracy, those guilty of premeditated murder were to be executed (Exod. 21:12–14; Num. 35:16–32; see also Rom. 13:3–4; 1 Peter 2:13–14). It should be noted that this important stipulation is not to be seen as relating only to Israel, that is, as part of the Mosaic covenant, for it predates even Abraham, the father of Israel. It was given to Noah, the father of all mankind in this new beginning after the flood. The stipulation, therefore, is timeless and is not limited to only certain peoples. The crime of murder has not only social implications but, more importantly, theological implications, **for in the image of God made He man** (see 1:26 and discussion). In killing a human being, a murderer demonstrates his contempt for God as well as for his fellow man.

c. A New Relationship (9:8–17)

9:8–11. I establish my covenant (v. 9). In this covenant, God sovereignly promised to Noah, his descendants, and all other living things (as a kind of gracious reward to righteous Noah, the new father of the human race; see 6:18) never again to destroy man and the earth until His purposes for His creation are fully realized ("While the earth remaineth," 8:22). For similar commitments by God, see His covenants with Abram (15:18–20), Phinehas (Num. 25:10–13), and David (2 Samuel 7; see chart, *KJV Study Bible*, p. 16).

Neither shall all flesh be cut off any more by the waters of a flood (v. 11). A summary of the provisions of the Lord's covenant with Noah follows—an eternal covenant, as seen in such words and phrases as "any more" (9:11, 15), "for perpetual generations" (9:12), and "everlasting" (9:16). Attention should be drawn to **the waters of** the **flood** (the Hebrew text has the definite article), which can refer only to a flood of global proportions, as just experienced by Noah. There have been many extensive, but local, floods since Noah's day that have claimed lives.

9:12–17. A covenant **token** (v. 12), or sign, was a visible seal and reminder of covenant commitments. Circumcision would become the sign of the covenant with Abraham (17:11), and the Sabbath would be the sign of the covenant with Israel at Sinai (Exod. 31:16–17). Rain and the rainbow doubtless existed long before the time of Noah's flood, but after the flood, the **bow** (v. 13) took on new meaning as the sign of the Noahic covenant.

d. A New Temptation (9:18–23)

9:18–19. Fulfillment of the instructions to fill the earth (9:1) is to be seen in Noah's sons, who **overspread** the earth (v. 19), and thus the table of nations (chap. 10) is anticipated (see discussion on 11:8).

9:20–21. Noah became **a husbandman** (lit., "a man of the ground"; v. 20). Like his father Lamech (see 5:29), Noah was a farmer, and for reasons unstated, he directed his attention to a vineyard. As one might expect, he partook of the grapes he had tended, and **he drank of the wine, and was drunken** (v. 21). The first reference to wine connects it with drunkenness. No reason is given why **he was uncovered within his tent**, but excessive use of wine led, among other things, to immodest behavior (see 19:30–35).

9:22–23. Of special note is the fact that Ham, who found Noah unclothed in his tent, was the **father of Canaan** (v. 22). Canaan is mentioned here because Ham, in acting as he did, showed himself to be the true father of Canaan (i.e., of the Canaanites; see discussion on 15:16). Rather than cover his father's immodesty, Ham **told his two brethren**; that is, he broadcast to his brothers their father's shame. They, however, wanted to avoid further disgrace to their father, so they covered him as they backed into his room, **and they saw not their father's nakedness** (v. 23).

9:24–25. When Noah awoke from his drunkenness caused by the wine, he learned what Ham had done. There is no need to assume that Ham had physically or sexually molested his father in any way, only disgraced him, for the action of his brothers in covering their father would not have corrected any sexual violation.

Cursed be Canaan (v. 25) is a prophetic statement. Some maintain that Ham's son Canaan (see 9:18, 22) was to be punished because of his father's sin (see Exod. 20:5), but Exodus 20:5 restricts such punishment to "them that hate me." It is probably better to hold that Canaan and his descendants were to be punished because they would be even worse than Ham (Lev. 18:2–3, 6–30). Canaan would be a **servant of servants.** Joshua's subjection of the Gibeonites (Josh. 9:27) is one of the fulfillments (see also Josh. 16:10; Judg. 1:28, 30, 33, 35; 1 Kings 9:20–21). Noah's prophecy cannot be used to justify the enslavement of blacks, since those cursed here were Canaanites, who were Caucasian.

9:26–27. Blessed be the LORD (v. 26). The Lord (instead of Shem) is blessed (praised) because He is the source of Shem's blessing. He is also the **God of Shem** (and his descendants, the Semites, which included the Israelites) in a special sense.

Japheth's blessing was to be enlarged (Japheth means "God will enlarge") as he stood related to Shem, that is, **in the tents of Shem** (v. 27). He would thus share in the blessings bestowed on Shem.

e. A Final Word (9:24–29)

9:28–29. As the tenth and last member of the genealogy of Seth (5:3–32), Noah is given an obituary that ends like those of his worthy ancestors (see discussion on 5:5).

H. The Spread of the Nations (10:1–11:26)

1. The Diffusion of Nations (chap. 10)

10:1. The generations of the sons of Noah is the fourth account to appear in Genesis (see discussion on 2:4). The links affirmed here may not all be based on strictly physical descent but may include geographical, historical, and linguistic associations (see discussion on 10:5). For example, the Hebrew for "sons" can mean "descendants," "successors," or "nations," and the Hebrew for "father" can mean "ancestor," "predecessor," or "founder." (See 1 Chronicles, Introduction: "Genealogies.")

10:2–4. Japheth (v. 2), the least involved in the biblical narrative and perhaps also the oldest of Noah's sons (see 10:21), has his descendants, or successors, listed first. The genealogy of Shem, the chosen line, appears last in the chapter (10:21–31; see also 11:10–26). The fourteen nations that came from Japheth plus the thirty from Ham and the twenty-six from Shem add up to seventy nations (the multiple of ten and seven, both numbers signifying completeness; see discussion on 5:5), perhaps in anticipation of the seventy members of Jacob's family in Egypt (46:27; Exod. 1:5; see also Deut. 32:8).

The Japhethites lived generally north and west of Canaan in Eurasia. The people of **Gomer** (the later Cimmerians; v. 2–3) and related nations lived near the Black Sea. **Magog** (v. 2) is possibly the father of a Scythian people who inhabited the Caucasus and adjacent regions southeast of the Black Sea. **Madai** is known later as the Medes. **Javan** (vv. 2, 4) is Ionia (southern Greece) and perhaps western Asia Minor. **Tubal, and Meshech** (v. 2) are not related to Tobolsk and Moscow in modern Russia. Together with Magog, they are mentioned in later Assyrian inscriptions (see also Ezek. 38:2). Probably Tubal was in Pontus, and Meshech was in the Moschian

Mountains. The movement of the Japhethites was from eastern Asia Minor north to the Black Sea. **Tiras** is possibly the Thrace of later times.

Ashkenaz (v. 3) is the later Scythians. All three names in verse 3 refer to peoples located in the upper Euphrates region.

Elishah (v. 4) is either Alashia (an ancient name for Cyprus) or a reference to Sicily and southern Italy. **Tarshish** is probably southern Spain. **Kittim** refers to a people living on Cyprus. **Dodanim** is found in some manuscripts as "Rodanim," a people whose name is perhaps reflected in Rhodes (a Greek isle). The Hebrew letters for *d* and *r* were easily confused by scribes (copyists) because of their similarity in form.

10:5. The terms **lands**, **tongue**, **families**, and **nations** (v. 5; see 10:20, 31) are geographic, ethnic, political, and linguistic terms, respectively. These several criteria were used to differentiate the various groups of people. They also anticipate the later event that so divided the people (chap. 11).

10:6 – 8. The sons of **Ham** (v. 6) were located in southwestern Asia and northeast Africa. **Cush** is the upper Nile region, south of Egypt. **Mizraim** means "two Egypts," a reference to Upper and Lower Egypt. **Phut** is either Libya (see discussion on "Lehabim," below) or the land the ancient Egyptians called Punt (modern Somalia). **Canaan** is a name that means "land of purple" (as does Phoenicia, the Greek name for the same general region), so called because Canaan was a major producer and exporter of purple dye, which was highly prized by royalty. The territory was much later called Palestine, named after the Philistim (v. 14).

The **sons of Cush** (i.e. the seven Cushite nations mentioned here; v. 7) were all in Arabia. Sheba and Dedan (or their namesakes) reappear as two of Abraham's grandsons (25:3). Together with Raamah, they are mentioned in Ezekiel 27:20 – 22.

The **Cush** (v. 8) listed here is probably not the same as that in 10:6 – 7. Located in Mesopotamia, its name may be related to that of the later Kassites. **Nimrod** has been variously identified but is possibly the Hebrew name of Sargon I, an early ruler of Accad (see 10:10).

10:10 – 12. Erech (v. 10) is the Hebrew name for Uruk (modern Warka), one of the important cities in ancient Mesopotamia. The **great city** (v. 12) is possibly Calah (or even Resen) but is most likely Nineveh (see Jonah 1:2; 3:2; 4:11), either alone or including the surrounding urban areas.

10:13 – 14. All the names listed here end in *-im*, indicating peoples or ethnic groups. **Ludim** is perhaps the Lydians in Asia Minor (v. 13; see discussion on 10:22). **Anamim** is located in north Africa, west of Egypt, near Cyrene. **Lehabim** is perhaps the Libyan desert tribes (see "Phut," in the discussion on 10:6). **Naphtuhim** are the people of Lower Egypt.

Pathrusim (v. 14) are the inhabitants of Upper Egypt (see discussion on v. 10:6). **Caphtorim** is Crete, known as Caphtor in ancient times, which was for a while the homeland of various Philistine groups (see Jer. 47:4; Amos 9:7). The Philistines were a vigorous Indo-European maritime people who invaded Egypt early in the twelfth century BC. After being driven out, they migrated in large numbers to southwest Canaan, later extending their influence over most of the land. The Philistines of the patriarchal period (see 21:32, 34; 26:1, 8, 14 – 15, 18) no doubt had earlier settled in Canaan more peacefully and in smaller numbers.

10:15. Sidon is an important commercial city on the northwest coast of Canaan. **Heth** is the progenitor of the Hittites, a powerful people centered in Asia Minor, who dominated much of Canaan from approximately 1800 to 1200 BC.

10:16 – 18. The Jebusite[s] (v. 16) inhabited Jerusalem at the time of Israel's conquest of Canaan. Jerusalem was also known as Jebus during part of its history (see Judg. 19:10 – 11; 1 Chron. 11:4). **Amorite** is a name that comes from an Akkadian word meaning "westerner" (west from the Babylonian perspective). The Amorites lived in the hill country of Canaan at the time of the Israelite conquest. Together with **the Girgashite[s]** (v. 16), the groups listed in verses 17 – 18 inhabited small city-states for the most part.

10:19 – 20. Sodom, and Gomorrah, and Admah, and Zeboim (v. 19) are four of the five cities of the plain (see 13:10; 14:2, 8). They were probably located east and/or southeast of the Dead Sea.

10:21. Unto Shem also … were children born. The descendants of Shem were called Shemites (later modified to Semites). Though **Eber** was a distant descendant of Shem (see vv. 24–25; 11:14–17), his importance as the ancestor of the Hebrews ("Eber" is the origin of the Hebrew word for "Hebrew") is already hinted at here. The Ebla tablets (see Introduction: "Background") frequently refer to a king named Ebrium, who ruled Ebla for twenty-eight years. It is possible that Ebrium and Eber were the same person.

10:22–24. Elam (v. 22) refers to the Elamites who lived east of Mesopotamia. **Asshur** is an early name for Assyria (see discussion on 2:14), in northern Mesopotamia. **Arphaxad** (see also 11:10–13) is perhaps a compound form of the Hebrew word for Chaldea, in southern Mesopotamia. **Lud** is probably the Lydians of Asia Minor (see "Ludim" in discussion on 10:13). **Aram** is located northeast of Canaan, the area known today as Syria.

10:25–31. Peleg (v. 25) is a name that means "division." Special attention is drawn to the fact that the **earth was divided** in his day. This apparently anticipates chapter 11 and places in his lifetime the dispersion of the people by new languages. **Joktan** (v. 26) is the predecessor of numerous southern Arabian kingdoms.

Sheba (v. 28) is in southwestern Arabia (roughly the area of Yemen). A later queen of Sheba made a memorable visit to King Solomon in the tenth century BC (see 1 Kings 10:1–13). **Ophir** (v. 29) was the source of much of King Solomon's gold (see 1 Kings 9:28; 10:11). Its location seems to have been south of Canaan, perhaps somewhere in Africa or south Arabia (but see discussion on 1 Kings 9:28).

10:32. In summary, this is the fourth time it is said that the sons and successors of Noah's three sons were **divided**, that is, dispersed, after the flood (due to language; see 10:5, 20, 31).

2. The Confusion of Tongues (11:1–9)

Chronologically earlier than chapter 10, this section provides the main reason for the scattering of the peoples listed there. The narrative is a beautiful example of inverted or hourglass structure (see Introduction: "Literary Features").

11:1–3. The whole earth (v. 1), that is, the whole human race, the descendants of the survivors of the flood (see 11:7–9; 10:1), spoke one language. They initially migrated eastward into the **land of Shinar** (v. 2), a reference to ancient Sumer, which was located in southern Mesopotamia. They decided on a building program of **brick for stone, and slime … for morter** (v. 3). Stone and mortar were used as building materials in Canaan. Stone was scarce in Mesopotamia, however, so mud bricks and slime were used (as indicated by archaeological excavations).

11:4. The people's plans were egotistical and proud, as seen in the multiple pronouns, **us … us … us … us … we**. The **tower** that they planned to build was likely similar to the typical Mesopotamian temple-tower, known as a *ziggurat*, which was square at the base and had sloping, stepped sides that led upward to a small shrine at the top. They intended that it would **reach unto heaven**. A similar ziggurat may be described in 28:12. Other Mesopotamian ziggurats were given names that demonstrate that they too were meant to serve as staircases from earth to heaven: "The House of the Link between Heaven and Earth" (at Larsa), "The House of the Seven Guides of Heaven and Earth" (at Borsippa), "The House of the Foundation-Platform of Heaven and Earth" (at Babylon), "The House of the Mountain of the Universe" (at Asshur). The people desired to make a **name** for themselves. In the Old Testament, "name" also refers to reputation, fame, or renown. (The giants [*nephilim*] were "men of renown [lit., 'name']," 6:4.) At Babel (see discussion on 11:9), rebellious humankind undertook a united and godless effort to establish for themselves, by a titanic enterprise, a world renown by which they would dominate God's creation (see 10:8–12; 2 Sam. 18:18). They hoped their efforts would prevent their being **scattered** (but see Gen. 11:8).

11:5–7. Described in anthropomorphic terms, the Lord came onsite to see the people's work. It can never be said that God judges capriciously and without necessary information.

The LORD said, Behold, the people is one (v. 6). If the whole human race were allowed to remained united in the proud attempt to take its destiny into its own hands and, by its man-centered efforts, to seize the reins of history, there would be no limit to its unrestrained rebellion against God. The kingdom of man would displace and exclude the kingdom of God.

God's **Go to, let us** from heaven (v. 7; see discussion on 1:26) counters proud man's "Go to, let us" (11:4) from earth. God purposed to prevent them from understanding **one another's speech**. Without a common language, joint effort became impossible (see 11:8).

11:8–9. God **scattered** (v. 8; see 11:4; 9:19) the people because of their rebellious pride. Even the greatest of human powers cannot defy God and long survive.

The place was named **Babel**, that is, Babylon (v. 9). The word is of Akkadian origin and means "gateway to a god" (Jacob's stairway was similarly called "the gate of heaven"; see 28:17). The Hebrew foot for **confound** (*balal*) sounds like "Babel," the Hebrew word for Babylon and the probable origin of the English word "babel." (The uncapitalized "babel" has as its meaning "the confusion of voices or sounds.")

3. The First Semitic Genealogy (11:10–26)

11:10–26. The generations of Shem (v. 10) is the fifth account to appear in Genesis (see discussion on 2:4). It is a ten-name genealogy, like that of Seth (see 5:3–31; see also discussion on 5:5). Unlike the Sethite genealogy, however, the genealogy of Shem does not give the ages of the men at their deaths and does not end each name with "and he died." It covers the centuries between Shem and Abram as briefly as possible.

The ten-name genealogy of Seth ended with Noah, who had three sons (5:32). Likewise, the ten-name genealogy of Shem ends with **Terah** (v. 26), who also had three sons: **Abram, Nahor, and Haran**.

As in the case of Shem, Ham, and Japheth, the names of the three sons may not be in chronological order by age (see 9:24; 10:21). Haran died while his father was still alive (see 11:28). Abram was 75 years old when he entered Canaan (12:4) after the death of his father, who died at the age of 205 (11:32), thus making Terah 130 years old when Abram was born. Abram is probably placed first in the list of sons due to his importance in the patriarchal account.

II. Patriarchal History (11:27–50:26)

A. The Life of Abraham (11:27–25:11)

1. Abraham's Background (11:27–32)

11:27–28. The generations of Terah (v. 27) is the sixth account to appear in Genesis (see discussion on 2:4).

The location of **Ur of the Chaldees** (v. 28) is debated. It is possibly the site on the Euphrates in southern Iraq that was excavated by Leonard Woolley between 1922 and 1934. Ruins and artifacts from Ur reveal a civilization and culture that reached high levels before Abram's time. King Ur-Nammu, who may have been Abram's contemporary, is famous for his law code. It is argued that since the moon-god was worshiped at both Ur and Haran (11:31), and since Terah was an idolater (see Josh. 24:2), he probably felt at home in both places. Another possible site is located in northern Mesopotamia, north of Haran. Haran seems to be too far north to be on the travel route from southern Ur to Canaan. Though etymology of names is not an exact science, it is worth noting that in addition to Haran (11:26), the names of Serug (11:21), Nahor (11:22), and Terah (11:24), all in the family line of Abraham, are represented in names of ancient sites in the vicinity of what has been identified as ancient Haran. Furthermore, 24:4–7, 10 defines northern Mesopotamia (Hebrew, *Aram-naharaim*; "Aram of the two rivers") as the land of Abraham's kindred.

11:29–30. The brothers all took wives (Haran had a son, Lot; see 11:31). Only Abram's wife **Sarai was barren** (v. 30). The sterility of Abram's wife (see 15:2–3; 17:17) emphasized the fact that God's people would not come by natural generation from the post-Babel peoples. God was bringing a new humanity into being, of whom Abram would be father (17:5), just as Adam and Noah were fathers of the fallen human race.

11:31. From the writer's perspective and for God's ultimate purpose, Abram left Ur of the Chaldees with his family to go to Canaan. According to Hebrews 11:8, however, Abram went out from Ur in faith, not knowing where God was taking him. The migrating family **came unto Haran**. In Hebrew, the name of the town is spelled differently from that of Abram's brother (11:26). Haran was a flourishing caravan city in the nineteenth century BC. In the eighteenth century BC, it was ruled by Amorites (see discussion on 10:16).

2. Abraham's Land (chaps. 12–14)

12:1. What Abram knew about God was not learned by tradition but by special revelation. According to Joshua 24:2, Abram's family served other gods. God had spoken to Abram "when he was in Mesopotamia, before he dwelt in Charran [Haran]" (Acts 7:2). God had said, **Get thee out ... unto a land that I will shew thee**. Abram had to leave the settled world of the post-Babel nations and begin a pilgrimage with God to a better world of God's making (see 24:7).

12:2–3. God's promise to Abram has a sevenfold structure: (1) **I will make of thee a great nation** (v. 2); (2) **I will bless thee**; (3) **and make thy name great**; (4) **thou shalt be a blessing** (v. 3); (5) **I will bless them that bless thee**; (6) **curse him that curseth thee**; and (7) **in thee shall all families of the earth be blessed**. God's original blessing on all mankind (1:28) would be restored and fulfilled through Abram and his offspring. In various ways and degrees, these seven promises were reaffirmed to Abram (11:7; 15:5–21; 17:4–8; 18:18–19; 22:17–18), to Isaac (26:2–4), to Jacob (28:13–15; 35:11–12; 46:3), and to Moses (Exod. 3:6–8; 6:2–8). The seventh promise is quoted in Acts 3:25 with reference to Peter's Jewish listeners (see Acts 3:12), Abram's physical descendants, and in Galatians 3:8, 16 with reference to Paul's Gentile listeners, Abram's

spiritual descendants. Both Peter and Paul show that ultimate fulfillment was found through Jesus Christ.

12:4–5. Abram departed, as the LORD had spoken unto him (v. 4; see Heb. 11:8). Prompt obedience grounded in faith characterized this patriarch throughout his life (see 17:23; 21:14; 22:3). **Lot went with him** (see 13:1, 5). Lot at first may have been little more than Abram's ward, but perhaps he chose to accompany Abram because of his God (2 Peter 2:7–8 describes him as a righteous man). Although **seventy and five years old**, quite advanced in age at the time of his call, Abram would live for another full century (see 25:7; see also discussion on 5:5).

Abram and Lot departed with all their possession and the **souls that they had gotten** (v. 5). Wealthy people in that age always had servants to help them with their flocks and herds (see 15:3; 24:2). Not all servants were slaves; many were voluntarily employed.

12:6–7. Abram's first stop in Canaan was **Sichem ... the plain of Moreh** (v. 6). Sichem (Shechem) was located in central Canaan and historically had religious significance (see 35:4; Josh. 24:26; Judg. 9:6, 37). "Plain" is better rendered "oak" or "terebinth." A large tree was often a conspicuous feature at such holy places. But Abram worshiped the Lord there, not the local deity. It was here that **the LORD appeared** (v. 7) to Abram for the first time in Canaan (v. 7). The Lord frequently appeared visibly to Abram and to others but not in all His glory (see Exod. 33:18–20; John 1:18). It was here also that Abram built **an altar**, the first of several that Abram built at places where he had memorable spiritual experiences (see 12:8; 13:18; 22:9). He acknowledged that the land of Canaan belonged to the Lord in a special way (see Exod. 20:24; Josh. 22:19). It was here that Abram is first promised that God would **give this land**, that is, Canaan, to his offspring.

12:8–9. Beth-el (v. 8) was located just north of Jerusalem and was an important town in the religious history of God's ancient people (see, e.g., 28:10–22; 35:1–8; 1 Kings 12:26–29). The only city mentioned more often than Bethel in the Old Testament is Jerusalem.

Abram continued traveling to the **south** (i.e., the Negev; v. 9), a term designating the dry wasteland stretching southward from Beersheba. The same Hebrew word, *negev*, is translated "southward" in 13:14.

12:10. Due to a famine in the land, Abram opted to go **down into Egypt ... for the famine was grievous**. Egypt's food supply was usually plentiful because the Nile's water supply was normally dependable.

12:11 – 13. Though Sarai was sixty-five at the time (compare 12:4; 17:17), she is described as **fair** (v. 11). The Genesis Apocryphon (one of the Dead Sea Scrolls) praises Sarai's beauty. Abram's experience in this episode foreshadows Israel's later experience in Egypt, as the author of Genesis, writing after the exodus, was very much aware. Abram was truly the father of Israel.

Fearing for his life, Abram instructed his wife in a half-truth. **Say, I pray thee, thou art my sister** (v. 13). Sarai was indeed his half sister (see 20:12), but the statement was meant to deceive. If Pharaoh knew that Sarai was Abram's wife and wanted to add her to his harem, Abram would have to be killed.

12:14 – 16. Indeed, **the Egyptians beheld** that Sarai was fair, and she **was taken into Pharaoh's house** (vv. 14 – 15). Pharaoh (probably not a personal name but a title) treated Abram well because of Sarai and gave him gifts (v. 16). Livestock was an important measure of wealth in ancient times (see 13:2), as were **menservants, and maidservants** (see 12:5). Although **camels** were not widely used until much later (see, e.g., Judg. 6:5), archaeology has confirmed their occasional domestication as early as the patriarchal period.

12:17 – 20. Though the disease that infected Pharaoh and his house is not stated, it made him aware that Sarai was Abram's wife. **Why saidst thou, She is my sister?** (v. 19). Egyptian ethics emphasized the importance of absolute truthfulness, and Abram was put in the uncomfortable position of being exposed as a liar. Abram was ordered to leave, but **Pharaoh commanded his men** (v. 20; see Exod. 12:31 – 32) to let Abram depart with his wife and all his possessions (including those newly acquired).

13:1 – 4. Abram left Egypt and returned to the **south** (i.e., the Negev; v. 1) with greater wealth than he had before, just as Israel would later leave Egypt laden with wealth from the Egyptians (Exod. 3:22; 12:36). Returning to Bethel, **Abram called on the name of the Lord** (v. 4), as he had done earlier at the same place (12:8).

13:5 – 7. Abram and Lot faced a critical problem. Livestock made up the greater part of their possessions, and the region around Bethel and Hai (Ai) did not have enough water or pasture for such large flocks and herds (see 13:10; 26:17 – 22, 32; 36:7). Compounding the problem was the presence of **the Canaanite and the Perizzite** (v. 7; see 12:6) who already lived in the area. "Perizzite" may refer to rural inhabitants in contrast to city dwellers.

13:8 – 9. Abram refused to be in conflict with his **brethren** (v. 8), that is, his relatives. Always generous, he gave his young nephew the opportunity to choose the land he wanted. He himself would not obtain wealth except by the Lord's blessing (see 14:22 – 24).

13:10 – 13. Lot saw the **plain of Jordan** (v. 10). The Hebrew for "plain" picturesquely describes this section of the Jordan Valley as oval in shape. It was **like the land of Egypt**. Because of its abundant and dependable water supply (see discussion on 12:10), Egypt came closest to matching Eden's ideal conditions (see 2:10). This description precedes the Lord's destruction of **Sodom and Gomorrah** (see 18:16 – 19:29). The names Sodom and Gomorrah became proverbial for vile wickedness and for divine judgment on sin. Archaeology has confirmed that prior to this catastrophe, the now dry area east and southeast of the Dead Sea (see discussion on 10:19) had ample water and was well populated.

Lot ... pitched his tent toward Sodom (v. 12). Since the men of Sodom were known to be wicked (see v. 13), Lot was flirting with temptation by choosing to live near them. Contrast the actions of Abram (13:18).

13:14 – 17. Lift up now thine eyes, and look (v. 14; see Deut. 34:1 – 4). Lot and Abram are a study in contrasts. The former looked selfishly and coveted (13:10); the latter looked as God commanded and was blessed. Though yet childless, the land he viewed was promised to his descendants, who would be **as the dust of the earth** (v. 16). The phrase is an appropriate simile (common in the ancient Near East) for the large number of Abram's offspring (see 28:14; 2 Chron. 1:9; see also Num. 23:10). Similar phrases are: "as the stars of the heaven" and "as the sand which is upon the sea shore" (22:17). Either to inspect the land or to exercise authority over it, demonstrating the promised ownership, Abram is instructed to **walk through the land in the length of it and in the breadth of it** (v. 17).

13:18. Abram returned to the **plain** (see discussion on 12:6) of **Mamre**, a site named after one of Abram's allies (see 14:13), located near **Hebron** (also known as Kirjath-arba; see discussion on 23:1–2). Here he built his second **altar** since entering Canaan (see discussion on 12:7).

14:1–4. An alliance of four eastern Mesopotamian kings led by **Amraphel king of Shinar** (ancient Sumer; v. 1) invaded the five cities of the plain. These were probably petty kings from the region, and thus they had need of an alliance. Though they and all their countries have not been positively identified from extrabiblical sources, Amraphel is not the great Babylonian king Hammurapi, as once thought. **Elam** refers to the Elamites east of Mesopotamia, but **nations** is obscure. The Hebrew word *goyim* means "Gentile nations" and may be used as a common noun here (as in Isa. 9:1).

Sodom and **Gomorrah** (v. 2) are the best known of the five cities that were overrun. These cities were located near the **salt sea** (v. 3). This is the Dead Sea, whose water contains a 25 percent concentration of chloride and bromide salts, making it the densest large body of water on earth.

14:5–7. The four eastern kings made a pass through the area south and west of the Dead Sea before attacking the five rebellious kings of the plain (14:2). In the process, the eastern kings **smote** (v. 5) a number of peoples and cities, some of which have been identified. The **Horites** (v. 6) were formerly thought to be cave dwellers (the Hebrew word *hor* means "cave"), but they are now known to have been

the Hurrians, a non-Semitic people widely dispersed throughout the ancient Near East. **En-mishpat** is another name for **Kadesh** (v. 7). It means "spring of judgment/justice." It is called Meribah-Kadesh, "quarreling/litigation at Kadesh," in Deuteronomy 32:51 (see Num. 27:14). It was located in the southwestern Negev (see discussion on 12:9), and was later called Kadesh-barnea (see Num. 32:8). The eastern alliance also smote the area later to be inhabited by **Amalekites**, a tribal people living in the Negev and in the Sinai peninsula in Moses' day.

14:8–12. The five kings of the plain did not fare well against the four eastern kings. They were forced to flee, and some fell in the area's **slimepits** (pits of asphalt or bitumen; v. 10). Lumps of asphalt are often seen, even today, floating in the southern end of the Dead Sea. Others fled to the **mountain** area that flanks both sides of the Dead Sea, the lowest body of water on earth (about 1,300 feet below sea level).

Among those taken captive was **Lot ... who dwelt in Sodom** (v. 12). He had moved into the town and was living among its wicked people (see 2 Peter 2:8). Though Lot was "righteous," he was now in danger of imitating the sensual conduct of wicked men (2 Peter 2:7).

14:13. Abram, the father of the Hebrew people, is the first biblical character to be called a **Hebrew** (see discussion on 10:21). Usually an ethnic term in the Bible, it was normally used by non-Israelites in a disparaging sense (see, e.g., 39:17). Outside the Bible, people known as the Habiru or Apiru (words probably related to "Hebrew") are referred to as a property-less, dependent, immigrant (foreign) social class rather than as a specific ethnic group. Negative descriptions of them are given in the Amarna letters (clay tablets found in Egypt). **Mamre** and his brothers allied themselves with Abram (14:24) to pursue and reclaim the captives taken by the eastern kings.

14:14. Three hundred and eighteen **trained servants** is a clear indication of Abram's great wealth. The Hebrew for "trained servants" is found only here in the Bible. A related word used elsewhere in very ancient texts means "armed retainers." Abram pursued as far as **Dan**. This well-known city in the north was formerly known as Laish and was not given the name Dan until the days of the judges (Judg. 18:29). The designation here is apparently an editorial updating subsequent to Moses' time.

14:15 – 17. Abram brought back the captives and was met by the king of Sodom at the **king's dale** (v. 17), a site thought to be near Jerusalem, probably to the east (see 2 Sam. 18:18).

14:18. Abram was met also by **Melchizedek king of Salem ... he was the priest**. In ancient times, particularly in non-Israelite circles, kingly and priestly duties were often performed by the same individual. Melchizedek means "my king is righteousness" or "king of righteousness" (see Heb. 7:2). "Salem" is a shortened form of Jerusalem (see Ps. 76:2) and is related to the Hebrew word for "peace" (see Heb. 7:2). The name Adoni-zedek, another king of Jerusalem (see Josh. 10:1), is very similar to that of Melchizedek and means "my lord is righteousness" or "lord of righteousness." **Bread and wine** was an ordinary meal (see Judg. 19:19) and is in no way related to the New Testament ordinance of communion. Melchizedek offered the food and drink as a show of friendship and hospitality.

14:19. He was priest of *El Elyon*, that is, the **most high God, possessor of heaven and earth**. The titles "most high," "lord of heaven," and "creator of earth" were frequently applied to the chief Canaanite deity in ancient times. Terminology and location (Jerusalem was in central Canaan) thus indicate that Melchizedek was probably a Canaanite king-priest. But Abram, by identifying Melchizedek's "most high God" with "the LORD" (14:22), bore testimony to the one true God, whom Melchizedek had come to know.

14:20. Abram **gave him tithes of all** the spoils (see Heb. 7:2, 4). Although Melchizedek's view of God was no doubt deficient, Abram's response to his blessing seems to indicate that he recognized that Melchizedek served the same God he did (see 14:18). So Abram took the occasion to offer him a tithe of his spoils for the **most high God**. One-tenth was the king's share (see 1 Sam. 8:15, 17). Melchizedek

is later spoken of as a type or prefiguration of Jesus, our "great high priest" (Heb. 4:14), whose priesthood is therefore in "the order of Melchizedek," not "after the order of Aaron" (Heb. 7:11; see Ps. 110:4).

14:21 – 24. Abram refused to accept for himself any of the spoils from the king of Sodom. **I have lift up mine hand** (v. 22). The raising of the hand when making an oath was common practice in ancient times (see Deut. 32:40; Rev. 10:5 – 6). In so doing, Abram acknowledged that everything he possessed was given him by the **most high God**, who possessed even **heaven and earth**.

I will not take any thing that is thine (v. 23). Abram refused to let himself become obligated to anyone but the Lord. Had he done so, this Canaanite king might later have claimed the right of kingship over Abram.

3. Abraham's People (chaps. 15 – 24)

15:1. Fear not Abram. What Abram fears has been interpreted variously: fear of retaliation from the eastern kings (chap. 14), fear of conversing with God (as here), fear of remaining childless (15:2). **I am thy shield**. The Hebrew word is literally "shield," thus promising Abram protection. However, it is sometimes used symbolically or figuratively as "sovereign" (e.g., Deut. 33:29; 2 Sam. 22:3; Pss. 7:10; 84:9). Whether "shield" or "sovereign" is meant, the reference is to the Lord as Abram's King, who would also be Abram's **exceeding great reward**. Though Abram was quite rich (13:2), God Himself was Abram's greatest treasure (compare Deut. 10:9).

15:2 – 4. Chapters 15 – 16 deal with Abram's continued childlessness, in spite of God's promises of descendants, and how Abram attempted to remedy the situation. **Eliezer of Damascus** (v. 2) is a servant, probably acquired by Abram on his journey southward from Haran (see 12:5). He may also be the unnamed "servant" of 24:2. Ancient documents uncovered at Nuzi (see chart, *KJV Study Bible*, p. xix) near Kirkuk on a branch of the Tigris River, as well as at other places, demonstrate that a childless man could adopt one of his male servants to be heir and guardian of his estate. Abram apparently contemplated doing this with Eliezer or perhaps had already done so. Abram learns that his heir will be one that he himself has fathered.

15:5. Look ... tell the stars ... number them (see 22:17). More than eight thousand stars are clearly visible in the darkness of a Near Eastern night. The promise **so shall thy seed be** was initially fulfilled in Egypt (see Exodus 1; Deut. 1:10; Heb. 11:12). Ultimately, all who belong to Christ are Abram's spiritual offspring (see Gal. 3:29).

15:6. Abram is the "father of all them that believe" (Rom. 4:11), and Genesis 15:6 is the first specific reference to faith in God's promises. Abram **believed**, and his faith was credited to him **for righteousness**. The apostle Paul (Rom. 4:10) notes that Abram's righteousness was credited before any "work" of circumcision, which came years later (see chap. 17). God graciously responds to a man's faith by crediting righteousness to him (see Heb. 11:7).

15:7–8. God is about to reaffirm His covenant with Abram, with a very solemn ritual. **I am the LORD that brought thee out** (v. 7). Ancient royal covenants often began with (1) the self-identification of the king and (2) a brief historical prologue, as here (see Exod. 20:2). Abram believed God's promise of a son, but he asked for a guarantee of the promise of the land: **whereby shall I know ...?** (v. 8).

15:9–11. For the prescribed ritual, Abram took select animals that were **three years old** (v. 9), the prime age for most sacrificial animals (see 1 Sam. 1:24). These he divided in half, but the selected **birds divided he not** (v. 10). Perhaps they were too small (see Lev. 1:17).

15:12–15. A deep sleep (v. 12; see 2:21) set Abram aside, while God spoke and acted. What God was about to do was unconditional. Abram could sense God's awesome presence in the darkness.

Abram learned that his descendants would be outside Canaan and in a **land that is not theirs** (v. 13; that the land would be Egypt is not revealed until later, 46:3–4) for **four hundred years**. This is a round number. According to Exodus 12:40, Israel spent 430 years in Egypt. Abram, however, would die first, **in a good old age** (v. 15; see 25:8).

15:16. His descendants would return to Canaan **in the fourth generation**, that is, after 400 years (see 15:13). A "generation" was the age of a man when his first son (from a legal standpoint) was born—in Abram's case, 100 years (see 21:5). The land was not given to Abram and his descendants immediately because **the iniquity of the Amorites is not yet full**. Just how sinful many Canaanite religious practices were is now known from archaeological artifacts and from their own epic literature, discovered at Ras Shamra (ancient Ugarit) on the north Syrian coast, beginning in 1929 (see chart, *KJV Study Bible*, p. xix). Their "worship" was polytheistic and included child sacrifice, idolatry, religious prostitution, and divination (Deut. 18:9–12). God was patient in judgment, even with the wicked Canaanites.

15:17. Abram witnessed a **smoking furnace, and a burning lamp**. This symbolized the presence of God (see Exod. 3:2; 14:24; 19:18; 1 Kings 18:38; Acts 2:3–4). The blazing torch **passed between those pieces** of the slaughtered animals (15:10). In ancient times, the parties solemnized a covenant by walking down an aisle flanked by the pieces of slaughtered animals (see Jer. 34:18–19). The practice signified a self-maledictory oath: "May it be so done to me if I do not keep my oath and pledge." Having credited Abram's faith as righteousness, God now graciously ministered to his need for assurance concerning the land. He granted Abram a promissory covenant, as He had to Noah (see 9:9 and discussion; see also chart, *KJV Study Bible*, p. 16).

15:18. Thus, God **made a covenant**. The Hebrew is literally "cut a covenant," referring to the slaughtering of the animals (the same Hebrew verb is translated "made" and "cut" in Jer. 34:18). The Lord initially fulfilled this covenant concerning the land through Joshua (see Josh. 1:2–9; 21:43; see also 1 Kings 4:20–21). The southern boundary of the land is the **river of Egypt**. This is probably the modern Wadi el-Arish in northeastern Sinai.

15:19–21. The people presently living in the land are listed in these verses. A similar list of ten peoples is found in 10:15–18 (see discussions there). The number ten signifies completeness.

16:1 – 3. Having been forbidden to adopt Eliezer, Abram now attempts to acquire children through another culturally acceptable means, through a surrogate mother, because Sarai still bore him **no children** (v. 1; see 11:30). Perhaps **Hagar**, the **Egyptian** maid introduced here, was acquired while Abram and Sarai were in Egypt (see 12:10 – 20).

Sarai faced the cultural stress of barrenness but blamed her inability on God: **the Lord hath restrained me from bearing** (v. 2). Some time had passed since the revelation of 15:4 (see 16:3), and Sarai impatiently implied that God was not keeping His promise. Therefore, she offered Hagar to Abram: **go in unto my maid.** Her offer reflects an ancient custom, illustrated in Old Assyrian marriage contracts, the Code of Hammurapi, and the Nuzi tablets (see discussion on 15:2 – 4), to ensure the birth of a male heir. Sarai would herself solve the problem of her barrenness. **Ten years** (v. 3) had passed since Abram had been promised children (12:4), and he was now eighty-five years old (see 16:16).

16:4 – 6. Once Hagar conceived, **her mistress was despised in her eyes** (v. 4). Peninnah acted similarly toward Hannah (see 1 Sam. 1:6). Sarai was offended and angry. Her hostility or suspicion toward her husband is seen in her statement, **the Lord judge between me and thee** (v. 5; see 31:53; 31:49).

16:7 – 8. Sarai's harsh treatment caused Hagar to flee, but the **angel of the Lord** (v. 7) intercepted her. Since the angel of the Lord speaks for God in the first person (16:10) and Hagar "called the name of the Lord that spake unto her, Thou God seest me" (16:13), the angel appears to be both distinguished from the Lord (in that he is called "messenger"; the Hebrew for "angel" means "messenger") and identified with Him. (Similar distinction and identification can be found in 19:1, 21; 31:11, 13; Exod. 3:2, 4; Judg. 2:1 – 5; 6:11 – 12, 14; 13:3, 6, 8 – 11, 13, 15 – 17, 20 – 23; Zech. 3:1 – 6; 12:8.) Traditional Christian interpretation has held that this angel was a pre-incarnate manifestation of Christ as God's Messenger-Servant. It may be, however, that as the Lord's personal messenger who represented Him and bore His credentials, the angel could speak on behalf of (and so be

identified with) the One who sent him (see especially 19:21; see also 18:2, 22; 19:2). Whether this angel was the second person of the Trinity therefore remains uncertain. Hagar was stopped on the road to **Shur**, located east of Egypt (see 25:18; 1 Sam. 15:7). Since Hagar did not yet know exactly where she was going, she answered only the first of the angel's questions: **I flee from the face of my mistress** (v. 8).

16:9 – 12. Hagar is promised descendants too numerous to count, a promise reaffirmed in 17:20 and fulfilled in 25:13 – 16. She is instructed to name her son **Ishmael** (meaning "God hears"; v. 11) since God had heard her misery. Her son would be a **wild man** (lit., a "wild donkey of a man"; v. 12). Away from human settlements, Ishmael would roam the desert like a wild donkey (see Job 24:5; Hos. 8:9). **In the presence of** his brethren is literally "to the face of," possibly suggesting "in defiance of." The hostility between Sarai and Hagar (see 16:4 – 6) would be passed on to their descendants (see 25:18).

16:13. Hagar's response to what she has been told is to call the Lord **Thou God seest me** (Hebrew, *El Roi*). **Have I also here looked after him that seeth me?** This question might be better rendered as a declarative or exclamatory statement in that she marvels that she is living, having just seen God (compare Exod. 33:23). To see God's face was believed to bring death (see 32:30; Exod. 33:20).

16:14 – 16. She named the place **Beer-lahai-roi** (v. 14). The name means "the well of the living one who sees me." Another possible translation that fits the context equally well is "well of the one who sees me and who lives."

Hagar thus produced a son for Abram, who was now eighty-six years old. Thirteen years later (see 17:1), Abram will learn that Sarai, his wife, will bear for him the promised covenant son (17:19).

17:1. Thirteen years had passed since Ishmael's birth (see 16:16; 17:24 – 25). Abram's faith was stretched when God **appeared** (see discussion on 12:7) and revealed new truth regarding Himself, His covenant, and His plans for Abram. **I am the Almighty God** (see discussion on 15:7). This was the special name by which God revealed Himself to the patriarchs (see Exod. 6:3). The name in Hebrew (*El Shaddai*) possibly means "God, the Mountain One," either highlighting the invincible power of God or referring to the mountains as God's symbolic home (see Ps. 121:1). Another, and perhaps more favorable, meaning finds the root of *Shaddai* in the verb *shadad*, "to destroy" or "to overpower." Thus, God is the "one who overpowers." Such meaning fits the context well. God introduced Himself to Abraham by this name before declaring that Sarai, who was barren and beyond the years of childbearing, would have her natural condition overpowered by God, and she would bear a son. *Shaddai* occurs thirty-one times in the book of Job and seventeen times in the rest of the Bible. **Walk before me, and be thou perfect** is perhaps equivalent to "Walk with me, and be blameless" (see discussions on 5:22; 6:9–12). After Abram's and Sarai's attempt to obtain the promised offspring by using a surrogate mother, God appeared to Abram. The Lord made it clear that if Abram was to receive God's promised and covenanted benefits, he must be God's faithful and obedient servant and accept what he is about to hear. His faith must be accompanied by "obedience to the faith" (Rom. 1:5; see Genesis 22).

17:2–3. God refers to the covenant with Abram as **my covenant** (v. 2; see 12:2–3; 13:14–16; 15:4–5). He calls it "my covenant" nine times in 17:2–21. He initiates (see 15:18), confirms (v. 2), and establishes (17:7) it. **I will ... multiply thee** (see 13:16 and discussion). Earlier God had covenanted to keep His promise concerning the land (chap. 15); here He broadens His covenant to include the promised offspring. (See chart, *KJV Study Bible*, p. 16.)

17:4–5. God begins with His own involvement: **As for me** (v. 4). Since Abram is to become the **father of many nations**, God will give him a new name. It will no longer be **Abram**, but **Abraham** (v. 5). The first name means "exalted father," perhaps in reference to God ("[God is] Exalted Father"); the second means "father of many," in reference to Abraham. By giving Abram a new name (see Neh. 9:7), God marked him in a special way as His servant (see discussions on 1:5; 2:19).

17:6. From Abraham would come **nations** and **kings**. This promise came also to Sarah (17:16) and was renewed to Jacob (35:11; see 48:19). It referred to the proliferation of Abraham's offspring, who, like the descendants of Noah (chap. 10), would someday become many nations and spread over the earth. Ultimately, it finds fulfillment in such passages as Romans 4:16–18; 15:8–12; Galatians 3:29; and Revelation 7:9; 21:24.

17:7–8. From God's standpoint, the covenant was **everlasting** (v. 7; see 17:13, 19), but from man's standpoint, it could be broken (see 17:14; Isa. 24:5; Jer. 31:32). **I will be a God unto thee.** This is the heart of God's covenant promise, repeated over and over in the Old Testament (e.g., Gen. 17:8; Jer. 24:7; 31:33; Ezek. 34:30–31; Hos. 2:23; Zech. 8:8). This is His pledge to be the protector of His people and the One who provides for their well-being and guarantees their future blessing (see 15:1).

The **land of Canaan** (v. 8; see 12:7; 15:18; Acts 7:5), though an **everlasting possession** given by God, could be temporarily lost because of disobedience (see Deut. 28:62–63; 30:1–10).

17:9. Having reviewed His covenanted commitment to Abraham (see 15:8–21) and having broadened it to include the promise of offspring, God now called upon Abraham to make a covenanted commitment to Him—to "walk before me, and be thou perfect" (17:1). **Thou** ("As for you") balances the "As for me" of 17:4. **Thou shalt keep my covenant.** Participation in the blessings of the Abrahamic covenant was conditioned on obedience (see 18:19; 22:18; 26:4–5).

17:10–14. Circumcision was God's appointed **token** (sign) **of the covenant** (v. 11), which signified Abraham's covenanted commitment to the Lord—that the Lord alone would be his God, whom he would trust and serve. It symbolized a self-maledictory oath (analogous to the oath to which God had submitted Himself; see discussion on 15:17): "If I am not loyal in faith and obedience to the Lord, may the sword of the Lord cut off me and my offspring [see v. 14] as I have cut off my foreskin." Thus, Abraham was to place himself under the rule of the Lord as his

King, consecrating himself, his offspring, and all he possessed to the service of the Lord. (For circumcision as signifying consecration to the Lord, see Exod. 6:12; Lev. 19:23; 26:41; Deut., 10:16; 30:6; Jer. 4:4; 6:10; 9:25 – 26; Ezek. 44:7, 9.) Other nations also practiced circumcision (see Jer. 9:25 – 26; Ezek. 32:18 – 19), but not for the covenant reasons that Israel did.

As the covenant sign, circumcision also marked Abraham as the one to whom God had made a covenant commitment (15:7 – 21) in response to his faith, which God "counted … to him for righteousness" (15:6). Paul comments on this aspect of the covenant sign in Romans 4:11.

The set age for circumcision was **eight days old** (v. 12; for the circumcision of Isaac, see Gen. 21:4 and Acts 7:8; John the Baptist, Luke 1:59; Jesus, Luke 2:21; Paul, Phil. 3:5). Abraham was ninety-nine years old when the newly initiated rite of circumcision was performed on him (see 17:24). The Arabs, who consider themselves descendants of Ishmael, are circumcised at the age of thirteen (see 17:25). For them, as for other peoples, it serves as a rite of transition from childhood to manhood, thus into full participation in the community.

For Abraham's male descendants, anyone who was not circumcised was to be **cut off from his people** (v. 14), that is, removed from the covenant people by divine judgment.

17:15 – 22. God's attention turns to Abraham's wife: **As for Sarai** (v. 15; see 17:4 and discussion on 17:9). Her name is changed from **Sarai** to **Sarah**. Both names evidently mean "princess." The renaming stressed that she was to be the mother of nations and kings (v. 16) and thus to serve the Lord's purpose (see discussion on 17:5).

Sarah, who had been barren, is promised a **son** (v. 16). In temporary disbelief she laughed (see 18:12; see also Rom. 4:19 – 21). The verb is a pun on the name Isaac, which means "he laughs" (see v. 19; 18:12 – 15; 21:3, 6).

Abraham's concern for Ishmael led God to reiterate His earlier promise to Hagar that He would **multiply him** (v. 20; see 16:10) and to add that Ishmael would father **twelve princes**. The fulfillment is recorded in 25:16. All the blessings of God's covenant with Abraham, however, are to be realized through Isaac (see 21:2 – 3). Paul cites the choice of Isaac (and not Ishmael) as one proof of God's sovereign right to choose to save by grace alone (see Rom. 9:6 – 13).

God's promise that Sarah would have a son **at this set time in the next year** (v. 21) was reiterated in 18:14 and fulfilled in 21:2. Then **God went up from Abraham** (v. 22), thus bringing a solemn conclusion to the conversation.

17:23 – 27. Abraham, like Noah (6:22), was characterized by prompt obedience (see discussion on 12:4), for in **the selfsame day** (v. 23), he, his son Ishmael, and all the men of his house were circumcised.

18:1. Within a short time (see 17:21; 18:14; 21:2), the Lord **appeared** again to Abraham (see 12:7; 17:2), who was resting outside his tent in **the heat of the day**, the early afternoon.

18:2 – 8. Abraham saw **three men** (v. 2). At least two of the "men" were angels (see 19:1; see also discussion on 16:7). The third may have been the Lord Himself (see 18:22, 1, 13, 17, 20, 26, 33).

The story in verses 2 – 8 illustrates Near Eastern hospitality in several ways: (1) Abraham gave prompt attention to the needs of his guests (vv. 2, 6 – 7). (2) He bowed low to the ground (v. 2). (3) He politely addressed one of his guests as **My lord** and called himself **your servant** (vv. 3, 5), a common way of speaking when addressing a superior (see, e.g., 19:2; 18 – 19). (4) He acted as if they would be doing him a favor if they allowed them to serve them (vv. 3 – 5). (5) He asked that water be brought to wash their feet (v. 4), an act of courtesy to refresh a traveler in a hot, dusty climate (see 19:2; 24:32; 43:24). (6) He prepared a lavish meal for them (vv. 5 – 8; a similar lavish offering was presented to a divine messenger in Judg. 6:18 – 19; 13:15 – 16). (7) He stood nearby (v. 8), assuming the posture of a servant (see 18:22), to meet their every wish. (The example of hospitality to strangers cited in Heb. 13:2 is probably a reference to Genesis 18:2 – 8 and 19:1 – 3.)

18:9 – 15. The previous promise that Sarah would bear a son (17:21) is repeated, this time in the hearing of Sarah, who was inside the tent. Paul quotes this promise of Isaac's birth (v. 14) in Romans 9:9 and relates it to Abraham's spiritual offspring (Rom. 9:7–8).

The eavesdropping Sarah **laughed** in disbelief (v. 12), as Abraham had (17:17). Her unvoiced question, **shall I have pleasure …?** expected the answer no. For the Lord's voiced response, **Is any thing too hard for the Lord?** (v. 14), the answer is also no, for Sarah as well as for her descendants Mary and Elisabeth (see Luke 1:34–37). Nothing within God's will, including creation (see Jer. 32:17) and redemption (see Matt. 19:25–26), is impossible for Him. Sarah had not yet realized that the one speaking was the omnipotent One who would enable her to conceive ("Is anything too hard?") and the omniscient One who knew her thoughts (**thou didst laugh**; v. 15).

18:16–19. As the three men prepared to leave on their journey to the notorious city of **Sodom** (v. 16; see discussion on 13:10), their conversation continued in Abraham's hearing. **Shall I hide from Abraham that thing which I do?** (v. 17). Abraham is considered a prophet (20:7), one to whom God revealed His secrets (Amos 3:7). As one destined to become **a great and mighty nation** through whom all nations would be blessed (v. 18; see discussion on 12:2–3), Abraham was indeed God's friend (v. 19; see 2 Chron. 20:7; James 2:23; see also discussion on Isa. 41:8). Because he was now God's covenant friend (see Job 29:4), God convened His heavenly council at Abraham's tent. There He announced His purpose for Abraham (18:10) and for the wicked of the plain (18:20–21)—redemption and judgment. He thus even gave Abraham opportunity to speak in His court and to intercede for the righteous in Sodom and Gomorrah. Here, in Abraham, is exemplified the great privilege of God's covenant people throughout the ages: God has revealed His purposes to them and allows their voice to be heard (in intercession) in the court of heaven.

I know him (v. 19). In Hebrew usage, "to know" sometimes connotes "to choose" (see, e.g., Amos 3:2). Abraham was chosen to pass on to his descendants the spiritual legacy of a covenantal relationship with God.

18:20–21. The **cry of Sodom and Gomorrah** (v. 20), two chief cities of the plain, is a cry of righteous indignation (compare 4:10, regarding the blood of Abel) that became one of the reasons for the destruction of the cities (see 19:13). The sin of Sodom (and probably of Gomorrah as well) was already proverbial (see 13:13) and remained so for centuries (see Ezek. 16:49–50).

I will go down (v. 21). On this occasion, the result would be judgment (as in 11:5–9), but God also comes down to redeem (as in Exod. 3:8). Going on location to **see** the sin is not a denial of God's infinite knowledge but a figurative way of stating that He does not act out of ignorance or based on mere complaints.

18:22–31. **Abraham stood yet before the Lord** (v. 22). This illustrates the mutual accessibility that existed between God and His servant. It is also the second time Abraham intervened for his relatives and for Sodom (see 14:14–16). His appeal is bold and frank in expressing his misgivings but is never presumptuous. He based his prayer on what he understood of God's character. **Shall not the Judge of all the earth do right?** (v. 25). Abraham based his plea on the justice and authority ("Judge" could be translated "Ruler") of God, confident that God would do what was right (see Deut. 32:4).

Abraham used the title **Lord** (v. 27), not the intimate name Lord, in his prayer. He was appealing to God as "Judge of all the earth." In contrast to God's exalted position, Abraham described himself as insignificant as **dust and ashes** (see Job 30:19; 42:6).

18:32. I will speak yet but this once. Abraham's earnest questioning in 18:23–32 did not arise from a spirit of haggling but from compassion for his relatives and wanting to know God's ways. Perhaps Abraham stopped at **ten** people because he had been counting while praying: Lot, his wife, possibly two sons (see 19:12), at least two married daughters and their husbands (see 19:14), and two unmarried daughters (see 19:8).

18:33. Having completed intercession with the Lord, Abraham returned to **his place**, that is, to his tent at Mamre (see 18:1). The next morning Abraham went back to see what God had done (see 19:27).

19:1. The **two angels** (the Hebrew text has the definite article) who had accompanied the Lord (see discussion on 18:2) came to Sodom in the evening. It is possible that Lot, who **sat in the gate of Sodom**, had become a member of Sodom's ruling council, since a city gateway served as the administrative and judicial center where legal matters were discussed and prosecuted (see Ruth 4:1–12).

19:2. The angels refused Lot's offer of hospitality, stating their intention to spend the night in the **street**, that is, in a large open space near the main city gateway (see 2 Chron. 32:6) where public gatherings were held. Important cities like Jerusalem could have two or more such places (see Neh. 8:16).

19:3. Knowing their potential danger, Lot persuaded them to accept the safety of his home and offered them a meal that included **unleavened bread**, which could be baked quickly (see 18:6; Exod. 12:39).

19:4–11. The horrific action recorded here with its disgusting details was sadly repeated among the Israelites in the time of the judges (see Judg. 19:22–25). What follows is not the performance of local hoodlums but reveals the debased character of the men, **old and young** from **every quarter** of the city (v. 4).

The men of the city demanded to have Lot's guests so that they could **know them** (v. 5). This is euphemistic language for sexual relations (see 4:1). Homosexuality was so characteristic of the men of Sodom (see Jude 7) that it is still often called sodomy.

Do not so wickedly (v. 7). Peter describes Lot as a righteous man who was tormented by the deeds of Sodom (2 Peter 2:7–8). He preferred to offer his virgin daughters to the wicked men rather than have them molest the men who were **under the shadow of** his roof (v. 8). Ancient hospitality obliged a host to protect his guests in every situation. To protect his guests, he was willing to sacrifice the virginity of his daughters, their safety, and their reputation.

This one fellow came in to sojourn, and he will needs be a judge (v. 9). To these wicked men, Lot, who stood in their way, was a moralist. Centuries later, Moses was also considered an outsider and ac-

cused of setting himself up as a judge (see Exod. 2:14; Acts 7:27). The angels "saved the day" by blinding the wicked men.

19:12–22. The intention of the angels is made known: **we will destroy this place** (v. 13). Sodom's wickedness had made it ripe for destruction (see Isa. 3:9; Jer. 23:14; Lam. 4:6; Zeph. 2:8–9; 2 Peter 2:6; Jude 7). Though Lot was given an opportunity to persuade loved ones to flee the city, **he seemed as one that mocked unto his sons in law** (v. 14). Lot had lost his power of moral persuasion even among his family members. Apparently, his words were inconsistent with his previous lifestyle.

Even Lot **lingered** (v. 16), perhaps because he was reluctant to leave his material possessions. The ten righteous people required to save Sodom (see 18:32) was reduced to four as the angels forcefully, but mercifully, removed Lot, his wife, and his two daughters from the city. Deliverance is due to divine mercy, not to human righteousness (see Titus 3:5). Mercy was granted even for Lot to flee to nearby **Zoar** (v. 22) rather than to more distant mountains. Lot's presence there apparently spared the city (see 14:2 and Deut. 29:23).

19:23–26. The LORD **rained … brimstone and fire** (v. 24). The conflagration may have resulted from a violent earthquake spewing up and raining down volatile asphalt (see discussion on 14:10), such as is still found in this region.

Sadly, Lot's **wife looked back … and she became a pillar of salt** (v. 26). Her disobedient hesitation (see 19:17) became proverbial in later generations (see Luke 17:32). Grotesque salt formations seen even today near the southern end of the Dead Sea are reminders of her folly.

19:27–29. To see if his prayer for the city had been answered, Abraham returned the next day to the place where he had petitioned the Lord, and he witnessed the telltale smoke of destruction. However, **God remembered Abraham** (v. 29; see discussion on 8:1). **God … sent Lot out of the midst of the overthrow.** Lot's deliverance was the main concern of Abraham's prayer (18:23–32), which God now answered on behalf of Abraham, his friend.

19:30–36. Out of sinful desperation, Lot's daughters contrived a way to conceive by their own father. **They made their father drink wine … and the firstborn went in, and lay with her father** (v. 33). Though Lot's role was somewhat passive, he bore the basic responsibility for the drunkenness and incest that eventually resulted in his two daughters' becoming pregnant by him (v. 36). Is their action any surprise after having been reared in Sodom and offered to wicked men (19:8)?

19:37–38. The sons born to Lot's daughters were the ancestors of the Moabites and Ammonites (see Deut. 2:9, 19), two nations that were to become bitter enemies of Abraham's descendants (see, e.g., 1 Sam. 14:47; 2 Chron. 20:1).

20:1–2. Abraham migrated from Mamre (18:1) southward (to the Negev) **between Kadesh and Shur** before settling for a while at **Gerar** (v. 1). This site was located at the edge of Philistine territory, about halfway between Gaza on the Mediterranean coast and Beersheba in the northern Negev. Here Abraham lied again about his relationship to Sarah (v. 2; see 12:12). **Abimelech** (v. 2), the Philistine king of the region (26:1), saw Sarah and, like Pharaoh in Genesis 12, took her into his harem.

20:3. This time by means of a **dream**, God once again intervened to spare the mother of the promised offspring (see 12:17–18). Dreams were a frequent mode of revelation in the Old Testament (see 28:12; 31:10–11; 37:5–9; 40:5; 41:1; Num. 12:6; Judg. 7:13; 1 Kings 3:5; Dan. 2:3; 4:5; 7:1). Abimelech learned not only that he had taken another man's wife but also that she was the wife of a covenant man, the friend of God.

20:4–8. Thinking Sarah was Abraham's sister, Abimelech had done what was culturally acceptable. Therefore, in his eyes what he had done was **in the integrity of** his **heart and innocency of** his **hands** (v. 5). Yet God had been at work. He had protected Sarah from the king by preventing him from touching her.

Abraham was the first man to bear the title of **prophet** (v. 7; see discussion on 18:16–19; Ps. 105:15). The one who had prayed for Sodom now,

as a prophet, was called upon to pray for Abimelech (see 20:17).

20:9–13. The covenant man is scolded by the pagan king. The one who was to be a blessing to others (12:2) had brought the rebuke and judgment of God instead (see 20:18).

Abraham's confession begins with a rationalization. **I thought, Surely the fear of God is not in this place** (v. 11). "The fear of God" is a conventional phrase equivalent to "true religion." Here "fear" has the sense of reverential trust in God that includes commitment to His revealed will (word). Abraham's true relationship to Sarah is now revealed. **She is my sister; she is the daughter of my father, but not the daughter of my mother** (v. 12). Abraham's half-truth was a sinful deception, not a legitimate explanation. What is worse, perhaps, is that the deception was a long-term agreement between them to protect Abraham at Sarah's expense.

20:14–16. Abimelech's generosity was a strong contrast to Abraham's fearfulness and deception. Abimelech gave to Abraham, Sarah's **brother** (a note of sarcasm?) a thousand **pieces** (i.e., shekels) **of silver** (v. 16). Originally, the shekel was only a weight, not a coin, since coinage was not invented till the seventh century BC. The silver was intended to be a **covering of the eyes**, that is, to remove Sarah's shame and embarrassment and to restore her reputation.

20:17–18. Abraham's prayer (see 20:7) for Abimelech and his wives reversed God's judgment upon them.

21:1–4. Isaac was indeed a son of "promise" (see Gal. 4:22–23, 28), for God **visited Sarah as he had said … as he had spoken**, and the ninety-year-old Sarah (v. 1; see 17:17) conceived and bore a son. As commanded, Abraham, who once laughed in God's presence, named his son **Isaac** (v. 3), meaning "he laughs" (17:19). On the eighth day, Abraham fulfilled his covenant obligation of circumcising his son (see 17:10–12).

21:5–8. Abraham, in fulfillment of the promise made to him (see 17:16), miraculously became a father at the age of one hundred years (see 17:17). Sarah, who also laughed in disbelief in God's presence (see 18:12), now laughs again, but this time it is a laugh of celebratory joy. It was a time of festivity when Isaac was weaned. The customary age for weaning in the ancient Near East was at age two or three.

21:9. Times of great blessing are often followed by severe testing. The birth of Isaac was a blessing, but what followed was a test. Ishmael, **the son of Hagar** (v. 9), who was in his mid to late teens at this time (see 16:15–16), was seen **mocking** Isaac. The Hebrew root of this word is the same as Isaac's name, "to laugh," but Ishmael's action was intense, for the New Testament says he was "persecuting" Isaac (Gal. 4:29). Sarah saw Ishmael as a potential threat to Isaac and his inheritance.

21:10–13. Sarah speaks with disdain. **Cast out this bondwoman and her son** (v. 10; see Gal. 4:21–31). Driving them out would have had the effect of disinheriting Ishmael. Such a demand **was very grievous in Abraham's sight** (v. 11). Both love and legal custom played a part in Abraham's anguish. He knew that the customs of his day, illustrated later in the Nuzi tablets (see chart, *KJV Study Bible*, p. xix), prohibited the arbitrary expulsion of a servant girl's son (whose legal status was relatively weak in any case).

Hearken unto her (Sarah's) **voice** (v. 12). God overruled in this matter, as He had done earlier (see 15:4), promising Abraham that both Isaac and Ishmael would have numerous descendants. It was not to be forgotten, however, that **in Isaac shall thy seed be called** (see Rom. 9:6–8 and Heb. 11:17–19 for broader spiritual applications of this statement).

21:14. Though Abraham would now be separated from Ishmael for the first time, he responded **early in the morning** to God's command, sending Hagar and Ishmael away, with prompt obedience (see discussion on 12:4). The general area of Hagar's wandering is the **wilderness of Beer-sheba**, but it is not named as such with significance until after a later event (see discussion on 21:31).

21:15–20. Hagar's expectation of her son's imminent death from thirst led her to weep in despair. Once again, God met her need where she was (see 16:7). **God heard … God hath heard** (v. 17). Twice the verb "heard" is used, thus drawing attention to

the pun on the name Ishmael, which means "God hears" (16:11). Ishmael will not die, for God promised to **make him a great nation** (v. 18; see 17:20).

21:21. Ishmael grew up in the **wilderness of Paran**, which is located in north-central Sinai. That **his mother took him a wife out of the land of Egypt** is not unusual, for parents often arranged their children's marriages (see chap. 24).

21:22–24. Abimelech (v. 22) may be the son or the grandson of the earlier king who bore the same name (see 20:2). **Phichol** is either a family name or an official title, since it reappears over sixty years later (25:26) in a similar context (26:26). The Philistine king recognized the blessing of God upon Abraham and requested an alliance with him. **Swear unto me … by God … the kindness that I have done … thou shalt do unto me** (v. 23). These phrases were commonly used when making covenants or treaties (see 21:27, 32). "Kindness" as used here refers to acts of friendship (see 21:27; 20:14). Such covenants always involved oaths.

21:25–31. Abraham used the occasion to complain of maltreatment from Abimelech's servants but complied with the request and provided the **sheep and oxen** (v. 27), animals probably to be used in the treaty ceremony (see 15:10). Seven ewe lambs were set apart as a gift for Abimelech, who then recognized Abraham's rights to the well he had dug. **Beer-sheba** became the name of the place **because there they sware both of them** (v. 31). Beersheba can mean "well of seven" or "well of the oath" (for a similar pun on the name, see 26:33). Beersheba, an important town in the northern Negev, marked the southernmost boundary of the Israelite monarchy in later times (see, e.g., 2 Sam. 17:11). An ancient well there is still pointed out as "Abraham's well" (see v. 25), but its authenticity is not certain.

21:32–33. Though history shows the Philistines migrating into the area largely around 1200 BC, earlier waves of migration could account for the **land of the Philistines** already present in Abraham's day.

Abraham planted a **grove** (v. 33), that is, a tamarisk tree, which is a shrub or small tree that thrives in arid regions. Its leafy branches provide welcome shade, and it is probably the unidentified bush under which Hagar put Ishmael in 21:15. There he invoked the name of the Lord, the **everlasting God**. Hebrew *El Olam* is a phrase unique to this passage. It is one of a series of names that include *El*, "God," as an element (see 14:19 and discussion; 17:1 and discussion; 33:20; 35:7).

22:1. After these things permits Isaac to have grown by this time into adolescence or young manhood, as implied also by 21:34 ("many days"). **God did tempt Abraham**; that is, He "tested" him. God does not tempt (James 1:13). Satan tempts (see 1 Cor. 7:5) to cause a fall; God tests to confirm faith (Exod. 20:20) or prove commitment (Deut. 8:2). The test was this: Would Abraham obey God's command to slay his son as a sacrifice when it contradicted God's promise that "in Isaac shall thy seed be called" (21:12)? Abraham answered with, **here I am**, the response of a servant, as did Moses and Samuel when God called them by name (see Exod. 3:4; 1 Sam. 3:4, 6, 8).

22:2. Take now thy son, thine only son Isaac, whom thou lovest. In the Hebrew text, Isaac's name is placed last in this sequence in order to heighten the effect. Though Abraham had two sons, Isaac was the "only son" of the promise (21:12). The **land of Moriah** is identified by the author of Chronicles as the area of the temple mount in Jerusalem (2 Chron. 3:1). Today Mount Moriah is occupied by the Dome of the Rock, an impressive Muslim structure erected in AD 691. It is believed that a large outcropping of rock inside the building still points to the traditional site of the intended sacrifice of Isaac. **Offer him there for a burnt offering**. Abraham had committed himself by covenant to be obedient to the Lord and had consecrated his son Isaac to the Lord by circumcision. The Lord put His servant's faith and loyalty to the supreme test, thereby instructing Abraham, Isaac, and their descendants as to the kind of total consecration the Lord's covenant requires. The test also foreshadowed the perfect consecration in sacrifice that another offspring of Abraham would undergo (see discussion on 22:15–16) to wholly consecrate Abraham and his spiritual descendants to God and to fulfill the covenant promises.

22:3–5. Once again prompt obedience, even under such trying circumstances, characterized Abraham's response to God, as he rose **early in the morning** (v. 3; see 21:14) to go the place God had instructed him to go. Three days would be necessary for the journey from Beersheba (see 22:19) to Jerusalem. His words to his servants, **I and the lad will ... come again to you** (v. 5), mark Abraham as a man of faith and "the father of all them that believe" (Rom. 4:11). He considered "that God was able to raise him [Isaac] up, even from the dead" (Heb. 11:19) if that were necessary to fulfill His promise. The Hebrew for "lad" has a wide range of meanings, from an infant (see Exod. 2:6) to a young man of military age (see 1 Chron. 12:28).

22:6–12. Isaac the "lad" (22:5) was old enough to be aware of the missing ingredient for sacrifice — the lamb. **God will provide himself a lamb** (v. 8). The immediate fulfillment of Abraham's trusting response was the ram of verse 13, but its ultimate fulfillment is the Lamb of God (John 1:29, 36). In obedience, Abraham **laid him on the altar upon the wood** (v. 9). Isaac is here a type (prefiguration) of Christ (see discussion on 22:15–16). Abraham's movement to kill Isaac is interrupted by the **angel of the Lord** (v. 11; see discussion on 16:7). The repetition of the name **Abraham, Abraham** indicates urgency (see 46:2; Exod. 3:4; 1 Sam. 3:10; Acts 9:4). Abraham had passed the test, showing that he feared God (see discussion on 20:11). He had **not withheld** his **only son** (v. 12). His faith was "made perfect" by what he had done (James 2:21–22).

22:13. Substitutionary sacrifice of one life for another, **in the stead of**, is here mentioned for the first time. As the ram died in Isaac's place, so also Jesus gave His life as a ransom "for" (lit., "instead of") many (Mark 10:45).

22:14. Therefore, Abraham called the place **Jehovah-jireh** (lit., "Jehovah will be seen," i.e., the "Lord will be seen" as a provider). During the Israelite monarchy, the phrase **the mount of the Lord** referred to the temple mount in Jerusalem (see Ps. 24:3; Isa. 2:3; 30:29; Zech. 8:3).

22:15–16. By myself have I sworn (v. 16). There is no greater name in which the Lord can take an oath (see Heb. 6:13). Abraham's devotion to God, seen in his not withholding his son, is paralleled by God's love expressed in Christ, as reflected in John 3:16 and Romans 8:32, which may allude to this verse.

22:17–19. God's analogies promising a multiplication of Abraham's seed (as the "dust of the earth," 13:16; as the "stars" of the heavens, 15:5) are expanded to include the **sand which is upon the sea shore** (v. 17). This is fulfilled, at least in part, during Solomon's reign (see 1 Kings 4:20). Taking possession of the **gate** of a city was tantamount to occupying the city itself (see 24:60). Once again the messianic implication (see Acts 3:25; Gal. 3:1) of the covenant is emphasized: **in thy seed shall all the nations of the earth be blessed** (v. 18; see discussion on 12:2–3).

22:20–24. Though these verses may at first appear intrusive to the narrative, they anticipate Isaac's need for a wife (chap. 24). Abraham's brother **Nahor** (see 11:26) became the father of eight sons by his wife, **Milcah** (v. 20), and four by his concubine, **Reumah** (v. 24). They would later become the ancestors of twelve Aramean (see v. 21) tribes, just as Abraham's grandson Jacob would become the ancestor of the twelve tribes of Israel (see 49:28).

23:1–2. Sarah, who conceived through faith (Heb. 11:11) and was cited as the model godly wife by Peter (2 Peter 3:6), died at age 127 at **Kirjatharba** (also known as Hebron; v. 2). The name means "the town of Arba." (Arba was the most prominent member of a tribe living in the Hebron area; see Josh. 14:15.) It can also mean "the town of four," referring to the place where Anak (see Josh. 15:13–14; 21:11) and his three sons lived (see Judg. 1:10, 20). Abraham **came to mourn**, meaning either that he came from Beersheba to Hebron or that he came into the place where Sarah's body was lying.

23:3–4. Sarah's death presented Abraham with a huge problem—where to bury his wife—because he didn't own land to be used for a burial plot. He was forced to appeal to the **sons of Heth** (v. 3), that is, the Hittites (see discussion on 10:15), who were apparently in control of the Hebron area at this time.

I am a stranger and a sojourner (v. 4). This and similar phrases were used often by the patriarchs and their descendants in reference to themselves (see 1 Chron. 29:15; Ps. 39:12; Heb. 11:13). On this earth, Abraham was dwelling in tents (Heb. 11:9), the most temporary of dwellings. He looked forward to the more permanent home promised him, which the author of Hebrews calls "a city which hath foundations, whose builder and maker is God" (Heb. 11:10).

23:5–9. The Hittites' response, **thou art a mighty prince** (v. 6), was probably intended as flattery, and they offered him burial privileges in their own sepulchers. Abraham, however, appealed to purchase the **cave of Machpelah** (v. 9), which was owned by Ephron. Though inaccessible today, the tombs of several patriarchs and their wives—Abraham and Sarah, Isaac and Rebekah, Jacob and Leah (see 23:19; 25:8–10; 49:30–31; 50:12–13)—are, according to tradition, located in a large cave deep beneath the Mosque of Abraham, a Muslim shrine in Hebron. The cave was situated at the **end of his** (Ephron's) **field**. Because buying the entire field would have made Abraham responsible for certain additional financial and social obligations, he wanted to buy only a small part of it. Hittite laws stipulated that when a landowner sold only part of his property to someone else, the original and principal landowner had to continue paying all dues on the land. If the landowner disposed of an entire tract, the new owner had to pay the dues.

23:10–16. In the audience of the children of Heth … at the gate (v. 10), Ephron negotiated the terms for selling the cave. The main gateway of a city was usually the place where legal matters were transacted and attested (see 23:18; and discussion on 19:1). Perhaps intending either to honor or to flatter Abraham by calling him **my lord** (v. 11), Ephron offered to **give** him (or "sell" to him) the entire field with the cave. He persisted, stating a price of **four hundred shekels of silver** (v. 15; see discussion on 20:16). Despite Ephron's pretense of generosity, four hundred shekels of silver was an exorbitant price for a field (see, e.g., Jer. 32:9). Ephron was taking advantage of Abraham during a time of grief and bereavement. He knew that Abraham had to deal quickly to obtain a place to bury Sarah, so he insisted that Abraham buy the entire lot and assume responsibility for the dues as well.

Abraham paid him **current money with the merchant** (v. 16); that is, he weighed out the silver according to the commercial standard, one that was subject to more variation and therefore greater dishonesty than the later royal standard (see 2 Sam. 14:26), which was carefully regulated and more precise.

23:17 – 20. The purchased land is described as **the field, and the cave which was therein, and all the trees** (v. 17). To be free of all obligations relating to the field in which the cave of Machpelah was located, Ephron had held out for the sale of the entire field and its contents (see discussion on 23:9).

In this cave, then, Abraham **buried Sarah his wife … in the land of Canaan** (v. 19). In that culture, people had a strong desire to be buried "with [their] fathers" (47:29 – 30) in their native land. By purchasing a burial place in Canaan, Abraham indicated his unswerving commitment to the Lord's promise. Canaan was his new homeland.

24:1. The events of this chapter occurred approximately three years after Sarah's death (see 24:67; 25:20). The issue Abraham now faced was finding a wife for Isaac. The precautions and stipulations he set forth for obtaining her is a paradigm against which the actions of Isaac and Jacob must be compared.

24:2. Though the **eldest servant of his house** is not named, it was probably Eliezer of Damascus (see discussion on 15:2). The strange command, **Put … thy hand under my thigh**, that is, near the organ of procreation, was probably meaningful to the culture because this oath was related to the continuation of Abraham's line through Isaac (see 47:29).

24:3 – 4. The majestic title used here by Abraham, **the Lord, the God of heaven, and the God of the earth** (v. 3), is similar to that used in an earlier oath (14:22). **Thou shalt not take a wife … of the Canaanites.** Isaac's wife must not be from a pagan people that might draw him away from the Lord after Abraham was dead (the same principle is stated years later in Exod. 34:15 – 16). She must

be from Abraham's **country** (v. 4), northern Mesopotamia (see discussion on 24:10), and from his kindred (see 22:20 – 24; Abraham's brother Nahor had a large family). The servant was to **take a wife** for Isaac from there (see discussion on 21:21). It was not a relative per se that Abraham sought for Isaac, but a woman who would leave her family to marry a stranger and, in becoming a wife to Isaac, identify totally with him and his God against the religious culture of Canaan. A relative who knew of Abraham would be most likely to leave the comfort zone of home and immediate family.

24:5 – 9. To the servant's question regarding a contingency plan, Abraham adamantly responded, **Beware thou shalt not bring my son thither again** (v. 6). Ever mindful of God's leading him (12:1), he would not permit his son to leave the land promised to him (12:7) and find himself among relatives that might persuade him, in order to marry their daughter, to remain with them outside the covenant land. The servant took the oath and accepted the challenge.

24:10. Setting out with **ten camels** (see discussion on 12:16) laden with gifts (24:53), the servant came to **Mesopotamia**. The Hebrew is *Aram-naharaim*, meaning "Aram of the two rivers," the Euphrates and the Tigris. Aram (see discussion on 10:22) Naharaim was the northern part of the area that the Greeks later called Mesopotamia, meaning "between the rivers." The **city of Nahor**, to which the servant came, was perhaps named after Abraham's brother (see 24:15; 11:26). It is mentioned in clay tablets excavated by the French beginning in 1933 at the ancient city of Mari on the Euphrates (see chart, *KJV Study Bible*, p. xix). Nahor was located in the Haran district (see discussion on 11:31) and was ruled by an Amorite prince in the eighteenth century BC.

24:11 – 14. The servant arrived **at the time of the evening** (v. 11), the coolest time of day, when women went **out to draw water**. His dilemma was to determine whom God had chosen for Isaac. **Thereby shall I know** (v. 14). Like his master Abraham, the servant asked God for a sign to validate his errand (see discussion on 15:8). In essence, the stipulations he set forth as a sign established the qualifications for

Isaac's bride: a woman who was courteous, cheerful, unselfish, and ready to serve. Nothing was said about physical beauty.

24:15-22. Before he had done speaking (v. 15), God had already begun to answer (see Matt. 6:8). **Rebekah**, who had the right pedigree, **born to Bethuel, son of ... the wife of Nahor, Abraham's brother** (see 22:20-24), appeared and fulfilled all the stipulations of the servant's prayer. Isaac would thus be marrying his father's grandniece (see 24:48). Before questioning the girl further, the servant gave her gifts for service already rendered.

24:23-27. Upon learning of Rebekah's pedigree and being invited to lodge in her father's house, the servant responded in a most exemplary manner. He immediately **bowed down his head and worshipped the Lord** (see 24:48, 52) in gratitude for answered prayer.

24:28-33. When the girl's brother, **Laban** (v. 29), saw the gifts that had been given her, he said, **Come in, thou blessed of the Lord** (v. 31). Though he himself did not know and serve the Lord, he recognized that the God Abraham obeyed and followed to Canaan had brought him blessing. (On the hospitality granted the servant in verses 32-33, see discussion on 18:2.)

24:34-49. The Lord hath blessed my master greatly (v. 35). Though all credit is given to the Lord, the prosperity and financial standing of his master had to be established first. Then the servant explained his mission to Rebekah's family. His speech, which summarizes the narrative of the earlier part of the chapter, is an excellent example of the ancient storyteller's art, which was designed to fix the details of a story in the hearer's memory.

24:50-53. The thing proceedeth from the Lord (v. 50). After hearing the servant's story, there was no denying that this was so. Rebekah's showing up at the well in answer to the servant's prayer was providential, not coincidental. Her father and brother could only respond, **Take her ... [to] be thy master's son's wife** (v. 51). The rich gifts bestowed on Rebekah and her family in verse 53 indicated the wealth of the household into which she was being

asked to marry—far from her loved ones and homeland. The family was assured their daughter would be well provided for.

24:54-60. The servant was ready to respond the next morning. **Hinder me not** (v. 56). He recognized the Lord's leading, and he knew Abraham was awaiting his return. The longer the servant waited, the more difficult it might become for Rebekah to leave her family. She parted with their blessing: **Be thou the mother of thousands of millions** (v. 60). Little did they know that their daughter was marrying into a "covenant family" and that their blessing unwittingly touched on the Abrahamic covenant (see 22:17).

24:61-67. In anticipation, Isaac went out as far as **the well Lahai-roi** (v. 62; see discussion on 16:14) to await the return of the servant. When Rebekah saw Isaac, **she took a veil, and covered herself** (v. 65). This was apparently a sign that she was unmarried (see 38:14, 19) or a sign of modesty and respect. Rebekah was courageous to come this far, but she was not bold in approaching her husband-to-be. Isaac brought her to his deceased **mother Sarah's tent** (v. 67), which was used as a bridal chamber (see Ps. 19:4-5).

4. Abraham's Last Days (25:1-11)

25:1-6. Abraham took a wife (v. 1); that is, he married another woman—his "concubine" (1 Chron. 1:32). If the order of events is chronological, Abraham would have been 140 years old at this time. **Keturah** provided him with six more sons. Abraham, however, **gave all that he had unto Isaac** (v. 5). The law of primogeniture provided that at least a double share of the father's property be given to the firstborn son when the father died (Deut. 21:15-17). Parallels to this practice come from Nuzi, from Larsa in the Old Babylonian period, and from Assyria in the Middle Assyrian period. Isaac was Abraham's firstborn son according to law.

Gifts (v. 6), doubtless representing a token inheritance, were left to Abraham's other sons of his two **concubines**, Hagar and Keturah. Concubines were secondary wives. Polygamy was practiced even by godly men in ancient times, though it was not the original divine intention (see discussion on 4:19). The other sons were dismissed from Canaan, and only Isaac was permitted to remain in the covenant land.

25:7 – 11. The writer jumps ahead to write the conclusion of Abraham's life. When Abraham died, Ishmael was eighty-nine years old, Isaac was seventy-five, and Isaac's twin sons, Esau and Jacob, were fifteen years old. Abraham had lived for a full century after "he departed out of Haran" (12:4), and he died at **an hundred threescore and fifteen years** of age (v. 7). Thus, as God had promised (15:15), he **died in a good old age ... and was gathered to his people** (v. 8); that is, he joined his ancestors in death (see 2 Kings 22:20; 2 Chron. 34:28). **Isaac and Ishmael** (v. 9) joined to bury their father. Isaac was legally the firstborn and thus is listed first.

B. The Descendants of Ishmael (25:12 – 18)

25:12 – 18. The generations of Ishmael (v. 12) is the seventh account to appear in Genesis (see discussion on 2:4). The list of the **names of the sons of Ishmael** (v. 13) contains Arab names, giving credence to the Arab tradition that Ishmael is their ancestor. Reference to **twelve princes** (v. 16), that is, "tribal rulers," indicate that twelve major tribes descended from Abraham's son Ishmael (as predicted in 17:20) — as was also true of Abraham's brother Nahor (see discussion on 22:20 – 24). **He died** (v. 18) is literally "he fell." It may have the meaning "he settled" or "he dwelt." **In the presence of all his brethren** (i.e., his relatives) has been interpreted variously: (1) He lived "close" to them, (2) he lived "in defiance of" them (see discussion on 16:10 – 12), or (3) he lived "to the east of" them (see 25:6).

C. The Life of Jacob (25:19 – 35:29)

1. Jacob at Home (25:19 – 27:46)

25:19 – 22. The generations of Isaac (v. 19) is the eighth account to appear in Genesis (see discussion on 2:4). His story begins with his marriage to Rebekah, who came from **Padan-aram** (v. 20), or the "plain of Aram," another name for Aram-naharaim (in northwest Mesopotamia; see discussion on

24:10). Isaac was **forty years old** when he married, and children were not born to him until he was sixty. Unlike his father, he did not resort to adoption or a concubine when Rebekah did not conceive; instead, he **intreated the LORD** on her behalf (v. 21).

Once Rebekah conceived, the children **struggled together within her** (v. 22). The struggle between Jacob and Esau began in the womb (see also 25:26). A perplexed Rebekah **went to enquire of the LORD**, perhaps at a nearby place of worship. Apparently, Isaac's God had become her God (see discussion on 24:3 – 4; compare Ruth 1:16).

25:23. Rebekah learned that **the elder shall serve the younger**. The ancient law of primogeniture (see discussion on 25:5) provided that, under ordinary circumstances, the younger of two sons would be subservient to the older. God's election of the younger son highlights the fact that God's people are the product not of natural or worldly development but of His sovereign intervention in the affairs of men (see discussion on 11:30). Part of this verse is quoted in Romans 9:10 – 12 as an example of God's sovereign right to do whatever He pleases (see Ps. 115:3), not in an arbitrary way (see Rom. 9:14) but according to His own perfect will.

25:24 – 25. The birth of the twins was unusual, somewhat like the birth of another set of twin boys at a later time (see 38:27 – 30). Wordplay was used in the naming of the two sons, one due to his appearance, the other due to his action. The first, Esau, was **red** (v. 25) when he was born. The Hebrew for "red" is a pun on Edom, one of Esau's other names (see 25:30). He was also **hairy**. The name Esau sounds somewhat like the Hebrew for "hairy."

25:26. At birth, the **hand** of the second son **took hold on Esau's heel**. He was named **Jacob**, meaning "heel grabber." His name became proverbial for the unsavory quality of deceptiveness (see Jer. 9:4). Hostility between the Israelites (Jacob's descendants) and Edomites (Esau's descendants) became the rule rather than the exception (see, e.g., Num. 20:14 – 21; Obadiah 9 – 10).

25:27 – 28. Isaac and Rebekah made the tragic parental mistake of having favorite sons. In spite of God's clear selection of the younger son (25:23), Isaac favored Esau, his firstborn, the **hunter** and **man of the field** (v. 27).

25:29–34. Catching Esau at a physically and emotionally weak moment, Jacob took advantage of his brother. **Sell me ... thy birthright** (v. 31). In ancient times, the birthright included the inheritance rights of the firstborn (see Heb. 12:16; discussion on Gen. 25:5). Jacob was ever the schemer, seeking by any means to gain advantage over others. It was by God's appointment and care, not by Jacob's wits, that he came into the blessing.

Jacob demanded, **Swear to me** (v. 33), knowing that a verbal oath was all that was required to make the transaction legal and the birthright his. All Esau gained was **pottage of lentiles** (v. 34). The lentil plant is a small pea-like annual, the pods of which turn reddish-brown when boiled. It grows well even in bad soil and has provided an important source of nourishment in the Near East since ancient times (see 2 Sam. 17:28; 23:11; Ezek. 4:9). **Thus Esau despised his birthright**, and in so doing, he proved himself to be "profane" (Heb. 12:16), since at the heart of the birthright were the covenant promises that Isaac had inherited from Abraham.

26:1–33. At first read, it might seem that the events of some of these verses (e.g., vv. 1–11) occurred before the birth of Esau and Jacob. Three times in this chapter, however, events are compared to **the days of Abraham** (vv. 1, 15, 18), seemingly assuming he is now deceased, and it was noted in 25:7 that Isaac's sons were fifteen years old when Abraham died. Also, it is assumed that Abraham is dead since Isaac moves about and makes decisions apart from his father's company and influence.

26:1. The famine Isaac faced is compared to **the first famine ... in the days of Abraham** (see 12:10). He joined **Abimelech**, probably the son or grandson of the earlier king who bore the same name (see 20:2), at **Gerar** (see discussion on 20:1).

26:2–6. Isaac may have gone to Egypt had the Lord not **appeared unto him** (v. 2; see discussion on 12:7) and prevented such a move. **I will be with thee** (v. 3). God's promise to be a sustainer and protec-

tor of His people is repeated often (see, e.g., 26:24; 28:15; 31:3; Josh. 1:5; Isa. 41:10; Jer. 1:8,19; Matt. 28:20; Acts 18:10; see also Gen. 17:7 and discussion). **The oath which I sware unto Abraham thy father** (see 12:2–3; 13:16; 15:5), perhaps most recently in Isaac's hearing (see 22:16–18), is now rehearsed to Isaac alone, but he reaps the benefit of his father's obedience (see discussion on 17:9). The terms **charge**, **commandments**, **statutes**, and **laws** (v. 5) are legal terms describing various aspects of the divine regulations that God's people were expected to keep (see Lev. 26:14–15, 46; Deut. 11:1). Addressing Israel after the covenant at Sinai, the author of Genesis used language that strictly applied only to that covenant. He emphasized to Israel that their father Abraham had been obedient to God's will in his time and that they must follow his example if they were to receive the covenant promises.

26:7–11. Like his father before him (see 12:11, 14), Isaac was concerned because his wife **was fair to look upon** (v. 7). He feared she would be viewed as a candidate for Abimelech's harem and thus his own life might be in jeopardy. Therefore, she was instructed to lie about their relationship. The truth was made evident when Isaac was seen **sporting** ("caressing") **with Rebekah** (v. 8). The word in Hebrew (a form of the verb translated "laugh" in 17:17; 18:12–13, 15; 21:6 and "mock" in 21:9) is yet another pun on Isaac's name. Once again God's covenant man is reprimanded by a pagan ruler for being less than truthful about his marriage relationship (see 12:18; 20:9).

26:12–16. The Lord's blessings on Isaac's crops and his many flocks and servants also caught the attention of the Philistines, so out of envy and fear of him, they filled in the wells that Abraham had dug years earlier and insisted that Isaac leave the area. They said, **Thou art much mightier than we** (v. 16). Here is a clear indication that the covenant promises were being fulfilled. Already in the days of the patriarchs, the presence of God's people in the land was seen as a threat by the peoples of the world. As the world's people pursued their own godless living, God's people aroused their hostility. A similar complaint was voiced by an Egyptian pharaoh hundreds of years later (Exod. 1:9).

26:17 – 22. Though Isaac left the immediate area, the Philistine resistance to him persisted. When **Isaac digged again the wells** (i.e., he reopened them; v. 18) his father had dug, the herdsmen of Gerar followed him and claimed, **The water is ours** (v. 20). In those arid regions, disputes over water rights and pasturelands were common (see 13:6 – 11; 21:25; 36:7). Isaac named each well he reopened according to the controversy he experienced. The first was named **Esek**, a word related to "contention"; the second was **Sitnah** (v. 21), related to the word "accusation"; and the third was **Rehoboth** (v. 22), related to "open spaces."

26:23 – 25. With Isaac's move to Beersheba came the Lord's second appearance to him and a reassurance of His presence and protection (see 26:2 – 4). Isaac's response was to build **an altar** (v. 25), the first attributed to him (see discussion on 12:7), where he **called upon the name of the LORD**; that is, he worshiped there.

26:26 – 33. At Beersheba, Isaac was visited by **Abimelech** and **Phichol** (v. 26; see discussion on 21:22), who apparently felt guilty and were uneasy about how Isaac had been mistreated (26:13 – 22). Therefore, they requested **an oath ... a covenant** (v. 28) with him to assure their peace and safety. So Isaac **made them a feast** (v. 30). Covenants were often concluded with a shared meal, signifying the bond of friendship (see 31:54; Exod. 24:11). That same day, his servants found water (see v. 25), and Isaac called the well **Shebah**, meaning "oath." This is the second event (see discussion on 21:31) that provided occasion for **the name ... Beer-sheba** (v. 33).

26:34 – 35. Like his father, Isaac, **Esau was forty years old** when he married (v. 34; see 25:20). Forty years was roughly equivalent to a generation in later times (see Num. 32:13). In addition to the two wives he married at this time, **Judith** and **Bashemath**, Esau also married Mahalath, who was the sister of Nebajoth and the daughter of Ishmael (28:9). The genealogy of Esau in chapter 36 also mentions three wives, but they are identified as "Adah the daughter of Elon the Hittite," "Aholibamah the daughter of Anah ... the Hivite," and "Bashemath, Ishmael's daughter, sister of Nebajoth" (36:2 – 3). Possibly the lists have suffered in transmission, or perhaps alternate names or nicknames are used. It may also be that Esau married more than three wives. Because these women **were a grief of mind**, Isaac and Rebekah were determined not to allow Jacob to make the same mistake of marrying Hittite or Canaanite women (see 27:46 – 28:2).

27:1 – 5. A comparison of measured times and people's ages (30:25 – 26; 31:41; 41:46 – 47; 45:6; 47:9) shows that thirty-seven years had passed since Esau married (26:34). Esau and Jacob were now 77 years old, and their aged father was 137. **His eyes were dim, so that he could not see** (v. 1). In ancient times, blindness and near blindness were common among elderly people (see 48:10; 1 Sam. 4:15). **I know not the day of my death** (v. 2). Having reached the age when his half brother Ishmael had died (see 25:17), Isaac anticipated his own death. His request for **savoury meat, such as I love** (v. 4) may indicate his need for a meal that would lift his spirit and give strength for the blessing or may show the dignity and importance of the occasion. His only stated purpose was **that my soul may bless thee before I die**. Oral statements, including deathbed bequests (see 49:28 – 33), had legal force in ancient Near Eastern law. The request was **heard** by Rebekah (v. 5), who was eavesdropping. She and Jacob took advantage of Isaac's love for a certain kind of food (see 27:9, 14).

27:6 – 10. Throughout the Jacob account, the author develops a wordplay on "birthright" (*bekorah*) and "blessing" (*berakah*), both of which Jacob seeks to obtain. **Rebekah** (*ribqah*) does her best to further the cause of her favorite son. Isaac had called his eldest son, Esau, and Rebekah **spake unto Jacob her son** (v. 6). The parental favoritism mentioned in 25:28 is about to bear its poisonous fruit. **My son, obey my voice according to that which I command thee** (v. 8). Rebekah proved to be just as deceitful as Jacob, whose very name signified deceit (see 27:36; 25:26 and discussion). She had devised a plan for

Jacob to receive Isaac's blessing, apparently also anticipating **his death** (v. 10).

27:11–17. For Jacob, deception was not an issue; being caught, exposed, and cursed by his father was. Thus, his mother's unprincipled encouragement: **Upon me be thy curse** (compare the similar self-imprecation in Matt. 27:25). Knowing that Isaac could not see, mother and son attempted to confuse his other senses: taste (young goat for venison), smell (wearing Esau's clothes), touch (applying goat's skin to make Jacob feel hairy). Only Isaac's hearing could not be misled (27:22).

27:18–29. Jacob's deception necessitated a series of lies. The ultimate lie was to credit **the LORD** (v. 20) for his quick return from hunting. The phrase **thy God** is consistent with Jacob's language elsewhere (31:5, 42; 32:9). Not until after his safe return from Haran did he speak of the Lord as his own God (see 28:20–22; 33:18–20).

Art thou my very son Esau? (v. 24). To the very end of the charade, Isaac remained suspicious. To the end, Jacob persisted in lying, believing in his own cause. Even a token of love was debased to deception. He approached his father and **kissed him** (v. 27). In his attempt to obtain the covenant blessing, Jacob, the father of Israel, betrayed with a kiss. Jesus, the great Son of Israel, who ultimately obtained the blessing for Israel, was betrayed with a kiss (Matt. 26:48–49; Luke 22:48).

Apparently believing that his hearing was also failing and that Esau was truly the one before him, Isaac blessed Jacob. **Be lord over thy brethren** (v. 29). He was unwittingly blessing Jacob and thus fulfilling God's promise to Rebekah in 25:23. Though the blessing conforms closely to the promise to Abraham (12:3), perhaps because Isaac thinks he is blessing Esau, he does not say, "In thee shall all families of the earth be blessed."

27:30–40. Isaac soon knew he had been deceived, and he **trembled very exceedingly** (v. 33). Why? In fear, because he knew that Jacob was indeed the son of promise (see 25:23)? Because he had attempted to bless Esau, who had "despised his birthright" and was a "profane person" (see 25:34;

Heb. 12:16)? Because Esau had married pagan wives (see 26:34)?

Esau's plea for a blessing showed repentance (i.e., a "change of mind") for having sold his birthright, but there was now no place for the blessing (Heb. 12:17). **Yea, and he shall be blessed** (v. 33). The ancient world believed that blessings and curses had a kind of magical power to accomplish what they pronounced. Isaac, as heir and steward of God's covenant blessing, acknowledged that he had solemnly transmitted that heritage to Jacob by way of a legally binding bequest (see discussion on 27:4). There would be no change, in spite of Esau's **great and exceeding bitter cry** (v. 34).

Is not he rightly named Jacob? (v. 36). Jacob means "he grasps the heel" (figuratively, "he deceives"; see 25:26 and discussion). **He took away my birthright … now he hath taken away my blessing**. The Hebrew for "birthright" is *bekorah*, and "blessing" is *berakah* (see discussion on 27:6). Though Esau tried to separate birthright from blessing, the former led inevitably to the latter since both involved the inheritance of the firstborn.

Thy dwelling shall be the fatness of the earth, and of the dew of heaven (v. 39). The Hebrew suggests that Esau would live "away from" the fatness of the earth, "away from" the dew of heaven, that is, outside Canaan (see 27:28). Isaac's secondary blessing of Esau could be only a parody of his primary blessing of Jacob. He concluded with a general reiteration of God's prediction to Rebekah (25:23).

27:41–46. The days of mourning for my father are at hand (v. 41). Esau also expected his father to die soon (see 27:2, 10), although Isaac lived on to reach the age of 180. Ever her son's guardian, Rebekah admonished Jacob, **Obey my voice** (v. 43). This was bad advice earlier (see 27:8, 13) but sensible counsel this time. Going to Haran to be with Laban **a few days** to escape Esau's revenge turned into a twenty-year venture (see 31:38, 41). She hoped to avoid losing **you both** (v. 45), a reference either to Jacob (a victim of murder) and Isaac (due to old age) or to Jacob and Esau, who would become a target for blood revenge if he killed Jacob (see 2 Sam. 14:6–7). Rebekah's plea to

Isaac sought two results: a wife for Jacob unlike Esau's wives (see 26:35) and escape from Esau's revenge.

2. Jacob Abroad (chaps. 28–30)

28:1–5. Isaac's instructions are reminiscent of his father's. Jacob was to go to **Padan-aram** (see 24:10; 25:20) to **take thee a wife from thence** (v. 2; compare Isaac's not being allowed to leave Canaan in search of his own wife, 24:3–4). Isaac officially and fully bestowed the Abrahamic covenant on Jacob (contrast 27:28–29), invoking the name of **God Almighty** (v. 3; see discussion on 17:1), who had the power to accomplish it. (For Paul's application of the **blessing of Abraham** (v. 4) to Christian believers, see Galatians 3:14. For Jacob's journeys, see map, *KJV Study Bible*, p. 48.)

28:6–9. Parenthetically, it is to be noted that Esau is aware of three things: (1) his father's blessing Jacob and instructing him not to marry from among the Canaanites, (2) his brother's obedience in going to Padan-aram for a wife, and (3) his father's displeasure with his wives. Therefore, Esau tried to appease his parents by taking a **daughter of Ishmael** as another wife, adding her **unto the wives which he had** (v. 9; see 26:34 and discussion).

28:10–15. Stopping to rest on his journey, Jacob **took of the stones ... for his pillows** (v. 11). In ancient times, people were used to sleeping on the ground, and headrests (e.g., in Egypt) were often quite hard, sometimes being made of metal. The **ladder** (v. 12) Jacob saw in his dream was probably not a ladder with rungs but was more likely a stairway such as mounted the sloping side of a ziggurat (see discussion on 11:4). He saw the **angels of God ascending and descending on it**, a sign that the Lord offered to be Jacob's God. Jesus told a disciple that he would "see heaven open, and the angels of God ascending and descending upon the Son of man" (John 1:51). Jesus Himself is the bridge between heaven and earth (see John 14:6), the only "mediator between God and men" (1 Tim. 2:5). He also saw that **the LORD stood above it** (v. 13). Mesopotamian ziggurats were topped with a small shrine where worshipers prayed to their gods.

In contrast, Jacob's God spoke to him and officially confirmed to him the promises and blessings of the covenant that had been given to Abraham and Isaac (see 12:3–4; 13:15–16; 20:17–18; 26:3–4). **I am with thee ... will keep thee ... will bring thee again ... I will not leave thee** (v. 15). Unlike the gods of pagan religions, in which the gods were merely local deities who gave protection only within their own territories, the one true God assured Jacob that He would always be with him wherever he went.

28:16–19. Sensing God's **dreadful** (i.e., awesome; v. 17) presence, Jacob saw the place as the **house of God ... the gate of heaven**. These are phrases that related Jacob's stairway to the Mesopotamian ziggurats (see discussion on 11:4, 9). He used his "pillows" (28:11) to make a **pillar** (v. 18), a memorial of worship or of communion between man and God, common in ancient times, and **poured oil upon the top of it** to consecrate it (see Exod. 30:25–29). The location, which had formerly been known as Luz, now became known as **Beth-el** (v. 19), the "house of God."

28:20–22. Is Jacob now striking a new deal by his **If God will ...** (v. 20)? Or might "if" have the nuance of "since"? **Then shall the LORD be my God** (v. 21). For the first time, Jacob considered acknowledging the God of Abraham and Isaac (see 28:13; 27:20) as his own. His full acknowledgment came only after his safe return from Haran. In the sense that **this stone** (v. 22) would memorialize Jacob's meeting with God at Bethel, it would **be God's house**. To acknowledge the Lord as his God and King, Jacob promised, **of all that thou shalt give me I will surely give the tenth to thee** (see discussion on 14:20).

29:1–6. God's providence directed Jacob to the very place where he would find one of the daughters of Laban (see 28:2). The first people he addressed were from Haran (see 11:31; 24:4, 10; 25:20; 28:2) who knew **Laban the son** (i.e., "grandson"; see 22:20–23; 24:15, 29) **of Nahor** (v. 5). Meanwhile, **Rachel** (v. 6), Laban's daughter, was coming into view.

29:7–12. Rachel was busy tending her **father's sheep: for she kept them** (v. 9). In the Middle East, men and women shared the task of caring for sheep and goats. Before formally introducing himself to Rachel, Jacob **rolled the stone** (v. 10) from the well to water the sheep for Rachel. This was a feat of unusual strength for one man, because the stone was large (see 29:2). Jacob's action was the reverse of 24:17-20, when Rebekah had watered the servant's camels. The servant had bowed to the ground when he learned of Rebekah's pedigree. Jacob **wept** (v. 11), however, apparently for joy, as he introduced himself as **her father's brother** (i.e., "relative").

29:13-14. Jacob's arrival was quite different from that of Abraham's servant in chapter 24: no camels bearing gifts, no prayers regarding the right damsel, no worship. Laban received him, however, as **my bone and my flesh** (v. 14), thus stressing his blood kinship with Jacob (see, e.g., 2:23).

29:15-20. Laban permitted Jacob to negotiate his wages, perhaps expecting him to bargain for one of his two daughters, **Leah** and **Rachel** (v. 16). He certainly knew why Jacob had come, for "he told Laban all these things" (29:13). The names Leah and Rachel mean "cow" and "ewe" respectively, appropriate in a herdsman's family. Since Jacob had no money for a dowry, he proposed **seven years** labor to marry **Rachel** (v. 18).

29:21-24. After seven years, and having reached eighty-four years of age (see discussion on 27:1), Jacob told Laban, **Give me my wife** (v. 21). If Jacob had said "Rachel," Laban would have had no excuse for giving him Leah. The appropriate **feast** (v. 22) was prepared. A wedding feast usually lasted seven days (see 29:27-28; Judg. 14:10, 12). **In the evening …he went in unto her** (v. 23). The darkness, or perhaps a veil (see 24:65), may have concealed Leah's identity. Parenthetically, giving one's daughter a **handmaid** (see 29:29) is a wedding custom documented in Old Babylonian marriage contracts.

29:25-30. Understandably upset, Jacob demanded, **wherefore then hast thou beguiled me?** (v. 25). Jacob, the deceiver in name (see discussion on 25:26) as well as in behavior (see 27:36), had himself been deceived. The one who had tried everything to obtain the benefits of the firstborn had now, against his will, received the firstborn (29:16,

26). After getting a commitment from Jacob for another seven years' labor, Laban **gave him Rachel his daughter** (v. 28). This was after Jacob's seven-day marriage festivities with Leah but before he worked another seven years. Jacob **loved also Rachel more than Leah** (v. 30), not only because Rachel had been his choice from the beginning but also, no doubt, because Laban had tricked Jacob into marrying Leah.

29:31-35. Leah, though unloved, nevertheless became the mother of Jacob's first four sons, including Levi (ancestor of the Aaronic priestly line) and Judah (ancestor of David and his royal line, and ultimately of Jesus).

At the birth of her firstborn, Leah **called his name Reuben** (meaning "See, a son"), saying, **Surely the LORD hath looked upon my affliction** (v. 32). Ishmael had received his name in similar circumstances (see 16:11). Over a seven-year period, Jacob had eleven sons and one daughter born to him by two wives and two concubines. All of his offspring had names significant to the circumstances of their births (e.g., **Simeon**, v. 33, is related to "hearing"; **Levi**, v. 34, is related to "attachment"; **Judah**, v. 35, is related to "praise").

30:1-2. Two sisters having the same husband caused friction and competition between them, for both wanted children and their husband's affection. **Rachel envied her sister** (v. 1), as Jacob envied his older brother. Her demand, **Give me children, or else I die**, is tragically prophetic (see 35:16-19). Jacob was equally frustrated. **Am I in God's stead …?** (v. 2). Jacob was forever trying to secure the blessing by his own efforts. Here he has to acknowledge that the blessing of offspring could come only from God (see 31:7-13 for the blessing of flocks). Joseph later echoed Jacob's words (see 50:19).

30:3-4. Rachel resorted to a surrogate and offered Jacob her maid, Bilhah, as a concubine, saying, **go in unto her** (v. 3; see 30:9; 16:2 and discussion). Apparently, the expression **upon my knees** is symbolic of adoption (see 48:10-16), meaning "as though my own" (see discussion on 50:23). Jacob complied with her wishes, taking Bilhah **to wife** (v. 4), that is, as a concubine.

30:5–13. Jacob's fifth, sixth, seventh, and eighth sons were born to him through his maidservant concubines: **Dan** (v. 6) relates to "vindication"; **Naphtali** (v. 8) relates to "wrestling"; **Gad** (v. 11) relates to "good fortune"; **Asher** (v. 13) relates to "happiness."

30:14–16. Reuben (v. 14) was a young boy when he brought his mother, Leah, **mandrakes** from the field. The mandrake is a plant bearing flowers and a fruit, but it also has fleshy, forked roots that resemble the lower part of a human body and were superstitiously thought to induce pregnancy when eaten (see Song 7:13). Therefore, Rachel demanded, **Give me … of thy son's mandrakes.** She, like Jacob (30:37–43), tried to obtain what she wanted by magical means. Leah traded the mandrakes for rights to Jacob's bed. Thus, Leah announced to Jacob, **I have hired thee** (v. 16). The verb "hired" will become a pun on the name of the son that is conceived, Issachar.

30:17–21. Jacob's ninth and tenth sons were born through Leah, who was thus the mother of half of Jacob's twelve sons. **Issachar** (v. 18) means "there is reward." **Zebulun** (v. 20) probably means "honor." Jacob's only daughter, **Dinah** (v. 21), is a feminine form of an earlier name, Dan, which relates to "vindication."

30:22–24. God remembered Rachel (v. 22; see discussion on 8:1), and she conceived. She saw her **reproach** (v. 23) lifted, since barrenness was considered to be shameful, a mark of divine disfavor (see 16:2; 30:2). She named her son **Joseph** (v. 24), which means "add," because, she said, **The Lord shall add to me another son.** The fulfillment of Rachel's wish would bring about her death (see 35:16–19).

30:25–27. In the year Dinah and Joseph were born, the fourteenth year Jacob had been with Laban, Jacob wished to return to Canaan. Laban begged him to stay because of what Laban had **learned by experience** (v. 27), that is, what he had divined. Divination is the attempt to discover hidden knowledge through mechanical means (see 44:5), the interpretation of omens (see Ezek. 21:21), or the aid of supernatural powers (see Acts 16:16). It was strictly forbidden for Israel (Lev. 19:26; Deut. 18:10, 14) because it reflected a pagan concept of the world

as being controlled by evil forces, and therefore obviously not under the sovereign rule of the Lord. Laban understood that **the Lord hath blessed me for thy sake** (see 21:22; 26:28–29). The offspring of Abraham were a source of blessing (see 12:2).

30:28–36. Laban tried to retain Jacob by allowing him to state his wages. Jacob asked simply that he could select and claim as his the multicolored animals in the flock and all such animals that would be born thereafter. Laban agreed, but **he removed** (v. 35) the animals himself, secretly and without telling Jacob, and placed them in the care of his sons so Jacob could not use them for breeding purposes.

30:37–43. Jacob continued to try to help himself. He had bartered for the birthright (25:31), deceived his father for the blessing (chap. 27), and now he attempted prenatal influence to get multicolored sheep and goats. While the cattle mated, he peeled back the bark on shoots of trees to expose white spots, intending to influence the breeding to produce spotted animals.

The Hebrew terms for **poplar** (*libneh*; v. 37) and **white** (*laban*) are puns on the name Laban. As Jacob had gotten the best of Esau (whose other name, Edom, means "red"; see discussion on 25:25) by means of red stew (25:30), so he now tried to get the best of Laban (whose name means "white") by means of white branches. In effect, Jacob was using Laban's own tactic (deception) against him.

The scheme worked (v. 39). Jacob later learned that it had worked only because of God's intervention (see Jacob's own admission in 31:9), not because of Jacob's superstition. So over a period of six years (see 31:41), Jacob **increased exceedingly** (v. 43) in cattle and servants. While in Haran, Jacob obtained both family and wealth.

3. Jacob at Home Again (chaps. 31–35)

31:1–3. Every sign Jacob was getting—from **the words of Laban's sons** (v. 1), from the **countenance of Laban** (v. 2), later from his wives (see 31:14–16), but now from God Himself, who said, **Return unto the land of thy fathers** (v. 3)—told him that it was time to return to Canaan. **I will be with thee** reiterates the promise spoken when he left Canaan (see 28:15).

31:4–9. Jacob used the privacy of the field to speak with his wives, **Rachel and Leah** (v. 4). At long last (see 31:14), Rachel, the younger, has been given precedence over Leah, but Rachel will soon become a deceiver like her husband (see 31:31, 35).

Jacob described a deteriorating relationship with their father, who had changed his wages **ten times** (v. 7). This could be a literal number, but it could also signify completeness. In effect, Jacob accused Laban of cheating him at every turn, while at the same time God had blessed Jacob with cattle.

31:10–16. In a dream, the **angel of God** (v. 11; see discussion on 16:7) showed Jacob how He had thwarted Laban's attempts to cheat him and identified Himself as the **God of Beth-el, where thou anointedst the pillar** (v. 13; see 28:18–19). At Bethel, Jacob had made his vow to God; now God told him to **return unto the land of his kindred**.

His wives showed no reluctance to leave their father but expressed bitterness. They resented his treating them like **strangers** and having **devoured also our money** (v. 15). Apparently, the wages of Jacob's fourteen years of labor had served as a dowry but had not been put in escrow for them, so they felt as if they had been sold.

31:17–21. While Jacob was secretly carrying away his possessions, Rachel was stealing her father's **images** (v. 19; Hebrew, *teraphim*). These were small portable idols, which she probably stole because she thought they would bring her protection and blessing. Perhaps she wanted to have something tangible to worship on the long journey ahead, a practice referred to much later in the writings of Josephus, a first-century Jewish historian. In any case, Rachel was not yet free of her pagan background (see 35:2; Josh. 24:2).

So he fled (v. 21), as he had fled earlier from Esau (27:42–43). Jacob's devious dealings produced only hostility from which he had to flee. His goal was to reach **mount Gilead**, the fertile hill country southeast of the Sea of Galilee.

31:22–29. Jacob's three-day head start took Laban seven days to overcome. **Speak not ... good or bad** (v. 24). Laban was to say nothing to alter the will of God, neither good, such as an irresistible bribe to return, nor bad, such as a threat forcing a return. Laban's charge against Jacob was: **thou hast stolen away unawares to me** (lit., "You have stolen my heart," i.e., "You have deceived me"; v. 26). Jacob's character, reflected in his name (see discussion on 25:26; 27:36), is emphasized in the narrative again and again. His quick, deceptive departure had deprived Laban of any normal parting festivities.

31:30–35. Though Laban could understand Jacob's desire to return to his kindred, he did not understand **wherefore hast thou stolen my gods?** (v. 30). Jacob resented the accusation and answered, **With whomsoever thou findest thy gods, let him not live** (v. 32). Though he made the offer in all innocence, Jacob almost lost his beloved Rachel. He had now been deceived by even his wife. Laban's search brought him to Rachel, who had hid the *teraphim* **in the camel's furniture** (i.e., saddle), **and sat upon them** (v. 34), thus indicating the small size and powerlessness of the household gods. **I cannot rise up before thee; for the custom of women is upon me** (v. 35). In later times, anything a menstruating woman sat on was considered ritually unclean (Lev. 15:20). Rachel had become not only a thief but also a deceiver.

31:36–42. Jacob's humiliation at being searched turned to anger. He made a strong case for his twenty years of faithful service in spite of Laban's unreliable labor contracts, claiming he would have gone away empty-handed had not the God of Abraham been watching over him. The **fear** (v. 42) of Isaac is here probably a surrogate for God, though some have thought the Hebrew for this word means "Kinsman," stressing the intimacy of God's relationship with the patriarch.

31:43–48. Before he parted from Jacob, Laban proposed a covenant. Sitting on a collected heap of stones, **they did eat** (v. 46) together, signifying that the covenant was made in friendship (see discussion on 26:30). Laban's name for the heap is **Jegar-sahadutha** (Aramaic for "witness heap"; v. 47), while Jacob called it **Galeed** (Hebrew for "witness heap";

v. 48) and **Mizpah** (Hebrew for "lookout point"; for the naming of an altar under somewhat different circumstances, see Josh. 22:10–12, 34).

31:49–55. In its context, the so-called Mizpah benediction, **The LORD watch between me and thee, when we are absent from one another** (v. 49), is in fact a denunciation or curse. Neither man trusted the other. The **heap** and **pillar** (v. 51) that they had erected were to be boundary markers between Laban's territory and Jacob's territory. God was witness that neither would cross over the line to harm the other.

There is an apparent contrast of deities here. Laban swore by **the God of their father** (v. 53), or possibly "the gods of their father [i.e., Terah]," reflecting Laban's polytheistic background (see Josh. 24:2). Jacob, however, swore by **the fear of his father Isaac** (see discussion on 31:42). Jacob had met the "God of Isaac" (28:13) at Bethel twenty years earlier.

To offer a **sacrifice** and to **eat bread** (v. 54) were two important aspects of the covenant-making process (see 31:44; Exod. 24:5–8, 11). Jacob's **brethren**, that is, his relatives with whom he had now entered into a covenant, joined him. The common meal indicated mutual acceptance (see discussion on 26:30). Then Laban **blessed** (v. 55), or "said farewell to," his grandsons and daughters (see 47:10).

32:1. Jacob had just left the region of the hostile Laban and was about to enter the region of the hostile Esau. He was met by the **angels of God**, whom he had seen at Bethel when he was fleeing from Esau to go to Laban (28:12). Thus, God was with Jacob, as He had promised (see 28:15; 31:3; see also discussion on 26:3).

32:2. The name **Mahanaim** means "two camps" and is located in Gilead (see discussion on 31:21), east of the Jordan and north of the Jabbok (see discussion on 32:22). Two camps had just met in hostility and separated in peace. Two camps were again about to meet (in hostility, Jacob thought) and separate in peace. Jacob called this crucial place "Two Camps" after seeing the angelic encampment, suggesting that he saw God's encampment as a divine assurance. God's host had come to escort him safely

to Canaan (see 33:12, 15). Yet he also feared meeting with Esau, so he divided his household into two camps (see 32:7, 10), still trying to protect himself by his own devices.

32:3–5. Seir (v. 3), another name for **Edom**, lay far to the south of Jacob's ultimate destination, but he assumed that Esau would come seeking revenge as soon as he heard that Jacob was on his way back. Jacob had seen God's angels (Hebrew, *mal'akim*; lit., "messengers"); now he sent his **messengers** (*mal'akim*) ahead to advise Esau of his return. He diplomatically called himself **thy servant** (v. 4), a phrase suggesting both courtesy and humility.

32:6–12. The announcement that Esau was approaching with **four hundred men** (v. 6) was one that was open to all kinds of interpretations. The number was probably a round number for a sizable unit of fighting men (see 1 Sam. 22:2; 25:13; 30:10). Jacob's fear and distress drove him to prayer. **Jacob said, O God** (v. 9). This is his first recorded prayer since leaving Bethel. Never before had he confessed his unworthiness of God's blessing. Never before did he demonstrate such a sense of need and dependency. He feared that Esau's wrath would extend to his family as well, **the mother with the children** (v. 11). He desperately reminded God of His earlier personal promises to him (28:14), to do him **good** and to make his **seed as the sand of the sea** earlier (v. 12).

32:13–23. Jacob's prayer did not result in inaction on his part. He prepared a **present** (v. 13). The Hebrew word for "present" is probably a wordplay: out of his "two companies" (Hebrew, *mahanayim*, 32:2; see 32:7–8, 10), Jacob selected a present (*minhah*) for his brother. The 520 animals Jacob selected was a sizeable gift and is a good indication of God's blessing him over the past six years. He left nothing to chance but instructed his servants what to say as they presented the gift to Esau in three installments. **I will appease him ... peradventure he will accept of me** (v. 20). Jacob hoped to blunt the force of Esau's past anger and deflect it with the gift, but interestingly, he never asked for forgiveness for what he had done.

The **Jabbok** (v. 22) is today called the Wadi Zerqa, flowing westward into the Jordan about twenty miles north of the Dead Sea.

32:24–27. Having sent his family across the brook, Jacob was **left alone** (v. 24), as he had been at Bethel (28:10–22). God **wrestled** (*ye'abeq*) with Jacob (*ya'aqob*) by the Jabbok (*yabboq*)—the author delighted in wordplay. Jacob had struggled all his life to prevail, first with Esau, then with Laban. Now, as he was about to reenter Canaan, he was shown that it was with God that he must "wrestle." It was God who held his destiny in His hands. Jacob wrestled with **a man**, but it was God Himself (as Jacob eventually realized; see 32:30) in the form of an angel (see Hos. 12:3–4 and discussion on Gen. 16:7).

The "man" **prevailed not against** Jacob and **touched the hollow of his thigh** (v. 25). God came to Jacob in such a form that he could wrestle with Him successfully, yet He showed him that He could disable him at will. Jacob's persistence, **I will not let thee go** (v. 26), was soon rewarded (32:29). **Except thou bless me** is Jacob's acknowledgment, finally, that the blessing must come from God.

32:28. Thy name shall be called no more Jacob. Now that Jacob had acknowledged God as the source of blessing and was about to reenter the promised land, the Lord acknowledged Jacob as His servant by changing his name (see 17:5 and discussion). **Israel** means "let God rule/strive," or perhaps "he struggles with God." In this event and in their father Jacob/Israel, the nation of Israel got her name and her characterization: they are the people who struggle with God (memorialized in the name Israel) and with men (memorialized in the name Jacob) and overcome. God later confirmed Jacob's new name (35:10).

32:29–32. Jacob's request, **Tell me … thy name** (v. 29), was an unworthy one and impossible to fulfill (see Judg. 13:17–18). The place was named Peniel, meaning "the face of God" because Jacob said, **I have seen God face to face, and my life is preserved** (v. 30; see discussion on 16:13; Judg. 6:22–23; 13:22). Only God's "back parts" (see Exod. 33:23) or "feet" (see Exod. 24:10) or "similitude" (see Num. 12:8), in a symbolic sense, may be seen.

God's touch disabled Jacob's hip socket (32:25). Therefore, the Israelites no longer ate **the sinew** (v. 32), probably the sciatic muscle that is attached to the hip socket. Mentioned nowhere else in the Bible, this dietary prohibition is found in the later writings of Judaism. Jacob retained in his body, and Israel retained in her dietary practice, a perpetual reminder of this fateful encounter with God.

33:1–4. In preparation for meeting Esau, Jacob separated his children according to concubines and wives but positioned **Rachel and Joseph hindermost** (v. 2). He wanted to keep his favorite wife and child farthest away from potential harm. As he approached Esau, Jacob **bowed himself to the ground seven times** (v. 3). This was a sign of total submission, which is documented also in texts found at Tell el-Amarna in Egypt, dating to the fourteenth century BC (see chart, *KJV Study Bible*, p. xix). All Jacob's fears proved unfounded. God had been at work and had so blessed Esau (33:9) that he no longer held a grudge against Jacob.

33:5–11. Having met Jacob's family, Esau questioned the purpose of all the animals presented to him. His generous and loving response, **I have enough, my brother** (v. 9), was in contrast to Jacob's cautious and fearful attempt to appease **my lord** (v. 8). Jacob urged Esau, **Take … my blessing** (v. 11). Though it is a reference to the **present** in verse 10, the Hebrew word is the same as that used for "blessing" in 27:35. The author of Genesis was conscious of the irony that Jacob now acknowledged that the blessing he had struggled for was from God. In his last attempt to express reconciliation with Esau, Jacob in a sense gave back the "blessing" he had stolen from his brother, doing so from the blessings the Lord had given him.

33:12–15. Jacob refused Esau's gracious offers to accompany and assist him on his journey, stating that his young children and the cattle would not be able to match Esau's pace. Interestingly, a rapid pace of travel had not been an issue when he fled from Laban. Jacob indicated that he would **come unto my lord unto Seir** (v. 14). Jacob, still the deceiver, had no intention of following Esau all the way to Seir.

Having been reconciled to his brother, he apparently now wanted to put a safe distance between them.

33:16–20. With Esau gone, Jacob reversed his path, heading back across the Jabbok, where he **made booths** (Hebrew, *Sukkoth*; v. 17), thus the name of that place. That he **built ... a house** may indicate a residence of several years before he moved and **came to Shalem** (v.18). The Hebrew for Shalem can be rendered adverbially, not as a noun; he "came safely to Shechem." Thus, it was the answer to Jacob's prayer of twenty years earlier (see 28:21). **Shechem** was an important city in central Canaan, first built and inhabited during the patriarchal period. Jacob followed in the footsteps of father Abraham (see 12:6–7), having arrived where Abraham was first promised the land and had built an altar. Jacob also dug a well there (see John 4:5–6), which can still be seen today.

Jacob purchased another foothold in the land (see 23:16–20). The Hebrew for **pieces of money** (v. 19) is *qesitah*, a unit of money of unknown weight and value, that is always found in patriarchal contexts (see Josh. 24:32; Job 42:11). The **altar** (v. 20) that he erected there was called **El-Elohe-Israel**, meaning "God, the God of Israel." Jacob formally acknowledged the God of his fathers as his God also (see 28:21). He lingered at Shechem and did not return immediately to Bethel (see 35:1), and that meant trouble (see chap. 34).

34:1–31. The name of God ends chapter 33 and begins chapter 35, but it is completely absent from this sordid chapter.

34:1–4. The inhabitants of the land seemingly regarded unattended women as legitimate prey (see 12:15; 20:2; 26:7), so **Dinah** (v. 1) was at risk by going off alone. **Shechem** (v. 2), the son of Hamor, who was a ruler in the area (33:19), was probably named after the city. He apparently felt he had special privileges with unattended girls. After violating Dinah, he demanded of his father, **Get me this damsel to wife** (v. 4).

34:5–7. Jacob withheld immediate reaction to the sordid news, waiting for the opinion of his sons. Though it was Dinah who was raped, the brothers viewed the offense in a corporate manner, against the whole clan of **Israel** (v. 7). In their moral judgment, Shechem had done something which **ought not to be done**. (Compare Tamar's plea to Amnon in a similar situation, 2 Sam. 13:12.)

34:8–12. Neither Hamor nor Shechem ever admitted guilt. No apology or excuse was made for what was done. They did, however, request of Jacob and his sons, **make ye marriages with us** (v. 9). Intermarriage was presented as providing an economical advantage for Israel, but the Canaanites wanted to absorb Israel (see 34:16) to benefit from the blessings Jacob had received from the Lord (both his offspring and his possessions; see 34:21–23). This was a danger Israel constantly faced from other peoples and nations—either absorption or hostility, both of which are perpetual threats to the people of God. Shechem was prepared to provide any **dowry and gift** (v. 12) asked of him (for an example of this marriage custom, see 24:53).

34:13–17. Like their deceitful father (see 27:19–24), **the sons of Jacob answered ... deceitfully** (v. 13). They agreed to intermarriage on the condition that all the men of Shechem **be circumcised** (v. 15) like them. They intended to use a sacred ceremony and covenant sign for a sinful purpose (see 34:24–25). No mere operation could make any people worthy to share with them their rich heritage. Jacob's sons were guilty of treating the covenant sign lightly and dishonoring it. For them, it was not a sign of a relationship with God, a sign which was to be cherished.

34:18–24. A less respected man might not have won the approval of the men of the city for the proposal, but the greed of the men of Shechem led to their destruction. The Canaanites were willing to submit to Israel's covenant rite to attain their purpose of gaining Israel's substance.

34:25–31. **Simeon and Levi** (v. 25), the full brothers of Dinah (all were Leah's children; see 29:33–34; 30:21), gained their purpose also, by slaughtering all the men when they were sore from their circumcision and too incapacitated to defend themselves. Because they slaughtered the men of Shechem, their own descendants would be scattered far and wide (see discussion on 49:7). They **slew all the males**. Shechem's crime, serious as it was, hardly warranted such brutal and extensive retaliation (see vv. 27–29).

Jacob saw their action as obnoxious and dangerous (v. 30). Though his sons have the last word here, Jacob's verdict was made on his deathbed: "Cursed be their anger" (49:5–7).

35:1–5. Go up to Beth-el (v. 1). Returning to the place where Jacob had met God and made his departure from the land (28:13–19) called for a time of general repentance and reconsecration.

Put away the strange gods that are among you (v. 2). Is Jacob now aware of Rachel's *teraphim* (see discussion on 31:19)? Were his servants and family already prone to syncretism (compare Josh. 24:23)? **Be clean**. Jacob ordered a ceremonial cleansing (including clean clothes), but it was to be indicative of a spiritual cleansing of their sinful environment.

Their strange gods and their **earrings** (v. 4), which were worn as amulets or charms as part of a pagan religious custom (see Hos. 2:13), were given to Jacob, who buried them under **the oak ... by Shechem**. This was obviously a well-known tree, perhaps the "oak" mentioned in 12:6 (see Josh. 24:26).

Though Jacob's sons' retaliation at Shechem could have brought revenge from other inhabitants of the land (see 34:30), **the terror of God** (v. 5) was on the neighboring cities, and He protected His servant from them as he traveled to Bethel.

35:6–8. Where he had once erected a stone pillar, Jacob now **built there an altar** (v. 7) and called it **El-beth-el**, meaning "God of Bethel."

After long years of faithful service, **Deborah Rebekah's nurse died** (v. 8; see 24:59). Jacob buried her **under**, that is, either "lower than" or "to the south of," an oak. Again, the oak is probably a well-known tree that is now named **Allon-bachuth**, the "oak of weeping."

35:9–15. The previous assignment to **Jacob** of the additional name **Israel** (v. 10; see 32:28) is here confirmed. (For similar examples of name confirmation, see 21:31 and 26:33; 28:19 and 35:15.)

Verses 11–12 are the climax of the Isaac-Jacob cycle (see Introduction: "Literary Features"). Now

that Jacob was at last back at Bethel, where God had begun His direct relationship with him, God confirmed to this chosen son of Isaac the covenant promises made to Abraham (17:1–8; see 28:3). His words echo His original benediction pronounced on man in the beginning (1:28) and renewed after the flood (9:1, 7). God's blessing on mankind would be fulfilled in and through Jacob and his offspring.

As before, Jacob erected a pillar in response (28:18). This time he poured a **drink offering** (liquid poured out as a sacrifice to a deity; v. 14) and oil on it and renamed it Bethel.

35:16. Ephrath is the older name for Bethlehem (see 35:19) in Judah (see Ruth 1:2; Mic. 5:2). Here Rachel went into labor with her second child.

35:17–20. Words meant to encourage, **Fear not; thou shalt have this son also** (v. 17), are an echo of Rachel's own plea at the time of Joseph's birth (30:24). Rachel named her son **Ben-oni** (meaning "son of my sorrow"; v. 18) as **she died** in childbirth, but Jacob renamed the son **Benjamin**, which means "son of the right hand," that is, a son of honor. **Rachel's grave** (v. 20) was marked, to be remembered (see 1 Sam. 10:2). The traditional, though not authentic, site is near Bethlehem.

35:21–26. Tower of Edar (v. 21) means "tower of the flock," doubtless referring to a watchtower built to discourage thieves from stealing sheep and other animals (see 2 Chron. 26:10). The same Hebrew phrase is used figuratively in Micah 4:8, where "flock" refers to the people of Judah (see Mic. 4:6–8). Reuben's act with **Bilhah** (v. 22) was more than sexually motivated. It was an arrogant and premature claim to the rights of the firstborn—here the right to inherit his father's concubine (for later attempts to take wives of deceased or absent kings, see 2 Sam. 3:7; 16:20–22; 1 Kings 2:22). For this act, Reuben would lose his legal status as firstborn (49:3–4; 1 Chron. 5:1; see discussion on Gen. 37:21).

Jacob's sons are listed with their mothers. **The sons of Jacob ... born to him in Padan-aram** (the "field" or "plain" of Aram, i.e. "Mesopotamia," v. 26; see 24:10; 25:20) is obviously a summary statement since Benjamin was born in Canaan (35:16–18).

35:27–29. Jacob returned to **Mamre, unto the city of Arba, which is Hebron** (v. 27; see discussions on 13:18; 23:2), in time to see his father yet alive. Isaac, who had anticipated his death at the age of 137 (see discussion on 27:1), lived to be 180.

Isaac's sons **buried him** (v. 29) in the family tomb, the cave of Machpelah (see 49:30–31).

D. The Descendants of Esau (36:1–37:1)

36:1. The generations of Esau is the ninth account to appear in Genesis (see discussion on 2:4). Though "generations" is repeated in 36:9, it does not mark the start of a new main section there since the information in 36:9–43 is merely an expansion of that in 36:1–8. **Esau** was also known as **Edom** (a pun on "red"; see discussion on 25:25). Reddish rock formations, primarily sandstone, are conspicuous in the territory of the Edomites, located south and southeast of the Dead Sea.

36:2–5. The names given here for Esau's three wives are **Adah, Aholibamah,** and **Bashemath** (v. 2), but they differ from those found in 26:34 and 28:9. It is possible that the lists have suffered in transmission, that alternate names are used here, or that Esau married more than three wives.

36:6–8. Prior to the events of 32:3 and 33:16, Esau had moved from Canaan with his wives (see discussion on 27:39) because **their** (Jacob's and Esau's) **riches were more than that they might dwell together** (v. 7; compare 13:6).

Seir (v. 8) is another name for Edom. The word is related to the Hebrew word meaning "hair," a possible meaning also for the name Esau (see discussion on 25:25). Esau's clan must have driven away the original Horite inhabitants of Seir (see 36:20; 14:6 and discussion). The descendants of Seir are listed in 36:20–28.

36:9–19. The list of Esau's descendants given in verses 9–14 (see 1 Chron. 1:35–37) is repeated in verses 15–19 as a list of **dukes** (v. 15), that is, as tribal chieftains or perhaps clan leaders.

Worthy of special note are **Eliphaz** and **Teman** (vv. 10–11). One of Job's friends was named Eliphaz the Temanite (Job 2:11), and Job himself was from the land of Uz (Job 1:1; see also Gen. 36:28, 34). Thus, Job probably lived in or near Edom. Esau's grandson **Amalek** (v. 12) became the father of the Amalekites, a tribal people living in the Negev and in the Sinai peninsula in Moses' day.

36:20–30. The list of Seir's descendants given in verses 20–28 (see 1 Chron. 1:38–42) is repeated in abbreviated form in verses 29–30 as a list of **dukes** (v. 29), tribal chieftains or perhaps clan leaders. These are the Horites who apparently were expelled from the region by Esau's clan.

36:31–39. The land of Edom had kings **before there reigned any king over the children of Israel** (v. 31). This statement presupposes the later Israelite monarchy and is evidently an editorial updating subsequent to Moses' time (see discussion on 14:14).

36:40–43. This list of **dukes** (v. 40), or clan leaders, overlaps the list given in 36:15–19 but with variation. The names are listed according to **their places,** the regions they settled, but the place-names are strangely lacking. **He is Esau the father of the Edomites** (v. 43). This is a summary statement for the whole chapter (just as 36:1 is a title for the whole chapter).

37:1. Jacob made **Canaan** his homeland and was later buried there (49:29–30; 50:13). His son Joseph also insisted on being buried in Canaan, which he recognized as the land the Lord had promised to Israel (50:24–25). The Jacob-Joseph cycle (see Introduction: "Literary Features") begins and ends with references to the Land of Promise.

E. The Life of Joseph (37:2–50:26)

1. Joseph's Career (37:2–41:57)

37:2–4. The generations of Jacob (v. 2; see discussion on 2:4) introduces the tenth and final main section of Genesis. The author immediately introduces **Joseph,** on whom the last cycle of the patriarchal narrative centers. In his generation, he, more than any other, represented Israel—as a people who struggled with God and with men and overcame (see discussion on 32:28) and as a source of blessing to the nations (see 12:2–3). It is, moreover, through the life of Joseph that the covenant family in Canaan becomes an emerging nation in Egypt, thus setting the stage for the exodus. The story of God's dealings with the patriarchs foreshadows the subsequent biblical account of God's purpose with Israel. It begins with the election and calling out of Abram from the post-Babel nations and ends with Israel in Egypt (in the person of Joseph), preserving the life of the nations (see 41:57; 50:20). So God would deliver Israel out of the nations (the exodus), eventually to send them on a mission of life to the nations (see Matt. 28:18 – 20; Acts 1:8).

Doubtless Joseph had opportunity to bring an **evil report** (v. 2), to report misdeeds, about all his brothers (as the later context indicates), not just about the sons of his father's concubines.

His **coat of many colours** (v. 3) was certainly a coat or tunic of distinction, and though the Hebrew is difficult, it probably was a tunic with long sleeves and a low hem rather than one of variegated colors. It was a mark of Jacob's favoritism, "for with such robes were the king's daughters that were virgins apparelled" (2 Sam. 13:18).

37:5 – 8. Was it out of arrogance or innocence that Joseph related his **dream** (v. 5; see discussion on 20:3) to those who hated him? **Your sheaves ... made obeisance** (v. 7). Joseph's dream would later come true (42:6; 43:26; 44:14), but at this time, he could not have known how it would unfold. His brothers, however, considered the implications. **Shalt thou indeed reign over us?** (v. 8). Joseph would later become the one "that was separated from his brethren" (Deut. 33:16) and receive "the birthright" (1 Chron. 5:2), at least the double portion of the inheritance (see discussion on 25:5), since his father, Jacob, adopted Joseph's two sons (48:5).

37:9 – 11. Jacob addressed the second dream with his own misgivings. He possibly referred to Leah as **thy mother** (v. 10), since Rachel had already died (see 35:19). His question, **Shall [we] bow down ourselves to thee?** is an unsettling echo of a hope expressed earlier to Jacob by his father, Isaac (see 27:29). Jacob **observed the saying** (v. 11). Here is a hint that he later recalled Joseph's dreams when events brought about their fulfillment. (Compare

Mary's equally sensitive response to events during Jesus' boyhood days, Luke 2:19, 51.)

37:12 – 17. Jacob's sons returned with the flocks to the region of **Shechem** (v. 12; see discussion on 33:18), where Jacob had purchased land and his sons had ravaged the city. To send Joseph alone to hateful brothers and a community with reason for revenge was potential trouble. He found his brothers at **Dothan** (v. 17), which was located about thirteen miles north of Shechem and was already an ancient city by this time.

37:18 – 22. The Hebrew for **dreamer** (v. 19) means "master of dreams" or "dream expert" and is here used with obvious sarcasm. Plans to kill Joseph were thwarted by **Reuben**, who **delivered him** (v. 21). As Jacob's firstborn, Reuben felt responsible for Joseph. He would later remind his brothers of this day (42:22). Initially, Reuben's attempts to influence events seemed successful (30:14 – 17). After his arrogant incest with Bilhah (see 35:22 and discussion), his efforts were always ineffective (see 42:37 – 38) — demonstrating his loss of the status of firstborn (see 49:3 – 4). Effective leadership passed to Judah (see 37:26 – 27; 43:3 – 5, 8 – 10; 44:14 – 34; 46:28; 49:8 – 12).

37:23 – 24. They stript Joseph out of his coat (v. 23). In Egypt, Joseph (though innocent of any wrongdoing) would similarly be stripped of his position of privilege and thrown into prison, also as a result of domestic intrigue (chap. 39). His cloak also would be torn from him and shown to Potiphar, but Joseph would be rescued (41:14).

37:25 – 28. The **Ishmeelites** (v. 25) are also called **Midianites** (v. 28; see Judg. 8:22, 24, 26) and Medanites (the literal Hebrew for "Midianites," in 37:36). These various tribal groups were interrelated, since Midian and Medan, like Ishmael, were also sons of Abraham (25:2). They came from **Gilead** (v. 25), the country southeast of the Sea of Galilee. **Balm** is an oil or gum with healing properties (see Jer. 51:8), exuded by the fruit or stems of one or more kinds of small trees. The balm of Gilead was especially effective (see Jer. 8:22; 46:11). **Myrrh** is probably to be identified as labdanum, an aromatic gum (see

Ps. 45:8; Prov. 7:17; Song 3:6; 5:13) exuded from the leaves of the cistus rose. Its oil was used in beauty treatments (see Est. 2:12), and it was sometimes mixed with wine and drunk to relieve pain (see Mark 15:23). As a gift fit for a king, myrrh was brought to Jesus after His birth (Matt. 2:11) and applied to His body after His death (John 19:39–40).

Joseph was sold as a slave for **twenty pieces of silver** (v. 28). In later times, this amount was the value of a male of Joseph's age who had been dedicated to the Lord (see Lev. 27:5).

37:29–35. The sale had occurred in Reuben's absence. They **killed a kid** (v. 31). A slaughtered goat again figured prominently in an act of deception (see 27:5–13).

Like Reuben (v. 29), Jacob **rent his clothes, and put sackcloth upon his loins** (v. 34). Wearing coarse and uncomfortable sackcloth instead of ordinary clothes was a sign of mourning. He was comforted by his **daughters** (v. 35), a term that can include daughters-in-law (e.g., a daughter-in-law of Jacob is mentioned in 38:2). According to some scholars, the Hebrew word *sheol*, translated here as **the grave**, can also refer in a more general way to the realm of the dead, the netherworld, where, it was thought, departed spirits live (for a description of *sheol*, see, e.g., Job 3:13–19).

37:36. In Egypt, Joseph was **sold** "for a servant" (Ps. 105:17). The peoples of the Arabian Desert were long involved in international slave trade (see Amos 1:6, 9). The Hebrew for **guard** can mean "executioners" (the captain of whom was in charge of the royal prisoners; see 40:4), or it can mean "butchers" (the captain of whom was the chief cook in the royal court; see 1 Sam. 9:23–24).

38:1–30. The unsavory events of this chapter illustrate the danger that Israel as God's separated people faced if they remained among the Canaanites (see 15:16 and discussion). In Egypt, the Israelites were kept separate because the Egyptians despised them (43:32; 46:34). While there, God's people were able to develop into a nation without losing their identity. Judah's actions contrasted with those of Joseph (chap. 39)—demonstrating the moral superiority of Joseph, to whom leadership in Israel fell in his generation (see 37:5–9).

38:1–5. Joseph was separated from his brothers by force, but **Judah went down from his brethren** (v. 1), voluntarily separating himself to seek his fortune among the Canaanites. He joined Hirah from Adullam, a town southwest of Jerusalem (see 2 Chron. 11:5, 7).

The daughter of Shua bore Judah three sons. The two eldest, **Er** and **Onan** (vv. 3–4), have names that also appear as designations of tribes in Mesopotamian documents of this time.

Chezib (v. 5) is probably the city Achzib (Josh. 15:44), three miles west of Adullam. The "men of Chozeba" (another form of the same word) were descendants of Shelah son of Judah (1 Chron. 4:21–22). The Hebrew root of the name Chezib means "deception" (see Mic. 1:14 and discussion), a theme running throughout the story of Jacob and his sons.

38:6–7. Judah took a wife for Er (v. 6), as parents often arranged their children's marriages (see chap. 24). Though the nature of Er's wickedness is not stated, it was so severe that **the Lord slew him** (v. 7).

38:8. A concise description of the custom known as "levirate marriage" (Latin *levir* means "brother-in-law") is given here. Details of the practice are given in Deuteronomy 25:5–6, where it is laid down as a legal obligation within Israel (see Matt. 22:24). The custom is illustrated in Ruth 4:5, though there it is extended to the nearest living relative (see Ruth 3:12; discussion on Ruth 2:20), since neither Boaz nor the nearer kinsman was a brother-in-law.

38:9–11. Onan knew that the seed should not be his (v. 9). Similarly, Ruth's nearest kinsman was fearful that if he married Ruth, he would endanger his own estate (Ruth 4:5–6). Taking advantage of sexual pleasure but avoiding responsibility to his deceased brother, he **spilled it** (his sperm) **on the ground**, a means of birth control sometimes called "onanism" (after Onan). His refusal to perform his levirate duty **displeased the Lord** (v. 10).

Judah showed reluctance to give Shelah to Tamar, **Lest peradventure he die also, as his brethren did**

(v. 11). Actually, he had no intention of giving Shelah to Tamar (see 38:14).

38:12–18. The exact location of **Timnath** (v. 12) and the sheep shearing is unknown, but it was somewhere in the hill country of Judah (see Josh. 15:48, 57). Tamar knew her father-in-law was sexually vulnerable, having been widowed himself, so she posed as a prostitute and **sat … by the way** (v. 14). Prostitutes customarily stationed themselves by the roadside (see v. 15; Jer. 3:2). She sat **in an open place**, literally, "the gate of Enaim," which means "two springs" and is probably Enam, in the western foothills of Judah (see Josh. 15:33–34).

Visiting a prostitute was not a moral issue for Judah. His concern was how to pay for her services. As a guarantee of payment, she asked for his **signet**, his **bracelets**, and his **staff** (v. 18). The signet was probably a small cylinder seal of the type used to sign clay documents by rolling them over the clay. The owner wore it around his neck on bracelets, that is, on a cord threaded through a hole drilled lengthwise through the signet.

38:19–23. Judah's friend who was sent to pay Tamar looked for a **harlot** (v. 21). The Hebrew here differs from that used for "harlot" in 38:15 and means "temple prostitute." Judah's friend perhaps deliberately used the more acceptable term, since ritual prostitutes enjoyed a higher social status in Canaan than did ordinary prostitutes. Such a person was not known in the area and could not be found.

38:24–30. When Judah learned Tamar was pregnant, he became a moralist and condemned her to **be burnt** (v. 24). In later times, burning was the legal penalty for prostitution (see Lev. 21:9). When she saved her life by producing **the signet, and bracelets, and staff** (v. 25)—items identifying Judah—he was forced to confess his moral failures.

Verses 28–30 describe the unusual birth of Tamar's twin sons (for a similarly unusual birth of twin boys, see 25:24–26). **Pharez** (v. 29), the firstborn of the twins, became the head of the leading clan in Judah and the ancestor of David (see Ruth 4:18–22) and ultimately of Christ (see Matt. 1:1–6).

39:1. Joseph's experiences in Egypt, as well as those of his youth in Canaan (see discussion on 37:23–24), are similar to Israel's national experiences in Egypt. Initially, because of God's blessing, Joseph attains a position of honor (in Potiphar's house); he is then unjustly thrown into prison, his only crime being his attractiveness and moral integrity; and finally he is raised up among the Egyptians as the one who, because God is with him, holds their lives in his hands. Similarly, Israel was first received with honor in Egypt (because of Joseph); then she was subjected to cruel bondage, her only crime being God's evident blessings upon her; and finally God raised her up in the eyes of the Egyptians (through the ministry of Moses) as they came fearfully to recognize that these people and their God did indeed hold their lives in their hands. The author of Genesis knew the events of the exodus and shows how the history of God and the patriarchs moved forward to and foreshadowed that event (see also 15:13–16; 48:21–22; 50:24–25).

39:2–6. The Lord was with Joseph (v. 2). This fact is echoed several times (39:3, 21, 23). Though Joseph's situation changed drastically, God's relationship with him remained the same (see Acts 7:9), and he was a recipient of the protection that God promised Isaac (26:3) and Jacob (28:15). Even Potiphar was conscious of it, for **the Lord blessed the Egyptian's house for Joseph's sake** (v. 5). The offspring of Abraham are becoming a blessing to the nations (see 12:2–3; 30:27).

Potiphar **left all that he had in Joseph's hand** (v. 6). Joseph had full responsibility for the welfare of Potiphar's house, as later he would have full responsibility in prison (vv. 22–23) and later still in all Egypt (41:41). Always this Israelite came to hold the welfare of his "world" in his hands—but always by the blessing and overruling of God, never by his own wits, as his father Jacob had so long attempted. In the role that he played in Israel's history and in the manner in which he lived it, Joseph was a true representative of Israel.

39:7–10. Having **cast her eyes upon Joseph** (v. 7), Potiphar's wife progressed to propositioning him. Responsibility of position often leaves one more vulnerable to temptation or sin, and one's accountability is often ignored; but not so with Joseph. **How can I ... sin against God?** (v. 9). He recognized that all sin is against God, first and foremost (see Ps. 51:4).

Her tempting was relentless **as she spake to Joseph day by day** (v. 10). However, **he hearkened not ... to be with her**. Joseph not only refused to sin with her but also avoided the possibility of sinning with her.

39:11–19. Being rejected by Joseph, Potiphar's wife forced herself upon him, only to be humiliated by further rejection. Her attitude turned hostile (compare Amnon's hostility toward Tamar, 2 Sam. 13:15–19), and she resorted to falsely accusing him. She called Joseph **a Hebrew** (v. 14), which is an ethnic term in the Bible usually used by non-Israelites in a disparaging sense.

39:20–23. Joseph was imprisoned **where the king's prisoners were bound** (v. 20; see Ps. 105:17–20). Though understandably angry (see 39:19), Potiphar put Joseph in the "house of the captain of the guard" (40:3)—certainly not the worst prison available. For a foreigner charged with raping an Egyptian official's wife, Joseph's sentence might be considered light. Not to be overlooked is the fact that **the LORD was with him** (v. 23).

40:1–4. Two of the Pharaoh's officers joined Joseph in prison. One, the **chief of the butlers** (v. 2), would later be the divinely appointed agent for introducing Joseph to Pharaoh (41:9–14). Providentially, Joseph is assigned to serve the two officers. He did not spend his time in prison being resentful and sulking over his own misfortune.

40:5–8. Each officer **dreamed a dream** (v. 5), each having its own meaning. Throughout the ancient Near East, it was believed that dreams had specific meanings and that proper interpretation of them could help the dreamer predict his future (see discussion on 20:3). God was beginning to prepare the way for Joseph's rise in Egypt. **Wherefore look ye so sadly to day?** (v. 7). In spite of his own circumstances, Joseph observed their changed countenance and kindly inquired of their personal distress.

Do not interpretations belong to God? (v. 8). Only God can interpret dreams properly and accurately (see 41:16, 25, 28; Dan. 2:28). **Tell me them** is not an arrogant statement. Joseph has not learned to interpret dreams by experience, for his own dreams (37:5–11) have not yet been realized. He presents himself as God's agent, through whom God will make known the revelation contained in their dreams. Israel is God's prophetic people, through whom God's revelation comes to the nations (see 18:17 and discussion; 41:16, 28, 32).

40:9–15. Joseph heard and interpreted the dream of the chief butler (vv. 9–11) first. Pharaoh will **lift up thine head, and restore thee unto thy place** (v. 13; compare Pss. 3:3; 27:6). For the meaning of the idiom "lift up thine head," see 2 Kings 25:27 and Jer. 52:31, where the Hebrew for "released" in the context of freeing a prisoner means literally "lifted up the head of."

Joseph's only request of the chief butler was, **think on me when it shall be well with thee** (v. 14). Unfortunately, the cupbearer did not remember Joseph (40:23) until two full years later (41:1, 9–13). **I was stolen** (v. 15) is a phrase depicting his loss of place, family, and rights. His mention of a **dungeon** is perhaps hyperbole to reflect his despair (see discussion on 39:20). Since the same Hebrew word is translated "pit" in 37:24, the author of Genesis has established a link with Joseph's earlier experience at the hands of his brothers.

40:16–20. The dream of the chief baker (vv. 16–17) had a bad interpretation. **Lift up thy head** (v. 19) is now a grisly pun based on the same idiom used in 40:13, for the baker's lot was to be released from prison only to be beheaded and then hung **on a tree**, probably a reference to being impaled on a pole.

Pharaoh's birthday (v. 20) served as a day for amnesties, and the interpretations of his officers' dreams were realized. Centuries later, the birthday of Herod the tetrarch would become the occasion for another beheading (see Matt. 14:6–10).

41:1–4. For **two full years** (v. 1), Joseph was forgotten by the chief butler. The events of this chapter jog his memory. The **Pharaoh dreamed** and saw **seven well favoured kine** (v. 2) coming up out of the river. Cattle often submerged themselves up to their necks in the Nile to escape the sun and insects. For cows to consume other cows may have seemed unusual, but considering the importance of the Nile to the life and economy of Egypt, it seems that the dream should have been readily understood.

41:5 – 8. In Pharaoh's second dream, which was perhaps even more unusual, he saw **seven thin ears** (v. 6), that is, heads of grain, **blasted with the east wind** spring up and consume seven good and healthy heads of grain. The Palestinian *sirocco* (Egyptian *khamsin*), which blows in from the desert (see Hos. 13:15) in late spring and early fall, often withers vegetation (see Isa. 40:7; Ezek. 17:10). Again, for a land whose crops were often threatened by desert winds, the meaning of the dream should have been obvious.

Like his imprisoned officials (see 40:6 – 7), Pharaoh's **spirit was troubled** (v. 8) by his dreams. The **magicians**, probably priests who claimed to possess occult knowledge, and **wise men** were called to interpret Pharaoh's dreams, but **none ... could interpret them unto Pharaoh** (see Dan. 2:10 – 11).

41:9 – 13. The butler advised Pharaoh about Joseph, who had interpreted his dream two years earlier in prison. **It came to pass, as he interpreted ... so it was** (v. 13), because his words were from the Lord (see Ps. 105:19).

41:14 – 16. Pharaoh sent and called Joseph (v. 14). This call effected Joseph's permanent release from prison (see Ps. 105:20). Before appearing before Pharaoh, Joseph **shaved** himself, because Egyptians were normally smooth-shaven, while Palestinians wore beards (see 2 Sam. 10:5; Jer. 41:5). Joseph is careful not to take any credit for abilities that were not his. **It is not in me: God shall give Pharaoh an answer of peace** (v. 16; see 40:8; Dan. 2:27 – 28, 30; 2 Cor. 3:5).

41:17 – 36. Both dreams were fully recounted to Joseph (vv. 17 – 24), who immediately informed Pharaoh that God had revealed **what he is about to do** (v. 25).

There would be **seven years of famine** (v. 27). Long famines were rare in Egypt because of the regu-

larity of the annual overflow of the Nile but not uncommon elsewhere (see 2 Kings 8:1). According to the New Testament, the great famine in the time of Elijah lasted three and a half years (James 5:17), thus half of seven years; it had been cut short by Elijah's intercession (1 Kings 18:42; James 5:18). Because of the famine's severity, **the dream was doubled ... twice** (v. 32). Repetition of a divine revelation was often used for emphasis (see 37:5 – 9; Amos 7:1 – 9; 8:1 – 3).

Joseph did not harbor resentment because of his years of unjust imprisonment and withhold advice but offered a plan that would prepare the Egyptians for the famine.

41:37 – 39. Pharaoh welcomed Joseph's advice because he identified him as a man indwelt by the **spirit of God** (v. 38). Perhaps "spirit of the gods" would be a better rendering, since Pharaoh was speaking. The word "spirit" should probably not be capitalized in such passages since reference to the Holy Spirit would be out of character in statements made by pagan rulers.

41:40 – 41. Thou shalt be over my house (v. 40). Pharaoh took Joseph's advice (41:33) and decided that Joseph himself should be "governor over Egypt" (Acts 7:10; see also Ps. 105:21). Pharaoh reasoned that the god who revealed the dream and this excellent plan would certainly enable him to carry it out. **According unto thy word shall all my people be ruled.** A more literal reading is, "At your command all my people are to kiss (you)," that is, kiss his hands or feet in an act of homage and submission (see Ps. 2:12 and discussion).

41:42 – 43. Three symbols of transfer and/or sharing of royal authority, **his ring ... vestures of fine linen ... a gold chain**, are referred to also in Esther 3:10 (ring), Esther 6:11 (apparel), and Daniel 5:7, 16, 29 (a gold chain). **And he made him to ride in the second chariot** (v. 43). Joseph's position was probably that of vizier, the highest executive office below that of the king himself. The Hebrew translated here as **Bow the knee** is difficult and may be an Egyptian imperative of a Semitic loanword calling attention to Joseph's position.

41:44 – 46. Joseph was given the name **Zaph-nath-paaneah** (v. 45) as part of his assignment to an official position within the royal administration (see discussion on 1:5). The meaning of Joseph's Egyptian name is uncertain. Pharaoh presumed to use this marvelously endowed servant of the Lord for his own royal purposes, as a later pharaoh would attempt to use divinely blessed Israel for the enrichment of Egypt (Exodus 1). He did not recognize that Joseph served a higher power, whose kingdom and redemptive purposes were being advanced. **Asenath** is an Egyptian name and probably means "she belongs to [the goddess] Neith." **Poti-phera** is not the same person as "Potiphar" (37:36; 39:1); the name (also Egyptian) means "he whom [the sun-god] Ra has given." **On**, located ten miles northeast of modern Cairo, was called Heliopolis ("city of the sun") by the Greeks and was an important center for the worship of Ra, who had a temple there. Poti-phera therefore bore an appropriate name.

At **thirty years** (v. 46) of age, in just thirteen years (see 37:2), Joseph had become second in command in Egypt.

41:47 – 49. As predicted, there were **seven plenteous years** (v. 47), and Joseph gathered and stockpiled grain **as the sand of the sea** (v. 49), a familiar simile, used earlier for the large number of offspring promised to Abraham and Jacob (22:17; 32:12).

41:50 – 52. Like his own name (see 30:24), the names of Joseph's two sons were significant wordplays. **Manasseh** (v. 51) is based on the Hebrew verb meaning "to forget," and **Ephraim** (v. 52) sounds like the Hebrew for "twice fruitful" and reflects the fact that God gave Joseph two sons.

41:53 – 57. The famine was severe **in all lands** (v. 57). With grain stored in Egypt, **all countries** came there to purchase it. "All countries" describes the known world from the writer's perspective (the Middle East).

2. Jacob's Migration (chaps. 42 – 47)

42:1 – 5. **Why do ye look one upon another?** (v. 1). Though a question, it depicts the despondency of Jacob's family, in need of food. Ten sons were sent to purchase grain from Egypt, but **Benjamin, Joseph's brother, Jacob sent not** (v. 4). Their mother, Rachel, had died (35:19), and Jacob thought Joseph also was dead (37:33). Jacob did not want to lose Benjamin, the remaining son of his beloved Rachel. The **famine** reached **the land of Canaan** (v. 5) and was reminiscent of the famine in Abram's day (see 12:10 and discussion).

42:6 – 8. As **governor over the land** (v. 6) and being responsible for the sale of grain to foreigners, Joseph was in a position to spot his brothers. In fulfillment of his dreams (see 37:7, 9), they **bowed down themselves before him**. Although at least twenty years had passed since he had last seen them (see 37:2; 41:46, 53 – 54), **Joseph knew his brethren** (v. 8) because they had been adults at the time and their appearance had not changed much, but **they knew not him**. Joseph, a teenager at the time of his enslavement, was now an adult in an unexpected position of authority, wearing Egyptian clothes and speaking to his brothers through an interpreter (see 42:23). He was, moreover, shaven in the Egyptian manner (see discussion on 41:14).

42:9 – 11. He accused them of being **spies** sent **to see the nakedness of the land** (v. 9), that is, the exposed and defenseless parts of the land due to famine. Unwittingly, Joseph's brothers again fulfilled his dreams and their own scornful fears (see 37:8) by addressing him as **my lord** (v. 10) and calling themselves **thy servants**. They affirmed that they were **all one man's sons** (v. 11). No one would send ten sons as a group to spy.

42:12 – 16. **By the life of Pharaoh** (v. 15) is an Egyptian oath. The most solemn oaths were pronounced in the name of the reigning monarch (as here) or of the speaker's deities (see Ps. 16:4; Amos 8:14) or of the Lord Himself (Judg. 8:19; 1 Sam. 14:39, 45; 19:6).

42:17 – 25. After three day's imprisonment, they were still rehearsing their past crime and how they had seen the **anguish of his** (Joseph's) **soul** (v. 21). A guilty conscience keeps the memory fresh. The brothers realized they were beginning to reap what they had sown (see Gal. 6:7) and began to cast blame (see 42:22; 37:21–22).

Joseph **took from them Simeon** (v. 24), Jacob's second son (29:32–33) and imprisoned him instead of the firstborn Reuben, perhaps because the latter had saved Joseph's life years earlier (37:21–22). By binding Simeon **before their eyes**, Joseph left a lasting impression—Simeon would not be released unless they returned with their younger brother Benjamin.

42:26–38. Their journey home only engendered more fear, as they discovered their money in their sacks. Jacob was distraught about losing **Simeon** (v. 36) and was adamant in his refusal to let **Benjamin** go with them. Reuben may have intended his offer to secure Benjamin's safety to be a generous one, but his words **Slay my two sons** (v. 37) were as rash as his earlier act with Bilhah (35:22, see discussion on 37:21).

43:1–9. When Jacob instructed his son to go to Egypt for more grain, **Judah spake unto him** (v. 3). From this point on, Judah became the spokesman for his brothers (see 43:8–10; 44:14–34; 46:28). His tribe would become preeminent among the twelve tribes (see 49:8–10), and he would be an ancestor of Jesus (see Matt. 1:2, 17; Luke 3:23, 33).

Judah recited two ultimatums. One was Joseph's: **Ye shall not see my face, except your brother be with you** (v. 3). The second was Judah's own: **if thou wilt not send him, we will not go down** (v. 5) to Egypt and buy food. He is not disrespectful, but under the circumstances, he is firm.

43:9–10. I will be surety for him ... let me bear the blame (v. 9). Having lost two sons of his own to death (38:7–10), and now having two very young twin sons (38:29–30), Judah fully understood his father's heart. Thus, he offered himself as security for Benjamin's safety—a more sane and generous gesture than that of Reuben (see 42:37 and discussion).

43:11–14. A resigned Jacob insisted that they **carry ... a present** (v. 11), a customary practice when approaching one's superior, whether political (see 1 Sam. 16:20), military (see 1 Sam. 17:18), or religious (see 2 Kings 5:15). The **balm** and **spices,**

and myrrh surely refreshed their memories of the caravan of the Ishmaelites that purchased Joseph (see 37:25 and discussion). The **honey** was either that produced by bees or an inferior substitute made by boiling grape or date juice down to a thick syrup. Pistachio **nuts,** mentioned only here in the Bible, are the fruit of a small, broad-crowned tree that is native to Asia Minor, Syria, and Canaan but not to Egypt.

Unwittingly, Jacob invoked the name of **God Almighty** (v. 14; see discussion on 17:1) to move the heart of his own son to release Simeon and Benjamin. **If I be bereaved of my children, I am bereaved.** (Compare Esther's similar phrase of resignation in Est. 4:16.)

43:15–23. The order to bring the brothers into the house of Joseph (the "man," 43:3; the "lord of the land," 42:30) was open to interpretation and left them fearful. The brothers' statement to Joseph's steward explaining their returned money compressed many details (see 42:27, 35). The steward spoke better than he knew when he assured them, **your God ... hath given you treasure** (v. 23).

43:24–28. Treated with utmost courtesy (water for their feet and fodder for their donkeys), the brothers prepared their present (see 43:11) for Joseph. When he arrived, they **bowed themselves to him to the earth** (v. 26), an additional fulfillment of Joseph's dreams (37:7, 9; see also 42:6; 43:28).

43:29–31. Having asked about his father's welfare, he saw **Benjamin, his mother's son** (v. 29). Joseph's special relationship to Benjamin is clear. **God be gracious unto thee.** Later blessings and benedictions would echo these words (Num. 6:25; Ps. 67:1). Though he once appeared harsh and insensitive (42:7–17), **Joseph** was both emotional and sensitive, and he **wept** often (v. 30; see 42:24; 45:2, 14–15; 46:29).

43:32–34. According to Egyptian custom, Joseph ate separately from his brothers because **Egyptians might not eat bread with the Hebrews** (v. 32). The taboo was probably based on ritual or religious reasons (see Exod. 8:26), unlike the Egyptian refusal to associate with shepherds (see 46:34), which was probably based on social custom. More amazing to his brothers, however, was that Joseph was able to seat them according to age. That **Benjamin's mess was five times so much** (v. 34) as his brothers reflected his special status with Joseph (see discussion on 43:29; see also 45:22) and was probably also a test to see how his brothers would react to his favoritism.

44:1–5. Returning their money and planting Joseph's silver cup in Benjamin's sack set up the brothers for their biggest test yet—a charge of theft. It happened when they had barely left **the city** (v. 4), one whose identity is unknown, though Memphis (about thirteen miles south of modern Cairo) and Zoan (in the eastern delta region) have been suggested. Joseph sent his steward after them and instructed him to say, **Is not this** the cup **in which my lord drinketh, and ... divineth?** (v. 5). Divining with a cup was culturally Egyptian but was forbidden for Israel (see discussion on 30:27), and it is doubtful that Joseph, who saw revelation of the future in God's hands (see 41:16, 25), would have done so.

44:6–12. The brothers were overtaken and charged with theft. They were so confident of their innocence that they offered, **With whomsoever of thy servants it be found, both let him die** (v. 9). Years earlier, Jacob had given Laban a similar, rash response (see 31:32 and discussion). The steward softened the penalty contained in the brothers' proposal, stating that only the guilty one **shall be my servant** (v. 10). The search **began at the eldest, and left at the youngest** (v. 12; for a similar build up of suspense, see 31:33).

44:13–17. They did not resort to accusation or cast blame on Benjamin but instead **rent their clothes** (v. 13), a sign of intense distress and grief (see 37:29). Then appearing before Joseph, they **fell before him on the ground** (v. 14), a further fulfillment of Joseph's dreams in 37:7, 9 (see 42:6; 43:26, 28). **God hath found out the iniquity of thy servants** (v. 16). Like Joseph's steward (see discussion on 43:23), Judah spoke better than he knew, or perhaps his words had a double meaning (see 42:21).

44:18–29. When Judah saw that Joseph was intent on holding Benjamin as a slave, he stepped up and spoke with the passion possible only of one who had shared grief with his father (see discussion on 43:3). He honored Joseph with terms such as **my lord** and **thy servant** (v. 18; see discussion on 42:10). The words **thou art even as Pharaoh** were more flattering than true (see 41:40, 43).

44:30–34. Though Judah spoke on behalf of Benjamin, he spoke more for his father, whose life was **bound up in the lad's life** (v. 30). The Hebrew underlying this clause is later used for "the soul of Jonathan" being "knit with the soul of David" (1 Sam. 18:1). True to his promise to Jacob (43:9), Judah begged to be Joseph's slave **instead of the lad** (v. 33). Judah's willingness to be a substitute for Benjamin helped make amends for his role in selling Joseph (see 37:26–27). He could not return without Benjamin and **see the evil** (v. 34) that would come on Jacob (v. 31). Judah obviously remembers an earlier scene (37:34–35).

45:1–2. The change in Joseph's temperament (harsh and accusatory, 42:7–17; kind and hospitable, 43:16, 26–34; again harsh and accusatory, 44:15; and now emotional and weeping) was psychologically unnerving to his brothers. Here he **wept** (v. 2; see also 45:14–15; 43:30), perhaps overjoyed at the change he had witnessed in his brothers, seeing their love and respect for their father and Benjamin, and being able to now identify himself to them and be reunited.

45:3–8. Joseph's **brethren ... were troubled** (v. 3) by the announcement of his identity, perhaps because they thought they were seeing a ghost, but probably because they were afraid of what Joseph would do to them. In the repeated announcement, **I am Joseph your brother** (v. 4), Joseph emphasized his relationship to them. **Ye sold me hither** was a painful reminder, but his added note, **God did send me** (v. 5), lessened the pain. God had a purpose to work through the brothers' thoughtless and cruel act (see Ps. 105:17; compare Acts 2:23; 4:28), and that was to preserve his brothers as **a posterity** (v. 7), that is, as a remnant. Although none had been lost, they had escaped a great threat to them all, so Joseph called them a remnant in the confidence that they would live to produce a great people. He could be used to accomplish this because of his position, **a father to Pharaoh** (v. 8). This was a title of honor given to viziers (see discussion on 41:43) and other high officials (in the Apocrypha, see 1 Maccabees 11:32). All three of Joseph's titles in verse 8, **father**, **lord**, and **ruler**, were originally Egyptian.

45:9–13. Haste you … tarry not (v. 9). Joseph was anxious to see Jacob as soon as possible (v. 13). Joseph selected **Goshen** (v. 10) as the place for them to live. A region in the eastern part of the Nile delta, it was very fertile (see 45:18) and remains so today. **It is my mouth that speaketh** (v. 12); that is, these were Joseph's personal promises in their language, not simply an aloof conversation through an interpreter as before (see 42:23). **All my glory in Egypt** (v. 13) was not a boast but evidence that he was able to assist his family in that land.

45:14–20. Weeping was unrestrained as he kissed his brothers. Then **his brethren talked with him** (v. 15) in intimate fellowship and friendship, rather than with hostility or fear, for the first time in over twenty years (see 37:2; 41:46, 53; 45:6; Joseph was now thirty-nine years old).

Pharaoh's offer that Joseph's family should **eat the fat of the land** (v. 18) was an echo of Isaac's blessing on Jacob (27:28). Providentially, Joseph had Pharaoh's full support to care for Jacob and his family in Egypt.

45:21–24. With Pharaoh's blessing, Joseph sent his brothers away equipped with wagons for transporting the family to Egypt, new clothing, money, and ten donkeys loaded with gifts and food from Egypt. Joseph's final word to his brothers was, **See that ye fall not out by the way** (v. 24). He wanted nothing to delay their return (see 45:9), and he wanted them to avoid mutual accusation and recrimination concerning the past.

45:25–28. Seeing is believing! Only after Jacob saw the wagons that Joseph had sent could he believe the good news that Joseph was indeed alive.

46:1–7. Israel took his journey (v. 1). The journey was to be a national venture, not a personal one; thus, the name Israel is used instead of Jacob. He probably left the family estate at Hebron (see 35:27).

En route, he **came to Beer-sheba, and offered sacrifices** where Abraham and Isaac had also worshiped the Lord (see 21:33; 26:23–25).

God spake unto Israel in the visions of the night (v. 2). This would be the last patriarchal vision. Just as God had once called to Abraham (22:11), He now called, **Jacob, Jacob**. The response was also the same: **Here am I**. When Isaac had considered a move to Egypt, God forbade him and instructed him to "sojourn in this land [Canaan]" (26:2–3). Now as Israel and his family were about to leave Canaan, he needed God's reaffirmation of His covenant promises.

I am … the God of thy father: fear not (v. 3). This is a verbatim repetition of God's statement to Isaac in 26:24. **I will there make of thee a great nation**, a reaffirmation of one aspect of His promise to Abraham (see 12:2), and it would happen "there," in Egypt (see Exod. 1:7). **I will go down with thee into Egypt** (v. 4). God would be with Jacob as he went south to Egypt just as He was with him when he went north to Haran, and He would again bring him back as He had done before (see 28:15; 15:16; 48:21). Thus encouraged, Jacob left Beersheba to take all that he had — family, cattle, and belongings — to Egypt.

46:8–15. These are the names of the children of Israel which came into Egypt (v. 8). The Hebrew here is repeated verbatim in Exodus 1:1, where it introduces the background for the story of the exodus (predicted in Gen. 46:4).

Jacob's sons (listed with their sons) that were born to his wife Leah were **Reuben** (v. 9), **Simeon** (v. 10), **Levi** (v. 11), **Judah** (v. 12), **Issachar** (v. 13), and **Zebulun** (v. 14). Judah's sons **Er and Onan** (v. 12) died in Canaan; his grandsons **Hezron** and **Hamul**, born after chapter 38, were probably born in Egypt.

The total number of descendants born by **Leah** was **thirty and three** (v. 15). There are thirty-four names in verses 8–15. To bring the number to thirty-three, the name **Ohad** (v. 10) should probably be removed, since it does not appear in the parallel lists in Numbers 26:12–13 and 1 Chronicles 4:24. The Hebrew form of Ohad looks very much like that of Zohar, listed in the same verse and in Exodus 6:15, and a later scribe probably added Ohad to the text accidentally.

46:16-18. Jacob's sons (listed with their sons) that were born to Leah's maid, **Zilpah** (v. 18), were **Gad** (v. 16) and **Asher** (v. 17). The total number of descendants was **sixteen** (v. 18).

46:19-22. Jacob's sons (listed with their sons) that were born to his favorite wife, **Rachel** (v. 19), were **Joseph** (v. 20) and **Benjamin** (v. 21). Joseph's sons were born in Egypt (41:51-52) and probably some of Benjamin's sons were as well, for he was a young man at the time of the move and could hardly have had ten sons already. The total number of descendants was **fourteen** (v. 22).

46:23-25. Jacob's sons (listed with their sons) that were born to Rachel's maid, **Bilhah,** (v. 25) were **Dan** (v. 23) and **Naphtali** (v. 24). The total number of descendants was **seven** (v. 25).

46:26-27. All the souls that came with Jacob into Egypt ... were threescore and six (v. 26). The total of thirty-three (see 46:15 and discussion), sixteen (46:18), fourteen (46:22), and seven (see 46:25) is seventy. To arrive at sixty-six, we must subtract Er and Onan, who "died in the land of Canaan" (46:12), and Manasseh and Ephraim (46:20), who **were born ... in Egypt** (v. 27).

Seventy, or **threescore and ten** (v. 27; see Deut. 10:22), is the ideal and complete number (see Introduction: "Literary Features"; see also discussions on 5:5; 10:2) of Jacob's descendants who would have been in Egypt if Er and Onan had not died earlier (see 38:7-10; for the number seventy-five in Acts 7:14, see discussion there).

46:28-32. Jacob **sent Judah before him** (v. 28), for he had emerged as the spokesman for his brothers (see discussion on 43:3), to inform Joseph of their coming. **Goshen** was the land Joseph selected for them (see 45:10).

After a tearful but joyful reunion with his father, Joseph instructed his brothers to state clearly to Pharaoh that they were shepherds, occupied with cattle. He further informed them that **every shepherd is an abomination unto the Egyptians** (v. 34; see discus-

sion on 43:32). He purposely created a situation in which once Pharaoh knew their occupation, hopefully he would mandate that Joseph's family (and flocks) should live isolated from the Egyptians — in the fertile area of Goshen.

47:1-6. When Pharaoh learned that Joseph's family had come as far as Goshen and wanted permission to live there with their flocks, he assigned the land to them: **in the land of Goshen let them dwell** (v. 6). Thus, when the famine became more severe and fertile land was needed, no Egyptian could fault Joseph, a foreigner, for having favored his family and placing them in the best of the land, because Pharaoh had made the decision.

47:7-10. Apparently out of gratitude to Pharaoh's kindness, Jacob **blessed** him (v. 7). Jacob referred to the itinerant nature of patriarchal life in general and of his own in particular as a **pilgrimage** (v. 9), as he hopefully awaited the fulfillment of the promise of a land (see Deut. 26:5). He considered the days of his life as **few** (he was only 130 years old, compared to Abraham, who lived to the age of 175 [25:7], and Isaac, who lived to 180 [35:28]) **and evil** (i.e., marked by deception, anger, anguish, and distress).

47:11-12. Israel took up residence **in the best of the land** (see discussion on 45:10), **in the land of Rameses** (v. 11). The city of Rameses is mentioned in Exodus 1:11; 12:37; and Numbers 33:3, 5. Though the name poses interpretative problems, it probably refers to the great Egyptian pharaoh Rameses II, who reigned centuries later (the designation here involves an editorial updating). In addition to being known as Goshen (47:27), the "land of Rameses" was called the "field of Zoan" in Psalm 78:12, 43 (see discussion on Gen. 44:4).

47:13-19. The famine was very sore (v. 13), that is, very severe. After the people used up all their money to buy corn (vv. 14-15), they traded their cattle (vv. 16-17), then their land (v. 20), and then themselves (v. 21).

47:20-22. The Egyptians sold their land to Joseph and were moved temporarily into the cities until seed could be distributed to them for planting. (The Septuagint says, "Joseph reduced the people to slavery." Regardless, the people were appreciative: "Thou hast saved our lives," 47:25). Only the priests were exempt from this policy.

47:23–26. Seed was distributed to the Egyptians on the condition that whatever it produced, **Pharaoh should have the fifth part** (v. 26). The same was true "in the seven plenteous years" (41:34), but now all the land on which the produce grew belonged to Pharaoh as well.

47:27–31. Israel … grew, and multiplied exceedingly (v. 27). In the additional seventeen years that Jacob lived, he began to see God's promises realized (see 35:11–12; 46:3 and discussions). Before he died, Jacob asked of Joseph, **Put … thy hand under my thigh** (v. 29). For this strange request, see discussion on 24:2. In both cases, an elderly man addresses a younger man, and ties of family kinship are being stressed. I will **lie with my fathers** (v. 30), a reference to joining his deceased ancestors in death (see discussion on 25:8). It was typical of the culture to desire to be buried with one's fathers in the homeland. **Bury me in their burying place**, that is, in the cave of Machpelah (see 50:12–13). As the "executor" of his father's will, Joseph **sware unto him** to do as asked (v. 31).

3. Jacob's Last Days (48:1–50:14)

48:1–4. With his aged father ill, Joseph knew that Jacob's time was short, so he made the trip with his two sons to visit him. Jacob **sat** up **upon the bed** (v. 2) for his final recorded personal conversation with Joseph.

Jacob identified the one who had spoken to him at Bethel as **God Almighty** (v. 3), the One who overpowers (see discussion on 17:1), perhaps because it was He who had taken Jacob, the deceiver who had struggled with God spiritually and physically (see 32:24–28), and had overpowered him so that he would experience His blessing. **Luz** is the older name for Bethel (see 28:19).

48:5. Thy two sons … are mine. Jacob was adopting Joseph's sons as his own. **Ephraim and Manasseh** are listed in reverse order of birth. (See 48:1 for the expected order since Manasseh was Jo-

seph's firstborn, 41:51). Jacob mentioned Ephraim first because he intended to give him the primary blessing and thus "set Ephraim before Manasseh" (48:20). Jacob called them **mine; as Reuben and Simeon**. Joseph's first two sons would enjoy equal status with Jacob's first two sons (35:23) and would in fact eventually supersede them. Because of an earlier sinful act (see 35:22 and discussion), Reuben would lose his birthright to Jacob's favorite son, Joseph (see 49:3–4; 1 Chron. 5:2), and thus to Joseph's sons (see 1 Chron. 5:1).

48:6. Any additional sons born to Joseph would be considered his and would take the place of Ephraim and Manasseh, whom Jacob had adopted. Ephraim and Manasseh **shall be called after the name of their brethren in their inheritance**; that is, their names would be perpetuated for purposes of inheritance (for a similar provision, see 38:8 and discussion; Deut. 25:5–6). Joseph's territory would thus be divided between Ephraim and Manasseh, but Levi (Jacob's third son; see 35:23) would not receive a share of the land (Josh. 14:4). The total number of tribal allotments would therefore remain the same.

48:7. On Jacob's return from **Padan** (short for Padan-aram, meaning "plain of Aram," another name for Aram-naharaim; see discussion on 24:10), **Rachel died** (see 35:16–19). Adopted by Joseph's father, Ephraim and Manasseh in effect took the place of other sons whom Joseph's mother, Rachel, might have borne had she not died on the way to **Ephrath** (see discussion on 35:16).

48:8–14. Either because he had never met his grandsons or because, being old, his eyes were **dim** (v. 10) and he could not see them clearly, **Israel … said, Who are these?** (v. 8). Jacob **kissed** and **embraced** his grandsons (v. 10) and took them to his knees (v. 12), an action probably symbolizing adoption (see discussion on 30:3). Joseph positioned his sons so that **Manasseh** was standing before **Israel's right hand** (v. 13). Joseph wanted Jacob to bless Manasseh, the firstborn, by placing his right hand on Manasseh's head.

48:15–16. As his father, Isaac, had blessed him (27:27–29), Jacob now **blessed Joseph** (v. 15).

Joseph's name is used here collectively and includes Ephraim and Manasseh (the Hebrew for "you" and "your" in 48:21 is plural). The phrase **fed me** (lit., "shepherded me") is an intimate royal metaphor for God (see Ps. 23:1), used in Genesis only here and in Jacob's later blessing of Joseph (49:24). It initiates the motif of God as a shepherd in Scripture, used later of the coming Messiah (Isa. 40:11) and Jesus (John 10:11; Heb. 13:20; 1 Peter 5:4).

The **Angel** (v. 16)—God Himself—who had earlier blessed Jacob (32:29; see also discussion on 32:24) is now invoked to bless his grandsons.

48:17-20. Contrary to Joseph's wishes, Jacob positioned his hands to bless Ephraim over the firstborn Manasseh. **His younger brother shall be greater than he** (v. 19; see discussion on 25:23). During the divided monarchy (930-722 BC), Ephraim's descendants were the most powerful tribe in the north. "Ephraim" was often used to refer to the northern kingdom as a whole (see, e.g., Isa. 7:2, 5, 8-9; Hos. 9:13; 12:1, 8). Thus, Jacob **set Ephraim before Manasseh** (v. 20). Jacob, the younger son had who struggled with Esau for the birthright and blessing and who preferred the younger sister (Rachel) above the older (Leah), now advanced Joseph's younger son ahead of the older.

48:21. I die: but God ... shall bring you again unto the land of your fathers. Years later, Joseph would conclude his life with these words to his brothers (50:24).

Joseph is promised **one portion above** his brothers. The Hebrew for this phrase is identical with the place-name Shechem, where Joseph was later buried in a plot of ground inherited by his descendants (see Josh. 24:32; see also Gen. 33:19; John 4:5). **I took out of the hand of the Amorite** is difficult to explain from history, but possibly it refers to the event at Shechem (34:25-29).

49:1-27. Jacob gathered his sons for his final words. Verses 2-27 contain the longest poem in Genesis, often called the "Blessing of Jacob." Its various blessings were intended not only for Jacob's twelve sons but also for the tribes that descended from them (see 49:28). For other poetic bless-

ings in Genesis, see 9:26-27; 14:19-20; 27:27-29; 27:39-40; 48:15-16; 48:20.

49:3-4. Reuben, **unstable as water** (v. 4), did rash things (35:22) and said rash things (42:37), and his descendants were characterized by indecision (see Judg. 5:15-16). **Thou shalt not excel; because thou wentest up to thy father's bed.** Jacob never forgot Reuben's incestuous deed (see 35:22 and discussion), and though he was the firstborn, he lost his birthright to Joseph's sons (see 1 Chron. 5:1; see also discussion on Gen. 48:5).

49:5-7. Simeon and Levi are brethren (v. 5), both born to Leah. They shared the traits of violence, anger, and cruelty (vv. 6-7), especially demonstrated at Shechem (see 34:13, 25-26). **I will divide ... scatter them** (v. 7) was fulfilled when Simeon's descendants were absorbed into the territory of Judah (see Josh. 19:1, 9) and when Levi's descendants were dispersed throughout the land, living in forty-eight towns and the surrounding pasturelands (see discussion on 48:6; see also Num. 35:2, 7; Josh. 14:4; 21:41).

49:8-12. Judah ... thy brethren ... shall bow down before thee (v. 8; see discussion on 43:3; 1 Chronicles 5:2). As those who would become the leading tribes of southern and northern Israel respectively, Judah and Joseph were given the longest (vv. 8-12 and 49:22-26) of Jacob's blessings. Judah was the fourth of Leah's sons and also the fourth son born to Jacob (29:35), but Reuben, Simeon, and Levi had forfeited their right of leadership. So Jacob assigned leadership to Judah (a son of Leah) but a double portion to Joseph (a son of Rachel).

Judah is a lion's whelp (v. 9), a symbol of sovereignty, strength, and courage. Judah (or Israel) is often pictured as a lion in later times (see Ezek. 19:1-7; Mic. 5:8; and especially Num. 24:9). Judah's greatest descendant, Jesus Christ (see discussion on 43:3), is Himself called "the Lion of the tribe of Judah" (Rev. 5:5).

Though difficult to translate, verse 10 has been traditionally understood as messianic. The promise of a **sceptre**, the symbol of kingship, in Judah (see discussion on Num. 24:17) was initially fulfilled in David and ultimately fulfilled in Christ. **Until Shiloh**

come is more difficult, but it probably means "until he comes to whom it belongs." It is a concept repeated in Ezekiel 21:27, in a section where Zedekiah, the last king of Judah, is told to "take off the crown" from his head because dominion over Jerusalem will ultimately be given to the one "whose right it is" (Ezek. 21:26–27).

Judah's descendants would someday enjoy a settled and peaceful life, marked by prosperity and abundance (vv. 11–12).

49:13. Though landlocked by the tribes of Asher and Manasseh, the descendants of **Zebulun** were close enough to the Mediterranean (within ten miles) to "suck of the abundance of the seas" (Deut. 33:19).

49:14–15. Issachar is a strong ass (v. 14). Apparently as a beast of burden, his descendants would submit to hard labor, supposedly engaged in agriculture in the pleasant land allotted them by Joshua. **Became as servant unto tribute** (v. 15) is difficult. Did Issachar's descendants, as some suppose, submit to the Canaanites instead of fighting? They are not listed among those who failed to drive out the Canaanites (Judges 1), and they are spoken of favorably for their bravery (Judg. 5:15).

49:16–17. Dan shall be a serpent (v. 17). The treachery of a group of Danites in later times is described in Judges 18:27. He will be **an adder … that biteth the horse heels**. Samson, from the tribe of Dan, would single-handedly hold the Philistines at bay (Judges 14–16).

49:18. Jacob paused midway through his series of blessings to utter a brief prayer for God's help.

49:19. Gad, a troop shall overcome him. Located east of the Jordan (see Josh. 13:24–27), the descendants of Gad were vulnerable to raids by the Moabites to the south, as the Mesha (see 2 Kings 3:4) stele (a Moabite inscription dating from the late ninth century BC) illustrates (see chart, *KJV Study Bible*, p. xix).

49:20. Out of Asher his bread shall be fat. Fertile farmlands near the Mediterranean (see Josh. 19:24–30) would ensure the prosperity of Asher's descendants.

49:21. Naphtali is a hind let loose. This is perhaps a reference to an independent spirit fostered in the descendants of Naphtali by their somewhat isolated location in the hill country north of the Sea of Galilee (see Josh. 19:32–38).

49:22–26. Joseph is a fruitful bough (v. 22). "Fruitful" is a pun on the name Ephraim (see discussion on 41:52), who Jacob predicted would be greater than Joseph's firstborn son, Manasseh (48:19–20). **Branches run over the wall** describes Ephraim's descendants, who tended to expand their territory (see Josh. 17:14–18).

His bow abode in strength (v. 24) describes the warlike Ephraimites (see Judg. 8:1; 12:1), who would often prove victorious in battle (see Josh. 17:18). Jacob uses three titles describing his God. **The mighty God of Jacob** stresses the activity of God in saving and redeeming His people (see Isa. 49:26). **The shepherd** (see discussion on 48:15) denotes His intimate care. **The stone of Israel** depicts Israel's sure defense (see Deut. 32:4,15,18, 30–31) and is a figure used often in Psalms and Isaiah.

The Almighty (v. 25; see discussion on 17:1) is the source of all blessings. **Blessings of heaven … of the deep** refers to the fertility of the soil watered by rains from above and springs and streams from below. **Blessings of the breasts, and of the womb** depicts the fertility of man and animals. For the later prosperity of Ephraim's descendants, see Hosea 12:8.

Joseph … him that was separate from his brethren (v. 26; see discussion on 49:8). Ephraim would gain supremacy, especially over the northern tribes (see Josh. 16:9; Isa. 7:1–2; Hos. 13:1).

49:27. Benjamin shall ravin as a wolf. See the exploits of Ehud (Judg. 3:12–30) and of Saul and Jonathan (1 Sam. 11–15). See Judges 19–21 for examples of the savagery that characterized one group of Benjamin's descendants.

49:28–33. After Jacob's blessing came his final charge: **bury me with my fathers** (v. 29; he had already received a commitment from Joseph in 47:29–31). Jacob does not forget that the land of his fathers is his God-appointed homeland. With the charge completed, he breathed his last and **was**

gathered unto his people (i.e., he joined his ancestors in death; v. 33).

4. *Joseph's Last Days (50:15–26)*

50:1–4. Professional embalmers could have been hired to attend to Jacob's body, but **physicians embalmed Israel** (v. 2), perhaps because Joseph wanted to avoid involvement with the pagan religious ceremonies accompanying their services. The two periods, **forty days** (for embalming; v. 3) and **threescore and ten days** (of mourning), probably overlapped.

50:4–6. To fulfill his obligation, Joseph had to appeal to Pharaoh. **My father made me swear** (v. 5; see 47:29–31). Jacob had asked to be buried in the grave he had **digged**, that is, in the grave he had prepared for himself. Permission was given to **go up** to Canaan, to Hebron, which has a higher elevation than Goshen.

50:7–14. The funeral procession to Canaan was made up of Pharaoh's servants, Joseph and his brothers, and a military escort. Arriving at the **threshing floor of Atad** (perhaps better transliterated from the Hebrew as a place-name, i.e., Goren ha-Atad; v. 10), they observed seven more days of mourning that were so intense that the locals who witnessed it called the place **Abel-mizraim** (v. 11), or the "mourning of Egypt." The procession ended at **Machpelah** (v. 13), where Jacob was buried.

50:15–21. With their father deceased, the brothers feared Joseph would **hate** and **requite** (v. 15) the evil they had done. Similarly, Esau had once planned to kill Jacob as soon as Isaac died (see 27:41). **Joseph wept** (v. 17; see 50:1 and discussion on 43:30) when he learned of their fear. He may have been saddened by the thought that his brothers might be falsely implicating their father in their story. He may have regretted his failure to reassure them sooner that he had already forgiven them. They **fell down before his face** (v. 18). This is the final fulfillment of Joseph's earlier dreams (see discussions on 37:7, 9–11). **We be thy servants**. They had earlier expressed a similar

willingness but under quite different circumstances (see 44:9, 33).

50:19–21. Joseph asked, **Am I in the place of God?** (v. 19). His question expects a negative answer. **God meant it unto good** (v. 20). Their act, out of personal animosity toward a brother, had been used by God to save life—the life of the Israelites, the Egyptians, and all the nations that came to Egypt to buy food in the face of a famine that threatened the known world. At the same time, God showed by these events that His purpose for the nations is life and that this purpose would be effected through the descendants of Abraham. **He comforted them** (v. 21), apparently assuring them of his forgiveness.

50:23–26. Joseph was blessed with long life; he saw Ephraim's children to **the third generation** (v. 23). **Machir**, Manasseh's firstborn son (second generation), became the ancestor of the powerful Gileadites (Josh. 17:1). The name Machir later became almost interchangeable with that of Manasseh himself (see Judg. 5:14). His children (third generation) were **brought up upon Joseph's knees**, probably inferring that Joseph adopted Machir's children (see discussion on 30:3; see also 48:12).

Before he died, Joseph addressed his **brethren** (v. 24), perhaps speaking here to more than his siblings. **God will … bring you out of this land**. Joseph did not forget God's promises (15:16; 46:4; 48:21) concerning "the departing" (Heb. 11:22). Therefore, he made his final request (for a similar request by Jacob, see 47:29–31). **Carry up my bones from hence** (v. 25). Centuries later, Moses did so to fulfill his ancestor's oath (see Exod. 13:19). Joseph's bones were eventually "buried … in Shechem, in a parcel of ground which Jacob bought of the sons of Hamor" (Josh. 24:32; see Gen. 33:19).

Joseph died, being an hundred and ten years old (v. 26). Ancient Egyptian records indicate that 110 years was considered to be the ideal life span; to the Egyptians, this would have signified divine blessing upon Joseph.

THE SECOND BOOK OF MOSES, CALLED EXODUS

INTRODUCTION

Title

The Hebrew titles for the books of the Bible are generally derived from their initial word or phrase. In Hebrew, Exodus is named after its first two words, *we'elleh shemoth,* meaning "these are the names." The same phrase occurs in Genesis 46:8, where it likewise introduces a list of the Israelite immigrants to Egypt, one manner in which the author consecutively linked these two books. The Hebrew title is generally shortened to just *Shemoth,* "names." The English title for the book, Exodus (meaning "departure"), is based on the Greek title, *Exodos,* which was assigned to the book by the translators of the Septuagint.

Author

The author of Exodus, in addition to the other four books of the Pentateuch, is Moses. Moses is the towering personality of the Hebrew Scriptures. His massive shadow falls over not only the five books he authored, the Pentateuch, but over the entirety of the Old Testament. This prince of Egypt, shepherd, prophet, mediator, and miracle worker is at the core of both Judaism, as a lawgiver, and Christianity, in his role as the typological progenitor of the Messiah, Jesus, the "prophet like unto Moses" (Deut. 18:15–18).

Within the story of the exodus is Moses, a man of great complexity, interest, humanity, and grandeur. The biblical text introduces him as a prince. Moses, in the prime of life, seems well aware of his unique destiny as the deliverer of his people. Boldly, yet prematurely, he acts to set that grand destiny in motion. A later version of this man, no longer royalty but an obscure shepherd, humbled by life and circumstance, seems reluctant to endorse his destiny even after a supernatural encounter and divine instruction. Within his narrative struggles, readers observe this man grow in faith, confidence, and power as he fulfills his divine destiny and finally becomes not only his people's deliverer but also their shepherd and mediator. Not once in the text does Moses' self-portrait yield to heroic caricature; he remains all too human throughout the Exodus narrative and the remainder of the Pentateuch.

Mosaic authorship, however, has been challenged by some scholars, who argue for a later date of composition (see "Date," below), and it remains a hotly contended issue.

Nonetheless, strong evidence contradicts the conclusion, postulated in certain arenas, that the book of Exodus or the Pentateuch as a whole is a literary monster created out of disparate literary parts. Evidence supporting Mosaic authorship is quite strong, for the following reasons: (1) The internal claims of the book itself (Exod. 17:14; 24:4; 34:27–28). (2) As a prince of Egypt, having been thoroughly educated in Egyptian arts and science (Acts 7:22), Moses was completely qualified to have written the books ascribed to him. (3) Other books of the Bible assume Mosaic authorship (Deut. 31:9; 24; Josh. 8:41, quoting Exod. 20:25; 1 Kings 2:3; Neh. 8:1; 13:1). (4) Jesus certainly accepted Mosaic authorship, quoting from Exodus and ascribing it to Moses (Mark 7:10, quoting Exod. 20:12; 21:17; and Mark 12:26, quoting Exod. 3:6). Therefore, reason supports that the initial composition of Exodus dates to the post-Egyptian wilderness wanderings.

Date

Of course, not only has the date of composition been a matter of controversy, but the date of the exodus event and the subsequent generation of wilderness wandering also has been subject to debate. The main question is whether the events described in Exodus date to the thirteenth century (1290 BC), the *late date*, or the fifteenth century (1446 BC), the *early date*.

Many scholars argue for a later date of composition, which would exclude Moses as the author. They believe that several layers of textual tradition — three, four, or even more — underlie the book's final form. These layers, which in some cases are separated from one another by several centuries, were later stitched together by a redactor or editor, at some point in time far distant from Moses. Proponents of this view believe that although some portions of the text as it exists today may be traced back to Mosaic authorship, orally preserved and transmitted over the centuries, it is impossible to separate historic fact from historical fiction.

Indeed, the movies that have shaped popular conceptions of these events are based on the late date. It is hard for some to overcome the media's powerful identification of Rameses as the pharaoh of the exodus. While the evidence for the late-date position is clear, it is certainly not compelling.

The "late daters" argue that archeological findings within Israel's fifteenth-century strata do not support accounts of devastating conquest throughout Canaan's ancient cities. Yet findings within thirteenth-century strata do evidence such widespread devastation. This fact, however, does not support a late date. Just the opposite; it supports an early date, for the biblical account does not record extensive destruction of the Canaanite cities, with the exception of Jericho, Hazor, and Ai (Josh. 11:13). The student of the biblical account would not expect the wholesale destruction found within thirteenth-century strata but rather the absence of destruction found within fifteenth-century strata.

The most common argument used by those holding to the late date is the reference to Hebrew slaves building the city of Rameses (1:11). This is taken as conclusive proof that the pharaoh whom they served was the son of Seti I, Rameses II, who reigned in the thirteenth century. However, since the account records that the building of the cities occurred prior to Moses' birth, and therefore, the exodus would have occurred some eighty years later, the pharaoh under whose rule that city was built could not have been

Rameses II. The origin of the name of the city of Rameses must lie elsewhere, presently lost in the mists of history. Perhaps the city name of Rameses is the result of later editorial updating of an earlier name, which would also explain the appearance of the same name in Genesis (Gen. 47:11).

Neither of the above late-date arguments, although interesting postulations, seems a particularly compelling reason to reject the early date of 1446 BC. On the contrary, the evidence for the early date is persuasive. The internal testimony of Scripture unambiguously records that the period between the exodus and the fourth year of Solomon's reign (when he began construction of the temple in Jerusalem) spanned 480 years (1 Kings 6:1). As it is generally agreed that construction of the temple began in approximately 966 BC, 480 years traces to approximately 1446 BC as the date for the exodus event. In addition, the book of Judges mentions Israel's dwelling in Israel for some three centuries (Judg. 11:26), a lengthy period that accords well with an early Exodus date but not at all with a later one.

Confidence for the early date is buttressed by Egyptian archaeological evidence. It is generally accepted that a non-Egyptian people known as the Hyksos ruled over Egypt from roughly 1730–1569 BC. When they were overthrown and the Egyptians returned to power with the Eighteenth Dynasty in 1569 BC, foreigners, in particular Semitic peoples, became forced labor to enable vast construction projects—precisely the scenario portrayed in the Exodus account.

A most remarkable and singular bit of additional evidence must be entertained as well. The pharaoh of the early-date Exodus, Amenhotep II, was not succeeded to the Egyptian throne by his eldest son but by a later one, Thutmose IV. Archaeology has uncovered a famous inscription recording the appearance to Prince Thutmose of an Egyptian god who promised that if the youth would restore the great Sphinx monument, he would one day become pharaoh. Of course, the implication of this inscription is that if Thutmose IV had been Amenhotep II's eldest son and logical heir, the dream would have been superfluous. Only if Thutmose IV was a later son could the dream be considered revelatory in any fashion. If one accepts the early date, the surprising ascension of Thutmose IV to power makes great sense in light of the death of Pharaoh's eldest son during the tenth plague.

Biblical Background

Genesis provides the foundation for interpreting Exodus. The Abrahamic covenant (Gen. 12:1–3; 15:1–21; 17:1–19) is the key to understanding many of the key events recorded in Exodus as well as every action of God in the account. One component of the Abrahamic covenant is a promise of reciprocal blessing or cursing in regard to behavior toward Abraham's covenant posterity: "I will bless them that bless thee, and curse him that curseth thee" (Gen. 12:3a). This explains why Egypt was blessed by God, since one pharaoh blessed Joseph and his family, and why Egypt was divinely smitten following a long succession of pharaohs who expressed quite a different disposition toward the Hebrews.

Nestled within the Abrahamic covenant's promise of the land of Canaan to Abraham's descendants is a divine warning that before the Hebrews would possess the Promised Land, they would first experience a four-century sojourn of affliction in a foreign land. Reassurance is given that upon the Hebrews' eventual departure, they will possess great wealth and their afflicters will be divinely judged. A reason for the Hebrews' four-hundred-year absence from the land God had given to Abraham is tacked on as a coda: "for the iniquity of the Amorites is not yet full" (Gen. 15:16b). The lengthy Egyptian sojourn would prove necessary, so that when the Hebrews returned to violently dispossess the inhabitants of Canaan, the Canaanites were certain to receive the divine justice that was their due for their abominable sins.

Genesis also provides reassurance to the Hebrews, through their father Jacob, that their time in Egypt is divinely superintended. It is for their benefit and is only temporary (Gen. 46:3–4). That this reassurance was clearly understood is evidenced by Joseph's deathbed request that his bones accompany the Hebrews upon their eventual exodus from Egypt and entry into the Land of Promise (Gen. 50:24–25).

Egyptian Background

While a great deal of fascinating material can be recounted concerning ancient Egypt's broad history, the background relevant to the Exodus account begins following the fall of the Twelfth Dynasty (1991–1786 BC), which was the pro-Semitic dynasty of Genesis' Joseph account (ca. 1876 BC). While the Hebrew people flourished under Egypt's Thirteenth and Fourteenth Dynasties, the glory of the Egyptian nation as a whole began to decline. This set the stage for the rise of the non-Egyptian Hyksos, a Semitic people who ruled Egypt during the Fifteenth through Seventeenth Dynasties. Apparently, the Hebrews continued to prosper under the rule of their fellow Semites, the Hyksos.

The Hyksos, however, were violently overthrown and expelled in 1569 BC, and the Egyptians again took power, ushering in the Eighteenth Dynasty. Under this ultra-nationalistic, expansive dynasty, the Hebrew nation's fortune dramatically capsized and the events described in the first chapter of Exodus commenced. Grand building projects were begun, and the local populace of Hebrews (and likely, other resident foreigners) was pressed into forced labor. Not only would the slavery of the Hebrews serve as a means to engineer the grand designs of the Egyptian architects, but their servitude would also serve as a prophylactic against their potential alliance in a possible Hyksos campaign to regain power.

The initial revolutionary pharaoh of the Eighteenth Dynasty was Ahmose I (1569–1546 BC). This is the king most likely described as the "new king over Egypt, which knew not Joseph" (1:8). He was followed by Amenhotep I (1546–1526 BC), most likely the initiator of the genocide described in 1:15–22. Interestingly, if Amenhotep I was indeed the pharaoh in question, the genocidal order was one of his final instructions; his successor, Thutmose I (1526–1512 BC), assumed the throne that very year, which incidentally, is the year of Moses' birth (2:1).

If Amenhotep I was not the initiator of the Hebrew genocide, then it was most certainly one of the first policies implemented by Thutmose I. Both Thutmose I and his daughter, the princess Hatshepsut, may have held central roles in the early Exodus narrative, as Moses' adoptive grandfather and mother (2:5–10). Moses' formative years in the Egyptian court (Acts 7:20–22) continued under the reign of his uncle, Thutmose II (1512–1504 BC). Moses was only twenty-two when Thutmose II died, and Hatshepsut, Thutmose II's sister and possibly Moses' adoptive mother, assumed the throne as queen in a coregency with her young nephew and stepson, Thutmose III (1504–1483 BC). Upon

Hatshepsut's death (1483 BC), Thutmose III became sole Egyptian ruler (1483–1449 BC) and began a systematic purge of anything and anyone connected with his hated aunt, stepmother, and by this time, mother-in-law. It is either just prior to or during this purge that Moses, possibly Hatshepsut's adopted son and Thutmose's stepbrother and cousin, was forced to flee Egypt for his life.

Only upon Thutmose III's death (2:23) was it safe for Moses to return to Egypt. Thutmose III was succeeded by his son, Amenhotep II (1449–1425 BC). This is the pharaoh of the Exodus, whose reign, contrasting with his father's rather distinguished record, was characterized by a marked lack of conquest and expansion—which makes perfect sense when one takes into account both the utter devastation of the land of Egypt following the ten plagues and the decimation of Amenhotep II's chariots and charioteers within the murky depths of the Red Sea.

Route of the Exodus

The route of the exodus is another area of the account that has been debated for some time. At least three routes of escape from Egypt have been proposed: (1) a *northern route* through the land of the Philistines, which would seemingly be ruled out by the Exodus narrative (13:17), (2) a *middle route* leading eastward across Sinai to Beersheba, and (3) a *southern route* along the west coast of Sinai to the southeastern extremities of the peninsula, which is the most commonly proposed and most likely option. Several of the sites in Israel's wilderness itinerary have been tentatively identified along the southern route, although in the absence of any definitive archaeological findings, coupled with a lack of biblical detail relating to the exact crossing point of the Red Sea, the route of the exodus remains educated speculation.

Theme

The purpose of Exodus is to provide an explanation and description of precisely how the Hebrews became "the chosen people." It is a redemptive roadmap that carries the reader along a journey from bitter bondage to glorious freedom as a nation is born by the power of God. The book provides a historical context to establish the redemptive connection between the divine promises of the Abrahamic covenant, made with Israel's patriarchs, and the stipulations of the covenant established through Moses at Sinai. The singular events of the Passover, the exodus, and the giving of the Torah are the monumental redemptive pillars on which Jewish history rests.

Yet Exodus does far more than serve as an extraordinary family history for the Jewish people. Exodus records a timeless and universal story of hope, liberation, and redemption. Moses' account provides, to Jews and Gentiles of every generation, conclusive proof of God's willingness and ability to intervene in the course of human history on behalf of His people and in fulfillment of His promises.

Theological Message

Throughout Exodus are profound insights into the nature of God. Beginning with the very assumption of God's existence as the I AM, the ultimate, eternal One (3:14), Moses paints a multifaceted portrait of a divine being with infinite power and inestimable attributes. The God of Moses controls the reins of history, turning them as He wills, adjusting historical events and the natural order by His command.

He is a holy God of such transcendence that to behold His glory would prove fatal (3:20). He demands that His people relate to Him in light of His holiness (3:5). He is a God of righteous absolutes, providing a legal roadmap for His people to follow in His paths (chaps. 20–23). Deviation from His standard of righteous demands His divine judgment (3:20; 4:22; 32:20–35).

He is the God who sees all, observes all, hears all (2:24). Yet He is no mere passive observer, content to view history from afar. He is the God who takes action, who intimately involves Himself in the affairs of men on behalf of His people whenever He so desires (3:7–10). His motivation for taking action is none other than His identity as the covenant-keeping God who remembers His promises and keeps His commitments (2:24).

The God of Moses is not inscrutable, but knowable, because He directly communicates with His people and makes His will known to them (see, e.g., 3:4–22, 20–23). He is a personal God who enters into an intimate relationship with his people, who passionately and emotionally responds to personal conversation, discussion, and argument (see, e.g., 3:11–4:17; 5:22–6:13; 32:9–14). Furthermore, He is the God who answers prayer, who responds to the intercession of His people (see, e.g., 8:12–13, 30–31; 9:33; 10:18–19; 32:9–14).

He is the God whose love for His people is so exceptional that He manifests Himself in their midst, that He Himself might personally and physically "dwell among the children of Israel" (29:45).

Interestingly, Moses also provides the insight that the focus of God's concern surpasses His own people and extends to the Gentile nations as well. In Exodus, the reader sees God concerned with creating and maintaining a reputation among the nations, specifically Egypt. He repeatedly acts and reacts to events with an eye toward how His actions will affect the Egyptians (see, e.g., 7:5, 17; 8:10, 22; 14:18).

Finally, Exodus reveals the monumental salvation of the Lord. The sequential events of the Passover, the exodus, and the parting of the Red Sea combine to become the second greatest redemptive act the world has ever known, surpassed in magnitude and consequence by only the sequential events of the death, burial, and resurrection of the Messiah, Jesus. Some fifteen centuries later, these events would lead to messianic redemption. In fact, both John the Baptist and the apostle Paul viewed the death of Jesus as the fulfillment of the Passover (John 1:29; 1 Cor. 5:7).

Outline

I. The Hebrews in Egypt (1:1–12:36)
    A. Oppression of the Hebrews (chap. 1)
        1. Genesis Recap (1:1–7)
        2. Enslavement and Genocide (1:8–22)
    B. Preparation of the Deliverer (2:1–4:31)
        1. The Prince of Egypt (2:1–15)
        2. The Shepherd of Midian (2:16–25)
        3. Moses Meets YHWH (3:1–4:17)

    5. Worship Regulations (chaps. 25–31)
       a. Elements of the Tabernacle (chaps. 25–27)
       b. Elements of the Priesthood (chaps. 28–29)
       c. Service Elements of the Tabernacle (chaps. 30–31)
   B. Rebellion in the Camp (chaps. 32–34)
    1. The Covenant Broken (32:1–33:6)
    2. The Covenant Renewed (33:7–34:35)
   C. Building the Tabernacle (chaps. 35–40)
    1. Preparation for Building the Tabernacle (35:1–36:7)
    2. Building the Tabernacle (36:8–39:31)
    3. Completing the Tabernacle (39:32–43)
    4. Inaugurating the Tabernacle (40:1–33)
    5. Indwelling the Tabernacle (40:34–38)

Bibliography

Cassuto, Umberto. *A Commentary on the Book of Exodus*. Jerusalem: Magnes, 1967.

Cole, R. Alan, *Exodus: An Introduction and Commentary*. The Tyndale Old Testament Commentaries 2. Downers Grove, IL: InterVarsity, 1973.

Davis, John J. *Moses and the Gods of Egypt*. Grand Rapids, MI: Baker, 1986.

Durham, John I. *Exodus*. Word Biblical Commentary 3. Waco, TX: Word, 1987.

Kaiser, Walter C., Jr. "Exodus." In *The Expositor's Bible Commentary*, edited by Frank E. Gaebelein, vol. 2. Grand Rapids, MI: Zondervan, 1990.

Kitchen, K. A. *On the Reliability of the Old Testament*. Grand Rapids, MI: Eerdmans, 2003.

Sarna, Nahum. *Exploring Exodus*. New York: Schocken, 1986.

EXPOSITION

Exodus divides nicely into four sections, as the narrative carries the children of Israel along a journey from slavery to freedom. The initial two sections record the conditions relating to the Hebrews' Egyptian bondage; the final two sections record Israel's progression toward becoming a free nation of God's chosen people.

I. The Hebrews in Egypt (1:1–12:36)

A. Oppression of the Hebrews (chap. 1)

1. Genesis Recap (1:1–7)

1:1–4. Moses' narrative in Exodus picks up exactly where he left off at the conclusion of Genesis. These four verses record the names of the sons of Jacob who came into Egypt with their families. From the outset, the text establishes the Hebrews' retention of their ancestry, heritage, and relation to God through His promises.

1:1. The expression **these are the names ... which came into Egypt** also appears in Genesis 46:8 at the head of a list of Jacob's descendants. **Israel ... Jacob**. Jacob had earlier been given the additional name Israel (Gen. 32:28).

1:2–4. Jacob's sons are grouped by birth seniority according to their mothers. The six sons of Leah, **Reuben ... Zebulun** (vv. 2–3; Gen. 35:23), are listed first, followed by Rachel's son, **Benjamin** (v. 3). Joseph is not included because the list notes those "which came into Egypt ... with Jacob" (Exod. 1:1). The list concludes with the four sons of Rachel and Leah's handmaids Bilhah, **Dan and Naphtali** (v. 4; Gen. 35:25), and Zilpah, **Gad and Asher** (Gen. 35:26).

1:5. These Jewish patriarchs, with their father, Jacob, moved their families to Egypt to be with Joseph. There is discrepancy as to the exact number of the Jewish population migrating to Egypt. Although the Masoretic text of Exodus lists a total Jewish population of **seventy** (Exod. 1:5), the number seventy-five is given by Stephen in Acts 7:14. There are two solutions to reconcile this discrepancy. The first is to assume that in addition to the **seventy** of Exodus 1:5, Stephen was also including Joseph's five grandsons (Gen. 50:23). The second solution is to simply assume that Stephen was quoting the Septuagint, which records the number seventy-five in two passages (Gen. 46:27; Exod. 1:5), contra the Masoretic text, or possibly that he was quoting an alternate Hebrew text, for example, the version of Exodus 1:5 found in the Dead Sea Scrolls, which also records the number seventy-five.

1:6. And Joseph died ... and all that generation. Since it is obvious that the original generation of immigrants had since died, the emphasis here seems to be that although several generations have passed between Joseph's generation and the events of the following narrative, no notable Hebrew leaders had yet arisen in that period.

1:7. The children of Israel were fruitful, and increased abundantly, and multiplied, and waxed exceeding mighty; and the land was filled with them. The original population of seventy Hebrews explodes during their Egyptian sojourn. Five descriptive terms are used here to emphasize their unique and rather sensational reproductive progress. By the time of their exodus, the adult Hebrew men totaled 600,000 (12:37). Conservatively adding to that number to include women and children creates a total Israelite population of possibly two million.

2. Enslavement and Genocide (1:8–22)

Having established a historical context, the narrative now moves into the thick of the action, with the Hebrews being subjugated first to slavery and then to genocide.

1:8. There arose up a new king over Egypt. In Stephen's brief recounting of the life of Moses, the implication from his use of the Greek term *heteros*, likely from the Septuagint, to describe the new pharaoh indicates not only a new ruler but a different dynasty as well (Acts 7:18). This accords well with the rise of Ahmose I and the rise of the Eighteenth Dynasty in approximately 1569 BC (see "Egyptian Background," above), some 307 years after the Hebrews entered Egypt and 123 years prior to their exodus. **Which knew not Joseph.** Three centuries and six dynasties after the fact, Ahmose I neither remembered Joseph's economic or political contributions to the land of Egypt nor felt any obligation to his progeny. Interestingly, none of the several pharaohs mentioned in the narrative are identified by name. Moses chooses to refer simply to each one with the simple, nonspecific title "king," as if they were all interchangeable generic royal pawns placed in their positions of authority to advance the plan and program of God.

1:9–10. The pharaoh identifies Israel's population explosion as a potential problem. While there was no danger of the Hebrews outnumbering the Egyptian nationals, nonetheless, the proportion of Jews to Egyptians was uncomfortable. Following the overthrow and expulsion of the hated Hyksos, the Egyptians distrusted all Semites remaining in their midst, which included the Hebrews. The Egyptians were threatened by the fact that for three centuries, the Hebrews had steadfastly resisted assimilation, avoided intermarriage, and managed to maintain their distinctive identity. **Let us deal wisely with them** (v. 10). This means to act with skill, to make a shrewd plan. The king's shrewd plan was to enslave the Hebrews.

1:11. Taskmasters to afflict them. Labor gangs were set over the Israelites to abuse, subjugate, and humiliate them. **They built for Pharaoh.** "Pharaoh," a word of Egyptian origin, means "great house" and is a royal title rather than a personal name. **Treasure cities, Pithom and Raamses.** Not only would the slavery of the Hebrews serve as a means to engineer the grand designs of the Egyptian architects for storehouse cities, but their servitude would also serve as a prophylactic against their potential fifth-column alliance in a possible Hyksos campaign to regain power. The Egyptian storehouse cities served as centers of Egyptian idolatry.

1:12. The implication here is that the pharaoh assumed that if he increased the Israelites' workload sufficiently, they would be too exhausted to procreate; thus the Hebrew population would be eventually reduced, or at least controlled. The text relays the Egyptians' frustration at seeing that, contrary to all expectation, the sexual potency of the Israelites increased in direct proportion to their amplified burdens. **They were grieved**. The increase in the Hebrew population unhinged the Egyptians, and their distrust of the Hebrews turned to loathing.

1:13–14. They made their lives bitter (v. 14). The term for bitter is *marar*, and the concept of the bitterness of their bondage will later be emphasized in the eating of bitter herbs at the Passover (12:8). The slaves' labors became progressively more arduous as their tasks expanded to encompass not only building but also farming and agricultural duties, such as pumping the waters of the Nile into the fields to irrigate them (Deut. 11:10).

1:15–21. After some forty years, it became clear to the Egyptian government that enslavement was ineffective at curbing the Hebrew population rate and that more drastic measures were needed to achieve the desired result. In 1526 BC, as either one of the final orders of Amenhotep I or an initial order of his successor, Thutmose I, a new policy of genocide was implemented against the Hebrews.

Shiphrah … Puah (v. 15). Considering the context, it is clear that these two women were the midwife overseers and not the sole midwives for the entire Israelite population. Their names are Hebrew, so there is no reason to question that they were Hebrews. **Upon the stools** (v. 16). It was customary to use two large stones as a birthing stool.

Pharaoh commissioned the midwives to carry out his new policy of genocide by murdering the Hebrew male children immediately upon birth. They were to achieve this goal by subtly making it appear as if the male babies were stillborn. The midwives' participation was necessary for this sinister task. (Later on, after the failure of this policy due to the midwives' deception [1:19], Pharaoh used far less subtle tactics in decimating the Hebrew male population.) The female babies were to be allowed to live. The rationale behind this insidious policy is that in the ancient world, nationality was determined through patrilineal descent. Hebrew identity could not be passed on if there was a dearth of fertile Hebrew men. It was a means to force an entire future generation of Hebrew women into a position of either remaining childless or assimilating by marrying Egyptians.

Pharaoh's grand extermination plan was frustrated, however, because the midwives **feared God** (v. 17) more than they feared Pharaoh. In a burst of dramatic foreshadowing, Moses reveals the midwives' insight into one of the great concepts of Exodus—that the Lord, being more powerful than Pharaoh, is therefore more worthy of obedience.

The midwives developed a shrewd plan of their own (vv. 18–19). Their outrageous yet plausible claim was that their genocidal mission failed because the Hebrew women, being a great deal more vigorous than Egyptian women, gave birth so quickly that the midwives simply could not arrive in time.

God blessed the midwives for their decision to protect the children. Through their deception, many Jewish lives were saved. **He made them houses** (v. 21). The midwives were divinely rewarded with prosperous families. In addition, the fertility of the Israelites was again divinely ratcheted up another level.

1:22. Pharaoh immediately implemented a malevolent plan. He dispensed with any pretext of subtlety and executed a general order to the Egyptian populace at large to exterminate every male Hebrew child. Every baby Jewish boy they could lay their murderous hands on was to be drowned in the Nile River.

B. Preparation of the Deliverer (2:1–4:31)

1. The Prince of Egypt (2:1–15)

At this critical turning point in the Israelites' history, probably in the year 1526 BC, Moses was born.

His entrance into the narrative is made at the least auspicious moment possible for any newborn Hebrew son, yet the text soon reveals that the Lord's orchestration of historical events will powerfully illuminate this dark hour.

2:1. The parents of Moses, Amram and Jochebed, are introduced here, but their names are not revealed until later in the narrative (6:20). Jochebed was Amram's aunt; the law against such interfamilial marriage had not yet been given by God at Sinai. At the time of Moses' birth, they already had two other children, Aaron and Miriam.

2:2. Jochebed realized that her son was **goodly**, a unique and special child of destiny. Therefore, she refused to subject him to the decree of Pharaoh and kept him hidden for three months.

2:3. After three months, it became clear that the baby could no longer be hidden or protected by his family. As did Noah, Jochebed built an **ark**, a vessel to preserve life. The boxy ark was constructed of the **bulrushes** that grew along the Nile River and made watertight with tar, **slime** and **pitch**. Irony abounds in the narrative, as Jochebed places the child in the homemade vessel and sets it adrift in the Nile, the very location into which Pharaoh had decreed the baby boys be thrown.

2:4. That this was not a mere random act of a mother's desperation but a well-considered plan is clear from Jochebed's instruction to her daughter, Miriam, to observe the basket's progress as it made its way down the river.

2:5–6. Through either providence or shrewd timing, the floating basket happened to capture the attention of Pharaoh's daughter, who had chosen this moment to bathe in the river. Whether it was her regular habit to wade in the Nile at this time of day is impossible to ascertain from the text. This could have been Princess Hatshepsut, daughter of Thutmose I. Egyptian pharaohs had numerous wives and daughters, so it is impossible to know her identity for certain. However, the details of Hatshepsut's life certainly can be correlated to these events. When the opened basket revealed its contents to the princess, a crying Hebrew baby boy, she was moved to **compas-**

sion (v. 6). This sympathy led the princess to spare the child from the royal decree of genocide.

2:7–9. There was, however, an obvious dilemma. No Egyptian woman, even if able, would nurse a Hebrew baby. The baby's sister, Miriam, immediately came out of hiding and revealed herself to the princess, offering to find a Hebrew woman to nurse the baby. She then introduced Jochebed to Hatshepsut. It is difficult to accept that the princess would have been so credulous as to believe that either the young Hebrew teen or the nursing-capable woman she brought to her attention was unaffiliated with the baby. The princess must have realized that they had all become silent coconspirators in a lifesaving operation. Interestingly, the narrative has now revealed five women who have purposely defied the edict of Pharaoh: the two Hebrew midwives, Jochebed, the princess, and Miriam. The use of the word **maid** (v. 8) indicates that Miriam was already a young woman of marriageable age, perhaps fourteen or fifteen years Moses' senior.

Irony of ironies, not only was Jochebed employed to nurse and care for her own child, but that child, with a decree of death hanging over his head, was now under the personal protection of the princess of Egypt. In the ancient world, it was customary to nurse children for at least the first three years of life, and it was not unusual for that to be extended until the age of four or five. These formative years under Jochebed's custody would likely have instilled a strong sense of Hebrew identity in the boy.

2:10. Sometime between the ages of three and five, Moses was adopted formally by the princess and accepted into the royal household of Pharaoh, his adopted uncle, Thutmose I. There he would have received an excellent, royal Egyptian education (Acts 7:22). Although the Hebrew Scripture does not comment on Moses' education, it is remarked upon by both Josephus and Philo, who records Moses' instruction in the subjects of arithmetic, geometry, music, literature, astronomy, writing, philosophy, and more.

Moses is a wordplay on the Hebrew term meaning "to draw out." The question arises, however, why an Egyptian princess would grant her adopted son a Hebrew name. Some argue that the name is actually based on the Egyptian word meaning "is born," which was commonly used as the second half of compound names, such as Thut-mose and Ah-mose. The possibility exists that, like these Egyptian names, Moses' given name was a longer compound, perhaps a name related to Egyptian deity. Such a name possibly would also indicate that his adoptive mother intended him to reign one day in the tradition of the other pharaohs in this dynasty. This is speculation, however, and whatever form Moses' original name took, the only form he recorded is the one with which we are familiar.

2:11–14. When Moses was grown (v. 11). Moses recorded nothing of his life until he reached the age of forty (Acts 7:23). Many conservative scholars believe that during the time span between his adoption by the princess (1522/21 BC) and the events described in verse 11, Hatshepsut had assumed the throne as queen of Egypt in a coregency with her young nephew and stepson, Thutmose III. Her rule would extend some twenty-one years (1504–1483 BC).

Upon Hatshepsut's death in 1483 BC, roughly three years following the events of verse 11, Thutmose III, Moses' stepbrother and cousin, became sole Egyptian ruler (1483–1449 BC). He began a systematic purge of anything and anyone connected with his hated aunt, stepmother, and by this time, mother-in-law. It was prior to or during this purge, as the reigns of power begin to slip from the elderly Hatshepsut to the vigorous Thutmose III, that Moses was forced to flee Egypt for his life because of events triggered in this passage.

Reading this passage through the insights revealed in Acts 7:22–25 and Hebrews 11:24–26, it can be conjectured that around the time he turned forty, Moses had an epiphany of identity. Once and for all refusing to be called an Egyptian prince, renouncing all political and royal aspirations (Heb. 11:24), Moses chose to identify with the oppression of his people, perhaps for the purpose of being the instrument of their deliverance from bondage (Acts 7:25).

Unfortunately, Moses' timing was not synchronized with God's timing. Moses' intervention in an Egyptian's physical abuse of a fellow Hebrew ended with Moses killing the Egyptian and hiding his corpse **in the sand** (v. 12). Moses believed that the Israelites would understand that he was the instrument God was going to use to deliver them from bondage and that they would welcome him in his role as their deliverer. Moses was mistaken, however. The Israelites neither understood his intentions nor accepted him as their deliverer.

The day after the murder, Moses tried to reconcile two Hebrew men who were fighting. However, the instigator of the conflict challenged Moses' authority and right to interfere, asking Moses who had appointed him **a prince and a judge** (v. 14) over the Israelites. God, of course, had appointed Moses to be ruler and judge of Israel, but ironically, the Hebrews rejected his leadership the first time it was offered. The very ones Moses attempted to help, his own nation, resolutely rejected their deliverer. Moses realized that, apparently, the murder he had done in secret was already common knowledge. Killing a freeman (nonslave) was punishable by death in Egypt at that time (Davis, *Moses*, pp. 51–58).

2:15. Fearful of Egyptian retribution, unable to rely on his mother as an ally, and rejected by his own people, Moses fled Egypt for **Midian**, a land beyond the borders of Egypt in the Sinai Desert, extending on both sides of the eastern arm of the Red Sea (Gulf of Aqaba) to the Arabian Peninsula.

2. The Shepherd of Midian (2:16–25)

2:16–22. In Midian, Moses took a wife and raised his family among the Gentiles. His father-in-law was **Reuel** (v. 18), meaning "friend of God." As the **priest of Midian** (v. 16), his title was Jethro (3:1; 18:1), possibly meaning "his excellency." In an act of gallantry, Moses had defended Jethro's seven daughters. While the daughters had reported Moses' heroic act, they had neglected to bring him to meet their father. Jethro extended typical Middle Eastern hospitality to Moses. In what is certainly an abbreviated description, the dinner invitation led to Moses' taking Jethro's daughter **Zipporah** (v. 21) in marriage. They had a son, whom Moses named **Gershom** (v. 22), a Hebrew wordplay indicating Moses' self-identification as **a stranger in a strange land**, one who has been banished from his proper place. There in Midian he remained, shepherding his flocks and growing familiar with the topography of the Sinai wilderness. It is interesting to note that the Egyptians considered shepherds as detestable (Gen. 46:34).

2:23–25. Moses allowed another forty years to go by (Acts 7:30) before he again picked up the narrative thread. The pharaoh, Moses' adopted cousin and brother-in-law, Thutmose III, had died and was succeeded by his son, Amenhotep II (1449–1425 BC). With the rise of a new king over their oppression, the Hebrews prayed to God for deliverance. The Hebrews **sighed** and **cried** (v. 23) out to God. This evoked a fourfold divine response. God **heard their groaning** (v. 24), meaning that He heard with an intent to act. He **remembered his covenant** with the Hebrew patriarchs, established with Abraham (Gen. 12:1–3; 15:18–21; 17:3–8) and later reiterated to **Isaac** (Gen. 17:21) and **Jacob** (Gen. 35:10–12). This was the basis of His intent to act. As the God who sees all, He **looked upon the children of Israel** and **had respect unto them** (v. 25), meaning He not only saw their plight but also would effect the termination of their suffering.

3. Moses Meets YHWH (3:1–4:17)

3:1–4. In the course of his shepherding duties, Moses, now eighty years of age, led his sheep to Mount **Horeb** (v. 1), a name used interchangeably with Mount Sinai. This is the same mountain where God will later give the Israelites His Torah (19:20–25). There Moses encountered the visible manifestation of God's presence, the Shekinah glory, in a flaming thorn bush. This is a small bush studded throughout the Sinai wilderness that, because of the intense desert heat and deficiency of rain, may sporadically and spontaneously combust. What Moses witnessed was truly unique, however, for the flame did not consume the bush. This strange sight arrested Moses' attention, and he moved closer to investigate.

The use of the term **angel of the LORD** (v. 2) indicates that this was a preincarnate appearance of the second person of the Trinity. The expression goes beyond reference to a mere angelic being and is used thus far in the Pentateuch to indicate a physical manifestation of God Himself (Gen. 16:7–13; 21:17; 22:11–18). Any ambiguity as to its reference is removed by the fact that, two verses later, Moses calls this individual both **God** and **the LORD** (v. 4).

When the Lord saw that He had aroused Moses' curiosity, He called out to him from within the burning bush. **Moses, Moses** (v. 4). In Scripture, there is a pattern of God's repeating a name to indicate an emphatic call for a specific commission. He does this here with Moses, and elsewhere with Abraham (Gen. 22:1), Jacob (Gen. 46:2), Samuel (1 Sam. 3:10), and Paul (Acts 9:4). Moses also responded as Abraham, Jacob, and Samuel responded to their divine calls, replying, **Here am I**.

3:5. As God had personally summoned Moses into His presence, He also instructed him in the appropriate manner in which to approach Him. In the biblical world, the removal of footwear was a sign of humility and respect. Moses was reminded of God's awesome holiness and that God's present manifestation in that place made the ground on which he stood **holy ground**.

3:6. The Lord revealed Himself to Moses as the God of Israel's fathers, **Abraham**, **Isaac**, and **Jacob**. This was no mere preamble before He introduced Moses to the topic at hand. The mention of the patriarchs would have served as an electrifying reminder that God had not forgotten the ancient promises He had made in the Abrahamic covenant. The Lord referenced the three patriarchs repeatedly throughout His dialogue with Moses. This reminder of God's splendor aroused fear in Moses that to behold this awesome God would result in death.

3:7. God reassured Moses that He had seen and heard the **affliction** and **sorrows** of His people and that His compassion toward them was now leading Him to decisive action on their behalf. The phrase **my people** is commonly used throughout the narrative to highlight God's identification of the Hebrews as His own personal possession (3:7, 10; 5:1; 7:4, 16; 8:1, 20–23; 9:1, 13, 17; 10:3–4; 22:25).

3:8. I am come down to deliver. God indicated His direct involvement in the rescue operation He envisioned. He would not only free His people from slavery but would also bring them out of Egypt and into their inheritance, the Land of Promise. **Land flowing with milk and honey**. The traditional descriptive shorthand for the Promised Land, indicating conditions of agricultural abundance (3:17; 33:3; Lev. 20:24; Num. 13:27; 14:8; 16:13–14; Deut. 6:3; 11:9; 26:9, 15; 27:3; 31:20; Josh. 5:6; Jer. 11:5; 32:22; Ezek. 20:6, 15). **Canaanites ... Jebusites**. The list of Canaanite nations inhabiting the Promised Land ranges from two names (Gen. 13:7), five names (Num. 13:29), six names (Judg. 3:5), seven names (Deut. 7:1), ten names (Gen. 15:19–21), to twelve names (see Gen. 10:15–18).

3:9–10. God reiterated His identity as the One who sees and hears His people and feels compassion for them. He then revealed that the method through which He would decisively intervene would be His chosen instrument of redemption, Moses. Moses is to return to Egypt to deliver the Hebrews. In a bit of literary foreshadowing, although there are two components to God's plan — deliverance from Egypt and entrance into Canaan — Moses specifies that his divine commission extends only to the Israelites' deliverance from Egypt and not to their deposition into the Promised Land (Deut. 32:48–52).

3:11. Surprisingly, Moses objected to his role in God's plan. Moses was all too aware that he was not the same man he was forty years ago. No longer an Egyptian prince but an obscure shepherd, he no longer possessed his former sense of divine destiny. His first of four objections was his personal inability to accomplish a task of this magnitude.

3:12. God responded to the first of Moses' objections with the assurance of His abiding personal presence, which would empower Moses' sufficiency. **Token**. A confirming sign. **Ye shall serve God**. A term equivalent to "worship." In the Torah, worship of God is equated with serving and obeying Him. Moses' ability to deliver Israel would be confirmed when he led

the Hebrews back to this same mountain for the purpose of worship. The Israelites would not go directly from Egypt to the Land of Promise but would first enjoy a roughly 150-mile detour to Mount Sinai.

3:13. In response, Moses raised his second objection. He reasoned that although arriving at Mount Sinai would prove confirmation of Moses' commission after the fact, until that point, what would motivate the Hebrews to trust that Moses could actually deliver them? While he himself might be aware of God's personal abiding presence, how would the people be certain of Moses' divine commission?

3:14–15. To this objection, God responded with the revelation of the essence and substance behind His personal name. He identified Himself as **I AM THAT I AM** (v. 14). The personal name of **the LORD** (v. 15) is YHWH, often presumed to be pronounced Yahweh, Yahveh, or Jehovah. The actual pronunciation of the Lord's personal name is today a matter of uncertainty; the ancient Hebrew priesthood so guarded the ineffable name of God that following the destruction of the temple in AD 70, knowledge of its correct articulation was lost with the passage of time. The uncertainty arises from the lack of vowels in the basic construction of Hebrew words. The name YHWH stems from a form of the Hebrew term "to be," indicating that the Lord is the timeless One, the Ultimate Cause, the ever-present One. This theological use of the term **I AM** (v. 14) is the designation Jesus used with reference to His divinity (John 8:58).

It is important to remember that this was not the first time the Hebrews learned God's name. After all, the name was placed in the mouths of speakers over thirty times throughout the events of Genesis. Israel was not worshiping a nameless deity known only by the mere descriptive El Shaddai and the like. In fact, it could be argued that coining a new name for God would not have authenticated Moses' commission to his people, but just the opposite. Moses was to remind his people, however, that this is the name by which God has always wished to be known and worshiped, the name that expresses His character as the God who both remembers His covenant and keeps His promises.

3:16–19. Moses was to relate this conversation to the Israelite leaders back in Egypt. The Hebrew for **elders** (v. 16) is "bearded ones," reflecting the age, wisdom, experience, and influence necessary for a man expected to function as a leader of his people. As heads of local families and tribes, "elders" had a recognized position also among the Babylonians, Hittites, Egyptians (Gen. 50:7), Moabites, and Midianites (Num. 22:7). Their duties included judicial arbitration and sentencing (Deut. 22:13–19) as well as military leadership (Josh. 8:10) and counsel (1 Sam. 4:3).

Moses was instructed to go to Pharaoh, together with the Hebrew leaders, and request of the king, not their wholesale freedom from slavery, but a minimal request. They were to petition him for a three-day vacation from their tasks in order to worship the Lord outside the borders of Egypt. God informed Moses that Pharaoh would not grant even this minimal request.

3:20–22. Therefore, God would demonstrate His authority. He would **stretch out** His **hand** (v. 20) to force Pharaoh's hand. After a demonstration of God's unspecified (at this point) **wonders**, the Hebrews would be free. The Egyptian people, however, would be so favorably disposed toward them that they would not allow the Israelites to leave empty-handed (v. 21). **Spoil the Egyptians** (v. 22). The Hebrews would receive from their taskmasters the recompense due for their labors. This would fulfill God's promise to Abraham that Israel would leave Egypt possessing great wealth (Gen. 15:14).

4:1. Despite the divine assurance of such a wondrous outcome, Moses raised a third objection to his role in the plan. He was still uncertain that he would be believed or would inspire the confidence of the Hebrews and be granted leadership authority over them. Perhaps rattling through his mind for the past four decades had been the lingering echo of the Hebrew's taunt, "Who made thee a prince and a judge over us?" (2:14).

4:2–9. To answer this objection, God enabled Moses to perform three authenticating supernatural signs to establish his credentials as the Lord's spokesman. First, Moses was empowered to change his **rod**

(v. 2), or shepherd's staff, into a snake and back again. A second **sign** (v. 8) was given just in case the first sign was insufficient to generate the people's trust: Moses was empowered to turn the flesh of his hand into that of a leper and back again to normal. A third sign was given in case the first two signs both proved insufficient to establish his credentials. Moses was empowered to turn the water of the Nile River into blood. Interestingly, unlike the first two signs, this one was not reversible. This sign, however, would serve as a warm-up for the first plague (7:17–21).

4:10. Remarkably, Moses raised a fourth and final objection, bemoaning to the Lord that he was not a commanding speaker, being **slow of speech, and of a slow tongue**. In light of Stephen's testimony of Moses' abilities (Acts 7:22), it would seem that a speech impediment was not the flaw that Moses has in mind. Rather, it was a fear of intimidation before the Egyptian court and apprehension that he lacked commensurate eloquence and adequate fluency for the task.

4:11–12. This objection evoked rapid reproof. The Lord reminded Moses that it was He who had created Moses' mouth and that Moses had precisely the mouth that the Lord had designed for him. Furthermore, God promised to overcome any of Moses' physical limitations, either perceived or real, by personally revealing the precise words he was to enunciate before both the Hebrews and Pharaoh.

4:13. Although every one of his four objections had been patiently addressed and answered by God, Moses was still not buying what the Lord was selling, and he raised a fifth objection. Ultimately, it came down to the fact that Moses simply did not care for the position being divinely offered and turned it down flat. He entreated the Lord to choose a replacement and send someone else.

4:14. The anger of the LORD was kindled. At this response from Moses, the Lord's patience finally ran out with His servant, and He lost his temper. No more gentle, reassuring answers were forthcoming.

4:15–16. The Lord answered Moses' request by bringing a third party into the equation, Moses' brother, Aaron. God begrudgingly indulged Moses' reluctance to expound the divine message. Although Moses was commissioned to serve as God's mouthpiece, Aaron was likewise commissioned to be Moses' mouthpiece. A three-way system was arranged whereby God would first speak to Moses. Moses would then convey the divine will to Aaron. Finally, Aaron would then publicly broadcast the message.

4:17. This rod, also called "the rod of God" (4:20). Whatever personal insecurities Moses continued to exhibit, he and Aaron possessed a visible totem of their ability to wield God's abiding power.

4. The Deliverer Returns to Egypt (4:18–31)

4:18. Moses immediately returned to Jethro to drop off the flock and ask permission to take his leave. His father-in-law granted the request.

4:19. God again communicated with Moses, reassuring him that it was finally safe for him to return to Egypt. In the forty years that had passed since he left Egypt as a fugitive, all who had previously wanted to kill him at that time were now themselves dead. Pharaoh Thutmose III had recently been succeeded by his son, Amenhotep II (1449–1425 BC).

4:20. Joining him on the journey back to Egypt were his wife, Zipporah (2:21), and his two sons, Gershom (2:22) and Eliezer (18:4). The narrative does not fail to note that Moses traveled holding **the rod of God** (see discussion on 4:17).

4:21. Along the way, the Lord communicated with Moses a third time. He prepared Moses for the fact that, due to divine intervention, Pharaoh would not be impressed by the three signs that Moses could perform. God is in complete control, and no man, not even the king of Egypt, is capable of resisting the divine will when it is exercised. **I will harden his heart**. An expression meaning "to strengthen his will." The text identifies the heart as the location of the volition, man's decision-making ability. On seven occasions in the narrative, God hardens Pharaoh's heart (9:12; 10:1, 20, 27; 11:10; 14:4, 8) or foretells that He will harden Pharaoh's heart (4:21; 7:3), and nine times in the text, Pharaoh hardens his own heart (7:13, 14, 22; 8:15, 19, 32; 9:7, 34–35). For the initial five plagues, the text registers Pharaoh as the

agent of hardening. Not until the sixth plague does God participate in the confirmation of Pharaoh's own volitional choices. Paul classically uses this specific situation to illustrate how the Lord places certain individuals in positions whereby He may utilize them to fulfill His larger purposes (Rom. 9:17–18).

4:22–23. From the outset of the mission, the Lord made clear to Moses His intention to exercise powerful leverage with Pharaoh. The highest of stakes would be in play: the future of the **firstborn** (v. 23) sons of Egypt (11:5; 12:12). This was appropriate, because in relation to God, Israel is His **son … my firstborn** (v. 22). This powerful term "my firstborn" is used elsewhere in Scripture (Jer. 31:9–20; Hos. 11:1) and illustrates the Hebrews' uniquely intimate relationship with God.

4:24–26. To illustrate the absolute necessity of obedience to the Lord's will, specifically in relation to the subject of sons, Moses recorded a peculiar interlude. One evening on **the way** (v. 24), as he and his family lodged overnight at an **inn, the LORD … sought to kill** Moses. The use here of the Lord's covenant name indicates that the issue is one of covenantal disobedience on the part of Moses. Apparently, Moses failed to circumcise his second son, Eliezer, in violation of the Abrahamic convenant (Gen. 17:9–14). It would have been flagrantly inappropriate for God's chosen representative, the deliverer of His people, not to comply with such a basic command, the very sign and symbol of the covenant relationship itself. God would consider only the circumcised as His firstborn.

In a way unspecified in the text, Moses and Zipporah identify the reason for the Lord's displeasure. With Moses violently ill and unable to act, Zipporah **took a sharp stone** (v. 25) and circumcised her son. Her reaction after so doing provides some insight into the motivation for their initial disobedience. She **cast it at his feet**, hurling her son's foreskin at her husband, thus assuaging God's anger and saving Moses' life. **A bloody husband** (v. 26). Although, for various reasons, circumcision was a common practice among many peoples of the ancient Near East, it was obviously repugnant to Zipporah. Although she had agreed to circumcision for her first son, Gershom, she had apparently objected to the practice for her second son. At this point, Moses decided that it was perhaps more prudent not to have his family accompany him on his mission. Zipporah and his sons were sent back to Midian, disappearing from the narrative until they rejoin Moses after the exodus from Egypt (18:2).

4:27–28. Prior to these incidents, God had commanded Moses' brother, Aaron, to trek into **the wilderness** (v. 27) to locate Moses. The brothers reunited at **the mount of God**, Sinai, and Moses caught Aaron up on all of the Lord's directives.

4:29–31. The brothers returned to Egypt. There, as divinely instructed, they revealed God's plan to the **elders of … Israel** (v. 29), punctuating the message with the three authenticating **signs** (v. 30). This resulted in a reverent and worshipful response from the Hebrews.

C. Battle of the Gods: Pharaoh vs. YHWH (chaps. 5–11)

As God had previously indicated to Moses, Pharaoh was not about to cooperate with the Lord's plan and program for the Hebrews. The events relayed in this portion of the narrative reveal not merely the surface conflict between Pharaoh and Moses but also the underlying and more potent conflict between the ultimate opponents: Pharaoh, the "god" of Egypt; and the Lord, the God of Israel.

1. Pharaoh versus YHWH: Round One (5:1–6:27)

5:1. Granted an audience with Pharaoh, Moses and Aaron, as previously instructed (Exod. 3:18), communicated to the king the Lord's minimal request to **let my people go** for the purpose of holding a religious **feast … in the wilderness**.

5:2. Pharaoh's antagonistic response to this basic appeal sets the tone and context for the remainder of his role in the narrative. He asks the text's key question, **who is the LORD …?** (lit., "Who is YHWH?"). This was no mere rhetorical question on the king's part. While there were some eighty ancient-Egyptian gods, none was known as YHWH. Although the Lord

had already provided Moses with the answer to this question at the burning bush, the remainder of Exodus' Egyptian chapters are dedicated to fleshing out the answer, for both the Hebrews and the Egyptians.

I know not the LORD. The events described throughout the following narrative, specifically, the ten plagues, are each divinely designed to remedy this self-identified problem, providing the king an unforgettable introduction to the Lord.

5:3. In a universal sense, God is the Lord of all, but in a specific sense, He may be designated as **the God of the Hebrews**. "Hebrews" is the self-designation of choice for the Israelite nation within Scripture. **Three days' journey**. This is the travel time for each leg of their journey beyond the border of Egypt, for a total travel duration of six days, not including the time spent in worship. **Pestilence**. Moses knows from personal experience (4:24–26) that the consequence of disobeying the Lord may be quite severe.

5:4–13. Pharaoh's immediate concern was to make known to Moses the severity of the consequences for those who challenge his royal authority. He complained that the Hebrews must have had too much time on their hands if they possessed the energy to desire worshiping their God. The workload of the Hebrews was significantly increased. The **taskmasters of the people** (the Hebrew foremen; v. 6) and **their officers** (the Egyptian overseers) were instructed to withhold the supply of **straw** (v. 7) for making their bricks while still requiring the same production quota. The straw was chopped and mixed in with the clay, both as a binding agent and to increase the bricks' durability. With this decrease in raw building materials, the Hebrews labors exponentially increased, as they were now required to gather straw before they produced the bricks. **Vain words** (v. 9). The main reason for this new policy of oppression was to discredit Moses is the eyes of his people by calling him a liar.

5:14–16. The Hebrew foremen **were beaten** (v. 14) when the people were unable to maintain their brick quota for several days running. Instead of praying to the Lord, the foremen complained to Pharaoh. They blamed their inability to maintain their brick quota on the Egyptians for unfairly with-holding raw construction material.

5:17–19. The king would not accept their excuses, again accusing the Hebrews of being **idle** (v. 17) and reiterating his burdensome policy.

5:20–21. The Hebrew leaders, having unproductively complained to the king, vented their complaint to **Moses and Aaron** (v. 20), who awaited their return from their audience with Pharaoh. **You have made** (v. 21). The Hebrews dumped the blame for their recent misfortunes squarely on the brothers. **A sword.** Moses and Aaron were accused of having given the Egyptians an excuse to execute the Hebrews and were told that any Hebrew blood spilled thereafter would be on Moses and Aaron's heads.

5:22–23. Moses (v. 22) acted as the Hebrews initially should have done and brought his people's complaints before **the Lord**. Since the Hebrews' situation had deteriorated so rapidly since his arrival on the scene, he questioned God as to his call and purpose as their deliverer, reminding the Lord that contrary to his expectation, the people had not yet, in any fashion, been delivered from bondage.

6:1. The Lord replied to Moses with immediate reassurance. **Now** Moses would **see** what God **will do to Pharaoh.** Since Pharaoh had rejected the Lord's initial request, He would now make the king an offer he could not refuse. This would result in Pharaoh not just passively letting the Hebrews go but forcefully driving them out of Egypt.

6:2–8. This solemn set of divine promises form an inclusion, beginning and ending with the statement, "I am YHWH," **I am the Lord** (v. 2). Moses was reminded of the Lord's identity as the covenant God and of His powerful, timeless commitment to the Israelites. The Lord would neither forget His promises nor ignore His covenantal obligations.

6:3. The Hebrew patriarchs, **Abraham ... Isaac ... Jacob**, had personally experienced the Lord only in His role as **God Almighty** (Hebrew, *El Shaddai*), the Divine King and powerful covenant maker. **By my name JEHOVAH was I not known.** Although they were well aware of God's sole personal name (see discussion on 3:14–15), it would have been

impossible for the patriarchs to have experienced the Lord in the way He was now revealing Himself. The patriarchs knew the Lord as the architect of the Abrahamic covenant and the guarantor of its promises. They had not lived long enough to witness those promises brought to fruition, as Moses' generation would soon have the privilege to realize. God was about to reveal much more of Himself and His power to the patriarch's descendants than the patriarchs themselves had ever experienced.

6:4–5. I have also established ... I have also heard ... and I have remembered (vv. 4–5). In three divine declarations, Moses was reassured of God's compassion toward His people and was once again reminded that God had not abandoned His covenantal promise to bring the Hebrews back into **Canaan**.

6:6–8. God continued with a sevenfold declaration of purpose, pledging Himself to seven related promises. (1) **I will bring you out from under** (v. 6) the burdens of Egypt. (2) **I will** deliver you from slavery. (3) **I will redeem you** with a magnificent display of power. (4) **I will** (v. 7) make you my people. (5) **I will be** your God, meaning that the relationship between the Lord and His people will be formalized and take on a new and deeper dimension. (6) **I will bring you in** (v. 8) to the Promised Land. (7) **I will give** you that land as an inheritance. The divine declaration, which began in 6:2, concludes as it began: "I am YHWH," **I am the Lord**.

The divine promises found in this passage form the basis for the names of the four cups that are consumed during the contemporary Passover seder meal. Each cup is named after one particular promise or set of promises: the cup of sanctification, the cup of deliverance, the cup of redemption, and the cup of consummation.

6:9. Moses' transmission of the divine reassurance to the dispirited Hebrews was neither accepted nor believed, however.

6:10–13. Moses was then divinely directed to return to Pharaoh's court and once again request that he release the Hebrews. As before, Moses again felt free to voice his concerns to God. If his own people had not believed his message, why should Pharaoh be expected to believe? **Uncircumcised lips** (v. 12). Moses refers again to his perceived inadequacy in public persuasion. God then reassured Moses of his and Aaron's commission as His personal team of representatives to two sets of unbelievers: **the children of Israel** and **Pharaoh** (v. 13).

6:14–27. The narrative flow is temporarily interrupted to provide the family lineage and pedigree of Moses and Aaron, serving to authenticate the brothers' genealogical qualifications for the task as divine spokesmen. **Reuben ... Simeon ... Levi** (vv. 14-16). In the genealogy contained in verses 14–25, only the first three of Jacob's twelve sons rate mention since Moses and Aaron were descended from the third-born son, Levi.

6:16. Moses and Aaron descended from Levi's son, **Kohath**.

6:20. Moses' father, **Amram**, and mother, **Jochebed**, who was not only Amram's wife but also his aunt, are listed. The law against such interfamilial marriage had not yet been given by God at Sinai.

It is a certainty that this genealogy is abbreviated, for it lists only two generations between Levi and Moses. The population explosion (emphasized in chap. 1) that occurred during approximately the 350 years prior to Moses' birth cannot be explained as the inclusive result of a total of four generations. In other words, the relationship of Moses to Levi must have been other than that of great-grandson. It is not uncommon for such genealogies to include only the most essential figures (and those whose inclusion is necessary to arrive at these essential figures) and omit the remainder.

6:21. Korah will play a significant role in the wilderness rebellion of Numbers 16.

6:23. Although **Aaron** married **Elisheba**, of the tribe of Judah (Num. 1:7; 2:3; 7:12; 10:14), their status as Levites and priests was accorded them through the biblical norm of patrilineal descent. **Nadab, and Abihu**, their eldest sons, would later be killed in divine judgment (Lev. 10:1–2). **Eleazar**, their third son, would eventually inherit the mantle of high priest upon Aaron's death (Num. 20:28).

6:24. See discussion on 6:21.

6:25. Phinehas, the son of **Eleazar**, would become high priest upon his father's death (Josh. 24:33).

6:26–27. Here the purpose of the genealogical listing is given: to establish that it is **that** same **Moses and Aaron** (v. 27) who play key roles in the narrative.

2. Pharaoh versus YHWH: Round Two (6:28–7:13)

6:28–30. Following the genealogical interruption, the narrative picks up again where the conversation between Moses and the Lord left off in 6:13, supplying a brief recap to reset the stage.

7:1–2. Moses' authority would be so great that it would seem he was **a god** before **Pharaoh** (v. 1). Aaron would play the role of prophet to Moses' role of divinity. A prophet is one who receives direct revelation from God and, as His spokesman, communicates that revelation to God's people. In the convoluted arrangement developed because of Moses' insecurities (4:15–16), just as God would transmit His word through His prophets to His people, so would Moses, functioning as a sort of divinely ordained middleman, then transmit God's message through Aaron to Pharaoh.

7:3–4. As they faithfully presented the message, God would act to **harden Pharaoh's heart** (v. 3; see discussion on 4:21). Moses' message would be confirmed through mighty and numerous **signs and ... wonders**. However, neither the message nor the authenticating signs would make a sufficient impression on Pharaoh for him to **hearken unto** them (v. 4). This will provoke the Lord to exercise **great judgments** of destruction upon Egypt.

7:5. The Egyptians shall know that I am the Lord, as a result of this great exercise of divine power and the subsequent deliverance of His people from their midst. The Egyptians would possess firsthand experience of Israel's covenant-keeping God.

Throughout the narrative, repeated emphasis is placed on how the Lord both acts and reacts to events with an eye toward how His actions will affect the Egyptians (see, e.g., 7:5, 17; 8:10, 22; 14:18). He is not unconcerned with establishing and maintaining His reputation among the Egyptians.

7:6 – 7. Just prior to the following confrontation, the ages of Moses, eighty, and Aaron, eighty-three, are provided.

7:8 – 10. Pharaoh challenged the brothers to publicly **Shew a miracle** (v. 9). As Moses had done with his staff at Sinai, so now Aaron did with his own staff. He cast it down before Pharaoh, and it became a serpent. **Take thy rod.** It is probably best to assume that Moses and Aaron shared one staff, "the rod of God" (4:20), rather than that they each possessed a different staff with which they performed signs.

7:11 – 12. Pharaoh summoned his **wise men** (sacred scribes educated in both human wisdom and supernatural secrets) **and the sorcerers** (the priests of the Egyptian religious cults), who served as **the magicians of Egypt** (v.11). Through the exercise of demonic power, they were able to duplicate God's sign and transform their rods into **serpents** (v. 12) as well. Jewish tradition records the names of two of the magicians who opposed Moses, Jannes and Jambres (2 Tim. 3:8). In this initial supernatural power encounter between God and the Egyptian deities, however, the superiority of the Lord was demonstrated when **Aaron's rod swallowed up their rods** (v. 12).

7:13. He hardened Pharaoh's heart. The agent of the hardening of Pharaoh's heart is ambiguous here and is probably best understood as Pharaoh hardening his own heart.

3. The Plagues (7:14 – 11:10)

While the Lord could have delivered the Hebrews from Egypt with one powerful and dramatic act, He chose to prolong the process through a series of ten plagues delivered over approximately six to nine months, spanning late summer or early fall 1445 BC through spring 1446 BC. With each plague, the intensity of God's judgment on Egypt escalates and markedly increases the peoples' suffering and the land's devastation.

The judgment of the ten Egyptian plagues served four divine purposes. The first and most obvious purpose for the plagues was to compel Pharaoh to release the Hebrews from bondage. The

second reason was to punish the Egyptians for their harsh treatment of the Hebrews. This purpose references the reciprocal-conduct clause of the Abrahamic covenant, that God would curse those who cursed Israel (Gen. 12:3a). The third purpose was to demonstrate God's sovereign power and absolute authority to both the Hebrews and the Egyptians (9:14, 16; 10:2).

The fourth purpose was to demonstrate the Lord's superiority over Egypt's voluminous number of false gods (12:12; 18:11; Num. 33:4). There were some eighty ancient-Egyptian gods, each one the personification of an animal or object. In addition, Pharaoh himself was considered to be the incarnation of the god Horus, with the court magicians serving as his priests. Each of the ten plagues was designed to challenge a specific god or gods within the Egyptian pantheon and ultimately to topple the credibility of Pharaoh's own divinity as well (see Davis, *Moses*, pp. 79 – 129).

The plagues are also distinctively ordered. With the final plague serving as a sort of grand finale, the first nine plagues can then be divided into three sets of three plagues each (7:14 – 8:19; 8:20 – 9:12; 9:13 – 10:29). The initial pair of plagues within each grouping (the first and second, the fourth and fifth, the seventh and eighth) were always introduced with a warning. Within each of these pairs, the initial plague's warning (the first, fourth, and seventh) was always delivered in the morning. The third plague in each set of three always arrived without warning.

a. The First Plague: Water Becomes Blood (7:14 – 25)

7:14 – 21. This section begins with the Lord warning Moses that Pharaoh will continue to refuse to let the Hebrews go. Moses was instructed to address the king again, **in the morning** (v. 15) at the Nile, having the rod of God at hand. Moses was to relate the divine command of YHWH, the Hebrew God, to let His people leave Egypt for a short duration for the purpose of worshiping Him **in the wilderness** (v. 16). As Pharaoh had not favorably responded to this request to date, the first plague was unleashed upon Egypt, turning the water of the Nile into **blood** (v. 17).

In this thou shalt know that I am the LORD (v. 17). This plague, as were they all, was meant to demonstrate the Lord's superiority over Pharaoh and his gods. The Nile River was considered sacred, the very bloodstream of the god Osirus. Other deities challenged by this particular plague were Khnum, the guardian of the Nile; Hapi, the spirit of the Nile; and Sepek, the crocodile god.

Some hold that the first nine plagues may have been a series of miraculous intensifications of natural events. For example, they hold that this initial plague could have resulted from large quantities of red sediment, algae, or fungus that caused the water to take on the appearance of blood. While possible, this is unlikely, for this and other similar theories do not explain the text's account of the immediate transformation of all water, including that which was previously stored in pools and containers.

Publicly, in front of Pharaoh and his servants, Aaron, at his brother's command, took **the rod, and smote the waters** (v. 20). The now completely crimson water **stank** (v. 21) with an inundation of dead fish and proved undrinkable. The magnitude of the sign's effect extended not merely to bodies of water but to every vessel that already contained drinking water.

7:22–25. The text records that the water remained in this toxic state for a period of **seven days** (v. 25). During this period, the sole source of fresh water throughout Egypt was the underground natural springs. The Egyptians now had to exert themselves. As the Hebrews had to gather their own straw, now the Egyptians were forced to dig **round about the river** (v. 24) for their own water.

And the magicians of Egypt did so with their enchantments (v. 22). Pharaoh's magicians were able to duplicate this sign supernaturally. The question is not by what means were they able to do so (the demonic), but what would have possessed them (the demonic) to waste this precious and hard-earned resource simply to demonstrate that their gods were able to match the power of YHWH. The real contest

of power would have been if the magicians could have changed the blood back into fresh water. The result of the first plague was that **Pharaoh's heart was hardened**.

b. The Second Plague: Frogs (8:1–15)

8:1–2. The second plague, as was the first one, is preceded by a warning. Once again, **Moses** (v. 1) communicated the Lord's request to **Let my people go** for the purpose of worshiping Him. In this instance, no duration is specified for the proposed leave. **Pharaoh** is presented with the choice either to allow the Hebrews to take their leave or to have his kingdom plagued with an inundation of **frogs** (v. 2). Egyptian deities challenged by this particular plague were Hapi, the spirit of the Nile, and Heqet, the frog-headed goddess of childbirth assistance, who also had the distinction of being the wife of Khnum, the guardian of the Nile.

8:3. Into thine house ... bedchamber ... bed ... the house of thy servants ... upon thy people ... into thine ovens, and ... kneading troughs. The frogs would swarm everywhere.

8:4. On thee ... thy people ... thy servants. The frogs would swarm over everyone, without exclusion.

8:5–7. Aaron once again stretched out his **rod** (v. 5) over the river and initiated the second plague. Immediately and on cue, the frogs **covered the land** (v. 6). Those who hold to the miraculous intensification of natural events theory of the plagues suggest that the red sediment, algae, or fungus, coupled with the dead fish, had so polluted the Nile that the frogs abandoned the river and swarmed over the land and into the houses to seek moisture. This explanation, however, does not sufficiently address the text's presentation of the abundance of frogs or their swarming at Moses' precise signal.

Again, the text records the Egyptian **magicians** (v. 7) supernaturally duplicating the miracle. As with their duplication of the first plague, the question must be raised as to why they would enact such a counterproductive measure. As the land teemed with a deluge of frogs, Pharaoh's priests increased the number of frogs. As noted with the previous plague, a demonstration of true supernatural power would have been to undo the plague of frogs. This power, however, the magicians did not possess.

8:8. As a result of the second plague, for the first time in the narrative, Pharaoh summoned Moses and Aaron. He acknowledged the existence of the Hebrew God and requested that they petition the Lord on Egypt's behalf to remove the plague. The king would then grant their request to allow the Hebrews to leave the land to worship the Lord.

8:9–11. That thou mayest know (v. 10). To demonstrate that it was done by the power of the Lord, Moses granted Pharaoh the honor of choosing the specific time for the frogs' removal. By this point, apparently, Pharaoh is so troubled by the plague that he is not thinking clearly. Instead of choosing to terminate the plague immediately, he chose for it to end on the following day.

8:12–14. Moses prayed, and the Lord favorably responded. The frogs all **died** (v. 13) on the following day, just as Pharaoh had specified. The land stank with **heaps** (v. 14) upon heaps of decomposing frog corpses.

8:15. When Pharaoh saw that there was a respite from the second plague, he again hardened his heart, just as the Lord had predicted.

c. The Third Plague: Lice (8:16–19)

8:16–17. The third plague within the first set of three plagues came completely without warning. **Aaron** stretched out his staff and struck the **dust of the land** (v. 16), and it **became lice throughout all the land of Egypt** (v. 17). Exactly which pesky flying insect is meant is unclear. Choices include lice, gnats, mosquitoes, or sand flies. Whichever insect it was that God chose, it swarmed over **man** and **beast** in exceptionally unpleasant quantities.

The Egyptian deities challenged by the third plague would have been Set, the desert god, and fly-like Uatchit, whose function was to divinely protect Egypt from insect swarms. It was also a successful swipe at the Egyptian priesthood who, concerned with maintaining ritual purity, frequently shaved themselves of all body hair to avoid lice.

8:18–19. For the first time in the narrative, the magicians' attempt to duplicate the sign meets with abject failure. Again, the question may be posed why they would attempt to create more lice (or gnats, etc.) instead of seeking to exercise some manner of divine fumigation power. From this point on in the narrative, the magicians are powerless to duplicate any of the remaining plagues. Their failure to perform led the magicians to conclude that this plague was enacted by **the finger of God** (v. 19). This admission is a powerful portrait of the Lord's sovereign power. Jesus quoted this same expression to associate His ability to drive out demons with YHWH's potent power (Luke 11:20).

This plague again resulted in **Pharaoh's heart** being **hardened** (v. 19).

d. The Fourth Plague: Flies (8:20–32)

8:20–24. The second set of three plagues commenced, as did the first set, with a warning. As he had done prior to the first plague, **Moses** (v. 20) appeared **before Pharaoh** at the Nile **early in the morning**. Again, the Lord's request was communicated for Pharaoh to **Let my people go** for the purpose of worshiping Him. Pharaoh was now presented with the choice to either allow the Hebrews to take their leave or have his kingdom plagued by **swarms of flies** (v. 21).

Upon thy servants and upon thy people, and into thy houses (v. 21). There would be no relief from these flies, for they would be everywhere throughout Egypt, with only one exception. No swarms would be found in **Goshen** (v. 22), the city of the Hebrews (Gen. 45:10). **A division between my people and thy people** (v. 23). From this plague forward, God makes a sharp distinction between Goshen and the rest of Egypt. This was not just to spare the Hebrews from the Egyptian judgments; it was also to be **a sign** for Pharaoh and his people so they would **know that I am the Lord** (v. 22). The Lord portrays this as a power contest between the gods of two people groups. One god would be proven to be the genuine article, and one would be proven false. By the final plague in this contest, only one god would be left standing.

The infestation of flies began on the following day. The Lord Himself, not Moses or Aaron, precipitated this plague, as He would the following plague. **The land was corrupted** (v. 24) as the Egyptians had their lives disrupted by the omnipresent, disease-bearing, biting flies. The Egyptian deity challenged by this plague would have been Uatchit, who looked like a fly and whose function was to divinely protect Egypt from insect swarms. This was the second time he had failed the Egyptians in his specialty.

8:25. Pharaoh called for Moses and for Aaron, requesting relief from this plague. He attempted to impose a restriction upon the Lord's request, however. He was willing to allow them to **sacrifice to** the Lord but said they had to remain within the Egyptian borders.

8:26–27. Moses refused to accept this compromise, for the Hebrews' worship would entail the sacrifice of either sheep or bulls or cows or all three, which he characterized as **the abomination of the Egyptians** (v. 26). The sacrifice of sheep was detestable to the Egyptians (Gen. 46:34). Bulls were considered the sacred representations of the Egyptian gods Apis and Mnevis. Cows were considered the sacred representations of their goddess Hathor. **Will they not stone us?** Moses was concerned that the Egyptians might consider the public sacrifice of these animals a blasphemous offense and be antagonized to a state of violence. For Moses, putting distance between the Egyptians and the Hebrews for their sacrifice was a nonnegotiable point. He reiterated the necessity of the **three days' journey into the wilderness** (v. 27).

8:28. Pharaoh viewed the point as negotiable and responded with a counter offer. He was willing to make a concession. **I will let you go.** He would allow the Hebrews to leave Egypt to worship God. **Ye shall not go very far away.** A three-day journey, however, was out of the question. They must not venture very far from the borders of Egypt. **Intreat for me.** Pharaoh concluded with a request that when the Hebrews sacrificed to their God, they pray specifically for him.

8:29–32. Moses promised to ask the Lord for the removal of the plague but solemnly warned Pharaoh not to play any games with the Lord by retracting his permission. He must keep his promise to let the Hebrews go. Moses prayed for the plague's removal, and God favorably responded. Pharaoh went back on his word, however, and **hardened his heart at this time also** (v. 32).

e. The Fifth Plague: Death of Egyptian Cattle (9:1–7)

9:1–6. The second plague of the second set began, as per the pattern, with a conditional warning. **Moses** (v. 1) again communicated to **Pharaoh** the request of **the LORD God of the Hebrews** to **Let my people go, that they may serve me.** The result of ignoring the request would be a **murrain** (v. 3), a noxious plague, on all Egypt's domesticated field animals: **cattle, horses, asses, camels, oxen**, and **sheep**.

Such a loss of livestock would be a body blow to both the Egyptians' economy and their religious sensibilities as masses of their sacred animals succumbed to the plague. The Egyptian deities challenged by this plague were Apis and Mnevis, both represented by the bull and associated with the gods Ptah and Ra, respectively; Hathor, the cow-headed goddess of love; and the ram-god Khnum, guardian of the Nile.

As with the initial plague in this second set, the precipitator of the fifth plague was neither Moses nor Aaron but was the Lord Himself. Once again, He made a clear distinction between the Egyptians and Hebrews. Only the Egyptian field animals were affected by the plague. **To morrow** (v. 5). This advance warning gave those Egyptians who feared God sufficient time to bring their livestock in from the fields and out of danger. **All the cattle of Egypt died** (v. 6), that is, all the unprotected livestock out in the fields, as remaining Egyptian cattle are affected by subsequent plagues.

Proponents of the miraculous intensification of natural events theory of the plagues posit that the livestock were infected by anthrax, carried by the flies of the previous plague. Again, the flaw of this position is that it accounts for neither the prediction of the specific time of the plague's onset nor the distinction it made between the Egyptians and the Hebrews.

9:7. Pharaoh sent representatives to investigate the livestock situation in Goshen. The accuracy of Moses' prediction of the distinction between Goshen and the remainder of Egypt was confirmed. The result was that instead of yielding to the power of the Lord, yet again **the heart of Pharaoh was hardened.** He continued to refuse to release of the Hebrews.

f. The Sixth Plague: Boils and Blains (9:8–12)

9:8–11. As per the pattern, the third plague of the second set arrived unannounced and without warning. The Lord commanded **Moses** (v. 8), in full view of Pharaoh, to take **handfuls of ashes** and **sprinkle it towards the heaven.** Once hurled into the air, the soot transformed into particles that caused boils to break out on both the Egyptians and their livestock. **A boil breaking forth with blains** (v. 9). A skin disease characterized by open sores, festering pustules, and/or blisters. The text emphasizes the helplessness of the population to defend themselves against the judgment of the Lord, in particular the magicians, whose gods were unable to protect them. Specific Egyptian deities challenged by this plague were a veritable pantheon: Typhon, the god of boil protection; Sekhmet, the lion-headed goddess of disease protection; Serapis and Isis, the god and goddess of healing; Imhotep, the medicine god; and Sunu, the pestilence god.

Proponents of the miraculous intensification of natural events theory propose that this plague was an advanced form of the anthrax that had been at the root of the previous plague, having now progressed to include people as well as livestock. The same objections to this theory apply, however, regarding the timing of the plague's commencement and termination, in addition to the distinction it makes between the Hebrew and Egyptian populace.

9:12. After a now well-established pattern of resistance of Pharaoh hardening his heart, the text now provides the first explicit instance of **the LORD** hardening **the heart of Pharaoh** (see discussion on 4:21).

g. The Seventh Plague: Hail and Fire (9:13–35)

9:13–17. The first plague of the third set began, as per the pattern (7:15; 8:20), with **Moses** (v. 13)

issuing an early **morning** ultimatum to **Pharaoh** to either let the **Hebrews** take their leave or face yet another divine judgment. **All my plagues** (v. 14). Through the unleashing of the final four plagues, Pharaoh was about to experience the full brunt of God's judgment. **Upon thine heart ... that thou mayest know that there is none like me.** These plagues were explicitly designed for the purpose of piercing the king's hardened, calloused heart and for demonstrating the uniqueness and supremacy of the Lord's power.

For now I will stretch out my hand, that I may smite thee ... with pestilence ... thou shalt be cut off (v. 15). This is hyperbolic language indicating that, figuratively, the Lord was removing the kid gloves. The previous plagues may have been brutal to endure, but the upcoming plagues would prove unprecedented in magnitude, severity, and ferocity.

For this cause have I raised thee up (v. 16). The divine king of Egypt was now exposed as a mere pawn in the Lord's hand, divinely positioned for the sole purpose of demonstrating God's divine power. God revealed Himself as the orchestrator behind great Pharaoh's rule. Paul uses this verse (v. 16) to effectively illustrate the sovereignty of God over small and great alike (Rom. 9:17). The contrasting **thy people** (v. 15) and **my people** (v. 17) serves to highlight the contest of the Egyptians' and the Hebrews' divine champions.

That my name may be declared throughout all the earth (v. 16). The term "earth" is perhaps better translated as "land." In the context of Exodus, the Lord's concern has been specifically with the Egyptians' recognition of His sovereign authority. This declaration, rather than a universal clarion call to worship the true God, was a specific call to the Egyptian people to acknowledge YHWH.

9:18–19. God's judgment was tempered with mercy. Allowing one days' advance warning of the coming devastation, the Lord directed the Egyptians to seek shelter for themselves and their animals. The following day would bring a torrent of **hail** (v. 18), the severity of which was unprecedented in Egypt's history.

9:20–21. The servants of Pharaoh (v. 20). Heretofore passive observers in the drama, the king's servants would now play an active role. Some servants heeded Moses' warning and thereby preserved their possessions. Some chose to ignore the warning, to their enormous loss.

9:22–24. Moses **stretched forth his rod toward heaven** (v. 23), and the cataclysm was unleashed. **Thunder … hail** (and "rain," 9:33) fell from heaven, and **fire** ran along the ground. **In all the land … upon man, and upon beast, and upon every herb** (v. 22). For those who had chosen not to make advance preparation, there was nowhere to escape from the powerful demonstration of the Lord's fury. The text again emphasizes the unprecedented nature of this disaster.

9:25. The devastation was total and unmitigated throughout the land. All who did not take shelter and all animals left exposed in the field were killed. **All that was in the field.** The landscape was pitted with the hail's fiery destructive power, with crops ruined and trees felled.

9:26. Yet the text reveals that God continued making a distinction between Egyptians and Hebrews, with **Goshen** the sole location in Egypt left unscathed, shielded from His judgment.

9:27. The seventh plague provoked a remarkable response from Pharaoh. **Pharaoh**, after sending for **Moses and Aaron**, confessed both his and his people's sinfulness. He also acknowledged the Lord's righteousness.

9:28. Having had his fill of God's newest demonstration of power, Pharaoh requested that Moses **intreat the Lord** to stay His hand. When the plague ceased, the Hebrews would be free to go.

9:29. Moses responded by providing reassurance that the moment he left the capital **city**, he would again intercede on the Egyptian's behalf before the Lord and cause the cessation of the plague. He would do this for the pedagogical purpose **that thou mayest know how that the earth is the Lord's.** As the plague's commencement served as a severe object lesson in God's sovereignty over the land, so too would the plague's cessation at the precise moment

Moses had specified. Egypt was the possession of neither Pharaoh nor any Egyptian deity; it belonged solely to the Lord.

The Egyptian deities challenged by the seventh plague would have been Shu and Nut, the respective sky god and goddess; Set and Isis, the respective god and goddess charged with providing weather conditions conducive to agriculture; and Osirus, the god charged with crop production.

9:30. Moses, however, perceived that although the Egyptians had begun to recognize the power of the Lord, they had not yet come to **fear** Him. Given all that the Egyptians had experienced those past few months, it is difficult to grasp their obtuseness. This exchange reveals an excellent example of man's extraordinary ability to question the extent of God's exclusive authority over His creation despite the overwhelming evidence of His authority's boundless parameters.

9:31–32. At this point, the text includes parenthetical information regarding the season in which this plague occurred, specifying that **flax** (v. 31), used for linen, and **barley**, used for bread and animal feed, comprised the bulk of the devastated crops. **Wheat** (v. 32) and **rye** (spelt), not yet being in season, were unaffected by the plague. This squarely places the seventh plague in January or February, as flax and barley began to blossom at that time, and wheat and spelt did not germinate until March or April.

9:33–35. As Moses had predicted, in response to his prayer, the **rain … hail … and the thunders were ceased** (v. 34). When Pharaoh realized that the danger had passed, he again **hardened his heart.** This time the passage reveals that his **servants** also hardened their hearts. He reneged on his word and refused to let the Hebrews go. Pharaoh is portrayed as a promise breaker, in contrast to the Lord, whom Moses, throughout the narrative, emphatically portrays as a promise keeper.

h. The Eighth Plague: Locusts (10:1–20)

10:1–2. The second plague of the third set of plagues, as per the pattern, was accompanied by a warning. Moses was again instructed by God to speak to Pharaoh, even though the king's heart had been divinely hardened, as had been **the heart of his servants** (v. 1). The Lord shared with Moses a previously undisclosed insight into the divine reasoning behind His hardening of Pharaoh's heart. The king's obstinate refusal to free the Hebrews provided the Lord with the opportunity to **shew these my signs before him**. Also, the memory of the Lord's powerful intervention on behalf of His people was to be orally passed on to each succeeding generation of Hebrews, from parent to child, as a legacy that would guarantee **that ye may know how that I am the Lord** (v. 2). God's mighty **signs** were to serve as foundation pegs to confirm the Hebrews' collective faith and strengthen their trust in the Lord (12:26–27; 13:8, 14–15; Deut. 4:9; Pss. 77:11–20; 78:4–6, 43–53; 105:26–38; 106:7–12; 114:1–3; 135:8–9; 136:10–15).

10:3. Once again, **Moses and Aaron** approached Pharaoh. On this occasion, the usual conveyance of the Lord's request to **let my people go** was preceded by the question, **How long wilt thou refuse to humble thyself before me?** Pharaoh's tenacity strained all reason.

10:4–6. The standard ultimatum followed God's request. On the following day, the eighth plague would commence with an infestation of **locusts** (v. 4). Locusts were a perpetual problem in the ancient world and were properly feared because of their ability to devour a region's entire food supply in mere moments, hours, or days (Joel 1:4–7; 2:1–11; Amos 7:1–3). An infestation was often viewed as divine judgment. The Egyptian deities challenged by this plague would have been Serapia, whose specialty was protecting the Egyptians from locust infestations; as well as the same gods challenged by the previous plague, Shu and Nut, the respective sky god and goddess; Set and Isis, the respective god and goddess charged with providing weather conditions conducive to agriculture; and Osirus, the god charged with crop production.

The face of the earth (v. 5) would be better translated as "the face of the land." Pharaoh was warned about the extensive damage that would be caused by the plague of locusts. **The residue of that which is escaped**. Whatever crops had survived the previous plague of hail were slated for total destruction. This would not be an average, run-of-the-mill locust invasion, such as they had previously experienced. This would a locust invasion unprecedented in Egyptian history.

He turned himself and went out (v. 6). In a graphic breach of Egyptian court protocol, without waiting for Pharaoh's royal dismissal, Moses dismissed himself with impunity.

10:7. Pharaoh's servants again play an increased role in the drama and implore Pharaoh to let the Hebrews leave. **Egypt is destroyed**. They questioned whether their king truly understood the extent to which the nation had already been devastated by the seven preceding plagues. **How long?** Ironically, the servants echo Moses' query to Pharaoh (10:3) and characterize Moses as **a snare** to them, responsible for the distress of the nation. They joined the Lord's prophet in urging their ruler to finally allow the Hebrews to leave Egypt.

10:8. Pharaoh was persuaded by his servants' arguments to again summon the Levite brothers and promise to allow the Hebrews temporary leave to worship God. He had another qualification to the Lord's plan in mind, however, and asked Moses to specify just how many of the Hebrews he intended to include in this excursion.

10:9. Moses responded that the **feast unto the Lord** that they intended to observe required not only the participation of every Hebrew, from the youngest to the eldest, but also of their entire flocks and herds.

10:10. Evil is before you. Many interpreters have stumbled over the explanation of this phrase. Pharaoh seems to be uncharacteristically warning Moses to beware of approaching evil. The difficulty of ascertaining Pharaoh's intent disappears, however, when one takes into account that the Hebrew word *ra*, usually translated as "evil," is also the name of the Egyptian sun god, Ra. Each pharaoh was considered to be Ra's divine son. The intent of Pharaoh may be conveyed as "My god Ra is before you; your god YWWH may be strong, but do not forget that Ra is just as strong." Ra, however, will have to wait to be challenged until the final two plagues, following locusts, are unleashed.

10:11. Therefore, Pharaoh decreed that Moses must be satisfied with taking just the Hebrew **men** on the journey. It was not to be a family outing, for the Hebrew women and children would be forced to remain in Egypt as collateral to ensure the Hebrews' return. Pharaoh then contemptuously drove them out from his royal presence. Pharaoh may have believed that his decree, however minimally, had satisfied YHWH's requirements and settled this bothersome matter once and for all. What the king failed to realize was that in attempting to force this compromise upon Moses, the king had once again compromised his nation.

10:12-14. The rod of Moses was yet again stretched out over the nation of Egypt, causing an **east wind** (v. 13) to blow throughout that afternoon and evening. By the next morning, the plague of **locusts** arrived with a vengeance; they destroyed everything in their wake. The unprecedented ferocity of the locust invasion is reiterated.

10:15. This plague proved to be an ecological and agricultural disaster for the Egyptians, as the locust infestation covered the land and left no fruit, no plant, and no crop uneaten.

10:16-17. Pharaoh quickly summoned Moses and Aaron. **I have sinned** (v. 16). Admitting that he had sinned against both YHWH and the Hebrews, he asked forgiveness of Moses and for one more chance to do the right thing. Again, he requested that Moses entreat YHWH to cease His powerful onslaught. **This death** (v. 17). If the locust infestation continued, there would be famine in the land.

10:18-19. Moses prayed, and God responded to His servant's petition for mercy. The locusts were blown by **a west wind** into the **Red sea** (v. 19). There is scholarly consensus that the Hebrew *yam suh*, which has traditionally been translated as "Red sea," is better rendered as "Reed Sea," or "Sea of Reeds." Increased accuracy of translation, however, has not improved scholars' ability to pinpoint the exact location of the Egyptian body of water indicated in the text.

10:20. The Lord hardened Pharaoh's heart. In what is, by this time, a quite anticipated literary outcome, it is revealed that, despite his promise to the contrary, Pharaoh never intended to allow the Hebrews to leave after all.

i. The Ninth Plague: Darkness (10:21-29)

10:21-23. The third plague of the third set, as per the pattern with the third plagues of the preceding two sets, struck unannounced and without warning. **Darkness over ... Egypt** (v. 21). The **thick darkness** (v. 22) was so oppressive to the Egyptians that the darkness could be **felt** (v. 21). This oppression lasted for **three days** (vv. 22-23).

Proponents of the miraculous intensification of natural events theory propose that the darkness resulted from the arrival of a blinding sandstorm. This does not take into consideration, however, that the darkness began at the discretion of Moses or the continued distinction the Lord made between Goshen and the remainder of Egypt. Although the entire nation suffered in suffocating, pitch-black darkness, the Hebrews in Goshen had retained the sunlight.

The chief Egyptian deity challenged by this plague was Pharaoh's own divine father, Ra, the sun god and high god of the pantheon. This is surely a response to Pharaoh's previous equation of YHWH's power with that of Ra (10:10). Shu and Nut, the respective sky god and goddess, would also have been (yet again) shown impotent before the Lord.

10:24. Pharaoh summoned Moses to propose another "generous" offer. Pharaoh was now willing to allow every Hebrew man, woman, and child to leave Egypt for the purpose of worship, but their flocks and herds had to remain behind as collateral.

10:25-26. Moses immediately conveyed just how objectionable this offer was. Pharaoh's deal was a nonstarter. The Hebrews had to be allowed to bring all their animals with them; **not a hoof** was to **be left behind** (v. 26). God had not yet revealed just which and how many animals he wanted sacrificed to Him; His people could not afford to come up short in their worship.

10:27–28. The Lord again hardened Pharaoh's heart, causing him to rescind the offer. The king expelled Moses and Aaron from his presence, forbidding any future return, with the promise of capital consequence for any infraction.

10:29. While they would indeed shortly see each other once again, it would be for the sole purpose of Pharaoh's humiliating admission of defeat before YHWH. Further details of the dialogue of 10:24–29 are provided in 11:4–8.

j. The Tenth Plague Announced: Death of the Firstborn (chap. 11)

11:1–3. These three verses form a parenthesis in the preceding conversation between Moses and Pharaoh, for the purpose of providing the reader with background information. Previously, the Lord had promised Moses that following the tenth and final plague, not only would Pharaoh let the Hebrews leave Egypt for a temporary sojourn, but he would passionately drive them out of Egypt permanently.

Moses was commanded to instruct the Hebrews to request **silver** and **gold** (v. 2) from their Egyptian neighbors. By this point in the narrative, the Hebrews have found **favour in the sight of the Egyptians** (v. 3). No longer were they loathed and reviled as slaves; they were now highly respected as the people of YHWH. Moses was likewise esteemed by the Egyptians and in the Egyptian court (**Pharaoh's servants**) as YHWH's representative. Most dramatically, Moses' reputation has been rehabilitated in the eyes of the Hebrews. The ones who had previously questioned his leadership (2:14; 5:21) now revered him as their deliverer.

11:4. This verse picks up the conversation between Moses and Pharaoh where it left off in 10:29. Moses announced the tenth and final plague to his adversary. Unlike the previous plague warnings, this was not attached to an ultimatum. God would not relent, nor stay His hand, nor exercise mercy under any circumstances. The decree is announced, and the fate of the Egyptians is sealed. **About midnight will I go out.** The Lord Himself would personally descend **into the midst of Egypt**.

11:5. The firstborn. Every firstborn son of the Egyptians would die, from the royal court of Pharaoh to the most humble village and hamlet. In addition, the firstborn of all the animals would be killed. Egyptian deities challenged by this concluding plague were Isis, the goddess of reproduction and the ostensible protector of Egyptian children; Min, the reproduction god; Ra, the divine father of every past, present, and future pharaoh; and Pharaoh himself, who was considered the divine incarnation of the falcon-headed god, Horus. With this plague, the pretense of the king's divinity would be forever shattered. The Egyptian king would definitively be shown powerless before YHWH.

11:6. A great cry. This plague would be the culmination of those preceding it and would result in the emotional devastation of the populace. The outpouring of mourning throughout Egypt would be unprecedented. Never again would Egypt experience such an intense tragedy.

11:7. Again, the Lord promises a stark distinction between **the Egyptians and Israel**, who would not be subjected to such horror.

11:8. Moses alerted Pharaoh that the time was nigh when his own servants would **bow down** before Moses and plead for the Hebrews to leave Egypt. Having been expelled from Pharaoh's presence (10:28), yet with nothing more to say to the suicidally hardened king, Moses departed the royal court **in a great anger**.

11:9–10. This is a summary statement of the entire narrative of the preceding plagues. The Lord encouraged Moses that it was His divine purpose for Pharaoh's **heart** to be **hardened** (v. 10) and that the king would stubbornly refuse to grant Moses' request. God's purpose for this refusal was so that the His power might be spectacularly displayed throughout Egypt.

D. The Passover (12:1–36)

12:1–2. Instructions are provided for observance of the Feast of Passover, the most frequently mentioned holiday in either the Old or the New Testament (see, e.g., Num. 9:1–5; Josh. 5:10; 2 Kings

23:21–23; 2 Chron. 30:1–27; 35:1–19; Ezra 6:19–22; Luke 2:41–43; John 2:13, 23; 6:4; 11:55–12:1). This is the initial festival in the annual cycle of seven (Leviticus 23). The holiday served as the catalyst for the inauguration of a new religious calendar system for the Hebrews (see chart, *KJV Study Bible*, p. 92). The month in which the Passover was observed was thereafter to be **the first month of the** new **year** (v. 2). This month was called Aviv at the time (13:41; 23:15; 34:18; Deut. 16:1), but following the Babylonian captivity, it would be called Nisan (Neh. 2:1; Est. 3:7). The reason for the institution of a religious calendar is that Passover was to serve as an annual celebration of new beginnings and as an annual reminder of the Hebrews' new identity as a people and nation.

12:3–5. On the tenth day of Aviv, each family was to select and set aside a lamb for their household. In the event that a particular family unit was too small to consume an entire lamb, they were to join with a neighboring family group. Jewish tradition, at some point, determined that ten was the minimum number of people required to constitute a household large enough to consume the Passover lamb. The reason for the minimum household number was that the entire lamb needed to be eaten in just the one holiday evening.

The qualifying requirements for the selection of the **lamb** (v. 5) were that it be either a **sheep** or a **goat** that was **without blemish** or physical imperfection of any sort and one year of age.

12:6. Each household's lamb was to be set aside for four days of observation and maintenance of its perfect condition. It was then to be killed on the fourteenth day of Aviv **in the evening**. The literal translation of this phrase is "between the evenings" and has been understood in Jewish tradition to mean either the time between sunset and full darkness (i.e., twilight) or between three o'clock in the afternoon and sunset. The second view was accepted and applied to the Passover sacrifices during the time of the temple, the lambs being slaughtered on the afternoon of the fourteenth of Nisan.

12:7. The **blood** of the sacrificed lamb was to be stained on **the two side posts and ... upper door post** of the home in which the lamb would be eaten that evening. At either corner where the side posts met the lintel, the bloody stain would have formed a cross. John, Peter, and Paul all use the imagery of the unblemished, sacrificed lamb to refer to Jesus (John 1:29; 1 Peter 1:19; 1 Cor. 5:7).

12:8–10. Specific instructions are enumerated for the eating of this sacred meal. **Flesh ... unleavened bread ... bitter herbs** (v. 8). Whatever additional liturgical elements have accrued to the Passover seder throughout the centuries, three indivisible elements are divinely commanded and nonnegotiable, regardless of individual or regional tradition. (1) The meal must be centered on the eating of the lamb and be accompanied by both matzo (unleavened bread; 12:34, 39) and some variety of bitter herb (horseradish, endive, etc.), symbolizing the bitterness of their slavery experience. (2) The animal must be roasted with fire, not eaten raw or cooked by boiling, and must be roasted whole with its head, legs, and inner parts intact. (3) **Let nothing of it remain** (v. 10). The lamb must be eaten that same evening; there were to be no leftovers. Anything left over had to be burned the following morning.

12:11–12. This meal was to be eaten with the Hebrews' **loins girded** (i.e., garment folds tucked into the belt; v. 12), sandals on, and staffs in hand. **Eat it in haste**. This is by no means a divine command or sanction for the Hebrews to rapidly wolf down their food. The term translated as "haste" simply means "with an attitude of trembling expectancy or trepidation." **The LORD's passover.** The term "passover," initially coined here, is used in Scripture to describe not only the festival but also the sacrificed lamb. It is also used to describe the event itself, the redemptive moment in history when the LORD executed **judgment** upon **all the gods of Egypt** (v. 12).

12:13–14. The blood shall be to you for a token (v. 13). When the Lord personally came to **destroy** the firstborn males of all Egypt, both human and animal, He would see **the blood** on the Hebrews' doors and would **pass over** them. The origin of the term Passover is a stark reminder that the Hebrews were not automatically exempt from the Lord's judgment simply because of their racial status. Although the Lord had chosen to automatically discriminate between the Egyptians and Hebrews in plagues four through nine, He changed that pattern here. From this point on in the collective life of Israel, Passover would serve as an annual object lesson and as a reminder of the necessity of blood to avert God's wrath; a lasting **memorial** (v. 14) to that night in Egypt was to be celebrated in perpetuity, that is, as long as the Torah was still in effect.

12:15. A second holiday was established in conjunction with Passover, the Feast of **unleavened bread**, to be celebrated immediately following Passover for the duration of another seven days. The combined observance of Passover and the Feast of Unleavened Bread lasts eight days. Although technically two separate holidays, the Bible usually links them together and often treats them as a single unit (see, e.g., Mark 14:12; Acts 21:3–4).

The observance of this holiday is characterized by the strict removal of **leaven out of your houses**. In the Bible, leaven (yeast) is frequently used as a powerful symbol of sin (see, e.g., Luke 12:1; 1 Cor. 5:8). With the removal of all leaven from the home and diet for the duration of the holiday, the home is symbolically purified and becomes a sin-free zone. This potent custom is still practiced in the homes of observant Jewish families.

In the event that anyone ate food containing leaven during the duration of the holiday, the penalty was quite severe: excommunication or even execution (**that soul shall be cut off from Israel**).

12:16–18. Both the **first** and **seventh** (v. 16) days of the **feast of unleavened bread** (v. 17) were to serve as days of rest. No work was to be done. This seven-day holiday, like the one-day holiday of Passover, was to be observed by Israel in perpetuity as an enduring memorial of the day of Hebrew liberation from Egyptian bondage.

12:19–20. The prohibition against eating food containing leaven during this period is reiterated, along with the severe consequences for either native Hebrew or **stranger** (v. 19), the sojourner of temporary residence.

12:21. The narrative is rejoined here as Moses instructs the Hebrew **elders** to ensure that all the families under their jurisdiction followed the divine instructions for the selection and slaying of the original Passover lambs.

12:22–23. Hyssop (v. 22) is a small plant that is indigenous to the Middle East, used elsewhere in the Torah for purification for sin (Lev. 14:4, 6, 49, 51–52; Num. 19:6, 18; Heb. 9:19; Ps. 51:7). Here it is to serve as the "paintbrush" for staining the Hebrews' doorposts and lintels with the lambs' blood. In most contemporary Passover seders, a sprig of parsley is used to symbolize the hyssop.

The application of blood created a zone of safety from God's judgment, and no one was to leave the "safe house" that evening until God's wrath had passed them over. **The destroyer** (v. 23). This is the angel of death. God moved throughout Egypt in the company of the death angel, the agent of God's judgment. The Lord would restrain the angel of death from entering any homes covered by the blood of the Passover lamb.

12:24–25. Again, the instruction is given that the Passover and the Feast of Unleavened Bread are to be annually observed in perpetuity, to be initiated upon entrance into **the land** (v. 25) of covenant promise.

12:26–28. As these holidays were to serve as a lasting memorial of the Lord's deliverance, emphasis is placed on the older generations passing down the significance of the observance to the younger generations. For some thirty-five hundred years, the events of Passover have been relayed, generation after generation, from Jewish parents to their children. The meal is an object lesson, a teaching tool for the purpose of recalling God's mercy, and children have always played a central role in its implementation.

12:29–30. At midnight (v. 29), the plague suddenly began to roil the nation. Not one home was left unaffected by the abrupt loss of all the **firstborn** males, from the royal court of Pharaoh to the prison house. **A great cry** (v. 30). Each family lost at least one member, as firstborn sons, fathers, and grandfathers were struck down. Even the firstborn of the

cattle (v. 29) were killed. Those holding to the miraculous intensification of natural events theory of the plagues cannot in any fashion explain the origin of a virus intelligent enough to select only firstborn males. The hand of the Lord is the only satisfactory explanation for this disaster. His promised judgment (4:23) had been rendered.

12:31 – 32. Before the sun rose after that horrific night, Pharaoh summoned Moses and Aaron for one final encounter, contradicting his previous oath to never again allow Moses into his presence (10:28). **Rise up … get you forth … go … take … and be gone** (vv. 31 – 32). His address to Moses is perforated with an urgent string of imperatives, all conveying the force of his desire that the Hebrews leave Egypt. Not only was he allowing the Hebrews to leave to worship the Lord; he actually demanded that they do so, without qualification or compromise, taking their flocks and herds with them.

Bless me also (v. 32). The king's final words to Moses were a request for his blessing — a final acknowledgment that Moses and his God are superior to Pharaoh and his pantheon of deities.

12:33. We be all dead men. The Egyptian people also urged the Hebrews to leave the land, presuming that if the Hebrews stayed any longer among them, the entire population of Egypt might eventually be exterminated.

12:34. The historical explanation of the centrality of unleavened bread in both the Passover ritual and the ensuing seven-day feast begins in verse 34 and continues in verse 39. Armies move on their stomachs, and in the Hebrews' haste to leave (on what was the first day of the seven-day festival), they grabbed the only food that was on hand: their as yet unleavened bread dough. They formed the dough into cakes and hoisted the pans onto their shoulders. The sun then baked the cakes into matzos, unleavened bread.

12:35 – 36. They borrowed (v. 35). The Hebrews had been instructed by Moses to ask their Egyptian neighbors for silver, gold, and clothing. This cannot be truly characterized as "borrowing," for the Hebrews did not intend to ever return, and so **they spoiled the Egyptians** (v. 36). The plunder was overdue back wages for all their slave labors.

II. The Exodus (12:37 – 15:21)

A. Departure (12:37 – 51)

12:37. Departing on the first day of the Feast of Unleavened Bread, the initial leg of the exodus spanned from the Egyptian treasure city **Rameses to Succoth** (perhaps present-day Tell el-Maskhutah). **Six hundred thousand … men.** This is a round figure; the total number of men aged twenty and older was 603,550 (38:26). Extrapolating from that number, assuming one wife and two children per man, one arrives at an exodus population of roughly two million people. Objections have been commonly raised over the possibility of such an extraordinary population. While enormous energy and scholarly creativity has gone into the development of alternative theories to explain why the population numbers should not be taken at their face value, none has proven definitively convincing. For the moment, other than simply accepting the narrative's record of 603,550 men, there is absolutely no way of knowing the total number of Hebrews who participated in the exodus.

12:38. A mixed multitude went with them. These were likely other, non-Hebrew, slaves and perhaps a few God-fearing Egyptians. This Gentile group would stir up trouble in the camp during the wilderness journey (Num. 11:4).

12:39. See discussion on 12:34.

12:40 – 41. The total duration of the Hebrews' sojourn in Egypt, as both freemen and slaves, was **four hundred and thirty years** (1876 – 1446 BC; v. 40). **Hosts of the Lord** (v. 41). The former slaves are pictured as the armies of YHWH, who have received their marching orders.

12:42. Night of the Lord. Another reminder that, as the seminal and epochal event in the history of the Jewish people, this night is to be a perpetual observance for Israel.

12:43 – 45. Rules are laid down concerning the participation of the previously mentioned mixed multitude in the Passover observance (12:38). First, as a national holiday, the Passover meal was not to be shared with a **stranger** (v. 43), a citizen of another nation. Also excluded from eating the meal was any non-Jewish **servant** (v. 45), unless the servant had been **circumcised** (v. 44) and thereby joined to the Israelite nation. Additionally, the Passover meal could not be eaten by a Gentile resident alien.

12:46–47. Two more general rules are laid down. First, the Passover meal was to be eaten by each household within the confines of **one house** (v. 46). There were to be no progressive Passover seders from home to home and no eating of the ritual meal out on the porch or in the backyard. In addition, the breaking of any of the lamb's bones was prohibited. The messianic significance of this rule is highlighted later in Scripture (Ps. 34:20; John 19:36). Second, the observance of Passover was to be obligatory for every Hebrew.

12:48–49. Again, concerning the permanent alien population of Israel, no **stranger** (v. 48), an uncircumcised Gentile, was to eat of the Passover. He was required to be **circumcised**, along with his family and servants, before he could eat the Passover meal as if he were a native Israelite. **One law … to him that is homeborn, and unto the stranger** (v. 49). God's standards were to apply equally to both the Hebrews and the permanent residents in the land, without exception.

12:50–51. The Hebrews' liberation by the hand of YHWH is again announced.

B. Consecration of the Firstborn (13:1–16)

13:1–2. In view of the Hebrews' supernatural liberation, laws are now enumerated concerning the consecration of the **firstborn** (v. 2) of Israel to YHWH. **Sanctify** means " to set apart, to dedicate or consecrate." Both the firstborn sons of the Hebrews and the firstborn males of their animals belong to God. The Lord considers the nation of Israel as a whole to be His firstborn (4:22). Jesus Himself was presented at the temple in accordance with this law (Luke 2:22–23).

13:3–10. Remember (v. 3). The reason that all the firstborn sons belong to God stems from His redemption of the Hebrew firstborn in Egypt. **Canaanites … land flowing with milk and honey** (v. 5). See discussion on 3:8. It is reiterated that once in the Land of Promise, the Hebrews are to meticulously keep the festivals of Passover and Unleavened Bread. The observance must be passed down to succeeding generations.

A sign unto thee upon thine hand, and for a memorial between thine eyes (v. 9). The literal interpretation of this passage is the origin of the ancient practice of wearing *tefillin* (phylacteries); little leather pouches that since biblical times, have been ritually bound around the foreheads and arms of observant Jewish men. These pouches, or boxes, contain a small parchment scroll on which is written four passages, including this one, in respective order: Deuteronomy 11:13–22; Deuteronomy 6:4–9; Exodus 13:11–16; and Exodus 13:1–10. Whether the Lord meant this instruction metaphorically or literally is a matter of interpretational dispute. Jesus, although He condemned the ostentatious proportions of some of His contemporaries' phylacteries (Matt. 23:5), left no other record of His opinion of the common practice of donning these tokens. The emphasis of this passage is that God's Torah is to be continually remembered throughout the day. Phylacteries can be a tool to achieve that end.

That the LORD's law may be in thy mouth (v. 9). The law was to be a constant topic of conversation and thought because of the Lord's deliverance of the Hebrews from Egyptian bondage.

13:11–12. The consecration of the firstborn males, both human and animal, was to be observed as soon as the Hebrews arrived in their **land** (v. 11).

13:13. Redeem. To obtain release by means of payment. God allowed for the exchange of the firstborn of an unclean, nonkosher domesticated animal (for example, **an ass**) with the offspring of a clean, kosher animal (for example, **a lamb.**) This was a handy law for most, as the agricultural value of a donkey was generally greater than that of a lamb. If, however, one did not wish to substitute the clean, kosher animal for the unclean, non-kosher firstborn (the lamb for the firstborn donkey) for some reason, then the unclean, nonkosher firstborn animal's neck was to be broken. No one could derive value from the animal, for it belonged to the Lord. No such substitutions were allowed for firstborn sons, however (nor could their necks be broken.) They were to be redeemed by their fathers at the price of five shekels (specified in Num. 18:15–16).

13:14–16. Moses again places great emphasis on passing the memory of this great redemptive act down through successive generations and reiterates that their liberation from bondage is the basis for the laws of the redemption of the firstborn.

A token upon thine hand, and for frontlets between thine eyes (v. 16). See discussion on 13:9.

C. The Red Sea (13:17–15:21)

1. Crossing the Sea (13:17–14:31)

13:17. Way of the … Philistines. The Lord did not guide the Hebrews from Egypt to Canaan via the most direct route, along the Mediterranean Sea. The Lord was concerned that seeing the numerous Egyptian military fortifications along this main highway would terrify the Hebrews and cause them to turn back. Therefore, He led them along a somewhat longer route.

13:18. Red sea. Whether translated as "Red sea" or "Reed sea," the exact location of this body of water is impossible to ascertain from the text (see discussion on 10:19). There is little reason to reject the possibility that the text refers to the "finger" of the Red Sea, the present-day Gulf of Suez. Many propose Lake Menzaleh as a more "reedy" alternative, one that would be deep enough and situated far enough north to meet the requirements of the narrative (see Kitchen, *Reliability*, pp. 265–74).

13:19. The Hebrews carried with them **the bones of Joseph.** Knowing the certainty of God's fulfillment of the promise of land in the Abrahamic covenant, the patriarch **had straitly sworn the children of Israel** to return his remains to the Promised Land (Gen. 50:25). Joseph's remains would eventually be buried in Shechem (Josh. 24:32).

13:20–22. The Lord visibly manifested His presence to His people as a **pillar of a cloud by day** and a **pillar of fire by night** (v. 22). The appearance of the Lord's Shekinah glory, His visible presence and leadership, spurred the multitude onward and very practically enabled them to travel both by day and by night.

14:1–2. The LORD (v. 1) directed **Moses** to change direction and lead the people to camp between the wilderness and the Red Sea.

14:3–4. For Pharaoh will say (v. 3). The Lord was well aware that Pharaoh's spies would see this apparently nonsensical, indeed suicidal, route and report back to the king that the Hebrews were wandering in circles. For a final time, Pharaoh's heart would again be hardened, causing him to change his mind concerning the Hebrews' freedom, and he would send his army to chase after them. **That the Egyptians may know that I am the LORD** (v. 4). Pharaoh's change of heart and mobilization of Egypt's great military machine would afford YHWH a final opportunity to impress His glory upon the Egyptian people.

14:5. The text reveals that both Pharaoh and his servants had a change of heart toward the Hebrews, and although they had forcefully expelled the Hebrews from their nation, by this point, the economic reality of what they had lost occurred to them. With their slave labor force set free and departed from their midst, the question arose as to just who would set about the task of rebuilding Egypt's cities from the monumental devastation wrought by the ten plagues of YHWH.

14:6–9. All the chariots of Egypt (v. 7). Pharaoh mobilized a vast military force, led by six hundred of his select charioteers (**chosen chariots**). The king and his army, traveling much faster by chariot than were the unwieldy two million Hebrews on foot, quickly overtook their former slaves as they camped by the seaside. **The children of Israel went out with a high hand** (v. 8). This phrase ironically notes that in the seminal stage of their freedom, the Hebrews were supremely confident.

14:10–12. The confidence of the **children of Israel** (v. 10) swiftly evaporated once they noticed the dramatic approach of Pharaoh's army in all its strength. In terror and surprise, they **cried out unto the Lord**. Their prayer, however, was not one of supplication but of protest. They complained to Moses that they would have been better off if they had remained as Egyptian property. They reminded Moses that they had initially rejected his leadership and had asked him not to upset the status quo. **Better for us to serve the Egyptians** (v. 12). They may have been slaves in Egypt, but it was better to be a living slave than a dead freeman.

Because there were no graves in Egypt (v. 11). Typical Jewish ironic humor is apparent even here, where the Hebrews ask Moses a rhetorical question about whether they needed to be buried in the desert for want of available graves in Egypt, a nation that prided itself on studding its landscape with the most extravagant and elaborate graves in the world, the pyramids.

14:13 – 14. Moses responded with a twofold command for his people, **Fear ye not** (v. 13) and **stand still**. In addition, they were to **hold** their **peace** (v. 14). The reason the Hebrews were to take courage was that not one approaching Egyptian would ever be seen by them again. They were to passively stand firm because **the Lord** Himself would **fight** this battle on their behalf. That day, they would witness **the salvation of the Lord** (v. 13), His mighty and unprecedented deliverance of His people.

14:15. The Lord said … Wherefore criest thou unto me? Apparently, Moses had turned to the Lord to intercede for the Hebrews but was interrupted in mid-intercession by YHWH. He directed Moses to stop praying and start instructing the Hebrews to press toward the sea.

14:16. The Lord commanded Moses to take his staff and stretch it out over the sea. This would cause the waters to divide and create a pathway of **dry ground** on which the Hebrews could cross through **the midst of the sea** and escape.

14:17 – 18. I will harden the hearts of the Egyptians (v. 17). The Lord hardened not only Pharaoh's heart but also the hearts of his charioteers and military so that they would be emboldened to follow the Hebrews into the midst of the sea. **The Egyptians shall know that I am the Lord** (v. 18). Their defeat would result in the Lord receiving **honour** over Pharaoh through the visceral impression of YHWH's sovereignty over the Egyptians.

14:19 – 20. Angel of God (v. 19). This is another term for the angel of the Lord, that is, the second person of the Trinity. His presence was within the Shekinah glory, the pillar of dark cloud, which then moved from its usual position before Israel to behind them, placing itself directly **between the camp of the Egyptians and the camp of Israel** (v. 20). **Darkness … light**. The side of the cloud that faced the Egyptian army brought darkness, but the opposite side, facing the rear of the Hebrew camp, shone brightly, enabling the Hebrews to keep traveling **all** through **the night**. This allowed the Hebrews time to escape — time for two million men, women, children, and their animals to cross the pathway through the Red Sea.

14:21. Moses' narrative description of how the Red Sea was parted is surprisingly terse. Rather than cultivating the high spectacle and drama of a climactic cinema scene, the narrative proceeds with matter-of-fact yet athletic prose. God's salvific activity betrays no hint of divine exertion or strain. When Moses stretched forth his staff over the water, **the Lord** simply caused **a strong east wind** to blow throughout the evening. This gale resulted in the division of the sea down the center.

The miracle recorded here is actually comprised of two components. First, there is the separation of the waters themselves. Second, the emergent pathway through the sea did not consist of the thick mud normally associated with the bottom of a seabed. The Hebrews would never have gotten very far in such muck. Instead, the parting of the waters revealed **dry land**, quite conducive to rapid travel.

14:22. Into this rift in the sea, which was perhaps one-eighth to one-quarter mile wide, the Hebrews proceeded. On either side of them stood a massive **wall** of water, held in check only by the power of God.

14:23 – 25. What follows in the narrative provides an excellent indication of just how hardened and **troubled** (v. 24) Pharaoh and the Egyptians had become by this time. In the dawning light of day (**the**

morning watch, from 2:00 a.m. to 6:00 a.m.), the Lord allowed the Egyptians to see beyond the pillar of cloud to the Hebrews crossing through the midst of the divided sea. The Egyptians incomprehensibly failed to realize that, yet again, mighty YHWH was supernaturally intervening on behalf of His people. Of course, they should have noticed the pattern that had developed over the course of the ten plagues. Each and every time the Egyptians had witnessed this sort of supernatural activity in the recent past, it had never worked out in their favor. Instead of concluding that when it came to standing toe-to-toe with YHWH, discretion was the better part of valor, they decided to pursue the Hebrews into the midst of the sea.

As the chariots proceeded along the pathway through the sea, in hot pursuit of their prey, the dry ground began to devolve into mud. Bogging down in the muck, the **chariot wheels** (v. 25) began to come off. To this chaos may have also been added either the thunderstorm or the earthquake poetically described in Psalms (see Ps. 77:16–19). Too late, the army comprehended what they should have perceived all along: the Hebrews possessed a powerful patron who **fighteth for them against the Egyptians**.

14:26–28. Regrettably for the Egyptians, this moment of insight arrived far too late. The Hebrews had safely arrived on the far shore of the sea. The Lord commanded Moses to again stretch out his staff over the divided sea so that the waters might reunite. The horror described in 14:27 is palpable. As the two walls of water began to collapse upon them, the Egyptians, realizing their impending doom, nonetheless attempted to escape their fate. **The waters returned** (v. 28). Escape proved impossible, however, as the deluge washed over Pharaoh's military force, covering them completely as the sea returned to its proper level, leaving no survivors.

14:29–30. In contrast to the Egyptians' unfortunate, soggy fate, the Hebrews remained both dry and secure. They camped long enough along the sea to witness the bodies of the Egyptian soldiers beginning to wash up on the shore.

14:31. This passage marks the historical conclusion of both the threat the Egyptian nation repre-

sented to the Hebrews as well as the true beginning of their status as a free people. The Lord's victory over Pharaoh was definitive; the battle of the gods was complete. This part of the narrative closes with a statement of the profound impression the Red Sea event made on the Hebrew nation's collective conscience. As they witnessed the power of YHWH, the Hebrews **feared the Lord** and **believed** in both Him and His representative, Moses. One need read only a bit further in the narrative, however, to learn that this new confident attitude would prove to be only temporary.

2. The Songs of Moses and Miriam (15:1–21)

The narrative is temporarily interrupted by the insertion of two poems: the songs of Moses and his sister, Miriam.

a. The Song of Moses (15:1–18)

15:1–18. Moses' "victory song" shares the characteristics of the classic psalms of Israel. It begins with an opening burst of praise (vv. 1–3), continues with an explanation for this praise (vv. 4–13) and concludes with yet more praise (vv. 14–18). The theme of the poem is the celebration of the Lord's spectacular victory over Pharaoh and his military force. The poem's main subject is God Himself; His covenant Name, YHWH, appears ten times. The first two sections (vv. 1–3, 4–12) retell the story of the Red Sea victory, and the third section (vv. 13–18) anticipates the future approach to and conquest of the Promised Land.

15:1–3. The psalm begins with an opening statement of purpose: to **sing unto the Lord** (v. 1). The motivation behind that purpose is also provided: His glorious triumph in casting the chariots of Pharaoh (**the horse and his rider**) into the Red Sea. This first section is studded with divine superlatives. **The Lord** is Moses' **strength and song ... my salvation ... my God ... my father's God** (v. 2). **The Lord is a man of war**. YHWH **is his name** (v. 3).

15:4–12. The second section relates God's total victory over the Egyptian military. They had been **cast into the sea ... drowned in the Red sea** (v. 4) ...

covered. They **sank into the bottom** (v. 5) and had been **dashed in pieces** (v. 6). The Lord had **overthrown them … consumed them** (v. 7) **… covered them**, and **they sank as lead** (v. 10). In a series of four "I will" statements (v. 9), the Egyptian army's unfulfilled desire for vengeance is revealed.

Yet while the Egyptians may have had the will to power, in this contest, only YHWH had the actual power. In a memorable image, the majestic act of parting the Red Sea is portrayed as taking no more divine effort than a **blast** of the Lord's **nostrils** (v. 8) or the stretching out of His **right hand** (v. 12). **Who is like unto thee, O Lord?** (v. 11). YHWH is peerless among other so-called deities, in **holiness** and power.

15:13–18. Moses moves his song from past victory to the certainty of the Lord's leadership of His people to their land. Other nations will be terrorized when they hear of the Lord's victory, which is exactly what came to pass later in Israel's history (Josh. 2:9–11, 24; 51). **Palestina … Edom … Moab … Canaan** (vv. 14–15). The order is roughly that along the route Israel would follow from Sinai to the Promised Land. The Hebrews' arrival in their land is assured. **The mountain of thine inheritance … the place … which thou hast made for thee to dwell in … the Sanctuary** (v. 17). This is a veiled reference to Jerusalem and Mount Zion.

b. The Song of Miriam (15:19–21)

15:19. This verse marks a brief return to the narrative to reestablish the purpose for the following song of praise.

15:20. Miriam the prophetess. Along with her brothers, Moses and Aaron, Miriam also participated in the "family business." She has the distinction of being the first of the rare, few women who are recognized as possessing the prophetic office (Num. 12:1–2). Other prophetesses in the Bible are Deborah (Judg. 4:4), Isaiah's wife (Isa. 8:3), Huldah (2 Kings 22:14), Noadiah (Neh. 6:14), Anna (Luke 2:36), and Philip's daughters (Acts 21:9). By this time, Miriam was well over ninety years old (see discussion on 2:6).

With timbrels and with dances. Music and dance were two common forms of victory celebration in the ancient world (see 1 Sam. 18:6; 2 Sam. 1:20).

15:21. The content of Miriam's brief song echoes the first line of her brother's song, telling of God's victory over the chariots of Egypt.

III. Journey to Sinai (15:22–18:27)

A. At Marah (15:22–27)

15:22–23. Three days in the wilderness (v. 22). This is not an indication of travel time but a measure of the distance traveled. Exactly how many days the Hebrews went without finding **water** is unknown. The phrase "three days in the wilderness" (Exod. 3:18; 5:3; 8:27) is the same phrase that Moses used in his many requests before Pharaoh. Instead of the Hebrews worshiping the Lord, however, they were about to murmur against Him. **The wilderness of Shur.** Located east of Egypt (see Gen. 25:18; 1 Sam. 15:7) in the northwestern part of the Sinai peninsula, elsewhere referred to as "the wilderness of Etham" (Num. 33:8), both names meaning "fortress wall," in Hebrew and Egyptian, respectively.

When they came to **Marah** (meaning "bitter"; v. 23), the local water supply proved undrinkable. This locale may possibly be modern Ain Hawarah, inland from the Gulf of Suez.

15:24. Having gone for some time now without drinkable water, the Hebrews **murmured against Moses.** This was an indication that their previously expressed trust in their leader was extremely shallow; their confidence in Moses was poised to evaporate at the first sign of trouble. During their wilderness wanderings, the Israelites grumbled against Moses and Aaron whenever Israel faced a crisis (16:2; 17:3; Num. 14:2; 16:11, 41).

15:25–26. Moses **cried unto the Lord** (v. 25), who instructed him to **cast** a particular tree **into the waters** to make the supply potable. **He proved them.** The purpose of this crisis was to test the people. **If thou wilt diligently hearken … I will put none of these diseases upon thee** (v. 26). Obedience to the Lord's **commandments** and **statutes** would immunize the Hebrews from the sort of judgments and plagues He had recently unleashed upon the Egyptians. Unstated, yet implied all the same, is the converse; disobedience would result in severe judgment. **I am the LORD that healeth thee**. The spiritual lesson to be learned by Israel was that although the Lord easily "healed" the water, it was their faith that was in need of healing.

15:27. That Marah was an object lesson is highlighted by Moses' casual notation that the next stop on their travel itinerary was the oasis of **Elim**. Elim, meaning "large trees," was an appropriate name, for Moses records this locale as having seventy **palm trees**. This is possibly the modern Gharandel valley, some seven miles south of Ain Hawarah.

B. In the Wilderness of Sin (chap. 16)

16:1. Continuing their journey to Sinai, they next came to **the wilderness of Sin**. This is possibly the present-day Debbet er-Ramleh, in the southwestern quadrant of the Sinai peninsula. Moses' notation that they arrived on **the fifteenth day of the second month** indicates that it has been exactly one month since the Hebrews departed Egypt (see 12:2, 6, 29, 31).

16:2–3. The whole congregation ... of Israel murmured against Moses and Aaron (v. 2). The phrase "whole congregation" indicates that this was not the shenanigans of a few troublemakers but a wholesale rebellion that was brewing. Even the casual reader of the exodus narrative is occasionally flummoxed by the level of intensity of the Hebrews' whining. They moan that they would have been better off if the Lord had "mercifully" wiped their nation out back in Egypt. **Flesh pots ... bread to the full** (v. 3). The reason they would have been better off dead in Egypt is that at least they would have been corpses with full bellies. Remarkably, they have the gall to accuse Aaron and Moses of having brought their nation **into this wilderness, to kill this whole assembly**.

The Hebrews had departed Egypt with an abundance of livestock in their possession, so the concern cannot be a perceived shortage of food. The problem seems to be that the Hebrews did not yet wish to begin utilizing their abundant food supply.

16:4–5. These verses serve as a preparatory statement to the event recorded in 16:9ff. The Lord made clear that if it was flesh and **bread** (v. 4) His people desired, He would certainly oblige them. He would provide by **rain[ing]** down **bread**, after a fashion, **from heaven**. The Lord's purpose in so doing was **that I may prove them**. This will be another divine object lesson for the Hebrews' benefit.

It will also serve as the Hebrews' introduction to God's revolutionary new concept of Sabbath. They were instructed to **gather on the sixth day ... twice as much** (v. 5) as they normally would on any other day (see discussion on 16:22–26).

16:6–8. At even, then ye shall know that the LORD ... And in the morning, then ye shall see the glory of the LORD (vv. 6–7). The Lord's daily provision for the Hebrews, of flesh in the evening and bread in the morning, would demonstrate that He was the covenant-keeping God; they would continually experience Him as YHWH.

The nation's attitude, however, was in dire need of improvement. Their disrespect for their divinely appointed leaders is indicated by Moses' question, **what are we?** (v. 7). The truth was that their **murmurings** were **not against** Moses and Aaron **but against the LORD** Himself.

16:9–10. He hath heard (v. 9). The covenant-making, promise-keeping God who had previously heard their wretched cries when they were still slaves now heard His people's pathetic murmuring. To dramatically punctuate His divine concern, **the glory of the LORD appeared in the cloud** (v. 10).

16:11–12. This is an reiteration of 16:6–8.

16:13–15. The Lord's provision begins that evening, as **the quails came** (v. 13), satisfying the people's desire for meat. The next morning, the Hebrews discovered a new, creative provision that would satisfy their need for **bread** (v. 15), and they said, **It is manna**.

They wist not what it was (v. 15). In Hebrew, manna means "What is it?" Although this passage and Numbers 11:7–9 attempt a physical description of manna, the language used is somewhat ambiguous, and the portrait of the substance remains unfocused for most readers. Manna is characterized as being a small and round flakelike substance, similar to coriander seed, that was the color of bdellium and tasted like fresh oil. It fell with the dew each morning, but exposure to the hot sun caused it to melt; leftovers stank and bred worms. It was somewhat flexible in its cooking use and could be ground up, baked, or boiled.

16:16–18. Gather of it every man according to his eating, an omer (v. 16). Whatever manna was, for forty years, sufficient quantities were generated daily to feed each person approximately two quarts worth. Each household gathered enough to meet the needs of their family. In this fashion, no one went hungry, and everyone's nutritional needs were met. It seems likely that Jesus had this illustration in mind when He taught His disciples to pray that the Lord would provide their daily bread (Matt. 6:11; Luke 11:3).

16:19–20. The flip side of God's perfect daily provision was an absolute prohibition of leftovers. Nonetheless, at the outset, some Hebrews **hearkened not unto Moses** (v. 20) and retained a supply until the following morning. **It bred worms, and stank. Moses was wroth.** Understandably, this flagrant violation of the Lord's command caused Moses to lose his temper. The text allows the reader a fleeting glimpse into Moses' humanity; this man of God is no holy automaton.

16:21. Uncollected manna **melted** in the heat of the afternoon **sun**.

16:22–26. The rest of the holy sabbath (v. 23). Detailed behavioral instructions are provided here for the gathering of manna on the Sabbath. These instructions were necessary because Israel had never heard of nor previously observed a **sabbath unto the Lord**, the fourth commandment having not yet been given at Sinai. The Hebrew word *shabbat* means, "to cease, desist, rest." Pharaoh was presumably not a big believer in granting his workforce a day off from their labors. Within the Hebrew Scriptures, the Sabbath is mentioned 111 times.

So as not to labor on the Sabbath, on the sixth day the Hebrews gathered twice as much manna as usual, a two-day supply, for **on the seventh day, which is the sabbath, in it there shall be none** (v. 26). The Lord would not provide manna on the Sabbath morning. Unlike the leftover manna on other days, leftover Sabbath-morning manna did not stink, nor did it breed worms.

16:27–30. Inevitably, some of the people ignored the instructions and, going out on Sabbath to gather manna, were surprised not to locate any. **How long refuse ye …?** (v. 28). The Hebrews could try even the Lord's inexhaustible supply of patience. That this desecration of the Sabbath did not result in capital consequence for the violators is another indication that it was a previously unknown concept. If Israel had been familiar with this practice, it is quite unlikely that as many Hebrews would have demonstrated such blatant ignorance. The leniency shown to the Sabbath breakers is strong evidence of the novelty of Sabbath. Later on, such leniency is in short supply concerning the violator who was caught gathering sticks on the Sabbath (Num. 15:32–36). Finally, **the people** got the message and **rested on the seventh day** (v. 30).

16:31. A description of manna is attempted here. See discussion on 16:15.

16:32–34. Moses instructed that two quarts of manna be set aside in a "golden pot" (Heb. 9:4) for posterity (**kept for your generations**; v. 32). Some time later, **Aaron laid it up before the Testimony** (v. 34). "The Testimony" refers to the two tablets of the law (25:16; 31:18; 32:15; 34:29), which were contained in the ark of the covenant and kept within the Holy of Holies.

16:35. The Hebrews **did eat manna forty years**. God's provision of manna finally ceased at the time the Israelites celebrated their first Passover in the Promised Land (Josh. 5:10–12).

Jesus made use of manna's powerful imagery in the Jewish imagination, connecting Himself with God's provision by referring to Himself as "the true bread from heaven" (John 6:32), "the bread of God" (John 6:33), "the bread of life" (John 6:35, 48), and "the living bread which came down from heaven" (John 6:51).

C. At Rephidim (17:1–18:27)

Three important events occur at Rephidim, all preparatory to the giving of the Torah at Sinai: (1) the waters of Meribah (17:1–7), (2) the war with Amalek (17:8–16), and (3) Moses' reunion with Jethro (18:1–27).

1. The Waters of Meribah (17:1–7)

17:1–2. The next stage of Israel's journey finds them having obeyed **the commandment of the LORD** (v. 1) to travel **from the wilderness of Sin** to **Rephidim**. This location, near Mount Sinai, may possibly be identified as the present-day Wadi Refayid or the Wadi Feiran. **There was no water.** Upon their arrival, they discovered that this was yet another desert locale with no water supply.

The Hebrews' reaction is a bit more abrasive than in previous accounts, with the narrative relating that **the people did chide with Moses** (v. 2). The force of the term translated "chide" indicates "striving, quarrels, contention." Moses challenged them to keep their attitude in check, asking them, **wherefore do ye tempt the LORD?** It was possible that YHWH might not tolerate their faithlessness much longer.

17:3. The people thirsted … and the people murmured. The Hebrews' attitude and behavior were predicated only on their unmet needs. By this time, they were irrational enough to have accused Moses of liberating them from Egypt for the purpose of killing **us and our children and our cattle with thirst**.

17:4–6. Moses apparently feared that the disgruntled crowd could easily transform into an angry mob. He **cried unto the Lord** (v. 4) that **this people … be almost ready to stone me**. Perhaps there is something to be read in Moses' use of "this people" instead of the usual "my people." Moses is told to approach the people, in the company of the elders, with the rod of God in hand. He is to stand before **the rock of Horeb** (v. 6) and **smite the rock** with his rod, which would result in water gushing forth from the rock. This rock, although called Horeb, is not on Mount Sinai itself but is merely within the region of the Horeb range. Paul would later use the

image of this rock in identifying Christ as the Rock (1 Cor. 10:4).

17:7. They tempted the LORD, saying, is the LORD among us, or not? Moses called this locale **Massah** ("proving") **and Meribah** ("strife"). A similar incident involving water and a rock occurred much later in Moses' career (Num. 20:13, 24; 27:14; Deut. 32:51; 33:8).

2. War with Amalek (17:8–16)

17:8. The origin of Israel's four-centuries-long antagonistic relationship with the nation of **Amalek** is presented here. The Amalekites were distantly related to the Hebrews, through their common patriarch, Isaac, descended through Esau's son Eliphaz (Gen. 36:12). Although they shared a familial bond as cousins of a sort, the Amalekites **fought with Israel in Rephidim**. Further details of the Amalekites' ignominious attack on Israel's vulnerable rear are provided in Deuteronomy 25:17–19.

17:9. This is the Torah's first mention of **Joshua**, Moses' personal assistant (24:13; 32:17; 33:11) and eventual successor (Deut. 1:38; 3:28; 31:14; 34:9; Josh. 1:5). His original name was Oshea, Hebrew for "savior," but Moses adapted his name to Joshua, Hebrew for "YHWH is savior" (Num. 13:16). Identified as the son of Nun, Joshua hailed from the tribe of Ephraim. The name Joshua is the Hebrew equivalent of the name Jesus.

Go out, fight with Amalek. Joshua was the Hebrews' commander in this, their initial military engagement.

17:10–12. Moses, Aaron, and Hur (v. 10) ascended a hilltop to observe the battle. Hur is possibly the son of Caleb and the grandfather of Bezaleel (1 Chron. 2:19–20), one of the tabernacle artisans (Exod. 31:2–5). This was no ordinary military campaign. It was, rather, a supernatural expression of Israel's complete dependence on God's provision and was the first of many holy wars to come. As Moses held up the rod of God, **Israel prevailed** (v. 11) in battle. Conversely, **when he let down his hand, Amalek prevailed.** The conflict was to be determined not by military prowess but by the power of God.

A problem arose when Moses' arms got tired and he had difficulty maintaining their lofty position. He was, after all, eighty years of age. **Aaron and Hur** (v. 12) solved this disability by providing Moses with a stone on which to sit and then taking a position on either side of him to hold up his arms for the remainder of the battle, which raged on until nightfall.

17:13–14. With Joshua's force victorious, the Lord instructed Moses to record **this for a memorial in a book** (v. 14). This would have been a scroll, a long strip of leather or papyrus on which scribes wrote in columns (Jer. 36:23) with pen (Isa. 8:1) and ink (Jer. 36:18), sometimes on both sides (Ezek. 2:10; Rev. 5:1). **Rehearse it in the ears of Joshua.** It was essential that Joshua, as military commander and Moses' successor, sustain his awareness of the perpetual enmity between Israel and Amalek. **For I will utterly put out the remembrance of Amalek.** From this point on, the Lord "has it in" for the Amalekites. His curse against them is reiterated in Numbers 24:20 and Deuteronomy 25:19.

17:15. Moses built **an altar** and honored the Lord by naming it **Jehovah-nissi,** "YHWH is my military banner, or standard."

17:16. War with Amalek from generation to generation. The enmity continues for approximately four centuries, acted on in various conflicts until the might of the Amalekites was definitively broken by King Saul (Num. 14:45; Judg. 6:33; 1 Sam. 14:48; 15:1–9, 32–33). The Lord effectively erased them from the world stage.

3. Moses and Jethro (chap. 18)

18:1–6. This chapter relates the reunion of Moses with his father-in-law, **Jethro, the priest of Midian** (v. 1; or "Reuel"; see discussion on 2:16–22). Somehow he had **heard of all that God had done** in bringing the Hebrews out from Egypt. The Hebrews were an unwieldy group, and Jethro had little trouble locating them in their camp near Sinai, **the mount of God** (v. 5; see discussion on 3:1). Traveling with Jethro was **Zipporah, Moses' wife** (v. 2) and his two sons, **Gershom** (v. 3; see discussion on 2:22) and **Eliezer** (v. 4). **After he had sent her back** (v. 2). It is

only now specified in the narrative that Moses had sent his family back to Jethro following the circumcision incident (see discussion on 4:24–26).

18:7–12. Moses ... did obeisance (v. 7) and showed great respect for Jethro in his position as both **his father in law** and priest of Midian, showing him appropriate hospitality. **Moses** (v. 8) then **told his father in law all that the** LORD **had** done in Egypt and thus far in the wilderness journey. In response, **Jethro rejoiced** (v. 9) and said, **Blessed be the** LORD (v. 10). He then acknowledged that **the** LORD **is greater than all gods** (v. 11). After offering **sacrifices** (v. 12), the Hebrew leadership shared a communal meal with Jethro. It is likely that Jethro had now become a true worshiper of YHWH. As the priest of Midian, however, Jethro may have merely exalted YHWH to the head of the Midianite pantheon.

18:13–23. The following day, Jethro had the opportunity to observe his son-in-law functioning in his capacity as the leader of the Hebrews. **Moses sat to judge the people** (v. 13). This was an all-day affair since crowds were continually lined up to bring their concerns before him. This is the origin of the concept of sitting in the "seat of Moses" (Matt. 23:2). When Jethro saw that **the people stood by Moses from the morning unto the evening,** he expressed concern for his son-in-law, asking him, **why sittest thou thyself alone?** (v. 14).

To inquire of God ... I judge ... I do make them know the statutes of God (vv. 15–16). Moses listed three reasons the people needed an audience with him: (1) in his capacity as prophet, the mouthpiece of God; (2) in his capacity as judge, to rule over conflicts; and (3) in his capacity as lawgiver, to teach the people God's righteous standards.

Jethro's response was, **The thing that thou doest is not good. Thou wilt surely wear away ... and this people that is with thee** (vv. 17–18). The quantity of people who were waiting to see Moses was unmanageable and overwhelming. It is more than any man could handle. Jethro advised Moses to **provide ... able men, such as fear God, men of truth, hating covetousness** (v. 21). The advice was to select men to whom he could delegate some of his responsibilities, creating a hierarchical system (**rulers of thousands ... hundreds ... fifties ... tens**) by which every matter, great and small, could be addressed at the appropriate level. While Moses himself needed to deal with certain areas and issues that could in no way be delegated, his caseload was lighter and the authority could indeed be shared. **Then thou shalt be able to endure** (v. 23). Implementation of this plan would enable Moses to avoid the inevitable burnout.

18:24–27. Moses hearkened ... Moses chose able men (vv. 24–25). The chapter concludes with the departure of Jethro and the implementation of his advice. While this chapter is appropriately placed thematically, it is possibly out of place chronologically. Three lines of evidence indicate that the events related in this chapter should actually be placed immediately following the giving of the law at Sinai: (1) Deuteronomy 1:9–18 specifies that Moses' delegation of authority was not implemented until after the law was given. (2) Although this chapter is sandwiched between two chapters that note the location of Rephidim (17:8; 19:1), a surface reading of chapter 18 has them camped at the "mount of God" (18:5), that is, Sinai. While Rephidim is certainly in the general vicinity of Sinai, they are not synonymous. (3) Moses is pictured here as already functioning in his capacity as lawgiver (18:16).

IV. At Sinai (chaps. 19–40)

The Hebrews would spend just under a year encamped at the broad, flat plain that comprises the base of Mount Sinai. All of the events spanning Exodus 19:1 to Numbers 10:10, including the entirety of Leviticus, occurred at this location. At Sinai, the Hebrews received God's law, the Torah, the Mosaic legislation was enacted, the Mosaic covenant was inaugurated, and the Hebrews were officially recognized as God's chosen people.

A. The Mosaic Covenant (chaps. 19–31)

1. Setting the Stage for the Covenant Gift (chap. 19)

19:1–2. In the third month (v. 1). The construction leaves some ambiguity as to precisely when the Israelites arrived at Sinai. Because the Hebrew grammar indicates a month-long period by referencing the new moon, four viable options are available. Their arrival may have occurred (1) exactly ninety days after the exodus, (2) sometime between the eleventh and thirteenth week (i.e., between seventy-one and ninety days after the exodus), or if the text is referencing the third month of Israel's liturgical calendar, either (3) exactly sixty days after the exodus or (4) as early as sometime between the seventh and the tenth week (i.e., between forty-two and seventy days from the exodus). Jewish tradition rejects the first three options, holding that the nation was given the law on Sivan 6, the holiday of Shabuoth (Pentecost), fifty days after the first day of the Feast of Unleavened Bread, the day of the exodus. Counting back three days, Jewish tradition's fifty days places the Hebrews' arrival at Sinai between forty-two and forty-seven days after the exodus event. Tradition notwithstanding, it is difficult to ascertain the date with any certainty based just on the text.

The wilderness of Sinai (v. 1). There is little reason to challenge the identification of this mountain with the traditional site, Jebel Musa, in the southern quadrant of the Sinai peninsula. Before the northwestern foot of this mountain is a vast plain, Er-Rahah, measuring approximately one and a half miles long by half a mile wide, which would have well suited the narrative's requirements of a one-year encampment.

19:3–6. Moses had now discharged his divine commission to return to Sinai with the liberated Hebrews. This was to have been a confirmation to Moses of the Lord's presence (3:12). All that remained was for the people to worship YHWH in this locale. The remainder of this chapter is concerned with the preparations for that corporate worship. **Moses went up** (v. 3). This is first of three ascensions Moses will make to the top of Sinai in this chapter (19:3, 8, 20).

On the mountain, the Lord gave Moses the first message he was to convey to the nation. In passionate language reminiscent of a groom charming his bride, the Lord reminded the Hebrews how He had rescued them and **brought you unto myself** (v. 4).

The Hebrews are described as the Lord's **peculiar treasure** (v. 5), meaning they are His personal property, His private possession. The Lord has specifically chosen this particular group of people with whom to maintain a covenant relationship. The reason the Hebrews were so valuable to God relates back to His initial sovereign choice of Abraham and the establishment of His covenant promises, made to both the patriarch and his descendants, the nation of Israel.

If ye will obey ... and keep ... then ... (v. 5). While the Mosaic covenant will be given as an unconditional gift to His people, the multiple **covenant** blessings are completely conditional, dependent on the people's obedience and response.

Israel is divinely identified as both **a kingdom of priests and a holy nation** (v. 6). Israel was to remain distinct and separate from all other nations and, at the same time, engage those nations on behalf of YHWH. Possessing a special relationship with YHWH and enjoying singular access to Him, they were to be His holy representatives on the international stage. Just as an individual priest's function is to act as an intermediary between God and man and to make intercession on behalf of others, this corporate nation of priests was commissioned to intercede on behalf of other nations.

19:7 – 8. Moses descended the mountain and communicated the Lord's message to Israel's leadership, and it was then broadcast to the people. The nation responds to the Lord's invitation with a resoundingly optimistic, **All that the Lord hath spoken we will do** (v. 8). For the second time, Moses ascended the mountain to relay the people's response to **the Lord.**

19:9. I come ... that the people may ... believe thee for ever. The Lord prepared Moses for a public demonstration of His establishment of him as Israel's mediator and intercessor. It was crucial that the entire nation both understand Moses and YHWH's unique relationship and accept Moses' divinely sanctioned authority. **A thick cloud.** The Shekinah glory would publicly appear before Moses and converse with him, firmly establishing Moses' credentials in the eyes of the people with this audiovisual object lesson.

19:10 – 15. In preparation for the divine manifestation of the Shekinah glory on Mount Sinai, the people required purification. The purification process required several essential components to be conscientiously communicated to the nation. First, they would have two days to prepare, for on **the third day the Lord will come down** (v. 11). Second, they needed to **wash** (v. 10) themselves and their clothing. Third, they were to abstain from sexual relations, to avoid the possibility of finding themselves ritually unclean (v. 15; Lev. 15:18; 1 Sam. 21:4 – 5). Fourth, Sinai was off-limits; a boundary line needed to be set around the mountain. Sinai would become holy while the Lord's presence was manifest upon it; it was His manifest holiness that instantly transformed any location into holy ground (see discussion on 3:5). The penalty for any person or animal making even minimal contact with the mountain was death via stoning or piercing with arrows. Having profaned God's holiness, the violator himself would be off-limits; hence the prescribed forms of noncontact capital punishment. The nation could approach the mountain only on the third day; a **trumpet** (the shofar, a ram's horn; v. 13) would sound the signal.

19:16 – 18. On the **morning** of **the third day** (v. 16), the people awoke to a frightening theophany on Mount Sinai. The Shekinah glory appeared in **thunders and lightnings ... a thick cloud** and the piercing blast of a **trumpet** (see Exod. 19:13), with descending **fire** (v. 18) and ascending **smoke ... and the whole mount quaked greatly**. The author of Hebrews characterizes this dramatic scene as one of absolute terror (Heb. 12:18 – 21). It is no wonder that **all the people ... trembled** (v. 16) violently with fear (the same Hebrew word is used in relation to both the people and the mountain's violent quaking). Moses led the terrified **people out of the camp to meet with God** (v. 17) and stood them at the foot of the mountain.

19:19. As the volume of **the trumpet** continued to increase, **Moses spake, and God answered him by a voice**. The manner of voice with which God responded is unclear. It is possible that God answered Moses as thunder or with the trumpet, yet contextually it seems best to conclude that the Lord spoke in an actual intelligible voice, a voice of inestimable force to have been understood over the violent storm.

19:20 – 25. For a third time, **the Lord** (v. 20) summoned **Moses … to the top of the mount**. As soon as Moses arrived, the Lord commanded that he descend immediately to yet again remind the people not to let their curiosity get the better of them **lest they break through unto the Lord to gaze, and many of them perish** (v. 21). Moses objected to the need to repeat the warning, as the people had already been alerted to the danger. The Lord knew the Hebrews just a bit better than did their leader, however, and was conscious of their propensity to rebellion.

Moses was sent down again, with instructions to return to the mountain with Aaron and with a final reminder to keep vigilance over the people's proximity to the mountain. **The priests also, which come near to the Lord** (v. 22). This phrase is a euphemism for those who lead in worship. As the Levitical priesthood had not yet been established, the Lord may have been referring to the firstborn males, who temporarily served as Israel's priests (13:1 – 2; 24:5).

2. The Ten Commandments (20:1 – 21)

20:1. These words. The Ten Commandments, or the "ten words" (Hebrew) or the Decalogue (Greek) are the preamble to the total of 613 positive ("Thou shalt") and negative ("Thou shalt not") commandments that comprise the Mosaic legislation. They serve as the foundation and core of God's Torah, the heart of the Mosaic covenant.

20:2 – 3. I am the Lord thy God, which have brought thee out (v. 2). The Ten Commandments are patterned according to the royal treaties of the ancient world. They establish the identity of YHWH as the monarch of Israel, and the Hebrews as His loyal and obedient subjects. **Thou shalt have no other gods before me** (v. 3). The first commandment demands the absolute allegiance of YHWH's people. He is to have the preeminent claim on their lives.

20:4 – 6. Thou shalt not make unto thee any graven image (v. 4) **… Thou shalt not bow down**

thyself to them … nor serve them (v. 5). The second commandment prohibits spiritual adultery. It is not a complete ban on the making of all images, for indeed, the tabernacle, the temple, and the ark of the covenant all contained images. Rather, it prohibits making images for the purpose of worshiping them or the gods they might represent. No image could ever accurately represent YHWH, who possesses no visible form. Therefore, it should never be attempted. Furthermore, the Egyptian practice of creating images of their gods according to the likenesses of animals whose habitations lie **in heaven above, or … in the earth beneath, or … in the water** (v. 4) is likewise condemned.

YHWH identifies himself as **a jealous God** (v. 5), equally capable of judgment and love. He views the Mosaic covenant as a marriage of sorts, and He will brook no rivals for His affections. His passion for His people is boundless, and to not have His ardor returned by His people would dishonor Him. **Unto the third and fourth generation of them that hate me.** Those Israelites who blatantly violated God's covenant demonstrated their disloyalty to and rejection ("hate") of their King. This demanded a divine response that would affect the entire multigenerational household. **Shewing mercy** (v. 6). Conversely, obedient and faithful Israelites would experience God's covenantal, loyal love.

20:7. Thou shalt not take the name of the Lord thy God in vain. The third commandment prohibits the frivolous or casual use of the divine, covenant name of YHWH (see discussion on 3:14 – 15). God's name might also be profaned by its invocation within an oath. YHWH is holy and demands that He be spoken of with both consideration and reverence.

20:8 – 11. Remember the sabbath day (v. 8). The fourth commandment is to set aside the **seventh day** (v. 10) of each week as a time to completely desist from all ordinary labor. Israel's remembrance of the Sabbath day was to be demonstrated through each household's diligent observance. By way of analogy, as the Lord Himself desisted from His labor on the **seventh day** (v. 11) of creation, so too was Israel to rest and follow God's example in appreciating and enjoying His creation. Paul teaches that Christians enjoy liberty in their participation in the Sabbath (Rom. 14:5–6).

20:12. Honour thy father and thy mother. The fifth commandment was designed to actively preserve the family by requiring appropriate parental honor, respect, obedience, and care. **That thy days may be long upon the land**. Compliance with this commandment is promised to result in Israel's prolonged residence in their land.

20:13. Thou shalt not kill. The sixth commandment prohibits the premeditated, deliberate, and unauthorized taking of human life, that is, murder. While it protects the sanctity of human life, it does not prohibit all killing and does not apply to the death penalty (Lev. 20:10; Num. 35:19) or to warfare (Deut.13:15).

20:14. Thou shalt not commit adultery. The seventh commandment prohibits the violation of the sanctity of marriage and the family unit, society's basic building block. This commandment pertains equally to men and women. To be correctly categorized as adultery (as opposed to other sexual immorality or fornication), at least one married participant must be involved.

20:15. Thou shalt not steal. The eighth commandment prohibits theft and protects private property.

20:16. Thou shalt not bear false witness. The ninth commandment prohibits perjury, with general reference to legal proceedings. It may or may not apply to deception or lying in general, depending on the situational context (see discussion on 1:15–21).

20:17. Thou shalt not covet. The tenth commandment is a prohibition, not of external action, but of internal motivation. The Israelites were to be content with their own lifestyles and property, reining in any avaricious eruptions of desire for someone else's possessions.

20:18–19. As the text returns to the narrative, the Hebrews are the terrified of God's pyrotechnic display of supernatural **thunderings … lightnings … trumpet, and … smoking** (v. 18). There was no danger that the Hebrews would approach the mountain; in fact, they ran in the opposite direction (**they removed, and stood afar off**). They had had enough of this direct access to YHWH. Fearful for their lives, the Hebrews wished to return to the previous system of Moses serving as their divine intercessor and intermediary. The author of Hebrews emphasizes Israel's request of a mediator to stand between them and God (Heb. 12:19–20). Moses was the first to serve in this capacity, followed by a succession of high priests, and finally, the role of Israel's divine mediator was ultimately and permanently filled by the Messiah (1 Tim. 2:5).

20:20–21. Moses told them, **Fear not** (v. 20), explaining that God had given them a brief exposure to His presence to serve as a corporate prophylactic against sin. While the nation maintained their distance from Sinai, **Moses drew near unto the thick darkness where God was** (v. 21).

3. The Mosaic Ordinances (20:22–23:33)

This section contains a lengthy series of assorted ordinances that involve Israel's basic civil rights and social relationships.

a. Worship (20:22–26)

20:22–26. Ye shall not make … thou shalt make (v. 23–24). The Lord provides two laws concerning worship: a negative command concerning idols and a positive command concerning an altar. Now that the people had personally witnessed the majestic power of the Lord's voice, they were to remember the second commandment's admonition to refrain from creating any idols. When they built their **altar** (v. 24) of worship, it could be constructed of either **earth** or unhewn **stone** (v. 25). Whether the altar was of earth or stone, however, it was to be devoid of **steps** (v. 26), to avoid any exposure of the ministering priest as he ascended.

b. Masters and Servants (21:1–11)

21:1–6. These verses concern the rights of a male **Hebrew servant** (v. 2). If an Israelite was forced to sell himself into indentured service because of an unpaid debt, he must be released from service at the onset of the **seventh** year. If both he and his wife were sold into service, his wife was also to be set free after their six years of labor. Conversely, if the Hebrew servant entered into service as a single man and then, during his service, was provided **a wife** (v. 4) by **his master**, **the wife** and any **children** must remain in service.

If a **servant** (v. 5) wished to extend his service permanently, **his ear** was to be pierced against a **door post** (v. 6) to symbolize the permanence of his service.

21:7–11. These verses concern the rights of the female Hebrew servant. If the girl was sold by her parents into service, she was, like the male servant, to be released at the onset of the seventh year. In the event that the **master** (v. 8) were to marry her, or if she functioned as his concubine while in his service and he no longer desired her, he must allow her to be **redeemed** from service early. He must not sell her into service to a Gentile master. In the event that she married the master's **son** (v. 9), she was to be treated the same as the other women of the household. If the master's son then takes an additional **wife** (v. 10), he is still obligated to provide sufficient **food**, clothing, and conjugal rights to his servant wife. If he were to fail to meet any of these three obligations, she must be set **free** (v. 11).

c. Personal Injury (21:12–32)

21:12–17. These verses concern capital punishment. If a man was found guilty of premeditated murder, he was to be executed. In the case of manslaughter, the guilty party had the option of seeking sanctuary by fleeing to a city of refuge. If he successfully arrived in the city of refuge, he was not to be punished. If a child either struck a parent or cursed a parent, the child was to be executed. Kidnapping, likewise, was a capital offense.

21:18–19. In the event of a quarrel that led to accidental injury, if the injured party subsequently recovered, no penalty was to be assessed to the one who caused the injury. The guilty party, however, was to make restitution for the injured party's **loss … of time** (v. 19) and medical expenses.

21:20–21. In the event that a master's beating caused a fatal injury to **his servant** (v. 20), the master

was to be **punished** only if the servant immediately died. If the servant died shortly thereafter, the master would **not be punished** (v. 21). His economic loss of his property was punishment enough.

21:22–25. So that her fruit depart from her, and yet no mischief follow (v. 22). There are two interpretive options for these verses, which deal with injury to a pregnant woman. The situation given is that a pregnant woman is caught in the middle of an argument between two men and is severely injured, affecting her pregnancy. It is unclear in the text, however, whether the injury triggers miscarriage or premature birth. If miscarriage is meant, then the verses teach that the party responsible for causing a miscarriage without also causing the loss of the mother's life shall be taken to court and assessed a fine. In the event of both miscarriage and the loss of the mother's life, the responsible party was to be executed, a **life for** a **life** (v. 23).

Alternatively, if premature birth is in view here, then the verses teach that the party responsible for triggering premature labor shall be taken to court and assessed a fine. In the event of either miscarriage or the loss of the mother's life, however, the responsible party was to be executed, a **life for** a **life** (v. 23).

Eye for eye, tooth for tooth (v. 24). Introduced here is the famous *lex talionis*, the law designed to restrict retaliation to punishment commensurate with the specific crime.

21:26–27. If a master permanently maimed his **servant** (v. 26), that servant was to **go free** (v. 27).

21:28–32. These verses concern injury caused by animals. If **an ox** (v. 28) gored a person to death, **the ox** was to be killed. If **the ox** (v. 29) was in the habit of goring, and **the owner** did not exercise adequate precaution to prevent his animal causing injury to others, he was held responsible and was to be killed along with his ox. The owner had the option of avoiding execution by paying financial compensation to the dead party's family.

In the event that **the ox** (v. 32) gored a servant, it was to be killed and the owner of the ox was to recompense the dead slave's owner **thirty shekels of silver**, the price of a servant. This was the exact sum paid to Judas for his betrayal of Jesus (Matt. 26:14 – 15; see also Zech. 11:12 – 13).

d. Property Rights (21:33 – 22:15)

21:33 – 36. In the event of livestock loss due to negligence, the negligent party was to recompense **the owner** (v. 34) and was allowed keep the dead livestock. In the event that the loss of livestock was due to its being gored by an ox, and that ox had no previous habit of goring, the owner of the ox was to sell it, dividing the profit with the owner of the dead livestock. The parties involved would **divide** (v. 35) the dead livestock between them. If, however, the ox had a previous habit of goring, the owner of the ox was required to replace the dead animal, and the dead livestock remained the property of its original owner.

22:1 – 4. These verses concern property loss due to theft. A livestock rustler must make restitution to the party he defrauded. If the animal has not yet been killed or sold, **restitution** (v. 3) is to be in kind: **five oxen** (v. 1) for the theft of one ox and **four sheep** for the theft of one sheep. If the the owner caught the **thief** (v. 2) in the act of stealing and killed him, it was considered an act of self-defense, and the owner went unpunished. If the thief was caught later and killed, it was no longer considered self-defense but rather premeditated murder. In the event that the thief was unable to make restitution, he was to **be sold** (v. 3) into indentured service until his debt was paid. If the thief was apprehended with the animal still in his possession, he was required to make restitution in kind, two animals for each one stolen.

22:5 – 6. In the event that one suffered the loss of crops due to negligence or arson, the offending party was to make restitution.

22:7 – 9. These verses concern **money** (v. 7) or property that had been entrusted to another and was later stolen. If the thief was caught, he was to **pay double.** If the thief was not caught, the **master of the house** (v. 8) was to go to court to ascertain whether he himself was the thief; if found guilty, he was **to pay double** (v. 9) to the wronged party.

22:10 – 13. These verses concern livestock entrusted to another. If entrusted livestock died or was injured or lost, the one taking care of it had to testify that he was not negligent or had to make restitution. If a wild animal had killed the livestock and the carcass could be produced, proving that it had not been stolen, no restitution was required.

22:14 – 15. These verses concern the destruction of borrowed property. In the event that borrowed property was damaged in the absence of **the owner** (v. 14), the borrower must provide restitution. If the property was damaged in the presence of **the owner** (v. 15), however, no restitution was required. The presumption is that the owner was negligent for not acting to prevent his property from being damaged and was ultimately responsible for his own loss.

e. Miscellaneous Evil Practices (22:16 – 23:9)

22:16 – 17. In the event that an unengaged virgin was seduced, the seducer was to pay the bride's dowry and marry her. **If her father** (v. 17) refused to allow his daughter to marry the seducer, the seducer was still required to pay the family her dowry price as compensation to the family for the loss of her virginity.

22:18 – 20. The following three offenses warranted capital punishment: practicing witchcraft, bestiality, and sacrificing to foreign gods. **He shall be utterly destroyed** (v. 20). The term indicating the punishment for sacrificing to foreign gods specifies not only the death penalty but also a devoted commitment to absolute obliteration (Num. 31:15 – 17; Deut. 7:2; 26:16 – 17; Josh. 6:21; 10;11; 11:12; Judg. 21:11; 1 Sam. 15:3; 27:9 – 11; Jer. 25:9).

22:21. This verse concerns the resident sojourner in the land, the *ger.* The Hebrews were not to **vex** or **oppress a stranger,** for they themselves had been **strangers** in **Egypt.**

22:22 – 24. These verses concern **widow[s]** (v. 22) and orphans. If they were mistreated, God would **hear their cry** (v. 23) and execute swift and equitable judgment upon the guilty parties, and their **wives shall be widows, and** their **children fatherless** (v. 24).

22:25 – 27. These verses concern appropriate lending practices. An Israelite was forbidden to charge any interest on a loan made to a fellow Israelite. No profit was to be generated from the misfortune of the poor. If a garment was taken from a borrower as collateral on a loan, it was to be returned to the owner at sundown, because it also served as his blanket. The fact that the borrower had been forced to surrender his cloak as **a pledge** (v. 26) would indicate his utter poverty. Not returning his cloak at evening was analogous to taking "the shirt off his back."

22:28–31. These verses concern propriety. Appropriate respect must be shown for both God and the **ruler of thy people** (v. 28). There must be no delay in presenting the firstfruits offering. The **firstborn** males of both men and animals belong to God (see discussion on 13:1–2). The meat from livestock that had been shredded by wild animals was not fit for human consumption.

23:1–9. These verses concern legal justice. An Israelite was never to bear false witness in a court of law. A judge was never to be pressured by the crowd to pervert justice. A judge was not to coddle the guilty party if he happened to be **poor** (v. 3). If a missing animal was located, the animal was to be returned to its master, even if he was the finder's enemy (v. 4). If an animal was found to be overburdened, the load must be eased. A judge was not to withhold justice from the **poor** (v. 6). Perversions of justice were to be avoided. Taking a bribe was forbidden. The resident sojourner in the land was not to be deprived of justice, since the Hebrews **were strangers in … Egypt** (v. 9).

f. Festivals (23:10–19)

23:10–12. These verses concern the sabbatical year and the Sabbath day. The Israelites' land was to be left uncultivated every **seventh year** (v. 11). Whatever then grew on the uncultivated land of its own accord was for the benefit of the poor, and what they left behind was for the benefit of **the beasts of the field**. Likewise, both people and their animals were to rest every seventh day, that they **may be refreshed** (v. 12). After all, the Sabbath was made for man, not man for the Sabbath (Mark 2:27).

23:13–19. These verses concern worship. The Israelites were never to **make … mention of the name of other gods** (v. 13). False gods were not to be acknowledged in even the most basic fashion.

Three times … in the year (v. 14), every Hebrew adult male was required to appear before God at Israel's central location of worship, originally the tabernacle and later on, the temple. The first of these three pilgrimage festivals was **the feast of unleavened bread** (which as used here is inclusive of the day of Passover; v. 15). The people were not to come empty-handed **before** the Lord but rather bearing the Passover sacrifice. The second pilgrimage feast was **the feast of harvest** (v. 16), held seven weeks after Passover. Also known as Shabuoth, this feast is called the "feast of weeks" in 34:22 and was called Pentecost in New Testament times. On this occasion, Israel was to come before the Lord with the firstfruits of the wheat harvest, baked into special loaves. The third pilgrimage festival was the eight-day **feast of ingathering** (also called the Feast of Booths and the Feast of Tabernacles), held every autumn. Israel was to appear before the Lord with the abundance of their crops at the climax of the year's agricultural cycle.

Sacrifices containing **leavened bread** (v. 18) were forbidden. **The fat** of the **sacrifice** was not to **remain until the morning**. All **firstfruits** (v. 19) belong to God and must be offered to Him. The practice of cooking a **kid** in **its mother's milk** was forbidden. This abominable and inhumane Canaanite practice was an idolatrous fertility rite. The prohibition is stated three times in the Torah (23:19; 34:26; Deut. 14:21) and is the basis for the Jewish practice of strictly separating the eating of meat and dairy. Observant Jewish homes always contain, at a minimum, two separate sets of dishes and cooking utensils, one set used exclusively for meat products, and the other used exclusively for dairy products.

g. The Promised Land (23:20–33)

23:20–23. I send an Angel before thee. In these verses, the angel of the Lord is again mentioned, a preincarnate manifestation of the second person of the Trinity. This angel will both protect Israel and deliver the nation into their land. **Beware of him … obey his voice** (v. 21). This angel must be diligently obeyed. **Provoke him not; for he will not pardon your transgressions**. Defiance of this angel will result in His refusal to forgive sin. **My name is in him**. This angel acts with an authority that belongs to God alone. He forgives sins and possesses the divine covenant name; He is a manifestation of YHWH. **If thou … then I** (v. 22). The reward for obedience to this angel is that He would **be an enemy unto thine enemies, and an adversary unto thine adversaries**. He would personally ensure the defeat of Israel's enemies.

23:24–26. Israel must never worship idols. Rather, the false gods of Canaan must be **utterly** (v. 24) destroyed. The five rewards promised for the Hebrews' unwavering allegiance to the true **God** (v. 25) were the provision of food, removal of **sickness**, avoidance of miscarriages, absence of barrenness, and personal longevity.

23:27–31. I will … will … I will … I will … I will not … I will … I will … I will (vv. 27–31). In a breathtaking crescendo of "I wills," God promised that He Himself would be responsible for the expulsion of **the Canaanites** (v. 28) from the Promised Land. He would be like a swarm of **hornets** from which **the Canaanites** would eventually flee. God would not **drive** (v. 29) the land's inhabitants **out** all at once, or even within **one year**, but in gradual stages, little by little, to prevent the land's desolation and its becoming overrun by wild animals. As the Israelites' presence in the land increased, the Canaanites would proportionately decrease until the Hebrews enjoyed their entire geographic inheritance. The seven-year campaign of Joshua (1406–1399 BC) would wipe out most, but not all, of the land's tenants. The ultimate boundaries of the Promised Land are provided here as **the Red sea** (v. 31) on the south, the Mediterranean on the west, **the desert** (likely present-day Jordan) on the east, and **the river** Euphrates on the north.

23:32–33. Israel is to establish no relationship whatsoever with the inhabitants of the land. There must be **no covenant** (v. 32) between them, no cohabitation in the land, and no commingled worship. God solemnly warned the Israelites that intimate contact between the nations would prove to be **a snare** (v. 33).

4. Covenant Affirmation (chap. 24)

The text again picks up where the narrative left off in 20:21, following Moses' ascent of Sinai to speak again with the Lord. This section relates the nation's acceptance and official ratification of the Mosaic covenant.

24:1–3. These verses specify the procedural order by which Israel's leadership was to approach the Lord's presence on Mount Sinai. **Aaron** (v. 1) and his two eldest sons, **Nadab and Abihu**, and the **seventy elders** were to preserve a certain distance. Moses alone, as the sole divinely sanctioned mediator of his people, was to ascend into the very presence of God. Aaron's son Nadab would have succeeded his father as high priest, but both he and Abihu were killed soon after this event because they offered unauthorized fire on the altar (Lev. 10:1–2; Num. 3:4).

Moses related to the people God's **words … and … judgments** (v. 3) that had been revealed thus far. Israel agreed to submit to the covenant, answering, **All the words which the Lord hath said will we do**.

24:4–8. Moses prepared for the covenant ratification with a flurry of activity. Springing into action, **Moses wrote all the words of the Lord** (v. 4) in a scroll. Then **early** the next **morning**, he had **an altar** built at the foot of Sinai and **twelve pillars** erected to represent **the twelve tribes of Israel**. Selected **young men** (v. 5), likely comprised of firstborn sons (13:1), **offered** several sacrifices. Moses sprinkled **half of the blood** (v. 6) from these sacrifices **on the altar**. After reading **the book of the covenant** to **the people** (v. 7), the congregation of Israel unanimously responded as they had upon their arrival at Sinai (19:8) as well as on the preceding day, declaring, **All that the Lord hath said will we do, and be obedient**. Now that the nation had officially consented to the covenant, **Moses took** (v. 8) the remainder of **the blood and sprinkled it** toward **the people**. This act symbolically bound the nation to the stipulations of the covenant, as it was now the most solemn of covenants, a covenant ratified by blood. The Mosaic covenant's successor and replacement, the new covenant, would later be ratified by the Messiah's superior blood (Matt. 26:28; Luke 22:20).

24:9–11. The seventy-four members of Israel's leadership then ascended Mount Sinai in the order prescribed in the previous verses (24:1–3). There **they saw the God of Israel** (v. 10); they were permitted an indirect or indistinct revelation of the Lord's glory. As no one could see God and survive the experience (33:11, 20), they were party to an event they could never have expected to witness. The only description the text renders is of the transparent blue **sapphire** pavement **under his feet**. In the glorious presence of God, the men shared a covenant meal together.

24:12–18. Following their descent from Sinai, Moses was again summoned into God's presence to receive the two **stone** (v. 12) tablets containing the ten **commandments ... that thou mayest teach them**. These tablets would serve as an enduring token of the ratified covenant and a tangible keepsake for posterity of their seminal national experience. Leaving **Aaron and Hur** (v. 14) in charge of the camp in his absence, **Moses went up into the mount** (v. 15). He was accompanied part of the way by his personal aid, Joshua, who waited on Sinai with Moses for seven days until God **called unto Moses out of the midst of the** Shekinah glory **cloud** (v. 16), which covered the mountain. **Moses went into the midst of the cloud** (v. 18) and would remain in God's presence for the next thirty-three days, for a total time of **forty days and forty nights** away from the camp. To the nation left behind in the distant camp, waiting pensively for their mediator to return, it appeared as if Moses disappeared into the midst of a **devouring fire on the top of the mount** (v. 17).

5. Worship Regulations (chaps. 25–31)

The vast majority of the remainder of Exodus contains regulations concerning the divinely sanctioned and acceptable means of worshiping the Covenant God. Thus, preparatory instructions for both the tabernacle and the priesthood occupy the following sections.

a. Elements of the Tabernacle (chaps. 25–27)

25:1–9. Moses (v. 1) was commanded to take up a strictly voluntary, freewill **offering** (v. 2) for the building of the tabernacle, a sanctuary in which God's Shekinah glory could take up permanent residence in Israel. Through revelation divinely granted to Moses, it was patterned after the true tabernacle in heaven.

Fifteen materials were to be collected, some of which were already in the Hebrews' possession as part of their Egyptian spoils, and some of which may have been acquired through trade. Throughout the following section, special note should be taken of not only the specific supply quantities required for the tabernacle construction but also the exceptional care taken in selecting the highest-quality materials. The place of God's residence and central location of Israel's worship was constructed in not only the most practical fashion but also the most sensuously aesthetic. The tabernacle was a perfect blend of form and function.

Quantities of three precious metals were needed: **gold, and silver, and brass** (v. 3), or more likely, bronze. Quantities of cloth (or yarn, to fashion into cloth) were needed, dyed **blue, and purple, and scarlet** (v. 4). The necessary blue dye was a dark, almost violet, hue made from the Mediterranean's shellfish (primarily the murex). The purple dye was also made from shellfish and was later imported from Phoenicia. The scarlet dye was a vibrant red-yellow hue derived from the eggs and carcasses of the worm *Coccus ilicis* (which attaches itself to the leaves of the holly plant), dried and ground into powder. Also required were quantities of **fine linen**, which was a white, tightly woven Egyptian cloth made from thread spun from the beaten fibers of flax. This silk-like fabric was the cloth of choice for the clothing of Egyptian officials, such as Joseph (Gen. 41:42), and numerous examples of it have been found in ancient Egyptian tombs. It is not surprising that former Egyptian slaves would have been skilled in the creation of this high-quality fabric.

Quantities of coarse, dark **goats' hair** were required, to be spun into yarn and woven to make the tent material. Also necessary were **rams' skins** (v. 5), tanned like leather and **dyed red**. The text mentions **badgers' skins**, but the underlying Hebrew word should be understood as indicating either the dolphin or, more likely, the dugong (sea cow), indigenous to the Red Sea.

Quantities of the durable and plentiful acacia (**shittim**) **wood** were required. Quantities of **oil** (v. 6), both for **anointing** and to burn for illumination, were needed. Quantities of spices (myrrh, cinnamon, cane, and cassia; 30:23–25) were necessary for both the **anointing oil** and the **incense** recipes. Quantities of **onyx** (v. 7) and various other precious **stones** were also required, **to be set in the ephod, and in the breastplate**.

In Scripture, five names are used to refer to the tabernacle, each name reflecting a specific purpose or function: (1) "the tabernacle" (25:9), emphasizing its main purpose as the place where God dwells among His people; (2) "[the] sanctuary" (25:8), emphasizing its holy character; (3) "the tent" (26:36), emphasizing its temporary character; (4) the tabernacle of the congregation (lit., "the tent of meeting" [27:21]), emphasizing its function; and (5) "the tabernacle of Testimony" (38:21) and "the tent of the Testimony" (Num. 9:15), both emphasizing its housing of the ark that contained the two tablets of the law.

25:10–16. These verses concern the details for constructing the **ark** (v. 10) of the covenant. This was the most important of the tabernacle elements because it served as God's throne (1 Sam. 4:4; 2 Sam. 6:2). The ark was an open-top chest constructed of acacia wood and overlaid inside and out with gold. It was rectangular, with dimensions of three feet nine inches in length and two feet three inches in both width and height, assuming a **cubit** length of eighteen inches.

An ornamental molding of gold ran along the top of the chest. Attached to the chest's **corners** (v. 12) were four **rings of gold**, into which two gold-

covered acacia-wood **staves** (v. 13), or poles, were permanently inserted on either side in order to transport it without having to make physical contact with the chest itself. The chest was to contain **the Testimony** (v. 16), the two stone tablets of the Ten Commandments, which Moses had yet to receive. The ark would also contain a golden jar of manna (16:33; Heb. 9:4–5) and Aaron's rod (Num. 17:10). It was common practice in the ancient world to house important documents, such as covenants, law codes, treaties, and so on, in specially constructed containers. A chest of similar dimensions, on which the same sort of carrying rings were attached, was one of the treasures discovered in the tomb of Tutankhamen.

25:17–22. The ark had a lid that fit over the open top, fashioned of solid **gold** (v. 17), with the same dimensions as the chest itself (three feet nine inches long by two feet three inches wide, assuming a **cubit** length of eighteen inches; v. 17). This was the **mercy seat**, the atonement cover, the throne of God's grace (Heb. 4:16), the place over which the Shekinah glory would dwell and where the Lord would **meet with** (v. 22) the high priest once a year, on the Day of Atonement, when he sprinkled blood on the lid for propitiation (Lev. 16:14). On each end, either attached or constructed with the golden cover as one solid piece, were **two cherubims of gold** (v. 18). These celestial beings faced each other, **their wings** (v. 20) spread toward one another, overshadowing the lid. God would thereafter be poetically pictured as the One enthroned between the cherubim (1 Sam. 4:4; Ps. 80:1–3).

25:23–30. These verses contain the specifications for constructing **the table** (v. 23) of **shewbread** (v. 30). This table, constructed of acacia wood and overlaid with gold, was designed to hold the twelve loaves of "shewbread" (lit., the "bread of the presence"), which were perpetually displayed and eventually eaten by the ministering priests, who replaced the bread each Sabbath (Lev. 24:5–9). The table's dimensions were three feet long by eighteen inches wide by two feet three inches high, assuming a **cubit** (v. 23) length of eighteen inches. An ornamental edging of gold ran around the four-footed table, and attached to the table's **corners** (v. 26) were four **rings of gold**, into which two gold-covered acacia-wood **staves** (v. 27), or poles, were inserted on either side in order to transport it. All **dishes ... spoons ... covers ... and bowls** (v. 29) used in conjunction with the table were fashioned **of pure gold**.

25:31–40. These verses contain the specifications for constructing the seven-branched **candlestick** (v. 31), the lampstand (Hebrew, *menorah*). It was constructed from one massive, solid piece of pure gold and weighed one **talent**, approximately one hundred twenty-five pounds (some sources estimate the talent at roughly seventy-five pounds). The ornate components of the menorah, the **shaft ... branches ... bowls ... knops** (an ornamental knob) **... flowers**, were patterned after the almond tree, the first of the Promised Land's trees to blossom in spring. The cups of the candlestick were designed to resemble either the calyx (the outer covering of the flower) or the almond nut. Coming out of the main shaft were **six branches** (v. 32), three on each side, together making seven branches. On top of the ornate branches were **seven lamps** (v. 37), with little pinch-ended bowls in which to hold olive oil and a wick. The menorah provided a perpetual light source within the windowless tabernacle. Tended morning and evening by the priests (Lev. 24:3–4), it was positioned opposite the table of shewbread and diagonally from the table of incense, in a triangular formation. The **vessels** (v. 39) used in conjunction with the menorah's maintenance were likewise made **of pure gold**.

26:1–6. The structure of the **tabernacle** (v. 1) was that of a reinforced, flat-roofed, rectangular tent with dimensions of forty-five feet in length by fifteen feet in width by fifteen feet in height. Always oriented eastward, the structure was divided into two sections, the larger Holy Place and the smaller Holy of Holies. Including the surrounding spacious outer courtyard, the tabernacle's total dimensions were one hundred fifty feet in length by seventy-five feet wide. The Egyptians used similarly designed portable structures during this period for both sacred

and secular use, and their royal tents were likewise subdivided into two rooms, with the outer chamber twice the length of the inner.

These verses contain the specifications for constructing **ten curtains** (v. 1), the innermost lining of the four-layer wall coverings of the tabernacle. These ten curtains were sewn of **fine twined linen**, fashioned into a tapestry with decorative cloth dyed in **blue, and purple, and scarlet** and artistically embroidered with images of **cherubims**. Each curtain measured forty-two feet in length by six feet in width. When woven together by **blue loops** (v. 4) and **gold** (v. 6) clasps, first into two sets of five curtains each and then into one lengthy piece, the combined dimensions totaled sixty feet in width by forty-two feet in length. Together, the curtains were of sufficient size to cover the tabernacle—the structure's top (forty-five feet long) and back (fifteen feet high) corresponding to the combined curtains' sixty feet in width, and the structure's top (fifteen feet wide) and two sides (each fifteen feet high) corresponding to the combined curtains' forty-two feet in length (the curtains did not extend all the way to the ground on either side.) As these magnificent, artistically rendered curtains were designed for the tabernacle's holy interior, they were exclusively for the enjoyment of the Levitical priesthood. Although the vast majority of Israelites would never glimpse the interior of the tabernacle, nonetheless every detail of the gold-covered wood and rich tapestry fabric was crafted to meticulous aesthetic perfection.

26:7–13. These verses contain the specifications for constructing the second interior layer of the four-layer wall coverings of the tabernacle, which was a protective, weather-resistant layer **of goats' hair** (v. 7). The **eleven curtains** (v. 8), each measuring forty-five feet in length by six feet in width, were sewn together by loops and bronze clasps first into one set of **five curtains** (v. 9) and one set of **six curtains** and then into one lengthy piece. When woven together, the combined curtains measured sixty-six feet in width by forty-five feet in length. Together, the goats'-hair curtains were of sufficient size to cover the tabernacle's innermost layer of fine embroidered linen (see discussion on 26:1–6). The sixty-six feet enveloped the tabernacle's top and back, leaving three feet of curtain to double over in front and back; the forty-five feet provided sufficient length for the covering to extend all the way to the ground on each side.

26:14. This verse contains the specifications for constructing the final two layers of the four-layer wall coverings of the tabernacle. These protective outer layers consisted of a layer of **rams' skins dyed red**, over which was laid the outermost layer of waterproof dugong (sea cow) skin (see discussion on 25:5).

26:15–30. These verses contain the specifications for constructing the frame of the tabernacle, on which the aforementioned wall coverings were hung and through which the embroidered inner layer of fabric could be seen. The frame was a three-walled structure of forty-eight gold-covered acacia-wood **boards** (v. 15), or more accurately, beams, forty-five feet in length by fifteen feet in width, strengthened and connected by **sockets of silver** (v. 19) with fifteen gold-covered acacia-wood crossbars inserted horizontally through **rings of gold** (v. 29). Each of the forty-eight beams measured fifteen feet in height by two feet three inches in width. Two sets of **twenty** (vv. 18, 20) beams, each separated by a space of about two feet, joined together to form each side of the frame, and **six** (v. 22) beams joined together to form the back side. Each corner was reinforced with an additional beam.

26:31–35. These verses contain the specifications for constructing the veil that divided the tabernacle into two areas: the larger **holy place** (v. 33) and the smaller inner sanctum, the **most holy** place, the Holy of Holies. The Holy of Holies was cube-shaped, measuring fifteen feet on each side and fifteen feet in height (as was the entire structure). The veil was made of **fine twined linen** (v. 31), interwoven with cloths vibrantly dyed in **blue, and purple, and scarlet** (see discussion on 25:1–9) in the same fashion as the tabernacle's innermost layer, with the identical embroidered rendering of **cherubims** (see discussion on 26:1–6). The veil was hung from **hooks … of gold** (v. 32) on gold-covered acacia-wood posts

set in **sockets of silver**. Here the instruction is given to set the **ark of the Testimony** (v. 33) in the Holy of Holies as its sole furnishing. Instructions are also given for furnishing the larger room with the table of shewbread, the menorah, and the table of incense.

26:36–37. These verses contain the specifications for constructing the **hanging for the door of the tent** (v. 36). This curtain was constructed in the exact fashion of the veil, **of blue, and purple, and scarlet, and fine twined linen**, with the exclusion of the embroidered cherubim. Like the veil, the door hanging was hung from **hooks … of gold** (v. 37) on gold-covered acacia-wood posts (five this time), but the posts were set in bronze, not silver, **sockets**.

27:1–8. This section, describes the courtyard of the tabernacle. These verses contain the specifications for constructing the **altar** (v. 1) of sacrifice, which was constructed of acacia wood and overlaid with bronze. It was a hollow square, with the same dimensions for both length and width, seven feet six inches; its height was four and a half feet. Projecting up from each of the **four corners** (v. 4) of the altar were chunky segments called **horns** (v. 2), which were symbols of help and refuge (see 1 Kings 1:50; 2:28; Ps. 18:2). The horns were smeared with blood on the Day of Atonement (Lev. 16:18) and during the consecration of priests (Exod. 29:1, 10–12; Lev. 8:14–15; 9:9).

All **vessels** (v. 3), the utensils used to handle the sacrificed meat and to collect its blood and ashes (the **pans … shovels … basons … fleshhooks … firepans**), were made of bronze. A bronze grating, on which the sacrifices were burned, was inserted halfway down inside the altar. Beneath the grating was a foundation of uncut stones (20:25), which were framed by the bronze altar. Attached to the altar were four bronze-covered acacia-wood rings, into which two bronze-covered acacia-wood **staves** (v. 6), or poles, were inserted on either side in order to transport it. The altar was placed between the entrance to the courtyard and the laver, in direct line with the entrance of the tabernacle.

27:9–19. These verses contain the specifications for constructing the **hangings** (v. 9) that enclosed the outer **court of the tabernacle**. These curtains were seven and one half feet high (half the height of the still-visible tabernacle proper) and, like the other curtains, were made of the **fine twined linen**, interwoven with **blue, and purple, and scarlet** (v. 16) material. They extended on the southern and northern perimeters for one hundred fifty feet and on the western and eastern perimeters for seventy-five feet, with a thirty-foot gap on the eastern side for the entrance. The total enclosed area of the rectangular tabernacle complex was roughly 11,250 square feet. In the court of the tabernacle, the Israelites would gather for worship, generation after generation, for over four centuries. Their worship was fueled, no doubt, by the knowledge that God's Shekinah glory was only yards away, separated from them by only a few layers of fabric.

The hangings were hung from silver hooks on twenty posts of bronze-covered acacia wood, set seven and one half feet apart in bronze **sockets** (v. 11) along the southern and northern perimeters, and on ten such posts along the western perimeter. The curtains were tightly secured with tent pegs. The entrance to the courtyard was a thirty-foot opening at the center of the eastern perimeter. The entrance was flanked on either side by curtains, each side supported by three posts, making a total of fifty-six posts.

27:20–21. These verses contain the specifications for maintaining the tabernacle menorah's undying flame. The fire, which was never to be completely extinguished, symbolized the presence of God among His people. Twice a day, **evening** and **morning** (v. 21), the priests were to clean the menorah's seven lamps, trimming the wicks and replenishing the olive oil. **Before the testimony.** The menorah, set in triangular formation with the tables of incense and shewbread within the Holy Place, was separated from the Holy of Holies by only a veil.

b. Elements of the Priesthood (chaps. 28–29)

As God's instructions for His dwelling were precise and detailed, so too were His specifications for the garments of His ministers, the priests.

28:1–5. These verses concern the clothing of the priesthood. The priests' role as Israel's religious leaders and mediators before God necessitated special uniforms. The priestly garments were to serve three purposes: holiness, **glory,** and **beauty** (v. 2). The distinctive clothing would **consecrate** (v. 3), or sanctify, Aaron's family for their unique role. In addition, they were skillfully crafted and were designed to inspire a sense of reverent awe in Israel's worshipers. The garments were sewn from the same material used for the tabernacle curtains, **fine linen** (v. 5) and **blue, and purple, and scarlet** cloth, with the addition of **gold** and precious stones.

Out of all of **the children of Israel** (v. 1), God chose only one family unit, that of **Aaron**, to serve, from generation to generation, as His priests. The Levitical priesthood originates with these five men: **Aaron** and his sons, **Nadab and Abihu, Eleazar and Ithamar.** In generations to follow, their sons, grandsons, and descendants will serve as priests. Aaron will be the initial high priest, and thereafter, that role will pass to his third son, **Eleazar** (Num. 3:4), and to his descendants in direct hereditary succession. The high priest's uniform had six components: **a breastplate … an ephod … a robe … a broidered coat, a mitre, and a girdle** (v. 4).

28:6–14. The **ephod** was the official emblem and symbol of the high priest's authority. It was a sleeveless outer garment worn over the torso and tied at the waist and was constructed of **fine twined linen** (v. 6) and **blue … purple … and scarlet** cloth, together with **gold**. It had two shoulder pouches, in which were placed **two onyx stones** (v. 9), one on each shoulder. The names of the twelve tribes were engraved on the stones, **six** on each stone, so that the high priest could **bear their names before the L**ORD **upon his two shoulders** (v. 12).

28:15–28. The high priest's **breastplate of judgment** (v. 15) was made of the same material as the ephod and was secured to it, top and bottom, by four **gold** (v. 22) chains. It was square, measuring nine inches on each side, and contained **gold** (v. 15) settings in which were embedded twelve precious **stones** (v. 17) in four rows of three. Engraved on each stone was the name of one of the **twelve tribes** (v. 21) of Israel, so that they would be represented before the Lord on the Day of Atonement, when the high priest entered the Holy of Holies. These were the same stones mentioned that were located in the garden of Eden (Ezek. 28:13).

28:29–30. The Scripture provides no physical description of the **Urim and Thummim** (v. 30), nor are instructions for their design or creation provided. This implies their prior existence; however, this is their initial mention in Scripture. Usually left untranslated, the Hebrew for "Urim and Thummim" literally means "lights and perfections." They were two stones, inserted into a pouch on the **breastplate of judgment** (which was attached to the ephod) and **continually resting upon Aaron's heart**, that were somehow used like lots for inquiring of the Lord. They were capable of answering only yes or no questions and were used for determining the Lord's will (28:30; Lev. 8:8; Num. 27:21; Deut. 33:8; 1 Sam. 28:6; 30:7–8; Ezek. 2:63; Neh. 7:65). Like the ark of the covenant, these two stones vanished following the Babylonian captivity.

28:31–35. Worn beneath the **ephod** (v. 31) was the high priest's **robe**. It was a loose, seamless, sleeveless, reinforced, **blue** pullover. Extending to just below the ankle, the bottom hem was fringed with alternating **pomegranates of blue, and of purple, and of scarlet** (v. 33) and golden **bells**. The pomegranates not only were beautifully decorative but also served to keep the robe adequately weighted down as the high priest went about his ministry. The bells served as an alarm system for the one day of the year, the Day of Atonement, when the high priest entered the Holy of Holies. As long as the bells tinkled, the priests standing outside the veil knew that the high priest was still alive. Jewish tradition speaks of tying a rope around the high priest's leg to pull him out of the Holy of Holies in the event that he had been struck dead and had to be removed.

28:36–39. The high priest's **mitre** (v. 37), his turban, was made of **fine linen** (v. 39) and had an engraved gold plate secured to it with **blue** (v. 37) cord. The plate read, **HOLINESS TO THE LORD** (v. 36), and was a continual reminder, to the high priest and to all others, of his unique position and extraordinary responsibility as Israel's mediator. These verses

also mention the remainder of the high priest's uniform, **the coat** (v. 39) and **the girdle**, as the text moves to articles also worn by ordinary priests.

28:40–43. The **coats** (v. 40) were worn next to the skin, were ankle length, and had long sleeves. The **girdles**, or sashes, were wide belts worn around the waist, with their ends hanging down. The **bonnets**, or priestly headwear, were bands of linen wrapped around the head. They were also to wear **linen** (v. 42) undergarments to keep from exposing themselves as they ministered. The priestly uniform, although less ornate than the high priest's, was also to be **for glory and for beauty** (v. 40; see discussion on 28:1–5). The priests were never to enter **the tabernacle** (v. 43) without their uniform, upon consequence of death. For Aaron and his sons to inaugurate their function as priests, Israel was to **anoint … consecrate … and sanctify them** (v. 41).

29:1–9. These verses describe the installation and consecration of the priesthood (see Leviticus 8). Moses was to take **one young bullock** (v. 1) and **two** unblemished **rams**, along with **unleavened bread, cakes unleavened** (v. 2) mixed **with oil, and wafers unleavened anointed with oil**, placing the bread, cakes, and wafers in a **basket** (v. 3). Aaron and his sons were to be brought before **the tabernacle** (v. 4) and symbolically purified by washing, after which their priestly garments were to be donned. Aaron, as high priest of Israel, was anointed with oil.

29:10–14. The installation ceremony continued with the sacrifice of the bull. **Aaron and his sons … put their hands upon** its **head** (v. 10) and slaughtered it as **a sin offering** (v. 14), or purification offering (see Lev. 4:1–3). **Blood** (v. 12) was applied to **the horns of the altar**, and the remainder of the blood was poured out at the base **of the altar** to purify it. **The fat** (v. 13) and the two kidneys were burned on the altar, and the remainder of the animal was taken and burned outside of **the camp** (v. 14).

29:15–18. This sacrifice was followed by that of the first of the two unblemished rams. Again, **Aaron and his sons … put their hand upon the head of the ram** (v. 15). Their sins would be transferred to the animal through this ritual. The ram's **blood** (v. 16) was sprinkled around **the altar**. As **a burnt offering … unto the** L**ORD** (v. 18) that needed to be entirely consumed on the altar, the carcass was butchered so that **the whole ram** would fit neatly within the dimensions of the altar grating and then washed to remove dung.

29:19–21. This sacrifice was followed by the sacrifice of the second unblemished **ram** (v. 19). After the laying on of hands, the ram was slaughtered. Its **blood** (v. 20) was applied on **Aaron and his sons**, on the tips of their right ears, right thumbs, and right big toes. The remainder of the blood was splattered on **the altar**. A mixture of **the blood** (v. 21) from **the altar** and **anointing oil** was splattered on Aaron and his sons and on their **garments**. The priests were thus **hallowed**, or consecrated, from head to toe.

29:22–28. As this third animal was neither a sin offering nor burnt offering but rather **a ram of consecration** (v. 22), it was not to be totally consumed. Certain portions, the breast and the leg, were to be eaten by the priests. First, though, the ram's **fat** and certain inner organ parts—together with one loaf of unleavened bread, one unleavened cake, and one unleavened wafer—were to be waved back and forth before the altar as **a wave offering** (v. 24) and burned on **the altar** (v. 25). Waved next was **the breast of the ram** (v. 26), which belonged to the priests. Waved and elevated before the altar next was **the heave offering** (v. 28), or presentation offering. This was the **shoulder** (v. 22), or thigh, of the animal, which along with the breast, also belonged to the priests. These meat portions were set apart for the nourishment and support of the priests (vv. 27–28).

29:29–30. In the future, the high priest will be ordained in the same manner. The original high priestly vestments created for Aaron were to be passed on to his son upon Aaron's death (Num. 20:22–29).

29:31–34. Instructions for eating **the ram** (v. 31) portions are provided. The meat was to be boiled, not roasted, and then eaten with the unleavened baked goods, in front of the tabernacle's entrance. These offerings, **because they are holy** (v. 33), were solely for the priests' consumption, and whatever leftovers remained had to be incinerated.

29:35–37. The consecration service spanned a period of seven days, with a bullock daily sacrificed as a sin offering to cleanse, anoint, and sanctify the **most holy** (v. 37) altar.

29:38–42. These verses refer to the regular responsibilities of the priesthood. In the **morning** (v. 39) and in the late afternoon, on a daily, perpetual basis, a lamb was to be sacrificed **upon the altar** (v. 38), along with two quarts of **flour** (v. 40) mixed with a quart of **oil**, and **a drink offering** of a quart of **wine**. The fire on the altar of sacrifice was never to be extinguished. The basic priestly responsibilities as given in the Torah were to burn incense (30:7–8); to make offerings (29:38–42; Lev. 6:13); to inspect the sacrificial animals (Lev. 27:11–12); to keep the menorah burning (Lev. 24:1–4); and to teach Israel God's requirements (Deut. 17:8–13; 19:15–20; 21:5).

29:43–46. These verses relay the tabernacle's main purpose: to serve as a location where God **will meet with the children of Israel** (v. 43). The **tabernacle** (v. 44), the **altar**, and the **priests** will all be sanctified by God's **glory** (v. 43). He **will dwell amongst the children of Israel** (v. 45) so that **they shall know** (i.e., by means of personal, multigenerational experience, v. 46) **that I am the** L**ORD their God**.

c. Service Elements of the Tabernacle (chaps. 30–31)

30:1–10. These verses contain the specifications for constructing the third and final piece of furniture for the tabernacle interior: the **altar** (v. 1) of **incense**. Placed directly in front of the veil, the altar for burning incense was made of gold-covered acacia **wood**, eighteen inches in both **length** (v. 2) and **breadth**, with a **height** of three feet. It had **horns** (v. 3) and an ornamental edging of gold. Attached to the table's **corners** (v. 4) were four **golden rings**, into which two gold-covered acacia-wood **staves** (v. 5), or poles, were inserted on either side in order to transport it. **Incense** (v. 7) was burned **every morning** and evening, in conjunction with the maintenance of the menorah. **Ye shall offer no strange incense** (v. 9). There was to be no deviation from the divine recipe for the incense to be burned on the table (30:34–38). Aaron's sons, Nadab and Abihu, would later commit that error (Lev. 10:1 – 2). In addition, nothing besides incense was ever to be offered on the table. Each **year** (v. 10) on the Day of Atonement, the high priest was to take the **blood of the sin offering** and apply it **upon the horns** of the table (see Lev. 16:18 – 19).

30:11 – 16. These verses relate to the support of **the tabernacle** (v. 16). Whenever a national census was taken, every male aged twenty or older was to pay a tax. The same amount, **half a shekel** (v. 13), was to be paid by both **rich** and **poor** (v. 15). God's ministry was to be supported by God's people. The Lord called this tax both **a ransom** (v. 12) and **an atonement for your souls** (v. 16). The idea was that if the newly inaugurated Levitical system were to break down through a paucity of contributions to its maintenance, there would be no forgiveness, and God's judgment would be incurred.

30:17 – 21. These verses contain the specifications for the construction of the **laver** (v. 18). This was a round, bronze basin to be filled with water and placed in line between **the altar** of sacrifice and the **tabernacle** tent. The priests were to use the laver to **wash their hands and their feet** (v. 19) before entering the **tabernacle** and before **offering** (v. 20) a sacrifice on the altar. The bronze for the laver is specifically recognized in the text as having been constructed from the mirrors of the Hebrew women (38:8).

30:22 – 33. These verses contain the formula for the special oil used to anoint the priests and the tabernacle furnishings for the purpose of sanctifying them and making them holy. **Pure myrrh** (balsam sap; v. 23), **sweet cinnamon** (bark of the cinnamon tree, a species of laurel), **sweet calamus** cane (pith from the root of a reed plant), and **cassia** (made from dried flowers of the cinnamon tree; v. 24) were four imported and very expensive **spices** (v. 23). They were skillfully processed together and blended with olive oil. As this **holy anointing oil** (v. 25) belonged uniquely to God, it was reserved for the exclusive use of the priesthood. Profane usage or unauthorized production were forbidden and were capital offenses.

30:34 – 38. These verses contain the formula for the incense. Four ingredients were blended and ground together: **stacte** (a rare and very expensive powder taken from the middle of hardened drops of myrrh; v. 34), **onycha** (made from mollusk shells), **galbanum** (a rubbery resin taken from the roots of a flowering plant that thrives in Syria and Persia), and **pure frankincense**. As with the anointing oil, profane usage or unauthorized production were forbidden and were capital offenses. **Tempered together** (v. 35). Salt was added to complete the recipe.

31:1 – 11. With the instructions for construction relayed, craftsmen could be now appointed to carry out those directives. God specifically appointed **Bezaleel** (v. 2) and his assistant, **Aholiab** (v. 6), **of the tribe of Dan**, to oversee the massive undertaking. They would be responsible for constructing and assembling the tabernacle, the tabernacle furniture, the priestly garments, and the oil and incense. **Bezaleel, of the tribe of Judah** (v. 2), was the grandson of **Hur** (17:10). The source of his skill was the Holy Spirit, who had supernaturally gifted him **in wisdom … understanding … knowledge … and in all manner of workmanship, to devise cunning works … in gold … silver … brass … in cutting of stones, to set them … and in carving of timber, to work in all manner of workmanship** (vv. 3 – 5).

31:12 – 17. With the tabernacle project now ready to get underway, a solemn warning was in order for the Hebrews. Under no circumstances were they to neglect keeping the **holy sabbath** (v. 14). Just as circumcision was the **perpetual** (v. 16) sign of the Abrahamic covenant, the **sabbath** was the **sign** (v. 17) of the Mosaic covenant; the loving relationship established between God and Israel that ratified their status as the chosen people. For that reason, YHWH identified Himself as the LORD **that doth sanctify you** (v. 13). Once a week, all **work** (v. 15) was to cease. Not even the construction of the holy tabernacle was sufficient reason to violate the Holy Sabbath laws. Disregarding this memorial day would result in capital consequences.

31:18. The text finally returns to the thread of the narrative where it left off (20:21). Forty days had passed since **Moses** ascended **Sinai**, and it was time for him to be given the **two tables of Testimony, tables of stone**. It was not that it took the combined space of two separate tablets to record the Ten Commandments; rather, it was common practice in the ancient world for two copies of a covenant document to be made, and one copy was given to each party for safekeeping. In this instance, both tablets would be kept together in the same location, the ark of the covenant, for safekeeping.

Written with the finger of God (see discussion on 8:18–19).

B. Rebellion in the Camp (chaps. 32–34)

1. The Covenant Broken (32:1–33:6)

32:1. During the period that **Moses** had been communing with the Lord, events were transpiring back at the Israelite camp that were not shaping up to be quite so spiritually oriented. The Hebrews, who had just ratified an unprecedented covenant with their God, became fearful when their mediator failed to return from Mount Sinai. By this time, Moses had been gone for at least thirty days. His absence from the camp began to unnerve his people, who had become quite dependent on him. The possibility began to occur to them that their mediator might not return. Perhaps some mishap had befallen him while in God's presence, and he had been stricken dead. The people came to **Aaron**, who, as Moses' brother and fellow prophet, was the logical choice to calm their fears. Instead of seeking solace and comfort from the man Moses had left in charge of the camp, however, they made an imprudent demand. They challenged him to manufacture for them **gods, which shall go before us**, hoping that he would provide them a tangible replacement mediator who would not desert them.

32:2–4. Aaron's resolve collapsed immediately, and he began organizing a collection of **golden earrings** (v. 2; doubtless part of their Egyptian spoils, 12:36) to fashion into a golden **calf** (v. 4), or bull. This was likely a wooden carving overlaid with **molten** gold plate. In a bizarre echo of the Lord's introductory words on Sinai (20:2), the people cried out, **These be thy gods, O Israel, which brought thee up out of the land of Egypt.** This declaration indicates that the people's actions were not merely a violation of the first commandment, prohibiting worship of a foreign god, but also a violation of the second commandment, prohibiting making a physical representation of the invisible God (20:4–6). Impossibly, Israel not only had failed to learn the lesson of the ten Egyptian plagues and the powerlessness of idols; they also did not retain the memory of the Lord's assertion of His commandments.

32:5–6. Aaron (v. 5), possibly attempting to make the best of an extraordinarily bad situation, then **built an altar before** the golden calf and proclaimed a festival to **the Lord**. The following morning, the people **rose up early ... and offered burnt offerings** (v. 6) and **peace offerings**. After eating together, the people **rose up to play**. The Hebrew verb translated "rose up to play" often has sexual connotations; it is possible that their worship involved immoral practices, likely involving fertility rituals.

32:7–10. The narrative cuts back to Moses on Mount Sinai, who, by this time, had been in God's presence for forty days and nights. The Lord dispatched Moses to descend the mountain immediately. So soon after the covenant ratification, the Lord complains, **thy people which thou broughtest out of the land of Egypt, have corrupted themselves** (v. 7). They have made a golden **calf** (v. 8) and not only have **worshipped it** and **sacrificed** to it, but they have given it credit for the exodus event. It is worth noting the pronoun change in God's surprising phrase, **thy people ... which thou broughtest out** (v. 7), instead of the previously ubiquitous "my people, whom I brought out" (see, e.g., 3:10). Apparently, when God was angry with the Hebrews, He disowned them, and they temporarily became Moses' people.

He then labeled the Hebrews a **stiffnecked** (v. 9), or obstinate, **people**, and His reference to them deteriorated from "thy people" to **this people**. The Lord continued, **Now therefore let me alone** (v. 10). God warned Moses ahead of time not to attempt to intervene or intercede on behalf of the people. **That my wrath may wax hot ... that I may consume them**. In a paroxysm of righteous anger, God threatened to completely annihilate the nation and start over with Moses. **I will make of thee a great nation**. Somehow, God intended to transfer the promises of the

Abrahamic covenant to Moses' descendants. Perhaps His allusion was His way of offering a subtle, if contradictory, cue for Moses to remember those promises and therefore intercede on Israel's behalf.

32:11-14. Despite the Lord's attempt at dissuasion, Moses immediately appealed to God, interceding on Israel's behalf through three lines of argument. First, Moses appealed to God's recent activity in delivering the Hebrews from Egypt. He reversed God's pronoun change, reminding Him that despite His current **fierce wrath** (v. 12), after all He had miraculously and powerfully done for them, the Hebrews were still His people. He would not have exerted all that power and effort if He did not love them and have a unique relationship with them.

Second, Moses appealed to God's reputation among the surrounding Gentile nations, Egypt in particular (v. 12). If God were to destroy the Hebrews so quickly after the exodus, the Egyptians might well conclude that He had removed the Hebrews from Egypt merely to destroy them. The Egyptians would not respect a god who behaved in that sort of cruel and arbitrary fashion.

Third, Moses appealed to God's solemn covenant oaths to **Abraham, Isaac, and Israel** (Jacob; v. 13), concerning both seed (Gen. 15:5; 22:17a; 26:4a; 28:14; 32:13) and land (Gen. 15:18–21; 22:17b; 26:4b; 28:13; 32:13). Throughout their relationship, from the burning bush onward, YHWH had always taken great pains to emphasize His identity as the promise-keeping God who remembers His covenants, not a promise breaker and capricious adjuster of covenants.

And the Lord repented (v. 14). YHWH responded favorably to Moses' petition and adjusted His course of action accordingly. This passage is an excellent reminder that while the Lord's character is unchanging, He is responsive to prayer and will amend even a divinely announced course of action, depending on the circumstance.

32:15–18. Having thus rescued his people from the dire consequences of God's wrath, **Moses** (v. 15) descended the mountain to confront them with his own fury, carrying with him **the two tables of the Testimony**. The tablets are here described for the first time. The Ten Commandments were **written on both their sides**, and the writing was **the writing of God** (v. 16). God Himself carved out these stone tablets and engraved them with His finger (31:18, see also discussion on 8:18–19).

Joshua (v. 17), who had been awaiting partway up the mountain for his master (24:13), thought that what he heard was disaster; the **noise of war in the camp**. Moses replied that it was not war they were hearing, but singing.

32:19–20. When Moses reentered the camp and saw the idolatrous rebellion of his people **dancing** (v. 19) around the golden **calf**, his **anger waxed hot**. It was Moses' turn to be offended by Israel's gross violation of their covenant. Moses graphically illustrated for his people that the Mosaic covenant had now been broken. He hurled the two tablets **out of his hands**, and broke them against the foot of Mount Sinai. He then destroyed the golden **calf**. After burning it, melting down the gold, and consuming the wood **in the fire** (v. 20), Moses took what remained of the idol and **ground it to powder**. Mixing the powder with **water**, he forced the rebels to **drink** the mixture. This was an object lesson in the utter folly of what Israel had done. They had been worried about what would happen to them if Moses did not return. Rather, they should have been worried about what would happen to them if he did return and found them engaged in idolatry. A god who would allow himself to be imbibed by his worshipers and subsequently evacuated from their bodies was not a very potent god.

32:21–24. Moses' next action was to investigate how this could have happened. He went to his brother, to whom he had entrusted the people in his absence. Not believing that **Aaron** would allow this without some manner of threat or coercion, Moses asked, **What did this people unto thee, that thou hast brought so great a sin upon them?** (v. 21) Aaron provided three excuses. First, he blamed the people's disposition toward **mischief** (lit., "evil"; v. 22). Second, he blamed the calf's creation on his responsibility as the Israelites' leader to comfort them in their fear that Moses was dead. Third, he blamed the creation of the calf on a miracle: **I cast the gold into**

the fire, and there came out this calf (v. 24). Moses' response to these laughable excuses remains unrecorded. Hur, who had also been left in charge of the camp (24:14), was not heard from at all. God, on the other hand, was angry enough with Aaron to have killed him (Deut. 9:20).

32:25–29. Moses, witnessing the utter anarchy in the camp, moved to punish the guilty parties. He would force Israel to make a very public choice. Standing **in the gate of the camp** (v. 26), he rallied the faithful to his side with the cry, **Who is on the LORD's side? let him come unto me.** Moses' own tribe, the Levites, were the ones who responded to his invitation. He commanded them to take their **swords** (v. 27) and **slay every man his brother … his companion … his neighbour**—every major participant in the rebellion. They executed **three thousand men.** Other rebels would soon be stricken by a plague (32:35). **That he may bestow upon you a blessing** (v. 29). This act of faithful zeal **consecrate[d]** the Levites from this sin and established their role as caretakers of the tabernacle (Num. 1:47–53; 3:5–9, 12, 41, 45; 4:2–3).

32:30–35. In the light of the following day, Moses addressed his people, informing them that they had **sinned a great sin** (v. 30). He informed them that he was leaving them again, this time to ascend Mount Sinai on their behalf, on a mission of intercession. He knew that God's divine judgment was only in the inaugural stage, and he would attempt to lessen the severity of the Lord's holy wrath. The extreme circumstance of the rebellion required a drastic strategy on Moses' part; he planned to offer his own life on their behalf, to **make an atonement** for them. Desperate times called for desperate measures.

Once again in the presence of the Lord, atop Sinai, Moses, in his role as mediator, formally confessed Israel's sin and begged for God's forgiveness. In a passionate plea for mercy, Moses made his own premature death the condition for God's destruction of the nation, praying that if the Lord refused to extend forgiveness, then Moses was to be blotted **out of thy book which thou hast written** (v. 32), that is, God's Book of Life (Pss. 9:5; 69:28). The Lord replied that only those who had **sinned against** (v. 33)

Him would be blotted out. Although Moses had previously averted God's utter destruction of Israel, his current offer of substitutionary atonement had been refused. Divine judgment, albeit less severe than annihilation, could not be forestalled for the guilty. Their sin would be punished with a plague. No description or symptoms of this epidemic are recorded, so one may only speculate as to its severity. Some take this mention of a plague as a reference to the preceding slaying of the three thousand.

Yet the Lord tempered the disappointment His message brought. He encouraged Moses by reaffirmed His commitment to the Abrahamic covenant, telling him to continue leading the Hebrews to the Land of Promise; His **Angel** (v. 34) would prepare the way in advance (see discussion on 23:20–23).

33:1–6. The Lord, using the language of the Abrahamic covenant, had reaffirmed His promises to deliver Israel to their land of inheritance and ensure the defeat of their enemies. However, although His **angel** (v. 2) would go before the Hebrews, the Lord Himself would be absent from their midst. **I will not go up in the midst of thee; for thou art a stiffnecked people: lest I consume thee in the way** (v. 3). As a result of the rebellion, He no longer planned to dwell with them. The idea was that if the Lord spent enough time with the Israelites, their rebellious tendencies would surely, yet again, tempt God to wipe them out of existence. The **people mourned** (v. 4) and **stript themselves of their ornaments** (v. 6) when they heard this news. **Canaanite … Jebusite … a land flowing with milk and honey** (v. 3). See discussion on 3:8.

2. The Covenant Renewed (33:7–34:35)

33:7–11. Since the Lord would no longer be in the midst of the camp, the whole motivation behind building the tabernacle was now eliminated. Moses moved to create a temporary substitute for the tabernacle in which to commune with God, one which would not involve the exertion of hiking up and down Mount Sinai. Moses relocated his personal tent some distance beyond the camp. His withdrawal left him close enough, nonetheless, for the people to witness the Shekinah glory, in the form of a pillar of cloud, take up residence outside his tent's entrance. The text records the nation's wistful worship at the cloud's appearance. **Tabernacle of the Congregation** (v. 7). The people could call on Moses at his tent to inquire of God; therefore, one of the names for the tabernacle was applied to his tent. In his role as Moses' personal aide and military general, **Joshua** (v. 11) guarded the tent. **The Lord spake unto Moses face to face.** An evocative idiom that signifies the singularly intimate friendship that existed between the Lord and His prophet (Num. 12:8; Deut. 34:10).

33:12 – 23. Moses petitioned the Lord to disclose His ways, allowing Moses to know Him with even greater intimacy. Moses shared his unqualified dissatisfaction with the idea of leading the multitude to their inheritance in the absence of YHWH's personal presence. After all, he petitioned, the Israelites were **thy people** (v. 13). In favorable response to Moses' petition, the Lord reconsidered His course of action, promising, **My presence shall go with thee** (v. 14).

Having thus far successfully received God's favor, Moses pressed his negotiation further. He desired confirmation of God's promised presence. As an authenticating sign of God's promise, Moses requested that the Lord reveal His **glory** to him (v. 18). The Lord consented to reveal as much of Himself and His majesty as Moses could endure. Although no human could survive the experience of seeing God's **face** (v. 20), His unfiltered glory, the Lord would allow Moses to see His **back** (v. 23). In this way, Moses would experience **all** (v. 19) of God's **goodness**, His covenant-keeping **name**, His grace, His **mercy**.

Moses will be placed in the cleft of **the rock** (v. 21) and hidden there. As the Lord, in His glory, passed by the rock, He would obscure Moses' view by covering the cleft with His **hand** (v. 22). The moment Moses was out of danger, the Lord would **take away** (v. 23) His **hand** and allow Moses to catch a brief glimpse of His glorious wake.

34:1 – 4. As a result of Moses' successful petition, God once again planned to personally accompany His people on their journey. It was now time to renew their covenant.

Moses was told to chisel out two new tablets of stone to replace the pair he had previously broken. While the first pair had been made by God, their replacement would be prepared by the hand of Moses. Nonetheless, the law would be engraved onto the tablets by God Himself. As per the divine directive, Moses **went up unto mount Sinai** (v. 4) alone.

34:5 – 9. Once Moses had ascended Sinai, God made good his promise and revealed His glory to Moses. God's Shekinah glory **descended in** a **cloud** (v. 5) and, through a sevenfold declaration of His character and attributes, proclaimed the sacred covenant name as He **passed by** (v. 6): (1) The covenant name of YHWH was divinely pronounced and repeated for emphasis. (2) His nature is **merciful and gracious.** (3) As for temperament, He was **longsuffering,** capable of extending a great deal of patience with His people. (4) He was **abundant in goodness and truth.** (5) As to judgment, His covenantal loving loyalty extends to multiple thousand generations. (6) He is ever ready to forgive the **iniquity and transgression and sin** (v. 7) of His people. (7) His judgment would be visited upon the entire family of **the guilty,** those who violate His covenant (see discussion on 20:5 – 6). This classic list of divine attributes is quoted or alluded to elsewhere throughout the Scriptures (Num. 14:18; Neh. 9:17; Pss. 86:15; 103:8; 145:8; Joel 2:13; Jonah 4:2; Nah. 1:3). Having seen the wake, or afterglow, of God's glory, **Moses worshipped** (v. 8). Confessing the **iniquity** (v. 9) and **sin** of the **stiffnecked people** of Israel, Moses petitioned the Lord's **pardon.** He again asked that the Lord manifest His presence in the midst of the people and personally escort them to the land of their **inheritance.**

34:10. The Lord formally agreed to Moses' requests and articulated the **covenant** renewal through His promise to perform greater **marvels** than they had yet experienced; the surrounding nations would **see the work of the Lord.**

34:11 – 17. To emphasize the covenant renewal, the Lord repeated select points, the highlights, of the Mosaic covenant. Canaan's inhabitants, **the Amorite ... the Jebusite** (v. 11; see discussion on 3:8) will be driven out to make room for the Israelites. Although they would be tempted to make agreements with the **inhabitants of the land** (v. 12), they must diligently refuse to do so. Rather than making covenants with these inhabitants, the Israelites were to **destroy their altars, break their images, and cut down their groves** (wooden fertility poles erected in honor of their goddess, Asherah; v. 13). Alliances with the Canaanites would inevitably ensnare the Israelites in idolatrous worship practices, including sexual rituals. Any such treaties and participation in pagan fertility rituals would naturally lead to intermarriage and the gradual but eventual erosion of Israelite identity. In case the people missed the main point of the golden-calf judgment, **the LORD** (v. 14) again reminded them that He is **a jealous God** (see discussion on 20:4–6) and would tolerate no rivalry for their affections; no **molten** images were to be found in their midst.

34:18–26. Having expressed what worship practices Israel must avoid, the Lord then enumerated the practices they must perform. They were to observe the three annual pilgrimage festivals: **the feast of unleavened bread** (v. 18) at the beginning of the year **in the month Abib** (23:15); **the feast of weeks** (Shabuoth, or Pentecost; v. 22) seven weeks later (23:16); **and the feast of ingathering**, also called the Feast of Tabernacles, **at the year's end** (23:17). During these festivals, no one was to worry about leaving their homes unguarded, for in their absence, God Himself would safeguard their property from theft.

Israel was to obey the law of the redemption of **the firstborn** (v. 20) of both humans and animals (see discussion on 13:11–13). Israel was never to appear **empty**-handed before the Lord in worship. Israel was to observe the Sabbath (see discussion on 20:8–11). No offerings of leavened bread were to be presented as a sacrifice (23:18). **The sacrifice of ... the passover** (v. 25) was to be completely consumed before **morning** (23:18). All **firstfruits** (v. 26) were to be brought to **the LORD** (23:19). The practice of cooking **a kid** in its **mother's milk** was forbidden (see discussion on 23:19).

34:27–28. Moses was instructed to record for Israel (v. 27) the **covenant** renewal laws. He remained in the presence of **the LORD** (v. 28) for another **forty**

days, fasting throughout the entire period. God Himself took Moses' two new tablets and engraved **the ten commandments upon** them.

34:29–35. When Moses descended Mount Sinai, carrying **the two** (v. 29) tablets, **his face shone** with the reflection of the Shekinah glory he had witnessed forty days earlier. Although at first unaware of this singular development to his complexion, he soon realized that something concerning his appearance was amiss when his people, including **Aaron** (v. 30), his own brother, **were afraid to come** near him. Moses called them back, explaining what had occurred and communicating all that God had commanded. Thereafter, **Moses** (v. 33) veiled **his face** when he was in public. Only in private, **before the LORD** (v. 34), did he remove the veil. As later explained by Paul, this policy was instituted because Moses, realizing that his glowing complexion was only a temporary reflection of God's glory and certain to dissipate with time, did not want to subject the people to the eventual sight of the fading radiance (2 Cor. 3:12–18).

Moses' face shone (vv. 29–30). The Hebrew for "shone," *qaran*, is similar to the term for "horn." The phrase was mistranslated as *cornuta*, "horns," in Jerome's Latin translation, the Vulgate. Therefore, Medieval and Renaissance art often depicted Moses with horns sprouting from his head, Michelangelo's superlative sixteenth-century marble sculpture of Moses being the preeminent example.

C. Building the Tabernacle (chaps. 35–40)

With the covenant renewed, the construction of the tabernacle needed to proceed immediately. The following sections are largely a repetition of the previously provided instructions for the building of the tabernacle (chaps. 25–31). Therefore, discussion will be relatively succinct concerning the areas already covered earlier in the commentary.

1. Preparation for Building the Tabernacle (35:1–36:7)

35:1–3. The **sabbath** (v. 2) laws are reiterated, emphasizing that they were to be obeyed even during the building of the holy tabernacle (31:15–17).

As they were the very last ordinances listed prior to Israel's covenant violation, here, following Israel's covenant renewal, they are the first ordinances listed. Any violation of the **holy day** was a capital offense. A new injunction against kindling fire was added to the earlier stipulations. The repeated placement of the Sabbath laws in proximity to the instructions for the construction of the tabernacle would later lead rabbis to conclude that the thirty-nine separate categories of labor involved in constructing the tabernacle were precisely the kind of work that was forbidden for Jews to do on the Sabbath.

35:4–9. The freewill **offering** (v. 5) of the fifteen items necessary for the tabernacle's construction that was previously commanded (see discussion on 25:1–9) was now collected.

35:10–19. The skilled craftsmen and artisans were gathered together to begin the construction of the necessary items for the tabernacle's operation.

35:20–29. All the congregation ... of Israel (v. 20), with **stirred** (v. 21) hearts and **willing** spirits, contributed to the freewill offering for the tabernacle. Items contributed by the men were **gold** (v. 22) jewelry, dyed cloth, and **fine linen** (v. 23), animal **skins, silver,** bronze, and acacia **wood.** Items contributed by the women were **gold** jewelry, woven cloth, **fine linen**, and animal **skins.** The wealthy Israelites gave contributions of **stones** (v. 27) **... spice, and oil** (v. 28).

35:30–36:1. Bezaleel (v. 30) was appointed as the project's overseer. The Lord **filled him with the spirit of God** (v. 31). Specific note is taken of Bezaleel's supernatural spiritual gifting in the areas of metalwork, stonework, woodwork, engraving, embroidery, and weaving. Both he and his assistant, **Aholiab** (v. 34), were enabled to pass on and **teach** their skills to the workers under their supervision (see discussion on 31:1–11).

36:2–7. Incredibly, so enthusiastic was the people's participation in the freewill offering that they eventually needed to be **restrained from bringing** (v. 6) any more material, for the supply was **more than enough** to meet the needs of the builders. Therefore, the order was broadcast **throughout the camp** for the cessation of **the offering.**

2. Building the Tabernacle (36:8–39:31)

36:8–38. The account of the building of the tabernacle structure is nearly identical to the corresponding instructions given in chapter 26: the construction of the inner layer of linen **curtains** (vv. 8–13; 26:1–6); the construction of the goats'-hair **curtains** (vv. 14–18; 26:7–13). The construction of the ram and dugong (sea cow) skin **curtains** (v. 19; 26:14); the construction of the wooden **boards,** or beams, and the wooden crossbars (vv. 20–34; 26:15–30); the construction of the veil (36:35–36; 26:31–35); and the construction of **tabernacle door** (vv. 37–38; 26:36–37).

37:1–38:8. The text moves from the construction of the tabernacle to the construction of its furnishings. **Bezaleel** (v. 1) himself **made the ark.** The account corresponds to the previous instructions: the construction of the **ark** of the covenant (vv. 1–9; 25:10–22); the construction of the **table** (v. 10) of shewbread (vv. 10–16; 25:23–30); the construction of the seven-branched **candlestick,** the menorah (vv. 17–24; 25:31–40); the construction of the **incense altar** (vv. 25–28; 30:1–5); the production of the **holy anointing oil** (v. 29; 30:22–33); the production of the **pure incense** (v. 29; 30:34–38); the construction of the **altar of burnt offering** (vv. 1–7; 27:1–8); and the construction of the bronze **laver** of burnt offering (v. 8; 30:17–21). **The looking-glasses of the women assembling.** Highly polished bronze was reflective and was used as mirrors in the ancient world. See discussion on 30:17–21.

38:9–20. The construction of the outer **court** of the tabernacle (38:9–20) corresponds to the previous instructions (27:9–19).

38:21–31. An inventory of all the materials used in the construction of the tabernacle was commissioned by Moses and carried out by Aaron's youngest son, **Ithamar** (v. 21). Staggering amounts of precious metals were collected and utilized: approximately one ton of **gold;** almost four tons of **silver** (v. 25); over two and a half tons of bronze. **The silver ... was an hundred talents, and a thousand seven hundred and threescore and fifteen shekels.** Each of the 603,550 men of military age (this figure agrees with the census figures in Num. 1:21–43) contributed **half a shekel** of **silver** (v. 26), the amount of the tabernacle tax (see discussion on 30:11–16).

39:1–31. The text moves to the construction of the final elements related to the operation of the tabernacle, the **holy garments** (v. 1) for the priests. Instructions are given for the construction of the **ephod** (vv. 2–7; 28:6–14); the **breastplate** (vv. 8–21; 28:15–28); the construction of the **robe** (vv. 22–26; 28:31–35); the construction of the **coats of fine linen**, the **mitre of fine linen**, or turban, the **fine linen** headwear, the **linen** undergarments, and the **girdle**, or sash (vv. 27–29; 28:39–42); and the construction of the golden **plate** for the turban (vv. 30–31; 28:36–37).

3. Completing the Tabernacle (39:32–43)

39:32–43. With **all the work of the tabernacle of the tent of the congregation finished** (v. 32), they presented the fruit their labors for Moses to inspect. When Moses saw that every item had been constructed according to the Lord's specifications, he **blessed** (v. 43) the congregation.

4. Inaugurating the Tabernacle (40:1–33)

40:1–15. On the first day of the first month (v. 2), the Lord directed Moses to inaugurate the tabernacle's operation, two weeks prior to the one-year anniversary of their exodus from Egypt. Assuming their arrival at Sinai occurred between seven and twelve weeks after the exodus, and accounting for the two forty-day periods Moses spent on Sinai as well as other brief periods noted throughout the narrative, the construction of the tabernacle took between five and seven months, from the autumn of 1446 BC to the spring of 1445 BC.

The placement of the tabernacle furnishings is noted, beginning with the inner sanctum and moving outward to the courtyard. Inside the Holy of Holies was placed **the ark of the Testimony** (v. 3). The veil was then hung to separate the Holy of Holies from the larger Holy Place, in which was placed the **table** (v. 4) of shewbread, the menorah, and **the altar** of **incense** (v. 5), arranged in a triangle, with the altar

of incense at the center, nearest the veil. The curtain over the entrance to the tabernacle was then hung to divide the tabernacle proper from the courtyard. In the courtyard, between the entrance to the tabernacle proper and the entrance to the courtyard, was positioned the **altar of the burnt offering** (v. 6). The **laver** (v. 7) was placed between the entrance to the tabernacle proper and the altar of the burnt offering. The outer curtains were then hung around the perimeter of the courtyard to separate the tabernacle's sacred area and the surrounding common area.

The **tabernacle** (v. 9), along with all of its interior and exterior furnishings and **vessels**, were anointed with **oil**, consecrating them for holy use. Then, to initiate the priesthood, **Aaron and his sons** (v. 12) were washed with water, dressed in the **holy garments** (v. 13) and anointed with oil.

40:16–33. The tabernacle was reared up (v. 17). With the tabernacle completed, the text emphasizes the conscientious obedience of Moses. It is noted in this section seven times that the work was accomplished just **as the Lord commanded Moses** (vv. 19, 21, 23, 25, 27, 29, 32), and the passage concludes, **So Moses finished the work** (v. 33).

5. Indwelling the Tabernacle (40:34–38)

40:34–38. In the narrative's momentous climax, **a cloud covered the tent … and the glory of the Lord filled the tabernacle** (v. 34). At last, God's promise to Moses that He would dwell with His people was fulfilled when the Shekinah glory saturated the tabernacle. So overwhelming was His presence that no one, not even Moses, could enter the tabernacle. From then on, God's Shekinah glory would fill both the interior of the Holy of Holies and manifest as **a cloud … upon the tabernacle by day** and as **fire** upon **it by night** (v. 38). The **journeys** of the Hebrews from their camp were thereafter signaled by whether the cloud remained stationary over the tent or had moved from its position. Until the tabernacle was replaced by Solomon's Temple (1 Kings 8:1–11), this portable complex, built by divinely liberated former slaves, would remain the central location of Israel's worship for the next four centuries.

THE THIRD BOOK OF MOSES, CALLED LEVITICUS

INTRODUCTION

Title

Leviticus receives its name from the Septuagint (the Greek translation of the Old Testament) and means "relating to the Levites." Its Hebrew title, *wayyiqra'*, is the first word in the Hebrew text of the book and means "and He [i.e., the Lord] called." Although Leviticus does not deal only with the special duties of the Levites, it is so named because it concerns mainly the service of worship at the tabernacle, which was conducted by the priests (who were the sons of Aaron), assisted by many from the rest of the tribe of Levi. Exodus gave the directions for building the tabernacle, and now Leviticus gives the laws and regulations for worship there, including instructions on ceremonial cleanness, moral laws, holy days, the Sabbath year, and the Year of Jubilee. These laws were given, at least for the most part, during the year that Israel camped at Mount Sinai, when God directed Moses in organizing Israel's worship, government, and military forces. The book of Numbers continues the history with the Israelites' preparations for moving from Sinai to Canaan.

Author

Leviticus contains the biblical regulations for priestly worship and Israel's sacrificial system. The first verse of Leviticus emphasizes that the contents of this book were given to Moses by God at Mount Sinai (see also the concluding verse, 27:34). In more than fifty places, it is said that the Lord spoke to Moses. Modern criticism has attributed practically the whole book to priestly legislation written during or after the exile. However, this is without objective evidence, is against the repeated claim of the book to be Mosaic, is against the traditional Jewish view, and runs counter to other Old and New Testament witness (Rom. 10:5).

Date

Many items in Leviticus are now seen to be best explained in terms of a second-millennium BC date, which is also the most likely time for Moses to have written the Pentateuch (see Genesis, Introduction: "Date"). There is no convincing reason not to take at face value the many references to Moses and his work.

Theme and Theological Message

The key thought of Leviticus is holiness (see *Zondervan KJV Study Bible* note on 11:44)—the holiness of God and man (man must revere God in "holiness"). In Leviticus, spiritual holiness is symbolized by physical perfection. Therefore, the book demands perfect animals for its many sacrifices (chaps. 1–7) and requires priests without deformity (chaps. 8–10). A woman's hemorrhaging after giving birth (chap. 12); sores, burns, or baldness (chaps.13–14); a man's bodily discharge (15:1–18); specific activities during a woman's monthly period (15:19–33)—all of these may be signs of blemish (a lack of perfection) and may symbolize man's spiritual defects, which break his spiritual wholeness. The person with visible skin disease was banished from the camp, the place of God's special presence, just as Adam and Eve were banished from the garden of Eden. Such a person could return to the camp (and therefore to God's presence) when he was pronounced whole again by the examining priests. Before he could reenter the camp, however, he had to offer the prescribed, perfect sacrifices (symbolizing the perfect, whole sacrifice of Christ).

After the covenant at Sinai, Israel was the earthly representation of God's kingdom (the theocracy), and as her King, the Lord established His administration over all of Israel's life. Her religious, communal, and personal life was regulated to establish her as God's holy people and to instruct her in holiness. Special attention was given to Israel's religious ritual. The sacrifices were to be offered at an approved sanctuary, which symbolized both God's holiness and His compassion. They were to be controlled by the priest, who by care and instruction would preserve them in purity and carefully teach their meaning to the people. Each particular sacrifice was to have meaning for the people of Israel but also had spiritual and symbolic import. (For the meaning of sacrifice in general, see the solemn ritual of the Day of Atonement, chap. 16. For the emphasis on substitution, see 16:21. For the meaning of the blood of the offering, see 17:11; Gen. 9:4.)

Some suppose that the Old Testament sacrifices were remains of old agricultural offerings—a human desire to offer part of one's possessions as a love gift to the deity. But the Old Testament sacrifices were specifically prescribed by God and received their meaning from the Lord's covenant relationship with Israel—whatever their superficial resemblances to pagan sacrifices. They indeed include the idea of a gift, but this is accomplished by other values such as dedication, communion, propitiation (appeasing God's judicial wrath against sin), and restitution. The various offerings have differing functions, the primary ones being atonement (see *KJV Study Bible* note on Exod. 25:17) and worship.

Outline

I. The Five Main Offerings (chaps. 1–7)
   A. The Content, Purpose, and Manner of Offering (1:1–6:7)
      1. The Law of Burnt Offerings (chap. 1)
      2. The Law of Meat Offerings (chap. 2)
      3. The Law of Peace Offerings (chap. 3)
      4. The Sin Offering (4:1–6:7)
   B. Additional Regulations (6:8–7:38)

Bibliography

Bonar, Andrew. *Leviticus.* Carlisle, PA: Banner of Truth, 1989.

Hertz, J. H., ed. *The Pentateuch and Haftorahs: Hebrew Text, English Translation, and Commentary.* Socino Books of the Bible. London: Soncino, 1971.

Lindsey, F. Duane. "Leviticus." In *The Bible Knowledge Commentary: Old Testament,* edited by John F. Walvoord and Roy B. Zuck. Wheaton, IL: Victor, 1987.

McGhee, J. Vernon. *Learning through Leviticus.* 2 vols. Los Angeles: Church of the Open Door, 1967.

Noordtzif, A. *Leviticus.* Translated by R. Togtman. Grand Rapids, MI: Zondervan, 1982.

Ross, Allen P. *Holiness to the Lord.* Grand Rapids, MI: Baker, 2002.

Unger, Merrill F. *Unger's Commentary on the Old Testament.* Chattanooga, TN: AMG, 2002.

Wenham, Gordon. *The Book of Leviticus.* The New International Commentary on the Old Testament. Grand Rapids, MI: Eerdmans, 1979.

Wolf, Herbert. *An Introduction to the Old Testament Pentateuch.* Chicago: Moody, 1991.

EXPOSITION

I. The Five Main Offerings (chaps. 1–7)

The book of Leviticus opens with a detailed description of the five main sacrificial offerings. Since this book focuses on the priestly functions and obligations, Moses, the author, wanted to make sure the priests had the importance of these sacrifices implanted in their minds. The five main offerings are the burnt offering (chap. 1:1–17; 6:8–13), the meat (grain) offering (2:1–16; 6:14–23), the peace offering (3:1–17; 7:11–34), the sin offering (4:1–5:13; 6:24–30), and the trespass offering (5:14–6:7; 7:1–6). Sometimes more than one kind of offering was presented (Num. 7:16–17). All together, these offerings included vow offerings, thank offerings, and voluntary offerings. The offerings pictured what God had to do to get rid of sin (the burnt offerings) and expiate, or inflict punishment for, sins (with the sin and trespass offerings). Of course, the innocent animals took the place of the one making the offering. They became the substitutes *in type* for sin, as would Christ at some point in the future at the cross.

A. The Content, Purpose, and Manner of Offering (1:1–6:7)

In great detail, Moses spells out how the offerings were to be handled and treated. He received his instructions from the Lord, who desires that all be done correctly, with order, respect, and holiness. The sacrifices were serious business because the issue of sin and redemption is so important. With orderly instructions, the Israelites would know exactly what the offerings were all about.

1. The Law of Burnt Offerings (chap. 1)

1:1–2. The first verses reinforce the fact of the inspiration of Holy Scripture. **The Lord** (v. 1) called **Moses** and spoke to him about these matters. The Lord addressed him **out of the tabernacle**, which is the Tent of Meeting, or the Holy Place in the tent. This is where God met with Israel (Exod. 27:21). The children of Israel were instructed to bring out from their own herds an offering of **cattle** (a bull; v. 2) or from the **flock** (sheep or goat). It was to be an offering **unto the Lord**. For those who were poor, the sacrifice could be made with birds (1:14–17).

1:3–4. The **burnt sacrifice** (v. 3) was to be a **male without blemish**, meaning it was not to be sick or deformed. The one making sacrifice was to do so **voluntarily** at the **door of the tabernacle**. The sacrifices foreshadow the perfect nature of the final great sacrifice, the Lord Jesus Christ, who was without blemish and sin (Mal. 1:8; Heb. 9:14).

The picture of substitution for sin is seen in the offerer putting his hand on the head of the animal. Then it was **accepted for him to make atonement for** sin (v. 4). The spiritual picture is that the sins of the one making the sacrifice, and even of his family, passed onto the animal that was about to be offered up. The word "atonement" (*kipper*) comes from the Hebrew verb *kapar*, meaning "to cover." The Hebrew word *koper* ("ransom") shows that a reconciliation has been accomplished between God and the Israelite. Sacrifice was required because sin disrupts the relationship between man and God. "So expiation had the effect of making propitiation—turning away divine wrath by a satisfactory, substitutionary sacrifice" (Lindsey, "Leviticus," p. 175). Such sacrifices were but shadows and had to be done over and over again until the coming of the Lord Jesus Christ. His sacrifice on the cross would finally and completely settle the issue of sin.

1:5–9. The details of how the animals were to be sacrificed are given here. The **bullock** (bull; v. 5) was to be slain **before the Lord** and before the priests, **Aaron's sons.** The priests were then to **sprinkle** the **blood** around the **altar** by the **door of the tabernacle of the congregation.** In a spiritual sense, the sprinkling of the blood is a presentation before the Lord, showing that something innocent has perished for the sins of the offerer. The offerer is publicly admitting that he is a sinner in need of God's forgiveness.

The offerer was then to **flay** (v. 6) the animal and cut it into **pieces.** The priests were to put **fire** (v. 7) fueled by **wood** upon the **altar.** Fire symbolizes the holiness of God in judgment (Heb. 12:29), by which He completely judges and condemns sin (Gen. 19:24; Mark 9:43–48; Rev. 20:15). The parts of the animal were to be placed on the wood **in order** and not in a helter-skelter manner (v. 8). The **inwards** (inner parts; v. 9) and **legs** were to be **wash[ed] in water** and offered as a burnt offering, which was as a **sweet savour unto the Lord.** While the stench of the burning flesh would have been repulsive to the priests, the offering was like a sweet aroma to God, prefiguring Christ as the beloved Son of God, who delighted His Father by doing His will in dying on the cross for sinners.

1:10–13. If the offerings were from the flocks of sheep or goats, they were to be slaughtered on the side of the altar **northward** (v. 11). Two reasons for this have been suggested: (1) While the wealthy Israeli could bring a bull for sacrifice, the average farmer or herdsman would bring a lamb or goat.

With thousands of lambs and goats being slaughtered, it only makes sense that the killing and dressing be done outside the tabernacle area. Since the prevailing winds in the desert are from the south to the north, the smell would be wafted away from the holy grounds. (2) Another theory is that Christ was crucified as the Lamb of God outside the Jerusalem city gates on the north side on the hill Golgotha (Mark 15:22), which means the "place of the skull."

1:14–17. An offering of **turtledoves** (v. 14) or **young pigeons** was permitted for those who could not afford to bring a larger animal for sacrifice. This was permitted for a burnt or a sin offering (5:7). The same birds were prescribed for some purification offerings (15:14–15, 29–30; Num. 6:10–11). The birds' small size meant the sacrificial ritual had to be simplified. But the blood had to be **wrung out** (v. 15) on the side of the **altar.** God is not satisfied until blood has been spilt for sin. In the final analysis, however, such offerings were only temporary "coverings" for sin until Christ would come to finish the issue that separated man from God.

The **crop with his feathers** (v. 16) was disposed of next to the **altar,** where the **ashes** were raked together into a pile. The impure inner parts were not seen as part of the sacrifice that was to be presented to the Lord. The priest was to **cleave** the bird, cut it open, but not split or **divide** it, and then it would be burned upon the altar as a **burnt sacrifice, an offering made by fire, of a sweet savour unto the Lord** (v. 17). Whether a large bull, a sheep, or a small bird was brought to sacrifice, all of the Jews stood equal before man and before God. They each had need of a sacrifice for sin. God treated their sacrifices in an equal manner, accepting each sacrifice regardless of size.

2. The Law of Meat Offerings (chap. 2)

2:1–3. What is rendered **meat offering** (v. 1) in seen from the context to refer to a "meal" or "grain" offering. This offering was made of grain or fine flour, shaped into small cakes or wafers. They were baked in a pan or cooked over a hot griddle. This was the only bloodless offering. Such flour offerings were expensive and time-consuming to bake and carry unspoiled to the tabernacle. These offerings took consideration and effort. **Oil** and **frankincense** were poured on the offerings and set before the Lord as a **memorial** (v. 2). Some have suggested that the "fineness" of the cereal offerings represented the perfection and the humanity of Christ, as the perfect Man. The oil foreshadows the anointing of the Holy Spirit (Luke 3:21–22; John 3:34). The frankincense, or perfume, is a reminder that the heavenly Father was well pleased with His Son when He came to earth to die for sinners (Matt. 3:17; 17:5; Mark 9:7). Part of the offering **remnant** (v. 3) was shared with Aaron and his sons, typifying Christ as the "bread of life" (John 6:51–54).

2:4–11. The fine cakes could be baked in an **oven** (v. 4), baked in a **pan** or skillet (v. 5), or cooked on a **frying pan** or griddle (v. 7). No **leaven** (which represents the pervasive corruption of sin; v. 11) or **honey** (which would represent some form of artificial additive) could be a part of these offerings (v. 11). Christ was sinless, and nothing covered or coated His righteous and holy nature before men. He was the perfect Divine Human with sinless "excellencies" as part of His character (Unger, *Commentary*, p. 152). Such grain offerings were **a thing most holy of the offerings of the LORD made by fire** (v. 10).

2:12–16. Besides offerings of grain, the Lord permitted offerings of the **firstfruits** (v. 12), or green vegetables, to be offered. Again, such offerings represented a form of sacrifice and labor. This does not speak of self-righteous acts of works to please God, but it does show struggle and costly labor that represent dedication in serving the Lord. The grain offerings and the **firstfruit** offerings were different from the burnt offerings in that there was the absence of any blood ritual. Firstfruits specifically represent the early spring crops, which assured a renewed food source following the winter season. Some have suggested that they represent the everyday life given to God. Or that they represent the fact that the Lord daily supplies such food out of His mercies (Lindsey, "Leviticus," p. 177). **Salt** (v. 13) is a life-sustaining mineral needed for survival. The human body cannot do without it. It has been suggested that **the salt of the covenant of thy God** constitutes a reminder of the covenants of mercies of the Lord, beginning with the Abrahamic covenant, which began the Jewish nation (Gen. 12:1–3).

3. The Law of Peace Offerings (chap. 3)

3:1–2. The **peace offering** (or fellowship offering, as it is sometimes called; v. 1) could be made with the **male** or the **female** animals of the herd. This offering was seen as optional. The Feast of Weeks (Pentecost) was the only yearly festival for which peace offerings were prescribed (23:19–20). They were also often prescribed for certain special ceremonies of covenant initiations (Exod. 24:5) or for spiritual renewal (Deut. 27:7), and for even special consecration times (Exod. 29:19–34; Lev. 8:22–32; 9:8–21; 1 Kings 8:63).

The word "peace" is *shalom* in Hebrew, meaning "wholeness." The picture is that God has provided peace between Himself and man, an inward tranquility that comes when the issues of sin, by sacrifice, have been addressed. Peace was made also between God and the priests who partook of these offerings (7:14–15, 31–34). As with the other sacrifices, the animals for peace offerings had to be **without blemish before the LORD** (v. 1). With other blood sacrifices, the offerer placed his hand on the head of the animal at the door of the tabernacle, and then the animal was killed. Its blood was sprinkled **upon the altar round about** (v. 2).

3:3–6. The worshiper had to prepare the offering by skinning, cleaning, dissecting, cutting apart, and washing the animal (v. 3). The **kidneys** (v. 4), the **fat**, the **caul** (the "midriff" portion that lies over the liver), and the **liver** had to be removed, and these **shall he take away**. These portions of the animals contained the most fat, and most of these functioned as filter organs. This prohibition also included the "whole rump," that is, the "fat tail" of some animal. As with other sacrifices, the offering was to be **without blemish** (v. 6). The animal was not to have sores, scales, cancers, running fluid from the eyes, and so on. Because hygienic measures were limited in the hot, waterless environment, God instructed that the fat parts of the animal and the diseased animals were to be rejected and certainly not consumed as food later.

3:7–15. Whether the worshiper was bringing to the Lord a **lamb** (v. 7) or a **goat** (v. 12), the instructions for the sacrifice are identical. All of the rules, procedures, and purposes are the same with all of the peace offerings. The animals were to be thoroughly cleaned and cut apart properly, with the fattier parts removed and discarded. The blood was to be sprinkled around the altar, and the offering was **unto the Lord** (v. 11). The Israelite sacrifices were not seen as food for the gods as in other ancient cultures (Ezek. 16:20; Ps. 50:9–13). Metaphorically, however, they were gifts to the Lord, which He would receive with delight (Lev. 21:6, 8, 17, 21, 22–25). The Lord God of Israel is not "hungry" for such food, but He responds with pleasure to what the offerings represent—personal trust, dedication, obedience—but also in the sacrifices themselves. The offerings were shadows of the true sacrifice of the Lord Jesus on the cross for sinners. Christ offered Himself, "called of God a high priest after the order of Melchisedec" (Heb. 5:10). It can be said of Him, that "neither by the blood of goats and calves, but by his own blood he entered in once into the holy place, having obtained eternal redemption for us" (Heb. 9:12). The prophet Micah made it clear: "For it is not possible that the blood of bulls and of goats should take away sins.... In burnt offerings and sacrifices for sin thou hast had no pleasure" (Heb. 10:4, 6, referring to Mic. 6:6–7).

3:16–17. All of the peace offerings were to be burned on the altar, and again, to the Lord, they were like a pleasant smell, **a sweet savour** (v. 16). These ordinances were given to Israel as a **perpetual statute** (v. 17) for all future **generations**. But the Jews were also commanded to **eat neither fat nor blood**. This is repeated in 17:11, with the reminder: "For the life of the flesh is in the blood ... for it is the blood that maketh an atonement for the soul." The blood shed in sacrifices was seen by the Lord in type as sacred. It epitomized the life of the sacrificial animal, whose blood was shed to spare the one bringing the offer-

ing. It was to be treated with respect (Gen. 9:5–6). Almost all of the sacrifices included the smearing of the blood, or sprinkling of the blood, on the altar. This foreshadows the shedding of the blood of the Lamb of God, who will obtain for His people "eternal redemption" (Heb. 9:12). Without the shedding of blood, there is no remission for sin (Heb. 9:22).

The prohibition against eating the fat or the blood had secondary importance. Both fat and blood are biological incubators of disease in a hot climate. The Jews were to drain the blood before preparing the animal for consumption. They, of course, did not understand the issue of germs, but the Lord did.

4. The Sin Offering (4:1–6:7)

4:1–3. The Lord **spake** (v. 1) again **unto Moses**, possibly in an additional revelation some days later (v. 1). The Lord spelled out what must be done if **a soul shall sin through ignorance** (v. 2) against any of God's commands. No Israelite was fully aware of all of his actions or forgetfulness about what the Lord had commanded. He may have forgotten what **ought not to be done**, or he may not have realized what he had sinned against. The **anointed priest** (v. 3), or the high priest, represented the people before the Lord. He too could sin and bring guilt on the people. He also had to bring a sacrifice to cover his waywardness. In this way, both the people and the priest stood equal before the Lord in their need of an offering. Christ was not like these priests because He "knew no sin" (2 Cor. 5:21). He offered Himself without blemish to God (Heb. 9:14). "For such a high priest became us, who is holy, harmless, undefiled, separate from sinners, and made higher than the heavens; who needeth not daily, as those high priests, to offer up sacrifice, first for his own sins, and then for the peoples: for this he did once, when he offered up himself" (Heb. 7:26–27).

4:4–7. The priest brought a bullock **unto the door of the tabernacle** (v. 4), laid his hand upon its head, and killed it **before the Lord**. He was then to **sprinkle** (v. 6) the **blood seven times ... before the vail of the sanctuary**. The number seven was probably symbolic of perfection and completeness. The great curtain that separated the Holy Place from the Most Holy Place, or the Holy of Holies, is here called **the vail**. The priest then placed blood on the four **horns** of the altar and poured the rest of it **at the bottom of the altar of the burnt offering** (v. 7). The four horns were symbolic of the atoning power of the sin offering (Exod. 30:1–3, 10).

4:8–10. The various inedible parts of the animal, already mentioned in 3:14–15, were then taken away and **burnt** (v. 10). By this act, the Jews were to see these parts as unclean and not worthy to be offered to the Lord as a sin offering or a peace offering.

4:11–12. The leftover **skin** (v. 11) and **flesh**, along with the **head** and **legs** and the **inwards**, or guts and intestines, and **dung** were to be carried **without the camp** (v. 12) and consumed **on the wood with fire**. Also the **whole bullock** was to be burned there at the place **where the ashes are poured out**. So also Jesus was crucified outside of the city of Jerusalem (Heb. 13:11–13). Since the sins of the offerer were symbolically transferred to the sacrificial bull, the animal had to be entirely destroyed and not thrown on the ash pile of 1:16.

4:13–15. If the **whole congregation** (v. 13) had sinned in **ignorance**, and the sin against the **commandments of the Lord** was **hid from the eyes of the assembly**, the **elders** (v. 15) were to be involved in the expiation. When the sin became known, the elders were called out to **lay their hands upon the head of the bullock before the Lord**. The young bullock was for a sin offering before **the tabernacle of the congregation** (v. 14). This shows that an entire people, along with their leaders, can be held culpable even when they sinned in ignorance.

4:16–21. The priests would then follow up with the ritual. A priest would **dip his finger** (v. 17) in the blood and **sprinkle it seven times** in front of the inner **vail** that separated the Holy Place from the Holy of Holies **before the Lord**. Many of the rituals mentioned before are repeated here: dipping the finger in the blood, sprinkling the blood seven times, pouring out the blood on the horns of the altar, pouring out the blood at the bottom of the **altar of the burnt offering** (v. 18), and burning the **fat** (v. 19).

Again, the order of the repetition is important so that the priests, and the people, would understand the solemnity of the offerings. All of these offerings portray God's wrath for transgressions but also His mercy and grace in forgiveness. With the offering, **an atonement** (v. 20) was made, which was followed by forgiveness. The burning of the animal was **a sin offering for the congregation** (v. 21).

4:22–26. No one escapes the need for an atonement, even the **ruler** (v. 22) who had sinned against **the commandments of the Lord his God**, though he may have sinned **through ignorance**. He was still **guilty**. Lack of knowledge of the sin is no excuse. He was to bring his offering of **a kid of the goats, a male without blemish** (v. 23). A larger animal, like a bullock, was not necessary. The sins of the ruler were transferred to the goat when he laid his hands on its **head** (v. 24). The goat was for a **burnt offering before the Lord** as a sin offering. The priest then followed through with the same rituals as before (v. 25). The **fat** (v. 26) is also consumed as is done when making **peace offerings**, with an atonement made for the forgiveness of his sins (v. 26). Whoever the ruler or leader, he was placed on the same level as all of the people, including the priests. All are sinners and have to come before the Lord for forgiveness in the same way.

4:27–35. If the **common people** (v. 27) sinned in **ignorance**, they were to approach God individually for forgiveness. Their sin done unknowingly still made them **guilty**. The rituals described here are virtually the same as before, yet with some differences. The guilty was to make an offering of **a kid of the goats, a female without blemish** (vv. 28, 32). A male animal more specifically represents the coming sacrifice of the Lord Jesus Christ, so why then is a female animal commanded here? The female animal is the breeder among the flocks and is therefore more valuable. It could be that this was a sign that the guilty "commoner" was forfeiting that which was more costly to atone for his personal sins of ignorance, but this is only speculation. Something else is added here that is mentioned only a few times, and that is that the sacrifice burned for a **sweet savour unto**

the LORD (v. 31; 1:9, 17). The sacrifice was a pleasing aroma before the Lord. He would accept the offering, and the man would be forgiven (v. 35).

5:1–5. The **voice of swearing** (v. 1) may be more than cursing here. It seems to have to do with someone making a public charge against someone else, against the priests, or against the Lord Himself. Unger calls this "Special Offenses," which could include refusing to testify as a witness or uttering a rash oath (Unger, *Commentary*, p. 154). The party was still guilty there whether this sin was known or unknown, and the man **shall bear his iniquity.** Included among such offenses is touching **any unclean thing** (v. 2), or a **carcase** of an unclean cow, or the **carcase** of an unclean **creeping thing**, such as a snake. The party was **guilty** (v. 3) even if this was done unknowingly. If one swore **with his lips** (v. 4) to do either evil or good and was unaware that he swore, he was still guilty. When it was brought to his attention that he was guilty, he was to **confess** (v. 5) such sins.

Such laws and commandments held the congregation of Israel to a higher standard of conduct. These rules were meant to make them aware of the sins that can slowly erode a culture that is dedicated to the Lord. Some of these commandments were also given to protect the people from disease or contamination.

5:6–13. The party guilty of the sins above was to bring a **trespass offering** (v. 6), a **sin offering,** for **an atonement** for what he has done. This could also be a female from the flock, **a lamb or a kid of the goats.** If the guilty party was poor, he could bring **two turtledoves, or two young pigeons** (v. 7). The Lord was looking for the act of confession, not the size of the offering. The expression **trespass offering** (v. 15) is often called the "guilt offering." It is very similar to the "sin offering" (7:7). The Hebrew words for these two offerings are often interchanged. The major difference between the trespass and sin offerings was that the trespass offering was brought in cases in which restitution for the sin was possible and therefore required (v. 16). Thus in cases of theft and cheating (6:2–5) the stolen property had to be

returned along with 20 percent indemnity. By contrast, the sin offering was prescribed in cases of sin in which no restitution was possible.

If birds were used for the sacrifice, the head of the bird was to be wrung (v. 8), and the priest would **sprinkle** (v. 9) the blood **upon the side of the altar** and wring out the rest of the blood **at the bottom of the altar** as a **sin offering.** The first little bird was for the sin offering, and the second was for a **burnt offering** (v. 10). Death (for sin) and punishment and wrath (for sin) are both pictured in these rituals. The offerer received **an atonement,** and the sin was **forgiven him.**

If the offerer was extremely poor, he could bring a **tenth part of an ephah of fine flour** (v. 11), with no oil or frankincense put on it, for **a sin offering** (see 2:1–3; Num. 5:15). God counted this as a sin offering. The priest was to burn part of the flour on the altar and take **the remnant** (v. 13) as a **meat offering** for himself. The Lord accepted the sacrifice, whether large or small, as a ransom payment for the particular sin which occasioned it, thus diverting His wrath from the sinner and (ultimately) to Christ on the cross (Lindsey, "Leviticus," p. 183).

5:14–19. The Lord spoke again in a definite manner to **Moses** (v. 14). In the laws given in these verses, the stakes are raised. If anyone committed a trespass through ignorance against **the holy things of the LORD** (v. 15), he was to bring a **ram without blemish out of the flocks** (v. 15) along with **thy estimation by shekels of silver, after the shekel of the sanctuary, for a trespass offering.** "Trespass" (Hebrew, *ma'al*) is better translated "violation." The violator was required to **make amends** (v. 16) for the **harm** he had done by giving 20 percent, or a **fifth part,** above the shekel price, which some believe was calculated in two shekels.

The sins mentioned here must have something to do with spiritual things and rituals that are part of the law and reflect on the ceremonies that God has commanded. Not only are sacrifices to be made, but monetary compensation was required, making the violations costly to the transgressor. Whether he recognized his sin or not, **he is guilty and shall bear**

7:19–21. Those who partook of these sacrifices and did not take follow the commandments could face death — **that soul shall be cut off from his people** (vv. 20–21; see also 7:25, 27; 17:4, 9; 18:29; 19:8) — or excommunication (Unger, *Commentary*, p. 156). The rule of thumb for partaking was that the sacrifice and the offerer must both be ceremonially **clean** (v. 19). Anyone who came to partake while ceremonially **unclean** (v. 21) would be punished (chaps. 11–15; 22). Anyone who touched someone who was unclean, or touched an unclean animal, or touched **any abominable unclean thing** would be judged (v. 21).

6. Forbidden Portions (7:22–27)

7:22–24. No animal that had simply died was to be eaten, and **fat** (v. 24) was never to be eaten. **Ye shall in no wise eat of it.**

7:25–27. Again the reminder: if the **fat** (v. 25) is eaten, the punishment could be severe, such as death. Also, **no manner of blood** (v. 26) was to be eaten (1 Sam. 14:33). Not only was the blood from the sacrificial animals not to be eaten or consumed, but the prohibition extended to any animal or bird killed **in any of your dwellings**. The Lord commanded that blood be drained from the animal after it was slain, whether for sacrifice or for consumption. Three reasons have been given why the blood was not to be eaten: (1) life is in the blood (Gen. 9:4), (2) the blood is precious to God because Christ's blood will be shed for sinners for the remission of their sins (Heb. 9:22; 1 Peter 1:19), and (3) blood left in the open is an incubator of disease.

7. The Portion for Priests (7:28–38)

7:28–34. The **breast** (v. 30) with the **fat** for **peace offerings** (v. 29) was to be brought by the offerer's own **hands** (v. 30) to the priest for sacrifice. Why with the fat when fat was prohibited? The fat helped cook the breast meat on the altar. The breast was then to **be Aaron's and his sons'** (v. 31) for food. The **right shoulder** (v. 32) of the animal was to be used for a **heave offering**, or wave offering, which was lifted up to the Lord. The priests were to receive

this meat as a **statute** (v. 34) that is a continual rule **among the children of Israel**.

7:35–38. The laws of the priesthood are important to the Lord. The priests have an **anointing** (v. 35) that goes all the way back to the first priest, Aaron. God presented **them to minister unto the Lord in the priest's office** (v. 35). Their work is assigned **for ever throughout their generations** (v. 36). That the priests would be provided for with the key sacrifices, from the major feasts, was a law **the Lord commanded Moses in mount Sinai** (v. 38). Though the priests will never be perfect, they are to be respected. Verses 37–38 are a summary of chapters 1–7.

II. The Ordination, Installation, and Work of Aaron and His Sons (chaps. 8–10)

These chapters, as well as 24:10–23, are considered the narrative sections of Leviticus. They tell the Jewish people specifically how to come to the Lord and how to worship Him. Not only was a sacrifice needed (chaps. 1–7), but the mediation of the priests was needed as well (Heb. 5:1–4). The priesthood needed to be in place to conduct sacrificial rituals. This was the first step in implementing Israel's communication and walk with the holy God. The priesthood was set in place through Aaron and his descendants (Exod. 29:9). All of the sacrifices, and even the priesthood, point forward to the coming death of Christ. With His death, Christ "now hath … obtained a more excellent ministry, by how much also he is the mediator of a better covenant, which was established upon better promises" (Heb. 8:6), that is, the new covenant (Heb. 8:7–13).

8:1–13. Here Moses rehearses the appointment of **Aaron and his sons** (v. 2) to the priesthood (Exod. 29:1–9). **The Lord spake unto Moses** (v. 1) is the divine formula (see Lindsey, "Leviticus," p. 186). This section also shows that Moses is the mediator of the Mosaic covenant (chaps. 8–10). He was told to bring Aaron and his sons along and to give them the priestly **garments** (v. 2) and the **anointing oil**. Also, a **bullock** and **two rams** were to be sacrificed, and a **basket of unleavened bread** would be part of the ordaining ritual. Moses was also to gather the **assembly** (v. 4) of the people, the **congregation** (v. 3), and tell them that this ordination was **the thing which the LORD commanded to be done** (v. 5).

Aaron and his sons were then ceremonially **washed** (v. 6), probably with the water of the brazen laver (Exod. 30:17–21), and given the clothes of the priesthood (vv. 7–9). This included the **Urim and the Thummim** (v. 8), worn on the breast. With these (probably two stones), the priests would make decisions for the Israelites (Exod. 28:22–28). The breastplate had a double fold (Exod. 28:16) that formed pockets for these objects. The Hebrew for "the Urim and the Thummim" possibly means "the lights and the perfections" (see discussion on Exod. 28:30; see also Num. 27:21; 1 Sam. 30:7–8). They were to be used by the priests to obtain answers from the Lord about important questions. They symbolized the authority of the high priests to receive direct divine messages when needed. The **ephod** (v. 7) was a blue sleeveless robe (Exod. 28:31–35), and the **mitre** (v. 9), or turban, made of linen (Exod. 28:39) pictured the authority of the priests to spiritually and ceremonially lead Israel. A **golden plate** was place upon Aaron's **forefront**, meaning his forehead. This was called **the holy crown**.

The **tabernacle** (v. 10) and the accoutrements were anointed with **oil**, as was the **altar** (v. 11), the altar **vessels**, and **both the laver and his foot**. All of these various instruments for worship were **sanctified** (v. 10) by these acts. Aaron was then sanctified with **anointing oil** (v. 12), and Moses then put the various **coats** (v. 13) of the priestly office on Aaron and his sons. The waist censures, or **girdles**, and the **bonnets** (the Hebrew means "to bound"), or the headdresses, were added. With all of this ornamentation and dress, the priests must have had a royal look about them. They represented God to the people, and the people to God.

8:14–30. Moses then performs the first rituals of sacrifice, which Aaron and his sons will later assume. Here they are simply ordinary citizens who are bringing their own sacrifices and receiving the blessings of the Lord. The sacrifices they will carry out

are listed here and in Exodus 29:10–34. The **bullock** (v. 14) offered for Aaron and his sons may indicate this was only for them and not for the common people, who were probably watching. Generally, this **sin offering** follows what was established in 4:3–12.

The first ram was for the **burnt offering** (v. 18). The second **ram** is called the **ram of consecration**. Aaron and his sons laid their hands **upon the head of the ram**, picturing that their sins went onto this animal, which would then be sacrificed. Moses was the one who **slew** (v. 23) the ram. The blood was then placed on their **right ear** (v. 24), their **right hands**, and **the great toes of their right feet**. The symbolism may be that they will carry out a sacred task in what they hear, what they do, and where they go. Other verses about sacrifice and the **unleavened bread** (v. 25) are similar to what is already mentioned. However, a **basket** of **unleavened bread**, a **cake**, and a **wafer** are **put all upon Aaron's hands, and upon his sons' hands, and waved ... for a wave offering before the LORD** (v. 27). The bread was then burned **on the altar** (v. 28). They were **consecrations for a sweet savour ... unto the LORD**. By these ceremonial rituals, **Aaron** (v. 30), his **garments**, and **his sons** were **sanctified**.

8:31–35. Aaron and all his sons shared in a sacrificial feast. Later, this would mean that the entire officiating priesthood would be fed together. The feast took place at the entrance, **the door** (v. 31), of the **tabernacle of the congregation**. The unleavened **bread** was shared by all, taken from **the basket of consecration**. "Consecration" refers to that which has been blessed. Nothing was to be wasted; what was left over was to be burned (v. 32). The consecration period would last **seven days** (v. 33), the number of completion. The partaking of the bread foreshadows Christians feeding spiritually upon Christ, who is the Bread of Life (John 6:50–55), and remembering the blessings that come from His death and sacrifice. As Moses set forth the pattern that day, **so the LORD hath commanded to do, to make an atonement for you** (v. 34), the priests. During the feast, the priests were to remain at the **door of the tabernacle** (v. 35) day and night for seven days. To disobey this command could mean death. Aaron and his sons complied with what **the Lord commanded by the hand of Moses** (v. 36). What Moses instructed was seen as the inspired, authoritative Word from the Lord.

A. The Offerings of Aaron (chap. 9)

9:1–7. On the **eighth day** (v. 1), after the seven days of consecration had passed, Moses assembled Aaron and his sons, and the **elders** for further instructions. This **sin offering** (v. 2) was for **thyself, and for the people** (v. 7). Aaron "needed an offering for himself. The high priest on all great public occasions began by making an offering for himself" (Mc-Ghee, *Learning through Leviticus*, 64). The offering was to be of an animal in its prime, **of the first year, without blemish** (v. 3), which would be for a **burnt offering**. The animals to be sacrificed were brought before the entrance to the **tabernacle** (v. 5), with the congregation standing **before the Lord**. As these offerings were being presented, **the glory of the Lord shall appear unto you** (v. 6). God was satisfied with their sincerity and obedience and made His presence known. Such an offering was **atonement** (v. 7) for the priesthood and for the people. The difference in this offering is that it was communal and served to atone for the whole nation. God saw the Israelites as individuals but also as a theocracy in which the people were blessed or judged collectively.

This sacrifice was similar to the Day of Atonement ritual because the offerings were for both the people and the priests. Unger sees this eighth-day feast as representing the millennial kingdom when Christ comes as the King-Priest in His second glorious advent (Unger, *Commentary*, p. 157). The Lord's declaration that the Jews will become "a kingdom of priests, and a holy nation" unto the Lord will be fulfilled (Exod. 19:6; see also Zech. 3:1–10; Isa. 61:6).

9:8–14. Aaron as the high priest was required of the Lord to make his own sacrifice and stands as an example of one who must humble himself before the Lord. Too, the fact that he was a sinner like all the rest was witnessed to everyone (v. 8). He had to dip his finger in the **blood** (v. 9) and smear it on the **horns** of the altar, then pour out the rest **at the bottom of the altar**. He also **sprinkled** the **blood round about upon the altar** (v. 12). The unused parts of the animal were **burnt upon the altar** (v. 10). The ritual followed is described in 4:3–12, except that the blood was smeared again (8:15) on the horns instead of on the altar of incense.

9:15–22. By making an **offering** (v. 15) of a **goat** for the sin offering for the people, a **calf** and a **lamb** (v. 3) for their **burnt offering** (v. 16) with a **meat offering** (v. 17), and the **bullock** (v. 18) and **ram** for their fellowship (**peace**) offering, Aaron was performing sacrificial observances with every kind of animal offering, except with birds, which were concessions for the poor people. "Aaron's benediction on the people at the completion of the sacrifices (v. 22) is linked in Jewish tradition with that in Numbers 6:24–26" (Lindsey, "Leviticus," p. 188). "Whenever the different sacrifices were offered together, the sin or guilt offering always came first, followed by the burnt and fellowship offering (Lev. 9:22; Num. 6:16–17). This order was important theologically, for confession for sin had to precede the consecration of the worshiper to God" (Wolf, *Pentateuch*, p. 170).

9:23–24. Moses and Aaron went together into the **tabernacle** (v. 23) as an act of first-time dedication and consecration, and when they came out and **blessed** the gathered throng, **the glory of the Lord appeared unto all the people**. What all the people witnessed is not fully described, except they did see the **fire** (v. 24) that came **out from before the Lord, and consumed upon the altar the burnt offering**. That in itself had to be a dramatic testimony and miraculous demonstration of God's presence. In either fear or awe, the people **shouted, and fell on their faces**. This generation could not deny that the God of creation was *their God* and that He was in their midst.

B. The Death of Nadab and Abihu (chap. 10)

10:1–7. The first testing of God's commands regarding sacrifice fell upon two of Aaron's sons, **Nadab** (v. 1) and **Abihu**, who **offered** the **incense of strange fire before the Lord**. They used their

censers, which were the vessels containing hot coals for burning the pleasant smells before God (Exod. 30:34–36; Lev. 16:12–13; 2 Chron. 26:19). The "strange fire" could have been ceremonial offerings that these two men had observed in Egypt. When they made their offering, the Lord **devoured** (v. 2) them immediately with **fire, and they died before the Lord**. While this was a tragedy, Moses told Aaron that the Lord was speaking, saying, **I will be sanctified in them that come nigh me, and before all the people I will be glorified** (v. 3). Though there are differences, some have compared their sudden deaths to the deaths of Ananias and Sapphira in Acts 5:1–11. The two sons of **Uzziel** (v. 4), the uncle of Aaron, were called to carry the bodies away from the **sanctuary**. Their bodies were carried outside the **camp** (v. 5), wrapped in their coats. "Whoever saw the dead bodies saw at once that it was the Lord's stroke! for the *coats*—the priestly coats—were left unconsumed" (Bonar, *Leviticus*, p. 197).

Aaron's other two priestly sons, Eleazar and Ithamar, were warned by Moses not to uncover their heads in respect for their dead brothers, **neither rend your clothes** (v. 6) in grief. However, the **whole house of Israel** was to **bewail** in mourning the **burning** and the fire that God had brought upon them. There could be no show of remorse or sadness because their punishment was just. They had defied the commandments of the Lord and tried to mix the worship of Him with some aspect of pagan worship. As priests, Eleazar and Ithamar were dutifully responsible to set an example for the people. They also could not leave their responsibilities as priests because **the anointing oil of the Lord is upon you** (v. 7). They could not give up their jobs and leave **from the door of the tabernacle**. They understood the seriousness of their responsibility and **did according to the word of Moses**.

10:8–11. With this tragedy as a backdrop, the Lord added additional moral imperatives upon the priesthood. The priests were not to be seen drinking when they went into the **tabernacle** (v. 9) to do service unto the Lord. This injunction was a **statute** for all generations to come. They had to live the example

of what was **holy** (v. 10) and **unholy**, and **unclean** and **clean** (v. 10). They had to teach such differences to **the children of Israel** (v. 11) and instruct them in all of the **statutes** given by the Lord through **the hand of Moses**.

10:12–15. Moses spoke assuring words to **Aaron**, **Eleazar**, and **Ithamar** (v. 12). He had them pick up their duties and go forward. They may have thought that their house was permanently cursed and their service to God was over. Moses brought some comfort in the face of the terrible judgment inflicted on their household. Some priests may fail; God never will. Believer-priests may be unfaithful; God remains faithful (2 Tim. 2:13). Therefore, the priests were to continue with their office of sacrifice. In a very real sense, the family was restored, **thy sons, and thy daughters with thee** (v. 14). They would again eat the meat sacrificed **in a clean place**.

10:16–20. While restoration for the family was certain, Eleazar and Ithamar did something not prescribed in God's sacrificial commandments. Moses was angry because they had burned up the entire sacrificial carcass of the people's **sin offering** (v. 16). In essence, Moses sensed that Aaron had deviated from the correct order of the sacrifice (v. 17). Either Aaron had a real fear of eating that which was "most holy" in the wake of his sons' deaths, or he was confused by grief and inadvertently mishandled the sacrificial procedure (Lindsey, "Leviticus," p. 189). In verse 19, Aaron is possibly saying that he should have brought his own **sin offering** (v. 17) for a ritual violation, though this fact is not fully made clear. Whichever, **when Moses heard that, he was content** (v. 20). At this stage, there seems to be a difference between out-and-out disobedience against what the Lord has said and misunderstandings about proper procedures. "Moses showed his appreciation of Aaron's comprehension of the spirit of the sacrificial laws" (Unger, *Commentary*, p. 159).

III. Laws of Cleanness — Food, Childbirth, Diseases, etc. (chaps. 11–15)

The dietary laws had twofold meaning for the Jews, especially in taking on the hardships of the wilderness wanderings. The first had to do with great spiritual lessons about moral cleanliness in approaching God. The second was that they gave Israel hygienic guidelines that could not have been fully understood in that ancient culture. The laws placed the Jews in a different class from the pagan world. The supreme motive of these laws was holiness, not as an abstract principle, but as a regulating guide in the everyday lives of Jewish men, women, and children. Whoever ate forbidden foods became imbued with the spirit of impurity and faced the Lord's judgments. The subject matter of chapter 11 is repeated in Deuteronomy 14 (*Pentateuch and Haftorahs*, p. 449).

A. Clean and Unclean Animals (chap. 11)

11:1–8. The Lord spoke directly to **Moses** (v. 1) and to **Aaron** and commanded them to present these laws to **the children of Israel** (v. 2). The first grouping covered which animals were edible and which were forbidden. The **beasts** that were acceptable for food are listed. The clean animals were the ox, sheep, goat, deer, gazelle, roe deer, wild goat, ibex, antelope, and mountain sheep, because they **parteth the hoof** (v. 3), thus were **clovenfooted**, and **cheweth cud**. The Israelites were not to eat these animals that **chew the cud** (v. 4): the camel, the **cony** (rock badger; v. 5), and the **hare** (v. 6), which **cheweth the cud, but divideth not the hoof**. A camel has a pad and does not have a cloven hoof. The **swine** (v. 7) or pig was also eliminated. These divisions give a demarcation between animals of prey and animals "of obnoxious habits from those suitable for human consumption" (*Pentateuch and Haftorahs*, p. 449). The unclean **carcase** (v. 8) was not even to be touched. The distinction between clean and unclean food was as old as the time of Noah (Gen. 7:2). These laws came down to govern the sanctity of God's holy people.

11:9–12. The second grouping has to do with water animals. Of the fish, only animals with **scales** (v. 9) could be eaten, whether they lived in the sea or in rivers. The other fish of soft skin, generally bottom dwellers, were considered scavenger animals. They were **an abomination** (v. 10) to the Jews. Because of limited water in the desert for cleaning, and because

of limited cooking with a shortage of firewood, these laws spared the Jews from eating fish that could not be properly prepared.

11:13–23. The third grouping includes the flying creatures. Both birds (vv. 13–19) and insects (vv. 20–23) are listed. Twenty species of birds are listed, including **the bat** (v. 19). Though left out of the list, clean birds that could be consumed were doves, pigeons, quail, and sparrows. Four species of flying insects, such as **locusts** (v. 22), could be for food. The prohibited birds were all part of the class denoted as birds of prey, including those that lived in the dark, swampy marshlands. Again, there is a twofold lesson here that has to do with holiness for the people but also with protection from birds that carried a greater risk of disease because of their feeding habits.

11:24–28. Touching the **carcase** (v. 24) of any animal that walked on its paws ("hands") made a person **unclean** (vv. 24, 27). The **unclean** state lasted **until the even** (vv. 24, 27–28). An example of these animals would be the cat, dog, and bear. While they may be creatures that capture their food, they are also to a large degree scavengers that may eat carrion. Germs that have a limited life span outside of the carcass of the host animal would have died off by evening. Too, the person made unclean had time to **wash his clothes** (v. 28) to remove the contamination.

11:29–47. More **unclean** (v. 29) animals are listed, such as the **weasel**, the **mouse**, and the **tortoise**. Also, the **ferret** (v. 30) and creepers such as the **chameleon** (gecko) and **lizard**, as well as the **snail** and the **mole** were unclean. These **creep** (v. 31) and are not to be touched when they are dead. If they were to **fall** on (v. 32) (possibly from a tree) or hid in any **vessel** or clothing or **sack**, the polluted items had to be rinsed off and were considered unclean **until the even**. Even the **vessel** or earthenware (v. 33) that these creatures fell into were made **unclean**, and **ye shall break it**. Any **meat** (v. 34) or **drink** that came into contact with such animals was unclean. If the **fountain** (v. 36) or **pit** they fell into was large, however, then the water was clean, though again, if anything touched the **carcase**, uncleanness followed.

If the **carcase** (v. 37) of such an animal touched **seed** about to be sown, that seed was clean, though if the water that was poured upon the seed had been contaminated by the dead **carcase** (v. 38), that water is **unclean unto you** for drinking. Even the carcasses of clean animals rendered a person who touched them **unclean** and in need of the "wash-and-wait" procedure, or the bathing and waiting **until the even** (vv. 39–40; see Lindsey, "Leviticus," p. 191). The animals that **creepeth upon the earth** (v. 41) and **upon their belly** (v. 42) were **an abomination**, and they **shall not be eaten** (v. 41).

The summary of and the reasons for such prohibitions and rules are given in verses 44–47: **For I am the LORD your God; ye shall therefore sanctify yourselves, and ye shall be holy; for I am holy** (v. 44). The Israelites were not to **defile** themselves because God brought them out of the pagan land of Egypt **to be** their **God** (v. 45). These laws were given to make a difference in how the Jews lived and survived in a very germ-ridden and hostile world. These laws separated them from pagan societies, which rarely made such distinctions. The Jews were to learn from the realm of *physical cleanliness* what God then also demanded in terms of *moral cleanliness.*

B. Purification after Childbirth (chap. 12)

12:1–5. There are marvelous protective principles in these verses, some of which may not be fully understood or appreciated today. The background is the giving of birth in a very hostile and unclean environment with limited hygiene and sanitation. While one may not fully understand these laws, cleanliness and medical protection is in view. When **a woman has conceived** (v. 2) and gives birth to a male child, she was unclean for **seven days**, plus another **three and thirty days**, thirty-three days (v. 4). When a daughter was born, a **maid child** (v. 5), the mother was unclean for **two weeks**, plus an additional **threescore and six days**. She was contagiously **unclean** as with her monthly period (15:19–24). Why is there a difference in uncleanness after the births of a male child and a female child? Some have speculated that the discharge from the womb lasts longer with a girl

than with a boy. Possibly, because a girl baby is often larger than a boy baby, the entrance of the womb was more open to infection or disease. Interestingly, the boy baby was to be **circumcised** (v. 3) on the **eighth day**, the day that vitamin K reaches it peak in the child. Medical science now knows that vitamin K wards off infection. Circumcision was for hygienic purposes, but it is a well-known fact that married women whose husbands have been circumcised have a lower rate of cervical cancer. Thus, circumcision was a great sign of physical cleanliness, but it was also a spiritual picture of the fact that Israel should be morally pure. It was also a sign of the Abrahamic covenant (Gen. 17:12).

12:6–8. Having a child was not a sin, whether male or female, as some critics have charged. Childbirth was a divine command (1:28). To make an **atonement** (v. 7) was a matter of ritual purification. After the period of purification, the woman was to bring a **lamb** (v. 6) for a **burnt offering**, although the poor could bring a **young pigeon** or a **turtledove**. The offering was to be brought **unto the door of the tabernacle, unto the priest**. These offerings were for an **atonement** (v. 8), and the woman **shall be clean**. While having children was not a sin, nevertheless, the sacrifice was a **sin offering** (vv. 6, 8) in that another child of Adam had been born, who would pass on the sin nature to another generation.

C. Laws about Skin Plagues (chap. 13)

13:1–8. In this chapter, twenty-one cases of skin aliments are mentioned (13:2, 7, 9, 12, etc.). Symptoms were to be inspected by the **priest** (v. 3) for a diagnosis. The diseased individual was to be isolated for **seven days** (v. 4) and then reexamined by the priest to see if the skin disease had been cured (v. 6). In a hot and dry germ-ridden environment with little sanitation, such skin problems were common. The symptoms were **a rising, a scab, or bright spot** (v. 2), something like **the plague of leprosy**. Leprosy was the most dreaded of infections, though some of these skin aliments may simply have looked like leprosy. Other symptoms included the hair turning **white** (v. 3) near the sore or the sore going deep into the **skin** (v. 3). The plague could **spread** (v. 5) on the skin, or the man could be cured and found clean. If the plague had not spread, he was instructed to **wash his clothes, and be** declared **clean** (v. 6). If, however, a spreading of **the scab** (v. 8) was seen, he was declared **unclean** because it was **a leprosy.**

13:9–17. In these verses, the examination of skin diseases continues with closer and more meticulous diagnoses made by the priests. Dangerous signs were **white … skin** (v. 10), the spreading of the disease (v. 12), the covering of the entire skin area with infection (v. 13), and open wounds with **raw flesh** (vv. 14–16).

13:18–28. Even where there was an indication of a past infection (v. 18) or other outward indications, the priest was called in to make an examination. Since **leprosy** (v. 20) is mentioned the most, it was considered the most serious because it could spread to others. A change in the color of a sore or in how deep the sore appeared within the skin was a worrisome sign (v. 25). Also, if a man had a sensation of burning, or **inflammation of the burning** (v. 28), on the skin, he was pronounced **unclean.**

13:29–37. More examinations are described, but this time regarding the symptoms of a **scall** (v. 34), the spreading of the **scall** (v. 36), the drastic change in color in the hair (vv. 36–37). One sign of a cure was if the hair of the individual had turned back to being **black** (v. 37). Also, it is mentioned again that the infected person was required to wash his clothes (v. 34). "What is the future of disease or illness? In the present world, death. But in the Lord's new creation, it will be done away with because of Christ's victory over the grave.… Because disease and death are incompatible with the glory of God" (Ross, *Holiness to the Lord*, p. 281).

13:38–46. A loss of **hair** (v. 40), a change in the color of the **sore** to **a white reddish** (v. 42), and the **rising of the sore** (v. 43) could all prove that leprosy was at work, and the man was **leprous** and **utterly unclean** (v. 44). A person who was declared **leprous** was to **rent** (v. 45) his clothes, **put a covering upon his upper lip, and … cry, Unclean, unclean.** The covering hanging from the upper lip was to keep spittle from falling on others, which could pass on the infection. Though such treatment seems harsh, it was a blessing in that it spared others from such a terrible disease. The leprous man was **defiled** (v. 46) and was required to live outside the camp **alone.** Until only recently, with the advent of medications, lepers had to be treated this way, with isolation. Modern medicines have changed this practice somewhat. This quarantine also symbolized the holiness of God. No unclean thing or person was to be present in the holy camp of the nation of Israel. Even in this tragedy of separation from the congregation, God was giving spiritual and moral lessons (Num. 5:1–4; Deut. 23:10–14).

13:47–59. The leprosy described in this chapter may not have been the strain of leprosy known today. There could well have been a different infection that had the symptoms normally associated with leprosy that is now dormant. Here the leprosy is described as a mold or mildew that could invade a **woollen garment** (v. 47), a **linen garment**, the **warp** (v. 48) and **woof** of the clothing, or anything made of **skin** (v. 49). The infected garment was to be isolated for **seven days** (v. 50). If the priest's examination showed that the infection was persistent, the article was finally to be burned **with fire** (v. 57). Some pieces of clothing had to be **washed the second time, and** (v. 58) then would **be clean.** These details were important to the Lord, and they were for the protection of His holy people. **This is the law of the plague of leprosy** (v. 59).

D. The Cleansing of Lepers (14:1–32)

14:1–2. These rules, regarding the cleansing of lepers, were important and were passed on to the priests directly from Moses. Sacrifice was required for the immediate cleansing of a leper. In such cases of leprosy was required an atonement, a sacrifice, to bring about cleansing. In this ceremony of cleansing from leprosy is seen the redemptive work of Christ as a sacrifice.

14:3–7. Two birds were to be taken out of the **camp** (v. 3) for sacrifice. The same ritual was used for the Day of Atonement (14:49–53). One bird was to be killed **in an earthen vessel over running water** (v. 5), and its blood **sprinkled upon him** (v. 7) that was unclean. The other bird was to be released **into the open field**. One bird was a type of substitution, and the other pictured sin (the leprosy) being taken away. The **cedar wood, and scarlet, and the hyssop** (v. 6) are not fully explained. It could be that the **cedar wood**, when burned, gave off a smell that was pleasant to the Lord. The **scarlet** (red threads or cloth) pictured sin, and the **hyssop** was used to sprinkle the blood **upon him that is to be cleansed from the leprosy** (v. 7).

14:8–20. The head of the sick was to be shaved, and he was then to wash in water. He then could return to the camp but was required to remain outside his tent for **seven days** (v. 8). On the **seventh day** (v. 9), the sick was to again wash himself and shave his head, beard, and even his **eyebrow**s. On the **eighth day** (v. 10), an offering of **two he lambs** and a **ewe without blemish** was to be made. Fine flour and a **meat offering, mingled with oil** were to be part of the ritual. The offering was made **at the door of the tabernacle of the congregation** (v. 11) as a **trespass offering** (v. 12), with the oil for a **wave offering before the LORD** (v. 12). Blood was smeared on the lobe of the **ear** (v. 14), on the **thumb** of the right hand, and on the toe of the right foot of the person to be cleansed (8:23–24). In this, the priest was making a **sin offering** (v. 19) for an **atonement** (v. 20) for the unclean. All blessings, even from illnesses, come through a redemption made by a sacrifice, all ultimately pointing to the sacrifice of the Lord Jesus Christ.

14:21–32. These verses describe the sacrifice for the **poor** (v. 21). It is similar to the sacrifice commanded and outlined in 14:10–20. The **two turtledoves, or two young pigeons** (v. 22) were used as a substitute for the lambs of the sin offering and the burnt offering. The rest of the verses are fairly repetitive of what was commanded earlier.

E. Leprosy in the House (14:33–57)

14:33–53. This section deals with the cleansing of a **house** (v. 34) infected with leprosy. The **leprosy**, or **plague,** was infectious and needed to be cleansed,

or the **house** (v. 35) was left **unclean** (v. 36). Again, **leprosy** (v. 34) here was probably a mildew or mold. While the Jews lived in tents in the desert, once in the Promised Land, they would be living in houses of **stone** or clay (v. 42; 14:24). If the plague was evident on the **walls** (v. 39), the stones had to be torn down, and the area **scraped within round about**, and the dust taken outside of the city **into an unclean place** (v. 41). If the mold returned, the walls were to be **scraped** (v. 43) and **plaistered** again. If the mold was extremely persistent (v. 44), the **house** (v. 45) was to be torn down. The resident who lived or ate in the house needed to **wash his clothes** (v. 47). If the treatment was successful and the leprosy was eradicated, the **house** (v. 48) was then purified with the ritual of the two birds (14:3–7).

14:54–57. These verses are a summary of what had been said about **the law for all manner of plague of leprosy, and scall** (v. 54). This law was given to **teach when it is unclean, and when it is clean: this is the law of leprosy** (v. 57). Two things stand out in these laws: repetition and detail. Often the Lord performed a healing and a restoration, but other times, illnesses and diseases were not cured. The individual then carried on with the ailment, or in the case of a home, it had to be destroyed to end the plague that had infected it.

F. Laws about Uncleanness (chap. 15)

15:1–15. The instructions from this divine revelation were again addressed to Moses and Aaron (v. 1). The first type of uncleanness to be addressed was **a running issue** (v. 2) or discharge that was chronic and ongoing. Many believe verses 1–2 describe the public disease of gonorrhea. The **uncleanness** (v. 3) was communicable and could infect whatever the sick one touched. Bathing and washing one's **clothes** (v. 8) were commanded. The discharge could infect even a **saddle** (v. 9). One who came in contact with the infected person was to rinse his hands, bathe, and **wash his clothes** (v. 11). Even an earthen **vessel** (v. 12) that the infected person touched had to be broken, and a wooden vessel was to be **rinsed in water**. The reason for the difference in the requirements for these vessels is not known. When and if the infected person was healed (v. 13), on the **eighth day** (v. 14), he was to offer sacrifices in the same way others have done who have been cured.

15:16–30. The husband who had a semen discharge during **copulation** (v. 16) needed to wash and was considered **unclean until the even** (vv. 16–17). The woman also needed to **bathe** (v. 18), though neither the man or the woman were required to bring a sacrifice. The woman who had **an issue** (v. 19), or flow of **blood**, had to take similar precautions as the man (vv. 20–23). A husband was not to have intercourse with his wife when she was in **her flowers** (v. 24), that is, when her menstrual period had begun. Again, blood can be a great incubator of germs. With limited hygiene and little available water, such precautions were important for health and purity. If a woman's flow was abnormally long, she was to be separated; she was **unclean** (v. 25). If the flow of blood stopped, then she was **cleansed of her issue** (v. 28) and was to count off **seven days** to make sure she was cured. On the **eighth day** (v. 29), she was to bring the sacrifices described over and over for those who had been healed, as **a sin offering** (v. 30) to make **an atonement for her before the LORD for the issue of her uncleanness**.

15:31–33. Here the Lord summarizes His instructions. Following these instructions would **separate the children of Israel from their uncleanness** (v. 31). Anyone with such chronic discharges would **defile** the tabernacle of the Lord. These laws brought hygienic principles to the Jewish people and set them far above the pagan world. The same laws also gave the nation a sense of God's holiness and of His demands that the world could never understand.

IV. The Day of Atonement and the Centrality of Worship at the Tabernacle (chaps. 16–17)

The ritual for the Day of Atonement (Yom Kippur, "the day of covering, or tenting") is spelled out in chapter 16. It is one of the most important days in the Jewish calendar. It comes in the fall, in the "seventh month" (16:29), the month of Tishri. Addi-

tional instructions are given in Exodus 30:10; Leviticus 23:26–32; 25:9; Numbers 29:7–11; see also Acts 27:9. The main reason for this day was the ceremonial cleansing of the sanctuary from the pollution brought about by the unclean worshipers (16:16, 19). This was a cleansing of "the holy place, and the tabernacle of the congregation, and the altar" (16:20). A slain goat died for the people (6:15–19), and the sin offering was completed when a live goat, in a substitutionary ritual, carried away the sins of the people into the wilderness (16:22). The Messiah would die as a substitute for sins, as prophesied in Isaiah 53. This was fulfilled in Christ (2 Cor. 5:21). In chapter 17, the significance of the blood in the sacrifices is explained.

A. The Day of Atonement (chap. 16)

16:1–10. After the death of the two sons of Aaron (v. 1), Nadab and Abihu, who had tried to sacrifice in an unauthorized way (10:1–2), the proper occasion and regulations were now given as commanded by **the LORD** (v. 1). God did not give the orders for the Day of Atonement directly to **Aaron** but gave them through **Moses** (v. 2). Aaron is not to enter into the **holy place** at just any time but only on the occasion God prescribes. He is to come into the Holy of Holies, before the **mercy seat**. At that specific time, the Lord would appear **in the cloud** (probably of incense; v. 2). A **young bullock** (v. 3) was to be presented for a **sin offering**, and a **ram** for a **burnt offering**. Before Aaron could minister as priest in the Holy Place for the people, he had to be cleansed (Heb. 5:1–3); but not so Christ, who is the believer's High Priest and Aaron's antitype (Heb. 7:26–28). Aaron had to **wash** (v. 4) and dress properly in the **holy** clothing of the high priest.

From the **congregation** (v. 5), Aaron was to take **two kids** from among the **goats** for a **sin offering** and a **ram** for a **burnt offering**. The one goat was to be killed; its blood was to be sprinkled in the Holy Place, and its body burned outside the camp (16:15, 27). The other goat was released in the **wilderness** (v. 10), symbolizing the removal of sin and guilt. This goat was the **scapegoat** (v. 8). The **bullock** (v. 6) offering was for Aaron **himself, and for his house**.

The two **kids** (v. 5) picture more than one aspect of the purging of sin. Christ made one offering of Himself and fulfilled every requirement to rid sin of its penalty against human beings. A **lot** (v. 9) was cast as to which goat would be for a **sin offering** and which one would be released into the **wilderness** (v. 10). The **scapegoat** was presented alive to the Lord **to make an atonement**. It was then let go into the **wilderness**. Sin must be punished and be removed from the presence of God.

16:11-22. The sprinkling of the blood of the **bullock** (v. 11) killed by the high priest was for his own **sin offering**. By this, the common people knew that the priests were sinners also. This ritual is like that given in 4:3-12. The difference is where the blood was to be sprinkled. Rather than being sprinkled in front of the great curtain and the incense altar (4:6-7), here it was sprinkled **with** the priest's **finger upon the mercy seat eastward ... seven times** (v. 14).

The **censer** (v. 12) full of burning coals from the altar created a cloud of smoke to prevent the priest from gazing at the Shekinah glory of God's presence over the atonement cover, thus preventing the Lord's wrath from falling on the priest (see also Exod. 30:34-36). The word *Shekinah* is the transliteration of a Hebrew word not found in scripture. It means "that which dwells," implying the presence of God, in the tabernacle or in an appearance to someone in a biblical account. The high priest had to be cleansed from the pollution of sin before he carried out his ministry to offer the **sin offering** (v. 15) for the people. The sin offering of the people had to do with the two male goats (16:5), one of which was chosen by lot to be the Lord's goat and the other to be the **scapegoat** (16:8). The selection of the goats is not mentioned here since it was explained in 16:7-8. However, the **scapegoat** is discussed again in verses 20-22.

The priest was also to make an **atonement** (v. 16) for the **holy place**. No one could go into the **tabernacle of the congregation** (Tent of Meeting) until the priest came out. The high priest acted alone, making an **atonement** (v. 17) for **his household** and **for all the congregation of Israel**. Much that has already been commanded is repeated in verses

18-21. Finally, Aaron, or some future high priest, was to place his **hands upon the head of the live goat, and confess over him all the iniquities of the children of Israel, and all their transgressions in all their sins** (v. 21). The scapegoat was then to be let loose into the wilderness, bearing **upon him all their iniquities unto a land not inhabited** (v. 22).

16:23-34. The Hebrew word for **scapegoat** (v. 26), *aza'zel*, is used in the Old Testament only in Leviticus 16. There are four views as to its meaning: (1) a reference to an "escaped goat" or to the goat that departed; (2) a reference to a proper name, *Azazel*, as a reference to the powers of evil, such as a wilderness demon or even Satan himself; (3) a term that means "rocky precipice," with some believing the goat is pushed over it to his death; (4) a totally meaningless term that has the idea of final destruction or total removal, as from the camp of the people. The actual etymology seems to be uncertain. The intent, however, cannot be ignored. The goat is bearing away the sins of the congregation into the wilderness, as clearly indicated in this chapter.

In conclusion, these commandments became **an everlasting statute** (v. 34) as an **atonement** for the nation, **for all their sins once a year**.

B. Laws about Special Sacrifices (chap. 17)

17:1-6. Outside of the environs of the tabernacle, the Jews were prohibited from making sacrifices without the official sanction and required ceremony attached to them. The **camp** (v. 3) was the larger area where the people lived in their tents by tribes. They could not simply go about offering sacrifices as they wished. The Lord had given detailed directions about how the offerings were to be administered and presented. This is made clear in verse 4. Sacrifices could not be renegade rituals. They were to be brought to the **door of the tabernacle of the congregation** (v. 4). Otherwise, the offering was an empty pursuit and only implied that blood had been shed. The offerer would be **cut off from among the people**. If, however, the intent was to butcher an animal in the field and then bring it to the **tabernacle** (v. 5) for an offering, this was acceptable. It would be

for **peace offerings unto the L**ORD (v. 5). The blood would be **sprinkle[d]** upon the altar and burned **for a sweet savour unto the L**ORD.

17:7–9. The people were further warned that they could not sacrifice **unto devils** (v. 7) as they did when they had **gone a whoring** after the pagan gods (20:5–6; Judges 2:17). The **house of Israel** (v. 8) and the **strangers** among them, those who were not Jews, could not on their own offer **a burnt offering or sacrifice** (v. 8). No one was to ritually make a sacrifice on his own and then bring it to the **door of the tabernacle** (v. 9) as an offering. Whoever did this would be **cut off from among his people**. No one wanted to be driven from the camp and have to try to survive in the hostile environment of the wilderness. The harshness of this penalty would cause many to think twice.

17:10–16. If blood were eaten or drunk, as the pagans did, God would set His face against that **soul** (v. 10), and he would also be cut off from the congregation. The reminder is given again that the life is in the blood, and it is not to be consumed as food. The **blood** (v. 11) is to be put on the altar for a sacrifice and an **atonement** for the **souls** of the people. **The blood … maketh an atonement for the soul**. Even when an animal was hunted and caught, its blood had to be poured out and covered with **dust** (v. 13). Every animal that died a natural death or was torn apart by **beasts**, or caused a fellow countryman or **stranger** who touched it to become **unclean** (v. 15). That person had to **wash his clothes** and **bathe in water**. He was **unclean until the even**, at which point he was **clean**. Dead animals corrupt quickly in a hot climate. Germs from the carcass multiply rapidly. Great care has to be taken so that disease does not spread to humans. If a Jew did not follow these important instructions, **he shall bear his iniquity** (v. 16), meaning he might be infected and become terribly ill.

V. Moral Laws Covering Incest, Honesty, Thievery, Idolatry, etc. (chaps. 18–20)

Chapter 18 sets out the important issues for the rest of Leviticus. It introduces how the entire nation of Israel is to be holy and responsible to the holy God. The nation was to be distinct, morally and spiritually, from the pagan nations surrounding it. This chapter contains specific instructions for the sanctity of marriage and the need for integrity in the family. It also prohibits illicit sexual practices found in pagan cultures and cultic prostitution, especially among the Canaanites, with whom Israel would be in contact.

In chapter 19, the basic tenants of the Ten Commandments are incorporated into the instructions, but not in the same order and often not with the same emphasis. Chapter 20 explains further the penalties for different crimes and offenses. This chapter is pointed about issues that the entire community must know and understand, especially about the punishments required for certain crimes.

A. Unlawful Sexual Relations (chap. 18)

18:1–5. The expression **I am the L**ORD **your God** (v. 2) is used five other times in this chapter (18:4–6, 21, 30) and was to serve as an incentive for keeping specific laws and commandments. A similar phrase introduces the Ten Commandments (Exod. 20:2; Deut. 5:6). The command to stay away from the sinful customs and practices of the other nations (particularly of **Egypt** and **Canaan**; v. 3) came from the fact that the Lord had a covenant relationship with the Jewish people not afforded the pagan peoples of the region. God's laws were meant to bring peace and a purpose to His redeemed people. His directives were summarized in His **judgments** and **ordinances** (v. 4). The people were **to walk therein** and **shall live in them** (v. 5).

18:6–18. Moses now gets specific about sexual sins. The Jews were not to even **approach to any that is near of kin** or **to uncover their nakedness** (v. 6). They were not to entice or go to bed with close relatives. The purpose here was to avoid promiscuity and even illicit marriages with near of kin. Also assumed is the avoidance of marriage with a non-Jew, which is forbidden in Deuteronomy 7:3–6 and 1 Kings 11:1–2. With a converted non-Israelite, such as Ruth, marriage was allowed.

The following prohibitions are listed here: a man could not have sexual relations with his **mother** (v. 7) (nor a woman with her **father**); stepmother (v. 8), **sister** (v. 9) or half sister, niece (v. 10), aunt (v. 14), daughter-in-law or stepdaughter (v. 17), or step-granddaughter (v. 17). Nor could he marry a sister-in-law, nor force and tempt her, nor take her to bed (v. 18). The moral lines in the family were to be kept straight.

18:19–23. Sex with a woman (exposing **her nakedness**; v. 19) during her period was forbidden (15:19–24; 20:18; 2 Sam. 11:4), as were relations with the **neighbour's wife** (v. 20). No one was to allow their son or daughter (**thy seed**; v. 21) to **pass through the fire to Molech. Molech** was the god of the Ammonites (1 Kings 11:7; see also 2 Kings 23:10; Jer. 32:35). Child sacrifice by burning (2 Kings 3:27) is in view here and would bring on the most severe punishment from the Lord (Lev. 20:2–5). The practice was to give a child as an offering or dedicate a child to cult prostitution by ritual fire. Homosexual relations were forbidden. **Thou shalt not lie with mankind, as with womankind: it is abomination** (v. 22). Bestiality (lying with an animal) brought defilement for a man or a woman who practiced such. **It is confusion** (v. 23); that is, it is unnatural and unclean.

18:24–30. If Israel committed these sins, they would be defiled—the same kind of impurity that was practiced by the nations that God was casting **out before you** (v. 24). If He was angry with those nations, how much more His rage against His covenant people who do the same things? By Israel's sins, the **land** (v. 25) would be **defiled**. God would **visit** their **iniquity**, and even **the land itself vomiteth out her inhabitants**. This is a warning that the Jews would be driven off the land for punishment if they violate God's ordinances. Moses later warned Israel that this was exactly what would happen. They would disobey the Lord, and He would "scatter thee among all people, from the one end of the earth to the other" (Deut. 28:64) because the Jews did not serve the Lord their God with joy and a glad heart, for the abundance of all things (Deut. 28:47).

Even the **stranger that sojourneth among you** (v. 26) was to keep the same laws, or the land would **spue** (v. 28) Israel out just as it had spued out the nations that had defiled the land before. **Whosoever** (v. 29) the **souls that commit** these things **shall be cut off from among their people. Therefore ye shall keep mine ordinance … I am the LORD your God** (v. 30).

B. Personal Conduct (chap. 19)

19:1–2. The purpose of this chapter is mentioned right up front: **Ye shall be holy: for I the LORD your God am holy** (v. 2). This was addressed to **all the congregation**. Personal ethics and morality are tied ultimately to the unchanging nature and holiness of God. All demands on human beings have a theological orientation.

19:3–4. The Jews were instructed to **fear** (v. 3), or honor, their **mother** and **father**, and to **keep my sabbaths**, because **I am the LORD your God**. It is interesting that honoring one's parents and keeping the Sabbath are mentioned together in the same verse. The apostle Paul reminded the Ephesians that the command to honor one's parents was the only command with a promise of long life on the earth (Eph. 6:3; Exod. 20:12; Deut. 5:16).

19:5–10. Moses repeats the warning (7:15–20) that meat used for the **peace offering** (fellowship offering; v. 5) must be consumed by the second day, or it must be **burnt in the fire** on the **third day** (v. 6). The reason for this is obvious: the meat would spoil and be contaminated. The spoiled meat **is abominable; it shall not be accepted** (v. 7). Anyone eating such meat **hath profaned the hallowed thing of the LORD** (v. 8) and would be **cut off from among his people**. From a modern perspective, such a prohibition seems harsh; but for an ancient people, such laws spared lives. The laws also gave invaluable lessons about God's holy demands. Spiritual lessons accompanied practical lessons.

When harvesting crops, such as grapes, the fallen fruit was to be left for the poor and the **stranger** (v. 10), the foreigner in the land who probably had no acreage. This was the Lord's way of providing for those less fortunate. The corners of the field were not to be wholly reaped.

19:11-18. Living in harmony with one's **neighbour** (v. 13) was important. It would be one of the signs of the critical cohesion required of Israel as a theocracy that followed the commands of the Lord. One should not **steal** (v. 11) from, or **deal falsely** with, his neighbour, nor **lie one to another**, nor give false oaths and **swear** (v. 12) by the name of God. This was profaning His name and His character. A **neighbour** (v. 13) was not to be defrauded or robbed, and the **wages** promised for labor were to be paid in the evening when the work was done. The **deaf** (v. 14) were not to be cursed, and a **stumblingblock** was not to be placed in a path where the **blind** might walk. Such helpless people were to be cared for because of a high view of God. The Jews were to **fear thy God: I am the LORD**. Justice was not to be subverted. Both the **poor** (v. 15) and the **mighty** were to be treated equally. **In righteousness shalt thou judge thy neighbour**. One was not to circulate the words of a **talebearer** (v. 16) or **hate thy brother** (v. 17), nor **rebuke thy neighbour, or suffer sin upon him,** or allow him to be treated unjustly. The Israelites were not to inflict vengeance or carry grudges against any of the **children of thy people, but thou shalt love thy neighbour as thyself: I am the LORD** (v. 18). The Lord is not calling here for self-love in the psychological sense but for treating one's neighbor as one would wish to be treated. No limits should be placed on caring for one's neighbor; instead, a person should love doing an abundance of good for his neighbor as he does for himself (Matt. 22:39; Mark 12:31; Luke 10:27; Rom. 13:9; Gal. 5:14).

19:19-25. A reminder is given here: **keep my statutes** (v. 19). Diverse breeds of cattle were not to be mixed, neither were various kinds of seed to be **mingled, neither shall a garment mingled of linen and woolen come upon thee**. Such mixing often weakens the line, or in the case of cloth, weakens the weave of the garment. While these may seem to be small or unimportant matters, they were issues that could weaken the productivity and economic strength of the nation. God cares for the small things as well as the large.

A man who committed adultery with another man's wife was to be put to death (20:10), but if he slept with a slave girl, a **bondmaid** (v. 20), the death penalty was not required, because she was still a slave and had not been ransomed or **redeemed** from her slavery, **nor freedom given her**. She was to be **scourged** as a warning, but the two would **not be put to death, because she was not free**. In other words, there is a question as to whether she was coerced and unable to resist the sexual advances. The man was to bring a **trespass offering unto the LORD** (v. 21) for the sin, and it would be forgiven him. An offering was not required of the **bondmaid** (v. 20) since she was, at least to a degree, helpless in the matter. Though the man was guilty of sin, the slave girl was not legally free, and while she may have been **betrothed**, she was not married.

19:23-25. When the Jews entered the Promised Land and planted **trees** (v. 23), they were not to partake of the **fruit** for **three years**, to allow the trees to flourish and not be harvested too early. The trees were to be considered **young** and **uncircumcised**, and the fruit was not to be eaten. In the **fourth year** (v. 24), the crops **shall be holy to praise the LORD withal**. The firstfruit law included crops (Exod. 23:19; Lev. 23:10; Deut. 26:1-15), animals (Exod. 34:19-20), and children (Exod. 13:2; Num. 8:16-18). In this way, the children of Israel were made to realize that everything pertaining to the people belonged to the Lord.

19:26-34. The prohibitions in these verses appear to have in mind the pagan religious customs, which were to be avoided. This included certain mourning rites (vv. 27-28) and cult religious prostitution (v. 29), in contrast to how **the LORD** (v. 30) was to be worshiped. Also prohibited were necromancy and the worship of **familiar spirits** (v. 31). Israel was not to seek advice from witches and warlocks (**wizards**). The Jews would be **defiled** by them. These verses give hints of how prevalent such practices were. Such prohibitions set the nation of Israel in contrast to the other peoples of the world.

Because the Jews had been strangers and slaves in Egypt, they were not to **vex** (v. 33) or trouble the foreigner or **stranger** (v. 34) who sojourned in their midst. He was to be treated **as one born among you**. He was to be loved **as thyself**, because **ye were strangers in the land of Egypt**. Again the reminder, **I am the LORD your God**.

19:35–37. Regarding weights, balances, and measurements, the Jews were not to do any **unrighteousness in judgment** (v. 35). They were to use **just** (v. 36) measures in the marketplace. Many other passages speak to the issue of fairness in economic dealings (Deut. 25:13–16; Prov. 11:1; 16:11; 20:10, 23; Amos 8:5). Verse 37 is a summary, similar to 18:4, 30.

C. Punishments for Sin (chap. 20)

Except for verses 19–21, this chapter deals with crimes that carried the death penalty. Though appearing to be harsh, these laws were necessary for preventing moral infection from destroying the community life of God's people. It is foolish to argue against deterrence of crime with such laws. They did hold in check the evil intentions of the criminal and of those who flirted with the evil of false religions that brought cruelty to its victims. The death sentence was generally carried out by stoning.

20:1–6. No one was to give his children, his **seed** (v. 2), to the worship of Molech. God said, **I will set my face against that man** (v. 3), and he would be cut off from the people. The Lord's **sanctuary** would be defiled, and His **holy name** profaned. If the people did not turn against the man, **and kill[ed] him not,** the Lord Himself would turn against him and against his family, and against all **that go a whoring after him, to commit whoredom with Molech** (v. 5). The soul that followed after the evildoer would also be **cut off from** the **people** (v. 6) by the Lord.

20:7–8. The Jews were to see themselves as a holy people. The Lord told them, **sanctify yourselves … keep my statutes, and do them.**

20:9–21. Death was the sentence for the man who **curseth his father or his mother** (v. 9). He would surely be put to death. Verses 10–21 are very similar to 18:6–20. These laws are repeated here because of

their importance to the sexual purity of the nation. However, the penalty in verses 19–21 is not clear.

20:22–27. Verses 22–24 are similar to those in 18:24–30, except for the mention of the blessings of the land **that floweth with milk and honey** (v. 24). God has given them the land **to possess it**, and He has separated Israel **from other people**.

Verses 25–27 are a summary of the law of clean and unclean animals. The **souls** (v. 25) of those who violate the Lord's rules about handling unclean animals for food or for sacrifice would be made **abominable**. The reason is repeated: **And ye shall be holy unto me: for I the LORD am holy** (v. 26). The chapter ends with a reminder about the danger of those having **a familiar spirit** (v. 27). They are to be put to death by stoning.

VI. Regulations for the Priests, the Offerings, and the Annual Feasts (21:1–24:9)

While some of the regulations presented here are similar to what has already been given, there are some differences and additions. Chapters 21–22 focus on the holiness of the priesthood. If it is important that the nation sees itself as holy, how much more important for the priests who stand and minister before the Lord at the altar (21:1–9). This is especially true of the high priest, who mediates between Israel and God (21:10–15). Chapter 23 looks at the various feasts of the Lord (see chart, *KJV Study Bible*, pp. 166–67), and 24:1–9 gives the commands concerning the use of the oil for the shewbread.

A. The Sanctity of the Priesthood (21:1–22:16)

21:1–9. Most of these verses contain instructions on the proper conduct for the priests. The priests were to set an example morally for the entire congregation of Israel. Like the common people, the priests were not to touch a **dead** body (v. 1; Num. 19:11) or enter a home where one had died (Num. 19:14), except in the case of the death of **kin** (v. 2) that is **near unto him.** (The exception for "touching" had to do with Nadab and Abihu, who died because of God's judgment against them.) The priest was not to **defile**

himself (v. 4), because he was **a chief man among his people**. The priests were to avoid pagan mourning customs, such as shaving their heads and the **corner of their beard, nor make any cuttings in their flesh** (v. 5), such as tattoos or slash marks; rather, **They shall be holy unto their God** (v. 6). Because they offered the ceremonial bread of the Lord, they were not to take a **whore** (v. 7) for a wife, nor a woman who was **put away from her husband** because of some kind of disease or indecency (Deut. 24:1–2). They were to remain sanctified, **for I the Lord, which sanctify you, am holy** (v. 8). A daughter of a priest was not to play the harlot; she would **profaneth her father** (v. 9). This prostitution may be cultic or at a pagan shrine. **She shall be burnt with fire**.

21:10–12. Here a higher standard is established for the priesthood. The high priest had received the **anointing oil** (v. 10) upon his head and had been **consecrated** to put on the priestly **garments**. Therefore, his head was never to be **uncover[ed]**, nor was he to **rend his clothes** in sorrow. He was to show that God is sovereign and rules over all of the disasters of life. The high priest was not to go out of the **sanctuary** (v. 12) even for a family funeral, nor leave it for frivolous purposes, because when officiating, he had **the crown of the anointing oil of his God … upon him**.

21:13–15. The high priest was to take a **wife in her virginity** (v. 13) **… of his own people** (v. 14). He was not to marry a **widow**, a **divorced woman**, or a **harlot**. Some argue that this was to ensure that any children born were his own. The first male child was potentially the next high priest. This rule guaranteed the priestly lineage. The priest was to remain pure and not be promiscuous, **for I the Lord do sanctify him** (v. 15).

21:16–24. The priest was not to have even a noticeable physical **blemish** (v. 17). A priest with a physical blemish was not to **approach to offer the bread of his God**. He was not to have outward physical limitations, such as blindness, lameness, a **flat nose, or any thing superfluous** (v. 18). Nor was he to have a broken limb (v. 19) or a deformation in the groin area (**stones broken**; v. 20). No man of the

seed of Aaron (v. 21) who had such physical deformities was to **offer the offerings of the Lord made by fire**, though he could **eat the bread of his God, both of the most holy, and of the holy** (v. 22). The Lord still had mercy on such an afflicted priest; he was able to participate in the priests' portions of the offerings. Yet he could not go into the Holy Place beyond the **vail** and come near the **altar** because of his blemish. He would be profaning the **sanctuaries. For I the Lord do sanctify them** (v. 23). These are the Lord's commands to be heeded by Aaron, his sons, and **all the children of Israel** (v. 24).

22:1–9. The instructions continue and are almost redundant. The Lord wanted to make sure the priests understood their limits. They were not to **profane** (v. 2) God's **holy name … I am the Lord**. Aaron's future seed **among your generations** (v. 3) was to keep God's **holy things … hallow** and not pollute them with their **uncleanness**. Again, **I am the Lord**. No priest could officiate who had become unclean as a **leper** (v. 4), or who had a **running issue** (discharge), or who had touched anything made **unclean by the dead**. He was not to touch **any creeping thing** (v. 5) or touch a man who might infect him. If the priest did, he had to **wash** (v. 6) with **water** and was considered **unclean** until the **sun is down** (v. 7). Then he could eat of the **holy food** (v. 7). Here again is another reminder not to eat an animal that had died of natural causes or had been torn apart by other animals (v. 8; 17:15). The priest who flagrantly violated these laws could lose his life (v. 9).

22:10–16. No foreigner, passerby, or **hired** (v. 10) servant was to eat of the **holy** food. However, if the **soul** (v. 11), or servant, had been purchased by the priest and had become part of his household, he could partake of the priest's **meat**. If the priest's daughter married **a stranger** (v. 12), better translated "a man," she was no longer in her father's house and could not eat of the food taken for the priests. If the daughter had fallen on hard times, she could come home and eat of **her father's meat** (v. 13). If a man **unwittingly** (v. 14), or unknowingly, picked up **holy** food meant for the priests and partook, he had to return a **fifth part** of the offering back to the priests for their sustenance. The priests were responsible for enforcing these rules so that the **holy things** (v. 15) would not be **profane[d]**. They were not to allow these laws to be broken; they could not let the offenders **bear the iniquity of trespass, when they** (the common people) **eat their holy things: for I the LORD do sanctify them** (v. 16).

B. Sacrifices of Blemished Animals (22:17–33)

22:17–25. The issue of blemished animals is repeated over and over. No one in the **house of Israel** (v. 18), nor a **stranger**, a Gentile dwelling in their midst, could bring a blemished offering to the Lord **for a burnt offering** (v. 18). This included **beeves** (chunks of beef; v. 19), **sheep**, and **goats**. Always, the animals had to be **without** blemish, then they were **acceptable for you** (v. 20). The animals had to **be perfect to be accepted** (v. 21). This rule included **peace offerings** and **freewill offering[s]**. When used as an **offering by fire unto the LORD** (v. 22) ... **upon the altar**, the animals were not to be deformed in any way or have a **wen** (a tumor) or **scurvy** or be **scabbed**. **It shall not be accepted** (v. 23). If the animal's testicles were **bruised, crushed**, or **broken** (v. 24) in any way, it could not be sacrificed as an offering anywhere **in your land**. Even the sacrifices from a **stranger's hand** (v. 25), even a sacrifice of **bread**, could not be accepted because he was not part of the nation, and his **corruption** was in him. "The sacrifices had to be physically perfect because they point to the moral perfections of Christ," and to His holy nature as well (Unger, *Commentary*, p. 172).

22:26–33. Young sacrificial animals (**under the dam**; v. 27) were to be observed for **seven days**, and after that, they could be accepted for **an offering made by fire unto the LORD.** A **cow** (v. 28) and her young were not to be killed on the same day. When a **sacrifice of thanksgiving** (v. 29) was offered, it had to be eaten that **same day** (v. 30), with none left over for the next day. This was meant not only to prevent spoilage but also to keep the Jews from seeing such sacrifices as "leftovers" to be consumed at will. All of these laws were to be honored without argument.

Therefore shall ye keep my commandments, and do them: I am the LORD (v. 31). God's name is not to be **profane[d]** (v. 32). It is **hallow**, or holy. The Lord brought the Israelites out of the **land of Egypt** (v. 33) to be their God.

C. Feasts of the Lord (chap. 23)

23:1–4. Here the Lord instructs His people to put into their calendar important national holidays and sacrificial feast days. These are the appointed **feasts** (v. 2), which are **holy convocations**. The first one is the **sabbath of rest** (v. 3) following **six days** of work. The **sabbath** remembers the Lord ceasing His creation activity. The seventh day is sanctified and holy because "in it he rested from all his work which God had created and made" (Gen. 2:1–3). This special day is incorporated into the holy convocations that are part of the law code for Israel (Exod. 16:23; 20:8–11). The Sabbath also recalled the Lord's redemption of the Israelites from Egyptian bondage (Deut. 5:15; Lev. 23:43).

23:5–8. The **LORD's passover** (v. 5) was to be observed on the **fourteenth day** of the **first month** of Abib, later named Nisan. It commemorated the nation's fleeing Egypt (Deut. 16:1–7) and the offering of the passover lamb (Exod. 12:1–13:10). Passover was held again at Sinai (Num. 9:1–5) but was not celebrated again until the Jews camped at Gilgal, across the Jordan River in the land promised to them (Josh. 5:10–12).

The **feast of unleavened bread** (v. 6) followed on the next day, the **fifteenth day**. No work was to be done and an **offering** (v. 8) was to be made for seven days. Unleavened bread pictures the holiness of the Lord Jesus, who is the "bread of life" (John 6:48–58). He is also "our passover" (1 Cor. 5:7) and the Lamb of God who brings redemption (John 1:36).

23:9–14. These verses seem to indicate another harvest festival, though they are often connected to the Feast of Unleavened Bread. This was barley grain, according to Unger (p. 173), of the firstfruits (first crops, v. 10) of the barley harvest before the Lord. A burnt offering of a **lamb without blemish** (v. 12) was to follow, and a **meat** (v. 13), or meal, **offering** burned upon the fire also was to take place **for a**

sweet savour, along with a **drink offering** of **wine, the fourth part of a hin**. (A hin was about one and a half gallons.) No **bread** (v. 14) or grain was to be eaten until the ceremony of the unleavened bread offering was complete. This period would be celebrated as **a statute for ever throughout your generations**.

23:15-22. The **new meat** (meal) **offering** (v. 16) became known as the Feast of Weeks (Num. 28:26; Deut. 16:10) and later as Pentecost (Greek, *pentekoste*; "fifty") in the New Testament. It was remembered for seven weeks plus one day (fifty days) after the harvest (Exod. 23:16; 34:22) and "the day of firstfruits" (Num. 28:26). It was the early-summer celebration of God's blessing of agriculture at the completion of the wheat harvest (Exod. 34:22). It pictured the sustaining of His people with harvest goodness. More animals were to be sacrificed as well for **peace offerings** (v. 19). Portions of the lambs were to be waved with **the bread of the firstfruits for a wave offering before the LORD** (v. 20). When the **harvest** (v. 22) was **reaped**, the people were not to **make clean riddance** of the corners of their fields. The leftover grain was for the poor and the **stranger**, the Gentile, in their midst who had no property. This was to show that everyone was to be blessed by God's sovereign provision and that this should be remembered by all.

23:23-32. The **day of atonement** (v. 27) falls in September or October, in the Jewish month of Tishri (see 16:1-34). It marked the end of the harvest period just before the two rainy seasons began, late fall and winter. This month marked the beginning of the new year in the Jewish civil calendar as calculated later in the postexilic period. Seven **trumpets** (v. 24) were to be sounded on the first day of the seventh month as a **sabbath** rest. Special offerings were to be brought before the Lord (Num. 29:1-6). God would **destroy from among his people** (v. 30) anyone who violated this day by working. **No manner of work** (v. 31) was to be done. This is the most holy day for all of Israel.

23:33-44. The word "tabernacles" refers to the booths or tents the Jews dwelt in when they came out of Egypt. The **feast of tabernacles** was "maybe the most important and joyful of the feasts at the last of the Jewish new year (*Unger's Commentary*, p. 174). It lasted

seven days. Sometimes called the Feast of Ingathering (Exod. 34:22; Deut. 16:13-15), it was an agricultural feast that finalized the fall **fruit** (v. 39) harvest. This festival was also meant to remind the Jews that they had rest when the Lord brought them up out of **Egypt** (v. 43). They sat down and rested in the shade of a covering made with tree branches or **boughs** (v. 40), in which they made a **booth[s]** (v. 42), or a lean-to (a *sukkah*), after their arduous journey from the land of the pharaohs (Deut. 31:13; Neh. 8:13-17). The good news preached to us about Christ now gives rest by faith; He is also now a Sabbath rest for the people of God (Heb. 4:1-10). These are the most important **feasts of the LORD** (v. 44) declared by Moses.

D. The Oil and the Shewbread (24:1-9)

24:1-4. The two most important objects in the Tent of Meeting, or the "holy place," were the seven **lamps** (v. 2), or seven lamp bowls, that continually burned with oil on the menorah, the **pure** golden **candlestick** (v. 4), or lampstand. **Pure oil** (v. 2) was to be **beaten** out of the fruit of the **olive** trees. The continual burning is a picture of Christ, who causes His own "to receive light and life daily through the Spirit in order to manifest it to a sin-darkened world (Matt. 5:14-16; 1 John 2:27)" (Unger, *Commentary*, p. 175).

24:5-9. The shewbread was made with **fine flour** (v. 5) and formed into **twelve cakes**. A measure of **two tenth deals** made one cake. The deal was probably an ephah, or roughly four quarts per cake. They were to be laid in **two rows, six on a row** (v. 6). They represented a **memorial** (v. 7) to the **everlasting covenant** (v. 8) the Lord had made with Israel. This bread was also called "the bread of the Presence" (Exod. 25:30), picturing God dwelling with His people. **Pure frankincense** (v. 7) was also placed on the table **upon each row** as a smell of acceptance by the Lord. Every Sabbath, the old bread was replaced with the new and was given to the priests as their portion, to be consumed at the week's end. The priests' portion was probably placed in small receptacles alongside the rows of bread. The **holy** (v. 9) bowls of oil were weekly **offerings of the LORD made by fire by a perpetual statute**.

VII. Punishment for Blasphemy, Murder, etc. (24:10–23)

Several issues are covered in this section. The two crimes that stand out, which were seen as equally heinous before God and before the congregation of Israel, are blasphemy against the Lord (24:10–16) and murder (24:17–23), though the killing of an animal was also serious, with restitution ordered for the offender. To curse God is a grievous sin. His name is holy, and the one who takes His name lightly was to be put to death (24:16).

24:10–16. Moses begins this section with an illustration about cursing the name of the Lord. A man whose mother was Jewish and whose father was an Egyptian **strove** (v. 10), or fought with, a full Israelite **in the camp**. The man who was part Jewish **blasphemed the name of the Lord, and cursed** (v. 11). The name of the man's mother was **Shelomith**, the daughter of **Dibri, of the tribe of Dan**. The man was **put ... in ward** (v. 12), or confined, so that **Moses** could wait for a distinct revelation of God concerning the issue (compare Num. 9:6–14; 15:32–36; 27:1–11). This person was only partly Jewish. Should he be held to the same standard concerning blasphemy as a full Jew, since he had cursed the covenant name of God, Yahweh? Moses received his answer.

The man was taken outside the **camp** (v. 14), and the people who had heard him curse placed their hands on his head, indicating that he would bear his own guilt and sin. He was then **stone[d]** (v. 16) by the congregation. This penalty was because he **blasphemeth the name of the Lord. Whosoever curseth his God shall bear his sin** (v. 15). To blaspheme the name of God was more than simply mentioning His name. It was a vile oath made toward His name and His person. It was a form of mocking God and His providence.

24:17–23. Anyone who killed another person was to be **put to death** (v. 17). Even killing another man's **beast** (v. 18) required costly restitution to **make it good; beast for beast**. Harming a **neighbour** (v. 19) by wounding him or causing **a blemish** required reciprocal measures. **As he hath done, so shall it be done to him**, with **breach for breach, eye for eye, tooth for tooth: as he hath caused a blem-**ish in a man, so shall it be done to him again (v. 20; Exod. 21:23–25; Deut. 19:21). If this is to be taken literally, it is a harsh retribution for injuring someone. Such countermeasures would certainly deter physical maiming and wounding. It would make a violent man think twice before attacking or hurting someone. However, some have taken this as hyperbole, or exaggeration, with the Lord saying that one who has injured someone else must pay back or restore in like kind, with the punishment gauged by the offense. Such heavy laws are "an expression of the Lord's grace to men, for by it He draws a fence around their lives to protect them from violence and death" (Unger, *Commentary*, p. 176).

If someone killed an animal, restitution was to be paid (v. 21). The same **law** (v. 22) was required both for the **stranger**, the outsider or the Gentile, and **for one of your own country**. God is fair. He is **the Lord your God**. Moses summarizes with the reminder that cursing the Lord brings on the death penalty by stoning, even for the **children of Israel** (v. 23).

VIII. The Sabbath Year, the Year of Jubilee, Land Tenure, and Reform of Slavery (chap. 25)

The first part of this chapter (25:1–7) deals with the sabbatical year for the land. The remaining verses spell out what is called the Year of Jubilee, which was meant to relieve those who had incurred heavy debts in their agricultural dealings. There are various rules that could be required to bring about land redemption. The same principles might be applicable to set free a Jewish farmer from slavery so that he might go back to working his land (25:41, 48–55). Another description of this chapter might be, "giving a person a second chance in financial matters in order to recover" from difficult economic situations.

25:1–7. The land needed a **sabbath** (v. 2) rest, just as people did. It was to be worked for six years and then rested in the seventh year. This is a Sabbath for human beings as well as for the land. It was seen as a rest, **a sabbath for the Lord** (v. 4). Both the people and the land belong to Him. (An additional proposal for the Sabbath year is given in Deut. 15:1–18, which included the canceling of all debts and the freeing of slaves; see also Exod. 21:2–6.) A **sabbath of the land** (v. 6) was a blessed event because the earth provides food for all. It was also a blessing for the **cattle** (v. 7) and the **beast ... in thy land**.

25:8–22. Every seventh sabbatical year (every forty-ninth year; v. 8) there was to be the **jubile** (*yobel*; v. 10), or the blowing of the ram's horn. This indicated a release from bondage. The **fiftieth year** (v. 10) was to be **hallow[ed]**, or holy, and in this year, **every man** was to be given back what he previously possessed, and **every man** who had enslaved himself for economic survival was to be returned **unto his family**. The shout was to **proclaim liberty** (v. 10) throughout all the land unto everyone. No work was to be done on that day (v. 11). It was a **holy** (v. 12) day. If a man needed to sell land, the price was to be fairly negotiated based on the number of years since the **jubile** (v. 15). The blessings that God brought about came when the people were obedient to His laws. Their obedience brought plenty at harvest time and freedom from war (v. 19; 26:3–13; Deut. 28:1–14). Some Israelites would be afraid that they could not forego planting in the seventh year and would cry out, **What shall we eat the seventh year?** (v. 20). But God would reward Israel with extra **blessing[s]** (v. 21). He said, **And ye shall sow the eighth year, and eat yet of old fruit until the ninth year; until her fruits come in ye shall eat of the old store** (v. 22). In other words, the Lord would reward their faithfulness to what He said by granting extra crops just before the sixth year ended.

25:23–34. The land was never to **be sold** (v. 23) in a final sense, because it belonged to the Lord. The Jews were to **grant a redemption for the land** (v. 24). For example, if a Jew was impoverished and had sold his land as a result, a relative (a *go'el*) was to **redeem** (v. 26), or buy back, the land from the one who bought it (Ruth 3:12–4:6; Jer. 32:7–12). The man could also simply redeem it himself, the value determined by referring to the Jubilee date (Lev. 25:16, 50–53).

"The Jubilee release did not apply to **a house in a walled city** (v. 29), and one could not redeem more

than a year after its sale" (Lindsey, "Leviticus," p. 211). It could not apply to the Levitical priesthood, who always had the right from the Lord to redeem their town property. This was covered in the release of the Jubilee.

25:35–38. If someone had fallen on hard times, **fallen in decay** (v. 35), whether an Israelite or a stranger, he is to be relieved, **that he may live with thee**. No excessive interest was to be charged, **usury** (v. 36), or unfair **increase**, but God was to be feared in this matter (v. 36). The one who was poor or struggling economically was not to be tempted with **money** (v. 37) that would build up **usury**, nor was he to be given loans with goods (**victuals**) that would bring about an increase of his debt. The Israelites were to be gracious because God was gracious in bringing them out of **the land of Egypt** (v. 38) to give them **the land of Canaan**.

25:39–55. While slavery was allowed in the Old Testament, there were guidelines that protected even pagan slaves, such as the Sabbath rest (Exod. 20:10; Deut. 5:14) and the rule that they were not to be mistreated (Exod. 21:20–21). The Israelites could not be enslaved to any other master (v. 55). A poor Hebrew, however, could indenture himself temporarily, which was a much better policy than the debtors' prisons of the nineteenth century.

A Jewish slave was to be treated as a hired hand (v. 43) and released during the Year of Jubilee. Gentile slaves were slaves for life and could be willed to one's inheritants (vv. 44–46). No matter how he was purchased, a Hebrew slave could be redeemed through laws similar to the laws of "redemption" (25:23–28). A near kinsman could also redeem a slave by paying owed debts (vv. 48–49), or if the slave had become able financially, he could redeem himself. Whichever, he would be redeemed during the Year of Jubilee. The Year of Jubilee is not mentioned anywhere outside of the Pentateuch, though it must have played a major role in the early stages of the nation of Israel.

IX. Blessings and Curses for Covenant Obedience and Disobedience (chap. 26)

Some have argued that the first part of chapter 26 is like a vassal treaty in the ancient Middle Eastern world, in which a blessing is pronounced for obedience. Other chapters in the Torah (and in the book of Joshua) do the same (Exod. 23:22–33; Deut. 28; Josh. 24:20). Judgment would follow, however, if the nation did not obey and hearken to the Lord's commands. The law is meant to rein in a people who had forgotten their heritage and who had been slaves in a very pagan environment in Egypt. Through the law, God was bringing the nation to certain spiritual truths, and He was also hedging them in and giving them protection by what He commanded. The Jews would fail because it is the nature of the human heart to rebel rather than to humble oneself under the laws of the Lord and under His grace.

A. The Blessings for Obedience (26:1–13)

26:1–2. Here the Lord sets forth the solemn warning against idolatry (v. 1; Exod. 20:1–7) and desecration of the **sabbath[s]** (v. 2). The Jews would be violating the "quintessential stamp of the Mosaic Covenant and the sign between the Lord and His people Israel (Exod. 31:12–17)" (Unger, *Commentary*, p. 177). They would also be dishonoring the **sanctuary** (v. 2), the tabernacle, and all it prefigures concerning God's grace and the foreshadowing of the work of Christ on the cross.

26:3–9. If the Israelites kept the Lord's **statutes** and **commandments** (v. 3), He would send the **rain** (v. 4) and bring **increase** to the land and the trees that yield its **fruit** in blessing. The **threshing** of the grain would be blessed, and **ye shall eat your bread to the full, and dwell in your land safely** (v. 5), with **peace** (v. 6) and with the **evil beasts** subdued. **The sword** would not **go through** their **land. Five** (v. 8) Jews would chase a **hundred** of the enemy, or a hundred Jews would chase **ten thousand** of the enemy from the land; the enemies would fall by the **sword**. The Lord would **have respect** (v. 9) for His people (Exod. 2:25) and would cause them to be **fruitful** and to **multiply** (Gen. 17:6–7; Ps. 107:38), establishing His covenant with them.

26:10–13. The ultimate covenant mentioned is the Abrahamic covenant (Gen. 17:7–8). Specifically, the laws are tied to the Mosaic covenant, which is set forth overall in Leviticus. God's continued presence in the middle of His people was manifested in His glory in the **tabernacle** (v. 11). He promises them, **I will walk among you, and will be your God, and ye shall be my people** (v. 12). He reminds them again that they were slaves in Egypt whom He brought out from bondage (25:55) and made them **go upright** (v. 13).

B. The Punishments for Disobedience (26:14–46)

26:14–15. If the Israelites broke the Lord's **commandments** (v. 14) and **covenant** (v. 15), however, there would be a price to pay. A breach of the covenant was the same as open rebellion against His statutes and precepts. At the end of the forty-year period of wandering in the wilderness, Moses would prophesy to the new generation, about to enter the Promised Land, that they would indeed do this. They would rebel and eventually be driven to all nations of the earth (Deut. 28), though a future restoration is assured for a far-off day (Deut. 30).

26:16–26. If God was not obeyed, He would **appoint** (v. 16) over His people **terror**, physical ailments, **sorrow of heart**, lack of productivity, with their enemies consuming their food production. As a king who shows disapproval toward a faithless servant, God would set His face against them with displeasure and cause them to **be slain** (v. 17) by their **enemies**. They would be punished **seven times more** (v. 18) for their sins; the Lord would break their **pride** (v. 19) in their **power**. He would bring natural disaster and drought by making their **heaven as iron, and** their **earth as brass,** with heat. Their **strength** (v. 20) would wane and the land would no longer yield its **fruits.**

Plagues (v. 21) would follow, and the **wild beasts** (v. 22) would roam freely and bring havoc upon the Israelites' **children** and their **cattle**. The Israelite population would be reduced, all because of their sin. If the Lord's people were under such heavy discipline because of their hostility toward Him, He would bring a sword of vengeance on the nation (Judg. 2:11–15) because they broke His covenant. A divinely sent **pestilence** (v. 25) would come, and they would be **delivered into the hand of the enemy**. Famine would follow, with scarcity of grain and with **bread** (v. 26) being weighed out for survival. They would **eat, and not be satisfied**.

26:27 – 39. God's anger would be great against His people (vv. 27 – 28), and they would be chastened. When the curse fell, even cannibalism would follow (v. 29; Deut. 28:49 – 57). This happened when Ben-hadad, king of Aram, invaded Samaria. Mothers were eating their own children (2 Kings 6:24 – 29). This was repeated at the destruction of Jerusalem by the Romans in AD 70. Moses reminded the people that the **cities** (v. 31) and **sanctuaries** would be destroyed and that the people would be dispersed **among the heathen** (v. 33). When they would be driven off the land, the land would rest with a **sabbath** (v. 34), probably implying that when they settled down in the land, they would mistreat it. Even the land needed the rest God had commanded for it.

A great fear would come upon the Lord's people, causing them to **flee** (v. 36) even when not pursued. They would **have no power to stand before** their **enemies** (v. 37). They would **perish among the heathen, and the land of your enemies shall eat you up** (v. 38). Those who survived in the **enemies' lands** would **pine away in their iniquity** (v. 39). They would also be punished with the **iniquities of their fathers**. The entire nation would suffer for not listening to the Lord.

26:40 – 45. If, however, the people would **confess** (v. 40) their sins and the **iniquity** of their **fathers**, and confess that they walked **contrary** with the Lord, and were **humbled** (v. 41) in **their uncircumcised hearts**, God would remember His **covenant** (v. 42) with Jacob, Isaac, and Abraham and would **remember the land** again. Despite their sins and how they mistreated the land, God would **not cast them away, neither will I abhor them, to destroy them utterly, and to break my covenant with them: for I am the LORD their God** (v. 44). Though they would someday be driven off the land for overworking it, as well as for their sins, God would not forsake them, nor break His promises with them. He would remember the **covenant of their ancestors** (v. 45) when He

brought them up out of the land of Egypt. He would again be their God.

26:46. For the time being, the children of Israel were to obey the Lord's **statues and judgments and laws**, which He gave at **mount Sinai by the hand of Moses**. Later, as divine discipline for their rebelliousness, the Lord would bring numerous deportations and dispersions on His people. Restoration is certain, culminating in the millennial kingdom with the second coming of Christ (Amos 9:11 – 15; Rom. 11:25 – 27).

X. Regulations for Offerings Vowed to the Lord (chap. 27)

This final chapter deals with the subject of **vows**. It seems to relate to the preceding chapter in that people are more likely to make rash vows in moments of terrible distress. Rash vows are prohibited in the Old Testament (Deut. 23:21 – 23; Prov. 20:25; Eccl. 5:4 – 5). The issue of inflated vows, false promises, gifts, and tithes for the tabernacle are very closely connected and so are rightly mentioned together in this last chapter.

27:1 – 8. A **singular vow** (v. 2), or a distinctive personal vow, was to be set by Moses and the later high priests. Such a vow was an offer to minister and serve the Lord, but it was to be accompanied by reasonable guidelines rather than an emotional outburst of dedication that had no basis in one's ability to carry it out. The vow, or pledge, could be made by one who was between **twenty years old** (v. 3) and **sixty years old**. For service, the offerer could sustitute money in the vow and **shekels of silver, after the shekel of the sanctuary**. Guidelines on how to evaluate the service rendered are spelled out in verses 5 – 7. For someone presenting himself **before the priest** (v. 8) for service, his **value** must be **according to his ability that vowed** thus **shall the priest value him**.

27:9 – 15. Specific guidelines regarding vows to give an animal to the Lord also had to be drawn. The priests needed to determine if the animal was acceptable for an offering or not. Nothing dedicated to the Lord was to be regretted. It was to be considered holy (v. 9), and the value could not be **changed** (v. 10) or **alter[ed]**. The offerer could not inflate his animal's value, nor could it be deflated in value. This protected the giver and the priests receiving the gift. It also removed any chance of bickering or taking pride in what was given.

An **unclean beast** (v. 11) not designated for **sacrifice** could be given **unto the LORD** after it was presented to the **priest** and evaluated. If the giver who made the vow and presented the **unclean** animal to the Lord wished to **redeem** (v. 13) it, retract it, or substitute it with another animal, he could do so. However, a fifth part of the value of the original gift had to be added to the animal substituted, because "declension is manifested and is treated somewhat like a trespass" (Unger, *Commentary*, p. 179). One could even **sanctify** (v. 14) his **house** and give it to the Lord. **The priest shall estimate it, so shall it stand**. The house could be purchased back, but the giver had to redeem it with a fifth added to the value, just as with the offering of animals.

27:16–21. Land that belonged to a family could also be offered as a vow to the Lord. The value was measured by **a homer of barley seed at fifty shekels of silver** (v. 16). (A homer was a little over five bushels.) This transaction was somewhat complicated and had to be synchronized with the laws of **the year of jubilee** (v. 18). The land was evaluated starting with the cost of the amount of **seed** (v. 16) needed to plant the field for forty-nine years "and then was discounted according to the number of harvests left until the next Year of Jubilee (27:17–19)" (Lindsey, "Leviticus," p. 213). Again, the giver could redeem the field, and he could even sell it to someone else for a redemption amount (v. 20). When the field was given, it was considered **holy unto the LORD, as a field devoted; the possession thereof shall be the priest's** (v. 21). They would be sustained by the crops produced.

27:22–29. Leased land could also be presented to the Lord. In the Year of **jubile** (v. 23), however, it had to revert back to the original owner. When the land was given, it was considered **a holy thing unto the LORD**. Animals that were the **firstlings** (v. 26) could not be vowed since they already belonged to God. Certain things could not be given. For example, no **devoted thing** (v. 28), something that was **devote[d] unto the LORD**, could be sold or **redeemed** (v. 29). The **death** (v. 29) penalty hung over anyone who violated this law. "Devoted" in Hebrew is *herem*, meaning "that which is placed under a ban." Whatever had been judged, or given over to destruction, could not be bought back, ransomed, or redeemed. Only what was worthy could be given to the Lord. All such banned gifts automatically became the property of the priests and could not be bought back (Num. 18:14; Ezek. 44:29).

27:30–34. The **tithe** (v. 30), or ten percent, of the land, the seed of the land, and the fruit was **holy unto the LORD**. There was not simply one tithe, or tenth. Many things, such as food crops and animals, were calculated as offerings based on the tenth. A **fifth** (v. 31) was also added if a man desired some of his crops back by redemption. A tenth of the animals that **passeth under the rod** (v. 32) was counted; these animals belonged to the Lord and were considered **holy**. Such an animal offering could **not be redeemed** (v. 33). The Lord seeks only what He is due. With these laws of the "vow" and the laws of the tithe, Israel could see that they had obligations to the Lord.

These **commandments** (v. 34) were given to **Moses for the children of Israel in mount Sinai**. Some of the laws seem harsh, but they were also merciful. They "reined" in the nation of Israel and gave to the Israelites a glimpse of God's holy and righteous demands. They brought a certain civilization to the Jewish people and almost instantly made them distinct from the heathen and pagan nations surrounding them. Some of these laws were repeated over and over to impress upon Aaron, other priests, and the congregation of Israel that the laws were important and could not be ignored. No nation has had such a blessed revelation as the children of Israel.

THE FOURTH BOOK OF MOSES, CALLED NUMBERS

INTRODUCTION

Title

The English name of the book comes from the Septuagint (the Greek translation of the Old Testament) and is based on the census lists found in chapters 1 and 26. The Hebrew title of the book (*bemidbar*, "in the wilderness") is more descriptive of its contents. Numbers presents an account of the thirty-eight-year period of Israel's wandering in the wilderness following the establishment of the covenant of Sinai (compare 1:1 with Deut. 1:1).

Author and Date

Numbers has traditionally been ascribed to Moses. This conclusion is based on (1) statements concerning Moses' writing activity (e.g., 33:1–2; Exod. 17:14; 24:4; 34:27) and (2) the assumption that the first five books of the Bible, the Pentateuch, are a unit and come from one author. (See Genesis, Introduction: "Author" and "Date.")

It is not necessary, however, to claim that Numbers came from Moses' hand complete and in final form. Portions of the book were probably added by scribes or editors in later periods of Israel's history. For example, the protestation of the humility of Moses (12:3) would hardly be convincing if it came from his own mouth. It seems reasonable to assume that Moses wrote the essential content of the book.

Theme

Numbers relates the story of Israel's journey from Mount Sinai to the plains of Moab on the border of Canaan. Much of its legislation for people and priests is similar to that in Exodus, Leviticus, and Deuteronomy. The book tells of the murmuring and rebellion of God's people and of their subsequent judgment. Those whom God had redeemed from slavery in Egypt and with whom He had made a covenant at Mount Sinai responded not with faith, gratitude, and obedience but with unbelief, ingratitude, and repeated acts of rebellion, which came to extreme expression in their refusal to undertake the conquest of Canaan (chap. 14). The community of the redeemed forfeited their part in the Promised Land. They were condemned to live out their lives in the wilderness. Only their children would enjoy the fulfillment of the promise that had originally been theirs (Heb. 3:7–4:11).

Theological Message

In telling the story of Israel's wilderness wanderings, Numbers offers much that is theologically significant. During the first year after Israel's deliverance from Egypt, she entered into a covenant with the Lord at Sinai to be the people of His kingdom, among whom He pitched His royal tent (the tabernacle)—this is the story of Exodus. As the account of Numbers begins, the Lord organizes Israel into a military camp. Leaving Sinai, she marches forth as His conquering army, with the Lord at her head, to establish His kingdom in the Promised Land, in the midst of the nations. The book graphically portrays Israel's identity as the Lord's redeemed covenant people and her vocation as the servant people of God, charged with establishing His kingdom on earth. God's purpose in history is implicitly disclosed: to invade the arena of fallen humanity and effect the redemption of His creation—the mission in which His people are also to be totally engaged.

Numbers also presents the chastening wrath of God against His disobedient people. Because of her rebellions (and especially her refusal to undertake the conquest of Canaan), Israel was in breach of the covenant. The fourth book of the Pentateuch presents a sobering reality: the God who had entered into a covenant with Abraham (Gen. 15; 17), who had delivered His people from bondage in the exodus (Exod. 14–15), who had brought Israel into a covenant with Himself as His "peculiar treasure" (Exod. 19:5), and who had revealed His holiness and the gracious means of approaching Him (Lev. 1–7) was also a God of wrath. His wrath extended to His errant children as well as to the enemy nations of Egypt and Canaan.

Not even Moses, the great prophet and servant of the Lord, was exempt from God's wrath when he disobeyed God. Chapter 20, which records his error, begins with the notice of Miriam's death (20:1) and concludes with the record of Aaron's death (20:22–29). Here is the passing of the old guard. Those whom God used to establish the nation died before the nation had come into its own.

The questions arose. Is God finished with the nation as a whole (Rom. 11:1)? Are His promises a thing of the past? In one of the most remarkable sections of the Bible—the account of Balaam, the pagan diviner (chaps. 22–24)—the reply was given. The Lord, working in a providential and direct way, proclaimed His continued faithfulness to His purpose for His people despite their unfaithfulness to Him.

Balaam was Moab's answer to Moses, the man of God. Balaam was an internationally known prophet who shared the pagan belief that the God of Israel was like any other deity and could be manipulated by acts of magic or sorcery. From the early part of the narrative, when Balaam first encountered the one true God in visions, and in the narrative of his journey on the donkey (chap. 22), he began to learn that dealing with the true God was fundamentally different from anything he had ever known. When he attempted to curse Israel at the instigation of Balak, the king of Moab, Balaam found his mouth unable to express the curse he desired to pronounce. Instead, from his lips came blessings on Israel and curses on her enemies (chaps. 23–24).

In his seven prophetic oracles, Balaam proclaimed God's great blessing for His people (23:20). Though the immediate enjoyment of this blessing will always depend on the faithfulness of His people, the ultimate realization of God's blessing is sure—because of the character of God (23:19). Thus, Numbers reaffirms the ongoing purposes of God. Despite His judgment on His rebellious people, God was still determined to bring Israel into the Land of Promise. His blessing to her rests in His sovereign will.

The teaching of the book of Numbers has lasting significance for Israel and for the church (Rom. 15:4; 1 Cor. 10:6, 11). God displays His wrath even against His errant people, but His grace is renewed as surely as is the dawn, and His redemptive purpose will not be thwarted.

Special Problem

The large numbers of men conscripted into Israel's army puzzle modern scholars (see, e.g., the figures in 1:46; 26:51). These numbers of men mustered for warfare demand a total population in excess of two million people. Such numbers seem to be exceedingly large for the time, for the locale, for the wilderness wanderings, and in comparison with the inhabitants of Canaan (see *Zondervan KJV Study Bible* note on 3:43).

Various possibilities have been suggested to solve this problem. Some have thought that the numbers may have been corrupted in transmission. The present text, however, does not betray textual difficulties with the numbers.

Others have felt that the Hebrew word for "thousand" might have a different meaning here from its usual numerical connotation. In some passages, for example, it has been proposed that the word is a technical term for a company of men (i.e., "family division" or "clan") that may or may not equal 1,000 (e.g., Josh. 22:14; 1 Sam. 23:23). Further, some have postulated that this Hebrew word means "chief" (or "duke," as in Gen. 36:15). In this way, the figure 53,400 (Num. 26:47) would mean "53 chiefs plus 400 men." Such a procedure would yield a greatly reduced total, but it would be at variance with the fact that the Hebrew text adds the "thousands" in the same way it adds the "hundreds" for a large total. Also, this would make the proportion of chiefs to fighting men top-heavy (59 chiefs for 300 men in Simeon).

Another option is to read the Hebrew word for "thousand" with the dual meaning of "chief" and "1,000," with the chiefs numbering one less than the stated figure. For example, the 46,500 of Reuben (1:21) is read as 45 chiefs and 1,500 fighting men, and the 59,300 of Simeon (1:23) is read as 58 chiefs and 1,300 fighting men, and so on. But in this case, as in the former, the totals of 1:46 and 2:32 must then be regarded as errors of understanding (perhaps by later scribes).

Still another approach is to regard the numbers as symbolic figures rather than as strictly mathematical figures. The numerical value of the Hebrew letters in the expression *bene yisra'el* ("all the congregation of the children of Israel," 1:2) equals 603 (the number of the thousands of the fighting men, 1:46); the remaining 550 (plus 1 for Moses) might come from the numerical equivalent of the Hebrew letters in the expression "all that are able to go forth to war in Israel" (1:3). This symbolic use of numbers (called *gematria*) is not unknown in the Bible (see Rev. 13:18), but it is not likely in Numbers, where there are no literary clues pointing in that direction.

While the problem of the large numbers has not been satisfactorily solved, the Bible does point to a remarkable increase of Jacob's descendants during the four centuries of their sojourn in Egypt (Exod. 1:7–12). With all their difficulties, these numbers also point to the great role of providence and miracles in God's dealings with His people during their life in the wilderness (see *KJV Study Bible* note on 1:46).

Literary Features

Numbers has three major divisions, based on Israel's geographical locations. Each of the three divisions has two parts, as the following breakdown demonstrates: (1) Israel at Sinai, preparing to depart for the Land of Promise (1:1–10:10), followed by the journey from Sinai to Kadesh (10:11–12:16); (2) Israel at Kadesh, delayed as a result of rebellion (13:1–20:13), followed by the journey from Kadesh to the plains of Moab (20:14–22:1); (3) Israel on the plains of Moab, anticipating the conquest of the Land of Promise (22:2–32:42), followed by appendixes dealing with various matters (chaps. 33–36).

Outline

I. Israel at Sinai, Preparing to Depart for the Promised Land (1:1–10:10)

   A. The Commands for the Census of the People (chaps. 1–4)

      1. The Numbers of Men from Each Tribe Mustered for War (chap. 1)

      2. The Placement of the Tribes around the Tabernacle and Their Order for March (chap. 2)

      3. The Placement of the Levites around the Tabernacle and the Numbers of the Levites and the Firstborn of Israel (chap. 3)

      4. The Numbers of the Levites and Their Tabernacle Service for the Lord (chap. 4)

         a. The Descendants of Kohath (4:1–20)

         b. The Descendants of Gershon (4:21–28)

         c. The Descendants of Merari (4:29–33)

         d. The Results of the Census (4:34–49)

   B. The Commands for Purity of the People (5:1–10:10)

      1. Concerning the Unclean (5:1–4)

      2. The Test for Purity in the Law of Jealousy (5:5–31)

      3. The Nazarite Vow (6:1–21)

      4. The Aaronic Benediction (6:22–27)

      5. The Offerings of the Twelve Leaders at the Dedication of the Tabernacle (7:1–88)

      6. The Setting Up of the Lamps (7:89–8:4)

      7. The Separation of the Levites (8:5–26)

      8. The Observance of the Passover (9:1–14)

      9. The Covering Cloud and the Silver Trumpets (9:15–10:10)

II. The Journey from Sinai to Kadesh (10:11–12:16)

   A. The Beginning of the Journey (10:11–36)

   B. The Beginning of the Sorrows: Fire and Quails (chap. 11)

      1. The People Complain (11:1–3)

      2. God Sends Quails (11:4–35)

   C. The Opposition of Miriam and Aaron (chap. 12)

III. Israel at Kadesh, the Delay Resulting from Rebellion (13:1–20:13)

A. The Twelve Spies and Their Mixed Report of the Good Land (chap. 13)
   1. Twelve Spies Sent to Canaan (13:1–25)
   2. The Spies Return (13:26–33)
B. The People's Rebellion against God's Commission and Their Defeat (chap. 14)
C. A Collection of Laws on Offerings, the Sabbath, and Tassels on Garments (chap. 15)
   1. Offerings Required of Israel (15:1–21)
   2. Offerings for Unintentional Sins (15:22–31)
   3. Stoning the Sabbath Breaker (15:32–36)
   4. The Fringes of Remembrance (15:37–41)
D. The Rebellion of Korah and His Allies (chap. 16)
E. The Budding of Aaron's Rod: A Sign for Rebels (chap. 17)
F. Concerning Priests, Their Duties, and Their Support (chap. 18)
   1. Duties of Priests and Levites (18:1–7)
   2. Tithes and Offerings (18:8–32)
G. The Red Heifer and the Cleansing Water (chap. 19)
H. The Sin of Moses (20:1–13)
IV. The Journey from Kadesh to the Plains of Moab (20:14–22:1)
A. Edom Refuses Israel Passage (20:14–21)
B. The Death of Aaron (20:22–29)
C. The Destruction of Arad (21:1–3)
D. The Serpent of Brass (21:4–9)
E. The Song of the Well and the Journey to Moab (21:10–20)
F. The Defeat of Sihon and Og (21:21–35)
G. Israel Returns to Moab (22:1)
V. Israel on the Plains of Moab, in Anticipation of Taking the Promised Land (22:2–32:42)
A. Balak of Moab Hires Balaam to Curse Israel (22:2–41)
   1. Balak Sends for Balaam (22:2–20)
   2. Balaam's Ass Speaks (22:21–41)
B. Balaam Blesses Israel in Seven Oracles (chaps. 23–24)
   1. Parable One (23:1–12)
   2. Parable Two (23:13–30)
   3. Parable Three (24:1–14)
   4. Parable Four (24:15–25)
C. The Baal of Peor and Israel's Apostasy (chap. 25)
D. The Second Census (chap. 26)
E. Instructions for the New Generation (chaps. 27–30)
   1. The Inheritance for Women (27:1–11)
   2. The Successor to Moses (27:12–23)
   3. Commands regarding Offerings (28:1–15)
      a. The Daily Burnt Offering (28:1–8)
      b. The Offering on the Sabbath (28:9–10)

Bibliography

Allen, Ronald B. "Numbers." In *The Expositor's Bible Commentary*, edited by Frank E. Gaebelein, vol. 2. Grand Rapids, MI: Zondervan, 1990.

Ashley, Timothy R. *The Book of Numbers*. The New International Commentary on the Old Testament. Grand Rapids, MI: Eerdmans, 1993.

Merrill, Eugene. "Numbers." In *The Bible Knowledge Commentary: Old Testament*, edited by John F. Walvoord and Roy B. Zuck. Wheaton, IL: Victor, 1987.

Harrison, R. K. *Numbers*. The Wycliffe Exegetical Commentary. Chicago: Moody, 1990.

Hertz, J. H., ed. *The Pentateuch and Haftorahs: Hebrew Text, English Translation, and Commentary*. Socino Books of the Bible. London: Soncino, 1971.

Smick, Elmer. "Numbers." In *The Wycliffe Bible Commentary*, edited by Charles F. Pfeiffer and Everett F. Harrison. Chicago: Moody, 1962.

Unger, Merrill F. *Unger's Commentary on the Old Testament*. Chattanooga, TN: AMG, 2002.

EXPOSITION

I. Israel at Sinai, Preparing to Depart for the Promised Land (1:1–10:10)

A little over two years after coming out of Egypt, the people were prepared to begin traveling in earnest from the Sinai wilderness in their journey across the desert. The Mosaic covenant was completed along with all of the law, the 613 commandments given. First, this mob of Israelites had to be organized to give to the nation mutual support and protection.

Numbers continues the history of the people as "a kingdom of priests, and a holy nation" (Exod. 19:6). Genesis is the book of beginnings; Exodus tells the story of release from Egypt and the preliminary giving of the law; Leviticus is the book that deals with worship and fellowship. Numbers is the book that tells about godly servitude and the walk of the redeemed of the Lord.

A. The Commands for the Census of the People (chaps. 1–4)

A census was important so that the numbers of all of the people would be known, including the men of fighting age. This task began with the Lord speaking directly to Moses, though both Moses and Aaron would minister together to complete this heavy task.

1. The Numbers of Men from Each Tribe Mustered for War (chap. 1)

1:1–16. Having been redeemed by blood out of Egypt (Exod. 12:12–36) and given the revelation of the law and the tabernacle (12:37–15:21), the nation now had to prepare for hostilities as it moved across the wilderness. The LORD spoke to Moses in the **tabernacle … on the first day of the second month, in the second year after they were come out of the land of Egypt** (v. 1). He instructed Moses to take a census, or the **sum** (v. 2) of all the **congregation**, at this time. It was to include the roll of families, the house of each father, and **every male** by their **polls**. Men **twenty years** (v. 3) of age and older were to be prepared to fight if necessary. Each **tribe** (v. 4) would have a representation and would form a war

council to advise Moses, even the head of **the house of his father**. The names of the **renowned** (v. 16) men and **princes** of their tribes are listed in verses 5–15. These men formed the army as the **heads of thousands in Israel**.

1:17–19. These men (v. 17) were then instructed to assemble the **congregation** (v. 18) and have the men of fighting age declare **their pedigrees** of their families. In this way, they were **numbered** (v. 19) in the wilderness of Sinai. This arduous process was done by the clan leaders and was not simply forced on the people by Moses and Aaron.

1:20–46. The counting began with the tribe of Reuben, **Israel's eldest son** (v. 20). The census differentiated the people of God by their tribal distinctions, but it also kept the order of the Aaronic priesthood intact. Also, it preserved the messianic lineage through the tribe of Judah, which was most numerous (Gen. 49:8–10). The count is as follows (Merrill, "Numbers," p. 216):

Reuben	46,500	1:21
Simeon	59,300	1:23
Gad	45,650	1:25
Judah	74,600	1:27
Issachar	54,400	1:29
Zebulun	57,400	1:31
Ephraim	40,500	1:33
Manasseh	32,200	1:35
Benjamin	35,400	1:37
Dan	62,700	1:39
Asher	41,500	1:41
Naphtali	53,400	1:43
Total	603,550	1:46

These are the ones that were able to go forth to **war in Israel** (v. 45).

1:47–54. The **Levites** (v. 47) were not to be **numbered** in the census. They were exempt from war because they had the responsibility of caring for the **tabernacle of Testimony** (v. 50) and all of its **vessels**. They alone were to **take it down** (v. 51) and set it up. Anyone else who **cometh nigh shall be put**

to death. The other tribes were to **pitch** (v. 52) their own **tents** in order of their tribes, that is, **by his own standard, throughout their hosts**. The Levites were to pitch their tents around the **tabernacle** (v. 53) to keep **the congregation of the children of Israel** away from the tabernacle so that they would not incur God's **wrath**. Again, the Levites were placed in charge of the tabernacle. It was holy and was not to be made unclean by the common citizens. The people followed what **Moses** (v. 54) said.

2. The Placement of the Tribes around the Tabernacle and Their Order for March (chap. 2)

The Lord set forth His rules and instructions for the encampments and for the journeys while in the wilderness. Specific positions were set forth, with the tribes forming an outer square around the **tabernacle** (v. 2). On the east were **Judah, Issachar**, and **Zebulun** (vv. 3–7), with Judah the leading tribe of the three. To the south were **Reuben, Simeon**, and **Gad** (vv. 10–14), with Reuben the leading tribe. On the west were **Ephraim, Manasseh**, and **Benjamin** (vv. 18–22), with Ephraim the leading tribe. To the north were **Dan, Asher**, and **Naphtali** (vv. 25–29), with Dan the leading tribe. Each tribe was identified by its own "standard," or flag, that had on it the "ensign," or representation, of the specific tribe. There is some indication, however, that the standard actually represented the camp or cluster, an army, of the three tribes on one side.

The tribe of Levi was to be divided by its major clans and placed immediately around the tabernacle. The tribes were set out in order as warriors, but they journeyed as a whole with all of the brothers, demonstrating their unity in battle. The number twelve shows a completeness of function. They all had to work together for survival.

2:32–34. The numbering of the congregation was for warfare purposes, and since the **Levites** (v. 33) were exempt from combat, they were not numbered. The people did as Moses **commanded** (v. 34) and arranged their camps **by their standards**. Each family was accounted for **according to the house of their fathers**.

3. The Placement of the Levites around the Tabernacle and the Numbers of the Levites and the Firstborn of Israel (chap. 3)

This chapter is expressly about the generations of the Levites, who were exempt from military service (chap. 1). The priests, the descendants of Aaron and his sons, are mentioned here in chapter 3 because the Levitical ministry to God governed and led the nation spiritually and set the pattern of the nation's identity. They were the people of God, and the nation was to function as a theocracy with the Lord as the governing Head.

3:1–4. This chapter lists the **generations** (v. 1) of Aaron and Moses because these families would be the heads, or spiritual fathers, of the whole Levitical tribe. The sons of Aaron are named, who are **anointed** (v. 3) and **consecrated** as holy to carry on after Aaron dies, excluding **Nadab** (v. 4) and **Abihu**, whom the Lord took because they had made a pagan offering that was offensive to God (Lev. 10:1–2). The priesthood was to reflect the highest spiritual standards because they represented the Lord to the people. Only Aaron and his descendants, and others of the tribe of Levi, could serve as priests (Exod. 28:1; 29:9; 40:15).

3:5–10. The entire body of Levites was given a charge by Aaron, and by **the whole congregation before the tabernacle of the congregation** (v. 7), to carry out the services of the tabernacle. The Levites were responsible for maintaining all **the instruments** (v. 8) for service. They functioned with the sole authority as representatives of God. Any **stranger** (v. 10), one not of the tribe of Levi, would be put **to death** if he came near the tabernacle.

3:11–13. The Lord had adopted the nation as His firstborn (Exod. 4:22), but the Levites were now to have that special place before Him. The Lord took the Levites from among the entire people instead of the firstborn of all the tribes. **The Levites shall be mine** (v. 12; 8:14; 1 Cor. 6:19–20). The Jews were reminded that no such favor had been given to the Egyptian **firstborn** (v. 13) who were slain with the most terrible plague, the tenth (Exod. 12:29).

3:14–26. Moses was specifically charged with numbering the sons of **Levi** (v. 15), by the **house**

of their fathers, by their families, from one month old upward. However, they were not seen as mature enough to serve until they turned thirty. Moses did as he **was commanded** (v. 16). The Levites were divided into three clans by their relationship with the sons of Levi—**Gershon, and Kohath, and Merari** (v. 17). The Gershonites were then divided again by the lines of **Libni, and Shimei** (v. 18), who all together numbered **seven thousand and five hundred** (v. 22). These families camped **westward** of the tabernacle and were in charge of the **tent** (v. 25), the **covering**, the **hanging for the door**, and the **hangings of the court, and the curtain for the door of the court** (v. 26).

3:27–32. From the **Kohathites** (v. 27) came the **families** of the **Amramites**, the **Izeharites**, and the **Hebronites**. They numbered **eight thousand and six hundred** (v. 28) and camped **southward** (v. 29) of the tabernacle. They were in charge of the **ark** (v. 31), the **table** of shewbread, the **altars**, and the **vessels of the sanctuary**.

3:33–37. The families of **Merari** (v. 33) were the **Mahlites** and the **Mushites**, who **numbered six thousand and two hundred** (v. 34). They pitched their tents **northwards** (v. 35) of the tabernacle and were in charge of the tabernacle's **boards** (v. 36), **bars, pillars**, and **sockets**. This included the **pillars of the court round about, and their sockets, and their pins, and their cords** (v. 37).

3:38–39. Moses and Aaron and his sons were to camp **toward the east** (v. 38) of the tabernacle and were to keep **the charge of the sanctuary for the charge of the children of Israel**. No **stranger** could take this position, lest they **cometh nigh** and **be put to death**. The total number of Levites was **twenty and two thousand** (v. 39).

3:40–51. The **firstborn males** (v. 43) came to 22,273, leaving 273 **firstborn** (v. 46) Israelites without Levitical **redemption**. The solution was solved by taking **five shekels apiece by the poll, after the shekel of the sanctuary** (v. 47). Some scholars try to argue that the 22, 273 firstborn of the twelve tribes was too small a number since all of the Israelite fighting men age twenty years and up totaled 603,550 (1:46). The answer seems to be that the count of the firstborn of the nation probably refers to only the ones born after the Levitical tribe was established as a sacred unit. "Only the firstborn males who were born between the time of the Exodus and the setting apart of Levi about two years later (Num. 1:1) would be counted. So a total of 22,273 would be in line for that period of time since there could hardly be more than that number of families that would give birth to their first sons during that time" (Merrill, "Numbers," p. 220).

4. The Numbers of the Levites and Their Tabernacle Service for the Lord (chap. 4)

a. The Descendants of Kohath (4:1–20)

The sons of Kohath had a very important task when it came to moving the tabernacle. They were responsible for taking it down in the prescribed way whenever Israel prepared to journey further into the wilderness.

4:1–4. The **sons of Kohath** (v. 2) were given a specific task that no other clan among the Levites could fulfill. The mature men, **from thirty years old and upward even until fifty years old** (v. 3), were to work together in their tabernacle service, **about the most holy things** (v. 4).

4:5–20. When Israel prepared to move, the Kohathites were to place a covering of **badgers' skins** (v. 6) over the ark, along with a **cloth** of **blue**, and then attach the **staves** to the ark for carrying it. A covering of **blue** (v. 7) was to be placed over the **table of shewbread**, along with its various articles of service, which was then to be covered with a **cloth of scarlet** (v. 8) and a **covering of badgers' skins**. The same was to be done with the **candlestick of the light** (v. 9) and its **vessels** (v. 10) and with the **golden altar** (v. 11). Other instruments were also covered with **badgers' skins** (v. 14), though the blue cloth is not mentioned. The badgers' skins would give cushioned protection, the blue is often said to represent God's glory, and the scarlet refers to blood and sacrifice. The items were not to be touched, even by the priests, under the pain of death (v. 15). Only the **Kohath** priests were to carry these instruments of the sacrificial system, and they were **the burden of the sons of Kohath** in their service to the Lord.

Aaron's son **Eleazar** (v. 16) had personal supervision over the items and the supplies of the sanctuary. The **oil**, the **incense**, the **daily meat** (meal) **offering**, and the **anointing oil** were all specially handled when the tabernacle was moved and transported. The families of the **Kohathites** (v. 18) could never be **cut off** from their special work among the Levites. Apparently, when covering these sacred items, the priests had to cover their eyes or walk in backward so that they would not look upon **the holy things** that **are covered, lest they die** (v. 20). "Even the most accidental contact with the sacred objects of the sanctuary would result in sudden death.... Even a momentary glance ... at the exposed sacred objects" would likewise result in the loss of one's life (Harrison, *Numbers*, p. 88). The tabernacle, and all of its workings, was most holy to the Lord because it represented the coming redemptive and sacrificial work of His Son on the cross for sinners.

b. The Descendants of Gershon (4:21–28)

4:21–26. The same requirements of age were placed on the **sons of Gershon** (v. 22). This **service** (v. 24) was their burden: they were responsible for the **curtains of the tabernacle** (v. 25) its **covering** and the **hanging for the door of the tabernacle**. This included the hangings for the **court** (v. 26) and for the **door of the gate** and **their cords ... so shall they serve**.

4:27–28. The **Gershonites** (v. 27) were given an **appointment ... in all their burdens, and in all their service**. The Gershonites were under **Ithamar** (v. 28), Aaron's son.

c. The Descendants of Merari (4:29–33)

4:29–33. The parts of the tabernacle made of metal and wood were delegated to the **sons of Merari** (v. 29). **Ithamar** (v. 33), however, was to supervise this part of the **tabernacle** when moved along with all of the nonwooden parts (4:28).

d. The Results of the Census (4:34–49)

4:34–49. The responsibilities and tasks of the Levites are summarized here so that there would be no question of the roles of the various families.

Nothing could be left to chance. No priest could shirk his responsibility and say that he did not understand his task. The total number of the Levites doing this work was 8,580 (v. 48), with 2,750 Kohathites (v. 36), 2,630 Gershonites (v. 40), and 3,200 Merarites (v. 44). "Levitical service was manifold and exceedingly varied, but it always depended upon and was efficaciously operative only as springing from priestly service" (Unger, *Commentary*, p. 190). The census of the Levites was carried out by the **hand of Moses** (v. 49), under the **commandment of the Lord**. Everyone was given a responsibility **according to his burden**. "The ordering, numbering, and structuring of the camp was completed at the end of chapter 4" (Allen, "Numbers," 2:737).

B. The Commands for Purity of the People (5:1–10:10)

This cluster of chapters deals with issues concerning separation from that which was unclean, both ceremonially and morally. The first few of these chapters contain rules and instructions about community life and commandments that must be obeyed specifically when the people settle in the land of Canaan. One of the main features is separation from every form of wickedness and corruption. God's authority, taught to the people by the priests, was to rule in the procedures to be observed. The Israelites were commanded to follow the Lord's injunctions meticulously.

1. Concerning the Unclean (5:1–4)

The instructions in these verses served as reminder to the nation of the Lord's attribute of holiness and of their requirement to be holy if they were to reside near His dwelling place. The nation's spiritual holiness and consecration was tightly tied to and symbolized by physical and interpersonal relations. Anyone who became ill was not only physically unclean but also unclean for fellowship with the Lord at the tabernacle.

5:1–2. Anyone who had been defiled physically was to be **put out of the camp** (v. 2), that is, anyone who had touched a **leper**, or who had **an issue** or flow of bodily secretions, or who had touched **the dead**. In any of these cases, germs could be transferred, bringing diseases upon the handler.

5:3–4. The discharges could be menstrual fluids or seminal emissions. **Male** (v. 3) or **female** had to be put **without the camp**. As Moses gave the Lord's commands to the Israelites, some had to be put **without the camp** at that moment; it could not wait.

2. The Test for Purity in the Law of Jealousy (5:5–31)

5:5–10. If a **man** (v. 6) or **woman** committed a sin **against the Lord**, that person was **guilty**. Sin is always first and foremost against God, though it generally also has repercussions and consequences against others. Confession was to be made, with full **recompense** (v. 7) for the sin plus 20 percent. Most scholars believe that this was monetary compensation but that a sacrifice for **atonement** (v. 8) also had to be made. A **ram** was to be sacrificed for the **recompense**. That **offering** (v. 9), made to the Lord but brought to the priest, **shall be his**, that is, the priest's. By this, the priests were supplied with victuals and necessities (v. 10). While adultery is not mentioned in these verses, many scholars believe that the gravity of the issue under discussion could have in mind certain gross or sexual sins, similar to what the apostle Paul calls "all filthiness of the flesh" (2 Cor. 7:1).

5:11–18. Adultery is clearly spelled out in these verses. A woman who committed a **trespass** (v. 12) against her husband in secret was **defiled** (v. 13), even if there was **no witness against her**. The issue of promiscuity and adultery could easily destroy the domestic fabric of the nation. Because of this, a test was devised to get to the truth of the matter if witnesses were not forthcoming. If the husband was suspicious and became **jealous** (v. 14), though the certainty of the matter was unclear, he could take his wife before **the priest** (v. 15). Since adultery was also a sin against the Lord, an offering of **barley meal** was made to bring **iniquity to remembrance** and to reveal the possible violation.

The **priest** (v. 17) was to place **holy** (consecrated) **water in an earthen vessel** and add to the water **dust** from the tabernacle **floor**. Holding this **bitter** (polluted) **water** (v. 18), he then approached the woman, who was set **before the Lord** (v. 16). The dissolved dust may relate to the fact that the serpent in the garden had been cursed by the Lord (Gen. 3:14).

5:19–31. The priest then charged the woman with **an oath of cursing** (v. 21), to which she was to respond, **Amen, amen** (v. 22). The rotting of her **thigh** or the swelling of her **belly** would be a sign that she was guilty. The **curse** (v. 27) shows that some physical disorder would become evident that would make the woman sterile. If the woman was innocent of adultery, her childbearing capacity would remain intact (vv. 27–28). This was the law of **jealousies** (v. 29), to be followed when **the spirit of jealousy** (v. 30) came upon a husband. Following this ordeal, which was unpleasant for all parties, the man would be **guiltless** (v. 31) of his accusations, but if the woman was found guilty, she would **bear her iniquity**.

The effect of the bitter potion is not to be attributed to pagan magic, nor to something inherent in the mixture of the water and dust, but to the Lord's role in these proceedings. In an extremely unsophisticated and backward society, as was the Jewish society coming out of Egypt, such dire measures were needed to extract the truth from a people who were quick to commit the vilest of sins. The procedure, promoted by the Holy Spirit, brought about conviction if the woman was guilty. If the woman was innocent, this fact was revealed to the priest and to the husband. Though this is not certain, this procedure was probably employed only in the harsh environment of the wilderness wanderings and may not have been practiced when the nation settled in the Promised Land. It may have been used only in extreme cases.

3. The Nazarite Vow (6:1–21)

In the Middle East, vows of religious dedication were commonly practiced. If it was to be practiced in Israel, it needed to be regulated by the Lord to promote the most spiritual of purposes. This chapter covers the Nazarite vow, which was not for the community life of the nation but for the individual. This vow was a solemn oath that set the person aside to serve the Lord for a specific period or for a lifetime. The vows could have to do with daily worship (Ps. 61:8) or with a specific festival or celebration (1 Sam. 1:21); sometimes they involved an act of thanksgiving for the Lord's special blessings (Ps. 116:12–14). The Nazarite vow was by far the most important personal oath or vow.

6:1 – 8. The word **Nazarite** (v. 2) comes from the Hebrew word *nazar*, meaning "to separate, abstain from, to consecrate." A man or woman could so **separate** himself or herself to be completely dedicated to the Lord (see 16:20–21; 2 Cor. 6:14–7:1). The person had to **separate** (v. 3) from **strong drink** and was not even to eat **moist grapes** or **dried** ones, which could be on the verge of fermentation. The person's **hair** (v. 5) was not to be cut off. Long hair is a natural reproach for men (1 Cor. 11:14), but for the Nazarite, it was the visible sign of his separation and his willingness "to bear worldly rejection and reproach for the Lord's sake" (Unger, *Commentary*, p. 191). The individual was to be **holy** (vv. 5, 8). The Nazarite could not touch a **dead body** (v. 6) or do anything his immediate family requested that would make him **unclean** (v. 7).

6:9 – 17. The Nazarite became **defiled** (v. 9) even if someone standing nearby suddenly died. In such a case, his head was to be shaved, and **on the eighth day he shall bring two turtles** (doves; v. 10) to the **tabernacle,** which were offered for a **burnt offering** (v. 11) and for **an atonement.** He was totally **consecrate[d]** (v. 12) all the days of his **separation** to the Lord. When his separation was completed, more sacrifices were to be brought to the **door of the tabernacle** (v. 13), along with **unleavened bread** (v. 15) and fine flour cakes. These were to be presented to the Lord, offered for **his sin offering, and his burnt offering** (v. 16), with a **ram** (v. 17) for a peace offering. This seems to indicate that after the Nazarite's religious dedication was ended, he again became an average Israelite who needed to continue offering sacrifices to the Lord because he was simply a sinner like others.

6:18 – 21. Another sacrificial ritual was to be followed when the Nazarite formally ended his vow of **separation** (v. 18). A ram's **shoulder** (v. 19), along with an **unleavened cake** and an **unleavened wafer,** was to be **put upon the hands** of the Nazarite, and his hair was to be **shaven.** After this ritual, the individual could drink **wine** (v. 20) again. Some have likened this to Christ's drinking the fruit of the vine again with His followers in the coming millennial kingdom (Matt. 26:29; Mark 14:25; Luke 22:18).

4. The Aaronic Benediction (6:22–27)

6:22 – 27. These verses are like a poetic pause in the narrative instructions. Through Moses, the Lord spoke to Aaron and his sons, saying, **On this wise ye shall bless the children of Israel** (v. 23). The priests were never to forget that they represented the people to God and God to the people. The great blessing contained in these verses has been quoted thousands of times as an ending to religious services that especially lifts up the people in remembrance before the Lord (vv. 24–26). With this sublime piece of poetry, the Lord's name was imprinted **upon the children of Israel** (v. 27), and the Lord would **bless them.**

5. The Offerings of the Twelve Leaders at the Dedication of the Tabernacle (7:1–88)

Chapter 7 is virtually a repetition of Exodus 40 (which describes the setting up of the tabernacle), ending with the report of the cloud-by-day covering and the very presence of the Lord Himself filling the tabernacle. This is a vivid audiovisual that graphically notes that God was with His people. Numbers 7 is the longest chapter in the Pentateuch and records the lavish and identical gifts the leaders of the twelve tribes offered to the Lord for the tabernacle service.

7:1 – 9. The **tabernacle** (v. 1) was **anointed** and **sanctified,** and the various tribal princes brought the **offerings** (v. 3), loaded in wagons, **before the tabernacle.** The Lord then instructed Moses to take the gifts and give them to the Levites **according to his service** (v. 5), dividing them up between the various priestly groups. No gifts were given to the **sons of**

Kohath (v. 9) because they were to bear the sacred objects **upon their shoulders** (see 4:15). Failure to follow these instructions later brought about immense grief for David and his servants when the ark of the covenant was moved from the house of Abinadab to Jerusalem (2 Sam. 6:3; 2 Sam. 6:7–8). The Merarites had to have more animal carts because they carried the heavy wooden and metal frameworks of the tabernacle (Num. 4:31–32). Often, what seems to be inequities (but really are not) brings emotional strife and carnality among those who should know better.

7:10–17. The various tribal leaders (see 1:5–15) brought their offerings to dedicate the altar. The word for leader is *nasi* and means "prince" or "elevated one." The first one to bear his gift was **Nahshon** (v. 12), the leader of the tribe of **Judah.** Including the carts and the **oxen** (v. 17), his tribe contributed silver plate of **one hundred and thirty** (v. 13) shekels in weight. Today this would be more than one thousand dollars in value. Nahshon also brought a **silver bowl** worth **seventy** shekels. The value of the gold and silver items offered was staggering. This represented the "bribe" given to the Jews by the Egyptians in order to urge them to leave the land (Exod. 12:35–36). Besides these gifts of wealth, Nahshon also contributed sacrificial animals (vv. 15–17).

7:18–88. In this extended section, the gifts given by each family and tribe are listed, including the sacrificial animals. All of the remaining tribal leaders brought the same gifts, each on consecutive days. It took twelve days to present the offerings, beginning on the first day of the first month of the second year after Exodus 40:17 and going on through the twelfth day of that month. "The order of their coming with their gifts corresponds exactly with the arrangement of the tribes around the tabernacle (cf. Num. 2:3–31)" (Merrill, "Numbers," p. 223). The purpose for such attention to detail and repetition of the same wording concerning the offerings and the gifts presented was so that later generations of Jews could look back and identify the names of their tribal ancestors and see the role they had in the establishing of the tabernacle worship. This section also adds to the historicity of the account of the exodus. These events actually took place.

6. The Setting Up of the Lamps (7:89–8:4)

7:89. After all of the presentations of the offerings, Moses went into the **tabernacle** to speak with the Lord. The Lord, however, began to speak first, **from the mercy seat,** and manifested His pleasure with Moses. Moses was standing before the **ark of Testimony … between the two cherubims: and he spake unto him.**

8:1. Through Moses, Aaron is instructed to light the oil **lamps** (v. 2) that are mounted on the **candlestick,** or lampstand (Exod. 25:37; 26:33; 27:21; 40:25).

8:2–4. The fine **beaten gold** (v. 4) represents the deity of Christ. As the prophesied High Priest, Christ entered the heavenly sanctuary to minister following His ascension. The author of Hebrews writes, "We have such a high priest, who is set on the right hand of the throne of the Majesty in the heavens; a minister of the sanctuary, and of the true tabernacle, which the Lord pitched, and not man" (Heb. 8:1–2; see also Ps. 110:1–3). In type, the Holy Spirit is the oil in the lamps, to bear witness of Christ (John 15:26–27) and to glorify Him (John 16:7, 14–15).

7. The Separation of the Levites (8:5–26)

After Aaron lit the lamps, the Lord gave Moses instructions concerning the role of the priests in the tabernacle. The remainder of chapter 8 focuses on the separation of the Levites and gives specific instructions for the purification of the priests.

8:5–16. The **Levites** (v. 6) were to be set aside and **cleanse[d]** (v. 7) by the sprinkling of water, by shaving, and by washing their clothes. They were then to bring **offering[s]** (v. 8) and be presented **before the tabernacle** (v. 9) and before the assembly of the people. The congregation was to put their hands on the **Levites** (v. 10), and Aaron was to **offer** (v. 11) them **before the Lord** to **execute the service of the Lord.** Both Aaron and the assembly were presenting the Levites to the work of the ministry. The Levites were separated from the people. The Lord concluded, **and the Levites shall be mine** (v. 14; see 3:45; 16:9). They were **wholly given** (v. 16) to the Lord, as the firstborn, **instead of such as opens every womb**.

8:17 – 26. When the ceremony of presentation was finished, the Levites were given as a **gift** (v. 19) to Aaron and went up to the tabernacle to begin their service. The Levites were set apart to serve as substitutes for the **firstborn of the children of Israel** (v. 17), who rightfully belonged to the Lord because He redeemed them from death at the time of the tenth **plague** (v. 19) in Egypt (see 3:11 – 13). Because the Levites were wholly dedicated to the Lord, He could give them as a gift to Aaron for **service in the tabernacle** (v. 22). They could begin their service at the age of **twenty and five years** (v. 24), though the ones who were to transport the tabernacle had to be thirty (4:3), and could serve up to the age of **fifty** (v. 25). Levites over the age of fifty were to minister as assistants to the younger priests (v. 26). These orders kept the service in the hands of men in the prime years of their lives.

8. The Observance of the Passover (9:1-14)

While the Day of Atonement (Yom Kippur) was an important feast, Passover seems to have dominated the Jewish festival calendar. Passover stands as the great example of redemption because of the great miracle associated with the Israelites' release from Egypt (Exod. 12:3 – 28; Lev. 23:4 – 5; Num. 28:16). After the first Passover in Egypt, it was not observed again until the children of Israel arrived in Canaan (Josh. 5:10 – 11).

9:1 – 8. These additional instructions for Passover were given in the **wilderness of Sinai, in the first month of the second year** (v. 1) after coming out of Egypt. It was to be kept in its **appointed season** (v. 2), just after the completion of the tabernacle (Exod. 40:17) and before the census taking. It was to be kept on the **fourteenth day of this month … according to all the ceremonies thereof** (v. 3). These new laws and instructions about Passover were given because some men had been **defiled** (v. 7) by the **dead body of a man** and had properly asked whether

they were allowed to partake in the ceremony. Moses instructed them to **Stand still** (v. 8) so that he could hear from the Lord in this matter.

9:9 – 14. Graciously, the Lord answered that if a man or his **posterity** (v. 10) was **unclean** from a dead body or was traveling **in a journey afar off**, he was still allowed to **keep the passover unto the LORD**. Though defilement was a serious issue, the Passover was a great sign of their miraculous redemption from a place of sin, Egypt. Therefore, this exception was to be made. At the Passover, **unleavened bread** (v. 11) and **bitter herbs** were to be eaten along with a lamb whose **bone[s]** (v. 12) were not to be broken (Exod. 12:46; Ps. 34:20). Jesus became the sacrificial Lamb, the crucified Passover for sins (Isa. 53; 1 Cor. 5:7; John 1:29). In fulfillment of Scripture, none of His bones were broken (John 19:36; Ps. 34:20). Breaking the bones of those being crucified was meant to speed their deaths. Jesus' life, however, was not taken from Him; He gave up His own spirit in death for His sheep (John 10:17 – 18; 19:30).

9. The Covering Cloud and the Silver Trumpets (9:15-10:10)

The cloud that covered the tabernacle had symbolic significance for the Israelites and was the Lord's way of guiding them as they moved in the wilderness. This certainly must have impressed upon this fledgling people that the God of nature was indeed leading them. It would be impossible to fake such a manifestation. It was not witnessed by a few, but by thousands, young and old, in the congregation.

9:15 – 18. When the **tabernacle** (v. 15) was finished and **reared up**, the special **cloud covered the tabernacle**, specifically the **tent of** the **Testimony**. At night, **at even**, an **appearance of fire** was upon it **until the morning**. Nothing could have shown more graphically that this people belonged to God. This was a perpetual miracle and sign of the Lord's personal presence (Exod. 13:21 – 22; 40:34 – 38). **So it was alway** (v. 16). The Lord used the cloud and the pillar of fire to indicate when the congregation was to move to a new location. It was **at the commandment of the LORD** (v. 18) that **they pitched**

their tents. Now the manifestation of the Lord's presence, and His guidance, is carried out by His Spirit through His Word (John 16:13; Acts 13:2–4).

9:19–23. If **the cloud tarried long upon the tabernacle many days** (v. 19), the children of Israel **journeyed not.** When the cloud moved, **they journeyed** (v. 20). The **cloud** (v. 21) and the fire represented God's marching orders for the congregation. The Israelites **rested in the tents** (v. 23) when the cloud remained over the tabernacle and traveled only at the Lord's direct command. Thus, **they kept the charge of the LORD** and obeyed Him in their journeying. The emphasis here is on God's mercy and the people's recognition of His grace. It is marked by their quick response to His leading. He gave them clear signs, and He demonstrated that Moses was the interpreter of His meaning. The emphasis on the sovereignty of God is also paramount in these verses (Allen, "Numbers," 2:778).

10:1–10. Two special silver trumpets were made to call the people together and to announce **the journeying of the camps** (v. 2). When these trumpets were sounded, all the assembly was to gather **at the door of the tabernacle of the congregation** (v. 3). Silver is a reminder of redemption and atonement (Exod. 30:12–16; 38:25–27; see also 1 Peter 1:18–19). When only one trumpet was sounded, the **princes** (v. 4) of Israel were to come to meet with Moses. When **an alarm** (v. 5) was blown, with certain distinct sounds, the congregation was to begin to move by courses and in a certain order. Different sounds were used for a call to assembly and an alarm. The ordering and sounding of these trumpets were to be well recognized and used **for an ordinance for ever throughout your generations** (v. 8). No one could be complacent when these trumpets were blown. If there was danger to the camp, both trumpets were to be sounded, and God would remember His people, **and ye shall be saved from your enemies** (v. 9). The trumpets were sounded for the defense of the people but also as an appeal to God to save them from their opponents.

The trumpets were also to be blown to start certain feasts and offerings. In such cases, the trumpets

were meant to announce holy days **for a memorial before your God: I am the LORD your God** (v. 10).

II. The Journey from Sinai to Kadesh (10:11–12:16)

This section deals with the first departure of the people from Sinai. It includes the order to march but also some of the problems that Moses had in guiding this mob through the desert. Problems of leadership and the people's complaining arose. When people make a commitment, often carnalities and weaknesses come to the surface. So it was with Israel as they began to work together as a redeemed congregation.

A. The Beginning of the Journey (10:11–36)

Israel set out on a journey that should have taken them, in only a few months, straight to Canaan and its conquest. This would not happen. The nation had to be diverted from its intended goal to rid the nation of certain rebels and to teach the assembly how to truly trust in the Lord. Their faith and resolve would be tested. As the Israelites began their journey, everything seemed to work in order, though some confusion or misunderstanding arose with Hobab, the brother-in-law of Moses, in 10:29–36. Some scholars see this incident as the beginning of problems in the camp.

10:11–17. These verses set forth the order of movement, which began on the **twentieth day of the second month, in the second year** (v. 11). The **cloud was taken up** from the **tabernacle** to lead the Israelites on their **journeys** (v. 12) as commanded by the Lord. The cloud had them halt in the wilderness of **Paran,** possibly the place called Et-tih in the north-central part of the Sinai peninsula (Gen. 21:21; Num. 12:16).

10:18–28. The movement of the travel and how the line of march was accomplished is set forth here. The tribes took their proper place as ordered by Moses. The various identifiable **standard[s]** (v. 18), or banners, for rallying and organizing the trip around the tribal leadership are mentioned. One would expect some stragglers had to look ahead for these banners to get back in line with their own tribe and clan. The importance of such order was to set the men **according to their armies** (v. 28) so that they would be prepared for defense if attacked. This seems to be the unvarying pattern of their journeys from this point on.

10:29-32. Some have seen this section as a weakening of Moses' resolve to totally trust God as the people began their journey. **Hobab** (v. 29) is the **son of Raguel** the **Midianite**, Moses' **father in law** (Exod. 2:18). Moses asked Hobab to help lead the people on the journey, which may imply that he was familiar with the route being undertaken. Hobab declines the first invitation (v. 30), though nothing is said about whether he declines the second request to lead Israel through the **wilderness** (v. 31), that **thou mayest be to us instead of eyes** (Judg. 1:16 indicates that Hobab acceded to Moses' request). In other words, Moses was saying, "We need your help; we do not know where we are going!" Or, "If you go with us, the Lord will be good to us, and **the same will we do unto thee**" (v. 32).

There is some question as to the exact identification of **Hobab** (v. 29). Judges 4:11 says Hobab was the "father in law [*hoten*] of Moses." However, the Hebrew root *htn* can often be translated as any "in-law." Hobab was a brother of Zipporah, the wife of Moses. He would play the role of the patriarch of the family, the role of Moses' father-in-law from the prevailing custom. "In light of all these factors it is reasonable to distinguish Hobab from Reuel and to identify Hobab as Moses' brother-in-law, precisely as Numbers 10:29 says" (Merrill, "Numbers," p. 226).

10:33-36. With the Levites carrying the **ark** (v. 33) leading, the congregation **departed from the mount of the LORD**, Mount Sinai. They journeyed **three days** with the cloud of the Lord **upon them** (v. 34). As the ark **set forward** (v. 35), Moses prayed that the Lord would **rise up** and defeat His enemies and scatter them. When the ark stopped, he prayed **Return, O LORD, unto the many thousands of Israel** (v. 36). In other words, "God, be with your people and protect them."

B. The Beginning of the Sorrows: Fire and Quails (chap. 11)

This chapter elaborates on the first chronic complaining and grumbling within the camp. While the Jews had it hard under the pharaohs in Egypt, they now forgot that experience and turned against Moses and against the Lord. The rabble and riffraff infected the true Israelites. Complaining often follows too many blessings and benefits. People generally forget "from whence they came."

1. The People Complain (11:1-3)

11:1-2. Here Moses writes bluntly, with no introduction: **the people complained** (v. 1). From this point forward, their murmurings and complaining were continual (Exod. 16:2-3; 17:3; 32:1-4; Num. 12:1-2). They grumbled about their hardships, when in reality, they were immeasurably blessed by God's provision and protection. The Lord's **anger was kindled**, and His **fire** was felt throughout the **uttermost parts of the camp** and **burnt** and destroyed the complainers. When the people **cried** (v. 2) unto Moses, he in turn **prayed unto the LORD**, and the fire was quenched.

11:3. Moses **called the name of the place Taberah**, meaning "burning." One can but imagine the disappointment of Moses. The law had been given, and the order of the tribes had been established, when suddenly, opposition was voiced about what the Lord, in His mercy, was doing.

2. God Sends Quails (11:4-35)

11:4-15. The **mixt multitude** (v. 4) included the rabble and the complainers who lusted and even **wept** for the **fish** (v. 5), fruit, **leeks,** and **onions** of Egypt. The people had a strong craving for the variety of foods in Egypt, a sharp contrast to the austere desert food with its staple of **manna** (v. 7), which looked like **coriander seed** and was grayish yellow in color. The Jews wept **again** (v. 4; see also Exod. 16:2-3). It was easy to forget the slavery and the cruelty of Egypt. The **manna** (v. 6) was plain and had to be gathered, ground, and baked, and it had the taste of **fresh oil** (v. 8). The people had lost their vision and wept at the doors of their tents. The Lord was angry, and Moses was **displeased** (v. 10).

With his faith tested, Moses complained to the Lord. He felt that the Lord had let him down. He felt God was treating him as a **nursing father** (v. 12) with a great burden, who could not supply the needs of his weeping children. **I am not able to bear all this people alone, because it is too heavy for me** (v. 14). Moses pleaded that if God would not relieve him, He would take his life: **kill me** (v. 15). Yet if the Lord wished to show him **favour**, Moses wanted to understand the full meaning of his **wretchedness**.

11:16–24. The Lord had mercy on Moses and commanded him to bring forth **seventy … elders** (v. 16) to stand with him before the **tabernacle**. The Lord took the **spirit** (v. 17) that was on Moses and placed it on these men. Many scholars believe this is actually the Holy Spirit, who would give guidance as was done for Moses. One of the most compelling reasons is that Moses later says of this spirit, "that the LORD would put his spirit upon them!" (11:29). Moses was then to command the people to **sanctify** (v. 18) themselves. They had **wept in the ears of the LORD**, and now they would have **flesh** to eat. They would have more than **twenty days** (v. 19) of eating meat, until they could stomach no more. In reality, their complaining was based on the fact that they **despised the LORD** (v. 20) and asked, **Why came we forth out of Egypt?** Moses asked the Lord where the meat for an entire **month** (v. 21) would come from. Maybe from the **flocks** (v. 22) and **herds** they had? God rebuked Moses and asked, **Is the LORD's hand waxed short?** (v. 23). In essence, "See whether I can provide or not." The people were told what the Lord said, and the **elders** (v. 24) were gathered around the tabernacle.

11:25–30. The Lord came down to Moses and spoke to him in the cloud. Then the **spirit** (v. 25) that was upon him came upon the seventy elders, whereupon they **prophesied, and did not cease.** What these men were able to predict, in speech or song, is not recorded. Some believe that it was prophecies of thanksgiving, as they realized the errors of the people, while God had poured mercy upon them rather than judgment.

Two of the men in the camp (v. 26), probably elders, **Eldad** and **Medad**, did not join the others before the tabernacle, yet they also were empowered to prophesy in the camp of the people. Two young men, including **Joshua** (v. 28), reported to Moses that these two elders had not joined the others and yet they were prophesying. Joshua urged Moses to **forbid them**. Moses suspected an attitude of envy and answered, **would God that all the LORD's people were prophets, and that the LORD would put his spirit upon them!** (v. 29). There was no reason to criticize **Eldad** (v. 27) and **Medad**, because God was using them.

11:31–35. To feed the people, the Lord sent forth a great **wind** (v. 31) that brought **quails from the sea, and let them fall by the camp**. It would have taken a day's journey in two directions to walk through all of the quail, which were piled **two cubits high** (about three feet deep) on the ground. The one who picked up the least number of quail still gathered **ten homers** (v. 32), or sixty bushels. They **spread** the birds on the ground, probably to dry in the sun. However, too much of a good thing can bring judgment. The people were stuffed. Many of them gluttonously devoured the meat so that the flesh was sticking between their teeth. The Lord sent upon them a **very great plague** (v. 33), possibly because they overstuffed themselves or because they had so much meat that some of it spoiled. The place was named **Kibroth-hattaavah** (v. 34), or the "graves of lust." The Israelites then pulled up camp and journeyed to **Hazeroth** (v. 35), which is somewhere northeast of the traditional Sinai.

C. The Opposition of Miriam and Aaron (chap. 12)

This chapter contains some deep undertones of criticism against Moses, which festered and finally boiled over. Moses' elder sister and brother, Miriam and Aaron, attacked his Ethiopian wife. This attack deflected the fact that they were jealous the Lord was so dramatically using Moses over them.

12:1–3. The identification of Moses' **Ethiopian** (or "Cushite"; v. 1) wife is somewhat of a puzzle. This woman was a Cushite from the line of Ham, who is mentioned in Genesis 10:6–7. Some believe the woman referred to here is Zipporah (Exod. 2:15–22). The term "Cushite" may have been used as a slanderous term and could have been used by Miriam in contempt of Zipporah's Midianite ancestry. "More likely, however, is the idea that Moses had taken a new wife, perhaps after the death of Zipporah (which is not recorded)" (Allen, "Numbers," 2:797–98). The attack was a pretext; the real reason for the attack was that Aaron and Miriam were jealous of Moses' prophetic gift and his special relationship with the Lord.

"Has God only spoken by Moses?" they asked. "Has He not spoken through us also?" (v. 2). Because he was basically shy, Moses apparently did not respond (v. 3).

12:4–10. The Lord responded quickly to their criticism and called them to come before His presence (v. 4). With His voice coming forth from the **pillar of the cloud** (v. 5), one can imagine the terror Miriam and Aaron must have experienced. He commanded them, **Hear now my words** (v. 6). With a **prophet**, the Lord generally would speak in a **vision** or a **dream**, but in faithful **Moses'** (v. 7) case, the Lord spoke **mouth to mouth** (better translated "face to face"; v. 8; Deut. 34:10), not **in dark speeches** but with clarity. "The Lord did not accommodate Himself to Moses through metaphors and other figurative devices" (Merrill, "Numbers," p. 228). **Wherefore then**, the Lord asked, **were ye not afraid to speak against my servant Moses?** Seeing God use their brother in such miraculous ways had become commonplace to them, and they became selfish, disgruntled, and envious.

The Lord's **anger** (v. 9) was **kindled against them; and he departed.** He had said enough, and no answers or self-justifications for their sin were required. When the **cloud departed** (v. 10), Miriam's skin instantly became **leprous** and **white as snow**.

12:11–13. Conviction came quickly to Aaron, and he admitted they had acted **foolishly** and had **sinned** (v. 11). While Aaron had rightly included himself in the transgression along with his sister, it is possible that she was more culpable in complaining

and criticizing Moses. As a result of the Lord's affliction of Miriam, the principal offender against her brother, she became a pariah, an outcast, since she now suffered an infectious skin disease that would exclude her from the camp of her people. Aaron pleaded for her because of her ghastly physical appearance (v. 12). Moses joined in the cry and, with urgency and simplicity, called upon the Lord to heal her. He cried out as with pain, **Heal her now, O God, I beseech thee** (v. 13).

12:14–16. The Lord responded by saying that if her father had spit **in her face** (v. 14), would she not have been unclean for **seven days**? Such public shame and rebuke (see Deut. 25:9) would have been scandalous. She would have been **ashamed** for seven days. In like manner, she was be put outside the **camp** for that same period but then **received** back into the fellowship of the congregation. Miriam was **shut out** (v. 15) for seven days, but the people did not journey until she **was brought in again**. This event showed that no one was able to do what was spiritually wrong and get away with it, not even the three who were most respected by the congregation. All of the people were detained in order to learn the lesson Miriam had to learn. Seeing Miriam judged, the people had an opportunity to judge their own thoughts, actions, and prejudices. The assembly then moved from **Hazeroth** (v. 16; 11:35; 33:18) and came to the **wilderness of Paran**, which is considered the southernmost region of the Promised Land. The opportunity to enter the land was near.

III. Israel at Kadesh, the Delay Resulting from Rebellion (13:1–20:13)

The tribes had reached the desert of Paran, where they would stay for some time. This is where the great oasis of Kadesh (13:26) is located, though technically it is in the desert of Zin (Merrill, "Numbers," p. 229). The people requested spies to be sent out (Deut. 1:22–23), and the Lord ordered it to be done, but in the end, it brought on a spirit of unbelief of the crowd. The Lord ordered it as a testing, so that the state of their hearts would be made known (Unger, *Commentary*, p. 200).

A. The Twelve Spies and Their Mixed Report of the Good Land (chap. 13)

The use of spies was a common practice in the Middle East (Josh. 2:1–24). The Lord's sending out spies was an act of grace, yet it revealed the fear that was smoldering deep in the hearts of most of the people.

1. Twelve Spies Sent to Canaan (13:1–25)

13:1–3. It is recorded in Deuteronomy 1:22 that the people said, "We will send men before us, and they shall search us out the land, and bring us word again by what way we must go up, and into what cities we shall come." Moses said yes and followed through with their request (Deut. 1:23). Here the Lord instructed Moses to send out men from **every tribe of their fathers** (v. 2). All the men sent were **heads of the children of Israel** (v. 3). Thus, all of the tribes had representatives to give their evaluation of the land of Canaan and its people.

13:4–15. In these verses, the tribes are listed along with the men who were to represent them. Mentioning all the men who traveled together into the land was important for later generations. The responsibility for the report, to go on and take the land or not, fell on these men. Their faith, or lack of it, was displayed and written down by Moses for all generations to see. The "land of Canaan" speaks figuratively of God's grace for His people. Failure to trust the Lord would be fraught with consequences more dire than could be imagined (see 14:32–33).

The names listed are somewhat different than those listed in chapters 1–2, 7, and 10, presumably because the tribal heads in the four earlier lists were older men. The job of the spies called for younger, more vigorous men who were respected by those in their tribes.

13:16–21. Verse 16 is a footnote about one of the spies, **called Oshea** (v. 16), meaning "salvation, deliverance," or **Jehoshua** (Joshua), which means "the Lord is salvation." The Greek word "Jesus" is from the Hebrew "Joshua" and means "the Lord saves." Along with the spy Caleb, Joshua gave a positive report about the land and urged the people to

trust God in delivering it into their hands (14:6–10). Joshua later took over the leadership of the congregation after the death of Moses (Deut. 34:9–12).

The spies were sent out, having been told to first **go up into the mountain** (v. 17), the central highland ridge that overlooked the land (3:17), and **see the land** (v. 18) and ascertain the strength of the people (v. 18). The scouts entered from the south (Negev) and traveled to the far northern limits, to **Rehob** (v. 21; 2 Sam. 10:6–8), near the outflow of the Jordan River. They continued to the area of **Hamath**, near Baalbek on the Orontes River.

The spies were to evaluate the **land** (v. 19) and the **cities**, whether the inhabitants live in **tents, or in strong holds**. They were also to judge whether the land **be fat or lean** (v. 20) and whether it had forests. Since it was August, the time of the **first ripe grapes**, they were told to bring back some of the **fruit of the land**.

13:22–25. They came to **Hebron** (v. 22), which would later become the inheritance of Caleb (Josh. 14:23–25) and, after that, the early capital of David when he reigned over Judah (2 Sam. 2:1–4). During the days of Moses, Hebron was the home of the Anakites, **the children of Anak**, the giants who would be continual enemies of Israel for many decades to come (Josh. 15:13–14). They came to the **brook (river) of Eshcol** (meaning, "a cluster of grapes"; v. 23), where they found grapes that had to be carried by two men on a **staff** because of the weight. They also found a rich harvest of **pomegranates** and **figs**. After **forty days** (v. 25), they returned to the camp.

2. The Spies Return (13:26–33)

13:26–29. The spies arrived at the camp, in **Kadesh** (v. 26), and showed the congregation the **fruit of the land**. Kadesh had plenty of water and was about eleven days' travel from Sinai (Deut. 1:2). The spies reported that the land **floweth with milk and honey, and this is the fruit of it** (v. 27). They added that the people of the land were strong and lived in **cities** (v. 28), which were **walled** and **very great**, but **moreover we saw the children of Anak there**. The fierce clans of the pagans were there

(v. 29). Despite the proof of the goodness of the Lord and the land He was giving them, ten of the twelve spies refused to trust in Him. Their unbelief took over and planted confusion, fear, and finally rebellion. They saw only the giants, the **Amalekites, Hittites, Jebusites, Amorites,** and **Canaanites**.

13:30 – 33. Caleb, however, quieted the people standing before Moses and spoke his confidence and faith. **We are well able to overcome** (v. 30) the people and the land. **Let us go up at once.** The other men countered his words, saying, **they are stronger than we** (v. 31). These spies brought an **evil report** (v. 32) and said the land **eateth up the inhabitants thereof; and all the people that we saw in it are men of a great stature.** Caleb stood on the promise that "if God be for us, who can be against us?" (Rom. 8:31).

Unbelief spread like an illness among the crowd of people and completely canceled out faith in God. Unbelief contradicts faith because it operates completely in the sphere of sight, of flesh, and of human endeavor, leaving the Lord out. Unbelief also canceled out the greatness of the land in the eyes of the people, causing them to see only the difficulties in conquering it. Their inheritance from God was replaced by the weakness of men. Unbelief becomes preoccupied with itself and blows up and magnifies problems, bringing on spiritual defeat (Romans 7). The rebels added that because of the giants, **we were in our own sight as grasshoppers, and so we were in their sight** (v. 33).

B. The People's Rebellion against God's Commission and Their Defeat (chap. 14)

The people repudiated Moses, and even the Lord, when the majority began to protest and declared that they would be better off in Egypt. The camp of God's own people turned into a place of hopelessness, with constant murmuring against what was happening to them. Against this unbelief and lack of trust and its dire results are directed all the "warnings of the book of Hebrews (2:1 – 4; 3:7 – 19; 5:11 – 6:12; 10:19 – 39; 12:25 – 29)" (Unger, *Commentary*, p. 202).

14:1 – 10. The people's crying and wailing lasted all **night** (v. 1), but in the morning, it turned to vi-

cious complaining against **Moses** (v. 2) and **Aaron**, with the declaration that it would have been better to die in Egypt than **in this wilderness**. Then the murmuring turned against the Lord, whom they said had led them into the desert **to fall by the sword** (v. 3), with their **wives** and **children** made a **prey**. Unbelievably, they argued that it was better to return to Egypt.

Rebellion was stirred when the crowd wanted to **make a** new **captain** (v. 4) and return to the land of slavery. Moses and Aaron fell on their faces ("facedown," also in 16:4, 22, 45; 20:6; 22:31) in front of the **assembly** (v. 5), and **Joshua** and **Caleb**, who had given the positive report to the people, **rent their clothes** (v. 6). They attempted to reason with the congregation (v. 7), saying that God had given them the land of **milk and honey** (v. 8), therefore **rebel not ye against the LORD ... the LORD is with us.** (v. 9). This provocation shows what disbelief really is all about and what it can do. As the assembly prepared to **stone** these leaders, the **glory of the LORD appeared in the tabernacle of the congregation before all the children of Israel** (v. 10).

14:11 – 25. The Lord revealed to Moses that the people were provoking Him despite all the **signs** (v. 11) He had displayed in their presence. The Lord declared that He would **smite** (v. 12) this generation of gripers with **pestilence** and **disinherit them**, and make a **greater nation**, or future generation, come up through the line of Moses, taking their place. Moses reminded the Lord that the Egyptians would hear of God's judgment, and after they had been made aware of His awesome dramatic power, they would think that He was **not able to bring this people into the land which he sware unto them** (v. 16). As Christ is now the Intercessor and Mediator before God for the believer (1 John 1:9 – 2:2), so Moses pleaded with the Lord, based on His power, longsuffering, mercy, and justice (vv. 17 – 18), to forgive His people (v. 19).

The Lord answered Moses, **I have pardoned according to thy word** (v. 20), but someday, He continued, **all the earth shall be filled with the glory of the LORD** (v. 21). In other words, God was saying, "The story is not over!" Despite human rebellion, the Lord will have the last say and accomplish all His plans even when it seems people are about to subvert His purposes. The people's actions had consequences. This crowd of grumblers would not enter Canaan, nor would they find rest (Heb. 3:18–19).

The people had seen God's **glory** (v. 22) and His **miracles** and had **tempted** Him **ten times**. "Ten times" may be an idiom for "many times." Because of this, the present generation would not **see the land** (v. 23). Caleb **had another spirit with him** (possibly referring to the Holy Spirit; v. 24); he would come **into the land … and his seed shall possess it**. As part of the Lord's punishment, when the people again began their travels, they would not go through **the valley** (v. 25) where the **Amalekites** and **Canaanites** dwelt but would instead make the long circuitous journey that would bring them to the plain of Moab, east of the city of Jericho. The longer trip would weed out the rebels and doubters, and it would take about thirty-eight years.

14:26–39. The Lord seemed to despair with the murmuring of the people, **which murmur against me** (v. 27). As Moses had asked, they would be spared an instant judgment (v. 28), yet their **carcases shall fall in this wilderness** (v. 29), and everyone **twenty years old and upward** would perish for their complaining. The Lord considered this the age division of who would be held accountable. The older generation would bear the consequences of their rebellion. Those who were younger would be spared (see Deut. 1:39).

Of the older generation, only Caleb and Joshua would enter the land because they had trusted in the Lord and gave to the people the good report (v. 30). The **little ones** (v. 31), who the people had said would be **prey** and die in the desert (14:3), would come into the Promised Land after the older generation died off (v. 32). They would **wander** for **forty years** (v. 33; Deut. 1:26–46) because of the older generation's **whoredoms**. The forty years of wandering corresponds to the **forty days** (v. 34) in which the land was spied out. The Lord called the people an **evil congregation** (v. 35) who would be **consumed**

by the **wilderness** because they murmured against Him and brought **a slander upon the land** (v. 36). The ten spies who were doubters had perished in the **plague before the Lord** (v. 37). **Joshua** (v. 38) and **Caleb**, however, would live. When Moses finished delivering the words of judgment, **the people mourned greatly** (v. 39). While this condemnation seems harsh, it must be remembered that the people had witnessed astounding miracles from the Lord up to this point in their journey. With great revelation comes great responsibility.

14:40–45. The people thought they could repent and restore their relationship with the Lord instantly. They ascended a high **mountain** (v. 40) and looked into the land, declaring, **Lo, we be here**, and we can go into the land the **Lord hath promised**: **for we have sinned**. Moses sensed they were trying to rescind the orders about their not going into the land (v. 41) and warns them that if they do, they will be **smitten** (v. 42) by Him **before your enemies**. The **Amalekites** (v. 43) and the **Canaanites** would destroy them because the Lord would not protect them. The people did not heed Moses' warning. It seems, however, that the Lord prevented the **ark of the covenant** (v. 44) and Moses from moving out of the camp. The enemy swept down the hill **and smote them, and discomfited them** (NASB, "beat them back"), **even unto Hormah** (v. 45). The name Hormah is from the Hebrew root *haram*, which implies "complete destruction." Hormah is eight miles southeast of Beersheba. The people changed their minds and tried to reclaim their blessing. They were more interested in the promises and were less concerned about their relationship with the Lord.

C. A Collection of Laws on Offerings, the Sabbath, and Tassels on Garments (chap. 15)

This chapter is divided into three sections, each of which begins with, **And the Lord spake unto Moses** (vv. 1, 17, 37). The congregation was now under a terrible judgment, and offerings were required to restore their position before Him. The offerings were also important to remind them that only with sacrifice could their sins be forgiven and their fortunes brought back in line with the will of the Lord.

1. Offerings Required of Israel (15:1–21)

15:1–16. Because the adults of this generation had been sentenced to perish in the desert, it became necessary for the younger generation to be shown the requirements for their covenant relationship with the Lord. The instructions speak of God's faithfulness in contrast to the unfaithfulness of the people. The words of these verses are addressed to those who will one day make their **habitations** (v. 2) in the land and give instructions for when they arrive in the land and make **a burnt offering, or a sacrifice in performing a vow, or in a freewill offering, or in your solemn feasts, to make a sweet savour unto the Lord** (v. 3). These offerings are spelled out in Leviticus 1–4. Also, these offerings were not sin or guilt offerings, "since their form and content were invariable (Lev. 4:1–6:7); these were votive, or 'fellowship' offerings (Lev. 1–3)" (Merrill, "Numbers," p. 233).

As the animal sacrifices became larger, from a ram up to a bull and oxen, so the people were to offer more grain, fine flour, and oil along with the animals (vv. 6–12). These passages are the first to indicate that wine offerings must accompany all burnt offerings and fellowship offerings (vv. 4–12). The instructions were for those born in the land but also for the **stranger** (v. 14) who was sojourning among them. The same **ordinance** (v. 15) for the sacrifices was for both.

15:17–21. When the new generation arrived in the land of Canaan and ate the bread of the land, they were to offer up a **heave** ("to lift up") **offering** (v. 19) as a sign of their gratitude for the blessings of the land. The **heave offering** (v. 20) was the **cake** made of bread that is first offered to God. This was to be a perpetual **offering** (v. 21) to Him.

2. Offerings for Unintentional Sins (15:22–31)

15:22–31. These passages differ somewhat from the instructions given in Leviticus 4:13–21 for offerings for sins of ignorance. In Leviticus, there is no burnt offering, "oblation, or drink offering" (Unger, *Commentary*, p. 204). Unintentional sins could be committed by the entire congregation (vv. 22–26) or by the individual Israelite (vv. 27–29). These instructions applied also for unintentional sins committed by the **stranger** (v. 26), or Gentile, that **sojourneth** in the land. The congregation was seen as being collectively guilty. A **she goat** (v. 27) was to be brought as a **sin offering** and as an **atonement** (v. 28) for the individual. The **soul** (v. 30) that sinned **presumptuously** ("with a high hand"), or knowingly or deliberately, **reproacheth**, or challenged, the Lord and would **be cut off** from the people. He had **despised** (v. 31) the word of God; **his iniquity shall be upon him**.

3. Stoning the Sabbath Breaker (15:32–36)

15:32–35. These verses seem to describe the first incident of someone breaking the Sabbath rest, by picking up **sticks** (v. 32) on that holy day. The penalty was clearly spelled out as death (Exod. 31:15; 35:2) because it was considered willful blasphemy (Lev. 24:10–16). By the time of Christ, Sabbath-keeping was distorted and turned into a meaningless legalistic exercise that was far from its original intention. The Sabbath was a reminder that the world was created uniquely by God and that He finished this marvelous work in six days (Gen. 2:1–2). It was a day that was especially blessed and sanctified (Gen. 2:3). For the Jews, it was to be not only a day of contemplation but also a day given over to physical rest. No other case of Sabbath-breaking was recorded up to this point, and the people questioned what was to be done with the guilty party (v. 34). The Lord commanded that he be stoned outside the **camp** (v. 35).

15:36. The man's sentence was carried out by the entire **congregation … as the Lord commanded Moses**. The law forbade picking up sticks for a fire on the Sabbath (Exod. 35:3). "The passage is to drive home how important it was for Israel to obey the Sabbath laws and maintain ceremonial holiness by obeying God's commandments" (Harrison, *Numbers*, p. 229).

4. The Fringes of Remembrance (15:37–41)

15:37–40. The Lord commanded the Jews to make **fringes** (Hebrew, *tzitzit*; v. 38 in the **borders**

of their clothing, overlaid with **a ribband of blue.** "Ribband" implies a cord of lace. These were swishing tassels that became auditory and visual reminders that everywhere the Jews went, they were to keep themselves clean. They were to watch what their heart sought after and what their eyes looked at, so that they would not go **a whoring** (v. 39). The blue reminded them of God's heavenly requirements. These were to remind them to do God's **commandments** (v. 40) and to **be holy unto your God.** Some have suggested that such swishing sounds would have made it harder for a Jewish man to sneak out into the night to commit a sin.

15:41. The Israelites' holiness was marked because God had brought them out of **Egypt, to be your God: I am the LORD your God.** "The true Israelite … arrayed in the sacred covering, reminding him of the Divine Presence, does not stray after the satisfaction of bodily pleasures; but is mindful that he is a member of a 'holy' People" (Hertz, *Pentateuch and Haftorahs*, p. 634).

D. The Rebellion of Korah and His Allies (chap. 16)

Earlier, Miriam and Aaron had brought on a rebellion against the leadership of Moses (chap. 12). Korah and his followers now did the same thing and attacked the leadership of both Moses and Aaron. Korah was descended from Levi through Kohath. As a Kohathite, he was responsible for serving the Lord in the tabernacle (see 4:1–20), but now he wanted more authority. He wanted to advance his priestly leadership.

16:1–7. Korah (v. 1) was the leading insurgent. As a Kohathite, he was assigned the honorable position of transporting the most holy things of the tabernacle. Korah had gathered a large group, and together they **rose up** (v. 2) against Moses. Among the rebellious group were **princes,** men **famous in the congregation, men of renown.** They accused Moses and Aaron of taking too much authority and lifting themselves above the **congregation** (v. 3). Moses was heartbroken and fell on **his face** (v. 4). He told **Korah** (v. 5) that God would show whom

He had **chosen** to lead the people. Korah was instructed to take **censers** (v. 6) and put **fire therein** (v. 7) along with **incense … before the LORD.** The Lord **doth choose** who shall be **holy** before Him.

16:8–35. Moses spoke strong words against Korah and his followers. He reminded them that God had separated them for **service** (v. 9) in the **tabernacle**; did they now seek **the priesthood also?** (v. 10). Moses then called for witnesses, **Dathan** (v. 12) and **Abiram**, but they refused to come forward to confirm Moses' words. Moses was then accused of bringing the people out of **a land of milk and honey** (v. 13), Egypt, **to kill us in the wilderness.** He did it by making himself a **prince** over them and by blinding them — **putting out the eyes of these men** (v. 14). Moses was **very wroth** (v. 15), greatly frustrated and angry. He reminded the Lord that he had not taken anything from these men or done anything to them to cause their rebellion.

Moses then instructed Korah and his followers to gather themselves before the **tabernacle** (v. 18) with their **censers.** Moses and Aaron would also be there. The glory of the Lord appeared to **all the congregation** (v. 19) and spoke to Moses and Aaron, telling them, **Separate yourselves** (v. 21) from the rebels **that I may consume them in a moment.** Moses and Aaron fell on their faces and questioned God, the Creator **of the spirits of all flesh** (v. 22). Would He be **wroth** with the entire congregation because of the sin of one man? The Lord did not reply to their question but instead told them to instruct everyone to remove themselves from the entrance to the tabernacle (vv. 23–27).

Moses reminded the people that all that he had done with the people was not done on his **own** (v. 28); rather, he was directed by the Lord to lead them. Moses told them that if God did nothing against these men and they lived natural lives and were not now judged, then **the LORD hath not sent me** (v. 29) to be the leader. If **the LORD make a new thing, and the earth open her mouth, and swallow them up** (v. 30), and they die quickly, then the people would know that these men had **provoked the LORD.** When Moses finished speaking, the earth opened and swallowed up Korah and his followers, along with their houses and all **that appertained to them**. They **went down alive into the** open **pit** and **perished from among the congregation** (v. 33).

All the people standing near the tabernacle saw this instant, visual judgment and fled, **Lest the earth swallow us up also** (v. 34). **Fire** (v. 35) came down from the Lord and **consumed the two hundred and fifty** rebels who had aligned themselves with Korah.

17:36 – 50. The **censers** (v. 37) that were left behind were collected and made into **broad plates** (v. 39), which were then used to cover the altar, because, though evil men had used them to worship before the Lord without proper authority, the censers were **hallowed** (v. 37), or holy, before Him. The covering for the altar that they made was to be a **memorial** (v. 40), or reminder, to the children of Israel that only the **seed of Aaron** could **come near to offer incense before the LORD.**

The people had not finished their grumbling. The **congregation** (v. 41) came before Moses and Aaron and accused them of killing **the people of the LORD.** The **glory of the LORD** (v. 42) appeared in the **cloud** covering the **tabernacle.** The wrath of God was kindled, and He was ready to **consume them as in a moment** (v. 45). But Moses and Aaron pled the people's case and quickly made an **atonement for them** (v. 46). God's wrath had gone out, however, and a **plague** began. **Incense** (v. 47) was waved before God, an atonement was made, and Aaron **stood between the dead and the living; and the plague was stayed** (v. 48). **Fourteen thousand and seven hundred** (v. 49) died that day **beside them that died about the matter of Korah**, and **the plague was stayed** (v. 50). The nature of the plague is not specified. Two words, however, are used to describe it: the "smiting" (vv. 46 – 47) and the "blow" (vv. 48 – 50). That the plague "was stayed" means "it was contained" (v. 48; Ashley, *Numbers*, p. 328).

This is a graphic and dramatic account of how God demonstrated that the authority of Moses and Aaron and his descendants was not to be questioned. The Lord had set the order of worship, and no one could change it through their own will. The leader-

ship of Moses and Aaron was confirmed and accompanied by judgment, but also by the fact that a blood atonement was made for their sins.

E. The Budding of Aaron's Rod: A Sign for Rebels (chap. 17)

Since Aaron's priestly role had been challenged by Korah and his followers, God now illustrated to the people that Aaron's authority was intact, to the exclusion of all others. The question broached by the rebels would be settled for all time.

17:1 – 12. A **rod** (v. 2), or staff, was brought from each house of the **fathers**, from all the **princes.** Representing the twelve tribes, **twelve** rods were gathered, each with the leader's name written on it. Aaron's name was inscribed upon the **rod of Levi** (v. 3). The rods were then laid **in the tabernacle of the congregation before the Testimony, where I will meet with you** (v. 4). The "Testimony" is the Holy Place, the inner sanctum. The leaders responded, and the rods were placed **in the tabernacle of Witness** (v. 7). On the following day, when Moses entered the **tabernacle of Witness** (v. 8), the rod of Aaron had **budded** and **bloomed blossoms** of **almonds.** The almond tree is the first to bloom after the winter. The rods were dead instruments with no life in them. Many see this miracle as a type of the resurrection of Christ. By His work at the cross, "we have not a high priest which cannot be touched with the feeling of our infirmities; but was in all points tempted like as we are, yet without sin. Let us therefore come boldly unto the throne of grace, that we may obtain mercy, and find grace to help in time of need" (Heb. 4:15 – 16).

In a sense, the rods of the leaders had "witnessed" the power of God with Aaron's rod of authority. Aaron's rod was to be **a token against the rebels** (v. 10), and it was also meant to stop the murmurings so that the people would not die. With this second miracle, after the swallowing up of the rebels in the ground, the people cried out, **Behold, we die, we perish, we all perish** (v. 12). Fear had swept the assembly, and they realized that the Lord was no longer patient with their foolishness.

17:13. The people finally got the point and said, **Whosoever** comes near **the tabernacle of the LORD shall die: shall we be consumed with dying?** In the larger picture, the tabernacle shows that there is only one way to come before a holy God. Only the proper priests could serve before Him. This is a type of Christ, the perfect Priest. He is the only one, as the Son of God, who can finally and completely bring redemption to lost sinners. Korah and his crowd had violated this prophecy in the tabernacle.

F. Concerning Priests, Their Duties, and Their Support (chap. 18)

Many scholars believe that this chapter is a reminder of the responsibilities of the Aaronic priesthood in light of the rebellion recorded in chapters 16 – 17. The priests' responsibilities and duties are restated and amplified. The tasks concerning the tabernacle are for the Levites alone. No other tribe is called to minister there because the tabernacle rituals were to be carried out by the Levites exclusively (Exod. 28:38). This chapter was written to make sure no unauthorized men intruded in the work of the sanctuary, as did those who rebelled with Korah.

1. Duties of Priests and Levites (18:1 – 7)

18:1 – 6. Aaron and his tribe were to **bear the iniquity of the sanctuary** (v. 1) and also of the **priesthood**. The Levites were responsible for any failure or neglect or unholy activity that might make the tabernacle unclean before the Lord. With their **charge** (v. 3), they were not to come near the **vessels of the sanctuary** in a flippant or unclean manner, or to the **altar, that neither they, nor you also, die.** The Levites were to work together and follow orders, **keep the charge** (v. 4), and not allow a **stranger** to come near the priests and detract them from their responsibilities. In this case, "stranger" refers to anyone not of the Levitical order. In keeping the common people of the children of Israel away, the Levites would ensure **that there be no wrath any more upon the children of Israel** (v. 5). The **Levites** (v. 6) are **a gift for the LORD.** These verses are the follow-through after

the recent negative events involving the rebels who had taken spiritual issues for granted.

18:7. It is repeated that there can be no violations of the **altar.** This would certainly include any violations against the Holy of Holies, the place where the ark was kept **within the vail.**

2. Tithes and Offerings (18:8 – 32)

18:8 – 24. The **heave offerings** (v. 8), or wave offerings, were presented or "waved" before the Lord, including the portions reserved for the priests because of their special **anointing** (Lev. 8:10 – 12, 30). These priestly laws became **an ordinance for ever.** The laws guaranteed that the priests would receive the offerings of grain, first fruits, wine, and oil, and the animals offered on the fire of the altar. They were **most holy** because they were rendered specifically for the Lord. The priests' sons and daughters were also provided for in these offerings. The command to do these offerings was **a statute for ever** (v. 11).

The priests could partake of these offerings. This included the best of the oil, wine, wheat, firstfruits **which they shall offer to the LORD, them have I given thee** (v. 12), along with other fruits, the **first ripe** (v. 13) of the land. Every thing that was **devoted** (v. 14), or presented, to the Lord belonged to the priests; they received a portion of the bounty. The firstborn of man and of the unclean animals must be redeemed by a payment of five shekels of silver. However, the firstborn of an ox, sheep, or goat was not redeemed but offered by fire as an aroma to the Lord. The clean animals were seen as ceremonially holy and were given as food for the priests and their families (vv. 17 – 18), "the portions being regulated according to the procedures of Leviticus 7:29 – 34. The idea of the redemption was that of transferring the ownership to another by paying a price of some kind" (Harrison, *Numbers*, pp. 249 – 50). The redemption money of **five shekels** (v. 16) was about two ounces of silver, amounting to five-months' pay for the average worker. "The ransom money was not only a means of providing for the tabernacle worship; it also was a somber reminder of the … necessity of a redemption of a fallen, lost race" (Unger,

Commentary, p. 140). This included **a covenant of salt for ever before the LORD** (v. 19; 2 Chron. 13:5). While this expression is not clear, it is somehow related to the provision of salt necessary for the diet. The priests were "worth their salt."

Though the priests would have **no inheritance in their land** (v. 20), God was their inheritance. The Levites were given **all the tenth in Israel** (v. 21), or a tithe, the giving of which had already been set in tradition with Abram (Gen. 14:20). Generally, the tithe could be made with foodstuffs, such as the **heave offering** (v. 24) or grain offering, rather than financial giving. Such substitution was legitimate.

18:25–32. The priests too were required to offer a tenth back to the Lord (vv. 28–29). What was offered was to be **the best** (v. 29), and it was considered **hallowed**, or holy. Wherever the camp of Israel moved, **in every place** (v. 31), the priests and their **households** were to be fed this way, **for it is your reward for your service in the tabernacle**. They **should bear no sin by reason of it** (v. 32), meaning that they should not take advantage of this blessing. They were not to force the people unduly in their giving or to **pollute** the gifts, which were considered **holy things** from the people, **lest ye die**.

G. The Red Heifer and the Cleansing Water (chap. 19)

The Jews were to bring to the tabernacle a young, unblemished, red-brown cow—probably the color of blood—that had never worked, to be committed, though not techincally a sacrifice, to the service of the Lord. It was thus a pure cow, meeting the high standards the Lord demanded for this unusual ritual. A priest by the name of Eleazar was to offer the animal outside the camp. The intense focus on this ceremony means that it was extremely important to God.

19:1–10. This ritual was a very important, standing **ordinance of the law** (v. 2) commanded for the children of Israel. The priest **Eleazar** (the son of Aaron; v. 3) was to bring the cow outside the **camp** and slay her himself. He was then to spread the **blood** (v. 4) with **his finger** and sprinkle it **before the tabernacle … seven times** (Lev. 4:6). In an

unusual command, the entire **heifer** (v. 5) was to be burned, with **cedar wood, and hyssop, and scarlet** (v. 6) thrown into the midst of the burning animal. The scarlet was probably a piece of red wool and more than likely symbolized blood. The hyssop may have been of the family of the labiate plants, such as thyme or marjoram. "The fact that sour vinegar was offered to the crucified Christ by means of a bunch of hyssop … attests to the ability of the plant to retain fluid in its foliage" (Harrison, *Numbers*, p. 256; see John 19:29). The three items may have given off a pleasant smell.

Of all of the offerings, this one may be the most illustrative of the sacrifice of Christ for sinners. He was slain outside the city walls at the place of the skull, Golgotha (John 19:17). Hebrews adds, "For if the blood of bulls and of goats, and the ashes of a heifer sprinkling the unclean, sanctifieth to the purifying of the flesh: how much more shall the blood of Christ, who through the eternal Spirit offered himself without spot to God, purge your conscience from dead works to serve the living God?" (Heb. 9:13–14).

After the bloodiness of the sacrifice, the priest was required to wash his clothes and bathe before returning to the camp. He would be unclean until **the even** (v. 7). Whoever helped burn the animal also had to wash his clothes and **bathe** (v. 8). The slaying of the red heifer was for all of Israel, including the **stranger** (v. 10) who was in their midst.

19:11–22. In some way, the ashes of the heifer, which had been placed in **a clean place** (v. 9) outside the camp, were to be used in the ritual cleansing of one who had touched a **dead body** (v. 11); otherwise, he would be defiled and was to be **cut off from Israel** (v. 13). Even going into a tent where one had died could make a person **unclean seven days** (v. 14). Any contamination caused by contact with the dead (v. 15) could be cleansed by the **ashes of the burnt heifer** as a **purification for sin** (v. 17), along with using water poured from a vessel. One who avoided this cleansing process was **unclean** (v. 20) and was to be **cut off** from **the congregation**. This law was **a perpetual statute unto them** (v. 21). The constant need for cleansing after contact with the dead is a reminder that there is no such thing as "personal" sins that do not affect others. All sin touches the entire family of God's people.

H. The Sin of Moses (20:1-13)

Miriam, the sister of Moses and Aaron, died in Kadesh and was buried there. Many scholars believe that a comparison of 20:22-29 with 33:38 leads to the conclusion that the events of this chapter began in the fortieth year after the exodus from Egypt. Most of the people who had rebelled years before would have already died (see chaps. 13-14). The greater part of the wilderness wandering is not recorded. It seems that Miriam's death gave the people another occasion to complain.

20:1-5. The **first month** (v. 1) seems to be the beginning of the fortieth year of the wilderness experience (14:33-35; 33:3, 37-39). The people are circling in the **desert of Zin** (see 13:21). The name **Miriam** means "bitterness." The narrative seems to indicate that her passing triggered more complaining, with the people rising up and confronting Moses and Aaron about the lack of **water** (v. 2). Miriam died almost within sight of the Promised Land, never entering into its rest (see Mic. 6:4; Heb. 4:1). The people **chode** (v. 3), or argued, with Moses and said, **Would God that we had died when our brethren died before the LORD!** The congregation poured contempt on Moses, arguing that the desert was not like Egypt with its physical "blessings" (vv. 4-5). The assembly, made up of younger Israelites, had quickly forgotten why they were taken out of Egypt. They had also lost sight of the Lord's miraculous dealings with them and the promises going back to Abraham.

20:6-13. In frustration, Moses and Aaron again fell on their faces before the Lord, and His **glory** (v. 6) appeared to them. Moses was commanded to strike the **rock before their eyes** (v. 8), and **water** would gush out for the people and their **beasts**. Moses was angry at this point and called the people **rebels** (v. 10). In a fit of rage, **he smote the rock twice** (v. 11), and the water came forth as the Lord had said it would. Moses' anger showed that he did

not trust what God had said. He was so frustrated that he went beyond the Lord's command and hit the rock a second time. Even Moses, the leader of the people, was required to follow the Lord's instructions. God charges him with lack of trust and with not holding Him holy before the people, with the penalty that Moses would not bring the congregation into the Promised Land (v. 12). The stream of water that came out of the rock was called **Meribah** (v. 13), meaning "contention," because here the people **strove with the LORD**. A similar event had happened forty years earlier (Exod. 17:7) at a place named Massah, meaning "testing" (see Ps. 95:8).

IV. The Journey from Kadesh to the Plains of Moab (20:14-22:1)

More trouble loomed ahead for Israel in the wilderness. For a long while, things did not get better; they only got worse. Israel was blocked from passing through Edom, Aaron died, and many people were killed when the Lord sent serpents among them as punishment for their complaining and mistrust of Him. The Israelites did experience some victories during this time, however. They overcame the Amorites and the people of Bashan. The Lord was with Israel in both of these encounters.

A. Edom Refuses Israel Passage (20:14-21)

The Edomites were the descendants of Esau, the brother of Jacob (Gen. 25:20-34). Esau, the older of the twins, had despised his birthright and his inheritance as the firstborn. Esau's descendants showed terrible cruelty to Israel in not letting them pass through their territory.

20:14-20. From **Kadesh** (v. 14), Moses appealed to **the king of Edom** and reminded him of all the **travail that hath befallen us**. Moses recounted how they were **vexed** (v. 15) in Egypt and how God heard their cry and **sent an angel** (v. 16) and brought the people **forth out of Egypt**. Moses pleaded that the people be allowed to pass through the Edomites' land **by the king's high way** (v. 17), not bothering their crops and vineyards, nor even drinking from **the water of their wells**. The king refused Moses' request and vowed to attack them **with the sword** (v. 18) if they attempted passage. No matter what Moses promised (v. 19), the king of **Edom** (v. 20) promised retaliation **with a strong hand** to keep them out.

20:21. Edom's show of hatred caused Israel to turn away to avoid conflict with this brother nation. The Lord forbade the Jews to take even a foothold in Edom (Deut. 2:4–6). Esau had operated from the natural and from the flesh, and his descendants did likewise. They could not see the hand of God in the deliverance of Israel from Egypt, nor did they wish to participate in blessing them.

B. The Death of Aaron (20:22–29)

Though Aaron never walked perfect before the Lord, he was still anointed as His servant. His death brought sadness to the people. It was also the closing chapter of their wilderness wanderings. From here on, Israel marched or encamped but was no longer simply wandering.

20:22–28. The congregation moved from **Kadesh** (v. 22) to **mount Hor**. Little is known of this mountain except that it is on the border of **Edom** (v. 23). Aaron would die, the Lord said, and he would not **enter into the land** (v. 24) because he had **rebelled** with Moses against the Lord's **word at the water of Meribah** (20:13). Aaron's high priestly **garments** (v. 26) were to be placed on his son **Eleazar**, and Aaron **shall be gathered unto his people, and shall die there**, on Mount Hor. The expression "gathered unto his people" is a euphemism for death (Gen. 25:8, 17; 35:29), meaning he would go home to heaven to be with his godly ancestors. A sad picture follows. Moses, Aaron, and Eleazar journey up Mount Hor, where Aaron dies. The priestly garments are placed on Eleazar, and the two men come down the **mount** (v. 28) after burying Aaron.

20:29. When the congregation saw the two men descending, they realized that Aaron was dead. **They mourned for Aaron thirty days, even all the house of Israel**. Though Aaron and all of the high priests to follow would die, it was prophesied that the last high priest, the Lord Jesus Christ, would be eternal.

"It is witnessed that he liveth" (Heb. 7:8). He would be a high priest "after the order of Melchisedec, and not be called after the order of Aaron" (Heb. 7:11).

C. The Destruction of Arad (21:1–3)

21:1–2. These verses may indicate that the passing of Aaron was traumatic for the congregation of Israel, so a quick and stunning military victory against the Canaanite forces of **king Arad** (v. 1) may have been a morale booster, letting the people know that the Lord had not deserted His people in the wilderness. This was a new day for Israel since they had been defeated by the Amalekites and the Canaanites a generation before (14:41–45). Pleading with the Lord as a voice of one, Israel vowed to destroy the cities of these pagan people if He delivered them into Israel's hands (21:2).

21:3. The Lord did so, and a great victory followed. The name of the place became known as **Hormah**, a word from the Hebrew *haram*, meaning "to utterly destroy as under a curse" (Unger, *Commentary*, p. 214). Numbers 14:45 probably reflects the incident recorded here.

D. The Serpent of Brass (21:4–9)

21:4–7. Leaving **mount Hor by the way of the Red sea** (v. 4), the people **compass[ed]**, or circled, **the land of Edom**. Each **soul** was **much discouraged** by this circular journey. Again, they spoke against God and against Moses, complaining about leaving Egypt **to die in the wilderness** (v. 5). They detested the lack of bread and water and loathed the **light bread**, the manna that fed them daily. For their mistrust of the Lord and Moses, God sent **fiery serpents among the people** (v. 6), and many Israelites died. The word "fiery" indicates the terrible sting and pain inflicted by the serpent bites. This judgment brought about conviction, and the people cried to Moses, **We have sinned** (v. 7) and have spoken against the Lord and you! They begged Moses to appeal for them in prayer that the snakes would be removed, which he did.

21:8–9. The Lord instructed Moses to make a **fiery serpent** (v. 8) of brass and mount it on a **pole**, saying that everyone who had been **bitten** and looked on it would **live**. As the Lord had said, **it came to pass** (v. 9). Some have likened the serpents' venom as the strike of death in the satanically inspired temptation in the garden (Gen. 3:1, 15; see Rev. 12:9). The brass serpent prefigures Christ, who was made to be sin for us (2 Cor. 5:21; cf. Ps. 22:1; Matt. 27:46). As the people were saved by faith by looking at the brass serpent, so Christ became the object of faith when He went to the cross. Jesus said, "And as Moses lifted up the serpent in the wilderness, even so must the Son of man be lifted up: that whosoever believeth in him should not perish, but have eternal life" (John 3:14 – 15).

E. The Song of the Well and the Journey to Moab (21:10 – 20)

21:10 – 13. The location of **Oboth** (v. 10) is not certain. **From Oboth** (v. 11), they journeyed to **Ije-abarim** ("the mounds of Abraham"), east of **Moab.** They moved to **Zared** (v. 12) and then to **the other side of Arnon** (v. 13), which **is the border of Moab.** The Zared valley forms the border between Moab and Edom, and the Arnon River borders Moab and the land of the Amorites. In degrees, Moses was leading the people closer and closer to the crossing point that would lead into the Promised Land.

21:14 – 20. The **book of the wars of the LORD,** mentioned only here, is probably the chronicles of the tactics that led up to the moment of invasion into the Promised Land (v. 14). **Ar** (*el Misna'*; v. 15) was a village or city in the northern part of Moab about ten miles south of **Arnon** (v. 13; see 22:36; Deut. 2:9, 18). The Israelites journeyed on to **Beer** ("well"; v. 16), so named because here the Lord provided a well. A poem was written about this blessing (vv. 17 – 18). This poem, or song, may also have been recorded in the "book of the wars." The poem says even the **princes** (v. 18) and the **nobles** dug the well, under the **direction of the lawgiver,** Moses. The journey then took them to **Mattanah** (Khirbet el-Medeiyinah), to **Nahaliel,** to **Bamoth** (v. 19), which lies eight miles south of Heshbon, and finally to **Pisgah** ("the hill"; v. 20), **which looketh toward Jeshimon** ("the wilderness"). "At last, Israel seemed to be on the verge of invasion and conquest of the Promised Land" (Merrill, "Numbers," p. 240). While the listing of these locations may seem tedious, it proves the historicity of the movement of the children of Israel as they finally stood poised to take the land promised to their fathers.

F. The Defeat of Sihon and Og (21:21 – 35)

Israel's journey, however, was not over. Sometimes spiritual victories seem so close yet remain illusive and distant. The people could see the land, yet more enemies lay in their path. Two pagan kings, Sihon and Og, stood to resist their arrival. In the conflicts that followed, the children of Israel grew stronger militarily and gained confidence in their preparation to invade Canaan. Spiritual conflicts should bring not defeat but further trust in the Lord and in His purposes.

21:21 – 30. At least for the moment, the Israelites were more trusting of their God. Greater victories were won, for the Lord's people now identified Him as the sovereign God who would lead them into battle, not defeat. **Sihon** (v. 21), the **king of the Amorites,** and Og, the giant king of the peoples of Bashan (21:33 – 35), were totally defeated, and their lands were possessed by the Israelites. Both rulers stand for complete resistance to the will of God. They were pagan dictators representing the powers of darkness and the desire to defeat God's people. **Sihon** (v. 23) was defeated at **Jahaz,** known as Khirbet Umm el-Idham, located about five miles north of Dibon. **Heshbon** (v. 26), originally a town in Moab, had been taken earlier by Sihon and made his royal city. At Edrei (21:33), the kingdom of the Amorites to the north of the Jabbok River was overrun.

21:31 – 35. These verses record the final strategy in which Moses and the people were victorious. In the ending phases of the conflict, the Lord assured Moses, **Fear Og not: for I have delivered him into thy hand, and all his people, and his land; and thou shalt do to him as thou didst unto Sihon king of the Amorites** (v. 34). Og and his two sons, who would have followed him, were slain, along with **all**

his people, until there was none left him alive: and they possessed his land (v. 35). It is a well-known historical fact that the peoples of Canaan were some of the most immoral and evil people in the Middle East. The Lord used Israel as the sword to bring justice upon these nations. The victory over Sihon and Og were recorded in song to commemorate God's victories and is recited in the celebration during the Passover season (Pss. 135:11; 136:19–20).

G. Israel Returns to Moab (22:1)

22:1. The Israelites returned to the **plains of Moab** and pitched their tents on the east side of the **Jordan** River **by Jericho**. More obstacles awaited them. Balak, king of Moab, was terrified because of what Moses and the people had done to the Amorites (21:21–35). He was overwhelmed at Israel's numbers and fighting strength. "Balak as king is closely identified with Moab, which represents unregenerate man's pride (Isa. 16:6; Jer. 48:42)" (Unger, *Commentary*, p. 215).

V. Israel on the Plains of Moab, in Anticipation of Taking the Promised Land (22:2–32:42)

These chapters contain more of the drama in Israel's preparation for taking the land of Canaan. More resistance is recorded concerning the Moabites Balak and Balaam. Since the Midianites were residing in Moab at this time, they also felt they were in peril from the Israelites. King Balak, however, was fearful without reason. The Moabites were kin to Israel (Gen. 19:26–37), as were the Ammonites, and were exempt from attacks by the congregation of Israel. Moses had previously been told to avoid harming the Edomites (Deut. 2:5–6), Moabites (Deut. 2:9), and Ammonites (Deut. 2:19). Even the Midianites, who were distantly related to Israel, had little to be afraid of because they were related to the children of Israel by Abaham's wife Keturah, whom he married following the death of Sarah (Gen. 25:1–4). These chapters also record a second census (chap. 26) and repeat many of the laws of the tabernacle (chaps. 28–31).

A. Balak of Moab Hires Balaam to Curse Israel (22:2–41)

King Balak realized that Israel had become a powerful force, too strong to be defeated by military might. Instead, he hired a well-known warlock or diviner (24:1; Josh. 13:22) to bring a curse upon Israel. Balak was the king of Moab and failed to realize that Israel had no plans to fight against him. Somehow he and his people may have realized that the true God was leading the Jews through the wilderness. Because they were an immoral people, they may have had a certain conviction about the sinful way they lived. At any rate, the Moabites did not trust the intention of the Israelites.

1. Balak Sends for Balaam (22:2–20)

22:2–8. The defeat of the Amorites was one of the causes of Balak's fright (v. 2). Out of fear, Balak made an alliance with the Midianites to oppose Israel (vv. 4, 7). Balak devised a plan to call upon the conjurer **Balaam** ("people's devourer"; v. 5). Balak rehearsed to him the story of Israel's flight from Egypt and asked him to come and **curse ... this people** (v. 6). The **elders of Midian** (v. 7) were sent **with the rewards of divination in their hand** to plead with Balaam to take on this assignment. Balaam told the elders to stay overnight, and the LORD (v. 8) would speak to him about the matter. Many scholars believe he was demonically inspired and may have "spoken" with demons, but not with the God of Israel. It is true, however, that the true God of Scripture did come and communicate with him in the following verses.

22:9–20. The Lord does not ask questions to get information. He inquires to bring out what is in the heart of the one He is addressing. God asked Balaam, **What men are these with thee?** (v. 9). **Balaam** (v. 10) answered honestly. This false prophet was dazzled by the rewards offered for his service of witchcraft (vv. 15–19), but the Lord pleaded with him to turn from his evil intentions. The Lord came to him by **night** (v. 20) and instructed him to go with the **princes** sent by Balak, **but yet the word which I shall say unto thee, that shalt thou do**. God had originally forbidden him to go with the elders, then allowed him to do so, provided he did what God said.

2. Balaam's Ass Speaks (22:21-41)

22:21-35. The next morning, Balaam saddled his ass and went with the **princes of Moab** (v. 21). The Lord was angry with him, probably because He knew that Balaam would capitulate and do what the king of Moab desired. The verses that follow have a tinge of humor in them. Unseen by Balaam, the **angel of the LORD** (the preincarnate Lord Jesus Christ; v. 22; see Judg. 2:1; Gen. 31:11-13) appeared with a **sword** (v. 23) to block his path (Josh. 5:13). Balaam's ass, however, saw the angel of the Lord and stumbled about, apparently attempting to escape the thrust of the sword. A ridiculous picture of a hapless Balaam takes place, with the ass twisting, turning, and falling down. The victim was not going to be the donkey!

In a furious state of frustration, Balaam told his donkey that she had **mocked** (v. 29) him and that he wished he had a **sword** with which to kill her. The angel of the Lord finally revealed Himself to Balaam, with the result that great conviction flooded him. He said, **I have sinned; for I knew not that thou stoodest in the way against me: now therefore, if it displeased thee, I will get me back again** (v. 34). Balaam was then instructed to go on his way with the men and **speak** (v. 35) what the Lord told him.

22:36-41. Balak came out to meet Balaam at one of the Moabite cities, **which is in the border of Arnon** (v. 36). Not knowing what had gone on up to this point, the king promised the prophet great **honour** (v. 37) for what he was about to do. Balaam stated that he could speak only what God put into his mouth (v. 38). The two traveled on together to what may have been a large Moabite city, **Kirjath-huzoth** (v. 39), meaning "the city of streets." **Oxen** (v. 40) and **sheep** were to be offered at the **high places of Baal** (v. 41). Balaam would have been a specialist in reading livers; liver divination was regularly practiced by the false prophets among the Canaanites.

B. Balaam Blesses Israel in Seven Oracles (chaps. 23-24)

Chapter 23 deals with Balaam's first prophecy, and chapter 24 gives his last two prophetic parables. These parables are prefaced with Balak's constant badgering and his zeal to bring a curse upon Israel (23:27-28). Chapter 24 also records Balaam's abandonment of his occult practice of omens and making enchantments, though this change was not permanent. Balaam is marked as the epitome of how a false prophet functions in deceiving those around him.

1. Parable One (23:1-12)

23:1-6. A **burnt offering** (v. 3) was prepared, which suggests that Balaam had some knowledge of the sacrifices that the Lord required to be **offered** (v. 4) by His people. Balaam expected God to meet him at the place of sacrifice, which was to be carried out at a **high place** (v. 3), where pagan rites were carried out. Indeed, the Lord came and spoke with him. Apparently to get God's attention, Balaam had prepared **seven altars** (v. 4) for sacrifice. The Lord **put a word in Balaam's mouth** (v. 5) and instructed him to return to Balak and speak that word, the first of seven poetic oracles.

23:7-12. In Balaam's first oracle, which has been described as exquisite poetry (vv. 7-10), he stated that he could not curse whom **God hath not cursed** (v. 8). From lofty heights, he saw God's work with Israel. They **shall dwell alone, and shall not be reckoned among the nations** (v. 9), nor could they be counted. Balaam wanted to die as one who is **righteous** (v. 10), not as one who defied God. Balak was furious at Balaam's refusal to curse Israel (vv. 11-12).

2. Parable Two (23:13-30)

23:13-24. Balak again begged Balaam to **curse** (v. 13) Israel. He took him to the field of **Zophim** (v. 14) and then to the top of mount **Pisgah**, where seven more **altars** were built for sacrifice. With audacious presumption, Balak now tried to **meet** (v. 15) with the Lord Himself. Instead, the Lord spoke again to **Balaam** (v. 16), with Balak inquiring, **What hath**

the Lord spoken? (v. 17). Through Balaam, the Lord told Balak to stand up and listen to what God had to say. **God is not a man, that he should lie; neither the son of man, that he should repent: hath he said, and shall he not do it? Or hath he spoken, and shall he not make it good?** (v. 19). God may stop the processes of judgment when people confess their sins, but His plans are unchangeable. The doctrine of the "immutability" of the Lord is stated in these sublime words. His integrity stands. God does not shift and change with the fickleness of people. With Him, there is "no variableness, neither shadow of turning" (James 1:17b).

Balaam could not **reverse** (v. 20) what he had been commanded to do. With the coming of the children of Abraham back to the land promised them, God did not see in this return **iniquity in Jacob, neither hath he seen perverseness in Israel: the LORD his God is with him** (v. 21). The children of Israel had a divine right to the land promised to them long ago. The Lord brought them out of Egypt (v. 22), and no **enchantment** ("omens"; v. 23) or **divination** ("divinations") could be placed upon them. God was behind the nation of Israel. Their coming into the land was His work: **What hath God wrought!** (v. 23). Israel was about to rise up **as a great lion** (v. 24) and devour its foes, like a lioness on the hunt (24:9; Gen. 49:9).

23:25–30. Balak tried to compromise and suggested that Balaam **neither curse them, all nor bless them all** (v. 25), to which Balaam replied, **Told not I thee … All that the LORD speaketh, that I must do?** (v. 26). Maybe if the location of the curse were changed, Balak suggested, God would from there curse this people (v. 27). Balaam was then taken to **Peor** ("the open place"; v. 28), which looked toward **Jeshimon** (21:10). Neither Pisgah nor **Peor** can be identified with certainty. **Peor** is probably near Baal-Peor (24:3, 5) and Beth-Peor, where Israel had encamped (Deut. 3:29; 4:46) and where Moses was buried (34:6; see Ashley, *Numbers*, p. 485). At Peor, Balaam suggested that building more altars and making additional sacrifices might cause the Lord to curse Israel (vv. 29–30). It is strange that he would

put forth such an idea since he seems so convinced that God would not curse Israel.

3. Parable Three (24:1–14)

24:1–3. Balaam finally fully realized that the Lord would not curse Israel and intended instead to bless the Israelites. Therefore, Balaam did not follow Balak to Peor to curse Israel with **enchantments** (v. 1) but instead **set his face toward the wilderness.** There he saw Israel abiding in their tents. **The spirit of God** (the Holy Spirit) then **came upon him** (v. 2), and his spiritual **eyes** were opened and he received a greater understanding of what the Lord was doing (22:31). Though the Holy Spirit would now control in a distinct way what Balaam said, it must not be thought that he was now a "believer" in God in a salvific way. Balaam would continue in his evil ways.

24:4–9. With his physical eyes open, not closed as in a **trance** (v. 4), Balaam both heard **the words of God** and saw **the vision of the Almighty** (v. 4). He saw Israel, **O Jacob** (v. 5), with **goodly … tents** and **tabernacles** spread out like **gardens by the river side** (v. 6). He prophesied that blessings would **pour** (v. 7) out like **many waters,** and Jacob's **king shall be higher than Agag, and his kingdom shall be exalted.** Agag was the name used in a general sense to describe Amalekite rulers (1 Sam. 15:8). Verse 7 is important because it is a key prediction of the far-off coming of the Messiah and His reign. Israel, which God had brought **out of Egypt** (v. 8), was strong and would conquer its enemies. **Blessed … and cursed** (v. 9). This refers to the blessings and curses of the Abrahamic promises (Gen. 12:1–3), which demonstrates that Balaam knew far more about the history of Israel than imagined.

24:10–14. Balak raged with anger because three times Balaam **blessed** (v. 10) Israel rather than **curse** the nation. He told Balaam to **flee** (v. 11) back home. The seer had forfeited the **honour** that he was to receive for cursing Israel, but more, **the LORD hath kept thee back from honour.** Balaam replied that if he were given a **house full of silver and gold** (v. 13), he could not **go beyond the commandment of the LORD.** He had to speak what the Lord told him to speak. Since he was leaving to go back to his own people, Balaam said he had to **advertise** (v. 14), or tell, what Israel would do to the Moabites **in the latter days**. Balaam foretold the ultimate victory of God's own people in the establishment of the millennial reign of Christ.

4. Parable Four (24:15–25)

24:15–24. In this final parable, the Lord gave to Balaam one of the most profound of the messianic prophecies. Similar to what happened to him in 24:3, Balaam's eyes were **open** (v. 15), and he **heard the words of God, and knew the knowledge of the most High** (v. 16). With **eyes open**, yet in a **trance**, he had a **vision of the Almighty**. The one he **shall see ... but not now** (v. 17) would be the future "king" mentioned in verse 24:7. Balaam could see Him, but He had not arrived yet. He is called the **Star** (Rev. 22:16), and He holds the **Sceptre** that **shall rise out of Israel**. He would bring judgment to **Moab** and would destroy the **children of Sheth** (see Isaiah 16; Jeremiah 48). The "children of Sheth" probably refers to the Shutu people, mentioned in early Egyptian records, who represent human pride.

The **Star out of Jacob** (v. 17) is a prophecy of the coming Messiah, who appears on the distant horizon. It is possible that the wise men (the magi) had access to the Hebrew Scriptures and associated this prophecy with the appearance of the Bethlehem star. From the east, the wise men (the magi) saw the star of Him "that is born King of the Jews" (Matt. 2:1–6). He is the Christ (the "anointed," Ps. 2:2), who was born in Bethlehem as prophesied (Matt. 2:4–6; Mic. 5:2). He would bring spiritual and personal salvation to His people by giving "the remission of their sins" (Luke 1:77) but also salvation "from our enemies, and from the hand of all that hate us" (Luke 1:71), such as the Moabites. The **Scepter** is the "rod of iron" by which He will rule the nations (Psalm 2). The lands of **Edom** (v. 18) and **Seir** would also be His possession, and His **dominion** (v. 19) would come **Out of Jacob** (v. 19), or Israel.

Part of the prophecy could happen before the time of the Messiah's reign. **Amalek** (v. 20) and the **Kenites** (v. 21) would be judged. Amalek was the first

to attack Israel (Exod. 17:8–13). **Asshur** (v. 22), or Assyria, would take the Kenites captive. Who would be able to **live** (v. 23) when God began this judgment? No one! God would use **Chittim** (v. 24), or Cyprus (Gen. 10:4), to **afflict Asshur** and **Eber** (Gen. 10:21–30), who would **perish for ever**.

24:25. Balaam and Balak went their own ways. Balaam returned to his home in Pethor (22:5), in Mesopotamia.

Some have wrongly thought that Balaam was converted to the Lord by his experience, but this is far from the truth. Balaam stands as the vilest of deceivers in Scripture. Though not stated in detail in Numbers 25, Balaam must have had some influence in the Moabite women's seduction of the Jewish men. When Balak urged Balaam to curse Israel, the Lord said, "I would not hearken unto Balaam; therefore he blessed you [Israel] still: so I delivered you out of his hand" (Josh. 24:10). According to the apostles Peter and Jude, Balaam would have taken the riches offered by Balak, "the wages of unrighteousness," but was "rebuked for his iniquity" by the "dumb" animal in the story (2 Peter 2:15–16; see also Jude 11).

The words of Christ to the church of Pergamos say this about Balaam: "Thou hast there [in Pergamos] them that hold the doctrine of Balaam, who taught Balac to cast a stumblingblock before the children of Israel, to eat things sacrificed unto idols, and to commit fornication" (Rev. 2:14). When Joshua led the Israelites into the land, he had Balaam, "the soothsayer," killed lest he again be used to deceive Israel (Josh. 13:22).

C. The Baal of Peor and Israel's Apostasy (chap. 25)

The satanic ploy involving the conjurer Balaam had not brought destruction upon Israel; the tactic of sexual sins was used next. Camping at Shittim, the people were seduced by the pagan women of Moab. The friendliness of the world is often more destructive than the open curses of a foe. What caused the Israelites to give in to the temptations instigated by Balaam (31:8, 16)? Possibly they were feeling flush with victory. "They perhaps felt superior to the moral laws that those commitments enshrined. During a period of inactivity the soldiers may have become somewhat restless and felt the need for adventure among the women of Moab" (Harrison, *Numbers*, p. 335).

25:1–15. Shittim (v. 1) is another name for the staging area on the Jordan River opposite the ancient city of Jericho (Josh. 2:1). Here, Israel began **to commit whoredom with the daughters of Moab**. The Israelites quickly began to sacrifice to the Canaanite gods with fertility rites of Baal. Sexual immorality was rampant among these pagan women. **Baal-peor** (v. 3) must have been the site of this immorality, and there, God's **anger … was kindled against Israel**. The **heads of the people** (v. 4), the princes, were to be hanged facing the **sun**. They were to be hanged **before the Lord**. The **judges** (v. 5) of Israel were to do the slaying. One of the men, **Zimri** (v. 14) brought a Midianite woman to **the tabernacle of the congregation** (v. 6) and showed her off to his family, to Moses, and to the entire congregation without any shame. **Phinehas** (v. 7), a grandson of Aaron, was incensed and took a **javelin** and killed both the man and the woman, who were intimate in the man's tent. **And he went after the man of Israel into the tent, and thrust both of them through** (v. 8). The **plague** of judgment **was stayed**, though **twenty and four thousand** (v. 9) died. The Lord said Phinehas **was zealous** (v. 11) for His sake; he cared about the holy reputation of God.

God made a **covenant of peace** (v. 12) and a **covenant of an everlasting priesthood** (v. 13) with Phinehas the priest because he was **zealous** for the Lord and **made an atonement for the children of Israel**. The "covenant of peace" (Isa. 54:10; Ezek. 34:25; Mal. 2:5) prefigures effecting "peace with God" in a "positional" sense, through atoning priestly sacrifice, as with the peace purchased by Christ in His death on the cross (Rom. 5:1; see Unger, *Commentary*, p. 220). The "covenant of an everlasting priesthood" may have been a badge of honor that would recognize for perpetuity the spiritual integrity of the priestly household of Phinehas. **Zimri, the son of Salu, a prince of a chief house among the Simeonites** (v. 14), brought a reproach upon his family and the tribe of Simeon. The Midianite woman slain,

Cozbi (v. 15), was a daughter of **Zur**, who was **head over a people, and of a chief house in Midian.** A blight would also hang over this family because of the brazen act of adultery.

25:16–18. Moses was instructed by the Lord to **vex** (Hebrew, *tzarar*; "harass, trouble, show hostility toward"; v. 17) **the Midianites** for using their women in immorally beguiling and seducing Israel. This later brought about a holy war (31:1–24).

D. The Second Census (chap. 26)

This second census is much like the first census (chap. 1), which listed 603,550 men of fighting age, from twenty years of age and up (1:46). The total from the second census was just a little less, 601,730 (26:51). The first census had been compiled just over thirty-eight years earlier. The aged Moses was joined in the task of this new census by his nephew Eleazar since Aaron had died (20:28). A second census was necessary because the Israelites were about to cross over the Jordan and take the land promised them by the Lord, and it was important to know the strength of their fighting force.

26:1–5. The census was to number all those who **are able to go to war in Israel** (v. 2). The people were encamped **in the plains of Moab by Jordan near Jericho** (v. 3). The **sum of all the congregation** (v. 2) represents the men ready for combat. The census began with the Reubenites, the **eldest** (v. 5) of the tribes of Israel.

26:6–51. This otherwise uneventful accounting contains some interesting side notes. **Er** (v. 19) and **Onan**, the two evil sons of Judah are listed. They had not been forgotten, though they had no heritage (Gen. 38:1–10). **Zelophehad** (v. 33), the son of **Hepher**, had no male heirs, so his daughters are listed but are not counted for combat. The daughters are **Mahlah, and Noah, Hoglah, Milcah, and Tirzah** (see 27:1–11; 36:1–13).

In addition to the list of the tribes, the leading family divisions are recorded, giving the names of the leading tribal patriarchs. Five tribes decreased in number since the last census: Reuben, Simeon, Gad, Ephraim, and Naphtali. The other tribes increased.

Simeon's large decrease came about because this tribe was more culpable in the moral defection at Baal-Peor and because of the severe punishment in the plague (25:14; see Unger, *Commentary*, p. 221).

26:52–62. The issue of territory of occupation is introduced in these verses. The division of land would be **for an inheritance according to the number of names** (v. 53). Larger tribes would receive larger territorial shares, but specific locations would be decided by lot (33:54; see Josh. 14:2). The Levites were counted separately, as in the first census (chap. 3), and they would not receive territory because they were to minister throughout the land, in various cities, to all of the people (26:57–62).

26:63–65. Leaving out the Levites, of those Israelites who were counted in the first census "in the desert of Sinai" (1:19), only two were still living, **Caleb** and **Joshua** (v. 65). All others had perished in the wilderness because of the revolt against Moses and their rebellious spirit (14:26–31). **There was not left a man of them**.

E. Instructions for the New Generation (chaps. 27–30)

This section, coming near the end of the book, is a potpourri of various issues, subjects, and events that prepare the people for the inevitable invasion of the Promised Land. It is almost like a wrap-up of topics that were especially important when the tribes began to move toward the Jordan River and when they took the land. Some of the topics are reviews of the offerings covered in other books of the Pentateuch (chaps. 28–29) and the laws about vows (chap. 30).

1. The Inheritance for Women (27:1–11)

The five daughters of **Zelophehad** (26:33) of the tribe of Manasseh, whose families came through Joseph (Gen. 50:22–26), brought before Moses a problem about family inheritance. Their father had died in the desert as part of the punishment of the generation of unbelief (14:28–29; 26:64–65). Since he had no male heirs, what would happen with the allotment of land for the family?

27:1–5. The daughters presented the problem before Moses and Eleazar the priest, but they also made their petition before **the princes and all the congregation** (v. 2) at the door of the tabernacle. The judgment for this case would become law for all similar situations in the future. The case was to be heard before all of Israel. The women admitted that their father who in the **company** (v. 3) of those who came **against the LORD in the company of Korah**. The results: he died in his own sin, and had no sons. The question then, **Why should the name of our father be done away from among his family, because he hath no son?** (v. 4). The daughters argued that they should have a possession among their father's brothers.

27:6–11. The Lord agreed and answered: **The daughters of Zelophehad speak right** (v. 7). This ruling would become law for all cases when there were no male heirs to take over the family **inheritance** (v. 8). If a man passed on without a son, his possession would go to his daughters; if he was childless, it would pass on to his brothers. If he had no brothers, his **inheritance** (v. 10) would go to his nearest relative. This ruling was to stand as a **statute of judgment** (v. 11) for all of Israel. This pronouncement by the Lord stands as a unique revelation for the ancient world. Women were not usually so blessed. Today the question might arise as to why the women were not originally included in the passing down of property and land. In the difficulty of existing in a hostile world, the strength of the male population was required to secure and keep possessions.

The action of the daughters in coming before Moses and Eleazar and the leaders of the nation was unprecedented; it was an act of boldness, forthrightness, and courage. What they asked for was only right. The response of the Lord shows His favor for the women who might find themselves in a similar problem in the future.

2. The Successor to Moses (27:12–23)

Moses and Aaron were denied entrance into the Promised Land because of the sin they committed at Meribah (20:12). The case of the daughters of Zelophehad brought to head the issue of Moses. He was to be excluded from entering the land because of his own personal failures.

27:12−23. Though Moses had sinned, the Lord was gracious to him and brought him up into **mount Abarim** (v. 12), in order to view the land that was about to be given to the children of Israel. God told Moses that when he had seen the land, he would **be gathered unto thy people** (v. 13) as his brother Aaron **was gathered**. Many scholars believe this is a confirmation that those who were pious and believed in the Lord were going together to heaven, as one people of faith. God reminded him that he had **rebelled** (v. 14) against His **commandment in the desert of Zin** and had failed to **sanctify** the Lord at the waters before the eyes of the congregation. Moses had failed in his leadership, though he had been terribly frustrated with the assembly of grumblers. Moses then asked that **the God of the spirits of all flesh** (v. 16) would set a man before the congregation so that they would not be as **sheep** (v. 17) without a **shepherd**.

The **spirit** (v. 18) in Joshua is the Holy Spirit, who would guide this man as the new leader after the death of Moses. Moses was to **lay** his **hand upon him** as a sign that he was picked to take the place of Moses upon his death. Joshua was set before the priest Eleazar and the congregation and given **a charge in their sight** (v. 19). As Moses and Aaron had needed to determine the true successor of Aaron before his death (20:22−29), so the one who would follow Moses also needed to be established. Joshua and Caleb were the only two spies who trusted God when the people previously were in the darkened hour of Israel's apostasy (chaps. 13−14).

Eleazar the priest was to ask to receive counsel for Joshua **after the judgment of Urim before the Lord** (v. 21). All of the children of Israel, with Joshua, **shall go out** and **come in** with the word of the Lord. Moses followed the Lord's instructions and **laid his hands upon** (v. 23) Joshua and gave him a solemn charge as commanded. The close relationship between the leader of the people and the priest shows how Christ stands in relation to the two offices He holds. In the case of the priest in this ac-

count, he could receive light from the mind of God through the Urim, which was kept in the breastplate that he wore (Exod. 28:30).

3. Commands regarding Offerings (28:1−15)

These chapters confirm the all-pervasiveness of sacrifice in the daily lives of the people. They also show the great responsibilities placed upon the priesthood. The burnt offering laws are repeated here, possibly as a further reminder of their importance, as previously given throughout this book, but especially in chapters 7 and 15. Perhaps the purpose of 28:1−15 was to maintain continuity during the transition from the leadership of Moses to that of Joshua (27:12−23).

a. The Daily Burnt Offering (28:1−8)

28:1−6. The Lord reminded Moses, **My offering, and my bread for my sacrifices made by fire, for a sweet savour unto me, shall ye observe to offer unto me in their due season** (v. 2). The key here may be the words "in their due season." The people were never to forget the order and the time of the calendar in which these rites are to be performed. God provided precise instructions that were to be followed without variation. **Two lambs of the first year without spot** (v. 3) were to be offered **day by day, for a continual burnt offering**. The lambs were to be offered in the **morning** (v. 4) and at even, with **a tenth part of an ephah of flour** (v. 5) for a **meat** (meal) **offering**, with **the fourth part of a hin** of **beaten oil**, or fine oil beaten out of olives. The burnt offering **was ordained** (v. 6) at Mount Sinai (Exod. 29:40). It would be a **sweet savour** to the Lord because it represented the coming sacrifice of Christ, who would give the believers rest (Heb. 4:3).

28:7−8. A **drink offering** (v. 7) of **strong wine** was also to be poured out before the Lord—**a fourth part of a hin for the one lamb**. A hin is approximately one gallon. Both the morning and evening sacrifices were **made by fire** (v. 8) and smelled as a **sweet savour** to the Lord, again, because they represented the death of His blessed Son at the cross—"as of a lamb without blemish" (1 Peter 1:19).

b. The Offering on the Sabbath (28:9–10)

28:9. On the Sabbath, two lambs were to be offered **without spot**, along with **two tenth deals of flour** mingled with **oil**, and the drink offering. These Sabbath offerings were in addition to the daily offerings.

28:10. While the Sabbath day was seen as a separate remembrance (Exod. 20:8–11), this is the first time that specific instructions are given for the Sabbath offerings. These rituals were to be done at every Sabbath. The Lord is due more on that day than on any other day of the week in terms of worship, praise, prayer, and testimony. A day of physical, spiritual, and even mental contemplation would allow for this.

c. The Offering at the New Moon (28:11–15)

28:11–13. At the **beginning** (v. 11) of each Jewish month, the new moon, every twenty-one days, special offerings were to be made. The requirements were virtually the same as the sacrifices listed earlier (vv. 12–13). These offerings were of great significance. The new moon was a time of celebration, and the trumpets were blown in worship (10:10). The pagan nations held that the moon, sun, and stars were astral deities in their new-moon celebrations, but Israel was permitted to worship no god but the Lord (Exod. 20:3–5). For the Jews, the new moon was not an object of superstition but a calendrical marker for ordering their lives and for planting and harvesting.

28:14–15. Again, the sacrifices for the new-moon celebrations are very similar to the offerings described earlier in the chapter.

4. Commands regarding Festivals (28:16–29:40)

Many of the instructions for the festivals and offerings are repeated in this section. Repetition would imprint on the people and the priests the importance of these ceremonies. They picture over and over again the issues of sin and redemption.

a. The Feast of Unleavened Bread (28:16–31)

28:16–25. These laws have to do with the Passover celebration as given earlier, but now there is the remembrance when the people were delivered from Egyptian bondage (Exod. 12:3–11; Lev. 23:5–8).

The **fourteenth day of the month** (Nisan; v. 16) was the **passover of the Lord**. The **feast** of **unleavened bread** (v. 17) followed on the next day. The Passover was a **holy convocation** (v. 18) in which no one was to do any work. The Passover lambs were to be slaughtered on **the first day**, and the feast was to last seven days, through the twenty-first of the month. The **offering[s]** (v. 22) made are similar to what has been described elsewhere, with **one goat for a sin offering, to make an atonement for you**. These offerings were to be made for **seven days** (v. 24). "The first of these seven days was a Sabbath and that day and each of the following six days required the same offerings as those of the New Moon (Num. 28:18–22, 24; cf. vv. 11–15)" (Merrill, "Numbers," p. 249). The second reminder: this is a **holy convocation** (v. 25), and no **servile work** is to be done.

28:26–31. The Feast of Weeks, or **firstfruits** (v. 26), came fifty days after the Feast of Unleavened Bread (Lev. 23:9–22). From this number comes the word "Pentecost" (meaning "fifty"), used in the New Testament (Acts 2:1). Christ is "our passover" (1 Cor. 5:7), "the living bread which came down from heaven" (John 6:51), and "the firstfruits," the first one to come forth by resurrection from the dead (1 Cor. 15:20–23).

b. The Feast of the Trumpets Offerings (29:1–6)

29:1–5. In the seventh month, on the first day of the month (v. 1), the Feast of the Trumpets was to be held, a **holy convocation**, with the blowing of the trumpets. Again, the offerings described here are very similar to those described earlier, including the **kid of the goats for a sin offering, to make an atonement for you** (v. 5). Almost all of the offerings were for an atonement, a "covering" or a "tent" placed over their sins. These offerings were prophetic of Christ's sacrifice, but the trumpets speak of the end-time regathering of Israel (Lev. 23:23–25; Isa. 11:10–16). Christ will come to the Jewish remnant preceding His second advent (Zech. 12:10–13; Rom. 11:25–36; see Unger, *Commentary*, p. 225).

29:2. The animals were to **be without blemish** in that they represent the holiness of Christ.

c. The Day of Atonement Offerings (29:7–11)

29:7–11. The Day of Atonement, **a holy convocation** (v. 7), was to be held on the **tenth day of this seventh month**. This day was to be a time of confession, contrition, and celebration (Lev. 16; 23:26–32). This day is known in the Jewish calendar as *Tishah b'ab*, or the "Tenth of Ab." The orthodox Jews usually read the book of Lamentations in its entirety on the ninth day of Ab, the traditional date of the destruction of the Solomonic temple in 586 BC as well as the date of the fall of Herod's temple in AD 70. Many Jews also read Lamentations each week at the Western Wall, once known as the "Wailing Wall" in the old city of Jerusalem. In the Old Testament, contrition was to be accompanied by sacrifice. Jews today do not offer any sacrifices before the Lord. The Lord Jesus Christ was their final offering before God, but today, the Jews reject His work on the cross for their sins.

The sacrifices on this occasion are virtually the same as described earlier. One line has been added in the text that is significant. The Jews are told, **ye shall afflict your souls: ye shall not do any work therein** (v. 7).

d. The Feast of Tabernacles Offerings (29:12–40)

29:12–34. The Feast of Tabernacles was to be **on the fifteenth day of the seventh month** (v. 12), and it too would be a **holy convocation** for Israel. This **feast** would last for **seven days**. Again, the offerings are almost the same as before, except in some cases, the numbers of animals sacrificed are increased, such as the **eleven bullocks** (v. 20) and **fourteen lambs** to be sacrificed on the third day. On each of the **seven days** (v. 12), different sacrifices were required, which are listed as follows: first day, verses 13–16; second day, verses 17–19; third day, verses 20–22; fourth day, verses 23–25; fifth day, verses 26–28; sixth day, verses 29–31; seventh day, verses 32–34. The bull, ram, and lamb offerings were to be accompanied by a grain offering (vv. 14–15), yet no drink offerings were commanded for that first day, except possibly what went with the normal **burnt offering** (v. 16) each day.

Though the sacrifices begin with large numbers of animals, it is noteworthy to see the decrease from **thirteen young bullocks** (v. 13) on the first day to just **seven bullocks** (v. 32) on the seventh day. This suggests a gradual deterioration in the kingdom age, Unger believes, as shown and revealed in Revelation 20:7–9 (Unger, *Commentary*, p. 225). The Feast of Tabernacles heralds the prophecy of the kingdom blessings and looks forward to the millennial reign of Christ. A final redemption awaits the Jewish people (Ps. 72:17–19; Hab. 2:14).

29:35–38. The **eighth day** (v. 35) was not part of the feast days, though no work was to be done on that day, as commanded for other ceremonial occasions. The priests were to call for a **solemn assembly**. "The eighth day of solemn rest points to the dawn of the eternal state. The precious work of Christ will never be forgotten throughout the eternal ages to come (cf. Rev. 22:1, 3)" (Unger, *Commentary*, p. 225).

29:39–40. These verses are the summary statements. Along with these **set feasts** (v. 39) and their vows, Israelites were to make all the offerings listed here. These offerings were due the Lord over and above the other set sacrifices and vows. "The recapitulation of each of these festivals was a necessary part of the transfer of power from Moses to Joshua. The new community would soon be in the Land of Promise wherein these festivals would take on their full meaning in the life of the people" (Allen, "Numbers," p. 955).

5. Commands regarding Vows (chap. 30)

Vows were binding verbal contracts that reflected on the integrity of those responsible for the vows. They were not to be spoken lightly, nor taken lightly. The commands regarding vows deal with practical and contractual issues that affected Jewish societal and business dealings. Here in this chapter, except for one verse that deals with men, the subject is women and vows. Because of the seriousness of the matter, unmarried women needed their father's approval on contractual matters, and married women needed the approval of their husbands. While these laws seem harsh or unfair in today's culture, they were necessary to stabilize the society in the beginning days of the nation.

30:1–5. Moses summoned the **heads of the tribes** (v. 1) to hear the Lord's commandments on these issues. If a man made a legal vow, it was an **oath** (v. 2) that was binding to his **soul**. He could not break his word, that which has gone **out of his mouth**. If a single woman who was still living at home made a **vow** (v. 3), it was subject to her father's approval. If he heard what she has vowed and **bound** (v. 4) with an oath and he let it stand, the agreement was binding. But if he hears her vow and he **disallow[ed]** (v. 5) it, or rejected it, it was not binding, and **the LORD shall forgive her**. Such agreements were not simply contracts that governed the society; they were oaths made to the Lord. These were not small business matters to be taken lightly.

30:6–8. The principle was the same for a married woman. Her husband could deny or confirm the agreement that she made, what has gone **out of her lips, wherewith she bound her soul** (v. 6). If the husband did indeed reject the agreement, it was **of none effect: and the LORD shall forgive her** (v. 8).

30:9. The vows or agreements made by a **widow** or a **divorced** woman **shall stand against her** and not be valid. Again, while this seems harsh, women in this condition did not have the economic ability to stand behind what they had promised. This commandment from the Lord is not prejudicial against women. It reflects the realities of the ancient world, when even the physical strength of men was necessary for family and societal stability. Without it, there would have been chaos.

30:10–15. Moses repeats these commandments, but he also reminds the reader what may happen if the husband **establisheth** (v. 14) all his wife's vows by holding **his peace** about her agreements. He would **bear her iniquity** (v. 15) if she failed in what she had agreed to do. A failure to keep one's agreements and promises was a serious matter with the Lord. Agreements were not to be entered into lightly. After an indeterminate period, "the vow was in force and could be abrogated only by an appropriate sin offering (Lev. 5:4–13)" (Merrill, "Numbers," p. 250).

30:16. These commands were permanent statutes, **which the LORD commanded Moses**, and they governed certain business issues that affected the relation between a man and his wife, between a father and his daughter yet in her youth in her father's house.

F. The War against Midian (chap. 31)

The war against Midian was one of the last official acts of Moses' leadership. He was instructed by the Lord to avenge the Israelites because they had been wronged by the Midianites. Whatever brought damage to the Lord's own people in their walk with Him, as what happened at Baal-Peor (25:1–3), was a serious issue with Him and required punishment (vv. 16–18).

1. The Killing of the Midianites (31:1–12)

31:1–6. The Lord told Moses, **Avenge the children of Israel of the Midianites: afterward shalt thou be gathered unto thy people** (v. 2). Not only was Israel to be **avenge[d]** (v. 2) but also the Lord. Israel was certainly not morally perfect, but they were God's people, whom He had nourished and to whom He made promises. This was a holy war and was not motivated by personal jealousy from Moses. The Midianites had seduced Israel to engage in sexual immorality and to worship Baal (25:16–18). A **thousand** (v. 6) from each tribe were gathered to go to war, except from the tribe of Levi (31:4). The total, however, was **twelve thousand** (v. 5) with the half tribes of Ephraim and Manasseh, who were the sons of Joseph. The army was led by **Phinehas the son of Eleazar the priest** (v. 6). The troop was led forth with the **holy instruments** and the war trumpets in the hand of Phinehas. The zeal of Phinehas had led him to execute Zimri and Cozbi (25:8).

31:7–12. It can be said that the Midianites were totally destroyed, with **all** of the **males** (v. 7) killed. The kings of Midian were also slain, along with the evil conjurer **Balaam** (v. 8), the seducer of Israel (chaps. 22–25). Joshua was the one who slew him with the sword (Josh. 13:22). The Midianite women who were virgins were taken, along with the children and the **spoil** (vv. 9, 18) of animals and goods. Their cities and **goodly castles** (v. 10), or fortifications, were destroyed and burned. The booty was brought before Moses, Eleazar, and the congregation **unto the camp at the plains of Moab, which are by Jordan near Jericho** (v. 12).

2. Purification of Those Who Killed (31:13–24)

31:13–20. When the army returned from the **battle** (v. 14), Moses was furious and **wroth** because the women who were the seductresses had been kept alive. It was because of them, **through the counsel of Balaam** (v. 16), that the men of Israel **committed trespass against the** LORD, which brought about **a plague among the congregation of the** LORD (29:5). The young boys (young men), **every male among the little ones** (v. 17), and the immoral women were to be killed. The teenage boys would grow up with bitter resentment and turn against the Israelite men. The immoral women, who had been with men sexually, would continue to ply their trade and would bring moral degeneration again to the camp. The young virgin women would be allowed to live, as servants **for yourselves** (v. 18). Because war is a dirty and filthy task, the warriors and their captives were to **abide without the camp seven days** (v. 19) and go through a purification. Their clothes, items made of skins and goat hair, and items of wood had to be cleansed. These items would have been bloody and therefore impure.

31:21–24. Eleazar the priest (v. 21) made certain the fighting men knew that the orders for cleansing were from the Lord to Moses. **Gold** (v. 22), **silver,** and other metal items that would survive the flame would be cleansed by **fire** (v. 23). Items that could not sustain the fiery ordeal were to be cleansed by water. This was a meticulous process that would take seven days to complete; then the men, after washing their clothes, could return to **the camp** (v. 24).

3. The Division of the Prey (31:25–54)

31:25–31. Eleazar (v. 26) and the **chief fathers of the congregation** were ordered to divide the spoil of captives and animals between the men who went to war and **all the congregation** (v. 27), the people and the priests. The warriors were to **levy a tribute** (v. 28) to the Lord, giving one of every **five hundred, both of the persons, of the beeves, and of the asses, and of the sheep.** The "beeves" were portions of meat that had probably already been butchered (Lev. 22:19). Thus, one-fifth of one percent of the warriors' portion was given to Eleazar, which went to the priests for their service to the Lord (vv. 29–30).

31:32–41. Thirty-two thousand virgins were captured (v. 35), along with **sixteen thousand** (v. 40) young men. The tabulations of the animals are in the rest of these verses (Merrill, "Numbers," p. 251).

The Israelites' Dividing of the Midianite Animal Spoils (Num. 31:25–47)				
	Sheep	**Cattle**	**Donkeys**	**Totals**
The soldiers' portion (½ of the total)	337,500	36,000	30,500	404,000
Minus the portion to the Lord (1/500 of the soldiers' portion	−675	−72	−61	−808
Soldiers' portion (net amount)	336,825	35,928	30,439	403,192
The people's portion (½ of the total)	337,500	36,000	30,500	404,000
Minus the portion to the Lord (1/50 of the people's portion)	−6,750	−720	−610	−8,080
People's portion (net amount)	330,750	35,280	29,890	395,920
Total	675,000	72,000	61,000	808,000

Table taken from Dallas Seminary Faculty, John F. Walvoord and Roy B. Zuck, eds., *The Bible Knowledge Commentary: An Exposition of the Scriptures, Old Testament* (Wheaton, IL: Victor Books, 1985), 251.

31:42–47. The people of the congregation were given the other half of the booty, with one-fiftieth of their portion given to the **Levites** (v. 47; see calculations in the table).

31:48–54. A moment of conviction struck the **officers** (v. 48) and the **captains** of the soldiers. The army leaders, after reviewing their troops and the various divisions, discovered to their great delight that not one man had died in combat. In gratitude, they brought 16,750 **shekels** (600 pounds; v. 52) of **gold** jewelry to present to the Lord. Because they were men of war, they brought these items **to make an atonement for our souls before the LORD** (v. 50). The conviction was brought about because each man had acted independently in taking the **spoil** (v. 53) and booty. As soldiers who had to fight with abandonment, they felt somewhat guilty and unclean and therefore wanted an atoning cleansing before the Lord. The gold was taken and presented before the tabernacle of the congregation, **for a memorial for the children of Israel before the LORD** (v. 54). The tabernacle already had a memorial of silver (Exod. 30:11–16; 38:25–27). This memorial of gold would be a continual reminder to the people of the awesome victory brought about by the Lord over the treacherous Midianites.

G. The Settlement of the Tribes East of the Jordan (chap. 32)

Because they were proficient in cattle raising and had great herds, the tribes of Reuben and Gad liked the land just conquered and found it extremely suitable for their purposes. They requested of Moses that this territory be given to them and asked not to cross the Jordan into the Promised Land.

32:1–15. The men of the tribes of **Reuben** and **Gad** (v. 1) looked at the land of **Jazer**, a plateau (21:32), and the land of **Gilead** and found it ideal for cattle raising. This land was between the Arnon and the Yarmuk rivers (Deut. 3:12; Josh. 12:2–5). The men of the tribes came to Moses, Eleazar, and the **princes** (v. 2) of Israel and listed off some of the territorial locations, the places that they were identifying between the Arnon River to the south and the

Jabbok to the north (v. 3). The abundance of fertile grazing land east of the Jordan caused the leaders of the two tribes to appeal to Moses to allow them to settle there and not cross the Jordan. This too was a gift from God and part of the land that was won by conquest.

Even the country which the LORD smote before the congregation (v. 4) was an ideal place for cattle raising. The men of the two tribes asked that the land be theirs and that they not be required to cross **over Jordan** (v. 5). At first Moses did not seem to understand and thought they were trying to shirk their responsibility of helping their brethren conquer the land west of the Jordan (v. 6), which would **discourage** (v. 7) the rest of the children of Israel from taking the land. Moses reminded these two tribes and their leaders how God brought them from Egypt to **Kadesh-barnea** (v. 8; 13:3, 26) and how the **LORD's anger** (v. 10) was kindled against the people for their mistrust of Him. The Lord swore to give this land to the descendants of **Abraham, Isaac**, and **Jacob** (v. 11), yet the people **have not wholly followed me**. The Lord made them wander for forty years in the wilderness, **until all the generation, that had done evil in the sight of the LORD, was consumed** (v. 13).

Moses argued, these two tribes have brought on **the fierce anger of the LORD toward Israel** (v. 14). **For if ye turn away from after him, he will yet again leave them in the wilderness; and ye shall destroy all this people** (v. 15). Moses' fear was that if these two tribes stayed on the east side of the Jordan, the community would abandon taking Canaan, and a general revolt would ensue.

32:16–33. The tribes of Reuben and Gad were willing to go armed into Canaan to help the other tribes take the land. Their cattle and their families and **little ones** (v. 16) they would leave protected in **fenced cities** (v. 17) because of the danger from the surrounding people. Then, they argued, when the land to the west was conquered, they would **return** (v. 18) to the east side of the Jordan. Moses agreed and said that if they were victorious and had conquered the land, they would be **guiltless before the LORD** (v. 22) and the land would be theirs, but if they would not go, **behold, ye have sinned against the LORD: and be sure your sin will find you out** (v. 23). Moses agreed to their proposal (v. 24).

The men of the tribes of **Reuben** and **Gad** (v. 25) concurred. Moses explained the agreement to the leaders of Israel (v. 28) and confirmed the details of the bargain (vv. 29–30). The tribes answered, **so will we do** (v. 31). Moses then formerly bequeathed the land to these tribes, including **unto half the tribe of Manasseh the son of Joseph** (v. 33). The area had belonged to **Sihon king of the Amorites** and **Og king of Bashan … with the cities thereof in the coasts, even the cities of the country round about**. The Reubenites occupied generally from **Hesbon** (v. 37) west and southwest to the Jordan and the Dead Sea (Merrill, "Numbers," p. 252). "The fact that part of the tribe of Manasseh claimed land outside of Canaan is explained by the conquest of Gilead by three clans from the tribe" (Unger, *Commentary*, p. 229). Later, Manasseh would also have a portion of the land west of the Jordan (Josh. 17:14–18).

32:34–42. The Gadites rebuilt the villages in southern Gilead from **Aroer** (v. 34) on the Arnon River to the south to **Jogbehah** (v. 35), along with **folds for sheep** (v. 36). The Reubenites built six other cities **and gave other names unto the cities which they builded** (v. 38). The sons of **Machir** (v. 39) went to Gilead and **dispossessed the Amorite which was in it.** Other small towns were also added to their possession. Some have seen the decision of Reuben and Manasseh as a worldly choice based on economics only. Others see this decision as wise in that these outer tribes became buffers of protection for the people who settled in Canaan.

VI. Appendixes Dealing with Various Matters (chaps. 33–36)

Chapters 33–36 conclude with a summary of God's leading the people from Egypt to the Land of Promise. Many geographical places are mentioned for which we have little information today. Chapter 36 deals with the question of what was to be done when a woman who had inherited land married into another family. These final chapters end with wrap-up issues that were important to Israel as the people prepared to enter Canaan and take the land promised to them by the Lord.

A. The Stages of the Journey (chap. 33)

Chapter 33 is an appropriate review of God's leading the people out of Egypt to the Promised Land, providing future readers with a bird's-eye view of what the Lord had done for His people. While this chapter may at first seem redundant, it serves as a somewhat detailed account of Israel's journey, condensed into fifty-six verses—an important summary for future generations, so that they could see the providence of God working in the children of Israel.

33:1–2. The introduction shows how God brought forth His people from Egypt **under the hand of Moses and Aaron** (v. 1) and then how Moses was instructed to compile an account of Israel's journeys **according to their goings out** (v. 2).

33:3–4. Leaving **Rameses** (Zoan-Tanis, v. 3; Exod. 1:11; 12:37) in Egypt **in the first month, on the fifteenth day of the first month** (Exod. 12:2; 13:4) they were led out by the Lord **with a high hand in the sight of all the Egyptians** (v. 3). "With a high hand" means "triumphantly." The Egyptians lost their **firstborn** under the curse of the Lord (Exod. 12:29), who also **executed judgments** (v. 4) upon the gods of Egypt.

33:5–15. The children of Israel **pitched in Succoth** (v. 5; Exod. 12:37), probably at Tel el Maskutah, southeast from Rameses, near the Egyptian Bitter Lakes, which are part of the Red Sea (Reed Sea). From there, they went to **Etham, which is in the edge of the wilderness** (v. 6). After moving from different locations (vv. 7–8), they arrived at the place of **twelve fountains of water** (v. 9), and the place of the forty **palm trees**. Moving away from the **Red sea** (v. 10), they **encamped in the wilderness of Sin** (v. 11). They arrived at **Rephidim where was no water for the people to drink** (v. 14). Finally, they **pitched in the wilderness of Sinai** (v. 15).

33:16–37. In these verses, all of the locations of Israel's movement are listed (most unrecognizable), with the people finally moving from **Kadesh** to **mount Hor, in the edge of the land of Edom** (v. 37).

33:38–49. The death of **Aaron** (v. 38) is recorded as having occurred in the **fortieth year after the children of Israel were come out from the land of Egypt**. He died at the age of 123 **years** (v. 39). The journey from Mount Hor is recorded, leading to the arrival **unto Abel-shittim in the plains of Moab** (v. 49). At Mount Hor, the king of Arad heard of their plan to travel to Atharim (21:1) and tried to defeat them by attacking. The children of Israel attacked and destroyed several Canaanite cities (21:3).

33:50–56. Moses records how the Lord spoke to him **in the plains of Moab by Jordan near Jericho** (v. 50). The instructions were to drive out the inhabitants of the land. They were to destroy **all their pictures** (plaques of the gods; v. 52), **all their molten images** (statutes), and **pluck down all their high places** (hillside groves with altars to Baal). Moses reviews the division of the land **by lot** (v. 54; 26:53–56), as instructed by the Lord. The larger tribes were to receive larger portions of the land, and the smaller tribes smaller portions. The land was taken according to the Lord's promises in the past (Gen. 13:17; 17:8; Exod. 6:2–5). If the Israelites failed to drive the enemy out from the Promised Land, those they allowed to remain would **be pricks in your eyes, and thorns in you sides** (v. 55). Because the Israelites did not completely drive out the people of the land, continuous trouble would haunt them, resulting finally in Israel being driven from Canaan (Josh. 23:13; 2 Kings 17:7–20). The Lord's words end with these sobering thoughts: **Moreover it shall come to pass, that I shall do unto you, as I thought to do unto them** (v. 56). If Israel sinned, though they are God's people, His justice would fall on them as it would even on pagan peoples.

B. The Land of Inheritance (chaps. 34–35)

In these chapters, the borders of the land are prescribed and delineated in reference to each tribe. The cities for the Levites are set forth, as well as the cities of refuge for those accused of crimes.

1. The Borders of Canaan (chap. 34)

34:1–15. The outer borders of Canaan are spelled out with the appropriate boundaries that encompass the various tribes. This has to do with **the land of Canaan** (v. 2) and not with the tribes living in the territory of Gilead (chap. 32). The Lord prescribes the southern border (v. 3), **the western border** (v. 6), the **north[ern]** border (v. 7), and the **east[ern]** border (v. 10). Though the children of Israel had not yet entered the land, God here gives them an appraisal of the boundaries of their inheritance. Though the Jews would not fully occupy the land God intended for them, they will in the coming millennial kingdom. The borders God had described delineated **the land which ye shall inherit by lot**, which was to be given **unto the nine tribes, and to the half tribe** (v. 13). Levi would not be given a land possession. The priests were to move about the land and dwell in various cities to minister to all of the people, though there would always be a large number ministering wherever the tabernacle was placed. The tribes of Reuben and Gad had their portions to the east. **Half** of **Manasseh** (v. 14) would have an inheritance in the Promised Land, and the other half would dwell in Gilead (see 32:33).

33:16–29. Eleazar the priest and **Joshua** (v. 17) would be responsible for assigning **one prince of every tribe, to divide the land by inheritance** (v. 18). This shows that God had a clear providential arrangement for the allocation of the tribal lands. Also, by assigning the task to certain men from each tribe, no one could accuse the leaders of unfairness. These assignments **the LORD commanded** to be done when the Israelites came into **the land of Canaan** (v. 29).

2. Cities for the Levites (35:1–8)

35:1–6. The children of Israel had not yet crossed the Jordan River, and Moses was still receiving important instructions from the Lord before the invasion began (v. 1). God commanded that the Levites have specific **cities** (v. 2) in which to dwell. For some specific cities, they were to live in **suburbs** that surround them. The "suburbs" would be pastureland for this tribe, who would not be given a particular territory to occupy (Lev. 25:32–34). The land given was **for their goods, and for all their beasts** (v. 3). The Levites were set aside for the Lord, presented to Him instead of the firstborn (see 3:40–51). They were particularly set apart for His service in the tabernacle. The land assigned to them was to extend 1,500 feet from each city and its walls and measure about 3,000 feet on every side (v. 5). Six of the cities were to be classified as **cities for refuge** (v. 6) so that a **manslayer**, a murderer, could find refuge until his case was fairly judged. The Levites would have a total of forty-eight cities, with six of those especially set aside for murder cases. The cities of refuge were a merciful provision for those accused of violent criminal acts because of the emotion stirred by such acts. Vengeful families would want to take justice into their own hands without a trial or hearing.

35:7–8. The dispersal of the Levites reminded Israel that they were to be a holy nation and were to live as a kingdom of priests to the Lord (Exod. 19:6). The distribution of the cities for the Levites was enacted in Joshua 21, where the cities are listed, though the appointment of all of these cities was never fully completed (Harrison, *Numbers*, p. 418).

c. The Cities of Refuge (35:9–34)

35:9–28. The **cities of refuge** (v. 11) were to be set aside as a haven for the **slayer** who may have killed **any person at unawares**, meaning "by error, accident." The Hebrew for "cities of refuge" (*are miqlat*) means "towns of asylum." The cities were to give refuge from the **avenger** (v. 12), to shield the slayer **until he stand before the congregation in judgment**. Three of the cities were to be on the east of **the Jordan** (v. 14), and three on the west side. They could also be used for refuge for the **stranger** (Gentile; v. 15) and the **sojourner** (traveler).

Specific rules regarding murder are laid out. The murderer was to be put to death if he had slain someone with an **instrument of iron** (v. 16), if he had killed someone by throwing a **stone** (v. 17), or if he smote someone with a **wood[en]** club (v. 18). If such a killing was obvious, then a family member, **the re-** venger (actually "the redeemer," *go'el* v. 19), could kill the perpetrator when he finds him. However, if the revenger was simply acting out **of hatred** (v. 20) or pounced on him while **laying of wait**, then he too was guilty of a crime and must die. If the revenger openly attacked and beat to death the one who was no doubt a murderer, **he is a murderer** and the avenger of blood can kill him if he finds him (v. 21), or if he used some instrument violently (v. 22) or a stone, and he did this without malice (v. 23), he was to be judged by the **congregation** (v. 24) as to the extent of his guilt. Both the slayer and the avenger were to be judged. The **slayer** (v. 25) found innocent of murder with malice intent could remain in a city of refuge until the acting **high priest, which was anointed with the holy oil** died. In other words, he was safe until another high priest was anointed. To be spared as a **slayer** (v. 26) had its limitations. If the **revenger of blood** (v. 27) found the slayer outside the city of refuge, he could be slain without impunity. The point seems to be letting enough time pass. The one who had killed someone and had lived for some time in the city of refuge could finally **return into the land of his possession** (v. 28), though such a journey might be perilous.

35:29–34. The death penalty was not to be carried out by the **witness** (v. 30) of only one person (Deut. 17:6; Matt. 18:16), nor was any pity, or **satisfaction** (v. 31), to be shown to a murderer who was found guilty; he must die. Carrying out the death penalty was a sign of justice. The shedding of blood by murder would **pollute** (v. 33) the land and **defileth** it. The Lord concludes, **Defile not therefore the land which ye shall inhabit, wherein I dwell: for I the LORD dwell among the children of Israel** (v. 34).

C. The Marriage of Heiresses (chap. 36)

The Old Testament shows a high regard for women. Israel was required to protect women in many ways. In no other ancient society were women afforded such fair laws that shielded them from prejudice. This chapter is almost a continuation of the special situation concerning the daughters of Zelophehad, a descendant of the tribe of Manasseh of Gilead (27:1–11).

36:1–9. These verses present a further development of the account given in 27:1–11. Since the Lord had commanded Moses that women could inherit their father's land, additional questions came up that needed to be settled. For example, what if Zelophehad's daughters **married** (v. 3) into a family of a different tribe? Would the property be taken from the tribal region of Manasseh and then belong to that other tribe? Would it remain with the other tribe when the **jubile** (v. 4), the Year of Jubilee, takes place? This special year followed forty-nine sabbatical years; it was the fiftieth year, when slaves were to be released and property was to return to the original owners (Lev. 25:8–38). "But marriage outside the tribe of Manasseh would mean that supposedly inalienable property could not even be redeemed in the jubilee year" (Harrison, *Numbers*, p. 426).

Through Moses, the Lord answered. The **chief fathers** (v. 1) had analyzed the problem correctly (v. 5). The daughters could **marry** (v. 6) whom they wished, but they had to remain within their tribe so that the inherited property would remain in the family **tribe** (v. 7). The property was not to be passed from **tribe** to **tribe** (v. 9). Though the issue was raised concerning the tribe of Manasseh, more than likely the principle would apply to the same problem in any tribe.

36:10–13. The **daughters of Zelophehad** (v. 10) did as the Lord instructed and **married into the families of the sons of Manasseh the son of Joseph** (v. 12). Thus, the property remained in the tribe of the family of their father. This law would spare all of the tribes from engaging in family feuds over land, but it would also allow the value of the property to increase and bless the original owners. Verse 13 seems to be a summary of all of the laws in the book of Numbers, certainly those given in the final chapters. They were given before Israel entered Canaan, **in the plains of Moab by Jordan near Jericho** (v. 13). Numbers was recorded during the lifetime of Moses, with the narration firmly established in the history of the nation of Israel. The completed book had as its goal the gradual movement of the people to the land God promised to Abraham and his children.

THE FIFTH BOOK OF MOSES,
CALLED DEUTERONOMY

INTRODUCTION

Title

In ancient times, books were generally named after their initial word or phrase. In Hebrew, the book of Deuteronomy is named *eileh haddebarim*, "These [are] the words," sometimes simply abbreviated as *debarim*, "words." Other popular Jewish designations are *sefer ha-zikaron*, "the book of remembrance," one of the text's major themes (1:1–4:43; 4:9–23; 5:15; 6:12; 8:2, 11, 18; 9:7; 24:9; 25:17) and *mishneh hatorah*, from 17:18, " a copy of the law," or "repetition of the law." The same verse gave rise to the title in the Septuagint Greek translation, *Deuteronomion*, meaning literally, "second law." The Latin Vulgate translation followed suit with *Deuteronomium*, from which was derived our English title, Deuteronomy. The title must be understood not in the sense of a "second" or additional law but as a restatement of the law for a new generation.

Author and Date

The author of Deuteronomy, in addition to the other four books of the Pentateuch, is Moses. The date of writing was 1406 BC, following the exodus and forty years of wilderness wanderings, and the place of composition was the plains of Moab (1:1; 29:1). Mosaic authorship was undisputed within Jewish tradition and, until fairly recently, by Christian tradition as well. Nonetheless, over the past two centuries, certain circles have argued against Mosaic authorship without arriving at any consensus as to a viable alternative author. Their only area of agreement is a mutual distrust of the book's ancient pedigree.

Critical arguments are based on four highly cynical assumptions. First, based on the accepted fact that Moses did not write Deuteronomy's final chapter (dealing with his death), it is assumed that he did not write any of the preceding chapters as well. This conclusion must be rejected as both unnecessary and unwarranted.

Second, it is assumed that King Josiah's discovery of the "book of the law" (2 Kings 22:1–20) in the seventh century BC was merely a charade designed to endorse religious reforms through passing off to the ignorant populace the freshly minted Deuteronomy as a conveniently rediscovered, "long lost" foundational document. While imaginative, this theory offers no credible supporting evidence and should be rejected.

Third, Deuteronomy presumes an unnamed, future, central location for Israel's worship (12:1–32; 14:23–26; 16:2–16; 17:8–10; 18:6; 26:2; 31:11). The assumption of some critics is that this concept could not have possibly derived from the time of the tabernacle but was, in fact, seventh-century pro-Jerusalem, pro-temple propaganda. Again, no evidence is brought forth to support this theory, nor is the city of Jerusalem mentioned by name even once within the text.

Fourth, due to these critics' extreme bias against accepting the validity of predictive prophecy, the presence the text's prophecies of Israel's dispersion (4:25–31; 28:20–68; 29:22–28; 30:1–10; 32:23–43) forces them to argue against Mosaic authorship, pedantically portraying the book as predicting something that, by the author's time, had already occurred. Regrettably for this theory's cheerleaders, anti-supernatural bias and presuppositions do not constitute evidence.

A substantial amount of both internal and external evidence supports Mosaic authorship. The text of Deuteronomy repeatedly attributes the book to Moses (1:1–5; 4:44–46; 5:1; 27:1, 9; 29:1–2; 31:1, 9, 22–24, 30; 33:1). Internally, there is no reason to suspect that anyone but Moses himself penned everything but the final chapter. Externally, other books within the Hebrew Scriptures assume Mosaic authorship (Josh. 1:7; Judg. 3:4; 1 Kings 2:3; 8:53; 2 Kings 14:6; 18:12; Ezra 3:2; Neh. 1:7; Ps. 103:7; Dan. 9:11; Mal. 4:4). In addition, Deuteronomy is the most frequently quoted Old Testament book within the New Testament, with almost one hundred quotations, citations, references, or allusions throughout (e.g., Acts 3:22–23; 7:37–38; Rom. 10:19). Further, Jesus Himself quoted Deuteronomy as authoritative (Matt. 4:4, 7, 10) and attributed the book to Moses (Matt. 19:7–8 and Mark 10:3–5, quoting Deut. 24:1–4; Mark 7:10, quoting Deut. 5:16; Luke 20:28, quoting Deut. 25:5; John 5:46–47, referencing Deut. 18:15–19).

Finally, there are patent parallels between the structures of Deuteronomy and the Hittite suzerain-vassal treaties of the middle of the second millennium BC, a format that would not have been utilized were the book the product of any other era. (See also Exodus, Introduction, especially "Author" and "Date.")

Theme

Deuteronomy represents a crucible of four major transitions for Israel. First, the book relates the emotional transition from the only leader the Israelites had ever known, Moses, to the leadership of Joshua. Second, the book was written following the transition from the liberated slave generation of the exodus to the generation that came of age in the wilderness. Third, the book prepares its audience for the geographic transition that will move a nation from the wilderness into the Land of Promise. This then leads to the fourth transition, that of progressing from the transient outlook of a nation of wanderers to the stationary mindset of permanent citizens in possession of their own land.

These states of transition created the need for a formal renewal of the covenant initially made at Sinai. For Israel's next generation to possess a solid sense of their identity, they first needed to know their storied history and their future destiny. Through the history, law, and prophecy contained in Moses' four addresses, Deuteronomy provided the theological perspective on Israel's past, present, and future that was necessary to prepare them to conquer the land and fulfill their covenantal obligations in their identity as God's chosen people.

Theological Message

In Deuteronomy, the reader is reminded of the Lord's distinctiveness and complete supremacy above all rival deities (4:12, 15, 35, 39, 39; 6:4–5; 7:9; 10:14–17; 12:29–31; 32:39). In addition, potent emphasis is placed on God's unique covenantal relationship with Israel (4:37; 6:5; 7:13; 10:12; 11:1; 30:6; 33:3). Israel is His chosen, elect nation (7:7–8: 14:2) and the focus of God's international program (32:8–9). As His unique chosen people (4:31; 7:12; 8:18; 26:16–19; 29:1), the Lord obligates Israel to an elevated standard of holiness (4:20; 7:6; 14:2–12; 26:18–19; 28:9) and sternly warns them against idolatry (6:14–15; 7:4; 8:19–20; 11:16–17, 28; 13:2, 6, 13; 17:3; 28:14, 36, 64).

Time and again, mention is made of the Lord's love for Israel (4:37; 7:7–11; 10:15; 25:3; 33:3) and His requirement that they love Him in return (6:5; 7:8; 10:12, 15; 11:1, 13, 22; 12:3; 19:9; 30:6, 16, 20). Israel's love is to be demonstrated through adherence to the Mosaic covenant, which is the basis for enjoying God's blessings, in particular, the Land of Promise (5:1–2). In relation to the land, Deuteronomy helps define the relationship between the Mosaic covenant and its predecessor, the Abrahamic covenant. While the land is Israel's unassailable inheritance through the unconditional promises of the Abrahamic covenant (1:8, 35; 4:27–31; 6:10, 18, 23; 7:8, 12–13; 8:1; 9:5; 26:3; 30:20), their entrance into and continued presence in their land is predicated on generational observance of the Mosaic covenant (30:15–20). The text of Deuteronomy uses the term "land" some two hundred times, highlighting the unparalleled bond between the nation of Israel and the land of their inheritance.

Literary Features

Deuteronomy is roughly patterned after the covenantal format of a typical Hittite suzerain-vassal (king-subject) treaty of the mid-second millennium BC. In fact, it may be that much of the repetition of legal material already developed in Exodus was for the purpose of restructuring it into the suzerain-vassal covenant format. The treaty format generally contained six identifiable components.

(1) A treaty would begin with a *preamble*, or introduction, in which the participating parties of suzerain and vassals are identified. Deuteronomy 1:1–5 serves this function.

(2) The preamble would be followed by a *historical prologue*, which relays the relationship of the vassals to the suzerain and extols the benevolence of the suzerain toward the vassal. Deuteronomy 1:6–4:49 serves this function, relaying Israel's exodus and wilderness history.

(3) *General stipulations* would be set forth, enumerating the mutual responsibilities of all parties to the treaty, whether suzerain or vassal. Emphasis here would be on the favor of the suzerain and the allegiance of the vassals. Stipulating Israel's obligation to love of God and holiness, Deuteronomy 5:1–11:32 serves this function.

(4) *Specific stipulations* would then be set forth, consisting of detailed means by which the vassals may tangibly express allegiance to their suzerain. The series of specific legal obligations of Deuteronomy 12:1–26:19 serve this function.

(5) A *witness* section would be set aside to specify the gods/goddesses who would serve as divine witnesses to the signing of the treaty. Since no other deities exist but the

Lord Himself, instead of false gods being called to witness the agreement, God instead calls heaven and earth as His witnesses (30:19; 31:28). Although the witness section was typically the fifth treaty element, in Deuteronomy, the conclusion of the book, chapters 31–34, serves this function.

(6) The treaty would then lay out a series of curses for disobedience to the treaty and blessings for obedience to the treaty. In the Lord's covenant, however, the blessings precede the curses. Deuteronomy reverses the standard order, listing the blessings in 28:1–14 and the curses in 28:15–68.

Outline

I. Introduction to the Covenant (1:1–5)

II. Message One — Past: Historical Prologue (1:6–4:49)
  A. Historical Review (1:6–3:29)
    1. The Command to Depart Sinai (1:6–8)
    2. The Delegation of Leadership (1:9–18)
    3. At Kadesh-barnea (1:19–46)
    4. From Kadesh-barnea to the Plains of Moab (2:1–25)
    5. Israel's Initial Conquests (2:26–3:22)
    6. The Appointment of Joshua and the Disappointment of Moses (3:23–29)
  B. Exhortation to Obedience (4:1–43)
    1. The Purposes of the Covenant (4:1–8)
    2. The Sinai Experience (4:9–14)
    3. Idolatry (4:15–24)
    4. The Future of the Covenant (4:25–31)
    5. One Israel, One God (4:32–40)
    6. Three Cities of Refuge (4:41–43)
  C. Historical Summary (4:44–4:49)

III. Message Two — Present: Covenant Responsibilities (5:1–26:19)
  A. General Covenant Responsibilities (5:1–11:32)
    1. The Ten Commandments (5:1–33)
      a. Introduction (5:1–5)
      b. The Ten Commandments (5:6–21)
      c. Israel's Response (5:22–27)
      d. The Lord's Response (5:28–33)
    2. Directives and Warnings (6:1–8:1–20)
      a. Directive to Obey and Remember (6:1–25)
      b. Warning against Idolatry and Intermarriage (7:1–5)
      c. Directives for Covenant Relationship (7:6–16)
      d. Directive for Holy War (7:17–26)
      e. Warning against Forgetfulness (8:1–20)
    3. The Stone Tablets (9:1–10:11)
      a. The Command to Conquer the Land (9:1–6)
      b. The Sin of the Golden Calf (9:7–21)

Bibliography

Craigie, Peter C. *The Book of Deuteronomy*. The New International Commentary on the Old Testament. Grand Rapids, MI: Eerdmans, 1976.

Kalland, Earl S. "Deuteronomy." In *The Expositor's Bible Commentary*, edited by Frank E. Gaebelein, vol. 3. Grand Rapids, MI: Zondervan, 1992.

Kline, Meredith. *Treaty of the Great King*. Grand Rapids, MI: Eerdmans, 1963.

Merrill, Eugene H. *Deuteronomy*. The New American Commentary 4. Nashville: Broadman & Holman, 1994.

Thompson, J. A. *Deuteronomy: An Introduction and Commentary*. The Tyndale Old Testament Commentaries 5. Downers Grove, IL: InterVarsity, 1974.

EXPOSITION

The first five verses of the book of Deuteronomy serve to introduce this re-presentation of the Mosaic covenant. Following the format of the Hittite suzerain-vassal treaties of the second millennium BC (see Introduction: "Literary Features"), this section is the brief preamble to the extended covenant treaty that follows.

I. Introduction to the Covenant (1:1–5)

1:1–5. Deuteronomy is identified as being a record of **the words** of **Moses** (v. 1), Israel's lawgiver, mediator, and initial prophet (34:10). The book records his final four public addresses to the nation, delivered over a period of roughly forty days, immediately prior to his death.

While a forty-day period, in which the entirety of Deuteronomy's events takes place, is not specified in the text, it is nonetheless easily arrived at through the careful analysis of certain dates recorded in Deuteronomy and Joshua. The first address was delivered **in the fortieth year, in the eleventh month, on the first day of the month** (v. 3). The date of the exodus was March or April 1446 BC (see Exodus, Introduction: "Author" and "Date"). The eleventh month of the fortieth year from the exodus would establish the date of this address as sometime during January–February 1406 BC. According to Joshua 4:19, Israel crossed over the Jordan River on the tenth day of the first month, sometime during March–April 1406 BC, some seventy days later. Subtracting the thirty-day period of mourning that followed Moses' death (Deut. 34:8) from the seventy days spanning Moses' initial speech and Israel's river crossing, the result is a forty-day period, which concludes with Moses' death on the tenth day of the twelfth month.

With the passing of Israel's exodus generation and the coming of age of its wilderness generation, and with the nation now poised and positioned to enter the Land of Promise, a renewal of the forty-year-old covenant was a crucial prerequisite to Israel's upcoming era of conquest.

Moses' message was addressed **unto all Israel** (v. 1), to the entire nation. The text's use of the phrase "all Israel," some thirteen times (1:1; 5:1; 11:6; 13:12; 18:6; 21:21; 27:9; 29:2; 31:1, 7, 11; 32:45; 34:12), is indicative of the Hebrews' deep unity as their corporate, national identity was forged in the wilderness experience.

Having identified both the party delivering the address and the party receiving it, Moses then provided the location of his message. Israel was camped **in the land of Moab** (v. 5), on the east bank of the **Jordan** River, **in the wilderness** (v. 1), the desert territory that comprises the Jordan rift valley, or Arabah. This region spans the Sea of Galilee in the north and the Gulf of Aqaba (the arm of the Red Sea between modern-day Israel and Jordan) in the south, running along the Dead Sea in its center.

Paran, Tophel, Laban, Hazeroth, and **Dizahab** (v. 1) were locations on the Israelites' itinerary as they had progressed from Mount Sinai to the territory of Moab.

Kadesh-barnea (v. 2) was to be Israel's initial entry point into Canaan. The distance from Mount **Horeb** (Moses' preferred designation for Sinai in Deuteronomy) to Kadesh-barnea is roughly one hundred forty-five miles. Through their rebellion (Num. 14:33–34), the Israelites had managed to prolong an eleven-day geographic journey into a forty-year theological trek. **The way of mount Seir** was the road the nation traveled as it had made its way to the territory of Edom.

Having established the text's author, audience, time, and location, that is, the *who*, *when*, and *where*, Moses now announced that the content of his message (the *what*) was **all that the LORD had given him in commandment unto them** (v. 3). The message was designed to reiterate all the commandments that YHWH had revealed to Israel, beginning at Sinai and extending through the remaining thirty-nine years of wilderness wandering. (For "the LORD," see discussion on Exod. 3:14–15.)

The historical context for the message was the previous conquest of **Sihon** and **Og**, the respective kings of **the Amorites** and **Bashan** (v. 4; see Num. 21:21–35; Deut. 2:26–3:11).

II. Message One — Past: Historical Prologue (1:6–4:49)

Following the format of Hittite suzerain-vassal treaties, this section is the second division, the historical prologue. This section of the treaty relayed the relationship of the vassals to the suzerain and extolled the benevolence of the suzerain toward his vassals. In this historical prologue, the first of his four discourses in the text, Moses summarized the covenant history of God's mighty deliverance of Israel.

A. Historical Review (1:6–3:29)

1. The Command to Depart Sinai (1:6–8)

1:6–8. The LORD our God (v. 6). Moses' historical discourse begins with a reminder that "the LORD," YHWH, has a uniquely personal, covenantal relationship with Israel. Following the receipt of the law and the construction of the tabernacle at Mount Sinai (**Horeb**), the Israelites had been divinely instructed that they had **dwelt long enough in this mount**. They had been encamped in that location for just over a year and were to begin their journey to the Land of Promise.

Moses listed the regions of the Promised Land by geographic area. **The mount of the Amorites** (v. 7) was the land's central and southern hill country, running along the east side of the Jordan. **The plain** was the Jordan rift valley, from the Gulf of Aqaba in the south to the Sea of Galilee in the north, and including the Dead Sea region in the center. **The hills** refers to the central mountain range that runs north and south along the west bank of the Jordan. **The vale** denotes the low hills that slope from the mountain range down to the Mediterranean coast. **The south** refers to the region of the Negev desert. **The sea side** refers to the Mediterranean coastal plain. **The land of the Canaanites** probably refers to the land's northern and northwestern regions. **Lebanon** is the land's northernmost region. **The river Euphrates** marked the northeastern border.

The Israelites had then been divinely commanded to **go in and possess the land** (v. 8). The basis for their possession of the land was the Abrahamic covenant. This unconditional covenant between the Lord and **Abraham, Isaac, and Jacob** (Gen. 15:18–21; 26:2–4; 35:11–12) is foundational to the context of Deuteronomy. References to the Abrahamic covenant and the patriarchs are studded throughout the text (Deut. 1:8, 35; 4:31; 6:10, 18, 23; 7:8, 12; 8:1, 18; 9:5, 27; 10:11; 11:9, 21; 13:17; 19:8; 26:3, 15; 28:11; 29:13; 30:20; 31:7, 20–23; 34:4). God's centuries-old promise of a homeland would not be neglected.

To give unto them and to their seed after them (v. 8). In the context of Deuteronomy, the key element of the Abrahamic covenant's promise of land was that the pledge extended beyond the initial Hebrew **fathers** to their posterity. Throughout their history, the Israelites were never able to conquer the totality of the territory described in this passage. For that matter, in their lifetimes, Abraham, Isaac, and Jacob were not granted the privilege of seeing God's promise fulfilled. Jesus revealed, however, that in the messianic age to come, both Israel and the resurrected patriarchs will finally enjoy the entirety of their geographic inheritance (Matt. 8:11).

2. The Delegation of Leadership (1:9–18)

1:9–18. The LORD God of your fathers (v. 11). The use of this phrase is yet another reminder of the Abrahamic covenant. One of the promised components of the Abrahamic covenant was the multiplication of the patriarchs' descendants. Indeed, by this point in Israel's history, they had become a mighty nation of over two million. Referencing the language of the covenant, Moses compared the **multitude** with **the stars of heaven** (see Gen. 15:5; 22:17; 26:4). **The LORD your God hath multiplied you ... as he hath promised** (v. 10–11). If God had fulfilled one element of the covenant, it made sense that He would fulfill the remainder as well.

1:16–18. At Mount Sinai, Moses had **charged** (v. 16) the leaders to hold court and exercise righteous judgment. They were to **judge righteously**, showing no favoritism, in the cases of Israelites and Israel's resident Gentiles and in the cases of **the small** and **the great** (v. 17), that is, the weak and the powerful, the poor and the wealthy. **You shall not be afraid of the face of man**. They were not to allow anyone to intimidate them when making their rulings, for ultimately they represented God in whatever **judgment** they made. **The cause that is too hard for you, bring it unto me**. While the majority of Israel's caseload could be shared, there were certain areas and issues that Moses alone needed to deal with and could in no way delegate to subordinates. Moses, possessing direct access to God as Israel's mediator, served as the nation's appellate court.

3. At Kadesh-barnea (1:19 – 46)

1:19. That great and terrible wilderness (v. 19). The journey from Mount Sinai to **Kadesh-barnea**, the gateway to the Promised Land, had taken the Israelites through one hundred forty-five miles of arid desert.

1:20 – 21. The mountain of the Amorites (v. 20). This phrase is used in Deuteronomy as a general reference to the Promised Land, just as the phrase "the Amorites" is used in Scripture as a general reference to the inhabitants of Canaan (e.g., Gen. 15:16). **The Lord our God doth give unto us**. God had been in the process of personally delivering the Land of Promise to the Israelites and had commanded the nation to **go up and possess it, as the Lord God of thy fathers hath said unto thee** (v. 21). Again, Moses emphasized that the foundational basis of the Israelites' claim to the land was the ancient promises of the Abrahamic covenant (see discussion on 1:8). Since their claim to the land rested on divine assurance, Israel was to **fear not, neither be discouraged**.

1:22 – 25. Prior to their impending military conquest, the Israelites had initiated a plan to first send out spies to **search us out the land** (v. 22; see Num. 13:1 – 2). This was to provide the military intelligence necessary to mount an appropriate offensive strategy. Moses had assented to the plan and selected one representative spy from each of the twelve tribes

(Num. 13:4 – 15). **The valley of Eshcol** (v. 24) was near Hebron (Num. 13:22 – 23), although the precise location is uncertain. *Eshcol* is Hebrew for "grape cluster," an appropriate name for this fertile region, for the spies had returned bearing great quantities of **fruit** (v. 25; see Num. 13:23 – 27).

1:26 – 28. The spies had also reported the intimidating magnitude of Canaan's fortified, **walled** (v. 28) cities, and that the general populace was **greater and taller** than the Hebrews. Seemingly most troubling had been the reported presence of **the Anakims**, a nation of giants, or perhaps better, of gigantic proportion (see Num. 13:22, 32 – 33). Evidence of the Anakim's existence is sketchy, although one thirteenth-century BC Egyptian source mentions the presence of eight-foot tall warriors in Canaan. In addition, two twelfth-century BC skeletons that are seven feet tall have been discovered in Jordan.

Israel had been so shaken by the report that they had **rebelled against the commandment of the Lord** (v. 26) and had refused to enter the land. Furthermore, not only had the nation allowed fear to overwhelm their faith, but they had **murmured** (v. 27) against God, purposely mischaracterizing His great love for them as hatred. Israel had ignored the Lord's previous command neither to fear nor be **discouraged** (1:21). So distorted was Israel's perception of theological reality that they had actually asserted that **the Lord ... hated** them enough to **destroy** them (v. 27). Indeed, the only reason He had rescued them from **Egypt** was **to deliver** them **into the hand of the Amorites**. Apparently, they reasoned that God had viewed the slavery of Egypt as being insufficiently onerous; what He really desired for the nation of Israel was their utter destruction.

1:29 – 33. Moses had responded with an attempt to restore Israel's resolve by reminding them that the events of the past two years more than demonstrated that **the Lord** (v. 30), who had powerfully rescued His people out of **Egypt**, would still exercise His power on their behalf. The power of Israel's God, thus far amply demonstrated both in **Egypt** and **the wilderness** (v. 31), would be no less potent in the

Promised Land. In this instance, past performance was an excellent gauge of future results. Their unbelief was irrational in light of their experience of God's personal presence among them **in fire by night ... and in a cloud by day** (v. 33).

1:34–36. The nation's murmuring had not escaped the attention of **the LORD** (v. 34). His anger kindled, He had pronounced a severe consequence upon the nation for their lack of faith, declaring that **surely there shall not one of these men of this evil generation see that good land** (v. 35). The exodus generation, the generation of divinely liberated slaves, the generation of the Sinai revelation, had at last gone too far. That generation would not receive their inheritance. The gift of the Land of Promise would instead be given to their children, a generation less inclined toward rebellion and unbelief.

Which I sware to give unto your fathers (v. 35). It is essential to bear in mind that the unbelief of one generation of Israel in no way invalidated the promises of the Abrahamic covenant. This passage demonstrates that God deals with the corporate entity of Israel on a generational basis. The actions of one unfaithful generation could not dissolve or dilute God's commitment to His people. Nonetheless, each generation's enjoyment of covenantal provisions was dependent on their level of obedience.

Two individuals of the exodus generation had been excepted from God's judgment, **Caleb** (v. 36) and Joshua, the two spies who had retained their faith (Num. 14:38). **To him will I give the land.** Caleb had attempted to rally the nation against their fear of the Anakim (Num. 13:30). Years later, Caleb's clan would single-handedly conquer the Anakim and receive the Anakim territory as their allotment (Josh. 14:6–15).

1:37–38. For your sakes (v. 37). The Lord's anger had also extended to Moses as the nation's representative leader. He had not been exempt from the contagion of his people's four-decade-long spirit of rebellion, having struck the rock at Meribah (Num. 20:9–13; 27:12–14). **Thou also shalt not go in thither.** The penalty for Moses was that he would die outside the Promised Land and be deprived of the

joy of leading his people, at long last, into their inheritance. That privilege would be enjoyed by Moses' successor, his aide **Joshua the son of Nun** (v. 38; see Exod. 17:9).

1:39–40. God's penalty had extended to all those who were age twenty years and older at the time of the Kadesh-barnea rebellion, thirty-eight years earlier. However, their **children** (v. 39), those who had not yet reached the age of twenty at the time of the rebellion, were not held accountable for their parents' sin. They would be the generation to **possess** the land. **Which ye said should be a prey.** Ironically, the parents had used their children as an excuse for unbelief (Num. 14:3, 31). The exodus generation had then been commanded to **turn** (v. 40) back from Canaan and return to **the wilderness.**

1:41–45. Incredibly, Israel had proceeded to add rebellion upon rebellion. **We will go up and fight, according to all that the LORD our God commanded us** (v. 41). Realizing their misjudgment and confessing their sin to **the LORD**, the nation had presumptuously seized for themselves a second chance to conquer the land. It was a second chance without divine authorization, however. **The LORD** had warned them through Moses not to attempt a conquest, **for I am not among you** (v. 42). God's presence was the necessary ingredient for military success. Any attempt at conquest in His absence would meet with certain defeat.

Israel had arrogantly disregarded the divine warning and plunged into battle. The exodus generation refused to accept their fate and were determined to take for themselves what God had withheld from them. They had first rebelled against the Lord's command to go into the land and then against His command not to enter the land. **The Amorites** (v. 44) had made short work of the overconfident Israelites, chasing them like a swarm of **bees** throughout the territory of Edom. Although the defeated nation **wept before the LORD** (v. 45) at the tabernacle, imploring Him to rescind His judgment, He had steadfastly refused to do so.

1:46. Many days. Having failed to enter the land, and unable to dissuade the Lord from His devastating decision, the nation had begun its wilderness wanderings.

4. From Kadesh-barnea to the Plains of Moab (2:1–25)

2:1–7. Israel had begun the final leg of their forty-year excursion through the **wilderness** (v. 1) of Sinai with their entrance into the southern tip of the territory of Edom, in the region of **mount Seir**. Some time later, **the LORD** (v. 2) relayed to Moses that they had been encamped there **long enough** (v. 3). They were now to travel north and pass through Edomite territory. **Your brethren the children of Esau** (v. 4). As the descendants of Esau, Jacob's brother, the Edomites were the nation with the closest familial ties to the Israelites.

Take ye good heed unto yourselves ... Meddle not with them (vv. 4–5). Since the Edomites would naturally **be afraid** (v. 4) of the considerable nation passing through their midst, Israel had been instucted to be especially careful to tread delicately and not arouse them to war. Even if the Edomites refused to treat the Israelites as family, Israel was not to take advantage of them. **I will not give you of their land** (v. 5). Israel had no claim to as much as **a foot breadth** of Edomite land. It had been a divine gift to **Esau**. This policy of protecting the territorial claims of Edom would have encouraged Israel that, in the future, the Lord would likewise protect their own territorial claims.

The Israelites were further instructed that whatever provisions they needed while en route were to be purchased, not taken, from the Edomites. **The LORD** (v. 7) had provided for all of Israel's needs during the previous **forty years**; they were to trust that He would continue to do so.

2:8. Earlier, Moses had requested passage through Edom but was refused (Num. 20:14–21). Therefore, Israel had carefully traveled along the eastern outskirts of Edomite territory, avoiding any arousal of local hostility, eventually arriving at the border of Moab **Elath ... Ezion-gaber** (v. 8) were seaports at the head of the Gulf of Aqaba.

2:9–13. Just as the Israelites had been instructed to tread delicately through the Edomite territory, the Lord instructed them to behave accordingly with the Moabites. Like the Edomites, the Moabites also were distantly related to the Israelites, through **Lot** (v. 9). Therefore, Israel was not to engage them in warfare. The Moabite territory was not divinely allocated to Israel and was, therefore, to remain untouched (**Ar** was a Moabite city).

Israel had then been commanded to cross **the brook Zered** (v. 13), the wadi at the southern end of the Dead Sea known today as Wadi al-Hesa, which served as the border between Moab and Edom.

2:14–15. With this crossing came the conclusion of the nation's thirty-eight-year-long wilderness wandering, and a de facto indication that by this point, the final members of the exodus generation had died (with the exception of Moses, Joshua, and Caleb; see Num. 14:30). **The hand of the LORD was against them, to destroy them** (v. 15). It is clearly stated that natural causes (i.e., old age) could not have accounted for the passing of the entirety of the generation, as those who had been but twenty years of age at the **Kadesh-barnea** (v. 14) rebellion (Num. 14:26–19) would have died at the still youthful age of fifty-eight. Their premature deaths served as a stark reminder to the conquest generation of the severity of the divine judgment that resulted from their parents' rebellion.

2:16–19. Just as Israel had been instructed to deal diplomatically and delicately with the Edomite and Moabite nations, so too they were told to treat the Ammonites. Like the Moabites, the **children of Ammon** (v. 19) were also distantly related to Israel, through **Lot**. Therefore, they were not to be dispossessed of their land. The Ammonite territory was just north of Moab, in the region of the Jabbok River.

2:20–23. Israel's imminent displacement of the Canaanites would be merely the latest chapter in the lengthy history of regional turnover. The Ammonites had displaced their local populace of giants (Hebrew, *Rephaim*), called **Zamzummims** (v. 20). The Edomites had displaced **the Horims** (v. 22; the Horites or Hurrians). **The Caphtorims** (v. 23; the Philistines, who originally hailed from Crete, or

Caphtor) had displaced the previous populace in **Azzah** (Gaza), **the Avims**.

2:24–25. At this point, the Lord had provided the "address" of the territory in which He was permitting Israel to declare war. The area of the **river Arnon** (v. 24), known contemporarily as the Wadi al-Mawjib, was the border between Moab on the south and Ammon on the north. However, upon **Sihon the Amorite, king of Heshbon**'s conquest, the region had become **Amorite** territory (Num. 21:26). As the territory was no longer Moabite or Ammonite, it was fair game for Israel. Israel had been commanded to **begin to possess** their land through conquest. **This day will I begin to put the dread of thee and the fear of thee upon the nations** (v. 25). Not only had God promised Israel His divine assistance in their battle; He had also declared that this conquest was the initial action He would utilize to make the fear of Israel permeate the land and demoralize their opposition.

5. Israel's Initial Conquests (2:26–3:22)

2:26–29. Prior to declaring war on the Amorites, Moses had sent diplomatic communiqués **of peace** to **Sihon** (v. 26; see Num. 21:26). In the proffered peace treaty, Moses had proposed that Israel remain on the main road (**the high way**) as they passed through Amorite territory (v. 27). Although both the Edomites and Moabites had refused passage through the center of their respective territories (Num. 29:20–21; Deut. 23:3–4), Israel had been permitted to navigate the territorial outskirts. Moses noted that Israel's ultimate destination was not the east bank of the **Jordan** (v. 29) but **the land which the LORD our God giveth us**, on the west bank of the river.

2:30–31. Sihon, however, had rejected Moses' offer of a treaty and **would not let us pass by him** (v. 30). As He had done with Pharaoh a generation earlier (see Exod. 4:21), **God hardened** Sihon's **spirit and made his heart obstinate** to create circumstances that would result in His chosen people's victory. **I have begun to give Sihon and his land before thee: begin to possess, that thou mayest inherit his land** (v. 31). The Lord Himself assured Israel a military triumph.

2:32–37. Sihon had marshaled his forces against Israel at **Jahaz** (v. 32), just east of Moab. Israel had defeated the Amorites (**our God delivered him before us**, v. 33), however, and their population—**men … women** (v. 34), and children—had been utterly **destroyed**. This was an example of the *haram* ("to give over to the Lord") judgment (sometimes translated as "the ban"), which declares that everyone and everything that can be destroyed should be destroyed, with no survivors (3:6; 7:2; 20:17; Josh. 6:17 provides the classic example of this divine curse). Moses reported that **there was not one city too strong for us** (v. 36). Whatever the fortifications of Sihon's cities, they had been no match for Israel's military. The text is clear that although Israel's victory was total, their conquest extended only to those cities and the territory that the Lord had allowed, which later contained the two and a half tribes on the east bank.

3:1–4. Once ensconced across the Jordan, Israel had strategically needed the territory of **Bashan** (v. 1), north of their newly conquered territory, to protect their right flank. Bashan, also called "the region of Argob" (3:13), was a fertile area, broadly encompassing the region surrounding the eastern half of the Sea of Galilee, extending northward through today's Golan Heights region to Mount Hermon. Israel's conquest had begun in **Edrei**, some thirty miles east of the southern tip of the Sea of Galilee, when the other Amorite king, **Og the king of Bashan**, had assembled his forces for battle. Israel was not to fear Og's military might, for the Lord promised to **deliver him … his people … his cities** (vv. 3–4) into Israel's hand, just as He previously had done with Sihon's forces.

3:5–11. Evidently, Bashan was highly populated, and Og ruled over an astounding sixty cities, both fortified (**fenced with high walls, gates, and bars**; v. 5) and unwalled farming communities. Again, the *haram* judgment had been applied (see discussion in 2:30–37). As in the victory over Sihon's cities, the populations of Og's sixty cities had been executed (**utterly destroying the men, women, and children, of every city**; v. 6). Once again, Israel had retained for itself **all the cattle, and the spoil of the cities** (v. 7). With the conquest of these two Amorite kings, Israel possessed a vast territory, extending from the **Arnon** River in the south to the snowcapped **mount Hermon** (v. 8) in the north.

3:12–17. The newly conquered Amorite territory had been distributed to the two and a half tribes who had received permission to remain east of the Jordan (Num. 32:28–42). Reuben received the territory from the **river Arnon** (v. 12) to Heshbon; Gad received the southern portion of **Gilead** to the **river Jabbok** (v. 16); **the half tribe of Manasseh** (v. 13) received the northern half of **Gilead** and **all Bashan**. Of special note for their territorial conquests were the **Jair** and **Machir** clans within the half tribe of **Manasseh** (vv. 14–15).

3:18–20. The territory east of the Jordan had been granted to the two and one half tribes contingent on their promise to participate with the remainder of their **brethren** (v. 18) in the conquest of Canaan. Moses now reminded the tribes of their commitment, specifying that the men of war were to leave their **wives** (v. 19) their children, and their numerous **cattle** behind, safely installed in the freshly conquered cities. **Which I have given you**. As the Lord Himself had delivered the cities into their hands, the warriors were not to fear for the safety of their families, being confident of their divine protection. Once Israel achieved victory and their fellow tribes were **given rest** by the Lord, through possession of the **land which the Lord your God hath given them beyond Jordan** (v. 20), they could return to their homes. This would turn into a seven-year separation for the two and a half tribes and their families, the time it would take Israel to conquer Canaan; only then would they be relieved from further military duty by Joshua.

3:21–22. Joshua, not Moses, would lead the conquest of Canaan. Therefore, Moses had encouraged his aide and successor, commanding him to remember what he had witnessed of the Lord's sovereign empowerment of Israel in their previous territorial conquests. Joshua was not to **fear** (v. 22) the inhabitants of the land, **for the Lord your God he shall fight for you**. The Lord's power, never Israel's military strength, would secure victory for Israel.

6. The Appointment of Joshua and the Disappointment of Moses (3:23–29)

3:23–25. Although the Lord had forbidden Moses to lead Israel's conquest of Canaan (Num. 20:12), He had allowed His servant to lead the conquest of the territory east of the Jordan. As a result, Moses had apparently become optimistic that the Lord would mercifully change His mind and allow him to oversee the entirety of Israel's conquest of the Promised Land. Opening his request with praise, Moses had beseeched the Lord that having shown him the beginning of the conquest (**thou hast begun to shew thy servant thy greatness**), he might also be witness to its conclusion (v. 24). He had requested that the Lord allow him to **go over**, to enter **the good land**, the Land of Promise.

3:26–27. But the Lord was wroth with me … and would not hear me (v. 26). The Lord had refused to grant Moses' request. (On **for your sakes**, see discussion on 1:37.) God had been furious with Moses for his failure as Israel's leader and His representative, who was held to the highest of standards. **Let it suffice thee; speak no more unto me of this matter**. Moses had been told to let the matter drop and never again bring it before the Lord. He was to be satisfied with His oversight of the Transjordanian conquest and seek nothing further for himself. Nonetheless, the Lord had extended a merciful gesture to His servant, commanding him to climb Mount **Pisgah** (v. 27) and view the Promised Land. From that elevation, it would be possible for Moses to see a vast portion of Canaan's territory in every direction.

3:28–29. Moses' responsibility now was not to oversee the conquest but to prepare the nation for the conquest and, in particular, for the transition from his leadership to that of Joshua. Moses had been commanded to **charge … encourage … and strengthen** (v. 28) his successor. **Beth-peor** (v. 29), also known as Baal-peor (Num. 25:3, 5), was the location of Balaam's blessings (Num. 23:28; 31:16) and of the exodus generation's final apostasy (Num. 25:1–18).

B. Exhortation to Obedience (4:1–43)

1. The Purposes of the Covenant (4:1–8)

4:1–2. Hearken, O Israel (v. 1). Calling His people to careful attention, the Lord enumerated two basic purposes of His gift of the covenant. Israel was to obey God's **statutes and … judgments … that ye may live, and go in and possess the land which the LORD God of your fathers giveth you**. The first purpose of the covenant was to enable Israel to achieve their full potential and enjoyment of life within their land as they exercised obedience to the God's law. The law was presented as an indivisible unit, and the text contains a stern admonition for Israel to neither add nor subtract from the Lord's Torah (v. 2). They were to resist both human nature's compulsion to create a more arduous legal system by accumulating extra legal layers as well as mankind's opposite tendency to "lower the bar" by removing or glossing over more cumbersome aspects of the law. This is a common refrain throughout both the Old and the New Testaments (12:32; Prov. 30:6; Jer. 26:2; Gal. 3:15; Rev. 22:18–19).

4:3–4. Because of Baal-peor (v. 3). The lesson of Baal-peor, the Moabite region referred to in the previous passage as Beth-peor (3:29), was that obedience to the Torah was not merely a lifestyle commitment but an indispensable component of Israel's very survival. Every adulterous Israelite who had violated the covenant through participation with the Moabite women in the idolatrous fertility rites at Baal-peor had been cut down and destroyed. Only those who had remained faithful to the covenant had been allowed to survive (Num. 25:1–9; Ps. 106:28–29; Hos. 9:10). Simply put, God judges sin and rewards obedience.

4:5–8. The second purpose of the covenant was evangelistic in nature. The Torah would set the nation apart as morally unique. This would serve to captivate the attention of neighboring nations and draw those nations to Israel's God. Israel was to both **keep … and do** (v. 6) the laws of God. This would result in the nations being impressed with Israel's reputation for **wisdom and … understanding**, their intimate relationship with their God, and the degree to which their laws reflect righteousness.

The terms **statutes and judgments** (v. 8) are idiomatically linked some seventeen times within Deuteronomy (e.g., 4:1, 5, 8, 14). They are basically synonymous and are used interchangeably throughout the text.

2. The Sinai Experience (4:9–14)

4:9. Take heed … and keep thy soul diligently, lest thou forget. Personal obedience to God's commandments was just the beginning of the Lord's requirements for His chosen people. The text of Deuteronomy is replete with emphases on Israel's timeless, corporate responsibility. The national culture was to be steeped in continual awareness and obedience to God's law. **Teach them thy sons, and thy sons' sons.** Vital to such national consciousness was the pedagogical efforts of each forthcoming generation's parents. Each generation's very survival depended on parents teaching their children God's law.

4:10–12. Of utmost importance was the corporate retention of the memory of the Lord's giving of the law at Sinai. **Thou stoodest** (v. 10). Although many present in Moses' audience were born during the wilderness wanderings, Moses nonetheless addressed the corporate identity of the contemporary generation standing before him as if they had all been personally present at Sinai.

The divine call for Israel to remember the Lord's past redemptive acts, in particular, how He delivered them from slavery in Egypt and brought them to Himself at Sinai, is a common theme in Deuteronomy (5:15; 7:18; 8:2, 18; 9:7, 27; 11:2; 15:15; 16:3, 12; 24:9, 18, 22; 25:17). That they had heard the Lord's awesome voice thundering from Sinai, in the midst of **fire … darkness, clouds, and thick darkness** (v. 11), was to be seared in the national consciousness.

4:13–14. He declared unto you his covenant (v. 13). Israel's God could powerfully manifest Himself, His **voice** and His power, but was nonetheless a nonvisible spirit, possessing **no similitude** or likeness (John 4:24; Isa. 31:3; see discussion on Exod. 19:16-20:21). This is the text's first use of the significant term "covenant," which Moses used some twenty-eight times in Deuteronomy. In this context, the covenant refers to the **ten commandments,** which God had presented directly to His people in His own voice. The remaining 603 commandments had been communicated to Israel through His servant Moses. **Two tables of stone.** See discussion on Exod. 31:18. **That ye might do them in the land whither ye go over to possess it** (v. 14). The vast majority of the Torah's 613 commandments were designed for and presuppose the nation's presence in their land. Many of the **statutes and judgments** could not be properly implemented outside the land of Israel. Deuteronomy presents obedience to the Torah and possession of the land as theologically inseparable concepts. Although Israel's ownership of the land, stemming from the Abrahamic covenant, was unconditional, each generation's enjoyment of their land, stemming from the Mosaic covenant, was contingent on their obedience to their covenantal obligations.

3. Idolatry (4:15-24)

4:15-18. Since YHWH had not manifested Himself in a specific visible form, Israel was strictly prohibited from representing Him in any manner of image. They were to **take ... good heed** (v. 15) not to **corrupt** (v. 16) themselves through the creation of **a graven image, the similitude of any figure ... male or female ... of any beast ... of any winged fowl ... of any thing that creepeth ... of any fish** (vv. 16-18). This was not a prohibition of all statues and artistic images of any kind for any purpose but merely a proscription of any images created for the purpose of worship, that is, idols. The Lord's essential nature was never to be thought of as being able to be contained or represented in a mere piece of art. (See discussion on Exod. 20:4-6.)

4:19. Furthermore, Israel was warned against worshiping any portion of the Lord's creation, specifically **the sun, and the moon, and the stars.** The cosmos has always elicited from man a measure of both awe and wonder. **Shouldest be driven to worship.** Although many of Israel's neighbors worshiped various astral deities, Israel was to resist the impulse to worship the creation along with the Creator.

4:20. YHWH alone was Israel's sovereign master. He alone had delivered His people from the oppressive, yet vitally formative, **iron furnace** of slavery in **Egypt** to take them for Himself as **a people of inheritance,** His own personal possession (9:26, 29; Pss. 28:9; 33:12; 68:9; 78:62, 71; 79:1; 94:14; Joel 2:17; 3:2; Mic. 7:14, 18).

4:21-24. Yet again, Moses commented on his inability to enter the Land of Promise. **For your sakes** (v. 21). Moses referred to himself as an object lesson from which His people could learn the severe consequence of disobedience. As Moses' moral failure had resulted in the loss of his enjoying **that good land,** so too future disobedience to the Torah would result in the nation's loss of enjoying their land. **Take heed unto yourselves, lest ye forget the covenant** (v. 23). Moses sternly warned Israel to be particularly wary of idolatry once they entered the land and were no longer under his leadership. He vividly described YHWH as **a consuming fire ... a jealous God** (v. 24), who had sole possession of His people and passionately refused to share their devotion or ardor.

4. The Future of the Covenant (4:25-31)

4:25-28. Despite the severity of his previous warning, Moses was aware that, centuries hence, future generations would neglect the covenant and allow themselves to be corrupted by idolatry. This would inevitably provoke the Lord **to anger** (v. 25). With **heaven and earth** (v. 26) as his witnesses (30:19; 31:28; 32:21; see Introduction: "Literary Features"), Moses declared that the product of Israel's future idolatry would be two stages of divine judgment. The initial stage would be characterized by the destruction of a great percentage of the people, the dispossession of their **land,** and their dispersion **among the nations** (vv. 26-27). Violation of the Torah would result in Israel's being reduced to a remnant (**ye shall be left few in number;** v. 27). The second stage of judgment for their idolatry would be that Israel's remaining remnant would be given over to serving the local idols of their host nations.

4:29–31. However, the **but if** of 4:29 provides a hopeful contrast to the preceding woes. In their dark hour of national distress, the Israelites would repent of their sins. **Thou shalt seek ... thou shalt find** (v. 29). Israel's future repentance was certain. **All thy heart and ... soul**. They would remember their former passion for their covenant God and once again fervently seek to obey Him. While Israel's repentance was predicated on the stipulations of the Mosaic covenant, the Lord's forgiveness was predicated on the timeless Abrahamic covenant (Gen. 15:18–21; 17:7–8; 26:3–5; 28:13–15; 35:12; see discussion on 1:6–8). The Lord **is a merciful God** (v. 31) who will not forever abandon His people but will remember **the covenant of thy fathers**.

Moses used three phrases to specify for Israel the time of this future national repentance. **When thou art in tribulation** (v. 30) describes the moment in history when all the judgments of Deuteronomy would befall Israel (**all these things are come upon thee**), which would occur during a period of time referred to in Scripture as **the latter days**, the period immediately preceding and leading into the millennial kingdom and the reign of the Messiah. Israel's future national repentance would occur outside of their land, while they were still dispersed among the nations. At that time, they would be returned to their land in conjunction with the inauguration of the millennium.

5. One Israel, One God (4:32–40)

4:32–34. Moses then contrasted the "latter days" with the **days that are past** (v. 32), the period spanning creation through Israel's experience at Sinai. Moses issued a challenge to his audience to inquire of the historical record, from the most distant to the most recent points, and of the geographical spectrum, **from the one side of heaven unto the other**, whether there was precedence for two events: (1) the Lord's awesome self-revelation to His people at Sinai, characterized by their hearing **the voice of God**

speaking out of the midst of the fire (v. 33), and (2) the exodus event, wherein God redeemed one **nation from the midst of another nation, by temptations ... signs ... wonders ... war ... a mighty hand ... a stretched out arm ... by great terrors** (v. 34). No other ethnic group in the history of the world shares an experience remotely similar to Israel's, either in their history or folk mythology. Israel's seminal experiences are both unique and unparalleled.

4:35–38. That thou mightest know that the LORD he is God (v. 35). God's purpose in conveying Israel through these unprecedented experiences was to create an innate and indelible corporate understanding that YHWH is the only true God; **there is none else beside him**. The awesome sound-and-light show at Sinai had in no way been mere sound and fury, signifying nothing. He revealed His words **out of the midst of the fire ... that he might instruct thee** (v. 36).

The basis for Israel's unique experience of both redemption and revelation was the Abrahamic covenant (see discussion on 1:6–8). **Because he loved thy fathers, therefore he chose their seed after them** (v. 37). The Lord's choice of Israel as His chosen people was based on nothing other than His covenantal love and commitment to one man, Abraham, and his extended family. That covenantal love and commitment was itself based on nothing other than God's own sovereign choice and would result in the Lord's driving **nations from before thee greater and mightier than thou ... to give thee their land for an inheritance** (v. 38). Israel had witnessed awesome spectacles over the past forty years, but more was still to come. The uniqueness of Israel's experience was to continue with the dispossession of stronger nations to make room for Israel in the land. As Israel was God's inheritance (4:20), so the land was Israel's God-given inheritance.

4:39–40. As a result of these unique experiences, Israel was both to **know** (i.e., understand; v. 39) and **consider** (continually contemplate) the uniqueness of the Lord and obey His **statutes and ... commandments** (v. 40). The motive for such obedience was **that it may go well with thee, and with thy chil-**

dren. A God-centered and Torah-structured lifestyle would lead to a more blessed life. Furthermore, obedience would prolong Israel's enjoyment of the land, **which the LORD thy God giveth thee, for ever**.

6. Three Cities of Refuge (4:41–43)

These verses are an editorial insertion (as indicated by the narrative's change from first person to third person) concerning Moses' designation of three cities of refuge (Num. 35:9–34) on the east side of the Jordan: **Bezer** (v. 43) for the tribe of Reuben, **Ramoth** for the tribe of Gad, **and Golan** for the tribe of Manasseh. In the cities of refuge, those guilty of manslaughter could find sanctuary from those seeking retribution (see discussion on 19:1–13).

C. Historical Summary (4:44–4:49)

This next section serves as both a historical summary of Moses' first sermon (1:6–4:40) and an introduction to his second, lengthier message (5:1–26:19). The Sinai covenant that **Moses now set before the children of Israel** (v. 44) on the east side of the Jordan is here designated as *torah*, **law** or instruction in a general sense, the contents of which were specific **testimonies ... statutes**, and **judgments** (v. 45). **The land of Sihon king of the Amorites ... the land of Og king of Bashan, two kings of the Amorites** (vv. 46–47). See discussions on 2:26–3:11.

III. Message Two — Present: Covenant Responsibilities (5:1–26:19)

A. General Covenant Responsibilities (5:1–11:32)

1. The Ten Commandments (5:1–33)

a. Introduction (5:1–5)

The third major division of Deuteronomy continues building on the literary structure of the ancient suzerain-vassal treaty (see Introduction: "Literary Features"). As the historical prologue section dealt with Israel's past, this section focuses largely on Israel's present responsibilities and those relating to the nation's imminent conquest of the Promised Land.

5:1–5. The section begins with the clear, corporate directive **Hear, O Israel** (v. 1), a solemn phrase that is repeated within Deuteronomy (6:4; 9:1; 20:3; 27:9). The forty-year-old covenant of Sinai, originally confirmed with the exodus generation, was now being reaffirmed with Israel's next generation, the generation of conquest. The purpose of capturing their national attention was so that Israel would hear **the statutes and judgments** of the covenant and **learn them, and keep, and do them**. Again referencing the nation in the timeless, corporate sense, Moses affirmed that the covenant was made **with us in Horeb ... all of us here alive** (vv. 2–3). It is reckoned as if every Israelite, including those of future generations, were present at the Sinai experience. To remove any ambiguity, Moses specified that it was the newer Sinai covenant to which he referred, not the older Abrahamic **covenant** (v. 3) made **with our fathers**. Scripture always treats these two foundational covenants as related yet distinct.

Moses reminded his audience that at the Sinai experience, the Lord Himself briefly **talked with you face to face in the mount out of the midst of the fire** (v. 4), long enough to orally deliver the Ten Commandments. However, this direct form of communication had been aborted at the request of the Israelites, who **were afraid by reason of the fire** (v. 5). This had led to Moses serving as mediator between YHWH and the nation (**I stood between the LORD and you at that time**) and to his uniquely intimate and direct pattern of communication with the Lord (Exod. 33:11; Deut. 34:10).

b. The Ten Commandments (5:6–21)

This section contains a reiteration of the Ten Commandments, which had first been announced at Sinai (see discussion on each element of the Decalogue in Exod. 20:1–20:21). On this occasion, however, it was Moses, not YHWH, who pronounced these foundational components of the covenant to the Israelites.

5:6–7. The first commandment corresponds to Exodus 20:2–3 and affirms the necessity of Israel's submission to the true God and establishes

His identity as YHWH, the covenant-making and covenant-keeping God. Inseparable from His identity is His redemptive activity in rescuing Israel **out of the land of Egypt, from the house of bondage** (v. 6). **None other gods before me** (v. 7). The first commandment goes beyond mere acknowledgment of YHWH's existence and demands complete repudiation of all other gods, deities, and divinities. Recognition of YHWH as the most potent of gods is unsatisfactory, for YHWH will accept nothing less than complete allegiance from His chosen people.

5:8–10. The second commandment corresponds to Exodus 20:4–6 and prohibits idols (see discussion on Deut. 4:15–18). Again, it is not artistic representations (i.e., statues, pictures, etc.) that are herein prohibited, for such images had been commissioned by God Himself—for example, the cherubim on the ark of the covenant (Exod. 25:19; 37:9) and the bronze serpent (Num. 21:9). **Any graven image, or any likeness ... Thou shalt not bow down thyself unto them, nor serve them** (vv. 8–9). The issue is the use of these artistic representations for the purpose of worship. The creation of images as an aid to worship was a widespread pagan custom and was never to be practiced or even attempted by Israel. The reason for this is not only the futility of attempting to contain the infinite majesty of YHWH in a finite representation, the invisible within the visible, but the Lord is **a jealous God** (v. 9) who will in no way tolerate the adulteration of His people's worship.

Visiting the iniquity of the fathers upon the children (v. 9). This does not refer to the concept of generational sin; rather, it is a euphemism conveying the severity and breadth of God's judgment upon His opposition, encompassing the entirety of a multigenerational household. **Them that love me and keep my commandments** (v. 10). YHWH desires to extend mercy (Hebrew, *hesed*), or covenant loyalty and faithfulness, and liberally does so to those who demonstrably love Him through their loyal obedience to His covenant (7:9).

5:11. The third commandment corresponds to Exodus 20:7 and prohibits the misuse of God's name, that is, taking **the name of the Lord thy God in vain**. This concept extends far beyond the popular conception of prohibiting the use of the word "god" as a profanity. It refers to the casual, cavalier, meaningless, or flippant use of YHWH's name; the use of the Lord's name in a manipulative fashion, such as using His name as an element of an incantation; as well as its use as a component of a false oath (Lev. 19:12). YHWH is holy and demands that He be spoken of with both consideration and reverence.

5:12–15. The fourth commandment corresponds to Exodus 20:8–11 and directs Israel to **keep the sabbath day to sanctify it** (v. 12); to observe the seventh day of the week and maintain its holiness, its separate nature from the common week. **As the Lord thy God hath commanded thee**. Whereas in the parallel Exodus account, Israel was commanded to remember the Sabbath (Exod. 20:8), here they are also directed to observe it. Forty years earlier, the Sabbath was a new concept, initially introduced to the nation of newly liberated slaves during their first few weeks of freedom (Exod. 16:23).

The basic stipulations of Sabbath observance are enumerated here for subsequent generations: the cessation on **the seventh day** (v. 14) of each week of the entire household's **labour**, extending beyond the primary family members to servants, guests, and livestock. Although the reason for the Sabbath provided in the parallel passage in Exodus was to follow the example of God in His cessation of labor following the creation of the world (Exod. 20:11), the additional reason for Sabbath observance provided here references Israel's personal experience, not the Lord's example. **The Lord thy God brought thee out thence** (v. 15). The exodus experience was to serve as the foundational template upon which Israel's observance of the Sabbath would be constructed. As circumcision had been divinely designated as the sign of the Abrahamic covenant (Gen. 17:10), so the Sabbath was now divinely designated as the sign of the Mosaic covenant (Exod. 31:12–17). The indication from this passage is that just as circumcision was intended exclusively for the chosen people, so too was the Sabbath. This is bolstered by the fact that observance of the Sabbath is the only one of the

Ten Commandments not repeated in the New Testament, and Paul's teachings clearly indicate the optional nature of participation in Sabbath observance for the church (Rom. 14:5–6; Col. 2:16–17), which functions not under the Mosaic covenant but within the parameters of the new covenant (Heb. 8:13).

5:16. The fifth commandment corresponds to Exodus 20:12 and contains the admonition to **honour** one's parents. The concept of such honor incorporates not only deference, obedience, and respect but also the proper care of one's parents as they enter their later years. Dishonoring one's parents inevitably leads to a wholesale covenantal breakdown in the larger community and, therefore, could not be tolerated. **That thy days may be prolonged, and that it may go well with thee, in the land which the LORD thy God giveth thee.** As Paul pointed out some fifteen centuries later, this is the first commandment to which a promise is attached (Eph. 6:2–3). The promise is longevity of Israel's residence within the Promised Land, another reminder that possession and enjoyment of the land was contingent on Israel's obedience.

5:17. The sixth commandment corresponds to Exodus 20:13, and although it is often misunderstood as a prohibition of all killing whatsoever, it actually proscribes premeditated murder, the deliberate and unauthorized taking of human life. While it protects the sanctity of human life, it does not prohibit all killing and does not apply to the death penalty (Lev. 20:10; Num. 35:19) or to warfare (Deut. 13:15).

5:18–19. The seventh commandment corresponds to Exodus 20:14 and prohibits **adultery** (v. 18), extramarital sexual relationships. This commandment prohibits the violation of the sanctity of marriage and the family unit—society's basic building block. The commandment pertains equally to both men and women, and to be correctly categorized as adultery (as opposed to other sexual immorality or general fornication), at least one married participant must be involved.

The sixth and seventh commandments reveal the high regard the Torah exhibits toward both human life and the societal institution of marriage. In the same way, the eighth commandment, corresponding to Exodus 20:15, emphasizes the Torah's high regard for personal property in prohibiting theft.

5:20. The ninth commandment, corresponding to Exodus 20:16, prohibits false accusation or perjury, whether in an official court of law or a less formal setting. It may or may not apply to deception or lying in general, depending on the situational context (see discussion on Exod. 1:18–21).

5:21. The tenth commandment, corresponding to Exodus 20:17, is a prohibition not of external action but of internal motivation (**desire … covet**). The Israelites were to be content with their own families, lifestyles, and properties, reining in any avaricious desire for someone else's possessions. Indeed, violation of the tenth commandment initiates the violation of the commandments seven through nine.

c. Israel's Response (5:22–27)

5:22–27. Moses reminded his audience that YHWH Himself had audibly spoken **these words … unto all your assembly in the mount out of the … fire … cloud, and … thick darkness, with a great voice** (v. 22). The elders and the leaders of the tribes, although impressed with the fact that they had **seen this day that God doth talk with man, and he liveth** (v. 24), had nonetheless been petrified at the experience, saying, **if we hear the voice of the LORD our God any more, then we shall die** (v. 25). Fearful for their very lives because of their exposure to God's **glory and … greatness** (v. 24), they had requested that from that point on, the Lord would address Moses exclusively on their behalf. Forty days later, on Mount Sinai, the Lord **wrote** the ten commandments **in two tables of stone, and delivered them unto me** (v. 22; see discussion on Exod. 31:18).

d. The Lord's Response (5:28–33)

5:28–30. The Lord had responded favorably to the Israelites' reverent response to His revelation and had directed Moses to dismiss them from the foot of the mountain to return to their **tents** (v. 30). At this point, the text allows the reader the merest glimpse into the heart of God, as YHWH expressed His passionate desire that the Israelites would always possess **such a heart** (v. 29) and **would fear me, and keep all my commandments**. The result of such continued reverence would be **that it might be well with them, and with their children forever**. The student of biblical history is well aware, however, how desperately and consistently Israel would fail to live up to YHWH's hopeful expectation.

5:31–33. Moses had been directed to ascend Sinai and absorb the Lord's personal tutoring concerning His remaining 603 **commandments … statutes, and … judgments** (v. 31), which Moses, in turn, conveyed to Israel. At that point, Moses' role had been formalized, not only as mediator of the covenant but as lawgiver to his people.

They may do them in the land which I give them to possess it (v. 31). Again, it is emphasized that adherence to the Torah is inexorably linked with dwelling within the Promised Land. Only in the context of the Land of Promise could the nation of Israel fulfill their divine destiny. They were to **walk in all the ways** of the LORD (v. 33) and not **turn aside to the right hand or to the left** (v. 32); no deviation from God's directives would be tolerated. Such obedience would yield three results: life (**that ye may live**; v. 33), prosperity (**it may be well with you**) and longevity in their land (**that ye may prolong your days in the land**).

2. Directives and Warnings (6:1–8:1–20)

a. Directive to Obey and Remember (6:1–25)

6:1. This section contains a catalog of directives and warnings that elaborate on the covenant details not expressed in the covenant's foundation, the Ten Commandments. As covenantal mediator and lawgiver, Moses had been commanded **to teach** the Israelites the remaining general **commandments**, **statutes**, and **judgments** to prepare Israel for their covenantal lifestyle in their new homeland.

6:2–3. This covenantal lifestyle and commitment to **fear the LORD** (v. 2) was a lifelong obligation (**all the days of thy life**) not only for the contemporary generation but for every one of Israel's generations to come thereafter. The result of covenantal faithfulness would be longevity in the land (**that thy days may be prolonged**), prosperity (**that it may be well with thee**; v. 3), and fertility (**that ye may increase mightily**). It is important to note that these promises of blessing upon Israel are completely contingent on Israel's faithful obedience to the covenant. **In the land that floweth with milk and honey** is the traditional descriptive shorthand for the Promised Land, indicating conditions of agricultural abundance and productivity (Exod. 3:8, 17; 13:5; 33:3; Lev. 20:24; Num. 13:27).

6:4. Hear, O Israel (v. 4) is a phrase specific to Deuteronomy that recurs throughout the text (5:1; 6:4; 9:1; 20:3; 27:9). **Hear, O Israel: The LORD our God is one LORD**. This particular verse, in Hebrew *sh'ma Yisrael Adonai Eloheinu Adonai echad*, is an amplification of the first commandment. The grammatical construction of the Hebrew text literally reads, "Hear, Israel, YHWH our God, YHWH one." Contemporary Judaism understands this passage as an affirmation of absolute philosophical monotheism, pointedly setting the Jewish faith apart from conventional trinitarian Christianity. Grammatically, however, the verse cannot teach YHWH's absolute unity because the word *echad*, "one," is a word often used of a compound unity (Gen. 2:24). Therefore, the passage certainly leaves the linguistic door open for YHWH's compound unity of essence and a personal plurality of identity.

The *Sh'ma* has always been central to the tenets of Jewish worship. By the time of the second temple, contemporaneous with the time of Jesus, this passage had already become Israel's fundamental confession of faith. Known as the *Sh'ma* (from the initial Hebrew word, "Hear"), it was recited by Jewish men both morning and evening and was taught to each Jewish boy from the moment he could speak. It was also to be every Jew's last recitation, immediately prior to death.

6:5. When Jesus was asked to rate the greatest commandment, He chose this text (Matt. 22:37–38). Israel was to **love the LORD**, to whom they were so uniquely related with passionately obedient devotion, with steadfast commitment and undivided allegiance (10:12; 11:1, 13, 22; 13:3; 30:6, 16, 20). **All thine heart**. In Hebrew thought, the heart, *levav*, encompasses both affection and intellect and represents the inner man—the mind—man's understanding, emotions, and passions. Because this term has a wide range of meanings, Jesus needed to add an additional word for "mind" when He quoted this verse (Mark 12:30).

All thy soul. The Hebrew word *nephesh* represents the self, one's vital life force. **All thy might**. The Hebrew *me'od*, normally a modifier carrying the force of the term "very" or "exceedingly," is uniquely used here in the Hebrew text as a substantive noun with the sense of "strength," "force," or "power," to underscore the total, loving commitment expected by the Lord.

6:6–7. The Lord's directives were to be communicated and faithfully passed down from one generation to the next. Furthermore, the transmission of spiritual truth from parent to child was not to be sporadically executed. **When thou sittest in thine house … when thou walkest by the way … when thou liest down … when thou risest up** (v. 7). Parents were to spontaneously seize various opportunities throughout the day to train their offspring in their covenantal responsibilities.

6:8–9. A sign upon thine hand … frontlets between thine eyes (v. 8). The literal interpretation of this passage is the origin of the ancient practice of wearing *tefillin* (Hebrew for *phylacteries*, from the Greek), little leather pouches that have been ritually bound around the foreheads and arms of observant Jewish men since biblical times. The emphasis of this passage is that God's Torah was to be continually remembered throughout the day (see discussion on Exodus 13:3–10). **Write them upon the posts of thy house** (v. 9). Likewise, the literal interpretation of this verse is the origin of the Jewish practice of affixing to the doorframe of each home a *mezuzah*, a small, rectangular, decorative wooden or metal box containing a diminutive parchment scroll on which is written both 6:4–9 and 11:13–21.

6:10–12. Israel's forthcoming conquest of the land would entail allowing most of the Canaanite cities to remain intact, complete with homes already prepared for their new tenants. Israel's promised prosperity carried with it an inherent danger: the natural human propensity to forget the source of divine blessing. **Lest thou forget the LORD** (v. 12). Israel was warned against developing an attitude of self-sufficiency and collective amnesia regarding their prosperity. They were to always maintain a sense of historical and theological equilibrium, remembering their recent status as powerless residents of **the house of bondage**.

6:13–19. Moses again stressed the necessity of worshiping YHWH alone. Although there would be tremendous peer pressure from the surrounding nations to worship foreign **gods** (v. 14) in addition to YHWH, that pressure had to be resisted at all costs, for it would result in YHWH's wrath and Israel's subsequent removal from their land. **A jealous God** (v. 15). See discussion on 5:8–10. **Destroy thee from off the face of the earth**. This verse should be understood not as Israel's being utterly destroyed from the face of **the earth** but as their being removed from their land. **Ye shall not tempt the LORD your God** (v. 16). Tempting God implies a disobedient lack of confidence in His capacity to make good His word, which was the sin of Israel at **Massah**, where water flowed from a rock (see discussion on Exod. 17:1–7). Jesus quoted both 6:13 and 6:16 during His temptation (Matt. 4:10 and Luke 4:8; Matt. 4:7 and Luke 4:12, respectively).

6:20–25. When children asked the significance and specific meaning of the Torah's **testimonies … statutes, and … judgments** (v. 20), parents were to seize those opportunities to pass on Israel's redemptive history, beginning with the exodus event and including the Abrahamic covenant and the conquest. **That he might preserve us alive, as it is at this day** (v. 24). The very fact that these parent-child dialogues arise is in itself evidence of God's faithfulness to His people. Israel's obedience regarding the **commandments** (v. 25) would result in their **righteousness**.

b. Warning against Idolatry and Intermarriage (7:1–5)

7:1–2. Having provided directives concerning home and family, Moses now moved to Israel's interaction with the surrounding cultures. During the impending conquest of the Land of Promise, the Israelites' relationships with their neighbors were to be severely restricted. First of all, the **Hittites, Girgashites, Amorites, Canaanites, Perizzites, Hivites,** and **Jebusites** (v. 1), all of whom were current occupants of Canaan (see discussion on Exod. 3:8), were to have their populations completely decimated by Israel's military. Israel was to be the instrument of divine judgment, as the Lord placed them under the *herem* curse of extermination (see discussion on 2:30–37). The history of rebellion and sin that those nations shared meant that if they were allowed to remain living side by side with the Israelites, they would inevitably prove to be a morally corrosive force to God's people. Therefore, Israel was to **make no covenant with them, nor shew mercy unto them** (v. 2).

7:3–5. Furthermore, Israel was to resolutely avoid establishing personal relationships, particularly marriages, with those of the surrounding nations. Social intermingling between Israel and other nations would be an impediment to covenantal obedience and entice them to idolatrous practices. **They will turn away thy son from following me, that they may serve other gods** (v. 4). Israel's preceding and subsequent biblical history demonstrates the inevitability of such moral corruption of the "kingdom of priests."

c. Directives for Covenant Relationship (7:6–16)

7:6. The basis of the imminent extermination of the Canaanite nations was that Israel had been chosen as **a holy people unto the Lord** (see Exod. 19:3–6), to be separated from the moral corruption so characteristic of other nations. **God hath chosen thee.** The text here is patently unambiguous in affirming that it was YHWH who chose Israel for His purposes, not the reverse. Israel had neither the capacity nor desire to initiate a relationship with YHWH. Israel is called YHWH's prized treasure, **a special people unto himself, above all** other nations.

7:7–8. The Lord's choice of Israel as His chosen people was not based on any intrinsic merit that Israel possessed or would eventually possess, for He

chose Israel prior to the nation's existence. He did this upon making **the oath which he had sworn unto your fathers** (v. 8). The Abrahamic covenant (Gen. 12:1–3; 15:13–16; 17:7–8; 26:3–5, 24; 28:13–15) was an everlasting commitment YHWH made to the patriarch's extended family, a commitment He had every intention of maintaining in perpetuity, most recently evidenced when He had **redeemed** Israel from **the house of bondmen** (see discussion on 1:6–8).

7:9–11. Based on both the committed choice of God and the redemptive actions of God, Israel was to **therefore keep the commandments** (v. 11). The consequence of rebellion against **the faithful God, which keepeth covenant and mercy** (v. 9), would be disastrous and self-destructive, as YHWH would **repay** (v. 10) the rebel **to his face. A thousand generations** (v. 9). A hyperbolic expression indicating "without end."

7:12–16. Israel's experience of the blessings contained within the Abrahamic covenant was contingent (**if ye;** v. 12) on their obedience to the **judgments** of the Mosaic covenant. The text enumerates two specific blessings: (1) the blessing of national fertility and agricultural productivity and (2) the blessing of physical health (see discussion on Exod. 15:25–26).

d. Directive for Holy War (7:17–26)

7:17–21. Knowing well the character of his people, Moses identified a potential danger. Moses reminded Israel that the conquest would not depend on numerical superiority or inferiority and encouraged Israel instead to **remember what the Lord thy God did unto … Egypt** (v. 18). Israel's enemies would be no more able to withstand YHWH's power than Pharaoh had been. YHWH had previously exercised power on Israel's behalf, and He would do so again. **The hornet** (v. 20). See discussion on Exod. 23:28.

7:22–26. God would ensure that the conquest of the land would be sufficiently gradual so that the land would not be too rapidly depopulated and overrun with **the beasts of the field** (v. 22). Nonetheless, as each nation under the *herem* judgment was conquered in turn, the citizens were to be completely exterminated, **their kings** (v. 24) in particular (Josh. 12:7–24). Their idols were to be immediately incinerated, without first stripping off the **silver or gold** (v. 25) plating. **It is an abomination**. The idols of Canaan were detestable to YHWH. Anyone foolish enough to bring such **an abomination into his house** (v. 26) opened the door to the community's corruption and would therefore likewise come under the *herem* curse of destruction. Achan is the premier biblical example of this particular folly (Josh. 6:17–19; 7:1, 20–25).

e. Warning against Forgetfulness (8:1–20)

8:1. Israel was reminded that their faithful implementation of YHWH's commandments would yield three benefits: long life, fertility, and enjoyment of the Land of Promise.

8:2–4. Israel was to **remember** (v. 2) their forty-year **wilderness** experience under YHWH's leadership (see discussion on 4:10–12). The Lord revealed two purposes for their lengthy sojourn: (1) their wanderings were the divine judgment for their faithlessness and rebellion; (2) the younger generation was to be YHWH's instrument of conquest. Israel was humbled and proven in the wilderness, where they were completely dependent on the leadership and provision of God. The Lord placed Israel in a position in which they were forced to trust Him for His miraculous provision of food and supernatural preservation of clothing. Indeed, Israel learned the sustaining truth that **man doth not live by bread only, but by every word that proceedeth out of the mouth of the LORD** (v. 3), a truth Jesus quoted in response to His temptation (Matt. 4:4; Luke 4:4).

8:5–6. This generation's response had been to follow the Lord's leadership. The Lord warned them to continue to **keep the commandments of the LORD thy God, to walk in his ways, and to fear him** (v. 6). Otherwise, just as a loving father disciplines his son (Prov.3:12), so the Lord would chasten Israel, His corporate son (see discussion on Exod. 4:22–23).

8:7–10. Israel is described as **a good land** (v. 7), for three reasons. It possessed an abundance **of water**, extraordinary agricultural productivity (**wheat, barley, vines, fig trees, pomegranates, oil, and honey**), and a wealth of natural resources (v. 8). **Iron** (v. 9) was located in various regions throughout Israel, and copper (**brass**) in the southern regions. There are still copperworks in Israel today at Timnah in the south Negev. It was essential that Israel retain an adequate perspective regarding their future prosperity and remember that as the Lord had blessed them, in return, they were to **bless the LORD**.

8:11–18. Which brought thee forth … from the house of bondage (v. 14). Israel was not to forget the power of YHWH, God of the exodus. **Who led thee through that great and terrible wilderness** (v. 15). Israel was not to forget that YHWH had preserved them. **Fiery serpents, and scorpions**. Israel was not to forget YHWH had protected them and **brought thee forth water out of the rock** (see discussion on Exod. 17:4–6). **Who fed thee … with manna** (v. 16). Israel was not to forget that YHWH had provided for them. Through His faithfulness to the blessings contained within the Abrahamic covenant, the Lord was responsible for their wealth. Indeed, Israel's prosperity would be a confirming sign of covenant blessings.

8:19–20. Nonetheless, if their forgetfulness eventually led the Israelites to idolatry, Israel would be expelled from their land as easily as were the Canaanites before them. **Before your face** (v. 20). The Lord's destruction of Israel's enemies would serve as an imposing object lesson as to the fate of those who neglect **the voice of the LORD your God**.

3. The Stone Tablets (9:1–10:11)

a. The Command to Conquer the Land (9:1–6)

9:1–3. The phrase **Hear, O Israel** (v. 1) is used in the same fashion as it was previously (Deut. 4:1; 5:1; 6:4), to call the nation to attention regarding a significant issue. In this context, the subject was the coming conquest of the Promised Land. Moses' concern was to prepare his people for what they would experience on the far side of the **Jordan**. They would encounter **nations greater and mightier** than Israel, nations that had built **cities great and fenced up to heaven** (in actuality, some thirty feet, no doubt an intimidating enough height) in which dwelt a people great and tall ... children of the Anakims (v. 2). Moses well remembered his people's previous response to such an encounter (Num. 13:26–14:4, see discussion on 1:26–28). **Who can stand before the children of Anak?** Although Israel might ask this rhetorical question, with the assumption that the obvious answer was that no one could do so, this would assuredly not be the case with Israel. Numerical strength or military prowess would not play a determinative role in the outcome; rather, it would be the power of YHWH Himself that would definitively settle the matter. Fighting on Israel's behalf, YHWH, **as a consuming fire**, would **destroy them ... drive them out, and destroy them quickly** (v. 3).

9:4–6. Israel's victory would be so devastating that Moses warned his people to beware of developing an ill-founded attitude of self-righteousness. The Israelites were to remember that they had been given the **land** (v. 4), not through their possession of any intrinsic **righteousness**, but for two reasons: (1) the staggering wickedness of the land's previous inhabitants and (2) God's faithfulness to carry out the promises contained within the Abrahamic covenant (Gen. 15:13–21). **Thou art a stiffnecked people** (v. 6). The land was YHWH's gracious gift to His people, not because of their righteousness, but rather, despite their rebelliousness (Exod. 32:9).

b. The Sin of the Golden Calf (9:7–21)

9:7–8. Elaborating on his previous mention of Israel's rebellious tendencies, Moses launched a rehearsal of Israel's greatest acts of rebellion thus far. Using both positive and negative vocabulary, he emphatically reminded his people to **remember, and forget not** (v. 7; see discussion on 4:10–12) their history of rebellion against YHWH **from the day that thou didst depart out of the land of Egypt,** from the wilderness to the plains of Moab. The first example Moses cited was that of the golden calf at Sinai (see discussion on Exod. 32:1–6), at which time **the LORD was** sufficiently **angry ... to have destroyed them** (v. 8).

9:9. To receive the tables of stone (see discussion on Exod. 31:18), **the tables of the covenant which** the LORD had just **made with** Israel, Moses **abode in the mount forty days and forty nights**. During this period, immediately following the divine declaration of the Ten Commandments, the people took advantage of Moses' absence to rebel. An interesting detail provided here is that during Moses' forty-day stay on Sinai, he had been supernaturally sustained by the presence of the Lord, having eaten neither **bread nor ... water**. In contrast, his people had been uncontrolled participants in idolatrous revelry.

9:10–11. At the conclusion of the period of **forty days and forty nights ... the LORD gave** Moses the **tables of the covenant** (v. 11), which had been **written with the finger of God** (v. 10; see Exod. 8:18–19; 31:18). Inscribed on them were the Ten Commandments, that is, **all the words, which the LORD spake with you in the mount out of the midst of the fire** (v. 10).

9:12–14. At that point, the Lord had dispatched Moses to immediately descend the mountain and return to camp. **Thy people which thou hast brought forth out of Egypt** (v. 12). See discussion on Exod. 32:7–10. Israel had **corrupted themselves** through their creation of **a molten image**. Labeling the Hebrews as **stiffnecked** (v. 13), God warned Moses ahead of time not to attempt to intervene or intercede on behalf of the people. **Let me alone, that I may destroy them, and blot out their name from under heaven: and I will make of thee a nation mightier and greater than they** (v. 14). See discussion on Exod. 32:7–10.

9:15–17. The nation's rebellion had been all the more heinous because during this period, **the mount** (v. 15) still **burned with fire**. YHWH's Shekinah glory was still visibly manifest. Moses had descended Sinai, carrying **the two tables of the covenant** (see discussion on Exod. 32:15–18). Overwhelmed by the nation's breaking of the covenant, Moses **took the two tables, and ... brake them** (v. 17) at the foot of Sinai, graphically and dramatically signaling the annulment of the covenant. See discussion on Exod. 32:19–20.

9:18–20. Moses had ascended Sinai again, immediately returning to the presence of the Lord for an additional forty-day period of fasting (making for an astonishing total of an eighty-day fast, coupled with the extraordinary vigor of an eighty-year-old man ascending and descending and ascending the mountain again). Moses, **afraid of the anger and hot displeasure** (v. 19) of the Lord, formally confessed Israel's sin and begged for their forgiveness in his role as Israel's mediator (9:26–29).

9:21. Moses then destroyed the golden **calf**. After burning it, melting down the gold, and consuming the wood with **fire**, Moses had taken what remained of the idol and **ground it** to powder.

c. The Sin at Kadesh-barnea (9:22–24)

9:22–24. Unfortunately, Israel's sin of creating the golden calf would prove to be not just an isolated incident but the beginning of a pattern. Moses continued his narrative recounting of Israel's greatest acts of rebellion, enumerating additional wilderness incidents, **at Taberah** (v. 22; see Num. 11:1–3), **at Massah** (see discussion on Exod. 17:1–7), and **at Kibroth-hattaavah** (Num. 11:31–34), culminating in their sin at Kadesh-barnea. In a statement reeking of a leader's unmitigated realistic appraisal of his charges, Moses declared that Israel had **been rebellious against the Lord from the day that I knew you** (v. 24).

d. Intercession of Moses (9:25–29)

9:25–29. Moses revealed a portion of the content of his intercessory prayer on Israel's behalf during his second forty-day fast (9:18–20). Moses had averted the Lord's wrath through four lines of argument: (1) Reversing God's pronoun change (see discussions on Exod. 32:7–10; Deut. 9:12–14), Moses had reminded YHWH that the Israelites not only continued to be **thy people** (v. 26) but were also **thine inheritance**. (2) Moses appealed to God's recent activity in delivering the Hebrews from **Egypt**. He would not have exerted all that **mighty power** (v. 29) and effort if He did not love them and have a unique relationship with them. (3) Moses appealed to God's solemn covenant oaths to **Abraham, Isaac, and Jacob** (v. 27). (4) Moses appealed to God's repu-

tation among the surrounding Gentile nations, in particular, Egypt. If God were to **to slay them in the wilderness** (v. 28) so quickly after the exodus, the nations might well conclude that He had removed Israel from Egypt either **because he hated them** (v. 28) or because He was incapable of bringing **them into the land which he promised**. Many of the Egyptian and Canaanite gods were similarly capricious, and all of them fell far short of omnipotence. Israel's destruction would do little to distinguish YHWH from every other sundry neighborhood deity. See discussion on 32:10–14.

e. The Second Pair of Tablets (10:1–11)

10:1–5. Having relented from His fury, the Lord had instructed Moses to carve two replacement **stone** (v. 1) tablets and again ascend Sinai. As He had done the first time, the Lord Himself inscribed **the ten commandments** (v. 4) on the tablets, recommitting Himself to the covenant (see discussion on Exod. 34:28). Moses also mentioned the Lord's later directive to create an **ark** of **shittim** (acacia) **wood** (v. 3) as a housing for the tablets, to be placed in the tabernacle, condensing the time frame of events for his thematic purpose (see discussions on Exod. 16:32–34; 25:10–16).

10:6–9. Elaborating on his previous mention of praying for his brother, Aaron, as well as the preceding mention of the ark, Moses noted Aaron's death, which came decades after the golden-calf incident, during the wilderness **journey** (v. 6; see Num. 20:28; 33:31–38). Aaron had been succeeded as high priest by his third son, **Eleazar**. The men of **Levi** (v. 8), the tribe of Moses, Aaron, and Eleazar, had been consecrated for the purpose of bearing **the ark of the covenant, to minister unto** YHWH in the tabernacle, and **to bless** the Israelites **in his name** (Num. 6:24–26). Alone among the tribes, **Levi** (v. 9) would receive no geographic **inheritance**, for **his inheritance** was **the Lord** (Num. 18:20, 24).

10:10–11. Returning to the topic of his intercession on Sinai, Moses reiterated the Lord's renewal of the Mosaic covenant and His commitment to the Abrahamic covenant.

4. Covenant Obligations (10:12–11:32)

a. The Obligation to Love God based on Election (10:12–22)

10:12–13. What doth the LORD thy God require of thee …? (v. 12). Along with the *Sh'ma* (see discussion on 6:4), this is the key passage of Deuteronomy. Moses eloquently summarized the 613 commandments of the covenant by reducing them to five simple obligations: (1) Israel was **to fear the LORD**, to possess an attitude of reverential awe; (2) they were **to walk in all his ways**, to express a lifestyle of obedience; (3) they were to **love him**; (4) they were to **serve the LORD … with … heart and … soul**, to exhibit steadfast commitment and undivided allegiance (10:12; 11:1, 13, 22; 13:3; 30:6, 16, 20; see discussion on 6:5); and (5) they were **to keep the commandments** (v. 13), to demonstrate their love through obedience to the covenant (Mic. 6:8). **For thy good.** The Mosaic covenant was divinely designed to preserve the lives of each Israelite and to maintain their practical enjoyment of the blessings of the Abrahamic covenant.

10:14–15. YHWH, as sovereign master of the universe, **had a delight in thy fathers to love them … he chose their seed** (v. 15). Israel's status as the chosen people was based on the Lord's love for the patriarchs and the promises He saw fit to make to them concerning their extended progeny (see discussion on 7:7–8).

10:16. Therefore. Based on the loving election of their God, Moses graphically called his people to put away their habitual attitude of rebellion and instead strive for loving obedience. He commanded them to **circumcise … the foreskin of your heart … be no more stiffnecked**. They were to carve away the heart's natural inclination to oppose God and expose their heart's spiritually sensitive core, thus enabling them to lead lives that conformed both outwardly and inwardly to the covenant.

10:17–22. Moses enumerated a series of divine titles to express YHWH's incomparable majesty, to drive home the point that rebellion would never amount to anything but sheer futility. Resist the will of the **God of gods and Lord of lords** (v. 17) would never be a logical choice. The only realistic response to the One who had **done for thee these great and terrible things** (v. 21) that they had witnessed was to **fear the LORD … serve** him, **cleave** to him, **and swear by his name** (v. 20). As encouragement, Moses noted that the Abrahamic covenantal promises were already beginning to be realized. Within a period of five centuries, the nation had numerically exploded from some seventy people (see discussion on Exod. 1:5) to their current status **as the stars of heaven for multitude** (v. 22; see Gen. 15:5; 22:17; 26:4; 1:10). In extolling the praises of YHWH, Moses had listed His concern for **the fatherless**, the **widow**, and **the stranger** (v. 18), the resident alien. Israel was to share in God's social concerns, in particular, to **love … the stranger** (v. 19), because they themselves had been resident aliens in **Egypt** (see discussion on Exod. 23:9).

b. The Obligation to Love God based on Experience (11:1–7)

11:1–7. Therefore. In light of the preceding catalog of YHWH's greatness and His blessings to Israel, Moses again repeated Israel's obligation to **love the LORD** (v. 1) and to demonstrate their love through unceasing obedience to **his charge … statutes … judgments, and … commandments** (6:5–6; 7:9; 10:12–13; 11:13, 22; 19:9; 30:6, 8, 16, 20). **The chastisement of the LORD … his greatness, his mighty hand, and his stretched out arm … his miracles, and his acts** (vv. 2–3) **… your eyes have seen all the great acts of the LORD** (v. 7). Moses charged the conquest generation with the significant responsibility of passing on to subsequent generations all that they had witnessed and experienced, from the **miracles … of Egypt** and **the Red sea**, to YHWH's provision in **the wilderness** (vv. 3–5), to the severe discipline meted out at Korah's rebellion (Num. 16:1–35).

c. The Obligation to Obey God for Longevity in the Land (11:8–12)

11:8–12. That ye may prolong your days in the land (v. 9). Obedience to the covenant was the crucial component not only in Israel's initial possession of the land but also in their maintaining that possession (4:40; 5:16; 25:15; 32:47; see discussion on 6:2–3). Although Israel's perpetual ownership of the land was a component of the Abrahamic covenant, each generation's enjoyment of it was predicated on their obedience to YHWH's **commandments** (v. 8). The **land ... flow[ing] with milk and honey** (v. 9; see discussion on Exod. 3:8) was an agricultural powerhouse whose productivity depended not on the seasonal overflow of the Nile, as did **Egypt** (v. 10), but on various rainy seasons throughout **the year. The eyes of the** LORD **thy God are always upon it** (v. 12). The Promised Land uniquely engenders the special regard of the Lord.

d. Obedience and Disobedience (11:13–25)

11:13–15. Diligent obedience to YHWH's **commandments** (v. 13) would yield agricultural blessing. **Love the** LORD **... with all your heart and ... soul.** See discussion on 6:5. **The first rain** (v. 14) in Israel occurs in early November, and **the latter rain** occurs in April. There is also an intermediate rainy season from December through January.

11:16–17. These agricultural blessings, however, would be replaced by drought and famine if the Israelites were not careful to avoid the **worship of other gods** (v. 16; see discussions on 6:10–12 and 8:11–18). They were not to permit themselves to **be deceived** into believing that their neighbor's pagan fertility rites were the source of the land's agricultural productivity. The teaching of the Torah is that the prosperity of the land directly correlates to the level of obedience displayed by the covenant people.

11:18–21. Bind them for a sign upon your hand ... as frontlets between your eyes (v. 18) is a restatement of 6:8. **Teach them your children ... when thou sittest ... when thou walkest ... when thou liest down, and when thou risest up** (v. 19) is a restatement of 6:7. **Write them upon the door posts** is a restatement of 6:9. (See discussion on 6:6–9.) Incorporating the covenantal obligations of the Torah into the fabric of communal lifestyle and ensuring covenantal commitment in succeeding generations

would result in Israel's permanent enjoyment of the land promised to the patriarchs.

11:22–25. Moses returned to the subject of Israel's coming conquest of the land. **Diligently keep ... love ... walk ... cleave** (v. 22). See discussion on 10:20. Although the conquest depended on Israel's covenantal faithfulness, the physical results of the conquest would rest on **the** LORD (v. 23), who would **drive out ... greater nations ... mightier than yourselves** (see discussion on 4:35–38). The geographic borders of the Promised Land are given, as they had been previously (see discussion on 1:7–8). **Fear of you and the dread of you** (v. 25). No nation would be able to withstand an army that had YHWH serving as its vanguard (2:25; 7:23–24).

e. A Blessing and a Curse (11:26–32)

11:26–32. This section concludes the general stipulations of YHWH's and Israel's suzerain-vassal treaty. **A blessing and a curse** (v. 26). Obedience to the covenant would yield **blessing** (v. 27), and covenantal disobedience would result in **a curse** (v. 28) on Israel. Once Israel crossed the **Jordan ... to possess the land** (v. 31), they were to ceremonially announce the covenant's blessings and curses antiphonally from the natural amphitheater between two centrally located mountains, Mounts **Gerizim** and **Ebal** (v. 29), some thirty-five miles north of Jerusalem, flanking Shechem in Israel's hill country. **The blessing** was to be pronounced from **mount Gerizim**, and **the curse** pronounced from **mount Ebal** (for the blessings and curses of the covenant, see discussion on 27:1–28:68).

B. Specific Covenant Responsibilities (12:1–26:19)

1. Ceremonial Laws (12:1–16:17)

a. Laws concerning the Sanctuary (12:1–14)

12:1. Moses now enumerated at length (12:1–26:19) the specific stipulations of the Mosaic covenant. While the previous section concentrated mainly on the general themes of loving YHWH, faithful obedience, and Israel's possession of the land, this section focuses on the Torah's particulars.

Which ye shall observe to do in the land. Much of the Torah's legislation could only be obeyed within the context of the Promised Land and was simply not applicable beyond Israel's borders.

12:2–3. As had previously been commanded (see discussion on 7:3–5), Israel, once in possession of the land, was to eradicate every last Canaanite outdoor shrine: **their altars ... their pillars, and ... their groves** (v. 3) found on **the high mountains and ... hills, and under every green tree ... hew down the graven images of their gods** (v. 2–3). Once these shrines were destroyed, Israel was then to erase all evidence of pagan worship having ever occurred in those places, wiping **the names** (v. 3) of the false gods from the historical record.

12:4–7. The total destruction of the Canaanite shrines was not merely for the purpose of cleansing the land from the defilement of pagan idols. What was at stake here was the possibility of any former shrines becoming worship attractions to rival **the place which the Lord your God shall choose** (v. 5), the central, authorized sanctuary that YHWH would establish. This sanctuary was the only location where the Israelites were to **bring ... burnt offerings ... sacrifices ... tithes ... heave offerings ... vows ... freewill offerings ... the firstlings of ... herds and ... flocks** (v. 6), as well as where the Israelites were to assemble for the pilgrimage festivals. Shiloh would serve as the initial location of authorized worship, the place where the tabernacle was erected (Josh. 18:1), followed by Nob (1 Sam. 21:1), Gibeon (1 Chron. 16:39), and finally, the holy city of Jerusalem (1 Kings 8:16), where Solomon built the temple. **Ye shall rejoice in all that you put your hand unto, ye and your households, wherein the Lord thy God hath blessed thee** (v. 7). A major component that has always flavored Jewish attitudes toward worship developed from the divine command for communal joy and public celebration of God's blessings (12:7, 12, 18; 14:26; 16:11; 16:14–15).

12:8–9. Ye are not as yet come to the rest and to the inheritance (v. 9). While the Israelites were still outside the Promised Land, the laws of the Torah were not yet being fully enforced. The practice of **every man** doing **whatsoever is right in his own eyes** (v. 8) was to terminate with Israel's entrance into the land. Unfortunately, the book of Judges reveals that the sin-redemption cycles that began once Israel settled into their land were fueled by the troublesome persistence of this attitude (Judg. 17:6).

12:10–14. Once Israel successfully completed the conquest of their homeland, and YHWH had given them **rest from all ... enemies ... so that ye dwell in safety** (v. 10), YHWH would chose a final location **to cause his name to dwell** (v. 11). Some four centuries would pass before Jerusalem would be revealed as God's choice for the site of His temple. The reason for the delay is that it could not be stated that Israel had peace and borders truly secure from hostile neighbors until the reign of David (2 Sam. 7:1) and Solomon (1 Kings 5:4).

b. Laws concerning Flesh and Blood (12:15–28)

12:15–16. The Torah makes a distinction between **flesh** (v. 15) that was permitted for Israelites to eat and that which was forbidden to them once they arrived in the land. If only intended for dinner and not for sacrifice, both wild game and domesticated animals could be eaten without the impracticality of their first being delivered to the central sanctuary. Ceremonially **clean** and **unclean** Israelites could eat such meat. Those who were unclean, however, were prohibited from eating sacrificial meat. In all circumstances, however, the consumption of **blood** (v. 16) was strictly forbidden (Gen. 9:4; Lev. 7:26–27). In the ancient world, blood was considered the life force (Lev. 17:11) and was always to be drained prior to preparation (Lev. 17:13).

12:17–19. Every **tithe** (v. 17) and sacrifice was to be eaten by the entirety of each household at the central sanctuary. Again, the command was repeated to **rejoice before the Lord** (v. 18; see discussion on 12:7; also discussions on 12:12; 14:26; 16:11; 16:14–15). This command was also again linked with providing for the needs of the local **Levite**, who, being dependent on the support of the community (14:27), was to be included in any ritual festivities.

12:20–28. All animals intended for sacrifice were to be delivered only to the central sanctuary and slaughtered in the prescribed ritual fashion. The admonition against eating **blood** (v. 23), identified as representing **the life** force (see discussion on 12:16), is again repeated. The reason for this prohibition was so **that it may go well with thee** (v. 28), because it **is good and right in the sight of the** LORD.

c. Laws concerning Idolatry (12:29–13:18)

12:29–31. Following Israel's successful conquest of the Promised Land, they were to always remember that idolatry was the underlying rationale for the Canaanites' dispossession and destruction. Israel was to **take heed** (v. 30) not to nourish their curiosity concerning the Canaanites' **gods** or related worship practices. **Every abomination … which he hateth** (v. 31). Although perhaps exotic or enticing, these abominable rituals could never be incorporated into the worship of YHWH. Particularly detestable was the practice of child sacrifice (prohibited in Lev. 18:21; 20:2–5). This was associated with the worship of the god Molech (Lev. 18:21; 20:2–5; 1 Kings 11:7; 2 Kings 23:10; Jer. 32:35).

12:32–13:5. Thou shalt not add thereto, nor diminish (v. 32). No one was to append or edit the written text of YHWH's revelation (see discussion on 4:1–2). Moses discussed three potential sources that could entice a community to modify YHWH's instructions: (1) an idolatrous false prophet (13:1–5), (2) an idolatrous friend or family member (13:6–11), and (3) an idolatrous town (13:12–18). In the first instance, that of a **prophet, or a dreamer of dreams** (v. 1) soliciting the community to idolatry, Moses warned the people to weigh the prophet's message against the written Word of God. They were not to be deceived by the performance of a miraculous **sign** or **wonder**. Certainly, the performance of signs and wonders was one validation of a true prophet (18:22). Regardless of supernatural abilities, however, a true prophet could never contradict the Word of God. Any prophet soliciting the worship of **other gods** (v. 2) was to be rejected as false.

God would allow such false prophets to arise in the midst of the community of faith as a test of Israel's loyalty and love (Gen. 22:1). **All your heart …**

all your soul (v. 3). See discussion on 6:5. **Ye shall walk … fear … keep … obey … serve … cleave** (v. 4; see 10:20; 11:22; 30:20). No deviation from YHWH's Torah was permissible. An Israelite was never to serve as a rival god's representative, contradicting YHWH and seeking to corrupt his fellow Israelites. This crime would necessitate the sentence of **death** (v. 5), for only then could Israel **put the evil away from the midst of thee**, that is, remove both the evil and the evildoer. The phrase "put the evil away from the midst of thee" is repeated eight more times in Deuteronomy (17:7, 12; 19:19; 21:21; 22:21–22, 24; 24:7) and is quoted by Paul in 1 Corinthians 5:13.

13:6–11. The second potential source of solicitation to idolatry was a close friend or family member. **Thy brother … son … daughter … wife … or thy friend, which is as thine own soul** (v. 6). Once compromised by idolatry, loved ones, those who generally exert the strongest influence, were a grave internal danger to the community. In contrast to the public bombast of a false prophet's signs and wonders, this would be a secret, intimate enticement to idolatry, implemented behind the closed doors of the family circle. The idolater was to be publicly exposed and brought forth for execution by stoning, a sentence to be carried out by the community. The accuser himself had the weighty responsibility of casting the initial stone. Stoning was a form of capital punishment unique to Israel, finding no mention in any other contemporary document of the ancient biblical world. Furthermore, only in Israel was the responsibility of capital punishment carried out by the general community rather than being limited to officially designated executioners. **All Israel shall hear, and fear, and shall do no more any such wickedness as this** (v. 11). The severity of such action would serve to deter further enticements to rebellion. **The** LORD **thy God, which brought thee out of the land of Egypt, from the house of bondage** (v. 10), would tolerate no rivals for His people's affection.

13:12–18. Finally, for the third potential source that could entice a community to modify YHWH's instructions, Moses related the case of the idolatrous city. In this example, if a rumor began circulating in Israel that **certain men** (v. 13) were teaching the citizens of their town to **go and serve other gods**, a thorough investigation would be undertaken to determine the certainty of the rumor's substance, since it was not an eyewitness account. **The children of Belial**. Worthless men (1 Sam. 1:16; 2:12; 10:27; 25:17; 30:22; 1 Kings 21:10, 13; Prov. 6:12). Belial was later used euphemistically for Satan (2 Cor. 6:15).

If the investigation determined that a town had indeed given itself over to the **abomination** (v. 14) of idolatry, that city was to be placed under the *herem* curse and destroyed (see discussion on 2:32–37). Every inhabitant and animal was to be annihilated. The city was to be burned, along with all **the spoil** (v. 16), and was to become **a heap for ever**, never to be rebuilt. **The LORD may turn from the fierceness of his anger** (v. 17). Failure to thoroughly comply with the excising of moral cancer from Israel's midst would result in the nation itself being subject to the *herem* curse.

d. Law concerning Disfigurement (14:1–2)

14:1–2. As the corporate son of God (8:5; see discussion on Exod. 4:22–23), Israel was to be set apart from the practices of its neighbors. **A holy people ... chosen ... a peculiar people ... above all the nations** (v. 2). Their identity as the chosen people meant that their appearance must also be recognizably different from their neighbors (7:6; 26:18; Lev. 11:44; Ps. 135:4; Mal. 3:17; see also Exod. 19:3–6). Israel was prohibited from disfiguring themselves by laceration, the mark of a false prophet (1 Kings 18:28), or by shaving their foreheads as a sign of mourning.

e. Laws concerning Clean and Unclean Foods (14:3–21)

14:3–8. The motivating force behind the seemingly arbitrary laws concerning clean and unclean foods have engendered much debate over the centuries. Of all the ancient Near Eastern biblical cultures, only Israel possessed such an advanced system of dietary restrictions. Many people believe the underlying reasons for the *kashrut* (kosher) laws are hygienic

in nature, though there is no indication of this in the text. The only reason provided in the text for the distinction between clean and unclean animals is that YHWH identified certain animals as **abominable** (v. 3), that is, detestable and abhorrent to Him, and they were to remain off-limits in the diet of His people. The term used for these animals, "abomination," is elsewhere used within the text in reference to idolatry (7:25), human sacrifice (12:31), blemished, imperfect sacrifices (17:1), occultism (18:9–14), and the use of false measures (25:13–16). No other reason or intrinsic distinguishing characteristics of these unclean animals is provided than that YHWH had rejected them for Israel's diet. Israel was to be set apart from their neighbors in every imaginable fashion; every facet of their lives was to publicly and privately reflect their devotion to the Lord.

The animals are divinely grouped according to their means of locomotion and physical characteristics. **Beasts** (v. 4) that Israel was permitted to eat were those that both possessed split hooves and **cheweth the cud** (v. 6), such as **the ox, the sheep, and the goat** (v. 4). Animals that were forbidden for Israel to **eat of their flesh** (v. 8) or make contact with their carcasses were those who failed to meet both criteria. They were **unclean** (vv. 7–8) because they either lacked cloven hooves, as do **the camel, and the hare** (v. 7), or did not **chew the cud** (v. 8), as **swine** do not. **Unclean unto you**. The kosher laws were specifically designed for implementation by the covenant people, Israel, within the confines of the Mosaic covenant's duration (Heb. 8:13). That these laws were never meant to be universally applied to every people at every time is clear from both Jesus' declaration of the cleanness of all foods (Mark 7:19) and Peter's threefold vision on the same topic (Acts 10:10–16).

14:9–20. Fish that Israel was permitted to eat were those that possessed both fins and scales. The absence of one or the other physical characteristic identified the fish as **unclean unto you** (v. 10). A list is provided of birds that Israel was forbidden to eat, mainly birds of prey, such as **the eagle** (v. 12). Flying insects were likewise off-limits.

14:21. Due to the prohibition against consuming blood (see 12:16), the eating of **any thing that dieth of itself** was forbidden for Israelites. The carcass of an animal that died a natural death, however, could be charitably given to **the stranger**, the resident Gentile living among them, or it could be sold to other Gentiles. Again, these laws were applicable only to Israel, **a holy people unto the LORD**. It was also forbidden to **seethe a kid in his mother's milk**, a detestable practice that epitomized the Canaanite paganism. Repeated three times in the Torah, this prohibition became determinative in the oral law's expansive view of forbidden foods (see discussions on Exod. 23:19; 34:26).

f. Laws concerning the Tithe (14:22–29)

14:22–27. In addition to the previously revealed legislation concerning the first tithe, the 10 percent of each household's personal income that was to be set aside to support the priesthood (Lev. 27:30–33; Num. 18:21–32), Moses now revealed legislation concerning a second **tithe** (v. 22). This tithe, an additional 10 percent of each household's personal income, was to be used for the purpose of worshiping God through fellowship meals at the central sanctuary during Israel's three annual pilgrimage festivals. If the central sanctuary was too distant to practically transport crops or livestock there, the crops or livestock could be converted into cash. **Thou shalt rejoice, thou and thine household** (v. 26). The **money** (v. 25) was to be used to purchase anything necessary to fulfill the divine mandate for each Israelite family to enjoy the feast: **for oxen, or for sheep, or for wine, or for strong drink, or for whatsoever thy soul desireth** (v. 26). **The place which he shall choose to place his name** (v. 23). See discussion on 12:4–7. No one family could consume the entirety of their tithe, so there would be plenty of provisions to share with the needy. A portion of this second tithe was also set aside for each community's **Levites** so that they also could worshipfully enjoy the three feasts. **He hath no part nor inheritance with thee** (v. 27). See discussion on 10:9; 18:1–8.

14:28–29. At the end of three years thou shalt bring forth all the tithe of thine increase the same **year** (v. 28). Moses then provided legislation concerning a third tithe, to be triennially collected, not at the central sanctuary but by each local community (**within thy gates**; v. 29). This was to be used as a food bank of sorts for the support of the local **Levite** as well as the needy: **the stranger, and the fatherless, and the widow** (see Exod. 22:22). Obedient collection of this tithe would result in divine blessing and provision.

g. Laws concerning the Sabbatical Year (15:1–11)

15:1–6. Every seven years thou shalt make a release (v. 1). The Torah provides three rationales for the sabbatical year: (1) for the sake of the poor (Exod. 23:10–11), (2) for the sake of the land (Lev. 25:2–7), (3) for the cancellation of debts. Every seven years, every **creditor** (v. 2) was to remit any debts owed him by fellow Israelites—not a postponement of debt payment during that year, but the permanent annulment of debt. This applied strictly to Israelites, not to the **foreigner** (v. 3) doing business in Israel. **There shall be no poor among you** (v. 4). Ideally, this seven-year cycle would serve to eliminate poverty in Israel. This statement, however, should be tempered with this text's additional realistic admission that **the poor shall never cease out of the land** (15:11; quoted by Jesus in Matt. 26:11). Indeed, perfect prosperity could only result from perfect obedience to all of YHWH's **commandments** (v. 5). The model of lending **unto many nations** and borrowing from none, of sovereignly reigning **over many nations** (v. 6) and not being reigned over, would have to await a more messianic age and climate.

15:7–11. The citizens of Israel were to exhibit enormous generosity, being particularly certain to lend the **poor … sufficient for his need** (vv. 7–8). The **thought** (v. 9) of withholding generosity because of the nearness of **the year of release** was never to be entertained. An act of such hardheartedness would **be sin**, resulting in the rejected Israelite crying **unto the LORD against thee. Thine eye be evil** is a Hebrew euphemism for stinginess (see Matt. 6:23). Giving openhandedly, as a gift, without thought of an approaching mandated cancellation of debt, would result in **the LORD ... bless[ing] thee in all thy works, and in all that thou puttest thine hand unto** (v. 10). God could be trusted to restore the financial balance.

h. Laws concerning Servants (15:12–18)

15:12–18. The sabbatical concept was also to be applied to **Hebrew** (v. 12) servants, both male and female. These would be Israelites for whom Israel's inherent anti-poverty system had broken down and who found themselves paying off their debt through a six-year term of indentured service (see discussion on Exod. 21:2–11). It is important to note that while Gentiles (to whom the sabbatical concept did not apply) could be pressed into permanent servitude in Israel, Israelites could not be so enslaved. The service of the indentured Israelite was contracted with his master for a set period, no longer than six years. **In the seventh year** of service, the servant was to be **free** to go. The servant was not to be released empty-handed but **liberally** (v. 14) supplied with provisions to enjoy his newfound freedom without fear of incurring additional debt and reinitiating the cycle of servitude. Israelites were to **remember** (v. 15) their history as Egyptian slaves and the Lord's redemption of them (see discussion on 4:10–12).

If the Israelite servant desired to remain in service to his master, either for the sake of loving affection or for financial security, his or her **ear** (v. 17) was to be pierced with **an aul**, a public indication of a lifetime commitment of service (see discussion on Exod. 21:5–6). If the servant choose instead to depart, the owner was to remember that six years of excellent value had been derived from his service and that releasing a servant would result in divine blessing.

i. Laws concerning the Firstborn (15:19–23)

15:19–23. The laws here concerning the dedication of firstborn animals parallel the legislation of Exodus 13:11–15; 22:29–30 (see discussion) and Numbers 18:11–18. **All the firstling males** of **herd and ... flock** (v. 19) were to be set apart for the Lord's use. Therefore, no personal benefit was to be derived from the firstborn. These were to be offered and eaten annually during one of the three pilgrimage festivals celebrated at the central sanctuary. If one of the firstborn animals was blemished or physically impaired, however, it was not to be sacrificed in the central sanctuary but slaughtered and eaten at home. As always, the animals' **blood** (v. 23) was to be poured out prior to consumption (see discussions on 12:16, 20).

j. Laws concerning Pilgrimage Festivals (16:1–17)

16:1–8. These verses contain legislation regarding the three annual pilgrimage festivals—the Passover, the Feast of Weeks, and the Feast of Tabernacles—when every Israelite was commanded to appear with their families to worship at the central sanctuary. See discussions on Exod. 23:10–19; 34:18–26. The first festival was **the passover** (v. 1), the anniversary of Israel's liberation from Egypt, occurring in **the month of Abib**, which was later changed to Nisan. (For Passover and its closely associated holiday, the Feast of Unleavened Bread, see discussions on Exod. 12:1–28.) The emphasis in this text is how Israel was to observe the Passover once settled in the Promised Land. **The place which the LORD shall choose to place his name** (v. 2). See discussion on 12:4–7. The Passover sacrifice was authorized to be offered only at the central sanctuary. Any other location was forbidden. The sacrifice was to be offered **at even, at the going down of the sun** (v. 6), the conclusion of Passover day.

The subsequent Feast of Unleavened Bread immediately followed the offering of the Passover, beginning with the waning of the Passover sun and the eating of the Passover seder (ritual meal). During this seven-day period, no **leavened bread** (v. 4) was to be found in any Israelite household. Unleavened bread was to be eaten in Israel for **seven days** to commemorate the nation's abrupt liberation and exodus. At the conclusion of the Passover seder meal, each household was to have completely consumed the meal; no leftovers were allowed. **In the morning, and go unto thy tents** (v. 7). When the meal would finally conclude, quite late in the evening, the pilgrims would disassemble and return to their temporary lodgings to sleep off the heavy meal.

16:9–12. The feast of weeks (Hebrew, *shavuot*; known as Pentecost in New Testament times; v. 10) was held **seven weeks** (v. 9) after Passover and the Feast of Unleavened Bread (see Exod. 23:13–19). Israelite families were commanded to bring an offering to the central sanctuary and **rejoice before the Lord** (v. 11; see discussion on 12:4–7; see also 12:12, 18; 14:26; 16:13–15). Amidst all the festivities, Israel was not to neglect the needs of the local **Levite**, nor the needs of the underprivileged, **the stranger, the fatherless, and the widow** (10:17–22; 14:28–29; see discussion on Exod. 22:22).

16:13–15. The feast of tabernacles (v. 13) was a seven-day celebration associated with the conclusion of the autumn harvest. Israelite households were to enjoy this feast through gathering for worship at the central sanctuary and building temporary structures, or booths, to commemorate their wilderness wanderings (Lev. 23:33–43). YHWH's blessing was cause for each family to **surely rejoice** (v. 15; see discussion on 12:4–7; see also 12:12, 18; 14:26; 16:11).

16:16–17. These verses reiterate and summarize the obligation to observe the three annual pilgrimage festivals, **the feast of unleavened bread … the feast of weeks … the feast of tabernacles** (v. 16; see Exod. 23:14, 17; 34:23). No one was to **appear before the Lord** at the central sanctuary empty-handed; all Israel was to give according to their ability and in accordance with the Lord's blessings.

2. Civil Laws (16:18–20:20)

a. Laws concerning Judges and Officials (16:18–17:13)

16:18–20. The text now turns to the tribal and local appointment of **judges and officers** (v. 18). Officers were to serve as secretaries to the judges and as record keepers of the adjudicated cases. The judges were to carefully pursue justice in all instances and circumstances (see 1:15–18; Exod. 18:13–23; 23:1–9). Justice in Israel's courts would result in the nation's longevity in the Promised Land.

16:21–17:1. Justice included the avoidance of idolatry in conjunction with Israel's worship of YHWH (see 7:3–5; 12:3; Exod. 34:13). Furthermore, every sacrifice offered to YHWH was to be a perfect specimen. The Lord considered a physically defective sacrifice to be an insult and an **abomination** (v. 1; 15:21; Mal. 1:6–8) as well as akin to idolatry.

17:2–7. As community leaders, judges were responsible for pronouncing sentences of capital punishment when necessary. If, following a diligent investigation, a **man or woman** (v. 2) were found guilty of **transgressing his covenant** by worshiping **other gods** (v. 3) or the cosmic elements (see 4:19), the transgressor was to be stoned to death by the local community (see discussion on 13:6–11). The testimony of one witness was insufficient in Israel's justice system (Num. 35:30). It took a minimum of **two or** (v. 6), preferably, **three witnesses** for capital convictions. The initial stones were always to be cast by **the witnesses** (v. 7) themselves, immediately followed by stones cast by the entire community. **So thou shalt put the evil away**. See discussion on 13:5.

17:8–13. If a judge was presented a controversial case for which arrival at a verdict was too difficult, the case was to be presented to Israel's highest court of appeal, at the central sanctuary (**the place which the Lord thy God shall choose**; v. 8). **The sentence** (v. 10) rendered by this "supreme court," composed of **Levites** (v. 9) and **the judge that shall be in those days** (i.e., the high priest), was binding and absolute. There was no higher authority in Israel to whom appeal could be made. Disobedience in carrying out their **sentence of judgment** was in itself a capital offense. **Thou shalt put away the evil from Israel** (v. 12). See discussion on 13:5. **And all the people shall hear, and fear, and do no more presumptuously** (v. 13). The swift and exacting implementation of justice would serve as a robust deterrent to further disobedience within the nation.

b. Laws concerning the King (17:14–20)

17:14–20. The Torah anticipates that Israel would eventually become a monarchy. Following the conquest and settlement of the Promised Land, Israel would desire a centralized government similar to that of their neighboring **nations** (v. 14; 1 Sam.

8:5, 20). Moses provided qualifications for the future king and guidelines for his behavior. Two qualifications were given for selecting a king: (1) the choice was to be made not by community standards but by YHWH's sovereign prerogative (**whom the Lord thy God shall choose**; v. 15), and (2) Israel's king was not to be a Gentile, **a stranger**, but was to be a Hebrew, chosen from among Israel's **brethren**.

Three prohibitions and two obligations were given as guidelines for the king's behavior. The prohibitions were: (1) the king was forbidden to **multiply horses to himself** (v. 16); that is, build up a large cavalry. Israel and her king were to depend on YHWH alone for their security. (2) The king was prohibited from multiplying **wives to himself** (v. 17). The majority of royal marriages generally found their basis in personal pleasure or political alliances. Israel's king was to avoid such indulgence and diplomatic entanglements, relying instead on the Lord. Foreign wives could especially entice the king's **heart** to **turn ... away** from YHWH. (3) The king was forbidden to acquire wealth and treasure. All three prohibitions required that the king remain dependent solely on the blessings of the Lord. Some four centuries later, the events of Solomon's reign would provide a graphic example of the disastrous result of a king's violating all three prohibitions (1 Kings 10:14–15, 23, 26–28; 11:1–6).

The obligations were: (1) At the commencement of a king's reign, he was to **write him a copy of this law in a book** (v. 18), that is, handwrite a personal copy of the entirety of the book of Deuteronomy. (2) The king was to habitually study his copy of the law **all the days of his life** (v. 19). Familiarity with the law would help the king **to fear the Lord his God, to keep all the words of this law and these statutes, to do them,** while keeping **his heart** (v. 20) from being **lifted up** in pride. Fear of YHWH and obedience to His commandments would result in a lengthy reign and an enduring dynasty.

c. Laws concerning the Priest (18:1–8)

18:1–8. The priests the Levites, and all the tribe of Levi (v. 1) possessed no designated tribal allotment of land. **The Lord is their inheritance** (v. 2). Their **inheritance** was the priestly ministry and sanctuary service. However, certain cities and surrounding fields were designated for the Levites' use (Num. 35:1–8; Josh. 21:41–42). They were also supported through Israel's tithes and portions of sacrifices (see discussions on 14:22–29; see also Lev. 27:30; Num. 18:21–29). **The priests** (v. 1) were a subset of **the tribe of Levi**, the direct descendants of Aaron, the original priest (Num. 10:8). All other males from the tribe were designated as **Levites** and served as the priests' support staff within the central sanctuary (Num. 18:1–7; 1 Chron. 23:28–32).

Certain portions of the animal and **firstfruit** (v. 4) sacrifices (Exod. 23:19), as well as **fleece**, were automatically designated as belonging to **the priests** (v. 3). This was to sustain the continual sanctuary ministry of the hereditary, professional priesthood specifically **chosen** (v. 5) by YHWH. If a Levite chose to supplement the compensation for his sanctuary ministry through **the sale of his patrimony** (v. 8), that is, by selling off a portion of his possessions or property (Lev. 25:32–34), he was still entitled to partake of his share of the compensation enjoyed by his fellow Levites.

d. Laws concerning Occult Practice (18:9–14)

18:9–14. These verses contain legislation prohibiting Israel's participation in occult activities that were habitually practiced by the Canaanites. Following the dispossession of the Canaanites, with Israel's successful conquest and resettlement of the land, Israel was to carefully avoid retaining any of the **abominations** (v. 9) of the land's former tenants. This text argues that the practice of these **abominations** corrupted the entire culture and had transformed the Canaanites into **an abomination unto the Lord** (v. 12). Indeed, it was these occult practices that caused YHWH to **drive** the **nations** from the land. Israel was to remember that these practices were unconditionally proscribed for the chosen nation called to **be perfect with the Lord** (v. 13).

To make a child **pass through the fire** (v. 10) refers to child sacrifice. **Divination** involved the attempt to influence future events or foresee the future through observation and interpretation of omens and signs, such as reading animal entrails, lunar eclipses, and so on (Num. 22:7; 23:23). **An observer of times** was a soothsayer, possessing the ability to summon spirits (Lev. 19:26). **An enchanter** was an omen interpreter, similar to the diviner. **A witch** was a practitioner of magic, a spell caster who sought to manipulate the natural realm through supernatural power (Lev. 19:26–31; 20:6; see discussion on Exod. 22:18). **A charmer** (v. 11) was similar to an enchanter, with special emphasis on magic incantations (Ps. 58:6; Isa. 47:9, 12). **A consulter with familiar spirits** was one who consulted the dead (Lev. 19:31; 20:6; 1 Sam. 28:7–9), similar to **a necromancer**, who was a medium that consulted the spirits of the dead (1 Sam. 28:7–14). **A wizard** was a general term for an occultist (Lev. 19:31; 20:6, 27; 1 Sam. 28:3, 9).

e. Laws concerning Prophets (18:15–22)

18:15–19. This section describes the **Prophet ... like unto** (v. 15) Moses. The common contemporary Jewish interpretation of these verses is that the "Prophet ... like unto [Moses]" is a collective reference to the successive line of prophets in Israel who followed Moses (Joshua, Samuel, etc.). Yet there is no reason to assume that the grammatically singular term "prophet" (Hebrew, *navi*) should be read as a collective singular. Nor was this the common interpretation in New Testament times (see John 1:21). The early church viewed the Messiah's identification with Moses as a key messianic element. To reject the prophetic messianic implications of this passage fails to recognize that in the history of Israel, no other person besides Jesus functioned with God or with the people of Israel in a fashion similar to Moses. The conclusion of Deuteronomy itself plainly rejects Moses' own prophetic successor, Joshua, as having fulfilled this prophecy (34:10).

Whosoever will not hearken unto my words which he shall speak in my name, I will require it of him (v. 19). The passage goes on to stress that obedience to the prophet like Moses would be of such importance to God that those who neither recognized this prophet nor obeyed him would suffer the severest penalty. God's harshest judgment would fall upon those who willingly disregarded this coming prophet.

18:20–22. As Israel was to watch for the coming ultimate prophet, in contrast, they were to beware of the false prophets who were to come. Any **prophet** (v. 20) who presumptuously proclaimed an unauthorized message, claiming to represent YHWH, or who possessed the audacity to **speak in the name of other gods**, was guilty of a capital offense and would be executed (see 12:32–13:5). By their actions, false prophets sought to usurp the authority of YHWH Himself. In the event that it was unclear whether a prophet was a true messenger of YHWH, the test of authenticity rested on the fulfillment or lack of fulfillment of what he had prophesied. If what he proclaimed failed to materialize, Israel was not to **be afraid of him** (v. 22) or any supposed power he claimed to possess. The false prophet was to be summarily executed.

f. Laws concerning Cities of Refuge (19:1–13)

19:1–13. These verses concern **three cities** (v. 2) of refuge to be established in addition to the three that had already been established on the east side of the Jordan (see discussion on 4:41–43). Following the successful conquest and resettlement of the Promised Land, Israel was to divide the geographic area of the nation into thirds and establish one centrally located city of refuge in each section. Any Israelite guilty of manslaughter could seek asylum from **the avenger of the blood** (v. 6), a victim's relative pursuing vengeance. These additional three cities would ensure that a city of refuge was accessible from every region of the nation, which would prevent the shedding of **innocent blood** (v. 10) in the **land**.

Although perpetrators of manslaughter could find sanctuary in these cities, perpetrators of premeditated murder could not. Murderers seeking asylum were to be extradited and delivered by the city **elders ... into the hand of the avenger of blood, that he may die** (v. 12). In this fashion, Israel was to

put away the guilt of (v. 13) unavenged, **innocent blood** and maintain an untainted presence in the Promised Land. This section summarizes legislation earlier presented in Numbers 35:9–34. Joshua 20:7–9 records the establishment of these refuge cities: Kedesh, Shechem, and Hebron.

g. Law concerning Boundaries (19:14)

19:14. The moving of a neighbor's landmark, a stone placed to mark a property boundary, entailed the theft of his property and usurpation of his inheritance (27:17; Job 24:2; Prov. 22:28–23:10; Hos. 5:10).

h. Laws concerning Witnesses (19:15–21)

19:15–21. These verses concern legislation governing trial witnesses. **One witness** (v. 15) was insufficient to convict anyone of anything (see discussion on 17:6). Criminal conviction required the testimony **of two ... or ... three witnesses**. Such a standard safeguarded justice in Israel. In the event that only one accuser provided testimony, the case was to be presented before a special panel composed of **priests and ... judges** (v. 17). Following a **diligent inquisition** (v. 18), if the panel determined that the testimony of a particular **witness** was false, the **false witness** was to receive a punishment equivalent to what the accused would have received had he been found guilty. In these cases, the punishment was certain to fit the crime. **So shalt thou put the evil away from among you** (v. 19). See discussion on 13:5. **Those which remain shall hear, and fear, and shall henceforth commit no more any such evil among you** (v. 20). The implementation of ironic justice against the false accuser would serve a prophylactic purpose, restraining further malicious activity and undermining morally corrosive influences. **Life shall go for life, eye for eye, tooth for tooth** (v. 21). This is *lex talionis*, the law of retribution (see discussion on Exod. 21:23–25).

i. Laws concerning Warfare (20:1–20)

20:1–4. These verses contain legislation concerning warfare. No matter how awesome the opposing forces arrayed against them were, Israel was not to **be ... afraid of them** (v. 1). The priests were to encourage Israel's military with the knowledge that **the LORD** fought alongside them. With the rallying call to attention, **Hear, O Israel** (v. 3), the priests were to remind them to **let not your hearts faint, fear not, and do not tremble, neither be ye terrified**.

20:5–7. Israel's victory was so certain that extensive exemptions could be made to excuse men from the responsibility of military service. **The officers** (v. 5) were to excuse anyone who had not yet had the opportunity to enjoy that which rightfully belonged to him, so that others might not usurp that privilege if he were to die in battle. One who had **built a new house** but had not yet **dedicated it** was temporarily excused from service to enjoy his new home. One who had **planted a vineyard** (v. 6) but had **not yet eaten of it** was also temporarily excused from service as well.

20:8–9. A final exemption from service was given to those who were **fearful and fainthearted** (v. 8). Fear was contagious and could demoralize an army. When the army had been accordingly pared down to its essential core, **captains** (v. 9) would then be appointed to lead the army into battle.

20:10–15. Israel's foreign warfare policy was always to first extend an offer of **peace** (v. 10). If the city accepted Israel's terms of surrender, the city's citizens were to serve as Israel's **tributaries** (v. 11), or vassals (Josh. 9:3–27). If, however, they rejected Israel's offer of peace, Israel was to **besiege** (v. 12) the city and upon victory, selectively apply the *herem* curse, destroying all the males of the city. **The women ... little ones ... cattle, and all that is in the city** (v. 14) were to be taken as spoils of war.

20:16–18. Israel had an alternate warfare policy regarding **the cities** (v. 16) within the Promised Land. Upon achieving victory, the *herem* curse was to be liberally applied to these cities. Not only the males but the entire populations were to be utterly annihilated. **The Hittites, and the Amorites, the Canaanites, and the Perizzites, the Hivites, and the Jebusites** (v. 17). See discussion on Exod. 3:8. **That they teach you not to do after all their abominations ... so should ye sin against the LORD** (v. 18). It was necessary to exterminate the populations of these cities to remove an idolatrous cancer from the midst of Israel's holy community (see discussion on 7:1–2). For the most part, the cities themselves were to be left intact for Israel's later residence (see discussion on 2:32–37).

20:19–20. YHWH laid down legislation that prevented His people from indiscriminately razing His creation. While Israel was allowed to freely utilize the wood of non-fruit-bearing trees for the machinery of warfare (siege works), they were to exercise a policy of restraint concerning fruit-bearing trees. These were to be conserved as a perpetual food source.

3. Communal Laws (21:1–26:15)

a. Laws concerning Unsolved Murders (21:1–9)

21:1–9. These verses contain legislation regarding an unsolved murder. If a corpse was discovered **lying in** a **field** (v. 1) and the murder was unsolvable, a panel of **elders and … judges** (v. 2) were to determine **the city** (v. 3) that was nearest to the body's location. **The elders of that city shall take a heifer** that had never been used for plowing, **bring down the heifer** (v. 4) into an uncultivated wadi with flowing water, and break its neck. Although this was a bloodless ritual performed outside of the central sanctuary's courts, **the priests** (v. 5) were to observe the ceremony. **The elders** (v. 6) were then to **wash their hands over the heifer** and symbolically declare that the community was innocent of the homicide (see Matt. 27:24). **The heifer that is beheaded**. More accurately, "the heifer whose neck is broken."

b. Laws concerning Marriage during War (21:10–14)

21:10–14. These verses contain legislation concerning the marriage of Israelite men to foreign women **taken … captive** (v. 10) in time of **war**. This relates exclusively to non-Canaanite foreign women, since intermarriage with them was strictly prohibited (see 7:1–4). If an Israelite man desired to take a **beautiful woman** (v. 11) as his **wife**, he was to bring her **home** (v. 12) with him. Following a month of mourning and symbolic preparation for this severe adjustment of lifestyle, during which the woman would **shave her head … pare her nails**, remove

the raiment of her captivity from off her … and bewail her father and her mother (v. 13), the Israelite could **go in unto her, and be her husband … If thou have no delight in her, then thou shalt let her go** (vv. 13–14). Following the consummation of the marriage, if the Israelite man changed his mind and desired to divorce his new wife (see 22:19, 29; 24:1–4), he was forbidden to **sell her** (v. 14) as if she were his property. **Thou hast humbled her**. The Hebrew word *anah*, translated "humbled," is commonly used for forced sexual relations (Gen. 34:2; Deut. 24:29; Judg. 19:24).

c. Laws concerning Sons (21:15–21)

21:15–17. These verses contain legislation concerning family obligations toward sons. The ancient primogeniture laws specified that **firstborn** (v. 17) sons were to receive **a double portion** of the family inheritance. In the case of a man with two wives, one of whom was favored above the other, the husband was forbidden to grant the right of firstborn inheritance to any son other than his firstborn. No matter the man's preference for one wife over another or one child over another, he could not confiscate what rightfully belonged to his firstborn son, **the beginning of his strength**, the initial example of his procreative abilities. **The beloved and the hated** (v. 15). The loved and the less loved, or rejected (Gen. 29:31, 33; Mal. 1:2–3).

21:18–21. The case of a family with **a stubborn and rebellious son** (v. 18), who was habitually and persistently disobedient despite parental discipline, called for drastic communal action. As this was a violation of the fifth commandment (see Exod. 20:12; Deut. 5:16) and therefore a direct attack on the family, the death penalty was warranted. The parents could only initiate the process of public discipline. Only **the elders of his city** (v. 19) had the authority to adjudicate the sentence.

d. Law concerning a Hanged Corpse (21:22–23)

21:22–23. Following the execution of a criminal for **a sin worthy of death** (v. 22), his corpse was often hung **on a tree** (or perhaps, "impaled on a pole") to serve as a graphic deterrent for the community. However, the **body** (v. 23) was not to be left overnight **upon the tree** but was to be buried **that day** to prevent the land's defilement by the exposed, decomposing corpse (Lev. 18:24–27; Num. 35:33–34). **For he that is hanged is accursed of God.** The criminal was not cursed through being impaled but rather was impaled because he was cursed through committing his crime. Paul quoted from this text to illustrate how Jesus came under God's curse to redeem us from "the curse of the law" (Gal. 3:13).

e. Laws concerning Lost Property (22:1–4)

22:1–4. These verses contain legislation concerning the responsibility of returning lost property. If a fellow Israelite's lost property was found, it was to be returned to its rightful owner. If the owner was unknown to the finder, the property was to be kept in trust until the owner could be identified. If another's animal were endangered, it was to be rescued. **Thou mayest not hide thyself** (v. 3). It was forbidden to shirk the responsibility of caring for the lost property of others, whether animal, clothing, or anything else (see Exod. 23:4).

f. Law concerning Clothing and Gender (22:5)

22:5. This verse legislates the visible distinction of gender through clothing, thereby prohibiting transvestism, homosexuality, and other sexual deviancy. It is to be noted that it is not the act of cross-dressing itself that the text identifies as an **abomination** but rather **all that** (i.e., "those who") engage in the activity.

g. Law concerning Birds and Chicks (22:6–7)

22:6–7. As with the legislation concerning the conservation of fruit trees, this law demands similar restraint regarding future sources of food supply. The mother bird would likely continue to produce more chicks. Perhaps a moral component is involved as well, demonstrating YHWH's reverence for the parent-child relationship even among animals (Lev. 22:27). Obedience would result in prosperity and longevity in the land.

h. Law concerning Parapets (22:8)

22:8. Make a battlement. The flat roofs of the ancient world were used as another room of the **house.** Parapets were required as a safety measure and to avoid liability for accidental deaths.

i. Law concerning Mixtures (22:9–11)

22:9–11. This legislation prohibits the mixture of **divers seeds** (v. 9), animals, and cloth. Only one type of seed was to be sown, **an ox and an ass** (v. 10) were not to be yoked **together**, and both **woollen and linen** (v. 11) material were not to be sewn together when making clothing. No reason for this prohibition of mixtures is provided, although the fact that mixed seeds would defile the vineyard's **fruit** (v. 9) indicates that it may be connected to unknown pagan practices (see Lev. 19:19).

j. Law concerning Tassels (22:12)

22:12. The command to **make ... fringes upon the four** corners of the Israelite males' garments parallels the command to wear the *tzitzit* of Numbers 15:37–41. These blue tassels were to serve as a visible reminder of God's commandments to the wearers and to the community to which they belonged.

k. Laws concerning Personal and Communal Purity (22:13–30)

22:13–21. This section contains legislation concerning sexual purity, both premarital and marital. The first example provided is that of a man who changes his mind and rejects his wife (**hate her**; v. 13) subsequent to their wedding night and then publicly sullies her reputation (**bring up an evil name upon her;** v. 14) by claiming that he discovered she was not a virgin on their wedding night. To accuse a woman of having engaged in premarital sex was a scandalous charge that not only gravely denigrated her integrity but also threatened her very life. The woman's reputation could be salvaged, however, by her parents' public display of **the tokens of the damsel's virginity unto the elders of the city in the gate** (v. 15). Although some interpret this to be her menstrual clothes, proving she was not pregnant on her wedding night, the context more closely aligns with the parents' proof being the bloodstained sheet from the wedding night. It would be an act of prudence for parents to obtain the sheet the morning after the wedding as a safeguard to family honor and their daughter's life.

If the parents could publicly produce such evidence of their daughter's purity, the husband's testimony would be completely discredited, and the accusation was to be dismissed. The assumption here is that the husband was willing to deliver his new wife to be executed and humiliate her family for the sake of a refund on his bride-price. Therefore, he was taken by the city elders and both flogged and fined **an hundred shekels of silver** (v. 19), double the bride-price (see 22:29). The fine was paid to the bride's father as compensation for having had the family name besmirched by the false accusation. If the parents were unable to produce evidence of their daughter's virginity on the wedding night, however, the wife was to be brought immediately **to the door of her father's house** (v. 21) and publicly executed there by **the men** of the community.

22:22. In the case of **a man** involved with a **married woman**, both parties were to be executed for adultery, a direct assault on the family, YHWH's building block for His holy community (see 5:18; Lev. 20:10). **So shalt thou put away evil from Israel.**

22:23–24. The next example concerns a man involved with an engaged woman (**a virgin ... betrothed**; v. 23). In the biblical world, betrothal was considered almost as binding as marriage, so the laws regulating adultery apply. If the relationship occurred within **the city** borders, it was automatically presumed that the sex must have been consensual since no one **in the city** had heard her cries of protestation. Both parties were to be brought **out unto the gate of that city** (v. 24) and executed by stoning for the crime of adultery. **So thou shalt put away evil from among you.**

22:25–27. However, in the case of the rape of **a betrothed damsel in the field** (v. 25), beyond the earshot of city residents, only the man was to be executed. The woman, a victim of rape, was to be presumed innocent of adultery, receiving the benefit

of the doubt about whether she had unsuccessfully protested the relationship.

22:28–29. In the case of **a man** (v. 29) who raped an unengaged **virgin** (v. 28), he was to pay the father a bride-price of **fifty shekels of silver** (v. 29) and marry her. In addition, his right to later divorce his wife was forfeited. This law served as both a deterrent to rape and a means of protecting the victim by providing security.

22:30. This law prohibits a man from marrying his stepmother upon the death of his father. Such a relationship was considered both dishonorable and incestuous (Gen. 9:20–24; Lev. 18:8; Deut. 27:20).

l. Laws concerning the Participation of Males in Public Worship (23:1–8)

These verses contain legislation regulating the participation of males in public worship at the central sanctuary (**the congregation of the LORD**; v. 1). Several groups—the sexually disfigured, the illegitimate, and certain nationalities—warranted exclusion; their participation was considered a violation of the sanctity of the tabernacle or, later, the temple.

23:1. Those who had become eunuchs, whether through accidental injury or intentional castration, were to be excluded from participation in corporate worship. However, the Lord later pronounced a unique blessing on eunuchs (Isa. 56:4–5).

23:2. A bastard (Hebrew, *mamzer*) could be an illegitimate child or the product of incest, a mixed marriage, or a cultic prostitute (Zech. 9:6). The exclusion of the *mamzer* was to continue for ten generations of his descendants (see Ruth 4:18–22).

23:3–6. Also to be excluded from participation in Israel's corporate worship were the Ammonites and Moabites. The exclusion of these incestuous descendants of Lot (Gen. 19:30–38) was to continue for ten generations of his descendants. The reason for their exclusion was both the lack of hospitality shown to Israel during their wanderings as well as the hostility exhibited by the hiring of **Balaam ... to curse** (v. 4) Israel (Num. 22:4–24:25). Although Balaam's curse resulted in the Lord's **blessing** (v. 5) Israel, nonetheless, Israel was not ever to wish **peace nor ... prosperity** (v. 6) on

Ammonites or Moabites. Again, this attitude extended only to Ammonite and Moabite males, which is why Ruth found immediate acceptance in Israel and why the exclusion from corporate worship could not apply to King David, her descendant.

23:7–8. In contrast to the Ammonites and Moabites, the Edomites were not to be hated. As the descendants of Esau (Gen. 36:40–43), they were the nation most closely related to the Hebrews. Egyptians were likewise not to be abhorred, in honor of Israel's sojourn in Egypt, which had initially been a positive experience (Gen. 37–50). The exclusion of Edomites and Egyptians from corporate worship was to be lifted **in their third generation** (v. 8).

m. Laws concerning Sanitation (23:9–14)

23:9–14. These verses contain legislation regulating the sanitation of Israel's camp during time of war. **Every wicked thing** (v. 9). In this context of holy war, reference is made to ceremonial uncleanness, not moral impurity. Ritual vigilance was to be strictly enforced. If a man were to experience a nocturnal emission, he was rendered unclean. He was to leave the **camp** (v. 10) premises until **evening** (v. 11), when he could return after bathing himself (Lev. 15:16–17). Every Israelite was to have a designated tool with which to bury his excrement outside the camp. Of note is the reason provided for such sanitary precaution: **For the Lord thy God walketh in the midst of thy camp ... therefore shall thy camp be holy: that he see no unclean thing in thee, and turn away from thee** (v. 14).

n. Law concerning Escaped Slaves (23:15–16)

23:15–16. This law permitted escaped Gentile slaves to find asylum within Israel's borders. Israel was to be a place of refuge, where the oppressed of other nations could experience the same freedom that YHWH had granted Israel, the nation of former slaves, upon their redemption from Egypt (Exod. 22:21).

o. Laws concerning Prostitution (23:17–18)

23:17–18. No whore of the daughters ... nor a sodomite of the sons ... a whore ... a dog (vv. 17–18). Prostitution, both female and male, whether in the general sense or within the context of religious ritual, was proscribed. Money gained through the abominable practice of prostitution was never to be donated to the treasury of the tabernacle or, later, the temple. **These are abomination** (v. 18). See discussions on 7:22–26; 14:3–8.

p. Laws concerning Usury (23:19–20)

23:19–20. This law prohibited Israelites from the practice of **usury** (v. 19), that is, charging interest. Prosperity within the covenant community was to be left to YHWH, not generated from those within the covenant community who were misfortunate enough to be forced into borrowing (see discussion on Exod. 22:25–27; Lev. 25:35–37). However, an Israelite could charge interest on a transaction made with a foreigner (**a stranger**; v. 20), who could otherwise easily take advantage of Israel's lenient fiscal policy.

q. Laws concerning Vows (23:21–23)

23:21–23. This law concerns the necessity of maintaining an individual's public commitments that were made in YHWH's name. Once made, it was essential to keep **a vow unto the Lord** (v. 21). Failure to fulfill the commitment was considered to **be sin**. This would instruct Israel to maintain a degree of circumspection regarding their pronouncements.

r. Laws concerning Property (23:24–25)

23:24–25. This law permitted eating of a neighbor's crops while passing through his property. Such gracious hospitality, however, had limits. The neighbor's crops could not be harvested or carted away for later use. That would be theft. Private property was to be respected within Israel's borders.

s. Laws concerning Divorce and Remarriage (24:1–4)

24:1–4. This section contains legislation regulating procedures for divorce and remarriage (Lev. 21:7, 14; 22:13; Num. 30:9). A man was entitled to divorce his wife if he became dissatisfied with her (**she find no favour in his eyes**; v. 1) through finding **some uncleanness in her**. This term indicates an impropriety of a sexual nature. It is unlikely that the impropriety was premarital sex or adultery, for both situations merited death, not divorce (see discussion on 22:20–22). The impropriety likely referenced a physical deformity of the wife, immodesty in her manner or conduct, or basic sexual incompatibility. He was then to **write her a bill of divorcement**. Personally placing the document in **her hand**, he was then to **send her out of his house**. The document was for the divorced wife's personal security, ensuring her ability to remarry.

If, however, her second husband either divorced her or died, she was forbidden to remarry her **former husband … after that she is defiled** (v. 4). This refers to the public humiliation the wife would experience through having been rejected by her first husband for an **uncleanness** (v. 1) that her second husband had not found objectionable. Note that the woman's defilement did not prohibit her from remarriage in general, only from specifically remarrying her original husband, which was considered an **abomination before the LORD** (v. 4), a means of causing **the land to sin**.

t. Law concerning New Marriages (24:5)

24:5. This law instructed the newly married **man** to devote the entire first **year** of his marriage to learning the means to **cheer up his wife**, a euphemism for enjoying sexual pleasure with his **new wife**. During the initial year of marriage, the man was to stay **at home … free** from both military and **business** responsibilities (see 20:7).

u. Law concerning Pledges (24:6)

24:6. In the biblical world, the **millstone** was a tool necessary for a household's survival. It was made of two basalt stones, with the larger, heavier flat one (**the nether**) serving as the base on which the grain would be placed and the smaller, lighter one (**the upper**) serving as the grain grinder. The millstone was used for the daily grinding of grain to prepare flour for the family's bread. To take either portion of the millstone as collateral for a **pledge** would render it useless and deprive the family of the daily means to feed itself.

v. Law concerning Kidnapping (24:7)

24:7. As the ultimate theft of one's personal property, stealing one's freedom, kidnapping was a capital offense in Israel (see Exod. 21:16). **Thou shalt put evil away from among you** (v. 7). See discussion on 13:5.

w. Law concerning Skin Diseases (24:8–9)

24:8–9. This is a command to **observe diligently** (v. 8) the instructions that Moses had previously delivered concerning leprosy and various other skin diseases (Lev. 13:1–46). Israel was to remember that, as with Miriam, leprosy could be used as divine judgment (Num. 12:10).

x. Law concerning Collection of Pledges (24:10–13)

24:10–11. This law forbids a lender from engaging in behavior that might shame the borrower or rob his family's dignity. The Torah preserves the debtor's honor, even in his humbling circumstance.

24:12–13. If a garment was taken as collateral on a loan, it was to be returned to the owner by sundown (see Exod. 22:26–27).

y. Law concerning Employees (24:14–15)

24:14–15. This legislation protected hired employees. No Israelite was to **oppress** (v. 14) an impoverished employee, whether the worker was a fellow Hebrew or a resident Gentile. Employees depended on their salaries to meet their family's needs and were therefore to be paid regularly and in a timely fashion. Any delay in the paying an employee would **be sin** (v. 15) and would cause the employee to **cry against thee unto the LORD** (Lev. 19:13).

z. Law concerning Family Guilt (24:16)

24:16. Every man shall be put to death for his own sin. The Torah teaches personal responsibility for the consequences of sin as a general principle. In other instances, corporate responsibility is the norm (see discussions on 5:8–10; 13:12–18 was 17; 21:1–9); usually more in relation to divine judgment than civic authority.

aa. Law concerning the Helpless (24:17–22)

24:17–22. These verses contain legislation that charge Israel to proactively care for the vulnerable of society, **the stranger ... the fatherless ... the widow** (v. 17). Israel was to remember their experience in Egypt as motivation to treat the needy with both fairness and kindness (see discussion on 4:10–12). Landowners were to leave a portion of their crops unharvested for the use of the poor. The poor could then rummage through the fields and gather food while maintaining the dignity of hard work and avoiding the dishonor of begging. This law was the basis of Ruth's actions in Boaz's fields (Ruth 2:3).

bb. Law concerning Corporal Punishment (25:1–3)

25:1–3. These verses contain legislation concerning corporal punishment administered as a result of the ruling of a criminal court. When the judges rendered the decision in a criminal case, if the guilty party was found to be deserving of corporal punishment, the flogging was to be meted out in the presence of **the judge** (v. 2). The number of prescribed lashes was variable, depending on the crime. However, the law sets **forty stripes** (v. 3) as the maximum sentence.

cc. Law concerning Working Oxen (25:4)

25:4. This law guarantees permission for **the ox** (v. 4) to eat while working, allowing the farm animal to glean some benefit from his labors and, indeed, to gain strength to continue in those labors. Paul applied this law to those laboring in ministry (1 Cor. 9:9–10; 1 Tim. 5:17–18).

dd. Laws concerning Levirate Marriage (25:5–10)

25:5–6. These verses contain legislation concerning the custom of levirate marriage. The term *levirate* is from the Latin word for "brother-in-law," *levir*. An ancient custom that significantly predates the Mosaic covenant (see Gen. 38:8–11), levirate

marriage served two necessary functions in the ancient biblical world. First, it provided vulnerable widows with economic and communal security. Second, it offered the means to protect a family inheritance by providing the circumstances necessary to generate an heir and guarantee the orderly transmission of property ownership. If a man died without a male heir, his widow was not to **marry ... a stranger** (v. 5). Rather, she was to be taken as wife by her brother-in-law, **her husband's brother** (or nearest male relative), providing the brothers had lived within reasonable proximity to each other. **The duty of a husband's brother** was to marry his brother's widow for the purpose of generating a male heir to inherit her first husband's property and to maintain his lineage.

25:7–10. If the brother refused to marry his sister-in-law, she was to publicly confront him in the presence of the **elders** (v. 7) gathered at the city **gate**. She was then to accuse him of failure to **perform the duty of my husband's brother**. If he still refused to agree to marriage following the elders' inquiry, the widow was to engage in a ritual meant to humiliate and shame her brother-in-law. Kneeling before her rejecter, she was to **loose his shoe from off his foot ... spit in his face ... and say, So shall it be done unto that man that will not build up his brother's house** (v. 9). Following the confrontation, the widow was free to marry outside the family, albeit without an heir to carry on her dead husband's **name** (v. 10). See Ruth 4:1–12 for an example of the levirate process.

ee. Laws concerning Intervention in a Fight (25:11–12)

25:11–12. These verses contain the only legislation within the Torah that not only permits physical mutilation but commands it. The proposed circumstance is that of two men fighting. During the altercation, the **wife** of **one** (v. 11) of the men, while attempting to come to the aid of her husband, grasped the genitals of the other man. Although her motive was noble in seeking to rescue her husband, the Torah does not consider the end to justify the means. In endangering the potential capacity of the man to produce future offspring, she had committed a grievous offense against the community and their values, and **thou shalt cut off her hand** (v. 12).

ff. Laws concerning Honest Commerce (25:13–16)

25:13–16. This legislation concerns honesty in Israel's commerce dealings. Prior to the coining of money, commerce was conducted through weights and measures, either stone or metal weights marked with standardized values. Israelites were not to be deceitful in their business dealings, having **divers weights ... divers measures, a great and a small** (vv. 13–14; see Prov. 11:1; 16:11; 20:10, 23; Hos. 12:7; Amos 8:5; Mic. 6:11). This was **an abomination unto the LORD** (v. 16). Every Israelite's weights and measures were to be **perfect and just** (v. 15). The exhibition of such integrity would result in Israel's longevity in the land (5:16; 6:2; 11:9; 32:47).

gg. Laws concerning Amalek (25:17–19)

25:17–19. This section legislates Israel's responsibility to **blot out the remembrance of Amalek from under heaven** (v. 19) following their successful conquest and settlement of the land. **Remember what Amalek did unto thee** (v. 17). See discussion on Exod. 17:8–16; Num. 14:39–45. The text lays two charges against the Amalekites. First, they cravenly attacked the weak stragglers bringing up Israel's rearguard. Second, they **feared not God** (v. 18); that is, while they were too cowardly to present a frontal attack against Israel, they had nevertheless recklessly provoked YHWH's wrath by attacking His chosen people at all.

Thou shalt not forget it (v. 19). The command to erase the Amalekites from both the world stage and history was a solemn charge from YHWH to His people.

hh. Laws concerning Firstfruits (26:1–11)

26:1–4. After Israel's conquest of the Promised Land and its successful resettlement, they were to initiate a special pilgrimage festival at the tabernacle, the central sanctuary, wherever it happened to be located at the time (**the place which the LORD thy God shall choose to place his name**; v. 2). The ceremony involved carrying **the first of all the fruit ... in a basket** and presenting it before a **priest** (v. 3). Each Israelite was to enact a short ritual with the priest, making a confession of YHWH's faithfulness to the Abrahamic covenant (**I am come unto the country which the LORD sware unto our fathers for to give us**), after which the priest would place the worshiper's basket of firstfruits **down before the altar of the LORD** (v. 4).

26:5–10. The brief confession was to be followed by a lengthy one, perhaps recited communally by the throng of Israelites. This confession was an acknowledgment of appreciation, recounting Israel's theological history, beginning with Jacob's entrance into Egypt, touching on the nation's growth, enslavement, and redemption in the exodus, and concluding with their triumphal conquest of the Promised Land. Throughout is a heavy emphasis on YHWH's goodness to Israel.

A Syrian ready to perish was my father (v. 5). The literal reading is "a wandering Aramean was my father." Jacob, the third of Israel's three patriarchs, had an Aramean mother, Rebecca (Gen. 24:10; 25:20, 26), and had lived for two decades in Aram (Gen. 31:41–42). His wives were also Aramean (Gen. 28:5; 29:16, 28). Israel's roots were nomadic, but they would now, at long last, be securely planted in their own land. **A few ... became ... a nation, great, mighty, and populous.** See discussion on Exod. 1:5, 7. **A land that floweth with milk and honey** (v. 9). See Exod. 3:8; Deut. 6:2–3.

26:11. Every Israelite family was to rejoice before the Lord (see discussion on 12:4–7) in a communal banquet, being conscientious to share their enjoyment of the first of the land's produce with those who owned no land, **the Levite, and the stranger** (v. 11; see 12:17–19; 14:21, 29).

ii. Laws concerning the Third-Year Tithe (26:12–15)

26:12–15. These verses expand on the previous legislation concerning the third-year tithe (see 14:28–29). **The Levite, the stranger, the fatherless, and the widow** (v. 12) enumerates the text's four categories representing the society's disadvantaged (see Exod. 22:22; Deut. 10:9; 12:10–14, 17–19; 14:21, 28–29) who were supported through the third-year tithe. Each Israelite family was to recite a confession **before the LORD** (v. 13) concerning their fulfillment of their responsibility to deliver the tithe for the use of the needy. **I have not eaten … in my mourning … taken away … for any unclean use, nor given … for the dead** (v. 14). The food dedicated as the tithe was undefiled and uncontaminated. The confession was to conclude with a prayer for YHWH's blessing on His **people** and their divinely bestowed **land … that floweth with milk and honey** (v. 15; see Exod. 3:8; Deut. 6:2–3).

C. The Covenant Is Ratified (26:16–19)

26:16–19. These verses conclude not only the section of the text containing the specific stipulations of the suzerain-vassal treaty between YHWH and Israel (12:1–26:19) but also bring to a close Moses' second sermon on Israel's covenant responsibilities, which began back in 5:1. Utilizing covenantal language and treaty terminology (**Thou hast avouched**; v. 17), both YHWH and Israel's conquest generation reaffirmed their mutual commitment to one another, formally ratifying the Mosaic covenant anew (see discussion on Exod. 19:7–8). **All thine heart … all thy soul** (v. 16). See discussion on 6:5. **His peculiar people** (v. 18). See discussion on Exod. 19:3–6; Deut. 14:1–2. Israel's duty was to demonstrate their love of God through obedience to **all his commandments**. YHWH's obligation was to elevate Israel **high above all nations … in praise … name … honour … that thou mayest be a holy people** (v. 19).

IV. Message Three — Future: Covenant Consequences (27:1–30:20)

A. The Covenant Is Renewed (27:1–26)

1. Writing the Law and Offering Sacrifice (27:1–8)

27:1–8. The transitional shift to Moses again being referenced in the third person, a shift last seen in the text at the commencement of his second message (5:1), indicates the beginning of a third address.

Having thus far provided the standard suzerain-vassal treaty elements of historical prologue (1:6–4:49), which focused on the past, and covenant stipulations both general (5:1–11:32) and specific (12:1–26:19), which focused on the present and immediate future, Moses now moved to covenant consequences, which emphasized Israel's distant future.

Together with Israel's **elders** (v. 1), Moses instructed the nation to observe a unique ceremony immediately upon their entrance into the Promised Land. They were to coat **great stones … with plaister** (v. 2; perhaps lime is meant) and, while the plaster was still pliable, clearly inscribe **all the words of this law** (v. 3). Most likely, the covenant's general and specific stipulations (Deut. 12–26) are meant here. The practice of inscribing plaster- or lime-covered stones was a common Egyptian practice, a skill with which the eldest members of the conquest generation would still be familiar.

The stones were to remain uncut and unadorned and were to be erected into **an altar** (v. 5) on **mount Ebal** (v. 4; see discussion on 11:26–32). On this special occasion, Israel was to offer sacrifices to the Lord on this altar and enjoy a festive communal meal. (See Josh. 8:30–35, which records the construction of this altar and the ceremony that was carried out.)

2. The Call to Obedience (27:9–10)

27:9–10. This day thou art become the people of the LORD (v. 10). Together with Israel's priests, Moses rehearsed the nation's declaration of covenant renewal to be made at the coming ceremony.

3. Blessings and Curses (27:11–26)

27:11–14. The recitation of covenant blessings and curses that was touched on earlier in the text (11:26–32) is here fully developed. Six tribes, the sons of Leah and Rachel (see Gen. 35:23–24), were to be stationed before **mount Gerizim** (v. 12) to affirm the blessings pronounced by the priests (who stood in the natural amphitheater between the mountains). The remaining six tribes, the remaining sons of Leah and Jacob's two concubines, Zilpah and Bilhah (see Gen. 35:23, 25–26), were to be stationed before **mount Ebal** (v. 13) to affirm the priests' pronouncement of curses.

27:15–26. The specific blessings are omitted from the text, and only a symbolic, representative sampling of twelve curses are included. Although eight of the twelve curses reference a violation of the Ten Commandments, it is difficult to definitively discern a pattern. **The Levites** (v. 14), that is, the priests, were to recite the covenantal violations that would generate a divine curse, and the tribes were to acknowledge and affirm their agreement with their oath of **Amen** (vv. 15–26). The first curse is for idolatry (see discussions on 5:8–9; Exod. 20:1). The second curse is for dishonoring one's parents (see discussions on 5:16 and 21:18–21). The third curse is for moving a **neighbour's landmark** (v. 17; see discussion on 19:14).

The fourth curse is for abuse of the disabled (see Lev. 19:14). The fifth curse is for the perversion of justice in the cases of the socially vulnerable. The sixth curse is for incest (see discussion on 22:30). The seventh curse is for bestiality (see Exod. 22:19; Lev. 18:23; 20:15). The eighth and ninth curses also regard incest (see Lev. 18:9, 18; 20:24). The tenth curse is for secret murder (see Exod. 20:13; 21:12; Deut. 5:17). The eleventh curse is for accepting money to commit murder, that is, for becoming a hit man (see Exod. 23:18; Lev. 19:15, 31; Deut. 1:17; 16:19). The twelfth and final curse is for general covenantal disobedience. Paul quoted this verse to demonstrate that no one whose adherence to the Mosaic covenant was less than perfect could avoid the curse of the Torah (Gal. 3:10).

B. Covenant Blessings and Curses (28:1–68)

1. The Blessings of Obedience (28:1–14)

This section begins the unabridged and complete catalog of the Mosaic covenant's blessings and curses. In line with other suzerain-vassal treaties of the time, the curses consume proportionately four times more space than do the blessings. Contrary to custom, however, in Deuteronomy, the blessings are listed prior to the curses, probably an indication of God's love for Israel and His desire to bless His people.

28:1–2. If thou shalt hearken diligently ... to observe and to do all his commandments (v. 1). Unlike the nature of the blessings attached to the unconditional Abrahamic covenant, the blessings of the conditional Mosaic covenant were dependent on Israel's obedience for their realization. God's ultimate goal concerning Israel was to elevate them **high above all nations of the earth,** but He would not indiscriminately bless them without their cooperation.

28:3–6. Blessed shalt thou be in the city, and ... in the field ... Blessed shall be the fruit of thy body ... thy ground ... thy cattle ... thy kine ... thy sheep ... Blessed shall be thy basket and thy store ... Blessed shalt thou be when thou comest in, and ... when thou goest out (vv. 3–6). The Lord offered a blessing in every area of life.

28:7–14. These verses elaborate on the immediately preceding summary of potential blessing (28:3–6). Israel was to experience the blessing of military superiority over their **enemies.** They were to experience material prosperity. YHWH would **establish** (v. 9) Israel as **a holy people unto himself,** a blessing of unprecedented relational intimacy. They would be blessed with the reputation of belonging to **the LORD** (v. 9), causing surrounding nations to **be afraid** (v. 10; see discussions on 2:25; 11:25). Israel was to be blessed by the agricultural productivity of their land and the biological fertility of their families. The enjoyment of each blessing, however, was necessarily dependent on Israel's obedience to the covenant through which the blessings emanated.

2. The Curses of Disobedience (28:15–68)

a. The Reversal of the Blessings (28:15–19)

28:15–19. If thou wilt not hearken ... all these curses (v. 15). Covenantal disobedience would yield the exact opposite of the previously enumerated blessings. Every curse was contingent on Israel's covenantal disobedience. Although Israel was to experience a limited measure of these curses during the Assyrian and Babylonian oppressions, Israel did not experience the totality of these curses until their two revolts against Rome in AD 70 and 135, respectively, following the Messiah's death, circa AD 30.

b. Curses of Disease and Drought (28:20–24)

28:20. As Moses had elaborated on the previous summary of blessings (28:3–6 and 28:7–14), so he now elaborated on the immediately previous summary of curses (28:15–19). **Cursing, vexation, and rebuke … whereby thou hast forsaken me** (v. 20). As a jealous God, YHWH would not brook being snubbed by His people. Every act of disobedience was a de facto declaration of God's inconsequentiality to the covenant violator.

28:21–24. Again, Moses included approximately four times more curses than blessings. **A consumption … fever … inflammation … extreme burning … the sword … blasting … mildew** (v. 22). The first category of curses was those of disease and drought. **Heaven … brass … earth … iron** (v. 23). The rain would be incapable of penetrating the sky, which would magnify the sun's heat; the land would be completely unproductive. **Powder and dust** (v. 24). Sandstorms would plague the land.

c. Curses of Defeat and Deportation (28:25–37)

28:25–26. If disobedient, Israel would experience military defeat, dispersion, and disgrace—military defeat in battle, dispersion from their land, and the disgrace of having their corpses eaten by animals instead of being properly buried.

28:27–29. If disobedient, Israel would be inflicted with a plethora of grave diseases. **The botch of Egypt** (v. 27) refers to the same type of boils that the Egyptians experienced in the sixth plague (Exod. 9.8–11). **Emerods** (hemorrhoids) **… the scab … the itch … madness … blindness, and astonishment of heart** (vv. 27–29), in other words, so afflicted by both physical and mental disease that Israel would lose all effectiveness in every area.

28:30–37. Disobedience would result in others enjoying Israel's possessions and the fruit of their labors. Israel's women would be raped, families displaced, and property destroyed or stolen. Ultimately, Israel would be exiled from the land and deported to foreign nations as spoils of war. There they would be oppressed and forced to **serve other gods** (v. 36). Israel's fall from power would be so dizzying that the nation would **become an astonishment, a proverb, and a byword, among all nations** (v. 37). Sadly, this prediction concerning Israel's worldwide reputation has unquestionably proven accurate for the past two millennia.

d. Curses of Economic Ruin (28:38–44)

28:38–44. Disobedience would lead to Israel's economy being wrecked by **locust** (v. 42) invasions, **worms** (v. 39), crop failures, and unproductive agriculture. Worse, Israel's children would be taken from the land **into captivity** (v. 41). **The head, and thou shalt be the tail** (v. 44). In a reversal of 28:13, Israel would experience a total loss of economic power. In this upside-down scenario, **the stranger** (v. 43), the resident alien, normally one of society's more vulnerable members, would be more prosperous than the Israelites around him.

e. The Reason for the Curses (28:45–48)

28:45–48. All these curses shall come upon thee (v. 45). Israel would eventually prove sufficiently disobedient that these prophetic curses were fulfilled. **For a sign and for a wonder** (v. 46). The phrase used here for the purpose of the curses is the same used of the Egyptian plagues (see Exod. 7:3–4), indicating that the curses would serve, as did the plagues for Pharaoh, as confirmation of YHWH's power and covenant commitment. Since Israel would neglect to joyfully serve the Lord in times of **abundance** (v. 47), He would ensure that they would **serve** (v. 48) their enemies **in hunger … thirst … nakedness, and in want.** Israel would suffer a complete reversal of fortune and again be enslaved, with **a yoke of iron upon thy neck.** Usually, yokes were made of wood; yokes constructed of iron would be exceptionally oppressive.

f. Curses of Invasion and Siege (28:49–57)

28:49–52. This section chronicles the invasion of Israel, who was to be besieged by a foreign **nation … from far, from the end of the earth** (v. 49). The oppressor nation is described as being one **whose tongue** Israel **thou shalt not understand.** Since the

Assyrians and the Babylonians spoke Semitic cognate languages related to Hebrew, those nations could not be in view here. The Latin-speaking Romans, however, are a different story. Indeed, Rome also fulfills the description of geographic distance (**from the end of the earth**; v. 49) and the reputation for brutal efficiency (**a nation of fierce countenance, which shall not regard the person of the old, nor shew favour to the young**; v. 50). The foreign military force would successfully **besiege** (v. 52) Israel's fortifications. **Wherein thou trustedst**. A further indication of why Israel's city defenses will fail; their trust will not be exclusively in YHWH to protect them. (Of course, those Israelites perceptive enough to understand the reasons behind their besiegement would realize that YHWH Himself was the instrumental cause of their calamity and that divine protection could not be expected.)

28:53–57. So lengthy would be the foreign military's siege that food supplies in the cities would be exhausted. This would eventually lead to the horrors of cannibalism. Since the invading army would devour the fruit of the land, Israelite parents would consume their children, **the fruit** (v. 53) of their womb. **His eye shall be evil … her eye shall be evil** (vv. 54, 56) is a Hebrew euphemism meaning stinginess. Even a man normally considered gentle and refined would be stingy in sharing **the flesh of his children** (v. 55) with the rest of his family. Indeed, **the tender and delicate woman** (v. 56), so refined that she would normally never consider going barefoot, would eat her newborn **secretly** to avoid sharing. (Examples of this curse being fulfilled in biblical history are found in 2 Kings 6:24–29; Jer. 19:9; Lam. 2:20; 4:10; and in the records of the post-biblical Roman siege of Jerusalem.)

g. Covenant Disaster (28:58–68)

28:58–68. As the Lord meted out these curses upon Israel, the blessings they had previously experienced would unravel one by one, until, in a reversal of the exodus, their status reverted to that of Egyptian slaves. **This glorious and fearful name, THE LORD THY GOD** (v. 58). See discussion on

Exod. 3:14–15. Israel would be devastated by interminable **plagues** and **sicknesses … of long continuance** (v. 59). **All the diseases of Egypt** (v. 60). See discussion on Exod. 15:26. **The book of this law** (v. 61). Moses would soon transcribe the oral messages of Deuteronomy into their final written form within a parchment scroll (31:9). Israel's population, formerly numerous **as the stars of heaven** (v. 62), would be decimated for want of the nation's obedience to the covenant. Israel would be exiled, divinely dispersed throughout all nations, **from the one end of the earth even unto the other** (v. 64), where they would **serve other gods**. They would find neither **ease** (v. 65) nor **rest … among these nations**. Rather, Israel would experience the distress of **a trembling heart …** and anguish **of mind**. Persecution would be the norm: **thy life shall hang in doubt before thee; and thou shalt fear day and night, and shalt have none assurance of thy life** (v. 66). Israel would enjoy none of the safety or security they had previously enjoyed within their own borders. Although a measure of these curses would be experienced by Israel following the Assyrian and Babylonian exiles (2 Kings 17:6; 25:21), only after Rome's final series of victories in AD 70 and AD 135, respectively, would Hebrew masses return via ship to Egypt as slaves (28:68).

C. The Land Covenant (29:1–30:20)

1. Covenant Introduction (29:1)

29:1. Once again, the text contains a grammatical shift, referencing Moses in the third person (see discussions on 27:1; 5:1). This shift indicates a transition from the previous address to a new message, although some incorrectly see 29:1 as the conclusion of the previous address. **The words of the covenant … beside the covenant which he made with them in Horeb** (v. 1). This verse not only relays the commencement of a fourth address but also the introduction to an additional, parallel covenant between YHWH and Israel. Moses clearly differentiates between the Mosaic covenant made at Sinai and this additional, contrasting covenant. What follows is not a mere recapitulation of what had already been set forth in detail but the description of Israel's national restoration following the devastating experiences they would incur for violation of the Mosaic covenant. The land covenant finds its basis in the unconditional promises contained within the Abrahamic covenant and functions in a parallel fashion with the Mosaic covenant, clearly and distinctly engaging only with Israel's experience of all the curses resulting from their extreme violation of the Mosaic covenant.

2. Covenant Background (29:2–9)

29:2–4. This additional covenant begins, as did the Mosaic covenant (1:6–4:49), with a historical prologue (see Introduction: "Literary Features"). **A heart to perceive, and eyes to see, and ears to hear** (v. 4). Moses explained to his people that although they had been personal witnesses to the redemptive exodus event and accompanying **miracles** (v. 3), they still retained an ignorant perspective, **unto this day** (v. 3). While technically referencing only those Israelites who were younger than twenty at the Kadesh-barnea rebellion (see Num. 14:29), he addressed Israel as a corporate unity. Paul later applied 29:4 to unbelieving Israel (Rom. 11:8).

29:5–9. Moses had been alongside his people for **forty years in the wilderness** (v. 5). During that period, their clothes and shoes had been miraculously preserved, and the Israelites' provisions had come from the Lord (see 8:2–4). **Sihon … and Og** (v. 7). See discussions on 2:26–3:11. **We took their land … for an inheritance** (v. 8).

3. Covenant Parties (29:10–15)

29:10–15. Ye stand this day all of you (v. 10). An indication of some sort of formal ratification ceremony. Moses addressed them as a participating party of the land covenant, outlining the covenant's general stipulations for the totality of Israel's population, both for the living generation and for the benefit of generations yet unborn (**also with him that is not here with us this day**; v. 15). **That he may establish thee to day for a people unto himself, and that he may be unto thee a God, as he hath said unto thee, and as he hath sworn unto thy fathers,** to Abraham, to Isaac, and to Jacob (v. 13). As was the Mosaic covenant, the land covenant was based on the Abrahamic covenant. Neither the Mosaic covenant nor the land covenant are comprehensible without a grasp of the blessings promised to the patriarchs (see discussion on 1:6–8).

4. The Results of Disobedience (29:16–29)

29:16–21. The nation's Egyptian experience and wilderness wanderings had exposed Israel to the bitter poison (**gall and wormwood**; v. 18) of idolatry (**their abominations**; v. 17). If the Mosaic covenant was violated in secret by a single "bad apple," that one individual's actions would corrupt the entire holy community. Therefore, he would be divinely dealt with accordingly: **all the curses that are written in this book** (see discussion on 28:61) **shall lie upon him, and the LORD shall blot out his name from under heaven** (v. 20).

29:22–28. The idolatry of future generations of Israel would likewise cause them to experience God's great **anger … wrath, and … great indignation** (v. 28). As had their fathers before them, the nation would forsake **the covenant of the LORD** (v. 25), leading to Israel's banishment from their land. **Brimstone, and salt, and burning** (v. 23). Israel would become a barren, agriculturally unproductive region, as if its soil was characterized by rich deposits of the detrimental elements sulfur and salt. **Sodom, and Gomorrah, Admah, and Zeboim.** See Genesis 14:12; 19:24–25. The Gentiles would be stupefied by what Israel's God had done **unto this land** (v. 24).

29:29. The secret things belong unto the LORD (v. 29). There were additional prophetic details pertaining to Israel's future that the Lord had yet to disclose. However, the voluminous content of prophetic revelation that He had chosen to divulge was given to encourage Israel's continued obedience to the Mosaic covenant.

5. The Restoration of Israel (30:1–10)

30:1–4. Moses was well aware that, in due time, future generations of his people would indeed experience both **the blessing** (v. 1) of enjoying their land **and the curse** of exile. During the distress of Israel's dispersion, however, the circumstances of the nation's accelerated tumble into ruin would inevitably cause the Israelites to reflect on the texts within Deuteronomy that prophetically foretold their situation. These texts would provide both the root cause of their punishment (national idolatry) and its antidote (national repentance), Israel's **return unto the LORD thy God** (v. 2).

30:3 – 6. Israel's repentance would be the trigger for God's reversal of the curses of the Mosaic covenant. Just as He had been the instrumental cause of their dispersion, so He would orchestrate their return to their land from the ends of the earth (Zeph. 3:20). **The LORD … will turn thy captivity … have compassion … will return and gather thee** (v. 3). When Israel returned to God, He would likewise return to them. God's return to His people in conjunction with their return to their land will literally be fulfilled by the Messiah's second coming (Isa. 59:20 – 62:12; Matt. 24:31; Mark 13:27). Once returned to the land, Israel will then finally possess all of the territory that God promised to the patriarchs. **Multiply thee above thy fathers** (v. 5). Indeed, the restored nation will experience blessings greater than those experienced by any of Israel's previous generations. It is at this time that **the LORD … will circumcise** (v. 6) their hearts, personally ensuring the spiritual sensitivity of that generation and all future generations (**the heart of thy seed**).

30:7 – 9. On them that hate thee (v. 7). Accompanying Israel's restoration will be judgment upon their enemies, which will fulfill the Abrahamic covenant's promise of reciprocal blessing for blessing and curse for curse (Gen. 12:3). **Thou shalt return and obey … the LORD … who will make thee plenteous in every work … in the fruit of thy body … of thy cattle … of thy land … the LORD will again rejoice over thee** (vv. 8 – 9). The time of Israel's restoration, that is, the kingdom reign of the Messiah, will be characterized by an abundance of divine blessings on Israel.

30:10. If thou shalt hearken. Sometimes the interpretation of an entire passage comes down to the translation of one ostensibly trifling preposition within a single verse. So it is in this instance. What is at stake here is whether Israel's restoration ultimately rests on the condition of their obedience or on the Lord's sovereign initiative. Specifically, there is no grammatical or contextual reason to translate, as does the KJV, the Hebrew preposition *ki* with the conditional "if." The use of *ki* generally indicates a degree of unconditional certainty and is typically translated as "for," "when," "then," "because," "indeed," "since," and the like — for example, as the KJV translates the same preposition a mere nine verses earlier, in 30:1.

The events spoken of within the land covenant are assured and unconditional, as are its promises of restoration, blessing, forgiveness, and spiritual circumcision. Just as certain as Israel's violation of the Mosaic covenant and experience of that covenant's curses is the divine promise to mercifully restore the nation from the profound depths of their misery. It is for that reason that the land covenant exists. It is a formal expression of the Abrahamic covenant's foundational truth, that while Israel's enjoyment of the land may be contingent on their adherence to the Mosaic covenant; the nation's perpetual ownership of the land is as unmitigated and unconditional as every other divine promise made to Abraham, Isaac, and Jacob.

6. The Appeal for Life (30:11 – 20)

30:11 – 14. Moses appealed to his people to live lives consistent with the Torah. God's law was not encoded, composed of **hidden** (v. 11) secrets, necessitating a seer to provide special interpretation. Neither was **it far off … in heaven … or … beyond the sea** (vv. 11 – 13), requiring the commissioning of emissaries in quest of God's will. Rather, the text of the Torah, the written revelation of divine will, was physically present in the midst of their community and easily committed to **mouth … heart** (v. 14), and deed. This verse was quoted by Paul in reference to the accessibility of the gospel (Rom. 10:6 – 8).

30:15 – 20. The land covenant concludes with Moses making it clear that what was at stake for

Israel was nothing less than a communal choice of **life** or **death, blessing** or **cursing** (v. 19). Adherence to YHWH's holy standards would yield communal blessing in the land and a protracted presence there. Spiritual infidelity, by contrast, would yield both divine denunciation and a truncated enjoyment of the land.

V. Covenant Continuity: Historical Epilogue (31:1–34:12)

A. Moses Prepares Israel for the Transition of Leadership (31:1–29)

1. Moses Charges Israel and Commissions Joshua (31:1–8)

31:1–5. While Moses may have continued to possess inordinate vigor for a man his age (14:7), nonetheless, as a man of **an hundred and twenty years** (v. 2), his physical capacity limited his ability to successfully lead the nation into the succession of battles that would characterize the next seven years of Israel's history. Despite Moses' absence, however, Israel would remain in the protective custody of both **the LORD** (v. 3), who would **destroy these nations** they would encounter, and Moses' aide and successor, **Joshua** (see 1:38; 3:21, 28).

31:6–8. Moses charged first the nation and then his successor to **be strong and of a good courage** (an often repeated charge of encouragement; v. 6; see 31:7, 23; Josh. 1:6–7, 9, 18; 10:25; 1 Chron. 22:13; 28:20; 2 Chron. 32:7), for **the LORD ... will not fail thee, nor forsake thee** (v. 8). Publicly commissioning Joshua as Israel's next leader, Moses instructed him to **fear not, neither be dismayed**, heartening his heir apparent with the news that he was God's chosen instrument to lead Israel's successful conquest of the Promised Land. **The land which the LORD hath sworn unto their fathers to give them** (v. 7). See discussion on 1:6–8.

2. Reading the Law (31:9–13)

31:9–13. In keeping with the customs of the suzerain-vassal treaties, YHWH instructed Moses to commit the Torah to writing (see 28:58). The writ-

ten record of the law was deposited with **the priests and elders** (v. 9) and was to be publicly read in the central sanctuary (**the place which he shall choose** (v. 11; see 12:4–7) to the entire community of Israel (**men ... women ... children ... thy stranger**; v. 12) during their mandatory pilgrimage **feast of tabernacles** (see 16:13–17) **every seven years ... the year of release** (v. 10; see discussion on 15:1–11; Exod. 23:10–12; Lev. 25:1–7). The public proclamation of the Torah was to ensure that each successive generation of Israel would have the opportunity to **hear ... learn ... fear ... and observe** (v. 12).

3. The Lord Commands Moses to Write a Song (31:14–23)

31:14–15. The Lord informed Moses that his life was drawing to a close and instructed Moses to come with Joshua for a private audience with Him outside the encampment at **the tabernacle of the congregation** (v. 14; see discussion on Exod. 33:7–11; Exod. 18:7–16; Num. 11:16, 24, 26; 12:4). **The LORD appeared in the tabernacle in a pillar of a cloud** (v. 15; Exod. 13:20–22; 33:7–11). This manifestation of YHWH's Shekinah glory reassured both leaders concerning the imminent transition of power.

31:16–23. God's message to the two leaders was that sometime following Moses' death, Israel would egregiously violate the **covenant** (v. 16). Israel's idolatry would cause YHWH to **hide** His **face** (v. 17) from them. Moses was to compose a **song** (v. 19) for the Hebrews to memorize as a prophylactic against future apostasy and as an antidote when their behavior provoked divine retribution and judgment and plunged them into the midst of **many evils and troubles** (v. 21).

4. Depositing the Law (31:24–29)

31:24–29. When Moses completed **writing the words of this law in a book** (v. 24) for Israel's posterity, the scroll was placed beside **the ark of the covenant** (see Exod. 16:34; 31:18), along with the jar of manna (Exod. 6:33–34) and Aaron's rod (Num. 17:10). The scroll would serve as **a witness against** (v. 26) Israel for their future **rebellion**. Moses said,

Ye have been rebellious ... and how much more after my death? (v. 27). Based on their previous **rebellious** uprisings under his leadership, Moses knew that without his restraining presence, Israel's apostasy was only a matter of time. **Call heaven and earth to record** (v. 28). The divine witnesses called for by the suzerain-vassal treaty formula.

B. The Song of Moses (31:30-32:44)

1. Introduction and Call to Witnesses (31:30-32:2)

31:30-32:2. This verse serves to introduce the covenant renewal **song** (v. 30) of Moses. The song portrays Israel's future as characterized by apostasy and the resulting divine judgment. The song is Hebrew poetry, which adds a unique hue to the rehearsal of themes common to the entire book of Deuteronomy. The song begins with a call to two witnesses; the **heavens** and the **earth** (v. 1).

2. God and Israel (32:3-14)

32:3-6. In this section, God's faithfulness is contrasted with Israel's infidelity. **He is the Rock** (v. 4) ... **without iniquity, just and right.** YHWH possesses both stability of character and constancy of personality. Moses repeats this metaphor within the song (32:15, 18, 20-31). By way of contrast, Israel was **corrupted ... a perverse and crooked generation** (v. 5).

32:7-9. As he had already done so many times within Deuteronomy, Moses called upon the nation's collective memory of their history (see discussion on 4:10-12). He refers to God as **the most High** (Hebrew, *Elyon* the only occurrence of this name for God in Deuteronomy; v. 8), emphasizing YHWH's sovereignty over all creation. An interesting fact is revealed here: because Israel was God's special **inheritance** (see 4:20), He **set the** territory of every nation **according to the number of the children of Israel**. This verse can be understood as teaching that God established every international boundary according to His geographic plan for Israel (see Gen. 10:1-11:9).

32:10-14. He found Jacob ... **led him ... instructed him ... kept him** (v. 10). YHWH's provi-

sion and care for Israel throughout their history had been unimpeachable. Israel is called **the apple of his eye,** a metaphor indicating that YHWH protects His people just as a person automatically protects the pupils of his eyes. Conversely, it indicates that when Israel is attacked or treated abusively, it is as if the attacker poked YHWH in the eye, which would automatically provoke a commensurate divine reaction (see Zech. 2:8). **The high places of the earth** (v. 13). Better, "the land's high places," that is, the secure hilltop cities that Israel would soon possess in the Promised Land. **Honey out of the rock, and oil out of the flinty rock.** Bees build their hives within the cleft of Israel's rocks (Isa. 7:18-19), and olive trees thrive on Israel's rocky hillside soil.

3. Israel's Rebellion (32:15-18)

32:15-18. Israel is referred to as **Jeshurun** (v. 15), a poetic and idealistic name meaning "upright one" (33:5, 26; Isa. 44:2), who would rebel against **the Rock** in the midst of their prosperity through idolatry. **They provoked Him to jealousy with ... abominations provoked they him to anger. They sacrificed unto devils** (vv. 16-17). Israel's idolatrous worship would not be confined to **strange gods** (v. 16); they would also worship demons (Hebrew, *sheidim*; winged cherubesque beings who were supposedly guardians of health, mentioned elsewhere only in Ps. 106:37). **New gods that came newly up, whom your fathers feared not** (v. 17). Israel would tire of worshiping only YHWH and would instead follow every latest religious fad.

4. God's Judgment (32:19-38)

32:19-22. Israel's idolatry would cause YHWH to **hide** his face (v. 20) from them. He would abhor His children, **in whom is no faith** (v. 19). Their actions would both move YHWH to **jealousy** (v. 21) and provoke Him to **anger** (see discussion on 4:21-24). Therefore, the Lord would punish them commensurately; He would **move them to jealousy with those which are not a people** and **provoke them to anger with a foolish nation.** Judgment would come upon Israel through a Gentile nation. This passage was quoted by Paul to illustrate Israel's failure to grasp the gospel (Rom. 10:19). He also alludes to its language of provocation to jealousy, albeit of a far more irenic variety, concerning the example believers in Messiah are to set before unbelieving Israel (Rom. 11:11). **The lowest hell ... the foundations of the mountains** (v. 22). This is poetic imagery for sheol, the abode of the dead, imagined as being far beneath the surface of the earth (where the foundations of mountains are located).

32:23–27. Israel's egregious violation of the Mosaic covenant would be answered by a variety of punishments set forth in poetic detail: **mischiefs** (v. 23) ... **arrows ... hunger** (v. 24) ... **burning heat ... bitter destruction ... the teeth of beasts ... the poison of serpents ... sword without** (v. 25) ... **terror within**. Furthermore, Israel would be scattered throughout the earth and their memory would almost be blotted out. YHWH admits, however, that He would restrain from the most severe venting of His wrath because of His fear that the Gentile nations would attempt to take credit for Israel's destruction.

32:28–33. A nation void of counsel (v. 28). Israel would reveal a shocking lack of discernment concerning the consequences of their behavior. Using the exaggerated imagery of **one** (v. 30) man chasing **a thousand** enemies and **two** men chasing **ten thousand**, Moses made the point that Israel's unprecedented prosperity had been supernaturally orchestrated by their **Rock** (v. 30). Israel is figuratively likened to **Sodom** (v. 32) and **Gomorrah**, ripe for divine judgment.

32:34–35. Sealed up among my treasures (v. 34) is poetic imagery indicating the security and certainty of God's prophetic plans. **To me belongeth vengeance, and recompence** (v. 35) was quoted by Paul to confirm the divine prerogatives (Rom. 12:19).

32:36–38. When YHWH perceived that Israel, having undergone divine judgment, was finally in a state of complete helplessness, He would then taunt His people concerning their misplaced trust in false,

dependent gods to make them realize that YHWH was their only hope for salvation and restoration.

5. Israel's Restoration (32:39–44)

32:39–43. The conclusion shifts the tone of the song as it climaxes with the divine restoration that Israel would experience following judgment. YHWH would use extreme circumstances to force Israel to realize that He is not just another god in a regional pantheon; He is the only God. There is no biblical truth more foundational than YHWH's claim that **there is no god with me** (v. 39; see 5:6–7). **I lift up my hand to heaven** (v. 40). A gesture that commonly accompanied a solemn oath. **Rejoice, O ye nations, with his people ... he will avenge ... will render vengeance ... and will be merciful unto his land, and to his people** (v. 43). YHWH would call upon the Gentile nations to join Israel in rejoicing at His people's restoration to His favor and to their land.

32:44. Moses and Joshua taught the newly composed **song** (v. 44) to the people. **Hoshea the son of Nun.** Joshua (see discussion on Exod. 17:9).

C. Moses Prepares for His Death (32:45–52)

32:45–47. Appealing to Israel on the basis of the alarming content of the poem he had just recited, Moses instructed his people, **Set your hearts unto ... all the words of this law** (v. 46). **It is your life** (v. 47). At stake was nothing less than Israel's posterity, prosperity, and longevity of presence in the land (see discussion on 30:15–20).

32:48–52. That selfsame day (v. 48), Moses received divine instructions concerning preparation for his death. He was to ascend **mount Nebo** (v. 49), in northwestern Moab's **Abarim** range. There, from an elevation of about 2,700 feet, he would be able to **behold the land of Canaan.** Moses would then **die in the mount ... and be gathered unto thy people** (v. 50). The failure of Moses at **Meribah-Kadesh** (v. 51), which resulted in the Lord's denying Moses permission to enter the land, is again mentioned. **Aaron ... died in mount Hor** (v. 50; see 10:6; Num. 20:22–29).

D. The Blessings of Moses (33:1–29)

1. Introduction and Historical Review (33:1–5)

33:1. In accord with ancient biblical custom, Moses, in his role as *pater familias*, pronounced a blessing upon the nation, just as Jacob had done prior to his death in Egypt (Gen. 49). The patriarch's blessing was prophetic in its revelation concerning the offspring's destiny (see Gen. 27:27–29). Moses' blessing was structured as Hebrew poetry, as was the previous song. **Moses the man of God** (v. 1). A title used of Moses only here and in the superscription of Psalm 90.

33:2–5. In a historical review of covenant history, rife with vivid imagery, Moses recounted YHWH's majestic sweeping in from the wilderness to give Israel the Torah at **Sinai** (v. 2; see Exod. 19:16–20:21; 24:1–11). The law is poetically portrayed as Israel's **inheritance** (v. 4). Better translated "holy ones," **ten thousands of saints** (v. 2) is a reference to the accompanying angels, whom the New Testament authors affirm as mediators of the law given to Moses (Acts 7:38, 53; Gal. 3:19; Heb. 2:2). **Jeshurun**. See discussion on 32:15.

2. Moses Blesses the Tribes (33:6–25)

In blessing the tribes, Moses mentioned every tribe by name with the exception, for reasons unknown, of Simeon. Moses began with three sons of Leah (Reuben, Judah, and Levi), moved to Rachel's two sons (Benjamin and Joseph), shifted back to two more of Leah's sons (Zebulon and Issachar), and concluded with the four sons of Jacob's two concubines (Gad, Dan, Naphtali, and Asher).

33:6. The blessing of **Reuben** was an expressed desire that their tribe continue in posterity.

33:7. The blessing of **Judah** concerned the tribe's future military success.

33:8–11. The blessing of **Levi** (v. 8) concerned the tribe's function as Israel's priests, teachers of the **law**, and worship leaders at the central sanctuary. **Thy Thummim and thy Urim**. (See discussion on Exod. 28:29–30.) **At Massah**. See Exodus 17:1–7; Deuteronomy 6:16; 9:22. **The waters of Meribah**.

See discussion on Exod. 17:7; Numbers 20:1–13; Deuteronomy 32:51. **Who said unto his father and to his mother, I have not seen him; neither did he acknowledge his brethren ... his own children: for they have ... kept thy covenant** (v. 9). A reference to the Levites' role at Sinai as the instruments of YHWH's wrath (see Exod. 32:25–29).

33:12. The blessing of **Benjamin** concerned the tribe's safety and security.

33:13–17. The blessing of **Joseph** (v. 13), including individual mention of its two subtribes, **Ephraim** and **Manasseh** (v. 17), concerned the tribe's economic prosperity, agricultural fertility, and military success. **Him that was separated from his brethren** (v. 16). See Genesis 37. **Him that dwelt in the bush**. See discussion on Exodus 3:1–6. **Bullock ... the horns of unicorns** (v. 17), poetic fertility symbols, is a reference to bulls and oxen.

33:18–19. The blessings of **Zebulon** and **Issachar** (v. 18) are linked together, likely based on the precedent set by Jacob's blessing (Gen. 49:13–15; see also Judg. 5:14–15), and concerned the future economic prosperity, derived from both land and sea, in the daily lives (**in thy going out ... in thy tents**) of those within these two tribes.

33:20–21. The blessing of **Gad** (v. 20) probably concerned the tribe's military prowess and courage.

33:22. The blessing of **Dan** portrayed the tribe as vigorously relocating their territory to Israel's northern borders, adjacent to **Bashan** (see discussion on 3:1–2).

32:23. The blessing of **Naphtali** concerned the tribe's possession of their territorial allotment.

32:24–25. The blessing of **Asher** (v. 24) concerned the tribe's abundant posterity and financial prosperity. **Let him dip his foot in oil** was an act of extreme economic extravagance. **Iron and brass** (v. 25). An indication of the tribe's military security.

3. Moses Blesses Israel (33:26–29)

33:26–29. The blessing concluded with Moses' final praise of YHWH's sovereign majesty and His **eternal** (v. 27) rule over creation. The prophet left Israel a reminder that the success of their coming military campaigns rested securely on YHWH's power, provision, and promises. Israel would **dwell in safety** (v. 28) in a land of agricultural abundance as a **people saved by the LORD** (v. 29). **Jeshurun** (v. 26). See discussion on 32:15. These are most likely the final words of Deuteronomy personally authored by Moses himself. The final chapter recounts the prophet's death.

E. The Death of Moses (34:1–12)

This last chapter is the work of someone other than Moses, as it recounts the circumstances of his death and burial from a post-conquest perspective. Whether the author of this concluding appendix was Joshua or a later, unnamed scribe is unknown, but the addition was nonetheless recognized as possessing the same authority and stature as God's Word as Deuteronomy's previous thirty-three chapters.

34:1–4. In obedience to the Lord's directive, Moses departed Israel's camp in the **plains of Moab** (v. 1), doubling back one day's journey to **the mountain of Nebo, to the top of Pisgah**, a specific ridge of Nebo, directly east of the city of **Jericho, the city of palm trees** (v. 3). From there, Moses viewed **all the land** (v. 1), beginning with the view in the north and proceeding counterclockwise. **Unto the utmost sea** (v. 2). The Mediterranean Sea is not usually visible from Nebo, which is about sixty miles inland, but apparently YHWH enabled Moses to view the entirety of **the land** (v. 4) that He had sworn **unto Abraham, unto Isaac, and unto Jacob, saying, I will give it unto thy seed**.

34:5–8. So Moses ... died (v. 5). This indomitable figure, who proved so integral to Israel's foundational history and whose shadow towers over the testimony of the Hebrew Scriptures, had successfully completed the course YHWH had laid out for him. **The servant of the LORD** is a title shared by many of YHWH's particularly valued representatives, such as Abraham (Gen. 26:24), Moses (Exod. 14:31), Joshua

(Josh. 24:29), and David (2 Sam. 7:5). The author of Hebrews alludes to this verse when he contrasts Moses' position as YHWH's servant with Jesus' position as YHWH's son (Heb. 3:1–6).

So beloved was Moses to God that the text reveals he was not buried by human hands. YHWH Himself buried Moses **in a valley in the land of Moab, over against Beth-peor** (v. 6; see discussion on 3:28–29). The New Testament letter of Jude alludes to the traditional account of a dispute between the angelic adversaries Michael and Satan over Moses' body (v. 9). Deuteronomy, however, reveals that **no man knoweth of his sepulchre unto this day**. Moses was **an hundred and twenty years old** when he died; **his eye was not dim, nor his natural force abated** (v. 7). Although Israel had mourned only seven days when Jacob died (Gen. 50:10), the nation had an extended, thirty-day period of mourning for Moses, their great prophet and lawgiver.

34:9. Joshua ... was full of the spirit of wisdom. Having been personally commissioned by Moses through the laying on of **hands**, Joshua was prepared and empowered to take on the heavy mantle of Israel's leadership. Israel was likewise ready to follow Joshua's lead with the same level of respect they had shown his predecessor.

34:10–12. The book of Deuteronomy concludes with the post-conquest author's recognition that since the time of the book's events, **there** had **arose not a prophet since in Israel like unto Moses, whom the LORD** (v. 10) intimately and uniquely **knew face to face** (see Exod. 33:11) and who uniquely performed unprecedented **signs and the wonders ... in the land of Egypt ... in all the that mighty hand and ... great terror** (vv. 11–12). Coupled with this recognition of Moses' unique status is a subtle, underlying note of pensive anticipation as the chosen community of Israel awaited the promised "second Moses" (the "Prophet ... like unto [Moses]" of 18:15–19)— the Messiah Himself.

THE BOOK OF JOSHUA

INTRODUCTION

Title

The book of Joshua is named after its principal character. Earlier in his life, Joshua was called simply Yeshua (Oshea) (Num. 13:8, 16), meaning "salvation." Moses later changed his name to Jehoshua (Joshua), meaning "the Lord saves" (or "the Lord gives victory"). When this same name (the Greek form of which is Jesus) was given to Mary's firstborn son, it became the most loved of names.

Author and Date

In the judgment of many scholars, Joshua was not written until the end of the period of the kings, some eight hundred years after the actual events. There are, however, significant reasons to question this conclusion and to place the time of composition much earlier. The earliest Jewish traditions (Talmud) claim that Joshua wrote his own book except for the final section about his funeral, which is attributed to Eleazar, the son of Aaron (the last verse must have been added by a later editor).

On at least two occasions, the text reports that events were recorded at Joshua's command or by Joshua himself. When the tribes received their territories, Joshua instructed his men, "Go and walk through the land, and describe it" (18:8). Then in the last scene of the book, when Joshua led Israel in a renewal of the covenant with the Lord, he "set them a statute and an ordinance" (24:25). On yet another occasion, the one telling the story appears also to have been a participant in the event; he uses the pronoun "us" (5:6).

Moreover, the author's observations are accurate and precise. He is thoroughly at ease with the antiquated names of cities, such as "the Jebusite [city]" (15:8; 18:16, 28) for Jerusalem, Kirjath-arba (14:15; 15:54; 20:7; 21:11) for Hebron, and "great Zidon" (11:8; 19:28) for what later became simply Sidon. Tyre is mentioned (19:29), but in the days of Joshua, it had not yet developed into a port of major importance.

If some features suggest Joshua's own lifetime, others point to a time somewhat later. The account of the long day when the sun stood still at Ajalon is substantiated by a quotation from another source, the book of Jasher (see discussion on 10:13). This would hardly be natural for an eyewitness of the miracle, writing shortly after it happened. Also, there are twelve instances where the phrase "unto this day" is employed by the author.

It seems safe to conclude that the book, at least in its early form, dates from the beginning of Israel's monarchy. Some think that Samuel may have had a hand in shaping or compiling the materials of the book, but in fact we are unsure who the final author or editor was.

The Life of Joshua

Joshua's remarkable life was filled with excitement, variety, success, and honor. He was known for his deep trust in God and for being "a man in whom is the spirit" (Num. 27:18). As a youth, he lived through the bitter realities of slavery in Egypt, but he also witnessed the supernatural plagues and the miracle of Israel's escape from the army of the Egyptians when God opened the waters of the sea before His people. In the Sinai peninsula, it was Joshua who led the troops of Israel to victory over the Amalekites (Exod. 17:8–13). He alone was allowed to accompany Moses up the holy mountain when the Tables of the Testimony were received (Exod. 24:13–14). And it was he who stood watch at the temporary tabernacle of the congregation that Moses set up before the tabernacle was erected (Exod. 33:11).

Joshua was elected to represent his own tribe of Ephraim when the twelve spies were sent into Canaan to look over the land. Only Joshua and his friend Caleb were ready to follow God's will and take immediate possession of the land (see Num. 14:26–34). The rest were condemned to die in the wilderness. Even Moses died short of the goal and was told to turn everything over to Joshua. God promised to guide and strengthen Joshua, just as He had Moses (Deut. 31:23).

Joshua proved to be not only a military strategist in the battles that followed but also a statesman in the way he governed the tribes. Above all, he was God's chosen servant (see 24:29 and *KJV Study Bible* note on Deut. 34:5) to bring Moses' work to completion and establish Israel in the Promised Land. In that role, he was a striking Old Testament type (foreshadowing) of Christ (see discussion on Heb. 4:1; *KJV Study Bible* note on Heb. 4:6–8).

Background

At the time of the Israelite migration into Canaan, the superpowers of the ancient Near East were relatively weak. The Hittites had faded from the scene. Neither Babylon nor Egypt could maintain a military presence in Canaan, and the Assyrians would not send in their armies until centuries later.

As the tribes circled east of the Dead Sea, only the stronghold of Edom offered any resistance. Moab was forced to let Israel pass through her territory and camp in her plains. When Og and Sihon, two regional Amorite kings east of the Jordan, tried to stop the Israelites, they were easily defeated and their lands occupied.

Biblical archaeologists call this period the Late Bronze Age (1550–1200 BC). Today thousands of artifacts give testimony to the richness of the Canaanite material culture, which was in many ways superior to that of the Israelites. When the ruins of the ancient kingdom of Ugarit were discovered at modern Ras Shamra on the northern coast of Syria (see chart, *Zondervan KJV Study Bible*, p. xix), a wealth of new information came to light concerning the domestic, commercial, and religious life of the Canaanites. From a language close to Hebrew came stories of ancient kings and gods that revealed their immoral behavior and cruelty. In addition, pagan temples, altars, tombs, and ritual vessels have been uncovered, throwing more light on the culture and customs of the peoples surrounding Israel.

Excavations at the ancient sites of Megiddo, Beth Shan, and Gezer show how powerfully fortified these cities were and why they were not captured and occupied by Israel in Joshua's day. Many other fortified towns were taken, however, so that Israel became firmly established in the land as the dominant power. Apart from Jericho and Ai, Joshua is reported to have burned only Hazor (11:13), so attempts to date these events by destruction levels in the mounds of Canaan's ancient cities are difficult undertakings. One must not forget that Israel had been promised a land with cities and houses that she did not build and accompanying vineyards and olive groves (Deut. 6:10–17), so one should not expect excessive destruction to date from Joshua's campaigns. It must also be remembered that other groups were involved in campaigns in the region about this time, among whom were the Egyptian rulers and the sea peoples (including the Philistines). There had also been much intercity warfare among the Canaanites, and afterward the period of the judges was marked by general turbulence.

Many scholars argue that the data from archaeology appears to support a date for Joshua's invasion of approximately 1250 BC. It is maintained that the evidence fits well with an exodus that would then have taken place forty years earlier under the famous Rameses II, who ruled from the Nile Delta at a city with the same name (Exod. 1:11). It also places Joseph in Egypt in a favorable situation. Four hundred years before Rameses II, the pharaohs were the Semitic Hyksos, who also ruled from the delta near the land of Goshen.

On the other hand, a good case can be made for the traditional viewpoint that the invasion occurred around 1406 BC. The oppression would have taken place under Amenhotep II after the death of his father Thutmose III, who is known to have used slave labor in his building projects. This earlier date also fits better with the two numbers found in Judges 11:26 and 1 Kings 6:1, which sets the date of the exodus from Egypt at 1446 BC, since it allows for an additional 150 years between Moses and the monarchy. See also Genesis, Introduction: "Date"; Exodus, Introduction: "Date"; and Judges, Introduction: "Background."

Theme

Joshua is a story of conquest and fulfillment for the people of God. After many years of slavery in Egypt and forty years in the wilderness, the Israelites were finally allowed to enter the land promised to their fathers. Abraham, always a migrant, never possessed the country to which he was sent, but he left to his children the legacy of God's covenant, which made them the eventual heirs of all of Canaan (see Gen. 15:13, 16, 18; 17:8). Joshua was destined to turn that promise into reality.

Where Deuteronomy ends, the book of Joshua begins: the tribes of Israel are still camped on the east side of the Jordan River. The narrative opens with God's command to move forward and pass through the river on dry land. Then it relates the series of victories in central, southern, and northern Canaan that gave the Israelites control of all the hill country and the Negev. It continues with a description of the tribal allotments and ends with Joshua's final addresses to the people. The theme of the book, therefore, is the establishment of Israel in the Promised Land.

Theological Message

In the Hebrew Bible, the book of Joshua initiates a division called the Former Prophets, which also includes Judges, Samuel, and Kings—all historical in content but written from a prophetic standpoint. These books do more than merely record the nation's development from Moses to the fall of Judah in 586 BC. They prophetically interpret God's covenant ways with Israel in history—how He fulfills and remains true to His promises (especially through His servants such as Joshua, the judges, Samuel, and David) and how He deals with the waywardness of the Israelites. In Joshua, it was the Lord who won the victories and "gave unto Israel all the land which he sware to give unto their fathers" (21:43).

Outline

2. The Forty-eight Cities of the Priests (chap. 21)

IV. Epilogue: Tribal Unity and Loyalty to the Lord (chaps. 22–24)
A. The Altar of Witness by the Jordan (chap. 22)
B. Joshua's Farewell Exhortation (chap. 23)
C. The Renewal of the Covenant at Shechem (24:1–28)
D. The Death and Burial of Joshua and Eleazar (24:29–33)

Bibliography

Boling, Robert G., and G. E. Wright, *Joshua: A New Translation with Notes and Commentary*. Anchor Bible 6. Garden City, NY: Doubleday, 1982.

Butler, Trent C. *Joshua*. Word Biblical Commentary 7. Waco, TX: Word, 1983.

Davis, John J., and John C. Whitcomb. *Israel: From Conquest to Exile: A Commentary on Joshua–2 Kings*. Grand Rapids, MI: Baker, 1989.

Hamlin, E. John. *Inheriting the Land: A Commentary on the Book of Joshua*. Grand Rapids, MI: Eerdmans, 1983.

Hess, Richard S. *Joshua: An Introduction and Commentary*. Tyndale Old Testament Commentaries 6. Downers Grove, IL: InterVarsity, 1996.

Howard, David M., Jr. *Joshua*. New American Commentary 5. Nashville: Broadman & Holman, 1998.

Madvig, Donald H. "Joshua," In *Expositor's Bible Commentary*, edited by Frank E. Gaebelein, vol. 3. Grand Rapids, MI: Zondervan, 1992.

Merling, David. *The Book of Joshua: Its Theme and Role in Archaeological Discussions*. Berrien Springs, MI: Andrews University Press, 1997.

Schaeffer, Francis A. *Joshua and the Flow of Biblical History*. Downers Grove, IL: InterVarsity, 1975.

Soggin, J. Alberto. *Joshua: A Commentary*. Old Testament Library. Philadelphia: Westminster, 1972.

Woudstra, Marten H. *The Book of Joshua*. New International Commentary on the Old Testament. Grand Rapids, MI: Eerdmans, 1981.

EXPOSITION

I. The Entrance into the Land (1:1–5:12)

A. The Exhortations to Conquer (chap. 1)

1:1–18. The Lord initiates the action by charging Joshua, His chosen replacement for Moses (see Deut. 31:1–8), to lead Israel across the Jordan and take possession of the Promised Land. He urges courage and promises success, but only if Israel obeys the law of God that Moses has given them. Chapter 1 consists of speeches significant in their content and order: the Lord commands Joshua as His appointed leader over His people (vv. 1–9); Joshua, as the Lord's representative, addresses Israel (vv. 10–15); Israel responds to Joshua as the Lord's representative and successor to Moses (vv. 16–18). Thus, the events of the book are set in motion, and the roles of the main actors are indicated.

1:1–5. The time and occasion of the action are immediately set forth, **after the death of Moses** (v. 1), showing that the story will continue where

Deuteronomy ended, with the death of Moses. In the same manner, the book of Judges begins with "after the death of Joshua" (Judg. 1:1).

Moses is remembered as the **servant of the LORD** (v. 1), a designation referring to him as one who had the status of a high official in the Lord's kingly court (Exod. 14:31; Deut. 34:5). Joshua is noted as **Moses' minister**, a title by which Joshua faithfully served for many years as second in command (Exod. 24:13; 33:11; Num. 11:28; Deut. 1:38).

Go over this Jordan (v. 2). The flow of the Jordan near Jericho was not large during most of the year (only 80–100 feet wide). At flood stage in the spring, the season of this occasion (see 3:15), it filled its wider bed, which at places was a mile wide and far more treacherous to cross. **The land which I do give to them** has been a central theme of the Pentateuch (Gen. 12:1; 50:24; Exod. 3:8; 23:31; Deut. 1:8). The book of Joshua records the fulfillment of this promise of God.

Every place ... your foot shall tread (v. 3) echoes God's earlier words to Abraham (Gen. 13:17), and verses 3–5 closely parallel Moses' promise regarding the land (Deut. 11:24–25). The dimensions of the land promised to Israel vary (v. 4; compare this text and Gen. 15:18 with Deut. 34:1–4), but these are the farthest limits—conquered and held only by David and Solomon. Canaan was still called "Hatti-land" centuries after the Hittites had withdrawn to the north. Joshua was to take all he set out to conquer; wherever he set his foot was his. His victories gave to the twelve tribes most of the central hill country and much of the Negev.

For Joshua, who had witnessed God's presence with Moses, hearing God say **I will be with thee** (v. 5) must have been reassuring. God would direct him, sustain him, and assure success.

1:6–9. Three times the Lord admonished Joshua to **be strong and of a good courage** (vv. 6–7, 9), and the two and a half tribes Joshua later addressed (1:12) echoed the same (1:18). In addition to conquering Canaan, Joshua was commissioned to divide the **land, which I sware unto their fathers** (v. 6). This was the long-awaited inheritance pledged to the descendants of Abraham (Gen. 12:7; 15:7, 18–21) and of Jacob (Gen. 28:13).

Observe to do according to all the law (v. 7). Success was not guaranteed unconditionally but was contingent on Israel's obedience to the Lord (Deut. 8:1; 11:8, 22–25). **This book of the law** (v. 8). A documentary form of the laws from Sinai and what Moses had rehearsed with Israel before he died was already extant (Deut. 31:9). It **shall not depart out of thy mouth**. The law, which was usually read orally (Deut. 17:19; 30:9–14; Acts 8:30), was to be so revered as to be constantly on their lips, to teach to the next generation (Deut. 4:9–10; 6:6–7; 11:19). **Thou shalt meditate therein** (see Ps. 1:2). Meditation not only keeps the law fresh in the memory but also ready on the lips to speak it and in the heart to obey it. Joshua learned of the importance of the revelation of God to His program. He was reminded that only his and Israel's obedience to the law would guarantee their success in the new land, not their strength in numbers or military strategy.

Have not I commanded thee? (v. 9). The rhetorical question not only emphasizes the authority of the speaker but also reinforces the reassuring promise of God's unfailing and abiding presence.

1:10–11. At this point, **Joshua commanded** (v. 10), thus fully assuming his role as leader. The **officers** he addressed to prepare Israel for departure may refer to those whom Moses had appointed over the divisions within the tribes (Exod. 18:21; Deut. 1:15). In Deuteronomy 20:5–9, they are those responsible for excluding the unqualified men from going to battle. **Victuals** (v. 11), or foodstuffs, were needed for the **three days** of marching to and across the Jordan (3:2), where they would then live off the food of the land (5:12).

1:12–15. The threat from the two kings **on this side Jordan** (v. 14) was overcome by military victory and the occupation of the lands north of Moab and east of the Jordan River (Num. 21:21–35). The two and a half tribes who asked to remain on the east side of the Jordan had been charged by Moses to send their fighting men across with the other tribes to conquer Canaan (Num. 32:1–27). God had given these eastern tribes **rest** (v. 13) in their land. Rest is an important Old Testament concept (see Deut. 3:20; Judg. 3:11; 2 Sam. 7:1, 11) implying secure borders, peace with neighboring countries, absence of threat to life, and well-being within the land (see discussion on 1 Kings 5:4).

The conquest of the Promised Land, however, was to be undertaken by all Israel. Moses' reminder to these two and a half tribes of their obligation to the others (Deut. 3:18–20) was repeated by Joshua. It was expected of them that **all the mighty men of valour** (v. 14), those over the age of twenty (see, e.g., Exod. 38:26), known for their valor and able to equip themselves with the weapons of war, would be armed to accompany their brothers across the Jordan.

1:16–18. The response of the two and a half tribes was gratifying. They not only promised their allegiance and support to Joshua but also issued a warning and agreed to the death penalty for any act of treason (e.g., the sin of Achan, 7:15). **Be strong and of a good courage** (v. 18) is repeated for the fourth time. This time, these are the people's words of encouragement to Joshua, and they echo and reinforce those from the Lord (1:6–7, 9).

B. The Reconnaissance of Jericho (chap. 2)

2:1–24. The mission of the two spies and the account of Rahab combine for a story of reconnaissance and espionage. It reveals a practice that is as old as war itself (see Judg. 7:10–11; 1 Sam. 26:6–12). Rahab became a convert to the God of Israel and a famous woman among the Hebrews. She is honored in the New Testament for her faith (Heb. 11:31) and for her good works (James 2:25).

2:1. Joshua selected two men to be **sent out of Shittim**. The invasion point was in the plains of Moab, facing toward the Jordan and Jericho (Num. 33:48–49). The Hebrew word *Shittim* means "acacia trees," which grow in the semi-arid conditions of the wilderness. The men were sent out **secretly**. Joshua had learned from experience (Num. 13:1–14:10) that a spy mission and its results should not be reported to the masses, who were incapable of evaluating an intelligence report. The primary focus of the spies was **Jericho**. It was a fortified city, well supplied by strong springs, which helped to make it an oasis, and it was located just five miles west of the Jordan. Its name probably means "moon city," and archaeological excavations there reveal continuous occupation back to at least 7000 BC.

They came into a harlot's house. Josephus and other early sources refer to Rahab as an "innkeeper," but the Hebrew *zonah* clearly refers to a prostitute (see Heb. 11:31; James 2:25). There is no evidence incriminating the spies of any immoral intentions. They were only gathering information. Having men come and go from her house would have been common, and her many encounters probably left her well informed of what was being said about the threatening Israelites. Going to her house provided the spies with good cover and potential intelligence.

2:2–3. That there was a **king of Jericho** (v. 2) affirms that the major cities of Canaan were in reality small kingdoms, each ruled by a local king with commanding authority (attested also in the Amarna letters of the fourteenth century BC; see chart, *KJV Study Bible*, p. xix). He demanded that the men who **search out the country** (v. 3) be brought out of Rahab's house.

2:4–7. Having hid the spies, she confessed that men had come. Her speech was convincing, for it accurately reflected her occupation: **There came men unto me ... the men went out** (vv. 4–5). She claimed innocence of knowing their identity and encouraged the king's men to pursue them.

She had **hid them with the stalks of flax** (v. 6). Rooftops in the Near East are still used for drying grain or stalks. Rahab's cunning saved the lives of the two Israelites but put her own life in jeopardy. It is worthy of note that she is commended for this act of preserving the spies' lives (James 2:25), not for her lie (Josh. 2:4). Her lie, told to protect the spies or herself for harboring them, must not be cited by Christians as scriptural support for situational ethics or license to misrepresent the truth. Rahab, though coming to faith in Israel's God, was still behaving as a Canaanite pagan and should not be seen as a model for the Christian who serves Him who is the Truth (John 14:6).

Sent on a wild goose chase, the king's men pursued the two spies to the **Jordan unto the fords** (v. 7). These were shallow crossings of the Jordan, where the depth of normal flow averages only three feet. At flood stage (3:15), however, even the fords would have been considerably deeper.

2:8-11. Rahab's confession has a significant concentric structure:

(a) **I know** (v. 9)

(b) **terror is fallen upon us ... the inhabitants of the land**

(c) **we have heard** (v. 10)

(bb) **our hearts did melt, neither did there remain any more courage in any man** (v. 11a)

(aa) **the LORD your God, he is God** (v. 11b)

Rahab's personal confession forms the outer frame (a–aa), and it reveals a confidence that Israel's God, the Lord, is the true God (compare Ruth's confession in Ruth 1:16–17). The inner frame (b–bb) offers the military intelligence that the spies report back to Joshua. The center (c) sums up the news about the Lord that occasioned both the Canaanite fear and Rahab's abandonment of Canaan and its gods for the Lord and Israel. Her confession of faith in the Lord and her accurate information about the Lord's triumphs over powerful enemies are astounding.

That the hearts of the Canaanites were **faint** (lit., "melted away"; v. 9), and **did melt** (a Hebrew synonym for "faint"; v. 11) was vital information to the spies. The Canaanites' lack of courage brings to mind Moses' description of the Israelites (Deut. 1:28) when the ten spies had discouraged them (lit., "melted [their] hearts") with the report of the strong people of Canaan and their walled and great cities (Num. 13:28).

2:12-14. Knowing that Jericho and its inhabitants were doomed for destruction, Rahab sought reward for her **kindness** (v. 12) to the spies. **Shew kindness unto my father's house**. The Hebrew for "kindness" or "kindly" is frequently translated "love" or "unfailing love" and often summarizes God's covenant favor toward His people or the love that people are to show to others. Rahab had acted toward the spies as though she were an Israelite, and she now

asked that Israel treat her and her family similarly. The **true token** that she requested was their oath to spare her whole family (v. 12).

Rahab was assured that her life would be spared **when the LORD hath given us the land** (v. 14). All were convinced of the inevitable victory of the Israelites over the city of Jericho. **We will deal kindly and truly with thee**. The terms of the pledge made by the spies echo Rahab's request (v. 12).

2:15-16. Rahab's **house was upon the town wall** (v. 15). Archaeological evidence shows that the people of Jericho occasionally built houses on the city wall. Although this evidence predates the time of Joshua, it may still serve to illumine this verse. Alternatively, the Late Bronze Age fortifications at Jericho may have included a casemate wall (a hollow wall with partitions), and Rahab may have occupied one or more rooms inside it.

Get you to the mountain ... and hide yourselves there three days (v. 16). Directly west of ancient Jericho were the high, rugged hills of the central mountain ridge in Canaan. These hills were honeycombed with caves, making the concealment and escape of the two spies relatively easy. There were ample places to hide until their pursuers (2:5) had returned in failure to Jericho.

2:17-21. The **line of scarlet thread in the window** (v. 18) was the "cord" by which Rahab had assisted the spies' escape over the wall (2:15). Had she previously used the cord for pulling the stalks of flax to her roof (2:6) or used it to mark her house for those seeking a prostitute? Now, however, the function of the red marker as prescribed by the spies was to be similar to that of the blood of the Passover lamb when the Lord struck down the firstborn of Egypt (Exod. 12:13, 22–23), to mark and identify for preservation her house and its inhabitants. The early church viewed the blood-colored cord as a type (symbol) of Christ's atonement.

The spies' oath required Rahab and her family to remain in her house. If any harm came to anyone in Rahab's house, **his blood shall be on our head** (v. 19). This was a vow that accepted responsibility for the death of another, with its related guilt and the retribution meted out by either relatives or the state. The oath was contingent, however, on Rahab's pledge to secrecy about the spies' mission even after they departed her premises.

2:22–24. Following Rahab's advice, they fled to **the mountain** (v. 22; see discussion on 2:16). Their report to Joshua concluded with exuberant optimism: **Truly the LORD hath delivered into our hands all the land** (v. 24; compare 1:2–3).

C. The Crossing of the Jordan (chaps. 3–4)

3:1–4:24. The great significance of this account of the river crossing and the memorial of twelve stones set up in the camp at Gilgal can hardly be overemphasized. It marks the crossing of the boundary into the Promised Land and parallels the miracle of the Red Sea crossing in the exodus (Exodus 14–15). The Israelites' faith in the God of their fathers was renewed and strengthened when it was about to be most severely challenged, while at the same time the Canaanites' fear was greatly increased (5:1). In this account, the author uses an "overlay" technique in which, having narrated the crossing to its conclusion (chap. 3), he returns to various points in the event to enlarge on several details: the stones for a memorial (4:1–9), the successful crossing by all of Israel (4:10–14), and the renewed flow of the river after the crossing was completed (4:15–18). The final paragraph of chapter 4 (vv. 19–24) picks up the story again from 3:17 and completes the account by noting Israel's encampment at Gilgal and the erecting of the stone memorial.

3:1–4. Israel was encamped at Shittim (see discussion on 2:1). Three days had passed since the officers commanded Israel to prepare for departure (1:11). The spies had been sent out from Shittim on their mission to Jericho, and since a three-day stay in the hills had delayed their return, it is possible that the events of chapter 2 actually preceded the preparations in 1:11.

The **ark of the covenant** (v. 3) was the most sacred of the tabernacle furnishings (Exod. 25:10–22). Since it signified the Lord's throne, the Lord Himself went into the Jordan ahead of His people as He led

them into the land of rest (see Num. 10:33–36). **A space** of **about two thousand cubits** (about 1,000 yards; v. 4) was to be maintained between the ark and the people. There was evidently a line of march, with the priests and ark leading the way. Reasons for the prescribed space include the following: (1) to show reverence for the sacred symbol of the Lord's holy presence (see 2 Sam. 6:6–7), (2) to enable the people to see the ark and understand that it was God who was leading them and not a military army, and (3) to permit Israel to see the faith of the priests as they stepped into the water and to witness the occurrence of the miracle.

3:5–6. Sanctify yourselves (v. 5). This was a spiritual preparation for the Israelites. Before their meeting with God at Sinai, such preparation had involved washing all their garments as well as their bodies, and also abstinence from sexual intercourse (Exod. 19:10, 14–15). Here it surely included a turning of the heart to God in faith and trust in His promise and in willing obedience to His commandments (1:8).

Take up the ark ... and pass over before the people (v. 6). The priests were told to lead the way. Obedience would necessitate faith. At this point, they did not know how they would cross the river. Very often God waits for the step of faith before He reveals His plans or opens the way.

3:7–8. This day will I begin to magnify thee (v. 7). God had already encouraged Joshua with the promise of His presence (1:5, 9), but a prime objective for the divine intervention at the Jordan was to validate the leadership of Joshua before the Israelites. With a miraculous event so much like that of the Red Sea crossing, Joshua's position as the Lord's servant would be shown to be comparable to that of Moses (see Exod. 14:31, where Israel witnessed a miracle and believed the Lord and Moses). God's objective for Joshua's elevation before Israel was realized by the event (4:14).

Ye shall stand still in Jordan (v. 8). At this point, the command seemed absurd, for God had not yet divulged to them what He intended to do (3:13) with the flooded river (3:15) once they stepped into it.

3:9–11. Hereby ye shall know … the living God (v. 10). The manner by which God was about to bring Israel across the Jordan River, the watery boundary of the Promised Land, would bring assurance that the one true God was with them and that He would surely dislodge the present inhabitants of Canaan. Two fundamental issues are at stake. First, who is the true and mighty God—the God of Israel or the god on whom the Canaanites depend (Baal, who was believed to reign as king among the gods because he had triumphed over the sea god)? By opening the way through the flooded Jordan, the Lord would show both Israel and the Canaanites that He is Lord over the waters (as He was at the Red Sea, at the flood, and at creation) and that He is able to establish His own order in the world. See 1 Kings 20:23; 2 Kings 18:32–35. Second, who has the rightful claim to the land—the Lord or the Canaanites? (For the juridical aspect of such wars, see Judg. 11:27.) By passing safely through the Jordan at the head of His army, the Lord showed the rightness of His claim on the land. In the ancient Near East, a common way for obtaining the judicial verdict of the gods was by compelling the accused to submit to a trial-by-water ordeal. This usually involved casting him into a river (if the accused drowned, the gods had found him guilty; if not, the gods had declared him innocent). In Israel, however, another form of water ordeal was practiced (see Num. 5:16–28). Significantly, **as Lord** (Hebrew, *'adon*; "master, sovereign") **of all the earth**, the Lord would enter the Jordan first and then remain there until His whole army had crossed safely over. Thus, His claim to the land was vindicated before all who heard about it. And it was His claim, not Israel's; she came through the Jordan only with Him and as His army, "baptized" to His service.

For the inhabitants of Canaan who were to be driven out, **Canaanites … Jebusites** (v. 10), see discussions on Genesis 9:25; 10:6, 15–16; 13:7; 15:16; 23:3; Exod. 3:8; Judg. 3:3; 6:10.

3:12–13. Either as a result of a previously received divine directive or in anticipation of the Lord's instructions, Joshua selected **twelve men** (v. 12) in advance to take stones from the river bed in preparation of building a stone monument of the event on the other side (4:2–3).

Simultaneously with the priests (who carried the ark of God) stepping into the Jordan, the waters would be **cut off** (v. 13), blocked or stopped in its flow, and **stand upon a heap**. The Hebrew for "heap" is found here, in 3:16, and in the poetic accounts of the Red Sea crossing (Exod. 15:8; Ps. 78:13).

It has been suggested by some that God used a physical means (such as a landslide) to dam up the Jordan near a city called Adam (3:16), near the entrance of the Jabbok. (As recently as 1927, an earthquake was recorded that dislodged cliffs overhanging the Jordan and created a blockage of the water that lasted over twenty hours.) Supporters of this explanation maintain that the miraculous element is not diminished (see Exod. 14:21). The reporting of the actual event (3:14–17), however, suggests a better interpretation.

3:15–17. As … the feet of the priests … dipped in the brim of the water (v. 15), the waters were stopped in their flow and piled up at **Adam** near **Zaretan**. Psalm 114:3, 5 says the water of the "Jordan was driven back" (lit., "turned back"). If the water stoppage was due to a landslide upriver, the priests who stepped into the flowing river would have stood there waiting for several hours while nearly twenty miles of river (this side of the blockage) flowed by before the Israelites had the opportunity to cross over. Also, it is unlikely that a landslide would have stopped the flow of a river that at this season **overfloweth all his banks**. It was the **time of harvest**, which took place in April and May. Following the harvest season, the spring rains and the melting of snow on Mount Hermon flooded the Jordan River.

The priests that bare the ark … stood firm on dry ground in the midst of Jordan (v. 17). It should be noted not only that the Lord Himself remained in the place of danger until all of Israel had crossed the Jordan but also that the place where the priests stood was dry riverbed (4:23). The Israelites crossed over on dry ground, not a muddy riverbed still containing puddles of water. A large stretch of river, from

Adam (where the river retreated) to the **salt sea** (for the water south of the priests had flowed on to the sea), was free of water and provided the Israelites relatively quick passage to the other side.

An interpretation of the event that accepts a miracle should be expected since the Lord is the "Lord of all the earth" (and water). He created an earth covered with water (Gen. 1:2), He separated water from water with the firmament (Gen. 1:6), He moved water for dry ground to appear (Gen. 1:9), He brought water from the "great deep" and the "windows of heaven" to flood the earth (Gen. 7:11), He turned the water of Egypt to blood (Exod. 7:19–20), He made walls of water at the Red Sea (Exod. 14:22), and twice He brought water out of a rock (Exod. 17:6; Num. 20:11). It should not be surprising that the Lord would temporarily reverse the course of the Jordan to allow Israel to cross over and "[magnify] Joshua in the sight of all Israel" (4:14).

4:1–9. The reason for Joshua's selection of twelve men (3:12) is now disclosed. The twelve stones removed from where the **priests' feet stood firm** (v. 3), in the middle of the Jordan, were remarkable evidence that the river had indeed stopped flowing to allow the Israelites to cross over. Indicating that the entire nation made the crossing in one day, the stones were to be carried and deposited **in the lodging place, where you shall lodge this night**. That place would later be designated as Gilgal (4:20; 5:9).

The specially placed stones were meant to elicit a question: **What mean you by these stones?** (v. 6). A stone monument was commonly used as a memorial to remind future generations of what had happened at that place (see 24:26; 1 Sam. 7:12). The question thus provided fathers the opportunity to recount to their children God's miraculous drying of the Jordan (4:21–23).

Apparently apart from any divine directive, **Joshua set up twelve stones in the midst of Jordan** (v. 9). This translation indicates that Joshua set up a second pile in the middle of the river. An alternative translation has been suggested: "Joshua set up the twelve stones that had been in the midst of the river"; that is, each tribe brought a stone for the monument

from the riverbed to the new campsite at Gilgal, and Joshua constructed the monument there (see 4:20).

4:10–14. The priests obediently maintained their position in the middle of the Jordan until all had successfully crossed over, and then they carried the **ark of the Lord** (v. 11) to the other side (4:16–18).

The two and a half tribes were faithful to their word (1:14, 16; Num. 32:17). The number of **about forty thousand** (v. 13) seems too few for the number of men listed in Numbers 26 for Reuben, Gad, and half of Manasseh. The contingents were very likely representative since it would have been imprudent to leave undefended the people who settled east of the Jordan (see 22:8, "Return … divide … with your brethren").

As promised (3:7), the events of the day were of such a nature that Israel knew that the Lord had truly elevated Joshua to replace Moses as leader, and **they feared him** (v. 14); that is, they revered him.

4:15–18. Not until they were commanded did the priests leave their post in the middle of the Jordan. Once they were safely on land with the ark of God, **the waters of Jordan returned** (v. 18) and overflowed its banks as before.

4:19–24. The narrative of 3:17 (which was expanded on in 4:1–18) is now resumed. The Israelites had crossed the Jordan and entered Canaan on **the tenth day of the first month** (v. 19), the very day the Passover lamb was to be selected (Exod. 12:3). Significantly, the forty-year experience of wandering was "bookended" with preparations for observing the Passover. Their campsite, **Gilgal** (so named in 5:9), is usually identified with the ruins at Khirbet el-Mafjer, two miles northeast of Jericho.

The lesson of the memorial stones is reiterated — to teach the next generation how **God dried up the waters of Jordan** (v. 23). Here is yet another descriptive phrase for the miracle, along with "the waters … stood," "rose up upon a heap," and "were cut off" (3:16). The purpose of the miracle was not for Israel alone but **that all … might know the hand of the Lord** (v. 24). The Lord's revelation of His power to the Israelites was a public event that all the Canaanites heard about (5:1), just as they had heard of the crossing of the Red Sea and the defeat of Sihon and Og (2:10). The miracle was also to evoke a response in Israel. To **fear the LORD** was to worship and serve Him according to His commandments.

D. The Consecration at Gilgal (5:1–12)

5:1–12. Two covenantal ceremonies were resumed at Gilgal in accordance with the laws from Sinai: the rite of circumcision and the Feast of the Passover. Both were significant preparations for the conquest of the Promised Land.

5:1. Usually interchangeable, the general names **Amorites** and **Canaanites** included the many smaller nations in the land. Amorite means "westerner," and Canaanite referred to the people living along the Mediterranean coast. This parenthetical verse perhaps concludes the account of the crossing since it notes the effect that event had on the peoples of Canaan (see discussion on 3:9–11). It also explains why the Israelites were undisturbed while performing the rite of circumcision and observing the Passover feast. The surgery of circumcision would have left the Israelites incapacitated and particularly vulnerable (see Gen. 34:24–25) if the Canaanites had been more "spirited" and aggressive in defense of their land.

5:2–8. Make thee sharp knives (lit., "flint knives"; v. 2). Metal knives were available, but flint made a more efficient surgical tool, as modern demonstrations have shown. Israel had to be consecrated to the Lord's service before she could undertake the Lord's warfare and take possession of the land (see Exod. 4:24–26). **Circumcise again ... the second time.** Circumcision marked every male as a son of Abraham (Gen. 17:10–11) bound to the service of the Lord, and it was a prerequisite for the Passover (Exod. 12:48). Due to the Israelites' failure to have their sons circumcised, a serious offense to God, who had required circumcision of Abraham's descendants, Joshua obeyed immediately. If the covenant people were to enjoy the Lord's blessing in the covenant land, they had to be willing to bear the sign of the covenant. The number of circumcisions accounted for the name **the hill of the foreskins**

(Hebrew, *Gibeath Ha'araloth*; v. 3), a grotesque memorial to Israel's laxity with the covenant sign.

The explanation for circumcising "the second time" appears in verses 4–7. No one was subjected to the surgical procedure of circumcision a second time. The males who had come out of Egypt had been circumcised, but the **men of war** (those age twenty and above; v. 4) had died in the wilderness. Those males who had been born during the wilderness experience, however, had not been circumcised. Apparently the Israelites had not taken circumcision, the covenant sign, seriously for **forty years** (v. 6). This is the total time between their departure from Egypt and the crossing of the Jordan. Only thirty-eight years had passed since they **obeyed not the voice of the LORD** and turned back at Kadesh-barnea (Num. 14:20–22; Deut. 2:14). It was this generation, then, that Joshua circumcised. Since circumcision involved the idea of dedicating one's offspring (children) to the Lord, it is possible that God refused to allow the disobedient generation that turned back to hypocritically practice this ritual. It was to be practiced again only when the new generation was in the Promised Land. No additional activity was required of Israel in the land until those who had been circumcised were healed (see discussion on 5:1).

5:9. I rolled away the reproach of Egypt. Although this reference may be to Egypt's enslavement of Israel, it is much more likely that the author had in mind the reproach the Egyptians would have cast on her and her God if Israel had perished in the wilderness (see Exod. 32:12; Num. 14:13; Deut. 9:28). Now that the wilderness journey was over and Israel was safely in the Promised Land as His special people consecrated to Him by circumcision, the reproach of Egypt was rolled away. **Gilgal**, interpreted as "rolling," is a pun on the Hebrew verb "to roll" (*galal*).

5:10–12. Israel ... kept the passover (v. 10). The Passover ceremonies took place in the month of Abib, the first month of the year (Exod. 12:2). At twilight on the fourteenth day of the month, the Passover lamb was to be slaughtered, then roasted and eaten that same night (Exod. 12:5–8). Israel had not celebrated Passover since Sinai, one year after her release from Egypt (Num. 9:1–5). Before the next Passover season, she had rebelled at the border of Canaan, and the generation of the exodus had been condemned to die in the wilderness (Num. 14:21–23, 29–35). For that generation, the celebration of Passover (deliverance from judgment) could have had little meaning. Part of the Passover meal was **unleavened cakes** (v. 11), bread baked without yeast. They were to be eaten during the seven feast days that followed (Exod. 12:15; Lev. 23:6).

That the **manna ceased** (v. 12) is especially noteworthy. This transition from eating manna to eating the "old corn of the land" (v. 11) ended forty years of dependence on God's special provision. Manna had been God's gift for the wilderness journey; from now on, He would provide Israel with food from the Promised Land.

II. The Conquest of the Land (5:13–12:24)

A. The Initial Battles (5:13–8:35)

1. The Victory at Jericho (5:13–6:27)

5:13–6:5. The narration of the conquest is introduced by the sudden appearance of a heavenly figure who calls himself the **captain of the host of the Lord** (5:14).

5:13–15. Joshua was by Jericho (v. 13). The leader of God's army went to scout the nearest Canaanite stronghold, but another warrior was already on the scene. **There stood a man over against him**. The "angel of the Lord" was sent on missions of this kind (Judg. 6:11; 13:3), and some angels were identified as captains over the heavenly armies (Dan. 10:5, 20; 12:1). However, the experience is taken by many to be an encounter with God in human form (theophany) or with Christ (christophany). If this indeed was Christ, then the encounter between the two Yeshuas involved a "savior" (Joshua) meeting the Savior (Jesus). Moses' preparation for leadership (Exod. 3:2) had begun similarly at the burning bush where he met the "angel of the Lord." In both accounts, Moses and Joshua were instructed to remove their shoes because they were standing on holy ground. Also, in both accounts, it was the Lord

who continued to speak. Here Joshua fell before the man and worshiped him without rebuke (see Acts 10:25–26; 14:11–15; Rev. 19:10; 22:7–8). **His sword was drawn in his hand**, symbolizing his participation in the coming battle. He would fight for Israel.

To Joshua's inquiry concerning the stranger's loyalties, the answer was, **Nay ... as captain of the host of the Lord am I now come** (v. 14). His response put things in perspective. Joshua and Israel must know their place. God is sovereign—it is not that He is on their side; rather, they must be on His side and fight His battles. The commander of His heavenly armies had come to take charge of the battle on earth. Joshua was to take orders from him (6:2–5), knowing that the armies of heaven are committed to this war, as later events confirm.

Joshua expressed his respect for his superior: **What saith my lord unto his servant?** (v. 14). Joshua was then commissioned to undertake the Lord's battles for Canaan (v. 15), just as Moses had been commissioned to confront Pharaoh (Exod. 3:5).

6:1. This verse is parenthetical to the conversation that began in 5:13 and will continue in 6:2. It explains why Joshua could draw near to Jericho without any threat of personal harm; it had been closed due to the presence of the Israelites now on the western side of the Jordan. **Jericho** is modern Tell es-Sultan, the site of more than two dozen ancient cities, built and destroyed one on top of the other. Many had powerful double walls. Though discussion continues on the identification of levels of the city's occupation, there is ample archaeological evidence of such destruction. The tell (mound) is roughly 400 yards by 200 yards. Since Jericho may have been a center for the worship of the moon god (Jericho probably means "moon city"), God was destroying not only Canaanite cities, but also Canaanite religion. (See Map 3 at the end of the *KJV Study Bible*.)

6:2–5. The words of the "captain of the host of the Lord" (5:14) continue here, but he had now been identified as **the Lord** (v. 2), and He ordered the first conquest of a Canaanite city. **I have given into thine hand Jericho**. The prophetic certainty echoes the encouraging promise to Joshua in 1:2–3 and introduces the course of action Joshua and Israel must take for its fulfillment.

The command to **compass the city** (v. 3) might be interpreted as a ritual act, signifying a siege of the city, which was to be repeated for six days. The central presence of the **ark** (v. 4) in the march around the city signified that the Lord was laying siege to the city. The **seven trumpets of rams' horns** to be carried by priests were instruments not of music but of signaling, in both religious and military contexts (which appear to come together here). The trumpets were to be sounded on the **seventh day** (6:4), announcing the presence of the Lord (see 2 Sam. 6:15; 1 Chron. 15:28; Zech. 9:14). The seventh day called for seven revolutions around Jericho. No note is taken of the Sabbath during this seven-day siege, but perhaps that was the day the Lord gave the city to Israel as the first pledge of the land of rest. To arrive at the goal of a long march on the seventh day is a motif found also in other ancient Near Eastern literature. In any event, the remarkable constellation of sevens (seven priests with seven trumpets, seven days, seven encirclements, on the seventh day) underscores the sacred significance of the event and is perhaps a deliberate evoking of the seven days of creation to signal the beginning of God's new order in the world.

A long blast (v. 5) and the **great shout** of the people would signal the onset of the attack. This was psychological warfare, intended to create panic and confusion (see Judges 7). In the Dead Sea Scroll "The War of the Sons of Light against the Sons of Darkness," the Levites are instructed to blow in unison a great battle fanfare to melt the heart of the enemy. The city wall would miraculously **fall down flat** (lit., "in its place"), and the Israelites would be able to advance, **every man straight before him**, into the city. There would not be a breach here and there but a general collapse of the walls, giving the surrounding Israelites access to the city from all sides.

6:6–7. Priests were immediately assigned their responsibilities for bearing the ark and seven trumpets. It might be expected that the ark would lead the procession (see 3:6, 8, 13), but instead, it was led by **him that is armed** (v. 7). The Hebrew for this term

differs from that in 6:3, "men of war," but is probably synonymous with it unless the present reference is to a kind of royal guard (but see 6:9 and discussion).

6:8–14. Throughout these verses, the focus is on the **ark of the LORD** (v. 11), highlighting the fact that it was the Lord Himself who besieged the city. It would appear that armed men led the procession, followed by the seven priests bearing the seven trumpets, then the priests bearing the ark of God, followed by the **rereward** (v. 9), the rear guard, which was made up of the final contingents of the army (see Num. 10:25). Whether the armed men (Josh. 6:7, 9) were equally divided before and after the ark is not specified.

The only noise to be heard during the march was the sound of the trumpets. The Israelites were to remain silent until the signal was given for all to shout (6:5).

In verses 12–14, literary repetition reflects repetition in action, a common feature in ancient Near Eastern literature.

6:15–19. After six days of faithful adherence to all instructions regarding the march around Jericho, Israel completed its seventh pass around the city on the seventh day and was given the order to **Shout** (v. 16; see 6:5). One critical detail remained, not to be overlooked. The city **shall be accursed** (Hebrew, *herem*; v. 17; see vv. 18; 6:21; 2:10), a term designating something as irrevocably and absolutely surrendered to the Lord, often by totally destroying it (for the verb form *haram*, which is usually translated "utterly destroy," see 6:21 and 2:10). This placed all of Jericho's inhabitants under the curse of death and all of the city's treasures that could not be destroyed under consignment to the Lord's house (v. 19). According to the law of Moses, this curse could be applied to animals for sacrifice, to property given to God, or to any person found worthy of death (Lev. 27:28–29). It was Moses himself who ruled that all the inhabitants of Canaan were to be "utterly destroyed" (i.e., "devoted"; see *KJV Study Bible* marginal note on 6:18) by execution for their idolatry and all its accompanying moral corruption (Deut. 20:16–18; see also *KJV Study Bible* note on Deut. 2:34).

Honoring the pledge made by the two spies (2:14), Joshua identified the only exceptions to *herem*. **Rahab ... shall live, she and all that are with her in the house** (v. 17).

Any violation of *herem* would **make the camp of Israel a curse** (v. 18). If Israel took for herself anything that was under God's curse, she would bring *herem*, the curse, upon Israel itself and would **trouble it** (see 7:25).

6:20-25. Explicit obedience on Israel's part brought down Jericho's walls, allowing the armed men to march straight in and "devote" the city to its intended destruction. The two spies, the only Israelites who could positively identify Rahab, were sent to fetch her to spare her life. With the people destroyed, the city was burned, but the valuables (things made of gold, silver, bronze, and iron) were dedicated to the treasury of the Lord.

Not only was Rahab's life spared, but **she dwelleth in Israel ... unto this day** (v. 25). The faith of Rahab is noted twice in the New Testament (Heb. 11:31; James 2:25), and she is honored by Matthew's inclusion of her name in his "book of the generations of Jesus Christ" (Matt. 1:5).

6:26-27. Joshua pronounced a curse: **Cursed be the man ... that ... buildeth this city** (v. 26). Jericho itself was to be devoted to the Lord as a perpetual sign of God's judgment on the wicked Canaanites and as a firstfruits offering of the land. This was a way of signifying that the conquered land belonged to the Lord. The curse was fulfilled in the rebellious days of King Ahab (1 Kings 16:34).

The Lord was with Joshua, just as He had promised (1:5), for without His presence, none of the miracles in chapters 3-6 would have been possible. Joshua's fame spread throughout the country, in addition to his being "magnified" in Israel (3:7).

2. The Failure at Ai because of Achan's sin (chap. 7)

7:1-26. The story of Achan, which stands in sharp contrast to the story of Rahab, is tragic. In the earlier event, a Canaanite prostitute, because of her courageous allegiance to Israel and her acknowledgment of the Lord, was spared and received

into Israel. She abandoned Canaan and its gods on account of the Lord and Israel and so received Canaan back. In the present event, an Israelite (of the tribe of Judah, no less), because of his disloyalty to the Lord and Israel, is executed as the Canaanites were. He stole the riches of Canaan from the Lord and so lost his inheritance in the Promised Land. This is also a story of how one man's sin adversely affected the entire nation. Throughout this account (as well as throughout much of the Old Testament), Israel is considered a corporate unity in covenant with and in the service of the Lord. Thus, even in the acts of one (Achan) or a few (the three thousand defeated at Ai), all Israel was involved (see 7:1, 11; 22:20).

7:1. This verse is also parenthetical to the main narrative (see 6:1). It provides an explanation of why Israel would fail at Ai (7:3-5). **The children of Israel committed a trespass**. Though one man stole from God, Israel bore corporate responsibility and guilt. Achan is identified as the culprit, and his sin was that he took of the **accursed thing**; that is, he misappropriated something considered sacred and belonging to God (see discussion on 6:17).

7:2-3. Riding the momentum of success, **Joshua sent men from Jericho to Ai** (v. 2), an uphill march of some fifteen miles through a ravine to the top of the central Palestinian ridge. Strategically, an advance from Gilgal to Ai would bring Israel beyond the Jordan Valley and provide them a foothold in the central highlands. Ai in Hebrew means "the ruin." It has usually been identified with et-Tell (meaning "the ruin" in Arabic), just two miles east of Bethel, but this precise identification is disputed (see discussion on 8:28). **Beth-aven** means "house of wickedness," a derogatory designation of either Bethel itself or a pagan shrine nearby (see 1 Sam. 13:5; Hos. 4:15; Amos 5:5). The men were to **view the country**, that is, spy out the area to bring a report to Joshua. It was learned that Ai was a relatively small and seemingly insignificant city, certainly not warranting an attack by all of Israel's men of war.

7:4-5. Without consulting the Lord or waiting instructions for taking Ai, Joshua dispatched a representative number, only **about three thousand men** (v. 4) to accomplish what was assumed would be an easy victory. Israel lost thirty-six men in the attempt, however, and was repelled and chased **unto Shebarim** (v. 5), a term that means "breaks" and is a fitting description for the landmark rocky bluffs overlooking the Jordan Valley. Israel's **hearts of the people melted** is a phrase that had previously described the Canaanites (2:11; 5:1). This incident shows how victory on the part of God's people can be quickly undermined by disobedience and sin on the part of a single individual (compare the jealousy of Miriam and Israel's delay, Num. 12:1–15).

7:6–9. As a sign of his great distress, **Joshua rent his clothes** (v. 6; see Gen. 37:29, 34; 44:13; Judg. 11:35). Joshua's dismay (and that of the people), as indicated by his prayer, arose from his recognition that the Lord had not been with Israel's troops in the battle. Without the Lord, the whole venture for which Israel had crossed the Jordan would be impossible. Moreover, the Canaanites would now judge that neither Israel nor her God was invincible. They would pour out of their fortified cities, combine forces, and descend on Israel in the Jordan Valley, from which Israel could not escape across the flooding Jordan.

Joshua pled on behalf of God's **great name** (v. 9), as Moses had (Num. 14:13–16; Deut. 9:28–29), knowing that God's honor in the eyes of all the world was at stake in the fortunes of His people.

7:10–12. Joshua's prayer was interrupted by God's rebuke: **Get thee up ... Israel hath sinned** (vv. 10–11). Joshua now learns what the reader has already learned (7:1). One soldier's theft of the devoted goods had brought collective guilt on the entire nation (see 22:20). They **transgressed my covenant** (v. 11; see 7:15, "he [Achan] hath transgressed the covenant"). This is the main indictment; what follows is further specification.

Because someone had **stolen** (v. 11) from God **and dissembled** (i.e., been deceptive), all the children Israel **were accursed** (v. 12; see discussion on 6:18). It would have been inconsistent of God to bless Israel with victory at Ai in view of her disobe-

dience at Jericho. Further blessing would not follow until what was to be devoted to God was found in Israel's possession and destroyed.

7:13–15. Sanctify yourselves against to morrow (v. 13) demands a series of purifications to be undertaken by every Israelite in preparation for meeting with God, as before a solemn religious feast or a special assembly called by the Lord (see discussion on 3:5). Here God summons His people before Him for His judgment.

The culprit harboring the **accursed thing** (v. 13) would be discovered in a search that began with the **tribe which the LORD taketh** (v. 14). When the lots were cast, one of the tribes would be "taken" by the Lord so that the search was narrowed (from clan, to family, to individual) until the Lord exposed the guilty person(s). The lots may have been the Urim and Thummim from the ephod of the high priest (see discussions on Exod. 28:30; 1 Sam. 2:28; see also 1 Sam. 14:41).

He hath wrought folly in Israel (v. 15). To appropriate for oneself what was to be surrendered to God, as Achan had done, was an act that within Israel, the covenant people of the Lord, was considered an outrage of utter folly (Deut. 22:21; Judg. 19:23–24; 20:6, 10; 2 Sam. 13:12).

7:16–19. The narrowing selection process revealed Achan to be the culprit. Joshua took a fatherly attitude toward Achan and addressed him as **My son** (v. 19), saying, **Give ... glory to the LORD ... make confession unto him** (lit., "give praise to him"). This was a solemn charge to tell the truth. If Achan denied his guilt, he would have called God a liar. If he confessed, he would honor God by acknowledging His omniscience.

7:20–21. Having confessed, **I have sinned** (v. 20), Achan chronicled the progressive steps of his sin: **I saw ... then I coveted them, and took them.** The items to which he referred were a **Babylonish garment, and ... silver, and ... gold** (v. 21). The garment was a valuable import from Shinar, the plain where Babel, later known as Babylon, had been constructed (Gen. 11:1–9). The **two hundred shekels** of silver would have weighed about five pounds, and the **fifty shekels** of gold would have weighed about one and one-fourth pounds.

7:22–24. Achan had thought he could hide his sin, but at his judgment, it was exposed for all to know. The stolen items were found where he described and were laid out **before the LORD** (v. 23), who here served as Judge. **Joshua, and all Israel** (v. 24) were God's agents for executing His judgment on both the Canaanites and this violator of the covenant. **All that he had**, family and possessions were destroyed. As the head of (and example for) his family, Achan involved his whole household in his guilt and punishment. This is in accordance with the principle of corporate solidarity—the whole community is represented in one member (especially the head of that community). The death of his family also suggests their knowledge of his theft and their role as accomplices in hiding the treasure, for Moses had instructed that the children were not to die for the sin of their fathers (Deut. 24:16).

7:25–26. Achan had **troubled** (v. 25) Israel, having ignored Joshua's warning (6:18). Now Achan faced **trouble** of his own from the Lord. Because he had been found guilty of violating the covenant of the holy Lord, all Israel **stoned him** and his family (see Exod. 19:13; Lev. 24:23; Num. 15:36). Afterward, the bodies were burned to purge the land of the evil. The **great heap of stones** (v. 26) that was raised over Achan's corpse constituted a second, but sad, monument in the land to the events of the conquest, alongside the memorial at Gilgal (4:20). **Achor** means "trouble" and is another name given to Achan (see 1 Chron. 2:7, where Achan is called "Achar," i.e., "the troubler").

3. The Victory at Ai (8:1–29)

8:1–29. After the short interlude dealing with Achan and his violation of the *herem*, which brought a curse upon all Israel, the account of the conquest and the taking of Ai is renewed.

8:1–2. Now that Israel had been purged, the Lord reassured Joshua once more: **Fear not** (v. 1; see 1:3–5; 3:11–13; 6:2–5). **I have given into thy hand ... Ai**. Though He had made a similar promise con-

cerning the whole of the land (1:3) and Jericho (6:2), God had not said this concerning Ai, for Joshua had sent men to Ai without consulting the Lord (7:2–4).

The Lord gave Israel a new provision: **the spoil ... take for a prey unto yourselves** (v. 2). In contrast to the instructions concerning Jericho (see 6:18–19), the Lord now assigned the wealth of Canaan to His troops who fight His battles. If Achan had only waited and not run ahead of God, how much greater and enjoyable might have been his share of the spoils.

The Lord also gave instructions for taking Ai. **Lay thee an ambush** (v. 2). Still in command, the Lord directed the attack. It is assumed that Joshua will know what to do after laying the ambush.

8:3–12. A contingent of **thirty thousand mighty men** (v. 3) were assigned to the ambush. Once Joshua and the rest of his army approached Ai and feigned a withdrawal, the troops of the ambush were to enter the city from the rear and set it on fire. There would also be another ambush of **five thousand men** (v. 12). Perhaps Joshua assigned two different units to the task to assure success. Or from the original 30,000, a unit of 5,000 may have been designated to attack Ai itself while the remaining 25,000 served as a covering force to block the threat from Bethel (see 8:17).

8:13–26. In full visibility, Joshua's main force, the **host ... on the north** (v. 13), approached the city from the north, then pretended to flee to the east, thus drawing out Ai's entire army of defenders. In spite of the ambush, which consisted of 5,000 Israelites, Bethel joined Ai in its defense (see v. 17). Their joint action indicates that the two cities were closely allied, though each is said to have had a king (12:9, 16). Previously, Ai had repelled 3,000 Israelites (see 7:5). Imagine Ai's temporary elation as an even larger number was seemingly routed.

The Lord's command that Joshua **Stretch out the spear** (v. 18) is seen by some as being reminiscent of Moses' holding the rod of God up in his hand when Israel fought the Amalekites (Exod. 17:9–12) and is apparently symbolic of an appeal to God for help. In light of the ambush's response of emerging from hiding, it was perhaps the signal used by Joshua for the ambush to attack. Joshua did not withdraw his spear until **he had utterly destroyed ... Ai** (v. 26). Trapped in the pincer movement caused by the ambush that had set the city on fire and Joshua's army that ceased retreating and returned to do battle, the men of Ai **had no power to flee** (v. 20). They apparently lost their will to fight when they realized their families and possessions were gone. Once again, obedience to God's directives had brought certain victory.

8:27–29. For the second time, Joshua ordered the holy curse on the inhabitants of a Canaanite city (see discussions on Num. 21:2; Deut. 2:34) and destroyed all the people, both women and men. Then, as he had done to Jericho (6:24) and would later do to Hazor (11:11), Joshua **burnt Ai** (v. 28) so that it was a heap, (Hebrew, *tel*; "a mound of ruins"). He made it **a desolation unto this day**, that is, the time of writing. If the ruins of Ai have been correctly identified (see discussion on 7:2), the site shows signs of later occupation only from circa 1200 to 1100 BC. Some archaeologists, however, have questioned proposed identifications of present-day et-Tell as biblical Ai and Beitin as biblical Bethel. Current excavations and research at Khirbet el-Maqatir are suggesting that el-Bireh was actually Bethel and Khirbet el-Maqatir was Ai, for recent discoveries fit better the geographical and historical description of these two ancient cities.

The king of Ai he hanged on a tree (v. 29). The Israelites did not execute by hanging. Here "tree" may refer to a pole on which the king's body was impaled after execution (see *KJV Study Bible* note on Deut. 21:22). This was a common treatment of defeated kings in the ancient Near East. Abiding by Mosaic instructions (see Deut. 21:22–23), the corpse of the king was allowed to hang only **until eventide.** Then a **great heap of stones** was placed over him. This was the third stone monument in the land (see discussion on 7:26, compare 10:27).

4. The Covenant Renewed at Shechem (8:30–35)

8:30–35. The renewal of the covenant with the Lord as Moses had ordered (Deut. 11:26–30; 27:1–8) concludes the account of the initial battles (see In-troduction: "Outline") and serves as a parenthetical interlude between 8:29 and 9:1–3. The conquest of Canaan has already been put into rich theological perspective. This final event (see also Joshua's final official act, chap. 24) underscores Israel's servant relationship to the Lord. In conquest and occupation, she must faithfully acknowledge her one identity as the people of the kingdom of God, subject to His commission and rule (see discussion on 5:14).

The Hebrew word *'az* (v. 31), normally translated "then" or "at that time," would assume that the journey to Mount Ebal followed immediately after the defeat and destruction of Ai. How Israel could assemble peacefully between Mount Ebal and Mount Gerizim without further conquest is a worrisome question to some interpreters and has led to some radical reconstructions of Israel's history. It must be noted, however, that biblical narrators at times followed a thematic, rather than a strictly chronological, order of events. That may be the case here, since it is clear that the story of the Gibeonite deception and submission (chap. 9) is included in the thematic development of how Israel came into possession of the rest of Canaan (see the author's introduction, 9:1–2). The Shechemites (Shechem was a major city lying between the two mountains mentioned) were Hivites (or were under Hivite domination; see Gen. 34:2) and thus were related to the people of the Gibeonite cities (Josh. 9:7; 11:19). Also, there was no important town between Gibeon and Shechem (Bethel and Ai had been subdued). Perhaps the treaty of submission established between Israel and the Gibeonites (chap. 9) applied also to the Hivites of Shechem, and the covenant renewal ceremony that concludes chapter 8 (and the previous narrative section) actually took place chronologically after the events narrated in chapter 9. If this suggestion is correct, the Gibeonites or their representatives might have been among the "strangers" who participated with Israel in the covenant event (vv. 33, 35).

The author assumes the reader's familiarity with Moses' directives, in Deuteronomy 11 and 27, that Joshua sets out to follow by going to the region of Mounts Gerizim and Ebal. Situated at the foot of mount **Ebal** (v. 30) and Mount Gerizim was the fortress city of Shechem, where Abraham had built an altar when he first entered the land (Gen. 12:6–7). The setting was an appropriate one for covenant renewal. On Mount Ebal, Joshua **built an altar ... an altar of whole stones** (vv. 30–31; see Deut. 27:6), that is, of uncut stones, thus following the guidelines of Exodus 20:25. There he offered **burnt offerings** (v. 31; see Lev. 1:1–17), and **peace offerings** (see Lev. 3:1–17; 7:11–18). These offerings also were ordered by Moses and replicate those he offered after he "wrote all the words of the LORD" following the giving of the covenant (Exod. 24:3–5).

Joshua **wrote ... upon the stones ... the law of Moses** (v. 32). Moses had ordered the people first to plaster the stones (not the altar stones), then to inscribe on them the words of the law (Deut. 27:2–4). These stones are the fourth monument in the land (see discussion on 8:29).

Joining the Israelites in this ceremony was the **stranger, as he that was born among them** (v. 33). Israel now included those who were part of the "mixed multitude" (Exod. 12:38) who had come out of Egypt, plus others who may have associated with them during the wilderness wanderings.

For reciting **the blessings and cursings** (v. 34; see Deut. 27–28 for a fuller listing of "blessings" and "cursings"), Moses had named the six tribes that would stand on Mount Gerizim to bless the people and the six tribes that would be positioned on Mount Ebal to pronounce the curses (see Deut. 27:12–13).

All was done in accordance with Moses' command. It was important that God's covenant people renew the covenant terms with Him, just as it been necessary for the covenant people to identify with their God through the covenant sign of circumcision and the Passover memorial once they entered the land (see 5:2–10), before they could experience further blessing from God.

B. The Campaign in the South (chaps. 9–10)

1. The Treaty with the Gibeonites (chap. 9)

9:1–27. This is the account of how the Gibeonites deceived the leaders of the tribes and obtained a treaty of submission to Israel. For Israel, it was a time of testing; times of blessing and success are frequently followed by testing. Joshua and Israel have shown that it is easy to run ahead of God after He has led one to success.

This account is the first of three sections telling how Israel came into possession of the bulk of the land. The three units are introduced in 9:1–2. In earlier chapters, the Israelites had chosen their agenda and military targets. They had been proactive and on the offensive. Now the cities of Canaan were awake to the threat of Israel and took the offensive, causing the Israelites to be more reactive than before.

9:1–2. The kings which were on this side Jordan (v. 1) ruled over small, independent city-kingdoms that were scattered throughout Canaan, which were inhabited by a variety of peoples who had come earlier from outside the land (compare vv. 1–2 with Gen. 15:19). Earlier, Rahab had noted that the Canaanites had "heard" how the Lord dried up the Red Sea for Israel (2:10), and they again "heard" how the Lord had dried up the waters of Jordan (5:1). Once again, they **heard** something, presumably of Joshua's fame (see 6:27) and that both Jericho and Ai had fallen to Israel and had been utterly destroyed and burned. Israel's one loss at Ai may have encouraged the Canaanites to believe that Israel could be defeated if the city-states combined their fighting resources in an alliance.

9:3–5. Gibeon (v. 3), a site just north of Jerusalem, presently known as el-Jib, shows the remains of a Late Bronze Age city with an excellent water supply. The Gibeonites were in league with a number of neighboring towns (9:17) but seem to have been dominant in the confederation. This smaller alliance chose to work independently of the other Canaanite city-states.

Motivated by their fear of Israel's God, the Gibeonites **did work wilily** (v. 4) and carefully organized a plan involving pretense to trick Joshua into a treaty that would allow them to live. They posed as a delegation from a far country, giving evidence of their distant travel.

9:6–13. Somehow the Gibeonites had learned of Moses' instructions (see 9:24) that no resident of

Canaan was to be spared (Deut. 7:1–5) and that Israel was permitted to make peace only with peoples who lived outside the boundaries of the Promised Land (Deut. 20:10–18). Thus, they came to Joshua at **Gilgal** (v. 6), the site that was Israel's base of operations throughout the years of conquest, claiming to be **from a far country** (see v. 9).

In their request, **make ye a league with us** (v. 6), they were offering to submit themselves by treaty to be subjects of the Israelites (see v. 11, where they call themselves **your servants**—unmistakable language in the international diplomacy of that day). They chose submission rather than certain death (9:24).

The **Hivites** (v. 7), possibly Horites, were an ethnic group living in Canaan that were related to the Hurrians of northern Mesopotamia (11:19; Gen. 10:17; Exod. 23:23; Judg. 3:3). Joshua's suspicions and questions called for an expanded explanation of the Gibeonites' identity and mission. They are deliberately vague in saying they are from **a very far country** (v. 9). They claim to have learned of the Lord **thy God** (v. 9) and **the fame of him**. They cite the same reports that had been heard in Jericho (2:10), carefully failing to mention the most recent victories of Israel at Jericho and Ai lest their knowledge of recent events be questioned. Once again, they put up for display their evidence of lengthy travel.

9:14–15. The performance of the Gibeonites was award-winning and convincing. Joshua and the elders only looked on the exhibits of travel and **asked not ... the Lord** (v. 14). Just as they had not asked counsel of the Lord before attacking Ai, they did not consult their King, whose mission they were charged to complete. This failure on Joshua's part was inexcusable, for he had been instructed that Eleazar the priest would seek counsel for him through the Urim and Thummim whenever needed (Num. 27:18–21; Exod. 28:30).

Israel **made peace** (v. 15) and **a league** with the Hivite delegation. A covenant to let them live was sworn by the heads of the tribes; that is, an oath was taken in the holy name of God. All such oaths were binding in Israel and could not be broken without casting aspersion on the character of God (Exod. 20:7; Lev. 19:12; 1 Sam. 14:24).

9:16–21. After three days, Israel **heard** (v. 16) something startling—the true identity of the delegation, that they were neighbors from Gibeon, located only about twenty miles away. All the cities (v. 17) in league with the Gibeonites were centrally located in the heart of the land, in the territory that would later be awarded to the tribe of Benjamin. Though it took only three days to detect the error of their decision, it took Israel a lifetime to live out the effects of that decision.

All the congregation murmured (v. 18) in response to the discovery. Perhaps the people feared the consequences of not following through on the earlier divine order to destroy all the Canaanites; but more likely, they grumbled because they had been outfoxed and could not take over the Gibeonite cities and possessions. Despite the deception, Israel reluctantly felt compelled to honor their treaty with the Hivites for she had **sworn unto them by the Lord God of Israel.** To renege on their oath would have brought the contempt of the Canaanites on the name of God (see Lev. 19:12). Israel had to prevent the sincerity of God from being rendered doubtful in the eyes of the Gibeonites. Therefore, it was decided that the Hivites would become **hewers of wood and drawers of water** (v. 21) for Israel. Though this is a conventional phrase for household servants, the Hivites' greatest contribution would be assisting the priests at the tabernacle (9:23). Years later, King Saul somehow violated the oath, and a three-and-one-half-year famine resulted. David corrected the situation by honoring the covenant with Gibeon (2 Sam. 21:1–9; 1 Sam. 22:18–19).

9:22–27. Joshua's rebuke for the scam was scathing: **ye are cursed** (v. 23). The Hebrew verb means "to be cursed" or "under a curse." It differs from the verb form "to be accursed" (see discussion on 6:17). Noah's prediction that Canaan would someday be the servant of Shem (Gen. 9:25–26) has part of its fulfillment in this event. Their sentence to serve **the house of my God** probably specifies how the Gibeonites were to serve "all the congregation"

(9:21). Worship at the tabernacle (and later at the temple) required much wood and water (for sacrifices and washing) and, consequently, a great deal of menial labor. From now on, that labor was to be supplied by the Gibeonites, perhaps on a rotating basis. In this way they entered the Lord's service. Interestingly, when Solomon became king, the tabernacle and altar were at Gibeon (2 Chron. 1:3, 5).

The Hivites' response, **as it seemeth good and right unto thee to do unto us, do** (v. 25), was not a simple statement of resignation to their fate but testimony to their confidence that Israel was duty bound to treat them kindly. So they were assigned their duties **for the congregation, and for the altar of the LORD … in the place which he should choose** (v. 27). Joshua later moved the tabernacle (and its altar) from Gilgal to Shiloh, and there it would reside at least until the days of Samuel (1 Sam. 4:3). Later, the Lord chose Jerusalem as the site of His tabernacle (1 Kings 9:3).

2. The Long Day of Joshua (10:1–15)

The army under Joshua came to the defense of Gibeon and defeated the coalition of southern kings at Ajalon (10:1–15), and then they subdued all the southern cities of Judah and the Negev (10:16–43).

10:1–2. When it was learned that Gibeon had defected from the Canaanite cause and had entered into a pact with the invading Israelites, it became a major concern for the cities in the central hill country, especially for **Adoni-zedek** (v. 1), the king of nearby Jerusalem. His name means "lord of righteousness" or "my (divine) lord is righteous." An earlier king of Jerusalem (Salem) had a similar name (Melchizedek; see Gen. 14:18 and discussion). **Jerusalem**, a city of the Jebusites, appears by this name for the first time in Scripture. It would not become an official Israelite city until the reign of David (2 Sam. 5:6–9).

Gibeon is noted here for being a **great city** (v. 2) and for its men, who were all considered **mighty**, that is, men famous for their courage in battle yet wise enough to have made peace with the Israelites. It was not only larger in size than Bethel or Ai but also closer to Jerusalem. With Bethel and Ai con-

quered and the Gibeonite league in submission, the Israelites were well established in the central highlands, virtually cutting the land in two. Naturally, the king of Jerusalem felt threatened, and he wanted to reunite all the Canaanites against Israel. Perhaps he also held (or claimed) some political dominion over the Gibeonite cities and viewed their submission to Israel as rebellion.

10:3–5. Adoni-zedek (v. 3) was the leader of the confederation of the **five kings of the Amorites** (v. 5). These kings ruled over five of the major cities in the southern mountains. The Amorites of the hills are here distinguished from the Canaanites along the coast. The intent of the confederation was not only to punish Gibeon for its alliance with Israel but also to warn and prevent any other city from doing likewise, wanting all the cities to maintain a united stance against the Israelites.

10:6–7. An urgent appeal for deliverance, **come … and save us** (v. 6), was sent to Joshua, whose name means "the Lord saves." A treaty such as Joshua had made with the Gibeonites usually obliged the ruling nation to come to the aid of the subject peoples if they were attacked, thus the immediate response to their desperate plea.

10:8–9. Once again, the Lord promised to be directly involved. **I have delivered them into thine hand; there shall not a man of them stand before thee** (v. 8; compare the assuring words "I have given," in 6:2; 8:1, and God's initial encouraging words to Joshua, "I will be with thee," in 1:5). God would bring triumph out of Israel's failure with the Gibeonites. By confronting the Amorite confederacy, many of the enemy would be drawn to one location for God to destroy at one time, thus leaving the supporting city virtually defenseless and removing the need for Israel to fight individually each city and its army.

Fortified by the promise of God's presence, Joshua **came unto them suddenly, and went up from Gilgal all night** (v. 9). He attacked early in the morning, perhaps while the moon was still up (10:12), having traveled from Gilgal, which was about twenty miles east of Gibeon. It would have been a strenuous, steep uphill climb for Joshua's men.

10:10–11. Few details are recorded regarding Israel's involvement in the initial stage of this campaign. It was the Lord's battle, for He **discomfited** (v. 10) the Amorite army. The Hebrew for this verb implies terror or panic that God produced, thus providing the Israelites with the opportunity to slay the enemy and pursue those attempting to escape through the Beth-horon ascent toward Azekah and Makkedah, two cities located in the Shephelah (the foothills region).

The escaping Amorites came to **the going down to Beth-horon** (v. 11). It was a long descent to the plain of Aijalon below (also known as the valley of Aijalon), a major route from the Shephelah to the hill country following the main east-west crossroad just north of Jerusalem. Here the Lord **cast down great stones** (hailstones) **from heaven**. This was truly a miraculous intervention, for apparently the stones were selective, finding only the Amorites as targets. (For the Lord's use of the elements of nature as His armaments, see Judg. 5:20; 1 Sam. 7:10; Job 38:22.)

10:12–15. Joshua addressed the Lord, requesting additional miraculous intervention regarding the sun. His appeal to God was recorded also in the **book of Jasher** (v. 13), apparently an early account of Israel's wars (perhaps all in poetic form; see 2 Sam. 1:18; see also discussion on Judg. 5:1–31) that was never a part of canonical Scripture and is no longer extant. **So the sun stood still ... and hasted not to go down**. This description is difficult. Some believe that God extended the hours of daylight locally for the Israelites to defeat their enemies. Others suggest that the sun remained cool (perhaps as the result of an overcast sky or eclipse) for an entire day, allowing the fighting to continue through the afternoon. It is uncertain what happened, except that it involved divine intervention and provided favorable conditions for the Israelites and enabled them to continue their task of destroying the Amorites. **The Lord fought for Israel** (v. 14), as He would do frequently, but it was a day that compared to no other.

A concluding statement, verse 15, matches verbatim the conclusion in 10:43 that Joshua and his men returned to their base camp at Gilgal. It is doubtful that Joshua would have returned east to Gilgal, only to turn about later to resume his pursuit of the five kings of the Amorite confederacy, who had taken refuge in a cave. Possibly verse 15 is the conclusion to the shortened version of the account that was to be found in the book of Jasher.

3. The Southern Cities Conquered (10:16–43)

10:16–23. Having defeated the Amorite confederacy, Joshua now had to capture the participating kings and visit their cities. **Makkedah** (v. 16), a site located near the town of Azekah (10:10) in the western foothills where Joshua's troops made their camp, provided a cave in which the escaping kings could hide. Though the cave was sought out for refuge, it became their prison (v. 18) and then later their tomb (10:27). Meanwhile, Joshua's challenge to his men was to **pursue after your enemies** (v. 19). Most of the fighting men defending the southern cities were caught and killed before they could reach the safety of their fortresses, for the Lord had indeed delivered them into the hand of Israel. As Joshua's men regrouped at Makkedah **in peace** (v. 21), that is, safely, **none moved his tongue against ... Israel**. The thought here appears to be that no one dared even to raise his voice against the Israelites anymore.

10:24–27. When the kings were brought out of their cave prison, Joshua ordered his men to **put your feet upon the necks of these kings** (v. 24). This symbolic public humiliation of the defeated enemy chieftains was the usual climax of warfare in the ancient Near East (see Ps. 110:1; for the implications of the Messiah's sovereign dominion over all things, see Ps. 8:6; Heb. 2:8).

After killing the kings, the Israelites **hanged them on five trees** (v. 26; see discussion on 8:29; *KJV Study Bible* note on Deut. 21:22). The public exposure of their corpses would have instilled fear in remaining enemies. After entombing the kings' corpses in their chosen cave, Israel **laid great stones** (v. 27) over its entrance. This became the fifth monument in the land to the events of the conquest (see discussion on 8:32).

10:28–39. Joshua set out on a campaign to visit and take some major cities of the south. Some of these cities had participated in the confederacy and the attack against Gibeon and had undoubtedly already lost the majority of their fighting men (see discussion on 10:8–9).

The description of Joshua's treatment of each city has a repetitive consistency. First, he **took** it (vv. 28, 32, 35, 37, 39), that is, captured it. Second, he **smote it with the ... sword ... and all the souls that were therein** (vv. 28, 30, 35, 37, 39), for God **delivered** (lit., "gave"; vv. 30, 32) it to Israel. These terms are significant, for many modern Bible scholars and archaeologists have denied a conquest of Canaan by Israel circa 1400 BC, citing the lack of any evidence of destruction. A lack of destruction is what should be expected, however, for God did not intend to give to His people as their inheritance a land full of destruction and debris but one with "great and goodly cities" intact, with "houses full of all good things" (see Deut. 6:10–11). Israel was instructed by Moses to utterly destroy the people and their pagan places of worship, not cities, buildings, trees, and vineyards (Deut. 7:1–5).

While still at Makkedah (see 10:21), Joshua **utterly destroyed ... all the souls** (v. 28). The holy curse (*herem*) was placed on the people there, meaning they were "devoted" to death for their wicked deeds (see discussion on 6:15–19; *KJV Study Bible* notes on Deut. 2:34; Num. 21:2). This same fate came to the other major cities of the south: **Libnah, Lachish, Eglon, Hebron,** and **Debir** (vv. 29–38).

Joshua's agenda was altered slightly by **Horam king of Gezer** (v. 33) and his army when he came to Lachish intending to help them but was defeated instead. This defeat is an important detail, for Horam was the king of the most powerful city in the area and the main site of the central Shephelah. Gezer was eventually taken over by the Egyptians and given to King Solomon as a wedding gift (see 1 Kings 9:16).

The defeat of Hebron also included **all the cities thereof** (v. 37), that is, the smaller satellite settlements around the walled city. Once a city's resistance was broken and it was taken, Joshua apparently moved on without leaving military behind to protect his claim on the city. Thus, after Israel's departure, it was possible for others to lay claims to the city, making it necessary for Caleb and Othniel to retake Hebron and Debir later (see 15:13–19). Identification of biblical cities with current place names is not always easy. In the past, **Debir** (v. 38), also known as Kirjath-sepher (15:15), was identified with Tell Beit Mirsim. More recently, however, it has been equated with Khirbet Rabud, about five miles southwest of Hebron.

10:40–43. Joshua claimed victory over all the south country: the **south** (the Negev; v. 40), the **vale** (the Shephelah or low hill region), and the **springs** (lit., "the slopes"). **Kadesh-barnea ... Gaza** (v. 41) are the south-to-north limits in the western part of the region. **Goshen** and **Gibeon** mark the south-to-north limits in the eastern part of the region. Goshen is a seldom-used name for the eastern Negev, not to be confused with the Goshen in the Egyptian delta; it is also the name of a town (15:51).

The southern campaign had begun with God's assurance, "I have delivered them into thine hand" (10:8). The author concludes the account by recording that **all these kings and their land did Joshua take ... because the Lord God of Israel fought for Israel** (v. 42). Thus, the Israelite army returned to its base camp at Gilgal.

C. The Campaign in the North (chap. 11)

11:1–23. Only the northern cities remained to be conquered. Chapter 11 describes the major battle for the hills of Galilee, which Israel fought and won against Hazor and the coalition of other northern city-states, though fewer details are provided than were given for the south. A summary follows of all Joshua's victories, including the southern and central regions.

11:1–5. Once again, the inhabitants of Canaan were reactionary (see 2:10; 5:1; 6:27; 9:1). **Jabin king of Hazor had heard those things** (v. 1). Jabin is perhaps a dynastic name, used again in the days of Deborah (Judg. 4:2). The archaeological excavation of Hazor (modern Tel el-Qedah) shows that it was the largest and best fortified of all the Canaanite cities. It was located in upper Galilee on a major trade route, and its lower city measured 175 acres.

The list of things Jabin heard continues to lengthen. Therefore, he requested help from nearby northern kings. The cities named **Madon, Shimron,** and **Achshaph** (v. 1) were presumably in the vicinity south of Hazor, perhaps located in the plain of Megiddo. **Cinneroth** (v. 2) means "harp" and is the Sea of Galilee, which is shaped like a harp. Jabin's muster extended as far as the **plains** (i.e., the Arabah) in the Jordan Valley and as far as **Dor**, on the Mediterranean and south of Mount Carmel.

This alliance was larger than the southern alliance had been and included many different peoples. The kings arrived with **much people ... as the sand ... upon the sea shore** (v. 4), a widely used figure of speech indicating large numbers (notably the description of Abraham's promised seed, Gen. 22:17), and **with horses and chariots.** Humanly speaking, the odds against Israel gaining a victory were getting greater. Previously, she had taken one city, Jericho, without battering rams or an organized military; in that campaign, she had taken on the foot soldiers of the combined forces of the southern alliance. Now the number of enemy soldiers was even greater, and they had the advantage of horses and chariots, military technology that, humanly speaking, was far superior to Israel's infantry. In each past event, however, the Lord had miraculously intervened. Now Israel, and the Canaanites, would learn that "there is no king saved by the multitude of a host ... [and] a horse is a vain thing for safety" (Ps. 33:16 – 17).

The **waters of Merom** (v. 5) is probably modern Meirun, just northwest of Safed near the source of the Wadi Ammud (Marun), some eight miles northwest of the Sea of Galilee. Since "Merom" appears to derive from the Hebrew for "height, elevation," this designation may specify a plain that was advantageous for the Canaanites in employing their chariots.

11:6 – 9. God promised His intervention, but details of the battle are limited. Israel was instructed to **hough** (i.e., hamstring) **their horses, and burn their chariots** (v. 6). Hamstringing was done by cut-

ting the tendon above the hock or ankle, crippling the horse so that it could not walk again (see 2 Sam. 8:4). Chariots as advanced implements of war were not used by the armies of Israel until the time of Solomon (1 Kings 9:22; 10:26 – 29). God was ensuring that Israel's boast would be in Him, not in horses and chariots (see Ps. 20:7).

The Lord **delivered** (v. 8) the enemy. Israel **smote** them and **chased** them as far as **great Zidon** and **Misrephoth-maim**, sites in the vicinity of Phoenicia.

11:10 – 15. Perhaps Joshua's greatest victory was taking **Hazor** (v. 10), for it was **the head of all those kingdoms**, thus demonstrating its supremacy in the north. The city's armed forces, however, had been defeated earlier at Merom. Returning to this city, Joshua **utterly destroy**ed (v. 11) its inhabitants and **burnt Hazor with fire**, thus rendering on it the full extent of *herem*, the curse of total destruction (see discussion on 6:15 – 19), with the exception that Israel claimed the spoils. The archaeological site reveals extensive damage and the burning of the Canaanite city in approximately 1400 BC, 1300 BC, and 1230 BC. Since the destruction level of 1300 BC probably indicates Pharaoh Seti I as the one who burned the city, this leaves the destruction levels of 1400 BC and 1230 BC for Joshua's conquest. Those who hold to the late date of the conquest opt for the 1230 BC level; those who hold to the early date opt for 1400 BC (see Introduction: "Background").

Joshua destroyed the population of each city he took; he did not destroy the city, however. With the exception of Hazor, Joshua did not burn the **cities that stood still in their strength** (lit., "on their *tel*"; v. 13). The Hebrew word *tel* (Arabic *tell*), is a hill formed by the accumulated debris of many ancient settlements, one above the other, over many years (see discussion on 7:2). Throughout the entire conquest, in all of the campaigns, only three cities were totally destroyed and burned: Jericho, Ai, and Hazor. In all places, however, Israel put the residents to the sword and took their possessions as spoil.

Joshua **left nothing undone** (v. 15). His success should be measured in the light of God's specific orders, which he carried out fully, rather than by the total area that would eventually have to be occupied by Israel. Joshua still had work to do. Having completed the first step of his mandate, conquering the land, he now turned his attention to the second step, dividing the land among the tribes as an inheritance (see 1:6).

11:16–17. Joshua took all that land (v. 16). A broad overview of the geography of Canaan follows (see Map 2 at the end of the *KJV Study Bible*), which includes the Negev, the land of Goshen (see discussion on 10:41), the Shephelah, the Arabah (the Jordan rift valley), the hill country, and the coastal plain. In this description, **mount Halak** (v. 17), a wilderness peak southeast of Beersheba and the east of Kadesh-barnea marks Israel's southern extremity. **Baal-gad**, the first valley west of Mount Hermon, marks the north boundary.

11:18–20. Joshua made war a long time (v. 18). An estimation of the duration of Joshua's conquests can be made from the life span of Caleb: seven years had elapsed from the beginning of the conquest (age seventy-eight; compare 14:7 with Deut. 2:14) until he took Hebron (age eighty-five; see 14:10). Throughout this period, Israel made an alliance with no one except the Gibeonites. **The LORD ... harden**ed **their hearts** (v. 20), just as He had the heart of Pharaoh (Exod. 8:32; 9:12), thereby allowing Joshua to succeed in destroying the Canaanites. Thus, God's patience with the Amorites (Gen. 15:16) was ended, and the curse of Noah began to be realized (Gen. 9:25), as Israel showed the Canaanites **no favour** and destroyed them **as the LORD commanded Moses** (Deut. 9:5; 20:16). God has sovereign control of history, yet His will never denies personal and moral freedom.

11:21–23. The pre-Israelite inhabitants of Canaan, the **Anakims** (v. 21), were renowned for their great stature (Num. 13:33). The twelve spies' report of them had caused the Israelites so much fear that they had refused to undertake the conquest. They were related to the Nephilim (see discussion on Gen. 6:4) and were named after their forefather, Anak. Joshua shared with Caleb his victory over the Anakim (14:12–15). That a remnant of the Anakim lived **in Gaza, in Gath, and in Ashdod** (v. 22), all

Philistine cities, may indicate that they were related peoples (the giant Goliath was from Gath, 1 Sam. 17:4). **And the land rested from war** (v. 23), allowing Joshua to begin assigning territories to the twelve tribes as an inheritance.

D. The Defeated Kings of Canaan (chap. 12)

12:1–24. The first section of Joshua concludes with a summary of the victories of the Israelites and the cities whose kings had been defeated (see Map 3 at the end of the *KJV Study Bible*).

12:1–6. By citing a list of kings and cities, the writer reiterates that the conquest was indeed complete. He begins with the land **on the other side Jordan** (v. 1) and the cities taken when Moses still led Israel. The unity of the nation is reaffirmed by the inclusion of this land **toward the rising of the sun**, that is, east of the Jordan. The **river Arnon** marked the border with Moab to the south, and **mount Hermon** denoted the upper limits of Israel's land to the north.

Sihon king ... in Heshbon (vv. 2–4) and **Og king of Bashan** (v. 4) both met defeat under the command of Moses (Num. 21:21–35), a long-remembered tribute to God's mighty power (see Neh. 9:22; Ps. 135:11). Og was a remnant of the giants (Hebrew, *Rephaim*, i.e., people apparently of great stature; see Deut. 2:20–21; 3:11). Bashan represents northern Transjordan, known today as the Golan Heights. This eastern land had already been assigned to two and a half tribes by Moses (Numbers 32).

12:7–24. These verses focus on Joshua's victories in **the country ... on the west** (v. 7) of the Jordan, in Canaan proper (9:1; 11:16–17; 24:11; Gen. 15:18–19), from **Baal-gad** in the north to **mount Halak** in the south (11:17). A total of thirty-one cities are listed, more than double the amount of cities noted in the conquest narrative. Once again, the reader learns that the writer was selective in the details presented, but one can never overlook the fact that God controlled the circumstances and the outcome of each battle and campaign of the conquest. Many of the cities cited here have not yet been positively identified with archaeological sites and are thus lacking on maps.

The kings and cities that were encountered in the central region and in the south, beginning with Jericho, are listed in verses 9–16. The kings and cities of the north follow in verses 17–24. The **king of Gezer** (v. 12) had been defeated in the siege of Lachish (10:33), but there is no record that his city was not visited by Joshua or captured; neither is it recorded that Joshua had taken the cities of Aphek, Taanach, Megiddo, or Dor (vv. 18–23). It will be learned later that Israel did fail to destroy the inhabitants of some of these cities (Judg. 1:27–31).

III. The Distribution of the Land (chaps. 13–21)

13:1–32. The heavenly King, who had conquered the land, began the administration of His realm by assigning specific territories to the tribes. Much of chapters 13–21 reads like administrative documents. The account begins (chap. 13) by noting the land not yet subdued (but to be allotted) and by recalling the assignments already made by Moses to the two and a half tribes east of the Jordan (see Map 4 at the end of the *KJV Study Bible*). The account continues (chaps. 14–19) with boundary descriptions, lists of towns, and brief interludes of narrative and explanatory material, all combined to instruct readers regarding each tribe's inheritance. The account is completed with the final allotments made for the cities of refuge (chap. 20) and the Levitical cities (chap. 21).

A. Areas Yet to Be Conquered (13:1–7)

13:1. This section is introduced by noting an aging leader. **Joshua was old**, but his exact age can only be surmised, perhaps between ninety and one hundred years of age since Caleb was eighty-five (14:10). At any rate, noting Joshua's age supports the fact that he "made war a long time" (see discussion on 11:18) and denotes a certain urgency in that there remained **yet very much land to be possessed**. This was not cited as criticism of Joshua (see 11:15) but as an indication that though the major military centers of Canaan (chap. 12) had been taken in the conquest, each tribe still needed to rid the land completely of Canaanites once they moved into their allotted territories.

13:2–7. These verses define **the land that yet remaineth** (v. 2) to be possessed. The **Philistines** controlled the southwestern coast, and the area of the **Geshuri** refers to the land east of the Sea of Galilee (see 13:13) or perhaps to an area south of the land occupied by the Philistines (see 1 Sam. 27:8).

Sihor (v. 3) is another name for the Wadi el-Arish, below Gaza at the northern entrance to the Sinai (see Jer. 2:18). The **five lords of the Philistines** ruled Gaza, Ashdod, Eshkalon, Gath, and Ekron (see map, *KJV Study Bible*, p. 313; for the five lords who came to Delilah, see Judg. 16:5). The Hebrew word (in the singular) for "lords" is *seren*, probably derived from the Greek word *tyrannos*, "tyrant," indicating the Aegean background of the Philistines. The **Avites** apparently were a people living south of the Philistines (Deut. 2:23).

The description of the land yet to be possessed continues on up the coast into Phoenicia, the very region where Israel had pursued escaping enemy soldiers in the northern campaign (see 11:8). The **Giblites** (v. 5) were inhabitants of the ancient city of Byblos, just north of modern Beirut. The Phoenicians and the Philistines held most of the territory still to be occupied by Israel, but though the tribes were commanded to take the land, God Himself promised to drive out the inhabitants before the children of Israel. The land was His to dispossess and to give to Israel as an inheritance. Even before the land was completely taken, Joshua was instructed to **divide this land** (v. 7) by lot **for an inheritance**. By casting lots, the assignment of land to the individual tribes fell to the choice of God (Prov. 16:33). It was His to give to the tribes as He chose, and no one could charge Joshua and the assisting elders with tribal favoritism.

B. The Land East of the Jordan for Reuben, Gad, and Half of Manasseh (13:8–33)

13:8–13. A general description is given of the land east of the Jordan, which Moses had already assigned to the two and a half tribes—Reuben, Gad, and half of Manasseh (see 1:13–15; Numbers 32). **Aroer** (v. 9), a town on the **river Arnon**, marked the southern boundary of Israel. From there, the land extended through **Gilead** (southeast of the Cinnereth, i.e., the Sea of Galilee; v. 11) to Maachah (northeast of the sea), Geshur, and **Bashan** (east of the sea), to the slopes of **mount Hermon** in the north. This was the territory once dominated by the two kings of the Amorites, **Sihon** (v. 10; Num. 21:21–30) and **Og** (v. 12; Num. 21:33–35).

Israel's unfortunate failure to rid these areas of certain peoples is not concealed. Chapters 13–21 state that not all of the conquered land was controlled by the Israelites (see Judg. 1:21–35).

13:14. The reader is reminded for the first time (see 13:33; 14:3–4; 18:7) that Moses had informed the Israelites that the Levites would receive no tribal allotment but would be dispersed among the other tribes, and their inheritance would be the **sacrifices of the LORD God** that the other tribes would bring (see Deut. 18:1–8). In the wake of the rebellion led by Korah, a Levite, and Dathan and Abiram, from the tribe of Reuben (Num. 16), the Lord had informed Aaron earlier that He had claimed the Levites for Himself to serve at the tabernacle (Num. 18:1–6). Therefore, they would receive no inheritance in the land, for the Lord Himself was their inheritance.

13:15–21. To the tribe of **Reuben** (and its clans; v. 15), Moses gave the land east of the Jordan between **Aroer** (v. 16) on the **river Arnon** (the boundary of Moab) and **Heshbon** (the old royal city of the kingdom of Sihon; v. 17; 13:9) and all its surrounding towns. As in other instances, Reuben, the firstborn son of Jacob (Gen. 29:32), is cited first (see Gen. 35:23; 46:8–9; 49:3).

13:22–23. **Balaam ... the son of Beor** (v. 22) was the soothsayer (i.e., one who practiced divination) who supposedly had influence with the gods (see Numbers 22–24). He was slain when the Lord punished the Midianites for their part in trying to seduce Israel into idolatry and sexual immorality (Numbers 25; 31:8, 16).

13:24–28. To **the tribe of Gad** (and its clans; v. 24), Moses gave the central area, beginning near **Heshbon** (v. 26) on the south and reaching along the Jordan to the southern end of the **sea of Cinnereth** (v. 27). It included most of Gilead and the rest of the kingdom of Sihon, but the exact boundary between Gad and the half tribe of Manasseh remains somewhat uncertain since not all of the places listed can be identified.

13:29–32. To **the half tribe of Manasseh** (v. 29), Moses **gave Bashan ... the kingdom of Og** (v. 30; see 13:12), the lands east and north of the Sea of Cinnereth. The allotment also included the upper part of Gilead. Descendants of **Machir** (v. 31), a son of Manasseh, led in the occupation of these lands (Num. 32:32, 39–42).

13:33. This section closes with the reminder that the Levites received no land allotment, for **the LORD ... was their inheritance** (see discussion on 13:14).

C. The Lands Given to Judah and "Joseph" at Gilgal (chaps. 14–17)

14:1–15. This short chapter serves as an introduction for chapters 15–19, providing a brief note on the men commissioned to divide the land, an explanation for the inclusion of Joseph's sons in the inheritance, and a special note on the Lord's faithfulness to Caleb.

14:1–5. A "committee" was commissioned to divide the land west of the Jordan to the remaining nine and a half tribes. **Eleazar the priest** (v. 1), who was the son of Aaron, and **Joshua** were assisted in this duty by **the heads of the fathers of the tribes**. The Lord Himself had selected these men before Moses died (see Num. 34:17–29 for a list of their names). Eleazar was now the high priest and the highest official over the casting of the lots. The Urim and Thummim (see Exod. 28:30; Num. 27:21) may have been used.

Manasseh and Ephraim (v. 4) were sons of Joseph who had been adopted by Jacob, and he had given them full status as his own sons before he died. They now constituted two separate tribes (see discussions on Gen. 48:5–7). The addition of these two "Joseph tribes" made possible the twelve-part nation, with the Levites serving as a nonpolitical tribe and receiving no inheritance except **cities to dwell in** (see Num. 35:2 for God's provision for the Levites' cities).

14:6–10. The tribe of **Judah** (v. 6) approached Joshua at **Gilgal**, still the base camp for Israel, apparently to support **Caleb**, one of their own, in his request for his inheritance. What follows is his personal testimony to his obedience and faithfulness to God. Caleb was a remarkable man. When he brought back a good report of the land and stood steadfast with Joshua against the ten spies who failed to trust God and thus rejected the Land of Promise, he had been noted as an exception to those who were destined to die in the wilderness (Num. 14:24, 30; Deut. 1:36). In the intervening years, he had lived in Joshua's shadow, apparently always loyal to him and never a rival for position (compare Aaron's and Miriam's rivalry with Moses, Numbers 12).

Caleb now recalled **the thing … the LORD said** (v. 6), the promise from the Lord earlier at Kadesh-barnea when Caleb had brought back a good report of the land (Num. 13:30; 14:6–9; Deut. 1:34–36). When he was **forty years old**, he had been sent from **Kadesh-barnea** to spy out the land of Canaan. When he returned, he had spoken with a conviction that derived from his relationship with God. In spite of the others, who made **the heart of the people melt** (i.e., they discouraged Israel; v. 8; see discussions on 2:9, 11), Caleb had **wholly followed the LORD his God**. Because of Caleb's firm stand, Moses had sworn that Caleb would acquire an inheritance in the land he had walked through as a spy (Deut. 1:36).

That had all happened forty-five years ago. His recollection of his age at that time and of the events of the intervening years is useful in approximating the length of the conquest. Caleb was now eighty-five years old. If the date of Israel's exodus from Egypt is set circa 1446 BC (see Introduction: "Background"), and Caleb was enlisted as a spy in the second year after Israel's exodus (after observing Passover at Sinai; see Num. 9:1), circa 1444 BC, with the wars ending (14:15) forty-five years after Caleb's good report at Kadesh-barnea (Num. 13:30), the year would be circa 1399 BC. If the conquest began

after forty years in the wilderness (thirty-eight years after the Kadesh-barnea experience), in 1406 BC, the conquest lasted approximately seven years.

14:11–12. I am as strong this day as when **Moses sent me** (v. 11). Caleb's claim to physical health and strength was matched by his courage and determination. Thus, he made his request: **give me this mountain** (v. 12), referring to Hebron, which is situated high in the Judahite hill country, about twenty-five miles south of Jerusalem. Caleb was well aware of the presence of the **Anakims** (see discussion on 11:21), for he had witnessed them firsthand as a spy (Num. 13:28–33), but he was confident that the Lord was with him: **I shall be able to drive them out**. At his age, Caleb sought a challenge and set the example not only for Judah but for all the tribes in taking their inheritance.

14:13–15. Caleb obtained his requested inheritance with Joshua's blessing. **Hebron** (v. 13) means "union." **Kirjath-arba** (v. 15) means "the town of Arba" and was named for Arba, the father of the Anakim (15:13; 21:11); it can also mean "the town of four." **And the land had rest from war**. Since the Judahites and Caleb approached Joshua concerning their territory while he was still headquartered at Gilgal, it may be that they did so shortly before the wars fought under Joshua were totally ended (see 11:23).

15:1–63. Judah is the first of the west-bank tribes to have its territory delineated. First the outer limits are listed (vv. 1–12), then the area apportioned to Caleb and Othniel (vv. 13–19), and finally the Canaanite cities allotted to the clans of Judah are named region by region (vv. 20–62), which is followed by a notice of failure (v. 63).

15:1–12. The first lot went to the clans of the **tribe of … Judah** (v. 1). Judah's priority in Israel is anchored in the oracle of Jacob (Gen. 49:8–12; see 1 Chron. 5:1–2) and upheld in the history of the nation (2 Kings 17:18).

The boundaries of Judah are laid out and described in a counterclockwise direction (vv. 1b–4), starting at the **south coast** (the southern boundary; vv. 1, 4). The points listed formed a curved line beginning at the lower tip of the **salt sea** (the Dead Sea;

vv. 2, 5) and moving through the **wilderness of Zin** (v. 1) under **Kadesh-barnea** (v. 3) to join the Mediterranean coast at the mouth of the **river of Egypt** (the Wadi el-Arish, southwest of Gaza; v. 4; see 13:3).

The description of Judah's territory proceeds north on the eastern boundary along the **salt sea** (v. 5b) to the **border in the north**. Judah's border with Benjamin ran in a westerly line from the mouth of the Jordan through the **valley of Hinnom** (v. 8), just south of **Jerusalem**, to **mount Seir** (not to be confused with Mount Seir of Edom; v. 10), over to **Timnah**, then northwest to the coastal city of **Jabneel** (later called Jamnia; v. 11), about ten miles south of Joppa. The western boundary (v. 12a) was the **great sea** (the Mediterranean Sea). Verse 12b is a summary statement.

15:13–20. These verses provide a brief interlude, focusing on one Judahite and how he claimed his inheritance. Caleb received Hebron, the city inhabited by the Anakim, at his request (14:6–15). Here three men of the Anakim are named, and Caleb expelled them (see Judg. 1:20).

He went up ... to ... Debir (v. 15), a neighboring city about five miles southwest of Hebron (see discussion on 10:38). Caleb led the attack but offered his daughter **Achsah** (v. 16) to whoever would capture the city (see Judg. 1:9–15 for the story with minor variants). **Othniel the son of Kenaz, the brother of Caleb** (v. 17; see Judg. 3:7–11 for Othniel's service as judge in Israel), accepted the challenge and took the city. Victory over the city served as the bride-price for Achsah. Othniel's relation to Caleb as "brother" is uncertain. Does "brother" imply "relative" or "blood brother"? It is possible that Othniel was Caleb's younger brother.

Caleb's daughter requested a **blessing** (v. 19), perhaps to be interpreted as a wedding gift. Since she had acquired **a south land**, that is, dry land of the Negev, water was needed. Therefore, Caleb gave her the **upper springs, and the nether** (i.e., lower) **springs** (v. 19). These springs still water the local farms in Hebron.

15:21–32. A long and detailed list of the cities located within Judah's territory follows, perhaps once again indicating Judah's leading role in Israel's history. The list begins with the **uttermost cities ... of Judah ... southward** (v. 21), that is, the towns at the lower end of Judah's allotted land. Most of the first twenty-nine villages listed were assigned later to the tribe of Simeon (19:1–9).

15:33–47. The list continues with towns in the **valley** (v. 33). The Hebrew for this term is *Shephelah*. This area, between the highlands of central Judah and the Philistine coast, was, for the most part, not occupied by Israel until the victories of King David. Some of the places listed here were reassigned to the tribe of Dan (19:41–43).

15:48–60. The cities in the **mountains** (v. 48) were those located in the high hill region south of Jerusalem. The Septuagint adds eleven names, including Tekoa and Bethlehem, to this list.

15:61–62. The towns in the **wilderness** (v. 61) were those in the chalky, dry region east and south of Jerusalem that borders the Dead Sea. Of these, only **En-gedi** (v. 62) can be positively located, though many believe the **city of salt** is Qumran, where, centuries later, the scribes who produced the Dead Sea Scrolls lived.

15:63. The list concludes sadly with a note of failure. The Judahites were unable to drive out the **Jebusites the inhabitants of Jerusalem**. A victory of men of Judah over the city of the Jebusites is recorded in Judges 1:8, but evidently this did not result in its permanent occupation. Benjamin and Judah both failed to take the Jebusite fortress of Jerusalem (Judg. 1:21).

16:1–17:18. These two chapters are devoted to the lands given to the **children of Joseph** (16:1), that is, Ephraim and the half tribe of Manasseh, who settled west of the Jordan. Following Judah, the Joseph tribes were given priority, and later, during the divided kingdom, they dominated the northern kingdom.

16:1–4. The **lot of ... Joseph** (v. 1) links Ephraim and western Manasseh in this introductory section, describing their southern boundary, which was actually Ephraim's southern border. It moved west from **Jericho** past **Beth-el**, down to **Gezer** (v. 3), and on to the Mediterranean coast. In verse 4, Manasseh and Ephraim are named in their birth order, though the order is reversed in the presentation that follows their individual allotments, perhaps showing that of the two, Ephraim would be dominant (see Jacob's blessing Ephraim over Manasseh, Gen. 48:13–20).

16:5–9. The list of Ephraim's towns is less detailed than that of Judah. With its southern border already delineated (vv. 1–4), the northern **border … of Ephraim** (v. 5) is now described (it was bordered by the Jordan on the east and the Mediterranean on the west). Ephraim's northern border began by the Jordan and ran west near Shiloh but south of Shechem, then followed the Wadi Kanah down to the Mediterranean Sea.

16:10. The short discussion of Ephraim's territory closes with another example of failure. **They drave not out the Canaanites … in Gezer.** Though Joshua had defeated its king and army in the southern campaign (see discussion on 10:33), there was no mention of the city being taken. Instead of destroying its residents or dispelling them, Ephraim made them **serve under tribute**, that is, become forced laborers. Since Gezer does not appear to have come under Israelite control until the days of Solomon (1 Kings 9:15–16), this may be a note added after that event (but see 2 Sam. 5:25).

17:1–18. Half of the tribe of Manasseh had received its inheritance from Moses on the eastern side of the Jordan (see 12:6 for a review of the event and 13:29–31 for a description of the land). In chapter 17, the western half of Manasseh is awarded its land.

17:1–2. Manasseh … was the firstborn of Joseph (v. 1). This may be a reminder to the proud Ephraimites that Manasseh had been the firstborn, though Jacob gave priority to Ephraim when he adopted Joseph's two sons (Gen. 48:14, 19). It is also learned that the tribe of Manasseh had its hero in **Machir the firstborn** because he was **a man of war**, even though he is usually linked to Transjordan **Gilead** and **Bashan**.

17:3–6. There is a brief break in the narrative to interject a special case involving **Zelophehad** who **had no sons, but daughters** (v. 3). Before Moses died, he promised Zelophehad's daughters an allotment along with their relatives (Num. 26:33; 27:1–7). The daughters appeared before **Eleazar the priest** (v. 4), **Joshua**, and **the princes** to remind them of Moses' special provision for them. Thus, Joshua awarded them a portion of the land for their inheritance.

Western Manasseh (apart from eastern Gilead and Bashan) had **ten portions** (i.e., districts or tracts of land; v. 5). Western Manasseh's territory was second only to Judah's in size. The ten portions went to the five brothers (minus Hepher) and to the five granddaughters of Hepher. (For the law protecting the inheritance rights of a daughter without brothers, see Num. 27:8–11.)

17:7–10. The description of Manasseh's boundaries is unclear at best. It shared a border with Ephraim to its south, with Manasseh claiming **En-tappuah** (v. 7), a town in **Ephraim** (v. 8), and Ephraim claimed some towns apparently within Manasseh's territory (v. 9). To the north, the Esdraelon plain was its boundary, but Manasseh claimed cities that lay within the borders of **Issachar** and **Asher** (v. 10).

17:11–13. Beth-shean (v. 11), **Ibleam, Dor, Taanach,** and **Megiddo** were powerfully fortified cities along Manasseh's common border with **Issachar** and **Asher**. These cities were not conquered until later. When King Saul died in battle, the victorious Philistines fastened his body to the wall of Beth-shean (1 Sam. 31:10), which suggests that that city was in league with the Philistines. **When the children of Israel were waxen strong** (v. 13), possibly referring to the days of David and Solomon, they put them **to tribute** (see 16:10) and did not drive them out.

17:14–18. The **children of Joseph** (v. 14) registered a complaint with Joshua. **I am a great people** (i.e., numerous). The reference is to both Ephraim and Manasseh (see v. 17). The allotment to the Joseph tribes is here handled as one (see 16:1, 4), though the two subdivisions have been described separately (16:5–17:11). The two tribes claim that their numbers are too great for the amount of land that has been awarded to them. In terms of square miles, the Joseph tribes had received disproportionately large allotments and some of the most fertile land. Joshua resisted their complaint and, based on their numbers, challenged them to go to the forested areas and **cut down for thyself** (v. 15). This region of Canaan was still heavily forested. It seems that the Israelites viewed their assigned territories primarily in terms of the number of cities with land cleared for farming and pasturage rather than in terms of the size of the region in which these cities were located. The region assigned to the Joseph tribes was at the time not as heavily populated as other regions. The forested land was inhabited by **the Perizzites and ... the giants** (Hebrew, *Rephaim*), who are listed here as neighboring peoples, though elsewhere the Perizzites are said to have lived on the west bank in Canaan (3:10; 12:8) and the Rephaites in the kingdom of Og, east of the Jordan (12:4; 13:12). **Mount Ephraim** denotes the territory of the Joseph tribes, under the name of the legal firstborn (see discussion on 17:1–2).

A further complaint of the Joseph tribes was that in addition to the hill country being inadequate for their people, Canaanites lived **in the land of the valley** (v. 16) and had at their disposal **chariots of iron**. These were chariots with certain parts made of iron, perhaps the axles; the use of iron was a new development (see discussion on 11:6). To take the land from the Canaanites would be to challenge them on their turf and at a decided disadvantage. Joshua gave no ground to their complaint but challenged them to deforest the hill country and to claim the plains from the Canaanites. Examples of valor have already been seen in Caleb (14:12–14), Othniel (15:16–17), and Machir (17:1). If Caleb could take Hebron, Othniel take Debir, and Machir take Gilead and Bashan, certainly the Joseph tribes should be able combine their forces to take their land.

D. The Lands Given to the Remaining Tribes at Shiloh (chaps. 18–19)

18:1–19:51. Seven tribes remained to be assigned land: Benjamin, Simeon, Zebulun, Issachar, Asher, Naphtali, and Dan. Their lots were cast at Shiloh, and their portions are described with considerably less detail than Judah and the Joseph tribes, again giving evidence of the prominence of these three tribes. The task of assigning allotments was completed with a portion awarded to Joshua.

1. The Tabernacle at Shiloh (18:1–10)

18:1–7. Israel assembled at **Shiloh** (modern Khirbet Seilun; v. 1), which is located in the heart of Ephraim about ten miles northeast of Bethel, a little east of the main road from Bethel to Shechem. Shiloh was the religious and political center of Israel for approximately three hundred years. The move from Gilgal to Shiloh is another indication that the wars of the conquest had ended. The **tabernacle of the congregation** (see *KJV Study Bible* note on Exod. 27:21) with its sacred ark of the testimony was set up, and it would remain at Shiloh until the time of Samuel (1 Sam. 4:3).

Joshua's sharp interrogation suggests that the seven tribes still without territorial assignments were lax about claiming an inheritance. They were **slack to ... possess the land** (v. 3). Conquest had to be followed by settlement, which required a survey, a fair distribution, and then a full occupation of the land. A distinction must therefore be made between the national wars of conquest (Joshua) and the tribal wars of occupation (Judges 1–2).

Joshua called for the formation of a new commission on land distribution, to be comprised of three men from each tribe, who would survey the remaining land and write a description of the features that would serve as natural boundaries for the remaining tribes. Judah's territory to the **south** (v. 5) was fixed, as was the allotment of the Joseph tribes to the **north**, that is, relative to the territory of Judah.

The findings of the team and their division of the unclaimed land into **seven parts** (v. 6) provided the basis for Joshua to **cast lots** for the remaining tribes (see discussion on 14:1). A final reminder was given that the Levites would not acquire any land as a result of this survey, for the **priesthood of the LORD is their inheritance** (v. 7; see discussion on 13:14), as well as a reminder that two and a half tribes had already received their inheritance in Transjordan.

18:8 – 10. The men completed their assignment and recorded their assessment in a **book** (v. 9). The actual form of the document was probably a scroll. **Joshua cast lots** (v. 10) for the remaining tribes **before the LORD**. Again, the assignment of land to the tribes was the Lord's decision.

2. The Allotments for Benjamin, Simeon, Zebulun, Issachar, Asher, Naphtali, and Dan (18:11–19:48)

18:11 – 28. The lot ... of Benjamin (v. 11) fell to a buffer zone between Judah and Ephraim, the two dominant tribes. Its northern line was the same as Ephraim's southern border (see discussion on 16:1), and its southern line the same as Judah's northernmost boundary (see discussion on 15:5). A description of its boundary (vv. 11–20) precedes a list of its cities (vv. 21–28).

19:1 – 9. The second lot came forth to Simeon (v. 1). All of the cities assigned to Simeon lay within the borders of Judah (see 15:1–12) in the Negev along Judah's southern border (see 1 Chron. 4:24–43) because the portion allotted to the people of **Judah was too much for them** (v. 9).

19:10 – 16. The third lot came up for the children of Zebulun (v. 10). To this tribe went a portion of lower Galilee, west of the Sea of Galilee and in the vicinity of New Testament Nazareth. Zebulun found itself wedged between four others tribes: Naphtali, Issachar, Manasseh, and Asher. Its borders are described (vv. 10–14), followed by a brief list of its cities (vv. 15–16).

19:17 – 23. The fourth lot came out to Issachar (v. 17). A brief list of Issachar's cities is given (vv. 18–21), followed by a rather vague description of its borders (vv. 22–23). Its portion lay southwest of the Sea of Galilee reaching down to Beth-shean and west to the Jezreel Valley. Mount Tabor marked its northern border.

19:24 – 31. The fifth lot came out for ... Asher (v. 24). Asher was given the coastal area of western Galilee as far north as Sidon in Phoenicia and as far south as Mount Carmel, though its eastern boundary is not well defined. Full possession of its allotment in Phoenicia was never realized.

19:32 – 39. The sixth lot came out to ... Naphtali (v. 32). Naphtali's area lay mostly to the north of the Sea of Galilee, taking in the modern Huleh Valley and the mountains that bordered on Asher, to Naphtali's west. Its southernmost point was at the lower edge of the Sea of Galilee, but its northern boundary is not defined in the text. The description of its borders (vv. 32–34) is followed by a list of its cities (vv. 35–39).

19:40 – 46. The seventh lot came out for ... Dan (v. 40). No description of Dan's boundaries is given, only a list of the cities within its borders. Its allotment was apparently an elbow of land squeezed between Ephraim and Judah, with Benjamin to the east. The port of Joppa marked the northwestern corner of Dan.

19:47 – 48. There is an addendum concerning Dan. **The coast of ... Dan went out too little for them** (lit., "went out from them"; v. 47), probably indicating they were not able to maintain control over it. The Amorites of this area "forced the children of Dan into the mountain" (Judg. 1:34), so most of the tribe migrated to the upper Jordan Valley, where they seized the town of Leshem (or Laish, Judg. 18:2–10, 27–29) and renamed it Dan (modern Tel Dan or Tel el-Qadi).

3. The Town Given to Joshua (19:49–51)

19:49 – 50. Israel gave an inheritance to Joshua (v. 49). In the account of the distribution of the Promised Land (the territory west of the Jordan), the assignment to Caleb is treated first (14:6–15), and the assignment to Joshua last. Thus, the allotment of inheritance to these two dauntless servants of the Lord from the wilderness generation (Num. 13:30; 14:6, 24, 30) frames the whole account. Both received the territory for which they asked. Appropriately, Joshua's allotment came last; he was not a king or a warlord but the servant of God commissioned to bring the Lord's people into the Promised Land.

Joshua asked for and received **Timnath-serah** (v. 50), which was located southwest of Shiloh in Ephraim. Caleb had asked for Hebron, a mountainous fortification, but Joshua asked for a mountainous site and built a fortification there. Joshua was later buried at this site (24:30).

19:51. In 11:15, 23, Joshua was commended for completing his first assignment—to take the land. Here it is noted that he had now completed his second assignment (1:6)—to divide the land among the tribes. The conclusion here (a rehearsal of those assigned the task of casting lots to determine God's choice of land for the tribes) and the introduction in 14:1 mirror each other and serve as bookends to the account of dividing the land among the tribes.

E. The Cities Assigned to the Levites (chaps. 20–21)

1. The Six Cities of Refuge (chap. 20)

20:1–9. Having distributed the land to the tribes, the Lord's next administrative regulation (see discussion on 13:1–32) provided an elementary system of government, specifically a system of regional courts to deal with capital offenses having to do with manslaughter. Thus, this most inflammatory of cases was removed from local jurisdiction, and a safeguard was created against the miscarriage of justice (with its potential for endless blood feuds) that occurred when retribution for manslaughter was left in the hands of family members. The cities chosen to be cities of refuge were among those assigned to the Levites (chap. 21), where ideally the law of Moses would especially be known and honored.

20:1–3. The **cities of refuge, whereof I spake unto you by ... Moses** (v. 2) refers first of all to God's initial promise of places of safety to which one could flee if he committed involuntary manslaughter (Exod. 21:13–14). The fullest description and explanation of these cities is found in Numbers 35:6–34. In Deuteronomy 4:41–43, Moses assigned three cities in the Transjordan to be cities of refuge and commanded that three more be assigned on the western side of the Jordan when the land had been taken (Deut. 19:2–13). It was now time to "separate three cities in the midst of the land" for this purpose.

The cities of refuge would provide asylum to anyone who was charged with involuntary manslaughter. There he would be protected from the **avenger of blood** (v. 3) until his case was tried. The "avenger" (Hebrew, *go'el*), also translated "near kinsman" (Ruth 3:9) and "redeemer" (Ps. 19:14), was a near relative who had the obligation of exacting retribution (see Lev. 24:17; Num. 35:16–28).

20:4–6. The one seeking asylum would state **his cause** (v. 4) at the **gate of the city**, the traditional place for holding trials, where the elders sat to hold court (see Ruth 4:1 and discussion; see also Job 29:7). The **slayer** (v. 5) would not be given over to the **avenger of blood** because the injury done to his victim was not premeditated. (In Num. 35:16–23 murder and manslaughter are defined, and instructions for handing the murderer over to the avenger of blood are given.)

The **congregation for judgment** (v. 6) was apparently made up of the adult males of the city. Their function in the trial before **the elders** (v. 4) is not clear, but perhaps they witnessed the trial to see that it was fair (closed courts are notoriously corruptible). The length of asylum was **until the death of the high priest** that was in office at the time of the offense (see Num. 35:25–28). The high priest's death either had an atoning effect, perhaps symbolically terminating the guilt incurred by the killer's careless act, or was a kind of amnesty, in essence a statute of limitations.

20:7–9. Three cities were appointed as cities of refuge (v. 7) in addition to those already established by Moses in the Transjordan (v. 8). **They appointed Kedesh** (v. 7) is a wordplay in the Hebrew: "they consecrated [the town of] consecration." The other two cities west of the Jordan, **Shechem** and **Hebron**, already had sacred associations. (For Shechem, see 8:30–35 and discussion; Gen. 12:6–7; for Hebron, the city claimed by Caleb, see Gen. 23:2; 49:29–32.) The geographical distribution of the cities was important: one in the north, one in the midlands, and one in the south. (See map, *KJV Study Bible*, p. 226.) In verse 8, the order of the three cities of refuge east of the Jordan is reversed: **Bezer** in the south, **Ramoth** in the midlands, and **Golan** in the north.

Justice for all was the issue. That these cities were appointed for all **Israel** (v. 9) and for **the stranger**

that sojourneth among them is evidence of the equal protection granted to the foreigners living in Israel (see Lev. 19:33–34; Deut. 10:18–19).

2. The Forty-eight Cities of the Priests (chap. 21)

21:1–45. Finally, the Levites were allotted their towns and adjoining pasturelands, with the priestly families being given precedence (21:10).

21:1–3. The author has noted repeatedly that the Levites would receive no tribal land (13:14, 33; 14:3, 4; 18:7). It is evident, however, that Moses made it quite clear that the Levites were to receive cities with the surrounding pastureland as their inheritance, for now the Levites cited Moses in their appeal to **Eleazar … Joshua … the heads of the fathers** (v. 1) for the cities that had been promised them.

21:4–40. The author methodically details the four lots that fell to Aaron and the sons of Levi, Kohath, Gershon, and Merari (Exod. 6:16; Num. 3:17). He lists each lot and the tribes in which the awarded Levitical cities were located (vv. 4–7), then follows with four lists of the names that comprise the forty-eight Levitical cities (vv. 9–41). The priests and Levites were to be given space in their assigned cities along with the other inhabitants.

The first lot fell to the **Kohathites** (v. 4), more specifically, the **children of Aaron the priest.** They were awarded thirteen cities within the boundaries of **Judah, Simeon**, and **Benjamin**, tribal areas close to Jerusalem, which would later be the site of the temple. A complete list of the thirteen cities is found in verses 9–19. Of special note is **Hebron** (v. 11), belonging to Judah, the city claimed by Caleb (14:13–15). It was selected to be a Levitical city (and a city of refuge, 20:7), and though Aaron's descendants were given space in the city to live, the fields and surrounding towns were given to Caleb for his possession (vv. 12–13).

The second lot fell to the remaining **children of Kohath** (v. 5). They were awarded ten cities within the boundaries of **Ephraim, Dan**, and **Manasseh**, adjoining tribes to the north of Judah and Benjamin. A complete list of the ten cities is found in verses 20–26. Noteworthy is the city of refuge, **Shechem** (v. 21), belonging to Ephraim (20:7).

The third lot fell to the **children of Gershon** (v. 6). They were awarded thirteen cities in the northern tribes of **Issachar, Asher**, and **Naphtali.** A complete list of the thirteen cities is found in verses 27–33. Of special note are the cities of refuge, **Golan in Bashan** (v. 27), belonging to eastern Manasseh (20:8), and **Kedesh** (v. 32), belonging to Naphtali (20:7).

The fourth lot fell to the **children of Merari** (v. 7). They were awarded twelve cities scattered over the territory belonging to **Reuben, Gad**, and **Zebulun.** A complete list of the twelve cities is found in verses 34–41. Of special note are the cities of refuge, **Bezer** (v. 36), belonging to Reuben, and **Ramoth in Gilead** (v. 38), belonging to Gad (20:8).

21:41–42. The total number of Levitical cities scattered throughout the tribes of Israel was forty-eight.

21:43–45. This concluding summary statement shows how the Lord had fulfilled His sworn promise to give Israel this land (Gen. 15:18–21). The occupation of the land was not yet complete (see Josh. 23:4–5; Judges 1–2), but the national campaign was over, and Israel was finally established in the Promised Land.

The LORD gave them rest round about (v. 44; see discussion on 1:13). No power was left in Canaan that could threaten to dislodge Israel. The Israelites were free to live in their land without fear of war with the surrounding nations.

IV. Epilogue: Tribal Unity and Loyalty to the Lord (chaps. 22–24)

A. The Altar of Witness by the Jordan (chap. 22)

22:1–34. The warriors from the two and a half tribes from east of the Jordan, faithful in battle, were commended by Joshua and sent to their homes. Their "altar of witness" (see 22:26–27, 34) was misunderstood, and disciplinary action against them was narrowly averted.

22:1–6. The exact time of Joshua's address to the warriors of Reuben, Gad, and eastern Manasseh is unclear but apparently occurs after the division of the land. It occurred after Israel's center had moved from Gilgal to Shiloh (22:9; 18:1) and after the Lord had given Israel **rest** (v. 4; 21:44).

Joshua's commendation of the warriors of the eastern tribes was deserved. **Ye have kept all that Moses … commanded you** (v. 2) does not refer to the totality of the law but to Moses' order that they join the other tribes in the conquest of Canaan (Num. 32:16–27; Deut. 3:18). They had remained until the conquest was completed. He instructed them to return to the Transjordan to their homes and possessions, but not before he gave them a personal charge.

His charge echoes the words of Moses to all Israel (Deut. 6:5; 10:12–13) and the words of the Lord to Joshua (1:8): **love the Lord your God … keep his commandments … serve him with all your heart** (v. 5). Both Moses and Joshua saw that obedience to the laws of God would require love and service from the heart; only then would His blessing follow. In the ancient Near East, "love" was also a political term, indicating truehearted loyalty to one's king.

22:7–8. The author adds a reminder that Manasseh was unique, having received land on both sides of the river: the land of Bashan from Moses (14:29–31) and land on the western side from Joshua (17:1–13).

Verse 8 appears to be an addendum to 22:2–5. Twice it is stated that the warriors returned to their tents after Joshua blessed them (22:6–7). Perhaps Joshua addressed these men twice, once publicly and once privately, thus sending them off to their homes with one last parting admonition. **Return with much riches … divide the spoil … with your brethren** (v. 8) is addressed to the men who were returning across the Jordan. Moses had set forth the principle for a fair sharing of the spoils of war (Num. 31:25–27). As they left for their homes, Joshua gave them a final reminder to share the spoils with those who had remained behind to guard their families.

22:9–10. After being dismissed and before entering Gilead to the east, the warriors **came unto the borders of Jordan** (v. 10) and **built there an altar**. The "borders of Jordan" is a term understood in the Septuagint to be Gilgal, next to Jericho. Some scholars have suggested that the Hebrew for "borders" should simply be transliterated as Geliloth, that is, the proper name of a site east of Shiloh along the Jordan River (see 18:17). The altar they built was **a great altar to see to**. Apparently, it was erected on the west side of the Jordan but was large enough to be seen from the eastern side.

22:11–12. And the children of Israel heard (v. 11). Anxiety about apostasy led to hasty conclusions. They thought the altar had been set up as a rival to the true altar at Shiloh. They **gathered … at Shiloh** (v. 12), that is, in the presence of God at the tabernacle, **to go up to war against them**. It is refreshing to see Israel take their obligation to God seriously and desire to maintain a pure worship of Him. They prepared to take disciplinary action against the eastern tribes.

22:13–14. A prestigious delegation was sent to search out the meaning of the new altar (see Deut. 13:12–18; Judges 20) and to try to turn the tribes east of the Jordan from their (supposed) act of rebellion against the Lord. Investigating carefully before taking action prevented the zealous Israelites on the west from engaging in civil war over the honor of God and the purity of worship. Leading the investigation was **Phinehas the son of Eleazar** (v. 13), who had already proven himself zealous for true worship when Israel had become involved in immorality and idolatry at Peor (22:17; Num. 25:1–15). Solidarity on the issue is seen in that all of the ten western tribes were represented, by the ten princes who accompanied Phinehas.

22:15–16. Thus saith the whole congregation of the Lord (v. 16) again shows Israel's solidarity on this theological and loyalty issue. **What trespass is this …?** The accusations were very grave: this breach of faith was an act of apostasy and rebellion.

22:17–20. Phinehas cited an example of apostasy and an example of rebellion. Both stemmed from events of relatively recent memory. One occurred at Shittim, east of Jordan, just before Moses died, and the other occurred on the western side right after the destruction of Jericho.

In the **iniquity of Peor** (v. 17). Some of the Israelites had been involved in the Moabite worship of Baal-Peor (Num. 25:1–5). Consequently, God had sent a plague that destroyed twenty-four thousand Israelites. Phinehas feared that God would **be wroth with the whole congregation of Israel** (v. 18) and would strike again.

He offered a passionate proposal. If the **land of your possession be unclean** (v. 19), that is, by pagan worship that corrupts its inhabitants, then **pass ye over unto the land of … the LORD**. Though God had given Israel the Transjordan (24:8), the Promised Land proper had never included territory east of the Jordan. Canaan was the land the Lord especially claimed as His own and promised to the descendants of Abraham, Isaac, and Jacob. Therefore, Phinehas invited the eastern tribes to join the tribes on the west, where the **LORD's tabernacle** was located. He begged them not to rebel by building an additional altar **beside the altar of the LORD**, knowing that God had commanded that Israel was to have only one altar (Lev. 17:8–9; Deut. 12:4–8, 11, 13, 26–27).

For his second example, Phinehas cited **Achan** (v. 20) and how God's wrath fell on **all the congregation of Israel** because of him, bringing defeat to Israel's army and the loss of thirty-six men (see discussion on 7:1–26). His argument was that if the sin of one man brought such dire consequences on Israel, how much more the sin of two and a half tribes?

22:21–29. The eastern tribes responded quickly. The repetition of the sacred names, **the LORD God of gods** (v. 22), gives an oathlike quality to this strong denial of any wrongdoing (see *KJV Study Bible* note on Ps. 50:1). They affirmed that the altar had not been constructed for offering any kind of sacrifice. They confessed to acting in **fear** (v. 24)—because it might be said to the next generation, **What have you to do with the LORD God of Israel?** They realized that the Jordan River valley served as a natural boundary, cutting the eastern tribes off from the western ones. While Joshua feared that the isolation caused by the Jordan might turn Transjordanian Israelites from the worship of the Lord (22:5), these same Israelites feared that the isolation might

eventually cause their descendants to be rejected by the western tribes.

The altar is a **witness between us and you** (v. 27). Presumably, the altar was made of uncut stones (see 8:31; Exod. 20:25) and was to serve as a testimony to the commitment of the tribes across the Jordan to remain loyal to the Lord and their continued right to worship the Lord at the tabernacle, even though they lived outside the Land of Promise. Therefore, the altar had been built after the pattern of the altar of the Lord; that is, it was a huge replica (see 22:10). Thus, this altar constituted the sixth monument in the land (see discussion on 10:27).

22:30–34. While the intentions of these tribes may have been good, their actions were needless. According to Mosaic law, all of Israel's males were to appear before the Lord at the tabernacle three times a year (Exod. 23:17). God's plan called for unity of the tribes by faithfully meeting before Him for centralized worship at the place He chose. At this time, it was Shiloh. Nevertheless, when Phinehas and his delegation heard the explanation, **it pleased them** (lit., "it was good in their eyes"; v. 30). **Ye have delivered the children of Israel** (v. 31). The eastern tribes' words prevented the terrible punishment that the other tribes were about to inflict as a divine act of judgment (consider the implications of 22:20).

Reuben and **Gad** (v. 34), the tribes located nearest the newly built altar, gave it a name. Though the name is lacking in the Hebrew, it undoubtedly was 'Ed because it was meant to signify "a witness" (the Hebrew is 'ed) that **the LORD is God** of all Israel.

B. Joshua's Farewell Exhortation (chap. 23)

23:1–16. Joshua, the Lord's servant, delivered a farewell address recalling the victories the Lord had given but also reminding the people of areas yet to be possessed and of the need to be loyal to God's covenant laws. Their mission remained: to be the people of God's kingdom in the world.

23:1–2. The precise time of Joshua's address cannot be determined, but the land had been experiencing **rest** (v. 1; see discussions on 1:13; 21:44), and Joshua was now **old and stricken in age**, approaching the age of 110 (24:29). Compare Moses' physical condition at the time of his death, at the age of 120 (Deut. 34:7). Joshua summoned all Israel and all its official representatives, indicating the importance of this address.

23:3–5. You have seen all that the LORD your God has done (v. 3). In the subsequent verses (3–16), "the LORD your God" appears thirteen times. Joshua assumes no credit, nor should Israel, for what had been accomplished in taking the land. **The LORD … fought for you.** The Lord had promised to give Israel the land (1:2–4), and Joshua was to divide the land among the tribes (1:6). This he had done. **I have divided unto you** (v. 4), but he reminded Israel that decisions had been made **by lot.** It was the Lord who deserved the credit (see discussion on 13:7), and it was He who would **expel** (v. 5) the remaining inhabitants of the land so Israel could **possess their land** as He had promised.

23:6–13. Be ye therefore very courageous to keep and to do all that is written (v. 6). This admonition echoes the Lord's instructions at the beginning of the book (1:7–8) and Joshua's earlier words to the eastern tribes (22:5). The **book of the law** is a reference to canonical written materials from the time of Moses (see Deut. 30:10, 19; 31:9, 24, 26).

With regard to the nations, Joshua forbade Israel to **make mention of the name of their gods** (v. 7; see Deut. 13:2, 6, 13). After all, it was **the LORD** (v. 8) who had driven out the nations and had given their land to Israel. Therefore, he summarized, **love the LORD your God** (v. 11; see 22:5).

If ye do in any wise go back (v. 12) is a serious warning. Remaining in the Promised Land was conditioned on faithfulness to the Lord and separation from the idolaters still around them. Failure to meet these conditions would bring Israel's banishment from the land (see 23:13, 15–16; 2 Kings 17:7–8; 2 Chron. 7:14–20). Israel was to **cleave unto the LORD your God** (v. 8) but forbidden to **cleave unto** (v. 12) and **make marriages** with the nations around them. The Lord prohibited alliances, either national or domestic, with the peoples of Canaan because such alliances would tend to compromise Israel's loyalty to

the Lord (see Exod. 34:15–16; Deut. 7:2–4). It was impossible for Israel to serve two masters (see Matt. 6:24). Disloyalty to God would be to forfeit His help in removing enemy nations. They would become **snares and traps** (v. 13) to Israel. Joshua's warning echoes Exodus 23:33; 34:12; Deuteronomy 7:16 and forecasts disastrous times ahead (see Judg. 2:20–3:4).

23:14–16. Joshua concluded with, **I am going the way of all the earth** (v. 14), a euphemism for "I am about to die" (compare David's words, 2 Kings 2:2). Joshua's final observation was that **not one thing hath failed of all the good things which the LORD your God spake concerning you,** but he attached a somber warning. God's faithfulness was not restricted to blessing. He would be just as faithful in punishing **until he have destroyed you from off this good land** (v. 15) if His covenant was transgressed (see 8:33–35 for the rehearsal of blessings and curses at Mounts Ebal and Gerizim). The anger of the Lord would burn, and Israel would perish quickly from off the land if the covenant were transgressed (see Deut. 4:26; 11:17).

C. The Renewal of the Covenant at Shechem (24:1–28)

24:1–33. Once more Joshua assembled the tribes at Shechem to call Israel to a renewal of the covenant (see 8:30–35). This was his final official act as the Lord's servant, mediator of the Lord's rule over His people. In this, he followed the example of Moses, whose final official act was also a call to covenant renewal, of which Deuteronomy is the preserved document.

24:1. The unity of the tribes and the importance of the occasion is emphasized. **All the tribes of Israel** and all its official representatives were summoned to Shechem, a centrally located site in Ephraim and a most important site in Israel's history thus far (Gen. 12:6–7; 33:18–20; 35:1–4; Josh. 8:30–35). This was the second time Joshua was privileged to lead Israel in covenant renewal with the Lord at this place (see 8:30–35).

24:2–13. Thus saith the LORD (v. 2). Only a divinely appointed mediator would dare to speak for

God with direct discourse, as in verses 2–13. In accordance with the common ancient Near Eastern practice of making treaties (covenants), after the king (the Lord) identified himself (v. 2a), a brief recital of the past history of the relationship preceded the making of covenant commitments (vv. 3c–13). Seventeen times in these verses, the personal pronoun **I** (i.e., God) appears to emphasize His past benevolent acts for His covenant people.

In verses 2–4, God focuses on His separation of Abraham from his polytheistic family and the establishment of the patriarchs and their families in Canaan. From **the other side of the flood** (lit., "the river," i.e., the Euphrates; v. 3), the homeland of Abraham, where his fathers had **served other gods** (v. 2; see 24:14), God had called Abraham to Canaan (Gen. 11:31–12:5) by His electing grace and through special revelation of Himself.

In verses 5–12, God reiterates His deliverance of Israel from Egypt by means of the plagues, their passage through the **Red sea** (v. 6), and the Lord's establishment of His people in Canaan. Enroute to Canaan, He had given them the **land of the Amorites** in the Transjordan and thwarted the attempts of Israel's enemies to stymie them. **I would not hearken unto Balaam** (v. 10). Not only did the Lord reject Balaam's prayers; He also turned Balaam's curse into a blessing (Num. 23–24). The inhabitants west of the Jordan had also been delivered to Israel. **I sent the hornet** (v. 12). Lower (northern) Egypt had long used the hornet as a national symbol, so Egypt's military campaigns in Canaan may have been in mind. "The hornet" may also refer to the reports about Israel that spread panic among the Canaanites (2:11; 5:1; 9:24; see discussion on Exod. 23:28). And now Israel was enjoying the **land** given them, with its **cities ... vineyards and oliveyards** (v. 13; see Deut. 6:10–11).

24:14–24. Now therefore (v. 14). This was the hinge. If the details of 24:2–13 were not true, there would be no basis for the appeal that follows (vv. 14–24). Historical validity was at the heart of the spiritual application Joshua was about to make.

Joshua began his appeal with **Fear the Lord** (v. 14); that is, trust, serve, and worship Him. The

gods which your fathers served on the other side of the flood, and in Egypt were again mentioned (see 24:2; but Joshua pled with the Israelites to **put away the gods** their forefathers had worshiped in Mesopotamia and Egypt). In Ur and Haran, Terah's family would have been exposed to the worship of the moon god, Nanna(r), or Sin. The golden calf of Exodus 32:4 may be an example of their worship of the gods of Egypt. It was probably patterned after Apis, the sacred bull of Egypt (see *KJV Study Bible* note on Exod. 32:4). This appeal to put away the gods is sadly indicative of the religious syncretism already present among the Israelites.

Joshua's appeal may not have been popular, but he "drew a line in the sand." **As for me and my house, we will serve the Lord** (v. 15). Joshua publicly announced his commitment, hoping to elicit the same from Israel.

The Israelites responded quickly. Beginning with **the Lord our God** (v. 17) and ending with **he is our God** (v. 18), their reply is a sort of creedal statement, based on the miraculous events of the exodus. Joshua may have questioned their sincerity. **Ye cannot serve the Lord** (v. 19). These were strong words meant to emphasize the danger of overconfidence, but the people insisted, **we will serve the Lord** (v. 21).

Ye are witnesses (v. 22; see 24:27). In the ancient Near East, a normal part of making a treaty or covenant was to appeal to the gods to witness the transaction. Such an action would have been most inappropriate for the Lord and Israel, so Joshua declared that the people themselves were witnesses, as was the stone that he erected (4:27; see Deut. 30:19). To this, the people agreed.

Put away ... the strange gods (v. 23). The other gods were represented by idols of wood and metal, which could be thrown away and destroyed. To this, the people also agreed.

24:25–28. Joshua made a **covenant with the people** (v. 25), consisting of the pledges they had agreed to and the decrees and laws from God. He set up **a great stone** (v. 26) as a witness to the covenant renewal that closed his ministry. This is the seventh monument in the land reminding Israel of what the Lord had done for them through His servant (see discussion on 22:27). To these memorials were added the perpetual ruins of Jericho (6:26). Thus, the Promised Land itself bore full testimony to Israel (seven being the number of completeness) — how she had come into possession of the land and how she would remain in the land only by fulfilling the covenant conditions.

The stone was set up **under an oak, that was by the sanctuary** (lit., "the sacred/holy place") **of the LORD** (v. 26), perhaps a temporary location of the Tent of Meeting. A large tree was often a conspicuous feature at such holy places, and centuries earlier, Abraham had worshiped the Lord by a terebinth tree at Shechem (see discussion on Gen. 12:6.)

With the covenant renewed, the people were dismissed to their inheritance, hopefully with a renewed commitment to expel the remnant in the land (see 23:5).

D. The Death and Burial of Joshua and Eleazar (24:29–33)

The book concludes with three burials. Since it was a deep desire of the ancients to be buried in their homeland, these notices not only mark the conclusion of the story and the close of an era but also underscore the fact that Israel had indeed been established in the promised homeland — the Lord had kept His covenant.

24:29–31. Joshua died at the age of **an hundred and ten** (v. 29), the same age at which his forefather Joseph had died (for the significance of this number, see discussion on Gen. 50:26). He was buried **in the border of his inheritance in Timnath-serah** (v. 30;

see 19:50 and discussion). The story told in Joshua is a testimony to Israel's faithfulness in that generation, **all the days of Joshua, and … of the elders that outlived Joshua** (v. 31), but it closes here on a rather ominous note. The author anticipates the quite different story that would follow, recorded in the book of Judges.

24:32. Returning **the bones of Joseph** to Shechem was significant not only because of the plot of land Jacob bought from Hamor (Gen. 33:19) but also because Shechem was to be the center of the tribes of Ephraim and Manasseh, the two sons of Joseph. Also, the return fulfilled an oath sworn to Joseph on his deathbed (Gen. 50:25; Exod. 13:19).

24:33. Eleazar had been the high priest who served Joshua as Aaron had served Moses. He was buried on the **hill** that belonged to his son **Phinehas** (the Hebrew for "hill" is *Gibeah*, not the Benjamite city but a place in Ephraim near Shiloh). Though it is not directly stated, it is implied that Phinehas would now assume the position of high priest (see Num. 25:7–13; Judg. 20:28).

To summarize, this book has focused on God's faithfulness to His covenant with Abraham in giving his descendants the land of Canaan (see Gen. 12:7), His faithfulness to the people of Israel, and the blessing of success when they are obedient to His commands (see 1:8). The book now has ended with notification that Joshua and Eleazar, the principal leaders, have died. It remains to be seen what will happen with the next generation (see comment on v. 31). Will Israel remain obedient and successful? The unfortunate sequel of failure that occurs in the next book will find its explanation in the compromise and apostasy that unfold there.

THE BOOK OF JUDGES

INTRODUCTION

Title

The title of this book describes Israel's leaders from the time of the elders who outlived Joshua until the time of the monarchy. These leaders' principal purpose is best expressed in 2:16: "Nevertheless the LORD raised up judges, which delivered them out of the hand of those that spoiled them." Since it was God who permitted the oppressions and raised up deliverers, He Himself was Israel's ultimate Judge and Deliverer (11:27; see also 8:23, where Gideon, a judge, insists that the Lord is Israel's true ruler).

Author

According to tradition, Samuel wrote the book of Judges, but authorship is actually uncertain. It is possible that Samuel assembled some of the accounts from the period of the judges and that such prophets as Nathan and Gad, both of whom were associated with David's court, had a hand in shaping and editing the material (see 1 Chron. 29:29).

Date

The date of composition is also unknown, but it was undoubtedly during the monarchy. The frequent expression "In those days there was no king in Israel" (17:6; 18:1; 19:1; 21:25) suggests a date after the establishment of the monarchy. The observation that the Jebusites still controlled Jerusalem (1:21) has been taken to indicate a time before David's capture of the city, circa 1000 BC (see 2 Sam. 5:6–10). The new conditions in Israel alluded to in chapters 17–21 suggest a time after the Davidic dynasty had been effectively established (tenth century BC).

Background

Fixing precise dates for the judges is difficult and complex. The dating system followed here is based primarily on 1 Kings 6:1, which speaks of an interval of 480 years between the exodus and the fourth year of Solomon's reign. This would place the exodus around 1446 BC and the period of the judges between 1380 BC and the rise of Saul, 1050 BC. Jephthah's statement that Israel had occupied Heshbon for 300 years (11:26) generally agrees with these dates.

Some scholars maintain, however, that the number 480 in 1 Kings 6:1 is somewhat artificial, arrived at by multiplying twelve (perhaps in reference to the twelve judges) by forty (a conventional number of years for a generation). They point out the frequent use of the round numbers ten, twenty, forty, and eighty in the book of Judges itself. A later date for the exodus would of course require a much shorter period of time for the judges and would render meaningless the numbers describing the lengths of the judgeships and times of rest from oppression (see Exodus, Introduction: "Date").

Theme and Theological Message

The book of Judges describes the life of Israel in the Promised Land from the death of Joshua to the rise of the monarchy. On one hand, it is an account of frequent apostasy, provoking divine chastening. On the other hand, it tells of Israel's urgent appeals to God in times of crisis, moving the Lord to raise up leaders (judges), through whom He threw off foreign oppressors and restored the land to peace.

After Israel was established in the Promised Land through the ministry of Joshua, her pilgrimage ended. Many of the covenant promises God had given to the patriarchs in Canaan and to the fathers in the wilderness had now been fulfilled. The Lord's land, where Israel was to enter into rest, lay under her feet; it remained only for her to occupy it, to displace the Canaanites, and to cleanse it of paganism. The time had come for Israel to be the kingdom of God in the form of an established commonwealth on earth.

In Canaan, however, Israel quickly forgot the acts of God that had given her birth and had established her in the land. Consequently, she lost sight of her unique identity as God's people, chosen and called to be His army and the loyal citizens of His emerging kingdom. She settled the land and attached herself to Canaan's peoples, morals, gods, and religious beliefs and practices as readily as to Canaan's agricultural and social life.

Throughout Judges, the fundamental issue is the lordship of God in Israel, that is, Israel's acknowledgment of and loyalty to His rule. His kingship over Israel had been uniquely established by the covenant at Sinai (Exodus 19–24), which was later renewed by Moses on the plains of Moab (Deuteronomy 29) and by Joshua at Shechem (Joshua 24). The author accuses Israel of having rejected the kingship of the Lord again and again. She stopped fighting the Lord's battles, turned to the gods of Canaan to secure the blessings of family, flocks, and fields, and abandoned God's laws for daily living. In the very center of the cycle of the judges (see "Outline," below), Gideon had to remind Israel that the Lord was her King (see discussion on 8:23). The recurring lament, and indictment, of chapters 17–21 is, "In those days there was no king in Israel, but every man did that which was right in his own eyes" (see discussion on 17:6). The primary reference here is doubtless to the earthly mediators of the Lord's rule (i.e., human kings), but the implicit charge is that Israel did not truly acknowledge or obey her heavenly King either.

Only by the Lord's sovereign use of foreign oppression to chasten His people — thereby implementing the covenant curses (see Lev. 26:14–45; Deut. 28:15–68) — and by His raising up deliverers when His people cried out to Him did He maintain His kingship in Israel and preserve the embryonic kingdom from extinction. Israel's flawed condition was graphically exposed; she continued to need new saving acts by God to enter into the promised rest (see discussion on Josh. 1:13).

Out of the recurring cycles of disobedience, foreign oppression, cries of distress, and deliverance (see 2:11–19; Neh. 9:26–31) emerges another important theme: the covenant faithfulness of the Lord. The amazing patience and long-suffering of God are no better demonstrated than during this unsettled period.

Remarkably, this age of Israel's failure, following directly on the redemptive events that came through Moses and Joshua, is in a special way the Old Testament age of the Spirit. God's Spirit enabled men to accomplish feats of victory in the Lord's holy war against the powers that threatened His kingdom (see 3:10; 6:34; 11:29; 13:25; 14:6, 19; 15:14; 1 Sam. 10:6, 10; 11:6; 16:13). This same Spirit, poured out on the church following the redemptive work of the second Joshua (Jesus), empowered the people of the Lord to begin the task of preaching the gospel to all nations and of advancing the kingdom of God (see discussions on Acts 1:2, 8).

Literary Features

Even a quick reading of Judges discloses its basic threefold division: (1) a prologue (1:1–3:6), (2) a main body (3:7–16:31), and (3) an epilogue (chaps. 17–21). Closer study brings to light a more complex structure, with interwoven themes that bind the whole into an intricately designed portrayal of the character of an age.

The prologue (1:1–3:6) has two parts, and each serves a different purpose. They are not chronologically related, nor does either offer a strict chronological scheme of the time as a whole. The first part (1:1–2:5) sets the stage historically for the narratives that follow. It describes Israel's occupation of the Promised Land, from her initial success to her large-scale failure and divine rebuke.

The second part of the prologue (2:6–3:6) indicates a basic perspective on the period from the time of Joshua to the rise of the monarchy, a time characterized by recurring cycles of apostasy, oppression, cries of distress, and gracious divine deliverance. The author summarizes and explains the Lord's dealings with His rebellious people and introduces some of the basic vocabulary and formulas he will use in the later narratives: "did evil in the sight of the LORD" (2:11; see 3:7, 12; 4:1; 6:1; 10:6); "delivered them into the hands of" (2:14; see 6:1; 13:1); and "sold them" (2:14; see 3:8; 4:2; 10:7).

The main body of the book (3:7–16:31), which gives the actual accounts of the recurring cycles (apostasy, oppression, distress, deliverance), has its own unique design. Each cycle has a similar beginning ("The children of Israel did evil in the sight of the LORD"; see discussion on 3:7) and a recognizable conclusion ("the land had rest ... years" or the particular judge "judged Israel ... years"; see discussion on 3:11).

The main body of Judges is constructed around six cycles of oppression, repentance, and deliverance. The first of these (3:7–11) provides the "report form" used for each successive story. The six cycles include:

1. Othniel (3:7–11), Caleb's nephew who leads the tribe of Judah against Aramean invaders from the northeast.
2. Ehud (3:12–30), a lone hero from the tribe of Benjamin who delivers Israel from the oppression of the Moabites.

3. Deborah (chaps. 4–5), a woman from one of the Joseph tribes (Ephraim, west of the Jordan) who judges at a time when Israel is being overrun by a coalition of Canaanites under Jabin and Sisera.

4. Gideon (from the other Joseph tribe, Manasseh, west of the Jordan) and his son Abimelech (chaps. 6–9), who form the central account. In many ways, Gideon is the ideal judge, evoking the memory of Moses, while his son is the very antithesis of a responsible and faithful judge.

5. Jephthah (10:6–12:7), a social outcast also from the Joseph of Manasseh (but east of the Jordan) who judges at a time when Israel is being threatened by a coalition of powers under the king of Ammon.

6. Samson (chaps. 13–16), a lone hero from the tribe of Dan who delivers Israel from the oppression of the Philistines.

The arrangement of these narrative units is significant. The central accounts of Gideon (the Lord's ideal judge) and Abimelech (the anti-judge) are bracketed by the parallel narratives of Deborah and the social outcast Jephthah, which in turn are framed by the stories of the lone heroes Ehud and Samson. In this way, even the structure focuses attention on the crucial issue of the period of the judges: Israel's attraction to the Baals of Canaan (shown by Abimelech; see discussion on 9:1–57) versus the Lord's kingship over His people (encouraged by Gideon; see discussion on 8:23).

The epilogue (chaps. 17–21) characterizes the era in yet another way, depicting religious and moral corruption on the part of individuals, cities, and tribes. Like the introduction, it has two divisions that are neither chronologically related nor expressly dated to the careers of specific judges. The events must have taken place, however, rather early in the period of the judges (see discussions on 18:30; 20:1, 28).

By dating the events of the epilogue only in relationship to the monarchy (see the recurring refrain in 17:6; 18:1; 19:1; 21:25), the author contrasts the age of the judges with the better time that the monarchy inaugurated, undoubtedly having in view the rule of David and his dynasty (see discussion on 17:1–21:25). The book mentions two instances of the Lord's assigning leadership to the tribe of Judah: (1) in driving out the Canaanites (1:1–2) and (2) in disciplining a tribe in Israel (20:18). The author views the ruler from the tribe of Judah as the savior of the nation.

The first division of the epilogue (chaps. 17–18) relates the story of Micah's development of a paganized place of worship and tells of the tribe of Dan abandoning their allotted territory while adopting Micah's corrupted religion. The second division (chaps. 19–21) tells the story of a Levite's sad experience at Gibeah in Benjamin and records the disciplinary removal of the tribe of Benjamin because it had defended the degenerate town of Gibeah.

The two divisions have several interesting parallels:

1. Both involve a Levite's passing between Bethlehem (in Judah) and Ephraim across the Benjamin-Dan corridor.

2. Both mention six hundred warriors—those who led the tribe of Dan and those who survived from the tribe of Benjamin.

3. Both conclude with the emptying of a tribal area in that corridor (Dan and Benjamin).

Not only are these Benjamin-Dan parallels significant within the epilogue; they also form a notable link to the main body of the book. The tribe of Benjamin, which in the epilogue undertook to defend gross immorality, setting ties of blood above loyalty to the Lord, was the tribe from which the Lord raised up the deliverer Ehud (3:15). The tribe of Dan, which in the epilogue retreated from its assigned inheritance and adopted pagan religious practices, was the tribe from which the Lord raised up the deliverer Samson (13:2, 5). Thus, the tribes that in the epilogue depict the religious and moral corruption of Israel are the very tribes from which the deliverers were chosen, whose stories frame the central account of the book (Gideon and Abimelech).

The whole design of the book from prologue to epilogue, the unique manner in which each section deals with the age as a whole, and the way the three major divisions are interrelated clearly portray an age gone awry—an age when "there was no king in Israel" and "every man did that which was right in his own eyes" (see discussion on 17:6). Of no small significance is the fact that the story is in episodes and cycles. It is given as the story of all Israel, though usually only certain areas are directly involved. The book portrays the centuries after Joshua as a time of Israelite unfaithfulness to the Lord and of her surrender to the allurements of Canaan. Only by the mercies of God was Israel not overwhelmed and absorbed by the pagan nations around her. Meanwhile, however, the history of redemption virtually stood still, awaiting the forward thrust of the Lord's servant David and the establishment of his dynasty.

Outline

Bibliograhy

Block, Daniel I. *Judges, Ruth.* New American Commentary 6. Nashville: Broadman & Holman, 2002.

Boling, Robert G. *Judges: Introduction, Translation and Commentary.* Anchor Bible 6A. Garden City, NY: Doubleday, 1975.

Cohen, A. *Joshua and Judges: Hebrew Text and English Translation, with an Introduction and Commentary.* Soncino Books of the Bible. Jerusalem: Soncino, 1976.

Cundall, Arthur, and Leon Morris. *Judges and Ruth: An Introduction and Commentary.* Tyndale Old Testament Commentaries 7. Downers Grove, IL: InterVarsity, 1968.

Davis, John J. *Conquest and Crisis: Studies in Joshua, Judges, and Ruth.* Grand Rapids, MI: Baker, 1969.

Gray, John. *Joshua, Judges, Ruth.* New Century Bible Commentary. Grand Rapids, MI: Eerdmans, 1986.

Hamlin, E. J. *At Risk in the Promised Land: Judges.* Grand Rapids, MI: Eerdmans, 1990.

Hindson, Edward E. "Judges." In *The King James Version Bible Commentary.* Edited by Edward E. Hindson and Woodrow M. Kroll. Nashville: Nelson, 1999.

———. *Philistines and the Old Testament.* Grand Rapids, MI: Baker, 1972.

Nordern, Rudolph. *Parables of the Old Testament.* Grand Rapids, MI: Baker, 1964.

Soggin, J. Alberto. *Judges: A Commentary.* Old Testament Library. Philadelphia: Westminster, 1981.

Wood, Leon. *Distressing Days of the Judges.* Grand Rapids, MI: Zondervan, 1975.

EXPOSITION

I. Prologue: Incomplete Conquest and Apostasy (1:1–3:6)

1:1–3:6. The book of Judges picks up the story of Israel's attempts to settle the Promised Land. The introduction is in two parts: (1) an account of Israel's failure to lay complete claim to the Promised Land as the Lord had directed (1:1–36) and of His rebuke for their disloyalty (2:1–5); (2) an overview of the main body of the book (3:7–16:31), portraying Israel's rebellious ways in the centuries after Joshua's death and showing how the Lord dealt with her in that period (2:6–3:6). See Introduction: "Literary Features."

A. First Episode: Israel's Failure to Purge the Land (1:1–2:5)

1:1–36. The Lord assigned Judah leadership in occupying the land (v. 2; see 20:18). The tribe's vigorous efforts (together with those of Simeon) highlight by contrast the sad story of failure that follows. Only Ephraim's success at Bethel (vv. 22–26) breaks the monotony of that story.

1:1–3. The opening words, **after the death of Joshua** (v. 1), are noteworthy. The book of Judges, like that of Joshua, tells of an era following the death of a leading figure in the history of redemption (see Josh. 1:1). Joshua probably died circa 1390 BC. The battles under his leadership broke the power of the Canaanites to drive the Israelites out of the land. The task that now confronted Israel was the actual occupation of Canaanite territory (see discussions on Josh. 18:3; 21:43–45). Presumably, Israel **asked the LORD** through the high priest, who used the Urim and Thummim (see discussions on Exod. 28:30; 1 Sam. 2:28) to obtain divine direction. The main Israelite encampment was at Gilgal, near Jericho in the Jordan Valley (about 800 feet below sea level), while the Canaanite cities were mainly located in the central hill country (about 2,500–3,500 feet above sea level). Therefore, the tribes had to **go up** to fight the Canaanites.

Judah shall go up (v. 2). The book begins and ends (see 20:18) with Judah going up first to battle. The selection of Judah was appropriate. It was the largest of the tribes (Num. 26:22) and was also the first to be assigned territory west of the Jordan (Joshua 15). The leadership role of the tribe of Judah had been anticipated in the blessing of Jacob (Gen. 49:8–12).

Simeon (v. 3) was invited to assist Judah since it was a full-brother tribe (Gen. 29:33–35) and Joshua had assigned it cities within the territory of Judah (Josh. 19:1, 9; see Gen. 49:5–7).

1:4–7. Canaanites (v. 4) is a term that includes all the ethnic groups in the land of Canaan. In Joshua's campaigns, Israel had visited and defeated the major fortified cities within the land. Now it remained for each tribe to complete the task of ridding the Canaanites from its own portion of land. **Perizzites** may refer to rural inhabitants in contrast to city dwellers. The location of **Bezek** is unknown. Saul marshaled his army there before going to Jabesh-gilead (1 Sam. 11:9).

The name **Adoni-bezek** (v. 5) means "lord of Bezek." When Adoni-bezek was captured, the Israelites **cut off his thumbs and his great toes** (v. 6). Physically mutilating prisoners of war was a com-

mon practice in the ancient Near East (see discussion on 16:21). Such treatment was humiliating and rendered them unfit for military service. Harsh and inhumane as it appears, here it was an act of mercy and disobedience, for Israel had been commanded to destroy totally all of the inhabitants and allow none to live (see Deut. 7:1–2; 20:16).

Canaan was made up of many small city-states, each of which was ruled by a king. **Threescore and ten kings** (v. 7) may be a round number, or it may be symbolic of a large number of kings that Adoni-bezek subjected to eating **under** his **table**, humiliating treatment like that given to a dog (see Matt. 15:27; Luke 16:21). **God has requited me.** Adoni-bezek acknowledged that he justly deserved such treatment, a classic example of *lex talionis*, the law of "an eye for an eye" (see discussion on Exod. 21:23–25).

1:8–15. Judah fought against Jerusalem (v. 8). Although the city was defeated, it was not occupied by the Israelites at this time (see 1:21). Israel did not permanently control the city until David captured it, circa 1000 BC (2 Sam. 5:6–10). Also attacked in this campaign were **Hebron**, that is, **Kirjath-arba** (v. 10; see discussion on Josh. 14:15), and **Debir** (v. 11; see discussion on Josh. 10:38).

Caleb (v. 12), who, with Joshua, had brought back an optimistic report about the prospects of conquering Canaan (Num. 14:6–9), received the city of Hebron for his inheritance. He promised his **daughter to wife** to whoever took neighboring **Kirjath-sepher**. Victory in battle was one way to pay a woman's bride-price (see 1 Sam. 18:25). **Othniel** (v. 13), Caleb's relative (and the first major judge), took the city and claimed the reward of marrying Caleb's daughter **Achsah**.

Achsah requested that Caleb give her **springs of waters** (v. 15) and was given **the upper springs and the nether** (i.e., lower) **springs**. These springs water the local farms in Hebron even today.

1:16. Descendants of **the Kenite, Moses' father in law** (see Exod. 2:16; 18:1–12), who had accompanied Israel through its wilderness journey (see Num. 10:29–32), were still residing among the Israelites but decided to move from **the city of palm trees,**

Jericho (see Deut. 34:3), to the vicinity of **Arad** in southern Judah. Interestingly, one man, Heber, chose not to move with his clan but moved northward near Kedesh and became an ally of Jabin, the Canaanite king of Hazor (see 4:11, 17).

1:17–20. Judah (v. 17) fulfilled its commitment (1:3) to **Simeon** by assisting that tribe in taking its territory. **Gaza, Askelon**, and **Ekron** were three of the five main cities inhabited by the Philistines (see map, *Zondervan KJV Study Bible*, p. 313).

What follows is a virtual roll call of the ten western tribes' failures to completely conquer their territories. Judah **could not drive out the inhabitants of the valley** (v. 19). Judah's military success was largely in the hilly regions of its territory. In the plains, the Canaanites had a decided advantage, humanly speaking, because of their employment of horse-drawn **chariots of iron**. These were wooden vehicles with certain iron fittings, perhaps axles. Though Joshua and Israel had had success against the chariot-equipped northern Canaanites (Josh. 11:1–9), Judah tended to fear and did not persist in defeating these enemies. The sons of **Anak** (v. 20), the gigantic people who had terrorized Israel decades earlier (see *KJV Study Bible* notes on Num. 13:22, 33), were expelled by Caleb.

Israel failed to comply with God's command (Deut. 7:1–5; 20:16–18) to drive the Canaanites out of the land. Five factors were involved in that failure: (1) the Canaanites possessed superior weapons (v. 19); (2) Israel disobeyed God by making treaties with the Canaanites (2:1–3); (3) Israel violated the covenant the Lord had made with their forefathers (2:20–21); (4) God was testing Israel's faithfulness to obey His commands (2:22–23; 3:4); (5) God was giving Israel, as His army, the opportunity to develop her skills in warfare (3:1–2).

1:21–26. The **children of Benjamin did not drive out the Jebusites** (v. 21), the residents of Jerusalem (see discussion on 1:8). Jerusalem lay on the border between Benjamin and Judah but was allotted to Benjamin (Josh. 18:28).

The **house of Joseph** (v. 22) refers to Ephraim and West Manasseh. In taking **Beth-el** (see Gen. 12:8;

28:10–19; 35:1–8), they sent people **to descry** (v. 23), that is, "to spy out," the city. Comparable to the kindness extended to Rahab, they **let go the man** (v. 25) who informed them of the entrance into the city. He thus escaped to the **land of the Hittites** (v. 26), a name for Aram (Syria) at the time of the conquest.

1:27–33. The tribes listed in these verses— **Manasseh** (v. 27), **Ephraim** (v. 29), **Zebulun** (v. 30), **Asher** (v. 31), and **Naphtali** (v. 33)—are indicted for failing to drive the Canaanites out of their territories. The backdrop for Manasseh's and Ephraim's failure is noted in Joshua 17:16–18. In time, **when Israel was strong** enough (v. 28), the tribes put the Canaanites to **tribute**, that is, forced labor. Israel was permitted to use residents of foreign cities as forced laborers only if they lived outside the boundaries of the Promised Land (Deut. 20:11–17). Perhaps Joshua's earlier treatment of the Gibeonites (Josh. 9:23, 27) had set a precedent that Israel followed here.

1:34–36. The **Amorites forced the children of Dan into the mountain** (v. 34; see discussion on Gen. 10:16). Joshua had defeated the Amorites earlier (Josh. 10:5–11), but they were still strong enough to withstand the Danites. For this reason, a large number of Danites migrated northward a short time later (see chap. 18).

Their dwelling, **mount Heres** (v. 35), means "mountain of the sun [god]"; it was probably the Beth-shemesh in Judah, which was also called Irshemesh, "city of the sun [god]" (Josh. 19:41). The **coast of the Amorites** (v. 36), that is, their southern boundary (see Josh. 15:2–3), extended from **Akrabbim** (i.e., "Scorpion Pass") to **the rock**, that is, Sela in Edom.

2:1–5. Because Israel had not zealously laid claim to the land as the Lord had directed (see 1:27–36), He withdrew His helping hand. On this note, the first half of the introduction ends. Although the actual time of the Lord's rebuke is not indicated, it was probably early in the period of the judges and may even have been connected with the event in Joshua 18:1–3, or perhaps it precipitated one or both of Joshua's final recorded messages before his death (Joshua 23–24).

The designation **angel of the Lord** (v. 1; see discussion on Gen. 16:7) is never used of a human messenger or a prophet. The presence of the angel of the Lord always highlights the importance of the occasion and message. His role in this passage parallels that of the unnamed prophet in 6:8 – 10 and the word of the Lord in 10:11 – 14, calling Israel to account. He came from **Gilgal**, the place where Israel first became established in the land under Joshua (Josh. 4:19 – 5:12), to **Bochim**, meaning "weepers." This is the name of the place where the Israelites demonstrated their distress over the Lord's message by weeping (v. 4). Whether this term was applied on the occasion to an already well-known site, such as Bethel or Shiloh, or to some other hitherto unnamed site is unknown.

Out of Egypt (v. 1) is the theme of Exodus and is frequently referred to as the supreme evidence of God's redemptive love for His people (see Exod. 20:2). Israel was now in **the land** that God had sworn to give them (see Gen. 15:18; 17:8; 24:7; 50:24), and they were to **make no league with the inhabitants of the land** (v. 2). To do so would break their covenant with the Lord (see Exod. 23:32; Deut. 20:10 – 19).

B. Second Episode: God's Dealings with Israel's Rebellion (2:6 – 3:6)

2:6 – 3:6. The second half of the introduction continues the narrative of Joshua 24:28 – 31. It is a preliminary survey of the accounts narrated in Judges 3:7 – 16:31, showing that Israel's first centuries in the Promised Land were a recurring cycle of apostasy, oppression, cries of distress, and gracious deliverance (see Introduction: "Literary Features"). The author reminds Israel that she will enjoy God's promised rest in the Promised Land only when she is loyal to Him and to His covenant.

2:6 – 10a. These verses parallel Joshua 24:28 – 31. Either they are to be viewed as retrospective, a flashback to the last days of Joshua, or they are complementary to Judges 2:1 – 5; that is, after this solemn message, Joshua called Israel together (Joshua 23 – 24) for his final challenges and then dismissed the people to **possess** their **land** (v. 6).

On one hand, verse 7 is positive, declaring that Israel **served the Lord all the days of Joshua, and … of the elders that outlived Joshua**, but it is also ominous, strongly suggesting that Israel would not serve the Lord once Joshua and the present leadership died. In his obituary, Joshua, like Moses, is called the **servant of the Lord** (v. 8) and is identified as the Lord's official representative (see *KJV Study Bible* note on Exod. 14:31; discussion on Josh. 1:1).

2:10b – 19. The events and stories of the narrative of the judges are cyclic in nature and align or nearly align to the formulaic pattern introduced here. The six stages set forth in this pattern are: (1) Israel does evil in the Lord's eyes; (2) the Lord's anger burns, and He gives (or sells) Israel into the hand of an oppressor; (3) Israel cries to the Lord in distress; (4) the Lord raises up a deliverer; (5) the oppressor is defeated, and Israel is delivered; and (6) the land has rest from the oppressor.

A new **generation … which knew not the Lord, nor … the works he had done for Israel** (i.e., they had no direct experience of the Lord's acts; v. 10b) arose and **did evil in the sight of the Lord** (v. 11). This phrase introduces an important theme. It will be said of the Israelites seven more times in this book (3:7, 12; 4:1; 6:1; 10:6; 13:1). They served **Baalim** (i.e., the many local forms of this Canaanite deity) and **provoked the Lord to anger** (v. 12; see Deut. 4:25; Zech. 1:2).

Baal (v. 13) means "lord." Baal, the god worshiped by the Canaanites and Phoenicians, was variously known as the son of Dagon and the son of El. In Aram (Syria), he was called Hadad, and in Babylonia, Adad. Believed to give fertility to the womb and life-giving rain to the soil, he is pictured as standing on a bull, a popular symbol of fertility and strength (see 1 Kings 12:28). The storm cloud was his chariot, thunder was his voice, and lightning was his spear and arrows. The worship of Baal involved sacred prostitution and sometimes even child sacrifice (see Jer. 19:5). The stories of Elijah and Elisha (1 Kings 17 – 2 Kings 13), as well as many other Old Testament passages, directly or indirectly protest Baalism (e.g., Pss. 29:3 – 9; 68:1 – 4, 32 – 34; 93:1 – 5; 97:1 – 5;

Jer. 10:12–16; 14:22; Hos. 2:8, 16–17; Amos 5:8). **Ashtaroth** refers to the female deities such as Ashtoreth (the consort of Baal) and Asherah (the consort of El, the chief god of the Canaanite pantheon). Ashtoreth was associated with the evening star and was the beautiful goddess of war and fertility. She was worshiped as Ishtar in Babylonia and as Athtart in Aram. To the Greeks, she was Astarte or Aphrodite, and to the Romans, Venus. Worship of the Ashtoreths involved extremely lascivious practices (see 1 Kings 14:24; 2 Kings 23:7).

2:14–15. Israel's problems were never political, but spiritual. Israel's apostasy brought the Lord's anger against them. He **delivered them** (v. 14; see 6:1; 13:1) and **sold them** (3:8; 4:2; 10:7), the very people He had "purchased" (Exod. 15:16) and redeemed (Exod. 15:13; see Ps. 74:2).

2:16–19. The Lord was merciful to His people in times of distress, sending deliverers to save them from oppression. Israel continually forgot these saving acts, just as she had forgotten those He had performed through Moses and Joshua. The deliverers are called **judges** (v. 16). See Introduction: "Title." There were six major judges (Othniel, Ehud, Deborah, Gideon, Jephthah, and Samson) and six minor ones (Shamgar, Tola, Jair, Ibzan, Elon, and Abdon). Never is it said of Israel that they served the Lord while the judge remained alive (see 2:7), only that Israel became more corrupt after the judge died. Why? Because they had not ceased **their stubborn way** (v. 19).

Went a whoring after other gods (v. 17) is a graphic phrase. Since the Hebrew for Baal (meaning "lord") was also used by women to refer to their husbands, it is understandable that the metaphor of adultery was commonly used in connection with Israelite worship of Baal (see Hos. 2:2–3, 16–17).

When Israel cried out in distress, God heard their **groanings** (v. 18) because they were **oppressed**. The language is reminiscent of the Egyptian bondage (see Exod. 2:24; 3:9; 6:5).

2:20–23. The second rebuke of the chapter (see 2:1–5) concludes with the Lord's decision to leave the remaining nations in the land to test Israel's loyalty, through the very nations they had failed to drive out.

3:1–6. The list of nations the Lord left in the land (see 2:23) roughly describes an arc along the western and northern boundaries of the area actually occupied by Israel at the death of Joshua (vv. 1–4). Within Israelite-occupied territory, there were large groups of native peoples (v. 5; see 1:27–36) with whom the Israelites intermingled, often adopting their religions (v. 6).

As His covenant servant, Israel was the Lord's army for fighting against the powers of the world that were settled in His land. Therefore, God purposed **to teach** the Israelites **war** (v. 2). In view of the incomplete conquest, succeeding generations in Israel needed to become capable warriors.

Five lords (v. 3) had control of a five-city confederacy: Ashdod, Ashkelon, Ekron, Gath, and Gaza. At one point, Judah had defeated three of these cities (1:18) but had been unable to hold them. The Hebrew for "lords" is related to the word "tyrant" (see discussion on Josh. 13:3) and is used only of Philistine rulers. The Philistines were also called "sea peoples" in nonbiblical texts. They controlled the coast of Israel during the period of the judges. **Sidonians** is used here collectively of the Phoenicians. **Hivites** is here identified with a region in northern Canaan reaching all the way to Hamath (see also Josh. 11:3). **Mount Baal-hermon** is probably Mount Hermon (see 1 Chron. 5:23).

Contrary to Moses' and Joshua's clear warnings (Deut. 7:2–4; Josh. 23:7, 12), **Israel dwelt among the Canaanites ... took their daughters ... and served their gods** (vv. 5–6). The degenerating effect of such intermarriage is well illustrated in Solomon's experience (1 Kings 11:1–8).

II. Oppression and Deliverance (3:7–16:31)

A. Othniel Defeats Mesopotamia (3:7–11)

3:7–11. In the account of Othniel's judgeship, the author provides the basic literary form he uses in his accounts of the major judges (i.e., beginning statement; cycle of apostasy, oppression, distress, deliverance; recognizable conclusion), adding only the brief details necessary to complete the report (see Introduction: "Literary Features").

Israel did evil in the sight of the LORD (v. 7). This recurring expression (see discussion on 2:11) is used to introduce the cycles of the judges. For **Baalim** and **the groves** (Hebrew, *Asheroth* [plural of *Asherah*]; female fertility deities often represented in wooden poles or tree trunks near altars or shrines; see discussion on 2:13; *KJV Study Bible* note on Exod. 34:13).

Chushan-rishathaim (v. 8) probably means "doubly wicked Cushan," perhaps a caricature of his actual name (see discussion on 10:6 regarding Baal-zebub), or perhaps a name given him by his enemies. Undoubtedly a petty king from **Mesopotamia**, Chushan-rishathaim has not been identified in extrabiblical sources.

Israel cried unto the LORD (v. 9). The Israelites' cries of distress due to their hardship occur in each recurring cycle of the judges. Never does it connote Israel's repentance. Only once in this book does Israel appear to repent (10:15–16), but even then, God questions their sincerity, and they select their own deliverer.

Othniel (v. 9) has already been recognized as a successful warrior (1:13). Here the **spirit of the LORD came upon him** (v. 10; see Num. 11:25–29) and empowered him to deliver His people, as He would do for Gideon (6:34), Jephthah (11:29), Samson (14:6, 19), and also David (1 Sam. 16:13).

A recognizable conclusion to the cycle of a judge is seen in the phrase **the land had rest ... years** (v. 11; noted only here and in 3:30; 5:31; 8:28). After the judgeship of Gideon, this formula is replaced by "judged Israel ... years" (12:7; 15:20; 16:31). Whether **forty years** is a literal number or a conventional round number of years for a generation is debated (see Introduction: "Background").

B. Ehud Defeats Moab (3:12–30)

3:12–30. The second cycle ends with Ehud's triumph over the king of Moab. Ehud, a left-handed Benjamite, was an authentic hero. All alone, and purely by his wits, he cut down the king of Moab, who had established himself in Canaan near Jericho. This account balances that of Samson in the five narrative units central to the book of Judges (see Introduction: "Literary Features").

Eglon the king of Moab (v. 12) brought the **children of Ammon and Amalek** (v. 13), the descendants of Esau (Gen. 36:12, 16) who lived in the Negev (Num. 13:29), into an alliance with him. (For the Moabites and the Ammonites, see discussion on Gen. 19:37–38.) After crossing the Jordan and smiting Israel, he set up his headquarters in **the city of palm trees**, Jericho (see Deut. 34:3).

The children of Israel (v. 14) most affected by Eglon's occupancy would have been Benjamin and Ephraim, the tribes located closest to Jericho. God's deliverer was Ehud, **a Benjamite, a man lefthanded** (lit., "restricted in his right hand"; v. 15). Lefthandedness was noteworthy among Benjamites (see 20:15–16), which is ironic since Benjamin means "son of [my] right hand." Being left-handed, Ehud could conceal his dagger on the side where it was not expected (see v. 21). He was a man of integrity, having been selected by Israel to carry a **present** (i.e., an annual payment; vv. 15, 18), perhaps of agricultural products, as the need of porters (v. 18) would attest (see 2 Kings 3:4).

Ehud made a dagger which had two edges (v. 16). During the period of the judges, Israelite weapons were often fashioned or improvised for the occasion (see 1 Sam. 13:19). Examples of this are Shamgar's ox goad (3:31), Jael's tent peg (4:22), Gideon's pitchers and lamps (7:20), the woman's millstone (9:53), and Samson's donkey jawbone (15:15).

Ehud returned to Eglon from the **quarries** (lit., "carved [stone] things"; v. 19), a Hebrew word frequently used for stone idols. Here the reference may be to carved stone statues of Eglon, marking the boundary of the territory he now claimed as part of his expanded realm—a common practice in the ancient Near East. Eglon was in a **summer parlour** (v. 20), that is, a roof chamber. Rooms were built on the flat roofs of houses (2 Kings 4:10–11) and palaces (Jer. 22:13–14), with latticed windows (2 Kings 1:2) that provided comfort in the heat of summer. Ehud's secret **errand** (v. 19) and **message from God**

(v. 20), different translations of the same Hebrew word, aroused the interest of Eglon, who rose from his seat and met his death.

Ehud's actions were calculated. He not only assassinated Eglon in secrecy; he also provided himself sufficient time to rouse an army. By the time the corpse of the king was discovered and confusion had broken out in the camp, Edud and his troops were in position to guard **the fords** (v. 28) of the Jordan. This move prevented the Moabites from sending reinforcements and also enabled the Israelites to cut off the Moabites fleeing Jericho.

1. First Minor Judge: Shamgar (3:31)

3:31. **Shamgar** is the first of six minor judges and a contemporary of Deborah (see 5:6–7). His name is foreign, so he may not have been an Israelite, or perhaps his name reflects religious syncretism. **Son of Anath** indicates either that Shamgar came from the town of Beth-anath (see 1:33) or that his family worshiped the goddess Anath. Since Anath, Baal's sister, was a goddess of war who fought for Baal, the expression "son of Anath" may have been a military title, meaning "a warrior." His weapon was an **ox goad**, which was a long, wooden rod, sometimes with a metal tip, used for driving draft animals (see 1 Sam. 13:21).

C. Deborah Defeats Canaan (chaps. 4–5)

4:1–5:31. The third cycle shows Deborah's triumph over Sisera (the commander of a Canaanite army), which is first narrated in prose (chap. 4) and then celebrated in song (chap. 5). At the time of the Canaanite threat from the north, Israel remained incapable of united action until a woman, Deborah, summoned them to the Lord's battle. Because the warriors of Israel lacked the courage to rise up and face the enemy, the glory of victory went to a woman, Jael—and she may not have been an Israelite.

4:1–3. Except for the Canaanites, Israel's enemies came from outside the territory she occupied. Nations such as Mesopotamia, Moab, Midian, and Ammon were mainly interested in plunder, but the Canaanite uprising of chapters 4–5 was an attempt to restore Canaanite power in the north. The Philistines engaged in continual struggle with Israel for permanent control of the land in the southern and central regions.

The name **Jabin** (v. 2) was possibly a royal name rather than a personal name. Joshua is credited with having earlier slain a king by the same name (Josh. 11:1, 10). **Hazor** was the original royal city of the Jabin dynasty; or perhaps it was thriving once again (see discussion on Josh. 11:10) because the Israelites had not prevented the Canaanites from returning and restoring the city. **Sisera**, who sought to recover the territory once ruled by the kings of Hazor, had a name that suggests he was not a Canaanite. The location of **Harosheth**, the camp of Sisera's chariot force, is uncertain, though it was probably situated toward the western end of the Esdraelon plain near Mount Carmel.

The number **nine hundred** (v. 3) likely represents the chariot force of a coalition rather than of one city. In the fifteenth century BC, Pharaoh Thutmose III boasted of having captured 924 chariots at the battle of Megiddo. **The children of Israel** most affected by Sisera were the tribes of Zebulun and Naphtali, but West Manasseh, Issachar, and Asher were also affected.

4:4–5. The name **Deborah** (v. 4) means "bee." She is the only judge said to have been a prophet(ess). Other women spoken of as prophetesses are Miriam (Exod. 15:20), Huldah (2 Kings 22:14), Noadiah (Neh. 6:14), and Anna (Luke 2:36), but see also Acts 21:9. The Hebrew text emphasizes Deborah's gender: she was a woman, a prophetess, and a wife. Normally, God called a man. At this particular time, however, godly male leadership must have been lacking in Israel, for Deborah was recognized by Israel as a judge, and it was necessary for her, a woman, to prod Barak, a man, into military duty. She lived in **mount Ephraim** (v. 5) about fifty miles south of the Esdraelon plain.

4:6–7. The name **Barak** (v. 6) means "thunderbolt," which suggests that he was summoned to be the Lord's "glittering sword" (Deut. 32:41). He is named among the heroes of faith in Hebrews

11:32. Kedesh-naphtali was a town affected by the Canaanite oppression. **Mount Tabor** was a conical shaped mountain about 1,300 feet high, situated on the northern edge of the Esdraelon plain and northeast of the proposed battle site. It was a prominent landmark, and its steep slopes provided safety from Sisera's chariots. Barak's troops were to be selected from **Naphtali and ... Zebulun.** Issachar, a near neighbor of these tribes, is not mentioned here but is included in the poetic description of the battle in 5:15. In all, six tribes are mentioned as having participated in the battle. Barak's hesitancy to raise troops is understandable since he lived nearby, yet his reluctance is inexcusable since the Lord had assured him a victory.

With the Israelites encamped on the slopes of mount Tabor, safe from chariot attack, the Lord's strategy was to draw Sisera into a trap. For the battle site, God chose the Valley of Jezreel along the Kishon River, where Sisera's chariot forces would have ample maneuvering space to range the battlefield and attack in numbers from any quarter. That was Sisera's undoing, for he did not know the power of the Lord, who would fight from heaven for Israel with storm and flood (see 5:20–21), as He had done in the days of Joshua (Josh. 10:11–14). Even in modern times, storms have rendered the plain along the Kishon virtually impassable. In April of 1799, the flooded Kishon River aided Napoleon's victory over a Turkish army.

4:8–9. Barak's timidity (and that of Israel's other warriors, whom he exemplified) was due to a lack of trust in the Lord, and he was thus rebuked.

Sisera would fall into the hand of **a woman** (v. 9). Barak probably assumed that since he demanded the company of Deborah, a confirmed prophet and judge, the honor of victory over Sisera would go to her.

4:11. The narrative is interrupted to introduce **Heber the Kenite.** Since one meaning of Heber's name is "ally," and since "Kenite" identifies him as belonging to a clan of metalworkers, the author hints at the truth that this man, a member of a people allied with Israel since the days of Moses, had moved from south to north to ally himself (see v. 17) with

the Canaanite king who was assembling a large force of chariots of iron. Possibly, Heber is the one who informed Sisera of Barak's military preparations. His clan, **the Kenites,** who had settled in the south not far from Kadesh-barnea in the Negev (see 1:16), were related to **Hobab,** Moses' father-in-law (Num. 10:29). Sisera was unaware that Jael, Heber's wife, had remained loyal to the Israelites (4:18–21).

4:12–16. As Sisera prepared for battle, Deborah instructed Barak to proceed to certain victory. **Is not the Lord gone out before thee?** (v. 14). The Lord was as a king at the head of His army (see 1 Sam. 8:20); He was "a man of war" (see also Exod. 15:3; Josh. 10:10–11; 2 Sam. 5:24; 2 Chron. 20:15–17, 22–24). **Barak,** the Lord's "thunderbolt" (see discussion on 4:6), **went down from mount Tabor** to attack the Canaanite army, and Sisera was **discomfited** (v. 15). The Hebrew for this word is also used of the panic that overcame the Egyptians at the Red Sea (Exod. 14:24) and the Philistines at Mizpeh (1 Sam. 7:10). Apparently, Sisera had been lured into battle near the river (vv. 7, 13) during ideal weather conditions, and then God brought a surprise cloudburst on the area, for "the river of Kishon swept them away" (5:21; see Ps. 83:9). The foot soldiers of Barak now had the advantage over the mud-clogged chariots of Sisera, so that even he fled for his life on foot.

4:17–19. Sisera fled to his ally, Heber, whose wife, **Jael** (v. 17), played the perfect hostess and invited him into her tent. Since ancient Near Eastern custom prohibited any man other than a woman's husband or father from entering her tent, Jael seemed to offer Sisera an ideal hiding place. **When he had turned in unto her ... tent** (v. 18), she covered him and offered him a **bottle** (i.e., a container made from the skin of a goat or lamb) **of milk** (v. 19; see discussion on 5:25). Jael, whose name means "mountain goat," gave him milk to drink, and it was most likely goat's milk (see Exod. 23:19; Prov. 27:27). It proved to be soporific, for he fell asleep.

4:20–21. Women commonly erected and took down tents, so Jael knew how to wield a mallet and tent peg. She **smote the nail** (i.e., tent peg) **into his temples, and ... into the ground** (v. 21). The laws of hospitality normally meant that one tried to protect a guest from any harm (see 19:23; Gen. 19:8). Jael remained true to her family's previous alliance with Israel (she may not have been an Israelite) and so undid her husband's deliberate breach of faith. Armed only with domestic implements, this dauntless woman destroyed the great warrior whom Barak had earlier feared, fulfilling Deborah's prediction that a woman would receive the honor of defeating Sisera (v. 9).

4:22–24. When the pursuing Barak arrived, **Sisera lay dead** (v. 22). With Sisera dead, the kingdom of Jabin was no longer a threat. The land "flowing with milk and honey" had been saved by the courage and faithfulness of "Bee" (see discussion on 4:4) and "Mountain Goat" (see discussion on 4:19).

5:1–31. Commemorating a national victory with songs was a common practice (see Exod. 15:1–18; Num. 21:27–30; Deut. 32:1–43; 1 Sam. 18:7). The "book of the wars of the LORD" (see *KJV Study Bible* note on Num. 21:14) and the "book of Jasher" (see discussion on Josh. 10:13) were probably collections of such songs.

The song commemorating Israel's victory over Sisera was probably written by Deborah (see v. 7) and is thus one of the oldest poems in the Bible. It highlights some of the central themes of the narrative (see Exod. 15:1–18; 1 Sam. 2:1–10; 2 Sam. 22; 23:1–7; Luke 1:46–55, 68–79). In particular, it celebrates before the nations (v. 3) the righteous acts of the Lord and of His warriors (v. 11). The song may be divided into the following sections: (1) the purpose of the song (praise) and the occasion of the deeds it celebrates (vv. 2–9); (2) the exhortation to Israel to act in accordance with her heroic past (vv. 10–11a); (3) the people's appeal to Deborah (vv. 11b–12); (4) the gathering of warriors (vv. 13–18); (5) the battle (vv. 19–23); (6) the crafty triumph of Jael over Sisera (vv. 24–27); (7) the anxious waiting of Sisera's mother (vv. 28–30); and (8) the conclusion (v. 31).

5:2–5. In her praise of the Lord, Deborah links Israel's most recent victory over the Canaanites to a poetic recalling of the Lord's terrifying appearance in a storm cloud many years before, when He had brought Israel from Sinai through **Seir** (i.e., Mount Seir in Edom; v. 4) to give His people the land of Canaan (see Deut. 33:2; Ps. 68:7–8; Hab. 3:3; see also Ps. 18:7–15). **The heavens … dropped water … the mountains melted** (vv. 4–5); that is, a thunderstorm and an earthquake had occurred when God appeared at Mount **Sinai** (v. 5; see Exod. 19:16–18; Ps. 68:8).

5:6. In the days of **Shamgar** (see discussion on 3:31), **the highways were unoccupied.** Because of enemy garrisons and marauding bands (see discussion on 4:1–3), the roads were unsafe, so fearful travelers and traders instead took circuitous routes to their destinations.

5:7–12. Due to oppressive conditions, **inhabitants of the villages ceased** (v. 7); that is, inhabitants of small villages fled to walled towns for protection. Deborah was **a mother** to more than her own children. Aware of the chaotic times and due to her role (see 4:4), she became a protector and guardian of Israel.

Because Israel **chose new gods** (v. 8; see 2:12, 17; 3:6–7), **war** began. **A shield or spear** was not **seen … in Israel**, either because Israel had made peace with the native Canaanites (3:5–6) or because she had been disarmed (see 1 Sam. 13:19–22) and could not defend herself.

Those **that ride on white asses** (v. 10) is an allusion to the nobles and the wealthy (see 10:4; 12:14). The Hebrew for **noise of archers** (v. 11) is difficult, and the meaning is uncertain. The leaders are encouraged by those at the watering places who rehearse the past heroic achievements of the Lord and His warriors.

Awake, awake (v. 12), normally a plea to take action (see Ps. 44:23; Isa. 51:9), indicates that Deborah may have needed rousing to become involved in Israel's deliverance from the Canaanites, and Barak was told: **lead thy captivity captive;** that is, take captive your captives. This is essentially a promise of success (see 4:7). The same action is applied to God in Psalm 68:18 and to Christ in Eph. 4:8.

5:13–18. Barak's call (4:10) did not go unheeded. A roll call of the Lord's warriors who gathered for the battle is given. The tribes who came were **Ephraim** (v. 14), **Benjamin**, Manasseh (**Machir** is possibly both East and West Manasseh; see Deut. 3:15; Josh. 13:29–31; 17:1), **Zebulun** (vv. 14, 18), **Issachar** (v. 15), and **Naphtali** (v. 18). Especially involved were Zebulun and Naphtali (v. 18; see 4:10), the tribes most immediately affected by Sisera's tyranny. **Reuben** (vv. 15–16) and **Gad** (referred to as **Gilead** in v. 17), from east of the Jordan, and **Dan** and **Asher** (v. 17), from along the coast, are rebuked for not responding. Judah and Simeon are not even mentioned, perhaps because they were already engaged with the Philistines. Levi is not mentioned because that tribe did not have military responsibilities in the theocracy (kingdom of God).

5:19. **Megiddo** and **Taanach** dominated the main pass that runs northeast through the hill country from the plain of Sharon to the Valley of Jezreel. Because of its strategic location, the "valley of Megiddo" (2 Chron. 35:22) has been a frequent battleground from the earliest times. There, Pharaoh Thutmose III defeated a Canaanite coalition in 1468 BC, and in AD 1917, British troops under General Allenby ended the rule of the Turks in Palestine by vanquishing them in the Valley of Jezreel, opposite Megiddo. In biblical history, the forces of Israel under Deborah and Barak crushed the Canaanites **by the waters of Megiddo** (v. 19). In the same locations, Judah's good king Josiah died in battle against Pharaoh Neco II in 609 BC (2 Kings 23:29). Revelation 16:16 refers to "a place called in the Hebrew tongue Armageddon" (i.e., "mount Megiddo") as the site of the "battle of that great day of God Almighty" (Rev. 16:14).

5:20–22. The stars … fought against Sisera (v. 20). Deborah uses an idea from Canaanite mythology, that the stars were the source of rain, to poetically describe how God's sudden thunderstorm **swept** the Canaanites **away** (v. 21; see discussions on 4:7, 12–16), who frantically tried to escape.

5:23. Special, but not honorary, mention is given to **Meroz**. Because of its refusal to help the army of the Lord, this Israelite town in Naphtali was cursed. Other cities were also punished severely for refusing

to participate in the wars of the Lord (see 8:15–17; 21:5–10).

5:24–27. Blessed above women shall Jael … be (v. 24). The honor predicted for a woman (4:9) belonged to Jael. She is praised for killing Sisera. He came asking for **water**; she put him to sleep by giving him **butter** (lit., "curds"; v. 25), that is, artificially soured milk made by shaking milk in a skin bottle and then allowing it to ferment (due to bacteria that remained in the skin from previous use). Verse 26–27, describing Jael striking Sisera, crushing his head, shattering and piercing his skull, add vivid and gruesome detail to the simple statement found in 4:21.

5:28–30. Only a woman and mother, like Deborah, could have understood the anguish of Sisera's mother as she awaited the return of her son from battle, encouraged by those who were confident of his victory but unaware of his defeat and death. This graphic picture of Sisera's anxious mother heightens the triumph of Jael over the powerful Canaanite general and presents a contrast between this mother in Canaan and the triumphant Deborah, "a mother in Israel" (5:7).

5:31. The song ends with a prayer that the present victory would be the pattern for all future battles against the Lord's enemies (see Num. 10:35; Ps. 68:1–2). **Enemies** and **them that love him** reflect the two basic attitudes of people toward the Lord. As Lord of the covenant and the royal Head of His people Israel, He demanded their love (see Exod. 20:6), just as kings in the ancient Near East demanded the love of their subjects.

D. Gideon Defeats Midian (chaps. 6–8)

6:1–9:57. The Gideon and Abimelech narratives are a literary unit and constitute the center account of the judges. They are bracketed by the stories of Deborah (from Ephraim, a son of Joseph; west of the Jordan) and Jephthah (from Manasseh, the other son of Joseph; east of the Jordan), which in turn are bracketed by the stories of the heroes Ehud (from Benjamin) and Samson (from Dan). In this center narrative, the crucial issues of the period of the judges are emphasized: the worship of Baal and the Lord's kingship over His covenant people Israel (see discussion on 8:23).

6:1–5. The fourth cycle of oppression was led by **Midian** (v. 1). The Midianites were descendants of one of the sons born to Abraham by Keturah (Gen. 25:2; see discussion on Gen. 37:25; *KJV Study Bible* note on Exod. 2:15). Since they were apparently not numerous enough to wage war against the Israelites alone, they often formed coalitions with surrounding peoples, as with the Moabites (Num. 22:4–6; 25:6–18), the Amalekites, and other tribes from the east (v. 3). Israel's defeat of Midian was an event long remembered in Hebrew history (see Ps. 83:9; Isa. 9:4; 10:26).

The **Amalekites** (v. 3), descendants of Esau's grandson (Gen. 36:12), were normally a people of the Negev, but they had assisted Eglon and the Moabites (3:12–13) and were now in a coalition with the Midianites and other eastern peoples, who were nomads from the desert east of Moab and Ammon.

The coalition's forces came in such hordes that they were likened to **grasshoppers for multitude** (v. 5), a vivid picture of the marauders who swarmed across the land, leaving it stripped bare (see 7:12; Exod. 10:13–15; Joel 1:4). Their camp was in the Valley of Jezreel (v. 33), so the tribes closest to that site (Manasseh, Asher, Zebulun, and Naphtali) were most affected by their presence. Their raids, however, were also experienced down the western coastal plain, as far the Philistine city of Gaza. The raids claimed Israel's crops and cattle, fulfilling Moses' prediction of what would happen if Israel disobeyed the Lord (see Lev. 26:14–16; Deut. 28:15, 31–33). This is the earliest Old Testament reference to the use of mounted **camels** in warfare.

6:6–10. The impoverished Israelites **cried unto the Lord** (v. 6) in their distress, but there is no evidence of repentance. Thus, an unnamed **prophet** (v. 8) rebuked Israel for forgetting that the Lord had saved them from Egyptian bondage and had given them the land. Note the contrast of God's constant care and Israel's ungrateful disobedience (vv. 9–10).

See the message at Bochim (2:1–3), which also cited the reason for Israel's misfortune. The reference to **Amorites** (v. 10) here probably includes all the inhabitants of Canaan (see discussion on Gen. 10:16).

6:11–12. For the **angel of the Lord** (v. 11), see discussion on 2:1. **Ophrah**, to be distinguished from the Benjamite Ophrah (Josh. 18:23), was located in northern East Manasseh, in the general area where the Midianites were gathered. The **Abi-ezrite[s]** (v. 11) were a clan from the tribe of Manasseh (Josh. 17:2). **Gideon threshed wheat by the winepress**. The threshing of one's grain normally was done in open areas where the wind could blow away the chaff (see discussion on Ruth 1:22). Gideon's presence at the winepress, probably a hollow carved out of rock, shows his awareness of the nearby Midianites and his determination to salvage some of his grain from their raids. He felt more secure threshing in this better-protected but very confined space.

The angel of the Lord called Gideon a **mighty man of valour** (v. 12) sarcastically to get his attention. Apparently, Gideon belonged to the upper class, perhaps a kind of aristocracy (see 6:27), in spite of his disclaimer in 6:15. His general sense of fear is evident throughout his initial encounters with God (6:27; 7:10–11).

6:13–18. Oh my lord (v. 13). The Hebrew for "my lord" is *Adoni*, a term used of man. Apparently, Gideon did not fully realize the identity of his visitor until later (see vv. 22–23). His complaint is that **all** God's **miracles which our fathers told us of** (v. 13) were only past memories.

The **Lord looked upon him** (v. 14). The name is now "Lord." Apparently, this appearance of the "angel of the Lord" (6:11) was a theophany (a manifestation of God), or more particularly a Christophany (appearance of Christ). **Go … have not I sent thee?** Gideon was commissioned to deliver Israel, as Moses had been (Exod. 3:7–10).

Wherewith shall I save Israel? (v. 15). Gideon regarded himself as the **least in my father's house**, someone of little significance. The Lord, however, usually calls the lowly, rather than the mighty, to act for Him (see discussion on 1 Sam. 9:21). **I will be**

with thee (v. 16). Like Barak (4:6–7), Gideon received the promise of God's presence and victory.

Shew me a sign (v. 17). More requests for signs would follow (see 6:36–40). Compare the signs the Lord gave Moses as assurance that He would be with him in his undertaking (Exod. 3:12; 4:1–17).

6:19–24. Gideon's offering was quite substantial for a time of oppression. Fire **consumed the flesh and ... the cakes** (v. 21) of his offering, indicating that it was accepted (see Lev. 9:24). **O Lord God!** (v. 22). Now Gideon knew the true identity of his visitor—the **angel of the Lord**, for he had seen him **face to face** (see Gen. 32:30). Having received assurance, **thou shalt not die** (v. 23; see 13:22), he named the place **Jehovah-shalom** (v. 24); that is, "Jehovah is peace."

6:25–30. Joash, Gideon's father, was involved in the Baal cult, and his altar apparently served the whole community. Gideon's first task as the Lord's warrior was to **throw down** (i.e., tear down) **the altar of Baal** (v. 25), as Israel had been commanded to do (see 2:2; Exod. 34:13; Deut. 7:5). For **Baal** and **the grove** (Hebrew, *Asherah*), see discussion on 2:13; *KJV Study Bible* note on Exodus 34:13. Gideon was to offer his father's special bull (which may have been reserved for Baal) on a newly erected altar to the Lord **in the ordered place** (v. 26), that is, a proper kind of altar (see Exod. 20:25). Assuming that such an action would be met with resistance, Gideon obeyed **by night** (v. 27), with the assistance of **ten ... servants.**

His fears were not unfounded. **The men of the city** (v. 30) ordered Gideon's father to **Bring out thy son, that he may die.** The Israelites were so apostate that they were willing to kill one of their own people for the cause of Baal (compare Deut. 13:6–10, where God told Moses that idolaters must be stoned).

6:31–32. After Joash scorned the men of the city for attempting to defend Baal, he called his son **Jerubbaal** (v. 32), a name that means "let Baal contend [for himself]." In other words, if Baal were a real god, he could defend himself. This name later occurs as Jerubbesheth (2 Sam. 11:21) by substituting a degrading term (Hebrew, *bosheth*; "shameful

thing") for the name of Baal, as in the change of the names Esh-baal and Merib-baal (1 Chron. 8:33–34) to Ish-bosheth and Mephibosheth (see discussions on 2 Sam. 2:8; 4:4). **Let Baal plead against him**; that is, let Baal defend himself against Gideon.

6:33–35. The oppressor's camp was in the **valley of Jezreel** (v. 33; see discussion on 5:19). **But the spirit ... came upon Gideon** (lit., the "Spirit ... clothed Himself with" Gideon; v. 34). This vivid figure, used only three times (here; 1 Chron. 12:18; 2 Chron. 24:20), emphasizes that the Spirit of the Lord empowered the human agent and acted through him (see discussion on 3:10). Gideon's army was to come from nearby tribes: **Manasseh** (i.e., West Manasseh; v. 35), **Asher**, a tribe that earlier had failed to answer the call to arms (5:17), Zebulun, and Naphtali.

6:36–40. Gideon was a man of wavering faith, but God knows human weakness (see Ps. 103:14) and was infinitely patient. Despite God's repeated promise (6:12, 14, 16), Gideon requested assurance by means of a sign. **I will speak but this once** (v. 39; compare Abraham's words in Gen. 18:32). Gideon then requested an additional sign, which, though similar to the first, demanded a more difficult miracle. He reasoned that the ground would naturally dry before the thick fleece would. His testing of God's will is not a practice for emulation. It is never honoring to God to question His clearly revealed directives and will.

7:1–8. As supreme commander of Israel, the Lord reduced the army so that Israel would know that the victory was by His power, not theirs, and not in the strength of numbers (see Ps. 33:16; Zech. 4:6).

7:1–3. Harod (v. 1) means "trembling" and may refer to either the timidity of the Israelites (v. 3) or the great panic of the Midianites when Gideon attacked (7:21). The Hebrew verb form of this name is translated "discomfited" in 8:12. **The hill of Moreh** was located across the Valley of Jezreel, approximately four miles from the Israelite army. **Let him return** (v. 3). Gideon's army was to be reduced according to the principle of fear. Those who were afraid to fight the Lord's battle were not to go out with His army so that they would not demoralize the others (Deut. 20:8). **Mount Gilead** is perhaps used here as another name for Mount Gilboa.

7:4 – 7. The second reduction of Gideon's army involved observing the troops as they drank from the spring (7:1). The **three hundred men** (v. 6) who **lapped** the water from their cupped hands were retained. The others were dismissed. The significance of this test is debated. Some would suggest that the three hundred men who lapped their water demonstrated a greater alertness; others contend that they stood, too timid to kneel and drink. Perhaps both suggestions are incorrect, for God said, **I will try them** (v. 4). The verb here is literally "to smelt, refine, test." The text does not state that the men's method of drinking was meant to be a test to determine their level of alertness or bravery. Perhaps it is best simply to see the ritual of drinking at the spring as the means God used to reveal to Gideon the men who were to help him carry out the divine plan.

7:8 – 14. The Lord provided Gideon with encouraging intelligence information for the battle. Although revelations by dreams are frequently mentioned in the Old Testament, here both the dreamer and the interpreter are non-Israelite. Contrast Joseph, who interpreted dreams in Egypt (Gen. 40:1 – 22; 41:1 – 32), and Daniel, who interpreted dreams in Babylon (Dan 2:1 – 45; 4:4 – 27).

Since barley was considered an inferior grain, with only one-half the value of wheat (see 2 Kings 7:1), **a cake of barley bread** (v. 13) is a fitting symbol for Gideon and for Israel, whose forces in this battle were inferior in numbers. **This is ... the sword of Gideon** (v. 14). The Midianites were aware of Gideon's activities, having surely witnessed men gathering to him and almost as many deserting him. With only a handful of men left, he would not have been considered a serious threat.

7:15 – 18. Though Gideon's dream was for his encouragement, it and its interpretation (v. 14) may have passed through the camp that night, preparing a setting for the panic and confusion created by Gideon's men.

Dividing the men into **three companies** (v. 16) was a strategy adopted by Israel on several occasions

(9:43; 1 Sam. 11:11; 2 Sam. 18:2). Gideon gave every man a **trumpet.** These trumpets were made from the horns of rams. They were used more often for making noise (see Josh. 6:4) and giving signals for battle (see Judg. 3:27; 6:34) than for making music. If only leaders normally signaled their troops with trumpets, the sound of three hundred trumpets must have suggested to the Midianites that they were surrounded by a very large army. The **pitchers** were clay jars that could be easily broken (v. 19) to expose the **lamps,** or torches, that had been hidden until needed.

7:19 – 25. The Hebrews divided the night into three watches (see discussion on Matt. 14:25). Gideon struck at **the beginning of the middle watch** (v. 19). The middle watch was approximately 10 p.m. to 12 a.m. He may have struck at the changing of the guard, while the rest of the camp was in a very deep sleep. No one suddenly awakened by a surprise attack would have been capable of thinking and acting coherently enough to defend himself.

Three hundred blew the trumpets (v. 22). Normally, only a comparatively small number of men in an army carried trumpets. The Lord set **every man's sword against his fellow.** God used Gideon and the trumpeters to scare the enemy. Those who had brought terror to Israel (see 6:2) were now terrorized. Undoubtedly, the clamor was only heightened by the probable stampeding of the Midianites' camels (see 7:12). A similar panic occurred among the Ammonites, Moabites, and Edomites (2 Chron. 20:23) and, on a somewhat smaller scale, among the Philistines at Gibeah (1 Sam. 14:20). See Ezekiel 38:21; Zechariah 14:13; see also discussion on Judges 4:15.

Encouraged by the turn of events, many of those who had departed now **gathered themselves together** (v. 23) and joined the battle. It is always easier to gather support when one is riding momentum.

Apparently, Gideon had not hitherto summoned Ephraim, the tribe just south of his own tribe, Manasseh. Now he called to **mount Ephraim** (v. 24) for aid from the Ephraimites to cut off the Midianites' retreat into the Jordan Valley. By controlling the **waters unto Beth-barah and Jordan,** probably the river crossings in the vicinity of Beth-shean, the Israelites could prevent the escape of the fleeing Midianites (see discussion on 3:28). The exact location of Beth-barah is unknown, but it must have been some distance down the river. Gideon's pursuit of the enemy across the river took him to Succoth, a town near the Jabbok River (8:5).

The heads of two slain Midianite princes, **Oreb and Zeeb** (v. 25), were brought to Gideon. Frequently, parts of the bodies of dead victims, such as heads, hands (8:6), and foreskins (1 Sam. 18:25), were cut off and brought back as a kind of body count.

8:1–3. Contrast the example of Gideon, who placates the wrath of the **men of Ephraim** (v. 1), with that of Jephthah, who brings humiliation and defeat to the tribe (12:1–6). Rivalry apparently existed between the tribes of Ephraim and Manasseh. Ephraim was proud to claim former leaders such as Joshua (2:9) and Deborah (4:5). So Gideon wisely defused a volatile confrontation with diplomacy and flattery and averted a potential civil war, which would have overshadowed a victory over the Midianites.

Here Gideon implied that Ephraim had accomplished more in **the gleaning** (i.e., leftovers) **of the grapes** (v. 2) than had the **vintage** of his clan, **Abiezer** (see discussion on 6:11), whose name means "My [divine] Father is helper" or "My [divine] Father is strong." Gideon went on to say that nothing he and his forces had accomplished in the initial attack compared to Ephraim's capture of **Oreb and Zeeb** (v. 3). Then Ephraim's **anger was abated**. Indeed, "a soft answer turneth away wrath" (Prov. 15:1).

8:4–9. Succoth (v. 5; see Gen. 33:17) lay east of the Jordan River, just north of the Jabbok River, and nearly forty miles from the hill of Moreh, where the surprise attack on the Midianites had occurred. **Zebah and Zalmunna**, the escaping **kings of Midian**, may have belonged to different Midianite tribes (see Num. 31:8).

Are the hands ... in thine hand, that we should give bread ...? (v. 6; for "the hands," physical evidence of a defeated enemy, see discussion on 7:25). The officials of Succoth doubted Gideon's ability to defeat the Midianite coalition and feared reprisal if they gave his army food, for their city was on the route the kings would take if they returned to retaliate.

The city at **Penuel** (v. 8), the place where Jacob had wrestled with God (Gen. 32:30–31), also was skeptical of Gideon's capability to capture the kings. Thus, it also refused him assistance. Gideon promised the men in both cities that they would be punished upon his return.

8:10–17. Gideon overtook the kings in the desert region of **Karkor** (v. 10), killing the remaining 15,000 Midianites, who had once numbered 135,000. It was vitally important that Gideon capture these two kings, not for personal pride (in the face of two cities' taunting), but to destroy the leadership of the Midianites and lessen the threat of future raids.

The capture of the kings provided Gideon with more than hands (see 7:25; 8:6) to show Succoth and Penuel as evidence of his victory. Both cities deserved and received severe punishment for their scornful refusal to assist Gideon.

8:18–21. Gideon had a personal score to settle—to avenge blood. These two kings were personally responsible for the death of his two full brothers, **sons of my mother** (v. 19). In an age when men often had several wives, it was necessary to distinguish between full brothers and half brothers. From Gideon's remarks, it seems doubtful that their deaths were the result of battle. Therefore, Gideon ordered his son to be the blood avenger.

Rise thou ... as the man is, so is his strength (v. 21). Dying at the hands of a boy may have been considered a disgrace (see 1 Sam. 17:42), but the kings undoubtedly were more fearful of a slow and painful death at the hands of a youth who was unable to wield a sword adequately. Gideon confiscated the **ornaments** (lit., "moon crescents"), probably crescent necklaces, that hung from their camels. This jewelry may have indicated their inclination for moon-god worship.

8:22–27. Gideon rejected Israel's offer to set up his house as rulers over Israel. **I will not rule ... the LORD shall rule** (v. 23). He, like Samuel (1 Sam. 8:4–20), rejected the establishment of a monarchy because he regarded it as a replacement of the Lord's rule. God's rule over Israel (theocracy) is a central issue in Judges.

He did, however, accept a gift of **golden earrings** (v. 24), or possibly "nose rings" (see Gen. 24:47; Ezek. 16:12) taken from the prey. The **Ishmaelites** were related to the Midianites (Gen. 25:1–2) and sometimes identified with them (vv. 22, 24; Gen. 37:25–28; 39:1). With the gold, Gideon made an **ephod** (v. 27).

The ephod was a holy garment usually associated with the priesthood (Exod. 28:6–30; 39:2–26; Lev. 8:7), but at times it was a pagan object associated with idols (17:5; 18:14, 17). Associated with the high priest's ephod were the Urim and Thummim, which were consulted to learn God's will (Num. 27:21). Two things remain unclear here: (1) What was the nature of Gideon's ephod? Was it a replica of the high priest's ephod but adorned with gold? Was it a freestanding image? (2) What was the purpose of Gideon's ephod? Had the priesthood degenerated and Gideon was purposing to assume the role of priest? Whatever his purpose was, whether or not he intended it for good, it proved to be the contrary, for it became another means of idolatry for Israel, who **went … a whoring after it** (i.e., the ephod; v. 27).

8:28–33. Jerubbaal (v. 29; see discussion on 6:32) — that is, Gideon — had **threescore and ten sons** (v. 30), a sign of power and prosperity (see 12:14; 2 Kings 10:1). Out of all Gideon's sons, only **Abimelech** (v. 31), born to a **concubine** who was originally a slave in Gideon's household (9:18; see discussion on Gen. 16:2) and who lived in another city, is mentioned by name. Abimelech appears elsewhere as a royal title (Gen. 20:2; 26:1; and title of Psalm 34) and means "My [divine] Father is King." Gideon, in naming his son, acknowledged that the Lord ("Father") is King. Thus, the central figure in the next chapter, Abimelech, is introduced.

Though Gideon's age is not given, he **died in a good old age** (v. 32), a phrase used elsewhere only of Abraham (Gen. 15:15; 25:8) and David (1 Chron. 29:28). After Gideon's death, Israel returned to **Baalim** (v. 33; see discussions on 2:11, 13) and **Baal-berith**

(i.e., "lord of the covenant"). The same deity is called "the god Berith" (meaning "god of the covenant") in 9:46. A temple was dedicated to him (see 9:4) in Shechem. The word "covenant" in his name probably refers to a solemn treaty that bound together a league of Canaanite cities whose people worshiped him as their god. Sadly and ironically, Shechem (v. 31), near Mount Ebal, was the site at which Joshua had twice renewed the Lord's covenant with Israel after they had entered Canaan (Josh. 8:30–35; 24:25–27).

8:33–35. The interesting juxtaposition of these verses shows that after Israel was delivered, neither God nor Gideon's family was treated favorably. Once again, Israel had turned to its God merely for help in a crisis.

9:1–57. The stories of Gideon and Abimelech form the literary center of Judges (see Introduction: "Literary Features"). Abimelech, who tried to set himself up like a Canaanite city king with the help of Baal (v. 4), stands in sharp contrast to his father Gideon (Jerubbaal), who had attacked Baal worship and insisted that the Lord ruled over Israel. Abimelech attempted this Canaanite revival in the very place where Joshua had earlier reaffirmed Israel's allegiance to the Lord (Josh. 24:14–27). In every respect, Abimelech was the antithesis of the Lord's appointed judges.

His unscrupulous actions, the support of Shechem, and the apparent disregard of the rest of Israel all provide a commentary for 8:35 (see v. 18). Previous oppressors had come from outside Israel. Now one of their own is an oppressor.

E. Abimelech, the Anti-Judge, (chap. 9)

9:1–5. Shechem (v. 1) was an important place in Israel's history. Abraham built his first altar in the land there (Gen. 12:6, 7). Jacob also built an altar there (Gen. 33:20) and later instructed his household to rid themselves of idols there (Gen. 35:1–4). It was in this region, (Mounts Gerizim and Ebal) that Joshua built an altar and rehearsed the terms of God's covenant with Israel (Josh. 8:30–35). And it was there that Israel had accepted Joshua's challenge to serve only the Lord (Josh. 24:1–28).

Now Shechem had its own temple, to **Baal-berith** ("Baal of the covenant"; v. 4). Ruins dating from the Canaanite era give evidence of a sacred area, probably to be associated with the temple of Baal-berith, or "the god Berith" (9:46). Archaeological evidence, which is compatible with the destruction of Shechem by Abimelech, indicates that its sacred area was never rebuilt after this time.

Abimelech was an opportunist and was about to claim kingship, something his father had refused (8:23). The people of Shechem apparently preserved a link to their Canaanite fathers (see 9:28; Genesis 34). Whether Abimelech's mother and the leaders of Shechem were Canaanites or not, their behavior was Canaanite.

The **men of Shechem** (v. 2) refers to the city's leaders. The singular form of the Hebrew word translated here as "men" is *ba'al*, which means "lord" or "owner," and the plural form probably refers here to the aristocracy or landowners of the city. **I am your bone and your flesh**. Being half Canaanite, Abimelech intimated that it was in their best interest to make him king rather than be under the rule of Gideon's seventy sons. The following he gathered was based on this relationship and became a threat to the people of Israel.

Ancient temples served as depositories for personal and civic funds. The payments of vows and penalties, as well as gifts, were also part of the temple treasury, so the men of Shechem took silver **out of the house of Baal-berith** (v. 4) to give to Abimelech. This temple is probably to be identified with a large building found at Shechem by archaeologists.

With this money, Abimelech hired mercenaries, described as **vain and light persons** (v. 4). Use of mercenaries to accomplish political or military goals was common in ancient times. Others who used them are Jephthah (11:3), David (1 Sam. 22:1–2), Absalom (2 Sam. 15:1), Adonijah (1 Kings 1:5), Rezon (1 Kings 11:23–24), and Jeroboam (2 Chron. 13:6–7). With the help of these paid assassins, Abimelech slaughtered his seventy brothers like sacrificial animals (see 13:19–20; 1 Sam. 14:33–34), all **upon one stone** (v. 5). In effect, he inaugurated his

kingship by using his Israelite half brothers as his coronation sacrifices (see 2 Sam. 15:10, 12; 1 Kings 1:5, 9; 3:4). Sadly, there is no record of Israel's angry reaction to the massacre.

9:6–7. The **house of Millo** (v. 6) is from the Hebrew *Beth-millo*. "Millo" is derived from a Hebrew verb meaning "to fill" and probably refers to the earthen fill used to erect a platform on which walls and other large structures were built. It may be identical to the "hold of the house" of 9:46 or the "tower of Shechem" of 9:47. The **plain** (lit., "oak"; see Josh. 24:25–26) may have been a landmark in Shechem. With the men gathered there, **Jotham** (v. 7), Gideon's surviving son, could address them from the **top of mount Gerizim**, perhaps from a ledge that overlooked the city. This was the very mountain where Israel had recited the blessings of God's covenant (see Deut. 11:26–29; Josh. 8:33–34). From there, Jotham delivered his fable of the trees, a story that was designed to teach a moral (see 2 Sam. 12:1–4, 7) and that served as a stinging rebuke for Shechem's foolish endorsement of Abimelech as king.

9:8–21. The **trees went forth** (v. 8). Parables of this type, in which inanimate objects speak and act, were popular among Eastern peoples of that time (see 2 Kings 14:9). This one has been called the "Parable of the Trees" (Nordern, *Parables*, pp. 44–48).

The **olive tree** (vv. 8–9), **the fig tree**, (vv. 10–11), and **the** grape **vine** (vv. 12–13) were all of value to the people of the Near East for their fruit and the products made from them.

The bramble (v. 14), however, is probably the well-known buckthorn, a scraggly bush common in the hills of Canaan and a constant menace to farming. This bush, which produces no timber, provides little shade, and burns very quickly in the heat and winds of summer, was an apt figure for Abimelech.

Ironically, in offering his **shadow** (i.e., shade to the trees; v. 15), the bramble symbolized the traditional role of kings as protectors of their subjects (see Isa. 30:2–3; 32:1–2; Lam. 4:20; Dan. 4:12). The **cedars of Lebanon** were the most valuable of Near Eastern trees, here symbolic of the leading men of Shechem (see v. 20).

Let fire come out ... and devour (v. 20). This is a grim prediction that Abimelech and the people of Shechem would destroy each other. Fire spreads rapidly through bramble bushes and brings about swift destruction (see Exod. 22:6; Isa. 9:18). Jotham's fable dripped with sarcasm. The city of Shechem thought it had a king; Jotham announced that it had a worthless "fire hazard."

9:22–25. Abimelech's rule **over Israel** (v. 22) was limited to those Israelites who recognized his authority, mainly in the vicinity of Shechem. Whether the **evil spirit** (v. 23; see 1 Sam. 16:14; 1 Kings 22:19–23) is to be explained as a supernatural being or simply a spirit of distrust and bitterness (the Hebrew for "spirit" is often used to describe an attitude or disposition), God was responsible for the estrangement **between Abimelech and the men of Shechem**, who **dealt treacherously with Abimelech**. The one who founded his kingdom by treachery is himself undone by treachery. The disruption of their relationship initiated the judgment that was to be theirs on account of the mass murder of Gideon's sons.

9:26–29. Just as the fickle population had followed Abimelech, so they were now swayed by the deceptive proposals of **Gaal** (nothing more is known of him; v. 26), and they **put their confidence in him**.

The vintage harvest was one of the most joyous times of the year (see Isa. 16:9–10; Jer. 25:30), but festivals and celebrations held at pagan temples often degenerated into debauched drinking affairs. So as Gaal and his crowd **made merry** (v. 27), he scorned Abimelech, Jerubbaal (i.e., Gideon), and Zebul. Gaal advised the people **to serve the men of Hamor** (v. 28), the Hivite ruler who had founded the city of Shechem (Gen. 33:19; 34:2; Josh. 24:32), and he made outrageous claims of leadership and what he would do to get rid of Abimelech.

9:30–41. Zebul (v. 30) served as a "fifth column" and reported Gaal's bravado to Abimelech and advised him how to retaliate: arrive early and **lie in wait** (v. 32), that is, set an ambush. An ambush had succeeded against Ai (Josh. 8:2) and against Gibeah in Benjamin (Judg. 20:37).

Abimelech's ambush consisted of **four companies** (v. 34). Smaller segments meant less chance of detection. Attacking from several directions was also good strategy. In the morning, Gaal saw two companies approaching, one from the **middle of the land** (Hebrew, *tabbur-eretz*; perhaps representing a landmark; v. 37) and the other from the **plain of Meonenim** (lit., "diviner's oak"), probably a sacred tree, perhaps in some way related to the temple of Baal-berith (see discussion on Gen. 12:6).

With his bluff called, Gaal was forced to back his talk with action and lead the residents of Shechem against Abimelech. He was defeated and forced to retreat to Shechem, but Zebul evicted him.

9:42–49. The following day, Abimelech divided his men into **three companies** (v. 43) and slew the residents who had gone to work their fields, and then he attacked the city. Symbolically, he **sowed it with salt** (v. 45), a ritual denoting that the city was condemned to perpetual barrenness and desolation (see Deut. 29:23; Ps. 107:33–34; Jer. 17:6; Zeph. 2:9). The men of the city retreated to the **hold of the house of the god Berith** (lit., Baal-berith; v. 46; see 9:4 and discussion on 9:6). Abimelech then **set the hold on fire** (v. 49), bringing fulfillment to Jotham's curse (v. 20).

9:50–55. Apparently, **Thebez** (v. 50) was an ally in Shechem's rebellion, so it also was subjected to Abimelech's revenge. While **the men** (v. 51) normally used bows, arrows, and spears to protect the tower, **the women** may have helped to defend it by dropping heavy stones on those who came near it. Attention is drawn to **a certain woman** (lit., "one woman"; v. 53). In view of the writer's use of "one" in this chapter (one man, 9:2; one stone, 9:5), it is likely that he is drawing attention to the fact that one woman alone, in contrast to the fearful men of the city, defended her city by "stoning" Abimelech.

The woman threw a **piece of a millstone** (v. 53), or the upper millstone (lit., the "riding stone"). This description fits the quern and muller. The bottom stone (averaging 13 inches wide by 25–30 inches long), called the "saddle quern" by archaeologists, had a concave depression in its top surface, worn through extended usage, that gave the stone the appearance of a saddle. The upper stone, the "muller," was a small hand stone (in the shape of a modern-day loaf of bread) that was used in washboard fashion, riding over the bottom stone. Grinding grain was women's work (see Exod. 11:5), usually considered too lowly for men to perform (see Samson's milling experience in Judg. 16:21). In this, the third example of improvised weaponry (see discussion on 3:16), a woman used her domestic implement to kill Abimelech.

A military leader usually had an **armourbearer** (v. 54), a young man to carry his shield and spear (see 1 Sam. 14:6; 31:4). Perhaps remembering Sisera's death at Jael's hand (4:21), Abimelech did not want it said of him that **A woman slew him**. It was considered a disgrace for a soldier to die at the hands of a woman. Abimelech's shameful death was long remembered (see 2 Sam. 11:21).

9:56−57. Thus God rendered the wickedness of Abimelech (v. 56). God was in control of the events. As Israel's true King, He brought Abimelech's wickedness to a quick and shameful end and repaid him and the men of Shechem for their evil. **The curse of Jotham** (v. 57; see 9:20) was fulfilled.

2. Second Minor Judge: Tola (10:1−2)

10:1−2. Tola the son of Puah (v. 1) was **a man of Issachar**. Tola and Puah bear names of two of the sons of Issachar (Gen. 46:13; Num. 26:23; 1 Chron. 7:1).

This man **arose to defend Israel**, but details of what he did and from whom or what he saved Israel are not given.

3. Third Minor Judge: Jair (10:3−5)

10:3−5. Since **Jair** (v. 3) came from Gilead (the territory assigned to Manasseh) and since a descendant of Manasseh bore the same name (Num. 32:41; Deut. 3:14; 1 Kings 4:13), it appears that Jair was a Manassite. All that is known of him is that he had **thirty sons ... thirty ass colts ... thirty cities** (v. 4), all apparently evidence of his wealth and position. The cities of his sons were known as **Havoth-jair**, that is, "towns of Jair."

F. Jephthah Defeats Ammon (10:6−12:7)

10:6−12:7. Israel now turned to Jephthah, a social outcast whom they had driven from the land, causing him to become an outlaw without an inheritance in Israel. The author notes this to Israel's shame. The account of Jephthah's judgeship balances that of Deborah in the story of the judges (see discussion on 4:1−5:31; see also Introduction: "Literary Features").

10:6−9. For the recurring phrase, **Israel did evil again in the sight of the** LORD (v. 6), see discussion on 3:7. Israel now engaged in wholesale apostasy; the list of false deities she served has lengthened (v. 6; see 2:11−13; 3:7). The chief **gods of Syria** were Hadad (Baal), Mot, Anath, and Rimmon. The **gods of Zidon** (the Sidonians) were essentially the same gods that the Canaanites worshiped (see discussions on 2:11, 13). Of the **gods of Moab**, the chief deity was Chemosh. Of the **gods of the children of Ammon**, Molech was the chief deity (see 1 Kings 11:7), who was sometimes worshiped by the offering of human sacrifice (Lev. 18:21; 20:2−5; 2 Kings 23:10). Molech is also called Milcom (see 1 Kings 11:5; 2 Kings 23:13; see also discussion on Lev. 18:21). Both Molech and Milcom are forms of a Semitic word for "king." While the Philistines worshiped most of the Canaanite gods, the most popular **gods of the Philistines** appear to have been Dagon and Baal-zebub. The name Dagon is the same as a Hebrew word for "grain," suggesting that he was a vegetation deity. He was worshiped in Babylonia as early as the second millennium BC. Baal-zebub was worshiped in Ekron (2 Kings 1:2−3, 6, 16). The name means "lord of the flies," a deliberate change by followers of the Lord (Yahweh) to ridicule and protest the worship of Baal-zebul ("Baal the prince"), a name known from ancient Canaanite texts (see Matt. 10:25; 12:24 and discussions).

Israel now faced a two-pronged, two-directional opposition: the Philistines from the west and the Ammonites from the east. Though introduced first, the account of the Philistine oppression is not resumed until 13:1. In addition, for the first time, the opposition from the west affected tribes on both sides of the Jordan River.

10:10 – 16. As usual, **Israel cried** in distress **unto the LORD** (v. 10), but her confession was empty and meaningless. The Lord rebuked Israel for forgetting that He had delivered them from their oppressors in Canaan (see discussions on 2:16 – 19; 6:8) and provided a list of her enemies to remind her. The **Maonites** (v. 12) are perhaps the same as the Mehunim, who, along with the Philistines and Arabs, opposed Israel (2 Chron. 26:7).

God's stern rebuke is most disturbing: **I will deliver you no more** (v. 13). Never before had He refused to raise up a deliverer for the Israelites or threatened to turn them over to the gods of their choosing for deliverance.

Despite Israel's confession of idolatry (vv. 10, 15) and her disposal of her foreign gods, that she truly repented remains questionable. The Lord's words in verses 12 – 13 may indicate that such actions had become routine. For the sake of convenience, Israel may have put away rival deities at other times of crises. Two things are noteworthy of this occasion: (1) As He had promised, God did not raise up a deliverer. Israel felt compelled to search for a volunteer to fight for them (10:18; 11:5 – 6). (2) This is the last time it is said in Judges that Israel "cried unto the Lord" in a time of distress. Israel's lack of sincerity does not prevent a merciful and compassionate God from being **grieved** (v. 16) at His covenant people's **misery.**

10:17 – 18. With the Ammonites encroaching, Israel set up camp at **Mizpeh** (v. 17). The name means "watchtower," and several places bore this name. Jephthah's headquarters was a town or fortress in Gilead (11:11) called "Mizpeh of Gilead" (11:29). It may have been the same as Ramath-mizpeh (Josh. 13:26), located about thirty miles east of Beth-shean. **The people and princes** (v. 18), that is, the troops and officers of the Gileadites, wanted to resist the Ammonite incursion but lacked the courageous military leadership to press their cause.

11:1 – 3. **Jephthah** (v. 1) lived in Gilead, the geographical area east of the Jordan, and was the son of a man with the same name. Born to a **harlot,** Jephthah was a social outcast and bore the stigma of

his illegitimacy. His half brothers ostracized him because he was **the son of a strange woman** (lit., "another woman," i.e., other than the brothers' mother; v. 2), thus forcing him to flee to **Tob** (v. 3), located northeast of Ramoth Gilead. The men of Tob later allied with the Ammonites against David (2 Sam. 10:6 – 8). The **vain men** (i.e., empty, idle, worthless men) who joined him were possibly also outcasts and social misfits.

11:4 – 6. Jephthah's call is a departure from that of past deliverers. The "LORD raised up a deliverer" in 3:9 (Othniel) and 3:15 (Ehud). In 4:4 – 7, the prophetess Deborah called Barak. The angel of the Lord appeared to Gideon in 6:12. Here, since no volunteer had come forward (see 10:18), the elders of Gilead offered Jephthah a position, **Come, and be our captain** (v. 6), apparently because he had established a reputation for leadership.

11:7 – 11. **Be our head over … Gilead** (v. 8). In addition to their initial offer of military command during the war with Ammon (11:6), the Gileadites now also offered to make Jephthah regional head once the fighting was over. Jephthah's reluctance to return to Gilead displays his fear of being rejected again even if he was successful against the Ammonites. On the human level, Jephthah did not want to be treated as Israel was accustomed to treating God — using Him for deliverance only to turn from Him and reject Him once again.

The elders swore to retain Jephthah as a leader, so the proposal of the elders was ratified by the people, a process followed in the election of Saul (1 Sam. 11:15), Rehoboam (1 Kings 12:1), and Jeroboam (1 Kings 12:20).

11:12 – 13. Jephthah first attempted to defuse the threat of war with Ammon through negotiations. The king of Ammon complained, **Israel took away my land** (v. 13). Actually, God had strictly forbidden Israel's harassing Ammon or taking its land (Deut. 2:19). When the Israelites had first approached Canaan, this area was ruled by the Amorite king Sihon, who had taken it from the Moabites (Num. 21:29). The Ammonites had since become dominant over Moab and now claimed all previous Moabite territory.

11:14–27. Jephthah responded in accordance with international policies of the time; his letter is a classic example of contemporary international correspondence. It also reflects, and appeals to, the common recognition that the god(s) of a people established and protected their political boundaries and decided all boundary disputes. Jephthah's defense of Israel's claim to the land is threefold.

First, Israel had taken the land from the **Sihon king of the Amorites** (v. 19), not from the Ammonites (vv. 15–22). If any one had a claim to the land, Moab did, for Sihon had taken the land from Ammon (Num. 21:29). Sihon and the Amorites had been delivered to Israel by the LORD **God of Israel** (v. 21). War was viewed not only in military terms but also as a contest between deities (see v. 24; Exod. 12:12; Num. 33:4).

Second, the LORD **God … dispossessed the Amorites** (v. 23) and gave the land to Israel. Ammon claimed the land as a gift from **Chemosh** (v. 24). Chemosh, normally thought to be the god of Moab (see discussion on 10:6), is Ammon's god here. Possible explanations include the following: (1) Jephthah may have confused the gods of Moab and Ammon, (2) Ammon had taken over some of Moab's land and therefore recognized its god, or (3) the Moabites had associated themselves once again with Ammon in a military confederacy against Israel (see 3:12–13). For **Balak** (v. 25) and his opposition to Israel, see Numbers 22–24.

Third, Israel had long possessed the land (vv. 26–27). **Three hundred years** (v. 26) had passed since Israel had entered the land and had taken Hesbon and her towns. Jephthah's question is this: Why did Ammon wait so long to reclaim the land under dispute? His appeal is to **the LORD the Judge** (v. 27; see 1 Sam. 24:15). As the Divine Judge, the Lord is the final court of appeal. It is significant that in the book of Judges, the singular noun "judge" is found only here, where it is used of the Lord, Israel's true Judge.

11:28–29. The king of Ammon rejected Jephthah's rationale. Then the **spirit of the LORD came upon Jephthah** (v. 29; see discussion on 3:10). In the Old Testament, the unique empowering of the

Spirit was given to an individual primarily to enable him to carry out the special responsibilities God had given him.

11:30–31. Jephthah had negotiated with the elders (11:7–11) and with the king of Ammon (11:12–28); in essence, he now negotiated with God, for he **vowed a vow unto the LORD** (v. 30). This was a common practice among the Israelites (see Gen. 28:20; 1 Sam. 1:11; 2 Sam. 15:8). If God would give him victory, **whatsoever cometh forth** (lit., the "coming one") **of the doors of** his **house** (v. 31) to greet him when he returned, he would offer to God as a whole **burnt offering**. That Jephthah had human sacrifice in mind seems evident, though such a view is repulsive. Therefore, many Christian interpreters have purposed instead that he had in mind either animal sacrifice or a perpetual dedication of someone to the Lord, depending on what (animal or person) came out to greet him. They argue that God had strictly forbidden human sacrifice (see Lev. 18:21; Deut. 12:31). However, idolatry was also strictly forbidden by Mosaic law (Exod. 20:3, 4), but it was a common practice in an era marked by everyone doing "that which was right in his own eyes" (see 17:6; 21:25) and by repeated occurrences of religious syncretism (see 3:7; 10:6). Is it unthinkable that Israel's religion might have degenerated to include features of paganism, such as human sacrifice? What sacrificial animal was known for rushing from a house to greet a hero returning from battle? Apparently, Jephthah was expecting that he would be greeted by a servant, not by his only daughter.

11:32–38. Jephthah's battle and victory receives minimal description. Emphasis is directed to his return home. His **daughter** (v. 34) greeted him with **dances**. It was customary for women to greet in this way armies returning victoriously from battle (see Exod. 15:20; 1 Sam. 18:6). Jephthah, however, **rent his clothes** (v. 35), which was a common practice for expressing extreme grief (see Gen. 37:34 and discussion).

A vow was not to be broken (see Num. 30:2; Deut. 23:21–23; see also Eccl. 5:4–5). Jephthah's daughter requested that his vow be kept after she had been given **two months** (v. 37) to mourn her

virginity with her **fellows**, that is, her girlfriends. To be kept from marrying and rearing children was a bitter prospect for an Israelite girl.

11:39 – 40. The story of Isaac being preserved from human sacrifice (Gen. 22:6 – 14) is replete with intimate details. Here the reader is spared any hideous detail. It is simply stated that he **did with her according to his vow which he had vowed** (v. 39). It became a **custom in Israel**, perhaps only locally, since no other mention of it is found in the Old Testament, that the girls of Israel would **lament** (perhaps "commemorate"; v. 40) Jephthah's daughter **four days in a year**.

12:1 – 3. As Gideon had (see 8:1 – 3), Jephthah faced the angry rivalry of the tribe of Ephraim because, they accused, he had failed to invite them to accompany him in the battle against Ammon. Their threat, **we will burn thine house upon thee** (v. 1), is similar to the threat the Philistines issued to Samson's wife (14:15). Jephthah was not as diplomatic as Gideon had been under similar circumstances (see discussion on 8:1 – 3). **When I called you, ye delivered me not** (v. 2). Jephthah was angry, because for eighteen years (see 10:8), Ephraim had not come to the Gileadites' rescue, and they had not responded to his call for help.

12:4 – 6. Apparently, West Manasseh and Ephraim had over time developed a hatred and disrespect for Transjordanian Gileadites. When the men of Ephraim uttered the derogatory statement **Ye Gileadites are fugitives** (v. 4), Jephthah was bent on punishing them before they escaped home to the western side of the Jordan. When the Ephraimites retreated to the fords of Jordan, they were required to say an innocent enough password, **Shibboleth** (v. 6), which in this context meant "flowing stream, floods" (see, e.g., Ps. 69:2, 15). Due to dialectical differences that had developed, the Israelites east of the Jordan pronounced its initial letter with a strong *sh* sound, while those in Canaan gave it a softer *s* sound. Thus, the Ephraimite men pronounced the password **Sibboleth** and exposed themselves as westerners (of Jordan) and opponents of Jephthah. Forty-two thousand men were thus screened out for destruction.

12:7. A new formula for closing out the account of the judge is introduced. Instead of the usual "the land had rest … years" (see discussion on 3:11; see also "Introduction: Literary Features"), the new formula now informs the reader that the judge "judged Israel … years." What Jephthah's continued role was as he **judged Israel for six years**, until his death, is not stated.

4. Fourth Minor Judge: Ibzan (12:8 – 10)

12:8 – 10. Ibzan (v. 8) came from **Beth-lehem**, which probably refers not to the Bethlehem of Judah but to the Bethlehem in western Zebulun, located about seven miles northwest of Nazareth (see Josh. 19:15 – 16). Having **thirty sons** (v. 9) is indicative of Ibzan's polygamy, and the fact that he arranged marriages for them with **thirty daughters from abroad** may indicate that he attempted to spread his influence in various areas through these marriages.

5. Fifth Minor Judge: Elon (12:11 – 12)

12:11 – 12. Elon (v. 11), though he bore the name of a clan in the tribe of Zebulun (Gen. 46:14; Num. 26:26), is a most obscure judge. Beyond his tribe (Zebulun), his length of judgeship (ten years), and his place of burial (Aijalon), nothing is known.

6. Sixth Minor Judge: Abdon (12:13 – 15)

12:13 – 15. Like Gideon, **Abdon** (v. 13) apparently was a judge from Ephraim. He too practiced polygamy, as evidenced by his **forty sons and thirty nephews** (lit., "sons of sons," i.e., grandsons; v. 14). He had a total of seventy descendants, who rode on donkeys — evidence of wealth (see discussions on 8:30; 10:4). His accomplishments are not noted. He was buried in Ephraim, presumably his tribe, **in the mount of the Amalekites** (v. 15). The background of this reference is unknown since the Amalekites are otherwise associated with the Negev (Num. 13:29).

G. Samson Checks Philistia (chaps. 13 – 16)

13:1 – 16:31. Samson (from the tribe of Dan), like Ehud (from the tribe of Benjamin), was a loner whose heroic exploits involved single-handed triumphs over powerful enemies. His story therefore balances that of Ehud (3:12–30). He typifies the nation of Israel—born by special divine provision, consecrated to the Lord from birth, and endowed with unique power among his fellowmen. The likeness is even more remarkable in light of his foolish chasing of foreign women, some of ill repute, until he was cleverly subdued by one of them. In this, he exemplified Israel, who constantly prostituted herself to Canaanite gods during the period of the judges, to her own destruction.

13:1. Israel did evil again in the sight of the Lord. This is the last time this recurring phrase appears (see discussion on 3:7). The two-directional and apparently simultaneous opposition from the Ammonites and Philistines was introduced in 10:6–9. The Ammonites were dealt with in chapter 11. Here the story of the Philistine domination of the coastal farmlands of Israel is resumed. Sadly, in the story of the Philistine oppression, there is no mention of Israel "crying unto the Lord" in her distress. The Lord does not raise up a deliverer who brings an end to Philistine oppression, only one who would "begin to deliver" Israel (13:5). Philistine opposition continues throughout the biblical accounts of Samson, Samuel, Saul, and David (see 1 Sam. 4–7; 13–17; 27–31; 2 Sam. 8:1; 23:8–17).

13:2–3. Zorah (v. 2) was a town in the Sorek Valley, which bordered Dan and Judah. The town was first assigned to Judah (Josh. 15:33) but later given to Dan (Josh. 19:41). It became the point of departure for the Danite migration northward (18:2, 8, 11).

Manoah (v. 2) and his wife were **Danites**. They were likely part of the remnant of the tribe of Dan that had remained in the area. Earlier, the Danites had felt pressure from the Amorites to move (1:34), probably due to the influx of Philistines, so a portion of the Danites had moved to the extreme north and relocated at the site of the Canaanite city of Laish (Judges 18 recounts the move).

Manoah's wife was **barren, and bare not** (v. 2), the same condition, before divine intervention, as that of Sarah, the mother of Isaac (Gen. 11:30; 16:1); Rebekah, the mother of Jacob (Gen. 25:21); Hannah,

the mother of Samuel (1 Sam. 1:2); and Elisabeth, the mother of John the Baptist (Luke 1:7).

The identity of the **angel of the Lord** (v. 3) was learned gradually over time. **The woman** (the name of Manoah's wife is not given) believed him to be a "man of God" (13:6) who had the appearance of an angel—"very terrible" (i.e., awesome). Her unwitting husband (see 13:16) learned that his name was "secret" (i.e., incomprehensible; 13:18) and that he "did wondrously" (13:19), for he ascended in the flame of the altar and vanished (13:20–21). Both man and wife would eventually learn that they had been in the presence of the Lord Himself (13:22).

The announcement **thou shalt … bear a son** (v. 3) compares to those of the births of Ishmael (Gen. 16:11), Isaac (Gen. 18:10), Immanuel (Isa. 7:14), John the Baptist (Luke 1:13), and Jesus (Luke 1:31).

13:4–5. Beginning immediately, the woman was to prepare for a son who would be a **Nazarite** (v. 5). The Hebrew for Nazarite means "separated" or "dedicated." A Nazarite was one who, in his devotion to God, voluntarily and for a set time took a vow embracing three regulations: (1) to refrain from eating grapes or any other product of the vine, (2) to refrain from cutting his hair, and (3) to avoid defilement by contact with a corpse. For the stipulations of this vow, see Num. 6:1–21 and *KJV Study Bible* notes. Samson's vow, however, was not voluntary, and it applied to his whole lifetime (v. 7). The same was true of Samuel (1 Sam. 1:11) and John the Baptist (Luke 1:15).

He shall begin to deliver Israel out of … Philistines (v. 5). Israel's deliverance from the Philistines, to begin with Samson, would be continued in the time of Samuel (1 Sam. 7:10–14) and completed under David (2 Sam. 5:17–25; 8:1). The Philistines were also called "sea peoples" in ancient inscriptions. They had migrated from Greece onto the Mediterranean coast of Israel in massive numbers during the period of the Judges. Their superior iron-age technology enabled them to dominate Israel during this time.

13:6–8. The expression **man of God** (v. 6) is often used of prophets (see Deut. 33:1; 1 Sam. 2:27; 9:6–10; 1 Kings 12:22), though it is clear from 13:3, 21 that this messenger was not a prophet but rather the angel of the Lord. Though the woman did not ask his name, she noted that his countenance was **terrible**, that is, beyond description. Manoah, not present when the "man of God" had come, entreated the Lord to **let the man of God return and ... teach us** (v. 8). This was not the usual parental concern but a special concern based on the boy's special calling.

13:9–14. Interestingly, the "man of God" appeared both times to the woman, who in turn informed her husband. **Now let thy words come to pass** (v. 12). This is a declaration of faith. To Manoah, it was a matter not of whether these events would occur but of when (13:17). Though the "man" returned the second time, no new information was imparted to Manoah, only a stern reminder to observe all the instructions pertaining to the Nazarite vow that had been commanded of his wife at the first visit (13:4–5).

13:15–18. Let us detain thee, until we ... have made ready a kid (v. 15). Such food was considered a special delicacy. Hospitality of this kind was common in the ancient Near East (see 6:18–19; Gen. 18:1–8). Manoah was still unaware of the visitor's identity. **What is thy name ...?** (v. 17). A messenger's identity was considered very important. Manoah wanted to know, To whom shall we give credit **when thy sayings come to pass?** Fulfilled prophecy was a sign of the authenticity of a prophet (Deut. 18:21–22; 1 Sam. 9:6). The name was **secret** (v. 18), that is, "incomprehensible, wonderful." In Isaiah 9:6, the Hebrew for this phrase (translated "Wonderful") applies to One who would come as "The mighty God."

13:19–23. When Manoah presented his offering to the Lord, **the angel did wondrously** (v. 19). The Hebrew root of "wondrously" is that of "secret" in 13:18. The angel did an "incomprehensible" thing: he **ascended in the flame of the altar** (v. 20). This finally made Manoah aware that he had been in the presence of the angel of the Lord, and he feared **We shall surely die, because we have seen God** (v. 22). Gideon had expressed the same fear (see 6:22–23, see also discussion on Gen. 32:30).

Manoah's wife's reasoning was more logical. If God intended to kill them, He would not have informed them of their future son who was to be set apart as a Nazarite (13:4–5, 14).

13:24–25. The name **Samson** (v. 24) is derived from a Hebrew word meaning "sun" or "brightness" and is used here either as an expression of joy over the birth of the child or as a reference to the nearby town of Beth-shemesh, which means "house of the sun [god]." Though nothing is told of his childhood, **the child grew, and the LORD blessed him**. Compare the similar statements regarding Samuel (1 Sam. 2:26) and Jesus (Luke 2:52). What occurred when **the spirit of the LORD began to move him** (v. 25) is not given (see discussions on 3:10; 11:29). The **camp of Dan** (Hebrew, *mahaneh-dan*) may indicate a proper name (see 18:12) or may refer to the smallness of what was left of the Danite community (see discussion on 13:2).

14:1–4. Timnath (v. 1) is identified as Tell Batash in the Sorek Valley, lying west of Beth-shemesh and a little more than four miles southeast of Zorah, Samson's hometown (13:2, 25). It was there, in Timnath, that he saw a woman **of the daughters of the Philistines**. The disappointment of Samson's parents (v. 3; compare the story of Esau, Gen. 26:35; 27:46; 28:1) is understandable in light of the prohibition against marriage with the peoples of Canaan (Exod. 34:11, 16; Deut. 7:1, 3; see also Judg. 3:5–6).

Samson's only recorded conversation with his parents was curt, demanding, and disrespectful: **get her for me** (v. 2; compare Shechem's demands, Gen. 34:4). As the head of the family, the father exercised authority in all matters, often including the choice of wives for his sons (see 12:9; Gen. 24:3–9; Neh. 10:30). But Samson's concerns were personal, not spiritual. Hence, his retort to their voiced dismay, **Get her for me; for she pleaseth me well** (v. 3), is even more emphatic in literal Hebrew terms: "Her, get for me, for she is right in my eyes." The Hebrew for "right" normally relates not to physical attributes but rather to conduct or cultural attractions. The prevailing attitude of the time of the judges, "every man did that which was right in his own eyes" (17:6; 21:25), now characterized the current judge-to-be.

Uncircumcised Philistines (v. 3) was a term of scorn, a contemptuous epithet for Israel's pagan coastal neighbors who were not bound by covenant to the Lord. Though Egypt and most of Israel's neighbors practiced circumcision (but not for covenantal reasons, as Abraham's descendants were commanded in Gen. 17:9–14), the Philistines did not. They were not among those with whom Israel was strictly forbidden to intermarry (Deut. 7:1–4), but they could be included under the umbrella term "Canaanites." Joshua had forbidden Israel from intermarrying with any of the nations that remained (Josh. 13:3; 23:12) and the angel of the Lord forbade any covenant with the inhabitants of the land (2:2). The cause and effect of marriage and apostasy remained (see Exod. 34:15–16; Judg. 3:5–7; 10:6), so Samson's marriage was clearly in violation of divine instruction.

It was of the Lord (v. 4; see Josh. 11:20; 1 Kings 12:15). The author wrote this after all the events of the story had occurred and the whole could be viewed with twenty-twenty theological hindsight. The Lord uses even the sinful weaknesses of men to accomplish His purposes and bring praise to His name (see Gen. 45:8; 50:20; 2 Chron. 25:20; Acts 2:23; 4:28; Rom 8:28–29). His parents, however, had no understanding of God's sovereignty working in the current events and were understandably disappointed.

14:5–9. The Sorek Valley, in which **Timnath** (v. 5) was located, and its surrounding areas were noted for their luxurious **vineyards**. Lions were once common in southern Canaan (see 1 Sam. 17:34; 2 Sam. 23:20; 1 Kings 13:24; 20:36). That a **young lion** should come upon Samson was perhaps God's way of providing him an escape from the temptation of the vineyard (see discussion on 13:5). When the **spirit ... came mightily upon him** (v. 6; see 13:25; 14:19; 15:14; see also discussions on 3:10; 11:29), Samson **rent** the lion. David (1 Sam. 17:34–37) and Benaiah (2 Sam. 23:20) later performed similar feats. On a second visit, Samson returned to the **carcase of the lion** (v. 8), a probable violation of the Nazarite vow. His silence concerning his whereabouts (v. 6) and activity (v. 9) strongly hints of his awareness of a broken Nazarite vow. The **honey** taken from the dead lion was considered unclean.

14:10–11. The special **feast** (Hebrew, *mishteh*; "drinking feast"; v. 10) Samson arranged was common in the ancient Near East (see Gen. 29:22) and here lasted seven days (14:12; see Gen. 29:27). Since it would have included drinking wine (the Hebrew root of "feast" relates to "drink"), Samson may have violated his Nazarite vow again (see 13:4, 7), for one would suppose the host would have imbibed with his guests. The **thirty companions** (v. 11) were the "attendants of the bridegroom" (see Matt. 9:15). They were probably charged with protecting the wedding party against marauders.

14:12–14. Samson proposed **a riddle** (v. 12). The use of riddles at feasts and special occasions was popular in the ancient world. **Thirty change of garments** would have been an attractive wager (garments are mentioned, together with silver, as gifts of great value in Gen. 45:22; 2 Kings 5:22; Zech. 14:14). The riddle was so enigmatic that it absolutely defied a solution from anyone who had not accompanied him near the vineyards of Timnath on those two occasions.

14:15–16. Embarrassed by the impossible riddle, the companions took advantage of the new bride and, with threats, forced her to be disloyal to Samson to learn its solution. Her accusation, **Thou ... lovest me not** (v. 16), was the same tactic that Delilah would later use (16:15). Sadly, the text never does say that Samson loved his new wife. She was obviously loyal to her people and her father, but to whom was Samson loyal?

14:17–18. Just before the deadline, having learned the answer from Samson's bride, the companions flaunted every detail of the riddle's solution. **If ye had not plowed with my heifer** (v. 18). Samson's term for his wife was anything but endearing. More importantly, since heifers were not used for plowing, Samson is accusing them of unfairness.

14:19–20. The spirit ... came upon him (v. 19) for the occasion, for God's purposes for Samson included humbling the Philistines. **Ashkelon**, one of the five principal cities of the Philistines (see map, *KJV Study Bible*, p. 313; see also discussion on 3:1–4), was located on the coast about twenty-three miles due west of Timnath. Other Philistine cities

Seven green withs (lit., "new cords"; v. 7) were cords made from moist tendons. Such cords were generally used for tent cords and bowstrings. The number seven had special significance to the ancients, symbolizing completeness or fullness. Note that Samson's hair was divided into seven locks (v. 13).

Men lying in wait (v. 9) is literally "the one lying in wait," that is, an ambush (vv. 9, 11). Apparently, the purpose of this ambush was to verify Samson's loss of strength and report to the Philistines.

The use of **new ropes** (v. 11) had already been attempted by Judah. Delilah apparently did not know that this method had already been tried and had failed (15:13–14), setting the Philistines up for disaster.

Samson's advice concerning weaving his hair was silly and irrelevant to his strength, but he was lowering his guard and was closer to telling Delilah the truth of his being a Nazarite. **She fastened it with the pin** (v. 14), probably from a weaver's shuttle. The details of this account suggest that the loom in question was the vertical type, with a crossbeam from which warp threads were suspended. Samson's long hair was woven into the warp and beaten up into the web with the pin, thus forming a tight fabric.

16:15–17. With her patience exhausted, Delilah tried a new ploy to gain the secret. She no longer commanded him to tell her his secret but complained that he had no affection for her: **How canst thou say, I love thee ...?** (v. 15). Her continual pressing (nagging) wore at his tolerance (see Prov. 27:15). Once Samson ran out of novel ideas (lies) to try the patience of Delilah, as she was trying his, he revealed that he was Nazarite (see discussion on 13:4–6) and that cutting his hair would deprive him of his strength. Even here, he was not entirely truthful. His hair was the only aspect of the Nazarite vow that he had not yet violated, but it was not the magical source of his strength. The repeated phrase "and the Spirit of the LORD came upon" (14:6, 19; 15:14) clearly indicates that his strength was supernatural, from the Lord Himself.

16:18–20. Having been duped three times (16:10, 13, 15) by Samson's false suggestions on how to "afflict" him, Delilah finally detected sincerity in his answer and apparently put in an immediate application for payment. Since Delilah had experimented with the first three suggestions to harm him, could Samson have been so naive that he believed she would not shave his head?

His strength went from him (v. 19). As a result of his disobedience and his broken vow, Samson was no longer usable for God's purposes. **The LORD was departed from him** (v. 20). The source of Samson's strength was ultimately God Himself, but He had withdrawn His empowering Spirit, and Samson **wist not**. This is one of the most tragic statements in the Old Testament. Samson was unaware that he had betrayed his calling. He had permitted a Philistine woman to rob him of the sign of his special consecration to the Lord. The Lord's champion lay asleep and helpless in the arms of his paramour. His lack of spiritual sensitivity reflects the poor quality of relationship with God that a man living in sin experiences.

16:21–22. The Philistines **put out his eyes** (v. 21). Brutal treatment of prisoners of war, to humiliate and incapacitate them, was common (see discussion on 1:6; see also 1 Sam. 11:2; 2 Kings 25:7). In shame and weakness, Samson was led **to Gaza**, the place where he had displayed great strength (16:1–3) and left in triumph. He had left Gaza in the darkness of night (16:3); now he returned in the darkness of blindness. **In the prison**, he was assigned to grinding, a task normally performed by women or slaves (see Exod. 11:5; and see discussion on 9:53).

16:23–24. Extrabiblical sources indicate that throughout Mesopotamia, **Dagon** (v. 23) was identified as a god of vegetation, grain (Hebrew, *dagan*), and fertility (see discussion on 10:6). Undoubtedly, this god retained the same attributes among the Canaanite and Philistines. Though unstated, it is not impossible that the Philistines intended to sacrifice Samson to Dagon at their celebration to show their gratitude for deliverance. **Our god hath delivered Samson ... into our hand**. It was common to attribute a victory to the national deities. Ironically, this time the Lord had delivered His judge into the hands of the oppressors.

16:25–30. Samson, who had once intimidated them with his inexplicable strength and ability to destroy persons and property, was reduced to being a blind, helpless entertainer, and thousands gathered to watch his performance, sitting even **upon the roof** (v. 27). The temple complex included Greek-style pillars surrounding an open court and had a flat roof, where a large number of people had gathered to get a glimpse of the fallen champion. A similar Philistine-style temple has been found at Tell Qasile (near modern Tel Aviv).

O Lord GOD, remember me … (v. 28; compare 1 Sam. 1:11; Luke 23:42). Samson's prayer was as sincere a cry as his thirsty call for water (15:18), for his prayer was answered. His request to be **avenged of the Philistines for my two eyes** contrasts our Lord's prayer from the cross (Luke 23:34) and Stephen's prayer for his stoners (Acts 7:60). His dying act, however, was more than revenge for eyes, for in his sacrifice of self, the Philistines suffered their greatest number of casualties at the hand of Samson and lost a number of their key leaders, **the lords** (vv. 27, 30).

Samson **bowed himself** (v. 30) and pushed the wooden pillars from their stone bases. Archaeologists have discovered a Philistine temple with a pair of closely spaced pillar bases. Samson previously had slain well over one thousand people (see 15:15; see also 14:19; 15:8), but now **he slew at his death** an even greater number.

16:31. His brethren … came down, and took him. The freedom of his family to secure his body and give it a burial indicates that the Philistines had no intention of further dishonoring him (contrast Saul's death, 1 Sam. 31:9–10).

III. Epilogue: Religious and Moral Disorder (chaps. 17–21)

17:1–21:25. In this section, two episodes form an epilogue to the story of the judges (see Introduction: "Literary Features"). The events narrated are not chronologically arranged and evidently took place fairly early in the period of the judges (see discussions on 18:30; 20:1, 28). They illustrate the religious and moral degeneracy that characterized

the age, in which "there was no king in Israel" and "every man did that which was right in his own eyes" (17:6; 21:25). Writing at a time when the monarchy, under the Davidic dynasty, had brought cohesion and order to the land and had reestablished a center for the worship of the Lord, the author portrays this earlier era of the judges as a dismal period of national decay, from which it was to be rescued by the house of David.

A. First Episode (chaps. 17–18)

1. Micah's Corruption of Religion (chap. 17)

17:1–18:31. The first episode (see 17:6; 18:1) illustrates corruption in Israelite worship by telling of Micah's establishment of a local place of worship in Ephraim, aided by a Levite claiming descent from Moses. This paganized worship of the Lord was taken over by the tribe of Dan when that tribe abandoned its appointed inheritance and migrated to Israel's northern frontier.

17:1–2. The setting is **mount Ephraim** (v. 1), the general area in which Shiloh, the religious center of Israel and home of the Mosaic tabernacle, was located.

Had Shiloh lost its moral influence on **Micah** (whose name means "Who is like Jehovah?"; v. 1), who, though religious, stole from his own mother? The missing **eleven hundred shekels of silver** (v. 2) was of significant value (see discussion on 16:5). Micah had overheard his mother curse the thief; fear of the curse seems to have motivated his confession and returning the stolen money, not a moral consciousness of what was right. **Blessed be thou … my son** was a blessing meant to counteract the curse.

17:3–6. Here is a classic example of religious syncretism. With their paganized view of the God of Israel, both **mother** and **son** (v. 3) were idolaters. To make a silver idol to the Lord was diametrically opposed to His will and Mosaic law (Exod. 20:4, 23; Deut. 4:16; 27:15) and invoked His curse. The **graven image** was probably made of wood overlaid with silver; the **molten image** was made of solid silver or of cheaper metal overlaid with silver. The silver was given to a **founder** (v. 4), a maker of idols, as in Acts

19:24 (see Isa. 40:19 and Jer. 10:9, where the Hebrew for this word is translated "goldsmith"). Micah had his own **ephod** (v. 5; see 8:27 and discussion on Exod. 28:6) and **teraphim**, household gods, used in this case for divining (see Ezek. 21:21; Zech. 10:2). Some of them were in human form (1 Sam. 19:13). He also engaged **one of his sons** (a non-Levite) as his personal priest. He had everything necessary for ritual—sanctuary, idols, and a priest—but lacked the Spirit of God.

There was no king in Israel (v. 6; see 18:1; 19:1; 21:25). The phrase suggests that Judges was written after the establishment of the monarchy (see Introduction: "Date"). **Every man did that which was right in his own eyes**. The expression implies that Israel had departed from the covenant standards of conduct found in the law (see Deut. 12:8) and reinforces the fact that "Israel did evil in the sight of the Lord" (see discussion on 2:11).

17:7–8. Beth-lehem-judah (v. 7) was not among the forty-eight designated Levitical cities (Joshua 21). The Levite (named in 18:20) **departed out of the city** (v. 8). His need to relocate to **find a place** is possibly indicative of the failure of the Israelites to obey the law, which probably resulted in a lack of support for the Levites (see Num. 18:20–24) and explains the man's wandering in search of his fortune.

17:9–11. Learning that the man was a Levite, Micah implored him to become a **father and a priest** (v. 10) to him. "Father" (see 18:19) is a term of respect used also for Joseph (Gen. 45:8), Elijah (2 Kings 2:12), and Elisha (2 Kings 6:21; 13:14). **Ten shekels** equals about four ounces. In the light of this remuneration for a year's service, the stated amounts in 16:5 and 17:2 take on special significance. The offer of wages, clothing, and food was more than this Levite could resist (v. 11). Clearly, material concerns were at the root of his decision, because he would later accept an even more attractive offer (18:19–20).

17:12–13. Micah consecrated the Levite (v. 12). This was an attempt to make his shrine legitimate and give it prestige. **The Lord will do me good** (v. 13). Micah was confident that he had improved

his standing with God by adding a Levite to his personal sanctuary. Though the newcomer was indeed a Levite, he did not qualify as God's priest, for he was not a descendant of Aaron (see Exod. 28:1), and deserved to die for assuming the role (Num. 3:10). The Levite probably replaced Micah's son, who had been the priest in Micah's shrine (see 17:5).

2. The Danites' Departure from Their Tribal Territory (chap. 18)

18:1–2. The Danites sought them an inheritance (v. 1). The Danite allotment was at the west end of the strip of land between Judah and Ephraim (Josh. 19:41–46), but due to the opposition of the Amorites (Judg. 1:34) and the Philistines, the Danites were unable to occupy that territory (see discussion on 13:2). Instead of resisting and claiming their inheritance, they chose to relocate. A five-member team was sent to **spy out the land** (v. 2; see Num. 13:2) to find a more accommodating place to live. They departed from Zorah, the town that would later become the home of Samson.

18:3–6. Their travels brought them to Micah's house, and they **knew the voice of … the Levite** (v. 3). Perhaps they recognized him by his dialect or accent. **Ask counsel … of God** (v. 5). The request is for an oracle, probably by using the ephod and the household gods (see discussion on 17:5). God had already revealed His will by the allotments given to the various tribes (Josh. 14–20). Ironically, they were searching for an oracle from God (through God-forbidden means) that would guarantee the success of their journey (to find a place other than God's choice for them). **Go in peace** (v. 6). The Levite gave them the message they wanted to hear. He was even careful to use the name of the Lord to give the message credibility and authority.

18:7–10. The journey northward to **Laish** (v. 7) was about one hundred miles from Zorah and Eshtaol (18:2). Laish is called Leshem in Joshua 19:47. After its capture by the Danites, Laish was renamed Dan (18:29), and it was Israel's northernmost settlement (see 20:1; 1 Sam. 3:20; 2 Sam. 3:10). Excavations there have disclosed that the earliest Israelite occupation of Dan was in the twelfth century BC and that the first Israelite inhabitants apparently lived in tents or temporary huts. Occupation of the site continued into the Assyrian period, but the town was destroyed and rebuilt many times. A large high place attached to the city was often extensively rebuilt and refurbished and was in use into the Hellenistic period.

Laish was located a safe distance from the **Zidonians** (v. 7), a peaceful Phoenician people who engaged in commerce throughout the Mediterranean world. The people of Laish **had no business with any man**; that is, they did not feel threatened by other powers and therefore sought no treaties for mutual defense. Laish afforded the lifestyle desired by the Danites.

The report to the Danites regarding Laish was, **God hath given it into your hands** (v. 10). Their claim to the land and God's approval, simply based on the Levite's blessing, was not justifiable.

18:11–16. What proportion of the tribe migrated to Laish is not clear, but apparently, part of the tribe did not participate in the move (see discussion on 13:2).

The **six hundred men** (v. 11) who were armed for war were presumably accompanied by family and may have been merely representative of the Danite population (the census of Num. 26:42–43 numbered the Danites at 64,400); compare the "six hundred men" who constituted the remnant of the tribe of Benjamin (20:47). The group passed Micah's house, where they were notified of all his religious paraphernalia.

18:17–21. The religious syncretism of the period is manifested in the Danites' thievery, stealing the gods of Micah (who was himself a confessed thief, 17:2) for their use at their new settlement. Also, the materialistic spirit of the Levite is evidenced when he accepted the Danites' offer to join them for a better life and larger "parish." For **be to us a father and priest** (v. 19), see discussion on 17:10.

Instead of serving one man, the Levite was invited to serve **a tribe and a family** (v. 19). Only one clan from the tribe of Dan is ever mentioned: Shu-

ham (Num. 26:42; called Hushim in Gen. 46:23). The Danites appealed to the Levite's vanity and materialism and won him over.

In their travel, the armed men placed **before them** (v. 21) the children, cattle, and possessions, presumably for protection in case of attack from the rear.

18:22–25. Micah's neighbors, who apparently also worshiped his god, joined his protest. **Ye have taken away my gods** (v. 24). Micah's concern about the loss of gods that could not even protect themselves underscores his theological confusion. **What have I more?** is the agonizing cry of one whose faith is centered in helpless gods. Contrast Micah's gods with the God who was his maker (Pss. 95:6; 100:3). **Let not thy voice be heard among us** (v. 25). Micah is warned not to fuss. The Danites were ready to take their sin to the next level, murder, if necessary.

18:26–29. As described earlier, the area of Laish was peaceful and unprotected. The Danites took the city without incident and renamed it in honor of their forefather.

18:30–31. The Levite who assumed the role of priest and assisted the Danites in establishing their city as a pagan and rival religious center to Shiloh (see Josh. 18:1) was **Jonathan** (v. 30), the grandson of **Manasseh**. However, the original reading appears to have been "Moses" (supported by an ancient Hebrew scribal tradition, some Greek Septuagint manuscripts, and the Latin Vulgate). The Levite Jonathan would then be identified as the son of Gershom, the son of Moses (Exod. 2:22; 18:3; 1 Chron. 23:14–15). In an effort to prevent desecration of the name of Moses, later scribes modified the name slightly, inserting the letter *nun* (*n*), making it read "Manasseh." If Jonathan was the grandson of Moses, the events in this chapter must have occurred early in the period of the judges (see discussions on 20:1, 28).

Jonathan and **his sons were** rival **priests** (v. 30) until the **captivity of the land**, a date that has not been determined (see discussion on 18:7 regarding Laish), and **Micah's graven image** (v. 31) was the focal point of worship **all the time that the house of God was in Shiloh**. (For Shiloh's destruction, see Ps. 78:60; Jer. 7:12, 14; 26:6.) Archaeological work at

Shiloh indicates that the site was destroyed circa 1050 BC and was left uninhabited for many centuries.

B. Second Episode (chaps. 19–21)

19:1–21:25. This is the second episode of the epilogue (see 19:1; 21:25; see also discussion on 17:1–18:31). It illustrates Israel's moral corruption by telling of the degenerate act of the men of Gibeah—an act remembered centuries later (Hos. 9:9; 10:9). Although that town showed itself to be as wicked as any Canaanite town, it was defended by the rest of the tribe of Benjamin against the Lord's discipline through the Israelites, until nearly the whole tribe was destroyed.

1. Gibeah's Corruption of Morals (chap. 19)

19:1–30. This chapter is an account of an Israelite town that revived the ways of Sodom (see Gen. 19).

19:1–9. As in the preceding episode, **a ... Levite** (v. 1), **mount Ephraim**, and **Beth-lehem-judah** are important details in the story. Unlike the Levite of chapters 17–18, this man is not named. He already lived in Mount Ephraim, but he would go to Bethlehem-judah to fetch his unfaithful concubine, that is, his secondary wife (see discussion on Gen. 25:6). His concubine played the whore; that is, she was morally unfaithful, before returning to her father. After four months' separation, the Levite pursued her to allow him to **speak friendly unto her** (lit., "speak to her heart"; v. 3), that is, to woo her and win her back.

Her father **rejoiced to meet him** (v. 3). Perhaps the separation of the concubine from the Levite was a matter of family disgrace, so his father-in-law was glad for the prospect of the two being reunited. The two "wined and dined" for five days until the Levite pulled himself away to return home with his concubine, accompanied by a servant.

19:10–15. Jebus (v. 10), or Jerusalem, lay about six miles north of Bethlehem. It was a **city of a stranger** (v. 12), that is, a city still controlled and inhabited by the Jebusites. The Levite was afraid he would receive no hospitality and might be in mortal danger. Thus, he dismissed any suggestion of spending the night in a non-Israelite city. He preferred to go on to Gibeah or Ramah for the night.

Gibeah (v. 14), where the trio stopped for the night, lay about four miles north of Jerusalem in **Benjamin** and is to be distinguished from the Gibeah in Judah (Josh. 15:20, 57) and the Gibeah in the hill country of Ephraim (Josh. 24:33; as the political capital of Saul's kingdom, it is called "Gibeah of Saul" in 1 Sam. 11:4; see also 1 Sam. 13:15.) The city lacked hospitality, for no one **took them into his house** (v. 15; see discussions on 13:15; Gen. 18:2), and the immoral behavior of the residents proved to be worse than might have been expected from pagan Jebus (v. 10).

19:16–21. Perhaps because he too was from Ephraim, **an old man** (v. 17) took in the traveling trio from Mount Ephraim. **I am now going to the house of the Lord** (v. 18). Was the Levite planning to go to Shiloh (see 18:31; Josh. 18:1) to present to the Lord a thank offering or a sin offering for himself and his concubine? Or was a "spiritual" mission stated so as to improve his chances for lodging? (The Septuagint has "my house," and he did indeed return to "his house," 19:29.)

Having been given lodging, **they washed their feet** (v. 21) before eating, a sign of hospitality in the ancient Near East, where travelers commonly wore sandals as they walked the dusty roads (see Gen. 18:4; 24:32; 43:24; Luke 7:44; John 13:5–14).

19:22–28. The Hebrew for the expression, **sons of Belial** (lit., "sons of no worth"; v. 22), refers to the morally depraved (see discussion on Deut. 13:13). Elsewhere the expression is associated with idolatry (Deut. 13:13), drunkenness (1 Sam. 1:16), and rebellion (1 Sam. 2:12). Here the reference is to homosexuality. **Bring forth the man.** The sexual perversion of these wicked men is yet another example of the decadence of an age when "every man did that which was right in his own eyes" (17:6; 21:25). A similar request had been made by the men of Sodom centuries earlier (Gen. 19:5). Homosexuality was common among the Canaanites.

Do not so wickedly (v. 23) is an expression of outrage at the willful perversion of what is right and natural (see Gen. 19:7; 2 Sam. 13:12; see also

Rom 1:27). What a compromise of morals is seen in the counteroffer: **here is my daughter a maiden, and his concubine** (v. 24). The tragedy of this story lies not only in the decadence of Gibeah but also in the callous selfishness of men who would betray defenseless women to be brutally violated for a whole night. (Compare Gen. 19:8, where Lot offered his two daughters to the men of Sodom.) For the old man, heterosexual rape was to be preferred over homosexual rape. What was "right" in the man's eyes was to choose what he considered to be the lesser of two evils. It is never right, however, to embrace one sin to avert another.

The Levite himself thrust his concubine out to the sinful crowd, who ravaged her physically until she died. Cold and uncaring, the Levite found her in the morning. Ironically, her immorality (19:2) had come full circle, and she died a victim.

19:29 – 30. The Levite **divided her ... into twelve pieces** (v. 29). Dismembering the concubine's body and sending parts to each of the twelve tribes was intended to awaken Israel from its moral lethargy and to marshal the tribes to face up to their corporate responsibility to serve judgment upon the sexual offenders. It is ironic that the one who issued such a call was himself so selfish and insensitive. (Compare Saul's similar action at Gibeah years later to muster an army, 1 Sam. 11:7.) The grisly act did indeed achieve its purpose.

2. The Benjamites' Removal from Their Tribal Territory (chaps. 20 – 21)

20:1 – 48. All Israel (except Jabesh-gilead; see 21:8 – 9) assembled before the Lord to deal with the moral outrage committed by the men of Gibeah. Having first inquired of God for divine direction, they marched against Gibeah and the Benjamites as the disciplinary arm of the Lord (see Josh. 22:11 – 34), following Him as their King.

20:1 – 2. Israel ... gathered together as one man (v. 1; see 20:8, 11; 1 Sam. 11:7). Though the reason for dismembering the corpse was not yet known to them, the Israelites sensed an indication of "wickedness" (20:3) and convened with unified purpose

to learn the meaning. They came from **Dan even to Beer-sheba**. This is a conventional way of speaking of the full length of the land of Israel from north, Dan, to south, Beersheba (see 1 Sam. 3:20; 2 Sam. 3:10; 24:2; 1 Chron. 21:2; 2 Chron. 30:5). The use of this expression, however, does not necessarily mean that the events of this chapter occurred after Dan's move to the north (18:27 – 29). Rather, it might indicate the author's perspective at the time of writing. Here the expression refers to the disciplinary action of all Israel (except Jabesh-gilead; see 21:8 – 9) against Gibeah and the rest of the Benjamites. Such a united response must have occurred early in the time of the judges, before the period of foreign domination of various parts of the land.

The exact location of **Mizpeh** (v. 1), the gathering place, remains uncertain, but it is generally believed to be near Gibeah, perhaps about three miles south of Bethel. It was also a gathering place of the tribes during the days of Saul (1 Sam. 7:5 – 17; 10:17). All of the tribes, with the exception of Benjamin (who was aware of the others' movements, 20:3), were represented at the assembly.

20:3 – 7. The Levite (v. 4) was given an opportunity to relate the shocking details of his concubine's murder. He implicated **the men of Gibeah** (v. 5; see 19:22), which here is literally the "lords" or "masters" of the city, that is, the leadership. The Levite conveniently omitted his part in thrusting her out to them (see 19:25). By dismembering his concubine's corpse, he had meant to arouse Israel's attention to Gibeah's **lewdness and folly** (v. 6). Now having the audience of Israel, he sought their advice.

20:8 – 11. The unity of Israel, **as one man** (v. 8; see v. 11), is noted as preparations are made to deal with Gibeah. Israel made plans to **go up by lot** (v. 9) against Gibeah (see 20:18). Casting lots was a common method of determining the will of God (see discussions on Exod. 28:30; Jonah 1:7; Acts 1:26).

Support for the large army had to be well organized and efficient. The formula **ten men ... hundred ... thousand** (v. 10) indicates that one man was responsible for providing food for nine men fighting at the front.

20:12–15. To avert a civil war, eleven tribes demanded that Benjamin admit to Gibeah's wickedness and **deliver us … the children of Belial** (v. 13; for Belial, see discussion on 19:22). The demand of Israel was not unreasonable. They wanted to punish only those directly involved in the crime and **put them to death**. The sin of the men of Gibeah called for the death penalty, and Israel had to punish the sin if she was to avoid guilt herself (see Deut. 13:5; 17:7; 19:19–20). Rather than complying, Benjamin's response was to prepare for battle, assembling 26,000 men.

20:16–17. Seven hundred (v. 16) selected Benjamites were **lefthanded**, like the earlier Benjamite judge Ehud (see discussion on 3:15). Each could **sling stones**. The sling was a very effective weapon, as David later demonstrated in his encounter with Goliath (1 Sam. 17:49), for a slingstone, weighing one pound or more, could be hurled at 90–100 miles an hour. They were extremely accurate and did **not miss**. Interestingly, in other contexts, the Hebrew for the verb "miss" is translated "to sin." The Benjamites prepared to face 400,000 fellow Israelites.

20:18–25. The **house of God** (v. 18) is probably better understood as a proper noun, for the Hebrew is *beth el*. At this time, the ark of the covenant and the high priest Phinehas were temporarily located at Bethel (see 20:26–28). It was there that Israel **asked counsel of God**, probably by priestly use of the Urim and Thummim (see discussions on Exod. 28:30; 1 Sam. 2:28). For eleven tribes to fight Benjamin, their brother tribe, was not an easy decision. **Which of us shall go up first …?** Compare 1:1–36, which begins with the same question. **Judah** was selected to go first, that is, to lead the others against the Benjamites, because of its place of prominence and leadership (see discussion on 1:2) or perhaps because the murdered concubine was from Bethlehem.

The first engagement was a rousing victory for the Benjamites, who numbered 26,700 and had slain **twenty and two thousand men** (v. 21) of the Israelites. Each Benjamite, therefore, had slain nearly one man apiece. In the second engagement, the Israelites lost **eighteen thousand men** (v. 25).

20:26–28. Why did the punishing tribes suffer such great losses of men? Is it possible that corporately the nation of Israel was no more righteous than Benjamin? The setback from Israel's two losses was humbling indeed, but it had a beneficial and healthy effect on the spiritual outlook of Israel, bringing them to a point of weeping, fasting, and sacrificing to the Lord. **Phinehas** (v. 28), the one who had been commended by the Lord for his zeal (Num. 25:1–15) and who had once helped mediate and avert a civil war (Josh. 22), was now the priest inquiring of the Lord and directing Israel in punishing Benjamin. The fact that Phinehas was still serving is further evidence that these events took place early in the days of the judges (see discussions on 20:1; 18:30).

20:29–48. Israel set liers in wait (v. 29), an ambush, around Gibeah, employing the same strategy that Joshua had used against Ai a few years earlier (Josh. 8:2). Sadly, Israel was now treating its own as if they were the enemy. In verses 29–36a, the narrative is brief and to the point, reporting that this third battle went to the eleven tribes, with Benjamin suffering a major defeat. Verses 36b–45, however, add fuller details to the battle, describing the placement of the ambush, the attack, the fake retreat, the burning of the city, and the pincer movement upon Benjamin.

The **twenty and five thousand** (v. 46) Benjamite men that were killed is probably a round number for 25,100 (see v. 35), but added to the 600 men who survived, the number still seems to contradict the number of 26,700 men in 20:15. The discrepancy of a thousand men might indicate the number that Benjamin lost while winning the first two battles against Israel.

Six hundred men (v. 47) were able to flee and survive. If these had not escaped, the tribe of Benjamin would have been annihilated (the same number of Danites went to Laish, 18:11). The tribe of Benjamin had defended the wicked deeds of Gibeah's men (20:12–14) and thereby became associated with their guilt. Thus, all the cities of Benjamin came under judgment, but Israel's zeal to punish Benjamin went unchecked. In putting each city to the sword and fire, no distinction was given to women and children.

21:1–25. Second thoughts about the slaughter of their Benjamite brothers caused the Israelites to grieve over the loss. Only six hundred Benjamites were left alive, and the men of Israel decided to provide wives for them to keep the tribe from disappearing. After slaughtering most of the people of Jabesh-gilead, the Israelites took four hundred girls from the survivors and gave them to four hundred Benjamites. Shortly afterward, each of the remaining Benjamites seized a wife from the girls of Shiloh, and Benjamin began to be restored.

21:1–4. The destiny of the tribe of Benjamin was complicated by the fact that Israel, in venting its anger, **had sworn** (v. 1) never to let their daughters marry Benjamites. This vow, probably taken in the name of the Lord, was not an ordinary vow but invoked a curse on oneself if the vow was broken (21:18; see Acts 23:12–15). With such an oath in place, the tribe of Benjamin was doomed to extinction.

Returning to the **house of God** (v. 2; see discussions on 20:18, 26–28), the Israelites **wept sore**. Earlier they wept because they had been defeated by the Benjamites (20:23, 26), but now they wept because the disciplinary action against the Benjamites had nearly annihilated one of the tribes (see v. 3). They built an altar for offerings, but it is not said that they inquired of the Lord concerning their dilemma (see 20:27).

21:5–7. Who ... came not up with the congregation unto the Lord? (v. 5). The tribes had a mutual responsibility in times of military action (see discussion on 5:13–18). Those who failed to participate were often singled out and sometimes punished (5:15–17, 23). Further complicating the situation for Israel was the fact that they had taken a second oath, **a great oath**, calling for the death of those who did not participate in the battle. The lingering problem was how to preserve Benjamin from extinction without violating their oath prohibiting marriages with that tribe.

21:8–15. The area of Gilead had sent representation (see 20:1), but **Jabesh-Gilead** (v. 8) had not participated. Therefore, **twelve thousand men** (v. 10), presumably a thousand from each tribe (see Num. 31:6), with 1,000 supplied to represent the tribe of Benjamin, were sent to Jabesh-Gilead to **smite the inhabitants ... women and children ... every male** (vv. 10–11). The punishment of Jabesh-gilead seems brutal, but the covenant bond between the tribes was extremely important. Even though delinquency on some occasions was not punished (5:15–17), the nature of the crime in this case, coupled with Benjamin's refusal to turn over the criminals, caused Israel to take this "great oath" (21:5).

Only **four hundred young virgins** (v. 12) were spared, who were then brought across the Jordan, from the east to **Canaan**, to be wives for the surviving Benjamites. Future events reveal a close tie between Gibeah and Jabesh-gilead. Years later, after the tribe of Benjamin revived, Gibeah was the home of Saul, Israel's first king. Saul's ancestress may have come from Jabesh-gilead. Shortly after Saul was made king, Jabesh-gilead was threatened by the Ammonites and called to him for help (see 1 Sam. 11:1–11). Also, it was the men of Jabesh-gilead who rescued Saul's body from disgraceful treatment when he was killed by the Philistines (see 1 Sam. 31:11–13).

21:16–22. Because two hundred Benjamites were still without wives (see v. 12; 20:47) and the Israelites' oath not to let their daughters marry Benjamites (21:1) was still in force, Israel devised a compromise involving the **feast of the Lord** (v. 19). In light of the mention of vineyards (v. 20), it is likely that this reference is to the Feast of Tabernacles (see discussion on 1 Sam. 1:3), though it may have been a local festival. The detailed description of Shiloh's location, **on the north side of Beth-el ... south of Lebonah** (v. 19), may indicate that this material was written at a time when Shiloh was in ruins, perhaps after its destruction during the battle of Aphek (1 Sam. 4:1–11).

Permission was granted for the remaining Benjamites to lie in wait during the festivities for each to **catch ... his wife** (v. 21). With the Benjamites securing wives in this manner, the other tribes were not actually "giving" their daughters to them and thus were not "guilty" of violating the oath. It was expected that the girls' **fathers or ... brethren** would **complain** (v. 22), and it was not uncommon for the brothers of a girl who had been abducted to demand satisfaction (see Gen. 34:7–31; 2 Sam. 13:20–38). It was therefore important that the elders anticipate complaints and be prepared to get cooperation from the girls' families.

21:23–24. The Benjamites took advantage of this "provision" and secured wives for themselves and began to rebuild. Meanwhile, Israel's soldiers, who had probably been away from home at least five months (see 20:47), returned to their **inheritance** (v. 24), that is, their respective tribe.

21:25. There was no king in Israel (see discussion on 17:6). The book of Judges ends with the reminder that Israel was still awaiting the arrival of its rightful King. Israel's spiritual and moral behavior in the book of Judges is generally disappointing and even repulsive. The author closes with a reminder that even the best man is capable of such behavior when his life is guided by his own standards rather than by the revealed will of God.

THE BOOK OF RUTH

INTRODUCTION

Title

The book is named after one of its main characters, a young woman of Moab, the great-grandmother of David and an ancestress of Jesus (Matt.1:1, 5). The only other biblical book bearing the name of a woman is Esther.

Author and Date

The author is unknown. Jewish tradition points to Samuel, but it is unlikely that he is the author because the mention of David (4:17, 22) implies a later date. Further, the literary style of the Hebrew used in Ruth suggests that it was written during the period of the monarchy.

Background

The story is set in the time of the judges, a time characterized in the book of Judges as a period of religious and moral degeneracy, national disunity, and general foreign oppression. The book of Ruth reflects a temporary time of peace between Israel and Moab (compare Judg. 3:12–30). Like 1 Samuel 1–2, Ruth gives a series of intimate glimpses into the private lives of the members of an Israelite family. It also presents a delightful account of the remnant of true faith and piety in the period of the judges, relieving an otherwise wholly dark picture of that era.

Theme and Theological Message

The author focuses on Ruth's unswerving and selfless devotion to desolate Naomi (1:16–17; 2:11–12; 3:10; 4:15) and on Boaz's kindness to these two widows (chaps. 2–4). Ruth and Boaz are striking examples of people who embody in their daily affairs the self-giving love that fulfills God's law (Lev. 19:18; Rom. 13:10). Such love also reflects God's love, in a marvelous joining of man's actions with God's (compare 2:12 with 3:9). In God's benevolence, such lives are blessed and are made a blessing.

It may seem surprising that one who reflects God's love so clearly is a Moabitess (see map, *Zondervan KJV Study Bible*, p. 347). Yet Ruth's complete loyalty to the Israelite family into which she has been received by marriage and her total devotion to her desolate mother-in-law mark her as a true daughter of Israel and a worthy ancestress of David. She exemplifies the truth that participation in the coming kingdom of God is decided not by blood and birth but by the conformity of one's life to the will of God through "obedience to the faith" (Rom. 1:5). Her place in the ancestry of David signifies that all nations will be represented in the kingdom of David's greater Son.

As an episode in the ancestry of David, the book of Ruth sheds light on his role in the history of redemption. Redemption is a key concept throughout the account; the Hebrew word in its various forms occurs twenty-three times. The book is primarily a story of Naomi's transformation from despair to happiness through the selfless, God-blessed acts of Ruth and Boaz. Naomi moves from emptiness to fullness (1:21; 3:17; see discussions on 1:1, 3, 5–6, 12, 21–22; 3:17; 4:15), from destitution (1:1–5) to security and hope (4:13–17). Similarly, Israel was transformed from national desperation at the death of Eli (1 Sam. 4:18) to peace and prosperity in the early days of Solomon (1 Kings 4:20–34; 5:4) through the selfless devotion of David, a true descendant of Ruth and Boaz. The author thus reminded Israel that the reign of the house of David, as the means of God's benevolent rule in Israel, held the prospect of God's promised peace and rest. This rest would continue only so long as those who participated in the kingdom — prince and people alike — reflected in their daily lives the selfless love exemplified by Ruth and Boaz. In Jesus, the great "son of David" (Matt.1:1), and His redemptive work, the promised blessings of the kingdom of God find their fulfillment.

Literary Features

The book of Ruth is a Hebrew short story, told with consummate skill. Among the historical narratives in Scripture, it is unexcelled in its compactness, vividness, warmth, beauty, and dramatic effectiveness — an exquisitely wrought jewel of Hebrew narrative art.

Marvelously symmetrical throughout (see "Outline," below), the action moves from a briefly sketched account of distress (1:1–5; seventy-one words in the Hebrew text), through four episodes, and on to a concluding account of relief and hope that is drawn with equal brevity (4:13–17; seventy-one words in the Hebrew text). The crucial turning point occurs exactly midway through the book (see discussion on 2:20). The opening line of each of the four episodes signals its main development (1:6, the return; 2:1, the meeting with Boaz; 3:1, finding a home for Ruth; 4:1, the decisive event at the gate), while the closing line of each episode facilitates transition to what follows (see discussions on 1:22; 2:23; 3:18; 4:12). Contrast is also used to good effect: pleasant (the meaning of "Naomi") and bitter (1:20), full and empty (1:21), the living and the dead (2:20). Most striking is the contrast between two of the main characters, Ruth and Boaz: the one is a young, alien, destitute widow, while the other is a middle-aged, well-to-do Israelite securely established in his home community. For each, there is a corresponding character whose actions highlight, by contrast, the main characters' selfless acts: Ruth and Orpah, Boaz and the unnamed kinsman.

When movements in space, time, and circumstance all correspond in some way, a harmony results that both satisfies the reader's artistic sense and helps open doors to understanding. The author of Ruth keeps his readers from being distracted from the central story:

Naomi's passage from emptiness to fullness through the selfless acts of Ruth and Boaz (see "Theme and Theological Message"). That passage, or restoration, first takes place in connection with Naomi's return from Moab to the Promised Land and to Bethlehem (meaning "house of bread"; see discussion on 1:1). It then progresses with the harvest season, in which the fullness of the land is gathered. All aspects of the story keep the reader's attention focused on the central issue. Consideration of these and other literary devices (mentioned throughout the notes) will aid the reader's understanding of the book of Ruth.

Outline

Bibliography

Atkinson, David. *The Wings of Refuge: The Message of Ruth*. Downers Grove, IL: InterVarsity, 1983.

Block, Daniel I. *Judges, Ruth*. New American Commentary 6. Nashville: Broadman & Holman, 2002.

Bush, Fredric. *Ruth, Esther*. Word Biblical Commentary 9. Waco, TX: Word, 1996.

Campbell, Edward F., Jr. *Ruth: A New Translation, with Introduction, Notes, and Commentary*. Anchor Bible 7. Garden City, NY: Doubleday, 1975.

Cundall, Arthur, and Leon Morris. *Judges and Ruth: An Introduction and Commentary*. Tyndale Old Testament Commentaries 7. Downers Grove, IL: InterVarsity, 1968.

Enns, Paul. *Ruth: Bible Study Commentary*. Grand Rapids, MI: Zondervan, 1982.

Hubbard, Robert. *The Book of Ruth*. New International Commentary on the Old Testament. Grand Rapids, MI: Eerdmans, 1988.

Huey, F. B., Jr. "Ruth." In *The Expositor's Bible Commentary*, edited by Frank E. Gaebelein, vol. 3. Grand Rapids, MI: Zondervan, 1992.

Leggett, Donald A. *The Levirate and Goel Institutions in the Old Testament, with Special Attention to the Book of Ruth*. Cherry Hill, NJ: Mack, 1974.

EXPOSITION

I. Introduction: Naomi Emptied (1:1–5)

1:1–2. This short story of Ruth finds its setting in the time **when the judges ruled** (v. 1), the period dating from approximately 1380 to 1050 BC (see Judges, Introduction: "Background"). By mentioning the judges, the author calls to mind that period of Israel's apostasy, moral degradation, and oppression. By contrast, the story of Ruth and Boaz adds a ray of light to the dark days of the judges. It is an important book, for it provides the family tree and background for David, God's choice of a king for Israel, and serves as a bridge from the period of the judges to David's reign.

As in the two stories in the epilogue to Judges (chaps. 17–21; see Judg. 17:7; 19:1), **Beth-lehem-ju-dah** (v. 1) plays an important role. In the final story of Judges, Gibeah, the future home of Saul, is cast in a bad light, whereas the story of Ruth focuses favorable attention on the future home of David (1 Sam. 16:18). Bethlehem was located about six miles south of Jerusalem.

In addition to the oppressors that God raised up in this period, Israel also experienced times of famine (see Lev. 26:14–16; Deut. 11:16–17; 28:15, 38–40). The name Bethlehem means "house of bread," but due to the **famine** (v. 1), Bethlehem was empty.

Moab lay east of the Dead Sea between the Arnon and Zered rivers. Though its people were descendants of Lot (Gen. 19:36–37), there were times when they were aggressively hostile to Israel (Num 22–24; Judg. 3:12–14).

The family personal names are significant: **Elimelech** (v. 2) means "(my) God is King" (see discussion on Judg. 8:23), and **Naomi** means "pleasant, sweetness." The names of the two sons, **Mahlon and Chilion**, are more difficult but may signify "weakling, sickly" and "failing, pining." Their names, if descriptive of their health, may offer a clue to their early deaths. They are called **Ephrathites**. This is probably because Bethlehem was originally known as Ephrathah (see 4:11; Gen. 35:19; 48:7; 1 Sam. 17:12; Mic. 5:2).

1:3–5. When **Elimelech Naomi's husband died** (v. 3), Naomi's "emptying" had begun (see 1:21). The prospect of continuing the family line remained, for her sons **took them wives of the women of Moab** (v. 4). Marriage with Moabite women was not forbidden, though no Moabite, or his sons to the tenth generation, was allowed to "enter into the congregation of the LORD" because of their past treatment of Israel (Deut. 23:3–6). The marriages of Naomi's sons were Mahlon to Ruth (see 4:10) and Chilion to Orpah. The name **Ruth** sounds like the Hebrew for "friendship." She is one of four women in Matthew's genealogy of Jesus. The others are Tamar, Rahab, and Bathsheba (Matt. 1:3, 5–6). Each one illustrates the magnitude of God's grace.

Naomi's emptiness was complete when she **was left of her two sons and her husband** (v. 5). With her sons and husband now deceased, she had only two young daughters-in-law, both of whom were foreigners and childless. The story opens with an announcement of the personal tragedies in the lives of Ruth and Naomi and then proceeds like a four-act play, unfolding the incredible account of their commitment to one another. The story also indicates the availability of God's grace to all people, as Ruth, a Moabitess (see Judg. 3:12–30)—a Gentile—is married into the family of Israel and, in particular, into the line of David and thereby into the line of Christ (Matt. 1:5).

II. Naomi Returns from Moab (1:6–22)

A. Ruth Clings to Naomi (1:6–18)

1:6–7. Naomi **arose ... that she might return** (v. 6) to her country. Though personally empty, she chose to return with her daughters-in-law to the newly filled Land of Promise because she had heard that **the LORD had visited his people**. The term "visited" is often used of divine activity. At several points in the account, God's sovereign control of events is acknowledged (v. 6; 1:13, 21; 2:20; 4:12–15). God had given His people **bread** (Hebrew, *lehem*; lit., "food"). Bethlehem ("house of bread") once again had bread, giving evidence that the famine had been God's judgment.

1:8-10. Go, return (v. 8). Desolate Naomi repeatedly urged her daughters-in-law to return to their original homes in Moab (1:11-12, 15); she had nothing to offer them. **The LORD grant you ... find rest** (v. 9). The "rest" that Naomi desired for her daughters-in-law was the settled life and security of a good marriage (see 4:10).

1:11-14. Are there yet any moe (i.e., more) **sons ... that they may be your husbands?** (v. 11). Naomi alluded to the Israelite law (Deut. 25:5-6) regarding levirate marriage (see discussions on Deut. 25:5-10; see also Mark 12:18-23), which was given to protect the widow and guarantee continuance of the family line. The law required the brother of a deceased, childless man to marry his widow in order to produce an heir for the deceased. (For a pre-Mosaic illustration of levirate marriage in a Canaanite context, see Gen. 38:8.)

Naomi explained, however, that the provision of the law was not feasible in their situation because her only sons were dead and so was her husband. **I am too old** (v. 12). Naomi could have no more sons; even her womb was empty. She had no hope of bearing additional sons for her widowed daughters-in-law.

The hand of the LORD is ... against me (v. 13). She expressed self-pity, feeling that God's hand had opposed her in judgment (see 1:5-6, 20-21). The choice of **Orpah** (v. 14) to turn back highlights Ruth's loyalty and selfless devotion to her desolate mother-in-law.

1:15-18. Naomi noted that Orpah had returned to **her gods** (v. 15). The chief god of the Moabites was Chemosh. The existence of gods other than the Lord (Yahweh) is never taken seriously in the Old Testament. It does assume, however, as Naomi does here, their reality as objects of worship. Ruth displayed genuine faith in Israel's God by rejecting the gods of her people.

Intreat me not to leave thee (v. 16). This classic expression of loyalty and love discloses the true character of Ruth. Her commitment to Naomi is complete, even though it holds no prospect for her

but to share in Naomi's desolation. (For a similar declaration of devotion, see 2 Sam. 15:21.)

The LORD do so to me, and more also (v. 17; see discussion on 1 Sam. 3:17). Ruth, a Gentile, swore her commitment to Naomi in the name of Israel's God, thus acknowledging Him as her God. So resolute was Ruth that Naomi stopped trying to persuade her to return to her home.

B. Ruth and Naomi Return to Bethlehem (1:19-22)

1:19-22. The city was moved about them (v. 19). Naomi's return to Bethlehem with Ruth had the town buzzing with curiosity. The women (**they** in Hebrew is a feminine pronoun) were asking, **Is this Naomi?** Apparently, the years in Moab and the loss of her husband and sons had taken their toll on Naomi's health and appearance.

Call me not Naomi, call me Mara (lit., "bitter"; v. 20). In the ancient Near East, a person's name was often descriptive. Here it is descriptive of Naomi's plight. In her self-pity, she felt **the Almighty** (see discussion on Gen. 17:1) had treated her **bitterly** (and **afflicted** her; v. 21) because she had gone away from Bethlehem **full** and had returned **empty**. These words highlight the central theme of the story: how the empty Naomi became full again.

Naomi undervalued the treasure that God had given her in the love and loyalty of her daughter-in-law, **Ruth the Moabitess** (v. 22). Several times the author reminds the reader that Ruth is a foreigner from a despised people (2:2, 6, 21; 4:5, 10; see 2:10). Naomi and Ruth arrived in Bethlehem just as the renewed fullness of the land was realized, at the **beginning** of the harvest—an early hint that Naomi will be full again. Reference to the **barley harvest** also prepares the reader for the next major scene in the harvest fields (see Introduction: "Literary Features"). The harvest of grain in ancient Canaan took place in April and May (barley first, wheat a few weeks later; see 2:23). The harvest was cut and bundled by men ("reapers"); the scraps that were left behind were gathered by the poor ("gleaners"). The sheaves of grain were transported to the threshingfloor, where the grain was loosened from the straw, or "threshed," and then tossed into the wind to blow away the chaff, or "winnowed." Threshingfloors, where both threshing and winnowing occurred, were hard, smooth, open places, prepared on either rock or clay and carefully chosen for favorable exposure to the prevailing winds. They were usually on the east side, that is, downwind, of the village.

III. Ruth and Boaz Meet in the Harvest Fields (chap. 2)

A. Ruth Begins Work (2:1 – 7)

2:1. There is a sign of hope: **a kinsman**. He was a relative who could redeem (purchase) someone from widowhood. The name **Boaz** probably means "in him is strength." He is included in both genealogies of Jesus (Matt.1:5; Luke 3:32).

2:2 – 3. Let me now go ... and glean (v. 2). Although Ruth was an alien and, as a young woman alone, obviously quite vulnerable in the harvest fields, she undertook to provide for her mother-in-law. Naomi would later undertake to provide for her daughter-in-law (3:1). Ruth wished to glean **corn** (i.e., grain) from whomever she might **find grace**. The law of Moses instructed landowners to leave what the harvesters missed so that the poor, the alien, the widow, and the fatherless could glean for their needs (Lev. 19:9; 23:22; Deut. 24:19). Thus, the poor were able to obtain food. Ruth was aware, however, that not all farmers were inclined to permit the poor among the reapers in their fields. **Her hap was to light on ... the field** of Boaz (v. 3). Her entrance into Boaz's field was not mere chance but divine providence at work (see Naomi's confession, 2:20).

2:4 – 7. The LORD be with you (v. 4). The exchange of greetings between Boaz and his laborers characterizes Boaz as a godly man with a kind spirit. To his question regarding the stranger in his field, he learns that **It is the Moabitish damsel** (v. 6). Her loyalty to Naomi was well known. Now she had graciously requested permission to **glean ... after the reapers** (v. 7).

B. Boaz Shows Kindness to Ruth (2:8 – 16)

2:8 – 10. Boaz entreated Ruth to remain in his fields with his servant girls and **go thou after them** (v. 9). It was customary for the men to cut the grain and for the servant girls to go behind them to bind the grain into sheaves. Then Ruth could glean what they had left behind (see discussion on 1:22). Boaz had already provided for her protection. Ruth humbly acknowledged that she had indeed **found grace** (v. 10; see 2:2).

2:11 – 13. Ruth's sacrificial love and her commitment to care for her desolate mother-in-law were well known in the community, and her reputation had preceded her to the fields. It remains the center of attention throughout the book. Boaz pronounced a blessing on her that the God of Israel, **under whose wings** (v. 12) she had come to trust (see 1:16), would reward her for her deeds of kindness. He employed the figure of a bird protecting her young under her wings (see Matt. 23:37; see also discussion on 3:9). Again Ruth was gracious, politely referring to herself as **thine handmaid** (v. 13) as she acknowledged Boaz's kind treatment of her.

2:14 – 16. Boaz provided Ruth a meal and **commanded his young men** (v. 15) not only to permit her to glean among them but to go beyond the requirement of the law in making sure that her labors were abundantly productive (see 3:15). There is dignity in working and earning one's food. Though Boaz insisted that Ruth remain in his field and he instructed his laborers to make her efforts worthwhile by purposely dropping grain, he did not provide for a freeloader. She worked for what she received.

C. Ruth Returns to Naomi (2:17 – 23)

2:17 – 23. Ruth **beat out** (v. 17) the grain that she had gleaned (see discussion on 1:22). In her case, as in that of Gideon (Judg. 6:11), the amount was small and could be threshed by hand simply by beating it with a club or a stick. Her efforts produced an **ephah** of grain, equivalent to about three-fifths of a bushel, an unusually large amount for one day's gleaning.

When Naomi saw the reward of Ruth's labors in gleaning and learned that the one who had taken generous notice of her had been Boaz, she responded, **Blessed be ... the LORD, who hath not left off his kindness** (v. 20; see 1:8). In 3:10, Boaz credits Ruth with demonstrating this same virtue.

Redemption is a key concept in Ruth (see Introduction: "Theme and Theological Message"). Naomi identified Boaz as **one of our next kinsmen** (v. 20). The next kinsman, also known as a "kinsman-redeemer," was responsible for protecting the interests of needy members of the extended family—for example, to provide an heir for a brother who had died (Deut. 25:5–10), to redeem land that a poor relative had sold outside the family (Lev. 25:25–28), to redeem a relative who had been sold into slavery (Lev. 25:47–49), and to avenge the killing of a relative (Num 35:19–21; Josh 20:6; "avenger" and "kinsman-redeemer" are translations of the same Hebrew word). Naomi was encouraged when she heard that the Lord had led Ruth to the fields of a relative who might serve as their kinsman-redeemer. This moment of Naomi's awakened hope is the crucial turning point of the story.

Naomi advised Ruth to accept the invitation of Boaz to remain in his fields. So she stayed by Boaz's servant girls until **the end of ... harvest** (v. 23). There is obviously a time lapse between her first entrance into his fields to the events of chapter 3, but this phrase rounds out the harvest episode and prepares the stage for the next major scene, on the threshingfloor (see Introduction: "Literary Features").

IV. Ruth Goes to Boaz at the Threshingfloor (chap. 3)

A. Naomi Instructs Ruth (3:1–5)

3:1–2. The life of a widow is not easy. Naomi's awakened hope of **rest** for Ruth (v. 1; see discussions on 1:8–13) now moved her to seek provision for Ruth's future (see discussion on 2:2). Knowing that a kinsman was available (see 2:20), she planned to alert him to his responsibilities. Naomi anticipated Boaz's activity. **He winnoweth ... to night** (v. 2; see discussion on 1:22). During the threshing season, it was customary for landowners to spend the night near the threshingfloor to protect their grain from theft.

3:3–5. Ruth was instructed to **wash ... and anoint** herself (v. 3), that is, to prepare herself like a bride (cf. Ezek. 16:9–12). **Get thee down to the** threshing **floor**, a place where women were not nor-

mally present during the evening revelries of the threshers (3:14). Harvest was a time of festivity, with **eating and drinking** (Isa. 9:3; 16:9–10; Jer. 48:33).

Although Naomi's instructions, **uncover his feet, and lay thee down** (v. 4), may appear forward, the moral integrity of Naomi and Ruth is never in doubt (see 3:11). Whether the instructions reflected an ancient custom or served a onetime event, Naomi's advice to Ruth was clearly for the purpose of appealing to Boaz for care and protection as her kinsman-redeemer. Ruth's actions were a request for marriage. Tamar, the mother of Pharez (4:12), had also laid claim to the provision of the levirate (or kinsman-redeemer) law (Gen. 38:13–30).

B. Boaz Pledges to Secure Redemption (3:6–15)

3:6–9. Ruth was careful to do all that Naomi had instructed her, waiting for her moment to lie at Boaz's feet. Discovered by a startled Boaz, she said, **I am Ruth ... spread therefore thy skirt over thine handmaid** (v. 9). It was a request for marriage (see Ezek 16:8); a similar custom is still practiced in some parts of the Middle East today. There is a play on the words "skirt" (lit., "wings") of the garment and "wings" of the Lord (2:12), both signifying protection. Boaz is vividly reminded that he must serve as the Lord's protective wing and watch over Ruth.

3:10–11. Thou hast shewed more kindness ... than at the beginning (v. 10). Apparently, Boaz was considerably older than Ruth and perhaps even flattered that she would want him to be her kinsman-redeemer. He considered the honor a kindness greater than she had shown to Naomi (see 2:11–12). All Bethlehem had come to know that Ruth was **a virtuous woman** (v. 11; see Prov. 31:10). The Hebrew for this expression is similar to that used of Boaz in 2:1; thus, the author maintains a balance between his descriptions of Ruth and Boaz.

3:12–13. Boaz admitted to Ruth that she had nearer kinsman, **a kinsman nearer than I** (v. 12). How Boaz was related to Ruth's former husband (Mahlon) is unknown, but the closest male relative had the primary responsibility to marry a widow. In this case, the nearer kinsman had to be granted first choice of refusal to the related obligations. Naomi had instructed Ruth to approach Boaz because he had already shown himself willing to be Ruth's protector. Boaz, however, would not bypass the directives of the law, which clearly gave priority to the nearest relative.

Boaz committed himself by oath, **as the LORD liveth** (v. 13; see 1:17), to redeem the family property and to arrange Ruth's honorable marriage if the nearest kinsman reneged on his obligations.

3:14-15. Ruth was "virtuous" (3:11) and Boaz was honorable. He carefully guarded against any improprieties that might soil either one's reputation, and he went beyond the requirement of the law in supplying Ruth with grain from the threshingfloor (see 2:15).

C. Ruth Returns to Naomi (3:16-18)

3:16-18. Who art thou ...? (v. 16) might be understood as "How is it with you?" (i.e., "How did it go?"). In giving Ruth barley, Boaz had said, **Go not empty unto thy mother in law** (v. 17). The author again emphasizes the empty-full motif (see discussion on 1:21). Naomi's advice: **Sit still** (i.e., wait; v. 18). The Hebrew underlying this phrase is translated "sat" in 4:1. Thus, the author prepares the reader for the next major scene, in which Boaz sits at the town gate to see the matter through.

V. Boaz Arranges to Marry Ruth (4:1-12)

A. Boaz Confronts the Unnamed Kinsman (4:1-8)

4:1-2. The **gate** (v. 1) of the city was the "town hall" of ancient Israel. It was the normal place for business and legal transactions and where justice was administered (see Deut. 21:19-21; 22:15; Josh. 20:4). With the flow of people to and from the city, it was not difficult to assemble witnesses for the various proceedings (4:9-12; see discussion on Gen. 19:1). The other kinsman is called simply **such a one** and remains unnamed. By assembling **ten men of the elders** (v. 2), Boaz had a full court for legal proceedings.

4:3-5. Boaz informed the relative that **Naomi ... selleth a parcel of land** (v. 3; see discussion on 2:20). Two interpretations are possible: (1) Naomi owned the land but was so destitute that she was forced to

sell. Thus, it was the duty of the kinsman-redeemer to buy any land in danger of being sold outside the family. (2) Naomi did not own the land—it had been sold by Elimelech before the family left for Moab—but by law, she retained the right of redemption to buy the land back. Lacking funds to do so herself, she was dependent on a kinsman-redeemer to do it for her. It was the right of redemption Naomi was "selling." Boaz called Elimelech **our brother** in the broader sense of "our relative."

The unnamed kinsman was given first opportunity to redeem the land, but if he bought the field, he **must buy it also ... the wife of the dead** (v. 5). Now Boaz revealed the other half of the obligation: the acquisition of Ruth. Levirate law (Deut. 25:5-6) provided that Ruth's firstborn son would keep Mahlon's name alive and would possess the right of ownership of the family inheritance.

4:6-8. The kinsman was willing to redeem Naomi's field until he heard the additional stipulation. **I cannot redeem it** (v. 6). Possibly he feared that if he had a son by her and that son were his only surviving heir, his own property would transfer to the family of Elimelech (see discussion on Gen. 38:9). He saw the entire arrangement as posed by Boaz as a financial liability, but his risk was no greater than that assumed by Boaz. This kinsman's refusal to assume the kinsman-redeemer's role highlights the kindness and generosity of Boaz toward the two widows, just as Orpah's return to her family highlights Ruth's selfless devotion and loyalty to Naomi.

The custom was that **a man plucked off his shoe** (v. 7). The process of renouncing one's property rights and passing them to another was publicly attested by taking off a sandal and transferring it to the new owner (see Amos 2:6; 8:6). The Nuzi tablets (see chart, *KJV Study Bible*, p. xix) refer to a similar custom. The act symbolically emphasized the sincerity of one's "walk" in life.

B. Boaz Buys Naomi's Property and Announces His Marriage to Ruth (4:9-12)

4:9-10. Ye are witnesses (v. 9). The role of public witnesses was to attest to all legal transactions and other binding agreements. Boaz publicly announced that he intended to fulfill his kinsman obligations to **raise up the name of the dead** (v. 10), that is, the name of Ruth's deceased husband, Mahlon, and fulfill his duties according to levirate law (see Deut. 25:6).

4:11-12. The elders joined to bless Boaz, invoking the Lord to make Ruth like **Rachel and like Leah ... which two did build the house of Israel** (v. 11). The Israelite readers of Ruth would have associated the house of Jacob (Israel), built up by Rachel and Leah, with the house of Israel, rebuilt by David (a descendant of Ruth and Boaz) after it had been threatened with extinction (1 Samuel 4). Israelite readers also knew that the Lord had covenanted to "build" the house of David as an enduring dynasty, through which Israel's blessed destiny would be assured (see 2 Sam. 7:27-29). For **Ephratah** and **Beth-lehem**, see discussion on 1:1-2.

Pharez, whom Tamar bare unto Judah (v. 12) was Boaz's ancestor (4:18-21; Matt.1:3; Luke 3:33). Pharez had been born to Judah out of a union that involved challenges arising from the levirate practice (Gen. 38:27-30; see discussion on 1:11). Despite these challenges, the descendants of Pharez had raised the tribe of Judah to a prominent place in Israel. So the blessing of the elders—that through the offspring Ruth would bear to Boaz, his family would be like that of Pharez—was fully realized in David and his dynasty. Thus, verse 12 prepares the reader for the events briefly narrated in the conclusion.

VI. Conclusion: Naomi Filled (4:13-17)

4:13-17. The conclusion of the story balances the introduction (1:1-5). In the Hebrew, both have the same number of words, both compress much into a short space, and both focus on Naomi. The introduction emphasizes Naomi's emptiness, and the conclusion portrays her fullness.

Once again God's sovereign control of events is acknowledged, for **the LORD gave her conception** (v. 13; see discussion on 1:6), and Ruth **bare a son**. In 1:19-21, the women of Bethlehem listened as Naomi expressed her bitterness over the "hand" that God had dealt her. Now they gathered to praise the Lord because His gracious hand had sovereignly provided a **kinsman** (v. 14). This was a reference to the child Obed, as verses 15-17 make clear. **That his name may be famous in Israel** (v. 14) is the same wish that was expressed concerning Boaz in 4:11.

The women acknowledged Ruth as **better to thee than seven sons** (v. 15; see 1 Sam. 1:8). Since seven was considered a number of completeness, to have seven sons was the epitome of all family blessings in Israel (see 1 Sam. 2:5; Job 1:2; 42:13). Ruth's selfless devotion to Naomi received its climactic acknowledgment. Naomi **laid** the infant **in her bosom** (v. 16), possibly symbolizing adoption (see discussion on Gen. 30:3). The women said, **There is a son born to Naomi** (v. 17). Through Ruth, aged Naomi, who could no longer bear children, obtained an heir in place of her deceased son Mahlon. The name **Obed** means "servant." In its full form, it possibly means "servant of the Lord."

VII. Epilogue: Genealogy of David (4:18-22)

4:18-22. Like the genealogies of Genesis 5:3-32; 11:10-26, this genealogy has ten names (see discussion on Gen. 5:5; see also 1 Chron. 2:5-15; Matt. 1:3-6; Luke 3:31-33). This may also reflect the author's response to Deuteronomy 23:2, in relation to the unusual nature of Pharez's birth. The ten names indicated David's right to rule as Israel's king. It brings to mind the reign of David, during which, in contrast to the turbulent period of the judges (recalled in 1:1), Israel finally entered into rest in the Promised Land (see 1 Kings 5:4). It signifies that just as Naomi was brought from emptiness to fullness through the selfless love of Ruth and Boaz, so the Lord would bring Israel from unrest to rest through their descendant David, who selflessly gave himself to fight Israel's battles on the Lord's behalf. The ultimate end of this genealogy is Jesus Christ, the great "son of David" (Matt.1:1), who fulfills prophecy and will bring the Lord's people into final rest.

THE FIRST BOOK OF SAMUEL

INTRODUCTION

Title

First and Second Samuel are named after the person God used to establish kingship in Israel. Samuel not only anointed both Saul and David, Israel's first two kings, but he also gave definition to the new order of God's rule over Israel that began when kingship was incorporated into its structure. Samuel's importance as God's representative approaches that of Moses (see Ps. 99:6; Jer. 15:1) since Samuel, more than any other person, provided for covenant continuity in the transition from the rule of the judges to that of the kings.

First and Second Samuel were originally one book. It was divided into two parts by the translators of the Septuagint (the Greek translation of the Old Testament), and this division was subsequently followed by Jerome (the Latin Vulgate) and by modern versions. The title of the book has varied from time to time, having been designated "The First and Second Books of Kingdoms" (Septuagint), "First and Second Kings" (Vulgate), and "First and Second Samuel" (Hebrew tradition and most modern versions).

Author, Date, and Sources

Many questions have arisen regarding the author, date, and sources of 1–2 Samuel. Who the author was cannot be known with certainty since the book itself gives no indication of his identity. Certain literary characteristics of the book suggest it was compiled with the use of a number of independent sources, which the author may have incorporated into his own composition, retaining as much as possible their original, unedited form.

Whoever the author was, he must have lived shortly after Solomon's death (930 BC) and the division of the kingdom (see references to Israel and Judah in 11:8; 17:52; 18:16; 2 Sam. 5:5; 24:1–9; and the expression "kings of Judah" in 1 Sam. 27:6). Some scholars have suggested the author may have been the son of Nathan the prophet, Zabud, who is referred to as King Solomon's "friend" in 1 Kings 4:5. Zabud would have had access to information about David's reign from Nathan and from court records; doubtless he also had access to written records of the lives and times of Samuel, Saul, and David. Explicit reference in 1–2 Samuel is made to only one such source ("the book of Jasher," 2 Sam. 1:18), but the writer of Chronicles refers to four other sources pertaining to this period ("the account of the chronicles of king David," 1 Chron. 27:24; "the book of Samuel the seer," "the book of Nathan the prophet," and "the chronicles of Gad the seer," 1 Chron. 29:29).

Theme

The primary theme of 1-2 Samuel is kingship and covenant. First Samuel relates the establishment of a monarchy in Israel. Before the author describes this momentous change in the structure of the theocracy (God's rule), he effectively depicts the complexity of its context. The following elements provide both the historical and theological context for the birth of the monarchy.

(1) The birth, youth, and calling of Samuel (chaps. 1–3). In a book dealing primarily with the reigns of Israel's first two kings, Saul and David, it is significant that the author chose not to include a birth narrative for either of these men but instead to describe the birth of their forerunner and anointer, the prophet Samuel. This accentuates the importance the author attached to Samuel's role in the events that follow. He seems to be subtly saying that flesh and blood were to be subordinated to Word and Spirit in the process of establishing the kingship. For this reason, chapters 1–3 should be viewed as integrally related to what follows, not as a more likely component of the book of Judges or as a loosely attached prefix to the rest of 1–2 Samuel. Kingship is given its birth and is nurtured by the prophetic word and work of the prophet Samuel. Moreover, the events of Samuel's nativity thematically anticipate the story of God's working that is narrated in the rest of the book.

(2) The "ark narratives" (chaps. 4–6). This section describes how the ark of God was captured by the Philistines and then, after God wreaked havoc on several Philistine cities, how it was returned to Israel. These narratives reveal the folly of Israel's notion that possession of the ark automatically guaranteed victory over her enemies. They also display the awesome power of the Lord (Yahweh, the God of Israel) and His superiority over the Philistine god Dagon. The Philistines were forced to confess openly their helplessness against God's power, by returning the ark to Israel. The entire ark episode performs a vital function in placing Israel's subsequent sinful desire for a human king in proper perspective.

(3) Samuel as a judge and deliverer (chap. 7). When Samuel called Israel to repentance and renewed dedication to the Lord, the Lord intervened mightily on Israel's behalf and gave her victory over the Philistines. The authority of Samuel as a divinely ordained leader was reaffirmed; at the same time, Israel was provided with evidence of the divine protection and blessing that was theirs when they placed their confidence in the Lord and lived in obedience to their covenant obligations.

All the material in chapters 1–7 serves as a necessary preface for the narratives of chapters 8–12, which describe the rise and establishment of kingship in Israel. The author has masterfully arranged the stories in chapters 8–12 to accentuate the serious theological conflict surrounding the historical events. Scholars have often noted the presence of tension or ambivalence in the attitude toward the monarchy. On one hand, Samuel is commanded by the Lord to give the people a king (8:7, 9, 22; 9:16–17; 10:24; 12:13). On the other hand, their request for a king is considered a sinful rejection of the Lord (8:7; 10:19; 12:12, 17, 19–20). These seemingly conflicting attitudes toward the monarchy must be understood in the context of Israel's covenant relationship with the Lord.

Moses had anticipated Israel's desire for a human king (Deut. 17:18–20), but Israelite kingship was to be compatible with the Lord's continued rule over His people as their Great King. Instead, when the elders asked Samuel to give them a king (8:5, 19–20), they rejected the Lord's kingship over them (8:7; 10:19; 12:17, 19). They desired a king such as the nations around them had, a king to lead them in battle and give them a sense of national security and unity. Their request for a king constituted a denial of their covenant relationship with the Lord, who was their King. Moreover, the Lord not only had promised to be their protector but had also repeatedly demonstrated His power in their behalf, most recently in the ark narratives (chaps. 4–6), as well as in the great victory won over the Philistines under the leadership of Samuel (chap. 7).

Nevertheless, the Lord instructed Samuel to give the people a king (8:7, 9, 22). By divine appointment, Saul was brought into contact with Samuel, and Samuel was directed to anoint him privately as king (9:1–10:16). Samuel subsequently gathered the people at Mizpah, where, after again admonishing them concerning their sin in desiring a king (10:18–19), he presided over the selection of a king by lot. The lot fell to Saul and publicly designated him as the one whom God had chosen (10:24). Saul did not immediately assume his royal office but returned home to work his fields (11:5, 7). When the inhabitants of Jabesh-gilead were threatened by Nahash the Ammonite, Saul rose to the challenge, gathered an army, and led Israel to victory in battle. His success placed a final divine seal of approval on Saul's selection to be king (see 10:24; 11:12–13) and occasioned the inauguration of his reign at Gilgal (11:14–12:25).

The question that still needed resolution, then, was not so much whether Israel should have a king (it was clearly the Lord's will to give them a king) but rather how they could maintain their covenant with God (i.e., preserve the theocracy) now that they had a human king. The problem was resolved when Samuel called the people to repentance and renewal of their allegiance to the Lord on the very occasion of Saul's inauguration as king (11:14–12:25; see discussion on 10:25). By establishing kingship in the context of covenant renewal, Samuel placed the monarchy in Israel on a radically different footing from that in the surrounding nations. The king in Israel was not to be autonomous in his authority and power; rather, he was to be subject to the law of the Lord and the word of the prophet (10:25; 12:23). This was to be true not only for Saul but also for all the future kings who would occupy the throne in Israel. The king was to be an instrument of the Lord's rule over His people, and the people as well as the king were to continue to recognize the Lord as their ultimate Sovereign (12:14–15).

Saul very quickly demonstrated that he was unwilling to submit to the requirements of his theocratic office (chaps. 13–15). When he disobeyed the instructions of the prophet Samuel in preparation for battle against the Philistines (13:13), and when he refused to totally destroy the Amalekites as he had been commanded to do by the word of the Lord through Samuel (chap. 15), he ceased to be an instrument of the Lord's rule over His people. These abrogations of the requirements of his theocratic office led to Saul's rejection as king (15:23).

The remainder of 1 Samuel (chaps. 16–31) depicts the Lord's choice of David as Saul's successor and then describes the long road by which David is prepared for accession to the throne. Although Saul's rule became increasingly antitheocratic in nature, David refused to usurp the throne by forceful means but left his accession to office in the Lord's hands. Eventually, Saul was wounded in a battle with the Philistines and, fearing capture, took his own life. Three of Saul's sons, including David's loyal friend Jonathan, were killed in the same battle (chap. 31).

Chronology

Even though the narratives of 1–2 Samuel contain some statements of chronological import (e.g., 1 Sam. 6:1; 7:2; 8:1, 5; 13:1; 25:1; 2 Sam. 2:10–11; 5:4–5; 14:28; 15:7), the data is insufficient to establish a precise chronology for the major events of this period of Israel's history. Except for the dates of David's birth and the duration of his reign, which are quite firm (see 2 Sam. 5:4–5), most other dates can only be approximated. The textual problem with the chronological data on the age of Saul when he became king and on the length of his reign (see discussion on 13:1) contributes to uncertainty concerning the precise time of his birth and the beginning of his reign. No information is given concerning the time of Samuel's birth (1:1) or death (25:1). His lifetime must have spanned, at least in part, that of Samson and that of Obed, son of Ruth and Boaz and grandfather of David. It is indicated that Samuel was well along in years when the elders of Israel asked him to give them a king (see 8:1, 5). That the author has not always arranged his material in strict chronological sequence also contributes to chronological uncertainty. It seems clear, for example, that 2 Samuel 7 is to be placed chronologically after David's conquests described in 2 Samuel 8:1–14 (see discussions on 2 Sam. 7:1; 8:1). The story of the famine that God sent on Israel during the reign of David because of Saul's violation of a treaty with the Gibeonites is found in 2 Samuel 21:1–4, though chronologically it occurred prior to the time of Absalom's rebellion, recorded in 2 Samuel 15–18 (see also discussions on 2 Sam. 21:1–2). The following dates, however, provide an approximate chronological framework for the times of Samuel, Saul, and David.

1105 BC	Birth of Samuel (1 Sam. 1:20)
1080	Birth of Saul
1050	Saul anointed to be king (1 Sam. 10:1)
1040	Birth of David
1025	David anointed to be Saul's successor (1 Sam. 16:1–13)
1010	Death of Saul and beginning of David's reign over Judah in Hebron (2 Sam 1:1; 2:1, 4, 11)
1003	Beginning of David's reign over all Israel and capture of Jerusalem (2 Samuel 5)
997–992	David's wars (2 Sam. 8:1–14)
991	Birth of Solomon (2 Sam. 12:24; 1 Kings 3:7; 11:42)
980	David's census (2 Sam. 24:1)
970	End of David's reign (2 Sam. 5:4–5; 1 Kings 2:10–11)

Outline

I. Historical Setting for the Establishment of Kingship in Israel (chaps. 1–7)

   A. Samuel's Birth, Youth, and Calling to Be a Prophet; Judgment on the House of Eli (chaps. 1–3)

   B. Israel Defeated by the Philistines; the Ark of God Taken and the Ark Restored; Samuel's Role as Judge and Deliverer (chaps. 4–7)

II. The Establishment of Kingship in Israel under the Guidance of Samuel the Prophet (chaps. 8–12)

   A. The People's Sinful Request for a King and God's Intent to Give Them a King (chap. 8)

   B. Samuel Privately Anoints Saul to Be King (9:1–10:16)

   C. Saul Publicly Chosen to Be King by Lot at Mizpeh (10:17–27)

   D. The Choice of Saul as King Confirmed by Victory over the Ammonites (11:1–13)

   E. Saul's Reign Inaugurated at a Covenant Renewal Ceremony Convened by Samuel at Gilgal (11:14–12:25)

III. Saul's Kingship a Failure (chaps. 13–15)

IV. David's Rise to the Throne; the Progressive Deterioration and End of Saul's Reign (chaps. 16–31)

   A. David Is Anointed Privately, Enters the Service of King Saul, and Flees for His Life (chaps. 16–26)

   B. David Seeks Refuge in Philistia; Saul and His Sons Are Killed in Battle (chaps. 27–31)

Bibliography

Baldwin, Joyce G. *1 and 2 Samuel: An Introduction and Commentary.* Tyndale Old Testament Commentaries 8. Downers Grove, IL: InterVarsity, 1988.

Bergen, Robert D. *1, 2 Samuel.* New American Commentary 7. Nashville: Broadman & Holman, 1996.

Davis, John J., and John C. Whitcomb. *Israel: From Conquest to Exile: A Commentary on Joshua–2 Kings.* Grand Rapids, MI: Baker, 1989.

Gordon, Robert. *1 and 2 Samuel: A Commentary.* Grand Rapids, MI: Zondervan, 1986.

Hertzberg, Hans Wilhelm. *1 and 2 Samuel: A Commentary.* Old Testament Library. Philadelphia: Westminster, 1964.

Kaiser, Walter C. *A History of Israel.* Nashville: Broadman & Holman, 1998.

Klein, Ralph W. *1 Samuel.* Word Biblical Commentary 10. Waco, TX: Word, 1983.

McCarter, P. Kyle, Jr. *I Samuel: A New Translation.* Anchor Bible 8. Garden City, NY: Doubleday, 1980.

Wood, Leon. *Israel's United Monarchy.* Grand Rapids, MI: Baker, 1979.

Youngblood, Ronald F. "1, 2 Samuel." In *Expositor's Bible Commentary*, edited by Frank E. Gaebelein, vol 3. Grand Rapids, MI: Zondervan, 1992.

EXPOSITION

I. Historical Setting for the Establishment of Kingship in Israel (chaps. 1–7)

A. Samuel's Birth, Youth, and Calling to Be a Prophet; Judgment on the House of Eli (chaps. 1–3)

1:1–3:21. The opening chapters of 1 Samuel are transitional, though they are integrally related to the rest of the book (see Introduction: "Theme"). Chapters 1–8 actually belong to the period of the judges, the intervening period between the death of Joshua (Josh. 24:29) and the installation of Saul as king (chaps. 9–10). They also close out that period, as Israel demanded a king to bring about what they considered a more stable form of government (chap. 8). In addition to their other roles, the two prominent people in these chapters, Eli and Samuel, serve as the period's final judges.

1:1–3. The name **Ramathaim-zophim** (lit., "twin heights of the Zuphites"; v. 1), occurs only here in the Old Testament and appears to be another name for Ramah (see 1:19; 2:11; 7:17; 19:18; 25:1). Its location is uncertain, but is perhaps to be identified with the Ramah of Benjamin (see Josh. 18:25), located in the hill country about five miles north of Jerusalem near the border of Ephraim and Benjamin. The suggested site is approximately a day's journey from Shiloh (see 1:3; 2:11). It is not entirely clear whether "-zophim" (or "a Zuphite") refers to the man or the place. If it refers to the man, it indicates he was a descendant of Zuph (see 1 Chron. 6:34–35). If it refers to the place, it designates the general area in which Ramathaim is located (see 9:5).

Although **Elkanah** (v. 1) is here called an **Ephrathite** (i.e., an "Ephraimite"), he was probably a Levite whose family belonged to the Kohathite clans that had been allotted towns in Ephraim (Josh. 21:20–21; 1 Chron. 6:22–26). He was apparently a man of some distinction; his lineage is traced back four generations. Elkanah had **two wives** (v. 2). Polygamy entered history with Lamech (see discussion on Gen. 4:19) and was practiced by several Old Testament notables: Abraham, Jacob, Gideon, and David. Though it departed from God's ideal of monogamy (Gen. 2:23–23; Matt.19:4–6), it is never explicitly condemned in the Old Testament (see Deut. 21:15–17). While polygamy was sometimes precipitated by a childless first marriage, it often brought unsettling complications into the marriage and home (see 1:6; Gen. 16:1–6; 30:1–2, 14–16).

This man went up ... yearly to worship (v. 3). Mosaic law required all Israelite men to meet before the Lord three times a year at the central sanctuary (Exod. 23:14–19; 34:23; Deut. 16:16–17). This sanctuary had been established by Joshua at **Shiloh** (Josh. 18:1), a site central to Israel and located in Ephraim between Bethel and Shechem. Throughout the period of the judges, with possible temporary exceptions (see Judg. 20:18; 21:19), Shiloh remained Israel's religious center, where the tabernacle and the ark of the covenant were located. The festival referred to here was probably the Feast of Tabernacles, which not only commemorated God's care for His people during the wilderness journey to Canaan (see Lev. 23:43) but more especially celebrated, with joy and feasting, God's blessing on the year's crops (see Deut. 16:13–15). On such festive occasions, Hannah's deep sorrow because of her barrenness was all the more poignant.

This is the first time in the Bible that God is designated by the title **the LORD of hosts** (v. 3). The Hebrew for "host[s]" can refer to (1) human armies (Exod. 7:4; Ps. 44:9); (2) the celestial bodies, such as the sun, moon, and stars (Gen. 2:1; Deut. 4:19; Isa. 40:26); or (3) the heavenly creatures, such as angels (Josh. 5:14; 1 Kings 22:19; Ps. 148:2). The title "the LORD of hosts" is perhaps best understood as a general reference to the sovereignty of God over all the powers in the universe. In the account of the establishment of kingship in Israel, this title became particularly appropriate as a reference to God as the God of armies—both of the heavenly army (Deut. 33:2; Josh. 5:14; Ps. 68:17; Hab. 3:8) and of the army of Israel (1 Sam. 17:45).

The ancestry of **Eli** (v. 3) the priest is not given, but a comparison of texts (1 Sam. 14:3; 21:20; 2 Kings 2:27; 1 Chron. 24:3) reveals that he was in the line of Ithamar, Aaron's fourth son. No information is given on how or when in the intervening years the priesthood passed from the line of Eleazar (Josh. 24:33; 1 Chron. 6:4–15) to the line of Ithamar. For Eli's **two sons**, see discussion on 2:12.

1:4–8. What **Elkanah offered** (v. 4) and gave to his wives and children refers to a sacrifice that was combined with a festive meal signifying fellowship and communion with the Lord and grateful acknowledgment of His mercies (see Lev. 7:11–18; Deut. 12:7, 17–18).

In contrast to the portions he gave to Peninnah and her children, he gave Hannah **a worthy portion** (v. 5) because **he loved** her (the Hebrew for "worthy" is difficult but perhaps means "double"; see the portion Joseph gave Benjamin, Gen. 43:34). Apparently, she was his favorite, but **the LORD had shut up her womb**. It is the Lord who gives and withholds children (see Gen. 18:10; 29:31; 30:2, 22). Perhaps her barrenness was the reason for his bigamy. This favoritism and Hannah's childlessness made Peninnah, who had children, Hannah's **adversary** (v. 6; see Gen. 16:1–6; 30:1–2, 14–16). The conflict between the wives was long term, **year by year** (v. 7), and her continued barrenness and Peninnah's provocations brought Hannah grief of heart that even **her husband** (v. 8) did not understand.

1:9–11. Hannah felt compelled to withdraw from the family to pray in isolation, near the place where **Eli the priest** (v. 9) was sitting. Here and in 3:3, the central sanctuary, the tabernacle (the temple in Jerusalem had not yet been built), is referred to as **the temple of the LORD**. It is also called "the house of the LORD" (1:7; 3:15), "the tabernacle of the congregation" (2:22), and "my [the Lord's] habitation" (2:32). The references to the tabernacle as a "house" and a "temple," as well as references to sleeping quarters and doors (3:2, 15), give the impression that the tabernacle was at this time part of a larger, more permanent building complex to which the term "temple" could legitimately be applied (see Jer. 7:12, 14; 26:6).

In her deep distress over her barrenness (1:2, 5–6), Hannah made a serious **vow** (v. 12) to the Lord. Making vows to the Lord was not uncommon (see Gen. 28:20–22; Num. 21:2; see discussion on 1:21), but vows made by women had certain regulations (see Num. 30:3–16). Her prayer, **remember me,** was more than asking God simply to recall that she existed. It was a request for action on her behalf (see 1:19; see also discussion on Gen. 8:1) in giving her a son. In contrast to the normal period of service for Levites, which was from age twenty-five to fifty (see Num. 8:23–26), she promised the Lord the service of her son **all the days of his life**. Hannah voluntarily vowed for her son that which God had required of Samson (Judg. 13:5). **There shall no rasor come upon his head.** Long hair was a symbol of dedication to the service of the Lord and was one of the characteristics of the Nazarite vow (see Num. 6:1–21). The Nazarite vow was normally taken for a limited time rather than for life.

1:12–18. Perhaps silent prayer was uncommon, for Eli, seeing her lips moving, accused Hannah of being **drunken** (v. 13). Eli's mistake suggests that in those days it was not uncommon for drunken people to enter the sanctuary. Further evidence of the religious and moral deterioration of the time is found in the stories of Judges 17–21.

Hannah made it clear that her anguish of soul and her praying lips were not to be misinterpreted as the drunkenness of a **daughter of Belial** (v. 16), that is, a "worthless" or wicked woman (see discussion on Deut. 13:13). Assurance that her prayer would be answered brought peace to her soul, and **her countenance was no more sad**.

1:19–23. That the Lord **remembered her** (v. 19) implies that He was about to intervene on Hannah's behalf (see Gen. 8:1; 30:22; Exod. 2:24; 6:5). She **conceived** (v. 20) and bore **a son**, whom she named **Samuel**. The name is a pun in Hebrew, but its meaning is uncertain. It derives from *El* (God) and possibly *sha'al* ("to ask," i.e., "asked of God"), or *shama'* ("to hear," i.e., "heard of God"), or *shem* ("name," i.e., "name of God"). Samuel's conception was of the Lord, he was dedicated to the Lord, and he was given a "godly" name.

Elkanah (v. 21) returned to Shiloh to offer his **yearly sacrifice, and his vow** (see discussions on 1:3–4). Making vows to God was a common feature of Old Testament piety, usually involving thank offerings and praise (see Lev. 7:16; Pss. 50:14; 56:12; 66:13–15; 116:17–18; Isa. 19:21). Elkanah no doubt annually made vows to the Lord as he prayed for God's blessing on his crops and flocks and then fulfilled those vows at the Feast of Tabernacles (see discussion on 1:3).

Hannah declined going to Shiloh until her **child be weaned** (v. 22). It was customary in the East to nurse children for three years or longer (in the Apocrypha, see 2 Maccabees 7:27) since there was no way to keep milk sweet.

Only the Lord establish his word (v. 23). Elkanah's statement is curious. No previous word from God is mentioned, unless this refers to the pronouncement of Eli in 1:17. The Dead Sea Scrolls, Septuagint (the Greek translation of the Old Testament), and Syriac version resolve this problem by reading "your word."

1:24–28. Hannah returned to Shiloh with her child and **three bullocks** (v. 24). The Septuagint and the Dead Sea Scrolls read "a three-year-old bull," which would explain why only one bull was sacrificed (v. 25). A bull of this age was of prime age, and perhaps corresponded to the age of Samuel. If Samuel was weaned at age three, indeed he **was young** (v. 24) when he was brought to the Lord.

As thy soul liveth (v. 26) is a customary way of emphasizing the truthfulness of one's words. **The Lord hath given** that **which I asked of him** (v. 27). Her words are the same as Eli's in 1:17, thus reminding him that his words had been fulfilled.

2:1–10. Hannah prayed (v. 1). Hannah's prayer is a song of praise and thanksgiving to God (see Ps. 72:20, where the psalms of David are designated "prayers").

2:1–3. This song has sometimes been termed the "Magnificat of the Old Testament" because it is so similar to the Magnificat of the New Testament (Mary's song, Luke 1:46–55). It also has certain resemblances to the "Benedictus" (the song of Zacharias, Luke 1:67–79). Hannah's song of praise finds many echoes in David's song in 2 Samuel 22. These two songs frame the main narrative, and their themes highlight the ways of God that the narrative relates—they contain the theology of the book in the form of praise. Hannah's prophetic words were spoken at a time when Israel was about to enter an important new period of her history, with the establishment of kingship through Hannah's son Samuel.

My heart rejoiceth in the Lord (v. 1). The supreme source of Hannah's joy is not in the child but in the God who has answered her prayer. **Mine horn is exalted in the Lord.** The horn is a symbol of strength, a metaphor probably drawn from oxen, whose strength is in their horns. To have one's horn lifted up by God is to be delivered from disgrace to a position of honor and strength (see Deut. 33:17; Pss. 75:5, 10; 92:10; 112:9; Luke 1:69).

The line **there is none beside thee** (v. 2) prevents any misunderstanding of the previous and following lines as saying that other gods might exist (see 2 Sam. 7:22; Deut. 4:39; Isa. 45:6). The **rock** is a metaphor depicting the strength and stability of the God of Israel as the unfailing source of security for His people (see 2 Sam. 22:32; Deut. 32:4, 31; Ps. 18:31). It is not uncommon to join the metaphors of horn (v. 1) and rock (see 2 Sam. 22:2–3; Ps. 18:2).

Talk no more so exceeding proudly (v. 3). Though the immediate context brings Peninnah, Hannah's rival, to mind (1:2, 6), this warning to the proud extends to all who might boast in the face of God. In the narratives of 1–2 Samuel, prime examples of such prideful behavior are Eli's sons, the Philistines, Saul, Nabal, Goliath, Absalom, Shimei, and Sheba. **The Lord is a God of knowledge** (see 16:7; 1 Kings 8:39; Ps. 139:1–6), and an arrogant heart cannot be hidden from Him.

2:4–5. In a series of general examples derived from everyday life, Hannah shows that God often works contrary to natural expectations and brings about surprising reversals. Such examples are seen frequently in the stories that follow. Hannah can identify with **the barren** (v. 5; see 1:2, 5). The number **seven** probably denotes in poetic terms an ideal number (see discussion on Ruth 4:15). In time, God gave Hannah a total of six children (see 2:21).

2:6–8. Hannah declares that life and death, prosperity and adversity, are determined by the sovereign power of God—another theme richly illustrated in the following narrative (see Deut. 32:39; 1 Kings 17:20–24; 2 Kings 4:32–35; John 5:21; 11:41–44). The Hebrew for **the grave** (v. 6) is *sheol*, that is, the netherworld (see discussion on Gen. 37:35). Her reference to the Lord's bringing one up from the grave may indicate Hannah's belief in resurrection after death (see Job 19:25–27), or it may affirm that God is sovereign over circumstances that bring one to the very brink of death (Pss. 18:4–6; 30:2–3; 86:13).

The **pillars of the earth** (v. 8) is a common figure in the Old Testament for the solid base on which the earth (the dry land on which man lives, not planet Earth; Gen. 1:10) is founded. The phrase does not teach a particular theory of the structure of the universe (see Job 9:6; 38:6; Pss. 75:3; 104:5; Zech. 12:1).

2:9–10. He will keep the feet of his saints (v. 9). Travel in ancient Israel was primarily by foot over trails that were often rocky and dangerous (see Pss. 91:11–12; 121:3). People who are faithful to the Lord are designated as "saints." The Hebrew root underlying this word is used of both God and His people in 2 Samuel 22:26 (see also Ps. 18:25) to characterize the nature of their mutual relationship. The word "saints" is also found in Psalms 12:1; 32:6; Proverbs 2:8.

The **Lord shall judge** (v. 10); that is, He will impose His righteous rule upon (see Pss. 96:13; 98:9), **the ends of the earth**, meaning upon all nations and peoples (see Deut. 33:17; Isa. 45:22). Hannah's prayer includes a prophetic reference to **his king**, an anticipation of the establishment of kingship in Israel and the initial realization of the messianic ideal in David (Luke 1:69). Ultimately, her expectation finds fulfillment in Christ and His complete triumph over the enemies of God. This is the first reference in the Bible to the Lord's **anointed**, that is, His anointed king. (Priests were also anointed for God's service; see Exod. 28:41; Lev. 4:3.) The word is often synonymous with "king" (as here) and provides part of the vocabulary for the messianic idea in the Bible. "Anointed" and "Messiah"

are the translation and transliteration respectively of the same Hebrew word. The Greek translation of this Hebrew term is *Christos*, from which comes the English word "Christ" (see discussion on Matt.1:17). A king (coming from the tribe of Judah) was first prophesied by Jacob (Gen. 49:10); kingship was further anticipated in the oracles of Balaam (Num. 24:7, 17). Deuteronomy 17:14–20 looked forward to the time when the Lord would place a king of His choice over His people after they entered the Promised Land. First and Second Samuel shows how this expectation of the theocratic king was realized in the person of David. Hannah's prophetic anticipation of a king at the time of the dedication of her son Samuel, who was to be God's agent for establishing kingship in Israel, is entirely appropriate.

2:11–12. In 2:11–3:21, the author contrasts Samuel and the sons of Eli. Samuel ministers before the Lord and gains favorable acclaim, but Eli's sons, renowned for their wickedness, lose respectability. Though a mere toddler (see discussion on 1:24), Samuel was left to **minister unto the Lord** (v. 11) and perform such services as a boy might render while assisting the high priest at the "house of the Lord" in Shiloh (1:7; 3:15). Hannah was careful to keep her commitment to the Lord (see 1:11), for though she lived probably only a day's journey from Shiloh, Samuel was given to the Lord and left in Eli's care without her frequent checking on his well-being. Apparently, she returned only yearly with new clothes for him (2:19–20).

With Eli's sons serving at the tabernacle, Samuel was left in an environment of potential wicked influence. They are described as **sons of Belial** (v. 12), a term denoting worthless or wicked character (see 1:16). **They knew not the Lord.** In Old Testament usage, to "know" the Lord is not just intellectual or theoretical recognition; it is to enter into fellowship with Him and acknowledge His claims on one's life. The term often has a covenantal connotation (see Jer. 31:34; Hos. 13:4).

2:13–17. These verses must be interpreted as referring to a peace offering (see Lev. 3:1–17; 7:11–34; 10:14–15; Deut. 18:1–5). A person making a peace offering could share the meat, but the portions for the Lord, the priest, and the offerer were carefully distinguished.

Apparently verses 13–14 describe the practice that had come to be accepted for determining the priests' portion of the peace offerings—a tradition presumably based on the assumption that a random thrust of the fork would providentially determine a fair portion.

Verses 15–16 then describe how Eli's sons arrogantly violated that custom and the law, claiming their portion **before they burnt the fat** (v. 15) on the altar as the Lord's portion, which He was to receive first (see Lev. 3:16; 4:10, 26, 31, 35; 7:28, 30–31; 17:6). **Give flesh to roast**. Boiling was the only form of cooking specified in the law for the priests' portion (Num. 6:19–20). Roasting this portion is nowhere expressly forbidden in the law, but it was specified only for the Passover lamb (Exod. 12:8–9; Deut. 16:7). The implication here seems to be that it was unlawful for the priests to roast their portion of the sacrifices. Presenting the priests' portion was to be a voluntary act on the part of the worshipers (see Lev. 7:28–36; Deut. 18:3), but **the priest's servant** threatened to take it **by force** (vv. 15–16).

2:18–21. But Samuel ministered before the LORD (v. 18). The series of sharp contrasts between Samuel and Eli's sons continues, and his service is evidenced by the **linen ephod** that he wore. This was a priestly garment worn by those who served before the Lord at His sanctuary (see 22:18; 2 Sam. 6:14). It was a close-fitting, sleeveless pullover, usually of hip length, and is to be distinguished from the special ephod worn by the high priest (see discussion on 2:28; see Exod. 39:1–26). His **little coat** (v. 19) was a knee-length, sleeveless garment that was worn over the undergarment and under the ephod (see 15:27; 18:4).

Hannah's love for her son endured, for she provided him a new coat every year when she came for the **yearly sacrifice** (v. 19; see discussion on 1:3). The Lord rewarded her commitment to her vow to Him by giving her five more children.

2:22–25. Eli's sons' hearts were hardened against God. They not only were irreverent with His sacrifices and disrespectful of fellow Israelite worshipers;

they also openly engaged in flagrant sexual promiscuity. They **lay with the women that assembled** (v. 22; see Exod. 38:8). There is no further reference to such women in the Old Testament. Perhaps these women performed various menial tasks, but certainly their service is not to be confused with that of the Levites, which is prescribed in the Pentateuch (Num. 1:50; 3:6–8; 8:15; 16:9; 18:2–3). The immoral acts of Eli's sons are reminiscent of the religious prostitution (fertility rites) at the Canaanite sanctuaries (see 1 Kings 14:24; 15:12; 22:46)—acts that were an abomination to the Lord and a desecration of His house (Deut. 23:17–18). With the report of their immoral conduct circulating, a sincere worshiper would have been reluctant to appear before the Lord when these men were present and perverting the worship of God.

Eli's rebuke of his sons was toothless, for he failed to remove them from office. God would do that. **Ye make the LORD's people to transgress** (v. 24). One's sin is most serious if it prevents or hinders others from worshiping or believing. **The judge shall judge him** (v. 25). The Hebrew for "judge" is *Elohim*, that is, "God." Eli's argument is that when someone commits an offense against another man, there is recourse to a third party to decide the issue (whether this be understood as God or as God's representatives, the judges; see Exod. 22:8–9 and *KJV Study Bible* note on Exod. 22:11), but when the offense is against the Lord, there is no recourse, for God is both the one wronged and the Judge. **The LORD would slay them**. This comment by the author of the narrative is not intended to excuse Eli's sons but to indicate that Eli's warning came much too late. Eli's sons had persisted in their evil ways for so long that God's judgment on them had already been determined (2:34; see Josh. 11:20).

2:26. The contrast between Eli's sons and Samuel continues. Samuel's reputation is the focus, for he **grew … in favour both with the LORD, and … with men.** (Compare Luke's description of Jesus, Luke 2:52.)

2:27–36. It is sad that an unnamed **man of God** (v. 27) had to appear to rebuke Eli, who was recognized as Israel's spiritual leader. "Man of God" denotes one closely related to God and is often a designation for a prophet (see 9:6, 10; Deut. 33:1; Josh. 14:6; 1 Kings 13:1, 6-8; 17:18, 24; 2 Kings 4:7). Eli's toleration of his sons' irreverent and immoral conduct disqualified him for that designation.

God's message to Eli contained three parts, concerning the past (vv. 27-28), the present (v. 29) and the future (vv. 30-36). In the past, God had selected the **house of thy father** (i.e., the tribe of Levi; v. 27), but more specifically the descendants of Aaron, **to be my priest** (v. 28). Three tasks of the priest are mentioned: (1) **to offer upon mine altar**, that is, to perform the sacrificial rites at the altar of burnt offering in the courtyard of the tabernacle; (2) **to burn incense** at the altar of incense in the Holy Place (Exod. 30:1-10); and (3) **to wear an ephod** (see discussion on 2:18). It would appear that the reference here is to the special ephod of the high priest (see Exod. 28:4-13). The breastplate containing the Urim and Thummim was attached to the ephod of the high priest. The Urim and Thummim were a divinely ordained means of communication with God, placed in the custody of the high priest (see Exod. 28:30 and discussion; see also 1 Sam. 23:9-12; 30:7-8).

In essence, Eli was trampling God's sacrifices and offerings by tolerating the unholy actions and behavior of his sons, thus honoring them over God (v. 29). In the past, God had said that Aaron's house would serve Him (see Exod. 29:9; Lev. 8-9; Num. 16-17; 25:13); now He said, **Be it far from me** (v. 30). This is not to say that the promise of the priesthood to Aaron's house had been annulled but that Eli and his house were to be excluded from participation in this privilege because of their sin. **Them that honour me I will honour**. Spiritual privileges bring responsibilities and obligations; they are not to be treated as irrevocable rights (see 2 Sam. 22:26-27).

In the future, four judgments would ensue. First, Eli's house (and the line of Ithamar; see discussion on 1:3) would be cut off from the priesthood. **Thine arm, and the arm of thy father's house** (v. 31) symbolizes the strength of Eli and the strength of his priestly family that would be cut off. **There shall not be an old man in thine house** is a prediction of the decimation of Eli's priestly family in the death of his sons

(4:11), in the massacre of his descendants by Saul at Nob (22:18-19), and in the removal of Abiathar from his priestly office (1 Kings 2:26-27). Eli would see an **enemy in my** God's **habitation** (v. 32). The Philistines would capture the ark (4:1-10), Shiloh would be destroyed (Jer. 7:14), and the tabernacle would be relocated to Nob (21:1-6; see discussion on 21:1). **The man of thine** (v. 33) apparently refers to Abiathar, who, although allowed to remain a priest for the time being, would later be expelled from office by Solomon (see 1 Kings 2:26-27) after an unsuccessful attempt to make Adonijah king as the successor to David.

Second, Eli's two sons would die the same day. The deaths of **Hophni and Phinehas** would be **a sign** (v. 34; see 4:11) confirming the longer-term predictions. Such confirmation of a prophetic word was not uncommon (see 10:7-9; 1 Kings 13:3; Jer. 28:15-17; Luke 1:18-20). Their deaths would precede that of their father (4:11), but Eli's house would continue as priests until the reign of Solomon (see 1 Sam. 14:3; 22:20; 1 Kings 2:26-27).

Third, **I will raise me up a faithful priest** (v. 35). This was initially fulfilled in the person of Zadok, who served as a priest during the time of David (see 2 Sam. 8:17; 15:24, 35; 20:25) and who eventually replaced Abiathar as high priest in the time of Solomon (see 1 Kings 2:35; 1 Chron. 29:22). **I will build him a sure house** (lit., "build for him a faithful house") signifies that the faithful priest would be given a "faithful" (i.e., sure, enduring) priestly family. Compare the similar word spoken concerning David, 25:28 (see also 2 Sam. 7:16; 1 Kings 11:38). This faithful priest would serve **mine** God's **anointed** (v. 35), that is, David and his successors (see discussion on 2:10). Zadok was a priest during David's reign, and his line, continued by his son Azariah (see 1 Kings 4:1), was still on the scene at the time of Israel's return from the exile (see 1 Chron. 6:14-15; Ezra 3:2). It continued in intertestamental times until Antiochus IV Epiphanes (175-164 BC) sold the priesthood to Menelaus (in the Apocrypha, see 2 Maccabees 4:23-50), who was not of the priestly line.

Fourth, no one of Eli's house who survived would serve as priests nor even be supported as

Levites. Instead, they would be forced to beg for **a piece of silver and a morsel of bread** (v. 36).

3:1–21. The events recorded in this chapter established Samuel as a prophet in the eyes of all the Israelites.

3:1–10. The **child Samuel** (v. 1; see 2:11, 18) continued to minister at the tabernacle. Samuel was now no longer a little child (see 2:21, 26). The Jewish historian Josephus places his age at twelve years, but he may have been older.

The word of the Lord was precious in those days (v. 1); that is, special revelation from God was rare during the entire period of the judges. This clause is explained by the next: **there was no open vision.** "Vision" technically denotes divine revelation that is disseminated by a prophet (lit., a "seer," i.e., one who sees the "vision"). Apart from the prophet of 2:27–36, there were only two known prophets (Judg. 4:4; 6:8) and five definite revelations (Judg. 2:1–3; 6:11–23; 7:2–11; 10:11–14; 13:3–21) during the period of the judges. This scarcity of prophets and divine revelation illustrate the truth of Proverbs 29:18: "Where there is no vision [i.e., divine revelation], the people perish [i.e., they cast off restraint]." The presence of a priest or a judge had not necessarily guaranteed a word from the Lord.

The time of this event was **ere the lamp of God went out** (v. 3). This reference is to the golden candlestick that stood opposite the table of shewbread (Exod. 25:31–40) in the Holy Place. It was still night, but the early morning hours were approaching, when the flame grew dim or went out (see Exod. 27:20–21; 30:7–8; Lev. 24:3–4; 2 Chron. 13:11; Prov. 31:18). For the lamp to be permitted to go out before morning was a violation of the Pentateuchal regulations. So it was just before dawn when Samuel heard the voice of God, but he would remain in bed until sunup. Eli's failure to recognize at once that the Lord had called Samuel (the Lord called him three times) may be indicative of Eli's own unfamiliarity with the Lord.

Samuel **did not yet know the Lord** (v. 7). He is not to be compared to Eli's sons, who did not know the Lord (see discussion on 2:12), but he had not yet directly experienced Him (see Exod. 1:8) by receiving a revelation from Him (as indicated by the last half of the verse), so he did not recognize the Lord's voice nor know how to respond.

3:11–14. The Lord's first revelation to Samuel repeated the warning Eli had already received from the anonymous "man of God" (2:27–36), which confirmed that the youth had indeed received a revelation from God. Thus, Samuel's prophetic career began by delivering a message of judgment and death (see his last message, given to Saul, 1 Sam. 28:16–20). The Lord's first warning to Eli had brought a mere reprimand to his sons, but he had taken no measures to curb their wicked deeds or relieve them of their duties and remove them from the premises of the tabernacle.

3:15–19. Samuel was hesitant to relay the vision to Eli and went about the duty of opening the **doors of the house of the Lord** (v. 15; see discussion on 1:9). Since the tabernacle itself did not have doors, this may refer to an enclosure in which the tabernacle stood. Eli demanded that Samuel relate all that God had said. **God do so to thee, and more** (v. 17). This is a curse formula (see 14:44; 20:13; 25:22; 2 Sam. 3:9, 35; 19:13; Ruth 1:17; 1 Kings 2:23; 2 Kings 6:31). Such curses were usually directed against the speaker, but here Eli directed it against Samuel if he concealed anything the Lord had said (see discussion on 14:24). After hearing the vision, Eli acknowledged it was from the Lord and accepted the judgment as righteous (see Exod. 34:5–7), saying, **let him do what seemeth him good** (v. 18). A literal translation would be, "Let him do what is good in his eyes," which contrasts the phrase used to describe the period of the judges, when "every man did that which was right in his own eyes" (Judg. 17:6; 21:25).

The Lord … let none of his words fall to the ground (v. 19). Because none of Samuel's words proved unreliable, he was recognized as a prophet who spoke the word of the Lord (see 3:20–21).

3:20–4:1a. That God had broken His silence once again and had spoken through Samuel quickly spread throughout the land. **From Dan even to Beer-sheba** (v. 20) is a conventional expression often used in Samuel, Kings, and Chronicles to denote the entire land (Dan was located in the far north, and

Beer-sheba in the far south). In contrast to 3:1, God continued to speak to all Israel through Samuel **in Shiloh** (v. 21). This would cease after the events in chapters 4–6, for Shiloh apparently was destroyed (see Jer. 7:12–14; 26:6).

B. Israel Defeated by the Philistines; the Ark of God Taken and the Ark Restored; Samuel's Role as Judge and Deliverer (chaps. 4–7)

4:1b–7:17. This section can rightly be called the "ark narrative," for the ark of the covenant is the main subject. The Philistines took the ark of God to their cities after defeating the Israelites in battle. The author briefly notes the death of Eli's sons, and then of Eli himself, but returns the focus to the movement of the ark among the Philistines. Because of the dreaded plague inflicted on the cities' residents, the Philistines eventually restored the ark to Israel, where it took up residence in the house of Abinadab. Only then does the author return to Samuel and his role as spiritual leader.

4:1b–2. The presence of the Philistines in the early days of Samuel is possibly related to their forty-year oppression of Israel, mentioned in Judges 13:1, 6, where it was predicted that Samson would "begin to deliver Israel out of the hand of the Philistines." Although Samson and Samuel appear in separate books and there is no record of their association with one another, it is possible that they were contemporaries. The Philistines' attack on Israel could have been their reaction to Samson's earlier forays against them.

Israel's army was camped at **Eben-ezer** (meaning "stone of help"; v. 1). The precise location is unknown, but it was probably a short distance (see 4:6) to the east of **Aphek**, a small town located about twelve miles northeast of the coastal city of Joppa, and approximately twenty miles northwest of Shiloh. The site of Israel's camp is probably not to be confused with the location of the stone, also named Eben-ezer, that was erected later by Samuel between Mizpeh and Shen (see 7:12) to commemorate a victory over the Philistines.

Philistine presence this far north suggests an attempt to spread their control over the Israelite tribes of central Canaan (see 4:9; Judg. 15:11). Some scholars attribute the success of the Philistines over Israel to their advanced metallurgy and weaponry (see 13:19–22), but it is better to see God's hand of judgment against His own people Israel as the real cause. Victory comes after repentance (7:3–14).

4:3–4. Wherefore hath the LORD **smitten …?** (v. 3). The elders understood that their defeat was more an indication of God's displeasure than it was of Philistine military might. Israel's pagan neighbors also believed that the gods decided the outcome of battles. **Fetch the ark of the covenant … it may save us.** In an attempt to secure the Lord's presence with them in the struggle against the Philistines, the elders sent for the ark of the covenant. Israel's move to bring the ark of God to the battle site was more an act of idolatry and superstition than of piety. They were correct in thinking there was a connection between God's presence with His people and the ark (see v. 4). No doubt they remembered the presence of the ark at notable victories in Israel's past history (see Num. 10:33–36; Josh. 3:3, 11, 14–17; 6:6, 12–20), but there is no evidence that the ark accompanied Israel on its campaigns of conquest or in routing the various oppressors in the period of the judges. They incorrectly believed that the Lord's presence with the ark was guaranteed, rather than subject to His free decision. They reflect the pagan notion that the deity is identified with the symbol of His presence and that God's favor could automatically be gained by manipulating the symbol.

The LORD **of hosts … dwelleth between the cherubims** (v. 4). On each end of the mercy seat of the ark of the covenant were golden cherubim with their wings spread upward over the ark (see Exod. 25:17–22). In the space between these cherubim, God's presence with His people was localized in a special way, so that the mercy seat of the ark came to be viewed as the throne of Israel's Divine King (see 2 Sam. 6:2; Pss. 80:1; 99:1). **Hophni and Phinehas,** Eli's sons and wicked priests (see 2:12), did not restrain the army from its improper use of the ark but actually accompanied the ark to the battlefield.

4:5–9. The exuberance of Israel over the arrival of the ark of the covenant is indicative of their misguided confidence. The Philistines nearby could hear the celebration of the **Hebrews** (v. 6) and were alarmed. "Hebrews" was an ethnic term often used by non-Israelites (see discussion on Gen. 14:13). **God is come into the camp** (v. 7). The Philistines, who had never had such an encounter before, identified the God of Israel with the symbol of His presence. They could think only in polytheistic terms. **These are the Gods that smote the Egyptians with ... plagues** (v. 8). The deliverance of Israel from Egypt had occurred centuries earlier, but the Philistines were well aware of the Lord's long-standing reputation for aiding His people with supernatural plagues. **Quit yourselves like men** (v. 9) is simply "Be men," **and fight**.

4:10–11. The Lord was not manipulated by Israel's use of the ark, and the results were disastrous. Israel lost 30,000 men to the Philistines, and **the ark of God was taken** (v. 11). This phrase or a variation of it occurs five times in the chapter (here, 4:17, 19, 21–22) and is the focal point of the narrative. In this calamitous event, God's word pronounced in 3:11 found swift fulfillment. One of God's judgments upon Eli and his house was also fulfilled: **Hophni and Phinehas, were slain** (see 2:34; 3:12).

4:12–18. The unfortunate messenger returned to **Shiloh** (v. 12) with **his clothes rent, and with earth upon his head**, a sign of his grief and sorrow, and here marking him as a bearer of bad news (see 2 Sam. 1:2; 13:19; 15:32). Eli was anxious over the outcome of the battle, and **his heart trembled for the ark of God** (v. 13). He had sufficient spiritual sensitivity to be aware of the danger inherent in the sinful and presumptuous act of taking the ark of God into the battle. He seems to have been even more concerned for the ark than for his sons (see v. 18). Perhaps he was resigned to the possibility that the predicted judgment on his sons might occur that day (2:24; 3:11–12).

The report of the battle's outcome, specifically the fate of the ark of the covenant, was too much for Eli, for having heard it, **he fell ... and he died** (v. 18). His death marked the end of the era that had begun with the death of Joshua and the elders who served with him (see Josh. 24:29, 31). Incapable of restraining Israel or his sons from their wicked ways and weakened and blinded by age, the old priest is an apt symbol of the flawed age that now came to a tragic close. He is also a striking contrast to the reign of David, which is the main focus of 1–2 Samuel. Eli was an old man (ninety-nine years old) and **heavy**. This bit of information not only helps explain why Eli's fall was fatal but also links his death with the judgment announced earlier: "Wherefore ... honourest thy sons above me, to make yourselves fat?" (2:29).

He had judged Israel forty years (v. 18). Eli is here included among the judges (see 2 Sam. 7:11; Judg. 2:16–19; Ruth 1:1), who served as leaders of Israel in the period between the deaths of Joshua and of the elders who outlived him and the establishment of the monarchy. It is likely that Eli's leadership of forty years overlapped that of Jephthah, Ibzan, Elon, and Abdon (Judg. 12:7–14), as well as that of Samson (Judg. 13–16).

4:19–21. The shock of the tragic news sent Phinehas's pregnant wife into premature labor. As her life ebbed away during the delivery of the child, she named him Ichabod, a name variously translated as "No glory" or "Where is the glory?" **The glory is departed from Israel** (v. 21). The glory of Israel was Israel's God, not the ark, and loss of the ark did not mean that God had abandoned His people — God was not inseparably bound to the ark (see Jer. 3:16–17). Yet the removal of the ark from Israel did signal estrangement in the relationship between God and His people, and it demonstrated the gravity of their error in thinking that in spite of their wickedness, they had the power to coerce God into doing their will simply because they possessed the ark.

5:1–2. The captured ark was taken to **Ashdod** (v. 1), one of the five major cities of the Philistines (Josh. 13:3). It was located near the Mediterranean coast about thirty-five miles west of Jerusalem. See map, *Zondervan KJV Study Bible*, p. 313. The fact that the ark was taken to Ashdod and not Ekron, which was closer to the battle site, may indicate that it was the leading Philistine city, or perhaps the main sanctuary to Dagon was located there. Due to subsequent circumstances, the ark would visit two more

Philistine cities (Gath, v. 8; Ekron, v. 10) before being returned to the Israelites.

In Canaanite mythology, **Dagon** (v. 2) was the son (or brother) of El and the father of Baal. He was the principal god of the Philistines and was worshiped in temples at Gaza (Judg. 16:21, 23, 26), Ashdod (here), and Beth-shan (31:10 – 12; 1 Chron. 10:10). Veneration of this deity was widespread in the ancient world, extending from Mesopotamia to the Aramean and Canaanite area and attested in nonbiblical sources dating from the late third millennium BC until Maccabean times (second century BC; in the Apocrypha, see 1 Maccabees 10:83 – 85). The precise nature of the worship of Dagon is obscure. Some have considered Dagon to be a fish god, but more recent evidence suggests he was either a storm god or a grain god. His name is related to a Hebrew word for "grain."

The Philistines viewed the ark of the covenant as Israel's god (see 4:7 – 8) and believed that defeating Israel and capturing her god clearly demonstrated the superiority of Dagon.

5:3 – 5. Dagon was fallen upon his face (v. 3). The Philistines had placed the ark next to the image of Dagon to demonstrate Dagon's superiority over the God of Israel, but the symbolism was reversed when Dagon was toppled to a position of homage before the ark of the Lord. On the second day, Dagon was found prostrate with his hands and head severed, which was even more disconcerting and humiliating, for this symbolized Dagon as vanquished before the superior God of Israel.

The priests do not **tread on the threshold** (v. 5). Apparently, the threshold was considered to possess supernatural power because of its contact with parts of the fallen image of Dagon. Zephaniah 1:9 appears to be a reference to a more general and rather widespread pagan idea that the threshold was the dwelling place of spirits. This belief continued until **this day**, that is, the time of the writing of 1 – 2 Samuel (see Introduction: "Author, Date, and Sources").

5:6 – 9. The hand of the LORD was heavy upon Ashdod (v. 6). Dagon's broken hand lay on the ground (5:4), but the Lord showed the reality and strength of

His own hand by bringing a plague (see discussion on 6:4) on the people of Ashdod and the surrounding area (see v. 9; 5:11). God would not be manipulated by His own people (see discussion on 4:3), nor would He permit the Philistines to think that their victory over the Israelites and the capture of the ark demonstrated the superiority of their god over the God of Israel. The nature of the Philistines' affliction is not clear. The Hebrew word for **emerods** denotes a "swelling," which has prompted various interpretations, primarily "boils" or "tumors." A suggested alternate Hebrew word would lend the meaning of "hemorrhoids," thus the KJV "emerods." A swelling such as a "tumor" matches the description of the disease (which was both deadly and of epidemic proportion; note also the reference to mice in 6:4), leading most scholars to conclude that what is reported here is an early occurrence of the bubonic plague.

The concerned citizens of Ashdod, concluding that the **God of Israel** (v. 7) was responsible for their physical dilemma, appealed to the **lords** (v. 8) of the five major cities of the Philistines (see 6:16; Josh. 13:3; Judg. 3:3) who suggested a quick remedy to the problem. **Let the ark of the God of Israel be carried … unto Gath**. Evidently, the leaders of the Philistines did not share the opinion of the Ashdodites that there was a direct connection between what had happened in Ashdod and the presence of the ark; they seem to have suspected that the sequence of events was merely coincidental (see 6:9). The removal of the ark to Gath put the matter to a test. The plague followed the ark of God.

5:10 – 12. Disastrous results forced the ark on to **Ekron** (v. 10), the northernmost of the five major Philistine cities, located eleven miles northeast of Ashdod and close to Israelite territory (see map, *KJV Study Bible*, p. 313). The bad reputation of the ark caused a panicky cry of distress, **They have brought about the ark of God … to slay us**, and prompted a second appeal to the five lords. **Send away the ark of the God of Israel** (v. 11). After three successive towns had been struck by disease upon the arrival of the ark, there was little doubt in the people's minds that the power of Israel's God was the cause of their distress.

6:1–9. After seven months, the **priests and ... diviners** (v. 2) were summoned. These experts on religious matters (priests) and discerners of hidden knowledge by interpretation of omens (diviners; see Deut. 18:10–11; Isa. 2:6; Ezek. 21:21) were expected to have the divine solution to correcting the Philistines' offense against Israel's God.

The priests and diviners advised returning the ark with a **trespass offering** (v. 3), a gift signifying recognition of guilt in taking the ark from Israel and compensation for this violation of the Lord's honor (see v. 5; for the trespass offering in Israel, see Lev. 5:14–6:7). The offering was of gold; Israel's God deserved something of value. It was comprised of **five golden emerods** (i.e., "tumors"; v. 4, corresponding to the symptoms of the plague; see 5:6), and **five golden mice**. The disease was accompanied by a plague of mice (v. 5). The Greek translation of the Old Testament (the Septuagint) includes this information earlier in the narrative (at the end of 5:6). It is likely that the mice were carriers of the disease, which may have been a form of bubonic plague. **Make images ... and ye shall give glory unto the God of Israel** (v. 5). The golden models were an acknowledgment that the disease and the mice were a judgment from the hand of the Israel's God, as well as a wistful display of sympathetic magic, a pagan belief that evil could be removed by presenting models of the disaster to the gods.

As a warning, the priests and diviners asked, **Wherefore then do ye harden your hearts ...?** (v. 6). The plagues that God inflicted on the Egyptians at the time of the exodus had made a lasting impression on the surrounding nations (see 4:8; Josh. 2:10). They recalled that the plagues on Egypt only intensified when **the Egyptians and Pharaoh** hardened their hearts against Israel's God.

The plan for returning the ark to Israel called for **two milch kine, on which there hath come no yoke** (v. 7), that is, two milk cows that had not been trained to pull a cart. **Bring their calves home from them**. Normally, cows do not willingly leave their suckling calves. The plan defied the natural instinct of the cows to return to their calves. A departure straight for Beth-shemesh would be clear confirma-

tion that the plagues had been ordered by Israel's God and had not happened by chance. Perhaps, however, the plan was contrived to provide undeniable proof that Israel's God was not involved in the Philistines' troubles, when the cows naturally turned to their calves. Thus, the priests and diviners would save face before Dagon's worshipers.

Beth-shemesh (v. 9) may have been selected as the site for returning the ark because it was a Levitical city within Judah's territory (see Josh. 15:10). It lay near the Philistine border about nine miles east and slightly south of Ekron and about two miles south of Zorah, Samson's hometown. Its name means "house [or sanctuary] of the sun [god]."

6:10–13. The cows took **the straight way ... to Beth-shemesh** (v. 12) as if they knew the way, **lowing as they went**. Against their will and instinct to return to their calves, the distressed cows traveled to Beth-shemesh as if directed and driven by the unseen angel of the Lord (see Num. 22:23) while the Philistine **lords** followed to verify the arrival of the cows at the proper destination (see 6:16). This event occurred at the time of the **wheat harvest** (v. 13), sometime between mid-April and mid-June.

6:14–18. The termination of the trip at Bethshemesh is just as much a revelation of the hand of God as the journey itself, because it was one of the towns of Judah that had been assigned to the priests, descendants of Aaron (Josh. 21:16), at the time of the conquest (see Josh. 21:13–16). The **cart** (v. 14) with the ark stopped by a **great stone**, which served as a display table for the golden gifts sent by the Philistines after the Levites used the wooden cart and cows for a **burnt offering**.

The components of the **trespass offering unto the Lord** (v. 17; see discussion on 6:3) are reviewed. They represented gifts from the lords of the Philistine cities in that area. The **great stone of Abel** (v. 18) is difficult to identify. It may be a proper name or a kind of monument to the event, or perhaps as some Hebrew manuscripts suggest, 'abel should read 'aben, that is, the "great stone" already mentioned in verse 15.

6:19–21. He smote the men ... because they had looked into the ark (v. 19). God judged the men of

Beth-shemesh (Levites and priests among them) for their irreverent curiosity. Mosaic law provided clear instructions for the proper handling of the ark (see Num. 3:30; 4:4–6, 15–20). Hence, the Levites' action was inexcusable, presumptuous, and disastrous. Because God had so closely linked the manifestation of His presence among His people with the ark, it was to be treated with great honor and respect (see 2 Sam. 6:7; Num. 4:17–20). This attitude of respect, however, is quite different from the superstitious attitude that led the elders to take the ark into battle against the Philistines, thus treating it as an object with magical power (see discussion on 4:3).

The actual and correct number of those who died is problematic. Some Hebrew manuscripts read **fifty thousand and threescore and ten** (v. 19), but a few Hebrew manuscripts (and the Jewish historian, Josephus) read "seventy." Most textual scholars believe the additional fifty thousand in most Hebrew manuscripts is apparently a copyist's mistake, because it is added in an irregular and ungrammatical way (the conjunction normally included in the number is lacking). Furthermore, it is doubtful that this small town could have contained so many inhabitants. Nevertheless, the point is clear in this verse: God would tolerate no irregularity in Israel's treatment of the ark (see 2 Sam. 6:6–7).

Who is able to stand ... to whom shall he go up from us? (v. 20). The deaths of the Beth-shemesh men instilled fear in the community. The inhabitants responded to God's judgment in much the same way as had the inhabitants of Ashdod, Gath, and Ekron (see 5:8–10). They too want to be rid of the ark of the covenant. Therefore, they appealed to Kirjath-jearim, a city on the Judah-Benjamin border (Josh. 18:14–15): **come ... fetch it up to you** (v. 21). For the next twenty years (7:2), the ark would remain in Kirjath-jearim until the events of 7:1–14. However, the ark remained in Abinadab's house for approximately fifty more years until David had it brought to Jerusalem (see discussion on 2 Sam. 6:3).

7:1. That the ark was not returned to Shiloh (4:4) was probably due to the site's destruction (possibly by the Philistines) around this time (proposed

by archaeology and presupposed by Ps. 78:60; Jer. 7:12–14; 26:6), although somehow the tabernacle of the congregation (and the altar of burnt offering) survived. Apparently, the tabernacle was first moved to Nob (21:1–9). In David's and Solomon's days, it was located at Gibeon (1 Chron. 16:39; 21:29; 2 Chron. 1:3, 13), the city whose people had been condemned to be menial laborers at the Lord's sanctuary (Josh. 9:23, 27). Later, Solomon brought the tabernacle of the congregation to the completed temple (see discussions on 1 Kings 3:4; 8:4).

The location of **Kirjath-jearim** (v. 1) is uncertain, though it is believed to have been about ten miles northeast of Beth-shemesh and about nine miles northwest of Jerusalem. At an earlier time, the city had been in league with the Gibeonites (see Josh. 9:3), but it had no significant religious history to Israel. Nothing more is known of **Abinadab** or his son **Eleazar**, the ark's caretaker.

7:2–6. The ark remained in relative obscurity at Abinadab's house until David brought it to Jerusalem (2 Sam. 6:2–3). **Twenty years** (v. 2) is the twenty-year interval between the return of the ark to Israel and the assembly called by Samuel at Mizpeh (see v. 5). The ark remained in Abinadab's house throughout the forty-year reign of Saul and well into the reign of David before he had it brought to Jerusalem (2 Sam. 6:2–4). During these silent years of the ark's obscurity, **all Israel ... lamented after the Lord**, apparently because the ark was separated from the tabernacle.

Samuel's urging, **put away the strange gods** (i.e., foreign gods; v. 3), is reminiscent of former pleas by Jacob (Gen. 35:2–4) and Joshua (Josh. 24:14, 23). **Ashtaroth** is the Hebrew plural of Ashtoreth, who was a goddess of love, fertility, and war and was worshiped in various forms by many peoples of the ancient Near East, including the Canaanites (see discussion on Judg. 2:13). The worship of Ashtoreth was frequently combined with the worship of Baal (see v. 4; 12:10; Judg. 2:13; 3:7; 10:6), in accordance with the common practice in fertility cults to associate male and female deities. **Return unto the Lord ... put away the strange gods ... prepare your hearts ...**

serve him only were all mandatory stipulations for God's deliverance from the Philistines.

All Israel gathered to **Mizpeh** (v. 5), a town in the territory of Benjamin (Josh. 18:26) and located about seven and a half miles north of Jerusalem. The Israelites had previously gathered in Mizpeh to undertake disciplinary action against Benjamin (Judg. 20:1; 21:1) after the abuse and murder of the concubine of a Levite traveling in Gibeah of Benjamin. Several other places bore the same name (see 22:3; Gen. 31:49; Josh. 11:3, 8; 15:38). **I will pray for you** (see 7:8–9; 8:6; 12:17–19, 23; 15:11). Samuel, like Moses, was later remembered as a great intercessor (see Ps. 99:6; Jer. 15:1). Both were appointed by God to mediate His rule over His people, representing God to Israel and speaking on Israel's behalf to God.

They drew water, and poured it out before the LORD (v. 6). No other reference is made to this type of ceremony in the Old Testament. It appears to have symbolized pouring out one's heart in repentance and humility before the Lord. (For related expressions, see 1:15; Ps. 62:8; Lam. 2:19.)

Samuel had been established as a prophet at a very young age (see 3:20), but here, for the first time, it is recorded that **Samuel judged the children of Israel** (v. 6; see 7:15; see also discussion on 4:18). Other than that he had a "circuit" (7:16), his role as a judge is not further described, although a comparison with his perverse sons (see 8:1–3) would suggest that Samuel held court, heard cases, and rendered justice.

7:7–11. With the Israelites gathered to one place, the Philistines saw an opportunity to attack. Samuel responded to Israel's plea for prayer by offering a **burnt offering … to the LORD** (v. 9). Though Samuel was not a descendant in Aaron's priestly line (see 1 Chron. 6:33–38), he did perform certain priestly duties, such as leading in the sacrifice. In light of past events (2:27–36; 3:11–21; 4:11–22), he was recognized as Israel's spiritual leader without peer.

The Philistines were soon to learn that it was not wise to interrupt God's people when they were of-

fering a sacrifice, clear evidence of repentance, by attacking them. The Lord made His presence known **with a great thunder** (v. 10). The Lord had promised to be the protector of His people when they were obedient to their covenant obligations (see Exod. 23:22; Deut. 20:1–4; see also 2 Sam. 5:19–25; Josh. 10:11–14; Judg. 5:20–21; 2 Kings 7:6; 19:35; 2 Chron. 20:17, 22), and He put the Philistines in disarray before Israel. Once more, the Philistines learned something of the true God (see 5:3–12).

7:12–14. In recognition of divine intervention, Samuel erected a stone monument and called it **Eben-ezer** (v. 12), that is, a "stone of help." Though this memorial probably did not mark the same site that earlier bore the same name (see discussion on 4:1), the second use of the name Eben-ezer showed how different the outcome of battle was when Israel was rightly related to God.

The subdued Philistines **came no more into the coast of Israel** (v. 13). Some interpreters see a contradiction between this statement and subsequent references to the Philistines in 9:16; 10:5; 13:3, 5; 17:1; 23:27. This statement, however, only indicates that the Philistines did not immediately counterattack. See 2 Kings 6:23–24 for a similar situation.

7:15–17. A summary statement marks the end of the author's account of Samuel's ministry as Israel's leader. In addition to his prophetic (3:21) and priestly (7:5, 9) roles, Samuel **judged Israel** (v. 15; see 7:6). His circuit was relatively small, limited to a few cities on the border of Benjamin and Ephraim and ending at his hometown of **Ramah** (v. 17; see discussion on 1:1). All the sites on the circuit had religious significance to Israel's history.

II. The Establishment of Kingship in Israel under the Guidance of Samuel the Prophet (chaps. 8–12)

8:1–12:25. The importance given to the founding of a monarchy is seen in the amount of space given to it. The transition from a judge to a king brought out theological tensions as the people demanded a king for the wrong reasons, and God commanded Samuel to satisfy their demands.

A. The People's Sinful Request for a King and God's Intent to Give Them a King (chap. 8)

8:1–5. The next recorded event occurs **when Samuel was old** (v. 1). It was perhaps about twenty years after the victory at Mizpeh, when Samuel was approximately sixty-five years old (see Introduction: "Chronology").

To assist him in judging, Samuel had enlisted his two sons, who served in **Beer-sheba** (v. 2). Samuel's success at rearing godly sons was hardly better than that of Eli, his spiritual predecessor, who also had served in the roles of priest and judge. Samuel's sons **took bribes, and perverted judgment** (v. 3). Perversion of justice through bribery was explicitly forbidden in Pentateuchal law (see Exod. 23:8; Deut. 16:19). Their conduct was known to Israel, for the elders informed Samuel, **thy sons walk not in thy ways** (v. 5). Samuel's own integrity was never questioned, and his character was always held in highest esteem (see 12:1–5).

After several centuries of failures and political instability (the period of the judges), Israel had come to look beyond their national apostasy and credited their troubles to their political organization (or lack thereof). Thus, they demanded, **make us a king to judge us like all the nations** (v. 5). The elders cited Samuel's age and the misconduct of his sons as immediate justifications for their request for a king. It soon became apparent, however, that the main reason for their request was a desire to be like the surrounding nations—to have a human king as a symbol of national power and unity, a human king who would lead them in battle and guarantee their security (see 8:20; 10:19; 12:12). If Israel had been true to their calling to be holy and separate from the nations (Lev. 20:26) and had not served false gods (Judg. 2:11–15), God's blessing would have remained on them, and they would have been successful regardless of the simplicity of their political structure.

8:6–9. Hearken unto the voice of the people in all that they say unto thee (v. 7). Anticipations of a monarchy in Israel are present in the Pentateuch. God had promised both Abraham (Gen. 17:16) and Jacob (Gen. 35:11) that kings would come from

them. In Jacob's prediction-blessing on his sons, he narrowed the kingship to Judah (Gen. 49:10). In his thwarted attempt to curse Israel, Balaam had predicted a future king for Israel (Num. 24:17). Before his death, Moses had given instructions that were to govern the selection of a king and regulations for his conduct in office (Deut. 17:14–20). All of this was in preparation for the reign of the future Son of David, Jesus the Messiah (Matt 1:1–18).

Samuel was therefore instructed to listen to the people's request (see v. 9; 8:22), but God put it in perspective: **they have not rejected thee, but ... me, that I should not reign over them** (v. 7; see Judg. 8:23). The sin of Israel in requesting a king (see 10:19; 12:12, 17, 19–20) did not rest in any evil inherent in kingship itself but in the kind of kingship the people envisioned and their reasons for requesting it. Their desire was for a form of kingship that denied their covenant relationship with the Lord, who Himself was pledged to be their Savior and Deliverer. In requesting a king "like all the nations" (8:20), they broke the covenant, rejected the Lord who was their King (12:12; Num. 23:21; Deut. 33:5), and forgot His constant provision for their protection in the past (10:18; 12:8–11).

8:10–18. Samuel depicted for Israel **the manner of the king** (v. 11). Using a description of the policies of contemporary Canaanite kings (vv. 11–17), Samuel warned the people of the burdens associated with the type of kingship they longed for, features of a monarchy that they had overlooked. A military draft of their **sons** would be necessary to maintain an army—charioteers, horsemen, runners, and commanders (v. 11; see 14:52)—and to harvest the king's crops and manufacture weapons for him (v. 12). Their **daughters** (v. 13) would be subjected to servitude, as confectionaries, cooks, and bakers. Private land, their **fields ... vineyards, and ... oliveyards** (v. 14), would be confiscated for royal purposes (see 1 Kings 21:7–16), and exorbitant taxes would be imposed, a **tenth** (v. 15) of their grain, vintage, and sheep. This king's portion would be over and above the tenth Israel was to devote to the Lord (Lev. 27:30–32; Num. 18:26; Deut. 14:22, 28; 26:12). In fact, the demands of the king would parallel all that Israel was to consecrate to the Lord as her Great King (persons, lands, crops, and livestock)—even the whole population (v. 17). Instead of crying out because of her enemies (see Judg. 3:9, 15; 6:6–7), Israel would **cry out ... because of your king** (v. 18; see 1 Kings 12:4; Jer. 22:13–17).

8:19–21. Israel was adamant in her demand for a king. **We will have a king over us** (v. 19). It is sadly ironic that the Jews in Jesus' day displayed the same spirit when they rejected the King who was their promised Messiah. When Pilate presented Jesus to them as the rightful king of the Jews, they said, "We have no king but Caesar" (John 19:15). **Our king may judge us ... and fight our battles** (v. 20). Israel was counting on a king to provide them with military preparedness and security. It will be seen that the threat of an Ammonite invasion precipitated their request for a king (12:12).

B. Samuel Privately Anoints Saul to Be King (9:1–10:16)

9:1–2. A brief background sketch of the king-select is given. His father was **Kish** (v. 1), a man from the tribe of **Benjamin**, a small tribe (9:21) that faced near extinction as a result of the civil war between the tribes during the early days of the judges (see Judg. 20:29–21:7). Kish's hometown was Gibeah (see 10:26), the very city whose perversion touched off the war of eleven tribes against Benjamin. He was **a mighty man of power**, perhaps indicating his wealth or influence. The name of his son **Saul** (v. 2) means "asked [of God?]." Israel had asked for a king (see 8:5, 10). Though God answered by selecting a king, Saul was not necessarily God's choice. Saul did, however, meet the worldly and physical criteria demanded by a people who wanted a king like the nations. Saul was **a choice young man ... goodly ... higher than any of the people** (see 10:23); that is, he was handsome and tall. Note Israel's reaction to Saul's physical appearance when Samuel introduced him to them (10:23–24). God's choice would later be seen in Saul's successor, David, a man after God's heart.

9:3–10. The asses of Kish ... were lost (v. 3). Saul is introduced as a donkey wrangler sent in search of donkeys that had strayed from home, perhaps symbolizing Saul and the rebellious people who had asked for a king (see Isa. 1:3). David would later be introduced as a shepherd caring for his father's flock and pictured as the shepherd over the Lord's flock (2 Sam. 5:2; 7:7–8; Ps. 78:71–72). Ironically, Saul went to find donkeys, found the prophet Samuel instead, and learned that he was to be a king.

The exact route Saul followed in search of his father's donkeys is not certain, but it ended in Samuel's neighborhood, in the **land of Zuph** (v. 5; see discussion on 1:1).

9:6–10. He said unto him. The perseverance of Saul's servant brought them in contact with Samuel. Perhaps Saul's ignorance of Samuel is indicative of his character. **This city** was probably Ramah (see 7:17), the hometown of Samuel, to which he had just returned from a journey (see 6:12; 7:16). Samuel is the **man of God** (see discussion on 2:27). **All that he saith cometh surely to pass** was evidence that Samuel was God's voice (see 3:19 and discussion).

Saul's concern was, **what shall we bring the man?** (v. 7). Other examples of gifts offered to prophets are found in 1 Kings 14:3; 2 Kings 4:42; 5:15–16; 8:8–9. Whether Samuel accepted the gift and whether he was dependent on such gifts for his livelihood are not clear. Elisha refused the gift of Naaman (2 Kings 5:16). In later times, false prophets adjusted their message to the desires of those who supported them (1 Kings 22:6, 8, 18; Mic. 3:5, 11). The servant had with him **the fourth part of a shekel** (i.e., about one-tenth of an ounce; v. 8) to pay Samuel if necessary. Before the use of coins, gold or silver was weighed out for each monetary transaction (see 13:21; Job 28:15). The value of that amount of silver in Saul's time is not known.

He that is now called a Prophet was beforetime called a Seer (v. 9). There was no essential difference between a "seer" and a "prophet." The term "seer" emphasized the receptive aspect of the prophet's ministry. With "spiritual eyes," he was granted to see and know what the natural eyes could not see and to receive God's revelation and will by dream or vision. The term "prophet" emphasized the proclamation aspect of his ministry as he became a spokesman for God by relaying what he had received as a "seer." Thus, Samuel learned of God's selection of Saul (9:15–16) and later made the public announcement to Israel. The person popularly designated a "prophet" at the time of the writing of 1–2 Samuel was termed a "seer" in the time of Saul. This need not mean that the term "prophet" was unknown in the time of Saul or that the term "seer" was unknown in later times (see Isa. 30:10). The reference is to popular usage.

9:11–14. Saul was directed to Samuel by some girls who apparently were quite familiar with the prophet's comings and goings. He was joining the people for **a sacrifice** (perhaps at the altar he had built; v. 12; see 7:17) in **the high place.** "High places" were elevations in or near a city that functioned as open-air sanctuaries for worship. After their entrance into the Promised Land, the Israelites often followed the custom of the Canaanites in building altars on hills. (At this time, the central sanctuary was not functioning because the ark of God had been separated from the tabernacle; Shiloh had been destroyed, and the priestly family, after the death of Eli's sons, was apparently still inactive.) In later times, worship at these "high places" provided a means for the entrance of pagan practices into Israel's religious observances and, for this reason, it was condemned (see discussion on 1 Kings 3:2).

He doth bless the sacrifice (v. 13). Samuel presided over the sacrificial meal (see 1:4; 2:13–16), at which he gave a prayer, probably similar to those referred to in the New Testament (see Matt. 26:26–27; John 6:11, 23; 1 Tim. 4:3–5).

9:15–19. This "coincidence" of meeting Samuel was indeed "providential," for the "seer" had already learned he was to meet God's choice for king (vv. 15, 17) and that it would be his responsibility to **anoint him** (v. 16). Priests were also anointed (see Exod. 29:7; 40:12–15; Lev. 4:3; 8:12), but from this point in the Old Testament, "the LORD's anointed" usually refers to the king (see discussion on 2:10; see 12:3; 24:6; 26:9, 11, 16; 2 Sam. 1:14, 16; 19:21; 22:51; 23:1; Ps. 2:2, 6; but see also Zech. 4:14). Anointing signified separation to the Lord for a particular task and

divine equipping for that task (see 10:1, 6; 16:13; Isa. 61:1). Saul's role was to be **captain over … Israel.** The Hebrew for "captain" indicates one designated (here by the Lord) to be the chief in rank. This useful term helped ease the transition between the time of the judges and that of the kings. Saul would continue the task of delivering Israel from the **Philistines** (see discussion on 7:13).

9:20–24. On whom is all the desire of Israel? (v. 20). The question is a reference to Israel's desire for a king. Saul modestly objected to being selected. He was a **Benjamite** (v. 21), from the **smallest of the tribes … the least of all the families.** Saul's origins were among the humblest in Israel (Benjamin was the last of Jacob's sons, and the tribe had been greatly reduced in the time of the judges; see Judg. 20:46–48). Saul's elevation to king shows that God "raiseth up the poor" (2:8), which is one of the central themes of Samuel. God's use of the powerless to promote His kingdom in the world is a common feature in the biblical testimony and underscores the truth that His kingdom is not of this world.

Samuel had prepared for Saul's coming as a guest of honor: a **parlour** (v. 22), the hall for the meal; the **chiefest place**, at the head of the guests; and a special reserved **portion** (v. 23) of meat. The Hebrew word for **shoulder** (v. 24) specifies the thigh, which was normally reserved for the Lord's consecrated priest (see Exod. 29:22, 27; Lev. 7:32–33, 35; Num. 6:20; 18:18). The presentation of this choice piece of the sacrificial animal to Saul was a distinct honor and anticipated his being designated the Lord's anointed.

9:25–27. Samuel had Saul spend the night with him, and they talked further. The Septuagint suggests that Samuel made a bed for Saul on the roof, where the night air was cool and pleasant. Rising at the **spring of the day** (v. 26), that is, early morning, Samuel prepared to send Saul home, but not before he arranged a private moment to reveal the **word of God** (v. 27) about his special anointing (10:1).

10:1. When Samuel was alone with Saul, he took **oil**, perhaps spiced olive oil (see Exod. 30:22–33). **Is it not because the LORD hath anointed thee …?** This special anointing solemnized the occasion and symbolized the coming of the Spirit (see 10:10) to empower Saul for his new responsibilities as leader of God's people. For **captain over his inheritance**, see discussion on 9:16. The Lord's inheritance includes both the people, "My people Israel" (compare 9:16 and 10:1; see also Exod. 34:9 for Israel as God's inheritance), and the land (see Exod. 15:17).

10:2-7. After departing from Samuel, Saul was to receive three signs to authenticate Samuel's words and to assure him that the Lord has indeed chosen him to be king. All of the signs occurred exactly as predicted on the same day. (Compare two earlier leaders, Moses [Exod. 4:1-9] and Gideon [Judg. 6:36-40], who also received confirmation by signs.)

The first sign: two men would meet Saul by **Rachel's sepulchre...at Zelzah** (v. 2) to inform him that his father's lost donkeys had been found. The location of Zelzah (and Rachel's tomb, marked in that day; see discussions on Gen. 35:16-20) is not known today.

The second sign: at the **plain of Tabor** (v. 3; "plain" is better rendered "oak" or "terebinth," a tree functioning as a landmark), Saul would meet three men. The place of meeting, their destination, and what they would be carrying were all specifically predicted.

The third sign: Saul would encounter some prophets at **the hill of God** (v. 5) and join them in prophesying. The "hill of God" can be translated "Gibeah of God." Gibeah was Saul's hometown (see 10:26; 11:4), located in the tribal area of Benjamin (Josh. 18:28; Judg. 19:12-14). It was usually called "Gibeah" or "Gibeah of Benjamin" (as in 13:2, 15) but twice was called "Gibeah of Saul" (15:34; 2 Sam. 21:6). The present designation (used only here) may have been Samuel's way of reminding Saul that the land of Canaan belonged to God and not to the Philistines (see Deut. 32:43; Isa. 14:2; Hos. 9:3).

The **company of prophets** (v. 5) he would meet was probably one of those with which Samuel was associated (similar to the "sons of the prophets" with whom Elijah and Elisha were associated; see discussion on 1 Kings 20:35). Apparently, small communities of men banded together in spiritually decadent times for mutual cultivation of their religious zeal. **Thou shalt prophesy**, in verses 5-6, 10:10-11, 13,

appears to designate an enthusiastic praising of God that was inspired by the Holy Spirit (for a similar use of the term, see Num. 11:24-30). When the signs occurred, Saul was to **do as occasion serve thee** (v. 7); that is, when the situation presented itself, he was to take whatever action was appropriate to manifest publicly his royal leadership (see 11:4-11).

10:8. Samuel instructed Saul that, at some unspecified future time, which perhaps they had previously discussed (see 9:25), **thou shalt go down before me to Gilgal** (v. 8). There he was to wait seven days for Samuel's arrival (see 13:7-14). This was a prediction for a separate and later occasion, but sadly, Saul would disregard the command and suffer rebuke from the prophet (see 13:8-14).

10:9-13. God gave him another heart (v. 9). This should not be understood as his conversion or spiritual regeneration, since no volitional decision concerning personal sin is evidenced. Instead, the Holy Spirit endued Saul with the leadship abilities that were not characteristically or inherently his.

Saul's prophesying raised eyebrows. **Is Saul also among the prophets?** (v. 11). This is an expression of surprise at Saul's behavior (see discussion on 10:5) by those who had known him previously—another subtle indication of his character (see discussions on 9:3, 6). **Who is their father?** (v. 12). Some understand this curious question as an expression of contempt for prophets generally; others see it as implying the recognition that prophetic inspiration comes from God and therefore could be imparted to whomever God chose. However, since leading prophets were sometimes called "father" (2 Kings 2:12; 6:21; 13:14), the speaker may have intended a disdainful reference to Samuel or an ironical gibe at Saul.

10:14-16. Saul recounted his search for the donkeys and his meeting with Samuel, but he divulged no information about **the kingdom** (v. 16), that is, his being chosen for kingship, not even to his relatives.

C. Saul Publicly Chosen to Be King by Lot at Mizpeh (10:17-27)

10:17-24. Samuel called the people ... to Mizpeh (v. 17). After the private designation and anointing of Saul to be king (9:1 – 10:16), Samuel called an assembly to make the Lord's choice known to the people (v. 21) and to define the king's task (10:25). **Mizpeh** had been the site of earlier convocations (see 7:5 and Judg. 20:1).

I brought Israel up … delivered you (v. 18). Speaking through Samuel, the Lord emphasized to the people that He had been their deliverer throughout their history. He brought them out of Egypt and delivered them from all their enemies during the time of the judges. Although the judges themselves are sometimes referred to as Israel's deliverers (see Judg. 3:9, 15, 31; 6:14; 10:1; 13:5), this was true only in a secondary sense, for they were instruments of the Lord's deliverance (see Judg. 2:18). It was the Lord who sent them (see 12:11; Judg. 6:14). After rehearsing the Lord's saving acts, Samuel solemnly reminded Israel that in their present action, **ye have … rejected your God** (v. 19; see discussion on 8:7).

Calling all the tribes forward, **the tribe of Benjamin was taken** (v. 20), probably by casting lots (see 14:41 – 42; Josh. 7:15 – 18). The Urim and Thummim were used for this purpose (see discussions on 2:28; Exod. 28:30). The process continued through the clans and families until Saul was selected, but still modest, the king-designate hid from the attention. Introduced as **him whom the LORD hath chosen** (v. 24; see discussion on 9:15 – 17; 10:1), the people joyously responded. **God save the king** reflects the English monarchial mindset of the KJV translators. The Hebrew is literally "let the king live" or "[long] live the king" (see 2 Sam. 16:16).

10:25 – 27. Samuel told … the manner of the kingdom (v. 25). Samuel took the first step toward resolving the tension between Israel's misdirected desire for a king (and their misconceived notion of what the king's role and function should be) and the Lord's intent to give them one. This description of the duties and prerogatives of the Israelite king was given for the benefit of both the people and the king-designate. It was intended to clearly distinguish Israelite kingship from that of the surrounding nations and to ensure that the king's role in Israel was compatible with the continued rule of the Lord over

Israel as her Great King (see Deut. 17:14 – 20). After writing it down, Samuel **laid it up before the LORD**. The written constitutional legal document defining the king's role in governing God's covenant people was preserved at the sanctuary (the tabernacle, later the temple; for other written documents defining Israel's covenant relationship with the Lord, see Exod. 24:7; Deut. 31:26; Josh. 24:26).

Like all leaders, Saul had supporters and detractors. Some, **whose hearts God had touched** (v. 26), accompanied Saul home to Gibeah, but others, **children of Belial** (v. 27; see discussion on 2:12), scoffed, **How shall this man save us?** Their question reflected the people's continued apostate idea that national security was to be sought in the person of the human king (see discussion on 10:18; see 8:20).

D. The Choice of Saul as King Confirmed by Victory over the Ammonites (11:1 – 13)

11:1 – 5. Saul's ability to lead was soon tested. **Nahash the Ammonite** (v. 1) was threatening **Jabesh-gilead**, a town east of the Jordan, in the tribal area of Manasseh. The Ammonites were descendants of Lot (see Gen. 19:38; Deut. 2:19) and lived east of the tribal territory of Gad, near the upper regions of the Jabbok River (see Deut. 2:37; Josh. 12:2). Previous attempts by the Ammonites to occupy Israelite territory are referred to in Judges 3:13; 11:4 – 32. The Philistine threat to Israel in the west presented the Ammonites with an opportunity to move against Israel from the east with supposed impunity. The Dead Sea Scroll 4QSam has an expanded introduction to this story that is helpful, if it is correct. It tells how Nahash had been terrorizing the eastern tribes of Gad and Reuben and had already subjected them to the barbaric treatment of gouging out the right eyes of the men. This seems to agree with a later criticism of Samuel that the frightening movements of Nahash had been the impetus for Israel's persistent demand for a king (see 12:12).

Moses had forbidden Israel to make a covenant with any of the nations living in the land God gave them for an inheritance (Deut. 7:1 – 2; 20:10 – 18). The tables had turned, however, and the inhabitants of Jabesh-gilead were desperate, for survival's sake, to make a covenant to serve the Ammonites. Nahash agreed to a covenant with Jabesh-gilead on one condition: **that I may thrust out all your right eyes** (v. 2). Besides causing humiliation (see Judg. 16:21), the loss of the men's right eyes would destroy the military capability of the archers.

Messengers came to **Gibeah of Saul** (v. 4; see 10:26 and discussion on 10:5) to appeal to the new king to defend Jabesh-gilead. Close family ties with the tribe of Benjamin (see Judg. 21:12–14) undoubtedly prompted the inhabitants of Jabesh-gilead to seek help from Saul. **Saul came ... out of the field** (v. 5). After Saul's public selection as the king-designate at Mizpeh (10:17–27), he returned home (10:26) to resume his normal activities and to wait for the Lord's leading for the next step in his elevation to the throne (see discussions on 11:15; 10:7).

11:6–11. In a fashion similar to His coming upon the judges who preceded Saul (Judg. 3;10; 6:34; 11:29; Judg. 14:6, 19; 15:14), **the spirit of God came upon Saul** (v. 6) to empower him to defend Jabesh-gilead.

Saul's quick response was to chop his oxen into pieces, and then he **sent them throughout ... Israel** (v. 7). Though military service was not yet compulsory, Saul's action sent a stern warning to all Israel. This is what would happen to anyone who ignored his solemn responsibility and failed to muster to defend Jabesh-gilead. (For a similar case, see Judg. 19:29.)

The men of Israel mustered at **Bezek** (v. 8). From this location, northeast of Shechem but west of the Jordan River, Saul was within striking distance of Jabesh-gilead. Having divided his men into three companies (compare Gideon's similar tatic, Judg. 7:16), Saul launched a surprise attack in **the morning watch** (v. 11), that is, the third watch, approximately 2:00 a.m. to 6:00 a.m. (see discussions on Judg. 7:19 and Matt.14:25), when the Ammonites would have still been sleeping soundly. Thus, he routed the enemy and defended Jabesh-gilead.

11:12–13. Saul wisely did not use the victory as an opportunity to avenge his detractors (see 10:27). **The Lord hath wrought salvation in Israel** (v. 13). Saul recognized Israel's true deliverer (see discussion

on 10:18). The victory, in combination with Saul's confession, placed yet another divine seal of approval on Saul as the man the Lord had chosen to be king.

E. Saul's Reign Inaugurated at a Covenant Renewal Ceremony Convened by Samuel at Gilgal (11:14–12:25)

11:14–15. Let us go to Gilgal, and renew the kingdom (v. 14). Samuel perceived that following Saul's success against the Ammonites, it was the appropriate time for the people to renew their allegiance to the Lord. Samuel was speaking of the Lord's kingship, not Saul's, and called for an assembly to restore the covenant relationship between the Lord and His people. Samuel wanted to inaugurate Saul's rule in a manner that demonstrated that the continued rule of the Lord as Israel's Great King was in no way diminished or violated in the new era of the monarchy (see Introduction: "Theme"). Verses 14–15 are a brief synopsis of the Gilgal assembly and are a preface to the more detailed account in chapter 12. **Gilgal**, located east of Jericho near the Jordan River, was a particularly appropriate place for Israel to renew her allegiance to the Lord (see Josh. 4:19–5:11; 10:8–15).

The people ... made Saul king before the Lord (v. 15). Saul had been anointed privately by Samuel at Ramah (10:1) and publicly selected as the king-designate at Mizpeh (10:17–27). In the subsequent Ammonite crisis (11:1–13), his leadership would not rest on public recognition of his royal authority but on the military victory. Now at Gilgal, Saul was inaugurated as God's chosen king and formally assumed the privileges and responsibilities of the office. **Peace offerings** were an important element in the original ceremony of covenant ratification at Sinai (Exod. 24:5, 11). It represented the communion, or peace, between the Lord and His people when the people lived in conformity with their covenant obligations (see Lev. 7:11–17; 22:21–23). **All ... rejoiced greatly**. Rejoicing was the reaction of the people, who had renewed their commitment to the Lord, confessed their sin (see 12:19), and been given a king.

12:1–5. Scholars commonly call these opening verses "Samuel's apologia," that is, his defense of his actions and character. Having **walked before** (v. 2) Israel since **childhood** (see 3:1, 19–21) as prophet, priest, and judge, his old age and Israel's acquisition of a king led Samuel to relinquish his role as judge. He was not retiring completely from ministering to Israel, for he would continue to be a spiritual leader (12:23) until his death (see 25:1).

After Samuel presented the newly inaugurated king to the people, he sought to establish publicly his own past faithfulness to the covenant as leader of the nation. **Witness against me** (v. 3). His purpose was to exonerate himself and provide an example for Saul in his new responsibilities. In stark contrast to his sons (see 8:3), Samuel's conduct as a judge had been exemplary. **Whose ox have I taken? or whose ass have I taken?** (See Exod. 20:17; 22:1, 4, 9; Num. 16:15.) He had not used his position for personal gain, nor had his sense of right and justice ever been "blinded" by bribery. **Whom have I defrauded ... of whose hand have I received any bribe ...?** (See Exod. 23:8; Lev. 19:13; Deut. 16:19; 24:14.)

12:6–17. Samuel said unto the people (v. 6). Samuel turned from consideration of his previous leadership to the matter of the people's request for a king, which he viewed as a covenant-breaking act and serious apostasy. The form of his appeal is similar to that of Joshua's earlier appeal (see Josh. 24:2–15). Verses 6–9 give a historical retrospect, contrasting God's gracious provision of deliverance and protection. Verses 10–12 show Israel's departure from Him for other gods and another king. Verses 13–17 present another contrast—the blessing of God upon them if they obey (v. 14) and the hand of God against them if they disobey (v. 15).

It is the Lord (v. 6). Samuel emphasized that the Lord had in the past provided the necessary leadership for the nation, beginning with **Moses and Aaron.** The terminology **I may reason with you** (v. 7) is that of a legal proceeding, as in 12:2–5, but here the relationship of the parties was reversed. This time Samuel was the accuser, the people were the defendants, and the Lord was the Judge. The **righteous acts of the Lord** (see vv. 8–11) demonstrated the constancy of the Lord's covenant faithfulness to-

ward His people in the past and, by way of contrast, serve as an indictment of their present apostasy. The language is reminiscent of Judges 2: **they forgat ... he sold ... they cried ... we have sinned ... and have served the Baalim and Ashtaroth** (vv. 9–10; see discussions on Judg. 2:11–19).

The Lord had repeatedly delivered Israel from her enemies, right up to Samuel's own lifetime, demonstrating again the people's apostasy in desiring a king. Samuel cited four men who led Israel during the judges period: **Jerubbaal** (v. 11; see discussions on Judg. 6:31–35), **Bedan** (found only here; the Septuagint and Syriac read "Barak"; see Judg. 4:10), **Jephthah** (Judg. 11:33), and **Samuel** himself (7:6–12).

When ye saw that Nahash ... came against you (v. 12; see discussion on 11:1). In the face of the combined threat from the Philistines in the west (9:16) and the Ammonites in the east (11:1–13), the Israelites sought to find security in the person of a human king. **The Lord your God was your king.** The Israelite desire for, and trust in, a human leader constituted a rejection of the kingship of the Lord and betrayed a loss of confidence in His care, in spite of His faithfulness during the time of the exodus, conquest, and judges (see discussion on 8:7).

Verse 13 is a hinge verse: **Now therefore behold the king whom ye ... have desired** (lit., "asked for"; Saul's name means "asked [of God?]"). **The Lord hath set a king over you** (v. 13). In spite of the sinfulness of the people's request, the Lord had chosen to incorporate kingship into the structure of the theocracy (His kingdom). Kingship was given by the Lord to His people and was to function as an instrument of His rule over them (see Introduction: "Theme").

If ye will fear the Lord (v. 14). Samuel related the old covenant condition (see Exod. 19:5–6; Deut. 8:19; 11:13–15, 22–28; 28; 30:17–18; Josh. 24:20) to the new era Israel was entering with the establishment of the monarchy. **Then shall both ye and also the king ... continue following the Lord your God.** Israel and her king were to demonstrate that although human kingship has been established, they would continue to recognize the Lord as their true King. In this new era, whenever the potential for divided loyalty between the Lord and the human king arose, Israel's loyalty to the Lord was to remain inviolate. (For similar use of the expression "to follow," see 2 Sam. 2:10; 15:13; 1 Kings 12:20; 16:21.)

If ye will not obey (v. 15). Samuel confronted Israel with the same alternatives Moses had expressed centuries earlier (see Deut. 28; 30:15–20). The introduction of kingship into Israel's sociopolitical structure had not changed the fundamental nature of Israel's relationship to the Lord. **See this great thing** (v. 16). Samuel called the people to observe as the Lord Himself demonstrated His existence and power and authenticated the truthfulness and seriousness of Samuel's words. **Is it not the wheat harvest to day?** (v. 17). Rains normally had ceased by the time of the wheat harvest, sometime between mid-April and mid-June. Thus, the **thunder and rain** (v. 18; see discussion on 7:10) was an unseasonable, supernatural reminder of God's displeasure over Israel's wickedness and served as a portent of the judgment they would experience if they continued in disobedience.

12:18–25. The sound of thunder was cause for alarm. **Pray ... unto the LORD thy God** (v. 19). Samuel's indictment (12:6–15) and the awesome sign of thunder and rain in the dry season (12:16–18) prompted the people to confess their sin and request Samuel's intercession for them.

Turn not aside from following the LORD (v. 20). Samuel again brought into focus the central issue in the controversy surrounding the establishment of kingship in Israel. Any alternates for the Lord were **vain things** (v. 21), and no rivals to the Lord could deliver or guarantee security. Since its initial presentation in Genesis 12:2–3, God had maintained His loyalty to the covenant that He had made with Abraham to make of him a great nation (see Gen. 17:6–8; 22:16–18; Deut. 7:6–9; Ps. 105:9–45). The Lord was not one to **forsake his people** (v. 22) or forget His covenant (Deut. 4:31; 31:6, 8), for His reputation was at stake. If God would not fail His people, then neither would His servant Samuel. **I will teach you the good and the right way** (v. 23). Samuel was not retiring from his prophetic role when he presented the people with their king. He would continue to intercede for the people (see v. 19; 7:8–9) and would instruct them in their covenant obligations (see Deut. 6:18; 12:28). Saul and all future kings were to be subject to instruction and correction by the Lord's prophets.

Fear the LORD (v. 24). Samuel summarized Israel's obligation of loyalty to the Lord as an expression of gratitude for the great things He had done for them. Again, he presented the alternative: **ye shall be consumed, both ye and your king** (v. 25). Should the nation persist in covenant-breaking conduct, it would bring upon itself its own destruction.

III. Saul's Kingship a Failure (chaps. 13–15)

13:1–3. Saul reigned one year ... two years over Israel (v. 1). The Hebrew reads: "Saul was ... years old when he became king, and he reigned two years over Israel." Compared to the frequently used formula for introducing a king's reign (see, e.g., 2 Sam. 2:10; 5:4; 1 Kings 14:21; 2 Kings 8:26), the Hebrew gives evidence of a possible scribal omission. Apparently, important numbers have been lost from the text in transmission, leaving the reading awkward and uncertain. Saul's age and length of reign are left to conjecture in the translations. The apostle Paul states, however, that Saul's reign was forty years (see Acts 13:21). It is possible that the events of this chapter occurred after Saul's second year as king.

Following his victory over the Ammonites (11:11), Saul had not entirely dispersed his army but had retained 3,000 men at two separate camps as he prepared to rebel against the Philistines. Saul had 2,000 men with him at **Michmash** (v. 2), which was located southeast of Bethel and northeast of Gibeah near a pass (see 13:23). Meanwhile, **Jonathan**, Saul's oldest son (see 14:49), who is mentioned here for the first time, had 1,000 men with him, and he attacked the Philistine outpost at **Geba** (v. 3), located across a ravine and south of Michmash.

13:4–5. Word went out that Jonathan's victory had made Israel an **abomination with the Philistines** (v. 4). The Hebrew for "abomination" is literally "make oneself odious, or a stench," a metaphor depicting an object of strong hostility (as in 2 Sam.

10:6; 16:21; Gen. 34:30; Exod. 5:21). Saul then returned to **Gilgal** (see discussion on 11:14) to muster more men. Saul had been instructed to wait for Samuel there (see discussions on 13:8; 10:8). The Philistines had a decided advantage with **thirty thousand chariots** (v. 5). This number seems exorbitantly high, especially in view of the hilly terrain of central Benjamin that these chariots would have had to encounter. Some consider the number 3,000, found in some Septuagint manuscripts, to be correct, although that number remains remarkably high. The Canaanites under Sisera (see Judg. 4:13) had 900 chariots. The Israelites did not acquire chariots until the time of Solomon (see 1 Kings 4:26).

13:6 – 12. The presence of large numbers of Philistines precipitated mass desertions from the army that had joined Saul at Gilgal. Saul waited the **set time that Samuel had appointed** (v. 8; see discussion on 10:8). He was fully aware that Samuel's previous instructions had reference to this gathering at Gilgal. The seven-day delay heightened the fear of the Israelite soldiers, and **the people were scattered**.

Due to his own anxiety over his dwindling army, Saul took matters into his own hands, and he **offered the burnt offering** (v. 9). Samuel had promised to make these offerings himself (see 10:8) before Israel went to battle (see 7:9), and he had directed Saul to await his arrival and instructions. Whether Samuel's delay was designed to test Saul's character is unstated.

13:13 – 14. Thou hast done foolishly (v. 13). Samuel did not rebuke Saul for assuming the role of priest. His sin was not the sacrifice per se. The foolish and sinful aspect (see 26:21; 2 Sam. 24:10; 1 Chron. 21:8; 2 Chron. 16:9) of Saul's act was that he thought he could strengthen Israel's chances against the Philistines while disregarding the instruction of the Lord's prophet Samuel. **Thou hast not kept the commandment of the LORD thy God**. Saul was to recognize the word of the prophet Samuel as the word of the Lord (see 3:20; 15:1; Exod. 20:18 – 19; see also discussion on Exod. 7:1 – 2). In disobeying Samuel's instructions, Saul had violated a fundamental requirement of his theocratic office. His kingship was not to function independently of the law and the

prophets (see discussions on 12:14, 23; 15:11). **Thy kingdom shall not continue** (v. 14). The self-will of Saul's heart, before known only to God, now became evident to all. Therefore, Saul would be set aside and would not be followed by his sons; there would be no dynasty bearing his name (contrast the Lord's word to David, 2 Sam. 7:11 – 16). The parallel in the word of the Lord to Eli is striking (see 2:30, 35). **The LORD hath sought him a man after his own heart**. (Paul quoted from this passage at Antioch, Acts 13:22.) As the Lord's **captain** (see 9:16), or ruler, this man would acknowledge God's rule over him.

13:15 – 18. The seven-day delay had greatly depleted Saul's forces (see 13:2, 4, 6 – 8), to a mere **six hundred men** (v. 15), so he returned home. His retreat allowed the unchecked activity of Philistine **spoilers** (v. 17), that is, raiding parties. The purpose of these Philistine contingents was not to engage the Israelites in battle but to plunder the land. As the Philistines branched out from their base at Michmash in three directions in Israel's heartland, they demoralized the Israelites living there.

13:19 – 22. There was no smith in Israel (v. 19). A Philistine monopoly on the technology of iron production placed the Israelites at a great disadvantage in fashioning and maintaining agricultural implements and military weapons. **They had a file for the mattocks** (v. 21). The Hebrew for "file" is *pim*, a word now known from archaeology to be a weight measurement, two-thirds of a shekel, and thus the Philistines' fee for sharpening Israel's farm implements. With no weapons, **neither sword nor spear** (v. 22), when the Israelites engaged in battle, they apparently fought with bows and arrows and slingshots.

13:23 – 14:5. The setting for the next Israel-Philistine encounter is established. The Philistines maintained their position at Michmash but also set up a camp at the pass that approached Michmash (see 13:11, 16). In a show of bravery, Jonathan again initiated action (see 13:3) by venturing into Philistine territory **on the other side** (v. 1). The Philistines were encamped to the north of the pass, and the Israelites remained to the south. Saul, however, was at home in **Gibeah under a pomegranate tree** (v. 2; see

13:16). His presence there may indicate his timidity (contrast Jonathan's actions, v. 1), or it may indicate a customary role of leaders in early Israel to hold court under well-known trees (see 22:6; Judg. 4:5).

The author's note on **Ahiah** (v. 3) is parenthetical to the story. Samuel was Israel's recognized spiritual leader, but the priestly family of Eli, albeit rejected by God, still remained (see 2:31–36; 3:14). Though Samuel offered sacrifices for Israel, he is not said to have worn the ephod of the high priest (see Exod. 39:2–21), which contained the Urim and Thummim (see Exod. 28:30). Either Ahijah, the current priest, was the brother and predecessor of Ahimelech son of Ahitub (referred to in 21:1; 22:9, 11), or his name is an alternate for Ahimelech. His father was **Ichabod's brother** (see 4:21). Ironically, the rejected Saul was keeping company with the rejected priestly family (see vv. 18–19) and one who was related to Ichabod, whose name means "no glory."

14:6–14. These uncircumcised (v. 6) is a term of contempt for the Philistines (see 17:26, 36; 31:4; 2 Sam. 1:20; Judg. 14:3; 15:18; 1 Chron. 10:4), which draws attention to Israel's covenant relationship to the Lord (see discussion on Gen. 17:10) and, by implication, to the illegitimacy of the Philistine presence in the land. Jonathan rightly understood that victory in battle was of the Lord and was not dependent on numbers of men, **by many or by few** (see discussion on 17:47; see also Lev. 26:8; Josh. 14:12; Judg. 7:4, 7; Ps. 33:16). His bold plan was undertaken as an act of faith (see Heb. 11:33–34) founded on God's promise (9:16).

This shall be a sign unto us (v. 10). Unaccompanied by a priest or prophet, Jonathan devised a sign to determine God's approval of his plan of attack. Unlike Gideon (see discussion on Judg. 6:36–40), however, Jonathan was not requesting a sign to confirm what God had already made known to him.

Behold, the Hebrews come forth (v. 11). The presumptuous Philistines, aware of Israel's past hiding and fear (see 13:6–8), belittled Jonathan and his attendant and carelessly invited them to **come up to us** (v. 12). Jonathan killed twenty men, which initiated a rout of the Philistines.

14:15–16. In addition to the Philistines' panic at the unexpected attack, **the earth quaked** (v. 15), and the disturbance caught Saul's attention in Gibeah. (For other instances of divine intervention in nature to bring deliverance to Israel, see 7:10; Josh. 10:11–14; Ps. 77:18.)

14:17–23. An inventory of Saul's men showed Jonathan to be missing. Saul was eager to join the chase, but he decided to seek God's will before entering into battle with the Philistines (see Num. 27:21; Deut. 20:2). The priest Ahiah was ordered to **Bring hither the ark of God** (v. 18). The Septuagint reads, "'Bring the ephod.' At that time he [Ahiah] wore the ephod before the Israelites." Here the Greek translation may preserve the original text for the following reasons: (1) In 7:1, the ark was brought to Kirjath-jearim, where it remained until David brought it to Jerusalem (2 Sam. 6), but the ephod was present in Saul's camp at Gibeah (see 14:3). (2) Nowhere else in the Old Testament is the ark used to determine God's will, but the ephod (with the Urim and Thummim) was given for that purpose (see 23:9; 30:7 and discussions on 2:18, 28). (3) The command to the priest to withdraw his hand (v. 19) is more appropriate with the ephod than with the ark.

Ahiah was issued a second command: **Withdraw thine hand** (v. 19). Due to the urgency of the moment, Saul decided that waiting for the word of the Lord might jeopardize his military advantage. As in 13:8–12, his decision rested on his own insight and determination rather than on dependence on the Lord and a commitment to obey Him.

With the Philistines on the run, some **Hebrews** (v. 21) who were in the service of the enemy found it safe to rejoin the Israelites in their battle. **So the Lord saved Israel that day** (v. 23). The writer attributes the victory to the Lord, not to Saul or Jonathan (see 14:6, 10, 15; 11:13).

14:24–46. Following the account of the great victory the Lord had given, the author relates the actions of Saul that strikingly illustrated his unfitness to be king. This foolish curse before the battle (see discussion on v. 24) made the army "distressed" (v. 24) and, as Jonathan tellingly observed, "troubled the land"

(v. 29) rather than contributed to the victory. Later, when hindered from taking advantage of the battle's outcome by the Lord's refusal to answer (v. 37), Saul was ready to execute Jonathan as the cause, though Jonathan had contributed most to the victory, as everyone else recognized (v. 45). Saul's growing egocentrism was turning into an all-consuming passion that threatened the very welfare of the nation. Rather than serving the cause of the Lord and His people, he was in fact becoming a king "like all the nations" (8:5).

14:24–30. In spite of victory, **the men of Israel were distressed** (v. 24). Saul's rash action in requiring his troops to fast, **Cursed be the man that eateth**, placed them at an unnecessary disadvantage in the battle (see vv. 29–30). To charge his men with an oath (v. 28) was a most serious matter because an oath directly invoked God's involvement, whether it concerned giving testimony (Exod. 20:7; Lev. 19:12), making commitments (Gen. 21:23–24; 24:3–4), or prohibiting action (as here; Josh. 6:24). It appealed to God as the supreme enforcement power and as the all-knowing Judge of human actions. **That I may be avenged on mine enemies.** Saul perceived the conflict with the Philistines more as a personal vendetta (see discussion on 15:12) than as a battle for the honor of the Lord and the security of the Lord's people (note the contrast between his attitude and that of Jonathan in 14:6, 10, 12). Saul's rash curse, then, derived from his self-centeredness and pride and proved to be detrimental to the welfare of his men and threatened Jonathan's life (compare the rash vow of Jephthah that affected his daughter; Judg. 11:30–31).

14:31–35. Saul's curse not only weakened his men physically but numbed them spiritually in that they disregarded God's instruction not to **eat** meat **with the blood** (v. 33; see Gen. 9:4; Lev. 17:11; 19:26; Deut. 12:16; Ezek. 33:25; Acts 15:20). It was reported to Saul that the men had **transgressed** (see *KJV Study Bible* marginal note; the same Hebrew term is translated "treacherous" in Jer. 3:8–11). To counter their sin, Saul erected an altar, the **first altar that he built unto the Lord** (v. 35). This is possibly another indication of Saul's personal lack of interest in religious matters (see discussions on 9:6; 10:11).

14:36–37. Saul was eager to press in pursuit of the Philistines, but the **priest** (v. 36), Ahiah (see 14:3), advised him to seek God first. So **Saul asked counsel of God** (v. 37). The means of ascertaining God's will appears to have been the ephod, with its Urim and Thummim (see 14:3 and discussion on 14:18). Because an oath had been broken in the battle, **he answered him not**; that is, God refused to answer Saul's inquiry concerning further military action.

14:38–46. A frustrated Saul was determined to learn who had caused God's silence. **As the Lord liveth** (v. 39) is an oath formula (see discussion on 14:24; see also 19:6; Jer. 4:2; Hos. 4:15). In the casting of the lots, he and Jonathan were **taken** (v. 41; see 10:20–21; Josh. 7:14–18; Prov. 16:33). Saul, humiliated by Jonathan's defiance of the curse (though done in ignorance), deemed his son's death necessary, invoking a curse formula once again (see discussion on 14:24; see also 3:17 and discussion). **He hath wrought with God this day** (v. 45). The men of Saul's army recognized the inappropriateness of taking the life of the one through whom God had delivered His people. Citing Saul's own oath formula, "as the Lord liveth" (v. 39), the army prevented their king from killing Jonathan. Thus, Saul had lost face before his own men.

14:47–48. This is a summary of Saul's military victories to the east (Moab and the Ammonites), south (Edom), west (Philistines), and north (Zobah). A detailed account of his spoiling the **Amalekites** (v. 48) is given in 15:2–9.

14:49–50. This is the first listing of the **sons of Saul** (v. 49; see 31:2; 2 Sam. 2:8, 10; 1 Chron. 9:39; 10:2). His daughters, **Merab and ... Michal**, would later be important in the story of David (see 18:17, 20, 27; 19:11–17; 25:44; 2 Sam. 6:16–23). **Ahinoam** (v. 50), a wife of Saul, is named only here. His concubine Rizpah is mentioned in 2 Samuel 3:7 and 21:8–11.

14:51–52. War against the Philistines all the days of Saul (v. 52) summarizes the main account of Saul's reign. He developed a special cadre of professional soldiers bound to himself (see 8:11), much as David would later do (see 22:2; 23:13; 25:13; 27:2–3; 29:2; 30:1, 9; 2 Sam. 2:3; 5:6; 8:18; 15:18; 23:8–39).

15:1–35. The author presents the event that occasioned Saul's rejection. Saul's dynasty had earlier been rejected (see 13:14), but here the rejection is applied to Saul himself. Although no time designation is given, this evidently occurred after the conflicts of 14:47, in a time of relative peace and security. It is likely that David was anointed (16:1–13) shortly after the rejection of Saul (vv. 22, 26, 28), thus around 1025 BC.

15:1–5. Samuel's opening line, **... now therefore hearken unto ... the words of the Lord** (v. 1), stressed Saul's obligation to obey what God was about to command concerning **Amalek** (i.e., the Amalekites; v. 2). The Amalekites were akin to the Edomites, a Bedouin people descended from Esau (see Gen. 36:12, 16) usually located in the Negev and Sinai regions (see 27:8; 30:1; Gen. 14:7; Exod. 17:8; Num. 13:29), who are almost always seen in an adversarial role to Israel. **I remember that which Amalek did to Israel**. When Israel was moving through the Sinai wilderness, the Amalekites had attacked from the rear (Exod. 17:8–16; Deut. 25:17–19). On that occasion, God had promised to destroy them and erase them from memory. During the intervening years of the judges, the Amalekites were inveterate enemies who seemingly joined themselves to any people in a position to harm Israel (see Judg. 3:13; 6:3–5, 33; 7:12; 10:12).

Go ... smite ... utterly destroy (v. 3). The Hebrew verb "destroy" denotes devoting something to God for judgment, often by total destruction (see *KJV Study Bible* notes on Lev. 27:28–29; Deut. 2:34). Two well-known cities, Jericho (see discussions on Josh. 6:17–18) and Ai (see Josh. 8:2, 22–24), experienced this kind of judgment. At Ai, an exception was made for Israel to preserve the livestock alive, but at Jericho, as here in Samuel's instructions concerning the Amalekites, all livestock was to be destroyed along with the people. Saul was given an opportunity as king to demonstrate his allegiance to the Lord by obedience in this assigned task.

Saul mustered an army at **Telaim** (v. 4), probably the same as the Telem in Joshua 15:24, a location in the southern part of Judah. The **city of Amalek** (v. 5), a settlement of Amalekites most likely located

between Telaim and Kadesh-barnea, was possibly the residence of their king.

15:6–9. The **Kenites** (v. 6) were a Bedouin people of the Sinai, closely related to the Midianites. Moses had married a Kenite woman (see Exod. 2:16, 21–22; Num. 10:29; Judg. 1:16; 4:11), and some of the Kenites had accompanied the Israelites when they settled in the land of Canaan (see 27:10; Judg. 1:16; 4:17–23; 5:24; 1 Chron. 2:55). These people were permitted to vacate the area before Saul smote the Amalekites from **Havilah ... to Shur** (v. 7). The location of Havilah is uncertain. Shur was on the eastern frontier of Egypt (see 27:8; Gen. 16:7; 20:1). Ishmael's descendants occupied this area (see Gen. 25:18).

Israel **utterly destroyed all the people** (v. 8), that is, all the Amalekites they encountered, for some Amalekites survived (see 27:8; 30:1, 18; 2 Sam. 8:12; 1 Chron. 4:43). Israel, however, disobeyed the Lord's command (15:3) by sparing **Agag the king** and the best livestock, and their holy war against the Amalekites degenerated into personal aggrandizement, much like that of Achan at the time of the conquest of Canaan (see Josh. 7:1). Giving to the Lord by destruction only what was despised and weak was a contemptible act (see Mal. 1:7–12), not to be excused (see 15:19) by the protestation that the best had been preserved for sacrifice to the Lord (15:15, 21).

15:10–11. It repenteth me that I have set up Saul to be king (v. 11). "Repentance," "regret," and "grieved" are various translations of God's attitude toward Saul. It does not indicate God's remorse over an error in His judgment in making Saul king, and thus a change of mind (see discussion on 15:29), but that He had changed His dealings with sinful Saul according to His sovereign purposes. Saul's willful disobedience grieved the Lord, as does the sin of anyone. **He is turned back from following me**, a violation of the fundamental requirement of his office as king (see discussions on 12:14–15).

15:12–15. Self-centered as always, Saul stopped at **Carmel** (v. 12), located about seven miles south of Hebron (see 25:2; Josh. 15:55). **He set him up a place**; that is, he erected a monument to himself. Saul's self-glorification here contrasts sharply with his self-abasement after the victory over the Ammonites (see discussion on 11:13; see v. 17; 2 Sam. 18:18).

Saul returned to **Gilgal** (v. 12), the place where he had been inaugurated and instructed in the responsibilities of his office (see 11:14–12:25). This was also where he had been told that he would not have a continuing dynasty because of his disobedience (see 13:13–14). Here he would receive his most severe reprimand yet and learn of God's rejection of him.

I have performed the commandment of the LORD (v. 13). Here and in 15:20, Saul was clearly less than honest in his statements to Samuel. **The people spared the best ... to sacrifice unto the LORD thy God** (v. 15). Saul attempted to shift responsibility from himself to the people and to excuse their action by claiming pious intentions. Sadly, Saul's use of the pronoun "thy" instead of "my" here and in 15:21, 30 indicates an awareness of his own alienation from the Lord (for a similar case, see 12:19), even though he spoke of obedience and the intent to honor God by sacrifice.

15:16–19. I will tell thee what the LORD hath said to me (v. 16). As a child, Samuel had gained recognition as God's spokesman when he delivered a judgment against Eli the priest's house (3:11–18); now he had to reprimand the king. **Thou wast little in thine own sight** (v. 17). Saul was humble when Samuel first met him and anointed him king (see 9:21; 10:22), but he had become arrogant (15:12), rebellious, and disobedient.

15:20–23. Samuel corrected Saul's protest, wherein he argued his compliance and obedience—with an exception for sacrifices. Samuel, as the other prophets who followed him, did not suggest that sacrifice was unimportant but that it was acceptable only when brought with an attitude of obedience and devotion to the Lord (see Ps. 15; Isa. 1:11–17; Hos. 6:6; Amos 5:21–27; Mic. 6:6–8). The sacrifice that is worthy of and acceptable to God comes from the worshiper whose faith, obedience, and moral conduct displays a life of spiritual reality and proper motivation. The **fat of rams** (v. 22) was the part of sacrificed animals that belonged to the Lord (see 2:15; Exod. 23:18; Lev. 3:14–16; 7:30).

Samuel charged Saul with **rebellion** (v. 23), that is, violation of the central requirement of the covenant condition given to him when he became king (see 12:14–15), which was equal to the **sin of witchcraft**. This was a serious offense against the Lord (see Lev. 19:26; Deut. 18:9–12), which Saul himself condemned (28:3, 9).

Thou hast rejected the word of the LORD (v. 23). Saul had set his own will above the command of the Lord and had ceased to be an instrument of the Lord's rule over His people, having violated the very nature of his theocratic office. **He hath also rejected thee from being king**. The judgment here goes beyond the earlier proclamation that his dynasty would not continue (see discussion on 13:14). Saul himself was now to be set aside as king. Although this did not happen immediately, as chapters 16–31 show, the process that led to his death began. It included in its relentless course the removal of God's Spirit and favor from him (16:14), the defection of his son Jonathan and daughter Michal to David, and the insubordination of his own officials (22:17).

15:24–33. Saul's confession, **I have sinned ... I feared the people, and obeyed their voice** (v. 24), retained an element of self-justification and a shift of blame (contrast David's confession, 2 Sam. 12:13; Psalm 51). Previously (15:15, 21), Saul had attempted to justify the actions of those under him.

Turn again with me (v. 25). Saul's greatest concern was not to worship God but to avoid an open break with the prophet Samuel, a break that would undermine his authority as king (see v. 30). In a desperate move to retain the prophet, Saul seized and tore Samuel's robe, an act that carried serious symbolic implications. The kingdom of Saul would be rent from him and given to a **neighbour** (v. 28). Chapter 16 reveals this person to be David (see discussion on 13:14).

The Strength of Israel (v. 29) is literally the "Eminence of Israel," or as some translations read, the "Glory of Israel." This is a title of God (see Mic. 1:15; see also discussion on 4:21; Pss. 89:17; 106:20). The Lord **will not lie nor repent**, that is, He is not fickle; He would not change His mind about Saul (see Num. 23:19; Ps. 110:4; Jer. 4:28; Mal. 3:6). There is no conflict between this statement and 15:11, 35, where the Lord is said to "repent" that He had made Saul king. God has real emotions (one of the marks of personality).

Saul repeated his confession, but in the face of rebuke and condemnation (presumably public), his plea, **honour me ... before Israel** (v. 30), shows him to have been more concerned with respect from Israel than with his relationship with God. **So Samuel turned again after Saul** (v. 31). Samuel's purpose in agreeing to Saul's request is not to honor Saul but to carry out the divine sentence on Agag and, in so doing, to reemphasize Saul's neglect of duty.

15:34–35. Prophet and king returned to their respective homes: Samuel to **Ramah** (v. 34; see 7:17), and Saul to **Gibeah of Saul** (see discussion on 10:5). **Samuel mourned for Saul** (v. 35). Samuel regarded Saul as if he were dead (see the use of "lamented" in 6:19). Even though his love for Saul remained (see 15:11; 16:1), he sought no further contact with him because God had rejected him as king. Saul did come to Samuel on one other occasion (see 19:24).

IV. David's Rise to the Throne; Progressive Deterioration and End of Saul's Reign (chaps. 16–31)

A. David Is Anointed Privately, Enters the Service of King Saul, and Flees for His Life (chaps. 16–26)

16:1–5. The Lord said unto Samuel (v. 1). When Samuel continued to mourn over Saul, the Lord directed him on a new assignment: anointing a replacement for Saul. This assignment probably occurred around 1025 BC (see discussion on 15:1–35). For the genealogy of **Jesse the Beth-lehemite**, see Ruth 4:18–22; Matthew1:3–6. Bethlehem was a town five miles south of Jerusalem, formerly known as Ephrath (Gen. 48:7). It was later to become renowned as the "city of David" (Luke 2:4) and the birthplace of Christ (Mic. 5:2; Matt. 2:1; Luke 2:4–7). **I have provided me a king among his sons**. Samuel had learned progressively that God would replace Saul as king with someone who was from a different family

and who had a spiritual heart (see 13:13; 15:26), but he had not known the identity of the new king.

Saul ... will kill me (v. 2). The road from Ramah (where Samuel was, 15:34) to Bethlehem passed through Gibeah of Saul. Saul already knew that the Lord had chosen someone to replace him as king (see 15:28), but Samuel wanted no charges of subversive activity. He feared that jealousy would incite Saul to violence if he knew that Samuel was appointing a successor to his throne. Later incidents (18:10–11; 19:10; 20:33) would demonstrate that Samuel's fears were well founded. God provided Samuel with a secondary reason for going to Bethlehem. **Say, I am come to sacrifice to the Lord**. This response was true but incomplete, and it was intended to deceive Saul. His preparation for sacrifice at Bethlehem aroused no suspicions in Saul. Perhaps it was not uncommon for Samuel to visit towns off his circuit (see 7:16), although the elders expressed some alarm at his arrival: **Comest thou peaceably?** (v. 4). Apparently, his unexpected visit portended trouble.

In preparation for the sacrifice, the elders were instructed, **sanctify yourselves** (v. 5). This involved preparing oneself spiritually as well as making oneself ceremonially clean by washing and putting on clean clothes (see Exod. 19:10, 14; Lev. 15; Num. 19:11–22). The requirement was extended to Jesse and his sons.

16:6–10. Beginning with **Eliab** (v. 6), Jesse's oldest son (see vv. 8–9; 17:13), Samuel considered which one was God's choice. **Look not on his countenance, or on the height** (v. 7). Samuel's initial inclination was a natural one and needed divine correction. He was not to focus on outward features, which had characterized Saul and turned the heads of all Israel (see 9:2; 10:23–24). **I have refused him**. The Lord "refused" Eliab just as He had "rejected" Saul (the Hebrew for "refuse" and "reject" is the same). **The Lord looketh on the heart**. Appearances may appeal (and deceive), but the Lord is concerned with man's inner disposition and character (see 1 Kings 8:39; 1 Chron. 28:9; Luke 16:15; John 2:25; Acts 1:24). None of Jesse's first seven sons met God's approval; **the Lord hath not chosen these** (v. 10).

16:11–13. Samuel then learned of the eighth and youngest son. **He keepeth the sheep** (v. 11). The one who was a shepherd was the Lord's choice to shepherd His flock (see discussion on 9:3; see also 2 Sam. 7:7–8; Ps. 78:71–72). Moses also had been a shepherd (see Exod. 3:1), and "shepherd" was a common characterization of kings in the ancient Near East.

Samuel **anointed** David **in the midst of his brethren** (v. 13; see discussion on 9:16). The small circle of witnesses assured confidentiality but also provided ample testimony for the future that David had been anointed by Samuel and that he was not merely a usurper of Saul's office. The coming of the **spirit of the LORD** upon David (see 10:5–6, 10; 11:6; Judg. 15:14) prepared him for a new role and gave him a new sense of purpose and destiny. He experienced no radical change in his behavior, as in Saul's case (see discussions on 10:11–13), for the Spirit of God had already been working in David's heart (see 13:14; 16:7). Juxtapositioned to this notice of God's Spirit coming upon David is the sad note that the Spirit of the Lord left Saul (16:14).

16:14–17:58. David was introduced to Saul's court and to Israel as a gifted musician and warrior. With these two gifts, he would become famous in Israel and would lead the nation to spiritual and political vigor (see 2 Sam. 22; 23:1–7). Also through these two gifts, Saul would become dependent on David.

16:14–23. The spirit of the LORD departed from Saul (v. 14; see Judg. 16:20). The removal of the Spirit from Saul and the giving of the Spirit to David (16:13) determined the contrasting courses of their lives. A correct understanding of the **evil spirit from the LORD** is difficult. Scripture indicates that evil spirits are subject to God's control and operate only within divinely determined boundaries (see Judg. 9:23; 1 Kings 22:19–23; Job 1:12; 2:6; compare 2 Sam. 24:1 with 1 Chron. 21:1), but explanations for Saul's judgment are various: (1) The evil spirit was an evil messenger who gave Saul incorrect advice (see 1 Kings 22:20–23). (2) The evil spirit was a disruptive spirit that severed Saul's relationship with Israel (see Judg. 9:23). (3) Saul was possessed by a demon who brought depression and insanity.

Regardless, Saul's disobedience continued to be punished by the assaults of this "evil spirit" (vv. 15–16, 23; 18:10; 19:9), for it **troubled him**. Saul's increasing tendencies to despondency, jealousy, and violence were no doubt occasioned by his knowledge of his rejection as king (see 13:13–14; 15:22–26; 18:9; 20:30–33; 22:16–18) and his awareness of David's growing popularity, but an "evil spirit" was also involved in these psychological aberrations.

For his periods of despondency, Saul was urged to search for a skilled musician, and **thou shalt be well** (v. 16). The soothing effect of certain types of music on a troubled spirit is a generally recognized phenomenon (see 2 Kings 3:15). Beyond this natural effect of music, it would appear that in this instance, the Spirit of the Lord was active in David's music to suppress the evil spirit temporarily (see v. 23). The search located the anointed son of Jesse. **Send me David thy son** (v. 19). Saul unknowingly invited to the court the person God had chosen to be his replacement. In this way, David was brought into contact with Saul, and his introduction to Israel began.

Almost a parenthetical thought, **David ... became** Saul's **armourbearer** (v. 21). This may refer to a later time, after David's victory over Goliath (see 18:2).

17:1–58. Probably no biblical story demonstrates better the triumph of faith over physical strength than the story of David fighting Goliath (see Zech. 4:6).

17:1–3. The scene was set for the next Philistine-Israel conflict. The Philistines had mustered their forces at **Shochoh** (v. 1), located about fifteen miles west of Bethlehem (see 2 Chron. 28:18) near their border, and then established camp at **Ephes-dammim** (Pasdammim in 1 Chron. 11:13; see 2 Sam. 23:9), somewhere near **Azekah**, which was located a little over a mile northwest of Shochoh.

Saul's men were also camped between Azekah and Shochoh, by the **valley of Elah** (i.e., the Wadi es-Sant; v. 2). A ravine separated the two armies, with the valley serving as the battleground between them.

17:4–7. Goliath, the Philistine **champion** (v. 4), is described in detail. His size and his home, **Gath,**

suggest he was related to the Anakim (see Josh. 11:21–22), a tall people that had caused the twelve spies great concern (see Num. 13:32–33). His **height was six cubits and a span**, that is, over nine feet. His strength was great; he could function with a brass coat of armor weighing **five thousand shekels** (v. 5), about 130 pounds, and he wielded a spear whose iron tip alone weighed **six hundred shekels** (v. 7), about 15 pounds.

17:8–11. Goliath called out to Israel's army, **Why are ye come out …?** (v. 8). He claimed to be the Philistine champion. **Am not I a** (lit., "the") **Philistine …?** For "forty days" (v. 16), he challenged Israel to representative warfare. The ancient Greeks, to whom the Philistines were apparently related, sometimes decided issues of war through chosen champions who met in combat between the armies. Instead of subjecting both armies to battle, with the potential of many casualties, one champion from each army would engage in a duel, and the winner would claim victory for his army and country. It was thought that through this economy of warriors, the judgment of the gods on the matter at stake was determined (i.e., trial by battle ordeal). Israel too may have known this practice (see 2 Sam. 2:14–16). This concept was known as "battle by champions."

Saul and all Israel … were … greatly afraid (v. 11). Israel's giant warrior (see 9:2; 10:23) quailed before the Philistine champion. The fear of Saul and the Israelite army (see 17:24; 32) betrayed a loss of faith in the covenant promises of the Lord (see Exod. 23:22; Deut. 3:22; 20:1–4). Their fear also demonstrated that the Israelite search for security in a human king (apart from trust in the Lord; see discussions on 8:5, 7) had failed. On the basis of God's covenant promises, Israel was never to fear her enemies but was to trust in the Lord (see 2 Sam. 10:12; Exod. 14:13–14; Num. 14:9; Josh. 10:8; 2 Chron. 20:17).

17:12–16. The author returns to the family of Jesse. The note that **David was the son of that Ephrathite** (v. 12) connects him to his genealogical roots in the book of Ruth (see Ruth 1:2; 4:18–22). One also learns that Jesse's three oldest sons were serving with Saul and that David was back home with his father's sheep. **David went and returned from Saul** (v. 15). His position at the court (see 16:21–23) was not permanent but was performed on an intermittent, as needed, basis. (For the relationship between chapters 16 and 17, see discussion on 17:55.) Meanwhile, **the Philistine** (v. 16) continued to present himself and his taunts.

17:17–23. The support of the troops was the responsibility of their families. A concerned father, Jesse sent David on a threefold mission: (1) to take food for his brothers (consisting of an ephah, about 21 quarts, of **parched corn … loaves**; v. 17), (2) to check on their welfare, and (3) to **take their pledge** (i.e., bring back a token of their welfare; v. 18).

Leaving early, David was able to travel the approximately fifteen miles to the **trench** (i.e., entrenchment or barricade; v. 20) just as the armies faced off that day. Leaving **his carriage** (i.e., his baggage; v. 22), he joined his brothers just in time to hear the taunt of Goliath.

17:24–30. The appearance of Goliath caused Saul's men who, were **sore afraid** (v. 24), to scatter (see discussion on 17:11). Saul's incentive plan was well known: **the king will enrich him with great riches** (v. 25; see 8:14; 22:7) and **give him his daughter** (see 18:17–26; see Josh. 15:16), but no man had been lured by these rewards to fight Goliath.

Who is this …? (v. 26). David was more than inquisitive. He was appalled that **this uncircumcised Philistine** (see discussion on Judg. 14:3) was permitted to defy God's army. David saw the issues clearly, which set him apart from Saul and all the other Israelites on that battlefield.

Eliab's anger was kindled (v. 28). David's question sparked Eliab's ire, and he was condescending to David as he charged him with youthful, irresponsible, and even wicked behavior. On the contrary, David had acted very responsibly in carrying out his father's mission. Eliab was the eldest brother; his anger may have arisen from jealousy of David and a sense of guilt for the defeatist attitude of the Israelites. He recognized, but did not comprehend, David's indomitable spirit (see 16:13).

What have I now done? (v. 29). David's question is not unlike the sibling talk of a younger brother being hassled and accused by a lording older brother. **Is there not a cause?** The Hebrew is literally, "Was it not a word?" The meaning, however, is that it was a significant word. A better paraphrase might be, "Did I not ask a good [or serious] question?" Thus, the idea of a "cause" was implied in David's response.

17:31–37. When David was called before Saul because of his comments, he encouraged the king, **Let no man's heart fail because of him** (i.e., Goliath; v. 32). David's confidence did not rest in his own prowess (see v. 37; 17:47) but in the power of the living God, whose honor had been violated by the Philistines and whose covenant promises had been scorned by the Israelites. When David enlisted himself, **thy servant will … fight with this Philistine,** Saul responded, **Thou art not able** (v. 33). He did not take into account the power of God (see v. 37; 17:47).

David argued his capabilities by citing two past experiences with dangerous beasts—a **lion** (v. 34) and a **bear.** (For the presence of lions in Canaan at that time, see 2 Sam. 23:20; Judg. 14:5–18; 1 Kings 13:24–26; Amos 3:1; and for bears, see 2 Sam. 17:8; 2 Kings 2:24; Amos 5:19.) For David, **this uncircumcised Philistine** (v. 36) was no greater a threat than those beasts (see discussion on 14:6). Though Goliath was an experienced warrior (from his youth), David's experience fighting wild animals had shown him God's protection then, and he was confident of that same protection now. **The Lord … will deliver me** (v. 37). Reliance on the Lord was essential for the true theocratic king (see discussions on 10:18; 11:13). Here David's faith contrasts sharply with Saul's loss of faith (for Saul's earlier fearlessness, see 11:6–7). **Saul said unto David, Go.** Saul was now dependent on David not only for his sanity (see discussion on 16:16) but also for the security of his realm.

17:38–40. Having refused Saul's armor, David approached the enemy with the three implements he knew: (1) **His staff** (v. 40)—God's newly appointed shepherd of His people (see 2 Sam. 5:2; 7:7; Ps. 78:72) went to defend the Lord's threatened and frightened flock. (2) **Stones**—usually the stones chosen were round and smooth and somewhat larger than a baseball. (3) **His sling**—the sling consisted of two cords attached to a leather pouch, into which the stone was placed. The sling was then twirled around the head, and the stone was released and projected with terrific force. When hurled by a master slinger, the stone probably traveled at close to 100 miles per hour. (For the Benjamites' skill with a sling, see Judg. 20:16.)

17:41–44. The well-armored champion was humiliated and angered to be matched in a fight with the boy David, who was equipped with sticks. **Am I a dog …?** (v. 43). To treat someone like a "dog" was to regard him with utmost disgust and contempt (see discussion on 2 Sam. 9:8). Saul **cursed David by his gods**, but David invoked the power and protection of his God.

17:45–47. David's retort was eloquent. **I come … in the name of the Lord of hosts** (v. 45). David's strength was his reliance on the Lord (see Ps. 9:10; Prov. 18:10; for comment on the Lord's "name," see also *KJV Study Bible* note on Exod. 3:13–14; Deut. 12:11). His trust in God gave him confidence. **All the earth may know** (v. 46). The victory that David anticipated would demonstrate to all the world the existence and power of Israel's God (see Exod. 7:17; 9:14, 16, 29; Deut. 4:34–35; Josh. 2:10–11; 4:23–24; 1 Kings 8:59–60; 18:36–39; 2 Kings 5:15; 19:19). **The battle is the Lord's** (v. 47). Both the Israelite and the Philistine armies would be shown the error of placing trust in human devices for personal or national security (see 2:10; 14:6; 2 Chron. 14:11; 20:15; Pss. 33:16–17; 44:6–7; Eccl. 9:11; Hos. 1:7; Zech. 4:6).

17:48–54. The unencumbered and nimble youth took his position quickly. Only one stone from his sling was needed to bring the champion down, but ironically, David finished the Philistine off with his own sword. **The Philistines … fled** (v. 51). Most likely, they saw the fall of their champion as the judgment of the gods, but they did not honor Goliath's original proposal (see 17:9).

David took the head … and brought it to Jerusalem (v. 54). This note is possibly parenthetical. Jerusalem had not at this time been conquered by the Israelites. David may have kept Goliath's head as a trophy of victory after presenting it to Saul (17:57) and brought the skull with him to Jerusalem when he took that city and made it his capital (see 2 Sam. 5:1–9). Or, having grown up almost under the shadow of the Jebusite city, he may have displayed Goliath's head to its defiant inhabitants as a warning of what the God of Israel was able to do and eventually would do. As his personal spoils of the battle, David **put his** (Goliath's) **armour in his tent**. Since Goliath's sword was later in the custody of the priest at Nob (see 21:9), David must have dedicated it to the Lord, the true victor in the fight (see 31:10).

17:55–58. Whose son is this youth? (v. 55). The seeming contradiction between verses 55–58 and 16:14–23 may be resolved by noting that prior to this time, David was not a permanent resident at Saul's court (see 17:15; 18:2; see also discussion on 16:21), so Saul's knowledge of David and his family may have been minimal. Further, Saul may have been so incredulous at David's courage that he was wondering if his family background and social standing might explain his extraordinary conduct.

18:1–5. It appears that David spoke with Saul at length, and he may have explained his actions as an expression of his faith in the Lord, thus attracting the love and loyalty of Jonathan (see v. 3; 14:6; 19:5). Jonathan's relationship with David developed in spite of a considerable age difference, which can be deduced as follows. Saul reigned for forty years (see Acts 13:21). After Saul was killed, David began to reign, at age thirty (see 2 Sam. 5:9), setting his birth year in Saul's tenth year as king. Early in Saul's reign, possibly his third year (see discussion on 13:1) and eight years before David's birth, Jonathan was old enough to be in charge of 1,000 soldiers (see 13:2). So Jonathan was possibly thirty years older than David. Their friendship endured even when it became clear that David was to replace him as the successor to his father's throne.

Saul ... would let him go no more home (v. 2). David's position in the court was no longer intermittent but permanent (see discussion on 17:15). **Jonathan and David made a covenant** (v. 3). The Hebrew indicates the initiative came from Jonathan.

The terms of the agreement are not specified here (for further details, see 19:1; 20:8, 13–16, 41–42; 23:18) but appear to have involved a pledge of mutual loyalty and friendship. At the very least, Jonathan accepted David as his equal. He **stript himself of the robe ... and gave it to David** (v. 4). Jonathan ratified the covenant in an act that symbolized giving himself to David. His act may have also signified his recognition that David was to assume his place as successor to Saul (see 20:14–15, 31; 23:17), a possibility that seems likely since he also gave David **his sword, and ... his bow, and ... his girdle** (see 13:22).

Whithersoever Saul sent him (v. 5) during the rest of the campaign, David **behaved himself wisely**; that is, he was successful (noted again in 18:14, 15, 30) and gained the respect of everyone.

18:6–9. It was common for women to greet victors with dancing and singing (see Exod. 15:20–21; Judg. 11:31, 34; 2 Sam. 1:20). Their reference to David's **ten thousands** of slain enemies (v. 7) is poetic and undoubtedly hyperbolic. In accordance with the normal conventions of Hebrew poetry, this was the women's way of saying, "Saul and David have slain thousands" (10,000 was normally used as the parallel of 1,000; e.g., see Deut. 32:30; Ps. 91:7; Mic. 6:7; also in Canaanite poetry found at Ugarit). It is a measure of Saul's insecurity and jealousy that he read their intentions incorrectly and took offense. His resentment may have been initially triggered by the mention of David's name alongside his own. (For the Philistines interpretation of this song, see discussion on 21:11.)

18:10–16. The evil spirit from God (v. 10; see discussion on 16:14) only exacerbated Saul's fragile mental state, and he **prophesied**. The Hebrew for this word is sometimes used to indicate uncontrolled ecstatic behavior, perhaps raving (see discussion on 1 Kings 18:29) and, in this context, is best understood in that sense (see also discussion on 10:5). Two factors contributed to Saul's envy of David: David's immense popularity (18:7–9) and the unmistakable fact that **the LORD was with him, and was departed from Saul** (v. 12). **Saul removed** David **from him, and made him his captain over a thousand** (v. 13). Saul's apparent motive for removing David was the hope that he would be killed in battle (see 18:17, 21, 25; 19:1). The result, however, was greater acclaim for David, for as he prospered, he stole the hearts of the people (see vv. 14, 16; 18:30).

18:17 – 19. Behold my elder daughter (v. 17). David was indeed entitled to have Saul's daughter as his wife because of his victory over Goliath (see 17:25). This promise had not been kept and was now made conditional on further military service, during which, Saul hoped, David would be killed. Israel's battles were addressed as **the LORD's battles** to enhance the offer. David responded in humility, and Saul reneged on his offer.

18:20 – 27. Michal's love for David gave Saul a new opportunity to set him up and have him killed by the Philistines. Saul's second proposal for David to become his son-in-law was not gracious but malicious. (Sadly, much later, David himself would resort to a similar tactic to eliminate a rival of another kind; see 2 Sam. 11:14 – 15.) Royal servants were engaged to persuade David of the king's favor, and, in light of David's poor economic standing, that Saul did not ask for **any dowry** (v. 25). Normally, the bridegroom paid a bride-price to the father of the bride (see Gen. 34:12; Exod. 22:16) as compensation for the loss of his daughter and as insurance for her support if she were widowed. Since David was poor, Saul required him instead to pass a test appropriate for a great warrior, hoping that he would "fall" (see 18:17, 21). Saul asked for a **hundred foreskins of the Philistines**. Foreskins were stipulated as needed evidence of his killing Philistines because they were an uncircumcised people (see discussions on 14:6; Judg. 7:25).

18:28 – 30. Michal ... loved him (v. 28). God's favor on David was revealed not only in his military accomplishments but also in Michal's love for him, now added to that of Jonathan. Everything Saul sought to use against David turned to David's advantage. **Saul was yet the more afraid of David** (v. 29). Saul's perception that God's hand was on David did not lead him to repentance and acceptance of his own lot (see 15:26) but to greater fear and jealousy toward David. As for David, his conduct and success only enhanced his reputation.

19:1 – 7. The irrational jealousy brought on by his dementia is most evident in Saul's giving orders to **kill David** (v. 1), his most successful fighter and the current celebrity in Israel. Saul abandoned his indirect attempts on David's life (see 18:13, 17, 25) and adopted a more direct approach, leading to David's departure from the court and from service to Saul (see 19:12, 18; 20:42). **Jonathan spake good of David** (v. 4). Jonathan did not let his own personal ambition distort his perception of David's true theocratic spirit (see v. 5 and discussions on 14:6; 17:11; 18:1). Jonathan's well-reasoned defense of David brought Saul to his senses temporarily. **Saul hearkened ... Saul sware** (v. 6) that David would live (see 14:24, 44 for previous oaths that Saul did not keep; see discussion on 14:39). David was thus able to return to Saul's court (see 18:2).

19:8 – 10. As David continued his success against the Philistines, the influence of the **evil spirit from the LORD** (v. 9) upon Saul became more unpredictable as to its timing and resultant behavior (see discussion on 16:14). Saul's new attempt to murder David **with the javelin** (v. 10) failed (see 18:10 – 11; 20:33), and David escaped.

19:11 – 17. The superscription of Psalm 59 cites this attempt of Saul to murder David as the setting for the psalm. Saul's open threat on David's life forced Michal to side with David and defend him against her own father. After helping David escape **through a window** (v. 12; see Josh. 2:15; Acts 9:25 for other window escapes), she found it necessary to lie and deceive Saul's men with an **image** (v. 13). The Hebrew word, *teraphim*, is plural and always refers to household gods (see discussion on Gen. 31:19). Since archaeology in Palestine has not produced any man-sized *teraphim*, perhaps Michal fashioned an appropriately sized dummy by placing several small images in the bed with an article made of goats' hair carefully arranged at the head.

19:18 – 24. David was now forced from his home, to become a fugitive from his king and father-in-law until Saul died. Instead of fleeing south to Bethlehem to his family, where Saul might look for him, he escaped north to **Ramah** (v. 18), the home of Samuel (see 7:17), the prophet who had anointed him (see 16:13). He stayed in **Naioth**, which means "habitations" or "dwellings." The term appears to designate a complex of houses in a certain section of Ramah where a **company of the prophets** (v. 20) resided (see vv. 19–20, 22–23), who were overseen by Samuel. This group may be the another example of what was later known as the "sons of the prophets" (see 10:5; 2 Kings 2:3–7, 15; 4:1, 38; 6:1).

Frustrated that three successive contingents of his messengers had failed to apprehend David because they were overcome by the Spirit and prophesied with the prophets instead, Saul took matters into his own hands. He fared no differently than the others. For the second time in his life, the Spirit of God caused him to prophesy with the prophets (see 10:11–13). This time, however, he alone stripped himself of his clothes, and he **lay down naked all that day and … night** (v. 24). Not only was such an act humiliating and shameful, but in casting aside his royal robes, he may have unwittingly symbolized the forfeiture of his claim to be king. He was so overwhelmed by the power of the Spirit of God that he was prevented from carrying out his intention to take David's life. His frustrated attempts to kill David—his own inability to harm David and the thwarting of his plans by Jonathan's loyalty, Michal's deception, and David's own cleverness—all reach their climax here. **Is Saul also among the prophets?** This second occasion reinforced the first (see 10:11). Its repetition underscores how alien Saul's spirit was from that of these zealous servants of the Lord.

20:1–42. The depth of Jonathan's friendship with David, which began in 18:1, is clearly demonstrated here. It was not affected by his knowledge that David's success would assure him of succeeding Saul to the throne instead of Jonathan.

20:1–4. With Saul at **Naioth in Ramah** (v. 1), David fled back to Jonathan, the only one in Saul's court whom he could trust. David's questions for his friend showed his emotional distress. Jonathan was mindful that his father had assured him that David "shall not be slain" (see 19:6), so it was difficult for him to accept David's analysis of Saul's intentions

and acknowledge that his father was indeed set on killing his close friend. David maintained that Saul kept his conspiracy from Jonathan to prevent him from grieving and claimed, **truly as the Lord liveth** (see discussion on 14:39) **… there is but a step between me and death** (v. 3).

20:5–8. Tomorrow is the new moon (v. 5). Each month of the year was consecrated to the Lord by special sacrifices (Num. 28:11–15) and blowing the trumpets (Num. 10:10; Ps. 81:3). Like the Sabbath, these observances involved cessation from normal work, especially at the beginning of the seventh month (Lev. 23:24–25; Num. 29:1–6; 2 Kings 4:23; Isa. 1:13; Amos 8:5). David knew that Saul would expect all of his servants to be in attendance, and he calculated that if Saul still bore ill-will against him, the discourtesy of his absence would bring it to the surface. Sadly, David's plan included a lie, another in a series to save his life (see 19:14; 21:2). He had no intention of returning to Bethlehem to celebrate a **yearly sacrifice** (v. 6). His statement indicates that it was customary for families to observe the new-moon festival together once in the year, but there is no other reference in the Old Testament to this practice.

David asked this favor on the basis of the **covenant** (v. 8) that Jonathan had initiated (see discussion on 18:3). He did not want to endanger himself by returning to Saul, as he had done once before with Jonathan's encouragement (see 19:7).

20:9–17. Jonathan was unaware of Saul's evil intentions. **O Lord God of Israel** (v. 12) is another oath formula, by which Jonathan assured David he would search out his father's intentions. **The Lord do so and much more to Jonathan** (v. 13) is a common curse formula (see discussion on 3:17). Jonathan assured David that he would inform him of Saul's evil intentions. **The Lord be with thee, as he hath been with my father.** Here is a clear indication that Jonathan expected David to become king. Having promised faithfulness to David, Jonathan wanted David to treat him and his descendants faithfully. **Shew me the kindness … that I die not** (v. 14). It was quite common in the ancient world for the first ruler of a new dynasty to secure his position by murdering all potential claimants to the throne from the preceding dynasty (see 1 Kings 15:29; 16:11; 2 Kings 10:7; 11:1). **Thou shalt not cut off thy kindness from my house** (v. 15). This request was based on the covenant previously concluded between Jonathan and David (see 18:3), and now he expanded it to include his offspring. It was subsequently honored in David's dealings with Jonathan's son Mephibosheth (see 2 Sam. 9:3, 7; 21:7).

Let the LORD even require it at the hand of David's enemies (v. 16). Jonathan aligned himself completely with David, calling for destruction of his enemies, even if that should include his father, Saul. For reassurance, he had David **swear again** (v. 17; see vv. 14 – 15; 20:42; 18:3). Jonathan's motivation for helping David was his deep love for him; **he loved him as he loved his own soul** (see 2 Sam. 1:26). He showed no trace of envy or desire to secure the throne for himself or his children.

20:18 – 23. Jonathan devised a plan for informing David of his father's intentions. He instructed David not to attend the **new moon** (v. 18) festivities (see discussion on 20:5) and to hide in **the place where thou didst hide** (v. 19), perhaps the place referred to in 19:2. Under the pretense of shooting arrows at a target, Jonathan planned to communicate to David his standing with Saul in case circumstances prevented them from actually conversing again. As it turned out, Jonathan and David had a few moments together before David had to flee (20:41 – 41). Regarding all their stated commitments (20:15 – 17), Jonathan concluded, **the LORD be between thee and me for ever** (v. 23). Thus, he invoked God to act as a witness and judge between them and ensure that their agreement would be kept.

20:24 – 34. At the meal of the new-moon festivities, David's absence was conspicuous, especially in view of the presence of Jonathan and **Abner** (v. 25), Saul's cousin and the commander of his army (see 14:50). Saul surmised David was absent because he was **not clean** (v. 26). Ritual meals demanded ritual purity of its participants (see discussion on 16:5; see Lev. 7:19 – 21; 15:16; Deut. 23:10). Upon learning of David's (deceitful) request to be away, and sens-

ing that Jonathan supported David, Saul flew into a rage: **Thou son of the perverse rebellious woman** (v. 30). The Hebrew idiom is obscene and was meant to characterize Jonathan, not his mother. **Thou shalt not be stablished, nor thy kingdom** (v. 31). Saul was now convinced that David would succeed him if David was not killed (see discussions on 18:13, 17, 29; 19:1), and he was incapable of understanding Jonathan's lack of concern for his own succession to the throne. He felt betrayed by his son's loyalty to David, and Jonathan's effort to intercede for David was to no avail. When Saul **cast a javelin** (v. 33; see 18:11; 19:10) at his own son, Jonathan became certain of his father's designs for David.

20:35 – 40. As prearranged (20:19 – 23), Jonathan went through the drill of shooting arrows to inform David secretly of Saul's intentions. The occasion did afford David one last opportunity to meet with Jonathan. He **bowed himself three times** (v. 41) to him, a sign of submission and respect (see Gen. 33:3; 42:6); then they embraced and parted after remembering their oath, **we have sworn both of us** (v. 42; see 20:14 – 15, 23; 18:3). Jonathan returned to **the city** (i.e., Gibeah; see 10:26), but David's life as a fugitive from Saul, which perhaps started out tentatively (see 19:10, 18), had become a confirmed reality.

21:1 – 9. Nob (v. 1) was a town northeast of Jerusalem and south of Gibeah and the site of the tabernacle after the destruction of Shiloh (4:2 – 3; Jer. 7:12). Although it appears that no attempt had been made to bring the ark to this sanctuary (see discussion on 7:1), **Ahimelech the priest** (see discussion on 14:3), eighty-five other priests (22:17 – 18), the ephod (v. 9), and the table of shewbread (v. 6) are all mentioned in connection with it. From 22:10, 15, it appears that David's purpose in coming to Nob was to seek the Lord's guidance by means of the Urim and Thummim (see discussions on 2:28; Exod. 28:30).

Why David resorted to deception in his response to Ahimelech is not clear (see also v. 8). Perhaps he suspected Ahimelech's loyalty to Saul, or possibly he was attempting to protect the priest from the charge of involvement in his escape from Saul. If so, his strategy was not successful (see 22:13 – 18).

Christians must not cite David's action as scriptural support for situational ethics or license to misrepresent the truth. Scripture simply records David's lie; it does not condone it. Scripture consistently condemns lying (see Lev. 19:11; Prov. 6:16–17; 12:22) and Christians, especially since they are being conformed to the image of Christ (see Rom. 8:29), who is the Truth (see John 14:6), are admonished to "put away lying" (see Eph 4:25).

Only **hallowed bread** (v. 4) was available for food. The shewbread (see v. 6; see *KJV Study Bible* note on Exod. 25:30), which was placed in the Holy Place in the tabernacle (and later in the temple) as a thank offering to the Lord, symbolized His provision of daily bread. There was one stipulation: **if the young men have kept themselves … from women.** Although the bread was to be eaten only by the priests (see Lev. 24:9), Ahimelech agreed to give it to David and his men on the condition that they were ceremonially clean (see Exod. 19:15; Lev. 15:18). Jesus used this incident to illustrate the principle that the ceremonial law was not to be viewed in a legalistic manner (see Matt. 12:3–4). He also taught that it is always lawful to do good and to save life (see Luke 6:9). Such compassionate acts are within the true spirit of the law.

Why **Doeg, an Edomite** (v. 7), was in Saul's employ is unclear. He may have been a proselyte to Israel's religion, or he may have been a mercenary who had been taken captive in Saul's campaign against Edom. His presence at the tabernacle, however, is parenthetically noted because of his importance to the story in chapter 22.

Having no weapon, David was given the **sword of Goliath** (v. 9), a weapon he could rightly claim as his own, since he had killed Goliath. How it came to be at the tabernacle is not stated (see discussion on 17:54).

21:10–15. According to the superscription of Psalm 34, David's encounter with **Achish the king of Gath** (v. 10) was the setting for the psalm (although Achish is called Abimelech; perhaps Achish was his personal name and Abimelech was his title). Gath was one of the five major towns of the Philistines

(Josh. 13:3). To seek refuge in Gath—the home of Goliath, whom David had killed—was risky. (See also the superscription of Psalm 56.)

The Philistines' designation of David as **king of the land** (v. 11) may be understood as a popular exaggeration expressing an awareness of the enormous success and popularity of David among the Israelite people. It is clear that the song of the women (18:7) had spread to the Philistines. Realizing he had been identified, David did not resort to verbal lies or denials. Instead, he acted a lie and pretended to be insane.

22:1–5. The **cave Adullam** (v. 1) was located in the border region between Judah and Philistia (see 2 Sam. 23:13; Gen. 38:1; Josh. 12:15; 15:35; 1 Chron. 11:15). Here David was joined by his family and **about four hundred men** (v. 2). It is unclear whether this cave experience or that of 24:3–8 provides the setting for Psalms 57 and 142 (see superscriptions of these psalms). David, officially an outlaw, was joined by others who were in similar circumstances, so that he began to develop the power base that would sustain him throughout his later years as king. A fugitive's life would have been too strenuous for his parents, so he sought asylum for them with the king of Moab. **Let my father and my mother … come … and be with you** (v. 3). The king of Moab was a natural ally for David because Saul had warred against him (see 14:47) and because David's great-grandmother was a Moabitess (see Ruth 4:13, 22).

The location of the **hold** (i.e., a stronghold; v. 4) where David stayed is uncertain. It was perhaps Adullam or a specific fortress but is more likely a reference to a geographical area in which it was easy to hide (see 23:14; 2 Sam. 5:17; 23:14).

David, the king-designate, was now served also by the **prophet Gad** (v. 5). Later, a priest would come to him (22:20) and complete the basic elements of a royal entourage—all of whom were refugees from Saul's administration. This is the first appearance of the prophet who would later assist David in musical arrangements for the temple services (see 2 Chron. 29:25), write a history of David's reign (see 1 Chron. 29:29), and confront David with the Lord's rebuke for his sin of numbering the Israelites (see 2 Sam.

24:11–25). The **forest of Hareth** was located in the tribal area of Judah.

22:6–8. Saul remained at **Gibeah** (v. 6; see discussion on 10:5) under a tamarisk **tree** (see discussion on 14:2). **In Ramah** is probably better rendered literally, "on a height" or "on a hill." He had his **spear in his hand**, a symbol that he was still ruler. Overcome by paranoia and self-pity, Saul felt abandoned by his own tribe, the **Benjamites** (v. 7; 9:1–2; 10:21). He sought to strengthen his position with his own officials by emphasizing tribal loyalty. David was from the tribe of Judah (see discussion on 16:1; 2 Sam. 2:4). Saul charged the Benjamites with presuming that David could give them something that he had not, **fields and vineyards**, and could put them in prestigious positions, **captains of thousands, and captains of hundreds**. He felt especially betrayed because no one had informed him of Jonathan's covenant with David.

22:9–19. Doeg (21:7), a loyalist and an opportunist, was quick to inform on Ahimelech the priest and cast suspicion on his allegiance to Saul. The superscription of Psalm 52 cites this event as the setting of the psalm.

Ahimelech the high priest and all the assisting priests were summoned to Saul and were charged with conspiracy. Ahimelech's attempt to justify his legitimate provision for the king's celebrated warrior only angered Saul. He intended to set an example that would deter others from conspiracy and ordered the priests to be killed, charging that **they knew when he** (David) **fled** (v. 17). How much the priests really knew is not clear. David himself had not told them (see 21:2–3, 8). Saul's **footmen**, probably his bodyguards, refused to kill the priests, perhaps having grown accustomed to Saul's irrational orders and acts. This is the second time clearer heads tried to prevail over a death sentence set by Saul (see 14:44–45).

The opportunistic Doeg, who was not an Israelite, was willing to execute the king's order and kill the priests. It is sadly ironic that Saul did to the priests of God and to the people of Nob and all their cattle what he disobediently neglected to do to the Amalekites (15:3, 4, 7–9). With the death of eighty-five persons

who wore a **linen ephod** (i.e., priests; v. 18; see discussion on 2:18), the prophecy of judgment against the house of Eli was nearer fulfillment (see 2:31).

22:20–23. One lone survivor from the priests, **Abiathar, escaped, and fled after David** (v. 20; see discussion on 22:5). Abiathar brought the high priestly ephod with him (see 23:6) and subsequently "inquired of the LORD" for David (see 23:2 and discussion; see also 23:4, 9; 30:7–8; 2 Sam. 2:1; 5:19, 23). Though David admitted his guilt in causing the priests' deaths, nothing could be undone. The impact of David's lies (see 21:2–8) and of the deaths of the priests on the spiritual climate of Israel is incalculable. Abiathar remained with David and served as high priest until he was removed from office by Solomon for participating in the rebellion of Adonijah (see 1 Kings 2:26–27).

23:1–26:25. These chapters chronicle David's life as a fugitive from Saul as he crisscrossed his homeland of Judah, always managing to stay a step ahead of his pursuers.

23:1–6. Though a fugitive from Saul, David learned of a Philistine raid on **Keilah** (v. 1) (probably modern Khirbet Qilah), which was located in Judah's foothills about eighteen miles southwest of Jerusalem. Ever loyal to Israel, **David inquired of the LORD** (v. 2), apparently by means of the Urim and Thummim through the high priest, Abiathar (see vv. 4; 23:10–12 and discussion on 2:28), to see if he should involve himself in protecting Keilah. Assured of God's deliverance, he obeyed. Verse 6 is parenthetical, informing the reader that when Abiathar had escaped Saul's massacre of the priests (see 22:18–20), he had salvaged the ephod (which contained the Urim and Thummim) and brought it with him. His father, Eli, had died for having consulted the Lord once for David; Abiathar would consult Him repeatedly for David.

23:7–13. When Saul learned that David was in a city that had **gates and bars** (v. 7), he figured David could be easily captured. **Bring hither the ephod** (v. 9; see discussion on 23:2). David knew that Saul meant him harm but consulted the Lord to learn of the intentions of Keilah. Thus, he discovered that their "thanks" for his having delivered them from the

Philistines would be to surrender him to Saul. The intentions of Keilah (and later the Ziphites, 23:19) indicate that David did not enjoy unanimous support from his own tribe, Judah, although it is possible that the residents of Keilah feared a massacre from Saul, similar to what he had ordered in Nob. In what appears to have been a relatively short time, the number of malcontents who had joined David (see 22:2) had grown significantly, to **about six hundred** (v. 13).

23:14–18. David took refuge in the **wilderness in strong holds** (v. 14), probably a reference to places inaccessible to Saul (see discussion on 22:4). The **wilderness of Ziph** was located south of Hebron. **God delivered him not into his hand.** The reality of God's protection of David contrasts sharply with the wishful thinking of Saul in 23:7.

Before reporting on the Ziphites' disloyalty to David, the author notes that Jonathan remained loyal to David and came to encourage him. **Thou shalt be king over Israel** (v. 17; see discussions on 18:4; 20:13, 16, 31). Jonathan stated plainly that he knew that God would not permit "his anointed" to be killed by Saul. **I shall be next unto thee.** Jonathan's love and respect for David enabled him to accept a role subordinate to David without any sign of resentment or jealousy (see discussions on 18:3; 19:4). Sadly, this is the last recorded meeting between Jonathan and David. **Saul ... knoweth**; that is, Saul also realized his throne would go to David (see 18:8 and discussion on 20:31). The parting words of the two friends were to reiterate their **covenant before the Lord** (v. 18; see discussions on 18:3; 20:14–15).

23:19–26. When David took refuge in the **strong holds** (v. 19; see discussion on 22:4), Saul found brief comfort because the Ziphites (i.e., residents in the wilderness of Ziph, southeast of Hebron) reported to him on the whereabouts of David. **Blessed be ye of the Lord** (v. 21) was a customary blessing. David, however, had relocated farther south, to the wilderness of Maon.

23:27–28. As Saul closed in on David, providential intervention came from the Philistines who invaded the land (the location is not stated) and diverted Saul's attention to "national security." The name **Sela-hammahlekoth** (v. 28) was derived from the occasion and is variously interpreted "rock of parting" or "rock of escape."

23:29–24:1–3. David moved farther east, to the **strong holds of En-gedi** (v. 29), and Saul resumed his pursuit. When Saul came to the **sheepcotes** (i.e., caves use to provide shelter for flocks from heat and cold; v. 3), he entered **to cover his feet**. This literal rendering is euphemistic for "to relieve himself." He was unaware that David and his men were already occupying the cave. A wonderful opportunity had been provided David to kill Saul and end his constant need to escape him.

24:4–7. Behold the day of which the Lord said (v. 4). There is no previous record of the divine revelation here alluded to by David's men. Perhaps this was their own interpretation of the anointing of David to replace Saul (see 16:13–14) or of the assurances given to David that he would survive Saul's vendetta against him and ultimately become king (see 20:14–15; 23:17). This clause may also be rendered "today the Lord is saying." Then the reference would be, not to a verbal communication from the Lord, but to the providential nature of the incident itself, which David's men understood as a revelation from God that David should not ignore.

David's smitten conscience over cutting Saul's robe may indicate his realization that his action was one of disrespect and rebellion. As much as he feared Saul and his malicious intent, David always maintained loyalty and respect for his **master, the Lord's anointed** (v. 6). Because Saul's royal office carried divine sanction by virtue of his anointing (see discussion on 9:16), David was determined not to wrest the kingship from Saul but to leave its disposition to the Lord who gave it (see 24:12, 15; 26:10).

24:8–15. In a fashion somewhat similar to Samuel (see 12:1–5), David maintained his innocence of any wrongdoing against Saul, and shamed the king for his vindictiveness. **My father** (v. 11) has been variously interpreted: (1) a title of respect (see v. 10; 24:6), (2) a suggestion that he has usurped Jonathan's "sonship" and now stood in line to be king (see 24:20), or (3) a reminder to Saul that he was David's father-in-law (see 18:27).

David held up the piece of Saul's robe that he had cut off, giving proof that he could have killed the king if he had so desired. When Saul had torn Samuel's garment (see 15:27), he had learned of the symbolic implication that his kingdom would be torn from him. Perhaps the sight of part of his robe in David's hand caused a flashback, and he surmised even further implications that his kingdom would be severed from him.

David cited a proverb: **Wickedness proceedeth from the wicked** (v. 13), but not from him, because he was innocent. He likened himself to a harmless **dead dog** (v. 14) and to a **flea**, expressions meant to depict his submissiveness to Saul. He concluded by placing his case in the hands of **the LORD** (v. 15) to judge and deliver him.

24:16–22. Saul lift up his voice, and wept (v. 16). Saul experienced temporary remorse (see 26:21) for his actions against David but quickly reverted to his former determination to kill him (see 26:2). **My son David** was a response to David calling Solomon "my father" (24:11).

I know well that thou shalt surely be king (v. 20) was a confession Saul made but not a reality he was willing to accept, indicated by his subsequent pursuit of David (see 26:2). **Sware … thou wilt not cut off my seed** (v. 21). His plea for David to extend kindness to his family is reminiscent of Jonathan's request (see discussions on 20:14–15).

David returned to the **hold** (v. 22), that is, the stronghold. Based on his previous experiences, David did not place any confidence in Saul's words of repentance.

25:1. Samuel died (v. 1). Samuel had been a man of integrity and was recognized as a leader of national prominence who had played a key role in restructuring the theocracy with the establishment of the monarchy (see chaps. 8–12). **All the Israelites … lamented him**. The loss of his leadership was mourned much like that of other prominent figures in Israel's past history, including Jacob (Gen. 50:10), Aaron (Num. 20:29), and Moses (Deut. 34:8). He was buried in his hometown of **Ramah** (see 7:17 and discussion on 1:1).

25:2–44. The account of Nabal effectively serves the author's purpose in a number of ways: (1) Nabal's general character, his disdainful attitude toward David though David had guarded his flocks, and his sudden death at the Lord's hand all parallel the account of Saul (whose "flock" David had also protected). This allows the author to characterize indirectly Saul as a fool (see 13:13; 26:21) and to foreshadow his end. (2) David's vengeful attitude toward Nabal displayed his natural tendency and highlighted his restraint toward Saul, the Lord's anointed (the account of Nabal is sandwiched between the two instances in which David, in spite of the urging of his men, spared Saul). (3) Abigail's prudent action prevented David from using his power as leader for personal vengeance (the very thing Saul had been doing). In this way, the Lord (who avenged His servant) kept David's sword clean, teaching him a lesson he did not forget. (4) Abigail's confident acknowledgment of David's future accession to the throne foreshadowed that event and even anticipated the Lord's commitment to establish David's house as a "sure house" (v. 28; see 2 Sam. 7:11–16). (5) Abigail's marriage to David provided him with a wise and worthy wife, while Saul gave away David's wife Michal to another man, illustrating how the Lord countered every move Saul made against David.

25:2–3. Nabal (v. 3), the "fool" (see 25:25 and discussion), lived south of Hebron near **Carmel**, where Saul had erected a monument in his own honor (15:12) and had committed the act that led to his rejection (15:26). Nabal was from the **house of Caleb** (i.e., a descendant of Caleb; v. 3; see Num. 14:24), who had settled at Hebron (see Josh. 14:13) after the conquest of Canaan. Since Caleb's name can mean "dog," Nabal is subtly depicted as a dog as well as a fool. He would soon be a dead dog (see discussion on 2 Sam. 9:8), when the Lord would avenge his acts of contempt toward David. The hint is strong that when the Lord avenged Saul's sins against David (see 24:12, 15), the king would no longer pursue a dead dog (see 24:14) but would himself become one—a case of biting irony.

25:4–8. Though a fugitive and an outcast, David had not behaved like an outlaw and appropriated others' property (especially food) for himself and his men. They had protected Nabal's servants (see 25:14–16) without remuneration. **Nabal did shear his sheep** (v. 4). Sheep shearing, the "harvest" for the shepherds, was a time of festivities (see v. 8; 2 Sam. 13:23–24), with lots of food on hand. Therefore, David figured it was **good day** (v. 8) to ask of Nabal for **whatsoever cometh to thine hand**. He and his men were asking for some remuneration for their protection of Nabal's shepherds and flocks against pillage (see 25:15–16, 21).

25:9–13. Nabal is described only in unfavorable terms (25:3, 17, 25, 36). His arrogant and ungrateful response to David's request matched his reputation (25:3). His retort, **Who is David?** (v. 10), showed his contempt, and he insulted David by likening him to a runaway slave.

David prepared to use violent force against Nabal. Three times it is said that he and his men girded on the **sword** (v. 13).

25:14–31. The author now shifts attention to **Abigail** (v. 14), Nabal's wife. A servant reminded her of Nabal's character, **such a son of Belial** (i.e., a worthless man, see 1:16; 2:12), **that a man cannot speak to him** (v. 17); that is, he was unreasonable. In this way too, Nabal was like Saul (see, e.g., 20:27–33).

Abigail, the total opposite of her husband, wisely averted disaster (note David's intentions, 25:13, 21–22) by bringing a gracious gift of provisions and diverting the blame of her foolish husband to herself (vv. 24–25). **She told not her husband** (v. 19) of what she planned to do (compare Michal's treatment of Saul, 19:11–14). By sending the provisions ahead, she hoped to placate David before she arrived to meet him face to face (see Jacob and Esau, Gen. 32–33).

David's intentions are defined: **So and more also do God unto the enemies of David** (v. 22; see discussion on 3:17). The sense may be, "As surely as God will punish my enemies, so surely will I kill every male in Nabal's household."

Abigail's speech was eloquent as she attempted to assume her husband's blame. She deferred to David by falling at his feet and repeatedly acknowledging him as **my lord** (v. 24). She concurred that Nabal was a **man of Belial** (v. 25; see v. 17), that **as his name is, so is he**. In ancient times, a person's name was believed to reflect his nature and character. **Nabal is his name**. In Hebrew, the name Nabal means "fool."

Citing an oath formula, **as the LORD liveth** (v. 26; see discussion on 14:39), she willed that David's **enemies … be as Nabal**, inferring that she thought her husband was going to die.

The LORD will certainly make … a sure house (v. 28). While the idea that David was destined to become king in place of Saul may have spread among the general populace, Abigail's assessment of David contrasts sharply with that of her husband (see 25:10). **My lord fighteth the battles of the LORD.** Abigail was familiar with David's victories over the Philistines, in which he sought to glorify the Lord rather than to advance his own honor (see 17:26, 45–47; 18:16–17). **Evil hath not been found in thee.** Abigail showed concern for the preservation of David's integrity in view of the office he was later to assume (see vv. 30–31; 25:39). **My lord shall be bound in the bundle of life** (v. 29) is a metaphor for long life. Using the figure of placing a valuable possession in a package carefully wrapped for safekeeping, Abigail assured David that the Lord would preserve his life in the midst of danger. **Them shall he sling out.** In a contrasting metaphor, she depicted David's enemies as being slung out from a sling.

Abigail told David that when he became **ruler** (v. 30; "ruler" and "captain" are from the same Hebrew word; see discussion on 9:16), he would not regret that he had not **shed blood causeless** (v. 31), that is, needlessly.

25:32–35. Blessed be the LORD … which sent thee (v. 32). David recognized the providential leading of the Lord in his encounter with Abigail (see 25:39). Though he had felt his determination to get revenge seemed justified, he was relieved he had not shed blood. Perhaps he realized that his reaction had been a bit hasty and intolerant, for later in his reign he would exhibit patience and tolerance on numerous occasions (e.g., 2 Sam. 16:11–12).

25:36–38. Nabal … held a feast … like the feast of a king (v. 36; see Prov. 30:21–22). Herein is another clue that the author is using Nabal as a subtle portrayal of Saul. The celebration ended, however, when Nabal learned of David's intentions and Abigail's intervention. His **heart … became as a stone** (v. 37). Whether he suffered a stroke or a heart attack is uncertain and unimportant, for his subsequent death was a divine act (see Deut. 32:35; Rom. 12:19). He who had been without moral sensitivity (was a *nabal*; see 25:25 and discussion) became as senseless as a stone. Several days later, the LORD **smote Nabal** (v. 38), and **he died**.

25:39–44. David's marriage to Abigail may have been the second of his polygamous marriages (see 2 Sam. 3:2–5; 5:13), because **Ahinoam** (v. 43), another of David's wives, is consistently listed first (see order of his wives in 27:3; 30:5; 2 Sam. 2:2; 3:2). Though there is no specific record, apparently while David was a fugitive from Saul, he had taken Ahinoam to be his wife and she was the mother of Ammon. Her hometown of **Jezreel** was located near Carmel (see 25:2; Josh. 15:55) and is not to be confused with the northern town of the same name, where Israel camped against the Philistines (see 29:1, 11) and where Ahab resided in later times (see 1 Kings 18:45–46). Since the only other known Ahinoam was the wife of Saul (1 Sam. 14:50), some have believed that even while in exile, David had taken Saul's wife to be his own, thus taking an early claim to the throne (see discussion on 2 Sam. 12:7–8; 16:21–22). However, such an interpretation seems questionable in that it is not said of Saul's wife that she was from Jezreel, and it would have been inconsistent of David, one who would not touch the LORD's anointed to take the throne, to have taken the king's wife before Saul had died.

26:1–5. For the second time, the **Ziphites** (v. 1; see discussions on 23:14, 19) were adversaries of David and informants for Saul. The superscription of Psalm 54 claims the Ziphites as the cause behind the psalm. **Gibeah** remained Saul's residence (see 10:26).

Though Saul had earlier admitted that David would become king (see 24:20), he had not lost his resolve to kill David. Thus, he led an intense search with **three thousand chosen men** (v. 2), apparently his standing army (see 24:2).

David arrived at Saul's camp during the night, when the men were sleeping, and located **the place where Saul lay** (v. 5). Saul's cousin, **Abner** (see 14:50), remained his captain. Saul was supposedly safe **in the trench**, that is, in the barricade provided by his surrounding troops.

26:6–12. Ahimelech the Hittite (v. 6) is not referred to elsewhere. Hittites had long resided in Canaan (see discussion on Gen. 10:15; see also Gen. 15:20; 23:3–20; Deut. 7:1; 20:17). Another Hittite in David's service was Uriah (see 2 Sam. 11:3; 23:39). **Abishai the son of Zeruiah, brother to Joab**. Zeruiah was an older sister of David (1 Chron. 2:16), so Abishai and Joab (and their brother Asahel, 2 Sam. 2:18) were David's nephews as well as trusted military leaders. Joab would long serve as the commander of David's army.

Accompanied by Abishai on the dangerous exploit, David entered Saul's camp. It was not difficult to locate Saul among the sleeping men because his spear, the sign of his royal rank, was stuck in the ground near his head. Abishai believed the time was right to end Saul's life and begged permission to kill Saul with his own spear. One stab would be sufficient.

As the LORD liveth (v. 10; see discussion on 14:39). David's respect for the Lord's anointed had not diminished or modified (see 24:6, 10), so permission to harm Saul was denied. Instead, **David took the spear and the cruse of water** (v. 12). In this way, he sought to prove again to Saul that he did not seek to kill him.

26:13–17. From a safe distance and in the dark, David shouted to Abner and publicly scolded him for being derelict in his duty to protect the king. Both Abner and the king tried to identify the voice, unable to see the one speaking.

26:18–20. David demanded that Saul identify the crime for which he was being pursued. He resented being alienated through no guilt of his own. **Let him accept an offering** (v. 19). David knew no reason why God should be angry with him, but if for some reason God was behind Saul's determined efforts to kill him, David appealed for God to accept an offering of appeasement (see 16:5)—in any event, to let the matter be settled between David and God, without Saul's involvement. **Cursed be they before the Lord.** David commited any such men to the judgment of God. David appealed to Saul's conscience by describing his present exclusion from **the inheritance of the Lord** (see discussion on 10:1), that is, the fellowship of God's people and living at peace in the Lord's land. **Go, serve other gods.** To be expelled from the Lord's land was to be separated from the Lord's sanctuary (an Old Testament form of excommunication) and left to serve the gods of whatever land one settled in (see Josh. 22:24–27).

David once again shamed the king for focusing so much attention on him. It was like seeking **a flea** (v. 20; see 24:14). He suggested that Saul was making a fool of himself in his fanatical pursuit of an innocent and undesigning man. David felt like a hunted **partridge**, a bird that made its escape by running rather than flying. Hence, it was pursued until fatigued and then clubbed to death.

26:21–24. I have sinned (v. 21) are words not often uttered by Saul (see 15:24). Contrast David, who had not sinned against Saul and caused the king to declare him more righteous (24:11, 17). **I have played the fool.** Saul confessed that his behavior had been not only unwise but also ungodly (see discussions on 13:13; 25:2–44).

Realizing that he could have been killed but was spared because, as David stated, **I would not stretch forth mine hand against the Lord's anointed** (v. 23; see 26:9 and discussion on 24:6), Saul made a veiled reference to his own conviction that David would replace him as king: **thou shalt … prevail** (v. 25; see 24:20). Their separation marked the end of David's confrontation with Saul. David would resort to political asylum among the neighboring Philistines.

B. David Seeks Refuge in Philistia; Saul and His Sons Are Killed in Battle (chaps. 27–31)

27:1–4. Sensing that the demented Saul would not cease the hunt for his life, David concluded, **I shall now perish … by the hand of Saul** (v. 1). David faltered in his faith (see 23:14; 25:29) and, under the pressure of Saul's superior forces, felt compelled to seek security outside Israel's borders. Besides his own safety, his responsibility for the 600 men, and their families, that were with him must have been a pressing burden. For the second time, David sought refuge in the **land of the Philistines** (see 21:10–15). In contrast to David's previous excursion into Philistia, **Achish … king of Gath** (v. 2; see 21:10–15) was now ready to receive him because he had become known as a formidable adversary of Saul. Any enemy of Saul was a friend of his. Moreover, under the circumstances, offering David sanctuary would obligate him and his men to serve Achish in any military venture (see 28:1). Asylum also included protection for David's two wives, **Ahinoam** (v. 3; see discussion on 25:43) and **Abigail** (see 25:39–42).

Saul **sought no more again for him** (v. 4). Saul did not have sufficient military strength to make incursions into Philistine territory, and with David out of the country, he no longer faced an internal threat to his throne.

27:5–7. Give me a place in some town in the country (v. 5). David desired more independence and freedom of movement than was possible while residing under the eye of the king of Gath. **Why should thy servant dwell in the royal city with thee?** David implied that he was not worthy of this honor. The location of **Ziklag** (v. 6) is unknown, but it is included in a list of towns in southern Judah (Josh. 15:31) and was probably south of Gath. It was given to the tribe of Simeon (Josh. 19:1–5) and was presumably occupied by them (Judg. 1:17–18), only to be lost to the Philistines at a later, undisclosed time. As a parenthetical note, Ziklag **pertaineth unto the kings of Judah unto this day**, that is, as royal property. This comment implies that the book of Samuel was written after the time of Israel's division into the northern and southern kingdoms—an important consideration in determining the date of the book's composition (see Introduction: "Author, Date, and Sources").

Though it is not stated how long he had been a fugitive from Saul, **David dwelt in the country of the Philistines ... a full year and four months** (v. 7). He would not move his residence from Ziklag (see 2 Sam. 1:1; 2:1–3) to Hebron until after the death of Saul.

27:8–12. Ziklag served as David's base of operations for forays into the southern parts of Judah. As a vassal of Achish, David was expected to make raids on Judah, but he raided only non-Israelite towns. Those affected were the **Geshurites** (v. 8), a people residing in the area south of Philistia who had not been defeated by the Israelites at the time of the conquest (Josh. 13:1–3) and who are to be distinguished from the Geshurites residing in the north, near the upper Jordan in Aram (see 2 Sam. 3:3; 13:37–38; Deut. 3:14; Josh. 12:5). Also affected were the **Gezrites** (or "Gerzites"), who are not mentioned elsewhere in the Old Testament, the **Amalekites** (see discussion on 15:2), and the inhabitants of **Shur** (see discussion on 15:7).

David ... left neither man nor woman alive (v. 9). Operating under the premise that "dead men tell no tales," David left no survivors to report on him to the Philistines. His action also conformed to that of Joshua in the conquest of Canaan (see, e.g., Josh. 6:21 and discussion on Josh. 6:17). Reporting to Achish, David told of forays against the **south of Judah** (v. 10). The Hebrew for "south" is *negeb* (commonly pronounced *negev*), which means "dry" and designates a large area from Beersheba to the highlands of the Sinai peninsula. The **Jerahmeelites** were descendants of Judah through Hezron (see 1 Chron. 2:9, 25). For the **Kenites,** see discussion on 15:6.

Achish believed David (v. 12). David led Achish to believe that he was raiding outposts of Israelite territory. Achish was delighted to have him defame himself among his own people, when in actuality, David was attacking the Geshurites, Gerzites, and Amalekites (see v. 8), all enemies of Judah and Israel.

28:1–2. David's deceit returned to haunt him, because a misinformed Achish (see discussion on 27:8–12) now expected David (his servant, 27:5, 12) to accompany him in active combat against Israel. **Know thou assuredly, that thou shalt go out with me to battle** (v. 1). In the ancient Near East, accepting sanctuary in a country involved obligations of military service (see discussion on 27:2). David's response, **thou shalt know what thy servant can do** (v. 2), was perhaps meant to be an ambiguous answer. **Therefore will I make thee keeper of mine head,** that is, his bodyguard. Very likely, this was conditional on David's proof of his loyalty and effectiveness in the projected campaign.

28:3. The reminder that **Samuel was dead** (see 25:1) informs the reader somewhat parenthetically that Saul could not turn to him, even in desperation. At some point early in his reign, Saul had **put away ... out of the land** (possibly a euphemism for "put to death," in agreement with Pentateuchal law; see Lev. 19:31; 20:6, 27; Deut. 18:11) all **those that had familiar spirits, and the wizards,** that is, all those involved with necromancy and the occult (see 28:9, 21). So these were not available for consultation either.

28:4–7. The Philistines assembled their forces far to the north, along the plain of Jezreel in the territory of Issachar at **Shunem** (v. 4; see Josh. 19:18). Saul encamped with Israel in **Gilboa,** a range of mountains east of the plain of Jezreel. Stricken by fear, Saul's **heart greatly trembled** (v. 5) because he was estranged from the Lord and was not performing his role as the true theocratic king (see discussion on 17:11).

Saul inquired of the LORD (v. 6), presumably through the agency of a (possibly illegitimate) priest. Saul seemed to sense disaster in the approaching battle and sought divine revelation concerning its outcome through three different means: (1) **dreams,** direct personal revelation (see Num. 12:6 and discussion); (2) **Urim,** revelation through the priest (see discussion on 2:28). Since the authentic ephod and its Urim were with Abiathar, who was aligned with David (see 23:2, 6, 9), either Saul had fabricated another ephod for his use or the author used a conventional statement including the three visual forms of revelation to underscore his point; and (3) **prophets**. David had a prophet (Gad, 22:5), but after Samuel's alienation from Saul (15:35), no prophet served Saul. In essence, Saul had been cut off from a word from God.

Seek me a woman that hath a familiar spirit (v. 7). In his desperation, Saul turned to a pagan practice that he himself had previously outlawed (28:3) in accordance with the Mosaic law (see Lev. 19:26, 31). Such a person was found at **En-dor**, located about six miles northwest of Shunem (see 28:4; Josh. 17:11).

28:8–14. Saul was forced to make his appeal under disguise and darkness. The woman was very cautious about practicing her trade with strangers, lest she be betrayed to Saul. **Wherefore then layest thou a snare for my life …?** (v. 9; see discussion on 28:3). Saul assured her with an oath, **As the LORD liveth** (v. 10; see discussion on 14:39), that there would be no trouble for her. He then instructed her to **Bring me up Samuel.**

When the woman saw Samuel (v. 12). This episode has been understood in many different ways, among them the following: (1) God permitted the spirit of Samuel to appear to the woman. (2) The woman had contact with an evil or devilish spirit, in the form of Samuel, by whom she was deceived and controlled. (3) By using parapsychological powers, such as telepathy or clairvoyance, the woman was able to discern Saul's thoughts and picture Samuel in her own mind. Whatever the explanation of this mysterious affair, the outcome was beyond what the medium expected, for she was frightened by the appearance of Samuel. In some way, the medium was used to convey to Saul that the impending battle would bring death, would dash his hopes for a dynasty, and would conclude his reign with a devastating defeat of Israel that would leave the nation at the mercy of the Philistines, the very people against whom he had struggled all his years as king. All this would occur, as Samuel had previously announced (15:26, 28), because of Saul's unfaithfulness to the Lord. **She cried … thou art Saul.** By whatever means,

the medium suddenly became aware that she was dealing with Saul.

I saw gods ascending (v. 13), though a literal rendering of the Hebrew, perhaps has the meaning of seeing a spirit coming up from the ground. She further described seeing **an old man … covered with a mantle** (v. 14). Saul remembered Samuel as customarily dressed in this apparel (see 15:27).

28:15–20. Saul poured out his despair to the prophet and asked him for a divine revelation. The first part of Samuel's message was review: the kingdom was being torn from Saul to be given to David because Saul had disobeyed God in not destroying the Amalekites (see 15:26–28). The second part of the message was new: the Philistines would defeat Israel, and Saul and his sons would be killed. It is noteworthy that the first and last prophetic messages that Samuel delivered were notices of judgment and death to two leaders of Israel (see 2:34; 3:11–14).

28:21–25. The woman came unto Saul (v. 21). This statement suggests that the woman had removed herself from Saul's view while she gave her oracles and the prophet addressed Saul. To encourage the despondent king, the woman provided him with a meal before he parted from her, though she had no means to reverse the prophet's message or its outcome.

29:1–5. The Philistines gathered … all their armies (v. 1). The narrative flow, broken at 28:2, is resumed. **Aphek** was in the vicinity of Shunem (28:4) and is to be distinguished from the Aphek referred to in 4:1 (see 1 Kings 20:26, 30; 2 Kings 13:17).

David's successful but deceptive predatory raids from Ziklag (see discussion on 27:8–12) had landed him in an uncomfortable predicament. He had been "drafted" by Achish to join in the battle against Israel (28:1). David's response had been nebulous. He neither welcomed nor rejected the idea. It is difficult to imagine that David would have participated in a battle to harm Saul, the Lord's anointed, especially since David had already passed up two opportunities to kill him. David undoubtedly would have used his presence to Israel's advantage by turning against Achish. Positioned at the rear as he was (v. 2), he could have aided Saul by catching the Philistines in a pincer movement, forcing Achish's troops to fight on two fronts. So the princes questioned the presence of the **Hebrews** (v. 3), David and his men, among them (see discussion on 4:6).

Achish defended David. **I have found no fault in him** (v. 3). David's tactics, described in 27:10–12, had been highly successful. The princes, however, insisted that David be returned to **his place, which thou hast appointed him** (v. 4; see 27:6). They feared that **in the battle he be an adversary to us**. The Philistines had experienced just such a reversal on a previous occasion (see 14:21).

29:6–11. As the LORD liveth (v. 6). Achish swore by the God of Israel, apparently as a means of proving his sincerity to David as he dismissed him. **But what have I done?** (v. 8). David pretended disappointment to keep intact his strategy of deception and registered a mild protest. In reality, this turn of events rescued David from a serious dilemma. **What hast thou found … that I may not go fight against the enemies of my lord the king?** David again used an ambiguous statement (see 28:2). To whom was he referring as "my lord the king"—Achish, Saul, or the Lord?

Achish enlarged upon his praise and endorsement of David. **Thou art … as an angel of God** (v. 9). This comparison would be said of David three more times (see 2 Sam. 14:17, 20; 19:27). As David departed, the Philistines moved on to **Jezreel** (v. 11), the place of Israel's camp (see 29:1), to prepare for battle.

30:1–31:13. Significant contrasts between Saul and David are presented in this narrative. While Saul went to his death at the hands of the Philistines, David, at approximately the same time, was drawn into and pursued the Lord's continuing war with the Amalekites (see 15:2–3 and discussions). David was able to consult the Lord before the pursuit, but Saul was not. David was victorious against the Amalekites, but Saul was defeated by the Philistines. David was able to rescue all the women and children, but Saul was killed in battle along with his own sons.

30:1–6. Returning to **Ziklag** (v. 1; see discussion on 27:6), David learned of the raid by the **Amale-kites** (see 27:8 and discussion on 15:2). The absence of David and his warriors gave the Amalekites an opportunity for revenge. That Ziklag, David's headquarters, was singled out for burning may indicate revenge for David's earlier raids against the Amalekites (see 27:8).

David shared everyone's grief, for his two wives, **Ahinoam** (v. 5; see discussion on 25:43) and **Abigail** (see 25:42), were among those taken captive, but he had the added stress of being blamed for the disaster. In times like these, as so many of his psalms affirm, he drew his strength from the Lord.

30:7–8. David did not make a hasty and foolish decision in the emotion of the moment; he immediately called for **Abiathar the priest** (v. 7; see discussion on 22:20) and the **ephod** (see discussion on 2:28) to consult the will of the Lord.

30:9–14. In his pursuit, two hundred of his men **were so faint** (v. 10) they had to drop out of the chase. Their exhaustion might be attributed to the three-day trip completed (30:1) just before this rescue mission began. An Egyptian slave who had been abandoned by the marauders due to his illness was found, and he served as an informant for David, relating details of the raid on the **south** (v. 14; see discussion on 27:10). **The Cherethites**, along with the Pelethites, later contributed contingents of professional warriors to David's private army (see 2 Sam. 15:18; 20:7; 1 Kings 1:38). The name may indicate that they originally came from the island of Crete (see discussion on Jer. 47:4). **South of Caleb** refers to the area south of Hebron (see Josh. 14:13).

30:15–20. The Egyptian boy directed David to the Amalekites. **David smote them** (v. 17) and recovered all the spoil. **There was nothing lacking** (v. 19); wives, children, possessions were all there. **David recovered all** and also took as his spoil **the flocks and the herds** (v. 20).

30:21–25. Dissension erupted over the division of the spoils when **wicked men and men of Belial** (i.e., worthless men; v. 22) opposed sharing with the two hundred exhausted men. David properly credited the Lord and His protection for the provisions— **that which the LORD hath given us** (v. 23). He gently but firmly rejected the idea that their victory was to be attributed to their own prowess. Because the Lord gave the victory, no segment of David's men could claim any greater right to the spoils than the other men. The two hundred men who had been left behind had not shirked their responsibilities to the others but had guarded the supplies. Centuries earlier, Moses had awarded spoils to the participants in battle as well as to those who remained at home (Num. 31:27).

30:26–31. As an expression of gratitude, David sent some of the plunder to the **elders of Judah, even to his friends** (v. 26), those who had assisted him during his flight from Saul. He thus reestablished contact with his tribe and affirmed his loyalty to them, building a bridge for future relationships and thus preparing the way for his later elevation to kingship in Judah. **Hebron** (v. 31), the most important city in the southern part of Judah, would be the city of David when Judah made him their king (see 2 Sam. 2:1–4). The other locations mentioned are to the southwest and southeast of Hebron.

31:1–13. Not only had Saul failed to liberate the Israelites from the Philistines; he died while being defeated by them.

31:1–6. No details of the battle are given, only the sad outcome. Saul had four sons (1 Chron. 8:33; 9:39). His three oldest sons, **Jonathan, and Abinadab, and Malchishua** (v. 2), died with him. (See 14:49, where Ishvi is listed instead of Abinadab— perhaps a different name for the same son.) Abner would later promote Saul's surviving son, called both Ish-bosheth and Esh-baal (see discussion on 2 Sam. 2:8; 1 Chron. 8:33; 9:39), who somehow survived the battle (or did not participate), to succeed his father as king (2 Sam. 2:8–9).

The wounded Saul feared humiliating abuse from **these uncircumcised** (v. 4), a deprecatory designation for the Philistines (see 14:6 and discussion). To abuse a victim was not an uncommon practice;

the Philistines had previously mutilated and humiliated Samson after his capture (Judg. 16:23–25). **Saul took a sword, and fell upon it,** an action that culminated a long process of self-destruction. The account given by the Amalekite (2 Sam. 1:9–10) was probably a fabrication and differs somewhat in the details.

31:7–13. The men of Israel fled (v. 7) when they saw that their king was dead (compare the Philistines' retreat when Goliath was killed, 17:51). Finding the fallen Saul, the Philistines **cut off his head** (v. 9), perhaps in retaliation for David's identical treatment of Goliath (17:51). Saul's head was **sent into the land of the Philistines.** Saul's head and armor served as proof and trophies of their victory. First Chronicles 10:10 states that Saul's head was put on display in the temple of Dagon. His **armour** (v. 10), likewise, was put in the temple of **Ashtaroth.** Clearly, displaying these "trophies" in the temples demonstrated their praise to their gods for their victory over Saul. Saul's corpse bore the ignominy of being fastened to **the wall of Beth-shan** for public viewing.

The valiant action of the men of **Jabesh-gilead** (v. 11) can be attributed to past events (see discussion on Judg. 21:8–15). They **took the body of Saul and the bodies of his sons** (v. 12). The men of Jabesh-gilead had not forgotten how Saul had come to their defense when they were threatened by the Ammonites (see chap. 11). Cremation was not customary in ancient Israel and here appears to have been done to prevent any further abuse of the bodies of Saul and his sons by the Philistines. Then they **took their bones, and buried them** (v. 13), a deed that did not escape the attention and praise of David (2 Sam. 2:4–7). He later had their remains removed from Jabesh and placed in the family burial grounds of Zela in Benjamin (see 2 Sam. 21:12–14). As an indication of their mourning for Saul, the people of Jabesh **fasted seven days** (see 2 Sam. 1:12; 3:35; 12:16, 21–23).

THE SECOND BOOK OF SAMUEL

INTRODUCTION

See Introduction to 1 Samuel.

Theme

Second Samuel depicts David as a true, though imperfect, representative of the ideal theocratic king. David was initially acclaimed king at Hebron by the tribe of Judah (chaps. 1–4) and was subsequently accepted by the remaining tribes after the murder of Ish-bosheth, one of Saul's surviving sons (5:1–5). David's leadership was decisive and effective. He captured Jerusalem from the Jebusites and made it his royal city and residence (5:6–14). Shortly afterward, he brought the ark of the Lord from the house of Abinadab to Jerusalem, publicly acknowledging the Lord's kingship and rule over himself and the nation (chap. 6; Ps. 132:3–5).

Under David's rule, the Lord caused the nation to prosper, to defeat its enemies and, in fulfillment of His promise (Gen. 15:18), to extend its borders from Egypt to the Euphrates (chap. 8). David wanted to build a temple for the Lord, as His royal house, as a place for His throne (the ark), and as a place for Israel to worship Him. The prophet Nathan told David that he was not to build the Lord a house (temple); rather, the Lord would build David a house (dynasty). Chapter 7 announces the Lord's promise that the Davidic dynasty would endure forever. This climactic chapter also describes the establishment of the Davidic covenant (see Ps. 89:34–37), a covenant that promises ultimate victory over the Evil One, through the offspring of Eve (see Gen. 3:15 and discussion). This promise—which had come to be focused on Shem and his descendants (see Gen. 9:26–27 and discussions), then on Abraham and his descendants (see Gen. 12:2–3; 13:16; 15:5 and discussions), and then on Judah and his (royal) descendants (see Gen. 49:8–11 and discussions)—now focused specifically on the royal family of David. Later, the prophets would make it clear that a descendant of David who sits on his throne would perfectly fulfill the role of the theocratic king. He would complete the redemption of God's people (see Isa. 9:6–7; 11:1–16; Jer. 23:5–6; 30:8–9; 33:14–16; Ezek. 34:23–24; 37:24–25), thus enabling them to achieve the promised victory with Him (Rom. 16:20).

After the description of David's rule in its glory and success, chapters 10–20 depict the darker side of his reign and describe David's weaknesses and failures. Even though David remained a king after God's own heart because he was willing to acknowledge his sin and repent (12:13), he nevertheless fell far short of the theocratic ideal and suffered the disciplinary results of his disobedience (12:10–12). His sin with Bathsheba (chaps. 11–12) and his leniency with both the wickedness of his sons (13:21; 14:1, 33; 19:4–6) and the insubordination of Joab (3:29, 39; 20:10, 23) led to intrigue, violence, and bloodshed within David's own family and within the nation. It eventually drove him from Jerusalem, at the time of Absalom's rebellion. Nonetheless, the Lord was gracious to David, and his reign became a standard by which the reigns of later kings were measured (see 2 Kings 18:3; 22:2).

The book ends with David's own words of praise to God, who had delivered him from all his enemies (22:31–51), and with words of expectation for the fulfillment of God's promise that a king would come from the house of David and rule over men righteously (23:3–5). These two songs echo many of the themes of Hannah's song (1 Sam. 2:1–10) and frame (and interpret) the basic narrative.

Outline

I. David's Becomes King (1:1–5:5)
   A. David Mourns for Saul and Jonathan (chap. 1)
   B. David Becomes King over Judah (chaps. 2–4)
   C. David Becomes King over All Israel (5:1–5)

II. David's Kingship in Its Accomplishments and Glory (5:6–9:12)
   A. David Conquers Jerusalem and Defeats the Philistines (5:6–25)
   B. David Brings the Ark to Jerusalem (chap. 6)
   C. God Promises David an Everlasting Dynasty (chap. 7)
   D. The Extension of David's Kingdom Externally and the Justice of His Rule Internally (chap. 8)
   E. David's Faithfulness to His Covenant with Jonathan (chap. 9)

III. David's Kingship in Its Weaknesses and Failures (chaps. 10–20)
   A. David Commits Adultery and Murder (chaps. 10–12)
      1. David's Victories over the Ammonites (chap. 10)
      2. David Commits Adultery and Murder (chap. 11)
      3. David's Repentance and Confession (chap. 12)
   B. David Loses His Sons Amnon and Absalom (chaps. 13–20)
      1. Amnon Defiles His Sister Tamar (13:1–22)
      2. Absalom Murders Amnon (13:23–36)
      3. Absalom's Exile, Return, and Revolt (13:37–15:12)
      4. David's Escape from Absalom (15:13–17:29)
      5. Absalom Killed by Joab; David Mourns (18:1–19:8)
      6. David Returns to Jerusalem (19:9–43)
   C. Sheba's Revolt (chap. 20)

IV. Final Reflections on David's Reign (chaps. 21–24)
   A. David Repays the Gibeonites (21:1–14)

B. David's Victories over the Philistines (21:15–22)

C. David's Concluding Song of Praise (chap. 22)

D. David's Last Words (23:1–7)

E. David's Mighty Men (23:8–39)

F. David's Sin in Taking a Census (chap. 24)

Bibliography

Anderson, A. A. *2 Samuel*. Word Biblical Commentary 11. Dallas: Word, 1989.

Baldwin, Joyce G. *1 and 2 Samuel: An Introduction and Commentary*. Tyndale Old Testament Commentaries 8. Downers Grove, IL: InterVarsity, 1988.

Bergen, Robert D. *1, 2 Samuel*. New American Commentary 7. Nashville: Broadman & Holman, 1996.

Davis, John J., and John C. Whitcomb. *Israel: From Conquest to Exile: A Commentary on Joshua–2 Kings*. Grand Rapids, MI: Baker, 1989.

Gordon, Robert. *1 and 2 Samuel: A Commentary*. Grand Rapids, MI: Zondervan, 1986.

Hertzberg, Hans Wilhelm. *1 and 2 Samuel: A Commentary*. Old Testament Library. Philadelphia: Westminster, 1964.

Youngblood, Ronald F. "1, 2 Samuel." In *Expositor's Bible Commentary*, edited by Frank E. Gaebelein, vol. 3. Grand Rapids, MI: Zondervan, 1992.

EXPOSITION

I. David Becomes King (1:1–5:5)

A. David Mourns for Saul and Jonathan (chap. 1)

1:1–5. After the death of Saul (v. 1; see Josh. 1:1; Judg. 1:1). The narrative thread of 1 Samuel is continued, since 1 and 2 Samuel were originally one book (see 1 Samuel, Introduction: "Title"). David's return **from the slaughter of the Amalekites** resumes the story begun in 1 Samuel 30:1–20. For **Ziklag**, see discussion on 1 Samuel 27:6.

The man's appearance, **his clothes rent, and earth upon his head** (v. 2), customary signs of anguish and distress (see Josh. 7:6; Job 2:12), was an indication that he bore bad news (see discussion on 1 Sam. 4:12). When David asked him where he had come from, the man replied, **Out of the camp of Israel am I escaped** (v. 3). He then conveyed the bad news in ascending order, arriving at the climax when he told of the deaths of Saul and Jonathan.

1:6–10. It is not necessary to conclude from verse 3 that this **Amalekite** (v. 8) was a member of Saul's army. His statement that he **happened by chance upon mount Gilboa** (v. 6) is probably not as innocent as it appears. He may have been there as a scavenger to rob the fallen soldiers of their valuables and weapons. It is ironic, however, that an Amalekite reported Saul's death.

I stood upon him, and slew him (v. 10). The Amalekite's story conflicts with 1 Samuel 31:3–6, which describes Saul taking his own life. An attempt to harmonize the two accounts, having the man end Saul's misery after a botched attempt at suicide, is not convincing in spite of the added irony that Saul, who failed to kill all the Amalekites (see 1 Samuel 15), especially their king, was finished off by an Amalekite. It seems more likely that the Amalekite fabricated this version of Saul's death, expecting David to reward him (see 4:10). His miscalculation of David's response cost him his life (see 1:15). **I took**

the crown. Apparently, he got to Saul before the Philistines did (see 1 Sam. 31:8–9).

1:11–16. David took hold on his clothes, and rent them (v. 11; see discussion on 1 Sam. 4:12). David and his men **mourned, and wept** (v. 12), expressing their grief in typical Near Eastern fashion (see Gen. 23:2; 1 Kings 13:30; Jer. 22:18), and they **fasted** (see 3:35; 1 Sam. 31:13).

I am ... an Amalekite (v. 13). The man was probably unaware of David's recent hostile encounters with the Amalekites (see 1:1; 1 Samuel 30; see also discussion on 1 Sam. 15:2). The Amalekite understood nothing of the deep significance that David attached to the sanctity of the royal office in Israel (see discussion on 1 Sam. 24:6) and **the LORD's anointed** (v. 14; see discussion on 1 Sam. 9:16).

Fall upon him (v. 15). David displayed no personal satisfaction over Saul's death and condemned to death the one he believed to be his murderer (see discussion on 1:10; see also 4:10). **Thy blood be upon thy head** (v. 16). The Amalekite's own testimony brought about his execution (see Josh. 2:19; 1 Kings 2:37). The man had claimed (whether truthfully or falsely) to have killed Saul, the Lord's anointed, something that David had twice refused to do.

1:17–27. David lamented with this lamentation (v. 17). It was a common practice in the ancient Near East to compose laments for fallen leaders and heroes.

The use of the bow (v. 18) could be rendered the "the song of the bow." Perhaps David taught his men to sing this lament while they practiced the bow (Israel's most common weapon; see, e.g., 22:35) as a motivation to master the weapon thoroughly so they would not experience a similar defeat (see discussion on Ezek. 21:9). **The book of Jasher** (lit., the book of "the upright") appears to be a collection of poems celebrating great events in Israel's national life (see discussion on Josh. 10:13).

The beauty of Israel (v. 19) is a reference to Saul and Jonathan as divinely designated leaders of God's covenant people, who had achieved many significant victories over Israel's enemies (see 1 Sam. 14:47–48 and discussion). They had been slain **upon the high places**, that is, the mountains of Gilboa (see vv. 21, 25; 1 Sam. 31:1). **How are the mighty fallen!** This is the theme of David's lament (see v. 27). It reflects David's sincere and deeply felt grief over Israel's loss. The nation would learn from this poem that though Saul had flaunted David as an enemy, the hostility had been one-sided. David's words contain no suggestion of bitterness toward Saul but rather recall the good qualities and accomplishments of Saul and Jonathan.

Tell it not in Gath ... Askelon (v. 20). As the major Philistine cities located the closest and the farthest from Israel's borders, Gath and Ashkelon represented the entire Philistine nation. David did not want the enemies of God's covenant people to take pleasure in Israel's defeat (as he knew they would; see 1 Sam. 31:9–10) and thus bring reproach on the name of the Lord (see Exod. 32:12; Num. 14:13–19; Deut. 9:28; Josh. 7:9; Mic. 1:10). **Uncircumcised** is a term of contempt directed against the Philistines (see discussion on 1 Sam. 14:6).

Ye mountains of Gilboa (v. 21). As an expression of profound grief, David rhetorically pronounced a curse on the place where Israel had been defeated and Saul and Jonathan had been killed (for other such rhetorical curses, see Job 3:3–26; Jer. 20:14–18). **The shield ... had not been anointed with oil**. Leather shields were rubbed with oil to preserve them (see Isa. 21:5).

In their death they were not divided (v. 23). Even though Jonathan had opposed his father's treatment of David, he gave his life beside his father in Israel's defense.

Thy love ... was wonderful, passing the love of women (v. 26). David was not suggesting that marital love is inferior to that of friendship, nor do his remarks have any sexual implications. He was simply calling attention to Jonathan's nearly inexplicable self-denying commitment to David, whom he had long recognized as the Lord's choice to succeed his father rather than himself (see discussions on 1 Sam. 20:13–16).

The weapons of war perished (v. 27) is probably a metaphorical reference to Saul and Jonathan.

B. David Becomes King over Judah (chaps. 2-4)

2:1-4. David inquired of the LORD (v. 1), apparently by means of the ephod (and the Urim and Thummim) through the priest Abiathar (see discussions on Exod. 28:30; 1 Sam. 2:28; 23:2). **Shall I go up into any of the cities of Judah?** Even though Saul was dead and David had many friends and contacts among the people of his own tribe (see 1 Sam. 30:26-31), David did not presume to return from Philistine territory to assume the kingship promised to him without first seeking the Lord's guidance. The Lord instructed him, **Go up ... Unto Hebron**. Hebron, a city of Judah, had patriarchal connections (Gen. 13:18; 23:2; 35:27). It was Caleb's inheritance (Josh. 14:14) but had been made a city of refuge (Josh. 20:7) and given to the Levites (Josh. 21:11). It was one of Judah's chief cities and had been a beneficiary of the spoils David took from the Amalekites (1 Sam. 30:26, 31). Situated on a hill in central Judah, it was located a safe distance from the Philistines.

David had connections to Hebron through two of his wives, **Ahinoam the Jezreelitess** (v. 2; see discussion on 1 Sam. 25:43) and **Abigail** (see 1 Samuel 25), who were from localities near Hebron. He brought with him to Hebron these women (Michal, daughter of Saul, was not with him; see 3:14-15) and the **men that were with him** (v. 3; see 1 Sam. 22:2; 23:13; 30:3, 9). **The men of Judah ... anointed David king** (v. 4; see discussions on 1 Sam. 2:10; 9:16). David had previously been anointed privately by Samuel in the presence of his family (see discussion on 1 Sam. 16:13). Here the anointing ceremony was repeated by his own tribe as a public recognition of his divine calling to be king **over the house of Judah**. Very likely, the tribe of Simeon was also involved (see Josh. 19:1; Judg. 1:3), but the Judahites dominated the area in every way. Then David learned that **men of Jabesh-gilead** (see discussions on 1 Sam. 11:1; 31:12) had **buried Saul** (see discussion on 1 Sam. 31:13).

2:5-7. David's message of commendation to the **men of Jabesh-gilead** (v. 5) was sincere, but it was also healthy diplomacy. The people of that Transjordanian city were loyal to Saul, so David desperately needed to establish a rapport with them. **Your master Saul is dead ... the house of Judah have anointed me king over them** (v. 7). David's concluding statement to the men of Jabesh-gilead is a veiled invitation to them to recognize him as their king, just as the tribe of Judah had done. This appeal for their support, however, was ignored (see 1 Sam. 2:8-9).

2:8-11. Abner (v. 8) remained captain over **Saul's host**, the small standing army of professionals loyal to Saul and his family (see 1 Sam. 13:2, 15; 14:2, 52). Saul's surviving son was **Ish-bosheth** (see discussions on 1 Sam. 14:49; 31:2). The name was originally Esh-baal (1 Chron. 8:33) but was changed by the author of Samuel to Ish-bosheth, meaning "man of shame" (see discussion on 4:4). Perhaps Baal (meaning "lord" or "master") was at the time still used to refer to the Lord, which was later discontinued because of confusion with the Canaanite god Baal, and the author of Samuel reflects the later sensitivity. Abner took the initiative in the power vacuum created by Saul's death, using the unassertive Ish-bosheth as a pawn for his own ambitions (see 3:11; see also discussion on 4:1). There is no evidence that Ish-bosheth had strong support among the Israelites generally. Abner **brought him over unto Mahanaim**, a Gileadite town east of the Jordan and thus beyond the sphere of Philistine domination after their victory at Gilboa. Mahanaim served as a kind of refugee capital.

As a relative of Saul (see 1 Sam. 14:50), Abner had both a family interest and a career interest in ensuring dynastic succession for Saul's house. Therefore, **he made** Ish-bosheth **king over Gilead ... and over all Israel** (v. 9). This delineation of Ish-bosheth's realm suggests that his actual rule, while involving territories both east and west of the Jordan, was quite limited and that the last entry ("all Israel") was more claim than reality. David ruled over Judah and Simeon, and the Philistines controlled large sections of the northern tribal regions.

David reigned in Hebron **seven years and six months** (v. 11). Compare Ish-bosheth's two-year reign in Mahanaim (v. 10). Because it appears that David was made king over all Israel shortly after

Ish-bosheth's death (5:1–5) and moved his capital to Jerusalem not long afterward (5:6–12), reconciling the lengths of David's and Ish-bosheth's reigns is difficult. The difficulty is best resolved by assuming that it took Ish-bosheth a number of years to be recognized as his father's successor and that the two years of his reign roughly correspond to the last two or three years of David's reign in Hebron.

2:12–17. Abner initiated an action to prevent David's sphere of influence from spreading northward out of Judah. **Gibeon** (v. 12) was located in the tribal area of Benjamin, to which Saul and his family belonged, an area the Philistines had not occupied. **Joab the son of Zeruiah** (v. 13; see discussion on 1 Sam. 26:6) would become a figure of major importance during David's reign as a competent but ruthless military leader (see 10:7–14; 11:1; 12:26; 1 Kings 11:15–16). David would be unable to control him at times (3:39; 18:5, 14; 1 Kings 2:5–6), and he would eventually be executed for his wanton assassinations and his part in the conspiracy to place Adonijah rather than Solomon on David's throne (1 Kings 2:28–34). Joab had with him the **servants of David**, at least some of David's small force of professionals that had gathered around him (see 1 Sam. 22:1–2; 23:13; 27:2; 30:9).

Abner proposed representative warfare (see discussion on 1 Sam. 17:8), in which twelve men from Judah would fight twelve men from **Benjamin** (v. 15). At this time, Ish-bosheth seems to have been supported mainly by his own tribesmen. **There was a very sore battle that day** (v. 17). Because the representative combat by twelve men from each side was indecisive, a full-scale battle ensued, and David's forces were victorious. The attempt to use representative combat to avoid the decimation of civil war failed (see 3:1).

2:18–24. David's men clearly had the upper hand, killing 360 Benjamites (see 2:31) while losing only 20 men (see 2:30). Joab's two brothers were engaged in the battle, but it was the youngest, Asahel, who pursued the retreating, but more experienced, Abner. **Turn thee aside from following me** (v. 22). Abner tried unsuccessfully to avoid the necessity of

killing Asahel. **How then should I hold up my face to Joab thy brother?** (v. 22). Abner did not want the hostility between himself and Joab to be intensified by the practice of blood revenge (see discussion on 3:27). Abner resorted to striking Asahel with **the hinder end of the spear** (v. 23). This might have been a backward thrust of the spear, using the sharpened butt of the spear to inflict the deadly blow.

2:25–31. With the Benjamites rallying behind him, Abner proposed an armistice as a means of avoiding the awful consequences of civil war. **Shall the sword devour for ever?** (v. 26).

As God liveth (v. 27) is an oath formula (see discussion on 1 Sam. 14:39). Joab agreed to call off any further engagement for battle. He **blew a trumpet** (v. 28), thus signaling the cessation of his pursuit. **Neither fought they any more**. For the time being, the open conflict ceased, but the hostility remained (see 3:1). Abner returned through the **plain** (v. 29). The Hebrew is *'Arabah*, a term which includes the Jordan Valley between the sea of Galilee and the southern end of the Dead Sea.

2:32. Asahel was honored by being buried in his father's tomb in Bethlehem.

3:1. No battles are recorded other than that of 2:14–31, so the **war between the house of Saul and … David** may refer to continual hostility. During his seven-and-a-half-year reign at Hebron, David continued to conduct himself wisely, showing himself to be a strong leader and gaining the confidence of all Israel, while Ish-bosheth lost support, even that of Abner, the one who had ensured his place on the throne (2:8–9).

3:2–5. Somewhat parenthetical to the narrative, the list of the six sons born to David in Hebron is given as evidence of the strengthening of David's house in contrast to that of Saul (3:1). That these six sons were each born of a different mother indirectly informs us that David married four additional wives (see 2:2) during his time in Hebron. The writer does not offer any direct criticism of this polygamous practice (see 5:13), which conflicts with Deuteronomy 17:17, but he lets the disastrous results in David's family life speak for themselves (see chaps.

13–19; 1 Kings 1–2). His firstborn, **Amnon, son of Ahinoam the Jezreelitess** (v. 2; see discussion on 1 Sam. 25:43), later raped his sister Tamar and was killed by his brother Absalom (see chap. 13). **Chileab** (v. 3), called Daniel in 1 Chronicles 3:1 (and otherwise unknown), was the son of **Abigail** (see 1 Sam. 25). **Absalom**, who later avenged the rape of Tamar by killing Amnon and conspired against his father, David, in an attempt to make himself king (see chaps. 13–18), was the son of **Maacah the daughter of Talmai king of Geshur**. Geshur was a small Aramean city kingdom (see 15:8) located northeast of the Sea of Galilee (see Josh. 12:5; 13:11–13). David's marriage to Maacah undoubtedly had political implications. With Talmai as David's ally on Ish-bosheth's northern border, in essence David's control now flanked both the northern and southern boundaries of the northern kingdom. **Adonijah** (v. 4), who attempted to take over the throne before Solomon could be crowned (see 1 Kings 1–2), was eventually put to death on charges of conspiracy.

3:6–11. Abner (v. 6) was the understood power behind Ishbosheth's throne. **Wherefore hast thou gone in unto my father's concubine?** (v. 7) is a reference to **Rizpah** (see 21:8–11). The wives of a deceased king were considered the property of his successor, so great significance was attached to taking the concubine of a former king (see discussion on 12:8; see also 16:21; 1 Kings 2:22). Ish-bosheth accused Abner of violating his royal rights by sleeping with the dead king's concubine, an act interpreted as part of a conspiracy to seize the kingship (see v. 6).

Abner spoke of himself in disparaging terms: **Am I dog's head, which against** (better rendered "belonging to" or "from") **Judah …?** (v. 8). He was angry that Ish-bosheth would think he had defected to Judah. He had not handed Ish-bosheth over to David, though he had the power to do so.

So do God to Abner, and more also (v. 9) is a curse formula (see discussion on 1 Sam. 3:17). **As the LORD hath sworn to David**. The knowledge of David's divine designation as successor to Saul had spread widely (see discussions on 2:4; 1 Sam. 16:13; 25:28) and was now clearly understood by Abner

also. Infuriated by Ish-bosheth's accusation and distrust, Abner vowed to **translate the kingdom** (v. 10), or "transfer" the kingdom, everything from **Dan even to Beer-sheba** (see discussion on 1 Sam. 3:20), to David.

3:12–16. Whose is the land? (v. 12) is possibly a rhetorical question that presumed the land belonged either to Abner or to David. That the land belonged to Abner seems more likely from the following sentence, since he had requested the opportunity to transfer it to David (see v. 10). **Make thy league with me**. Abner wanted assurance from David that he would face no reprisals for his past loyalty to the house of Saul.

David's acceptance of Abner's offer was conditional on the return of his first wife, **Michal Saul's daughter** (v. 13). Although Saul had given Michal to David (1 Sam. 18:27), he later gave her to another man after David fled from his court (1 Sam. 25:44). In the minds of the northern elders, the reunion of David and Michal would strengthen David's claim to the throne, as a legitimate son-in-law of Saul, for it symbolized outwardly the unification of two royal families.

David sent messengers to Ish-bosheth (v. 14). David wanted Michal returned as an open and official act of Ish-bosheth himself rather than as part of a subterfuge planned by Abner. David knew that Ish-bosheth would not dare to defy Abner's wishes (see 3:11). **An hundred foreskins of the Philistines** (see 1 Sam. 18:25; discussion on Judg. 7:25) was what Saul had required of David for the privilege of marrying Michal. David had gone beyond Saul's demand and presented him with two hundred foreskins (1 Sam. 18:27).

Michal was wrenched from her current husband, Phaltiel, who followed weeping as far as **Bahurim** (v. 16), the last Benjamite city on the way to Hebron (see 16:5; 17:18).

3:17–21. Abner proved to be a capable diplomat. He convinced the **elders of Israel** (v. 17), the collective leadership of the various tribes that comprised an informal national ruling body (see discussion on Exod. 3:16; *Zondervan KJV Study Bible* note on Joel

1:2; discussions on Matt. 15:2; Acts 24:1; see also 1 Sam. 8:4; 2 Sam. 5:3; 1 Kings 8:1, 3; 20:7; 2 Kings 10:1; 23:1), to support David. **Ye sought for David ... to be king**. Apparently, Ish-bosheth's support came mainly from the tribe of Benjamin (see 2:15 and discussion) and from Gilead, across the Jordan (see 2:8; 1 Sam. 11:9–11; 31:11–13).

The LORD hath spoken of David (v. 18). By this time, Samuel's anointing of David must have become common knowledge (see 5:2). Abner probably interpreted the anointing as a promise from the Lord, since Samuel was the Lord's much-revered prophet.

Abner also spake in the ears of Benjamin (v. 19). Because Saul and his family were from the tribe of Benjamin, Abner was careful to consult the Benjamites concerning the transfer of kingship to the tribe of Judah. Apparently, they consented, but Abner was not above representing matters in a way that was favorable to his purpose.

Abner negotiated also with David. He obtained an audience with David and promised to bring all Israel into **a league with** him (v. 21; see 5:3 and discussion).

3:22–27. David's negotiations with Abner occurred in the absence of Joab, who charged David with being naive about Abner's intentions: **he came to deceive thee** (v. 25). Joab despised Abner for killing his brother (2:18, 23; 3:27) and sought to discredit him in David's eyes as a mere opportunist. Undoubtedly, Joab also sensed that his own position of leadership would be threatened if Abner joined forces with David, since Abner was obviously a power among the northern tribes.

Joab took matters into his own hands and arranged a meeting with Abner. **Joab ... smote him there under the fifth rib, that he died** (v. 27). Joab's murder of Abner is not to be excused either as an act of war or as justifiable blood revenge (see Num. 35:12; Deut. 19:11–13). Abner had killed Asahel in the course of battle (see 2:23; see also discussion on 2:21).

3:28–30. Abner's assassination could have been interpreted as a plot David set in motion to seize the power. After disclaiming any personal or official involvement in Abner's assassination (v. 28), David cursed Joab and thereby called on God to judge his wicked act. **Let it rest on the head of Joab, and on all his father's house** (v. 29). In this crucial hour, when David's relationship to the northern tribes hung in the balance, he apparently did not feel sufficiently secure in his own position to bring Joab to justice publicly (see 3:39). The crime went unpunished until early in the reign of Solomon (1 Kings 2:5–6, 29–35).

3:31–39. David's mourning for Abner seems to have been sincere. **Joab** (v. 31) also was compelled to join the mourners. It may be that Joab's involvement was not widely known, and David hoped to keep the matter secret for the time being. Abner was buried in **Hebron** (v. 32), David's royal city at the time. **The king lift up his voice, and wept at the grave of Abner**. Because Abner's murder had the potential of destroying the union of the nation under David's rule, David did everything possible to demonstrate his innocence to the people. In this, he was successful, for **all Israel** (v. 37) exonerated him of any personal involvement in the senseless murder. **So do God to me, and more also** (v. 35) is a curse formula (see discussion on 1 Sam. 3:17). David refused to eat that day while he mourned Abner's death.

The **sons of Zeruiah** (v. 39), that is, Joab and his brothers, were a loyal and zealous but bloodthirsty threesome (see 2:18–21; 1 Sam. 26:6–8) and were a source of embarrassment to David. Perhaps because these men were his nephews (see 2:18; 1 Chron. 2:16), he left their punishment to God. **The LORD shall reward the doer of evil** (see discussion on 3:29).

4:1–3. With Abner, the power behind the throne, dead, Ish-bosheth's **hands were feeble** (v. 1); that is, he lost courage. He was very much aware of his dependence on Abner (see discussion on 2:8). **All the Israelites were troubled**. They were painfully aware that the weak Ish-bosheth was incapable of reigning alone. Civil strife now threatened, and the northern tribes were without a strong leader.

Baanah and Rechab (v. 2), brothers and captains of raiding bands, are introduced as Benjamites, members of Saul's tribe, from **Beeroth**, one of the

Gibeonite cities (Josh. 9:17) assigned to Benjamin (Josh. 18:25). Thus, one would expect them to have been loyal to the Saulide dynasty, not the opportunistic assassins they turned out to be. The original **Beerothites** (v. 3) had fled to **Gittaim**, a location that is not known (but see Neh. 11:33), leaving their town to Benjamin.

4:4. This parenthetical note provides vital information that serves also as an introduction to chapter 9. **Jonathan, Saul's son, had a son that was lame of his feet.** The writer emphasizes that with the death of Ish-bosheth (see 4:6), there was no other viable claimant to the throne from the house of Saul. **When the tidings ... of Saul and Jonathan** came (see 1:4; 1 Sam. 31:2–4), the child **Mephibosheth** had been rushed to safety but had been dropped and made lame for life (see 9:1–13; 16:1–4; 19:24–30; 21:7–8). The name was originally Merib-baal (apparently meaning "opponent of Baal"; see 1 Chron. 8:34), perhaps to be spelled "Meri-baal" (meaning "loved by Baal"), but was changed by the author of Samuel to Mephibosheth (meaning "from the mouth of the shameful thing"). See discussion on 2:8.

4:5–8. Baanah and Rechab found Ish-bosheth resting and killed him in the same manner that Abner had killed Asahel, by striking him **under the fifth rib** (v. 6), that is, in the belly (see 2:23). Then they **beheaded him** (v. 7). They traveled through the night from the Transjordan across the **plain** (see discussion on 2:29) to reach David.

The **head of Ish-bosheth** (v. 8) was brought to David as certain evidence of the rival king's death, but it became incriminating evidence of the two captains' wickedness and murder. **The LORD hath avenged my lord the king ... of Saul.** Rechab and Baanah depicted their assassination of Ish-bosheth in pious terms, expecting David to commend them for their act—a serious miscalculation.

4:9–12. As the LORD liveth (v. 9) is an oath formula (see discussion on 1 Sam. 14:39). They had come expecting a reward, but David quickly sized up their opportunistic motives and rewarded them with a death sentence (see 1:14–16). **Shall I not ... require his blood of your hand ...?** (v. 11). Declar-

ing his judgment of the death penalty (see Gen. 9:5–6), David here does what he had been unable to do with Joab (see discussion on 3:29). Having executed the men, they cut off the men's **hands and ... feet** (v. 12), the hands that had assassinated Ish-bosheth and the feet that had run with the news, and then hung the bodies up for public display. The **head of Ish-bosheth** was given an honorable burial alongside Abner.

C. David Becomes King over All Israel (5:1–5)

5:1–24:25. Beginning with chapter 5, certain sections of 2 Samuel have parallel passages in 1 Chronicles. In some instances, these parallel accounts are nearly identical; in others, the accounts have variations.

5:1–5. All the tribes of Israel (v. 1), that is, representatives of each tribe, including elders and armed soldiers (see 1 Chron. 12:23–40), came to David. **We are thy bone and thy flesh.** The representatives of the various tribes cited three reasons for recognizing David as their king. First was their acknowledgment that David was an Israelite. Even though national unity had been destroyed in the civil strife following Saul's death (2:8–3:1), this blood relationship had not been forgotten. Second was that **thou was he that leddest out and broughtest in Israel** (v. 2); that is, he had led Israel in war (see 1 Sam. 18:5, 13–14, 16, 30). Third, and most important, was that **the LORD said to thee ... feed my people Israel.** The former shepherd of his father's sheep (1 Sam. 16:11; 17:28, 34) was the first to be called the shepherd of his people. Like the patriarch Jacob, David would acknowledge the gentle and caring shepherding of God (see Gen. 48:15; Psalm 23), and he would have a descendant greater than he, the Good Shepherd, who would give His life for His sheep (John 10:11).

King David made a league with them ... before the LORD (v. 3). David and Israel entered into a covenant in which both the king and the people obligated themselves before the Lord to carry out their mutual responsibilities (see 2 Kings 11:17 and discussion). Thus, while David became king over Judah when his tribe anointed him to be king and would become king over Jerusalem through conquest (5:6–10), his rule over the northern tribes was by virtue of a treaty (covenant) of submission. That treaty was not renewed with David's grandson Rehoboam because he refused to negotiate its terms at the time of his accession to the throne (1 Kings 12:1–16). **They anointed David king over Israel.** This was the third time David had been anointed (see discussion on 2:4).

David had reigned **in Hebron** for **seven years and six months** (v. 5; see 2:11). He would reign an additional thirty-three years over **Israel and Judah.** Though they were now united into one kingdom, the specific relationship of David to these two segments of his realm appears to have remained distinct (see discussion on v. 3).

II. David's Kingship in Its Accomplishments and Glory (5:6–9:12)

A. David Conquers Jerusalem and Defeats the Philistines (5:6–25)

5:6–10. One of the most significant accomplishments of David's reign was the establishment of **Jerusalem** (v. 6) as his royal city and the nation's capital (see Introduction: "Theme"). The site was first occupied in the third millennium BC and was a royal city in the time of Abraham (see discussion on Gen. 14:18). It was located on the border between Judah and Benjamin but was controlled by neither tribe. At the time of the conquest, both Judah and Benjamin had attacked the city (see discussions on Judg. 1:8, 21), but it was quickly lost again to the Jebusites (Josh. 15:63) and was sometimes referred to by the name Jebus (see Judg. 19:10; 1 Chron. 11:4). The city David conquered covered somewhat less than eleven acres and could have housed not many more than 3,500 inhabitants. By locating his royal city in a more centrally located and newly conquered town on the border between the two segments of his realm, David had chosen a site that was virtually neutral. Thus, he united the kingdom under his rule without seeming to subordinate one part to the other. Also, such a historically impregnable city was ideal for his own defense. The **Jebusites** were a Canaanite people (Gen. 10:15–16) inhabiting the area

in (Josh. 15:8; 18:16) and around (Num. 13:29; Josh. 11:3) Jerusalem. They boastfully claimed, **the blind and the lame, thou shalt not come in hither.** Jerusalem was a natural fortress because of its location on a rise surrounded on three sides by deep valleys, so the Jebusites were confident that their walls could easily be defended.

David took the strong hold (v. 7), probably a reference to the fortified city itself. This is the first occurrence of the name **Zion** in the Old Testament (its meaning is unknown). The name appears to have been given to the southernmost hill of the city on which the Jebusite fortress was located. As the city expanded (from the days of Solomon onward), the name continued to be applied to the entire city (see Isa. 1:8; 2:3).

David said on that day (v. 8). First Chronicles 11:6 may be combined with this verse for a more complete account. Joab's part in the conquest of the city again demonstrated his military prowess and reconfirmed him in the position of commander of David's armies. **Whosoever getteth up to the gutter.** Although the Hebrew for "gutter" is obscure, it appears that David knew of a secret tunnel—perhaps running from the Gihon spring outside the city into the fortress—that gave the city access to water when it was under siege (see 2 Chron. 32:30). Some have proposed this to be the tunnel known today as Warren's shaft, which Warren discovered in 1867. Apparently, Joab gained access to the city by means of this tunnel (1 Chron. 11:6). **The lame and the blind** is an ironic reference to the Jebusites (see v. 6). **The blind and the lame shall not come into the house.** This proverb may mean that the Jebusites did not have access to the royal palace, or the temple, though they were allowed to remain in the city and its environs.

The term **Millo** (v. 9) is difficult. It derives from the Hebrew for "to fill." Some archaeologists believe the "Millo" was the system of stone terraces on the steep slope of Jerusalem's hill, which created additional space for buildings (see discussions on Judg. 9:6; 1 Kings 9:15).

5:11–12. Hiram king of Tyre sent ... to David (v. 11). This Phoenician king was the first to accord the newly established King David international recognition. It was vital that the king of Tyre have good relations with the king of Israel since Israel dominated the inland trade routes to Tyre. **Tyre** was an important Phoenician seaport on the Mediterranean coast north of Israel (see Ezek. 26–27) and was dependent on Israelite agriculture for much of its food (which was still true in the first century AD; see Acts 12:20). A close relationship existed between these two realms until the Babylonian invasions.

Having built himself a house, **David perceived that the Lord had established him king** (v. 12). In the ideology of the ancient Near East, the king's possession of a palace was the chief symbolic indication of his status. David acknowledged that his elevation to kingship over all Israel was the Lord's doing, that it was **for his people Israel's sake,** and that it was an integral part of His continuing redemptive program for Israel—just as the ministries of Moses, Joshua, the judges, and Samuel had been.

5:13–16. David took him mo (i.e., more) **concubines and wives** (v. 13; see discussion on 3:2–5). That David's additional marriages were due to political alliances (see 1 Kings 3:1; 11:1) is possible, though not indicated in the text. A large harem was a sign of wealth and prestige and was common among ancient Near East royalty, yet it was a clear violation of Mosaic instruction pertaining to Israel's king (Deut. 17:17). Though David's polygamy was not singled out for condemnation, he would suffer dearly from troubles that arose later in his royal court. Of the sons that are named, **Shammua, and Shobab, and Nathan, and Solomon** (v. 14) are designated as sons of Bathsheba (see 1 Chron. 3:5).

5:17–21. When the Philistines heard that they had anointed David king (v. 17). Chronologically, it is likely that the Philistine attack immediately followed the events of 5:3 and preceded the capture of Jerusalem in 5:6–14. (The author arranged his narrative by topics; see discussion on 7:1.) The Philistines had not been disturbed by David's reign over Judah when he appeared to be in opposition to the house of Saul. Perhaps they considered him to be their servant. Once he was made king over all Israel

and unification was assured, they saw him as an opponent. They acted to protect their interests in the north, much of which they had dominated after the defeat of Saul (1 Sam. 31). Their search for David sent him into the **hold,** probably a reference to the wilderness area in southern Judah where David had hidden from Saul (see discussions on 1 Sam. 22:4; 23:14). David's reaction suggests that he had not yet taken Jerusalem.

As he had done before, **David inquired of the Lord** (v. 19; see discussions on 2:1; 1 Sam. 2:28; 22:20; 23:2) to learn His will for fighting the Philistines.

David's victory over the Philistines gave new meaning to the battle site's name. **The Lord hath broken forth … Baal-perazim** (v. 20). The literal meaning of Baal, the name of a Canaanite god, is "lord" or "master." Thus, in this situation, Baal-perazim (i.e., the "master of a breakthrough") is a reference to the Lord. As a true theocratic king, David attributed the victory to the Lord and did not claim the glory for himself (see discussions on 1 Sam. 10:18, 27; 11:13; 12:11; 14:23; 17:11, 45–47).

There they left their images (i.e., idols; v. 21). As the Israelites had taken the ark into battle (see discussion on 1 Sam. 4:3), so the Philistines carried images of their deities into battle in the hope that this would ensure victory. His men **burnt them.** A literal translation of the Hebrew is, "they carried them off." David's capture of their idols was a reversal of when the Philistines had captured the ark of the covenant after a stunning victory over Israel (see 1 Sam. 4:11). In compliance with the instruction of Deuteronomy 7:5, David's men also burned the idols (see 1 Chron. 14:12).

5:22–25. David inquired of the Lord regarding a second encounter with the Philistines and received different instructions but a similar result. **Thou shalt not go up** (v. 23). As had been true in the case of the conquest under Joshua, the Lord ordered the battle, and He Himself marched against the enemy with His heavenly host (see Josh. 6:2–5; 8:1–2; 10:8, 14; 11:6). David's wars were a continuation and completion of the wars fought by Joshua. When David heard **the sound of a going in the … trees** (v. 24), it was the heavenly host of the Lord going into battle and smiting the Philistines for Israel.

B. David Brings the Ark to Jerusalem (chap 6)

6:1–2. David desired to make Jerusalem Israel's religious center in addition to its being her political capital. He gathered his chosen men to **Baale of Judah** (v. 2), that is, Kirjath-jearim (see Josh. 15:60; 18:14; 1 Sam. 6:21; 7:1; see also discussion on 1 Chron. 13:6). The **ark of God** (see Exod. 25:10–22; see also discussions on 1 Sam. 4:3–4, 21) had remained at Kirjath-jearim in the house of Abinadab (1 Sam. 7:1) during the reign of Saul. The phrase **called by the name** is used elsewhere to designate ownership (see 12:28; Deut. 28:10; Isa. 4:1; 63:19). **The LORD of hosts** (see discussion on 1 Sam. 1:3) **dwelleth between the cherubims** (see discussion on 1 Sam. 4:4; see also 1 Chron. 28:2, the "footstool of our God"). David recognized the great significance of the ark as the earthly throne of Israel's God. As a true theocratic king, he wished to acknowledge the Lord's kingship and rule over both himself and the people by restoring the ark to a place of prominence in the nation.

6:3–5. The ark was placed on a **new cart** (v. 3). David followed the example of the Philistines (see 1 Sam. 6:7) rather than the instructions of Exodus 25:12–14 and Numbers 4:5–6, 15, which required that the ark be carried on poles over the shoulders of the Levites, specifically by the Kohathites (see 1 Chron. 15:13–15). It was brought **out of the house of Abinadab** (see 1 Sam. 7:1). **Uzzah and Ahio, the sons of Abinadab.** In 1 Samuel 7:1, Eleazar is referred to as the son of Abinadab. The Hebrew word for "son" can have the broader meaning of "descendant." The ark was transported with much fanfare and celebration.

6:6–11. **Uzzah** (v. 6), apparently following the ark (his brother Ahio led the way, 6:4), reached out **to the ark of God, and took hold of it** to stabilize it on the shifting cart. Uzzah died on account of **his error** (v. 7). Although Uzzah's intent may have been good, he violated the Lord's clear instructions for handling the ark (see discussion on 6:3; Exod. 25:15; Num. 4:5–6, 15; 1 Chron. 15:13–15; see also discussion on 1 Sam. 6:19). At this important new begin-

ning in Israel's life with the Lord, the Lord gave a shocking and vivid reminder to David and Israel that those who claim to serve Him must acknowledge His rule with absolute seriousness (see Lev. 10:1–3; Josh. 7:24–25; 24:19–20; Acts 5:1–11).

David was displeased (v. 8). David's initial reaction was resentment that his attempt to honor the Lord had resulted in a display of God's wrath. His anger was unfounded. A proper conveyance of the ark would have prevented Uzzah's death. Not even the Kohathites, whose responsibility it was to carry the ark, were permitted to touch it, for it was holy, and any infraction of God's holiness would result in death. No matter how noble Uzzah's intentions, God's holiness would permit no irregularities.

Perez-uzzah (v. 8) means "the breakthrough of Uzzah." The place-name memorialized a divine warning that was not soon forgotten (see Josh. 7:26 and discussion), for it was remembered **to this day**, that is, until the time of the writing of 2 Samuel.

David was afraid of the LORD (v. 9). David's anger was accompanied by fear — not the wholesome fear of proper honor and respect for the Lord (1 Sam. 12:24; Josh. 24:14) but an anxiety arising from an acute sense of his own guilt (Gen. 3:10; Deut. 5:5). His fear caused a change of plans for the ark, and it was diverted to the house of **Obed-edom** (v. 10), whose name perhaps means "servant of man." He was a **Gittite**. He appears to have been a Levite (see discussion on 1 Chron. 13:13; see 1 Chron. 15:18, 24; 16:5; 26:4–8, 15; 2 Chron. 25:24), though many think the term "Gittite" fixes his place of birth at the Philistine city of Gath (see 15:18). However, Gittite may be a reference to the Levitical city Gath-rimmon, which was probably located in either Dan or Manasseh. Apparently both Dan and Manasseh had a city by the name of Gath-rimmon (Josh. 21:20–25).

6:12–16. God's blessing on the household of Obed-edom showed David that God's anger had been appeased. So **David ... brought up the ark** (v. 12). David had become aware of his previous error, and he exercised great care to see that it was carried exactly according to Mosaic instruction (1 Chron. 15:13–15).

When they that bare the ark ... had gone six paces (v. 13), a sufficient distance to show that God's blessing was on the Levites (see 1 Chron. 15:26), David sacrificed to the Lord. He was clothed in a **linen ephod** (v. 14) for the occasion (see discussion on 1 Sam. 2:18). When Michal saw David, **she despised him** (v. 16). She had no appreciation for the significance of the event and deeply resented David's public display as being unworthy of the dignity of a king (see 6:20-23).

6:17-19. The Mosaic tabernacle was standing at Gibeon at this time (1 Chron. 21:29). The ark was brought to a tent especially erected for it until a more permanent structure, the temple, could be built. After offering **burnt offerings** (v. 17; see Leviticus 1) and **peace offerings** (see discussion on 1 Sam. 11:15), David **blessed the people** (v. 18), as Solomon would later do at the dedication of the temple (1 Kings 8:55-61).

6:20-23. Michal had despised David for his celebration behavior (6:6), believing it too undignified for royalty. David had danced to the honor of the Lord, who had put him on the throne. For David, the honor of God outweighed his personal dignity. Michal spoke to him with scorn: **How glorious was the king ... who uncovered himself** (v. 20), an allusion to David's having worn only a linen ephod (6:14) rather than his royal robe. Michal's opposition to David, God's choice for king, resulted in her barrenness. That **Michal ... had no child** (v. 23) was probably a punishment for her pride and was at the same time another manifestation of God's judgment on the house of Saul. She, the daughter of the rejected Saul, would not produce a possible heir to David's throne.

C. God Promises David an Everlasting Dynasty (chap. 7)

7:1-29. Countering David's desire to build God a house, God issued His great promise to David (see Introduction: "Theme"). Although it is not expressly called a covenant here, it is elsewhere (23:5; Ps. 89:3, 28, 34, 39; see Ps. 132:11), and David responded with language suggesting his recognition that a covenant had been made (see discussions on vv. 20, 28).

7:1-3. The conversation recorded in this chapter occurred **when the king sat in his house** (v. 1; see discussions on 5:12). **The LORD had given him rest ... from all his enemies.** Chronologically, the victories noted in 8:1-14 probably preceded the events of this chapter. The arrangement of material is topical—chapter 6 records David's bringing the ark to Jerusalem; chapter 7 tells of his desire to build a temple in Jerusalem in which to house the ark.

Though **Nathan** (v. 2) is mentioned here for the first time, the prophet probably had served in David's court prior to this occasion, for he was one of the chroniclers of David's reign (1 Chron. 29:29). His hasty approval of David's proposal to construct a temple for God should not be interpreted as fawning (see 1 Kings 22:6-13). Nathan would later have an important role in the story of David and Bathsheba (12:1ff.) and in installing David's successor to the throne (1 Kings 1:11-44).

God dwelleth within curtains (v. 2), that is, tent curtains (see 7:6; 6:17). Now that he himself had a royal palace (symbolic of his established kingship), David did not think a tent was an appropriate place for the throne of Israel's divine King (see discussion on 6:2; see also Ps. 132:2-5; Acts 7:46). He wanted to build Israel's heavenly King a royal house in the capital city of his kingdom. David's plan to build God a house was not humanly unreasonable, for in the ancient Near East, it was not uncommon for kings to erect and maintain temples to their gods.

Nathan said ... Go, do (v. 3). In consulting a prophet, David sought God's will, but Nathan boldly voiced approval of David's plans in the Lord's name before he had received a revelation from the Lord.

7:4-7. First Nathan, then David, learned that permission from God to build a temple had been withheld. The decision to build the temple was to be God's initiative, not David's. **Shalt thou build me a house?** (v. 5). David's desire was commendable (1 Kings 8:18-19), but other Scriptures affirm that David was too occupied with wars and the shedding of blood (see 1 Kings 5:3; 1 Chron. 22:8; 28:3). On a positive note, however, his gift and mission were to fight the Lord's battles until Israel was securely at rest in the Promised Land (see 7:10; 1 Kings 5:3).

Spake I a word ... saying, Why build ye not me a house ...? (v. 7). David was not reprimanded for his desire to build the temple, but he had misunderstood the Lord's priorities. He perhaps reflected the pagan notion that the gods were interested in human beings only as builders and maintainers of their temples and as practitioners of their cult. Instead, the Lord had raised up rulers in Israel only to shepherd His people (which is also why he had brought David "from the sheepcote [i.e., pasture]," 7:8).

7:8 – 10. Thus saith the Lord of hosts, I took thee. David was reminded of God's calling. He had indeed been taken from one flock (1 Sam. 16:11 – 13) to shepherd another (2 Sam. 5:2). Various scholars have likened God's covenant with David to the ancient Near Eastern royal grant, in which the king promised to show favor to and protect the rights of his servants. Promises experienced in David's lifetime are seen in 7:8 – 11a. Promises fulfilled after his death are given in 7:11b – 16.

I ... have cut off all thine enemies (v. 9) is a backward look (see discussion on 7:1). There is also a look forward: **I will appoint a place for my people Israel** (v. 10). For this purpose, the Lord made David king, and through David, He accomplished that purpose. It has been David's calling to establish God's people Israel safely and securely in their land, where they would not be harassed by oppression **as beforetime**, that is, in Egypt (see 7:6).

7:11 – 17. I commanded judges (v. 11) refers to the leaders God raised up during the period of the judges (see Judges, Introduction: "Title"). **And I have caused thee to rest from all thine enemies** (see 7:1, 9). David is promised complete victories over the threatening powers, so that the rest already enjoyed would be assured for the future. **The Lord ... will make thee a house**. Compare this statement with the rhetorical question of 7:5. In a beautiful play on words, God said that David was not to build Him a house (temple); rather, God would build David a house (royal dynasty) that would last forever (v. 16). God had been building Israel ever since the days of Abraham; now

He commited Himself to building David's royal house so that the promise to Israel could be fulfilled — rest in the Promised Land. It is God's building that effects His kingdom. This covenant with David was unconditional, like those with Noah, Abram, and Phinehas (see discussion on Gen. 9:9; see also chart, *KJV Study Bible*, p. 16), grounded only in God's firm and gracious purpose. It would find its ultimate fulfillment in the kingship of Christ, who was born of the tribe of Judah and the house of David (see Ps. 89:30 – 38; Isa. 9:1 – 7; Matt. 1:1; Luke 1:32 – 33, 69; Acts 2:30; 13:23; Rom. 1:2 – 3; 2 Tim. 2:8; Rev. 3:7; 22:16).

I will set up thy seed after thee (v. 12). The royal line of David, in contrast to that of Saul, would continue after David's death by dynastic succession. **He shall build a house for my name** (v. 13). God's priorities were that His own royal house, where His throne (the ark) could finally come to rest (1 Chron. 6:31; 28:2), would wait until Israel was at rest and David's dynasty (in the person of his son) was secure. "My name" is equivalent to the "me" of verse 5 (see discussion on 1 Sam. 25:25).

I will be his father, and he shall be my son (v. 14). This familial language expresses the special relationship God promised to maintain with the descendant(s) of David whom He would establish on David's throne. It marked him as the one God had chosen and enthroned to rule in His name as the official representative of God's rule over His people (see discussions on Pss. 2:7; 45:6; 89:27). In Jesus Christ, this promise comes to ultimate fulfillment (see Matt. 1:1; Mark 1:11; Heb. 1:5). The unconditional nature of this covenant is clearly seen here. The covenant would not be contingent on the obedience of David's son. God would discipline him as His own son, but His **mercy** (v. 15), that is, God's special and unfailing favor, would never be withdrawn, and the throne would never be in danger of being forfeited to another.

Thy throne shall be stablished for ever (v. 16; see Ps. 89:3 – 4, 19 – 34; see also Introduction: "Theme"). The promise of an everlasting kingdom for the house of David became the focal point of many later prophecies and powerfully influenced the development of the messianic hope in Israel.

The immediate fulfillment of God's covenant with David was witnessed in Solomon, David's successor, who indeed built the temple. He and his descendants often felt the chastening but loving hand of God, even to the point of having the kingdom divided, but the "scepter" never departed from the tribe of Judah (Gen. 49:10). The ultimate fulfillment is realized in the messianic Son of David. In the face of Judah's exile, Jeremiah was assured of God's unfailing commitment to the Davidic covenant (Jer. 33:17–26). In captivity, Ezekiel looked forward to a future restoration of Israel that would be shepherded by David (Ezek. 34:17–26). Matthew was quick to inform that Jesus was the son of David (Matt. 1:1). Mary learned from the angel that her son would assume the throne of his father David to reign forever (Luke 1:31–32), and Peter's first sermon declared that Jesus was the Messiah and ultimate heir to the throne of David (Acts 2:29–36).

7:18–24. David's prayer expressed his wonder that God would make such commitments to him and his descendants. He also acknowledged that what God had pledged to him was for Israel's sake, that its purpose was the fulfillment of God's covenanted promises to His people, and that its ultimate effect would be the honor and praise of God throughout the world.

Then went king David in (v. 18), presumably into the tent (6:17) in which the ark was kept. He **sat before the Lord**. The ark was the symbol of God's presence with His people (see Exod. 25:22; see also discussions on 1 Sam. 4:3–4, 21).

And is this the manner of man, O Lord God? (v. 19). The Hebrew for this clause is difficult, and thus its meaning is uncertain (see 1 Chron. 17:17). Some scholars have taken it to be an exclamation ("This is Your law for man, O Lord God!" or "This is your charter for humanity!") and see it as a summation of the divine decree concerning David and his house.

Thou … knowest thy servant (v. 20); that is, you have "especially acknowledged" or "have chosen" (see Gen. 18:19, "I know him"; Amos 3:2, "you only have I known"). David recognized God's promise to him as a covenant (23:5).

For thy word's sake … hast thou done all these great things (lit., "this great thing"; v. 21). The "word" is probably God's covenant word of promise to His people concerning a lasting dynasty, which David now represented. Overwhelmed by the magnitude of God's favor being poured out on Israel and humbled that God had established his posterity to be blessed forever, David could only exclaim, **there is none like thee** (v. 22; see 22:32; 1 Sam. 2:2). **What one nation … whom God went to redeem for a people to himself** (v. 23). Israel's uniqueness did not consist in her national achievements but in God's choice of her to be His own people (see Deut. 7:6–8; 33:26–29). The basis for God's electing love, revealed in His dealings with Israel, did not lie in any meritorious characteristic of the Israelite people but in His own sovereign purposes, **to make him a name** (see Deut. 7:6–8; 9:4–5; 1 Sam. 12:22; Neh. 9:10; Isa. 63:12; Jer. 32:20–21; Ezek. 36:22–38). **Thou, Lord, art become their God** (v. 24). David acknowledged that what God had pledged to him, He had pledged as the God of Israel. Central to the Old Testament is the idea that Israel is the Lord's people and He is their God (see Exod. 6:7).

7:25–29. Having extolled God for His deeds for Israel (7:22–24), David returned to the subject of his own dynasty (see 7:18–21) and entreated God to fulfill His promise. Because of God's revealed promises, David confessed, **thy servant found in his heart to pray this prayer unto thee** (v. 27). His prayer laid claim to God's promise, especially **this goodness unto thy servant** (v. 28). "Goodness" is a common summary expression for covenant benefits from God (see also, e.g., Num. 10:29; Josh. 23:14, "good [words]"; Num. 10:32; Isa. 63:7, "goodness"; Deut. 26:11; Josh. 21:45, "good thing"; Jer. 29:32; 32:40–41; 33:9, "good").

D. The Extension of David's Kingdom Externally and the Justice of His Rule Internally (chap 8)

8:1–14. The author provides a summary of David's success in battles on all fronts: with the Philistines to the east (v. 1), the Moabites to the west (v. 2), the Syrians (Arameans) to the north (vv. 3–12), and the Edomites to the south (vv. 13–14).

8:1–2. After this it came to pass (v. 1). Chronologically, the events of this chapter, or many of them, are probably to be placed between chapters 5 and 6 (see 7:1 and discussion). The meaning of **Metheg-ammah** is debated, and its location is uncertain. It is possibly another name for Gath (1 Chr. 18:1) or another nearby site.

The people of **Moab** (v. 2) were descendants of Lot (Gen. 19:37) who occupied territory east of the Dead Sea. Saul had fought with the Moabites (1 Sam. 14:47), and David had sought refuge in Moab for his parents during his exile from Israel (see discussion on 1 Sam. 22:3–4). What interrupted the friendly relations with Moab and precipitated a war is unknown. Neither is it known why David chose two-thirds of his prisoners of war for execution by the use of a line-lot, a method not mentioned elsewhere.

8:3–12. In David's day, Syria (Hebrew, *Aram*) was fragmented by rival Aramean kings. The leading petty kingdoms were Zobah (v. 3), Damascus (v. 5), and Hamath (v. 9). **Hadadezer** (v. 3) means "Hadad is [my] help." Hadad was an Aramean deity equivalent to the Canaanite god Baal. Hadadezer ruled at **Zobah.** Saul had previously fought against the kings of Zobah (1 Sam. 14:47), whose territory apparently was located in the Beqaa Valley between the Lebanon and Anti-Lebanon mountains, thus on Israel's northern border. David fought against Hadadezer, who had gone **to recover** land that Saul's earlier victories over the kings of Zobah had brought under Israelite control, if only briefly. This land extended as far as the fringes of the valley of **the river Euphrates.** The land promised to Abraham had included borders from Egypt to the Euphrates River (Gen. 15:18–21; Deut. 1:7; 11:24; Josh. 1:4). Here is another, at least provisional, fulfillment of this promise (see 1 Kings 4:21–24; see also Gen. 17:8; Josh. 21:43–45). See Map 5 at the end of the *KJV Study Bible.*

Of the spoils of victory, David **houghed** (i.e., hamstrung) **all the chariot horses** (v. 4; see Josh. 11:6 and discussion), making them unfit for military use.

No reason is offered for hamstringing (i.e., cutting the tendons of the leg) the horses. David possibly may not have understood the value of the chariot as a military weapon, but perhaps the Mosaic instructions that the king was not to acquire great numbers of horses is in view (Deut. 13:18), and he refused to keep horses lest he be tempted to place his trust in them rather than in the Lord (see Ps. 33:17). Warriors from **Damascus came to succour** (i.e., help) **Hadadezer** (v. 5). They feared Israelite expansion to the north, but David defeated them with the Lord's help. He stripped Hadadezer's men of their **shields of gold** (v. 7), that is, shields adorned with gold (the phrase is similar to "chariots of iron"; see Josh. 17:16 and discussion), and deposited them in Jerusalem. From other cities, he took **brass** (i.e., bronze; v. 8), which Solomon would later use in the construction of the temple (1 Chron. 18:8).

A third king, Toi of **Hamath** (v. 9), whose kingdom was centered on the Orontes River, north of Zobah (see v. 3 and discussion), congratulated David for his victories over his rival Hadadezer and sent him presents. David dedicated the plunder to the Lord, thus acknowledging Him as the giver of his success.

8:13–14. David also fought enemies to the south. The reference to the **Syrians** (Hebrew, *Aram*; v. 13; see discussion on 8:3) requires textual comment. In Hebrew, only a slight variation, one letter, distinguishes *Aram* (Syria) from *Edom.* The Hebrew equivalents for *r* and *d* are similar and are easily confused. Apparently, a copyist made an error in the Hebrew, writing *Aram* for *Edom* (here and in 8:12). Obviously, Edom is in view (see 1 Chron. 18:12 and Psalm 60 superscription), because Edom, not Syria, was located near the **valley of salt**, the region of the Salt Sea (i.e., the Dead Sea). Some Hebrew manuscripts, the Septuagint, and the Syriac Peshitta support the reading of *Edom.*

8:15–18. David executed judgment and justice (v. 15). As a true theocratic king, David's reign was characterized by adherence to God's standards of right rule (see discussions on 1 Sam. 8:3; 12:3), as no doubt laid down in Samuel's "manner of the kingdom" (see 1 Sam. 10:25 and discussion; 1 Kings 2:3–4).

The names and offices of members of David's administration are given. **Joab the son of Zeruiah was over the host** (v. 16), that is, the army (see discussions on 2:13; 5:8). **Jehoshaphat ... was recorder.** The precise duties of this official are not indicated, though the position was an important one in the court and was maintained throughout the period of the monarchy (see 2 Kings 18:18, 37; 2 Chron. 34:8; Isa. 36:3, 11, 22). He may have been a kind of chancellor or a chief administrator of royal affairs, responsible, among other things, for the royal chronicles and annals.

Zadok the son of Ahitub (v. 17) is first mentioned here. He was a descendant of Eleazar son of Aaron (see 1 Chron. 6:4–8, 50–52; 24:1–3). His father, Ahitub, is not to be identified with Ichabod's brother of the same name (1 Sam. 14:3). Zadok remained loyal to David throughout his reign (15:24–29; 17:15–16; 19:11) and eventually anointed Solomon as David's successor (1 Kings 1:8, 45; 2:35; 4:4). It appears that a copyist's error may have occurred here in the reference to **Ahimelech the son of Abiathar** (repeated in 1 Chron. 24:3, 6, 31) in which these two names have been transposed. Abiathar is referred to as the son of Ahimelech in 1 Samuel 22:20. While it is true that the Abiathar of 1 Samuel 22:20 could have had a son named Ahimelech (after his grandfather), such a person does not appear elsewhere in the narratives of Samuel and Kings as a colleague of Zadok, but Abiathar consistently does (15:29, 35; 17:15; 19:11; 20:25; 1 Kings 1:7–8, 19; 2:27, 35; 4:4). Abiathar was a descendant of Aaron through Ithamar (1 Chron. 24:3) in the line of Eli (see discussions on 1 Sam. 2:31, 33). **Seraiah**, also called Sheva (20:25), Shisha (1 Kings 4:3), and Shavsha (1 Chron. 18:16), was a **scribe**. His duties presumably included domestic and foreign correspondence, perhaps keeping records of important political events, and various administrative functions (2 Kings 12:10–12).

Under the leadership of **Benaiah** (v. 18), the **Cherethites and the Pelethites** (see discussion on

1 Sam. 30:14) formed a sort of special royal guard for David (23:22–23). "Pelethite" is probably an alternate form of "Philistine." It was not uncommon for royal bodyguards to be foreigners, whose loyalties to the king would not be conditioned by local or national politics. The Hebrew for **chief rulers** is the common word for "priests" (see also 20:26), but the usage is obscure since that sense appears unlikely. Chronicles has "chief about the king" (1 Chron. 18:17), which supports the meaning "chief ministers," or perhaps "chief advisors."

E. David's Faithfulness to His Covenant with Jonathan (chap 9)

9:1–20:26. These chapters, together with 1 Kings 1:1–2:46, are often referred to as the "court history of David" or the "succession narrative" and are hailed as one of the finest examples of historical narrative produced in the ancient world. Their intimate and precise detail marks them as the work of an eyewitness.

9:1–13. The events of this chapter cannot be dated precisely, but they occurred a number of years after David's capture of Jerusalem. Mephibosheth was five years old at the time of his father's death (4:4); now he had a son of his own (v. 12).

9:1–6. David inquired concerning any remaining descendants of Saul so that he could **shew him kindness for Jonathan's sake** (v. 1). David had not forgotten his promise to Jonathan. Thus, he wished to show Saul's descendants "kindness," a term that is variously translated "lovingkindness," "steadfast love," and "unfailing love" and is often used in the context of a covenant (see Jonathan's covenant of steadfast love with David, 1 Sam. 20:8, 14–15). From **Ziba** (v. 2), the chief steward of Saul's estate, which had been inherited by Mephibosheth son of Jonathan, Saul's firstborn (see 16:1–4; 19:17), it was learned that **Jonathan hath yet a son** (v. 3). Saul had other descendants (see 21:8), but Ziba mentioned only the one in whom David would be chiefly interested.

Jonathan's son Mephibosheth (see discussion on 4:4) lived with **Machir** (v. 4), apparently a wealthy benefactor of Mephibosheth. Machir would later come to David's aid (17:27). He lived at **Lo-debar**, a town in Gileadite territory east of the Jordan (Josh. 13:26, "Debir") whose location is uncertain. It was probably in the general vicinity of where Ishbosheth's headquarters had been located, far from the family estate and from David's court (see discussion on 2:8).

9:7–8. I … will restore thee all the land (v. 7). Apparently, the property that Saul had acquired as king had either been taken over by David, or Ziba as steward had virtually taken possession of it and was profiting from its income (see 16:1–4; 19:26–30). David also promised, **thou shalt eat bread at my table continually.** This was a matter more of high honor than of economic assistance (see 1 Kings 2:7; 18:19; 2 Kings 25:29–30). Mephibosheth's general financial needs were to be cared for from the produce of Saul's estate (v. 10).

What is thy servant … a dead dog as I? (v. 8). Mephibosheth expressed his submission to David with an expression of deep self-abasement. The author has used the "dead dog" motif with great effect. First Goliath, scornfully disdaining the young warrior David, asked, "Am I a dog …?" (1 Sam. 17:43) and unwittingly foreshadowed his own end. Then David, in a self-deprecating manner, described himself as a "dead dog" (1 Sam. 24:14) to suggest to Saul that the king of Israel should not consider him worthy of so much attention. In the Nabal episode, that "dog" (a Calebite) and his sudden death characterized Saul and foreshadowed his unhappy end (see discussion on 1 Sam. 25:3). A similar description is used here for a grandson of Saul and in 16:9 for a relative of the dead king who had cursed David. For the author, "dead dog" fittingly characterized those who foolishly scorned or opposed the Lord's anointed, while David's own self-deprecation (see 1 Sam. 18:18; 2 Sam. 7:18) was conducive to his exaltation.

9:9–13. David assigned **Ziba** (v. 9) to be a steward over Mephibosheth's property. Though Ziba was apparently wealthy (he had fifteen sons) and had servants of his own (v. 10), he was now required to work for Mephibosheth. Having been crippled at age five (4:4), Mephibosheth would have been only twelve

years old when David moved to Jerusalem about seven years later. Considerable time must have elapsed, for Mephibosheth himself now had a son, **Micha** (v. 12; for Micha's descendants, see 1 Chron. 8:35–39).

III. David's Kingship in Its Weaknesses and Failures (chaps. 10–20)

A. David Commits Adultery and Murder (chaps. 10–12)

1. David's Victories over the Ammonites (chap. 10)

10:1–6. The king of the children of Ammon died (v. 1). The Ammonites were descendants of Lot (see Gen. 19:38; Deut. 2:19) and lived east of the tribal territory of Gad near the upper regions of the Jabbok River (see Deut. 2:37; Josh. 12:2). The king is identified as **Nahash** (v. 2), who had terrorized the eastern tribes in the early days of Saul's reign (see 1 Sam. 11). Although specific details are lacking, at some point in the past, perhaps when David had ascended the throne of Saul, Nahash, Saul's enemy, had extended some kindness to David, perhaps even congratulated him. Hearing of Nahash's death, David reciprocated by extending sympathy to his son and successor, Hanun. **I will shew kindness.** The Hebrew for this expression suggests that a formal treaty existed between the Israelites and the Ammonites. Perhaps this explains why there is no account of a war against the Ammonites in chapter 8 and why the Ammonites did not come to the assistance of the Moabites (8:2). Hanun's officials misinterpreted David's motives, suspecting that his servants had come to spy on their city, that is, Rabbah, their capital (11:1; 12:26).

The Ammonites treated David's representatives shamefully. They **shaved off the one half of their beards** (v. 4). In the Eastern world of that time, this was considered a most serious insult. Men shaved their beards only as a sign of deep mourning (see Isa. 15:2; Jer. 41:5; Ezek. 5:1). They **cut off their garments … even to their buttocks**, a customary way of degrading prisoners of war (see Isa. 20:4), making them objects of ridicule and sending them away indecently exposed.

David permitted his humiliated men to remain in isolation at **Jericho** (v. 5; see discussions on Josh. 6:1, 26; 1 Kings 16:34) until their beards grew back. Jericho was on the border of Israel and Ammon and remained unrestored during the centuries between Joshua's conquest and the time of Ahab.

10:6–14. Instead of making restitution, Hanun behaved even more foolishly by preparing to fight David with the help of hired Syrian mercenaries from **Beth-rehob** (v. 6; see Num. 13:21; Judg. 18:28), from **Zoba** (see discussion on 8:3), and from **king Maacah** (see Deut. 3:14; Josh. 12:5; 13:13), and from **Ish-tob** (the marginal note reads "the men of Tob," i.e., people of Tob; also rendered "land of Tob").

David's army was led by Joab, who divided the men into groups, one comprised of the choicest under his own command and the rest under the command of his brother **Abishai** (v. 10; see discussion on 1 Sam. 26:6). They fought simultaneously on two fronts: Abishai against the Ammonites, and Joab against the Syrians coming from the north. Both were able to rout their opponents.

10:15–19. The retreating Syrians regrouped, however. Strengthened by the additional troops he recalled from across **the river** (i.e., the Euphrates River; v. 16), **Hadarezer** (Hebrew, *Hadadezer*; see discussion on 8:3) prepared to fight once again Israel's army, which had now been joined by David. They met at **Helam**, a Transjordanian town close to the northern border of Gilead and about forty miles east of the Sea of Galilee. The Syrians were routed once again, as David smote **seven hundred** (v. 18) charioteers (in 1 Chron. 19:18, the figure is 7,000, indicating a copyist's mistake in one of the accounts). The former vassals of Hadadezer **made peace with Israel** (v. 19) and became their subjects. There is no indication that Hadadezer himself made peace with Israel as his vassals did in the aftermath of this defeat. These events represent David's last major campaign against combined foreign powers.

2. David Commits Adultery and Murder (chap. 11)

11:1–27. The sad story of David's adultery with Bathsheba and his murder of her husband, Uriah, is embedded in the larger account of his wars with the Ammonites.

11:1–6. The story occurs **after the year was expired** (v. 1), that is, in the spring of the year following the events reported in chapter 10. The time must have been about ten years after David became established in Jerusalem. It was **the time when kings go forth to battle**. Kings normally launched their military campaigns in the spring, after the winter rains had stopped and the roads were passable. Not only was the weather more favorable then, but it was directly after the grain harvest in April and May, and the armies could expect to live off the land they raided. The army **besieged Rabbah** (see discussion on 10:3). Though now alone without the help of allies (see 10:19), the Ammonites had not yet been subjugated.

In contrast to the involvement of **all Israel** (i.e., the whole army; v. 1), David remained at home. His idleness and inactivity left him vulnerable to temptation. **David … walked upon the roof** (v. 2), which was flat (see 1 Sam. 9:25). David had probably gone there to enjoy the cool evening air. While there, he saw a woman who stimulated a lust that drove him to inquire about her.

She was Bath-sheba, the daughter of Eliam (v. 3), perhaps the same Eliam who was a member of David's personal bodyguard (23:34) and a son of his counselor Ahithophel. Her husband, **Uriah**, was also listed among those comprising David's royal guard (23:39). His name suggests that even though he was a **Hittite** (v. 3; see discussion on 1 Sam. 26:6), he had adopted the Israelite faith (Uriah means "my light is the Lord").

David sent messengers, and took her (v. 4). Through this action, David would eventually become guilty of breaking the sixth, seventh, ninth, and tenth commandments (see Exod. 20:13–17). His first sin was not one of additional polygamy but of adultery, and it was not done in ignorance, for he had learned that the woman was Bathsheba, the wife of Uriah. Neither was it done in secret, for he had ordered others to bring her to him. So the royal court was aware that their king was guilty of a crime that was punishable by death (Lev. 20:10). **She came in unto him, and he lay with her.** Bathsheba appears to have been an unprotesting partner in this adulterous relationship with David, but if it were questionable whether she protested against the desires of the king, his crime could be considered royal rape. **She was purified from her uncleanness.** She had just ceremonially purified herself from the uncleanness of her menstrual cycle (see Lev. 15:19), so she later knew with certainty that she was pregnant by David.

I am with child (v. 5). Bathsheba left the next step up to David. The law prescribed the death penalty for both David and Bathsheba (Lev. 20:10; Deut. 22:22), as they well knew. David acted quickly. **Send me Uriah** (v. 6). Under the pretense of seeking information about the course of the war, David brought Uriah back to Jerusalem.

11:7–13. Ostensibly, Uriah was brought home to report on the battle, but David's questions were meant to disguise his true intent, to send Uriah to his wife so that everyone would suppose she had conceived by him, thus covering David's adultery. **Go down to thy house, and wash thy feet** (v. 8). In essence, David told Uriah to go home and relax. What he did not say specifically was that which was most important, and which was well understood by Uriah (v. 11). **There followed him a mess of meat from the king.** The Hebrew word for "mess" (i.e., "portion") has the meaning of "food" in Genesis 43:34 ("mess" from the king's table). David wanted Uriah and Bathsheba to enjoy their evening together. To David's surprise and dismay, **Uriah slept at the door of the king's house** (v. 9), not with his wife as David had planned.

The ark, and Israel, and Judah abide in tents (v. 11). Uriah's statement suggests that the ark was in the field camp with the army rather than in the tent that David had set up for it in Jerusalem (6:17). If so, it was probably there for the purposes of worship and seeking guidance for the war. The circumstances are even more damning for David; the Lord was in the field with His army while David stayed at home in leisure. **Shall I then go into mine house …?** Uriah's devotion to duty exposed by sharp contrast David's dalliance at home while his men were in the field. **As thou livest, and as thy soul liveth** was a customary way of emphasizing the truthfulness of one's words. Uriah emphatically refused to go to his wife. Uriah's loyalty to and solidarity with his fellow soldiers, who remained in the field, shamed David. Then David **made him drunk** (v. 13), hoping that in this condition, he would relent and go to Bathsheba. The drunken Uriah, however, was still more honorable than the sober but sinful David.

11:14–17. The desperation of David's sinful heart was revealed when he stooped to a tactic of Saul (see 1 Sam. 18:25): having Uriah, one of his thirty best soldiers (23:39), killed. His letter to Joab ordered, **Set ye Uriah … that he may be smitten, and die** (v. 15). Unsuccessful in making it appear that Uriah was the father of Bathsheba's child, David plotted Uriah's death so that he himself could marry Bathsheba as quickly as possible.

The strategy implemented by Joab was not exactly what David had prescribed. Other soldiers were needlessly killed as well, but the primary mission for the moment was accomplished. Uriah lay dead.

11:18–21. Joab sent a real report (see discussion on 11:7) to David, comparing the most recent event—that is, Uriah's death—with the end of **Abimelech the son of Jerubbesheth** (v. 21), that is, the son of Gideon. (Another possible spelling is "Jerubbosheth.") In Judges, Gideon is called Jerubbaal (see discussion on Judg. 6:32; for similar name changes by the author of Samuel, see discussions on 2:8; 4:4). Abimelech had been killed by a piece of **millstone** thrown from the wall (Judg. 9:52–53). In a somewhat similar manner, **Uriah** was **dead.** Joab knew that this news was of great importance to David, and he used it to squelch any criticism David might otherwise have had of the battle tactics.

11:22–25. Joab's messenger reported to David, concluding with what David most wanted to hear: **Uriah … is dead also** (v. 24). David hid his satisfaction over the news with a hypocritical statement that war was war, and the death of Uriah should not be a discouragement. It is disheartening to see how callous and cold-blooded the once warm and compassionate David had become in his effort to hide his sin.

11:26–27. David permitted Bathsheba to mourn her husband, but **when the mourning was past** (v. 27), presumably a period of seven days (Gen. 50:10; 1 Sam. 31:13), **she became his wife** (see discussions on 3:2–5; 5:14). David knew that if he quickly took Bathsheba as a wife, the public would believe that the child she would bear was legitimately his. **The thing that David had done displeased the LORD.** David had not only brazenly violated God's laws (see discussion on 11:4), but even worse, he had shamelessly abused his royal power, which the Lord had entrusted to him to shepherd the Lord's people (5:2; 7:7–8). The Lord's attitude toward David's action is ominous and leads the reader to expect the reproof and discipline that follows.

3. David's Repentance and Confession (chap. 12)

12:1–25. Ancient Near Eastern records customarily glossed over moral failures of the kings, perhaps even accepting such behavior as normal or the privilege of royalty. In contrast, Scripture brings all men's unholy actions under scrutiny. David's sin and confession are given in detail. His efforts to conceal his sin are indicative that he was struggling against God's Spirit and his own moral consciousness, which convicted him.

12:1–6. The LORD sent Nathan unto David (v. 1). Prophets were messengers from the Lord. Here the Great King sent His emissary to rebuke and announce judgment on the king that He had enthroned over His people. For an introduction to Nathan, see discussion on 7:2. His visit to David occurred after Bathsheba's son had been born (see 11:27; 12:14–15), so David apparently had concealed his sin for nearly a year.

There were two men (v. 1). Nathan began one of the most striking parables in the Old Testament. It captivated David's attention and stirred his emotions and sense of justice. The parable demanded that David render a verdict in the case, and unwittingly, his verdict fell upon himself. **As the LORD liveth** (v. 5) is an oath (see discussion on 1 Sam. 14:39). Justice

would be served, and repayment would be **fourfold** (v. 6). David knew the Mosaic law and was ready to apply it to the fullest extent (see Exod. 22:1). Most important, David's righteous outburst indicted himself.

12:7–12. I anointed ... I delivered ... I gave ... thy master's wives (v. 8). God rehearsed David's indebtedness for what He had done for him. Earlier narratives refer to only one wife of Saul (Ahinoam, 1 Sam. 14:50) and one concubine (Rizpah, 2 Sam. 3:7; 21:8). This statement suggests that there were others. Since it was customary for new kings to assume the harem of their predecessors (see discussion on 3:7), it may be that Nathan merely used conventional language to emphasize that the Lord had placed David on Saul's throne. **I ... gave thee the house of Israel and of Judah.** See 2:4; 5:2–3.

David's sin had been blatant. He had **despised the commandment of the LORD** (v. 9; see discussions on 11:4, 27), going so far as to commit murder. **Thou ... hast slain him.** David was held directly responsible for Uriah's death even though he fell in battle (see 11:15).

Though David would obtain forgiveness immediately upon confessing his sin, the judgments that fell upon his household were long-term reminders that a moment of pleasurable sin had long-lasting effects. **The sword shall never depart from thine house** (v. 10). Three of David's sons would come to violent deaths: Amnon (13:28–29), Absalom (18:14), and Adonijah (1 Kings 2:24, 25). **I will raise up evil against thee out of thine own house** (v. 11). David would be driven from Jerusalem by Absalom's conspiracy to seize the kingship from his own father (15:1–15). **He shall lie with thy wives in the sight of this sun.** This also would be fulfilled at the time of Absalom's rebellion (see discussion on 16:22).

12:13–14. A clear contrast is made between David's confession and Saul's confession (see discussion on 1 Sam. 15:24). David made no excuses for his actions. He recognized his guilt and confessed his sin in response to Nathan's rebuke (see Psalm 51 superscription) and pled for forgiveness. **I have sinned against the LORD** (v. 13). Although David had sinned against Bathsheba and Uriah, and his own wives, and had betrayed the moral trust of the nation, he fully understood that his sin was ultimately against God (see Gen. 39:3). **The LORD also hath put away thy sin**. David experienced the joy of knowing that his sin was forgiven (see Ps. 32:1, 5; see Ps. 51:8, 12). **Thou shalt not die**. The Lord, in His grace, released David from the customary death penalty for adultery and murder (Lev. 20:10; 24:17), but his son born to Bathsheba would die.

12:15 – 23. Although Nathan said the child would die (12:14), David agonized in prayer and fasting for his son's life. When the Lord took his son, David was bereft but not bitter. He accepted God's will in contentment and **came into the house of the LORD, and worshipped** (v. 20). In this way, David clearly demonstrated his humble acceptance of the disciplinary results of his sin. A contrast is again made between David's attitude and Saul's (see discussions on 12:13; 1 Sam. 15:25).

David's servants were puzzled that the king would **fast and weep for the child, while it was alive** (v. 21) and then end his fast when the child died. David's fasting and weeping were not signs of grief but expressions of his repentance and supplication to God that He would spare the child's life. When the child died, David accepted the will of the Lord. **I shall go to him** (v. 23). David knew he could not bring his son back from the dead, but he, like the child, would die and join him in the grave (see discussion on Gen. 37:35). Many see this verse as an expression of David's confidence that he would join his son in God's presence in the afterlife.

12:24 – 25. David gave his second son born to Bathsheba the name **Solomon** (v. 24). The name derives from the Hebrew word for "peace" (see 1 Chron. 22:9 and discussion), therefore perhaps meaning "peaceful" or "man of peace." Of David's sons, Solomon was loved by God and chosen to succeed his father. Therefore, Nathan named him **Jedidiah** (v. 25), a name meaning "beloved of the Lord," which suggests that the Lord's special favor rested on Solomon from his birth. And since the name also contained an echo of David's name, it

provided assurance to David that the Lord loved him also and would continue his dynasty.

12:26 – 31. Joab fought against Rabbah (v. 26). The writer now returns to the outcome of the attack against the Ammonites (11:1, 25), which provided the background for the story of David and Bathsheba. Even while the Lord was displeased with David, He gave the Israelites victory over a people who had abused them. Just before the Ammonite city fell, Joab had requested David's presence in the final assault. The meaning of **the city of waters** (v. 27) is uncertain. Perhaps it means Joab had found and cut off the city's water supply (see 5:8 and discussion). All that was left to do was to actually take the city, and Joab wanted David, the king, present to claim credit.

Their king's crown … was set on David's head (v. 30). A crown of such weight (about seventy-five pounds) would have been worn only briefly and on very special occasions. Perhaps it was worn only once in a symbolic act of transferring to David sovereignty over Ammon. David's treatment of the captives of Rabbah, to **put them under saws … through the brickkiln** (v. 31) may refer to the customary practice in the Near East of subjecting captives to forced labor. An alternative interpretation is that he had them tortured and/or killed in keeping with their own cruel practices (see 1 Sam. 11:2; Amos 1:13).

B. David Loses His Sons Amnon and Absalom (chaps. 13 – 20)

1. Amnon Defiles His Sister Tamar (13:1 – 22)

13:1 – 39. The trouble within David's family begins (see discussion on 12:10). In general, David reaped a harvest of rivalry between the children of his multiple wives (3:2 – 5), but more specifically, he experienced the effects of his adultery with Bathsheba (12:10 – 12).

13:1 – 5. Tamar (v. 1) was David's daughter by Maacah of Geshur (3:3) and the full sister of David's third son, **Absalom**. David's oldest son was **Amnon** (3:2), and by ancient Near East standards of royal succession, he was the heir apparent to the throne. Amnon was infatuated by his half sister Tamar's beauty and received scheming advice on how to gain physical access to her from his cousin Jonadab, the son of **Shimeah** (v. 3; called Shammah in 1 Sam. 16:9), the third older brother of David (see 1 Chron. 2:13).

13:6 – 14. Amnon requested that Tamar be allowed to attend him at his sickbed. David innocently sent her into a dangerous situation, in which Amnon seized her and tried to compromise her. Tamar vigorously objected, **Nay … do not force me** (v. 12). She attempted reasoning with him. **As for thee … be as one of the fools** (v. 13). This act would jeopardize Amnon's position as crown prince and heir to the throne. She offered an alternate proposal: speak **unto the king, for he will not withhold me from thee**. This was possibly a futile attempt by Tamar to escape Amnon's immediate designs, rather than a serious proposal, since such a marriage was prohibited in Israel (see Lev. 18:9; 20:17; Deut. 27:22). Seeing that Tamar spurned his wicked advances, he raped her for his self-gratification. Then his infatuation and lust turned to revulsion (see Gen. 39:7 – 18).

13:15 – 20. Amnon hated her (v. 15). The turnabout in Amnon's feelings toward Tamar demonstrated that his former "love" (13:1) had been nothing but sensual desire. **Arise, be gone** is a direct reversal of his earlier "Come lie with me" (13:11). Tamar's humiliation and rejection was intense. **This evil in sending me away is greater** (v. 16). No longer a virgin, she could not be offered by her father to any other potential husband (see 13:21 and discussion).

She donned a **garment of divers colours** (v. 18). The Hebrew for "colours" is uncertain, but it was perhaps a long-sleeved or embroidered garment (see Gen. 37:3 and discussion). As a sign of great mourning, she **put ashes on her head** (v. 19). She also **rent her garment of divers colours**, thus expressing her anguish and announcing that her virginity had been violated. She **laid her hand on her head**, also a sign of grief (see Jer. 2:37).

Her full brother Absalom offered shallow comfort. **Hold now thy peace, my sister … regard not this thing** (v. 20). Absalom urged his sister not to make the matter a public scandal and attempted to quiet her by minimizing its significance. As subsequent verses prove, he was inwardly seething with anger and was formulating his own secret plans for revenge (see 13:22, 28, 32).

13:21 – 22. He was very wroth (v. 21). Although David was incensed by Amnon's rape of Tamar, he himself had naively compromised his daughter. There is no record that David took any punitive action against Amnon. Perhaps the memory of his own sin with Bathsheba adversely affected his judicious handling of the matter, for he had compromised his own moral integrity by his adultery (11:4) and murder (11:14). Whatever the reason, David abdicated his responsibility both as king and as father. This disciplinary leniency toward his sons (see discussions on 14:33; 1 Kings 1:6) would eventually lead to the death of Amnon and the revolts of Absalom and Adonijah.

Absalom … hated Amnon (v. 22). Absalom did not converse with Amnon concerning this incident. He simply bided his time quietly, waiting for his moment to avenge his sister's rape.

2. Absalom Murders Amnon (13:23 – 36)

13:23 – 27. Absalom understood that his father would inflict no punishment, so after a period of two years, he took matters into his own hand. He devised a scheme that would avenge Tamar's rape and improve his own chances to succeed to his father's throne instead of Amnon. **Absalom invited all the king's sons** (v. 23). The time of sheepshearing was a festive occasion (see 1 Sam. 25:4, 8). The invitation was extended to his father also, whom Absalom expected would refuse to come. **Let my brother Amnon go with us** (v. 26). Upon David's refusal of the invitation, Absalom diplomatically requested that Amnon, the crown prince and oldest son, be his representative. **Why should he go with thee?** David's question suggests some misgivings because of the strained relationship between the two half brothers (see 13:22), but he granted permission for Amnon to attend.

13:28 – 29. Smite Amnon … kill him (v. 28). Absalom arranged for the murder of his half brother in violation of Eastern hospitality. In the wicked acts of Amnon and Absalom, David's oldest sons became guilty of sexual immorality and murder, as their father had before them. With the murder of Amnon, Absalom not only avenged the rape of his sister but also secured for himself the position of successor to the throne (see 3:3; 15:1–6). Chileab, David's second son (3:3), may have died in his youth since there is no reference to him beyond the announcement of his birth.

David's other sons in attendance, fearing that they too were destined to die, each fled on his **mule** (v. 29) to survive. The mule was apparently the normal mount for royalty in David's kingdom (see 18:9; 1 Kings 1:33, 38, 44; see also discussion on 1 Kings 1:33).

13:30–36. David's response to the first report, that all his sons had been murdered, was to **tare his garments, and lay on the earth** (v. 31), common ways of expressing grief (see Josh. 7:6; 1 Kings 21:27; Est. 4:1, 3; Job 1:20; 2:8). Jonadab, who had offered Amnon wicked advice, now offered David shallow comfort: **Amnon only is dead** (v. 32). David's grief was intense and sincere. His judgment had been clouded. He had unwisely ordered Tamar to Amnon's house, where she was raped. Then he had sent Amnon to Absalom's sheepshearing festivities, where he was murdered. David undoubtedly understood that he was reaping the harvest of his own sin.

3. Absalom's Exile, Return, and Revolt (13:37–15:12)

13:37–39. Meanwhile, Absalom had fled across the Jordan River to his grandfather, **Talmai, the son of Ammihud, king of Geshur** (v. 37; see 3:3), where he remained for three years as a fugitive from his own father. **David longed to go forth unto Absalom** (v. 39). With Absalom a refugee, David had lost both of his oldest living sons.

14:1–3. Joab the son of Zeruiah (v. 1; see discussion on 2:13) sensed that David's mind, torn between anger and love, was so preoccupied with what to do about Absalom (13:39) that he might be rendered an ineffective leader and thus demoralize the nation. Joab may have also surmised that Absalom was now the heir apparent to the throne

(Scripture is silent regarding Chileab, David's second son; see 3:3); hence, it was necessary to recall Absalom to Jerusalem and pardon him. Therefore, Joab took the initiative and **sent to Tekoah** (v. 2), a town a few miles south of Bethlehem (and from which the prophet Amos originated, Amos 1:1), for a **wise woman** who would follow his instructions explicitly in speaking to the king. Joab, motivated by a concern for the political implications of the unresolved dispute between David and his son in line for the throne, attempted to move David to action by means of a story designed to elicit a response that was clearly applicable, by analogy, to David's own predicament. A similar technique had been used by Nathan the prophet (12:1–7; see 1 Kings 20:38–43).

14:4–7. The woman's dialogue with the king was lengthy as she related her fictitious story. She was a widow, and one of her two sons was guilty of murdering the other—thus her dilemma. **The whole family is risen against thine handmaid** (v. 7). It was customary in Israel for a murder victim's next of kin to avenge the blood of his relative by putting the murderer to death (see discussion on 3:27; Num. 35:12; Deut. 19:11–13). In the case the woman presented, however, blood revenge would wipe out the family line, which was something Israelite law and custom tried to avoid if at all possible (see discussions on Deut. 25:5–6; Ruth 2:20). **We will destroy the heir also.** The woman suggested that the motivation for blood revenge was more a selfish desire to acquire the family inheritance than a desire for justice (see Num. 27:11). **They … shall not leave to my husband neither name nor remainder.** The implication was that it would be a more serious offense to terminate the woman's family line than to permit a murder to go unpunished by blood revenge. Apparently, Joab hoped to suggest subtly to David that if he did not restore Absalom, a struggle for the throne would eventually ensue.

14:8–9. I will give charge concerning thee (v. 8). David's judicial action may have rested on the legal ground that the murder was not premeditated (see Deut. 19:4–6). David seemed to dismiss her without addressing the crime; it had not been expiated (see

Num. 35:31–33). **The iniquity be on me** (v. 9). The woman asked that the blame or guilt for the unpunished crime be charged to her. Since she was innocent, she was attempting to force the king to declare a pardon for her son's crime on her account.

14:10–11. Let the king remember the Lord thy God (v. 11). The woman wanted David to confirm his promise by an oath in the Lord's name. **As the Lord liveth** was an oath formula (see discussions on Gen. 42:15; 1 Sam. 14:39) that solemnly bound David to his commitment.

14:12–17. The woman departed momentarily from her fabrication to make a royal application. **Wherefore then hast thou thought such a thing against the people of God?** (v. 13). The woman's suggested that David had done to Israel the same thing that her family members had done to her. The people of Israel wanted their crown prince returned safely to them. **The king doth speak ... as one which is faulty.** Her argument was that when David had exempted the fictitious murderer from blood revenge, he had in effect rendered himself guilty for not doing the same in the case of Absalom. The analogy placed David in the position of the blood avenger, unwilling to extend the same mercy to his son. David and Joab, his accomplice in Uriah's murder, both knew that he was in no position to punish his son for a crime for which he too was guilty.

As water spilt on the ground (v. 14) speaks of blood revenge. It would not return the victim of murder to life, just as water spilled on the ground cannot be recovered. **Neither doth God respect any person** is literally "God does not take away life." In the suggestion that avenging blood was contrary to God's ways of dealing with people, the woman apparently distorted the biblical teaching of God's justice (see discussion on Gen. 9:6). She dwelt on the mercy of God, who would rather preserve life than take it (see Ezek. 18:23, 32; 33:11). David's own guilt and subsequent experience of God's mercy appear to have given added weight to the woman's argument (see discussions on 12:13; 13:21).

The woman feared that David might get angry and punish her, so she reverted to her fabricated story. **The people have made me afraid** (v. 15). "The people" are evidently those of her family who were seeking blood revenge. She came to David hoping that he would grant her request and desired that his **word ... be comfortable** (v. 17), that is, "bring comfort" or "rest" to her, for David was as **an angel of God ... to discern good and bad.** In flattering terms, she described David as possessing superhuman powers of discernment—as a king ideally should possess (see 14:20; 19:27).

14:18–20. The woman never betrayed the confidence of Joab, but when David detected **the hand of Joab** (v. 19) in her presentation of the impressive fictitious story, she did not deny his involvement. Seeing that David was not fooled, she complimented him again that he had **the wisdom of an angel of God** (v. 20).

14:21–24. Joab (v. 21), who appears to have been present the whole time, was commissioned to **bring ... Absalom again.** Joab **went to Geshur** (v. 23), the place of Absalom's asylum (see 13:37), and brought him back to Jerusalem, where he was sent to his own house. **Let him not see my face** (v. 24). David still vacillated (see discussion on 14:1) and refused to see him; he did not offer Absalom forgiveness and restoration.

14:25–27. In Israel ... none ... so much praised (v. 25). Absalom's handsomeness brought him attention and popular favor, which he would soon cultivate. Attention was given to the **hair of his head** (v. 26) and even to the details of his haircuts. For the people of that time, hair apparently was a sign of vigor. Kings and heroic figures were usually portrayed with abundant locks, while baldness was a disgrace (see 2 Kings 2:23). In this too, Absalom seemed destined for the throne. He apparently took great pride in his hair, for each time he cut it, he weighed the large quantity of it according to the **king's weight.** The royal shekel was perhaps heavier than the sanctuary shekel (see Exod. 30:13; Lev. 5:15; Num. 3:47).

Absalom had **three sons** (v. 27), but their names are unknown; 18:18 suggests that they died in their youth. Absalom named his daughter **Tamar** after his sister (13:1). Maachah, who is named in 1 Kings 15:2, was probably a daughter of Tamar and Absalom's granddaughter (see discussion on 2 Chron. 11:20).

14:28–33. Though recalled to Jerusalem, Absalom remained estranged from his father for two more years. When his appeal to Joab did not produce results, he proved that drastic measures did get results (see Judg. 15:4–6). Absalom showed his vicious side and proved to Joab that he was not one to be snubbed. **If there be any iniquity in me, let him kill me** (v. 32). Absalom demanded either full pardon and restoration or death, but he still gave no sign of repentance.

A meeting of father and son was arranged, and **the king kissed Absalom** (v. 33), which signified his forgiveness and Absalom's reconciliation with the royal family. David sidestepped repentance and justice, and in this way, he probably contributed to the fulfillment of the prophecy of Nathan (12:10–12). The events of chapter 15 show that Absalom's reconciliation was superficial indeed.

15:1–6. Absalom's years of estrangement provided an incubation period for a conspiracy against his father. He **prepared him chariots** (lit., "a chariot") **and horses** (v. 1). As far as is known, Absalom was the first Israelite leader to acquire a chariot and horses (see Deut. 17:16). The **fifty men** who ran before him probably functioned as bodyguards and provided a display of royal pomp, which appealed to the masses. Adonijah later followed Absalom's example (1 Kings 1:5).

Proving to be politically adept, Absalom stationed himself outside the city gate. There he had access to discontented citizens (see 1 Sam. 22:2) before they reached the city to register their complaint in hopes of a favorable judgment from the king. **Thy matters are good** (v. 3). Absalom sought to ingratiate himself with the people by endorsing their grievances apart from any investigation into their legitimacy.

Oh that I were made judge in the land (v. 4). One of the king's primary functions was to administer justice (see 12:1–6; 1 Kings 3:16–28; 2 Kings 8:1–6). Absalom presented himself as the solution to the people's legal grievances. In the case of Amnon, Absalom had taken matters into his own hands because of his father's laxity. He had found, he believed, the weakness in his father's reign, and he capitalized on it with political astuteness. His feigned interest in the people's cause **stole the hearts of the men of Israel** (v. 6).

15:7–9. After **forty years** (v. 7), Absalom was set to launch his rebellion. Some ancient manuscripts read "four years," that is, four years after Absalom's return to the court (14:33). By this time, he must have been about thirty years old, so his revolt must be dated early in the last decade of David's reign. **Hebron** was where David had first been proclaimed king (see discussions on 2:1, 4; 5:3, 5) and where Absalom had been born (3:2–3). Absalom may have had reason to believe that he could count on some local resentment over David's transfer of the capital to Jerusalem (5:6–9). Hebron was also the site of an important sanctuary.

Absalom asked his father for permission to fulfill in Hebron a vow that he had made while a fugitive in **Geshur** (v. 8; see 13:37). Once again, the unsuspecting king fell prey to his blind trust in a deceitful son (see 13:6–7, 26–27). **Go in peace** (v. 9). Though David sent him away in peace, he departed to prepare for rebellion and war.

15:10–12. Absalom was joined in Hebron by **men out of Jerusalem** (v. 11), who apparently were not suspecting a revolt from David. **Ahithophel** (v. 12), Bathsheba's grandfather (see 11:3; 23:34) and a wise and respected counselor (16:23), was consulted. He appears to have secretly aligned himself with Absalom's rebellion in its planning stage, perhaps in retaliation against David for his treatment of Bathsheba and Uriah. This unsuspected betrayal by a trusted friend may have prompted David's statements in Psalms 41:9; 55:12–14. Ahithophel was a **Gilonite**; that is, he was from Giloh, a town near Hebron (see Josh. 15:51).

4. David's Escape from Absalom (15:13–17:29)

15:13–16. Upon hearing of Absalom's revolt, David said, **Arise ... flee ... we shall not else escape**

from Absalom (v. 14). Uncertain of the extent of Absalom's support (v. 13), David feared being trapped in Jerusalem, and he wanted to spare the city a bloodbath and the loss of innocent lives. According to its superscription, Psalm 3 was composed on this occasion.

The king left ten women ... concubines, to keep the house (v. 16; see 5:13; see also discussion on 3:2). That he left these women behind may indicate David's intention to return soon (note also that he returned the ark, 15:25), but in leaving them behind, David unknowingly arranged for the fulfillment of one of Nathan's prophecies (see discussion on 12:11; see also 20:3).

15:17–23. As David departed the city, he was joined by the **Cherethites ... Pelethites** (v. 18; see discussion on 8:18). The six hundred **Gittites** were Philistine soldiers from **Gath** under the command of **Ittai** (v. 19), a mercenary, foreigner, and exile who had for some unknown reason joined David's personal military force (see 18:2). David encouraged him to **return ... and abide with the king,** thus releasing the Philistine contingent from further obligations to him. **As the LORD liveth** (v. 21) is an oath of loyalty and devotion taken in the name of Israel's God (see discussion on 1 Sam. 14:39; for a similar oath, see Ruth 1:16–17). Ittai's loyalty to David was proven when he chose to accompany David despite his questionable future.

15:24–29. Zadok (v. 24; see discussion on 8:17), **Levites ... bearing the ark,** and **Abiathar** (see 8:17; 1 Sam. 22:20–23) prepared to accompany David as he departed the city. **Carry back the ark of God into the city** (v. 25). David revealed a true understanding of the connection between the ark and God's presence with His people. He knew that possession of the ark did not guarantee God's blessing (see discussions on 1 Sam. 4:3, 21). He also recognized that the ark belonged in the capital city as a symbol of the Lord's rule over the nation (see discussion on 6:2), no matter who the king might be. **Let him do to me as seemeth good to him** (v. 26). David confessed that he had no exclusive claim to the throne and that Israel's Divine King was free to confer the kingship on whomever He chose.

Art not thou a seer? (v. 27). The question is perhaps an allusion to the high priest's custody of the Urim and Thummim as a means of divine revelation (see discussions on Exod. 28:30; 1 Sam. 2:28; 9:9). David enlisted the priests to be informants on Absalom's activities. Their sons would serve as runners to David.

In the meantime, David's plan was to stay in **the plain** (lit., "fords") **of the wilderness** (v. 28), that is, the fords that crossed the Jordan in the vicinity of Gilgal, and await further word on Absalom's actions.

15:30–31. Leaving Jerusalem was sorrowful for David, who **wept as he went** (v. 30). His grief was displayed in other ways as well. He **had his head covered** (see Est. 6:12; Jer. 14:3–4), and **he went barefoot** (see Isa. 20:2, 4; Ezek. 24:17; Mic. 1:8). It was then that he learned the sad news that **Ahithophel** (v. 31; see discussion on 15:12), who was known for his wisdom (see 16:23), had joined the rebellion.

15:32–37. David was joined by another trusted advisor, **Hushai the Archite** (v. 32). The Archites were a clan (some think non-Israelite) that inhabited an area southwest of Bethel (Josh. 16:2). Since Hushai was a trusted member of David's court, his appearance was the beginning of an answer to David's prayer (15:31) that the Lord would thwart the counsel of Ahithophel. Therefore, David sent Hushai back to Jerusalem to "advise" Absalom and work with Zadok and Abiathar. Hushai is called **David's friend** (v. 37). First Chronicles 27:33 calls him the "king's companion," which seems to be an official title for the king's most trusted adviser (see 1 Kings 4:5).

16:1–23. This chapter gives evidence that David's efforts to unify the kingdom had been somewhat superficial. In some areas, a pro-Saul sentiment remained, which surfaced when David found himself in political trouble.

16:1–4. Ziba (v. 1; see 9:2, 9), servant of **Mephibosheth** (see discussion on 4:4), met David with a **couple of asses saddled** for the king's use, foodstuffs, and a pretentious display of loyalty. Since David had assumed control of Saul's estate (9:7–10), Ziba, always the opportunist, sought to profit from the political crisis. **Where is thy master's son?** (v. 3).

"Son" here means "grandson," that is, Mephibosheth (see 9:2–3, 9). Ziba slandered his master, who reportedly had remained in Jerusalem to seek a political recovery for the house of Saul should David be overthrown. Ziba's report would later be declared false (see 19:26–27), and David's hasty decision to reward Ziba would be altered (see 19:29). **Thine are all that pertained unto Mephibosheth** (v. 4). Because the revolt was so widespread and loyalties so uncertain, David was quick to assume the worst.

16:5–8. Bahurim (v. 5) is a site on the eastern slope of the Mount of Olives (see discussion on 3:16). A man **of the family of the house of Saul** (from the clan of Matri; see 1 Sam. 10:21) accosted David as he fled. **Shimei, the son of Gera**, whose exact relation to Saul is unknown (see discussion on 1 Kings 2:8), exposed his pent-up hostilities by pelting David and all the **people and ... mighty men** (v. 6) who were with him with stones and calling out slanderous and disparaging epithets. The "mighty men" were the Cherethites, Pelethites, and six hundred Gittites who had joined David (see 15:18).

Shimei called David a **bloody man** and a **man of Belial** (v. 7, that is, a worthless man; see discussion on Deut. 13:13). His charge that David was a "bloody man" was possibly an accusation that David had murdered Abner (3:27–30) and Ish-bosheth (4:1–7) to seize Saul's throne or a reference to Uriah's murder. **The blood of the house of Saul** (v. 8) may have been another reference to these murders or a reference to the executions reported in 21:1–14, but the time of that event is uncertain (see discussion on 21:1).

16:9–14. An intolerant and impatient **Abishai** (v. 9; see discussion on 1 Sam. 26:6) was ready to kill **this dead dog**, an expression of absolute contempt (see discussion on 9:8). In contrast to his much earlier experience with Nabal (1 Sam. 25:2–12, 2–34), David showed remarkable tolerance and restraint, denying Abishai permission to execute Shimei. **Let him curse ... the LORD hath said unto him, Curse David** (v. 10). David left open the possibility that God had seen fit to terminate his rule; the verdict was not yet determined (see 15:26; for David's later

actions regarding Shimei, see 19:18–23; 1 Kings 2:8–9). David put the event in balance. **Behold my son ... of my bowels** (v. 11). What Absalom was doing to David through his rebellion was far worse than anything Shimei could do to him.

16:15–23. Absalom (v. 15) entered Jerusalem with all his supporters, including Ahithophel (see discussion on 15:12). There **Hushai the Archite, David's friend** (v. 16; see discussions on 15:32, 37) joined them. Absalom, knowing of Hushai's loyalty to David, had to be convinced that Hushai had returned to support him. Thus, the contest began between two men, Ahithophel and Hushai, to gain Absalom's confidence and counsel him.

Ahithophel counseled, **Go in unto thy father's concubines** (v. 21). This would signify Absalom's assumption of royal power; it would also be a definitive and irreversible declaration of the break between father and son (see discussions on 3:7; 12:8; 1 Kings 2:22). **Absalom went in unto his father's concubines** (v. 22), fulfilling Nathan's prophecy (12:11–12), perhaps on the very roof where David had first observed Bathsheba.

17:1–3. From the standpoint of Absalom's attempted coup, Ahithophel's advice to Absalom was brilliant (16:23): pursue immediately and strike David before he could organize his supporting troops. Ahithophel envisioned a cheap and easy victory that would not leave the nation weakened.

17:4. All the elders of Israel (v. 4) were pleased by Ahithophel's counsel. Absalom's rebellion appears to have gained extensive backing from prominent but fickle tribal leaders who had already shifted their loyalty from David (see discussions on 3:17; 5:1) to Absalom.

17:5–14. Hushai the Archite (v. 5), who had returned to counter Ahithophel's wise counsel (see discussions on 15:32–37), was called by the unsuspecting Absalom, who thought Hushai also had abandoned his loyalty to David (see 16:16–19).

Hushai's counteradvice subtly capitalized on Absalom's uncertainty, fear, and egotism and was meant to benefit David. He reminded Absalom of David's experience and military prowess. To prevent a humiliating defeat, he recommended that Absalom should wait until he had amassed a much larger number of troops representing all tribes between Israel's boundary cities, from Dan to Beersheba. To play on Absalom's arrogance, Hushai suggested that the rebel himself lead his troops against David. Hushai carefully linked himself with the revolt through a careful use of pronouns: **we … we will light upon him** (i.e., David; v. 12).

Absalom and the men of Israel agreed that Hushai's counsel was best, because **the LORD had appointed to defeat the good counsel of Ahithophel** (v. 14). This was indeed an answer to David's prayer (see 15:31; see Ps. 33:10; Prov. 21:30).

17:15–23. Hushai's counsel bought time for David, who was waiting at the fords (see 15:28) for the word advising him to cross the Jordan River and prepare for Absalom's pursuit. Hushai instructed **Zadok and … Abiathar** (v. 15; see 15:24–29, 35–36) on what information to relay to David, who waited by the **plains of the wilderness** (v. 16; see 15:28 and discussion). **Pass over.** Hushai advised David to cross the Jordan River at once, knowing that Absalom might change his mind and immediately set out after him.

Jonathan and Ahimaaz (v. 17), the priests' sons (see 15:36), waited at **En-rogel**, a spring in the Kidron Valley just outside the walls of Jerusalem, for any messages that needed to be carried to David (15:27–29). Using **a wench**, a maidservant, as an intermediary, because a servant girl going to the spring for water would attract no attention, a warning was delivered to the priests' sons, who carried it on to David. Their movements were spotted and reported to Absalom, but with the help of a man and his wife at **Bahurim** (v. 18; see discussion on 16:5) who hid them in a well, they were preserved and escaped to David.

The humiliation of having his counsel rejected brought Ahithophel to suicide. He retired to Giloh, **his city** (v. 23; see discussion on 15:12), where he **hanged himself**. Ahithophel may have been convinced that the rebellion would fail and that he would be found guilty of treason as a co-conspirator.

17:24–26. Crossing over the Jordan River, David came to **Mahanaim** (v. 24), a walled city (see. 18:24), which ironically was where Ish-bosheth had sought refuge after Saul's death (2:8).

Absalom replaced Joab as captain of the army with **Amasa** (v. 25), a nephew of David and cousin of both Absalom and Joab son of Zeruiah. Amasa was the son of **Abigail the daughter of Nahash, sister to Zeruiah**. Zeruiah was David's sister (1 Chron. 2:16). Since the father of Abigail and Zeruiah was Nahash rather than Jesse, it would appear that their unnamed mother married Jesse after the death of Nahash.

17:27–29. David was joined by three Transjordanian benefactors who supplied him with foodstuffs. **Shobi the son of Nahash** (v. 27) apparently was the brother of Hanun (see 10:2–4), whom David had defeated earlier in his reign (12:26–31) at **Rabbah of the children of Ammon** (see discussion on 10:3). Earlier, **Machir** had accommodated Mephibosheth in his home (see discussion on 9:4). **Barzillai**, not previously mentioned, is remembered for his generosity (see 19:32; 1 Kings 2:7). After the Babylonian exile, there were claimants to the priesthood among his descendants (see Ezra 2:61–63; Neh. 7:63).

5. Absalom Killed by Joab; David Mourns (18:1–19:8)

18:1–5. Organizing the army into smaller units and into three divisions seems to have been a conventional military maneuver (see Judg. 7:16; 1 Sam. 11:11; 13:17). The three divisions were under the headship of Joab, his brother Abishai, and **Ittai the Gittite** (v. 2). Ittai had joined David earlier and, out of loyalty to the king, had refused to be dismissed to go home (15:18–22). Joab was apparently in overall command in the field (see 18:10–16, 20–2; 19:13).

Knowing that Absalom's primary ambition would be to kill David and thus defeat the army, David's men insisted that he not participate in the field. **Thou shalt not go forth** (v. 3). In addition to the reason given, David was growing old and was no longer the warrior he had been (see discussion on 15:7), which is essentially the same idea that Ahithophel had expressed to Absalom (17:2).

David's final order to the three commanders, given in the hearing of all (18:12), was not a word of military strategy from the commander in chief but a plea of compassion from a loving father. **Deal gently for my sake with ... Absalom** (v. 5). David's love for his (now) oldest son was undying, and was almost his undoing (see 19:5–7).

18:6–8. The battle between **the people** (i.e., David's men; v. 6) and **Israel** (i.e., Absalom's army; see 15:13; 16:15; 17:4, 11, 24–26) began in an open field and moved to the **wood of Ephraim**. The battle site apparently was located in Gilead, east of the Jordan (see 17:24, 26). Why this area was termed the "wood of Ephraim" is not clear. Perhaps the term stemmed from an Ephraimite claim on the area (see Judg. 12:1–4). The terrain apparently was very rugged (see 18:17), for it proved unkind to Absalom's troops. **The battle was there scattered** (v. 8). The armies apparently became dispersed, and many of the men got lost in the forest.

18:9–17. Unlike David, his father, Absalom participated in the battle, as Hushai had counseled him (17:11). Absalom was riding **a mule** (v. 9; see discussion on 13:29) when he encountered some of David's men, and **his head caught hold of the oak**. Whether by the entanglement of his abundant hair (14:26) or by some other means is not stated, but in the end, his pride in his handsome head (see 14:25) was, ironically, his undoing.

Joab was displeased that Absalom had been found but not killed. **I would have given thee ten shekels of silver** (v. 11). Joab must be referring to an announced intent on his part to reward anyone that killed Absalom. The unscrupulous Joab's actions and interests did not always coincide with David's wishes (see discussion on 2:13). After Joab had stabbed Absalom with **three darts ... through the heart** (v. 14) and he continued to live, ten other men beat him and **slew him** (v. 15). Killing Absalom was the easiest and most certain way of ending the rebellion, but the brutal overkill was indicative of the deep animosity that David's men felt toward Absalom. Their contempt for Absalom was also shown by dumping his body **into a great pit** (v. 17) and then piling a **great heap of stones upon him**. This mound of rocks mocked the monument that Absalom himself had erected (18:18). With a leader fallen, **all Israel** (v. 17; see discussion on 18:6) fled the scene.

18:18. To perpetuate his own memory, Absalom had **reared up for himself a pillar** (as Saul had done, 1 Sam. 15:12) in the **king's dale**, that is, a valley thought to be located near Jerusalem (see Gen. 14:17; Josephus *Antiquities* 7.10.3). **I have no son**. Apparently, Absalom's three sons (see 14:27 and discussion) had all died early in life. The pillar was called **Absalom's place**, but it is not to be confused with the monument of the same name that was erected much later and that is still visible today in the valley east of Jerusalem.

18:19–32. Ahimaaz the son of Zadok (v. 19; see 15:27; 17:17–21) was an eager runner and wished to run to David with news of the battle's outcome. **Thou shalt not bear tidings this day** (v. 20). The choice of a messenger depended on the content of the message (see v. 27 and discussion). Joab's reluctance to send Ahimaaz may indicate that he feared a reaction similar to when David received word concerning Saul's death (see 1:2–16) and Ish-bosheth's death (4:8–12).

Cushi (v. 21), not a personal name, but "the Cushite," was an unnamed alien from Cush (see discussions on Gen. 10:6–8) whom Joab dispatched, instead of Ahimaaz, with the official news of Absalom's defeat.

Ahimaaz ... cometh with good tidings (v. 27). David presumed that Joab would not have sent someone like Ahimaaz to carry bad news (see v. 20 and discussion). **All is well** (v. 28). While Ahimaaz evaluated the result of the battle, David awaited word concerning Absalom and asked directly about his welfare. Ahimaaz's answer, **I saw a great tumult** (v. 29), avoided a direct answer to David's question, though he knew Absalom was dead. When the Cushite arrived, his message was indirect, but it was clearly intended to reveal that Absalom was dead.

18:33. O my son Absalom ... my son. David's personal lament differed from his public laments for Saul and Jonathan (1:9–27) and Abner (3:33–34).

It was simply a cry of grief, calling out the name of his son. This is one of the most moving expressions in all literature of a father's love for a son—in spite of all that Absalom had done. Unquestionably, David's grief was compounded by his knowledge that Absalom's death was one of the continuing tragic consequences of his sin with Bathsheba.

19:1–8. David's mourning the death of his rebel son probably came as no surprise to Joab, who had earlier witnessed David's curious and unexpected reaction the deaths of his rivals (1:15–27; 3:31–39; 4:12). This time, however, Joab took offense at David's mourning. **Joab came ... to the king** (v. 5), apparently confident that the king was unaware of his part in Absalom's death. David never indicated that he had learned of it (see 1 Kings 2:5).

Thou hast shamed ... the faces of all thy servants (v. 5). Joab boldly rebuked David for allowing his personal grief to keep him from expressing his appreciation for the loyalty of those who risked their lives to preserve his throne. Joab warned David that his love for Absalom could still undo him. If he did not quickly honor those who had endangered their lives for him, he was at risk of an even greater insurrection (perhaps led by Joab himself?). David yielded to Joab's most emphatic political warning and assumed his royal position **in the gate** (v. 8) to be near his men.

6. David Returns to Jerusalem (19:9–43)

19:9–10. With Absalom dead, the northern tribes found themselves in an awkward situation, having sided with the rebel against David. **The king saved us** (v. 9). Remembering David's former accomplishments on their behalf (see 3:17–18; 5:2), the northern tribes realized that the only sensible thing to do was to restore him to power.

19:11–15. Judah was slow to receive David back. They were shamed by the fact that the northern tribes welcomed him back before his own tribe and kin did. They were undoubtedly embarrassed that they had withdrawn their loyalty from David to promote Absalom's rebellion. The priests Zadok and Abiathar were called on to help bring reconciliation.

Speak unto the elders of Judah (v. 11). The rebellion had begun in Hebron, in Judah (see 15:9–12). Now David rebuked the elders of his own tribe for being the last to restore him to the throne in Jerusalem (see 2:4; 1 Sam. 30:26). This appeal produced the desired result, but it also led to the arousal of tribal jealousies (see 19:41–42).

David made a conciliatory move to the former supporters of Absalom. Although **Amasa** (v. 13; see 17:25 and discussion) deserved death for treason, David appointed him commander of his army in place of Joab. Knowing that Amasa had great influence in Judah, David hoped to secure the allegiance of those who had followed Amasa. **God do so to me, and more also** is a curse formula (see discussion on 1 Sam. 3:17) emphasizing his resolve to demote Joab, who had disregarded David's orders to treat Absalom gently.

He bowed (i.e., "he won over") **the heart ... of Judah** (v. 14). It is unclear who did the winning over, David or Amasa. It is possible that Amasa immediately used his influence to win back support for David. Judah responded favorably and met David at **Gilgal** (v. 15; see discussion on Josh. 4:19) to assist him in crossing the Jordan River.

19:16–23. Accompanying the men of Judah who welcomed David's return was the Benjamite Shimei, who had cursed David (16:5–13), and **a thousand men of Benjamin** (v. 17). No doubt they feared that their tribe might be implicated in Shimei's deed and be suspected of conspiracy against the king. **Thy servant doth know that I have sinned** (v. 20). Shimei's guilt was common knowledge; he could only seize the most appropriate time to plead for mercy. He tried to be first to welcome David home, ahead of those from **the house of Joseph**, which was a common way of referring to the northern tribes (see 1 Kings 11:28; Ezek. 37:19; Amos 5:6; Zech. 10:6), of which Ephraim and Manasseh (sons of Joseph) were the most prominent (see Num. 26:28; Josh. 18:5; Judg. 1:22).

Abishai (v. 21; see 16:9; see also discussion on 1 Sam. 26:6) was ready to avenge by death Shimei's earlier maltreatment of **the LORD's anointed** (see discussion on 1 Sam. 9:16; 1 Sam. 24:6; 26:9–11; Exod. 22:28; 1 Kings 21:10). David seized the opportunity to heal the breach between Judah and the other tribes, especially Benjamin, and ignored the revengeful Abishai and permitted Shimei to live. **Shall there any man be put to death this day in Israel?** (v. 22). It was to be a day for general amnesty (see 1 Sam. 11:13). **Thou shall not die** (v. 23). David kept his pledge; he would not himself avenge the wrong committed against him (see discussion on 1 Sam. 25:2–44). On his deathbed, however, he instructed Solomon to take Shimei's case in hand (1 Kings 2:8–9, 36–46).

19:24–30. An unkempt **Mephibosheth** (v. 24; see 9:6–13) also arrived, his appearance depicting his concern for David's safety and welfare. **Wherefore wentest not thou with me ...?** (v. 25). David remembered Ziba's previous allegations (see 16:3). Mephibosheth explained that he had been confined to Jerusalem because he was **lame** (v. 26; see 4:4; 9:3) and that Ziba **hath slandered thy servant** (v. 27; see 16:3). With a mixture of flattery and appeal, he addressed the king **as an angel of God** (see 14:17 and discussion), asking David to **do therefore what is good in thine eyes**. Mephibosheth discreetly requested David to reconsider the grant of his property to Ziba (see 16:4).

Divide the land (v. 29). Faced with conflicting testimony that could not be corroborated, David withheld judgment as to who actually lied and ordered the division of Saul's estate. His compromise of two earlier decisions (9:9; 16:4) indicates certain uneasiness about both men's integrity.

19:31–40. Barzillai (v. 31; see discussion on 17:27), who had generously supplied David with food in his temporary exile, also greeted David upon his return. He declined David's invitation, however, to accompany him to Jerusalem, where he would be cared for in his old age. **Can I discern between good and evil ...?** (v. 35). Being eighty years old, he would be indifferent to all the pleasures of the court. He asked that the favor be granted instead to **Chimham** (v. 37), who likely was a son of Barzillai (see 1 Kings 2:7).

19:41–43. Unfortunately, David's efforts at reconciliation promoted quarreling between Judah and the other tribes as to who was the most loyal to the king or who had the greater claim on him. **Why have ... the men of Judah stolen thee away, and have brought the king ... over Jordan?** (v. 41). It seems that the Jordan was a kind of psychological border of the land of Israel (see Josh. 22:19, 25; Judg. 12:4), which may also explain why Ish-bosheth (2:8), Mephibosheth (9:4), and even David himself (17:22) had sought refuge on the other side. That being the case, the protest of the Israelites may have been that the Judahites had not waited for all Israel to assemble before bringing David across the Jordan, thus leaving the Israelites in a bad light, as though they were reluctant to receive the king back (see v. 43).

The ten tribes, excluding Judah and Simeon (see discussion on 2:4), claimed, **We have ten parts in the king ... more right in David** (v. 43). The grounds for this assertion may be that the Lord had chosen David to reign in the place of Saul (see 3:17–18; 5:2). Sadly, the tension would lead to another rebellion.

C. Sheba's Revolt (chap. 20)

20:1–2. The dispute over the claim to David (19:41–43) led to a new rebellion. Present at that time in Gilgal (19:40–43) was **Sheba** (v. 1), one who is described as a **man of Belial**, that is, a worthless fellow (see discussion on Deut. 13:13). He was a descendant of **Bichri**, Benjamin's second son (Becher, Gen. 46:21; 1 Chron. 7:6–9), and was a **Benjamite**. Tribal jealousy still simmered over the transfer of the royal house from Benjamin (Saul's tribe) to Judah. **We have no part in David**. Sheba angrily appealed to the Israelite suspicion that David favored his own tribe, Judah, over the other tribes (see 1 Kings 12:16). His appeal was so effective that **every man of Israel** (v. 2), that is, those referred to in 19:41–43, followed him, leaving only the tribe of Judah supporting David. A new rebellion had indeed broken out.

20:3. This verse is parenthetical to Sheba's rebellion. After his exile from Jerusalem, David returned to his house. His **ten ... concubines** whom he had left behind and with whom Absalom had publicly engaged in intercourse (see discussions on 15:16; 16:22) continued to receive David's protection and support, but he no longer cohabited with them.

20:4–11. David bypassed Joab and assigned **Amasa** (v. 4; see discussions on 17:25; 19:13) the task of mustering an army from Judah to squelch Sheba's rebellion. When Amasa acted too slowly, David bypassed Joab a second time and turned to **Abishai** (v. 6), Joab's brother, to complete the assignment. **Take thou thy lord's servants**, that is, Joab's men. The intent was to prevent Sheba from escaping to fortified cities.

Joab's men (v. 7; see 18:2) were accompanied by the soldiers. It becomes clear that, although not in command (by the king's order), Joab was obviously the leader recognized by the soldiers (see vv. 7, 11; 20:15). Once more, in a time of crisis, David depended mainly on the small force of professionals, the **Cherethites, and the Pelethites** (see discussion on 8:18) and **the mighty men** (see 23:8–39), many of them non-Israelite, who made up his private army.

20:8–13. The great stone (v. 8) apparently was a well-known landmark in **Gibeon** (see discussion on 2:12). **Amasa went before them**; that is, he also came or arrived later to join the already assembled men (20:7), apparently with some troops (see v. 11). Undoubtedly simmering with anger over his humiliating demotion from his position as captain of the army (19:13), Joab seized an opportunity to reclaim his position. Pretending to embrace his cousin Amasa (1 Chron. 2:16–17), he stabbed him **in the fifth rib** (v. 10; see 2:23; 3:27). For the second time, Joab committed murder to secure his position as commander of David's army (see 1 Kings 2:5–6). Leaving Amasa to wallow in his own blood until he died (v. 12), and in defiance of David's order, Joab reassumed command on his own initiative (see 20:23). **Joab and Abishai his brother** then continued their quest to put down Sheba's rebellion.

He that favoureth Joab, and he that is for David … go after Joab (v. 11). To dispel any idea that Joab was aligned with Sheba's conspiracy, one of Joab's men appealed to Amasa's troops to support Joab if they were truly loyal to David.

20:14–15. Joab pursued Sheba as far as **Abel, and … Beth-maachah** (v. 14), which were located to the north of Dan (see 1 Kings 15:20; 2 Chron. 16:4). Sheba's strategy was to gather as many volunteers for his revolt as possible, but he was obviously afraid to assemble his ragtag army anywhere within close reach of David's men. **The Berites** are otherwise unknown.

20:16–22. A woman from the city informed Joab that the wisdom of the inhabitants of Abel was proverbial. It had often been said that **They … ask counsel at Abel** (v. 18), apparently because it was famous for offering solutions to difficult situations. **I am one of them … a mother in Israel** (v. 19) could refer either literally to the woman speaking to Joab or metaphorically to Abel as a town that produced faithful Israelites; cities were commonly personified as women (see Jer. 50:12; Gal. 4:26). Perhaps unaware of Sheba's presence in the city and of his intentions, the woman rebuked Joab for his attack on a reputable city to destroy **the inheritance of the** Lord (i.e., His people; see discussion on 1 Sam. 10:1).

Joab informed her that Abel was harboring a rebel from **mount Ephraim** (v. 21). Either Sheba, a Benjamite (see 20:1), lived in the tribal territory of Ephraim or this was the designation of a geographical, rather than a strictly tribal, region. Therefore, to save the city and stop a civil war, the woman wisely advised the residents to behead the insurrectionist (for another woman who saved her city, see Judges 9:53). Joab was then able to return **to Jerusalem unto the king** (v. 22), having accomplished his mission.

20:23–26. These royal officials apparently served David during most of his reign (see 8:15–18). **Joab was over all the host of Israel** (v. 23). Though in some disfavor, he held this position until he participated in Adonijah's conspiracy (1 Kings 1:7; 2:28–35). For the **Cherethites and … Pelethites**, see discussion on 8:18.

Adoram was over the tribute (v. 24). This position was not established in the early years of David's reign (see 8:15–16). Adoram (a variant of Adoniram) must have been a late appointee of David since he continued to serve under Solomon (1 Kings 4:6; 5:14) and was eventually killed in the early days of the reign of Rehoboam (1 Kings 12:18; 2 Chron. 10:18). **Tribute** refers to forced labor that was performed primarily by prisoners of war from defeated nations (see Josh. 9:21; 1 Kings 9:15, 20–21). For the position of **recorder**, see discussion on 8:16.

For **Sheva** (v. 25) the **scribe**, also called Seraiah, see discussion on 8:17. For **Zadok and Abiathar** the **priests**, see discussion on 8:17. **The Jairite** (v. 26) is a reference either to Jair of the tribe of Manasseh (Num. 32:41) or to a judge from Gilead (Judg. 10:3, 5). For the term **chief ruler**, see discussion on 8:18.

IV. Final Reflections on David's Reign (chaps. 21–24)

A. David Repays the Gibeonites (21:1–14)

21:1–24:25. This concluding section forms an appendix to 1–2 Samuel and contains additional materials (without concern for chronology) relating to David's reign. While its topical arrangement is striking, it also employs a literary pattern, a-b-c/c-b-a, frequently found in Old Testament literature. The first and last units (21:1–14; 24:1–25) are narratives of two events in which David had to deal with God's wrath against Israel (the first occasioned by an act of Saul, the second by his own act). The second and fifth units (21:15–22; 23:8–39) are accounts of David's warriors (the second much longer than the first). At the center (22:1–23:7) are two songs of David (the first much longer than the second), one of which celebrates David's victories as warrior-king, while the other recalls his role as psalmist (see discussion on 1 Sam. 16:14–17:58). Whether the motivation for this arrangement went beyond aesthetic considerations is unknown. The triumph song of chapter 22 and the song of Hannah in 1 Samuel 2:1–10 clearly form a literary frame enclosing the main composition (see discussion on 1 Sam. 2:1).

21:1–14. This event whereby David will atone for Saul's bloodguilt against the Gibeonites appears to have occurred after David extended kindness to Mephibosheth (chap. 9) and before Absalom's rebellion (16:7–8). This may be the event Shimei referred to in his charge against David regarding the "blood of the house of Saul" (see comment on 16:8).

21:1–3. There was a famine … three years (v. 1). Famines were not uncommon in Palestine (see Gen. 12:10; 26:1; Ruth 1:1), but David sensed a divine reason behind this one and inquired of the Lord (apparently through Zadok and Abiathar, the priests, and the Urim and Thummim; see Num. 27:21). He learned that he had inherited the bloodguilt of something Saul had done: **he slew the Gibeonites**.

The Gibeonites (v. 2) were a **remnant of the Amorites**, a comprehensive name sometimes used to designate all the pre-Israelite inhabitants of Canaan (Gen. 15:16; Josh. 24:18; Judg. 6:10; Amos 2:10). More precisely, the Gibeonites were called Hivites (Josh. 9:7; 11:19). **The children of Israel had sworn unto them**; that is, they had made a pledge in the name of the Lord (Josh. 9:15, 18–26). After Joshua and Israel had destroyed Jericho and Ai, the Gibeonites had deceived Joshua and the elders into entering a covenant relationship (Joshua 9). Saul's action against the Gibeonites is not recorded elsewhere. Could it have occurred early in his reign, when, motivated by an excessive nationalism, if not tribalism, he attempted to rid the territory of Benjamin of the Gibeonites? The Gibeonites did indeed occupy territory partly assigned to Benjamin, and Saul's great-grandfather was known as the "father of Gibeon" (see 1 Chron. 8:29; 9:35).

Could the action which incurred Saul's guilt be the one when in retaliation he attempted to destroy the priests at Nob and ended up smiting the entire city (1 Sam. 22:18–19)? The Gibeonites had earlier been assigned to cut wood and carry water for the altar (Josh. 9:27), and since they were probably in the area, many of them may have fallen victim to Saul's massacre. **Saul sought to slay them** (v. 2). The reason Saul was unsuccessful is not known.

Since the oath sworn to them had been violated, the Gibeonites could rightly call down God's curse on the land. So David wanted to atone for Israel's sin against them so that they could **bless the inheritance of the LORD** (v. 3), that is, bless His people (see discussion on 1 Sam. 10:1).

21:4–6. The Gibeonites did not desire expiation by material payment. **Neither for us shalt thou kill**

any man in Israel (v. 4) might be more clearly rendered, "It is not for us to put to death a man in Israel." Bloodguilt could only be redressed by the shedding of blood, but as subject aliens, the Gibeonites had no right to legal redress against an Israelite. This restriction must have been Saul's since it is contrary to the Mosaic law (see Exod. 22:21; Lev. 19:34; 24:22; Deut. 1:16–17; 24:17; 27:19).

They demanded payment from **the man** (v. 5), that is, Saul, who had tried to destroy them and had driven them from their towns and lands. They specifically asked for **seven of his sons** (i.e., his descendants; v. 6) — seven, because it would represent a full number (seven symbolized completeness) — though many more Gibeonites had been slain. They also asked to hang the bodies of these men for display in **Gibeah**, the place of Saul's residence (see 1 Sam. 10:26).

21:7–9. Saul had violated Israel's oath to the Gibeonites, but because **of the Lord's oath ... between David and Jonathan** (v. 7; see 4:4; 9:1–13; 1 Sam. 18:3; 20:15), David was careful to spare Jonathan's son Mephibosheth. He selected the two sons of **Rizpah** (v. 8), who had been Saul's concubine (see 3:7), and five sons of **Michal** (but see 6:23; the *KJV Study Bible* marginal note on 21:8 reads "Michal's sister"), which she bore to **Adriel**. Two Hebrew manuscripts read "Merab" (see 1 Sam. 18:19). **Barzillai the Meholathite** is not to be confused with Barzillai the Gileadite (17:27; 19:31).

They fell all seven together (v. 9). This nearly extinguished the house of Saul, which God had rejected (see 1 Sam. 13:13–14; 15:23–26). In 1 Chronicles 8:29–39; 9:35–44, no descendants of Saul are listed other than from the line of Jonathan. Killing Saul's grandsons would have helped prevent a possible political revolt later, but this certainly was not David's motivation for compliance with the Gibeonites' demands. Eliminating potential rivals was contrary to David's manner for establishing his throne and to his oath to Saul not to destroy his descendants (1 Sam. 24:21–22). The executions occurred at **the beginning of barley harvest** (v. 9), around the middle of April (see discussion on Ruth 1:22).

21:10–14. Rizpah's **sackcloth** (v. 10) signified her intense mourning (see discussion on Gen. 37:34). She remained by the decomposing corpses of her sons until **water dropped ... out of heaven**, which indicates that drought had been the cause of the famine. Some interpret the rain as the seasonal (early or "first"; see Deut. 11:14) rains that came in November-December. However, it was probably an unseasonable shower that God sent as evidence that the bloodguilt had been expiated and that the judgment on Israel for breaking the oath sworn to the Gibeonites (see 21:1) was now over, and the drought ended.

Impressed by the report of Rizpah's vigil, David had the **bones of Saul and ... Jonathan his son** (v. 12; see 1 Sam. 31:11–13) exhumed and brought to the family tomb in Benjamin. David's final act toward Saul and Jonathan was a deed of deep respect for the king he had honored and the friend he had loved. Perhaps the seven descendants of Saul were buried there also.

B. David's Victories over the Philistines (21:15–22)

21:15–22. These four Philistine episodes (vv. 15–17, 18, 19, 20–21) cannot be chronologically placed with any certainty (see discussion on 21:1–24:25). Each involves a heroic accomplishment by one of David's mighty men, resulting in the death of "the sons of the giant" (see vv. 16, 18, 20, 22).

21:15–17. The giant (v. 16) is *rapha* in Hebrew. In saying the four formidable enemy warriors referred to in this series were "born to the giant in Gath" (21:22), the writer may have been linking them to Deuteronomy 2:10–11, 20–21. In that case, they may have been related to the Anakim (see Josh. 11:21–22). See Genesis 15:19–20, which in its list of ten peoples of Canaan mentions Rephaim but not Anakim, though the Anakim (but not the Rephaim) figure significantly in the accounts of the conquest (Num. 13:22, 28, 33; Deut. 1:28; 9:2; Josh. 14:12, 15; Judg. 1:20).

In the first battle, David was heroically spared by his nephew **Abishai** (v. 17; see 1 Chron. 2:16; discussion on 1 Sam. 26:6). His men determined then that David would no longer join them on the field, **that thou quench not the light of Israel**. Here is a striking metaphor depicting Israel's dependence on David for its security and continuing existence as a nation—its national hope (see 22:29; 23:3–4; 1 Kings 11:36).

21:18. The second battle occurred at **Gob**, probably in the near vicinity of Gezer, where 1 Chronicles 20:4 locates this same battle. **Saph** (called Sippai in 1 Chron. 20:4), another son of the "giant," was killed.

21:19. There is confusion concerning the Philistine hero of the third battle. **Elhanan ... slew the brother of Goliath**. The Hebrew does not include "the brother of." Since it is clear from 1 Samuel 17:50–51 that David killed Goliath, and it is equally clear from 1 Chronicles 20:5 that Elhanan (named here) killed "Lahmi the brother of Goliath," it is possible that an early copyist misread the Hebrew for "Lahmi the brother of " (see 1 Chron. 20:5) as "a Beth-lehemite."

21:20–22. In the fourth battle, another man from Gath **defied Israel** (v. 21), as Goliath had done (1 Sam. 17:10, 25). This time another nephew of David was Israel's hero. His father **Shimea** is also called Shammah (1 Sam. 16:9; 17:13).

C. David's Concluding Song of Praise (chap. 22)

22:1. This song, with minor variations, is preserved also as Psalm 18 (see discussions there). Here it appears as part of the historical narrative of David's reign. Besides an introduction (22:2–4) and conclusion (22:47–51), the song consists of three major sections. The first describes David's deliverance from mortal danger at the hands of his enemies (22:5–20), the second sets forth the moral grounds for God's saving help (22:21–30), and the third recounts the help that the Lord gave him (22:31–46). The song was probably composed shortly after David's victories over foreign enemies (8:1–14) and before his sin with Bathsheba (compare 22:21–25 with 1 Kings 15:5). Despite the reference to his deliverance **out of the hand of all his enemies** (see 8:1–14) and **out of the hand of Saul** (see 1 Sam. 18–31), it

is impossible to determine the precise event that occasioned this psalm.

22:2–4. David was careful to acknowledge that his ultimate security was found in the Lord his God. Nine short synonymous epithets are derived from David's experience in battle and depict God as his protection. Note the personalized "my" with each epithet.

My rock (v. 2) is a figure particularly appropriate to David's experience (see 22:32, 47; 23:3; Deut. 32:4, 15, 18, 31; Pss. 28:1; 31:2; 61:2; 78:35; 89:26; 94:22; 95:1). He had often taken refuge among the rocks of the wilderness (1 Sam. 23:25; 24:2), but he realized that true security was found only in the Lord. The Hebrew word for **fortress** occurs in 5:17; 23:14; 1 Sam. 22:4–5; 24:22, referring to places where David sought refuge.

For **my shield** (v. 3), see 22:31, 36; Genesis 15:1; Deuteronomy 33:29. The **horn** is a symbol of strength (see Deut. 33:17; 1 Sam. 2:1–2; Jer. 48:25; Luke 1:69).

22:5–20. In verses 5–6, David depicts his experiences in poetic figures of mortal danger: **the waves of death** (v. 5) and its parallel, **the floods of ungodly men** (Hebrew for "ungodly men" is *belial*, probably having the meaning of "destruction" here); **the sorrows** (better rendered "cords") **of hell** (v. 6; Hebrew, *sheol*, the place of the dead; see Jonah 2:2) and its parallel, **the snares of death**.

22:7. David's cry was heard by the Lord from **his temple**, that is, from heaven, where He is enthroned as King (see Ps. 11:4; Isa. 6:1; Jonah 2:7).

22:8–16. Like Deborah, who linked Israel's victory over the Canaanites to God's marching out to assist Israel in the conquest (see Judg. 5:4–5), David attributed his deliverance to the theophanic presence and power of God (for other examples, see Deut. 3:2; Ps. 68:7–8; Hab. 3:3–16). As the Creator marched through the land, the earth trembled at the sight of His anger. At His appearance, storms responded, bringing rain, lightning, and thunder to defeat and scatter the enemies of His people.

There went up a smoke out of his nostrils (v. 9). God's power is portrayed in terms similar to those applied to the awesome beast, the Leviathan (Job 41:19–21). **He rode upon a cherub** (v. 11). See Ezekiel 1 and 10, where cherubim are said to be the bearers of the throne of God; see also discussions on Genesis 3:24; 1 Samuel 4:4; Ezekiel 1:5. **The Lord thundered** (v. 14). The reference to thunder as the voice of God is common in the Old Testament (see Psalm 29; Job 37:2–5). Thunder is particularly suited to expressing God's power and majesty.

22:17–20. He sent from above, he took me (v. 17). In these verses, David describes his deliverance, initially in figurative terms (see 22:5) and subsequently in more literal language (vv. 18–20). Summarizing his deliverance, he attributed it to the fact that the Lord **delighted in** him (v. 20). The Hebrew underlying this expression is used in 15:26 and Psalm 22:8 (see Matt. 3:17, "well pleased") and expresses the idea of the sovereign good pleasure and favor of God toward His anointed one (22:51).

22:21–30. In verses 21–25, David refers to the Lord's deliverances as a reward **according to my righteousness** (v. 21). While these statements may give the impression of self-righteous boasting and a meritorious basis for divine favor, in their context, they should be understood as: (1) David's desire to please the Lord in his service as the Lord's anointed (see discussion on 22:51); (2) his recognition that the Lord rewards those who faithfully seek to serve Him. David certainly does not boast of moral perfection, but of devotion and a clear conscience before God. Though David was known to commit grievous sin, God's own final analysis was that David had followed Him "with all his heart," doing "only which was right" (1 Kings 14:8).

Because God responds to man in kind (see Job 34:11; Prov. 3:34), David acknowledges in verses 26–30 that he has experienced the Lord's favor.

Thine eyes are upon the haughty, that thou mayest bring them down (v. 28). These words fit well with David's experience in his conflict with Saul (compare Hannah's song, 1 Sam. 2:3–8).

In 21:17, David is called the "light of Israel," the one through whom God had brought prosperity to the whole land. Here he rightfully declares, **thou art my lamp** (v. 29), for it was truly the Lord who had caused David's life and undertakings to flourish (see Job 18:5–6; 21:17; see also discussion on Ps. 27:1).

22:31–46. His way is perfect (v. 31). The remainder of the song (vv. 31–51) accentuates David's praise to God for His deliverances. Verse 32 is a powerful affirmation of monotheism: there is no God except **the Lord**, and no **rock** (see discussion on 22:2) like Israel's God. He is the one who strengthens, guides, supports, defends, and saves David (vv. 33–37). In verses 38–43, the contrasting pronouns "I" and "thou" are to be noted. David's boast of aggression and prowess in battle derives from his confidence that the Lord would permit no enemy to stand up successfully against His anointed.

22:47–51. The Lord liveth (v. 47). God's interventions and blessings on David's behalf have shown Him to be the living God (see Deut. 5:26). **Blessed be my rock.** David returns full circle in his song to praise the Lord his God, his Rock, his Savior (see 22:2–3). **I will give thanks unto thee, O Lord, among the heathen** (v. 50). For Paul's reference to this vow, see Romans 15:9.

For comments on **his king … his anointed** (v. 51), see discussions on 1 Sam. 2:10; 9:16; 10:25. David refers to himself in the third person in a way that acknowledges the covenantal character of his kingship. The entire song is to be read and understood in the context of David's official capacity as the Lord's anointed (see discussion on 22:21). The mercy shown to David extends to **his seed for evermore.** David speaks here of God's promise through Nathan (see 7:12–16).

D. David's Last Words (23:1–7)

23:1–7. The last words of David (v. 1) are probably to be understood as David's last poetic testimony (in the manner of his psalms), perhaps composed at the time of his final instructions and warnings to his son Solomon (for other "last words," see 1 Kings 2:1–9 and 1 Chron. 23:27).

The Spirit of the Lord spake by me (v. 2). David was conscious of God's Spirit at work in him, enabling him to speak under the Spirit's guidance (see discussions on 2 Tim. 3:16; 2 Peter 1:21). In the New Testament, both Jesus and Peter state that the Spirit of the Lord spoke through His prophet David (Matt. 22:43; Acts 2:29–30).

Identifying God as his **Rock** (v. 3) is consistent with David's theology and experience (see discussions on 22:2, 32) and with the songs of Moses (Deut. 32:4, 15, 18, 30–31) and Hannah (see also 1 Sam. 2:2). **He that ruleth over men must be just.** In brief and vivid strokes, David portrays the ideal theocratic king—to be fully realized only in the rule of David's greater son, Jesus Christ. This prophetic utterance complements that of 7:12–16 and anticipates those of Isaiah 9:7; 11:1–5; Jeremiah 23:5–6; 33:15–16; and Zechariah 9:9.

David contrasts a righteous, God-fearing king—who is likened to the **light of the morning** (v. 4; see Pss. 27:1; 36:9) that appears after the beneficial **rain**—with the wicked ones, who are compared to unwanted thorns (23:6).

Although my house be not so with God (v. 5) is an awkward statement, perhaps better rendered as a question: "Is not my house so with God?"

David views himself as ruling justly and **in the fear of God** (v. 3), and therefore he directs attention to God's covenant with him and his dynasty (see 7:12–16). It is an **everlasting covenant** (v. 5). David expressly calls God's promise to him a covenant that will not be abrogated (see discussions on 7:20, 28; Isa. 55:3; see also Pss. 89:3, 28, 34, 39; 132:11). David is confident that God will be true to His covenant, and he follows with what is probably intended to be another rhetorical question. Concerning his **salvation** and **desire**, will God **make it not to grow?** that is, through David's promised descendants.

But the sons of Belial shall be … thrust away (v. 6). Godless people who have no interest in the righteous king will be destroyed like worthless thorns (see Pss. 2:9; 110:5–6).

E. David's Mighty Men (23:8–39)

23:8–39. See discussion on 21:1–24:25. This list of thirty-seven (see v. 39) of David's most valiant warriors and the description of some of their exploits are paralleled in 1 Chronicles 11:11–41. There the list is expanded by sixteen names (1 Chron. 11:41–47).

23:8–12. The first select group David's men was known as "the three" (v. 9). Foremost was **the Tachmonite that sat in the seat** (v. 8). This phrase should probably be translated as a name, that is, Josheb-basshebeth, a Tachmonite (1 Chron. 11:11 reads "Jashobeam, an Hachmonite," derived from an unknown place-name). **He was chief among the captains.** The Hebrew word rendered "captains" is similar to the word for "three," thus allowing for the translation of "chief among the three," that is, chief of the three men in this most elite group of soldiers. Two groups of three warriors (vv. 8–12; 23:13–23) and one group of thirty warriors (23:24–39) are mentioned (see discussion on 23:39 for the total number of warriors). Perhaps the Tachmonite achieved his ranking by killing **eight hundred** in one encounter. On separate occasions, **Eleazar … the Ahohite** (i.e., a descendant of Ahoah from the tribe of Benjamin; v 9; see 1 Chron. 8:4) and **Shammah** (v. 11) stood their ground while the rest of the troops fled.

23:13–17. On another occasion, **three** men (v. 13), unnamed here, not the same as the "three mighty men" of 23:9 but members of the **thirty chief** (v. 13; see 23:23–24, 39), risked their lives to bring David a drink from the well at Bethlehem. The circumstances of this event suggest that it happened shortly after David had fled from Saul, when men first began to gather to his cause (see 1 Sam. 22:1–4), or shortly after his conquest of Jerusalem (see 2 Sam. 5:17–18). They had come to him at **harvest time** (see 11:1 and discussion) when he had been in the **cave of Adullam** (see 1 Sam. 22:1) and the Philistines were in the valley of **Rephaim** (see 5:18). When David was in the strong**hold** (v. 14; see discussion on 1 Sam. 22:4), his men had overheard his yearning for water from Bethlehem and fetched some for him. Upon receiving the water, however, David did not consider himself worthy of such devotion and sacrifice and made the water a drink offering to the Lord (see Gen. 35:14; 2 Kings 16:13; Jer. 7:18; Hos. 9:4).

23:18–23. Two other men performed extraordinary feats of heroism. **Abishai** (v. 18; see 10:10, 14; 18:2; see also discussion on 1 Sam. 26:6), who killed **three hundred**, was chief among **three**, presumably those referred to in 23:13–17.

Benaiah the son of Jehoiada (v. 20) was commander of the Cherethites and Pelethites, the royal bodyguard (v. 23; 8:18; 20:23), and of the division of troops for the third month of the year (1 Chron. 27:5). He would support Solomon's succession to the throne (1 Kings 1–2) and eventually replace Joab as commander of the army (1 Kings 2:35).

23:24–39. The heroic deeds that gained an entrance for these men into "the thirty" are not mentioned. Though the number is **thirty** (v. 24), only twenty-nine names are listed in verses 24–39. Since the three of 23:13–17 are also included in the thirty (see 23:13), the total number of warriors mentioned is thirty-two. First Chronicles 11:26–47 lists sixteen additional names for this group, so it appears that the list includes the names of replacements for warriors who either dropped out or died. Notable for their appearance here are **Asahel** (v. 24; see 2:18–23), who was killed by Abner (see 2:23); **Eliam** (v. 34), the father of Bathsheba (see 11:3) and the son of David's counselor Ahithophel, who joined in Absalom's conspiracy (see 15:12, 31, 34; 16:20–23; 17:1–23); and **Uriah** (v. 39), the husband of Bathsheba (see 11:3–27). The total of **thirty and seven** is the total number of warriors referred to in 23:8–39, including the three of 23:8–12, the three of 23:13–17, Abishai (23:18–19), Benaiah (23:20–23), and the twenty-nine men whose names are recorded in verses 24–39. Surprisingly absent from any list of David's military elite is his captain Joab.

F. David's Sin in Taking a Census (chap. 24)

24:1–4. Again (v. 1) seems to connect this chapter to chapter 21, where the Lord revealed His anger against Israel in a three-year famine. **The anger of the LORD was kindled against Israel**. The specific reason for the Lord's displeasure is not stated. Because the anger is said to be directed against Israel rather than against David, some have concluded that it was occasioned by the widespread support among the people for the rebellions of Absalom and Sheba against David (see 15:12; 17:11, 24–26; 18:7; 20:1–2), the divinely chosen and anointed theocratic king. This would mean that the events of this chapter are to be placed chronologically shortly after those of chapters 15–20, thus after 980 BC (see discussion on 15:7). **The LORD ... moved David against them**. First Chronicles 21:1 says that Satan inspired David to take the census. Although Scripture is clear that God does not cause anyone to sin (James 1:13–15), it is also clear that man's, and Satan's, evil acts are under God's sovereign control (see Exod. 4:21; 7:3; 9:12; 10:1, 20, 27; 11:10; 14:4; Josh. 11:20; 1 Kings 22:22–23; Job 1:12; 2:10; Ezek. 3:20; 14:9; Acts 4:28).

Go, number Israel and Judah (v. 1). David's military census (see vv. 2–3) does not appear to have been prompted by any immediate external threat. Since he wanted to **know the number of the people** (v. 2), it is evident that his action was motivated either by pride in the size of the empire he had acquired or by reliance for his security on the size of the manpower he could muster in an emergency or, more likely, both. The mere taking of a census was hardly sinful (see Num. 1:2–3; 26:2–4), but in this instance, it represented an unwarranted glorying in, and dependence on, human power rather than the Lord (not much different from Israel's initial desire to have a king for their security; see 1 Sam. 8–12). Knowing the number of available troops would give David cause to boast and give him a sense of self-sufficiency. The act was uncharacteristic of him (see 1 Sam. 17:26, 37, 45–47; 2 Sam. 22:2–4, 47–51). The census was to be thorough, stretching from **Dan even to Beer-sheba**, two geographical sites often used in Samuel, Kings, and Chronicles to denote the entire land (Dan was located in the far north, and Beersheba in the far south).

Why doth ... the king delight in this thing? (v. 3). David's directive did not go unchallenged. The fact that David did not answer suggests that he knew his reasons were highly questionable. In any event, for once, Joab appears more noble than David, and his challenge rendered David all the more guilty.

24:5–8. Joab's tour for the military census began east of the Jordan, first in the south, then northward, then back across the Jordan, moving from north to south.

24:9. The sum Joab presented to David was **eight hundred thousand ... and ... five hundred thousand**. These figures differ from those of 1 Chronicles 21:5 and have spawned a variety of speculative explanations from scholars, but none that is entirely satisfactory (see discussions on 1 Chron. 21:5–6).

24:10–14. Smitten with conviction over his grave error of judgment, David confessed, **I have sinned greatly** (v. 10; see discussion on 24:1). For discussions on **the prophet Gad, David's seer** (v. 11), see 1 Samuel 9:9; 22:5.

Go and say unto David (v. 12). See 12:1 and discussion. **I offer thee three things**. Few people in history have been given the opportunity to choose their judgment. The three alternative judgments were all included in the curses that Moses said would come on God's people when they failed to adhere to their covenant obligations (see Deut. 28:15–25).

None of the choices—experiencing famine, fleeing from his enemies, or facing pestilence—could be considered inviting. David had already experienced famine (chap. 21) and had fled from Saul and, most recently, from his own son (chap. 16). **Let me not fall into the hand of man** (v. 14). David, who knew both God and war, knew that even in His anger, God is more merciful than man let loose in the rampages of war (see Ps. 30:5).

24:15–17. The **pestilence** (v. 15) destroyed Israelites from **Dan even to Beer-sheba** (see discussion on 24:2), and then the **angel stretched out his hand upon Jerusalem to destroy it** (v. 16). Angels appear elsewhere in Scripture as instruments of God's judgment (see Exod. 33:2; 2 Kings 19:35; Pss. 35:5–6; 78:49; Matt. 13:41; Acts 12:23). **The LORD repented him of the evil** (see discussion on 1 Sam. 15:29). The Lord was indeed grieved by the calamity upon

His people and stopped the plague. The **threshing-place of Araunah** was located on Mount Moriah, immediately north of David's city and overlooking it. It would later become the site of the temple (see 1 Chron. 22:1; 2 Chron. 3:1). Araunah was a **Jebusite**, a remnant of the people who once occupied the fortified city of Jerusalem (see discussion on 5:6).

Let thine hand ... be against me, and against my father's house (v. 17). Although the people of Israel were not without guilt (see 24:1), David had to come to grips with the far-reaching consequences of his personal sin. He assumed full blame for his own act and acknowledged his responsibility as king for the well-being of the Lord's people. The Lord had entrusted to him the role of shepherd (see 5:2; 7:7–8), but he had betrayed that trust by endangering the very lives of his sheep.

24:18–25. Directed by God to build an altar on Araunah's threshing floor, David went to do **as the LORD commanded** (v. 19). The Lord Himself appointed the atoning sacrifice in answer to David's prayer. David went **to buy the threshingfloor** (v. 21) from Araunah; he did not simply expropriate the property for his royal purposes (see 1 Sam. 8:14). For the purpose of offering **burnt offerings** (v. 24; see Lev. 1:1–17), David bought the threshing floor. He would not accept it as a gift from Araunah. Thus, the later site of the temple (see discussion on 24:16) became the royal property of the house of David. David also purchased **the oxen** from Araunah. In his haste, David could not wait for oxen to be brought from his own herds, some distance away. On the apparent discrepancy of the **fifty shekels of silver** paid to Araunah and the six hundred shekels of gold recorded in 1 Chronicles, see discussion on 1 Chronicles 21:25.

David offered burnt offerings and peace offerings (v. 25; see discussion on 1 Sam. 11:15). Reconciliation and restoration of covenant fellowship were obtained by the king's repentance, intercessory prayer, and offering of sacrifices.

THE FIRST BOOK OF THE KINGS

INTRODUCTION

Title

First and Second Kings (like 1 and 2 Samuel and 1 and 2 Chronicles) are actually one literary work, called in Hebrew tradition simply "Kings." The division of this work into two books was introduced by the translators of the Septuagint (the Greek translation of the Old Testament) and subsequently followed in the Latin Vulgate and most modern versions. In 1448, the division into two sections also appeared in a Hebrew manuscript and was perpetuated in later printed editions of the Hebrew text. Both the Septuagint and the Latin Vulgate further designated Samuel and Kings in a way that emphasized the relationship of these two works (Septuagint: First, Second, Third, and Fourth Book of Kingdoms; Latin Vulgate: First, Second, Third, and Fourth Kings). Together, Samuel and Kings relate the whole history of the monarchy, from its rise under the ministry of Samuel to its fall at the hands of the Babylonians.

The division between 1 and 2 Kings has been made at an appropriate but somewhat arbitrary place, shortly after the deaths of Ahab of the northern kingdom (22:37) and Jehoshaphat of the southern kingdom (22:50). Placing the division at this point causes the account of the reign of Ahaziah of Israel to overlap the end of 1 Kings (22:51–53) and the beginning of 2 Kings (chap. 1). The same is true of the narration of the ministry of Elijah, which for the most part appears in 1 Kings (chaps. 17–19). However, Elijah's final act of judgment and the passing of his cloak to Elisha at the moment of his ascension to heaven in a whirlwind are contained in 2 Kings (1:1–2:17).

Author, Date, and Sources

There is little conclusive evidence as to the identity of the author of 1–2 Kings. Although Jewish tradition credits Jeremiah, few today accept this as likely. Whoever the author was, it is clear that he was familiar with the book of Deuteronomy, as were many of Israel's prophets. It is also clear that he used a variety of sources in compiling his history of the monarchy. Three such sources are named: "the book of the acts of Solomon" (11:41), "the book of the chronicles of the kings of Israel" (14:19), "the book of the chronicles of the kings of Judah" (14:29). It is likely that other written sources were also employed (such as those mentioned in Chronicles; see below).

Although some scholars have concluded that the three sources specifically cited in 1–2 Kings are to be viewed as official court annals from the royal archives in Jerusalem and Samaria, this is by no means certain. It seems at least questionable whether official court annals would have included details of conspiracies such as those referred to in 16:20 and 2 Kings 15:15. It is also questionable whether official court annals would have been readily accessible for public scrutiny, as the author clearly implies in his references to them. Such considerations have led some scholars to conclude that these sources were probably records of the reigns of the kings of Israel and Judah compiled by the succession of Israel's prophets spanning the kingdom period. First and Second Chronicles makes reference to a number of such writings: "in the book of Samuel the seer, and in the book of Nathan the prophet, and in the book of Gad the seer" (1 Chron. 29:29), "the prophecy of Ahijah the Shilonite" and "the visions of Iddo the seer" (2 Chron. 9:29), "the book of Shemaiah the prophet" (2 Chron. 12:15), "the book of Jehu the son of Hanani" (2 Chron. 20:34), "the story of the book of the kings" (2 Chron. 24:27), the "acts of Uzziah [Hezekiah] ... did Isaiah the prophet, the son of Amoz, write" (2 Chron. 26:22; see also 2 Chron. 32:32) — and there may have been others. It is most likely, for example, that for the ministries of Elijah and Elisha, the author depended on a prophetic source (perhaps from the eighth century) that had drawn up an account of those two prophets in which they were already compared with Moses and Joshua.

Some scholars place the date of composition of 1–2 Kings in the time subsequent to Jehoiachin's release from prison (562 BC; 2 Kings 25:27–30) and prior to the end of the Babylonian exile (538 BC). This position is challenged by others on the basis of statements in 1–2 Kings that speak of certain things in the preexilic period that are said to have continued in existence "unto this day" (e.g., the poles used to carry the ark, 8:8; conscripted labor, 9:20–21; Israel in rebellion against the house of David, 12:19; Edom in rebellion against the kingdom of Judah, 2 Kings 8:22). From such statements, it is argued that the writer must have been a person living in Judah in the preexilic period rather than in Babylon in postexilic times. If this argument is accepted, one must conclude that the original book was composed about the time of the death of Josiah and that the material pertaining to the time subsequent to his reign was added during the exile, circa 550 BC. While this "two-edition" viewpoint is possible, it rests largely on the "unto this day" statements.

An alternative is to understand these statements as those of the source used by the author rather than as statements of the author himself. A comparison of 2 Chronicles 5:9 with 1 Kings 8:8 suggests that this is a legitimate conclusion. Chronicles is clearly a postexilic writing, yet the wording of the statement concerning the poles used to carry the ark ("there it is unto this day") is virtually the same as it is in Kings. Probably the Chronicler was simply quoting his source, namely, 1 Kings 8:8. There is no reason that the author of 1–2 Kings could not have done the same thing in quoting from his earlier sources. This explanation allows for positing a single author living in exile and using the source materials at his disposal.

Theme

First and Second Kings describes the history of Israel's monarchy from the closing days of the rule of David until the time of the Babylonian exile. After an extensive account of

Solomon's reign, the narrative records the division of the kingdom and then, by means of its synchronistic accounts, presents an interrelated picture of developments within the two kingdoms.

Kingship in the northern kingdom was plagued with instability and violence. Twenty rulers represented nine different dynasties during the approximately 210 years from the division of the kingdom (930 BC) until the fall of Samaria (722–721 BC). The southern kingdom also had twenty rulers, but these were all descendants of David (except Athaliah, whose usurping of the throne interrupted the sequence for a few years) and spanned a period of about 345 years, from the division of the kingdom until the fall of Jerusalem in 586.

First and Second Kings contain no explicit statement of purpose or theme. Reflection on its content, however, reveals that the author has selected and arranged his material in a manner that provides a sequel to the history found in 1–2 Samuel—a history of kingship regulated by covenant. In general, 1–2 Kings describes the history of the kings of Israel and Judah in the light of God's covenants. The guiding thesis of the book is that the welfare of Israel and her kings depended on their obedience to their obligations as defined in the Mosaic covenant.

It is clearly not the author's intention to present a socio-politico-economic history of Israel's monarchy in accordance with the principles of modern historiography. The author repeatedly refers the reader to other sources for more detailed information about the reigns of the various kings (see, e.g., 11:41; 14:19, 29; 15:7, 31; 16:5, 14, 20, 27), and he gives a covenantal rather than a social, political, or economic assessment of their reigns. From the standpoint of a political historian, Omri would be considered one of the more important rulers in the northern kingdom. He established a powerful dynasty and made Samaria the capital city. According to the Moabite Stone (see chart, *Zondervan KJV Study Bible*, p. xix), Omri was the ruler who subjugated the Moabites to the northern kingdom. Long after Omri's death, Assyrian rulers referred to Jehu as the "son of Omri" (either mistakenly or merely in accordance with their literary conventions when speaking of a later king of a realm). Yet in spite of Omri's political importance, his reign is dismissed in six verses (16:23–28), with the statement that he "wrought evil in the eyes of the LORD, and did worse than all that were before him" (16:25). Similarly, the reign of Jeroboam II, who presided over the northern kingdom during the time of its greatest political and economic power, is treated only briefly (2 Kings 14:23–29).

Another example of the writer's covenantal rather than merely political or economic interest can be seen in the description of the reign of Josiah of Judah. A detailed description is given of the reformation and renewal of the covenant that he promoted in his eighteenth year as king (2 Kings 22:3–23:28), but nothing is said about the early years of his reign. Nor is anything said of the motives leading Josiah to oppose Pharaoh Nechoh of Egypt at Megiddo, or of the major shift in geopolitical power from Assyria to Babylon, which was connected with Josiah's opposition to Nechoh (see discussions on 2 Kings 23:29–30).

It becomes apparent, then, that the kings who receive the most attention in 1–2 Kings are those whose reigns saw either a notable deviation from or a notable affirmation of the covenant (or a significant interaction between a king and God's prophet; see below). Ahab son of Omri is an example of the former (17:1–22:39). His reign is given extensive treatment, not so much because of its extraordinary political importance but because of the serious threat to covenant fidelity and continuity that arose in the northern kingdom during his reign. Ultimately, the pagan influence of Ahab's wife, Jezebel, through Ahab's daughter Athaliah (whether she was Jezebel's daughter is unknown), nearly led to the extermination of the house of David in Judah (see 2 Kings 11:1–3).

Manasseh (2 Kings 21:1–18) is an example of a similar sort. Again, in the account of his reign, a deviation from the covenant is emphasized rather than political features, such as involvement in the Assyrian-Egyptian conflict (mentioned in Assyrian records but not in 2 Kings). The extreme apostasy characterizing Manasseh's reign made exile for Judah inevitable (2 Kings 21:10–15; 23:26–27).

On the positive side, Hezekiah (2 Kings 18:1–20:21) and Josiah (2 Kings 22:1–23:29) are given extensive treatment because of their involvement in covenant renewal. These are the only two kings given unqualified approval by the writer for their loyalty to the Lord (2 Kings 18:3; 22:2). It is noteworthy that it is said of all the kings of the northern kingdom that they "did evil in the eyes of the LORD" and "walked in the ways of Jeroboam," who caused Israel to sin (see, e.g., 16:26, 31; 22:52; 2 Kings 3:3; 10:29). Jeroboam established the golden-calf worship at Bethel and Dan shortly after the division of the kingdom (see 12:26–33; 13:1–6).

While the writer depicts Israel's obedience or disobedience to the Sinai covenant as being decisive for her historical destiny, he also recognizes the far-reaching historical significance of the Davidic covenant, which promised that David's dynasty would endure forever. This is particularly noticeable in references to the "lamp" (or "light") that the Lord had promised David (see 11:36; 15:4; 2 Kings 8:19; see also discussion on 2 Sam. 21:17). It also appears in more general references to the promise to David (8:20, 25) and its consequences for specific historical developments in Judah's later history (11:12–13, 32; 2 Kings 19:34; 20:6). In addition, the writer uses the life and reign of David as a standard by which he measures the lives of later kings (see, e.g., 9:4; 11:4, 6, 33, 38; 14:8; 15:3, 5, 11; 2 Kings 16:2; 18:3; 22:2).

Another prominent feature of the narratives of 1–2 Kings is the emphasis on the relationship between prophecy and fulfillment in the historical developments of the monarchy. On at least eleven occasions, a recorded prophecy is later said to have been fulfilled (see, e.g., 2 Sam. 7:13 and 1 Kings 8:20; 1 Kings 11:29–39 and 1 Kings 12:15; 1 Kings 13 and 2 Kings 23:16–18). The result of this emphasis is that the history of the kingdom is presented not as a chain of chance occurrences or as the mere interplay of human actions but as the unfolding of Israel's historical destiny under the guidance of an omniscient and omnipotent God—Israel's covenant Lord, who rules all history in accordance with His sovereign purposes (see 8:56; 2 Kings 10:10).

The author also stresses the importance of the prophets themselves in their role as official emissaries from the court of Israel's covenant Lord, the Great King to whom Israel and her king were bound in service through the covenant. The Lord sent a long succession of such prophets to call the king and the people back to covenant loyalty (2 Kings 17:13). For the most part, the prophets' warnings and exhortations fell on deaf ears. Many of these prophets and prophetesses are mentioned in the narratives of 1–2 Kings (see, e.g., Ahijah, 11:29–40; 14:5–18; Shemaiah, 12:22–24; Micaiah, 22:8–28; Jonah, 2 Kings 14:25; Isaiah,

2 Kings 19:1–7, 20–34; Huldah, 2 Kings 22:14–20), but particular attention is given to the ministries of Elijah and Elisha (1 Kings 17–19; 2 Kings 1–13).

Reflection on these features of 1–2 Kings suggests that it was written to explain to a people in exile that the reason for their condition of humiliation was their stubborn persistence in breaking the covenant. In bringing the exile upon His people, God, after much patience, imposed the curses of the covenant, which had stood as a warning to them from the beginning (see Lev. 26:27–45; Deut. 28:64–68). This is made explicit with respect to the captivity of the northern kingdom in 2 Kings 17:7–23; 18:10–12, and to the southern kingdom in 2 Kings 21. The reformation under Josiah in the southern kingdom is viewed as too little, too late (see 2 Kings 23:26–27; 24:3).

The book, then, provides a retrospective analysis of Israel's history. It explains the reasons both for the destruction of Samaria and Jerusalem and their respective kingdoms and for the bitter experience of being forced into exile. This does not mean, however, that there was no hope for the future. The writer consistently keeps the Lord's promise to David in view as a basis on which Israel in exile could look to the future with hope rather than with despair. In this connection, the final four verses of the book, reporting Jehoiachin's release from prison in Babylon and his elevation to a place of honor in the court there (2 Kings 25:27–30), take on added significance. The future would remain open for a new work of the Lord, in faithfulness to His promise to the house of David.

It is important to note that, although the author was undoubtedly a Judahite exile, and although the northern kingdom had been dispersed for well over a century and a half at the time of his writing, the scope of his concern was all Israel—the whole covenant people. Neither he nor the prophets viewed the division of the kingdom as an excommunication of the ten tribes, nor did they see the earlier exile of the northern kingdom as a final exclusion of the northern tribes from Israel's future.

Chronology

First and Second Kings presents the reader with abundant chronological data. Not only is the length of each king's reign given, but during the period of the divided kingdom, the beginning of each king's reign is synchronized with the regnal year of the ruling king in the opposite kingdom. Additional data, such as the age of the ruler at the time of his accession, is often provided as well.

By integrating biblical data with that of Assyrian chronological records, the year 853 BC can be fixed as the year of Ahab's death, and the year 841 as the year Jehu began to reign. The years in which Ahab and Jehu had contacts with Shalmaneser III of Assyria can also be given definite dates (by means of astronomical calculations based on an Assyrian reference to a solar eclipse). With these fixed points, it is then possible to work both forward and backward in the lines of the kings of Israel and Judah to give dates for each king. By the same means, it can be determined that the division of the kingdom occurred in 930 BC, that Samaria fell to the Assyrians in 722–721 BC, and that Jerusalem fell to the Babylonians in 586 BC.

The synchronistic data correlating the reigns of the kings of Israel and Judah present some knotty problems, which have long been considered nearly insoluble. In more recent times, most of these problems have been resolved in a satisfactory way through recognizing such possibilities as overlapping reigns, coregencies of sons with their fathers, differences in the time of the year in which the reign of a king officially began, and differences in the way a king's first year was reckoned (e.g., see discussions on 15:33; 2 Kings 8:25; see also chart, *KJV Study Bible*, pp. 478–79).

Outline

First and Second Kings can be broadly outlined by relating their contents to the major historical periods they describe and to the ministries of Elijah and Elisha. See also 2 Kings, Introduction: "Outline."

5. Elijah Condemns Ahab for Seizing Naboth's Vineyard (chap. 21)
6. Micaiah Prophesies Ahab's Death; Its Fulfillment (22:1-40)
   B. Jehoshaphat of Judah (22:41-50)
   C. Ahaziah of Israel (22:51-53)

Bibliography

Davis, John J., and John C. Whitcomb. *Israel: From Conquest to Exile: A Commentary on Joshua-2 Kings.* Grand Rapids, MI: Baker, 1989.

DeVries, Simon J. *1 Kings.* Word Biblical Commentary 12. Waco, TX: Word, 1985.

Gray, John. *I and 2 Kings: A Commentary.* Old Testament Library. Philadelphia: Westminster, 1963.

House, Paul R. *1, 2 Kings.* New American Commentary. Nashville: Broadman and Holman, 1995.

Jones, Gwilym H. *1 and 2 Kings.* Century Bible Commentary. Grand Rapids, MI: Eerdmans, 1984.

Long, Burke O. *1 Kings, with an Introduction to Historical Literature.* Forms of the Old Testament Literature 9. Grand Rapids, MI: Eerdmans, 1984.

Patterson, R. D., and Herman Austel. "1, 2 Kings." In *The Expositor's Bible Commentary,* edited by Frank E. Gaebelein, vol. 4. Grand Rapids, MI: Zondervan, 1992.

Provan, Iain W. *1 and 2 Kings.* New International Biblical Commentary. Vol. 7. Peabody, MA: Hendrickson, 1995.

Thiele, Edwin R. *The Mysterious Numbers of the Hebrew Kings.* New revised edition. Grand Rapids, MI: Zondervan, 1983.

Wiseman, Donald J. *1 and 2 Kings: An Introduction and Commentary.* Tyndale Old Testament Commentaries 9. Downers Grove, IL: InterVarsity, 1993.

EXPOSITION

I. The Solomonic Era (1:1-12:24)

A. Solomon's Succession to the Throne (1:1-2:12)

1:1-12:24. The narrative of the Solomonic era is an exquisite example of literary inversion, in this case consisting of nine sections. The first and last are parallel, as well as the second and eighth, and so on. The fifth section, which occupies the central position in the structure, is the longest of the nine and describes Solomon's building projects (see Introduction: "Outline").

1:1-4. David was old and stricken in years (v. 1), and his health began to fail. Second Samuel 5:4 indicates that David died at about seventy years of age (see 1 Kings 2:11). The form of diatherapy recommended by his servants, whereby a healthy body was used to warm a sickly one, was not uncommon. The **young virgin** (v. 2) that was brought to David was **Abishag a Shunammite** (v. 3); that is, she was from Shunem (2 Kings 4:8; Josh. 19:18; 1 Sam. 28:4; probably to be identified with modern Solem), which was located near the plain of Jezreel in the tribal territory of Issachar. Abishag is called a concubine in 2:13 – 25, but her relationship to the king was as his companion and personal nurse. He **knew her not** (v. 4); that is, he had no intimate relations with her. This is significant in connection with Adonijah's request to be given Abishag as his wife after the death of David (see discussions on 2:17, 22).

1:5 – 6. Adonijah (v. 5) was the fourth son of David (see 2 Sam. 3:4), who was at this time approximately thirty-five years of age. It is likely that he was the oldest surviving son of David (see discussion on 2 Sam. 13:28; see also 2 Sam. 18:14). Since no precedent had been set in Israel for succession to the throne, on the grounds of primogeniture, Adonijah **exalted himself**. This was a unilateral attempt to usurp the throne, bypassing King David's right to designate his own successor (Adonijah must have at least known that his father favored Solomon; see 1:10). If successful, it would have thwarted God's and David's choice of Solomon (see 1:13, 17, 30; 1 Chron. 22:9 – 10; see also discussion on 2 Sam. 12:25). Following the example of Absalom before him, Adonijah had **chariots ... horsemen ... and fifty men to run before him** (see discussion on 2 Sam. 15:1).

Three reasons are given for his behavior: (1) He was a spoiled child because his father **had not displeased him** (v. 6). David appears to have been consistently negligent in disciplining his sons (see discussions on 2 Sam. 13:21; 14:33). (2) Like Absalom, he was **very goodly**. Attractive physical appearance was an important asset to an aspirant to the throne (see 1 Sam. 9:2; 16:12; 2 Sam. 14:25). (3) He was next in line as heir because he was born **after Absalom**.

1:7 – 10. Adonijah's plot was supported by **Joab the son of Zeruiah** (v. 7; see discussions on 1 Sam. 26:6; 2 Sam. 2:13; 19:13; 20:10, 23). Joab's alignment with Adonijah may have been motivated by a struggle for power with Benaiah (see v. 8; 2 Sam. 8:18; 20:23; 23:20 – 23). Joab held his position more by his standing with the army than by the favor and confidence of David (see 2:5 – 6). **Abiathar the priest** (v. 7), one of the two priests serving at that time (see discussion on 2 Sam. 8:17; 1 Chron. 15:11), also supported Adonijah.

Remaining loyal to David were **Zadok the priest** (v. 8; see discussion on 2 Sam. 8:17), **Benaiah the son of Jehoiada** (see discussion on 2 Sam. 23:20), **Nathan the prophet** (see 2 Sam. 12:1 – 25), and **Shimei, and Rei**. This is not the Shimei of 2:8, 46 (and 2 Sam. 16:5 – 8) but is perhaps the same as "Shimei the son of Elah" (4:18). "Rei" may mean "and his friends," that is, the friends of Shimei. If Rei is a proper name, this is its only occurrence in the Old Testament. **The mighty men which belonged to David** (see 2 Sam. 23:8 – 39) also remained true.

1:9. Adonijah slew sheep (v. 9). Adonijah's self-coronation was solemnized by the sacrificing of animals on the **stone of Zoheleth** (i.e., the "serpent's stone") near **En-rogel** (i.e., "the spring of Rogel"), which was located just south of Jerusalem, about two hundred yards south of where the Hinnom and Kidron valleys meet. Choosing a site frequented by those coming for water provided him with an audience for the proceedings. His younger brothers were invited, but Nathan, Benaiah, and Solomon — his rival to the throne — were not invited.

1:11 – 14. That David was unaware of Adonijah's scheme prompted Nathan's intervention on behalf of **Bath-sheba the mother of Solomon** (v. 11). The queen mother held an important and influential position in the royal court (see 2:19; 15:13; 2 Kings 10:13; 2 Chron. 15:16), so he informed her that **Adonijah ... doth reign**. Although the preceding narrative does not relate the actual proclamation of Adonijah's kingship, it can be assumed (see 1:25; 2:15; see 2 Sam. 15:10). **Save thine own life, and the life of thy son Solomon** (v. 12). It was common in the ancient Near East for a usurper to liquidate all potential claimants to the throne in an attempt to secure his own position (see 15:29; 2 Kings 10:6, 11; 11:1). Nathan instructed her to ask of David, **Didst not thou ... swear unto thine handmaid ...?** (v. 13). Although 2 Samuel does not record David's oath concerning the succession of Solomon, it does suggest that Solomon was the son through whom the Lord's promise to David of an eternal dynasty would be carried forward (see discussion on 1:5). That Nathan was aware of the promise supports the opinion that Adonijah and Joab also knew of the promise and were perhaps trying to force the king's hand. Once Adonijah was crowned, perhaps David would renege on his promise to Bathsheba.

1:15–21. As instructed by Nathan, Bathsheba approached David in his chamber. **Thou swarest by the LORD thy God unto thine handmaid** (v. 17). An oath taken in the Lord's name was inviolable (see Exod. 20:7; Lev. 19:12; Josh. 9:15, 18, 20; Judg. 11:30, 35; Eccl. 5:4–7). She explained that Adonijah had already proclaimed himself king. Unless David intervened, Adonijah would retain the kingship. She encouraged David to make an immediate public proclamation that Solomon was to succeed him. She feared that when David would **sleep with his fathers** (v. 21), a conventional expression for death (see Gen. 47:30; Deut. 31:16), she and Solomon would be **counted as offenders**, that is, as criminals, and the consequences would be severe.

1:22–27. At the appropriate moment, Nathan entered and approached David diplomatically by raising a question that revealed the dilemma. Either David had secretly encouraged Adonijah to claim the throne and thereby had broken his oath to Bathsheba and Solomon (see v. 27) or he had been betrayed by Adonijah.

Already the usurper had supporters proclaiming, **God save king Adonijah** (lit., "May the king Adonijah live!"; v. 25), an expression of recognition and acclamation of the new king (see 1 Sam. 10:24; 2 Sam. 16:16; 2 Kings 11:12). Nathan's appearance brought confirmation from a second source and lent credibility to Bathsheba's report.

1:28–31. David recalled Bathsheba and assured her by oath that **Solomon … shall reign after me** (v. 30). In the stereotypic, hyperbolic language of the court (see Neh. 2:3; Dan. 2:4; 3:9; 5:10; 6:21), Bathsheba expressed her gratitude: **Let my lord king David live for ever** (v. 31).

1:32–37. David's quick and firm resolution indicates that despite his ailing physical health, he remained sharp of mind. He called his trusted supporters Zadok, Nathan, and Benaiah (see discussion on 1:8) and charged them, **Take with you the servants of your lord** (v. 33). These presumably included the Cherethites and Pelethites (see 1:38). **Cause Solomon … to ride mine own mule.** Although crossbreeding was forbidden in the Mosaic law (Lev. 19:19), mules (perhaps imported; see Ezek. 27:14) were used in the time of David, at least as mounts for royalty (see 2 Sam. 13:29; 18:9), while commoners rode donkeys. To ride on David's own mule was a public proclamation that Solomon's succession to the throne was sanctioned by David (see Gen. 41:43; Est. 6:7–8). **Gihon** was a spring on the eastern slope of Mount Zion (see discussions on v. 9; 2 Sam. 5:8), a few hundred yards north of where Adonijah was celebrating. This spring was the major water source for the city and a natural place for people to congregate.

Anoint him there king (v. 34; see discussions on 1 Sam. 2:10; 9:16), **blow ye with the trumpet** (see 2 Kings 9:13; 2 Sam. 15:10; 20:1), and proclaim **God save king Solomon** (see discussion on 1:25). David's order thus instituted a temporary coregency. He was making Solomon king **over Israel and over Judah** (v. 35). The distinction between Israel and Judah was rooted in the separate arrangements by which David had become king over these two tribal units (see 2 Sam. 2:4; 5:3).

David's commands met with a hearty approval. **Amen: the LORD … say so too** (v. 36; see Jer. 28:6). Benaiah's stated desire to see Solomon's **throne greater than the throne of … David** (v. 37) was not a deprecation of David's accomplishments but an expression of total loyalty to David and Solomon. Benaiah shared David's own desire for his chosen successor (see 1:47–48).

1:38–40. The Cherethites, and the Pelethites (v. 38), apparently David's personal bodyguards (see discussion on 2 Sam. 8:18), brought Solomon to Gihon, where **Zadok … anointed Solomon** (v. 39). Kings chosen by God who were not in a line of dynastic succession were anointed by prophets (Saul, 1 Sam. 9:16; David, 1 Sam. 16:12; Jehu, 2 Kings 9). Kings who assumed office in the line of dynastic succession were anointed by priests (Solomon, here; Joash, 2 Kings 11:12). The distinction seems to be that the priest worked within the established order, while the prophets introduced new divine initiatives. The **horn of oil**, perhaps containing the anointing oil described in Exodus 30:22–33, was taken from the **tabernacle**, that is, the tent that David had erected in Jerusalem to house the ark (see 2 Sam. 6:17) rather than the tabernacle at Gibeon (see 3:4 and discussion; 2 Chron. 1:3). The blowing of the trumpet alerted the people (see 1:20) that David's choice had been anointed.

1:41–49. Adonijah ... heard it (v. 41). Although Gihon may not have been visible from En-rogel, the distance was not great, and the sound would have carried down the Kidron Valley to where Adonijah's celebration was still in progress. **Joab**, the seasoned warrior, sensed trouble immediately.

Jonathan the son of Abiathar (v. 42), who had served in David's behalf during Absalom's revolt (see 2 Sam. 17:17–21), arrived to report on the noise and happenings at Gihon. Solomon had been anointed king, and David's servants desired to see Solomon's name **better than** David's **name** (v. 47; see discussion on 1:37). David had **bowed himself upon his bed** (see Gen. 7:31) and blessed God for giving him **one to sit on** his **throne** (v. 48). In Solomon's succession to the throne, David saw a fulfillment of the promise given to him in 2 Samuel 7:12, 16.

Upon hearing such an alarming report, all of Adonijah's guests **went every man his way** (v. 49). No one wanted to be identified with Adonijah's abortive coup now that it appeared certain to fail.

1:50–53. Adonijah himself fled and **caught hold on the horns of the altar** (v. 50). The horns of the altar were vertical projections at each corner. The idea of seeking asylum at the altar was rooted in the Pentateuch (see Exod. 21:13–14). The priest smeared the blood of the sacrifice on the horns of the altar (see Exod. 29:12; Lev. 4:7, 18, 25, 30, 34) during the sacrificial ritual. Adonijah thus sought to place his own destiny under the protection of God.

Solomon graciously granted Adonijah a pardon on the condition that **he shew himself a worthy man** (v. 52), that is, that he would recognize and submit to Solomon's office and authority. **If wick-edness shall be found in him,** if he showed evidence of continuing opposition to Solomon's succession to the throne, he would surely die.

2:1–4. The length of Solomon's coregency with David cannot be determined, but before David died, **he charged Solomon his son** (v. 1). Moses (Deut. 31:1–8), Joshua (Josh. 23:1–16), and Samuel (1 Sam. 12:1–25), as representatives of the Lord's rule, had all given final instructions and admonitions shortly before their deaths.

I go the way of all the earth (v. 2), that is, to the grave (see Josh. 23:14). **Be thou strong** (see Deut. 31:7, 23; Josh. 1:6–7, 9, 18). David's successes were all due to his obedience to the word of God; therefore, he admonished his successor to **keep the charge of the Lord thy God** (v. 3; see Gen. 26:5; Lev. 18:30; Deut. 11:1). **Walk in his ways** is a characteristic expression of Deuteronomy for obedience to covenant obligations (Deut. 5:33; 8:6; 10:12; 11:22; 19:9; 26:17; 28:9; 30:16). **His statutes ... commandments ... judgments ... testimonies** are four generally synonymous terms for covenant obligations (see 6:12; 8:58; 2 Kings 17:37; Deut. 8:11; 11:1; 26:17; 28:15, 45; 30:10, 16). Therefore, David challenged Solomon to prosper by observing the requirements of God (see Deut. 29:9; Josh. 1:8).

That the Lord may continue his word ... concerning me (v. 4). David was alluding to the covenanted promise of an everlasting dynasty given to him by God through Nathan the prophet (see discussions on 2 Sam. 7:11–16). Although the covenant promise to David was unconditional, individual participation in its blessing on the part of David's royal descendants was conditioned on obedience to the obligations of the Mosaic covenant (see 2 Chron. 7:17–22). Thus, the condition, **If thy children ... walk before me ... with all their heart and ... soul** (see Deut. 4:29; 6:5; 10:12; 30:6), followed by the promise, **there shall not fail thee ... a man on the throne of Israel.** Sadly, both Solomon and his descendants would fall short of their covenant obligations, which would lead to the division of the kingdom and eventually to the exile of both the northern and southern kingdoms. Only in the coming of Christ would the fallen tent of David be restored (see discussions on Amos 9:11–15; Acts 15:16) and the promise of David's eternal dynasty ultimately fulfilled. When the nation and its king turned away from the requirements of the Sinai covenant, they would experience the covenant curses rather than blessings, but God would remain faithful to His covenant promises to Abraham and to David (see Lev. 26:42–45; Isa. 9:6–7; 11:1–16; 16:5; 55:3; Jer. 23:5–6; 30:9; 33:17, 20–22, 25–26; Ezek. 34:23–24; 37:24–28).

2:5–9. David did not turn vindictive on his deathbed. However, two individuals who were wicked and had disrupted David's reign needed to be punished to guarantee Solomon's success. One was **Joab the son of Zeruiah** (v. 5; see discussion on 1:7). He had murdered **Abner the son of Ner** (see discussions on 2 Sam. 3:25–32) and **Amasa the son of Jether** (see 2 Sam. 20:10). Out of revenge and jealousy, Joab had **shed the blood of war in peace.** His actions had been unlawful assassinations (see Deut. 19:1–13; 21:1–9) and had served only his own self-interest. He had also killed Absalom against David's orders (see 2 Sam. 18:5, 14) and most recently had supported Adonijah's attempt to seize the throne.

In contrast, David instructed Solomon to show kindness to the **sons of Barzillai** (v. 7; see discussion on 2 Sam. 17:27), that they be granted to **eat at thy table,** that is, having a position of honor that brought other benefits as well (see 18:19; 2 Kings 25:29; 2 Sam. 9:7; 19:28; Neh. 5:17).

The other wicked person that needed to be dealt with was **Shimei the son of Gera, a Benjamite** (v. 8) who had cursed David when he fled Absalom (see 2 Sam. 16:5–13). Gera was probably the ancestor of Shimei's particular line of descent rather than his immediate father (see Gen. 46:21; Judg. 3:15). The Hebrew for "son" may mean "descendant," "successor," or "nation." David instructed Solomon, **hold him not guiltless** (v. 9). The Mosaic law prohibited cursing a ruler (21:10; Exod. 22:28). It is clear that Shimei had bitterly rebelled against God in rejecting David, God's anointed, in favor of the house of Saul, whom God had publicly rejected.

2:10–11. David slept with his fathers (v. 10; see discussion on 1:21). The **city of David** is Jerusalem, the Jebusite stronghold that he had conquered and fortified for his centralized government (see 2 Sam. 5:7 and discussion). Peter implied that David's tomb was still known in his day (Acts 2:29). David had reigned for **forty years** (v. 11; see 2 Sam. 5:4–5), having ruled approximately 1010–970 BC (see 1 Samuel, Introduction: "Chronology").

B. Solomon's Throne Consolidated (2:13–46)

2:13–18. Having ascended the throne as the sole monarch, Solomon soon experienced his first test. **Adonijah the son of Haggith** (v. 13; see discussion on 1:5) made an appeal to Solomon through the king's mother. Her question was, **Comest thou peaceably?** The question (see 1 Sam. 16:4; 2 Kings 9:22) reveals Bathsheba's apprehension concerning Adonijah's intention (see 1:5).

The kingdom was mine (v. 15; see 1:11). By right of primogeniture, Adonijah claimed that the kingdom had been his. In his estimation, Israel had been prepared to support him as king. **All Israel set their faces on me, that I should reign.** This was a gross exaggeration (see 1:7–8). He admitted to divine intervention, however. **It was his from the LORD.** Adonijah professed to view Solomon's kingship as God's will and to have no further intentions of seeking the position for himself.

Adonijah's request was simple: **Give me Abishag the Shunammite to wife** (v. 17). From our cultural perspective, Adonijah's request had the appearance of being innocent (but see discussion on 2:22) since Abishag had remained a virgin throughout the period of her care for David (see 1:1–4; Deut. 22:30). Bathsheba agreed to present the request to Solomon.

2:19–21. When his mother approached him, Solomon seated her at his **right hand** (v. 19), the position of honor (see Ps. 110:1; Matt. 20:21). From there, she made her **one small petition** (v. 20). Did Bathsheba not attach any great significance to Adonijah's request, or did she understand his request and was eager to initiate his undoing?

2:22–25. Ask for him the kingdom also (v. 22). Solomon immediately understood Adonijah's request as another attempt to gain the throne. Possession of the royal harem was widely regarded as signifying the right of succession to the throne (see discussions on 2 Sam. 3:7; 12:8; 16:21). Although Abishag was a virgin, she would be regarded by the people as belonging to David's harem, so marriage to Abishag would greatly strengthen Adonijah's claim to the throne. **Ask ... for Abiathar the priest, and for Joab the son of Zeruiah** (see discussion on 1:7). Solomon assumed that Abiathar and Joab continued to be involved in Adonijah's treacherous schemes.

God do so to me, and more also (v. 23) is a curse formula (see discussion on 1 Sam. 3:17), showing Solomon's resolve to have Adonijah killed. Adonijah's request nullified the pardon he had received from Solomon (see 1:52) and forfeited his chance to live. **As the LORD liveth** (another oath formula), **which hath established me** (lit., "has made me a house") ... **as he promised** (v. 24; see 2 Sam. 7:11 and discussion; 1 Chron. 22:9–10). Solomon's own son and successor, Rehoboam, had been born shortly before Solomon became king (see 11:42; 14:21).

Benaiah the son of Jehoiada, who had been head of David's personal bodyguard (see discussions on 1:8; 2 Sam. 23:20), had been promoted to Joab's position as captain of the army in Solomon's administration. It now fell to Benaiah to execute Adonijah for conspiracy.

2:26–27. Abiathar (v. 26), one of the priests and a supporter of Adonijah, was deposed and banned to **Anathoth**, a little Levitical city located within the tribe of Benjamin (see Josh. 21:18), about three miles north of Jerusalem. Much later, this city was the home of the prophet Jeremiah (Jer. 1:1). Abiathar was not executed because of his earlier service to the Lord (**thou barest the ark**; see 2 Sam. 15:24–25, 29; 1 Chron. 15:11–12) and his support of David (**thou hast been afflicted in all wherein my father was afflicted**; see 1 Sam. 22:20–23; 23:6–9; 30:7; 2 Sam. 17:15; 19:11).

During David's reign, two priests had been serving concurrently. One, Zadok, traced his lineage to Aaron's third son, Eleazar (1 Chron. 24:3); the other, Abiathar, traced his lineage through Eli (1 Sam. 1:3) to Aaron's fourth son, Ithamar (see 1 Sam. 14:3; 22:20; 1 Chron. 24:3). From Ezekiel 44:15 and 48:11, it would appear that Zadok (the line of Eleazar) was God's choice for high priest. Solomon's action fulfilled God's promise of punishment **which he spake concerning the house of Eli in Shiloh** (v. 27; see discussions on 1 Sam. 2:30–35).

2:28–35. The **tidings** (v. 28) of Adonijah's death and Abiathar's banishment reached Joab, who had **turned after Adonijah**, that is, supported Adonijah (see 1:7). Joab fled to the **tabernacle of the LORD** (see discussion on 1:39), where he **caught hold on the horns of the altar** (see discussion on 1:50), assuming he would be granted asylum. Solomon commanded Benaiah to **fall upon him** (v. 29), that is, in execution. The right of asylum was extended only to those who had accidentally caused someone's death (see Exod. 21:14). Solomon was completely justified in denying this right to Joab, not only for his complicity in Adonijah's conspiracy but also for his murder of Abner and Amasa (see vv. 31–33). In this incident, Solomon found a suitable occasion for carrying out his father's instruction (see 2:5–6).

Joab's crimes are rehearsed. He **fell upon two men ... and slew them** (v. 32; see 2 Sam. 3:27; 20:9–10). His two victims had been two captains: **Abner ... of the host of Israel** (see 2 Sam. 2:8–9) and **Amasa ... of the host of Judah** (see 2 Sam. 20:4).

Joab **was buried in his own house** (v. 34). The tomb of Joab's father was located near Bethlehem (see 2 Sam. 2:32) in the **wilderness** of Judah, east of Bethlehem.

Solomon then installed **Benaiah the son of Jehoiada** (v. 35; see discussion on 2 Sam. 23:20) as captain to replace Joab, and he made **Zadok the priest** (see discussions on 1 Sam. 2:35; 2 Sam. 8:17).

2:36–46. One last political threat remained: **Shimei** (v. 36; see discussion on 2:8–9). Therefore, Solomon stipulated that Shimei **build ... a house in Jerusalem** and stay there. Confinement to Jerusalem would keep him under surveillance and greatly reduce the possibility of Shimei's (see 2:8) conspiring with any remaining followers of Saul against Solomon's rule. Consequently, Shimei was cut off from his hometown, Bahurim (see 2 Sam. 16:5), and from his tribe of Benjamin.

Shimei submitted to the restriction imposed on him until he pursued his runaway slave to **Achish son of Maachah king of Gath** (v. 39). Gath was a major Philistine city (see Josh. 13:3; 1 Sam. 6:16–17). It is likely that Gath was ruled successively by Maoch, Achish the elder (1 Sam. 27:2), Maachah, and Achish the younger (here). One can only conjecture why Shimei did not seek Solomon's permission to pursue what ostensibly was a legitimate venture.

Shimei, like Adonijah, had forfeited his gracious pardon and therefore suffered punishment according to the exact terms of his oath to Solomon (vv. 37–38). **Benaiah ... fell upon him, that he died** (v. 46). This was the third execution carried out by Benaiah (see 2:25, 34), and it brought to completion the tasks assigned to Solomon by David just before his death (2:6, 9).

C. Solomon's Wisdom (chap. 3)

3:1. Solomon made affinity with Pharaoh; that is, he made a marriage alliance. It appears likely that Solomon established his marriage alliance with either Siamun or Psusennes II, the last kings of the Twenty-first Dynasty (the first Egyptian pharaoh mentioned by name in the Old Testament is Shishak [11:40; 14:25–26], who established the Twenty-second Dynasty, circa 945 BC). Such an alliance attests to Egyptian recognition of the growing importance and strength of the Israelite state. Apparently, at the time of his daughter's marriage to Solomon, the pharaoh gave her the Canaanite town of Gezer as a dowry (see 9:16). Gezer was located near the crossing of two important trade routes. One, to the west of Gezer, went from Egypt to the north and was very important for Egypt's commercial interests. The other, to the north of Gezer, went from Jerusalem to the Mediterranean Sea and the port of Joppa and was important to Solomon as a supply line for his building projects. The marriage alliance enabled both Solomon and the pharaoh to accomplish important economic and political objectives. No precise date is given for the conclusion of the marriage alliance, though it appears to have occurred in the third or fourth year of Solomon's reign (see 2:39). Solomon began construction of the temple in his fourth year (6:1), and control of the Gezer area was important for the beginning of this project. The Egyptian princess was given a temporary residence in the **city of David**, in the old fortress (see 2 Sam. 5:7 and discussion), until a separate palace of her own could be constructed, some twenty years later (7:8; 9:10; 2 Chron. 8:11).

3:2–4. At that time, Israel **sacrificed in high places** (v. 2). Upon entering Canaan, the Israelites often followed the Canaanite custom of locating their altars on elevated platforms (Hebrew, *bamoth*) or high hills, probably on the old Baal sites. The question of the legitimacy of Israelite worship at these high places has long been a matter of debate. It is clear that the Israelites were forbidden to take over pagan altars and high places and use them for the worship of the Lord (Num. 33:52; Deut. 7:5; 12:3). It is also clear that altars were to be built only at divinely sanctioned sites (Exod. 20:24; Deut. 12:5, 8, 13–14). It is not so clear whether multiplicity of altars was totally forbidden provided the above conditions were met (see 19:10, 14; Lev. 26:30–31; Deut. 12; 1 Sam. 9:12). It seems, however, that these conditions were not followed even in the time of Solomon, and pagan high places were being used for the worship of the Lord. This would eventually lead to religious apostasy and syncretism and was strongly condemned (2 Kings 17:7–18; 21:2–9; 23:4–25). According to the author, Israel utilized the high places **because there was no house built**. Worship at a variety of places was apparently considered normal prior to the building of the temple (see Judg. 6:24; 13:19; 1 Sam. 7:17; 9:12–13).

Solomon loved the LORD ... only he sacrificed ... in high places (v. 3). Solomon's one major fault early in his reign was inconsistency in meeting the Mosaic requirements concerning places of legitimate worship. He **went to Gibeon to sacrifice there** (v. 4). The Gibeonites had tricked Joshua and Israel into a peace treaty at the time of the conquest of Canaan (Josh. 9:3–27). The city was subsequently given to the tribe of Benjamin and set apart for the Levites (Josh. 18:25; 21:17). David had avenged Saul's violation of the Gibeonite treaty by the execution of seven of Saul's descendants (see 2 Sam. 21:1–9). At Gibeon (modern El-jib) was the **great high place**. The reason for Gibeon's importance was the presence of the Mosaic tabernacle and the ancient bronze altar (see 1 Chron. 21:29; 2 Chron. 1:2–6). These must have been salvaged after the destruction of Shiloh by the Philistines (see discussion on 1 Sam. 7:1) and taken to Gibeon after Saul had the priestly community at Nob destroyed (see 1 Sam. 21:1–2; 22:6–23). The ark, however, resided in Jerusalem in the special tent that David had erected for it (see Sam. 6:12–17).

3:5–15. The Lord appeared … in a dream (v. 5). Revelation through dreams is found elsewhere in the Old Testament (Gen. 28:12; 31:11; 46:2; Num. 12:6; Judg. 7:13; Dan. 2:4; 7:1), as well as in the New Testament (see, e.g., Matt. 1:20; 2:12, 22).

Thou hast shewed … David … mercy (v. 6). The Hebrew for "mercy," often translated "lovingkindness," refers to God's covenant favors (see discussion on 2 Sam. 7:15). Solomon praised the Lord for faithfulness to His promises to David (2 Sam. 7:8–16) **according as he walked … in righteousness** (see discussion on 2 Sam. 22:21).

I am but a little child (v. 7). The birth of Solomon is generally placed in approximately the middle of David's forty-year reign, meaning that Solomon was about twenty years old at the beginning of his own reign (see 2:11–12). Therefore, his comment is probably a humble confession of his lack of experience in assuming the responsibilities of his office. Saul, who had stood head and shoulders over everyone else (see 1 Sam. 10:23), had been small in his own eyes when he began to reign (see 1 Sam. 15:17; see also Jer. 1:6).

Solomon saw Israel as **a great people, that cannot be numbered … for multitude** (v. 8). From the small beginnings of a single family living in Egypt (see Gen. 46:26–27; Deut. 7:7), the Israelites had increased to an extent (see 4:20) that approached the promise given to Abraham (Gen. 13:16; 22:17–18)

and Jacob (Gen. 32:12). Therefore, he asked for **an understanding** (lit., "hearing") **heart** (v. 9). This can be understood as (1) hearing God's voice and following Him in obedience or (2) having the patience to hear a case and understand it fully. Both qualities are needed in making good judgments.

In a time of opportunity, Solomon did not seek **long life … riches … life of thine enemies** (v. 11), that is, personal gain and acclaim, typical desires of ancient Near Eastern monarchs. Instead, he requested wisdom. God was pleased, therefore, and promised to distinguish Solomon so that none would compare to him (see 4:29–34; 10:1–13). **I have also given thee that which thou hast not asked** (v. 13; compare Jesus' promise in Luke 12:31). God rewarded him with riches and honor.

If thou wilt walk in my ways … I will lengthen thy days (v. 14). This promise echoes Deuteronomy 6:2; 17:20; 22:7. Unfortunately, Solomon would not remain obedient to the covenant as his father David had (11:6); therefore, he would not live to be much more than sixty years of age (see discussion on v. 7; see 11:42).

Returning to Jerusalem, he stood before the **ark of the covenant of the Lord** (v. 15; see discussions on 6:19; 2 Sam. 6:2, 17) to offer **burnt … and peace offerings**.

3:16–28. Solomon's wisdom was soon tested when he was compelled to determine the truth of two harlots' stories and which woman was the true mother of a child in question. That the two harlots **came … unto the king** (v. 16) and had an audience with him shows that it was possible for Israelites (and others within the realm) to bypass lower judicial officials (Deut. 16:18) and appeal directly to the king (see 2 Kings 8:3; 2 Sam. 15:2). It also helps explain why Solomon's judicial responsibilities weighed on him (see 3:9). It is not known if these two harlots were Israelites or Jebusites, possibly the latter. They claimed to **dwell in one house** (v. 17). Brothels were common in ancient Near Eastern cities. Each had given birth to a child; during the night, one child had died, and each woman claimed to be the mother of the **living** child (v. 22).

Solomon staged a confrontation in which the true identity of the child's mother became apparent when she pleaded for the preservation of her child's life. This judicial decision convinced all Israel **that the wisdom of God was in him** (v. 28). This episode strikingly demonstrated that the Lord had answered Solomon's prayer for a discerning heart (3:9, 12).

D. Solomon's Reign Characterized (chap. 4)

4:1–6. Solomon was king over all Israel (v. 1); that is, he ruled over an undivided kingdom, as his father had before him (see 2 Sam. 8:15). One does well to compare this list of Solomon's high-ranking officials with that of David's (2 Sam. 20:23–26). Apparently, the service of some of David's officials drew Solomon's attention, and he retained them in his administration. It will be noted, however, that Solomon later found it necessary to enlarge his staff. This list was probably compiled early in Solomon's reign, for it includes Abiathar as priest (v. 4), who was later removed from this position (see 2:26–27).

According to 2 Samuel 15:27, 36 and 1 Chronicles 6:8–9, Azariah was the son of Ahimaaz and the grandson of Zadok (see discussion on 2:8). Here he is listed as the **son of Zadok** (v. 2). Apparently, Zadok's son Ahimaaz had died, so Zadok was succeeded by his grandson Azariah. For Zadok, see discussions on 2:27, 35.

Shisha (v. 3), a veteran scribe for David (see discussion on 2 Sam. 8:17), now had two sons who served as **scribes** for Solomon, presumably conducting domestic and foreign correspondence, perhaps keeping records of important political events, and various administrative functions. **Jehoshaphat the son of Ahilud**, who had served in David's court, retained his position as **recorder** (see discussion on 2 Sam. 8:16).

Benaiah (v. 4) replaced Joab as commander of the army (see 2:35; 2 Sam. 8:18). **Zadok and Abiathar** were priests during David's reign, but Abiathar was banished at the beginning of Solomon's reign (2:27, 35), and Zadok was succeeded by his grandson Azariah (v. 2).

Nathan (v. 5), either the prophet (1:11) or the son of David (2 Sam. 5:14), had two sons who served. One was over the **officers** (see 4:7–19), and the other was a **principal officer** (see "chief rulers" in discussion on 2 Sam. 8:18). For the designation **the king's friend**, see discussion on 2 Sam. 15:37.

Over the household (v. 6) is a designation appearing here for the first time in the Old Testament. It is a reference to an office mentioned frequently in 1–2 Kings (1 Kings 16:9; 18:3; 2 Kings 18:18, 37; 19:2). It is likely that this official was administrator of the palace and steward of the king's properties. **Adoniram** served not only under Solomon but also under David before him (2 Sam. 20:24) and Rehoboam after him (1 Kings 12:18). He was over the **tribute**, that is, the forced labor (see discussions on 9:15; 2 Sam. 20:24).

4:7–19. Solomon had twelve officers (or governors; v. 7) who administered twelve districts that were not identical to the tribal territories, possibly because the tribes varied greatly in agricultural productivity. Solomon's administrative decision violated traditional tribal boundaries and may have intended to weaken the authority of the tribes and make Jerusalem more central in its authority. If so, his plan seemed to backfire and probably stirred up ancient tribal loyalties, eventually contributing to the disruption of the united kingdom. A distinction is made between "Judah" and "Israel" (see 4:20), and it will be seen that the twelve districts did not include Judah. Unfortunately, this apparent favoritism to Solomon's tribe, Judah, would provide a reason for discontent with Solomon's rule.

The governors and their districts are enumerated, but the boundaries are not defined; only principal cities are named. Most of the governors are noted as "the son of" (Hebrew, *ben*), which could actually be part of their name (e.g., **The son of Hur** [v. 8] could be rendered "Ben-hur"). Some of the governors were sons of men previously noted in the narrative of 1–2 Samuel.

The son of Abinadab (Hebrew, *ben-abinadab*; v. 11) was most likely the son of David's brother Abinadab (see 1 Sam. 16:8; 17:13), making him Solomon's first cousin (he was also Solomon's son-in-law). **Baana the son of Ahilud** (v. 12) was probably a brother of Jehoshaphat the recorder (4:3). **Baana the son of Hushai** (v. 16) was perhaps the son of David's trusted adviser (see discussions on 2 Sam. 15:32, 37). **Shimei the son of Elah** (v. 18) was perhaps the same Shimei mentioned in 1:8.

4:20-21. As the sand which is by the sea (v. 20), a descriptive phrase originally used to depict the multitude of Abraham's descendants (see Gen. 22:17), frequently portrays great numbers, sometimes used of Israel (2 Sam. 17:11; Isa. 10:22; Jer. 33:22; Hos. 1:10), sometimes her enemies (Josh. 11:4; Judg. 7:12), and sometimes grain (Gen. 41:49) and birds (Ps. 78:27). The large numbers of people and the **eating and drinking, and making merry** are all indications that Judah and Israel had prospered (see 5:4).

The borders of Solomon's empire extended **from the river** (i.e., the Euphrates River; see discussion on 2 Sam. 8:3) **unto the land of the Philistines, and unto the border of Egypt** (perhaps the Wadi el-Arish; v. 21). These were the limits originally promised to Abraham (Gen. 15:18). Rebellion was brewing, however, in Edom (11:14-21) and Damascus (11:23-25).

4:22-25. The amount of food that comprised **Solomon's provision for one day** (v. 22), that is, for his entire household—his palace servants and his court officials and their families—was enormous and gives an indication of how large a family, staff, and administration he supported.

Two cities, **Tiphsah** (v. 24), a city on the west bank of the Euphrates River, and **Azzah** (i.e., Gaza), the southernmost city of the Philistines on the Mediterranean coast, marked the general extremes of Solomon's empire.

4:26-28. Solomon had forty thousand stalls of horses (v. 26). The number 40,000 is probably a copyist's error, for one manuscript reads 4,000, as does the parallel passage in 2 Chronicles 9:25. First Kings 10:26 and 2 Chronicles 1:14 indicate that Solomon had 1,400 chariots, meaning he maintained stalls for two horses for each chariot, with places for up to 200 reserve horses. By way of comparison, an Assyrian account of the battle of Qarqar in 853 BC (about a century after Solomon) speaks of 1,200 chariots from

Damascus, 700 chariots from Hamath, and 2,000 chariots from Israel (the northern kingdom).

4:29-34. The descriptive phrase **as the sand ... on the sea shore** (v. 29; see discussion on 4:20) is now used to describe Solomon's vast wisdom, insight, and understanding. His wisdom had no rival, excelling that of the **children of the east country** (v. 30). The phrase is general and appears to refer to the peoples of Mesopotamia (see Gen. 29:1) and Arabia (see Jer. 49:28; Ezek. 25:4, 10)—those associated with Israel's northeastern and eastern horizons, just as Egypt was the main region on her southwestern horizon. Many examples of Mesopotamian wisdom literature have been recovered. Solomon's wisdom excelled also the **wisdom of Egypt** (see Gen. 41:8; Exod. 7:11; Acts 7:22). Examples of Egyptian wisdom literature are to be found in the proverbs of Ptahhotep (ca. 2450 BC) and Amenemope (see Proverbs, Introduction: "Date").

Until Jesus came (see Luke 11:31), Solomon **was wiser than all men** (v. 31), including some notable men such as **Ethan the Ezrahite** (see Psalm 89 superscription), **Heman, and Chalcol, and Darda** (see discussion on 1 Chron. 2:6). **Three thousand proverbs** (v. 32) were attributed to Solomon. Only some of these are preserved in the book of Proverbs. Psalms 72 and 127 are attributed to him, but most of his 1,005 songs are lost. His knowledge was broad, permitting him to write about **beasts, and of fowl, and of creeping things, and of fishes** (v. 33). Examples of Solomon's knowledge of these creatures are found in Proverbs 6:6-8; 26:2-3, 11; 27:8; 28:1, 15. His reputation was so widespread that **all people ... all kings of the earth** (v. 34) came to hear him, a general statement referring to the Near Eastern world (see Gen. 41:57).

E. Solomon's Building Projects (5:1-9:9)

1. Preparation for Building the Temple (Chap. 5)

5:1-6. Hiram king of Tyre (v. 1) ruled circa 978-944 BC. He may have also served as coregent with his father, Abibaal, as early as 993 BC. Before Solomon was born, Hiram had enjoyed a friendly relationship with David and had provided timber and workmen for the building of David's palace (see 2 Sam. 5:11). Here he apparently sent Solomon his greetings and congratulations.

My father could not build a house (v. 3). Although David had been denied the privilege of building the temple, he had not remain idle. He made plans and provisions for its construction (see 1 Chron. 22:2–5; 28:2; see also Psalm 30 superscription). Hiram, therefore, was not unaware of David's unfulfilled intentions.

Solomon described his **rest** (v. 4) as having **neither adversary nor evil occurrent** (i.e., "disaster" or "misfortune"). God's promises to His people (see Exod. 33:14; Deut. 25:19; Josh. 1:13, 15) and to David (2 Sam. 7:11) had now been fulfilled (see 8:56), so the Israelites were free to concentrate their strength and resources on building their Great King's royal house (see discussion on 2 Sam. 7:11).

Solomon now proposed to build a house for the **name of the LORD his God** (v. 5). "Name" signifies God's revealed character or self-revelation as a person (see, e.g., 8:16; Exod. 20:24; Deut. 12:5; 2 Sam. 6:2; 7:13). Achieving this goal would fulfill what **the LORD spake unto David** his **father** (see 2 Sam. 7:12–13; 1 Chron. 22:8–10). So Solomon asked that Hiram **command** (v. 6) his servants to cut **cedar trees out of Lebanon**. Cedar was widely used in the ancient Near East to construct royal houses and temples. Both the timber from Lebanon and the craftsmen of Phoenicia were renowned and were necessities to Solomon. A more detailed account of Solomon's request is found in 2 Chronicles 2:3–10.

5:7–9. Blessed be the LORD (v. 7). In polytheistic cultures, it was common practice for the people of one nation to recognize the deities of another nation (see 10:9; 11:5) and even to ascribe certain powers to them (see 2 Kings 18:25; see also 2 Chron. 2:12).

Hiram agreed to have rafts of timber floated by sea to the **place that thou shalt appoint me** (v. 9). Second Chronicles 2:16 identifies this seaport as Joppa (see discussion on 1 Kings 3:1), the nearest port to Jerusalem. There they would be broken up and transported overland to Jerusalem. In exchange, Hiram asked of Solomon, **accomplish my desire ...**

food for my household. Provision of food for Hiram's court personnel appears to have covered only the cost of the wood itself. In addition, Solomon would have to provide for the wages of the Phoenician laborers (5:6). A comparison of 5:11 with 2 Chronicles 2:10 indicates that besides wheat and olive oil for Hiram's court, Solomon also sent barley and wine for labor costs. Hiram may have sold some of these provisions to pay the laborers.

5:10–12. The **twenty thousand measures** (i.e., "kors") **of wheat** (v. 11) amounts to about 125,000 bushels. By way of comparison, Solomon's court received 10,950 kors of flour and 21,900 kors of meal annually (see 4:22). Solomon's whole grain payment to Hiram of 20,000 kors of wheat and 20,000 kors of barley (2 Chron. 2:10) probably yielded about 26,666 kors of refined flour and meal, or about 20 percent less than the requirements of Solomon's own court.

Hiram and Solomon ... made a league together (v. 12). The peaceful relation between these two kings would be strained somewhat when Hiram was later dissatisfied with the twenty cities that Solomon gave him as payment (9:10–13), but the relationship apparently was mended as they later cooperated in naval operations (9:26–27).

5:13–18. David had compelled foreigners in the land to cut stone for him, but **Solomon raised a levy** (v. 13); that is, he imposed forced labor on the Israelites (see discussions on 9:15; 2 Sam. 20:24). His action was the very thing about which Samuel had warned Israel when they demanded a king (see 1 Sam. 8:16). If **all Israel** is to be interpreted as it was in 4:7 (see discussion there), it is conceivable that Judah was favored and was excluded from the labor force, leaving the ten northern tribes to supply the 30,000 men for hard labor. Resentment among the people about this sort of forced labor would eventually lead to a civil uprising and the division of Solomon's kingdom immediately after his death (12:1–18).

There were **threescore and ten thousand that bare burdens ... fourscore thousand hewers** (v. 15). These workers were conscripted from the non-Israelite population that David had subdued and incorporated into his kingdom (see 2 Chron. 2:17–18). The **mountains** were the limestone hills of the Holy Land where the stone was quarried.

Three thousand and three hundred (v. 16) supervised the people in the work. First Kings 9:23 refers to 550 chief officers. If these are two different categories of supervisory personnel, the total is 3,850 men. Second Chronicles 2:2 refers to 3,600 supervisors, and 2 Chronicles 8:10 speaks of 250 chief officers, which again yields a total of 3,850 men in a supervisory capacity.

Great stones, costly stones (v. 17; for the size of the stones, see 7:10) were needed for the foundation. Transportation of such stones to Jerusalem would have required enormous manpower. The term **stone-squarers** (v. 18) is more accurately rendered "Giblites" or "Gebalites," who shaped the stones. Gebal is also known as Byblos (see discussion on Ezek. 27:9).

2. Building the Temple (chap. 6)

6:1–38. See drawing, *KJV Study Bible*, p. 458.

6:1. The data presented in this verse is extremely important to biblical students, for it serves as a benchmark in biblical chronology. Not only is the commencement date of the temple construction given, but from that date, the year in which Israel came out of Egypt can be calculated. Critical is the **four hundred and eightieth year ... fourth year**. Synchronizations between certain events in the reigns of later Israelite kings and Assyrian chronological records fix the fourth year of Solomon's reign at circa 966 BC (see Introduction: "Chronology"). If Israel's exodus is placed 480 years prior to 966, it would have occurred circa 1446 BC, during the rule of the Eighteenth-Dynasty Egyptian pharaoh, Amunhotep II. On the basis of Exodus 1:11 and certain other historical considerations, however, some have concluded that the exodus could not have occurred prior to the rule of the Nineteenth-Dynasty pharaoh, Rameses II — thus, not until approximately 1290 (see discussion on Gen. 47:11). This would mean that the 480 years of verse 1 would be understood as either a schematic (perhaps representa-tive of twelve generations multiplied by the conventional, but not always actual, forty-year length of a generation) or an aggregate figure (the combined total of a number of subsidiary time periods, which in reality were partly concurrent, examples of which are to be found in Egyptian and Mesopotamian records).

6:2–6. David had desired to build God a "house," something more permanent than a "tent" (2 Sam. 7:2). **The house which king Solomon built** (v. 2), that is, the temple, was patterned after the tabernacle (and in general, after other temples of the time) and was divided into three major areas: the Most Holy Place, the Holy Place, and the outer courtyard. The Most Holy Place in the temple was cubical, as it probably was in the tabernacle. The dimensions of the temple in most instances seem to be double those of the tabernacle (see Exod. 26:15–30; 36:20–34).

A **porch** (or foyer; v. 3) extended another fifteen feet in front of **the temple of the house**. "Temple" here refers to the first main room or hall, the Holy Place (as opposed to the "innermost room," where the ark of the covenant would reside, 6:19), rather than the whole building.

The description of the **windows** (v. 4) is unclear. Framed windows with immovable latticework have been suggested. Presumably, their construction would provide circulation of air but would tone down the direct, bright rays of light.

Around three sides of the house was a three-storied complex of rooms (vv. 5–6). The width of the bottom story (seven and a half feet) was successively increased by one and a half feet on each side of the two stories. To avoid boring holes in the temple wall, for inserting beams to support the ceilings for the lower stories and floors for the upper ones, the thickness of the walls was successively reduced by one and a half feet in the second and third stories. Thus, it was on these **narrowed rests** (v. 6), a series of ledges, that the beams for the three floors of side chambers rested. The description of the construction accounts for the different widths of the rooms on each floor and gives some indication of the needed thickness of the walls at their bases. The rooms were presumably used for storage or perhaps for accommodations for the priests.

6:7. Remarkably, the stones were so well prepared at the quarry that no tools for dressing them were required on the construction site.

6:8 – 10. Access to the storage rooms was through an entrance on the right side of the building, which revealed a winding staircase to the second and third floors.

6:11 – 13. As the temple neared completion, **the word of the LORD came to Solomon** (v. 11), perhaps through an unnamed prophet (but see 3:5, 11 – 14; 9:2 – 9). Did the task of building prove to be a greater undertaking than Solomon had anticipated? At any rate, during the process of building, he received divine encouragement and assurance of blessing, conditioned on his obedience. **If thou wilt walk in my statutes … then will I perform my word with thee** (v. 12). In words similar to those spoken by David (see discussions on 2:1 – 4), the Lord assured Solomon of a continuing dynasty (see 2 Sam. 7:12 – 16) if he remained faithful to the covenant. **I will dwell among the children of Israel** (v. 13), that is, in the present context, in the temple being built (see 9:3). To avoid any apprehension among the Israelites concerning His presence with them (see Ps. 78:60; Jer. 26:6, 9; see discussion on 1 Sam. 7:1), the Lord gave assurance that He would dwell in their midst (see 8:10 – 13; Lev. 26:11).

6:14 – 22. As Solomon finished the construction of the temple, he turned to decorating the interior. The interior walls were totally paneled with cedar boards and overlaid with gold. The **oracle** (v. 16) refers to what was known as the **most holy place**, that is, the innermost room of the house of God. Similar terminology was used for the inner sanctuary housing the ark in the tabernacle (see Exod. 26:33 – 34; Lev. 16:2, 16 – 17, 20, 23). The cedar panels of this room were decorated with carved gourds and open flowers. This room was prepared to house **the ark of the covenant of the LORD** (v. 19). The Ten Commandments are called "the words of the covenant" in Exodus 34:28, and the stone tablets on which the Ten Commandments were inscribed are called "the

tables of the covenant" in Deuteronomy 9:9. The ark in which the tablets were kept (see Exod. 25:16, 21; 40:20; Deut. 10:1 – 5) is thus sometimes called "the ark of the covenant of the LORD" (see Deut. 10:8; 31:9, 25; Josh. 3:11). Elsewhere, the ark is variously designated as "the ark of the LORD" (Josh. 3:13; 4:11), "the ark of the Testimony" (Exod. 30:6; 31:7), and "the ark of God" (1 Sam. 3:3; 4:11, 17, 21; 5:1 – 2).

The extensive use of gleaming **pure gold** (v. 20) probably symbolized the glory of God and His heavenly temple (see Rev. 21:10 – 11, 18, 21). The **chains of gold** (v. 21), which partitioned off the Most Holy Place, probably supported the curtain that covered the entrance (see 2 Chron. 3:14; Matt. 27:51; Heb. 6:19). Due to the striking similarities between this house and the tabernacle, the **altar that was by the oracle** (i.e., the inner sanctuary; v. 22) probably refers to the incense altar that stood before the veil that divided the Most Holy Place from the Holy Place in the tabernacle (see 7:48; Exod. 30:1, 6; 37:25 – 28; Heb. 9:3 – 4).

6:23 – 36. Within the innermost room, **two cherubims** (v. 23) stood as sentries on either side of the ark (8:6 – 7; 2 Chron. 3:10 – 13), each cherub standing **ten cubits high**. They are not to be confused with the two cherubim that stood over each end of the mercy seat of the ark of the covenant (see *KJV Study Bible* note on Exod. 25:18), which would eventually be placed in this room. The Most Holy Place, where the cherubim stood, was twenty cubits high (6:16). Their presence enhanced the impression of the awesome holiness of God, who chose to dwell among His people and could be approached in this place.

In addition to the aforementioned cherubim, **he carved all the walls … with … cherubims** (v. 29). This was not a violation of the second commandment, which prohibits making anything to serve as a representation of God and worshiping it (see discussion on Exod. 20:4). Additional decorations were **palm trees and open flowers**. Early Jewish synagogues were adorned with similar motifs. The depiction of cherubim and beautiful trees and flowers is reminiscent of the garden of Eden, from which man had been driven as a result of sin (Gen. 3:24). In a symbolic sense, readmission to the paradise of God was now to be found only by means of atonement for sin at the sanctuary.

Even the doors into the innermost room, the Most Holy Place, were adorned with carvings of cherubim, palms, and open flowers that were overlaid with gold, thus introducing the grandeur of the room within.

Mention of an **inner court** (v. 36) suggests that there was an outer courtyard (see 8:64). Second Chronicles 4:9 refers to the "court of the priests" (inner) and the "great court" (outer). The inner court is also called the higher court (Jer. 36:10) because of its higher position on the temple mount.

The description of the walls, three rows (i.e., "courses") of hewed stone and a row of cedar beams (see Ezra 6:4), is a construction feature attested to at various archaeological sites. The layer of wood apparently was meant to be a bonding agent between every three courses of stone.

6:37–38. The house of God was begun in the **fourth year** (v. 37) of Solomon's reign (see 6:1 and discussion), and it was completed in the **eleventh year** (v. 38) of his reign (959 BC). Its construction took a total of **seven years**.

3. Building the Palace (7:1–12)

7:1–12. Solomon spent **thirteen years** (v. 1), almost twice as long building his own house as he did building the Lord's house (see 6:38; see also Hag. 1:2–4). Several reasons may be offered: (1) extensive preparations had not been previously made for the palace (see 5:9); (2) the palace was much larger than the temple, requiring more time for construction; (3) he had prioritized his labor forces, thus accelerating the construction on the temple but delaying the construction of his residence.

7:2–12. Part of his palace complex was **the house of the forest of Lebanon** (v. 2). This consisted of cedar beams laid on four rows of cedar pillars (from Lebanon, see 5:6) in the palace, which created the impression of a great forest. **The length ... an hundred cubits, and the breadth ... fifty cubits, and the height ... thirty cubits** is equivalent to about 150

feet long, 75 feet wide and 45 feet high. (Compare these measurements with those of the temple; 6:2.) The building included a storage area for weaponry (see 10:16–17).

The porch of pillars (v. 6) apparently was an entrance hall to the palace of the forest of Lebanon. The length of the porch (fifty cubits) corresponded to the width of the palace. It may have served as a waiting room for those awaiting an audience with the king before they were admitted into the next specified room, the **porch for the throne** (v. 7), where Solomon sat in judgment. It is not clear whether the throne hall, the hall of judgment, Solomon's own living quarters (**his house**, v. 8), and the **house** (palace) **for Pharaoh's daughter** were separate buildings or locations within the palace of the forest of Lebanon. His private quarters, that is, his royal residence and his Egyptian wife's quarters, are simply noted without description.

The buildings (the temple and the palace complex) were constructed of expensive and carefully surfaced stones that had been **sawed with saws** (v. 9). The pinkish white limestone of the Holy Land is easily cut when originally quarried but gradually hardens with exposure. Some of the foundation stones were comparable in size to some of those in the lower courses of the western wall (the "Wailing Wall") of Herod's construction.

The walls of the **great court** (v. 12), that is, the courtyard, apparently encompassed all of Solomon's buildings—the temple (and the "inner court," 6:36), and the palace complex. The great court was constructed in the same way as the inner court of the temple (see 6:36).

4. The Temple Furnishings (7:13–51)

7:13–14. Prior to the completion of the temple and the construction of Solomon's palace (see 2 Chron. 2:7, 13–14), **Solomon sent** for **Hiram** (v. 13), an artisan from Tyre (in 2 Chron. 2:13, he is called Huram, a variant of Hiram). He is not to be confused with the king of Tyre (see 5:1), for he was a **widow's son of the tribe of Naphtali** (v. 14). Second Chronicles 2:14 indicates that Hiram's mother was from Dan. Apparently, she had been born in the city of Dan in northern Israel, close to the tribe of Naphtali, from which came her first husband. After he died, she married a man from Tyre. Hiram was skilled in **all works in brass** (i.e., "bronze"). According to 2 Chronicles 2:7, 14, Hiram had a much wider range of skills as well. The description of his skills is strikingly similar to that of Bezalel in Exodus 31:1–5.

7:15–22. Positioned at the front of the "porch," or portico, were two (apparently freestanding) molded **pillars of brass** (i.e., "bronze"; v. 15). One was placed on each side of the main entrance to the temple (v. 21). Each pillar had a large, molded bronze, bowl-shaped **chapiter** (v. 16), that is, a capital, that was elaborately ornamented with **nets of checker work** (v. 17), that is, nets of latticework or meshwork, **wreaths of chain work,** with additional artistic touches of **pomegranates** and **lily work** (vv. 18–20). Surely decorative, they may also have embodied an unknown symbolism not known to us. It has been suggested that they were not actually freestanding (as supposed by some) but supported a roof (forming a portico to the temple) and an architrave.

The pillars were assigned names. **The right pillar** (v. 21) was called **Jachin** (i.e., "He has established"), and **the left pillar** was called **Boaz** (i.e., "in Him is strength"). These names seem to be Solomon's testimony of dependence on God, who had established him to perpetuate the covenant He had made with David (see discussions on 2 Sam. 7:14–16).

The temple, like the tabernacle before it, faced east (see Ezek. 8:16).

7:23–26. The **molten sea** (v. 23) was an enormous reservoir of water that corresponded to the bronze laver made for the tabernacle (see Exod. 30:17–21; 38:8). Its water was used by the priests for ritual cleansing (2 Chron. 4:6). Its circumference was **thirty cubits.** Technically speaking, this should be 31.416 cubits because of the 10-cubit diameter of the circular top. Thirty may be a round number here, or perhaps the measurement was taken a bit below the rim or on the inside circumference (see v. 26). The rim was adorned with **knops** (i.e., "gourds") **… ten in a cubit** (v. 24). With ten gourds to a cubit, it took

three hundred gourds to span the entire reservoir, or six hundred gourds counting both rows. The "sea" was mounted on four groups of three bronze oxen, facing the four directions of the compass.

7:27–39. The **ten bases** (i.e., stands; v. 27) were movable bronze (**brass**) stands designed to hold water basins (**lavers**; v. 38) of much smaller dimensions than the molten sea. The water from the basins was used to wash certain prescribed parts of the animals that were slaughtered for burnt offerings (see Lev. 1:9, 13; 2 Chron. 4:6). These carriage-like bases were mounted on wheels and axles for mobility and were decorated with engraved **cherubims, lions, and palm trees** (v. 36; see discussion on 6:29).

7:40–47. In addition to what has already been described, Hiram made **the lavers** (v. 40). Suggestions for their use are several. Perhaps they were used for cooking meat to be eaten in connection with the peace offerings (see Lev. 7:11–17; 22:21–23). More attractive, however, is the suggestion that they were small **pots** (v. 45) used to carry away ashes from the altar (see the "pots" used for this purpose in 2 Kings 25:14; 2 Chron. 4:11). **The shovels** were used for removing ashes from the altar. **The basons** were used by the priests in various rites involving the sprinkling of blood or water (see Exod. 27:3).

Verses 41–45 are a summary itemization of what Hiram had designed and built. The mention of **two networks** (v. 41) summarizes his work of 7:17. The **four hundred pomegranates** (v. 42) summarizes 7:18, 20. The construction of the **ten bases, and ten lavers** (v. 43) was detailed in 7:27–37. For the construction of the **sea, and twelve oxen** (v. 44), see the details in 7:23–26. And **the pots, and the shovels, and the basons** (v. 45) were briefly mentioned in verse 40.

Of special interest is the fact that Hiram was exceptionally skilled in the very complicated process of making ornate molds of special clay found along the Jordan, into which the molten bronze was poured. This was done somewhere between **Succoth and Zarthan** (v. 46). Succoth was located on the east side of the Jordan (Gen. 33:17; Josh. 13:27; Judg. 8:4–5), just north of the Jabbok River. Excavations in this area have confirmed that Succoth was a center of metallurgy during the period of the monarchy. Zarthan was located near Adam (see Josh. 3:16) and Abel-meholah (4:12).

7:48–51. In contrast to all of the bronze implements that were made for use in the courtyard, the temple furnishings were made of gold, to match the gold-adorned room into which they were placed.

The altar of gold (v. 48) is the incense altar (see discussion on 6:22). **The table of gold** was the table on which the **shewbread** was placed (see Exod. 25:23–30; 1 Chron. 9:32; 2 Chron. 13:11; 29:18). Ten such golden tables are mentioned in 1 Chronicles 28:16 and 2 Chronicles 4:8, 19, five on each side of the temple.

There were ten **candlesticks** (lit., "lampstands") **of pure gold** (v. 49). Only one lampstand had stood in the tabernacle; it had seven arms and was placed opposite the table of shewbread (Exod. 25:31–40; 26:35). The ten lampstands in the temple, five on the right side and five on the left, created a lane of light in the Holy Place. The lampstands were decorated with **flowers ... of gold** (see Exod. 25:33), and the **lamps** (i.e., "bowls" for oil) were of gold also (see Exod. 25:37). The **tongs** were used for handling coals (see 2 Chron. 4:21; Isa. 6:6).

The **censers** (v. 50) were "firepans" used for transferring live coals (see 2 Kings 25:15; 2 Chron. 4:22; Jer. 52:18–19).

To summarize, all the utensils were made of gold. Even the doors pivoted on hinges (i.e., "sockets" or "door fittings") of gold.

Solomon concluded his work by bringing into the temple all the things **which David his father had dedicated** (v. 51). These were valuable objects of silver and gold, either taken as booty in war or received as tribute from kings seeking David's favor (see 2 Sam. 8:9–12; 1 Chron. 18:7–11; 2 Chron. 5:1). These objects were **put among the treasures of the house of the LORD** (see 15:18; 2 Kings 12:18; 1 Chron. 9:26; 26:20–26; 28:12).

5. Dedication of the Temple (chap. 8)

8:1–2. Representatives of all Israel were summoned to join the celebration of installing the ark

in the new temple. **Bring up the ark of the covenant** (v. 1). David had previously brought the ark from the house of Obed-edom to Jerusalem (see 2 Sam. 6:10) to **the city of David, which is Zion** (see 2 Sam. 5:7), where he had prepared a tabernacle (i.e., "tent") for it (see 2 Sam. 6:17).

The time chosen for the installation of the ark was the **feast in the ... seventh month** (v. 2). Since Solomon completed building the temple in the eighth month of the eleventh year of his reign (see 6:38), it is probable that he waited eleven months to dedicate the temple during the Feast of Tabernacles, which began on the fifteenth day of the seventh month of the year and continued for seven days (Lev. 23:34; Deut. 16:13–15). Thus, he chose to have his celebration coincide with an existing and significant yearly festival, in the twelfth year of his reign.

8:3–5. The priests carried the ark (recall the sad events of 2 Sam. 6:3–7) from its special tent (2 Sam. 6:17) to the temple. **The tabernacle of the congregation** (v. 4), that is, the Mosaic tabernacle, which had been preserved at Gibeon (see discussions on 3:4; 1 Sam. 7:1; see also 2 Chron. 5:4–5), and all its sacred objects were brought to the temple in preparation for the sacrifices.

8:6–9. The ark (v. 6) was placed in the **oracle**, (i.e. the Most Holy Place; see 6:16) **under the wings of the cherubims** (see 6:23–28), which overspread the ark. **The ends the staves were seen** (v. 8), that is, the carrying poles (which were always to remain in the gold rings of the ark; Exod. 25:15) were visible from the adjoining room, the sanctuary, or the Holy Place. **There they are unto this day.** These are probably the words of the author of the source from which this description of the dedication of the temple was taken rather than those of the final compiler of the books of Kings (see Introduction: "Author, Date, and Sources"; see also 2 Chron. 5:9). **The two tables of stone** (v. 9; see Exod. 25:16; 40:20), from the time **when the LORD made a covenant with ... Israel** (see Exod. 24), were all that remained in the ark. It is pointless to speculate what may have happened to the other items listed in Hebrews 9:4 (the pot of manna and Aaron's staff). The tables of stone (i.e., the Ten Commandments) were enough to remind Israel of her covenant relation to God as a kingdom of priests, God's holy nation (see Exod. 19:6).

8:10–13. Symbolizing God's glorious presence, **the cloud filled the house of the Lord** (v. 10). Just as a visible manifestation of the presence of the Lord had descended on the tabernacle at Sinai, so now the Lord came to take up His abode in the temple (see Exod. 40:33–35; Ezek. 10:3–5, 18–19; 43:4–5). Solomon reminded the congregation that God had said **he would dwell in the thick darkness** (v. 12; see Exod. 19:9; 24:15, 18; 33:9–10; 34:5; Lev. 16:2; Deut. 4:11; 5:22; Ps. 18:10–11). He recognized that God had now taken up residence in the house that he had built for Him.

8:14–21. In the audience of his people, Solomon extolled God, who had not only spoken to David (see 2 Sam. 7:5–15) but had **fulfilled** (v. 15) His words. God, who had not chosen a house for His **name** (v. 16), a term equivalent to the Lord Himself (see discussion on 5:5), had, however, **chosen David to be over … Israel.** It had been David's desire to build the Lord a house. God was seen to be faithful to David in at least two respects: David's desire to build a house for God had been realized (in what Solomon had been permitted to accomplish; vv. 17–19), and Solomon, David's son, had succeeded him to the throne (v. 20). Now the very ark of God was in its place in the temple.

8:22–26. Solomon stood before the altar of the Lord (v. 22). This altar presumably was the bronze altar that stood before the bronze sea (see discussions on 7:23–26) in the courtyard. Though its construction is not mentioned in Kings, details are found in 2 Chronicles 4:1. According to 2 Chronicles 6:13, Solomon had a bronze platform erected, upon which he stood and prayed his prayer of dedication, so that he could be seen and heard by all who were present. In his prayer, he enumerated many conditions and circumstances in which Israel (and foreigners, 8:41–43) might be found, and he petitioned God specifically on the basis of each one.

Solomon's first observation in prayer was this: as for keeping covenant, **There is no God like thee** (v. 23). No other god had acted in history as had the God of Israel, performing great miracles and directing the course of events so that His long-range covenant promises were fulfilled (see Exod. 15:11; Deut. 4:39; 7:9; Ps. 86:8–10). He specifically applauded God for keeping with **David my father that thou promisedst him** (v. 24; see 8:15; 2 Sam. 7:5–16). Solomon was particularly concerned with God's promise that related to David's successors occupying the throne **so that** (i.e., "if") **thy children … walk before me** (v. 25; see 9:4–9; 2 Chron. 7:17–22; see also discussion on 1 Kings 2:4).

8:27–30. Solomon prayed concerning the newly constructed temple. **Heaven cannot contain thee … how much less this house that I have builded?** (v. 27). There is no theological contradiction in 8:12–13 and verse 27. With the construction of the temple and the appearance of a visible manifestation of the presence of God within its courts, the erroneous notion that God was irreversibly and exclusively bound to the temple in a way that guaranteed His assistance to Israel no matter how the people lived could very easily arise (see Jer. 7:4–14; Mic. 3:11). Solomon confessed that even though God had chosen to dwell among His people in a special and localized way, He far transcended containment by anything in all creation. The temple would only serve as a point of contact between Israel and her omnipresent and transcendent God.

Solomon prayed that God, from His dwelling place in heaven, would always keep His eyes turned to this place of worship and prayer, because He had promised, **My name** (i.e., "I the Lord") **shall be there** (v. 29; see discussions on 8:16; 5:5). When Israelites were unable to pray in the temple itself, they would **pray towards this place** (v. 30), directing their prayers toward the place where God had pledged to be present among His people (see Dan. 6:10). Solomon entreated God to hear from **heaven** His **dwelling place** these prayers also.

8:31–32. The king then prayed concerning one person sinning against another. **If … an oath be laid upon him to cause him to swear** (v. 31). In cases such as default in pledges (Exod. 22:10–12) or alleged adultery (Num. 5:11–31), when there was insufficient evidence to establish the legitimacy of the charge, the supposed offender was required to take an oath of innocence at the sanctuary. Such an oath, with its attendant blessings and curses, was considered a divinely given means of determining innocence or guilt since the consequences of the oath became apparent in the life of the individual by his experiencing either the blessing or the curse or by direct divine revelation through the Urim and Thummim (see Exod. 28:29–30; Lev. 8:8; Num. 27:21). **Hear thou in heaven** (v. 32). It is clear that Solomon viewed the oath as an appeal to God to act, rather than as an automatic power that worked in a magical way.

8:33–40. Solomon prayed concerning his people when they would repent. That they would be **smitten down before the enemy, because they have sinned against thee** (v. 33) was Solomon's expectation. Defeat by enemies was listed in Deuteronomy 28:25 as one of the curses that would come on Israel if she disobeyed the covenant. Solomon's prayer reflects an awareness of the covenant obligations the Lord had placed on His people and a knowledge of the consequences that disobedience would bring. However, if they should repent, he prayed that God would **bring them again unto the land** (v. 34), a reference to prisoners taken in battle.

Solomon prayed that if there was **no rain** (v. 35; drought was another of the covenant curses listed in Deuteronomy 28:22–24) and the people repented, God would teach them the **good way … they should walk** (v. 36), that is, in accordance with covenant obligations (see Deut. 6:18; 12:25; 13:18; 1 Sam. 12:23).

In verse 37, Solomon listed all the forms of judgment God has promised Israel if they disobeyed: **famine** (see Deut. 32:24), **pestilence** (see Deut. 28:21–22; 32:24), **locust, or … caterpillar** (see Deut. 28:38, 42), **their enemy besiege them in the land of their cities** (see Deut. 28:52), **plague** (see Deut. 28:61; 31:29; 32:23–25), and **sickness** (see Deut. 28:22).

Solomon prayed that when an Israelite was conscious of his guilt before God; that is, he knew **the plague of his own heart** (v. 38), and had an attitude

of repentance and the desire for God's forgiveness and grace (see 2 Chron. 6:29; Ps. 38:17–18; Jer. 17:9), the Lord would **give to every man according to his ways** (v. 39). This is not to be viewed as a request for retribution for the wrong committed (forgiveness and retribution are mutually exclusive). Solomon expressed a desire for whatever discipline God in His wisdom saw fit to use to correct His people and to instruct them in the way of the covenant (see Prov. 3:11; Heb. 12:5–15) so **that they may fear thee** (v. 40), that is, honor and obediently serve God (see Deut. 5:29; 6:1–2; 8:6; 31:13; 2 Chron. 6:31; Ps. 130:4).

8:41–43. Solomon prayed for the **stranger, that is not of thy people Israel** (v. 41). Here he was referring to one who might come from a foreign land to pray to Israel's God at the temple, as distinguished from a resident alien. **They shall hear of thy great name … thy strong hand … thy stretched out arm** (v. 42). Foreign nations generally knew of Israel's God (see 9:9), but there are multiple examples of non-Israelites who acknowledged Israel's God: Rahab (see Josh. 2:9–11), the Philistines (see 1 Sam. 4:6–8), and the queen of Sheba (10:1). God's great power was demonstrated by His interventions in the history of His people (see Deut. 4:34; 5:15; 7:19; 11:2; 26:8). Solomon asked that the temple might be a place of worship for all who feared God, just as Moses had permitted foreigners to bring their sacrifices to the tabernacle (see Num. 15:14).

8:44–45. Solomon prayed for warriors who would **go out to battle … whithersoever thou shalt send them** (v. 44). He was referring to military initiatives undertaken with divine sanction (see, e.g., Lev. 26:7; Deut. 20; 21:10; 1 Sam. 15:3; 23:2, 4; 30:8; 2 Sam. 5:19, 24). Solomon asked that God would hear and protect the warriors if they prayed **toward the city which thou hast chosen** (see discussion on 8:30).

8:46–53. Solomon prayed for Israelites who repented of their sin while in captivity. On the basis of Leviticus 26:33–45 and Deuteronomy 28:64–68; 30:1–5, Solomon knew that stubborn disobedience would lead to exile from the Promised Land, that God would deliver them to **the enemy, so that they carry them away captives** (v. 46). Solomon entreated God to forgive them and show them compassion as He had when he brought Israel out of Egypt, from the **furnace of iron** (v. 51; see Deut. 4:20 and discussion).

Thou didst separate them ... to be thine inheritance (v. 53). Solomon began his prayer with an appeal to the Davidic covenant (8:23–30), and he closed with an appeal to the Sinaitic covenant (see Exod. 19:5; Lev. 20:24, 26; Deut. 7:6; 32:9).

8:54–61. Solomon closed his lengthy dedicatory prayer with a benediction. Having been **kneeling on his knees** (v. 54; see 8:22; 2 Sam. 7:18; 2 Chron. 6:13; Luke 22:41; Eph. 3:14), he arose to bless God. First Chronicles omits this benediction but includes the spectacular falling of fire from heaven to ignite the burnt offering (1 Chron. 7:1).

Blessed be the LORD (v. 56). Solomon understood this historic day to be a testimony to God's covenant faithfulness. He **hath given rest unto his people.** After the conquest of Canaan under the leadership of Joshua, the Lord gave the Israelites a period of rest from their enemies (see Josh. 11:23; 21:44; 22:4), even though there remained much land to be possessed (see Josh. 13:1; Judg. 1). Only with David's victories was the rest made durable and complete (see 2 Sam. 7:1; see also discussion on 1 Kings 5:4).

The LORD ... be with us ... to incline our hearts unto him (vv. 57–58). Solomon asked for a divine work of grace within his people that would enable them to be faithful to the covenant (see Deut. 30:6; Ps. 51:10; Phil. 2:13).

Solomon the king, the Lord's anointed, saw himself as **his servant** (v. 59) who served as the earthly representative of God's rule over His people (see discussions on Ps. 2:2, 7). Solomon prayed that God would bless him, not so that he would receive the praise of men, but so **that all ... may know that the LORD is God** (v. 60; see discussion on Ps. 46:10).

8:62–66. Solomon offered a sacrifice of peace offerings (v. 63), sacrifices that involved a communion meal (see discussion on 1 Sam. 11:15). Although the numbers of **two and twenty thousand oxen, and an hundred and twenty thousand sheep** may seem large, vast numbers of people participated

in the dedication ceremony, which lasted fourteen days (see 8:1–2; see also v. 65). The number was so large, however, that the bronze altar (note its size in 2 Chron. 4:1) was inadequate, so Solomon consecrated the center of the temple court and utilized it as a huge altar for the sacrifices.

The **congregation** (v. 65) of Israelites represented those from as far as the **entering in of Hamath** (see discussion on Ezek. 47:15) and the **river of Egypt,** probably Wadi el-Arish (see discussion on Gen. 15:18). People came to Jerusalem for the dedication of the temple from nearly the entire area of Solomon's dominion (see discussion on 4:21). The feast lasted for **seven days and seven days, even fourteen days.** It appears that the seven-day celebration for the dedication of the temple was followed by the seven-day Feast of Tabernacles (see discussion on 8:2), which was observed from the fifteenth to the twenty-first of the seventh month. According to Chronicles, this was followed by a final assembly on the next day (in accordance with Leviticus 23:33–36); then on the twenty-third of the month, the people were sent to their homes (see 2 Chron. 7:8–10).

6. The Lord's Response and Warning (9:1–9)

9:1–2. The narrative continues after **Solomon had finished** (v. 1) his initial major building projects. At the earliest, this would have been in the twenty-fourth year (4 + 7 + 13 = 24) of Solomon's reign, 946 BC (see 6:1, 37–38; 7:1; 9:10). **The LORD appeared ... the second time** (v. 2). God had first appeared to Solomon at Gibeon (see 3:4–15). Scripture records one more such "appearance" (11:11), this time not for encouragement but for reprimand.

9:3–5. Contextually, **I have heard thy prayer** (v. 3) seems to refer to the petitions of Solomon's dedicatory prayer in 8:22–53. It is curious, however, why God would have waited thirteen years to answer in this manner (see discussions on 9:2 and 8:1–2). God had already answered immediately with fire from heaven (see 2 Chron. 7:1), so it is not inconceivable that God now responded again because Solomon was at a spiritually critical point in his life. **I have hallowed this house ... to put my name there**

for ever (see 8:10 – 13). The Lord continued, **mine eyes and mine heart shall be there perpetually**, thus answering Solomon's earlier request that God's "eyes be open toward this house" (see 8:29). After twenty-four years of building and blessing (see 6:1; 9:1, 10), perhaps Solomon needed a reminder that the blessings of the Davidic covenant would continue on God's house.

If thou wilt walk before me ... in integrity of heart ... I will establish the throne of thy kingdom upon Israel for ever (vv. 4 – 5; see 8:25 and discussion on 2:4). The Lord reemphasized that to experience the covenant's blessings rather than its curses, Israel's obedience to the covenant was necessary. Obedience would be particularly important as Solomon's kingdom grew in influence and wealth, with all the potential for covenant-breaking that prosperity brought (see Deut. 8:12 – 14, 17; 31:20; 32:15).

9:6 – 9. David is held up as a godly example for the kings that would follow him. He sinned, but he never served other gods as Solomon would (see 11:4 – 8). Thus, a warning was necessary: if you **turn from following me ... and serve other gods, and worship them** (v. 6). The warning would go unheeded.

The prediction that Israel would become **a proverb and a byword among all people** (v. 7) closely parallels Moses' covenant curse on Israel for serving other gods (see Deut. 28:36 – 37). Sadly, other nations would look at Israel and understand that **the LORD** their God **brought upon them all this evil** (v. 9; see Deut. 29:22 – 28; Jer. 22:8 – 30).

F. Solomon's Reign Characterized (9:10 – 10:29)

9:10 – 28. See Map 5 at the end of the *KJV Study Bible.*

9:10 – 14. At the end of twenty years (v. 10). This number includes the seven years of building the temple (see 6:38) and the thirteen years of building his palace (see 7:1). **Then king Solomon gave Hiram twenty cities in the land of Galilee** (v. 11). Comparison of verses 10 – 14 with 5:1 – 12 suggests that during Solomon's twenty years of building activity,

he became more indebted to Hiram than anticipated in their original agreement (see discussion on 5:9), which had provided for payment for labor (5:6) and wood (5:10 – 11). From verses 11 and 14, it is evident that in addition to wood and labor, Solomon had also acquired great quantities of gold from Hiram. It appears that Solomon gave Hiram the twenty towns in the Phoenician-Galilee border area as a surety for repayment of the gold. Second Chronicles 8:1 – 2 indicates that at some later date when Solomon's gold reserves were increased, perhaps after the return of the expedition to Ophir (1 Kings 9:26 – 28; 10:11) or after the visit of the queen of Sheba (10:1 – 13), he settled his debt with Hiram and recovered the twenty towns held as collateral.

9:15 – 23. Solomon's **levy** (i.e., forced labor; v. 15) refers to non-Israelite slave labor of a permanent nature (in contrast to the temporary conscription of Israelite workmen, described in 5:13 – 16). **Millo** (lit., "filling") has generally been interpreted by scholars to refer to terrace-like structures on the hillside, probably Solomon's expansion of Jerusalem on the ridge north from David's city, to provide more space for buildings and additional fortifications (see discussion on 2 Sam. 5:9). Solomon's building activity at Hazor, Megiddo, and Gezer (v. 15) was intended to strengthen the fortifications of these ancient, strategically located towns (Solomonic gates, probably built by the same masons, have been found at all three sites). **Hazor** was the most important fortress city in the northern Galilee area, controlling the trade route running from the Euphrates River to Egypt. **Megiddo** was another fortress city along the great north-south trade route; it commanded the pass through the Carmel range, from the plain of Jezreel to the coastal plain of Sharon. For the location and importance of **Gezer**, see discussion on 3:1.

Although Joshua had killed the king of Gezer at the time of the conquest (Josh. 10:33; 12:12), the tribe of Ephraim had been unable to drive out its inhabitants (Josh. 16:10; Judg. 1:29). Now the pharaoh of Egypt was credited with having **slain the Canaanites ... in the city** (v. 16) to present the city to **his daughter, Solomon's wife**.

Solomon rebuilt and fortified key cities for commercial and defensive purposes (vv. 17–19). **Beth-horon the nether** (i.e., lower Beth-horon; v. 17) was located about eight miles northwest of Jerusalem at a pass giving entrance to the Judahite highlands and Jerusalem from the coastal plain. **Baalath** (v. 18) is to be identified with either the Bealoth of Joshua 15:24, located to the south of Hebron in the tribe of Judah, or the Baalath southwest of Beth-horon in the tribe of Dan (Josh. 19:44). A city known as **Tadmor** (Hebrew, *Tamor*; a site in the Negev on the border of Edom) was located north of Damascus in Syria (see 2 Chron. 8:4).

Solomon conscripted forced labor from the **people of ... the Amorites ... and Jebusites** (v. 20) still in the land (see Deut. 7:1; 20:17; see also discussions on Gen. 10:15–18; 13:7; 15:16; 23:9; Josh. 5:1; Judg. 3:3; 6:10; 2 Sam. 21:2), but **of the children of Israel did Solomon make no bondman** (v. 22). No Israelite was reduced to slavery. Instead, Israelites served as Solomon's warriors and filled official positions. There were **five hundred and fifty, which bare rule** (v. 23), that is, that held supervisory positions over the slave labor (see discussion on 5:16).

9:25. Three times in a year, Solomon led his people in observing the three important annual festivals: the Feast of Unleavened Bread, the Feast of Weeks, and the Feast of Tabernacles (see Exod. 23:14–17; Deut. 16:16; 2 Chron. 8:13).

9:26–28. Phoenicia was famous for its shipping on the Mediterranean Sea. Solomon built a fleet of **ships** (v. 26) that were used in a large trading business, which brought great wealth to Solomon's court (see v. 28; 10:11). They ported at **Ezion-geber**, located at the northern tip of the Gulf of Aqaba (see 22:48; Num. 33:35; Deut. 2:8), on the **Red sea.** The Hebrew for this term, normally read as *Yam Suph* ("sea of reeds"), refers to the body of water through which the Israelites passed at the time of the exodus (see *KJV Study Bible* notes on Exod. 13:18; 14:2). It can also be read, however, as *Yam Soph* ("sea of [land's] end"), a more likely reading when referring to the Red Sea, and especially (as here) to its eastern arm (the Gulf of Aqaba). **Hiram** (v. 27), the king of

Tyre, supplied experienced mariners, and the two kings shared a prosperous commercial venture.

Ophir (v. 28) is known as a source for gold (2 Chron. 8:18; Job 28:16; Ps. 45:9; Isa. 13:12), almug trees, precious stones (10:11), silver, ivory, and apes and baboons (10:22). Its location is disputed. Southeastern Arabia, southwestern Arabia, the northeastern African coast (in the area of Somalia), India, and Zimbabwe have all been suggested. If Ophir was located in Arabia, it was probably a trading center for goods from farther east as well as from East Africa. The three-year voyages of Solomon's merchant vessels (10:22) suggest a more distant location than the Arabian coast.

10:1. That Solomon's wisdom was unexcelled and of widespread fame (see 4:29–31) is illustrated by the visit from an unnamed **queen of Sheba**. Archaeological evidence suggests that Sheba is to be identified with a mercantile kingdom that flourished in southwest Arabia (see discussion on Gen. 10:28; *KJV Study Bible* note on Joel 3:8) circa 900–450 BC. It profited from the sea trade of India and East Africa by transporting luxury commodities north to Damascus and Gaza on caravan routes through the Arabian Desert. It is possible that Solomon's fleet of ships threatened Sheba's continued dominance of this trading business.

It is not stated how the queen of Sheba came to know of Solomon's wisdom, but perhaps she learned of it from caravans traveling through the area. Establishing trade with Solomon might have been a secondary motive for visiting him (note that the gifts she brought Solomon were samples of products that were indigenous to Sheba), but her primary reason for visiting him was to test firsthand the reports of his wisdom. In addition to reports of Solomon's wisdom, she had **heard of the fame of Solomon concerning the name of the Lord**. The queen of Sheba recognized a connection between the wisdom of Solomon and the God he served.

10:2–7. No hint concerning the nature of the queen's **questions** is given, but apparently she was quite sincere. Jesus used her example to condemn the people of His own day who had not recognized that "a greater than Solomon" was in their midst (Matt. 12:42; Luke 11:31). She was duly impressed with the exhibition of Solomon's wisdom and the open display of the luxuries of his kingdom. She confessed not only that the reports of Solomon's wisdom and glory were true but also that what she had observed far exceeded any of those reports.

10:8–9. The queen declared what the servants of Solomon (and all Israel) may have taken for granted: **Happy are** they that **hear thy wisdom** (v. 8). A wise and just king was a blessing to his people, and the God who established such a king was to be praised. **Blessed be the Lord thy God** (v. 9). The queen of Sheba's confession was beautifully worded and reflected a profound understanding of Israel's covenant relationship with the Lord. It does not necessarily imply, however, anything more than her recognition of the Lord as Israel's national God, in conformity with the ideas of polytheistic paganism (see discussion on 5:7; see also 2 Chron. 2:12; Dan. 3:28–29). There is no confession that Solomon's God had become her God to the exclusion of all others.

10:10–13. The queen's gifts to Solomon included **an hundred and twenty talents of gold** (v. 10; see discussions on 9:11, 28) and other products from her country. He reciprocated by giving to her **all her desire, whatsoever she asked** (v. 13). The exchange of gifts between Solomon and the queen may have signified a trade agreement (see discussion on 10:1). There is no basis for the idea, as some have suggested, that she desired offspring fathered by Solomon and left Jerusalem carrying his child.

Verses 11–12 are parenthetical. The products imported from Ophir, and their use in Jerusalem, are introduced here in the context of the costly gifts the queen presented to Solomon to inform the reader that the king was acquiring precious commodities from various sources. **The navy also of Hiram** (v. 11; see 9:26–28) provided Solomon with gold. Hiram had supplied the wood, the sailors, and the expertise in construction that Israel lacked. Among the goods imported from Hiram were **almug trees**, perhaps a variant of "algum trees" (2 Chron. 9:10–11). The identity of this tree is unknown, though some sug-

gest it is juniper. It was apparently available from Lebanon as well as from Ophir (2 Chron. 2:8). The wood was useful for decorative **pillars** (v. 12) and for making musical instruments.

10:14–17. In addition to the 666 talents of gold that Solomon received each year was the revenue he took from caravans of merchants passing through Israel and tribute from **all the kings of Arabia** (v. 15), that is, the Bedouin sheiks, who may have sponsored trade into Israelite territory. **The governors of the country** probably were the officers who administered the twelve districts in Israel (see discussion on 4:7–19).

Solomon made two sizes of ornamental shields from gold. **Targets** (v. 16), that is, "large shields" were rectangular in shape and were designed to afford maximum protection, while smaller, round **shields** (v. 17) were used to protect the archers (see 2 Chron 14:8). These gold "targets" and "shields," likely made of wood and overlaid with gold, were probably intended not for battle but for ceremonial use, symbolizing Israel's wealth and glory. Thus, they were hung on display in **the house of the forest of Lebanon** (see discussion on 7:2). Shishak of Egypt would later carry them off as plunder, in the fifth regnal year of Solomon's son Rehoboam (see 14:25–26).

10:18–20. There was not the like made in any kingdom (v. 20) summarizes the description of the imposing throne that Solomon had erected for himself. Perhaps it was meant to demonstrate the prestige bestowed on him by God, but perhaps it was meant to emphasize the justice that would emanate from his throne due to his God-endowed wisdom.

10:21–25. Due to the abundance of gold available to Solomon, silver was virtually devalued (v. 21).

Solomon **had at sea a navy** (lit., "ships") **of Tharshish** (v. 22; see 2 Chron. 9:21). Scholars have usually identified Tharshish with one of two ports named Tartessus (one in Spain, the other in Sardinia) or Tarsus in Cilicia. Some scholars believe Solomon may have had two fleets: the fleet that sailed the Red Sea to Ophir (see discussions on 9:26–28), and the fleet noted here that sailed the Mediterranean. However, the fleet may be the same one referred to in 10:11

and 9:26–28, since "ships of Tharshish" does not necessarily denote ships that sailed to Tarshish (see discussion on Jonah 1:3), but can simply refer to large oceangoing vessels capable of carrying heavy cargo.

10:26–29. In Deuteronomy 17:16–17, Moses had strictly warned any future king of Israel against four matters: (1) accumulating many horses, (2) returning to Egypt for horses, (3) taking many wives, and (4) amassing great wealth. It is clear that Solomon ignored the first two directives, for he **gathered together chariots and horsemen** (v. 26; see discussion on 4:26), and he became a horse trader, buying horses out of Egypt. **Linen yarn** (v. 28) is *Kew* in Hebrew, a word that has been discovered to refer to Cilicia. Thus, he purchased horses from the north (Cilicia) and the south (Egypt). Many of his purchases were for his own armies. Through his agents, however, he was the middleman in lucrative commercial transactions with the **Hittites** (v. 29; see discussion on Gen. 10:15) and with **Syria**, a people who occupied a large area north and east of the Sea of Galilee (see "Aram" in discussion on Gen. 10:22). Concerning Moses' other two directives, Solomon's wealth can be credited to God's blessing. His taking many wives (see 11:1–3), however, can only be attributed to disobedience.

G. Solomon's Folly (11:1–13)

11:1–2. Sadly, the wise Solomon used the gifts and blessings of God in a foolish and careless manner for his own self-gratification. His wealth, fame, and power gave him seemingly limitless opportunity to acquire wives. **Solomon loved many strange** (i.e., "foreign") **women** (v. 1). Many of Solomon's marriages were no doubt for the purpose of sealing international relationships with various kingdoms, large and small. A common and effective way of confirming a treaty was for one king to give his daughter to another, presumably more powerful and influential, king for a wife. What king would offend his father-in-law by breaking his commitment to a treaty?

Solomon's taking many foreign wives violated not only the prohibition against taking many wives

(Deut. 17:17) but also the prohibition against taking wives from the pagan peoples among whom Israel had settled (see Exod. 34:16; Deut. 7:1–3; Josh. 23:12–13; Ezra 9:2; 10:2–3; Neh. 13:23–27). Solomon's wives came from among the **Moabites** (v. 1; see discussion on Gen. 19:36–38), **Ammonites** (see discussion on Gen. 19:36–38; see also 14:21; Deut. 23:3), **Edomites** (see discussions on Gen. 25:26; 36:1; Amos 1:11; 9:12; see also Deut. 23:7–8), **Zidonians** (see 16:31), and **Hittites**. Based on the number of wives Solomon had (11:3), it is conceivable that they came from a wide range of countries, perhaps even more countries than those listed here.

The wives also came from among peoples about which God had warned Israel, **surely they will turn away your heart after their gods** (v. 2; see Deut. 7:3). An example of this happening in Israel's earlier history is found in Numbers 25:1–15.

11:3–4. Solomon's **seven hundred wives, princesses, and three hundred concubines** (v. 3) promoted what was predicted in 11:2. Solomon's foreign wives served foreign deities, which they brought with them, and they diverted his attention from the Lord to their gods. **His heart was not perfect with the LORD his God** (v. 4; see 8:61). The atmosphere of paganism and idolatry introduced into Solomon's court by his foreign wives gradually led Solomon himself into syncretistic religious practices.

11:5–6. Sadly, Solomon began to serve **Ashtoreth** (v. 5), the Hebrew name for the Phoenician Ashtarte and Babylonian Ishtar, the consort of Baal and a goddess of fertility (see 11:33; 14:15; 2 Kings 23:13; see also discussion on Judg. 2:13). **Milcom**, commonly known as Molech, was the god of the Ammonites to whom children were offered as human sacrifices (see 2 Kings 23:10, 13). Worship of this god not only severely jeopardized the continued recognition of the absolute kingship of the Lord over His people but also involved (on rare occasions) the abomination of child sacrifice (see 2 Kings 16:3; 17:17; 21:6; Lev. 18:21; 20:2–5; see also discussion on Judg. 10:6).

Solomon … went not fully after the LORD, as did David his father (v. 6). Although David had committed grievous sins, he had been repentant, and he was never involved in idolatrous worship.

11:7 – 8. Solomon became accustomed to these gods, and they found public acceptance when he built shrines for them, thus the **high place** (v. 7; see discussion on 3:2) for **Chemosh** (see discussion on 2 Kings 3:27) and **Molech** and other foreign gods. These were erected in relatively close proximity to the temple that he had built for the Lord. In spite of subsequent reformations by Asa and Hezekiah, these shrines were permitted to stand for nearly three centuries, until the reign of Josiah (see 2 Kings 23:13 – 15).

11:9 – 13. On two earlier occasions, the Lord had **appeared unto him** (v. 9; see 3:4 – 5; 9:1 – 9) and had given Solomon personal promises of blessing for obedience, but now he lived in disobedience. **Thou hast not kept my covenant** (v. 11). Solomon had broken the most basic demands of the covenant (see Exod. 20:2 – 5) and had thereby severely undermined the entire covenant relationship between God and His people. **I will surely rend the kingdom from thee**; that is, "I forecast a division of the kingdom." The division would not occur during Solomon's reign, **for David thy father's sake** (v. 12), that is, in honor of David's unwavering loyalty to the Lord and to God's covenant with him (see 2 Sam. 7:11 – 16).

One tribe (v. 13), Judah (see discussion on 11:31 – 32; see also 12:20), would remain **for David ... for Jerusalem's sake, which I have chosen**. Now that Jerusalem contained the temple built by David's son, in accordance with 2 Samuel 7:13, the destiny of Jerusalem and the Davidic dynasty were closely linked (see 2 Kings 19:34; 21:7 – 8; Psalm 132). The temple represented God's royal palace, where His earthly throne (the ark) was situated and where He had pledged to be present as Israel's Great King (9:3).

H. Solomon's Throne Threatened (11:14 – 43)

11:14 – 22. Solomon's disobedience also brought more immediate consequences. Early in his reign, he had no enemies (see 5:4), but now God provided for him an enemy in **Hadad** (v. 14), an **Edomite** of royal blood. Hadad was a familiar name among Edomite kings (see Gen. 36:35, 39).

11:15 – 22. Hadad had survived the time **when David was in Edom** (v. 15; see 2 Sam. 8:13 – 14). David had waged a military campaign in Edom, and Joab had remained **for six months** (v. 16), until he had slaughtered **every male in Edom**. As **a little child** (v. 17), probably in his early teens, Hadad had escaped to Egypt with some of his father's servants.

He had fled from **Midian** (v. 18). At that time, the Midianites inhabited a region on the eastern borders of Moab and Edom. Hadad came to **Paran**, a wilderness area southeast of Kadesh in the central area of the Sinai peninsula (see Num. 10:12; 12:16; 13:3), before continuing on to Egypt. There he won the favor of **Pharaoh king of Egypt** (see discussion on 3:1), who **gave him a house, and ... victuals, and ... land**, and Hadad then became connected to Egyptian royalty through marriage. In a time of Israel's growing strength, it was in Egypt's interest to befriend those who would harass Israel and keep her power in check.

Let me depart (v. 21). Upon learning of David's death, Hadad apparently had sought permission from the pharaoh to return to Edom during the early days of Solomon's reign. **What hast thou lacked with me ...?** (v. 22). Because Egypt had by this time established relatively good relations with Israel (see discussion on 3:1), perhaps the pharaoh was reluctant to see Hadad return to Edom and provoke trouble with Solomon. How Hadad opposed Solomon is not told. Guerilla attacks against the garrisons David had established in Edom (see 2 Sam. 8:13) is a possibility, but Hadad's success must have been somewhat limited since there is no indication that shipment of goods from the port city, Ezion-geber, through Edomite territory was hindered in Solomon's day.

11:23 – 25. Another enemy was **Rezon** (v. 23), who had been an ally of **Hadadezer**, the Aramean **king of Zobah**. When David had invaded Zobah (2 Sam. 8:12), Rezon had fled and became **captain over a band** (v. 24) of men, as David had been (1 Sam. 22:1 – 2) and Jephthah before him (Judg. 11:3). Rezon and his men **went to Damascus, and dwelt therein, and reigned**. Presumably this took place in the early part of Solomon's reign (for the situation in Damascus during the time of David, see 2 Sam. 8:6). It is likely that Solomon's expedition (2 Chron. 8:3) against Hamath-zobah (the kingdom formerly ruled by Hadadezer, 2 Sam. 8:3–6) was provoked by opposition led by Rezon. Even though Solomon was able to retain control of the territory north of Damascus, to the Euphrates (4:21, 24), he was not able to drive Rezon from Damascus itself.

11:26–28. A third enemy was Jeroboam, Solomon's own capable servant. **He lift up his hand** (i.e., "rebelled") **against the king** (v. 26; see discussion on 11:40). What form this rebellion took is not stated, but 11:27–39 provides the background of the revolt. When **Solomon built Millo** (v. 27; see 9:15 and discussion), he had made Jeroboam, because of his ambition and leadership abilities, **ruler over all the charge of the house of Joseph** (v. 28), that is, a supervisor over the conscripted laborers (see 5:13–18; 9:15) in Ephraim and Manasseh. Jeroboam's supervisory role had made him aware of smoldering discontent among the people because of Solomon's policies (see 12:4).

11:29–32. The prophet **Ahijah**'s (v. 29) symbolic act of tearing Jeroboam's **new garment** (v. 30) was prophetic of the kingdom's division. Jeroboam would receive **ten tribes** (v. 31) to rule over, while the Davidic line would retain **one tribe** (v. 32). This one tribe, Judah, may have included the tribe of Simeon (see Josh. 19:9), which possibly had been absorbed into Judah years earlier, unless it, like the tribe of Dan (see Judg. 18), had migrated to the north. It is interesting, however, that the tribe of Benjamin was usually aligned with Judah (see 12:21, 23).

The tradition of considering the ten northern tribes as a unit distinct from the southern tribes (Judah and Simeon; Levi had received no territorial inheritance, see Joshua 21) began in the period of the judges (see Judg. 5:14–16). The reason, no doubt, was the continuing presence of a non-Israelite corridor (Jerusalem, the Gibeonite league, and Gezer) that separated the two Israelite regions (see Map 4 at the end of the *KJV Study Bible*). Political division along the same line during the early years of David's reign and the different arrangements

that brought the southern and northern segments under David's rule (see 2 Sam. 2:4; 5:3) reinforced this sense of division. With the conquest of Jerusalem by David (2 Sam. 5:6–7) and the pharaoh's gift of Gezer to Solomon's wife (9:16–17), all Israel was for the first time territorially united. (Once Jerusalem and Gezer were under Israelite control, the Gibeonite league, which had already submitted to Joshua [see Joshua 9], could be effectively absorbed politically.) In the division announced in 11:31–32, the "one tribe" refers to the area dominated by Judah (but including Simeon; see Josh. 19:1–9), and the "ten tribes" refers to the region that came under David's rule at the later date (Ephraim and Manasseh, Joseph's sons, being counted as two tribes; see Gen. 48:5; see also discussion on Josh. 14:4). For further refinement of the new boundaries that would come about, see discussion on 12:21.

11:33–40. Jeroboam was advised that idolatry was the reason that much of the kingdom would be torn from Solomon: they have **forsaken me** (v. 33; see 11:5–8) and **have not walked in my ways** (see 11:1–2; 3:14). Jeroboam, however, would later lead his ten northern tribes, "Israel," into sin by introducing a new form of idolatry (see 12:26–33).

I will make him prince all the days of his life (v. 34; see 11:12–13). To be faithful to His covenant with David, God promised to retain one tribe for the Davidic dynasty when He took the kingdom **out of his son's hand** (v. 35), that is, from Solomon's son Rehoboam (see 12:1–24). **That David … may have a light alway before me in Jerusalem** (v. 36) symbolizes the continuance of the Davidic dynasty in the city where God had chosen to cause His name to dwell (see 11:13 and discussion). In a number of passages, the burning or snuffing out of one's lamp signifies the flourishing or ceasing of one's life (Job 18:6; 21:17; Prov. 13:9; 20:20; 24:20). Here (and in 15:4; 2 Kings 8:19; 2 Chron. 21:7; Ps. 132:17) the same figure is applied to David's dynasty (see especially Ps. 132:17, where "ordained a lamp for mine anointed" is parallel to "make the horn of David to bud"). Through David's royal sons, his "lamp" would continue to burn before the Lord in Jerusalem.

Through the prophet Ahijah, the Lord promised Jeroboam that he would be king over **Israel** (v. 37), that is, over the northern ten tribes. **If thou wilt hearken unto all that I command thee … I will be with thee** (v. 38). Jeroboam was placed under the same covenant obligations as were David and Solomon before him (see 2:3–4; 3:14; 6:12–13).

I will … afflict the seed of David, but not for ever (v. 39). The division of the kingdom would considerably reduce the status and power of the house of David. This promise anticipates a restoration (announced also in the messianic prophecies of Jer. 30:9; Ezek. 34:23; 37:15–28; Hos. 3:5; Amos 9:11–12), in which the nation would be reunited under the rule of the house of David.

Solomon sought therefore to kill Jeroboam (v. 40). Having learned of God's promise that he would be king of Israel, and perhaps because of his sympathy for those subjected to the burden of forced labor (11:28), Jeroboam, being indifferent to the timing announced by Ahijah (vv. 34–35), apparently rebelled and made an abortive attempt to wrest the kingdom from Solomon (11:26). To save the throne for his own son Rehoboam, Solomon's reaction was to attempt to kill Jeroboam. Jeroboam was forced to flee to **Shishak king of Egypt** (see 14:25–26), where he found political asylum. This first Egyptian pharaoh to be mentioned by name in the Old Testament was the Libyan founder of the Twenty-second Dynasty (945–924 BC). Solomon's marriage ties were with the previous dynasty (see discussion on 3:1).

11:41–43. The book of the acts of Solomon (v. 41) was a written source concerning Solomon's life and administration, which was used by the writer of 1–2 Kings (see Introduction: "Author, Date, and Sources"; see also 15:7, 23). After a reign of **forty years** (v. 42), Solomon **slept with his fathers** (v. 43; see discussion on 1:21).

I. Rehoboam's Succession to the Throne (12:1–24)

12:1–5. Shechem (v. 1) was a city of great historical significance located in the hill country of northern Ephraim (see Gen. 12:6–7; 33:18–20; Josh. 8:30–35 and discussion on Josh. 8:30; see also Josh. 20:7; 21:21; 24:1–33). **All Israel** refers to the representatives of the northern tribes (see 12:16). That David had become king over the northern tribes on the basis of a covenant (see 2 Sam. 5:3) suggests that their act of submission was to be renewed with each new king and was subject to negotiation. Why this site was selected for Rehoboam's coronation is not stated, but it may be that the northern tribes (see discussion on 5:13) had already lent support to Jeroboam's revolt (see 11:26) and would have refused to go to Jerusalem for the occasion. Therefore, Rehoboam risked going into hostile surroundings, hoping to win support.

Jeroboam … heard of it (v. 2); that is, he heard of the death of Solomon (11:43). Since fleeing from Solomon, he had **dwelt in Egypt** (see 11:40; 2 Chron. 10:2). The northern tribes called Jeroboam home from Egypt, apparently to be at Shechem when Rehoboam arrived. Conceivably, Jeroboam was the spokesman on behalf of the northern tribes. Who could have represented them better? He had been involved in Solomon's forced labor program (see 11:28) and understood the people's grievance.

Thy father made our yoke grievous (v. 4). Smoldering discontent with Solomon's heavy taxation and conscription of labor and military forces flared into strong expression (see 4:7, 22–23, 27–28; 5:13–14; 9:22; see also discussions on 9:15; 11:28). Conditions had progressively worsened since the early days of Solomon's rule (see 4:20). There is no reason to doubt the word of these tribes. A lighter load would have brought loyalty to Rehoboam.

12:6–11. Rehoboam consulted with the old men, that stood before Solomon (v. 6). These were the officials of Solomon's government, such as Adoniram (4:6) and the district governors (4:7–19), who had had ample opportunity to witness the schism that was developing among the tribes and that would ultimately divide the nation if critical grievances were not addressed. These men reminded Rehoboam, **If thou wilt be a servant …** (v. 7). Authority in the kingdom of God is for service, not for personal aggrandizement.

Rehoboam turned to the **young men** (v. 8), that is, young in comparison to the officials who had served Solomon. (Rehoboam was forty-one years old when he became king; 14:21.) These peers of Rehoboam were probably opportunists and status seekers who appealed to the king's ego. They already **stood before him**. Apparently, Rehoboam had quickly established new administrative positions for his friends and associates of his own generation.

Their advice encouraged him to wield the same power and enjoy the same standard of living that his father had. **My little finger shall be thicker than my father's loins** (v. 10). This is a proverb claiming that Rehoboam's weakest measures would be far stronger than his father's strongest measures.

Scorpions (v. 11) were leather lashes with metal spikes. Not only would governmental burdens on the people be increased, but the punishment for not complying with the government's directives would be intensified.

12:12-15. After three days, the northern tribes learned that Rehoboam had accepted **the counsel of the young men** (v. 14). His answer reflects a despotic spirit completely contrary to the covenantal character of Israelite kingship (see Deut. 17:14-20; see also discussion on 1 Sam. 10:25).

The cause was from the Lord (v. 15). The writer of Kings does not condone either the foolish act of Rehoboam or the revolutionary spirit of the northern tribes, but he reminds the reader that all of these things occurred to bring about the divinely announced punishment on the house of David for Solomon's idolatry and breach of the covenant (11:9-13). The sovereign God of history was directing the events of the rebellion to accomplish His purpose and to fulfill the prophetic word **which the Lord spake by Ahijah … unto Jeroboam** (see 11:29-39). For the relationship between divine sovereignty over all things and human responsibility for evil acts, see the discussion on 2 Samuel 24:1.

12:16-19. The response of **all Israel** (v. 16), that is, the northern tribes (see discussion on 12:1), was essentially that of Sheba, the earlier Benjaminite rebel (2 Sam. 20:1-22). **What portion have we in David?**,

that is, the Davidic dynasty (compare Sheba's earlier expression of the same sentiment, 2 Sam. 20:1). The developing schism among the tribes had now severed Israel from Judah. Israel had rejected the dynasty of their former hero and God's covenant king.

The children of Israel which dwelt in the cities of Judah (v. 17) possibly were Judahites loyal to Rehoboam but more likely were people originally from the northern tribes who had settled in Judah. They would later be joined by others from the north who desired to serve the Lord and worship at the temple (see 2 Chron. 11:16-17).

Rehoboam underestimated the gravity of the political situation. In sheer folly, he sent **Adoram, who was over the tribute** (i.e., forced labor; v. 18), to the northern tribes. Adoram (a variant of Adoniram) had served in the same capacity under both David (2 Sam. 20:24) and Solomon (1 Kings 4:6; 5:14). This man, who would become a most vivid reminder of the reason for the rebellion, was sent either to quell the rebellion, to enroll more laborers, or to exact taxes. Israel **stoned** Adoram, which gave Rehoboam cause to escape to Jerusalem for safety.

The rift between the tribes was never mended, so the rebellion continued **unto this day** (v. 19), that is, until the time of the source from which the author of 1 Kings derived this account (see Introduction: "Author, Date, and Sources").

12:20-24. Although only **the house of Judah** (v. 21) remained loyal to the Davidic dynasty, a curious reference is made here to the **tribe of Benjamin**. While the bulk of Benjamin was aligned with the northern tribes (see discussion on 11:31-32), the area around Jerusalem remained under Rehoboam's control (as did the Gibeonite cities and Gezer). The northern boundary of Judah must have reached almost to Bethel (twelve miles north of Jerusalem), which Abijah, Rehoboam's son, would later hold for a short while (see 2 Chron. 13:19). The **hundred and fourscore thousand … warriors** of Rehoboam probably included all support personnel along with those who would actually be committed to battle.

Shemaiah (v. 22) wrote a history of Rehoboam's reign (2 Chron. 12:15). Another of his prophecies is recorded in 2 Chronicles 12:5–8. He is noted here as being a **man of God**, a common way of referring to a prophet (see, e.g., 13:1; Deut. 18:18; 33:1; 1 Sam. 2:27; 9:9–10). He was sent to address **Judah and Benjamin, and … the remnant of the people** (v. 23; see discussion on 12:17) to prevent them from beginning a civil war with the northern tribes. Duly warned, Judah and Benjamin obeyed and **returned to depart** (v. 24) from the planned invasion. Although full-scale civil war was averted, intermittent skirmishes and battles between Israel and Judah would continue throughout the reigns of Rehoboam, Abijah, and Asa. Political instability in Israel after the death of Baasha would finally bring the conflict to a halt. Asa's son Jehoshaphat would enter into an alliance with Ahab and seal the relationship by the marriage of his son Jehoram to Ahab's daughter Athaliah (see 14:30; 15:6, 16; 22:2, 44; 2 Kings 8:18).

II. Israel and Judah from Jeroboam I and Rehoboam to Ahab and Asa (12:25–16:34)

A. Jeroboam I of Israel (12:25–14:20)

12:25–33. The writer's attention shifts to Jeroboam, whose first course of action was to fortify Shechem to serve as his administrative center. His later move across the Jordan to **Penuel** (v. 25), a town east of the Jordan (see Gen. 32:31; Judg. 8:9, 17), may have coincided with the Egyptian Shishak's invasion, circa 924 BC (see 14:25). It would also have been of strategic importance for defense against the Arameans of Damascus (see 11:23–25) and the Ammonites.

A people unified around religion tend to be united politically also. According to Mosaic law, three times a year, all Israel was to make the pilgrimage to God's appointed place (Jerusalem at this time) to worship (Exod. 23:17; Lev. 23:1–44). Jeroboam knew that if the northern tribes were permitted to return three times annually to Jerusalem, their loyalty might **return to the house of David** (v. 26). He did not have confidence in the divine promise given to him through Ahijah (see 11:38) and thus took action (his tactics are outlined in verses 28–33) that forfeited the theocratic basis for his kingship.

Jeroboam changed the symbols of worship. The ark of God resided in the temple (see 8:6–8), but now Jeroboam fashioned **two calves of gold** (v. 28). Two views are advanced concerning these calves. First, it is proposed that Canaanite influence is in view, since the pagan gods of the Arameans and Canaanites were often represented as standing on calves or bulls as symbols of their strength and fertility (see discussion on Judg. 2:13). Hence, the calves were not intended to be idols of worship but merely a throne upon which the invisible God, Yahweh, stood. Second, and the preferred view, is that the calves indicated Egyptian influence, for the sacred bull was worshiped in Egypt as a symbol of the goddess Hathor. Possibly Jeroboam had become acquainted with this cult during his stay in Egypt, after he fled from Solomon (see 11:40), and was now inclined to set up calf worship from what he had observed. His statement, **behold thy gods, O Israel, which brought thee up out of the land of Egypt**, is reminiscent of Aaron's words in Exodus 32:4–5. Was Jeroboam attempting to combine the pagan calf symbol with the worship of the Lord? No attempt was made to represent the Lord physically; that is, no "god" stood on the backs of his calves. In fact, no mention is made of the Lord at all.

Jeroboam also changed the center of worship. To discourage pilgrimages to Jerusalem, he appointed **Beth-el** (v. 29) and **Dan**, two border cities, as worship sites and appealed to convenience for attending there. Bethel was located about twelve miles north of Jerusalem, close to the border of Ephraim but within the territory of Benjamin (Josh. 18:11–13, 22). It held a prominent place in the history of Israel's worship of the Lord (see Gen. 12:8; 28:11–19; 35:6–7; Judg. 20:26–28; 1 Sam. 7:16). Dan was located in the far north of the land, near Mount Hermon. A similarly paganized worship had been practiced here during the period of the judges (Judg. 18:30–31). **This thing became a sin** (v. 30). Jeroboam's royal policy promoted violation of the second commandment (Exod. 20:4–6). It inevitably led to Israel's violation of the first commandment also (Exod. 20:3) and opened the door for the entrance of fully pagan practices into Israel's religious rites (especially in the time of Ahab). Jeroboam foolishly abandoned religious principle for political expediency and, in doing so, he forfeited the promise given him through the prophet Ahijah (see 11:38).

Jeroboam went on to change the priesthood. After establishing **high places** (v. 31; see discussion on 3:2), he **made priests ... which were not of the sons of Levi**. According to 2 Chronicles 13:9, anyone who could consecrate himself with a young bull and seven rams qualified to be a priest. Consequently, many of the priests and Levites of the northern kingdom migrated to Judah because Jeroboam bypassed them when appointing cult personnel in the north. This migration ultimately strengthened Rehoboam's kingdom (see 2 Chron. 11:13–17).

He altered the religious calendar by instituting **a feast in the eighth month, on the fifteenth day ... like unto the feast that is in Judah** (v. 32). Apparently, Jeroboam intended to duplicate, one month later, the Feast of Tabernacles, observed in Judah on the fifteenth to the twenty-first of the seventh month (see 8:2; Lev. 23:34). Conceivably, his celebration was intended to surpass the festivities at Jerusalem so that the festival at Jerusalem would in time cease to be attractive, and pilgrimages there would cease.

Jeroboam overstepped the limits of his prerogatives as king and assumed the role of a priest and **offered upon the altar, and burnt incense** (v. 32; see 2 Chron. 26:16–21). All of his religious activity in opposition to the worship of the Lord at Jerusalem gained him the epitaph of the one "who made Israel to sin" (see 14:16).

13:1–2. God was gracious and sent an unnamed **man of God out of Judah ... unto Beth-el** (v. 1; for "man of God," see discussion on 12:22). This prophet came from the southern kingdom to Bethel, in the northern kingdom, to issue a warning to the wicked Jeroboam, who had come to **the altar to offer incense**. Possibly the man of God did this to emphasize that the divinely appointed political division (11:11, 29–39; 12:15, 24) was not intended to establish rival religious systems in the two kingdoms. Two centuries later, the prophet Amos from Tekoa (in Judah) would also go to Bethel (in the northern kingdom) to pronounce God's judgment, on Jeroboam II (Amos 7:10–17).

The unnamed prophet announced that **Josiah** (v. 2), a Davidic king from Judah, would one day desecrate the bones of **the priests of the high places** upon that very altar. This prophecy is remarkable in that it specifically names Josiah nearly three hundred years before the actual event (see the fulfillment in 2 Kings 23:15–20). Such predictions are unique features of Old Testament prophetic Scripture (see Isaiah 44, where Cyrus is likewise called by name). Modern scholarship that denies this prophetic element in Scripture, falsely insisting that the prediction concerning Josiah is a *vaticinium post eventum* (prophecy after the event) or a later gloss must be rejected.

13:3–6. The prophet **gave a sign** (v. 3) to Jeroboam. The immediate fulfillment of a short-term prediction would serve to authenticate the reliability of the longer-term prediction concerning Josiah (for this principle, see Deut. 18:21–22).

The altar also was rent, and the ashes poured out from the altar (v. 5). Attempting to explain this miracle (the cracked altar) by suggesting natural causes (e.g., cold water was spilled on the hot altar stones, and they split open) is unacceptable. Quite visibly, God demonstrated His power to fulfill the words of the prophet (see discussion on v. 3) and provided a clear sign that Jeroboam's offering was unacceptable to the Lord (see Lev. 6:10–11).

It is probably going beyond the author's intent to assume that Jeroboam's reference to **thy God** (v. 6) should be taken as implying that he no longer considered the Lord as his own God (see 2:3; Gen. 27:20). Rather, it probably suggests that he recognized the prophet as his superior in the theocratic order. He recognized the event as an undeniable miracle and the prophet as unquestionably a man of God. He begged for another miracle, which was immediately granted, and **the king's hand was restored**. The Lord's gracious response to Jeroboam's request is to be seen as an additional sign (see v. 3) that was given to confirm the word of the prophet and to move Jeroboam to repentance.

13:7–10. Come home with me (v. 7). Jeroboam's invitation to the prophet was not motivated by repentance. He attempted to renew his prestige in the eyes of the people by creating the impression that there was no fundamental break between himself and the prophetic order (for a similar situation, see 1 Sam. 15:30). Perhaps he had other ulterior motives as well, such as hoping to persuade the prophet to soften his pronounced judgment or perhaps to bribe him to remain on in the king's service. Had the prophet accepted the Jeroboam's invitation, he could have created in the mind of anyone present the impression that the pronounced judgment could be avoided or lightened.

Eat no bread (v. 9). The prophet's refusal of Jeroboam's invitation rested on a previously given divine command and underscored God's extreme displeasure with the apostate worship at Bethel. Also, to **turn again by the same way** he had come, provided the possibility of forming some social acquaintance or being waylaid by those who had seen him arrive at Bethel.

13:11–19. Scripture does not clarify whether the **old prophet in Beth-el** (v. 11) was a true or false prophet (he is simply called an "old prophet," not a "prophet of the LORD") or, if he was a man of God, why he remained at Bethel in the midst of Jeroboam's apostasy. His subsequent action certainly demonstrated spiritual compromise.

One can only speculate if **the man of God** (v. 11) would have been found by the "old prophet" if he had been more diligent in his retreat from Bethel and had not stopped to rest under an oak tree.

I am a prophet also as thou art (v. 18). This was a half-truth only if the old prophet in Bethel had faithfully proclaimed the word of the Lord in former days, but those days had long since passed. The old prophet did not claim a communication direct from God but through an angel. Nevertheless, he lied, and why he did is another matter for speculation.

He went back with him (v. 19). Neither his own need nor the old prophet's lie justified the man of God's disobedience to the direct and explicit command of the Lord. His public action in this matter

undermined respect for the divine authority of all he had said at Bethel.

13:20–22. During the course of the meal, **the word of the LORD came unto the prophet** (v. 20), which was a message of judgment on the man of God for his disobedience to the clear commands of God. The fundamental distinction between a true and a false prophecy here becomes apparent. The false prophecy arises from one's own imagination (Jer. 23:16; Ezek. 13:2, 7), while the true prophecy is from God (Exod. 4:16; Deut. 18:18; Jer. 1:9; 2 Peter 1:21). Even if the old prophet was indeed a false prophet, one need not doubt that God could have chosen to speak through him (see Num. 2:28–30, where God caused even a donkey to speak).

Thy carcase shall not come unto the sepulchre of thy fathers (v. 22). The man of God from Judah would die far from his home and his family burial plot. One may be disposed to feel sorry for the man who was judged so severely after being deceived by a "prophet." The man of God, however, had clearly understood God's initial prohibition and should have known that God never contradicts His own word.

13:23–32. A lion … slew him (v. 24). This was a stern warning to Jeroboam that God takes His word very seriously. **The ass stood by it, the lion also**. The remarkable fact that the donkey did not run and the lion did not attack the donkey or disturb the man's body (v. 28) clearly stamped the incident as a divine judgment. This additional miracle was reported in Bethel (v. 25) and provided yet another sign authenticating the message that the man of God from Judah had delivered at Jeroboam's altar. Jeroboam still was not moved to repentance (13:33).

Upon hearing of the death of the disobedient **man of God** (v. 26), **the old prophet** took it upon himself to tend to the body. **He laid his carcase in his own grave** (v. 30; see 13:22). The old prophet did the only thing left for him to do to make amends for his deliberate and fatal deception. He instructed his sons to bury him in the **sepulchre wherein the man of God is buried** (v. 31). The old prophet chose in this way to identify himself with the message that the man of God from Judah had given at Bethel, that is, in anticipation of the prediction concerning Josiah (see 13:2 and 2 Kings 23:17, 18). He wanted to be associated with the man of God and not have his bones desecrated with those of the wicked priests.

As the capital of the northern kingdom, **Samaria** (v. 32) is used to designate the entire territory of the ten northern tribes (see discussion on 16:24). Samaria, however, was not established until about fifty years after this (16:23–24); the use of the name here reflects the perspective of the author of Kings. (For a similar instance of the use of a place-name, Dan, of later origin than the historical incident with which it is connected, see discussion on Gen. 14:14.)

13:33–34. The incident did not bring a change of heart to Jeroboam. He continued to make **of the lowest of the people priests** (v. 33; see 12:31 and discussion).

This thing became sin (v. 34). The sin in 12:30 was the establishment of a paganized worship; here it is persistence in that worship, with all its attendant evils.

14:1–3. At that time (v. 1) probably indicates a time not far removed from the event narrated in chapter 13. **Abijah** means "My (divine) Father is the Lord," suggesting that Jeroboam, at least to some degree, at the time of his child's birth and naming, had desired to be regarded as a worshiper of the Lord.

Disguise thyself (v. 2). Jeroboam's attempt to mislead the prophet Ahijah into giving a favorable prophecy concerning the sick boy indicates (1) his consciousness of his own guilt, (2) his superstition that prophecy worked in a magical way, and (3) his confused but real respect for the power of the Lord's prophet. For **which told me that I should be king over this people**, see 11:29–39. The prophet Ahijah appears at the beginning and the end of the Jeroboam narrative. Jeroboam's first encounter with the prophet brought good news. Now he hoped for good news from the prophet regarding his son. That he sent his wife instead of going himself and that he instructed her to disguise herself may indicate that Ahijah had broken off communication with Jeroboam due to his religious policies. Recognition of the king or his wife might have resulted in a condemning message from the prophet.

In keeping with custom, she took the prophet a gift of simple food: **ten loaves … cracknels** (i.e., wafers, probably hardtack) **… honey** (v. 3). This was the gift of a commoner (compare Saul's gift in 1 Sam. 9:7–8), not royalty.

14:4–5. Old age may have impaired Ahijah's vision, but his spiritual sight remained keen, and his ears were tuned to the voice of God. **The Lord said unto Ahijah** (v. 5). Jeroboam was indeed pagan in his theology if he thought he could deceive the omniscient God. (For other examples of divine revelation concerning an imminent visit, see 1 Sam. 9:15–17; 2 Kings 6:32.)

14:6–16. To Jeroboam's wife's amazement, she was greeted by the blinded prophet "seeing" through her disguise. **Come in, thou wife of Jeroboam** (v. 6). Ahijah's recognition of the woman and his knowledge of the purpose of her visit served to authenticate his message as truly being the word of the Lord. He rebuked her for her deception and delivered a message of judgment and doom.

The Lord God … exalted thee … made thee prince … rent the kingdom away (vv. 7–8). Jeroboam was first reminded of the gracious acts of the Lord on his behalf (see 11:26, 30–38). He was also reminded that he had been chosen to be a "prince," a term often used of spiritual leaders, but in his effort to be king, he had led his people into spiritual disaster. **Thou hast not been as my servant David** (v. 8). Jeroboam had not responded to God's gracious acts and had ignored the requirements given when Ahijah told him he would become king (see 11:38).

But thou **hast done evil above all that were before thee** (v. 9). Jeroboam's wickedness surpassed that of Saul, David, and Solomon in that he implemented a paganized system of worship for the entire populace of the northern kingdom, even to the point of making **other gods** (see discussions on 12:28, 30).

God's judgment was that He would **cut off from Jeroboam** (v. 10) every male (**him that pisseth against the wall**) and **him that is shut up and left in Israel** (i.e., the bond and the free without exception; see 21:21; 2 Kings 9:8; 14:26). **Him that dieth in the field shall the fowls of the air eat** (v. 11). The covenant curse of Deuteronomy 28:26 was applied to Jeroboam's male descendants, none of whom would receive an honorable burial (and is repeated in 16:4 regarding Baasha).

The child shall die (v. 12). The Hebrew for "child" allows for wide latitude in age (the same term is used for the young advisers of Rehoboam; see 12:8 and discussion). Although the death of Abijah was a severe disappointment to Jeroboam and his wife, it was an act of God's mercy to the prince, sparing him the disgrace and suffering that were to come on his father's house (see Isa. 57:1–2). **All Israel shall mourn for him, and bury him** (v. 13), perhaps indicates that Abijah was the crown prince and was well known and loved by the people. He alone of Jeroboam's descendants would receive an honorable burial in a **grave**.

The prophet Ahijah looked beyond the brief reign of Nadab, Jeroboam's son (15:25–26), to the revolt of Baasha (15:27–16:7), **a king ... who shall cut off the house of Jeroboam** (v. 14). God would raise up Baasha to cut off Jeroboam's dynasty. The phrase **as a reed is shaken in the water** (v. 15) is descriptive of the instability of the royal house in the northern kingdom, which would be characterized by assassinations and revolts (see 15:27–28; 16:16; 2 Kings 9:24; 15:10, 14, 25, 30). **He shall root up Israel**. The list of curses for covenant breaking found in Deuteronomy climaxes in the forced exile of God's people from the Land of Promise (Deut. 28:63–64; 29:25–28). The Hebrew for **groves** is *asherim*. Ahijah perceived that Jeroboam's use of golden bulls in worship would inevitably lead to the adoption of other elements of Canaanite nature religion. The goddess Asherah was the consort of El (see *KJV Study Bible* note on Exod. 34:13; discussion on Judg. 2:13), and the Asherim were probably wooden representations of the goddess.

Whereas the fidelity of David was the exemplar against which the spiritual qualities of Judah's kings were compared, **the sins of Jeroboam** (v. 16; see 12:26–33; 13:33–34) were the standard for measuring the wickedness of Israel's kings. **Who made Israel to sin** is an oft-repeated phrase in 1–2 Kings

(see, e.g., 15:26; 16:2, 13, 19, 26). What a horrible epitaph by which to be remembered in the royal chronicles and in the pages of Scripture.

14:17–18. Tirzah (v. 17), used by the kings of Israel as the royal city until Omri purchased and built up Samaria to serve that purpose (16:24), was apparently Jeroboam's third and final residence. It is probably modern Tell el-Far'ah, about seven miles north of Shechem (see discussion on Song 6:4). Abijah died when Jeroboam's wife returned home, fulfilling the prophet's prediction. The fulfillment of this short-term prediction (14:12) assured fulfillment of the long-term prediction concerning Israel (14:14–15; see discussions on 13:3–6).

14:19–20. The chronicles of the kings of Israel (v. 19) was a record of the reigns of the kings of the northern kingdom that the author of 1–2 Kings used as a source and apparently was accessible to those interested in further details of the history of the reigns of the Israelite kings. It is not to be confused with the canonical book of 1–2 Chronicles, which was written later than 1–2 Kings and contains the history of the reigns of the kings of Judah only (see Introduction: "Author, Date, and Sources"). Jeroboam reigned for **two and twenty years** (v. 20), 930–909 BC, and **he slept with his fathers** (see discussion on 1:21). For the reign of **Nadab**, see 15:25–32.

B. Rehoboam of Judah (14:21–31)

14:21–24. Rehoboam the son of Solomon reigned in Judah (v. 21). Rehoboam's mother was from Ammon, where Molech was worshiped (see 11:1, 5–7). Undoubtedly, Rehoboam followed his mother and father in the worship of this god. Based on his age, **forty and one years old**, and the length of his father's reign (forty years), Rehoboam was born shortly before David's death (see 11:42; see also discussion on 2:24). Therefore, Solomon apparently had engaged in a foreign marriage prior to his becoming king. Rehoboam reigned for **seventeen years** (930–913 BC) **in Jerusalem, the city which the Lord did choose ... to put his name** (see 9:3; Ps. 132:13).

Judah did evil in the sight of the Lord (v. 22). The priests and Levites who immigrated to Judah from the north led the country to follow the way of David and Solomon for the first three years of Rehoboam's reign (see 12:24; 2 Chron. 11:17). In later years, however, Rehoboam and the people of Judah turned away from the Lord (2 Chron. 12:1). The reign of Rehoboam is described in greater detail in 2 Chronicles 11–12.

For the **high places** (v. 23), see discussion on 3:2. The **images** (i.e., "sacred pillars") were stone pillars, bearing a religious significance, that were placed next to the altars. The use of such pillars was common among the Canaanites and was explicitly forbidden for the Israelites in the Mosaic law (Exod. 23:24; Lev. 26:1; Deut. 16:21–22). It is likely that the pillars were intended to be representations of the deity (2 Kings 3:2). For legitimate uses of stone pillars, see Genesis 28:18; 31:45; Exodus 24:4. For **groves**, see discussion on 14:15.

The **sodomites** (v. 24) were male cult prostitutes. Ritual prostitution was an important feature of Canaanite fertility religion. The Israelites had been warned by Moses not to engage in this abominable practice (see Deut. 23:17–18; see also 1 Kings 15:12; 2 Kings 23:7; Hos. 4:14).

14:25–28. The glory of Solomon's state was short lived. **In the fifth year of king Rehoboam** (926 BC), **… Shishak king of Egypt came up against Jerusalem** (v. 25; (see discussions on 3:1; 11:40). Shishak's invasion is described in more detail in 2 Chronicles 12:2–4 and is also attested in a victory inscription found on the walls of the temple of Amun at Karnak (Thebes), where numerous cities that Shishak plundered in both Judah and the northern kingdom are listed. Second Chronicles 12:5–8 indicates that fear of the impending invasion led to a temporary reformation in Judah. While it appears Shishak plundered the treasures of the temple and the palace, Rehoboam himself may have despoiled the temple and palace to pay a ransom to save Jerusalem. **The shields of gold which Solomon had made** (v. 26; see 10:16–17) were also taken, and Rehoboam replaced them with **brasen shields** (v. 27). The reduced realm could not match the great wealth that Solomon had accumulated in Jerusalem (see 10:21, 23, 27).

14:29–31. The information of this concluding summary is quite standard for the kings of Judah (see 11:41–43; 15:23–24). **The chronicles of the kings of Judah** (v. 29) was a record of the reigns of the kings of Judah, similar to the one for the kings of the northern kingdom, that the author of 1–2 Kings used as a source (see discussion on 14:19; see also Introduction: "Author, Date, and Sources"). The **war between Rehoboam and Jeroboam** (v. 30) was not open warfare. The Lord had forbidden the children of Israel to engage in war with each other (see 12:24). Minor conflicts and threats involving the territory of Benjamin, since both kings would have wanted control of that buffer zone, were always possible.

C. Abijam of Judah (15:1–8)

15:1–2. Dating Rehoboam's son to the **eighteenth year of king Jeroboam** (v. 1) is the first of numerous synchronisms in 1–2 Kings between the reigns of the kings in the north and those in Judah (see, e.g., 15:9, 25, 33; 16:8, 15, 29; see also Introduction: "Chronology"). **Abijam** is a variant of Abijah (see 2 Chronicles 13 and discussion on 1 Kings 14:1) and may possibly indicate Canaanite influence, for it means "my father is Yam" (Yam was the Canaanite sea god). Both Rehoboam and Jeroboam had sons by this name.

Abijam reigned **three years** (913–910 BC; v. 2). He was not Rehoboam's oldest son but the son of his favorite wife, **Maachah** (Rehoboam had eighteen wives and sixty concubines; see 2 Chron. 11:18–22), **the daughter of Abishalom** (Absalom in 2 Chron. 11:20). Abijah's mother was a daughter of Uriel of Gibeah (2 Chron. 13:2.) It is likely that Maachah was the granddaughter of Absalom and the daughter of a marriage between Tamar (Absalom's daughter; see 2 Sam. 14:27) and Uriel. Absalom's mother was also named Maacah (2 Sam. 3:3).

15:3–8. Abijam followed **in the sins of his father** (v. 3; see 14:22–24). **His heart was not perfect with the LORD his God, as the heart of David his father**. Although David had fallen into grievous sin, his heart was never divided between serving the Lord and serving the nature deities of the Canaanites.

Only because of David's righteousness did God extend His grace to this wicked descendant to allow him to reign as long as he did and to give David a **lamp in Jerusalem** (v. 4), that is, continue David's dynasty (see discussion on 11:36). The most serious blot on David's career had been **in the matter of Urijah the Hittite** (v. 5; see 2 Sam. 11).

The rest of the acts of Abijam (v. 7; see 2 Chron. 13) were recorded in the **chronicles of the kings of Judah** (see discussion on 14:29). **There was war between Abijam and Jeroboam** (see v. 6; 14:30). From 2 Chronicles 13, it is clear that the chronic hostile relations of preceding years flared into serious combat, in which Abijam defeated Jeroboam and took several towns from him, including Bethel (2 Chron. 13:19).

D. Asa of Judah (15:9–24)

15:9–10. The reign of **Asa over Judah** began **in the twentieth year of Jeroboam** (910 BC; v. 9; see discussion on 14:20). He reigned **forty and one years** (910–869 BC; v. 10). For his [grand]mother, **Maachah, the daughter of Abishalom,** see discussion on 15:2.

15:11–15. It is refreshing to see the grace of God touching the life of one who had been reared in a wicked environment and establishing him as a righteous king. Unfortunately, his life would have a sad ending. For a fuller account of Asa's life and reign, see 2 Chronicles 14–16.

Asa removed the **sodomites** (v. 12; see discussion on 14:24) and **all the idols that his fathers had made** (see 14:23). How serious Asa was in his religious reform is evidenced by his deposing his grandmother **Maachah** (v. 13) from her honored position as queen mother. Second Chronicles 14:1–15:16 indicates a progression in Asa's reform over a period of years. Although Asa had destroyed pagan idols and altars early in his reign (2 Chron. 14:2–3), it was not until after a victory over Zerah the Ethiopian (2 Chron. 14:8–15) that Asa responded to the message of the prophet Azariah son of Oded by calling for a covenant-renewal assembly in Jerusalem, in the fifteenth year of his reign (2 Chron. 15:10). After this assembly, Asa deposed his grandmother (the Hebrew

for "mother" here means "grandmother," a common usage) Maachah because of her idolatry (2 Chron. 15:16). **She had made an idol in a grove**; that is, she had made an idol for Asherah (see discussion on 14:15). It appears that Maachah's action was a deliberate attempt to counter Asa's reform.

The high places were not removed (v. 14). The reference here and in 2 Chronicles 15:17 is to those high places where the Lord was worshiped (for the question of the legitimacy of worship of the Lord at high places, see discussion on 3:2). Second Chronicles 14:3 indicates that Asa removed the high places, but this is a reference to the high places that were centers of pagan Canaanite worship (see 2 Chron. 17:6; 20:33 for the same distinction). This same statement of qualified approval that is made of Asa is made of five other kings of Judah prior to the time of Hezekiah (Jehoshaphat, 22:43; Joash, 2 Kings 12:3; Amaziah, 2 Kings 14:4; Azariah, 2 Kings 15:4; Jotham, 2 Kings 15:35). For **Asa's heart was perfect with the LORD,** see discussion on 15:3.

The things which Asa **himself had dedicated ... silver, and gold** (v. 15) most likely consisted of war booty that Abijam had taken from Jeroboam (2 Chron. 13) and that Asa acquired from Zerah the Ethiopian (2 Chron. 14:8–15).

15:16–17. During Asa's reign, there was change of dynasties in Israel (see 15:27–30), and there was **war between Asa and Baasha king of Israel all their days** (v. 16). This again refers to the chronic hostile relations that had existed ever since the division of the kingdom rather than to full-scale combat (see discussions on 15:7; 12:24; see also 2 Chron. 15:19).

Baasha ... built (i.e., "fortified") **Ramah** (v. 17). Baasha had recaptured the territory Abijam had previously taken from Jeroboam (see discussion on 15:7; see also 2 Chron. 13:19). Now Baasha fortified Ramah since it was located south of Bethel and only about five miles north of Jerusalem. This was his response to Asa's reforms. Many from the tribes of Manasseh, Ephraim, and Simeon were touched by Asa's reforms in Judah and were leaving Israel to join Asa at Jerusalem (see 2 Chron. 15:9–10). Therefore, Baasha was attempting to close the border crossing so that **he might not suffer any to go out or come in to Asa**. Thus, the security of Judah was threatened.

15:18–22. Asa panicked. Forgetting God's former protection (see 2 Chron. 14:9–15), he foolishly took **the silver and the gold that were left ... in the house of the LORD** (v. 18), that is, that which remained after Shishak of Egypt plundered Jerusalem (see 14:25), to buy protection from **Ben-hadad**. It is not clear whether **Hezion** is to be identified as Rezon of Damascus (see 11:23–25) or as the founder of a new dynasty.

There is a league ... between my father and thy father (v. 19). Apparently, this is a reference to a previously unmentioned treaty between Abijam and Tabrimmon of Syria. When Tabrimmon died, Baasha had succeeded in establishing a treaty with his successor, Ben-hadad. Asa had seen no hope for success against Baasha without the assistance provided by a renewal of the old treaty with Syria. Although his plan seemed to be successful, it was condemned by Hanani the prophet as a foolish act and a denial of reliance on the Lord (see 2 Chron. 16:7–10). The true theocratic king was never to fear his enemies but to trust in the God of the covenant for security and protection (see discussion on 1 Sam. 17:11). Ahaz would later follow Asa's bad example and seek Assyria's help when he was attacked by Israel and Syria (see 2 Kings 16:5–9; Isa. 7).

The cities that Ben-hadad conquered in **Naphtali** (v. 20) were of particular importance because the major trade routes west, from Damascus to Tyre, and southwest, through the plain of Jezreel to the coastal plain and Egypt, transversed this area. This territory would later be seized by the Assyrian ruler Tiglath-pileser III (2 Kings 15:29). Ben-hadad's invasion from the north forced Baasha to leave his southern border and return to **Tirzah** (v. 21), his royal city (see discussion on 14:17).

Asa's **proclamation throughout all Judah** (v. 22) was an action reminiscent of the labor force conscripted by Solomon (5:13–14; 11:28). He used the forced labor to destroy Baasha's fortifications at Ramah. Then he used the materials from the ruins to fortify **Geba ... and Mizpah**, two border fortresses,

to check Baasha's desire to expand his territory southward. Geba was east of Ramah, and Mizpah was southwest of Ramah.

15:23–24. The rest of all the acts of Asa (v. 23; see 2 Chron. 14:2–16:14) were written in **the chronicles of the kings of Judah** (see discussion on 14:29). In his final days, Asa became **diseased in his feet**. As grave as his physical condition was, he refused to seek God but consulted only physicians (see 2 Chron. 16:12). When he **slept with his fathers** (v. 24; see discussion on 1:21), **Jehoshaphat his son reigned in his stead**. For the reign of Jehoshaphat, see 22:41–50; 2 Chronicles 17:1–21:1.

E. Nadab of Israel (15:25–32)

15:25–26. These verses begin where 14:20 ended. The biblical historian must turn once again to the kings of Israel, because during the forty-one-year reign of Asa, eight kings of Israel came and went. Judah had only one dynastic family (David's) in its history. Israel to the north, however, had eight different dynasties (nine, if one counts Zimri's seven-day reign as a dynasty; see 16:15).

Nadab the son of Jeroboam began to reign ... in the second year of Asa (v. 25). The second year of Asa of Judah corresponded to the twenty-second and last year of Jeroboam of Israel (see 15:9; 14:20). Nadab reigned only **two years** (909–908 BC) before being killed by Baasha, and he continued in the sin of Jeroboam **his father ... wherewith he made Israel to sin** (v. 26; see discussion on 14:16). Although Abijam of Judah occupied Bethel during the reign of Jeroboam (see discussion on 15:7), it is probable that the paganized worship Jeroboam initiated was continued elsewhere until control of Bethel was regained by Baasha.

15:27–30. Baasha conspired against Nadab and killed him at **Gibbethon** (v. 27), a town located between Jerusalem and Joppa (probably a few miles west of Gezer), in the territory originally assigned to Dan (Josh. 19:43–45). This Levitical city (Josh. 21:23) probably had fallen into Philistine hands at the time of the Philistine expansion in the period of the judges. Nadab's death occurred in the **third year**

of Asa (908 BC; v. 28; see discussion on 15:10). It is likely that Baasha was a commander in Nadab's army and was able to secure the support of the military for his revolt. Though his murderous elimination of Jeroboam's dynasty is not necessarily approved by the writer, Baasha's action is seen as providential fulfillment of the divine prediction the Lord had spoken **by his servant Ahijah** (v. 29; see 14:10–11; Ahijah the prophet is not to be confused with Baasha's father, v. 27). This judgment occurred **because of the sins of Jeroboam … which he made Israel sin** (v. 30; see discussion on 14:16).

15:31–32. Details of Nadab's reign were also recorded in **the chronicles of the kings of Israel** (v. 31; see discussion on 14:19). The demise of Jeroboam's dynasty did not improve relations between the two kingdoms of Israel and Judah, for **there was war between Asa and Baasha … all their days** (v. 32; see discussion on 15:16).

F. Baasha of Israel (15:33–16:7)

15:33–34. Baasha's reign began **in the third year of Asa** (908 BC; v. 33; see discussion on 15:10) at **Tirzah** (see discussion on 14:17), and he reigned for **twenty and four years** (908–886 BC). His official years were counted as twenty-four, though his actual years were twenty-three (see 16:8; see also Introduction: "Chronology"). **He did evil … and walked in the way of Jeroboam** (v. 34). Sadly, the destruction of Jeroboam's family had not destroyed the seed of sin he had sown. The assessment of Baasha's reign indicates no improvement over the reign of Nadab, whom he replaced (see 15:26).

16:1. Jehu the son of Hanani brought God's word of condemnation to the king, as his father before him had (see 2 Chron. 16:7–10). Much as the man of God from Judah (see discussion on 13:1) and later the prophet Amos, Jehu was sent from the south to a northern king. If he pronounced his judgment at the beginning of Baasha's reign, the prophet must have been a relatively young man at the time, because his ministry continued for about fifty years, until the reign of Jehoshaphat of Judah (2 Chron. 19:2). If his prophecy was delivered shortly before

the fulfillment, his ministry still may have spanned thirty-five years. This prophet's work as a historian was included in "the book of the kings of Israel" (2 Chron. 20:34).

16:2–4. I exalted thee out of the dust (v. 2) depicts Baasha's lowly origin (see 14:7). His walking **in the way of Jeroboam** denotes his continuance in the sin of Jeroboam (see discussion on 14:16), which would terminate in the same judgment Jeroboam and his family had suffered. **I will take away the posterity of Baasha, and … his house** (v. 3; compare 14:10, the house of Jeroboam; and 21:21, the house of Omri and Ahab). Even the description of death is identical to the prophecy against Jeroboam's dynasty (14:11).

16:5–7. For the purposes of the writer of Kings (see Introduction: "Theme"), it was not necessary to list any of Baasha's achievements. While he may have been a very successful ruler from a military and political point of view, only **his might** (v. 5) was mentioned in **the chronicles of the kings of Israel** (see discussion on 14:19). He is remembered for the **evil that he did … like the house of Jeroboam** (v. 7; see 16:2; 15:34). **He killed him** is literally "he struck it" (i.e., he struck Jeroboam's house). Although Baasha fulfilled God's purpose (14:10, 14) in destroying the house of Jeroboam, he remained responsible for this violent and unlawful act (see Gen. 50:20; Isa. 10:5–7, 12).

G. Elah of Israel (16:8–14)

16:8–10. Elah the son of Baasha began to reign **in the twenty and sixth year of Asa** (886 BC; v. 8; see discussion on 15:10; see also Introduction: "Chronology"). He reigned only **two years** (886–885 BC). His **drinking himself drunk** (v. 9) depicts his carousing at Tirzah while the army was laying siege to Gibbethon (16:15) and indicates that he had little perception of his responsibilities as king. Elah was killed by **Zimri** (v. 10), **in the twenty and seventh year of Asa** (885 BC).

16:11–14. Zimri was thorough. **He slew all the house of Baasha** (v. 11; see 15:29; 2 Kings 10:1–7; 11:1). Zimri's extermination went beyond Baasha's immediate family. In addition to the royal descendants, he killed Elah's **kinsfolks** (lit., "redeemers," who would have been obliged to avenge the murder: see Deut. 19:12; Josh. 20:3) and **friends** (i.e., those would be opposed to Zimri, the murderous usurper). Among his friends was probably the chief adviser to the king (see discussion on 2 Sam. 15:37).

Zimri's actions fulfilled the **word of the LORD ... by Jehu the prophet** (v. 12; see 16:1–4). Zimri did not consciously decide to fulfill Jehu's prophecy, but he unwittingly became the instrument by which Jehu's prediction was fulfilled (see discussion on 16:7) when he conspired against Elah and destroyed the dynasty of Baasha.

As it was with Jeroboam, **the sins of Baasha, and ... Elah his son, by which they sinned** (v. 13), brought the judgment of God upon them (see 15:34). The **vanities** of Israel refers to all the paganism in Israel's religious observances, including the use of the golden calves in worship (see 12:28; 14:9). The acts of Elah were also recorded in **the chronicles of the kings of Israel** (v. 14; see discussion on 14:19).

H. Zimri of Israel (16:15–20)

16:15–20. Zimri reigned only briefly, **in the twenty and seventh year of Asa** (885 BC; v. 15; see discussions on 15:1, 10). He had only seven days to accomplish his dastardly deed. He did not have the support of the populace or the military. When word reached the military at **Gibbethon** (see discussions on 16:9; 15:27) that Zimri had **conspired, and ... slain the king** (v. 16; see 16:9–12), Israel promptly appointed **Omri, the captain of the host**, as king to oppose and dethrone Zimri. Omri had held a higher rank than Zimri did under Elah (16:9). With Omri's new appointment and support, he went to **Tirzah** (v. 17), the royal residence (see 16:8–10; see also discussion on 14:17), and besieged it. Zimri took his own life, however, having walked **in the way of Jeroboam** (v. 19; see discussion on 14:16).

I. Omri of Israel (16:21–28)

16:21–22. For four years, Israel divided her loyalties between Omri and Tibni, another military rival. **Tibni died** (v. 22). It is not clear whether Tib-

ni's death was due to natural causes or to the military struggle for control of the land.

16:23–24. In the thirty and first year of Asa (880 BC; v. 23; see discussion on 15:10; see also Introduction: "Chronology") **began Omri to reign;** that is, he became sole king. The struggle for control of the northern kingdom between Omri and Tibni lasted four years (compare this verse with 16:15). The **twelve years** of Omri's reign (885–874) included the four years of struggle between Omri and Tibni (see 16:15, 29). **Tirzah** (see discussion on 14:17), which Omri had been able to capture in a matter of days (16:15–19), was his royal city for six years.

Seven miles northwest of Shechem, **Samaria** (v. 24) rose about three hundred feet above the surrounding fertile valleys (and is referred to as a "crown" in Isa. 28:1). The original owner may have been persuaded to sell his property (see 21:3) on the condition that the city be named after him (see Ruth 4:5). The site provided an ideal location for a nearly impregnable capital city for the northern kingdom (see 20:1–21; 2 Kings 6:25; 18:9–10). With the establishment of this royal city, the kings of the north came to possess a royal citadel-city like that of the Davidic dynasty (see 2 Sam. 5:6–12). Archaeologists have discovered that Omri and Ahab adorned it with magnificent structures to rival those Solomon had erected in Jerusalem. From this time on, the northern kingdom could be designated by the name of the royal city, just as the southern kingdom could be designated by its capital, Jerusalem (see, e.g., 21:1; Isa. 10:10; Amos 6:1).

16:25–28. Omri wrought evil ... and did worse than all ... before him (v. 25). His alliance with Ethbaal of Tyre and Sidon (Omri's son Ahab married Ethbaal's daughter Jezebel to seal the alliance) led to widespread Baal worship in the northern kingdom (16:31–33) and eventually to the near extinction of the Davidic line in the southern kingdom (see 2 Kings 11; see also discussion on 2 Kings 8:18). This marriage alliance must have been established in the early years of Omri's reign (see discussion on 16:23), perhaps to strengthen his hand against Tibni (see 16:21–22). He even exceeded the sin of Jeroboam and his **sin wherewith he made Israel to sin** (v. 26; see 12:26–33; see also discussion on 14:16). For Israel's **vanities**, see discussion on 16:13.

16:27. Though not reported in Scripture, **his might that he shewed** (v. 27) was recorded in **the chronicles of the kings of Israel** (see discussion on 14:19). Omri's military and political accomplishments were not of importance for the purposes of the writer of Kings (see Introduction: "Theme"). Apart from his establishing Samaria as the capital of the northern kingdom, about all that is known of Omri is that he organized a governmental structure in the northern kingdom that was in place during the rule of his son Ahab (see 20:14–15). Omri's dynasty, however, endured for over forty years. A century and a half later (732 BC), Tiglath-pileser III of Assyria referred to Israel as "the house of Omri" in his annals.

J. Ahab of Israel (16:29–34)

16:29–33. Ahab the son of Omri began to reign **in the thirty and eighth year of Asa** (874 BC; v. 29; see discussions on 15:9–10), and he reigned for **twenty and two years** (874–853 BC). He **did evil ... above all that were before him** (v. 30). Omri had sinned more than those before him (see 16:25), and Ahab sinned even more than his father had. Evil became progressively worse in the royal house of the northern kingdom. Nearly a third of the narrative material in 1–2 Kings concerns the thirty-four-year period of the reigns of Ahab and his two sons, Ahaziah and Joram. In this period, the struggle between the kingdom of God (championed especially by Elijah and Elisha) and the kingdom of Satan was especially intense.

Ahab **took to wife Jezebel the daughter of Ethbaal** (v. 31). The Jewish historian Josephus refers to Ethbaal as a king-priest who ruled over Tyre and Sidon for thirty-two years. Ahab had already married Jezebel during the reign of his father (see discussion on 16:25). **Baal** is perhaps Melqart, the local manifestation of Baal in Tyre, whose worship was brought to Israel by Jezebel. It is probable that Ahab participated in the worship of this deity at the time

of his marriage. The names of Ahab's sons (Ahaziah, "the Lord grasps"; Joram, "the Lord is exalted") may suggest, however, that Ahab did not intend to replace the worship of the Lord with the worship of Baal but to worship both deities in a syncretistic way.

Ahab imported the Phoenician Baal worship of his wife Jezebel into the northern kingdom and erected **an altar for Baal in the house of Baal** (v. 32) in the royal city of **Samaria** and then added a **grove** (v. 33; see discussion on 14:15). Solomon had erected the temple of the Lord in Jerusalem, but then he built shrines for the gods of his wives (see 11:4–8). Ahab's pagan temple and its sacred stone (see discussion on 14:23) were later destroyed by Jehu (2 Kings 10:21–27). By elevating the worship of Baal to an official status in the northern kingdom at the beginning of his reign, **Ahab did more to provoke the Lord ... than all the kings of Israel that were before him**.

16:34. During Ahab's reign **did Hiel ... build Jericho**. This does not mean that Jericho had remained uninhabited since its destruction by Joshua (see Josh. 18:21; Judg. 1:16; 3:13; 2 Sam. 10:5) but that it had remained an unwalled town or village. During the rule of Ahab, Hiel fortified the city by reconstructing its walls and gates (for a similar use of "rebuilt," see 9:17), perhaps at Ahab's instruction. This violated God's intention that the ruins of Jericho (Josh. 6:26) be a perpetual reminder that Israel had received the land of Canaan from God's hand as a gift of grace. Whether Hiel deliberately sacrificed his two sons as part of a ritual in laying the foundation or lost them to accidental deaths, the curse that Joshua had pronounced on the one who would rebuild Jericho was realized.

III. The Ministries of Elijah and Elisha and Other Prophets, from Ahab and Asa to Ahaziah and Jehoshaphat (17:1–22:53)

A. Elijah (and Other Prophets) in the Reign of Ahab (17:1–22:40)

1. Elijah and the Drought (chap. 17)

17:1. Elijah appeared providentially on the historical scene as a shining light whose rays pierced the darkness of wicked Ahab's reign. Ahab had so totally committed himself to Baalism that Elijah and his successor, Elisha, never addressed the issues of the gold calves and the rival worship at Dan and Bethel but devoted their ministries to denouncing Baal. Interestingly, their ministries involved a new outburst of miracles, such as had not been witnessed since the exodus from Egypt and the conquest of Canaan. Truly, all indications show that Israel stood at a major spiritual crossroad.

Information concerning Elijah's background is scanty. The name **Elijah** means "The Lord is my God," which was the essence of his message (18:21, 39). He was sent to oppose vigorously, by word and action, both Baal worship and those who engaged in it. He was **of the inhabitants of Gilead**, a phrase that could possibly be rendered "from Tishbe of Gilead." Gilead was in the northern area across the Jordan. The precise location of Tishbe, however, is unknown. His recorded ministry begins with an address to Ahab.

Before whom I stand is a technical expression indicating one who stands in the service of a king. Kings and priests in Israel were supposed to be anointed to serve as official representatives of the Lord, Israel's Great King, leading Israel in the way of faithfulness to the Lord and channeling His covenantal care and blessings to them. Since the days of Jeroboam, the northern kingdom had not had such a priest (12:31), and its kings had all been unfaithful. Now, in the great crisis brought on by Ahab's promotion of Baal worship, the Lord sent Elijah (and after him, Elisha) to serve as His representative (instead of king and priest), much as Moses had done long ago. The author of Kings highlights many parallels between the ministries of Elijah and Moses. **There shall not be dew nor rain**. The drought was not only a divine judgment on a nation that had turned to idolatry but also a demonstration that even though Baal was considered the god of fertility and lord of the rain clouds, he was powerless to give rain (see Lev. 26:3–4; Hos. 2:5, 8).

17:2–7. God's first directive to Elijah was **Get thee hence** (v. 3). With this command, God withdrew His prophet from His land and people, to leave them isolated from His word and blessings. The absence of the prophet confirmed and intensified the judgment. The location of the **brook Cherith** is uncertain. Perhaps it was a gorge formed by one of the northern tributaries to the Yarmuk River that lay on the eastern side of the Jordan. **I have commanded the ravens to feed thee there** (v. 4). The Lord's faithful servant Elijah was miraculously sustained beyond the Jordan (as Israel had been in the wilderness, in the time of Moses), while Israel was going hungry in the Promised Land—a clear testimony against Israel's reliance on Baal. That Elijah was sustained in a miraculous way demonstrated that the word of God was not dependent on the people, but the people were dependent on the word of God.

17:8–16. God's second directive sent Elijah to **Zarephath, which belongeth to Zidon** (v. 9), a coastal town located between Tyre and Sidon, in the territory ruled by Jezebel's father, Ethbaal (16:31). Elijah was commanded to go and reside in the heart of the very land from which the Baal worship being promoted in Israel had come. **I have commanded a widow woman there to sustain thee**. Elijah, as the bearer of God's word, was now to be sustained by human hands, but they were the hands of a poor widow facing starvation (v. 12). She was, moreover, from outside the circle of God's own people (see Luke 4:25–26); in fact, she was from the pagan nation that at that time (much like Egypt earlier and Babylon later) represented the forces arrayed against God's kingdom.

So he arose and went (v. 10). Elijah's reliance on the Lord demonstrated the faith in the Lord that all Israel should have been living by. The woman too was subjected to a severe test of faith by Elijah's request for food, and she responded with a tremendous demonstration of faith. **As the LORD thy God liveth** (v. 12). Her oath in the name of the Lord was either an accommodation to Elijah, whom she recognized as an Israelite (see discussions on 5:7; 10:9), or a genuine expression of previous knowledge of and commitment to the God of Israel.

As a prophet, Elijah's words were the command of the Lord. **Make me thereof a little cake first …**

and after make for thee and for thy son (v. 13). The widow was asked to give all she had to sustain the bearer of the word of God. The demand to give her all was in essence the demand of the covenant that Israel had broken. **Thus saith the LORD God of Israel** (v. 14). Elijah could tell the widow, **Fear not** (v. 13), because the demand of the covenant was not given without the promise of the covenant. The Lord does not ask more than He promises to give.

By an act of faith, the woman **did according to the saying of Elijah** (v. 15) and received the promised blessing. Israel had forsaken the covenant and followed Baal and Asherah in search of prosperity. In the midst of a pagan kingdom, a widow realized that trustful obedience to the word of God was the way leading to life. **The barrel of meal wasted not** (v. 16). God miraculously provided for this non-Israelite who, in an act of faith in the Lord's word, had laid her life on the line. Any other explanation, such as her generosity triggered the consciences of her more wealthy neighbors to give also, must be rejected. God gave her "manna" from heaven even while He was withholding food from His unfaithful people in the Promised Land. The warning of Deuteronomy 32:21 was being fulfilled (see Rom. 10:19; 11:11, 14).

17:17 – 24. When the woman's son became ill and died, in her grief, she questioned the presence of the prophet and the purpose of God. **Art thou come … to call my sin to remembrance, and to slay my son?** (v. 18). The widow concluded that Elijah's presence in her house had called God's attention to her sin and that the death of her son was a divine punishment for her sin. Although her sense of guilt seems to have been influenced by pagan ideas, both she and Elijah were confronted with the question, Why did the God who promised life bring death instead?

Taking the child, Elijah **stretched himself upon the child three times** (v. 21). The apparent intent of this physical contact was to transfer the prophet's bodily warmth and stimulation to the child. Elijah's prayer, however, makes it clear that he expected the life of the child to return as an answer to prayer, not as a result of bodily contact. **Let this child's soul come into him again**. Moved by a faith like that of

Abraham (Rom. 4:17; Heb. 11:19), Elijah prayed for the child's return to life so that the veracity and trustworthiness of God's word might be demonstrated. **The soul of the child came into him again** (v. 22). This is the first instance of raising the dead that is recorded in Scripture. This non-Israelite widow was granted the supreme covenant blessing, the gift of life rescued from the power of death. The blessing came in the person of her son, the only hope for a widow in ancient society (see 2 Kings 4:14; Ruth 1:11 – 12; 4:15 – 17; Luke 7:12).

When Elijah presented her a living child, the woman exclaimed, **I know that thou art a man of God** (v. 24). The widow had addressed Elijah as a "man of God" previously (v. 18), but now she knew in a much more experiential way that he truly was a prophet of the Lord (see discussion on 12:22). **The word of the LORD in thy mouth is truth**. God used this experience to convince the widow that His word was completely reliable. Her confession was one that the Lord's own people in Israel had failed to make.

2. Elijah on Mount Carmel (chap. 18)

18:1 – 2. In the third year (v. 1), apparently of the drought, the Lord spoke again to Elijah. Three may be a round number, for later Jewish tradition indicates that the drought lasted three and a half years (see Luke 4:25; James 5:17). It is possible that three and a half represents a symbolic number for a drought cut short (half of seven years; see Gen. 41:27; 2 Kings 8:1). Elijah's new directive was **shew thyself unto Ahab; and I will send rain upon the earth**. Elijah's return to Israel was not occasioned by repentance in Israel but by the command of the Lord, who in His sovereign grace determined to reveal Himself anew to His people. By the time Elijah returned, the **famine** (v. 2) in the land was severe.

18:3 – 6. Obadiah (v. 3), a common Old Testament name meaning "servant of the Lord," served Ahab as **governor of his house** (lit., "over the household"; see discussion on 4:6). True to his name, Obadiah feared and served the Lord, even risking his life to protect the true prophets of God, hiding them from **Jezebel** (v. 4), who was committed to abolishing the worship of the Lord and promoting Baalism. The **hundred prophets** (v. 4) may be the same as the "sons of the prophets" in 2 Kings 2:3–4.

The famine did not move Ahab to repentance (contrast Ahab's response to the famine with that of David years earlier, 2 Sam. 21:1). When his military strength seemed to be jeopardized, he scoured the land for food and water (see 10:26; according to the annals of the Assyrian ruler Shalmaneser III, Ahab had a force of at least 2,000 chariots). Ahab and Obadiah went separate ways in search of water.

18:7–16. While apart from Ahab, Obadiah encountered the returning prophet Elijah and was instructed, **go, tell thy lord, Behold, Elijah is here** (v. 8). This action would publicly identify Obadiah with Elijah, in contrast to Obadiah's previous clandestine support of the prophets Jezebel sought to destroy (see 18:4, 13). Obadiah's reluctance to announce Elijah's return to Ahab is understandable. Ahab had thoroughly, but unsuccessfully, searched all the neighboring regions (except for Phoenicia) for Elijah. Ahab's growing wrath and hatred for Elijah might be vented on Obadiah if the prophet should suddenly disappear, as he had a reputation for doing, and fail to make his appearance at the appointed meeting. **The spirit of the LORD shall carry thee whither I know not** (v. 12). Elijah's earlier disappearance and his sudden reappearance suggested to Obadiah that God's Spirit was miraculously transporting the prophet about (see 2 Kings 2:16).

Obadiah informed Elijah, **Jezebel slew the prophets** (v. 13). Her action was possibly an attempt to please Baal so that he would send rain. **The prophets of the LORD** that Obadiah had hidden were probably members of the communities of "prophets" that had sprung up in Israel during this time of apostasy (see discussion on 20:35).

18:17–20. Art thou he that troubleth Israel? (v. 17). Ahab held Elijah accountable for the drought and charged him with a crime against the state worthy of death (he called Elijah a "trouble bringer"; see Josh. 7:25). Elijah reversed the charges, telling Ahab, **ye have forsaken the commandments of the LORD, and ... followed Baalim** (v. 18). The source of Israel's trouble was not Elijah, or even the drought, but the breach of covenantal loyalty.

After three years of drought, Israel should have had serious doubts about the abilities of Baal, the storm and fertility god (see discussions on Judg. 2:11–13), to send the much needed rains. All Israel was invited to **mount Carmel** (v. 19), where Elijah would publicly discredit Baal and expose the futility of worshiping him. Mount Carmel was a high ridge next to the Mediterranean Sea, where the effects of the drought would be least apparent (see Amos 1:2) and the power of Baal to nurture life would seem to be strongest. Theoretically, if Baal were a true god, he would have had a decided advantage since **the prophets of Baal ... and the prophets of the groves** (see discussion on 14:15) were invited to invoke his response by fire, whereas only one prophet called upon the Lord. These pagan prophets, persons of privilege in the kingdom, all ate **at Jezebel's table** (see discussion on 2:7).

18:21–24. How long halt ye between two opinions? (v. 21). The Hebrew for "halt" is the same as that used for "leapt" in 18:26 (see discussion there). Elijah spoke with biting irony. In her religious ambivalence, Israel was but engaging in a wild and futile religious "dance," merely "hopping about" without making a decisive choice of whom to serve. **If the LORD be God, follow him: but if Baal, then follow him.** Like Joshua, who had challenged, "Choose ... whom you will serve" (Josh. 24:15), Elijah placed a clear choice before the people. He drew a sharp contrast between the worship of the Lord and that of Baal, to eliminate the apostate idea that both deities could be worshiped in a syncretistic way. Baalism would accommodate other gods, but the Lord demanded total and uncompromising loyalty and worship. **I, even I only, remain** (v. 22). Elijah was the only one to stand boldly and publicly against the king and the prophets of Baal (but see 18:4; 19:10, 14; 20:13, 28, 35; 22:6, 8; see also 19:18 and discussion). Perhaps the "hundred prophets" (18:4) were still hidden away and inactive.

The God that answereth by fire, let him be God (v. 24). Both the Lord and Baal were said to ride the thunderstorm as their divine chariot (see Ps. 104:3 and discussion); thunder was their voice (see Ps. 29:3–9 and discussion), and lightning ("fire") their weapon (see Ps. 18:14 and discussion). Elijah's challenge was direct and was understood by the people.

18:25–29. To prevent any complaints of an unfair advantage, Elijah permitted the prophets of Baal to select the bull of their choice and to proceed first. When Baal did not respond, **they leapt upon the altar** (v. 26). The ecstatic cultic dance was part of the pagan ritual intended to arouse the deity to perform some desired action.

Cry aloud: for … either he is talking, or … he sleepeth (v. 27). Elijah ridiculed the prophets of Baal, but as he did, he showed knowledge of the Baal myths. His taunts cast Baal in extremely bad light; Baal was too preoccupied to hear his prophets' cries. Contrast Israel's God, whose presence cannot be escaped (see Ps. 137:7–10) and who never sleeps (see Ps. 121:3–4).

Hoping to arouse Baal's attention, the desperate prophets submitted themselves to self-inflicted torture **till the blood gushed out** (v. 28). Self-inflicted wounds (that caused blood to flow) were symbolic of self-sacrifice, an extreme method of arousing the deity to action. Such mutilation of the body was strictly forbidden in the Mosaic law (Lev. 19:28; Deut. 14:1). **And they prophesied** (v. 29). This is indicative of ecstatic raving, in which the ritual reached its climax (see discussions on 1 Sam. 10:5; 18:10). Elijah permitted them to continue until the **time of the … evening sacrifice** (see Exod. 29:38–41; Num. 28:3–8). In the time permitted, Baal had not responded with fire. There was **neither voice … nor any that regarded.** The demonstration of Baal's impotence was dramatic (see Pss. 115:5–8; 135:15–18; Jer. 10:5).

18:30–35. The united monarchy of David and Solomon had been broken, and Israel's covenant with the Lord had been broken by idolatry. So Elijah's action to repair **the altar of the LORD that was broken down** (v. 30) was symbolic indeed. It was also an implicit condemnation of the existence of a separate northern kingdom and her idolatry. It is possible that the altar had been built by people of

the ten northern tribes after the division of the kingdom (see discussion on 3:2) and that it had been destroyed by the agents of Jezebel (18:4, 13; 19:10, 14). **Elijah took twelve stones, according to the number of the tribes** (v. 31). In this way, Elijah called attention to the covenant unity of Israel as the people of God, in spite of her political division. What was about to happen concerned the entire nation, not just the ten northern tribes. After repairing the altar and preparing the bullock, but before calling upon the Lord for fire, Elijah drenched the whole installation **with water** (v. 33), thus showing to all that he was using no tricks.

18:36–40. Elijah … came near and said (v. 36). Elijah's simple but earnest prayer stood in sharp contrast to the frantic shouts and "dancing" and self-mutilation of the Baal prophets. His appeal to the **LORD God of Abraham, Isaac, and of Israel** was a plea to the Lord to remember His ancient covenant with the patriarchs and a plea to Israel to remember all that the Lord had done for her since the days of her forefathers. As the fire had come out and consumed the first sacrifice on the altar at the tabernacle (see Lev. 9:24; see Chron. 21:26; 2 Chron. 7:1), **the fire of the LORD fell** (v. 38), proving that the Lord was the true God. The manner in which the whole altar of stone was consumed prohibits any notion that this fire was merely a strike of lightning that preceded a rainstorm. This demonstration of divine visitation was so overwhelming that all the people could only exclaim in reverential awe, **The LORD, he is the God** (v. 39; see discussion on 18:24). Elijah, acting on the authority of the Lord, who had sent him, carried out the sentence pronounced in the Mosaic law for prophets of pagan deities (Deut. 13:1–5, 13–18; 17:2–5). He took **the prophets of Baal** (v. 40) to the **brook Kishon** (in the Esdraelon plain, just north of Mount Carmel), and he **slew them there.**

18:41–46. There is a sound of abundance of rain (v. 41). Now that Baal worship had been struck a devastating blow, there was the promise of rain (see 17:1). Significantly, Ahab had taken no action; he had neither moved to carry out the Mosaic sentence nor halted Elijah. **Elijah … cast himself down**

upon the earth, and put his face between his knees (v. 42). Now that the people had confessed that the Lord alone was God, Elijah prayed for the covenant curse to be lifted (see discussion on 17:1) by the coming of rain (see 8:35; 2 Chron. 7:13–14). **Seven times** (v. 43), the number symbolic of completeness, the servant of Elijah was sent to scan the sea for a sign of a cloud. On the seventh time, he saw a small cloud arising **out of the sea** (v. 44), that is, appearing on the western horizon. The Lord's last proof of His supremacy over Baal was to do what the storm god could not do—send the rain God had shut off three and a half years earlier. Recognizing that a great rain was about to fall, Elijah **ran before Ahab to the entrance of Jezreel** (v. 46). Divinely energized by extraordinary strength, Elijah ran before Ahab's chariot to Jezreel. This dramatic scene, with the Lord's prophet running before the king and the Lord Himself racing behind him, riding His mighty thundercloud chariot (see discussion on 18:24), served as a powerful appeal to Ahab to break once and for all with Baal and henceforth to rule as the servant of the Lord.

3. Elijah's Flight to Horeb (chap. 19)

19:1–3. Any hope that the Lord's victory over Baal and his prophets might produce a change in Jezebel's attitude and character was quickly shattered. She promptly threatened to kill Elijah. **So let the gods do to me, and more also** (v. 2). This is a curse formula (see discussion on 1 Sam. 3:17). She expressed her intent to make Elijah like **one of them**, that is, like one of the dead prophets of Baal.

When he saw that, he arose, and went for his life (v. 3). In spite of Elijah's great triumph in the trial on Mount Carmel and the dramatic demonstration that Elijah's God was the Lord of heaven and earth and the source of Israel's blessings, Jezebel was undaunted. Hers was no empty threat, and Ahab had shown that he was either unwilling or unable to restrain her. So Elijah knew that one of the main sources of Israel's present apostasy was still spewing out its poison and that his own life was in danger. He fled to **Beer-sheba**, the southernmost city in

Judah (see discussions on Gen. 21:31; see also Judg. 20:1), which was out of Ahab's jurisdiction and out of range of Jezebel's vindictive pursuits. At a time when prospects for a nationwide spiritual revival were conceivably the greatest, the prophet himself spoiled them by fleeing in fear and discouragement, abandoning the nation and leaving them without spiritual leadership. He sought instead only to protect himself.

19:4–8. Elijah rested **under a juniper tree** (a broom tree; v. 4), a wilderness shrub that may reach a height of twelve feet and is thus large enough to offer some shade. **He requested for himself that he might die** (compare Jonah 4:3, 8). Elijah concluded that his work was fruitless and, consequently, life was not worth living. He had lost his confidence in the triumph of the kingdom of God and was withdrawing from the arena of conflict.

That **the angel of the LORD** (v. 7) encouraged the prophet to eat food because **the journey is too great for thee** indicates that Elijah had intentions to press further south. (For "the angel of the LORD," see discussion on Gen. 16:7.) God, in His mercy, provided sustenance and rest for His discouraged servant. Evidently, Elijah had already determined to go to Mount Horeb, where God had established His covenant with His people. There is no indication that the Lord had instructed him to do this, as He had previously directed him to go to Cherith (17:2–3), to Zarephath (17:8–9), and to meet Ahab (18:1).

For Elijah to have spent **forty days and forty nights** (v. 8) en route to Horeb, he must have been despondent. He was sustained, however, by the Lord, as Moses had been for the same length of time on Mount Sinai (Exod. 24:18; 34:28) and as Jesus would be in the wilderness (Matt. 4:2, 11). **Horeb the mount of God**, probably an alternate name for Mount Sinai (where God had first appeared to Moses and where He gave the Ten Commandments; see Exod. 3:1, 12; 19:1–3), was located in the wilderness about 250 miles south of Beersheba.

19:9–14. He came to **a cave** (v. 9). The parallels between Elijah's experience in this cave and Moses' experience in the "clift of the rock" where God had sheltered him (see Exod. 33:13 – 23) are striking. **What doest thou here, Elijah?** The question implies that Elijah had come to Sinai for his own misguided reasons and not because the Lord had sent him. It provided an opportunity for Elijah to state his case and for God to rebuke him gently.

Elijah did not give a direct answer to the Lord's question but implied that the work the Lord had begun centuries earlier with the establishment of the Sinai covenant had now come to nothing. Whereas Moses had interceded for the Israelites when they sinned with the golden calf (Exod. 32:11 – 13), Elijah condemned the Israelites for breaking the covenant and bitterly complained over the fruitlessness of his own work. **I, even I only, am left** (v. 10). Elijah's despair clouded his memory of Obadiah and the hundred prophets (see 18:3 – 4; and discussion on 18:22) and all those who had assisted him in slaying the prophets of Baal (18:39 – 40).

The series of phenomenal acts of nature was significant, because such acts were sometimes precursors of God's judgment on His enemies. In this situation, however, God spoke in **a still small voice** (v. 12), a loving, gracious, and gentle whisper. In the symbolism of these occurrences (vv. 11 – 12), the Lord appears to be telling Elijah that although His servant's indictment of Israel was a call for God to judge His people with windstorm, earthquake, and fire, it was not God's will to do so now. Elijah was to return and continue God's mission to His people, and Elisha would carry it on for another generation (19:16). When Elijah heard the voice of God, **he wrapped his face in his mantle** (v. 13; compare Moses' action in Exod. 3:6).

What doest thou here, Elijah? (v. 13). After demonstrating His presence in the gentle whisper rather than in the wind, earthquake, or fire, the Lord gave Elijah an opportunity to revise the answer he had previously given to the same question (vv. 9 – 10). Elijah's unrevised answer demonstrated that he did not understand the significance of the divine revelation he had just witnessed.

19:15 – 18. The LORD said unto him (v. 15). God's instructions to Elijah revealed His sovereign power over people and nations. Even though Israel would experience divine judgment through Hazael, Jehu, and Elisha, God would continue to preserve a remnant faithful to Himself among the people. **Return … to the wilderness of Damascus**. Apparently, Elijah was to go back by way of the road east of the Dead Sea and the Jordan River. Elijah was to anoint three men through whom God would render His judgment. (As it turned out, all three anointings took place east of the Jordan, though it was Elisha who effected the anointing of the two kings.) On the international level, Elijah was to **anoint Hazael to be king over Syria**. "Anoint" appears to mean here no more than "designate as divinely appointed." This anointing would be done by Elijah's successor, Elisha (see 2 Kings 8:7 – 15). Hazael would subsequently become a serious threat to Israel during the reigns of Joram, Jehu, and Jehoahaz (see 2 Kings 8:28 – 29; 10:32 – 33; 12:17 – 18; 13:3, 22).

On the national level, Elijah was to anoint **Jehu … to be king over Israel** (v. 16). Jehu was a military commander under Ahab and Joram, Ahab's son (2 Kings 9:5 – 6). He would be anointed king over Israel by "one of the sons of the prophets," at the instruction of Elisha (2 Kings 9:1 – 16) and given a mandate to destroy the house of Ahab. On the spiritual level, Elijah was to anoint **Elisha** as his prophetic successor. As with Elijah (see discussion on 17:1), Elisha's name (meaning "God is salvation" or "God saves") was the essence of his ministry. His name evokes memory of Joshua ("the Lord saves"). Here the Lord provided Elijah with a successor who would finish his work, just as the Lord had done for Moses. Elisha would channel the covenant blessings to the faithful in Israel, just as Joshua had brought Israel into the Promised Land (see the account of Elisha's ministry in 2 Kings 2:19 – 8:15; 9:1 – 3; 13:14 – 20). In the New Testament, John the Baptist ("Elijah," Matt. 11:14; 17:12) was followed by Jesus ("Joshua"; see discussion on Matt. 1:21) to complete God's saving work. Elisha was **the son of Shaphat**. *Shaphat* means "He judges," which was also in accordance with Elisha's ministry. For the location of **Abel-meholah**, see map, *KJV Study Bible*, p. 489.

Him that escapeth the sword of Hazael shall Jehu slay (v. 17) apparently was a prediction of Hazael's warring against Israel and wounding of Joram (see 2 Kings 8:28–29) before Jehu subsequently killed him (see 2 Kings 9:24). **Him that escapeth from the sword of Jehu shall Elisha slay** is more difficult. How this may have been fulfilled is unknown, but see 2 Kings 2:24; 8:1 (see also Hos. 6:5).

The remnant of **seven thousand** (v. 18) is probably a round number and is perhaps symbolic of the fullness or completeness of the divinely preserved godly remnant (Rom. 11:2–4). In any case, Elijah had been mistaken in his conclusion that he alone had remained faithful (see 19:10, 14; 18:22 and discussion). There were many who had **not bowed unto Baal, and** had **not kissed him** (see Hos. 13:2).

19:19–21. The reader is introduced to Elijah's successor, Elisha, but the details of his time of apprenticeship are not given; Scripture records only Elijah anointing his successor. **Elijah found Elisha … and cast his mantle upon him** (v. 19). Elisha understood the symbolism of the act and recognized his call. He immediately slew **a yoke of oxen** to provide a quick farewell feast, then assumed his new role as a prophet in training. Elisha's break with his past vocation was complete, though he obviously came from a wealthy family. **He … went after Elijah, and ministered unto him** (v. 21). In Hebrew, the same designation ("minister") is used for Joshua's relationship to Moses (Exod. 24:13; 33:11).

4. A Prophet Condemns Ahab for Sparing Ben-hadad (chap. 20)

20:1. Ben-hadad the king of Syria invaded Israel and **besieged Samaria.** Chronological considerations suggest that this was Ben-hadad II, either a son or a grandson of Ben-hadad I, who had ruled Syria as early as 900–895 BC (see discussions on 15:9–10, 18–20, 33). The events of this chapter span parts of two years (see 20:22–26), followed by three years of peace between Israel and Syria (see 22:1). Since Ahab died at the conclusion of the three years of peace, in a battle against the Syrians (22:37) in

853 BC, the events of this chapter are to be dated circa 857 BC. With Assyria to the north strengthening itself (on the international scene), Ben-hadad saw a possible invasion impending, so he headed up an Aramean alliance with **thirty and two kings,** that is, tribal chieftains or city-state kings who were vassals to him. To strengthen himself further, he invaded Israel and held Samaria in siege, either to prevent any future threat from this southern neighbor or to coerce Ahab into becoming a vassal and joining the coalition against Assyria.

20:2–9. Ben-hadad demanded an exorbitant ransom of royal possessions (wives, children, and valuables) from Ahab, wishing to humiliate him thoroughly. **I am thine, and all that I have** (v. 4). Ahab's submission to Ben-hadad's demand suggests that Israel saw little hope for the possibility of a military victory over the Aramean forces. The negotiated settlement would end the siege on Samaria, spare Ahab's life, and avoid the plundering of the city.

Ben-hadad then raised the ante: **I will send my servants unto thee … search thine house, and the houses of thy servants** (v. 6). Ben-hadad's new demand required the surrender of the city to his forces. Though Ahab replied in language conceding Ben-hadad's superiority (**my lord the king … thy servant;** v. 9; see also v. 4), he was adamant in refusing to surrender the city. **This thing I may not do** (v. 9).

20:10–12. Ben-hadad responded with a curse formula: **The gods do so unto me, and more also** (v. 10; see discussion on 1 Sam. 3:17). He also boasted that Samaria would be so utterly pulverized by his army that the city would be carried away as **handfuls** of dust.

Ahab replied, **Let not him that girdeth on his harness boast himself as he that putteth it off** (v. 11). This saying was proverbial and is comparable to the familiar "Don't count your chickens before they hatch." This reply incited Ben-hadad and his allies to advance on Samaria.

20:13–15. An anonymous **prophet** (v. 13) delivered to Ahab God's promise of victory, affirming, **thou shalt know that I am the LORD.** Although Ahab had not sought God's help in the crisis confronting the city, the Lord graciously chose to reveal Himself yet another time (see 18:24, 36–39) to the king and people, this time through a deliverance. Ahab, however, was to initiate an attack **by the young men of the princes of the provinces** (v. 14). Organizational details of the provincial government of the northern kingdom are unknown (see discussion on 16:27), but apparently Ahab had expected deliverance to come through them. **The young men … were two hundred and thirty two … all the children of Israel, being seven thousand** (v. 15). This was not a large military force (though a significant number for a city under siege), but its size is appropriate for demonstrating that the imminent victory was from the Lord rather than from Israel's own military superiority (see Judg. 7:2).

20:16–21. Ben-hadad was drinking himself drunk (v. 16). It is not clear whether Ben-hadad's excessive drinking with his allies was meant to lift their spirits and fortify their courage or was an overconfident, premature celebration of what they thought would be certain victory. Learning of Ahab's approaching men, Ben-hadad arrogantly commanded, **take them alive** (v. 18).

Ahab's young men **slew every one his man** (v. 20). Apparently, they were met by a small advance force like their own (see 2 Sam. 2:15–16). **Ben-hadad … escaped on a horse with the horsemen**. Since fighting on horseback did not come until later, this must refer to the chariot horses and charioteers. The Syrians seem to have withdrawn to Damascus after their defeat.

20:22–27. The king of Syria will come up against thee (v. 22). The anonymous prophet (see 20:13) warned Ahab against undue self-confidence. The prophet's announcement of an impending, renewed attack by Ben-hadad should have driven Ahab to more complete reliance on the God who had revealed Himself on Mount Carmel and in the recent military victory.

Meanwhile, Ben-hadad was ill-advised, on the basis of theological error. The Syrians presumed Israel's God was a provincial god. **Their gods are gods of the hills** (v. 23) was an expression of the pagan idea

that a deity's power extended over only the area of his particular jurisdiction. **Therefore they were stronger than we**. The Syrians believed that the outcome of military conflicts depended on the relative strength of the gods of the opposing forces rather than on the inherent strength of the two armies. For this reason, their strategy was to fight the next battle in a way that advantageously maximized the supposed strengths and weaknesses of the deities involved.

Several sites were named Aphek. This **Aphek** (v. 26) is presumably the one located a few miles east of the sea of Galilee. The battle apparently took place in the Jordan Valley, near the juncture of the Yarmuk and Jordan rivers.

20:28–30. The **man of God** (v. 28) is apparently the same prophet mentioned in 20:13, 22. **Ye shall know that I am the LORD** (see discussion on 20:13). With Israel so outnumbered by the Syrians, victory, which would come from the Lord, would demonstrate once again that He was the sovereign ruler over all nature and history and that the pagan nature deities were powerless before Him. His power was not restricted to the hills as the Syrians had surmised.

After a seven-day delay, Israel engaged in battle and **slew … an hundred thousand footmen** (v. 29). This number probably included all those who were driven from the field and the Syrian encampment, including support personnel. A remnant escaped to Aphek, where a **wall fell** (v. 30). Scripture does not clarify whether the wall collapsed due to poor construction, to Israel's use of a battering ram, or to divine intervention. Regardless, the God of Israel not only gave Israel's army a victory in battle but also brought an additional disaster to the Syrian army, claiming **twenty and seven thousand** more men. Aphek was not a large city, so it is doubtful that its wall could have literally collapsed on so many. Perhaps this is the number of troops that had taken refuge in Aphek and were left defenseless when the city wall gave way.

20:31–34. The kings of the house of Israel are merciful (v. 31). The Syrians recognized that Israel's kings were different from, for example, the ruthless Assyrian kings. Ben-hadad's servants appealed to

Ahab's sympathy with clothes of mourning, **sack-cloth … and ropes**, though here they were perhaps symbolic of humility and submission (compare another such charade, Josh. 9:3–15). In the diplomatic language of the time, Ben-hadad acknowledged his inferiority and subordination to Ahab by referring to himself as **thy servant** (v. 32; see discussion on 20:9). Ahab disregarded Ben-hadad's concession and responded in terminology used by rulers who considered themselves equals, calling him **my brother** (see 9:13). In doing this, Ahab gave much more than Ben-hadad had asked or expected. Ahab probably hoped that his leniency would lead to peace with Ben-hadad and a common front against the Assyrians (see discussion on 20:1).

Ahab **caused him to come up into the chariot** (v. 33), where the terms of Ben-hadad's new status as Ahab's ally must have been discussed. This was not the treatment normally accorded a defeated military opponent. Ben-hadad promised to return to Israel **the cities, which my father took from thy father** (v. 34). These were perhaps Ramoth-gilead (see 22:3) and some of the cities that Ben-hadad I had taken from Baasha (15:20) at an even earlier time. **Thou shalt make streets for thee in Damascus** apparently refers to outlets for engaging in the lucrative international trade, a distinct economic advantage; such privileges were usually a jealously guarded local monopoly. Ahab **made a covenant with him, and sent him away.** This was a parity treaty (a peace treaty between equals) that included among its provisions the political and trade agreements proposed by Ben-hadad.

20:35–40. Ahab's treaty called for a divine reprimand. It was not his prerogative to dictate terms of peace for a victory that God had won. An anonymous **man** (v. 35) received a message from God for Ahab and was to deliver it in a most unusual way. (Josephus [*Antiquities* 7.14.5] says the "man" was Micaiah; see 22:8). **The sons of the prophets** is an expression designating members of prophetic companies (see 2 Kings 2:3, 5, 7, 15; 4:1, 38; 5:22; 6:1; 9:1). "Son" is not to be understood here as a "male child" or "descendant" but as a member of a group.

These companies of prophets apparently were religious communities that sprang up in the face of general indifference and apostasy, for the purpose of mutual edification and cultivation of the experience of God. It seems likely that they were known as "prophets" because their religious practices (which were sometimes ecstatic) were called "prophesying" (see 18:29; Num. 11:25–27; 1 Sam. 10:5–6, 10–11; 18:10; 19:20–24), which is to be distinguished from "prophet" in the sense of one bringing ("prophesying") a word from the Lord. The relationship of the Lord's great prophets (such as Samuel, Elijah, and Elisha) with these communities was understandably a close one; the Lord's prophets probably were viewed as their spiritual mentors.

The **neighbour** (v. 35) who refused to strike the unnamed man was also reprimanded and condemned. **As soon as thou art departed from me, a lion shall slay thee** (v. 36). This penalty is reminiscent of what happened to the "man of God" from Judah (13:23–24). **Another man** (v. 36) was found to inflict an injury on the "man of the sons of the prophets."

By pretending to be a wounded soldier, the "prophet" induced Ahab to render his own judgment. The man claimed that he had lost a hostage he had been ordered to guard and that it would cost him a **talent** (i.e., about seventy-five pounds) **of silver** (v. 39) or his life. Because few soldiers could have paid such a large sum, it would have appeared to Ahab that the man's life was at stake. **So shall thy judgment be** (v. 40). Ahab refused to grant clemency. Little did he know that he was pronouncing his own death sentence (compare the similar technique used by Nathan the prophet, 2 Sam. 12:1–12).

20:41–43. With his disguise removed, the man, identified now as **of the prophets** (v. 41; see discussion on 20:35), identified Ben-hadad from God's perspective, **a man whom I appointed to utter destruction** (v. 42). The Hebrew refers to the irrevocable giving over of things or persons to the Lord, often by totally destroying them (see *KJV Study Bible* note on Lev. 27:28; discussion on Josh. 6:17). It is not clear whether Ahab had violated a previous revelation or had erred by simply neglecting to inquire of the Lord before releasing Ben-hadad. In any case, the Lord had given Ben-hadad into Ahab's hand (see 20:28), and Ahab was responsible to the Lord for his custody. Ahab's motive for sparing Ben-hadad revealed a lack of trust in God to exercise His power against Assyria, as he had done against the Syrians (see discussion on 20:32). **Thy life shall go for his life, and thy people for his people**. Because Ahab sinned in his official capacity as king, the sentence fell not only on Ahab personally but also on the people of the northern kingdom. Ahab would soon die in battle against the Syrians (22:29-39), and Israel would be severely humiliated by them during the reigns of Jehu and Jehoahaz (2 Kings 10:32; 13:3).

5. Elijah Condemns Ahab for Seizing Naboth's Vineyard (chap. 21)

21:1-4. In the previous story, Ahab had hoped to profit by not putting a deserving person to death. In contrast, in this story, he intended to profit by allowing a corrupt court to put to death an innocent person.

Naboth (v. 1) is introduced as a man who owned **a vineyard ... hard by the palace of Ahab**. Ahab maintained a residence in **Jezreel** in addition to his official palace in Samaria (see 18:45; 2 Kings 9:30). **Samaria**, though the capital city (see discussion on 16:24), here represents the entire northern kingdom.

Give me thy vineyard (v. 2). Because royal power in Israel was limited by covenantal law (see Deut. 17:14-20; 1 Sam. 10:25), Ahab was unable simply to confiscate privately held land, as was customary with Canaanite kings (see discussion on 21:7; see also 1 Sam. 8:9-17). Naboth's refusal to dispose of his land was based on his conviction that the land was the Lord's, that He had granted a perpetual lease to each Israelite family, and that this lease was to be jealously preserved as the family's permanent inheritance in the Promised Land. If Ahab understood Naboth's reason for refusal, he certainly could not have related it to Jezebel, his Phoenician wife (see 16:31), without facing ridicule. His chosen recourse was to sulk like a child.

21:5-10. Even when pressed by his wife for the reason of his sadness, Ahab said only that Naboth refused to sell him land, without offering any explanation that might be based on covenantal law.

Dost thou now govern the kingdom of Israel? (v. 7). Here is a sarcastic remark of incredulity spoken by one accustomed to the despotic practices of the Phoenician and Canaanite kings, who would not hesitate a moment to use their power to satisfy their personal interests. Whatever or whomever the king wanted, he got (contrast the attitude and practice of Samuel in the exercise of his civil power, 1 Sam. 12:3-4).

Jezebel acted with royal swiftness, sending out letters with **Ahab's name, and ... seal** (v. 8) to provide evidence of royal authorization. **Proclaim a fast** (v. 9). She attempted to create the impression that the people were threatened by a disaster that could be averted only if they would humble themselves before the Lord and remove any person whose sin had brought God's judgment on them (see Judg. 20:26; 1 Sam. 7:5-6; 2 Chron. 20:2-4).

To implicate Naboth falsely, she demanded **two men** (v. 10). Mosaic law required two witnesses for capital offenses (Num. 35:30; Deut. 17:6; 19:15). They are characterized as **sons of Belial** (see discussion on Deut. 13:13). Their purpose was **to bear witness** unscrupulously against Naboth. The entire scenario was designed to give an appearance of legitimate judicial procedure (see Exod. 20:16; 23:7; Lev. 19:16). The trumped-up charge was, **Thou didst blaspheme God and the king**. For this offense, the Mosaic law prescribed death by stoning (Lev. 24:15-16).

21:11-16. Jezebel's evil scheme was quickly carried out. Naboth was framed and condemned on false charges, then taken **out of the city** (v. 13) to be stoned, all in accordance with Mosaic law (Lev. 24:14; Num. 15:35-36). He was stoned on his own field (compare 21:19 with 2 Kings 9:21, 26), and his sons were stoned with him (see 2 Kings 9:26; compare the case of Achan, Josh. 7:24-25), thus also eliminating Naboth's heirs.

Jezebel ordered Ahab, **Arise, take possession of the vineyard** (v. 15). Either custom provided for property of slain criminals to be forfeited to the crown or Ahab illegally confiscated the property.

21:17–24. At this point, Elijah is reintroduced into the narrative (see 19:21). He was instructed to ask Ahab, **Hast thou killed, and also taken possession?** (v. 19). Ahab's willing compliance with Jezebel's scheme made him guilty of murder and theft.

Elijah appeared at the most inopportune times for Ahab (see 18:17). Had they not faced each other since their parting in 18:46? Ahab knew that Elijah never came to commend him but rather to condemn him. Elijah's denunciation led to three doom-filled predictions: **dogs ... shall ... lick thy blood** (v. 19; fulfilled in 22:38), **thy posterity ... will** be **cut off** (v. 21; fulfilled in 2 Kings 10:11, 17), and **dogs shall eat Jezebel** (v. 23; fulfilled in 2 Kings 9:33–36).

Ahab's subsequent repentance (21:29) occasioned the postponement of certain aspects of this prophecy until the time of his son Joram, whose body would one day be thrown on the field of Naboth (2 Kings 9:25–26). Ahab himself would be killed in battle at Ramoth-gilead (22:29–37) and his body would be brought to Samaria, where the dogs would indeed lick his blood as it was washed from his chariot (22:38).

When Ahab's descendants were cut off, it would affect both **him that is shut up and left in Israel** (v. 21), that is, both bond and free (see discussion on 14:10). Ahab was the third king of Israel to hear the curse of annihilation placed on his sons. His house would become **like the house of Jeroboam** (v. 22; see 14:10; 15:28–30) and **the house of Baasha** (see 16:3–4, 11–13). None of his descendants would receive an honorable burial (see discussions on 14:11; 16:4). This curse would not be fully accomplished until Jehu's purge (2 Kings 9:4–10:17).

21:25–26. The author now comments on Ahab's idolatrous behavior, **whom Jezebel his wife stirred up** (v. 25; see 16:31; 18:4; 19:1–2; 21:7). She was specifically named in the curse on Ahab's sons (21:23) because she had influenced her husband to behave even more wickedly. His idolatry exceeded that of **the Amorites** (v. 26), noted here as a designation for the entire pre-Israelite population of Canaan (see Gen. 15:16; Deut. 1:7).

21:27–29. Ahab outwardly demonstrated his remorse by donning **sackcloth** (v. 27; see discussion on Gen. 37:34). Because he "humbled" himself before the Lord (it is not stated that he repented of his idolatry), God promised the judgment would come **in his son's days** (v. 29). The judgment was postponed but not rescinded (see discussion on 21:19). Ahab would be permitted to die without seeing all the horrors of God's judgment (on his family) in his lifetime.

6. Micaiah Prophesies Ahab's Death; Its Fulfillment (22:1–40)

22:1–4. Three years (v. 1) passed after Israel's last battle with Syria (see discussion on 20:1). In the meantime, there had been no **war between Syria and Israel**. The annals of the Assyrian ruler Shalmaneser III (859–824 BC) record the participation of both "Ahab the Israelite" and Hadadezer (Benhadad) of Damascus in a coalition of twelve rulers who fought against Assyrian forces at Qarqar on the Orontes River in 853. According to the Assyrian records, Ahab contributed two thousand chariots and ten thousand foot soldiers to the allied forces. Assyrian claims of victory appear exaggerated since they withdrew and did not venture westward again for four or five years. With the threat of an Assyrian invasion somewhat abated, Ahab felt more at liberty to wage war on Syria to reclaim Ramoth in Gilead. Apparently, Ben-hadad had reneged on his agreement to return all of Israel's cities (see 20:34).

Jehoshaphat the king of Judah came down to the king of Israel (v. 2), perhaps to congratulate him on the success of the western alliance against the Assyrian threat (see discussions on v. 1; 2 Chron. 18:2).

Ramoth in Gilead (v. 3) was located near the Yarmuk River, east of the Jordan; it had been an Israelite city since the days of Moses (see 4:13; Deut. 4:43; Josh. 20:8). Ahab said the city **is ours**. Israel could lay claim to Ramoth-gilead also by virtue of the treaty concluded with Ben-hadad a few years earlier (see 20:34), the provisions of which he had apparently failed to honor.

Wilt thou go with me ...? (v. 4) Even though Ahab had just been allied with the Syrians against the Assyrians, now that the Assyrian threat was over, he did not hesitate to seize an opportunity to free Ramoth-gilead from Syrian control but felt he needed Jehoshaphat's help to guarantee success. **I am as thou art, my people as thy people, my horses as thy horses.** Jehoshaphat would later be condemned by the prophet Jehu (2 Chron. 19:2) for violating the Lord's will by joining forces with Ahab. In this alliance, Jehoshaphat completely reversed the policy of his father, Asa, who had entered into an alliance with the Syrians against Baasha of the northern kingdom (see 15:17–23).

22:5–9. Inquire ... at the word of the Lord to day (v. 5). Jehoshaphat hesitated to proceed with the planned action without assurance of the Lord's favor (see 1 Sam. 23:1–4; 2 Sam. 2:1). Four hundred **prophets** (v. 6) were consulted. Since their identity is not given, two options are possible: (1) they were false prophets who may have been (but not necessarily) Jezebel's new prophets of Asherah (see discussions on 18:19–20); (2) they were associated with the paganized worship at Bethel (see discussions on 12:28–29) and exercised their "office" by proclaiming messages designed to please the king (see Amos 7:10–13).

Is there not here a prophet of the Lord ...? (v. 7). Jehoshaphat recognized that the four hundred prophets were not to be relied on (see Ezek. 13:2–3) and asked for consultation with a true prophet of the Lord. There was one, **Micaiah** (v. 8), who refused to rubber-stamp Ahab's plans as the other prophets did. **He doth not prophesy good concerning me.** Ahab's assessment of a prophet depended on whether his message was favorable to him (see 18:17; 21:20).

22:10–14. While the two kings awaited Micaiah's arrival, **Zedekiah** (v. 11), evidently the spokesman for the four hundred prophets, dramatically acted out the promised victory through the symbolic use of **horns of iron**, a symbol of power (see Deut. 33:17).

The messenger who had been sent for Micaiah cautioned him, **Let thy word ... be like the word of one of them** (v. 13), a bit of advice that reflected the view that all prophets were merely self-serving. Mi-

caiah, however, committed himself to speaking **what the Lord saith** (v. 14).

22:15–18. Shall we go against Ramoth-gilead ...? (v. 15). Does "we" indicate a subtle shift (see 22:6) that sought a favorable response by including Jehoshaphat as a co-sponsor of the enterprise? **Go ... the Lord shall deliver it into the hand of the king.** Perhaps Micaiah's tone of voice betrayed that he sarcastically mimicked the four hundred false prophets (see 22:12).

Tell me nothing but that which is true (v. 16). Micaiah apparently betrayed his lack of seriousness, and Ahab immediately recognized this. When pressed for the truth, Micaiah uttered a sobering prediction: **I saw all Israel ... as sheep that have not a shepherd ... These have no master** (v. 17). Using the imagery of shepherd and sheep (see Num. 27:16–17; Zech. 13:7; Matt. 9:36; 26:31), Micaiah depicted Ahab's death in the upcoming battle. His words were indeed unfavorable to Ahab.

22:19–23. I saw the Lord sitting on his throne (v. 19). A true prophet was one who had, as it were, been made privy to what had transpired in God's heavenly throne room and could therefore truthfully declare what God intended to do (see Isa. 6:1; Jer. 23:16–22).

The Lord hath put a lying spirit in the mouth of all these thy prophets (v. 23). Some view the "lying spirit" as Satan or one of his agents. Others have suggested a spirit of God who undertakes the task of a lying spirit (but see 1 Sam. 15:29). Still others understand the lying spirit as a symbolic picture of the power of the lie. The Lord had given the four hundred prophets over to the power of the lie because they did not love the truth and had chosen to speak out of their own hearts (see Jer. 14:14; 23:16, 26; Ezek. 13:2–3, 17; see also discussion on 2 Sam. 24:1; 2 Thess. 2:9–12). Ahab had hardened his heart and had used the prophets for his own purposes; now he was being led to his ruin by their prophecy.

22:24–28. Which way went the spirit of the Lord from me to speak unto thee? (v. 24). By this sarcastic question, Zedekiah suggested that one prophet could be a liar just as well as another. Micaiah's answer was sobering: **Thou shalt see ... when thou shalt go into an inner chamber to hide** (v. 25), the place where Zedekiah would seek refuge (see 20:30). This would vindicate Micaiah's prophetic authority.

Because of his prediction, Micaiah was to be confined in prison until Ahab returned from battle and proved the prophet wrong. Micaiah's retort is reminiscent of Moses' test of a prophet's authenticity (Deut. 18:20–22). A true prophet's predictions come true.

22:29–30. Strangely, neither Ahab nor Jehoshaphat heeded Micaiah's warning. Ahab, somewhat shaken, displayed a pagan concept that God's knowledge is limited. Before entering battle, he took a precaution. **I will disguise myself** (v. 30). By this strategy, Ahab thought he could direct attention away from himself to Jehoshaphat, who was dressed as a king, and so minimize any chance for fulfillment of Micaiah's prediction to come true.

22:31–33. The king of Syria instructed his **captains** to **Fight ... only with the king of Israel** (v. 31). If a leader was killed or captured, armies usually fell apart (see 22:35–36). Ahab's plan to misdirect the enemy to Jehoshaphat almost worked, but God spared Jehoshaphat when the Syrians realized he was not Ahab.

21:34–38. A randomly shot arrow providentially found its target between the plates of Ahab's armor, mortally wounding him and necessitating that **the driver of his chariot** change course (v. 34). A war chariot normally carried two men, a fighter and a driver. It appears that chariots sometimes carried three men, but the third seems to be an officer who commanded a chariot unit (see 9:22; 2 Kings 9:25; Exod. 14:7; 15:4). After much loss of blood, Ahab **died at even** (v. 35), thus fulfilling Micaiah's prophecy (21:17, 28).

Ahab's body was returned to Samaria for burial, and his chariot was washed. **And they washed his armour** (v. 38) is better translated, "the prostitutes bathed there," that is, in the place where the chariot was washed. To whom was the greater indignity: to Ahab or to the prostitutes who bathed there? Dogs licked his blood **according unto the word of the** LORD, thus partially fulfilling Elijah's prophecy concerning Ahab's death (see discussion on 21:19).

22:39–40. The ivory house which he made (v. 39) has become better understood through archaeological discovery. Excavators of Samaria have found ivory inlays in some of the buildings dating from this period of Israel's history. Ahab's use of ivory in this way is indicative of the realm's economic prosperity during his reign. With reference to the **cities that he built,** that is, "rebuilt," excavators have found evidence that Ahab strengthened the fortifications of Megiddo and Hazor. Ahab's other accomplishments were recorded in **the chronicles of the kings of Israel** (see discussion on 14:19), and **Ahaziah his son reigned in his stead** (v. 40). For the reign of Ahaziah, see 22:51–53; 2 Kings 1.

B. Jehoshaphat of Judah (22:41–50)

22:41–42. The introduction to Jehoshaphat's reign at this point is virtually parenthetical. Beginning with 22:51, attention is directed once again to the Omride dynasty, and the writer concentrates on the northern kingdom until the end of Jehu's reign (2 Kings 10:36). **Jehoshaphat ... began to reign over Judah in the fourth year of Ahab** (v. 41). This detail appears to refer to the beginning of Jehoshaphat's reign as sole king, in 869 BC (see discussions on v. 42; 16:29; see also Introduction: "Chronology"). He reigned **twenty and five years** (872–848 BC; v. 42). The full span of Jehoshaphat's reign dates from the thirty-ninth year of King Asa, when he became coregent with his father (see discussion on 15:10; see also 2 Chron. 16:12).

22:43–45. Though his association with Ahab somewhat clouded his image, Jehoshaphat was characterized as a good king, but though he did what was right, **the high places were not taken away** (v. 43; see discussions on 3:2; 15:14). **He made peace with the king of Israel** (v. 44), probably to be understood in the collective sense and as including Ahab, Ahaziah, and Joram, all of whom ruled in the north during the reign of Jehoshaphat in the south (see discussion on 22:4). Additional details of his reign were recorded in **the chronicles of the kings of Judah**

(v. 45; see discussion on 14:29). A fuller biblical account of Jehoshaphat's life is to be found in 2 Chronicles 17:1–21:1.

22:46–49. Other items of interest are mentioned. Jehoshaphat removed the **sodomites** (v. 46), that is, the male prostitutes (see discussion on 14:24), that remained in the land from his father's reign. That there was **no king in Edom** (v. 47) suggests that Edom was subject to Judah (see 2 Sam. 8:14; 2 Kings 8:20).

Jehoshaphat allied himself to Ahaziah, wicked Ahab's son, to develop a shipping fleet comparable to that of Solomon's and that sailed as far as **Ophir** (v. 48; see discussions on 9:26–28; 10:22). The prophet Eliezer denounced this alliance with Ahaziah and predicted that his fleet of ships would be destroyed (see 2 Chron. 20:35–37). Indeed, **the ships were broken at Ezion-geber,** a judgment of God on Jehoshaphat for entering into an alliance with Ahaziah of the northern kingdom (see 2 Chron. 20:35–37). Ahaziah apparently offered to assist Jehoshaphat a second time, but this time he wisely refused.

22:50. After Jehoshaphat's death, **Jehoram his son reigned in his stead** (v. 50). The reign of Jehoram is introduced again in 2 Kings 8:16–24 (see also 2 Chron. 21).

C. Ahaziah of Israel (22:51–53)

22:51–53. The **seventeenth year of Jehoshaphat** (v. 51) was 853 BC (see discussions on 22:41–42). Ahaziah reigned **two years** (853–852; see discussion on 2 Kings 1:17).

He followed in the evil **way of his father, and … his mother** (v. 52; see 16:30–33) and in the notorious **way of Jeroboam … who made Israel to sin** (see 12:28–33).

THE SECOND BOOK OF
THE KINGS

Introduction

See Introduction to 1 Kings.

Outline

G. Amaziah of Judah (14:1–22)
H. Jeroboam II of Israel (14:23–29)
I.   Azariah of Judah (15:1–7)
J.   Zachariah of Israel (15:8–12)
K. Shallum of Israel (15:13–16)
L. Menahem of Israel (15:17–22)
M. Pekahiah of Israel (15:23–26)
N. Pekah of Israel (15:27–31)
O. Jotham of Judah (15:32–38)
P. Ahaz of Judah (chap. 16)
Q. Hoshea of Israel (17:1–6)
R. Exile of Israel; Resettlement of the Land (17:7–41)

III. Judah from Hezekiah to the Babylonian Exile (chaps. 18–25)
A. Hezekiah (chaps. 18–20)
1. Hezekiah's Good Reign (18:1–8)
2. The Assyrian Threat and Deliverance (18:9–19:37)
3. Hezekiah's Illness and Alliance with Babylon (chap. 20)
B. Manasseh (21:1–18)
C. Amon (21:19–26)
D. Josiah (22:1–23:30)
1. Repair of the Temple; Discovery of the Book of the Law (chap. 22)
2. Renewal of the Covenant; End of Josiah's Reign (23:1–30)
E. Jehoahaz Exiled to Egypt (23:31–35)
F. Jehoiakim: First Babylonian Invasion (23:36–24:7)
G. Jehoiachin: Second Babylonian Invasion (24:8–17)
H. Zedekiah (24:18–20)
I.   Babylonian Exile of Judah (25:1–21)
J.   Removal of the Remnant to Egypt (25:22–26)
K. Elevation of Jehoiachin in Babylon (25:27–30)

Bibliography

Davis, John J., and John C. Whitcomb. *Israel: From Conquest to Exile: A Commentary on Joshua–2 Kings.* Grand Rapids, MI: Baker, 1989.

DeVries, Simon J. *1 Kings.* Word Biblical Commentary 12. Waco, TX: Word, 1985.

Gray, John. *1 and 2 Kings: A Commentary.* Old Testament Library. Philadelphia: Westminster, 1963.

House, Paul R. *1, 2 Kings.* New American Commentary. Nashville: Broadman and Holman, 1995.

Jones, Gwilym H. *1 and 2 Kings.* Century Bible Commentary. Grand Rapids, MI: Eerdmans, 1984.

Long, Burke O. *1 Kings, with an Introduction to Historical Literature.* Forms of the Old Testament Literature 9. Grand Rapids, MI: Eerdmans, 1984.

Patterson, R. D., and Herman Austel. "1 and 2 Kings." In *Expositor's Bible Commentary,* edited by Frank E. Gaebelein, vol. 4. Grand Rapids, MI: Zondervan, 1992.

Provan, Iain W. *1 and 2 Kings*. New International Biblical Commentary. Vol. 7. Peabody, MA: Hendrickson, 1995.

Thiele, Edwin R. *The Mysterious Numbers of the Hebrew Kings*. New revised edition. Grand Rapids, MI: Zondervan, 1983.

Wiseman, Donald J. *1 and 2 Kings: An Introduction and Commentary*. Tyndale Old Testament Commentaries 9. Downers Grove, IL: InterVarsity, 1993.

EXPOSITION

I. The Ministries of Elijah and Elisha and Other Prophets from Ahaziah of Israel and Jehoram of Judah to Joram of Israel (1:1 – 8:15)

A. Ahaziah of Israel; Elijah's Last Prophecy (1:1 – 1:18)

1:1. Moab rebelled. Moab had been brought into subjection by David (see 2 Sam. 8:2), but when the northern tribes and those east of the Jordan rebelled and made Jeroboam their king, political domination of Moab probably also shifted to the northern kingdom. An inscription of Mesha, king of Moab (see chart, *Zondervan KJV Study Bible*, p. xix), indicates that during the reign of Omri's "son" (probably a reference to his grandson Jehoram, not to Ahab), the Moabites were able to free the area of Medeba from Israelite control (see Map 5 at the end of the *KJV Study Bible*). This parenthetical note is probably positioned here because **after the death of Ahab** (see 1 Kings 22:37), his son Ahaziah reigned for only two years (see 1 Kings 22:51). Second Kings opens with the event that would lead to Ahaziah's death. The Moabites would rebel when his brother Joram was ruling (3:4 – 6).

1:2 – 4. After sustaining an injury, Ahaziah sent to inquire of **Baal-zebub** (v. 2), the local god of **Ekron**, the northernmost and closest of the five major Philistine cities (see Josh. 13:3; 1 Sam. 5:10 and discussions). The name Baal-zebub means "lord of the flies" and is apparently one of Hebrew ridicule (see discussion on Judg. 10:6). The original name was probably Baal-zebul, "Baal is prince," a name sup-

ported in the New Testament (see Mark 3:22; Luke 11:15). **Inquire … whether I shall recover**. Ahaziah apparently feared that his injury would be fatal. He turned to the pagan deity for a revelatory oracle, not for healing.

On this occasion, **the angel of the LORD** (v. 3; see 1 Kings 19:7; see also discussion on Gen. 16:7) spoke to **Elijah the Tishbite** (see discussion on 1 Kings 17:1). The Lord usually spoke directly to the consciousness of a prophet (1 Kings 17:2, 8; 18:1; 19:9; 21:17). Perhaps the means of revelation was changed in this instance to heighten the contrast between the messengers of Ahaziah (vv. 2 – 3; 1:5) and the angel (which means "messenger," same Hebrew word) of the Lord. For **the king of Samaria**, see discussion on 1 Kings 21:1. Ahaziah's messengers learned from Elijah, **Thou … shalt surely die** (v. 4). Ahaziah received the oracle he sought, but it came from the Lord through Elijah, not from Baal-zebub.

1:5 – 8. Why are ye now turned back? (v. 5). Ahaziah realized the messengers could not have traveled so quickly to Ekron and back. Their answer, **There came a man** (v. 6), and the message he bore, led Ahaziah to ask another question: **What manner of man was he …?** (v. 7). His query concerning the appearance of the man who had interrupted the mission of his messengers might have been prompted by recollections of his father's encounter with Elijah. **He was a hairy man** (v. 8); that is, he wore a garment (probably his cloak; see 1 Kings 19:19) made of sheepskin or camel's hair, tied with a simple leather thong (see Matt. 3:4). His dress contrasted sharply with the fine linen clothing (see Jer. 13:1) of his wealthy contemporaries and constituted a protest against the materialistic attitudes of the king and the upper classes (see Matt. 11:7–8; Luke 7:24–25). **It is Elijah the Tishbite.** Ahaziah was familiar with Elijah's appearance because of the prophet's many encounters with Ahab, his father.

1:9–10. The king sent unto him a captain of fifty with his fifty (v. 9). Feeling insulted by Elijah, who had not only challenged his royal command but had also issued a sentence of death, Ahaziah ordered Elijah to be taken into custody.

The pagan people of that time thought that the magical power of curses could be nullified either by forcing the pronouncer of the curse to retract his statement or by killing him so that his curse would go with him to the netherworld. It appears that Ahaziah shared this view and desired to take Elijah prisoner to counteract his pronouncement of Ahaziah's death.

The captain in charge of this mission spoke disrespectfully, emphasizing his own commission over the prophet's commission. **Thou man of God, the king hath said, Come down** (v. 9). Ahaziah attempted to place the prophet under the authority of the king. This constituted a violation of the covenant nature of Israelite kingship, in which the king's actions were always to be placed under the scrutiny and authority of the word of the Lord spoken by His prophets (see discussions on 1 Sam. 10:25; 12:23).

Elijah demonstrated the superiority of his authority by calling down fire, and **there came down fire from heaven, and consumed him and his fifty** (v. 10; see 1 Kings 18:38). Here is another link between the ministries of Elijah and Moses (see Lev. 10:2; Num. 16:35). At stake in this incident was the question of who was sovereign in Israel. Would Ahaziah recognize that the king in Israel was only a vice-regent under the authority and kingship of the Lord, or would he exercise despotic power, like the pagan kings did (see discussions on 1 Sam. 12:14–15)? At Mount Carmel, the Lord had revealed Himself and had authenticated His prophet by fire from heaven (see 1 Kings 18:38–39). This previous revelation was now confirmed to Ahaziah. Jesus' rebuke of His disciples for suggesting that fire be called

down from heaven to destroy the Samaritans (Luke 9:51–56) is not to be understood as a disapproval of Elijah's action but as an indication that the disciples failed to discern the difference between the issue at stake in Elijah's day and the unbelief of the Samaritans in their own day.

1:11–14. Again also he sent unto him another captain of fifty with his fifty (v. 11). Ahaziah refused to submit to the word of the Lord in spite of the dramatic revelation of God's power and risked sacrificing another captain and his men. The second captain was sent with a more insolent message, demanding that Elijah **Come down quickly.** This captain's fate also was death by fire from heaven.

The third captain **fell on his knees before Elijah** (v. 13). Recognizing that Elijah was the bearer of the word of the Lord, he feared for his life and bowed before him with a humble request.

1:15–16. The angel of the LORD (see discussion on 1:3) **said … Go down … be not afraid of him** (v. 15). Standing before the king did not frighten Elijah or influence him to modify the severity of his message (see 1:3–4, 6).

1:17–18. He died according to the word of the LORD (v. 17). In the end, Ahaziah was punished for turning away from the God of Israel to a pagan deity, and the word of the Lord was shown to be both reliable and beyond the power of the king to annul. **Jehoram**, Ahaziah's younger brother (see 3:1; 1 Kings 22:51), began to reign in Israel **in the second year of Jehoram the son of Jehoshaphat** in Judah. For a few years, two Jehorams (or Jorams) reigned contemporaneously: one, the son of Ahab, reigned in the north; the other, the son of Jehoshaphat (1 Kings 22:50) and the son-in-law of Ahab (see 8:18), reigned in the south. (For consistency and clarification, *Joram* will designate the northern king of Israel, and *Jehoram* the southern king of Judah.)

The southern Jehoram's reign overlapped that of his father, Jehoshaphat, from 853 to 848 BC (see discussion on 8:16). The reference here is to the second year of that coregency. The eighteenth year of Jehoshaphat (3:1) is therefore the same as the second year of Jehoram's coregency (852 BC).

For **the chronicles of the kings of Israel** (v. 18), see discussion on 1 Kings 14:19.

B. Elijah's Translation; Elisha's Inauguration (2:1–18)

2:1–5. The following narrative indicates that Elijah was aware of his imminent departure, probably having learned of it by revelation. Either he had informed Elisha, who was still accompanying him (see 1 Kings 19:21), and the "sons of the prophets," or they had separate prophetic premonitions. The story indicates a smooth transition from one prophet to the next.

I will not leave thee (v. 2). Aware that Elijah's ministry was almost finished and that his departure was near (v. 5), Elisha was determined to accompany him until the moment the Lord took him. His commitment to Elijah and to Elijah's ministry was unfailing (see 2:9). His persistence in remaining with Elijah, demonstrated here, passed the test of faithfulness, characterizing him as a suitable successor to Elijah.

For **the sons of the prophets** (v. 3), see discussion on 1 Kings 20:35. During the days of Elijah and Elisha, companies of prophets were located at Bethel (where Jeroboam had set up cultic calf worship; see discussion on 1 Kings 12:28–29), Jericho (v. 5), and Gilgal (4:38). It appears that Elijah journeyed by divine instruction to Gilgal (v. 1), Bethel (v. 2), and Jericho (v. 4) for a last meeting with each of these companies of prophets. Elisha's consistent response to their informative questioning, **Yea, I know it; hold you your peace** (vv. 3, 5), seems comparable to saying, "Yes, I am knowledgeable; do not be a distraction."

2:6–8. When Elijah and Elisha went to the Jordan River, **fifty men** (v. 7), sensing that something extraordinary was about to happen, followed and were present to witness the miracle by which Elijah and Elisha crossed the river.

Elijah took his mantle ... and smote the waters (v. 8). Elijah used his cloak much as Moses had used his staff at the time of Israel's passage through the Red Sea (Exod. 14:16, 21, 26). Over five centuries earlier, the Jordan had offered a similarly miraculous dry passage to all of the Israelites (Josh. 3:14–17).

2:9–10. Elisha's request was specific: **Let a double portion ... be upon me** (v. 9). He was not expressing a desire for a ministry twice as great as Elijah's, but he was using terms derived from the inheritance laws to express his desire to carry on Elijah's ministry. Israel's inheritance laws assigned a double portion of a father's possessions to the firstborn son (see Deut. 21:17 and discussion). He wanted to be a worthy successor in the prophetic ministry.

Thou hast asked a hard thing (v. 10). Although Elijah had previously been told to anoint Elisha as his successor (1 Kings 19:16, 19–21), Elijah's response clearly showed that the issue rested solely with the Lord's sovereign good pleasure. **If thou see me ... it shall be so ... but if not, it shall not be so.** Elijah left the answer to Elisha's request in the Lord's hands.

2:11–12. There appeared a chariot of fire, and horses of fire (v. 11). Elijah did not ride into heaven on a chariot of fire. It and the horses first isolated Elijah from Elisha, and then the whirlwind snatched Elijah up. The Lord's heavenly host had accompanied and supported his ministry (as it had that of Moses; see Exod. 15:1–10), and now at his departure, Elisha was allowed to see it (see 6:17). **Elijah went up by a whirlwind into heaven.** Elijah, like Enoch before him (Gen. 5:24), was bodily taken up to heaven without experiencing death; as Moses had been (Deut. 34:4–6), he was taken away outside the Promised Land.

My father, my father (v. 12). In respect and devotion, Elisha called Elijah his spiritual father. **The chariot of Israel, and the horsemen thereof.** War chariots and horsemen were sought after by Israel's kings for national security measures, but Elisha depicted Elijah as embodying the true strength of the nation. He, rather than the apostate king, was the Lord's representative. The same description would later be used of Elisha as well (13:14).

2:13–15. He took up also the mantle (v. 13). Possession of Elijah's cloak symbolized Elisha's succession to Elijah's ministry (see 1 Kings 19:19). Returning to the Jordan, he called, **Where is the Lord God of Elijah?** (v. 14). His question did not seek information but confirmation. Had the divine power so evident in Elijah's ministry been transferred to him? And **when he also had smitten the waters, they parted** (see 2:8). The Lord authenticated Elisha's succession to Elijah's ministry and demonstrated that the same divine power that had accompanied Elijah's ministry was now operative in the ministry of Elisha. In crossing the Jordan as Joshua had before him, Elisha was shown to be Elijah's "Joshua" (Elisha and Joshua are very similar names; Elisha means "God saves," and Joshua means "the Lord saves"). **The sons of the prophets ... bowed themselves to the ground before him** (v. 15), indicating their recognition of Elisha's succession to Elijah's position. Elisha was now the Lord's official representative in this time of royal apostasy.

2:16 – 18. Peradventure the spirit of the LORD hath taken him up, and cast him upon some mountain (v. 16). Did these fifty prophets also witness Elijah's spectacular ascension? They either doubted or did not understand the permanence of Elijah's departure. Obadiah had expressed a similar idea years earlier (see 1 Kings 18:12). **Ye shall not send.** Elisha knew their search would be fruitless. **Send** (v. 17). When the company of prophets refused to be satisfied with Elisha's answer, he eventually agreed to their request and permitted them to go so that the authority and truth of his words would be confirmed to them.

C. Elisha in the Reign of Jehoram (2:19 – 8:15)

1. Elisha's Initial Miraculous Signs (2:19 – 25)

2:19 – 22. A public miracle involving the purification of water promptly confirmed Elisha's prophetic succession (recall Moses at Marah, Exod. 15:23 – 25).

The inhabitants of **the city** (v. 19), evidently Jericho (see 2:18), were experiencing the effects of the covenant curse. **The water is naught** (i.e., bad)**, and the ground barren** (contrast Deut. 28:15 – 18 with Exod. 23:25 – 26; Lev. 26:9; Deut. 28:1 – 4). Jericho had been cursed by Joshua (see Josh. 6:26) but had been rebuilt by Hiel in Ahab's day (see 1 Kings 16:34).

Elisha asked for **a new cruse** (v. 20), a small vessel for holding liquid. That which was to be used in the service of the Lord was to be undefiled by profane

use (see Lev. 1:3, 10; Num. 19:2; Deut. 21:3; 1 Sam. 6:7). **Put salt therein.** Elisha may have used salt because of its known preservative qualities, but it is more likely that he used it to symbolize the covenant faithfulness of the Lord (see *KJV Study Bible* note on Num. 18:19; see also 2 Chron. 13:5).

I have healed these waters (v. 21). Any idea of a magical effect of the salt in the purification of the water is excluded by the explicit statement that the Lord Himself healed the water. In this symbolic way, and as the first act of his ministry, Elisha was able to proclaim to the people that in spite of their disobedience, the Lord was merciful and was still reaching out to them in His grace (see 13:23).

2:23 – 25. Bethel (v. 23) was the royal cult center of the northern kings (see 1 Kings 12:29; Amos 7:13); and Elijah and Elisha had been known to frequent Samaria (perhaps even as their main residence; see discussion on 5:3). The **little children** that came from the city were not innocent children. The Hebrew word here can depict youths. They were undoubtedly a band of rowdy, irresponsible, young men who taunted Elisha. **Go up.** Perhaps the youths from Bethel assumed that Elisha was going up to Samaria to continue Elijah's struggle against royal apostasy. Perhaps, as some believe, the youths were making a mockery of Elijah's translation to heaven. They may have regarded the reports about Elijah with skepticism or wished to be rid of Elisha in a similar manner; thus in their mocking, they were telling Elisha to ascend to heaven as Elijah had done. **Thou bald head** depicts contempt. Baldness was uncommon among the ancient Jews, and luxuriant hair seems to have been viewed as a sign of strength and vigor (see discussion on 2 Sam. 14:26). By calling Elisha "bald head," the youths from Bethel expressed that city's utter disdain for the Lord's representative, who, they felt, had no power. Therefore, Elisha **cursed them in the name of the LORD** (v. 24), pronouncing a curse similar to the covenant curse of Leviticus 26:21 – 22. The result, **there came forth two she bears ... and tare forty and two children,** gave a warning of the judgment that would come on the entire nation should it persist in disobedience and apostasy (see

2 Chron. 36:16). Thus, Elisha's first acts were indicative of his ministry that would follow: God's covenant blessings would come to those who looked to Him (2:19–22), but God's covenant curses would fall on those who turned away from Him.

2. Elisha during the Campaign against Moab (chap. 3)

3:1–3. Joram the son of Ahab began to reign … the eighteenth year of Jehoshaphat (v. 1; see discussion on 1:17). His reign of **twelve years** extended from 852–841 BC. Though wicked, he was **not like his father, and like his mother** (v. 2), that is, not as wicked as Ahab (see discussions on 1 Kings 16:30–34) and Jezebel (see 1 Kings 18:4; 19:1–2; 21:7–15). **The image of Baal that his father had made** is apparently a reference to the stone representation of the male deity (see discussion on 1 Kings 14:23) that Ahab placed in the temple he had constructed for Jezebel in Samaria (see 1 Kings 16:32–33). Joram removed this image, but from 10:27, it appears that this stone was later reinstated, perhaps by Jezebel. Jehoram persisted, however, in **the sins of Jeroboam** (i.e., calf worship) **… which made Israel to sin** (v. 3; see discussion on 1 Kings 14:16).

3:4–5. For the rebellion of **Mesha king of Moab** (v. 4), see discussion on 1:1. From this vassal state of Moab, Israel had required the heavy annual tribute (see Isa. 16:1) of **an hundred thousand lambs, and an hundred thousand rams, with the wool.** It was against this heavy demand that **the king of Moab rebelled** (v. 5).

3:6–10. To recover this source of tribute, Joram prepared for battle against Moab. Just as his father, Ahab, had done, he recruited the assistance of Judah's king, Jehoshaphat (see 1 Kings 22:4). **Wilt thou go with me against Moab to battle?** (v. 7). Joram wished to attack Moab from the rear (see v. 8), but to do that, his army had to pass through Judah. **I am as thou art, my people as thy people, and my horses as thy horses** (v. 7). Though Jehoshaphat had already been condemned by prophets of the Lord for his alliance with the northern kings Ahab (see 2 Chron. 18:1; 19:1–2) and Ahaziah (2 Chron. 20:35–37), his response was the same (see 1 Kings 22:4). He agreed

to join with Joram against Moab. Perhaps he was disturbed by the potential danger the growing strength of Moab posed to Judah (see 2 Chronicles 20), and he may have considered Joram less evil than his predecessors (see 3:2).

Joram chose to attack Moab by **the way through the wilderness of Edom** (v. 8). This route of attack took the armies of Israel and Judah south of the Dead Sea, enabling them to circumvent the fortifications of Moab's northern frontier and to avoid the possibility of a rearguard action against them by the Arameans of Damascus. The Edomites, who were subject to Judah, were in no position to resist the movement of Israel's army through their territory. Although here designated a king, **the king of Edom** (v. 9) was in reality a governor appointed by Jehoshaphat (see 8:20; 1 Kings 22:47) and was obligated to assist in this campaign.

The success of Joram's southern strategy was dependent on adequate water in the area to support his forces. **They fetcht a compass** (i.e., they made a circuit) **of seven days' journey** (v. 9), possibly around the southern end of the Dead Sea, and when no water was to be found, Joram assumed that God opposed his plan.

3:11–15. Despite his disposition to ally himself to pagan kings, Jehoshaphat is presented as a godly king who consistently sought divine counsel prior to a military engagement (see 1 Kings 22:7; 2 Chron. 20:3–12). **Is there not here a prophet of the LORD …?** (v. 11; see 1 Kings 22:7). Only after the apparent failure of their own strategies did the three rulers seek the word of the Lord (v. 12). **Here is Elisha the son of Shaphat.** Since Elijah is reported to have sent a letter to Jehoshaphat's son Jehoram after his father's death (2 Chron. 21:12–15), it seems that Elisha accompanied the armies on this campaign as the representative of the aged Elijah. The event is narrated here after the account of Elisha's initiation as Elijah's successor and the two events that foreshadowed the character of his ministry. Following the introduction to Elisha's ministry, the present episode is topically associated with the series of Elisha's acts that now occupies the narrative.

Elisha addressed the Israelite king rudely but to the point: **Get thee to the prophets of thy father, and ... mother** (v. 13; see 1 Kings 22:6). Elisha, like Jehoram, was from Israel, but it was only for the sake of Jehoshaphat, the godly king from Judah, that Elisha sought divine instruction. **Were it not that I regard ... Jehoshaphat ... I would not look toward thee** (v. 14). Joram would share in the blessing of the word of God only because of his association with Jehoshaphat.

Bring me a minstrel (v. 15). The musician was not called for magical purposes. Music soothes the troubled mind (see 1 Sam. 16:23), and Elisha desired the right atmosphere to create a disposition conducive to receiving the word of the Lord.

3:16–20. Make this valley full of ditches (v. 16). The Israelite armies were encamped in the broad valley (the Arabah) between the highlands of Moab on the east and those of Judah on the west, just south of the Dead Sea.

God promised, **Ye shall not see wind, neither ... rain; yet that valley shall be filled with water** (v. 17). The word of the Lord contained a promise and a directive. The Lord would graciously provide for His people, but they must respond to His word in faith and obedience (v. 16). God promised that the two Israelite armies would defeat Moab and devastate the rebellious country.

In the morning, when the meat offering was offered (v. 20; see Exod. 29:38–39; Num. 28:3–4), **there came water by the way of Edom**. Either by divinely produced water or divinely timed flash floods in the distant mountains of Edom, water flowed north through the broad, usually dry, valley that sloped toward the Dead Sea (see discussion on v. 16).

3:21–25. As the Moabites prepared for battle, they looked toward the valley, which should have been dry. Seeing it full of water and the rising sun's rays giving it a reddish tint, the Moabites imagined the water was bloody and suspected a fallout among their enemies. **The kings are surely slain ... smitten one another** (v. 23). The Moabites would have good reason to suspect that an internal conflict had arisen between the parties of an alliance whose members had previously been mutually hostile.

Coming to the camp of the Israelites, the Moabites fell prey to a surprise attack. They were defeated, pursued, and their cities were destroyed. Only **Kir-haraseth** (v. 25) was left intact. This was the capital city of Moab (see Isa. 16:7, 11; Jer. 48:31, 36) and is usually identified with present-day Kerak, located about eleven miles east of the Dead Sea and fifteen miles south of the Arnon River.

3:26–27. The king of Moab attempted to **break through even unto the king of Edom** (v. 26), hoping desperately to induce Edom to turn against Israel and Judah. In the face of certain defeat, King Mesha resorted to child sacrifice. **He took his eldest son** (v. 27), the crown prince, **and offered him for a burnt offering upon the wall** (see 16:3; Jer. 7:31) to the Moabite god Chemosh (see 1 Kings 11:7; Num. 21:29; Jer. 48:46) in an attempt to induce the deity to come to his aid. **There was great indignation against Israel**. The Hebrew underlying this clause would normally refer to a visitation of God's wrath. It may be that just when total victory appeared to be in Israel's grasp, God's displeasure with Ahab's dynasty showed itself in some way that caused the Israelite kings to give up the campaign. Comparing the Hebrew with later Aramaic usage, a few scholars suggest that the Hebrew here can be translated, "There was great dismay upon/in Israel"; that is, the Israelites found his action so repulsive that they lost interest in seeing their sure victory to its completion and returned home.

3. Elisha's Ministry to Needy Ones in Israel (chap. 4)

4:1–7. The prophets were not celibates. They had wives, children, and social obligations. Here one of **the wives of the sons of the prophets** (v. 1; see discussions on 2:3; 1 Kings 20:35), a widow, had a serious problem. **The creditor is come to take unto him my two sons to be bondmen**. Servitude as a means of debt payment was permitted in the Mosaic law (Exod. 21:1–2; Lev. 25:39–41; Deut. 15:1–11). It appears the practice was much abused (see Neh. 5:5, 8; Amos 2:6; 8:6), even though the law limited the term of such bondage and required that those so held be treated as hired workers. Here the creditor was threatening to take the woman's sons.

Learning that she had only **a pot of oil** (v. 2), Elisha instructed her, **Go, borrow thee vessels … borrow not a few** (v. 3). The increase of her oil would be proportionate to her faith and obedience. **Shut the door upon thee and upon thy sons** (v. 4). The impending miracle was not intended to be a public sensation but to demonstrate privately God's mercy and grace to this widow (see Ps. 68:5).

She did not hesitate to respond to the instructions of the Lord's prophet in faith and obedience, and she was richly rewarded. Not even Elisha was present, so the increase of oil could be attributed to nothing but the power of God.

4:8–11. The next story, whose chronology spans several years, occurred at **Shunem** (modern Solem; v. 8; see discussion on 1 Kings 1:3), which lay near Jezreel, on a route that Elisha frequented. Residing there was **a great woman**, one apparently known for her influence, wealth, or hospitality. She told her husband concerning Elisha, **This is a holy man of God** (v. 9). The woman recognized that Elisha was a person set apart for the Lord's work in a very special sense. Nowhere else in the Old Testament is the term "holy" applied to a prophet. She desired to build accommodations for Elisha so that **when he cometh to us … he shall turn in thither** (v. 10). This room, which was built especially for the prophet, was situated on the flat roof and probably had a private entrance from the outside. Through her hospitality, the woman was able to assist in sustaining the proclamation of God's word through Elisha.

4:12–14. Elisha's servant **Gehazi** (v. 12) is referred to here for the first time; he appears to have served Elisha in some of the same ways that Elisha had served Elijah, though Elisha and Gehazi were of drastically different character (see 5:19–27; 6:15). Elisha wished to reciprocate the kindness of the woman from Shunem. **Wouldest thou be spoken for to the king?** (v. 13). Had Elisha's assistance in the war against Moab (see 3:11–27) gained him prestige with the king and the military? Knowing that her husband was old, Elisha offered his influence to provide her and her property with royal protection. **I dwell among mine own people**. The Shunammite woman felt secure and content in the community of her own family and tribe and had no need or desire for favors from high government officials.

Gehazi noted, however, **She hath no child, and her husband is old** (v. 14). This would have been a great disappointment because it meant that the family's name would cease, and its land and possessions would pass on to others. It was also a great threat to this young wife's future because she faced the likelihood of many years as a widow with no provider or protector; children were a widow's only social security in old age (see 8:1–6; see also discussion on 1 Kings 17:22).

4:15–17. The woman was notified that she would have a son **about this season, according to the time of life** (v. 16), that is, at this time next year (see Gen. 17:21; 18:14). **Thou man of God, do not lie unto thy handmaid**. The woman's response revealed the depths of her desire for a son and her fear of disappointment more than it showed a lack of confidence in the word of Elisha. The woman conceived and bore a son as **Elisha had said unto her** (v. 17). The trustworthiness of Elisha's word was confirmed, and the birth of the son was shown to be the result of God's gracious intervention on her behalf.

4:18–21. Several years transpired. When the child was old enough to accompany his father (but still young enough to sit on his mother's knees), he suddenly suffered from what may have been sunstroke, judging from the season (harvest time) and his complaint. He was carried to his mother, whereupon **he sat on her knees … and then died** (v. 20). The child, given as evidence of God's grace and the reliability of His word, was suddenly taken from the woman in a severe test of her faith. Her subsequent actions demonstrated the strength of her faith in the face of great calamity. She told no one, not even her husband, but she **laid him on the bed of the man of God** (v. 21). In this way, the woman concealed the child's death from the rest of the household, committing him to God while she went to seek the prophet at whose word the child had been born.

4:22–23. Her husband thought it strange that she would inexplicably rush to the prophet. **Wherefore**

wilt thou go to him to day? (v. 23). The question suggests that it was not uncommon for the woman to go to Elisha, but on this occasion, the timing of her visit was unusual, for there were no religious celebrations or holy days to occasion the visit. **It is neither new moon, nor sabbath.** The sabbath and new moon were observed by cessation from work (see discussions on Gen. 2:3; 1 Sam. 20:5; *KJV Study Bible* notes on Exod. 16:23; 20:9–10; see also Lev. 23:3).

4:24–28. The woman rode urgently **to mount Carmel** (v. 25). **The man of God** (i.e., Elisha) recognized her from a distance and sent Gehazi to meet her. **It is well** (v. 26). Though intercepted by Elisha's servant, the woman was determined to share her distress with no one but the prophet from whom she had received the promise of the birth of her son. Kneeling before the prophet, the grieving woman reminded him, **Did I not say, Do not deceive me?** (v. 28). The woman struggled with the question of why the Lord would take from her that which she had been given as a special demonstration of His grace and the trustworthiness of His word.

4:29–30. Elisha instructed Gehazi, **Lay my staff upon the face of the child** (v. 29). It appears that he expected the Lord to restore the boy's life when the staff was placed on him. This does not suggest that Elisha attributed magical power to the staff but that he viewed it as a representation of his own presence and a symbol of divine power (see discussion on 2:8; see Exod. 14:16; Acts 19:12). The mother persisted, **I will not leave thee** (v. 30). She was not convinced that Gehazi's mission would be successful and insisted that Elisha himself accompany her to Shunem.

4:31–39. Though Gehazi had done as instructed, the child did not awake. When Elisha arrived, he entered his room, where the mother had laid her child, and **shut the door upon them twain, and prayed** (v. 33). Just as Elijah had done in a similar situation years before (see 1 Kings 17:20–22), Elisha first turned to the Lord in earnest prayer for the dead child's restoration to life. His prayer is clear evidence that his subsequent actions were not intended as a magical means of restoring life. **He … lay upon the child** (v. 34). His action should be compared to some

modern forms of artificial resuscitation (see discussion on 1 Kings 17:21). Perhaps Elisha was familiar with Elijah's earlier, similar action.

When the child was revived, the anxious mother was called to take her son. Seeing her son alive, she **fell at his** (Elisha's) **feet, and bowed herself to the ground** (v. 37). The woman gratefully acknowledged the special favor granted to her by the Lord through Elisha and silently reaffirmed the verbal confession of the widow of Zarephath (see 1 Kings 17:24).

4:38–41. There was a dearth in the land (v. 38). Perhaps this was the same famine mentioned in 8:1. Famine was a covenant curse (see Lev. 26:19–20, 26; Deut. 28:18, 23–24; 1 Kings 8:36–37) and evidence of God's anger with His people's disobedience to their covenant obligations. Due to the famine, **the sons of the prophets** (see discussion on 2:3) were forced to make a stew from whatever herbs could be found. One prophet included some unfamiliar **gourds** (v. 39) from **a wild vine.** The precise type of plant is not specified, though a possibility is the colocynth, a cucumber-like fruit that was bitter and fatally poisonous if eaten in large quantities. It is doubtful that the **meal** (v. 41), or flour, that Elisha added to the stew reversed the poisonous effects and made the stew edible (see 2:21 and discussion). His act was more likely symbolic of the miraculous means by which the Lord provided for those who were faithful to the covenant, at a time when others suffered under the covenant curse.

4:42–44. According to Mosaic law, the firstfruits belonged to God (Exod. 23:19; Lev. 23:10) and were given to the priests for food (Num. 18:12–13). **A man from Baal-shalisha** (v. 42) brought to Elisha food of **the firstfruits.** Instead of bringing the firstfruits of the new harvest (see Lev. 2:14; 23:15–17; Deut. 18:3–5) to the apostate priests at Bethel and Dan (see 1 Kings 12:28–31), godly people in the northern kingdom may have contributed their offerings for the sustenance of Elisha and those associated with him (see 4:38 and discussion on famine). Thus, they looked upon Elisha, rather than the apostate king and priests, as the true representative of their covenant Lord.

Though there was not enough food to feed the **hundred men** (v. 43) present, Elisha ordered that the food be given to them. **Thus saith the LORD, They shall eat**. The bread was multiplied at the word of the Lord through Elisha, apart from any intermediate means (compare 4:41; 2:20; see Mark 6:35–43).

4. Elisha Heals Naaman (chap. 5)

5:1–3. This account begins outside Israel, but Naaman, the recipient of God's grace, would go to the prophet of God in Israel for healing. **Naaman, captain of the host … of Syria was a great man … because by him the LORD had given deliverance unto Syria** (v. 1). This is probably a reference to an otherwise undocumented Aramean victory over the Assyrians in the aftermath of the battle of Qarqar, in 853 BC (see discussion on 1 Kings 22:1). In the narrator's theological perspective, this victory was attributable to the sovereignty of the God of Israel, who is the ruler and controller of the destinies of all nations, not just that of Israel (see Ezek. 30:24; Amos 2:1–3; 9:7). For all Naaman's greatness, he bore the stigma of being a **leper**. The Hebrew word for "leper" was used for various diseases affecting the skin, some more serious than others, not necessarily leprosy. That his wife's maid and the king displayed such concern for Naaman may indicate that his "leprosy" was of the fatal variety. There is no indication that lepers were social outcasts in Syria, as they were in Israel (see Lev. 13–14), but if Naaman died, his expertise would be lost to the military. Though not specifically named, the king of Syria at his time was probably Ben-hadad II (see discussions on 8:7; 13:3; 1 Kings 20:1).

The Syrians had gone out by companies (v. 2). Although Israel had concluded a peace treaty with the Arameans during the reign of Ahab (see 1 Kings 20:34), minor border skirmishes continued between the two states in the aftermath of the battle for control of Ramoth-gilead, in which Ahab had been killed (see discussion on 1 Kings 22:4; see also 1 Kings 22:35). They **brought … out of the land of Israel a little maid**. In sharp contrast to the Israelite king in Samaria, this young girl being held captive in Damascus was very much aware of God's saving

presence with His people through His servant Elisha, and she selflessly shared that knowledge with her Aramean captors. She notified her mistress of **the prophet that is in Samaria** (v. 3), Elisha, who maintained a residence in Samaria (see 5:9; 2:25; 6:19). The maid had great confidence in Elisha's ability even though he was not renowned for healing lepers (see Luke 4:27).

5:4–7. Having been informed of the prophet in Israel, the king of Syria declared, **I will send a letter unto the king of Israel** (v. 5). The border skirmishes apparently had not nullified the official peace between the two nations as established by treaty. The king of Israel is unnamed, but he was probably Joram (see 1:17; 3:1; 9:24). Part of the payment to the king was **ten talents of silver**, equivalent to about 750 pounds of silver. An idea of the relative value of this amount of silver can be seen by comparing it with the price Omri paid for the hill of Samaria (see 1 Kings 16:24). The weight of the gold and the value of the garments cannot be determined.

I have … sent Naaman … that thou mayest recover him of his leprosy (v. 6). Ben-hadad assumed that the prophet the Israelite slave girl had described was subject to the authority of the king and that his services could be bought with a sufficiently large gift. He thought he could buy with worldly wealth one of the chief blessings of God's saving presence among His people. On the other hand, Joram concluded that the entire incident was an attempt by Ben-hadad to create a pretext for a declaration of war and that he was subtly seeking to expose Joram's human frailties by asking him to heal a leper. **He seeketh a quarrel against me** (v. 7). So blind was Joram to God's saving presence through Elisha that he could think only of international intrigue.

5:8–14. Wherefore hast thou rent thy clothes? (v. 8). Elisha chided Joram for his fear (see discussion on 1 Sam. 17:11) and for his failure to consult the Lord's prophet (for evidence of the tension that existed between Joram and Elisha, see 3:13–14). **Let him come now to me**. Only then would Naaman learn that there was a **prophet** of the Lord **in Israel** (see 5:3).

Naaman arrived at Elisha's door **with his horses and with his chariot** (v. 9). This proud pagan would command the healing by his lordly presence. There was no magic, however, no exorcism, not even the touch or personal appearance of the prophet. Elijah's messenger instructed Naaman to **wash in Jordan seven times** (v. 10). The instruction was designed to demonstrate to Naaman that healing would come by the power of the true and living God of Israel, but only if he obeyed the word of the Lord's prophet. The prophet himself was not a healer. Ritual washings were practiced among Eastern religions as a purification rite, and the number seven was generally known as a symbol of completeness. Naaman was to wash in the muddy waters of the Jordan River, demonstrating that there was no natural connection between the washing and the desired healing. Perhaps it also suggested that one needed to pass through the Jordan, as Israel had done (Joshua 3–4), to obtain healing from the God of Israel.

I thought, He will … strike his hand over the place, and recover the leper (v. 11). Naaman expected to be healed by the magical technique of the prophet rather than by the power of God in conjunction with his own obedient response to God's word. **Are not Abana and Pharpar … better?** (v. 12). The Abanah was termed the Golden River by the Greeks. It is usually identified with the Barada River of today, rising in the Anti-Lebanon mountains and flowing through the city of Damascus. The Pharpar River flows east from Mount Hermon, just to the south of Damascus. An angry Naaman was ready to walk away unhealed, but his servant rationalized that if he had been asked to do some great thing commensurate to his status, he would have complied readily.

After Naaman obeyed completely, **his flesh came again like unto the flesh of a little child, and he was clean** (v. 14). Physically, Naaman was reborn (see also 5:15 and discussion). As he obeyed God's word, he received the gift of God's grace. Naaman was a sign to disobedient Israel that God's blessing was to be found only in the path of trustful obedience. When His own people turned away from covenant faithfulness, God would raise up those who would follow His word from outside the covenant nation (see discussions on 1 Kings 17:9–24; see also Matt. 8:10–12; Luke 4:27).

5:15–19. Naaman returned to Elisha a changed man, healed and converted. **There is no God in all the earth, but in Israel** (v. 15). Naaman's confession put to shame the Israelites who continued to waver in their opinion on whether Baal and the Lord (Yahweh) were both gods or whether Yahweh alone was God (see discussion on 1 Kings 18:21). God's miracles and blessings are not for sale. Acceptance of a gift on Elisha's part might have made it seem otherwise to Naaman. **I will receive none** (v. 16). Neither did Elisha seek monetary gain for proclaiming the word of the Lord (see Matt. 10:8). Naaman was healed solely by divine grace, not by the power of Elisha.

Naaman still associated Israel's God, the Lord, with the land of Israel. **Shall there not then … be given to thy servant two mules' burden of earth** (v. 17). In the ancient world, it was commonly thought that a deity could be worshiped only on the soil of the nation to which he was bound (see v. 15). For this reason, Naaman wanted to take Israelite soil with him in order to have a place in Damascus for the worship of the Lord.

That Naaman's faith was genuine is evidenced two ways: (1) his decision to sacrifice only to the Lord (v. 17); (2) his concern that he might be regarded as an idolator when he returned to Syria and assisted his king (as his servant) in worshiping his god (v. 18). Therefore, he asked for the Lord's pardon whenever this would occur. Naaman's **master** (v. 18) was probably Ben-hadad (see discussion on 5:1), whose god was **Rimmon,** also known as Hadad (and as Baal in Canaan and Phoenicia). This Aramean deity was the god of storm (Rimmon means "thunderer") and war. The two names were sometimes combined as Hadadrimmon (see *KJV Study Bible* note on Zech. 12:11).

Go in peace (v. 19). Elisha did not directly address Naaman's problem of conscience (v. 18) but commended him to the leading and the grace of God as he returned to his pagan environment and official responsibilities.

5:20-27. This delightful story has a sad ending, clouded by covetousness and deception. The sin of **Gehazi** (v. 20), Elisha's servant, was fivefold: (1) He coveted the wealth that Elisha was allowing to slip away. Using an oath formula, **as the Lord liveth** (see discussion on 1 Sam. 14:39), he decided to **take … somewhat of him.** (2) He lied to Naaman concerning needed assistance to accommodate two young prophets. (3) He exploited an unsuspecting, new convert on the pretext of aiding a religious cause, receiving gifts for **the sons of the prophets** (v. 22; see discussion on 2:3). **Give them, I pray thee, a talent of silver, and two changes of garments.** Gehazi deceived Naaman to satisfy his desire for material gain. (4) He distorted the picture of God. The evil of his lie obscured the gracious character of the Lord's work in Naaman's healing and blurred the distinction between Elisha's function as a true prophet of the Lord and the self-serving actions of false prophets and pagan soothsayers. (5) He lied to Elisha about his whereabouts. After he deposited the gifts in the **house** (v. 24) of Elisha (see 5:9), he told Elisha that he **went no whither** (v. 25).

Is it a time to receive money …? (v. 26). Gehazi sought to use the grace of God, granted to another individual, for his own material advantage. This was equivalent to making merchandise of God's grace (see *KJV Study Bible* note on 2 Cor. 2:17). "Money" here and elsewhere in 2 Kings refers to gold or silver in various weights, not to coins, which were a later invention. The things listed in this verse, **garments … maidservants,** evidently were what Gehazi secretly hoped to acquire with the two talents of silver (see discussion on 5:5).

Gehazi had confused his priorities. In an effort to gain some external things, he had lost sight of the real and eternal values of life. Therefore, along with Naaman's gift, he would receive Naaman's **leprosy** (v. 27; see discussion on 5:1). It **shall cleave unto thee, and unto thy seed for ever.** (For the extension of punishment to the children of an offender of God's law, see *KJV Study Bible* note on Exod. 20:5; see also discussion on Josh. 7:24.) Gehazi departed **a leper as white as snow** (see Exod. 4:6).

5. Elisha's Deliverance of One of the Prophets (6:1-7)

6:1-7. In this simple yet delightful story, one learns that no circumstance or incident was unimportant or insignificant to Elisha or to God. **The sons of the prophets** (v. 1) complained, **the place where we dwell with thee is too strait for us;** that is, it was too limited or too cramped. They asked that they be allowed to go to the Jordan and **make us a place there, where we may dwell** (v. 2). Some have suggested that the company of prophets lived in a communal housing structure. The Hebrew for this phrase, however, could be translated "a place there for us to sit," referring to some type of assembly hall. It is implied in 4:1-7 that the members of the prophetic companies had separate dwellings (see discussion on 1 Sam. 19:18).

When one man accidentally lost an ax head in the process of felling timber, his first concern was that **it was borrowed** (v. 5). At that time, an iron ax head was a costly tool, too expensive for the members of the prophetic company to purchase. Having lost it, the borrower faced the prospect of having to work off the value as a bondservant. Both Elisha and God showed concern and compassion for the man's predicament. Elisha symbolically **cut down a stick, and cast it in thither; and the iron did swim** (v. 6). The Lord demonstrated here His concern for the welfare of His faithful ones by causing the ax head to float miraculously to the surface of the water so that it could be retrieved.

6. Elisha's Deliverance of Joram from Aramean Raiders (6:8-23)

6:8-12. In the following story, neither opposing king is named, but undoubtedly the **king of Syria** (v. 8) was Ben-hadad II (see discussion on 5:1). He **warred against Israel,** a reference to border clashes rather than to full-scale hostility (see 6:23; see also discussion on 5:2). Some indication of Israelite weakness and Syrian strength is seen, however, in the ability of the Syrians to send forces to Dothan (only about eleven miles north of Samaria) without apparent difficulty (see 6:13-14). The new tactic of the Syrian king was to set up a secret camp to be used as an ambush.

The man of God (v. 9), Elisha (see v. 10), warned the **king of Israel**, probably Joram (see 1:17; 3:1; 9:24), not to travel on the route of the ambush. When this happened several times, a frustrated Syrian king demanded, **which of us is for the king of Israel?** (v. 11). Repeated evidence that Israel possessed advance knowledge of Syrian military plans led the king of Syria to suspect that there was a traitor among his top officials. He learned that the culprit was the prophet Elisha, who was able to inform Joram of every private detail of Ben-hadad's life.

6:13–20. Go and spy ... that I may send and fetch him (v. 13). The king of Syria thought he could eliminate Elisha's influence by denying him contact with Israel's king. Did he not consider that the prophet would have known also of the plans for his capture? Elisha was at **Dothan**, a town located on a hill about halfway between Jezreel and Samaria, where the main royal residences were (see 1:2; 3:1; 8:29; 9:15; 10:1; 1 Kings 21:1). The array of **horses, and chariots, and a great host** (v. 14) of men reveal Ben-hadad's determination to capture Elisha.

Elisha assured his servant, **they that be with us are moe** (more) **than they that be with them** (v. 16). He knew that there was greater strength in the unseen reality of the hosts of heaven than in the visible reality of the Syrian forces (see 2 Chron. 32:7–8; Ps. 34:7; 1 John 4:4). Then **he saw ... the mountain was full of horses and chariots** (v. 17). In response to Elisha's prayer, his servant was able to see the protecting might of the heavenly hosts gathered about Elisha (see Gen. 32:1–2; Pss. 34:7; 91:11–12; Matt. 18:10; 26:53; see also discussion on 2 Kings 2:11).

Smite this people ... with blindness (v. 18). Elisha had prayed for the eyes of his servant to be opened to the unseen reality of the heavenly hosts; now he prayed for the eyes of the Syrian soldiers to be closed to earthly reality (see Gen. 19:11).

This is not the way, neither is this the city (v. 19). Elisha's statement led the Syrian soldiers to believe that they were being directed to the city where Elisha could be found. Technically, this state-

ment was not an untruth, since Elisha accompanied them to Samaria. It was, however, a means of deceiving the Syrian soldiers into a trap inside Samaria, the fortress-like capital city of the northern kingdom (for other instances of deception recorded in the Old Testament, see Exod. 1:19–20; Josh. 2:6; 1 Sam. 16:1–2). When their eyes were opened, they learned that **they were in the midst of Samaria** (v. 20). The power of the Lord operating through Elisha turned the intended captors into captives.

6:21–23. The king of Israel (v. 21) appears to have been unsure of what to do next with his unscheduled visitors. **Thou shalt not smite them** (v. 22). In reality, the Syrian soldiers had been taken captive by the power of the Lord, not by Joram's military prowess. They were given the most unusual treatment: they were fed and released to return to Syria. The Lord's purpose was to demonstrate to them and their king and to the Israelites and their king that Israel's national security ultimately was grounded in the Lord, not in military forces or strategies. **The bands of Syria came no more into the land of Israel** (v. 23; see discussions on 6:8; 5:2). Temporarily, the Syrians recognized the futility of opposition to the power of the God of Israel.

7. The Aramean Siege of Samaria Lifted, as Elisha Prophesied (6:24–7:20)

6:24–25. Ben-hadad (v. 24) is the same king who had besieged Samaria on a previous occasion (see discussions on 13:3; 1 Kings 20:1). This siege is probably to be dated circa 850 BC. The siege resulted in an extreme food shortage and desperate circumstances. An **ass's head** (v. 25) sold for an exorbitant price, **fourscore pieces of silver**, about two pounds of silver (see also discussion on 5:5). According to Pentateuchal law, the donkey was unclean and was not to be eaten (see Lev. 11:2–7; Deut. 14:4–8). The severity of the famine caused the inhabitants of Samaria not only to disregard the laws of uncleanness but also to place a high value on the least edible part of the donkey. Even **dove's dung** (by the **kab**, a dry measure equal to about two pints) was sold, probably for fuel and not for food (although some have suggested "dove's dung" should be interpreted as "carob pods," which might have been eaten).

6:26–33. To a desperate woman crying for help, Joram responded, **If the Lord do not help thee, whence shall I help thee?** (v. 27). He correctly recognized his inability to assist the woman if the Lord Himself did not act on Israel's behalf, but he wrongly implied that the Lord was to be blamed for a situation that had been brought on by Israel's own disobedience and idolatry. The woman replied, **We will eat my son to morrow** (v. 28). Even mothers were reduced to becoming cannibals, and this mother appealed to the king to enforce an agreement whereby she could eat her friend's son. The sins of the king and the people were so great that the covenant curses of Leviticus 26:29 and Deuteronomy 28:53, 57 were being inflicted (see Lam. 4:10).

Joram could but **rent his clothes** (v. 30). This was probably more an expression of anger toward Elisha and the Lord (see v. 31) than one of repentance and sorrow for the sins that had provoked the covenant curse. He also donned **sackcloth**, a coarse cloth usually worn as a sign of mourning (see discussion on Gen. 37:34). It is not clear why he hid his sackcloth under his royal robe. Perhaps it was a testing of the Lord, a private ritual to attempt to gain divine favor.

God do so and more also to me (v. 31). Horrified and frustrated by his inability to do anything about the famine, Joram uttered a curse formula (see discussion on 1 Sam. 3:17). **If the head of Elisha ... shall stand on him this day.** Joram considered Elisha in some way responsible for the conditions in the city (compare Ahab's attitude toward Elijah, 1 Kings 18:10, 16; 21:20) and vowed to kill him.

The elders (v. 32), that is, the leaders of the city (see discussions on Exod. 3:16; 2 Sam. 3:17), joined Elisha and sat with him rather than with the king. They were present when the king's messenger arrived to behead Elisha. The prophet commanded, **shut the door, and hold him fast at the door.** Elisha knew that Joram was following his messenger, apparently having had a change of mind and now wishing to prevent Elisha's death. The king arrived and said, **this evil is of the Lord; what should I wait**

for the Lord any longer? (v. 33). Joram felt himself deceived by Elisha and abandoned by the Lord, whom he blamed for the disastrous conditions in the city.

7:1–2. Elisha's words were meant to bring encouragement to the despairing king (6:33). In just one day, the siege would be lifted, the famine would end, and food would be in abundance. **A measure** (Hebrew, *seah*) **of fine flour be sold for a shekel** (v. 1). A seah was about seven quarts, and a shekel was about two-fifths of an ounce. This was about double the normal cost of flour but was a phenomenal improvement over the highly inflated prices the famine had caused. The high-ranking official assisting the king lacked faith and thought Elisha's words were absurd, doubting the possibility of their fulfillment even **if the Lord would make windows in heaven** (v. 2; see 7:19; Gen. 8:2; Isa. 24:18).

7:3–5. Only those enclosed by Samaria's walls were starving. The Syrians holding siege lived off the land and fared well. The narrative introduces four lepers, **at the entering in of the gate** (v. 3). Pentateuchal law prohibited persons with skin diseases from residing within the community (Lev. 13:46; Num. 5:2–3). Outcasts of society, who by virtue of their disease were destined to die, they decided to risk entering the Syrian camp to beg for food. They reasoned that no evil consequence could be worse than the death to which they were already doomed.

7:6–7. They found the camp deserted, for in the silence of the night **the Lord had made the ... Syrians to hear a noise** (v. 6; see 2 Sam. 5:24 and discussion). Hearing the sound of advancing horses and chariots, they assumed that **the kings of the Hittites**, kings of small city-states ruled by dynasties of Hittite origin, which had arisen in northern Syria after the fall of the Hittite empire circa 1200 BC, **and the kings of the Egyptians**, from the south, had converged on Samaria to aid the Israelite king. In a panic, the Syrians had fled, leaving everything behind.

7:8–11. The lepers fared sumptuously—food, silver and gold, clothing—until their consciences reminded them of the starvation within the city. **We**

do not well (v. 9). In fear of divine punishment for withholding such wonderful news, they promptly reported their discovery to the city.

7:12–15. I will now shew you what the Syrians have done to us (v. 12). The king's unbelief caused him to conclude that the report of the four leprous men was part of a Syrian war strategy rather than evidence of the fulfillment of Elisha's prophecy (7:1). Suspecting a ruse to draw Israel out of the city for an ambush, Joram sent several brave men on a reconnaissance mission to search out the whereabouts of the Syrians. Clothing and equipment found strewn along the escape route were convincing evidence that the Syrians had indeed made a hasty withdrawal.

7:16–20. The author repeatedly reminds readers that the events all occurred **according to the word of the LORD** (v. 16) ... **as the man of God had said** (v. 17) ... **as the man of God had spoken** (v. 18) ... **so it fell out unto him** (v. 20), thus emphasizing the trustworthiness of the prophetic word spoken by Elisha. In the fulfillment of Elisha's prophecy, Israel was reminded that deliverance from her enemies was a gift of God's grace and that rejection of God's word provoked the wrath of divine judgment.

The king's official (7:2) was appointed to control the crowd as it rushed from the city for the spoils. He witnessed the miracle and the excitement it generated, but he was unable to participate in eating. He was trampled by the crowd he could not control, **and he died** (v. 20).

8. The Shunammite's Land Restored (8:1–6)

8:1–2. The narrative returns to the woman from Shunem (see 4:8–37), for whom Elisha continued to care for. **The LORD hath called for a famine** (v. 1). The famine should have been perceived by the people of the northern kingdom as a covenant curse sent on them because of their sin (see discussion on 4:38). Elisha predicted the famine would last **seven years**. It is not clear whether this famine began before or after the Syrian siege of Samaria (see 4:38; 6:24–7:20).

In the face of this impending food shortage, Elisha warned the woman to move temporarily for the duration of the famine. **She went with her house-**

hold (v. 2). Her obedience to Elisha's instruction enabled the woman and her family to escape the privations of the famine.

8:3–6. When she returned to her land, she found that someone had illegally occupied her property during her absence (whether a relative or strangers is not known), or perhaps it had fallen to the domain of the king by virtue of its abandonment. **She went forth to cry unto the king for her house** (v. 3). Had her husband died (see 4:14), so that she pled her own case? The king providentially was engaged at that very moment in listening to a report on the accomplishments of Elisha.

The king had asked **Gehazi** (v. 4; see 5:27), **Tell me ... all the great things that Elisha hath done.** The king's lack of familiarity with Elisha's ministry is perhaps an indication that this incident occurred in the early days of the reign of Jehu rather than in the time of Joram, who had had numerous contacts with Elisha (see 3:13–14; 5:7–10; 6:10–23; 6:24–7:20; but see discussion on 5:7). **As he was telling the king** (v. 5). The woman's approach to the king providentially coincided with Gehazi's story of her son's miraculous restoration to life through the ministry of Elisha. Her association with the prophet apparently influenced the king to return her land (see discussion on 4:13). **Restore all that was hers** (v. 6). The (supposed) widow and her son were living examples of the Lord's provision and blessing for those who were obedient to the word of the Lord through His prophets.

9. Elisha Prophesies Hazael's Oppression of Israel (8:7–15)

8:7–11. Elisha came to Damascus (v. 7). The purpose of Elisha's visiting Damascus is not stated. The time apparently had come, however, for Elisha to carry out one of the three tasks originally given to Elijah at Mount Horeb (see discussions on 1 Kings 19:15–16).

The annals of the Assyrian ruler Shalmaneser III record Assyrian victories over Ben-hadad (Hadadezer) of Damascus in 846 BC and Hazael of Damascus in 842 BC. Therefore, Elisha's visit to

Damascus is to be dated circa 843 BC. His reputation had preceded him (see Naaman's healing, 5:1–19). A very sick Ben-hadad sent **Hazael** (v. 8) to present a gift to Elisha and to **inquire of the LORD by him**. In a reversal of the situation described in 1:1–4, a pagan king was seeking an oracle from Israel's God. **Shall I recover …?** The question is the same as that of Ahaziah in 1:2.

The gift presented to Elisha consisted of **every good thing of Damascus, forty camels' burden** (v. 9). Damascus was the center for trade between Egypt, Asia Minor, and Mesopotamia. Ben-hadad evidently thought a generous gift would favorably influence Elisha's oracle. The king's use of father-son terminology, **thy son Ben-hadad,** was a tacit acknowledgment by Ben-hadad of Elisha's superiority (see 6:21; 1 Sam. 25:8).

Elisha instructed Hazael, **Go, say unto him, Thou mayest certainly recover** (v. 10), an assertion that Ben-hadad's illness was not terminal (see 8:14). Elisha continued, **Howbeit … he shall surely die.** Elisha's words appear contradictory but can be interpreted in a couple of ways: (1) Hazael already planned to tell Ben-hadad that he would live, but the Lord declared that Ben-hadad would die; or (2) Ben-hadad would survive his illness, but he would die nonetheless (by the hand of Hazael).

8:11–15. Elisha explained his weeping: **I know the evil that thou wilt do unto the children of Israel** (v. 12). The Lord gave Elisha a clear picture of the severity of the judgment He was about to send on Israel by the hand of Hazael (see 9:14–16; 10:32; 12:17–18; 13:3, 22). **Their strong holds wilt thou set on fire … and rip up their women with child.** These actions were characteristic of victorious armies at that time (see 15:16; Hos. 10:14; 13:16; Amos 1:13). Elisha's words did not sanction such acts but simply described Hazael's future attacks on Israel.

What, is thy servant a dog, that he should do this great thing? (v. 13) Hazael did not show repulsion at these violent acts but saw no possibility of gaining the power necessary to accomplish them (for this metaphorical use of "dog," see discussion on 2 Sam. 9:8). If Hazael had not known he was destined to be king (see discussions on 1 Kings 19:15), it should have been evident now. **Thou shalt be king over Syria.** Elisha's prophecy suggests that Hazael was not a legitimate successor to Ben-hadad. In an Assyrian inscription, Hazael is designated "the son of a nobody" (i.e., a commoner) who usurped the throne.

The next day, Hazael smothered Ben-hadad, and **he died** (v. 15). Elisha's prophecy of Hazael's kingship did not legitimize the assassination. Hazael's murder of Ben-hadad and his future acts of violence against Israel were wicked acts arising out of his own sinful heart (see Isa. 10:5–19). His reign extended from around 842 BC to 806 or 796 BC, and he was followed by a son he had named Ben-hadad (13:24).

II. Israel and Judah from Joram and Jehoram to the Exile of Israel (8:16–17:41)

A. Jehoram of Judah (8:16–24)

8:16–19. The fifth year of Joram the son of Ahab was 848 BC. Jehoram, the son of Jehoshaphat and brother-in-law to Israel's king (he had married Athaliah, the daughter of Ahab; see v. 18), had been coregent with his father since 853 (see discussion on 1:17), but he now began his reign as sole king. **He reigned eight years in Jerusalem** (v. 17). Jehoram's sole reign is to be dated 848–841 BC.

The long-lasting impact of the alliance between Ahab and Jehoshaphat (see discussion on 1 Kings 22:4) is now seen. Jehoram did not walk in the godly ways of his father but was influenced by his wife to walk in the ways of the Israelite kings, **as did the house of Ahab** (v. 18). Jehoram introduced Baal worship in Judah, as Ahab had done in the northern kingdom (see 11:18). Baal worship now spread to the southern kingdom at the same time it was being restricted in the northern kingdom by Ahab's son Joram (see 3:1–2). **The daughter of Ahab was his wife.** Jehoram's wife was Athaliah, a daughter of Ahab but probably not of Jezebel (see 8:26; 2 Chron. 18:1). Athaliah's influence on Jehoram, however, paralleled that of Jezebel on Ahab (see 1 Kings 16:31; 18:4; 19:1–2; 2 Chron. 21:6; for the evil measures Jehoram took to assure his position as king, see 2 Chron. 21:4).

The Lord had promised David **to give to him alway a light** (v. 19; see discussion on 1 Kings 11:36; see also Ps. 132:17). The Lord spared Judah and its royal house the judgment He had brought on the house of Ahab because of His covenant with David (see 2 Sam. 7:16, 29; 2 Chron. 21:7).

8:20–22. Edom, Judah's former vassal, revolted and **made a king over themselves** (v. 20). Previously, Edom had been ruled by a deputy (see discussion on 3:9; see also 1 Kings 22:47). Although Jehoram and his army were able to break through an encirclement of Edomite forces, they were soundly defeated, and **the people** (Israelites) **fled** (v. 21); that is, they were forced to retreat to their own territory. The Edomite revolt persisted **unto this day** (v. 22), until the time of the source from which the author of 1–2 Kings derived the account of Jehoram's reign (see 1 Kings, Introduction: "Author, Date, and Sources"; see also discussion on 1 Kings 8:8). Later, Amaziah of Judah was able to inflict a serious defeat on Edom (14:7), and his successor, Azariah, regained control of the trade route to Elath through Edomite territory (see 14:22; 2 Chron. 26:2). **Libnah revolted at the same time.** Libnah appears to have been located close to the Philistine border near Lachish (see 19:8). It is likely that the revolt of Libnah was connected with that of the Philistines and Arabs (described in 2 Chron. 21:16–17).

8:23. The rest of the acts of Joram (Jehoram; v. 23; see also 2 Chron. 21:4–20) were recorded in **the chronicles of the kings of Judah** (see discussion on 1 Kings 14:29). For the term **slept with his fathers** (v. 24), see discussions on 1 Kings 1:21; 2 Chronicles 21:20.

B. Ahaziah of Judah (8:25–29)

8:25–27. The twelfth year of Joram was 841 BC. The apparent contradiction with the years given in 9:29 can be explained thus: in 9:29, the first year of Joram's reign was counted as his accession year, and his second year was counted as the first year of his reign, whereas here his accession year was counted as the first year of his reign (see 1 Kings, Introduction: "Chronology"). Ahaziah was **two and twenty**

years old … when he began to reign in Judah (v. 26; see discussion on 2 Chron. 22:2). His mother was **Athaliah, the** grand**daughter of Omri** (see discussion on 8:18), so it was not surprising that **he walked in the way of the house of Ahab** (v. 27; see 2 Chron. 22:3–5).

8:28–29. In a concerted effort to regain the Israelite city of Ramoth-gilead, Ahaziah **went with Joram … to the war against Hazael … in Ramoth-gilead** (v. 28). As Jehoshaphat had joined Ahab in battle against the Syrians at Ramoth-gilead (1 Kings 22), so now Ahaziah joined his uncle Joram in a similar venture. On the previous occasion, Ahab had met his death (1 Kings 22:37). On this occasion, Joram was wounded, and while recuperating in Jezreel (see discussion on 1 Kings 21:1), both he and his nephew Ahaziah were assassinated by Jehu (see 9:14–28).

C. Jehu's Revolt and Reign (chaps. 9–10)

1. Elisha Orders Jehu's Anointing (9:1–13)

9:1–6. While Joram was convalescing and Ahaziah was visiting him, Elisha sent **one of the children** (i.e., "sons") **of the prophets** (v. 1) to the battle at Ramoth-gilead to anoint Jehu, the son of Jehoshaphat (not to be confused with Jehoshaphat, former king of Judah). Joram was instructed to find Jehu, take him from his comrades to an inner room, pour oil on his head, and speak the words of the Lord: **I have anointed thee king … over Israel** (v. 3; see discussions on 1 Sam. 2:10; 9:16; 1 Kings 19:16).

9:7–10. Jehu's inaugural commission was to **smite the house of Ahab** (v. 7). Jehu learned that he was the divinely appointed agent to inflict the judgment Elijah had pronounced many years earlier, in Jehu's hearing, against the house of Ahab (see 9:25–26; 1 Kings 21:21–24). **That I may avenge … the blood of all the servants of the LORD, at the hand of Jezebel** is a reference to people such as Naboth and his family (1 Kings 21:13), who had been unjustly put to death through Jezebel's influence. Ahab's whole house was to perish. For **him that is shut up and left in Israel** (v. 8), see discussion on 1 Kings 14:10. Ahab's house was destined to become **like the house of Jeroboam** (v. 9; see 1 Kings

14:7–11; 15:27–30) and **like the house of Baasha** (see 1 Kings 16:1–4, 8–12), two other dynasties that had ended tragically. Elijah had spoken the same words to Ahab years earlier (see 1 Kings 21:21–24).

9:11–13. After accomplishing his mission, Elisha's messenger had run from the house. **Wherefore came this mad fellow to thee?** (v. 11). The epithet "mad fellow" betrays a scornful attitude on the part of the military officers of the northern kingdom toward members of the prophetic companies. With an anti-prophetical description, **Ye know the man and his communication**, Jehu tried to conceal the prophet's purpose. Perhaps the tone of his voice or the oil dripping from his head suggested he was suppressing the truth.

Upon learning the truth, his comrades (other captains, 9:5) immediately declared, **Jehu is king** (v. 13). Either these men were moved by the prophet's message, or Jehu's popularity among them was greater than their loyalty to the wounded Joram.

2. Jehu's Assassination of Joram and Ahaziah (9:14–29)

9:14–15. The first command of Jehu's conspiracy was, **Let none go forth nor escape ... to go to tell it in Jezreel** (v. 15). For the success of Jehu's revolt, and to avoid a civil conflict, it was important for him to reach Jezreel before word of his revolt reached Joram so that Jehu could take him totally by surprise. **Jezreel** (v. 16) lay about forty-five miles to the west of Ramoth-gilead.

9:16–20. Both kings were at Jezreel at the time, for **Ahaziah ... was come down to see Joram** (v. 16; see 8:29). Jehu must have been spotted from a great distance away; two different horsemen left the city to meet him before he was properly identified by Joram by his notorious driving.

9:21–22. Noting that Jehu would not address his couriers, Joram supposed that Jehu's message was of great importance, and he went out personally (with Ahaziah) to meet him. The author notes that providentially (and ironically?) the kings met Jehu **in the portion of Naboth** (v. 21; see discussions on 1 Kings 21:2–3, 13, 19). **Is it peace, Jehu?** (v. 22).

In his answer, Jehu played on the word "peace." How could there be peace for the people of God when **the whoredoms ... of Jezebel and her witchcrafts are so many?** Both of these evils were punishable by death (see Deut. 13; 18:10–12). As long as they were promoted in the northern kingdom, there could be no peace.

9:23–26. Joram now recognized Jehu's revolt. **There is treachery** (v. 23). Before he could escape, Jehu shot him with an arrow and killed him, and his body was dumped in the field of Naboth, **according to the word of the Lord** (v. 26). Jehu was providentially placed in the position of fulfilling the prophecy of Elijah given years before (see 1 Kings 21:18–24). Even though Ahab's own blood was not shed on Naboth's field (see 1 Kings 21:29 and discussion), Jehu saw in Joram's death the fulfillment of Elijah's prophecy (see discussion on 1 Kings 21:19).

9:27–29. Ahaziah the king of Judah ... fled but was mortally wounded near Ibleam, about five miles south of Jezreel. Then **he fled to Megiddo, and died there** (v. 27). It may be questioned whether Jehu was justified in extending the purge of Ahab's house (see Hos. 1:4) to the descendants of David's house through Ahab's daughter Athaliah (see 8:18, 26). Suggested reasons for his actions are several: (1) Ahaziah was an ally of Joram; (2) he was a grandson of Ahab, and as Ahab's descendant, God's judgment extended to him also; (3) if all of Ahab's children were killed, Ahaziah, a nephew of Joram, would have remained as the nearest kinsman and blood avenger. For any of these reasons, Jehu could have counted Ahaziah worthy of death.

3. Jehu's Execution of Jezebel (9:30–37)

9:30–37. Jehu initiated one of the most thorough "cleanup" campaigns in history, beginning with Jezebel, who demonstrated composure as she prepared for her death, which she knew was imminent. **Had Zimri peace, who slew his master?** (v. 31). With bitter sarcasm, Jezebel called Jehu by the name Zimri. About forty-five years earlier, Zimri had seized the throne from Elah by assassination and had then destroyed the whole house of Baasha. Zimri ruled for only seven days, however, before Omri seized power (see 1 Kings 16:8 – 20).

Throw her down (v. 33). Jehu's cold, callous indifference to the death of Jezebel resulted in the fulfillment of another aspect of Elijah's prophecy (see 1 Kings 21:23). When the dogs had finished dismembering and eating Jezebel, there was not enough of her corpse remaining to make a positive identification of her. Jehu's summary observation was, **This is the word of the Lord, which he spake by his servant Elijah** (v. 36). In the manner of Jezebel's death, the word of the Lord was confirmed — the word she had defied during her life (see 1 Kings 21:23).

4. Jehu's Slaughter of Ahab's Family (10:1–17)

10:1–5. The purge of Ahab's house continued. **Ahab had seventy sons** (v. 1). While the number of Ahab's wives is unknown (see 1 Kings 20:5), his "seventy sons" presumably included both sons and grandsons, and their need for guardians denotes their youth and immaturity. To consolidate his coup and establish control of the northern kingdom, Jehu still faced the formidable problems of taking the nearly impregnable fortress of **Samaria** (see discussion on 1 Kings 16:24) and then of completing the destruction of Ahab's house. Jehu wrote to **the rulers**, that is, officers appointed by the king (see 1 Kings 4:1 – 6); to **the elders**, that is, local leaders by virtue of their position in the tribal and family structure (see discussions on Exod. 3:16; 2 Sam. 3:17), and to **them that brought up Ahab's children**, that is, those entrusted with the care and upbringing of the princes in the royal family.

Jehu issued an invitation to the officials: **fight for your master's house** (v. 3). The strategy of his first letter was to induce the leaders of Samaria into submission to his rule by bluffing a military confrontation to determine the right to the throne of Israel. **They were exceedingly afraid** (v. 4). The leaders of Samaria were completely intimidated by Jehu's challenge, knowing that no one was a match for Jehu. All surrendered their destiny to his terms. **He that was over the house** (v. 5; see discussion on 1 Kings 4:6), **he that was over the city**, probably an official

appointed by the king who served as commander of the militia of the capital city, **the elders also, and the bringers up of the children** (see discussion on v. 1) declared, **We are thy servants**.

10:6 – 11. Jehu's second letter contained his terms. **Take ye the heads of the men your master's sons, and come to me** (v. 6). Jehu's command contained what appears to be a deliberate ambiguity. The "heads of the men your master's sons" could be understood as a reference to the leading figures among the seventy descendants of Ahab, such as the crown prince and several other sons of special ability and standing. On the other hand, the expression could be taken as a reference to the literal heads of all seventy princes.

They … slew seventy persons (v. 7). The leaders of the city understood the communiqué in the literal sense, as Jehu most certainly had hoped they would, and they **put their heads in baskets, and sent him them**. The leaders of Samaria did not carry the heads of the princes to Jezreel themselves, as they had been ordered to do by Jehu (see v. 6). It is likely that they feared for their lives.

Lay ye them in two heaps at the entering in of the gate (v. 8). This gruesome procedure imitated the barbaric practice of the Assyrian rulers Ashurnasirpal and Shalmaneser III, whose reigns were characterized by acts of terror. Perhaps he intended for these grisly stacks to discourage any counterrevolution.

I conspired … and slew him (v. 9). Jehu openly confessed his own part in the overthrow of the government of Joram. **Who slew all these?** Because of the ambiguous communiqué Jehu had sent to the leaders of Samaria (see discussion on v. 6), he could now deny any personal responsibility for the slaughter of the seventy sons of Ahab and could lay the blame on the leaders of Samaria.

Jehu warned that nothing would be left undone **which the Lord spake concerning the house of Ahab … by his servant Elijah** (v. 10) (see 1 Kings 21:20 – 24, 29). Jehu implied a divine sanction not only for what had already been done but also for his intent to continue the purge of Ahab's house and associates. **He**

slew all that remained ... all his great men, and his kinsfolks, and his priests (v. 11). Jehu went beyond the responsibility given to him (see 9:7; Hos. 1:4) and acted solely on grounds of political self-interest. Jehu himself had been in the service of Ahab (see 9:25).

10:12–14. En route to Samaria, **at the shearing house** (probably a place name, i.e., Beth-eked; v. 12), Jehu encountered **brethren of Ahaziah** (v. 13), that is, relatives of Ahaziah (see 2 Chron. 21:17). They were traveling to pay respects to **the children of the king** (i.e., their cousins) and **the queen** (i.e., the queen mother). These were members of the royal family from Judah, who had not yet heard of the deaths of Joram and Jezebel. **Take them alive** (v. 14). He then killed all forty-two of them. Did Jehu have eventual designs on the throne of Judah also?

10:15–17. Jehu then met **Jehonadab the son of Rechab** (v. 15). Jehonadab was the leader of a conservative movement among the Israelites that was characterized by strong opposition to Baalism as well as to various practices of a settled agricultural society, including the building of houses, the sowing of crops, and the use of wine. His followers still adhered to these principles over two hundred years later and were known as Rechabites (see Jer. 35:6–10). Jehu **made him ride in his chariot** (v. 16). Public association with Jehonadab gave Jehu added credentials among the rural populace as a follower of the Lord.

5. Jehu's Eradication of Baal Worship (10:18–36)

10:18–21. Ahab served Baal a little; but Jehu shall serve him much (v. 18). After settling in Samaria, Jehu gave the appearance of having previously appealed to the word of the Lord only as a political maneuver. His lie alleviated any suspicions that might have arisen when all the prophets and worshipers of Baal were ordered to the temple of Baal to be led in worship of Baal by the new king himself. He promised, **whosoever shall be wanting** (i.e., fails to come), **he shall not live** (v. 19). Jehu's reputation made this no idle threat.

10:22–28. Jehu issued special robes to those who worshiped Baal. These robes would help identify all the adherents of Baalism a little later. Anyone who worshiped the Lord was denied entrance to the temple. Eighty men were appointed to prevent anyone from escaping the temple when the signal was given for the execution to begin. The worshipers were cut down by the sword and dragged out of the temple. **The city of the house of Baal** (v. 25) may refer to the inner room of the temple, from which **images** (v. 26) were removed and **burnt**. These images may refer to the Asherim (see discussion on 1 Kings 14:15) that usually accompanied a sacred pillar (see 1 Kings 16:32–33). They broke **the image of Baal** (v. 27; see discussion on 1 Kings 14:23), destroyed the temple, and disgraced it by making it a latrine **unto this day** (see discussion on 8:22).

10:29–31. Jehu was God's man (i.e., he accomplished his assigned task), but he was not a man of God (i.e., he had no spiritual relationship with God). Though he purged Baalism from Israel, he still remained an idolator. He did not renounce the **sins of Jeroboam ... who made Israel to sin** (v. 29; see 1 Kings 12:26–32; 13:33–34; 14:1) but served the golden calves at Bethel and Dan. **Because thou hast done ... unto the house of Ahab according to all that was in mine heart** (v. 30). Jehu was the Lord's instrument for bringing judgment on the house of Ahab, for which he was commended. The prophet Hosea would later condemn Jehu for killing all of Ahab's associates, as well as Ahaziah of Judah and the forty-two Judahite princes—the "blood of Jezreel" (Hos. 1:4). His dynasty would reign until **the fourth generation**. The restriction of this blessing to four generations is reflective of the qualified approval given to Jehu's reign. Nevertheless, his dynasty lasting nearly one hundred years, longer than any other dynasty of the northern kingdom. It included the reigns of Jehoahaz, Jehoash, Jeroboam II, and Zechariah (see discussion on 15:12).

Even with the prediction of a restricted dynasty, Jehu **took no heed to walk in the law of the LORD ... with all his heart** (v. 31). He seems to have been driven more by a political desire to secure his own position on the throne of the northern kingdom than by a desire to serve the Lord. In this, he was guilty of using God's judgment on the house of Ahab to satisfy his self-interest.

10:32–33. The LORD began to cut Israel short (v. 32); that is, He reduced the size of Israel's land. The climax of the covenant curses enumerated in Leviticus 26 and Deuteronomy 28 was Israel's expulsion from Canaan. During the rule of Jehu, the northern kingdom experienced the beginnings of this curse (for its full realization, see 17:7–18). All the land east of the Jordan was lost to Hazael and the Syrians of Damascus.

10:34–36. The rest of the acts of Jehu were recorded in **the chronicles of the kings of Israel** (v. 34; see discussion on 1 Kings 14:19). Interestingly, the Black Obelisk of the Assyrian ruler Shalmaneser III informs us that Jehu paid tribute to the Assyrians shortly after coming to the throne of the northern kingdom in 841 BC. In the Assyrian inscription, Jehu is incorrectly called the "son of Omri," but this may simply be Shalmaneser's way of identifying Jehu with Samaria (or Israel). There is no reference to this payment of tribute in the biblical narratives of Jehu's reign.

When Jehu died, **Jehoahaz his son reigned in his stead** (v. 35). For the reign of Jehoahaz, see 13:1–9. The length of Jehu's reign was **twenty and eight years** (v. 36), that is, 841–814 BC.

D. Athaliah and Joash of Judah; Repair of the Temple (chaps. 11–12)

11:1–3. Athaliah (v. 1) was the daughter of Ahab (see discussion on 8:18, 26). When she learned that **her son was dead** (see 9:27), **she ... destroyed all the seed royal** to secure the throne in Judah for herself. By this time, the royal family in Judah had already been reduced to a mere remnant. Jehoram, the late husband of Athaliah and the father of Ahaziah, had killed all his brothers when he succeeded his father, Jehoshaphat, on the throne (see 2 Chron. 21:4). Jehu had slain another forty-two members of the royal house of Judah, perhaps including many of the sons of Jehoram's brothers (10:12–14; 2 Chron. 22:8–9), and the brothers of Ahaziah had been killed by marauding Arabs (2 Chron. 22:1). It is likely that

Athaliah's purge focused primarily on the children of Ahaziah, that is, on her own grandchildren. Ahaziah had died at the young age of twenty-two (see 8:26). This attempt to destroy completely the house of David was an attack on God's redemptive plan— a plan that centered in the Messiah—which the Davidic covenant promised (see discussions on 2 Sam. 7:11, 16; 1 Kings 8:25).

Jehosheba (v. 2) was **the daughter of King Jehoram, sister of Ahaziah**. It is likely that Jehosheba was the daughter of Joram by a wife other than Athaliah, and thus she was a half sister of Ahaziah. She was married to the godly high priest Jehoiada (see 2 Chron. 22:11). Jehosheba **took Joash the son of Ahaziah ... and hid him ... and his nurse**. The child was not more than a year old and had not yet been weaned (compare v. 3 with 11:21); thus, he was probably the easiest child to hide. He was hidden and protected **in the house of the LORD** (v. 3), the temple, for six years.

11:4–12. In **the seventh year** (v. 4) of Athaliah's rule, Jehoiada the priest decided to present the legitimate royal heir to the people. First he secured an oath of allegiance from several ranks of bodyguards. Among these were the **rulers over hundreds** (2 Chron. 23:1 lists the names of five commanders, all native Israelites) and **captains** (Hebrew, *Cari*; i.e., "Carites"). These were mercenary soldiers from Caria, in southwest Asia Minor, who served as royal bodyguards. He **brought them to him into the house of the LORD** to enter into a covenant with them and to introduce them to the king's son. Second Chronicles 23:2 includes the Levites and the family leaders of Judah in the conspiracy.

Jehoiada chose a most opportune time for presenting the boy for coronation, at the changing of the temple guard, when the most protection would be present with the least disturbance. He armed the captains over hundreds with **king David's spears and shields, that were in the temple of the LORD** (v. 10). David had probably taken the spears and gold shields as plunder in his battle with Hadadezer and then dedicated them to the Lord (see 2 Sam. 8:7–11).

With the armed guards in their places, Jehoiada brought out the royal heir and presented him with **the Testimony** (v. 12). This was either (1) the Ten Commandments, (2) the entire Mosaic covenant, or (3) a document dealing more specifically with the covenant responsibilities of the king (see Deut. 17:14–20; see also discussion on 1 Sam. 10:25). The third option is most likely. **They made him king, and anointed him** (see discussions on 1 Sam. 2:10; 9:16; 1 Kings 1:39), and said, **God save the king** (lit., "Let the king live"; see discussion on 1 Sam. 10:24; see also 1 Kings 1:34, 39).

11:13–16. Hearing the noise of celebration, Athaliah came inquiring, and **the king stood by a pillar** (v. 14). This pillar was apparently one of the two bronze pillars of the portico of the temple, which were named Jachin and Boaz (see 23:3; 1 Kings 7:15–22; 2 Chron. 23:13). **All the people of the land rejoiced.** It is likely that Jehoiada had chosen to stage his coup on a Sabbath during one of the major religious festivals, when many from the realm who were loyal to the Lord would be in Jerusalem. With all the royal offspring supposedly dead, Athaliah thought she had the only legitimate right to the throne. She **rent her clothes and cried, Treason, Treason**. Undoubtedly, she had cold memories of the murderous revolt in Israel just years before that had wiped out her father's house. To prevent desecration of the temple, Athaliah was removed and then put to death.

11:17–21. Jehoiada (v. 17) should not be underrated as the spiritual force and counselor for the young king (see 12:2). Until Joash was mature, Jehoiada was the real power behind the throne, while Joash was a figurehead. Here Jehoiada mediated **a covenant between the Lord and the king and the people, that they should be the Lord's people**. This was a renewal of the Mosaic covenant, by which Israel had been constituted as the Lord's people (see Exod. 19:5–6; Deut. 4:20). The years of apostasy, involving both the royal house and the people of Judah, necessitated a renewal of allegiance to the Lord at the time of an important new beginning for the southern kingdom (see discussions on 1 Sam.

11:14–15; 12:13–15, 24–25; where Samuel led Israel in renewing their covenant loyalty to the Lord when Saul was made king). He mediated **between the king also and the people**; that is, he defined responsibilities and mutual obligations of king and people that were compatible with Israel's covenant relationship with the Lord (see discussions on 1 Sam. 10:25; 2 Sam. 5:3).

The house of Baal (v. 18) in Jerusalem is mentioned here for the first time. Apparently, it had been established by Athaliah in the interregnum, or perhaps when her husband Jehoram reigned (see 8:18). With Athaliah deposed and dead, the pagan sanctuary was destroyed, its altars and all of its **images**, that is, the stone pillars (see discussion on 1 Kings 14:23) and Asherim (see discussion on 1 Kings 14:15), were smashed, and its priest was killed.

Jehoash ... began to reign (v. 21) at age seven. (Jehoash is an alternate name for Joash; see 11:2. Both Israel and Judah had a king by the name of Jehoash, with Joash as an alternate spelling. For consistency and clarity, *Jehoash* will designate the northern king of Israel, and *Joash* will designate the southern king of Judah.) Due to Jehu's purge of the descendants of Ahab and his jealous murder of the descendants of Jehoshaphat, and because of the intermarriage between the royal families of Ahab and Jehoshaphat, Joash was the last living remote descendant of Ahab and the last seed of David. God was faithful to His covenant with David (see 2 Sam. 7:16) and had preserved a light for David in Jerusalem (see 1 Kings 11:36).

12:1–3. The reign of **Jehoash** (v. 1) began **in the seventh year of Jehu** (835 BC; see discussion on 10:36), and he reigned **forty years** (835–796 BC). He did **that which was right ... all his days wherein Jehoiada the priest instructed him** (v. 2). This notation, though initially encouraging, is ominous. Sadly, it intimates what was to come. After Jehoiada died, Jehoash turned away from the Lord (see 2 Chron. 24:17–27).

The high places were not taken away (v. 3). This refers to high places where the Lord was worshiped rather than pagan deities (see discussion on 1 Kings

15:14). Nevertheless, they were potential sources for the entrance of pagan practices into Israel's worship (see discussion on 1 Kings 3:2).

12:4 – 5. The temple was in dire need of repair (**breaches** are noted in v. 5) and refurbishing. Construction of the temple had been completed 124 years before the beginning of the reign of Joash (see discussions on 12:1; 1 Kings 6:38). In addition to deterioration due to age, the temple had fallen into disrepair and abuse during the rule of Athaliah (see 2 Chron. 24:7). Joash determined to correct the situation by using **all the money of the dedicated things ... brought into the house of the** LORD (v. 4). The money was derived from three sources: (1) **Money of every one that passeth the account**, that is, money collected in the census. At the age of twenty, Israelite youths were required to register for military service and to make an offering of half a shekel (see discussion on 5:26) for use in the service of the central sanctuary (see Exod. 30:11 – 16; 38:25 – 26; Num. 2:32). (2) **Money that every man is set at**, that is, money received from personal vows. Various types of vows and their equivalence in monetary assessments are described in Leviticus 27:1 – 25. (3) **Money that cometh into any man's heart to bring into the house of the** LORD, that is, money brought voluntarily to the temple. (For voluntary offerings, see Lev. 22:18 – 23; Deut. 16:10.)

Take it (the money) **... of his acquaintance** (v. 5). "Acquaintance" may refer to one's "benefactor" or, more likely, to the "treasurer," a temple functionary who handled financial matters for the priests relative to the people's sacrifices and offerings.

12:6 – 12. Exactly how long the priests were in charge of collecting money for repairs is not stated, but Joash was clearly dissatisfied with their progress. No accusation of misappropriation of funds was made, but Joash's first arrangement had not been successful, so a change was made in **the three and twentieth year of king Jehoash** (v. 6). Joash may have instituted his plan for restoration of the temple a few years before the twenty-third year of his reign. Now, at age thirty, he asserted his royal authority and took charge of the temple repairs.

Receive no more money of your acquaintance (v. 7). The proceeds from the sources of revenue mentioned in 12:4 were no longer to be given to the priests. **The priests consented** (v. 8). Apparently, a compromise was reached: the priests would no longer take the money from the people, but neither would they pay for the temple repairs from the money they had already received. A collection chest was prepared and placed by the entry for the use of **the priests that kept the door** (v. 9), that is, those three high-ranking priests charged with protecting the temple from unlawful (profane) entry (see 25:18; Jer. 52:24). These priests **put therein all the money** brought by worshipers. When the people were assured that all their offerings would be used for the temple restoration, they responded with greater generosity. (For the continuation, or renewal, of this practice in the reign of Josiah, see 22:3 – 7.)

When much money accumulated in the chest, **the king's scribe** (v. 10; see discussion on 2 Sam. 8:17) removed it. Joash thus arranged for direct royal supervision of the temple's monetary affairs. The money was then given to **them ... that had the oversight** (v. 11) over the work of restoration. Again, the whole matter was taken out of the hands of the priests.

12:13 – 16. **There were not made for the house of the** LORD **... vessels of gold, or ... silver** (v. 13). All the money was initially designated for the restoration of the temple. When the restoration was completed, additional funds were used for the acquisition of silver and gold articles for use in the temple service (see 2 Chron. 24:14).

Joash made sure the gifts that, according to Mosaic law, were to provide for the priests, were not misappropriated for temple repair. **The trespass money and sin money ... was the priests'** (v. 16). For references to priestly income in connection with the bringing of a guilt offering, see Lev. 5:16; 6:5; Num. 5:7 – 10. There is no Pentateuchal reference to priestly income in connection with the sin offerings (but see Lev. 7:7).

12:17 – 18. **Then Hazael ... went up, and fought against Gath** (v. 17). These events must have taken place toward the end of Joash's reign. From

2 Chronicles 24:17–24, it is clear that the Syrian attack was occasioned by Joash's turning away from the Lord after Jehoiada's death. Jehoash's apostasy reached its climax in the stoning of Jehoiada's son Zechariah (2 Chron. 24:22). Probably because of Joash's earlier zeal for the temple, the author of Kings chose not to relate these matters. For Hazael, see 8:7–15; 10:32–33; 13:3, 22. Gath was one of the major Philistine cities (see Josh. 13:3) that David had conquered (1 Chron. 18:1) and that continued to be subject to Judah during the reign of Rehoboam (2 Chron. 11:8). In the latter years of the reign of Joash of Judah (835–796 BC) and during the reign of Jehoahaz of Israel (814–798 BC; see 13:3, 7), the Syrians had virtually overrun the northern kingdom, enabling them to advance against the Philistines and the kingdom of Judah with little resistance. After taking Gath, **Hazael set his face to go up to Jerusalem**.

After first suffering defeat (see 2 Chron. 24:23–24), Joash **took all the hallowed things … gold … and sent it to Hazael** (v. 18), thus paying tribute to Hazael for the protection of Jerusalem. Years earlier, Asa had sought to secure assistance from the Syrians with a similar gift (see 1 Kings 15:18).

12:19–21. The acts of Joash (v. 19) were recorded in **the chronicles of the kings of Judah** (see discussion on 1 Kings 14:29). A fuller account of the reign of Joash (Jehoash) is also found in 2 Chronicles 22:10–24:27.

His servants … made a conspiracy (v. 20). The conspiracy was a response to Joash's murder of Zechariah, son of Jehoiada (see 2 Chron. 24:25). **The house of Millo**. For the meaning of "Millo," see discussion on Judges 9:6. Here the reference may be to a building (perhaps a kind of barracks) built on the "Millo" in the old City of David (see 2 Sam. 5:9 and discussion; 1 Kings 11:27). Perhaps the king was staying there temporarily with his troops at the time of his assassination; Chronicles says he was killed "on his bed" (2 Chron. 24:25). **Silla** may refer to a steep descent from the City of David down into the Kidron Valley.

The named **servants** (v. 21) who assassinated Joash were sons of Ammonite and Moabite mothers (2 Chron. 24:26), suggesting that they may have been mercenary military officers, whose services could have been bought by others. **They buried him with his fathers** (but see 2 Chron. 24:25), and **Amaziah his son reigned in his stead**. For the reign of Amaziah, see 14:1–22.

E. Jehoahaz of Israel (13:1–9)

13:1–3. In the three and twentieth year of Joash (v. 1), the year of Joash's second effort to repair the temple (i.e., 814 BC; see discussions on 12:1, 6; see also 1 Kings, Introduction: "Chronology"), Jehoahaz began his reign of **seventeen years** (814–798 BC). Since he continued in the **sins of Jeroboam** (v. 2; see 1 Kings 12:26–32; 13:33–34; 14:16), God delivered him to **Hazael** (v. 3; see discussions on 8:12–13, 15; 10:33) and to **Ben-hadad** (see 13:24), whose reign began in either 806 or 796 BC.

13:4–9. Jehoahaz's prayer is reminiscent of Israel's cry of distress during the days of the judges (see discussion on Judg. 3:9) and is not an indication of repentance. He and Israel continued in their sin. **The LORD hearkened unto him** (v. 4). Although deliverance did not come during the lifetime of Jehoahaz (see 13:22), the Lord was merciful to His people in spite of their sin, because of His covenant with Abraham, Isaac, and Jacob (13:23). **The LORD gave Israel a saviour** (v. 5), that is, a "deliverer." Though not identified, he was probably either (1) the Assyrian ruler Adadnirari III (810–783 BC), whose attacks on the Syrians of Damascus in 806 and 804 BC enabled the Israelites to break Syrian control over Israelite territory (see 13:25; 14:25), (2) Jehoash, son of Jehoahaz (13:17, 19, 25), or (3) Jeroboam II, who was able to extend Israel's boundaries far to the north (see 14:25, 27) after the Assyrians had broken the military power of the Syrians.

There was no spiritual change in Israel, and **there remained the grove** (Hebrew, *asherah*; v. 6). This idol had been set up by Ahab (see 1 Kings 16:33) and had either escaped destruction by Jehu when he purged Baal worship from Samaria (see 10:27–28) or had been reintroduced during the reign of Jehoahaz.

Jehoahaz was left with but **ten chariots** (v. 7). In effect, this was merely a small police force. According to the Assyrian annals of Shalmaneser III, Ahab had contributed 2,000 chariots to the coalition of forces that opposed the Assyrians at the battle of Qarqar, in 853 BC (see discussion on 1 Kings 22:1). Jehoahaz had **ten thousand footmen**. At the battle of Qarqar, Ahab had supplied 10,000 foot soldiers to the coalition opposing the Assyrians. At that time, this would have represented only a contingent of Israel's army, while now it represented the entire Israelite infantry. In 857 BC, Ahab had inflicted 100,000 casualties on the Syrian foot soldiers in one day (see 1 Kings 20:29).

The other acts of Jehoahaz were recorded in **the chronicles of the kings of Israel** (v. 8). When he died, his son **Joash** (v. 9) assumed the throne.

F. Jehoash of Israel; Elisha's Last Prophecy (13:10–25)

13:10–13. Jehoash (Joash; v. 10), not to be confused with Judah's king by the same name (for a short time, they reigned concurrently), assumed the throne of Israel **in the thirty and seventh year of Joash** (of Judah, in 798 BC) and **reigned sixteen years** (798–782). He duplicated his father and grandfather in not departing from **the sins of Jeroboam** (v. 11; see 1 Kings 12:26–32; 13:33–34; 14:16). For the battle that Jehoash **fought against Amaziah** (v. 12), see 14:8–14; 2 Chronicles 25:17–24. He too was remembered in **the chronicles of the kings of Israel**. When he died, his son **Jeroboam sat upon his throne** (v. 13). For the reign of Jeroboam II, see 14:23–29.

13:14–19. Elisha was fallen sick (v. 14). The last previous reference to Elisha was in chapter 9. Since Jehu had been anointed in 841 BC (see discussion on 10:36) and Jehoash began to reign in 798 (see discussion on 13:10), there is at least a forty-three-year period in which we are told nothing of Elisha's activities. Based on his relationship with Elijah, Elisha must have been born prior to 880 and must have lived to be more than eighty years of age. Jehoash paid a visit to the sick prophet. **O my father ... the chariot of Israel, and the horsemen thereof**. He expressed his recognition that Elisha was of greater significance for Israel's military success than Israel's

military forces were (see discussions on 2:12; 6:13, 16–23). Jehoash was undoubtedly aware that he was about to lose the man of God who had been his only contact with God in time of emergency.

Elisha instructed, **Take bow and arrows** (v. 15). These weapons were Jehoash's means of defense. From his deathbed, Elisha had Jehoash symbolically enact his final prophecy. He **put his hands upon the king's hands** (v. 16). By this symbolic act, Elisha indicated that Jehoash was to engage the Syrians in battle with the Lord's blessing on him. **Open the window eastward** (v. 17), that is, in the direction facing across the Jordan, which was controlled by the Syrians (see 10:32–33). **He shot** an arrow that represented a future victory over the Syrians at **Aphek**. About sixty years earlier, Ahab had won a decisive victory at Aphek over the Syrians and Ben-hadad II (see 1 Kings 20:26–30; discussion on 1 Kings 20:26). **Smite upon the ground ... he smote thrice, and stayed** (v. 18). Jehoash's less than enthusiastic response to Elisha's directive reflected insufficient zeal for accomplishing the announced task. **Thou shalt smite Syria but thrice** (v. 19). Jehoash's moderate enthusiasm in striking the ground with arrows symbolized the moderate success he would have against the Syrians. It would be left for Jeroboam II, the son of Jehoash, to gain complete victory over them (see 14:25, 28).

13:20–21. Elisha died (v. 20) and was buried. **At the coming in of the year**, the interment of another man was interrupted when a band of Moabite raiders was spotted nearby. The man's corpse was hurriedly cast into the sepulchre of the prophet. **When the man ... touched the bones of Elisha, he revived, and stood up on his feet** (v. 21). The life-giving power of the God Elisha represented was demonstrated once again in this last Old Testament reference to Elisha (for previous demonstrations of this power, see 4:32–37 and 1 Kings 17:17–24; for Elijah's translation to heaven without dying, see 2:11–12). In Elisha's life and death, fourteen miracles were associated with him.

13:22–25. Though **Hazael** (v. 22) was able to oppress Israel, God would not let him defeat them.

Because of His covenant with the patriarchs, He **would not destroy them, neither cast he them from his presence** (v. 23). In His mercy and grace, the Lord was long-suffering toward His people and refrained from full implementation of the covenant curse of exile from Canaan (see discussion on 10:32). This postponement of judgment provided Israel with the opportunity to repent and return to covenant faithfulness. **As yet** (lit., "until now") refers to the time of the source from which the author derived this account (see discussion on 1 Kings 8:8; see also 1 Kings, Introduction: "Author, Date, and Sources").

After the death of Hazael and during the reign of **Ben-hadad** (v. 24; see discussion on 13:3), Jehoash regained the **cities, which he** (Ben-hadad) **had taken out of the hand of Jehoahaz** (v. 25). These were probably towns west of the Jordan, since the area east of the Jordan had been lost already in the time of Jehu (see 10:32 – 33). Israel would not fully recover the area east of the Jordan until the time of Jeroboam II (see 14:25). In fulfillment of Elisha's prophecy (13:19), Jehoash defeated Ben-hadad **three times**, thus reclaiming Israel's cities.

G. Amaziah of Judah (14:1 – 22)

14:1 – 4. The reader once again must distinguish Joash of Israel from Joash of Judah. **In the second year of Joash** (of Israel, 796 BC; v. 1; see discussion on 13:10), **Amaziah the son of Joash king of Judah** began his reign of **twenty and nine years** (796 – 767; v. 2). His twenty-nine-year reign included a twenty-four-year coregency with his son Azariah (see discussions on 4:21; 15:1 – 2). Though Amaziah did that which was right, he did not compare to **David his father** (i.e., his "ancestor"; v. 3). He did not remain completely free from involvement with the worship of pagan deities (see 2 Chron. 25:14 – 16). His loyalty to the Lord fell short of that of Asa and Jehoshaphat before him (see 1 Kings 15:11, 14; 22:43; see also 1 Kings 9:4; 11:4). **The high places were not taken away** (v. 4; see discussion on 1 Kings 15:14).

14:5 – 7. Once Amaziah established himself on the throne, he punished his father's assassins, Jozachar and Jehozabad (12:21), by death, but because

of Moses' instruction in Deuteronomy 24:16, he spared their sons.

Amaziah was able to regain temporarily (see 2 Chron. 28:17) some of Judah's control over the Edomites when **he slew of Edom … ten thousand** (v. 7). Control over Edom had been lost during the reign of Jehoram (see 8:20 – 22). **The valley of salt**, the same battlefield on which David had defeated the Edomites (see 2 Sam. 8:13; 1 Chron. 18:12; Psalm 60 superscription), is generally identified with the Arabah, directly south of the Dead Sea. **Selah** means "rock" and is often regarded as the Edomite stronghold presently known as Petra (a Greek word meaning "rock"; see Judg. 1:36; Isa. 16:1; 42:11; Obadiah 3). **Unto this day** refers to the time of the source from which the author of 1 – 2 Kings derived the account of Amaziah's reign (see discussion on 1 Kings 8:8; see also 1 Kings, Introduction: "Author, Date, and Sources").

14:8 – 16. After defeating Edom and receiving foolish advice (see 2 Chron. 25:17), Amaziah arrogantly issued a challenge to **Jehoash … king of Israel** amounting to a declaration of war: **Let us look one another in the face** (v. 8). Perhaps Amaziah's challenge was provoked by the hostile actions of mercenary troops from the northern kingdom after their dismissal from Judah's army (see 2 Chron. 25:10, 13) and by Jehoash's refusal to establish a marriage alliance with Amaziah (v. 9).

Jehoash … sent to Amaziah … saying (v. 9). For his reply, Jehoash used a "thistle" fable (see Judg. 9:8 – 15), in which he represented himself as a strong cedar and Amaziah as an insignificant thistle that could easily be trampled underfoot. In essence, Jehoash warned Amaziah that he would be fighting out of his league, all because of his pride. While the fable was probably true, it did more to anger Amaziah than to alter his thinking.

Amaziah would not hear (v. 11; see 2 Chron. 25:2). He faced off with Jehoash at **Beth-shemesh**, a town about fifteen miles west of Jerusalem, near the border between Judah and Dan (see Josh. 15:10; 1 Sam. 6:9). The results of the battle were disastrous for Amaziah. Judah was soundly defeated, and

Jehoash ... took Amaziah (v. 13). It is likely that Amaziah was taken back to the northern kingdom as a prisoner, where he remained until being released to return to Judah after the death of Jehoash (see vv. 15–16; see also discussion on 14:21). The wall of Jerusalem was broken from **the gate of Ephraim unto the corner gate**. The corner gate (see Jer. 31:38; Zech. 14:10) was at the northwest corner of the wall around Jerusalem. The Ephraim gate was on the north side of Jerusalem (see Neh. 12:39), six hundred feet east of the corner gate. This northwestern section of the wall of Jerusalem was the point at which the city was most vulnerable to attack. The palace and temple were plundered of their **gold and silver, and all the vessels** (v. 14). The value of the plundered articles was probably not great because Joash had previously stripped the temple and palace to pay tribute to Hazael of Damascus (see 12:17–18). **Hostages** were taken also. The hostages were probably taken to secure additional payments of tribute in view of the meager war booty.

14:15–16. Jehoash's other activities were recorded in **the chronicles of the kings of Israel** (v. 15; see discussion on 1 Kings 14:19). When he died, Jehoash **was buried in Samaria** (v. 16).

14:17–20. Amaziah outlived his captor (see 14:13), having **lived after the death of Jehoash ... fifteen years** (v. 17). Jehoash died in 782 BC, and Amaziah in 767 BC. He too had his other activities recorded in **the chronicles of the kings of Judah** (v. 18).

Amaziah was the second king of Judah to die by **a conspiracy against him** (v. 19; see 12:20). Second Chronicles 25:27 connects the conspiracy against Amaziah with his turning away from the Lord, but it did not serve the purpose of the author of Kings to note this. Amaziah fled to **Lachish**, where he was pursued and killed. Lachish was a fortress city in southern Judah, fifteen miles west of Hebron, presently known as Tell ed-Duweir (see 18:14; 2 Chron. 11:9).

14:21–22. Azariah (v. 21) was a popular appointee to the throne. **All the people of Judah took Azariah ... and made him king instead of his father Amaziah**. Azariah (meaning "the Lord has helped"),

who is also called Uzziah (meaning "the Lord is my strength"; see 15:13), began to reign at age sixteen. It is likely that this occurred after Amaziah had been taken prisoner by Jehoash (see 4:13). Thus, Azariah's reign substantially overlapped that of his father, Amaziah (see discussions on 14:2; 15:2). **He built Elath, and restored it to Judah** (v. 22). Azariah extended the subjection of the Edomites begun by his father (see 14:7) and reestablished Israelite control over the important port city on the Gulf of Aqaba (see 1 Kings 9:26).

H. Jeroboam II of Israel (14:23–29)

14:23–27. The fifteenth year of Amaziah (782 BC; v. 23; see discussion on 14:2) marked the beginning of the sole reign of **Jeroboam**. He had previously served as coregent with his father, Jehoash. He reigned in Samaria **forty and one years** (793–753 BC), which included the coregency with his father.

Jeroboam II was not a godly king, following in **the sins of Jeroboam [I]** (v. 24; see 1 Kings 12:26–32; 13:33–34; 14:16; Amos 3:13–14; 4:4–5; 5:4–6; 7:10–17). He was, however, the last strong king of Israel. He restored Israel's Davidic borders north of Damascus as far as the **entering of Hamath** (probably a place-name, Lebo-hamath; v. 25). Jeroboam II was able to free the northern kingdom from the oppression it had suffered at the hands of Hazael and Ben-hadad (see 10:32; 12:17; 13:3, 22, 25). He also extended Israelite political control over the Syrians of Damascus, an undertaking that had been begun by his father, Jehoash (see 13:25). Assyrian pressure on the Syrians, including attacks on Damascus by Shalmaneser IV in 773 BC and Ashurdan III in 772 BC, had weakened the Syrians enough to enable Jeroboam II to gain the upper hand over them. Meanwhile, Assyria as well had become too weak to suppress Jeroboam's expansion. Jeroboam also restored Israel's borders east of the Jordan as far south as **the sea of the plain** (Hebrew, *arabah*; i.e., the Dead Sea). According to Amos 6:14, the southern limit of Jeroboam's kingdom east of the Jordan was the "river of the wilderness," probably to be connected with the Valley of Salt (see discussion on

14:7). If so, Jeroboam had also subdued Moab and the Ammonites.

This success was stirred by **Jonah … the prophet … of Gath-hepher** (v. 25; see Jonah 1:1). Gath-hepher was located in the tribe of Zebulun, northeast of Nazareth ("Gittah-hepher," Josh. 19:13). This reference to Jonah helps date the ministry of the prophet. Perhaps Jeroboam was encouraged to be aggressive soon after Jonah's mission to Nineveh, while the Ninevites were repentant, and the Assyrians would not have been a threat to Israel or a help to the Syrians.

God continued to hear His people in distress (see Exod. 2:25; 3:7; Judg. 2:16–17; 2 Kings 13:4–7), and He saw their **affliction** (v. 26) at the hands of the Syrians (see 10:32–33; 13:3–7), the Moabites (13:20), and the Ammonites (Amos 1:13). For the phrase **not any shut up, nor any left**, see discussion on 1 Kings 14:10. The prophecies of Amos and Hosea (both lived during Jeroboam II's reign) depict the sad moral and religious character of Israel that stemmed from the prosperity of this time. **The Lord said not that he would blot out the name of Israel** (v. 27). The sin of the Israelites had not yet reached its full measure, and the Lord mercifully extended to the nation an additional period of grace, in which they had opportunity to repent (see discussion on 13:23). Persistence in apostasy, however, would bring certain judgment (see Amos 4:2–3; 6:14). **He saved them by the hand of Jeroboam**; that is, God used the king to spare Israel from their neighbors (see discussion on 13:5).

14:28–29. The acts of Jeroboam … all that he did (v. 28) were many indeed. During his reign, the northern kingdom enjoyed greater material prosperity than at any time since the rule of David and Solomon. Unfortunately, it was also a time of religious formalism and apostasy as well as social injustice (see the books of Amos and Hosea, who prophesied during Jeroboam's reign). He reclaimed **Damascus, and Hamath** (see discussion on 14:25), which belonged to **Judah**. Damascus and Hamath were once included in territory ruled by David and Solomon (see 2 Sam. 8:6; 2 Chron. 8:3). Further details of Jeroboam's reign were recorded in **the chronicles of the kings of Israel**. After he died, **Zachariah his son**

reigned in his stead (v. 29). For the reign of Zachariah, see 15:8–12.

I. Azariah of Judah (15:1–7)

15:1–7. Azariah (v. 1) began his reign in the **twenty and seventh year of Jeroboam** (767 BC). This year is based on dating the beginning of Jeroboam's coregency with Joash in 793 BC (see discussion on 14:23). Azariah began his sole reign after a twenty-four-year coregency with his father, Amaziah (see discussions on v. 2; 14:2, 21). Counting the years of his coregency (792–767 BC), Azariah reigned for a total of **two and fifty years** (792–740 BC; v. 2).

As his father had done before him, Azariah **did that which was right in the sight of the Lord** (v. 3; see discussion on 14:3), but as before, **the high places were not removed** (v. 4; see 14:4).

Sadly, **the Lord smote the king, so that he was a leper** (v. 5). This incurable disease was a punishment for usurping the priestly function of burning incense on the altar in the temple (see 2 Chron. 26:16–21; see Lev. 13:46). Though Azariah retained his office as king for the remainder of his life (750–740 BC; see discussion on 15:33), his son Jotham was elevated to coregent, so Jotham ruled for his father, **judging the people of the land.**

All that he did (v. 6) was recorded in the **chronicles of the kings of Judah** (see discussion on 1 Kings 14:29). A more detailed account of Azariah's accomplishments is found in the canonical book of 2 Chron. 26:1–15. When Azariah died of his leprosy, **Jotham his son reigned in his stead** (v. 7). For the reign of Jotham, see 15:32–38.

J. Zachariah of Israel (15:8–12)

15:8–12. Zachariah (v. 8) became king in Israel **in the thirty and eighth year of Azariah** (753 BC; see discussion on 15:2). He too followed in **the sins of Jeroboam** (v. 9), and his brief reign of only six months ended when he was publicly killed by **Shallum** (v. 10). There is no indication that the people called for retribution.

The word of the Lord (v. 12) had promised Jehu a son on the throne for four generations after him (see 10:30), **and so it came to pass**. With the downfall of Jehu's dynasty, the northern kingdom entered a period of political instability (see Hos. 1:4). The remaining five kings of the northern kingdom would all be assassinated, with the exception of Menahem, who would reign ten years, and Hoshea, who would be imprisoned by the Assyrians. From the strength and wealth of the reign of Jeroboam II, the northern kingdom would swiftly decline and fall.

K. Shallum of Israel (15:13–16)

15:13–16. Shallum (v. 13) took the throne **in the nine and thirtieth year of Uzziah** (752 BC; see discussion on 15:2) and reigned a mere month.

Menahem … went up from Tirzah … to Samaria (v. 14). The Jewish historian Josephus states that Menahem was the commander of a military garrison at Tirzah, the former capital of the northern kingdom (see 1 Kings 14:17; 15:21, 33). Menahem apparently believed that with Zachariah's death, the throne should go to the captain of the army. Therefore, he killed Shallum, usurped the throne (as Shallum had), and **reigned in his stead**. For the reign of Menahem, see 15:17–22. Other details of Shallum's conspiracy were recorded in **the chronicles of the kings of Israel** (v. 15).

Then Menahem smote Tiphsah (v. 16). A city named **Tiphsah** was located far to the north of Hamath (see 14:25) on the Euphrates River (see 1 Kings 4:24). It is unlikely, however, that such a distant city was intended. Some interpreters prefer the reading "Tappuah," as in the Septuagint. Tappuah was a city on the border between Ephraim and Manasseh (Josh. 16:8; 17:7–8). Perhaps there was a Tiphsah in Israel, near Tirzah, not otherwise mentioned. Menahem employed the barbarous tactics of the Syrians and the Ammonites in that **all the women … that were with child he ript up** (see 8:12 and discussion). Such cruelty would have demoralized any opposition.

L. Menahem of Israel (15:17–22)

15:17–22. Menahem (v. 17) began to reign **in the nine and thirtieth year of Azariah** (752 BC), and he reigned for **ten years** (752–742 BC). As his evil predecessors had, he followed in **the sins of Jeroboam** (v. 18).

Pul (v. 19) is the Babylonian name (see 1 Chron. 5:26) of the Assyrian ruler who assumed the longer name Tiglath-pileser III when he came to power (745–727 BC). Two years into his reign, he **came against the land** of Israel. Assyrian annals of Tiglath-pileser III indicate that he marched west with his army in 743 BC and took tribute from, among others, Carchemish, Hamath, Tyre, Byblos, Damascus, and Menahem of Samaria (see Maps 6 and 8a at the end of the *KJV Study Bible*). He exacted tribute (extortion) of **a thousand talents of silver** from Menahem. This is equivalent to about 37 tons of silver, an enormous sum of money. By way of comparison, Omri bought the hill of Samaria for about 150 pounds of silver (see 1 Kings 16:24). **That his** (Pul's) **hand might be with him** (Menahem) **to confirm … his** (Menahem's) **hand**. It appears that as a usurper, Menahem still felt insecure on the throne. Therefore, in exchange for Assyrian support to his claim on Israel's throne, Menahem became a vassal to Assyria at a huge price. The opposition to his rule may have come from those following the leadership of Pekah, who favored an alliance with the Syrians of Damascus to resist the Assyrian threat (see discussion on 15:27). Hosea denounced the policy of seeking aid from the Assyrians and predicted that it would fail (Hos. 5:13–15).

To pay Assyria, Menahem exacted **fifty shekels** (about one and one-fourth pounds; v. 20) of silver from each Israelite of means. A simple calculation reveals that it would require approximately 60,000 men of means to provide the 1,000 talents of tribute. This gives some indication of the prosperity the northern kingdom had enjoyed during the time of Jeroboam II.

M. Pekahiah of Israel (15:23–26)

15:23–26. Apparently, Menahem died a natural death, and his son **Pekahiah** (v. 23) began to reign **in the fiftieth year of Azariah** (742 BC), but he reigned only **two years** (742–740 BC). He too followed in **the sins of Jeroboam** (v. 24; see 1 Kings 12:26–32; 13:33–34; 14:16).

Pekah (v. 25), Pekahiah's captain, was probably the ranking official in the provinces east of the Jordan, but his allegiance to Menahem and Pekahiah may well have been more apparent than real (see discussion on 15:27). Pekah **conspired against him** (Pekahiah)**, and smote him**. Differences over foreign policy probably played an important role in fomenting Pekah's revolution. Pekahiah undoubtedly followed the policy of his father, Menahem, in seeking Assyria's friendship (see 15:20). Pekah advocated friendly relations with the Syrians of Damascus to counter potential Assyrian aggression (see 16:1–9; Isa. 7:1–2, 4–6).

N. Pekah of Israel (15:27–31)

15:27–31. Pekah (v. 27) assumed the throne **in the two and fiftieth year of Azariah** (740 BC) and reigned for **twenty years** (752–732 BC). The years of his reign are based on the following assumptions (which the data seem to require): (1) when Menahem assassinated Shallum (see discussions on 15:17, 19, 25), Pekah had established east of the Jordan virtually a rival government to that of Menahem and (2) the number of regnal years given here includes this period of rival rule. Pekah also followed in **the sins of Jeroboam** (v. 28).

During Pekah's reign (ca. 733 BC) **came Tiglath-pileser king of Assyria** (v. 29; see discussion on 15:19) into Israel, apparently because of Pekah's anti-Assyrian position and Ahaz's appeal to Assyria. The historical background for this attack is found in 16:5–9; 2 Chronicles 28:16–21; and Isaiah 7:1–17. Assyria's invasion into northern Israel resulted in the capture of **Ijon … Naphtali**. Over 150 years earlier, Ben-hadad I of Damascus had taken this same territory from the northern kingdom in response to an appeal by a king of Judah (see discussions on 1 Kings 15:19–20). Many northern Israelites were carried **captive to Assyria** (see 1 Chron. 5:26). This forced exile of Israelites from their homeland was a fulfillment of the covenant curse (see discussion on 10:32).

Hoshea … made a conspiracy against Pekah (v. 30) and killed him. Hoshea probably represented the faction in the northern kingdom that favored cooperation with Assyria rather than resistance. In one of his annals, Tiglath-pileser III claims to have placed Hoshea on the throne of the northern kingdom and to have taken ten talents of gold and one thousand talents of silver as tribute from him. Hoshea then assumed the throne of Israel **in the twentieth year of Jotham** (732 BC; see discussions on 15:32–33).

O. Jotham of Judah (15:32–38)

15:32–38. Jotham (v. 32) began to reign **in the second year of Pekah** (750 BC; see discussion on 15:27). Godly Jotham is credited for reigning **sixteen years** (750–735 BC; v. 33). This included the period he was coregent with his father, Azariah (750–740 BC; see discussion on 15:5). Jotham's reign was in some sense terminated in 735 BC, and his son Ahaz took over. However, Jotham continued to live until at least 732 BC (see discussions on 15:30, 37).

He was godly king and did right, as **his father Uzziah had done** (v. 34; see discussion on 15:3; see also 2 Chron. 27:2), however, **the high places were not removed** (v. 35) in his day (see 15:4; see also discussion on 1 Kings 15:14). He rebuilt **the higher** (i.e., "upper") **gate of the house of the LORD** (see 2 Chron. 23:20; Jer. 20:2; Ezek. 8:3; 9:2). Additional information on Jotham's building activities is given in 2 Chronicles 27:3–4.

More of **the acts of Jotham** (v. 36) were recorded in **the chronicles of the kings of Judah** (see discussion on 1 Kings 14:29) and in canonical 2 Chronicles 27:1–6.

The author states that **Rezin** (v. 37) of Syria and **Pekah** of Israel banded together in an anti-Assyrian alliance. Judah refused to join the alliance and consequently suffered reprisal from the two northern kings and came under attack (see Isa. 7:1). This parenthetical statement concerning Jotham's reign supports the idea of an overlap of the reigns of Jotham and Ahaz (see discussion on v. 33), since 16:5–12; 2 Chronicles 28:5–21; and Isaiah 7:1–17 all place the major effort of Rezin and Pekah in the time of Ahaz. When Jotham died, his son **Ahaz** (v. 38) **reigned in his stead** as sole king.

P. Ahaz of Judah (chap. 16)

16:1-4. Ahaz (v. 1) began to reign **in the seventeenth year of Pekah** (735 BC; see discussion on 15:27). His reign apparently overlapped that of Jotham, with Ahaz serving as a senior partner beginning in 735 BC (see discussions on 15:33, 37; see also discussions on v. 2; 17:1). He was **twenty years old ... when he began to reign** (v. 2), perhaps the age at which he became a senior coregent with his father, Jotham, in 735 BC. Otherwise, according to the ages and dates provided, Ahaz would have been eleven or twelve, instead of fourteen or fifteen, when his son Hezekiah was born (see 18:1-2). Ahaz **reigned sixteen years in Jerusalem**. The synchronizations of the reigns of Ahaz and Hezekiah of Judah with those of Pekah and Hoshea of the northern kingdom present some apparent chronological difficulties (see discussions on v. 1; 17:1; 18:1, 9-10). It seems best to take the sixteen years specified here as the number of years Ahaz reigned after the death of Jotham, thus 732-715 BC (see discussions on 15:30, 33). The beginning of his reign appears to be dated in a variety of ways in the biblical text: (1) in 744/743 BC, which presupposes a coregency with his grandfather Azariah when Ahaz was eleven or twelve years old (see 17:1); (2) in 735 BC, when Ahaz became senior coregent with Jotham (see v. 1); and (3) in 732 BC, when Ahaz began his sole reign after the death of Jotham. Ahaz **did not that ... like David his father**. He was a disappointing contrast to his immediate predecessors and did not even receive the qualified approval given to Amaziah (14:3), Azariah (15:3), and Jotham (15:34). Instead, he ranked with Judah's wicked kings, Jehoram (8:18), Manasseh (21:2), Jehoiakim (23:37), and Zedekiah (24:19). **He walked in the way of the kings of Israel** (v. 3). It is unlikely that Ahaz adhered to the calf worship introduced by Jeroboam I at Bethel and Dan (see 1 Kings 12:26-32; 13:33-34; 14:16). The reference here is probably to Baal worship in the spirit of Ahab (see discussions on 1 Kings 16:31-33; see also 2 Chron. 28:2). He **made his son to pass through the fire**. Israel had been warned by Moses not to engage in this pagan rite (see Lev. 18:21; Deut. 18:10). In Israel, the firstborn son in each household was to be consecrated to the Lord and redeemed by a payment of five shekels to the priests (see Exod. 13:1, 11-13; Num. 18:16; see also 3:27; 17:17; 21:6; 23:10; 2 Chron. 28:3; Jer. 7:31; 32:35). **He sacrificed ... in the high places ... under every green tree** (v. 4; see 15:4, 35; see also discussion on 1 Kings 15:14). These high places appear to be those assimilated from pagan Baal worship and used for the worship of the Lord in a syncretistic fashion. Large trees were viewed as symbols of fertility by the pre-Israelite inhabitants of Canaan. Immoral pagan rites were performed at shrines located under such trees. Contrary to the explicit prohibition of the Mosaic covenant, the Israelites adopted this pagan custom (see 17:10; 1 Kings 14:23; Deut. 12:2; Jer. 2:20; 3:6; 17:2; Ezek. 6:13; 20:28; Hos. 4:13-14).

16:5-9. Because Ahaz was uncooperative with their anti-Assyrian policy **Rezin ... and Pekah ... came up to Jerusalem to war** (v. 5; see discussions on 15:25, 37). Though they were able to besiege Ahaz, they **could not overcome him**. While he was surrounded by enemies, God assured him that they would fail and offered him the opportunity to seek a sign from Him (see Isa. 7:1-17; 2 Chron. 28:5-21). Rezin and Pekah desired to replace Ahaz on the throne of the southern kingdom with the son of Tabeal (Isa. 7:6) to gain another ally in their anti-Assyrian political policy (see discussions on 15:19, 25). The Lord delivered Judah and Ahaz from this threat, in spite of their wickedness, because of the promises of the Davidic covenant (see 1 Kings 11:36; 2 Sam. 7:13; Isa. 7:3-7, 14).

Rezin king of Syria recovered Elath (v. 6; see discussion on 14:22). **The Syrians came to Elath**. The Hebrew reads "Edomites." The word for "Syrians" ("Arameans") is sometimes confused for "Edomites," (the *d* and *r* being written so similarly) and may have occurred here (see 2 Chron. 28:17). Thus, there is an indication that the Edomites moved into what the Syrians had conquered. **Unto this day**, that is, until the time of the source from which the author of 1-2 Kings derived this account (see discussion on 1 Kings 8:8). The Philistines also took this opportunity to avenge previous defeats (compare 2 Chron. 26:5-7 with 2 Chron. 28:18).

Thoroughly frightened by Rezin and Pekah's threats, Ahaz appealed to **Tiglath-pileser** (v. 7; see discussions on 15:19, 29). **I am thy servant and thy son.** Ahaz preferred to seek security for Judah by means of a treaty with Assyria rather than by obedience to the Lord and trust in His promises (see Exod. 23:22; Isa. 7:10-16). To pay for the Assyrian king's assistance, he took **silver and gold ... found in the house of the LORD** (v. 8). The temple treasure must have been restored to some degree by Jotham (see 12:18; 14:14). The name "Jehoahaz of Judah" (Ahaz) appears on a list of rulers (including those of the Philistines, Ammonites, Moabites, and Edomites) who brought tribute to Tiglath-pileser in 734 BC.

Tiglath-pileser III obliged and **went up against Damascus, and took it** (v. 9). In 732 BC, he moved against Damascus and destroyed it (see the prophecies of Isa. 7:16; Amos 1:3-5) and killed Rezin. He then **carried the people of it captive to Kir.** The Syrians were sent back to the place from which they had come (Amos 9:7), in fulfillment of the prophecy of Amos (Amos 1:5). The location of Kir is unknown, though it is mentioned in connection with Elam in Isaiah 22:6. Syria had served as a buffer state between Assyria and Israel, but with Syria defeated, Israel also became an easy victim for Assyria and it too was invaded (see discussion on 15:29).

16:10-16. Ahaz went to Damascus to meet Tiglath-pileser (v. 10). As a vassal king, Ahaz went either to express his gratitude and loyalty to the victorious Assyrian ruler or to pay more tribute. **The altar** that he saw **at Damascus** was perhaps that of the god Rimmon (see 5:18; 2 Chron. 28:23) but more likely was a royal altar of Tiglath-pileser. Ahaz probably would not have reproduced an altar of people who had just been defeated. Ahaz's reproduction of such an altar would have been a further sign of submission to the Assyrians.

Solomon's bronze altar was set aside so that Ahaz could use the reproduction for his own **burnt offering ... meat offering ... drink offering ... peace offerings** (v. 13). With the exception of the drink offering, these same sacrifices had been offered at the dedication of the temple (1 Kings 8:64). He removed the bronze altar from its prominent place in front of the temple and gave it a place alongside the new stone altar **on the north side** (v. 14). Even though fire from heaven had inaugurated and sanctioned the use of the bronze altar for the worship of the Lord (see 2 Chron. 7:1), Ahaz now replaced it with a **great altar** (v. 15) built on the pattern of the pagan altar from Damascus. And although the bronze altar was quite large (see 2 Chron. 4:1), the new altar was larger. The priest Uriah was instructed to offer on the new altar the **morning burnt offering** (see 3:20; Exod. 29:38-39; Num. 28:3-4), the **evening meat offering** (see discussion on 1 Kings 18:29), **the king's burnt sacrifice, and his meat offering.** There is no other reference to these special offerings of the king in the Old Testament, with the possible exception of Ezekiel's depiction of the offerings of a future prince (Ezek. 46:12). **The brasen altar shall be for me to inquire by.** Ahaz reserved the right to use Solomon's altar for divination. Seeking omens by the examination of the entrails of sacrificed animals is well attested in ancient Near Eastern texts. Here Ahaz was stating his intention to follow an Assyrian divination technique in an attempt to secure the Lord's guidance.

16:17-18. Ahaz pillaged the temple by stripping the furnishing of their valuable ornamentation. He **cut off the borders of the bases, and removed the laver** (v. 17); that is, he dismantled the portable bases and their basins (see 1 Kings 7:27-39), and he **took down the sea from off the brasen oxen**; that is, he confiscated the bronze oxen that supported the "sea" (see 1 Kings 7:23-26). Perhaps the bronze was needed for the tribute required by Tiglath-pileser III.

He even altered the structure of the temple, removing **the covert for the sabbath** (v. 18), that is, the "covered passage," to give it to **the king of Assyria.** As a vassal of Tiglath-pileser, Ahaz was forced to relinquish some of the symbols of his own royal power.

16:19-20. See 2 Chronicles 28, where, among other things, it is said that Ahaz even "shut up the doors of the house of the LORD" (2 Chron. 28:24). **Ahaz slept with his fathers** (v. 20), but he was not honored with a burial among the former kings (see

2 Chron. 28:27). **Hezekiah his son reigned in his stead**. For the reign of Hezekiah, see 18:1–20:21.

Q. Hoshea of Israel (17:1–6)

17:1–2. Hoshea (v. 1) gained the throne by conspiracy **in the twelfth year of Ahaz** (732 BC; see discussion on 15:30). This date is based on the assumption that Ahaz began a coregency with Azariah in 744/743 BC (see discussions on 16:1–2). Some interpreters prefer to place the beginning of Ahaz's reign in 735 BC, on the assumption that the "twelfth" year of his reign in this text is a copyist's error for the "fourth" year of his reign (i.e., 732 BC). He reigned **nine years** (732–722 BC; see 1 Kings, Introduction: "Chronology"). Tiglath-pileser III took credit for placing Hoshea on the throne, so from the beginning, Hoshea was a vassal to the Assyrian king. Hoshea was an evil king, but he did not rank with his predecessors.

17:3–6. Tiglath-pileser III died in 727 BC, and his son **Shalmaneser [V]** (v. 3) succeeded him and ruled from 727–722 BC. Hoshea paid him tribute for a time, then declared himself free of Assyrian control and sought support from Egypt. The identity of **So king of Egypt** (v. 4) is unclear. The name So may refer to the Egyptian city Sais, where Tef Nekht had founded the Twenty-fourth Dynasty, or to king Osorkon of the Twenty-second Dynasty. Hoshea was to learn that once one became a vassal of Assyria, it was unwise to renege. Shalmaneser V had Hoshea imprisoned. While Israel was without a functioning king, the Assyrians came through the land, apparently taking the smaller towns until they reached Samaria, the capital city. Samaria was a strongly fortified city and was extremely difficult to subdue (see discussion on 1 Kings 16:24), for it was held in siege for **three years** (725–722 BC; v. 5) before it fell.

In the ninth year of Hoshea (722 BC; see discussion on 17:1), **the king of Assyria took Samaria** (v. 6). In the winter (December) of 722–721 BC, Shalmaneser V died (possibly by assassination), and the Assyrian throne was seized by Sargon II (722–705 BC). In his annals, Sargon II lays claim to the capture of Samaria at the beginning of his reign, but it was hardly more than a mopping-up operation. He **carried Israel away into Assyria**. Because the northern kingdom refused to be obedient to their covenant obligations, the Lord brought on them the judgment pronounced by Ahijah during the reign of the northern kingdom's first king, Jeroboam I (see discussion on 1 Kings 14:15). In his annals, Sargon II claims to have deported 27,290 Israelites. He then settled other captured people in the vacated towns of the northern kingdom (see 17:24). The location of **Halah** is uncertain. **Habor by the river of Gozan** should more likely be translated, "Gozan, on the river of Habor." Gozan was an Assyrian provincial capital located on a tributary of the Euphrates River. **The cities of the Medes** refers to towns located in the area south of the Caspian Sea and northeast of the Tigris River.

R. Exile of Israel; Resettlement of the Land (17:7–41)

17:7–23. A theological explanation for the downfall of the northern kingdom is necessary at this point. Israel had repeatedly spurned the Lord's gracious acts, had refused to heed the prophets' warnings of impending judgment (vv. 13–14, 23), and had failed to keep her covenant obligations (v. 15). The result was the implementation of the covenant curse precisely as it had been presented to the Israelites by Moses before they entered Canaan (Deut. 28:49–68; 32:1–47). What follows is a sordid list of Israel's theological failures.

17:7. Samaria did not fall to Assyria because God was helpless to rescue her. His deliverance of Israel from Egypt was proof enough of His might. **The LORD ... had brought them up out of the land of Egypt** (v. 7). The deliverance from Egypt was the fundamental redemptive event in Israel's history. She owed her very existence as a nation to this gracious and mighty act of the Lord (see Exod. 20:2; Deut. 5:15; 26:8; Josh. 24:5–7, 17; Judg. 10:11; 1 Sam. 12:6; Neh. 9:9–13; Mic. 6:4). She **had feared other gods**, a violation of the fundamental obligation of Israel's covenant with the Lord (see 17:35; Deut. 5:7; 6:14; Josh. 24:14–16, 20; Jer. 1:16; 2:5–6; 25:6; 35:15).

17:8. Israel's sin fell into two related categories: (1) following the religious practices of the Canaanites and (2) idolatry supported by her kings. Israel had **walked in the statutes of the heathen** (v. 8; see Deut. 18:9; Judg. 2:12–13) and in the statutes **of the kings of Israel, which they had made** (see, e.g., 10:31, Jehu; 14:24, Jeroboam II; 1 Kings 12:28–33, Jeroboam I; 16:25–26, Omri; 16:30–34, Ahab).

17:9–12. The Israelites had practiced idolatry everywhere, in flagrant disobedience to God's explicit prohibition. They built **high places in all their cities** (v. 9; see 14:4; 15:4, 35; see also discussions on 16:4; 1 Kings 3:2; 15:14). They had erected **images** (see discussion on 1 Kings 14:23)] **and groves** (i.e., "Asherah"; see discussion on 1 Kings 14:15) **in every high hill, and under every green tree** (v. 10; see 16:4; 1 Kings 14:23; Jer. 2:20; 3:6, 13; 17:2).

That they did **wicked things** (v. 11) is perhaps a reference to ritual prostitution (see discussion on 1 Kings 14:24; see also Hos. 4:13–14). Their idolatry violated specific prohibitions: **Ye shall not do this thing** (v. 12; see Exod. 20:4–5; see also Exod. 23:13; Lev. 26:1; Deut. 5:6–10).

17:13–15. God had graciously and repeatedly sent His prophets to warn Israel. He **testified against Israel, and against Judah, by all the prophets** (v. 13). Israel had not only violated the requirements of the Sinai covenant; she had also spurned the words of prophets that the Lord had graciously sent to call His people back to the covenant (see, e.g., 1 Kings 13:1–3; 14:6–16; Judg. 6:8–10; 1 Sam. 3:19–21; as well as the ministries of Elijah, Elisha, Amos, and Hosea). For **the seers,** see discussion on 1 Samuel 9:9.

The Israelites had **hardened their necks** (v. 14), a figure derived from the obstinate resistance of an ox being placed under a yoke (see Deut. 10:16; Jer. 2:20; 7:26; 17:23; 19:15; Hos. 4:16). **They followed vanity** (v. 15), that is, they were deluded by worthless idols (see Deut. 32:21; Jer. 2:5; 8:19; 10:8; 14:22; 51:18).

17:16–17. The assortment of Israel's paganism is further detailed. They made **molten images, even two calves** (v. 16), referring to the golden calves of Bethel and Dan (see 1 Kings 12:28–30). They **worshipped all the host of heaven**. Israel had been commanded not to follow the astral cults of her pagan neighbors (see Deut. 4:19; 17:3). Although

this form of idolatry is not mentioned previously in 1–2 Kings, the prophet Amos apparently alludes to its practice in the northern kingdom during the reign of Jeroboam II (see *KJV Study Bible* note on Amos 5:26). It was later introduced in the southern kingdom during the reign of Manasseh (see 21:3, 5) and abolished during the reformation of Josiah (see 23:4–5, 12; see also Ezek. 8:16).

They caused their sons and their daughters to pass through the fire (v. 17; see discussion on 16:3) and relied on **divination and enchantments**. Such practices were forbidden in the Mosaic covenant (see discussion on 16:15; see also Lev. 19:26; Deut. 18:10).

17:18–23. Having summarized Israel's sin (17:8–17), the writer now summarizes the consequences of her sin. **Therefore the LORD ... removed them out of his sight** (v. 18), by means of the exile of the northern kingdom (see 17:6; 23:27). **There was none left but the tribe of Judah**. The southern kingdom included elements of the tribes of Simeon and Benjamin, but Judah was the only tribe in the south to retain its complete integrity (see discussions on 1 Kings 11:31–32; see also discussion on 2 Kings 19:4). He **afflicted them, and delivered them into the hand of spoilers** (v. 20; see 10:32–33; 13:3, 20; 24:2; 2 Chron. 21:16; 28:18; Amos 1:13). He **rent Israel from the house of David** (v. 21; see 1 Kings 11:11, 31; 12:24). The division of the kingdom was of the Lord, but it came to the nation as a punishment for their sins. **Jeroboam ... made them sin a great sin** (see 1 Kings 12:26–32; 13:33–34). All that happened was fulfilled just as the Lord **had said by all his servants the prophets** (v. 23; see 1 Kings 14:15–16; Hos. 10:1–7; 11:5; Amos 5:27).

17:24–26. The writer now introduces a reverse deportation, in which **the king of Assyria** (v. 24) brought foreigners to Samaria. This was done primarily by Sargon II (722–705 BC), though later Assyrian rulers, including Esarhaddon (681–669 BC) and Ashurbanipal (669–627 BC), settled additional non-Israelites in Samaria (see Ezra 4:2, 9–10). **Babylon** and **Cuthah** (located about eight miles northeast of Babylon) were forced to submit to Assyrian rule by Sargon II in 709 BC. **Ava** is probably the same as

Ivah (see 18:34; 19:13). Its association with Hamath, Arpad, and Sepharvaim suggests a location somewhere in Syria. **Hamath** was located on the Orontes River (see 14:25; 18:34; see also discussion on Ezek. 47:15). In 720 BC, Sargon II made the kingdom of Hamath an Assyrian province. **Sepharvaim**, perhaps located in Syrian territory, was possibly situated between Damascus and Hamath. **Samaria** is here a designation for the entire northern kingdom (see discussion on 1 Kings 13:32).

These displaced foreigners did not fare well in the land. **They feared not the LORD** (v. 25) but worshiped their own national deities. **The LORD sent lions among them**. Lions had always been present in Canaan (see 1 Kings 13:24; 20:36; Judg. 14:5; 1 Sam. 17:34; Amos 3:12). In the aftermath of the disruption and depopulation caused by the conflict with the Assyrians, the lions greatly increased in number (see Exod. 23:29). This was viewed by the inhabitants of the land and by the writer of Kings as a punishment from the Lord (see Lev. 26:21–22).

The king of Assyria (v. 26), probably Sargon II, was informed that the people did not know **the manner of the God of the land**. According to the religious ideas of that time, each regional deity required special ritual observances, which, if ignored or violated, would bring disaster on the land.

17:27–28. The king ordered that **one of the priests** (v. 27), that is, a priest from the golden-calf cult that Jeroboam I had established in the northern kingdom (see 1 Kings 12:31 and discussion), be sent to teach the people. The priest **came and dwelt in Beth-el** (v. 28). Bethel continued to be the center for the apostate form of Yahweh worship that had been promoted in the northern kingdom since the time of Jeroboam I (see discussions on 1 Kings 12:28–30).

The mixed population of the former territory of the northern kingdom, with its mixed ancestry, eventually intermarried with the remaining Israelites, and the mixed population came to be known as **Samaritans** (v. 29). In later times, the Samaritans rejected the idolatry of their polytheistic origins and followed the teachings of Moses, including monotheism. In New Testament times, Jesus testified to a Samaritan woman (John 4:4–26), and many Samaritans were converted under the ministry of Philip (Acts 8:4–25).

17:29–41. The religion of Samaria and its vicinity was extremely syncretistic. The Lord (Yahweh) was viewed as the local deity, but all the transported peoples continued to worship their native gods. The writer repeatedly states that **They feared the LORD, and served their own gods** (v. 33), a classic statement of syncretistic religion.

Such syncretism persisted **unto this day** (v. 34), that is, until the time of the writing of 1–2 Kings. **They fear not the LORD** is here used in the sense of faithful worship. **Feared the Lord** (vv. 32–33) refers to a paganized worship.

Ye shall not fear other gods (v. 35). The Mosaic covenant demanded exclusive worship of the Lord (Exod. 20:5; Deut. 5:9). This was the first and greatest commandment, and it was to distinguish Israel from all other peoples. The first commandment is irrevocably connected to the phrase **the LORD, who brought you up out of the land of Egypt … him shall ye fear** (v. 36; see Exod. 20:2–3). Here, as in 17:7, the deliverance from Egypt is cited as the gracious act of the Lord par excellence that entitled Him to exclusive claim on Israel's loyalty. God graciously reminded Israel, the Lord **shall deliver you out of the hand of all your enemies** (v. 39; see Exod. 23:22; Deut. 20:1–4; 23:14). Sadly, in spite of all that God said, **these nations** (v. 41) persisted in their syncretism **unto this day**, that is, until the time of the writing of 1–2 Kings.

III. Judah from Hezekiah to the Babylonian Exile (chaps. 18–25)

A. Hezekiah (chaps. 18–20)

1. Hezekiah's Good Reign (18:1–8)

18:1–3. That three complete chapters are devoted to godly Hezekiah is an indication of how important his reign was. **In the third year of Hoshea … Hezekiah … began to reign** (729 BC; v. 1; see 17:1). Hezekiah was coregent with his father, Ahaz, from 729–715 BC (see discussion on 16:2; Isa. 36:1).

Hezekiah was twenty-five years old when he became sole king of Judah, and he reigned for **twenty and nine years** (715–686 BC; v. 2). See 2 Chronicles 29–32 and Isaiah 36–39 for a description of the events of his reign, including a more detailed account of the reformation he led (2 Chronicles 29–31). One of Hezekiah's first acts was to reopen the temple, which had been closed by his father, Ahaz (see discussion on 16:19; see also 2 Chron. 29:3).

He did that which was right ... according to all that David his father did (v. 3). Hezekiah was one of the few kings who was compared favorably with David. The others were Asa (1 Kings 15:11), Jehoshaphat (1 Kings 22:43), and Josiah (2 Kings 22:2). A qualification, however, was introduced with both Asa and Jehoshaphat: they did not remove the high places (see 1 Kings 15:14; 22:43).

18:4–8. Hezekiah initiated a large-scale reform to rid the land of the idolatrous practices of Ahaz, his father (for an expanded account, see 2 Chron. 29:3–31:21). **He removed the high places** (v. 4). Hezekiah was not the first king to destroy high places (see discussions on 1 Kings 3:2; 15:14), but he was the first to destroy the high places dedicated to the worship of the Lord (see 12:3; 14:4; 15:4, 35; 17:9; 1 Kings 22:43). This became known even to the Assyrian king, Sennacherib (see 18:22). He **brake the images** (see 3:2; 10:26–27; 17:10; see also discussion on 1 Kings 14:23) and **cut down the groves** (see 13:6; 17:10, 16; 1 Kings 16:23; see also discussion on 1 Kings 14:15). Almost seven hundred years after Moses had erected the bronze serpent for Israel to see (see Num. 21:8–9), this object remained and was now superstitiously reverenced. **The children of Israel did burn incense to it.** It is unlikely that the bronze serpent had been an object of worship all through the centuries of Israel's existence as a nation. Just when an idolatrous significance was attached to it is not known, but perhaps it occurred during the reign of Hezekiah's father, Ahaz (see chap. 16). Snake worship of various types was common among ancient Near Eastern peoples. Hezekiah, however, reduced this object of veneration to scrap metal and contemptuously **called it Nehushtan,** "a piece of bronze."

He trusted in the LORD ... after him was none like him ... nor any that were before him (v. 5). A difference of emphasis is to be seen in this statement when compared to that of 23:25. Hezekiah's uniqueness is to be found in his trust in the Lord, while Josiah's uniqueness is to be found in his scrupulous observance of the Mosaic law.

Judah had become a vassal to Assyria under Ahaz (see 16:7), which required at least formal recognition of Assyrian deities. Hezekiah reversed the policy of his father, Ahaz. **He rebelled against the king of Assyria** (v. 7) and sought independence from Assyrian dominance. It is likely that sometime shortly after 705 BC, when Sennacherib replaced Sargon II on the Assyrian throne, Hezekiah refused to pay the annual tribute due the Assyrians. He was probably able to do this because during the last years of Sargon II, Assyria had been preoccupied with affairs in southern Mesopotamia.

In a reversal of the conditions that existed during the time of Ahaz, in which the Philistines captured Judahite cities in the hill country and the Negev (see 2 Chron. 28:18), Hezekiah now **smote the Philistines** (v. 8) and was able once again to subdue them. Probably Hezekiah tried to coerce the Philistines into joining his anti-Assyrian policy. In one of his annals, Sennacherib tells of forcing Hezekiah to release Padi, king of the Philistine city Ekron, whom Hezekiah held prisoner in Jerusalem. This occurred in connection with Sennacherib's military campaign in 701 BC.

2. The Assyrian Threat and Deliverance (18:9–19:37)

18:9–12. The writer reviews the events of chapter 17, synchronizing Hezekiah's reign with Israel's final years. The Assyrians besieged Samaria **in the fourth year of king Hezekiah** (725 BC; v. 9), that is, in the fourth year of Hezekiah's coregency with Ahaz (see discussions on 18:1; 17:1). **Three years** later (v. 10; see discussion on 17:5), in **the ninth year of Hoshea,** Samaria fell to Assyria, **and the king of Assyria did carry away Israel** (v. 11; see discussion on 17:6). These were the serious consequences for having disobeyed the Lord and having **transgressed his covenant** (v. 12; see 17:7–23).

18:13-16. In the fourteenth year (v. 13) of Hezekiah's sole reign (701 BC; see discussion on 18:2), **Sennacherib king of Assyria** came up against the cities of Judah. Verses 13-16 correspond very closely with Sennacherib's own account of his 701 BC campaign against Phoenicia, Judah, and Egypt. **He took them.** In his annals, Sennacherib claims to have captured forty-six of Hezekiah's fortified cities, as well as numerous open villages, and to have taken 200,150 people captive. He says he made Hezekiah "a prisoner in Jerusalem, his royal residence, like a bird in a cage," but he does not say he took Jerusalem.

Sennacherib's campaign brought him to Lachish, only about thirty miles southwest of Jerusalem. Hezekiah quickly admitted his guilt and offered to pay whatever Sennacherib demanded, who imposed payment of **three hundred talents of silver and thirty talents of gold** (v. 14), equivalent to about eleven tons of silver and one ton of gold. The Assyrian and biblical reports of the amount of tribute Hezekiah paid to Sennacherib agree with respect to the thirty talents of gold, but Sennacherib claims to have received eight hundred talents of silver rather than the three hundred specified in the biblical text. This discrepancy may be the result of differences in the weight of Assyrian and Israelite silver talents, or it may simply be due to the Assyrian propensity for exaggeration. (For the relative value of this amount of silver and gold, see discussion on 15:19.) Hezekiah made the payment by emptying the coffers of **silver … in the house of the LORD, and in the treasures of the king's house** (v. 15; see 12:10, 18; 14:14; 16:8; 1 Kings 7:51; 14:26; 15:18) and stripping gold from the temple.

18:17-19:37. The following account of Sennacherib's threat on Hezekiah and Jerusalem, the prophet Isaiah's counsel and encouragement, and the Lord's supernatural intervention is paralleled in Isaiah 36-37 (see also 2 Chron. 32). Some of the narrative is verbatim, indicating that the writer of Kings drew on the work of the prophet or that both writers consulted a common historical source.

18:17-18. Sennacherib had set up camp at **Lachish** (v. 17), an important city southwest of Jeru-

salem that guarded the main approach to Judah's capital from that direction. He sent three high-ranking officials to Jerusalem, **Tartan and Rabsaris and Rab-shakeh,** where they were met by three representatives of Hezekiah. They met at the **conduit … field** (its precise location is unknown). It is ironic that the Assyrian officials demanded Judah's surrender on the very spot where Isaiah had warned Ahaz to trust in the Lord rather than rely on an alliance with Assyria for deliverance from the threat issued by Syria and the northern kingdom of Israel (see 16:5-10; Isa. 7:1-17). Hezekiah's three representatives were Eliakim, who **was over the household** (v. 18; see discussion on 1 Kings 4:6), **Shebna the scribe** (see discussion on 2 Sam. 8:17), and **Joah … the recorder** (see discussion on 2 Sam. 8:16).

18:19-25. Thus saith the great king (v. 19). The following address is a masterpiece of calculated intimidation and psychological warfare designed to demoralize and break the resistance of the inhabitants of Jerusalem (see 18:26-27). "The great king" was a frequently used title of the Assyrian rulers, and occasionally of the Lord (Pss. 47:2; 48:2; 95:3; Mal. 1:14; Matt. 5:35).

What confidence is this wherein thou trustest? … thou trustest upon … Egypt (vv. 19, 21). Within Jerusalem's walls was a pro-Egypt party that wanted to seek help from Egypt. Isaiah condemned such a move (Isa. 30:1-5; 31:1-3), and Sennacherib correctly warned that Egypt was totally unreliable and incapable of offering any assistance.

Is not that he, whose high places and whose altars Hezekiah hath taken away …? (v. 22). The Assyrians cleverly attempted to drive a wedge between Hezekiah and the people. They attempted to exploit any resentment that may have existed among those who opposed Hezekiah's reformation and his destruction of the high places (see discussion on 18:4). Sennacherib, however, had completely misunderstood Hezekiah's reform. His pagan thinking was this: Why would God help the king who so sacrilegiously had destroyed all the altars for worship?

I will deliver … horses, if thou be able … to set riders upon them (v. 23). With this sarcastic taunt, the Assyrians undoubtedly suggested accurately that the Judahites were so weak in military personnel that they could not even take advantage of such a generous offer. In contrast with the Assyrians, the army of Judah at the time consisted largely of foot soldiers. The city under siege would have contained few chariots, and it is not known whether the Israelites ever employed mounted men in combat.

The LORD said to me (v. 25). Sennacherib claimed he was on a divine mission. This may have been mere pretense, or possibly Assyrian spies had informed Sennacherib of the prophecies of Isaiah and Micah.

18:26–27. Hezekiah's representatives requested, **Speak … in the Syrian language** (Hebrew, *Aramith*; i.e., Aramaic; v. 26). It had become the international language of the Near East, known and used by those experienced in diplomacy and commerce. It is surprising that the Assyrian officials were able to speak the Hebrew dialect of the common people of Judah (see 2 Chron. 32:18). **Rab-shakeh** (v. 27) responded, **hath he not sent me to the men which sit on the wall …?** The Assyrian strategy was to negotiate in the hearing of the people to demoralize them and turn them against Hezekiah. Refusal to surrender would result in terrible famine. The gross description of eating and drinking was meant to be a vivid portrayal of the potential hardship of a prolonged siege (compare past famine conditions in Samaria, 6:24–29).

18:28–35. Thus saith the king (v. 29). The Assyrian officials now addressed their remarks directly to the populace rather than to the officials of Hezekiah, as in verses 19–27. **Let not Hezekiah deceive you.** Here and in verses 30–31, the people are urged three times to turn against Hezekiah.

Neither let Hezekiah make you trust in the LORD, saying … this city shall not be delivered into the hand of the king of Assyria (v. 30). Hezekiah could say this on the basis of God's promise to him (see 20:6).

Rab-shakeh continued, **Eat ye every man of his own vine, and every one of his fig tree, and drink … of his cistern** (v. 31). He depicted the peaceful and prosperous times (see 1 Kings 4:25; Mic. 4:4; Zech. 3:10) that could be Judah's if they would surrender.

The phrase **until I come and take you away to a land like your own** (v. 32) indicates that ultimately surrender would mean deportation, but Sennacherib, through his representative, pictured it as something desirable. The Assyrians, however, had a horrific reputation for leading their "guests" away on a leash, with hooks through their noses. **That ye may live, and not die** presented a false hope. The alternatives depicted for the people are: (1) trust in the Lord and Hezekiah and die, or (2) trust in the Assyrians and enjoy prosperity and peace. These words directly contradicted the alternatives placed before Israel by Moses in Deuteronomy 30:15–20.

Hath any of the gods of the nations delivered at all his land out of the hand of the king of Assyria? … Who are they … that the LORD should deliver Jerusalem out of mine hand? (vv. 33, 35). The flaw in the Assyrian reasoning was to equate the one true and living God with the no-gods (Deut. 32:21) of the pagan peoples the Assyrians had defeated (see 19:4, 6; 2 Chron. 32:13–19; Isa. 10:9–11). As proof of his power over the gods, Sennacherib cited the cities that had already fallen due to their gods' incapability to defend them: **Hamath** (v. 34; see discussions on 14:25; 17:24), **Arpad** (a city located near Hamath and taken by the Assyrians in 740 BC; see 19:13; Isa. 10:9; Jer. 49:23), **Sepharvaim** (see discussion on 17:24), **Hena** (probably located in the vicinity of the other cities mentioned), and **Ivah** (see discussion on 17:24). Sennacherib's rationalization was this: If the gods that protected cities greater than Jerusalem had been ineffective against him, what god could possibly save Jerusalem?

18:36–37. The king's commandment was … Answer him not (v. 36). The Assyrian attempt to stir up a popular revolt against the leadership and authority of Hezekiah had failed. Hezekiah's representatives returned to him **with their clothes rent** (v. 37), an outward expression of great emotion (see 6:30; 1 Kings 21:27). Perhaps in this instance it was motivated by the Assyrians' blasphemy against the true God (see 19:4, 6; Matt. 26:65; Mark 14:63–64).

19:1–2. Clothed in **sackcloth** (v. 1), garments of grief and mourning (see discussion on 6:30),

Hezekiah presented himself in humility to the Lord. He sent two of his representatives (see discussion on 18:18) and **the elders of the priests** (v. 2), probably the oldest members of various priestly families (see Jer. 19:1), for counsel. The crisis involved not only the city of Jerusalem but also the temple. They were sent to **Esai** (i.e., Isaiah) **the prophet**. This is the first reference to Isaiah in the book of Kings, though he had been active in the reigns of Uzziah, Jotham, and Ahaz (see Isa. 1:1). Hezekiah now consulted him, hoping for an encouraging word.

19:3–5. Hezekiah's appeal was that the besieged people of Jerusalem were completely demoralized. **The children are come to the birth, and there is not strength to bring forth** (v. 3). This depicted the critical nature of the threat facing the city. He suggested that the Lord rebuke the Assyrian king for his blasphemy and scorn of **the living God** (v. 4), in contrast to the no-gods of 18:33–35. (See 1 Sam. 17:26, 36, 45 for another example of ridiculing the living and true God.) He asked of Isaiah, **lift up thy prayer**. Intercessory prayer was an important aspect of the ministry of the prophets (see, e.g., the intercession of Moses and Samuel, Exod. 32:31–32; 33:12–17; Num. 14:13–19; 1 Sam. 7:8–9; 12:19, 23; Ps. 99:6; Jer. 15:1). **The remnant** refers to those left in Judah after Sennacherib's capture of many towns and numerous people (see discussion on 18:13; see Isa. 10:28–32). Archaeological evidence reveals that many Israelites fled the northern kingdom during the Assyrian assaults and settled in Judah, so that the nation of Judah became the remnant of all Israel.

19:6–7. Isaiah's answer was comforting. Sennacherib would return to Assyria in fear and would die there. **I will send a blast** (v. 7). The Hebrew for "blast" means "spirit," referring to a spirit of insecurity and fear. **He shall hear a rumour.** Some interpreters link this "rumor" to the challenge made to Sennacherib by Tirhakah of Egypt (19:9). Others regard it as disturbing information from Sennacherib's homeland. He **shall return ... to fall by the sword** (see 19:37). Here the eventual murder of Sennacherib is connected with his blasphemy against the living God.

19:8–13. Meanwhile, Sennacherib was battling **Libnah** (v. 8; see discussion on 8:22) about six miles north of **Lachish** (see 18:17). Rumors were that **Tirhakah** (v. 9; see *KJV Study Bible* note on Isa. 37:9) of **Ethiopia** (Hebrew, *Cush*; i.e., the upper Nile region) was coming from Egypt to fight Sennacherib. Tirhakah was probably the crown prince and general at the time, but he became the pharaoh of Egypt's Twenty-fifth Dynasty.

Sennacherib reminded Hezekiah of his track record of conquest, giving a long list of conquered cities: **Gozan** (v. 12; see discussion on 17:6); **Haran** (see discussion on Gen. 11:31; it is not known just when the Assyrians took Haran); **Rezeph**, located south of the Euphrates River and northeast of Hamath; **Eden**, a district along the Euphrates River, south of Haran, which was incorporated into the Assyrian empire by Shalmaneser III in 855 BC (see Ezek. 27:23; Amos 1:5); **Thelasar**, location unknown; and **Hamath ... Ivah** (v. 13; see discussion on 18:34). Once again, Hezekiah was warned that no god has been able to stand in Sennacherib's way. Hezekiah should not be deceived by his god to think his situation would be any different (see 18:33–35; see also 2 Chron. 32:17).

19:14–19. Hezekiah took **the letter** (v. 14) to the Lord in prayer. His prayer included four points: (1) God is sovereign, exercising complete authority over what He had created. He **dwellest between the cherubims** (v. 15; see *KJV Study Bible* note on Exod. 25:18; discussion 1 Sam. 4:4). **Thou art the God, even thou alone** (see discussions on 18:33–35; Deut. 6:4). (2) The pagan Sennacherib had defied the living and sovereign God. **Hear the words ... to reproach the living God** (v. 16). (3) Sennacherib had indeed destroyed many peoples and their gods, but his claims (18:33–35; 19:11–13) only proved that pagan gods were not gods at all **but the work of men's hands** (v. 18; for the foolishness and futility of idolatry, see Pss. 115:3–8; 135:15–18; Isa. 2:20; 40:19–20; 41:7; 44:9–20). (4) Hezekiah requested that God save His people and show the world that the Lord was the only true God.

19:20–35. Thus saith the LORD ... I have heard (v. 20). On this occasion, Isaiah's message to

Hezekiah was unsolicited (compare 19:2). This message is found almost verbatim in Isaiah 37:22-35 (see *KJV Study Bible* notes there).

19:21-28. The arrogance of the Assyrians and their ridicule of the Israelites and their God were countered with a derisive pronouncement of judgment (see Psalm 2) on the misconceived Assyrian pride (see Isa. 10:5-34).

19:21-22. The virgin the daughter of Zion (v. 21) is a personification of Jerusalem and its inhabitants. She had not been violated or conquered since the days of David. **Hath shaken her head at thee.** Shaking one's head was a gesture of derision (see Ps. 22:7). Sennacherib had not mocked Jerusalem but its God, **the Holy One of Israel** (v. 22). This designation of the God of Israel is characteristic of Isaiah (see Isa. 1:4).

19:23-24. In metaphorical terms, Sennacherib had boasted of his easy victories, claiming even to have **dried up all the rivers of besieged places** (v. 24). This was a presumptuous boast for one who had not even conquered Egypt.

19:25-26. I have formed it ... Now have I brought it to pass (v. 25). The God of Israel is the ruler of all nations and history. The Assyrians attributed their victories to their own military superiority. However, Isaiah said that God alone ordained these victories (see Isa. 10:5-19; see Ezek. 30:24-26).

19:27-28. I know thy abode ... thy rage against me (v. 27). The omniscient God knew Sennacherib's every movement and his blasphemy against God. Sennacherib had planned to lead Judahites shamefully back to Assyria (see 18:32), but he himself would return shamefully, humbled by the God he had reviled. **I will put my hook in thy nose** (v. 28). At the top of an Assyrian obelisk, an Assyrian king (probably Esarhaddon, 681-669 BC) is pictured holding ropes attached to rings in the noses of four of his enemies. Isaiah portrayed the same thing happening to Sennacherib (see discussion on Isa. 37:29; see Ezek. 38:4; Amos 4:2).

19:29. Ye shall eat this year such things as grow of themselves (v. 29). Sennacherib had apparently either destroyed or confiscated the entire harvest that

had been sown the previous fall. The people would have use of only the later, second growth that came from seeds dropped from the previous year's harvest (see Lev. 25:5). This suggests that Sennacherib came to Judah in March or April, around the time of harvest. **In the second year that which springeth of the same** indicated that Sennacherib's departure would be too late in the fall (October) for new crops to be planted for the coming year. In the Holy Land, crops are normally sown in September and October. **In the third year sow ye, and reap** indicated that the routine times for sowing and harvesting could be observed in the following year. **The third year** is likely a reference to the third year of harvests detrimentally affected by the Assyrian presence.

19:30-31. Out of Jerusalem shall go forth a remnant (v. 31; see discussion on 19:4). For use of the term "remnant" as a designation for those who will participate in the future unfolding of God's redemptive program, see Isaiah 11:11, 16; 28:5; Micah 4:7; Romans 11:5.

19:32-34. He shall not come into this city (v. 32). Sennacherib, who was presently at Libnah (see 19:8; see also discussion on 8:22), would not be able to carry out his threats against Jerusalem (see discussion on 18:13). God Himself would defend Jerusalem, **for my servant David's sake** (v. 34; see discussion on 1 Kings 11:13).

19:35-37. The angel of the LORD (v. 35; see discussion on Gen. 16:7) destroyed **an hundred fourscore and five thousand** Assyrians in one night. The Greek historian Herodotus attributes this huge loss of life to a bubonic plague, but the author of Kings clearly attributes it to divine intervention.

A humiliated Sennacherib returned to **Nineveh** (v. 36), the capital of the Assyrian empire, where he had made empty boasts of his success (see discussion on 18:13). Twenty years later (681 BC), while he was worshiping his god **Nisroch** (the name of this deity does not appear in preserved Assyrian records; v. 37), **Adrammelech and Sharezer his sons** killed him. Ancient records refer to the murder of Sennacherib by an unnamed son on the twentieth of the month of Tebet in the twenty-third year of Sennacherib's reign. His assassins escaped to **Armenia** (Hebrew, *Ararat*; see discussion on Gen. 8:4). **Esarhaddon his son reigned in his stead** (681–669 BC). Assyrian inscriptions speak of a struggle among Sennacherib's sons for the right of succession to the Assyrian throne. Sennacherib's designation of Esarhaddon as heir apparent, even though he was younger than several of his brothers, may have sparked the abortive attempt at a coup by Adrammelech and Sharezer.

3. Hezekiah's Illness and Alliance with Babylon (chap. 20)

20:1–3. In those days (v. 1) is probably a general term for Hezekiah's reign. His illness (20:1–11) as well as his reception of envoys from Babylon (20:12–19) must have preceded the Assyrian campaign in 701 BC (see 20:6; see also discussions on 20:12–13). It is unlikely that Hezekiah would have been able to show his Babylonian visitors all his treasures (see 20:13) if he had just given them to Sennacherib for tribute (see 18:15). Babylonian records indicate that Berodach-baladan (20:12) died in Elam after being expelled from Babylon in 703 BC. **Set thine house in order.** Arrangements of a testamentary nature needed to be made, especially with respect to throne succession. **Thou shalt die.** Assuming that Hezekiah was twenty-five years old in 715 BC, when he began his sole reign (see 18:2), and that his illness occurred a little more than fifteen years prior to his death (see discussion on 20:6), he would have been about thirty-seven or thirty-eight years old at this time.

I have walked before thee in truth … and have done that which is good (v. 3). Hezekiah's prayer was not an appeal for divine favor based on good works, but it expressed the realization that the Lord graciously favors those who earnestly serve Him (see discussion on 2 Sam. 22:21). Isaiah 38:10–20 relates a longer prayer, in which Hezekiah expressed the anguish of his soul when he thought he was about to die and his gratitude when he learned his life had been extended.

20:4–7. I will heal thee (v. 5). God is the one who sovereignly ordains all that comes to pass (Ps.

139:16; Eph. 1:11). Hezekiah's petition and God's response demonstrate that (1) divine sovereignty does not make prayer inappropriate but, on the contrary, establishes it, and (2) both prayer and the divine response to prayer are to be included in one's conception of God's sovereign plan (see 1 Kings 21:29; Ezek. 33:13–16).

I will add unto thy days fifteen years (v. 6). Hezekiah died in 686 BC. The beginning of the extension of his life is thus to be placed no later than 702 BC. For the phrase **for mine own sake, and for my servant David's sake,** see 19:34 (see also discussion on 1 Kings 11:13).

A poultice of **a lump of figs** (v. 7) was apparently the medication of that day for boils. The Lord healed Hezekiah (see v. 5), but divine healing does not necessarily exclude the use of known remedies. Apparently, the application of the poultice and Hezekiah's recovery followed the confirming sign (20:8–11), for what need would there have been for a sign if he had already recovered from his deathly illness (20:1)?

20:8–11. The word translated **dial** (i.e., sundial; v. 11) should probably be rendered "staircase." God's sign to Hezekiah involved the shadow returning **ten degrees** ("stairs" or "steps"; v. 9). The shadow did not move across a sundial but rather backed up a series of ten steps. This was obviously caused by the miraculous intervention of God.

Opinions differ over the nature of this miracle. Although it is not impossible that this was a universal phenomenon, it was more likely a local miraculous prolongation of light in Judah. In the account of the same event in 2 Chronicles, Hezekiah was promised a "sign" (see 2 Chron. 32:24), but the Babylonian ambassadors later inquired of the "wonder that had been done in the land" (2 Chron. 32:31). If "land" referred to Judah, it would have been a local phenomenon.

20:12–13. Hezekiah received ambassadors from **Berodach-baladan** (v. 12). Some manuscripts and ancient versions read "Merodach-baladan" (see Isa. 39:1). The name means "[the god] Marduk has given me a son." Berodach-baladan ruled in Babylon from 721–710 BC before being forced to submit to Assyrian domination by Sargon II of Assyria. Sometime after Sargon's death in 705 BC, Berodach-baladan briefly reestablished Babylonian independence and ruled in Babylon until Sennacherib forced him to flee in 703 BC (see discussion on 20:1). He **sent letters and a present unto Hezekiah** (see 2 Chron. 32:31; Isaiah 39). Ostensibly, the delegation came to congratulate Hezekiah on his recovery and to inquire of his "sign," but it is likely that Berodach-baladan was attempting to draw Hezekiah into an alliance against Assyria. Although Hezekiah rejected the pro-Assyrian policies of his father, Ahaz (see 16:7), and rebelled against Assyria (see 18:7), he erred in seeking to strengthen Israel's security through friendship with Babylon and Egypt (see 2 Chron. 32:31; Isaiah 30–31; see also discussions on 1 Sam. 17:11; 1 Kings 15:19).

Hezekiah hearkened unto them, and shewed them all (v. 13). His reception of the delegation from Babylon was overly hospitable. Perhaps it was an attempt to bolster Judah's security by impressing the Babylonians with the wealth and power of his kingdom as a basis for mutual cooperation against the Assyrians. In principle, this was a denial of the covenantal nature of the royal office in Israel (see discussion on 2 Sam. 24:1). He showed them **his precious things ... his treasures**. The presence of these treasures in Jerusalem is evidence that this incident occurred before the payment of tribute to Sennacherib in 701 BC (see 18:15–16).

20:14–15. What said these men ...? (v. 14). Hezekiah gave no response to Isaiah's question concerning the diplomatic purpose of the Babylonian envoys. **What have they seen in thine house?** (v. 15). Possibly because of God's promise to defend Jerusalem (see 20:6), Hezekiah had confidently showed all his treasure to the Babylonians.

20:16–19. All that is in thine house ... shall be carried unto Babylon (v. 17). Hezekiah's reception of the Babylonians would bring the exact opposite of what he desired and expected. Isaiah's prediction of Babylonian exile at least 115 years before it happened is all the more remarkable because at the time of his prediction, it appeared that Assyria, rather than Babylon, was the world power from whom Judah had the most to fear.

Thy sons ... shall they take away (v. 18). Hezekiah's own son Manasseh was taken by the Assyrians and held prisoner for a while in Babylon (see 2 Chron. 33:11); later, many more from the house of David would follow (see 24:15; 25:7; Dan. 1:3).

Good is the word (v. 19). Although it is possible to understand Hezekiah's statement as a selfish expression of relief that he himself would not experience the announced adversity, it seems better to take it as a humble acceptance of the Lord's judgment (see 2 Chron. 32:26) and as gratefulness for the intervening time of peace that the Lord in His mercy was granting to His people.

20:20–21. He made a pool, and a conduit (v. 20). Hezekiah built a tunnel from the Gihon spring (see 1 Kings 1:33, 38) to a cistern (2 Chron. 32:30) inside the city's walls (see Map 10 at the end of the *KJV Study Bible*). This greatly reduced Jerusalem's vulnerability to siege by guaranteeing a continuing water supply. In 1880, an inscription (the Siloam inscription; see chart, *KJV Study Bible*, p. xix) was found in the rock wall at the entrance to this tunnel, describing the method of its construction. The tunnel, cut through solid rock, is over 1,700 feet long; it varies from 3 feet to 11½ feet in height and averages 2 feet in width.

When Hezekiah died, his son **Manasseh** (v. 21) followed him on the throne.

B. Manasseh (21:1–18)

21:1. Manasseh (v. 1) began to reign when he was **twelve years old**. He was born after Hezekiah's serious illness (see 20:6), and he reigned **fifty and five years** (697–642 BC), including a ten-year coregency (697–686 BC) with his father, Hezekiah. This was the longest reign of any king in either Israel or Judah. His godly father had little spiritual impact on him, for Manasseh was the most wicked king of Judah.

21:2–9. Manasseh went **after the abominations of the heathen** (v. 2) and reversed the religious policies of his father, Hezekiah (see 18:3–5), and in open defiance, exceeded the syncretism of Ahaz (see 16:3). He rebuilt **the high places ... Hezekiah ... had destroyed** (v. 3; see discussion on 18:4; see also 2 Chron. 31:1) and made a **grove** (see 1 Kings 14:15, 23; 15:13; 16:33), **as did Ahab.** Manasseh was the "Ahab of Judah" (see 1 Kings 16:30–33). He **worshipped all the host of heaven** (see discussion on 17:16) and built altars for them in the temple **in Jerusalem** (v. 4), where the Lord chose to place His name (see 1 Kings 8:20, 29; 9:3).

He sacrificed his own son—he **made his son pass through the fire** (v. 6; see discussion on 16:3; see also 17:17). He was heavily involved in demon-energized occultism—he **observed times, and used enchantments** (see discussions on 16:15; 17:17) and **dealt with familiar spirits and wizards** which had been emphatically prohibited by Moses (see Lev. 19:31; Deut. 18:11; and see 1 Sam. 28:3, 7–9 and discussions).

Manasseh defied the Lord by setting up **a graven image of the grove** (v. 7; see discussion on 1 Kings 14:15) in God's house. God had promised **David** that his son would build "a house for my name" (2 Sam. 7:13) and had promised **Solomon** that He had "hallowed this house" and would "put my name there for ever" (1 Kings 9:3).

Manasseh did all these things in Jerusalem, a city that had been **chosen out of all tribes** (v. 7) for God's name (see 1 Kings 11:13, 32, 36). Thanks to Manasseh, Judah became more heathen than **the nations whom the LORD destroyed** (v. 9) under the leadership of Moses and Joshua (see 1 Kings 14:24; Deut. 12:29–31; 31:3).

21:10–13. Manasseh's actions were not committed without warning from God's **servants the prophets** (v. 10; see 2 Chron. 33:10). Because he did **wickedly above all that the Amorites did** (v. 11; see discussion on 1 Kings 21:26), God determined to bring **evil upon Jerusalem and Judah** (v. 12). Three metaphors follow: (1) **Whosoever heareth of it, both his ears shall tingle** (see Jer. 19:3); that is, the news of Jerusalem's terrifying punishment would make one's ears hurt as a discordant note does. (2) **I will stretch ... line ... plummet** (v. 13). Instruments

normally associated with construction are used here as symbols of destruction (see Isa. 34:11; Amos 7:7–9, 17). Jerusalem would be judged by the same standard used against Samaria and Ahab. (3) **I will wipe Jerusalem as ... a dish**; that is, the city would be depopulated.

21:14–15. I will forsake the remnant of mine inheritance (v. 14). This is to be taken in the sense of giving them over to judgment (see Jer. 12:7), not in the sense of abrogation of the covenant (see 1 Sam. 12:22; Isa. 43:1–7). Upon the destruction of the northern kingdom, Judah had become the remnant of the Lord's inheritance (see 1 Kings 8:51; Deut. 4:20; 1 Sam. 10:1; Ps. 28:9; see also discussion on 2 Kings 19:4). The history of Israel was a history of covenant breaking. With the reign of Manasseh, the cup of God's wrath overflowed, and the judgment of exile from the Land of Promise (see discussion on 17:7–23) became inevitable (see 24:1–4).

21:16. Manasseh was guilty also of shedding **innocent blood** (v. 16). This is a reference to godly people, and perhaps even prophets, who were martyred for opposition to Manasseh's evil practices (see 21:10–11). According to a Jewish tradition (not otherwise substantiated), Isaiah was sawed in two during Manasseh's reign (see Heb. 11:37).

21:17–18. The rest of the acts of Manasseh (v. 17), for example, his captivity, humbling, and repentance, all of which apparently occurred late in his reign (see 2 Chron. 33:12–19), are not mentioned here, perhaps because they left no lasting impression. When he died, Manasseh was buried **in the garden of Uzza** (v. 18). Uzza is probably a shortened form of Uzziah (see 14:21–22 and 15:1–7, Azariah; 2 Chronicles 26, Uzziah).

C. Amon (21:19–26)

21:19–22. Amon (v. 19) reigned only **two years** (642–640 BC). That Manasseh's wickedness, and not his life after his repentance, influenced his son is evidenced in that Amon **did ... evil** (v. 20). He did not share in the change of heart that characterized his father, Manasseh, in the last days of his life (see 2 Chron. 33:12–19). Amon must have restored the idolatrous practices that Manasseh had abolished, because these were again in existence in the time of Josiah (see 23:5 – 7, 12).

21:23 – 26. As had happened to Joash (12:20 – 21), Amon's servants **conspired against him** (v. 23) and killed him. Whether this palace revolt was motivated by religious or political considerations is not known. The conspiracy was not a popular overthrow, for **the people of the land** (v. 24), the citizenry in general (see 11:14, 18; 14:21; 23:30), **slew all them that had conspired against king Amon**. It is not clear whether this counterinsurgency was motivated simply by loyalty to the house of David or by other factors. Tragic though his death was, God graciously spared Judah from having another wicked king reign longer than two years. When Amon died, he was buried in the same burial site as his father (see discussion on 21:18).

D. Josiah (22:1 – 23:30)

1. Repair of the Temple; Discovery of the Book of the Law (chap. 22)

22:1 – 2. Josiah (v. 1) was only eight when he began to reign, and he reigned **thirty and one years** (640 – 609 BC; see discussion on 21:19). **He walked in all the way of David his father** (v. 2; see discussion on 18:3). Josiah was the last godly king of the Davidic line prior to the exile. Jeremiah, who prophesied during the time of Josiah (see Jer. 1:2), spoke highly of him (Jer. 22:15 – 16). Zephaniah also prophesied in the early days of Josiah's reign (Zeph. 1:1).

22:3 – 7. Due to his young age, Josiah's first few years as king were probably under the guardianship of the elders or priests (see discussion on 11:17). He began to serve the Lord faithfully at the age of sixteen (the eighth year of his reign, 2 Chron. 34:3), and when he was twenty years old (the twelfth year of his reign, 2 Chron. 34:3), he had already begun to purge the land of its idolatrous practices. Now in his **eighteenth year** (622 BC; v. 3), Josiah was twenty-six years old (see 22:1), and he initiated new reform measures. He sent **Shaphan ... the scribe** to the priest to instruct him to oversee the offering of the people for repairs on the temple. (For the du-

ties of such a scribe, see discussion on 2 Sam. 8:17.) In 2 Chronicles 34:8, two additional individuals are mentioned as having accompanied Shaphan.

Since Joash had repaired the temple (see 12:4 – 16), there had been ample occasions for deterioration (see the wicked reigns of Ahaz and Manasseh; and Hezekiah's stripping the temple of valuables to pay tribute, 18:15 – 16).

The high priest (v. 4) was **Hilkiah**, the father of Azariah and grandfather of Seraiah, the high priest who would be executed at the time of the Babylonians' destruction of Jerusalem (see 25:18 – 20; see 1 Chron. 6:13 – 14). It is unlikely that this Hilkiah was also the father of Jeremiah (see Jer. 1:1). Hilkiah was instructed to oversee **the silver ... the keepers of the door have gathered** for distribution to the supervisors, **doers of the work, that have the oversight** (v. 5; for names of the workers, see 2 Chron. 34:12 – 13). Josiah used the method that Joash had devised for collecting funds for the restoration of the temple (see 12:1 – 16; 2 Chron. 34:9).

22:8 – 14. Regrettably, the consensus of liberal scholarship maintains that **the book of the law** (v. 8) that was found had no connection to Moses but was a forgery written just prior to 622 BC and was used as the basis for Josiah's reform. According to this erroneous thinking, the recovered book underwent a series of editorial changes, eventually becoming what is known as Deuteronomy. Internal biblical evidence does not support this notion at all.

It cannot be determined with certainty whether or not this recovered book contained the whole Pentateuch, but in light of the following, it seems possible. (1) Josiah's reaction of horror (v. 11) and his zeal for removing idolatry (see 23:4 – 20) seem to indicate that Shaphan had read from a section of God's judgment (e.g., Leviticus 26; Deuteronomy 28). (2) Josiah's passion for observing the Passover (see 23:20 – 23; 2 Chron. 35:1 – 19) shows an understanding of Exodus 12. Some interpreters, however, believe the book was a copy of part or all of Deuteronomy only (see Deut. 31:24, 26; 2 Chron. 34:14).

When Josiah heard the reading of the book, **he rent his clothes** (v. 11; see discussion on 18:37).

Contrast Josiah's reaction with Jehoiakim's reaction to the words of the scroll written by Jeremiah (see Jer. 36:21–24). Perhaps the covenant curses of Leviticus 26 and/or Deuteronomy 28, climaxing with the threat of exile, were the statements that especially disturbed Josiah.

So horrified was Josiah at his people's neglect of God's commandment and their impending judgment as the consequence, he sent five men to inquire of the Lord by the prophetess Huldah. Two of the men are mentioned again later. **Ahikam** (v. 12) was the father of Gedaliah, who would later be appointed governor of Judah by Nebuchadnezzar (see 25:22; Jer. 39:14). He was also Jeremiah's protector when his life was threatened during the reign of Jehoiakim (see Jer. 26:24). The son of **Achbor**, Elnathan, is mentioned in 24:8 and in Jeremiah 26:22; 36:12. Josiah's purpose in consulting the prophetess was to learn if hope remained for Judah.

Why the delegation sought out **Huldah the prophetess** (v. 14) rather than Jeremiah or Zephaniah is not known. Perhaps it was merely a matter of her accessibility in Jerusalem. She was the wife of **Shallum ... keeper of the wardrobe**, perhaps the same Shallum who was the uncle of Jeremiah (see Jer. 32:7). She lived **in Jerusalem in the college**. The Hebrew here is *mishneh*, which literally means "in the second [quarter]." This was a section of the city probably located in a newly developed area between the first and second walls in the northwest part of Jerusalem (see 2 Chron. 33:14; Zeph. 1:10).

22:15–20. Huldah's words were sobering. Judah was so deeply entrenched in apostasy that God's wrath would not be repealed. **I will bring evil on this place** (v. 16), that is, Jerusalem. On a positive note, however, **because thine heart was tender** (v. 19), because Josiah was receptive to the law, he would be spared this judgment.

Thou shalt be gathered into thy grave in peace (v. 20). This prediction refers to Josiah's death before God's judgment on Jerusalem through Nebuchadnezzar and therefore is not contradicted by his death in battle with Pharaoh-nechoh of Egypt (see 23:29–30). Josiah was assured that the final judgment on Judah and Jerusalem would not come in his own days.

2. Renewal of the Covenant; End of Josiah's Reign (23:1–30)

23:1–3. Josiah had begun his purge of idolatry in his twelfth year (see 2 Chron. 34:3), but in his eighteenth year (see 22:3), the purge had taken on new intensity after the book of the law had been found. His purge proved to be more extensive than Hezekiah's, and he needed the support of all levels of Judah's leadership. Thus, he called **the elders of Judah and of Jerusalem** (v. 1), that is, local leaders by virtue of their position in the tribal and family structure. He read to them **the book of the covenant** (v. 2). Although this designation is used in Exodus 24:7 with reference to the contents of Exodus 20–23, it is here applied either to all or part of the book of Deuteronomy or to the entire Mosaic law. Whatever else the scroll contained, it clearly included the covenant curses of Leviticus 26 and/or Deuteronomy 28 (see discussions on 23:21; 22:8, 11). Standing by a **pillar** (v. 3), which may have been the official place for authoritative declarations (but see discussion on 11:14), he **made a covenant**. Josiah carried out the function of covenant mediator; compare Moses (Exod. 24:3–8; Deut. 1–34), Joshua (Joshua 24), Samuel (1 Sam. 11:14–12:25), and Jehoiada (2 Kings 11:17). Josiah personally covenanted **to walk after the LORD** (see discussions on 1 Sam. 12:14, 20). **All the people stood to the covenant**. It is likely that some sort of ratification rite was performed, in which the people participated and pledged by oath to be loyal to their covenant obligations. Whether this was done symbolically (see Jer. 34:18) or verbally (see Deut. 27:11–26) is not clear.

23:4–7. Josiah authorized Hilkiah the priest and **the keepers of the door** (v. 4; see 12:9) to rid the temple of every trace of paganism. Vessels that had been **made for Baal, and for the grove** (see discussion on 1 Kings 14:15) and **the host of heaven** (see discussion on 17:16) **he burnt** outside Jerusalem, then **carried the ashes of them unto Beth-el** (see 23:15–16). Bethel was located just over the border, between Judah and the former northern kingdom in territory nominally under Assyrian control. With a decline in Assyrian power, Josiah was able to exert his own influence in the north. He apparently deposited the ashes at Bethel to desecrate (see discussion on 23:14) the very place where golden-calf worship had originally polluted the land (see discussions on 1 Kings 12:28–30). He did away with **the idolatrous priests** (v. 5; see Hos. 10:5; Zeph. 1:4) that **the kings of Judah** (a reference to Manasseh and Amon, and perhaps to Ahaz before them) had appointed for burning incense on **the high places** (see discussion on 18:4).

Josiah removed **the grove** (v. 6), that is, the Asherah (see discussion on 1 Kings 14:15). The Asherah destroyed by Hezekiah (18:4) was reintroduced by Manasseh (21:7). When Manasseh turned to the Lord, it is likely that he too got rid of the Asherah (see 2 Chron. 33:15) and that it was then reintroduced by Amon (2 Kings 21:21; 2 Chron. 33:22). Having burned it and ground it to powder, Josiah **cast the powder thereof upon the graves of the children of the people.** This was intended as a defilement of the goddess, not as a desecration of the graves of the poor (see Jer. 26:23). **And he tore down the houses of the sodomites** (v. 7), that is, male cult prostitutes (see discussion on 1 Kings 14:24).

23:8–9. All the priests throughout Judah were recalled to Jerusalem, and they **defiled the high places** (v. 8) where they had been making offerings, **from Geba to Beer-sheba.** Geba was on the northern border of the southern kingdom (see 1 Kings 15:22), and Beersheba was on its southern border (see discussion on 1 Sam. 3:20). Those who had participated at these pagan shrines were declared ineligible to perform priestly duties in the temple. Although they were not permitted to serve at the temple altar, these priests were to be sustained by a share of the priestly provisions; that is, **they did eat of the unleavened bread among their brethren** (v. 9; see Lev. 2:10; 6:16–18). They occupied a status similar to that of priests with physical defects (see Lev. 21:16–23).

23:10–14. He defiled Topheth (v. 10). This is the name of an area in the valley of Hinnom where altars used for child sacrifice were located (see Isa. 30:33;

Jer. 7:31; 19:5–6). He prevented anyone from making **his son or his daughter to pass through the fire** (see 17:17; 21:6; see also discussion on 16:3) to the Ammmonite god **Molech** (see discussion on 1 Kings 11:5).

He removed **the horses ... given to the sun** (v. 11). If live horses are implied here, they may have been used to pull chariots bearing images of a sun god in religious processions. Small images of horses have recently been found in a cult location just outside one of the ancient walls of Jerusalem. **Nathan-melech** may have been the official in charge of the chariots.

The altars ... on the top of the upper chamber (v. 12) were altars dedicated to the worship of all the starry hosts (see Jer. 19:13; Zeph. 1:5), which had been erected by Ahaz (2 Kings 16:3–4, 10–16), Manasseh (21:3), and Amon (21:21–22). These Josiah tore down. **And the high places ... Solomon ... had built** (v. 13) for the gods of his foreign wives (see discussion on 1 Kings 11:5), which, having survived Hezekiah's reform, were still standing, Josiah defiled and shattered the images that stood on them. Then he **filled their places with the bones of men** (v. 14). The bones would defile these sites and make them unsuitable for cultic use in the future (see Num. 19:16).

23:15–20. Josiah's reform was not limited to Judah but extended to Bethel, the southern site for Jeroboam's calf worship. He tore down **the altar that was at Beth-el** (v. 15; see 1 Kings 12:32–33). Nothing is said of the golden calf, which perhaps had been sent to Assyria as tribute at the time of the captivity of the northern kingdom (see Hos. 10:5–6).

Spotting **the sepulchres** (v. 16) of the priests of the Bethel sanctuary (see 1 Kings 13:2), Josiah exhumed their bones **and burnt them upon the altar, and polluted it** (see discussions on 23:6, 14). This fulfilled the prophecy of **the man of God ... who proclaimed these words** (see 1 Kings 13:1–2, 32). The bones of the "man of God" from Judah and **the prophet that came out of Samaria** (v. 18; see 1 Kings 13:31–32) were not disturbed. Here Samaria is not to be understood as the city by that name since the prophet came from Bethel (see 1 Kings 13:11), and the city Samaria did not yet exist (see 1 Kings 16:24). Rather, it is to be taken as a designation for the entire area of the former northern kingdom (see discussions on 17:24, 29; 1 Kings 13:32).

He slew all the priests of the high places (v. 20). These were non-Levitical priests of the apostate worship that was practiced in the area of the former northern kingdom (see discussions on 17:27–28, 33–34). They were treated like the pagan priests of Judah (see 23:5), in contrast to Josiah's treatment of the priests at the high places in Judah (see 23:8–9). Josiah's actions in this matter conformed to the requirements of Deuteronomy 13; 17:2–7.

23:21–23. **Keep the passover … as it is written in the book of this covenant** (v. 21; see discussion on 23:2). This observance appears to refer to Deuteronomy 16:1–8, where the Passover is described in a communal setting at a sanctuary (see Exod. 23:15–17; 34:23–24; Lev. 23:4–14) rather than in the family setting of Exodus 12:1–14, 43–49. A more complete description of this observance is found in 2 Chronicles 35:1–19. The uniqueness of Josiah's Passover celebration seems to be that all the Passover lambs were slaughtered exclusively by the Levites (for the Passover observed in the time of Hezekiah, see 2 Chron. 35:1–19; see 2 Chron. 30:2–3, 17–20). The writer reminds readers that this occurred in Josiah's **eighteenth year** (622 BC; v. 23), when he was twenty-six (see discussion on 22:3).

23:24–25. Josiah's reforms included occult practices that were carried out in homes. He did away with necromancers and mediums and all the things on which they relied. **The images** (Hebrew, *teraphim*; v. 24) were family household gods (see discussion on Gen. 31:19). Josiah was intent on being obedient to **the words of the law** (see discussions on 23:2; 22:8). Thus, it could be summarized of him: **like unto him was there no king before him** (see discussion on 18:5), **that turned to the LORD with all his heart … soul, and … might** (v. 25; see Deut. 6:5).

23:26–28. **Notwithstanding the LORD turned not from the fierceness of his great wrath** (v. 26). The judgment against Judah and Jerusalem was postponed, but not rescinded, because of Josiah's reformation (see discussions on 21:15; 22:20). Sadly, it must be observed that, like Hezekiah's reforms, Josiah's were superficial in that Judah immediately returned to its sinful ways when Josiah was killed and his son Jehoiakim began to reign. As God had **removed Israel** (v. 27; see 17:18–23), He promised likewise to deal with **this city Jerusalem which I have chosen** (see 21:4, 7, 13), **and the house of which I said, My name shall be there** (see discussion on 1 Kings 8:16).

23:29–30. During Josiah's reign, **Pharaohnechoh king of Egypt went up against** (better translated "to," i.e., for the purpose of assisting) **the king of Assyria** (v. 29). Pharaoh-nechoh (who ruled from 610–595 BC) intended to help Ashur-uballit II, the last Assyrian king, in his struggle against the rising power of Babylon under Nabopolassar. The Assyrian capital, Nineveh, had already fallen to the Babylonians and Medes in 612 BC (see the book of Nahum). The remaining Assyrian forces had regrouped at Haran, but in 609 BC, they were forced west of the Euphrates. Apparently, the Egyptians under Nechoh were at this time coming to the Assyrians' aid. **King Josiah went against him**. Perhaps Josiah opposed the passage of Nechoh's army through the pass at Megiddo (see 2 Chron. 35:20–24) because he feared that the growth of either Egyptian or Assyrian power would have adverse results for the continued independence of Judah.

Josiah was killed, and his servants **buried him in his own sepulchre** (v. 30; see 2 Chron. 35:24–25). **The people of the land** (see discussion on 21:24) made **Jehoahaz the son of Josiah** king in his place. Jehoahaz's name was originally Shallum (see 1 Chron. 3:15; Jer. 22:11), which was probably changed to Jehoahaz (meaning "the Lord sustains") at the time of his accession to the throne. Perhaps the people chose Jehoahaz (Josiah's fourth son) over Jehoiakim (Josiah's second-born son, who would later replace Jehoahaz) because it was known that Jehoiakim favored a pro-Egyptian policy instead of the anti-Egyptian policy of Josiah and Jehoahaz. (For the anointing of a king, see discussion on 1 Sam. 9:16.)

E. Jehoahaz Exiled to Egypt (23:31-35)

23:31-35. Jehoahaz (v. 31) reigned only **three months** (in 609 BC). His mother was the daughter of **Jeremiah** (not the prophet; see Jer. 1:1) from **Libnah** (see discussion on 8:22). Jehoahaz's short reign was characterized by doing **evil ... according to ... his fathers** (v. 32; see 16:3; 21:2, 21; Ezek. 19:3). When Nechoh returned from the north (see discussion on 23:29), he **put him** (Jehoahaz) **in bands at Riblah** (v. 33). By either deception or overt force, the Egyptians were able to take Jehoahaz captive and impose tribute on Judah (see 2 Chron. 36:3). Jehoahaz was imprisoned at Nechoh's military headquarters, established at Riblah on the Orontes River. Nebuchadnezzar would later make his headquarters at the same place (see 25:6, 20).

Nechoh made **Eliakim the son of Josiah** (v. 34) king instead. Eliakim was an older brother of Jehoahaz (see 1 Chron. 3:15). Perhaps he had been bypassed earlier as a successor to Josiah because of a pro-Egyptian political stance. Nechoh then **turned his name to Jehoiakim**. The meaning of these two names is similar (Eliakim, "God has established"; Jehoiakim, "Yahweh has established"). Perhaps Nechoh wanted to use the name change to imply that his actions were sanctioned by the Lord (Yahweh), the God of Judah (see 18:25; 2 Chron. 35:21). In any case, the change in name indicated that Jehoiakim was subject to Nechoh's authority. Jehoahaz was taken **to Egypt, and died there** (see 2 Chron. 36:4; Jer. 22:10-12).

To pay tribute to Nechoh, Jehoiakim **exacted the silver and the gold of the people of the land** (v. 35). The tribute for Nechoh was raised by a graduated tax placed on the very people who had supported the kingship of Jehoahaz (see 23:30). Menahem of the northern kingdom had used a similar method of raising funds for tribute (see 15:20).

F. Jehoiakim: First Babylonian Invasion (23:36-24:7)

23:36-37. Jehoiakim (v. 36) reigned **eleven years** (609-598 BC) and is remembered for doing **evil in the sight of the LORD** (v. 37), just like **his fathers** before him, namely Manasseh (21:1-18) and Amon (21:19-26). He was responsible for the murder of the prophet Uriah from Kirjath-jearim (Jer. 26:20-24), and his rule was characterized by dishonesty, oppression, and injustice (see Jer. 22:13-19). He reintroduced idolatrous worship in the temple (see Ezek. 8:5-17) and refused to accept the word of the Lord through Jeremiah (see Jeremiah 36).

24:1-7. During the reign of Jehoiakim, **Nebuchadnezzar ... came up** (v. 1) to Jerusalem. Nebuchadnezzar's name means "O [god] Nabu, protect my son."

Nebuchadnezzar was the son of Nabopolassar (see discussion on 23:29) and became the most powerful king of the Neo-Babylonian empire (612-539 BC), reigning 605-562 BC (see Daniel 1-4). In 605 BC, as the crown prince and commander of the Babylonian army, he defeated Pharaoh Nechoh and the Egyptians at the battle of Carchemish, and again at Hamath (see 23:29; Jer. 46:2). These victories had far-reaching implications in the geopolitical power structure of the eastern Mediterranean world. Nebuchadnezzar went on to conquer all of the "Hatti-country," which, according to Babylonian records, included the "city of Judah." When his plans for taking Jerusalem and Jehoiakim (see 2 Chron. 36:6-7) were altered by news of his father's death, demanding his immediate return to Babylon, he made Jehoiakim his vassal. Daniel and his three friends were among the Judahite hostages taken at this time (see Dan. 1:1). Perhaps as early as September 6, 605 BC, Nebuchadnezzar acceded to the Babylonian throne upon the death of his father. Jehoiakim served Nebuchadnezzar for **three years**, probably 604-602 BC. In 604 BC, Nebuchadnezzar returned to the west and took tribute from "all the kings of Hatti-land." It is likely that Jehoiakim was included among these kings. Jehoiakim, however, **turned and rebelled**. In 601 BC, Nebuchadnezzar again marched west against Egypt and was repulsed by strong Egyptian resistance. This may have encouraged Jehoiakim's rebellion, even though Jeremiah had warned against it (see Jer. 27:9-11).

The LORD sent against him ... Chaldees ... Syrians ... Moabites ... Ammon (v. 2). Reaction to Jehoiakim's rebellion was swift. Chaldean (Babylonian) troops, perhaps garrisoned in Syria, along with troops of other loyal vassals, were sent to put down the Judahite rebellion. All of this came upon Judah as the Lord's punishment for the past **sins of Manasseh** (v. 3; see 21:11–12; 23:26–27; Jer. 15:3–4), who had shed **innocent blood** (v. 4; see discussion on 21:16), something the Lord **would not pardon** (see 22:17).

In 597 BC, Nebuchadnezzar himself came to deal with the rebellious Jehoiakim. Jehoiakim **slept with his fathers** (v. 6); that is, he died shortly before Jerusalem fell to the Babylonian siege (see 24:8–12). Whether his death was due to natural causes or political intrigue is not indicated. He was so wicked, however, that when he died, he was neither mourned nor given an honorable burial (see Jer. 22:18–19; 36:30).

The king of Egypt came not again any more out of his land (v. 7). This was due to the Egyptian defeat at Carchemish (Nechoh's second attempt to assist Assyria; see Jer. 46:2) in 605 BC, and it explains why Jehoiakim received no help from Egypt in his rebellion against the Babylonians. The Babylonians had extended their control of the land between the **river of Egypt** (i.e., probably the Wadi el-Arish) **unto the river Euphrates**.

G. Jehoiachin: Second Babylonian Invasion (24:8–17)

24:8–9. Jehoiachin (v. 8) reigned a mere **three months** (598–597 BC). Babylonian records place the fall of Jerusalem to Nebuchadnezzar on March 16, 597 BC. This means that the three-month and ten-day reign (see 2 Chron. 36:9–10) of Jehoiachin began in December 598 BC. In that short time, he characterized himself by the evil he did (see Jer. 22:20–30).

24:10–17. In the eighth year of his reign (April 597 BC; v. 12; see 2 Chron. 36:10; see also *KJV Study Bible* note on Jer. 52:28, where a different system of dating is reflected), **Nebuchadnezzar king of Babylon ... came up against the city** (v. 11), Jerusalem. Babylonian records say that Nebuchadnezzar "en-camped against the city of Judah, and on the second day of the month of Addaru (i.e., March 16, 597 BC), he seized the city and captured the king."

As the LORD had said (v. 13), that is, as He had predicted would happen (see 20:13, 17), Nebuchadnezzar stripped the temple and the palace of their remaining valuables, all to be taken to Babylon. He led away **ten thousand** (v. 14) leading citizens as **captives**. This figure may include the 7,000 fighting men and 1,000 craftsmen mentioned in verse 16 (see *KJV Study Bible* note on Jer. 52:28, where a different number of captives is mentioned). **And he carried away Jehoiachin to Babylon** (v. 15), fulfilling Jeremiah's prophecy (Jer. 22:24–27; see 2 Kings 25:27–30). Ezekiel was probably taken to Babylon in this deportation.

Having removed Jehoiachin from the throne, Nebuchadnezzar exercised his rights as conquering king and made **Mattaniah his** (Jehoiachin's) **father's brother** (v. 17) king instead. Mattaniah was a son of Josiah (see 1 Chron. 3:15; Jer. 1:3) and a brother of Jehoiachin's father, Jehoiakim. Nebuchadnezzar **changed his name to Zedekiah**. Mattaniah's name (meaning "gift of Yahweh") was changed to Zedekiah ("righteousness of Yahweh"). Perhaps Nebuchadnezzar wanted to imply that his actions against Jerusalem and Jehoiachin were just. In any case, the name change signified subjection to Nebuchadnezzar (see discussion on 23:34).

H. Zedekiah (24:18–20)

24:18–20. Though **Zedekiah reigned eleven years** (597–586 BC; v. 18), he was never recognized as king by the prophet Ezekiel (who dated his ministry in terms of Jehoiachin's reign), for the last legitimate king, Jehoiachin, was still living, though in captivity. For **Jeremiah**, Zedekiah's maternal grandfather, see discussion on 23:31.

Just as his brother Jehoiakim had been, Zedekiah was evil, seemingly having learned nothing from the punishment of Jehoiakim and Jehoiachin's. During Zedekiah's reign, idolatrous practices continued to increase in Jerusalem (see 2 Chron. 36:14; Ezek. 8–11). He was a weak and indecisive ruler (see Jer.

38:5, 19) who refused to heed the word of the Lord given through Jeremiah (2 Chron. 36:12).

Zedekiah rebelled against the king of Babylon (v. 20). This rebellion was the last straw for the Babylonians and would consequently lead to Judah's ultimate disaster. Most interpreters link Zedekiah's revolt with the succession to the Egyptian throne of the ambitious pharaoh Apries (Hophra) in 589 BC. Zedekiah had sworn allegiance to Nebuchadnezzar (Ezek. 17:13), he had sent envoys to Babylon (see Jer. 29:3), and he had made a personal visit (see Jer. 51:59). He seems to have capitulated, however, to the seductive propaganda of the anti-Babylonian and pro-Egyptian faction in Jerusalem (see Jer. 37:5; Ezek. 17:15–16) in a tragically miscalculated effort to gain independence from Babylon.

I. Babylonian Exile of Judah (25:1–21)

25:1–7. In the ninth year ... tenth month ... tenth day (January 15, 588 BC; v. 1; see Jer. 39:1; 52:4; Ezek. 24:1–2), **Nebuchadnezzar ... came ... against Jerusalem** to besiege it. Earlier, he had subdued all the fortified cities in Judah except Lachish and Azekah (see Jer. 34:7). A number of Hebrew inscriptions on potsherds were found at Lachish in 1935 and 1938. These Lachish ostraca (or letters; see chart, *KJV Study Bible*, p. xix) describe conditions at Lachish and Azekah during the Babylonian siege. Approximately two and a half years later, in **the eleventh year ... ninth day ... fourth month** (July 18, 586 BC; vv. 2–3; see Jer. 39:2; 52:5–7), Nebuchadnezzar breached the city's walls to take it. Some scholars follow a different dating system and place the fall of Jerusalem in the summer of 587 BC.

Due to the long siege, **famine prevailed in the city** (v. 3). When strength, provisions, and all hope were gone and the city was breached, Zedekiah attempted to escape to cross over the Jordan at a ford near Jericho. At Jericho, he was captured and then taken to stand before **the king of Babylon to Riblah** (v. 4; see discussion on 23:33; see also Jer. 39:5; 52:9). **They slew the sons of Zedekiah ... put out the eyes of Zedekiah ... carried him to Babylon** (v. 7; see Jer. 32:4–5; 34:2–3; 38:18; 39:6–7; 52:10–11). The last

thing Zedekiah was permitted to see before being blinded was the slaughter of his sons. Thus, he left no claimant to the throne. Ezekiel (12:13) had predicted that Zedekiah would be brought to Babylon but that he would not see it. Zedekiah could have spared his own life and prevented the destruction of Jerusalem if he had listened to Jeremiah (see Jer. 38:14–28).

25:8–12. In the fifth month ... seventh day ... nineteenth year (August 14, 586 BC; v. 8; see Jer. 52:12), **Nebuzar-adan**, the king's servant, came to Jerusalem to burn **the house of the LORD** (v. 9; see 2 Chron. 36:19; Jer. 39:8; 52:13) and the king's palace, and in general, to render the defeated city uninhabitable, even for **the poor**, who were not taken captive (v. 12). Recall the prediction of 23:27.

25:13–17. Anything pertaining to the temple that was made of gold, silver, or bronze was taken as spoil: **pillars of brass** (v. 13; see 1 Kings 7:15–22), **bases** (see 1 Kings 7:27–39), **the brazen sea** (see 1 Kings 7:23–26), **all the vessels of brass** (v. 14; see 1 Kings 7:40, 45), and **the chapiter** (i.e., "capital"; v. 17) of the pillars (see 1 Kings 7:16–20). Truly, the physical "glory" (see Ezekiel's vision of the Lord's glory, Ezek. 8–11) had departed.

25:18–21. Prominent citizens of Jerusalem, who had probably been leaders in resisting Nebuchadnezzar, were also killed. Among them was **Seraiah the chief priest** (v. 18). Seraiah was the grandson of Hilkiah (see discussion on 22:4; see also 22:8; 1 Chron. 6:13–14). His son Jehozadak was taken captive to Babylon. Ezra was one of Jehozadak's descendants (see Ezra 7:1). These persons were brought **to the king of Babylon to Riblah** (v. 20; see 25:6). Their execution probably coincided with the execution of Zedekiah's sons (see Jer. 52:10).

Judah was carried away out of their land (v. 21). This was now the third deportation of Judah's population (see 24:1 and discussion; 24:14–16 and discussion). Judah's exile from Canaan fulfilled the prediction of judgment given during the reign of Manasseh (see 23:27). Exile was the most dire of the covenant curses (see Lev. 26:33; Deut. 28:36; see also Jer. 25:8–11).

J. Removal of the Remnant to Egypt (25:22–26)

25:22–24. Nebuchadnezzar could no longer trust the word or loyalty of members of Judah's royal family, so he appointed **Gedaliah ... ruler** (v. 22; see discussion on 22:12). Gedaliah, however, shared Jeremiah's nonresistance approach to the Babylonians (see v. 24) and won their confidence so that he could be trusted as governor of Judah (see Jer. 41:10).

With Jerusalem destroyed, Gedaliah apparently made **Mizpah** (v. 23) his administrative city. It had been a town of important political significance in the time just before the establishment of the monarchy (see discussion on 1 Sam. 7:5). Jeremiah found Gedaliah there (see Jer. 40:1–6).

Upon Gedaliah's appointment, the remaining captains gathered to him. Gedaliah's statement (v. 24) leads one to believe that these men were pro-Egypt and were advising him to find refuge for everyone in Egypt (see 25:26). Among these men was **Ishmael the son of Nethaniah** (v. 23; for a fuller genealogy, see 25:25). Elishama, Ishmael's grandfather, had been the royal secretary under Jehoiakim (Jer. 36:12). Also among the men was **Jaazaniah the son of a Maachathite.** In 1932, an agate seal was found at Tell en-Nasbeh (Mizpah) bearing the name of Jaazaniah (perhaps the man mentioned here), with the inscription: "Belonging to Jaazaniah the servant of the king."

Gedaliah urged submission to the Babylonians as the judgment of God. He advocated the restoration of the normal pursuits of a peacetime society (see Jeremiah 27). A similar message had been given by Jeremiah to the captives taken to Babylon in 597 BC (see Jer. 29:4–7).

25:25–26. In the seventh month (October 586 BC; v. 25), Ishmael **smote Gedaliah.** (For a more complete account of the assassination of Gedaliah, see Jer. 40:13–41:15.) Ishmael appears to have had personal designs on the throne, to have resented Gedaliah's ready submission to the Babylonians, and to have been manipulated by the Ammonites, who also chafed under Babylonian domination (see Jer. 40:14; 41:10, 15). In fear of Nebuchadnezzar's certain retribution, all who remained in the area **came to Egypt** (v. 26). Pharaoh Apries (Hophra) was then ruler in Egypt (see discussion on 24:20).

K. Elevation of Jehoiachin in Babylon (25:27–30)

25:27–30. In Jehoiachin's thirty-seventh year as a captive in Babylon, in the **twelfth month ... seven and twentieth day** (v. 27) of that year (March 22, 561 BC), **Evil-merodach** began to reign (some scholars place Evil-merodach's succession to the throne in October 562 BC). His name means "man of [the god] Marduk."

Evil-merodach began his rule on a reconciliatory note and gave the captive king some freedom and privileges. He **did lift up the head of Jehoiachin ... out of prison** (v. 27). Babylonian administrative tablets (see chart, *KJV Study Bible*, p. xix), recording the payment of rations in oil and barley to prisoners held in Babylon, mention Yaukin (Jehoiachin) king of Iahudu (Judah) and five of his sons (see 24:15). No reason is given for Jehoiachin's release. Perhaps it was part of a general amnesty proclaimed at the beginning of Evil-merodach's reign. **Evil-erodah spake kindly to him, and set his** (Jehoiachin's) **throne above the throne of the kings** (v. 28). The book of Kings ends on a hopeful note. The judgment of exile would not destroy the people of Israel or the line of David. God's promise concerning David's house remained (see 2 Sam. 7:14–16).

THE FIRST BOOK OF
THE CHRONICLES

INTRODUCTION

Title

The Hebrew title (*dibre hayyamim*) of Chronicles can be translated "the events [or annals] of the days [or years]." The same phrase occurs in references to sources used by the author or compiler of Kings (translated "chronicles" in, e.g., 1 Kings 14:19, 29; 15:7, 23, 31; 16:5, 14, 20, 27; 22:45). The Septuagint translators (who translated the Old Testament into Greek) called the book "the things omitted," indicating that they regarded it as a supplement to Samuel and Kings. Jerome (AD 347–420), translator of the Latin Vulgate, suggested that a more appropriate title would be "chronicle of the whole sacred history." Luther took over this suggestion in his German version, and others have followed him. Chronicles was first divided into two books by the Septuagint translators.

Author, Date, and Sources

According to ancient Jewish tradition, Ezra wrote Chronicles, Ezra, and Nehemiah (see to Ezra, Introduction: "Author and Date"), but this cannot be established with certainty. A growing consensus dates Chronicles in the latter half of the fifth century BC, thus possibly within Ezra's lifetime. It must be acknowledged that the author, if not Ezra himself, at least shared many basic concerns with that reforming priest—though Chronicles is not so narrowly "priestly" in its perspective as was long affirmed.

Some believe the text contains evidence here and there of later expansions that were added after the basic work had been composed. While editorial revisions are not unlikely, all specific proposals regarding them remain tentative.

In his recounting of history long past, the Chronicler relied on many written sources. About half his work was taken from Samuel and Kings; he also drew on the Pentateuch, Judges, Ruth, Psalms, Isaiah, Jeremiah, Lamentations, and Zechariah (though he used texts of these books that varied somewhat from those that have been preserved in the later standardized Hebrew texts). There are frequent references to still other sources: "the book of the kings of Israel" (2 Chron. 20:34; 2 Chron. 33:18), "the account of the chronicles of king David" (27:24), "the book of the kings of Judah and Israel" or " ... of Israel and Judah" (1 Chron. 9:1; 2 Chron. 16:11; 25:26; 27:7; 28:26; 32:32; 35:27; 36:8), and "the story of the book of the kings" (2 Chron. 24:27). It is unclear whether these all refer to the same source or to different sources and what their relationship is to Samuel and Kings or to the royal annals referred to in Kings. In addition, the author cites a number of prophetic writings: those of "Samuel the seer" (29:29), "Nathan the prophet" (29:29; 2 Chron. 9:29), "Gad the seer" (29:29), "Ahijah the Shilonite" (2 Chron. 9:29), "Iddo the seer" (2 Chron. 9:29; 12:15; 13:22), "Shemaiah the prophet" (2 Chron. 12:15), "Isaiah the prophet" (2 Chron. 26:22), and "the seers" (2 Chron. 33:19). All these he used, often with only minor changes, to tell his own story of the past. He did not invent, but he did select, arrange, and integrate his sources to compose a narrative "sermon" for postexilic Israel as she struggled to reorient herself as the people of God in a new situation.

Theme

Just as the author of Kings had organized and interpreted the data of Israel's history to address the needs of the exiled community, so the Chronicler wrote for the restored community. The burning issue was the question of continuity with the past: Is God still interested in us? Are His covenants still in force? Now that there is no Davidic king and the people are subject to Persia, do God's promises to David still have meaning for us? After the great judgment (the dethroning of the house of David, the destruction of the nation, of Jerusalem, and of the temple, and the exile to Babylon), what is the nation's relationship to Israel of old? Several elements go into the Chronicler's answer.

(1) Continuity with the past is signified by the temple in Jerusalem, rebuilt by the Lord's sovereign influence on a Persian imperial edict (2 Chron. 36:22–23). For a generation that had no independent political status and no Davidic king, the author takes great pains to show that the temple of the Lord and its service (including its book of prayer and praise, an early edition of the Psalms) were supreme gifts of God given to Israel through the Davidic dynasty. For that reason, the account of the reigns of David and Solomon is largely devoted to David's preparations for the temple, Solomon's building of the temple, and David's instructions for the temple service (with the counsel of Gad the seer and Nathan the prophet, 2 Chron. 29:25; and the Levites Asaph, Heman, and Jeduthun, 2 Chron. 35:15). The temple of the Lord in the ancient holy city and its service (including the Psalms) were the chief legacy the house of David left to the restored community.

(2) The value of this legacy is highlighted by the author's emphasis on God's furtherance of His gracious purposes for Israel through His sovereign acts of election, including His election (a) of the tribe of Levi to serve before the ark of God (15:2; see 23:24–32), (b) of David to be king over Israel (28:4; 2 Chron. 6:6), (c) of Solomon, David's son, to be king and to build the temple (28:5–6, 10; 29:1), (d) of Jerusalem (2 Chron. 6:6, 34, 38; 12:13; 33:7) and of the temple (2 Chron. 7:12, 16; 33:7) to be the place where His Name would be present among His people. These divine acts gave assurance to postexilic Israel that her rebuilt temple in Jerusalem and its continuing service marked her as God's people, whose election had not been annulled.

(3) In addition to the temple, Israel had the law and the prophets as a major focus of her covenant life under the leadership of the house of David. Neither the Davidic kings nor the temple had in themselves assured Israel's security and blessing. All had been conditional on Israel's and the king's faithfulness to the law (28:7; 2 Chron. 6:16; 7:17; 12:1;

33:8). In the Chronicler's account, a primary feature of the reign of every faithful Davidic king was his attempt to bring about compliance with the law: David (6:49; 15:13, 15; 16:40; 22:12–13; 29:19), Asa (2 Chron. 14:4; 15:12–14), Jehoshaphat (2 Chron. 17:3–9; 19:8–10), Joash (2 Chron. 24:6, 9), Hezekiah (2 Chron. 29:10, 31; 30:15–16; 31:3–4, 21), and Josiah (2 Chron. 34:19–21, 29–33; 35:6, 12, 26). Heeding God's prophetic word was no less crucial (see 2 Chron. 36:15–16). The faithful kings, such as David, Asa, Jehoshaphat, Hezekiah, and Josiah—and even Rehoboam (2 Chron. 11:4; 12:6) and Amaziah (2 Chron. 25:7–10)—honored His prophetic word; the unfaithful kings disregarded it to their destruction (Jehoram, 2 Chron. 21:12–19; Joash, 2 Chron. 24:19–25; Amaziah, 2 Chron. 25:15–16, 20; Manasseh, 2 Chron. 33:10–11). Chronicles, in fact, notes the ministries of more prophets than do Samuel and Kings. Jehoshaphat's word to Israel succinctly expressed the Chronicler's view: "Believe in the Lord your God, so shall you be established; believe his prophets, so shall ye prosper" (2 Chron. 20:20). In the Chronicler's account of Israel's years under the kings, her response to the law and the prophets was more decisive for her destiny than were the reigns of the kings.

Thus, the law and the prophets, like the temple, were more crucial to Israel's continuing relationship with the Lord than the presence or absence of a king, the reigns of the Davidic kings themselves being testimony of this.

(4) The Chronicler further underscores the importance of obedience to the law and to the word of the prophets by emphasizing the theme of immediate retribution. See the express statements of David (28:9), of the Lord (2 Chron. 7:14), and of the prophets (2 Chron. 12:5; 15:2, 7; 16:7, 9; 19:2–3; 21:14–15; 24:20; 25:15–16; 28:9; 34:24–28). In writing his accounts of individual reigns, the Chronicler never tires of demonstrating how sin always brings judgment in the form of disaster (usually either illness or defeat in war), whereas repentance, obedience, and trust yield peace, victory, and prosperity.

(5) Clearly, the author of Chronicles wished to sustain Israel's hope for the promised Messiah, the son of David, in accordance with the Davidic covenant (2 Samuel 7) and the assurances of the prophets, including those near to him (Haggai, Zechariah, and Malachi). The Chronicler is careful to recall the Lord's pledge to David (1 Chronicles 17) and to follow this with many additional references to it (see especially his account of Solomon's reign and 2 Chron. 13:5; 21:7; 23:3). Perhaps even more indicative of his wish to sustain Israel's hope are his idealized depictions of David, Solomon, Asa, Jehoshaphat, Hezekiah, and Josiah. While not portrayed as flawless, these kings are presented as prime examples of the messianic ideal, that is, as royal servants of the Lord whose reigns promoted godliness and covenant faithfulness in Israel. They were crowned with God's favor toward His people in the concrete forms of victories, deliverances, and prosperity. These kings sat, moreover, on the "throne of the Lord" (29:23; see 28:5; 2 Chron. 9:8) and ruled over the Lord's kingdom (17:14; 2 Chron. 13:8). Thus, they served as types, foreshadowing the David to come, of whom the prophets had spoken, and remembrance of these kings nurtured hope in the face of much discouragement (see the book of Malachi). See also "Portrait of David and Solomon," below.

(6) Yet another major theme of the Chronicler's history is his concern with "all Israel" (see, for example, 9:1; 11:1–4; 12:38–40; 16:1–3; 18:14; 21:1–5; 28:1–8; 29:21–26; 2 Chron. 1:1–3; 7:8–10; 9:30; 10:1–3, 16; 12:1; 18:16; 28:23; 29:24; 30:1–13, 23–27;

34:6–9, 33). As a matter of fact, he views the restored community as the remnant of all Israel, both north and south (9:2–3). This was more than theological conceit. His narrative makes frequent note of movements of godly people from Israel to Judah for specifically religious reasons. The first were Levites in the time of Rehoboam (2 Chron. 11:14). In the reign of Asa, others followed from Ephraim and Manasseh (2 Chron. 15:9). Shortly after the Assyrian destruction of the northern kingdom, many from that devastated land resettled in Judah at Hezekiah's invitation (2 Chronicles 30). Presumably, not all who came for Hezekiah's great Passover remained, but archaeology has shown a sudden large increase in population in the region around Jerusalem at that time, and the Chronicler specifically mentions "children of Israel … that dwelt in the cities of Judah" (2 Chron. 31:6). He also speaks of the people of "Manasseh and Ephraim, and of all the remnant of Israel" who joined with the people of "Judah and Benjamin" and the inhabitants of Jerusalem in restoring the temple in the days of Josiah (2 Chron. 34:9). These groups were also present at Josiah's Passover (2 Chron. 35:17–18). So the kingdom of "Judah" had absorbed many from the northern kingdom through the years, and the Chronicler views it as the remnant of all Israel from the time of Samaria's fall.

(7) The genealogies also demonstrate continuity with the past. To the question, "Is God still interested in us?" the Chronicler answers, "He has always been." God's grace and love for the restored community did not begin with David or the conquest or the exodus but with creation (1:1). See also "Genealogies," below.

(8) The Chronicler often introduces speeches not found in Samuel and Kings, using them to convey some of his main emphases. Of the 165 speeches in Chronicles of varying lengths, only 95 are found in the parallel texts of Samuel and Kings. See, for example, the speeches of Abijah (2 Chron. 13:4–12), Asa (2 Chron. 14:11), and Jehoshaphat (2 Chron. 20:5–12).

Portrait of David and Solomon

The bulk of the Chronicler's history is devoted to the reigns of David (chaps. 11–29) and Solomon (2 Chron. 1–9). His portraits of these two kings are quite distinctive and provide a key to his concerns.

(1) The Chronicler has idealized David and Solomon. Anything in his source material (mainly Samuel and Kings) that might tarnish his picture of them is omitted. He makes no reference to David's seven-year reign in Hebron before the uniting of the kingdom, the wars between Saul's house and David, the negotiations with Abner, the difficulties over David's wife Michal, or the murders of Abner and Ish-bosheth (2 Samuel 1–4). The Chronicler presents David as being immediately anointed king over all Israel after the death of Saul (chap. 11) and enjoying the total support of the people (11:1–12:40; see discussion on 11:1–3). Subsequent difficulties for David also are not recounted. No mention is made of David's sin with Bathsheba, the crime and death of Amnon, the fratricide by Absalom and his plot against his father, David's flight from Jerusalem, the rebellions of Sheba and Shimei, and other incidents that might diminish the glory of David's reign (2 Samuel 11–20). David is presented without blemish, apart from the incident of the census (the Chronicler had a special purpose for including it; see chap. 21 and discussions).

The Chronicler handles Solomon similarly. Solomon is specifically named in a divine oracle as David's successor (22:7–10; 28:6). His accession to the throne is announced publicly by David and is greeted with the unanimous support of all Israel (chaps. 28–29). No mention is made of the bedridden David, who must overturn the attempted coup by Adonijah at the last moment to secure the throne for Solomon. Nor is it mentioned that the military commander Joab and the high priest Abiathar supported Adonijah's attempt (1 Kings 1). Solomon's execution of those who had wronged David (1 Kings 2) is also omitted. The accession of Solomon is presented as proceeding without competition or detracting incident. The account of his reign is devoted almost wholly to the building of the temple (2 Chronicles 2–8), and no reference to his failures is included. No mention is made of his idolatry, his foreign wives, or the rebellions against his rule (1 Kings 11). Even the blame for the schism is removed from Solomon (1 Kings 11:26–40; 12:1–4) and placed on the scheming of Jeroboam. Solomon's image in Chronicles is such that he can be paired with David in the most favorable light (2 Chron. 11:17). The David and Solomon of the Chronicler, then, must be seen not only as the David and Solomon of history but also as types for the messianic king of the Chronicler's expectation.

(2) Not only has the Chronicler idealized David and Solomon, but he also appears to have consciously adopted the account of the succession of Moses and Joshua as a model for the succession of David and Solomon: (a) Both David and Moses failed to attain their goals—one to build the temple and the other to enter the Promised Land. In both cases, the divine prohibition was related to the appointment of a successor (22:5–13; 28:2–8; Deut. 1:37–38; 31:2–8). (b) Both Solomon and Joshua brought the people of God into rest (22:8–9; Josh. 11:23; 21:44). (c) The appointments of Solomon and Joshua have a number of verbal parallels (compare 22:11–13, 16; 28:7–10, 20; 2 Chron. 1:1 with Deut. 31:5–8, 23; Josh. 1:5, 7–9). (d) Both private and public announcements were made of the appointment of the successors (private, 22:6; Deut. 31:23; public, made "in the sight of all Israel," 28:8; Deut. 31:7). (e) Both David and Moses enjoyed the immediate and wholehearted support of the people (29:23–24; Deut. 34:9; Josh. 1:16–18). (f) It is twice reported that God "magnified" or "magnified … exceedingly" Solomon and Joshua (29:25; 2 Chron. 1:1; Josh. 3:7; 4:14).

The Chronicler also uses other models from Pentateuchal history in his portrayal of David and Solomon. Like Moses, David received the plans for the temple from God (28:11–19; Exod. 25:9) and called on the people to bring voluntary offerings for its construction (29:1–9; Exod. 25:1–7). Solomon's relationship to Huram-abi, the craftsman from Tyre (2 Chron. 2:13–14), echoes the role of Bezaleel and Aholiab in the building of the tabernacle (Exod. 35:30–36:7; see also discussion on 2 Chronicles 1:5).

Genealogies

Analysis of genealogies, both inside and outside the Bible, has disclosed that they serve a variety of functions (with different principles governing the lists), that they vary in form (some being segmented, others linear) and depth (the number of generations listed), and that they are often fluid (subject to change).

Genealogies function in three general areas: the familial or domestic, the legal or political, and the religious. In the domestic area, an individual's social status, privileges, and obligations may be reflected in his placement in the lineage (see 7:14–19); the rights of the firstborn son and the secondary status of the children of concubines are examples from the Bible. In the political sphere, genealogies substantiate claims to hereditary office or settle competing claims to the office. Land organization and territorial groupings of social units may also be determined by genealogical reckoning—for example, the division of the land among the twelve tribes. In Israel, military levies also proceeded along genealogical lines; several of the genealogies in Chronicles reflect military conscription (5:1–26; 7:1–12, 30–40; 8:1–40). In the religious sphere, genealogies function primarily by establishing membership among the priests and Levites (6:1–30; 9:10–34; Neh. 7:61–65).

As to form, some genealogical lists trace several lines of descent (segmented genealogies), while others are devoted to a single line (linear genealogies). Comparison of genealogical lists of the same tribal or family line often brings to light surprising differences. The fluidity of the lists may reflect variation in function. Sometimes changes in the status or relations of social structures are reflected in genealogies by changes in the relationships of the names (see discussions on 1:35–42; 6:22, 27) or by the addition of names or segments to a lineage (see discussions on 5:11–22; 6:27; 7:6–12). The most common type of fluidity in biblical materials is telescoping, the omission of names from the list. Unimportant names are left out to relate an individual to a prominent ancestor, or possibly to achieve the desired number of names in the genealogy. Some biblical genealogies, for example, omit names to achieve multiples of seven. For the period from David to the exile, Matthew cites fourteen generations (2 times 7), while Luke cites twenty-one (3 times 7), and the same authors cite similar multiples of seven in the period from the exile to Jesus (Matt 1:1–17; Luke 3:23–38).

The genealogies of Chronicles show variation in all these properties. The arrangements often reflect the purpose for which the genealogies were composed prior to their being adopted by the Chronicler as part of his record.

Outline

H. Organization of the Temple Service (chaps. 23–26)

I. Administrative Structures of the Kingdom (chap. 27)

J. David's Final Preparations for Succession and the Temple (28:1–29:20)

K. Succession of Solomon; Death of David (29:21–30)

Bibliography

Coggins, R. J. *The First and Second Books of Chronicles.* London: Cambridge University Press, 1976.

DeVries, Simon J. *1 and 2 Chronicles.* Forms of the Old Testament Literature 11. Grand Rapids, MI: Eerdmans, 1989.

Keil, C. F. "The Books of the Chronicles." In *Biblical Commentary on the Old Testament.* Translated by Andrew Harper. Grand Rapids, MI: Eerdmans, 1957.

Payne, J. Barton. "1, 2 Chronicles." In *Expositor's Bible Commentary*, edited by Frank E. Gaebelein, vol. 4. Grand Rapids, MI: Zondervan, 1992.

Selman, Martin J. *1 Chronicles: An Introduction and Commentary.* Tyndale Old Testament Commentaries 10A. Downers Grove, IL: InterVarsity, 1994.

Slotki, I. W. *Chronicles: Hebrew Text and English Translation, with an Introduction and Commentary.* Soncino Books of the Bible. London: Soncino, 1952.

Williamson, H. G. *Israel in the Book of Chronicles.* London: Cambridge University Press, 1977.

EXPOSITION

I. Genealogies: Creation to Restoration (chaps. 1–9)

1:1–9:44. The genealogies succinctly show the restored community's continuity with the past. The great deeds of God on Israel's behalf prior to the rise of David are passed over in silence, but the genealogies serve as a skeleton of history to show that the Israel of the restoration stands at the center of the divine purpose from the beginning (from Adam, v. 1). And the genealogies also serve the very practical purpose of legitimizing the present. They provide the framework by which the ethnic and religious purity of the people can be maintained. They also establish the continuing line of royal succession and the legitimacy of the priests for the postexilic temple service. (See Introduction: "Genealogies").

A. The Patriarchs (chap. 1)

1:1–54. Here the Chronicler covers the period from Adam to Jacob, and the materials are drawn almost entirely from Genesis. The subsidiary lines of descent are presented first: Japheth and Ham (vv. 5–16) are given before Shem (vv. 17–27), the sons of Shem other than those in Abraham's ancestry (vv. 17–23) before that line (vv. 24–27), the sons of Abraham's concubines (vv. 28–33) before Isaac's line (v. 34), the descendants of Esau and the Edomite ruling houses (vv. 35–54) before the sons of Israel (2:1). In each case, the elect lineage is given last.

Several features of this genealogy are striking when compared with nonbiblical materials. The genealogy begins without an introduction. Two sections of the genealogy have no kinship terms and are only lists of names: the first thirteen names in verses 1–4 (see discussion on v. 4) and the ten names in verses 24–27. In verses 5–16 (and following v. 27), kinship terms are used. Both segmented (those tracing several lines of descent) and linear (those tracing a single line) genealogies are included. This identical structure is found in a copy of the Assyrian King List:

there is no introduction, and the scribe has drawn lines across the tablet to divide it into four sections, two of which are lists of names without kinship terms, alternating with two lists in which relations are specified; both segmented and linear genealogies are used. This suggests that the Chronicler was following a known literary pattern for his composition.

1:1–4. The names listed here extend from creation to the flood. This list is taken from an abbreviated version of Genesis 5:1–32 (see discussions there). The omission of Cain and Abel demonstrates the Chronicler's interest in the chosen line (see Gen. 4:17–25).

The list concludes with **Noah, Shem, Ham, and Japeth** (v. 4). The last three names are not successive generations that follow Noah (as one might expect from the pattern in vv. 1–3) but are his three sons, though they are not identified as such. The Chronicler's readers would have known that **Shem, Ham, and Japheth** were the sons of Noah and would not have needed a kinship notice in the text. The Septuagint (the Greek translation of the Old Testament) and some modern translations read "the sons of Noah" to clarify the relationship of the four names.

1:5–23. This genealogy is drawn from the table of nations in Genesis 10:2–29 (see discussions there). The arrangement is primarily geographical and cultural rather than biological. Omitting **the Philistines** (v. 12) as a parenthesis, a total of seventy nations is achieved: Japheth, fourteen; Ham, thirty; Shem, twenty-six (see discussion on Gen. 10:2). This is an example of a genealogy that is telescoped to attain multiples of seven (see Introduction: "Genealogies").

On **the sons of Japheth** (v. 5), the widest dispersed of Noah's sons, see Genesis 10:2–5. On **the sons of Ham** (v. 8), see Genesis 10:6–20. The special attention to **Nimrod** (v. 10) reproduces comments from there. Special attention is drawn to the messianic line through Shem by placing **the sons of Shem** (v. 17) last (see Gen. 10:21–31).

1:24–27. The line of **Shem** (v. 24) is traced from **Arphaxad** to **Abraham** (v. 27), the father of God's covenant people (see discussions on 1:1–2:1; Gen. 11:10–26).

1:28–34. Abraham's descendants through his concubines (see Gen. 25:6) are listed first: **Ishmael** (v. 29; Gen. 25:12–16), born to Hagar (Genesis 16), and **the sons of Keturah** (v. 32, Gen. 25:1–4). Primary attention is reserved for **Isaac** (v. 34), the son of promise and his sons, **Esau** (vv. 34–54) and Israel (i.e., Jacob). Jacob (i.e., Israel) and his sons follow in 2:1–9:44.

1:35–37. In Genesis 36:10–14, Esau's sons are arranged according to his wives, Adah and Aholibamah.

The sons of Eliphaz (v. 36) correspond to Genesis 36:11–12, with one difficulty: listing **Timna** and **Amalek** as sons of Eliphaz is in apparent conflict with Genesis 36:12, where Timna is the concubine of Eliphaz and the mother of Amalek. The Septuagint (the Greek translation of the Old Testament) assumes a mistake in the Hebrew text and lists Amalek as Eliphaz's son by Timna. Perhaps the Chronicler has once again omitted kinship terminology (see discussions on 1:1–2:1; 1:4). Alternatively, some regard this as an example of genealogical fluidity (see Introduction: "Genealogies") — since the name Timna also became the name of a chiefdom in Edom (1:51; Gen. 36:40), over time Timna was "promoted" in the Edomite genealogies to the position of a son of Eliphaz and a brother of Amalek.

1:38–42. Seir (v. 38), sometimes a place-name for the mountain south of the Dead Sea, is here and in Genesis 36:20 a reference to the Horite inhabitants who were expelled from the region by Esau's descendants.

1:43–54. The Chronicler continues with extensive coverage of **Edom** (v. 43; see Gen. 36:31–43). This is striking in contrast to his omission of the line of Cain and his brief treatment of the line of Ishmael. It probably reflects the fact that the Edomites were important in the Chronicler's own day (see 18:11–13; 2 Chron. 8:17; 21:8; 25:20; 28:17).

B. The Twelve Sons of Jacob/Israel (2:1–2)

2:1–2. Although numerous lists of the twelve tribes are given in the Old Testament, only four are given in genealogical form: (1) Genesis 29:31–30:24; 35:16–20; (2) Genesis 35:22–26; (3) Genesis 46:8–27; (4) here. Other lists of the tribes are found in 12:24–37; 27:16–22; Exodus 1:2–5; Deuteronomy 27:12–13; 33; Ezekiel 48:31–34. In other lists, the tribe of **Levi** (v. 1) is omitted, and the number twelve is achieved by dividing **Joseph** (v. 2) into the tribes of Ephraim and Manasseh (Num. 1:5–15; 1:20–43; 2:3–31; 7:12–83; 10:14–28; 13:4–15; 26:5–51). In this passage, the Chronicler appears to follow Genesis 35:22–26 except for the position of the tribe of **Dan**, which is found in seventh instead of ninth place. The list here does not set the order in which the Chronicler will take up the tribes; rather, he moves immediately to his major concern with the house of David and the tribe of **Judah** (v. 1; 2:3–4:23), even though Judah is fourth in the genealogy. In the other lists of these chapters, the Chronicler maintains the number twelve, but with the following names: Judah, Simeon, Reuben, Gad, half of Manasseh, Levi, Issachar, Benjamin, Naphtali, Ephraim, Manasseh, and Asher. Zebulun and Dan are omitted.

C. The Family of Judah (2:3–4:23)

2:3–9. The lineage of **Judah** (v. 3) is traced to **the sons of Hezron** (v. 9), whose descendants are given in 2:10–3:24. Of Judah's five sons, the first two (**Er and Onan**) died as the result of sin (see Genesis 38). The lineage of the third son, **Shelah**, is taken up in 4:21; this section focuses on the remaining two sons (see Gen. 46:12; Num. 26:19–22).

Zimri (v. 6) is not otherwise known, unless his name appears in a variant form (Zabdi) in Joshua 7:1. **Ethan, and Heman, and Calcol, and Dara** (v. 6) are known, but they were not immediate descendants of **Zerah**; rather, they were from the later period of the reign of Solomon (1 Kings 4:31). A Heman and an Ethan were David's musicians (see 15:19; Psalms 88–89 superscriptions), but whether these are the same individuals is uncertain. If they are the same, the fact that Heman and Ethan are assigned to the tribe of Levi in 6:33–42 and 15:19 may be another example of genealogical fluidity, in which these men's musical skills brought them into the Levitical lineage. The reverse may have occurred: as Levites associated with Judah, they were brought into that lineage.

The name **Achar** (v. 7) means "trouble." He is called Achan in Joshua 7; 22:20. The change from Achan to Achar is probably an intentional play on words reflecting the trouble that Achan brought to Israel.

2:10–3:24. That the Chronicler's primary concern in the genealogy of Judah is with the line of David is seen in his arrangement of this section's material as an inversion:

> Descendants of Ram (David's ancestry), 2:10–17
> Descendants of Caleb, 2:18–24
> Descendants of Jerahmeel, 2:25–33
> Supplementary material on Jerahmeel, 2:34–41
> Supplementary material on Caleb, 2:42–55
> Supplementary material on Ram (David's descendants), chapter 3

The Chronicler has structured this central portion of the Judah genealogy in a way that highlights the Davidic ancestry and descent, which frame this section and emphasize the position of David, in line with the Chronicler's interests in the historical portions that follow (see discussion on 4:1–23).

2:10–17. Verses 10–12 are a linear genealogy from **Ram** (v. 10) to **Jesse** (v. 12). Jesse's lineage is then segmented, reminiscent of 1 Samuel 16:1–13. The source for most of this material is Ruth 4:19–22. In 1 Samuel 16:10–13, **David** (v. 15) was the eighth of Jesse's sons to appear before Samuel. In this passage, only seven sons are named (perhaps because one of the sons died or was childless), enabling David to occupy the favored place of **the seventh** son (see Introduction: "Genealogies"). David was the half uncle of his famous warriors **Abishai ... Joab ... Asahel** (v. 16), and **Amasa** (v. 17; 11:6, 20, 26; 2 Sam. 2:13, 18; 17:25; 19:13).

2:18–24. This **Caleb** (v. 18) is not to be confused with Joshua's associate, Caleb the son of Jephunneh (see Num. 13:30ff; Josh. 14:6–14; 1 Chron. 4:15). For the Chronicler, the important name in this genealogy of the Calebites is **Bezaleel** (v. 20), the wise master craftsman who supervised the building of the tabernacle (Exod. 31:1–5). He is mentioned in the Bible only in Exodus and Chronicles. The Chronicler uses Bezaleel and Aholiab (Exod. 31:6) as a model for his portrait of Solomon and Huram in the building of the temple (see discussion on 2 Chron. 1:5). By inserting a reference to the builder of the tabernacle next to the genealogy of David (2:10–17), the Chronicler characteristically juxtaposes the themes of king and temple—themes so important to his historical narrative.

2:25–33. This section is identified as an entity separate from the supplementary material by its opening and closing formulas: **The sons of Jerahmeel** (v. 25) and **These were the sons of Jerahmeel** (v. 33). The clan is little known. The information in 2:25–41 is the only genealogical material on the Jerahmeelites in the Bible. First Samuel 27:10 and 30:27–29 place their settlements in the Negev, and David repaid this clan's kindness to him with spoils taken from the Amalekites.

2:34–41. This is supplementary material on the line of **Sheshan** (v. 34; see 2:31); it is a linear genealogy to a depth of thirteen generations. The generation of **Elishama** (v. 41) would be the twenty-third since Judah (2:3), if this lineage has not been telescoped. If no names have been omitted, David was likely a contemporary of Elishama, though nothing is known about him.

2:42–55. The same opening and closing formulas noted in 2:25, 33 occur again here: **Now the sons of Caleb** (v. 42) and **These were the sons of Caleb** (v. 50a). The list in this section is a mixture of personal names and place-names; the phrase "father of" can be understood not only as "ancestor" or "predecessor" but also (as is likely here) as "founder of" or "leader of" a city.

Verses 50b–55 resume the genealogy of **Hur** (v. 50; see 2:20). The same formulas for identifying the genealogical sections in 2:25, 33 and in verses 42 and 50a are used here, **the son[s] of Hur** (v. 50b), and in 4:4, "These are the sons of Hur." The presence of these formulas suggests that this section and 4:1–4 were once a unit; the Chronicler has inserted his record of the Davidic descent (chap. 3) in the middle of this genealogy, apparently to balance the sections of his material (see discussions on 2:10–3:24; 4:1–23). Otherwise, the disruption of the genealogy of Hur may have already occurred in the Chronicler's sources.

The Tirathites, the Shimeathites, and Suchathites (v. 55) may refer to three families, as translated here, or to three different classes of scribes, perhaps those who (1) read, (2) copied, and (3) checked the work. **The Kenites** were originally a foreign people, but many of the Kenites were incorporated into Judah (see Num. 10:29–32; Judg. 1:16; 4:11).

3:1–24. See discussion on 2:10–3:24.

3:1–9. This list of David's children is largely drawn from 2 Samuel 3:2–5; 5:13–16; 13:1 (see discussions there). The sons born **in Jerusalem** (vv. 5–8) are repeated in 1 Chronicles 14:3–7. The name **Eliphelet** occurs twice (vv. 6, 8). In 14:5, 7, two spellings of the name are given (only one son having this name is mentioned in 2 Sam. 5:14–16). The reference to David's seven-year rule **in Hebron** (v. 4) is repeated in 29:27, though the Chronicler does not deal with this period in his narrative. The references to **Absalom** (v. 2), **Tamar** (v. 9), **Adonijah** (v. 2), **Amnon** (v. 1), and **Bath-shua** (i.e., Bathsheba; v. 5) all recall unhappy incidents in the life of David, incidents the Chronicler has omitted from his later narrative (see 2 Sam. 11–15; 17–18; 1 Kings 1).

3:10–16. Solomon was clearly God's choice of David's sons to be his successor and recipient of the covenant (see 2 Sam. 12:24; 1 Chron. 22:9–10). Here Solomon's lineage is traced through the reign of Zedekiah and the beginning of the exile. The reigns of each of these descendants are recorded in some detail in 2 Chronicles. Verse 10: **Rehoboam** (see 2 Chron. 10–12); **Abia** (see 2 Chron. 13:1–14:1); **Asa** (see 2 Chron. 14–16); **Jehoshaphat** (see 1 Kings 22; 2 Chron. 17–20). Verse 11: **Joram** (see 2 Chron. 21); **Ahaziah** (see 2 Chron. 22:1–22); **Joash** (see 2 Chron. 23–24). Verse 12: **Amaziah** (see 2 Chron. 25); **Azariah** (Uzziah; see 2 Chron. 26); **Jotham** (see 2 Chron. 27). Verse 13: **Ahaz** (see 2 Chron. 28); **Hezekiah** (see 2 Chron. 29–32); **Manasseh** (see 2 Chron. 33:1–20). Verse 14: **Amon** (see 2 Chron. 33:21–25); **Josiah** (see 2 Kings 22:1–23:30; 2 Chron. 34:1–36:1).

At this point, the genealogy is segmented rather than linear, as in verses 10–14. **The firstborn Johanan** (v. 15) is not mentioned elsewhere and may have died before **Josiah**. Since Josiah's other three sons would all occupy the throne, the succession was not uniformly father to son. **Shallum** (Jehoahaz; 2 Chron. 36:2–4; 2 Kings 23:30–35) was replaced by **Jehoiakim** (v. 16; 2 Chron. 36:5–8; 2 Kings 23:34–24:6). Jehoiakim was succeeded by his son Jehoiachin (2 Chron. 36:9–10; 2 Kings 24:8–16). After Jehoiachin was taken captive to Babylon by Nebuchadnezzar, Josiah's son **Zedekiah** (2 Kings 24:17–25:7; 2 Chron. 36:11–14) became the last king of Judah.

3:17–20. What follows is the royal line after the exile. Seven sons are attributed to **Jeconiah** (Jehoiachin; v. 17), but not one succeeded him (see discussions on 3:15–16; Jer. 22:30). Tablets found in Babylon dating from the tenth to the thirty-fifth year of Nebuchadnezzar (595–570 BC), listing deliveries of rations, mention Jeconiah and five sons as well as other Judahites held in Babylon. Jeconiah received similar largesse from Nebuchadnezzar's successor, Evil-merodach (562–560 BC; see 2 Kings 25:27–30).

Shenazar (v. 18) may be another spelling of the name Sheshbazzar. If so, the treasures of the temple were consigned to his care for return to Judah (Ezra 1:11). He also served for a short time as the first governor of the returnees and made an initial attempt at rebuilding the temple (Ezra 5:14–16). Little is known of him; he soon disappeared from the scene and was overshadowed by his nephew **Zerubbabel** (v. 19), who assumes much importance in Ezra, Haggai, and Zechariah. (But see discussion on Ezra 1:8.)

Zerubbabel, a leader of the exiles who returned to Jerusalem, is shown here to be the son of **Pedaiah** (v. 19). Other texts name Shealtiel (**Salathiel**, v. 17) as Zerubbabel's father (Ezra 3:2, 8; Neh. 12:1; Hag. 1:12, 14; 2:2, 23). Suggestions offered to resolve this difficulty are: (1) Shealtiel may have died early, and Pedaiah became the head of the family; (2) Pedaiah may have married the childless widow of Shealtiel, in which case, Zerubbabel would be regarded as the son of Shealtiel according to the law of levirate marriage (Deut. 25:5–6). In Luke 3:27, Neri instead of Jehoiachin ("Jeconiah," v. 17) is identified as the father of Shealtiel. Suggestions similar to those above could be made in this instance as well. It is interesting to note that the genealogies of Jesus in Matthew 1 and Luke 3 both trace his descent to Zerubbabel, but none of the names subsequent to Zerubbabel (3:19–24) is found in the New Testament genealogies.

The other **five** listed in verse 20 may have been sons of Zerubbabel, but no kinship terms are provided. Since the sons of **Hananiah** (v. 19) are specified in 3:21, perhaps the "five" could be the sons of **Meshullam**.

3:21–24. The sons of Rephaiah … Shechaniah (v. 21) are not connected in the Hebrew to the previous names and are not said to be descendants of Zerubbabel. They were probably other Davidic families in the time of Zerubbabel (3:19) or **Pelatiah** and **Jesaiah**. If they are understood as contemporary with Zerubbabel, his genealogy was carried only two generations (his sons and grandsons), and a date for Chronicles as early as 450 BC is possible (see Introduction: "Author, Date, and Sources").

Five names appear in the list of **the sons of Shemaiah** (v. 22), not **six**. Perhaps a copyist accidentally omitted one name.

4:1–23. None of the genealogies of Judah in this section appear elsewhere in Scripture. Although this section may have the appearance of miscellaneous notes, the careful shaping of the Chronicler is evident in light of the overall inverted structure of the genealogies of Judah.

2:3	Shelah
2:4–8	Pharez
2:9–3:24	Hezron
4:1–20	Pharez
4:21–23	Shelah

This balancing of the material in inverse order shows the centrality of the lineage of Hezron and the house of David; the same balancing in inverse order is observed in the Hezron section (see discussion on 2:10–3:24). The record of Judah's oldest surviving son, Shelah, frames the entire genealogy of Judah. There are fifteen fragmentary genealogies in this section, with two to six generations in each. The connection of these genealogies to one another (or other genealogical lists) is often difficult to determine.

4:1–8. These verses at times supplement the genealogy of **Hezron** (v. 1) that is given in chapter 2.

The descendants of Judah here (vv. 1–2) are not brothers. Rather, the genealogy is linear; they are descendants of successive generations. **Carmi** (v. 1) is either a scribal confusion or an alternative name for Chelubai (2:9); the confusion may have been induced by 2:7. **Reaiah** (v. 2) is a variant of Haroeh (2:52). **The sons of Hur** (v. 4) supplement in some way 2:19, 50. Verses 5–8 provide supplementary information on the family of **Ashur** (v. 5; 2:24).

4:9–10. The practice of inserting short historical notes into genealogical records is amply attested in nonbiblical genealogical texts from the ancient Near East as well as in other biblical genealogies (Gen. 4:19–24; 10:8–12). **Jabez** (meaning "he causes pain"; v. 9) is a place-name in 2:55 but a personal name here. The parenthetical note on Jabez emphasizes that God answers the prayer of faith, for Jabez was able to triumph over his name.

4:11–20. The following—**Chelub** (v. 11), **Kenaz** (v. 13), **Caleb** (v. 15), **Jehaleleel** (v. 16), **Ezra** (v. 17), **Hodiah** (v. 19), **Shimon** (v. 20), and **Ishi**—are all heads of genealogies. The connections of these men is not readily apparent.

In 1:36, 53, Kenaz is a descendant of Esau (see Gen. 36:11, 42). **Othniel** (v. 13), the first of Israel's judges (see Judg. 3:9–11), was the nephew of Caleb (see Josh. 15:17; Judg. 1:13). **Caleb the son of Jephunneh** (v. 15; not the Caleb of 2:18, 42, 50), Joshua's associate, was also a Kenezite (Josh. 14:14). So Kenaz's relation to Judah is not clear. Apparently, part of this one family from Esau's line joined the tribe of Judah (perhaps by adoption or marriage).

Verses 16–20 present a portion of the genealogy from preexilic times; several of the places named were not included in the province of Judah during the restoration period—for example, **Ziph** (v. 16) and **Eshtemoa** (v. 19).

Bithiah the daughter of Pharaoh, which Mered took (v. 18) is otherwise unknown; the fact that Mered married a daughter of Pharaoh suggests his prominence. The event may be associated with the fortunes of Israel in Egypt under Joseph.

4:21–23. The list of **The sons of Shelah** (v. 21; see Gen. 8:5, 11) is supplementary to 2:3. This section accurately reflects a feature of ancient Near Eastern society. Clans were often associated not only with particular localities but also with special trades or guilds, such as **linen** workers (v. 21), **potters** (v. 23), royal patronage (v. 23), and scribes (2:55).

D. The Sons of Simeon (4:24–43)

4:24–43. The genealogy of **Simeon** (v. 24) is also found in Genesis 46:10; Exodus 6:15; and Numbers 26:12–13. Simeon settled in part of the territory of Judah; the list of occupied towns should be compared with Joshua 15:26–32, 42; 19:2–7. Since Simeon occupied areas allotted to Judah, this tribe was politically incorporated into Judah and appears to have lost much of its own identity in history (see Gen. 34:24–31; 49:5–7; see also discussions on Gen. 34:25; 49:7). Geographical and historical notes are inserted in the genealogy (see discussion on 4:9–10).

Apparently, two genealogies are included here. The first (vv. 24–33) ends with the formula, **and their genealogy** (v. 33). This brief list extends the genealogies found in parallel passages (Gen. 46:10; Exod. 6:15; Num. 26:12–14). Attached to the genealogy is a list of the cities Simeon inhabited (see Josh. 1:1–9).

The second genealogy (vv. 34–43) records names found nowhere else in the Bible. Overpopulation (v. 38) caused these people to expand toward **Gedor** (v. 39) and east toward Edom in the time of **Hezekiah** (v. 41).

The long hostility between Israel and **the Amalekites** (v. 43) surfaced once again (see Exod. 17:8–16; Deut. 25:17–19; 1 Samuel 15; see also Esther, Introduction: "Theme and Theological Message").

E. Reuben, Gad, and the Half Tribe of Manasseh (chap. 5)

5:1–26. Chapter 5 presents the genealogical records of the tribes east of the Jordan: Reuben, Gad, and half of Manasseh (see Num. 32:33–42). Because of the Chronicler's concern with "all Israel," he includes the genealogical records of these tribes, which were no longer significant entities in Israel's life in the restoration period, having been swept away in the Assyrian conquests.

5:1–10. The initial statement in verse 1 is interrupted by an explanation of why the birthright of the firstborn did not remain with **Reuben** (v. 1; for Reuben's sin with his father's concubine, see Gen. 35:22; 49:4). After this explanation, the initial statement is repeated in verse 3. The parenthetical material (vv. 1–2) shows the writer's partiality for **Judah** (v. 2), even though **Joseph** (v. 1) received the double portion (Ephraim and Manasseh) of the firstborn.

Judah was singled out for prominence (Gen. 49:8–9) and produced for Israel a ruler, David, through whose lineage its ultimate ruler, the Messiah, would come. The Hebrew term translated **chief ruler** (v. 2) is used of David in 11:2; 17:7; 2 Samuel 5:2; 6:21; 7:8 (see also 1 Chron. 28:4). The use of military titles (vv. 6–7) and a battle account (v. 10) suggest that this genealogy may have functioned in military organization (see Introduction: "Genealogies").

The source for some of this material on Reuben is Numbers 26:5–11. The Chronicler has omitted reference to Eliab and his three sons, who perished in the rebellion of Korah (see Num. 26:8–10) and so were not relevant to the author's purpose.

Tilgath-pilneser (v. 6) is a variant of Tiglath-pileser. This Assyrian king (745–727 BC) attacked Israel (5:26; 2 Kings 15:29) and also imposed tribute on Ahaz of Judah (2 Chron. 28:19–20; 2 Kings 16:7–10).

The Hagarites (v. 10; see 5:19–22) are named among the enemies of Israel (Ps. 83:6). This tribe is apparently associated with Hagar, the mother of Ishmael (Genesis 16; but see *Zondervan KJV Study Bible* note on Psalm 83:6).

5:11–22. The materials in this list for the tribe of **Gad** (v. 11) have no parallels in the Bible. The other genealogies of Gad are organized around his seven sons (Gen. 46:16; Num. 26:15–18); here four names are given, none of which are found in the other lists. So how **Joel** (v. 12) and the following leader are connected to Gad is not known. The Chronicler states that these records came from the period of **Jotham king of Judah** (750–732 BC; v. 17) and **Jeroboam king of Israel** (793–753 BC). The presence of military

titles and narratives (vv. 12, 18–22) suggests that this genealogy originated as part of a military census. The territory of Gad is delineated in Deuteronomy 3:12.

Verses 18–22 are the first example of the Chronicler's theme of immediate retribution (see Introduction: "Theme"). Sometime during Saul's reign (see 5:10), the Transjordanian tribes engaged in a war in which the opposition was led by the Hagarites. The tribes' success in warfare is attributed to their crying out to God (v. 20; see 2 Chron. 6:24–25, 34–39; 12:7–12; 13:13–16; 14:9–15; 18:31; 20:1–30; 32:1–23).

5:23–26. Manasseh (v. 23) is treated further in 7:14–19; **the half tribe** that settled east of the Jordan is dealt with here since it shared the same fate as Reuben and Gad, and possibly also so that the Chronicler could keep the total of twelve for his tribal genealogies (see discussion on 2:1–2). Again, immediate retribution is apparent: just as trust in God can bring victory (5:18–22), so also defeat comes to the unfaithful (vv. 25–26). The use of the retributive theme in these two accounts argues for the unity of the genealogies with the historical portions of Chronicles.

The list of names given here (v. 24) is not properly a genealogy but rather a list of clans. The connection of these clan leaders to the descendants of Manasseh listed elsewhere is not indicated. Since these leaders are described as brave warriors in connection with a battle report (vv. 24–26), this section is likely derived from records of military conscription (see discussion on 5:1–10; see also 2 Kings 15:19, 29; 17:6; 18:11).

The idolatry of these Transjordanian tribes (Reuben, Gad, Manasseh; v. 26) resulted in divine punishment by exile. For the historical setting and the Assyrian whom God chose to execute this punishment, see discussions on 2 Kings 15:17–19. The Assyrian **Pul** is probably Tilgath-pilneser's (Tiglath-pileser's) throne name in Babylon (the Babylonians called him Pulu; see discussion on 2 Kings 15:19).

F. Levi (chap. 6)

6:1–81. This chapter is devoted to a series of lists, all pertaining to the tribe of Levi. The first section (vv. 1–15) records the line of the high priests up to the exile; the clans of Levi follow (vv. 16–30). David's appointees as temple musicians came from the three clans of Levi: Gershon (Gershom), Kohath, and Merari (vv. 31–47). The generations between Aaron and Ahimaaz are given a separate listing (vv. 49–53), reinforcing the separate duties of priests and Levites (see *KJV Study Bible* note on Exod. 32:26). The listing of the Levitical possessions among the tribes concludes the chapter (vv. 54–81).

6:1–15. Of **the sons of Levi** (v. 1), **Kohath** is singled out because it was from his clan that God selected **Aaron** (v. 3) and his sons to be priests.

Verses 1–3 introduce a short segmented genealogy that narrows the descendants of Levi to the lineage of **Eleazar** (v. 3), in whose line the high priests are presented in linear form (vv. 4–15). "The sons of Levi" always appear in this order, based on age (6:16; Gen. 46:11; Exod. 6:16; Num. 3:17; 26:57). Of Aaron's four sons, the first two, **Nadab** and **Abihu** (v. 3), died as a result of sacrilege (Lev. 10:2; Num. 26:61); succeeding generations of priests would trace their lineage to either Eleazar or **Ithamar**.

Verses 4–15 present a list of high priests, from the time of **Eleazar** (v. 4) to the time of the exile, that has been sharply telescoped. The Ithamar line of priests (e.g., Eli and Abiathar; see discussions on 1 Sam. 2:27–36; 1 Kings 2:26–27) constitute an interlude in Eleazar's line and are omitted. The following high priests known from the Old Testament are not mentioned: Jehoiada (2 Kings 12:2), Urijah (2 Kings 16:10–16), possibly two other Azariahs (2 Chron. 26:17, 20; 31:10–13), Eli (1 Sam. 1:9; 14:3), and Abiathar (2 Sam. 8:17). The list is repeated with some variation in Ezra 7:1–5 (see discussions there).

Ahitub begat Zadok (v. 8). Following the Ithamar interlude, the Eleazar line of priests was reinstated with Zadok. This Zadok was one of David's two priests (18:16; 2 Sam. 8:17). When David's other priest, Abiathar (see discussion on vv. 4–15), supported the rebellion of Adonijah, Zadok supported Solomon (1 Kings 1). After the expulsion of Abiathar (1 Kings 2:26–27), Zadok alone held the office (1 Chron. 29:22), which continued in his line (1 Kings 4:2). The Ahitub mentioned here (v. 7)

should not be confused with the priest who was the grandson of Eli (1 Sam. 14:3) and grandfather of Abiathar (1 Sam. 22:20); the line of Zadok replaced the line of Eli (1 Sam. 2:27–36; 1 Kings 2:26–27). For the importance of the line of Zadok, see Ezekiel 40:46; 43:19; 44:15; 48:11. Ezra was concerned to trace his own priestly lineage to this house (Ezra 7:1–5).

Hilkiah (v. 13) was the one who discovered the book of the law in the temple at the time of Josiah (2 Kings 22; 2 Chronicles 34).

Seraiah (v. 14) was executed by the Babylonians after the conquest of Jerusalem in 586 BC (2 Kings 25:18–21). **Jehozadak** was the father of Jeshua, the high priest in the first generation of the restoration. His name is also spelled "Jozadak" (Ezra 3:2, 8; 5:2; 10:18; Neh. 12:26) and "Josedech" (see Hag. 1:1; 2:2; Zech. 6:11).

6:16–30. The clans of Levi follow: **Gershom** (vv. 17–21), **Kohath** (vv. 22–28), and **Merari** (vv. 29–30).

Much of the clan of Gershom (vv. 17–19a) is repeated from Exodus 6:16–19 and Numbers 3:17–20; 26:57–61.

The arrangement of names from the clan of Kohath (vv. 22–28) is clearly a reverse, but modified, listing of the almost parallel genealogy of Heman's ancestors found later in this chapter (6:33–38). The appearance of the name **Amminadab** (v. 22) is curious. Verse 38 lists Izhar in the place of Amminadab, who is nowhere else listed as a son of Kohath, while every other list includes Izhar (vv. 2, 37–38; Exod. 6:18, 21). Either Amminadab is an otherwise unattested alternative name of Izhar or an otherwise unknown son. Or this may be another example of genealogical fluidity, in which the Levites are linked with the tribe of Judah and the lineage of David (see Ruth 4:18–22; see also Matt. 1:4; Luke 3:33) in view of Aaron's marriage to the daughter of Amminadab of Judah (Exod. 6:23; see 1 Chron. 2:10).

Korah (v. 22) was swallowed up by the earth because of his part in a rebellion against Moses and Aaron (see Num. 16:1, 32), but his children survived.

Exodus 6:24 names **Assir...Elkanah...Ebiasaph** (vv. 22–23) as sons of Korah, but here they are presented in the form ordinarily used for a linear genealogy of successive generations (see vv. 20–21, 25–26, 29–30). Either this is another example of genealogical fluidity, or one must understand "his son" as referring to Kohath and not to the immediately preceding name.

Uriel (v. 24) is possibly the one who led the Kohathites in David's day (15:5). **Zophai … Nahath … Eliab** (vv. 26–27) are apparently variant names for Zuph, Toah, and Eliel, which appear later (6:34–35).

The lineage of **Samuel** (v. 28) is also given in 1 Samuel 1:1, where his family is identified as Ephraimite (see discussion there). Either this is an example of genealogical fluidity, in which Samuel's involvement in the tabernacle (1 Samuel 3) and performance of priestly duties (9:22; 1 Sam. 2:18; 3:1) resulted in his incorporation into the Levites, or the term "Ephraimite" is to be understood as a place of residence, not as a statement of lineage.

6:31–48. Each of the three Levitical clans contributed musicians for the temple: **Heman** (v. 33) from the family of Kohath, **Asaph** (v. 39) from Gershom, and **Ethan** (v. 44) from Merari. The Chronicler makes frequent reference to the appointment of the musical guilds by **David** (v. 31; 15:16, 27; 25:1–31; 2 Chron. 29:25–26; see Neh. 12:45–47). The frequent mention of the role of the Levites has led many to assume that the author was a member of the musicians. Nonbiblical literature also attests to guilds of singers and musicians in Canaanite temples. This genealogy appears to function as a means of legitimizing the Levites of the restoration period (see Ezra 2:40–41; Neh. 7:43–44; 10:9–13, 28–29; 11:15–18; 12:24–47).

6:49–53. All Levites were not priests. Only **Aaron** (v. 49), a member of the Kohath clan, and his male descendants had the sacred duty of serving the Lord and Israel as priests. The present verses repeat 6:4–8 but presumably serve a different function: to legitimize the line of **Zadok** (v. 53), which is traced up to Solomon's time, as the only Levitical division authorized to offer sacrifices.

6:54–81. This list of Levitical possessions is taken from Joshua 21 with only minor differences (see discussions there). The Levites, who were not given a territory of their own, were distributed throughout Israel to occupy the forty-eight cities awarded them.

G. Issachar, Benjamin, Naphtali, Manasseh, Ephraim, and Asher (chaps. 7–9)

7:1–5. Parts of the genealogy of **Issachar** (v. 1) are taken from Genesis 46:13; Numbers 1:28; 26:23–25, though many of the names are otherwise unattested. Why the clan of **Tola** (v. 2) is singled out is not stated. He may have been the ancestor of the judge who bears his name (Judg. 10:1), though a direct connection can not be established. This list of the clans appears to come from a military muster (vv. 2, 4–5) from the time of David (v. 2), perhaps reflecting the census of chapter 21 and 2 Samuel 24.

7:6–12. There is considerable fluidity among the biblical sources listing **the sons of Benjamin** (v. 6). Variations occur in each account. This list gives three sons; Genesis 46:21 records ten; Numbers 26:38–39 and 1 Chronicles 8:1–2 both list five (the only name appearing in all these sources is **Bela**, the firstborn). The variations apparently reflect the different origins and functions of these genealogies. The list here appears to function in the military sphere (vv. 7, 9, 11).

7:13. This genealogy of **Naphtali** repeats Genesis 46:24; Numbers 26:48–50. Dan and Naphtali were **sons of Bilhah**; that is, they were the actual sons of Jacob's concubine Bilhah (Gen. 30:3–8), so Naphtali's sons are Bilhah's "sons."

7:14–19. See discussion on the line of **Manasseh** (v. 14) in 5:23–26. The sources for this genealogy are Numbers 26:29–34; Joshua 17:1–18. The daughters of **Zelophehad** (v. 15) prompted the rulings on the inheritance rights of women (Num. 26:29–34; 27:1–11; 36:1–12; Josh. 17:3–4). Of the thirteen different clans of the tribe of Manasseh known from these genealogies, seven are mentioned in the Samaria ostraca (about sixty-five inscribed potsherds containing records of deliveries of wine, oil, barley, and other commodities in the eighth century BC). The prominence of women in this genealogy is unusual and suggests that it may have functioned in the domestic sphere, perhaps as a statement of the social status of the various clans of Manasseh (see Introduction: "Genealogies").

7:20–29. The source for part of the genealogy of **Ephraim** (v. 20) is Numbers 26:35. If **Rephah** (v. 25) is the grandson of Ephraim, ten generations are recorded from Ephraim to Jehoshuah (v. 27), a number that fits very well the four-hundred-year interval when Israel was in Egypt. Joshua's Ephraimite ancestry (v. 26) is also mentioned in Numbers 13:8 (where he is called "Oshea"; see Num. 13:16). The raid against **Gath** (v. 21) must have taken place well before the conquest of Canaan and must have originated in Egypt. Concerning his sons **Ezer** and **Elead**, ambiguous pronouns make it difficult to determine whether they were killed by livestock thieves or while they themselves were attempting to steal livestock. The list of settlements (vv. 28–29) summarizes Joshua 16–17.

7:30–40. The genealogy of **Asher** (v. 30) follows Genesis 46:17 for the first three generations; it is also parallel to Numbers 26:44–46, except that the name **Isuah** is missing there. This genealogy reflects a military function (v. 40).

8:1–40. The inclusion of a second and even more extensive genealogy of **Benjamin** (v. 1; see discussion on 7:6–12) reflects both the importance of this tribe and the Chronicler's interest in **Saul** (v. 33). Judah, Simeon, and part of Benjamin had composed the southern kingdom (1 Kings 12:1–21), and their territory largely comprised the restoration province of Judah in the Chronicler's own time. The genealogy of Benjamin is more extensive than that of all the other tribes except Judah and Levi. The Chronicler is also concerned with the genealogy of Saul (vv. 29–38), to set the stage for the historical narrative that begins with the end of his reign (chap. 10); Saul's genealogy is repeated in 9:35–44. Several references suggest that this genealogy also originated in the military sphere (vv. 6, 10, 13, 28, 40).

8:1–5. This list of names varies from previous lists (see Gen. 46:21–22; Num. 26:38–41). Even the Chronicler's former list (see 7:6–12) offers many divergences.

8:6–28. Beginning with **the sons of Ehud** (v. 6) and ending with the **sons of Jeroham** (v. 27), this list is unique to Chronicles, having no parallel in Scripture, and its connection to Benjamin's immediate de-

scendants (8:1–5) is not stated. The identity of **Ehud** is uncertain since his father is not named. If his father (ancestor) is **Gera** (v. 5), then he is possibly the left-handed judge who killed Eglon (Judg. 3:15–22).

Presumably, the leaders referred to in verse 28 are those listed in verses 14–27. Since Jerusalem lay just within the original boundary of Benjamin's tribal territory (see Josh. 18:11, 28), one should expect to find a large Benjaminite population there during the monarchial period, just as Nehemiah describes in the postexilic period (see Neh. 11:4, 7, 31, 36).

8:29–38. This list is essentially the same as the list in 9:35–44. There Jehiel is the one who is married to **Maachah** (v. 29) and is the first father in the list.

Saul (v. 33) was Israel's first king (see 1 Sam. 9–10). For the sons of Saul, see 1 Sam. 14:49; 31:2. **Jonathan** was the firstborn and the best known of Saul's sons, both for his military prowess and for his friendship with David (1 Samuel 13–14; 18:1–4; 19:1–7; 20:1–42; 23:16–18; 2 Sam. 21:13–14). Jonathan, **Malchishua**, and **Abinadab** all died with Saul in his battle against the Philistines (10:2; 1 Sam. 31:2). **Eshbaal** is Ish-bosheth in 2 Samuel and had a short reign after Saul was killed (see also discussion on 2 Sam. 2:8).

Merib-baal (v. 34) is Jonathan's son Mephibosheth in 2 Samuel 4:4, whom David befriended (see 2 Samuel 9).

9:1. All Israel were reckoned by genealogies. The Chronicler's concern with "all Israel" is one key to why he included the genealogies (see Introduction: "Theme").

9:2–34. This list of the members of the restored community reflects the Chronicler's concern with the institutions of his own day, especially the legitimacy of officeholders.

9:2–9. The Chronicler lists **Israelites** (i.e., "laity," v. 2) in verses 3–9, **priests** in 9:10–13, and **Levites** in 9:14–34. He mentions a fourth class of returnees—**Nethinims** (lit., "given ones," i.e., the "temple servants") but does not give them a separate listing in the material that follows. They may have originally been non-Israelites who were incorporated into the Levites (Josh. 9:23; Ezra 8:20) and so are not listed apart from that tribe. Perhaps they traced their ancestry to the Gibeonites (see Josh. 9:16–27) or to others who had been enslaved by Israel. A similar office is known to have existed in the temple at ancient Ugarit. The list here is related to the one in Nehemiah 11, but less than half the names are the same in the two lists.

Among the "laity" living in Jerusalem were those from the tribes of **Ephraim, and Manasseh** (v. 3). Again reflecting his concern with "all Israel," the Chronicler shows that the returnees were not only from Judah and Benjamin but also from the northern tribes.

The returnees of **Judah** (vv. 4–6, see 2:3–6; 4:21) are traced to all three of Judah's sons **Pharez** (v. 4), **Zerah** (v. 6) and Shelah—if the word **Shilonites** (v. 5) is read as "Shelanites" (Num. 26:20). If the reading "Shilonites" is retained, the reference is to Shiloh, the important sanctuary city (Judg. 18:31; Jer. 7:12–14; 26:9).

9:10–13. The list of **priests** (v. 10) is essentially the same as that in Nehemiah 11:10–14. Since it is tied to the list of priests earlier in the genealogies (6:1–15, 50–53), contemporary Israel's continuity with her past is shown. **Jedaiah, Jehoiarib, Jachin, Malchijah,** and **Immer** (vv. 10, 12) are all names associated with the twenty-four priestly groupings that David established (see 24:7–18).

9:14–34. This section lists the nonpriestly responsibilities of the Levites and some of the men who fulfilled them.

9:14–16. Among those in the first list of Levites are **Asaph** (v. 15) and **Jeduthun** (v. 16). These men were leaders of musical groups (6:39; 16:41). Later, the Chronicler again lists the musicians (chap. 25) before the gatekeepers (chap. 26). This group of Levites lived among the **Netophathites,** a name given to those from Netophah, a town of Judah near Bethlehem (see discussion on Neh. 12:28).

9:17–21. **Shallum** (v. 17) was the head over the group of Levites known as **porters,** that is, "gatekeepers." The Chronicler gives four names, while Nehemiah 11:19 mentions only two. The chief of the gatekeepers had the honor of being responsible for the gate used by the king (Ezek. 46:1–2). The gatekeepers are also listed in chapter 26 and Ezra 2:42. These officers traced their origin to **Korah** (v. 19).

Though Korah was destroyed, his family continued (see Num. 26:11) and was important to the clan of Kohath (see discussion on 6:22, where the clan of Kohath is traced through Korah). In the early days of the tabernacle, the gatekeepers had reported to **Phinehas the son of Eleazar** (v. 20; 6:4; Num. 3:32; 25:6–13).

9:22–27. Twenty-four guard stations were manned around the clock, in three shifts; 72 men were needed for each week. With a total of 212 men, each man would have had a tour of duty approximately every three weeks (26:12–18). Additional responsibilities of the gatekeepers were varied (see 26:1–19). Some guarded the entrance to the temple (v. 23), others guarded the **treasuries** (v. 26; see 2 Chron. 31:11–12), and still others provided security for the furnishings and supplies (9:28–29).

9:28–34. The Levites not only were responsible for the temple precincts and for opening the gates in the morning; they also had charge of the chambers and supply rooms (23:28; 26:20–29) as well as the implements, supplies, and furnishings (28:13–18; Ezra 1:9–11). In addition, they were responsible for the preparation of baked goods (Exod. 25:30; Lev. 2:5–7; 7:9). The priests alone prepared the perfumed anointing oil and spices (Exod. 30:23–33).

9:35–44. The genealogy of **Saul** (v. 39) is duplicated here (see 8:29–38) as a transition to the short account of his reign, which begins the Chronicler's narration (chap. 10), and to show how his dynasty came to an end.

II. The Reign of David (chaps. 10–29)

A. The Death of Saul (chap. 10)

10:1–12. This account of Saul's dying with his sons in battle with the Philistines provides the background for David's ascent to the throne. For Saul's death, see the nearly identical passage in 1 Samuel 31:1–13.

The Philistines followed hard after Saul (v. 2). In this battle, the Philistines were intent on getting to Saul. If the leader was killed or captured, ancient armies usually fell apart (vv. 6–7; see discussion on 1 Kings 22:31). Saul died with **his three sons** (v. 6; see v. 2) and **all his house,** that is, his three sons and his chief officials (his official "house"), not all his descendants (see 8:33–34 and discussions; 1 Sam. 31:6). Ish-bosheth survived to reign for a short time (see discussion on 2 Sam. 2:10).

First Samuel 31:10 records that the Philistines fastened Saul's body to the wall of Beth-shan. Here it is stated that **his head** (v. 10), apart from his body, was fastened to the wall of the **temple of Dagon**.

10:13–14. These verses are not paralleled in the Samuel account; their inclusion here reflects the Chronicler's concern with immediate retribution (see Introduction: "Theme"). Seeking mediums was forbidden (Deut. 18:9–14) and brought death to Saul. The Chronicler is obviously writing for an audience already familiar with Samuel and Kings, and he frequently assumes that knowledge. Here the consultation with the medium at En-dor is alluded to (see 1 Samuel 28), but the Chronicler does not recount the incident.

B. Capture of Jerusalem; David's Power Base (chaps. 11–12)

11:1–29:30. See 2 Chronicles 9:31. See also Introduction: "Portrait of David and Solomon."

11:1–3. Then all Israel gathered themselves to David (v. 1). The material here parallels that in 2 Samuel 5:1–3 (see discussions there) but is recast by the Chronicler in accordance with his emphasis on the popular support given David by "all Israel." While the Chronicler twice mentions the seven-year reign at **Hebron** before the death of Ish-bosheth and the **covenant** (v. 3) with the northern tribes (3:4; 29:27), these incidents are bypassed in the narrative portion of the book. Most striking is the elimination of the information in 2 Samuel 5:4–5. The Chronicler instead paints a picture of David's immediate accession over "all Israel," followed by the immediate conquest of Jerusalem (see Introduction: "Portrait of David and Solomon"). The author once again assumes the reader's knowledge of the parallel account.

11:4–9. See 2 Samuel 5:6–10 and discussions. "All Israel" appears in verse 4 as a substitute for "the king and his men" (2 Sam. 5:6).

Verse 6 supplements the narrative of 2 Samuel. In response to David's challenge, **Whosoever smiteth**

the Jebusites first shall be chief and captain (v. 6), David's nephew **Joab** (see 2:16; 2 Sam. 17:25) was the first to enter Jerusalem, the Jebusite city, to take it (see discussion on 2 Sam. 5:8). As a reward, he retained the position that he had with David at Hebron.

11:10–41a. See 2 Samuel 23:8–39 and discussions. In the Samuel account, this list of David's "mighty men" is given near the end of his reign. The Chronicler has moved the list to the beginning of his reign and has greatly expanded it (11:41b–12:40).

11:10–14. See 2 Samuel 23:9b–11a. Again the Chronicler emphasizes the broad support of "all Israel" for the kingship of David (v. 10). These **mighty men** (v. 10) supported David and made him strong. While it is not necessary to believe that these men had performed all their heroic feats before David became king, it is likely that many had accompanied him in his exile, had been supportive of him in his rise to the throne in Hebron, and had helped secure recognition of his kingship over "all Israel."

The first in the list, **Jashobeam, a Hachmonite** (v. 11), is the Tachmonite in 2 Samuel 23:8 (see discussion there). The **three hundred slain** is probably accurately recorded as eight hundred in 2 Samuel 23:8. "Three hundred" here is apparently a copyist's mistake, perhaps influenced by the same number in 11:20.

11:15–19. Knowing that his men had put their lives at great risk to bring him **water** from **Bethlehem** (v. 17), David recognized that he was not worthy of such devotion and made the water a drink offering to the Lord (see Gen. 35:14; 2 Kings 16:13; Jer. 7:18; Hos. 9:4).

11:20–41a. Abishai ... was chief of the three (vv. 20–21). In addition to his heroism here, he accompanied David into Saul's camp when David was a fugitive from the king (see 1 Sam. 26:6–12). For "the three," see discussion on 2 Samuel 23:8. He was a noted leader in battles against the Ammonites (2 Sam. 10:10), Absalom (2 Sam. 18:2–5), and Sheba (2 Sam. 20:6). The heroics of **Benaiah the son of Jehoahaz** (vv. 22–25) listed here and his continued loyalty to the house of David placed him in good stead when Solomon became sole ruler. It was Benaiah who was ordered to kill Joab, David's long-time captain, for his bloodshed, and then Solomon made him his new captain of the army (1 Kings 2:5–6, 28–35).

The roster of "the thirty" (2 Sam. 23:13, 23) begins in verse 26 (some names appear with variant spellings in parallel text, 2 Sam. 23:24–39; see discussion there). The inclusion in this list of **Asahel** (v. 26), who was killed (see 2 Sam. 2:18–23) before David became king over all the tribes, would indicate that this list of loyal and capable men was formulated very early in David's reign.

11:41b–12:40. See discussion on 11:10–41a. The list in 2 Samuel 23 ends with **Uriah the Hittite** (v. 41; see 2 Samuel 11); the source for the sixteen additional names is not known, and no explanation is given for their inclusion. Perhaps they were included when some of the original members retired or died. The emphasis, however, continues to be on the support of "all Israel"; even Saul's own kinsmen recognized the legitimacy of David's kingship before Saul's death (12:1–7, 16–18, 23, 29).

12:1–7. Chapter 12 has no parallel in 1–2 Samuel. It emphasizes the broad-based support that had developed for David even while he was in exile from Saul. The Chronicler assumes the reader's knowledge of the events at **Ziklag** (v. 1; see 1 Samuel 27; 12:19–20), the city on Judah's border that had fallen to the Philistines. Achish, king of Gath, gave the city to David for his residence while he was in exile from Saul.

Among those who assisted David were kinsmen of Saul, from the tribe of **Benjamin** (v. 2). Perhaps the inadequacies of Saul's rule had fostered discontent among his own tribe so that some deserted him and took refuge with David (see Saul's distrust of the Benjaminites, 1 Sam. 22:7–8).

12:8–15. The defection of the men of Gad, from across the Jordan, probably occurs chronologically before David fled to Ziklag. The most appropriate time for this incident would have been in the period of David's wandering in the region of the Dead Sea (1 Sam. 23:14; 24:1; 25:1; 26:1). Identification of the stronghold is uncertain, but the strongholds of En-gedi (1Sam 23:29) would have been more convenient for contact and seems likely. So dedicated

were these men to David's cause that they crossed the **Jordan** (v. 15) river at flood time. Melting snows to the north would have brought the Jordan to flood stage **in the first month** (March–April) at the time of their crossing (see Josh. 3:15).

12:16–18. David's suspicions were aroused when certain ones from **Benjamin and Judah** (v. 16) came to him, as evidenced by his saying, **If ye be come peaceably unto me** (v. 17). He had experienced four previous betrayals: by Doeg the Edomite (1 Sam. 21:7; 22:9–10), by the residents of Keilah (1 Sam. 23:1–12), and twice by the residents of Ziph (1 Sam. 23:19ff; 26:1ff).

The spirit came upon Amasai (v. 18) is literally "the Spirit clothed Himself with Amasai." This Amasai probably should not be confused with Amasa, David's nephew, for it seems unlikely that this Spirit-empowered man would desert David to support Absalom's rebellion (2 Sam. 17:25).

12:19–22. The defection of these captains from **Manasseh** (v. 20) must have occurred just prior to the Philistines' battle with Saul at Gilboa (see 1 Samuel 29). As the Philistines prepared for battle, the lords became suspicious of David's presence among them. They mistrusted his loyalty, so he was sent back to Ziklag. En route, he would have passed through Manasseh, where he apparently was joined by these seven captains.

12:23–37. This account is peculiar to 1 Chronicles and is an enlargement of the event described in 11:1–3 (see 2 Sam. 5:1–3). The emphasis remains on "all Israel" (12:38). Armed bands from each of the tribes **came to David to Hebron** (v. 23) to entreat him to rule over a once again united monarchy. Though thirteen tribes are named including the Levites (v. 26), they are grouped in a way that maintains the traditional number of twelve (see discussion on 2:1–2). The northernmost tribes and those east of the Jordan sent the largest number of men (vv. 33–37), reinforcing the degree of support that David enjoyed not only in Judah and Benjamin but throughout the other tribes as well. The special mention of **Zakok** (v. 28) may refer to the Levite who was later made a priest, along with Abiathar (see 2 Sam.

20:25; cf 1 Kings 2:26). The decision to make David king was one of unity indeed.

The numbers in this section seem quite high. Essentially, two approaches are followed on this question: (1) It is possible to explain the numbers so that a lower figure is attained. The Hebrew word for "thousand" may represent a unit of a tribe, each having its own commander (13:1; see Num. 31:14, 48, 52, 54). In this case, the numbers would be read not as a total figure but as representative commanders. For example, the 6,800 from **Judah** (v. 24) would be read either as six commanders of 1,000 and eight commanders of 100 (see 13:1), or possibly as six commanders of thousands and 800 men. Reducing the numbers in this fashion fits well with 13:1 and with the list of commanders alone found for the family of **Zadok** (v. 28) and the tribe of **Issachar** (v. 32). Taking the numbers as straight totals would require the presence of 340,800 persons in Hebron for a feast at the same time. (2) Another approach is to allow the numbers to stand and to view them as hyperbole on the part of the Chronicler to achieve a number "like the host of God" (12:22). This approach would fit well with the Chronicler's glorification of David and with the banquet scene that follows.

12:38-40. This portrait of David is influenced by the Chronicler's messianic expectations (see Introduction: "Theme"). In the presence of a third of a million people (see discussion on 12:23-37), David's coronation banquet typifies the future messianic feast (Isa. 25:6-8). The imagery of the messianic banquet became prominent in the intertestamental literature (Apocalypse of Baruch 29:4-8; Enoch 62:14) and in the New Testament (see Matt. 8:11-12 and Luke 13:28-30; Matt. 22:1-10 and Luke 14:16-24; see also Matt. 25:1-13; Luke 22:28-30; Rev. 19:7-9). The Lord's Supper anticipates that coming banquet (Matt. 26:29; Mark 14:25; Luke 22:15-18; 1 Cor. 11:23-26).

C. Return of the Ark; Establishment of David's Kingdom (chaps. 13-16)

13:1-14. The Chronicler's material is arranged thematically; therefore, he does not always present

his material in chronological order. The events of this chapter did not occur immediately after David's coronation but at some point after his capture of Jerusalem (11:4-9), when he decided to make Jerusalem the religious center in addition to his political center. The Chronicler abandons the chronological order as given in 2 Samuel 5-6. For him, the transfer of the ark to Jerusalem takes precedence. Thus, he delays his account of the construction of the palace and the Philistine campaign until later (chap. 14). This is in accordance with his portrayal of David. David's concern with the ark was expressed immediately upon his accession; his consultation with the leaders appears to be set in the context of the coronation banquet (12:38-40). See 2 Samuel 6:1-11 and discussions.

13:1-4. These verses are not found in Samuel and reflect the Chronicler's own concerns with "all Israel." The semi-military expedition to retrieve the ark in 2 Samuel 6:1 is here broadened by consultation with and support from the whole assembly of Israel, **all the land of Israel** (v. 2), including **the priests and Levites**—an important point for the Chronicler since only they were allowed to move the ark (15:2, 13; 23:25-27; Deut. 10:8).

We inquired not at it in the days of Saul (v. 3; for details regarding the ark's safe storage at Kirjathjearim, see discussions on 1 Sam. 7:1-2). First Samuel 14:18 (see discussion there) may be an exception; for on one occasion, Saul requested that the ark be brought to him, but there is no record that his command was obeyed or that he in fact inquired of the Lord if, indeed, it was brought to him.

13:5-6. The emphasis remains on the united action of **all Israel** (v. 5). Israelites came to participate in this venture all the way from **Shihor of Egypt** in the south and from **the entering of Hemath** (i.e., Lebo Hamath, near the Orontes River) in the north. "Shihor" is an Egyptian term meaning "the pool of Horus." It appears to be a part of the Nile or one of the major canals of the Nile (see discussion on Josh. 13:3; *KJV Study Bible* note on Isa. 23:3; see also Jer. 2:18).

The ark of God (v. 5) was brought from **Baalah** (v. 6), the Canaanite name for **Kirjath-jearim** (also known as Kirjath-baal; see Josh. 18:14). The

Chronicler assumes that his readers are familiar with the account of how the ark came to be at Kirjath-jearim (1 Sam. 6:1–7:1).

13:7–14. The intention of David and Israel was commendable, but the method chosen to remove the ark from **the house of Abinadab** (v. 7) violated God's prescribed instructions for carrying it. In transporting the ark of God to Jerusalem, **Uzza and Ahio** (sons or descendants of Abinadab; see 2 Sam. 6:3) drove the ox cart. **The anger of the LORD was kindled against Uzza … because he put his hand to the ark** (v. 10). The ark was to be moved only by Levites, who carried it with poles inserted through rings in the sides of the ark (Exod. 25:12–15). None of the holy things were to be touched, on penalty of death (Num. 4:15). These strictures were observed in the second, and successful, attempt to move the ark to Jerusalem (15:1–15). It cannot be known whether Uzza and Ahio were Levites; the Samuel account does not mention the presence of Levites, but the Chronicler's careful inclusion of Levites in this expedition suggests that they were present (see discussion on 13:1–4). In any case, the ark should not have been moved on a cart (as done by the Philistines, 1 Samuel 6) or touched.

The ark was housed temporarily at the home of **Obed-edom** (v. 13). He is perhaps the same man mentioned in 15:18, 21, 24. In 26:4, God's blessing on Obed-edom included numerous sons. This reference also establishes that Obed-edom was a Levite and that the ark was properly left in his care.

14:1–17. The Chronicler backtracks to pick up material from 2 Samuel 5 that he has deferred to this point (see discussion on 13:1–14). The three-month period that the ark remained with Obed-edom (13:14) was filled with incidents showing God's blessing on David: the building of his royal house (vv. 1–2), his large family (vv. 3–7), and his success in warfare (vv. 8–16)—all because of the Lord's blessing (vv. 2, 17).

14:1–2. These opening verses closely follow the account in 2 Samuel 5:11–12 (see discussions there). **Hiram** (v. 1) later provided materials and labor for building the temple (2 Chronicles 2). His mention here implies international recognition of David's rise as king over Israel and a treaty between David and Hiram.

14:3–7. On David's polygamy, see discussions on 2 Samuel 5:13–16. For an earlier listing of his children born **at Jerusalem** (v. 3), see 3:5–9. David's children born in Hebron are omitted (see 3:1–4; 2 Sam. 3:2–5; discussion on 11:1–3). **Beeliada** (v. 7) is Eliada in 3:8 and 2 Samuel 5:16.

14:8–12. David's two early encounters with the Philistines (vv. 8–12 and 14:13–16), whereby he gained Israel's independence from them, find their parallel in 2 Samuel 5:17–25 (see discussions there).

Success against the Philistines led David to declare, **God hath broken in upon mine enemies … therefore they called the name … Baal-perazim** (v. 11). The Hebrew underlying the name of this place where the Lord broke out against the Philistines is literally "master of the breakthrough." It is the same as that underlying the word used in 13:11 when the Lord broke out against Uzza. Perez-uzza means "breakthrough of Uzza."

David gave a commandment, and they (the Philistine's "gods") **were burnt** (v. 12). Second Samuel 5:21 does not mention burning but says that David and his men carried the idols away. Many have seen here an intentional change on the part of the Chronicler in order to bring David's actions into strict conformity with the law, which required that pagan idols be burned (Deut. 7:5, 25). However, some Septuagint (the Greek translation of the Old Testament) manuscripts of Samuel agree that David burned the idols. This would indicate that the Chronicler was not innovating for theological reasons but was carefully reproducing the text he had before him, which differed from the Masoretic (traditional Hebrew) text of Samuel.

14:13–17. For a parallel account, see 2 Samuel 5:22–25 and discussions. The Chronicler concludes his account with, **the LORD brought the fear of him upon all nations** (v. 17). This statement must not be interpreted as an exaggeration made by the Chronicler to glorify David in the eyes of his readers. David's victory over the Philistines was indeed significant. He was now fully established as king, and Israel was recognized as a nation with which to be reckoned. More important, however, here and elsewhere, the Chronicler uses an expression that refers to an incapacitating terror brought on by the sense that the awful power of God was present on behalf of His people (see Exod. 15:16). Thus, David was seen by the nations as the very representative of God (compare Asa, 2 Chron. 14:14; Jehoshaphat, 2 Chron. 17:10; 20:29).

15:1 – 16:3. The story of Israel's bringing the ark to Jerusalem, which was begun in chapter 13, is resumed. Obed-edom had enjoyed blessings from the Lord during the three months when the ark was stored in his house (13:14), obviously indicating that God had not been opposed to the moving of the ark but rather to the manner in which it had been moved. This account of the successful attempt to move the ark to Jerusalem is greatly expanded compared to the material in 2 Samuel. Only 15:25 – 16:3 has a parallel (see 2 Sam. 6:12 – 19); the rest of the material is unique to the Chronicler and reflects his own interests, especially in the Levites and cultic musicians (15:3 – 24; see Introduction: "Theme"). Psalm 132 should also be read in connection with this account.

15:1. David made him houses. Preparing a place in Jerusalem for the ark followed the construction of David's own house (see 14:1 – 2 and discussion on 13:1 – 14). He **prepared a place for the ark of God … a tent.** The tent David prepared for the ark was not the Mosaic tabernacle, for it was located at Gibeon (see 21:29). No explanations are given for why the tabernacle was at Gibeon, when or how it was taken there, or why David erected another tent for the ark instead of bringing the tabernacle to Jerusalem.

15:2 – 3. In his first attempt to move the ark, David may have chosen to transport it on a new cart (see 13:7) because it was the method successfully employed by the Philistines (who were ignorant of God's instructions; see 1 Sam. 6:7 – 15). David learned through Uzza's death that God's blessing follows obedience to specific revelation (see Num. 4:4 – 15; 7:9). This time, therefore, David ordered that **None … but the Levites** (v. 2) were to transport the ark (see discussion on 13:10).

15:4 – 10. At David's summons, Levites from six clans assembled: the three well-known clans of **Kohath** (v. 5), **Merari** (v. 6), and **Gershom** (v. 7; see 6:1, 16 – 19) as well as three distinct subgroups within Kohath — **Elizaphan** (v. 8), **Hebron** (v. 9), and **Uzziel** (v. 10) — that apparently had gained the prestige to be named here. In all, 862 Levites were present.

15:11 – 15. David addressed the Aaronic priests. **Zadok** (v. 11), representing the line of Eleazar, and **Abiathar**, representing the line of Ithamar, were both priests at this time (see discussions on 6:3 – 15 and 1 Kings 2:26). **Sanctify yourselves** (v. 12). Both priests were to cleanse themselves through ritual washings and avoidance of ceremonial defilement (Exod. 29:1 – 37; 30:19 – 21; 40:31 – 32; Lev. 8:5 – 35). After properly preparing themselves, the Levites followed the prescribed manner for transporting the ark. The Chronicler provides the explanation for the failure in the first attempt to move the ark, an explanation not found in the Samuel account.

15:16 – 24. Israel's bringing the ark to Jerusalem was a joyous occasion. David arranged for the procession to be accompanied by music. A choir of Levites led by **Chenaniah** (v. 22) was joined by instrumentalists led by **Heman, Asaph, and Ethan** (v. 19), representatives of each of the Levite clans (see 6:33, 39, 44). **Obed-edom** (vv. 18, 21, 24; see discussion on 13:13) was part of the glorious procession, and **the priests, did blow with the trumpets** (v. 24; see 16:6; Num. 10:1 – 10).

15:25 – 26. Included in the procession were also **elders** (i.e., civil administrators; v. 25) and **captains** (i.e., military leaders), but it is emphasized that the Levites carried the ark.

15:27 – 28. Both 2 Samuel 6:14 and the Chronicler mention David's wearing **an ephod of linen** (v. 27), a garment worn by priests (1 Sam. 2:18; 22:18). The Chronicler adds, however, that David (as were the rest of the Levites in the procession) was wearing **a robe of fine linen**, further associating him with the dress of the cultic functionaries. Apparently, the Chronicler viewed David as a priest-king, a kind of messianic figure (see Psalm 110; Zech. 6:9 – 15).

15:29. This verse is parallel to 2 Samuel 6:16, but the Chronicler omits the remainder of the incident recorded there (2 Sam. 6:20–23). Some interpreters regard this omission as part of the Chronicler's positive view of David, whereby a possibly unseemly account is omitted. On the other hand, it is equally plausible that the Chronicler here simply assumes the reader's knowledge of the other account (see discussions on 10:13–14; 11:1–3; 12:1; 13:6).

16:1–3. When the ark was placed within the tent prepared for it, the occasion was solemnized by sacrifices. The **burnt sacrifices and peace offerings** (v. 1) showed the people's devotion to God and their fellowship with Him. David is further associated with the priests in his supervision of these sacrifices and in his exercising the priestly prerogative of blessing the people (see Num. 6:22–27; discussion on 15:27). The baked goods provided by David were for the sacrificial meal that followed the peace offerings (Lev. 3:1–17; 7:11–21, 28–36).

16:4–6. David organized certain Levites for a continuing ministry of music before the Lord. This was done in obedience to God's revelation to him through the prophets Gad and Nathan (see 2 Chron. 29:25). The Levites had appointed **Asaph** (v. 5) to be one of the leaders of music (15:17), but David now appointed him to minister before the ark in thanksgiving and praise to the Lord as part of his daily duties (see 16:37).

16:7–36. The song that follows embodies various parts of three anonymous psalms from the book of Psalms (for vv. 8–22, see Ps. 105:1–15; for vv. 23–33, see Psalm 96; for vv. 34–36, see Ps. 106:1, 47–48). The song is not here explicitly attributed to David; neither is this song found in the Samuel account.

16:8–22. The use of this lengthy historical portion from Psalm 105 (16:1–15 is very similar but not identical), emphasizing the promises to Abraham, would be particularly relevant to the Chronicler's postexilic audience, for whom the faithfulness of God was a fresh reality in their return to the land. Verses 8–12 are a call to God's people, **Israel** (v. 13), to worship Him by making known to the world the **wondrous works** (v. 9) God had performed. Verse

14 identifies Israel's God as **the LORD** (Yahweh), who entered into a covenant with Abraham and had been faithful to maintain it with his descendants throughout their wanderings (vv. 15–22).

16:23–33. Except for several minor variations, these verses parallel Psalm 96:1–13. David admonishes the whole world to join Israel in praise of the God who is indeed worthy of praise. He is the true God and He created heaven and earth. He is to be worshiped **in the beauty of holiness** (v. 29; see Ps. 29:2). All creation is called on to issue forth His praise.

16:34–36. These verses expand on Psalm 106:1, 47–48. This citation from Psalm 106 would also be of immediate relevance to the Chronicler's audience, those who had been gathered and delivered from the nations (v. 35). The song closes with thanksgiving for God's faithful love, a petition for His deliverance, and a short doxology. The people responded to the song with a confirmatory **Amen** (v. 36) and praise to the Lord.

16:37–42. David's commitment to continued worship is reiterated. **Asaph** (v. 37) was put in charge of ministry before the ark. **Zadok** (v. 39) was assigned to the **tabernacle … at Gibeon**. The tabernacle remained at Gibeon until Solomon's construction of the temple in Jerusalem (2 Chron. 1:13; 5:5), when it was placed within the temple. The existence of these two shrines—the tabernacle and the temporary structure for the ark in Jerusalem (16:1)—accounts for the two high priests: Zadok in Gibeon and Abiathar in Jerusalem (18:16; 27:34; see discussion on 6:8). **Hemen and Jeduthun** (v. 41) led the singing with the accompaniment of the **trumpets and cymbals** (v. 42).

D. Dynastic Promise (chap. 17)

17:1–27. See 2 Samuel 7 and discussions.

17:1–15. This narrative concerns David's ambition to build a house for the Lord (v. 1), Nathan's immediate approval (v. 2), and the Lord's response (vv. 2–15). God prohibited David from building (vv. 4–6) but promised David an everlasting dynasty (vv. 7–14). In this context, the words of verses 12–14 refer to Solomon, though the New Testament applies them to Jesus (Mark 1:11; Luke 1:32–33;

Heb. 1:5). Nathan delivered the Lord's message to David (v. 15). These verses are virtually identical to 2 Samuel 1–17, with some notable omissions.

In verses 1 and 10, the Chronicler omits the statement that David had rest from his enemies (2 Sam. 7:1, 11). Several factors may be at work in this omission: (1) The account of David's major wars is yet to come (chaps. 18–20). Chronologically, this passage should follow the account of the wars (v. 8), but the author has placed it here to continue his concern with the ark and the building of the temple (vv. 4–6, 12). (2) The Chronicler views David as having been a man of war through most of his life (22:6–8), in contrast to Solomon, who was the man of "rest" (22:9) and who would build the temple (22:10). For the Chronicler, David had rest from enemies only late in his life (22:18). (3) As part of his concern to parallel David and Solomon to Moses and Joshua, Solomon (like Joshua) brings the people to rest from enemies (see Introduction: "Portrait of David and Solomon").

In verse 13, the Chronicler omits from his source (2 Sam. 7:14) any reference to chastening "with the rod" or "with the stripes of the children of men" as discipline for Solomon. This omission reflects his idealization of Solomon as a messianic figure, for whom such punishment would not be appropriate (see Introduction: "Portrait of David and Solomon").

The Chronicler introduces his own concerns by changing the pronouns found in his source (2 Sam. 7:16); instead of "thine house and thy kingdom," the Chronicler says **in mine house and in my kingdom** (v. 14). This same emphasis on theocracy (God's rule) is found in several other passages unique to Chronicles (28:5–6; 29:23; 2 Chron. 1:11; 9:8; 13:4–8).

17:16–27. David ... sat before the Lord (v. 16). Aside from the parallel verse in 2 Samuel 7:18, the only other reference in the Old Testament to sitting as a posture for prayer is 1 Kings 19:4. In his prayer, David revealed no hint of disappointment that his ambition had been denied but rather confessed that he was overwhelmed and humbled to be chosen by God for His purpose (vv. 16–19). He proclaimed that none can compare with Israel's God (v. 20), nor could any other nation boast of His redemptive acts,

which Israel experienced at His hand. The references to the exodus from Egypt would have reminded the Chronicler's audience of the second great exodus, the release of the restoration community from the period of Babylonian captivity (vv. 21–22; see Deut. 4:32–39). David could do nothing more or less than yield himself to the will of God and thank Him for His goodness (vv. 23–27). For the parallel passage, see 2 Sam. 7:18–29 and discussions.

E. David's Conquests (chaps. 18–20)

18:1–20:8. The accounts of David's wars serve to show God's blessing on his reign; God kept His promise to subdue David's enemies (see 17:10). These accounts are also particularly relevant to a theme developed in the postexilic prophets: that the silver and gold of the nations would flow to Jerusalem; the tribute of enemy peoples would build the temple of God (18:7–8, 11; 22:2–5, 14–15; see Hag. 2:1–9, 20–23; Zech. 2:7–13; 6:9–15; 14:12–14). While this passage of Chronicles portrays God's blessing on David, it simultaneously explains the Chronicler's later report (22:6–8; 28:3) that David could not build the temple because he was a man of war. The material in these chapters essentially follows the Chronicler's source, 2 Samuel. The major differences are not changes the Chronicler introduces into the text, but items he chooses not to deal with—in particular 2 Samuel 9; 11:2–12:25, where accounts not compatible with his portrait of David occur.

18:1–13. See 2 Samuel 8:1–14 and discussions. This summary of David's wars with **the Philistines** (v. 1), **the Moabites** (v. 2), **the Syrians** (vv. 3–11), and **the Edomites** (vv. 12–13) contain only a few variations and additions not found in 2 Samuel 8.

In verse 2, the Chronicler omits the harsh treatment of the Moabites recorded in 2 Samuel 8:2, perhaps so that no unnecessary cruelty or brutality would tarnish his portrait of David.

The Syrians were mentioned also among the enemies of Saul (1 Sam. 14:47, "Zobah"). By the time of David, they were united north (Zobah) and south (Beth-rehob, 2 Sam. 10:6) under Hadarezer. They persisted as a foe of Israel for two centuries, until they fell to Assyria shortly before the northern kingdom likewise fell (2 Kings 16:7–9).

Tibhath and **Chun** (v. 8) are additional sites (or variations of names) of those named in 2 Samuel 8:8. These cities were located in the valley between the Lebanon and Anti-Lebanon mountain ranges. From these sites, David acquired bronze **wherewith Solomon made the brasen ... vessels**. This reference to Solomon is peculiar to Chronicles. The Chronicler, who is concerned with details relating to the temple, notes that the bronze David confiscated was later used by his son for constructing the bronze sea, pillars, and other utensils (see 2 Chron. 4:2–5, 18; 1 Kings 7:15–47).

Abishai (v. 12) is recognized for his feat over **the Edomites**, but 2 Samuel 8:13 speaks only of David. Actually, a third also receives recognition, Joab, Abishai's brother (see Psalm 60 superscription; 1 Kings 11:15–16).

18:14–17. The titles and duties of these officers at David's court appear to be modeled on the organization of Egyptian functionaries serving Pharaoh.

For the account of how **Joab** (v. 15) attained his position over the army, see 11:4–6; 2 Samuel 5:6–8. For **Zadok ... Abimelech the son of Abiathar** (v. 16), see discussions on 6:8; 16:39; 2 Samuel 8:17.

The Cherethites and the Pelethites (v. 17) apparently were a group of foreign mercenaries who constituted part of the royal bodyguard (2 Sam. 8:18; 20:23; see discussion on 1 Sam. 30:14). They remained loyal to David at the time of the rebellions of Absalom (2 Sam. 15:18) and Sheba (2 Sam. 20:7) and supported the succession of Solomon against his rival, Adonijah (1 Kings 1:38, 44). **The sons of David were chief about the king**. For "chief," the earlier narrative at this point uses the Hebrew *cohen*, a term ordinarily translated "priests" (see discussion on 2 Sam. 8:18). The Chronicler has used a term for civil service instead of sacral service. Two approaches to this passage are ordinarily followed: (1) Some scholars see here an attempt by the Chronicler to keep the priesthood restricted to the Levitical line as part of his larger concern with the legitimacy of cultic institutions in his own day. (2) Others argue that the Hebrew term used in 2 Samuel 8:18 could earlier have had a meaning broader than "priest" and could be used of some other types of officials (see 2 Sam. 20:26; 1 Kings 4:5). The Chronicler used an equivalent term, since by his day the Hebrew term for "priest" was restricted to cultic functionaries. The Septuagint, Targum, Old Latin, and Josephus all translate the term in Samuel by some word other than "priest."

19:1–20:3. The Chronicler follows 2 Samuel 10–12 closely (see discussions there), apart from his omission of the account of David's sin with Bathsheba (2 Sam. 11:2–12:25). The Ammonites were a traditional enemy of Israel (2 Chron. 20:1–2, 23; 27:5; Judg. 3:13; 10:7–9; 10:17–11:33; 1 Sam. 11:1–13; 14:47; 2 Kings 10:32–33; Jer. 49:1–6; Zeph. 2:8–11). Even during the postexilic period, Tobiah the Ammonite troubled Jerusalem (Neh. 2:19; 4:3, 7; 6:1, 12, 14; 13:4–9).

19:1–19. Following the death of **Nahash** (v. 1), possibly the same as Saul's foe (1 Sam. 11:1) or perhaps his descendant, David's act of kindness to the Ammonites was reciprocated with insult when David's ambassadors were humiliated (vv. 1–5).

David retaliated for the ill treatment by sending Joab against the Ammonites (vv. 6–15). To help defend themselves, the Ammonites hired charioteers and horsemen from **Mesopotamia, and out of Syria-maachah, and out of Zobah** (v. 6). Second Samuel 10:6 also mentions Beth-rehob and Tob. All these states were north and northeast of Israel and formed a solid block from the region of Lake Huleh through the Anti-Lebanons to beyond the Euphrates.

These Syrian recruits assembled at **Medeba** (v. 7), a town in Moab apparently controlled by Ammon. This is a detail not given in 2 Samuel 10. The battle occurred at the entrance to **the city** (v. 9), that is, the capital city, Rabbah, to which Joab would lay siege the following year (20:1–3).

The Syrians were routed (vv. 16–19). Rather than the **seven thousand** (v. 18) charioteers noted here, 2 Samuel 10:18 has 700 charioteers. And instead of **forty thousand** foot soldiers, 2 Samuel has 40,000 horsemen. Apparently, over time and in the course of transcription, some confusion occurred in the Hebrew text that makes a precise determination of some details difficult. First Chronicles 18:4–5 confirms the 7,000 charioteers. Also listed there are 20,000 foot soldiers and 22,000 horsemen ("men"), leading to the conclusion that the "forty thousand" here is perhaps a combination of both horsemen and foot soldiers, and a round number besides.

20:1. This verse corresponds to 2 Samuel 11:1 but does not continue the account of David's sin. **The time that kings go out to battle** refers to the time immediately following the spring harvest, when there was some relaxation of agricultural labors and armies on the move could live off the land. Joab besieged **Rabbah,** the site of an earlier battle (see discussion on 19:9). Rabbah is the site of modern Amman, Jordan.

20:2–3. The Chronicler assumes that the reader is familiar with 2 Samuel 12:26–29; he does not offer an explanation of how David, who had remained in Jerusalem (20:1), came to be at Rabbah.

20:4–8. Of the four campaigns against the Philistines listed in 2 Samuel 21:15–22 (see discussions there), the Chronicler mentions only the last three. The two accounts have some minor variations. In 2 Samuel 21, the site of the second and third battles was Gob, which may have been near **Gezer** (v. 4) or may have been a less familiar name for the same site. In the first battle, **Sibbechai,** one of David's valiant men (see 11:29; 27:11), was the hero who killed **Sippai ... the giant** (Hebrew, *Rephaim*; v. 4; see Gen. 14:5; Deut. 2:10–11; see also discussion on 2 Sam. 21:16).

Lahmi (v. 5) is unnamed in 2 Samuel 21:19 (see discussion there). **Weaver's beam** (see 11:23; 1 Sam. 17:7) refers to a heavy shaft on a loom and thus depicts the size of the Lahmi's massive spear.

At the battle **at Gath** (v. 6), David's nephew **Jonathan** (v. 7) was the hero, for he killed **the giant** (lit., "man of stature"; v. 6).

F. The Census (chap. 21)

21:1–22:1. See 2 Samuel 24 and discussions. Although the story of David's census is quite similar in both narratives, the two accounts function differently. In Samuel, the account belongs to the appendix (2 Samuel 21–24), which begins and ends with accounts of the Lord's anger against Israel during

the reign of David because of actions by her kings (in 2 Samuel 21, an act of Saul; in 2 Samuel 24, an act of David; see discussion on 2 Sam. 21:1–24:25). The Chronicler appears to include this story to account for the purchase of the ground on which the temple would be built. The additional material in Chronicles that is not found in Samuel (21:28–22:1) makes this interest clear. The census is the preface to David's preparations for the temple (chaps. 22–29).

21:1. See discussion on 2 Sam. 24:1. **Satan** means "adversary" or "accuser" (see discussions on Job 1:6; Zech. 3:1), but it was no mere adversary who prompted David to number the people. Here Satan is the personal name of the Devil, the Prince of Evil, who stands in opposition to God. In 2 Samuel, David's act is attributed to God's prompting. The two accounts are not contradictory but complementary. God was indeed the ultimate cause in that He was bringing justly deserved punishment upon Israel (see the context in 2 Samuel, where the census follows several rebellions against David that had gained Israel's support). Satan, though a created angel of God, is a rebel and evil, and he has only as much power as God has entrusted to him (see Job 1:6–12; 2:1–6). Here Satan is God's minister and an instrument fulfilling God's purposes.

21:2–4. Joab (v. 3) protested the wisdom of David's decision to take the census (for David's possible motivation, see discussion on 2 Sam. 24:3), but **the king's word prevailed** (v. 4). The Chronicler abridges the more extensive account of Joab's itinerary found in 2 Samuel 24:4–8; he does not mention that the census required nine months and twenty days (2 Sam. 24:8).

21:5–8. All they of Israel were a thousand thousand and an hundred thousand men ... Judah was four hundred threescore and ten thousand (v. 5). Second Samuel 24:9 has 800,000 in Israel and 500,000 (which could be a round number for 470,000) in Judah. The reason for the difference is unclear. Perhaps it is related to the unofficial and incomplete nature of the census (see 27:23–24), with the differing figures representing the inclusion or exclusion of certain unspecified groupings among the people (see v. 6). Perhaps it is simply due to a copyist's mistake.

The Chronicler adds the note that Joab exempted **Levi and Benjamin** (v. 6) from the counting. This additional note reflects the Chronicler's concern with the Levites and with the worship of Israel. The tabernacle in Gibeon and the ark in Jerusalem both fell within the borders of Benjamin.

21:9–13. Gad (v. 9) was David's longtime friend and personal **seer** (see discussion on 1 Sam. 9:9), having been with him when he was a fugitive from Saul (1 Sam. 22:3–5; see 1 Chron. 29:29; 2 Chron. 29:25). Gad presented to David his options for punishment. The first option, **three years' famine** (v. 12), is "seven years of famine" in 2 Samuel 24:13, but the Septuagint reads "three years" there.

21:14–17. The divinely sent **pestilence** (v. 14) killed 70,000 Israelites, and God's angel was poised to destroy it. Verse 16 has no parallel in the traditional Hebrew text of 2 Samuel 24, so some scholars regard it as an addition by the Chronicler reflecting the more developed doctrine of angels in the postexilic period. However, a fragmentary Hebrew text of Samuel from the third century BC, discovered at Qumran, contains the verse. It now appears that the Chronicler was carefully copying the Samuel text he had at his disposal, which differed in some respects from the Masoretic (traditional Hebrew) text. Josephus, who appears to be following the text of Samuel, also reported this information. Presumably, Josephus used a text of Samuel similar to that followed by the Chronicler.

21:18–27. The destroying **angel of the LORD commanded Gad** (v. 18) to instruct David to build **an altar ... in the threshingfloor of Ornan**. The Chronicler reports that **Ornan** (a variant of Araunah; see 2 Sam. 24:16) **was threshing wheat** (v. 20) as the king approached, having just seen the angel himself—information not found in 2 Samuel 24:20. However, Josephus and the fragmentary text of Samuel from Qumran both mention this information (see discussion on 21:16).

David paid Ornan **six hundred shekels of gold** (v. 25). Second Samuel 24:24 says fifty shekels of silver were paid for the threshingfloor and oxen. The difference has been explained by some as the Chronicler's attempt to glorify David and the temple by inflat-

ing the price. The difference is more likely explained, however, by the Chronicler's statement that this was the price for the "site" (**the place**), that is, for a much larger area than the threshingfloor alone.

God answered David **from heaven by fire** (v. 26). This underscores the divine approval and the sanctity of the site (see 2 Chron. 7:1; Lev. 9:24; 1 Kings 18:37–38). God's answering by fire would be repeated in answer to Solomon's prayer (2 Chron. 7:1) and Elijah's prayer (1 Kings 18:38).

21:28–22:1. This material is not found in 2 Samuel 24 and reflects the Chronicler's main concern in this narrative (see discussion on 21:1–22:1). Seeing that God had answered him on the site of the threshingfloor, David sacrificed there, and apparently continued to sacrifice there from that time forward.

Verses 29–30 are a parenthetical explanation of why David sacrificed at the threshingfloor. His fear of the angel of the Lord and a direct command through Gad (21:18) prevented him from going to **the tabernacle** (v. 29) and **the high place at Gibeon**.

G. Preparations for the Temple (chap. 22)

22:1–29:30. This material is unique to Chronicles and displays some of the Chronicler's most characteristic interests: the preparations for the building of the temple, the legitimacy of the priests and Levites, and the royal succession. The chapters portray a theocratic "messianic" kingdom as it existed under David and Solomon.

22:1. David dedicated this property (21:18–30) as the site for the temple (see 22:2–6; see *KJV Study Bible* note on Psalm 30 title). Compare the building site for Solomon's temple (2 Chron. 3:1).

22:2–19. Solomon's appointment to succeed David was twofold: (1) a private audience, with David and some leaders in attendance (vv. 17–19), and (2) a public announcement to the people (chap. 28), similar to when Joshua succeeded Moses (see Introduction: "Portrait of David and Solomon").

22:2–5. David's preparations for building included **strangers** (v. 2), that is, resident aliens or tolerated sojourners. From these, he appointed **masons**. Second Samuel 20:24 confirms David's use of forced labor but does not specify that these laborers were aliens and not Israelites. Solomon used Israelites in conscripted labor (1 Kings 5:13–18; 9:15–23; 11:28), but the Chronicler mentions only his use of aliens (2 Chron. 8:7–10). Though aliens were personally free, they were without political rights and could be easily exploited. The Old Testament contains frequent warnings that they were not to be oppressed (Deut. 24:14; Jer. 7:6; Zech. 7:10). Isaiah prophesied the participation of foreigners in the building of Jerusalem's walls (Isa. 60:10–12).

Among materials that David stockpiled for Solomon's future use was **brass** (i.e., bronze; v. 3), which was already noted in 18:8. David undoubtedly purchased the **cedar wood** (v. 4) through Hiram, king of Tyre (see 14:1), and also prepared the way for Solomon's future dealings with the Phoenicians (see 1 Kings 5:1–12; 2 Chron. 2:3–16).

Solomon my son is young (v. 5). Solomon's age at this time cannot be determined with certainty, though he probably was not much younger than when he became sole ruler (see discussion on 1 Kings 3:7). He came to the throne in 970 BC and was likely born circa 991 BC.

22:6–8. David **called for Solomon … and charged him** (v. 6). It does not appear that this charge is the one David issued Solomon in 1 Kings 2:1–9. **The word of the LORD came to me** (v. 8). The prophet Nathan had informed David that he was not to build a house for God (see 17:3–15; 2 Sam. 7:4–17). No written account cites David's war experience as a reason for God's denial to David's desire to build a house for Him. In 1 Kings 5:3, however, Solomon explained that David could not build the temple because he was too busy with wars. The Chronicler's nuance is slightly different—not just that wars took so much of David's time but that he was in some sense defiled by them because of the bloodshed.

22:9–11. These verses parallel somewhat 17:11–13 (see discussion; see 2 Sam. 7:12–14). A pun on Solomon's name is woven into the divine oracle ("Solomon" sounds like and may be derived from the Hebrew word for "peace"). Not only does the play on words contrast David as a man of war,

but the idea of **peace** (v. 9) implies that the whole Israelite community would experience God's blessing and attendant prosperity during Solomon's rule.

22:12–13. See Introduction: "Portrait of David and Solomon." Perhaps David's fatherly concern and desire that his son have wisdom came to Solomon's mind when he made his request for an understanding mind (see 1 Kings 3:9) and wisdom and knowledge (2 Chron. 1:10). Verse 13 is reminiscent of God's charge to Joshua (Josh. 1:7).

22:14–16. David had taken great pains to amass an extraordinary amount of supplies and wealth for the construction of the temple (see 22:3–4). Solomon was without excuse if he failed to complete the project his father had initiated.

22:17–19. David also commanded all the princes of Israel to help Solomon (v. 17; see 2 Chron. 5:1–7). All the civil and military leaders were ordered to render their full support to young Solomon, to encourage him as he endeavored to build the temple in fulfillment of David's ambition.

H. Organization of the Temple Service (chaps. 23–26)

23:1–27:34. David's preparations for the temple were not restricted to amassing materials for the building; he also arranged for its administration and worship. Unique to Chronicles (see discussion on 22:1–29:30), these details of the organization of the theocracy (God's kingdom) were of vital concern in the Chronicler's day. Characteristically, the Chronicler gives precedence to the details about religious and cultic matters (chaps. 23–26), over those that are civil and secular (chap. 27). David's arrangements provided the basis and authority for the practices of the restored community.

23:1. David was old and full of days. The reference to David's age is an allusion to 1 Kings 1, when he was about seventy years of age and in failing health (see discussion on 1 Kings 1–4). **He made Solomon his son king over Israel.** The account of Solomon's succession is resumed in chapters 28–29. The Chronicler omits the accounts of disputed succession and bloody consolidation that are recorded in 1 Kings 1–2 (see discussion on 28:1–29:30) since these would not be in accord with his overall portrait of David and Solomon (see Introduction: "Portrait of David and Solomon").

23:2–5. The Levites had been not counted in the census that had provoked the wrath of God (21:6–7), but **Now the Levites were numbered from the age of thirty years and upward** (v. 3). The census of the Levites presumably was made first in accordance with the Mosaic prescription, that is, of those ages thirty to fifty-five (Num. 4:1–3). These 38,000 Levites were divided into four groups: (1) 24,000 to supervise the work of the temple, that is, the priests and their assistants (see 24:1–19); (2) 6,000 officials and judges (see 26:29–32); (3) 4,000 **porters**, that is, gatekeepers (see 9:22–29); and (4) 4,000 musicians (see 25:1–31).

23:6–23. David grouped the Levites according to their clans: **Gershon** (vv. 7–11), **Kohath** (vv. 12–20), **and Merari** (vv. 21–23; see chap. 6; Exod. 6:16–19; Numbers 3). This list of names parallels those in 6:16–30; 24:20–30.

23:24–27. The sons of Levi … were counted by number … from the age of twenty years and upward (v. 24). Apparently, soon after the first count (23:3), David had instructed that the age be lowered to twenty years (vv. 24, 27). A similar adjustment to age twenty-five had been made under Moses (Num. 8:23–24). Perhaps the two ages here (23:3, 27) should be viewed as corresponding to the two ages in Numbers 4:3 and 8:24, where the younger age of twenty-five seems to be the age of enlistment. After a five-year apprenticeship and time of maturing, the Levites carried out full responsibilities at age thirty. Another possibility is that David simply lowered the minimum age. Perhaps he thought that once worship was centralized at Jerusalem in the temple there would be a need for a greater number of Levites to maintain the ritual at the temple.

23:28–32. Though of critical importance to the ritual at the temple, the role of the Levites was subsidiary to the priests, for their function was to assist the priests. In addition to the care of the precincts and implements, baked goods, and music (mentioned as Levitical duties in 9:22–34; see discussions there), the Chronicler adds details on the role of the Levites assisting in sacrifices (see Exod. 29:38–41; Num. 28:3–8).

24:1–19. In these verses, several lists of priests from the postexilic period are given (see 6:3–15; 9:10–13; Ezra 2:36–39; Neh. 10:1–8; 11:10–12; 12:1–7, 12–21).

24:2. Aaron's sons **Nadab and Abihu died**. The Chronicler alludes to the tragic events recorded in Leviticus 10:1–3 (see discussion on 6:1–3). They **had no children** (see Num. 3:4), so only the descendants of **Eleazar and Ithamar**, Aaron's remaining sons, were divided into groups for service.

24:3. David was assisted in dividing the priests by **Zadok**, descendant of Eleazar, and **Ahimelech**, descendant of Ithamar. Zadok and Abiathar had served as David's high priests. Here, late in David's life, Abiathar's son Ahimelech appears to have taken over some of his father's duties (see discussion on 6:8, but see also discussion on 2 Sam. 8:17).

24:4–6. Due to the greater numbers of **chief men** (i.e., leaders; v. 4) among Eleazar's descendants, David assigned **sixteen** leaders to Eleazar's line and **eight** leaders to Ithamar's line. A total of twenty-four divisions was selected **by lot** (v. 5). This would allow for service either in monthly shifts, as was done by priests in Egyptian mortuary temples, or in two-week shifts once each year, as found in New Testament times. The names of the first, second, fourth, ninth, and twenty-fourth divisions have been found in a Dead Sea scroll from the fourth cave at Qumran.

24:7–19. The twenty-four leaders of the divisions of priests are listed in the order determined by lot. According to the order in which these divisions of priests were drawn, they served in the temple on a rotating basis, presumably under the direction of Zadok and Ahimelech.

Jehoiarib (v. 7) was drawn in the first lot. Mattathias, father of the Maccabees, was a member of the Jehoiarib division (in the Apocrypha, see 1 Maccabees 2:1). **Abijah** (v. 10) was in the seventh lot. The father of John the Baptist was "of the course of Abia [Abijah]" (Luke 1:5). **Hezir** (v. 15) was in the seventeenth lot. The division from the family of Hezir was prominent in intertestamental times; the name appears on one of the large tombs in the Kidron Valley, east of Jerusalem.

24:20–31. This list supplements 23:7–23 by extending some of the lines mentioned there. Presumably, they too assisted the priests, but it is not specifically stated if these Levites were included among the twenty-four divisions and if their work was assigned on a rotating basis (see discussion above) as determined by the lot that was cast (v. 31).

25:1–6. Verse one introduces and summarizes the chapter, which recaps David's interest in and concern for the inclusion of music in the worship of God at Jerusalem (see 6:31–48; 15:16–24; 16:4–7, 37, 41, 42; 23:5). Here even the **captains of the host** (v. 1) assist him. David often sought the counsel of military leaders (11:10; 12:32; 28:1), even in cultic affairs (13:1; 15:25).

David appointed from the Levites the descendants of **Asaph ... Heman, and ... Jeduthun** (v. 1) to be official musicians in the worship services (see discussion on 6:31–48). Their purpose was to **prophesy.** There are several passages in Chronicles, largely in portions unique to these books, where cultic personnel are designated as prophets (here; 2 Chron. 20:14–17; 29:30; 35:15; see 2 Kings 23:2; 2 Chron. 34:30). Zechariah the priest also appears to function as a prophet, though he is not so named (2 Chron. 24:19–22). This may reflect the postexilic interest in the prophet-priest-king figure of messianic expectation: in Chronicles, not only do priests prophesy, but kings function as priests (see discussions on 15:27; 16:1–3). The particular prophesying of the musicians may have been their proclaiming God's message in song and accompaniment, or perhaps their writing hymns (psalms).

Heman is called **the king's seer in the words of God** (v. 5) here and in 2 Chronicles 35:15. Gad (1 Chron. 21:9) and Asaph (2 Chron. 29:30) were also called "seers." Since "seer" is comparable to "prophet" (see discussion on 1 Sam. 9:9), the role of these musicians is emphasized. Heman had **fourteen sons and three daughters.** Numerous progeny were a sign of divine blessing (see Job 1:2; 42:13; see also 1 Chron. 3:1–9; 14:2–7; 26:4–5; 2 Chron. 11:18–21; 13:21;

21:2; 24:3). This is stated specifically for Heman as the result of God's promises to exalt him.

The organization of these musicians was done according to divine command through his prophets Gad and Nathan (2 Chron. 29:25). David's organization of the temple musicians certainly reflects also his overall interest in music (1 Sam. 16:23; 18:10; 19:9; 2 Sam. 1:17–27; 6:5, 14).

25:7–8. So the number of them (v. 7), that is, Levites that were trained and skilled in music, was 288. These were divided into twenty-four groups (25:9–31). Lots were cast to determine the order in which each group would serve its term. Apparently joining these skilled musicians were the remaining 4,000 Levites who were musicians (23:5) but evidently were not considered to be as skillful.

25:9–31. The twenty-four groups of musicians are listed in the order in which they were selected to serve.

26:1–19. David's preparations for the temple included organizing **the porters** (v. 1), that is, gatekeepers. This is the most extensive of the Chronicler's lists of porters (see 9:17–27; 16:37–38). A list of porters in the postexilic period is found in Ezra 2:42 (Neh. 7:45). Their responsibilities included guarding temple property and, apparently, restricting entrance to those unqualified to enter the temple.

26:1–11. The porters listed here were the descendants of Korah (v. 1), who rebelled against Moses (see Num. 16:1–11, 16–35), and **Merari** (v. 10).

The name **Asaph** (v. 1) appears to be an abbreviation of Ebiasaph (6:23; 9:19); he should not be confused with Asaph the temple musician (25:1–2, 6).

Obed-edom (v. 4) had cared for the ark when it was left at his house (see discussion on 13:13); later, he had assisted the celebrated proper moving of the ark (16:5) and had been appointed to be a musician to minister before the ark (15:21; 16:38). Numerous sons are again a sign of divine blessing (see discussion on 25:5).

26:12–19. These divisions of porters were assigned **wards** (i.e., "duties"; v. 12; see 9:22–29) for ministering in the temple. Lots were cast to determine the place of service (i.e., at which gate), not the time or rotation of service, as was done earlier for the musicians (25:8).

The lot **eastward** (v. 14) refers to the east gate, which was the main entrance; it had six guard posts, as opposed to four at the other gates (v. 17).

The lot **southward** (v. 15) refers to the southern gate. The palaces of David and Solomon were south of the temple mount. The southern gate would have been the main one used by the king, and this assignment probably reflects particular honor for Obed-edom (see discussions on 26:4–5; see also Ezek. 46:1–10).

The gate **Shallecheth** (v. 16) is referred to only here. Presumably, it was located on the western side. The Chronicler's audience was familiar with these topographical details.

26:20–28. Another important responsibility that fell to the Levitical porters (gatekeepers) was guarding the two treasuries. The first treasury contained **the treasures of the house of God** (v. 20). The Levites in charge of these treasuries received the offerings of the people and cared for the valuable temple utensils used in worship (9:28–29).

The second treasury contained **the treasures of the dedicated things** (v. 20), that is, valuables received as gifts or plunder from warfare (vv. 27–28). Texts from Mesopotamian temples confirm the presence of temple officers who served as assayers to handle and refine the precious metals received as revenue and offerings. The Levites' handling of the offerings of the people may be seen in the reign of Joash (2 Chron. 24:4–14; 2 Kings 12:4–16). Numerous passages reflect on the wealth collected in the temple (see, e.g., 29:1–9; 2 Chron. 4:1–22; 34:9–11; 36:7, 10, 18–19; 1 Kings 14:25–28; 15:15, 18; 2 Kings 12:4–18; 14:14; 16:8; 25:13–17). **Shelomith** (v. 26) was assigned to guard **the dedicated things, which David … had dedicated** (see discussion on 18:1–20:8; see also 2 Chron. 5:1) **Out of the spoils won in battles** (vv. 26–27).

26:29–32. These verses designate the six thousand officials and judges (23:4) who would work outside Jerusalem; they were drawn from two subclans of Kohath (6:18). Deuteronomy 17:8–13 envisages a judicial function for the priests and Levites

(see 2 Chron. 19:4–11). A summary of these Levites' responsibilities is given: their duties were **in all the business of the LORD, and in the service of the king … pertaining to God, and affairs of the king** (vv. 30, 32). In the theocracy (kingdom of God), there is no division between secular and sacred, no tension between serving God and serving the king (see Matt. 22:15–22; Luke 16:10–13; Rom. 13:1–7; 1 Tim. 2:1–4; 1 Peter 2:13–17).

In David's **fortieth year** (v. 31), that is, the last year of David's reign, a search was conducted among one of the Amram clans (see 26:23), **the Hebronites**, to find capable men to serve in the above duties.

I. Administrative Structures of the Kingdom (chap. 27)

27:1–15. The names of the commanders of David's army are the same as those found in the list of his mighty men (see 11:11–47; see also 2 Sam. 23:8–39 and discussions). Those who had served David while he fled from Saul became commanders in the regular army.

27:1–8. David's military organization was comprised of twelve divisions of **twenty and four thousand** (v. 1). Questions have arisen over the large numbers of men in David's militia (see discussion on 12:23–37). Although a national militia consisting of twelve units of 24,000 each (a total of 288,000) is not unreasonable, the emphasis on unit commanders and divisions suggests that here again the Hebrew word for "thousand" perhaps represents a military unit. To designate a division as "one thousand" would be to give the upper limit of the number of men in such a unit, though such units would ordinarily not have a full complement of men. If this approach is followed, the figures in the following verses would be read as "twenty-four units" instead of "twenty and four thousand [men]."

Each division served one month out of the year and was then relieved by the next division. Over each division was a commander who had distinguished himself in the military and who was listed among David's mighty men (see 11:10–47; 2 Sam. 23:8–39) as one of either "the three" or **the thirty** (v. 6). Four of the first five captains are especially noteworthy. **Jashobeam** (v. 2) was the outstanding figure who ranked first among David's most notable heroes (see 11:11). **Dodai** (v. 4) was notable in that he was the father of Eleazar, who was one of David's prestigious "three" (see variant name Dodo in 11:12). **Benaiah** (v. 5) was among "the thirty" and almost ranked with "the three" (see 11:22–25; 18:17). He was the son of Jehoida, a priest (12:27). This was a surprisingly different role for the son of a priest, especially when it is noted that he served as Solomon's executioner (see 1 Kings 2:25, 29, 34, 46). **Asahel** (v. 7) was either an early commander as David's military organization developed or was an honorary commander (see 11:26), for he was killed when David was still king in Hebron (see 2 Sam. 2:18–23).

27:9–15. The remainder of the commanders were selected from among "the thirty" (see 11:25 and the names listed in 11:27–31).

27:16–22. The civil and tribal leaders are now listed. The Chronicler's interest in "all Israel" appears in this list of officers who were over the twelve tribes (see Introduction: "Theme"). The arrangement of the tribes as it appears here is peculiar to 1 Chronicles in that **the Levites** (v. 17) and **the Aaronites** are both listed as tribes, and both eastern and western Manasseh are listed. The number is kept at twelve, however, by excluding Gad and Asher, for which no explanation is given (see discussion on 2:1–2).

Since the tribe of Levi was represented twice, **Hashabiah** (v. 17) represented the tribe in general, while **Zadok** the priest (see discussion on 6:8; see also 12:28; 16:39) represented Aaron's family. **Elihu** (v. 18) is not named elsewhere among the brothers of David. Perhaps he is the unnamed son from the list in 2:10–17 (see discussion there). Elihu could also be a variant of the name of Jesse's oldest son, Eliab, or the term "brother" could be taken in the sense of "relative," in which case Elihu would be a more distant kinsman.

Abner (the father of Benjamin's officer, **Jaasiel**; v. 21) was a relative of King Saul (see 26:28; 1 Sam. 14:50–51), the captain of Saul's army, and the power supporting Ish-bosheth after Saul was killed (17:55–58; 26:5–16; 2 Sam. 2:8–4:1).

27:23–24. That **David took not the number of them** (v. 23) is a reference to the census narrative in chapter 21 (2 Samuel 24). In keeping with Numbers 1:3, those who were **twenty years old and under** had not been counted; that is, the figures reported in chapter 21 and 2 Samuel 24 were the numbers of those older than twenty years. **The Lord had said he would increase Israel like to the stars.** The patriarchal promises of numerous descendants (Gen. 12:2; 13:16; 15:5; 22:17) appear to have been the basis for the objections of **Joab** (v. 24) to the census (21:3; 2 Sam. 24:3). He **finished not** the census in that he did not include the tribes of Levi and Benjamin in the census (21:6).

27:25–31. A list of twelve administrators of David's property, **the substance** (v. 31), is given here. Every area of David's royal possessions was carefully supervised. The large cities of the ancient Near East had three basic economic sectors: royal, temple, and private. There is no evidence of direct taxation during the reign of David; his court appears to have been financed by extensive landholdings, commerce, plunder from his many wars, and tribute from subjugated kingdoms.

27:32–34. This list of David's cabinet members is supplementary to that in 18:14–17. **Ahithophel** (v. 33), one of the king's counselors, was replaced after he committed suicide following his support of Absalom's rebellion (2 Sam. 15:12, 31–37; 16:20–17:23). **Jehoiada the son of Benaiah** (v. 34; see discussion on 27:5) replaced him.

28:1–29:30. The account of the transition from the reign of David to that of Solomon is one of the clearest demonstrations of the Chronicler's idealization of their reigns when it is compared with the succession account in 1 Kings 1–2. The Chronicler makes no mention of the infirmities of the aged David (1 Kings 1:1–4), the rebellion of Adonijah and the king's sons (1 Kings 1:5–10), the court intrigue to secure Solomon's succession (1 Kings 1:11–31), or David's charge to Solomon to punish David's enemies after his death (1 Kings 2:1–9). The Chronicler's selection of material presents a transition of power that is smooth and peaceful and that receives the support of "all Israel" (29:25), the officials and the people (28:1–2; 29:6–9, 21–25). Instead of the bedridden David who sends others to anoint Solomon (1 Kings 1:32–35), David himself is present and in charge of the ceremonies (see 23:1 and discussion).

J. David's Final Preparations for Succession and the Temple (28:1–29:20)

28:1. For the public presentation of Solomon as David's successor, all civil and military leaders were called to Jerusalem. The assembly was composed largely of the groups named in chapter 27. Any reference to the priests and Levites is strangely omitted here (but see 32:2, where both are mentioned). This public announcement (28:5) followed the private announcement of Solomon's succession (chap. 22; see discussion on 22:2–19).

28:2–7. David related what all Israel must have known—that he had a burning desire **to build a house of rest for the ark of the covenant** (v. 2), God's "footstool" (i.e., the mercy seat or place of atonement; 28:11; Exod. 25:19–25). Israel surely would have known this because David was already making preparations for the building (see 22:2–19). David now explained publicly why he was unable to build the temple (he had privately informed Solomon earlier; see 2:7–8): **thou hast been a man of war, and hast shed blood** (v. 3; see discussion on 22:6–8).

Verses 4–6 are a clear reference to the Davidic covenant (see 17:11–14; and discussions on 2 Sam. 7:11–16). To be a king forever indicates that David's everlasting reign would culminate in the millennial reign of David's son, the Messiah (Jesus). David, God's chosen king, presented God's chosen successor. **He hath chosen Solomon my son** (v. 5; see v. 6, 28:10; 29:1). These are the only uses in the Old Testament of the Hebrew verb for "chosen" with reference to any king after David (see Introduction: "Theme"). The Chronicler's application of this term to Solomon is consistent with his depiction of him. Solomon was chosen **to sit upon the throne of the kingdom of the LORD**, a theocratic designation (see discussion on 17:14). The Chronicler does not state

the precise time and place of God's revelation to David that Solomon would succeed him. The reader has learned earlier, however, that Solomon was from birth the object of God's love (2 Sam. 12:24–25). Here David presented Solomon as God's choice both to reign and to build the temple (see 22:9–10). The Lord had said to David, **I have chosen him to be my son, and I will be his father** (v. 6).

28:8–10. Keep and seek for all the commandments of the LORD ... serve him with a perfect heart (vv. 8–9). David charged both the assembly and Solomon to obey the Lord. Obedience would be the test and security of the nation. David's fatherly admonition to Solomon does not entirely correspond to his private charge in 1 Kings 2:2–4, but the spirit of the charge is the same. This charge resumes in 28:20. See Introduction: "Portrait of David and Solomon."

28:11–19. Although Solomon is remembered as the king who built the temple, David provided Solomon with the plans for the temple. This reflects the Chronicler's modeling David after Moses: just as Moses received from God the plans for the tabernacle (Exodus 25–30), so also David received the plans for the temple (v. 19). The information recorded here shows how inclusive the details of the plans were. Listed are not only the different items of furnishings but also their weight and whether they were made of gold or silver. By the phrase **in writing by his hand upon me** (v. 19) the Chronicler may intend no more than the ordinary process of inspiration, whereby David wrote under divine influence. On the other hand, he may imply a parallel with Moses, who also received documents from the hand of the Lord (Exod. 25:40; 27:8; 31:18; 32:16).

28:20–21. Be strong and of good courage (v. 20). David's final admonition to his son is reminiscent of God's encouraging word to Joshua when he assumed the role of leader after Moses' death (Josh. 1:7, 9).

29:1. David continued his appeal to the gathered assembly to assist and support Solomon because he was inexperienced in the work **God** had **chosen** (see discussion on 28:5) him to perform. On Solomon's **young and tender** age, see discussion on 22:5.

29:2-5. David did not ask of his subjects what he himself was unwilling to do. He donated an enormous gift from his own fortune. On the basis of his example, he then appealed to the people for their voluntary gifts.

29:6-9. The Chronicler again appears to be modeling his account of David on the life of Moses (Exod. 25:1-8; 35:4-9, 20-29). The willing response of the people aided the building of both the tabernacle and the temple.

The use of the term **drams** (i.e., "darics"; v. 7) may appear anachronistic. The daric was a Persian coin, apparently named for Darius I (522-486 BC), in whose reign it first appeared (see Ezra 8:27). Since the Chronicler's readers were familiar with this coin, he could use it as an up-to-date standard of value for an earlier treasure of gold.

29:10-20. David spontaneously lifted a prayer of blessing and thanksgiving to God (note his earlier prayer of thanks, 17:16-27). The Lord is addressed as the sovereign God who is the source of all blessing (v. 12). The understanding of David needs to be that of every believer. Everything believers have comes from God. Anything that Christians give to God is merely returning to Him what is already His (v. 14).

David knew that the true measure of his people's giving was the willingness with which they gave, and he prayed that they might never lose the generosity and devotion that they now exhibited (vv. 16-18).

David closed by inviting the whole assembly to join in blessing God and worshiping Him.

K. Succession of Solomon; Death of David (29:21-30)

29:21-25. David's prayer was followed by sacrifices and offerings. The people **did eat and drink before the LORD** (v. 22; see 12:38-40 and discussion). The anointing of both Solomon and Zadok portrays the harmony between them (see Zech. 4:14; 6:13 and discussions). They **made Solomon ... king the second time** (for another notice of this event, see 23:1). Perhaps Solomon's first anointing was that recorded in 1 Kings 1:32-36 but omitted by the Chronicler

(see discussion on 28:1-29:30). However, the phrase "second time" is missing in the Septuagint, suggesting that a scribe may have added it to the Hebrew text of this passage after the Septuagint had already been translated, to harmonize the Chronicles account with that of Kings. Multiple anointings are found in the cases of both Saul (1 Sam. 10:1, 24; 11:14-15) and David (1 Sam. 16:13; 2 Sam. 2:4; 5:3).

Zadok (v. 22) was confirmed as the solitary high priest because Abiathar had disqualified himself by his participation in Adonijah's plot (1 Kings 1:7; Abiathar was later deposed as priest, 1 Kings 2:26-27).

All the princes ... and all the sons ... submitted themselves unto Solomon the king (v. 24). Compare the rebellion of Adonijah, in which the officers and sons of the king had assisted the attempted coup (1 Kings 1:9, 19, 25). The Chronicler certainly knew of Adonijah's coup and knew that Adonijah had feared for his life (1 Kings 1:50-53), but again the author bypasses a negative event that would tarnish his image of David and Solomon.

Returning to his theme of **all Israel** (v. 25), the Chronicler shows that the Lord elevated Solomon in the eyes of Israel and that he was unanimously accepted just as David had been (see 11:1, 10; 12:38-40; see also Introduction: "Theme").

29:26-30. For the length of David's reign, see 2 Samuel 5:4-5; 1 Kings 2:11 (see also discussions on 3:1-9). **A good old age** (v. 28) for David was seventy years (see discussion on 1 Kings 1:1-4; the full time of life, see Ps. 90:10). His life was **full of days, riches, and honour.** As a feature of the Chronicler's theme of immediate retribution (see Introduction: "Theme"), the righteous enjoy these blessings (see Psalm 128; Prov. 3:2, 4, 9-10, 16, 22, 33-35).

All **the acts of David** (v. 29), that is, the events of his reign, and **all the kingdoms of the countries** (v. 30), those immediately surrounding David's kingdom, were recorded in three noncanonical books: **the book[s] of Samuel ... of Nathan ... of Gad** (v. 29), which are no longer extant. Undoubtedly, the Chronicler was led by the Holy Spirit to consult these annals for his inspired record (see Introduction: "Author, Date, and Sources").

THE SECOND BOOK OF
THE CHRONICLES

INTRODUCTION

See Introduction to 1 Chronicles.

The Building of the Temple in Chronicles

The Chronicler uses the Pentateuchal history as a model for his account of the reigns of David and Solomon. Similarly, the Pentateuchal record of the building of the tabernacle affects his account of the building of the temple.

(1) The building of the tabernacle had been entrusted to Bezaleel and Aholiab (Exod. 35:30–36:7), and they provide the Chronicler's model for the relationship of Solomon and Huram (2 Chron. 2:13). It is significant that the only references to Bezaleel outside the book of Exodus are in Chronicles (1 Chron. 2:20; 2 Chron. 1:5).

Solomon is the new Bezaleel: (a) God designated both Solomon and Bezaleel by name for their tasks; they were the only workers on their projects to be chosen by name (Exod. 31:2; 35:30–36:2; 38:22–23; 1 Chron. 28:6). (b) Both were from the tribe of Judah (Exod. 31:2; 35:30; 1 Chron. 2:20; 3:10). (c) Both received the Spirit to endow them with wisdom (Exod. 31:3; 35:30–31; 2 Chron. 1:1–13), and Solomon's vision at Gibeon (2 Chron. 1:3–13) dominates the preface to the account of the temple construction (2 Chronicles 2–7). (d) Both built a brasen altar for the sanctuary (2 Chron. 1:5; 4:1; 7:7). Significantly, the brasen altar is not mentioned in the summary list of Huram's work (4:12–16). (e) Both made the sanctuary furnishings (Exod. 31:1–10; 37:10–29; 2 Chron. 4:19–22).

Similarly, Huram becomes the new Aholiab: (a) In the account of the temple building in Kings, Huram is not mentioned until after the story of the main construction of temple and palace has been told (1 Kings 7:13–45); in Chronicles, he is introduced as having been involved in the building work from the beginning, just as Aholiab worked on the tabernacle from the beginning (Exod. 31:6; 2 Chron. 2:13). (b) Kings speaks only of Huram's skill in works of brass (1 Kings 7:14); in Chronicles, however, his list of skills is the same as Aholiab's (Exod. 31:1–6; 35:30–36:2; 38:22–23; 2 Chron. 2:14). (c) Kings reports that the mother of Huram was a widow from the tribe of Naphtali (1 Kings 7:14); Chronicles, however, states that she was a widow from the tribe of Dan (2 Chron. 2:14), thus giving Huram the same ancestry as Aholiab (Exod. 31:6; 35:34; 38:23). See discussion on 2 Chron. 2:13.

(2) The plans for both the tabernacle and the temple were given by God (Exod. 25:1–30:37; see Exod. 25:9, 40; 27:8; see also 1 Chron. 28:11–19 — not mentioned in Samuel and Kings).

(3) The spoils of war were used as building materials for both the tabernacle and the temple (Exod. 3:21–22; 12:35–36; see 1 Chron. 18:6–11 — not mentioned in Samuel and Kings).

(4) The people contributed willingly and generously for both structures (Exod. 25:1–7; 36:3–7; see 1 Chron. 29:1–9 — not mentioned in Samuel and Kings).

(5) The glory cloud appeared at the dedication of both structures (Exod. 40:34–35; 2 Chron. 7:1–3).

Outline

Bibliography

Coggins, R. J. *The First and Second Books of Chronicles.* London: Cambridge University Press, 1976.

DeVries, Simon J. *1 and 2 Chronicles.* Forms of the Old Testament Literature 11. Grand Rapids, MI: Eerdmans, 1989.

Dillard, Raymond B. *2 Chronicles.* Word Biblical Commentary 15. Waco, TX: Word, 1987.

Keil, C. F. "The Books of the Chronicles." In *Biblical Commentary on the Old Testament.* Translated by Andrew Harper. Grand Rapids, MI: Eerdmans, 1957.

Payne, J. Barton. "1 and 2 Chronicles." In *Expositor's Bible Commentary,* edited by Frank E. Gaebelein, vol. 4. Grand Rapids, MI: Zondervan, 1992.

Selman, Martin J. *2 Chronicles: An Introduction and Commentary.* Tyndale Old Testament Commentaries 10B. Edited by D. J. Wiseman. Downers Grove, IL: InterVarsity, 1994.

Slotki, I. W. *Chronicles: Hebrew Text and English Translation, with an Introduction and Commentary.* Soncino Books of the Bible. London: Soncino, 1952.

Williamson, H. G. *Israel in the Book of Chronicles.* London: Cambridge University Press, 1977.

EXPOSITION

I. The Reign of Solomon (chaps. 1–9)

1:1–9:31. Beginning with Solomon's reign, the parallels between 2 Chronicles and 1–2 Kings abound, but there are significant differences to be noted. In 2 Chronicles, the account of the reign of Solomon is primarily devoted to his building of the temple (chaps. 2–7); his endowment with wisdom is mainly to facilitate the building work. Much of the material in Kings that does not bear on building the temple is omitted by the Chronicler; for example, he does not mention the judgment between the prostitutes (1 Kings 3:16–28) or the building of the royal palace (1 Kings 7:1–12).

A. The Gift of Wisdom (chap. 1)

1:1. Solomon ... was strengthened. This expression, or a variation of it, is common in Chronicles (12:13; 13:7–8, 21; 15:8; 16:9; 17:1; 21:4; 23:1; 25:11; 27:6; 32:5; 1 Chron. 11:10; 19:13). Here and in 21:4, it includes the elimination of enemies and rivals to the throne (see 1 Kings 2, especially 2:46). Not to be overlooked, however, is the fact that **the LORD his God was with him, and magnified him exceedingly.**

1:2–13. See 1 Kings 3:4–15 and discussions.

1:2–6. These verses are largely unique to Chronicles and show some of the author's concerns: (1) The support of "all Israel" (v. 2) is emphasized (see 1 Chronicles, Introduction: "Theme"). (2) While the author of Kings is somewhat apologetic about

Solomon's visit to "high places" (1 Kings 3:3), the Chronicler adds the note that this was the location of the tabernacle made by Moses in the wilderness (v. 3), bringing Solomon's action in line with the provisions of the law (Lev. 17:8–9).

Solomon ... went to the high place ... at Gibeon (v. 3). Gibeon, a small city located about seven miles northwest of Jerusalem, had become the home of the Mosaic tabernacle. From the time of Joshua (see Josh. 18:1) until the time of Eli (see 1 Sam 1:3; 4:3–4), the tabernacle resided at Shiloh. With Israel's defeat by the Philistines and the consequent loss of the ark of the covenant (1 Sam. 4:10–11), the ark and the tabernacle became separated. The ark eventually came to reside in **Kirjath-jearim** (v. 4), until David had it brought to Jerusalem (see discussions on 1 Samuel 6 and 1 Chronicles 15). The tabernacle, however, was apparently moved to Nob (see discussion on 1 Sam. 21:1) and finally came to be located at Gibeon. What precipitated the moving of the tabernacle is never stated.

The brasen altar (v. 5) from Moses' time, upon which the burnt offerings were sacrificed, was still positioned before the tabernacle. Solomon's going to Gibeon to sacrifice indicates that this was the official place of worship, even though the ark had been brought to Jerusalem. It is specifically in connection with his offering on the altar built by **Bezaleel** (Exod. 31:1–11; 38:1–2) that Solomon received the wisdom from God to reign. In the account that follows, Solomon devotes his gift of wisdom primarily to building the temple, just as Bezaleel had been gifted by God to serve as the master craftsman of the tabernacle.

1:7–13. God ... said unto him (v. 7). Both David and Solomon functioned as prophets (7:1; 29:25; 1 Chron. 22:8; 28:6, 19). **Ask what I shall give thee.** The Chronicler abridges somewhat the details of Solomon's request as they appear in 1 Kings 3:6–15 (see discussions). In acknowledging God's faithfulness to David, Solomon stated that he had been made a **king over a people like the dust of the earth in multitude** (v. 9). This was a provisional fulfillment of the promise to Abraham (Gen. 13:16; 22:17; see discussion on 1 Chron. 27:23; see Gen. 28:14).

1:14–17. The Chronicler does not include the material in 1 Kings 3:16–4:34. He moves rather to the account of Solomon's wealth in 1 Kings 10:26–29; part of this material is repeated in 2 Chronicles 9:25–28. Recounting Solomon's wealth at this point shows the fulfillment of God's promise (v. 12).

For Solomon's trade with **Egypt** (v. 16), see discussions on 1 Kings 10:26–29.

B. Building the Temple (2:1–5:1)

2:1. Solomon resolved **to build a house for the name of the Lord, and a house for his kingdom**. Although the Chronicler frequently mentions the palace Solomon built (7:11; 8:1; 9:11), it is always viewed as secondary in importance to the temple, and he gives no details of its construction (see 1 Kings 7:1–12).

2:2. The Chronicler does not mention the 30,000 Israelites under Adoniram's supervision who were conscripted for hard labor (see discussion on 1 Kings 5:13–14). His total number of foremen (3,600) exceeds the number in 1 Kings by 300 (see discussions on 2:17–18; 1 Kings 5:15–16).

2:3–10. The Chronicler's theological interests appear in his handling of Solomon's correspondence with **Huram the king of Tyre** (v. 3). In the Kings account, the correspondence was initiated by Huram (a variant of Hiram, see 1 Kings 5:1). The Chronicler omits this (and also the material in 1 Kings 5:3–5)

but adds his own material, reflecting his concerns with the temple worship (vv. 3–7).

2:4. Solomon projected the activities that would occur regularly (daily and seasonally) in the house built for his God. David had already numbered and assigned the Levites to assist in these activities (1 Chron. 23:28–31).

2:5–6. The same theological consideration of God's omniscience and transcendence is included in Solomon's letter as is shown in Solomon's later dedicatory prayer (6:18). **Great is our God above all gods** (v. 5). In a rare occurrence, an Israelite king gave witness to a heathen king of the greatness and supremacy of his God the Lord (Yahweh), the one true God.

2:7–10. See Introduction: "The Building of the Temple in Chronicles." In the Kings account, Solomon's request for a master craftsman is found late in the narrative (1 Kings 7:13). To carry out his parallel between Aholiab and Huram, the Chronicler includes it in the initial correspondence. Furthermore, here and in 2:13–14, the list of Huram's skills is expanded and matches that of Bezaleel and Aholiab (Kings is concerned only with casting bronze, or "brass").

The payment here (v. 10) differs from that reported in 1 Kings 5:11, but the texts speak of two different payments. In Kings, the payment is an annual sum delivered to the royal household of Hiram, while Chronicles speaks of one payment to the woodsmen. The goods paid are also not identical; the oil specified in Kings is of a finer quality.

2:11–16. Hiram's return letter is an expanded version of its parallel in 1 Kings 5:7–9 (see discussions there; see also 7:13–14 and discussions).

Huram my father's (v. 13) can be rendered as a personal name, "Huram-abi" (see discussion on 2:7). Perhaps the compound name (Huram-"my father") indicates that he was Hiram's chief craftsman. Kings reports that the ancestry of Huram was through a widow of Naphtali (1 Kings 7:14); Chronicles strengthens the parallel between Huram and Aholiab by assigning Huram Danite ancestry (see Exod. 31:6; 35:34). These statements are not necessarily contradictory: (1) the mother's ancestry may have been Danite, though she lived in the territory of

Naphtali, or (2) her parents may have been from Dan and Naphtali, allowing her descent to be reckoned to either. The Danites had been previously associated with the Phoenicians (Judg. 18:7).

2:17–18. See 1 Kings 5:13–18 and discussions. The Chronicler specifies that this levy of forced laborers was from **strangers** (i.e., "aliens"; v. 17) resident in the land, not from Israelites. This is not stated in the parallel passage in Kings, though 1 Kings 9:20–22 confirms that alien labor was used (see 8:8).

There were **three thousand and six hundred overseers** (v. 18; see 2:2). The number given in 1 Kings 5:16 is 3,300; however, some manuscripts of the Septuagint (the Greek translation of the Old Testament) also have 3,600. The Chronicler may have been following a text of Kings that differed from the present Masoretic (traditional Hebrew) text at this point (but see discussion on 1 Kings 5:16).

3:1–17. The Chronicler has considerably curtailed the description of the temple's construction found in Kings, omitting completely 1 Kings 6:4–20. This abridgment probably indicates that the Chronicler's audience was familiar with the details of the earlier history and that the temple of the restoration period was less elaborate than the original Solomonic structure (Hag. 2:3). On the other hand, the Chronicler goes into more detail on the furnishings and implements (3:6–9; 4:1, 6–9).

3:1–2. The Chronicler specifies the location of the construction site — in Jerusalem on **Mount Moriah** (v. 1). This is the only passage in the Old Testament in which Mount Zion is identified with Mount Moriah. The only other appearance of this name is Genesis 22:2, where Abraham was commanded to offer Isaac on one of the mountains in "the land of Moriah." The temple was to be built **in the place that David had prepared in the threshing floor of Ornan**, the very site where God had demonstrated His presence and acceptance of David's offering by igniting his sacrifice with fire from heaven (see 1 Chron. 21:18–22:1).

The commencement date was **the second month, in the fourth year** (v. 2), that is, in the spring of 966 BC (see discussion on 1 Kings 6:1).

3:3–9. The description of **the house of God** (v. 3) matches that of the "temple of the house" in 1 Kings 6:3, 19–21 (see discussions there). It was the main room between **the porch** (i.e., portico; v. 4) and **the most holy house** (v. 8). **The greater house** (v. 5) was the temple proper, that is, "the house of God" (v. 3). It was **overlaid with ... gold** (v. 5). The term "inlaid" perhaps gives a more correct picture: not that the entire interior was covered with gold leaf but that designs (**palm trees, chains**) were inlaid with gold leaf. That **the gold was gold of Parvaim** (v. 6) designates either the source of the gold (the geographical location is debated, perhaps in southeast Arabia) or a particular quality of fine gold.

The length and breadth of "the most holy house" (i.e., the Holy of Holies) is given here as **twenty cubits, and ... twenty cubits** (v. 8). It was also twenty cubits high (1 Kings 6:20), making the dimensions of the Most Holy Place a perfect cube, as probably were the dimensions of the tabernacle. In the new Jerusalem, there will be no temple (Rev. 21:22); rather, the whole city will be in the shape of a cube (Rev. 21:16), for the whole city will be the Most Holy Place.

The fact that gold is such a soft metal would make it unlikely that **nails** (v. 9) were made **of gold**. It is probable that this small amount, only fifty shekels weight (i.e., only one and a quarter pounds), represents gold leaf or sheeting used to gild the nail heads.

3:10–14. The **cherubims** (v. 10) mentioned here, though located in the Most Holy Place, are not to be confused with the cherubim above the ark of the covenant (see 5:7–8). The thirty-foot wingspan of these two cherubim extended from wall to wall in this sacred room (see discussion on 1 Kings 6:23–27).

3:14. The vail, that is, the linen curtain, is not mentioned in 1 Kings. Presumably, it hung between the temple proper and the Most Holy Place, thus corresponding to the curtain that separated the two rooms of the tabernacle (Exod. 26:31–33). Wooden doors could also be closed across the opening (4:22; 1 Kings 6:31–32; see Matt. 27:51; Heb. 9:8).

3:15–17. For the front of the temple, Solomon made **two pillars of thirty and five cubits high** (v. 15). Since 1 Kings 7:15 indicates the pillars were each eighteen cubits high (confirmed by 2 Kings 25:17; Jer. 52:21, though Jer. 52:21 in the Septuagint has thirty-five), the thirty-five cubits here probably refers to the combined height of both. Alternatively, thirty-five may be the result of a copyist's mistake. Remains of such pillars have been found in the excavations of numerous temples in the Holy Land. The pillars were given names: **Jachin, and ... Boaz** (v. 17; see Rev. 3:12). Jachin probably means "He establishes," and Boaz probably means "in Him is strength" (see 1 Kings 7:21–22).

4:1. The parallel text in Kings does not mention the construction of the main altar, the **altar of brass,** of the temple described here (1 Kings 7:22–23), though several other passages in Kings do refer to it (1 Kings 8:64; 9:25; 2 Kings 16:14). This altar, measuring about thirty feet square and fifteen feet high, dwarfed the altar at the tabernacle, which was about seven and a half feet square and four and a half feet high (Exod. 27:1). The height of this altar would have necessitated some form of ascent to it, either as an incline or steps. In spite of its large size, it still proved to be inadequate for the number of sacrifices at the temple's dedication (see 7:4–7; 1 Kings 8:62–64). Interestingly, the main altar of Solomon's temple was similar to the altar with steps that is described in Ezekiel 43:13–17.

4:2–6. The **molten sea** (v. 2) replaced the brass laver of the tabernacle (Exod. 30:18); it was used by the priests for their ceremonial washing (v. 6; Exod. 30:21). The New Testament views these rituals as foreshadowing the cleansing provided by Christ (Titus 3:5; Heb. 9:11–14). In the temple of Ezekiel, the sea, which was on the south side in front of the temple (4:10), was replaced by a life-giving river that flowed from the south side of the temple (Ezek. 47:1–12; see Joel 3:18; Zech. 14:8; John 4:9–15; Rev. 22:1–2).

Apparently circling the rim were two rows of **oxen** (v. 3; 1 Kings 7:24 has "knops"). The Hebrew for the two words is quite similar, so the difference may well be due to a copyist's mistake. Supporting this massive "sea" were **twelve oxen** (v. 4). The number is possibly symbolic of the twelve tribes, which encamped three on each side of the tabernacle during the wilderness journeys (Numbers 2; see Ezek. 48:30–35). The "sea" held **three thousand baths** (v. 5) of water (1 Kings 7:26 has "two thousand baths"). These figures could easily have been misread by the ancient scribes.

While the "sea" was for the priests' ceremonial washing, **ten lavers** (i.e., "basins"; v. 6) were made for rinsing the offerings. These lavers were placed five on each side of the "sea" (see 1 Kings 7:38–39).

4:7–10. The construction of **ten candlesticks** (i.e., lampstands) **of gold** (v. 7) is mentioned only here, although 1 Kings 7:49 lists them in the summary of furnishings and describes their location more precisely. The Mosaic tabernacle had only one lampstand (see Exod. 25:31–40). **According to their form** (see 1 Chron. 28:15) may indicate that these lamps were not necessarily of the same shape as those described in Exodus 25:31–40; possibly they resembled the style of lamp depicted in Zechariah 4:2–6. These were positioned five to each side of the room.

He made **ten tables** (v. 8) instead of one, as in the tabernacle (Exod. 25:23–30; 40:4; Lev. 24:5–9; 1 Sam. 21:1–6; Ezek. 41:22; Heb. 9:2; see 2 Chron. 13:11; 29:18). However, 1 Kings 7:48 mentions only one table of shewbread, so perhaps the ten lampstands were placed on these ten tables.

The court of the priest (v. 9) was an inner court to which only the priests had access. The larger outer courtyard was for Israel's worshipers. The tabernacle had only one courtyard.

4:11–4:22. These final verses provide a summarizing inventory of the articles Huram made and closely follow 1 Kings 7:40–50. For the articles made of **bright brass** (v. 16), that is, "polished bronze" (vv. 11–18), see discussions on 1 Kings 7:40–47 (see also 1 Chron. 18:8). The **clay** (v. 17) beds of the Jordan plain made it possible to dig molds for these bronze ("brass") castings. For the articles made of gold (vv. 19–22), see discussions on 1 Kings 7:48–50 (see also 1 Chron. 28:14–18).

5:1. Having completed all the work, Solomon collected **all the things that David his father had dedicated** and had them brought to the temple. (See discussions on 1 Chron. 18:1–20:8; 22:2–16; 29:2–5; see also 1 Chron. 26:26.)

C. Dedication of the Temple (5:2–7:22)

5:2–10. See 1 Kings 8:1–9 and discussions.

5:2–3. Solomon assembled the leadership of all the tribes (see 1 Chron. 15:25), to celebrate transporting **the ark** (v. 2) from the tent David had provided for it when he brought it to Jerusalem (as a temporary dwelling, perhaps forty years earlier; see 1 Chron. 15:1–16:6) to the new temple prepared for it. The move coincided with **the feast … in the seventh month** (v. 3), that is, the Feast of Tabernacles. In 1 Kings 8:2, the month is designated by its Canaanite name, Ethanim; the Hebrew name is Tishri. According to 1 Kings 6:38, the temple was completed in the eighth month of Solomon's eleventh year, that is, September–October 959 BC. This celebration of dedication took place either a month before the completion of the work or eleven months after, probably the latter (see discussion on 1 Kings 8:2).

5:4–10. The Chronicler notes twice (vv. 4–5) that the priests and Levites followed Mosaic directives (see Num. 4:4–15; 7:9) and carried the ark to the temple (compare David's bringing of the ark to Jerusalem, 1 Chron. 15:26; 16:1–3).

It was placed in **the oracle of the house** (v. 7), that is, **the most holy place.** The Hebrew root for "oracle" is the same as the verb "to speak," and it was in the Most Holy Place that God promised to dwell among His people and, from there, to give them guidance. The ark is there **unto this day** (v. 9), that is, unto the day of the writing of the Chronicler's source (for this oft-used phrase, see discussion on 1 Kings 8:8; see also 8:8; 10:19; 20:26; 21:10; 35:25; 1 Chron. 4:41, 43; 5:26; 13:11; 17:5).

The two tables which Moses put therein (v. 10) were all that remained in the ark of the covenant (see *Zondervan KJV Study Bible* note on Exod. 31:18; see also Exod. 32:15–16). The ark had earlier contained also the pot of manna (Exod. 16:32–34) and Aaron's rod (Num. 17:10–11; Heb. 9:4). These items were presumably lost, perhaps while the ark was in Philistine hands (see discussion on 1 Kings 8:9).

5:11–14. These verses supplement 1 Kings 8:10–11. The priests had been organized into groups to serve at the temple on a rotating basis

(see 1 Chronicles 24). The solemn occasion of the temple's dedication was of such importance that all the priests who were there purified themselves to serve. They **did not then wait by course** (v. 11); that is, they prepared to serve without regard to their place in the rotation. Likewise, all the Levites who were musicians (1 Chronicles 25) participated under the leadership of **Asaph, Heman,** and **Jeduthan** (v. 12; see discussion on 1 Chron. 6:31–48), while the **priests** blew the trumpets (see 1 Chron. 15:25; Num. 10:8).

They **praised the LORD, saying, For he is good** (v. 13). While praise was ascending, **the cloud … the glory of the LORD** (v. 14) descended and filled the temple (see 7:1–3). The glory cloud represented the presence of God. It had guided Israel out of Egypt and through the wilderness and was present above the tabernacle (Exod. 13:21–22; 40:34–38; see Ezek. 43:1–5; Hag. 2:9; Zech. 1:16; 2:10; 8:3).

6:1–11. In the audience of all Israel, Solomon gave recognition to the presence of the Lord, which was observed in the glory cloud (5:14) and **the thick darkness** (v. 1). Then he gave a brief testimony to the faithfulness of God before offering his prayer of dedication. This account's only variation from 1 Kings 8:12–21 (see discussions there) is the statement, **I chose no city … neither chose I any man … But I have chosen Jerusalem … and have chosen David** (vv. 5–6). Until David, God had not chosen any man to rule over His people in a city that He chose to be associated with by name. For verses 8–9, see David's speech in 1 Chronicles 28:2–3.

6:12–42. This lengthy section is given wholly to Solomon's prayer of dedication. Verses 12–39 are drawn almost verbatim from 1 Kings 8:23–50a. However, the Chronicler omits a portion of the prayer that is recorded in 1 Kings 8:50b–53.

6:12–21. The only major variation from the same prayer in Kings is verse 13 and the reference to the **brasen scaffold** (v. 13), or platform, that was erected for Solomon for the occasion. Some think that the Chronicler may have wished to clarify the fact that Solomon was not **before the altar** (v. 12) exercising priestly duties. On the other hand, the verse may have been dropped from Kings by a copyist's error. The phrase **spread forth his hands** occurs in verses 12–13; it is possible that the scribe copying Kings looked back to the second occurrence of the phrase and thus omitted the verse. The verse would then be present in Chronicles because it was in the particular text of Kings used by the Chronicler.

Solomon stood **before the altar of the LORD** (v. 6) and invoked the God of heaven (v. 18) who keeps His covenant with Israel to answer the prayers of His people (see discussions on the parallel passage in 1 Kings 8:22–30).

6:22–39. Solomon's prayer pertained to every foreseeable circumstance that might cause his people to cry out to the Lord. For each, he asked God to hear from heaven (see discussions on 1 Kings 8:31–46). The smaller segments of this section draw on Solomon's knowledge of Mosaic law. He prayed regarding the Israelite and the **oath … to make him swear** (v. 22; see Exod. 22:10–11; Lev. 6:3–5). He prayed regarding Israel's repentance in face of the enemy (vv. 24–25; see Lev. 26:17, 23; Deut. 28:25, 36–37, 48–57, 64; Josh. 7:11–12). He prayed concerning Israel's repentance in drought (vv. 26–27; see Lev. 26:19; Deut. 11:10–15; 28:18, 22–24) and in the face of additional afflictions (vv. 28–31; see Lev. 26:16, 20, 25–26; Deut. 28:20–22, 27–28, 35, 42). Solomon envisioned Gentiles coming to Jerusalem to worship the Lord, something the later prophets also envisaged (vv. 32–33; see Isa. 56:6–8; Zech. 8:20–23; 14:16–21; see Psalm 87). He addressed Israel's going **out to war** (v. 34; see Lev. 26:7–8; Deut. 28:6–7). The Chronicler repeatedly demonstrates God's answer to prayer in time of battle (chap. 13; 14:9–15; 18:31; 20:1–29; 25:5–13; 32:20–22). Solomon prayed for those who might repent after having been carried **captives unto a land far off** (v. 36; see 36:15–20; Lev. 26:33, 44–45; Deut. 28:49–52; 2 Kings 17:7–20; 25:1–21). To preface this last section, Solomon noted the sinful state of mankind: **There is no man which sinneth not** (see Jer. 13:23; Rom. 3:23).

6:40–42. The Chronicler replaces the ending of Solomon's prayer in 1 Kings 8:50–53 with a repetition of Psalm 132:8–10, a psalm that deals with

bringing the ark to the temple, the event that introduces the dedication of the temple in Chronicles (5:2–14). The prayer in Kings ends with an appeal based on the exodus deliverance under Moses, while in Chronicles, the appeal is based on the eternal promises to David.

7:1–22. See 1 Kings 8:54–9:9 and discussions.

7:1–3. The material in these verses is not found in 1 Kings 8. At the conclusion of Solomon's prayer, God responded immediately and climatically with a display of **fire** that **came down from heaven** (v. 1) to consume the sacrifices on the altar. This provided the same sign of divine acceptance as was given at the dedication of the tabernacle (Lev. 9:23–24) and at David's offering at the threshing floor of Ornan (a variant of Araunah; see 2 Sam. 24:16) the Jebusite (1 Chron. 21:26; see 1 Kings 18:38). While verses 1–3 are unique to Chronicles, the Chronicler has omitted Solomon's blessing of the congregation (1 Kings 8:55–61).

Once again **the glory of the LORD** (v. 1) filled and overwhelmed the place (see 5:14 and discussion). Recall also the experience of Moses following the completion of the tabernacle's construction (Exod. 40:34–35). Israel's words of praise, **For he is good; for his mercy endureth for ever** (v. 3), are identical to those they proclaimed when the ark was brought into the temple shortly before (see 5:13). Then too the glory of the Lord had filled the place and had prevented the priests from attending to their tasks.

7:4–7. For the dedication feast and the subsequent Feast of Tabernacles (4:8–10), see discussions on 1 Kings 8:62–66.

Verse 6 is unique to Chronicles and reflects the author's overall interest in **the Levites** (v. 6), especially the musicians (see 29:26–27; see discussion on 1 Chron. 6:31–48). The Chronicler then turns his attention to **all Israel** (see 1 Chronicles, Introduction: "Theme"), who stood to join in praising the Lord.

7:8–11. All Israel (v. 8) was represented at Solomon's feast, people **from the entering in of Hamath unto the river of Egypt.** The patriarchal promises of descendants were provisionally fulfilled under David and Solomon (see 1:9; 1 Chron. 27:23–24 and discussions), as well as the promises of land (Gen. 15:18–21).

In the eighth day they made a solemn assembly (v. 9). The Feast of Tabernacles was observed immediately after the dedication of the altar. At first glance, the days appear difficult to reconcile with 1 Kings 8:65–66. The **seven days** of dedication occurred in the seventh month (see 5:3), ending on the fourteenth day in order for the week of the Feast of Tabernacles (days 15–21, see Lev. 23:33–36) to be completed in fourteen days (see 1 Kings 8:65) and on the twenty-first day of the month. Apparently, at the end of the eighth day of the Feast of Tabernacles (see Lev. 23:36), that is, the twenty-second day of the month, the people were released to return to their homes (1 Kings 8:66). The people did not actually depart, however, until the twenty-third day. The Day of Atonement was on the tenth day of the seventh month (see Leviticus 16).

7:12. The LORD appeared to Solomon. This is the second time God appeared to Solomon; the first was at Gibeon (see 1:3–13; 1 Kings 9:2) when his request for wisdom was granted. This time God assured Solomon that He had heard his prayer and had accepted the temple as a place for sacrifice.

7:13–15. These verses are unique to Chronicles. Israel belonged to God. It was the only nation upon which His name had been placed. Therefore, His requirement for national blessing was national repentance and obedience. Only then would He remove their guilt and restore them to usefulness (see, e.g., 12:6–7, 12).

Once again the Chronicler's emphasis on immediate retribution is apparent (see 1 Chronicles, Introduction: "Theme"). He subsequently portrays the kings in a way that demonstrates this principle (see v. 22).

7:17–22. These verses reproduce 1 Kings 9:4–9 (see discussions there). Such words as those in verses 17–18 reinforced ancient Israel's Messianic hopes.

D. Solomon's Other Activities (chap. 8)

8:1–18. See 1 Kings 9:10–18 and discussions. Verses 13–16 are unique to Chronicles and underscore the Chronicler's concern to show continuity with the past and his association of David with Moses (see 1 Chronicles, Introduction: "Theme").

8:1–2. Twenty years (v. 1) was the time spent in building the house of the Lord (seven years) and Solomon's house (thirteen years; see 1 Kings 6:38; 7:1). The details of the construction of Solomon's own house (see 1 Kings 7:1–8) are omitted in Chronicles.

In 1 Kings 9:10–14, Solomon gave **the cities** (v. 2) to Hiram ("Huram" in Chronicles), whereas the reverse is true in Chronicles. Perhaps as part of his effort to idealize Solomon, the Chronicler does not record the fact that Hiram found these cities to be unacceptable payment (1 Kings 9:11–13) and mentions only the sequel to the story, the return of the cities to Solomon and their subsequent improvement. They may also have served as a kind of collateral against the monies owed Hiram, who returned them when the debt was satisfied (see discussion on 1 Kings 9:11). The Chronicler also says nothing about Pharaoh's gift of Gezer to Solomon (1 Kings 9:16).

8:3–6. The Chronicler records a military campaign to the north against **Hamath-zobah** (v. 3), which is not mentioned in Kings. David had also campaigned in the north against Zobah (see 1 Chron. 18:3–9; 19:6; 2 Sam. 8:3–12; 10:6–8; see 1 Kings 11:23–24). Solomon's campaign was probably retaliation for breaking a voluntary peace agreement that had been made with David.

The two cities named **Beth-horon** (v. 5) were situated on a strategic road from the coastal plain to the area just north of Jerusalem. For notes on the other cities Solomon rebuilt for defensive purposes (vv. 4–6), see discussion on 1 Kings 9:17–18.

8:7–10. There remained in the land people who **were not of Israel** (v. 7; see 2:17; 1 Chron. 22:2). For Solomon's dealings with them, see discussions on the parallel passage in 1 Kings 9:20–23. The tribute he exacted from them persisted **until this day** (v. 8), that is, until the day of the writing of the Chronicler's source.

8:11. Of special interest is the Chronicler's supplementary note on Solomon's Egyptian wife. Though he does not record Solomon's marriage to Pharaoh's daughter (see 1 Kings 3:1), the context indicates that his statement here was made in reference to her. Both 1 Kings 9:24 and Chronicles record the transfer of Pharaoh's daughter to special quarters, but only Chronicles adds the reason: not only the temple but also David's palace was regarded as **holy** because of the presence of the ark. Even though Solomon was not obedient to God's command forbidding foreign wives, his apparent sensitivity at the start led him to remove this idolatrous wife from close proximity to the holy places in Jerusalem.

8:12 – 16. In line with his overall interests, the Chronicler elaborates considerably on the sacrificial and temple provisions made by Solomon. While 1 Kings 9:25 mentions only the sacrifices at the three annual feasts, the Chronicler adds the offerings on sabbaths and new moons to conform these provisions fully to Mosaic prescription (Lev. 23:1 – 37; Num. 28 – 29).

This summary of Solomon's temple construction is fitting here (v. 16), because apart from a completed temple, Solomon's worship at Jerusalem was impossible.

8:17 – 18. See 1 Kings 9:26 – 28. This joint venture between Solomon and Huram secured for these kings the lucrative trade routes through the Mediterranean to the south Arabian Peninsula; Solomon became the middleman between these economic spheres. **Huram sent him ... ships** (v. 18), presumably ships crafted in Phoenicia and assembled at the port of Ezion-geber after being shipped overland (see 9:21).

E. Solomon's Wisdom, Splendor, and Death (chap. 9)

9:1 – 12. See 1 Kings 10:1 – 13 and discussions. The visit of the queen of Sheba portrays the fulfillment of God's promise to give Solomon wisdom and wealth (1:12). Although the themes of Solomon's wisdom and wealth are here put to the fore, a major motive for the queen's visit may have been commercial, perhaps prompted by Solomon's naval operations toward southern Arabia (8:17 – 18). On the geographical location of **Sheba** (v. 1), see discussion on 1 Kings 10:1 (see also Job 1:15; 6:19; Ps. 72:10 – 11, 15; Isa. 60:6; Jer. 6:20; Ezek. 27:22; 38:13; Joel 3:8).

The most significant variation from the account of the queen's visit in 1 Kings is found in her statement, **Blessed be the LORD thy God, which ... set thee on his throne, to be king for the LORD thy God** (v. 8; 1 Kings 10:9 has "the throne of Israel"). The queen's speech becomes the vehicle for the Chronicler's conviction that the throne of Israel is the throne of God, for whom the king ruled (see 13:18; see also discussion on 1 Chron. 17:14).

9:13 – 28. This summary of Solomon's trade and wealth reinforces the description of his trade in 1:14 – 17. See discussions on 1 Kings 10:14 – 29. Though verse 26 is not found in 1 Kings 10, the summary statement reiterates 1 Kings 4:21 (see also 2 Chron. 7:8 and discussion). Verse 27 affirms God's promise of wealth (see 1:12, 15).

9:29 – 31. See 1 Kings 11:41 – 43. As the Chronicler chose not to report on David's sin with Bathsheba, so he omits the accounts of Solomon's wives and the rebellions at the end of his reign (1 Kings 11:1 – 40), both of which would detract from his uniformly positive portrayal of Solomon. The prophets **Nathan, Ahijah,** and **Iddo** (v. 29) recorded further details of Solomon's reign. Kings refers to the "book of the acts of Solomon" (1 Kings 11:41), a noncanonical book that is no longer extant.

II. The Schism, and the History of the Kings of Judah (chaps. 10 – 36)

10:1 – 36:23. The material covering the divided monarchy in Chronicles is considerably shorter than that in Kings: twenty-seven chapters compared to thirty-six (1 Kings 12 – 2 Kings 25). Moreover, about half of this material is unique to Chronicles and shows no dependence on Kings. The most obvious reason for this is that the Chronicler has written a history of the Davidic dynasty in Judah; the history of the northern kingdom is passed over in silence except where it impinges on that of Judah. At least two considerations prompt this treatment of the divided kingdom: (1) The Chronicler is concerned to trace God's faithfulness to His promise to give David an unbroken line of descent on the throne of Israel. (2) At the time of the Chronicler, the restored community was confined to the returnees of the kingdom of Judah, who were actually the remnant of all Israel (see 1 Chronicles, Introduction: "Theme").

A. Rehoboam (chaps. 10 – 12)

In approximately 930 BC and subsequent to Rehoboam's foolish decision to follow bad counsel, the united monarchy, which had been established by David and strengthened by Solomon, divided into the northern kingdom (Israel) and the southern kingdom (Judah). In the remaining chapters, the Chronicler concerns himself with reporting on Judah's political and religious history.

10:1 – 19. See the nearly verbatim account in 1 Kings 12:1 – 20 (and discussions there). Somewhat in line with his idealization of Solomon, the Chronicler places most of the blame for the schism on the rebellious Jeroboam (see 13:6 – 7).

10:1 – 5. Rehoboam (v. 1) would reign for seventeen years (ca. 930 – 913 BC; see 12:13). For a possible reason for Rehoboam's journey to **Shechem** to receive the support of all Israel, and their petition for him to lessen the tax burden, see discussions on 1 Kings 12:1 – 5. This is the second mention of **Jeroboam** (v. 2) in Chronicles (see 9:29). The Chronicler assumes the reader's familiarity with 1 Kings 11:26 – 40.

10:6 – 11. On the **counsel** (v. 6) that Rehoboam sought, the good that he rejected and the bad that he accepted, see discussions on 1 Kings 12:6 – 11.

10:12 – 15. For Rehoboam's announcement of his decision to follow the advice of his opportunistic peers, see 1 Kings 12:12 – 15. The Chronicler reminds readers that the event was of the Lord, who was fulfilling the prophetic word of **Ahijah** (v. 15). He assumes the reader's familiarity with 1 Kings 11:29 – 33.

10:16 – 19. On the rebellion of the northern tribes and Rehoboam's senseless decision that sent Hadoram to his death, see 1 Kings 12:16 – 19. **Hadoram that was over the tribute** (i.e., the forced labor; v. 18) had held the same office under Solomon (see 1 Kings 4:6; 5:14, where he is called Adoniram). The rebellion of Israel continued **unto this day** (v. 19; see discussion on 5:9).

It appears that the Chronicler intentionally omitted any mention that Jeroboam (see 10:2) was made king over the northern tribes (see 1 Kings 12:20).

11:1 – 23. Verses 1 – 4 are parallel to 1 Kings 12:21 – 24; verses 5 – 23 are largely unique to Chronicles. The Chronicler's account of Rehoboam is a good example of his emphasis on immediate retribution (see 1 Chronicles, Introduction: "Theme"). Chapter 11 traces the rewards for obedience to the command of God (vv. 1 – 4): Rehoboam enjoys prosperity and power (vv. 5 – 12), popular support (vv. 13 – 17), and numerous progeny (vv. 18 – 23). Chapter 12 demonstrates the reverse: disobedience brings judgment.

11:1 – 4. Rehoboam's reaction to the northern tribes' rebellion was to prepare for military retaliation. The godly **Shemaiah** (v. 2) delivered God's directive opposing such a measure **to all Israel in Judah and Benjamin** (v. 3), and civil war was averted. In accordance with the Chronicler's interest in "all Israel," a variation is seen here; the parallel passage in 1 Kings 12:23 has, "the house of Judah and Benjamin, and to the remnant of the people." The function of the prophets as guardians of the theocracy (God's kingdom) is prominent in Chronicles; most of Judah's kings are portrayed as receiving advice from prophets (see 1 Chronicles, Introduction: "Theme").

God again reminded the people that His purpose is being fulfilled. **This thing is done of me** (v. 4). See 10:15.

11:5 – 10. This list of cities is not found in Kings. Rehoboam fortified his eastern, western, and southern borders but not the northern border, perhaps demonstrating his hope of the reunification of the kingdoms. He undoubtedly hoped to protect his small kingdom from the threat of an invasion from Egypt (see 12:2 – 9). All of the listed fortifications comprised a fortification line blocking all roads leading into Judah.

11:13 – 17. The Chronicler assumes the reader's familiarity with 1 Kings 12:26 – 33 (see discussions there) and has thus omitted the background of the action of **the priests and Levites** (v. 13). Jeroboam had changed the symbols of worship, the center of worship, the priesthood, and at least one of the scheduled feasts. With the initiation of these changes, the priests and Levites had two options: (1) forsake the Lord and serve Jeroboam's golden calves or (2) migrate to Judah, where the Lord was still worshiped. They chose the latter. Thus, the Levites **left their suburbs** (i.e., pasture lands) **and their possession** (v. 14; see 1 Chron. 6:54-80; Lev. 25:32-34; Num. 35:1-5; see also 1 Chronicles, Introduction: "Theme"). The record of their move to Judah is unique to Chronicles and reflects the author's concern both with the temple and its personnel and with showing that the kingdom of Judah was the remnant of all Israel.

Jeroboam, however, chose his own priests to serve **devils** (i.e., goat idols)**, and ... calves** (v. 15). The account in Kings mentions only the golden calves (for the worship of "devils," or satyrs, see Lev. 17:7).

The priest and Levites were not the only ones who migrated to Judah for religious reasons. Loyalists from all the tribes of Israel who desired to remain true to the Lord joined the migration. Israel's loss was Judah's gain because the migration of the pious ones **strengthened the kingdom of Judah** (v. 17), and the southern kingdom **walked in the way of David and Solomon**. Characteristically, the Chronicler idealizes Solomon, but contrast the portrait of Solomon in 1 Kings 11:1-13. Unfortunately, Judah apparently apostatized after **three years** (see discussion on 12:2).

11:18-22. The report on the size of Rehoboam's family is placed here as part of the Chronicler's effort to show God's blessing on his obedience (see discussion on 11:1-23). The material is not in chronological sequence with the surrounding context but summarizes events throughout Rehoboam's reign. The Chronicler uses numerous progeny as a sign of divine blessing (see 13:21; see also discussions on 21:2; 1 Chron. 25:5).

On Rehoboam's favorite wife, **Maachah the daughter of Absalom** (v. 20), and his son **Abijah** (Abijam in 1 Kings), see discussion on 1 Kings 15:2. Maachah was likely the granddaughter of Absalom, through his daughter Tamar (2 Sam. 14:27; 18:18), who was married to Uriel (2 Chron. 13:2).

Verses 21-22 explain why Rehoboam's eldest son was not appointed to be his successor.

11:23. Rehoboam **dealt wisely, and dispersed of all his children**. He may have sought to secure the succession of Abijah by assigning other sons to outlying posts, perhaps to avoid the difficulties faced by David, whose sons at court (Adonijah and Absalom) had attempted to seize power. Perhaps Rehoboam dispersed his sons throughout the country as his agents. He was thus able to maintain a firm grip on the people in the more distant parts of his kingdom.

12:1-14. See discussion on 11:1-23. Whereas obedience to the prophetic word (11:1-4) had brought blessing (11:5-23), the prophet Shemaiah now came to announce judgment for disobedience (see 1 Kings 14:25-28). While the author of Kings also reports the attack of Shishak, the Chronicler alone adds the rationale that the invasion was because Israel had forsaken the commands of God (vv. 1-2, 5).

12:1. He forsook the law of the LORD. Rehoboam did the opposite of seeking the Lord (12:5, 14; see also discussions on 24:18, 20, 24). Details of Rehoboam's and Judah's apostasy, which consequently led to divine punishment at the hand of the invading Egyptian pharaoh, Shishak, are omitted here but are given in 1 Kings 14:22-24 (see discussions there). **All Israel** sinned with Rehoboam. The term "all Israel" is used in a variety of ways in 2 Chronicles: (1) of both kingdoms (9:30), (2) of the northern kingdom (10:16; 11:13), or (3) of the southern kingdom alone (as here; 11:3).

12:2-4. The fifth year of king Rehoboam (v. 2), when **Shishak** invaded Judah, was 925 BC. The Chronicler often introduces chronological notes not found in Kings (e.g., 11:17; 15:10, 19; 16:1, 12-13; 17:7; 21:20; 24:15, 17, 23; 26:16; 27:5, 8; 29:3; 34:3; 36:21). These become a vehicle for his emphasis on immediate retribution by dividing the reigns of individual kings into cycles of obedience-blessing and disobedience-punishment. This sequence is clear for Rehoboam: three years of obedience and blessing (11:17) are followed by rebellion, presumably in the fourth year (12:1), and punishment in the fifth year (here). Shishak was the founder of the Twenty-second Dynasty of Egypt, and he ruled circa 945-924

BC. The Bible mentions this invasion only as it affected Jerusalem, but Shishak's own inscription on the wall of the temple of Amun at Karnak (Thebes) indicates that his armies swept as far north as the plain of Jezreel and Megiddo. Joining him in his campaign, among others, were the **Sukkiims** (v. 3), who were probably a group of mercenary soldiers of Libyan origin who are known from Egyptian texts.

12:5–8. In the face of the Egyptian invasion, **Shemaiah** (v. 5; see 11:1) announced judgment for Judah's disobedience, whereupon both the princes and Rehoboam humbled themselves before the Lord (see 12:12). The Chronicler has in mind God's promise in 7:14. Even after the people of Judah humbled themselves, God permitted them to remain subject to Egypt so that they might learn that it was better to serve Him than to serve pagan kings.

12:9–12. The glory of the kingdom that had been Solomon's had already begun to fade, symbolized now by the temple and palace being stripped of their gold articles, which were replaced with bronze ones.

In spite of Judah's spiritual lapse, it had not been seized totally by Canaanite religious influence, in contrast to the northern kingdom.

12:13–16. Rehoboam reigned for **seventeen years** (v. 13; see discussion on 10:1), a reign characterized by the king's doing **evil** (v. 14). **Shemaiah the prophet** (v. 15), who denounced him and warned of judgment, and **Iddo the seer** wrote of his other acts. For verses 15–16, compare 1 Kings 14:29–31.

B. Abijah (13:1–14:1)

13:1–14:1. The Chronicler's account of Abijah's reign is about three times longer than that in 1 Kings 15:1–8, largely due to Abijah's lengthy speech (13:4–12; see discussion on 28:1–27). The most striking difference in the accounts of Abijah's reign in Kings and in Chronicles is the evaluation given in each: Kings offers a negative evaluation (1 Kings 15:3), for which there was no doubt warrant, while the assessment in Chronicles is positive, in view of what the Chronicler is able to report of him. The kings' reigns, like the lives of common people, were often a mixture of good and evil.

13:1–2. The name **Abijah** ("my father is Yah," i.e., Yahweh; v. 1), is Abijam in 1 Kings (see discussion on 1 Kings 15:1). He reigned for only **three years** (913–910 BC; v. 2). **Michaiah** is a variant of Maachah (see discussion on 11:20).

13:3–4a. What incited the conflict is not stated. In the case of Rehoboam, God had forbidden war with Israel. Here God did not interfere, perhaps because Jeroboam's flagrant idolatry deserved judgment. Abijah's army of **four hundred thousand ... men** (v. 3) and Jeroboam's army of **eight hundred thousand ... men** are surprisingly large figures, but they are in line with those in 1 Chronicles 21:5 (see discussion there). Apparently, this was all-out war (contrast the "war" between Rehoboam and Jeroboam; see discussion on 1 Kings 14:30).

The precise location of **mount Zemaraim** (v. 4) in Ephraim is uncertain. The town Zemaraim was in the territory of Benjamin (Josh. 18:22), located a few miles south of Bethel; presumably, the battle was along the common border of Benjamin and Israel.

13:4b–12. Abijah's speech is unique to Chronicles and demonstrates the Chronicler's emphasis. Abijah's address is surprising. He sounds like a devout and godly king speaking with deep conviction. Yet 1 Kings 15:3 portrays him as walking "in all the sins of his father." Perhaps the Chronicler shows that Abijah was capable of acts of faith even though his life was generally characterized by disobedience to God. It is possible, however, that he used his religious arguments for political purposes, hoping to discourage Jeroboam from launching his military attack.

Hear me ... all Israel (v. 4). Here and in 13:15, the reference is to the northern kingdom (see discussion on 12:1), whereas **the kingdom** of **Israel** (v. 5), which had been given to David, refers to a united Israel of all twelve tribes (see 7:17–18; 1 Chron. 17:13–14).

Abijah represents God's covenant with David (see 1 Chron. 17:10–14) as **a covenant of salt** (v. 5). Since salt is a preservative, it would seem that the term is descriptive of a permanent covenant (see Num. 18:19).

Jeroboam's rebellion (v. 6; see discussion on 10:1–19) was followed by rotten rule. Not all in the northern kingdom are rebuked, only the leadership—a subtle appeal to those in the north who had been led into rebellion (v. 7). Abijah described Jeroboam's supporters as **children of Belial** (i.e., worthless men; see *KJV Study Bible* note on Deut. 13:13), while he described his own father, Rehoboam, as **young and tender hearted** (see 1 Chron. 22:5; 29:1), that is, immature and inexperienced, not necessarily young in years. Rehoboam was forty-one years old at the time of the schism (12:13).

Abijah properly ridiculed Jeroboam and Israel for taking on **the kingdom of the** LORD (v. 8). The house of David represented the kingdom of God (see 9:8 and discussion), but Jeroboam's objects of worship were man-made golden calves (see 1 Kings 12:25–33). Furthermore, he had **cast out the priests of the** LORD (v. 9) and staffed the sacred offices with any non-Levite who could **consecrate himself** (see 11:13–15; see Exod. 29:1).

In contrast, Abijah claimed that Judah still served the Lord, even though his own allegiance appears to be momentary and merely token. In addition to legitimate Aaronic priests (v. 9), it appears that Abijah may have claimed possession and continued use of the articles that Moses had made for the tabernacle (v. 10). It is clear, however, that the Chronicler's concern was with acceptable worship since he focuses on the legitimate priests and the observance of prescribed worship (see 1 Chron. 23:28–31).

As for the battle at hand, God was Judah's **captain** (v. 12; see Josh. 5:14–15), and the priests blowing the trumpets were God's appointed pledges that He would remember them in war (see Num. 10:9).

13:13–20. Jeroboam was unmoved by Abijah's address. His army encircled Abijah and attacked from the front and the rear. Whether God delivered Judah supernaturally through divine intervention or providentially through Abijah's army is not indicated. Interestingly, one of Israel's cities that Abijah captured was **Bethel** (v. 19), Jeroboam's southernmost site for a shrine to golden calf worship (see 1 Kings 12:28–29).

13:21–22. As the Chronicler closes his profile of Abijah's reign, he draws attention to his wives and children. Thus he continues to emphasize numerous progeny as a sign of divine blessing (see discussion on Rehoboam's children, 11:18–22).

14:1. The land was quiet ten years. For the Chronicler, peace and prosperity go hand in hand with righteous rule.

C. Asa (14:2–16:14)

14:2–16:14. This first decade of the reign of Asa (910–900 BC) preceded the invasion by Zerah (14:9–15) and was followed by twenty more years of peace, from the fifteenth (15:10) to the thirty-fifth years (15:19) of Asa's reign. Contrast this account with the statement that there was war between Asa and Baasha throughout their reigns (see 1 Kings 15:16 and discussion). The tensions between the two kingdoms may have accounted for Asa's fortifications (14:7–8), though actual combat was likely confined to raids until the major campaign was launched in Asa's thirty-sixth year (16:1). See 15:8 and discussion. Here the account of Asa's reign (910–869 BC) greatly expands on the one in 1 Kings 15:9–24. The expansions characteristically express the Chronicler's view concerning the relationship between obedience and blessing, disobedience and punishment. The author introduces chronological notes into his account to divide Asa's reign into these periods (see discussion on 12:2). For ten years, Asa did what was right and prospered (14:1–7), and an invasion by a powerful Cushite (Ethiopian) force was repulsed because he called on the Lord (14:8–15). There followed further reforms (15:1–9) and a covenant renewal in Asa's fifteenth year (15:10–18), so he enjoyed peace until his thirty-fifth year (15:19). Then came a change. When confronted by an invasion from the northern kingdom in his thirty-sixth year (16:1), Asa hired Syrian reinforcements rather than trusting in the Lord (16:2–6), and he imprisoned the prophet who rebuked him (16:7–10). In his thirty-ninth year, he was afflicted with a disease (16:12) yet steadfastly refused to seek the Lord. In his forty-first year, he died (16:13).

14:2–7. Asa did … good and right in the eyes of the LORD (v. 2). For one reared by a wicked father (see 1 Kings 15:3–4), Asa's establishment as a righteous king is a display of the grace of God.

Asa acted radically to remove rival cultic objects from the land. **The high places** (v. 3) were elevated platforms upon which cultic objects were placed and worshiped (see 1 Kings 3:2 and discussion). **The images** were free standing stones symbolizing a deity (see discussion on 1 Kings 14:23). **The groves** (Hebrew, *asherim*) were Asherah poles, that is, wooden symbols of the goddess Asherah (here and throughout 2 Chronicles; see discussions on Judg. 2:11–13; 3:5–7).

He took away … the high places (v. 5; see Deut. 12:2–3). First Kings 15:14 states that Asa did not remove the high places. This difficulty is best resolved by the Chronicler's own statement in 15:17, which is properly parallel to 1 Kings 15:14: early in his reign, Asa did attempt to remove the high places, but pagan worship was extremely resilient, and ultimately his efforts were unsuccessful (15:17). Statements that the high places both were and were not removed are also found in the account of the reign of Jehoshaphat (17:6; 20:33).

Asa's rebuilding and fortifying **cities in Judah** (v. 6) duplicated Rehoboam's efforts (11:5–12). However, Asa recognized that the peace that he and Judah enjoyed, that is, **rest on every side** (v. 7; see discussion on 15:15), was the direct result of their obedience in serving the Lord (vv. 2–5).

14:8–15. The raid by **Zerah the Ethiopian** (v. 9) is not mentioned in 1 Kings. He is literally "Zerah the Cushite." Many identify him with Pharaoh Osorkon I, second pharaoh of the twenty-second Egyptian dynasty. However, since he is not called "king" or "pharaoh" and is known as the "Cushite" or "Nubian," some prefer to identify him as an otherwise unknown general serving the pharaoh. The invasion appears to have been an attempt to duplicate the attack of Shishak thirty years earlier (12:1–12), but the results against Asa were quite different.

The place of confrontation was **the valley of Zephathah** (v. 10), which marked the entrance to a road leading to the hills of Judah and Jerusalem. **Mareshah** was one of the cities fortified earlier by Rehoboam (11:8) to protect the route mentioned here.

Asa's prayer was a remarkable display of faith. He knew he was hopelessly outnumbered (by human calculation), but more important, he knew God's victories did not depend on the number or strength of men (compare Jonathan's statement, 1 Sam. 14:6).

Details are omitted concerning Asa's victory over Zerah (see discussion on Abijah's God-given victory over Jeroboam in 13:13–20), but he pursued Zerah to **Gerar** (v. 13; see discussion on Gen. 20:1), taking **much spoil**. Much of this booty (v. 14) made its way to the storehouses of the temple (15:18; see discussion on 1 Chron. 18:1–20:8). The Chronicler attributes Asa's success in spoiling neighboring towns to **the fear of the LORD** that **came upon them** (v. 14; see discussion on 1 Chron. 14:17).

15:1–19. This chapter appears to recount a second stage in the reforms introduced by Asa, beginning with the victory over Zerah and encouraged by the preaching of Azariah (v. 1).

15:1–7. The prophet **Azariah** (v. 1), who is not mentioned elsewhere, went out to meet Asa, apparently as he returned with spoils after his victory over Zerah (14:9–15). **The LORD is with you** (v. 2). Azariah explains the reason for Asa's success, and the key to any future success: he was rightly aligned with the Lord, who blessed him.

Israel hath been without … a teaching priest (v. 3). In the Hebrew Bible, this verse has no verb, so it is difficult to determine exactly what period of history Azariah had in mind. The duties of the priests were not only to officiate at the altar but also to teach the law (see 17:7–9; Lev. 10:11).

Be ye strong therefore (v. 7). In view of his recent reform (14:3–5), his dependence on the Lord (14:11), and Israel's record of failure, Asa was encouraged to remain firm in loyalty to God and to continue strong in his work for God. It would not go unrewarded.

15:8–11. Encouraged by the prophet, Asa rid **the land of Judah and Benjamin** (v. 8) of **abominable idols** (lit., "detestable things," a term that includes anything associated with idolatry, such as shrine prostitution; see 1 Kings 15:12). The reference to **cities which he had taken from … Ephraim** is a tacit admission that there had been some fighting between Baasha and Asa prior to Asa's thirty-sixth year (16:1; see 17:1 for implied conflict between Judah and Israel). Asa's repairing **the altar of the LORD** implies that some form of desecration had occurred at the temple.

Asa's reform movement sparked a revival that was not limited to Judah. A notable number — **they fell to him … in abundance** (v. 9) — from three other tribes joined Asa when they recognized God's presence with him (compare the defection from the northern kingdom that occurred under Rehoboam, 11:13 – 17). This influx of believers from the north alarmed Baasha and caused him to take preventive measures (16:1; 1 Kings 15:17).

This gathering **in the third month, in the fifteenth year of Asa** (v. 10) would have occurred in the spring of 895 BC, the year after Zerah's invasion; see 5:19. The Feast of Weeks (or Pentecost), one of the three required pilgrimage feasts (see Exod. 23:14 – 17; Deut. 16:9 – 12), was held in the third month (Lev. 23:15 – 21) and may have been the occasion for this assembly.

15:12 – 15. They entered into a covenant to seek the LORD. This was a renewal of the covenant made at Sinai, similar to the covenant renewals in the land of Moab (Deut. 29:1), at Mount Ebal (Josh. 8:30 – 35), at Shechem (Josh. 24:25), and at Gilgal (1 Sam. 11:14; see discussion there). Later, the priest Jehoiada (23:16), as well as Hezekiah (29:10) and Josiah (34:31), would also lead in renewals of the covenant — events of primary significance in the view of the Chronicler. A major stipulation was that **whosoever would not seek the LORD** (v. 13) but would turn to other gods, that one **should be put to death** (see this basic element of covenant law, Exod. 22:20; Deut. 13:6 – 9). Asa's method of enforcing his reforms was in line with Moses' command in Deuteronomy 17:2 – 6. **All Judah rejoiced at the oath** (v. 15). Due to the threat of death for breach of the covenant, undoubtedly there were those who complied as a matter of expediency, not out of heartfelt conviction.

The LORD gave them rest round about (v. 15). Rest from enemies is part of God's blessing for

obedience in Chronicles (14:5 – 7; 15:15; 1 Chron. 22:8 – 9, 18).

15:16 – 19. Maachah … made an idol in a grove (v. 16) is literally, "Maachah made for Asherah a horrid thing" (see discussion on 14:3). For Asa's deposing of Maachah, see discussions on 1 Kings 15:13 – 15. **The high places were not taken away** (v. 17). See 14:5 and discussion.

For the chronological issues related to **the five and thirtieth year of Asa's reign**, see discussion on 16:1.

16:1. The six and thirtieth year of the reign of Asa Baasha poses a chronological problem. According to Kings, Baasha ruled for twenty-four years and was succeeded by Elah in the twenty-sixth year of Asa (1 Kings 15:33; 16:8). Obviously, Baasha could not have been alive in the thirty-sixth year of Asa, where this passage places him; he had been dead for a decade. To solve this difficulty, some suggest that here and in 15:19, the Chronicler is dating from the schism in Israel rather than from the year number of Asa's reign. Since Rehoboam had reigned seventeen years and Abijah reigned three years, twenty years are deducted, with the result that the thirty-fifth and thirty-sixth years of Asa are in fact the fifteenth and sixteenth years of his reign. This would make Baasha's attack a possible response to the defections from the northern kingdom (15:9). While this solution may be possible, it has not been met with general acceptance. The action described here is not dated in 1 Kings 15:17. Perhaps the dates here and in 15:19 are the result of a copyist's error (possibly for an original "twenty-fifth year" in 15:19 and a "twenty-sixth year" here in 16:1).

For Baasha's motivation for rebuilding Ramah, see discussion on 1 Kings 15:17.

16:2 – 6. For Asa's panic-stricken, God-abandoning reaction and the immediate results, see discussions on 1 Kings 15:18 – 22. His hiring of foreign troops brought him into a foreign alliance, which showed a lack of trust in the Lord. Other examples of condemned foreign alliances are found in the reigns of Jehoshaphat (20:35 – 37), Ahaziah (22:1 – 9), and Ahaz (28:16 – 21). By hiring **Ben-hadad** (v. 2) to the north, Asa opened a two-front war for Baasha and forced his withdrawal.

16:7-10. The corresponding account in 1 Kings 15 lacks this severe four-point rebuke that **Hanani the seer** (v. 7; see 1 Sam. 9:9) sent to Asa. (1) If Asa had trusted God, he could have defeated not only Israel but Syria as well. (2) Asa should have trusted God because he had already seen God destroy **the Ethiopian and the Lubims** (i.e., Lybians; v. 8; see 14:12). (3) The Lord eagerly watches for opportunities to help those who trust Him. (4) Due to Asa's foolish and deliberate sin in not trusting God, he was destined to **have wars** (v. 9).

Asa was wroth with the seer (v. 10). Instead of being repentant, Asa took out his anger on Hanani and imprisoned him. Those citizens whom Asa had oppressed may have been those who sought the prophet's release.

16:11-14. During the last three years of his reign, Asa **was diseased in his feet** (v. 12). For other examples of disease as punishment for sin see 21:16-20; 26:16-23; 2 Kings 15:5; Acts 12:23. **He sought not to the LORD, but to the physicians.** The Chronicler does not necessarily condemn Asa for consulting physicians, but he is amazed that Asa was so hardened that he did not seek the Lord even when he was seriously ill.

They made a very great burning for him (v. 14). This does not refer to cremation subsequent to ritual burial but to the burning of spices in honor of a worthy king (see Jer. 34:5).

D. Jehoshaphat (17:1-21:3)

17:1-21:3. The Chronicler's account of Jehoshaphat's reign is more than twice as long as that in Kings (17:1-19 is unique). In Kings, the interest in Ahab and Elijah overshadows the space allotted to Jehoshaphat (1 Kings 22:1-46). The Chronicler uses Jehoshaphat's reign to again emphasize immediate retribution. This theme is specifically announced in 19:10 and is illustrated in the blessing of Jehoshaphat's obedient faith and in the reproof for his wrongdoing (19:2-3; 20:35-37). Jehoshaphat reigned from 872 to 848 BC. From 872 to 869 BC, he likely was coregent

with his father, Asa (see 20:31 and discussion). The details of Jehoshaphat's reign may not be in chronological order; the teaching mission of 17:7-9 may have been part of the reforms noted in 19:4-11.

17:1-2. To protect Judah from an attack by the northern kingdom, which was ruled by wicked Ahab at this time, Jehoshaphat stationed troops in fortified **cities of Judah ... cities of Ephraim** (v. 2; see discussion on 15:8). Abijah (13:19), Asa (15:8), and now Jehoshaphat had managed to hold these cities; they would be lost under Amaziah (25:17-24).

17:3-6. He walked in the first ways of his father David (v. 3). The Septuagint (the Greek translation of the Old Testament) says Jehoshaphat followed the example of his father's (i.e., Asa's) early years. The Hebrew Bible cites the example of "his father David." Whichever text is preferred (Hebrew or Greek), the Chronicler notes that the latter days of David (or Asa) were less exemplary than the former.

Jehoshaphat **sought not unto Baalim ... walked ... not after the doings of Israel** (vv. 3-4). He did not worship Baal, who had been introduced wholesale in Israel by Ahab and Jezebel (see 1 Kings 16:29-33 and discussions). The "doings" of Israel certainly included the idolatrous worship of the golden calves at Dan and Bethel (1 Kings 12:28-30).

His heart was lift up in the ways of the LORD (v. 6). The Hebrew is literally, "His heart was lofty," a phrase that usually has the negative nuance of being haughty (see 26:16; 32:25; Ezek. 28:2, 5, 17). Here it is positive. Jehoshaphat took pride or was encouraged in the ways of the Lord. **He took away the high places.** Just as his father Asa had attempted to remove the high places, only to have them be restored (14:5; 15:17), so also Jehoshaphat removed them initially, only to have them revive and persist (20:33; see 1 Kings 22:43). But see discussions on 1 Kings 3:2; 15:14. For the **groves** (Hebrew, *asherim*), see discussion on 14:3.

17:7-9. This incident may have been part of the reform more fully detailed in 19:4-11. Jehoshaphat was in effect initiating the first itinerate Bible teaching team to be sponsored by the crown. These laymen accompanied certain Levites and priests to teach the book of the law, that is, the law of Moses, in Judah (see 15:3; Lev. 10:11). In the theocracy, the law of the Lord was supposed to be an integral part of the law of the land; the king and his officials, as well as the priests and prophets, were representatives of the Lord's kingship over His people.

This occurred **in the third year of his reign** (v. 7), perhaps the first year of Jehoshaphat's sole reign after a coregency of three years with his father, Asa (see 20:31 and discussion).

17:10–19. The author of Kings does not record Jehoshaphat's growth in prestige, prosperity, and power. The Chronicler notes that Jehoshaphat's success was due to the fact that **the fear of the Lord fell** (v. 10) on neighboring nations (see discussion on 1 Chron. 14:17) and they left Jehoshaphat undisturbed. Some even honored him with gifts and tribute.

Questions have arisen about the number of Jehoshaphat's **mighty men of valour** (v. 13). If the Hebrew *'eleph* is translated as "thousand," as this version is rendered, then Jehoshaphat assembled an enormous army for protection: **three hundred thousand** (v. 14), **two hundred and fourscore thousand** (v. 15), **two hundred thousand** (v. 16), **two hundred thousand** (v. 17), **an hundred and fourscore thousand** (v. 18). If, however, the Hebrew is seen as *'alluph*, then perhaps the Chronicler was reporting on "leaders" over units of men, thus: "300 units," "280 units," "200 units," "200 units," "180 units" (see discussions on 1 Chron. 12:23–37; 27:1).

18:1–19:3. See 1 Kings 22:1–40 and discussions. To conform to his interest in the southern kingdom and Jehoshaphat, the Chronicler omits elaboration on the death of Ahab and his succession (1 Kings 22:36–40) and adds the material on the prophetic condemnation of Jehoshaphat's involvement (19:1–3).

18:1. The Chronicler enhances the status of Jehoshaphat by mentioning that he was blessed with wealth for his fidelity, something not found in 1 Kings 22, and also sets the stage for an entangling foreign alliance, condemned by the prophet in 19:2–3. When Jehoshaphat acquired his riches and honor, however, he became careless in his diplomatic relations with Israel. That he **joined affinity with**

Ahab refers to an alliance by marriage. This marriage alliance to Athaliah, daughter of Ahab, would later result in an attempt to exterminate the Davidic line (22:10–23:21).

18:2–3. The Chronicler further enhances the status of Jehoshaphat by noting the large number of animals Ahab slaughtered in his honor, a note not found in 1 Kings 22. That Ahab **persuaded him to go … with him to Ramoth-gilead** (v. 2) is also not found in the parallel text. The Hebrew for the verb "persuade" is often used in the sense of inciting to evil (see, e.g., 1 Chron. 21:1) and may express the Chronicler's attitude toward Jehoshaphat's involvement.

18:4–34. Before accompanying Ahab, Jehoshaphat insisted, **Inquire … at the word of the Lord to day** (v. 4). This request fits the Chronicler's overall positive portrait of Jehoshaphat.

For the four hundred prophets that were called (v. 5), the call for Micaiah, Ahab's response to the man of God (vv. 6–27), and Ahab and Jehoshaphat's battle against Ramoth-gilead (vv. 28–34), see the virtually identical narrative in 1 Kings 22:5–38.

That Ahab disguised himself while directing Jehoshaphat into battle in royal regalia (v. 29), thus making Jehoshaphat the logical target for attack, was consistent with Israel's dominant position at this time (see discussion on 1 Kings 22:29–30).

When Jehoshaphat came under attack by the Syrians, who thought they had found the king of Israel, he cried out, **and the Lord helped him; and God moved them to depart from him** (v. 31). This information is not found in 1 Kings 22:32. However, some Septuagint manuscripts of Kings do contain the statement that "the Lord helped him," which suggests that the Chronicler was following a Hebrew text of Kings.

19:1–3. This rebuke by **Jehu the son of Hanani the seer** (v. 2) is not found in 1 Kings 22. **Shouldest thou help the ungodly …?** Jehu's father, Hanani, had earlier given Jehoshaphat's father, Asa, a similar warning for his distrust in God (see 16:7–9 and discussion). Now Jehu had to reprimand Jehoshaphat for his bad decision. Jehoshaphat was rebuked for helping "the ungodly" (i.e., Ahab) and loving **them that hate**

the LORD (i.e., Israel). Jehoshaphat would later commit the same sin again and would suffer for it (see 20:35–37). **Wrath is upon thee from ... the LORD.** The Lord's anger may have been manifested in the form of the Moabite and Ammonite invasion in 20:1–4.

Nevertheless there are good things found in thee (v. 3). Jehoshaphat received commendation for his good (i.e., his past) reforms, notably removing the **groves** (see discussion on 14:3) and teaching (17:4–7).

19:4–11. Jehoshaphat did not react in a mean-spirited manner to the prophet's rebuke, as Asa had done (16:10). Instead, he accepted the rebuke and launched new reforms, something not mentioned in 1 Kings.

Jehoshaphat ... went ... through the people (v. 4). The king personally traveled throughout the realm to promote religious reformation. **And he set judges in the land** (v. 5). The name Jehoshaphat (meaning "the Lord judges") is appropriate for the king who instituted this judicial reform. He instructed his appointed judges in a most important principle: they were to be mindful that they were not judging for man but for the Lord Himself. **Let the fear of the LORD be upon you** (v. 7); that is, let a terrifying sense of God's presence restrain you from any injustice (see discussion on 1 Chron. 14:17). Then there would be no impartiality or bribery leading to a biased court decision (see Deut. 16:18–20; 17:8–13). This arrangement of the courts under Jehoshaphat (vv. 5–11) would be of particular interest to the Chronicler's postexilic audience in the postexilic period, when the courts of the restored community would have their own existence and structure legitimized by this precedent.

He appointed **Levites, and ... priests ... for the judgment of the LORD** (v. 8; see discussion on 1 Chron. 26:29–32). One effect of this judicial reform appears to have been that the traditional system of justice, administered by the elders of the city, was brought under closer royal and priestly supervision. Apparently, these judges in centrally located Jerusalem served as a court of appeals in religious and civil cases. In certain cases, they would have also decided whether a killing had been premeditated murder or involuntary manslaughter.

Amariah (v. 11), the high priest, and **Zebadiah**, a judge from Judah, heard final appeals **in all matters of the LORD ... all the king's matters**, that is, in religious and civil cases respectively. This division of the affairs of religion and the affairs of the king reflects the postexilic structure of the Chronicler's day. Compare the anointing of Solomon and Zadok (1 Chron. 29:22) and the administration of the postexilic community by Zerubbabel, a Davidic descendant, and Joshua, the high priest (Zech. 4:14; 6:9–15).

20:1–30. This episode holds special interest for the Chronicler since the restored community of his day was being harassed by the descendants of these same peoples (see Neh. 2:19; 4:1–3, 7–9; 6:1–4; 13:1–31). He uses it to encourage his contemporaries to trust in the Lord and His prophets, as Jehoshaphat, son of David, had exhorted (v. 20). The account is significantly structured. Apart from the outer frame, which highlights the reversal of circumstances (vv. 1–4, 28–30), it falls into three divisions: (1) Jehoshaphat's prayer (vv. 5–13), (2) the Lord's response (vv. 14–19), and (3) the great victory (vv. 20–27). At the center of each is its crucial statement, all of which are linked by a key word: "we *stand* before this house, and in thy presence" (v. 9); "*stand* ye still, and see the salvation of the LORD with you" (v. 17); "the children of Ammon and Moab *stood* up against the inhabitants of mount Seir, utterly to slay and destroy them" (v. 23).

20:1–4. Both **the children of Moab, and the children of Ammon** (v. 1) lived east of the Jordan River. **Other beside the Ammonites** is probably better rendered "Meunites," that is, a people from the region of Mount Seir in Edom (26:7; 1 Chron. 4:41; see 2 Chron. 20:10, 22–23). As these groups prepared to do battle with Jehoshaphat, he learned that they were being joined by **Syria** (v. 2). Most Hebrew manuscripts read *Aram* (the word translated "Syria"); one Hebrew manuscript reads *Edom*. The Arameans/Syrians were well to the north and are not mentioned among the attackers named in verse 1, so "Edom" may be the correct reading (20:10 refers to Mount Seir, which is synonymous with Edom).

The difference between *Aram* and *Edom* in Hebrew is only one letter, which is very similar in shape and was often confused in the process of copying manuscripts. This invading army came up the west side of **the sea** (i.e., the Dead Sea) as far as **En-gedi**, a place where Saul had pursued David (1 Sam. 24:1).

In spite of his own large army (see 17:14–18), **Jehoshaphat feared** (v. 3), perhaps because of Jehu's earlier warning of God's wrath (see 19:2).

20:5–13. In the face of attack, Jehoshaphat led his people Judah in a prayer to God. His prayer shows him to be a true theocratic king, a worthy son of David and a type (foreshadow) of the awaited Messiah (see 1 Chronicles, Introduction: "Theme"). **The new court** (v. 5), where Jehoshaphat stood, evidently refers to the outer court that had been renovated, or perhaps it was an innovation since Solomon's time.

Jehoshaphat's knowledge of God was sound. He rehearsed God's sovereignty and omnipotence (v. 6), His faithfulness to Israel and Abraham (v. 7), and His promise to hear His people in their affliction (vv. 8–9; note the apparent reference to Solomon's prayer and the divine promise of response; 6:14–42; 7:12–22). Jehoshaphat earnestly described Judah's plight to God. Three nations whom Israel was not permitted to invade were about to dispossess Judah from its God-given land (vv. 10–11) unless God intervened (v. 12; for God's prohibition concerning disturbing Edom, Moab, and Ammon, nations all related to Israel, see Deut. 2:4, 9–10).

Demonstrating their utter dependence on divine intervention, the people of Judah (wives and children included) stood before the Lord, awaiting His answer (v. 13).

20:14–19. God's answer through **Jahaziel** (v. 14) was assuring, reminiscent of earlier confident utterances: (1) **Be not afraid nor dismayed** (v. 15; recall God's encouragement to Joshua, Josh. 1:9); (2) **The battle is not yours, but God's** (compare David's words to Goliath, 1 Sam. 17:47); (3) **Stand ye still, and see the salvation of the Lord** (v. 17; compare Moses' words at the parting of the Red Sea, Exod. 14:13–14); (4) **Fear not ... for the Lord will be with you** (compare God's words to Joshua, Josh. 1:5, 9; 3:7).

Jehoshaphat was advised that the enemies would begin their approach the next day by the way of **the cliff** (i.e., "ascent, pass") **of Ziz** (v. 16), which was seven miles north of En-gedi and wound inland, emerging west of Tekoa. They would be found at the valley in **the wilderness of Jeruel**, a site located southeast of Tekoa.

Jehoshaphat bowed his head (v. 18), the people **fell before the Lord** to worship, **and the Levites ... stood up to praise the Lord** (v. 19). Note the Chronicler's apparent interest in the priests and Levites throughout the account (v. 14; 20:21–22, 28).

20:20–30. Judah's army approached the enemy with Jehoshaphat's encouraging reminder: **Believe in the Lord your God ... believe his prophets** (v. 20). This was a particularly apt word for the Chronicler's contemporaries to hear from this son of David—at a time when their only hope for the future lay with the Lord and the reassuring words of His prophets. Singers led the way, singing, **Praise the Lord; for his mercy endureth for ever** (v. 21; recall this refrain in 5:13; 7:3).

The Lord set ambushments against (v. 22) the enemy, but no further explanation is given. Whether He employed supernatural agents or surprised the enemy with an unexpected attack from inhabitants of the area is not certain. What is clear is that the Lord inflicted the enemy nations with panic and turned them on each other so that Israel's foes destroyed each other in the confusion of battle, similar to Israel's victory under Gideon (Judg. 7:22).

Judah arrived too late to do battle, for the enemy was already defeated and dead, but they arrived right on time to collect the spoils, an effort that took **three days** (v. 25). **The fourth day** (v. 26) was devoted to blessing the Lord in a valley that was named **Berachah** (the Hebrew means "blessing") because of the occasion. The Chronicler notes that the name persisted **unto this day** (see discussion on 5:9).

The people of Judah had departed Jerusalem to do battle armed with trust in their God; they returned rejoicing in a victory He had accomplished against their enemies without their involvement. **The fear of God** (v. 29) was on all the kingdoms (see discussion on 1 Chron. 14:17), for they heard how the LORD **fought against the enemies of Israel**. God then gave Jehoshaphat **rest round about** (v. 30; see discussion on 15:15). Righteous kings had victory in warfare (Abijah, Asa, Jehoshaphat, Uzziah, and Hezekiah), while wicked rulers experienced defeat (Jehoram, Ahaz, Joash, and Zedekiah).

20:31-34. Jehoshaphat reigned **twenty and five years** (v. 31). Kings reports twenty-two years (eighteen years in 2 Kings 3:1 and four more in 8:16). These figures are reconciled by suggesting a coregency with his father, Asa, for three years, probably due to the severity of his father's illness and the need to arrange for a secure succession (16:10-14). The author of Kings speaks only of Jehoshaphat's years of sole reign after his father's death.

The high places were not taken away (v. 33). The best intentions of a godly king's reforms could not change the hearts of the people. Though Jehoshaphat officially destroyed the religious shrines (see discussion on 17:6), the people persisted in resorting to them.

Jehu the son of Hanani (v. 34; see discussion on 19:2) was responsible for writing the annals of Jehoshaphat's reign.

20:35-37. On Jehoshaphat's alliance with **Ahaziah king of Israel** (v. 35) for shipping, see discussion on 1 Kings 22:48. The lucrative maritime trade through the Gulf of Aqaba no doubt tempted Jehoshaphat to enter into this improper alliance (see 19:2 and discussion). Solomon's earlier alliance for the same purpose had been with a non-Israelite king (8:17-18). Ahaziah was the son of Ahab, and he reigned from 853 to 852 BC (for the account of his reign, see 1 Kings 22:51-2 Kings 1:18).

21:1-3. When Jehoshaphat died, Jehoram, his firstborn son, reigned in his place. Special attention is drawn to **the sons of Jehoshaphat** (v. 2). The Chronicler shows the blessing of God on Jehoshaphat by mentioning his large family, particularly his seven sons (see 11:18-22; 1 Chron. 25:5 and discussions). Jehoshaphat's large number of sons is in striking contrast to the wicked Jehoram, who, after murdering his brothers (21:4), was left with but

one son (21:17). Jehoram's wife Athaliah would later perform a similar slaughter (22:10).

Jehoshaphat gave his sons **great gifts ... with fenced cities** (v. 3) in Judah. Though specific details are lacking, it appears he may have been following the example of Rehoboam with his sons (see 11:23).

E. Jehoram and Ahaziah (21:4-22:9)

21:4-20. See 2 Kings 8:16-24 and discussions.

21:4. To ensure his position on the throne, Jehoram **slew all his brethren** (see Judg. 9:2-5). This bloody assassination of all potential rivals is not reported in Kings, but it fits the pattern of the northern kings; the purge may have occurred at the instigation of his wife, Ahab's daughter, because the Chronicler notes that Jehoram walked in the way of her father (21:6). **The princes of Israel** may have been leading men in the southern kingdom who opposed having a king married to a daughter of Ahab. For this use of "Israel," see discussion on 12:1.

21:5-7. Jehoram reigned for **eight years** (848-841 BC; v. 5). The period 853-848 BC was probably a coregency of Jehoram with his father, Jehoshaphat; Jehoshaphat's eighteenth year was also Jehoram's second year (see 2 Kings 1:17; 3:1). Jehoram **had the daughter of Ahab to wife** (v. 6). This is probably the marriage referred to in 18:1, used to cement the alliance between Jehoshaphat and Ahab. Such political marriages were common. Many of Solomon's marriages sealed international relationships, as did Ahab's marriage to Jezebel.

The long-lasting impact of the alliance between Ahab and Jehoshaphat (see discussion on 1 Kings 22:4) becomes evident. Jehoram did not walk in the godly ways of his father, but was influenced by his wife to walk **in the way of the kings of Israel ... as did the house of Ahab** (v. 6).

21:8-11. The Edomites revolted from ... Judah (v. 8; see 1 Kings 8:20-22 and discussion). The pious Jehoshaphat had enjoyed victory over Edom (see discussion on 20:2), while the wicked Jehoram was defeated in his attempt to keep Edom in subjection to Judah (see discussion on 20:30), and the revolt persisted **unto this day** (v. 10; see discussion on 5:9).

For the revolt of **Libnah**, a city located between Judah and Philistia, see discussion on 1 Kings 8:22. With the phrase **because he had forsaken the LORD** (not found in 2 Kings 8:22), the Chronicler introduces this judgment as an indication of immediate retribution (see discussions on 12:1–14; 12:2; see also 1 Chronicles, Introduction: "Theme"). The Chronicler adds that Jehoram aggressively attempted to undo his father's reforms by building shrines in opposition to the Lord and by causing Judah **to commit fornication** (or spiritual adultery; v. 11), that is, going after false gods.

21:12–20a. These verses find no parallel in 2 Kings 8.

21:12–15. This reference to a letter from **Elijah** (v. 12) is the only mention in Chronicles of the prophet Elijah, to whom the books of Kings give so much attention (see 1 Kings 17–2 Kings 2). Elijah's letter specifically announces the immediate consequences of Jehoram's disobedience—further defeat in war, which would cost Jehoram his wives and sons, and disease, which would lead to his death (see discussion on 16:12). Compare the foot disease of Asa (16:12–14) and the leprosy of Uzziah (26:16–23). Kings does not mention the nature of Jehoram's death. Some have argued that this letter could not have been authentic because, they claim, Elijah was taken to heaven before Jehoram became king. This is not a necessary conclusion (see 2 Kings 1:17; see also discussion on 2 Kings 3:11). Elijah's translation may well have taken place as late as 848 BC.

21:16–17. Earlier, the Philistines and Arabians had paid tribute to Jehoshaphat (see 17:11), but now, with the aid of the **Ethiopians** (lit., "Cushites," i.e., people from the upper Nile region; v. 16), they made a raid on Judah. This foray was devastating and humiliating. Ironically, the one who began his reign by slaughtering his brothers was now deprived of all but one of his sons. The sole son left to Jehoram was Ahaziah (called here by a variant name, Jehoahaz [v. 17], but see Ahaziah throughout chapter 22, with one exception, an alternative name, Azariah in 22:6). Both Jehoahaz and Ahaziah mean "the Lord has grasped."

21:18–20. With Jehoram's infliction of **an incurable disease** (v. 18), the prophecy of Elijah (21:15)

was fulfilled. This disease of the bowels may have been some form of dysentery. When he died, after **eight years** (v. 20) of reigning (see discussion on 21:5), he was not honored with the burning of spices (see discussion on 16:14) or burial **in the sepulchres of the kings**. Only the Chronicler mentions the refusal of the people to accord Jehoram the customary burial honors of a tomb with the other kings of Judah (see 24:25). Interestingly, this is the first time that the Chronicler does not refer his readers to other sources for additional details on the reign of a king.

22:1–9. The Chronicler's account of Ahaziah's reign is much shorter than the parallel in 2 Kings 8:24–9:29, probably due to the fact that the Kings account focuses on the rebellion of Jehu and the downfall of the dynasty of Omri (see 2 Kings 8:26; see also 1 Kings 16:21–28)—events in the history of the northern kingdom, in which the Chronicler is not interested. The Chronicler's account again shows his interest in immediate retribution: Ahaziah's personal wickedness and his involvement in a foreign alliance result in immediate judgment and a reign of only one year (see discussion on 16:2–9; see also 1 Chronicles, Introduction: "Theme").

22:1–5. Ahaziah (v. 1), Jehoram's youngest and sole remaining son was made king. In his emphasis on divine retribution, the Chronicler notes that an invading **band of men ... with the Arabians ... had slain all the eldest** of Jehoram's sons. He who had murdered all his brothers had to watch the death of his own sons (21:4, 13, 16–17).

Ahaziah's age of **forty and two years** (v. 2) is apparently a copyist mistake. The Hebrew reading of "forty-two" would make Ahaziah older than his father (see 21:20). The Septuagint (the Greek translation) reads "twenty-two" and appears to be correct. He reigned only **one year** (841 BC).

Ahaziah's mother was **Athaliah the daughter of Omri** (v. 2). Athaliah is connected to her wicked grandfather, Omri, the founder of a dynasty (see 1 Kings 16:23). Perhaps it was he who arranged for the marriage of her father Ahab to Jezebel to seal a political alliance with Phoenicia (see 1 Kings 16:29–33 and discussions). Her own marriage to Jehoram also seemed to have political ramifications (see discussions on 18:1 and 21:6). Each of these marriages led to spiritually disastrous results. The great influence of the dynasty of Omri in Judah is indicated by the power of Athaliah and the presence of advisers from the northern kingdom (see discussion on 18:29). Bad counsel, perhaps his mother's, led Ahaziah into an alliance that would shortly destroy him, with Jehoram, son of Ahab and brother to his mother.

Ahaziah **went with Jehoram ... to war** (v. 5). This was an action similar to that for which Jehoshaphat had been rebuked (see 19:2 and discussion). They went to fight Syria's king **Hazael**, who had been anointed by Elisha; he later killed his master in a coup to seize the throne (2 Kings 8:13–15; see 1 Kings 19:15 and discussion). The site of the battle was **Ramoth-gilead**, located across the Jordan, in the border area between Israel and Syria. More than ten years earlier, Jehoshaphat had participated with Ahab in a battle there, which cost Ahab his life (chap. 18; 1 Kings 22).

22:6–9. When Jehoram was wounded, **he returned to ... Jezreel** (v. 6). Jehoram apparently recovered Ramoth-gilead and left Jehu in charge (2 Kings 8:28–9:28). On the series of events that followed Jehoram's being wounded, see discussion on 2 Kings 9:1–26.

The destruction of Ahaziah was of God (v. 7). Ahaziah's association with Jehoram made him a deserving target for judgment also (compare Jehu's instructions after his anointing, 2 Kings 9:6–10). The Chronicler assumes the reader's familiarity with the account of Jehu's anointing and the additional details of the coup, which resulted in the deaths of Jehoram and Ahaziah (2 Kings 8:28–9:28). While the author of Kings primarily portrays the end of the dynasty of Omri as a result of the judgment of God (1 Kings 21:20–29; 2 Kings 9:24–10:17), the Chronicler notes that the assassination of Ahaziah was also brought about by God.

The account of Ahaziah's death appears to be somewhat different in the two histories (see 2 Kings 9:21–27; 10:12–14). Since the author of Chronicles presumes the reader's familiarity with the other account (see discussion on v. 7), it is best to take the details of Chronicles as supplementary, not contradictory, to Kings, though it is difficult to know the precise sequence and location of events. A harmonized reconstruction of the two accounts is possibly as follows: Upon witnessing Jehu's murder of Jehoram (2 Kings 9:23–24), Ahaziah fled to Samaria, where he hid until found by Jehu's men. They brought him to Jehu, who fatally wounded him near Ibleam. He was able to flee once again, this time to Megiddo, where he died. His was then brought back to Jerusalem. Apart from the Chronicler's statement that Ahaziah received a decent burial because of his father's piety rather than his own, the apparent differences in the two accounts do not appear to be theologically motivated. Neither account offers a summary statement about the reign of Ahaziah.

F. Joash (22:10–24:27)

22:10–12. On Athaliah's usurpation of the throne of Judah, her attempted purge of all the royal heirs, and the protection plan for the infant Joash, see discussion on 2 Kings 11:1–3. In the history of Judah, Athaliah represents the only break in the continuity of the Davidic dynasty; she was the only queen of Judah to rule in her own name (841–835 BC). Her attempt to wipe out the royal family repeated the action of her husband, Jehoram (21:4). It threatened the continuity of the Davidic dynasty, and if she had succeeded, Judah might have been claimed by the dynasty of Omri in the north since Athaliah was from that dynasty and had no living son and heir.

Kings notes that Jehoram's daughter Johosheba (not necessarily the daughter of Athaliah) spared Joash; it does not mention, however, that she was **the wife of Jehoiada the priest** (v. 11), one who had access to the temple, where the infant royal son was hidden.

23:1–24:27. See 2 Kings 11:4–12:21 and discussions. The Chronicler divides the reign of Joash (835–796 BC) into three parts: (1) the recovery of the throne for the house of David (chap. 23); (2) Joash and Jehoiada—the good years (24:1–16); (3) Joash alone—the bad years (24:17–27). The last section is largely unique to Chronicles and further develops the theme of immediate retribution: Once again, chronological notes provide the framework for cycles of obedience and disobedience (24:15–17, 23; see discussions on 12:2; 14:2–16:14).

23:1–21. See 2 Kings 11:4–20. The Chronicler follows his source rather closely but introduces material reflecting his own concerns in three areas: (1) The account in Kings has more to say about the participation of the military in the coup; the Chronicler adds material emphasizing the presence of temple officials and their role (vv. 2, 6, 8, 13, 18–19). (2) The Chronicler stresses the widespread popular support for the coup by mentioning the presence of large groups of people, such as "all the congregation," "all the people," or "all Judah" (vv. 3, 5–6, 8, 10, 16–17). (3) The Chronicler shows additional concern for the sanctity of the temple area by inserting notes showing the steps that were taken to ensure that only qualified personnel entered the temple precincts (vv. 5–6, 19).

23:1–3. The Chronicler's account of Jehoiada's preparatory steps to introduce the crown prince is fuller than that of Kings. Jehoiada **took the captains … Azariah … Elishaphat** (v. 1). The Chronicler names the commanders, which was not done in Kings, but he does not mention the Carites, mercenaries who served as a royal guard (see discussion on 2 Kings 11:4). Verse 20 exhibits the same omission (see 2 Kings 11:19), the motive for which may have been the Chronicler's concern to show that only authorized persons entered the temple precincts.

Jehoiada issued a call to **the Levites … and the chief of the fathers of Israel** (v. 2) throughout Judah to come to Jerusalem to participate in the celebration when he would bring Joash out to be introduced and crowned king. Again, this detail, unique to the Chronicler, reflects his concerns with both the temple personnel and the widespread support for the coup against Athaliah. **The king's son shall reign, as the Lord hath said** (v. 3) harks back to God's covenant with David (see 2 Sam. 7:11–16).

23:4–11. For the details of Jehoiada's revelation of Joash as the legitimate royal heir, see 2 Kings 11:5–11. **Then they … gave him the Testimony**

(v. 11). This may refer to the covenant sworn by the assembly (23:1, 3; see 23:16) or to the law of God, by which the king was to rule (see Deut. 17:18–20). See discussion on 2 Kings 11:12.

23:12–15. The noise of the celebration aroused the attention of Athaliah, who came and found **the king … the princes and … also the singers with instruments of musick** (v. 13), a note the Chronicler adds (not found in 2 Kings 11:14) about the presence of Levitical musicians, who were leading the praises (see discussions on 1 Chron. 6:31–48). On Athaliah's reaction and accusation of treason and her death outside the temple, see 2 Kings 11:13–16 and discussions.

23:16–19. On Jehoiada's leadership, see discussions on 2 Kings 11:17–18. Jehoiada not only attempted a purge of Baalism; he also restored worship as prescribed by Moses and organized by David. The Chronicler includes additional information on the cultic ritual and the guards at the gates (see discussion on 23:1–21).

23:20–21. They … set the king upon the throne of the kingdom (v. 20). Joash was the last living remote descendant of Ahab and the last seed of David. God was faithful to His covenant with David (see 2 Sam. 7:16) and had preserved a light for David in Jerusalem (see 1 Kings 11:36). **All the people of the land rejoiced** (v. 21). Perhaps no Old Testament event illustrates better the essence of Proverbs 28:12: when the godly succeed, everyone is glad.

24:1–14. See 2 Kings 12:1–17.

24:1–3. As a mere seven-year-old, **Joash** (v. 1) began his reign of **forty years** (835–796 BC). The Chronicler provides notice that Joash's conduct was initially pleasing to the Lord but also an ominous hint that a change will follow after the death of **Jehoiada the priest** (v. 2). He thus presents the outline for his treatment of Joash—the good years while Jehoiada was alive (24:1–16), and the turn to evil after his death (24:17–27; see discussion on 25:2).

Jehoiada seems to have functioned as the young king's parent and guardian, but his taking **two wives** (v. 3) for Joash is inexplicable since it clearly violates Mosaic regulations for a king (see Deut. 17:17). The notice of Joash's multiple **sons and daughters**, however, is another expression of the Chronicler's conviction that large families represent the blessing of God (see 24:27; see also discussion on 1 Chron. 25:5).

24:4–14. Joash was minded to repair the house of the LORD (v. 4). The vandalism and atrocities of Athaliah (v. 7) required the refurbishing of the temple.

24:5. The author of 2 Kings mentions three different sources of revenue (see 2 Kings 12:4–5 and discussion), whereas the Chronicler mentions only the census tax (see Exod. 30:14; 38:26; Matt. 17:24). He adds that the Levites were dispersed throughout Judah to collect money also. **See that ye haste the matter.** Joash wanted the repairs on the temple to be completed quickly. The reason for the tardiness of the priests is not stated (see 2 Kings 12:6–8). The author of Kings notes that the Joash's audience with the priests took place in the twenty-third year of his reign, when he presumably was no longer the ward of Jehoiada. Resistance on the part of the priests to the reassignment of the temple revenues for repair work may have been the underlying cause for their delay of temple repairs. On Joash's dissatisfaction with the progress of repairs, see discussion on 2 Kings 12:6–12.

When Joash believed his procedure for collection and repairs was moving too slowly, he ordered a new policy (24:8–10). **They made a chest** (v. 8), a special collection box, and its purpose was publicized throughout Judah. Mesopotamian texts speak of a similar offering box placed in temples. Representatives of both the king and the temple officials administered temple revenues (see discussion on 1 Chron. 26:20). All money that was received was expeditiously presented to the various workers for repairs (24:11–12). The reference to **spoons, and vessels of gold and silver** (v. 14) need not be considered contradictory to 2 Kings 12:13. Apparently, 2 Kings refers to a time in the repair work when there was no surplus for making vessels, and the Chronicler notes a later time when a surplus had developed.

Burnt offerings (v. 14) were offered in the temple **all the days of Jehoiada**. This is an additional note on the part of the Chronicler to introduce the kingdom's turn for the worse upon Jehoiada's death, during the reign of Joash (24:15–16).

24:15–22. This section is unique to the Chronicler and shows his emphasis on immediate retribution (see discussion on 23:1–24:27). After a period of righteous rule, until the death of Jehoiada, Joash turned to idolatry and murdered Jehoiada's son. In the following year, he was invaded and defeated by Syria because Judah, under his leadership, "had forsaken the LORD" (24:24).

24:15–16. The godly priest Jehoiada was honored as the statesman that he truly was. **They buried him … among the kings** (v. 16) of Judah, an honor that was not granted even to King Joash (see 24:25).

24:17–19. After Jehoiada's death, **the princes of Judah** (i.e., the leaders; v. 17) gained Joash's ear by flattery (they **made obeisance to the king**) and persuaded him to return to the **groves** (Hebrew, *asherim*) **and idols** (v. 18), with all their fertility rites (see Judg. 3:5–7). **They left the house of the LORD** (v. 18) **… ye have forsaken the LORD … he hath also forsaken you** (v. 20) **… they had forsaken the LORD** (v. 24). The Hebrew word is the same for "left" and "forsake" in these verses; it is a verb the Chronicler frequently uses to denote the reason for divine punishment (see discussion on 12:1; see also 7:19, 22; 12:5; 13:10–11; 15:2; 21:10; 24:18, 20, 24; 28:6; 29:6; 34:25; 1 Chron. 28:9, 20).

Yet he sent prophets (v. 19). God graciously sought those who turned from Him, but they rejected His message through His prophets. Israel's failure to heed the Lord's prophets ultimately led to her destruction (see 36:16; see 20:20; see also 1 Chronicles, Introduction: "Theme").

24:20–22. The spirit of God came upon Zechariah (v. 20). A literal rendering is, "The Spirit of God clothed Zechariah." Therefore, Zechariah the priest, who was Jehoiada's son and Joash's cousin (see 22:11; 2 Kings 11:2), was empowered to confront the idolators with boldness. Joash's peers killed Zechariah at the king's command **in the court of the house of the LORD** (v. 21; see discussion on Matt. 23:35), perhaps on the basis of some trumped-up charge (compare the case of Naboth, 1 Kings 21:8–13). Joash owed his life, his throne, and his past spiritual successes to Jehoiada, but he **remembered not the kindness**

which Jehoiada ... had done to him (v. 22). All was disregarded when Joash had Zechariah murdered, the one who dared to challenge his wicked ways (compare Asa's treatment of the prophet Hanani, 16:10).

24:23–27. The king of the Syrians at Damascus was Hazael (see discussion on 2 Kings 12:17–18). The army of the Syrians was **a small company of men** (v. 24). Just as God had helped the small army of Judah against overwhelming odds when the king and people were faithful to Him (14:8–9; 20:2, 12), so now they were defeated by a much smaller force of invaders when they were unfaithful to Him (see discussion on 20:30).

The Syrian attack on Jerusalem destroyed its leadership and left Joash seriously wounded and bedridden. **His own servants conspired against him for the blood of the sons of Jehoiada ... and slew him** (v. 25; see discussions on 2 Kings 12:20–21). Only the Chronicler mentions that this assassination was revenge for the murder of Zechariah. **They buried him not in the sepulchres of the kings.** Burial in the tombs of the kings was an honor accorded to Jehoiada (24:16) but withheld from his rebellious ward Joash (see discussion on 21:20).

That the two assassins were born to non-Israelite women, one **an Ammonitess** (v. 26), the other **a Moabitess**, is information not given in Kings but important to the Chronicler (see discussion on 20:1–30).

G. Amaziah (chap. 25)

25:1–28. Characteristically, the Chronicler divides the reign of Amaziah into two parts: (1) the good years, marked by obedience, divine blessing, and victory (vv. 1–13), and (2) the bad years, marked by idolatry, defeat, and regicide (vv. 14–28). See 2 Kings 14:1–20 and discussions.

25:1–4. Coming to the throne at age twenty-five, Amaziah reigned for **twenty and nine years** (796–767 BC; v. 1).

The Chronicler does not indicate that Amaziah failed to remove the high places, which the people continued to used as places for sacrifice (see 2 Kings 14:4; also compare 24:2 with 2 Kings 12:4, and 26:4 with 2 Kings 15:4). The author appears to be moti-

vated by his outline, which covered the good years first and then the **reversion** to evil. Those kings of Judah that the Chronicler has described as "doing right in the sight of the Lord" he holds off making negative comments on until the second half of the account of their reigns, whereas in Kings, the summary judgment about their reigns and the high places is given immediately.

On Amaziah's treatment of his father's assassins and their children, see discussion on 2 Kings 14:5–7.

25:5–16. These verses are a considerable expansion on 2 Kings 14:7. The author of Kings mentions the successful war with Edom only as a prelude to Amaziah's challenge to Joash, but the Chronicler sets it in the framework of his emphasis on immediate retribution: obedience brought victory over Edom, while the subsequent idolatry (vv. 14–16) brought defeat in the campaign against Israel. By expanding his account, the Chronicler gives the theological reason for both the victory over Edom and the defeat before Israel.

The numbers of Amaziah's army show a marked decrease since the time of Asa (14:8) and Jehoshaphat (17:14–18), perhaps indicating Judah's disastrous defeat by the Syrians in the days of Joash (24:24). Because of his military deficiencies, Amaziah hired mercenaries from the northern tribe of Ephraim. However, an unidentified **man of God** (v. 7) instructed him, **let not the army of Israel go with thee**. This is another instance of the Chronicler's condemnation of alliances that imply lack of trust in the Lord (see discussions on 16:2–9; 22:5; compare other prophetic speeches that called on the people to trust in God, 20:15–17, 20; 32:7–8). The man of God made it clear that the Lord would not bless Amaziah with the mercenaries present because they represented a godless Israel. Though Amaziah had already paid the mercenaries and risked the possibility of humiliating Ephraim, who might threaten retaliation, he obeyed the word of the Lord (see 25:2).

Amaziah took his army to **the valley of salt** (v. 11), that is, the valley south of the Dead Sea. There he smote **the children of Seir**, the Edomites (see 2 Kings 14:7), who had revolted in Jehoram's reign (see discussions on 21:8–10; 2 Kings 8:20–22). The mercenaries from Ephraim did indeed retaliate. Instead of returning directly home, they attacked the cities of Judah, killing **three thousand of them** (v. 13), perhaps civilians. This may have been the inciting incident for the later war with the north. The cities of Judah that were ravaged by the returning soldiers of Ephraim included **Samaria**. A town by this name in the southern kingdom is not otherwise known. The reference may be a copyist's error.

Amaziah … brought the gods … of Seir … to be his gods (v. 14). Amaziah's action was unbelievably senseless. His own defeat of Edom had just proved these gods powerless to save even their own worshipers. Therefore, Amaziah stood condemned by the unnamed prophet.

25:17–24. The Chronicler's account of the war with the north closely parallels 2 Kings 14:8–14 except for some additions in line with his theme of immediate retribution. The Chronicler mentions Amaziah's foolish idolatry and the prophetic speech of judgment, neither of which is found in Kings. In verse 20 (and in 25:27), he also adds notes to emphasize that the idolatry of Amaziah was being punished.

On Joash's parable of the **thistle** (v. 18), see discussion on 2 Kings 14:9. Compare the parable in Judges 9:8–15.

On the battle and its results, see 2 Kings 14:11b–14. Joash of Israel severely damaged Jerusalem's wall **from the gate of Ephraim to the corner gate** (v. 23). Both gates were located in the northern wall of the city, the area most vulnerable to attack—the Ephraim gate in the northwest and the corner gate in the northeast. He also took as spoil the gold and silver vessels from the temple. The family of **Obed-edom** (v. 24) was the Levitical family who had been entrusted with the care of the temple storehouse (1 Chron. 26:15).

25:25–28. On the death of Amaziah, see discussion on 2 Kings 14:17–20. See also discussion on 25:17–25.

H. Uzziah (chap. 26)

26:1–23. See 2 Kings 15:1–7 and discussions. The Chronicler characteristically divides his account

of Uzziah's reign into two parts: the good years, then the bad (compare his treatment of Uzziah's father, Amaziah, and Uzziah's grandfather, Joash; see discussions on 24:2; 25:1–28). The Chronicler elaborates on the blessings and divine help that flowed from Uzziah's obedience and fidelity (vv. 4–15), whereas the author of Kings only alludes to his fidelity (2 Kings 15:3). Whereas Kings only mentions Uzziah's leprosy (2 Kings 15:5), the Chronicler gives additional details to show that the disease was a result of unfaithfulness (vv. 16–21). Under Uzziah and his contemporary in the north, Jeroboam II, the borders of Israel and Judah briefly reached the extent they had attained under David and Solomon (vv. 6–8; 2 Kings 14:25). In part, this flourishing of the two kingdoms was facilitated by the removal of the Syrian threat by Assyria under Adadnirari III (802 BC), following which Assyria herself went into a period of weakness.

26:1–4. Uzziah (v. 1) is also called Azariah (see 2 Kings 15:6–7; 1 Chron. 3:12). It is likely that Uzziah was a throne name, while Azariah was his personal name. He began his reign at age sixteen and reigned **fifty and two years** (792–740 BC; v. 3), including a coregency with his father, Amaziah (792–767 BC).

The Chronicler has constructed his account of Uzziah's reign to give it the same outline as that for Amaziah and Joash (see discussion on 26:1–23). Uzziah is the third king in succession who began his reign doing **right in the sight of the Lord** (v. 4; see 24:2; 25:2) and later became willful and commited serious sin before he died. As he did in the accounts of the other two kings (see discussion on 25:2), the Chronicler once again bypasses the statement in the parallel account that the king did not remove the high places (2 Kings 15:4).

26:5. He sought God in the days of Zechariah. The author again uses chronological notes to portray the cycles of blessing and judgment associated with a king's response to God's commands (see discussion on 12:2). All that is known of Zechariah, Uzziah's mentor, is stated here. He is not to be confused with the later prophet of the book that bears his name.

26:6–15. These verses are unique to 2 Chronicles.

26:6–8. The years in which Uzziah's reign coincided with that of Jeroboam II of Israel (ca. 790–750 BC) were opportune ones for Judah. While Jeroboam II was preoccupied with fighting the Syrians and restoring his borders (see 2 Kings 14:23–27), Uzziah was free to extend his borders toward the southeast and the southwest. For the **Mehunims** (or "Meunites"; v. 7), see discussion on 20:1. The tribute Uzziah received and the spread of his fame are reminiscent of the days of Jehoshaphat (see 17:10–11).

26:9–10. Uzziah strengthened the defense of Jerusalem, erecting towers at two gates, **the corner gate, and ... the valley gate** (v. 9). These gates were positioned in northeastern and southwestern portions of the walls. That he **fortified** these gates may reflect, in part, repair of the damage done by Joash (of Israel) during the reign of Amaziah (25:23). In the desert, Uzziah **built towers** (v. 10) and **wells** (i.e., "cisterns"). Towers and cisterns have been found in several excavations (Qumran, Gibeah, Beersheba). A seal bearing Uzziah's name has been found in a cistern at Tell Beit Mirsim.

26:11–15. Uzziah had a host of fighting men (v. 11). Compared to the armies of past kings, Uzziah's army was not large, but it was well equipped and efficient. Tiglath-pileser III of Assyria states that in his advance toward the west (743 BC), he was opposed by a coalition headed by "Azriau of Yaudi," perhaps Azariah (Uzziah) of Judah. Uzziah made **engines ... to shoot arrows and great stones** (v. 15). Since the catapult was not known in the military technology of the period, and since torsion-operated devices for shooting arrows did not appear for approximately another three centuries, the devices mentioned here may refer to defensive constructions to protect those shooting arrows and hurling stones from the tops of the walls. Whatever their construction or function, they seemed to be the latest in military equipment.

26:16–21. When he was strong, his heart was lifted up to his destruction (v. 16). Unfortunately, Uzziah's pride in his strength and capabilities led to further sin (see discussion on 26:5). He attempted to perform a duty in the temple reserved exclusively for the priests (v. 18; see Exod. 30:7–8). Apparently, he

had become dissatisfied with his role as mere king and desired to be a divine king, something similar to contemporary pagan priest-kings. What Uzziah desired, however, was the unique position that God had reserved for the Lord Jesus Christ, our Priest-King.

Nothing more is known of **Azariah the priest** (v. 17; the name appears in the list of priests in 1 Chron. 6:10, perhaps Azariah II). His attempt to restrain the king and his condemnation of him did not motivate Uzziah to repent; it infuriated him. Therefore, he was judged by God and smitten with **leprosy** (v. 19) and remained a leper until **the day of his death** (v. 21; see *KJV Study Bible* note on Isa. 6:1; for disease as a punishment for sin, see discussions on 16:12; 21:12–15). **He dwelt in a several** (i.e., "separate") **house,** or a "house where he was relieved of responsibilities"; the same phrase in the Canaanite texts from Ugarit suggests a kind of quarantine or separation. Uzziah was subjected to a form of quarantine demanded by the law (Lev. 13:45–46). He remained a figurehead, but his son Jotham was elevated to coregent and carried out the royal duties during Uzziah's last eleven years (see 2 Kings 15:5).

26:22–23. The other acts of Uzziah were recorded by **Isaiah the prophet** (v. 22). This is not a reference to the canonical book of Isaiah, but to some other work no longer in existence. Uzziah was **buried ... in the field ... which belonged to the kings** (v. 23; see 2 Kings 15:7). Apparently due to his leprosy, Uzziah was buried in a cemetery belonging to the kings, though not in the tombs of the kings.

I. Jotham (chap. 27)

27:1–9. See 2 Kings 15:32–38 and discussions.

27:1. Jotham's reign of **sixteen years** (750–735 BC; v. 1) included a coregency with Uzziah (750–740 BC). His reign also overlapped that of his successor, Ahaz, from 735 to 732 BC. Jotham imitated his father's virtues, not his faults. It is noteworthy that **he entered not into the temple** (v. 2). The Chronicler commends Jotham for not making the same error Uzziah had made, underscoring the point that Jotham continued in divine favor, in contrast to his father who had forfeited it by his presumptuous action

(26:16). However, **the people did yet corruptly**. This notation appears to refer to the high places, which continued to flourish (see 2 Kings 15:35).

27:3–6. These verses are unique to the Chronicler and are an elaboration of his thesis that fidelity to God's commands brings blessing: in construction, military victory, and prosperity—all **because** Jotham **prepared his ways before the LORD his God** (v. 6). Judah's relationship with the Ammonites held particular interest for the Chronicler (see discussions on 20:1–30; 24:26). Apparently, the Ammonites had rebelled and ceased paying tribute (see 26:8). Therefore Jotham brought them once again under subjection and required them to pay tribute in silver and grain for at least three years.

27:7–9. On **all his wars** (v. 7) with Rezin of Syria and Pekah of Israel, see 2 Kings 15:37. Upon Jotham's death, he received an honorable burial **in the city of David** (v. 9).

J. Ahaz (chap. 28)

28:1–27. See 2 Kings 16:1–20 and discussions, though only the introduction and conclusion in the two accounts are strictly parallel. The reign of Ahaz is the only one for which the Chronicler does not mention a single redeeming feature. The Chronicler appears to adopt explicit parallels from Abijah's speech condemning the northern kingdom (13:4–12) to show that under Ahaz, the southern kingdom sunk to the same depths of apostasy. Judah's religious fidelity, of which Abijah had boasted, was completely overthrown under Ahaz.

28:1–4. Ahaz took the throne at age twenty and **reigned sixteen years** (732–715 BC; v. 1), not including his coregency with Jotham (735–732 BC). The spiritual description of Ahaz is characteristic of the northern kingdom's kings. He **made also molten images for Baalim** (v. 2; see 13:8) and **burnt incense in the valley of the son of Hinnom**, or the "valley of Ben-hinnom" (v. 3; see 33:6). *Ge-ben-hinnom* in Hebrew is a term that was shortened to *Ge-hinnom*, from which "gehenna," the New Testament word for eternal punishment, is derived. He **burnt his children in the fire** (see Lev. 20:1–5; Jer. 7:31–32). Second Kings 16:3

has the singular "son." Some have regarded the plural as a deliberate inflation on the part of the Chronicler to heighten the wickedness of Ahaz. However, some manuscripts of the Septuagint (the Greek translation of the Old Testament) also have a plural in 2 Kings 16:3, suggesting that the Chronicler may have faithfully copied the text before him. Later, Manasseh (33:6) would also sacrifice his children at this site, but Josiah would put an end to the pagan practices observed there. He defiled the valley and reduced it to a place of refuse (see 2 Kings 23:10).

28:5–8. God delivered Ahaz **into the hand of the king of Syria** (v. 5; see 13:16–17). According to the Chronicler's view on immediate retribution, defeat in war is one of the results of disobedience (see discussion on 20:30). **He was also delivered into the hand of the king of Israel**. Second Kings 16:5–6 and Isaiah 7 make it clear that Rezin (king of Syria) and Pekah (king of Israel) acted together against Judah. The Chronicler has chosen either to treat them separately or to report on two different episodes of the Syria-Israel coalition.

Pekah (v. 6) reigned over the northern kingdom from 752 to 732 BC (see 2 Kings 15:27–31). He became an ally of Syria, and when Ahaz persistently refused to join him and Rezin in their resistance to Assyria, Judah was invaded. Thousands of men were killed, including **Maaseiah**, Ahaz's own son, and thousands were taken captive **because they had forsaken the LORD**. This was the same charge that Abijah had made against the northern kingdom (see 13:11).

28:9–15. Oded (v. 9) was a prophet in Samaria (Israel) who is otherwise unknown. He intercepted Pekah's army with a message from God (vv. 9–11). Israel had been an instrument of God to punish Judah for her sin and had accomplished its mission. It dared not go beyond that mission and enslave its kinsmen to the south.

The leadership of the northern tribes took Oded's message seriously and determined not to hold and enslave their defeated **brethren** (v. 11) whom they had taken captive from the south or to claim their spoils but instead to release them. The kindness of the northern captors to their captives from Judah, especially as recorded in verses 14–15, may have been the background for Jesus' parable of the good Samaritan (see Luke 10:25–37). Oded's attitude to the south is shown by his willingness to call them "brethren." In this case too, the record of chapter 13 has been reversed: the northern tribes were more righteous than the south (see discussion on 28:1–27).

28:16–19. Pekah and Rezin had also threatened to remove Ahaz from his throne (see discussion on 2 Kings 16:5–9). Ahaz appealed to Assyria for help because additional trouble came his way. **The Edomites had ... smitten Judah ... Philistines also had invaded** (vv. 17–18). Foreign alliances (v. 16) led to further defeats for Ahaz (see discussions on 16:2–10). **The LORD brought Judah low because of Ahaz** (v. 19). This is the same formula used to describe the defeat of the northern tribes in 13:18, though under Ahaz, it was Judah that was subdued.

28:20–21. **Tilgath-pilneser** (v. 20) is a variant of Tiglath-pileser, king of Assyria 745–727 BC (see 1 Chron. 5:26 and discussion). This king **distressed him** (Ahaz), **but strengthened him not**. On the surface, this comment appears to contradict the statement in 2 Kings 16:9 that Tiglath-pileser III responded to Ahaz's request by attacking and capturing Damascus, exiling its population, and killing Rezin. The Chronicler assumes the reader's familiarity with the other account and knows of the temporary respite for Judah gained by Assyrian intervention against Damascus and the northern kingdom of Israel. He focuses on the long-range results, in which Judah herself was reduced to vassalage to Assyria. Assyria's help was temporary and stressful. Ahaz found himself obligated to serve Assyria and pay tribute. He also set the stage for Assyria's campaigns against Israel (see discussion on 2 Kings 15:29; 17:3–6) and ultimately for Sennacherib's campaign against Judah in 701 BC (see discussions on 2 Kings 18:13–16).

28:22–23. Ahaz's distress did not bring him to repentance, but in his hardness of heart, he sinned further against the Lord. The Chronicler presumes the reader's familiarity with Ahaz's trip to Damascus and his copying of the altar and practices there (2 Kings 16:10–16). He began to worship foreign gods at a foreign altar in the house of the Lord. Of course, his syncretistic worship led to the neglect of true worship and the actual abandonment of the temple because of the rival altar there.

28:24–25. Additional details on Ahaz's alterations are found in 2 Kings 16:17–18. The Chronicler adds to his description of Hezekiah's reforming activities his corrections of some of the abuses under Ahaz. At the sanctuary, not only had the doors been shut but the lamps had been put out, and offerings were not made (29:7). The altar and utensils had been desecrated, and the table for the consecrated bread had been neglected (29:18–19). It is precisely these accoutrements of proper temple service about which Abijah had boasted when he had proclaimed the faithfulness of Judah in contrast to that of the northern kingdom (13:11). Now these orthodox furnishings were lacking under Ahaz and made the southern kingdom just like the north (see discussion on 28:1–27).

28:26–27. When Ahaz died, **they brought him not into the sepulchres of the kings** (v. 27). Ahaz was the third king whose wickedness resulted in the loss of this honor at death. The others were Jehoram (21:20) and Joash (24:25). Uzziah's sin and leprosy brought the same result, though it is not reported in exactly the same terms (26:23). See also Manasseh (33:20).

K. Hezekiah (chaps. 29–32)

29:1–32:33. The Chronicler devotes more attention to Hezekiah than to any other post-Solomonic king. Although the parallel text (2 Kings 18–20) has approximately the same amount of material, only about a fourth of the total relates the same or similar material; only a few verses are strict literary parallels (29:1–2; 32:32–33). In Kings, preeminence among the post-Solomonic kings is given to Josiah (2 Kings 22–23; see 1 Kings 13:2), and the record of Hezekiah is primarily devoted to his confrontation with Sennacherib of Assyria. By contrast, the Chronicler highlights almost exclusively Hezekiah's religious reforms and his devotion to matters of ceremony and ritual. The parallel passage (2 Kings 18:1–6) touches the religious reforms only briefly. The numerous parallels in these chapters with the account of Solomon's reign suggest that the Chronicler viewed Hezekiah as a "second Solomon" in his celebration of the Passover (30:2, 5, 23, 25 – 26), his cultic arrangements (29:7, 18, 35; 31:2 – 3), his wealth (32:27 – 29), the honor accorded him by the Gentiles (32:23), and the extent of his dominion (30:25).

29:1 – 2. At the age of twenty-five, **Hezekiah** (v. 1) began his reign of **nine and twenty years** (715 – 686 BC; but see discussion on Isa. 36:1), including a fifteen-year extension of life granted by God (2 Kings 20:6) but not mentioned by the Chronicler. Hezekiah's righteous reign, in contrast to his father's extremely wicked one, is testimony to the grace of God in his life (compare Asa, 14:1 – 2 and discussion).

29:3 – 30:27. This account of Hezekiah's purification of the temple and celebration of the Passover is not found in Kings.

29:3 – 4. While 2 Kings 18 – 19 concentrates mainly on the political struggles of Hezekiah, 2 Chronicles 29 – 32 deals primarily with the positive aspects of his religious reforms. In the beginning of his reign, he immediately endeavored to reestablish the true worship of the Lord. Noting Hezekiah's **first year** (715 BC; v. 3) is another example of the Chronicler's practice of introducing chronological materials into his narrative (see discussion on 12:2). He **opened the doors of the house of the Lord, and repaired them.** Opening the doors of the temple was a necessary move after the actions of Ahaz (28:24). The repairs to the doors included new gold overlay (see 2 Kings 18:16).

29:5 – 11. Sounding more like a prophet than a king, Hezekiah instructed the priests and Levites in the course of action they were to take to initiate the necessary reforms. **Sanctify now yourselves, and sanctify the house of the Lord** (v. 5). Attention was to be given to personal purification before attending to the cleansing of the temple. The impurity to be removed probably relates more specifically to the pollution due to the practice of idolatry in the sacred place.

Our fathers have trespassed (v. 6). Hezekiah's speech demonstrates again the Chronicler's convictions about the coherence of action and effect: the sins of the past brought difficulty and judgment,

but renewed fidelity brought relief. He notes all the temple arrangements that Hezekiah's father and others had stopped. These Hezekiah would reinstitute — following the pattern of Solomon (see 2:4; 4:7). The Chronicler also notes, **The wrath of the Lord was upon Judah ... he hath delivered them to trouble, to astonishment, and to hissing** (v. 8). This observation echoes the language of the prophets, especially Jeremiah (see Jer. 19:8; 25:9, 18; 29:18; 51:37). The Lord's wrath probably alludes to a series of past, but not so distant, events: the war with Syria and Israel (28:5 – 6) and the resultant demanding alliance with Assyria (see 28:16). Though Israel had returned the captives (see 28:15), Judah's other enemies (see 28:17) had not followed suit, and some of Judah's population was still held captive.

29:12 – 14. All three clans of the Levites (see 1 Chron. 6:1), **the Kohathites ... sons of Merari ... the Gershonites** (v. 12), had representatives overseeing the purification of the temple. Joining them were **Elizaphan** (v. 13), a leader of the Kohathites (Num. 3:30) whose family had achieved status almost as a subclan (see 1 Chron. 15:8; discussion on 1 Chron. 15:4 – 10), and **Asaph ... Heman ... Jeduthun** (vv. 13 – 14), founders of the three families of Levitical musicians (see 1 Chron. 6:31 – 48; 25:1 – 31).

29:15 – 19. Only the priests entered the temple to bring out **the uncleanness** (v. 16), that is, the impure things that they found there. The Levites then carried these things out **into the brook Kidron** for disposal. Asa had burned pagan cult objects at this site (see 15:16; see also 30:14). When the work was completed, the priests and Levites reported to Hezekiah that the temple was now cleansed and ready for use. Their report mirrors somewhat Solomon's stated purpose for building the temple (see 2:4).

29:20 – 22. The remainder of the chapter concerns the appropriate sacrifices that were offered. **A sin offering** (v. 21; see Lev. 4:1 – 5:13) was made for **the kingdom** (perhaps a reference to the royal house), **the sanctuary** (the temple), and **Judah** (i.e., the southern kingdom in contrast to all Israel). The priests **sprinkled the blood** (v. 22) of the sacrificial animals upon the altar (see Lev. 17:6; Num. 18:17).

29:23–24. They laid their hands upon them (i.e., the he goats; v. 23; see Lev. 4:13–15; 8:14–15; Num. 8:12). To lay their hands on the goats for the sin offering symbolically denoted the animals as the substitutionary offering for their sin (see Lev. 1:4). These offerings were for **all Israel** (v. 24). Since Samaria, the capital of the northern kingdom, had already fallen in 722 BC, about seven years before Hezekiah became king, this reference to "all Israel" may reflect Hezekiah's anticipation of drawing the remnant people of the north into his religious reforms (see 30:1).

29:25–29. The temple musicians, which appear to be a Davidic institution in 1 Chronicles 25, are rightly shown here to have been organized through **the commandment of David, and of Gad ... and Nathan ... his prophets** (v. 25). The Chronicler associates David among the prophets (see discussions on 1:7; 1 Chron. 28:19). For **the instruments of David** (v. 26), see 1 Chronicles 23:5.

29:30–35. The Levites were commanded **to sing praise unto the LORD with the words of David, and of Asaph** (v. 30). This may be a reference to the psalms of David and Asaph that had been collected and were already being used in the worship of the Lord at the temple.

Hezekiah encouraged the offering of sacrifices, and the response was overwhelming, for the number of available priests was inadequate. Perhaps Urijah the priest, who had cooperated with Ahaz (see 2 Kings 16:10–16), had drawn many other priests into idolatry. **The burnt offerings were in abundance ... peace offerings ... drink offerings** (v. 35). All that was done was reminiscent of the dedication of the temple under Solomon (7:4–6). For the laws regarding the peace offerings, see Leviticus 3; 7:11–21; for the drink offerings, see Numbers 15:1–12.

So the service of the house of the LORD was set in order (v. 35). This summary statement is similar to the formula used in 8:16 with reference to Solomon's work.

30:1–27. Hezekiah's celebration of the Passover is unique to the Chronicler; compare the famous Passover under Josiah (35:1–19; 2 Kings 23:21–23).

Hezekiah allowed two deviations from the law (see Exodus 12; Deut. 16:1–8) in this observance: (1) the date in the second month (v. 2) and (2) exemption from some ritual requirements (vv. 18–19).

30:1–5. Hezekiah saw the observance of Passover as a golden opportunity to reunite all the tribes religiously. Thus, he **sent to all Israel and Judah** (v. 1; see 1 Chronicles, Introduction: "Theme"). With the northern kingdom now ended as the result of the Assyrian invasion and deportation (which, surprisingly, is not mentioned), the Chronicler shows "all Israel" once again united around the Davidic king and the temple (see v. 5; 30:18–19, 25). Ephraim and Manasseh, two major tribes in the north, received special invitations.

After taking counsel with the princes, Hezekiah decided to celebrate Passover in the **second month** (v. 2). After the division of the kingdom, Jeroboam deferred the sacral calendar of the northern kingdom by one month (1 Kings 12:32), possibly to wean further the subjects in the north away from devotion to Jerusalem. By delaying the celebration of Passover one month, Hezekiah not only allowed time for the priests to consecrate themselves (v. 3) and for the people to gather (v. 3; 30:13) but also achieved unity between the kingdoms on the date of the Passover for the first time since the schism, more than two centuries earlier. Delaying the date reflects Hezekiah's concern to involve "all Israel." For the first time since the days of Solomon, the entire nation observed Passover together, reflecting the Chronicler's view that Hezekiah was a "second Solomon." Passover was prescribed for the fourteenth day of the first month (Exod. 12:2, 6; Deut. 16:1–8), but a delay of one month was permitted by Mosaic law for extenuating circumstances of uncleanness (Num. 9:10–11). Here the Passover could not be celebrated in the proper month due to the defilement of the temple and the purification rites that were under way (29:3, 17). In addition, **the priests had not sanctified themselves sufficiently** (v. 3), and the people had not yet arrived at Jerusalem. For the celebration of Passover by the restored community shortly after the dedication of the rebuilt temple, see Ezra 6:16–22.

Beer-sheba and **Dan** (v. 5) were the traditional southern and northern boundaries of united Israel. With the division of the monarchy in 931 BC, the northern tribes no longer worshiped at Jerusalem (see 1 Kings 12:26–33). Of the southern tribes, probably only the pious minority actually observed the Passover. **Of a long time** is literally, "of/for great ...," perhaps referring to "great numbers" of participants observing the Passover, thus providing another comparison with the time of Solomon (see 30:26). At the time of its inception, Passover was primarily a family observance (Exodus 12). It later became a national celebration at the temple (30:8; see Deut. 16:1–8).

30:6–9. Once again, Hezekiah's passionate plea was more characteristic of a prophet than a king (see 29:5–11). Addressing the remnant of the northern tribes who had escaped Assyrian captivity, he pled with them to avoid the sins of their fathers and return to the Lord, Israel's God. **Enter into his sanctuary** (v. 8). Passover was one of three annual pilgrim feasts requiring attendance at the temple (see Num. 28:9–29:39). **If ye turn again unto the LORD, your brethren ... shall find compassion before them that lead them captive** (v. 9). In Solomon's prayer in 6:39, the Chronicler omitted the phrase found in the parallel account (see 1 Kings 8:50) stating that their conquerors would "have compassion on them." Here the phrase is found in the speech of Hezekiah, again portraying him as a kind of "second Solomon" (see Lev. 26:40–42). **They shall come again into this land.** Hezekiah's plea to the northern remnant implied that their repentance would move the heart of God and the Assyrians to return their captives back to Israel.

30:10–12. Hezekiah's couriers traveled as far north as **Zebulun** (v. 10). The northern tribes of Asher, Naphtali and Dan probably had been subdued, first by Syria, and then by Assyria, leaving Zebulun to be the extreme northern tribe at this time. Though some from Zebulun **laughed ... and mocked** the couriers, many others had a positive response.

30:13–17. As the priests had purified the temple, in like manner, the people who assembled in Jerusalem cleansed the city of the rival altars, **and cast them into the brook Kidron** (v. 14; see 29:16 and discussion). **The priests and the Levites ... sanctified themselves** (v. 15). The reproach previously directed against the priests (30:3; 29:34) was broadened to include also the Levites—an exhortation to the priests and Levites of the restored community to be faithful. **The Levites had the charge of the killing of the passovers** (v. 17; see Exod. 12:6; Deut. 16:6). According to the law, the heads of families were to slay the Passover sacrifice. The Levites perhaps acted for the recent arrivals from the northern kingdom who were not ceremonially clean (see John 11:55).

30:18–20. Faith and obedience take precedence over ritual (see Mark 7:1–23; John 7:22–23; 9:14–16). Some from the northern tribes were not properly purified. They had responded to Hezekiah's invitation but had not had time to prepare themselves. Their presence at Jerusalem was evidence enough that their hearts were right before God. Therefore, Hezekiah prayed, **The good LORD pardon every one** (v. 18). The Lord's response to Hezekiah's prayer recalls the prayer of Solomon (7:14).

30:21–24. The feast of unleavened bread (v. 21) commenced on the fifteenth day of the month, the day after Passover, and continued through the twenty-first day (Exod. 12:15–20). Participation in the sacrifice and confession of sin was so overwhelming that the feast was extended an **other seven days** (v. 23). The festival was observed for two weeks, just as the observance of the dedication of Solomon's temple had been (7:8–9).

30:25–27. The spiritual blessings of the feast were enjoyed by all, including **the strangers that came out of the land of Israel** (evidently proselytes; v. 25; see Exod. 12:48). Certainly such a spirit of unity in worship of the Lord brought joy to Jerusalem unlike anything **since the time of Solomon** (v. 26) at the dedication of the temple (see 7:9–10). This again is an explicit indication of the Chronicler's modeling of the reign of Hezekiah after that of Solomon (see discussion on 29:1–32:33). The priests' **prayer came up to his holy dwelling place, even unto heaven** (v. 27). This is another echo of Solomon's dedication prayer (6:21, 30, 33, 39).

31:1–21. Apart from verse one, which parallels 2 Kings 18:4, the material in this chapter is unique to the Chronicler, whose interest in the Levites and the temple predominates. Hezekiah's efforts to ensure the material support of the Levites (v. 4) probably had relevance to the postexilic audience for whom the Chronicler wrote.

31:1. Hezekiah's reforms were destructive, calling for the removal of idolatry from the land, and **all Israel** became involved. The Chronicler's interest in "all Israel" as united under Hezekiah is again apparent. The destruction of the **images** (see discussion on 1 Kings 14:23) and the **groves** (Hebrew, *asherim*; see discussions on 14:3 and 2 Kings 18:4) spread north from Judah and Benjamin into Ephraim and Manasseh. Since the movement to destroy the images and the groves was supported by a minority (see 30:10–11), it need not be supposed that Hezekiah made a clean sweep of idolatry there.

31:2–4. David's organizational structure for the priests and Levites ministering at the temple (see 1 Chron. 23–26), which Solomon had put in operation for the first time (see 8:14), was now re-instituted by Hezekiah. The Chronicler continues to model Hezekiah as a "second Solomon" (see discussions on 29:7, 18). With the priests and Levites in place to serve, Hezekiah himself **appointed also the king's portion … for the burnt offerings** (v. 3). The king's giving from his own wealth prompted a generous response from the people, as it had also under David (1 Chron. 29:3–9). The offerings and feasts that were required **in the law of the LORD** are set forth in Numbers 28–29.

Hezekiah also commanded the support of the priests and Levites. **The portion of the priests and the Levites** (v. 4) came from parts of the sacrifices (see Lev. 6:16, 18, 26, 29; 7:6, 33) and the firstfruits of Israel's produce (Exod. 23:19; Num. 18:12). The portion of the Levites also came from the tithes of the other tribes (Num. 18:21–24). With these remunerations, the priests and Levites were able to devote themselves to **the law of the LORD.**

31:5–10. See Deut. 12:5–19; 14:22–27. The **corn** (i.e., "grain"; v. 5), new **wine**, and **oil** had to be brought to the temple (Deut. 12:17). Those coming from a distance, however, could bring the value of their offerings and purchase them on arrival (Deut. 14:24). Only those who actually lived in Judah brought the tithe of their herds and flocks, a difficult procedure for those who lived farther away. For the restored community's commitment to bring their **firstfruits**, tithes, and offerings, see Nehemiah 10:35–39. For their failure to do so, see Nehemiah 13:10–13; Malachi 3:8–10.

The people began to pile up their tithes and offerings in the **third month** (i.e., May–June, the time of the Feast of Weeks and the corn harvest; v. 7). This continued through the **seventh month** (i.e., September–October, the time of the Feast of Tabernacles and the fruit and vine harvest; see Exod. 23:16). The immediate and generous response of the people in their giving was staggering. Noting the reaction of the priests, it is apparent that support of the priests had long gone unpracticed.

31:11–15. Hezekiah commanded to prepare chambers (v. 11) for storage. The storerooms that Solomon built (see 1 Kings 6:5–6 and discussion) apparently needed repair or cleaning. Certain Levites were given the responsibility of overseeing the storing and distribution of **the offerings and the tithes and dedicated things** (v. 12) that had been brought to the temple.

31:16–19. Age thirty had once been the age the priests were inducted into service (see 1 Chron. 23:3). David had lowered the age to twenty (see discussion on 1 Chron. 23:24–27). Levites males now began receiving support from the offerings **from three years old and upward** (v. 16). Though all ancient manuscripts read "three years," this is possibly a copyist's mistake for "thirty years," the age at which duties were assigned in the temple (1 Chron. 23:3).

Based on genealogical records (to establish their Levite lineage), the Levites and their families in their cities (away from Jerusalem and the temple) were also distributed their portion of support.

31:20–21. Hezekiah … wrought that which was good … and prospered (vv. 20–21). His reforms with respect to the service at the temple were pleasing to the Lord. Hezekiah was zealously committed to the law and to God. Therefore, he prospered. Here is another brief indication of the Chronicler's emphasis on immediate retribution: Not only does disobedience bring immediate chastening, but obedience and seeking God bring prosperity.

32:1–23. The record of Sennacherib's invasion is much more detailed in 2 Kings and Isaiah (see discussion on 29:1–32:33).

32:1. The Chronicler omits the date of the invasion (701 BC, Hezekiah's fourteenth year; see 2 Kings 18:13; Isa. 36:1).

32:2–8. Hezekiah's defensive measures are unique to the Chronicler but were normal preparations for an invasion. Hezekiah reasoned that he would not contribute to Sennacherib's siege of Jerusalem by providing an adequate water supply. He stopped **all the fountains, and the brook that ran through the midst of the land** (v. 4). This is probably a reference to the Gihon Spring (see 32:30; and discussion on 2 Kings 20:20).

Though Hezekiah set military captains in place, he kept a proper perspective, and he encouraged his people by reminding them of their ultimate and true defense. Sennacherib may have had with him a multitude, a mere **arm of flesh** (v. 8), but, Hezekiah assured the people of Jerusalem, **with us is the Lord our God to help us, and to fight our battles**.

32:9. The Chronicler bypasses 2 Kings 18:14–16, which records Hezekiah's suit for peace, with its accompanying bribe stripped from the temple treasures. These acts were apparently out of accord with the Chronicler's portrait of Hezekiah. He also omits 2 Kings 18:17b–18.

32:10–15. The Chronicler omits 2 Kings 18:20–21 (and Isa. 36:5–6), which contain a portion of the Assyrian commander's speech ridiculing Hezekiah and the citizens of Jerusalem for trusting in Egypt and Pharaoh. This too may have been theologically motivated, in light of the Chronicler's attitude toward foreign alliances (see discussion on 16:2–9). The same concern with foreign alliances is also likely the reason for his omission of the material in 2 Kings 18:23–27 (and Isa. 36:8–12), where mention is

again made of the hope of Egyptian intervention (see 2 Kings 19:9 for the incursion of Tirhakah). The Chronicler does include Sennacherib's ridicule directed at Hezekiah's attempt to encourage his people in the Lord their God after having destroyed (as Sennacherib wrongly assumed) His altars, when in fact he had destroyed the altars of those nonexistent gods that Israel had made rival to the Lord.

32:16–19. His (Sennacherib's) **servants spake yet more against the Lord God** (v. 16). The Chronicler appears to assume his reader's familiarity with the longer account of the Assyrian taunts found in Kings and Isaiah. Sennacherib's taunts were committed to writing, and his servants **cried with a loud voice in the Jews' speech** (v. 18). This assumes knowledge of the fuller story (2 Kings 18:26–28; Isa. 36:11–13) and Hezekiah's representatives requesting that all dialogue be done in the "Syrian language" so as not to dishearten the residents of Jerusalem who might hear.

32:20. This brief reference to the prayers of Hezekiah and Isaiah abridges the much longer narrative in 2 Kings 19:1–34 (and Isa. 37:1–35) and is the Chronicler's only reference to the activity of the prophet Isaiah. Hezekiah had begged him to pray for those left in Jerusalem (see 2 Kings 19:3–4); here the prophet joined Hezekiah in prayer, though the words of his prayer are not recorded. Perhaps he shared the words of Hezekiah (see 2 Kings 19:15–19).

32:21–23. The Chronicler omits God's encouragement to Hezekiah through the prophet Isaiah's message of condemnation for Sennacherib (see 2 Kings 19:20–28) and promise of protection for Jerusalem (see 2 Kings 19:29–34). Then God took action against the Assyrians (see 2 Kings 19:35–37; Isa. 37:36–38). The Chronicler and the parallel accounts telescope events somewhat: Sennacherib's invasion of Judah was in 701 BC, while his death at the hand of his sons was in 681 BC.

Hezekiah ... was magnified in the sight of all nations (v. 23). Here is another effort to compare Hezekiah with Solomon (see 9:23–24).

32:24. The Chronicler again abridges the narrative of Hezekiah's illness (2 Kings 20:1–11; Isa.

38:1–8), assuming the reader's familiarity with the role of Isaiah and the miraculous sign of the shadow reversing ten steps.

32:25–30. Hezekiah recovered from his fatal illness, but the following account of his pride is not found in the parallel texts. **His heart was lifted up ... pride** (vv. 25–26). The Chronicler does not specify the nature of Hezekiah's pride (but see 32:31; 2 Kings 20:12–13; Isa. 39:1–2). Even for a "second Solomon" like Hezekiah, disobedience brought anger from the Lord. The evidence of God's wrath on Hezekiah is probably seen in Sennacherib's invasion, for the invasion is probably to be positioned in time after Hezekiah's illness (for the time of Hezekiah's illness, see discussion on 2 Kings 20:1).

Hezekiah's accumulation of wealth is summarized, and though the Chronicler is careful to give God His due credit, he again likens Hezekiah to Solomon, this time by recounting his wealth (see 9:13–14).

For Hezekiah's manipulation of water from the Gihon Spring, see 32:2–4 and discussions on 2 Kings 20:20.

32:31. See 32:25. The Chronicler assumes the reader's knowledge of the fuller account in 2 Kings 20:12–19 (and Isa. 39:1–8). The envoys from Babylon were apparently interested in joint efforts against the Assyrians, hoping to open two fronts against them simultaneously.

32:32–33. Isaiah's account of the acts of Hezekiah was incorporated **in the vision of Isaiah the prophet** (v. 32; see Isa. 1:1; 36–39). In contrast to his wicked father (see 28:27), Hezekiah received a royal and honorable burial.

L. Manasseh (33:1–20)

33:1–20. See 2 Kings 21:1–18 and discussions. **Manasseh** (v. 1) had the longest reign of any of the kings of Judah, a total of fifty-five years. The emphasis in the two accounts differs. While both histories report at length the evil done in Manasseh's reign, only the Chronicler mentions his journey to Babylon and his repentance and restoration to rule. For the author of Kings, the picture is only a bad one, in which Manasseh could be considered almost

single-handedly the cause of the exile (2 Kings 21:10–15; 23:26). Some scholars regard the record of Manasseh's repentance in Chronicles as motivated by the author's emphasis on immediate retribution: length of reign is viewed as a blessing for obedience, so the Chronicler deliberately records some good in Manasseh as a ground for his long reign. It must be noted, however, that length of reign is not elsewhere used by the Chronicler as an indication of divine blessing. The usual indicators for such blessing in his account are peace and prosperity, building projects, success in warfare, and large families.

33:1–9. At the age of twelve, **Manasseh** (v. 1) began his reign of **fifty and five years** (697–642 BC). He so aggressively indulged in Baalism that he could legitimately be touted as the "Ahab of the southern kingdom" (see 1 Kings 16:32–33; 21:25). All that Hezekiah had destroyed, Manasseh endeavored to rebuild, including the **groves** (Hebrew, *asheroth*; v. 3; see discussion on 14:3), and **he caused his children to pass through the fire** (v. 6; see discussion on 28:3–4).

33:10. See discussion on 33:1–20. The Chronicler abridges what the Lord said to Manasseh and the people through the prophets; the fuller record is found in 2 Kings 21:10–15 (see discussions there).

33:11–17. This account of Manasseh's humbling is unique to the Chronicler, showing his stress on immediate retribution: Manasseh's evil brought invasion and defeat, while his repentance brought restoration to rule.

The king of Assyria ... carried him to Babylon (v. 11). In extant nonbiblical records, no reference has as yet been found to Manasseh's being taken to Babylon by an Assyrian king. Esarhaddon (681–669 BC) lists Manasseh among twenty-two kings required to forward materials for his building projects, and Ashurbanipal (669–627) names him as one of a number of vassals supporting his campaign against Egypt. The fact that an Assyrian king would have him taken to Babylon suggests that this incident may have taken place during the rebellion of Shamash-shum-ukin against his brother and overlord Ashurbanipal. This rebellion lasted from 652 to 648 BC, and Manasseh may have joined the rebellion, or at least have been suspected of assisting the Babylonian defection from Assyria. Manasseh may have been found innocent, or he may have been pardoned on the basis of a renewed pledge of loyalty. Egypt had also bolted from the Assyrian yoke under the new Twenty-sixth Dynasty, and the return of Manasseh to rule may reflect the Assyrian need of a vassal near the border of Egypt.

Manasseh's affliction drove him to repentance. That his repentance was genuine is evidenced by his actions following his release from captivity and return to Jerusalem (vv. 15–16). The language of his prayer of repentance is reminiscent of Solomon's prayer (see 7:14).

How much of Manasseh's reign and life remained after his repentance and release is not told. He attempted to do something constructive: **he built a wall without the city** (v. 14), that is, an outer wall. For the Chronicler, such building programs are a sign of divine blessing (see 8:1–6; 11:5–12; 14:6–7; 26:9–10, 14–15; 32:1–5, 27–30; 1 Chron. 11:7–9; 15:1).

It is evident that the trends Manasseh had set were not easily reversed. Whatever the precise nature of Manasseh's reforms, Josiah would later still need to remove "the altars which Manasseh had made in the two courts of the house of the LORD" (see 2 Kings 23:12). Sadly, it was his wickedness, not his repentance and changed life, that would be emulated by his people and his own son Amon.

33:18–20. It is unfortunate that Manasseh's reign was so clouded by his wickedness that even the Chronicler remembered him more for his sin than for his repentance and the good that he subsequently performed.

When Manasseh died, **they buried him in his own house** (v. 20; see 2 Kings 21:18). His burial in the palace garden makes him the fifth king the Chronicler names who was not buried in the tombs of the kings (see discussion on 28:27).

M. Amon (33:21–25)

33:21–25. The reign of Amon was a compact duplication of his father's evil rule. The Chronicler's account of the reign of Amon (642–640 BC) is quite similar to that in Kings, apart from (1) the additional note that Amon was not repentant like his father, Manasseh, a note based on a passage unique to the Chronicler (33:12–13), and (2) the absence of the death formula. For Amon's reign, see discussions on 2 Kings 21:19–26.

N. Josiah (34:1–35:27)

34:1–36:1. See 2 Kings 22:1–23:30 and discussions. The two accounts of Josiah's reign are about the same length and treat the same subjects but have considerable variation in emphasis. Both deal with three different aspects of Josiah's reform: (1) the removal of foreign cults, (2) the finding of the book of the law and the covenant renewal that followed, and (3) the celebration of Passover. On the second item, the two histories are quite similar. On the first item, the author of Kings goes to great lengths (2 Kings 23:4–20), while the Chronicler summarizes it only briefly (34:3–7, 33). The account of the Passover is greatly expanded in Chronicles (35:1–19), while only alluded to in 2 Kings (23:21–23). Not only are these items treated at different lengths but also the order is changed. In Kings, the finding of the book of the law in the temple in Josiah's eighteenth year is the first incident mentioned. The author appears to have organized his material geographically, that is, beginning with the temple and spreading through the city, then into the rest of the nation. The Chronicler, on the other hand, has arranged the incidents in order of their occurrence and has characteristically introduced a number of chronological notes into the text: 34:3 (two notes without parallel in Kings); 34:8 (see 2 Kings 22:3); 35:19 (see 2 Kings 23:23; see also discussion on 2 Chron. 12:2). Chronicles makes it clear that the reform began in Josiah's twelfth year (34:3), six years before the discovery of the book of the law.

34:1–2. See 2 Kings 22:1–2 and discussion. At the age of eight, **Josiah** (v. 1) began his reign of **one and thirty years** (640–609 BC).

34:3–7. The author of Kings covers this aspect of Josiah's reform in much greater detail (2 Kings 23:4–20). He also delays his account of the removal of pagan cults until after the discovery of the book of the law, while the Chronicler places it before.

Due to his young age, Josiah undoubtedly began his reign under the guardianship and tutelage of the elders or the priests. From his **eighth year** (age sixteen; v. 3), when **he began to seek after the God of David**, until his **twelfth year** (age twenty), his religious instruction created within him the desire to restore the worship of the Lord. Therefore, he began to purify Judah of all the defilements initiated by Manasseh and Amon, spending six years (see 34:8) on this endeavor.

Some scholars have sought to tie the events of Josiah's **eighth** (v. 3), **twelfth** (v. 3), and **eighteenth** (34:8) years to stages in the progressive decline and fall of the Assyrian empire, which had dominated the area for about two centuries. The demise of Assyrian control in Syria and Israel undoubtedly facilitated and encouraged Josiah's reassertion of Davidic authority over former Assyrian provinces (vv. 6–7). However, one must not undercut religious motives in Josiah's reforms. Otherwise, the reform is reduced to merely a religious expression of an essentially political rebellion.

On Josiah's purge of idolatry, compare Asa's similar actions in 14:3–5 and Hezekiah's in 31:2. On his removal of the **groves** (Hebrew, *asherim*; v. 7), see discussion on 14:3. In purifying Judah and Jerusalem, Josiah desecrated the bones of pagan priests. He moved north to the pagan shrine at Bethel and repeated the procedure there (see discussion on 2 Kings 23:15–20). He enforced reforms as far north as **Manasseh, and Ephraim, and Simeon, even unto Naphtali** (v. 6), showing his movement to be even more far-reaching than Hezekiah's (see 31:1). The Chronicler's concern for "all Israel" (see 1 Chronicles, Introduction: "Theme") is apparent in his recording the northern tribes' involvement in Josiah's reform (see also 34:9, 21, 33). The Chronicler again shows all Israel united under a Davidic king, just as he did under Hezekiah (see discussion on 30:1). The reference to **Simeon** (v. 6) positions this tribe strangely in the north. Perhaps some Simeonites had migrated from Judah to the north. Josiah's campaign

of destroying images and idols **throughout all the land of Israel** (v. 7) is defined by the list of tribes in verse 6.

34:8–21. See 2 Kings 22:3–13 and discussions. In Josiah's **eighteenth year** (age twenty-six; v. 8), he directed his attention to the repair of the temple. Hezekiah had repaired the doors and purified the temple in 29:3–17. Second Kings notes Josiah's instructions to collect money for repairs, while the Chronicler emphasizes the implementation of these instructions. Money for repairs was received from **Manasseh and Ephraim, and of all the remnant of Israel** (v. 9). Again, as part of his concern with "all Israel," the Chronicler notes that worshipers from the north also brought gifts to the temple (not explicitly indicated in 2 Kings 22:4). Josiah's collecting of money and its distribution to the workmen (vv. 10–13) is comparable to Joash's repairs and payment years earlier (see 24:8–12).

For Hilkiah's discovery **of the law of the LORD** (v. 14), its presentation to Josiah, and his reaction to hearing it read (vv. 14–21), see discussions on 2 Kings 22:8–13.

34:22–28. For **Huldah the prophetess** (v. 22) and the prophetic word of the Lord, the evil He would bring on Jerusalem, and His promise to Josiah that judgment would not come in his day, see 2 Kings 22:14–20 and discussions.

34:29–31. For Josiah's **covenant before the LORD** (v. 31) to keep all the requirements of the law, see 2 Kings 23:1–3.

34:32–33. Josiah obligated all Judah and Benjamin to observe **the covenant of God** (v. 32). Then he removed the detestable things from **all the countries that pertained to the children of Israel ... all that were present in Israel** (v. 33; see discussion on 34:6; 2 Kings 23:4–20, 24 and discussions).

35:1–19. The Chronicler gives much more extensive coverage to Josiah's Passover celebration than is found in the brief allusion in Kings (see 2 Kings 23:21–23).

35:1–6. In the same year in which he repaired the temple, Josiah celebrated the Passover (see 34:8 and 35:19) **on the fourteenth day of the first month**

(v. 1), the prescribed date (see Exod. 12:6), whereas Hezekiah had needed to delay its observance by one month (see 30:15). Josiah's observance of the Passover confirmed his obedience to the newly found law.

Josiah's charge to the Levites, **Put the holy ark in the house which Solomon ... did build** (v. 3), implies that it had been removed from the temple. Possible reasons: (1) it had been removed from the Most Holy Place during the reign of one of the preceding wicked kings, either by the king himself or perhaps by the priests to protect it from the king by hiding it, or (2) it had been removed while the temple was being repaired.

Prepare yourselves ... according to the writing of David ... Solomon (v. 4). The Chronicler specifically parallels David and Solomon in three cases: 7:10 (compare 1 Kings 8:66, where only David is mentioned), 11:17, and here. This tendency reflects his glorification and idealization of both (see 1 Chronicles, Introduction: "Portrait of David and Solomon").

Kill the passover, and sanctify yourselves (v. 6). In his first year (715 BC; see 29:3–4), Josiah's great-grandfather Hezekiah had observed the Passover as it had not been observed "since the time of Solomon" (see 30:26). The Chronicler noted that there was apparently some confusion then in the preparation of the priests and Levites for celebrating the Passover (see 30:15–17). Here Josiah, about ninety-three years later, in his eighteenth year (35:19; 622 BC), commanded the Levites to be purified for the task of slaughtering the Passover lambs.

35:7–9. Josiah set the example by supplying numerous bullocks, presumably for peace offerings for the seven-day Feast of Unleavened Bread, which was to follow (compare the example of Hezekiah, 31:2–4). Then **his princes gave willingly unto the people** (v. 8). The emphasis in Chronicles on voluntary and joyful giving (24:8–14; 29:31–36; 31:3–21; 1 Chron. 29:3–9) presumably had direct relevance to the postexilic readers for whom the Chronicler wrote.

35:10–14. The Passover was prepared as prescribed by the law (see Exod. 12:6–10). The actual Passover sacrifice was offered, but the animals for the burnt offerings (i.e., possibly peace offerings) were apparently set aside for the following week of the Feast of Unleavened Bread.

35:15–17. The musicians (see 1 Chron. 25) assumed their role as commanded by David (see 1 Chron. 29:25), and the **porters** (i.e., gatekeepers; v. 15) took their stations to serve in the festivities of the occasion.

35:18–19. Josiah's Passover was observed by Judah and the remnant of Israel. No observance of the Passover since **the days of Samuel the prophet** (v. 18; instead of "from the days of the judges," 2 Kings 23:22) compared to it. Not even Hezekiah's great Passover compared because it had been delayed one month (see 30:17–18) and there were fewer participants (compare the 17,000 lambs slain in Hezekiah's day [30:2] to the 30,000 slain in Josiah's day).

Josiah's **eighteenth year** (v. 19) was the same year as the discovery of the book of the law (34:8, 14).

35:20–27. See 2 Kings 23:29–30 and discussion. In 609 BC, Pharaoh Necho "went up against the king of Assyria to the river Euphrates" (2 Kings 23:29) against the Babylonians. He went **up to fight against Carchemish** (better rendered "at Carchemish"; v. 20). This geographical note is not found in Kings.

Verses 21–22 are unique to the Chronicler, showing his view on retribution once again: Josiah's death in battle comes as a result of his disobedience to the word of God, as heard even from the mouth of the pagan pharaoh. Necho warned Josiah not to interfere, for to do so would be to interfere with his fulfilling God's command. Necho's statement cannot be lightly dismissed as diplomatic propaganda, for the Chronicler condemns Josiah for rejecting a divine prophecy (v. 22). Necho was not a prophet but a pagan king who momentarily served as God's spokesman (for another pagan king who was directly addressed by God, see Gen. 20:3–7). Further evidence of the validity of Necho's warning was Josiah's death.

The house wherewith I have war (v. 21) is a reference to the Babylonians; Nabopolassar was on the throne of Babylon, while his son Nebuchadnezzar was commanding the armies in the field. Nebuchadnezzar would succeed his father after another battle at Carchemish against Egypt, in 605 BC. Josiah may have been an ally of Babylon (see 32:31; 33:11 and discussions).

Josiah **disguised himself** (v. 22) to go into battle (compare Ahab and Jehoshaphat; see 18:29 and discussion) **in the valley of Megiddo**. See discussion on Judges 5:19.

This note (vv. 24b–25) is unique to Chronicles. Josiah's death came as a shattering blow to all Judah. One mourner who is named was Jeremiah, the prophet of the book bearing his name: **Jeremiah lamented for Josiah** (v. 25). Jeremiah held Josiah in high esteem (Jer. 22:15–16). The **lamentations** he composed for Josiah are no longer extant and are not to be confused with the canonical book of Lamentations. The statement that Jeremiah composed laments, however, is one of the reasons the book of Lamentations has been traditionally associated with him. For the phrase **to this day**, see discussion on 5:9.

35:26–27. Though the action that led to Josiah's death is criticized, this summary statement concerning Josiah is indeed favorable.

O. Josiah's Successors (36:1–14)

36:1–14. Josiah was the only king of Judah to be succeeded by three of his sons (Jehoahaz, Jehoiakim, and Zedekiah). The number of Josiah's sons and the order in which they assumed the throne present minor difficulties. The Chronicler states that Josiah had four sons (1 Chron. 3:15); the firstborn, Johanan, is otherwise unknown, and the fourth is Shallum (apparently an alternate name for Jehoahaz; see Jer. 22:11). Of the three sons who reigned after Josiah, however, Jehoahaz appears to have been the middle son (Jehoahaz was twenty-three when he reigned, v. 2; three months later, Jehoiakim was twenty-five when he reigned, v. 5; and Zedekiah was twenty-one when he reigned, v. 11). No explanation is given here why Jehoahaz reigned first (see discussion on 2 Kings 23:30). The Chronicler's account of the reigns of the remaining kings of Judah is quite brief.

36:1–4. See 2 Kings 23:31–35. With the death of Josiah at the hands of Pharaoh Necho, Judah slipped into a period of Egyptian domination (vv. 3–4). Jehoahaz reigned a mere **three months** (v. 2). In 609 BC, Necho's assertion of authority over Judah ended the brief twenty years of Judahite independence under Josiah. The Chronicler makes no moral judgment on this brief reign, though the author of Kings does (see 2 Kings 23:32).

Just as Necho took Jehoahaz into captivity and replaced him with **Eliakim** (v. 4), whose name he changed to **Jehoiakim**, so also Nebuchadnezzar would later take Jehoiachin to Babylon, replacing him with Mattaniah, whose name he changed to Zedekiah (2 Kings 24:15–17). Each conqueror wanted to place his own man on the throne; the change of name implied authority over him.

36:5–8. For Jehoiakim's reign of **eleven years** (609–598 BC; v. 5), see 2 Kings 23:36–24:7. Jehoiakim persecuted the prophets and was the object of scathing denunciation by Jeremiah (see Jeremiah 25–26; 36). After the Egyptian defeat at Carchemish (Jer. 46:2) in 605 BC, Jehoiakim transferred allegiance to Nebuchadnezzar of Babylon (see discussion on 2 Kings 24:1–7). When he later rebelled and again allied himself with Egypt, Nebuchadnezzar sent a punitive army against him. But Jehoiakim died before the army arrived, and Nebuchadnezzar took his son Jehoiachin into captivity.

36:9–10. For Jehoiachin's reign of **three months and ten days** (598–597 BC; v. 9), see 2 Kings 24:8–17; see also Jeremiah 22:24–28; 24:1; 29:2; 52:31. Although Jehoiachin was taken into captivity (597 BC) with a large retinue, including the queen mother and high officials, and was succeeded by Zedekiah, the exiles continued to fix dates in terms of his reign (see Jer. 52:31; Ezek. 1:2; see also Est. 2:5–6).

36:11–14. For Zedekiah's reign of **eleven years** (597–586 BC; v. 11), see 2 Kings 24:18–20; Jeremiah 52:1–3. **He did ... evil ... and humbled not himself before Jeremiah the prophet** (v. 12). This is the Chronicler's second reference to Jeremiah (see 35:25), who is not mentioned in 2 Kings. For the prophet's encounters with Zedekiah, see Jeremiah

37–38. Verses 13b–14 are unique to the Chronicler (see Jer. 1:3; 21:1–7; 24:8; 27:1–15; 32:1–5; 34:1–7, 21; 37:1–39:7). Zedekiah succumbed to the temptation to look to Egypt for help and rebelled against Nebuchadnezzar. The Babylonian reaction was swift. Jerusalem was besieged (Jer. 21:3–7) in 588 BC and held out for over two years before being destroyed in the summer of 586.

Not only had Zedekiah **hardened his heart** (v. 13) against **the Lord God of Israel**, but the core of spiritual leadership, **the priests** (v. 14), were corrupt and had **polluted the house of the Lord**. For the desecration of the temple, compare the corruption in the temple as witnessed by Ezekiel (Ezekiel 8).

P. Exile and Restoration (36:15–23)

36:15–19. They mocked the messengers of God, and despised his words, and misused his prophets (v. 16; see 24:19 and discussion; see also Jer. 26:20–24; 37:15–21; 38:6). Therefore, God could no longer exercise mercy. He had to take drastic measures of judgment against His people, who persisted in their rebellion against Him. He permitted the destruction of them, their city, and their temple and permitted their captivity in Babylon.

36:20–21. Them that had escaped from the sword carried he away to Babylon (v. 20). "He" in this sentence is "the king of the Chaldees," 36:17. The Babylonian captivity would last until the Persian overthrow, a period of approximately seventy years (see Jer. 25:12). Apparently since the beginning of the monarchy Israel had not observed the Sabbatical years as prescribed by the Law (see Lev. 25:1–7; 26:33–35). Therefore the captives from Judah would remain in Babylon until their land was compensated for its unobserved sabbaths.

The conclusion of the two biblical histories is interestingly different. The author(s) of Samuel and Kings had sought to show why the exile occurred and had traced the sad history of Israel's disobedience to the exile, the time in which the author(s) of those books lived. With the state of Israel at an end, he could still show God's faithfulness to His promises to David (2 Kings 25:27–30) by reporting the favor bestowed on his descendants. The Chronicler, whose vantage point was after the exile, was able to look back to the exile not only as judgment but also as containing hope for the future. For him, the purified remnant had returned to a purified land (vv. 22–23), and a new age was beginning. The exile was not judgment alone but also blessing, for it allowed the land to catch up on its sabbath rests (Lev. 26:40–45). God remembered His covenant (Lev. 26:45) and restored His people to the land (see next discussion).

36:22–23. The author of Kings concluded his history before the restoration, so this text is not paralleled in his account. It is repeated, however, at the beginning of Ezra (1:1–4), which resumes the history at the point where Chronicles ends—indicating that Chronicles and Ezra may have been written by the same author.

Though the Chronicler related an unhappy ending to Judah and Jerusalem, he closes on a more encouraging note. Judah's punishment had run its course (see the prophecy of Jeremiah; Jer. 25:11–14; 29:10–14; see also Daniel 9). **Cyrus king of Persia** (v. 22), whom Isaiah called the Lord's "anointed" (Isa. 45:1), took Babylon in 539 BC. A year later, he issued a decree that released all of Babylon's prisoners and allowed them to return to their homelands. Under God's sovereignty, this effort by a Persian king to win the favor of peoples treated harshly by the Babylonians also inaugurated the restoration period. Thus, the Jews were permitted to return to Jerusalem and rebuild their place of worship (see discussions on Ezra 1:1–4).

THE BOOK OF EZRA

INTRODUCTION

Title

Although the caption in Nehemiah 1:1, "The words of Nehemiah the son of Hachaliah," indicates that Ezra and Nehemiah were originally two separate compositions, they were combined as one work in the earliest Hebrew manuscripts. Josephus (ca. AD 37–100) and the Jewish Talmud refer to the book of Ezra but not to a separate book of Nehemiah. The oldest manuscripts of the Septuagint (the Greek translation of the Old Testament) also treat Ezra and Nehemiah as one book.

Origen (AD 185–253) is the first writer known to distinguish between the two books, which he called 1 Ezra and 2 Ezra. In translating the Latin Vulgate (AD 390–405), Jerome called Nehemiah the Second Book of Esdrae (Ezra). The English translations by Wycliffe (1382) and Coverdale (1535) also called the two books 1 Esdras (Ezra) and 2 Esdras (Nehemiah). This separation first appeared in a Hebrew manuscript in 1448.

Author and Date

Certain materials in Ezra are first-person extracts from Ezra's memoirs: 7:27–28; 8:1–34; 9. Other sections are written in the third person: 7:1–26; 10 (see also Nehemiah 8). Linguistic analysis has shown that the first-person and third-person extracts resemble each other, making it likely that the same author wrote both.

Most scholars conclude that the author-compiler of Ezra and Nehemiah was also the author of 1–2 Chronicles. This viewpoint is based on certain characteristics common to both Chronicles and Ezra-Nehemiah. The verses at the end of Chronicles and at the beginning of Ezra are virtually identical. Both Chronicles and Ezra-Nehemiah exhibit a fondness for lists, for the description of religious festivals, and for such phrases as "chief of the fathers" and "the house of God." Especially striking in these books is the prominence of Levites and temple personnel. The words for "singer," "porter," and "Nethinims" (i.e., temple servants) are used almost exclusively in Ezra-Nehemiah and Chronicles. See 1 Chronicles, Introduction: "Author, Date, and Sources."

Ezra was composed circa 440 BC and the Nehemiah memoirs circa 430.

Chronology

According to the traditional view, Ezra arrived in Jerusalem in the seventh year (7:8) of Artaxerxes I (458 BC), followed by Nehemiah, who arrived in the king's twentieth year (445 BC; Neh. 2:1).

Some have proposed a reverse order, in which Nehemiah arrived in 445 BC, while Ezra arrived in the seventh year of Artaxerxes II (398 BC). By amending "seventh" (7:8) to either "twenty-seventh" or "thirty-seventh," others place Ezra after Nehemiah but maintain that they were contemporaries.

These alternative views, however, present more problems than the traditional position. As the text stands, Ezra arrived before Nehemiah, and they are found together in Nehemiah 8:9 (at the reading of the law) and Nehemiah 12:26, 36 (at the dedication of the wall). See chart, *Zondervan KJV Study Bible*, p. 635.

Literary Features

As in the closely related books of 1 and 2 Chronicles, one notes the prominence of various lists in Ezra and Nehemiah, which have evidently been obtained from official sources. Included are lists of (1) the temple vessels (1:9–11), (2) the returned exiles (chap. 2, which is virtually the same as Neh. 7:6–73), (3) the genealogy of Ezra (7:1–5), (4) the heads of the clans (8:1–14), (5) those involved in mixed marriages (10:18–43), (6) those who helped rebuild the wall (Nehemiah 3), (7) those who sealed the covenant (Neh. 10:1–27), (8) residents of Jerusalem and other towns (Neh. 11:3–36), and (9) priests and Levites (Neh. 12:1–26).

Also included in Ezra are seven official documents or letters (all in Aramaic except the first, which is in Hebrew): (1) the decree of Cyrus (1:2–4), (2) the accusation of Rehum and others against the Jews (4:11–16), (3) the reply of Artaxerxes I (4:17–22), (4) the report from Tatnai (5:7–17), (5) the memorandum of Cyrus's decree (6:2b–5), (6) Darius's reply to Tatnai (6:6–12), and (7) the authorization given by Artaxerxes I to Ezra (7:12–26). The documents compare favorably with contemporary nonbiblical documents of the Persian period.

Ezra and Nehemiah were written in a form of late Hebrew with the exception of Ezra 4:8–6:18; 7:12–26, which were written in Aramaic, the international language during the Persian period. Of these sixty-seven Aramaic verses, fifty-two are in records or letters. Ezra evidently found these documents in Aramaic and copied them, inserting connecting verses in Aramaic.

Outline

I. First Return from Exile and Rebuilding of the Temple (chaps. 1–6)
- A. First Return of the Exiles (chap. 1)
  1. The Edict of Cyrus (1:1–4)
  2. The Return under Sheshbazzar (1:5–11)
- B. List of Returning Exiles (chap. 2)
- C. Revival of Temple Worship (chap. 3)
  1. The Rebuilding of the Altar (3:1–3)

Bibliography

Breneman, Mervin. *Ezra, Nehemiah, Esther*. New American Commentary 10. Nashville: Broadman & Holman, 1993.

Fensham, F. Charles. *The Books of Ezra and Nehemiah*. New International Commentary on the Old Testament. Grand Rapids, MI: Eerdmans, 1982.

Kidner, Derek. *Ezra and Nehemiah*. Tyndale Old Testament Commentaries 11. Downers Grove, IL: InterVarsity, 1979.

McConville, J. Gordon. *Ezra, Nehemiah, and Esther*. Daily Study Bible. Philadelphia: Westminster, 1985.

Williamson, Hugh. *Ezra, Nehemiah*. Word Biblical Commentary 16. Waco, TX: Word, 1985.

Yamauchi, Edwin. "Ezra." In *Expositor's Bible Commentary*, edited by Frank E. Gaebelein, vol. 4. Grand Rapids, MI: Zondervan, 1988.

———. *Persia and the Bible*. Grand Rapids, MI: Baker, 1990.

EXPOSITION

I. First Return from Exile and Rebuilding of the Temple (chaps. 1–6)

A. First Return of the Exiles (chap. 1)

1. The Edict of Cyrus (1:1–4)

1:1–3a. These verses are virtually identical with the last two verses of 2 Chronicles. This fact has been used to argue that Chronicles and Ezra-Nehemiah were written and/or edited by the same person, the so-called Chronicler. However, the repetition may have been a device of the author of Chronicles (or less probably of Ezra) to dovetail the narratives chronologically.

1:1. **The first year** of the reign of Cyrus over Babylon began in March 538 BC, after he captured Babylon in October 539 BC. Cyrus, the founder of the Persian Empire, reigned over the Persians from 559 until 530 BC. Isaiah 44:28 and 45:1 speak of him as the Lord's "shepherd" and His "anointed." **Jeremiah** prophesied a seventy-year Babylonian captivity (Jer. 25:11–12; 29:10). The first deportation began in 605 BC, the third year of Jehoiakim (Dan. 1:1). In 538 BC, approximately seventy years later, the people began to return.

1:2–4. This oral proclamation of Cyrus's decree was written in Hebrew, the language of the Israelite captives, in contrast to the copy of the decree in 6:3–5, which was an Aramaic memorandum for the archives. Of the twenty-two Old Testament occurrences of the phrase **God of heaven** (v. 2), seventeen occur in Ezra, Nehemiah, and Daniel. God's **house** (v. 3) and **Jerusalem** are prominent subjects in Ezra and Nehemiah.

Cyrus instituted the policy of placating the gods of his subject peoples instead of carrying off their cult images, as the Assyrians and the Babylonians had done earlier. His generosity to the Jews allowed them to return to Jerusalem. Those who did not wish to leave Mesopotamia were permitted to remain, but they were encouraged to give **a freewill offering** (v. 4), which was key to the restoration of God's temple and its services (see 2:68; 3:5; 8:28).

2. The Return under Sheshbazzar (1:5–11)

1:5–7. Chief of the fathers (v. 5). In ancient times, families were extended families, more like clans than modern nuclear families. The authority figure was the patriarch, who was the "head of the household" (see 10:16; see also 2:59; Neh. 7:61; 10:34). **Judah and Benjamin** were the two main tribes of the kingdom of Judah, which the Babylonians had exiled (see 1 Kings 12:21). The **Levites** were those entrusted with the menial tasks of temple service (see Leviticus, Introduction: "Title").

It was the custom for conquerors to carry off the images of the gods of conquered cities. Since the Jews did not have an image of the Lord (see Exod. 20:4), Nebuchadnezzar carried away only the temple articles (v. 7).

1:8. Mithredath is a Persian name meaning "given by/to Mithra," a Persian god who became popular among Roman soldiers in the second century AD. **Sheshbazzar** is a Babylonian name meaning either "Sin, protect the father" or "Shamash, protect the father." Sin was the moon god, and Shamash (Shashu is a variant) was the sun god. In spite of his

Babylonian name, Sheshbazzar was probably a Jewish official who served as a deputy governor of Judah under the satrap in Samaria (see 5:14). Some believe that Sheshbazzar and Zerubbabel were the same person and give the following reasons: (1) both were governors (5:14; Hag. 1:1; 2:2), (2) both are said to have laid the foundation of the temple (3:2–8; 5:16; Hag. 1:14–15; Zech. 4:6–10), (3) Jews in Babylon were often given "official" Babylonian names (see Dan. 1:7), and (4) Josephus (*Antiquities* 11.1.3) seems to identify Sheshbazzar with Zerubbabel.

Others point out, however, that the Apocrypha distinguishes between the two men (1 Esdras 6:18). Furthermore, it is likely that Sheshbazzar was an elderly man at the time of the return, while Zerubbabel was probably a younger contemporary. Sheshbazzar also may have been viewed as the official governor, while Zerubbabel served as the popular leader (3:8–11). Whereas the high priest Jeshua is associated with Zerubbabel, no priest is associated with Sheshbazzar. Although Sheshbazzar presided over the foundation of the temple in 536 BC, so little was accomplished that Zerubbabel had to preside over a second foundation some sixteen years later (see Hag. 1:14–15; Zech. 4:6–10).

Still others hold that Sheshbazzar is to be identified with Shenazar (1 Chron. 3:18), the fourth son of King Jeconiah. Zerubbabel would then have been Sheshbazzar's nephew (compare 3:2 with 1 Chron. 3:18).

1:9–11. When Assyrian and Babylonian conquerors carried off plunder, their scribes made a careful inventory of all the goods seized. The total of the figures in verses 9–10 adds up to 2,499 rather than the 5,400 of verse 11. It may be that only the larger and more valuable vessels are specified here.

No details are available of Sheshbazzar's journey, which probably took place in 537 BC. Judging from Ezra's later journey (7:8–9), the trip took about four months. See Map 8 at the end of the *KJV Study Bible*; see also map, *KJV Study Bible*, p. 631.

B. List of Returning Exiles (chap. 2)

2:1–70. The list of returning exiles in chapter 2 parallels almost exactly the list in Nehemiah 7:6–73

(in the Apocrypha, see 1 Esdras 5:4–46). The list of localities indicates that people retained the memories of their homes and that exiles from a wide background of tribes, villages, and towns returned. In comparing this list with that in Nehemiah 7, one notes many differences in the names and numbers listed. About 20 percent of the numbers, for example, are not the same in Ezra and Nehemiah. Many of these differences may be explained, however, by assuming that a cipher notation was used, with vertical strokes for units and horizontal strokes for tens, which led to copying errors.

2:1. The province is probably Judah. Compare 5:8, where the Aramaic word for "province" occurs (see also Neh. 1:3).

2:2–20. Zerubbabel (v. 2) was the appointed governor (see discussion on 1:8; 3:2; Hag. 1:1). The names listed with Zerubbabel were apparently leaders who accompanied him to assist him. The name of the priest was **Jeshua,** which means "the Lord saves," and is an Aramaic variant of the Hebrew name Joshua. Jesus is the Greek form of this name. Jeshua is the same person as the Joshua of Haggai 1:1, the son of the high priest Jehozadak (Jozadak in Ezra 3:2), who was taken into exile (1 Chron. 6:15). **Nehemiah** is not the Nehemiah of the book by that name. **Mordecai** is a Babylonian name based on that of Marduk, the god of Babylon (see Jer. 50:2). Esther's cousin had the same name (Est. 2:7). Several members of the families named in verses 6–14 also returned with Ezra (8:3–14).

2:21–35. Whereas the names in 2:3–20 are of families, verses 21–35 present a series of villages and towns, many of which were in Benjamite territory, north of Jerusalem. It is significant that there are no references to towns in the Negev, south of Judah. When Nebuchadnezzar overran Judah in 597 BC (Jer. 13:19), the Edomites (see the book of Obadiah) took advantage of the situation and occupied that area.

Significantly, at the head of the list are the **children of Beth-lehem** (v. 21; see 1 Sam. 17:12; 20:6; Mic. 5:2; Luke 2:4), for the ancestors of Jesus may have been among these returnees.

Towns such as Bethel, Mizpah, Gibeon, and Gibeah seem to have escaped the Babylonian assault. **Beth-el** (v. 28), however, was destroyed in the transition between the Babylonian and Persian periods. Archaeological excavations reveal that there was a small town on the site in Ezra's day.

The largest number of returnees, 3,630 (3,930 in Neh. 7:38), is associated with **Senaah** (v. 35). It has therefore been suggested that they did not come from a specific locality or family but represented the poorer and lower classes of people, as inferred from the meaning of the name Senaah, "the hated one."

2:36–39. These four clans of priests, numbering 4,289, represent about one-tenth of the total number of priests (see 2:64).

2:40. The number of **Levites** who returned was relatively small (see 8:15). Since the Levites had been entrusted with the menial tasks of temple service, many of them may have found a more comfortable way of life in exile.

2:41. Asaph was one of the three Levites appointed by David over the temple singers (1 Chron. 25:1; 2 Chron. 5:12; 35:15), whose duties are detailed in 1 Chronicles 15:16–24.

2:42. The **porters** (i.e., "gatekeepers") were usually Levites (1 Chron. 9:26; 2 Chron. 23:4; 35:15; Neh. 12:25; 13:22). They are mentioned sixteen times in Ezra-Nehemiah and nineteen times in Chronicles. Their primary function was to tend the doors and gates of the temple (1 Chron. 9:17–27) and to perform other menial tasks (1 Chron. 9:28–32; 2 Chron. 31:14).

2:43–57. The **Nethinims** (i.e., "temple servants"; v. 43) and the descendants of Solomon's servants together numbered 392 (2:58), which was more than the total of the Levites, singers, and gatekeepers together (2:40–42).

Sophereth (v. 55), more fully *Hassophereth* in Hebrew, probably means "the scribal office/function" and may have once been an official title.

2:58. The children of Solomon's servants is a phrase that occurs only here and in Nehemiah 7:57, 60; 11:3. These may have been the descendants of the Canaanites whom Solomon enslaved (1 Kings 9:20–21).

2:59–63. Some who returned with Zerubbabel were individuals who lacked evidence of their ancestry and were thus unable to prove they were from Israel. The sites listed are places in Mesopotamia where the Jews had been settled by their Babylonian captors. The Hebrew word **Tel** (v. 59) designates a hill-like mound formed by the remains of a ruined city. The Jewish exiles had been settled along the Chebar River (Ezek. 1:1), perhaps near Nippur, a city in southern Mesopotamia that was the stronghold of rebels. The Jews had probably been settled on the mounds of ruined cities that had been depopulated by the Babylonians.

Tirshatha (v. 63) is a transliteration of the Hebrew word for "governor." It probably refers to either Sheshbazzar or Zerubbabel (see 1:8), who excluded these individuals from the priesthood until their pedigree could be established. The high priest's vesture included a place for the **Urim and ... Thummim**, sacred lots that were often used to determine God's will (see Exod. 28:30).

2:64. The number of the congregation is considerably more than the sum of the other figures given.

Categories	Ezra	Nehemiah	1 Esdras
Men of Israel	24,144	25,406	25,947
Priests	4,289	4,289	5,288
Levites, singers, gatekeepers	341	360	341
Temple servants, descendants of Solomon's servants	392	392	372
Men of unproven origin	652	642	652
Totals	29,818	31,089	32,600

It is difficult to account for the difference of about 10,000–12,000 people. The figure may refer to an unspecified 10,000–12,000 women and/or children, and it doubtless includes the priests of unproven origin (2:61–63). Some suggest that the groups explicitly counted were returnees from Judah and Benjamin, while the remainder was from other tribes.

2:65. The ratio of **servants and ... maids** to others (one to six) is relatively high. That so many returned with their masters speaks highly of the benevolent treatment of servants by the Jews. The **singing men and ... women** listed here may be secular singers who sang at social events, such as weddings and funerals (2 Chron. 35:25), as distinct from the temple singers of 2:41, who were all male.

2:66–67. The **horses** (v. 66) were perhaps a donation from Cyrus for the nobility. **Mules** were often used by royalty and the wealthy (1 Kings 1:33; Isa. 66:20). **Asses** (v. 67) were used to carry loads, women, or children. Sheep, goats, and cattle are not mentioned. They would have slowed the caravan.

2:68–69. The parallel passage in Nehemiah (7:70–72) gives a fuller description than the account in Ezra. In Ezra, the gifts came from the heads of the families (v. 68), while in Nehemiah the gifts are credited to three sources: the governor, the heads of the families, and the rest of the people. **Drams** (i.e., "drachmas"; v. 69) were Greek silver coins. Some believe, however, that the coin intended here was the Persian daric, a gold coin. **Pound** is literally "minas." In the sexagesimal system (based on the number sixty), which originated in Mesopotamia, there were sixty shekels in a mina, and sixty minas in a talent. A shekel, which was about two-fifths of an ounce of silver, was the average wage for a month's work. Thus, a mina would be the equivalent of five years' wages, and a talent would be three hundred years' wages.

For the route of the return to **Jerusalem** (v. 68) from exile, see Map 8 at the end of the *KJV Study Bible*.

2:70. Later, Nehemiah (11:1–2) would be compelled to move some of these returnees, by lot, to reinforce the population of Jerusalem.

C. Revival of Temple Worship (chap. 3)

1. The Rebuilding of the Altar (3:1–3)

3:1–3. The seventh month (v. 1), Tishri (September–October), occurred about three months after the arrival of the exiles in Judah (537 BC). The

time was most fitting for the event, for Tishri was one of the most sacred months of the Jewish year (see Lev. 23:23–43 and discussions). In view of the nature of the occasion (compare 3:8; 4:3; 5:2; Hag. 1:1), the high priest, **Jeshua** (v. 2), took precedence over the civil leader, **Zerubbabel**. With the altar restored, even though the temple was not yet rebuilt, the sacrifices prescribed by the law could be offered.

2. The Feast of Tabernacles (3:4–6)

3:4–6. The seventh month was the set time for **the feast of tabernacles** (v. 4), the commemoration of how they had lived when they came out of Egypt (see Lev. 23:33–43 and discussions). With the altar in place, they were able to offer all the daily offerings, the offerings for consecrating the **new moons** (i.e. the first day of the month; v. 5), and all of the other fixed feasts. The **freewill offering** was often offered with other sacrifices and feasts but could be brought for no other reason than love for God. It is noteworthy that the restoration of the sacrifices preceded the erection of the temple itself.

3. The Beginning of Temple Reconstruction (3:7–13)

3:7–9. As in the case of the first temple, the Phoenicians cooperated by sending timber, **cedar trees** (v. 7), and workmen (1 Kings 5:6–12). Since the Jews probably returned to Judah in the spring of 537 BC, **the second year** (v. 8) would have been the spring of 536. **The second month** is the same month (April–May) in which Solomon had begun his temple (1 Kings 6:1). In earlier times, the lower age limit for Levites to serve was thirty (Num. 4:3) or twenty-five years (Num. 8:24). It was later reduced to **twenty years** (1 Chron. 23:24, 27; 2 Chron. 31:17), probably because there were so few Levites.

3:10–13. The construction was accompanied by **trumpets** (v. 10) and **cymbals**. The trumpets were probably made of hammered silver (see Num. 10:2). According to Josephus (*Antiquities* 3.12.6, written ca. AD 93), the trumpet was "in length a little short of a cubit; it is a narrow tube, slightly thicker than a flute." With the possible exception of their use at the coronation of Joash (2 Kings 11:14; 2 Chron.

23:13), the trumpets were always blown by priests. They were most often used on joyous occasions, such as here and at the dedication of the rebuilt walls of Jerusalem (Neh. 12:35; see 2 Chron. 5:13; Ps. 98:6). The instruments were joined with the voices of a choir divided into two groups, probably singing antiphonally a common refrain, **he is good … his mercy endureth for ever** (v. 11; see, e.g., 1 Chron. 16:34; 2 Chron. 5:13; Ps. 100:5). Accompanying **the shout of joy** (v. 13) was **the noise of the weeping**. The people of Israel were accustomed to showing their emotions in visible and audible ways (10:1; Neh. 1:4; 8:9). The same God who had permitted judgment had now brought them back and would enable them to complete the project. A Babylonian cornerstone reads: "I started the work weeping, I finished it rejoicing." See Psalm 126:5–6.

D. Opposition to Rebuilding (4:1–23)

4:1–23. Chapter 4 is a summary of various attempts to thwart the efforts of the Jews. In verses 1–5, the author describes events in the reign of Cyrus (559–530 BC); in verse 6, the reign of Ahasuerus (486–465 BC); and in verses 7–23, the reign of Artaxerxes I (465–424 BC). In verse 24, he reverts to the time of Darius I (522–486 BC), during whose reign the temple was completed (see 5:1–2; 6:13–15; Haggai; Zech. 1:1–17; 4:9).

1. Opposition during the Reign of Cyrus (4:1–5)

4:1–5. The people who offered "help" (v. 2) to **Judah and Benjamin** (v. 1; see 1:5) were from Samaria and were considered **adversaries**. After the fall of Samaria in 722–721 BC, the Assyrian kings brought in people from Mesopotamia and Aram. These people served their own gods but had also taken up the worship of the Lord as the god of the land (2 Kings 17:24–41) in the days of **Esar-haddon** (v. 2; see 2 Kings 19:37). **The people of the land … troubled them** (v. 4). Josephus (*Antiquities* 11.2.1) singles out especially the Cutheans (see 2 Kings 17:24, 30). The Hebrew for the verb "troubled" often describes the fear aroused in a battle situation (see Judg. 20:41; 2 Sam. 4:1; 2 Chron. 32:18). For

the hiring of **counsellers against them** (v. 5), see the hiring of Balaam (Deut. 23:4–5; Neh. 13:2) and the hiring of a prophet to intimidate Nehemiah (Neh. 6:12–13).

2. Opposition during the Reign of Ahasuerus (4:6)

4:6. When Darius died in 486 BC, Egypt rebelled, and **Ahasuerus** (see the book of Esther), the son of Darius, had to march west to suppress the revolt.

3. Opposition during the Reign of Artaxerxes (4:7–23)

4:7. Three Persian kings bore the name **Artaxerxes**: Artaxerxes I (465–424 BC), II (404–358), and III (358–338). The king here is Artaxerxes I. Near Eastern kings employed an elaborate system of informers and spies. Egyptian sources speak of the "ears and eyes" of the pharaoh. Sargon II of Assyria had agents in Urartu whom he ordered: "Write me whatever you see and hear." The officials listed here were the king's "eye and ears," who reported to the Persian monarch.

4:8–6:18. For this passage, the author draws on Aramaic documents. In the original text of Ezra, this section is written in Aramaic; a further Aramaic section is 7:12–26.

4:8–10. Rehum (v. 8) was an official who had the role of **chancellor**, that is, commanding officer or commissioner. Perhaps he dictated, and **Shimshai** wrote the letter in Aramaic. (Alternatively, Shimshai may have been a high official rather than a scribe.) The letter would later be read before the king in a Persian translation (see 4:18). According to Herodotus (3.128), royal scribes were attached to each governor to report directly to the Persian king.

One of the striking characteristics of Persian bureaucracy was that each responsibility was shared among **companions** (v. 9), that is, colleagues (see 4:17, 23; 5:3, 6; 6:6, 13). Among these were **Archevites** (i.e., men of Erech) and **Babylonians**. During the reign of the Assyrian king Ashurbanipal (669–627 BC), a major revolt had taken place (652–648 BC) involving Shamash-shum-ukin, the brother of the king and the ruler over Babylonia. After a long siege, Shamash-shum-ukin hurled himself into the flames.

Doubtless these men of Babylon and the other cities mentioned were the descendants of the rebels, whom the Assyrians had deported to the west. **Susanchites** were men of Susa, the major city of Elam (in southwest Iran). Because of Susa's part in the revolt, Ashurbanipal brutally destroyed it in 640 BC (two centuries before Rehum's letter). **Asnappar** (v. 10) is to be identified as "Ashurbanipal," the last great Assyrian king, famed for his library at Nineveh. He is not named elsewhere in the Bible, but he is probably the king who freed Manasseh from exile (2 Chron. 33:11 – 13). Ashurbanipal may be the unnamed Assyrian king who **brought** people to Samaria according to 2 Kings 17:24. It was characteristic of such deportations that the descendants of these populations, removed from their homelands nearly two centuries earlier, still stressed their origins. The earlier murder of Amon king of Judah (642 – 640 BC; see 2 Kings 21:23; 2 Chron. 33:24) was probably the result of an anti-Assyrian movement inspired by the revolt in Elam and Babylonia. The Assyrians may then have deported the rebellious residents of **Samaria** and replaced them with the rebellious Elamites and Babylonians. **This side the river** is literally "beyond the river" (i.e., the Euphrates River). From Israel's point of view the land "beyond the river" was Mesopotamia (Josh. 24:2 – 3, 14 – 15; 2 Sam. 10:16). From the Mesopotamian point of view, the land "beyond the river" included the areas of Aram, Phoenicia, and Israel (1 Kings 4:24).

4:12 – 13. As Isaiah had foretold (see Isa. 58:12), the Jews had **set up the walls … and joined the foundations** (v. 12). The accusers hoped that the king would fear the loss of revenue if the city were rebuilt, for most of the gold and silver coins that came into Persia's treasury were melted down to be stored as bullion. Very little of the taxes returned to benefit the provinces.

4:14 – 16. We have maintenance from the king's palace (v. 14) is literally, "We eat the salt of the palace." Salt was made a royal monopoly by the Ptolemies in Egypt and perhaps by the Persians as well. These accusers maintained that since they were supported by the king, they were duty bound to report

on the Jews. Several repositories of documents existed in the major capitals, where **the book of the records** (v. 15) were preserved (see 5:17; 6:1; Est. 2:23; 6:1 – 2). These royal archives preserved documents for centuries. In the third century BC, the Babylonian priest Berossus used the Babylonian Chronicles in his history of Babylon, which covered events from the Assyrian to the Hellenistic (beginning with Alexander's conquest of Babylon, 330 BC) eras.

4:17 – 18. The letter was **plainly read** (v. 18), that is, translated from Aramaic into Persian (see discussion on 4:8 – 6:18). Since the king probably could not read Aramaic, he would have had the document read to him.

4:19 – 20. There was some truth in the accusation of **rebellion** (v. 19). Jerusalem had rebelled against the Assyrians in 701 BC (2 Kings 18:7) and against the Babylonians in 600 and 589 BC (2 Kings 24:1, 20).

4:21 – 23. As a result of the intervention of the provincial authorities, Artaxerxes I (see 4:11 and discussion on 4:7) ordered that the Jews stop rebuilding the walls of Jerusalem (see discussion on Neh. 1:3). The events of 4:7 – 23 probably occurred prior to 445 BC. The forcible destruction of these recently rebuilt walls rather than destruction by Nebuchadnezzar would then be the basis of the report made to Nehemiah (Neh. 1:3).

E. Completion of the Temple (4:24 – 6:22)

1. Resumption of Work under Darius (4:24)

4:24. After the long digression describing the opposition to Jewish efforts, the writer returns to his original subject of the rebuilding of the temple (4:1 – 5). According to Persian reckoning, **the second year of the reign of Darius [I]** began on Nisan 1 (April 3), 520 BC, and lasted until February 21, 519 BC. In that year, the prophet Haggai (Hag. 1:1 – 5) exhorted Zerubbabel to begin rebuilding the temple on the first day of the sixth month (August 29). Work began on the temple on the twenty-fourth day of the month, September 21 (Hag. 1:15). During his first two years, Darius had to establish his right to the throne by fighting numerous rebels, as recounted in his famous Behistun (Bisitun) inscription. It was only after the stabilization of the Persian empire that efforts to rebuild the temple could be permitted.

2. A New Beginning Inspired by Haggai and Zechariah (5:1–2)

5:1–2. Beginning on August 29 (520 BC; Hag. 1:1) and continuing until December 18 (Hag. 2:1, 10, 20), the prophet **Haggai** (v. 1) delivered a series of messages to stir up the people to resume work on the temple. Two months after Haggai's first speech, **Zechariah** joined him (Zech. 1:1). **Zerubbabel** (v. 2) is a Babylonian name meaning "offspring of Babylon," referring to his birth in exile. He was the son of Shealtiel and the grandson of Jeconiah (1 Chron. 3:17), the next-to-last king of Judah. Zerubbabel was the last of the Davidic line to be entrusted with political authority by the occupying powers. He was also an ancestor of Jesus (Matt. 1:12–13; Luke 3:27). For **Jeshua**, see discussion on 2:2.

3. Intervention of the Governor, Tatnai (5:3–5)

5:3–5. Another attempt to prevent the building was initiated by the governor, **Tatnai** (v. 3), probably a Babylonian name, and **Shethar-boznai**, perhaps a Persian official. The Persian governor, however, gave the Jews the benefit of the doubt by not stopping the work while the inquiry was proceeding.

4. Report to Darius (5:6–17)

5:6–7. Texts found in the royal city of Persepolis vividly confirm that such inquiries were sent directly to the king himself, revealing the close attention he paid to minute details.

5:8–17. The report of Tatnai and Shethar-boznai cited the **timber** (v. 8), perhaps referring to interior paneling (1 Kings 6:15–18) or to logs that were alternated with the brick or stone layers in the walls (see discussion on 6:4). Their report also included the explanation made by the **elders** (v. 9) that the temple had been built by **the great king of Israel** (v. 11). According to 1 Kings 6:1, Solomon began building the temple in the fourth year of his reign (966 BC). The project lasted seven years (1 Kings 6:38).

The elders confess that their sin had brought God's judgment on them, at **the hand of Nebuchadnezzar the king of Babylon, the Chaldean** (v. 12). The Chaldeans were the inhabitants of the southern regions of Mesopotamia who established the Neo-Babylonian Empire (612–539 BC). Their origins are obscure. In the late seventh century BC, the Chaldeans, led by Nebuchadnezzar's father, Nabopolassar, overthrew the Assyrians.

Cyrus (v. 14) the Persian king, however, had made **Sheshbazzar** governor and granted permission to rebuild the temple (see discussion on 1:8).

5. Search for the Decree of Cyrus (6:1–5)

6:1–2. A search for the decree in question was made **in the house of the rolls, where the treasures were laid up in Babylon** (v. 1). Many documents have also been found in the so-called treasury area of Persepolis (see map, *KJV Study Bible*, p. 545). **Achmetha** (i.e., Ecbatana; v. 2) was one of the four capitals (along with Babylon, Persepolis, and Susa) of the Persian Empire. Located in what is today the Iranian city of Hamadan, its remains have not yet been excavated. This is the only reference to the site in the Old Testament, though there are numerous references to it in the Apocryphal books (Judith 1:1–4; Tobit 3:7; 7:1; 14:12–14; 2 Maccabees 9:3). The **Medes** were a people whose homeland was Media, in northwestern Iran. They were an Indo-European tribe related to the Persians. After the rise of Cyrus in 550 BC, they became subordinate to the Persians. The name of the area was retained as late as the New Testament era (see Acts 2:9).

6:3–5. Compare this Aramaic memorandum of the decree of Cyrus with the Hebrew version in 1:2–4. The Aramaic is written in a more sober administrative style and does not contain any references to the Lord (Yahweh). A similar memorandum pertaining to permission to rebuild the Jewish temple at Elephantine in Upper Egypt was found among fifth-century BC Aramaic papyri recovered at that site.

The dimensions given in verses 3–4, which contrast with those of Solomon's temple (see 1 Kings

6:2 and discussion), are probably not specifications of the temple as built but of the outer limits of a building the Persians were willing to subsidize. The second temple was not as grandiose as the first (3:12; Hag. 2:3). The same kind of construction, **great stones ... timber** (v. 4; see 5:8), is mentioned in 1 Kings 6:36; 7:12. Such a design possibly was intended to cushion the building against earthquake shocks. **The expences** were to come from the king's treasury. In 1973, archaeologists discovered at Xanthos, in southwestern Turkey, a religious foundation charter from the late Persian period that provides some striking parallels with this decree of Cyrus. As in Ezra, amounts of sacrifices, names of priests, and the responsibility for the upkeep of the cult are specified. The Persian king seems to have known details of the cult.

6. Darius's Order for the Rebuilding of the Temple (6:6–12)

6:6–8. That of the king's goods ... expences be given (v. 8). Persian kings had a consistent policy of helping to restore sanctuaries in their empire. For example, a memorandum concerning the rebuilding of the Jewish temple at Elephantine was written by the Persian governors of Judah and Samaria. Also noted from nonbiblical sources, Cyrus repaired temples at Uruk (Erech) and Ur. Cambyses, successor to Cyrus, gave funds for the temple at Sais in Egypt. The temple of Amun in the Khargah Oasis was rebuilt by order of Darius.

6:9. That the Persian monarchs were interested in the details of foreign religions is clearly shown by the ordinances of Cambyses and Darius I regulating the temples and priests in Egypt. On the authority of Darius II (423–404 BC), a letter was written to the Jews at Elephantine concerning the observation of the Feast of Unleavened Bread.

6:10. Darius's request for prayer is consistent with the inscription on the Cyrus Cylinder (made of baked clay), in which the king asks, "May all the gods whom I have resettled in their sacred cities ask Bel and Nebo daily for a long life for me." The Jews of Elephantine offered to pray for the Persian governor

of Judah. The daily synagogue services included a prayer for the royal family (see 1 Tim. 2:1–2).

6:11–12. At the end of decrees and treaties, it was customary to append a long list of curses against anyone who might disregard them. The threat of being **hanged thereon** (or "impaled"; v. 11) was not an idle one. According to Herodotus (3.159), Darius I impaled three thousand Babylonians when he took the city of Babylon (see Est. 2:23). At the end of his famous Behistun (Bisitun) inscription, Darius I warned: "If you see this inscription or these sculptures, and destroy them and do not protect them as long as you have strength, may Ahuramazda strike you, and may you not have a family, and what you do ... may Ahuramazda utterly destroy." Here, however, Darius acknowledged the Jews' God, who had **caused his name to dwell** (v. 12) at Jerusalem (see Deut. 12:5).

7. Completion of the Temple (6:13–15)

6:13–14. Earlier, the Jews had made little progress in their work on the temple, not only because of opposition but also because of the returnees' preoccupation with their own homes (Hag. 1:2–9). Because they had placed their own interests first, God sent them famine as a judgment (Hag. 1:5–6, 10–11). Spurred on by the preaching of Haggai and Zechariah, and under the leadership of Zerubbabel and Jeshua, a new effort was begun (Hag. 1:12–15).

The reference to **Artaxerxes** (v. 14) seems out of place because he did not contribute to rebuilding the temple. He may have been inserted here since he contributed to the work of the temple at a later date under Ezra (7:21–24).

6:15. On March 12, 516 BC, almost seventy years after its destruction, God's **house was finished**. The renewed work on the temple had begun on September 21, 520 BC (Hag. 1:15), and sustained effort had continued for almost three and a half years. According to Haggai 2:3, the older members, who could remember the splendor of Solomon's temple, were disappointed when they saw the smaller size of Zerubbabel's temple (see Ezra 3:12). Yet in the long run, the second temple, though not as grand as the first, enjoyed a much longer life. The general plan of the second temple was similar to that of Solomon's, but the Most Holy Place was left empty because the ark of the covenant had been lost during the Babylonian conquest. According to Josephus, on the day of atonement, the high priest placed his censer on the slab of stone that marked the former location of the ark. The Holy Place was furnished with the table for the shewbread, the incense altar, and one candlestick (in the Apocrypha, see 1 Maccabees 1:21-22; 4:49-51) instead of Solomon's ten candlesticks (1 Kings 7:49).

8. Dedication of the Temple (6:16-18)

6:16-18. The returnees from **the captivity** (v. 16) participated in the **dedication** of the temple. (Compare the dedication of Solomon's temple, 1 Kings 8.) The leaders of those who had returned from exile had been responsible for the completion of the temple. "Dedication" is translated from the Aramaic word *hanukkah*. The Jewish holiday in December that celebrates the recapture of the temple from the Seleucids and its rededication (165 BC) is also known as Hanukkah.

The number of animals sacrificed (v. 17) was small in comparison with similar services in the reigns of Solomon (1 Kings 8:5, 63), Hezekiah (2 Chron. 30:24), and Josiah (2 Chron. 35:7), when thousands rather than hundreds of animals were offered.

The priests were separated into twenty-four **divisions** (v. 18; see 1 Chron. 24:1-19), each of which served at the temple for a week at a time (see Luke 1:5, 8). In 1962, fragments of a synagogue inscription listing the twenty-four divisions were found at Caesarea. All was done **as it is written in the book of Moses**, perhaps referring to such passages as Exodus 29; Leviticus 8; and Numbers 3; 8:5-26; 18.

9. Celebration of the Passover (6:19-22)

6:19-22. The passover (v. 19) was observed on **the fourteenth day of the first month**. The date would have been around April 21, 516 BC. To participate, **the priests and Levites** (v. 20) had to be ceremonially clean so that they could fulfill their ritual

functions (see Lev. 4:12). The returning exiles were willing to accept those who **had separated themselves** (v. 21) from the paganism of the foreigners who had been introduced into the area by the Assyrians. **King of Assyria** (v. 22) is a surprising title for Darius, the Persian king. Even after the fall of Nineveh in 612 BC, the term "Assyria" continued to be used for former territories the Assyrians had occupied (even Syria is an abbreviation of Assyria). Persian kings adopted a variety of titles, including "king of Babylon" (see 5:13; Neh. 13:6).

II. Ezra's Return and Reforms (chaps. 7-10)

A. Ezra's Return to Jerusalem (chaps. 7-8)

1. Introduction (7:1-10)

7:1-5. The genealogy of Ezra lists sixteen ancestors back to Aaron, the brother of Moses. The events of the preceding chapter concluded with the completion of the temple in 516 BC. The identity of the king mentioned in this chapter has been disputed. If this was Artaxerxes I, which seems likely, Ezra would have arrived in Judah in 458 BC, and there would be a gap of almost sixty years **after these things** (v. 1), that is, between the events of chapter 6 and those of chapter 7. The only recorded event during this interval is the opposition to the rebuilding of Jerusalem in the reign of Ahasuerus (486-465 BC) in 4:6.

Ezra (v. 1) is perhaps a shortened form of Azariah, a name that occurs twice in the list of his ancestors. The Greek form is Esdras, as in the Apocrypha. **Seraiah** was the high priest under Zedekiah and was killed in 586 BC by Nebuchadnezzar (2 Kings 25:18-21), some 128 years before Ezra's arrival. Therefore, Seraiah was the ancestor rather than the father of Ezra; "son" often means "descendant" (see 1 Chron. 6:14-15). **Hilkiah** was the high priest under Josiah (2 Kings 22:4). **Zadok** (v. 2) was a priest under David (2 Sam. 8:17). Solomon had appointed Zadok as high priest in place of Abiathar, who supported the rebel Adonijah (1 Kings 1:7-8; 2:35). Ezekiel regarded the Zadokites as being free from idolatry (Ezek. 44:15). They held the office of high priest until 171 BC. The Sadducees may have been named after Zadok, and the Qumran community (see "Social Developments" in the essay "The Time between the Testaments" in *KJV Study Bible*, p. 1346) looked for the restoration of the Zadokite priesthood. **Ahitub** was actually the grandfather of Zadok (Neh. 11:11).

7:6. Ezra is described as a **ready** (translated "diligent" in Prov. 22:29) **scribe** (v. 6; see Neh. 8:1, 4, 9, 13; 12:26, 36). Earlier, scribes served kings as secretaries, such as Seraiah under David (see 2 Sam. 8:17, where the Hebrew word for "scribe" is translated "secretary"). Other scribes took dictation, such as Baruch, who wrote down what Jeremiah spoke (Jer. 36:32). From the exilic period on, the "scribes" were scholars who studied and taught the Scriptures (see "scribes" and "doctors [teachers] of the law" in the New Testament; Matt. 2:4; Luke 5:17). In the New Testament period, the scribes were addressed as "Rabbi" (Matt. 23:7). Ezra had been blessed by **the hand of the Lord** upon him, a striking description of God's power and favor (see also v. 9, 7:28; 8:18, 22, 31; Neh. 2:8, 18).

7:7–9. Ezra began his journey on the first of Nisan (April 8, 458 BC), and he arrived in Jerusalem on the first of Ab (August 4, 458 BC). The journey took four months, including an eleven-day delay (indicated by comparing verse 9 with 8:31). Spring was the most auspicious time for such journeys; most armies went on campaigns at this time of the year. Although the actual distance between Babylon and Jerusalem is about 500 miles, the travelers had to cover a total of about 900 miles, going northwest along the Euphrates River and then south. The relatively slow pace was caused by the presence of the elderly and children. See Map 8b at the end of the *KJV Study Bible*.

7:10. Ezra had prepared his heart to **seek the law** so that he could **do it** and minister, that is, **teach** it (see also Nehemiah 8).

2. The Authorization by Artaxerxes (7:11–26)

7:11. Many regard the **letter** of Artaxerxes I to Ezra as the beginning point of Daniel's first sixty-nine "weeks" (Dan. 9:24–27). Others regard the commission of Nehemiah by the same king as the starting point of Daniel's prophecy (Neh. 1:1, 11; 2:1–8). By using either a solar calendar with the former date (458 BC) or a lunar calendar with the latter date (445 BC), one can arrive remarkably close to the date of Jesus' public ministry.

7:12. The text of 7:12–26 is in Aramaic (see discussion on 4:8–6:18). The phrase **king of kings** was originally used by Assyrian kings, since their empires incorporated many kingdoms. It was then used by the later Babylonian (Ezek. 26:7; Dan. 2:37) and Persian kings. The grandest application was to the Lord (see 1 Tim. 6:15; Rev. 17:14; 19:16).

7:13–14. It is noteworthy that the inclusive term **the people of Israel** (v. 13) is used rather than "Judah." It was Ezra's aim to make one Israel of all who returned. The markedly Jewish coloring of this decree may have resulted from the king's use of Jewish officials, quite possibly Ezra himself, to help him compose it.

Esther 1:14 refers to the "seven princes" who had access to the king's presence. The mention here of **seven counsellers** (v. 14) corresponds with Persian practice, as reported by the early Greek historians Herodotus and Xenophon. **The law of thy God** is perhaps the complete Pentateuch (the five books of Moses) in its present form (see 7:6).

7:15–23. The Persian treasury had ample funds, and benevolence was a well-attested policy of Persian kings. Here Ezra was provided **silver and gold** (v. 15; see Hag. 2:8), which the king and his counselors had **freely offered**.

An **offering of the people** (v. 16) for the service at Jerusalem was encouraged. The custom of sending gifts to Jerusalem from the Jews who lived outside the Holy Land continued until the Jewish-Roman War, when the Romans forced the Jews to send such contributions to the temple of Jupiter instead (Josephus *Antiquities* 18.9.1). Such directives have close parallels in the contemporary letters from the Jewish garrison at Elephantine in Egypt, including a papyrus in which Darius II ordered: "Let grain offering, incense, and burnt offering be offered" on the altar of the god Yahu "in your name."

Whatever else was needed for the temple was to come **out of the king's treasure house** (v. 20). Texts from the treasury at Persepolis also record the disbursement of supplies and funds from the royal purse.

An hundred talents of silver (v. 22) was an enormous amount, about three and three-fourths tons of silver. **An hundred measures** (i.e., cors) **of wheat** equaled about 600 bushels. The wheat would be used in grain offerings. **Salt** (see 4:14) was provided as needed. A close parallel is the benefaction of Antiochus III, as recorded by Josephus (*Antiquities* 12.3.3): "In the first place we have decided, on account of their piety, to furnish for their sacrifices an allowance of sacrificial animals, wine, oil, and frankincense to the value of 20,000 pieces of silver, and sacred artabae of fine flour in accordance with their native law, and 1,460 medimni of wheat and 375 medimni of salt."

Egypt had revolted against the Persians in 460 BC and had expelled the Persians with the help of the Athenians in 459 BC. In 458 BC, when Ezra traveled to Jerusalem, the Persians were involved in suppressing this revolt. With this problem at hand, Darius wished to avoid God's **wrath against the realm of the king and his sons** (v. 23). It is not known how many sons the king had at this time, but he ultimately had eighteen, according to Ctesias (a Greek physician who wrote an extensive history of Persia).

7:24–26. Priests (v. 24) and other temple personnel were often given exemptions from enforced labor or taxes. A close parallel is found in the Gadates inscription of Darius I to a governor in western Turkey, granting exemptions to the priests of Apollo. Antiochus III granted similar exemptions to the Jews: "The priests, the scribes of the temple, and the temple singers shall be relieved from the poll tax, the crown tax, and the salt tax that they pay" (Josephus *Antiquities* 12.3.3).

The extensive powers that were given to Ezra against **whosoever will not do the law of … God** (v. 26) are striking and extended to secular fields as well. Perhaps the implementation of these provisions involved Ezra in a great deal of traveling, which would explain the silence about his activities between his arrival and the arrival of Nehemiah,

thirteen years later. A close parallel to the king's commission of Ezra may be found in an earlier commission by Darius I, who sent Udjahorresenet, a priest and scholar, back to Egypt. He ordered the codification of the Egyptian laws by the chief men of Egypt—a task that took from 518 to 503 BC.

3. Ezra's Doxology (7:27–28)

Beginning with 7:27, the remainder of the book is again written in Hebrew (see discussions on 4:8–6:18 and 7:12–26). Ezra personalized his prayer with the pronoun **me** (v. 28), the first occurrence of the first person for Ezra—a trait that characterizes the "Ezra Memoirs," which begin in verse 27 and continue to the end of chapter 9.

4. List of Those Returning with Ezra (8:1–14)

8:1–14. Ezra lists those who accompanied him in his return from Mesopotamia, including the descendants of fifteen individuals. The figures of the men given total 1,496 in addition to the individuals named. There were also women and children (see 8:21). About 40 Levites (8:18–19) are also included, as are 220 temple servants ("Nethinims," 8:20).

Though the names Phinehas and Ithamar are names of Aaron's descendants (see Exod. 6:23, 25), Ezra does not indicate directly that these men are Aaronic priests.

5. The Search for Levites (8:15–20)

8:15. Ezra gathered his group together at **the river that runneth to Ahava**, which was probably a canal that flowed into either the Euphrates or the Tigris (the Chebar "River" of Ezek. 1:1 was also a canal). Remaining there for **three days**, perhaps from the ninth to the twelfth day of Nisan; the journey began "on the twelfth day" (8:31). Among the people assembled, Ezra found **none of the sons of Levi**. Since the Levites were entrusted with many menial tasks, they may have found a more comfortable way of life in exile. A rabbinic midrash (commentary) on Psalm 137 relates the legend that Levites were in the caravan but that they were not qualified to officiate because when Nebuchadnezzar had ordered them to sing for him the songs of Zion, "they refused and bit off the ends of their fingers, so that they could not play on the harps." In the Hellenistic era (following Alexander's conquest of the Holy Land in 333 BC), the role of the Levites declined sharply, though the "Temple Scroll," found among the Dead Sea Scrolls in Qumran (see "The Dead Sea Scrolls," *KJV Study Bible*, p. 1345) assigns important roles to them.

8:16–20. Because of the lack of Levites, Ezra sent leaders and **men of understanding** (v. 16; lit., "those who cause to understand," the Hebrew for this word is also used in Neh. 8:7) to Iddo, who was the leading man at **Casiphia** (v. 17), to find some Levites. Casiphia must have had a strong settlement of Levites. Some have located it at the site that was later to become the Parthian capital of Ctesiphon on the Tigris River, north of Babylon. Only about 40 Levites from two families (vv. 18–19) and 220 **Nethinims** (i.e., temple servants; v. 20; see 2:43–57) were found who were willing to join Ezra's caravan.

6. Prayer and Fasting (8:21–23)

8:21–23. Ezra prayed for a **right way** (lit., "straight way"; v. 21), that is, a safe journey, unimpeded by obstacles and dangers (see 8:31; Prov. 3:6), because the children in the group and the vast treasures his people were carrying with them would be a huge temptation for robbers.

Scripture speaks often of unholy shame (Jer. 48:13; 49:23; Mic. 3:7) and on occasion, as here, of holy shame. Ezra was quick to blush with such shame (see also 9:6). Having proclaimed his faith in God's ability to protect the caravan, he **was ashamed** (v. 22); that is, he was embarrassed to ask for human protection. Grave dangers faced travelers going the great distance between Mesopotamia and the Holy Land. Some thirteen years later, Nehemiah was accompanied by an armed escort. The difference, however, does not mean that Nehemiah was a man of lesser faith (see Neh. 2:9). Because of Ezra's concern for safety, all those returning to Jerusalem **fasted and besought ... God** (v. 23). For the association of fasting and prayer, see Nehemiah 1:4; Daniel 9:3; Matthew 17:21; Acts 14:23.

7. The Assignment of the Sacred Vessels (8:24–30)

8:25–30. Ezra was bearing **the offering** (lit., "what is lifted," or dedicated; v. 25; see Exod. 25:2; 35:5; Lev. 7:14) of the Persian king. In Deuteronomy 12:6, the Hebrew for this word is translated "offerings of your hand." There were enormous sums of gold and silver, and products made from each, worth millions of dollars today (see also 7:22). On **drams** (v. 27), see discussion on 2:69. The **fine copper** vessels may have been made of orichalc, a bright yellow (the Hebrew for "yellow" in Lev. 13:30, 32, 36 is related to the Hebrew word used here) alloy of copper that resembles gold and was highly prized in ancient times.

8. The Journey and Arrival in Jerusalem (8:31–36)

8:31–36. On the twelfth day (v. 31; see 7:7–9). After an eleven-day delay, Ezra continued his journey and arrived in Jerusalem, and he **abode there three days** (v. 32) before conducting any business. Nehemiah also took a similar rest period after his arrival in Jerusalem (Neh. 2:11). Then the offering from Artaxerxes was deposited with **Meremoth the son of Uriah** (v. 33), probably the same man who repaired two sections of the wall (Neh. 3:4, 21). The weight of all the gold, silver, and vessels was **written** (v. 34), that is, recorded. According to Babylonian practice (e.g., in the Code of Hammurapi; see chart, *KJV Study Bible*, p. xix), almost every transaction, including sales and marriages, had to be recorded in writing. Ezra may have had to send Artaxerxes a signed certification of the delivery of the treasures.

Except for an identical number of male goats, the **offerings** (v. 35) here were far fewer than those presented by the returnees under Zerubbabel (6:17), who brought with him a far greater number of families.

B. Ezra's Reforms (chaps. 9–10)

1. The Offense of Mixed Marriages (9:1–5)

9:1. Ezra had reached Jerusalem in the fifth month (7:9). The measures dealing with the problem of intermarriage were announced in the ninth month (10:9), or four months after his arrival. Those who brought the problem to Ezra's attention were probably the ordinary members of the community rather than the leaders, who were themselves guilty (9:2). Malachi, who prophesied around the same time as Ezra's mission, indicates that some Jews had broken their marriages to marry daughters of a foreign god (Mal. 2:10–16), perhaps the daughters of influential landholders. One of the reasons for such intermarriages may have been a shortage of returning available Jewish women. What happened to Jewish communities that were lax concerning intermarriage can be seen in the example of the Elephantine settlement in Egypt, which was contemporary with Ezra and Nehemiah. There the Jews who married pagan spouses expressed their devotion to pagan gods in addition to the Lord. The Elephantine community was gradually assimilated and disappeared. **The people of the lands** are the eight groups mentioned, representative of the original inhabitants of Canaan before the Israelite conquest (see discussion on Exod. 3:8). Only the Ammonites, Moabites, and Egyptians were still living there in the postexilic period (see 2 Chron. 8:7–8).

9:2–5. The phrase **holy seed** (v. 2) appears also in Isaiah 6:13, but here it refers to Israel as a race set apart for God's purposes. The priests and Levites had led the Israelites in the wrong direction (see 10:18) and had **been chief** (i.e., foremost) in a serious **trespass**. Marrying those who did not belong to the Lord was an act of infidelity for the people of Israel.

When Ezra heard of the intermarriages, he **rent** his **garment** (v. 3). A common way to express grief or distress was to tear one's garments (see v. 5; Gen. 37:29, 34; Josh. 7:6; Judg. 11:35; 2 Sam. 13:19; 2 Chron. 34:27; Est. 4:1; Job 1:20; Isa. 36:22; Jer. 41:5; Matt. 26:65). Ezra's plucking the **hair** of his head and **beard** is unique in the Bible. Elsewhere grief is expressed by the shaving of one's head and/or beard (Job 1:20; Jer. 41:5; 47:5; Ezek. 7:18; Amos 8:10). When Nehemiah was confronted with the same problem of intermarriage, instead of pulling out his own hair, he pulled out the hair of the offending parties (Neh. 13:25).

Every one that trembled (v. 4; see Exod. 19:16; Isa. 66:2; Heb. 12:21) at the word of God joined Ezra, who sat **astonied** (or "appalled," see v. 3; Dan. 4:19; 8:27) until the **evening sacrifice** (see Exod. 12:6). The informants had probably visited Ezra in the morning, so he must have sat appalled for many hours. The time of the evening sacrifice, usually about 3:00 p.m., was also the appointed time for prayer and confession (Acts 3:1). Ezra then rose from his **heaviness** (v. 5; the Hebrew for this word later meant "fasting," see Lev. 16:29, 31), fell on his **knees** (see 1 Kings 8:54; Ps. 95:6; Dan. 6:10), and spread out his **hands** (see Exod. 9:29). Ezra's prayer (9:6–15) may be compared with those of Nehemiah (Neh. 9:5–37) and Daniel (Dan. 9:4–19).

2. Ezra's Confession and Prayer (9:6–15)

9:6–7. Ezra felt both an inner shame before God (see 8:22; Luke 18:13) and an outward humiliation before the people for his own sins and the sins of his people. He was **ashamed and blush[ed]**. These two Hebrew verbs often occur together ("ashamed" and "confounded"; Ps. 35:4; Isa. 45:16; Jer. 31:19). Though their **iniquities** and **trespass** (see also v. 7; 9:13, 15; 10:10, 19; 1 Chron. 21:3; 2 Chron. 24:18; Ps. 38:4) were exceedingly great, God's love is more than a match for anyone's guilt (Ps. 103:11–12).

The Israelites were conscious of their corporate solidarity with their ancestors and reviewed their spiritual history **since the days of** their **fathers** (v. 7). **The sword** refers to judgment. In Ezekiel 21, "the sword of the king of Babylon" (21:19) is described as an instrument of divine judgment. The ultimate humiliation before God, however, was **confusion of face** (lit., "shame of faces"; see Dan. 9:7–8; 2 Chron. 32:21).

9:8–9. God graciously had spared a **remnant** (v. 8; see Gen. 45:7; Isa. 1:9; 10:20–22). The rebuilt temple, like **a nail** driven into a wall (see Isa. 22:23) or a stake driven into the ground (Isa. 33:20; 54:2), upheld the community, bringing with it enlightened **eyes,** that is, an increase in vitality and joy (Ps. 19:8; Eccl. 8:1).

The Achaemenid **kings of Persia** (v. 9) were favorably disposed to the Jews: Cyrus (539–530 BC) gave them permission to return (chap. 1); his son Cambyses (530–522 BC), though not named in the Bible, also favored the Jews, as evidenced by the Elephantine papyri; Darius I (522–486 BC) renewed the decree of Cyrus (chap. 6); his son Ahasuerus (486–465 BC) granted privileges and protection to Jews (Esther 8–10); his son Artaxerxes I (465–424 BC) gave authorizations to Ezra (chap. 7) and to Nehemiah (Nehemiah 2). That the Jews were permitted to **repair the desolations thereof** fulfilled Isaiah's prophecy that the Lord would restore Jerusalem's ruins (Isa. 44:26), which would burst into singing (Isa. 52:9; see 58:12; 61:4). The Hebrew for **wall** is used of a city wall only in Micah 7:11. The use here is metaphorical (see Zech. 2:4–5), similar to "nail" in verse 8.

9:10–15. The references to the land in verses 11–12 are not to a single Old Testament passage but to several passages, such as Deuteronomy 11:8–9; Isaiah 1:19; and Ezekiel 37:25. Canaanite idolatry and the immoral practices associated with it (Lev. 18:3; 2 Chron. 29:5; Lam. 1:17; Ezek. 7:20; 36:17) are depicted here as **filthiness** (v. 11). The degrading practices and beliefs of the Canaanites are described in texts from ancient Ugarit (see chart, *KJV Study Bible*, p. xix). Ezra acknowledged that God's anger (v. 14) came upon the Israelites because they had violated His covenant with them (Deut. 7:4; 11:16–17; 29:26–28; Josh. 23:16; Judg. 2:20). God is **righteous** (v. 15), and Ezra's people could not stand before Him. A proper sense of God's holiness makes one aware of his unworthiness (see Isa. 6:1–5; Luke 5:8). For comparable passages of national lament, see Psalms 44; 60; 74; 79–80; 83; 85; 90; 108; 126; 129; 137.

3. The People's Response (10:1–4)

10:1. The prophets and other leaders used object lessons, even bizarre actions, to attract people's attention (Isa. 7:3; 8:1–4, 18; Jer. 13:1–11; 19; 27:2–12; Ezek. 4:1–5:4). Here Ezra's **weeping**, not silently but out loud (see 3:13; Neh. 1:4; Joel 2:12), and **casting himself down** were heartfelt responses of remorse.

10:2–4. Ezra, as a wise teacher, waited for his audience to draw their own conclusions about what

should be done. If **Shecaniah** was the son of the same **Jehiel** mentioned in 10:26, since he was also of the family of Elam, he was doubtless grieved that his father had married a non-Jewish woman. Six members of the clan of Elam were involved in intermarriage (10:26). Shecaniah proposed making **a covenant** (v. 3) with God **to put away all the wives, and such as are born of them**. Mothers were given custody of their children when marriages were dissolved. When Hagar was dismissed, Ishmael was sent with her (Gen. 21:14). In Babylonia, divorced women were granted their children and had to wait for them to grow up before remarrying, according to the Code of Hammurapi (see chart, *KJV Study Bible*, p. xix). In Greece, however, children from broken homes remained with their fathers.

Shecaniah's proposal was radical in light of God's hatred of divorce (Mal. 2:16), but gross sin calls for emphatic measures of repentance for restoration. Therefore, he exhorted all the guilty to **arise** (v. 4) and do what was necessary (compare David's exhortation, 1 Chron. 22:16).

4. The Calling of a Public Assembly (10:5–15)

10:5. Ezra reinforced the Israelites' commitment with an oath. The implied curse attendant on nonfulfillment of a biblical oath was often expressed with the vague statement, "God do so to thee, and more also, if ..." (see 1 Sam. 3:17). On rare occasions, the full implications of the curse were spelled out (Num. 5:19–22; Job 31; Ps. 7:4–5; 137:5–6).

10:6–8. Ezra retired to a **chamber** (v. 6) to fast. Such temple chambers were used as storerooms (8:29; Neh. 13:4–5). Complete fasting from both food and drink was rare. Moses did it twice (Exod. 34:28; Deut. 9:18), and the Ninevites also did it (Jonah 3:7). Ordinarily, fasting involved abstaining only from eating (1 Sam. 1:7; 2 Sam. 3:35). Ezra could not eat or drink, for he **mourned** because of the people's sin. The Hebrew for "mourning" often describes the reaction of those who are aware of the threat of deserved judgment (Exod. 33:4; Num. 14:39).

While Ezra continued to fast and pray, the officials and elders ordered all the exiles to assemble in Jerusalem (vv. 7–8). Although Ezra had been invested with great authority (7:25–26), he used it sparingly and influenced the people by his example.

Since the territory of Judah had been much reduced, the most distant people were not more than fifty miles from Jerusalem, so all who were called were able to arrive **within three days** (v. 8). See chart, *KJV Study Bible*, p. 635. The borders were Bethel in the north, Beersheba in the south, Jericho in the east, and Ono in the west (see Neh. 7:26–38; 11:25–35). Those who refused to come **forfeited** their property. The Hebrew for forfeit means "to ban from profane use and to devote to the Lord," either by destruction (see Exod. 22:20; Num. 21:2; Deut. 2:34; 13:12–18) or by giving it to the Lord's treasury (see Lev. 27:28; Josh. 6:19; 7:1–15).

10:9–15. The men of Judah and Benjamin (v. 9; see 1:5) gathered in **the street**, a reference either to the outer court of the temple or to the open space before the Water Gate (Neh. 8:1). The Hebrew for the word **rain** is here a plural of intensity, indicating heavy torrential rains. The ninth month, Kislev (November–December), is in the middle of the rainy season (see v. 13), which begins with light showers in October and lasts until mid-April. December and January are also cold months, with temperatures in the 50s and even the 40s in Jerusalem. The people shivered not only because they were drenched but perhaps also because they sensed divine displeasure in the heavy rains (see 1 Sam. 12:17–18; Ezek. 13:11, 13).

The sins and failures of the exiles were great enough, but they had added insult to injury by marrying pagan women, which served to **increase the trespass of Israel** (v. 10). Therefore, Ezra admonished them to separate themselves from their marriages with the people of the land (see Num. 16:21; 2 Cor. 6:14). In response, the people concurred, **with a loud voice** (v. 12; see Neh. 9:4). Then **the elders of every city, and the judges** (v. 14) were put in charge

to enforce the separations (see Deut. 16:18; 19:12; 21:3, 19; Ruth 4:2). Only four men opposed the measure, perhaps because they wanted to protect themselves or their relatives, or they may have viewed it as being too harsh. If **Meshullam** (v. 15) is the Meshullam of 10:29, he himself had married a pagan wife (see 8:16). Fortunately, those who took a stand for separation and righteousness prevailed.

5. Investigation of the Offenders (10:16–17)

10:16–17. The committee completed its work in three months, discovering that about 110 men were guilty of marrying pagan wives.

6. The List of Offenders (10:18–43)

10:18–22. Even some of **the priests** (v. 18) had married foreign wives, but these **gave their hands** (v. 19) in pledge to put away their wives. (For the symbolic use of the handshake, see 2 Kings 10:15; Ezek. 17:18.) Trespass offerings were to be made for sins committed unintentionally (Lev. 5:14–19) as well as intentionally (Lev. 6:1–7), and a **ram** was the appropriate offering in either case (Lev. 5:15; 6:6).

10:23–24. The Levites (v. 23) also were involved. It is striking that only one singer and three gatekeepers were involved. No temple servants (2:43–54) or descendants of Solomon's servants (2:55–57) sinned through intermarriage.

10:25–43. The list of offenders is completed without any further personal comment.

7. The Dissolution of Mixed Marriages (10:44)

10:44. Both the list of offenders and the book end quite abruptly. Some of the marriages had produced children, but if righteousness and adherence to God's law were to prevail, this could not be accepted as a reason for halting the divorce proceedings. While these measures seem harsh, Ezra was attempting to preserve the identity of the Jewish people to secure their place in the Promised Land.

THE BOOK OF NEHEMIAH

INTRODUCTION

See Introduction to Ezra.

Outline

Bibliography

Breneman, Mervin. *Ezra, Nehemiah, Esther*. New American Commentary 10. Nashville: Broadman & Holman, 1993.

Fensham, F. Charles. *The Books of Ezra and Nehemiah*. New International Commentary on the Old Testament. Grand Rapids, MI: Eerdmans, 1982.

Kidner, Derek. *Ezra and Nehemiah*. Tyndale Old Testament Commentaries 11. Downers Grove, IL: InterVarsity, 1979.

McConville, J. Gordon. *Ezra, Nehemiah, and Esther*. The Daily Study Bible. Philadelphia: Westminster, 1985.

Myers, Jacob. *Ezra, Nehemiah*. Anchor Bible 14. Garden City, NY: Doubleday, 1965.

Williamson, Hugh. *Ezra, Nehemiah*. Word Biblical Commentary 16. Waco, TX: Word, 1985.

Yamauchi, Edwin. "Ezra." In *Expositor's Bible Commentary*, edited by Frank E. Gaebelein, vol. 4. Grand Rapids, MI: Zondervan, 1988.

———. *Persia and the Bible*. Grand Rapids, MI: Baker, 1990.

EXPOSITION

I. Nehemiah's First Administration (chaps. 1–12)

A. Nehemiah's Response to the Situation in Jerusalem (chap. 1)

1. News of the Plight of Jerusalem (1:1–4)

1:1–4. Though the books of Ezra and Nehemiah appear as a single work from earliest times (see Ezra, Introduction: "Title"), **the words of Nehemiah** (v. 1) served originally as an introduction to the title of a separate composition (see Jer. 1:1; Amos 1:1). Nehemiah means "the Lord comforts." **Hachaliah** perhaps means "wait for the Lord," though an imperative in a Hebrew name is quite unusual. The name occurs only here and in 10:1. **In the month Chisleu, in the twentieth year** is equivalent to November–December, 445 BC. See chart, *KJV Study Bible*, p. 635. Nehemiah lived in Shushan (i.e., Susa), the winter residence of the Persian kings. See discussions on Ezra 4:8–19 and Esther 1:2.

Hanani (v. 2) is probably a shortened form of Hananiah, which means "the Lord is gracious." The Elephantine papyri mention a Hananiah who was

the head of Jewish affairs in Jerusalem. Many believe that he is to be identified with Nehemiah's brother (see 7:2) and that he may have governed between Nehemiah's first and second terms (see discussion on 7:2). Nehemiah immediately showed concern for the **Jews that had escaped**, that is, the remnant who had returned from captivity (see Ezra 9:8; 2 Kings 19:30–31).

The report concerned the **province** (v. 3) of Judah (see Ezra 2:1; 5:8), and the **wall of Jerusalem** that was **broken down**. The lack of a city wall meant that the people were defenseless against their enemies. Thucydides (1.89) describes the comparable condition of Athens after its devastation by the Persians in 480–479 BC. Excavations at Jerusalem during 1961–67 revealed that the lack of a wall on the eastern slopes also meant the disintegration of the terraces there. When Nebuchadnezzar assaulted Jerusalem, he battered and broke down the walls around it (2 Kings 25:10). Most, however, do not believe that Nehemiah's distress was caused by Nebuchadnezzar's destruction in 586 BC but by the episode of Ezra 4:7–23. The Jews had attempted to rebuild the walls earlier in the reign of Artaxerxes I, but after the protest of Rehum and Shimshai, the king ordered the Jews to desist (see discussion on Ezra 4:21–23.

Nehemiah was overwhelmed by the news. He **sat down** (v. 4; see Ezra 9:3), **wept** (see 8:9), **mourned** (see Ezra 10:6; Dan. 10:2), **fasted, and prayed**. During the exile, fasting became a common practice, including solemn fasts to commemorate the fall of Jerusalem and the murder of Gedaliah (see Est. 4:16; Dan. 9:3; 10:3; Zech. 7:3–7; 8:19). Nehemiah directed his prayer to the sovereign God, **the God of heaven**, a phrase that occurs twenty-two times in the Old Testament, seventeen of which are in Ezra, Nehemiah, and Daniel.

2. Nehemiah's Prayer (1:5–11)

1:5–6. Nehemiah's prayer began with an appeal to God's **mercy** (v. 5), or "faithful love," the quality that honors a covenant through thick and thin. This was the basis for Nehemiah's prayer. His prayer was consistent, **day and night** (v. 6; see Ps. 88:1; Luke 2:37; 2 Tim. 1:3). In his confession of sins (see Ezra 9; Daniel 9), he included himself and the members of his own family, **my father's house**. A true sense of the awesome holiness of God reveals the depths of personal sinfulness (see Isa. 6:1–5; Luke 5:8).

1:7–8. Nehemiah knew the Scriptures, the **commandments ... statutes ... judgments** (v. 7; for the prominence of the law of Moses in Ezra and Nehemiah, see Ezra 3:2; 6:18; 7:6; Neh. 1:8; 8:1, 14; 9:14; 10:29; 13:1). He knew that dispersion (v. 8) was the inescapable consequence of the people's unfaithfulness. By the New Testament period, there were still more Jews in the Diaspora (dispersion) than in the Holy Land.

1:9–10. God's promise to gather Israel from abroad if she repented (v. 9; see Deut. 30:1–5) is a frequent promise, especially in the prophets (see, e.g., Isa. 11:12; Jer. 23:3; 31:8–10; Ezek. 20:34, 41; 36:24; Mic. 2:12), for He had chosen to set His name in Zion (see Deut. 12:5; Ps. 132:13). Nehemiah understood that although his people had sinned and failed, they were still God's people by virtue of His redeeming them (v. 10; see Deut. 4:34; 9:29).

1:11. Nehemiah's prayer turned personal, **prosper ... thy servant this day**, for he was about to make an appeal to the king. He had access to the king, for he was his **cupbearer** (lit., "one who gives [someone] something to drink"). The Hebrew for this word occurs eleven other times in the Old Testament in the sense of "cupbearer" (Gen. 40:1–2, 5, 9, 13, 20–21, 23; 41:9; 1 Kings 10:5; 2 Chron. 9:4). According to the Greek historian Xenophon (*Cyropaedia* 1.3.9), one of the cupbearer's duties was to choose and taste the king's wine to make certain that it was not poisoned (see 2:1). Thus, Nehemiah had to be a man who enjoyed the unreserved confidence of the king. The need for trustworthy court attendants is underscored by the intrigues that characterized the Achaemenid court of Persia. Ahasuerus, the father of Artaxerxes I, had been killed in his own bedchamber by a courtier.

B. Nehemiah's Journey to Jerusalem (chap. 2)

1. The King's Response (2:1–8)

2:1–2. In the month Nisan, in the twentieth year (v. 1) was March–April, 444 BC. Four months passed from the time Nehemiah first heard the news (Chisleu, 1:1) to when he approached the king. Various reasons have been suggested: (1) The king may have been in his other winter palace at Babylon. (2) Perhaps the king was not in the right mood. (3) Even though Nehemiah was a favorite of the king, he would not have rashly blurted out his request. Whatever one's personal problems were, the king's servants were expected to keep their feelings to themselves and to display a cheerful disposition before him. Since Nehemiah had not been **sad** in the king's presence before, he was fearful when he realized that his countenance had betrayed his inner feelings.

2:3–6. Let the king live for ever (v. 3) was a common form of address to kings. Nehemiah did not mention his **city**, Jerusalem, by name (see v. 5); he may have wished to arouse the king's sympathy by stressing first the desecration of ancestral tombs. Not having anticipated the king's question, Nehemiah uttered a brief, spontaneous prayer to **the God of heaven** (v. 4) before turning to answer the king.

One of Nehemiah's striking characteristics was his frequent recourse to prayer (1:4; 4:4, 9; 5:19; 6:9, 14; 13:14, 22, 29, 31).

The presence of **the queen** (v. 6) is noteworthy. The Hebrew for this word is used only here and in Psalm 45:9. It is a loanword from Akkadian and means literally "[woman] of the palace." The Aramaic equivalent is found only in Daniel 5:2–3, 23, where it is translated "wives." Ctesias, a Greek who lived at the Achaemenid court, records that the name of Artaxerxes' queen was Damaspia and that Artaxerxes had at least three concubines. The Achaemenid court was notorious for the great influence exercised by the royal women. Especially domineering was Amestris, the cruel wife of Ahasuerus and mother of Artaxerxes I. Like Esther, Damaspia may have used her influence with the king (see Esther 5), who granted Nehemiah a leave to Jerusalem.

For how long shall thy journey be? (v. 6). Nehemiah probably asked for a brief leave of absence, which he then had extended. It can be inferred from 5:14 that his first term as governor of Judah lasted twelve years. In the thirty-second year of Artaxerxes, Nehemiah returned to report to the king and then came back to Judah for a second term (13:6–7).

2:7–8. Nehemiah requested **letters** (v. 7) authorizing his mission. A contemporary document from Arsames, the satrap of Egypt who was at the Persian court, to one of his officers who was returning to Egypt, orders Persian officials to provide him with food and drink on the stages of his journey. Nehemiah needed protection traveling through the provinces **beyond the** Euphrates **river** (see discussion on Ezra 4:10) before arriving at Jerusalem.

Another letter was to Asaph, keeper of the **king's forest** (v. 8). Some believe that this forest was in Lebanon, which was famed for its forests of cedars and other coniferous trees (see discussions on Judg. 9:15; Ezra 3:7). A more plausible suggestion is that it should be identified with Solomon's gardens at Etham, about six miles south of Jerusalem (see Josephus *Antiquities* 8.7.3). For the city gates, costly imported cedars from Lebanon would not be used but rather indigenous oak, poplar, or terebinth (Hos.

4:13). **The palace** probably refers to the fortress north of the temple, the forerunner of the Antonia fortress built by Herod the Great (Josephus *Antiquities* 15.11.4; see Acts 21:34, 37; 22:24).

2. The Journey (2:9–10)

2:9–10. In striking contrast to Ezra (see discussion on Ezra 8:22), Nehemiah was accompanied by an armed escort, **captains of the army and horsemen** (v. 9), since he was officially Judah's governor. His arrival in Jerusalem was not met with a welcome from nearby governors.

Sanballat (v. 10) is a Babylonian name meaning "Sin [the moon god] has given life." He was a **Horonite**, which identifies him as coming from (1) Hauran (Ezek. 47:16, 18), east of the Sea of Galilee, (2) Horonaim, in Moab (Jer. 48:34), or, most probably, (3) either Upper or Lower Beth-horon, two key cities twelve miles northwest of Jerusalem, which guarded the main road to Jerusalem (Josh. 10:10; 16:3, 5; 1 Macc. 3:16; 7:39). Sanballat was the chief political opponent of Nehemiah (v. 19; 4:1, 7; 6:1–2, 5, 12, 14; 13:28). He was the governor over Samaria (see 4:1–2). An Elephantine papyrus letter of the late fifth century BC written to Bagohi (Bigvai), governor of Judah, refers to "Delaiah and Shelemiah, the sons of Sanballat, governor of Samaria." In 1962, a fourth-century BC papyrus was found in a cave north of Jericho, listing the name Sanballat, probably a descendant of Nehemiah's contemporary. **Tobiah**, the name of the Ammonite official, means "the Lord is good." He was probably a worshiper of the Lord (Yahweh), as indicated not only by his name but also by that of his son Johanan (6:17–18), which means "the Lord is gracious." Johanan was married to the daughter of Meshullam, son of Berechiah, the leader of one of the groups repairing the wall (3:4, 30; 6:18). Tobiah also had a close relationship with Eliashib the priest (13:4–7). Tobiah probably served under the Persians as the governor of the area east of the Jordan River. The reasons for the opposition of Sanballat and Tobiah were not basically religious but political. The authority of the Samaritan governor in particular was threatened by Nehemiah's arrival.

3. Nehemiah's Nocturnal Inspection of the Walls (2:11–16)

2:11–16. After **three days** rest (v. 11; see Ezra 8:32), Nehemiah cautiously and discreetly inspected the city's fortifications at night while riding on his **beast** (v. 12), probably a mule or donkey. He did not make a complete circuit of the walls (see v. 13) but only of the southern area. Jerusalem was always attacked from the north because it was most vulnerable there, so the walls had probably been completely destroyed in that part of the city. Nehemiah, however, drew attention to several key locations on the southern side of the city.

He went out **the gate of the valley** (v. 13). According to 2 Chronicles 26:9, Uzziah fortified towers in the west wall, which overlooked the Tyropoeon Valley, that is, the central valley between the Hinnom and Kidron valleys. Excavations in 1927–28 uncovered the remains of a gate from the Persian period, which has been identified as the Valley Gate.

Many scholars suggest that **the dragon well** (v. 13) was En-rogel (Josh. 15:7–8; 18:16; 2 Sam. 17:17; 1 Kings 1:9), a well that was situated at the junction of the Hinnom and Kidron valleys, 250 yards south of the southeast ridge of Jerusalem. Others suggest that it was the Pool of Siloam.

The dung port (v. 13) was perhaps the gate leading to the rubbish dump in the Hinnom Valley (see 3:13–14; 12:31; 2 Kings 23:10). It was situated about five hundred yards south of the Valley Gate (3:13).

The gate of the fountain (v. 14) was possibly in the southeast wall, facing toward En-rogel (see 3:15; 12:37). **The king's pool** may have been a pool into which Hezekiah may have diverted the overflow from his Siloam tunnel (see 2 Kings 20:20; 2 Chron. 32:30) to irrigate the royal gardens (2 Kings 25:4) located outside the city walls at the junction of the Kidron and Hinnom valleys. The king's pool was probably, therefore, the Pool of Siloam ("Siloah," 3:15) or the adjacent Birket el-Hamra. Possibly because of the collapse of the supporting terraces (see 2 Sam. 5:9; 1 Kings 9:15, 24), there was **no place ... to pass** on the east side of the city. So he returned by the brook, that is, the Kidron, to his point of departure from the city. All had been surveyed without the knowledge of the cities' officials.

4. Nehemiah's Exhortation to Rebuild (2:17–18)

2:17–18. Lieth waste (v. 17) described the condition of the walls and gates of the city since their destruction by Nebuchadnezzar in 586 BC, in spite of abortive attempts to rebuild them. The leaders and people had evidently become reconciled to this sad state of affairs. It took an outsider to assess the situation and to rally them to renewed efforts.

With an awareness of God's **hand** (v. 18) upon him and with the king's support, Nehemiah could personally attest both that God was alive and active in his behalf and that he had come with royal sanction and authority.

5. The Opposition of Sanballat, Tobiah, and Geshem (2:19–20)

2:19. Sanballat and **Tobiah** were joined by **Geshem** in their opposition to Nehemiah. Inscriptions from Dedan in northwest Arabia and from Tell el-Maskhutah, near Ismailia in Egypt, bear the name of Geshem, who may have been in charge of a north Arabian confederacy that controlled vast areas from northeast Egypt to northern Arabia, including the southern part of the Holy Land. Geshem may have been opposed to Nehemiah's development of an independent kingdom because he feared that it might interfere with his lucrative spice trade, since he is identified as a **Arabian** (see 2 Chron. 9:14; Isa. 21:13). Arabs became dominant in this area from the Assyrian to the Persian periods. Sargon II of Assyria resettled some Arabs in Samaria in 715 BC. Classical sources reveal that the Arabs enjoyed a favored status under the Persians.

C. List of the Builders of the Wall (chap. 3)

3:1–32. This is one of the most important chapters in the Old Testament for determining the topography of Jerusalem (see Map 10 at the end of the *KJV Study Bible*; see also map, *KJV Study Bible*, p. 655). The narrative begins at the Sheep Gate (northeast corner of the city) and proceeds in a counterclockwise direction around the wall. About forty key men are named as participants in the reconstruction of about forty-five sections. The towns listed as the homes of the builders may have represented the administrative centers of the province of Judah. Ten gates are named: (1) the Sheep Gate (v. 1), (2) the Fish Gate (v. 3), (3) the Old Gate (v. 6), (4) the Valley Gate (v. 13), (5) the Dung Gate (v. 14), (6) the Gate of the Fountain (v. 15), (7) the Water Gate (v. 26), (8) the Horse Gate (v. 28), (9) the East Gate (v. 29), and (10) the Gate Miphkad (i.e., "the inspection gate"; v. 31). The account suggests that most of the rebuilding was concerned with the gates, where the enemy's assaults were always concentrated. Not all the sections of the walls or buildings in Jerusalem were in the same state of disrepair. A selective policy of destruction seems to be indicated by 2 Kings 25:9.

1. The Northern Section (3:1-7)

3:1-7. It was fitting that **Eliashib the high priest** (v. 1) should set the example. Among the ancient Sumerians, the king himself would carry bricks for the construction of a temple. **The sheep gate** (see 3:32; 12:39) was known in New Testament times (John 5:2) as being located near the Bethesda Pool (in the northeast corner of Jerusalem). Even today a sheep market is held periodically near this area. The Sheep Gate may have replaced the earlier gate of Benjamin (Jer. 37:13; 38:7; Zech. 14:10). **The tower of Meah** (Hebrew for "hundred") may refer to (1) its height (100 cubits), (2) the number of its steps, or (3) a military unit (see Deut. 1:15). The two towers mentioned (see also **the tower of Hananeel**) were associated with the "palace which appertained to the house [i.e., the temple]" (2:8), protecting the vulnerable northern approaches to the city.

During the days of the first temple, **the fish gate** (v. 3; see 12:39) was one of Jerusalem's main entrances (2 Chron. 33:14; Zeph. 1:10). Merchants brought fish from either Tyre or the Sea of Galilee to the fish market (13:16) through this entrance, which may have been located close to the site of the present-day Damascus Gate.

Meremoth (v. 4; see Ezra 8:33) and **Meshullam** repaired a second section (3:30). Nehemiah com-

plained that Meshullam had given his daughter in marriage to a son of Tobiah (see 6:17–18; discussion on 2:10).

The Tekoites (v. 5) were from the small town of Tekoa, about six miles south of Bethlehem and eleven miles from Jerusalem. It was the hometown of the prophet Amos. The **nobles,** that is, the aristocrats (the Hebrew means means "mighty" or "magnificent"), disdained manual labor and **put not their necks to** the work. This expression (lit., "put the back of the neck to") is drawn from the imagery of oxen that refuse to yield to the yoke (Jer. 27:12).

The old gate (v. 6) was in the northwest corner. Its Hebrew name (the *Jeshanah* Gate) has also been interpreted as "the gate to Jeshanah" (which was on the border between Judah and Samaria, 2 Chron. 13:19) or as a corruption of *Mishneh* Gate (Hebrew for "Second Quarter" or "New Quarter"; see Zeph. 1:10). In any case, it may be another name for the gate of Ephraim (see 12:39), which otherwise is not mentioned in chapter 3. **The throne** (v. 7) was the official seat that symbolized the governor's authority here.

2. The Western Section (3:8-13)

3:8-13. The broad wall (v. 8) may be the wall west of the temple area, which archaeologists uncovered in Jerusalem in 1970–71. It is dated to the early seventh century BC and was probably built by Hezekiah (2 Chron. 32:5). The expansion to and beyond the broad wall may have become necessary because of the influx of refugees fleeing from Samaria after its fall in 722–721 BC.

Jedaiah (v. 10) repaired the wall near **his house** (see 3:23, 28–30). It made sense to have him and others repair the sections of the wall nearest their homes.

The tower of the furnaces (v. 11) was on the western wall, perhaps in the same location as one of those built by Uzziah (2 Chron. 26:9). The furnaces may have been those situated in the "bakers' street" (Jer. 37:21).

The reference to **daughters** (v. 12) is unique in that women were working on the wall. When the Athenians attempted to rebuild their walls after the Persians had destroyed them, it was decreed that "the whole population of the city—men, women and, children—should take part in the wall-building" (Thucydides 1.90.3).

Those assigned to **the valley gate** (v. 13; see discussion on 2:13) repaired the wall for **a thousand cubits**, that is, five hundred yards. This is an extraordinary length; probably most of this section was relatively intact.

3. The Southern Section (3:14)

3:14. For **the dung gate**, see discussion on 2:13. **Beth-haccerem** means "house of the vineyard." It was a fire-signal point (Jer. 6:1) and is identified with Ramat Rahel, two miles south of Jerusalem. It may have been the residence of a district governor in the Persian period.

4. The Eastern Section (3:15–32)

3:15–32. For **the gate of the fountain** (v. 15), see discussion on 2:14. **The pool of Siloah** (a variant of Shiloah, i.e., "Siloam") was perhaps the lower pool of Isaiah 22:9 (see discussion on Isa. 8:6). **The city of David** is Jerusalem, the Jebusite city captured by David (2 Sam. 5:7).

Beth-zur (v. 16) was a district capital, thirteen miles south of Jerusalem. Excavations in 1931 and 1957 revealed that occupation was sparse during the early Persian period but was resumed in the fifth century BC. **The sepulchres of David** refers to the area in the city where David was buried (1 Kings 2:10; 2 Chron. 21:20; 32:33; Acts 2:29). The so-called Tomb of David, on Mount Zion, which is venerated today by Jewish pilgrims, is in the Coenaculum building, which was erected in the fourteenth century AD. Such a site for David's tomb is mentioned no earlier than the ninth century AD. **The house of the mighty** may have been the house of David's mighty men (see 2 Sam. 23:8–39), which perhaps served later as the barracks or armory.

The residences of the high priest and his fellow priests (vv. 20–21) were located inside the city, along the eastern wall. **The king's high house** (v. 25) is perhaps the old palace of David (see 12:37). Like

Solomon's palace, it would have had a guardhouse (Jer. 32:2).

Ophel (v. 26) is a word that means "swelling" or "bulge" (the word is rendered "strong hold" in Mic. 4:8 in reference to Jerusalem), and here it describes specifically the northern part of the southeastern hill of Jerusalem, which formed the original City of David, just south of the temple area (2 Chron. 27:3). **The water gate** was so called because it led to the main source of Jerusalem's water, the Gihon Spring. It must have opened onto a large area, for the reading of the law took place there (8:1, 3, 16; 12:37). **The tower that lieth out** refers to a "projecting" tower, such as the large tower whose ruins were discovered by archaeologists on the crest of the Ophel hill in 1923–25. Excavations at the base of the tower in 1978 revealed a level dating to the Persian era.

The common people of Tekoa, **the Tekoites** (v. 27), did double duty, whereas the nobles of Tekoa shirked their responsibility (see discussion on 3:5).

The horse gate (v. 28) was where Athaliah had been slain (2 Chron. 23:15). It may have been the easternmost point in the city wall—a gate through which one could reach the Kidron Valley (Jer. 31:40).

The east gate (v. 29) may have been the predecessor of the present Golden Gate. **The gate Miphkad** (v. 31) was the inspection gate in the northern part of the eastern wall, and the **sheep gate** (v. 32) brings the reader back to the point of departure in describing the repairs (see 3:1).

D. Opposition to Rebuilding the Wall (chap. 4)

1. The Derision of Sanballat and Tobiah (4:1–5)

4:1–3. Disputes between rival Persian governors were frequent. Sanballat's (2:10) address to his people asked several derisive questions meant to taunt the Jews and to discourage them in their efforts. The efforts of the Jews were considered futile, for fire had damaged the stones, which were probably limestone, and had caused many of them to crack and crumble.

Sanballat's ally, Tobiah (2:10) added that **a fox** (v. 3) could destroy the unstable wall. The Hebrew for this word may also mean "jackal," an animal that normally hunts in packs, whereas the fox is usually a nocturnal and solitary animal.

4:4–5. Nehemiah did not himself take action against his opponents but called down on them redress from God (as in the so-called imprecatory psalms, Pss. 79:12; 83; 94:1–3; 109:14; 137:7–9). In verse 5, Nehemiah's prayer echoes the language of Jeremiah 18:23.

2. The Threat of Attack (4:6–15)

4:6–9. When the work continued, **the Ashdodites** (the residents of Ashdod, a Philistine city that became a district capital under Persian rule; v. 7) joined Sanballat's and Tobiah's resistance to the Israelites' repair of the walls. In spite of the conspiracy against them, Nehemiah's workers prayed and **set a watch** (v. 9). Prayer and watchfulness blend faith and action and emphasize both the divine side and the human side.

4:10–15. A weary and discouraged **Judah** (v. 10) described its strength as **decayed**. The picture is of a worker staggering under the weight of his load and ready to fall at any step.

Nehemiah knew what the **adversaries said** (v. 11). Either he had friendly informants, or the enemy was spreading unsettling rumors. After being warned by Jews of the enemies' threats **ten times** (v. 12), Nehemiah posted men conspicuously in the areas that were the most vulnerable, **in the lower places … and on the higher places** (v. 13) along the wall, and armed them with **spears**. Nehemiah encouraged everyone: **Be not ye afraid of them: remember the Lord** (v. 14). The best way to dispel fear is to remember the Lord, who alone is to be feared (see Deut. 3:22; 20:3; 31:6).

3. Rebuilding the Wall (4:16–23)

4:16–20. Nehemiah found it necessary to have **half** (v. 16) of his workers defend **the other half**. The **shields** were made primarily of wood or wickerwork and therefore were combustible (see Ezek. 39:9), while the **habergeons** are designated by the Hebrew as being primarily breastplates of metal or

coats of mail. The builders were armed also. They either carried their materials with one hand and their weapons with the other or simply kept their weapons close at hand (v. 17). Nehemiah was prepared to use **the trumpet** (v. 18) to summon the workers to any point of attack (Isa. 18:30) but noted that **our God shall fight for us** (v. 20; for the concept of holy war, in which God fights for His people, see Josh. 10:14, 42; Judg. 4:14; 2 Sam. 5:24).

4:21–23. That the workers labored at the wall **till the stars appeared** (v. 21) indicates the earnestness of their efforts, since the usual time to stop working was at sunset (Deut. 24:15). At **night** (v. 22), the workers stayed within the city, even men from outside Jerusalem, so that some of them could serve as sentries. Constant preparedness was the rule (v. 23). According to Josephus (*Antiquities* 11.5.8), Nehemiah "himself made the rounds of the city by night, never tiring either through work or lack of food and sleep, neither of which he took for pleasure but as a necessity."

E. Social and Economic Problems (chap. 5)

5:1–19. During his major effort to rebuild the walls of Jerusalem, Nehemiah faced an economic crisis. Since the building of the wall took only fifty-two days (6:15), it is surprising that Nehemiah called a "great assembly" (v. 7) in the midst of such a project. Perhaps the economic pressures created by the rebuilding program brought to light problems that had long been simmering and that had to be dealt with before work could proceed. Among the classes affected by the economic crisis were (1) the landless, who were short of food (v. 2); (2) the landowners, who were compelled to mortgage their properties (v. 3); (3) those forced to borrow money at exorbitant interest rates and sell their children into slavery (vv. 4–5).

1. The Complaints of the Poor (5:1–5)

5:1–5. The situation was so serious that the **wives** (v. 1) joined in the protest as they ran short of funds and supplies to feed their families. They complained not against the foreign authorities but against their own countrymen who were taking advantage of their poorer brothers at a time when all were needed for the defense of the country. There was a desperate need for **corn** (i.e., grain, v. 2). About six to seven bushels was needed to feed a family for a month.

Even those who had considerable property were forced to mortgage it (v. 3), which benefited the wealthy few (see Isa. 5:8). In times of economic stress, the rich got richer and the poor got poorer. The economic situation was aggravated by the natural conditions that had produced a famine. Some seventy-five years earlier, the prophet Haggai had referred to a time of drought, when food was insufficient (Hag. 1:5–11). Such times of distress were considered to be expressions of God's judgment (Isa. 51:19; Jer. 14:13–18; Amos 4:6). Famines were common in Canaan. They occurred in the time of Abraham (Gen. 12:10), Isaac (Gen. 26:1), Joseph (Gen. 41:27, 54), Ruth (Ruth 1:1), David (2 Sam. 21:1), Elijah (1 Kings 18:2), Elisha (2 Kings 4:38), and Claudius (Acts 11:28).

Others had **borrowed money for the king's tribute** (v. 4). It is estimated that the Persian king collected the equivalent of 20 million darics a year in taxes. Little was ever returned to benefit the provinces; most of it was melted down and stored as bullion. Alexander the Great found at Susa alone 9,000 talents (about 340 tons) of coined gold and 40,000 talents (about 1,500 tons) of silver stored as bullion. As coined money was increasingly taken out of circulation by taxes, poverty increased dramatically. The acquisition of land by the Persians and its removal from production also helped produce a 50 percent rise in the prices of everything during the Persian period.

In times of economic distress, families would borrow funds, using family members as collateral. If a man could not repay the loan and its interest, his children, his wife, or even the man himself could be sold into **bondage** (v. 5). An Israelite who fell into debt, however, would serve his creditor as a "hired servant" (Lev. 25:39–40). He was to be released in the seventh year (Deut. 15:12–18), unless he volun-

tarily chose to stay. During the seven-year famine in Egypt, Joseph was approached by people who asked him to accept their land and their bodies in exchange for food (Gen. 47:18–19). The irony for the Israelites was that as exiles in Mesopotamia, at least their families had been together, but now, because of dire economic necessity, their children were being sold into slavery.

2. The Cancellation of Debts (5:6–13)

5:6–8. Nehemiah **was very angry** (v. 6) because of the report. Sometimes it becomes necessary to express indignation against social injustice (see Mark 11:15–18; Eph. 4:26). Mosaic law forbid **usury** (v. 7) of fellow Israelites (see Exod. 22:25–27; Lev. 25:36; Deut. 23:20). Josephus (*Antiquities* 4.8.25) explains: "Let it not be permitted to lend upon usury to any Hebrew either meat or drink; for it is not just to draw a revenue from the misfortunes of a fellow countryman. Rather, in consoling him in his distress, you should reckon as gain the gratitude of such persons and the recompense that God has in store for an act of generosity."

An impoverished brother could be hired out as a servant, but he was not to be sold as a slave (Lev. 25:39–42), and selling fellow Hebrews as slaves to foreigners was forbidden (Exod. 21:8). These Jews had redeemed their fellow **Jews, which were sold unto the heathen** (i.e., "the nations"; v. 8), but had then sold impoverished Jews to Jews. Nehemiah's audience held **their peace** because their guilt was so obvious that they had no rebuttal or excuse (see John 8:7–10).

5:9–13. Failure to treat others, especially fellow believers, with compassion is **not good** (v. 9). It is an insult to one's Maker and a blot on one's testimony (see Prov. 14:31; 1 Peter 2:12–15). The Old Testament condemns the greed that seeks a profit at the expense of people (Ps. 119:36; Isa. 57:17; Jer. 22:13–17; Ezek. 22:12–13). In view of the economic crisis facing his people, Nehemiah urged the creditors to **leave off this usury** (v. 10), that is, relinquish their rights to repayment with interest and return **the corn, the wine, and the oil** (v. 11) that they were exacting.

Nehemiah **shook** his **lap** (v. 13), thus symbolizing the solemnity of an oath and reinforcing the attendant curses for its nonfulfillment. The people responded with **Amen**, a solemn assertion to accept the terms just stated (see 8:6).

3. Nehemiah's Unselfish Example (5:14–19)

5:14–18. From the **twentieth year unto the** thirty-second **year of Artaxerxes** (from April 1, 444 BC, to April 19, 432; v. 14), Nehemiah served his first term as governor, twelve years, before being recalled to court (13:6). Then he returned to Jerusalem (13:7) for a second term, the length of which cannot be determined. Provincial governors normally assessed the people in their provinces for their support, that is, **the bread of the governor** (v. 18). Nehemiah, like Paul (1 Corinthians 9; 2 Thess. 3:8–9), sacrificed even what was normally his to serve as an example to the people.

The Hebrew for **governors** (v. 15) is used of Sheshbazzar (Ezra 5:14) and Zerubbabel (Hag. 1:1, 14; 2:2) as well as of various Persian officials (Ezra 5:3, 6; 6:6–7, 13; 8:36; Neh. 2:7, 9; 3:7). Nehemiah was not referring here to men of the caliber of Zerubbabel. Some believe that Judah did not have governors before Nehemiah and that the reference here is to governors of Samaria. New archaeological evidence, in the form of seals and seal impressions, confirms the reference to the previous governors of Judah.

It was customary Persian practice to exempt temple personnel from taxation, which increased the burden on laypeople. If the governors themselves used extortion, their underlings, that is, **their servants** (v. 15), often proved even more oppressive (see Matt. 18:21–35; 20:25–28). Nehemiah was the exception because of his **fear of God**. Those in high positions are in danger of abusing their authority over their subordinates if they forget that they themselves are servants of a superior "Master in heaven" (Col. 4:1; see Gen. 39:9).

Nehemiah's behavior as governor was guided by principles of service rather than by opportunism. Neither he nor his servants took advantage of position to purchase land (v. 16).

At my table (v. 17). As part of his social responsibility, a ruler or governor was expected to entertain lavishly. A text found at Nimrud has Ashurnasirpal II feeding 69,574 guests at a banquet for ten days. When Solomon dedicated the temple, he sacrificed 22,000 cattle and 120,000 sheep and goats and held a great festival for the assembly for fourteen days (1 Kings 8:62–65). How many people this fed (see 1 Kings 4:27) is not recorded. The meat listed here for Nehemiah's **daily** (v. 18) use would provide one meal for 600–800 persons, including the 150 Jews and officials of verse 17. (Compare Solomon's provisions for one day, 1 Kings 4:22–23.)

5:19. Think upon me (lit., "remember me") is a key element of Nehemiah's prayers (see 1:8; 6:14; 13:14, 22, 29, 31). Perhaps Nehemiah's memoirs (see Ezra, Introduction: "Author and Date") were inscribed as a memorial that was set up in the temple. A striking parallel to Nehemiah's prayer is found in a prayer of Nebuchadnezzar: "O Marduk, my lord, do remember my deeds favorably as good [deeds]; may these my good deeds be always before your mind." Certainly, the sovereign God of Heaven does not overlook the good deeds of His saints (see Heb. 6:10).

F. The Wall Rebuilt Despite Opposition (chap. 6)

1. Attempts to Snare Nehemiah (6:1–9)

6:1–4. Sanballat, and Tobiah, and Geshem (v. 1; see discussions on 2:10, 19) were disturbed by reports of Nehemiah's progress. They requested a meeting with Nehemiah in **the plain of Ono** (v. 2). Ono was located about seven miles southeast of Joppa, near Lod (Lydda), in the westernmost area settled by the returning Jews (Neh. 7:37; 11:35). It may have been proposed as neutral territory, but Nehemiah recognized the invitation as a trap (see Jer. 41:1–3).

His sharp reply (v. 3) may seem like a haughty response to a reasonable invitation, but he correctly discerned the insincerity of his enemies. He refused to be distracted by matters that would divert his energies from rebuilding Jerusalem's wall. Nehemiah's foes were persistent, however, requesting his presence **four times** (v. 4), but he was equally persistent in resisting them.

6:5–9. During this period, a letter was ordinarily written on a papyrus or leather sheet, which was rolled up, tied with a string, and sealed with a clay bulla (seal impression) to guarantee the letter's authenticity. Sanballat sent **an open letter** (v. 5), apparently wanting the contents of his letter to be made known to the public. The letter charged that Nehemiah intended to **be their king** (v. 6) at Jerusalem once the walls were completed. The Persian kings did not tolerate the claims of pretenders to kingship, as is evident from the Behistun (Bisitun) inscription of Darius I. In New Testament times, the Roman emperor was likewise suspicious of any unauthorized claims to royalty (John 19:12; see Matt. 2:1–13). Nehemiah did not mince words. He called the report a lie (v. 8). He may have sent his own messenger to the Persian king to assure him of his loyalty. Nehemiah recognized the charge as a scare tactic. His enemies thought the Jews' **hands shall be weakened from the work** (lit., "their hands will get too weak for the work"; v. 9), figurative language to express the idea of discouragement. The Hebrew for this phrase is used also in Ezra 4:4 and Jeremiah 38:4, as well as on an ostracon from Lachish dated circa 588 BC.

2. The Hiring of False Prophets (6:10–14)

6:10–14. Shemaiah … was shut up (v. 10) in his own home. Perhaps this was a symbolic action to indicate that his life was in danger and to suggest that both Nehemiah and he should flee for safety to the temple (for other symbolic actions, see 1 Kings 22:11; Isa. 20:2–4; Jer. 27:2–7; 28:10–11; Ezek. 4:1–17; 12:3–11; Acts 21:11). Since Shemaiah had access to the temple, he may have been a priest. He was clearly a friend of **Tobiah** (v. 12) and was therefore Nehemiah's enemy. It was at least credible for Shemaiah to propose that Nehemiah take refuge in the temple area at the altar of asylum (see *KJV Study Bible* notes Exod. 21:13–14), but not in the **house of God** (v. 10), the temple building itself.

Even if the threat against his life was real, Nehemiah was not a coward who would run into hiding

(v. 11). Nor would he transgress the law to save his life. As a layman, he was not permitted to enter the sanctuary (Num. 18:7). When King Uzziah had entered the temple to burn incense, he was punished by being afflicted with leprosy (2 Chron. 26:16–21).

The fact that Shemaiah proposed a course of action contrary to God's word revealed him as a false prophet (v. 12; see Deut. 13:1–5; 18:20; Isa. 8:19–20). Other "prophets" tried to intimidate Nehemiah, including the **prophetess Noadiah** (v. 14), who is mentioned only here.

If Nehemiah had wavered in the face of the threat against him, his leadership would have been discredited (v. 13), and morale among the people would have plummeted.

3. The Completion of the Wall (6:15–19)

6:15. The wall was completed on **the twenty and fifth day of the month Elul**, around September 21, 444 BC. The walls that had lain in ruins for nearly a century and a half had been rebuilt in less than two months, only **fifty and two days**, once the people were galvanized into action by Nehemiah's leadership. Archaeological investigations have shown that the circumference of the wall in Nehemiah's day was much reduced. Josephus states (*Antiquities* 11.5.8) that the rebuilding of the wall took two years and four months, but he is doubtless including such additional tasks as further strengthening of various sections, embellishing and beautifying, and the like. The dedication of the wall is described in 12:27–47.

6:16–18. Nehemiah's enemies recognized in his success the work of God. Yet **Tobiah** (v. 17), who was related to an influential family in Judah (his son Johanan was married to the daughter of Meshullam, who had helped repair the wall of Jerusalem; see 3:4, 30) and whose deeds were well-spoken of, continued his attempts of intimidation.

G. List of Exiles (7:1–73a)

1. Provisions for the Protection of Jerusalem (7:1–3)

7:1–2. When the wall and gates were completed and proper personnel were appointed, Nehemiah gave his **brother Hanani, and Hananiah** (v. 2), who was commander of **the palace**, that is, the northern fortress (see discussions on 2:8; 3:1), **charge over Jerusalem**. Hananiah was well recognized for his faithfulness and fear of God. These two trusted men were placed over Rephaiah and Shallum, who were over sections of the city (3:9, 12).

7:3. Nehemiah gave orders for the gates to be closed **until the sun be hot**. Normally, the gates were opened at dawn, but their opening was to be delayed until the sun was high in the heavens to prevent the enemy from making a surprise attack before most of the people were up.

2. Nehemiah's Discovery of the List of Returnees (7:4–5)

7:4–5. With a spacious city enclosed by a newly restored wall but a sparse population of people, Nehemiah hoped to obtain new residents for the city. To ensure that they were pure Jews, unadulterated by mixed marriages (see Ezra 9:1–2), he searched for and found the registry of people who had returned in 536 BC with Sheshbazzar.

3. The Returnees Delineated (7:6–72)

7:6–73. This section is essentially the same as Ezra 2. For the nature of the list and the reasons for the numerous variations in names and numbers between the two lists, see discussions on Ezra 2.

4. Settlement of the Exiles (7:73a)

7:73a. These returnees **dwelt in their cities**, not in Jerusalem. Later, Nehemiah (11:1–2) would be compelled to move some of these returnees, by lot, to reinforce the population of Jerusalem.

H. Ezra's Preaching and the Outbreak of Revival (7:73b–10:39)

1. The Public Exposition of the Scriptures (7:73b–8:12)

7:73b. The seventh month was September–October 444 BC. Though this concluding clause is the same as Ezra 3:1, which introduced an event approximately ninety-three years earlier, here it introduces the events that follow.

8:1–18. According to the traditional view, Ezra's reading of the law is the first reference to him in almost thirteen years, since his arrival in 458 BC. Since he had been commissioned to teach the law (Ezra 7:6, 10, 14, 25–26), it is surprising that there was such a long delay in its public proclamation.

8:1. As in Ezra 3:1, which also refers to an assembly called in the seventh month (Tishri), the beginning of the civil year (see chart, *KJV Study Bible*, p. 92), **all the people gathered** in the **street** (i.e., the square) **... before the water gate** (see discussions on 3:26). Open squares were normally located near a city gate (2 Chron. 32:6). The people requested that **Ezra the scribe** (see discussion on Ezra 7:6) **bring the book of the law of Moses**. Four views have been proposed concerning the extent of this book: (1) a collection of legal materials, (2) the priestly laws of Exodus and Leviticus, (3) the laws of Deuteronomy, and (4) the Pentateuch. Surely Ezra could have brought back with him the Torah, that is, the entire Pentateuch.

8:2. The presence of **women** is noteworthy (see 10:28). Women did not usually participate in assemblies (see *KJV Study Bible* note on Exod. 10:11) but were included, as were the children, on such solemn occasions (see Deut. 31:12; Josh. 8:35). This special occasion fell on **the first day of the seventh month**. This was the New Year's Day of the civil calendar (see *KJV Study Bible* note on Lev. 23:24) and was celebrated as the Feast of Trumpets (Num. 29:1–6), with cessation of labor and a sacred assembly.

8:3–5. Ezra **read** (v. 3) the law (see Exod. 24:7) **from the morning until midday**, apparently for five or six hours. When he **opened the book** (v. 5; i.e., the scroll; see *KJV Study Bible* note on Exod. 17:14), **all the people stood up** and apparently remained standing, listening attentively to the reading and exposition (8:7–8, 12) of the Scriptures. The rabbis deduced from this verse that the congregation should stand for the reading of the Torah.

8:6. With uplifted **hands** (see Pss. 28:2; 134:2; 1 Tim. 2:8), the people responded with a solemn **Amen, Amen**, the repetition conveying the intensity of feeling behind their affirmation (for other repetitions, see 2 Kings 11:14; Luke 23:21). **They**

bowed their heads, and worshipped. In its original sense, the Hebrew for "worship" meant "to prostrate oneself on the ground," as the frequently accompanying phrase **to the ground** indicates. Private acts of worship often involved prostration "to the ground," as in the case of Abraham's servant (Gen. 24:52), Moses (Exod. 34:8), Joshua (Josh. 5:14), and Job (Job 1:20). There are three cases of spontaneous communal worship in Exodus (4:31; 12:27; 33:10). In 2 Chronicles 20:18, Jehoshaphat and the people "fell before the LORD, worshipping the LORD" when they heard His promise of victory.

8:7–8. As Ezra read throughout the morning from the scroll, he wanted the people **to understand** (v. 7; see Ps. 119:34, 73; Isa. 40:14), so he **read … distinctly** (v. 8), perhaps translating the text before explaining it. Rabbinic tradition understands the Hebrew for this expression as referring to translation from Hebrew into an Aramaic Targum. But there is no evidence of Targums (free Aramaic translations of Old Testament books or passages) from such an early date. The earliest extensive Targum is one on Job from Qumran, dated circa 150–100 BC. Targums exist for every book of the Old Testament except Daniel and Ezra-Nehemiah.

8:9–12. Here **Nehemiah … and Ezra** (v. 9) appear together, an explicit reference showing that they were contemporaries (see 12:26, 36). Upon hearing the word of God, the people began to weep, but they were admonished to **mourn not** (see Est. 9:22; Isa. 57:18–19; Jer. 31:13), **nor weep** (see 1:4; see discussions on Ezra 3:13; 10:1). Nehemiah told them instead to **Go your way, eat the fat**. Delicious festive food prepared with much fat is in view. The fat of sacrificial animals was offered to God as the tastiest element of the burnt offering (Lev. 1:8, 12), the peace offering (Lev. 3:9–10), the sin offering (Lev. 4:8–10), and the trespass offering (Lev. 7:3–4). The fat was not to be eaten in these cases. Nehemiah's additional instruction was, **send portions unto them for whom nothing is prepared**. It was customary for God's people to remember the less fortunate on joyous occasions (2 Sam. 6:19; Est. 9:22; compare 1 Cor. 11:20–22; James 2:14–16).

2. The Feast of Tabernacles (8:13–18)

8:13–15. A reading **on the second day** (v. 13) reminded the people that they should live **in booths** (v. 14) to celebrate the Feast of Tabernacles (Exod. 23:16; Lev. 23:34, 42; John 7:37), which was observed from the fifteenth to the twenty-second of the seventh month, when the produce and vines had been harvested. It also commemorated Israel's wilderness wanderings. The reminder gave them ample time to prepare for the occasion (see 8:2).

Booths were to be made from branches of diverse trees. The **olive** (v. 15) tree was widespread in Mediterranean countries. It was growing in Canaan before the conquest (Deut. 8:8). Because it takes an olive tree thirty years to mature, its cultivation requires peaceful conditions. **Pine** (lit., "tree of oil") is commonly regarded as the wild olive tree. This is questionable since the "tree of oil" was used as timber (1 Kings 6:23, 31–33), whereas the wood of the wild olive tree would have been of little value for use in the temple's furniture. Also, the wild olive tree contains very little oil. The reference may be to a resinous tree like the fir. The **myrtle** is an evergreen bush with a pleasing odor (Isa. 41:19; 55:13; Zech. 1:8, 10–11). The **palm** (i.e., the date palm) was common around Jericho (Deut. 34:3; 2 Chron. 28:15). Later Jewish celebrations of the Feast of Tabernacles included waving the *lulav* (made of branches of palms, myrtles, and willows) with the right hand and holding branches of the *ethrog* (a citrus native to Canaan) in the left.

8:16–18. The booths that the Jews constructed were visible to all, erected on their housetops, in their courts, **in the courts of the house of God** (v. 16), and in the open squares. The temple that Ezekiel saw in his visions had an outer and an inner court (see map, *KJV Study Bible*, p. 1202). Ezekiel's temple was to some extent patterned after Solomon's, which had an inner court of priests and an outer court (1 Kings 6:36; 7:12; 2 Kings 21:5; 23:12; 2 Chron. 4:9; 33:5). The temple of the New Testament era had a court of the Gentiles and an inner court, which was subdivided into the courts of the women, of Israel, and of the priests. The Temple Scroll from Qumran has

God setting forth in detail an ideal temple. Column 42 describes the outer court as follows: "On the roof of the third story are columns for the constructing of booths for the Feast of Tabernacles, to be occupied by the elders, tribal chieftains, and commanders of thousands and hundreds."

Since the days of Jeshua ... unto that day (v. 17) does not mean that the Feast of Booths (i.e., Tabernacles) had not been celebrated since Joshua's time, because such celebrations took place after the dedication of Solomon's temple (2 Chron. 7:8–10) and after the return of the exiles (Ezra 3:4). What apparently is meant is that the feast had not been celebrated before with such great joy (see 2 Chron. 30:26; 35:18). The feast was concluded with **a solemn assembly** (v. 18), as prescribed in Numbers 29:35.

3. A Day of Fasting, Confession, and Prayer (9:1–5a)

9:1–37. The ninth chapters of Ezra, Nehemiah, and Daniel are devoted to confessions of Israel's national sin of rebellion (in spite of God's gracious acts of promise, provision, and deliverance) and to prayers for God's extended grace.

9:1–5a. On **the twenty and fourth day** (v. 1), that is, two days following the Feast of Tabernacles, the Jewish leadership led the Israelites in a day of penance, in the spirit of the Day of Atonement, which was held on the tenth day (Lev. 16:29–30). There was the outward display of inner sorrow for sin, that is, **fasting ... sackclothes ... earth** (see Ezra 8:23; 10:6). The day began with a reading of the law of God for **one fourth part of the day** (v. 3), that is, for about three hours; then they confessed their sins and worshiped for **another fourth part**.

4. A Recital of God's Dealings with Israel (9:5b–31)

9:5b–37. This is one of the most beautiful prayers in the Bible, outside the Psalms. It reviews God's grace and power (1) in creation (v. 6), (2) in the Abrahamic covenant (vv. 7–8), (3) in Egypt and at the Red Sea (vv. 9–11), (4) in the wilderness and at Sinai (vv. 12–21), (5) during the conquest of Canaan (vv. 22–25), (6) through the judges ("saviours,"

vv. 26–28), (7) through the prophets (vv. 29–31), and (8) in the present situation (vv. 32–37). For other historical reviews of God's gracious acts and Israel's fickleness, see Psalms 78; 105–106.

9:6. Though **thou, even thou, art LORD alone** is not found in the words of Deuteronomy 6:4, which expresses the central monotheistic conviction of Israel's faith, this prayer began with a similar affirmation (see 2 Kings 19:15; Ps. 86:10). As Creator of **the heaven of heavens ... the earth ... the seas** (see Exod. 20:11; Deut. 10:14; Ps. 148:4), all **the host of heaven** rightfully worships Him (see Ps. 89:5–7).

9:7–8. God called **Abram** (v. 7) from **Ur of the Chaldees** (see discussion on Gen. 11:28) **and gave him the name of Abraham** (see discussion on Gen. 17:5). Because he was **faithful** (v. 8; compare Rom. 4:16–22 with James 2:21–23), God made **a covenant with him** (see discussion on Gen. 15:18) and gave him the land of **the Canaanites ... the Girgashites**.

9:9–11. Perhaps the turning point of Israel's history was their arrival at **the Red sea** (v. 9; see Exod. 13:18; 14:2), after her deliverance from Egypt, and watching God **divide the sea** (v. 11; see Exod. 14:21–22).

9:12–21. God led Israel to **mount Sinai** (v. 13), where He gave her His **laws**. The singular form of the Hebrew for this word is *Torah*, which means "instruction," "law," and later was used to refer to the Pentateuch, the five books of Moses. He gave Israel the **holy sabbath** (v. 14; see Exod. 20:11) as a special sign of His covenant relationship to her (Exod. 31:15–17). According to the rabbis, "the sabbath outweighs all the commandments of the Torah" (see 10:31–33; 13:15–22). God provided **bread from heaven** (v. 15), that is, manna (Exod. 16:4), and **water ... out of the rock** (Exod. 17:6), in bringing her to the land He had **sworn** to give her (Gen. 22:15–17; Exod. 6:8). Yet they **hardened their necks** (v. 16); that is, they became stubborn (Exod. 32:9) and **appointed a captain** (v. 17) to return them to Egypt. Their intention to do so is recorded in Numbers 14:4. Though God was **gracious ... and of great kindness** (see Exod. 34:6–7), they committed the ultimate blasphemy by attributing their deliverance to a molten calf (v. 18; see Exod. 32:4). With **manifold mercies** (v. 19), that is, a tender, maternal kind of love, God guided them and instructed them. Another evidence of God's special providence was that their **clothes waxed not old** (v. 21; see Deut. 8:4); neither did their feet swell (or "blister").

9:22–25. Beginning with the land of **Sihon** and **Og** (v. 22; see Num. 21:21–35), God gave Israel the Promised Land, ready for occupation (see Deut. 6:10–12; Josh. 24:13). It was described as **fat land**, that is, fertile land (v. 25; see 9:35; Num. 14:7; Deut. 8:7; Josh. 23:13), with **wells digged** already. Because of the lack of rainfall during much of the year, almost every house had its own well or cistern in which to store water from the rainy seasons (2 Kings 18:31; Prov. 5:15). By 1200 BC, the technique of water-proofing cisterns was developed, permitting greater occupation of the central hills of Judah. **Vineyards, and oliveyards, and fruit trees** were abundant (see Deut. 8:8). The Egyptian text *Sinuhe's Story* (ca. 2000 BC) describes Canaan as follows: "Figs were in it, and grapes. It had more wine than water. Plentiful was its honey, abundant its olives. Every [kind of] fruit was on its trees." With these abundant blessings, Israel **became fat**. Elsewhere, the Hebrew for "fat" always implies physical fullness and spiritual insensitivity.

9:26–28. In spite of all the blessings God had given her, Israel was rebellious (see discussion on Judg. 2:6–3:6), and when God sent oppressors, He then sent **saviours** (v. 27; see Judges, Introduction: "Title") to deliver them.

9:29–31. Israel's predicament was due to her disobedience to God's commandments, for if **a man do [them], he shall live in them** (v. 29; see Lev. 18:5). Israel **withdrew the shoulder** and turned from God in continued resistance to His will.

5. Confession of Sins (9:32–37)

9:32–37. Israel had faced trouble since the time **of the kings of Assyria** (v. 32), a list which included Tiglath-pileser III, also known as Pul (1 Chron. 5:26), Shalmaneser V (2 Kings 18:9), Sargon II (Isa. 20:1), Sennacherib (2 Kings 18:13), Esarhaddon (Ezra 4:2), and Ashurbanipal ("Asnappar," Ezra 4:10). The Isra-

elites confessed that though they were back in their land, they still experienced Persian **dominion over** (v. 37) them. The Persian rulers drafted their subjects into military service. Some Jews may have accompanied Xerxes on his invasion of Greece in 480 BC.

6. A Binding Agreement (9:38)

9:38. Israel's covenant commitment became a legal document with the personal seal of the leaders, Levites, and priests.

7. A List of Those Who Sealed the Covenant (10:1–29)

10:1–27. What follows is a legal list, bearing the official seal and containing a roster of eighty-four names of members of the Jewish leadership. Notably, as governor, Nehemiah set the example, and his name appears first on the list.

10:2–8. About half of the names in this list of priests occurs again in 12:1–7.

10:9–13. Most of the names in this list of Levites appear also in the lists of Levites in 8:7 and 9:4–5.

10:14–27. Almost half of the names of leaders in this category are also found in the lists of 7:6–63 and Ezra 2:1–61.

10:28–29. The rest of the people, though they did not fix their names to any legal document, aligned themselves with **their wives, their sons, and their daughters** (v. 28) by **curse** (v. 29) and **oath** to abide by the Mosaic law.

8. Provisions of the Agreement (10:30–39)

10:30–33. These verses perhaps constitute a code drawn up by Nehemiah to correct the abuses listed in 13:15–22.

The Israelites promised not to make any purchases **on the sabbath day** (v. 31) even though Exodus 20:8–11 and Deuteronomy 5:12–15 do not explicitly prohibit trading on the sabbath (but see the prohibitions listed in Jer. 17:19–27). They promised to **leave the seventh year … every debt**, that is, forgo working the land every seventh year (see *KJV Study Bible* note on Lev. 25:4). The Romans misrepresented the sabbath and the sabbath year as being caused by laziness. According to Tacitus, the

Jews "were led by the charms of indolence to give over the seventh year as well to inactivity."

Exodus 30:13–14 speaks of "half a shekel" as an "offering to the Lord" from each man who was twenty years old or more as a symbolic ransom. Later, Joash had used the annual contributions for the repair of the temple (2 Chron. 24:4–14). In the New Testament period, Jewish men from everywhere sent an offering of a half shekel (actually two drachmas, its equivalent; see Josephus *Antiquities* 3.8.2) for the temple in Jerusalem (Matt. 17:24). The pledge of **the third part of a shekel** (v. 32) in Nehemiah's time may have been due to economic circumstances. The collected money was used for the support of the temple.

10:34. The Israelites **cast the lots** (see discussion on 11:1) to determine who would bring **the wood offering** to the temple. Though there is no specific reference to a wood offering in the Pentateuch, the perpetual burning of fire on the sanctuary altar (Lev. 6:12–13) would have required a continual supply of wood. Josephus mentions "the festival of wood offering" on the fourteenth day of the fifth month (Ab). The Jewish Mishnah (rabbinic interpretations and applications of Pentateuchal laws) lists nine times when certain families brought wood and stipulates that all kinds of wood were suitable except the vine and the olive. The Temple Scroll from Qumran describes the celebration of a wood offering festival for six days following a new oil festival.

10:35–39. A string of commitments follow. **The firstfruits** (v. 35) would be brought to the sanctuary, to support the priests and Levites (see Exod. 23:19; Deut. 26:1–11; Ezek. 44:30) and stored in **the chambers** (v. 38) in the courts of the temple. These were rooms used as storage areas for silver, gold, and sacred articles (see 12:44; 13:4–5, 9; Ezra 8:28–30). Also, **the firstborn** (v. 36) children and livestock (see Exod. 13:12–13) would be presented to God. **Tithes** (v. 37) meant for the support of **the Levites** (13:12–13; Lev. 27:30; Num. 18:21–32) would be brought to the temple. **The tithe of the tithes** (v. 38) was the tenth that the Levites would give for the support of the priests (Num. 18:26–28).

The Israelites close with a promise: **we will not forsake the house of our God** (v. 39). In earlier years, Haggai (Hag. 1:4–9) had accused the people of neglecting the temple, and Nehemiah would later condemn the people for failure once again (see 13:11).

I. New Residents of Judah and Jerusalem (chap. 11)

1. New Residents for Jerusalem (11:1–24)

a. Introductory Remarks (11:1–4a)

11:1–4a. It was Nehemiah's desire to expand the population of Jerusalem (7:4). This was accomplished by selecting new residents to live in Jerusalem. These residents were chosen by casting **lots** (v. 1). Lots were usually made out of small stones or pieces of wood. Sometimes arrows were used (Ezek. 21:21). It was decided that **one of ten** would be selected to **dwell in Jerusalem**. Josephus (*Antiquities* 11.5.8) asserts: "But Nehemiah, seeing that the city had a small population, urged the priests and Levites to leave the countryside and move to the city and remain there, for he had prepared houses for them at his own expense." The practice of redistributing populations was also used to establish Greek and Hellenistic cities. It involved the forcible transfer from rural settlements to urban centers. Tiberias, located on the Sea of Galilee, was populated with Gentiles through such a process, undertaken by Herod Antipas in AD 18. **The holy city** is another name for Jerusalem because the temple of God was there (see Isa. 48:2; Dan. 9:24; Matt. 4:5; Rev. 11:2).

In addition to those chosen by lot, some volunteered out of a sense of duty (v. 2). Evidently most preferred to stay in their hometowns. The census roster that is introduced in verse 3 parallels 1 Chronicles 9:2–21, a list of the first residents in Jerusalem after the return from Babylonia. About half of the names in the two lists are the same.

b. Residents from Judah (11:4b–6)

11:4b–6. Whereas Chronicles lists 690 descendants of Judah's second son, Zerah (see Gen. 38:29–30), the roster here focuses on 468 of Judah's first son, **Perez** (v. 4b).

Nehemiah attacked the offenders and **pluckt off their hair** (v. 25) and made them swear not to give or take daughters in intermarriage. Nehemiah's action was clearly designed to prevent future intermarriages, whereas Ezra dissolved the existing unions.

13:26–27. Solomon (v. 26) had been Israel's outstanding king in terms of wealth and political achievements (1 Kings 3:13; 2 Chron. 1:12). He began his reign by humbly asking for wisdom from the Lord (1 Kings 3:5–9), but **even him did … women cause to sin**. In later years, his foreign wives had led him to worship other gods, so that he built a high place for Chemosh, the god of the Moabites (1 Kings 11:7).

13:28. One of the grandsons of **Eliashib the high priest** had become a **son in law to Sanballat**. According to Leviticus 21:14, the high priest was not to marry a foreigner. The expulsion of Eliashib's grandson followed either this special ban or the general prohibition against intermarriage. The union described in this verse was especially rankling to Nehemiah in the light of Sanballat's enmity (see 2:10). Josephus (*Antiquities* 11.7.2) records that an almost identical episode, involving a marriage between the daughter of a Sanballat of Samaria and the brother of the Jewish high priest, took place a little over a century later, in the time of Alexander the Great.

4. Provisions of Wood and Firstfruits (13:30–31)

13:30–31. Nehemiah appointed **wards** (v. 30) or "divisions," referring to the assignment of particular duties to groups of priests and Levites, possibly on a rotating basis (see discussion on 12:9), to supply the **wood offering** (v. 31; see discussion on 10:34) and oversee the **firstfruits** (see discussion on 10:35).

Remember me, O my God, for good (v. 31). The last recorded words of Nehemiah recapitulate a theme running through the final chapter (13:14, 22; see discussion on 1:8). His motive throughout his ministry was to please and to serve his Divine Sovereign.

THE BOOK OF ESTHER

INTRODUCTION

Author and Date

Although the author of the book of Esther is unknown, from internal evidence, it is possible to make some inferences about the author and the date of composition. It is clear that the author was a Jew, both from his emphasis on the origin of a Jewish festival and from the Jewish nationalism that permeates the story. The author's knowledge of Persian customs, the setting of the story in the city of Susa, and the absence of any reference to the land of Judah or to Jerusalem suggest that he was a resident of a Persian city. The earliest date for the book would be shortly after the events narrated, circa 460 BC (before Ezra's return to Jerusalem; see discussion on 8:12). Internal evidence also suggests that the festival of Purim had been observed for some time prior to the writing of the book (9:19). Several scholars have dated the book in the Hellenistic period. The absence of Greek words and the style of the author's Hebrew dialect, however, suggest that the book must have been written before the Persian Empire fell to Greece in 331 BC.

Theme and Theological Message

The author's central purpose in writing the book was to record the institution of the annual festival of Purim and to keep alive for later generations the memory of the great deliverance of the Jewish people during the reign of Ahasuerus. The book accounts for both the initiation of that observance and the obligation for its perpetual commemoration (see 3:7; 9:24, 28–32).

Throughout much of the story, the author calls to mind Israel's ongoing conflict with the Amalekites (see discussions on 2:5; 3:1–6; 9:5–10), a conflict that began during the exodus (Exod. 17:8–16; Deut. 25:17–19) and continued through Israel's history (1 Samuel 15; 1 Chron. 4:43; and, of course, Esther). As the first to attack Israel after their deliverance from Egypt, Israel viewed the Amalekites—and the author of Esther views them—as the epitome of all the powers of the world arrayed against God's people (see Num. 24:20; 1 Sam. 15:1–3; 28:18). Now that Israel had been released from captivity, Haman's edict was the final major effort in the Old Testament period to destroy them.

Closely associated with Israel's conflict with the Amalekites is the rest that had been promised to the people of God (see Deut. 25:19). With Haman's defeat, the Jews enjoyed rest from their enemies (9:16, 22).

The message of the book of Esther is expressed in Mordecai's confidence that the Jews would be delivered, based on God's sovereignty in working out His purposes and fulfilling His promises. Their deliverance would come, even if through some means other than Esther. The author highlights the relationship between divine sovereignty and human responsibility. Unless Esther recognized her providential placement in the palace and exercised her individual responsibility, she and her family would perish.

Literary Features

The author draws on the remnant motif, which recurs throughout the Bible (natural disasters, disease, warfare, or other calamities threaten God's people; those who survive constitute a remnant). Events in the Persian city of Susa threatened the continuity of God's purposes in redemptive history. The future existence of God's chosen people, and ultimately the appearance of the Redeemer-Messiah, were jeopardized by Haman's edict to destroy the Jews. The author of Esther patterned much of his material on the events of the Joseph narrative (see discussions on 2:3–4, 8–10, 21–23; 4:12–17; 6:1–2, 7–12, 13–14; 8:3–6), in which the remnant motif is also central to the narrative (Gen. 45:7).

Feasting is another prominent theme in Esther (see "Outline"). Banquets provide the setting for important plot developments. There are ten banquets: (1) 1:3–4, (2) 1:5–8, (3) 1:9, (4) 2:18, (5) 3:15, (6) 5:1–8, (7) 7:1–10, (8) 8:17, (9) 9:17, (10) 9:18–32. The three pairs of banquets that mark the beginning, middle, and end of the story are particularly prominent: the two banquets given by Ahasuerus, the two prepared by Esther, and the double celebration of Purim.

Recording duplications appears to be one of the favorite compositional techniques of the author. In addition to the three groups of banquets that come in pairs, the author records two lists of the king's servants (1:10, 14), two reports that Esther concealed her identity (2:10, 20), two gatherings of the women (2:8, 19), two houses for the women (2:12–14), two fasts (4:3, 16), two consultations of Haman with his wife and friends (5:14; 6:13), two unscheduled appearances of Esther before the king (5:2; 8:3), two investitures for Mordecai (6:7–11; 8:15), two coverings of Haman's face (6:12; 7:8), two references to Haman's sons (5:11; 9:6–10, 13–14), two appearances of Harbona (1:10; 7:9), two royal edicts (3:12–14; 8:1–13), two references to the subsiding of the king's anger (2:1; 7:10), two references to the irrevocability of the Persian laws (1:19; 8:8), two days for the Jews to take vengeance (9:5–15), and two letters instituting the commemoration of Purim (9:20–32).

An outstanding feature of this book, and one that has given rise to considerable discussion, is the complete absence of any explicit reference to God, worship, prayer, or sacrifice. This "secularity" has produced many detractors, who have judged the book to be of little religious value. It appears, however, that the author has deliberately refrained from mentioning God or any religious activity as a literary device to heighten the fact that it is God who controls and directs all the seemingly insignificant coincidences (see, e.g., discussion on 6:1) that make up the plot and that issue in deliverance for the Jews. God's sovereign rule is assumed at every point (see discussion on 4:12–16), an assumption made all the more effective by the total absence of reference to Him.

Outline

I. The Feasts of Ahasuerus (1:1–2:18)
    A. Vashti Deposed (chap. 1)
    B. Esther Made Queen (2:1–18)
II. The Feasts of Esther (2:19–7:10)
    A. Mordecai Uncovers a Plot (2:19–23)
    B. Haman's Plot (chap. 3)
    C. Mordecai Persuades Esther to Help (chap. 4)
    D. Esther's Request to the King: The First Banquet (5:1–8)
    E. A Sleepless Night (5:9–6:14)
    F. Haman Hanged: The Second Banquet (chap. 7)
III. The Feasts of Purim (chaps. 8–10)
    A. The King's Edict in Behalf of the Jews (chap. 8)
    B. The Institution of Purim (chap. 9)
    C. The Promotion of Mordecai (chap. 10)

Bibliography

Baldwin, Joyce G. *Esther*. Tyndale Old Testament Commentaries 12. Downers Grove, IL: InterVarsity, 1984.

Berg, Sandra Beth. *The Book of Esther: Motifs, Themes and Structure*. Missoula, MT: Scholars Press, 1979.

Bush, Fredric. *Ruth, Esther*. Word Biblical Commentary 9. Waco, TX: Word, 1996.

Clines, David J. A. *Ezra, Nehemiah, Esther*. Grand Rapids, MI: Eerdmans, 1984.

Hess, Margaret. *Esther: Courage in Crisis*. Wheaton, IL: Victor, 1980.

Huey, F. B. "Esther." In *Expositor's Bible Commentary*, edited by Frank E. Gaebelein, vol. 4. Grand Rapids, MI: Zondervan, 1988.

Whitcomb, John C. *Esther: Triumph of God's Sovereignty*. Everyman's Bible Commentary. Chicago: Moody, 1979.

Wright, J. Stafford. "The Historicity of the Book of Esther." In *New Perspectives on the Old Testament*, edited by J. Barton Payne. Waco, TX: Word, 1970.

EXPOSITION

I. The Feasts of Ahasuerus (1:1–2:18)

A. Vashti Deposed (chap. 1)

1:1. Ahasuerus (also known as Xerxes, a Greek form of the Persian name Khshayarshan) succeeded his father Darius and ruled from 486 to 465 BC. The Greek historian Herodotus (3.89) records that Ahasuerus's father, Darius, had organized the empire into twenty satrapies. (Satraps, the rulers of the satrapies, are translated "lieutenants" in 3:12; 8:9; 9:3.) The **hundred and seven and twenty provinces** were smaller administrative units (see also 8:9).

1:2. Shushan the palace was the fortified acropolis and palace complex; it is distinguished from the surrounding city in 3:15; 4:1–2, 6; 8:15. Several archaeological investigations have been made at the site since the mid-nineteenth century. Ahasuerus had made extensive renovations in the palace structures. Shushan (i.e., Susa, the city) was the winter residence of the Persian kings; the three other capitals were Ecbatana (Ezra 6:2), Babylon, and Persepolis. One of Daniel's visions was set in Susa (Dan. 8:2); Nehemiah also served there (Neh. 1:1).

1:3–4. The year (483–482 BC), the persons in attendance, and the length of the meeting suggest that the purpose of the gathering may have been to plan for the disastrous campaigns against Greece, 482–479 BC. Herodotus (7.8) possibly describes this assembly, which culminated in a **feast**.

1:5–6. The excavations at Susa have unearthed a text in which Ahasuerus's father, Darius, describes in some detail the building of his palace. Ahasuerus continued the work his father had begun.

1:9. Vashti the queen was deposed in 484/483 BC; Esther became queen in 479/478 BC (see 2:16–17). The Greek historians call Ahasuerus's queen Amestris; they record her influence during the early part of his reign and as queen mother during the following reign of her son Artaxerxes (Ezra 7:1, 7, 11–12, 21; 8:1; Neh. 2:1; 5:14; 13:6) until the time of her own death circa 424 BC. Artaxerxes came to the throne when he was eighteen years old; therefore,

he was born circa 484/483 BC, approximately at the time of Vashti's deposal. Since he was the third son of Amestris, the name Amestris cannot be identified with Esther and must be viewed as a Greek version of the name Vashti. Comparatively little is known of the late portions of Ahasuerus's reign, nor is it possible to determine the subsequent events of the life of Esther. Apparently, after Esther's death or her fall from favor, Vashti was able to reassert her power and to exercise a controlling influence over her son.

1:13–14. Both Ezra 7:14 and the Greek historian Herodotus indicate that seven men, **wise men, which knew the times** (i.e., court astrologers; v. 13), functioned as the immediate advisers to the king.

1:19. The irrevocability (**be not altered**) of the Persian laws is mentioned in 8:8 and Daniel 6:8. The punishment awarded Vashti corresponded to the crime: Since she refused to appear before the king, it was decreed that she **come no more before** him. Furthermore, from this point on, the author no longer refers to her with the title "queen."

1:21–22. It **pleased the king** to depose his wife Vashti and make her such an example that husbands throughout the kingdom would not fear having their authority in their homes questioned. Since the kingdom was composed of peoples of differing languages, the king was careful to distribute his decrees by letters in every language spoken by his subjects.

B. Esther Made Queen (2:1–18)

2:1–2. After these things (v. 1), that is, after the dispersal of the king's letters (1:22) and the Greek wars (see discussion on 1:3–4), a search was made for **fair young virgins** (v. 2) to be added to the king's harem. Esther was taken to Ahasuerus "in the seventh year of his reign" (2:16), in December 479 BC or January 478 BC.

2:3–4. The phraseology here is similar to that in Genesis 41:34–37. This and numerous other parallels suggest that the author of Esther modeled his work after the Joseph narrative. Both accounts are set in the courts of foreign monarchs and portray Israelite heroes who rise to prominence and provide the means by which their people are saved (see discussions on 8–10, 21–23; 4:12–17; 6:1–2, 7–12, 13–14; 8:3–6).

2:5–7. As far back as the fall of the northern kingdom in 722–721 BC, Israelites had been exiled among the cities of the Medes (2 Kings 17:6). After the conquest of Babylon by King Cyrus of Persia in 539 BC, some of the Jewish population taken there by the Babylonians (605–586 BC) probably moved eastward into the cities of Medo-Persia. Only fifty thousand of them returned to Israel in the restoration of 538 BC (Ezra 2:64–67). The presence of a large Jewish population in Medo-Persia is confirmed by the discovery of an archive of texts in Nippur (southern Mesopotamia) from the period of Artaxerxes I (465–424 BC) and Darius II (424–405 BC). This archive contains the names of about one hundred Jews who lived in that city. Some had attained positions of importance and wealth. Similar Jewish populations probably lived in many other Medo-Persian cities. **In Shushan the palace** (v. 5) was **a Jew** named **Mordecai.** His name is derived from that of the Babylonian deity Marduk. There are numerous examples in the Bible of Jews having double names—a Hebrew name and a "Gentile" name. Mordecai likely had a Hebrew name, as did Esther (v. 7), Daniel and his friends (Dan. 1:6–7), Joseph (Gen. 41:45), and others, but the text does not mention Mordecai's Hebrew name. A cuneiform tablet from Borsippa, near Babylon, mentions a scribe by the name of Mardukaya; he was an accountant or minister at the court of Susan in the early years of Ahasuerus. Many scholars identify him with Mordecai, who was the **son of Jair, the son of Shimei, the son of Kish.** The persons named could be immediate ancestors, in which case Mordecai would have been the great-grandson of Kish, who was among the exiles with Jehoiachin in 597 BC. It is more likely, however, that the names refer to his remote ancestors in the tribe of Benjamin (see 2 Sam. 16:5–14 for Shimei, 1 Sam. 9:1 for Kish). This association with the tribe and family of King Saul sets the stage for the ongoing conflict between Israel and the Amalekites (see discussions on 3:1–6). If the names were those of remote ancestors, the clause **who had been carried away** (i.e., into exile; v. 6) in the days of **Jeconiah king of Judah** (see 2 Kings 24:8–17; 2 Chron. 36:9–10) would not apply to Mordecai, who would have been over one hundred years old in that case. Rather, it would have to be taken as an elliptical construction in the sense of "whose family had been taken into exile." Esther's Hebrew name, **Hadassah** (v. 7), means "myrtle." The name Esther is likely derived from the Persian word for "star," though some derive it from the name of the Babylonian goddess Ishtar (see discussion on Jer. 7:18).

2:8–10. Esther was brought ... unto the king's house (v. 8) and had no choice in the matter (compare 2 Sam. 11:4). She was given items for purification and **such things as belonged to her** (lit., "her portions," i.e., her food; v. 9). Unlike Daniel and his friends (Dan. 1:5–10), Esther did not observe Hebrew dietary laws, perhaps in part to conceal her Jewish identity, a fact that is recorded twice (v. 10; 2:20). Giving such portions was a sign of special favor (1 Sam. 9:22–24; 2 Kings 25:29–30; Dan. 1:1–10; negatively, Jer. 13:25); compare the Joseph narrative, Genesis 43:34. The motif of giving portions appears later as a practice in observing Purim (9:19, 22).

2:14–18. After each of the maidens had her audience with the king, she returned **into the second house of the women** (v. 14), the chambers of the concubines. **In the tenth month** (v. 16) of **the seventh year,** that is, December 479 BC or January 478 BC (see discussions on 1:3–4; 2:1), Esther was chosen to be the new queen. Her tenure as queen continued through the events of the book, through 473 BC (see 3:7 and discussion; see also 8:9–13; 9:1). She may have died or fallen from favor shortly thereafter (see discussion on 1:9). Part of the celebration included a **release** (v. 18). The Hebrew word used here is unique to this verse and may imply a remission of taxes, an emancipation of slaves, a cancellation of debts, or a remission of obligatory military service.

II. The Feasts of Esther (2:19–7:10)

A. Mordecai Uncovers a Plot (2:19–23)

2:19. The enlargement of the harem apparently continued unabated. Perhaps there was a causal connection between the second gathering of women and the assassination plot (2:21–23); some have suggested that it reflects palace intrigue in support of the deposed Vashti.

Mordecai sat in the king's gate. The gate of an ancient city was its major commercial and legal center. Markets were held in the gate; the court sat there to transact its business (see Deut. 21:18–20; Josh. 20:4; Ruth 4:1–11; Ps. 69:12). A king might hold an audience at the gate (see 2 Sam. 19:8; 1 Kings 22:10). Daniel was at the king's gate as ruler over all Babylon (Dan. 2:48–49). Mordecai's sitting at the king's gate confirms he held a high position in the civil service of the empire (see discussion on 2:5). From this vantage point, he could overhear any plans for the murder of the king.

2:21–23. Another point of comparison with the Joseph narrative is the involvement of **two ... chamberlains** (v. 21; Gen. 40:1–3; see discussion on 2:3–4).

The conspirators, **Bigthan and Teresh** (v. 21), were **hanged on a tree** (v. 23), that is, impaled on poles. Among the Persians, this form of execution was impalement, as is confirmed in pictures and statues from the ancient Near East and in the comments of the Greek historian Herodotus (3.125, 129; 4.43). According to Herodotus (3.159), Darius I impaled three thousand Babylonians when he took Babylon, an act that Darius himself recorded in his Behistun (Bisitun) inscription. In Israelite and Canaanite practice, hanging was an exhibition of the corpse and not the means of execution itself (Deut. 21:22–23; Josh. 8:29; 10:26; 1 Sam. 31:8–10; 2 Sam. 4:12; 21:9–10). The execution of a chamberlain in the Joseph narrative also appears to have been by impalement (Gen. 40:19). The sons of Haman were later killed by the sword, and then their corpses were displayed in this way (9:5–14).

The concern of the author of Esther with rhetorical symmetry is seen in his mentioning **the chronicles** (v. 23) in the beginning (here), middle (6:1), and end (10:2) of the narrative. The episode dealing with the plot of Bigthan and Teresh is a good example of the many "coincidences" in the book that later take on crucial significance in the story.

B. Haman's Plot (chap. 3)

3:1. Four years had elapsed since Esther's selection as queen (3:7; 2:16–17). That no reason is given for the promotion of Haman provides an ironic contrast between the unrewarded merit of Mordecai (2:21–23; see 6:3) and the unmerited reward of Haman. There is some debate about the ancestry of Haman, **son of Hammedatha the Agagite**. The name Hammedatha appears to be Persian and probably refers to an immediate ancestor. The title "Agagite" could refer to some other immediate ancestor or to an unknown place; however, it is far more likely that it refers to Agag, king of Amalek (1 Sam. 15:20). The Amalekites had attacked Israel after she fled from Egypt (Exod. 17:8–16; 1 Sam. 14:47–48). For this reason, the Lord would have "war with Amalek from generation to generation" (Exod. 17:16). Israel was not to forget; they were to "blot out the remembrance of Amalek from under heaven" (Deut. 25:17–19). Saul's attack on Amalek (1 Samuel 15) resulted in the death of most, though not all (1 Chron. 4:42–43), of the city's population and later in the death of King Agag. In Esther, about five hundred years after the battle led by the Benjamite Saul, the Benjamite Mordecai (see discussion on 2:5) continued the war with the Amalekites.

3:2–6. Obedience to the second commandment (Exod. 20:4) was not the issue in Mordecai's refusal to bow down to Haman, for the Jews were willing to bow down to kings (see 1 Sam. 24:8; 2 Sam. 14:4; 1 Kings 1:16) and to other persons (see Gen. 23:7; 33:3; 44:14). Only the long-standing enmity between the Jews and the Amalekites accounts both for Mordecai's refusal and for Haman's intent to destroy all the Jews (vv. 5–6). The threat against the Jews **throughout the whole kingdom** (v. 6) was a threat against the ultimate issue of redemptive history.

3:7. In the first month of **the twelfth year**, that is, April or May 474 BC, the fifth year of Esther's reign, **they cast pur**, perhaps the astrologers who assisted Haman (5:10, 14; 6:12–13). "Pur" (see 9:24, 26) is a word found in Akkadian texts with the same meaning, **the lot**. The celebration known as Purim takes its name from the plural of this noun (see 9:23–32).

Ironically, the month of the Jews' celebration of the Passover deliverance from Egypt was also the month that Haman began plotting their destruction (Exod. 12:1–11). With the lot providentially falling on **the twelfth month**, there would be an eleven-month delay between the securing of the decree and the execution of it in **the month Adar** (February–March).

3:8–9. The name of the people Haman wished to destroy was slyly omitted in his blend of the true and the false. The Jews did have their own customs and laws, but they were not disobedient to the king (see Jer. 29:7). They were indeed a people **scattered abroad and dispersed** (v. 8; see 8:11, 17; 9:2, 2, 16, 19–20, 28). Herodotus (3.95) records that the annual income of the Persian empire was 15,000 talents. If this figure is correct, Haman's offer of **ten thousand talents** (v. 9) was two-thirds of that amount—a huge sum. Presumably, the money would have come from the plundered wealth of the victims of the decree. In 3:13, it is implied that those who took part in the massacre would be allowed to keep the plunder, perhaps adding financial incentive to the execution of the decree since Ahasuerus later disavowed taking the money (3:11). On the other hand, 4:7 and 7:4 may imply that the king had planned on collecting some of the money. **Those that have the charge of the business** may represent the title of revenue officers who would bring the money to the treasury, or it may refer to those who would carry out the decree. The Amalekites had plundered Israel once before (see discussion on 3:1); Haman planned a recurrence.

3:12–13. On the thirteenth day of the first month (v. 12), that is, April 17, 474 BC, in the twelfth year of Ahasuerus's reign (3:7), Haman's decree was prepared for distribution. Its call for Israel's destruction was the same that had earlier been decreed against Amalek (1 Sam. 15:3). The decree was to be carried out on **the thirteenth day of the twelfth month** (v. 13), that is, March 7, 473 BC (see 8:12).

3:15. Ironically, Haman and the king would drink together again when the fate of the Jews was once again being decided (7:1–2), but then it would signify the dissolution of their relationship and the

reversal of the decree here celebrated. The celebration here is in sharp contrast to the fasting and mourning of the Jews (4:1–3, 15–16).

C. Mordecai Persuades Esther to Help (chap. 4)

4:1–3. The prominence of feasting throughout the book of Esther sets the mourning and fasting of verse 3 and 4:16 in sharp relief; a pair of fasts matches the prominent pairs of banquets.

4:4–11. The dialogue of Esther and Mordecai was mediated by **Hatach** (v. 5), which reflects the prohibition against Mordecai's entering the royal citadel dressed in mourning (4:2) and the isolation of Esther in the harem quarters. That Mordecai was aware of the amount **Haman had promised to pay** (v. 7) the king (see 3:9) is a reminder of his high position in the bureaucracy at Susa (2:21–23).

Esther's fears (v. 11) were founded. Herodotus (3.118, 140) notes that anyone approaching the Persian king unsummoned would be killed unless the king gave immediate pardon.

4:12–17. The theme of the book of Esther is most clearly expressed in this passage. Mordecai's confidence that the Jews would be delivered was based on God's sovereignty in working out His purposes and fulfilling His promises. Their deliverance would come, even if through some means other than Esther. Yet that sovereignty was not fatalistic: unless Esther recognized her providential placement in the palace **for such a time as this** (v. 14; compare the Joseph narrative, Gen. 45:5–7) and exercised her individual responsibility, she and her family would perish. (For similar treatments of the relationship between divine sovereignty and human responsibility, see Matt. 26:24; Acts 2:23.) Esther called for local Jews to **fast** (v. 16). Prayer, which usually accompanied such fasting, is not mentioned but may have been a part of this fast as well (see Judg. 20:26; 1 Sam. 7:6; 2 Sam. 12:16; Ezra 8:21–23; Neh. 9:1–3; Isa. 58:3; Jer. 14:12; Joel 1:14; 2:12–17; Jonah 3:6–9). The omission of any reference to prayer or to God is consistent with the author's intention; absence of any distinctively religious concepts or vocabulary is a rhetorical device used to heighten the fact that it is indeed God who has been active in the whole narrative. **I also and my maidens will fast**. Note the rhetorical symmetry: where once Esther and her maids had received special foods (2:9), now they shared a fast.

D. Esther's Request to the King: The First Banquet (5:1–8)

5:1–7. Esther's steps to intervene give occasion for an example of divine providence influencing a king's heart (see Prov. 21:1). One can only speculate regarding Esther's reasons for delaying her answer to the king's question until he had asked it a third time (vv. 3, 6–7; 7:2). The author uses these delays as plot retardation devices to sustain the tension and permit the introduction of new material on Haman's self-aggrandizement (5:11–12) and Mordecai's reward (6:6–11).

E. A Sleepless Night (5:9–6:14)

5:9–11. Haman's rage was kindled when Mordecai **stood not up** (v. 9) in his presence (an ironic contrast to Mordecai's earlier refusal to bow, 3:2–6), but Haman **refrained himself** (v. 10) and took pride in his wealth and the **multitude of his children** (v. 11; he had ten sons, 9:7–10). Herodotus (1.136) reports that the Persians prized a large number of sons second only to valor in battle; the Persian king sent gifts to the subject with the most sons (see Ps. 127:3–5).

5:12–14. Haman's pride of position motivated him to eliminate Mordecai early, and also set Haman up for humiliation (see Prov. 16:18; 29:23). There may be a note of hyperbole in the gallows of **fifty cubits** height (seventy-five feet; v. 14). Some have suggested that the gallows was erected atop some other structure to achieve this height, for example, on the city wall (see 1 Sam. 31:10; see also discussion on 2:23).

6:1–2. These verses mark the literary center of the narrative. When things could not look worse, a series of seemingly trivial coincidences marks a critical turn that brings resolution to the story. The king's inability to sleep, his requesting the reading of the chronicles, the reading of the passage reporting Mordecai's past kindness, Haman's noisy carpentry in the early hours of the morning (5:14), his sudden entry into the outer court, and his assumption that he was the man the king wished to honor—all testify to the sovereignty of God over the events of the narrative. Circumstances that seemed incidental earlier in the narrative take on crucial significance. Just as in the Joseph narrative (Gen. 41:1–45), the hero's personal fortunes are reversed because of the monarch's disturbed sleep (see Dan. 2:1; 6:18).

When the king could not sleep, the scribe read from **the chronicles** (v. 1) records of events that had occurred five years earlier (compare 3:7, the king's "twelfth year," with 2:16, his "seventh year"). **It was found written that Mordecai had told** (v. 2) the king about the two **chamberlains** who had sought to kill him.

6:4–6. Again, irony is evident. Just as Haman had withheld from the king the identity of the "certain people" (3:8), so now the king unintentionally kept from Haman the identity of the **man whom the king delighteth to honour** (v. 6).

6:7–12. Great significance was attached to the king's garment in ancient times; being allowed to wear his garments was a sign of unique favor (1 Sam. 18:4). To wear another's garments was to partake of his power, stature, honor, or sanctity (compare the Joseph narrative, Gen. 41:41–43.2; see 2 Kings 2:13–14; Isa. 61:3, 10; Zechariah 3; Mark 5:27). Haman's suggestion that the honoree be dressed in **royal apparel ... which the king useth to wear** (v. 8) would be a great honor for the recipient, but it was also considerably flattering to the king: wearing his garment was chosen instead of wealth.

6:13–14. As a special guest, Haman was escorted to the feast according to custom (compare the Joseph narrative, Gen. 43:15–26; see Matt. 22:1–14).

F. Haman Hanged: The Second Banquet (chap. 7)

7:1–3. Esther was now ready to state her **petition** (v. 2) and plead for her life (see 5:3, 6) if she had indeed **found favour** (v. 3) from the king (see 2:15, 17).

7:4-5. Esther declared herself **sold** (v. 4) as she referred to the bribe Haman had offered to the king (3:9; 4:7); she also paraphrased Haman's edict (3:13). The Hebrew word translated **enemy** can also mean "distress," perhaps a better rendering here. The statement probably means either (1) that the affliction of the Jews would be less injurious to the king if slavery was all that was involved or (2) that Esther would not trouble the king if slavery was the only issue.

7:6-8. The king left the banquet **in his wrath** (v. 7), setting the stage for the final twist that would seal Haman's fate. Meals were customarily eaten while reclining on a couch (Amos 6:4-7; John 13:23), so the king returned to find Haman **fallen upon the bed whereon Esther was** (v. 8), to beg for his life. It is ironic that Haman, who had been angry when the Jew Mordecai would not bow down (which set the whole story in motion), now fell before the Jewess Esther (see 6:13).

7:9-10. Before this moment, there is no evidence that Esther knew of Mordecai's triumph earlier in the day (6); she had pled for the life of her people. Harbona's reference to **the gallows** in effect introduces a second charge against Haman: his attempt to kill the king's benefactor. Harbona was one of the seven chamberlains who had been sent to bring Vashti before the king (1:10-11), thus setting in motion the events that led to her fall and the choice of Esther; now he was instrumental in the fall of Haman and the rise of Mordecai. For the second time, the author notes that the king's anger was **pacified** (v. 10; see 2:1).

III. The Feasts of Purim (chaps. 8-10)

A. The King's Edict in Behalf of the Jews (chap. 8)

8:1-17. The author achieves considerable literary symmetry by recapitulating much of 3:1-4:3 in almost identical terms.

8:1-2. That same day, the king **did ... give the house of Haman ... unto Esther the queen** (v. 1). Herodotus (3.128-29) and Josephus (*Antiquities* 11.17) confirm that the property of a traitor reverted to the crown; Ahasuerus presented Haman's wealth

(5:11) to Esther. Earlier, the king's offer of **his ring** (v. 2; see 3:10) had included Haman's keeping the money; now Mordecai received the office and the estate of Haman.

8:3-6. Esther and Mordecai were secure (7:4-5), but the irrevocable decree (see 1:19) was still a threat to the rest of the Jews. Drawing on the fact that she had received favor (see 4:11; 5:2), Esther pled for the lives of her people (compare the Joseph narrative, Gen. 44:34).

8:7-8. The dilemma was the same as the one that confronted Darius the Mede in Daniel (Dan. 6:8, 12, 15). The solution (v. 8) was to issue another decree that in effect countered the decree of Haman without formally revoking it (see discussion on 9:2-3).

8:9-13. The phraseology in these verses is taken from the parallel in 3:12-14. The extent of the destruction was the same as that earlier decreed against Amalek (see discussion on 3:12-13). In Ahasuerus's twelfth year, **in the third month ... on the three and twentieth day** (v. 9), that is, June 25, 474 BC, two months and ten days after the proclamation of Haman's edict (see discussion on 3:13), a new edict was authorized by the king and put into effect. On the very day that the Jews were to have perished, **the thirteenth day of the twelfth month**, March 7, 473 BC (see 3:13-14), the Jews were permitted to defend themselves. Some fifteen years after this first Purim, Ezra would lead his expedition to Jerusalem (Ezra 7:9).

8:14-17. The phraseology here is taken from 3:15-4:3. The royal couriers dispatched the new edict with equal speed. Whereas the first edict had brought mourning to the Jews (4:3), the new edict brought joy. For the second time, meanwhile, Mordecai was dressed in **royal apparel** (v. 15), indicating his newly bestowed rank and authority (see discussion on 6:7-12).

B. The Institution of Purim (chap. 9)

9:1. The Jews carried out the edict of Mordecai eight months and twenty days later, and the plot of their enemies **turned to the contrary**. This statement that the opposite happened points to the author's concern with literary symmetry: he balances most of the details from the first half of the story with their explicit reversal in the second half.

9:2-4. The events that followed illustrate the promise of Genesis 12:3. Confronted with two conflicting edicts issued in the king's name—the edict of Haman and the edict of Mordecai—the governors followed the edict of the current regime.

9:5-10. The Jews attended to the unfinished business of "blotting out the name of the Amalekites" (Exod. 17:16; Deut. 25:17-19; see discussions on 3:1-6). This incident is presented as the antithesis of 1 Samuel 15. The narrator emphatically states that the Jews did not take plunder (v. 10), in spite of the king's permission to do so (8:11). Seizing the plunder five hundred years earlier in the battle against Amalek had cost Saul his kingship (1 Sam. 15:17-19); here, not taking the plunder brought royal power to Mordecai (9:20-23; see 9:15-16; Gen. 14:22-24).

In self-defense, the Jews in Susa killed **five hundred men** (v. 6), the most noteworthy of whom were **the ten sons of Haman** (v. 10).

9:11-14. Once again, the king gave Esther the opportunity to present her **petition** (v. 12; see 5:3, 6; 7:2). Her request that **Haman's ten sons be hanged** (v. 13) in this case refers to the display of their corpses, not to the means of their execution (see 9:7-10 and discussion on 2:21-23).

9:15-17. The author again emphasizes that the Jews' purpose was self-defense, not aggression. They were careful to take no plunder (v. 15). Twice the author notes that the Jews **had rest from their enemies** (v. 16; 9:22). Closely associated with the vengeance on their enemies is the rest promised to Israel (Deut. 25:19). The defeat of Haman brought rest to the Jews (see 1 Chron. 22:6-10; Ps. 95:8-11; Isa. 32:18; Heb. 3:11-4:11).

9:18-19. The author accounts for the tradition of observing Purim on two different days: It was observed on the **fourteenth** (v. 19) in most towns, but the Jews of Susa observed it on the **fifteenth** (v. 18). Today it is observed on the fourteenth, except in Jerusalem, where it is observed on the fifteenth.

9:20-28. Some take the phrase **Mordecai wrote these things** (v. 20) as indication that Mordecai wrote the book of Esther. However, the more natural understanding is that he recorded the events in the letters he sent. Mordecai authorized the Jews to celebrate with feasting and exchanging **portions** of food (v. 22; see discussion on 2:9; see Neh. 8:10, 12), and the Jews agreed to celebrate **Purim** (v. 26; the significance of this term is reiterated in vv. 24, 26; see discussion on 3:7). It is also noted that **all such as joined themselves unto them** (v. 27) were invited to celebrate Purim. While some refer this phrase to a period of Jewish proselytism and regard it as important in dating the book, it is more likely that it refers to those mentioned in 8:17.

9:29-32. No date is assigned for **the fastings** (v. 31) mentioned here. Jews traditionally observe the thirteenth of Adar, Haman's propitious day (see 3:7, 13), as a fast ("the fast of Esther") before the celebration of Purim. These three days of victory celebration, on the thirteenth to the fifteenth of Adar, rhetorically balance the three days of Esther's fasting prior to interceding with the king (4:16).

C. The Promotion of Mordecai (chap. 10)

10:1-2. The reference to this taxation may represent material in the author's source, **the book of the chronicles of the kings of Media and Persia** (v. 2), to which he directs the reader for additional information and confirmation (see discussion on 2:23). The book ends with the affirmation of Mordecai and Esther's influence in sustaining the Jewish people during the time of their postexilic dispersion.

THE BOOK OF JOB

INTRODUCTION

Author

Although most of the book consists of the words of Job and his counselors, Job himself was not the author. The author no doubt was an Israelite, since he (not Job or his friends) frequently uses the Israelite covenant name for God ("LORD"; Yahweh). In the prologue (chaps. 1–2), the divine discourses (38:1–42:6), and the epilogue (42:7–17), "LORD" occurs a total of twenty-five times, while in the rest of the book (chaps. 3–37), it appears only once (12:9).

The unknown author probably had access to oral and/or written sources from which, under divine inspiration, he composed the book. Of course, the subject matter of the prologue had to be divinely revealed to him, since it contains information only God could know. While the author preserved much of the archaic and non-Israelite tone of the language of Job and his friends, he also revealed his own style as a writer of Wisdom Literature. The literary structures and the quality of the rhetoric used display the author's literary genius.

Date

Two dates are involved: (1) the date of the man Job and his historical setting and (2) the date of the inspired author who composed the book. The latter could be dated anytime from the reign of Solomon to the exile. Although the author was an Israelite, he mentioned nothing of Israelite history. He had a written and/or oral account about the non-Israelite sage Job (1:1), who appears to have lived during the second millennium BC (2000–1000 BC; see discussion on 19:24). Like the Hebrew patriarchs, Job lived more than one hundred years (42:16). His wealth was measured in livestock (1:3), and he acted as priest for his family (1:5). The raiding of Sabean (1:15) and Chaldean (1:17) tribes fits the second millennium, as does the mention of qesitah, "a piece of money," in 42:11 (see Gen. 33:19; Josh. 24:32). The discovery of a Targum (Aramaic paraphrase) on Job dated to the first or second century BC (the earliest written Targum) makes a very late date for authorship highly unlikely.

Theme and Theological Message

The book provides a profound statement on the subject of theodicy (the justice of God in light of human suffering). The manner in which the problem of theodicy is conceived and the solution offered (if it may be called that) is uniquely Israelite. The theodicy question in Greek and later Western thought has been, How can the justice of an almighty God be defended in the face of evil, especially human suffering and, even more particularly, the suffering of the innocent? In this form of the question, three assumptions are possible: (1) God is not almighty, (2) God is not just (there is a "demonic" element in His being), and (3) man may be innocent. To the ancient Israelites, however, it was indisputable that God is almighty, that He is perfectly just, and that no human is wholly innocent in His sight. These three assumptions were also fundamental to the theology of Job and his friends. Simple logic, then, dictated the conclusion: every person's suffering is indicative of the measure of his guilt in the eyes of God. In the abstract, this conclusion appeared inescapable, logically imperative, and theologically satisfying. Hence, in the context of such a theology, theodicy was not a problem because its solution was self-evident.

What was thus theologically self-evident and unassailable in the abstract was often, as in the case of Job, in radical tension with actual human experience. Some people lived lives of genuine godliness, had upright moral character, and though not sinless, had kept themselves from great transgression but were nonetheless made to suffer bitterly. For such people, the self-evident theology brought no consolation and offered no guidance; it only gave rise to a great enigma. The God to whom the sufferer was accustomed to turn in moments of need and distress became the overwhelming enigma. The speeches of chapters 3–37 outline, on the one hand, the flawlessly logical but wounding thrusts of those who insisted on the "orthodox" theology and, on the other hand, the writhing of the soul of the righteous sufferer who struggled with the great enigma. In addition, Job suffered from the wounds inflicted by his well-intended friends (see discussion on 5:27). Here, then, is a graphic portrayal of the unique form of the problem of theodicy as experienced by righteous sufferers within orthodox Israel.

The "solution" offered is also uniquely Israelite—or, better said, biblical. The relationship between God and man is not exclusive and closed. A third party intrudes, the Great Adversary (see chaps. 1–2). Incapable of contending with God hand to hand, power pitted against power, he is bent on frustrating God's enterprise, embodied in the creation and centered on the God-man relationship. As tempter, he seeks to alienate man from God (see Gen. 3; Matt. 4:1); as accuser (one of the names by which he is called, Satan, means "accuser"), he seeks to alienate God from man (see Zech. 3:1; Rev. 12:9–10). The Adversary's all-consuming purpose is to drive an irremovable wedge between God and man, to effect an alienation that cannot be reconciled.

In the story of Job, the author portrays the Adversary in his boldest and most radical assault on God and the godly man and the special and intimate relationship that was dearest to them both. When God called up the name of Job before the Accuser and testified to the righteousness of this one on the earth—this man in whom God delighted—with one crafty thrust, Satan attempted both to assail God's beloved and to discredit God as a fool. True to one of Satan's modes of operation, he accused Job before God. He charged that Job's godliness was evil. The very godliness in which God took delight was void of all integrity; it was a terrible sin. Job's godliness was self-serving; he was righteous only because it benefited him. If God would only let Satan tempt Job by breaking the link between righteousness and blessing, he would expose the righteous man for the sinner he was.

It was the Adversary's ultimate challenge. For if the godliness of the righteous man in whom God delighted could be shown to be a terrible sin, a chasm of alienation would stand between them that could not be bridged. Then even redemption would be unthinkable, for the godliest of men would be shown to be the most ungodly. God's whole enterprise in creation and redemption would be shown to be radically flawed, and God could only sweep it all away in awful judgment.

The accusation, once raised, could not be removed, not even by destroying the Accuser. So God let the Adversary have his way with Job (within specified limits) so that God and the righteous Job would be vindicated and the Great Accuser silenced. Thus came the anguish of Job, robbed of every sign of God's favor so that God became for him the great enigma. Also, his righteousness was assailed on earth through the logic of the "orthodox" theology of his friends. Alone, he agonized. Job knew in his heart that his godliness had been authentic and that someday he would be vindicated (see 13:18; 14:13–17; 16:19; 19:25–27). In spite of all that had befallen him, though he cursed the day of his birth (chap. 3) and chided God for treating him unjustly (9:28–35) — the uncalculated outcry of a distraught spirit — he would not curse God (as his wife, the human nearest his heart, proposed; see 2:9). In fact, what pained Job most was God's apparent alienation from him.

In the end, the Adversary was silenced. The astute theologians, Job's friends, were silenced. Job was silenced. God was not, and when He spoke, it was to Job that He spoke, bringing the silence of regret for hasty speech in days of suffering and the silence of repose in the ways of the Almighty (see 38:1–42:6). Furthermore, as his heavenly friend, God heard Job's intercessions for his associates (42:8–10), and He restored Job's beatitude (42:10–17).

In summary, the author's pastoral word to the godly sufferer is that his righteousness has such supreme value that God treasures it most of all. The Great Adversary knows that if he is to thwart the purposes of God, he must assail the righteousness of man (see 1:21–22; 2:9–10; 23:8, 10; see also Gen. 15:6). At stake in the suffering of the truly godly is the outcome of the struggle in heaven between the Great Adversary and God, with the all-encompassing divine purpose in the balance. Thus, the suffering of the righteous has a meaning and value commensurate with the titanic spiritual struggle of the ages.

Literary Features

In many places, Job is difficult to translate because of its many unusual words and its style. For that reason, modern translations frequently differ widely. Even the early translator(s) of Job into Greek (the Septuagint) seems often to have been perplexed. The Septuagint of Job is about four hundred lines shorter than the accepted Hebrew text, and it may be that the translator(s) simply omitted lines he (they) did not understand. The early Syriac (Peshitta), Aramaic (Targum), and Latin (Vulgate) translators had similar difficulties.

Like some other ancient compositions, the book of Job has a sandwich literary structure: prologue (prose), main body (poetry), and epilogue (prose), revealing a creative composition, not an arbitrary compilation. Some of Job's words were lament (see chap. 3 and many shorter poems in his speeches), but the form of lament is unique to Job and often unlike the regular format of most lament psalms (except Psalm 88). Much of the book takes the form of legal disputation. Although the friends came to console Job, they ended up arguing over the reason for his suffering. The argument broke down (chap. 27), and Job then proceeded to make his final appeal to God for vindication (chaps. 29–31). The Wisdom poem in chapter 28 appears to be the words of the author, who sees the failure of the dispute as evidence of lack of wisdom. So in praise of true wisdom, he centers his structural apex between the three cycles of dialogue and dispute (chaps. 3–27) and the three monologues: Job's (chaps. 29–31), Elihu's (chaps. 32–37), and God's (38:1–42:6). In his monologue, Job turned directly to God for a legal decision: that he was innocent of the charges his counselors have leveled against him. Elihu's monologue—another human perspective on why people suffer—rebuked Job but moved beyond the punishment theme to the value of divine chastening and God's redemptive purpose in it. God's monologue gave the divine perspective: Job was not condemned, but neither was a logical or legal answer given for why Job had suffered. That remained a mystery to Job, though the reader is ready for Job's restoration in the epilogue because he has had the heavenly vantage point of the prologue all along. Thus, the literary structure and the theological significance of the book are beautifully tied together.

Outline

I. Prologue (chaps. 1–2)
   A. Job's Happiness (1:1–5)
   B. Job's Testing (1:6–2:13)
      1. Satan's First Accusation (1:6–12)
      2. Job's Faith Despite Loss of Family and Property (1:13–22)
      3. Satan's Second Accusation (2:1–6)
      4. Job's Faith during Personal Suffering (2:7–10)
      5. The Arrival of the Three Friends (2:11–13)
II. Dialogue and Dispute (chaps. 3–27)
   A. Job's Opening Lament (chap. 3)
   B. First Cycle of Speeches (chaps. 4–14)
      1. Eliphaz (chaps. 4–5)
      2. Job's Reply (chaps. 6–7)
      3. Bildad (chap. 8)
      4. Job's Reply (chaps. 9–10)
      5. Zophar (chap. 11)
      6. Job's Reply (chaps. 12–14)
   C. Second Cycle of Speeches (chaps. 15–21)
      1. Eliphaz (chap. 15)
      2. Job's Reply (chaps. 16–17)
      3. Bildad (chap. 18)

Bibliography

Andersen, Francis I. *Job: An Introduction and Commentary*. Tyndale Old Testament Commentaries 13. Downers Grove, IL: InterVarsity, 1976.

Barnes, Albert. *Barnes' Notes*. Vol. 3. Grand Rapids, MI: Baker, 1973, 1983.

Cohen, A., ed. *Job: Hebrew Text and English Translation, with an Introduction and Commentary*. Soncino Books of the Bible. New York: Soncino, 1985.

Ellison, H. L. *From Tragedy to Triumph: The Message of the Book of Job*. Grand Rapids, MI: Eerdmans, 1958.

Hartley, John E. *The Book of Job*. New International Commentary on the Old Testament. Grand Rapids, MI: Eerdmans, 1988.

Lawson, J. Steven. *Job*. New American Commentary 11. Nashville: Broadman & Holman, 2004.

Smick, Elmer B. "Job." In *Expositor's Bible Commentary*, edited by Frank E. Gaebelein, vol. 4. Grand Rapids, MI: Zondervan, 1988.

Thomas, David. *The Book of Job*. Minneapolis, MN: James & Klock, 1976.

Unger, Merrill F. *Unger's Commentary on the Old Testament*. Chattanooga, TN: AMG, 2002.

Zuck, Roy B. "Job." In *Bible Knowledge Commentary: Old Testament (BKC)*, edited by John F. Walvoord and Roy B. Zuck. Wheaton, IL: Victor, 1987.

EXPOSITION

I. Prologue (chaps. 1–2)

This great poetic drama seems to be one of the oldest statements of the continual problem of man's destiny and God's inscrutable providential ways with him here on earth. Can humanity have a pure love for its Maker? How is evil reconciled with a God who is sovereign? Are circumstances that fall on every human being to be taken as a test of one's moral character?

Job was a historical figure who lived in a distinct place (Jer. 25:20; Lam. 4:21), just as definite as Tema (Job 6:19), Sheba (6:19), Ethiopia (28:19), and the area of the Jordan River (40:23). The specific location was the land of Uz in Syria, known as Aram. The man listed as Uz in Genesis 10:23 more than likely is the one who established a home in this area. The book was written during the period of Abraham or during the pre-Abrahamic age. The two men named Uz in Genesis (10:23; 22:20–24; 36:28) had long passed from the scene when this book was penned. The name Uz may mean "replacement."

The first two chapters of Job provide a proper introduction to this somewhat complicated but important work.

A. Job's Happiness (1:1–5)

Job and his family were extremely blessed in the material sense, and Job walked with admirable integrity before the Lord and before others. Job's wealth was great, but he had a problem with his immoral older children, something that haunts many older parents. These verses quickly get to the heart of the struggle that must have vexed Job's soul as a pious believer in God.

1:1–2. The name **Job** (Hebrew, *Iyyob*; v. 1) can mean "where is my father?" or "no father" and may indicate that Job was an orphan or that he was illegitimate. Job is described as **perfect** (Hebrew, *tam*; "blameless") **and upright**, from *yashar*, from a root meaning "to be upright, straight." Job walked with integrity before people and before God. The story of Job reveals that many people in ancient times trusted in and walked with the true God. While most people in this period had turned away from the revelation of the Lord, a remnant had retained the truth about Him. Job **eschewed evil**, meaning he turned away from sin. He was blessed with **seven sons and three daughters** (v. 2).

1:3–5. Job was a wealthy man. **His substance** (v. 3) consisted of great flocks of animals; he also had hundreds of servants, **a very great household**. In fact, he was **the greatest of all the men of the east**, meaning among the people of northern Arabia, identified with Kedar (Jer. 49:28). The problem was his children, who on certain feast days banqueted in **their houses** (v. 4) with their sisters, and more than likely, many unsavory characters joined them. Though not stated, this implies that his sons also had luxurious homes with many slaves to serve them.

These **feasting** (v. 5) days, which may have lasted a week (Gen. 29:27; Judg. 14:12) and which were celebrated before the feasts of the law given by Moses, may have been ceremonial feasts held as a remembrance of the true God. When these feast days were over and Job's sons had spent themselves, Job **sanctified them** before the Lord with **burnt offerings** for all of them. He rightly assumed that they had **sinned, and cursed God in their hearts**. Being a pious believer in the Lord, Job did this **continually**. The Lord had slain the first animal and made the first sacrifice to cover the sins of Adam and Eve (Gen. 3:21). Those who followed their ancestors knew that such an offering was to be continued. The ancient people who believed in the Lord followed this pattern of slaying an animal and offering it to Him as a burnt offering (see 22:2–3, 6–8, 13; Exod. 18:12).

B. Job's Testing (1:6–2:13)

The focus of these verses is on the man Job. He was considered "upright" (1:1) and one of the wealthiest men in the region (1:3). What would happen to his piety and his honor if he were placed in the vise of a terrible and troubling test? Satan was one of the key players in the drama, along with Job's wife, who fell into a deep pit of despondence. God's goodness was questioned because He allowed Satan to bring poverty to Job, who was considered such a pious believer.

1. Satan's First Accusation (1:6–12)

1:6–12. The drama moved to heaven, where **the sons of God** (the host of angels) **came to present themselves before the LORD** (v. 6). **Satan** (lit., "the adversary/accuser"; see Rev. 12:10), came along with the heavenly angelic council to stand in the presence of God (1 Kings 22:19; Ps. 89:5–7; Jer. 23:18, 22). Satan is not simply a representation of evil or an evil force; he was the highest of the created beings, but he rebelled and took with him a large number of angels, who joined him in his rebellion against God. In Isaiah 14:12–17, using the king of Babylon as an illustration, the fall of Satan is put in poetic form and described. Satan, represented by the king of Babylon, proclaimed his rise "into heaven," where he would set himself "above the stars of God." He is called "Lucifer, sun of the morning" (Isa. 14:12–13). His fall is further dramatized through the king of Tyre in Eze-

kiel 28:11–17, where he is pictured as having been "in Eden the garden of God" (Ezek. 28:13).

How could such a sinful being as Satan come before the Lord in heaven? The answer seems to be that he cannot enjoy spiritual fellowship with God, in that sense he cannot be with God, but he can appear in God's presence to present petitions.

While the Lord does not need to ask questions for information, He often asks questions to draw out the motives of His created beings. The Lord asked Satan, **Whence comest thou?** (v. 7), with Satan replying that he had been roaming throughout the **earth**. The answer implies that Satan is a powerful creature who can travel great cosmic distances and appear in many locations, though he certainly is not omnipresent as God is.

The Lord brought up Job's name and rehearsed his goodness, noting that he **feareth God, and escheweth evil** (v. 8). Satan instantly brought a charge against Job's motive for being **upright**. He said that the Lord had **made a hedge about him, and about his house … on every side** (v. 10). Everything Job did was **blessed,** and **his substance is increased in the land**.

Now came the challenge and the test: if God **put forth** His **hand** (v. 11) and touched all that Job had, **he will curse thee to thy face** (v. 11). After all, if God is sovereign, He can do what He wishes, and surely such a test would reveal Job's true motives for worshiping the Lord. The Lord responded to the challenge and told Satan, **all that he hath is in thy power; only upon himself put not forth thine hand** (v. 12). Satan did not discuss the matter further but quickly responded and **went forth from the presence of the LORD**.

2. Job's Faith Despite Loss of Family and Property (1:13–22)

1:13–19. Satan waited for the right day, when Job's sons and daughters were banqueting, and more than likely were drunk with **wine**, in the **eldest brother's house** (v. 13). Satan orchestrated various tragedies that tumbled one upon another. **The Sabeans fell upon** (v. 15) Job's oxen and his donkeys

JOB 2:9 – 10

and carried them off, and the servants tending them were killed by the **sword**. These people were probably marauding Arabians from the south, from Sheba, who were wealthy traders in spices, gold, and precious stones. Another servant rushed in and reported that **The fire of God** (v. 16) fell from heaven and **consumed** Job's sheep and the servants who were tending them. Three bands of **Chaldeans** (v. 17), or Babylonians, set upon Job's herds of **camels** and took them away and also killed the servants tending them. Again, another servant arrived and told Job that a **great wind** (v. 19), possibly a tornado, came and destroyed the house where all his children were feasting. All of Job's children had perished.

While God is not the author of evil, He can and does allow evil for His own mysterious, providential reasons. Without a doubt, He allows Satan to do terrible things against humanity. The Lord is allowing sin and evil to run their course but will ultimately bring them to an end in His universe. Two things are certain: Satan is not omnipotent; nor is God helpless. In the Lord's overall providence, all things take place. No human can adequately explain this from such a limited perspective.

1:20 – 22. Listening to the torrent of bad news that came all at once, **Job arose** (v. 20) and tore **his mantle** (coat), **and shaved his head, and fell down ... and worshipped** God. Job's statement of trust is one of the greatest recorded in Scripture (v. 21):

> Naked came I out of my mother's womb,
> And naked shall I return thither:
> The LORD gave, and the LORD hath taken away;
> Blessed be the name of the LORD.

Job's faith led him to see God's sovereign hand at work, and this gave him comfort even in the face of calamity and suffering. He did not charge God **foolishly** (v. 22).

3. Satan's Second Accusation (2:1 – 6)

2:1 – 3. Satan again came **before the LORD** (v. 1), and the Lord again asked him, **From whence comest thou?** (v. 2), with the same answer before. The answer may seem somewhat casual, as if Satan had not

planned to come to God with another diabolical plan against Job. The dialogue is similar to that in 1:8 but with the added statement that Job **holdeth fast his integrity, although thou movedst me against him, to destroy him without cause** (v. 3). Another revelation is stated in verse 3. Although Satan is active, as in this drama, he is still dependent on what God does. The Lord was the one who "movedst" against Job. It is not always clear in the events of life what is happening and why; nevertheless, everything that takes place is part of God's divine plan, for purposes often unknowable on this side of glory (see 38:2).

2:4 – 8. Satan replied, **Skin for skin** (v. 4), which means "like for like" or "hide for hide," a Bedouin proverb implying that one responds in a human way to adversity. No one sits by idly while troubles pour down upon them. Man reaches a point when he has to react. Therefore, Satan added, if God **put forth His hand** (v. 5) against Job and touched **his bone and his flesh ... he will curse thee to thy face**. The Lord again granted Satan the opportunity to act, only **save** Job's **life** (v. 6).

4. Job's Faith during Personal Suffering (2:7 – 10)

Satan went forth and **smote Job with sore boils from the sole of his foot unto his crown** (his head; v. 7). Job and his wife were now destitute, having lost everything, including their children. They sat **among the ashes** (v. 8) to keep warm and had no other place to go. To sit on the ash heap was a sign of utter poverty and despair. Job scraped his skin with a broken piece of pottery (a **potsherd**) to remove the sores and the loose flesh.

2:9 – 10. Another blow followed with the bitter outpouring of Job's wife. She advised him, **curse God, and die** (v. 9). Essentially, "How can you take this?" In calling her **foolish** (v. 10), Job was using the word in the sense of "wicked." Her response is understandable, however, in light of how such a tragedy would break a mother's heart. Job delivered his second great statement of faith: **What? shall we receive good at the hand of God, and shall we not receive evil?** Only one with absolute reliance on and trust in God's sovereignty could make such a proclamation.

In all this did not Job sin with his lips. So far Satan was still unsuccessful.

5. The Arrival of the Three Friends (2:11–13)

2:11–13. The narrative now introduces what are called **three friends** (v. 11) of Job. **Eliphaz** was a **Temanite** (Teman was a village in northern Edom; see Gen. 36:11; Jer. 49:20; Ezek. 25:13); the Temanites were famed for their wisdom (Jer. 49:7). **Bildad** was a **Shuhite**, descended from Shuah, who was a son of Abraham by Keturah, a brother of Midian, and the uncle of Sheba and Dedan (Gen. 25:2–3). Bildad was from the east country, known for its great wise men who were counselors, the great "men of the east" (1:3). **Zophar the Naamathite** apparently was from the same place. The three men had heard of Job's problems and decided **to come to mourn with him and to comfort him**. When they saw him from afar sitting in the ash heap, they began to respond emotionally and cried aloud, wept, tore their clothes, and threw dust on their heads—Middle Eastern responses to grief (v. 12, see Josh. 7:6; 1 Sam. 4:12; Ezek. 27:30; Acts 22:23). Their emotional response may also indicate that they truly cared for and respected Job. Seated by him, they said nothing for **seven days and seven nights … for they saw that his grief was very great** (v. 13). For at least a week, they realized there was nothing they could say to comfort Job, though they were indeed his friends.

The names of two of these men may be significant: Eliphaz means "my God's strength," and Bildad means "the Lord loves." The meaning of Zophar's name is uncertain. Some scholars have conjectured that all three men may have come from godly families.

II. Dialogue and Dispute (chaps. 3–27)

This is the heart of the book of Job and is the longest section. It narrates the debate between Job and his friends. After "seven days and seven nights" (2:13), Job began to speak with the passion of the soul. Again and again, his friends attempted to counter what he said and to lay blame on Job. The dialogue continued between truth and error and between accusation and denial. Job's frustration cannot be overlooked. He often lashed out, as in 21:3: "Suffer me that I may speak; and after that I have spoken, mock on." Job had the last word in this section of the book. No matter what his "friends" said, he still clung to his integrity. "My lips shall not speak wickedness, nor my tongue utter deceit. God forbid that I should justify you: till I die I will not remove my integrity from me" (27:4–5).

A. Job's Opening Lament (chap. 3)

In the dialogues recorded in chapters 3–12, Job employed emotional anguish about the day he was born. Nothing in ancient or modern poetry equals the depth of feelings expressed here. It is a sublime portion of Scripture, for the picture it paints of pain and sorrow. Some have compared it to the Jeremiah's poetry in Jeremiah 20:14–15.

3:1–10. After a week of silence, Job opened his mouth and **cursed his day** (v. 1). He wanted the day on which he was born and the night on which it was known that he had been conceived to **perish** (v. 3). The day he was born was a **day** of **darkness** (v. 4) that God should have forgotten, a day when the light should not have shined. **The shadow of death** (v. 5) should have **stain[ed]**, or challenged, the day of his birth, and a cloud should have overshadowed it and made it like **blackness** that would bring terror. That day should not have been **joined unto the days of the year** (v. 6). That day should not have been **joyful** (v. 7) but instead a day of cursing and **mourning** (v 8). That day of his birth should have no **dawning** (v. 9). While Job did not contemplate suicide, he wished that the days of his conception and birth had never happened. With great bitterness, Job wished that the day of his birth had closed **the doors of** his **mother's womb** (v. 10). The doors had not been shut, however; he had been born. Now terrible **sorrow** had come upon him.

3:11–19. Since he had been born into this world, he wished that he had been stillborn. Job asked, **Why did I not give up the ghost** (the spirit) **when I came out of the belly?** (v. 11). Why did his mother's **knees** (v. 12), which were bent in childbirth, not **prevent**

his coming forth from the womb? It would have been better if he had died, fallen asleep at birth; then he would have had peace and **rest** (v. 13) and would not have experienced the pain he was now suffering. He would have been in the company of **kings and counselors** (v. 14) and rich rulers who had died and who had great wealth, such as gold and silver. Again Job wished that he had been stillborn (v. 16). Death would have been far better than what he was now experiencing. In death, the **wicked** (v. 17), the **weary**, the **prisoners** (v. 18), the **small** (v. 19), the **great**, the **servant**, and the **master** are **at rest** (v. 17) and no longer hear **the voice of the oppressor** (v. 18).

3:20–23. Wherefore, or "why" (v. 20), marks the fifth of the six times Job asked God why He was doing what He was doing (3:11–12, 16, 23). "Why?" often comes from one whose heart or body is racked with pain and sorrow, but the source of the question often is doubt about the providence of God. Job believed it was better to **long for death** (v. 21) and even to **dig** or search for it, as if looking for **hid treasures**. When death or the grave is found, the weary sufferer **rejoice[s]** (v. 22) and is **glad**. Job felt that God, who had put a hedge of protection around him (see 1:10), had now hemmed him in with turmoil (v. 23, 3:26).

3:24–26. Before taking a bite of food, Job began to sigh or groan within, followed by **roarings** (v. 24), an outpouring of emotion like the rushing waters of a torrential stream. He tried to eat but began instead to cry and weep. Verses 25–26 provide an interesting study on the man Job. Most scholars believe that when the first news was brought to him about the loss of his animals and children (1:13–19), he perhaps was apprehensive or terrified that something catastrophic was going to happen to him. Possibly he had the normal fears of the wealthy, who know that someday their fortunes could disappear. Did his fears display a lack of trust in the Lord, or were they a rich man's premonition that he could lose all that he had? (see *Barnes Notes*, 3:139). Possibly he realized that both good and evil could come upon him, for reasons he would never know. He voiced this in 1:21. Whichever the case, Job said, **I was not in safety, neither had I rest, neither was I quiet; yet trouble came** (v. 26).

B. First Cycle of Speeches (chaps. 4–14)

In chapters 4–14, the first round of confrontations and speeches begin. These include the messages of Eliphaz (4:1–27), Bildad (8:1–22), and Zophar (11:1–20), each followed by Job's response. The speeches of Job's friends contain elements of truth, but they must be carefully interpreted within their context. The problem was not so much what they said but what they did not know. God, in His mysterious providence and for His higher purposes, was allowing Satan to buffet Job.

1. Eliphaz (chaps. 4–5)

Eliphaz charged Job to be confident that his righteousness would count with God, that though the Lord was now chastening him for some sin, it was to a good end (5:17). And he could count on the fact that God would not destroy him along with the wicked. His friends began with the assumption of Job's innocence but later changed their minds and charged him with personal sins, which were bringing about his suffering.

4:1–11. Eliphaz (v. 1) probably was the oldest of the friends and was the most sympathetic. He politely asked Job if they could **commune** (v. 2) with him, but warned him that if they did, they could not hold back from speaking. He reminded Job that he had been a teacher, had strengthened many **weak hands** (v. 3), and had held up many with his **words** (v. 4). Now, Eliphaz said, trouble **is come upon thee, and thou faintest; it toucheth thee, and thou art troubled** (v. 5). Job's **uprightness** (v. 6) should support him, because as he should remember, the **innocent** (v. 7) never perish. Those who **plow ... and sow wickedness, reap the same** (v. 8). **By the blast of God they perish** (v. 9) and are **consumed** by the **breath of his nostrils**. The thought and presumption here is that only the wicked suffer, and Job was certainly righteous. Just as strong and **young lions** (v. 10) die, so the wicked eventually are destroyed.

4:12–16. Eliphaz stated that he had received revelations that supported his theological viewpoint on this matter. He had received a frightening dream (vv. 13–14) that had caused **trembling, which made**

all his **bones to shake** (v. 14), a sign of great fear and distress (see Jer. 23:9; Hab. 3:16). **A spirit passed before** his **face** (v. 15), and a whispered voice had given him a message (v. 16). Later, Elihu would claim the same kind of vision (33:15). Many scholars believe Eliphaz's dream was not a true vision or mystical experience, that it was not a divine revelation. He simply used hyperbole and fiction to bolster his powers of wisdom in this matter. Some scholars believe that what he had pondered during the day became his absorbing thoughts during the night, reproduced in strange visions (see Thomas, *The Book of Job*, p. 57).

4:17–21. Since all human beings are sinful, God has the right to punish them for their sins. Men cannot **be more pure than** their **Maker** (v. 17). God does not fully trust those who serve Him, nor does He put confidence in His angels. He even charges them with **folly** (v. 18), as when He cast Satan to the ground (Ezek. 28:17b). How much less those who **dwell in houses of clay** (v. 19) and **whose foundation is in the dust**, who **perish for ever** (v. 20)? **Doth not their excellency go away?** (v. 21; lit., "Is not their tent cord pulled up?"). **They die … without wisdom** (v. 21). Eliphaz told Job that he should be thankful the Lord was now correcting him for his good (5:17).

5:1–5. Eliphaz continued his tirade against what he perceived as Job's sinfulness, telling him that his flagrant sin would ruin him in the eyes of public opinion. Believing that Job was complaining against the providence of God, Eliphaz told Job, **Call now** (v. 1) and see if anyone **will answer thee … to which of the saints** or righteous ones can you turn? He accused Job of being **foolish** (v. 2) and **silly**, and his **wrath** and **envy** would ultimately slay him. Though he did not say so in so many words, Eliphaz was arguing that Job resented God and that this would eventually bring great harm to him. The word "foolish" is *e'wil* and refers to an arrogant and hardened fool, someone who seeks his own purposes without thought of God. "Silly" is *poteh* and means "one who is naive" (Hartley, *The Book of Job*, p. 117). Eliphaz implied that this was how Job was acting.

Eliphaz then backed up his argument, saying, **I have seen the foolish** (v. 3) burrow in, **taking root**. It

is as if they destroy and infect all those around them. Eliphaz resented such a foolish man and responded by cursing **his habitation**. His home and family will pay the price for his stupidity. He puts his children in jeopardy. They are resented and persecuted. **They are crushed in the gate** (v. 4). Equally as bad, no one will defend them or come to their aid. There is no one **to deliver them**.

A foolish man's children can no longer prosper. He has set their course for failure. Others who are **hungry eateth up** (v. 5) the **harvest** that would normally belong to them. Barnes sees "the hungry" as **the robber**, who takes the crops **even out of the thorns**. He takes the entire harvest all the way down to the thistles and chaff, and no grain is left for the foolish man's children (Barnes, *Barnes' Notes*, 3:158). For the foolish man, nothing goes right, and even his family and children pay the price for his stubbornness.

5:6–11. **Affliction** (v. 6) and **trouble** do not come about by accident. They do not simply come upon people automatically, as if rising out **of the dust** or **spring[ing] out of the ground**. Unlike weeds, trouble must be sown and cultivated by people and their foolish actions. Eliphaz was implying, "Job, this lesson is for you!"

For a moment, in verse 7, Eliphaz seems to have let up on Job. Eliphaz made a general statement about the universal sinfulness of human beings and argued that all must turn to God. **Man is born unto trouble, as the sparks fly upward** (v. 7) is an awesome truth about human depravity. People were born for affliction "as the sparks fly upward." Trouble is now the natural condition. Humans should expect problems and should submit themselves to the wise and good Being they can trust. If affliction came to him, Eliphaz said, **I would seek unto God, and unto God would I commit my cause** (v. 8). It is true that troubles are "ordered in infinite wisdom, and that they always have a design" (Barnes, *Barnes' Notes*, 3:159). Troubles do not spring out of the ground by accident.

God can be counted on to do **great** (v. 9) and **unsearchable** things, **marvellous things without**

number. His works are vast and boundless. Believers can therefore commit themselves to what He is doing and can have confidence that He knows what is right. For example, He sends **rain upon the earth, and ... waters upon the fields** (v. 10). Since He controls all things, He can **set up on high those** people **that be low** (v. 11). For those who cry, they may be rescued and **exalted to safety**. Though it may not have been Eliphaz's main intention, here he presented a biblical balance between the responsibility of limited humanity and the sovereignty of God. People are 100 percent responsible, and God is 100 percent sovereign. This is an inscrutable fact.

5:12–16. Eliphaz continued to argue how great and benevolent God is toward His creatures. He can foil the schemes of the wise and **the crafty** (v. 12) so that they cannot carry out their plans; **their hands cannot perform** the wishes they set out to establish. "The crafty" (*a'rumim*) refers to those who want to carry out cunning activities.

God thwarts the plans of **the wise** (v. 13) with their own **craftiness** and brings about confusion. "He makes these crafty people so anxious about their plans they they lack the patience to carry them out. As they flounder about in confusion, their plans fall apart without acheiving their purpose" (Hartley, *The Book of Job*, p. 121). Verse 13 is the only clear and specific verse from Job quoted in the New Testament (see 1 Cor. 3:19). These evil men live in **darkness** (v. 14). They are so blinded, it is as if they **grope** about **in the noonday as in the night**. The apostle Paul described the lost as those who are "in darkness" and as the children who "sleep in the night" (1 Thess. 5:4–7).

At this point, Eliphaz changed direction in his argument, saying that God will **saveth the poor from the sword** (v. 15), will deliver them from the **mouth** that spews out condemnation, and rescue them from the oppressive **hand of the mighty**. In His providence, God will turn around the fortunes of those who are poor, who have no other defender. Because of God's intervention, now **the poor hath hope** (v. 16). Personifying **iniquity** as a scurrilous, evil woman, **her mouth** is stopped because of God's

work of deliverance. "God's providence often confounds the reasonings of the ungodly, and smites with speechlessness the slanderer and the skeptic" (Thomas, *The Book of Job*, p. 71).

5:17–21. Eliphaz implied that Job deserved God's discipline and that he should accept it as a wound intended to make him whole. The person whom God **correcteth** (v. 17) is made **happy**. One should not **despise** such discipline and **chastening** from the **Almighty** (*Shaddai*). God knows what He is doing when He corrects us. Often He has to "spank" us and bring pain to cause us to change course. Quoting Proverbs 3:11–12, the writer of Hebrews said, "For whom the Lord loveth he chasteneth, and scourgeth every son whom he receiveth. If ye endure chastening, God dealeth with you as with sons; for what son is he whom the father chasteneth not?" (Heb. 12:6–7). This providential work of God in disciplining is repeated in 1 Samuel 2:6 and Hosea 6:1.

In discipline, God can **maketh sore** (v. 18) and **woundeth** us, but He then **bindeth up** the wounds and makes us **whole** again. It is certain that God wants to **deliver** (v. 19) His own from **troubles**. With a Hebrew idiom using the number **six**, in reference to the number of **troubles** that can come upon a man, Eliphaz showed that God goes beyond what is expected, **Yea, in seven there shall no evil touch thee**. The righteous may be disciplined, but they will be restored. This includes deliverance when **famine** (v. 20) sweeps the land; God will **redeem thee from death** and will even hide His people from the danger of **the sword**.

Eliphaz again mentioned the pain that the mouth can inflict as criticism and judgment (see 5:15–16). God will hide His people from the whipping that comes from the mouth, **the scourge of the tongue** (v. 21). The apostle James reminds believers that "the tongue is a fire, a world of iniquity: so is the tongue amongst our members" (James 3:6). "How often the slanderous tongue cuts and lacerates the soul" (Thomas, *The Book of Job*, p. 75). The last stanza of verse 21 seems to still be referring to the power of the tongue. Eliphaz reminded Job and others who trust in God that they should not be afraid when the tongue's **destruction** comes. God will finally make right what is wrong.

5:22–26. Eliphaz reminded Job that he should be defiant and not fear when **destruction and famine** (v. 22) come. Neither should he be **afraid of the beasts of the earth.** In Job's day, the deserts of Arabia were overrun with wild animals, which were always objects of fear. In Scripture, references to wild animals are often used figuratively to represent human enemies. The words here in Job are similar to Psalm 91, which describes the protection of God from the wicked and from the wild animals: "Thou shall tread upon the lion and adder: the young lion and the dragon shalt thou trample under feet. Because he [the believer] hath set his love upon me, therefore will I deliver him" (Psalm 91:13–14).

Eliphaz told Job that if he trusted God, he would not **be in league with the stones of the field** (v. 23). This was a figurative way of saying that the rocks will "be at peace with you." With God's protection, the righteous can be unafraid "of the beasts of the earth" (v. 22). The **tabernacle** (v. 24) of the righteous, his tent or home, will be at **peace.** Only with God reigning in the household can there be contentment, calmness, and quietness of spirit. Too often in the home, confusion and dissension rule.

Many commentators believe that **and shalt not sin** (v. 24) is a mistranslation. Barnes says, "Here the original sense of the Hebrew word [*hata*] should be retained, meaning that he would not *miss* the way of his destiny; that is, that he would be permitted to return to [his home] in safety" (Barnes, *Barnes' Notes,* 3:169). The thought may be that when the head of the house returns, he will find all is well at home. This seems to fit the context.

The righteous who cling to the Lord **shalt know … that** their **seed shall be great** (v. 25). Their offspring shall be as numerous **as the grass of the earth.** The one who is righteous shall be blessed with many children, and children provide security, especially in old age. They will be like weapons, the arrows in the "quiver" (Ps. 127:5). The one who trusts God, who has been disciplined by Him, as Eliphaz said previ-

ously, will die **in a full age** (v. 26). Under normal circumstances, he will not die prematurely. He will be like **a shock of corn** that reaches the right period for ripening. He will **cometh in in his season.** Eliphaz's prediction about Job was more accurate than he realized (see 42:16–17).

5:27. Eliphaz concluded that what he had just said was observed as true in the past. It was common knowledge, and **so it is.** He exhorted Job, **Hear it, and know thou it**; this factual information was **for thy good.** "With this mild but firm exhortation, Eliphaz shows that his counsel is designed to offer Job hope in order that he may come through his suffering to a new, richer life" (Hartley, *The Book of Job,* p. 128).

2. Job's Reply (chaps. 6–7)

Eliphaz had much to say about Job's anguish, grief, and vexation (5:2). In reply, Job asked that his pain be properly weighed over against his troubles (6:2), which then would cause his words to cease, to be "swallowed up" because God's chastisement (His arrows) is even more painful (6:3b–4). Job spoke to Eliphaz but also to his other friends, as the plural verbs and nouns show. Eliphaz had completely and utterly failed to show Job what moral wrongdoing he had committed to deserve God's chastisement. Though Eliphaz had chided him for his murmuring, the question still remained, why was Job suffering? Eliphaz had not touched on this matter.

6:1–4. Job was immediately concerned that the words of Eliphaz had not properly weighed his **grief** (v. 2) or used the **balances** of justice to fully comprehend his **calamity.** Job's problems were like the weight of sea sand that **swallowed up** (v. 3) his **words.** God's **arrows** (v. 4) had brought **poison** to his **spirit,** and His **terrors** were arrayed against him. Job traced his anguish to Jehovah. His pains were as poisoned arrows that stuck fast into his very being and into his soul, bringing instant death. It was as if the Lord was trying to undo him (7:20; 16:12–13).

6:5–10. Just as **the wild ass** (v. 5) does not **bray** and **the ox** does not **loweth** (bellow) when they have food, so Job would not have complained if his situation were more tolerable and not so extreme.

A meal goes together with salt, and **the white of an egg** is tasteless without a yolk (v. 6). To the ancients, salt was essential for creating taste and an egg white would probably never be separated from the yolk. In like manner, "a man afflicted with such sores from the sole of his foot to the crown of his head could not relish any food" (v. 7; Thomas, *Job*, p. 81). Job exclaimed, **O that God would grant me** death (v. 8) and **destroy me** (v. 9), that the Lord **would let loose his hand, and cut me off!** If God would not **spare** (v. 10) him, he could **have comfort**. Verse 10 is better translated, "That I might still have consolation, and rejoice in the pain He spares not, for I have not denied the words of the Holy One" (Thomas, *Job*, pp. 81–82). If Job had been permitted to die, he could have exulted in his sufferings, knowing that he had been faithful to his Creator.

6:11–13. Job asked his friends how he could have **hope** (v. 11) in his situation. If his life continued in this way, why **should** I **prolong my life?** he asked. His strength was pulled down like the dead weight of a stone, and his **flesh** (v. 12) was as hard as **brass**. There was no **help** (v. 13) for him, and all human **wisdom** was gone. He was ready to give way to this heavy pressure and deep sorrow of heart.

6:14–23. When one is distraught, friends should respond with gentleness, but Job's friends instead seem to be saying that he had forsaken **the fear of the Almighty** (v. 14). His **brethren** (v. 15), his friends, were like dried-up **brooks** that **pass away**. In the winter, brooks are frozen and look **blackish** (v. 16) from **the ice**, but when it gets warm, the brooks dry up and **vanish** (v. 17). The passing **troops of Tema** (where Eliphaz was from; v. 19; 21:14) and **of Sheba** (1:15) waited and searched for the waters but saw their mistake; when they arrived at waters, they looked at each other with shame and confusion (v. 20; see Thomas, *The Book of Job*, p. 87).

Job turned to his friends with scorn and disappointment and said, **For now ye are nothing; Ye see my casting down, and are afraid** (v. 21). Did I ask anything of you? he inquired. He had not asked of them a **reward** (v. 22), nor deliverance or redemption **from the hand of the mighty** (v. 23) enemy.

6:24–30. With tongue in cheek, Job begged his friends, **Teach me** (v. 24) to **hold my tongue** and give understanding **wherein I have erred**. After all, they had spoken **forcible** (v. 25) and **right words**. It was as if, in their criticisms, they wanted to **overwhelm** (lit., "casting lots for") **the fatherless** (v. 27) and **dig a pit** to entrap their **friend**.

Job pleaded with his friends to rethink their position. He implored them, **look upon me** (v. 28); they would see he was not lying about his pain. He wanted them to revisit the issue and see that his problem was not iniquity; he was a righteous man (v. 29). He appealed to their consciences and to the fact that they had known him for some time. He asked them, **Is there iniquity in my tongue? Cannot my taste discern perverse things?** (v. 30). He was not faking his pain and sorrow and argued that he was genuine and sincere, not a hypocrite.

7:1–3. Job then broadened the conversation to include other people **upon earth** (v. 1). Are people not like hired hands in their sojourn on earth? he asked. The servant **earnestly desireth the shadow**, or looks for sunset and the end of the workday, and the reward for his labor. Though Job's longing as a human being on earth was hopeful, he was **made to possess months of vanity, and wearisome nights are appointed to me** (v. 3). His life had not turned out as he had expected. Instead, it had turned out empty ("vanity") and meaningless. Job was forgetting about God. He had taken Him out of the equation, and thus could find no purpose for existence now that trouble had come.

7:4–11. When he tried to sleep, Job found himself **tossing to and fro unto the dawning of the day** (v. 4). Sitting in the ashes, his skin was **clothed with worms and clods of dust**, with scabs and sores that were **loathsome** (v. 5). In this condition, the days passed swiftly and without meaning. They were **spent without hope** (v. 6). His life was tossed about like the capricious **wind** (v. 7), and he could no longer see any good in living.

The **eyes** (v. 8) of those who had known him looked for him, but he was no more. **I am not**, he proclaimed. As the **cloud** (v. 9) in the sky evaporates and disappears, so is the one who dies and **goeth down to the grave**. They will come up no more. The Mesopotamians believed the netherworld was the "land of no return." From his depressed viewpoint, Job believed he would **return no more to his house** (v. 10), his present earthly body. Why then should he not open his mouth and **speak in the anguish of** his **spirit** (v. 11) and **complain in the bitterness of** his **soul**?

But later, by God's divine revelation, Job would speak words of encouragement. It would be revealed to him that his Redeemer (*Go'el*) lives and would stand someday upon the earth (see 19:25). Though Job's skin be destroyed, someday his flesh would see God, "Whom I shall see for myself, and mine eyes shall behold, and not another" (19:27). The God-man, the Lord Jesus, would come to raise the dead (see Matt. 5:8; John 11:17–44; 1 John 3:2). He is "the resurrection, and the life" (John 11:25).

7:12–19. Job hated being watched like a **whale** (or "sea monster"; v. 12), like a "leviathan" (Hebrew, *tannin*). When he tried to find comfort on his bed (v. 13), his friends scared him with **dreams** and **visions** (v. 14). He would have chosen **strangling, and death rather than … life** (v. 15). He pleaded, **Let me alone; for my days are vanity** (v. 16), or empty. Here Job seems to have addressed God, asking why He had set His heart on such humanity (v. 17). This is similar to Psalm 8. How can God's majestic greatness stoop so low as to take notice of insignificant, sin-cursed man? Why would He come to man **every morning** and then **try him every moment** (v. 18)? Job was never free from the Lord's gaze, not even long enough to **swallow** (v. 19).

7:20–21. After this bitter outcry, Job confessed that he had **sinned** (v. 20). He added that God alone is the **preserver of men**. Why then had God set **a mark against** him? (v. 20). If the problem was with him, why did God **not pardon** his **transgression, and take away** his **iniquity** (v. 21)? Job wanted to **sleep in the dust** so that God could not find him in the morning. Thinking that he was a terrible sinner and that he could not find redemption, Job wanted to simply die. However, "The glorious revelation in Scripture is that

God himself is the one who in his compassionate love bears human sin" (Hartley, *The Book of Job*, p. 153). "The LORD, The LORD God, merciful and gracious, longsuffering, and abundant in goodness and truth, keeping mercy for thousands, forgiving iniquity and transgression and sin" (Exod. 34:6–7a).

3. Bildad (chap. 8)

Bildad restated the argument of Eliphaz but gave it a new edge and clearness. He affirmed the law of divine providence, stating that it renders good to the good, and evil to the evil. He followed the ancient wisdom of his day. Bildad branded the words coming out of Job's mouth as "a strong wind" (8:2), tempestuous thoughts that were empty. Bildad was outspoken, discourteous, and unemotional, which suggests he was a younger, more immature "friend" of Job.

8:1–7. Bildad answered Job by asking, **how long shall the words of thy mouth be like a strong wind?** (v. 2). **Doth God pervert judgment** and **justice?** (v. 3). If those who had **sinned** (v. 4) sought God, they should make **supplication to the Almighty** (v. 5). Bildad was suggesting that Job was rash and spoke foolish words that were destructive and sinful, like the "strong wind" (v. 2) that had killed his children. Generally speaking, Bildad was right. As the writer of Ecclesiastes said, "I saw under the sun the place of judgment, that wickedness was there; and the place of righteousness, that iniquity was there" (Eccl. 3:16). Bildad continued, if Job was **pure and upright** (v. 6), God would **awake** and return his prosperity (Job 8:6); from a small **beginning … thy latter end should greatly increase** (v. 7). If Job would confess, his prosperity would return.

8:8–10. Bildad urged Job to look back to times past, **the former age** (v. 8), and search out what **their fathers** had done. Since the duration of life is so brief, it would be presumptuous to judge by mere human experience what is going in the world; the past should be consulted (v. 9). He believed that the best instructor is not one's own experience but rather the wisdom of the forefathers and the experience of history (v. 10).

8:11–19. Bildad illustrated his point with a lesson from nature. The **rush** (papyrus; v. 11) cannot flourish without the wet mud of the marshes, nor can the **flag** (reed) grow **without water**. They would surely dry up and die. So is the fate of **all that forget God** (v. 13), Bildad reasoned, including Job. In some ways, Bildad was attempting to be subtle, but he was also aiming his criticisms at Job.

Bildad believed that those who forgot God were hypocrites, **and the hypocrite's hope … shall be cut off** (v. 13), like one who trusts in **a spider's web** (v. 14). The hypocrite **shall hold it** (i.e., the web) **fast, but it shall not endure** (v. 15). The wicked man is like a plant that comes up in the midst of a **heap** (v. 17) of **stones**, rubbish, or old ruins and fails because it is not growing in fertile soil. Bildad sarcastically added, **Behold, this is the joy of his way** (v. 19a), meaning that this is all he receives. The joy of hypocrites is here only for a little while. **Out of the earth shall others grow** (v. 19b), others who are honorable and not wicked.

8:20–22. God would not throw away a **perfect** ("true, upright"; v. 20) man (see 1:1), nor would He come to the aid of **the evil doers**. Since Job is a righteous man, in time God would restore him to favor and fill his **lips with rejoicing** (v. 21). If Job returned to the Lord, He would yet fill him with joy, while those who hated Job would be filled **with shame** (v. 22). God brings reproach on **the dwelling place of the wicked**; they **shall come to nought**. Bildad believed that Job must have done something wrong because his home had been destroyed. If he repented, he would be restored, and others who were wicked would find their houses demolished by the Lord.

4. Job's Reply (chaps. 9–10)

9:1–4. How could someone plead with a sovereign God? Man cannot **be just** (v. 2) in God's sight. He cannot **contend with** (v. 3) the Lord because **He is wise in heart, and mighty in strength** (v. 4). No one can be **hardened** against the Lord and prosper. No human can give a defense for his sins. God is so far above humans that He cannot be deceived by

simple sophistry and conniving. When God brings retribution, no one can resist Him.

9:5–10. How can humans contend with God when He is so great? He **removeth the mountains** (v. 5), **shaketh the earth** (v. 6), **commandeth the sun** (v. 7), and **sealeth up the stars**. He causes the **heavens** (v. 8) to spread out and **treadeth upon the waves of the sea**. He is the one who moves the natural courses of His creation. He made **Arcturus** (the Bear), **Orion, and Pleiades** (v. 9). These three constellations are referred to again in 38:31–32, and the last two are mentioned also in Amos 5:8. Though they had a limited understanding of astronomy, the ancient Israelites were rightly awed by the fact that it was God who had created the constellations. They were not simply astral gods, as the pagans surmised. God **doeth great things past finding out** (v. 10), astounding things, **and wonders without number**.

9:11–15. God is near and is in all of the unseen operations of nature (v. 11). No one can ask Him, **What doest thou?** (v. 12). Since no one can stand up under the wrath of God, even the **proud helpers** ("helpers of pride"; v. 13) have to **stoop under him**. This probably means that everything that contributes to pride, or those who ally together to maintain pride on the earth, must sink into the wrath of God (Barnes, *Barnes' Notes*, 3:215). Job asked, **How much less shall I answer him, and choose out my words to reason with him?** (v. 14). No one can debate, argue, or fight with God. Even if he were righteous, Job reasoned, he could not answer God; he would instead **make supplication to my judge** (v. 15). God is a better judge of character than humans can ever be. That He regards humans as sinners is proof that humans are such, "whatever may be our view to the contrary" (Thomas, *The Book of Job*, p. 125).

9:16–24. Even if Job **had called** upon the Lord, **and he had answered** (v. 16), Job would **not believe that he had hearkened unto my voice**. God could **breaketh** Job **with a tempest** (v. 17) and multiply his **wounds without cause**. He did not have to allow Job to breathe but could fill him **with bitterness** (v. 18). If Job spoke of **strength** (v. 19), God was stronger; if he talked about **judgment**, he would not be given time **to plead** his case. If he tried to **justify** (v. 20) himself or to say he was **perfect** (upright), he would condemn himself and be proven as **perverse**. Job continued, **Though I were perfect, yet would I not know my soul; I would despise my life** (v. 21). God can destroy **the perfect and the wicked** (v. 22). With poetic hyperbole, Job said that it appeared as if God mocks those who suffer and that He **laugh[s] at the trial of the innocent** (v. 23). It seemed that **the earth** (v. 24) had been turned over to the **wicked** and that God was covering **the faces of the judges** so that they would ignore the plight of those who were suffering. If this was not a just view of God, what was? Job asked.

9:25–28. Job saw his days moving **swifter than a post** (v. 25), probably a reference to the courier, runner, or camel or horse rider used to deliver messages. **They flee away, they see no good.** Job saw nothing good in his life. He found no happiness; life was only misery. His days seemed to have **passed away as … ships: as the eagle that hasteth to the prey** (v. 26). He wished he could forget his **complaint** (v. 27) so that his **heaviness** would leave him and he would be comforted, but he was afraid to forget his **sorrows** because they must have been caused by his sins, and he knew that God **wilt not hold me innocent** (v. 28). Some scholars believe that Job was sarcastically saying that the continuation of his sufferings was giving his friends the evidence they needed to prove that he was guilty as charged.

9:29–35. If he was guilty as charged, why should he **labour … in vain** (v. 29) to deny it? If he washed himself (v. 30), God would overwhelm him with consciousness of his guilt, so that even his **own clothes** (v. 31) would **abhor** him. God **is not a man** (v. 32) that Job **should answer him** or could **come together in judgment** with him. No **daysman** (Hebrew, *mokiah*; "judge, decider") stood between Job and God to **lay his hand upon us both** (v. 33). Job felt he needed an umpire, an arbiter, or a mediator to act as a go-between. This is one of the first times Job mentions the need for a mediator to plead his case (see 16:20–21; 19:25–26). The New Testament reveals that such a mediator did indeed come, the

Lord Jesus Christ. Because He died for the sins of humanity, He can now act as our Divine Mediator. Paul wrote, "For there is one God, and one mediator between God and men, the man Christ Jesus; who gave himself a ransom for all" (1 Tim. 2:5). Only Christ, the God-man, can represent both parties, divine and human.

Job pleaded for the Lord to remove **his rod** (v. 34) of judgment and to **let not his fear terrify me**. Then he could **speak** (v. 35) with God and **not fear him; but it is not so with me.** This is the plea of all sinners under conviction. If Job were a gross sinner, his cry would have been appropriate, but this was not the case, though he seems to have thought so.

10:1–7. Job had asked the Lord to remove His wrath from him (9:34–35) so that he could speak his mind without fear. Here he went further and stated that while suffering under his pains, he would give free course to his words. Even if the worst happened, he would not mind losing his life, which had become such a heavy burden.

My soul is weary (v. 1), Job declared, and he spoke with **the bitterness of** his **soul**. He pleaded with God to **not condemn** him, but if He did, to show him why He **condendest** with him (v. 2). Job asked the Lord if it is agreeable to Him to **oppress** (v. 3). Is it part of His nature? Does the Lord see **as man seeth** (v. 4), with **eyes of flesh**, and are His **days** and **years as man's** (v. 5)? Job asked, Is this why **thou inquirest after mine iniquity, and searchest after my sin?** (v. 6). These questions were raised out of Job's frustration. Because God is sovereign, He knew that Job was **not wicked; and there is none that can deliver out of thine hand** (v. 7). By saying that he was not wicked, Job did not mean that he was not a sinner before his Maker but that he was not a gross, evil man and was not a hypocrite, as his friends implied.

10:8–12. Job continued to question God as if He were his adversary in court. Since God **made** (v. 8) him, why would He **destroy** him? Job reminded God that he was made of **clay** and asked why the Lord would **bring** him **into dust again** (v. 9). Job felt like he was **milk** (v. 10) that had been poured out and cruddled, or curdled, divided and separated like cheese. Job knew, however, that the Lord had created him with skin and flesh (v. 11; see Ps. 139:13, 15), bones and sinews, that He had granted him favour (v. 12), and that thy visitation hath preserved my spirit. After giving him life, why would God turn against him?

10:13–17. In his distraction, Job felt that these things (v. 13) the Lord had hid in His heart, as if He were trying to be someone other than who He really was to Job (see Unger, Commentary, p. 692). He thought that God would markest (v. 14), or take note, of him and would probably acquit him. If he was wicked (v. 15), it would be bad for him (woe unto me), but if he was righteous, still he could not lift up my head. He was saying that he could not win with God: I am full of confusion; therefore see thou mine affliction. It seemed as if the pressure from God increaseth (v. 16). God hunted him as if he were a fierce lion. It seemed as if God had more evidence against him, thus, ever-increasing indignation (v. 17) toward him. With changes and war ... against him, Job thought of his troubles as having come upon him as a succession of soldiers in a battle. "When one is worn out and crushed, another battalion appears" (Thomas, The Book of Job, p. 141).

10:18–22. Job again asked why he had been created and why he had not died at birth (v. 18; 3:11), again stating that it would have been better if he had been stillborn (v. 19). Since his days were few (v. 20), he pleaded for God to leave him alone. He saw death as the land of darkness (v. 21) and believed that death is without any order (v. 22), meaning it has no arrangements and makes no distinction between rich and poor, king and servant. All are equal in death. No light is to be found in the place of the dead, and even if there were light, it would be as darkness.

5. Zophar (chap. 11)

Zophar was one of the weaker counselors among Job's friends. He was also one of the most straightforward; he had little tact. Evidently, Job words had stretched Zophar's patience and had irritated him.

He was the last and the least in the debate. He had a mean spirit and was insolent, labeling Job "a wild ass's colt" (11:12) and, in essence, a windbag.

11:1–6. Zophar showed no mercy to Job. He could not put himself in Job's place. He called Job a man full of talk (v. 2) and a liar. In Zophar's eyes, Job could not be justified. Shall no man make him who is a mocker ashamed? (v. 3). He accused Job of claiming that his doctrine (v. 4), his teaching, was pure and that he was clean. Zophar said, O that God would speak, and open his lips against thee (v. 5). God needed to show to Job the secrets of wisdom (v. 6), secrets which are double to that which is. The word "to double" is keh'phel and carries the idea "to fold" (41:13). It is not plain but is "infolded" and must be unrolled to be understood. God's wisdom is about that which is seen and that which is hidden. Zophar told Job he was fortunate that God exacteth of thee less than thine iniquity deserveth. He believed that Job was not getting all the punishment he deserved.

11:7–12. In verse 7, it seems as if Zophar unwittingly anticipated the Lord's discourses in 38:1–42:6. No one by searching (v. 7) can find out God, discover who He is, unto perfection or completion. The knowledge of God is as high as heaven (v. 8) and Deeper than hell, or sheol, the place of the dead (see Psalm 139). The Septuagint renders verse 7: "The heaven is high, what can thou do? And there are things deeper than in Hades." It is impossible to attempt to investigate the knowledge of God fully. The believer looks into the Word of God for such understanding of Him. The knowledge of God measured out is longer than the earth, and broader than the sea (v. 9). To the ancients, this was tantamount to saying that the knowledge of God is infinite.

Since the Lord is absolutely sovereign, who can restrain Him if He chooses to cut off, and shut up, or gather together (v. 10), as "calling an assembly," for the purpose of judging an evildoer (see Prov. 5:14; Ezek. 16:40; 23:46). God knows vain men (v. 11) and wickedness ... will he not then consider it? With sarcasm and resentment, Zophar added that a vain (fake) man (v. 12) would obtain common sense when he is born like **the wild ass's colt**, that is born tame, for example, "signifying the weakness and dullness of the human understanding" (Barnes, *Barnes' Notes*, 3:240). These stinging barbs were aimed at Job, whom Zophar disdained with biting words.

11:13–15. If Job would only **prepare** his **heart** (v. 13), **stretch out** his **hands** to God, **put** iniquity **far away** (v. 14), stop **wickedness** from being in his **tabernacles** (or tents), then he could **lift up** his **face without spot** (v. 15) or blemish, then he would **be steadfast** and would **not fear.** While there was truth to what Zophar said, he missed the fact that Job was innocent, though certainly not perfect. Zophar spoke of the glittering rewards of repentance (see also 5:17–27). After confessing, Job would then be able to face the world fearlessly and unashamedly without confusion (see 10:15).

11:16–20. If Job repented, his **misery** (v. 16) would pass away like evaporated water. His life would shine like **noonday** (v. 17) and he would **be as the morning.** He would be **secure** with **hope** (v. 18), he would **dig** (i.e., "to search") and find **rest in safety,** and he would **lie down** (v. 19) unafraid. Many would **make suit** of him (lit., "make soft his face"), meaning they would petition him or ask favors of him as a superior, wise man. If Job would only repent, his life would be restored. He would be happy and elevated as a prosperous sage in the community. **The eyes of the wicked shall fail** (v. 20), however; they will **not escape** punishment, and **their hope** will turn to death **as the giving up of the ghost,** or spirit. The conclusion of Zophar's discourse was similar to Bildad's (8:22). Zophar "was a legalist, presuming to know what God would do in any case, why He would do it, and what His thoughts were about it" (Unger, *Commentary*, p. 693).

6. Job's Reply (chaps. 12–14)

Chapter 12 begins Job's reply, addressed to all three of his friends. His answer extends to the end of chapter 14 and is divided into two parts: (1) his argument with his friends (12:1–13:20) and (2) his appeal to the God of heaven (13:21–14:22). Job pointed out that they had tried to overwhelm him with their numbers and with the unanimity of their opinions, namely, that he must be a great and wicked sinner. All three friends assumed that Job was totally ignorant of his evilness and guilt. In his reply, Job resorted to biting sarcasm in light of the harsh treatment he was receiving from his would-be comforters.

12:1–6. Job responded to the attacks of his friends. He replied that they had the upper hand, **ye are the people** (v. 2), and what is right, **wisdom,** would die with them. He added, however, that he was not stupid and was **not inferior** (v. 3) to them. His friends had wrongly accused him of sins for which he was not guilty. He was **as one mocked** by **his neighbour** (v. 4). God used to answer his prayers, but now, though he was guiltless (1:1, 8; 2:3; 9:21–22), it was as if the Lord had let him become a laughingstock. He was like one walking confidently and **at ease** (v. 5) in the dark, one who **despised** the **lamp** in his hand. Though he thought he was secure, he was **ready to slip with his feet.** To Job, things seemed opposite from what was right. The **robbers prosper[ed]** (v. 6) in their **tabernacles,** or tents, and the people who **provoke[d]** God were **secure.** It seemed that God had put abundance in their hands.

12:7–13. These verses deal with the providence of God. Is He passive in His creation, or does He allow things to happen, even in the natural world, that are painful yet part of His dealing with life on earth? **Ask now the beasts ... fowls** (v. 7), even **the earth ... and the fishes** (v. 8). **They shall teach thee** (v. 7). Has not His hand **wrought** (worked) **this?** (v. 9). It seemed to Job that God does not interfere to protect the weak from the strong and that He is passive, not interfering in the material world to prevent the lion from destroying the lamb; likewise, Job thought, God does not interfere in human affairs to treat men according to their character. Animals and **the soul of every living thing, and the breath of all mankind** (v. 10) are in His hand. Here "soul" (Hebrew, *nephesh*) means "life."

The Lord is the one who made the human organs (v. 11). With age comes **wisdom** (v. 12); with **length of days** comes **understanding.** Job may have been older than his friends were, and he was saying that with his age came **wisdom and strength** (v. 13) in knowledge, as well as **counsel and understanding**. Some believe the **him** in verse 13 is referring to God. No matter whether the reference is to **the ancient wise ones** or to God, it is still a fact that ultimately all wisdom comes from God and is imparted to the wise. Rabbinical observation says, "With Him—God alone—is wisdom, and also might, for one can be wise without being mighty" (Cohen, *Job*, p. 58).

12:14–25. It impossible to escape God's absolute sovereignty and providence in these verses. God is sovereign in His created world and in its history. In many ways, humans cannot respond to the thoughts written here. They are inscrutable and incomprehensible to the limited human mind.

God can **breaketh down** (v. 14) and build up again anything He wishes, and He can shut and open as He pleases. He can hold back the rain or flood the earth (v. 15). **With Him** (v. 16) are both **strength and wisdom**, and **the deceived and the deceiver are his**. He is the God who is in charge of both the good and the bad. God can **leadeth counsellers away** (v. 17) and can **maketh the judges fools**. He can loosen the **bond** (Hebrew, *musar*; "control") of rulers, **kings**, and He can grant them strength with **a girdle** (v. 18) around their waists. He can make the invincible **princes** (v. 19) a part of the spoils of war and can **overthroweth the mighty**. He can silence the **speech of the trusty** (or "the trusted"; v. 20) and can take **away the understanding of the aged**. He can make **princes** (v. 21) contemptuous and weaken **the strength of the mighty**.

The Lord can bring to light hidden plots and conspiracies that were planned in **darkness** (v. 22), and He **bringeth out to light the shadow of death**. The expression "shadow of death" is best expressed as "deep darkness." God causes **the nations** (v. 23) to grow, and He can destroy them. He can make them large and then **straiteneth** (lead) **them** where He wishes. He can cause **the chief of the people of the earth … to wander** (v. 24) and take away their heart. He can cause them to wander endlessly **in a wilderness where there is no way**. He can make the rul-

ers of the world to **grope in the dark without light** (v. 25) and make them **stagger like a drunken man**, meaning He can deprived them of reason and cause them to weave aimlessly in confusion. The same imagery is used of Egypt in Isaiah 19:14. God is the Sovereign Lord and does what is good in His sight. Job's point was that God does not always treat men based on their moral character but rather based on His own mysterious purposes.

13:1–6. Job felt that his counselors had become completely untrustworthy (see 13:12). He had **seen** (v. 1) what was happening and had **heard** and **understood it**. What they thought they knew about life and God's ways, he also knew, for **I am not inferior unto you** (v. 2). He could speak with the Lord and lay his cause before Him, for **I desire to reason with God** (v. 3). He claimed that his "friends" were **forgers of lies** (v. 4) and fake **physicians of no value**. They would be wise to hold their peace (v. 5; see Prov. 17:28). They needed to stop talking and listen to his **reasoning** (v. 6) and **hearken to the pleadings of** his **lips**. Again, Job attempted to make them understand correctly what was happening. If they would only give him a hearing, they would see he was not the evil person they had implied he was.

13:7–11. Job then issued a strong argument. Would they advocate false positions in the cause of God and **talk deceitfully** (v. 7), in order to present fallacious arguments to denounce what He is doing with humanity? Would they accept Him as He is and **contend for God** (v. 8)? How would they fare if God were to examine them? Were they mocking God (v. 9)? God would severely **reprove** them if they **secretly accept[ed] persons** (v. 10), that is, "covertly curry favor" or show partiality (see Unger, *Commentary*, p. 696). God's **excellency** (Hebrew, *nasa*; "majesty") should make them fearful, **And his dread fall upon you** (v. 11). The Lord's majesty should always fill the mind with awe and produce proper fear and veneration.

13:12–16. Job's friends' boasting passed away like **ashes** (v. 12) and like **bodies** that turned back to **clay**. Their great spiritual proclamations and maxims were like dust blowing in the wind. They needed to keep quiet because they were of no help; they needed to leave him **alone** (v. 13). Job asked why he should bite his flesh to keep silent and **put my life in mine hand** (v. 14). He asked why he should risk his life in speaking his convictions (see Thomas, *The Book of Job*, p. 175). Job then set forth a great attitude of trust in God with his famous words, **Though he slay me, yet will I trust in him** (v. 15), and he added, **But I will maintain mine own ways before him**. He would not vary his opinions about God. No matter what happened, Job intended to seek vindication from Him and believed that he would receive it (see 13:18). He then added, **He also shall be my salvation** (v. 16). These are not the words of a guilty man. Job realized that God would save him; he was not a hypocrite.

13:17–22. Job asked his friends to listen to what he was going to say to God (v. 17). He had prepared his case and he knew that he would **be justified** (v. 18). He then spoke the words of a plaintiff challenging his adversary to come to court (v. 19; see Isa. 1:18). If he held his **tongue** (v. 19) and did not speak out, he would **give up the ghost**, or die.

13:23–28. If all of Job's problems had come about because he was a terrible sinner, he wanted God to tell him **how many ... iniquities and sins** (v. 23) he had committed. He needed to know of his **transgression** and **sin**. Why did God **hidest** His **face** (v. 24) from him and withhold His blessings? Why did God **holdest**, consider, him an enemy? Would God trample on him as if he were **dry stubble** (v. 25), as one already prostrate and crushed who did not have any strength left? It was as if God was writing **bitter things against** (v. 26) him (see Ps. 130:3; Hos. 13:12) and was bringing up the **iniquities of** his **youth**, holding his past sins over him. God was confining him by putting his feet in **stocks** (v. 27) and scrutinizing his every move, looking **narrowly unto all my paths**. As a marked slave, his heels had been burned and slashed so that he could not escape. The Babylonian Code of Hammurabi (eighteenth century BC) mentions such a practice. With God so confining him, he was as **a rotten thing** (v. 28), as an old **garment that is moth-eaten** and worthless.

He found himself under the heavy hand of the Lord, who had laid a heavy affliction on him.

14:1–6. Job reminded his friends that all humans, **born of a woman** (v. 1), live but a **few days, and full of trouble**. Like a flower that blooms quickly and then is **cut down**, man is but a **shadow** (v. 2) that **fleeth ... and continueth not**. How could God look upon such as Job and still bring him **into judgment with** (v. 3) Himself? If Job was so bad and so **unclean** (v. 4), how could God make him **clean**? It was impossible. Yet God's sovereignty prevails because man's **days are determined, the number of his months are with thee, thou hast appointed his bounds that he cannot pass** (v. 5). Whether wicked or righteous, no one can live beyond the time that God has set for that person. Job then pleaded for the Lord to **turn from him** (v. 6) so that **he may rest** and not be hounded. Man must fulfill his tenure as a hired laborer on earth.

14:7–12. In contrast to humanity, **there is hope** for **a tree** (v. 7) when it is cut down. The root remains in the ground, and if it is supplied water, **it will sprout again**. Not so for people; if **man dieth, and wasteth away: Yea, man giveth up the ghost, and where is he?** (v. 10). The righteous in Job's day knew that God would somehow take care of them after death, but the details were not made clear by revelation. Here Job was looking at death simply from the human standpoint. No one knew specifically where the human spirit went in the afterlife. Job would later be given the great and blessed revelation of a Redeemer and of the resurrection of the body (19:23–27), a revelation that David expanded on (Ps. 73:24). Here, however, Job became more and more depressed as he thought of death. Just as **the waters** (v. 11) of **the sea** are limited, and **the flood decayeth** (subsides) **and drieth up**, so those who die will not rise up, **nor be raised out of their sleep** (v. 12). From earth's perspective, Job's belief was that no one ever comes back from the dead.

14:13–16. Again from a human viewpoint, Job pleaded for God to **hide** him **in the grave** and forget him **until thy wrath be past** (v. 13). On the other hand, he pleaded, **appoint me a set time, and**

remember me. It seems that as he continued to speak, God gave him a new revelation; he posed the question, **If a man die, shall he live again?** (v. 14) and declared that in his **appointed time,** he would **wait, till my change come.** His heartfelt desire became a living conviction. In Hebrew, the word "change" is *haliphah,* meaning "change, relief, or substitute." The resurrection is clearly in view here. Job would exchange his old body for a new one (see 1 Corinthians 15). God would someday call Job forth from the grave, and he would answer. God has **a desire** (v. 15) for receiving the work of His hands, but **for now** (v. 16), Job said, **thou numberest my steps,** and pleaded that the Lord not look upon his **sin** (see 13:27).

14:17-22. Job wished that his **transgression[s]** (v. 17) were hidden, **sealed up in a bag** and concealed from view. Human hope disintegrates like a crumbling **mountain** (v. 18), an eroding **rock,** and plans that are washed away by the rain (v. 19). In the disintegration of all things, the hope of the existence of humanity is destroyed in death. God is stronger than man; He wins every time. He is **forever against him** (v. 20). The Lord simply changes His facial features, shows His displeasure, and **sendest him away.** When a man dies, another generation follows, and **his sons come to** (i.e., receive) **honour** (v. 21), but the man **knoweth it not.** Finally, that generation passes on, **but he perceiveth it not of them.** Because of the shortness of life, one will not know of the good or bad that happens in his own family. One thing is sure, however: at the end of life is **pain, and** man's **soul within him shall mourn** (v. 22).

C. Second Cycle of Speeches (chaps. 15-21)

With his pride damaged, Job's three "friends" continued to accuse him of being a guilty sinner. The duel continued, with Eliphaz, Bildad, and Zophar hammering away with their theory that pain and suffering always come from transgressions. In this section, they became more vocal and vicious than before. They issued no call for repentance, however, but instead spoke of the pitfalls facing the unrepentant sinner (Eliphaz, chap. 15), the terrible things awaiting those who practice evil (Bildad, chap. 18), and the

elusive prosperity of the sinner (Zophar, chap. 20). Job responded after each of their discourses.

1. Eliphaz (chap. 15)

Eliphaz began his first diatribe with some semblance of calm and sympathy, but here he lost patience with the bereaved Job and denounced him severely. He argued that Job was a conniving and hardened sinner, who had failed to heed the warnings of his friends and who was defiant of the Lord.

15:1-6. Eliphaz argued that Job was trying to speak like **a wise man** (v. 2) but only uttered **vain** (i.e., empty) **knowledge** and filled **his belly** with hot air, that is, **the east wind.** Job reasoned with **unprofitable talk** (v. 3) that could **do no good.** He blustered without **fear** (v. 4) and was irreverent toward God. His mouth spoke his **iniquity** (v. 5), and his **tongue** uttered the words **of the crafty** to conceal his guilt. When he opened his mouth, he condemned himself (v. 6) and exposed himself as a hypocrite.

15:7-10. Eliphaz accused Job of presuming to be wise enough to sit among the members of God's council in heaven (see 1:6), where secrets are spoken (v. 8), when in reality, he was no wiser than ordinary elders and sages on earth (v. 9). **With us,** Eliphaz said, are some **very aged men, much older than thy father** (v. 10). This could imply that Job's father was still alive or that he was old when he died.

15:11-16. Did Job consider the Lord's mercies, His **consolations** (v. 11), to be **small?** Did Job know a great divine **secret** that others did not know? To Eliphaz, Job appeared to be condescending, snooty, and arrogant (v. 12) and even to have turned his **spirit against God** (v. 13) with pompous words. Why did Job think that **he which is born of a woman** (v. 14) could be **clean?** Even God puts **no trust in his saints** (i.e., "holy ones"; v. 15), referring to the angels of heaven, which is **not clean in His sight.** In comparison, the Lord holds **man** (v. 16) as **much more abominable** than the best of those in heaven. Eliphaz insinuated that Job was detestable and drank **iniquity like water.**

15:17-19. Eliphaz virtually commanded Job to listen to him, saying that he would **declare** (v. 17) to

Job what **wise men have told** (v. 18), which is open and not secret. This wisdom was uncorrupted and not polluted by the foreigners (the **stranger**; v. 19), the pagans. This great wisdom had escaped Job.

15:20–24. The wicked man (v. 20), like Job, has **pain all his days.** He hears **in his ears** (v. 21) troubles coming; **In prosperity the destroyer shall come upon him.** "The destroyer" could be death, though the parallel thought in Exodus 12:23 may shed some light on this. There "the destroyer" is God's agent who brings His wrath on the Egyptians. That event is described in Psalm 78:49, where "evil angels" are mentioned (lit., "angels of evil ones"; i.e., "adversities"). God has often used angels to bring destructive plagues (see 2 Sam. 24:15–16; 2 Kings 19:35).

The wicked man ends up wandering about **for bread** (v. 23), with **Trouble and anguish** (v. 24) making him afraid. The enemy rushes upon him and **shall prevail against him, as a king** who leads his troops to battle. The wicked are incessantly tossed about by calamity (see Isa. 22:18).

15:25–30. Eliphaz composed a poem about "the wicked man" who believes he is stronger than **the Almighty** (v. 25). He attacks God (v. 26), though he will ultimately get what he deserves, like a fat (v. 27) and poverty-stricken (v. 29) wicked man. His **substance** (i.e., accumulated wealth; v. 29) will not **continue,** and he will never **depart out of darkness** (v. 30). These verses describe, in strong figurative language, the ruin to which the wicked will ultimately be reduced.

15:31–35. Vanity (Hebrew, *shawa*; "worthless"; v. 31) comes back to the one who trusts in it. Vanity and destruction fall on the wicked man before his days are fulfilled (v. 32). The **branch** (v. 32) that could have turned green and budded and the **unripe grape** (v. 33), which could have been good for him, does not develop. The crowd of **hypocrites shall be desolate, and fire shall consume the tabernacles** (i.e., tents; v. 34) that have been given over to **bribery.** They conceive evil, **and bring forth vanity** (v. 35). Their **belly** (i.e., womb) **prepareth** to birth **deceit.** The words of Eliphaz reveal his cruelty toward Job. He insinuated that Job was a wicked merchant and a deceiver of the highest order. It is true that God judges sinners, but the whole story of Job shows that hard times can come upon the righteous. Eliphaz and his friends could not believe that Job was righteous. In their minds, if he were righteous, he could not have suffered so severely.

2. Job's Reply (chaps. 16–17)

Eliphaz's second speech was ruthless and totally without comfort. The complete callousness of one who was supposed to be his friend had deeply wounded Job, who expected more understanding and sympathy. Resentment burned in his heart, like a volcano about to explode. His three friends babbled along with long-winded diatribes against him and only added to his pain. They certainly were not kind counselors who consoled and listened to what he had to say.

16:1–5. Job replied that he was hearing the same old thing with which they had begun, to which he answered that they were **miserable comforters** (v. 2), literally, "comforters of trouble." This is the same expression Eliphaz had just used (15:35). Job asked if such **vain words** (v. 3) would ever end and why they were so emboldened to answer this way. If the situation were reversed, he said, **I also could speak as ye do ... and shake mine head at you** (v. 4), but instead of heaping pain, **I would strengthen you with my mouth, and the moving of my lips should assuage your grief** (v. 5).

16:6–9. Job answered further that in the present impasse, whether he spoke out or remained silent, his pain was not **eased** (v. 6). Instead of sharing friendship, God had **made desolate all my company** (v. 7) because his entire household had been wiped out. Instead of being lifted up, he had been **filled ... with wrinkles, which is a witness against me** (v. 8). **Leanness** of body and face were also a **witness** against him; that is, he was made thin and gaunt by the troubles that had come upon him. It would be fair to add that his leanness was also of a spiritual nature. With bitter words, Job pictured God as a fierce lion attacking and tearing at his flesh (v. 9; see 10:16; 19:11). While he spoke harsh words,

Job still did not curse God, as his wife had earlier advised him (2:9).

16:10–14. Here Job appears to be saying that God Himself had made him a target. His enemies (possibly his Satan-influenced friends) had **gaped** at him **with their mouth** (v. 10; see Ps. 22:13; 35:21), **smitten** him **upon the cheek**, and **gathered themselves together against** him. It seemed God had **delivered** (v. 11) him, turned him over, **to the ungodly** and wicked men. Though he had lived **at ease** (v. 12) before, now God had **broken** him **asunder**. As a lion grabbing the **neck** of its prey, the Lord had **shaken** him **to pieces, and set** him **up for his mark**, or target. Job saw himself as a target for **archers** (v. 13) who **doth not spare**. God was breaking him **with breach upon breach** (from the Hebrew root *parats*, referring to a severe beating; v. 14), and **like a giant**, God was running upon Job and knocking him down.

16:15–22. The Lord had inflicted Job with so many wounds that he had to sew **sackcloth upon** his **skin** (v. 15) as a sign of mourning. He had **defiled** his **horn in the dust**, possibly meaning he had been facedown, on his "brow," in the dirt. His face was dirty from the wetness of his **weeping** (v. 16), and his eyelids were half closed with despair. But none of this was because he had **any injustice in** his **hands** (v. 17), and even his **prayer** continued to be **pure**. He was as innocent, just as guiltless, as Abel, who had been killed by his brother Cain (v. 18; see Gen. 4:10). Job declared, **behold my witness is in heaven, and my** righteous **record is on high** (v. 19). While his friends continued to **scorn** him (v. 20), he **poureth out tears unto God**. He wished that God could understand as a human being, just as **one might plead for** (v. 21) another human being, such as a **neighbour. When a few years are come** (v. 22), however, Job would die and **not return**. Regardless, nothing was going to change; death would end all of this.

17:1–5. Looking at himself as one who had but limited days, Job reflected on the harsh treatment he had received from his friends. His **breath** (v. 1) was **corrupt**, which could mean he had bad breath because of his condition. Some translate this passage, "My spirit is spent, and growing weak." **The**

graves were waiting for him. Job was continually forced to look at his accusers and endure their hostile words and attitudes (v. 2). Job asked God to give him **a surety** (v. 3), a guarantee, that he was right in his plea and was not guilty of the sins with which his friends had charged him. **Their heart** (v. 4) did not understand; therefore, God should **not exalt them**, or honor what they said. Seeming to quote a proverb, Job reminded God that if his friends were spoken to with **flattery** (v. 5), were or allowed to think they were right, it would someday affect their **children**.

17:6–10. Job felt God was responsible for making him **a byword** (v. 6), an object of scorn, and **a tabret**, literally, "one in whose face people spit" (see Unger, *Commentary*, p. 702). His eyes had been dimmed **by reason of sorrow** (v. 7), and his **members**, or thoughts of the past, were but **as a shadow**. The Jewish rabbis hold that the word "members" refers to the "limbs" of his body, which had become very thin (Cohen, *Job*, p. 87). People who were **upright** (v. 8) would be **astonied**, astonished, at what they saw, and **the innocent** would be angry with the **hypocrite. The righteous** (v. 9) would remain steady, have **clean hands**, and grow morally stronger. The meaning of this verse is simple, but the question is, About whom was Job speaking? Some scholars think he was talking about himself. By stating, **do you return, and come now**, Job may have been inviting his friends to renew their arguments. With directness, he added, **For I cannot find one wise man among you** (v. 10).

17:11–16. Job commented that his days were **past** (v. 11), ended, and the **purposes** of his life and **the thoughts of** his **heart** were **broken off**. Everything was convoluted and turned upside down. Neither **night** (v. 12) nor **day** seemed natural to him. He found no comfort and peace (see Barnes, *Job*, 3:302). Only **the grave** and **the darkness** (v. 13) of death remained for him. **Corruption** (v. 14) was all around him, as intimate as his **father**, and **the worm** in the ground was as his **mother** and **sister**. He had no pleasant recollections. His **hope** (v. 15) was gone; no one could find it. The pronoun **They** (v. 16) refers to his hopes, which had gone **down to the bars of the**

pit, the prison bars or gates of sheol. Job's hopes were abandoned, lost, and buried, never to be resurrected. They would go with him **in the dust**. Job, as well as his friends, had cut God out of the equation of life.

3. Bildad (chap. 18)

Bildad the Shuhite did not have much that was new to say to Job and could offer nothing to help him. He assumed that Job was evil, but his words on the fate of the unrighteous could have no meaning for the real situation in which Job found himself. Interestingly, Bildad spoke to Job in the plural, maybe to ignore him as an individual and to categorize him as being part of sinful humanity.

18:1–7. Bildad seemed frustrated that Job continued to defend himself with his **words** (v. 2). Bildad resented what he perceived as a belittling attitude in Job and considered his emotional responses to be self-centered and irrational. In his responses, Job was treating his friends as if they were **beasts** (v. 3) and **vile** in his sight. He seemed to be flailing about **in his anger** (v. 4) and unreasonable in how he expected them to react. Job appeared self-righteous. Bildad then expounded on the fate of the wicked. **The light of the wicked shall be put out, and the spark of his fire shall not shine** (v. 5). This metaphor, "the light [or lamp] of the wicked," was commonly used in Wisdom Literature (see Prov. 13:9; 20:20; 24:20). Like an old man whose stride is reduced to a few tottering **steps**, the fortunes of the wicked wane (Ps. 18:36; Prov. 4:12). **His own counsel** (v. 7), his schemes, **shall cast him down**.

18:8–11. Job's own words had **cast** him **into a net** (v. 8) and made him to walk **upon a snare**. **The grin** (i.e., the trap; v. 9) would **take him by the heel**, and **the robber** would subdue him. He would be terrified **on every side** (v. 11). **Terrors** would **drive him to his feet** (lit., "scatter his feet"); he would be harassed and bothered at every step. The idea in these verses is that the evil man is suddenly seized by calamities as a wild animal is trapped in snares.

18:12–15. Bildad went on to say that the wicked man will be **hunger-bitten** (v. 12), his lack of **strength** will overcome him. Hunger will **devour**

the strength of his skin (v. 13), meaning his evil will bring him down, and he will be unable to provide his daily food and will become shriveled and thin. **The firstborn of death** is a metaphor for a deadly disease or even a description of the malady that afflicted Job (see Unger, *Commentary*, p. 703). **His confidence** will disappear, which would **bring him to the king of terrors** (v. 14), meaning terror would reign over him. Terror will **dwell in his tabernacle** (tent; v. 15). **Brimstone**, or volcanic rocks, will **be scattered** about his home; that is, he will live with terror and destruction until he himself is consumed.

18:16–21. Furthermore, the **roots** (v. 16) of the wicked man will dry up, his **branch** will be **cut off**, and he will no longer be remembered on **the earth** (v. 17). **He shall be driven from** (v. 18) places of **light**, of good, and **chased** from the earth. He will have no relatives left **among his people, nor any remaining in his dwellings** (v. 19). Those who come after him will be appalled at his fate (v. 20). All of this horror will come upon **the wicked** (v. 21) and fall upon **him that knoweth not God**. This speech on the fate of the wicked was, of course, aimed at Job. Bildad believed that Job must have been evil for such calamity to have descended on him, his family, and his wealth.

4. Job's Reply (chap. 19)

Job retaliated with charges against his friends. He accused them of tormenting him with their words and of reproaching him at least ten times. He charged them with shaming him and making themselves strangers to him. He added that they made God a God of injustice by saying that God was bringing judgment against him when he had done no wrong.

19:1–6. Job struck back with strong, emotional words. **How long will you vex my soul, and break me in pieces with words?** (v. 2). He accused them of reproaching him **ten times** (v. 3), and still they were not **ashamed** for making themselves a stranger to him. Job said that if he had **erred** (v. 4), the **error** was his own. They were using what they perceived as his evil to **magnify** (v. 5) themselves against him. Job did not mind admitting that it was God who had overthrown (v. 6) him and **compassed** him with a **net** of affliction. He was telling his friends, "If God has brought all of these troubles upon me, you should have compassion rather than triumph over my pain."

19:7–12. Job felt he was **not heard** (v. 7) when he cried **aloud** for justice. God had **fenced** (v. 8) him in and had **set darkness in** his **paths**. Though Job was once respected, God had **stript** (v. 9) him of his **glory** and had removed **the crown** of honor from his **head. On every side** (v. 10), God had **destroyed** him and pulled him up like a **tree**. It was as if God had **kindled his wrath** (v. 11) and **counteth** Job **as one of his enemies**, as if God had sent His armies to rise against him and had encamped about his **tabernacle** (tent; v. 12). Who could fight against the Lord or defeat His adversarial purposes?

19:13–20. Job's friends and acquaintances were now **estranged** (v. 13) from him, and his **kinsfolk** had **failed** (v. 14), or deserted him, as had his closest companions. His household and his maiden servants who had survived the onslaught of destruction had also left him. Even they now counted him as a **stranger** (v. 15). When he had called for his head **servant** (v. 16), the man had not responded, though Job **intreated him with** his **mouth**. His **breath** (Hebrew, *ruach*) was offensive to his wife, though he had pleaded with her for sympathy for the sake of the children they had conceived (v. 17). *Ruach* could refer to Job's inner "spirit," meaning his wife no longer related to him and his personal sorrow of heart. **Young children** (v. 18) who knew him **despised** him, and when he arose from the ash heap to speak with them, they tormented him with their words. His **inward friends** (v. 19), or dearest friends, hated him and had turned against him. Job had become very thin, with his bones sticking out and clinging to his skin. He had **escaped with the skin of** his **teeth** (v. 20), which could mean his teeth were gone and only his gums remained.

19:21–27. Here Job changed his mode and called for his friends to **have pity** (v. 21) on him, **for the hand of God hath touched me**. They were persecuting him as God had been doing (v. 22). His dilemma was such that he wished his words were

recorded **in a book** (scroll; v. 23) and **were graven**, engraved or chiseled on a rock, **for ever** (v. 24; see 20:24; 28:2; 40:18; 41:27).

Verses 25–27 form a profound prophecy of redemption and salvation, of resurrection and glory. These words form the medium or the basis of Handel's great composition *Messiah*. Job realized he needed an advocate in heaven who could plead with the Lord on his behalf (9:33–34; 16:18–21). The word **Redeemer** (v. 25) is from the Hebrew word *go'el*, meaning a "vindicator" who would free him from guilt. **Liveth** is the present-tense form (*hai*) of the Hebrew verb *hayah*. He presently exists. Christ as God is eternal (John 1:1–3, 14). The **Redeemer**, of course, is the ever-existing Lord, who provided all believers, of all generations, with redemption (Rom. 3:24) through His blood on the cross (Eph. 1:7). Someday (**at the latter day**), **he shall ... stand upon the earth**, literally "upon dust." This redemption provides the forgiveness of sins (Col. 1:14) and is for eternity (Heb. 9:12). By the inspiration of the Holy Spirit, Job was here acting as an ancient prophet (see 2 Peter 1:20–21). His prophecy of redemption would be applied back to him. Though Job would die, by resurrection, his **flesh shall ... see God** (v. 26; see Matt. 5:8; 1 John 3:2). Job would later reaffirm his belief in the resurrection (42:5). His eyes, following his resurrection, **shall behold** (v. 27) Him, **and not another**, though his **reins**, his kidneys or heart (his bodily organs), **be consumed**.

19:28–29. Job told his friends they should ask themselves, **Why persecute we him?** (v. 28), adding, since **the root of the matter is found in me?** He warned them of the **punishments** (v. 29) that might come for their mistreatment of him. His friends could be the recipients of God's **wrath** for continually harassing an innocent victim. Certain that his friends were wrong, Job "was able to look beyond death to his being acquitted by God and fellowship with Him," his Redeemer (Zuck, *BKC*, p. 742).

5. Zophar (chap. 20)

Zophar ignited with exasperation at Job's charges against God and against his friends. Like his partners before him, Zophar could not remain silent. He was troubled by what he perceived as Job's harsh words. He felt he had to respond and fired back the notion that Job had dishonored *him*.

20:1-5. Zophar felt he had to answer Job quickly (v. 2) because he detected Job checking his **reproach** (v. 3). **The spirit of** his **understanding** caused him to respond. He chided Job for not understanding, saying, **since man was placed upon earth** (v. 4) ... **the triumphing of the wicked is short, and the joy of the hypocrite but for a moment** (v. 5). Zophar was reacting because he had taken Job's words as an affront. His statements reflected the theology of the day.

20:6-11. The wicked one has pride (**his excellency**; v. 6) that rises **to the heavens** and has his head in **the clouds; yet he shall perish for ever like his own dung** (vv. 6-7), and no one will be able to find him anymore. He is **as a dream** (v. 8) and **shall be chased away as a vision of the night.** He will not be seen or found anymore (v. 9), though **His children** (v. 10) will have to repay the wrong done to **the poor** whom he oppressed (see Amos 2:6-8; 8:4-8). Later, Job would not argue over this issue (Job 31:16-23). A wicked man's **bones** (v. 11), which will go down to the grave with him, are sinful even from **his youth.**

20:12-16. The **wickedness** (v. 12) of the sinner is **sweet in his mouth** yet is hidden deep within his inner parts. Much of his evil is accomplished through the ill-gain of riches; God will **cast them out** (v. 15), and the wicked man **shall vomit them up again.** As if he swallowed **the poison of asps** (v. 16), he will die from the venom of his unrighteousness. He will suffer a premature death (see Ps. 55:23).

20:17-25. The wicked person will not see the blessings of his land (v. 17). He will return his ill-gotten gain unused and will not live to enjoy his accumulated wealth, which has been amassed dishonestly (vv. 18-19; see 20:10). He will not find peace from his gain, nor be able to keep what he has plundered (v. 20). None of his **meat** (v. 21), substance, will remain and no one will try to find any of his fortune, for it will have disappeared. He will heap troubles upon himself, and the **hand** (v. 22) of others who are **wicked shall come upon him.** When he thinks

he has arrived with plenty (**to fill his belly**; v. 23), God will bring **the fury of his wrath upon him.** God's wrath will fall **upon him while he is eating.** Evil forces will come upon him (v. 24), and it will be as if he is pierced through, with the shaft of a **bow of steel** coming out of his back (**out of his gall** bladder; v. 25), broadly meaning through his entrails (see 16:13). He will not escape such judgment.

20:26-29. All darkness shall be hid in his secret places, meaning literally, "All darkness shall hide his treasures" (v. 26). Death will prevent him from enjoying his wrongly accumulated gain. Everything he has will **go ill with him** that he has brought into **his tabernacle,** or tent. Even **heaven** (v. 27) and **earth** will **rise up against him** and expose **his iniquity.** His fortunes **shall depart** (v. 28) and **shall flow away in the day of his wrath.** This is the fate of a **wicked man** (v. 29), Zophar concluded; it is **the heritage appointed** by the Lord. But Job was not **a wicked man.** Zophar's great speech, while true in the larger sense, and eloquent, was totally misapplied concerning Job. This gave Satan an open door for tormenting Job (see 1:12; 2:6).

6. Job's Reply (chap. 21)

Unlike in his previous speeches, Job had nothing to say to the Lord in his reply to Zophar's speech. Many of his comments in 21:7-33 were aimed directly at refuting what Zophar had said (chap. 20). In some ways, Job may have been demonstrating that he had the higher argument, the upper hand, and that he was meeting the views of his friends in their accusations of him. He begged them to "hear diligently" (21:2) what he had to say. In his third reply, Job again argued that his great sufferings were not caused by his terrible wickedness. He pleaded for the facts but also for the sake of the suffering he was enduring.

21:1-6. Job pleaded for his friends to listen (v. 2) and hear him **speak** (v. 3), and after that, they could **mock on.** He told his friends, **Mark me** (v. 5), that is, "Look at me," **and lay your hand upon your mouth.** When he thought of these things, he was troubled and his body was seized with **trembling** (v. 6). In other words, he was saying, "Surely you, my friends, can see my anguish."

21:7–11. While Job's counselors had argued the fate of the wicked (8:11–19; 15:20–35; chap. 20), his experience was just the opposite. The wicked have children (v. 8) and are safe in their houses, and God's **rod** (v. 9) of punishment does not come upon them. Their animals multiply (v. 10), their children are numerous, and the children are happy and **dance** (v. 11). The general idea is that the wicked in this world prosper no more or less than the pious do.

21:12–21. While the wicked enjoy life (v. 12), they still must **go down to the grave** (v. 13). **They say unto God, Depart … For we desire not the knowledge of thy ways** (v. 14). Why should we serve **the Almighty** (v. 15) and **pray unto him?** Job added, **their good** (i.e., property) **is not in their hand** (v. 16); that is, they did not get wealth on their own. It was provided by God. **The counsel of the wicked is far from me.** Job proclaimed that he was not like these people. **God distributeth sorrows in his anger** (v. 17), and **the wicked** are destroyed. They are blown away like **stubble** (v. 18) and **chaff** in **the storm**, and they receive the punishment for their sins (v. 19) and **shall drink of the wrath of the Almighty** (v. 20). When the wicked man dies, **his house** (v. 21) and posterity have no more **pleasure**. In his sins, he does not think of his children.

21:22–26. God judges **those that are high** (v. 22) and seemingly mighty. Death falls on those who seem to have it all together, who **are full of milk** (v. 24) and have healthy **bones. Another dieth in the bitterness of his soul** (v. 25). Both, however, **shall lie down … in the dust** (v. 26).

21:27–31. Job declared that he knew the **thoughts** (v. 27) of his three friends, who **wrongly imagine against me.** They had asked, **Where is the house of the** wicked **prince** (v. 28) and **the dwelling places of the wicked?** The **tokens** (v. 29), the eyewitness accounts, of travelers found the wicked thriving. **The wicked** (v. 30) are spared for **the day of destruction** and **the day of wrath.** Will God not bring the wicked to account and **repay him what he hath done** (v. 31)?

21:32–34. God will bring the wicked **to the grave** (v. 32), and he **shall remain in the tomb.** Job knew that there would be judgment (v. 30), but here he was looking at the sinner's death from the standpoint of history. The wicked are given no second chance on earth. It is as if the wicked are placed in a comfortable grave, where they are at rest. Others will follow, and others have gone before (v. 33). **How then** (v. 34), Job asked, do you **comfort me in vain,** while **in your answers there remaineth falsehood?** Their consolations (see 21:2), Job evaluated, were only **vain** (Hebrew, *hebel*; "empty, futile, useless"), with no meaning. Job could not buy their explanation of suffering (Zuck, *BKC*, pp. 744–45).

D. Third Cycle of Speeches (chaps. 22–26)

This third cycle of discourses, unlike the first (chaps. 4–14) and second (chaps. 15–21), is truncated and abbreviated. Bildad's speech is very brief (25:1–6), and Zophar does not talk at all. The dialogue between Job and his friends did not convince Job that he was guilty. Job refused to acknowledge what was not true.

1. Eliphaz (chap. 22)

In this speech, Eliphaz used odd reasoning. He stated that since all things have their origin in God, man's giving back what God has given him does not enhance God in any way—as if the Lord is indifferent to what good people do, because goodness is expected of them. When men become wicked, however, God is wrathful. Eliphaz held out recovery for Job if only he would repent. The God of Eliphaz seems like a heartless automaton whose absoluteness separates Him from His concerns about mankind.

22:1–4. As a man is **profitable** (v. 2) to himself, can he in the same way be **profitable** to God? Since all things have their origin from Him, can a human being enhance Him or give back to Him? Does God have **pleasure** (v. 3) or **gain** in human righteousness? Does He **fear** (v. 4) human beings or **enter with** them **into judgment?** God is absolutely independent of human conduct; He will not condescend to enter into discussion with humanity. One cannot bargain with God.

22:5–9. In his earlier discussions, Eliphaz had been the least caustic, but he now reprimanded Job for gross social sins against the needy. He asked Job, **Is not thy wickedness great?** (v. 5) and accused him of having **taken a pledge … for nought**, which probably refers to having held a debtor liable by keeping his coat for a debt without returning it before nightfall (see Exod. 22:26–27; Deut. 24:10–13). He further accused Job of having **stripped** (v. 6) his debtors **of their clothing**, having failed to give a drink of **water to the weary** (v. 7), and having withheld **bread from the hungry**. He had not, however, harmed **the mighty man** (v. 8) and **the honourable man**. He had **sent widows away empty** (v. 9) and had broken **the arms of the fatherless**. Saying that he had broken "the arms of the fatherless" was hyperbole but pointed at Job for his supposed mistreatment of the helpless.

22:10–14. Because of Job's sins, Eliphaz stated, he was close to retribution, which was all around him (vv. 10–11). God is greater than humans; He is **in the height of heaven** (v. 12) and **the height of the stars**. How could anyone pretend to say they understand God? Can He not see through the **clouds** (v. 13) and **judge**? Verse 14 is written as if this is what Job was saying and is an absurd charge that Job thought God could not see through the clouds and was hiding in them.

22:15–20. Eliphaz questioned whether Job had followed in the steps of the sinners that had died in the **flood** (v. 16). Had he **marked** (v. 15), or noted, their ways? **Out of time** (v. 16) means "before that time." Since the men of the deluge had said to God, **Depart from us** (v. 17), the Lord could do no more for them (see Genesis 6).

22:21–25. Eliphaz made one last effort to reach Job and fully convince him that he was wicked. He told Job to **Acquaint** (v. 21) himself with God, or "submit" to God, to find **peace**, and good would then come to him. In saying, **Receive … the law** (or "rule") **from his mouth** (v. 22), Eliphaz was not referring to the Mosaic law, which was yet to be given

to the children of Israel. If Job would **return to the Almighty** (v. 23) and **put away iniquity far from his tabernacles**, he would find prosperity (v. 24). **The gold of Ophir** was the finest gold (see 1 Kings 9:28; 10:11; Ps. 45:9; Isa. 13:12). He would also be rewarded with **plenty of silver** (v. 25).

22:26–30. If Job repented, he would **delight in the Almighty** (v. 26) and be able to **lift up** his **face unto God**. The Lord would hear his prayers, and he would be able to **pay** his **vows** (v. 27). "Vows" more than likely refers to his spiritual agreements and promises made to God. Whatever **decree** (v. 28) or petition Job made with the Lord, He would do. The **light** of wisdom would **shine upon** his **ways**. One who had confessed his sins and been restored would lift others up and **save the humble** (v. 29). He would rescue him who was **innocent** (v. 30) **by the pureness of** his **hands**. Many may be suffering for their own sins. God forgives the sinful when they turn to Him. It is also true that God will save him in answer to the prayers of a righteous man (Zuck, *BKC*, p. 746). While there may be some truth here, the words were put forth in an artificial and mechanical way. Eliphaz did not see all of the issues, and again, he still believed that all of Job's problems were his own fault. All things would automatically go well for Job if he would simply confess and respond in a certain way.

2. Job's Reply (chap. 23–24)

Job did not deny Eliphaz's unfounded judgments against him. Neither did he agree, however; rather, he maintained an attitude of dispassionate calm and ignored Eliphaz's comments until later (chap. 31). Job answered by reflecting primarily on two issues: injustices he was experiencing and injustices that others had experienced. Job wished to present his case before the Lord (23:1–7), though it seemed God was inaccessible and sometimes unfair (23:8–17). The Lord also seemed quiet about the sins of others (chap. 24). Such unfairness, along with the silence of the Lord, troubled Job.

23:1–9. Job responded that the pain of God's **stroke** (i.e., the hand of calamity and affliction; v. 2) is heard with his **groan**. His sighs bear no proportion to his suffering; there are no adequate expressions for his pains. He longs to find God and come before Him, **to his seat** (v. 3). If he could see God, he would present his **cause** (v. 4), his **arguments**. If he could but speak with God, he would hear His **answer ... and understand what he would say unto me** (v. 5). The Lord would not **plead against** (v. 6) him but **would put strength in** him. In God's presence, **the righteous** (v. 7) can **dispute with him** and **be delivered** from Him as **judge**. But wherever Job turned, he could not find God because He had hidden Himself so **that I cannot see him** (v. 9). In all directions of the compass, wherever Job turned, he could not find the Lord. All his efforts were fruitless.

23:10 - 13. Job nonetheless maintained that God knew him. When he was **tried** (v. 10) as in a smelting cauldron, he would **come forth as gold**. He had tried to follow God, to trod in the footsteps of Him who was his Guide (v. 11). He had kept the Lord's **commandment** (v. 12) and had **esteemed the words of his mouth more than my necessary food**. Job closed this paragraph with a sublime statement about the sovereignty of God. **He is** of **one mind, and who can turn him? And what his soul desireth, even that he doeth** (v. 13). God carries out what He has foreordained with apparent disregard of merit or demerit (Unger, *Commentary*, p. 712).

23:14 - 17. The sovereignty of God extends down to the human level, and it had touched Job. **He performeth the thing that is appointed for me** (v. 14), Job stated. **Many such things are with him.** A necessary part of Job's faith was fear of God, who does what He pleases. His presence can be troubling (v. 15; 21:6). Job said, **God maketh my heart soft** (or "faint"), **and the Almighty troubleth me** (v. 16) and added that he could be dismayed before the Lord and recoil from Him, not because of **the darkness** or the gloom that **covered** Job's **face** but because he had failed to reconcile God's providence with His justice (v. 17; see Unger, *Commentary*, p. 712).

24:1 - 4. Job posed a perplexing problem. **Why, seeing times and events are not hidden from the Almighty, do they that know him not see his days**

of judgment? (v. 1). There are those who steal land (**remove the landmarks**; v. 2), **take away flocks**, and **drive away the ass of the fatherless** (v. 3). **They take the widow's ox for a pledge** and **turn the needy out of the way** (v. 4) and make **the poor of the earth hide**. These are wicked crimes at which the Almighty (*Shaddai*, as in 6:4) seemed to wink (Acts 17:30; 2 Peter 3:9).

24:5 - 8. The wicked are thieves who find food like **wild asses** (v. 5), who strip **the desert** (the steppe). These donkeys **reap** and **gather** even from **the wicked** (v. 6). They take what is not theirs and cause others to suffer. The poor are alone and **naked** (v. 7), shivering in the **cold** nights, seeking **shelter** (v. 8) in the crevices of the rocks.

24:9 - 17. Those who are evil kidnap **the fatherless** infant (v. 9), make **the poor** give them **a pledge** of exorbitant payments, leave their victims **without clothing** (v. 10), and take food from their mouths. They make the poor work **their winepresses** (v. 11) and then leave them thirsty, causing the poor to cry out, yet it is as if **God layeth not folly to them**; the wicked are not punished (v. 12). The evil **rebel against the light** (v. 13) and do not know the right **ways** or **paths**. They murder in the day, **killeth the poor** (v. 14), and act as thieves **in the night**. They **waiteth for the twilight** (v. 15) in order to tempt as an **adulterer ... saying, No eye shall see me**. They stake out houses in the day and break into them at night. They are like mold; **They know not the light** (v. 16). The daylight and the morning is to them **the shadow of death** (v. 17) because they are exposed. If they are recognized, they are terrified.

24:18 - 21. Verse 18 is difficult to interpret. Job seems to agree with his counselors. Verse 18 may mean that the wicked are as quick **as the waters; their portion** (what they own) **is cursed** and not blessed, and they do not know how to work, that is, to keep **vineyards**. It is as if **drought and heat** (v. 19) burn up (**consume**) their blessings of the **snow waters**, and so does **the grave**. The infancy of the wicked is forgotten, he will soon be eaten by **the worm** (v. 20; see 17:14; 21:26), and he will soon **be no more remembered**. The wicked mistreat **the**

barren (v. 21) women who are alone and **doeth not good to the widow**, that is, they prey on the helpless.

24:22–25. But God **draweth** (v. 22), drags away, the wicked to judgment. When God **riseth up** to judge, **no man is sure of life.** God gives them rest, and they are sustained **in safety** (v. 23), yet His eyes always see **their ways.** They may be **exalted for a little while** (v. 24), but they are soon **gone and brought low ... cut off as the tops of the ears of corn**, a symbol of judgment. Job boldly challenged his friends: Could they prove otherwise? Could they **make** his **speech nothing worth?** (v. 25).

3. Bildad (chap. 25)

In this speech, Bildad added nothing new but described the greatness of God, His infinite and absolute nature, and how no one can contend with Him or claim to be pure in His sight. Zophar, who had admitted how emotionally disturbed he was about what was being said (20:2), did not even comment.

25:1–6. God is great! **Dominion and fear are with him** (v. 2). The Almighty is the Universal Ruler, and as such should be regarded with reverence and fear. **His armies** (v. 3) are uncountable, and He is omniscient, for **upon whom doth not his light arise?** All are exposed to His view. Because this is so, **How then can man be justified with God? Or how can he be clean that is born of a woman?** (v. 4). Here Bildad echoed the earlier statements of Eliphaz about human depravity (see 4:17–19; 15:14–16). This is reminiscent of David's cry in Psalm 51:10: "Create in me a clean heart, O God; and renew a right spirit within me." A parallel idea is also found in 14:1–3 and is quoted by Paul: "As it is written, There is none righteous, no, not one" (Rom. 3:10). God is so great that even the heavenly lights of **the moon** (v. 5) and **the stars** pale in comparison to God's glory. What hope then has man, **that is a worm** (v. 6) because he is so lowly, morally and spiritually (Ps. 139:8)?

Bildad tried to humiliate Job by focusing on his lowliness and degradation. This short and unkind speech did nothing since Job had already admitted the greatness of God's glory and the failure of sinful humanity.

4. Job's Reply (chap. 26)

With emotional sarcasm, Job replied to Bildad alone, using the Hebrew singular pronoun "you" in 26:2–4. This seems to indicate that Eliphaz and Zophar were for the moment silenced and had nothing to add to Bildad's criticisms. This chapter is an introduction to the longest section in the book in which Job is answering his three friends. His defense follows their accusations and runs through chapters 27–31.

26:1–4. Job asked Bildad how his words had **helped** (v. 2) the helpless and saved the one who has **no strength.** How had his counseling helped him who supposedly had **no wisdom** (v. 3)? Who had Bildad tried to reach, **and whose spirit came from thee?** (v. 4). Was God speaking through him or some other source? Bildad's words were of no value. He and his friends were like worthless physicians (13:4) and were "miserable comforters" (16:2).

26:5–10. Job added that **dead things** (better translated "the dead"; v. 5) inhabit the underworld (see 3:13–15, 17–19). They **are formed** (lit., "tremble") even **under the waters.** They are in anguish, they and other **inhabitants thereof. Hell ... and destruction** (v. 6) are **naked before Him** and have **no covering**; that is, they are continually before Him. God is awesome in His sovereignty over the natural world. **He bindeth** (or "holds") **up the waters in his thick clouds** (v. 8), and they are not torn. **He holdeth back** (v. 9) the openness of **his throne** (i.e., His grandeur and splendor are not always seen), or rules as He pleases, and covers it as if by a **cloud** (Ps. 18:11). He encircles **the waters** (v. 10) of the earth and gives them **bounds**, in which they stay, even when **the day and night come to an end.** This suggests the cure of the circle of the earth, and to some extent, the turning of the earth on its axis, a phenomenon discovered by scientists only a few centuries ago.

26:11–13. When God brings **reproof** (v. 11) on His world, **The pillars of heaven tremble.** God **divideth the sea** (v. 12), which probably refers to the movement of the ocean currents with the tides. By His great and unfathomable knowledge and wisdom, **he smiteth through the proud**, or reduces to ignorance those who think they can understand Him. **By His spirit** (probably the Holy Spirit; v. 13), He **garnished the heavens**, and **His hand hath formed the crooked serpent** (Hebrew, *nahash*). This is a description of the leviathan, the great sea monster of the ocean (see 3:8; Isa. 27:1).

26:14. These are parts of his ways is better translated "These are the edges of His ways." What God has revealed of His world and His dominion over natural and supernatural forces amounts to no more than a whisper: **How little a portion is heard of him?** No one **can understand** the **thunder of his power**. If Job's so-called friends had fully comprehended the limitation of their understanding, they might not have misinterpreted his plight and given him such shallow advice.

E. Job's Closing Discourse (chap. 27)

The dispute between Job and his friends begins in chapter 3, continues through the three cycles of speeches and arguments (chaps. 4–14; 15–21; 22–26), and ends here with Job's closing discourse, in which he reasserts his innocence (vv. 2–6) and clearly describes his understanding of the justice denied him. With his friends and counselors now quiet, Job addressed all three of them.

27:1–7. Job began his closing discourse with the most solemn of oaths: **As God liveth** (v. 2). His faith in the Lord continued despite his perception that he had been denied justice: **God ... hath taken away my judgment; and ... hath vexed my soul**. Though he had been "vexed" ("made bitter"), he proclaimed, **my breath is in me, and the spirit of God is in my nostrils** (v. 3). "Breath" (Hebrew, *ruach*) may refer to Job's life force or to the Holy Spirit, who was giving him comfort (see 10:12; 12:10; 34:14–15). In the Old Testament, the Spirit of God could come upon a righteous person for specific purposes and then depart (see, e.g., Exod. 31:3; Ps. 51:11). In the New Testament, the Holy Spirit seals the believer in Christ and is the "earnest," or guarantor, of the final and ultimate redemption (Eph. 1:13–14).

Job could not back off and speak with **wickedness** (v. 4) or **deceit** about his situation; he could not **justify** (v. 5) the words of his friends. He would **die** before allowing his **integrity** to be taken away. He would not let go of his **righteousness** (v. 6), nor let his **heart** be **reproach[ed] ... so long as I live**. His **enemy** (v. 7), presently his friends, were **as the wicked** and **the unrighteous** (see Pss. 109:6–15; 137:8–9).

27:8–18. The wicked are hopeless if God takes away their life. In contrast, Job had pleaded with God for a Helper (see 9:32–33; 10:4–5; 13:21–22). The wicked man is a **hypocrite** (v. 8), though for awhile he may look prosperous (**he hath gained**). **Will God hear his cry** (v. 9) when trouble comes, and **Will he delight himself in the Almighty** and **always call upon God?** (v. 10). Job declared that he would **teach** (v. 11) his friends by truth, that is, **by the hand of God**, that which was **not conceal[ed]** by **the Almighty**. His friends had **seen** (v. 12) the truth; why were they denying it?

The wicked man has a **heritage** (v. 13) from God: **his children** will die by **the sword** (v. 14), and **his offspring** will have no food to eat. His children **that remain** (v. 15) will die, and his many wives, **widows**, will be so hardened and bitter that they will **not weep**. He will **heap up silver as the dust** (v. 16); he will have great wealth. He will accumulate clothes like one accumulates cheap and dispensable clay pots. His end will come, however, and **the just** (v. 17) will wear his garments, and **the innocent** will **divide** his **silver**. His home will not last; it is as fragile as the cocoon of **a moth** (v. 18) and as **a booth**, or lean-to shack, used by **the keeper** guarding his crops in the field. The old saying fits these verses: Here today, gone tomorrow.

27:19–23. **The rich man** (v. 19) thinks he is secure, but he is not. **Terrors take hold on him** (v. 20) as one who cannot swim in deep **waters**. He is swept away as one caught in the winds of a storm because God will fall upon him and will **not spare** (v. 22) him. When he loses everything he has, people will be merciless. They will **clap their hands** (v. 23) and chase him **out of his place** with hisses and taunts.

III. Interlude on Wisdom (chap. 28)

Here Job stopped his self-defense and gave a dialogue that some call a striking wisdom poem, which answered the question, "Where shall wisdom be found?" (vv. 12, 20). This poem is divided into three parts: (1) precious stones and metals are found only in the deepest mines (vv. 1–11); (2) wisdom is not found in these mines, nor can it be bought with such riches (vv. 12–19); and finally (3) wisdom is found only in the Lord and in the fear of Him (vv. 20–28). This chapter sets up the book for the theme of God's speeches (38:1–42:6). God alone could answer the question that Job and his friends sought to fathom.

28:1–4. Job used an analogy of the wealth of the earth, which has to be mined. **Silver, gold, iron,** and **brass** (vv. 1–2) have to be searched for in the earth. The miner has to enter the recesses of the darkened earth to search for such wealth, **all perfection: the stones** (v. 3), which are buried as if in **the shadow of death.** In the mine, the floodwaters are **dried up ... gone away** (v. 4), literally, "they dangle (or slosh) away from men as the streams swing back and forth." Job probably had in mind the Nubian mines of the Egyptians, which were not far from where he lived, and the mines of the Sinai peninsula at Serabit el Khadem, which were more remote and hard access.

28:5–12. As for **the earth** (v. 5), it gives forth **bread** but has **fire** beneath its surface, referring to volcanoes or the heat that can be felt in a mine. In **the stones** (v. 6) and the dirt are **sapphires** and **gold.** Up above, the birds do not see this wealth (v. 7), nor have **the lion's whelps** (v. 8) walked upon it. Miners lay hold of **the rock** (v. 9), turn over **the mountains** as if **by the roots,** and cut flowing **rivers among the rocks** (v. 10) to see the **precious thing,** that is, the gems and valuable metals. They control the underground **floods** (v. 11) of water to expose that which is hidden and bring it **to light.** Job then asked, **But where shall wisdom be found?** (v. 12). It cannot be found with such a physical pursuit. **Where is the place of understanding?**

28:13–19. Wisdom is priceless and is not found **in the land** (v. 13); it is not found in **the depth** (v. 14) of the sea, nor can it be purchased with **silver** and **gold** (v. 15). It is more valuable than **the gold of Ophir** (see 1 Kings 9:26–28; 10:11) and **the precious onyx, or the sapphire** (v. 16). This was Job's way of saying that God's wisdom is priceless, and nothing that is valued on this earth can compare — not **crystal** (glass; v. 17) and **jewels of fine gold,** nor the baubles of **coral, pearls, rubies, topaz,** or **pure gold** (vv. 18–19). With poetic eloquence, Job added, **For the price of wisdom is above rubies** (v. 18).

28:20–24. Job again asked, **Whence then cometh wisdom? And where is the place of understanding?** (v. 20). Humans cannot find it; neither can **the fowls of the air** (v. 21). Even personified **destruction and death** (v. 22) do not know, but the Lord knows and **understandeth the way thereof** (v. 23). He **looketh to the ends of the earth** (v. 24) and can **seeth under the whole heaven.** He is omniscient and knows the source of wisdom (see 9:4; Prov. 8:22–36). He perceives all things within His universe (see Pss. 11:4; 33:13; 66:7; Prov. 15:3).

28:25–28. It is He who created air pressure, **the weight for the winds** (Ps. 135:7) and gave weight to water; **he weigheth the waters by measure** (v. 25; see 12:15; 38:8–11). **He made a decree for the rain** (see 37:6, 11–12; 38:26–28), **and a way for the lightning of the thunder** (v. 26; see 37:3; 38:25). He saw the goodness of His plan, declared it, **prepared it ... and searched it out** (v. 27). These natural laws are God's domain, and He is in charge of His universe. As for humans, **Behold, the fear of the Lord, that is wisdom; and to depart from evil is understanding** (v. 28).

These final verses serve as a link to chapter 29, in which Job presented evidence that he deeply revered and feared the Lord, and to chapter 31, in which he brought forth further evidence that he was not wicked and that he had repudiated evil.

IV. Monologues (29:1–42:6)

In these final chapters, Job spoke to God from his heart, except in chapters 32–37, which present the speeches of a fourth and younger counselor by the name of Elihu. As an attorney summarizing his arguments before a jury panel, Job spoke of his past life and its goodness (chap. 29), reflected on his deep gloom and affliction (chap. 30), and finally gave his concluding words with an oath of innocence (chap. 31). The Lord's answer is recorded in chapters 38–41, followed by Job's response in 42:1–6.

A. Job's Call for Vindication (chaps. 29–31)

Job submitted his legal brief, in which he cited his final argument and protestation of his innocence. He was not timid in expressing his feelings; his words are charged with emotion.

1. Job's Past Honor and Blessing (chap. 29)

This chapter is a classical example of Semitic rhetoric. Job followed symmetrical patterns: blessing (vv. 2–6), honor (vv. 7–10), benevolence (vv. 11–17), blessing (vv. 18–20), honor (vv. 21–25). Although this chapter starts out with "Job continued his parable" (v. 1), it is rightly seen as the beginning of a new section.

29:1–6. Job **continued his parable** (v. 1) and looked back at the **months past … when God preserved** (v. 2) him, whereby he earlier said, "I was at ease" (16:12). The **candle** of the Lord **shined upon** his **head**, by which he could walk safely **through darkness** (v. 3). As a **youth** (v. 4), he had been blessed in his **tabernacle**, or tent, with **the secret of God**, meaning he had great understanding of hidden spiritual truths. He was blessed with **the Almighty** (*Shaddai*, v. 5; 6:4) and with his **children** all about him. His steps were coated **with butter** (or cream), **and the rock poured me out rivers of oil** (v. 6, see Deut. 32:13; 33:24; Ps. 81:16). Some believe "oil" could here refer to petroleum oozing from the ground, but others hold it is simply another expression of the wealth and fertility of his environment.

29:7–10. Job had been esteemed at the city **gate** (v. 7), where the wise gave their opinions. **The young men** (v. 8) had respected him, and the **aged … stood up** in his presence. Even the rulers, **the princes** (v. 9) and **the nobles** (v. 10), were quiet when he spoke. Job remembered the honor that had been shown to him when he would go out to the gate of the city and the square of the town, where the city courts met and held judicial proceedings.

29:11–14. Those who **heard** (v. 11) Job's wisdom had **blessed** him. When people saw him coming, they witnessed to others of his understanding. He was known for his charity to **the poor** (v. 12), **the fatherless**, the dying (v. 13), and the widow. His **righteousness** was seen by all, as if he wore it like a coat, and his judgment was like the splendor of a royal **robe and a diadem** (v. 14).

29:15–20. Job had been **eyes to the blind, feet … to the lame**, and **a father to the poor** (v. 16). If a problem needed solving, a **cause**, he tackled it and **searched out** the solution. He described with hyperbole he had been quick with justice, breaking **the jaws of the wicked** (v. 17) and taking back **the spoil**, as removing bits of food out of the mouths of the robbers. Musing on what might have been if calamity had not befallen him, Job said he had hoped to live long in his **nest** (v. 18; see Deut. 32:11; Isa. 16:2), in the land in which he had been raised and where he was comfortable. His life had been stable and established with firmness, like the **root** (v. 19) of a tree nourished by **the waters**, with **dew** covering the **branch** in the morning (see 8:16; 18:16; Ps. 1:3; Jer. 17:8; Ezek. 31:7). His glory had been undiminished, **fresh** (v. 20), and his **bow**, as the bow of a warrior, had been **renewed**, or strong and sturdy in his hand. If a soldier's bow was broken, he was impotent and helpless (see Jer. 49:35; Hos. 1:5).

29:21–25. Job's words had commanded attention and respect (vv. 21–22). Men sought him out and longed for his counsel as one opens his mouth for the refreshing **latter rain** (v. 23) of the spring wet season. They were astonished when someone of Job's importance smiled and jested with them. They longed for his approval, his smile, and they accepted and relished **the light of** his **countenance** (v. 24). He **sat chief**, that is, in the most respected place in the civic seat of leadership; he had been **as a king** followed by his army, as one who could comfort **the mourners** (v. 25).

2. Job's Present Dishonor and Suffering (chap. 30)

Job returned to speaking about his gloom and bewailed his misery, which it seemed would never go away. This is a stark contrast to his description of his pre-disease days. He was no longer respected socially

(vv. 1–15), was in continual suffering (vv. 16–19), seemed to be alone and abandoned spiritually (vv. 24–26), and was drained in body and in emotions (vv. 27–31).

30:1–8. Younger (v. 1) men who saw Job's predicament now put him in **derision**, though he knew of the foibles of their fathers and would not have trusted them enough to be the watchdogs of his **flock**. Those who made sport of Job were those whose vigor and strength had been dissipated by scarcity and lack (vv. 2–3) and who ate the **mallows**, the marsh saltwort, and the scrub of the **juniper roots** (v. 4; see 1 Kings 19:4; Ps. 120:4). **They were driven** (v. 5) away from the cities and shouted after as if they were thieves. They dwelled **in the clifts … in caves … and in the rocks** (v. 6), and **they brayed** (v. 7) like donkeys among **the nettles**. Like donkeys, they were senseless and stubborn. **They were children of fools** (v. 8), that is, **children of base men**, meaning "sons of those who have no name." **They were viler than the earth**, or "lower than the low."

30:9–15. The tables were now turned, however. These men now sing ditties about Job; he was a **byword** (v. 9) among them. They hated him, ran from him, and **spit in** his **face** (v. 10). God had **loosed** (or "cut"; v. 11) the **cord** of his bow (see 29:20), had afflicted him, and had **let loose the bridle**, so those who taunted him were unrestrained. The young men, **the youth** (v. 12), now teased and tormented him, blocked his path, tripped him, and were **no helper** (v. 13) to him in his need. They came on him like a flood (v. 14) and terrorized and **pursue[d]** (v. 15) his soul like a rushing **wind**. They did not have his **welfare** or need in mind.

30:16–23. Job's **soul** was **poured out** (v. 16) like water, and **the days of affliction** had gripped him. He was so thin that his **bones** (v. 17) jabbed him at night, and his **sinews** ached and gave him no rest. As he tossed about at night, his coat bound him and choked him around the neck as a **collar** (v. 18). God had **cast** (v. 19) Job about like **mire** on the seashore and had made him **like dust and ashes**. He cried out to God, but God did not hear him. He would **stand up** (v. 20), and the Lord did not pay attention to him.

God had **become cruel** (v. 21) to him, as if by His **strong hand**, He had become Job's enemy. The Lord had lifted up Job up to a tornadic **wind** (v. 22) and had left him **to ride** the currents. It seemed to him that he was living simply to be dashed about and tormented by the Lord. Job was certain that God planned to **bring** him **to death** (v. 23) and to the grave, **the house appointed for all living**.

30:24–31. Job had not turned against the poor when they were in need (vv. 24–25). He had **looked for good** (v. 26), why then had evil come to him? He had **waited for light**, but **darkness** had come to him. Why was the Lord treating him differently from how he had treated the helpless? His **bowels boiled** (v. 27), meaning he was torn up emotionally and found no peace (see Lam. 1:20; 2:11). The intestines were considered the center of affections and feelings. His **days of affliction prevented** him from finding peace and kept him continually upset. He went about **mourning** (blackened; v. 28) even when it was not day, and he stood up in the public assembly and **cried** vainly for help (see 19:7). He lived with the wild creatures, the **dragons** (lizards; v. 29) and the **owls**. His body was sunburned from being outdoors; his bones were **burnt with heat** (v. 30), or fever. His **harp** (v. 31), the lyre, once used for rejoicing, had **turned to mourning**, and his **organ**, the pipe, once used for celebrations, had turned **into the voice of them that weep**. Such misery took Job down the pathway of terrible depression and despair. God and people had turned away from him. He had nothing left to live for.

3. Job's Protestations of Innocence and Final Oath (chap. 31)

This is the final climatic section of Job's summation. It is negative in that Job denied all the sins listed against him, but it is positive in that he attested his loyalty to God as his sovereign Lord. In the strongest "legal" terms, and using a series of self-maledictory oaths, Job completed his defense. Nothing more could be uttered (v. 40). It is as if he affixed his signature to the document (v. 35) and let his final defense of proof that he was a contrite sinner rest with God.

31:1–8. Job had previously vowed (**made a covenant with** his **eyes;** v. 1) that he would not even look upon **a maid**. Did God reward **the wicked** (v. 3), and did He not see Job's **ways, and count all** his **steps** (v. 4)? Elihu would later echo verse 4 (34:21). Job was asking how he could have gotten away with sinning before God. If he had **walked with vanity** (v. 5), or went quickly to deceive, he desired to **be weighed in an even balance** (with honest scales; v. 6) and let the Lord judge him. If he had misstepped and had wanderlust or hands dirty from sin (v. 7), he would accept the punishment of having his prosperity (his sowing) be consumed by another and his **offspring be rooted out** (v. 8), or lose their inheritance. Job was putting his moral actions on the line and challenging his friends to point out his flaws.

31:9–12. Job declared that he had never seduced **a woman** (v. 9), **laid wait** to harm his neighbor, and if he had, **Then let my wife grind** (v. 10) corn for another and **bow down** as a servant to another, or sleep with another for favors or for survival. If he so sinned, it was **a heinous crime** (v. 11) and should be punished. Such sins are like **a fire that consumeth to destruction** (v. 12) and would cancel out **all** his **increase**, destroy his prosperity.

31:13–15. Job had never **despise[d] the cause** (v. 13) of his servants when they had just complaints because he knew God might bring a similar challenge to him. **When he visiteth, what shall I answer him?** (v. 14). Job had to be kind and fair with his servant staff because the Lord was watching. The same God created both master and servant **in the womb** (v. 15). For Job's time, this was a profound statement about the equality of the human race, which answers to the same Maker. Everyone should be respected as God's creature (see Prov. 17:5; 22:2; Eph. 6:9).

31:16–23. Job continued his challenge. He had never **withheld the poor from** (v. 16) what they needed or robbed **the widow** so that her **eyes** failed. He had never selfishly fed himself while **the fatherless** (v. 17) went hungry. He had always been kind to the less fortunate (v. 18) and had been generous to those who needed clothing (v. 19). **If his loins have not blessed me** (i.e., if the poor had not blessed him

for such provisions; v. 20), and if he had lifted up **his hand against the fatherless** (v. 21), **Then let mine arm fall from my shoulder blade, and mine arm be broken from the bone** (v. 22).

Job kept from sinning because he feared God. He knew that the Lord was aware of his motives and saw his actions. Being judged by God **was a terror to** (v. 23) him; because He was so far above, Job could not survive or endure His scrutiny. Therefore, Job could not bring himself to commit such cowardly sins in the presence of so majestic a being as God (Thomas, *The Book of Job*, p. 347).

31:24–28. Job had never placed his **confidence** (v. 24) in **fine gold**. "Fine gold" was specially refined for creating very expensive jewelry. He had never **rejoiced** (v. 25) in his **wealth** or worshiped **the sun** (v. 26) and **the moon**. He had never been **secretly enticed** (v. 27) or **kissed** his **hand**, which was possibly a ritual in some pagan religions and may have been forbidden in the region where Job lived. This was **punished** (v. 28) by some judges because it was a denial of **the God that is above**. Being a respected influential man, Job might have been able to get away with this, but he would not do it because he truly loved and honored the true God.

31:29–34. Job had never **rejoiced at the destruction of** those **who hated** (v. 29) him. He had never cursed the **soul** (v. 30) of one who hated him. He had never agreed with those in his **tabernacle** (tent) who called for satisfaction against the one who hated Job (v. 31). He was always charitable to **the stranger** (v. 32) and to **the traveller** who needed a place to stay. He did not try to hide his sin **as Adam** (v. 33; see Gen. 3:8–10; Hos. 6:7) by keeping his **iniquity** secreted away in his **bosom**. Neither **fear** of **a great multitude** (or "mob"; v. 34) nor **families** who were excitable with grievances had kept Job from saying what was right. He was never fearful of going before such people and answering.

31:35–40. After his outbursts of vindication, Job pleaded, **O that one would hear me!** (v. 35). His **desire** was that **the Almighty would answer**. If he was such a sinner, he wished that his **adversary** would have recorded the grievances in **a book** (scroll).

"Adversary" is not the same word used to refer to Satan in 1:6. Here the Hebrew word is *ish riv*, referring to a lawyer who makes a charge in a legal case (see Isa. 41:11, 21). Job stated that he would take the charge seriously and be forthright, carrying it as it were on his **shoulder** (v. 36) and binding it around his head **as a crown**, or turban. He would be not afraid to give an account of his actions (v. 37). With a climatic oath, Job called for a curse on his land if he had not been fully committed to justice (vv. 38–40; see 31:13–15).

B. Elihu's Speeches (chaps. 32–37)

This section introduces a fourth counselor, named Elihu ("He is my God"), who was younger than the other three (see 32:4, 6–7, 9). He apparently had been on the sidelines, giving deference to the age of the other men and listening carefully to the debate. Now he stepped forward to show Job and his three friends that they were all wrong. This section consists of a prose introduction (32:1–4) written by the author of the book, followed by Elihu's four poetic speeches (32:5–33:33; chap. 34; chaps. 36–37).

1. Introduction (32:1–5)

Elihu must have thought his purpose was to answer the question of why the righteous suffer and to open the door for the Lord to appear, remove the self-righteousness from Job, and then reinstate him to his blessings. Elihu may have been a mediating influence in bringing about the impasse that was now at hand.

32:1–5. The three men ceased talking because they felt Job was so self-righteous, **righteous in his own eyes** (v. 1). Elihu stepped forward to speak. He was a **Buzite** (v. 2) from the land of Buz, which was a desert region in the east (see Jer. 25:23). His father, **Barachel** ("God has blessed"), was of the family of **Ram**. Buz is the eponymous ancestor of an Aramaean tribe and was Abraham's nephew (see Gen. 22:20–21) and the brother of Uz, the presumed founder of Job's tribe (see Gen. 10:22–23; Unger, *Commentary*, p. 722). Elihu was furious with Job because he believed Job had **justified himself rather**

than God. His **wrath** (v. 3) was also **kindled** against the three friends, who had come up with **no answer**, though they had **condemned Job**. He waited for Job to finish his speech because he was older (v. 4). Some scholars consider Elihu brash, but his deference should be seen as commendable.

2. The Speeches (32:6–37:24)

Elihu's speeches were powerful but sometimes conciliatory to Job and his situation (33:1). He pleaded for Job to listen to him, as if he had finally found the answers to all the questions being bantered around.

a. First Speech (32:6–33:33)

32:6–10. Elihu began by reminding his audience that he was **young** (v. 6) and was reluctant to show his **opinion**. Age should be respected because it gives forth **wisdom** (v. 7). However, every man has a **spirit** (v. 8) that is inspired **of the Almighty** and **giveth … understanding**. This is not a reference to divine biblical "inspiration" but to the fact that man supposedly has sensibility because he is created by God. **Great men are not always wise** (v. 9), however; **neither do the aged** always **understand judgment**. This was a slam against Job and his counselors. **Therefore** (v. 10), Elihu said, they should listen to him though he was young.

32:11–14. Elihu had held back his words and had listened to and contemplated the three friends' **reasons** (v. 11), though it was clear they had not **convinced Job, or … answered his words** (v. 12). They could not claim to have **found out wisdom** (v. 13) in the matter. Only God could **thrusteth** Job down, not man. Something important had been left out, something that age had missed. Their understanding had not supplied the right answers (v. 14).

32:15–22. Earlier, the three friends had been **amazed** (v. 15) and had quit talking with Job. Elihu said he had **waited** (v. 16) for more but finally decided to answer himself and **shew mine opinion** (v. 17). He then added that he was **full of matter** (v. 18), meaning he was full of words and ready to speak. The **spirit within** him **constraineth** him, meaning that his human spirit had held him back from talking (see 33:4). He was like **new bottles** (wineskins; v. 19), **as wine which hath no vent**, ready to burst. He needed to **speak** (v. 20) so that he could be **refreshed**. He added, **Let me not ... accept any man's person** (v. 21), meaning literally, "lift up the face." He did not want flattering words to be given to anyone; only God honors and calls (see Isa. 44:5; 45:4). He did not want to give **flattering titles**, as if he would be considered wise after his speech. If that happened, his **Maker** (v. 22; see 4:17; 9:9; 35:10; 36:3; 40:19) **would soon take** him **away**, meaning God might end his life for his vanity and pride.

33:1–7. Elihu again pleaded to be heard (v. 1; see 32:10). He would speak with his **mouth** (v. 2) from **the uprightness of** his **heart** (v. 3), uttering **knowledge clearly**. He declared, **The Spirit of God** (see Gen. 2:7; Ps. 139:15–17) **hath made me, and the breath of the Almighty hath given me life** (v. 4). Elihu thought that his arguments were foolproof (v. 5) and that he was like the mouth of God before them, though he was but **formed out of the clay** (v. 6) as they were. He thought his words carried the same weight as God's. Job was not to be terrorized or afraid of Elihu's **heavy hand**, his strong word upon him (v. 7; see 23:2; 1 Sam. 5:6). His attitude of superiority showed through.

33:8–12. Elihu pointed out that he had listened to them (v. 8) and had not sinned against them. He was **innocent** (v. 9). He quoted what Job had said about how God had treated him, that God had put his **feet in the stocks** (v. 11) and marked all his **paths** (see 13:27). Job was wrong to accuse God in this way because **God is greater than man** (v. 12). Job had never denied this but had magnified God's great and awesome power and wisdom (see 9:1–13; 12:13–25). This was not a problem for Job (see 9:14–20; 13:13–16).

33:13–18. Why was Job striving against God? Elihu asked (v. 13), since He often makes Himself clear, speaking to man at least **twice** (v. 14). He comes and speaks through **a dream, in a vision ... in slumberings upon the bed** (v. 15). He opens **the ears of men** (v. 16) and **sealeth** up His instruction that He

wants them to have. God speaks to man to deter him from his sinful intentions (v. 17) and thus guides him, keeping **his soul from the pit, and his life from perishing by the sword** (v. 18). God uses the conscience to give inner conviction to the one tempted to sin.

33:19–24. The Lord may chasten man with sicknesses, **pain upon his bed** (v. 19), wracking **his bones with strong pain** so that he is too ill to eat, especially dainty (or "rich"; v. 20) food. **His flesh is consumed away** (v. 21), which may be a reference to cancer or some skin disease. The patient grows thin, with **his bones** sticking out. **His soul** (Hebrew, *nephesh*; possibly "his breath"; v. 22) comes near **the grave,** and **the destroyers** (Hebrew, *memitim*; "killers"), those who bring death, are about to take his life.

Elihu then spoke of **a messenger** (Hebrew, *melits*; "mediator, interpreter"), **one among a thousand,** to show a man God's **uprightness** (v. 23). The Lord **is gracious** (v. 24) and says, **Deliver him from ... the pit: I have found a ransom**, a redemption based on a mediator (see 5:1). "Ransom" (Hebrew, *koper*) literally means a "covering" for sin in the sight of a holy God. Christ is now the one who gives permanent forgiveness of sin (Rom. 3:25). God is gracious to the sinner.

33:25–33. Though Elihu was still ignorant of the true nature of Job's relationship with God, he spoke of the possibility of redemption based on repentance. Elihu said that the sinner who is redeemed and who is suffering physically for his sins will be restored to health (v. 25) and **shall pray unto God** (v. 26) and **will be favourable**. The Lord will restore **his face with joy** because He will repay the restored one according to **his righteousness**. Confession of sin will bring relief when the sinner realizes that sinning brought no profit (v. 27). The soul will be delivered, and the restored one **shall see the light** (v. 28). God **oftentimes** (v. 29) does this to bring the soul of the sinner back **from ... the pit, to be enlightened with the light of the living** (v. 30).

These words of Elihu were meant for Job. Elihu told Job to hold his **peace** (v. 31) and listen. Job was not to resist Elihu's words, though he could speak, probably words of a confession, so that he can be justified (v. 32). If Job did not confess, he was to be quiet so that Elihu could **teach** him **wisdom** (v. 33). Again, Elihu's presupposition was that Job was guilty and could only repent; otherwise he was doomed.

b. Second Speech (chap. 34)

The second of Elihu's four speeches is divided into three sections: (1) addressed to all wise men, including the three friends (vv. 2–15), (2) addressed to Job (vv. 16–33), and (3) addressed to himself (vv. 34–37; as was done in 32:15–22).

34:1–9. Elihu called all **wise men** (v. 2) to listen, those **that have knowledge.** In verse 3, Elihu echoed Job's words in 12:11. Discernment was to be applied to what was said (v. 3), to **choose** (v. 4) right **judgment,** to **know … what is good.** Job was standing up for himself and said, **I am righteous**; therefore Elihu declared, God must have taken away **my judgment** (v. 5). With indignation, Elihu exclaimed that he could not lie against what he knew to be **right** (v. 6). He proclaimed that Job was gulping **up scorning** mockery **like water** (v. 7) and that he must have kept **company** with wicked men (v. 8) because he found no profit in **delight[ing] himself with God** (v. 9) and obeying Him. Job never claimed to be perfect, and verse 9 is not a direct quotation of Job but only an imagined picture that Elihu applied to him.

34:10–15. Elihu then appealed to **men of understanding** (v. 10). God cannot be wicked. The Almighty cannot be charged with doing **wickedness.** People reap what they sow (v. 11; see Ps. 62:12). Even believers will be called to account for their actions (see 2 Cor. 5:10). Elihu was zealous for God's sovereignty and His glory as the Sustainer who shows His grace every moment by granting life and breath to human beings (vv. 13–15).

34:16–23. In the Hebrew, the singular pronoun shows that Elihu was addressing Job here, who was to **hearken to** (v. 16) him. Elihu asked, should Job live, he who **hateth right** (v. 17) and who **condemn[s] him** (God) **that is most just** (see 2 Sam. 23:3)? Should Job resist the rule of law and the principles of right that God has established? Would Job ever say **to a king** (v. 18) or **to princes** that they are **wicked**

or **ungodly?** To criticize those whom God has appointed to rule is dangerous, **For they all are the work of his hands** (v. 19). How much worse to question the Lord! The ruler, the rich, as well as any other person, can be taken away suddenly in death (v. 20), for God is in charge, and He sees **the ways** (v. 21) of all. **There is no darkness, nor shadow of death, where the workers of iniquity may hide themselves** (v. 22) from Him. The Lord will not be unfair with human beings. He will not demand from them what they cannot do. He does not wish to bring people **into judgment** (v. 23) with Him.

34:24–28. Yet God is sovereign. He can **break in pieces** the **mighty** and put **others in their stead** (v. 24). **He knoweth their works** (v. 25) and can destroy them suddenly **in the night.** He can bring them down in the sight of everyone (v. 26) **because they turned back from him, and would not consider any of his ways** (v. 27; see 1 Sam.15:11). In their injustice, they cause **the poor** (v. 28) to turn to the Lord, **and he heareth the cry of the afflicted** (see James 5:4). Those who are wealthy and turn their back on God are callous to human suffering; "so the oppressed have no resort but God" (Unger, *Commentary*, p. 727).

34:29–32. Elihu attempted to answer Job's complaints about God's silence (see chap. 23). If the Lord remains quiet, who can condemn Him (v. 29; see 1 Chron. 22:9)? If He hides His face, who can get a glimpse of Him? In His omniscience, He watches over the nations and over individuals, so no godless man may reign except when divine justice will be vindicated, either in time or eternity (Unger, *Commentary*, p. 727). Elihu indirectly called for Job to repent. If Elihu was wrong, it needed to be shown to him (vv. 31–32).

34:33–37. Job needed to understand that God rewards on his own terms, not Job's (v. 33). Elihu accused Job of speaking **without knowledge** (v. 35) and claimed that his words were **without wisdom** (Hebrew, *haskel*; "discernment"). Job did not know what he was talking about. His arguments were but foolishness. Elihu felt that Job had not been sufficiently tried in the heat of affliction, and thus he said that Job needed to **be tried unto the end** (to the limit; v. 36) for talking as a **wicked** man who **addeth rebellion unto his sin** (v. 37; see 7:11; 10:1; 1 Sam. 15:23). Elihu accused Job of exuberance in clapping **his hands** before his friends and then brazenly multiplying **his words against God**.

c. Third Speech (chap. 35)

In his third speech, Elihu continued his address to Job and his exposition of the fact that God is exalted beyond measure, above any and all temptation to be unfair and unrighteous, but Job's complaints implied the opposite.

35:1-8. Elihu continued speaking, **moreover** (v. 1), and jumped on the fact that he thought Job had said earlier that his **righteousness is more than God's** (v. 2; see 19:6-7). Elihu thought it was unjust for Job to expect vindication from God and at the same time imply that God does not care whether humans are righteous (v. 3). It is human to wonder what God is doing. The psalmist who thirsted for God (Ps. 42:1-2) also questioned why God had forgotten him (Ps. 42:9) and had rejected him (Ps. 43:2).

Elihu declared that he would now provide the answer for Job and his **companions** (v. 4). He told them to look upward to **the heavens** (v. 5) and see **the clouds** that are higher than humans (see 22:12; Gen. 15:5; Ps. 8:3). God is so far beyond humans, if one sins, what does this do to God (v. 6)? Or if humans are **righteous** (v. 7), what does this recompense Him? Expressing **wickedness** (v. 8) and **righteousness** may affect humans, but it does not move God.

35:9-16. The oppressed ... cry out (v. 9). Elihu said that those, like Job, who pray for help when suffering innocently never seem to get around to trusting the justice of their **Maker** (v. 10), who is also the Giver of wisdom and joy (v. 11). Such failure is a sign of arrogance (v. 12), so Job's complaints about God's justice and His silence were meaningless jabber. Elihu declared, **God will not hear vanity**, as Job had spoken (vv. 13-16).

d. Fourth Speech (chaps. 36-37)

Elihu defended God's justice in his second speech (chap. 34) and God's sovereignty in his third speech

(chap. 35). In his final speech, he again spoke of both of these attributes—first of God's justice and power (36:1-26) and then of His omnipotence and charity in His providence with nature (36:27-37:24). In this, Elihu tried to answer both Job (32:2; 33:10-12) and his three elderly friends (32:3, 12; see Zuck, *BKC*, p. 762).

36:1-7. Elihu went further in his arguments by daring **to speak on God's behalf** (v. 2). He declared he would reach deep into his treasury of **knowledge** (v. 3) and **ascribe righteousness** to the Lord and brazenly added, **my words shall not be false** (v. 4). God is **perfect**, absolute, in His **knowledge. God is mighty** (v. 5), all-powerful, **and despiseth not any** of His creatures. He punishes **the wicked** (v. 6) but defends **the poor**. He sees the activities of **the righteous** (see Pss. 33:18; 34:15) and **establish[es]** (v. 7) the godly kings, exalts them, on their throne **for ever**. God is powerful and mighty and does not lack mercy for His creatures.

36:8-12. If kings transgress and become puffed up against God (see 15:25), He will pull them down and put them in chains (v. 8). Through their troubles, He will guide and discipline them to **return from iniquity** (v. 10). If they listen to Him, He will restore them and return their **prosperity** (v. 11). If they scorn His punishment and continue in their wicked ways, they will **perish by the sword** (v. 12) and **die without knowledge.** This is similar to the New Testament doctrine of committing the "sin unto [physical] death" (1 John 5:16; see 1 Cor. 5:5; 11:30-32).

36:13-15. But **the hypocrites** (v. 13) who pretend to be righteous will not **cry out** when the Lord **bindeth them.** Some **die** (lit., "the soul dies") **in youth** (v. 14), and live **their life ... among the unclean** (lit., "cult prostitutes," the sodomites; see 1 Kings 14:24). However, God **delivereth the poor** (v. 15) who are afflicted; they hear the voice of God in their **oppression**.

36:16-21. Those who repent are taken out of the confines of **the strait** (v. 16) wherein they have been squeezed and are brought **into a broad place**, where they are liberated. God sets the repentant free. Their provisions shall again be plenty, **full of fatness**.

Elihu claimed that Job had brought all his problems on himself; **the judgment of the wicked** (v. 17) had befallen him, but if **judgment and justice take hold on** him, he could find restoration. Job needed to be careful, lest **wrath** (v. 18) allure him into taking God and men lightly. If he committed this error, Elihu declared, even **a great ransom cannot deliver thee** (see 34:33; Jonah 4:4, 9). Job's cry would not save him. Neither his **riches** (v. 19) of gold nor **strength** would release him from God's judgment. Job was wrong to desire **the night** (v. 20) of death, **when people are cut off** where they are. Elihu urged Job to turn from his **iniquity** (v. 21) because he had **chosen** it and not the **affliction** that he was experiencing. Elihu's evaluation of Job was the opposite of God's (see 1:8; 2:3).

36:22-29. God is powerful, and who can instruct like Him (v. 22)? Who can accuse God of wrong or say to Him, **Thou hast wrought iniquity** (v. 23)? Human beings **magnify his work** (v. 24), which **Every man may see**, even from **afar off** (v. 25). **God is great** (v. 26), and **the number of his years** cannot **be searched out.** He makes the **rain** (v. 27), which the **clouds ... drop and distil upon man abundantly** (v. 28). No one can understand how **the clouds** (v. 29) work or comprehend **the noise**, the thunder, that comes from His dwelling, or **tabernacle.**

36:30-33. God's lightning is so powerful that it lights up even **the bottom of the sea** (v. 30) and is used (1) to judge **the people** (v. 31) and (2) to provide **meat** (food) **in abundance.** Concerning the provision of food, when lightning strikes, nitrogen is released into the atmosphere, which then settles into the ground as needed vegetation fertilizer. The lightning is hidden in the clouds but also comes forth from them (v. 32). All of this shouts aloud God's glory (see Ps. 19:1-6; Rom. 1:19-20). Verse 33 is difficult. The idea is that His thunder announces His presence. **The cattle** (Hebrew, *miqneh*) in the context is also hard to explain. Some have assumed that the verse means the cattle are alerted to an approaching storm and announce its coming (see Hartley, *The Book of Job*, p. 477).

37:1-5. Humans also tremble and listen **attentively** (v. 2) to God's **voice** in the thunder. Through-

out Job, anthropomorphisms (something described as having human characteristics) are used, such as speaking of God's tabernacle or His voice in the thunder. The Bible gives a pristine view of the eternal God, however. He is not like men; He is Spirit and is an eternal being. Anthropomorphisms help the reader understand and visualize some concepts by putting them in human, physical terms. God directs **his voice ... under the whole heaven** (vv. 2-3) and **his lightning unto the ends of the earth** (v. 3), from one horizon to another. The lightning **roareth** (v. 4), gives forth thunder, as **the voice of his excellency.** He **thundereth marvellously** (v. 5), doing **great things ... which we cannot comprehend.** People are subdued with terror in a thunderstorm. Such displays of God in His natural world bring humans down to size.

37:6-10. God sends **the snow** (v. 6), **the small rain**, and **the great rain.** They display His strength in His world. When God is sending forth a storm, people have to fold their hands and look at **his work** (v. 7), and even the animals are frightened and have to go into their **dens** (v. 8). From **the south** (v. 9) come the winds, even **the whirlwind**, or tornado, and from **the north** comes the **cold.** Here, **The breath of God** (v. 10) is a metaphor for the chilling wind.

37:11-13. God **wearieth** ("burdens or loads down") **the thick cloud.** He can disperse **his bright cloud** (lit., "the cloud of His light"; v. 11). By the Lord's **counsels**, His decrees, the clouds **do whatsoever he commandeth them upon ... the earth** (v. 12). Elihu echoed his statement in 36:31, that God does these things (1) **for correction** (v. 13), (2) for His earth, or (3) to be merciful to His creation.

37:14-16. Elihu again addressed Job directly. He told Job to listen and **stand still, and consider the wondrous works of God** (v. 14) he had just described. Did Job understand how God flashes **light** (v. 15) from His clouds or balances **the clouds** (v. 16) from the heights down to the earth? The Lord does these things with perfection **in knowledge** (see also 36:4). His knowledge is infinite, and He knows what He is doing. No human being can fully comprehend gravity or the workings of climatology.

37:17 – 20. Elihu continued to question Job. Did he know how heat works? The Lord makes **garments ... warm** (v. 17) when **the south wind** blows. He can **spread out the sky** (v. 18) and make it like bronze, **as a molten looking glass**. No one can argue with Him **by reason of darkness** (v. 19). This may mean that He sends forth light and darkness every day, or it may mean that like darkness, no one can figure out how and why He does what He wishes in His natural world. No one can argue with God (v. 20).

37:21 – 24. It is as if **the clouds** (v. 21) cover **the bright light** of sunshine, **but the wind passeth** and clears the clouds away. The cold dry air from **the north** (v. 22) brings **fair weather**. Verse 22 can be literally translated, "from the north God comes with gold" (as golden splendor) (see Ps. 48:2). His **terrible majesty** is seen in this sudden change in climate. We can not trace out **the Almighty** (v. 23); **He is excellent in power ... judgment, and ... justice**, and **he will not afflict** without reason. Everything has a purpose, and nothing in nature happens capriciously or by accident. This should cause humanity to **fear him** (v. 24), knowing that He does not consult the **wise of heart**; that is, God does not need human advice.

C. Divine Discourses (38:1 – 42:6)

Job had begged for answers (31:35), and the silence from heaven was finally broken. The Lord answered Job out of the whirlwind (the tornado). He answered by showing Job that he was finite and had audacious pride in questioning God's actions and government in His universe. The name "LORD," or Jehovah (Yahweh), is His redemptive designation (see Exod. 6:3 – 4), which is used in both the prologue and the epilogue, though not during the dialogue. The name is used here as well (as in Job 40:1, 3, 6; 42:1). The holy God can converse with fallen man.

1. God's First Discourse (38:1 – 40:2)

Finally, Job's plea for the Lord to answer him was fulfilled. Over and over again, Job had beseeched heaven, begging for an answer from God (see 13:22; 31:35). He had pleaded for an arbiter, a counselor (9:33), an advocate, or an intercessor (16:19 – 20),

who would represent him and speak on his behalf. God's response, however, was nothing like what Job had anticipated. Job's charges about the injustices of the Almighty were set aside, and instead of answering Job's subpoena, God issued the same charges against Job. The Lord asked Job seventy questions that he could not answer and rebuked him for thinking he could challenge what God was doing.

38:1 – 3. Out of a raging storm, **the whirlwind**, the Lord answered Job (v. 1): **Who is this** (v. 2) who is bringing darkness to **counsel** without knowing what he is saying? Job was ordered to stand up **like a man** (v. 3), prepare for combat (**Gird up now thy loins**), and be ready to answer—a command that is repeated in 40:7 and 42:4. As the Lord began to answer, He said nothing about Job's suffering.

38:4 – 7. The Lord began by asking Job questions about creation. Had Job been there when He had **laid the foundations of the earth** (v. 4) or set the boundaries for creation (drafted its dimensions; v. 5)? Tell me if you know, God commanded. Did Job know how **the foundations** (v. 6) hang in space or how **the morning stars sang together, and all the sons of God shouted for joy** (v. 7; see Pss. 64:13; 148:2 – 3)? Many scholars believe "the morning stars" are part of the angelic host, as well as "the sons of God." Others believe "the morning stars" refer to the bright stars Venus and Mercury. Their "singing" may refer to what appears as their blinking in the early dawn. The point was that Job certainly had not been there. What did he know?

38:8 – 11. Had Job been there when the Lord established the boundaries of **the sea** (v. 8), and did he know how **it brake forth** with sudden waves, as a baby comes forth from **the womb**? Had Job been present when God had created **the cloud[s]** (v. 9), which sometimes look like **swaddling band[s]** and which **brake up** (v. 10) when He decreed? God set the natural **bars and doors** that limited and confined nature to go only as far as He planned (v. 11). The waters can go only so far, and the **proud waves** are **stayed**, or held back, by His commands.

38:12 – 15. God commands **the morning** (v. 12) and the day, **that it might take hold of the ends of**

the earth during daylight hours. As dawn spreads, **the wicked** (v. 13) hide, whose activities are in the night (see 24:14−17; John 3:19). With the morning light, the earth's features become visible, like the impression made on a **clay ... seal** (v. 14), and the light causes the earth to have patterns, as a beautifully designed **garment**. In the night, **the wicked** (v. 15) are at work; the Lord would break their **high arm**, which does evil. Because Job had nothing to do with establishing the day and the night, which were created by God, how could he question what God was doing in His world?

38:16−21. The Lord asked Job if he knew anything about what is under **the sea** (v. 16) or if he understood what **death** (v. 17) is. Did Job know **the breadth** (size) **of the earth** (v. 18)? If he knew, why did he not speak out? Where do **light** (v. 19) and **darkness** come from, and how does one get to the source, **the bound** (v. 20), and **the paths to the house thereof?** Did Job know such things because he was **born** (v. 21) at that time, or because he was old in age? Job had to keep silent because he was a mere mortal. No one can trace out God's providential workings with His world.

38:22−27. The Lord continued with His questions. Did Job understand the details of the climate? Did he know of **the treasures** (v. 22), where **the snow** and **the hail** come from, which God has **reserved** as ammunition against His enemies (v. 23)? How does God make a division in **the light** (v. 24) and make the **east wind** (see 15:2) blow **upon the earth**? How does God move the water currents, make the tides (**the overflowing of waters**; v. 25), and **cause it to rain on the earth** (v. 26) where no people dwell, **to satisfy** (v. 27) the land and make **the bud** and **the herb to spring forth?**

38:28−30. Job knew nothing of how water works. He knew nothing about what forms **dew** (v. 28), **ice** (v. 29), and **frost**. He was unaware of **the waters** (v. 30) that come out of **stone** and of how the **face of the deep is frozen**. What did Job know about God's storehouses of the elements, which act as His instruments to effect life on earth? What could he comprehend about the production of water, with all of its facets and change in form?

38:31−33. What about the planets and stars above? Job could not figure out how to **bind** (tie with fetters) **the sweet influences** (Hebrew, *ma'adannot*; "to be delightful") **of Pleiades** (v. 31), **Orion** (the hunter), and **Arcturus** (v. 32; see 9:9; Amos 5:8). God listed the constellations that could be seen by humans on earth, who certainly could not understand how these great lights worked. **Mazzaroth** may possibly refer to the twelve zodiacal signs. **With his sons** designates the constellation Boötes, which appears to follow the Great Bear (Arcturus) in the sky. Though the Lord spoke of these heavenly bodies in terms Job knew, He was not assigning them the pagan mythical meanings that were part of pagan culture. **The ordinances** (v. 33) refer to the laws God created to control the movements of the stars and planets. Their **dominion** has to do with how these distant bodies guide the seasons and all life on earth.

38:34−41. Still questioning Job, the Lord returned to the issue of **the clouds** (v. 34) and the **lightnings** (v. 35). Can anyone be like God? Who can **put wisdom** in the **inward parts** (possibly meaning the "mind"; v. 36) and **given understanding to the heart** (see 9:4; Ps. 51:6; Eccl. 2:26)? With **wisdom** (v. 37), could Job **number the clouds** or **stay** (lit., "make to lie down") **the bottles of heaven?** "The bottles" means "the jars" of moisture-filled clouds that release rain on the earth to break the drought (v. 38). Could Job help feed **the lion** (v. 39) or **fill the appetite of the young lions** who crouch in their **dens** (v. 40)? Of course not; neither could he provide for **the raven** (v. 41). The **young** ravens did not cry to Job but to God, and without His provision, **they wander for lack of meat**. Only God can give food to the wildlife that roam the earth (see Pss. 104:27−28; 147:9; Matt. 6:26; Luke 12:24).

39:1−4. Did Job understand how the **wild goats** (v. 1) live among the rocks and give birth to their young ones? No, he did not know of the time of their gestation (v. 2), how they struggle to birth **their young ones** (v. 3) in **sorrows**, with the pains of birthing, or how the little goats **grow up** (v. 4) so rapidly, leave their mother, and **return not**. Did Job understand how these processes work?

39:5–8. Did Job know the patterns of **the wild ass** (donkey; v. 5) that roams and lives in **the wilderness** (v. 6)? **He scorneth** (shies away from; v. 7) the cities and will not obey **the driver** who attempts to control him. He **range[s]** (v. 8) through the mountains and **searcheth** out **green** vegetation. He needs no help from humans. God gives him the urge to survive without the assistance of people.

39:9–12. The Lord asked, Who can govern **the unicorn** (the wild ox; v. 9)? He cannot be tamed or gated in a **crib**; he will not **harrow** (plow) **the valleys** (v. 10) with a human driver. He cannot be trusted because of his great strength, nor will he work by himself (v. 11). He will not harvest nor bring the crops into the **barn** (v. 12). He is wholly independent, a creature of God, but he is not a servant of humans.

39:13–18. Who gave the **goodly wings unto the peacocks** (v. 13) and **the ostrich?** The ostrich is dumb and leaves her eggs in the **dust** (v. 14) and sometimes steps on them herself or leaves them for **the wild beast** (v. 15) to **break them**. She is callous to **her young** (v. 16) and works **in vain** to birth her chicks because it seems she easily forgets them. It is no accident that the ostrich is dumb **because God hath deprived her of wisdom, neither hath he imparted to her understanding** (v. 17). While she cannot fly, she lifts her head high and races faster than **the horse and his rider** (v. 18). Though God made her without sense, the ostrich still has abilities beyond her apparent limitations. God creates His creatures with differences that humans cannot fathom, for purposes that are hidden to the mind.

39:19–25. God also created **the horse** (v. 19) with its **strength**. He cannot be made afraid, as if he were **a grasshopper** (v. 20). His **glory**, what makes him so strong, is **terrible** when snorted through his **nostrils**. **He paweth** (v. 21) the ground to show his power and is unafraid to go to battle against **armed men**. No instruments of war make him fearful (vv. 22–23). It is as if he swallows up **the ground** (v. 24) with his **fierceness and rage** in combat. He does not run away at the sound of the war **trumpets** (v. 25) but seems to laugh at them. He relishes the battle, which he smells **afar off**, and its noise and **shouting**.

39:26–30. Where did **the hawk** (v. 26) get its wisdom? Did **the eagle** (v. 27) rise up at Job's **command, and make her nest on high?** She dwells in **the rock[s]** (v. 28) and sees **prey** (v. 29) with her **eyes** from far away. **Her young … suck up blood** (v. 30) and eat **where the slain are**. This could refer to those killed on a battlefield.

The animal world attests to God's sovereignty, power, and loving care for that which He created. He made the animals and gave them their unique characteristics, which Job was unable to understand. He made the lion (38:39–40), the raven (38:41), the wild goat (39:1–4), the wild ass (39:5–8); the unicorn (wild ox; 39:9–12), the ostrich (39:13–18), the horse (39:19–25), the hawk (v. 26), and the eagle (vv. 27–30). They all have a purpose in His providential plan.

40:1–2. The conclusion of the first divine discourse is given in these two verses. Once again God challenged Job. Can the one **that contendeth with the Almighty instruct him?** (v. 2). If Job could reprove God, then **let him answer**, let him vindicate himself if he dared (see 13:3; 23:4; 31:35).

2. Job's Response (40:3–5)

All of Job's self-vindication vanished. He was humbled in the dust before the voice of the Lord, who revealed His infinite omnipotence before this frail and erring creature. Observing that human beings are not master of the earth and that the Lord is in charge of His creation, Job could do nothing but acknowledge how vile he was.

40:3–5. Job answered the Lord (v. 3) with the only words he could utter: **I am vile; what shall I answer thee?** (v. 4). He put his hand over his mouth and agreed that having answered **twice** (v. 5), he could **proceed no further**. To say he had answered "twice" may be a poetic expression, like "six" and "seven" in 5:19.

3. God's Second Discourse (40:6–41:34)

Again the Lord answered Job out of the storm and again told him to gird up his loins and prepare to do battle with Him once more. Job had yet to be completely silenced and vanquished. The debate and the contest continued. This time, the Lord spoke with strong irony to bring Job to his senses.

40:6–9. The Lord commanded Job to stand up **like a man** (v. 7), a man prepared for (verbal) combat, with his **loins** girded. The Lord again began to question Job. Did Job have the nerve to **disannul** (v. 8) the **judgment** of God or to **condemn** Him so that he might appear **righteous?** Did Job, **like God** (v. 9), have **an arm** of strength, or could he blast forth **thunder with a voice like him?** If Job could not act like God and sound like God, who did he think he was? Job could not condemn the Lord (see 10:3, 7; 16:11; 19:6; 27:2) to justify himself (13:18; 27:6).

40:10–14. If Job was so great, could he dress himself **with majesty and excellency ... with glory and beauty** (v. 10)? Could he cause the proud to be abased, with the **wrath** (v. 11) of a sovereign ruler? With just a glance, could Job bring **the proud ... low** (v. 12) and trample **the wicked in their place** and put their faces **in the dust** (v. 13)? If Job could do these things, the Lord would assure him that his **own right hand can save** (v. 14) him. In other words, the Lord would be admitting that Job was godlike and powerful. This was, of course, hyperbole and had the opposite intention of the words. Job was but a mortal and would never even begin to possess the authority and power of God the Almighty. No one can be compared with Him.

40:15–18. The Lord told Job to look at the **behemoth** (v. 15), which some believe refers to the elephant, or possibly the hippopotamus or rhinoceros. This animal was created by the Lord just as Job had been. He eats **grass** (v. 16) and has **strength ... in his loins** (the hips; v. 16) and **force** in the area of his stomach and body. His tail swishes about like the bending of the **cedar** (v. 17) tree in the wind. **His stones** refers to the animal's genitals and its virility and strength (see Hartley, *The Book of Job*, p. 525). **His bones are as strong** (v. 18) and heavy as **pieces of brass** and **are like bars of iron**. From the small hawk to this monster creature, God is the Maker of them all. They do His bidding and serve their purpose in His world.

40:19–24. The chief of the ways of God (v. 19) may refer to His awesome wisdom. The Hebrew underlying this phrase is translated "the beginning of his way" in Proverbs 8:22. The behemoth was used as an example of a huge animal under the control of God's sovereignty. Only God would ever think of engaging this creature in combat. The grasses of **the mountains** (v. 20) give him **food**, in the place where the other animals **play**. He lays under **the shady trees** (v. 21) in the hiding place **of the reed, and fens**, the marshy areas where there are **willows of the brook** (v. 22), where he can drink the waters of the river **Jordan** (v. 23). Many believe this could have been in the headwaters of the Jordan, in the Huleh region, north of the Sea of Galilee. The phrase **He taketh it with his eyes** (v. 24) is puzzling. Many suggest it means that a hunter cannot approach this animal while in its line of sight; he would run (see Barnes, *Barnes' Notes*, 3:252). His nose and his head could not be held in **snares**, traps. He is too powerful.

41:1–9. God's questioning continued. Could Job catch the **leviathan with a hook** (v. 1) or **a cord**? The word "leviathan" is used in a figurative sense in 3:8 but is generally used in the literal sense to describe a large marine animal, probably the crocodile (see 41:1; Ps. 104:26). The indication here is that this animal is more terrifying than the behemoth (see 40:15–18). Not even **a hook** (v. 2) through **his nose** or **a thorn** drilled through **his jaw** will subdue him. With irony, the Lord asked, **Will he** plead with you or **speak soft words unto thee?** (v. 3). **Will he make a covenant** or become your **servant for ever?** (v. 4). Can you **play with him as with a bird** (v. 5) or put a string on him as a plaything for young girls?

Can the leviathan be easily captured for food, sold to **merchants** (v. 6), vanquished by **spears** (v. 7), or wrestled into submission by **hand** (v. 8)? To hope to control him **is in vain** (v. 9). The Lord used this fierce amphibian to illustrate how unable humans are to oppose God, to stand against Him. If the crocodile's power went beyond the strength of Job, certainly Job was impotent before God, who made such an animal.

41:10–17. Since no one can **stir ... up** (v. 10) the leviathan, neither are they **able to stand before** God. Can anyone **prevent** God, or hinder Him, that He has to respond and **repay him? Whatsoever is under the whole heaven is mine** (v. 11), the Lord answered. He then reminded Job of the crocodile's anatomy and strength (v. 12). He has protective skin and armor of tough hide (v. 13), and **His teeth are terrible round about** (v. 14). **His scales** (v. 15) are daunting and add to **his pride.** He has no fear of humans. His scales are strong, **with a close seal.** Nothing, not even **air** (v. 16), can go **between** his scales; **they cannot be sundered** (v. 17) or breeched.

41:18–21. By his neesings **a light doth shine, and his eyes** (v. 18) reflect light as the brightness **of the morning.** "Neesings" means "sneezing, snorting." The passage can be translated, "His sneezings, light shines," or "His sneezing is like a glistening fire" (Barnes, *Barnes' Notes*, 3:261). Verses 19–21 are poetic exaggeration and are highly figurative, showing how fearful the breathing and snorting of the crododile sounds to frail humans. The movements of the crocodile's eyes, nose, and mouth cause people to panic. When the animal comes up from the river bottom, it sprays air and water, as if **His breath kindleth coals** (v. 21) with smoke.

41:22–29. Much of the leviathan's **strength** (v. 22) is **in his neck,** and people who see him run in fear. The expression **sorrow is turned into joy before him** is better translated, "terror dances, leaps, before him." His brisk and rapid movements strike fear in those nearby (see Barnes, *Barnes' Notes*, 3:262). His **flakes** (v. 23), the folds of his skin, **are joined together** and **are firm** and **cannot be moved.** His skin cannot be penetrated; even the flabby parts are strong. **His heart is as firm as a stone** (v. 24), or solid in that he can exert great strength suddenly and cannot be easily quieted. **His heart is as firm as a stone ... the nether millstone,** which is hewn out of deep, hard rock and is the hardest rock used for millstones. When the crocodile rises up, even the **the mighty are afraid** (v. 25). With their **breakings,** they **purify** themselves; that is, they void their body, losing their bowels and urinating with fear in

their leap to safety. One who dares to approach **him cannot hold** (v. 26) on to his weapons. He drops his **spear,** arrow, and **habergeon** (breastplate) because the crocodile has no fear; he sees **iron as straw, and brass as rotten wood** (v. 27). He is not afraid of **the arrow** (v. 28) or **slingstones,** and **he laugheth at the shaking of a spear** (v. 29).

41:30–34. Sharp stones (v. 30) do not deter the crocodile, and he makes **the deep** water **to boil like a pot ... of** hot **ointment** (v. 31). When he moves, he makes **a path** (v. 32) of shiny waves through the water. From the way he stirs the waves, **one would think** the water in **the deep** is **hoary,** white, at its bottom. **Upon earth** (v. 33), there is no creature like him, **who is made without fear.** This last clause best reads, "who behaves himself without fear." He fears no one. From his vantage point in the water, he has to look up at all creatures that are higher than he is, yet he has no fear. For **He is a king over the children of pride** (v. 34), that is, those who walk upright and think they can subdue him. Humans cannot subdue such a creature; nor can they overcome evil, which this creature symbolizes. Only God can do that.

4. Job's Repentance (42:1–6)

These are the last recorded words of Job. Before the Sovereign Lord, he abandoned his arguments. He could not argue anymore. He admitted his limits before the display of the Lord's numerous wonders of nature above, on, and below the earth and sea. Job confessed God's great power and his own sinfulness and pride in his second reply to the Lord.

42:1–4. Job admitted that the Lord is sovereign, He can **do every thing** (v. 2), and **no thought** is hidden from Him. Quoting the Lord (38:2), Job confessed that he had obscured His **counsel without knowledge** (v. 3) and uttering that which he did not understand. Elihu had reminded him that he did not know what he was saying (34:35; 35:16). Job was unable to comprehend wonders that were too great for him, **things too wonderful.** He begged the Lord to answer him, while quoting what He had said at the start of each of His two discourses (38:3; 40:7). He pleaded with God to let him **speak** (v. 4) what was right.

42:5–6. These are some of the most well-known verses of Scripture. While Job knew God and had heard of Him **by the hearing of the ear** (v. 5), now his eye **seeth thee**, meaning that because of all he had gone through, he now had a more comprehensive view of who God is. When Job looked through the dark clouds of the events coming against him, he could see God. Job's friends could speak about the Lord, but Job was enlightened with greater personal understanding. His only response was to hate what he saw in himself, though he was not a gross sinner. Sitting **in dust and ashes** (v. 6), he repented. The best of believers are but detestable when compared to His glory.

V. Epilogue (42:7–17)

God now spoke to Eliphaz and showed His anger. Along with Job's other friends, Eliphaz had not spoken correctly about God. These men made an assumption that they needed to defend God, His judgment, and His grace. They had wrongly accused Job, and as he had predicted (13:7–9), it did not turn out well for them. These verses form the conclusion of the narration.

A. God's Verdict (42:7–9)

42:7–9. Almost immediately after He finished speaking to Job, the Lord addressed Eliphaz, saying, **My wrath is kindled against thee, and against thy two friends** (v. 7). They had not spoken what was right as His **servant Job** had. For their sins, they were to offer sacrifices for themselves in front of Job. Job would in turn pray for them and intercede for their arrogance. God would **accept** the prayers of Job, and maybe the Lord would not deal with them in their **folly** (v. 8) in their false accusations. They had defended God's justice but struck Job down. While they had uttered many things that were correct about God, they had failed to realize that suffering is not always caused by one's sins. Eliphaz, Bildad, and Zophar did as God **commanded them** (v. 9). **The Lord also accepted Job** for obeying Him.

B. Job's Restoration (42:10–17)

42:10–11. The captivity of Job (v. 10), his pain and suffering, were turned around. God rewarded him with **twice as much as he had before**. When he was restored, all his family and acquaintances came to his house to eat, and they **comforted him over all the evil that the Lord had brought upon him** (v. 11). Interestingly, they even gave some of their wealth to Job, possibly as some sort of appeasement. While Satan was the instrument of the torment that came upon Job (1:6–2:10), nothing can happen in God's universe without His permission. While this is an inscrutable teaching in the Bible, it should comfort the believer to know that God has purposes in mind that cannot be seen; the believer must simply trust God.

42:12–17. The Lord's blessing on Job was greater than before. The number of animals he was given was twice as much as he had previously (see 1:3). The Lord replaced the children he had lost earlier (vv. 13–14; see 1:2, 18–19). His daughters grew to be the fairest in the land, and each was given an equal **inheritance** along with their brothers (v. 15) — something almost unheard of in ancient times. The Lord honored Job with longevity. If Job was around seventy when calamity befell him, he would have lived to be about 210 years old. Jewish tradition says his age was doubled, in the same way the Lord doubly rewarded him in other areas. He lived to see **four generations** (v. 16) of his offspring. **Job died, being old and full of days** (v. 17), years that were a blessing.

Job's misfortunes were not a sign that the Lord had left him. He has purposes that the sufferer may never understand. God is in charge. His love remains though the believer may be suffering in a tormented and evil world. Job's friends are not mentioned at the end of the story. Satan disappears as well. Job did not receive explanations for everything he went through, though he did gain a greater understanding of the majesty and providence of God. Though God's plans are mysterious, inexplicable, and mysterious, they are benevolent and beneficial (see Zuck, *BKC*, p. 776).

THE BOOK OF PSALMS

INTRODUCTION

Title

The titles "Psalms" and "Psalter" come from the Septuagint (the Greek translation of the Old Testament) and originally referred to stringed instruments (such as harp, lyre, and lute), then to songs sung with their accompaniment. The traditional Hebrew title is *tehillim* ("praises"), even though many of the psalms are *tephillot* ("prayers").

Authors

Opinions regarding the authors of the psalms vary widely. The notations of names are ambiguous since the Hebrew phraseology used to indicate authorship, generally meaning "belonging to," can also be taken in the sense of "concerning," "for the use of," or "dedicated to." The names may refer to the title of a collection of psalms that had been gathered under a certain name (such as "of Asaph" or "for the sons of Korah"). As for Davidic authorship, there can be little doubt that the Psalter contains psalms composed by that noted singer and musician and that there was at one time a "Davidic" psalter (see 1 Sam. 16:16–18). This, however, may have also included psalms written concerning David, psalms concerning one of the later Davidic kings, or even psalms written in the manner of those David authored.

Date, Collection, and Arrangement

The Psalter is a collection of collections of psalms and represents the final stage in a process that spanned centuries. It was put into its final form by postexilic temple personnel, who completed it probably in the third century BC. As such, it served as the prayer book for the second (Zerubbabel's and Herod's) temple and for use in the synagogues. By the first century AD, it was referred to as "the book of Psalms" (Luke 20:42; Acts 1:20). At that time, "Psalms" was also used as a title for the entire section of the Hebrew Old Testament canon known as "the Writings" (see Luke 24:44).

Many collections preceded this final compilation of the Psalms. In fact, the formation of psalters probably goes back to the early days of the first (Solomon's) temple (or even to the time of David), when the temple liturgy began to take shape. The earlier collections expressly referred to in the present Psalter include: (1) "the prayers of David the son of Jesse" (72:20), (2) the songs and/or psalms "for the sons of Korah" (Psalms 42–49; 84–85; 87–88), (3) the psalms and/or songs "of Asaph" (Psalms 50; 73–83), and (4) the "Song[s] of degrees" (the Psalms of Ascent, Psalms 120–134).

Other evidence points to further compilations. Psalms 1–41 (book 1) make frequent use of the divine name Yahweh ("LORD"), while Psalms 42–72 (book 2) make frequent use of Elohim ("God"). The reason for the Elohim collection in distinction from the Yahweh collection remains unexplained, but both of them date, at least essentially in their present form, from the period of the monarchy. Moreover, Psalms 93–100 appear to be a traditional collection (see "The LORD reigneth" in 93:1; 96:10; 97:1; 99:1). Other apparent groupings include Psalms 111–117 (a series of Hallelujah Psalms), Psalms 138–145 (all of which include "David" in their titles, often referred to as the Davidic Psalms), and Psalms 146–150 (with their frequent "Praise the LORD"). Whether the "Great Hallel" (Psalms 120–136) was already a recognized unit is not known.

In its final edition, the Psalter contained 150 psalms. On this, the Septuagint and Hebrew texts agree, though they arrive at this number differently. The Septuagint has an extra psalm at the end (but not numbered separately as Psalm 151); it also unites Psalms 9–10 (see introduction to Psalm 9) and Psalms 114–115 and divides Psalm 116 and Psalm 147 each into two psalms. Strangely, both the Septuagint and Hebrew texts number Psalms 42–43 as two psalms, whereas they were evidently originally one.

The Psalter was divided into five books (Psalms 1–41; 42–72; 73–89; 90–106; 107–150), and each was provided with an appropriate concluding doxology (see Pss. 41:13; 72:18–19; 89:52; 106:48; Psalm 150). The first two books were probably preexilic. The division of the remaining psalms into three books, thus attaining the number five, was possibly in imitation of the five books of Moses.

Superscriptions (Titles)

Of the 150 psalms, only 34 lack superscriptions of any kind (only 17 in the Septuagint). These so-called orphan psalms are found mainly in books 3–5 and tend to occur in clusters: Psalms 91; 93–97; 99; 104–107; 111–119; 135–137; 146–150. (In books 1–2, only Psalms 1–2; 10; 33; 43; and 71 lack titles, and Psalms 10 and 43 are actually continuations of the preceding psalms.)

The contents of the superscriptions vary but fall into a few broad categories: (1) author, (2) name of collection, (3) type of psalm, (4) musical notations, (5) liturgical notations, and (6) brief indications of the occasion of composition. (For details, see discussions on the superscriptions of the various psalms.)

Students of the Psalms are not agreed on the antiquity and reliability of the superscriptions. That many of them are at least preexilic appears evident from the fact that the Septuagint translators were no longer certain of their meaning. Furthermore, the practice of attaching titles, including the name of the author, is ancient. On the other hand, a comparison of the Septuagint and the Hebrew texts shows that the content of some titles was still subject to change well into the postexilic period.

As for the superscriptions regarding the occasion of composition, many of these brief notations of events read as if they had been taken from 1–2 Samuel. Moreover, they are sometimes not easily correlated with the content of the psalms they head. The suspicion therefore arises that they are later attempts to fit the psalms into the real-life events of history. But then why the limited number of such notations, and why the apparent mismatches? The arguments cut both ways.

Psalm Types

Superscriptions to the Psalms acquaint us with an ancient system of classification: (1) *mizmor* ("psalm"); (2) *Shiggaion* (see *Zondervan KJV Study Bible* note on Psalm 7 title); (3) *Michtam* (see *KJV Study Bible* note on Psalm 16 title); (4) *shir* ("song"); (5) *Maskil* (see *KJV Study Bible* note on Psalm 32 title); (6) *tephillah* ("prayer"); (7) *tehillah* ("praise"); (8) *lehazkir* ("to bring to remembrance"; i.e., before God, a petition); (9) *letodah* ("of praise"); (10) *lelammed* ("to teach"); and (11) *shir yedidot* ("Song of loves"; i.e., a wedding song). The meaning of many of these terms, however, is uncertain. In addition, some titles contain two of these terms (especially *mizmor* and *shir*), indicating that the types are diversely based and overlapping.

Analysis of content has given rise to a different classification that has proven useful for study of the Psalms. The main types that can be identified are: (1) prayers of the individual (e.g., Psalms 3; 7–8); (2) praise from the individual for God's saving help (e.g., Psalms 30; 34); (3) prayers of the community (e.g., Psalms 12; 44; 79); (4) praise from the community for God's saving help (e.g., Psalms 66; 75); (5) confessions of confidence in the Lord (e.g., Psalms 11; 16; 52); (6) hymns in praise of God's majesty and virtues (e.g., Psalms 8; 19; 29; 65); (7) hymns celebrating God's universal reign (Psalms 47; 93–99); (8) songs of Zion, the City of God (Psalms 46; 48; 76; 84; 122; 126; 129; 137); (9) royal psalms—by, for, or concerning the king, the Lord's anointed (e.g., Psalms 2; 18; 20; 45; 72; 89; 110); (10) pilgrimage songs (Psalms 120–134); (11) liturgical songs (e.g., Psalms 15; 24; 68); (12) didactic (instructional) songs (e.g., Psalms 1; 34; 37; 73; 112; 119; 128; 133).

This classification also involves some overlapping. For example, "prayers of the individual" may include prayers of the king (in his special capacity as king) or even prayers of the community speaking in the collective first-person singular. Nevertheless, it is helpful to study a psalm in conjunction with others of the same type. Attempts to fix specific liturgical settings for each type have not been very convincing.

Of the twelve psalm types, the prayers (both of the individual and of the community) are the most complex. Several modes of speech combine to form these appeals to God: (1) address to God, (2) initial appeal, (3) description of distress, (4) complaint against God—"Why?" or "How long?" (5) petition, (6) motivation for God to hear, (7) professions of trust, and (8) vows to praise God for answers to prayer and deliverance.

Though not all of these modes of speech appear in every prayer, they all belong to the conventions of prayer in the Psalter, with petition itself being but one (usually brief) element among the rest. On the whole, they reflect the conventions of the court, the psalmist(s) presenting his/their case before the heavenly King/Judge. When beset by wicked adversaries, the petitioner describes his situation, pleads his innocence ("righteousness"), lodges an accusation against his adversaries, and appeals for deliverance and judicial redress. When the petitioner is suffering at the hands of God (when God is his adversary), he confesses his guilt and pleads for mercy. Giving attention to the various modes of speech in the prayers and to their functions in the judicial appeals they present will significantly aid the reader.

Literary Features

The Psalter is from first to last poetry—even though it contains many prayers, and not all Old Testament prayers were poetic (see 1 Kings 8:23–53; Ezra 9:6–15; Neh. 9:5–37; Dan. 9:4–19), nor was all praise poetic (see 1 Kings 8:15–21). The Psalms are impassioned, vivid, and concrete; they are rich in images, in simile and metaphor. Assonance, alliteration, and wordplays abound in the Hebrew text. Effective use of repetition and the piling up of synonyms and complements to fill out the picture are characteristic. Key words frequently highlight major themes in the prayer or song. Enclosure (repeating at the end a significant word or phrase that occurs at the beginning) frequently wraps up a composition or a unit within it. The notes on the structure of the individual psalms in this work often call attention to literary frames within which the psalm has been set.

Hebrew poetry lacks rhyme and regular meter. Its most distinctive and pervasive feature is parallelism. Most poetic lines are composed of two (sometimes three) balanced segments (the balance is often loose, with the second segment commonly somewhat shorter than the first). The second segment either echoes (synonymous parallelism), contrasts (antithetic parallelism), or syntactically completes (synthetic parallelism) the first. These three types are generalizations and are not wholly adequate to describe the rich variety that the creativity of the poets achieved within the basic two-segment line structure. They can serve, however, as rough distinctions that will assist the reader.

Close study of the Psalms discloses that the authors often composed with an overall design in mind. This is true of the alphabetic acrostics, in which the poet devoted to each letter of the Hebrew alphabet one line segment (as in Psalms 111–112), or a single line (as in Psalms 25; 34; 145), or two lines (as in Psalm 37), or eight lines (as in Psalm 119). In addition, Psalms 33, 38, and 103 each have twenty-two lines in the Hebrew, no doubt because of the number of letters in the Hebrew alphabet (see Lamentations, Introduction: "Literary Features"). The oft-voiced notion that this device was used as a memory aid seems culturally prejudiced and quite unwarranted. It is much more likely that the alphabet, representing all that could be expressed in human speech, commended itself as a framework on which to hang significant phrases.

Other forms of composition were also used. Psalm 44 is a prayer fashioned after the design of a ziggurat (a Babylonian stepped pyramid; see discussion on Gen. 11:4). A sense of symmetry is pervasive. Many Psalms begin and end with the same call to praise ("Praise ye the LORD," Psalms 113; 135; "O LORD our Lord ...," Psalm 8). A particularly interesting device is the placement of a key thematic line at the very center, sometimes constructing the whole or part of the poem around that center (see 6:6). The authors of the psalms crafted their compositions very carefully. They were heirs of an ancient art (many details show that they had inherited a poetic tradition that goes back hundreds of years), and they developed it to a state of high sophistication. Their works are best appreciated when carefully studied and pondered.

The word "Selah" is found in thirty-nine psalms, all but two of which (Psalms 140 and 143, both "Davidic") are in books 1–3. It is also found in Habbukuk 3, a psalm-like poem. Though the meaning of this term is not clear, it is most likely a liturgical notation. The common suggestions that it calls for a brief musical interlude or for a brief liturgical response from the congregation are plausible.

Theme and Theological Message

The Psalter is for the most part a book of prayer and praise. It speaks to God in prayer, and it speaks of God in praise. Although occasionally didactic in form and purpose, the Psalter is not a catechism of doctrine. Therefore, its theology is not abstract or systematic but confessional and doxological. So a summation of that theology impoverishes it by translating it into an objective mode.

Furthermore, attempting any such summation poses a still greater problem. The Psalter is a large collection of independent pieces of many kinds, serving different purposes and written over the course of many centuries. Not only must a brief summary of its theology be selective and incomplete; it will also of necessity be somewhat artificial. It will suggest that each psalm reflects or at least presupposes the theology outlined, that there is no theological tension or progression within the Psalter. Manifestly, this is not so.

Still, the final editors of the Psalter were obviously not eclectic in their selection. They knew that many voices from many times spoke here but none that in their judgment was incompatible with the Law and the Prophets. No doubt they also assumed that each psalm was to be understood in the light of the collection as a whole. Hence, something can be said, after all, concerning major theological themes that, while admittedly a bit artificial, need not seriously distort and can be helpful to the student of the Psalms.

At the core of the theology of the Psalter is the conviction that the gravitational center of life (of right human understanding, trust, hope, service, morality, adoration) and also of history and of the whole creation (heaven and earth) is God (*Yahweh*, "the LORD"). He is the Great King over all, the One to whom all things are subject. He created all things and preserves them; they are the robe of glory with which He has clothed Himself. Because He ordered them, they have a well-defined and "true" identity. Because He maintains them, they are sustained and kept secure from disruption, confusion, or annihilation. Because He alone is the Sovereign God, they are governed by one hand and held in the service of one divine purpose. Under God, creation is a cosmos — an orderly and systematic whole. What is distinguished as nature and history had one Lord, under whose rule all things worked together. Through the creation, the Great King's majestic glory is displayed. He is good (wise, righteous, faithful, benevolent, and merciful — evoking trust), and He is great (His knowledge, thoughts, and works are beyond human comprehension — evoking reverent awe). By His good and lordly rule, He is shown to be the Holy One.

As the Great King by right of creation and enduring absolute sovereignty, He ultimately will not tolerate any worldly power that opposes, denies, or ignores Him. He will come to rule the nations so that all will be compelled to acknowledge Him. This expectation is no doubt the root and broadest scope of the psalmists' long view of the future. Because the Lord is the Great King beyond all challenge, His righteous and peaceable kingdom will come, overwhelming all opposition and purging the creation of all rebellion against His rule — such will be the ultimate outcome of history.

As the Great King on whom all creatures depend, He opposes "the proud," those who rely on their own resources (and/or on the gods they have contrived) to work out their own destiny. These are the ones who ruthlessly wield whatever power they possess to attain worldly wealth, status, and security—those who are a law unto themselves and exploit others as they will. In the Psalter, this kind of pride is the root of all evil. Those who embrace it, though they may seem to prosper, will be brought down to death, their final end. "The humble" and "the poor and needy," those who acknowledge their dependence on the Lord in all things, are the ones in whom God delights. Hence, "the fear of the LORD"—that is, humble trust in and obedience to the Lord—"is the beginning of [all] wisdom" (111:10). Ultimately, those who embrace it will inherit the earth. Not even death can hinder them from seeing the face of God.

The psalmists' hope for the future—the future of God and His kingdom and the future of the godly—was firm, though somewhat generalized. None of the psalmists expressed a two-age vision of the future (the present evil age giving way to a new age of righteousness and peace on the other side of a great eschatological divide). Such a view began to appear in the intertestamental literature—a view foreshadowed by Daniel (see especially Dan. 12:2–3) and Isaiah (see Isa. 65:17–25; 66:22–24)—and it later received full expression in the teaching of Jesus and the apostles. This revelation, however, was only a fuller development that was consistent with the hopes expressed by the psalmists.

Because God is the Great King, He is the ultimate executor of justice among men (to avenge oneself is an act of "the proud"). God is the court of appeal when persons are threatened or wronged, especially when no earthly court that He has established has jurisdiction (as in the case of international conflicts) or is able to judge (as when one is wronged by public slander) or is willing to act (out of fear or corruption). He is the mighty and faithful Defender of the defenseless and the wronged. He knows every deed and the secrets of every heart. There is no escaping His scrutiny, and no false testimony will mislead Him in judgment. He hears the pleas presented to Him. As the good and faithful Judge, He delivers those who are oppressed or wrongfully attacked and redresses the wrongs committed against them (see 5:10). This is the unwavering conviction that accounts for the psalmists' impatient complaints when they boldly, yet as ones "poor and needy," cried to Him, Why have You not yet delivered me? How long, O Lord, before You act?

As the Great King over all the earth, the Lord had chosen Israel to be His servant people, His "inheritance" among the nations. He had delivered them by mighty acts out of the hands of the world powers, He had given them a land of their own (territory He took from other nations as His own "inheritance" in the earth), and He had united them with Himself in covenant as the initial embodiment of His redeemed kingdom. Thus, both their destiny and His honor were bound up in this relationship. To them, He also gave His word of revelation, which testified of Him, made specific His promises, and proclaimed His will. By God's covenant, Israel was to live among the nations, loyal only to her heavenly King. She was to trust solely in His protection, hope in His promises, live in accordance with His will, and worship Him exclusively. She was to sing His praises to the whole world, which, in a special sense, revealed Israel's anticipatory role in the evangelization of the nations.

As the Great King, Israel's covenant Lord, God chose David to be His royal representative on earth. In this capacity, David was the Lord's "servant." The Lord Himself anointed him and adopted him as His royal "son" to rule in His name. Through the Davidic ruler, God made His people secure in the Promised Land and subdued all the powers that threatened them. Moreover, He covenanted to preserve the Davidic dynasty. Henceforth the kingdom of God on earth, while not dependent on the house of David, was linked to it by God's decision and commitment. And since the Davidic kings were God's royal representatives in the earth, in concept seated at God's right hand (see 110:1), the scope of their rule was potentially worldwide (see Psalm 2).

The Lord's anointed, however, was more than a warrior king. He was to be endowed by God to govern His people with godlike righteousness: to deliver the oppressed, defend the defenseless, suppress the wicked, and thus bless the nation with internal peace and prosperity. He was also an intercessor with God on behalf of the nation, the builder and maintainer of the temple (as God's earthly palace and the nation's house of prayer), and the foremost voice calling the nation to worship the Lord. It is perhaps with a view to these last duties that he was declared to be not only king but also "priest" (see Psalm 110 and discussion).

As the Great King, Israel's covenant Lord, God also chose Jerusalem (the City of David) as His own royal city, the earthly seat of His throne. Thus, Jerusalem (Zion) became the earthly capital (and symbol) of the kingdom of God. There in His palace (the temple), He sat enthroned among His people. There His people could meet with Him to bring their prayers and praise and to see His power and glory. From there, He brought salvation, dispensed blessings, and judged the nations. With Him as the city's great Defender, Jerusalem was the secure citadel of the kingdom of God, the hope and joy of God's people.

God's goodwill and faithfulness toward His people were most strikingly symbolized by His pledged presence among them at His temple in Jerusalem, "the city of the great King" (48:2). No manifestation of His benevolence was greater than His readiness to forgive the sins of those who humbly confessed them and whose hearts showed Him that their repentance was genuine and that their professions of loyalty to Him had integrity. As they anguished over their own sinfulness, the psalmists remembered the ancient testimony of their covenant Lord: I am Yahweh ("the Lord"), "the Lord God, merciful and gracious, longsuffering, and abundant in goodness and truth, keeping mercy for thousands, forgiving inquity and transgression and sin" (Exod. 34:6–7). Only with this remembrance did they dare to submit to Him as His people, to "fear" Him (see 130:3–4).

Unquestionably, the supreme kingship of Yahweh is the most basic metaphor and most pervasive theological concept in the Psalter, as in the Old Testament generally. It provides the fundamental perspective in which man is to view the Lord, the whole creation, events in nature and history, and the future. The whole creation is His one kingdom. To be a creature in the world is to be a part of His kingdom and under His rule. To be a human being in the world is to be dependent on Him and responsible to Him. To proudly deny that fact is the root of all wickedness—the wickedness that now pervades the world.

God's election of Israel and subsequently of David and Zion, together with the giving of His word, represents the renewed inbreaking of God's righteous kingdom into this world of rebellion and evil. It initiates the great divide between the righteous nation and the wicked nations and, on a deeper level, between the righteous and the wicked, a more significant distinction that cuts even through Israel. In the end, this divine enterprise will triumph. Human pride will be humbled, and wrongs will be redressed. The humble will be given the whole earth to possess, and the righteous and peaceable kingdom of God will come to full realization. These theological themes, of course, have profound religious and moral implications. Of these, too, the psalmists spoke.

One question that ought yet to be addressed is, do the Psalms speak of the Christ? Yes, but in a variety of ways and not as the prophets do. The Psalter is not a book of prophetic oracles and was never numbered among the Prophetic Books. When the Psalms speak of the king on David's throne, they speak of the king who was being crowned (as in Psalms 2 and 72) or was reigning (as in Psalm 45) at the time. They proclaim his status as God's anointed and declare what God would accomplish through him and his dynasty. Thus, they also speak of the sons of David to come. In the exile and the postexilic era, when there was no reigning king, they spoke to Israel only of the great Son of David, whom the prophets had announced as the One in whom God's covenant with David would yet be fulfilled. So the New Testament quotes these psalms as testimonies to Christ, which, in their unique way, they are. In Him, they are truly fulfilled. Thus, they are often called Messianic Psalms, since they portray aspects of the coming Messiah.

In the Psalms, when righteous sufferers—who are "righteous" because they are innocent, not having provoked or wronged their adversaries, and because they are among "the humble" (or "the poor") who trust in the Lord—cry out to God in their distress (as in Psalms 22; 69), they give voice to the sufferings of God's servants in a hostile and evil world.

These cries became the prayers of God's oppressed "saints," and as such, they were included in Israel's book of prayers. When Christ came in the flesh, He identified Himself with God's "humble" people in the world. He became for them God's righteous servant par excellence, and He shared their sufferings at the hands of evil men. Thus, these prayers became His prayers also—uniquely His prayers. In Him, the suffering and deliverance of which these prayers speak are fulfilled (though they continue to be the prayers also of those who take up their cross and follow Him).

Similarly, in speaking of God's covenant people, of the city of God, and of the temple in which God dwells, the Psalms ultimately speak of Christ's church. The Psalter is not only the prayer book of the second temple; it is also the enduring prayer book of the people of God. Now, however, it must be used in the light of the new era of redemption that dawned with the first coming of the Messiah and that will be consummated at His second coming.

Outline

Book 1: Psalms 1–41
Book 2: Psalms 42–72
Book 3: Psalms 73–89
Book 4: Psalms 90–106
Book 5: Psalms 107–150

Bibliography

Allen, Leslie C. *Psalms 101–150*. Word Biblical Commentary 21. Waco, TX: Word, 1983.

Alter, Robert. *The Art of Biblical Poetry*. New York: Basic, 1985.

Anderson, Bernhard W. *Out of the Depths: The Psalms Speak for Us Today*. 3rd edition. Louisville: Westminster John Knox, 2000.

Bellinger, W. H. *Psalms: Reading and Studying the Book of Praises*. Peabody, MA: Hendrickson, 1990.

Broyles, Craig C. *Psalms*. New International Biblical Commentary. Peabody, MA: Hendrickson, 1999.

Brueggemann, Walter. *The Message of the Psalms*. Minneapolis: Augsburg, 1984.

Bullock, C. Hassell. *Encountering the Book of Psalms: A Literary and Theological Introduction*. Grand Rapids, MI: Baker, 2001.

Craigie, Peter C. *Psalms 1–50*. Word Biblical Commentary 19. Waco, TX: Word, 1983.

Gunkel, Hermann. *The Psalms: A Form-Critical Introduction*. Translated by T. M. Horner. Philadelphia: Fortress, 1967.

Holladay, William L. *The Psalms through Three Thousand Years*. Minneapolis: Fortress, 1993.

Kidner, Derek. *Psalms 1–72*. Tyndale Old Testament Commentaries 14A. Downers Grove, IL: InterVarsity, 1973.

———. *Psalms 73–150*. Tyndale Old Testament Commentaries 14B. Downers Grove, IL: InterVarsity, 1975.

Kirkpatrick, A. F. *The Book of Psalms*. Cambridge: Cambridge University Press, 1957.

Longman, Tremper III. *How to Read the Psalms*. Downers Grove, IL: InterVarsity, 1988.

Mays, James L. *Psalms*. Interpretation: A Bible Commentary for Teaching and Preaching. Louisville: John Knox, 1994.

McCann, J. Clinton, Jr. *A Theological Introduction to the Book of Psalms: The Psalms as Torah*. Nashville: Abingdon, 1993.

Miller, Patrick D. *The Psalms and the Life of Faith*. Minneapolis: Augsburg Fortress, 1995.

———. *They Cried to the Lord: The Form and Theology of Biblical Prayer*. Minneapolis: Fortress, 1994.

Murphy, Roland. *The Gift of the Psalms*. Peabody, MA: Hendrickson, 2000.

Ross, Allen P. "Psalms." In *The Bible Knowledge Commentary: Old Testament*, edited by John F. Walvoord and Roy B. Zuck. Wheaton, IL: Victor, 1985.

Tate, Marvin E. *Psalms 51–100*. Word Biblical Commentary 20. Waco, TX: Word, 1990.

Terrien, Samuel. *The Psalms: Strophic Structure and Theological Commentary*. Eerdmans Critical Commentary. Grand Rapids, MI: Eerdmans, 2003.

Weiser, Artur. *The Psalms*. Old Testament Library. Philadelphia: Westminster, 1962.

Westermann, Claus. *Praise and Lament in the Psalms*. Translated by K. R. Crim and R. N. Soulen. Atlanta: John Knox, 1981.

Wilson, Gerald H. *Psalms, vol. 1*. The NIV Application Commentary. Grand Rapids, MI: Zondervan, 2002.

EXPOSITION

Book 1: Psalms 1–41

Psalm 1. This wisdom psalm contrasts the final outcome of the two "ways": "the way of the ungodly" (v. 1) and "the way of the righteous" (v. 6; see 34:19–22; 37).

As an introduction to the book, this psalm is a reminder that the one who truly desires to worship the Lord must be characterized by righteousness. Sinners have no place in the worshiping community (v. 5; see Psalms 15; 24). In its essence, godly piety is a faithful response to God's revealed (and written) directives for life, which is the path that leads to blessedness. The fivefold division of the Psalms perhaps recalls the five books of the Mosaic law and demonstrates that fidelity to the law and praiseful worship are perfect complements.

1:1–4. The psalmist begins with a description of the righteous man (vv. 1–3). **Blessed** (v. 1) is the happy condition of those who revere the Lord and do His will (94:12; 112:1; 119:1–2; 128:1), who put their trust in Him (40:4; 84:5, 12) and therefore are blessed by God (41:1–3; 144:12–14; Matt. 5:3–12). Godliness has both negative and positive dimensions. Negatively, the righteous refuse to participate in the ways of ungodliness. The verbs **walketh not** (v. 1), **standeth**, and **sitteth** portray the progressively corrupting influence of the wicked, which the righteous man avoids. Positively, the righteous man seeks guidance for life in God's **law** (v. 2) rather than in the deliberations of the wicked. The simile **like a tree ... shall not wither** (v. 3) describes the blessedness of the righteous. Such a tree withstands the buffeting of the winds, and flourishing, it blesses man, animals, and birds with its unfailing fruit and shade.

1:4–6. The fate of the ungodly is precisely the opposite of the righteous. They are like **chaff** (v. 4), which is carried away by the lightest wind, and its removal brings about cleansing by extracting what is utterly useless (see Ruth 1:22). They will **not stand** (v. 5) against God's wrath when He judges (see 76:7; 130:3; Matt. 25:31–46; Rev. 6:17). The wicked are also excluded from **the congregation of the righ-**teous who worship at God's sanctuary (see 22:25; 26:12; 111:1; 149:1). The judgment of the wicked in the Psalms includes not only the final judgment but also their destruction in this life as well (see 73:18–20; 92:7–9). The image of the two "ways" in verse 6 refers both to the contrasting lifestyles of godliness and wickedness and to their contrasting destinies.

Psalm 2. A psalm celebrating the special relationship between the Lord and the Davidic king and proclaiming the ultimate dominion of the Davidic king over the nations.

This royal psalm was originally composed for the coronation of Davidic kings, in light of the Lord's covenant with David (see 2 Samuel 7). The author and date of this psalm is unknown. Peter and John ascribed it to David in Acts 4:25, possibly in accordance with the Jewish practice of honoring David as the primary author of the Psalter. As a coronation song, the psalm expresses the wishes and aspirations associated with the reign of each individual ruler in the Davidic line. Later prophetic announcements of God's future redemption of His people through an exalted royal son of David highlighted the messianic import of this psalm. As the second half of a two-part introduction to the Psalms, it proclaims the blessedness of all who acknowledge the lordship of God and His anointed and "put their trust in him" (v. 12). This psalm is frequently quoted in the New Testament, where it is applied to Christ as the great Son of David and God's Anointed.

2:1–6. The nations rebel **against the LORD, and ... his anointed** (v. 2). The "anointed" refers to the Davidic king and is ultimately fulfilled in Christ. The English word "Messiah" comes from the Hebrew word for "anointed one," and the English word "Christ" comes from the Greek word (*christos*) for "anointed one." To rebel against the Lord's anointed is also to rebel against the One who anointed Him. In the ancient Near East, the coronation of a new king was often the occasion for the revolt of peoples and kings who had been subject to the crown. The newly anointed king is here pictured as a ruler over an empire. The Lord mocks the rebels who dare to challenge His authority (vv. 4–6). With derisive laughter, the Lord meets the confederacy of rebellious world powers with the sovereign declaration that it is He who has established the Davidic **king** (v. 6) in His own royal city of **Zion** (Jerusalem).

2:7–9. The Lord's king himself proclaims the Lord's coronation decree: **Thou art my Son; This day have I begotten thee** (v. 7). In the ancient Near East, the relationship between a great king and one of his subject kings, who ruled by his authority and owed him allegiance, was expressed not only by the words "lord" and "servant" but also by "father" and "son." The Davidic king was the Lord's "servant" and His "son" (2 Sam. 7:5, 14). The word "begotten" indicates the initiation of this relationship on the day of the king's coronation. This passage does not teach that Jesus the Son is "begotten" (created/born) of the Father or that the Father eternally generates the Son. The New Testament applies this proclamation to the resurrection of Jesus in Acts 13:33; the resurrection demonstrates the divine sonship of Jesus and initiates a new aspect of Christ's rule and reign. The Lord promises the Davidic ruler dominion over the uttermost parts of the earth. Ultimately, the rule of Christ will extend as far as the rule of God Himself. According to Revelation 12:5; 19:15, this promise will be fulfilled in the triumphant reign of Christ.

2:10–12. The rebellious rulers are given a final warning. They are to **Serve the Lord** (v. 11) by joyfully acknowledging the Davidic king as His human vice-regent. They are to **Kiss the Son** (v. 12) as a sign of honor and submission (see 1 Sam. 10:1; 1 Kings 19:18). Submission to an ancient king was often expressed by kissing his feet.

Psalm 3. Though threatened by many foes, the psalmist confidently trusts in the Lord and prays for deliverance from his enemies.

References to events in David's life are found in the superscriptions of thirteen psalms (3; 7; 18; 34; 51–52; 54; 56–57; 59–60; 63; 142); all but one (Psalm 142) of these are in books 1 and 2 of the Psalter. David is presented as a model worshiper who turns to the Lord when facing various forms of adversity, and David's flight from Absalom provides the backdrop for this psalm (see 2 Sam. 15:13–17:22).

3:1–6. When describing their oppression by the wicked (vv. 1–2), the psalmists frequently quote their wicked oppressors to portray how they mock God and His servants (see 22:7–8; 71:10–11). **Selah** (vv. 2, 4, 8) is a word of uncertain meaning, occurring frequently in the Psalms—possibly a musical term; see Introduction: "Literary Features."

Despite his troubles, David is confident that God will not fail to answer his prayers (vv. 3–4). It is frequently asserted that the Lord is the **shield** (v. 3) of His people (see 18:2, 30; 28:7; 33:20; 119:114; 144:2), and the idea of a king as one's shield (protector) was a common concept in ancient Israel (see 7:10; 47:9; 59:11; 84:9; 89:18; Gen. 15:1). The Lord will lift up David's **head** in victory over his enemies (see 110:7). David has absolute security in the Lord's protection (vv. 5–6). Even while his own watchfulness is surrendered to sleep, the watchful Lord preserves him (see 4:8).

3:7–8. David's prayer is for the Lord to quickly **Arise** (v. 7) and **save** him from his enemies. Hebrew idiom frequently prefaces an imperative asking for immediate action with the call to "arise" (see Exod. 12:31; Deut. 2:13; Judg. 7:9). David is so certain of the defeat of his enemies that he speaks as if it has already happened. The statement that God has **broken the teeth of the ungodly** likens the enemies to wild animals (see 7:2). A common feature in the prayers of the Psalter is a concluding expression of confidence that the prayer will be or has been heard: **Salvation belongeth unto the Lord** (v. 8; as in 6:8–10; 7:10–17; 10:16–18; 12:7; 13:5–6 and elsewhere). Here David's confidence becomes a testimony to God's people.

Psalms 3 and 4 are linked by references to "glory" (see v. 3; 4:2) and to the psalmist's sleep at night (see v. 5; 4:8). In verse 5, David speaks of the assurance of his waking in the morning because the Lord will keep him while he sleeps; in 4:8 he speaks of the inner quietness with which he goes to sleep because of the Lord's care. This juxtaposition of prayers with references to waking (morning) and sleeping (evening) at the beginning of the Psalter suggests that God's faithful care sustains the godly day and night, whatever the need or circumstances, many of which are mentioned in this book of prayers.

Psalm 4. A prayer for relief when some calamity (possibly drought; see v. 7) has befallen the nation and many are turning from the Lord to the gods of Canaan.

4:1–4. After an initial request to be heard (v. 1), David rebukes those who turn away from his God to seek relief from the counterfeit gods; he assures them that the Lord will hear him (vv. 2–3). The question **how long** (v. 2) expresses David's anguish over not (yet) being delivered from his enemies and exhibits the boldness with which the psalmists would question and wrestle with God. Though deliverance is delayed, the Lord will preserve the **godly** (v. 3) because of His special relationship with them. The Hebrew *hasid* for "godly" is one of several Hebrew words for God's people, referring to them as people who are or should be devoted to God and faithful to Him. This term is often translated "saint" in the KJV.

4:5–8. Following this statement of confidence, the psalmist exhorts the godly not to give way to exasperation or anxiety but to look to the Lord, to continually reflect on His greatness, and to persevere in their **sacrifices of righteousness** (v. 5). Right worship comes from having a right heart toward God (see 51:9). While adversity causes many to turn to other gods, which they believe will bring them **good** (v. 6), the righteous recognize that the **light** of God's **countenance** is their only source of blessing (vv. 6–8). The light of God's face is a common expression of favor, reminiscent of the Aaronic benediction (see Num. 6:25–26). The Lord rewards the faith of the godly with **gladness** (v. 7) of contentment and the **peace** (v. 8) of security.

Psalm 5. This morning prayer, perhaps offered at the time of the morning sacrifice, is the psalmist's cry for help when his enemies spread malicious lies to destroy him.

5:1–8. The psalmist makes an initial cry to God as King (vv. 1–3) and then appeals to the righteousness of God's rule over mankind in his request that the Lord deliver him from his enemies (vv. 4–6). The Lord has a righteous hatred for the wicked and will destroy those who **speak leasing** ("lies, falsehood"; v. 6).

David presents his plea to the Lord in humble reverence, trusting in the Lord's great **mercy** (v. 7) and **righteousness** (v. 8). Very often, the "righteousness" of God in the Psalms (and frequently elsewhere in the Old Testament) refers to the faithfulness with which He acts. This faithfulness is in full accordance with His commitments (both expressed and implied) to His people and with His status as the Divine King, to whom the powerless may look for protection, the oppressed for redress, and the needy for help. In his request, **Make thy way straight**, David is asking that the Lord would lead him on a path that is straight, level, and free from the obstacle of temptation. He prays that God will so direct him that his enemies will have no grounds for their malicious accusations (see 25:4; 27:11; 139:24; 143:8–10).

5:9–10. In providing the motivation for the Lord to act on his behalf, David levels an accusation against his enemies (a common element in the prayers of the Psalter) and calls for a redress. The most frequent weapon used against the psalmists is the tongue (see 10:7; 12). The speech of the wicked is like an **open sepulchre** (v. 9), reflecting their inward corruption. (For the plots and intrigues of enemies, usually involving lies to discredit the king and bring him down, see Psalms 17; 25; 27–28; 31; 35; 41; 52; 54–57; 59; 63–64; 71; 86; 109; 140–141.) Frequently, such attacks come when the king is "low" and seemingly abandoned by God (as in Psalms 25; 35; 41; 71; 86; 109). In that case, he is viewed as no longer fit to be king—God is no longer with him (and so he can no longer secure the safety of the nation; see 1 Sam. 8:20; 11:12; 2 Sam. 3:18; 7:9–11). In any event, he is an easy prey at such times (see 3:2; 22:7–8; 71:11).

The psalmist pray for God to **Destroy** (v. 10) the wicked who slander him. The presence of these so-called imprecations (curses) in the Psalms has occasioned endless discussion and has caused many Christians to wince, in view of Jesus' instructions to turn the other cheek and to pray for one's enemies (see Matt. 5:39, 44) and of His own example on the cross (see Luke 23:34). Actually, these "imprecations" are not that at all; rather, they are appeals to God to redress wrongs perpetrated against the psalmists, by imposing penalties commensurate with the violence done (see 28:4). They had devised destruction for David through their words; they should receive that destruction themselves. In calling for the Lord to redress the wrong done to him, David leaves the execution of justice to the Lord rather than taking vengeance into his own hands (see Deut. 32:35; Prov. 20:22; Rom. 12:19). The psalmist calls for God to **Cast ... out** the wicked from His presence, thus from the source of blessing and life (see Gen. 3:23). They deserve this punishment because they have **rebelled against** the Lord. When they attack the Lord's anointed, it is as if they are attacking the Lord Himself.

5:11 – 12. The psalmist expands his prayer to include all the godly who **love** the **name** (v. 11) of the Lord. The name of the Lord is the manifestation of His character (see Exod. 3:14 – 15; 34:6 – 7) and is synonymous with the Lord Himself in His gracious manifestation and accessibility to His people. Hence, the Jerusalem temple is the earthly residence of His name among His people (see 74:7; Deut. 12:5, 11; 2 Sam. 7:13), and His people can pray to Him by calling on His name (see 79:6; 80:18; 99:6; 105:1; 116:4, 13, 17). The Lord saves by His name (see 54:1); and His saving acts testify that His name is good (see 52:9). Accordingly, the godly trust in His name (20:7; 33:21), hope in His name (see 52:9), "sing praise" to His name (7:17; 9:2; 18:49), and "rejoice" in His name (89:16). The character of God, reflected in His name, gives the psalmist confidence that the Lord will **bless** (v. 12) and protect the **righteous**.

Psalm 6. A prayer offered in time of severe illness, an occasion David's enemies seize to vent their animosity.

6:1 – 3. In this prayer, the initial cry of the psalmist is a plea for mercy. Though the Lord has sent him illness to chastise him for his sin (see 32:3 – 5; 38:1 – 8, 17 – 18), the psalmist asks that God would not **in ... anger** (v. 1) impose the full measure of the

penalty for sin. David has suffered greatly under the Lord's chastisement. The **bones** (v. 2), as the inner skeleton, represent the whole body. Similarly, the **soul** (v. 3) refers not to a spiritual aspect distinct from the physical, nor to the "inner" being in contrast to the "outer" being, but rather to the very self as a living, conscious, personal being. Thus, "bones" and "soul" are two ways of referring to himself—his suffering has afflicted his entire person. His agony leads to his impatient cry, **O Lord, how long?**

6:4 – 5. David makes an earnest prayer for deliverance from death. If the Lord imposes the full measure of His anger, death will surely come. Rather than wrath, the psalmist asks for mercy (v. 4). "Mercy" in Hebrew denotes befriending and can be translated "lovingkindness" or "unfailing love." Appeal to God's mercy is frequent in the Old Testament since it summarizes all that the Lord covenanted to show to Israel (see Deut. 7:9, 12) as well as to David and his dynasty (see 89:24, 28, 33; 2 Sam. 7:15; Isa. 55:3). The psalmist urges that God's praise, not just his physical life, is at stake (v. 5). It is the living, not the dead, who remember and celebrate God's mercies.

The Israelites usually viewed death as they saw it, as the very opposite of life, and resurrection was not yet a part of their communal experience with God. The grave brought no escape from God (see 139:8), but just how they viewed the condition of the godly dead is not clear. Nonbiblical documents from the ancient Near East indicate a general conception that the dead continued to have some kind of shadowy existence in the dismal netherworld. The Old Testament writers knew that man was created for life and that God had power over life and death. They also knew that death was every man's lot, and at its proper time, the godly rested in God and accepted it with equanimity (see Gen. 15:15; 25:8; 47:30; 49:33; 1 Kings 2:2). Death could even be a blessing for the righteous, affording escape from the greater evil that would overtake the living (see 2 Kings 22:20; Isa. 57:1 – 2). Furthermore, the death of the righteous was reputedly better than that of the wicked (see Num. 23:10). It seems clear that there was an awareness that death is not the end for the righteous, that God had more in store for them (see 16:9–11; 17:15; 49:14–15; 73:24; see Gen. 5:24). When the psalmists wrestled with God for the preservation of life, it was death, in its radical contradiction to life, that was evoked.

6:6–10. David's lament expresses in vivid detail his nightly anguish because of the prolongation of the illness and the barbs of the enemies (vv. 6–7). **I am weary with my groaning** (v. 6) stands at the very center of the poem, thus underscoring the pathos of this prayer. This literary device—placing a key thematic line at the very center of the psalm—is frequently used (see 8:4; 21:7; 23:4; 34:8–14; 42:8; 47:5–6; 48:8; 54:4; 71:14; 74:12; 76:7; 82:5a; 86:9; 92:8; 97:7; 113:5; 138:4–5; 141:5). The dimming of the **eye** (v. 7) is a powerful figure for David's loss of physical health and vitality (see 31:9; 38:10; Jer. 14:6). The psalm concludes with an expression of buoyant confidence (vv. 8–10). The psalmist is certain of the Lord's response to his **prayer** (v. 9), and when he is restored, his **enemies** (v. 10) will be disgraced.

Psalm 7. An appeal to the Lord's court of justice when enemies attack.

The superscription makes reference to **Cush**, a figure otherwise unknown but, as a **Benjamite**, likely a supporter of Saul, thus associating this psalm with the time of Saul's determined attempts on David's life.

7:1–5. In David's initial summation of his appeal, he compares the attack of his enemy to that of a **lion** (v. 2). As a young shepherd, David had been attacked by lions (see 1 Sam. 17:34–35), but it is also a convention in the Psalms to liken the attack of enemies to that of ferocious animals, especially the lion (see 10:9; 22:12–13, 16, 20–21). David pleads his innocence; he has given his enemy no cause to attack him (vv. 3–5). He invites the Lord to allow his enemy to put him to death if he is guilty of wrongdoing.

7:6–9. The petition proper is an appeal to the Judge of all the earth to execute His judgment over all peoples, and particularly to adjudicate David's cause. David asks the Lord to **awake for me** (v. 6). The Lord does not sleep while evil prevails (see 121:4), but the psalmists' language of urgent prayer vividly expresses their anguished impatience with God's inaction

in the face of their great need (see 80:2; Isa. 51:9). When asking the Lord to judge him on the basis of his **righteousness** (v. 8), the psalmist is not claiming sinless perfection but rather is claiming the rightness of his cause against his enemies. The Lord knows what is right in this conflict between David and his enemies because He tests **the hearts and reins** (lit., "hearts and kidneys"; v. 9) of all men. The Israelites used these two words as virtual synonyms (but used "heart" most often) to refer to man's innermost center of conscious life (see 4:7). Speaking of searching the mind and heart was a conventional expression for God's examination of man's hidden character and motives (see Jer. 11:20; 17:10; 20:12).

7:10–17. David has absolute confidence that his prayer will be heard (vv. 10–13). The Lord delivers those who are **upright in heart** (v. 10) but is **angry with the wicked every day** (v. 11). God's judgments are not all kept in store for some future day. David further comforts himself with the common wisdom that under God's rule, "crime does not pay" (vv. 14–16). The psalm concludes with a vow to **praise** (v. 17) the Lord. Many prayers in the Psalter include such vows in anticipation of the expected answer to prayer. They reflect Israel's religious consciousness that praise must follow deliverance as surely as prayer springs from need—if God is to be truly honored. Such praise was usually offered with thank offerings and involved celebrating God's saving act in the presence of those assembled at the temple (see 50:14–15, 23). Rather than being a bargain with God or an attempt to manipulate Him, these vows are expressions of confidence in the answer to prayer before it arrives.

Psalm 8. A hymn in praise of the Creator, expressing wonder over His sovereign ordering of the creation and the exalted role given to humanity in the creation.

In this reflection on God as Creator, two matters especially impress the psalmist: (1) the glory of God reflected in the starry heavens and (2) the astonishing condescension of God to be mindful of puny man, to crown him with almost godlike glory, and to grant him lordly power over His creatures.

The psalm's chiastic structure reflects the primacy of these two themes.

8:1–5. The mighty God, whose **glory** (v. 1) is displayed across the face of the **heavens**, appoints and evokes the praise of little children to silence the dark powers arrayed against Him (vv. 1–2; for a New Testament application, see Matt. 21:16). As Judge, He silences **the avenger** (v. 2), the one who strikes back in malicious revenge against the righteous (see 44:16). The vastness and majesty of the **heavens** (v. 3) as the handiwork of God (see 19:1–6; 104:19–23) evoke wonder for what their Maker has done for little man, who is here today and gone tomorrow (vv. 3–5; see 19:1–6; 104:19–23). The Hebrew for **What** (v. 4) is translated "how" in verses 1 and 9 and begins the line focusing on humanity's place in creation, which serves as the center of the psalm. The Lord attends to and takes care of (**visitest**; v. 4) the needs of humanity. The Lord has also given man an exalted place of honor that is only **a little lower than the angels** (v. 5). The word 'elohim can be translated either "God" or "angels," and the KJV follows the Septuagint (the Greek translation of the Old Testament) in reading the latter. If "God" is taken as the correct translation, the point is related to Genesis 1:26–27 and the fact that man bears the image of God. If "angels" are in view, the point is that man, an earthly creature, bears a glory that is only slightly less than the heavenly beings in the presence of God. Whichever option is chosen, the idea is that feeble humans are **crowned** with the greatest possible **glory**. Hebrews 2:6–8, quoting the Septuagint, applies these verses to Jesus, who as the incarnate Son of God is both the representative Man and the One in whom man's appointed destiny will be fully realized. The author of Hebrews thus makes use of the eschatological implications of these words in his testimony of Christ. Paul does the same with verse 6 in 1 Corinthians 15:27 (see also Eph. 1:22). Christ's work of redemption for sinful humanity will ultimately restore man to his exalted position.

8:6–9. The key component of man's exaltation is his position of **dominion over** (v. 6) the creation (vv. 6–8; see Gen. 1:26–27). Man's rule is real—a

part of his "glory and honour" (v. 5)—and it is his destiny that will be realized in the future kingdom of God. It is not, however, absolute or independent. It is participation, as a subordinate, in God's rule; and it is a gift, not a right. After focusing on humanity, the psalm closes by returning to the theme of God's greatness; verse 9 repeats verse 1a verbatim.

Psalm 9. Praise for God's deliverance from the enemies that have attacked the king and his people.

That Psalms 9 and 10 were sometimes viewed (or used) as one psalm is known from the Septuagint (the Greek translation of the Old Testament). Whether they were originally composed as one psalm is not known, though a number of indicators point in that direction. Psalm 10 is the only psalm from Psalms 3 to 32 that has no superscription, and the Hebrew text of the two psalms together appears to reflect an incomplete (or broken) acrostic structure. The first letter of each verse or pair of verses tends to follow the order of the Hebrew alphabet near the beginning of Psalm 9 and again near the end of Psalm 10. The thoughts also tend to be developed in two-verse units throughout. Psalm 9 is predominantly praise (by the king) for God's deliverance from hostile nations. It concludes with a short prayer for God's continuing righteous judgments (see v. 4) on the haughty nations. Psalm 10 is predominantly prayer against the rapacity of unscrupulous men within the realm—as arrogant and wicked in their dealings with "the poor" (10:2) as the nations were in their attacks on Israel (10:2–11). The attacks of "the wicked" (9:5; 10:4), whether from within or from without, on the godly community are equally threatening to true Israel. Praise of God's past deliverances is often an integral part of prayer in the Psalter (see 25:6; 40:1–5), as also in other ancient Near Eastern prayers. Such praise expressed the ground of the psalmist's hope that his present prayer would be heard, and it also functioned to motivate the Lord to act once more on His people's (or His servant's) behalf.

9:1–9. The initial announcement of praise (vv. 1–2) reflects the psalmist's desire to **shew forth** (v. 1) the greatness of the Lord. Praise of God in the Psalter is rarely a private matter between the psalmist and the Lord. It is usually a public celebration (at the temple) of God's holy virtues, His saving acts, or His gracious bestowal of blessings. In his praise, the psalmist proclaims to the assembled throng God's glorious attributes or His righteous deeds. To this, he usually adds a call to praise, summoning all who hear to acknowledge and joyfully celebrate God's glory, His goodness, and all His righteous acts. This aspect of praise in the Psalms has rightly been called the Old Testament anticipation of New Testament evangelism. The focus of praise here is God's **marvellous works**, His saving acts that demonstrate His sovereign power. The Lord has **turned back** (v. 3) the enemy nations that have attacked His people.

In destroying the enemies, God has redressed the wrongs they committed against David (and Israel; vv. 3–6). He has **put out** the **name** (v. 5) of the wicked, blotting it out as if from a register of mankind written on a papyrus scroll (see Num. 5:23; see also Deut. 9:14; 25:19; 29:20; 2 Kings 14:27). Their defeat is final and irreversible. The Lord's victory causes the psalmist to celebrate God's righteous rule, which evokes trust in those who look to the Lord (vv. 7–10). The permanence of the Lord's sovereignty provides a **refuge for the oppressed** (v. 9).

9:10–14. David calls the assembly at the temple to praise God for His righteous judgments (vv. 11–12). In executing His righteous judgment, the Lord makes **inquisition for blood** (lit., "seeks blood"; v. 12). God "seeks" justice for **them that seek** (v. 10) him. The Lord functions as the kinsman redeemer, who had the responsibility of avenging the death of a family member (see Num. 35:9–34). In his praise, David recalls how the Lord had answered his prayer by delivering him from death (vv. 13–14). Having been thrust down by the attacks of his enemies to **the gates of death** (v. 13), David prays to be lifted up so he can celebrate his deliverance **in the gates of ... Zion** (v. 14).

9:17–20. Under the Lord's just rule, those who wickedly attack others bring destruction on themselves, and their end will be the grave (**hell**; v. 17). Those who are attacked do not trust in the Lord in vain. David and Israel are counted among **the needy** (v. 18) and **the poor** because of the threat from the enemies. At the conclusion of praise is a prayer asking that the Lord may ever rule over the nations as He has done in the event here celebrated so that those who **forget God** (v. 17) may know that they are only men, not gods, and cannot withstand the God of Israel (vv. 19–20).

Psalm 10. A prayer for rescue from the attacks of unscrupulous men. This psalm contains a classic Old Testament portrayal of "the wicked."

10:1–11. Under attack from his enemies, the psalmist impatiently cries for the Lord to act on his behalf (v. 1). It appears as if the Lord is hiding when the wicked go unpunished. A lengthy accusation is lodged against the psalmist's oppressors (vv. 2–11). Both their deeds and words betray the arrogance with which they defy God. They greedily seek to glut their unrestrained appetites by victimizing others, not considering that they have to contend with God (v. 4; see also 14:1; 36:1; 53:1). The three most common weapons of their tongues are **cursing and deceit and fraud** (v. 7). The ancient Near Eastern peoples thought that pronouncing curses on someone could bring down the power of the gods (or other mysterious powers) on that person and they had a large conventional stock of such curses. The wicked employ slander and false testimony for malicious purposes (see, e.g., 1 Kings 21:8–15). The arrogance with which the wicked speak, especially their easy dismissal of God's knowledge of their evil acts and His unfailing prosecution of their malicious deeds, is frequently noted by the psalmists (see v. 13; 12:4; 42:3, 10; 59:7; 64:5; 71:11; 73:11; 94:7; 115:2; see also Isa. 29:15; Ezek. 8:12).

10:12–18. The psalmist prays that God will call the wicked to account and deliver **the humble** (v. 12) who trust in Him and are at the mercy of the oppressors (vv. 12–15). The wicked are deserving of judgment because they have contempt for God and arrogantly claim that He will not punish their sinful actions. **Break thou the arm** (v. 15) is a request for God to destroy the strength that allows them to oppress others. The psalmist is confident in the answer to his prayer because of God's righteous reign (vv. 16–18). The conclusion to this psalm expands the vision of God's just rule to its universal scope and sets the purging of the Lord's **land** (v. 16) of all nations (**The heathen**) that do not acknowledge Him alongside God's judicial dealing with the wicked oppressors. Both belong to God's assertion of His righteous rule in the face of man's arrogant denial of it.

Psalm 11. A confession of confident trust in the Lord's righteous rule, at a time when wicked adversaries seem to have the upper hand.

11:1–3. David testifies of his unshakable trust in the Lord (his refuge) to the apprehensive people around him. These people, under attack from a powerful and ruthless enemy, fear that the **foundations** (v. 3) of the world order, in which good triumphs over evil, are crumbling (see 82:5). The only recourse is flight to a **mountain** (v. 1) refuge. David dismisses their fearful advice with disdain.

11:4–7. The psalmist replies to the fearful that the Lord is still securely on His heavenly **throne** (v. 4). The Lord examines and judges the character, motives, and actions of all men. He discerns **the righteous** (v. 5) to give them a place in His presence, while His judgment will **rain** (v. 6) on **the wicked**. The image of **fire and brimstone** (a slight emendation of the text would also render "burning coals" for **snares**) appears to recall God's judgment on Sodom and Gomorrah (see Gen. 19:24, 28; see Rev. 20:10; 21:8). The promise that **His countenance doth behold the upright** (v. 7) literally reads, "the upright will see His face." The Hebrew for "see the king's face" is an expression denoting access to the king (see Gen. 43:3, 5; 44:23, 26; 2 Sam. 3:13; 14:24, 28, 32). Sometimes it referred to those who served before the king (see 2 Kings 25:19; Est. 1:14). Here David speaks of special freedom of access before the heavenly King. He is no doubt referring to His presence at the temple (God's earthly royal house), which is nonetheless the presence of the One who sits on the heavenly throne. Ultimate access to the heavenly temple may also be implied (see 16:11; 17:15; see also 23:6; 140:13).

Psalm 12. A prayer for help when it seems that all men are faithless and every tongue false (see Mic. 7:1–7).

12:1–8. The psalmist turns to God in distress over the absence of **godly** (v. 1) and **faithful** people

who maintain moral integrity (vv. 1–2). Lying and falsehood pervaded the culture of his day. David's prayer is that God will put an end to (**cut off**; v. 3) the **proud** who believe that they can accomplish whatever they will through their clever speech (vv. 3–4). The Lord responds to David's prayer with a reassuring word (vv. 5–6).

Such words of assurance following prayer in the Psalms were perhaps spoken by a priest (see 1 Sam. 1:17) or a prophet (see 51:8; 2 Sam. 12:13). It may be that abrupt transitions from prayer to confidence in the Psalms presuppose such priestly or prophetic words, even when they are not contained in the psalm. Here the Lord promises that He will preserve and protect the godly from the hateful and maligning words of their enemies. **The words of the Lord** (v. 6) in their purity and perfection, as flawless as thoroughly refined **silver**, are set in sharp contrast with the boastful words of the adversaries. The number **seven** signifies fullness or completeness—here thoroughness of refining. The psalmist remains fully confident in the Lord's protection, even though the wicked think they have the upper hand and strut about with pride and arrogance (vv. 7–8).

Psalm 13. A cry to the Lord for deliverance from a serious illness that threatens death, which would give David's enemies just what they wanted.

13:1–6. The psalm opens with an anguished complaint concerning a prolonged illness (vv. 1–2). In moments of need, the psalmists frequently ask God why He hides His **face** (v. 1; see 30:7; 44:24; 88:14), or they plead with Him not to do so (see 27:9; 69:17; 102:2; 143:7). When He hides His face, those who depend on Him can only despair (see 30:7; 104:29). When His face shines on a person, blessing and deliverance come (see 4:6; 31:16; 67:1; 119:135). Following his lament, the psalmist appeals for deliverance from **death** (v. 3). Unless the Lord intervenes, David's death will cause his enemies to exult and to believe in the rightness of their unjust cause. The concluding expression of confidence (vv. 4–6) expresses David's trust in the **mercy** (v. 5) of the Lord. It is David who will **rejoice**, not his enemies.

Psalm 14. A testimony concerning the folly of evil men who refuse to acknowledge God.

This psalm has many links with Psalms 10 and 12. It shares the view of Psalm 11, that the righteous Lord is on the throne, and it stands in contrast with Psalm 15, which describes those who are acceptable to God. Psalm 53 is a somewhat revised duplicate of this psalm.

14:1–3. The psalmist opens with a characterization of the wicked. The Hebrew words rendered "fool" in Psalms denote one who is morally deficient. This deficiency stems from the belief that **There is no God** (v. 1), a practical atheism in which one chooses to live as if God does not exist and one is not ultimately accountable to Him (see 10:4, 6, 11, 13; 36:1). **The Lord** (v. 2) is emphatically contrasted with **The fool** (v. 1). No matter how much such people try to put God out of their consciousness, their lives stand under His evaluation. The statement **There is none that doeth good** (vv. 1, 3) further describes those who take no account of God and do not hesitate to show their malice toward the godly—as in 9:19–20; 10:2–11; 12:1–4, 7–8. Elsewhere the psalmists include themselves among those who are not righteous in God's eyes (130:3; 143:2; see 1 Kings 8:46; Job 9:2; Eccl. 7:20). Paul uses these verses (Rom. 3:10–12) to demonstrate that all humanity lives under the power of sin.

14:4–7. The folly of the wicked is exposed in verses 4–6. They live by the violence of their own hands and do not rely on the Lord. The two lines in verse 5 contrast the wicked and the righteous. The wicked live **in great fear** (v. 5), a dread of God's coming judgment that is real despite their pretense of self-sufficiency. **The generation of the righteous** have no such fears because they know God is with them. Though the righteous may become **poor** (v. 6) as the victims of injustice, God will ultimately be their **refuge.** The psalmist longs for Israel's complete deliverance from her enemies, which will come when God deals with the wicked in defense of their victims (v. 7). The closing statement looks beyond the individual psalmist to the exilic community in Babylon, who long for the Lord to **bringeth back the captivity of his people** (see 126:1).

Psalm 15. Instruction to those who wish to have access to God at His temple (see also 24:3–6).

15:1–5. The psalm opens with a question as to who may **abide** (v. 1) as God's guest in His holy, royal house, the temple (see 23:6; 27:4–6; 84:10; 2 Sam. 12:20). The answer is that it is not sacrifices or ritual purity that grants access to the Lord (as among the religions of the ancient Near East) but rather moral righteousness (vv. 2–5; see Isa. 1:10–17; 33:14–16; 58:6–10; Jer. 7:2–7; Ezek. 18:5–9; Amos 5:21–24; Mic. 6:6–8). This moral righteousness includes integrity, proper conduct, truthful speech, concern for others, and hatred of evil. Those who reverence (**fear**; v. 4) God order their lives in accordance with His will. They keep their promises even when it costs or is inconvenient (**sweareth to his own hurt**). In accordance with the Mosaic law, the righteous are not to charge interest on loans (**putteth not out … to usury**; v. 5; see Exod. 22:25–27) or take bribes against innocent persons (see Deut. 27:25). The reward for the godly is that they will never be moved; they enjoy fellowship with God and the security that comes from living in His presence.

Psalm 16. A prayer for safekeeping, pleading for the Lord's protection against the threat of death. It could also be called a psalm of trust.

16:1–3. The petition is brief and to the point: **Preserve me, O God** (v. 1). The petition element in prayer psalms is often relatively short (see 3:7; 22:19–21; 44:23–26). The basis of the petition—David's loyal commitment to God (**Thou art my Lord**; v. 2)—is elaborated on in the remainder of the psalm. The Lord is David's one and only good thing (see 73:25, 28). The statement **My goodness extendeth not to thee** should be read, "I have no good apart from you." David will have nothing to do with the counterfeit gods to whom others pour out the **blood** (v. 4) of sacrifices on their altars. He will not speak the names of other gods to appeal to them or worship them.

16:4–6. In contrast to the multiplied **sorrows** (v. 4) of those who worship idols, David is filled with joy over the **inheritance** (v. 5) received from the Lord. This "inheritance" refers to what the Lord bestowed on His people in the Promised Land, either to the gift of fields there (see Num. 16:14) or to the Lord Himself (as in 73:26; 119:57), who was the inheritance of the priests (see Num. 18:20) and the Levites (see Deut. 10:9). The **cup** is a metaphor referring to what the host offers his guests to drink. To the godly, the Lord offers a cup of blessings (see 23:5) or salvation (see 116:13); to the wicked, He offers a cup of wrath (see Jer. 25:15; Rev. 14:10; 16:19). Just as each Israelite's family inheritance in the Promised Land was to be secure (see Leviticus 25; Num. 36:7), David is confident that the Lord will preserve and maintain his **lot**, and the boundary **lines** (v. 6) of his inheritance are pleasing to him. With the Lord's blessing, the psalmist is like a wealthy landowner; he has no need for other gods because the Lord has given him everything that he could possibly want.

16:7–11. The psalmist praises the Lord for counseling and keeping him (vv. 7–8). Through this **counsel** (v. 7), He has shown the way that leads to life. David's "mind" (**reins**; lit., "kidneys"; see 7:9) reflects on the truth he has learned from God. The Lord is always at David's **right hand** (v. 8), as Sustainer and Protector (see 73:23; 109:31). The joy of this total security in the Lord's protection is described in verses 9–11. Here, as in the rest of his psalms, David speaks first of all of the life he enjoys by the gracious provision and care of God. The Lord has led him on **the path of life** (v. 11) and will not abandon him to the grave (**hell**; v. 10). Implicit in these words of assurance is the confidence that, with the Lord as his refuge, even the grave cannot rob him of life (see 17:15; 73:24). If this could be said of David, how much more of David's promised Son. So Peter quotes verses 8–11 and declares that with these words, David prophesied of Christ and His resurrection (Acts 2:25–28; see Acts 13:35).

Psalm 17. The psalmist appeals to the Lord as Judge when under attack by ungodly foes.

17:1–5. The psalm reflects many of the Hebrew conventions of lodging a judicial appeal before the king and opens with an initial appeal for justice (vv. 1–2). David asks for the Lord's help because his case is truly just (**right**; v. 1), not a clever misrepresentation by deceitful lips. He then presents an extended claim of innocence in support of the rightness of his case (vv. 3–5). He is not guilty of the ungodly ways of his attackers. God's testing and examination of his heart has demonstrated the purity of his life (see 139:23–24). The psalmist has lived his life in accordance with **the word** (v. 4) of the Lord, by which He has made known the **paths** (v. 5) that people are to walk.

17:6–9. David petitions the Lord to hear his prayer, expressing his confidence that the Lord will answer him. He appeals to the Lord's unfailing righteousness, which will move the Lord to take up his cause. The psalmist asks for God to protect him as if he were **the apple** ("pupil"; v. 8) of His **eye** (see Deut. 32:10). David longs to rest in the security of **the shadow of** God's **wings**, using the metaphor of a bird protecting its young (see 36:7; 91:4; Ruth 2:12; Matt. 23:37).

17:10–15. The accusation lodged against the vicious adversaries is that they are **inclosed in their own fat** (lit., "have closed their fat"; v. 10); they have closed their calloused hearts to the Lord. They are proud and arrogant and stalk David like a **lion** (v. 12) hunting its **prey**. Returning to petition, the psalmist requests that the Lord deal with the two parties in the conflict (vv. 13–14a). He prays for God to wield His **sword** (v. 13) as Warrior, to deliver him by striking down his enemies. The opening line of verse 14 is difficult and should be read as suggested in the KJV marginal note: "From men by thine hand." David is asking the Lord Himself to directly intervene and defeat his enemies. The **men of the world** (v. 14) who oppose David **have their portion in this life** alone, and he is asking the Lord to take away the blessings of life (wealth and posterity) that they presently enjoy.

In his concluding confession of confidence (vv. 14b–15), David affirms that he will experience the blessings that come from seeing God's **face** (v. 15) and having access to the Lord as King. The righteous Judge will acknowledge and vindicate the innocent. David will be **satisfied** by seeing God's

likeness, as Moses, the servant of the Lord, had seen it (see Num. 12:8).

Psalm 18. The king's celebration of the Lord's protection and deliverance from death at the hands of his enemies.

The superscription identifies David as **the servant of the LORD** (see 78:70; 89:3, 20, 39; 132:10). This title designates David in his royal office as an official in the Lord's own kingly rule over His people—as were Moses (see *KJV Study Bible* note on Exod. 14:31), Joshua (see Josh. 24:29), and the prophets (Elijah, 2 Kings 9:36; Jonah, 2 Kings 14:25; Isaiah, Isa. 20:3; Daniel, Dan. 6:20). It appears that David composed this song shortly after his victories over his foreign enemies (see 2 Sam. 8:1–14).

This song of David occurs also (with minor variations) in 2 Samuel 22 (see discussions there). Apart from the introduction (vv. 1–3) and the conclusion (vv. 46–50), the song has three major divisions: (1) the Lord's deliverance of David from his mortal enemies (vv. 4–19), (2) the moral grounds for the Lord's saving help (vv. 20–29), and (3) the Lord's help recounted (vv. 30–45).

18:1–3. This prelude of praise emphasizes the fervor of David's **love** (v. 1) for the Lord. The LORD is [a] **rock** (v. 2) of security for David, which is a common poetic figure for God, symbolizing His unfailing strength as a **fortress** refuge (see vv. 31, 46; 31:2–3; 71:3; Isa. 17:10) or as deliverer (see 19:14; 89:26; 95:1; Deut. 32:15). This figure is particularly appropriate for David's experience, since he had often evaded his enemies by hiding out in the rocks (see 1 Sam. 23:14, 25; 24:2, 22; 26:20). The image of the Lord as **buckler** ("shield"; v. 2) also pictures the protection that the Lord provides for David. Just as a **horn** is the source of strength for many animals, the Lord gives strength to David (see Deut. 33:17; Jer. 48:25).

18:4–15. David gave an extended report of how the Lord had saved him and delivered him from his enemies (vv. 4–29). God heard David's cry when he was in mortal danger, which is described in highly poetic language (vv. 4–6). He had, as it were, been snared by **death** (personified; vv. 4–5) and bound as a prisoner of the grave (see Job 36:8). **The sorrows**

of hell (lit., "cords of Sheol," the grave; v. 5) were wrapped around him. God heard his prayer from His heavenly **temple** (v. 6) and responded to his cry as he was being carried away.

The Lord came to the aid of His servant, and His intervention is depicted as a fearful theophany (divine manifestation) of the heavenly Warrior descending in a wrathful attack on David's enemies (see 68:1–8; 77:16–19; Mic. 1:3–4; Nah. 1:2–6; Hab. 3:3–15). **He rode upon a cherub** (v. 10) refers to the Lord riding across the sky on His chariot-throne. The cherub is a symbol of royalty that often adorned the thrones of ancient Near Eastern kings (see 80:1; 99:1; Exod. 25:18; Ezek. 1:8–12; 10:9–12). The Lord covered Himself with the dark storm clouds and swept down on the enemy like a fierce thunderstorm (see Josh. 10:11; Judg. 5:20–22; 2 Sam. 5:24). The shafts of lightning were like the **arrows** (v. 14) of God (see 77:17; 144:6). God's awesome majesty is further portrayed in terms similar to those applied to the awesome leviathan (v. 15; see Job 41:19–21).

18:16–29. The Lord's deliverance was like a rescue at sea, with David about to drown in the midst of **many waters** (v. 16). The Lord removed him from danger and placed him in **a large place** (v. 19), where he was free to roam unconfined by the threats and dangers that had constrained him (vv. 4–6, 16–18). God rescued David because He delighted in David as "a man after his own heart" (1 Sam. 13:14; 15:28; 1 Kings 14:8), a man with whom He had made a covenant assuring him of an enduring dynasty (2 Samuel 7).

David's rescue demonstrates that the Lord rewards the righteous (vv. 20–24). The psalmist's assertion of his **righteousness** (v. 20; like that of Samuel, 1 Sam. 12:3; Hezekiah, 2 Kings 20:3; Job, Job 13:23; 31; see also Pss. 17:3–5; 26; 44:17–18) is not a pretentious boast of sinless perfection. Rather, it is a claim that, in contrast to his enemies, he has devoted his life to the service of the Lord and has lived a life of godly integrity. David's claim is not boasting in self because he acknowledges elsewhere that his integrity is the fruit of God's gracious working in his heart (see 51:10–12). David has experienced the Lord's favor, because God responds to man in kind (vv. 25–29; see Job 34:1; Prov. 3:34). He is **merciful** (v. 25) and **upright** to the godly, but He also shows Himself cunning to the **froward** ("crooked, perverse"; v. 26). God responds to their perverse dealings thrust for thrust, like a wrestler countering his opponent. Though David has been afflicted by his enemies, God has caused his life and undertakings to flourish.

18:30–45. By God's blessing, David the king has thrived. The Lord's **way is perfect** (v. 30) and does not fail; therefore, because of His blessing, David's way has not failed. The Lord provides David with **strength** (v. 32), agility (**feet like hinds' feet**; v. 33), and the skill to make **war** (v. 34) so that he triumphs over his enemy. With God's help, David has crushed all his foes. Unlike David, they had no one to **save them** (v. 41) when they cried out for help. God has made David **the head** (v. 43) of nations (see 2 Sam. 5; 8; 10)—he who had been on the brink of death and sinking into the depths (see vv. 4–5, 16).

18:46–50. In the concluding doxology, David declares that God's interventions and blessings on his behalf have shown Him to be the living God. The Lord's deliverance leads David to vow to praise the Lord among the nations. David views himself as the Lord's chosen and **anointed** (v. 50) ruler, and his words here recall the Lord's covenant with him (see 2 Sam. 7:8–16). The whole song is to be understood in the context of David's official capacity and the Lord's covenant with him. What David claims in this grand conclusion—as, indeed, in the whole psalm—has been and is being fulfilled in Jesus Christ, David's great descendant.

Psalm 19. A hymn extolling "the glory of God" (v. 1), as revealed to all by the starry heavens (see vv. 1–6), and "The law of the LORD" (v. 7), which has been given to Israel (see vv. 7–13).

19:1–6. Placed after Psalm 18, this psalm completes the cycle of praise—for the Lord's saving acts, for His glory reflected in creation, and for His law. The silent **heavens** (v. 1) speak as the work of God's hands, declaring the **glory** of their Maker to all who are on the earth (vv. 1–4a). The heavenly lights are not divine (see Deut. 4:19; 17:3), nor do they control

or disclose man's destiny (see Isa. 47:13; Jer. 10:2; Dan. 4:7). Their glory instead testifies to the righteousness and faithfulness of the Lord who created them (see 50:6; 89:5–8; 97:6; see also Rom. 1:19–20). The heavens are the divinely pitched **tabernacle** ("tent"; v. 4) for the lordly **sun**, which was widely worshiped in the ancient Near East (see Deut. 4:19; Jer. 8:2; Ezek. 8:16) but here is a mere creature of God (see 136:7–8; Gen. 1:16). Of the created realm, the sun is the supreme metaphor for the glory of God (see 84:11; Isa. 60:19–20), as it makes its daily triumphant sweep across the whole extent of the heavens and pours out its heat (its felt presence) on every creature.

19:7–14. Like the heavens, the law of the Lord also reflects His perfection and glory (vv. 7–13). The Lord's commands produce life-nurturing effects for those who follow them (vv. 7–10). They provide wisdom for the **simple** (v. 7), whose childlike understanding and judgment have not yet matured (see 119:98–100; Prov. 1:4; 2 Tim. 3:15; Heb. 5:13–14). They bring joy to **the heart** (v. 8), and the one who fears God enough to obey His commands will live in purity and righteousness. Those who follow what the law requires will find it to be even **Sweeter … than honey** (v. 10), the sweetest of all substances in the ancient Near East. By contrast, those who abandon the law turn justice into bitterness (see Amos 5:7; 6:12).

The law marks the way that leads to life (vv. 11–13; see Deut. 5:33). Man's moral consciousness remains flawed and imperfect; hence, he errs without realizing it and has reason to seek pardon for **secret faults** (v. 12; see Lev. 5:2–4). Willful sins, however, are open rebellion; they are **the great transgression** (v. 13) that leads to being cut off from God's people (see Num. 15:30–31). The psalmist presents this hymn as a praise offering to the Lord, desiring to live a life that is pleasing to the Lord and thankful for the Lord's protection in his life (v. 14).

Psalm 20. A liturgy of prayer for the king just before he goes out to battle a threatening force (see 2 Chron. 20:1–30).

20:1–53. The people (perhaps his assembled army) address the king, adding their prayers to his prayer for victory over his enemies, as he prepares to go to war (vv. 1–5). They ask the Lord to help the king from His **sanctuary** (v. 2) in **Zion**, reminding the Lord of the sacrifices the king has offered with his prayers. The worshipers further request that God grant the desires of the king's **heart** (v. 4) and that the king's battle **counsel** is successful in execution. When the victory is won, the people will **rejoice** (v. 5) in their God.

20:6–9. As part of the liturgy, a participant, perhaps a Levite (see 2 Chron. 20:14), declares assurance that the king's prayer will be heard (v. 6). The army following the king into battle also confess their trust in the Lord rather than in chariot corps (vv. 7–8); the enemy perhaps came reinforced by such a prized corps. David made a similar confession of confidence when he faced Goliath (1 Sam. 17:45–47). The army makes a final petition for victory in verse 9. The first line of this verse should read, "Save, O LORD, the king," asking God, not the king, to answer their petition. With the verb **hear** in the second line, the psalm ends as it began (see v. 1).

Psalm 21. A psalm of praise for victories granted to the king.

This psalm is linked with Psalm 20, but whether both were occasioned by the same events is unknown. Here the people's praise follows that of the king (see v. 1); there (Psalm 20) the people's prayer was added to the king's. In its structure, the psalm is framed by verses 1 and 13 ("in thy strength, O LORD" and "LORD, in thine own strength") and is centered around verse 7, which proclaims the king's trust in the Lord and the security afforded him by God's unfailing love.

21:1–7. The people celebrate the Lord's many favors to the king (vv. 1–6). The Lord has granted the king **his heart's desire** (v. 2) in answering his prayer. The warrior's helmet is exchanged for a **crown** (v. 3), possibly the captured crown of the defeated king (see 2 Sam. 12:30). David's **life** (v. 4) has been spared, to live **for ever and ever**—poetic hyperbole for longevity (see 1 Kings 1:31; Dan. 2:4; 3:9; 1 Kings 1:34, 39). The king is given **glory** (v. 5) and **majesty** like that belonging to his heavenly Overlord (see 45:3; 96:3) and enjoys an unending flow

of blessings. God's **countenance** (v. 6), the favor of His presence, is the supreme cause of joy because it is the greatest blessing and the wellspring of all other blessings. At the center of the psalm, verse 7, a participant in the liturgy (perhaps a priest or Levite) proclaims the reasons for the king's security: he has put his trust in **the most High** (v. 7) God, whose power and sovereignty is unrivaled.

21:8–13. The people hail the future victories of their triumphant king (vv. 8–12). They credit the king's victories to the Lord's fierce **wrath** (v. 9) against His enemies. The king's royal enemies will be left no descendants to rise against him again, and their plots to overthrow the king will not succeed. They will instead **turn their back** (v. 12) when the king rains his arrows down upon them. The conclusion returns to the opening of the psalm. The people pray for the Lord to assert His **strength** (v. 13; see v. 1) so that they will ever praise His might.

Psalm 22. The anguished prayer of David as a godly sufferer victimized by the vicious and prolonged attacks of enemies whom he has not provoked and from whom the Lord has not yet delivered him.

While David is describing his own sufferings in highly figurative language, no other psalm quite so aptly fits the circumstances of Jesus at His crucifixion. Hence, on the cross, He takes it to His lips (see Matt. 27:46 and parallels), and the Gospel writers, especially Matthew and John, frequently allude to it (as they did to Psalm 69) in their accounts of Christ's passion (Matt. 27:35, 39, 43; John 19:23–24, 28). They see in the passion of Jesus the fulfillment of this cry of the righteous sufferer. The author of Hebrews places the words of verse 22 on Jesus' lips (Heb. 2:12). No psalm is quoted more frequently in the New Testament.

22:1–11. In his agony, David feels as if God has **forsaken** (v. 1) him and ignored his prayers for help (v. 1–2), but he takes comfort in recalling what the Lord has done for Israel in the past (vv. 3–5). The Lord is intimately related to His people and dwells where they praise Him in celebration of His saving acts. He has been faithful in answering their prayers.

In contrast, David laments that he is like a **worm** (v. 6) because of the scorn and abuse he receives from his enemies. They mock and taunt him because the Lord does not **deliver** (v. 8) him, even though he claims to be the object of God's favor. When enduring these taunts, the psalmist recalls what the Lord has been for him (vv. 9-11). David has been committed to God since the time he was nursed as an infant at his **mother's breasts** (v. 9) and even since the time he was inside his **mother's belly** (v. 10), hyperbole stressing that David has trusted in God all his life.

22:12-18. Yet the psalmist is in deep distress. Images are piled on top of one another to depict the intensity of the attack of his enemies. He is attacked by wild animals (**bulls**, v. 12; **lion[s]**, v. 13; **dogs**, v. 16). **Bashan** (v. 12) was noted for its good pasturage and hence for the size and vigor of its animals (see Deut. 32:14; Ezek. 39:18; Amos 4:1). The psalmist feels an inner sense of powerlessness under these fierce attacks (vv. 14-15). His pain is like that of a man with his **bones ... out of joint** (v. 14). His **heart** melts within him, and his mouth is dried by thirst. The wild animals and/or evil men wound his **hands and ... feet** (v. 16) as he tries to ward off their vicious blows. David is like one attacked by highway robbers or enemy soldiers, who strip him of his garments so that all of his **bones** (v. 17) are visible. They take his clothing and **cast lots** (v. 18) for it as the reward for their robbery.

The suffering of David points prophetically to the sufferings of Christ on the cross as the ultimate son of David. Rather than providing a detailed and specific prediction of how Christ would die, however, this figurative language portrays more the degree of suffering endured by the righteous sufferer, Jesus being the supreme example. Certain details (piercing, casting of lots) refer very directly to things Jesus suffered; other details (the attack of wild animals) do not.

22:19-31. The psalmist's prayer for deliverance in verses 20-21 recalls in reverse order the images used to describe his attackers in verses 12-18—the **sword** (v. 20; evoking the robbery scene in vv. 16b-18); **dog** (v. 20), **lion** (v. 21), and **unicorns** ("wild oxen"; corresponding to the earlier "strong bulls"). While making his petition, the psalmist experiences the assurance of having been **heard**. Confident of the ultimate outcome, David vows to praise the Lord when the Lord's sure deliverance comes (vv. 22-31). The vows proper appear in verses 22 and 25—**I will declare ... will I praise** (v. 22); **My praise shall be ... I will pay my vows** (v. 25). Verses 23-24 anticipate the calls to praise that will accompany the psalmist's praise. Verses 26-31 describe the expanding company of those who will take up the praise. The worshipers who will gather with the psalmist will **eat and be satisfied** (v. 26) as they share in the ceremonial festival of praise (see Lev. 7:11-27). Ultimately, **All the ends of the world** (v. 27) will hear of God's saving acts, and the good news that the God of Israel hears the prayers of His people and saves them will move them to turn from their idols to the true God. No psalm or prophecy contains a grander vision of the scope of the throng of worshipers who will join in the praise of God's saving acts. This throng will include the most prosperous (**they that be fat**; v. 29) and those on the brink of death (**they that go down to the dust**), as well as those whose life situations falls in between these two extremes.

Psalm 23. A psalm of confidence professing joyful trust in the Lord as the good Shepherd-King.

This psalm may have accompanied a festival of praise at "the house of the LORD" (v. 6) following a deliverance, such as is contemplated in 22:25-31. Two kingship metaphors describe the blessing and security that the Lord provides for His people: the Shepherd-King (vv. 1-4) and the Host of the royal banquet (vv. 5-6). The image of "shepherd" (v. 1) is a widely used metaphor for kings in the ancient Near East and also in Israel (see 78:71-72; 95:7; 2 Sam. 5:2; Isa. 40:11; Ezek. 34:11-16). Here David the king acknowledges that the Lord was his Shepherd-King. The New Testament also presents Jesus as the shepherd of His people (see John 10:11, 14; Heb. 13:20; 1 Peter 5:4; Rev. 7:17).

23:1-6. The Shepherd performs several key roles for His flock. First, He is their Provider (v. 1b-3a). The psalmist does **not want** (v. 1). On the contrary, he will enjoy **goodness** (v. 6) all his life. The flocks **lie down** (v. 2) in contented and secure rest (see Ezek.

34:14–15) and feed **in green pastures**, a metaphor for all that makes life flourish (see Ezek. 34:14; John 10:9). They have **still waters** from which they can drink deeply and satisfy their thirst (see Isa. 49:10).

The Shepherd is also the Leader of the flock (v. 3b). A shepherd has to know the land to keep his sheep from getting lost and must lead them in paths that offer safety and well-being. David's Shepherd-King guides him in ways that cause him to be secure and prosperous. **Righteousness** (v. 3) has a double meaning, picturing both level and safe paths (see Prov. 8:18, 20–21) and a way of life that conforms to God's moral will. The prosperity of the Lord's flock brings honor to the Lord's name (v. 3) and to His reputation as Shepherd (see 1 Kings 8:41–42; Isa. 48:9).

The Shepherd is also the Protector of the flock in dangerous circumstances. The phrase **valley of the shadow of death** (v. 4) could also be read "the valley of darkness" and pictures the flock traversing through a deep ravine, where steep cliffs and attacks from predators threaten the sheep. The Lord uses His **rod** to count, guide, rescue, and protect His sheep (see Lev. 27:32; Ezek. 20:37) and employs His **staff** as an instrument of support (see Exod. 21:19; Zech. 8:4).

The psalmist directly addresses the Lord (**Thou;** v. 5) and transitions into the image of the heavenly Shepherd-King receiving David as a guest at His **table**. David is the Lord's vassal king and lives under the protection of the Lord as His suzerain. In the ancient Near East, covenants were often concluded with a meal, expressive of the bond of friendship (see 41:9; Gen. 31:54; Obadiah 7); in the case of vassal treaties or covenants, the vassal was present as the guest of the overlord (see Exod. 24:8–12). Having his head anointed **with oil**, David receives the customary treatment of an honored guest at a banquet (see also 2 Sam. 12:20; Eccl. 9:8; Luke 7:48). The covenant benefits of **goodness** and **mercy ... follow** (v. 6) after David, an arresting figure in that the verb "follow" has the meaning of "pursue" and frequently refers to stalking an enemy. The idea is that God is relentlessly committed to blessing His people. David will enjoy these blessings as he **dwell[s] in the house of the Lord for ever**. The Hebrew suggests "through-

out the years," but the Psalms also anticipate a relationship with the Lord that carries on beyond the boundaries of this life (see 11:7; 16:9–11).

Psalm 24. A processional liturgy (see Psalms 47; 68; 118; 132) celebrating the Lord's entrance into Zion and describing those who have the right to enter into God's presence.

This psalm was likely composed either for the occasion when David brought the ark to Jerusalem (see 2 Samuel 6) or for a festival commemorating that event. It was probably placed next to Psalm 23 because it prescribes who may enter the sanctuary (see 23:6). The church has long used this psalm in celebration of Christ's ascension into the heavenly Jerusalem and into the sanctuary on high.

24:1–2. The prelude (perhaps spoken by a Levite) proclaims that the Lord is the Creator, Sustainer and Possessor of the whole world and is therefore worthy of worship and reverent loyalty. The Lord **founded** (v. 2) and **established** the earth as Creator, a metaphor taken from the building of a city or temple (see Josh. 6:26; 1 Kings 16:24; Ezra 3:6–12). Like a temple, the earth was depicted as having foundations and pillars (see 18:15; 82:5; 1 Sam. 2:8; Isa. 24:18). In the ancient Near East, temples were thought of as microcosms of the created world, so language applicable to a temple could readily be applied to the earth. The Lord's work as Creator establishes His right of rulership.

24:3–6. The psalmist delivers instruction (probably spoken by a priest) concerning those who may enter the sanctuary (see Psalm 15). Admission is granted only to those whose life is characterized by moral integrity, including guiltless actions (**clean hands**; v. 4), right attitudes and motives (**pure heart**), a refusal to worship false gods (**lift up his soul unto vanity**), and honest dealings (**sworn deceitfully**). Jesus likewise promised that the "pure in heart ... shall see God" (Matt. 5:8). The reward of those who are morally upright is that they will receive **righteousness** (v. 5) from God, that is, the fruits of vindication honoring their godly lifestyle.

24:7–10. The final section of the psalm heralds the approach of **the King of glory** (v. 7) and was perhaps spoken by the king at the head of the assembled Israelites, with responses by the keepers of the gates. The Lord's arrival at His sanctuary in Zion completes His march from Egypt. The personified **gates** of the city of Jerusalem are commanded to open in jubilant reception of the victorious **King of glory** (v. 9). **The LORD of Hosts** (v. 10) and **the LORD mighty in battle** (v. 8) has triumphed over all His enemies and comes now in victory to His own city (see Psalms 46; 48; 76; 87). Henceforth, Jerusalem is the royal city of the kingdom of God.

Psalm 25. The psalmist prays for God's covenant mercies when suffering affliction for sins and when enemies seize the occasion to attack, perhaps by trying to discredit the king through false accusations.

25:1–7. David prays for relief from his distress or illness and the slander of his enemies that it occasions (vv. 1–3). The attacks of the adversaries are unfair because David has given no **cause** (v. 3) for their hostilities. He then prays for guidance and pardon from the Lord (vv. 4–7). He seeks guidance in the **truth** (v. 5) so that he might continue to walk in the ways of the Lord and seek forgiveness for his past failures. He calls for the Lord to **Remember** (v. 6) His long-standing **tender mercies** and to **Remember not** (v. 7) David's long-standing sins of his **youth**. David's life of integrity will refute the false accusations of his enemies.

25:8–15. In his prayer, David expresses his confidence in the Lord's covenant favors. In this context of prayer for pardon, David implicitly identifies himself with **sinners** (v. 8) as well as with the **meek** (v. 9)—those who keep God's covenant and those who fear the Lord (vv. 10–14). As a sinner, he is in need of forgiveness, and God's forgiveness will express itself in removing his affliction. His enemies will then no longer have occasion to slander him. With God guiding him, he will no longer wander into sin. The promise that the righteous **shall inherit the earth** (v. 13) means that they will retain their family portion in the Promised Land (see 37:9, 11; Isa. 60:21). The Lord also takes into His confidence as friends those who **fear him** (v. 14; see Gen. 18:17–19).

25:16–22. David again petitions the Lord for relief from distress or illness and from the attacks of his enemies (vv. 16–21). Appealing to the Lord's

mercy, he describes the depth of his affliction. Pardon for past failures is not enough; David also prays that God will enable him to live a life of moral purity. The virtues of **integrity and uprightness** (v. 21) are personified as his protectors. David's integrity is the reason God should defend his cause against the wicked. The psalm closes with a prayer for deliverance on behalf of all God's people (v. 22).

Psalm 26. A prayer for God's discerning mercies to spare His faithful and godly servant from the death that overtakes the wicked and ungodly.

26:1–8. Judge me (v. 1) is a prayer for vindication and suggests that the king is threatened by violent enemies. David appeals for God to take account of his moral **integrity**, his unwavering trust, and his genuine delight in the Lord as the grounds for his vindication (vv. 1–8). David is claiming that he lives an upright life rather than boasting of sinless perfection. Obedience and trust are the two sides of godliness. The psalmist's godliness involves a refusal to associate with the wicked. **Vain persons** (v. 4) and **dissemblers** refer to those who speak and deal fraudulently (see Prov. 6:12–14). David's love for the temple and his public devotion to the Lord provides further proof of his piety (vv. 6–8). **I will wash mine hands in innocency** (v. 6) likely refers to a ritual claiming innocence. "Clean hands" and "a pure heart" are requisite for those who come to worship the Lord (see 24:4). He joins with those who offer praise and **thanksgiving** (v. 7) at the Lord's altar.

26:9–12. Having made his claim of moral purity, David prays that God will not bring on him the end (death) that awaits the wicked (vv. 9–11). He affirms his commitment to **walk in mine integrity** (v. 11), as he has done in the past (see v. 1). The psalm concludes with a confession of confidence and a vow of praise. Because the Lord gives him protection and security, David will **bless the LORD** (v. 12) before the **congregations** that gather for worship.

Psalm 27. David's triumphantly confident prayer to God to deliver him from all those who conspire to bring him down.

27:1–6. The king finds security in the Lord in spite of all that his enemies can do to him. This prayer presupposes the Lord's covenant with David (see 2 Samuel 7). The Lord is his source of **light** (v. 1), a symbol of well-being, life, and salvation (see Job 18:5–6; Isa. 9:2). Therefore, he does not fear the **enemies** (v. 2) that seek to destroy him. The Lord's **temple** (or tabernacle; v. 4) is the king's stronghold because the Lord Himself is present there with His people. **The beauty of the Lord** (v. 4) is the unfailing benevolence enjoyed by those who make the Lord their refuge (see 90:17). The king promises to present **sacrifices** (v. 6) and to **sing praises** in response to deliverance from his enemies.

27:7–14. David's confident reliance on the Lord, expressed in the first half of the psalm, leads to his prayer for deliverance from his enemies (vv. 7–12). The chief weapon of these treacherous enemies is false charges that seek to discredit the king. David has faithfully sought the Lord in his life and now asks that God not abandon him in his time of need. He is confident that the Lord's concern for him is even greater than that of a human parent. In addition to praying for deliverance, David also asks **Teach me thy way** (v. 11). Only those who know and do the Lord's will can expect to receive favorable response to their prayers. In the concluding note of confidence (vv. 13–14), the psalmist affirms that his confidence in **the goodness of the Lord** (v. 13) keeps him strong as he waits for the Lord to answer his prayer. His words are an example of faith encouraging faith (see 42:5, 11; 43:5; 62:5).

Psalm 28. A prayer for deliverance from deadly peril at the hands of malicious and God-defying enemies.

28:1–9. In the initial appeal, the psalmist pleads for the Lord to act to deliver him from **the pit** (v. 1), a metaphor for death. David directs his prayer toward the Lord's **holy oracle** (lit., "holy sanctuary"), the temple that served as God's throne room on earth. Expanding on his plea for help, David prays for God to deliver His servant and deal judgment to those who harbor malice toward the king and God's people and defy God Himself (vv. 3–5). He asks the Lord to pay back his enemies for their wicked designs against him. These wicked men oppose the king **Because they regard not the works of the Lord** (v. 5), which include the establishment of Israel as His kingdom (see Exod. 19–24) and the appointment of the house of David as His earthly regent (see 2 Sam. 7). The Lord will ultimately **destroy** the wicked for opposing His people and His chosen ruler. The psalmist gives joyful praise, in confidence of his request being heard (vv. 6–7). The song closes with a prayer for God to **Save … And bless** (v. 9), the two primary acts by which He effects His people's well-being: He saves from time to time as circumstances require; He blesses day by day to make their lives and labors fruitful. David also issues a call for the Lord to **feed** (or "shepherd") His people, a request that receives a lasting and complete answer in the ministry of the "good shepherd," Jesus Christ (see John 10:11, 14).

Psalm 29. A hymn in praise of the King of Creation, whose majesty and power are trumpeted by the thunderbolts of the rainstorm.

The glory of the Lord is not only visible in the creation (see 19:1–6; 104); it is also audible in creation's most awesome voice, the thunderstorm. This song pictures a storm that rises above the Mediterranean (v. 3), sweeps across the Lebanon range (see vv. 5–6), and rolls over "the wilderness of Kadesh" (v. 8). This hymn to Yahweh served as a testimony and protest against the worship of the Canaanite god Baal, who was thought to be the divine power present in the thunderstorm. The name Yahweh ("the Lord") is sounded four times in both the introduction (vv. 1–2) and the conclusion (vv. 10–11), and it is heard ten times in the body of the psalm (vv. 3-9). "The voice of the Lord" (vv. 3–5; 7–9) is repeated seven times, representing the seven thunders of God.

29:1–2. The introduction is a summons to all beings in the divine realm to worship the Lord. The **mighty** (lit., "sons of God"; v. 1) perhaps refers to the angelic host (see 103:20; Job 1:6; 2:1), or possibly to all those foolishly thought to be gods (see 97:7). The Lord alone must be acknowledged as the Divine King. It is not clear if the phrase **in the beauty of holiness** (v. 2) describes God Himself, the sanctuary, or the (priestly) garb the worshipers are to wear when they approach God. The use of an almost identical

Hebrew phrase in 110:3 appears to support the last alternative.

29:3–9. The psalmist's praise of the Lord portrays the crashing thunder as a reflection of the power and glory of Israel's God. The thunder breaks the **cedars of Lebanon** (v. 5), the mightiest of trees (see Isa. 2:13), and an earthquake shakes the mountains of **Lebanon and Sirion** (v. 6). The Lord sends the forked lightning across the sky, which has devastating effects on the **wilderness** (v. 8) and the **forests** (v. 9). This powerful display of God's power causesd the worshipers at the Jerusalem temple to testify of **his glory**.

29:10–11. The conclusion to the psalm affirms that the Lord's absolute and everlasting rule is committed to His people's complete salvation and blessedness. **The LORD sitteth upon the flood** (v. 10) as the One who by His word brought the ordered creation out of the formless "deep" (Gen. 1:2, 6–10) and who thus controls the forces of nature in a world where threatening tides seem to make everything uncertain. The Lord is not capricious in the use of His infinite strength but graciously shares His **strength** (v. 11) with **his people** for their blessing and prosperity.

Psalm 30. A song of praise publicly celebrating the Lord's deliverance from the threat of death, probably brought on by illness.

If **of David**, in the superscription, indicates authorship, the most probable occasion for the psalm is recorded in 1 Chronicles 21:1–22:6. In 1 Chronicles 22:1–6, David dedicated both property and building materials for the temple, and he may well have intended that this song be used at the dedication of the temple itself. If this is the case, the reference to healing and deliverance from death vv. 2–3 refers to David's predicament described in 1 Chronicles 21:17–30, when he was punished by God for numbering the people of Israel.

30:1–5. This psalm is framed by promises to praise the Lord (vv. 1, 12). The occasion for praise is that the Lord has **healed** (v. 2) the psalmist of a life-threatening illness (vv. 1–3). The vivid imagery associating distress with the need to be **lifted** (v. 1) out

of trouble is common in Old Testament poetry (see 69:2, 15; Lam. 3:55). The depths are often linked, as here, with sheol (**the grave**; v. 3) and the pit (see 18:5; Jonah 2:2). The Lord's healing rescued the psalmist from the brink of death. The psalmist calls for the gathered worshipers to praise God (vv. 4–5). They are to testify to the Lord's graciousness, which causes discipline to be temporary (**endure for a night** literally reads, "come in at evening to lodge"; v. 5) but **joy** to be the continual experience of the godly.

30:6–12. The psalmist provides an expanded recollection of the Lord's gracious deliverance (vv. 6–10). In his security, he has grown arrogant, forgetful of who has **made** his **mountain to stand strong** (v. 7), but the Lord reminds him through his adversity (vv. 6–7). Since he spoke with the arrogant pride of the wicked (**I shall never be moved**; v. 6), he lost the blessing of the righteous. The Lord ultimately restored David but only after sweeping away all his self-reliance (vv. 8–10). The Lord responded to his cries when he was about to die. Because of God's answer, David vows to prolong his praise forever (vv. 11–12). **Dancing** (v. 11) and joy replace wailing and **sackcloth** so that songs of praise, not silence, may attend the acts of God.

Psalm 31. A prayer for deliverance when confronted by a conspiracy so powerful and open that all David's friends abandoned him.

31:1–5. The psalmist makes his initial appeal to the Lord, the faithful refuge, basing his prayer for deliverance on the Lord's reputation (**for thy name's sake**; v. 3). God's honor is at stake in the safety of His servant, who is now under attack. He asks the Lord to **lead** and **guide** him because his enemies have set a **net** (v. 4) to trap him. **Into thine hand I commit my spirit** (v. 5) is the climactic expression of trust in the Lord. Jesus prayed these words on the cross as He prepared to die (see Luke 23:46), and the New Testament encourages those who share in His sufferings at the hands of anti-Christian forces to hear and use these words in a new light (see Acts 7:59; 1 Peter 4:19).

31:6–8. David confesses his trust in the Lord, a confidence arising from the Lord's past mercies to him when threatened by enemies. Because of his faith, David refuses to associate with the wicked and waits for the Lord's deliverance. The Lord has **set his feet in a large room** (v. 8), or place, where he is able to escape his attackers (see 18:19).

31:9–13. While confident in the Lord, David also experiences deep distress. He is utterly drained, physically and emotionally. All his friends have abandoned him as a piece of broken pottery because the conspiracy against him is so strong (v. 13). Being abandoned by one's friends was a common experience at times when God seemed to have withdrawn His favor (see 69:8; Job 19:13–19; Jer. 12:6).

31:14–18. The theme of confidence and joy returns in these verses, as David confesses that his trust in the Lord is unwavering. His defense against his powerful enemies is his reliance on God's faithfulness and discerning judgment. He finds comfort in the fact that all the events and circumstances of life are under God's control (**My times are in thy hand**; v. 15). He prays for the favor of God's **face** (v. 16) upon his life and for the **lying lips** (v. 18) of his enemies to be silenced in the grave.

31:19–24. David confidently anticipates God's saving help and deposits his life in the hands of God to share in the covenant benefits that God has stored up for His faithful servants (vv. 19–20). The Lord delivers His servants **Before the sons of men** (v. 19), thus showing His approval of their lives in contrast to the accusations of their adversaries. The Lord provides protection for the righteous in the **strong** (or besieged) **city** (v. 21) by cutting off their enemies (vv. 21–22). The psalm concludes by encouraging the **saints** (v. 23) to **love the Lord** and to **Be of good courage** (v. 24) because the Lord has promised to bless those who live in humble reliance on Him. In contrast, the Lord will recompense **the proud** (v. 23), who arrogantly try to make their way in the world either as a law unto themselves or by relying on false gods.

Psalm 32. A grateful testimony of joy for God's gift of forgiveness toward those who confess their sins with integrity and are receptive to God's rule in their lives.

32:1–5. This psalm appears to be a liturgical dialogue between David and God in the presence of the worshipers at the sanctuary. David addresses the worshipers at the sanctuary and makes an exuberant proclamation of the happy (**Blessed**; vv. 1–2) state of those who experience God's forgiveness. Forgiveness involves the covering of sin so that God does not impute the sin against the person who is truly repentant. Only those who are honest with God receive pardon.

David gave testimony of a personal experience of God's forgiveness (vv. 3–5). Brought down **day and night** (v. 4) on the stubborn silence of unacknowledged sin, God's **hand was heavy upon** him and had filled his life with groaning, but full confession brought blessed relief. Under God's heavy hand, David wilted like a plant in the heat of **summer**. Neither the sin nor the form of suffering is identified, but it would be uncharacteristic of the Psalms to speak of a mere emotional disturbance brought on by suppressed guilt. Some affliction, perhaps illness, was the instrument of God's chastisement (see Psalm 38).

32:6–7. As a result of his experience, David makes the chastened confession that life is secure only with God. Though addressed to God as confession, these words are also intended for the ears of fellow worshipers. David admonishes them to seek the Lord in prayer and not to foolishly provoke His withdrawal as he had done. A God who forgives is a God one can trust when threatened by **the floods of great waters** (v. 6). This powerful imagery for threatening forces or circumstances is borrowed from ancient Near Eastern creation myths. In many of these, a primal mass of chaotic waters (their threatening and destructive forces were often depicted as a many-headed monster of the deep) had to be subdued by the creator-god before he could fashion the world and/or rule over the earth (see 74:13–14). Though in these myths the chaotic waters were subdued when the present world was created, they remained a constant threat to the security and well-being of the present order on earth. Hence, by association, they were linked with anything in human experience that endangered or troubled that order. Even in the midst of these difficulties, David looks forward to being surrounded by the **songs of deliverance** (v. 7) sung by the people of the Lord in celebration of His saving acts.

32:8 – 11. The priestly word of instruction in verses 8 – 10 calls the worshipers to learn from David's experiences and to make obedience to the Lord the priority in their lives. God's servant must be wiser than beasts, more open to God's will than horses and mules are to the will of their masters. Those who obey the Lord will be surrounded by His covenant mercy. David's final word to the assembled worshipers is a call to allow the praise of God to resound (v. 11). A God who graciously forgives is worthy of worship.

Psalm 33. A liturgy in praise of the Lord, the sovereign God of Israel.

33:1 – 3. The psalmist calls for praise and celebration to the Lord. Though the original occasion is unknown, the reference to a **new song** (v. 3) suggests a national deliverance, such as Judah experienced in the time of Jehoshaphat (see 2 Chronicles 20) or Hezekiah (see 2 Kings 19).

33:4 – 19. The content of the praise is expressed in two eight-verse parts. The focus in verses 4 – 11 is on the Lord as Creator. Since by His power, He has imposed His order on the creation, no power or combination of powers can thwart His plan and purpose to save His people. God governs all things by His royal **word** (v. 4) in a manner that is righteous and that promotes what is good. The Lord is not despotic in how He exercises His absolute power. His absolute power is demonstrated in the way that He gathered **the waters of the sea … as a heap** (v. 7), like a householder storing up his olive oil and grain (see Gen. 1:9 – 10; Job 38:8 – 11). All mankind, not only Israel, are to **fear** (v. 8) and **stand in awe** of the Lord, for all experience the goodness of His sovereign rule. As the Sovereign King, the Lord foils the plans of those who stand in opposition to Him.

The second half of the praise turns to the consequence of the Lord's absolute rule: Israel is safe and secure as the people of God under His protection (vv. 12 – 19). They are blessed as His **chosen** (v. 12) people and have a special place among all the na-

tions. The Lord is ultimately in control of all nations and rulers on the earth, and His plans rather than military strength determine the outcomes of human history. The Lord extends blessing and protection to Israel as they **fear him** (v. 18) and **hope in his mercy**. He will **deliver** (v. 19) them from all calamities.

33:20 – 22. The people respond with their confession of faith and trust in the Lord. They wait for the Lord and trust in Him as their Protector. While anticipating the joy they will experience in the Lord's deliverance, they pray for His **mercy** (v. 22) to be upon them.

Psalm 34. Praise of the Lord for deliverance in answer to prayer, and instruction in godliness.

The superscription assigns this psalm to the occasion narrated in 1 Samuel 21:10 – 15, when David, in fear for his life, feigned insanity before the Philistine king. The name **Abimelech** (rather than "Achish," as in 1 Samuel 21) was perhaps a traditional dynastic name or title for Philistine kings (see Genesis 20; 21:22 – 34; 26).

34:1 – 7. David offers praise for the Lord's deliverance in answer to prayer. He is committed to continually praising the Lord so that the godly who are experiencing hardship will be encouraged. God's answer to prayer and deliverance has brought David joy, which he feels the need to share with others in the context of public worship. The psalmist calls himself **poor** (v. 6) not because he lacks possessions, but because he is without resources to effect his own deliverance, and thus is completely dependent on God. David declares that **The angel of the** Lord (v. 7) surrounds His people individually and collectively. The "angel of the Lord" is God's heavenly representative sent to carry out His will on earth. This figure is closely identified with the Lord, though distinct from Him (see Gen. 16:7 – 9). This verse is not teaching a doctrine of individual "guardian angels."

34:8 – 22. The praise of verses 1 – 7 leads into godly instruction which develops three major themes. The first theme is instruction in the fear of the Lord (vv. 8 – 14). A symmetrical development of the theme "good" dominates the stanza: Because **the** Lord **is good** (v. 8), those who trust in Him will lack nothing

good (v. 10), but to experience **good** (v. 12) days, they must shun evil and **do good** (v. 14). A series of imperatives in this section emphasizes that the fear of the Lord involves trust and obedience: **taste** (v. 8), **fear** (v. 9), **Come** (v. 11), **Keep** (v. 13), and **Depart** (v. 14).

The second theme in the instruction section is the assurance that the Lord hears the prayers of the righteous (vv. 15–18). His concern for the righteous is contrasted to His opposition to the wicked. The Lord so thoroughly thwarts those who **do evil** (v. 16) that they are forgotten. The third theme is another assurance that the Lord is the unfailing deliverer of the righteous and condemns the wicked for their hostility toward the righteous (vv. 19–22). The promise **He keepeth all his bones** (v. 20) is a figurative expression for God's protection of the whole person (see 6:2). It appears that John's gospel applies this word to Jesus (see John 19:36; Exod. 12:46; Num. 9:12), a reminder that the Lord watches over His righteous ones even in death. The warning that the wicked **shall be desolate** (v. 21) literally reads, "shall be guilty," and they will be dealt with according to their guilt.

Psalm 35. An appeal to the heavenly King, as Divine Warrior and Judge, to come to the defense of "his servant" (v. 27), who is being maliciously slandered by those toward whom he had shown only the most tender friendship.

35:1–10. The attack against David seems to have been occasioned by some "hurt" (v. 26) that had overtaken the king, perhaps an illness (see v. 13; Psalm 6). The initial appeal to the Lord as Divine Warrior (vv. 1–3) is followed by a threefold elaboration of David's petition to the Divine Judge, each concluding with a vow to praise Him (vv. 4–10, 11–18, 19–28). David asks the Lord to deal with his attackers by matching His judgment with their violent intent (vv. 4–10). He prays for them to **be confounded** (v. 4), or humiliated, through their judgment and his vindication. The request for them to travel down a **dark and slippery** (v. 6) path, where they will fall is appropriate because they have set a trap to bring David down into the **pit** (v. 7).

35:11–18. David accuses his enemies of repaying his friendship with malicious slander. They have **rewarded** (v. 12) him with **evil for good**. In contrast to their abuse, the king had provided a living example of Jesus' command to pray for one's enemies (vv. 13–14; Matt. 5:44). They in turn **rejoiced** (v. 15) over his affliction and acted like drunkards at a pagan feast as they heaped on him their vicious and profane derision (vv. 15–16). David renews his petition for deliverance and vows to praise the Lord (vv. 17–18). The term **My darling** (v. 17) literally reads, "My only one," and refers to David's soul or life.

35:19–28. The psalmist continues his prayer for judgment. His enemies are worthy of judgment because they conspire against him with their secretive gestures and words (see Prov. 6:13) and have hated him **without a cause** (v. 19; see John 15:25). David boldly prays for the Lord to act on his behalf and to vindicate him because of the rightness of his cause. If the Lord fails to act, David's enemies will see their desire to destroy the king come to pass. He prays that they will be **ashamed and brought to confusion** (v. 26) so that their judgment will match their evil intent. Confident that the Lord will act on behalf of **his servant** (v. 27), David offers a final vow of **praise** (v. 28).

Psalm 36. A prayer for God's unfailing protection, offered as the psalmist reflects on the godlessness of the wicked and the goodness of God.

36:1–4. The contrast between the wicked and the godly is a dominant theme in this psalm. **The wicked** (v. 1) are foolish and haughty in their disregard for the Lord (vv. 1–4). They take no account of His all-seeing eye, His righteous judgment, and His power to deal with them. The wicked person **flattereth himself** (v. 2) with the smug, conceited notion that he is accountable to no one. He is unable to recognize and hate the sinfulness in his own heart and has stopped even trying to do what is right. Rather than meditating on God's law "day and night" (1:2), he is absorbed with ways to practice evil.

36:5–9. The evil of the wicked is contrasted with the goodness of the Lord, who shows His benevolence toward all His creatures. His **mercy** (v. 5), **faithfulness**, and **righteousness** (v. 6) encompass all realms of creaturely existence, and the righteous are wise to put their trust in Him. God's blessings are pictured as rich food and life-giving water. The earth is God's **house** (v. 8), or estate, from which springs the abundance of food for all living things. **The river of thy pleasures** is vivid imagery, depicting God's control over, and gift of, the waters from heaven, which feed the rivers and streams of earth to give life and health wherever they flow (see Ezek. 47:1–12; Rev. 22:1–2).

36:10–12. The psalmist prays that God will **continue** (v. 10) to show His mercy and righteousness to all who acknowledge Him and are upright in their lifestyle. On the other hand, the wicked will be **cast down** (v. 12) because of their **pride** (v. 11).

Psalm 37. Instruction in godly wisdom, contrasting the wicked and the righteous.

Continuing the thought of Psalm 36, the central issue addressed in this psalm is, who will "inherit the earth" (vv. 9, 11, 22, 29), or live on to enjoy the blessings of the Lord in the Promised Land? Will the wicked, who scheme (vv. 7, 12, 32), default on debts (v. 21), use raw power to gain advantage (v. 14), and seem thereby to flourish (vv. 7, 16, 35)? Or will the righteous, who trust in the Lord (vv. 3, 5, 7, 34) and are humble (v. 11), blameless (vv. 18, 37), generous (vv. 21, 26), peaceable (v. 37), and wise (vv. 30–31)?

37:1–11. The main theme is developed in these verses and further elaborated in the rest of the psalm. The whole is framed by statements contrasting the brief career of the wicked (vv. 1–2) and the Lord's sustaining help of the righteous (vv. 39–40). The psalmist begins by urging the reader not to worry but to **Trust** (v. 3) and **Delight** (v. 4) in the Lord. The righteous will receive their **desires** because they live in conformity to the will of God. The Lord will vindicate them against their enemies and cause their righteousness to shine as a light for all to see (vv. 5–6). They have no need to worry or be angry over the temporary prosperity and success of the wicked (vv. 7–8). The righteous will receive from the Lord secure entitlement to the Promised Land, for them and their children, while **evildoers shall be cut off** (v. 9). Their destruction will occur in **a little while** (v. 10), the shortness of time serving as a figure

for the certainty of the event (see Job 20:5–11). God will so completely destroy the wicked that they will not be found even with a careful search.

37:12–22. The psalm elaborates on the fate of the righteous and the wicked with a series of contrasts. The wicked are deserving of judgment because of their hatred of the righteous (vv. 12–15). They plot against the righteous with malice, but the Lord laughs in derision at their schemes and will destroy them with their own **sword** (v. 15) and **bows**. The righteous are better off with their limited resources, because the wealth of the wicked will not last (vv. 15–17). The Lord will break **the arms** (v. 17) of the wicked, returning their violence upon them, while upholding **the righteous**. The Lord will allow the **upright** (v. 18) to perpetually enjoy their inheritance, but **the wicked shall perish** (v. 20). The wicked are like "the beauty of the fields" (read instead of **the fat of lambs**), that is, the grass and flowers, and like **smoke** that is here and gone. **The wicked** (v. 21) refuse to repay their debts, but **the righteous** are blessed because of their generosity (vv. 21–22).

37:23–31. The Lord watches over **the righteous** (v. 25) and directs their lives. He sustains them and provides them with food. This section promises that God will never abandon the righteous but does not guarantee that they will never experience difficulties. Paul, for example, suffered physical hunger because he made the righteous choice to be a messenger of Christ (see 1 Cor. 4:11; 2 Cor. 11:27). Whatever the circumstances, the unchanging reality is that **the Lord loveth judgment** (justice; v. 28) and always does what is right.

37:32–40. **The wicked** (v. 32) seek to destroy **the righteous**, but their evil designs cannot thwart God's blessing. **The Lord will not leave** (v. 33) the upright person in the **hand** of the wicked nor allow a miscarriage of justice. **The wicked** (v. 35) may have power and success temporarily, but they will pass away in death. The Psalms focus primarily on judgment in this life, and the fate of the wicked is that their lives on earth are cut short (see vv. 25–26; 49:13–14; 55:15, 23). **The righteous** (v. 39) have a hope that endures, and the Lord will save them out of **trouble**. The Lord makes secure their inheritance in the Promised Land, in spite of all that the wicked do.

Psalm 38. An urgent appeal for relief from a severe and painful illness, which is God's "rebuke" (v. 1) for a sin David has committed.

Neither the specific occasion behind this psalm nor the illness can be identified. David's suffering is aggravated by the withdrawal of his friends (v. 11) and the unwarranted efforts of his enemies to seize this opportunity to bring him down (vv. 12, 16, 19–20).

38:1–8. The psalm begins with a plea for relief from the Lord's **rebuke** (v. 1). The Lord's discipline is like **arrows** (v. 2) piercing David's body (see Job 6:4; 34:6). His illness has had devastating physical and psychological effects (vv. 5–8). His body was covered with festering sores, and he groans in agony.

38:10–16. The psalmist makes a renewed appeal for deliverance, with further elaboration of his troubles: his illness (v. 10), the abandonment by his friends (v. 11), and the hostility of his enemies (v. 12). His dialogue with God involves a detailed and passionate description of his affliction. David further requests that the Lord answer his enemies (vv. 13–16). Like a deaf-mute, David will not reply to his enemies, but instead waits for the Lord to act on his behalf (vv. 15–16).

38:17–22. As David's health declines, the vigor of his many enemies increases (vv. 17–20). He is about to collapse (**ready to halt**; v. 17), and death seems near. The positive effect of David's affliction is that he is **sorry** (v. 18) for the **sin** he has committed against the Lord. At the same time, he is innocent of any wrongdoing against those attacking him. Despite his sin, the direction of his life has been to **follow** (v. 20) after what is morally **good**. David concludes the psalm with a final appeal for God to help him and deliver him from his affliction (vv. 21–22).

Psalm 39. The poignant prayer of a soul deeply troubled by the fragility of human life.

Like Psalm 38, this song is a prayer offered at a time of illness. Both psalms acknowledge sin and express deep trust in God.

39:1–3. Having determined to keep silent, David can no longer suppress his anguish. He has kept a muzzle on his mouth for fear that rebellious words would escape in the hearing of the wicked, but his **silence** (v. 2) only intensified his agony.

39:4–6. Not merely praying for relief from his suffering, the psalmist asks for understanding and patient acceptance of the brief span of human life (vv. 4–6). David's illness has reminded him of how brief and transient life really is. He compares his life span to **a handbreadth** (v. 5), the length of four fingers, and a vapor (**vanity**) that is here and gone. His statement that **every man walketh in a vain shew** (v. 6) acknowledges that humans walk around like shadow images. **They are disquieted in vain** because they hurry and worry over things that do not ultimately matter. The psalmist's message could almost serve as a summary of Ecclesiastes.

39:7–13. Having learned from his illness, David prays for relief from the Lord's rebuke (vv. 7–11). If the Lord does not restore him, he will be mocked by **the reproach of the foolish** (v. 8). The Lord's discipline has brought correction, but David is nearly **consumed** (v. 10) by the severity of his punishment. He presents his request while modestly acknowledging that he lives his life before God only as a pilgrim passing through (vv. 12–13). Without the Lord's help, he will **be no more** (v. 13). Here there is no glimpse of what lies beyond the horizon of death, a hope that becomes clear with later revelation.

Psalm 40. A prayer for help when troubles abound.

This psalm does not specify the causes of distress, but David acknowledges that they are occasioned by his sin (see v. 12), as in Psalms 38–39. His afflictions are aggravated by the gloating of his enemies.

40:1–5. David begins his prayer with praise of God for His past mercies and recounts through a **new song** (v. 3) how God has helped him in his time of trouble so that others will be moved to trust the Lord. He gives testimony of the Lord's benevolence to all who trust in Him (v. 4) and to His people Israel (v. 5).

40:6–10. David affirms his faithfulness to the Lord. His devotion goes beyond the performance of sacrifice and includes the more important commitment of obedience to God's will (vv. 6–8; see 1 Sam. 15:22; Isa. 1:10–17; Amos 5:21–24). God has **opened** (v. 6) his **ears** so that he might be able and eager to hear God's law. **Lo, I come** (v. 7) probably reflects David's promise to obey the Lord, given at the time of his enthronement, and **In the volume … it is written of me** likely refers to the personal copy of the law that the king took at the time of his enthronement to serve as the covenant charter of his administration (see Deut. 17:18–20). These verses concerning David's obedience are applied to Christ in Hebrews 10:5–10. David's life is filled with praise, he proclaims God's faithful and loving acts on behalf of His people (vv. 9–10). David's piety forms the basis for the prayer that follows.

40:11–17. The psalmist prays for the Lord's help and for deliverance from the divine discipline that has come into his life because of his **iniquities** (v. 12). His troubles are innumerable, and in the midst of his affliction, his enemies harass him (vv. 14–15). He asks that those who wish to put him to shame be put to shame themselves. He concludes with the request that he experience the joy of the Lord's deliverance, acknowledging that he is dependent on God as one who is **poor and needy** (v. 17).

Psalm 41. David's prayer for mercy, offered when he is seriously ill.

This psalm forms the conclusion to book 1 of the Psalms. Book 1 begins and ends with a "Blessed" psalm. As in Psalms 38–40, David acknowledges that his affliction is related to his sin. The first and last sections (vv. 1–3, vv. 10–12) frame the prayer with a note of confidence.

41:1–3. As he opens his prayer, David expresses his confidence that the Lord will restore him. The Lord will help him because as king he has fulfilled his duty to defend the poor (see 72:2, 4, 12–14). **Thou wilt make all his bed in his sickness** (v. 3) is a promise that the Lord will "restore him from his sickbed."

41:4–9. David then prays for God to show mercy and to heal him. His enemies visit, pretending to be concerned for him but looking forward to his demise. Even a **familiar friend** (v. 9), who shared the king's table as a trusted confidant, has turned against him. Jesus applies this verse to himself when He was betrayed by Judas (John 13:18). In fulfilling the role of His royal ancestor as God's anointed king over Israel, the great Son of David also experienced the hostility of men and the betrayal of a trusted associate and thus fulfilled His forefather's lament.

41:10–13. The tone of confidence returns in David's closing prayer, as he asks that he be able to requite (v. 10) his enemies by paying them back for their evil (vv. 10–12). He is confident in the Lord's favor and that he will enjoy the blessing of God's presence as His royal servant **for ever** (v. 12). Because of God's covenant promises (see 2 Sam. 7:15–16), David is never to be rejected. Verse 13 is actually not part of this psalm but rather contains the doxology with which the worshiping community is to respond to the contents of book 1 (see 72:18–19; 89:52; 106:48; 146–150).

Book 2: Psalms 42–72

Psalm 42. A prayer for deliverance from "the oppression of the enemy" (42:9; 43:2) and for restoration to the presence of God at His temple.

Structure and common themes indicate that Psalms 42 and 43 form a single prayer. The same refrain appears in 42:5, 11; 43:5. The prayer may have been separated into two psalms for a particular liturgical purpose.

Psalm 42 begins book 2 of the Psalter, a collection that is distinguished from book 1 primarily by the predominance of the Hebrew word for "God" (*Elohim*), whereas in the first book, the Hebrew word for "the LORD" (*Yahweh*) predominates. This song is also the first of a collection of seven psalms ascribed to **the sons of Korah** (Psalms 42–49); four more occur in book 3 (Psalms 84–85; 87–88). "The sons of Korah" refers to the Levitical choir made up of the descendants of Korah appointed by David to serve in the temple liturgy (see 1 Chron. 6:31–47).

42:1–5. The psalmist begins by expressing his longing to be with God at the temple (vv. 1–4). His desire for God is like that of a thirsting deer, but circumstances prevent him from being at the temple, where he is able to enter God's presence and commune with Him.

The psalmist remembers the past processions to Jerusalem on the holy feast days, which he is presently unable to enjoy. The refrain **Hope thou in God** (v. 5) is an example of faith encouraging faith in the midst of difficulty.

42:6–11. The reason for the psalmist's troubled soul is that he is exiled from the land of Israel and Judah (vv. 6–10). He locates himself at Mount **Mizar** (a small peak or village, not otherwise known; v. 6) on the flanks of Mount Hermon somewhere near the headwaters of the Jordan. Separation from his homeland and the temple is like being overwhelmed by the waters of the sea. The **Deep** (v. 7) and **noise of thy waterspouts** appear to allude to the waterfalls by which the waters from God's storehouse, the "Deep" above, pour down into the streams and rivers that empty into the seas, the "deep" below (see 36:8). The imagery continues in the parallel statement that God's **waves** and **billows** are sweeping over the psalmist (see 32:6; Jonah 2:3, 5).

The vivid description of anguish in verse 8 is followed by the confession of faith that stands at the center of Psalms 42–43. Day and night, the Lord directs His love to the psalmist and provides a **song** (v. 8) of hope. The phrase **command his lovingkindness** personifies God's love as a messenger sent to do His will. Nevertheless, the fact that God's hand is involved in David's suffering, at least to the extent that He has allowed this catastrophe, only adds to the intensity of his suffering. It appears as if God has **forgotten** (v. 9) him, so the psalmist again exhort himself to **Hope thou in God** (v. 11).

Psalm 43. The prayer of Psalm 42 continues in Psalm 43.

43:1–5. David prays for deliverance from the enemy and for restoration to God's presence. Using the language of the courts, he pleads the justice of his cause against **an ungodly nation** (v. 1). His continued exile makes it appear that the Lord has **cast** (v. 2) him **off.** Echoing 42:8, the psalmist personifies God's

light (v. 3) and **truth** as God's messengers who will bring deliverance and safely guide him back to the temple, where he will enjoy God's presence and offer **praise** (v. 4). The refrain (repeated from 42:5, 11) is a final reminder of the need for continued trust while waiting for God's answer to his prayer.

Psalm 44. Israel's cry for help after suffering a devastating defeat at the hand of an enemy.

This psalm is a national lament at a time of military defeat. In the light of verses 17–22, it is difficult to associate this defeat with any announced by the prophets as judgments on Israel's covenant unfaithfulness. It probably relates to an experience of the kingdom of Judah, perhaps during the reign of Jehoshaphat or Hezekiah.

44:1–8. The psalm opens with praise to the Lord for Israel's past victories (vv. 1–8). These victories established Israel in the land (vv. 1–3) and kept them secure in the land (vv. 4–8). The first-person singular references throughout this psalm refer to the nation corporately. Israel's success in battle came not from military strength (**bow** and **sword**; v. 6) but from the Lord fighting on behalf of His people.

44:9–16. The second section of the psalm provides a vivid description of Israel's present defeat and its consequences. The Israelites cannot understand why God has allowed them to suffer defeat (vv. 9–12) and shame before their enemies (vv. 13–16). They are like butchered sheep because the Lord has not protected them as their Shepherd-King. The Lord has stopped fighting on behalf of His people and has sold them like chattel no longer valued. The enemy nations look on Israel's pathetic condition with scorn and contempt.

44:17–22. The people plead their innocence before God and argue that they have done nothing to deserve punishment. They have not **forgotten** (v. 17) the Lord or been unfaithful to His **covenant.** God Himself knows **the secrets of the heart** (v. 21) and is their witness that they have not turned to other gods (vv. 20–22). In fact, from the time of her stay in Egypt, Israel has suffered the hostility of the nations because of her relationship with the Lord.

44:23–26. Having protested their innocence, the people pray for God's help and deliverance. They boldly call for God to **Awake** (v. 23) and hide not His **face** (v. 24), because it appears that He is ignoring their suffering (vv. 23–24). They pray for God to intervene because they are **bowed down to the dust** (v. 25) and about to sink away into death (vv. 25–26).

Psalm 45. A song in praise of the king on his wedding day.

The king in this psalm undoubtedly belonged to David's dynasty, and the song was probably used at more than one royal wedding. Since the bride is a foreign princess (vv. 10, 12), the wedding reflects the king's standing as a figure of international significance. Accordingly, he is addressed as one whose reign is to be characterized by victories over the nations (vv. 3–5; see Psalms 2; 110). As a royal son of David, the king is a type (foreshadowing) of Christ. After the exile, this psalm was applied to the Messiah, the promised Son of David who would sit on David's throne. For the application of verses 6–7 to Christ, see Hebrews 1:8–9.

45:1–9. The psalmist is stirred by the majesty of **the king** (v. 1) on his wedding day and pledges to perpetuate the king's memory throughout the generations (vv. 1–2). The king is honored because he is **blessed** (v. 2) by God. The first section of the psalm contains words addressed to the king (vv. 3–9). The psalmist exhorts the king to go forth with his sword in the service of all that is right. The king's reign of justice and **righteousness** (v. 4) will become an even greater adornment than the royal garb he wears at his wedding. The king's glory is such that he is addressed as **God** (v. 6). This exalted language does not attempt to deify the king but rather reflects the special relationship between the Lord and the Davidic ruler, who was adopted as a "son" of God at the time of his enthronement. His earthly throne is a reflection of God's heavenly rule. Such a description of the Davidic king attains its fullest meaning when applied to Christ (see Heb. 1:8–9). God has blessed the king by anointing him with **the oil of gladness** (v. 7), a figure for the joy that is even more delightful than the aromatic oils with which his head and body were anointed on his

wedding day. The splendor of the king's wedding is a visual demonstration of God's blessing.

45:10–15. The psalmist addresses the royal bride and exhorts her to be totally loyal to her adoring king (**worship thou him**; v. 11). The glory of the royal bride is described with lavish imagery. The great trading center of **Tyre** (v. 12) is personified as presenting a wedding **gift** to the bride. The king of Tyre was the first foreign ruler to recognize the Davidic dynasty (see 2 Sam. 5:11), and Solomon maintained close relations with that city-state (see 1 Kings 5; 9:10–14, 26–28). Wealthy individuals desire to be in the bride's good graces since she is the wife of the king. She is beautifully adorned and accompanied by her attendants at the wedding.

45:16–17. The psalm concludes with an expression of confidence that God will continue the family line of the king (vv. 16–17). **Instead of thy fathers shall be thy children** (v. 16) perhaps suggests that the sons to come will surpass the fathers in honor. This continual succession will cause the **name** (v. 17) of David **to be remembered in all generations**.

Psalm 46. A celebration of the security of Jerusalem as the city of God.

46:1–3. The first stanza of the psalm is a triumphant confession of fearless trust in God and portrays the Lord as a **refuge and strength** (v. 1) in the midst of natural disaster (vv. 1–3). God's people have no need to **fear**, even if an earthquake breaks up the continents and causes them to sink beneath the resurging waters of the seas. God provides security even if the creation itself seems to become uncreated and all appears to be going down into the primeval deep.

46:4–6. The middle stanza describes the security of Zion because of God's mighty, sustaining presence. Unlike other great cities of the ancient world, Jerusalem had no natural river, so God's presence is metaphorically portrayed as a **river** (v. 4) that continually flows with sustaining and refreshing blessing. **The city of God** becomes like the Garden of Eden (see Gen. 2:10; Isa. 33:21; Ezek. 31:4–9). The Lord protects Zion from enemy assault and defeats her enemies **right early** (i.e., at dawn; v. 5), when attacks against cities were likely to be launched.

The nations **raged** (v. 6), which is the same verb as that used for the "roar" of the seas in verse 3; both threaten Zion's security. God destroys His enemies with the power of His **voice**, which causes the **earth** to melt as though struck by lightning.

46:7–11. The third stanza offers the people's glad response to the Lord's protective presence (vv. 7–9). God's triumph over the nations brings peace to Zion, a preview of the universal peace that will be enjoyed when the Messiah will rule over the earth (see Isa. 9:2–7). God responds to the people with the command, **Be still** (v. 10); the Hebrew for this phrase carries the meaning of "Enough!" (as in 1 Sam. 15:16, "Stay"). God instructs the people to cease seeking security in their own actions and strength and to look to Him. **I will be exalted in the earth**: God's mighty acts on behalf of His people will bring Him universal recognition, a major theme in the Psalter (see 47:9; 66:1–7; 67:2–5; 86:9; 98:2–3; 99:2–3) and elsewhere in the Old Testament (see Exod. 14:4, 18; 1 Kings 8:41–43; Ezek. 36:23; Hab. 2:14).

Psalm 47. A celebration of the universal reign of Israel's God and a testimony to the nations.

This psalm belongs to a group of hymns to the Great King, elsewhere found clustered in Psalms 92–100. Here it serves to link Psalms 46 and 48.

47:1–4. The God who reigns in Zion is identified as **a great King over all the earth** (v. 2; see v. 7; 48:2). The nations are called to rejoice in the God of Israel, the Lord over all the earth. Their celebration with clapping and singing suggests their inclusion in the blessings of salvation; thus, this song serves as an Old Testament anticipation of the evangelization of the nations. The Lord has blessed Israel above all nations because of His special love for His people. He has promised Israel dominion over the nations and has given them the inheritance of the Promised Land.

47:5–9. The center of the poem (vv. 5–6) portrays the liturgical ascension of God to the temple, perhaps represented by the processional bearing of the ark into the temple. The ark is symbolic of God's throne; the temple is the earthly symbol of His heavenly palace. This procession was likely connected to one of Israel's major festival days, perhaps the Feast of Tabernacles (see Lev. 23:34). The **trumpet** (a ram's horn; v. 5) announces the presence of God as King and the declaration is made that **God is the King of all the earth** (v. 7).

The Lord is enthroned in the Most Holy Place of the temple, and the nations acknowledge the God of Israel to be the Great King (vv. 8–9). **The princes** (v. 9) of the nations becoming **the people of the God of Abraham** fulfills the covenant promises made to Abraham (see Gen. 12:2–3; 17:4–6; 22:17–18). This psalm anticipates the messianic kingdom, when all nations will recognize the Lord's sovereignty over the earth.

Psalm 48. A celebration of the security of Zion (as viewed with the eyes of faith) in that it is "the city of the Great King" (v. 2).

48:1–3. The opening stanza describes the beauty of Zion as God's impregnable citadel. Zion is **the city of our God** (v. 1). Though **mount Zion** (v. 2) was only a small hill, its significance as the mountain of God makes it the "highest" mountain in the world (see 68:15–16; see Isa. 2:2). Because of the admiration of other nations, Zion is **the joy of the whole earth** (see 1 Kings 10:1–13). God Himself, not her walls, is her defense.

48:4–8. The attacks of hostile nations against Zion are futile (vv. 4–7). They fled in panic when they saw that the Great King was in Zion. Events such as the destruction of the confederacy in the days of Jehoshaphat (see 2 Chronicles 20) or the slaughter of the Assyrians in the time of Hezekiah (see 2 Kings 19:35–36) may have been in the psalmist's mind. The armies of the world may be as impressive as the great merchant **ships of Tarshish** (v. 7), but the Lord destroys them. Past generations have recounted the great acts of God in their days, but the psalmist and his fellow worshipers have **seen** (v. 8) for themselves (in experience and in the liturgy of the temple) the greatness of God's power.

48:9–14. The worshipers meditate at the temple with joy because of God's mighty acts on Zion's behalf (vv. 9–11). God's saving acts are a reflection of His covenant love for Israel. In response, the praise of God reaches from the temple to **the ends of the earth** (v. 10). The people contemplate Zion's defense and acknowledge that the strength of Zion's **towers** (v. 12), **bulwarks** (v. 13), and **palaces** is the presence of God (vv. 12–13). The opening and closing verses frame this psalm with a comforting confession concerning Israel's God. The Lord will protect and **guide** (v. 14) Israel for all time.

Psalm 49. A word of instruction concerning rich fools who proudly rely on their great wealth to assure their security in the world.

49:1–5. The psalmist offer wisdom for all to hear (vv. 1–4), wisdom he first heard from God and now shares with others. This wisdom is a **dark saying** ("riddle"; v. 4) that requires deep reflection and spiritual sensitivity to the mysterious ways that God works in the world. The use of **the harp** to convey this wisdom offers a further hint of the author's sense of inspiration (see 1 Sam. 10:5–6; 2 Kings 3:15).

49:6–12. The wisdom instruction focuses on the problem of the prosperity of the wicked. Those of little means or power need not be unsettled when surrounded by rich fools who threaten and **boast** (v. 6) of their wealth. Wealth cannot buy escape from death, even if one has a redeemer willing to pay the **ransom** (v. 7; see Exod. 21:30; Lev. 25:47–49). Anyone can see that even the wise die and leave their wealth to others (see Eccl. 2:18, 21; 7:2; 9:5). Only fools refuse to accept the inevitability of death or attempt to perpetuate their memory by attaching their names to their large landholdings.

49:13–15. True wisdom understands the ultimate fate of the wicked and the righteous. The fool thinks he is secure because of his wealth. He may gain large estates in this life (see v. 11), but his final dwelling place will be the **grave** (v. 14). **Death** is already his shepherd, leading him to the grave so that he may consume him. For the imagery of death (or the grave) as an insatiable monster feeding on its victims, see 69:15; Proverbs 30:15–16; Isaiah 5:14; Jonah 2:2. The imagery is borrowed from Canaanite mythology, which so depicts the god Mot (death). As one Canaanite document reads, "Do not approach divine Mot, lest he put you like a lamb into his mouth." The contrasting fate of the righteous is that God delivers them from **the power of the grave** (v. 15). The earthly

focus suggests the psalmist refers to deliverance from physical death so that the righteous might live a full and blessed life, but this promise at least anticipates the hope of resurrection and eternal life in the presence of God, which is made clear in later revelation.

49:16–20. Understanding their final destiny, the righteous are not to allow the present state of the wealthy to captivate them. The **rich** (v. 16) will not take their wealth with them when they die. They may be praised by **men** (v. 18) as enjoying life's ultimate good, but the spiritually wise recognize that wealth is fleeting and transitory.

Psalm 50. The Lord calls His covenant people to account as they meet before Him in worship at the temple.

The superscription ascribes this song to **Asaph** (or it was written for him or his descendants who functioned in his place). Asaph was one of David's three choir leaders (see 1 Chron. 16:5, 7). This song may have been separated from the other psalms of Asaph (Psalms 73–83) because of its thematic links with Psalms 46–49.

The psalm depicts a courtroom scene in which God comes to judge His people and may have been part of a temple liturgy in which Israel reaffirms her commitment to God's covenant. Its rebuke of a false understanding of sacrifice reflects an affinity with the prophecies of Amos, Micah, and Isaiah (see Amos 5:21–24; Mic. 6:1–6; Isa. 1:10–17).

50:1–6. The psalm begins with an announcement of the coming of Israel's covenant Lord to call His people to account. The Lord calls **the earth** (v. 1) as a witness to the courtroom proceedings. When Moses renewed the covenant between the Lord and Israel on the plains of Moab, he called on heaven and earth to serve as third-party witnesses to the covenant (Deut. 30:19; 31:28). The Lord will ultimately come as a consuming **fire** to **judge** Jerusalem (vv. 3–4), a warning fulfilled when the Babylonians destroy the city in 586 BC. Israel has been unfaithful despite solemnly confirming their covenant commitment to the Lord through their sacrifices.

50:7–15. The Lord also has words of correction for His people (vv. 7–15). The problem is not that

Israel had failed to bring enough **sacrifices** (v. 8) but rather that she was ever tempted to think that sacrifices were of first importance to God. God is not dependent on their sacrifices because He already possesses the animals they offer to Him. The sacrifices are more for the people's benefit than for God's. The Lord wants Israel to acknowledge her dependence on Him, by giving thank offerings for His mercies (v. 14) and by praying to Him in times of need (v. 15).

50:16-23. The Lord's rebuke of the wicked in these verses is a reminder of the priority He places on obedience to His moral law as the ultimate expression of covenant faithfulness. The wicked affirm their loyalty to God and claim His blessings (**take my covenant in thy mouth**; v. 16), but their worship is nothing more than empty words. They participate in the rituals of worship but hate **instruction** (v. 17) and reject God's law as the rule for life outside the ritual. Their deeds and words are evil, and they view God's patient and merciful silence toward their sins is viewed as tacit approval of their lifestyle. Their perception of God could not be more wrong, and He warns that He will **reprove** (v. 21) the wicked and **tear** them **in pieces** (v. 22). The wicked will have no part in the **salvation** (v. 23) that God provides for His people.

Psalm 51. David's humble prayer for forgiveness and cleansing.

The superscription connects this prayer for forgiveness to David's sin with **Bath-sheba** (see 2 Sam. 11:1–12:25).

51:1-2. The psalmist makes an initial plea for the Lord to show mercy in granting pardon for his sin. He piles up synonyms for grace (**mercy**; v. 1, **lovingkindness, tender mercies**), for the act of granting forgiveness (**blot out, wash**; v. 2), and for his sinful act (**transgressions**, v. 1; **iniquity … sin**, v. 2) as a means of reflecting his desperation and the largeness of his request. The image behind the request to "blot out" is that of a papyrus scroll on which God had recorded David's deed. The other figure for forgiveness is the washing of a filthy garment.

51:3-6. David confesses his sin. **Against thee, thee only** (v. 4) is an acknowledgment that his sin

is preeminently against God, but he is not denying the effect that his sin had on others. He cannot plead that this sin was a rare aberration in his life; it sprang from what he is and has been from birth. The contrast in verse 6 is that David has acted contrary to what God desires and to what God has been teaching him, but it is God's desire for **truth** (v. 6) and His teaching that gives David hope that God will help him change and become a person of **wisdom**.

51:7-9. David renews his prayer for pardon. The Hebrew for **Purge me** (v. 7) literally reads, "Un-sin me." **Hyssop** is a plant used in ritual cleansing (see Exod. 12:22). **I shall be clean** and **Wash me** again compare David's life to a filthy garment (see v. 2). If God washes him, he will be **whiter than snow**, so pure that no figurative word can describe him (see Isa. 1:18; Dan. 7:9; Rev. 7:14). **Make me to hear joy** (v. 8) is David's request to hear a prophetic oracle of forgiveness that will result in joy. He asks God to **Hide** His **face** (v. 9) from what is **ever before** (v. 3) David.

51:10-17. Not merely desiring forgiveness, David also prays for a pure **heart** (v. 10) and a steadfast **spirit** of faithfulness (vv. 10–12). God's work of transformation will be the creation of something new that only He can fashion. The requests **Cast me not away** (v. 11) and **take not thy holy Spirit from me** are essentially one (see 139:7; Ezek. 39:29). David's prayer recalls the rejection of Saul (see 1 Sam. 16:1, 14; 2 Sam. 7:15) and pleads for God not to take away His Spirit, by which He had equipped and qualified David for his royal office (see 1 Sam. 16:13; see 2 Sam. 23:1–2).

David makes a vow to praise the Lord in response to the forgiveness of his sin (vv. 13–17). His praise for God's forgiveness and purification will be accompanied by instruction for **sinners** (v. 13). Praise will follow God's forgiveness, but David realizes that what pleases God more than sacrifices is a humble **heart** (v. 17) that looks to Him when troubles abound and that penitently pleads for mercy when sin has been committed.

51:18-19. The conclusion, a prayer for **Zion** (v. 18), is an addition to the original psalm. The reference to **the walls of Jerusalem** suggests that these verses originated after the exile. The restoration of Zion will result in God's people offering true worship in the form of **the sacrifices of righteousness** (v. 19), in which ritual and right behavior are joined together.

Psalm 52. An expression of fearless confidence in God, when attacked by an arrogant and evil enemy.

According to the superscription, Doeg's act of treachery against David, which led to Saul's slaughter of the priests at Nob, provides the setting for this psalm (see 1 Sam. 22:9–10).

52:1–9. David stands in the presence of God and, from the high tower of that refuge, hurls his denunciation into the face of his attacker. The enemy views himself as a **mighty man** (v. 1) but is nothing next to God, whose enduring **goodness** prevails over the evil of men (vv. 1–4). The enemy has a perverted sense of right and wrong and is arrogant in both word and deed. God will destroy the wicked and remove them from the land (vv. 5–7), and the righteous will mock the wicked in their demise. David's security rests in God (vv. 8–9). The Lord will establish him **like a green olive tree** (v. 8), which lives for hundreds of years. David vows to praise the Lord, knowing that He has and will again deliver him "out of all his troubles" (34:6).

Psalm 53. A testimony concerning the folly of evil men.

This psalm serves as a further commentary on the kind of arrogant fool denounced in Psalm 52 and is a somewhat revised duplicate of Psalm 14 (see discussion there).

53:1–6. The fool (v. 1) is morally **corrupt** because he lives as if God does not exist. His disregard for God translates itself into hatred of the righteous. The promise is that God will overwhelms the godless who attack His people (v. 5). The destruction of the wicked is expressed in the past tense, likely to stress the certainty of their downfall. The wicked fall victim to fear when, humanly speaking, they are not even threatened. God's curse falls on them rather than on Israel (see Lev. 26:36–37). Over the battlefield of their defeat, God leaves their bodies **scattered** and unburied, like something loathsome (see

Isa. 14:18–20; Jer. 8:2). David closes with a prayer for God to deliver His people from **captivity** (v. 6) and restore them.

Psalm 54. A prayer for deliverance from enemies who want to have David killed.

According to the tradition reflected in the superscription, David turns to God when he was fleeing from Saul and was betrayed by the Ziphites (see 1 Sam. 23:19). When man has failed him, David turns to God.

54:1–7. David prays for God to judge his case and to vindicate him before his enemies (vv. 1–2). The case against his enemies is that they live without regard for God (see 53:1). At the center of this poem, David expresses his confidence that the Lord is his helper and will deal justly with his enemies (vv. 4–5). Following his deliverance, David will fulfill his vow of praise and will **freely sacrifice** (v. 6) to the Lord. David's call for vindication (v. 1) and his assurance that he will look in triumph on his foes frame this prayer.

Psalm 55. A prayer for God's help when threatened by a powerful conspiracy in Jerusalem under the leadership of a former friend.

The situation described here is like that of Absalom's conspiracy against the king (see 2 Sam. 15–17): the city is in turmoil, and there is uncertainty as to who can be trusted. Rumors, false reports, and slander are circulating freely. Under such circumstances, David casts his cares on the Lord. The prayer is framed by a plea for help (v. 1) and a simple confession of faith: "I will trust in thee" (v. 23).

55:1–14. David makes an initial appeal for God to hear because his enemies seek to harm him (**cast iniquity upon me**; v. 3). His **heart** (v. 4) is in anguish because danger is everywhere, a danger so great that it is as if death itself were stalking him (vv. 4–8). David longs for a quiet retreat, away from treacherous and conniving people. Turning to petition, David prays for God to foil the plot of his enemies (vv. 9–11). He desires for God to **divide their tongues** (v. 9) and paralyze the conspirators with conflicting designs, as at Babel (see Gen. 11:5–9; 2 Sam. 17:1–14). The situation is desperate because

Mischief ... and sorrow (v. 10), **Deceit and guile** (v. 11) patrol the city streets, looking for an opportune moment to attack the righteous.

The insults and plots of an enemy are difficult, but those of a treacherous friend are nearly too much for David to bear (vv. 12–14). In the past, he and his betrayer had enjoyed fellowship (**sweet counsel;** v. 14), and their ties of friendship had been a bond hallowed by common commitment to the Lord and sealed by its public display in the presence of God at the temple.

55:15–23. David prays for **death**(v. 15) to **seize** the conspirators that are seeking his death. His prayer that they would **go down quick into hell,** or "alive unto sheol," expresses his desire that they go to the grave before life has run its normal course (see Num. 16:29–33). In the remainder of the psalm, David moves between confidence in the Lord's answer to his prayer and continued sorrowful reflection over the treachery of his former friend (vv. 16–23). Knowing that the Lord will answer, David continually expresses his prayer for deliverance (vv. 16–19). The Lord will not disappoint in the same way as his flattering friend, whose words proved deceptive (vv. 20–21). Giving testimony to all who are assembled at the temple, David exhorts the faithful that the Lord will **sustain** (v. 22) them when they give their burdens to Him. In contrast, He will destroy the wicked so that they **shall not live out half their days** (v. 23).

Psalm 56. A prayer for help, offered when the psalmist is attacked by enemies and his very life is threatened.

The superscription connects this psalm to David's flight from the Philistine king at Gath (see 1 Sam. 21:10–15 and Psalm 34 title). The contrast between David's fear in the narrative of 1 Samuel 21 and his absolute confidence in the Lord in this psalm serves as a reminder that the life of faith is never without doubt and struggle. Ultimately, the psalmist's faith wins out over his fear.

56:1–9. After an initial appeal for God's help (vv. 1–2), David confesses his trust in the Lord in the face of fear (vv. 3–4). He has nothing to fear because of God's promise to come to the aid of his people when they call to Him. Man in his feebleness, compared with God in His power, can do nothing to harm him.

David accuses his enemies of conspiring against him and calls for redress while appealing to God's sense of justice (vv. 5–7). The rhetorical question, **Shall they escape by iniquity?** (v. 7), asks if the wicked will get away with their wrongdoing. The psalmist also appeals for God to take special note of his troubles (vv. 8–9). He reminds the Lord that his troubles are recorded in His **book** (v. 8), or the heavenly royal records, as matters calling for His action. He also calls on the Lord to **Put** his **tears** in a **bottle.** The figure of David's tears being stored in a skin bottle as were liquids (water, wine, or milk) used for drinking in a hot and arid climate indicates God's great regard for the cries of His people. If God takes such note of David's tears that He collects them in a bottle and records them in His book, He will surely respond to David's call for help. The use of "tear bottles" is not attested elsewhere.

56:10–13. The confession of trust in verses 10–11 and verses 3–4 provides a frame of **I will not be afraid** (v. 11) around David's petition. He has no fear because he is confident that God will hear him (vv. 12–13). Speaking as if his prayer has already been answered, David acknowledges that he now needs to keep the **vows** he made to God when he was in trouble. God's answer allows David to **walk before God in the light of the living** (v. 13), enjoying the full blessedness of life.

Psalm 57. A prayer for deliverance when threatened by fierce enemies.

The tradition reflected in the superscription states that David offered this prayer while hiding in a cave from King Saul (see 1 Sam. 24:1–3). This psalm is thematically linked to Psalm 56 and is composed of two parts (vv. 1–5 and vv. 6–11) that end with the refrain, "Be thou exalted, O God" (vv. 5, 11). The imagery of the psalm reflects a movement from the night of danger (v. 4) to the morning of salvation (v. 8).

57:1–5. David presents his prayer in the first half of the song. He cries for God's merciful help and is confident of being heard. The Hebrew for **that performeth all things for me** (v. 2) can also be read, "who makes an end [of troubles] for me." God **send from heaven ... mercy and ... truth** (v. 3) as His messengers to save His servant. David employs standard imagery to describe his threatening situation. He lies as a sheep among **lions** (v. 4). The psalmists often compare their enemies to ferocious beasts (see 7:2; 22:12–13, 21). Because of his enemies, the psalmist prays for God to show His exalted power and glory by coming to his rescue (v. 5).

57:6–11. In the second half of the psalm, David turns to praise for God's saving help, confidently anticipating the desired deliverance. The enemies will suffer the calamity they have plotted for David; the lions themselves will be caught in their own traps. David's heart is steadfast and secure (**fixed**; v. 7); all cause for fear has been removed. The **psaltery and harp** (v. 8), here personified, join to accompany the praise of the Lord in celebration of deliverance. **I myself will awake early** literally reads, "I will awaken the dawn." Dawn is also personified as taking part in the rejoicing over David's salvation. David vows to praise and to sing to others of the greatness of the Lord's **mercy** (v. 10) and **truth**. His praise will exalt the Lord and spread His **glory** (v. 11) through the earth.

Psalm 58. A prayer for God, the Supreme Judge, to set right the affairs of men, judging those rulers who corrupt justice and championing the cause of the righteous.

This psalm reflects a concern for the proper use of judicial power, which is pervasive in the Old Testament. This was the primary agency in the ancient Near East for the protection of the innocent, usually the poor and powerless, against the assaults of unscrupulous men, usually the rich and powerful. Israelite society was troubled with the corruption of this judicial power from the days of Samuel to the end of the monarchy (see, e.g., 1 Sam. 8:3; Amos 5:7, 10–13; Mic. 3:1–3, 9–11; 7:2). The early church applied this psalm to Jesus' trial before the Sanhedrin (see Matt. 26:57–68 and parallels).

58:1–5. The psalmist accuses wicked judges of perverting justice with their mouths, hearts, and **hands** (v. 2). The term **congregation** (v. 1) used for these judges is the word for "gods" or "mighty ones" (see Exod. 22:8–9). This title signifies that these officials hold administrative positions that call them to act as earthly representatives of God's heavenly court. Rather than carrying out this sacred responsibility, these judges issue decisions that result in cruel injustice. Their actions are in accordance with their wicked nature.

58:6–8. Employing imagery drawn from conventional curses of the ancient Near East, David prays for God to purge the land of such perverse judges (vv. 6–8; see 5:10). He prays for the **teeth of the young lions** (v. 6) to be broken so that they will no longer be able to prey on the needy. He calls for the Lord to quickly put the wicked judges to death, that they would be like **waters which run continually** (v. 7) and are absorbed by the ground, like a slug that appears to dry up to nothing as it moves over stone in the hot sun, and like a miscarriage (**the untimely birth**; v. 8).

58:9–11. The psalmist assures the people that God will judge the wicked who have abused their positions of authority. **Before your pots can feel the thorns** (v. 9) speaks of the speed and severity of God's judgment. God's judgment will come more quickly than thorns can heat a fire for cooking. The Lord will right the wrongs that have been inflicted on the **righteous** (v. 10), who will **rejoice** in their vindication. The image of washing **feet in the blood** uses vivid imagery from the battlefield to portray the triumph of the righteous. The climax is a promise that all people will see that right ultimately prevails under God's just rule. The righteous can be confident that **there is a reward** (v. 11) for them.

Psalm 59. A prayer for deliverance when endangered by enemy attacks.

The superscription relates the original setting of the psalm to David's narrow escape when Saul and his men watched over David's house (see 1 Sam. 19:11).

59:1–9. The psalmist cries for deliverance and prays that the Lord will protect him from his **enemies** (v. 1). The enemies justify their attacks with curses and lies, but David protests his innocence and pleads with God to judge those who wrong him (vv. 3–5). They set an ambush against him, but he has done nothing to deserve their attacks. The appeal to the Lord as **the God of Israel** (v. 5) demonstrates that the attack on the psalmist involves an attack by the nations on Israel. The psalmist is confident that God mocks these enemies, who besiege the city like dogs at night on the prowl for food (vv. 6–8). In the danger of the night, he will **wait upon** (lit., "watch for"; v. 9) the morning of salvation.

59:10–17. With assurance that the Lord will hear his prayer, David renews his petition (vv. 10–15). He prays that God will not sweep them away suddenly but will prolong their punishment so that Israel will not forget God's acts of salvation. He asks the Lord to **Scatter** (v. 11) his enemies so that they wander like vagabonds constantly having to search for food. These defeated foes will become a continual reminder of what happens to those who oppose God, and the enemies themselves will acknowledge that Israel's God is the Judge of all the earth. When God delivers him, the psalmist **will sing** (v. 16) for joy in the Lord's protection (vv. 16–17).

Psalm 60. A national prayer for God's help after Israel suffers a severe blow from a foreign nation, presumably Edom (see v. 9).

The superscription connects this psalm to David's military struggles with the nations surrounding Israel (see 2 Samuel 8; 1 Chronicles 18; and perhaps also 2 Samuel 10). If this tradition is correct, it must be supposed that our knowledge of the events is incomplete, since the narratives do not mention Edom. The Israelite war against Edom at this time of great northern battles may have been occasioned by an attack on the part of Edom, trying to take advantage of Israel's preoccupation elsewhere, an attack in which Edom succeeded in overrunning the garrisons that guarded Judah's southern borders.

60:1–3. The psalmist laments that God has cast off His people and no longer accompanies their armies to battle (see Psalm 44). Defeat by the enemy is interpreted as a sign of God's anger. Their defeat is like a devastating earthquake, and God has made

them drink from **the wine of astonishment** (or "wine that makes us stagger"; v. 3) rather than from His cup of blessing and salvation.

60:4–8. Speaking for the nation, the psalmist pleads for help from the Lord, a prayer that is grounded in reasons for confidence (vv. 4–8). The Lord's promises of protection and victory are like **a banner** (v. 4) used to rally the troops in preparation for battle and to lead them into action (see Isa. 5:26; Jer. 4:21). The Lord delivers Israel and their king because they are His **beloved** (v. 5), a word of special endearment (see 127:2; 2 Sam. 12:25).

The Lord comforts His people with an oracle of salvation, perhaps an already ancient word from the time of the conquest (vv. 6–8). The Lord is Israel's triumphant Warrior-King, and He will **divide** (v. 6) His conquered territory among His servant people. **Shechem** and **Succoth** (see Gen. 33:17–18; 1 Kings 12:25) and **Gilead … and Manasseh** (v. 7; see Josh. 13:29–31; 17:5–11) are places representative of the territory west and east of the Jordan that was taken over by the Lord and Israel. **Ephraim** and **Judah** are the two leading tribes of Israel, representing the northern and southern kingdoms of Israel. The Lord gives His people victory over **Moab … Edom … Philistia** (v. 8), their perpetual enemies on Israel's eastern, southern, and western borders. Moab will become a **washpot** in which the Lord washes His feet.

60:10–12. The psalmist is confident that Israel's being **cast … off** (v. 10) by the Lord is only temporary. The Lord will give **help** (v. 11) to His people and enable them to **do valiantly** (v. 12) on the battlefield so that they will triumph over their enemies.

Psalm 61. A prayer for deliverance from a hostile enemy and for restoration to God's presence.

Psalms 61–64 form a series linked by the common theme of trust in God when under threat. David may have composed this prayer at the time of his flight from Absalom (see 2 Sam. 17:21–29).

61:1–3. The song opens with a plea for God to hear (v. 1) and a prayer for protection from the threats of an enemy (vv. 2–3). **The end of the earth** (v. 2) perhaps refers to the brink of the underworld, as the psalmist feels he is near death. The place of security that David seeks is beyond his reach; only God can bring him to it. He appeals to God because God has never failed him as a refuge.

61:4–8. In the midst of danger, David longs for the security of God's sanctuary (vv. 4–5). If the Absalom crisis is in view, David desires to return to Jerusalem and to **abide in** (v. 4) the Lord's presence at the **tabernacle.** God's protective presence is the inheritance (**heritage;** v. 5) of **those that fear** the Lord. God's promises lead to a prayer for the king's long **life** (v. 6). The king himself may have offered this prayer, or it may have been the prayer of the people. The Lord's attributes of **mercy and truth** (v. 7) are personified as David's guardians. The psalmist vows to **sing praise** (v. 8) to the Lord when He delivered him from danger.

Psalm 62. The psalmist commits himself to God when threatened by the assaults of conspirators who wish to dethrone him.

62:1–8. David expresses his confidence in God in the face of conspiracy (vv. 1–4). The circumstances here could well have been the efforts of the family of Saul to topple David from power. He quietly waits for the Lord's deliverance. **Ye shall be slain** (v. 3) reads as a statement of confidence in the ultimate demise of his enemies. However, the context of verses 3–4 would suggest that David is describing his own fragile condition: "Would you slay him— this **bowing wall** (v. 3) and **tottering fence?**" His enemies are seeking to cast him down from his exalted position or throne (**his excellency;** v. 4). David exhorts himself to trust in God and to **wait** (v. 5) for God's deliverance (vv. 5–7). Faith must encourage faith in times of difficulty. He then exhorts God's people to trust in the Lord and **pour out** (v. 8) their hearts to Him in earnest prayer.

62:9–12. People of faith recognize that frail, misguided men who may oppose them are nothing compared to their powerful and trustworthy God. The parallel **men of low degree … men of high degree** (v. 9) signifies persons of every condition. In reality, the rich and powerful are nothing more than a puff of wind (**vanity**) next to God. Man's insig-

nificance also serves as a warning against trusting in oneself for security rather than turning to God. **God hath spoken once; twice have I heard** (v. 11) is a figure emphasizing the certainty of God's promises and His power to accomplish them (see Amos 1:3). Ultimately, every person will experience God's righteousness, either in judgment or in salvation.

Psalm 63. A confession of longing for God and for the security of His presence, offered when deadly enemies threaten.

The superscription refers to **David … in the wilderness of Judah,** most likely connecting this song to David's flight from Absalom since the psalmist is referred to as a king in verse 11 (see 2 Sam. 15:23–28; 16:2, 14; 17:16, 29).

63:1–8. In a time of need, David expresses his intense longing for God through the metaphor of thirst and hunger (vv. 1–5). His affliction places him **in a dry and thirsty land** (v. 1) so that he needs to be satisfied by the **marrow and fatness** (v. 5) of God's presence. He has **seen** (v. 2) God at the sanctuary and recognizes God's presence as life's ultimate good. The psalmist's night reflections on God's presence and **help** (v. 7) in times past motivates his pursuit of God (vv. 6–8). He is confident that the Lord's **right hand** (v. 8) will sustain him.

63:9–11. In contrast, David's enemies will receive what they deserve (vv. 9–10). In seeking his life, they forfeit their own lives. His foes will go down **into the lower parts of the earth** (v. 9), or the underworld (see 61:2). Their unburied bodies will become **a portion for foxes** (v. 10), which adds to their disgrace. **The king** (v. 11) and those who revere and trust God will have cause for celebration when God destroys those who live by falsehood.

Psalm 64. A prayer to God for protection when threatened by a conspiracy.

64:1–6. The psalmist prays for protection from his enemies, who attack him like an angry mob intent on **insurrection** (v. 2). It is not clear whether the conspirators come from within or outside of Israel, but their primary means of attack is their vicious words (vv. 3–6). Their tongues are like weapons, and they feel secure from exposure and retaliation. Their depravity has perverted their intellectual capacities, and the **deep** (v. 6) thoughts of these wicked men are cunning and devious as they plot evil.

64:7–10. The psalmist is confident in God's righteous judgment (vv. 7–8). The Lord will turn the words of the wicked against them and do to them what they had intended to do to David. Their self-confidence will turn to fear. The Lord's judgment will bring a reversal of David's present distress (vv. 9–10). All mankind will **fear** (v. 9) the Lord and **declare** His righteous works, while **The righteous** (v. 10) rejoice, take refuge in the Lord's protection, and **glory** in His deliverance. In verse 10, the Hebrew for **be glad** is a wordplay on the Hebrew for "hear," which is the first word of the psalm, a wordplay framing the psalm and highlighting the reversal that is central to its message.

Psalm 65. A hymn in praise of God's great goodness to His people.

65:1–3. The psalmist expresses his commitment to praise God (vv. 1–2). **Praise waiteth for thee** (v. 1) appears to personify praise as a permanent resident of the temple, lying quietly at rest, whom the people will awaken when they come to make good their vows. **The vow** refers to the promises made to God in conjunction with their prayers in times of need (see 7:17; 66:14). All mankind is called to praise God because He answers prayer.

65:3–13. The specific grounds for praise in this psalm are three great blessings that God has conferred on His people. The first and primary blessing is that He pardons the sins of His people so that they continue to enjoy the **goodness** (v. 4) of fellowship with Him at His temple (vv. 3–4). The second blessing is that God orders the affairs of the world so that international turbulence is put to rest and Israel is secure in her land (vv. 5–8). God has performed **terrible things** (v. 5), or "awesome works," on Israel's behalf (see Deut. 10:21; 2 Sam. 7:23). The God who brought order out of chaos at creation establishes a peaceful order among the nations. The Old Testament poets often compared God's mighty acts in redemption with His mighty acts in creation (see 74:12–17; 89:9–18; Isa. 27:1; 51:9–11). Israel

enjoyed God's blessing as His chosen people, but this psalm anticipates when all peoples will recognize the Lord's sovereignty. The demonstrations (**tokens**; v. 8) of the Lord's infinite power will move the nations to reverence Him. Turning to the Lord, they will have as much cause as Israel to celebrate His answers to prayer and His goodness (see vv. 2, 12–13).

The third blessing is that God turns the Promised Land into a veritable Garden of Eden (vv. 9–13). Israel is blessed with prosperity and agricultural bounty. Keeping with the universal focus of this psalm, the creation itself (**hills**, v. 12; **pastures** and **valleys**, v. 13) is personified as joining in the celebration of the goodness of God.

Psalm 66. A psalm of praise for God's answer to prayer.

It seems that God has saved the author, probably a king, from an enemy threat, and his deliverance has involved also that of the whole nation. It has often been suggested that this psalm speaks of Judah's remarkable deliverance from the Assyrians (see 2 Kings 19).

66:1–4. The psalmist begins with a call for all the earth to joyfully praise the Lord. Because of the Lord's awesome (**terrible**; v. 3) deeds, even His **enemies** will one day acknowledge Him and give Him the worship He deserves.

66:5–7. The cause for praise is God's deliverance of Israel at the Red Sea as a sign of His power to rule over the nations (vv. 5–7). The psalmist portrays his own deliverance as similar to the Red Sea rescue in its manifestation of God's saving power and as a continuation of God's same saving purposes. With **Come and see** (v. 5), the psalmist calls the people to behold God's saving acts of old as they are continually celebrated and retold in the liturgy at the temple. Just as God subdued the waters of **the** Red **sea**, the Lord continues to hold in check **the nations** (v. 7) that rebel against His rule.

66:8–12. The Lord's new deliverance of His people is as much cause for celebration as are His works in the past. The worshipers at the temple are to **praise** (v. 8) God for His protection. Their affliction was a time in which God **proved** (v. 10) and

tried them. Times of distress constitute a testing of His people's trust in and loyalty to Him. The metaphor is borrowed from the technology of refining precious metals, which included heating the metals in a crucible to see if all impurities had been removed (see 12:6; 17:3).

Even when enemies attack His people for malicious purposes, God is not a mere passive observer but has His own holy purposes in it (vv. 11–12; see Isa. 45:7; Amos 3:6). Several metaphors describe Israel's suffering and its intensity; they are like captives thrown into prison, prisoners of war turned into slaves, defeated troops overrun by chariots. The images of **fire and ... water** (v. 12) are conventional figures for severe trial. God brought them out of their distress into overflowing well-being (**into a wealthy place**).

66:13–20. The king, as representative of the people, will fulfill the **vows** made to God by presenting sacrifices and offerings (vv. 13–15). The offerings will be accompanied by the proclamation of what God has done (vv. 16–20). The call to **Come and hear** (v. 16) parallels "Come and see" in verse 5.

Psalm 67. A communal prayer for God's blessing.

The content, form, and brevity of this psalm suggest that it served as a liturgical prayer of the people, offered at the conclusion of worship, perhaps just prior to (or immediately after) the priestly benediction.

67:1–7. The prayer (vv. 1–2) asks that God's favors to His people be so obvious that all the world takes notice. The wording of this prayer echoes the priestly benediction (see Num. 6:24–26). The motivation for God to answer is that the praise of the nations will be added to that of Israel in a worldwide concert of worship (vv. 3–5). The nations will rejoice in the Lord when they see the benevolence of God's rule (see 98:4–6; 100:1). God's blessing will become evident through the agricultural abundance of the Promised Land (vv. 6–7). The blessing of Israel will cause the nations to **fear him** (v. 7; see 65:9–13).

Psalm 68. A processional liturgy celebrating the glorious and triumphant rule of Israel's God.

This psalm describes God's triumphal march from Mount Sinai (in the days of Moses) to Mount Zion (in the days of David). The events at Mount Sinai marked the birth of the kingdom of God among His people; the establishment of the ark of the covenant in Jerusalem marked the establishment of God's redemptive kingdom on earth, with Jerusalem as its royal city. The early church, taking its cue from Ephesians 4:8–13, understood this psalm to foreshadow the resurrection, ascension, and present rule of Christ and the final triumph of His church over the hostile world.

68:1–6. The procession begins as God marches from Sinai with His people in army formation (vv. 1–3). With God at the head of Israel's army, her enemies will **be scattered** (v. 1). The psalmist calls the people to praise God for the benevolence of His rule (vv. 4–6). The title **him that rideth upon the heavens** (or "clouds"; v. 4) employs an epithet of Baal found in Canaanite literature to make the point that the Lord (Yahweh, not Baal) is the exalted One who truly makes the storm cloud His chariot and provides the rains (see v. 33; 18:9; 104:3; Isa. 19:1; Matt. 26:64). **JAH** is a shortened form of Jahweh (Yahweh), the personal name of God, normally translated "LORD" (see Exod. 3:14). God is the defender of the powerless and meets their needs (see 10:14; 146:7–9; 147:6; Deut. 10:18).

68:7–14. Leaving Sinai, God marched through the wilderness to the Promised Land (vv. 7–10). The thunderstorm and earthquake announced God's **presence** (v. 8) at Sinai. He provided rains that refreshed the people on their journey through the barren wilderness (see Judg. 5:4, though the Pentateuch preserves no tradition of rain during the wilderness wanderings). In the land, God provided for Israel from the produce of Canaan (see Josh. 5:11–12). God also defeated the kings of Canaan, who fled because they were no match for Him (vv. 11–14). Through God's decree, Israel's victories were won before they ever went to battle. While still in camp, Israel, as God's **dove** (v. 13; see 74:19; Hos. 7:11), was enriched with the **silver** and **gold** of plunder from the kings of Canaan. The reference to **white as snow** (v. 14) in connection with the scattering of the kings may refer to their abandoned weapons that littered the field from which they fled. **Salmon** was a mountain near Shechem (see Judg. 9:46–48).

68:15–18. Israel celebrates God's ascent to Mount Zion following His great triumph. The mountains surrounding **Bashan** (v. 15), including the towering Mount Hermon, are portrayed as being jealous because God has chosen Mount Zion as the seat of His rule, making it the "highest" of mountains (see 48:2 and discussion). **Why leap ye?** (v. 16) could be translated, "Why do you look enviously?" The great heavenly host accompanying God are likened to a vast chariot force (see 2 Kings 6:17). God ascends His throne as a victorious king with captives and tribute as the prizes of war. **The rebellious** (v. 18) who had opposed His rule are compelled to submit to Him. Paul applies verse 18 (as translated in the Septuagint) to the ascended Christ (see Eph. 4:8–13), thereby implying that Christ's ascension was a continuation, and fulfillment, of God's establishment of His kingdom in His royal city, Jerusalem.

68:19–23. In light of God's triumphant ascent, the people joyously confess their hope that God's victorious campaigns will continue until the salvation of His people is complete (vv. 19–23). The Lord takes the gifts received from His vanquished enemies and heaps them upon His people. He also is the source of **the issues from death** (v. 20), or "escape from death," as He protects His people from their enemies, including death itself as the last great enemy. He will crush those who oppose Him.

68:24–27. The liturgical procession celebrating God's ascent approaches the temple (see Psalms 24, 47). Music is played as the ark representing God's presence is brought into the temple. All Israel is represented, from **little Benjamin** (v. 27) to powerful **Judah,** and from tribes from the north as well as the south. **Benjamin with their ruler** seems to refer to the fact that the first king (Saul), who began the royal victories over Israel's enemies (see 1 Sam. 11:11; 14:20–23), came from the tribe of Benjamin.

68:28–35. The psalmist prays for God to continue His conquest of the threatening powers (vv. 28–31). The **kings** (v. 29) of the earth will **bring presents** to Him as subjected rulers bringing tribute

to their conqueror (see 2 Sam. 8:2, 6, 10; 2 Kings 3:4). Egypt is singled out as representative of the hostile nations because of Israel's past experiences with that world power and because it was the one great empire on Israel's immediate horizons at the time the psalm was composed. The climax of the liturgical procession is a call for all kingdoms to hail with praise the God of Israel as the God who reigns in heaven and who has established His earthly throne in the temple in Jerusalem (vv. 32–35). The Lord of all has made Israel His people, and His rule among them makes them participants in His victorious **strength and power** (v. 35; see 29:10–11).

Psalm 69. The prayer of a godly king for God to have mercy and to save him from a host of enemies, offered when under vicious attack by a widespread conspiracy, at a time when God disciplined him for sin in his life.

David may have originally authored this psalm, but in its present form, the prayer suggests a later son of David who ruled over the southern kingdom of Judah (see v. 35). That king may have been Hezekiah (see 2 Kings 18–20; 2 Chronicles 29–32). The authors of the New Testament viewed this cry of a godly sufferer as foreshadowing the sufferings of Christ. Other than Psalm 22, no psalm is quoted more frequently in the New Testament.

69:1–4. In his initial plea for God to save him, the psalmist uses the conventional imagery of the flood to describe his great distress. This distress is the result of God's "wounding" (see v. 26) and especially of the attacks of his enemies (see vv. 14–15, 29). His many enemies have hated him **without a cause** (v. 4). Because of the false accusations that his enemies have been spreading about him, he has become like a person forced to pay restitution for something he has not stolen.

69:5–12. David prays that God's discipline of him will not bring disgrace on all those who trust in the Lord (vv. 5–12). He acknowledges that his affliction has been occasioned by the **sins** (v. 5) in his life, but he has not sinned against those who have become his enemies. His suffering has caused his enemies to mock his deep commitment to the Lord, and even those nearest him dissociate themselves from him. The psalmist reminds God of his devotion and **zeal** (v. 9). His weeping and **fasting** (v. 10) are tokens of his humility and repentance, but he continues to be an object of mockery and ridicule for everyone, from the elders of the city to the town drunks. In describing his plight, David implicitly asks God to have mercy on him and vindicate him before his enemies.

69:13–21. Though the enemies continue to mock him, the psalmist prays to God and waits for his deliverance **in an acceptable time** (v. 13). He prays that his troubles will not overwhelm him and that God will not continue to withhold His favor. His enemies are deserving of judgment because of the abuse they have heaped on him (vv. 19–21). The images of **gall** (v. 21) and **vinegar** are vivid metaphors for the bitter scorn they made him eat and drink when his whole being craved for the nourishment and refreshment of comfort. The Gospels suggest that the psalmist's suffering foreshadowed Christ's suffering on the cross (see Matt. 27:34, 48; Mark 15:23, 36; Luke 23:36; John 19:29).

69:22–29. Continuing his prayer, David prays for God to redress the wrongs that are committed against him. **Let their table become a snare** (v. 22) is a request for God to overturn the conspiracy of David's enemies, which have been sealed with a covenant meal. David prays that God's divine **anger** (v. 24) will bring physical affliction upon his enemies. Since they have sought to remove him from his place, David prays that the conspirators be removed from their places of influence and authority. Peter applies the judgment of verse 25 to Judas (Acts 1:20). David's foes have falsely accused him of crimes he has not committed; he prays that they will be punished for their real crimes against him. They are deserving of death because they have plotted his death. **The book of the living** (v. 28) refers to God's royal list of **the righteous**, whom God blesses with life (see 92:12–14; 140:13). In the New Testament, "the book of life" refers to God's list of those destined for eternal life (see Phil. 4:3; Rev. 3:5; 13:8; 12, 15; 21:27).

69:30–36. Out of assurance that his prayer will be heard, the psalmist vows to **praise** (v. 30) the Lord (vv. 30–33). His sincere gratitude will be more pleasing to the Lord than the offering of any animal sacrifice. The closing call to praise (vv. 34–36) gives this psalm a more nationalistic focus: God is worthy of praise because He will restore Judah and assure His people's inheritance in the land. In its final form, this royal prayer was used at a time when not only the king was in trouble but also the kingdom of Judah had suffered devastating defeat.

Psalm 70. An urgent prayer for God's help when threatened by enemies.

This psalm is a somewhat revised duplicate of 40:13–17 (see discussion there). The prayer is framed by pleas for God to "make haste" (vv. 1, 5) with His help. The rest of the prayer focuses on the effects of God's saving help.

70:1–5. On the one hand, those who are **seeking** (v. 2) David's life will be judged. David's enemies wish to disgrace him, but they are the ones who will be put to **shame** (v. 3). On the other hand, **all those that seek** (v. 4) the Lord will be blessed. God's deliverance of His servant will give joy to all who trust in the Lord, because they see in it the assurance of their own salvation. **God** is to **be magnified** because His saving help is sure and effective.

Psalm 71. A prayer for God's help when enemies threaten because they see that the king's strength is waning in his old age.

71:1–8. The psalmist appeals for God to deliver him from **the hand of the unrighteous and cruel man** (v. 4). He confesses that the Lord has sustained him throughout his life and has always been his hope (vv. 5–8). David is **a wonder** (v. 7), or a "mystery," to others because he claims to follow the Lord but experiences great difficulties in his life. While God has not promised to exempt His people from hardship, the psalmist is unshaken in his confidence that God will remain his **strong refuge**.

71:9–18. The psalmist prays for God's continuing help in the waning years of his life (vv. 9–13). The enemies who plot against the king believe that God has abandoned him, so he asks God to act quickly in redressing the situation. When God delivers him, his enemies will be put to shame. The psalmist confesses his unfaltering trust in the Lord (v. 14) and vows to praise the Lord when he receives the answer to his prayer (vv. 15–18). Even in the midst of trouble, he joyfully acknowledges that He is unable to measure (**know not the numbers thereof**; v. 15) the fullness and richness of God's salvation. He will publicly rehearse to other worshipers how God has delivered him when he fulfills his vows at the temple.

71:19–24. David's hope in the Lord is fostered by a recognition of God's greatness (vv. 19–21). There is no one **like** (v. 19) God, who has the power to give His people life by rescuing them from the realm of the dead (**the depths of the earth**; v. 20). For a final time, the psalmist vows to praise God in confident anticipation of His help (vv. 22–24). He will never cease to speak of God's **righteousness** (v. 24), His saving acts on behalf of His people in accordance with His covenant promises.

Psalm 72. A prayer for the king, a son of David who rules on David's throne as God's earthly regent over His people.

The superscription attributes this psalm to Solomon (either by him or for him), and this song was undoubtedly used in Judah as a prayer for later Davidic kings. This prayer may have been used at the time of the king's coronation (as were Psalms 2 and 110) and expresses the nation's desire that the king's reign will be characterized by justice and righteousness, the supreme virtues of kingship. The prayer reflects the concept of the ideal king and the glorious effects of his reign. Later Jewish tradition saw in this psalm a description of the Messiah, as did the early church.

72:1–7. The people pray that their king will be endowed with a gift for and love of justice and righteousness so that his reign reflects the rule of God Himself (vv. 1–7). Solomon asked for wisdom so that he might be this kind of ruler (see 1 Kings 3:9, 11–12; see Prov. 16:12). **Righteousness** (v. 3) in the realm will be like fertilizing rain on the land, for then the Lord will bless His people with abundance (see 65:9–13; Lev. 25:19; Deut. 28:8). The statement that the king's reign will endure **as long as the sun** (v. 5) is hyperbole but finds fulfillment in the eternal reign of the Davidic dynasty and Jesus Christ as the Messiah.

72:8–17. The domain of the Davidic ruler will extend to all the world (vv. 8–11). The tribes of the Arabian Desert, to the east, will yield to him. His **enemies … lick[ing] the dust** (v. 9) pictures them bowing in obeisance to him (see Mic. 7:17). The kings whose lands border the Mediterranean Sea, to the west, will acknowledge him as overlord, as will those who rule in southern Arabia and along the eastern African coast. As God's earthly regent, the Davidic king possesses royal authority that extends on earth as far as God's authority. No historical ruler in the Davidic dynasty came close to realizing this idea, but this expectation is fulfilled in Christ. The king's worldwide domain is the direct result of his righteous rule (vv. 12–14). He will be a protector and defender of **the poor and needy** (v. 13). The concluding summation of this psalm is a prayer for the king to enjoy a long and prosperous reign that brings blessing to the **nations** (v. 17) of the earth (vv. 15–17). The inclusion of the "nations" in the blessing recalls the promise to Abraham (see Gen. 12:13) and suggests that it will be fulfilled through the royal son of David, ultimately the Messiah.

72:18–20. Verses 18–19 serve as a doxology at the conclusion of book 2 of the Psalter (see 41:13). It is the people's response, their **Amen, and Amen** (v. 19), to the contents of book 2.

Verse 20 is an editorial notation probably carried over from an earlier collection of psalms ascribed exclusively to **David** (v. 20).

Book 3: Psalms 73–89

Psalm 73. A word of godly wisdom concerning the destinies of the righteous and the wicked.

This psalm is ascribed to Asaph, the leader of one of David's Levitical choirs. It begins a collection of eleven Asaphite psalms (Psalms 73–83), to which Psalm 50 at one time probably belonged. The collection clearly contains prayers from a later date (e.g., Psalms 74; 79; 83); therefore, references to Asaph in these titles must sometimes include descendants of Asaph who functioned in his place. The Asaphite psalms are dominated by the theme of God's rule over His people and the nations. This psalm addresses one of the most disturbing problems of the Old Testament saints: How is it that the wicked so often prosper while the godly suffer so much? Thematically, the psalm has many links to Psalm 49. The psalm is divided into two sections of fourteen verses each.

73:1-14. The first section describes Asaph's almost-fatal trial of faith: in his troubles, he has nearly stumbled from the path of truth and godliness when he saw how much the wicked prospered. His observations on life are hardly objective; he provides an exaggerated picture of the prosperous state of the wicked that effectively reflects the envy he feels in his own heart (see Job 21). From his jaded perspective, it appears that those who disregard God live free of pain or difficulty. Their haughty **pride** (v. 6) is like an expensive necklace they wear for all to see. They have full faces that show they are prosperous and well-fed. They are not called to account for their threatening words and proud boasts. The meaning of the phrase **his people return hither** (v. 10) is uncertain but perhaps suggests that God's people are so impressed by the wicked who prosper that they turn to the wicked rather than to the Lord as their source of provision. The comfort and security of the wicked are most troubling to Asaph when he compares their state with his own troubled lot (vv. 12-14). He feels as if he has lived a pure life **in vain** (v. 13) and that it has brought him only trouble.

73:15-28. The second half of the psalm portrays Asaph's renewal of faith. In the temple, the godly man sees the destiny that God has appointed for the wicked. Asaph recognizes that publicly expressing his envy of the wicked would have been a betrayal of God's children, but the crisis in his own soul was **painful** (v. 16) to bear. The resolution to his crisis came when he went to the temple to worship (v. 17). He realized that though the wicked seem to prosper, God has made their position precarious, and they are swept away without warning (vv. 18-20). They are here but **a moment** (v. 19) and then vanish like the shadowy characters of a dream. The psalmist does not reflect on the state of the wicked after death but leaves it as his final word that the wicked fall utterly and inevitably from their state of proud prosperity.

Asaph recognizes that his envy of the wicked was **foolish** (v. 22), but though he had almost fallen to the level of beastly stupidity, God will never let him go (vv. 22-27).

God's counsel has overcome his folly and will guide him through all the pitfalls of life (see 16:7; 32:8; 48:14). From the limited perspective of the Old Testament, the phrase **afterward receive me to glory** (v. 24) is probably not a promise of heaven but rather a reference to the honor and blessing enjoyed by the righteous when God delivers them from trouble and brings about their vindication. This passage and others in the Psalms (see 16:11; 49:14-15) certainly point to the promise of eternal life for the righteous. Though Asaph has envied the prosperity of the wicked, he now confesses that nothing in heaven or earth is more desirable than God. As a Levite, the Lord was his **portion** (v. 26) in the Promised Land in that he lived by the people's tithes dedicated to the Lord (see Num. 18:21-24; Deut. 10:9; 18:1-2). Here the Lord is even more to Him—sustainer, preserver, and his very life. The psalmist concludes with a vow to praise God for all His mercies (v. 28).

Psalm 74. A prayer for God to come to the aid of His people and defend His cause in the face of the enemies' mocking.

This psalm dates from the time of the exile, when Israel had been destroyed as a nation, the Promised Land had been devastated, and the temple had been reduced to ruins (see Psalm 79; Lamentations 2).

74:1-8. The first half of the psalm is framed by **Why ...?** (vv. 1, 11). In their initial complaint, the people ask why God has rejected the people that He **redeemed** (v. 2) to be His **inheritance**. The Babylonian destruction of **Zion** seems to be the undoing of God's great victory over Egypt.

The psalmist asks the Lord to hurry to restore (**Lift up thy feet unto;** v. 3) Jerusalem, which Babylon destroyed in a proud and high-handed manner (vv. 3-8). The Babylonians destroyed the temple like woodcutters chopping trees in the forest. They burned the temple to the ground though it was **the dwelling place** (v. 7) of God. The reference to **all the synagogues of God** (v. 8) is not clear. At the time of the Babylonian attacks, there may have been a number of (illegitimate) places in Judah where people went to worship God (see discussions on 1 Kings 3:2; 2 Kings 18:4).

74:9–17. The psalmist renews his complaint and petition (vv. 9–11). The people do not **see** (v. 9) the **signs** of God's wondrous power as they did at the time of the exodus, and there is no longer a **prophet** among the people to speak for God. Jeremiah had been taken to Egypt (see Jer. 43:6–7), but whether Ezekiel was no longer prophesying is unknown. The psalmist cannot understand why God remains inactive when the destruction of His people causes the enemy to **blaspheme** His **name** (v. 10).

The center verse of the psalm (v. 12) confesses the truth that underlies this entire prayer: God is Israel's **King** (v. 12) and Savior; Israel is God's people (kingdom). This accounts for both the complaint and the prayer. The Lord is the mighty God of salvation and creation, who delivered His people from Egypt (vv. 13–17). The imagery describing the exodus is borrowed from ancient Near Eastern creation myths, in which the primeval chaotic waters were depicted as a many-headed dragon that the creator-god overcame as a means of establishing world order (see 89:10; Job 9:13; 26:12–13; Isa. 51:9). The poet employs this imagery to celebrate that the Lord is able to overcome all hostile powers to redeem His people and bring order out of chaos.

74:18–23. Having reflected on God's past deliverance, the psalmist longs for and prays for God to save His people in the present (vv. 18–23). **The enemy** (v. 18) has attacked God's **turtledove** (v. 19), a term of endearment for Israel (see 68:13; Song 2:14; 5:2; 6:9). He prays for God to act in accordance with His **covenant** (v. 20) promises to make Israel blessed and secure in the Promised Land (see 105:8–11; Lev. 26:44–45; Deut. 28:1–14). God's rescue will give **the poor and needy** (v. 21) reason to **praise** His name, and His judgment will bring fitting retribution on the **enemies** (v. 23) who have mocked God for not protecting His own people.

Psalm 75. A song of reassurance, composed when arrogant worldly powers threaten Israel's security.

This psalm is framed by thanksgiving (v. 1) and praise (vv. 9–10). The two stanzas in the body of the psalm contain a reassuring word from heaven (vv. 2–5) and a triumphant response from earth (vv. 6–8).

75:1–5. The congregation offers thanksgiving, praising God's character (**name**; v. 1) and His **wondrous works**. The word from heaven is that God will not fail to call the arrogant to account (vv. 2–5). **When I shall receive the congregation** (v. 2) literally reads, "When I shall set the time," and promises that God will judge in His own time. This promise brings comfort when the upsurge of evil appears to have crumbled the moral order of the world. God guarantees that He upholds **the pillars** (v. 3) that provide stability for His world. The wicked are arrogant and foolish to **Lift … up the horn** (v. 4) like an attacking bull in defiance of God's rule.

75:6–10. The worshipers on earth respond with a joyful affirmation of the comforting word from God (vv. 6–8). The issue of **promotion** (v. 6), or who is exalted on earth, is determined by God as **judge** (v. 7) over all. He brings down and exalts as He chooses. He causes the wicked to drink the wine of His judgment, **a cup** (v. 8) that is **full of mixture**, that is, mixed with spices to increase the intoxicating effect. Because of God's promised victory, the psalmist offers a concluding vow to praise God forever (vv. 9–10). The strength (**horns**; v. 10) of the **wicked** will be **cut off**, and the **righteous** are **exalted**.

Psalm 76. A celebration of the Lord's invincible power in defense of Jerusalem, His royal city.

This song of Zion is thematically related to Psalms 46, 48, and 87, and the ancient tradition may well be correct that the psalm was composed after the Lord's destruction of Sennacherib's army when it threatened Jerusalem (see 2 Kings 19:35).

76:1–3. Because of the Lord's crushing defeat of the enemy in defense of Zion, the psalmist declares, **In Judah God is known** (v. 1). The reference to **his tabernacle** (v. 2) perhaps speaks of the temple as the Lord's campaign tent (see 2 Sam. 11:11; 1 Kings 20:12, 16). He destroyed the weapons of the enemy attacking Zion.

76:4-10. God is worthy of praise because of His awesome majesty, and His mighty judgment evokes fearful reverence (vv. 4-10). He is more majestic than the great **mountains** (v. 4) that are rich with animals to be hunted. He puts His enemies to death, and they cannot even lift their **hands** (v. 5) to defend themselves against Him. God is victorious through the power of His word, which **rebuke[s]** (v. 6) and turns back His enemy. Though God is present in Zion, He sovereignly rules from **heaven** (v. 8). **The wrath of man** (v. 10) in opposition to God ultimately brings **praise** to God when the righteous observe His sovereign power and experience His deliverance. **The remainder of wrath** indicates that particular judgments do not exhaust His wrath.

76:11-12. The Lord's majesty and power demand a response. Israel is to acknowledge God's help with grateful vows. The nations are to bring tribute (**presents**; v. 11) in recognition of His sovereign rule. Any nation or ruler in opposition to Him will ultimately be destroyed.

Psalm 77. Comforting reflections in a time of great distress.

77:1-9. In the first half of the psalm, the psalmist expresses anguished perplexity over God's apparent inaction, when He fails to respond to unceasing and urgent prayers. The distress appears to be personal rather than national. **My sore ran** (v. 2) literally reads, "My hand was stretched out" (in prayer), but God has not answered." Remembrance of His past mercies intensifies the psalmist's perplexity. God's failure to act on his behalf now is so troubling that he cannot sleep. He wonders if God will ever again show His **tender mercies** (v. 9) to him.

77:10-20. The prayer moves from anguished bewilderment to comforting recollection of God's mighty acts on Israel's behalf in the exodus (vv. 10-20). Faith looks beyond the present troubles to draw hope anew from God's saving acts of old. The Lord as Warrior demonstrated the power of His **right hand** (v. 10) in the exodus (see Exod. 15:6, 12). **Thy way ... is in the sanctuary** (v. 13) reflects how God's great saving acts of the past were continually

rehearsed and recalled in the temple liturgy. In the exodus event, it was the God of thunderstorm and earthquake who made His majestic way through the mighty **waters** (v. 16) of the sea to bring His people out of bondage (vv. 16-19). The waters are personified as the forces of chaos that oppose God but flee at the sight of His awesome presence (see 65:6-7; 74:13-15; 89:10). Following the exodus, the Lord brought His people through the wilderness under the leadership of **Moses and Aaron** (v. 20). The psalmist implicitly anticipates that God will continue to shepherd and protect His people.

Psalm 78. A psalm of instruction — of warnings not to repeat Israel's sins of the past but to remember God's saving acts and to keep faith with Him and His covenant.

Asaph exhorts obedience to God's law. Faith and obedience, which are Israel's central covenant responsibilities, result from remembering and focusing on God's mighty saving acts. The psalm serves as a warning not to fall away from the Lord. Unfaithfulness is especially blameworthy because it contemptuously disregards all God's wonderful acts on His people's behalf (see Psalms 105-106).

78:1-8. Asaph writes in the style of a wisdom writer, describing his teaching as **my law** (v. 1), **a parable** (v. 2), and **dark sayings**. The substance of his teaching is that the people must listen to what they have heard from their fathers so that they may be faithful to the Lord. Each **generation** (v. 4) must give special attention to the Lord's saving acts and His covenant commands and must past them on to **their children** (v. 5) as the focal point of faith and obedience. The people must guard against the rebellion that has characterized Israel's past.

78:9-16. The northern kingdom of **Ephraim** (v. 9) is a prime example of this rebellion, but Israel's history of disobedience began in the wilderness during the time of Moses. Since neither the tribe of Ephraim nor the northern kingdom had a reputation for cowardice or ineffectiveness in battle (see, e.g., Deut. 33:17), verse 9 is best understood as a metaphor for Israel's betrayal of God's covenant. Israel had rebelled in the wilderness despite seeing

God's awesome works in the exodus and experiencing His miraculous provision of food and water.

78:17–39. The two cycles (vv. 17–39, 40–64) that follow elaborate on the events in the wilderness, further intensifying the indictment of Israel's rebellion. God became angry with Israel's constant complaints and lack of faith. When He provided water for them, they complained that He was not able to give them food (vv. 17–20). He sent the **fire** (v. 21) of divine judgment down upon them, but He also graciously gave them manna, referred to as **angels' food** (v. 25) because it was sent from heaven (vv. 21–25). He gave them a large harvest of quails, but then He destroyed those who had lusted after meat (vv. 26–31). The exodus generation was condemned to die in the wilderness because they refused to believe that God could give them victory over the Canaanites (vv. 32–39; see Numbers 14). Reflecting a cycle that would occur later in the period of the judges, they would temporarily return to God in times of hardship, only to turn from Him when the difficulties were over. They refused to be **stedfast in his covenant** (v. 37).

78:40–64. The second cycle stresses that Israel's rebellion in the wilderness occurred because she did not remember how she had been **delivered** (v. 42) from oppression by God's plagues on **Egypt** (v. 43) and His deliverance at **the** Red **sea** (v. 53). Despite their unfaithfulness, God safely brought His people through **the wilderness** (v. 52) and gave them possession of the Promised Land, described as God's **sanctuary** (v. 54), or dwelling place.

Rebelliousness continued to be Israel's way of life in the Promised Land, so God rejected Israel (vv. 56–64). Israel has been to the Lord as a **deceitful bow** (v. 57) that could not be relied on in battle. God **greatly abhorred Israel** (v. 59) and abandoned her to her enemies. Nevertheless, the psalmist does not speak of a permanent casting off of Israel, not even of the ten northern tribes. When Israel worshiped at their **high places** (v. 58), God destroyed **Shiloh** (v. 60), the center of worship from the conquest through the period of the judges (see Josh. 21:1–2; Judg. 18:31; 1 Sam. 1:3). Shiloh was apparently destroyed by the Philistines when they captured the ark

or shortly afterward (see 1 Samuel 4). Many in Israel died at that time, and Israel's devastation at this was so great that both the wedding songs of brides and the wailing of widows were silenced in the land.

78:65–72. After judging His people, God awoke to save Israel from their troubles. He chose **Judah** (v. 68) rather than **Ephraim** (v. 67) as the leading tribe in Israel (see Gen. 49:8–12) and Mount **Zion** (v. 68) rather than Shiloh as the place of His sanctuary (vv. 65–72). **David** (v. 70) became His **servant** and His regent to shepherd the people. David's military victories with the Lord's empowerment securely established Israel in the Promised Land, following the long period of Israel's struggles from the death of Joshua to the death of Saul. At Zion, the Lord **built his sanctuary like high palaces** (v. 69), making His dwelling place as impregnable as a mountain fortress. Under David's leadership, God blessed Israel in spite of their long history of unfaithfulness. The Davidic king leads and shepherds the people, and Israel under the care of the future royal shepherd from the house of David (the Messiah) was for the prophets the hope of God's people (see Ezek. 34:23; 37:24; Mic. 5:4). This hope is fulfilled in Jesus Christ (see Matt. 2:6; John 10:11; Rev. 7:17).

Psalm 79. Israel's prayer for God's forgiveness and help and for His judgment on the nations that have so cruelly destroyed her.

This psalm dates from the time of the exile and shares many thematic links with Psalm 74.

79:1–4. Israel acknowledges that the Lord has used the nations to punish her for her sins, so she pleads for pardon. She knows too that the nations have acted out of their hostility to and disdain for God and His people, warranting God's judgment against them. The nations have attacked the land of Israel, God's **inheritance** (v. 1) and domain. They have **defiled** the **temple** and slaughtered God's people. The armies of the nations have degraded God's **servants** (v. 2) in death by leaving their bodies as carrion for birds and beasts (vv. 2–4).

79:5–8. Asaph prays for God to relent and deal with the nations that do not acknowledge Him. He prays that in the same way the enemies have shed the blood of God's people **like water** (v. 3), God would **Pour out** His **wrath** (v. 6) on them. The exiles plead with God to redress the wrongs committed against them and to forgive their **former iniquities** (v. 8). Israel suffered exile because of the accumulated sins of the nation (see 2 Kings 17:7–23; 24:3–4; Dan. 9:4–14), from which she did not repent until the judgment of God had fallen on her. The exiles here pray that God will take notice of their penitence and not continue to hold the sins of past generations against His now repentant people. God's **tender mercies** are personified as the agent that will bring relief to His people.

79:9–13. Asaph prays for Israel's deliverance and the judgment of their enemies for the sake of God's **glory** (v. 9). As the desolation of God's people brings reproach on God (see v. 10), so their salvation and prosperity bring Him glory. The nations will no longer be able to say, **Where is their God?** (v. 10). The exiles are described as prisoners **that are appointed to die** (v. 11). As captives in Babylonia, they are not actually in prisons but are under the threat of death if they seek to return to their homeland. Asaph requests that Israel's enemies receive a full and complete (**sevenfold**; v. 12) retribution.

The enemies' violent action against Israel was above all a high-handed reviling of God (see 2 Kings 19:10–12, 22–23). The concluding vow of **praise** (v. 13) looks forward to Israel expressing their gratitude for their deliverance from the bondage of exile.

Psalm 80. Israel's prayer for restoration when she had been ravaged by a foreign power.

The recurring petition "Turn us again, O God … and we shall be saved" (vv. 3, 7, 19) reflects the urgency of Israel's cry for restoration.

80:1–3. The psalm opens with Israel's appeal for God to arouse Himself and go before His people again with all His glory and might as He did in days of old in the wilderness (vv. 1–3). It seems likely that **Ephraim and Benjamin and Manasseh** (v. 2) here represent the northern kingdom and that the Assyrian campaign that swept the northern kingdom away serves as the backdrop for this prayer (see 2 Kings 17:1–6). Recent archaeological surveys of

the Holy Land have shown that Jerusalem and the surrounding countryside experienced at this time a dramatic increase of population, no doubt the result of a massive influx of displaced persons from the north fleeing the Assyrian army. This could account for the presence of the northern tribes at the Jerusalem sanctuary and for a national prayer for restoration with special focus on these tribes.

80:4–15. The psalmist laments the Lord's severe punishment of His people (vv. 4–7). He asks **How long** (v. 4) the Lord will continue to be **angry** with His **people** and states that He has now given them **tears** as their food and water. Israel is nothing more than a laughingstock to the surrounding nations.

The poet employs the vine-vineyard metaphor to describe Israel's changed condition (vv. 8–16; see Isa. 5:1–7; Ezek. 17:6–8; Matt. 20:1–16). Israel was once God's flourishing transplanted **vine** (v. 8), which had grown to the height of **the goodly cedars** (v. 10), but now the vineyard has been ravaged and destroyed. The psalmist prays for God to renew His care for His ruined **vine** (v. 14), which had once been so **strong** (v. 15).

80:16–19. Reminding the Lord of Israel's devastation, the psalmist makes a final plea for the favor and empowerment of God's **hand** (v. 17) to be upon **the man of thy right hand**, most likely a reference to the Davidic king as the Lord's anointed and the one in whom the hope of the nation rested. Having experienced restoration, Israel will be loyal to God and will look to Him alone as their source of security (vv. 18–19).

Psalm 81. A festival song celebrating God's deliverance of His people.

This psalm of rejoicing seems most closely connected to the Feast of Tabernacles (v. 3; see Lev. 23:34; Num. 29:12). The festivals were central to Israel's religious life because they functioned as memorials of God's saving acts and called Israel to celebrate God's faithfulness and to recommit themselves to Him. In this psalm, Israel is addressed by a Levite, speaking on behalf of God.

81:1–6. The psalm opens with a summons to celebrate the appointed sacred feast (vv. 1–5). The

solemn feast day (v. 3), the Feast of Tabernacles, is often simply called "the feast" (see 1 Kings 8:2, 65; 12:32; 2 Chron. 5:3; 7:8; Neh. 8:14, 18). As the great seven-day autumn festival, beginning on the fifteenth of the month (the full moon), it followed shortly after the Day of Atonement (observed on the tenth of the month, Lev. 16:29) and recalled God's care for His people during the wilderness journey (see Lev. 23:43). Linking past with present, it also served as a feast of thanksgiving for the harvest (see Lev. 23:39–40; Deut. 16:13–15) and marked the conclusion of the annual cycle of religious festivals. Every seventh year, the covenant law was to be read to all the people during this festival (see Deut. 31:9–13; Neh. 8:2, 15). Israel had much to celebrate because of all that God had done for His people.

81:6–16. The Lord's past deliverance of Israel from bondage in Egypt demands a present response of loyalty and obedience on the part of His people (vv. 6–10). Just as God had listened to their cries of distress, they must now listen to Him. **Open thy mouth wide** (v. 10) is a call for Israel to renounce all idols and to trust in the Lord alone for all of life's needs so that He might bless them with every good thing.

The sad reality is that Israel often had not listened to the Lord, and He had allowed them to suffer the consequences of where their stubborn hearts had led them (vv. 11–16). Israel could have experienced victory over their enemies, abundant prosperity, and every covenant blessing if they had only followed the Lord instead of going their own way (see Exod. 23:22–27; Lev. 26:3–13; Deut. 7:12–26; 28:1–14).

Psalm 82. A word of God's judgment on unjust rulers and judges.

82:1–5. The psalmist evokes a vision of God presiding over His heavenly court (see 1 Kings 22:19; Job 1:6; Isa. 6:1–4) before the **congregation** (v. 1) in the great hall of judgment. He issues an indictment against the **gods** (Hebrew, *'elohim*) who are responsible for defending the weak and oppressed on earth (vv. 2–5). While some understand these "gods" (*'elohim*) to be the angels who form God's heavenly council, the more likely interpretation is

that the term refers to unjust rulers and judges in Israel (see John 10:34–35). In the language of the Old Testament and in accordance with the conceptual world of the ancient Near East, Israel's leaders, as deputies of the heavenly King, could be given the honorific title "god" (see 45:6; 58:1) or be called "son of God" (see 2:7).

Assembled before God, these rulers and judges are charged with practicing injustice and giving preference to the **wicked** (v. 2) and are ordered to fulfill their responsibility to **Defend** (v. 3) the oppressed. In the Old Testament, a first-order task of kings and judges was to protect the powerless against all who would exploit or oppress them (see 72:2, 4, 12–14; Prov. 31:8–9; Jer. 22:3, 16). While these leaders ought to have shared in the wisdom of God, they are utterly devoid of true understanding concerning moral issues and the moral order that God's rule sustains. When such rulers are the wardens of justice, the whole world order crumbles (**the foundations … are out of course**; v. 5).

82:6–8. I have said, Ye are gods (v. 6) is a reminder that those who rule do so by God's appointment and thus are His representatives. They are accountable to God for how they carry out this important responsibility, and they will **die** (v. 7) because they have abused their power in mistreating the poor. However exalted their position, these corrupt "gods" will be brought low by the same judgment as other men. Having seen what the future holds, the psalmist prays for God's judgment to hasten and for the perfect reign of God to come quickly to **all nations** (v. 8).

Psalm 83. Israel's prayer for God to crush His enemies when it appears that the whole world is arrayed against His people.

Neither Kings nor Chronicles tells of a confederacy as extensive as that described here. Perhaps only some of the nations mentioned were actually attacking, while the rest of Israel's historic enemies were more passively supporting the campaign. If so, the occasion may have been that reported in 2 Chronicles 20, when Moab, Ammon, Edom, and their allies were invading Judah.

83:1–8. The psalm opens with an appeal to God to act in the face of Israel's imminent danger (vv. 1–4). **Keep not thou silence** (v. 1) is a plea for God to not remain inactive as the enemy armies seek to destroy Israel. The psalmist expects God to act on behalf of Israel because they are His treasured people, whom He keeps **hidden** (v. 3) from the enemy. Numerous nations have allied themselves against Israel, including **Edom** (v. 6), **Moab, the Hagarenes** (descendants of Ishmael), **Gebal** (an important Phoenician city, also called Byblos; v. 7), **Ammon, Amalek**, and **Assur** (or Assyria; v. 8).

83:9–12. The psalmist petitions God to destroy His enemies as He did in the time of the judges (vv. 9–12). He makes specific reference to Gideon's great victory over the **Midianites** (v. 9; see Judges 7) and Barak's defeat of the Canaanite coalition led by **Sisera** (see Judges 4). **Oreb** (v. 11), **Zeeb, Zebah**, and **Zalmunna** were leaders of the Midianite host destroyed by Gideon. Those who hurl themselves against the kingdom of God to destroy it from the earth must be crushed if God's kingdom of righteousness and peace is to come and be at rest.

83:13–18. As he continues to pray for Israel's deliverance, the psalmist uses vivid imagery of fleeing armies and of God's fearsome power (vv. 13–16). He prays that the enemy armies will become **like a wheel** (v. 13), or like tumbleweed blowing in the wind. God as the heavenly Warrior will attack His enemies out of the thunderstorm (see 18:7–15; Exod. 15:7–10; Judg. 5:4, 20–21). The ultimate goal of God's warfare is not merely the security of Israel and the destruction of Israel's enemies but also the worldwide acknowledgment of the true God and of His rule (vv. 17–18).

Psalm 84. A prayer of longing for the house of the Lord.

This psalm is similar to Psalm 42 in tone and perspective and appears to reflect a time when the psalmist is barred from access to the temple (perhaps when Sennacherib was ravaging Judah; see 2 Kings 18:13–16).

84:1–4. The poet voices his longing for the nearness of God in His temple, which he had known in the past. His entire being longs for God, and he is jealous of the small birds that have unhindered access to the temple and the altar. They are able even to build their nests there for their young—in the place where Israel was to enjoy communion with God.

84:5–8. The psalmist describes the blessedness of those who have the freedom to make a pilgrimage to Zion for worship (vv. 5–7). The pilgrims face toils and hardships on their journey, but they are sustained by their resolve and commitment to observe the religious festivals at Jerusalem. The joyful expectations of the pilgrims transform even the arid stretches of the journey, like the unknown and perhaps figurative **valley of Baca** ("valley of weeping"; v. 6), into places of refreshment. Through the **rain**, God's saints on their way to Zion experience anew the bountiful hand of God, just as their ancestors did on their way through the wilderness of Sinai to the Promised Land (see 78:15–16).

84:9–12. The psalmist prays for God's blessing on the king (**look upon the face of thine anointed**; v. 9). Only as God blesses the king in Jerusalem will the psalmist once more realize his great desire to return to his accustomed service in the temple (v. 10). The humble role of **doorkeeper** (v. 10) at the temple, perhaps the psalmist's normal service, is preferable to anything that dwelling **in the tents of wickedness** could ever offer. The psalmist desires God's presence at the temple so intensely because the Lord, who withholds nothing from those who trust in Him, is Israel's source of blessing and protection (vv. 11–12).

Psalm 85. A communal prayer for the renewal of God's mercies to His people at a time when they are once more suffering distress.

Many believe this psalm refers to the return from exile (vv. 1–3). Verse 12 suggests that a drought has ravaged the land and may reflect the drought with which the Lord chastened His people in the time of Haggai (see Hag. 1:5–11). The reference to "captivity," however, does not necessitate a specific historical event (see Job 42:10). The psalmist's purpose is to remind his listeners that the God who has delivered His people in the past can do it again.

85:1–7. The first half of the psalm is a prayer for the renewal of God's favor and the revival of God's people. Israel begins her prayer by appealing to the Lord's past mercies, recalling how He has **forgiven** (v. 2) and restored them. The prayer acknowledges that the present troubles are indicative of God's displeasure but asks that His anger with Israel come to an end. The people pray for God's **mercy** (v. 7) and **salvation.**

85:8–13. God's reassuring answer to Israel's prayer, conveyed through a priest or Levite, is recorded in the second half of the psalm. The Lord **speak[s] peace** (v. 8) by promising that He will again bless His people. The people, however, are warned to **not turn again to folly** and so provoke God's wrath in the future. God reveals His **glory** (v. 9) by displaying His saving power on Israel's behalf (see 72:18–19; Exod. 14:17–18; Isa. 66:19). **Mercy and truth … Righteousness and peace** (v. 10), the expressions of God's favor to Israel, are personified, and the vivid portrayal of their meeting and embracing offers one of the most beautiful images within Scripture of God's gracious dealings with His covenant people. The Lord's blessing will bring abundance and prosperity to Israel and her land (vv. 11–12). This blessing is only possible because of God's attribute of **Righteousness** (v. 13), His perfect faithfulness to His covenant promises.

Psalm 86. A prayer for God's help when David is attacked by enemies, whose fierce onslaughts betray their disdain for the Lord.

This is the only psalm in book 3 of the Psalter (Psalms 73–89) that is ascribed to David. It is perhaps placed among the Korahite psalms for thematic reasons (see v. 9 and 87:4). David's reference to himself as God's "servant" (vv. 2, 4, 16) suggests his royal status and thus his special relationship with the Lord (see 2 Sam. 7:5, 8). Therefore, the enemies may be either those within the kingdom who refuse to acknowledge him as the Lord's anointed or foreign powers that are attempting to remove him from the international scene.

86:1–10. The psalmist presents an initial prayer for God to have mercy and protect his life (vv. 1–4). David's devotion to God and God's commitment to him are deliberately juxtaposed. David trusts in the Lord as one of His saints (Hebrew, *hasid*; "faithful ones"), and the Lord has chosen David as His **servant** (v. 2). David longs to experience the joy of deliverance. He presents his prayer because he recognizes that the Lord is a God of mercy and love (vv. 5–7). The God to whom David appeals is the only true God (vv. 8–10). No other "god" acts with such sovereign power (see 115:3–7; 135:13–17). **All nations** (v. 9) will one day recognize the Lord and worship Him.

86:11–13. Teach me thy way (v. 11) and **Unite my heart to fear thy name** reflect that David prays for godliness as much as he does for deliverance. What would be the benefit if God saved him from his enemies but abandoned him to his own waywardness? David's dependence on God is complete, and so is his devotion to God. He is asking God to save him from the enemy without but also from his frailty within (see 25:5; 51:7, 10). Anticipating the answer to his prayer, David vows to praise the Lord for saving him from death (**from the lowest hell**, or "the depths of sheol"; v. 13).

86:14–17. The psalmist renews his petition and asks for God's deliverance from **violent men** (v. 14). In attacking David, the wicked dismiss the heavenly Warrior who is David's defender. The Lord's deliverance will serve as a **token** (v. 17), or sign, of God's covenant favor, which will shame David's enemies when they see that the Lord is with him.

Psalm 87. A celebration of Zion as the "city of God" (v. 3), the special object of His love and the royal city of His kingdom.

87:1–7. This song of Zion (see Psalms 46; 48; 76) not only celebrates the glory of Jerusalem in the psalmist's time but also foresees the ingathering of the nations into Zion as fellow citizens with Israel in the kingdom of God (see Isa. 2:2–4; 19:19–25; 56:6–8; Mic. 4:1–3; Zech. 14:16). Zion is exalted because the Lord Himself has laid her **foundation** (v. 1) and chosen her as His dwelling place. As the chosen city of His rule, Zion is the Lord's most cherished city, even among the towns of Israel (vv. 2–3; see 78:68; 132:12–14).

At a future time, God will list foreigners in His royal register as those who are native (**born**; vv. 4–6) citizens of His royal city, having all the privileges and enjoying all the benefits and security of such citizenship (vv. 4–6; see 9:5; 51:1; 69:28). The nations listed are representative of all Gentile peoples. **Rahab** ("Boistrous One"; v. 4) is a name applied elsewhere to the mythical monster of the deep (see 32:6; 89:10; Job 9:13), but here it is a poetic name for Egypt (as in Isa. 30:7; 51:9). These verses anticipate a widespread conversion to the Lord among the peoples who from time immemorial had been hostile to Him and to His kingdom (see Isa. 19:21). Zion will be a place of music and singing for all peoples because of the **springs** (v. 7) of God's blessing that will flow out from the city (see 36:8; 46:4).

Psalm 88. A cry out of the psalmist's depths, the prayer of one on the edge of death, one whose whole life has been lived, as it were, in the vicinity of the grave.

This song is perhaps the most anguished prayer in the Psalter; it contains no expressions of hopeful expectation or any vow of praise. **Heman** (superscription; see 1 Chron. 15:19; 16:41–42) is so troubled that he seems to have known only the back of God's hand (v. 7), and even those nearest him have withdrawn themselves as from one with an infectious skin disease (v. 8). The psalm recalls the fact that although godly persons sometimes live lives of unremitting trouble (see 73:14), they can still grasp the hope that God is Savior.

88:1–5. Heman appeals to the LORD (v. 1) as the **God of my salvation** because he is living on the brink of death. Even in his despair, Heman has the faith to pray urgently and to recognize God as the only source of deliverance. Whether the psalmist lies mortally ill or experiences some analogous trouble or peril cannot be known. He is about to go down to the grave, where he will no longer be remembered (see 6:5). From the perspective of this life, death cuts one off from God's care in that God no longer provides for the dead person or actively delivers from danger and distrust (see 25:7; 106:4). In his dark mood, the author portrays his situation in the bleakest colors.

88:6–18. Heman makes a series of statements that attribute his circumstances directly to God

(vv. 6–8). The psalmist does not know why he is suffering, but he knows God's hand is in it (see Ruth 1:20–21; Amos 3:6). That his Savior-God shows him **wrath** (v. 7) deepens his anguish and helplessness. He does not try to resolve the dark enigma; he simply pleads his case to God. The Lord has not responded to his cries, but Heman appeals for God to help him before he sinks into **the land of forgetfulness** (v. 12). Heman will continue to cry out for deliverance, even though it appears that God is unresponsive to his prayers (vv. 13–14). Fitting with the overall tone of the psalm, Heman concludes by reminding the Lord that he has suffered His **terrors** (v. 15) all his life. The psalmist turns to God for help because everyone else has abandoned him to his anguish.

Psalm 89. A prayer mourning the downfall of the Davidic dynasty and pleading for its restoration.

Ethan (superscription) was a Levite (see 1 Chron. 15:17–18) and voices this agonizing prayer as a spokesman for the nation. This psalm is a prayer offered to God at a time when the removal of the Davidic king from his throne in Jerusalem seems to indicate that the Lord has abandoned His firm covenant with David. The bitter shock at this turn of events evokes from the psalmist a lament that borders on reproach (see vv. 38–45). The event behind this psalm may have been the attack on Jerusalem by Nebuchadnezzar and the exile of King Jehoiachin in 597 BC (see 2 Kings 24:8–17). As with the communal lament in Psalm 44, a massive foundation is laid for the psalm's concluding prayer.

89:1–4. The introduction sings of God's love and faithfulness and of His covenant with David. God's **mercies** (v. 1) and **faithfulness** appear to have failed in His rejection of the Davidic king; the author repeats each of these words precisely seven times in the psalm. God's **covenant** (v. 3) with **David** is clearly presented as a covenant that will last **for ever** (v. 4; see 2 Sam. 7:8–16).

89:4–18. Ethan expands on the theme of God's faithfulness (vv. 5–18). The Lord's faithfulness and awesome power set Him apart among all the powers in the heavenly realm (vv. 5–8). **The congregation** (v. 5), **the assembly of the saints** (lit., "holy ones";

v. 7), and **the sons of the mighty** (v. 6) are references to the angelic beings who belong to the Lord's heavenly council (see 29:1). These powerful beings in the heavenly realm give praise and reverence to the Lord because **faithfulness** (v. 8) surrounds Him as an essential attribute.

The Lord is able to keep His promises because He is the all-powerful Creator (vv. 9–13). The psalmist employs imagery borrowed from ancient Near Eastern myths of creation to celebrate God's power in ordering the primeval chaotic waters so that the creation order could be established (see 65:6–7; 74:13–14; see Gen. 1:6–10). **Rahab** (v. 10) is a mythical monster of the deep (see 32:6; 87:4), also referred to as Leviathan in other passages (see 74:14; 104:26). **The north and the south** (v. 12) likely are references to two mountains (Zaphon and Amana) because of the parallel to **Tabor and Hermon**.

Ethan declares that the Lord's goodness guarantees that His infinite power will be exercised benevolently on Israel's behalf (vv. 14–18). Righteousness and justice are the foundation stones of God's throne. **Mercy and truth** (v. 14) are personified as angelic attendants that herald His royal movements and decrees. Israel rejoices in her privileged position as God's royal subjects.

89:19–37. The psalmist focuses on the special covenant between the Lord and David (vv. 19–37). The Lord's covenant with David involves five specific promises: (1) He has anointed David as His servant and will sustain him (vv. 20–21), (2) He will crush all David's foes (vv. 22–23), (3) He will extend his realm (vv. 24–25), (4) He will make him first among all the kings (vv. 26–27), and (5) He will cause David's dynasty to endure forever (vv. 28–29), a promise fulfilled in the eternal reign of Jesus Christ. David's rule will extend from the Mediterranean Sea to the Euphrates River as a reflection of God's rule over the earth (v. 25). The title **firstborn** (v. 27) refers to David's position as a royal son with the highest privilege and position in the kingdom of God (see 2:7–12; 45:6–9; 72:8–11; 110), making David the most exalted of the kings of the earth. The Lord's covenant with David and his dynasty is everlasting and unconditional, but if any of David's royal descendants is unfaithful, he will individually suffer under God's **rod** (v. 32), to the detriment of the entire nation (vv. 30–37). No act of unfaithfulness, however, will ever cause the Lord to abandon His covenant with the house of David.

89:38–45. The psalm then turns from jubilation to lament (vv. 38–45). God's present rejection of David's son (**thine anointed**; v. 38), with all its fearful consequences, is the undoing of all that had been promised and assured by the **covenant** (v. 39). Instead of triumphing over his enemies, the Davidic king is now subject to them and has been removed from his seat of power and authority.

89:46–52. The climax of the psalm is a petition and appeal for God, in spite of all that has happened, to restore the Davidic dynasty in accordance with His covenant promises (vv. 46–51). Because of the Lord's faithfulness, Ethan is hopeful that His anger toward the house of David will not last forever. The Lord will act to restore the Davidic king to his throne. The closing verse (v. 52) is a brief doxology, with which the final editors concluded book 3 of the Psalter.

Book 4: Psalms 90–106

Psalm 90. A prayer to the everlasting God to have compassion on His servants, who live their lives under the rod of divine wrath and under His sentence of death.

The superscription ascribes this song to **Moses**, which would make this one of the earliest compositions in the Psalter. No other psalm depicts so poignantly the dismal state of mortal man before the face of God, holy and eternal. That Israel's forty years of enforced sojourn in the "great and terrible wilderness" (Deut. 8:15) on its pilgrimage to the Promised Land (see Num. 14:26–35) should evoke such a prayer ought not to be surprising. Yet the prayer in this psalm expresses neither defiance nor despair. Moses honestly acknowledges sin that warrants God's "anger" (v. 7) and pleads for God's "mercy" (v. 14), which brings joy in the midst of life's difficulties.

90:1–12. The Lord is the protective **dwelling place** (v. 1) of His people **in all generations** because

He is the eternal God (vv. 1–2), yet humans are mortal and live under God's sentence of death (vv. 3–6). For God, a thousand years are like a **watch in the night** (v. 4), but He cuts man's life short like new **grass** (v. 5) that shows itself at dawn's light but withers in the hot Canaanite sun before evening falls. Adding to the difficulty of man's plight is the fact that even life's short span of seventy or eighty years is filled with trouble (vv. 7–10). God ferrets out man's every sin and makes him feel His righteous anger (v. 7). No one has taken the measure of God's anger, but everyone ought to know the measure of his (few) days. Only an arrogant fool takes no thought of his mortality or of his accountability to God (see Psalms 49; 73:4–12).

90:13–17. Taking account of his mortality, Moses prays for God's compassion (vv. 13–17). He requests that God not delay in delivering his **servants** (v. 13) from trouble and that His love shine **early** (v. 14) in the morning to provide relief from the long, dark night of His anger. Perhaps Moses pleads for the anticipated rest of the Promised Land (see Exod. 33:14; Deut. 12:9). The final answer to his prayer comes with the resurrection (see Rom. 5:2–5; 2 Cor. 4:16–18).

Psalm 91. A glowing testimony to the security of those who trust in God.

91:1–8. The first half of the psalm affirms the security of the godly, who **abide under the shadow of the Almighty** (v. 1). Like those of a mother bird, the Lord's protective wings shelter His children. They are safe from four specific threats: the hunter's **snare** (enemies; v. 3), deadly plague (**noisome pestilence**), **terror** (v. 5) of war, and destructive diseases. The Lord protects the righteous in the most dangerous of circumstances, but He recompenses the **wicked** (v. 8) with destruction.

91:9–16. The second half of the psalm echoes the theme of the absolute security of those who trust in the Lord, using hyperbole to promise that the **angels** (v. 11) watch over the godly to keep them from even dashing their feet **against a stone** (v. 12). They are assured of triumph over menacing beasts in the double reference to **the lion** (v. 13) and poisonous snakes (**adder** and **dragon**). With the dangers mentioned in verses 5–6, these predators are figurative of any mortal threat that the godly may face. Employing the form of a prophetic oracle in verses 14–16, the psalmist offers climactic assurance of the security of the godly by recalling God's promises to those who truly love and trust Him. Because of these promises, the godly can look forward to deliverance from **trouble** (v. 15) and **long life** (v. 16).

In the New Testament, the Devil applied the promises of verses 11–12 to Jesus (see Matt. 4:6; Luke 4:10–11). Satan's misapplication is a reminder of the danger of presumptuously claiming God's protection or of taking His promise to mean that believers never endure sickness or suffering. God's people will face all kinds of adversity, but their assurance is that God will protect and preserve them in all circumstances.

Psalm 92. A joyful celebration of the righteous rule of God.

The testimony of this psalm to the prosperity of the righteous, links it thematically with Psalm 91, while its joy over God's righteous reign relates it to the cluster of psalms that follow (Psalms 93–100). The psalmist here may be the king, whose triumph in battle brings blessing to all of God's people (see vv. 10–11).

92:1–16. The psalmist calls the people to praise the Lord for His exalted position (**most High; v. 1**) and His righteous attributes (vv. 1–3). The people of God rejoice because of God's saving acts (vv. 4–5), but the **fool** (v. 6) does not recognize that the Lord rules righteously (vv. 6–7). Such folly is fatal because the fool sees the wicked flourishing but does not **understand** the ways of the Lord or foresee the end He has appointed for him. The prosperity of the wicked is only temporary.

God's eternal exaltation assures the destruction of His enemies and the exaltation of the righteous (vv. 8–15). The righteous triumph and are securely **planted in the house of the LORD** (v. 13), unlike the wicked, who **spring as the grass** (v. 7) but wither under God's judgment. Through the Lord's blessing, the godly retain the vigor of youth into **old age** (v. 14). The contrasting fates of the righteous and the wicked demonstrate the discriminating justice of God's rule.

Psalm 93. A hymn to the eternal, universal, and invincible reign of the Lord.

The Kingship Psalms (or Enthronement Psalms) in Psalms 47 and 93–100 offer a majestic confession of faith in and hope for the kingdom of God on earth. These hymns were composed for the liturgy of a high religious festival in which the kingship of the Lord—over the cosmic order, over the nations, and in a special sense, over Israel—was annually celebrated. Implicitly, where not explicitly, the Lord's kingship is hailed in contrast to the claims of all other gods; He is "a great King above all gods" (95:3).

93:1–5. The Lord's reign, by which the creation order has been and will be secure throughout the ages, is from eternity (vv. 1–2). Though Israel as a nation has come late on the scene, her God has been King since before the creation of the world. **The Lord reigneth** (v. 1) is the ultimate truth, and first article, in Israel's creed. Since His founding of the world, the Lord has shown Himself to be mightier than all the forces of disorder that threaten His kingdom (vv. 3–4). The **floods** (v. 3) refer to the primeval chaotic waters, tamed and assigned a place by the Lord's creative word (see 104:7–9; Gen. 1:6–10; Job 38:8–11). Implicitly, the floods symbolize the spiritual powers and enemy nations that oppose the coming of the Lord's kingdom (see 65:6–7; 74:13–14). The roar of these chaotic waters is no match for the power of the Lord's creative decrees.

The Lord, whose indisputable rule has made the world secure, has also given His people life directives (**testimonies**; v. 5) that are stable and reliable (see 19:7). The people honor God as their holy King by following His commands.

Psalm 94. An appeal to the Lord, as "judge of the earth" (v. 2), to redress the wrongs perpetrated against the weak by arrogant and wicked men who occupy seats of power.

94:1–11. The initial appeal to God, the Judge, acknowledges that the right to execute **vengeance** (v. 1) belongs to the Lord (vv. 1–3). The psalmist prays that God will repay **the proud** (v. 2) and not allow **the wicked** (v. 3) to succeed in carrying out their evil schemes. Evil men in positions of authority are guilty of mistreating the poor and needy (**the widow … the stranger … the fatherless**; v. 6) yet arrogantly believe they will not have to answer to God for their sins (vv. 4–7). The psalmist warns the arrogant evildoers that they are **fools** (v. 8) to believe God will not punish them for their sinful behavior (vv. 8–11). The Lord created them and knows all about their evil intentions, and He keeps man in line by chastising his sinful behavior. They will not get away with flaunting God's standards of righteousness.

94:12–15. Though oppressed by the wicked, those whose lives are directed by God's **law** (v. 12) are the blessed ones. Rather than leading to judgment (see v. 10), God's correcting and teaching provide positive direction that guides the righteous into a life of **rest** (v. 13) and security. The Lord will not abandon the powerless among His people to the injustice of their oppressors. When injustices exist, He will act to "restore righteousness" (**return unto righteousness**; v. 15).

94:16–23. The Lord is the only sure court of appeal (vv. 16–19). Without God's help, the wicked would have silenced the psalmist in the grave. Now, however, it is the wicked for whom **the pit** (v. 13) will be dug. When the psalmist feels he is about to be overwhelmed by the wicked, he is strengthened by his confidence in the Lord's faithful mercy. The Lord's justice will ultimately prevail (vv. 20–23). Though corrupt leaders may hold positions of authority that allow them to abuse their power by passing unjust laws, God will protect **the righteous** (v. 21) and repay the wicked according to their sins.

Psalm 95. A call to worship the Lord as "a great God, and a great King above all gods" (v. 3). This psalm was likely spoken by a priest or Levite to the assembled Israelites at the temple.

95:1–15. The first part of this psalm is a call to praise the Lord of all the earth (vv. 1–5). The call to praise is given in verses 1–2, and the cause for praise is expressed in verses 3–5. Israel is called to praise the Lord because He is **above all gods** (v. 3), and there is no corner of the universe that is not under His sovereign control. The ancient pagan world had different gods for different peoples, different geographical areas, different cosmic regions (heaven, earth, netherworld), and different aspects of life (e.g., war, fertility, crafts), but the Lord rules over all. **The deep places** (v. 4), **the strength of the hills ... the sea** (v. 5), and **the dry land** represent the whole world, over which God rules.

95:6–11. The second part of the psalm is a call for the people to acknowledge the Lord's kingship by submissive attitude and obedient heart (vv. 6–11). They submit to the Lord by kneeling before Him. They acknowledge Him as their **Maker** (v. 6), both as Creator of all things and as Israel's Redeemer. Since kings were commonly called "shepherds" of their people, Israel recognizes herself as **the people of his pasture** (v. 7; see 100:3; Jer. 25:36; Ezek. 34:21).

It is not enough for Israel to confess the Lord's rule over them, however; they must also demonstrate their submission to the Lord by obeying **his voice** (v. 7). They must decisively choose **To day** not to follow the example of the wilderness generation, who rebelled against the Lord at Meribah ("quarreling," or **provocation**; v. 8) and Massah ("testing," or **temptation**) (see Exod. 17:7; Num. 20:3). The climax of Israel's rebellion came when she faithlessly refused to undertake the conquest of Canaan and considered returning to Egypt (see Num. 14:1–4). The experiences of the wilderness generation demonstrate the terrible consequences of refusing to submit to the Lord. That generation was condemned to a forty-year stay in the wilderness (see Num. 14:34) and never entered into the **rest** (v. 11) of the Promised Land (see Num. 14:30; Josh. 1:13, 15). "Rest" here is a fertile concept indicating Israel's possession of a place with God on earth where she is secure from all external threats and internal calamities (see 1 Kings 5:4).

Psalm 96. A call to all nations to praise the Lord as the only God and to proclaim the glory of His reign throughout the world.

The psalms envision a time when all peoples will submit to the Lord and give Him the worship that He deserves (see also 22:27–30; 145:10–13), an Old Testament anticipation of the world mission of the New Testament people of God (see Matt. 28:16–20). This psalm appears in slightly altered form in 1 Chronicles 16:23–33.

96:1–6. The first part of this psalm calls for all nations to **sing** (vv. 1–2) praise to the Lord. The triple repetition of "sing" reflects a common feature in Old Testament liturgical calls to worship (see vv. 7–9; 103:20–22; 118:2–4; 135:1; 136:1–3). That the nations are to sing **a new song** (v. 1) indicates that, like Israel, they have access to the Lord's mercy and salvation (see 33:3). Israel's responsibility is to proclaim the Lord's greatness and **glory** (v. 3) to the nations so that they will know that deliverance comes from the Lord. All peoples are to praise the Lord because He alone is God (vv. 4–6). The idols of the nations are nothing, but God is the Creator who **made the heavens** (v. 5). As the Maker of the heavenly realm, which pagans considered the abode of the gods, the Lord is greater than all the gods. Two pairs of divine attributes, **Honour and majesty** (v. 6) and **Strength and beauty**, are personified as throne attendants whose presence before the Lord heralds the exalted nature of the one, universal King.

96:7–13. Worship is the only appropriate response to the greatness of God, and the second half of the psalm calls on all nations to worship the Lord and to declare the glory of His righteous rule (vv. 7–13). The threefold **give** (vv. 7–8) balances out the threefold "sing" of verses 1–2. As part of their worship, the nations are called to come to the temple at Jerusalem to present **an offering** (v. 8) to the Lord. While such tribute was presented on a limited scale during the reigns of David and Solomon, the future millennial kingdom will be a time when the wealth of the nations flows into Jerusalem in recognition of the Lord's universal reign (see Isa. 61:6). The nations are to broadcast the Lord's universal and righteous rule through their praise (vv. 10–13). Because God's kingdom is one, all His creatures will **rejoice** (v. 11–12) when God's rule over mankind brings righteousness to full expression in His cosmic kingdom. The future aspect of God's eternal kingdom rule over the earth will be established through His righteous judgment of all peoples. Israel lived in hope of God's future acts in which He would decisively deal with all wickedness and establish His **righteousness** (v. 13) on earth.

Psalm 97. A joyful celebration of the Lord's righteous reign over all the earth.

97:1–6. This psalm reminds the nations that they have seen God's majesty displayed in the creation and should rejoice with Israel that the Lord reigns supreme (vv. 1–6). Through general revelation and common grace, even the peoples of the distant lands are able to see the Lord's majestic glory revealed in the sky's awesome displays, especially in the thunderstorm (see 18:7–15; 29). The dark storm clouds that hide the sun are dramatic visual reminders that the fierce heat and brilliance of God's glory must be veiled from creaturely eyes. God's glory is such that it destroys **his enemies** (v. 3) and melts the earth. While God rules in power, His reign is also founded on righteousness and justice, which the heavens also proclaim. The stable order of the vast array of **the heavens** (v. 6) declares God's **righteousness** in that it is a mirror image of the moral order that God has also placed within His creation.

97:7–12. The center verse of the psalm (v. 7) provides the counterpoint of the psalm. There is joy for all who acknowledge the Lord but shame and disgrace for those who trust in false gods. With biting irony, the psalm calls on **all ye gods** (v. 7), all the gods that people foolishly worship, to bow before the Lord. **Zion** (v. 8) rejoices that their LORD (v. 9) is the God who reigns over all (vv. 8–9). The psalmist provides a reminder, however, that only those who hate evil have real cause to rejoice in the Lord's righteous rule (vv. 10–12). The benefits of God's rule are reserved for **the upright in heart** (v. 11) because He is a God of **holiness** (v. 12).

Psalm 98. A call to joyfully celebrate the righteous reign of the Lord.

In the three stanzas of this psalm, the call to praise the Lord is progressively extended to ever-widening circles.

98:1–3. In the first stanza, the worshiping congregation at the temple is called to celebrate the **marvellous things** (v. 1) that God has done, specifi-

cally His saving acts on behalf of His people. God's powerful acts of deliverance for Israel are also His self-revelation to the nations. In this sense, God acts as His own evangelist. God's saving acts reveal His **righteousness** (v. 2), because He is just in keeping the covenant promises He has made to Israel.

98:4–6. In the second stanza, the psalmist calls on **all the earth** (v. 4) to join in the celebration. The peoples of the earth are to worship the Lord with music, and the command **Make a joyful noise** frames this section of the psalms.

98:7–9. In the final stanza, the psalmist extends to all of creation the call to celebrate before the Lord. **The sea** (v. 7), **the world**, and **the floods** ("the rivers"; v. 8), and **the hills** are merisms representing every feature of the whole earth. The imagery of the personified elements of nature giving praise to the Lord adds to the celebratory tone of this psalm and also highlights that every individual in God's creation exists to give Him worship. The Lord is worthy of praise because He is coming to **judge** (v. 9) and to establish **righteousness** on earth. In faith, Israel lived between the past (see vv. 1–3) and the future righteous (saving) acts of God.

Psalm 99. A hymn celebrating the Lord as the Great and Holy King in Zion.

In developing the theme of God's absolute sovereignty, the poet makes striking use of the symbolic significance (completeness) of the number seven: seven times he speaks of "the LORD," and seven times he refers to Him by means of independent personal pronouns (Hebrew). The refrain calling for the Lord to be exalted for His holiness (vv. 5, 9) marks the two halves of this psalm.

99:1–5. The psalmist calls the nations to acknowledge that Israel's God, enthroned in Zion, is the ruler over all (vv. 1–3). The Lord is seated on His throne **between the cherubims** (v. 1) standing over the ark of the covenant, which serves as **his footstool** (v. 5; see Exod. 25:18; 2 Chron. 9:18). The nations are to **tremble** (v. 1) before the Lord, giving Him the reverence and honor that are His due. The Lord has shown the quality of His rule by what He has done for Israel (vv. 4–5). **Strength** (v. 4) and judgment ("justice") are the chief characteristics of God's reign. God's absolute power is in harmony with His perfect justice.

99:6–9. The benevolent nature of God's reign is especially demonstrated by His merciful and patient treatment of Israel throughout their history (vv. 6–8). The Lord provided priestly intermediaries who were appointed to intercede with Him on behalf of His faltering people and were given knowledge of His will so they could instruct Israel. **Moses ... Aaron ... and Samuel** (v. 6) serve here as representatives of all those the Lord used as intermediaries for His people in times of great crises. The **priests** of Israel had interceded for the sinful people, and the Lord had **answered** their prayers (see Exod. 32:11–13; Num. 14:13–19; 1 Sam. 12:19, 23). The Lord had communicated His will and directive by speaking to them **in the cloudy pillar** (v. 7), recalling the times that God had spoken with Moses (see Exod. 33:9) and Aaron (see Num. 12:5–6). However imperfectly, Israel lived by God's righteous statues and decrees, and their obedience was possible only because God had revealed His commands to them. The Lord had also been gracious in forgiving Israel's sins when they repeatedly failed to live up to His righteous standard. The remembrance of God's gracious dealings with Israel leads to the closing refrain, which calls for the Lord to be exalted for His holiness (v. 9).

Psalm 100. A call to praise the Lord for His special relationship with Israel and for His enduring goodness, mercy, and truth.

The superscription **A Psalm of Praise** ("Thanksgiving") perhaps indicates that this song was composed as an accompaniment for a thank offering (see Lev. 7:12). The final editors of the Psalter used this song to close the series of Kingship (or Enthronement) Psalms, which begin with Psalm 93.

100:1–5. The psalm contains two separate calls to praise the Lord, with explanations of why He is to be praised (vv. 1–3, 4–5). The first main division calls for the whole world to praise the Lord because of His special relationship with Israel, reflecting the idea that the covenant between the Lord and Israel brings benefit and blessing to all peoples

(see 96:1–4; Gen. 12:1–3). The second call to praise (vv. 4–5) focuses on God's attributes of goodness, **mercy** (v. 5), and **truth**. These attributes are unfailing through all time.

Psalm 101. A king's pledge to reign righteously (see 2 Kings 23:3).

If this psalm was authored by David (see superscription), it may have been composed for Solomon's use at his coronation (see superscription; 1 Kings 2:2–4; 2 Sam. 23:1–7). Only Christ, the great Son of David, has perfectly fulfilled these commitments.

101:1–8. The psalmist begins by celebrating the **mercy and judgment** ("justice"; v. 1) of God's reign, which the king uses as the model for his own reign (vv. 1–2a). The king vows to rule **in a perfect way** (v. 2), pledging to act blamelessly rather than implying sinless perfection. His rhetorical question, **O when wilt thou come unto me?** is an urgent prayer for God to come and sustain him in his pledge. The essential commitment of the psalmist is one of keeping his **heart** and his **eyes** (v. 3) pure. In Old Testament understanding, a person follows the dictates of the inner man (the "heart") and/or the external influences and attractions of external influences (the "eyes").

The king's promise to act righteously also includes a repudiation of evil deeds and those who promote them (vv. 3b–4). The term **froward** ("perverse"; v. 4) refers to that which is the opposite of "perfect" (see 18:26; Prov. 11:20; 19:1). A "froward" heart and a deceitful tongue are root and fruit (see Prov. 17:20), so the king will remove from his presence all slanderous and arrogant persons. While avoiding the influence of the wicked, the king will surround himself with godly persons who will influence the administration of his kingdom in a positive direction (vv. 6–7). He will look upon **the faithful** (v. 6), those who maintain moral integrity, with favor. He will choose his servants, advisors, and officials from among the blameless and not from among those **that telleth lies** (v. 7). The king will fulfill his responsibility to remove all the wicked from the Lord's kingdom with diligence and persistence. It was probably the custom for kings to hear cases **early** (v. 8) in the morning.

Psalm 102. The prayer of an individual in a time of great distress.

The superscription for this psalm is unique in that it identifies only the life situation in which the prayer is to be used: it is for **the afflicted, when he is overwhelmed.** It appears that the distress of the psalmist, while described as a physical illness, is the result of sharing in a national disaster such as the exile (see vv. 12–22, 28). Some have suggested that the prayer was originally that of a Davidic king or a member of the Davidic royal house while in Babylonian exile.

102:1–11. The psalmist urgently prays for God to hear his prayer and to not withhold the favor of His presence (vv. 1–2). His distress is a suffering so great that it withers his body and spirit (vv. 3–11). The complaint that his life is wasting away frames this stanza. The combination of **bones** (v. 3) and **heart** (v. 4) refers to the whole man. It is as if a fire is consuming his physical frame, and his heart is withering **like grass** scorched by the hot sun. He is weakened because his agony leaves him with no appetite, and he feels abandoned like a lonely bird. Seeing his suffering, his **enemies reproach** (v. 8) him, viewing his suffering as divine abandonment. They use his name as a curse (**sworn against me**), perhaps saying to others, "May you become like him." **Ashes** (v. 9) and tears are his food and drink because his sorrow is constant. The writer feels as if he is about to be consumed because of God's unrelenting **wrath** (v. 10).

102:12–26. Despite the enormity of his pain, the psalmist is certain that the King eternal will hear the prayer of the destitute and restore Zion (vv. 12–17). The references to **Zion** (vv. 13, 16) suggest that the psalmist's distress was occasioned by the Babylonian exile. The Lord's **servants** (v. 14) love Zion, and the psalmist is confident of her restoration because the Lord must love her even more. The Lord will be glorified among the nations and their rulers through the restoration and rebuilding of Zion.

The psalmist desires God's certain deliverance of His people to be recorded so that future generations may hear of it and give continual praise to the Lord. The Lord's deliverance of the exiles will be like the rescue of **prisoner**[s] (v. 20) condemned to **death**. In the final restoration of Zion in the last days, the **people** (v. 22) of Israel **and the kingdoms** of the earth will gather **to serve the Lord** at Jerusalem. The expectation expressed here may be influenced by such prophecies as Isaiah 2:2–4 and Micah 4:1–3. In the concluding recapitulation (vv. 23–28), the psalmist returns to his suffering and how he has called on God to spare his life. He knows that God is able to keep his **days** (v. 23) from being **shortened** because He is the eternal Creator and more enduring than the creation. Because the Lord does not change, Israel has a secure future.

Psalm 103. A hymn celebrating God's love and His compassion toward His people.

The length of this psalm has been determined by the number of letters in the Hebrew alphabet, as with the hymn found in Psalm 33. Calls to praise frame the body of the hymn (vv. 1–2, 20–22) and set its tone.

103:1–5. The recital of praise in verses 3–5 contains a celebration of personal blessings the psalmist has received. The **tender mercies** (v. 4) of the Lord include forgiveness of sin, healing of physical illness, and rescue from death. "The pit" (**destruction**; v. 4) is a metaphor for the grave (see 30:1). The Lord's blessing restore the vigor of youth, to match the proverbial unflagging strength of the eagle (see Isa. 40:31).

103:6–19. Here the recital of praise turns to a recollection of God's mercies to His people Israel. The Lord has righteously intervened for Israel when they have been **oppressed** (v. 6) by other peoples. He has had compassion on Israel when they have sinned and failed to live by the laws that He revealed through **Moses** (v. 7). The Lord's mercy is so vast that He removes the sins of His people, **As far as the east is from the west** (v. 12). The Lord shows pity to Israel because they are frail mortals whose **days are as grass** (v. 15). The infinite span of God's **everlasting** (v. 17) love and **mercy** overarches man's little time here on earth.

103:20–22. The psalm concludes with a fourfold call to **Bless the Lord** (vv. 20–22), which is directed to all creatures. The **angels** (v. 20) and the **hosts**

(v. 21) of heaven are to praise Him. Though they are heavenly creatures of great power, they were created to worship and to serve the Lord. The angels serve as a model for all of the **works** (v. 22) of God's creation, which are personified so that they may give praise to the Lord as well. Ultimately, the praise of the entire creation reminds the psalmist that he himself is to praise the Lord.

Psalm 104. A hymn to the Creator, celebrating God's power in creation and His providential care for the world He has created.

Obviously influenced by Genesis 1, the psalmist has adapted that account to his different purpose and has subordinated its sequence somewhat to his own design. Whereas Genesis 1 recounts creation as God's first work at the beginning, the poet views the creation displayed before his eyes and sings of the glory of its Maker and Sustainer. Surprisingly, he only hints at the angelic world (v. 4) and mentions man only in passing (vv. 14, 23). His theme is the visible creation around him, through which the invisible Creator has demonstrated His glory.

104:1–4. The psalmist calls for praise to the Lord for His greatness and majesty, which is reflected in the creation. The light made on the first day of creation is portrayed as the radiant and stately robe of the Sovereign Lord. The Lord is great because He rules over the earth from His heavenly abode. The heavens formed on the second day of creation are like a curtain over the earth and the luminaries that give it light. The Lord Himself dwells in the **chambers** (v. 3) of the heavens, and the term "chamber" normally refers to the upper-level room of a house (see 1 Kings 17:19; 2 Kings 1:2). This chamber is above the waters of the firmament (the **curtain** of v. 2; see Gen. 1:7). From these waters, the Lord provides life-giving rains as He rides across **the clouds** (v. 3) that form **his chariot** (see 18:7–15; 68:4). The winds (**spirits;** v. 4) and lightning bolts (**flaming fire**) of the thunderstorm are personified as the agents of God's purposes.

104:5–9. As Creator, the Lord has also made the realm of the earth secure. The earth, referring to the land in distinction from sky and seas, is solidly established on foundations. It is firmly founded so that **it should not be removed for ever** (v. 5). The Lord caused the land to emerge from the waters on the third day of creation, and He placed boundaries so that the land will never be overwhelmed by the sea. Life is possible because the Lord brought the waters of chaos under His control.

104:10–26. Because of the Lord's continuing providential care, the earth is a flourishing garden of life (vv. 10–18). The Lord gives water from below, which water the ravines of the Negev (vv. 10–12), and He gives the rains from above, which water the uplands of Israel with their cultivated fields (vv. 13–15). These waters produce food for both animals and man. Well-watered Lebanon, with its great trees, its hordes of birds, and its alpine animals, is a prime example of the blessing and fertility that the Lord provides (see 72:16; Hos. 14:7). He has also established the orderly cycles of life on earth, governed by the moon and sun, which were put in place on the fourth day of creation (vv. 19–23).

The greatness of the Lord's sovereignty is magnified by the diversity of His creation, including the creatures belonging to the nautical realm, which were made on the fifth day of creation (vv. 24–26). The **leviathan** (v. 26) was the fearsome mythological monster of the deep (see Job 3:8) but here seems to represent an actual animal created by God. Even this powerful animal is merely God's harmless pet playing in the ocean.

104:27–35. Through God's benevolent care, the earth flourishes like a zoological garden (vv. 27–30). Recalling the creation of the land animals on the sixth day, the psalmist highlights God's provision of food for these creatures and His control over life and death.

The creation reflects **The glory of the Lord** (v. 31), but He is so much greater than His creation that with a look or a touch He could undo it (vv. 31–32). The psalmist concludes with a vow to **praise** the Lord (v. 33) and the expression of his desire that **the sinners** (v. 35) and **the wicked** be destroyed so that the earth may be purged of sin, which alone mars the beauty of God's handiwork.

Psalm 105. An exhortation to Israel to worship and trust in the Lord because of all His saving acts in fulfillment of His covenant with Abraham to give his descendants the land of Canaan.

This psalm was composed for one of Israel's annual religious festivals, most likely the Feast of Weeks (see Lev. 23:15–21; Deut. 16:9–12; 26:1–11).

105:1–7. The introduction consists of two parts: (1) an exhortation (with ten imperatives) to worship the Lord (vv. 1–4); and (2) a call to remember what the Lord has done (vv. 5–7). Israel is to celebrate the Lord's past saving acts and to trust in Him for future deliverance and blessing.

105:8–45. The main body of the psalm (vv. 8–45) highlights the theme that the Lord has remembered His covenant with Abraham. The promise to **Abraham** (v. 6) that he will become a great nation and that his descendants will possess the land of Canaan was **confirmed** (v. 10) with **Isaac** (v. 9) and **Jacob** (v. 10) and became a **law**, or a fixed policy governing the Lord's future actions (vv. 8–11). The author recites at length God's saving acts on Israel's behalf, from the granting of the covenant to its fulfillment (vv. 12–45). The Lord protected Abraham's family **When they were but a few men in number** (v. 12), and Abraham made his journeys to Canaan from Mesopotamia and from Canaan to Egypt and back (vv. 12–15; see Gen. 12–20). The Lord providentially sent **Joseph** (v. 17) ahead of the Israelites into Egypt and exalted him to a position of leadership so that the Israelites would have food in a time of famine (vv. 16–22; see Gen. 37–47).

While the Israelites were in Egypt, they became a numerous people, and the Lord used even the hatred of the Egyptians to bring about Israel's deliverance (vv. 24–25). He sent **Moses** (v. 26) and **Aaron** as deliverers and carried out **signs** (v. 27) and **wonders** through the terrible plagues that were inflicted on Egypt (vv. 26–36). The seven plagues (symbolizing completeness) of this poetic recollection represent the ten plagues of Exodus 7–11. Apart from omissions (the plagues of livestock disease and boils), the poet follows the order of Exodus except that he combines the third and fourth plagues (lice and flies)—

in reverse order—to stay within the number seven. He also places the ninth plague (darkness) first to frame his recital with the two plagues that climaxed the series. The climatic event leading to Israel's departure from Egypt was the killing of Egypt's **firstborn** (v. 36). The plagues made the Egyptians so **glad** (v. 38) to see the Israelites leave their land that they gave them **silver and gold** (v. 37) when they departed.

The Lord also protected and provided for Israel in the wilderness when they left Egypt (vv. 39–42). He gave the **cloud** (symbolic of His presence; v. 39) as a protective **covering** so that the sun would not harm them by day (see 121:5–6). The **fire** of God's presence gave **light** in the darkness of night. Time and again, God provided food in miraculous ways. The concluding summary (vv. 43–45) repeats the theme of God's covenant faithfulness. He gave them the land of Canaan so that they might live there in obedience to Him. God has kept His **law** (v. 10) so that Israel might keep **his statutes** (v. 45)—the Hebrew word is the same. God's redemptive work in fulfillment of His covenant promise has as its goal the creation of a people on earth who conform their lives to His holy will.

Psalm 106. A confession of Israel's long history of rebellion and a prayer for God to once again save His people.

In length, poetic style, and shared themes, this song has much affinity with Psalm 105 even while it contrasts with it by reciting the past as a history of rebellion (see Psalm 78; Neh. 9:5–37).

106:1–5. In the introduction, the psalmist calls the people to praise the Lord for His mighty acts. He raises the question as to **Who can** (v. 2) recite the Lord's great **acts** and then answers that it is those who practice justice and **righteousness** (v. 3); only they can worship with integrity because their lifestyle matches their confession. The psalmist also prays that the Lord will **Remember** (v. 4) him as one committed to the way of life described in verse 3 and that the Lord will include him as one of the recipients of His blessing.

106:6–43. The main body of the psalm narrates at length Israel's many rebellions during their history (vv. 6–43). This recital of rebellion opens with a general confession of sin (**We have sinned**; v. 6) in which the author identifies himself with Israel in her rebellion even as he prays for inclusion in God's mercies toward His people (see Ezra 9:6–7). Israel sinned at the Red Sea when they failed to remember the **wonders** (v. 7) God had used to deliver them from Egypt, yet God **saved them for his name's sake** (v. 8) and performed an even greater miracle in drying up the sea (vv. 7–12; see Exod. 12–14).

Israel celebrated her deliverance from Egypt but forgot again and repeatedly tempted the Lord in the wilderness wanderings (vv. 13–33). They resisted the leadership of **Moses** (v. 16) and **Aaron**, which led to the death of **Dathan** (v. 17) and **Abiram** (vv. 16–18; see Numbers 16). They worshiped the golden calf and would have been destroyed were it not for the intercession of Moses (vv. 19–23; see Exodus 32). The Israelites **despised the pleasant land** (v. 24) at Kadesh Barnea by believing the majority report of the spies rather than trusting in God's promise to give them the land (vv. 24–27; see Numbers 13–14). This lack of faith caused God to **overthrow them in the wilderness** (v. 26) and to keep the disobedient generation from entering the land. Israel also angered the Lord with their worship of **Baal-peor** (v. 28), resulting in a **plague** (v. 29) that was stopped when **Phinehas … executed judgment** (v. 30; see Numbers 25). The zealous act of Phinehas **was counted unto him for righteousness** (v. 31; see Gen. 15:6) **for evermore**, referring to "the covenant of an everlasting priesthood" (Num. 25:13) that the Lord granted Phinehas as a gracious reward. Israel's sin **at the waters of strife** (or "Meribah"; v. 32) cost Moses the opportunity to enter the Promised Land when **he spake unadvisedly** (v. 33) and dishonored the Lord in front of the people (vv. 32–33; see Numbers 20).

The psalmist follows with a general description of Israel's sins, applicable from the time of the judges to the Babylonian exile (vv. 34–39). Failure to **destroy the nations** (v. 34) in Canaan led to Israel worshiping **their idols** (v. 36). The Hebrew for the word **devils** (v. 37) occurs elsewhere in the Old Testament only in Deuteronomy 32:17, where it refers to false gods. It is related to a Babylonian word referring to (pagan) protective spirits. Their shedding of **innocent blood** (v. 38) through the heinous practice of child sacrifice had defiled the very **land** itself (see Num. 35:33). They had committed spiritual prostitution (v. 39) by joining themselves with false gods (see Ezek. 23:3, 5–8; Hos. 5:3; 6:10).

God had taken stern measures against His rebellious people (vv. 40–43). In His **wrath** (v. 40), He had brought upon them the covenant curse of military defeat throughout their history, climaxing in the Babylonian exile (see Lev. 26:25–26, 33, 38–39; Deut. 28:25, 36–37, 48–57, 64–68).

106:44–46. Yet, despite His anger, God had graciously remembered His covenant and had repeatedly delivered them from their enemies when they cried out to Him in repentance. God had often **repented** (v. 45), or relented from sending judgment. God does not "repent" in the sense that he alters His decrees out of a limited knowledge of the future. At the same time, God has entered into a give-and-take relationship with human beings so that human responses to Him and His word do have an effect on His decisions and actions (see Jer. 18:7–10; Jonah 3:9). The Lord had even taken pity on the exiles when they were taken away as **captives** (v. 46; see 1 Kings 8:50; 2 Chron. 30:9; Ezra 9:9; Jer. 42:12).

106:47–48. The psalm concludes with a communal prayer for deliverance and restoration from dispersion (v. 47). When the Lord has regathered His people from exile, they will be able to triumphantly celebrate. The doxology in verse 48 provides the closing statement of book 4 of the Psalter (see 41:13).

Book 5: Psalms 107–150

Psalm 107. An exhortation to praise the Lord for His unfailing love in that He hears the prayers of those in need and saves them.

107:1–3. Having experienced anew God's mercies in her return from Babylonian exile (v. 3), Israel celebrates God's unfailing benevolence toward those who have cried to Him in the crises of their lives. In its recitational style, the psalm is closely related to

Psalms 104–106. The introduction to the psalm calls for those **redeemed ... out of the lands** (v. 2–3) of exile to **give thanks** (v. 1) to the Lord.

106:4–32. The body of the psalm uses four prevailing images to portray the Lord's rescue of His people from exile. The deliverance of the exile is like the rescue of those lost in a trackless **wilderness** (v. 4). Since Israel had journeyed through the wilderness on her way to Canaan, she had firsthand experience of the terrors of the wilderness. She was, moreover, bounded on the east by the great Arabian Desert, across which her merchant caravans traveled. The wanderers in the wilderness are rescued by the Lord when wracked by hunger and thirst. He sets them on the **right way** (v. 7), or the "level way," a direct route clear of dangerous and difficult obstacles. The Lord brings them into **a city of habitation**, where their hunger is satisfied.

The psalmist next portrays the deliverance of the exiles as rescue from a dark dungeon or prison (vv. 10–16). The prisoners **sit in darkness** (v. 10), which is like **the shadow of death**, and are bound by **iron** fetters as punishment for their sin. They are crushed in spirit, and their strength fails until they cry out to the Lord. God even delivers those who cry to Him when their distress is a result of His discipline for their sins. In rescuing the prisoners, the Lord breaks the **gates of brass** (v. 16) and **bars of iron**, the seemingly impregnable defenses of a powerful enemy.

The third image used to portray Israel's salvation is that of deliverance from the punishment of a wasting disease (vv. 17–22). The nation of Israel acted as **Fools** (v. 17) in disregarding the commands of the Lord and had received their just punishment. The effects of sin, which destroy the soul, are here compared to a physical illness that ravages the body (see Isa. 1:5–6). Their disease was such that they were at **the gates of death** (v. 18). The realm of the dead was sometimes depicted as a netherworld city with a series of concentric walls and gates to keep those descending there from returning to the land of the living (see 9:13; Job 38:17; Matt. 16:18). In their hopeless condition, they cried to the Lord

and He provided healing. They will offer **thanksgiving** (v. 22) offerings and **declare his works** as the appropriate response to their deliverance (see Lev. 7:12–15; 22:29–30).

The fourth image portraying the exiles' deliverance (vv. 23–32) is that of being rescued from a shipwreck at **sea** (v. 23). Israel's merchants braved the sea in pursuit of trade (see Gen. 49:13; Judg. 5:17; 1 Kings 9:26–28; 10:22). The storm portrayed here is of such severity that those on the ship melt with fear and are tossed about like drunken men by the waves of the sea. Their cries to the Lord are answered as He saves them and calms the storm. Since the peoples of the eastern Mediterranean coastlands associated the sea with the primeval chaotic waters (see 32:6), the Lord's total control of them was always a cause of wonder and a sense of security for Israel.

107:33–43. The final section of the psalm (vv. 33–42) is a twofold instructive supplement reminding the people how the Lord has disciplined them in the past but also how He has rescued and saved them. The Lord sometimes disciplined His people by turning the **fruitful land** (v. 34) into a virtual **wilderness** (v. 35) but then restored the land again so that **the hungry** (v. 36) could live there and prosper in the midst of plenty (v. 33–38). At other times, the Lord sent against them powerful armies that devastated the land and deported its people. Yet afterward, He once again restored the needy (vv. 39–43). In the manner of the wisdom teachers, the poet generalizes Israel's past experiences to teach the people that they must remain faithful to the Lord and trust in His **lovingkindness** (v. 43).

Psalm 108. Praise of God's love and a prayer for His help against the enemies.

With slight modifications, this psalm is a combination of 57:7–11 and 60:5–12.

108:1–13. The song opens with a praise of God's love that also serves as an expression of trust in God (vv. 1–5). The Lord is worthy of love and trust because He is a God of **mercy** (v. 4) and **truth**. The psalmist then prays for God's help against enemies. The Lord will help David because he is the Lord's **beloved** (v. 6), and He will help Israel because they are

His chosen people. The Lord will defeat the enemy nations attacking Israel and give strength to David as he fights his battles (see discussion on 60:5–12).

Psalm 109. A prayer for God to judge a case of false accusation.

109:1–5. This psalm is framed by an opening (vv. 1–5) and closing (vv. 26–29) petition. In the opening petition, David appeals for God to deliver him from his false accusers. **Hold not thy peace** (v. 1) is a request for God to not be inactive in righting the wrong done against him. While the enemies attack David with their speech, he gives himself **unto prayer** (v. 4), perhaps calling attention to how he has even prayed for his enemies (see 35:13–14).

109:6–20. The psalmist continues his appeal by asking that the Lord deal with his enemies in accordance with their malicious intent against him, matching the punishment with the crime. Since the enemy falsely accused him, he prays that the enemy himself be confronted by an "accuser." The Hebrew word for **Satan** (v. 6) literally means "accuser," and the lack of the definite article seems to indicate that Satan himself is not in view. David further asks that his enemy be put to death (**Let his days be few;** v. 8) and that **another take his office.** The enemy held some official position and was perhaps plotting a coup. Because of the close identity of a man and his children in ancient society (see Exod. 20:5), the psalmist also prays that the consequences of the enemy's sin to be passed on to his posterity (vv. 9–15). David asks that the false accuser be deprived of all his property so that he has no inheritance to pass on to **his children** (v. 10) and that his family line would ultimately be **cut off** (v. 13) and **blotted out.** Looking backward as well as forward, the psalmist even asks for the **iniquity** (v. 14) of the accuser's ancestors to **be remembered** and held against them.

While these requests are harsh, they reflect David's intense longing for the execution of justice. The enemy is deserving of this terrible judgment because he has **persecuted the poor and needy** (v. 16). Since the accuser lived by curses against others as his food and clothing, it is only fitting that those curses be turned against him.

109:21–31. David prays for deliverance because his suffering is intense (vv. 21–25). The Hebrew for **is wounded** (v. 22) sounds like the Hebrew for **cursing** (vv. 17–18), a wordplay demonstrating that his hurt is directly related to the attacks of those who conspire against him. David'd affliction is such that he feels as if he is fading or passing away (**I am gone;** v. 23). He presents a concluding petition (vv. 26–29) that echoes many of the preceding themes found in the psalm. He prays for deliverance because he is the Lord's **servant** (v. 28) and then vows to **praise the LORD** (v. 30) when He delivers him from his troubles.

Psalm 110. Oracles concerning the messianic King-Priest.

This psalm (specifically vv. 1, 4) is frequently referred to in the New Testament testimony regarding Christ. Like Psalm 2, it has the marks of a coronation psalm, composed for use at the enthronement of a new Davidic king. Before the Christian era, Jews already viewed this psalm as messianic. Because of the manner in which it was interpreted in the New Testament—especially by Jesus (see Matt. 22:43–45; Mark 12:36–37; Luke 20:42–44) but also by Peter (see Acts 2:34–36) and the author of Hebrews (see Heb. 1:13; 5:6–10; 7:11–28)—Christians have generally held that it is the most directly prophetic of all the psalms. If so, David, speaking prophetically (see 2 Sam. 23:2), composed a coronation psalm for his great future Son, the Messiah. This psalm falls into two precisely balanced halves (vv. 1–3, 4–7). Each of the two brief oracles (vv. 1, 4) is followed by thematically similar elaboration.

110:1–3. The psalm opens with the Lord's decree, promising that the Messiah will rule over all His enemies (vv. 1–3; see 2:7–12). By referring to this future Son as "my Lord" (v. 1), David acknowledges the superiority of the future king to himself (see Matt. 22:44–45; Mark 12:36–37; Luke 20:42–44; Acts 2:34–35; Heb. 1:13). In the New Testament, Jesus specifically uses this verse to refer to His divine origin (Matt. 22:41–45). The **right hand** (v. 1) refers to the place of honor beside a king (see 45:9; 1 Kings 2:19); thus, the authority of the Messianic Son of David will be second only to that of God Himself.

New Testament references to Jesus' exaltation to this position are many (see Matt. 26:64; Mark 14:62; 16:19; Luke 22:69; Acts 2:33; 5:31; 7:55–56; Rom. 8:34). God's Messiah will ultimately defeat His **enemies** and use them as His **footstool**. Ancient kings often had themselves portrayed as placing their feet on vanquished enemies (see Josh. 10:24). The authority of the Lord's anointed expands in ever-widening circles until no foe remains to oppose His rule.

In response to the Messiah's authority, the **people** (v. 3) of Israel will present themselves as "freewill offerings" (**shall be willing**) to their king. They will offer themselves as dedicated warriors to support the king on the battlefield. In the New Testament, Paul speaks of Christ's followers offering their bodies as "a living sacrifice" (Rom. 12:1) and of himself as being "offered upon the sacrifice and service of your faith" (Phil. 2:17). The phrases **in the beauties of holiness** and **dew of thy youth** are descriptive of the Lord's Messiah and depict Him as being clothed in the beauty of royal majesty and perpetually preserving the bloom of youth even as the **womb of the morning** gives birth each day to the dew.

110:4–7. The Lord issues an oath establishing His Messiah as king-priest in Zion and assuring Him victory over all powers that oppose Him (vv. 4–7). The Messiah will be **a priest** (v. 4) belonging to **the order of Melchizedek**. David and his royal sons, as chief representatives of the rule of God, performed many worship-focused activities, such as overseeing the ark of the covenant (see 2 Sam. 6:1–15; 1 Kings 8:1), building and overseeing the temple (see 1 Kings 5–7; 2 Kings 23:4–7; 2 Chron. 29:3–11), and overseeing the work of the priests and Levites and the temple liturgy (see 1 Chron. 16:4–42; 23:3–31). In all these duties, they exercised authority over even the high priest. They could not, however, engage in those specifically priestly functions that had been assigned to the Aaronic priesthood (see 2 Chron. 26:16–18). Melchizedek was the king-priest of God Most High at Jerusalem in the days of Abraham (see Gen. 14:18). As such a king-priest, He was appointed to a higher order of priesthood than that of Aaron and his sons. Jesus as Messiah belongs to this higher order of priesthood and also offered a superior sacrifice than the Aaronic priesthood through His death on the cross (see Hebrews 7–8).

When the Messiah will go into battle, **The Lord** (v. 5) will be at His **right hand**, near to assist and empower Him for warfare. With the Lord's help, He will defeat and put to death His enemies (v. 6). Even in the heat of battle, He will find refreshment from **the brook** (v. 7) and will **lift up** His **head** with undiminished vigor.

Psalm 111. Praise of God for His unfailing righteousness.

This psalm combines hymnic praise with wisdom instruction, as its first and last verses indicate. Close comparison with Psalm 112 shows that these two psalms are twins, probably written by the same author and intended to be kept together. Both Psalm 111 and Psalm 112 are alphabetic acrostics and introduce a series of Hallelujah psalms that extend to Psalm 117.

111:1–9. I will praise the Lord (v. 1) introduces the praise that follows (vv. 2–9). The hymn focuses especially on **The works of the Lord** (v. 2), what God has done for His people. These powerful and benevolent acts are a reflection of God's righteous character. The provision of food (v. 5a) is illustrative of His bountiful provisions for the daily needs of His people (see Matt. 6:11). He is faithful to His **covenant** (v. 5) promises, and His word is absolutely trustworthy (**sure**; v. 7), based in **truth and uprightness** (v. 8). The Lord redeemed Israel from death and bondage because of His **covenant** (v. 9) promises. The Lord's works on behalf of Israel demonstrate His holiness.

111:10. The concluding word of godly wisdom is that **fear of the Lord is the beginning of wisdom** (v. 10), which is the classic Old Testament statement concerning the religious basis of what it means to be wise (see Job 28:28; Prov. 1:7; 9:10). This reverential awe of God provides the resolve to obey **his commandments**.

Psalm 112. A eulogy for the godly man, written in the spirit of Psalm 1 but formed after the pattern of Psalm 111 and likely intended as its complement (see discussion on Psalm 111).

112:1-7. The basic theme of the psalm, introduced in verse 1, is the blessing of the individual who fears the Lord and keeps **his commandments** (v. 1). The godly man brings blessing to his children and is blessed through them (v. 2). They will become persons of influence and reputation because of his example. The righteous man will enjoy physical prosperity, which is not a guarantee that wealth is the reward of righteousness but a promise that he will be blessed with godly success in his endeavors (v. 3; see 1:3; 128:2).

Even in times of adversity, the godly man will have the **light** (v. 4) of God's protection and favor. The godly man will be rewarded for the generosity that he shows to others and will be blessed with discernment in how to direct his life (v. 5). He will be firmly established in life and faith in that his righteousness will erect an enduring memorial in the memory of both God and man (v. 6). Because his trust in God is steadfast, he will **not be afraid** (v. 7) when facing calamity. Trust in and obedience to God's righteous will is the sum of true godliness (see 34:8-14).

112:8-10. The promise that the righteous individual will **see his desire upon his enemies** (v. 8) does not reflect a desire for personal revenge but rather a trust in the execution of God's perfect justice. Because the godly man is willing to share with **the poor** (v. 9), others will honor his memory, just as God's name is held in holy awe (see 111:9).

The counterpart to the blessing of the godly is the cursing and judgment of **the wicked** (v. 10). Rather than enjoying God's blessing, the wicked man will be left to **gnash with his teeth**, a figure for the bitter regret of the wicked over their fate. The wicked will ultimately not prevail over the righteous.

Psalm 113. A hymn to the Lord, celebrating His majesty and His mercies to the lowly (see 138:6).

This psalm begins the "Egyptian Hallel" (Psalms 113-118), which came to be used in Jewish liturgy at the great religious festivals (see Leviticus 23; Num. 10:10; John 10:22). At Passover, Psalms 113 and 114 were sung before the meal and Psalms 115-118 after the meal.

113:1-3. The psalm opens with a fourfold call to praise. Such repetition was a liturgical convention. The praise of those who truly worship the Lord cannot rest content until it fills all time and space.

113:4-6. The Lord is to be praised because He is enthroned on high, exalted over all creation (vv. 4-6). He is **above all nations** (v. 4) and, implicitly, over all their gods. The rhetorical question, **Who is like unto the LORD our God?** (v. 5) forms the center of the psalm. The Lord demonstrates His grace in His condescending to become involved in the affairs of men.

113:7-9. The final section of the psalm promises that the Lord exalts the lowly. The God of highest majesty does not ally Himself with the high and mighty of the earth but stands with and raises up **the poor** (v. 7) and **the needy** (see 1 Sam. 2:3-8; Luke 1:46-55). The Lord rescues them from **the dust** and **the dunghill**, which are symbolic of humble status but here probably also of extreme distress and need (see Job 30:19; 42:6; Isa. 47:1; Jer. 25:34). The Lord also causes **the barren woman** (v. 9) to give birth. In the ancient world of the Old Testament, barrenness was for a woman the greatest disgrace and the deepest tragedy (see Gen. 30:1; 1 Sam. 1:6-7, 10). Examples of God blessing the barren with a child include Sarah (see Gen. 21:2), Rebekah (see Gen. 25:21), Rachel (see Gen. 30:23), Hannah (see 1 Sam. 1:20), the Shunammite (see 2 Kings 4:17), and others.

Psalm 114. A hymn celebrating the exodus.

This psalm is one of the most exquisitely fashioned songs of the Psalter. The first two stanzas (vv. 1-4) recall the great events of the exodus; the last two (vv. 5-8) celebrate their continuing significance. The exodus from Egypt was the great Old Testament act of redemption, through which the nation of Israel was formed. The crucial event was the establishment of the covenant at Sinai, where Israel became bound to the Lord as a "kingdom of priests, and a holy nation" (Exod. 19:3-6).

114:1-4. With the establishment of the Mosaic covenant, Israel as a people became a **sanctuary** (v. 2) in which God took up residence in the world, a fact symbolized by the tabernacle and later by the temple. In Exodus 15:17, the Promised Land is similarly called God's "sanctuary." Israel was also the Lord's **dominion**, the special realm over which He ruled as King.

In portraying the exodus, the psalmist evokes a fearsome scene similar to that portrayed by other biblical poets (vv. 4–6; see 18:7–15; 68:7–8; 77:16–19; Judg. 5:4–5). **The** Red **sea** (v. 3) and the **Jordan** River, through which the Lord brought His people, are here personified to highlight the sense of wonder at God's saving acts. The sea and river **saw** the mighty God approach in His awesome pillar of cloud and **fled. The mountains** (v. 4) and **the little hills** quaked at God's approach.

114:5–8. The psalmist reminds Israel that the Lord of yesterday—the God of Jacob—is still with His people (vv. 7–8) and that His awesome presence calls for a response of reverential respect. The reference to the Lord's act of providing water from the rock during Israel's wilderness wanderings (see Exod. 17:6; Num. 20:11) provides one final reminder of how great Israel's God truly is.

Psalm 115. Praise of the Lord, the one true God, for His love and faithfulness toward His people.

This psalm was composed as a liturgy of praise for the temple worship and may have been written for use at the dedication of the second temple, when Israel was beginning to revive after the disruption of the exile (see Ezra 6:16). The song is structured as an exchange between the people and the worship leaders: (1) verses 1–8, the people; (2) verses 9–11, the choir leader; (3) verses 12–13, the people; (4) verses 14–15, the priests; (5) verses 16–18, the people.

115:1–8. The people that have assembled for worship praise God's love and faithfulness toward them, which silences the taunts of the nations. Israel's existence and her anticipated revival are not her own achievements but are due to the **mercy** (v. 1) and faithfulness of the Lord. The nations have taunted, **Where is … God?** (v. 2) when Israel has been decimated by natural disasters or crushed by enemies, especially when the temple of the Lord was destroyed in 586 BC (v. 2). **God is in the heavens** (v. 3) and remains sovereign over all. If Israel is decimated or destroyed,

it is God's doing; it is not His failure or inability to act, nor is it the achievement of the idols that the nations worship. When Israel is revived, that will also be God's doing, and no other god can oppose Him. Whatever glory and power the false gods are thought to have (as symbolized in the images made to represent them), they are mere figments of human imagination and utterly worthless (vv. 4–7). The power of the nations that taunt Israel is similarly illusory (v. 8).

115:9–15. The response of the choir leader to the people is a call to trust in the Lord, not in idols. The triple repetition of **He is their help and their shield** (vv. 9–11) is a liturgical formula highlighting God's protection of His people. Because of the security the Lord provides, the people confess their trust in the Lord (vv. 12–13). They are mindful of His past faithfulness and confident of His future blessing. The priestly blessing in verses 14–15 promises that the Lord will **increase** (v. 14) Israel in numbers, wealth, and strength.

115:16–18. The people deliver a closing doxology. The Lord's sovereignty extends over heaven and earth. As long as the worshipers live, they will devote themselves to praising the Lord, and they are confident of His protection from death at the hands of their enemies. **The dead praise not the LORD** (v. 17) because the dead no longer live on earth but descend to the silent realm below, where blessings are no longer enjoyed and hence praise is absent (see 6:5; 30:1). Because of further revelation and the resurrection of Jesus from the dead, the New Testament places greater emphasis on the eternal blessings that the redeemed will enjoy in God's presence (see Revelation 21–22).

Psalm 116. Praise of the Lord for deliverance from death.

This psalm may have been written by a king and recalls Hezekiah's thanksgiving when the Lord spared him from a life-threatening illness (see Isa. 38:10–20). This thanksgiving song falls into three main divisions (vv. 1–6, 7–14, 15–19). In each of these major sections, the psalmist expresses his intention to "call upon" (vv. 2, 13, 17) the Lord as his source of help in all circumstances.

116:1–6. In the opening section, the psalmist declares his **love** (v. 1) for the Lord because the Lord has **heard** his prayer and saved him. The Lord intervened to rescue him from **The sorrows of death ... and the pains of hell** (or the "grave"; v. 3). Death is personified here as stalking the psalmist, and the Lord rescued him when he was in death's grasp. Because of God's deliverance, the writer wishes to recount his experience to God's people (note **our God;** v. 5). Thanksgiving in the Old Testament is not only a personal experience but also involves sharing with others the goodness and faithfulness of the Lord. The psalmist reminds the congregation that the Lord protects the simple, that is, the person who is childlike in his dependence on and trust in the Lord (see discussion on 19:7).

116:7–14. The writer gives further testimony to the Lord's goodness and expresses how he will repay the Lord for His goodness. Because the Lord has delivered him from death, he enjoys **rest** (v. 7), a state of unthreatened well-being (see 1 Kings 5:4; Jer. 6:16). His life is a gift from the Lord, and he determines to **walk before the Lord** (v. 9) and to live his life for Him. The threat of death from which the psalmist had been delivered was brought on by the false accusations of enemies. He characterizes his accusers as **liars** (v. 11; see 5:9–10; 35:11; 109:2–4).

The psalmist considers what he **could render** (v. 12) as an expression of devotion to the Lord (vv. 12–14; see 50:14–15). He promises thank offerings in honor of the Lord's deliverance. **The cup of salvation** (v. 13) likely refers to the cup of wine drunk at the festal meal that climaxed a thank offering (see 22:26, 29; Lev. 7:11–21). In presenting the thank offerings, the psalmist will fulfill the **vows** (v. 14) he has made to praise the Lord.

116:15–19. The psalmist is thankful that the Lord has counted his life as precious. **Precious ... is the death** (v. 15) does not convey that the believer's death is a joyous experience to God but rather that it is something of great importance to the Lord so that He carefully watches over the believer's life and will not allow him to die before his time. The psalmist concludes by again affirming his intention to offer

the sacrifice of thanksgiving (v. 17) in connection with the fulfillment of his **vows** of praise.

Psalm 117. A call for all people to give praise to the Lord.

This psalm, the shortest psalm in the Psalter and the shortest chapter in the Bible, is an expanded hallelujah that may have originally served as the conclusion to the series of Hallelujah Psalms (beginning at Psalm 111). All nations and peoples are called on to praise the Lord (as in 47:1; 67:3–5) for His great love and enduring faithfulness toward Israel. Thus, the hallelujahs of the Psalter, when fully expounded, express that great truth, so often emphasized in the Old Testament, that what God was doing in and for His people Israel involved the destiny of all peoples (see, e.g., 2:8–12; 47:9; 110; Gen. 12:3; Deut. 32:43; 1 Kings 8:41–43; Isa. 2:2–4; 25:6–7; 60:3; 66:18–24; Jer. 16:19–21; Amos 9:11–12).

117:1–2. The psalm opens with the call, **O praise the Lord, all ye nations** (v. 1). This verse is quoted in Romans 15:11 as proof that the salvation of Gentiles and their glorifying God was not a divine afterthought. The reason for the praise is that the Lord is a God of **merciful kindness** (v. 2) and **truth.**

Psalm 118. A hymn of thanksgiving for deliverance from enemies.

A Davidic king leads the nation in this liturgy of thanksgiving for deliverance and victory after a hard-fought battle with a powerful confederacy of nations (see 2 Chron. 20:27–28). In the postexilic liturgy developed for the annual festivals, the song was used as a thanksgiving for national deliverance. As the last song of that liturgy, it may have been the hymn sung by Jesus and His disciples at the conclusion of the Last Supper (see Matt. 26:30).

118:1–21. The king calls the people to praise the Lord because of His enduring **mercy** (v. 1) and covenant faithfulness toward Israel (vv. 1–4). The king's song of thanksgiving for deliverance and victory follows (vv. 5–21). The Lord answered the king's prayer in battle and **set** him **in a large place** (v. 5), a place where he could effectively maneuver, free from the threats of his enemies (vv. 5–6; see 18:19). Because of the Lord's help, he is confident that his desire (v. 7) to **destroy** (v. 10) his enemies will be realized. The psalmist addresses the enemies that viciously attacked him—**Thou hast thrust sore at me** (v. 13)—but even in its brutality, the strength of the enemy was nothing compared to the Lord's protection (v. 14). The Lord's protection brings rejoicing among **the tabernacles** (tents or dwellings) **of the righteous** (v. 15) in celebration of His power and strength. While the king is certain of deliverance, he also recognizes that the grave threat through which he has passed has also served God's purpose: to discipline him and teach him humble godliness (v. 18).

Open to me (v. 19) suggests a liturgical procession in which the king approaches the inner court of the temple at the head of the jubilant worshipers (see Psalms 24; 68). It is possible that the procession began outside the city and that **the gates of righteousness** are the gates of Jerusalem, the city of God. The king promises to lead the people in **praise** (v. 21) for the Lord's **salvation**. The closing verse of the thanksgiving song (v. 21) echoes the **give thanks** of verse 1, the **answered me** of verse 5, and the testimony of verse 14.

118:22–27. The people's exultation in the Lord follows (vv. 22–27). **The stone which the builders refused** (v. 22) is most likely a reference to the king, who had been viewed with disdain by the kings invading his realm—the builders of worldly empires. The enemy kings were unable to realize that this rejected ruler would become **the head stone of the corner,** likely a large stone used to anchor and align the corner of a wall. This imagery portrays the Davidic ruler as the most important stone in the structure of the new world order that God is bringing about through Israel. Jesus applied this verse (and v. 23) to Himself (see Matt. 21:42; Mark 12:10–11; Luke 20:17; Eph. 2:20; 1 Peter 2:7). The Lord alone had **made** (v. 24) possible this **day** of rejoicing for Israel and their king. In their celebration, the people pray for the Lord to continue to save and sustain them (vv. 25–27).

The crowds who greeted Jesus at His triumphal entry into Jerusalem used the words of verses 25–26 (see John 12:13), which are fitting because Jesus is the son of David who brings God's ultimate deliverance to His people. The command to **Bind the sacrifice with cords** (v. 27) is apparently a call to bring to completion the liturgy of the thank offering being presented to the Lord (see Lev. 7:11–21).

118:28–29. The king speaks his final word of praise (v. 28), and a liturgical conclusion (v. 29) repeats the opening call to praise, thus framing the whole service.

Psalm 119. A devotional on the Word of God.

The author of this psalm was an Israelite of exemplary piety who (1) was passionately devoted to the Word of God as the word of life; (2) humbly acknowledged, nevertheless, the errant ways of his heart and life; (3) knew the pain, but also the fruits, of God's corrective discipline; and (4) had suffered much at the hands of those who arrogantly disregarded God's Word and made him the target of their hostility, ridicule, and slander. It is possible that he was a priest (see vv. 23, 57), and the psalm might well be a vehicle for priestly instruction in godliness.

This psalm forms a massive alphabetic acrostic (the verses of each stanza begin with the same letter of the Hebrew alphabet) that demands patient, meditative reading. The alphabetic acrostic form may appear arbitrary and artificial to a modern reader, but a sympathetic and reflective reading of this devotional will compel a more favorable judgment. The author had a theme that filled his soul and that ranged the length and breadth and height and depth of a person's walk with God. Nothing less than the use of the full power of language would suffice, and for that, the alphabet was a most apt symbol.

Devotion to the Word of God (and the God of the Word) is the dominant theme. The Word as God's directives for life demands obedience and as God's promises for the righteous demand faith. In referring to God's Word, the psalmist makes use of eight Hebrew terms: *torah,* "law" (v. 1); *'edot,* "testimonies" (v. 2); *piqqudim,* "precepts" (v. 4); *mitswot,* "commandments" (v. 6); *mishpatim,* "judgments" (v. 7); *huqqim,* "statutes" (v. 5, 8); *dabar,* "word" (v. 9); *'imrah,* "word" (v. 11). These terms highlight the covenantal nature of God's Word, and the use of these varied terms is another poetic device for highlighting the centrality of God's law.

119:1–8. The introduction to this psalm (vv. 1–3) focuses on the blessedness of those who walk in obedience to God's commands, and the remainder of the psalm develops in many ways the specifics of what this blessing entails. Those who obey God's law can hope for God's help (vv. 4–8). They will **not be ashamed** (v. 6) by suffering poverty, sickness, or humiliation at the hands of their enemies, because the Lord will not forsake them in their times of need.

119:9–16. The **word** (v. 9) of God keeps the righteous from being corrupted by sin and its consequences. Some consider **young man** (v. 9) to be a characterization of the author, but more likely, it indicates instruction addressed to the young, after the manner of the wisdom teachers (see Prov. 1:4; Eccl. 11:9; 12:1). The psalmist is devoted to the Lord's commands because of their cleansing effect on his life. He stores the Word in his inner person and publicly declares his covenant commitment to the Lord for others to hear. He loves the Word of God more than even **riches** (v. 14; see vv. 72, 111, 162).

119:17–24. Devotion to God's law characterizes the Lord's **servant** (v. 17) but alienates him from the arrogant of the world. Out of gratitude for God's care and blessing, the psalmist keeps His law. The term **wondrous** (v. 18) usually describes God's redeeming acts (see 9:1), but His law contains matters just as wonderful for the righteous. The righteous are **stranger[s] in the earth** (v. 19) because of their devotion to the Lord, while **the proud** (v. 21) who stand in opposition to God and His people are a law unto themselves (see 10:2–11). Because of his zeal for God and His commands, the writer has suffered much from the hostility of the arrogant. Because he states that **Princes** (v. 23) oppose him (see v. 46) and also mentions speaking **before kings** (v. 46), it is possible that the psalmist was a priest, one of whose functions would have been to teach God's law (see Lev. 10:11; Ezra 7:6; Neh. 8:2–8). These kings and rulers probably are either Israelite rulers in the time of the monarchy or Persian rulers in the postexilic period. As they share their worldly counsels, they speak derisively of the one who stands apart because he delights in God's statutes and makes them his **counsellers** (v. 24).

119:25–32. Regardless of his difficult circumstances, the psalmist is determined to cling to God's Word. The phrase **cleaveth unto the dust** (v. 25) indicates despair and nearness to death. The author speaks much of his sorrow, suffering and affliction that bring ridicule and slander from his adversaries (see vv. 28, 50, 67, 71, 75, 83, 92, 107, 143, 153). His suffering only intensifies his desire to know and live by God's commands, which are the hope of his life. The psalmist asks God to keep him **from … the way of lying** (v. 29), the way that seems right but leads to death, and to **enlarge** his **heart** (v. 32), or increase his understanding of the Lord's commandments (see 1 Kings 4:29), so that he might be able to follow them.

119:30–40. Expanding on this idea of increased understanding, the psalmist prays for instruction in God's will because of his intense longing to live by His precepts (vv. 33–40). He asks not only for greater knowledge but also for the resolve to walk **in the path of thy commandments** (v. 35). He prays that God will do His part by fulfilling the promises He has made to those who **fear** (v. 38) Him. The Lord's saving acts in fulfillment of His promises contribute to the recognition that He is the true God (see 130:4; 2 Sam. 7:25–26; 1 Kings 8:39–40; Jer. 33:8–9).

119:41–48. The psalmist further petitions the Lord to deliver him so that he will have the opportunity to honor His law in life as he walks about **at liberty** (v. 45), unconfined by affliction or oppression. His deliverance, which would allow him to live and serve the Lord, will also give him the opportunity to share God's **testimonies** (v. 46) with others and to **speak … before kings.** His love for God's word is too great for him to remain silent concerning its benefits and blessings.

119:49–64. The psalmist moves from petition to testimony that God's Word is his comfort and guide at all times (vv. 49–56). The Word brings him **comfort** (v. 50) when his enemies mock him. He finds special hope in the fact that God's law is **of old** (v. 52); it is not fickle but is firmly grounded in God's unchanging moral character. The permanence of God's commands is one of the main reasons the psalmist cherishes the law so highly (see vv. 89, 144, 152, 160). **Horror hath taken hold upon me** (v. 53) refers to his zeal for God's commands, which awakens righteous anger against those who reject the law (see vv. 113, 115, 158) and brings abhorrence of all that is contrary to it. The law of God directs the psalmist as he lives **In the house of my pilgrimage** (lit., "my temporary house"; v. 54) as a stranger on earth (see v. 19).

The Lord is the psalmist's true homestead (**portion**; v. 57) because it is God's law that fills the earth with all that makes life secure and joyous. The psalmist has not turned from keeping God's commands, even though **the wicked** (v. 61) have mistreated and persecuted him. He is thankful for God's **mercy** (v. 64) and that he can live in fellowship with those who also order their lives by God's Word.

119:65–80. Turning again to petition, the psalmist asks God to deal favorably with him in accordance with His goodness, even if that means affliction (vv. 65–72). Affliction has been good for him because it has kept him from sin and taught him **good judgment** (v. 66) from God's law. In contrast, **the proud** (v. 69) have a callous disregard for God's law, and their hearts are **as fat as grease** (v. 70; see Isa. 6:10; Jer. 5:28). The psalmist has learned through his difficulties the inestimable value of God's Word. He also requests for his will to be conformed to God's righteous precepts so that the arrogant may be put to shame and those who **fear** (v. 74) the Lord may rejoice with him (vv. 73–80). Those who love the Lord and keep His commands can expect Him to intervene when they call out to Him for deliverance.

119:81–88. The last stanza of the first half of this psalm is a prayer for God's help, with the psalmist asking God to save him from his affliction and persecutors. The psalmist bears the marks of his afflictions, just as a wineskin (**bottle**; v. 83) hanging **in the smoke** and heat above a fire becomes smudged and shriveled. He does not know how much more he can endure, so he pleads with God to **execute judgment** (v. 84) on his enemies. God's gracious deliverance will lead the psalmist to even greater resolve to obey His commands.

119:89–96. Like the opening verses of the psalm, the first three verses of the second half of the psalm (vv. 89–91) teach a general truth: God's sovereign and unchanging Word governs and maintains all creation. The secure order of **heaven** (v. 89) and **the earth** (v. 90) declares the reassuring truth that God's Word is enduring and trustworthy. This larger truth confirms the godly man's confidence in the trustworthiness of God's special revelation given in the Scriptures. The psalmist has experienced the reliability of God's Word, as it has sustained him in his affliction (vv. 92–96). He prays for God's deliverance because he has kept His commands. There is a reciprocal faithfulness between the Lord and the righteous man throughout this psalm. Everything in life has boundaries and limitations (**I have seen an end of all perfection**; v. 96), but the Word of God is an inexhaustible source of wise counsel for life.

119:97–112. Meditation on God's law yields the highest wisdom (vv. 97–104). This truth is lost on the proud **enemies** (v. 98) of the psalmist, who place their confidence in their worldly wisdom. The precepts of God's law give the psalmist a greater understanding than that of the best of human **teachers** (v. 99) and the old men who have learned much through the experiences of life. The law of God is **sweeter than honey** (v. 103) to the psalmist because it keeps him from walking in the ways of evil, which lead to destruction.

The Word of the Lord is a **lamp** (v. 105) that keeps the righteous man from groping about in the darkness (vv. 105–112). The psalmist takes an oath to keep God's commands and to rejoice in them even in the midst of persecution. He takes his life into his own hand (**My soul is continually in my hand**; v. 109) by publicly honoring God's law in the face of threats and hostility but is confident that his trust in God's Word is not misplaced. God's **testimonies** (v. 111) are his **heritage**, the possession that he has received from God as his homestead and that provides all he needs for life.

119:113–129. The psalmist mixes testimony and petition in the remainder of his song. God's precepts provide clear moral direction so that the godly man knows to separate himself from the deceitful thoughts and actions of the wicked (vv. 113–120). The psalmist prays that he might remain obedient so that he can live and not be destroyed by the judgment that will fall on the ungodly. **The wicked** (v. 119) are like **dross**, the scum removed from molten ore or metal. Understanding the judgment that befalls the wicked, the godly fear the Lord and quiver in deep reverence for Him.

The psalmist prays for deliverance because of his faithfulness to the Lord (vv. 121–128). Since he has kept God's commands, he prays for God to **Be surety for thy servant** (v. 122), or to take the responsibility for his safety. He argues that **It is time** (v. 126) for the Lord to work in his defense, or possibly in the judgment on those who have broken His commands. The psalmist is not arguing that he has earned God's favor or demanding that God owes him for his obedience; rather, he is appealing to God's covenant promise to bless those who keep His commands. The blessing that comes from keeping God's commands makes them more valuable than **fine gold** (v. 127).

119:129–144. The psalmist confesses that God's Word is **wonderful** (v. 129) because it provides **light** (v. 130) and direction for his life (vv. 129–136). He prays for God to be merciful to him **as thou usest to do** (lit., "according to the judgment"; v. 132), or in accordance with the way that God has customarily acted toward His people. The consistency of God's character gives the psalmist confidence that the Lord will deliver him from his enemies and bless him with His favor. The psalmist further acknowledges that the Lord and His laws are **Righteous** (v. 137–138), completely true and trustworthy (vv. 137–144). He loves the Word of God because it is **pure** (lit., "refined"; v. 140) and contains nothing worthless or useless. Because the Word and all its promises are **everlasting** (v. 144), he is sustained through his time of temporary affliction.

119:145–168. As the psalm draws to a close, the prayers for deliverance become more dominant and persistent. The psalmist prays that God will deliver him, basing his appeal on his faithfulness to God's commandments (vv. 145–160). He rises before dawn and stays awake during **the night watches** (v. 148; see Judg. 7:19; Lam. 2:2) so that he might meditate on God's law. He refuses to **forget** God's precepts, recognizing that **Salvation is far from the wicked** (v. 155). The psalmist remains obedient even when he is being persecuted by powerful enemies (vv. 161–168). He fears God so that he remains unmoved by the opposition of men and continues to trust that the Lord will deliver him.

119:169–176. The closing section of the psalm contains one final plea for God to hear his prayer for deliverance so that he might **praise** (v. 171) the Lord and continue to testify of the excellence of God's Word to others. He has **chosen** (v. 173) to follow God's **precepts** and longs for God's **salvation** (v. 174). While affirming his commitment and devotion to the Lord, the psalmist acknowledges, **I have gone astray like a lost sheep** (v. 176; see Isa. 53:6). For all his devotion to God's law, he has again and again wandered into other (deceitful) ways and, like a lost sheep, must be brought back by his heavenly Shepherd. For one who has made God's law the guide and dearest treasure of his life, the last word can only be such a confession, and such a prayer.

Psalm 120. A prayer for deliverance from enemies so that the psalmist might live in peace.

Psalms 120–134 represent a collection of psalms known as the Songs of Degrees. (**degrees**, or "ascents"; see superscription). Some have thought that the Hebrew for "ascents" refers to stairs leading to the temple, hence "a song of the stairs," to be used in the temple liturgy (probably at the Feast of Tabernacles). Most believe it refers to the annual religious pilgrimages to Jerusalem (see 84:5–7; Exod. 23:14–17; Deut. 16:16; Mic. 4:2), which brought the worshipers singing to Mount Zion (Isa. 30:29). The themes of trust in the Lord, longing for God's presence, and the Lord's blessings on the worshipers who come to celebrate before Him pervade these songs. Whether a thematic (or some other) scheme controls the arrangement of Psalms 120–134 is unclear, though it is probably not coincidental that they begin with a prayer that evokes the experience of one far from home and beset by barbarians and end with a call to praise in the sanctuary.

120:1–7. In this song, the psalmist prays for deliverance from his enemies, who assail his character with lies and deceit (vv. 1–2), and then expresses his assurance that God will act (vv. 3–4). The lies of his enemies were like **Sharp arrows** (v. 4; see 57:4; Prov. 25:18) and **coals** of searing fire (see Prov. 16:27; James 3:6), and God's judgment against them will answer in kind. Returning to his lament, the psalmist expresses his weariness over the prolonged harassment he receives from those who are continually stirring up conflict. Beseiged by slanderers, he feels as if he were far from home, surrounded by the barbarians of **Mesech** (v. 5) and **Kedar**. The former was in central Asia Minor (see Gen. 10:2), the latter in Arabia (see Isa. 21:16).

Psalm 121. A dialogue (perhaps liturgical) of confession and assurance of the Lord's help and protection.

The use of this psalm as a pilgrimage song provides the key to its understanding. The comforting assurance it expresses is equally appropriate for individuals making pilgrimage to Jerusalem in a caravan and for the pilgrimage of life to the "glory" into which the faithful will be received. The psalm is composed of four (Hebrew) couplets, each having an introductory line, which the rest of the couplet develops. The key terms in this psalm are "the LORD" and "keep" ("preserve" in vv. 7–8), each occurring five times.

121:1–8. The pilgrim psalmist opens by confessing his trust in the Lord (vv. 1–2). He looks to the **hills** (v. 1) in the vicinity of Jerusalem, of which Mount Zion is one, because of the Lord's presence in Zion. The God who dwells there and meets there with His people is the one true God, the King of all creation. The psalmist receives assurance (from a Levite or priest) that the Lord, as the unsleeping guardian of Israel, will give him and his fellow travelers safety in their journey (vv. 3–4). The Lord will not allow his foot to slip even when the way is narrow and treacherous. The Lord does not slumber like the pagan god Baal (see 1 Kings 18:27). The next couplet (vv. 5–6)

elaborates on the Lord's unfailing protection. The Lord is a **shade** (v. 5) of protection from **the sun** (v. 6) and **the moon**, figures for all that threaten the pilgrim by day or night. The final assurance affirms that the Lord's protection of His people extends to all of life (vv. 7–8). The phrase **thy going out and thy coming in** (v. 8) is an expression indicating all of life.

Psalm 122. A hymn of joy, celebrating Jerusalem (see Psalms 42–43; 46; 48; 84; 87; 137).

This psalm was sung by a pilgrim in Jerusalem, very likely at one of the three annual festivals (see Deut. 16:16), expressing his deep joy regarding the city and his prayer for its welfare. As the third of the Pilgrimage Psalms (Psalms 120–134), it shares many dominant themes with Psalm 132, the third from the end of this collection—possibly a deliberate arrangement. Structurally, a two-verse introduction locates the worshiper with the festival throng in the city of his joy, and the major themes are developed in two stanzas of four (Hebrew) lines each. References to "the house of the LORD" (vv. 1, 9) frame the song.

122:1–5. After expressing his joy for having joined the pilgrimage to Jerusalem (vv. 1–2), the psalmist reflects on the significance of Jerusalem for the faithful (vv. 3–5). His statement that **Jerusalem is ... a city that is compact together** (v. 3) refers to the city's well-knit construction but perhaps, and more significantly, also recalls the construction of the tabernacle (see Exod. 26:11, "couple ... that it may be one"). Jerusalem is being celebrated as the earthly residence of God. The tribes of Israel gather together at Jerusalem to **give thanks** for God's saving acts and blessings on behalf of the nation. Additionally, Jerusalem is the royal city of His chosen dynasty, **the house of David** (v. 5), through which He (ideally) protects and governs the nation (see 2:2, 6–7; 89:3–4, 19–37; 2 Sam. 7:8–16). In postexilic times, it remained the city of David, though now in hope of a future Messiah.

122:6–9. The final section of the psalm contains prayers for Jerusalem's peace and security. In Hebrew, a beautiful wordplay tightly binds together **Pray** (*sha'al*; v. 6), **peace** (*shalom*), **Jerusalem** (*yerushalayim*), and **prosper** (*yishlayu*). All who are devoted to Jerusalem constitute a loving brotherhood, who worship together, pray together, and seek each other's welfare as the people of God (see Psalm 133). Because Jerusalem is the place supreme where God and His people meet together in fruitful union, the psalmist vows to seek the city's peace.

Psalm 123. A prayer of God's humble people for Him to show mercy and thereby foil the contempt of the proud.

123:1–4. The psalmist looks to the Lord for help because the same God whose earthly throne is in the temple on Mount Zion dwells **in the heavens** (v. 1) and is above all. The faithful in Israel, men and women alike, present themselves as humbly dependent on God. Like **servants** (v. 2), they rely on the Lord for their every need. The psalmist prays that the Lord will **Have mercy** (v. 3) on Israel because they are mocked and ridiculed by their enemies (vv. 3–4). **The proud** (v. 4), who live by their own wits and strength, pour contempt on those who humbly rely on God, especially when those who rely on God suffer or do not prosper (see 10:2–11).

Psalm 124. Israel's praise of the Lord for deliverance from powerful enemies—an appropriate sequel to Psalm 123.

Not all ancient witnesses to the text contain "of David" in the superscription, and both language and theme suggest a postexilic date. This song may have been assigned to David because of supposed echoes of Psalms 18 and 69.

124:1–8. Very likely, a Levite speaks in verses 1–5, calling on Israel to acknowledge that the Lord alone has saved her from extinction. **If it had not been the LORD who was on** Israel's **side** (vv. 1–2), her proud enemies would have destroyed her. These enemies sought to swallow Israel (**swallowed**; v. 3), just as death itself is a swallower (see 49:14; 69:15; Isa. 25:8). In their **wrath** (v. 3), the hostile nations would have poured over Israel like a flood of **proud waters** (v. 5).

The worshipers answer with a response of praise for their deliverance, which is described with vivid imagery. Without the Lord's help, their enemies would have torn them with **their teeth** (v. 6) like wild beasts. Israel's release from Babylonian captivity was

like a bird's escape from the hunter's **snare** (v. 7). The Creator God has acted and delivered Israel.

Psalm 125. A proclamation of the security of those who trust in the Lord's protection and reward of the righteous.

The psalm is most likely postexilic and was probably spoken in the temple liturgy by a Levite.

125:1–2. The opening affirms the solid security of God's people. They are described as people of faith and integrity (see 34:8–14). The Lord surrounds His people as substantially and immovably as **the mountains … round about Jerusalem** (v. 2). Though Jerusalem is not surrounded by a ring of peaks, the city is located in what Old Testament writers called a mountainous region (see 2 Kings 6:17; Zech. 2:5).

125:3–5. Wicked rulers, whether by example or by oppression, tend to corrupt even the righteous, but the Lord will preserve His people from this corrosive threat also (vv. 3–5). **The rod of the wicked** (v. 3), probably referring to Persian rule, would not beat Israel into submitting to a wicked lifestyle. **The lot of the righteous** refers specifically to the Promised Land (see 78:55). The righteous are confident of their reward and the punishment of the wicked because God renders to each according to what he is and does. They assert that **peace shall be upon Israel** (v. 5), perhaps citing a concise form of the priestly benediction (see Num. 6:24–26).

Psalm 126. A song of joy, celebrating Israel's restoration to Zion.

If not composed for those who returned from Babylonian exile (see Ezra and Nehemiah)—the place of exile is not named—this psalm surely served to voice the joy of that restored community (see Psalms 42–43; 84; 137). The psalm has two stanzas of four (Hebrew) lines each, with their initial lines sharing the theme of the "turn[ing]" of Israel's "captivity" (vv. 1, 4). Thematic unity is further served by repetition (see vv. 2–3) and other key words ("the LORD," "singing," "bearing … bringing"). References to God's action (vv. 1, 3) frame the first stanza.

126:1–3. The opening verses describe Israel's joy over the nation's restoration. The wonder and joy of the restoration from **captivity** (v. 1) were so marvelous that the returnees hardly dared to believe it. It seemed more like a **dream**, with which they had so long been tantalized. The twofold effect of the restoration was joy for those who returned and honor for God among the nations (see discussion on 46:10).

126:4-6. The people pray for the restoration to be completed (vv. 4-6). **Turn again our captivity** (v. 4) is a request either to complete the repatriation of exiles or to fully restore the security and prosperity of former times. The people ask to be like **the streams in the south**, which are bone-dry in the summer until the winter rains renew their flow. The contrast between the difficulty in sowing and the joy of harvest is an apt metaphor for the reversal that the people have both experienced and anticipated. Even when sowing is accompanied by sorrow, harvest brings joy.

Psalm 127. A wisdom psalm expressing the need for reliance on God in the realm of home and family.

The wisdom focus of this pilgrimage song fits with its ascription to **Solomon** in the superscription. The theme of this psalm is timeless; it reminded the pilgrims on their way to Jerusalem that all of life's securities and blessings are gifts from God rather than their own achievements (see Deut. 28:1-14). Two balanced stanzas (vv. 1-2, 3-5) develop, respectively, two distinct but related themes.

127:1-2. The first stanza reminds us that it is the Lord who provides shelter, security, and food. All human effort—the building of a **house** (v. 1), the guarding of a **city**, the harvesting of a crop— is futile without the Lord's help. With His blessing, those that trust in the Lord enjoy **sleep** (v. 2) and are free of anxiety.

127:3-5. The second stanza teaches that **children** (v. 3) are a gift of God and a sign of His favor; they are not merely the product of virility and fertility. The depiction of children as a **heritage** emphasizes the idea of gift rather than possession. Perhaps more is implied. In the Old Testament economy, an Israelite's "heritage" (inheritance) from the Lord was first of all property in the Promised Land (see Num. 26:53; Josh. 11:23; Judg. 2:6). Without children, however, that inheritance would be lost (see Num. 27:8-11), so offspring were a heritage in a double

sense. Children provide security, like **arrows ... in the hand** (v. 4) of a warrior. Fathers with many sons have many defenders when falsely accused in court. **The gate** (v. 5) of the city was a judicial site for legal proceedings (see Deut. 17:5; Ruth 4:1; Amos 5:12). A father's many sons are considered a **reward** (v. 3) that testifies to God's favor toward him. In effect, they are God-provided character witnesses.

Psalm 128. A wisdom psalm describing the blessing of the home of a godly man (see also Psalm 127).

The concluding benediction of this psalm suggests that it originally served as a Levitical (or priestly) word of instruction to those who left their homes to assemble in Jerusalem for worship.

128:1-4. Structurally, the frame (**that feareth the LORD**; vv. 1, 4) distinguishes verses 1-4 as the main body of the psalm. These verses set forth the specific ways in which God blesses the man who fears Him. His labor is blessed so that he enjoys prosperity—**it shall be well with thee** (v. 2). He will also enjoy life with a faithful and fruitful **wife** (v. 3). The **vine** is a symbol of fruitfulness (see Gen. 49:22), and perhaps also of sexual charms (see Song 7:8-12) and festivity (see Judg. 9:13). His wife remains at home (**By the sides of thine house**), unlike the faithless wife, whose "feet abide not in her house" (Prov. 7:11). The godly man will raise children that enjoy both long life and productivity, like **olive plants**. The vine and the olive tree are frequently paired in the Old Testament (see, e.g., Exod. 23:11). Both were especially long-lived, and they produced the wine and the oil that played such a central role in the lives of the people.

128:5-6. The psalmist pronounces a benediction in the closing verses, completing the scope of true blessedness. The godly will enjoy unbroken prosperity, a secure relationship with God, and peaceful national existence.

Psalm 129. Israel's prayer for the continued withering of all her powerful enemies.

129:1-4. This psalm celebrates that the wicked oppressors of Israel **have not prevailed** (v. 2). From the time Israel was enslaved in Egypt, she has suffered much at the hands of hostile powers. The figure of these enemies plowing upon Israel's **back**

(v. 3) reflects the intensity of the oppression. Nevertheless, these enemies have not succeeded in their efforts to destroy Israel or to hold her permanently in bondage. The rescue celebrated here, in which God **cut asunder the cords of the wicked** (v. 4), is probably from Babylonian exile.

129:5-8. The psalmist prays that all who hate Zion will similarly become destitute and cursed (vv. 5-8). He asks that those who would "plow" the backs of Israel (see v. 3) would wither like the **grass** (v. 6) that sprouts on the flat, sunbaked **housetops**, where no plow can prepare a nurturing soil to sustain the young shoots. Whoever passes by the harvesters in the fields of the enemy will not exchange joyful greetings because the hands of the harvesters will be empty (see Ruth 2:4). This prayer for the cursing of the wicked contrasts to the promises of blessing for the righteous in the immediate context of Psalms 124-128.

Psalm 130. A testimony of trust in the Lord, offered by one who knows that even though he is a sinner, the Lord hears his cry out of the depths.

130:1-4. The psalmist prays that the Lord would have mercy on him in spite of his many sins—either a reference to personal sin or the national sins of Israel that have resulted in exile or some other form of judgment (see v. 8). Chastisement for this sin causes the psalmist to cry out for rescue from the depths (see 30:1; 32:6; 69:2). No one could **stand** (v. 3) if the Lord kept a record of sins, but the Lord is a God of **forgiveness** (v. 4).

130:5-8. With this assurance, the psalmist exhorts the people of Israel to trust in the Lord and to confidently wait for His deliverance. The psalmist's personal testimony expands into a reassuring invitation for the entire nation. He anticipates the Lord's rescue like the watchman looking for the first rays of the **morning** (v. 6) sun. **Israel** (v. 7) can trust in the Lord because of His **mercy**, knowing that He will redeem His people from all their **iniquities** (v. 8). This greatest of all hopes has been fulfilled in Christ.

Psalm 131. A confession of humble trust in the Lord—appropriately placed next to Psalm 130.

131:1-3. The psalmist reminds the Lord that he has renounced the ways of the proud and the arrogant (v. 1). More than anything else, it is human pride that pits man against God. He has not devoted himself to heroic exploits or achievements (**great matters ... too high for me**; v. 1) for the purpose of self-promotion, which diminishes the glory of God. He has refused to claim godlike powers or to view himself as self-sufficient. Instead, he has trusted in the Lord like **a child that is weaned** (v. 2), a child of four or five who walks trustingly beside his mother. In the same manner, **Israel** (v. 3) is to put her **hope in the LORD** for all time.

Psalm 132. A prayer for God's favor on the son of David who reigns on David's throne.

The language of this psalm suggests a date early in the monarchy. The venerable belief that it was composed for the dedication of the temple may be correct (compare vv. 8-10 with 2 Chron. 6:41-42), but the possibility cannot be ruled out that it was used in the coronation ritual (see Psalms 2; 72; 110). The author of Chronicles places the prayer, or a portion of it, on the lips of the king himself. As part of the postexilic liturgy, it testifies to the stubborn persistence of the messianic hope when there is no current Davidic ruler on the throne.

Two verses of petition (vv. 1, 10) are each followed (in Hebrew) by two four-line stanzas, all having an identical form: an introductory line followed by a three-line quotation. A final couplet brings the prayer to its climactic conclusion.

132:1-9. The people first of all pray that the LORD (v. 1) would **remember** David's past devotion to Him and reward the king accordingly. They appeal to David's oath to the Lord that he would not rest (**I will not give sleep to mine eyes**; v. 4) until he had found **a place for the LORD** (v. 5) by bringing the ark to its place of rest. David had brought the ark of the covenant to Jerusalem (see 2 Samuel 6) and had desired to build the temple as a permanent dwelling place for the ark (see 2 Samuel 7). The special relationship between David and the Lord is epitomized in this psalm by their mutual oaths to each other (see vv. 11-12). In the narratives of 2 Samuel 6-7, David's oath is not specifically mentioned.

Recalling the events when David brought the ark to Jerusalem, the congregation remembers hearing the news of the ark being in **Ephratah** (v. 6), the region around Bethlehem, at Kiriath-jearim (which means **the fields of the wood**; see 1 Sam. 7:1; 2 Sam. 6:2). When the ark returned to Jerusalem, the people determined to worship the Lord at **his tabernacles** (v. 7), where He had chosen to dwell among His people. They called for the Lord to **Arise** (v. 8) and to take up His **rest** at the sanctuary David had provided. As the Promised Land was Israel's place of rest at the end of her wanderings (see Num. 10:33; Josh. 1:13), so the temple was the Lord's resting place after He had been moving about in a tent (see 2 Sam. 7:6; 1 Chron. 28:2). This expression and the reference to the Lord's **footstool** (v. 7) suggest that the Jerusalem sanctuary was the place of God's throne. The congregation prayed for the Lord's blessing on the **priests** (v. 9) who would lead worship at the sanctuary, asking that their ministry would truly bear the character of **righteousness** as an inner quality, not merely as something associated with their priestly garb. They asked for themselves that they would be filled with joy as God's devoted and faithful people (**saints**; see 4:2). They prayed that God would always show His favor to the Davidic ruler by answering his prayers. The events surrounding the establishment of the sanctuary at Jerusalem are presented as grounds for the Lord to continue showing His favor to the house of David. In the postexilic context of the Psalms of Ascent (Psalms 120–134), this prayer becomes a petition for God to restore the Davidic throne by sending the promised Messiah.

132:11–18. In the second half of the psalm, the psalmist appeals to the Lord's oath to David and His election of Zion as His dwelling place as the grounds for the people's prayer for the Lord's blessing on the descendants of David. The Lord made a covenant promise that David's descendants would rule over Israel (see 89:28–34; 2 Sam. 7:8–16; 2 Sam. 23:5). The Lord had also stipulated that the Davidic kings were obligated to keep the statutes of the Sinai **covenant** (v. 12), which all Israelites were to keep.

The Lord had also **chosen Zion** (v. 13) as His dwelling place (vv. 13–18). God had determined to dwell there, enthroned at His resting place. The Lord's presence brings assurance that He will **bless** (v. 15) the land, providing food for His people. The assurance of the threefold blessing on the priests, the saints, and David corresponds to the petition in verses 9–10. The image of the animal **horn** (v. 17) refers to the strength of the Davidic ruler. He will **bud** like a plant or branch (see Isa. 11:1; Jer. 23:5–6; Zech. 3:8; 6:12). The promise of **a lamp** for David guarantees the continuity of the dynasty (see 1 Kings 11:36), which will endure forever under the reign of Messiah. The Lord will cause all of the enemies of the king to be put to **shame** (v. 18). The exile and the removal of the Davidic ruler from the throne only intensified the messianic hopes associated with the house of David.

Psalm 133. A song in praise of brotherly unity among the people of God.

If David authored this psalm, his motivation to write it may have been an occasion such as when, after many years of conflict, all Israel came to Hebron to make him king (2 Sam. 5:1–3). This idea of unity was also especially appropriate for the pilgrims who journeyed together to Jerusalem and then assembled with the entire nation as one people in worshiping the Lord.

133:1–3. The opening affirms the goodness of God's people living together in **unity** (v. 1). Two striking similes help to illustrate this basic principle. The oil of anointing (Exod. 29:7; Lev. 21:10) saturated **Aaron's beard** (v. 2; see Exod. 29:7; Lev. 21:10) and ran down on his priestly robes, signifying his total consecration to holy service. Similarly, brotherly harmony sanctifies God's people. **Dew** (v. 3) as profuse as that of Mount **Hermon** would make **the mountains of Zion** (or Mount Zion) richly fruitful (see Gen. 27:28; Hag. 1:10; Zech. 8:12). So would brotherly unity make Israel richly fruitful. The two similes (vv. 2–3) are well chosen: God's blessings flowed to Israel through the priestly ministrations at the sanctuary (see Exod. 29:44–46; Num. 6:24–26) and through heaven's dew, which sustained life in the fields.

Psalm 134. A liturgy of praise, calling for the Levites to bless the Lord and for the Lord to bless His people.

This psalm concludes the Songs of Degrees. This song most likely represents a brief exchange between the worshipers, as they are about to leave the temple after the evening service, and the Levites, who kept the temple watch through the night.

134:1–3. The departing worshipers call on the Levites to continue the praise of the Lord through the **night** (v. 1; see 1 Chron. 9:33). One of the Levites responds with a benediction on the worshipers (see 121:2; 124:8; 128:5). The psalm demonstrates the connection between Israel's faithfulness in **bless[ing] the LORD** (v. 2) through worship and their reception of blessing from the Lord.

Psalm 135. A call to praise the Lord, the one true God: Lord of all creation, Lord over all the nations, Israel's Redeemer.

This psalm echoes many lines found elsewhere in the Old Testament. No doubt postexilic, clearly it was composed for the temple liturgy.

135:1–7. The psalm is framed by calls to praise (**Praise ye the LORD,** vv. 1, 21). The Lord's goodness in choosing Israel to be His personal and prized **treasure** (v. 4; see Exod. 19:5) is the central reason for giving praise (vv. 3–4). The Lord is **great** (v. 5) in power as well as good (vv. 5–7). He is the absolute Lord in all creation. The **heaven ... earth ... seas** (v. 6) are the three great domains of the visible creation, as the ancients viewed it (see Gen. 1:8–10). The assertion that **He causeth the vapours to ascend** (v. 7) is a reminder that the Lord, not Baal or any other god, causes clouds to bring the life-giving rains.

135:8–13. The Lord's goodness to Israel and His greatness in power are recalled through a recital of God's saving acts for Israel in Egypt and Canaan (vv. 8–12). The Lord struck down **the firstborn of Egypt** (v. 8) as the culmination of the plagues (see Exodus 7–14), defeated the **mighty kings** (v. 10) that opposed Israel as they prepared to enter the Promised Land (see Num. 21:21–35), and gave the Promised Land to Israel as their **heritage** ("inheritance"; v. 12) in the conquest (see Joshua 1–10).

The Lord's reputation (**name;** v. 13) and fame (**memorial**) are perpetuated by the praise of His people. Israel celebrates that **the LORD will judge his**

people (v. 14); that is, He will uphold Israel's cause and her claim that the Lord is the only true God. **Will repent himself** means that the Lord "will show compassion" to Israel as He defends her.

135:15–21. In contrast, the false gods and those who trust in them are powerless. Unlike the Lord, who does whatever He pleases (v. 5), these gods are unable to **speak** (v. 16), **see,** or **hear** (v. 17). The Lord sends **the wind** (*ruach*) **out of his treasuries** (v. 7), but the idols do not even have **breath** (*ruach*) **in their mouths** (v. 17). With this reminder of the goodness of God and the impotence of idols, the psalmist concludes with a call to praise the Lord addressed to all who are assembled at the temple (vv. 19–21).

Psalm 136. A liturgy of praise to the Lord as Creator and as Israel's Redeemer.

The theme of this psalm and many of its verses parallel much of Psalm 135.

136:1–26. Most likely, a Levitical song leader led the recital, while the Levitical choir or the worshipers responded with the refrain, **For his mercy endureth forever** (vv. 1–26; see 106:1; 107:1; 118:1–4). Following the initial call to praise (vv. 1–3), the recital includes six verses to God's creation acts (vv. 4–9), six to His deliverance of Israel out of Egypt (vv. 10–15), one to the wilderness journey (v. 16), and six to the conquest (vv. 17–22). The four concluding verses return to the same basic themes in reverse order: God's action in history on behalf of His people (vv. 23–24), God's action in the creation order (v. 25), and a closing call to praise (v. 26).

Psalm 137. A plaintive song of the exile of one who has recently returned from Babylon but in whose soul lingers the bitter memory of the foreign land and the cruel events that led to that enforced stay.

137:1–6. The psalmist begins his song by reflecting on the sorrow and torment of the years in exile in Babylon (vv. 1–3). While in Babylon, the exiles had mourned over their forced separation from **Zion.** They refused to play their **harps** (v. 2) because the callous Babylonians demanded exotic entertainment with the joyful **songs of Zion** (v. 3). Expressing an oath of total commitment to **Jerusalem** (v. 5), the psalmist prayed that he would never play the harp again or sing another syllable if untrue to his beloved city (vv. 4–6).

137:7–9. The psalmist prays for God to execute vengeance (**Remember**; v. 7) on Edom and Babylon in retribution for the destruction of Jerusalem (vv. 7–9). The Edomites had rejoiced in the destruction of Jerusalem and may have even contributed troops to the Babylonian forces attacking Jerusalem. The Old Testament gives witness to the agelong animosity that existed between Israel and Edom, the descendants of Esau, and the prophets announce God's judgment against this people (see Isa. 63:1–4; Jer. 49:7–22; Ezekiel 35; Obadiah). The psalmist curses **Babylon** (v. 8) with the harshest possible language possible, pronouncing a blessing on the enemy soldiers who commit atrocities against the children of Babylon (v. 9). War was as cruel then as now; women and children were not spared (see 2 Kings 8:12; Amos 1:13; Nah. 3:10). The harsh language against Babylon is justified in part because the attack on God's people and His holy city was an attack against God Himself (see Psalm 5). The psalmist may have known the Lord's announced judgments against Babylon (see Isa. 13; 21:1–10; 47; Jeremiah 50–51; Hab. 2:4–20; for the final announcement of the destruction of the "Babylon" that persists in its warfare against the City of God, and the joy with which that announcement is greeted, see Rev. 18:1–19:4).

Psalm 138. A royal song of praise for God's saving help against threatening foes.

This psalm begins a collection of eight Davidic Psalms (Psalms 138–145)—six prayers framed by two psalms of praise.

138:1–8. David expresses praise for God's faithful love, shown in His answer to prayers for help (v. 1–3). Without reserve, he gives praise to the Lord **Before the gods** (v. 1), either pagan kings or the gods they claimed to represent (see 82:1). God's display of love and faithfulness in His answers to prayer has made His **name** (v. 2) and promises more precious than anything that even a king may possess. The center of this psalm are a wish and hope that **All the kings of the earth** (v. 4) may come to join him in his **praise** of the Lord's words and ways (vv. 4–5). God's

words and His ways are in harmony, and together they display His great glory.

David gives further testimony to God's condescending and faithful love (vv. 6–8). The Lord shows favor to **the lowly** (v. 6) that recognize their need for Him, but He rejects **the proud**. He recognizes them from **afar off** for what they are and does not allow them into His presence. Based on his confidence that the Lord will **perfect** ("accomplish"; v. 8) what he has asked, David concludes with a prayer for God to not abandon him in the midst of his difficulty. Though the Lord has promised to protect him, the psalmist still recognizes his responsibility to pray in faith for the fulfillment of that promise.

Psalm 139. A prayer for God to examine the heart of the psalmist to see its true devotion.

Like Job, the author firmly claims his loyalty to the Lord. Nowhere outside Job does one find such profound awareness of how awesome it is to ask God to examine not only one's life but also his soul— God, who knows every thought, word, and deed, from whom there is no hiding, who has been privy even to one's formation in the dark concealment of the womb. References to God's searching and knowing begin and end the prayer.

139:1–6. David opens by expressing his wonder that God knows him perfectly, far beyond his own understanding of himself (vv. 1–6). The Lord knows his every action (v. 2a), his thoughts before they are fully crystallized (v. 2b), his every undertaking (v. 3), and his words before they are uttered (v. 4). The Lord keeps him under constant scrutiny and has **laid** His **hand upon** (v. 5) him so that he does not escape. The Lord's knowledge of the psalmist **is too wonderful** (v. 6), or beyond human capacity, to fully grasp. The Hebrew term for "wonderful" regularly applies to God's wondrous acts (see 77:11, 14; Exod. 15:11).

139:7–12. The psalmist acknowledges that there is no hiding from the Lord, expressing not an abstract doctrine of divine omnipresence but an awed confession that God cannot be escaped (vv. 7, 12). The vertical extremes of **heaven** (v. 8) and **hell** (Hebrew, *sheol;* "the grave") and the horizontal extremes of east (**wings of the morning**; v. 9) and west (**the**

sea) denote the totality of spatial reality, demonstrating that God is present in all of creation. Just as the whole creation offers no hiding place, neither does even the **darkness** (vv. 11–12). While God's omnipresence brings comfort to the believer, the dominant idea here is a reverential sense of accountability to God. Since God is everywhere, the psalmist is responsible to God for how he lives every moment of his life.

139:13–18. God exercised His sovereign control over the psalmist before he was even born. As his Creator, the Lord has intimate knowledge of every aspect of David's person. The Lord had formed his **reins** (lit., "kidneys; v. 13), which in Hebrew idiom refers to the innermost center of emotions and moral certainty. Though it is not visible to the physical eye, the Lord sees and knows David's **substance** (lit., "bones"; v. 15), referring to the substantial part of his physical being.

Poetic imagery stresses God's sovereign activity in human conception (**I was made in secret … in the lowest parts of the earth**; v. 15). The womb is a "secret" place because it normally conceals (see 2 Sam. 12:12), and it shares with the "lowest parts of the earth" associations with darkness, dampness, and separation from the visible realm of life. Moreover, both phrases refer to the place of the dead (63:9; Job 14:13), with which, on one level, the womb appears to have been associated: Man comes from the dust and returns to the dust (90:3; Gen. 3:19; Eccl. 12:7). The word for **substance** (Hebrew, *golem*; v. 16) is not the same term translated "substance" in verse 15 and refers to something that is "wrapped together" in an unformed mass. The context indicates that the embryonic mass is fashioned daily in fetal form as God's blueprint for life is clearly charted from the moment of conception. This blueprint includes even the span of the psalmist's life, which was written in God's **book**, the heavenly register of God's royal decisions (see 56:8). The phrase **my members were written … were fashioned** literally reads, "all were written down, the days that were planned." These verses clearly teach that human life begins at conception and is sacred to God.

139:19–24. Because of God's intimate knowledge of him and concern for him, David has a zeal for God that sets him against all of God's enemies (vv. 19–22). **Surely thou wilt slay the wicked** (v. 19) expresses David's desire for God to judge the wicked, a jealous impatience with His patience toward them, whose end will come. The psalmist leaves this judgment to God. For the Christian, Jesus has elevated the law of love so that believers are to pray for their enemies (see Matt. 5:44), with a recognition that God is "not willing that any should perish" (2 Peter 3:9). At the same time, Christians will rejoice in the fairness and justice of God's judgment when it falls on the wicked (see 2 Thess. 1:7–10).

David issues a declaration of loyalty to the Lord that echoes the pledge ancient Near Eastern kings required of their vassals (vv. 21–22). The psalmist has a righteous hatred for those that **hate** (v. 21) the Lord. To stress the sincerity of his pledge, David invites God to examine his **heart** (v. 23) to see the integrity of his devotion. At the same time, he recognizes his own tendency to sin and prays that God will keep him true to **the way everlasting** (v. 24).

Psalm 140. A prayer for deliverance from the plots and slander of unscrupulous enemies.

140:1–13. In his opening cry, David prays for deliverance from his **violent** (v. 1) enemies, who attack him like venomous serpents with their poisoned speech (vv. 1–3). In his lament, the psalmist further compares his adversaries to proud and wicked hunters who have set **a snare** (v. 5) and **a net** to bring him down (vv. 4–5). In his desperate situation, he asks God not to allow the wicked to attain their evil desires against him (vv. 6–8). If they are successful, they will only become more proud and arrogant. Turning to the language of imprecation, David asks that the harm his enemies plot against him recoil upon their heads (vv. 9–11; see Psalm 5). He prays that God will bring down **burning coals** (v. 10) on them and cast them into a fiery pit. The combination of **fire** and **deep pits** suggests the idea that the fire of God's judgment reaches even into the realm of the dead (see Job 31:12 and discussion on Ps. 30:1). He is praying for their physical death so that they will **rise not up again** (see 36:12; Isa. 26:14). David is confident in God's just judgment and is certain that the Lord will intervene on his behalf as one of **the afflicted** (v. 12) and **the righteous** (v. 13).

Psalm 141. A prayer for deliverance from the wicked and their evil ways.

141:1–7. The psalmist makes an initial appeal for God to hear him, comparing his prayer to the **incense** (v. 2) and **evening sacrifice** that were presented to God daily at the Jerusalem temple (vv. 1–2). So that he can continue to present his requests to God as a righteous man, David also pleads that God will keep him from speaking, desiring, or doing evil (vv. 3–4). He asks that God will keep his **heart** (v. 4) from yielding to the example and urgings of the wicked and from acquiring an appetite for the luxuriant **dainties** that the wicked acquire from their unjust gains. The psalmist views even the disciplining blows and rebukes of **the righteous** (v. 5) as **a kindness** (Hebrew, *hesed*; "faithful love") and anointing **oil** that will help keep him on the right path. David's commitment to righteousness leads him to pray for the destruction of the wicked. He prays for calamities to befall the ungodly (v. 5c) and anticipates corrupt judges being thrown down upon **stony places** (v. 6). The bones of the wicked will be **scattered at the grave's mouth** (v. 7) because the Lord will put them to death.

141:8–10. The psalmist prays that the Lord will protect him from the enemies who seek his harm. He asks that he not be left alone and that God keep him from **the snare** (v. 9) and **grins** (or "traps") that the wicked have laid for him. His final request is that the wicked will **fall** (v. 10) by their own designs.

Psalm 142. A plaintive prayer for deliverance from powerful enemies, offered when the psalmist is powerless, alone, and without refuge.

The superscription reflects the tradition that David offered this prayer while hiding **in the cave** from Saul (see 1 Sam. 24:1–3 and introduction to Psalm 57).

142:1–7. David recounts presenting his appeal to the Lord (vv. 1–2) and describes the desperate circumstances that caused him to seek the Lord's help

(vv. 3–4). The Lord was the only one David could turn to for help. His spirit was overwhelmed as evil men plotted against him, and there was no one at his right hand to be a helper or defender. In the midst of this difficulty, the Lord knew David and took notice of his situation. With the Lord as his sole source of help, the psalmist prayed for rescue (vv. 5–7). The Lord was his **refuge** (v. 5) who provided protection. The Lord was also his **portion**, all that he had and needed in life (see 73:26). He prayed that God would rescue him from his **persecutors** (v. 6) and the **prison** (v. 7) of affliction so that he could give **praise** to the Lord. When celebrating the Lord's saving help, the man who had been all alone in his time of difficulty would be securely surrounded by **the righteous**. The conclusion to this psalm expresses expectant confidence.

Psalm 143. A prayer for deliverance from enemies and for divine leading.

Appeal to God's "righteousness" (vv. 1, 11) and David's self-identification as "thy servant" (vv. 2, 12) enclose this prayer for divine help.

143:1–6. In the first half of this psalm, David makes his appeal and describes his situation. As he begins his prayer, he pleads on the basis of God's **faithfulness** (v. 1) and **righteousness** that God not sit in **judgment** (v. 2) over His servant but that He focus His judicial attention on the enemy's harsh and unwarranted attacks. The psalmist knows his failings, but his cause is just when compared to his evil enemies, who cause him great distress. David **dwell[s] in darkness** (v. 3), as one cut off from the enjoyments of life, and his **spirit** (v. 4) is **overwhelmed**. Despite his anguish, remembrance of God's past acts of deliverance encourages him in his appeal. The act of stretching out his **hands** (v. 6) and the imagery of his **soul** thirsting for God demonstrates the intensity of David's cry for the Lord's help.

143:7–12. In the second half of the psalm, David presents his prayer to the Lord. His **spirit** (v. 7) is failing and he pleads that God not withhold the blessing of His presence, lest he die. This deliverance will bring a new demonstration of God's loyal love and will turn the darkness of his present situation into **the morning** (v. 8) of salvation. Deliverance from the enemy is not enough; the psalmist also prays that the Lord would help him **to know the way** in which he should live and instruct him in how to do His **will** (v. 10). Through the Lord's direction, David will be allowed to live in the **land of uprightness**. The concluding summary of the prayer returns to the themes of God's righteousness (v. 11) and David's relationship to the Lord as His servant (v. 12). It is just and right for the Lord to deliver David and destroy his enemies because of his devotion to the Lord.

Psalm 144. A royal prayer for victory over treacherous enemies.

144:1–4. David's opening praise in verses 1–2 functions both as an initial appeal for God to answer his prayer and as a confession of confidence that his prayer will be heard. The psalmist acknowledges that God is his source of strength on the battlefield and uses a series of epithets to describe all that God means to him. The reference to God as **My goodness** (v. 2) indicates that the Lord is the source of benevolent acts of love on David's behalf. David acknowledges his own insignificance, which drives him to rely on God's help (vv. 3–4). **Man is like to vanity** (v. 4) compares humans to a breath or vapor that is here and gone (see Job 7:7; James 4:14).

144:5–10. Having demonstrated his trust in and reliance on the Lord, the psalmist prays for God to **come down** (v. 5) to deliver him from his enemies (vv. 5–8). He uses the language of theophany to describe the Lord's intervention as Divine Warrior; smoking **mountains** (v. 5) and flashing **lightning** (v. 6) announce the presence of the Lord (see Exod. 19:16–18). David's enemies are powerful, so deliverance from them is like being rescued from death out of the strong **waters** (v. 7). These enemies are identified as **strange children**, or foreigners from the bordering kingdoms. David battled against these neighboring states in establishing his kingdom (see 2 Sam. 8). The psalmist vows to praise the Lord after receiving the answer to his prayer, by singing **a new song** (v. 9) celebrating the Lord's deliverance (vv. 9–10; see 33:3).

144:11–15. Verse 11 repeats the prayer of verses 7–8, apparently to serve as a transition to what follows. If God will deliver David, his kingdom will prosper and be secure (vv. 12–15). This prosperity is described in highly figurative language. The **sons** (v. 12) of Israel will be like fertile **plants,** and their **daughters** like the ornately decorated pillars (**corner stones**) of the temple. Their "barns" (**garners**; v. 13) will be full of their harvested crops, and their animals will reproduce and multiply greatly. There will be **no breaking in** (v. 14) of enemy armies and no **going out** into captivity. Israel will be truly blessed (**Happy;** v. 15) because the Lord is their God.

Psalm 145. A hymn to the Lord, the Great King, for His mighty acts and benevolent virtues, which are the glory of His kingly rule.

Psalms 145–150 comprise a final doxology for the entire Psalter. The word "praise" appears forty-six times in these six psalms, and these psalms are likely postexilic. This psalm fully exploits the traditional language of praise and, as an alphabetic acrostic, reflects the care of studied composition. Between the two-line introduction (vv. 1–2) and the one-line conclusion (v. 21), four poetic paragraphs develop as many themes, each introduced with a thematic line (see vv. 3, 8, 13b, 17).

145:1–7. The psalmist initially expresses his commitment to **praise** (v. 2) the Lord (vv. 1–2), and references to the Lord's **name** (v. 1–2; v. 21) frame this psalm. The psalmist praises God's mighty acts in creation, providence, and redemption, which display His **greatness** (v. 3) and His **goodness** (v. 7). These references to two of God's attributes enclose this section.

145:8–21. The next section elaborates further on God's benevolent virtues, which move all creatures to celebrate the glory of His kingdom (vv. 8–13a). The Lord's perfection is reflected in the fact that His **compassion** (v. 8) and **tender mercies** (v. 9) work in complete harmony with His **power** (v. 11) and **mighty acts** (v. 12). The saints rejoice that they are able to live under the rule of His **everlasting kingdom** (v. 13). Verses 14–16 praise God's faithfulness: He provides for the needs **of every living thing** (v. 16). Verses 17–20 praise His righteousness, which is reflected in how He responds to the cries of those who **call upon him in truth** (v. 18), whose lives are characterized by godly integrity. The conclusion states that **the praise of the LORD** (v. 21) must continue, and every creature must take it up, **for ever and ever**.

Psalm 146. An exhortation to praise and trust in the Lord, Zion's King.

This psalm continues the theme of praise introduced in the previous psalm; this and the remaining four psalms, as part of the closing doxology for the book, are all framed with hallelujahs, which may have been added by the final editors (see Psalms 105–106; 111–117).

146:1–10. The psalmist delivers an opening call for praise (**Praise ye the LORD**—Hebrew *halleluyah*; v. 1) and makes a vow to praise the Lord—as long as life continues (vv. 1–2). He then calls the people to put their trust in the Lord (vv. 3–4). The call to trust in the Lord is heightened by the contrast between God and mortal man, whose spirit departs from him (**breath goeth forth**; v. 4) at death. While those who trust in man will be disappointed, those who trust in the covenant God of Jacob are truly blessed (vv. 5–9). He is the Creator God and Lord over all. He is the Faithful One who defends the defenseless and provides for the needy. He is the Righteous One who shows favor to **the righteous** (v. 8) but checks **the wicked** (v. 9) in their pursuits. In response to the words of the psalmist, the citizens of **Zion** (v. 10), God's royal city, offer exultant testimony concerning the Lord's eternal kingship.

Psalm 147. Praise of God, the Creator, for His special mercies to Israel; possibly composed for the Levitical choirs on the joyous occasion of the dedication of the rebuilt walls of Jerusalem (see Neh. 12:27–43).

The Septuagint (the Greek translation of the Old Testament) divides this work into two separate psalms (vv. 1–11, 12–20), but it is actually a three-part song (vv. 1–6, 7–11, 12–20), bound together by the frame (vv. 2–3, 19–20), in which the Lord's unique favors to Israel are celebrated.

147:1–6. The psalmist bases his opening call to praise (*halleluyah*, see Psalm 146) on how the Lord has blessed His people in bringing about the postexilic restoration of Jerusalem and Israel (vv. 1–3). He

has provided healing for **the broken in heart** (v. 3), such as the exiles (see Psalms 126; 137) and for those who struggled in the face of great opposition to rebuild Jerusalem's walls (Neh. 2:17–20; 4:1–23). He whose **power** (v. 5) and **understanding** are such that **He telleth the number of the stars** (He counts them; v. 4) and **names** them is able to sustain His humble ones and bring **the wicked down** (v. 6; see also Isa. 40:26–29).

147:7–11. The God who governs the **rain** (v. 8) and thus provides food for **beast** (v. 9) and bird is not pleased by man's reliance on his own capabilities or those of the animals he has domesticated. He is pleased when people serve Him and trust His loving care.

147:12–20. The Lord of all creation is also Zion's God, and He secures the defenses of the city, bringing **peace** (v. 14) and prosperity to His people (vv. 12–18). This psalm mentions **clouds** and **rain** (v. 8); **snow**, frost, and hail (vv. 16–17); icy winds and warm breezes (vv. 17–18)—the whole range of weather that God governs and controls. God's **commandment** (v. 15) and **word** are personified as messengers commissioned to carry out the divine decrees concerning the elements. A God who possesses this kind of power is a God who can be trusted. God's most unique gift to Israel is His other **word** (v. 19), His redemptive word, by which He makes known His program of salvation and His holy will (vv. 19–20; see Deut. 4:8).

Psalm 148. A call for all creation to praise the Lord.

Whatever its original liturgical purpose, this psalm's placement serves to complete the scope of the calls to praise with which the Psalter concludes. Two balanced (Hebrew) stanzas of six verses each are followed by a two-verse conclusion.

148:1–6. In the first stanza, all creatures in the heavens are called to praise the Lord. Joining with the **angels** (v. 2), the heavenly bodies (**sun and moon ... stars of light**; v. 3) and the **waters** (v. 4) of the firmament **above the heavens** (see Gen. 1:7) are personified so that they might worship the Lord. They are to praise the Lord because He has **created** (v. 5) them and made their existence secure (**stablished them for ever and ever**; v. 6).

147:7-12. In the second stanza, all creatures beneath the heavens are called to join in the praise and worship of the Lord. Likely with Genesis 1 in mind (see Gen. 1:7, 10, 21), the call begins with the sea creatures (**dragons, and all deeps**; v. 7) and moves toward the human components (**Kings ... children**; vv. 11-12). The pairs appearing in these poetic lines employ a figure of speech known as *merism*, which refers to all reality pertaining to the sphere to which they belong. All creatures, great and small, are to join in giving praise to the Lord.

148:13-14. The conclusion focuses on the motivation for the praise. The excellence of the Lord's power and **glory** make Him deserving of all praise. The glory of the Creator is greater than the glory of the creation. The Lord has also exalted **the horn of his people** (v. 14). "Horn" here symbolizes a person of strength, that is, the king of Israel (see 89:17). The king is God's instrument for saving Israel from her enemies. Thus, the Lord is to be praised for both His works in creation and redemption.

Psalm 149. Praise of God for the high honor bestowed on His people.

This postexilic psalm focuses on two aspects of Israel's unique honor: she has been granted salvation (in fact and in promise), and she has been armed to execute God's sentence of judgment on the world powers that have launched their attacks against the kingdom of God—she is the earthly contingent of the armies of the King of heaven (see 68:17; Josh. 5:14; 2 Sam. 5:23-24; 2 Chron. 20:15-17, 22; Hab. 3:3-15). This next-to-last psalm should be read in light of the promise in Psalm 2 of Israel's ultimate dominion over the nations through the rule of Messiah.

Following an introductory verse, the two main themes are developed in two balanced (Hebrew) stanzas of four verses each. References to God's "saints" enclose the song (vv. 1, 5, 9). A common pair of synonyms, "glory" (v. 5) and "honour" (v. 9), effectively link the two stanzas.

149:1-5. In the first stanza, the psalmist calls for Israel to **Sing ... a new song** (v. 1; see 33:3), rejoicing

in their King, who has crowned them with the honor of **salvation** (v. 4). This salvation is for the **meek**, who acknowledge that they are without resources apart from the Lord.

149:6-9. In the second stanza, Israel is called to praise their God because He has given them the glory of bearing the sword as His army in service. They **execute vengeance** (v. 7) and carry out His firmly determined **judgment** (v. 9) on the nations that have attacked His kingdom. The Old Testament speaks often of this divine retribution (see 58:10; 79:10; 94:1; Num. 31:2; Deut. 32:35; Isa. 63:4; Jer. 46:10; 51:6; Nah. 1:2). In the New Testament age, however, God's people are armed with the "sword of the Spirit" for spiritual warfare against the powers arrayed against God's kingdom (see 2 Cor. 6:7; 10:4; Eph. 6:12, 17; Heb. 4:12). Rather than defeating the nations, they go into all the world to "teach the nations" (Matt. 28:19) and proclaim the gospel of peace. Their participation in God's retribution on the world awaits the final judgment (see 1 Cor. 6:2-3).

Psalm 150. The final great Hallelujah calls for "every thing that hath breath" (v. 6) to praise to the Lord.

This psalm was likely composed specifically to close the Psalter (see the conclusions to the first four books of the Psalms: 41:13; 72:18-19; 89:52; 106:48).

150:1-6. This final call to praise moves powerfully by stages from place to themes to orchestra to choir, framed by **Praise ye the Lord** (*halleluyah*; v. 1, 6). The people's praise goes up to God **in his sanctuary** (v. 1) in heaven. **The firmament** (see 19:1; Gen. 1:6) is the expanse of the sky that displays or symbolizes His power or in which His power resides. God is to be praised specifically for **his mighty acts** (v. 2) in creation and redemption. God should be praised with music and dancing (vv. 3-5). The whole orchestra (eight instruments: wind, string, percussion) is mentioned, with dancing aptly placed at the middle of this concert. The closing verse (v. 6) calls for all living things to join in the celebration of God's mighty acts and surpassing greatness.

THE PROVERBS

INTRODUCTION

Authors

This great collection of proverbs begins with a title that ascribes the major responsibility for the creation of the book to Solomon. Most of the book is closely linked with Solomon. The headings in 10:1 and 25:1 assign authorship to him, though 25:1 states that these proverbs were transcribed by "the men of Hezekiah," indicating that a group of wise men or scribes compiled these proverbs as editors and added chapters 25–29 to the earlier collections. Solomon's ability to produce proverbs is specified in 1 Kings 4:32, where three thousand proverbs are attributed to him. Coupled with the statements about his unparalleled wisdom (1 Kings 4:29–31), it is reasonable to assign authorship of most of the proverbs to Solomon. It is clear from later chapters that he was not the only author who contributed to the production of the book. The presence of an introduction in 22:17–21 indicates that these sections stem from a wider circle of wise men, not from Solomon himself. In 24:23, we are introduced to additional sayings that are attributed simply "to the wise." Chapter 30 is attributed to Agur son of Jakeh, and 31:1–9 is attributed to King Lemuel.

The book contains a short prologue (1:1–7) and a longer epilogue (31:10–31), which may have been added to the other materials. It is possible that the discourses in the large opening section (1:8–9:18) were the work of a compiler or editor, but the similarities of this section with other chapters (compare 6:1 with 11:15; 17:18; 20:16; 27:13; compare 6:19 with 14:5, 25; 19:5) fit a Solomonic origin equally well. The emphasis on the "fear of the LORD" (1:7) throughout the book ties the various segments together.

Date

Since Solomon is credited with authorship of most of the book of Proverbs, most of Proverbs likely stems from the tenth century BC during the time of Israel's united kingdom. The peace and prosperity that characterized that era accord well with the development of reflective wisdom and the production of literary works. Moreover, several scholars have noted that the thirty sayings of "the wise" in 22:17–24:22 contain similarities to the thirty sections of the Egyptian *Amenemope's Wisdom*, an instructional piece that is roughly contemporary with the time of Solomon (see chart, *Zondervan KJV Study Bible*, p. xix).

Likewise, the personification of wisdom, so prominent in chapters 1–9 (see 1:20 and discussion; 3:15–18; 8:1–36), can be compared with the personification of abstract ideas in both Mesopotamian and Egyptian writings of the second millennium BC.

The role of Hezekiah's men (see 25:1) indicates that important sections of Proverbs were compiled and edited from 715 to 686 BC. This was a time of spiritual renewal led by the king, who also showed great interest in the writings of David and Asaph (see 2 Chron. 29:30). Perhaps this was also when the sayings of Agur (chap. 30) and Lemuel (31:1–9) and the other "words of the wise" (22:17–24:22; 24:23–34) were added to the Solomonic collections, though it is possible that the task of compilation was not completed until after the reign of Hezekiah.

The Nature of a Proverb

The Hebrew word translated "proverb" is also translated "parable" (Num. 23:7, 18; Ezek. 17:2) and "byword" (Ps. 44:14); so its meaning is considerably broader than the English term. This may help explain the presence of the longer discourse sections in chapters 1–9. Most proverbs are short, compact statements that express truths about human behavior. Often a word or sound is repeated to aid memorization. In 30:33, for example, "churning" and "wringing" are translations of the same Hebrew verb.

In the largest section of the book (10:1–22:16), most of the proverbs are two lines long, and those in chapters 10–15 almost always express a contrast. Sometimes the writer simply made a general observation, such as "Even in laughter the heart is sorrowful" (14:13), but usually he evaluated conduct: "Lying lips are abomination to the LORD" (12:22). Many proverbs, in fact, describe the consequences of a particular action or character trait: "A wise son maketh a glad father" (10:1). Since the proverbs were written primarily for instruction, often they were given in the form of commands: "Love not sleep, lest thou come to poverty" (20:13). Even where the imperative form is not used, the desired action is quite clear (see 14:5).

A common feature of the proverbs is the use of figurative language: "As cold waters to a thirsty soul, so is good news from a far country" (25:25). In chapter 25 alone, nine verses contain similes introduced by the words "like" or "as." These similes make the proverbs more vivid and powerful. Occasionally, the simile is used in a humorous or sarcastic way: "As a jewel of gold in a swine's snout, so is a fair woman which is without discretion" (11:22; see 26:9), or, "As the door turneth upon his hinges, so doth the slothful upon his bed" (26:14). Equally effective is the use of metaphors: "The law of the wise is a fountain of life" (13:14) and "A wholesome tongue is a tree of life" (15:4). According to 16:24, "Pleasant words are as a honeycomb." The figure of sowing and reaping is used in both a positive and a negative way (see 11:18; 22:8).

To develop a proper set of values, a number of proverbs use direct comparisons: "Better is the poor that walketh in his uprightness, than he that is perverse ... though he be rich" (28:6). This "better ... than" pattern can be seen also in 15:16–17; 16:19, 32; 17:1; a modified form occurs in 17:12; 22:1. Another pattern found in the book is the so-called numerical proverb. Used for the first time in 6:16 (see discussion there), this type of saying normally has the number three in the first line, and the number four in the second (see 30:15, 18, 21, 29).

The repetition of entire proverbs (compare 6:10–11 with 24:33–34; 14:12 with 16:25; 20:16 with 27:13) or parts of proverbs may serve a poetic purpose. A slight variation allowed the writer(s) to use the same image to make a related point (as in 17:3; 27:21) or to substitute a word to achieve greater clarity or a different emphasis (see 19:1; 28:6). In 26:4–5, the same line is repeated in a seemingly contradictory way, but this was designed to make two different points.

At times, the book of Proverbs is very direct and earthy (see 6:6; 21:9; 25:16; 26:3, 11). This is the nature of the Wisdom Literature; the writer sought to use truth to compel sinners to forsake their associations with wicked ways and walk the path of wisdom.

Theme and Theological Message

According to the prologue, Proverbs was written to give "subtilty to the simple, to the young man knowledge and discretion" (1:4) and to make wise men wiser (1:5). The frequent references to "My son" (1:8, 10; 2:1; 3:1; 5:1) emphasize instructing the young and guiding them into happy and prosperous lives. Acquiring wisdom and knowing how to avoid the pitfalls of folly leads to health and success. Although Proverbs is a practical book dealing with the art of living, it bases wisdom solidly on "the fear of the LORD" (1:7). Throughout the book, reverence for God is set forth as the path to life and security (see 3:5; 9:10; 22:4). People must trust in the Lord (3:5) and not in themselves (28:26). The references to the "tree of life" (3:18; 11:30; 13:12) recall the joyful bliss of the garden of Eden and figuratively say that the one who finds wisdom will be greatly blessed.

In chapters 1–9, the writer contrasted the way of wisdom with the path of violence (1:11–18) and immorality (2:16–18). With her seductive words, the adulteress tries to lure a young man to her and ultimately to death (see chap. 5; 6:24–35; 7; 9:13–18). Sexual immorality is thus an example of and a symbol for the antithesis of wisdom (see 22:14; 23:27; 30:20).

At the same time, Proverbs condemns the quarrelsome wife and her unbearable ways (19:13; 21:9, 19). The home is supposed to be a place of love, not dissension (see 15:17; 17:1). Quarrelsome, quick-tempered men are also denounced (see 14:29; 26:21), and gossiping is viewed as a source of great trouble (11:13; 18:8; 26:22). A man who is able to control his tongue is a man of knowledge (see 10:19; 17:27). At the same time, the tongue must be used to instruct one's children (see 1:8; 22:6; 31:26), and discipline is necessary for their well-being (see 13:24 and discussion).

Proverbs strongly encourages diligence and hard work (see 10:4 and discussion; 31:17–19) and holds the sluggard in contempt for his laziness (see 6:6 and discussion). A son "that sleepeth in the harvest … causeth shame" (10:5), and those who love sleep are sure to grow poor (see 20:13). Generally, wealth is connected to righteousness (see 3:16), and poverty to wickedness (see 22:16), but some verses link riches with the wicked (15:16; 28:6). Honesty and justice are praised repeatedly, and it is expected that a king will defend the rights of the poor and needy (see 31:5). Those who are kind to the needy will be richly blessed (see 14:21 and discussion), but several warnings are issued against putting up security for a neighbor (see 6:1 and discussion).

The proud and the arrogant are sure to be destroyed (see 11:2; 16:18), especially "the scorners" with their insolent pride (see discussion on 1:22). A drunkard is depicted as the epitome of the fool (see 20:1), and his woes and miseries are described in graphic terms in 23:29–35.

Although Proverbs is more practical than theological, God's work as Creator is especially highlighted. The role of wisdom in creation is the subject of 8:22–31 (see discussions there), where wisdom as an attribute of God is personified. Twice God is called the Maker of the poor (14:31; 17:5). He also directs the steps of a man (see 16:9; 20:24), and His eyes observe all a man's actions (see 5:21; 15:3). God is sovereign over the kings of the earth (21:1), and all history moves forward under His control (see discussions on 16:4, 33).

Literary Features

A short prologue (stating the purpose and theme, 1:1–7) opens the book, and a longer epilogue (identifiable by its subject matter and its alphabetic form, 31:10–31) closes it. The first nine chapters contain a series of discourses that contrast the way and benefits of wisdom with the way of the fool. Except for the sections in which personified wisdom speaks (1:20; 8:1, 22; 9:1), each discourse begins with "My son" or "Hear, ye children." These units are similar to the discourses found in Job and Ecclesiastes, which also contain speeches given in poetic form.

A key feature in the introductory discourses of Proverbs is the personification of both wisdom and folly (as women), each of whom (by appeals and warnings on the part of Lady Wisdom, by enticements on the part of Lady Folly) seeks to persuade "simple" youths to follow her ways. These discourses are strikingly organized. Beginning (1:8–33) and ending (chaps. 8–9) with direct enticements and appeals, the main body of the discourses is made up of two nicely balanced sections, one devoted to the commendation of wisdom (chaps. 2–4) and the other to warnings against folly (chaps. 5–7). In these discourses, the young man is depicted as being enticed to folly by men who try to get ahead in the world by exploiting others (1:10–19) and by women who seek sexual pleasure outside the bond of marriage (chap. 5; 6:20–25; 7). In the social structures of that day, these were the two great temptations for young men. The second is especially illustrative and emblematic of the appeal of Lady Folly.

The main collection of Solomon's proverbs (10:1–22:16) consists of individual couplets, many of which express a contrast. On the surface, no discernible arrangement can be seen in this collection, though occasionally two or three proverbs deal with the same subject. For example, 11:24–25 deals with generosity, 16:12–15 mentions a king, and 19:4, 6–7 talks about friendship. The second Solomonic collection (chaps. 25–29) continues the pattern of two-line verses but also contains proverbs with three (25:13; 27:10, 22) or four (25:4–5, 21–22; 26:18–19) lines. The last five verses of chapter 27 (vv. 23–27) present a short discourse on the benefits of raising flocks and herds.

In "the words of the wise" (22:17–24:22) and the collection introduced by "These things also belong to the wise" (24:23–34), there is a prevalence of two- and three-verse units and something of a return to the style of chapters 1–9 (see 23:29–35 especially). These sections function as an appendix to the main collection of Solomon's proverbs (10:1–22:16) and contain some similar proverbs (compare 24:6 with 11:14; 24:16 with 11:5). Even stronger are the links with chapters 1–9 (compare 23:27 with 2:16; 24:33–34 with 6:10–11).

The last two chapters of the book serve as an appendix to chapters 25–29. The words of Agur are dominated by numerical proverbs (30:15, 18, 21, 24, 29) and include, in 30:5, a close parallel to Psalm 18:30 (also compare 30:6 with Deut. 4:2). After the nine verses attributed to King Lemuel (31:1–9), Proverbs concludes with an epilogue, an impressive acrostic poem honoring a worthy woman. She demonstrates, and thus epitomizes, many of the qualities and values identified with wisdom throughout the book. The lengthy description of the worthy woman is primarily addressed to young men on the threshold of mature life, and its purpose may be twofold: (1) to offer counsel on the kind of wife a young man ought to seek and (2) in a subtle way, to advise the young man (again) to marry Lady Wisdom, thus returning to the theme of chapters 1–9 (as climaxed in chap. 9; compare the description of Lady Wisdom in 9:1–2 with the virtues of the wife of noble character). In any event, the concluding epitome of wisdom in the wife of noble character forms a literary frame with the opening discourses, where wisdom is personified as a woman.

Outline

Bibliography

Alden, Robert L. *Proverbs: A Commentary on an Ancient Book of Timeless Advice.* Grand Rapids, MI: Baker, 1983.

Archer, Gleason L. *An Encyclopedia of Bible Difficulties*. Grand Rapids, MI: Zondervan, 192.

Bridges, Charles. *An Exposition of Proverbs*. 1846. Grand Rapids, MI: Zondervan, 1959.

Buzzel, Sid S. "Proverbs." In *The Bible Knowledge Commentary: Old Testament*. Edited by John F. Walvoord and Roy B. Zuck. Wheaton, IL: Victor, 1985.

Delitzsch, Franz. *Biblical Commentary on the Proverbs of Solomon*. 1873. Grand Rapids, MI: Eerdmans, 1986.

Harris, R. Laird. "Proverbs." In *The Wycliffe Bible Commentary*. Edited by Charles F. Pfeiffer and Everett F. Harrison. Chicago: Moody, 1982.

Jensen, Irving L. *Proverbs*. Everyman's Bible Commentary. Chicago: Moody, 1982.

Kidner, Derek. *The Proverbs: An Introduction and Commentary*. Tyndale Old Testament Commentaries 15. Downers Grove, IL: InterVarsity, 1964.

Lange, John P. *Proverbs of Solomon*. A Commentary on the Holy Scriptures.

McKane, William. *Proverbs: A New Approach*. Philadelphia: Westminster, 1970.

Rylaarsdam, J. *The Proverbs, Ecclesiastes, Song of Solomon*. Layman's Bible Commentary 10. Richmond: John Knox, 1964.

Scott, R. B. Y. *Proverbs, Ecclesiastes: A New Translation with Introduction and Commentary*. Anchor Bible 18. Garden City, NY: Doubleday, 1965.

Smith, John Pye. *The Scripture Testimony to the Messiah*. London: R Fenner, 1818.

Toy, Crawford C. *A Critical and Exegetical Commentary on the Book of Proverbs*. International Critical Commentary. New York: Charles Scribner's Sons, 1902.

Whybray, R. N. *The Book of Proverbs*. Cambridge: Cambridge University Press, 1972.

EXPOSITION

I. Prologue: Author, Purpose, and Theme (1:1–7)

Proverbs was designed to assist everyone seeking to meet the challenges related to the intellectual and moral development of Israel's youth. Generations of parents, educators, statesmen, and preachers have found an invaluable resource in Proverbs. Fallen and redeemed persons who embrace the wisdom contained in the proverbs are empowered for living lives that are pleasing to God, which leads to living life skillfully. The ultimate objective of the wisdom teacher is the creation of a people who fear God, keep His commandments, and embrace the salvation that is found alone in Him who is the wisdom of God, even Jesus Christ (1 Cor. 1:30).

1:1. Proverbs begins by introducing **Solomon** (v. 1) as the primary author of the book. His wisdom and prolific production of proverbs and songs are mentioned in 1 Kings 4:32 and uniquely qualified him for writing this important book. His authorship is affirmed again in the headings of 10:1 and 25:1. Although Solomon is the primary author and compiler of the proverbs found in this book, others also contributed to the collection and writing of these proverbs (see Introduction, "Authors").

The term **proverbs** (v. 1) not only provides the title for this important book but also designates the primary literary form that the author used to communicate his message. The *mashal* (proverb) is designed to communicate a profound truth with an economy of words.

Solomon's collection of proverbs and those contributed by others to the book were designed to equip fathers for the skillful instruction of their sons. Sons who heed the **instruction** (v. 2) conveyed in the proverbs will be equipped with **wisdom** (see

10:9–10). "Wisdom" (Hebrew, *hokmah*) is a key term in Proverbs and occurs over forty times in the book. The authors urged people to acquire wisdom (4:5), for it is worth more than silver or gold (3:13–14). Wisdom provides one with the skills for living life successfully (Eccl. 10:9–10). Those who follow the directives of wisdom possess an ability to create beauty in this world to the glory of God. The craftsman guided by wisdom creates beauty as well and can also be called a wise man (see Exod. 31:3). Additionally, those who embrace the instruction of wisdom are able to follow God's design and thus avoid the moral pitfalls that ensnare those who refuse wisdom's instruction. The New Testament refers to Christ as "wisdom" from God (1 Cor. 1:30; see Col. 2:3).

1:2–5. Disciples of wisdom are able **to perceive the words of understanding** (v. 2) and **to receive the instruction of wisdom, justice, and judgment, and equity** (v. 3; see 2:9). **The simple** (v. 4) who follow the instruction of wisdom are able to move forward in this fallen world with **subtilty**. "Subtilty" implies good judgment or good sense (see 15:5; 19:25). Outside Proverbs, the Hebrew word for "subtilty" is used in a negative sense for craftiness or shrewdness (see Gen. 3:1; Job 5:13). Wisdom prepares people to interact with sin in a way that parallels the artful shrewdness of the evil man. Such persons are not like "the simple," which is another key word in Proverbs, occurring some fifteen times. It denotes those who are easily persuaded and lack "understanding" (9:4, 16), who are immature and inexperienced (see Ps. 19:7). Generally speaking, the Hebrew term for "simple" denotes one without moral direction and inclined to evil (see 1:22).

1:6–7. Solomon wished to accomplish two more objectives through his communication of the wisdom contained in the proverbs. He aimed to equip the young men of Israel with the ability to understand **dark sayings** (v. 6). The Hebrew for this word can sometimes refer to riddles or allegories (see Ezek. 17:2). Solomon had amazed the queen of Sheba with his ability to solve difficult questions (1 Kings 10:1–7). When using the term "dark sayings," Sol-

omon had such difficult questions in mind. Those instructed in wisdom will amaze others with their ability to answer the hard questions. Perhaps Solomon's highest purpose in Proverbs was to lead Israel's sons to embrace **The fear of the Lord** (v. 7), which we may say is the theme of the book (see 9:10; 31:30; see Job 28:28; Ps. 111:10). "The fear of the Lord" is a loving reverence for God that includes submission to His lordship and to the commands of His Word (Eccl. 12:13). Whybray suggests that a real understanding of the term *fear* in the Wisdom Literature is dependent on observing the close connection between the fear of Yahweh and education. In many passages the fear of Yahweh is to be taught and learned as in Ps. 34:11–14; Deut. 17:18–20; 2 Kings 17:25–38 (Whybray, *Wisdom in Proverbs*, p. 97). God is the king (Mal. 1:14), but even as believers stand in awe of Him, they can rejoice (see Ps. 2:11; Isa. 12:6). **Fools**, those who "hate knowledge" (v. 22) and correction of any kind (12:1), who are ready to argue (20:3) and make no effort to restrain their anger (29:11), who are complacent (1:32), and who trust in themselves (28:26) rather than in God (see Ps. 14:1) **despise wisdom and instruction** (see also 5:12).

II. The Superiority of the Way of Wisdom (1:8–9:18)

A. Appeals and Warnings Addressed to Youth (1:8–33)

1. Enticements to Secure Happiness through Violence (1:8–19)

1:8–9. Coming from the heart of a father, the proverbs were designed to be delivered within the context of a loving relationship. **My son** (v. 8) is a typical introduction to an instruction speech in Proverbs, evoking a domestic situation of a father preparing his son for life in the world. Here and in 6:20, the mother is also depicted as a teacher. Wisdom is like **an ornament** (v. 9) or precious jewelry. Those who follow wisdom add beauty and honor to their lives.

1:10–14. Sinners entice (v. 10). Wisdom has competitors in this fallen world. Peers often speak words that are contrary to wisdom and the instruction of the law (*torah*). These sinners **lay wait for blood** (v. 11). Their goal is personal enrichment by theft or oppression (vv. 13, 19), even if they have to commit murder. Solomon cited two major enticements that sinners in that culture utilized to lure young men away from wisdom. They drew them into folly by enticing them to (1) get rich by exploiting others (here) and (2) be drawn into illicit sexual pleasure with immoral women who refuse to honor their marriage vows (5:1–6; 6:24; 7:5; see 2:12–19). Sinners abuse others in their pursuit of gain. They **swallow … as the grave** (v. 12); poetic imagery for their shameless victimization of others (see discussion on Ps. 49:14). By contrast, Proverbs teaches that wisdom brings the greatest riches man could ever gain (3:14–16; 16:16; see also Job 28:12–19).

1:15–19. Beginning with verse 15, the destructive path (**the way**; v. 15) of the adulteress is the focus of instruction. Avoiding this path is a particular challenge for young men and is in view again in 2:18 and 7:25. The wicked are quick **to shed blood** (v. 16; see Prov. 6:17–18; the same is said of them in the first two lines of Isa. 59:7 and is partially quoted in Rom. 3:15). The wicked's **net is spread** (v. 17), like nets used in ancient Israel to catch unwary birds and animals (see 6:5; 7:23; Eccl. 9:12; Isa. 51:20; Jer. 5:26), but in reality, **they lurk privily for their own lives** (v. 18). The wicked unintentionally spread a net for their own feet (see 29:6; Ps. 35:8), so they are less intelligent than birds (see 7:22–23). According to Isaiah 17:14, the lot of those who plunder God's people is destruction, while long life will be enjoyed by those who hate ill-gotten gain (28:16).

2. Warnings against Rejecting Wisdom (1:20–33)

1:20–21. Wisdom crieth without (v. 20). Here, in 3:15–18; 9:1–12, wisdom is personified, a poetic device common also in Isaiah (see 55:12; 59:14). Wisdom pleads for the souls of people **in the streets**, or in the town square, an open area inside the gate of a fortified city. Wisdom has the heart of an evangelist; like Jesus, she goes where the people are. Wisdom goes to the masses and goes to the leaders who sit **in the … gates** (v. 21), where the leaders of the city

met to hold court (see 31:23; Ruth 4:11; Job 29:7) and where the marketplace was located (2 Kings 7:1).

As a young man confronts life in its social context, two voices appeal for his allegiance and seek to shape his life: (1) the voice of wisdom (as exemplified in the instructions of the wisdom teachers) and (2) the voice of folly (as exemplified by the sinners of vv. 10–14 and the adulteress of 5:3; 6:24; 7:5). Consequently, the young must learn to exercise discretion. Here and in chapters 8–9, wisdom makes her appeal. She speaks neither out of heaven (by special revelation, as do the prophets) nor out of the earth (through voices from the dead, necromancy; see Lev. 19:31; Deut. 18:11; 1 Sam. 28:7–19). Rather, she speaks out of the center of the life of the city, where man's communal experience of the creation order (established by God's wisdom, 8:22–31) is concentrated (see, e.g., 11:10 and discussion) and where the godly, the truly wise, test human experience in the crucible of faith and afterward give divine wisdom a human voice in their wise instructions, as in Proverbs.

1:22–33. Wisdom demands to know **How long … the scorners** (v. 22), those who are proud and arrogant (21:24), who are full of insults, hatred, and strife (9:7–8; 22:10; 29:8), and who resist correction (13:1; 15:12) even though they deserve flogging (19:25; 21:11), will refuse knowledge and **delight in** their sin. To such rebels, wisdom offers the gift of her **spirit** (v. 23), which is life, and the gift of her instruction, which leads to the fear of the Lord and the path of true profit, success, and skill in this life. How sad that they have often **refused** (v. 24) such a gracious offer, even as Israel refused God (see Isa. 1:4; 5:24) and the people of Jerusalem refused Jesus (Matt. 23:37). In spite of their refusal, God **stretched out** His **hand** (v. 24; see Isaiah 65:2, where God held out His hands all day long to a stubborn people) to those who **set at nought all** His **counsel** (v. 25; see 8:33). Because these rebels have rejected God, He will no longer stretch out His hand to them in grace but will **laugh at** their **calamity** (v. 26). This is not an expression of heartlessness but a reaction to the absurdity of fools, who laugh at wisdom, choose folly, and bring disaster on themselves (see Ps. 2:4 for the Lord's response to kings who think they can rebel against Him). Those who reject God's gracious gifts will experience angst of soul as **fear cometh** upon them. These foolish men will experience the calamities that they secretly dread, and when they reach out to God, He **will not answer** (v. 28), just as God refused to listen to Israel when the people sinned (Deut. 1:45; Isa. 1:15). Though those who reject wisdom may seek the God who gives it as gift, **they shall not find** Him. Rather, they will be left to **eat of the fruit of their own way, and be filled with their own devices** (v. 31). The consequences depend on their actions (18:20; 31:31; Isa. 3:10). "Whatsoever a man soweth, that shall he also reap" (Gal. 6:7). These fools think that their **prosperity** (v. 32) will protect them from everything. In the writings of the prophets, the false sense of security that prosperity provides is frequently exposed as foolishness (see Isa. 32:9; Amos 6:1; Zeph. 1:12). Solomon could not close this important teaching session without focusing on the celebration believers experience in their spirits when they realize that the spirit of wisdom indwells them. Having embraced the fear of the Lord, they receive the gift of wisdom and **dwell safely** (v. 33; see Isa. 32:18; Ezek. 34:27).

B. Commendation of Wisdom (chaps. 2–4)

1. Benefits of Accepting Wisdom's Instructions (chap. 2)

2:1–4. Wisdom continues pointing to the path that the young should travel. Just as the psalmist urged young men to avoid sin by hiding God's word in their hearts (Ps. 119:11), so the wisdom teacher urged the young to hide wisdom's teachings in their hearts. Eight strong verbs are used in verses 1–4: **receive … and hide** (v. 1), **incline … and apply** (v. 2), **criest … and liftest up** (v. 3), **seekest … and searchest** (v. 4). The objects of this intense activity are the words and commands of the wisdom teacher. **Incline thine ear** (v. 2) implies attentiveness and obedience (see Isa. 55:3; Jer. 13:15). The Hebrew word translated **heart** here (and in 4:21; 1 Kings 3:9) can sometimes be translated "mind" or "understand-

ing" (see Job 12:3). **Silver, and … hid treasures** (v. 4) describes ancient mining techniques and compares the search for wisdom to mining (see Job 28:12).

2:5–11. The results of obedience to the command to pursue wisdom vigorously are introduced in verses 5 and 6. Perhaps the most desired outcome is **the fear of the Lord** (v. 5; see discussion on 1:7). **Knowledge of God** involves knowing God as a person (see Phil. 3:10) and knowing what He is teaching us. The Hebrew word used here for God, *Elohim* (see discussion on Gen. 2:4), occurs elsewhere in Proverbs only in 2:17; 3:4; 25:2; 30:9. To those who are attentive to the commands of wisdom, the Lord gives **sound wisdom** (v. 7), or the power for victory and advancement. He is the **buckler,** or shield associated with victory, for all who **walk uprightly** (see 19:1). The Lord **keepeth … and preserveth** (v. 8; see Ps. 91:3–7, 11–12) those who know Him and gives them wisdom to know what course of action to follow (see Heb. 5:11–14). They shall be able to discern **every good path** (v. 9; see "the paths of righteousness," Ps. 23:3). In addition, He will cause them to know **righteousness, and judgment, and equity** (see 1:3; Phil. 4:8). Such knowledge will be **pleasant unto thy soul** (v. 10), just as the words of a wise man are "sweet to the soul" of another (16:24; see 3:17). Following the paths commended by wisdom will **preserve** and **keep** (v. 11) followers on their journey because God guards the faithful (see v. 8).

2:12–15. Wisdom will also save one from the enticements of men to follow perverse ways (vv. 12–15) and from the enticements of the adulteress (vv. 16–19; see discussion on 1:11). The young are always in danger before those who **speaketh froward things** (v. 12) or use perverse and dishonest speech (see v. 14). The deceitfulness of men's speech is also mentioned in 8:13; 10:31–32; 17:20. These persons abandon **the paths of uprightness** (v. 13; see 3:6; 9:15–16) and pursue **the ways of darkness.** Men love darkness instead of light (see John 3:19–21; see also Job 24:15–16; Isa. 29:15; Rom. 13:12). Such men **rejoice to do evil, and delight in … the wicked** (v. 14). Their **ways are crooked** (v. 15; see Isa. 59:7–8).

2:16–19. Here **the strange woman** (v. 16) and her ability to entice one into sexual sin is the focus of wisdom's instruction. The Hebrew for this phrase and for **the stranger** occur again in 5:20 and 7:5. The two terms literally mean "foreigner," implying an "adulteress," because anyone other than one's own wife was to be considered off limits, like a foreigner who worshiped another god (see 1 Kings 11:1). "Stranger" is parallel to "evil woman" in 6:24 and "whore" in 23:27. **Her words** are equal to the "flattering of the tongue" of 6:24 and the "fair speech" of 7:21 (see 5:3). She breaks covenant with **the guide of her youth** (v. 17), her husband, whom she married when she was a young woman (see Isa. 54:6). She abandons **the covenant of her God**, perhaps the marriage covenant, spoken in God's presence (see Ezek. 16:8; Mal. 2:14). Here, however, the "covenant of her God" more likely refers to the breaking of the seventh commandment (Exod. 20:14). Her very surroundings **inclineth unto death** (v. 18). A life of immorality leads to the destruction and death of all who are involved (see 5:5; 9:18). All who walk with such a woman are walking with **the dead** (see Job 26:5).

2:20–22. Solomon contrasted those who walk in the ways of death with those who **dwell in the land** (v. 21). Israel had been promised the land of Canaan, and Psalm 37:29 says that "The righteous shall inherit the land" (see also Ps. 37:9, 11; Matt. 5:5). The dead shall not partake of Israel's promise and will be **cut off from the earth, and … rooted out of it** (v. 22). The Hebrew word for "earth" can also be translated "land" and here refers to removal from the Promised Land of Israel. In Deuteronomy 28:63, God warned that if the people refused to obey Him, they would be "plucked from off the land." Evil men and their offspring will be cut off (see Ps. 37:9, 28).

2. Wisdom's Instructions and Benefits (chap. 3)

3:1–4. The instruction on wisdom's benefits continues. Remembering and obeying God's commandments will bring **length of days, and long life … shall they add to thee** (v. 2). The fear of the Lord (see 10:27; 19:23) brings health to the body (v. 8) and "prolongeth days" (10:27; see also 9:10–11).

When Solomon prayed for wisdom, God promised him riches as well as long life if he would obey His commands (1 Kings 3:13–14). Such powerful truths must never be forsaken, and we must **bind** (v. 3) such treasure **about** our **neck[s]** like a beautiful necklace (see 1:9; 3:22). We must also **write them upon the table of** our **heart[s]**, and in so doing, we will **find favour** (v. 4) with **God and man** (see Luke 2:52; Rom. 12:17; 2 Cor. 8:21).

3:5–6. Assent to these truths requires a wholehearted commitment of their entire lives to the Lord. They must follow on with hearts that wholly **Trust in the LORD** (v. 5). Believers must commit their way to the Lord (see Ps. 37:5), as did Israel's forefathers, who trusted in God and were rescued (see Ps. 22:4–5). David challenged Solomon to serve God with wholehearted devotion (1 Chron. 28:9). One also must **acknowledge him** (v. 6) and serve Him with a willing and faithful heart (see 1 Chron. 28:9; Hos. 4:1; 6:6). Then believers may rest peacefully with the assurance that He will **direct** their **paths** and bring them to their appointed goal (see 11:5; Isa. 45:13).

3:7–10. Commitment to these truths must also awaken a resolve to **Fear the LORD, and depart from evil** (v. 7). Rejecting dependence on human wisdom and committing to doing what aligns with the truth will bring health to one's **bones** (v. 8), which stand for the whole body. Elsewhere, good news and pleasant words are said to bring health to the bones (15:30; 16:24; see 17:22). The presence of total trust in the living God will always manifest itself in one's stewardship. When men love God in spirit and in truth, they will always give Him the **firstfruits of all** their **increase** (v. 9). The Israelites were required to give to the priests the first part of the olive oil, wine, and grain produced each year (see Lev. 23:10; Num. 18:12–13). Such careful attention to the stewardship of God's gifts has a marvelous upside. For all who honor Him with the firstfruits, God will ensure that their barns and lives are **filled with plenty** (v. 10). For those who bring to the Lord His tithes and offerings, God promises to pour out more blessings than they have room to receive (see Mal. 3:10; see also Deut. 28:8, 12; 2 Cor. 9:8).

3:11–12. A word of caution is required at this point. Life does not always correspond to neat formulas. Because life is experienced in a fallen world and because people are sinners, there will certainly be times when difficulties challenge. Here the reader finds the warning that the righteous are not always prosperous (see 3:2 and discussion). Times of testing and affliction serve a purpose, however, for God is always teaching them (see 12:1; Job 5:17; 36:22; Ps. 119:71). In Hebrews 12:5–6, both of these verses are quoted to encourage believers to endure hardship (Heb. 12:7). God **as a father** (v. 12) often disciplines his children even as He disciplined Israel by testing the nation in the wilderness for forty years (Deut. 8:2–5). In such times, one must trust God's heart and guard against fleshly tendency to despise or grow weary of His loving correction, which always effects some larger purpose attached to His glory and the greater good.

3:13–20. A short poem in praise of wisdom is offered here. The poem continues the celebration of the benefits of wisdom. The first and last verses suggest that happiness attends those whose find wisdom and that the possession of it **is better than … silver, and … gold** (v. 14). The psalmist made the same claim for the commands and precepts of the Lord (see Pss. 19:10; 119:72, 127). Wisdom is personified here, and her possession **is more precious than rubies** (v. 15; as in Job 28:18, "the price of wisdom is above rubies"; and Prov. 31:10, "a virtuous woman … her price is far above rubies"). **Length of days is in her right hand** (see discussion on 3:2); **and in her left hand riches and honour** (v. 16; see 8:18; 22:4). Furthermore, **her paths are peace** (Hebrew, *shalom*; v. 17; see 3:2; 16:7; Ps. 119:165), which surrounds all of her relationships, and **She is a tree of life** (v. 18), a source of life to all who companion with her. This may allude to the tree in the garden of Eden (see Gen. 2:9 and discussion; see Prov. 11:30; 13:12; 15:4). The reference to the tree of life points back to creation and the time when the Lord **founded the earth** (v. 19). God's work in creation is compared to the construction of a building (see 1 Kings 5:17; 6:37; see also 8:29; Job 38:4–6; Ps. 104:5; Zech. 12:1). God

opened up springs and streams (see Gen. 7:11; 49:25; Ps. 74:15). Alternatively, though perhaps less likely, this is a reference to the dividing of the waters above from the waters below (see Gen. 1:7; Ps. 42:7 and discussion). The role of wisdom in creation is described more fully in 8:22–31. Divine wisdom guided the Creator and now permeates the whole creation. "Surely this is a reference to that One who upholds all things by the word of His power: the Lord Jesus Christ. Wisdom is the divine mediatrix between God and men" (Keil and Delitzsch, *Proverbs of Solomon*, p. 41). To live by wisdom is to imitate the Lord and conform to the divinely appointed creation order.

3:21–26. Wisdom's role in the conception of all things in this universe qualifies it to serve as our guide in all things related to living life well on the planet. Wisdom personified pleads that the **son** (v. 21) embrace **sound wisdom and discretion**. The son should value her highly, for she is **grace to thy neck** (v. 22), like a beautiful necklace (see 3:3), and **life unto thy soul**. Keeping sound wisdom and discretion at the center of one's life requires consistent effort. **Depart from thine eyes** (v. 21) refers to the ease with which a person may allow wisdom to slip away. The required effort is well spent, for cleaving to wisdom assures that one will dwell in safety: **thy foot shall not stumble** (v. 23; see 10:9. 3:24) and **When thou liest down, thou shalt not be afraid** (v. 24), which is also listed among the covenant blessings (see Lev. 26:6; Job 11:18–19; Mic. 4:4; Zeph. 3:13; see also Prov. 1:33). For **Thy sleep shall be sweet**, see 6:22; Psalm 4:8. The Lord shields the godly from deadly arrows and plagues (see 10:25; Ps. 91:3–8; Job 5:21), and He will **keep thy foot from being taken** (v. 26). Contrast the fate of the fool, stated in 1:18; 7:22–23.

3:27–35. Here attention is drawn to relationships with others. Four instructional offerings containing the word **not** are given. Those who are wise live according to the dictates of wisdom. They will not **Withhold … good from them to whom it is due** (v. 27; see Acts 9:36; Gal. 6:10; 1 John 3:17–18). They will not harm a **neighbour** (v. 28; see Luke 11:5–8; James 2:15–16). They will not **devise … evil against**

their **neighbour** (v. 29). "Devise" is from the same Hebrew root word as "plow," signifying a high level of intentional planning to harm one's neighbor. They will not **Strive ... without cause** (v. 30; see Job 2:3). They will not **Envy ... the oppressor** (v. 31; see 24:19; Ps. 37:1, 7). Four reasons are given for why the person who cleaves to wisdom will not practice any of these "do nots." The practice of any of these is an **abomination to the LORD** (v. 32). This phrase expresses God's abhorrence of pagan practices and immorality (see Deut. 18:9, 12) and is common in Proverbs (see, e.g., 6:16; 8:7; 11:20). In contrast, **his secret is with the righteous.** God takes the righteous into His confidence by revealing His plans to them (see Gen. 18:17–19; Job 29:4; Ps. 25:14; John 15:15). This contrast is seen also in Deuteronomy 11:26–28. Additionally, **The curse of the LORD is in the house of the wicked** (see Josh. 7:24–25; Zech. 5:3–4): **But he blesseth the habitation of the just** (v. 33; see Job 42:12–14) and **giveth grace unto the lowly** (v. 34). This section closes with the assurance once again that the Lord will honor **The wise** (v. 35; see Prov. 3:16). **Fools** will be promoted, something they deeply desire, but it will not be **the promotion** they envisioned; rather, it will be a promotion to **shame.**

3. Challenge to Hold on to Wisdom (chap. 4)

4:1–9. The appeal given here to hear and hold on to wisdom, similar to other appeals in Proverbs (e.g., 1:8–9; 2:1–6; 3:1; 4:10; 5:1; 7:24), is addressed to **ye children** (v. 1) and once again was issued from the heart of a concerned and loving father. The father was a man of conviction and knew the law of God to be an enduring and faithful guide for living the life of honor. His appeal is addressed to the **Tender** (v. 3), who are youthful, inexperienced, and yet **beloved** (see David's words about Solomon, 1 Chron. 22:5; 29:1). This is part of an autobiographical statement, such as was sometimes used by the wisdom teachers (see 24:30–34; see also the book of Ecclesiastes). Solomon spoke as the only son of David and Bathsheba, and thus, one deeply loved (see Gen. 37:3; Zech. 12:10). Solomon quoted the words

of David and desired to pass the fatherly advice he had received on to his sons. David's admonition to Solomon to **Let thine heart retain my words** (v. 4) and **Get wisdom** (v. 5) was undoubtedly responsible in large part for the request Solomon laid before the Lord for the gift of wisdom, which formed the foundation for his ultimate fame as a leader (1 Kings 3:5–14). David had taught his son, and now David's son taught his sons that **Wisdom is the principle thing** (v. 7) and will **preserve thee** (v. 6) and **keep thee.** In the Hebrew, these two verbs are used together also in 2:8, 11. Solomon continued, **with all thy getting get understanding** (v. 7). Acquiring wisdom must be man's top priority (see 1:7; see also the parable of the merchant who sold everything to buy a pearl of great price, Matt. 13:45–46). One's relationship with wisdom is to be not merely intellectual but rather relational and full of affection. Solomon admonishes the reader to **Love her** (v. 6), for to love wisdom is to prosper (8:21), and to hate wisdom is to "love death" (8:36). When wisdom is heard and loved, she bestows a life dazzling with **grace** (v. 9) and crowned with **glory.** Wreaths or crowns were always worn at joyous occasions, such as weddings or feasts (see Ezek. 16:12; 23:42).

4:10–19. Here the way of wisdom is contrasted with the ruinous **path of the wicked** (v. 14). Careful instruction has been given regarding **right paths** (v. 11; see discussions on 3:6; Ps. 23:3). Those sons who heed this instruction **shalt not stumble** (v. 12), because of their lack of light (see v. 19; 3:23; 10:9; Ps. 18:36; Isa. 40:30–31). "The path of the wicked" may well refer to the destructive path of the adulteress (see 2:18; 7:25; Pss. 1:1; 17:4–5). The adulteress and all who do evil are malicious and aggressive in their destructive efforts. **They sleep not, except they have done mischief** (v. 16; see Ps. 36:4; Mic. 2:1). Contrast the attitude of David, who would not sleep until he found a permanent place for God's house (Ps. 132:3–5). These evildoers **eat the bread of wickedness, and drink the wine of violence** (v. 17). They thrive on wickedness and violence (see 13:2; Job 15:16). The evil walk on a path of **darkness** (v. 19) and stumble ignorantly in their bondage. This darkness is like a fog enshrouding a dangerous path that leads to destruction (see discussion on 2:13; see also Isa. 59:9–10; Jer. 23:12; John 11:10; 12:35). The path pursued by those who follow the directives of wisdom is remarkably different, for **the path of the just is as the shining light** (v. 18). The godly have all the guidance and protection they need (see vv. 11–12) and are able to lead others to righteousness (see Dan. 12:3).

4:20–27. The words of wisdom must be continuously before the eyes of the **son** (v. 20), and more than that, they should be gladly received into the heart, the place of our deepest desires and thoughts (see 3:1, 3). The heart needs to be guarded, for out of it proceed the issues of life. If one stores up good things (see 2:1) in one's heart, one's words and actions will be good. "For out of the abundance of the heart the mouth speaketh" (Matt. 12:34; see Mark 7:21). Careful attention to the **heart** (v. 21) will lead to **health** (v. 22), referring to physical, psychological, and spiritual (see 3:8 and discussion) health. The guarded heart leads to behavioral transformations that extend to the tongue and the words used by wisdom's sons. Followers of wisdom will **Put away ... a froward mouth** (v. 24), or lying and deceit (see discussion on 2:12; see also 19:1). They will put away **perverse lips**, another reference to deceitful speech (see 6:12; 19:28; Eph. 4:29; James 3:6). Sons who are attentive to wisdom will **Let thine eyes look right on** (v. 25), straight ahead, not at worthless things (see Ps. 119:37). They will continuously **Ponder the path of** their **feet** (v. 26), pay attention to what is good and remove every moral hindrance (see 4:11–12; Isa. 26:7). They will **Turn not to the right hand nor to the left** (v. 27). This warning is also found in Deuteronomy 5:32–33; 28:14; and Joshua 1:7. Such careful behavior will lead one to diligently **remove** his **foot from evil** (see 1:15). "Proverbs provides both a goal and a route. The goal is successful living and the route is the way of wisdom" (Alden, *Proverbs*, p. 48). The wisdom teacher is patiently contending for the souls of Israel's sons and pleading with them to embrace a vision of success that glorifies God by faithful adherence to the directives of wisdom.

C. Warnings against Folly (chaps. 5–7)

1. Warning against Adultery (chap. 5)

Solomon issued a sharp warning against the peril of involvement with the adulteress (vv. 1–6), cited the tragic consequences that attend infidelity (vv. 7–14), and extolled the blessings of marital love (vv. 15–20).

5:1–6. Sons are again exhorted to listen to the words of their fathers. **Discretion, and ... knowledge** (v. 2) are the possessions of sons who give their ears and hearts to wisdom's instruction. Careful attention to the father's instruction is the son's best protection against the words, or **lips** (v. 3), of the adulteress, which **drop as a honeycomb**. This is probably a reference to the pleasant-sounding talk (see 16:24) of the adulteress, though some explain it as kisses (see Song 4:11; 5:13; 7:9). She is the **strange woman** whose words are **smoother than oil** (see 2:16). Her words are soothing (see Ps. 55:21) but full of flattery (see Prov. 29:5) and hypocrisy (see Ps. 5:9). What seems attractive and irresistible will all too soon turn to **wormwood** (v. 4), a bitter herb (see Deut. 29:18; Lam. 3:15, 19; Amos 6:12). Her words will ultimately cut a man asunder like a **twoedged sword** (see Judg. 3:16; see also Pss. 55:21; 149:6; Heb. 4:12; Rev. 1:16). She leads men **down to death** (v. 5). Her immorality hastens her end (see discussion on 2:18). **Her ways are moveable** (v. 6), or shaky and unstable (see 2:15; 10:9).

5:7–14. The father (teacher) continues to warn the son (student) about the consequences of immorality and admonishes his son to stay **far from** (v. 8) the adulteress (see Gen. 39:12; 2 Tim. 2:22). Wise sons will not go near **the door of her house** (see 7:25; 9:14). Failure to heed this instruction will expose the son to many dangers. He will lose the opportunity to honor God and his parents with his life, and he will give the days of his life to **the cruel** (v. 9), possibly a reference to the vengeful husband (see 6:34–35), or perhaps to the ravages of Satan and sin to which sexual addiction will expose him. Sober reflection on these devastating losses may serve to keep the son from the door of the adulteress, but there is more to contemplate. **Strangers** will **be filled with thy wealth** (v. 10). Contrast the riches and honor that come to the man who embraces wisdom (3:16–18). Immorality eventually reduces a man "to a piece of bread" (6:26). The young man's **flesh and ... body are consumed** (v. 11), possibly because of the debilitating effects of immorality (see 1 Cor. 6:18; Prov. 3:8; 4:22) but more likely because of the loss of vigor that accompanies old age. In old age, he will look back and sadly acknowledge that he has played the fool (see 1:7, 22, 29–30). He **hated instruction ... despised reproof** (v. 12) and had **not obeyed** (v. 13). In spite of the repeated urging to "hear" or "attend unto" wisdom's instruction (1:8; 3:1; 4:1; 5:1), at the end of his days, he will find himself encased **in all evil** (v. 14). Total calamity—physical, financial, and social ruin—will be his lot, and all shall see. **In the midst of the congregation**. The offender was subject to "a wound and dishonour" (6:33) or even death (see Deut. 22:22).

5:15–23. The wisdom teacher called his son to consider the unfathomable blessings to be experienced within the bonds of covenantal marriage, a stark contrast to the tragic losses sustained through involvement with the adulteress. Wisdom counsels the young to drink deeply from **thine own cistern ... thine own well** (v. 15). A man's wife is to be a source of pleasure for him, as water to a thirsty man. Wells and cisterns were privately owned and of great value (see 2 Kings 18:31; Jer. 38:6). In light of what the teacher has said, the young man is instructed to maintain devout fidelity to the wife with whom he is in covenant and make certain his sperm, or **fountains** (v. 16), is never shared with another outside the covenantal relationship. Wisdom instructs the young man to **rejoice with the wife of thy youth** (v. 18), whom he chose when he was young to be as the **hind and ... roe; Let her breasts satisfy thee at all times** (v. 19; see Song 7:7–8). He is admonished to be intoxicated with or captivated by her beauty and hers alone. Marital love is portrayed as being better than wine in Song of Solomon 4:10 (see Song 7:9). Wisdom now asks a painful question: **why ...?** (v. 20). In light of the sheer joy found within the

bonds of marriage and the calamity encountered with infidelity, why commit adultery? Why embrace the **strange woman** (see 5:3; 2:16 and discussion)? One must remember that all that is done is done **before the eyes of the Lord** (v. 21; see 15:3; Job 31:4; 34:21; Jer. 16:17). **He pondereth all** one's **goings** (see Job 7:18; 34:23; Pss. 11:4; 26:2; 139:23; Jer. 17:10). The eyes of the Lord behold both covenantal faithfulness and adultery, and He rewards men according to their deeds. In Ecclesiastes 7:26, the sinner is captured by a woman "whose heart is snares and nets." He is held in bondage by the **cords of his sins** (see Job 36:8; Eccl. 4:12; Isa. 5:18). The death of the fool is described in similar terms in 1:29–32; 7:21–25 (see also Job 36:12). He refuses **instruction** (v. 23), and in what he views as a grandiose engagement of all that is anti-God, he lives his life and ends his journey in desolation and Hell. "McKane compares this foolish person to a corpse that has been wrapped in a shroud. The shroud in this case is his sexual folly" (McKane, *Proverbs*, p. 313).

2. Warning against Perverse Ways (6:1–19)

The issues in view here continue to be those that can lead a young man to the loss of his honor and ultimately shame. Counsel is offered regarding the dangers of foolish financial alliances and laziness. Once again the counsel is offered to "My son," and the term of endearment is used again in verses 3 and 20.

6:1–5. The warning against **be[ing] surety** (v. 1) for another is offered many times in Proverbs (11:15; 20:16; 22:26; 27:13). Severe consequences attended the decision to be surety or to strike **thy hand** for another. These actions refer to the willingness to assume responsibility for someone else's debt (see 22:26), often a very high-interest loan or some other obligation. Taking responsibility for the debt of another can end in abject poverty if you cannot repay the loan (see 22:27). In ancient Israel, it could even result in slavery. For example, Judah volunteered to personally guarantee the safe return of Benjamin to Jacob (Gen. 43:9), and when this seemed impossible, Judah had to offer himself to Joseph as a slave

(Gen. 44:32–33). Such an arrangement was sealed by "striking hands," equivalent to our handshake (see 11:15; 17:18; 20:16; 22:26; Job 17:3). Unwisely taking responsibility for the debt of another may lead to being **snared … taken** (v. 2; see v. 5; 5:22). The father's wise advice to a son whose words have led him into this snare is, **deliver thyself** (v. 3), or gain release from the obligation as quickly as possible. Haste is necessary, for to **come into the hand of thy friend** symbolizes that control of the young man's future no longer belong to him but to the friends for whom he has co-signed the loan or obligation. Losing control of one's future is devastating and must be rectified as quickly as possible. **Go** is the mandate. **Make sure thy friend** means that one should be as persistent as the man in Luke 11:8 in getting out of this responsibility. Do whatever is necessary to get free of this enslavement; **humble** yourself and do **not sleep … nor slumber** (v. 4) until you have broken free as the bird breaks free **from the hand of the fowler** (v. 5; see Ps. 124:7).

6:6–11. The little ant models some laudable virtues for the young who desire to acquire wisdom. The ant is the opposite of the **sluggard** (loafer; v. 6), who is the object of heavy criticism in Proverbs. This lazy individual refuses to work, and his desires are not met (see 10:26; 13:4; 15:19; 19:24; 22:13; 24:30; 26:13–16). The ant has **no … ruler** (v. 7) and is mastered by an internal motivation to industry (compare the locust of 30:27). Wisdom internalized can serve this vital role in the life of a young man. The lazy sleeper provides a stark contrast to the industrious ant. Wisdom's instructor cries out, **How long wilt thou sleep, O sluggard?** (v. 9). His love for sleep is described also in 26:14. Sleep in proper measure and at the right time is a good thing, but too much sleep and sleeping at the wrong times will lead to poverty and actual endangerment. Poverty will come upon the lazy person with the suddenness and devastation of a highway bandit who plunders and leaves a wake of destruction behind him. **Poverty … want** (v. 11) are connected with too much sleep also in 10:5; 19:15; 20:13. Hard work is an antidote to poverty (see 12:11; 14:23; 28:19).

6:12–16. Here is a vivid description of one who uses his mouth, eyes, feet, and fingers (all a person's means of communication) in devious ways to achieve the deceitful plots of his heart, here especially to spread slander about someone to destroy him. Such a person is **a naughty person** (v. 12), or a "worthless person" (for the use of this term, see Judg. 19:22; 1 Sam. 25:25; Job 34:18; see also discussion on Deut. 13:13). This person is also characterized by **a froward mouth** (see 19:28; 2:12 and discussion). **He winketh with his eyes** (v. 13); making insinuations (see 10:10; 16:30). **He deviseth mischief** (v. 14; see v. 18; 3:29; Mic. 2:1). **He soweth discord.** Through slander, he creates distrust, which culminates in alienation and conflict. He causes lots of problems for God's people through his words and gestures, but his end is disastrous, and **his calamity come[s] suddenly** (v. 15) as a sign of God's judgment (see 1:26; 24:22; Job 34:20). He will **suddenly … be broken without remedy** and will suffer the same fate he thought to bring upon another; his punishment will fit his crime. He, and all like him, will come to destruction because the Lord hates all who practice such behaviors and is committed to pressing His judgment upon them. **Six … yea, seven** (v. 16) is a way of handling numbers in synonymous parallelism in Hebrew poetry (see Introduction: "The Nature of a Proverb"). Such catalogues of items are frequent in the Wisdom Literature of the Old Testament (see 30:15, 18, 21, 29; see also Job 5:19). Solomon here enumerated those actions that particularly **are an abomination** to our Lord (see 3:32 and discussion).

6:17–19. God hates **a proud look** (v. 17), which reflects a proud heart, and He will judge those with such an attitude (see 21:4; 30:13; Pss. 18:27; 101:5). **A lying tongue** too is an abomination to Him (see 2:12 and discussion; 12:19; 17:7; 21:6). He hates **hands that shed innocent blood** (see 1:11, 16 and discussions; 28:17) and **a heart that deviseth wicked imaginations** (v. 18; see 1:31; 24:2; Gen. 6:5). He promises His stern judgment against **Feet that be swift in running to mischief** (see 1:16 and discussion) and lips that bear **false witness** (v. 19).

Proverbs emphasizes the damage done by the false witness (12:17–18; 25:18; see discussion on Ps. 5:9) and the punishment God reserves for all who **speaketh lies** (see discussion on 6:15; see also 19:5, 9; 21:28) and **soweth discord** (see 14:5, 25 and discussion on 6:14).

3. Cost of Committing Adultery (6:20–35)

6:20–25. Having stated clearly the actions that God hates, Solomon reissued the call for obedience to the commandments given in the law. The law of God will find a place of lodging in the hearts of the young who seek to honor their father and **mother** (v. 20). God's law firmly implanted in the hearts of the young is their best protection against sexual sin. Those who follow wisdom add beauty and honor to their lives. Wisdom guides and protects the godly at all times, when awake and when asleep. **When thou sleepest** (see discussion on 3:24)**, it shall keep thee** (v. 22; see 4:6). The Torah in the heart of the young and old alike is **a lamp** (v. 23) and **light**, just as the Word of God "is a lamp unto my feet, and a light unto my path" (Ps. 119:105; see Ps. 19:8). These commandments brighten the path and are an invaluable help in keeping one on the path that is **the way of life** (see 3:22; 4:22; contrast the way of death for the one who hates discipline, 5:23). **The evil woman** (v. 24) with her **flattery of the tongue** has led innumerable young men into the way that leads to death. Such knowledge should lead all men who read these words to run to wisdom, get it in their minds and hearts, and render radical obedience to its demands lest they fall under her spell and abandon the way that leads to life and honor. Jesus showed the close connection between lust and adultery (Matt. 5:28; see Exod. 20:17). When passion for something other than the law of the Lord takes hold of our hearts, it can **take thee** (v. 25; see 5:20) just as inevitably as focusing on the beautiful eyes of the "whorish woman" (6:26) will lead you surely to her imprisoning embrace.

6:26–35. Wisdom knows all too well the tragic pain in store for the young man who falls under the spell of the evil woman. It is perhaps noteworthy that these verses contain an acknowledgment that

evil really does exist; it **hunt[s] for the precious life** (v. 26) and seeks to destroy all that is pure and honoring to God. A man who practices such evil is **brought to a piece of bread**, and in the end, all that is good in him will be **burned** (vv. 27, 28) away. Both the prostitute (29:3) and the adulteress (5:10) reduce a man to poverty (see 1 Sam. 2:36). The man who plays with this fire will pay a terrible price, and **whosoever** (v. 29) practices such evil **shall not be innocent** and will not go unpunished (see vv. 33–34 and discussion on 5:14). The ordinary thief will be required to repay **sevenfold** (v. 31). Hebrew law demanded no more than fivefold payment as a penalty for any theft (see Exod. 22:1–9). The number seven is symbolic here; he will pay in full. This requirement is simple when compared to the consequences attached to adultery. Whoever **committeth adultery … destroyeth his own soul** (v. 32; see 5:14 and discussion; 7:22–23). To participate in adultery is to inflict upon the self **A wound and dishonour … and [a] reproach** that **shall not be wiped away** (v. 33). Consider the dishonour that followed Amnon's raping of Tamar (2 Sam. 13:13, 22) and the heart cry of Joseph in his perilous encounter with the evil woman: "how then can I do this great wickedness, and sin against God?" (Gen. 39:9). "A wound" may well refer to the blows that such a man will receive from the husband against whom the adulterous offender has so callously sinned. The **jealousy** (v. 34) of the offended one will burn like a fierce prairie fire (for the destructive force of jealousy see also 27:4; Song 8:6). No amount of **ransom** (v. 35) or **gifts** will remedy the offense or appease the jealousy. The offended party will not **rest content**, nor will he **spare in the day of vengeance** (v. 34). A man thus offended will, apart from a remarkable work of the Holy Spirit, commit all of his energies to the destruction of the enemy who ravaged his home and committed adultery with the wife who is his by covenant.

4. Warning against the Enticements of an Adulteress (chap. 7)

7:1–5. The exhortation to vigorous engagement with the words and commandments of the father are heard once again. The verbs in this section are vigorous and represent a call to vigilance. **Keep … and lay up** (v. 1), **Bind … write** (v. 3), **Say … and call** (v. 4) all represent a call to action on the part of the young. The young are commanded to keep these laws **as the apple of thine eye** (v. 2). Literally, they are to be protected "as the little pupil in thine eye" (Lange, *Proverbs of Solomon*, p. 90). The pupil is where light enters the eye and is to be cared for and protected because of its great value (see Deut. 32:10 and discussion). To neglect to care for and protect the pupil could result in a life spent in darkness. Neglect of the father's commandments is equally precarious, for it can lead to darkness in this life and the next. Therefore, we are told, **Bind them upon thy fingers** (v. 3), as a reminder (see 6:21; Deut. 6:8) so that the words might always be right in front of us and before our eyes. This reminder is meant to serve a higher purpose, for the ultimate relationship with the words of the law is one of heart, not merely of eye and mind. The words are to be encoded **upon the table of thine heart** (see Jer. 31:33). **Wisdom** (v. 4) is described with terms of endearment. She is **my sister … kinswoman**. Wisdom must be one's most intimate companion. "Sister" may be used here in the sense of "bride" (see Song 4:9 – 10, 12; 5:1 – 2). This intense respect for and internalizing of the commandments is the best protection against **the strange woman … which flattereth with her words** (v. 5).

7:6 – 21. After once again calling attention to the danger represented by the adulterous woman, Solomon once again visited the tragedy of her wiles and destructive work. From his **window** (v. 6) above the street, he watched **the simple ones** (v. 7; see discussion on 1:4). He viewed a certain young man among the group who was **void of understanding** (see 6:32; 9:4, 16). Although sin is the vice of the masses, it always comes down to the one who breaks his parents' hearts and brings destruction, death, and hell down upon himself. The one who is eager to expand his engagement with the vices of the world finds **the way to her house** (v. 8; see 5:8) **in the black and dark night** (v. 9). The young man hoped no one would see him (see 2:13 and discussion). There in

the blackness, he met the destroyer in **the attire of a harlot** (v. 10), perhaps dressed in a gaudy manner (see Ezek. 16:16) and heavily veiled (see Gen. 38:14 – 15). **She … lieth in wait** (v. 12), ready to catch her prey (see 7:22). She **kissed him** (v. 13), a bold greeting (see Gen. 29:11). How deceptive and duplicitous this adulteress was. She had recently made her **peace offerings** (v. 14), of which part of the meat could be eaten by the offerer and his (or her) family (Lev. 7:12 – 15). **This day have I payed my vows.** One of her peace offerings had been made in fulfillment of a vow, and the meat had to be eaten on the first or second day (see Lev. 7:15 – 16). So the young man had an opportunity to enjoy a real feast, one that ironically had religious significance (see Amos 5:21 – 22). Neither he nor the adulteress was bothered by the fact that their vile conduct was preceded by a religious act. She had prepared sumptuous surroundings, including a banquet of food and **fine linen of Egypt** (v. 16) upon which to lay their naked bodies. Linen is associated with the wealthy in 31:22. Egyptian linen was of great value (see Isa. 19:9; Ezek. 27:7). In preparation for the unleashing of their passions, she had perfumed her bed with **myrrh, aloes, and cinnamon** (v. 17). These fragrant perfumes are linked with lovemaking also in Psalm 45:8; Song 4:14; 5:5. The trap had been set and now the invitation was boldly extended: **Come, let us take our fill of love** (v. 18). Lovemaking is compared to eating and drinking also in 9:17; 30:20; Song 4:16; 5:1. She proposed that they gorge themselves with sexual pleasure, for **the goodman** (v. 19), her husband, was **not at home.** He would never know (see 6:34 – 35), she reasoned, for he was on **a long journey.** Perhaps he was a wealthy merchant. He had taken with him **a bag of money** (v. 20). Pieces of silver of various weights were a common medium of exchange, but not in the form of coins until a later period. This young man, who was void of understanding, who never took the time to implant the Word of God in his heart, and for whom these words were not the pupil of his eye, found himself in a dance with the Devil, and the light of wisdom was all but gone from him. She **with her much fair speech … with the flat-**

tering of her lips (v. 21; see discussions on 2:16; 5:3; see also 6:24; 7:5) **caused him to yield** (see 5:23).

7:22–23. Tragically, the young man was totally oblivious to the unspeakable damage he did to his own soul in consenting to her invitation. He was **as an ox goeth to the slaughter** (v. 22) and totally oblivious of the fate that awaited him. This action would cost him **his life** (v. 23), for **a dart** would **strike through his liver**. The terrible fate of the wicked is similarly described in Job 20:24–25. In his ignorance, he **hasteth to the snare** (see discussions on 1:17–18; 5:22). Possibly the husband of the adulteress would bring the young man to his death, or perhaps he would die as a consequence of a life of debauchery, but this young man was on a path that leads to death, as are all who follow his ways.

7:24–27. This stark tragedy warranted another plea for the salvation of Israel's young and the young of all peoples and all times. **Let not thine heart decline to her ways** (v. 25) was the cry of our wisdom teacher. **Her paths** will take all who enter them astray (see 1:15). **She hath cast down many wounded** (v. 26; see 9:18; Isa. 5:14). Her embrace is certain to put a young man on **the way to hell** (v. 27; see discussions on 2:18; 5:5; see also 14:12; 16:25; Matt. 7:13; 1 Cor. 6:9–10). Wisdom is ever in the battle for the souls of men. The battle is about the tragedy of wasted lives and eternal damnation in the everlasting fires of hell. Hence, wisdom observes what is happening in the streets to our young men and women and passionately cries out with instruction, seeking to rescue those who are in peril and put them on the path that leads to life.

D. Appeals Addressed to Youth (chaps. 8–9)

1. Wisdom's Appeal (chap. 8)

8:1–5. Wisdom is here again personified (see discussion on 1:20) as she addresses mankind in preparation for the final plea from both wisdom and folly in chapter 9. Although the precise reasons for wisdom being personified as a female in Proverbs will probably never be totally understood, it is indeed a poignant reminder of the valuable place of women in the fulfillment of the program God laid out for humans in Genesis and beyond. The feminine is presented in all of her beauty and holiness, crying out for the souls of God's post-Edenic and fallen creation. In contrast to the adulteress, wisdom does not come under cover of darkness or with a seductive voice. She stands in the higher parts of the city and proclaims truth wherever the masses are to be found. She is not willing to allow any to perish and aggressively seeks to rescue all within the reach of her voice (see 2 Peter 3:9). She cries out to all; the rescue of even the **simple** (v. 5) and the **fools** is a burden she gladly sustains.

8:6–11. The words of wisdom are focused on **excellent things … right things** (v. 6), and **wickedness is an abomination to** her **lips** (v. 7; see 3:32; 12:22). Wisdom is consumed with a passion for personal holiness and pledges before God and men that **nothing froward or perverse** (v. 8) shall issue from her mouth (see 2:15; Phil. 2:15). She conducts herself in a manner that provides a stark contrast to that of the evil woman, whose destructive words and actions are thoroughly discussed in chapter 7. In the providence of God, there exists a community of men who **understandeth** (v. 9). The wiser a person is, the more he appreciates words of wisdom, and for those **that find knowledge**, especially the knowledge of God (see discussion on 2:5), these words are of greater value than **gold** (v. 10) and **rubies** (v. 11; see 8:19; 2:4; 3:14 and discussion).

8:12–21. **Wisdom dwell[s] with prudence** (v. 12; see Job 28:20). "Prudence" signifies a unique **knowledge** that leads to **witty inventions** (see 1:4 and discussion). Wisdom is an invaluable ally and empowers a man to respond to the challenges of life with well-thought-out plans that will assure him a place of prominence in the affairs of the city. Wisdom is eager to offer herself as ally to all who would pursue the glory of God. She reminds all who seek her services that **The fear of the Lord is to hate evil** (v. 13; see 1:7; 3:7 and discussions; see also 9:10; 16:6). Additionally, wisdom will serve only those who put away from themselves **pride, and arrogancy**, which the Lord hates, and forsake **the evil way, and the froward mouth** (see 16:18; 1 Sam. 2:3;

Isa. 13:11; see also Ps. 10:2 – 11). To all who will for-sake that which wisdom hates, she pledges **Counsel ... sound wisdom ... understanding ... strength** (v. 14; on "Counsel," see 1:25; 19:20; on "strength," see Eccl. 9:16). These attributes characterize the Lord (see 2:6 – 7; Job 12:13, 16; Isa. 40:13 – 14; Rom. 16:27) and the Spirit of the Lord (see Isa. 11:2). Through wisdom, **kings reign** (v. 15; see 29:4). Solomon prayed for wisdom to govern Israel (see 1 Kings 3:9; 2 Chron. 1:10). She **love[s]** (v. 17) and pours out her benefits on (see 4:6 and discussion; see also John 14:21) **those that seek** her, whom, she declares, **early shall find me** (v. 17; see 2:4 – 5; Isa. 55:6; James 1:5). An incentive for such "early" seeking is found in the fact that enduring **Riches and honour are with** her (v. 18; see 3:16; 22:4). She focuses our attention on her **fruit** (v. 19); she is called "a tree of life" in 3:18 (see discussion there). Again she focuses on **fine gold ... choice silver** (see 3:14; 8:10; Job 28:15). Wisdom leads in **the way of righteousness ... and the paths of judgment** (v. 20), and to all who heed her direc-tion, she promises, **I will fill their treasures** (v. 21; see discussion on 3:10; see also 24:4).

8:22 – 31. Wisdom welcomes those who would follow her ways into the sanctuary to participate in worshiping our God by reflecting on the words of a hymn describing wisdom's role in creation. Wis-dom is again personified, as in 1:20 – 33; 3:15 – 18; 9:1 – 12. These verses provide part of the back-ground for the New Testament portrayal of Christ as the Divine Word (John 1:1 – 3) and as the Wis-dom of God (1 Cor. 1:24, 30; Col. 2:3). Here wisdom is an attribute of God that was involved with Him in creation. The God of creation **possessed** (v. 22) wisdom when He commenced His great works re-corded in Genesis 1. The Hebrew for the verb "pos-sessed" is also used in Genesis 4:1; 14:19, 22. Wisdom here tells part of her story; she is **from everlasting** (v. 23). She existed before **ever the earth was.** Wis-dom existed before God began to create the world (see Christ's statement in John 17:5). Wisdom **was brought forth** (v. 24). Elsewhere it is stated that the sea "brake forth" (Job 38:8 – 9), and the hills and mountains "were brought forth" (Ps. 90:2). She was

"brought forth" before the creation of the **fountains abounding with water** (see Ps. 104:10) and before the **mountains** (v. 25) stood with grandeur in their appointed place. Wisdom was there when God **pre-pared the heavens** (v. 27), that is, **set a compass upon the face of the depth** and **strengthened the fountains of the deep** (v. 28), Earth's springs and streams (see discussion on 3:20; see Gen. 7:11). She was there when God gave **the sea his decree** (v. 29) and, by the word of His mouth, established the sea's boundaries and **appointed the foundations of the earth** (see discussion on 3:19; see Gen. 1:9; Job 38:10 – 11; Ps. 104:9). **Then** she **was by him** and was **... his delight** (v. 30). Wisdom was **as one brought up with him,** or "as a master workman." A workman was sometimes called a wise man (see, e.g., Bezaleel, who designed and built the tabernacle; Exod. 31:3). Here the term stresses the skill demonstrated in cre-ation. Verse 22 points to the story of wisdom, and this marvelous hymn celebrates her incomparable privilege and history. It is significant that the journey now leads to wisdom's celebratory announcement that such participation led her to **rejoicing always before him** and **in the habitable part of his earth** (vv. 30 – 31). Can the experience of joy be any less strong considering the privilege of companioning with her and ultimately with Christ, whom God has made to be wisdom and redemption (1 Cor. 1:30)? Consider also that as she was by the Creator and wit-nessed the creation of Adam and Eve, her **delights were with the sons of men** (v. 31; see v. 4). Man, made in the image of God, represented the climax of creation (see Gen. 1:26 – 28), and Wisdom delighted in witnessing God's work and God's word as He pro-nounced humanity good and commissioned them to fulfill His purposes.

8:32 – 36. It seems an understatement to say **blessed** (v. 32) are those who **hearken** to the voice of wisdom and **keep** her **ways.** The blessings associ-ated with gaining wisdom are also given in 3:13 – 18 (see also Pss. 119:1 – 2; 128:1). Surely the benefits of cleaving to wisdom will awaken the desire to be **watching daily at** wisdom's **gates** (v. 34). Contrast the warning not to go near the door of the adulteress's house (5:8). Such diligent watchfulness brings great reward, for all who are so single-minded **findeth life, and ... obtain favour of the** Lord (v. 35; see 3:4; 12:2; 18:22). Wisdom has recounted her story and her joy as a witness to the Lord's mighty works. Consider carefully the joy that can be realized when one, like wisdom, journeys with the Lord as a witness to all the mighty works of God in this generation. Who could possibly turn away from wisdom's gracious invitation? Some will, and for them, wisdom has a parting lament: **All they that hate me love death** (v. 36; see 1:28–33; 5:12, 23; 7:27 and discussions). Sin makes no sense; it is nonsense. Wisdom, the companion of God from eternity, speaks a message of life and offers blessing to all who will receive it, yet so often men choose another way and wend their way to death and destruction.

2. Invitations of Wisdom and Folly (chap. 9)

9:1–2. Chapter 7 outlined the house of the harlot, perfumed and arranged for the seduction of the young simple ones. In contrast, wisdom also **hath builded her house** (v. 1). Both wisdom and folly have a house to which mankind is invited (see v. 14; 7:8; 8:34). Wisdom's house has **seven pillars**, perhaps referring to seven major aspects of wisdom. Wisdom has prepared a banquet that contrasts with the perfumed bed the adulteress prepared in 7:17 and has **mingled her wine** (v. 2) with spices, to make it tastier (see Song 8:2).

9:3–6. Wisdom's banquet is not meant to be a private party for a few elite. Wisdom sends her maidens, and **she crieth upon the highest places of the city** (v. 3). Her invitation is to the **simple** (v. 4) and to those who **wanteth understanding.** The same invitation is given by folly in 9:16. Folly's invitation is also to the "simple" and those who "wanteth understanding" (see 9:16; 7:7). As in 9:2, wisdom's gifts to mankind are described symbolically as a great banquet (see Isa. 55:1–2; John 6:27, 35). The banquet serves as the backdrop, while wisdom, as the evangelist-teacher, proclaims her message: **Forsake the foolish** (see 1:22), **and live** (v. 6; see 9:11; 8:35; see also discussion on 3:2).

9:7–9. Wisdom advises discernment in the proclamation of her message. The scorner is not a worthy recipient of wisdom's pearls, and **He that reproveth a scorner getteth to himself shame** (v. 7; see 1:22 and discussion; see 1:30). The scorner is incorrigible, like the dogs and the swine before whom Jesus refused to cast His pearls (Matt. 7:6). In discerning who the scorner is, wisdom's guidance is greatly needed. To attempt proclamation in the scorner's presence is not advisable, **lest he hate thee** (v. 8; see 15:12, 32). The wise will focus on the **rebuke** of the **wise man, and he will love thee** (see 10:8; 17:10). The wise man not only loves wisdom and all who teach it, but **he will be yet wiser** (see 18:15; 21:11) **... he will increase in learning** (v. 9). Such a person brings delight to the wisdom teacher and is a testament to the fulfillment of God's purpose in this world.

9:10–12. Here wisdom summarizes the heart of the message she proclaimed in chapters 1–9. **The fear of the** Lord **is the beginning of wisdom: and the knowledge of the holy** results in **understanding** (v. 10; see discussion on 2:5). Through the practice of these principles, **the years of thy life shall be increased** (v. 11; see discussion on 3:2; see also 3:16; 10:27; 14:27; 19:23) and **thou shalt be wise for thyself** (v. 12). The wise person reaps the benefits of wisdom. Some of wisdom's rewards are listed in 3:16–18; 4:22; 8:35; 14:14. Wisdom is ever alert to the possibility that one might depart from her counsel and feels the need to issue warnings because if for any reason a man **scornest** her counsel (see 9:7; discussion on 1:22), he **shalt bear** tragic consequences (see 1:26; 19:29). Huge benefits accrue to the account of those who heed wisdom's teachings, and huge consequences are borne by those who reject her advances and instruction.

9:13–18. Wisdom separates herself from the scorner and the foolish woman and counsels all who would companion with her to do the same. **A foolish woman is clamorous** (v. 13). "Clamorous" links the "foolish woman" with the adulteress and the **simple**, who **knoweth nothing** and lack good judgment, prudence, and the fear of the Lord (see 1:3–4, 22, 29; 5:6). Companioning with her cannot possibly result in good. Such a woman **sitteth at the door of her house** (v. 14) so as **To call passengers** (v. 15). Her invitation is identical to wisdom's (v. 4; see discussion on 1:21), but the foolish woman has a message infused with thievery. She speaks of **Stolen waters ... and bread eaten in secret** (v. 17). The banquet prepared by folly seems poorer than the wine and meat provided by wisdom (9:2), and it is illicitly taken. The "meal" she offers is about stolen pleasures, exemplified by the illicit sex offered by the adulteress (see 7:18 and discussion; 5:15–16). The food may seem **sweet** (Job 20:12–14), but **the dead are there; and ... her guests are in the depths of hell** (v. 18; similar to 2:18; 5:5; 7:27). How different the outcomes as men listen to the voices of the women in their lives. The words of a woman of wisdom brings knowledge and long life to her listeners, while the words of a woman of folly leads the receptive heart straight into the fires of hell.

III. The Main Collection of Solomon's Proverbs (10:1–22:16)

This section begins the second division of the book of Proverbs, consisting of a collection of individual proverbs that stand alone and are not connected to any larger context. This is a gathering of the Solomon's shorter proverbs as opposed to his discourse on wisdom in the first nine chapters.

10:1. These are **The proverbs of Solomon,** and this collection of individual proverbs extends through 22:16. The numerical values of the consonants in the Hebrew word for "Solomon" total 375—the exact number of verses in 10:1–22:16; 375 of Solomon's proverbs were selected from a much larger number (see 1 Kings 4:32). Here the young man is described as the **wise son** (see 10:5; 15:20; 17:21, 25; 29:3, 15). In later collections, he is described as "righteous" (23:24–25) and as one "who keepeth the law" (28:7).

10:2–7. Here the earthly lots of the wicked and the righteous are compared. The **Treasures of wickedness profit nothing** (v. 2), for the ill-gotten gain of the wicked is fleeting (21:6) since they incur God's judgment (see 1:19; 10:16; Ezek. 7:19). In contrast,

the **righteousness** of those who walk with wisdom pays large dividends and **delivereth from death** (see 2:16–18; 3:2; 13:21). **The LORD will not suffer the soul of the righteous to famish** (v. 3). He will not allow the righteous to go hungry (see 13:25; 28:25; Pss. 34:9–10; 37:19, 25). The Lord **casteth away the substance of the wicked.** He does not give the wicked their desires (see Num. 11:34; Ps. 112:10). **The hand of the diligent maketh rich** (v. 4). Many proverbs praise diligence and the profit it brings and condemn laziness as a cause of hunger and poverty (see 6:6–11 and discussions; 12:11, 24, 27; 13:4; 14:23; 18:9; 27:23–27; 28:19). The son who **sleepeth in harvest** (v. 5) is always condemned. Sleeping when there is work to be done is condemned also in 6:9–11; 19:15; 20:13. The slumbering son **causeth shame** (see 17:2; 19:26; 28:7; 29:15). God's gifts and favors (see 3:13–18; 28:20; Gen. 49:26; Deut. 33:16) **are upon the head of the just** (v. 6), while **violence covereth the mouth of the wicked,** for the trouble caused by their lips will eventually ruin them (see Ps. 140:9; Hab. 2:17; but see Prov. 2:11).

10:8–10. Three proverbs are now given that contrast the way of the wise with the way of the fool. **The wise ... receive commandments** (v. 8; see 9:8–9) and are established, while the **prating fool,** or person who babbles on without wisdom (see v. 10; 10:14, 18–19), will fall. The wise **walketh surely** (v. 9), or confidently (see 2:7; 3:23; 13:6; Ps. 23:4; Isa. 33:15–16), while **he that perverteth his ways shall be known,** or exposed (see 26:26; Luke 8:17; 1 Tim. 5:24–25; 2 Tim. 3:9). The fool **winketh with the eye** (v. 10) and will bring sorrow upon himself and all who must deal with him.

10:11–14. The contrast here is between the mouth of the wicked and the mouth of the righteous. **The mouth of a righteous man is a well of life** (v. 11), or a source of life-giving wisdom (see 13:14; 14:27; 16:22; see also Ps. 37:30). **Violence covereth the mouth of the wicked,** and their words **stirreth up strifes** (v. 12; see discussion on 6:14). The righteous **covereth all sins.** They promote forgiveness (see 17:9) and stir up **love,** which provides a covering for sins. This line is quoted in James 5:20 and

1 Peter 4:8. In contrast, the sins of the wicked will not be covered but will be punished with **a rod ... for the back** (v. 13; see 14:3; 19:29). The wise **lay up knowledge** (v. 14) rather than babbling folly, so the wise prosper. The foolish man, who is quick with his mouth, brings only ruin upon himself (see 10:8, 10; 13:3).

10:15–22. These verses present Solomon's observations on wealth and poverty. The rich man finds that **wealth is his strong city** (v. 15), and his wealth brings him friends (14:20; 19:4) and power (18:23; 22:7). Ultimate security, however, is found only in God (Ps. 52:7). **The destruction of the poor is their poverty,** for the poor have no influence (18:23), no friends (19:4, 7), and no security. **The labour of the righteous tendeth to life** (v. 16). Not wealth (v. 15), but righteousness, assures life (see discussion on 3:2; see also 3:16; 4:22). In contrast, **the fruit of the wicked** is **sin** (v. 16). The righteous, on the other hand, hear instruction and stay **in the way of life** (v. 17; see discussion on 6:23). Those who have Christ's righteousness imputed to them keep their ears attuned to the instruction of wisdom and continue to experience the abundant life God desires for them. In contrast, **he that refuseth reproof** (see 5:12; 15:10) is sure to inherit the devastating consequences of his error. The words of the righteous are not filled with lies but are like **choice silver** (v. 20). What the righteous say has great value (see 3:14; 8:10; 25:11) and is not to be compared with the lies flowing from **the heart of the wicked,** whose thoughts and schemes (see 6:14, 18) are self-serving and lead ultimately to death. The words of the righteous, however, set a banquet in the presence of all who will hear and **feed many** (v. 21; see 10:11 and discussion). This may not be said of fools, for they **die for want of wisdom** (see 5:23 and discussion; see also 7:7; 9:16). The righteous, who hear the instruction of wisdom and practice its precepts, know that **The blessing of the Lord, it maketh rich** (v. 22). Wealth is a gift from God, not a product of human attainment (see discussions on 10:6; 3:10; see also 8:21; Gen. 24:35; 26:12). The Lord **addeth no sorrow with** the gifts He gives.

10:23–32. It is as sport to a fool to do mischief (v. 23; see 2:14; 15:21; 26:19), while the **man of understanding** cleaves to wisdom. The calamity and distress that the fool dreads shall surely be his inheritance, while **the desire of the righteous shall be granted** (v. 24; see Pss. 37:4; 145:19; Matt. 5:6; 1 John 5:14–15). This outcome is inevitable because we have a God who assures that justice will always be done. The wise man always builds his house on a rock, and the foolish man always builds his on the sand (Matt. 7:24–27). Just as **the whirlwind** (v. 25) roars and is no more, **so is the wicked no more** (see Ps. 37:10; Isa. 28:18). In contrast to the quickly disappearing wicked, **the righteous** are built on a solid **foundation.** They are unshakable, unmovable (see 3:25 and discussion; see also 12:3, 7; 14:11; Ps. 15:5; 1 Cor. 15:58). Like **vinegar** on **the teeth ... is the sluggard to them that send him** (v. 26). As a messenger, the sluggard is a constant source of vexation for those who send him on a mission. He knows nothing of the fear of the Lord that **prolongeth days** (v. 27), and his **years ... shall be shortened** (see Job 22:16; Pss. 37:36; 55:23). The expectations of the sluggard **shall perish** (v. 28; see 11:7, 23), but the **hope of the righteous** will result in **gladness.** The sluggard lacks the discipline to bring his hopes to fulfillment, but the righteous stay at it until the dream becomes reality. **The way of the Lord** (v. 29) and commitment to its practice is a source of strength for the righteous. **Destruction** is the gift God gives **to the workers of iniquity** since they refuse God's way (see 21:15; 2 Cor. 2:15–16; 2 Peter 2:21). In contrast, **The righteous shall never be removed** (v. 30), or shaken from their security (see 2:21 and discussion; 10:25; 12:3; Ps. 125:1). The righteous will inherit with Jesus Christ the privilege of ruling on earth with their Lord, but the wicked are destined for hell and will **not inhabit the earth** or dwell in the Promised Land (see discussion on 2:22).

11:1–9. These proverbs address the world of commerce and the relationship that wisdom counsels between neighbors. The **abomination** (v. 1) attached to **A false balance** (see also 16:11; 20:10, 23) is also found in the Law (see Lev. 19:35 and discussion) and the Prophets (Amos 8:5; Mic. 6:11). Silver was weighed on scales balanced with a stone weight, which could be labeled dishonestly. Commerce flourished during Solomon's prosperous reign, and prosperity often brings out the worst in people. Wisdom calls for integrity in the midst of affluence. **When pride cometh, then cometh shame** (v. 2). For those who heed wisdom; even in the midst of plenty, **integrity ... shall guide them** (v. 3; see the actions of Joseph in Gen. 39:6–12). The lot of the transgressor is different, and their **perverseness ... shall destroy them**. The transgressor motivated by pride and greed has an appointment with the **day of wrath** (v. 4; see Isa. 10:3; Zeph. 1:18). How different the lot of the righteous, who will find that their **righteousness delivereth from death** (see 2:16–18; 3:2; 10:2; 13:21). Righteousness is the possession of **the perfect** (v. 5) and **shall direct his way** and enable him to reach his goals (see discussion on 3:6; see also v. 3; 10:9). His **righteousness ... shall deliver** (v. 6) him, while the wicked man will be **taken** in his naughtiness (see the rescue of Mordecai and the execution of Haman, Est. 5:14; 7:10). The wicked **destroyeth his neighbour** (v. 9) by spreading slander (see 10:18), but the just are delivered **through knowledge**, perhaps the knowledge of the schemes and distortions of the godless (see John 2:25).

11:10–14. Here the effect of the righteous and the wicked on their communities is discussed. Through God's blessing and **the blessing of the upright** (v. 11), the city prospers. Their good influence and desire for justice as well as their prosperity (v. 10) bring honor to the city. The city is **overthrown by the mouth of the wicked** (v. 11). Their deceit, dishonesty, and sowing of discord (see 11:9; 6:12–14) bring the city to ruin. The wicked bring to their community a style of relating that is characterized with the words **despiseth his neighbour** (v. 12). They express their contempt for others openly (see 10:18; 14:21). The wise man **holdeth his peace**. He keeps silent and promotes peace in his community (see 10:19). The wicked love to spread rumors, while the man with a faithful spirit conceals matters that will only produce division and unrest among neighbors. A community

requires **counsellors** (v. 14) who are careful with their words and protect others from hearing unnecessary information (see the close parallels in 15:22; 20:18; 24:6) and who promote safety and harmony in the community. Their absence exposes the community to grave danger (see 2 Sam. 16:23; Isa. 1:26).

11:15–21. Once again (as in 6:1–5), the focus here is on avoiding co-signing for those whose integrity is questionable. The wise man will escape the anxiety fully developed in 6:1–5 if he simply makes it a practice to avoid co-signing for the debts of another; particularly one who is not well known to him (see discussion on 6:1). Assuming that "a good name is rather to be chosen than great riches" (22:1), the observation is made that a woman who is **A gracious woman** (v. 16) will be accorded more respect than wealthy men who are "strong" (i.e., "ruthless"; see 31:28, 30). A man who exhibits abundant wisdom in his dealings with others **doeth good to his own soul** (v. 17), or benefits himself (see Matt. 5:7). In like manner, the man who is cruel to others **troubleth his own flesh**, or does himself harm. Both men reap what they sow (see Gen. 34:25–30; 49:7). The works of the wicked do not endure, for they **worketh a deceitful work**. The wicked receive passing rewards for wrongdoing because the benefits do not last (see discussions on 10:2, 16; see also Hag. 1:6). In contrast, the benefits achieved by the righteous **shall be a sure reward** (see 10:24; Gal. 6:8–9; James 3:18). Everything the righteous undertake **tendeth to life** (v. 19; see 10:16; 12:28; 19:23). What the righteous gain from their righteous labor lasts for eternity. In contrast, the activities of the wicked are motivated by selfishness and involve them in activities that lead to **death** (see 5:23; 21:16; Rom. 6:23; James 1:15). The wicked are directed by a **froward heart** (v. 20), which is an **abomination** to the Lord (see 3:32 and discussion; 16:5). The **upright** are those whose bondage to Adam's sin has been broken. They are persons of faith who walk in the ways of righteousness and cleave to wisdom's directives. Their commitments and deeds are the opposite of those of the wicked, who, though they join together to overthrow righteousness, **shall not be unpunished** (v. 21; see 6:29).

The righteous and their **seed ... shall be delivered** (see Ps. 118:5). Nothing can separate this righteous seed from the protection of God's providence, which is their possession in all the fiery furnaces and lions' dens the world can prepare for their destruction.

11:22–31. How incongruous the sights illustrated in verse 22. **A jewel of gold** (v. 22), commonly worn by women on their noses (see Gen. 24:47; Ezek. 16:12), is seen in the nose of a pig. This is as bizarre as beholding a beautiful women who is **without discretion**. David praised Abigail for her display of discernment (1 Sam. 25:33), and she epitomizes the beauty that is woman. Women lacking the discretion that wisdom bestows as a gift are vessels destined to experience the **wrath** (v. 23) and just judgment of God (see 11:4; Isa. 10:3; Zeph. 1:18; Rom. 2:8–9). Generosity is the path to blessing and further prosperity (see 3:9–10 and discussions; Eccl. 11:1–2 and discussions; Ps. 112:9; 2 Cor. 9:6–9). In contrast, the stingy person does not make any friends and, in the long run, will experience **poverty** (v. 24; see 21:13). **The liberal soul shall be made fat** (v. 25). A generous person will experience prosperity, for "he which soweth bountifully shall reap also bountifully" (2 Cor. 9:6; see Luke 6:38). **He that watereth shall be watered** (see Rom. 15:32). **He that withholdeth corn** (i.e., grain; v. 26), probably in times of scarcity to raise the price, will be cursed by his neighbors. In contrast, **blessing shall be upon the head** of the person who feels empathy for his neighbors in need and **selleth** his corn to them. Like Joseph during the famine in Egypt (Gen. 41:53–57), the men **that diligently seeketh good procureth favour** (v. 27). Such a man reaps what he sows, like the man in verse 25 (see Matt. 7:12). **He that seeketh mischief, it shall come unto him** (v. 27), for his wicked schemes will backfire (see 11:8 and discussion; 1:18). **He that trusteth in his riches** (v. 28), usually said of the wicked (see Pss. 49:6; 62:10; but see Mark 10:25; 1 Tim. 6:17), will fall. The man who trusts in righteousness **shall flourish as a branch** and is like a healthy tree sprouting vegetation (see Ps. 1:3). The man **that troubleth his own house shall inherit the wind** (v. 29; see 15:27 and discussion). The inheritance of Levi

and Simeon was affected because of their cruelty to Shechem (Gen. 34:25–30; 49:7). Though the wicked man may prosper for a season, in the long run, he will become **servant to the wise of heart** (see 14:19; see 17:2). God equips the righteous for a life of blessing. It is important for the righteous to remember that God delights in **The fruit of the righteous** (v. 30). What a wise man produces as fruit is for the glory of God (8:18–19), who has grafted him into the **tree of life** (see discussion on 3:18). The righteous man's attempt to **winneth souls** leads many out of darkness into the experience of abundant and eternal life. He that is wise turns people to wisdom and righteousness (see Dan. 12:3; 1 Cor. 9:19–22; James 5:20). The righteous are always under the watchful eye of their God and will be disciplined by their heavenly Father when they sin. **The righteous shall be recompensed in the earth** (v. 31). Even Moses and David were punished for their sins (see Num. 20:11–12; 2 Sam. 12:10). God will discipline every son whom he receives (Heb. 12:6). **Much more the wicked and the sinner** will be recompensed for the evil they do in the sight of God, and they will have no mediator to appease God's wrath against them (see 1:18, 31 and discussions; Pss. 11:6; 73:18–19; 1 Peter 4:17).

12:1–3. The one who **hateth reproof is brutish** (v. 1) and is like a wild animal that is of no value in the world of men. He should be sought out and put to death. The person who hates correction is foolish (see 1:22; 5:12 and discussion). The man who **loveth instruction loveth knowledge** (see 1:7; 10:17; see also 6:23 and discussion). Such a person will **obtaineth favour** (v. 2) with God, while **a man of wicked devices will he condemn** (see 3:4; 8:35; Job 5:12–13; 1 Cor. 3:19). **Man shall not be established by wickedness** (v. 3; see 11:5). The evil may appear to succeed at times, but their success will be short-lived. In contrast, **the root of the righteous shall not be moved** (see 2:21; discussions on 10:25, 30; 12:12). The righteous are committed to obeying God's directives, and they will rest in the protection of His sovereignty.

12:4–11. A virtuous woman is a crown to her husband (v. 4). Here Solomon was referencing someone like Ruth (Ruth 3:11) and fully described this woman of virtue in 31:10–31. She brings her husband honor and joy (see 4:9 and discussion). The wife who brings shame upon her husband is like **rottenness** (see Hab. 3:16) **in his bones** (see discussion on 3:8). **The counsels of the wicked are deceit** (v. 5), and they **lie in wait for blood** (v. 6; see discussion on 1:11; see also 1:16). **The mouth of the upright shall deliver them,** and they will be **commended** (v. 8; see 3:4 and discussion; 1:3–4, 6, 9; Hab. 3:16. 1). However, **he that is of a perverse heart shall be despised** (see Deut. 32:5; Titus 3:11).

In Solomon's day, even people of moderate means had servants (see Judg. 6:15, 27). **He that is despised, and hath** one **servant, is better than** (v. 9) the man who has so many servants he cannot care for all of them yet thinks he **honoureth himself** by having so many servants (see 13:7). This man brings himself to such poverty that he cannot even afford to buy **bread** for himself. Absence of wisdom and dominance of pride have directed his dealings, and he will pay a high price for his lack of wisdom. The wise **regardeth the life of his beast** (v. 10; see 27:23; Deut. 25:4; see also chart, *KJV Study Bible*, p. 256). **The tender mercies of the wicked are cruel** to both man and beast. The wicked **followeth vain persons** (v. 11). The Hebrew reads, "follows vain [worthless] things." Here the honest pursuits of the wise, who faithfully **tilleth his land**, are contrasted with the dishonest schemes of the fool.

12:12–23. The wicked desireth the net of evil men (v. 12). The wicked will seek to trap the righteous; the wicked desire ill-gotten gain (see 1:13 and discussion; 21:10). In contrast to the fruitlessness of the wicked, **the root of the righteous yieldeth fruit** (see 12:3, 7; 11:30; 10:25 and discussion; Ps. 1:3). The wicked man is **snared by the transgression of his lips** (v. 13; see 1:18 and discussion; 29:6), while **the just shall come out of trouble** (see 11:8–9 and discussions; 21:23; 2 Peter 2:9). The man who speaks with wisdom will reap a harvest from his words, just as a farmer enjoys the crops he planted (see 1:31 and discussion; Job 34:11). **The way of a fool is right** (v. 15) in his twisted way of thinking, but it

ends in death (see 1:25, 30; 14:12; 16:25). The fool practices foolishness in the presence of all, while the man of wisdom seeks to **coMereth shame** (v. 16). The companion of wisdom possesses self-control, which keeps him from doing shameful things (see 29:11; 2 Sam. 16:11–12). The **false witness** (v. 17) lives a life that is best described by the word **deceit** (see discussion on 6:19). He **speaketh like the piercings of a sword** (v. 18). The words of the wicked hurt and injure like a sword piercing the body (see Ps. 106:33; discussion on Ps. 5:9). In contrast, **the tongue of the wise is health**. The wise promote healing by speaking soothing, comforting words (see 4:22; 15:4). Deceit confuses, separates friends, and angers God, but it **is but for a moment** (v. 19), for the lies will be refuted and the liar punished (see 19:9; Ps. 52:4–5). **Deceit is in the heart** (v. 20; see 6:14 and discussion; see also 1:31; 24:2; Gen. 6:5). The only remedy for deceit is a remedy that changes the heart of a man. Only when the peace of God, in the person of the Prince of Peace, takes up residence in men through regeneration are they in a position to overcome deceit, become **counsellors of peace**, and experience the result of peace, which **is joy**. "Blessed are the peacemakers" (Matt. 5:9). **No evil** (v. 21) will overtake those in whom Christ dwells, for the righteous are under the protection of the Lord of Peace (see 1:33 and discussion; 2:8; Pss. 91:10–12; 121:7). The sovereign God will see to it that the lives of the wicked are **filled with mischief** (see 1:31 and discussion; 11:5, 8; 22:8; Job 4:8). Much of what they find to be troubling is the result of God's attempt to turn them toward Him and salvation. Although the **Lying lips** (v. 22) of the wicked are an **abomination to the Lord**, He goads and troubles the wicked for the purpose of turning their hearts toward Him (see discussion on 3:32; see the Lord's goading of Saul in Acts 9). God seeks to turn men to righteousness and delights in **they that deal truly** (see 16:13). The Lord delights in those who **concealeth knowledge** (v. 23). Such a person stores up knowledge (see 10:14) and loves deeply enough to practice controlled silence when others experience failure. In contrast, the fool **proclaimeth foolishness** (see v. 16; 13:16; 15:2;

29:11). The fool loves to uncover the faults and failures of others. Rumor peddling is food for the soul of the fool.

12:24 – 28. Wisdom counsels devotion to self control and diligence. **The hand of the diligent shall bear rule** (v. 24; see 17:2). To rule well requires the ability to put others before self — the capacity for self-discipline and self-denial. **The slothful** possess little or no capacity for self-denial in the service of others. They will certainly wind up paying **tribute** to others and may even be subjected to forced labor (see Judg. 1:28; discussion on 2 Sam. 20:24).

Heaviness in the heart (v. 25) is unavoidable for all who live in this broken world. Anxiety, depression, and other negative feelings are unavoidable through this earthly journey (see Ps. 94:19). However, **a good word maketh it glad** (see 15:23). The word of God's grace and the words of His marvelous book, the Bible, secure the pilgrim, and words of encouragement from others banish negative emotions from the heart and fill one with joy. Cleaving to these words and to the Hoy Spirit who empowers them is an important discipline for the righteous because the wicked constantly lay in wait to **seduceth them** (v. 26). We are in a war, and Satan and his evil followers constantly attempt to lead the unwary down the wrong path (see 5:23; 14:22).

Satan has fostered in the evil man a disdain for the principle of stewardship. He will go hunting, kill his prey, and **roasteth not that which he took in hunting** (v. 27). This kind of waste characterizes his life, and he is too lazy to lift the food from the dish to his mouth (19:24). The diligent man thinks much of the stewardship of his life and all of his resources. He wastes nothing, for **the substance of a diligent man is precious** to him. **The way** or path **of righteousness** (v. 28) does not lead to death. The way of the righteous, who live under the discipline of a stewardship that honors God, **is life** (see 3:2; 11:4). **There is no death** for them since death has been emptied of its power in their lives (see the identification of wisdom with the "tree of life," 3:18 and discussion; see 14:32). R. B. Y. Scott translates verse 28, "on the road of righteousness there is life and the treading of its path (reading *Netibato* for Mount *Netigah*) is deathlessness" (Scott, *Proverbs*, p. 91).

13:1 – 7. This section presents the kind of teaching that a father would give to his son, or a teacher to his pupil. **A wise son heareth his father's instruction** (v. 1; see 1:8; 4:1). The **scorner heareth not rebuke** (see 1:22; 9:7 – 8 and discussions). The wise man uses his mouth in a manner that brings life to all who hear his words, while **the soul of the transgressors shall eat violence** (v. 2; see 4:17 and discussion). The man who **keepeth his mouth keepeth his life** (v. 3). The ability to control the tongue is one of the clearest marks of wisdom, and "Death and life are in the power of the tongue" (18:21; see 10:19; 21:23; James 3:2). The man **that openeth wide his lips shall have destruction** (see 12:18 and discussion; see also 10:14; 18:7; 2 Tim. 3:3 – 4). **The sluggard** (v. 4) is never satisfied yet refuses to work (see 21:25 – 26). **The soul of the diligent shall be made fat** because diligence yields a profit (see 6:6; see also discussions on 10:4, 24). The **wicked man is loathsome, and cometh to shame** (v. 5). The contrast between the righteous and the wicked here repeats the thought of 2:21 – 22; 10:9; 11:3, 5 (see discussions there; see also 21:12; Ps. 25:21). At times, the wicked man feigns riches and then poverty to match his diabolical plans. Both pretenses are folly and lead to folly (see 14:8 and discussion; see also 11:24; 12:9).

13:8 – 12. Those who have riches trust in them for their deliverance. They see in their riches **The ransom of a man's life** (v. 8). The rich have the means to pay off robbers or enemies (see 10:15 and discussion; Jer. 41:8). **The poor heareth not rebuke.** Poverty has its advantages. The poor do not need to worry about threats as the rich do, for their poverty makes them unlikely targets. **The light** (v. 9) and **the lamp** are symbols of life (see Job 3:20), and their presence causes the righteous to **rejoiceth**. Joy and prosperity (see discussion on 4:18) await those who walk in the light of the lamp God provides. There is no light for the wicked, for **the lamp of the wicked shall be put out**, and their lives will end (see 20:20; 24:20; Job 18:5; 21:17). Contention follows the man whose heart is wrapped up in **pride** (v. 10; see 11:2

and discussion). Vanity and pride go together, and all the **Wealth** (v. 11) a man gains in his pride and **vanity shall be diminished** (see discussion on 10:2; see also Jer. 17:11). In contrast, wealth gained through diligent labor and thoughtful stewardship **shall increase** (see discussion on 10:4). Life can be frustrating, particularly for the vain. Continuous frustrations of a person's dreams can produce sickness, for **Hope deferred maketh the heart sick** (v. 12; see Gen. 30:1). However, **when the desire cometh, it is a tree of life**, for the realization of dreams revives and strengthens (see discussion on 3:18; see also 10:28; 13:19). The realization of a person's dreams is far more likely to be achieved if the dream is wrapped up in the glory of God and born in the midst of a faithful allegiance to wisdom.

13:13-15. Humanity is divided. There are those who love wisdom and the God who gives it, and there are those who despise God and His gifts. These verses provide a warning on the fate of these despisers of wisdom: **Whoso despiseth the word shall be destroyed** (v. 13; see 1:29-31; see also 5:12 and discussion). In contrast, those who love His wisdom and **feareth the commandment shall be rewarded** with the benefits wisdom gives (see 3:2 and discussion; 3:16-18; 13:21). The law that comes from God **is a fountain of life** (v. 14; see discussion on 10:11). In the precepts given in God's Word, one finds the truth that delivers **from the snares of death** (see discussions on 1:17; 5:22; see also 7:23; 22:5). The **understanding** (v. 15) acquired through embracing the teachings of wisdom **giveth favour** with God and man (see 3:4; 8:35). The one who chooses to ignore or openly rebel against the commandments handed down by God in His Word will find again and again that **the way of transgressors is hard.**

13:16-25. The thoughtful lifestyle of the prudent man is compared with the thoughtless lifestyle of the fool. The folly of the foolish ambassador is open for all to see, and all can behold that he **falleth into mischief** (v. 17), perhaps by misrepresenting those who sent him. The **faithful ambassador is health** since his tactful, honest approach benefits all he serves (see 25:13; 12:18; 15:4). **Poverty and**

shame (v. 18) are the inheritance of those who refuse instruction (see 5:10-12 and discussions). In contrast, **he that regardeth reproof shall be honoured** (see 13:1; 3:16-18; 8:35; 10:17). Those who walk with wisdom will frequently see their **desire accomplished** (v. 19; see 13:12). Those who despise wisdom's teachings and who think it an **abomination ... to depart from evil** will surely be destroyed (see their hatred of correction in 5:12). Man must must make a choice. **He that walketh with wise men shall be wise** (v. 20), while the **companion of fools shall be destroyed** (see 1:10, 18; 2:12; 16:29; 22:24-25). The fool will leave nothing as an inheritance for his children, and what he might have gained ultimately **is laid up for the just** (v. 22). Job teaches that this is often what happens to a wicked man's possessions (Job 27:16-17; see Prov. 28:8). The man who walks with wisdom will lay up **an inheritance** for **his children's children**. The poor show better judgment and concern for stewardship of their land than the rich do. They till every inch of their little farms and maximize productivity. The rich are frequently **destroyed for want of judgment** (v. 23). Mesmerized by their abundance, they squander their land and fail to appreciate how quickly their abundance can turn to poverty. The protection of the family can be assured if parents understand that **He that spareth his rod hateth his son** (v. 24). Parents are encouraged to apply the rod of punishment to drive out folly (22:15) so that the child will not follow a path that leads to destruction (see 19:18; 23:13-14). "The rod and reproof give wisdom" (29:15) and promote a healthy and happy family (29:17). Discipline is rooted in love (see 3:11-12 and discussion). "The rod" is a figure of speech for loving and corrective discipline of any kind.

13:25. Instruction on stewardship—stewardship of instruction, land, and children—begins here. The man who heeds the call and follows wisdom's teachings to practice Godly stewardship over these important elements of life will **eateth to the satisfying of his soul** and know great peace and satisfaction during his journey through life. All who refuse to consider their lives as a gift from God's hand

and carefully steward His gifts to them will never be filled and will always be in want.

14:1. Once again attention is focused on stewardship as illustrated by what the wise woman does with her house. The **wise woman buildeth her house**, and she is a source of strength and an example of diligence for her family (see 31:10–31; see the house built by wisdom in 9:1). The foolish woman tears her house apart with her own **hands.**

14:2. He that **feareth the LORD** walks in **uprightness.** Faith without works is dead; so too the man who professes the fear of God while avoiding the responsibility to walk in His statutes is deluded (see discussion on 1:7).

14:3. The fool speaks, and all can tell that his tongue is held in place by **a rod of pride.** His proud and arrogant words get him into trouble with God and men (see 10:13; 19:29; 26:3). The wise man is preserved by the words of his mouth. He turns away wrath with a soft answer and is swift to hear and slow to speak, especially in situations requiring a wise response.

14:4. Oxen are certainly a challenge since their stalls require consistent cleaning and their mouths consistent feeding. They can do so much to increase a man's productivity that they are worth the trouble, however. Consider all the things in life that require work yet produce blessings through their presence and assistance. Thus, one should not complain about work connected with the attainment of the blessing.

14:5–9. Faithfulness and truthfulness go together. One may never think of himself as faithful if he has lying lips (see discussion on 6:19). Just as faithfulness and lies cannot go together, so **a scorner** (v. 6) and **wisdom** cannot abide in the same space (see 1:22 and discussion). Though the scorner **seeketh wisdom,** he **findeth it not.** The scorner cannot gain wisdom because he refuses to fear the Lord or accept any correction. The fool believes he can find wisdom whenever he wants, but his is the way of deceit, for **the folly of fools is deceit** (v. 8) and they **mock at sin** (v. 9). What a fool believes to be prudent (but is really folly) does not bring success; instead, it leads toward his ruin. Wisdom directs men into the way that brings success, and **among the righteous,** the **favour** of God is experienced (see 11:27).

14:10. Every man **knoweth his own bitterness,** and another man cannot fix the sadness of our hearts with his joy (see 1 Kings 8:38; see the experience of Hannah, 1 Sam. 1:10). Another who is filled with joy cannot fix the heart; he cannot **intermeddle with his joy.** Both sorrow and joy have a personal dimension that cannot be fully shared with another individual (see Matt. 13:44; 1 Peter 1:8).

14:11–14. There is a way which **seemeth right unto a man, but the end thereof are the ways of death** (v. 12; see 5:4, 23; 7:21–27; Matt. 7:13–14). The wicked think they shall prevail, but they **shall be overthrown** (v. 11). **Even in laughter the heart** of the wicked **is sorrowful** (v. 13). One can never fully escape the harsh realities of life in a fallen world (see Ezra 3:11–12). **The backslider** (v. 14), like the wicked man, will not find joy that lasts. Only the man who cleaves to the righteousness God provides will find satisfaction for his soul, in the rest that comes from being in the arms of the sovereign and gracious God (see 1:31; 12:14 and discussions; see also 11:5, 8; 18:20; 22:8; Job 4:8).

14:15–19. The **simple** (v. 15) man is naive and believes everything he is told (see discussion on 1:4). In contrast, **the prudent man looketh well to his going.** He approaches life with caution and discernment (see 4:26 and discussion; 21:29). The **wise man feareth, and departeth from evil** (v. 16) and avoids sin because he fears the consequences of his actions (see discussions on 1:7; 3:7). **The fool rageth** and has a presumptuous confidence that causes him to be careless in his words (see 12:18; 13:3) and actions (see Judg. 9:4).

The fool is too **soon angry** (v. 17), quick-tempered, and filled with **wicked devices** (see 12:2; Job 5:12–13; 1 Cor. 3:19). He is hated for his evil deeds. The prudent man is **crowned with knowledge** (v. 18), or adorned and blessed with knowledge (see discussion on 4:9; see also 14:24; 12:4; Ps. 103:4). Ultimately, **The evil bow before the good** (v. 19) and come to **the gates of the righteous** to beg for some favor (see 1 Sam. 2:36).

14:20–22. The rich hath many friends (v. 20) who vie for his favors. The poor, on the other hand, **is hated even of his own neighbor** (v. 20) and sometimes by his relatives (see 19:7).

Wisdom admonishes one to have **mercy on the poor** (v. 21). Sharing food (22:9), lending money (28:8), and defending their rights (31:9) are ways one can show kindness to the poor. A person honors God with these deeds (14:31; see 17:5) and will lack nothing (28:27; see 21:13; Ps. 41:1). Those who teach otherwise **err** (v. 22) and **devise evil** (see 3:29; 6:14, 18; Mic. 2:1). **Mercy and truth** will be the reward of all who treat the poor with grace and kindness. Those who have mercy on the poor will receive the support and care of faithful friends (see 3:3; 16:6; 20:28); perhaps God's support and care are also implied here.

14:23–28. In all labour there is profit (v. 23; see discussion on 10:4; see also 21:5). Those who spend their time talking about work but never getting around to it will reap only poverty. **The wise** (v. 24) labor much, talk less, and obtain wealth, which adorns them like a **crown** (see 10:22).

The wise practice consistent **fear of the LORD** (v. 26; see 1:7; 3:7 and discussions). In reverent fear, the wise experience **strong confidence** and create **a place of refuge** for their children. This means either that the father's godliness will result in blessings for himself and his children (see 20:7) or that "the fear of the LORD" will be a strong tower where the children also can find refuge (see 18:10; Ps. 71:7; Isa. 33:6). The fear of the Lord is a fountain of life for all who practice it (see discussion on 10:11; see also 13:14).

14:29–35. He that is slow to wrath (v. 29) has, through the work of the wisdom of God within him, attained a measure of control over his inner life. He is a man who understands the way of righteousness and is empowered by faith and the work of the Holy Spirit to live a life of self-control (see 15:18; 16:32; 19:11; James 1:19). Such men are in possession of **a sound heart** (v. 30), which is **the life of the flesh** and brings health to the body (see 3:7–8 for the healthy effects of fearing the Lord and walking in wisdom).

In comparison, the haste of spirit and **envy** found in the life of the fool produces **rottenness of the bones**. Envy leaves physical and emotional scars (see discussion on 3:8; see also 12:4; Ps. 37:7–8). When a man oppresses the poor, he **reproacheth his Maker** (v. 31) because God created both the rich and the poor in His image (see 22:2; Job 31:15; James 3:9). **He that honoureth him hath mercy on the poor.** Practicing generosity honors God and in a sense is giving to God Himself (see discussion on 14:21; 19:17; Matt. 25:40). The wicked think they have a grip on life and are convinced that they will achieve success. In God's time, however, **The wicked is driven away** (v. 32), into an experience of God's wrath and judgment (see 1:26–27 and discussion; 11:5; 24:16). **The righteous hath hope in his death.** His faith in God gives him hope beyond the grave (see discussion on 12:28; see also Pss. 49:14–15; 73:24). Over time, **that which is in the midst of fools is made known** (v. 33). A foolish person's lack of wisdom is unveiled through their words and actions. **Righteousness exalteth a nation** (v. 34; see discussion on 11:11). Israel was promised prosperity and prestige if she obeyed God's laws (see Deut. 28:1–14). In the context of the Wisdom Literature, this basic principle applies to all nations. In contrast, **sin is a reproach to any people**. The Canaanites were driven out because of their terrible sin (see Lev. 18:24–25), and Israel later received the same curse (see Deut. 28:15–68; see 2 Sam. 12:10). In guarding the nation, the king's **wrath is against** (v. 35) those who cause shame, and his favor is directed toward the wise servant (see 16:14; 19:12; Dan. 2:12).

15:1–2. The Holy Spirit empowers a person to achieve a measure of self-control, which makes possible the **soft answer** that **turneth away wrath** (v. 1; see the way Gideon calmed the anger of the men of Ephraim in Judg. 8:1–3; see also Prov. 15:18; Eccl. 10:4). The unbridled emotions of the wicked produce **grievous words** that **stir up anger**. Remember how Nabal's sarcastic response put David in a fighting mood (1 Sam. 25:10–13). Knowledge is a good thing, but when it is combined with a passion for glorifying God, it becomes wisdom in action.

15:3. The eyes of the LORD are in every place. The man of wisdom knows that God is watching his every action. This knowledge serves as a filter through which he presses every thought and behavior. The Lord is ever ready to come to the aid of the righteous man. In Psalm 25:15–17, the psalmist took comfort in this reality (see 5:21; Job 31:4; 34:21; Jer. 16:17).

15:4–5. A wholesome tongue is a tree of life (v. 4; see discussion on 12:18). The garden of Eden was provisioned with the **tree of life** (see discussion on 3:18). Imagine a tree that imparted life to those who partook of its fruit. The tongue of the righteous can impart life to those who are blessed by its fruit. No wonder Paul cautioned the Ephesians to let no corrupting word come from their mouths (Eph. 4:28). **Perverseness therein is a breach in the spirit**. Wicked speech, especially false testimony in court (see 6:19; 22:22) or slander in the community, hurts others and is as far from being life-giving as words can get. The fool has no appreciation for the value of life-giving words, and he **despiseth his father's instruction** (v. 5). The **prudent** listen carefully to instruction and seek to find in it that which enhances their ability to glorify God and fulfills His purposes in their lives.

15:6–7. The blessing of God is upon **the house of the righteous** (v. 6). **Much treasure** is found where the righteous abide (see 8:18, 21; 24:4; Zech. 8:12; see also discussion on 3:10). This treasure is both material and spiritual, with the spiritual possessions of those in the house holding the supreme value. Their words are a part of their treasure and are a great blessing to those who hear them. In contrast, the **revenues** and words **of the wicked** are trouble. The wicked trade in a currency that stirs up trouble for all who traffic with them (see 10:2, 16, 22 and discussions).

15:8–9. The sacrifice of the wicked is an abomination (v. 8). Those whose hearts are not right with God gain nothing by offering sacrifices (see 21:3, 27; Eccl. 5:1; Isa. 1:11–15; Jer. 6:20). "The term abomination is found only in Proverbs and Deuteronomy (Deut. 7:25, 26; 18:12). Abomination (Hebrew, *to'ebah*) denotes something that is abhor-rent or repulsive" (McKane, *Proverbs*, p. 486). **The prayer of the upright** is a delight to the Creator. God delights in hearing from His people. Far too often, God seems distant and disengaged. Nothing could be further from the truth. He loves His children who **followeth after righteousness** (v. 9) and delights in visiting with them (see 3:32; 21:21; 1 Tim. 6:11).

15:10–15. The way (v. 10) is the right path, which leads to the glory of God and the growth of the saint (see 2:13). Correction is not grievous to those who walk on this path. Those who choose the broader path, which leads away from God, hate correction, and all who **hateth reproof shall die** (see 5:12, 23 and discussions). Lest any of the wicked think they will get by with their lack of attention to the glory of God, all are reminded that **Hell and destruction are before the LORD** (v. 11). Not even the grave, the netherworld, is inaccessible to God (see Job 26:6; Ps. 139:8). Therefore, He knows the secrets of man's innermost being, and every person will be called to give an account to Him for all things done in this life (see 1 Sam. 16:7). The **scorner** (v. 12; see discussion on 1:22) avoids the wise and distances himself from all who advise him to pursue the right (see 1:30; 10:8; 13:1; 17:10). The fool **feedeth on foolishness** (v. 14), while **he that is of a merry heart hath a continual feast** (v. 15). Life is as joyful and satisfying as the days of a festival (see v. 13; 14:30; Lev. 23:39–41) for those who pursue the knowledge of and fear of God. They rest in the wisdom that the God who observes all is absolutely sovereign and makes all things beautiful in His time (Eccl. 3:11).

15:16–17. The little that the righteous have is to be preferred to the **great treasure and trouble** (v. 16) that is often the experience of the wicked. The ill-gotten gains of the wicked and their inability to deliver from the trouble that comes with them is also discussed in 10:2. The **stalled ox** (v. 17) refers to a fattened cow, whose meat was something of a luxury and was reserved for special occasions (see 7:14; Matt. 22:4; Luke 15:23). When such a delicacy is served in a home where hatred fills the air, those having a humble meal of herbs in a home saturated with love are enjoying the better meal.

15:18–22. Men who are filled with anger **stirreth up strife** (v. 18; see discussion on 6:14). The person who is **slow to anger** enjoys the ability not only to control his own emotions but also to assist others with controlling theirs. Such a person is able to win the peace in situations in which others with lesser abilities might enflame the situation (see 14:29; 16:32; 19:11; James 1:19). **The slothful man** (v. 19) walks in a way that is characterized **as a hedge of thorns** (see discussion on 6:6). His way is overgrown with thorns because he was too lazy to remove them (see 24:30–31; Hos. 2:6). **The way of the righteous is made plain** (lit., "lifted up") like a smooth path or highway, meaning that the upright are able to make progress and reach their goals (see discussion on 3:6). The child who honors God and his parents by walking in the way of the righteous is a particular cause of joy for his parents (see 10:1 and discussion). Other parents will experience intense pain as they watch their children find **joy in Folly** (v. 21) because they are **destitute of wisdom** (a variation of 10:23). For verse 22, see the close parallels in 11:14; 20:18; 24:6.

15:23–24. The person who companions with Christ finds true **joy** (v. 23) in knowing that he has ministered grace to another with **the answer of his mouth** by his speaking in the right way (see Isa. 50:4). The experience of ministering grace to another through the spoken word causes all who experience it to utter, **a word spoken in due season, how good is it!** (see 24:26). The wise know that **The way of life** (v. 24) has its origins in that which **is above.** Wisdom found in the Word of God and in the Son of God leads upward along the highway (15:19), the straight course (15:21) that leads to life. Those whose affections are set on that which is above **depart from hell beneath** (see discussion on 2:18).

15:25–26. **The LORD will destroy the house of the proud** (v. 25; see 2:22; 14:11; see also 10:25 and discussion). The world is badly broken and evil often seems so strong. The righteous, however, may find great comfort in the knowledge that the omnipotent God is watching the works of all men and will destroy the wicked and bring them into everlasting damnation. The just and loving God will also **establish the border of the widow.** In ancient times, boundary stones marked a person's property. Anyone who moved such a stone was in effect stealing land (see 22:28; Job 24:2; Ps. 68:5; Deut. 19:14 and discussion). The widow may seem powerless, but God watches over her and pledges His strength for her protection. The evil deeds that the wicked perform find their origins in **thoughts ... that are an abomination to the LORD** (v. 26; see 15:8–9). In contrast, **the words of the pure are pleasant words** (see 22:11; Ps. 24:4).

15:27. The balanced pursuit of gain is a good thing, but **He that is greedy of gain troubleth his own house** (see 1:19; 11:29; 28:25). Achan's whole family perished because of his greed at Jericho (Josh. 7:24–26). Greed leads to a disposition that is open to accepting bribes, but **he that hateth gifts shall live.** The use of the term "gifts" is a reference to bribes (see 17:8; 28:16; Deut. 16:19; 1 Sam. 12:3; Eccl. 7:7; 1 Tim. 6:10).

15:28–29. **The righteous** (v. 28) are known not only by their attention to moral actions but also by the fact that they **studieth to answer.** They think before speaking (see 10:32; 1 Peter 3:15). **The mouth of the wicked** is controlled by a mind obsessed with self and **poureth out evil things** (see 15:2; see also 15:7; 12:23). The righteous will make it their practice to stay **far from the wicked** (v. 29), for the Lord is never encountered in their presence (see 1:28 and discussion).

15:30–33. **The light of the eyes rejoiceth the heart** (v. 30). The righteous should always remember that a cheerful attitude brings joy (see 15:13; 16:15; Job 29:24). Such control of one's attitude coupled with **a good report maketh the bones fat** (see 3:8 and discussion; see also Phil. 2:19). The wise will carefully listen for good reports and take responsibility for maintaining truth and peace in their lives. The righteous possess an **ear that heareth the reproof of life** (v. 31; see 1:23; 6:23 and discussion). They know that the person who **refuseth instruction despiseth his own soul** (v. 32; see discussion on 5:12; see also 1:7; 5:23; 8:36), and they understand that few things are more important than a willingness to **heareth reproof** (v. 32; see 15:5, 31). This willingness is born in the heart of the person who lives under the influence of **The fear of the Lord** (v. 33; see discussion on 1:7). The righteous understand that **before honour is humility** (see 22:24; 25:6–7; Matt. 23:12; Luke 14:11; 18:14; 1 Peter 5:6). Wisdom companions with humility and the willingness to put oneself under the authority of others (see 11:2; 13:10).

16:1–5. People like to make plans and often assume that they have the control required to bring their plans to fulfillment. An important part of growing as a follower of Jesus Christ is recognizing that **the answer of the tongue, is from the Lord** (v. 1) and fully appreciating the fact that God must give us the ability to articulate and accomplish plans (see 19:21). **The Lord weigheth the spirits** (v. 2). God examines the motives behind desires and blesses or distances Himself from plans based on His assessment of motives (see 24:12; Ps. 139:23; 1 Cor. 4:4–5; Heb. 4:12). The righteous **Commit** (v. 3; see 1 Peter 5:7) their works to the glory of God, and God promises that their **thoughts shall be established**. Goals and plans will be achieved when the motivation behind them is the glory of God and the benefit of others (see 3:5–6 and discussions; Pss. 1:3; 55:22; 90:17). **The Lord hath made all things for himself** (v. 4). God is sovereign in every life and in all of history (see Eccl. 7:14; Rom. 8:28). He sees all, weighs all, and in the end, judges all. Even the wicked have a role in the divine program, and God keeps **the wicked for the day of evil**. R. B. Y. Scott sums up well the thrust of this Proverb when he says, "Man proposes but God disposes" (Scott, *Proverbs*, p. 106). God displays His power even through wicked men (see Exod. 9:16), and all evil will be judged (see Ezek. 38:22–23; Rom. 2:5–11). This passage is not teaching that God is the author or creator of evil but rather that even those who practice evil serve His sovereign pleasure. Though the wicked join forces, **though hand join in hand** (v. 5), their combined power will not begin to match the power of God, who will visit upon them His justice and judgment (see 11:20–21 and discussions).

16:6. By mercy and truth iniquity is purged. The moral quality of conduct that God desires is summed up by two Hebrew terms often translated "mercy" and "truth" (see 3:3; Hos. 4:1). When His people repent of sin and bring their lives into accord with His will, God forgives them and withdraws His judgment (see Isa. 1:18–19; 55:7; Jer. 3:22; Ezek. 18:23, 30–32; 33:11–12, 14–16; Hos. 14:1–2, 4). Thus, it can be said that mercy and truth "purge" sin; that is, they turn away God's wrath against sin.

16:7–9. Pleasing and glorifying God should always be the highest motivation for the righteous. When this aspiration dominates a man's desires, God **maketh even his enemies to be at peace with him** (v. 7). This truth is illustrated again and again in the history of Israel, as in the reigns of godly Asa and Jehoshaphat (2 Chron. 14:6–7; 17:10). Peace is God's special gift to all who humble themselves before Him and seek Him with all their hearts (see 3:17 and discussion; Rom. 12:18; Heb. 12:14). Those who fear God believe that **a little** (v. 8) is much when God is in it and that it is to be preferred to **great revenues** gained without the desire to glorify God in word and action (see 10:2 and discussion). The fear of the Lord teaches a man that **the Lord directeth his steps** (v. 9). God's control of men's lives is also emphasized in 16:1, 3–4 (see discussions there; 19:21; 20:24; Ps. 37:23; Jer. 10:23).

16:10–15. In judging cases brought before him, a king functioned as God's representative (see Deut. 1:17). Therefore, he needed the divine gift of wisdom to discern between right and wrong and render God's judgment (see 1 Kings 3:9). When he did so, his judgment was tantamount to a divine oracle for the people (see 1 Kings 3:28; 2 Sam. 14:17, 20; 19:27). The ruler whose heart is intent on honoring God through his judgments can be assured that the **divine sentence** (v. 10) flows from the **lips of the king**. This king will be mindful that a **just weight and balance** (v. 11) are always required in the administration of commerce for those who profess to be **the Lord's** (see 21:2; 24:12; Job 6:2; 31:6). **All the weights of the bag** refers to the stones of different sizes that merchants carried in a bag with them to weigh and measure quantities of silver for payment (see Mic. 6:11). The godly king is mindful that his **throne is established by righteousness** (v. 12). When the king "faithfully judgeth the poor" (29:14), refuses to take bribes (29:4), and removes any wicked advisers (25:5), he can be assured of God's blessing and support as he carries out the responsibilities attached to his leadership of the nation (see 14:34; Deut. 17:19–20; Isa. 16:5; Rom. 13:3). Such a king values **Righteous lips** (v. 13). The lips of the righteous speak the truth in the presence of the king rather than sugarcoat errors or bad leadership decisions. Even when the stakes are high, the righteous will tell the king the truth (like Nathan before David), and the king will ultimately value highly those who are the protectors of his integrity (see 20:28). Kings have the power of life and death in their lips, and their words may serve as **messengers of death** (v. 14). An angry king can pronounce death quickly and effectively (see 19:12; Est. 7:7–10; Matt. 22:7; Luke 19:27). The **wise man will pacify** as quickly as possible the angry words of the king (see Daniel's response to the rage of Nebuchadnezzar, Dan. 2:12–16). However, **In the light of the king's countenance is life** (v. 15), which refers to the king's favorable disposition toward a person (see Num. 6:25). The king's **favor is as a cloud of the latter rain**. The spring rain was essential for the full development of barley and wheat; it was therefore a sign of good things to come (see the "dew" of 19:12; see Ps. 72:6).

16:16–20. Gold may secure much for a person in this life, but **wisdom** (v. 16) enriches a man's soul for this life and for eternity; hence, it is more valuable than **gold** or **silver** (see 3:14 and discussion; 8:10, 19). Wisdom allows followers to travel on **The highway of the upright** (v. 17; see discussion on 15:19). The upright **depart from evil** and avoid becoming entangled in the thorns and snares that fill the paths traveled by the wicked (see 22:5). **Pride ... and a haughty spirit** (v. 18) are the dominant characteristics of those who reject the counsel of wisdom (see 11:2 and discussion). Prideful persons are headed for a great fall, so it is better for a man **to be of an humble spirit** (v. 19; see 3:34; Isa. 57:15; Matt.

5:3). Those who **divide the spoil with the proud** will ultimately experience God's judgment and condemnation (see 1:13–14; Judg. 5:30). Those who follow after wisdom will, unlike the proud, **find good** (v. 20; see 13:13). This good will include the experience of inner joy, for **whoso trusteth in the LORD, happy is he** (see 16:3; 3:5–6; 28:25; Pss. 34:8; 37:4–5).

16:21–24. Sweetness of the lips increaseth learning (v. 21). People are more willing to listen to someone who uses pleasant speech (see also v. 23b). "Sweetness" is expanded in verse 24 (compare the persuasive but destructive words of the adulteress in 7:21). The willingness to receive this kind of instruction is a **wellspring of life** (v. 22) for those who receive it (see discussion on 10:11). **The instruction of fools** does not lead to life but to folly (see 13:13 and discussion; see also 7:22; 13:15; 15:10). Wisdom in the heart of a person **teacheth his mouth** (v. 23) to make responses to difficult circumstances that bring blessing to those who listen and obey (see 22:17–18). These **Pleasant words are as a honeycomb** (v. 24). They are good for those who speak them and for those who receive them (see 24:13–14). They taste good (see 2:10; Ps. 19:10) and bring **health to the bones** (see discussion on 3:8) of the speaker and the recipients (see discussions on 4:22; 12:18; 15:30).

16:25–30. Sinners will always offer advice that appeals to many, but **the end thereof are the ways of death** (v. 25). Only the wisdom of God, which is ultimately incarnated in the Son of God, leads to life (see 5:4, 23; 7:21–27; Matt. 7:13–14; 1 Cor. 1:30). The sinner counsels laboring for the self alone. Labor for the sake of labor alone meets the need for physical food but leaves an emptiness in the spirit that causes a man to feel hollow. The **ungodly man** (v. 27) can be identified through the bad counsel he gives (see discussions on 6:12; Deut. 13:13). The ungodly are not content to give their earthbound wisdom but are driven to move forward to **diggeth up evil** (see 3:29; 6:14; Mic. 2:1). While digging up evil, they utter words that are like **a burning fire**; their speech is inflammatory and destructive (see James 3:6). They **soweth strife** (v. 28; see discussion on 6:14). They are like the **whisperer** who whispers slander and gossip about others (see 11:13). The whisperer **shutteth his eyes** (v. 30). His winking eye signals his insincerity (see discussion on 6:13). The whisperer is constantly **moving his lips;** he incessantly makes insinuations (see discussion on 6:12–14).

16:31–32. The hoary head is a crown of glory (v. 31). The elderly are to receive deep respect (see Lev. 19:32); especially when they manifest an affection for the way of righteousness (see 3:1–2, 16). **He that is slow to anger is better than the mighty** (v. 32; see 14:29; 15:18; 19:11; James 1:19). "Wisdom is better than weapons of war" (Eccl. 9:18). **He that ruleth his spirit** is better **than he that taketh a city.** Although one who practices righteousness, patience, and self-control receives far less attention and acclaim than a warrior who takes a city, he accomplishes better things. This person comes to old age and incarnates that which pleases God, in contrast to the sinner, who arrives at old age broken in body and in spirit.

16:33. Discerning direction in the ordinary affairs of life is not always easy. The ancients often resorted to the practice of casting **The lot ... into the lap.** Here the lot may have been several pebbles held in the fold of a garment and then drawn out or shaken to the ground. This practice was commonly used to make decisions (see Exod. 28:30; Num. 26:53; Neh. 11:1; Ps. 22:18; Jonah 1:7; Acts 1:26). For those who companion with wisdom, however, it is essential to affirm that **the whole disposing thereof is of the LORD.** God, not chance, is in control, and God rules in sovereignty over all the affairs of men (see 16:1, 3–4, 9).

17:1–5. The teaching in verse 1 is similar to the instruction given in 15:17. It is better to enjoy a simple meal in peace than to have a sumptuous feast with contention. **A wise servant shall have rule over a son that causeth shame** (v. 2; see 10:5; 19:26; 28:7; 29:15). The wise servant may receive the inheritance originally intended for the son. Such a rise in position and good fortune is due solely to the shameful behavior of the son and the faithful attention to duty that has characterized the servant. This observation is designed to call attention to wisdom's emphasis on

faithfulness and the fact that God watches, evaluates, and ultimately assigns rewards for faithfulness. **The fining pot ... the furnace** (v. 3) is the place where **silver** and **gold** were refined to remove their impurities (see Isa. 1:25; Mal. 3:3). The servant in verse two discovered that there is a Master who **trieth the hearts** (see 15:11; 16:2 and discussions; Jer. 17:10). Every follower of Christ should remember that the Father watches, evaluates, and rewards faithfulness. The Father is deeply interested in one's attitude regarding the poor, and **Whoso mocketh the poor reproacheth his Maker** (v. 5; see 14:31). **He that is glad at calamities shall not be unpunished** by the watching Father. The people of Edom were condemned for gloating over the collapse of "brother" Israel ("thy brother Jacob," Obadiah 10; see Ezek. 35:12, 15; see also Prov. 24:17).

17:6–7. Grandchildren are a special source of joy for the elderly and are viewed as **the crown of old men** (v. 6; see the "hoary head" of 16:31). To live to see one's grandchildren was considered a great blessing (see Gen. 48:11; Ps. 128:5–6). A deep appreciation for the value of family characterizes those who walk with wisdom, and **the glory of children are their fathers** (see Gen. 47:7). Notice the intergenerational appreciation for the family, which starts with godly grandparents and flows down to children who honor their parents and hold them in deep affection. These children eschew the speech patterns of the fool and understand that **lying lips** and **a prince** (v. 7) do not fit well together. The right of the prince to rule depends on honesty and justice (see 12:22; 16:12–13).

17:8–9. In this text, **A gift** that **is as a precious stone** (v. 8) is a reference to a bribe. Greed brings people under the influence of bribery, a sad commentary on human behavior (see 18:16; 21:14; Eccl. 10:19). Bribes are also condemned elsewhere (see v. 23; 15:27; 28:16; Deut. 16:19; 1 Sam. 12:3; Eccl. 7:7; Isa. 1:23; Amos 5:12; 1 Tim. 6:10). The wise will run away from bribes and run toward opportunities to help an erring brother, for **He that covereth a transgression seeketh love** (v. 9; see 10:12 and discussion). The evil person fuels the rumor mill by uncovering the transgression of another and seeking to discredit him.

17:10–13. One only has to speak softly to get the attention of a wise person because **reproof entereth more into a wise man than an hundred stripes into a fool** (v. 10). The wise humble themselves before the instruction of God and man, while fools deserve and will receive a flogging (see 10:13; 19:25, 29; 26:3; Deut. 25:3). A fool, that is, **an evil man** (v. 11), follows after **rebellion**, and he deserves and will experience the pain inflicted by **a cruel messenger** (see the dispatching of Abishai and Joab to end Sheba's rebellion against David, 2 Sam. 20:1–22; see also 1 Kings 2:25, 29, 46; Prov. 16:14). A man would do better to meet **a bear robbed of her whelps** (v. 12), who is certain to attack him and rip him open (see 2 Sam. 17:8; Hos. 13:8; compare the raging of the fool in Prov. 29:9) than to companion with a fool in his folly. Robert Alden suggests, "Consider meeting a fool with a knife, or gun, or even behind the wheel of a car; a mother bear could be less dangerous" (Alden, *Proverbs*, p. 134). These fools and ambassadors of evil **rewardeth evil for good** (v. 13), like Nabal, who refused to pay David's men (1 Sam. 25:21; see Ps. 109:5; Rom. 12:17–21). Retribution awaits such men, and **evil shall not depart from his house**.

17:14–16. The wise will not allow the sun to set on wrath without seeking to resolve the problem at hand (Eph. 4:26). They will **leave off contention** (v. 14), or seek peace, as soon as possible. The fool will seek to **justifieth the wicked** (v. 15), perhaps motivated by his willingness to receive a bribe (see 17:8; 24:24). These fools are an **abomination to the Lord**. Even when the fool has the money in his hand to pay for schooling, he will not gain wisdom through his attendance, for he has **no heart** (v. 16) for it.

17:17–18. Friends are extremely valuable, for **A friend loveth at all times** (v. 17; see David's friendship with Jonathan, 2 Sam. 1:26; see also 18:24; Ruth 1:16; 1 Cor. 13:4–7). A brother like Jonathan will stand beside his friend in all the **adversity** and joys of life. One should proceed with great caution before co-signing a loan for a friend, however, because that can cause the loss of at least two valuable pos-

sessions: your friend and your money (see 6:1 and discussion).

17:19–22. People who love **transgression** (v. 19) also **loveth strife**. A hot-tempered man commits many sins (29:22), chief among them being that he **exalteth his gate**. The person who stirs up strife is motivated primarily by pride (see 16:18; 29:23). The "gate" (lit., "opening") in this context may be a figure for the mouth ("he who opens his mouth wide"), meaning "he brags too much" and so "seeketh destruction," including his own. Such a person **findeth no good** (v. 20; compare 16:20). These people are easy to identify because they have a perverse tongue and go from one self-imposed crisis to another (see discussion on 2:12). Pity the parents who beget these liars and deceivers, for their lives are filled with **sorrow** (v. 21) and they experience little or **no joy** (see 17:25; 19:13). This is a sad state of affairs since **A merry heart** (v. 22) is the source of untold blessing for those who experience it (see 14:30; 15:13, 30; 16:15; Job 29:24). The **broken spirit** that is the daily experience of those who parent and befriend sowers of deception **drieth the bones** (see discussion on 3:8; see also 12:4; 14:30; Pss. 32:3; 37:7–8).

17:23–25. The wicked man readily **taketh a gift** (v. 23), or a bribe (see discussion on 17:8). These wicked people are fools, and their eyes **are in the ends of the earth** (v. 24). They chase fantasies, lack understanding, and are interested in everything except wisdom (see 12:11; Deut. 30:11–14). They have no settled purpose and flit from one thing to another like a bee moving from flower to flower in search of some sweet extract. These persons are **bitterness** (v. 25) to the mothers who bore them and grief to the fathers who instructed them (see 14:10 and discussion).

17:26. When people **punish the just** (see 17:10 and discussion) and **strike princes** (see the beating and disgrace endured by Jeremiah, Jer. 20:2), they are participating in actions that are an abomination to God. Rulers are to be a terror to those who do evil, not to those who do good (Rom. 13:1–4).

17:27–28. The person who walks with wisdom **spareth his words** (v. 27; see 10:19). Such people possess **an excellent spirit** and are clearly distinguishable from those who are hot-tempered (see KJV marginal note; see also 16:32). **Even a fool, when he holdeth his peace, is counted wise** (v. 28), for then he does not expose his lack of wisdom (see Job's sarcastic comment in Job 13:5).

18:1 – 3. Through desire a man, having separated himself (v. 1) refers to someone who alienates himself from others through the pursuit of his selfish desires. This person **intermeddleth with all wisdom**. The selfish person rejects wisdom and has an argumentative spirit. Such a man is a fool who finds **no delight ... but that his heart may discover itself** (v. 2). This fool has no desire for wisdom but is driven by only the selfish desires of his heart (see Eccl. 10:3). He will find for himself only **contempt ... ignominy** and **reproach** (v. 3; see 3:35; 6:33; 10:5; 11:2; Ps. 31:17; Isa. 22:18).

18:4 – 5. The wise man's words are like **deep waters** (v. 4). The wise speak with a profound wisdom (see 20:5) that originates in an internal **wellspring of wisdom** that moves through them to others like **a flowing brook**. A wise man's words are refreshing and a source of life to all who receive them (see 1:23; 13:14; see also 10:11 and discussion). The wicked speak from another internal source; their words are deeply rooted in their sinful self-serving nature. **To accept the person of the wicked** (v. 5), or to willingly cooperate with the ungodly in the overthrow of the righteous, is a wicked thing. **To overthrow the righteous in judgment** is to participate in an action that is wicked (see 17:26; 31:5; Mal. 3:5).

18:6 – 9. In the New Testament, James expands on the **contention** (v. 6) that the tongue is capable of stirring up. Proverbs reminds the reader again and again that the fool is quick to quarrel (see 17:14, 19; 20:3). His actions **calleth for strokes**, and he deserves the rod on his back (see 10:13; 19:29). His mouth provides ample evidence that he deserves destruction (see 10:14 and discussion). The mouth of the fool is filled with **The words of a talebearer** (v. 8). A gossip's words are as pleasant as a wise man's words (see 16:21, 23), but they promote dissension (see 11:13; 26:20, 22). Such words are **as wounds** (lit., "as bits greedily swallowed"). Gossip is like tasty food but has disastrous consequences. These words **go down into the innermost parts of the belly**, where they are thoroughly digested and so are carried about and live on to continue destroying. This tragic waste of energy reminds one of **He ... that is slothful in his work** (v. 9; see 10:4 and discussion). The slothful person is a brother to the wasteful talebearer. The talebearer squanders the opportunity to bless others with the fruit of his words, while the slothful person squanders the opportunity to bless others with the fruit of his labor.

18:10 – 12. He who is wise will companion with neither the slothful nor the talebearer. He will find himself constantly relying on **The name of the Lord** (v. 10). The name equals the Person, since it expresses His nature and qualities (see *KJV Study Bible* notes on Exod. 3:14 – 15). In the name of the Lord, the righteous will find **a strong tower** to which they may flee for encouragement, provisioning, and protection in all of life's circumstances (see Pss. 18:2; 91:2; 144:2). In this tower, refugees are **safe** from all that alarms and potentially harms (see 29:25; Ps. 27:5). The rich contemplate a safety of their own construction: they believe that wealth can be their **high wall** (v. 11) and make them safe. God can bring it down (see Isa. 25:12). Their plans will end in their **destruction** (v. 12; see 15:33 and discussion).

18:13 – 15. Pride is once again the theme in these verses (see 15:13; 17:22). The height of arrogance is to answer another before he has been graced with the gift of a respectful hearing, which may wound his spirit and may be the last straw that leads him to despair. Listening carefully and seeking to heal the wounded strengthens their spirit and gives them a refreshed ability to deal with their infirmities. **The ear of the wise seeketh knowledge** (v. 15), for knowledge allows them to minister well to the needs of others and to glorify their Maker.

18:16 – 21. The gifted man will never need to force himself on others, for he understands that his **gift maketh room for him** (v. 16). The responsibility of those gifted by God is to use their gifts to serve others. In so doing, they glorify God and endear themselves to those they serve. Judges use their gifts well when they hear both sides of a case (see Deut. 1:16). Often when a dispute was particularly difficult, the lot would be cast for the purpose of causing **contentions to cease** (v. 18). Reaching a decision through the casting of lots was one way of settling a dispute (see discussion on 16:33; Matt. 27:35). Contention between brothers is always a serious matter, and **A brother offended** (v. 19) is difficult to win over (see Esau's anger when Issac blessed Jacob, Gen. 27:41). **The tongue** (v. 21) possesses great power for good and ill. Good words flowing from the lips are like wonderful **fruit** filling a man's being with refreshment and joy (see discussion on 13:3).

18:22-24. In the beginning, God created man and said it was not good for him to be alone. Here Solomon reminds us that **Whoso findeth a wife findeth a good thing, and obtaineth favour of the Lord** (v. 22). The statement here is identical to 8:35, where finding wisdom brought similar favor. Friends are another gift from God to ward off the perils of aloneness, but **A man that hath friends must shew himself friendly** (v. 24). Men should choose friends carefully (see 12:26 and discussion; 17:17). We are blessed when we find **a friend that sticketh closer than a brother**. True friends do not turn away in tough times. It is better to have a true friend than many false friends.

19:1-3. Here the discussion turns to **integrity** (v. 1; see discussion on 2:7). In wisdom's view, the poor man who walks before God with integrity is superior to the man of great wealth who gives little or no attention to the cultivation of his character (see 28:6). People who are **without knowledge** (v. 2) or an appreciation for its value are a foolish lot and are devoid of integrity (see Rom. 10:2). The man who **hasteth with his feet** is equally foolish, for haste can lead to poverty (21:5) or folly (29:20). The man who in **his heart fretteth against the Lord** (v. 3) is the man who rages in anger as he blames God for his troubles (see Gen. 4:5; Isa. 8:21; Lam. 3:39). This angry man will find himself far from the integrity that is so highly valued by God and those who walk with wisdom.

19:4-5. Befriending the poor often seems to have no immediate advantage. Pursuing friendship with the wealthy is the preferred pastime of many. The poor often find themselves unable to keep up with the lifestyle of the rich and famous, are left behind by their wealthy neighbors, and struggle with feeling separated from the wealthy (see 19:7; 14:20). It helps when the poor remember that God watches all and that false witnesses and liars will not go unpunished, nor will the poor always be poor. God will one day bring into heaven all the poor who cleave to wisdom and integrity (see 6:19 and discussion).

19:6-10. Many will intreat the favour (v. 6) of the powerful prince and seek to be a **friend to him that giveth gifts**. Generosity (see 19:4) or bribery (see 18:16) could be in view here. The contrast once again is between the wealthy and the poor, whose **brethren ... do hate him** (v. 7; see 19:4; 14:20; Job 19:19; Ps. 38:11). The man who pursues instruction in wisdom **loveth his own soul** (v. 8) and **shall find good** (see 8:35-36; 13:13 and discussion). The lover of wisdom is a radically different person from the man who bears false witness and speaks lies. This man may glory in his lack of integrity, but such **Delight is not seemly for a fool** (v. 10). Nor is it an honor (see 26:1) **for a servant to have rule over princes**. Servants typically lack the wisdom required for such leadership and tend to become tyrants (see 17:2; 29:2; Isa. 3:4).

19:11-14. The wise man has self-control and **deferreth his anger** (v. 11; see 14:29; 15:18; 16:32; Eccl. 7:9; James 1:19). He will also **pass over a transgression** rather than demand a pound of flesh for every infraction of the rules. He has compassion for the failures of others (see 12:16; 29:11; 2 Sam. 16:11-12).

Everyone fears the roar of the man-eating lion. **The king's wrath is as the roaring of a lion** (v. 12), and all who are within earshot of its expression would do well to give him the same wide berth they would afford the roaring lion (see 16:14). The king's approval is another matter, and all who experience his benevolence will affirm that **his favour is as** refreshing as the morning **dew** (see 16:15 and discussion).

Home is the place where God intended the incubation of the godly seed that would fulfill His purpose and bring Him glory (see Mal. 3:14–16). The **foolish son** (v. 13) and the **contentio[us] wife** are contrary to the divine intention and are a source of great pain for the father and husband (see 17:21, 25). These violators of the divine intention are also denounced in 21:9, 19; 25:24; 27:15, and stirring up dissension is condemned throughout Proverbs (see 6:14 and discussion). An Arab proverb says, "Three things make a house intolerable: *tak* (the leaking through of rain), *nak* (a wife's nagging), and *bak* (bugs)" (Toy, *Exegetical Commentary on Proverbs*, p. 373). The home that God describes in Malachi represents a rich inheritance for any father, and a good wife is one of God's greatest gifts (see 12:4 and discussion; see also 18:22).

19:15–17. Slothfulness (v. 15), in view of all that God created mankind to do, is a great sin (see 6:11; 10:4). So also disregard for His commandments is a grievous sin. The person who keeps Yahweh's commandments is doing himself a great good, for he is also investing in his own growth and protection. He that despises the commandments will surely find himself in the way of death (see 13:13; 15:10; 16:17). The man **that hath pity upon the poor lendeth unto the Lord** (v. 17). The Lord regards these gifts as a gift to Him (see Matt. 25:40).

19:18–23. There is no shortage of commandments regarding the discipline of children. Here wisdom counsels, **Chasten thy son** (v. 18) and do not **spare for his crying**. Parents should be sensitive to the pain their discipline inflicts on the child, but noise that is out of proportion to the discipline should not keep a parent from following through with disciplining the child. "We have here a caution against that cruel kindness that kills by withholding reasonable correction" (Lange, *Proverbs of Solomon*, p. 173). Gleason L. Archer points out that this Hebrew verb is similar to the Egyptian *h-n-k*, which means "to give to the gods" or "to set up something for divine service." He suggests that this gives verse 6 "the following range of possible meanings: 'Dedicate the child to God,' 'Prepare the child for his future responsibilities,'

'Exercise or train the child for adulthood'" (*Archer Encyclopedia of Bible Difficulties*, p. 252). The **man of great wrath** (v. 19) should be careful to monitor his actions, whether he is disciplining his children or engaging in a confrontation with friend or foe. Such a man will be punished if his anger continues untamed. One should practice care when dealing with such persons. The responder will eventually have to draw the line and cease coming to their rescue (see 14:16–17, 29; 15:18). Such persons would do well to **Hear counsel** (v. 20) so that in the end they may finish well. Men will propose many ways to achieve good endings, but the only true way to come to a good end is to hear and obey the commandments of the Creator (see 16:1, 9). A good-hearted person has a **desire** (v. 22) to practice **kindness**, but such goodness is difficult to find (see 3:3; 14:22). **A poor man** who practices kindness **is better than a liar** (see 19:1, 28; 6:12). Kindness is often motivated by the **fear of the Lord** (v. 23; see discussion on 1:7), which **tendeth to life** (see discussion on 10:11). Practitioners of godly fear may rest assured that they will **not be visited with evil**. When evil does touch their lives, it must first be filtered through the fatherly watchfulness of the Sovereign God (see 3:2; 14:26).

19:24–29. The **slothful man** (v. 24) provides a stark contrast to the man who fears God (see discussion on 6:6). He is so lazy that he will not even nourish himself when food is supplied. Even when wisdom is available to him, he discounts its pursuit as a task unworthy of him. The scorner is equally unaffected by the presence of instruction. **Smite a scorner** (v. 25), and he will not heed your instruction (see v. 29; 14:3; see also discussions on 1:22; 17:10). The **simple**, however, who are witnesses to this process and are not to be confused with the mocker (see discussion on 1:4), will often heed the advice rejected by the scorner. The man who emulates the slothful **wasteth his father, and chaseth away his mother** (v. 26; see 10:5; 13:5). He steals from and is abusive toward his parents. Children are expected to take care of their parents when they are sick or old (see Isa. 51:18). Robbing them (see Judg. 17:1–2) and attacking them (Exod. 21:15, 17) are serious crimes. The **ungodly witness** (v. 28) is also an abomination to the Lord (see v. 5; see also 6:19). This witness, like the wicked son, **devoureth iniquity** (see the description of man as one who "drinketh iniquity like water," Job 15:16; see also Job 34:7). These evil men will not go unpunished, for **Judgments ... for scorners, and stripes for the back of fools** (v. 29) fits with the divine plan (see 10:13; 14:3; 26:3).

20:1-3. Various principles are discussed in this section that, when followed, lead to a life of integrity. While focusing on those who bring shame to the covenant community, Solomon reminded the young that **Wine is a mocker, strong drink is raging** (v. 1). Those who overindulge become mockers and brawlers (see Hos. 7:5). Proverbs associates drunkenness with poverty (23:20-21), strife (23:29-30), and injustice (31:4-5). **Deceived** is the best word to describe the person who drinks heavily and expects to live a life characterized by integrity (see Gen. 9:21; Isa. 28:7). Like wine, the **anger** (v. 2) of **a king** represents a grave danger. Fools **will be meddling** (v. 3). The fool is quarrelsome and argumentative and will risk the wrath of the king (see 6:14; 17:14, 19; 18:6). The wise man will cease from strife before he endangers **his own soul** (v. 2).

20:4-7. **The sluggard** (v. 4) is always ready to abandon hard work and will do so with the slightest encouragement (see 6:6; 13:4; 21:25-26). He will never secure integrity, but the man who values **Counsel** (v. 5), a reference to plans or motives, will secure a reputation for integrity. He will see the counsel of others as **deep water** and **will draw it out**. He will treat the counsel he receives as something of value, and when needed, he will draw on it as one draws life-giving water from a well. The **goodness** (v. 6) of such a man is rooted in faithfulness to God (see 19:22). Such men are rare, and **a faithful man who can find?** (see Eccl. 7:28-29). The faithful man is one who **walketh in his integrity** (see 2:7): **His children are blessed** (v. 7; see 13:22; 14:26).

20:8-15. The wise king **scattereth away all evil** (v. 8; see 16:10; Ps. 11:4). Rulers are appointed by God to aid the righteous and vex the evildoer. All men, like the wise king, should be able to say they strive to keep their hearts **clean** (v. 9) and **pure from ... sin**. No one is without sin (see Job 14:4; Rom. 3:23), but those whose sins have been forgiven have "clean hands, and a pure heart" (Ps. 24:4; see also 51:1-2, 9-10). Cheating is far from the mind and heart of the man who seeks to honor God (see 11:1; 16:11). Men should take great care to hear God and order their deeds according to His laws. Men who do so will not love sleep, for those who love **sleep ... come to poverty** (v. 13; see 24:33-34). Hard work leads to satisfaction with bread purchased through toil. The wise man avoids securing gain at the expense of others or bargaining in a manner that leads to boasting. The important objective in this life is the acquisition of wisdom, not **gold** (v. 15) or **rubies**. Earlier, wisdom was valued more highly than gold or jewels (3:14-15; 8:10-11).

20:16-18. **Take his garment** (v. 16). A garment could be taken as security for a debt (Deut. 24:10-13). Anyone who foolishly assumes responsibility for the debt of a stranger, whose reliability is unknown, or that of a wayward woman, whose unreliability is known, ought to be held accountable, even to the degree of taking his garment as a pledge. The **bread of deceit** may be **sweet to a man** (v. 17) for a brief season, but the sweetness will not endure (see the sweet "bread" prepared by the adulteress in 9:17). Zophar observes that evil is sweet in the mouth of a wicked man, but it turns sour in his stomach (Job 20:12-18). Men are well served if they seek **counsel** (v. 18) and **advice** before they participate in activities that on the surface appear profitable but actually may end in disaster (see 15:22; Luke 14:31).

20:19-21. A person who seeks to companion with wisdom will practice great care when it comes to his speech. He will certainly never **curseth his father or his mother** (v. 20). In Israel, such action was punishable by death (see Lev. 20:9; Prov. 30:11, 17), and the **lamp** of such a sinner **shall be put out**. The wise will distance themselves from all who **flattereth** (v. 19). Wisdom counsels caution in all things. Get-rich-quick tactics are always to be avoided, for **An inheritance may be gotten hastily at the beginning; but the end thereof shall not be blessed** (v. 21).

20:22–25. Speech is again the focus here. No man should ever say, **I will recompense evil** (v. 22). Vengeance is God's prerogative. He will repay the wicked for their actions (see Deut. 32:35; Ps. 94:1). It is the way of wisdom to **wait on the LORD** for the administration of justice (see Pss. 27:14; 37:34). Men need to practice great care in their dealings with one another and with Yahweh. **Vows** (v. 25) to God must always be honored. **It is a snare** for a man to make a vow rashly. The vow was a promise to make a special gift to the Lord if He answered an earnest request (see Lev. 27:1–25; Deut. 23:21; Judg. 11:30–31, 34–35; 1 Sam. 1:11). Sometimes such a vow was made hastily and was not carried out (see Eccl. 5:4–6).

20:26–30. The wise leader **bringeth the wheel** (v. 26) over the evildoer. The wheel of the threshing cart separated the grain from the husk (see Isa. 28:27–28). The wise ruler will see to it that the wicked are separated from the righteous and duly punished. All men must remember that **The spirit of man is the candle of the LORD** (v. 27). The soul of man has a God-consciousness and moral awareness of right and wrong (see Rom. 2:14–15). The Creator endowed man with a conscience designed to search **all the inward parts of the belly** (see discussion on 15:11). **Mercy and truth preserve the king** (v. 28), for kindness and moral uprightness endear a king to his people and encourage them to be loyal subjects (see 3:3; 14:22; 16:12; 29:14). **The glory of young men is their strength** (v. 29; see Jer. 9:23). **The beauty of old men is the gray head** (see discussion on 16:31). **The blueness of a wound** (v. 30) is a means that leads to integrity and the development of character in the young. Stern punishment is necessary to restrain evil. Several verses refer to fools whose backs are beaten (10:13; 14:3; 19:29), but even then, because they are fools, they may not change their ways (see 17:10; 27:22).

21:1–4. God is an omnipotent God who rules over all things that take place on planet earth. Even the **king's heart is in the hand of the LORD** (v. 1). God controls the lives and actions even of kings, such as Nebuchadnezzar (Dan. 4:31–32, 35) and Cyrus (Isa. 45:1–3; see Ezra 6:22). He **turneth** the hearts and hands of all human beings **whithersoever**

he will (see 16:9; see also 16:1; 19:21; 20:24). Men have always defended their actions and pronounced them **right** (v. 2; see 14:12; 16:2). The Lord of Israel **pondereth the hearts**, however, and judges the actions of all against the standard of His unalterable truth (see 24:12; Job 31:6; Ps. 139:23; 1 Cor. 4:4–5; Heb. 4:12). God values personal righteousness and the active pursuit of justice in relationships **more ... than sacrifice** (v. 3). This theme is found in the Prophets (Hos. 6:6; Mic. 6:7–8; see Prov. 21:27; discussion on 15:8). **A high look** (v. 4), a proud and haughty look, renders all participation in ceremonial worship meaningless from God's point of view (see discussion on 6:17; see also 16:5, 18).

21:5–8. The thoughts of the diligent tend ... to plenteousness (v. 5; see 10:4). The diligent are able to develop courses of action that lead to blessing for all who come under their influence. The **hasty** are those who counsel rash actions or desire to get rich quick (see 13:11; 20:21; 28:20). These persons will end badly and experience great emptiness and want. They may know momentary success, but only those who practice righteousness will inherit the kingdom of God. Those who have **a lying tongue** (v. 6; see discussion on 10:2; see 19:1) and practice **vanity** are like a vapor that is here and gone (see 13:11 and discussion; Eccl. 1:14). Such persons **seek death** (see 5:22; 7:23). **The robbery of the wicked shall destroy them** (v. 7; see 1:18–19 and discussions).

21:9–12. A corner of the housetop (v. 9) refers to a small room on the roof that was used to house guests. Roofs were flat, and small rooms could be built there (see Deut. 22:8; 2 Kings 4:10). It is better to retreat to such a little place than to stay in a large house with a spacious bedroom when these quarters must be shared with **a brawling woman** (see discussion on 19:13). **The wicked desireth evil** (v. 10; see 4:16; 10:23). Pity the **neighbour** of the wicked, for he **findeth no favour** in the eyes of the wicked man, who is critical of his every move (see 14:21). **The house of the wicked** (v. 12) will surely be overthrown by the Lord (see 10:25 and discussion; 14:11).

21:13–18. In 19:17, Solomon provided instruction on the proper response of the righteous to the

cry of the poor (v. 13; see discussion on 14:21; see also 28:27). Those who ignore this instruction shall also cry **but shall not be heard**. The punishment fits the crime (see discussion on 1:28; compare the fate of the rich man, Luke 16:19–31, and the unmerciful servant, Matt. 18:23–34). The **gift** (v. 14) or **reward** (see discussion on 17:8; see also 18:16; 19:6) given **in secret pacifieth** the **anger** of an offended party (see 6:34–35). Doing good brings **joy to the just** (v. 15; see 11:10 and discussion). God has established justice in His dealings with men, and **destruction** is His reward **to the workers of iniquity** (see 10:29 and Rom. 13:3). The man who refuses the understanding that comes from wisdom will receive this reward and will dwell eternally **in the congregation of the dead**. This is graphically illustrated by the man who succumbed to the adulteress (see 2:18; 5:23; 7:22–23; 9:18). **Wine and oil** (v. 17) here are associated with lavish feasting (see 23:20–21; Amos 6:6). Oil was used in various lotions or perfumes, some of which were very expensive (John 12:5). Persons who are in love with these expensive lotions and indulge in too much wine will find themselves impoverished. These **wicked shall be a ransom for the righteous** (v. 18). In Isaiah 43:3–4, God gave three nations to Persia in exchange for Persia's willingness to release the exiles of Judah (see discussion on Isa. 43:4).

21:19–26. The contentious woman mentioned in 21:9 is once again the subject for consideration. **It is better to dwell in the wilderness** (v. 19) without her quarrelsome presence than to dwell in a palace if it has to be shared with her (see 19:13). The wise will always have a store of the valuable **treasure** (v. 20) that enriches and ennobles life. We will find **oil in the dwelling of the wise** (see 3:10 and discussion; 8:21; on the value and use of olive oil, see 21:17 and Deut. 7:13). Those who **followeth after righteousness** (v. 21) will find **life, righteousness, and honour**. These are among the most important benefits for those who seek wisdom (see discussion on 3:2; see also 3:16; 8:18; 22:4). Those who companion with wisdom **scaleth the city of the mighty** (v. 22). This is another way of saying, "Wisdom is better than strength" (Eccl. 9:16; see Prov. 24:5; 2 Cor.

10:4, where spiritual weapons are "mighty through God to the pulling down of strong holds"). Those who companion with wisdom are careful stewards of their speech and avoid many of the pitfalls that befall those who speak foolishly (see 13:3 and discussion; 18:21). The scorner is defined here. He is garbed in the clothing of the **Proud ... scorner is his name** (v. 24; see discussion on 1:22). God mocks and punishes him for his **proud wrath** (see 3:34; 19:25, 29; 21:11). **The desire of the slothful** (v. 25) is spread over many things but is never coupled with wisdom or hard work (see discussions on 6:6; 13:4). The righteous companion with wisdom, and they **giveth and spareth not** (v. 26). The righteous are prosperous, so they can share with those in need (see Pss. 37:26; 112:9; Eph. 4:28). The wicked can never find right standing before God, for **The sacrifice of the wicked is abomination** (v. 27; see discussions on 21:3; 15:8). Wisdom counsels good listening and a faithful accounting of what has been heard and seen because the **false witness shall perish** (v. 28; see 19:5, 9; see 6:19). The wicked man heeds not this counsel of wisdom and **hardeneth his face** (v. 29). The upright heed the counsel of wisdom and follow the prescribed path, which leads to **life, righteousness, and honour** (v. 21). The wicked believe their counsel and strength is superior to that of the Lord. They do not bow to the reality that no **counsel against the LORD** (v. 30) will prevail. The Lord is sovereign and controls all peoples and nations (see 16:4, 9 and discussions; 19:21; 21:1; 1 Cor. 3:19–20). Wisdom once again cautions against trusting in horses and chariots for victory (see e.g., Ps. 20:7; Hos. 1:7; Deut. 17:16). Wisdom now offers a summary of one of her greatest themes: **safety is of the LORD** (v. 31). Victory in battle as well as security in this world are found in walking with the God who created humanity and trusting in His words and works (see 1 Sam. 17:47; Ps. 3:8).

22:1–5. Those who companion with wisdom place a high value on their **good name** (v. 1). Its value is recognized also in 3:4; 10:7 (see also Eccl. 7:1). Those who wish to protect their reputation would rather have the **loving favour** of God and others, which accompanies a good reputation, **than silver and gold**. All humans should share this passion for the favor of God because God is **the Maker of them all** (v. 2; see 14:31). The God who is the Creator is also the God who is the Judge, and everyone will eventually appear in His courtroom for an evaluation of the work done while in the body. In light of this, one ought to seek to aid and honor others, for God is favorably disposed to all who do so. **A prudent man** (v. 3) senses impending problems before they are upon him and **hideth himself** (see 14:8). **The simple** never comprehend the problems that are just around the corner and walk right into their own destruction; never knowing what hit them (see discussion on 1:4; see also 9:16). **Humility and the fear of the** LORD (v. 4) characterize those who embrace wisdom and seek always to glorify God in their words and actions. These character traits are associated also in 15:33 (see discussion on 1:7). **Riches, and honour, and life** are some of the benefits experienced by those who seek wisdom (see 3:2; see also 3:16; 8:18; 21:21). **Thorns and snares** (v. 5; see 15:19), evil, **shall be far from them** because they have chosen to travel on "the highway of the upright" (16:17).

22:6–11. To **Train up a child** (v. 6) is one of the highest privileges and responsibilities given to parents. The responsibility is timeless and embraced by all enduring cultures. In Scripture, "training" implies the need to "dedicate," as in 1 Kings 8:63, or "start" the instruction (1:8) and discipline (22:15) of the child. Each of these activities carries with it the understanding that the parent knows the **way** the child **should go**. The parent is convinced that there is a right way, the way prescribed by biblical wisdom (see 4:11 and discussion). Parents who companion with wisdom are also convinced that if children are trained within these guidelines, they will adopt these principles for the shaping of their own identities and lifestyles when they become adults.

Borrowers need to practice caution, for during the lifetime of the loan, **the borrower is servant to the lender** (v. 7). This is one of the reasons why putting up security for someone else (22:26) is frowned

on (see Neh. 5:4–5). Problems are one of the inevitable consequences of sin. Persons who **soweth iniquity shall reap vanity** (v. 8; see 12:21). **The rod of … anger**, or the ability to oppress others, which is central to the character and agenda of the wicked, will ultimately fail (see Ps. 125:3; Isa. 14:5–6). In contrast to the tragic fate of the oppressor, **He that hath a bountiful eye shall be blessed** (v. 9; see 11:25). The person who **giveth of his bread** to the poor will secure the blessing of God for himself in time and eternity (see 14:21; Deut. 15:8–11). The scorner will never embrace any of these teachings of wisdom. Therefore, wisdom counsels that one **Cast out the scorner** (v. 10; see 1:22; Gen. 21:9–10). The benefit of heeding wisdom's counsel is that **contention shall go out** with the scorner, and **strife … shall cease** (see 17:14; 18:3; 20:3). When a person has **pureness of heart** (v. 11), it will be evidenced by **the grace of his lips**. Gracious speech is characteristic of the wise man in Ecclesiastes 10:12. Grace in speech will bring many benefits to those who practice it, not the least of which might include that **the king shall be his friend** (see 22:29; Eph. 4:28–30).

22:12. How tender and securing are the words, **The eyes of the** LORD **preserve** (see 5:21; 15:3; Job 31:4; 34:21; Jer. 16:17; Heb. 4:13). God protects those who have knowledge (see Pss. 1:6; 34:15). God **overthroweth the words of the transgressor** and overrules their plans and desires (see 16:9; see also discussion on 21:30).

22:13–16. The sluggard creates excuses to avoid work; it matters not how deceitful or absurd the reasons are. Wisdom advises that one avoid friendship and an alliance with such a person. **The mouth of strange women** (v. 14), like the mouth of the scornful sluggard, is filled with deceit. The seductive speech of the adulteress (see discussion on 5:3; see also 2:16; 7:5) is the opening to a **deep pit**. Perhaps a well or a hunter's trap is implied here (see 5:22 and discussion; 7:22). This kind of sinful foolishness lies **bound in the heart** (v. 15) of all humans, even the **child**. **The rod of correction** is God's tool and the parent's tool for separating such foolishness from the immature before it finds a permanent lodging place in their minds and becomes permanently attached to their behavioral preferences. The desire here is never for the destruction or hurt of the child but for the deliverance of the child from practices that could bring destruction both in this life and in the life to come (see discussion on 13:24; Heb.12:6–11). **He that oppresseth the poor** (v. 16) has never experienced or given heed to the rod of correction. Such persons are in bondage to self and labor only for their own benefit. They oppress the poor and will ultimately experience the rod of God's correction and condemnation (see 14:31; 17:8; 18:16; 19:6; 21:5; 28:3; 28:22).

IV. The Thirty Sayings of the Wise (22:17–24:22)

A new section opens here, one that returns more to the style encountered in chapters 1–9. Proverbs 22:17–21 introduces the thirty proverbial sayings of the wise. The thirty sayings are: (1) 22:22–23; (2) 22:24–25; (3) 22:26–27; (4) 22:28; (5) 22:29; (6) 23:1–3; (7) 23:4–5; (8) 23:6–8; (9) 23:9; (10) 23:10–11; (11) 23:12; (12) 23:13–14; (13) 23:15–16; (14) 23:17–18; (15) 23:19–21; (16) 23:22–25; (17) 23:26–28; (18) 23:29–35; (19) 24:1–2; (20) 24:3–4; (21) 24:5–6; (22) 24:7; (23) 24:8–9; (24) 24:10; (25) 24:11–12; (26) 24:13–14; (27) 24:15–16; (28) 24:17–18; (29) 24:19–20; (30) 24:21–22.

22:17–21. The introduction to the thirty sayings opens with the plea to **Bow down thine ear, and hear** (v. 17; see 4:20; 5:1). The author challenges the reader to be mentally alert and to prepare to accept the truth that is communicated in the sayings of the wise. **The words of the wise** forms the title for the section, as did "The proverbs of Solomon" in 10:1. "Wise" is plural here and suggests that this section contains proverbs written by others and collected by Solomon. It is **a pleasant** (v. 18) experience to internalize the wisdom taught here, for it bears a blessed fruit in the soul in which it is engrafted (see 2:10; 16:24). The Lord has given this repository of divine wisdom **That thy trust may be in the LORD** (v. 19; see discussion on 3:5). To all who will hear, the Lord has given marvelous **counsels and knowl-edge** (v. 20) so that they might answer with **words of truth** (v. 21) the questions of **them that send unto thee** (see 1 Peter 3:15). All who view themselves as the commissioned of God may speak with certainty to the needs of any situation because they have a word from the Lord in the proverbs they have read, received as truth, and sought to incarnate in their lives and relationships.

22:22–23. God has a passion for justice and mercy (see Mic. 6:8; Isa. 5:4–8). Wisdom exhorts its followers to never plunder or **Rob ... the poor** (v. 22; see 22:16; 14:31). The wise will never oppress the afflicted **in the gate** (see Isa. 1:17). The gate was where court was convened. The wise will see to it that the poor are given proper assistance in defending their cause when they are pulled into court. Ultimately, **the LORD will plead their cause** (v. 23; see 23:11; Pss. 12:5; 140:12; Isa. 3:13–15; Mal. 3:5). The Lord will **spoil the soul of those that spoiled them**. The Lord will put to death those that oppress the poor (see Exod. 22:22–24). Surely, all who companion with the God of Israel, and ultimately with the God who creates His church on the foundation of His risen Son, will share His passion for justice and mercy.

22:24–25. Following the teachings of wisdom requires that a person give careful thought to the subject of friendships. The wise will **make no friendship with an angry man** (v. 24; see 12:26). The characteristics of persons with whom to avoid relationships are given in 14:16–17; 15:18; 29:22. Anyone who chooses to disobey this admonition will find himself imitating the behaviors of these persons and may become involved in a situation from which he cannot easily dislodge himself. He will have placed himself in **a snare to** his **soul** (v. 25; see discussion on 5:22; see also 12:13; 13:14; 29:6).

22:26–27. The danger involved in becoming **one of them ... that are sureties for debts** (v. 26) of another has come up several times in Proverbs (see discussion on 6:1). **Strike hands** indicates the confirmation of an agreement. If the borrower fails to pay, the co-signer will be responsible, and if the co-signer cannot pay, they may **take away** the co-signer's **bed from under** him (v. 27). One should beware of such foolish activity, or be reduced to poverty as a consequence of good-hearted willingness to become responsible for the debt of another.

22:28–29. The Scriptures often mention the sin of moving property boundary stones, or **the ancient landmark** (v. 28; see discussion on 15:25; 23:10; Deut. 19:14; Hos. 5:10). This action represents a subtle way of stealing from one's neighbor. Diligence in business is applauded by wisdom, not stealing from one's neighbor. **A man diligent in his business** (v. 29) is worthy of honor. Such men will **stand before kings**, for they work hard and are skilled in their craft. Craftsmen were considered to be wise (see discussion on 8:30; see also Exod. 35:30–35). Like Joseph, an administrator (Gen. 41:46), David, a musician (1 Sam. 16:21–23), and Hiram, a worker in bronze (1 Kings 7:13–14), craftsmen often found themselves in the presence of the rich and famous.

23:1–3. Each of the appetites are a gift from God, but if a man is controlled by any of his appetites, it may eventually lead to his destruction (see the similar warning in 23:20–21). A man given to the desire for food should always carefully consider the cost of consuming too much. Wisdom counsels such a man to **Be not desirous of his dainties** (v. 3). Lavish foods were served at the king's table. This admonition is repeated in a different context in 23:6. Eating too much under the influence of unbridled desire may prove to be a **deceitful** enterprise. Perhaps the meaning here is that the ruler wants to obligate his guest in some way, even to influence him to support a wicked scheme (see Ps. 141:4). In any event, what seemed filled with only pleasure is discovered to contain the seeds of the participant's destruction.

23:4–5. If a man wants to grow in his relationship with wisdom, he will not **Labour** (v. 4) simply **to be rich**. The desire to get rich can ruin a person physically and spiritually, "For the love of money is the root of all evil" (1 Tim. 6:10; see 15:27; 28:20; Heb. 13:5). Riches are hard to hold on to, and frequently **they fly away** (v. 5). One's trust must be in God, not in riches (see Jer. 17:11; Luke 12:21; 1 Tim. 6:17).

23:6–8. A host who is evil is in view here. He has **an evil eye** (v. 6). He is a stingy man who is eager to get rich (see 28:22). **His heart is not with thee** (v. 7; see 26:24–25). He encourages you to receive from him but only so that he may ensnare you and obligate you to support him in some evil cause. You will ultimately wish to **vomit** (v. 8) all you ingested at his table, from disgust at the host's attitude.

23:9. Wisdom cautions against verbal interaction with a fool, **for he will despise the wisdom of thy words**. Fools despise wisdom (1:7), hate knowledge and correction (1:22; 12:1), and heap abuse on those who rebuke them (9:7).

23:10–11. Anyone who seeks to remove **the old landmark** (v. 10), or boundary stones, in the **fields of the fatherless** will reap a terrible consequence (see discussion on 15:25; see also 22:28). Oppressing the widow and the fatherless is strongly denounced in Scripture (see Isa. 10:2; Jer. 22:3; Zech. 7:10). The fatherless have a **Redeemer** (v. 11) who watches over them. The kinsman-redeemer was someone who helped a close relative regain land (see *KJV Study Bible* note on Lev. 25:25) or who avenged his death (Num. 35:12, 19). God is "A father of the fatherless, and a judge of the widows" (Ps. 68:5; see discussions on Ruth 2:20; Jer. 31:11; see also Jer. 50:34). Ultimately, God is the Redeemer of the fatherless, and **he shall plead their cause** (see Pss. 12:5; 140:12; Isa. 3:13–15; Mal. 3:5).

23:12. Godly wisdom does not come to the casually attentive. Wisdom is received when seekers **Apply** their **heart[s]** and seek it with fervor. Paul reminded Timothy of this responsibility when he exhorted him to give great energy to the study of God's Word (2 Tim. 2:15).

23:13–14. Children require **correction** (v. 13) to engender the kind of discipline in view in 23:12. The momentary unpleasantness that accompanies correcting the child is well worth the discomfort experienced by the parent and the child. Applied by a loving parent, such discipline may save the child from a life of self-indulgence, which would land him in **hell** (v. 14).

23:15–16. In Hebrew poetry, **reins** (v. 16) represents the place of the deepest affections in humans (see 10:1 and discussion; see also 23:24; 27:11; 29:3).

The **son** (v. 15) whose **heart** is **wise** and whose **lips speak right things** (v. 16) is the cause of great rejoicing in the deepest parts of his parents' being. Such joy is beyond expression (see 1:8, 10).

23:17–18. At one time or another, most people face the temptation to admire the sinner for his apparent gain. Wisdom counsels **not ... to envy sinners** (v. 17; see 3:31; 24:1, 19). One ought rather to practice always **the fear of the Lord** (see discussions on 1:7; 3:7). This fear will help one to trust that in the **end** (v. 18) God will make all things right and that He will reward all human beings for the good and evil they have done while in the body. In the future, God will reward those who fear Him (see Ps. 37:37; Jer. 29:11).

23:19–21. Wisdom counsels the **son** (v. 19) to practice diligent control of his heart and to cultivate an affection for walking in **the way** (see 4:25–26). The way of wisdom is not the way of **winebibbers** (v. 20). Drunkenness is also condemned in 23:29–35; 20:1 (see also Deut. 21:20; Matt. 24:49; Luke 21:34; Rom. 13:13; Eph. 5:18; 1 Tim. 3:3). The wise son will not companion with men who destroy themselves with wine. The wise will also refuse to companion with **the glutton** (v. 21) or those who love excessive sleep (see 23:2; 28:7; Matt. 11:19). These persons will all **come to poverty** (see 21:17; see also the poverty that overtakes the sluggard, 6:9–11).

23:22–25. The young may forget to listen carefully to their aging parents, thinking they are too old to offer them anything of much value. Wisdom counsels the young to **Hearken unto thy father ... and despise not thy mother** (v. 22; see 15:20; 30:17). These aged godly sages will be of great value to the young when they seek to **Buy the truth ... also wisdom ... and understanding** (v. 23; see 4:5; see also 4:7 and discussion). The request and the bestowal of such wisdom from aged, godly parents to their children will be a source of great joy for the parents (see 23:15; 27:11; see also 10:1 and discussion).

23:26–28. The young are in need of godly advice from the aged, for there are many **deep ditch[es]** (v. 27) into which they may fall (see discussion on 22:14). The **strange woman** is one of these ditches

(see discussion on 2:16; see also 5:20; 7:17–23). She **lieth in wait** (v. 28; see 6:26; 7:12; Eccl. 7:26) and has a powerful and toxic ability to **increaseth the transgressors** (see 7:26). The son's **eyes** (v. 26) as well as his lips (22:18) and ears (23:12) are important. What one sees, says, and hears should be pleasing to the Lord. The urgency of the father's appeal is related to the dangers of sexual waywardness (see 5:20; 6:24; 7:5; 20:16).

23:29–35. A vivid description of the physical and psychological effects of drunkenness is found in these proverbs. Those who give themselves to wine **hath woe** (v. 29; see the woes pronounced on drunkards in Isaiah 5:11, 22) and **contentions** (see 20:1). They have **wounds** (see "stripes for the back of fools," 19:29). Wisdom counsels all to not **tarry long at the wine** (v. 30; see 1 Sam. 25:36). Wisdom counsels as well the avoidance of **mixt wine**, probably wine mixed with spices (see 9:2; Ps. 75:8). When the wine is well-fermented, **it biteth like a serpent** (v. 32), and death may result from consuming the befuddling liquid (see Num. 21:6). The drunkard loves to **behold strange women** (v. 33), or "strange things" (the noun is not supplied in the original). In the delirium that afflicts the alcoholic, the carnal desire for loose women and all manner of strange experiences consumes him. He becomes like one **that lieth down in the midst of the sea** (v. 34). His head will be spinning like the proverbial top. He will not even be aware of injuries from beatings he received while in his drunken stupor (compare the condition of Israel in Jer. 5:3). The greatest tragedy in the life of the alcoholic is his resolve to **seek it yet again** (v. 35) as soon as he can get his feet back under him. His woe and misery do not prevent him from repeating his folly (see 26:11; 27:22; Isa. 56:12).

24:1–2. The tendency to admire the prosperity and fame of the rich and famous has always been a problem for the righteous. Wisdom advises that one **Be not ... envious** (v. 1; see 24:19; Ps. 37:1). Additionally, wisdom counsels that one also not **desire to be with them** (see 1:15; 12:26; 23:20). Evil persons may seem to prosper for a season as they **studieth destruction** (v. 2), but in the end, they themselves will experience eternal destruction (see 1:10–11; 6:14; Job 15:35; Ps. 38:12).

24:3–4. Building a house requires skill and commitment. Here **house** (v. 3) may be symbolic of the life of an individual or a family. The man of **understanding** will fill his mind with wisdom. His house will be **builded** on that firm foundation and furnished well with the **precious and pleasant riches** (v. 4) wisdom promises to bestow on those who love her (see 8:21).

24:5–6. Wisdom serves not only to build a strong house but also to build a **strong** (v. 5) person (see discussion on 21:22). The man who receives the counsel of wisdom and places himself in a circle of persons who offer counsel from wisdom will dwell in **safety** (v. 6) and will wage **war** successfully.

24:7. The mind of **a fool** is filled with his own ideas and has no room for the counsel of wisdom. He thinks of wisdom as nonsensical and otherworldly, not practical enough for the challenges faced in the real world. He is not able to offer anything of substance **in the gate**. This was the normal meeting place for official business. In such arenas, wisdom shines in its power to offer direction in solving great challenges (see discussion on 1:21).

24:8–9. The person who **deviseth to do evil** (v. 8) is **a mischievous person** (see 24:2; see also 1:10–11; 6:14; Job 15:35; Ps. 38:12). This person is a schemer and is called a "man of wicked devices" in 12:2 and 14:17. He spends his time plotting to do evil (see 1:11–16; 9:13–18). Such people are **an abomination to men** (v. 9). They are proud, dishonoring (9:7), contentious (22:10), and their every thought is shrouded in **sin.**

24:10. The day of adversity will surely come to all, and in that day, the measure of a man is taken. There is a wordplay here, with the Hebrew terms for **adversity** and **small** being very similar. Heeding wisdom will enable a man to stand tall in adversity so that adversity and smallness will not follow one another in his life (see Jer. 12:5; Gal. 6:9).

24:11–12. Here one encounters situations in which the character of a man is tested. It is always easier to pass by **them that are drawn unto death** (v. 11) than it is to engage their cause and work for justice. This phrase perhaps refers to innocent men condemned to die (see 17:15; Isa. 58:6–7). Wisdom reminds that **he that pondereth the heart consider[s] it** (v. 12). God knows even one's thoughts and motives and will not hold one guiltless if the suffering of the innocent is ignored and one offers no challenge to the oppressor (see 16:2; 21:2; Ps. 94:9–11).

24:13–14. Honey…is good (v. 13), and wisdom counsels the enjoyment of good things. A person's experience of honey provides a rich frame of reference for appreciating the value of **the knowledge of wisdom…unto thy soul** (v. 14). Wisdom nourishes and brings healing (see 16:24 and discussion). Wisdom also gives birth and sustains **expectation**, or hope for the future (see Pss. 9:18; 37:37; Jer. 29:11).

24:15–16. A righteous man is hard to keep down. He may fall, but he will surely rise again, for he is energized by the strength of the living God. The wicked are advised to **Lay not** in **wait** (v. 15) for the destruction of the righteous, for their waiting will be in vain (see 1:11; 12:6; Ps. 10:9–10). The righteous man may fall **seven times** (v. 16; see 6:16; *KJV Study Bible* note on Job 5:19), but he **riseth up again**. God promises to uphold and rescue the righteous (see Pss. 34:19; 37:24; Mic. 7:8). **The wicked shall fall into mischief;** their demise is certain (see 24:22; 4:19; 6:15; 11:3, 5).

24:17–18. The righteous must **Rejoice not** (v. 17) when calamity befalls the wicked. Wisdom takes no comfort in the destruction of the wicked, for she wishes only their redemption (see 17:5). The Lord is always displeased with gloating and may **turn away his wrath from** (v. 18) the wicked and visit punishment upon the gloater instead. Edom was made desolate because she rejoiced over Israel's destruction (see Ezek. 35:15).

24:19–20. This proverb is almost identical to Psalm 37:1 (see 24:1; 23:17). The righteous must not fret over the prosperity of the wicked. These persons have **no reward** (v. 20) that is lasting, either for themselves or for their posterity (see Ps. 37:2, 28, 38; contrast 24:14; 23:18). **The candle of the wicked shall be put out** (see discussion on 13:9).

24:21 – 22. Wisdom counsels the young to **fear … the LORD and the king** (v. 21). Submission to civil authority is also commanded in Ecclesiastes 8:2 – 5. In 1 Peter 2:17, Peter counsels, "Fear God. Honour the king," and Romans 13:1 – 7 urges the same obedience. These passages all view the king and the Lord as a terror to the wicked (see 20:8, 26). Some men are given to rebellion and want to overthrow the king, but **their calamity shall rise suddenly** (v. 22). God's judgment of such people is certain (see 6:15; 11:3, 5), and the power of the king to bring swift judgment upon the rebellious is seen in 20:26.

V. Additional Sayings of the Wise (24:23 – 34)

These proverbs offer additional sayings of the wise and may be an appendix to 22:17 – 24:22.

24:23 – 25. Showing partiality when judging disputes is condemned in Deuteronomy 16:19 and in Proverbs 17:15; 18:5; and 28:21. Here this truth is reinforced with the admonition that **it is not good to have respect of persons in judgment** (v. 23), that is, to show favoritism or partiality. Anyone who says to the wicked **Thou art righteous; him shall the people curse** (v. 24). Just as they will curse the man who "withholdeth corn" (11:26), so the people will curse the one who perverts justice. Bearing witness to the truth may be costly at times, but **a good blessing** (v. 25) is the reward of those who seek to assure that the truth is always heard, regardless of the station in life of those involved (see 10:6; Deut. 16:20).

24:26. As a sincere kiss between lovers is a cause of delight, so it is to **kiss** the **lips** of one who habitually speaks words that are upright and truthful (see 16:24, "pleasant words" are "sweet to the soul").

24:27. The issue of priorities is clearly under discussion here. Wisdom counsels that a person **make it fit … in the field**, or plan carefully and acquire the means, as he builds his **house** (see discussion on 24:3).

24:28 – 29. The person who companions with wisdom will never seek the destruction of his neighbor or **witness … without cause** (v. 28) against him (see 3:30). Wisdom counsels, **deceive not with thy lips** (see 6:19 and discussion; 12:17; 25:18). Neither should

one ever seek to repay evil for evil and say, **I will do so to him as he hath done to me** (v. 29). A spirit of revenge is discouraged also in 20:22 (see discussion there; see also 25:21 – 22; Matt. 5:43 – 45; Rom. 12:17).

24:30 – 32. A journey to **the field of the slothful** (v. 30) or **the vineyard of the man void of understanding** is a depressing yet profitable experience. Viewing the **thorns, and nettles** (v. 31), and the broken **stone wall** presents a sad picture of what can happen when a farmer fails in his duty to the land and serves as a reminder of what can happen to one's life when tempted to be similarly inattentive to walking in the way of wisdom (see discussion on 6:6; see also 20:4; 15:19; Isa. 34:13).

24:33 – 34. People must make choices in this life. Here the choice is between **sleep** and **folding of the hands** (v. 33) or constant attention to duty, with its accompanying requirement for hard work and weariness in the body. Wisdom challenges all to consider well that one choice leads to **poverty** (v. 34) and the other leads to "delight, and a good blessing" (24:25; see 6:10 – 11).

VI. Hezekiah's Collection of Solomon's Proverbs (chaps. 25 – 29)

This section contains another collection of Solomon's proverbs, similar to those found in 10:1 – 22:16.

25:1. These are also proverbs of Solomon (see discussions on 1:1; 10:1). **The men of Hezekiah … copied out** these proverbs to preserve them and restore them to a position of influence in Hezekiah's reign (ca. 715 – 686 BC), during which a great revival occurred and the king restored the singing of hymns to its proper place (2 Chron. 29:30). Hezekiah's interest in the words of David corresponds to his support of a compilation of Solomon's proverbs. Solomon was the last king to rule over all Israel during the united monarchy; Hezekiah was the first king to rule over all Israel (then restricted to the southern kingdom) after the destruction of the divided monarchy's northern kingdom.

25:2 – 7. In these verses, wisdom's instruction on the role of the king in Israel or any society is revealed.

While **It is the glory of God to conceal a thing** (v. 2), it is the glory of a king to diligently search out the answers related to solving vexing problems encountered in his reign. God receives glory because man cannot understand His universe or the way He rules it (see Deut. 29:29; *KJV Study Bible* note on Job 26:14; Isa. 40:12–24; Rom. 11:33–36). A king receives glory if he can uncover the truth and administer justice (see 1 Kings 3:9; 4:34). Like God's ways, the ways of the king are **unsearchable** (v. 3). The judgments of kings often cannot be understood (like the four things in 30:18–19). Yet God controls the hearts of kings (see discussion on 21:1). Achieving peace in this life requires coming to terms with the fact that neither God nor kings feel compelled to explain what they are doing. This often leads humans to frustration and complaining, but wisdom counsels trust in the One who is over the king and works all things together for good.

Every leader needs trustworthy advisors who will tell him the truth and serve him faithfully. The absence of such persons will surely result in the crippling of the king. **Take away the dross from the silver** (v. 4) is a metaphor for a process that is necessary for the purification of society in general and rulers in particular (see Isa. 1:22–25; Ezek. 22:18; Mal. 3:2–3). Only when thoughtful attention is given to personal purity will **his throne ... be established in righteousness** (v. 5; see discussion on 16:12; see also 20:26).

Humility and caution are good traits to practice when in the presence of the king. Wisdom counsels, **Put not forth thyself in the presence of the king** (v. 6). Jesus gave a similar warning about taking the place of honor at a wedding feast (Luke 14:7–11). It is always better to wait and hear the king say, **Come up hither** (v. 7), and sit in the place designated under his authority than to be embarrassed when asked to take a lesser seat (see "Friend, go up higher," Luke 14:10; contrast Isa. 22:15–19).

25:8–10. Go not forth hastily to strive (v. 8) is a warning about the seriousness of disputes (see 17:14) and the need to exercise caution when initiating a dispute (see 24:28). The enjoinder to **discover not a secret** (v. 9) applies to uncovering information a neighbor has shared in confidence in a court of law. One who uncovers and repeats such information is a gossip (see 11:13; 20:19), and his **infamy** (v. 10) may become a permanent part of his reputation. A gossip gets a bad reputation. This is a serious issue because a good name is one of life's most valuable possessions (see 22:1 and discussion).

25:11–12. Few things in this world are more powerful than an appropriate and well-timed word, even if it is a word of correction. Such a word is more valuable than **gold ... silver** (v. 11; see 8:19). It is more precious than **an earring of gold** (v. 12). This valuable word and the **wise reprover** who delivers it are comparable to the beautiful wreath and necklace that represent the adornment of wisdom and sound teaching (see 1:9; 3:22; 4:9; see "the reproof of life," 15:31).

25:13. Few refreshments were as enjoyable as the drink cooled by **snow** from the mountains and delivered to those sweltering in the heat of the **harvest** (see 26:1; contrast 10:26). In like manner, the **faithful messenger ... refresheth the soul of his masters** (see 13:17 and discussion).

25:14. Clouds and wind normally signify the coming of a rainstorm, and if the rain does not come, farmers are disappointed. In like manner, the person who promises a gift and does not deliver it is **like clouds ... without rain**. This image is applied to unproductive men in Jude 12.

25:15. Judicious words softened by gentleness and kindness can overcome great resistance. **By long forbearing**, even **a prince is persuaded** (see 14:29). The idea that **a soft tongue** is able to break a **bone** is used to show how the most difficult of matters can sometimes be resolved by using gentle words.

25:16–17. Too much of a good thing often turns into a bad thing. Eating too much sweet **honey** (v. 16) can sicken you, just as too many visits to your **neighbour's house** (v. 17) will most certainly cause him to resent your presence. Balance and self-control are valuable allies when it comes to eating your favorite foods and visiting your favorite people.

25:18. Giving **false witness** in court (see discussion on 6:19; see also 24:28; Exod. 20:16) against a **neighbour** can cause a person to be viewed as a

maul, and a sword, and a sharp arrow (see Ps. 57:4; Jer. 9:8). The tongue here is likened to a weapon of war spreading death and destruction.

25:19. One ought never to place confidence in a man who has demonstrated that he is unfaithful. Such a man is like **a broken tooth** or **a foot out of joint**. When you need such a person to accomplish something weighty, they will always let you down. Israel discovered that relying on Egypt was like leaning on a crushed reed (Isa. 36:6), just as all who rely on the faithless will discover.

25:20. Offering only a song for those who are in deep need is like taking away a man's garment when it is the only thing separating him from the biting cold of the night air. It is also like pouring **vinegar on nitre**, probably sodium carbonate (see Jer. 2:22). A vigorous reaction is produced when vinegar is poured on this substance. One may expect the same kind of reaction from a person whose human needs are dismissed with a song.

25:21–22. Paul quoted this passage in his instruction to the righteous on how to overcome evil with good (Rom. 12:20). Kindness to one's enemy is encouraged in 20:22 and Exodus 23:4–5. Here wisdom counsels that one should **give** the enemy **bread** (v. 21) and **water**. In keeping with this wisdom, at Elisha's request, a trapped Aramean army was given a great feast and then sent home (2 Kings 6:21–23; see 2 Chron. 28:15). This practice will **heap coals of fire upon** the enemy's **head** (v. 22), which was a horrible punishment reserved for the wicked (see Ps. 140:10). Here, however, it is kindness that will hurt the enemy (see the broken bone of 25:15) but perhaps win him over. Alternatively, the expression may reflect an Egyptian expiation ritual, in which a guilty person, as a sign of his repentance, carried a basin of glowing coals on his head. The meaning here, then, would be that in returning good for evil and being kind to your enemy, you may cause him to repent or change. In any event, **the LORD shall reward** the kindness even if the enemy remains hostile (see 11:18; 19:17).

25:23. Just as **The north wind driveth away rain** (see Luke 12:54), so the **backbiting tongue** produces **an angry countenance** (see 10:18). Some things logi-

cally follow one another. Hence, some things should be avoided and other things embraced because of the consequences that flow from them.

25:24. Tight quarters on a **housetop** with solitude are to be preferred to life in spacious quarters that must be shared with **a brawling woman** (see 21:19).

25:25. Communication between persons in distant countries was difficult in the days of Solomon. The feelings derived from receiving **good news from a far country** may be likened to the feelings derived from downing a cold drink on a very hot day after being hard at work (see Gen. 45:25–28).

25:26. A righteous man who begins to practice sin is like **a troubled fountain**. The pure water that flowed from an untroubled spring becomes contaminated with mud or other impurities and is unfit for human consumption. So the man who pollutes himself with sin is of little value to God or man, even if he was once noted for his righteousness (see Ezek. 34:18–19).

25:27. For men to search their own glory is to abandon the primary reason for man's existence, which is to glorify God. To seek glory for oneself is thus to turn the creation order on its head and worship the created more than the Creator. Man has always been good at doing this, but always to his shame (see 25:6–7).

25:28. Ancient cities depended on their walls for safety and security. Wisdom counsels that men should depend on self-control for their safety and security. **He that hath no rule over his own spirit** is lacking in self-control (see 16:32). Such a person **is like a city that is … without walls**, defenseless and surely to be disgraced (see Neh. 1:3).

26:1. The fool is the subject for consideration in 26:1–12. All of the elements in verse 1 are connected in an illogical manner. **Snow in summer … rain in harvest** and **honor … for a fool** are all illogical pairings. In the Holy Land, it rarely rains between June and September (but see 1 Sam. 12:17–18). It is never logical to honor a fool, and doing so could hurt others who might choose to follow his foolish ways (see 26:8; 30:22).

26:2. A curse has no effect when it is aimed at an innocent person. Hence, **the curse causeless shall**

not come to fruition. It shall fly about as ineffectually as a fluttering bird. When David was cursed by Shimei, David realized that the curse would not take effect because he was innocent of the charge of murdering members of Saul's family (see 2 Sam. 16:8, 12).

26:3. The horse and donkey are not controlled by reason but rather by bridle and whip. So the fool does not listen to reason, and a rod for the fool's back is necessary to bring him under control (see 14:3; 19:29).

26:4–5. These two proverbs are meant to complement one another. The wise must never descend to the level of the fool. Hence, Answer not a fool according to his folly (v. 4); do not stoop to his level (see 23:9; Matt. 7:6). At times, however, the wise feel constrained to Answer a fool according to his folly (v. 5), for sometimes folly must be plainly exposed and denounced. Wisdom is required in discerning when to apply verse 4 and when to apply verse 5.

26:6–7. A man who entrusts the carrying of an important message to a fool (v. 6) may drinketh damage to his business and perhaps to his own life. The fool cannot be trusted with the simplest of tasks, and at times it seems that his feet and mind have been severed from his body (see 4:17; Job 34:7). Even if the fool gets where he has been sent, he will likely misrepresent the one who sent him or in some other manner frustrate the sender's purpose (see 13:17).

26:8. To promote a fool to a position of honor is a grievous error. The man who does so is as foolish As he that bindeth a stone in a sling. A fool with authority wields a formidable weapon, but it is useless in his hands—as useless as a stone that is tied, not placed, in the sling. The man who promoted the fool is like a man who would go to war with that sling, clearly showing that he is a fool.

26:9. In 26:7, a proverb in the mouth of a fool is of no value. Here it is compared to a thorn bush in the hand of the drunkard. A fool reciting a proverb will do as much damage to himself and others as a drunkard wielding a thornbush.

26:10. When the fool and transgressors have achieved their twisted, self-serving ends, they will probably be surprised to learn that one more reward will most certainly to be theirs. The great God that formed all things has reserved an everlasting reward for both the fool and the transgressor. The Creator God has reserved a day when all will receive their just rewards, every person according to his or her deeds.

26:11. The fool never learns, and like the drunkard who returns to his drink, he repeats the same foolish acts over and over again (see 23:35). A fool returneth to his folly, no matter how disgusting his actions, just as a dog returneth to his vomit. This passage is quoted in 2 Peter 2:22, where it refers to false teachers.

26:12. This verse concludes this section of instruction on the fool (26:1–12). There is one who is a little worse than a fool: a man wise in his own conceit. Conceit is applied to the sluggard in 26:16 and to the rich in 28:11 (see also 26:5). Conceit is extremely dangerous because it blinds a person to the great needs in his life, especially to his need for God.

26:13–16. Here wisdom offers her views on the sluggard. The sluggard loves to sleep and seems to be attached to his bed as a door is to its hinges. He is extremely creative when it comes to offering excuses for absenting himself from work. The streets are filled with danger, he insists, There is a lion is in the way (v. 13). He is so lazy that he will not even bring his hand to his mouth (v. 15). No man can change the sluggard's views on life, for in his conceit (v. 16), he imagines himself to be wiser than seven men.

26:17–21. Wisdom next offers counsel on disputes, deceit, and lying. A man has to be foolish indeed to taketh a dog by the ears (v. 17). The dog in view here is a wild dog, and to grab hold of him is to risk great harm to oneself. Mixing in the disputes of others when it is not directly related to one's personal concerns is equally filled with the potential for harm. It is better to stay away from wild dogs and wild people.

The wise will also stay far from the mad man (v. 18) whose sport (v. 19) is casting firebrands, arrows, … death (v. 18) and deception at his neighbor (see the archer in 26:10). The firebrands could easily ignite sheaves of grain (see Zech. 12:6). This mad man asks, Am not I in sport? (v. 19). He claims that he is joking or playing a prank. There are truly evil people in this world, and one should make an effort to stay as far away from them as possible.

A quarrel will die out if no gossip fuels it, just as **a fire goeth out** (v. 20) if it is not regularly fueled with **wood**. When hot coals are added to dry wood, fire quickly blazes. In the same way, it takes a **contentious man to kindle strife** (v. 21; see 6:14). Evil men are like hot coals, and with their seditious gossip and slander, they enflame many and keep dissension and hatred ablaze.

26:22. Gossip here performs the same evil purpose as in 26:20–21 (see also 18:8).

26:23. The speech of the adulteress is seductive (2:16; 5:3) and is like **silver dross** (v. 23), or "glaze." Her **Burning lips** are like the attractive glaze coating of a piece of pottery. The pottery is attractive on the outside, but inside, it is as empty as the empty and **wicked heart** of the adulteress (see the "clean outside" of the cup and dish, Luke 11:39; see also Matt. 23:27).

26:24–28. The central idea of 26:23 is explored in verses 24–26. There is one who is evil like the adulteress. He keeps up an outer appearance and says he hates sin, but he **layeth up deceit within him** (v. 24; see 12:20). **He speaketh fair** (v. 25) and uses gracious speech to deceive, but he is evil through and through (see Jer. 9:8). He is filled with **seven abominations** (see *KJV Study Bible* note on Job 5:19; for seven things the Lord detests, see 6:16–19). In time, **His wickedness shall be shewed before the whole congregation** (v. 26; see 5:14; Luke 8:17). The righteous can count on his unveiling, for **Whoso diggeth a pit shall fall therein** (v. 27). "His mischief shall return upon his own head" (Ps. 7:16; see Prov. 1:18 and discussion; 28:10; 29:6; Est. 7:10; Ps. 7:15; Eccl. 10:8–9). This certainty should give some solace to the righteous, who are often wounded by the **lying tongue** that **hateth those that are afflicted by it** (v. 28) and the **flattering mouth** that **worketh ruin** (see 29:5; 16:13). God can be depended on to affect a great work on behalf of the righteous when he delivers them from those evil persons who truly hate them and are committed to their ruin.

27:1. Here, the focus is on arrogance that leads one to imagine he is in control of his destiny. The prohibition **Boast not thyself of to morrow** is found also in James 4:13–16. This type of boasting reveals pride in one's ability to control the future and a lack of submission to God's sovereignty. Compare the words of the rich fool in Luke 12:19–20 (see also Prov. 16:9; Isa. 56:12).

27:2. Praising one's self also betrays a pride in self that runs contrary to the humility commended by wisdom. Wisdom counsels all to **Let another man praise thee** (see 2 Cor. 10:12, 18).

27:3–6. Jealousy, anger, and deceit have a devastating impact on relationships. **Who is able to stand before envy** (v. 4), bear up under the heavy weight of anger, or deal with the deceitful lies of an enemy (see 6:34; Song 8:6)? These ingredients weigh on relationships with the heaviness of a great stone. **Open rebuke** (v. 5) can benefit a relationship and is called "the reproof of life" in 15:31 (see Gal. 2:14). Friends will be open and honest in relationships, and although they may issue challenging words at times, their words are beneficial because **Faithful are the wounds of a friend** (v. 6). These wounds are called a sign of kindness in Psalm 141:5.

27:7. Having too much can sometimes destroy the ability to enjoy the little things in life. When a man is full, he **loatheth a honeycomb**, even though he may love honey and would have welcomed it if he had been hungry. **To the hungry soul every bitter thing is sweet** (see 25:16, 27). Gratitude for all things and the cultivation of a spirit of giving may keep hunger alive in the soul and help a man hold on to his ability to practice moderation and retain the ability to find joy in all things.

27:8. The **man that wandereth from his place**, or leaves home too early, may find himself in big trouble (Luke 15:11–32). By leaving home, he has lost his security and may be vulnerable to temptation (see 7:21–23). The dangers surrounding him are similar to those surrounding a little bird who leaves the nest prematurely.

27:9. The counsel of a good friend is as valuable as **Ointment** (see discussion on 21:17) **and perfume**

(see the one "perfumed with myrrh and frankincense," Song 3:6). A relationship with such a **friend** brings great **sweetness** (see 16:21, 24).

27:10. Here the value of friendship is extolled. Wisdom counsels that one not fail a friend in need. When in need, sometimes one can rely on friendship rather than on mere family relationships. **Thine own friend, and thy father's friend, forsake not**. A true friend will prove of more value when facing challenges **than a brother far off**, whose affections and willingness to aid may have been diluted by time and distance.

27:11. The son is always in some measure the reflection of the father. Hence, the father pleads, **My son, be wise** (see 10:1). A wise son (or student) serves as a powerful testimony that the father (or teacher) who has shaped him is a man of worth. When people attack the character of the father, he **may answer him that reproacheth** by pointing to the son he has raised, which may serve to end the attack.

27:12. The simple pass on, and are punished. They go their own way, disregarding wise counsel, and their punishment is certain (see 7:22 – 23; 9:16 – 18).

27:13. Here is an example of the prudent man discussed in 27:12. This is a repetition of 20:16 (see discussion there).

27:14. The wise man **blesseth his friend** but not too **early in the morning**. Perhaps the blesser seeks to win his friend's favor but has failed to remember that timing and tone are everything. Arousing his friend too early and loudly sabotages his intent, angers his friend, and ruins their friendship (see Ps. 12:2).

27:15 – 16. In Solomon's era, the rain soaked the earthen roofs and then dripped everywhere inside the houses. The **contentious woman** (v. 15) is similarly annoying (see 19:13). The poison of her words saturates the house and continuously drips on everything. She is completely unmanageable and as difficult to control as **the wind** (v. 16). Woe to the man who is married to such a contentious, soggy, and dripping woman.

27:17. In stark contrast to the contentious woman and the havoc she produces, a positive person **sharpeneth the countenance of his friend**. Positive people can contribute much to the development and molding of their companions' characters, as **Iron sharpeneth iron**.

27:18. The fig tree requires thoughtful and consistent attention before it will bear its luscious fruit. The man who cares well for the fig tree **shall eat the fruit thereof** and **shall be honoured** (see 2 Tim. 2:6; Gen. 39:4; see also Matt. 25:21; Luke 12:42 – 44; John 12:26). Working hard to secure good outcomes for employers often pays off with honor and abundance.

27:19. The condition of a man's **heart** indicates his true character, as one's **face** is reflected in a pool of **water** (see Matt. 5:8). To know what is in **the heart of man**, one need only to watch how he treats others. In his treatment of his neighbor, his heart is unveiled.

27:20. Hell and destruction are never full (see 15:11; discussion on Job 26:6). Their appetites are insatiable (see Isa. 5:14). **So the eyes of man are never satisfied** and long to behold new and exciting things (see Eccl. 4:8). Sin causes vacillation in commitments. The wise will rigorously control their desires and hold fast to godly commitments. This is not easy but is doable through the power of the Holy Spirit.

27:21. The fining pot was necessary to bring out the highest value of **gold** and **silver**, which were refined to remove their impurities (see Isa. 1:25; Mal. 3:3). **Praise** represents an opportunity for the unveiling of what is truly in the heart of a man. How a person responds to praise is a reflection of one's character. One must not become proud, and one must be wary of flattery (see 12:8; Luke 6:26). Satan has destroyed many of God's servants with success and praise.

27:22. In spite of severe punishment, fools refuse to change (see discussion on 20:30; see also 26:11; Jer. 5:3). Even **a pestle**, a clublike tool used for pounding grain, cannot cause **his foolishness** to **depart from him**.

27:23 – 27. Here wisdom praises the basic security afforded by agricultural pursuits, reflecting the agricultural base of the ancient economy. Farmers should **Be ... diligent** (v. 23) in caring for their **herds**, which are a good investment, unlike monetary **riches** (v. 24) that do not last **for ever**. Like money, **the crown** does not **endure to every generation**, but **flocks** bear offspring from generation to generation (see Job 19:9; Lam. 5:16). It is important to consider the lasting power of investments of time. A cycle begins when **the hay appeareth, and the ... grass sheweth itself** (v. 25). This cycle provides food for sheep and goats, which sometimes served as tribute payments (see 2 Kings 3:4). The **goats' milk** (v. 27) and flesh provided food and sustenance year-round for one's family and **maidens**. Goats' hides and lambs' wool provided clothing and warmth for all the members of the household. Hard work and attention to the resources nature provides are to be preferred to chasing after money or worldly power.

28:1. Chapters 28 and 29 return to the use of the antithetical literary device. As in chapters 10–15, the writer sets up a contrast in which the second line begins with the use of "but." The **wicked flee** (see Lev. 26:17, 36; Ps. 53:5) **... but the righteous are bold as a lion** (like David in 1 Sam. 17:46; see Ps. 18:33–38). God gives to the righteous courage that the wicked can never know.

28:2. Israel's rebellion often brought **many ... princes** and rapid changes in leadership (see 1 Kings 16:8–28; 2 Kings 15:8–15), but **a man of understanding ... shall be prolonged**. A ruler who companions with wisdom will be successful and may expect a longer reign (see 8:15–16; 24:5; 29:4).

28:3. They **that oppresseth the poor** are **like a sweeping rain**. This language is used to describe the destructive power of Assyria's army in Isaiah 28:2. The gentle rain that nourishes the crops and provides sustenance for the farmer is compared to a righteous king in Psalm 72:6–7. There will always be men and armies who are empty of compassion and destroyers of good, and they are a terror to any people.

28:4. The oppression of the poor is a violation of **the law**. Here "the law" is either the teachings of wisdom (3:1; 7:2) or the law of Moses (Ps. 119:53). Turning from God's law, people may **praise the wicked** (see Rom. 1:32). Those who **keep the law** will **contend with** the wicked (see 28:7, 9; 29:18;

Eph. 5:11; Rom. 1:32). The righteous will always contend with lawbreakers and speak out for right and justice.

28:5. The wicked are openly disobedient to the law of God and have become perverted in their minds and lifestyles. **They that seek the LORD understand all things**. Those who fear the Lord **understand all things** that are necessary for living a godly and successful life. They know "righteousness, and justice, and equity" (2:9).

28:6. It is better to be poor and **walketh in ... uprightness** than to be rich and perverse in one's dealings with man and God (see 2:7).

28:7. Whoso keepeth the law displays a concern for the glory of God and will not lose his reward. Such a person will not be **a companion of riotous men** who pursue a hedonistic lifestyle without regard for God. Separation from the ungodly is the ageless responsibility of the righteous.

28:8. The person who charges excessive interest to pile up **unjust gain** will not go unpunished. This practice is prohibited in Exodus 22:25; Leviticus 25:35–37; Deuteronomy 23:19–20; Ezekiel 22:12. The Lord will see to it that a redistribution of wealth takes place, and He will **gather it for him that will pity the poor** (see 14:31).

28:9. Avoiding **the law** of God has tragic consequences. The **prayer** of the lawbreaker **shall be** an **abomination** to God. The prayers of lawbreakers will receive the same condemnation that the sacrifices of the wicked received in 15:8 (see also Ps. 66:18; Isa. 1:15; 59:1–2).

28:10. The man who deliberately seeks to turn the righteous away from God **shall fall ... into his own pit**. The Lord has pledged that He will cast these wicked persons into the pits they have dug for others (see Num. 31:15–16). In contrast, **the upright shall have good things** (see 3:35; Heb. 6:12; 1 Peter 3:9).

28:11. The rich and the poor are once again compared. **The rich man is wise in his own conceit**. He is like the fool (26:5) or the sluggard (26:16). In contrast, **the poor** can discern this fatal flaw in the rich and proceed to move forward with godly understanding.

28:12. When the righteous are in power, the people rejoice and **there is great glory**. When the wicked are in power, **a man is hidden**. He hides to avoid the tryanny of the wicked ruler. Obadiah hid one hundred prophets during the reign of Ahab (see 1 Kings 18:13), and Joash was hidden for six years while the wicked Athaliah ruled (see 2 Kings 11:2–3). How different the environment in a kingdom when the righteous are in power.

28:13. He that covereth his sins shall not prosper. When a man tries to hide his wrongdoing, the physical and psychological pain referred to in 3:7–8 and Psalm 32:3 results. When a man **confesseth and forsaketh** his sin, however, he **shall have mercy**. Note the joy of forgiveness in Psalm 32:5, 10–11. Men cover sin, and God covers sin. God covers sin on the heels of confession, and the result is joy. Men cover sin out of guilt, and the results are conceit, shame, and pride.

28:14. The wise man **feareth** God **alway** and experiences joy (see 1:7; 23:17). **But he that hardeneth his heart**, as did Pharaoh (Exod. 7:13) and the Israelites who tested the Lord at Horeb (Exod. 17:7; see Ps. 95:8; Rom. 2:5), continuously falls into ruin.

28:15–16. The oppressive reign of the **wicked ruler** (v. 15) is compared to the presence of **a roaring lion, and a ranging bear**. This ruler is full of rage and murderous intent (see 19:12; Matt. 2:16; 1 Peter 5:8). He is like an angry bear on the attack (see 17:12; 28:12). **He that hateth covetousness shall prolong his days** (v. 16). Unlike the wicked ruler, this person values understanding and detests the use of power for personal gain. Such a person will enjoy long life.

28:17. A man that doeth violence to the blood … shall flee to the pit. The murderer will experience an early death as punishment for his sin. Murder was punishable by death (see Gen. 9:6; Exod. 21:14). No one should seek to prevent his punishment.

28:18. Salvation belongs to those who live **uprightly**, for they walk with God and are in His keeping. Those who are twisted or **perverse** will **fall at once**, or suddenly (see 11:5). They too are in the hand of God, and He will bring them to a swift and damning end (see 28:6; 19:1).

28:19–20. The undisciplined **followeth after vain persons** (v. 19). They follow after unprofitable things and are obsessed with schemes for making easy money. The disciplined farmer provides a dramatic contrast. He is committed to tilling his land, planting the seeds, and a prayerful waiting for the harvest. He will have **plenty of bread**, while the vain will be filled with poverty. Wisdom counsels all to follow the way of the tiller of the ground. The way to become rich is to practice the self-discipline and **faithful[ness]** (v. 20) of the farmer. This is the way to **abound with blessings** and receive God's gifts and favors (see 3:13–18; 10:6; Gen. 49:26; Deut. 33:16). **He that maketh haste to be rich shall not be innocent** and will not go unpunished for the wrongdoings he practices in pursuit of his riches (see similar warnings in 20:21; 23:4).

28:21. To have respect of persons is not good (see 18:5 and 24:23). In court cases, a judge might render a favorable verdict **for a piece of bread**. How unthinkable that a man would transgress the law and accept a bribe as small as a piece of bread when the acceptance of bribes was so clearly condemned in the law (see Ezek. 13:19).

28:22. Again a warning is given to anyone who **hasteth to be rich** (see similar warnings in 20:21; 23:4; 28:20). Such a person **hath an evil eye**; he has impure motives and is stingy (see 23:6). Wisdom insists that **poverty shall come upon** this stingy man (see 23:6), for it is the generous man who will prosper.

28:23. He that rebuketh a man, afterwards shall find … favour (see 15:31; 25:12; Gal. 2:14). It is not easy to deliver a loving challenge to a sinning brother. It is far easier to **flattereth with the tongue** (see 16:13; 26:28; 29:5). In the end, however, the maturing brother will bless those who aided his growth with their challenging words. One should endure the unpleasantness attached to confrontation, knowing wise rebukers are instruments in God's hand for the perfecting of their brothers and should be confident that God is using all of their efforts to mature others.

28:24. Whoso robbeth his father or his mother … is the companion of a destroyer. This type of thievery was refined in the day of Jesus, but the person who practices it has always been "a destroyer" (a murderer) in God's eyes. Such a man destroys the spirits of his parents, who look to him in their old age for protection and security. He is an abomination (see discussion on 19:26; see Matt. 15:4–6; Mark 7:10–12).

28:25–26. A man who is consumed with the desire to advance himself will always **stirreth up strife** (v. 25), but **he that putteth his trust in the LORD shall be made fat.** Men who are not obsessed with self will become prosperous, as will those who are generous (11:25) and diligent (see 13:4, "the soul of the diligent shall be made fat"). **Whoso walketh wisely** (v. 26) equals "whoso putteth his trust in the LORD" in 29:25 (see also 3:5). These are the men who will know the deliverance of the Lord in times of trouble. Those who trust in self are fools.

28:27. The man who **giveth unto the poor shall not lack.** Generosity is the path to blessing (see 11:24; 14:21; 19:17). In contrast, the man who **hideth his eyes** from the needs of the poor will hear **many a curse** from those whose needs he ignores, but ultimately he will hear the curse of God (see 21:13).

28:28. Men must often **hide themselves** when the wicked are in power (see 28:12). When the wicked perish, and they most certainly will, the **righteous** may **increase** (see 11:10; 29:2). They will no longer need to be in hiding.

29:1. The person who is **often reproved** and still **hardeneth his neck** is headed for a terrible end. Eli's sons died because of their stubbornness (see 1 Sam. 2:25; Deut. 9:6, 13). He **shall suddenly be destroyed, and that without remedy** (see the fate of the mockers in 1:22–27).

29:2. Power in the hands of the righteous creates a nation in which **the people rejoice** (see 11:10). **When the wicked ... rule, the people mourn** (see 28:12; Judg. 2:18). The Israelites groaned in Egypt (see Exod. 2:23–24).

29:3. Whoso loveth wisdom brings joy to his father (see 10:1). In contrast, the companion of **harlots** wastes his money (see 5:10; 6:26). Wisdom protects the young from adultery.

29:4. The king may bring stability to **the land** through the practice of justice (see 16:12). The king who is greedy for **gifts**, or bribes, will soon destabilize his kingdom (see 17:8).

29:5–7. Flattery frequently involves deception. A wicked man uses flattery to spread **a net** (v. 5) or set **a snare** (v. 6), intending to imprison the naive. **The righteous** are in possession of a wisdom that allows them to discern this evil intent and go on their way in freedom, singing and rejoicing (see 1:18 and 22:5). **The righteous** (v. 7) do not just go on their way singing. They **considereth ... the poor** and use resources available to them to relieve the suffering of the poor (as Job did, see Job 29:16; see also Prov. 29:14; 19:17; 22:22).

29:8–11. These verses contrast the angry fool and the wise man. **Scornful men** (v. 8) may bring an entire city **into a snare** (see 6:14; 11:11; 26:21). In contrast, **wise men** are often used by God to bring about the deliverance of a city. They are able to **turn away wrath** (see James 3:17–18). This deliverance is no easy process since it often involves dealing with the fool, who practices anger and ridicule in his attempt to disrupt justice. The fool is like an angry bear (17:12) or the tossing sea (Isa. 57:20–21). Fools are also **bloodthirsty** (v. 10). They **hate the upright** and design elaborate schemes to kill them (such schemes are described in 1:11–16; see Ps. 5:6). The fool says whatever he feels when he loses his temper (see v. 9; 14:16–17). The wise man has his hands full when dealing with the fool but has cultivated self-control, timing, and confidence in God's wisdom and power, which allows him to still the raging fool and overcome his evil schemes (see 16:32).

29:12. If a ruler prefers lies to the truth, **all his servants** will become **wicked** and will tell him nothing but lies (see Isa. 1:23). Leaders will beget followers who are much like themselves and who value what they value.

29:14. God is pleased with rulers who **faithfully** care for the poor and seek justice in all things. The kingdom of such a ruler will be **established for ever** since it finds its origin and sustenance in the kingdom of the eternal God (see 16:12; see also 29:4; Isa. 9:7).

29:15. A child has a sinful nature, and left to himself, he will choose behaviors rooted in that nature and bring shame to his parents and community.

Parents employ the **rod and reproof** because they love the child and wish to prepare him to glorify God and love his neighbor. Discipline consists of physical and verbal elements (see discussion on 13:24).

29:16. When wicked leaders govern a nation, sin is rampant (see 29:2; 11:11; 28:12, 28). In time, however, **the righteous shall see** the wicked leaders' **fall** (see 10:25; 14:11; 21:12).

29:17. Parents who want to delight in their adult children must teach and train them while they are young (see 13:24 and 22:6). The correction of children is a sacred responsibility God entrusts to parents. Parents who ignore this responsibility will reap a tragic harvest.

29:18. In Hebrew, the term **vision** refers to a revelation or message from God given through a prophet (see 1 Sam. 3:1; Isa. 1:1; Amos 8:11–12). S. S. Buzzell, commenting on the text, states: "The word 'vision' is the revelation (*hazon*) a prophet receives. Also the KJV translation 'the people perish' does not refer to unsaved people dying in sin. The verb *para'* means to cast off restraint. So the verse is stating that without God's Word people abandon themselves to their own sinful ways. On the other hand keeping (obeying) God's law (see 28:4, 7) brings happiness" (Buzzell, "Proverbs," p. 968). The text may allude to the sinful actions of the Israelites while Moses was on Mount Sinai (see Exod. 32:25). **Happy is he** who lives in obedience to the restraining yet freeing dictates of the revelation received from God in His message to mankind (see 28:4; 8:32; 28:14).

29:19. Servants, like sons (see 29:15, 17), must be disciplined (see 22:6). Sometimes words are not enough for the servant who willfully chooses to disregard the directions of his master. Sterner measures may be required to get the attention and compliance of one who is unwilling to heed directions.

29:20. The man who is **hasty in his words** often speaks before he listens (see 18:13; see also 10:19; 17:27–28; James 1:19). **There is more hope of a fool than of him** is identical to 26:12. The man is conceited and will create problems everywhere he goes.

29:21. The warning here is against pampering one's servants. If one treats **his servant** too delicately, he **shall have him become his son at the length**. The Hebrew literally reads, "the end shall be trouble." The word translated "trouble" in this reading appears only here. The admonition is to maintain a level of discipline that assures that servants comply with requests and get their work done.

29:22. An angry man stirreth up strife. The man who is dominated by his passions **aboundeth** is rich **in transgressions** (see 6:14; 15:18). The list of his many sins is hard to keep up with. The wise will do well to stay far from him and pray that he will be divinely enabled to live a very different lifestyle, one characterized by kindness, holiness, and peace.

29:23. When observing the opposing effects of pride and humility, the godly should pray for growth in humility and deliverance from pride (see 15:33; 18:12). An irony is discovered in this proverb. Pride, which is designed by a man to exalt himself, in the end brings him low; and humility, which seemingly brings a man down, actually brings about his exaltation.

29:24. The **partner** of **a thief** is setting himself up for trouble. When the thief is apprehended, the partner will have to testify against him and swear an oath in the courtroom to tell the truth. If he says nothing, he will be held responsible for failing to testify against the thief and will be required to share in the thief's punishment (see Lev. 5:1). Men will do well to consider carefully with whom they join up.

29:25. A person's actions are controlled to a significant extent by what they fear and what they love. **The fear of man** enslaves a man to the opinions and directions of those whom the man fears. Such a man is in bondage to others, and his end will not be a good one unless he is released from the bondage created by his fear (see 1 Sam. 15:24; Isa. 51:12; John 12:42–43). In stark contrast to this bondage is the freedom and joy that comes with putting our trust in the Lord, for **whoso putteth his trust in the LORD shall be safe** (see 18:10; 3:5–6).

29:26. Many seek the ruler's favour, for they imagine that if they can just gain his protection, all will go well for them. Their social-security program is his favor. They fail to realize how fickle and changeable that favor can be (see 2 Sam. 14:22; 16:4; Est. 4:8;

5:2; 7:3; 8:5). The wise discern that **every man's judgment cometh from the LORD** and understand that God controls all of the circumstances of life, including the actions of the king (see discussion on 21:1), and defends the cause of the poor and the just (see Job 36:6). When you are right with the God of the universe, you need fear no one and nothing, and you can be eternally secure in the arms of His protecting love. God's love is not fickle, and He changes not.

VII. The Words of Agur (chap. 30)

This is the first of the two chapters that serve as an appendix to Proverbs.

30:1-3. The identity of **Agur the son of Jakeh** (v. 1) is not certain. He was probably a wise man like Ethan and Heman (see 1 Kings 4:31). The use of the term **prophecy** is intended to indicate the authority and importance of the forthcoming message. This message was written for **Ithiel and Ucal**, who were perhaps Agur's students. The messenger's confession, **I am more brutish than any man** (v. 2), undoubtedly was an exaggerated expression of his ignorance, serving to accentuate his humility. Paul described himself as the "chief" of sinners (1 Tim. 1:16). Agur's message did not arise from his own intelligence but was the byproduct of **the knowledge of the holy** (v. 3), or "of the Holy One" (God), which he had received as a gift from God. This phrase, "the holy," occurs elsewhere in Proverbs only in 9:10.

30:4. The use of rhetorical questions to express God's greatness as Creator occurs also in Job 38:4-11 and Isaiah 40:12. The answer to these questions is God, for only He has **gathered the wind** (see Ps. 135:7) and **bound the waters in a garment** (see Job 26:8; 38:8-9). Few questions are more important than this one: **What is his name, and what is his son's name, if thou canst tell?** or "Do you know who this God is?" God similarly challenged Job (Job 38:4). The questions conclude with an inquiry into the deeper subject of "the son's name." Some have found here a reference to plurality in the Godhead and a parallel to the messianic psalms and their revelation of the Coming One who would embody wisdom, the Lord Jesus Christ (see Smith, *Scripture Testimony*, p. 496).

30:5-6. This verse is almost identical to Psalm 18:30. When trusting God, He becomes a protective **shield** (v. 5; see 14:32; 18:10). Every word received from God is flawless; it is like fine, smelted or purified gold. It is wise to take great care to **Add ... not unto his words** (v. 6; see Moses' warning to the Israelites in Deut. 4:2). No one can improve on the flawless truth given in the Bible, and one should beware of all who seek to elevate their views to a level equal to that of God's inspired Word.

30:7-9. Agur petitioned the Lord for **Two things** (v. 7). In keeping with his humility and the confession of his limitations, Agur asked the Lord (1) to keep away from him the temptation to live a life of **vanity and lies** (v. 8) and (2) to provide him with **food** for his daily physical sustenance (see Job 23:12; and the Lord's Prayer, Matt. 6:11). Agur's petition was related to two fears. First, the fear that he might **be full, and deny** (v. 9) his Lord. Moses predicted that Israel would forget God when their food was plentiful and their herds were large (Deut. 8:12-17; 31:20). Second, the fear that he might **be poor, and steal**. Surely, if he became a thief, he would bring dishonor to himself and to his God.

30:10. Accuse not a servant. A man should never suppose that he can take advantage of a servant and falsely accuse him of wrongdoing. To practice such an injustice and to **be found guilty** will bring the curse of the servant's master on the false accuser. Since the accusation is false, the master's curse will be effective (see 26:2), so do not suppose you can take advantage of a servant's lowly position.

30:11-14. The term **generation** (vv. 11-14) occurs four times in these verses and is meant to designate a group of persons who embody the evil traits mentioned in 30:7-9. The first group is composed of those who **curseth their father** (v. 11). This evil behavior was punishable by death (see Exod. 21:17; Lev. 20:9; see Prov. 30:17). The second evil generation is composed of men who are **pure in their own eyes** (v. 12). This self-righteous generation is like the Pharisees, who thought themselves the most righteous of men but in reality were **not washed from their filthiness** (Luke 18:11; see Isa.

65:5). Of the third generation, Proverbs remarks on **how lofty are their eyes!** (v. 13; see discussion on 6:17; see also Isa. 3:16). The fourth generation has **teeth** that **are as swords ... as knives** (v. 14). This circle of evil persons is like ravenous beasts that devour their prey (see Job 29:17). They delight **to devour the poor ... and the needy** (see Ps. 14:4; Mic. 3:2–3).

30:15–16. Four things are never satisfied. First is **The horseleach** (v. 15), which sucks the blood from a horse with an insatiable appetite that is never satisfied. Second is **The grave** (v. 16), whose appetite for the broken, dead bodies of those resting under the curse of the Adamic fall is never satisfied (Isa. 5:14; Hab. 2:5). Third is **the barren womb**. In ancient Israel, a wife without children was desolate, even desperate (see Gen. 16:2; 30:1; Ruth 1:11–13, 20–21; 1 Sam. 1:6, 10–11; 2 Kings 4:14). Fourth is **fire**, which devours everything in its path and asks only for more to destroy and devour.

30:17. Perhaps this proverb is placed here to remind all who read it that disrespect for one's parents has the same devastating impact on a person and on a nation as do the horseleach, the grave, the barren womb, and fire. The haughty and disdainful **eye that mocketh at his father, and despiseth to obey his mother** (see 30:11; 15:20), **the ravens ... shall pick it out.** The loss of an eye was a terrible curse (see the story of Samson, Judg. 16:21). Since vultures normally devoured the dead (see Jer. 16:4; Matt. 24:28), the meaning may be that the body of a disgraceful son will lie unburied and exposed.

30:18–20. These verses focus on four amazing things, or four "ways," that are difficult to understand because they are wrapped up in great power, make a great impression, and yet leave no tracks that can be readily followed. Consider **the way of an eagle** (v. 19) soaring and swooping majestically (see Job 39:27; Jer. 48:40; 49:22) and the mesmerizing movement of **a serpent upon a rock**. Consider **the way of a man with a maid**. The focus here is on the mystery of courting and how it leads to consummation. Consider **the way of an adulterous woman as she eateth, and wipeth her mouth**. Here the sexual act is compared to eating food (see discusssions on 9:17; 7:18).

30:21–23. The attention is now directed to four things that cause the people on the earth to tremble and that create for them troubled times. First, disasterous times will befall the people when **a servant ... reigneth** (v. 22) (see 19:10). A king needs great wisdom, such as will not be found in the lowly servant. Second, **a fool** who is filled with himself causes trouble for all who come in contact with him. Third, trouble is caused by **an odious woman when she is married** (v. 23) is probably one of several wives, who is miserable because her husband does not love her (see Leah in Gen. 29:31–32). Fourth, trouble is also caused by **a handmaid that is heir to her mistress**. She replaces the wife in the affections of the husband, perhaps because she was able to bear a child, whereas the wife was barren (see the story of Hagar and Sarah, Gen. 16:1–6). Each of these four are the cause of great trouble for all with whom they associate.

30:24–26. Wisdom is greater than physical strength, and these verses point to four instances in which this maxim holds true. **The ants** (v. 25) model careful thought for the future and industry. **The conies** (v. 26), or rock badgers, model the ability to find a hiding place in troubled times. They secure themselves **in the rocks** (see Ps. 104:18). **The locusts have no king** (see 6:7), **yet go they forth ... by bands** (v. 27). Locusts are portrayed as a mighty army in Joel 2:3–9 and epitomize a commitment to order as they advance. **The spider** (v. 28) ascends **in kings' palaces**. Spiders climb stone walls easily and thus share sumptious surroundings.

30:29–31. In contrast to the small creatures of 30:25–28, the focus is now directed to some of the greatest of God's creations, those that move with a stateliness that arouses admiration. The first focus is the majestic **lion which is strongest among beasts** (v. 30; see 2 Sam. 1:23; Mic. 5:8). His boldness has earned him the admiration of successive generations. The **greyhound** (v. 31) perhaps refers to a "rooster," who also moves swiftly and is mighty for his size. Next is the **he goat**, which was used to lead flocks of sheep (see Jer. 50:8; Dan. 8:5) and whose stately demeanor induced caution in all who drew near. Last, is the **king**, whose great power and armies cause foes to tremble.

30:32–33. Agur concluded with a word for anyone who might be tempted to **lifting up thyself** (v. 32). This journey into pride will lead to tragic consequences and is condemned in 8:13; 11:2; 16:18. To the young man who acted with pride or **hast thought evil** (see 6:14; 16:27) and is about to speak **foolishly,** Agur counsels, **lay thine hand upon thy mouth.** In other words, "Stop your plotting immediately!" (see Job 21:5; 40:4). As certainly as **churning of milk bringeth forth butter, and the wringing of the nose bringeth forth blood: so the forcing of wrath bringeth forth strife** (v. 33; see discussions on 6:14; 15:1; see also 29:22). Men who are arrogant and run their mouths put pressure on those around them, which ultimately may produce anger that fuels an initiative directed at their undoing.

VIII. The Words of King Lemuel (31:1–9)

31:1–7. This brief section was written by **King Lemuel,** who is unknown apart from this contribution. Here a mother warns her son about the perils of companioning with evil women, rebellious men, and those who drink wine. She exhorts her son to avoid that which destroys and to instead champion justice and the good. This entire chapter emphasizes the role and significance of wise mothers and women in general. The queen mother was an influential figure (see 1 Kings 1:11–13; 15:13). The wise mother is focused on her children; they are of great importance to her. Her love for her children causes her to make vows to God on their behalf; hence, he is the **son of my vows** (v. 2; see Hannah and the vow she made as she prayed for a son, 1 Sam. 1:11). The wise mother instructs her son to avoid giving his **strength unto women** (v. 3). This is a warning against sexual immorality (see 5:9–11 and discussions; 1 Kings 11:1; Neh. 13:26). The mother who companions with wisdom reminds her son that **it is not for kings to drink wine** (v. 4). Woe to the land whose rulers are drunkards (see Eccl. 10:16–17; Prov. 20:1 and discussion;

Hos. 7:5). Consuming wine can skew a man's judgment and lead him to **pervert the judgment of any of the afflicted** (v. 5; see 30:14; 17:15; Isa. 5:23; 10:2). The proper use of wine is medicinal, and it should be used primarily to relieve human suffering.

31:8–9. The greatest attribute a king can possess is love for justice. This explains why for a second time (see 31:5) the mother reminds her son of the need to promote justice. In her view, the king represents God as the defender of **the poor and needy** (v. 9; see 16:10; Ps. 82:3; Lev. 19:15; Job 29:12–17; Isa. 1:17). She exhorts her son to be kingly at all times, avoiding the potentially destructive things in life and always promoting justice and good for all, regardless of their station in life.

IX. Epilogue: The Worthy Woman (31:10–31)

This epilogue is in the form of an acrostic poem (each verse begins with a successive letter of the Hebrew alphabet) praising the "virtuous woman" (v. 10). It corresponds to 1:1–7 (the prologue), as it describes a "woman that feareth the LORD" (v. 30; see discussion on 1:7). Such a woman is a personification of wisdom, "her price is far above rubies" (v. 10; see 3:15; 8:11), and he who finds her will "obtain favour of the LORD" (8:35; 18:22).

31:10–11. The **virtuous woman** (v. 10) is priceless, and although she exists, she is something of a rarity. Like Ruth (see Ruth 3:11), she is "a crown to her husband" (12:4) and is a capable companion who always provides strength and comfort as they experience the reward that comes from solving the challenges of life together. She is always "for him" in spite of his weaknesses, and he can always **trust** (v. 11) her commitment to the marital covenant. This trust moves him to place under her supervision much of their worldly resources, over which she exercises a careful stewardship that results in them experiencing no lack of abundance (**no need**).

31:12. She will do him good as long as she lives, and her husband will experience much good in his life that is directly attributable to the energies she expends on his behalf (see 18:22; 19:14).

PROVERBS 31:24 – 31

31:13. This woman enjoys her work and is not given to complaining. She seeks **wool, and flax** and makes fine linen from its fibers (see 31:19, 22, 24; Isa. 19:9). She takes the coarse substance, labors willingly over it, and makes something of beauty for herself, her husband, and their family to enjoy.

31:14. She is a careful and discerning shopper. **She is like the merchant's ships** that go to distant places and bring back helpful and interesting items. She is an enterprising person (see 31:18) who loves to go out and look for things that can be brought into her home to enrich the lives of all who dwell there.

31:15. She riseth also while it is yet night. She is energetic and is the opposite of the sluggard (see 6:9 – 10; 20:13). She is kind and gives **a portion to her maidens** (see 27:27; Luke 12:42).

31:16 – 17. This woman has a mind for business, and her husband supports her incursions into the world of commerce. **She considereth a field, and buyeth it** (v. 16). Then **she planteth a vineyard**. She shows good judgment, unlike the sluggard, whose vineyard is overgrown with thorns and weeds (see 24:30 – 31). **She girdeth her loins with strength** (v. 17). She is not afraid of hard work. She pitches in to assure the vineyard will be a success (see 10:4 and discussion).

31:18 – 20. Her merchandise is good (v. 18). Again, this is a woman who is of great value; like wisdom, "her price is far above rubies" (31:10; 3:15; 8:11). The profit of wisdom "is better than the merchandise of silver" (3:14). She is at **the distaff** (v. 19), using **the spindle**, late into the night when necessary (v. 18). Spinning thread was women's work. **She stretcheth out her hand to the poor** (v. 20; see 22:9; Job 31:16 – 20). Perhaps the nobelest feature in this woman's character is her generosity.

31:21 – 23. She prepares ahead for the cold of the winter **snow**. She prepares garments, and her family is **clothed with scarlet** (v. 21). Scarlet garments were of high quality, probably made of wool (see 2 Sam. 1:24; Rev. 18:16). This woman is remarkable for her ability to give attention to her own attractiveness while she cares so extensively for the needs of others.

Her clothing is silk and purple (v. 22). Her clothing makes her both pleasing in her husband's eyes and speaks of the high esteem she has for herself. Silk was associated with nobility (see discussion on 7:16; Gen. 41:42), and purple was linked with kings (see Judg. 8:26; Song 3:10) and the rich (Luke 16:19; Rev. 18:16). She enhances her husband's standing **in the gates** (v. 23). Others value her husband's opinion a little more and think better of him because of his marriage to such an outstanding woman.

31:24 – 31. Her skill with **fine linen** (v. 24) has already been mentioned (see Judg. 14:12 – 13; Isa. 3:23). Her productivity leads her to deal with **the merchant** (see 31:18). Beyond the temporal clothing she wears, this woman is clothed with **Strength and honour** (v. 25; see Isa. 52:1; 1 Tim. 2:9 – 10). The opposite is to be "clothed with shame and dishonour" (Ps. 35:26). Joy is wrapped up in the demeanor of this woman of virtue. She is free of anxiety and worry concerning the future (see Job 39:7). **The law of kindness** (v. 26) governs her speech. She is a wise and loving counselor (see 1:8; 6:20) to her children and friends. She blesses her household with her words, her joy, and her activities. She is seldom idle and **looketh well to the ways of her household** (v. 27). Her children cannot help but understand the benefits she bestows upon them, and they **call her blessed** (v. 28) because of the happy environment she creates and the joy she radiates to others (see Gen. 30:13; Ps. 72:17; Song 6:9; Mal. 3:12; Ruth 4:14 – 15). Her husband understands that while many wives and mothers **have done virtuously** (v. 29; see Isa. 32:8), she **excellest them all**. He knows that **Favour is deceitful** (v. 30; see 5:3), **beauty is vain** (see Job 14:2; 1 Peter 3:3 – 5), and the woman **that feareth the Lord** is worthy of the highest praise and admiration. Physical beauty is fleeting, but a character infused with the fear of the Lord endures for eternity. **The fruit of her hands** (v. 31) should be returned to her, and all should **praise her in the gates**. It would be unusual for a woman to be so honored in the gates, but through "humility and the fear of the Lord" (22:4), she has lived a life worthy of such an honor.

ECCLESIASTES OR THE PREACHER

INTRODUCTION

Author and Date

No time period or author's name is mentioned in the book, but several passages strongly suggest that king Solomon is the author (1:1, 12, 16; 2:4–9; 7:26–29; 12:9; see also 1 Kings 2:9; 3:12; 4:29–34; 5:12; 10:1–8). On the other hand, the author's title ("Preacher"; Hebrew, *qoheleth*; see discussion on 1:1), his unique style of Hebrew, and his attitude toward rulers (suggesting that of a subject rather than of a monarch; see, e.g., 4:1–2; 5:8–9; 8:2–4; 10:20) may point to another person and a later period.

Theme

With his life largely behind him, the author takes stock of the world as he has experienced it between the horizons of birth and death—the latter a horizon beyond which man cannot see. The world is seen as being full of enigmas, the greatest of which is man himself.

From the perspective of his own understanding, the Preacher takes measure of man, examining his capabilities. He discovers that human wisdom, even that of a godly person, has limits (1:13, 16–18; 7:24; 8:16–17). It cannot find out the larger purposes of God or the ultimate meaning of man's existence.

As the author looks about at the human enterprise, he sees man in mad pursuit of one thing and then another, laboring as if he could master the world, lay bare its secrets, change its fundamental structures, break through the bounds of human limitations, and master his own destiny. He sees man vainly pursuing hopes and expectations that in reality are "vanity and vexation of spirit" (1:14; 2:11, 17, 26; 4:4, 16; 6:9; see also 1:17; 4:6).

Faith, however, teaches him that God has ordered all things according to His purposes (3:1–15; 5:19; 6:1–2; 9:1) and that man's role is to accept these, including his limitations, as God's appointments. Man, therefore, should be patient and enjoy life as God gives it. He should know his limitations and not vex himself with unrealistic expectations. He should be prudent in everything, living carefully before God and the king and, above all, fearing God and keeping His commandments (12:13).

Theological Message

Life not centered on God is purposeless and meaningless (see discussions on 1:2; 2:24–25). Without Him, nothing else can satisfy (2:25). With Him, all of life and His other good gifts are to be gratefully received (see James 1:17) and used and enjoyed to the full (2:26; 11:8). The book contains the philosophical and theological reflections of an old man (12:1–7), most of whose life was meaningless because he had not himself relied on God as he should have.

Outline

I. Author (1:1)

II. Theme: The Vanity of Man's Efforts on Earth apart from God (1:2)

III. Introduction: Working to Accumulate Things to Achieve Happiness Is without Profit (1:3–11)

IV. Discourse, Part 1: In Spite of Life's Apparent Enigmas and Vanity, It Is to Be Enjoyed as a Gift from God (1:12–11:6)

V. Discourse, Part 2: Since Old Age and Death Will Soon Come, Man Should Enjoy Life in His Youth, Remembering That God Will Judge (11:7–12:7)

VI. Theme Repeated (12:8)

VII. Conclusion: Reverently Trust and Obey God (12:9–14)

Bibliography

Bridges, Charles. *An Exposition of the Book of Ecclesiastes.* London: Banner of Truth, reprinted, 1960.

Eaton, Michael A. *Ecclesiastes: An Introduction and Commentary.* Tyndale Old Testament Commentaries 16. Downers Grove, IL: InterVarsity, 1983.

Ginsberg, C. D. *The Song of Songs and Coheleth.* New York: KTAV, 1970.

Goldberg, Louis. *Ecclesiastes.* Bible Study Commentary. Grand Rapids, MI: Zondervan, 1983.

Kaiser, Walter C., Jr. *Ecclesiastes: Total Life.* Everyman's Bible Commentary. Chicago: Moody, 1979.

Kidner, Derek. *The Message of Ecclesiastes.* The Bible Speaks Today. Leicester: InterVarsity, 1976.

Laurin, John Peter, ed. "Ecclesiastes." In *Wycliffe Bible Commentary,* edited by Charles F. Pfeiffer and Everett F. Harrison. Chicago: Moody, 1962.

Leupold, N. C. *Exposition of Ecclesiastes.* Grand Rapids, MI: Baker, 1966.

Murphy, Roland E. "Ecclesiastes." In *Wisdom Literature: Job, Proverbs, Ruth, Canticles, Ecclesiastes, Esther.* Forms of the Old Testament Literature. Vol. 13. Grand Rapids, MI: Eerdmans, 1981.

Wardlaw, Ralph. *Expository Ecclesiastes.* 1868. Minneapolis: Klock and Klock, 1982.

EXPOSITION

I. Author (1:1)

1:1. The author is **the Preacher** of wisdom (12:9). The Hebrew for "preacher" (*qoheleth*) is related to that for "assembly" (possibly meaning "leader of the assembly"; also in 1:2, 12; Exod. 16:3; Num. 16:3). Perhaps the Preacher, whose work is described in 12:9–10, also held an office in the assembly. The Septuagint (the Greek translation of the Old Testament) word for "Preacher" is *ekklesiastes*, from which most English titles of the book are taken, and from which such English words as "ecclesiastical" are derived. **The son of David** suggests Solomon, though his name occurs nowhere in the book. The Hebrew word for "son" can refer to a descendant (even many generations removed), or even to someone who follows in the footsteps of another (see Gen. 4:21; see also Introduction: "Author and Date").

II. Theme: The Vanity of Man's Efforts on Earth apart from God (1:2)

1:2. Here the author's theme is briefly stated (see 12:8). The author makes extensive use of the word **vanity**, which is used about twenty-two times in Ecclesiastes and only a few other places in the Old Testament (see 2 Kings 17:15; Ps. 62:9; Isa. 49:4). The Hebrew for "vanity" originally meant "breath" (see Pss. 39:5, 11; 62:9; 144:4). The basic thrust of Ecclesiastes is that all of life is meaningless, useless, hollow, futile, and vain if it is not rightly related to God. Only when based on God and His word is life worthwhile. **All** things undertaken apart from dependence on God lead to vanity (see 1:8).

III. Introduction: Working to Accumulate Things to Achieve Happiness Is without Profit (1:3–11)

1:3–11. In this section, the author elaborates his theme that human activity apart from a real commitment to the glory of God is without lasting benefit or purpose. On the issue of "profit," Stedman maintains that "this is the right question to ask. It is a question

we all are asking. Is there anything that will minister continually to my need—the summum bonum, that highest good which, if I find it, I do not need to look any further? Is there a key to continual pleasure, to delight and joy in life?" (Stedman, p. 12). The question of **profit** (v. 3) is expanded on by Jesus in Mark 8:36–38. The phrase **under the sun**, another key expression (used twenty-nine times) in this book, refers to this present world and the limits of what it offers. The phrase "under heaven," though it occurs less frequently (1:13; 2:3; 3:1), is used synonymously. The author wishes to remind all people that the **earth abideth for ever** (v. 4) and, by contrast, man's life is fleeting. **All things** (v. 8) on earth, everything mentioned in verses 4–7, speaks of a cycle that is attached to earthly things that are beyond man's control. The emphasis here is on the limitation that is tied to being human and to the oppressive cyclical nature of life on the fallen planet. Additionally, man is troubled by the fact that in this repetitive cycle, nothing truly **new** (v. 10) is ever to be experienced. Many things seem to be new simply because the past is easily and quickly forgotten, but in reality, the "new" is only the old ways reappearing in new guises.

IV. Discourse, Part I: In Spite of Life's Apparent Enigmas and Vanity, It Is to Be Enjoyed as a Gift from God (1:12–11:6)

1:12–18. Having set forth his theme that all human striving seems futile (see especially 1:3, 11, which frame the section), the Preacher shows that both human endeavor (vv. 12–15; see 2:1–11) and the pursuit of human wisdom (vv. 16–18; see 2:12–17) are futile and meaningless. Here the author shifts to the use of the first-person **I** (v. 12), returning to the use of the third person only in the conclusion (12:9–14). The only Hebrew word the author uses for **God** (v. 13) is *Elohim* (used almost thirty times), which emphasizes God's absolute sovereignty. He does not use the covenant name *Yahweh* (translated "LORD"; see discussion on Exod. 3:15). God has determined to exercise fallen humanity through the things done **under heaven** (v. 13). This exercising is a **vexation of spirit** (v. 14) for the descendants of Adam, literally "a striving after wind," a graphic illustration of futility and meaninglessness (see Introduction: "Theme"). "Vexation of spirit" is used nine times in the first half of the discourse (here; v. 17; 2:11, 17, 26; 4:4, 6, 16; 6:9; see also 5:16). Because of the unalterableness of events (v. 15), human effort is meaningless and hopeless. One should therefore learn to happily accept things as they are and to accept a divinely appointed lot in life, as the Preacher later counsels. One should listen carefully to this message because the author has worked to develop a better acquaintance with wisdom **than all they that have been before me in Jerusalem** (v. 16; see 2:7, 9). This does not necessarily exclude Solomon as the Preacher; rather it argues for his authorship of Ecclesiastes. The reference could include kings prior to David, such as Melchizedek (Gen. 14:18), Adonizedek (Josh. 10:1), and Abdi-khepa (mentioned in the Amarna letters from Egypt; see chart, *Zondervan KJV Study Bible*, p. xix).

1:18. Humanistic **wisdom** — wisdom without God — leads to grief and sorrow.

2:1 – 11. Now the Preacher attempts to show that mere pleasure cannot give meaning or satisfaction (see 1:12 – 15; see also discussion on 1:12 – 18). **I said in mine heart** (v. 1) introduces the reader to an interesting exercise undertaken by the author (see 2:15; see also 1:16). Since life is so difficult, he pursued pleasurable things while **yet acquainting mine heart with wisdom** (v. 3). From first to last (v. 9), the author used wisdom to discover the good (v. 1) and the worthwhile (v. 3). Yet he walked a fine line as he flirted with alcohol, materialism, and sex to enhance meaning in life and dull the vexation. See 1 Kings 4 – 11, which tells of Solomon's splendor and of his wives **of all sorts** (v. 8). The Hebrew for this word occurs only here in Scripture, and its meaning is uncertain. The meaning seems to be indicated in an early Egyptian letter that uses a similar Canaanite term for concubines. It fits the situation of Solomon, who had three hundred concubines in addition to seven hundred wives (1 Kings 11:3). Beyond the women,

he had extensive pleasures, and his **labour** (i.e., the gain from his enterprises; v. 10) allowed him to have everything he desired. In all these things, however, he found no lasting **profit under the sun** (v. 11). This expression represents a key thought in Ecclesiastes. All the things a man may gain apart from God are **vanity**. "Toil," "labour," and "work" are words that occur more than twenty-five times in the book, and they are always associated with **vexation of spirit** for persons whose labors do not take place within the larger context of the fear of God.

2:12 – 17. In this section, the Preacher again returns to the folly of trying to find satisfaction in merely human wisdom (see 1:16 – 18). He is certain that **wisdom excelleth folly** (v. 13). In his view, even secular wisdom is better than folly, but in the end, it is of no value since one fate befalls them both (i.e., befalls both the wise believer and the foolish unbeliever, v. 14; see Ps. 49:10). Wisdom is better than folly, for the wise man's **eyes** (v. 14) are filled with understanding, while the fool walks about in **darkness**. There is value in the possession of wisdom, but it is a cause of sadness to realize that people tend to soon forget even their wisest leaders and heroes (v. 16; see 1:11).

2:18 – 23. A second sobering reality is that the fruit of a man's labor must ultimately be left **unto the man that shall be after me** (v. 18; see v. 21; Ps. 39:6; Luke 12:20). The preacher asks the sobering question, **who knoweth …?** (v. 19). The question addresses the reality that the recipient of the inheritance may squander all of it. For a more searching "Who knoweth …?" for secular man, see 3:21. These sobering realities may cause a man to spend many a sleepless night.

2:24 – 26. In this section, the Preacher repeats the theme at the heart of Ecclesiastes (repeated again in 3:12 – 13, 22; 5:18 – 20; 8:15; 9:7 and climaxed in 12:13). He affirms that only in God does life have meaning and true pleasure. Without Him, nothing satisfies; with Him, we find satisfaction and enjoyment. True pleasure comes only when we acknowledge and revere God (12:13). Men who walk with wisdom know that God is in control. He ultimately gives travail **to the sinner** (v. 26) and joy to those who are **good in His sight**. For exceptions to this general principle, see 8:14; Psalm 73:1–12.

3:1–22. In this section, the Preacher shows that humans are subject to times and changes over which they have little or no control and contrasts this state with God's eternity and sovereignty. He is certain that God sovereignly predetermines all of life's activities and that, ultimately, man's ability to experience profit in this life hinges on his ability to rest by faith in that sovereignty (e.g., the fourteen opposites of vv. 2–8).

3:1–11. Events in this world are not rooted in happenstance. Everything that occurs **under the heaven** (v. 1) is tied to God's purposes. Hence, because He is a wonderful God, everything that He purposes to bring to pass does come to pass and is wrapped up in the beauty of His person and His purposes. All things happen in their divinely appointed **time** (v. 2; see Ps. 31:15; Prov. 16:1–9). Kidner, in commenting on verse 11, says, "Qoheleth in verse 11 enables us to see perpetual change not as something unsettling but as an unfolding pattern, scintillating and God-given. The trouble for us is not that life refuses to keep still, but that we see only a fraction of its movement and of its subtle, intricate design. Instead of changelessness, there is something better: a dynamic, divine purpose, with its own character and its period of blossoming and ripening, beautiful in its time and contributing to the over-all masterpiece which is the work of one Creator" (Kidner, *The Message of Ecclesiastes*, pp. 38–39). Since humans were made for eternity, temporal things cannot fully and permanently satisfy.

3:12–14. In these verses, the author points to the book's conclusion. God's people find meaning in life when they cheerfully accept all of life as a **gift** (v. 13) from the hand of God.

Whatever God does with mortals has to do with **for ever** (v. 14) since He is the eternal God and has planted eternity in the heart of men and women. In light of this, the "eternity" of 3:11 becomes clearer. The forever God arranges all the events in a man's life so that he may learn to fear God. The author's challenge to **fear** God sums up the message of the book (see 12:13). The fear that is commended here is not fear of God himself but fear of the consequences that God's nature will require Him to impose on those who violate His law and forsake the duties attached to His covenants.

3:15–22. Life on the fallen planet is hard. In these verses, the Preacher laments the pervasiveness of evil and its influence on even **the place of righteousness** (v. 16). He is able to cope with this reality because of his conviction that God will ultimately **judge** (v. 17) both **the righteous and the wicked**. God's true judgments are the answer to human cynicism about man's injustices. **That which hath been** (v. 15) is not meaningless (as people dismiss it as being, 1:11), and God will override the perverse judgments (v. 16) of men (see 12:14).

The Preacher affirms this truth in the face of the stark reality that man is of **one breath** (v. 19; see Ps. 104:27–30), like the **beasts** (v. 18), and both **go unto one place** (v. 20). The author is not speaking of heaven or hell but of man's observable destination: men will **all turn to dust again**, just as the animals do. Death is the great leveler of all living things (see Gen. 3:19; Ps. 103:14). Man **under the sun** (man on his own; v. 16) is as mortal as any animal. Unlike the animals, however, man is an eternal being who will, at some point in his future, stand before God. Man on his own cannot know fully what is in his future; he can only guess. The answer to the question; **who knoweth** (v. 21; see 2:19 and discussion; 12:7) the eternal destiny of the spirit of man, revealed at first in glimpses (e.g., Pss. 16:9–11; 49:15; 73:23–26; Isa. 26:19; Dan. 12:2–3), was only brought fully "to light through the gospel" (2 Tim. 1:10). The Preacher's message on eternity is not informed by the richness of the gospel of redemption in Jesus Christ, which is fully unfolded in the pages of the New Testament. The Preacher does understand that as an end in itself, work is meaningless (see 4:4; 9:9) and that only when it is received as a "gift of God" (v. 13) does the opportunity to work have enduring worth (v. 14).

4:1–3. The hurt experienced because of **oppressions** (v. 1) creates a real challenge to joy for those living **under the sun**. This theme has already been touched on by the Preacher (3:16) and is one more ingredient in the human tragedy. To struggle with life's meaningfulness is sad enough, but to taste its cruelty is bitter beyond words. This struggle can lead a man to think that the dead are actually better off **than the living** (v. 2; see Job 3; Jer. 20:14 – 18; for faith that sees a bigger picture, see Rom. 8:35 – 39). The author introduces a series of comparisons with the terms **better … than** (v. 3), reminding the reader that despite the difficulties of life, some things are better than others. This is a further indication that all may not be hopeless after all.

4:4 – 6. Hard work is frequently commended by the Preacher, but neither hard work (motivated by envy) nor idleness brings happiness, meaning, or fulfillment. A man may give himself to **every right work** (v. 4) and reap the envy and ill will of **his neighbour**. This work may prove meaningless unless done with God's blessing (see 3:13; compare the selfless success of Joseph, Genesis 39). Work is to be preferred to laziness, and the ruin of the idle person is vividly pictured in verses 5 and 10:18 (see also Prov. 6:6 – 11; 24:30 – 34). In the end, **quietness** (v. 6) in the human spirit represents the highest value (see Prov. 30:7 – 9). Paul says the last word on this subject (Phil. 4:11 – 13).

4:7 – 12. Another item to be highly valued in this world is found within the context of relationships. The loner has a meaningless and difficult life. Profit or meaning in this life is only achieved by those who push out of isolation into connection with the **two** (v. 12) and live their lives within the context of the **threefold cord**. Here is where a man finds lasting reward and assistance with meeting the challenges confronted on the fallen planet. **When he falleth … another** will **help him up** (v. 10). When he succeeds, he will know the **reward** (v. 9) of God's blessing and sharing with another who truly cares and desires to celebrate his successes with him.

4:13 – 16. The Preacher has established that reward is the portion of those who walk with wisdom. The **wise child** (v. 13) is better off than the **foolish king** who will not receive instruction. The wise child who comes from prison may rule well for a season, but all must remember that advancement without God is another example of the **vanity** (v. 16) of secularism.

5:1 – 7. The theme of this section is the vanity of superficial religion, as reflected in making rash vows. The admonition is given to **keep thy foot** (v. 1) when participating in worship. Eaton affirms that this charge "refers to demeanour and preparedness as one comes to worship, particularly readiness to obey, for *listen* refers to heeding as well as hearing (see Luke 8:18)" (Eaton, *Ecclesiastes*, pp. 97 – 98). Worshipers must think carefully about what they ought to say and do. They should **be more ready to hear** than to speak. The Preacher admonishes, **Be not rash with thy mouth** (v. 2). First Samuel 15:22 uses the same Hebrew verb used in "keep thy foot" and makes the same contrast between real and superficial worship. Words can be a form of **sacrifice** (v. 1), and those who seek to worship in spirit and in truth will be very careful with what they promise God. Verse 3 is a proverb. In this context, it suggests that in the midst of cares, a person dreams of bliss (as a starving man dreams of a banquet), and in anticipation of **the multitude of dreams**, he may offer rash vows (**many words**; v. 7) to God. **A vow unto God** (v. 4) is a serious matter (see Deut. 23:21 – 23; 1 Sam. 1:11, 24 – 28). The fool is hasty with his vows, and God takes **no pleasure in fools**. In Scripture, the fool is not one who cannot learn but one who refuses to learn due to moral deficiency (see Prov. 1:7, 20 – 27). The **mouth** (v. 6) may be the instrument used to accomplish great sin. A man should never tell **the angel** or messenger that the promise was an error. He should rather **fear … God** (v. 7), recognize and repent of the reality that he has sinned with his rash words, repent, and make good on his promise or duty (see Mal. 2:7).

5:8 – 17. For other frank appraisals of human society, see 4:1 – 3. Like Jesus, who "knew what was in man" (John 2:25), this teacher had no illusions or utopian schemes. He instructs readers to **marvel not** (v. 8) at the perversion of justice but remember that all are called to fear God and trust in His **judgment**

and justice. Some might think that greater wealth would deliver them from meaningless lives. The Preacher insists that greater wealth does not bring satisfaction (see 1 Tim. 6:9–10). Quite the contrary: greater wealth brings greater anxiety. While the man who has little but has quietness of spirit often sleeps extremely well, the man who has much often spends his nights worrying about the loss of his riches. The wealthy often keep their riches to their own **hurt** (v. 13). They worry about preserving their possessions and having to leave them to a worthless son who will squander everything in the pursuit of pleasure. This worry causes the wealthy to lose any joy that might be derived from their wealth. In addition to all of these woes, the wealthy man knows that he **shall take nothing** (v. 15) with him to the grave. Monetary riches have no value after death (see Luke 12:14–21). Such dark realities produce **much sorrow and wrath with ... sickness** (v. 17) for the poor rich man.

5:18–20. The challenges associated with wealth and possessions have been explored by the Preacher. Now he turns to the **good and comely** (v. 18) that is associated with the fruit of **labour**. The man who recognizes that things and the ability to enjoy them are alike **the gift of God** (v. 19) is in a position to find great delight **in his labour**. He partakes of all things with **joy** in **his heart** (v. 20), with which **God answereth** to the man's proper view of things and their use.

6:1–6. All men are not fortunate enough to have the inner joy that comes as a gift from God. Some men have great possessions, but God does not give them the **power to eat thereof** (v. 2). These tragic figures must watch as **a stranger eateth** the fruit of all their labor. Comparing verse 2 with 5:19 demonstrates that the ability to enjoy God's blessings is a bonus—a gift of God, not a right or guarantee (see also vv. 3, 6). God calls the person who forgets this truth a "fool" (Luke 12:20). The man who lives a long life but knows not the inner joy that comes as a gift from God and dies unlamented or dishonored, like King Jehoiakim (Jer. 22:18–19), might better have had **an untimely birth** (v. 3). For the secularist, life is a pointless journey to extinction, to which miscarriage is the quickest and easiest route (see Job 3:16; Ps. 58:8). In their view, **all go to one place** (v. 6). The Preacher is still talking in terms of what we can observe (that all men die), not of what lies beyond death (see 6:12; 3:21).

6:7–12. In view of these sobering realities, it is easy to see why many become cynical and pessimistic about life on the fallen planet. The Preacher gives several reasons why such cynicism abounds: the short-lived (v. 7), debatable (v. 8), and elusive (v. 9) rewards of life; the limits of creativity, power, and wisdom (vv. 10–11); and the unreliability of merely human values and predictions (v. 12). In the midst of these vexing realities, one truth dominates: **That which hath been is named** (v. 10), that is, predetermined by God. All that humanity experiences has been foreknown by God, and it is He that is **mightier than** man, who spends his life **as a shadow** (v. 12). God alone **can tell a man what will be after him under the sun** (see 1 Chron. 29:15).

7:1–7. The preceeding section closed with the question, "Who knoweth what is good for man in this life?" (6:12). The Preacher now proceeds to give some answers to that question. It is a good thing for a man to guard his **good name** (v. 1). It is a good thing for a man to **lay ... to his heart** (v. 2) the reality of his impending death. It is better to reflect on **the day of death than** on **the day of one's birth** (v. 1) because such reflection leads to the fear of God and responsible living. The Christian has ample reason to say this (2 Cor. 5:1–10; Phil. 1:21–23). The Preacher's point is valid, as explained in verses 2–6, namely, that happy times generally teach one less than hard times do. The section closes with the admonition **to hear the rebuke of the wise** (v. 5), for the frivolous **gift** (v. 7) or nonsubstantive commendations of the fool will only appeal to a man's vanity and hasten his destruction (see Matt. 28:11–15; Luke 22:4–6).

7:8–10. The devastating consequences of impatience and **anger** (v. 9) are pointed out here. This is an issue frequently addressed in the Scriptures (see, e.g., Prov. 16:32; 17:14; 1 Cor. 13:4–5). The Preacher also points out the peril of extolling **the former days**

(v. 10) or living in the past. Profit in this life is found only by those who are truly alive to the present and who depend on God for the wisdom and power to impact people now.

7:11–14. Another **good** (v. 11) to be pursued in this life is **wisdom**. Wisdom carries with it **an inheritance. Wisdom is a defence**, as is **money**, but the advantage of wisdom is that it **giveth life to them that have it** (v. 12; see Prov. 3:13–18; 13:14). Wisdom also teaches one to rely on God's assistance, **for who can make that straight, which he hath made crooked?** (v. 13). This is not fatalism but a reminder of who is God. Man cannot change what God determines (see discussion on 1:15). God **hath set the one over against the other** (v. 14). God uses both prosperity and adversity to accomplish His purposes (see Rom. 8:28–29). There is purpose in all that God does, and His ultimate purpose is **that man should find nothing after him**. No one knows the future, whether it will hold prosperity or adversity, but in all things, God desires that man look to Him for ultimate profit in this life and the next. God structures events with the intent "that men might be sensible of their entire dependence, the lesson being brought home to their minds by their felt inability to alter, in the smallest degree, what he has done before, and fixed" (Wardlaw, *Expository Ecclesiastes*, p. 221).

7:15–25. Another **good** (v. 18) to **take hold of** is now considered. Those who are righteous face a vexing dilemma: **there is a just man that perisheth in his righteousness** (v. 15), while **a wicked man … prolongeth his life**. Righteousness is no sure protection against hard times or an early death, so what is a righteous man to do in the presence of such a dilemma? The answer is found in verse 18. The righteous man finds his rest in the reality that as long as he **feareth God** (v. 18), he will triumph over all. Such wisdom is empowering, so the righteous must never aspire to be **righteous over much … over wise** (v. 16). If true righteousness and wisdom do not necessarily prevent ruin, then extreme, legalistic righteousness and wisdom will surely not help. The issue of balance is here advocated, for wisdom counsels also that one **be not over much wicked** (v. 17).

Extreme wickedness is even more foolhardy than extreme pride in one's righteousness. It is good for the righteous and the wicked to remember that **there is not a just man upon earth** (v. 20). This is a sobering biblical truth (see Rom. 3:10–20).

For verse 24, see Job 28:12–28; 1 Corinthians 2:9–16. The reality of fallen man's sinfulness demands that even the most godly walk with great humility. At best, knowledge of God and oneself is hindered by identification with the fallen Adam.

7:26–29. The Preacher now reflects on the impact of sin on his relationships with men and women. **Counting one by one, to find out the account** (v. 27), he has not had a relationship with a **woman** (v. 28) who is **upright** (v. 29). His experience with women has been **more bitter than death** (v. 26). The women he has had relationships with had hearts that were **snares and nets** (see Prov. 7:6–27). This evaluation argues for the fact that the author is Solomon, or one like him, who never experienced the biblical pattern of marriage but rather replaced it with hundreds of concubines and wives. Solomon forfeited the opportunity to personally experience the beauty of marital love outlined in the Song of Solomon and other biblical passages. His summative insight is: **God hath made man upright; but they have sought out many inventions** (v. 29). Hence, relationships that end in the reward of the threefold cord (see chap. 4) are rare, and God is often grieved by the actions of His people (see also Gen. 3:1–6; Rom. 5:12).

8:1–11. Though men live in an upside-down world and must constantly cope with their own limitations and the injustices of others, wisdom, when heeded, produces dramatic change for the good in a man. It not only causes him to think and behave differently; it also changes his appearance. **The boldness** (v. 1) of a man's face goes away, for wisdom causes a man's **face to shine**. Wisdom also produces caution in the choice of companions, and thoughtful compliance with **the king's commandment** (v. 2). Those who heed wisdom practice both principle (v. 2) and prudence (vv. 3–6), and this sets limits on their freedom. They honor always **the oath** (v. 2) of loyalty that they have taken to the king (as seen, e.g., in 1 Chron. 29:24). They appreciate the fact that no one may say to the king, **What doest thou?** (v. 4; see Isa. 45:9; Rom. 9:20). Men who walk with wisdom understand that their safety on the fallen planet is somewhat linked to a cheerful compliance with the commandments of the king. Wisdom allows a man to discern the right place and the right **time** (v. 6) for all his words and actions. One should put the king's command above his own misery because **he knoweth not** (v. 7) what is going to happen and **no man ... hath power** (v. 8) to control his circumstances (see Ps. 31:15; 2 Cor. 5:1–10; James 4:13–16). This limitation of power is felt most keenly in the matter of death. Death comes for all in its own time, and no man can obtain a **discharge in that war**. Men must also deal with the fact that the **wicked** (v. 10) are often **buried** with undeserved respect (see discussion on 6:3; see also Job 21:28–33; Luke 16:22) and that punishment for evil deeds is often **not executed speedily** (v. 11). This delayed punishment tends to induce more wrongdoing.

8:12–17. Many enigmas confront the man who seeks to walk with God during his journey under the sun. Yet some certainties stabilize the man who walks with wisdom. These certainties empower the man to practice the fear of God and to keep His commandments. In keeping with these certainties, the Preacher now says, **I know that it shall be well with them that fear God** (v. 12). He speaks from mature faith, not as one who "seeketh" without coming to the truth (7:28). For similar declarations, see 3:17; 11:9; 12:14. This affirmation does not solve the problem of the prosperity of the wicked and the suffering of the righteous, but it allows the man of faith to proceed with inner peace during his days under the sun. Job 21–24 enlarges on this; Psalm 73 removes its sting and John 5:28–29 provides the final explanation. The Preacher returns to the fact that all the good that a man receives in this life is the gift of God. The opportunity to **eat ... drink, and ... be merry** (v. 15) is a great gift. Here these words reflect the confession of a grateful heart (see 5:19; 9:7; Deuteronomy 8). The same words are spoken arrogantly

in Luke 12:19–20 and 1 Corinthians 15:32. In summation, the Preacher returns to the reality that **man cannot find out** (v. 17) what God is up to, nor does he have the power to control the circumstances of his life. Deuteronomy 29:29 sums up what humans are allowed and not allowed to know.

9:1–6. The Preacher once again shares his conviction regarding God's ultimate control of all events. In spite of man's limited knowledge, one may rest secure in the knowledge that **the righteous, and the wise, and their works, are in the hand of God** (v. 1). The future is always under God's control, and no one but He knows whether that future will bring blessing or trial. One certainty awaits both the righteous and the unrighteous: death, which comes **alike to all** (v. 2). Not only the wise and the foolish (2:14) but also the good and the bad are leveled, in the sense noted in 3:20. For the Preacher's conviction (beyond mere observation) that God ultimately will see justice done, see discussion on 8:12. This apparently common destiny (both the righteous and the wicked die) encourages some people to sin since the dead have lost all opportunity in this life for enjoyment and reward from labor (see v. 6).

9:7–10. The Preacher counsels a different course of action in view of impending death. He believes time should be viewed as a gift from God and used to accomplish good things. People should go about their lives **with joy** (v. 7), rooted in the reality that the God who has all things under control is open to **accept[ing] their works** when they bear certain characteristics. These accepted works are performed by those whose **garments** are **white** (v. 8) and whose **head[s] lack no ointment** (i.e., have been anointed), symbols of purity and festivity. Joy in the days of one's life is also available for those who practice covenantal faithfulness to the wife God has given them as gift. The joy derived from the love of a godly woman stands in stark contrast to the words of 7:27–28. Life can be good even in view of the reality of death. A man is wise to discover that goodness and fill his days with the joy of these things. He is also wise to do **with** all his **might** (v. 10) whatever task he engages (see Col. 3:23).

9:11–18. Once again, the Preacher reflects on **time and chance** (v. 11). The fact that success is uncertain is always unsettling but is also further evidence that man does not ultimately control events. Man does not know when **his time** (v. 12) of disaster will come, and it is beyond the scope of humans to control the times when **men** are **snared**. Here again the emphasis is on unpredictablity of success, because man is not wise enough to know when misfortune may overtake him. The wise man enjoys the gift of joy celebrated by the Preacher in 9:7–10, but that cannot erase the sobering reality that his wisdom gets an uneven reception among humans. When his wisdom is received and he has thereby **delivered the city** (v. 15), he is often soon forgotten. Despite the best efforts of the man of wisdom to create righteous community, **one sinner destroyeth much good** (v. 18). These vexing realities serve as further warnings against placing too much faith in one's wisdom. Its reputation fades, its good is soon undone (see v. 18b), and it has no answer to death (2:15–16).

10:1–11. In spite of these sobering reflections on the often limited impact of wisdom and the words and works of men, the Preacher advises continuous attention, rooted in wisdom, to the performance of one's duty. The **wise man's heart is at his right hand; and not at his left** (v. 2). These metaphors stand for the greater and the lesser good (see Gen. 48:13–20), or perhaps here, as in some later Jewish writings, for good and evil. The wise man knows that it is as easy to destroy one's reputation for goodness as it is to destroy a batch of valuable perfume. A small fly in the ointment will ruin the whole batch; likewise, a small sin can destroy the **reputation** (v. 1) of a great man. A man who is not **yielding** (v. 4) in the presence of the word of the king may find himself in grave danger, while appropriate yielding may **pacifieth great offenses**. A man who reflects too deeply on the inequities of life may also find himself in grave danger of depression and thereby lose the joy commended by the Preacher. Rulers often elevate men of questionable character, and **princes** (v. 7) are often afoot in this

upside-down world. This is **an error ... from the ruler** (v. 5) that mortal men cannot make right. For the Preacher's observations on human regimes, see vv. 4, 6–7, 16–17, 20; 3:16; 4:1–3, 13–16; 5:8–9; 8:2–6, 10–11; 9:17. In this post-Edenic world, **folly is set in great dignity** (v. 6), and the man who chews too much on this evil will surely lose his joy and find all things soured to his taste. The anecdote for this sobering reality is total confidence in the God who makes all things beautiful in His time (3:11). The Preacher has some more sobering advice regarding ways to preserve joy and ways to lose it. Men should be careful when they dig pits, break hedges, remove stones, and work with dull axes, for all these activities may result in injury. Such impending danger may be avoided, however. The way of safety is found in listening to **wisdom** (v. 10), for it **is profitable to direct**. Men who follow the directives of wisdom will avoid much harm as they move through activities fraught with the potential to harm them.

10:12–15. Words (v. 12) are a favorite topic in the Wisdom Literature (see, e.g., Proverbs 15). A wise man is known for the gracious quality of his speech. The fool, on the other hand, is in endless trouble because of his mouth and may actually get himself killed as a consequence of his babbling. The fool also **knoweth not how to go to the city** (v. 15). In Scripture, a "fool" is one who refuses God's teaching (see discussion on 5:4), so this caustic saying (probably proverbial) refers to more than mere stupidity.

10:16–20. The **king** who **is a child** (v. 16) is a small-minded upstart, not "a poor and a wise child," as in 4:13. (See 2 Kings 15:8–25; Hos. 7:3–7, which portray some of the short-lived usurpers and vicious courtiers who hastened the downfall of Israel.) **Woe** to the land that is led by such evil persons. On the contrary, **blessed** (v. 17) is the land whose leaders are characterized by nobility and a self-control that despises **drunkenness**. The childish ruler leads his land into corruption and decay (v.18). In this evil kingdom, meals are prepared for drunkenness, and **money answereth all things** (v. 19).

11:1–8. The Preacher has offered sage advice on the value of hard work. He has sought in all his counsel to cultivate a deep affection for industriousness in those who seek wisdom. He has equally strong convictions about what a man should do with the fruit of his labor. The wise man is a giver. He gives a portion of the abundance gained through his efforts to those who are in need. He heeds the counsel of the Preacher to **cast thy bread upon the waters** (v. 1). His giving will even be adventurous, like those who accept the risks and reap the benefits of seaborne trade. He will not always play it safe (see Prov. 11:24). He will **give a portion to seven, and also to eight** (v. 2). He will be generous while he has plenty and before unforeseen disasters make him dependent on the generosity of others. He will give knowing that his time for giving will come to an end and that when **the tree fall[s] there it shall be** (v. 3). The giver will not observe **the clouds** (v. 4) or **the wind** and offer up excuses for not giving. He will not toy with the "maybe" and the "might have been." He will start where he can, recognize how limited his knowledge and time is, and busy himself with meeting others' needs. He will not try to distinguish who is worthy of his investment, because he does not know **the way of the spirit** (v. 5) in producing life in the womb. Therefore, he does not know how and in whom the Spirit will choose to begin a great work on the foundation of the "bread" (v. 1) he shares.

V. Discourse, Part 2: Since Old Age and Death Will Soon Come, Man Should Enjoy Life in His Youth, Remembering That God Will Judge (11:7–12:7)

11:7–10. In view of this exciting calling to invest in the lives of others, man has reason to value his days under the sun. It is good **to behold the sun** (v. 7), celebrate the sweet light, and live life to the fullest. Being headed for death should spur us on to full engagement in the activities promoted in the preceeding verses. The emphasis on **vanity** (vv. 8, 10) again serves as a warning against letting the wonderful gifts mentioned in verses 7–10 dazzle and distract. Verse 9 sets the true course. **Judgment** (v. 9) and the prospect of divine praise or blame makes every detail of life significant rather than meaning-

less. Awareness of impending judgment gives direction to the heart and discrimination to the eyes. The stage is now set for the Preacher's conclusion, in chapter 12.

12:1–8. In commenting on verse one, Kidner affirms, "At last we are ready—if we ever intend to be—to look beyond earthly vanities to God, who made us for Himself. The title Creator is well chosen, reminding us from earlier passages in the book that He alone sees the pattern of existence whole (3:11); that His was the workmanship we have spoilt by our 'devices' (7:29); and that His creativity is continuous and unsearchable (11:5). To remember Him is no perfunctory or purely mental act—it is to drop our pretense of self-sufficiency and commit ourselves to Him" (Kidner, *The Message of Ecclesiastes*, p. 100). The Preacher now asks the reader to look ahead and understand even better his admonitions to labor and give. Man's ultimate destiny is death, but before he dies, he participates in a process that severely limits his opportunities for work and giving. The Preacher presents a graphic description of man's progressive deterioration, an allegory of aging. The metaphors used by the Preacher may refer to parts of the body (hands, legs, etc.). The imagery is surrounded by rich poetic language, which moves freely between figures such as darkness, a storm, a house in decline, a deserted well, and such literal descriptions as in verse 5a. **The keepers of the house** (v. 3) are the hands and the arms, whose major function is the protection of the body. **The strong men** is undoubtedly a reference to the legs, which contain the strongest muscles in the human body. **The doors** (v. 4) are the ears, and **the almond tree** (v. 5) with its pale blossom possibly suggests the white hair of age. **The grasshopper**, which is normally agile and yet moves slowly on a cold morning (see Nah. 3:17), recalls the stiffness of old age. The **long home** is literally "his eternal home." In context, this probably points simply to the grave, not beyond it (see Job 10:21; 17:13). **The silver cord** (v. 6) and **the golden bowl** represent a hanging lamp suspended by a silver chain. If even one link snaps, the light and beauty will perish, suggesting how fragile life is.

VI. Theme Repeated (12:8)

12:8. Such is life "under the sun" (on earth, apart from God), ending in brokenness. But with a relationship with the Creator already demanded (12:1), and with the fact of His judgment affirmed (11:9), **Vanity** is not the last word.

VII. Conclusion: Reverently Trust and Obey God (12:9–14)

12:9–11. The closing words from **the Preacher** (v. 9) serve to enforce the message that vanity is not the last word on man's life in this world. The Preacher reveals the source for this conclusion: he has immersed himself in **words** (v. 10) found in a book **given from one shepherd** (v. 11), who is Yahweh. The book is the Holy Scriptures, in which the **proverbs** (v. 9) are found. The Preacher **gave good heed, and sought out, and set in order** the proverbs from the sacred Scriptures given by Yahweh. This language is designed to describe the rigorous process required of the man who seeks wisdom; no pains must be spared when seeking truth and comprehension. The Scriptures contain **goads** and **nails** (v. 11), literally, "prods" or "pegs." Wisdom both prods one to seek for truth and serves as a peg on which to hang one's thoughts. Since these are given from the One Shepherd, Scripture is in a class of its own. The Preacher searched this material, given by God, to find **words of truth** (v. 10) designed to meet the need of the moment in a particular situation or person's life. The Preacher insists that the proverbs are sufficient to meet every need and that readers are to **be admonished** (v. 12) by these proverbs and accord them an authority superior to that of all other books. While reading many books will result in **weariness of the flesh**, immersion in the Scriptures will result in refreshment and renewal.

12:13–14. The Preacher concludes with a summary statement on the chief end of man: **Fear God, and keep his commandments** (v. 13). Loving reverence is the foundation of wisdom (Ps. 111:10; Prov. 1:7; 9:10), as well as its content (Job 28:28), its goal, and its conclusion. This is the whole duty of man. To "fear God" is our fulfillment and our all—a far cry from "vanity." His commandments provide guidance for our activity under the sun, and He will **bring every work into judgment** (v. 14). This truth is emphasized at intervals in the book: 3:17; 8:12–13; 11:9 (see also discussion on 11:9; Matt. 12:36; 1 Cor. 3:12–15; 2 Cor. 5:9–10; Heb. 4:12–13). Along with the certainty of judgment for every work performed in the open is the more sobering reality that God will bring into judgment also **every secret thing**, everything done in secret (see Rom. 2:16), **whether it be good, or whether it be evil.**

SONG OF SOLOMON

INTRODUCTION

Title

The title in the Hebrew text is "Solomon's Song of Songs," meaning a song by, for, or about Solomon. The phrase "Song of Songs" means the "greatest of songs" (as in "God of gods, and Lord of lords," Deut. 10:17; and in "King of kings," 1 Tim. 6:15).

Author and Date

Verse 1 appears to ascribe authorship to Solomon (see discussion on 1:1; but see also "Title," above). Solomon is referred to seven times (1:1, 5; 3:7, 9, 11; 8:11–12), and several verses speak of the "king" (1:4, 12; 7:5), but whether Solomon was the author remains an open question.

To date the Song in the tenth century BC, during which Solomon reigned, is not impossible. In fact, mention of Tirzah and Jerusalem in one breath (6:4) has been used to prove a date prior to King Omri (885–874 BC; see 1 Kings 16:23–24), though the reason for Tirzah's mention is not clear. On the other hand, many have appealed to the language of the Song as proof of a much later date, but based on present evidence, the linguistic data is ambiguous.

Consistency of language, style, tone, perspective, and recurring refrains seems to argue for a single author. However, many who have doubted that the Song came from one pen, or even from one time or place, explain this consistency by ascribing all the Song's parts to a single literary tradition, since Near Eastern traditions were very careful to maintain stylistic uniformity.

Theme and Theological Message

In ancient Israel, everything human came to expression in words: reverence, gratitude, anger, sorrow, suffering, trust, friendship, commitment, loyalty, hope, wisdom, moral outrage, repentance. In the Song, it is love that finds words — inspired words that disclose its exquisite charm and beauty as one of God's choicest gifts. The voice of love in the Song, like that of wisdom in Proverbs 8:1–9:12, is a woman's voice, suggesting that love and wisdom draw men powerfully with the subtlety and mystery of a woman's allurements.

This feminine voice speaks profoundly of love. She portrays its beauty and delights. She claims its exclusiveness ("My beloved is mine, and I am his," 2:16) and insists on the necessity of its pure spontaneity ("stir not up, nor awake my love, till he please," 2:7). She also proclaims its overwhelming power—it rivals that of the fearsome enemy, death; it burns with the intensity of a blazing fire; it is unquenchable even by the ocean depths (8:6–7a). She affirms its preciousness: all a man's possessions cannot purchase it, nor (alternatively) should they be exchanged for it (8:7b). She hints, without saying so explicitly (see 8:6), that it is a gift of the Lord to man.

God intends that such love—grossly distorted and abused by both ancient and modern people—be a normal part of marital life in His good creation (see Gen. 1:26–31; 2:24).

Interpretation

To find the key for unlocking the Song, interpreters have looked to prophetic, wisdom, and apocalyptic passages of Scripture, as well as to ancient Egyptian and Babylonian love songs, traditional Semitic wedding songs, and songs related to ancient Mesopotamian fertility cults. The closest parallels appear to be those found in Proverbs (see Prov. 5:15–20; 6:24–29; 7:6–23). The description of love in 8:6–7 (compare the descriptions of wisdom in Proverbs 1–9 and Job 28) seems to confirm that the Song belongs to biblical Wisdom Literature and that it is wisdom's description of an amorous relationship. The Bible speaks of both wisdom and love as gifts of God, to be received with gratitude and celebration.

This understanding of the Song contrasts with the long-held view that the Song is an allegory of the love relationship between God and Israel, or between Christ and the church, or between Christ and the soul (the New Testament nowhere quotes from or even alludes to the Song). The Song may indeed picture Christ's love by the example of a marital relationship, but that is not its primary purpose. This understanding is also distinct from more modern interpretations of the Song, such as those that see it as a poetic drama celebrating the triumph of a maiden's pure, spontaneous love for her rustic shepherd lover over the courtly blandishments of Solomon, who sought to win her for his royal harem. Rather, it views the Song as a linked chain of lyrics depicting love in all its spontaneity, beauty, power, and exclusiveness—experienced in its varied moments of separation and intimacy, anguish and ecstasy, tension and contentment. The Song shares with the love poetry of many cultures its extensive use of highly sensuous and suggestive imagery drawn from nature.

Literary Features

No one who reads the Song with care can question the artistry of the poet. The subtle delicacy with which he evokes intense sensuous awareness while avoiding crude titillation is one of the chief marks of his achievement. This he accomplishes largely by indirection, by analogy, and by bringing to the foreground the sensuous in the world of nature (or in food, drink, cosmetics, and jewelry). To liken a lover's enjoyment of his beloved to one who "feedeth among the lilies" (2:16), or her breasts to two fawns that "feed among the lilies" (4:5), or the beloved herself to a garden filled with choice fruits inviting the lover to feast (4:12–16)—these combine exquisite artistry and fine sensitivity.

Whether the Song has the unity of a single dramatic line linking all the subunits into a continuing story is a matter of ongoing debate among interpreters. There do appear to be connected scenes in the love relationship (see "Outline," below).

Virtually all agree that the literary climax of the Song is found in 8:6–7, where the unsurpassed power and value of love — the love that draws man and woman together — are finally expressly asserted. Literary relaxation follows the intenseness of that declaration. A final expression of mutual desire between the lovers brings the Song to an end, suggesting that love goes on. This last segment (8:8–14) is in some sense also a return to the beginning, as references to the beloved's brothers, to her vineyard, and to Solomon (the king) link 8:8–12 with 1:2–6.

In this song of love, the voice of the beloved is dominant. It is her experience of love, both as the one who loves and as the one who is loved, that is most clearly expressed. The Song begins with her wish for the lover's kiss and ends with her urgent invitation to him for love's intimacy.

Outline

    I. Title (1:1)
   II. The First Meeting (1:2–2:7)
  III. The Second Meeting (2:8–3:5)
  IV. The Third Meeting (3:6–5:1)
   V. The Fourth Meeting (5:2–6:3)
  VI. The Fifth Meeting (6:4–8:4)
 VII. The Literary Climax (8:5–7)
VIII. Conclusion (8:8–14)

Bibliography

Carr, G. Lloyd. *The Song of Solomon: An Introduction and Commentary.* Tyndale Old Testament Commentaries 17. Downers Grove, IL: InterVarsity, 1984.

Deere, Jack. "Song of Solomon." In *The Bible Knowledge Commentary: Old Testament,* edited by John F. Walvoord and Roy B. Zuck. Wheaton, IL: Victor, 1985.

Delitzsch, Franz. *Commentary on the Song of Songs and Ecclesiastes.* 1885. Grand Rapids, MI: Eerdmans, 1950.

Ginsberg, Christian D. *The Song of Songs and Coheleth.* New York: KTAV, 1970.

Glickman, S. Craig. *A Song for Lovers.* Downers Grove, IL: InterVarsity, 1976.

Gordis, Robert. *The Song of Songs and Lamentations.* Revised edition. New York: KTAV, 1974.

Lehrman, S. M. "The Song of Songs." In *The Five Megilloth.* Soncino Books of the Bible. London: Soncino, 1946.

Provan, Iain. *Ecclesiastes/Song of Songs.* The NIV Application Commentary. Grand Rapids, MI: Zondervan, 2001.

EXPOSITION

I. Title (1:1)

1:1. According to 1 Kings. 4:32, Solomon wrote 1,005 songs. This is the **song of songs**, or the greatest of **Solomon's** songs. See Introduction: "Title" and "Author and Date." In this song, the people of God of all ages are called to a celebration of the love that God has purposed for men and women within the context of covenantal marriage.

II. The First Meeting (1:2–2:7)

1:2–4. Here begins a section in the Song (1:2–3:5) that represents the courtship phase of love and is filled with both restraint and expressions of deep sexual desire between the lovers. The pronouns **him … his … thy** (v. 2) all refer to the same person, the lover (Solomon). **The kisses … thy love … thy good ointments** (vv. 2–3) are expressions of love—caresses, embraces, and consummation (see v. 4; 4:10; 7:12; see also Prov. 7:18; Ezek. 16:8; 23:17). These are **better than wine** (v. 2; see v. 4). In 4:10, the lover speaks similarly of the beloved's love. The "ointments" are aromatic spices and gums blended in cosmetic oil, which permeate the air around the lover and enhance his desirability. The very mention of the lover's **name** (v. 3) fills the air as with a pleasant aroma. The Hebrew words for "name" and **savour** sound alike. The **virgins** are probably young women of the court or of the royal city (see 6:8–9). **The king** (v. 4) who brings her into **his chambers** or private quarters is Solomon. **We** is likely a reference to the maidens of verse 3. They will all **remember thy love more than wine** for the reason given in verse 2.

1:5–6. She is **black** (v. 5) or deeply browned by the sun (see v. 6). She expresses concern over her appearance and enjoins the **daughters of Jerusalem** (v. 5), probably the maidens of verse 3, **look not upon me** (v. 6). She feels she is rather unsightly, like **the tents of Kedar** (v. 5; see discussion on Isa. 21:16), but also as beautiful as **the curtains** of Solomon's dwellings. She has been so busy in the vineyard that her **own vineyard** (v. 6), or her body, she has not

kept (see 8:12 and 2:15). A vineyard is an apt metaphor since it yields wine, and the excitements of love are compared with those produced by wine (see discussion on 1:2). The beloved is also compared to a garden, yielding precious fruits for the lover (see discussion on 4:12).

1:7–8. The focus shifts from her concerns about herself to her desire to be near the one **my soul loveth** (v. 7; see 3:1). She desires to know **where thou feedest … thy flock**. The lover is portrayed as a shepherd. In verse 8, the beloved is depicted as a shepherdess. **Noon** is the time of rest in warm climates. Ginsburg suggests that **turneth aside by the flocks** be translated "roams/wanders among the flocks" (*Song of Songs*, p. 136). The beloved does not wish to look for her lover among the shepherds, not wanting to appear as though she were a prostitute (see Gen. 38:14–15). The ladies of the court address the beloved as the **fairest among women** (v. 8; see also 1:15; 2:10, 13; 4:1, 7; 5:9; 6:1, 4, 10). The lover is also called "fair" in 1:16 (the masculine form of the same Hebrew word). The beloved is pictured as a shepherdess (v. 7) and is advised by the court ladies to learn where the lover is by joining her **kids** (v. 8) to the herds of the shepherds in the fields. In doing so, she justifies her presence and can seek her lover and yet refrain from any appearance of evil.

1:9–11. Solomon speaks as the lover here. Like all lovers, he cannot keep from speaking of his great admiration and affection for **my love** (v. 9), a term that is used only of the beloved (see discussion on 1:13). To see her as **a company of horses** is meant obviously to be a flattering comparison, similar to Theocritus's praise of the beautiful Helen of Troy (*Idyl* 18.30–31). Her beauty attracts attention the way a mare would attention among the Egyptian chariot stallions. According to 1 Kings 10:28, Solomon imported many of these beautiful horses from Egypt. It is only fitting that a woman of such beauty be given splendid gifts. Necklaces of **gold** and **silver** (vv. 10–11) are some of his many gifts to his beloved and will add to her already overwhelming beauty.

1:12–15. While **the king** (v. 12) reclines at his table with his circle of friends, her **spikenard** calls his mind and heart to her. Nard is an aromatic oil extracted from the roots of a perennial herb that grows in India (see 4:13–14; Mark 14:3; John 12:3). **Myrrh** (v. 13) is an aromatic gum exuding from the bark of a balsam tree that grows in Arabia, Ethiopia, and India. It was commonly used as an alluring feminine perfume (Est. 2:12; Prov. 7:17). It was also used to perfume royal nuptial robes (Ps. 45:8). The wise men brought myrrh to the young Jesus as a gift fit for a king (Matt. 2:2, 11). Myrrh was an ingredient in the holy anointing oil (Exod. 30:23). Adorned with her perfumes, she is an intoxicating presence for the king, whose love for her overwhelms him. She is equally in love with him, and he is to her **my well-beloved.** This is a phrase that is only used by her to describe her affection for the lover. He is also like **a cluster of camphire** (v. 14) to her. This is a shrub of the Holy Land (perhaps the cypress) with tightly clustered, aromatic blossoms. **En-gedi** is the oasis watered by a spring, located on the west side of the Dead Sea. David sought refuge there from king Saul (1 Sam. 24:1). Her rapturous affection for her lover causes a similar response in him. He responds, **thou art fair, my love** (v. 15; see 4:1; 6:4; see also 1:16). **Doves' eyes** are symbolic of gentleness, and doves have only one mate for life (see 4:1). "According to Rabbinic teaching, a bride who has beautiful eyes possesses a beautiful character; they are an index to her character" (Lehrman, "The Song of Songs," p. 4).

1:16–17. The Shulamite (see discussion on the meaning of the name in commentary on 6:13) responds to these terms of endearment with an expression of her equal affection and admiration for the king. He too is **pleasant** (v. 16), and the place of their meeting **is green,** or "luxuriant." The lovers lie together in the field under the trees and exalt in the wonder and ecstasy of the gift God has given to them in each other.

2:1. The instruction on the art of communication between lovers is rich in this section. She states that she thinks of herself as **the rose of Sharon** (see Isa. 35:1–2). This flower is a member of the crocus family that grows everywhere on the fertile coastal plain south of Mount Carmel. She also compares herself to **the lily of the valleys,** which also are found in abundance. These flowers are beautiful, but they are found in abundance everywhere and hence are not as special as some other flowers.

2:2–6. The lover disagrees with her assessment of her beauty and value. He exclaims **my love** (v. 2) is like a **lily among thorns.** To the lover, she is special and is like a lily in a field of thorns. She replies that he is like **the apple tree among the trees of the wood** (v. 3). He is a source of shade and great sweetness for her. Married couples do well to remember that words are for edification, and in this interchange between the lovers, one sees that process at work. Verbal interaction of this sort puts a **banner** of love (v. 4) over a relationship for all to clearly see (see 6:4; Num. 2:2; Ps. 20:5). The king's love for her is displayed for all to see, like a large military banner. Little wonder they are **sick** with **love** (v. 5) and in need of nourishment. Some things in life so enthrall one that it is easy to forget to eat. She asks for **flagons** and **apples,** which were known for their power to revive.

2:7. Although love is difficult to manage, it is necessary that lovers control the feelings they have for one another. She now issues a **charge** to the **daughters of Jerusalem,** or attempts to place them under oath. Perhaps in the imaginative language of love, **the roes** (or gazelles) and **hinds** are portrayed as witnesses to the oath. She petitions that they **stir not up** love until the time is appropriate. This is a recurring refrain in the Song (see 3:5; 8:4; see 5:8). It is always spoken by the beloved and always in a context of physical intimacy with her lover. It is best translated, "Do not arouse love until it is proper." Out of the beloved's experience of love comes the wise admonition that love is not to be stimulated by one's friends, or by stimulants. Physical intimacy is for the marital bed and is not to be engaged in outside of the covenant of marriage.

III. The Second Meeting (2:8–3:5)

2:8–9. The eager lover tries to catch sight of the beloved while she is still preparing for their meeting.

He looketh forth at the windows (v. 9) beyond which she prepares herself, hoping to catch a glimpse of her. Like all lovers, his eyes cannot behold the beloved too often. He comes to his beloved like **a roe**, which is celebrated for its form and beauty, or like **a young hart**, or "deer," an apt simile for youthful vigor (see Isa. 35:6).

2:10 – 15. Glimpses will never suffice for young lovers or for old ones either. Physical presence and companionship is always eagerly sought. The lover cries out to his beloved, **Rise up … my fair one … and come away** with me (v. 10; see v. 13; 7:11 – 13). The first signs of spring are appearing everywhere (see 6:11; 7:12). It is the time of love, and he cannot bear to be out of her presence. Sequestered in her quarters, or **the secret places of the stairs** (v. 14; see Ps. 55:6 – 8; Jer. 48:28), she is like the **dove** hidden in the unreachable **clefts of the rock,** and he agonizes to **hear** her **voice,** touch her, and share time and space with her. Additionally, the desire is expressed that the lovers be kept safe from whatever **foxes** (v. 15) might mar their mutual love for one another. Their love is like **tender grapes.** Their attraction to one another is in its prime, and the potential for its ruin looms ominously before them. Hence, the desire that they might be together to fend off any **little foxes** that might seek to insidiously harm their budding relationship. "The foxes represent as many obstacles or temptations as have plagued lovers throughout the centuries. Perhaps it is the fox of uncontrolled desire which drives a wedge of guilt between a couple. Perhaps it is the fox of mistrust and jealousy which breaks the bond of love. It may be the fox of selfishness and pride which refuses to let one acknowledge his fault to another. It may be an unforgiving spirit which will not accept the apology of the other. These foxes have been ruining vineyards for years and the end of their work is not in sight" (Glickman, *A Song for Lovers,* pp. 49 – 50).

2:16 – 17. Lovers know moments when they are anxious over the possible loss of the relationship and need reassurance. This is one of those moments. The Shulamite senses her lover's need for her words of encouragement and says, **My beloved is mine, and I am his** (v. 16; see 6:3; 7:10). She insists that they belong to each other exclusively, in a relationship that allows no intrusion and that cannot be destroyed by the little foxes. Though **he feedeth among the lilies,** she bids him **turn** (v. 17) and make haste at **day break** to come to her. The lover is compared to **a roe,** which is famous for its speed (see v. 17; 2:9). She bids him to close the distance between them and end their separation. **Bether** means separation or division.

3:1 – 5. Few forces in this world are stronger than love. She has bid her lover to come in the morning. However, she cannot get him out of her mind, and as she lays on her bed at night. the vision of him fills her longing heart. **By night** (v. 1), with its freedom from the distractions of the day, her heart is filled with her preoccupations. She dreams and, in her dream, determines that she **will rise** (v. 2) and go in pursuit of her lover. She encounters the **watchmen** (v. 3) who were stationed at the city gates (see Neh. 3:29; 11:19; 13:22) and on the walls (see 5:7; 2 Sam. 13:34; 18:24 – 27; 2 Kings 9:17 – 20; Ps. 127:1; Isa. 52:8; 62:6). Apparently, they also patrolled the streets at night (see 5:7). She presses them for information regarding the whereabouts of **him whom my soul loveth.** Dreaming that she finds him, she brings him into her **mother's house** (v. 4). It is a matter of interest that mothers are referred to frequently in the Song, while fathers are never mentioned. Though the moment is filled with loving affection for the pair, she keeps the standard of morality high, and once again she issues a **charge** to the **daughters of Jerusalem** at the moment of intimacy (see 2:7). This is not the time for physical intimacy, although the couple may desire it. Physical intimacy is to be reserved for its right time, and that time is within the sacredness of the marital union and covenant. This verse marks the end of the section on courtship.

IV. The Third Meeting (3:6 – 5:1)

3:6 – 11. The marriage ceremony is fully in view in this section of the poem. First the account of the wedding processional is given (vv. 6 – 11), and then the details of the wedding night are shared (4:1 – 5:1).

The wedding processional was a significant part of the Jewish wedding tradition. On the great day of the wedding, the bridegroom would lead a processional to the bride's home and then escort her back to their new home. As the community looks on at this splendid processional led by the king, they ask, **Who is this that cometh out of the wilderness** (v. 6) in such splendor. The **smoke** refers to the imported and expensive incense that will engulf the procession. The **bed** (v. 7) is a richly adorned royal conveyance, a palanquin (see vv. 9–10). The processional is totally secure because of the presence of swordsmen who accompany the group **because of fear in the night** (v. 8; see Ps. 91:5). The processional is an open show for all to see the great wealth and love that Solomon has immersed himself in and now shares with his bride. **The pillars** (v. 10) supporting the canopy are constructed of Lebanon wood and are overlaid with **silver** and **gold**. The royal conveyance is wrapped in the **purple** of royalty and engulfed in the love that this couple shares (see discussion on 7:5; *Zondervan KJV Study Bible* note on Exod. 25:4). The **daughters of Zion** (v. 11) are invited to view this regal event and to behold **the crown**, or wedding wreath (see Isa. 61:10), that was given to the bridegroom by **his mother**. Here the reference is to Bathsheba.

4:1–7. Now that the wedding night has arrived, the lover speaks to his beloved of his enthrallment with her physical beauty. He launches into expressions of appreciation for her physical beauty, which assures her of the favor she has found in his eyes and heart. For other exuberant descriptions of the beloved's beauty, see 6:4–9; 7:1–7. The godly are herein granted permission to celebrate the human body as one of God's good gifts to His creation. Within the bounds of the marital covenant and the exclusivity of the monogamy championed in Scripture, this type of adulation for the body of one's lover is not only allowed but encouraged. While he notices all that is **fair** (v. 1) in his **love**, his initial focus is on her **eyes** (see 1:15). With the rest of her face concealed by a veil, the lover's attention is focused on the **dove**-like gentleness in the beloved's eyes. From her eyes, his attention moves to his lover's hair, which was black like the **flock of goats, that appear from mount Gilead**. The beloved's black tresses flowing from her head remind the lover of a flock of sleek black goats streaming down one of the hills of Gilead (noted for its good pasturage). Her teeth are clean and white, which reminds him of **a flock of sheep that are even shorn** (v. 2), glistening as they **came up from the washing**. Her lips are like a **thread of scarlet** (v. 3). Perhaps the beloved painted her lips, as Egyptian women did. Her **temples**, or the upper part of her cheeks, are like the inside of a **piece of a pomegranate**. They are blushed with red. The beloved's erect, bespangled **neck** (v. 4) is like a **tower** on the city wall adorned with warriors' **shields** (see 7:4). Her **breasts** (v. 5) resemble **young roes**, or fawns, representing tender, delicate beauty and promise rather than full growth (see 8:8). The simile of the "roe" (gazelle) is used of the lover in 2:9. The lovers envision a night of rapturous love, and his fascination with her breasts, which are described as **the mountain of myrrh** (v. 6) and **the hill of frankincense**, is once again expressed.

4:8–11 The beloved has been taken from her home in the remote mountains of **Lebanon, Amana,** and **Hermon** (v. 8). Her lover asks her to erase this past place of safety from her mind and find her safety in his presence. These are mountain peaks on the northern horizon. **Shenir** is the Amorite name for Mount Hermon (Deut. 3:9). For lovers to address each other as "brother" and **sister** (v. 9) was common in the love poetry of the ancient Near East (see v. 10; 4:12; 5:1). She has ravished his heart **with one of** her **eyes**, or with a single glance (see 6:5 and discussion). He is surely smitten, and her love is to him **better ... than wine** (v. 10; see discussion on 1:2). **The smell of ... ointments** on her body surpasses the enticement of all the **spices** he has ever smelled (see 4:14; 5:1, 13; 6:2; 8:14). Spice was an imported luxury item (see 1 Kings 10:2, 10, 25; Ezek. 27:22). Spices were used for fragrance in the holy anointing oil (Exod. 25:6; 30:23–25; 35:8) and for fragrant incense (Exod. 25:6; 35:8) as well as for perfume. Her **lips ... drop as the honeycomb** (v. 11); they drip with honey. The beloved speaks to him of love (see Prov. 5:3; 16:24).

People in the ancient Near East associated sweetness with the delights of love. **Honey and milk** are perhaps reminiscent of the description of the Promised Land (see discussion on Exod. 3:8), and they **are under thy tongue** (see Job 20:12; Ps. 10:7).

4:12. She surely represents **a garden** to him, a place of sensual delights (see 4:16; 5:1; 6:2). This delightful garden is **inclosed ... shut up ... sealed**. These are metaphors for the beloved's virginity, or perhaps for the fact that she had kept herself exclusively for her husband. That she is a **spring** or **fountain** speaks of the reality that she was designed by God to be such a rich source of refreshment for her husband. These terms are employed as metaphors for the beloved as a sexual partner, as in Proverbs 5:15–20.

4:13–15. Verses 13–14 elaborate on the garden metaphor of verse 12a, and verse 15 elaborates on the fountain metaphor of verse 12b. The trees and spices in verses 13–14 are mostly exotic, referring to the beloved's charms. **Thy plants** (v. 13) represent all the beloved's features that delight the lover. **Orchard** is from the Hebrew term *pardes*, from which the English word "paradise" comes and is a loanword from Old Persian meaning "enclosure" or "park." Nehemiah 2:8 and Ecclesiastes 2:5 refer to royal parks and forests. For **camphire** and **spikenard**, see discussions 1:14 and 1:12. **Saffron** (v. 14) is a spice made of dried stigmas from a crocus plant that bears purple or white flowers. **Calamus** was an imported (see Jer. 6:20), aromatic spice cane, used also in the holy anointing oil and incense (see "cane" in Exod. 30:23, 25; Isa. 43:23–24). **Cinnamon** was used in the holy anointing oil (Exod. 30:23, 25). **Myrrh and aloes** were used to perfume royal nuptial robes (Ps. 45:8). Proverbs 7:17 says that the adulteress perfumed her bed "with myrrh, aloes, and cinnamon."

The lover has not finished with his torrent of praise for her. In addition to praising the overwhelming appeal of her ointments, he compares her to **living waters** (v. 15). She is ever fresh, never stagnant. She is like the **streams from Lebanon**, ever refreshing him with cool, sparkling water from the snowfields on the Lebanon Mountains.

4:16. She knows the power of her beauty and offers herself only to her lover. Her desire is that the fragrance of her charms waft about and draw her lover to her so that they may enjoy love's intimacies. She is **his garden**. She belongs to him, and she delights in sharing the powers of her feminine persona and body with her lover (see 6:2).

5:1. Such a powerful invitation from one who is so overwhelming beautiful cannot be ignored. The lover claims the beloved as his garden and enjoys the delight of their sexual experience. Pairing the phrases **my sister** and **my spouse** may serve to accentuate the friendship and covenantal dimensions of their relationship. **Eat, O friends** sets the context of their meeting within that of a circle of friends, who applaud the couple's enjoyment of love.

V. The Fourth Meeting (5:2–6:3)

5:2–8. Love holds sway even in sleep, just as a new mother sleeps with an ear open to her baby's slightest whimper. Though the beloved is deep in **sleep,** her **heart waketh** (v. 2) to the voice of her beloved. In her dream, her instinctive reaction raises a complaint before the language of love takes over. She moves to admit him and reaches to the lock with **fingers** (v. 5) dripping **with sweet smelling myrrh.** Love's eager imagination has moved her to extravagantly lotion her hands with perfume. Alas, at her rebuff, he has withdrawn. She dreams of pursuing him through the city streets and meets with ill treatment from the **keepers of the walls** (v. 7), who take from her the **vail** covering her head. This dream speaks of separation, distance, and danger for the maturing relationship between the lovers. It may signify that the relationship between the lovers had encountered a troubled period, and she was frantic to resolve it. Lovers, young and old, are sometimes guilty of foolish attitudes, words, and actions. The section closes with a plaintiff cry to her friends: **If ye find my beloved ... tell him, That I am sick of love** (v. 8). In 2:5, the Shulamite was "sick [with] love" because of the joy derived from his presence, while here she is overcome with the sickness of love because of the pain of his absence. Little wonder

Paul says the greatest force in human relationships is love (1 Corinthians 13).

5:9-16. The daughters ask, **What is thy beloved more than another beloved ...?** (v. 9). The daughters' question provides an opportunity for the beloved to describe the beauty of her lover, which she does only here. Her delight in his physical body serves as a reminder that both men and women are sensual beings who were created by God to celebrate and commend the physical beauty of their counterpart in creation. To her, he stands out even as the standard-bearer is clearly distinguishable from the **ten thousand** (v. 10) regular soldiers who surround him. His face is **ruddy**, and his hair is **black as a raven** (v. 11). His eyes too are **the eyes of doves by the rivers of waters** (v. 12). The lover's eyes sparkle and are **washed with milk**, a description of the white of the eye. The similes she uses—**a bed of spices ... lilies, dropping sweet smelling myrrh ... gold rings set with the beryl ... ivory overlaid with sapphires ... pillars of marble, set upon sockets of fine gold** (vv. 13-15)—are probably used to compare sensuous effects rather than appearances. Each of these in their turn contribute to the arousal of love's pleasant excitements. Their cumulative effect results in one whose **countenance is as Lebanon** (v. 15), awesome, majestic, and as **excellent as the cedars**. The cedars of Lebanon were renowned throughout the ancient Near East, and their wood was desired for adorning temples and palaces. The lover's kisses and loving speech are given within the context of covenantal fidelity and friendship. The question raised by the "daughters of Jerusalem" has been fully answered, and they can only wish that they should be so blessed.

6:1. The question asked by her friends forms a transition from the beloved's description of the lover to her delighted acknowledgment of his intimacy with her and the exclusiveness of their relationship. The beloved has spoken so positively of her lover that the daughters of Jerusalem would love to meet him and are more than willing to assist in her search for him. Lovers should only speak positively of one another in the presence of others.

6:2-3. She expresses her devotion to her lover and her confidence in his devotion to her with the words **I am my beloved's, and my beloved is mine** (v. 3). She believes that he has gone to **his garden, to the beds of spices** (v. 2).

VI. The Fifth Meeting (6:4-8:4)

6:4-10. When united, the lover again ventures forth in praise of the beauty he finds in his beloved. She is to his eyes as pleasant as **Tirzah** (v. 4). Tirzah was an old Canaanite city in the middle of the land (see Josh. 12:24). It was chosen by Jeroboam I (930-909 BC) as the first royal city of the northern kingdom (1 Kings 14:17; see 1 Kings 15:21; 16:23-24). The meaning of its name ("pleasure, beauty") suggests that it was a beautiful site, perhaps explaining why the author here sets it alongside Jerusalem (though what constituted the beauty of Tirzah is not known). Comparison of the beloved's beauty to that of cities was perhaps not so unusual in the ancient Near East, since cities were regularly depicted as women (see discussion on 2 Kings 19:21). She is as **terrible** (i.e., awesome) **as an army with banners** (see 6:10). The beloved's noble beauty evokes in the lover emotions like those aroused by a troop marching under its banners. Her **eyes ... have overcome** (v. 5) him and have awakened in him such intensity of love that he is held captive (see 4:9). She is more beautiful than all the **queens ... concubines, and virgins** (v. 8), all the beautiful women of the realm. She is **undefiled** (v. 9) and is **the only one of her mother**. Not literally an only child, but the one uniquely loved (see Gen. 22:2; Judg. 11:34; Prov. 4:3). **The daughters ... blessed her**, and all the other women praised her beauty (see 1:8; 5:9; 6:1). The rising **morning** (v. 10), with its red light looking down from heaven and over the mountains, the beautiful and placid complexion of the **moon**, and the grandiose and resplendent appearance of the **sun** have often afforded, to both the Oriental and the Greek and Latin writers, exquisite similes for beauty and grandeur (Ginsburg, *Song of Songs*, p. 174). The lover employs all of these to attempt a description of the beauty he finds in her.

6:11-13. She has made her way **down into the garden of nuts** (v. 11) to see if her lover was there and if his love for her still **flourished**. She will soon have evidence that his love for her indeed flourishes, when he speaks to her in 7:1–9. Before she **was aware** (v. 12) of the feelings his praise evoked in her, she " became enraptured" and was beside herself with joy (Deere, "Song of Solomon," p. 1022). Solomon, who was famous for his **chariots** (1 Kings 10:26), heightened the joy of the encounter by placing her on his chariot and leading his entourage in a processional from the garden. The inhabitants of the area were unhappy with their hasty departure and begged her to stay. Four times they expressed their desire to gaze on the **Shulamite** (v. 13). This term is either a variant of "Shunammite" (see 1 Kings 1:3), that is, a young woman from Shunem (see Josh. 19:18), or a feminine form of the word "Solomon," meaning "Solomon's girl." In ancient Semitic languages, the letters *l* and *n* were sometimes interchanged. Asked why they want to gaze upon her beauty longer, they respond that beholding her is like beholding **the company of two armies**. The text is literally, "We look upon the Shulamite as one looks upon the dance of the Mahanaim." They see in her a resemblance of the dance of the Mahanaim, the magnificent and transporting dance of the angel host that occurred east of the Jordan during Jacob's return to the Promised Land (Gen. 32:1–3).

7:1-6. This portion of the Song illustrates the maturing of marital intimacy. The images used to describe the beauty of the beloved are bolder and more intimate than those employed in 4:1–11. Here the description moves up from the **feet** (v. 1) rather than down from the head (see 5:11–15). Her curvaceous **thighs** are of such beauty that they resemble the work of a master craftsman. The allusion to the **prince's daughter** is a reference to the nobility of her beauty (see Ps. 45:13). The **goblet** (v. 2) is a large, two-handled, ring-based bowl (see Exod. 24:6; Isa. 22:24; see also Amos 6:6) that would hold a large amount of the intoxicating wine. The emphasis here is on the excitement awakened in the lover by the sight of this beautiful part of her anatomy, which he compares to the excitement derived from drinking

deeply of the mixed wine. Her **belly is … set about with lilies**. The beloved perhaps wore a loose garland of flowers around her waist. For her breasts, see discussion on 4:5. Her **neck is as a tower of ivory** (v. 4). This is mixed imagery, referring to shape as well as to color and texture. The beloved's **eyes** reflect like the surface of **fishpools**; the imagery may depict serenity and gentleness. **Heshbon** was once the royal city of king Sihon (Num. 21:26); it was blessed with an abundant supply of spring water. **Bath-rabbim** means "daughter of many," perhaps a popular name for Heshbon. **The tower of Lebanon** was perhaps a military tower on the northern frontier of Solomon's kingdom but more likely was the beautiful, towering Lebanon mountain range. **Carmel** (v. 5) was a promontory midway along the western coast of the kingdom, with a wooded top, and was known for its beauty. **Purple** is a reference to the purple royal cloth (as in 3:10; see *KJV Study Bible* note on Exod. 25:4). The **king** (Solomon) **is held in the galleries** (lit., "bound by the locks"), captivated by the beauty of her hair. Solomon begins to conclude his praise of her beauty with the exclamation, **O love** (v. 6).

7:7-9. Solomon summarizes his rationale for such extensive praise by comparing the beloved to the the stately date **palm tree** (v. 7). The sight of this tree awakened joy, for it promised the presence of both water and fruit to assuage the thirst and hunger of the weary traveler. She is such a welcome sight to him. Her **breasts** are equally filled with promise for his delight. They are as desirable as sweet **clusters of grapes**. He wants to **take hold of the boughs** (v. 8) of his palm tree and cover her mouth with kisses, for her breath smelled with the sweetness of **apples**, or the fragrance of apple blossoms. Her kisses are **like the best wine** (v. 9), sweet to the taste and loosening to the spirits of the imbiber. The beloved offers the wine (see 5:1) of her love freely to her lover.

7:10. Once again the Shulamite exclaims, **I am my beloved's** (see discussions on 2:16; 6:3). She is confident that his sexual **desire** is totally focused on her (see Gen. 3:16).

7:11-12. In 2:10–13, the beloved reported a similar invitation from her lover. In 7:1–10, he took the lead in the expression of desire for sexual intimacy. Now in 7:11–13, she takes the initiative and petitions the lover for sexual intimacy, with the words **give thee my loves** (v. 12). She offers herself completely to her lover and requests that they **go ... into the field** (v. 11) and **lodge in the villages**. It is spring, and the fields are alive with symbols of fertility. **The mandrakes** (v. 13) are short-stemmed herbs associated with fertility (see discussion on Gen. 30:14). The **gates** where the lovers meet may be a metaphor for the delights the beloved has for her lover from her "garden" (see 4:13–14). In this place of sexual intimacy, they will experience the **new and old**. They will experience the thrill of sexual pleasures already shared and those still to be enjoyed. The Song has led us to the celebration of sexuality unencumbered by the smut of this world and fully enjoyed within the context of covenantal marriage. Truly, sex is one of God's greatest gifts to humans.

8:1–4. So grand is this gift of sexuality that the beloved wishes they could have been together many more years than they have. She now considers their relationship as multifaceted across time and suggests ways in which her wish could have been realized. Her desire could have been accomplished if the lover had been her **brother** (v. 1). She could then have openly showed her affection for her brother and she would **not be despised**. The beloved could have openly given her brother **kiss[es]** without any public disgrace. Her desire could have been fulfilled if she could have filled the role of his older sister. She could have led him and **cause[d] thee to drink**. If her lover had been a guest in the home of her mother, she could have offered him the delights of intoxicating juices. In her role as wife, however, she could enjoy his caresses. Surely this is a superior role to the others, for with **his right hand** (v. 3), he shall **embrace me**. This amorous action should be motivated by his desire and not by the prodding of the **daughters of Jerusalem** (v. 4).

VII. The Literary Climax (8:5–7)

8:5. The section begins with the question, **Who is this that cometh up from the wilderness, lean-**

ing upon her beloved? The question is not answered since the answer is obvious. It is the lovers, around whose experiences the entire Song has been constructed. "The wilderness" may stand for the curse God has placed on the world as a consequence of Adam's sin. They are a picture of what can be when lovers commit to God's plan for marriage even though the world is fallen. **The apple tree** was often associated with sexual union and birth in the biblical world. The image here refers to the beginning of their love. "The beloved roused (better, 'awakened') her lover to love. The 'awakening' is a metaphor for new life or rather a new way of perceiving life, which her love had brought to him. Much as he was the product of his parents' love and was brought into the world by physical birth, the lover had now received a second 'birth' or 'awakening' through the love of his beloved" (Deere, "Song of Solomon," p. 1024). Such is the awesome power of love.

8:6–7. The three wisdom statements contained in these verses characterize marital love as the strongest, most unyielding, and most invincible force in human experience. With these statements, the Song reaches its literary climax and discloses its purpose. The **seal** (v. 6) was precious to it's owner, as personal as his name (see discussion on Gen. 38:18) and represented ownership, responsibility, and protection. The Shulamite requests that her lover think of her as precious and remember always his responsibility to honor and protect her. A positive response to this request will require that he place her name over his heart, for the purpose of informing all of his decisions, and on his **arm**, as an external witness to her prominence in his affections. Nothing less than this type of action on the part of the husband would be appropriate, since **love is strong as death**, and only a symbol as fitting as the seal speaks adequately to its character. A lesser action may serve to awaken **jealousy** in the beloved, with its potential to damage love. To comply with her request is to experience a love that cannot be extinguished by **many waters** (v. 7). These words suggest not only the ocean depths (see Ps. 107:23) but also the primeval waters that the people of the ancient Near East regarded as a permanent threat to the world (see discussion on Ps. 32:6). Love cannot be overcome even by so great a threat. Love is also beyond price, and **if a man** were to seek to purchase it, all the gold he could offer would be **contemned**. This is a fourth wisdom statement, declaring love's unsurpassed worth. Riches are "contemned" (despised) in comparison to love.

VIII. Conclusion (8:8–14)

8:8–14. In the closing lines of the Song, the words of the brothers (vv. 8–9), the beloved's reference to her vineyard (v. 12), and her final reference to Solomon (vv. 11–12) suggest a return to the beginning of the Song (see 1:2–7). The lines may recall the beloved's development into the age for love and marriage and the blossoming of her relationship with her lover.

8:8–10. In the ancient Near East, brothers often were guardians of their sisters, especially in matters pertaining to marriage (see Gen. 24:50–60; 34:13–27). While she was a young girl and under their care, they had wondered what they would do **in the day when she shall be spoken for** (v. 8). Marriage was often contracted at an early age, and these imaginative verses probably express the brothers' determination to defend the honor of their young sister (the beloved) and their concern that she might be promiscuous before her proper time for love and marriage had come. If she was **a wall** (v. 9), practicing caution and manifesting character in her relationship with males, they were determined to reward her; but if the opposite was true and she was frivolous, they intended to **inclose her with boards of cedar**. The Shulamite announced that she was ready for marriage; her breasts were **like towers** (v. 10). The beloved rejoiced in her maturity (see Ezek. 16:7–8).

She came to the marriage ceremony as one who had found absolute **favour** in **his** the lover's **eyes.**

8:11–12. The lovers first meeting was apparently in a vineyard owned by Solomon and leased to her brothers for the price of **a thousand pieces of silver** (v. 11). Whether these figures are to be taken literally (see Isa. 7:23) is uncertain. The location of **Baal-hamon** is unknown. The Hebrew *hamon* sometimes means "wealth" or "abundance"; hence, "Baal [i.e., 'lord'] Hamon" could mean "lord of abundance," bringing to mind Solomon's great wealth. **My vineyard** (v. 12) is a metaphor for her body (see discussion on 1:6). As Solomon is master of his vineyard, so the beloved is mistress of her attractions, to dispense them as she will. She offers Solomon the owner's portion of her vineyard. In 7:11–12, the beloved invited her lover to accompany her to the countryside and the vineyards. Here the imagery places her appropriately **in the gardens** (v. 13) Intimacy requires that they speak often and tenderly to one another, hence her petition, **Cause me to hear ... thy voice** (see 2:14). Intimacy requires proximity, hence her petition, **be thou like to a roe or to a young hart** (v. 14). She petitions her lover for a display of his virile strength and agility for her delight, as he performs **upon the mountains of spices**. The Song of Songs closes with an allusion once again to the joy of physical intimacy. There is no shame attached to the human body and the awesome enjoyment to be derived from sharing its delights within the context of covenantal marriage. It is for this very reason that the New Testament pictures the relationship of Christ to the believer as one of bridegroom and bride (Eph. 5:22–33; Rev. 19:7–9). Christians are to love Him as He loves them, with the same kind of passion and commitment as that of a married couple.

THE BOOK OF THE PROPHET ISAIAH

INTRODUCTION

Author

Isaiah son of Amoz is often thought of as the greatest of the writing prophets. His name means "the Lord saves." He was a contemporary of Amos, Hosea, and Micah, beginning his ministry in 740 BC, the year King Uzziah died (see discussion on 6:1). According to an unsubstantiated Jewish tradition (the ascension of Isaiah), Isaiah was sawed in half during the reign of Manasseh (see Heb. 11:37). He was married and had at least two sons, Shear-jashub (7:3) and Maher-shalal-hash-baz (8:3). He probably spent most of his life in Jerusalem and enjoyed his greatest influence under King Hezekiah (see 37:1–2). Isaiah is also credited with writing a history of the reign of King Uzziah (2 Chron. 26:22).

Many scholars today challenge the claim that Isaiah wrote the entire book that bears his name. Yet his is the only name attached to it (see 1:1; 2:1; 13:1). The strongest argument for the unity of Isaiah is the expression "the Holy One of Israel," a title for God that occurs twelve times in chapters 1–39 and thirteen times in chapters 40–66. Outside Isaiah, this title appears in the Old Testament only six times. There are other striking verbal parallels between chapters 1–39 and chapters 40–66. Compare the following verses: 1:2 with 66:24; 1:5–6 with 53:4–5; 5:27 with 40:30; 6:1 with 52:13 and 57:15; 6:11–12 with 62:4; 11:1 with 53:2; 11:6–9 with 65:25; 11:12 with 49:22; 35:10 with 51:11. Altogether, at least twenty-five Hebrew words or forms are found in Isaiah (i.e., in both major divisions of the book) that occur in no other prophetic writing.

Isaiah's use of fire as a figure of punishment (see 1:31; 10:17; 26:11; 33:11–14; 34:9–10; 66:24), his references to "the mountain of the Lord" of Jerusalem (see discussion on 2:2–4), and his mention of the highway to Jerusalem (see discussion on 11:16) are themes that recur throughout the book.

The structure of Isaiah also argues for its unity. Chapters 36–39 constitute a historical interlude, which concludes chapters 1–35 and introduces chapters 40–66. Several New Testament verses refer to the prophet Isaiah in connection with various parts of the book: Matthew 12:17–21 (Isa. 42:1–4); Matthew 3:3 and Luke 3:4 (Isa. 40:3); Romans 10:16, 20 (Isa. 53:1; 65:1); and especially John 12:38–41 (Isa. 53:1; 6:10).

Date

Most of the events discussed in chapters 1–39 occurred during Isaiah's ministry (see 6:1; 14:28; 36:1), so it is likely that these chapters were completed not long after 701 BC, the year the Assyrian army was destroyed (see discussion on 10:16). The prophet lived until at least 681 BC (see 37:38) and may have written chapters 40–66 during his later years. In his message to the exiles of the sixth century BC, Isaiah was projected into the future, just as the apostle John was in Revelation 4–22.

Background

Isaiah wrote during the stormy period marking the expansion of the Assyrian Empire and the decline of Israel. Under King Tiglath-pileser III (745–727 BC), the Assyrians swept westward into Aram (Syria) and Canaan. About 733 BC, the kings of Aram and Israel tried to pressure Ahaz king of Judah into joining a coalition against Assyria. Ahaz chose instead to ask Tiglath-pileser for help, a decision Isaiah condemned (see 7:1). Assyria did assist Judah and conquered the northern kingdom in 722–721 BC. This made Judah even more vulnerable, and in 701 BC, King Sennacherib of Assyria threatened Jerusalem itself (see 36:1 and discussion). The godly King Hezekiah prayed earnestly, and Isaiah predicted that God would force the Assyrians to withdraw from the city (37:6–7).

Nevertheless, Isaiah warned Judah that her sin would bring captivity at the hands of Babylon. The visit of the Babylonian king's envoys to Hezekiah set the stage for this prediction (see 39:1–6). Although the fall of Jerusalem did not take place until 586 BC, Isaiah assumed the demise of Judah and proceeded to predict the restoration of the people from captivity (see 40:2–3 and discussions). God would redeem His people from Babylon just as He had rescued them from Egypt (see discussions on 35:10; 41:14). Isaiah predicted the rise of Cyrus the Persian, who united the Medes and Persians and conquered Babylon in 539 BC (see 41:2 and discussion). The decree of Cyrus allowed the Jews to return home in 538 BC, a deliverance that prefigured the greater salvation from sin through Christ (see 52:7 and discussion).

Theme and Theological Message

The central theological concept in the book of Isaiah is that the Lord is "the Holy One of Israel" (1:4; 5:19, 24; 49:26; 55:5). Isaiah's understanding of God was rooted in the vision he received from the Lord when he was first called to the prophetic ministry (chap. 6). The Lord is perfect in power and purity but graciously entered into a covenant relationship with Israel. Isaiah's conception of the Lord as "the Holy One" caused him to stress that God is the true King and must be exalted above all (6:1; 12:6; 33:15–16), through Israel's faith and obedience. The primary sin of Israel and Judah was that they had put man in the place of God and God in the place of man (2:11–18; 10:20; 17:7; 31:1). Isaiah called the future exiles to recognize the Lord as the all-powerful Creator and Redeemer who is superior to the Babylonians and their gods (40:7–8, 12–17; 46–47). The Lord will ultimately defeat His enemies and rule over all in the messianic kingdom (60:1–3; 63:1–6).

The book of Isaiah unveils the full dimensions of God's judgment and salvation. As "the Holy One of Israel," God had to punish His rebellious people (1:2) but would afterward redeem them (41:14, 16). Israel was a nation blind and deaf (6:9–10; 42:7), a vineyard that would be trampled (5:1–7), a people devoid of justice or righteousness (5:7; 10:1–2). The awful judgment that would be unleashed on Israel and all the nations that defied God is called "the day of the LORD." In the Old Testament prophets, the Day of the Lord in some texts refers to the judgment that is near in the form of invasion by the Assyrian or Babylonian armies; in other texts, it refers to the final judgment that God will unleash on the earth in the last days. Because of the way that the prophets describe even the imminent judgment in cataclysmic terms, it is often difficult to determine if they are referring to the Day of the Lord that is "near" or "far." Although Israel had a foretaste of that day (5:30; 42:25), ultimately the nations will bear its full power (see 2:11, 17, 20). The future day of the Lord is associated with Christ's second coming and the accompanying judgment (see 24:1, 21; 34:1–2 and discussions). Throughout the book of Isaiah, God's judgment is pictured as a consuming fire (see 1:31; 30:33 and discussions). He is "the Lord GOD" (25:8), far above all nations and rulers (40:15–24).

Yet God would have compassion on His people (14:1–2) and would rescue them from both political and spiritual oppression. Their restoration would be like a new exodus (43:2, 16–19; 52:10–12) as God redeemed them (see 35:9; 41:14) and saved them (see 43:3; 49:8). Israel's mighty Creator (40:21–22; 48:13) would make streams spring up in the desert (32:2) as He graciously led them home. The theme of a highway for the return of exiles is prominent in both major parts of the book (see 11:16; 40:3). The Lord would raise an "ensign" (banner; 5:26) to summon the nations to bring Israel home.

The Lord's work of salvation on behalf of Israel is portrayed in the book of Isaiah as the transformation of Zion. The city is personified as a woman to represent the nation as a whole. In chapter 1, Zion is judged (vv. 8–9) so that it might be purged (vv. 22–25) and ultimately restored as "the city of righteousness" (vv. 26–29). In the first half of the book, the old Jerusalem of Isaiah's day stands under judgment as an unfaithful "harlot" (1:21). In the second half of the book, however, the promise is that the new Jerusalem of the messianic age will become the pure and holy bride of the Lord (49:14–18; 50:1; 54:1, 5–8; 65:17–19).

Peace and safety will mark the messianic age (11:6–9). A king descended from David will reign in righteousness (9:7; 32:1), and all nations will stream to the holy mountain of Jerusalem (see 2:2–4). God's people will no longer be oppressed by wicked rulers (11:14; 45:14), and Jerusalem will truly be "the city of the LORD" (60:14).

The Lord calls the messianic King "my servant" in chapters 42–53, a term also applied to Israel as a nation (see 41:8–9; 42:1). It is through the suffering of the Servant that salvation in its fullest sense would be achieved. Cyrus was God's instrument for delivering Israel from Babylon (41:2), but Christ delivered mankind from the prison of sin (52:13–53:12). He became "a light [to] the Gentiles" (42:6) so that the nations that faced judgment (chaps. 13–23) could find salvation (55:4–5). These Gentiles also became "servants of the LORD" (54:17).

The Lord's kingdom on earth, with its righteous Ruler and His righteous subjects, is the goal toward which the book of Isaiah steadily moves. The restored earth and the restored people will then conform to the divine ideal, and all will result in the praise and glory of the Holy One of Israel for what He has accomplished.

Literary Features

Isaiah contains both prose and poetry; the beauty of its poetry is unsurpassed in the Old Testament. The main prose material is found in chapters 36–39, the historical interlude that unites the two parts of the book (see Introduction, "Author"). The poetic material includes a series of oracles in chapters 13–23. A taunting song against the king of Babylon is found in 14:4–23. Chapters 24–27 comprise an apocalyptic section stressing the last days (see 24:1–27:13). A wisdom poem is found in 28:23–29 (see also 32:5–8). The parable of the vineyard (5:1–7) begins as a love song as Isaiah describes God's relationship with Israel. Hymns of praise are given in 12:1–6 and 38:10–20, and a national lament occurs in 63:7–64:12. The poetry is indeed rich and varied, as is the prophet's vocabulary (e.g., he uses nearly 2,200 different Hebrew words—more than any other Old Testament writer).

One of Isaiah's favorite techniques was personification. The sun is ashamed and the moon is confounded (24:23), while the wilderness and desert rejoice (see 35:1), and the mountains and forests burst into song (44:23). The trees "clap their hands" (55:12). A favorite figure is the vineyard, which represents Israel (see 5:7). Treading the winepress is a picture of judgment (see 63:3), and to drink God's "cup of ... fury" (51:17) is to stagger under His punishment. God is described as a "rock" (17:10), and animals such as the Leviathan and Rahab represent nations (see 27:1; 51:9).

The power of Isaiah's imagery is seen in 30:27–33, and he made full use of sarcasm in his denunciation of idols in 44:9–20. A forceful example of wordplay appears in 5:7, and one finds chiasm (inversion) in 6:10 (see also 16:7) and alliteration and assonance in 24:17. The "overflowing scourge" of 28:15, 18 is an illustration of a mixed metaphor.

Isaiah often alluded to earlier events in Israel's history, especially the exodus from Egypt. The crossing of the Red Sea forms the background for 11:15 and 43:2, 16–17, and other allusions occur in 4:5–6; 31:5; 37:36. The overthrow of Sodom and Gomorrah is referred to in 1:9, and Gideon's victory over Midian is mentioned in 9:4; 10:26 (see also 28:21). Several times Isaiah drew on the song of Moses (Deuteronomy 32; compare Isa. 1:2 with Deut. 32:1; Isa. 30:17 with Deut. 32:30; Isa. 43:11, 13 with Deut. 32:39). Isaiah, like Moses, called the nation to repentance and to faith in a holy, all-powerful God (see discussion on 49:8).

Outline

Part 1: The Book of Judgment (chaps. 1–39)
    I. Messages of Rebuke and Promise (chaps. 1–6)
        A. Introduction: Charges against Judah for Breaking the Covenant (chap. 1)
        B. The Future Discipline and Glory of Judah and Jerusalem (chaps. 2–4)
            1. Jerusalem's Future Blessings (2:1–4)
            2. The Coming Day of the Lord (2:5–22)
            3. The Judgment of Judah and Its Leaders (3:1–15)
            4. The Judgment of Judah's Wealthy Women (3:16–4:1)
            5. The Restoration of Zion (4:2–6)
        C. The Nation's Judgment and Exile (chap. 5)
            1. The Parable of the Vineyard (5:1–7)
            2. God's "Woe" Judgments against Judah (5:8–30)

Bibliography

Alexander, Joseph A. *Commentary on the Prophecies of Isaiah*. Grand Rapids, MI: Zondervan, 1970.

Childs, Brevard. *Isaiah: A Commentary*. The Old Testament Library. Philadelphia: Westminster, 2001.

Delitzsch, Franz. *Biblical Commentary on the Prophecies of Isaiah*. 2 vols. Translated by James Denney. Grand Rapids, MI: Eerdmans, 1965.

Hindson, Edward E. *Isaiah's Immanuel*. Philadelphia: Presbyterian & Reformed, 1978.

Motyer, J. Alec. *The Prophecy of Isaiah: An Introduction and Commentary*. Downers Grove, IL: InterVarsity, 1993.

Oswalt, John N. *Isaiah*. The NIV Application Commentary. Grand Rapids, MI: Zondervan, 2003.

———. *Isaiah 1–39*. NICOT. Grand Rapids, MI: Eerdmans, 1986.

———. *Isaiah 40–66*. NICOT. Grand Rapids, MI: Eerdmans, 1988.

Watts, John D. W. *Isaiah 1–33*. Word Biblical Commentary 24. Waco, TX: Word, 1985.

———. *Isaiah 34–66*. Word Biblical Commentary 25. Waco, TX: Word, 1987.

Wolf, Herbert M. *Interpreting Isaiah: The Suffering and Glory of the Messiah*. Grand Rapids, MI: Zondervan, 1985.

Young, E. J. *The Book of Isaiah*. 3 vols. Grand Rapids, MI: Eerdmans, 1964–72.

EXPOSITION

Part 1: The Book of Judgment (chaps. 1–39)

Judgment is the focus of chapters 1–39. Isaiah warned the people of Judah that the Lord would use the Assyrians as His "rod of ... anger" (10:5) to punish them for their covenant unfaithfulness. After using Assyria to discipline Judah, the Lord would deliver Jerusalem from the Assyrian army, when Hezekiah turned to the Lord for protection and deliverance (chaps. 36–37). The conclusion of this section points to the judgment of Judah and Jerusalem at the hands of the Babylonians (chap. 39). Isaiah's messages in this section also speak of the judgment that would fall on the nations surrounding Judah (chaps. 13–23) and on all peoples in the last days prior to the establishment of God's kingdom on earth (chaps. 24–27). Despite the emphasis on judgment, Isaiah issued numerous promises concerning Israel's future restoration, the coming of the Messiah, and the future messianic kingdom, which indicate that judgment is not the Lord's final word for His people (see 2:2–4; 4:2–6; 7:14; 9:2–7; 11:1–16; 25:7–9; 33:17–24; 35:1–10).

I. Messages of Rebuke and Promise (chaps. 1–6)

A. Introduction: Charges against Judah for Breaking the Covenant (chap. 1)

1:1–6. The book of Isaiah begins and ends (66:24) with a condemnation of those who rebel against God. The prophet depicted a courtroom scene in which God presented a covenant lawsuit charging Israel with unfaithfulness. The lawsuit began with the prophet, as the Lord's prosecuting attorney, bringing the charge or accusation of the specific crime that Israel had committed (vv. 2–4). The prophet called on the **heavens** (v. 2) and **earth** to testify to the truth of God's accusation against Israel because they were the witnesses of the original covenant that God established with Israel (see Deut. 30:19; 31:28; 32:1). The specific charge was that the people of Israel were rebellious **children** who had refused to recognize the Lord as their Father (v. 2) and Master (v. 3). Their sin had provoked the Lord to anger as the **Holy One of Israel** (v. 4). This name for God appears twenty-five times in Isaiah and only six times elsewhere in the Old Testament. This title stresses the willingness of a morally perfect God to commit Himself to a covenant relationship with a morally flawed people and heightens Israel's sin in failing to give proper recognition to the Lord as their covenant partner. The Lord appealed to Israel to turn from their sinful ways by reminding the people of the painful consequences of their sin. The image of a beaten and wounded individual ravaged by illness effectively portrays what Israel had already suffered as a result of the Lord's judgment against them (vv. 5 – 6). Later in the book, the pitiable moral and spiritual condition of Israel is transferred to the suffering Servant (53:4 – 5), who would suffer to provide atonement for Israel's sin.

1:7 – 9. The Assyrian invasion of Sennacherib in 701 BC had left the land **desolate** (v. 7). Isaiah personified Jerusalem and its inhabitants as a young woman and portrayed the city as vulnerable and alone. Jerusalem was like **a cottage** (v. 8) or **a lodge** in a field, temporary structures (shelters or huts) used by watchmen who were on the lookout for thieves and intruders (see Job 27:18). Sennacherib boasted in his annals that he captured forty-six cities in Judah and had trapped Hezekiah in Jerusalem as a "caged bird." Jerusalem appeared to have no defense against its attackers. The Lord had left only **a very small remnant** (v. 9) of survivors of the attack. Isaiah often referred to the "remnant" that would survive God's judgment and take possession of the land (see 4:3; 10:20 – 23; 11:11, 16; 46:3). In a somewhat shocking manner, Isaiah associated Judah with the cities of **Sodom** and **Gomorrah**, classic examples of sinful cities that were completely destroyed by the Lord (see 3:9; Gen. 13:13; 18:20 – 21; 19:5, 24). Isaiah attempted to awaken his complacent countrymen to the depths of their evil and depravity.

1:10 – 15. The prophet appealed to the people of Judah to change their ways, pointing to the hypocrisy of their religious practices. Isaiah and the Old Testament prophets were not opposed to the sacrificial system but confronted the people with the fact that the sincerity of the worshiper, not the number of religious activities, is what is most important to God (see 66:3; Jer. 7:21 – 26; Amos 5:21 – 24; Mic. 6:6 – 8). The Lord was tired of their meaningless **sacrifices** (v. 11) and their empty observances of special days. The **new moons** (vv. 13 – 14) were celebrated on the first day of each Hebrew month and included special sacrifices and feasts (see Num. 28:11 – 15). Their **appointed feasts** included the annual feasts, such as Passover, the Feast of Weeks (Pentecost), and the Feast of Tabernacles (see Exod. 23:14 – 17; 34:18 – 25; Leviticus 23; Deut. 16:1 – 17). The hypocrisy of the people was such that they were like murderers stretching out their bloodstained **hands** (v. 15) in prayer to the Lord, and the Lord's response was to **hide** His face (i.e., to withhold the blessings of His presence) from Judah (see 8:17; 59:2; Mic. 3:4).

1:16 – 20. Isaiah exhorted the people to cleanse themselves and to **put away** (v. 16) their sinful practices (vv. 16 – 20). The prophet focused specifically on the practice of social justice. They were to defend and take care of **the fatherless** (v. 17) and **the widow**, representatives of the weak and often oppressed part of society (see Jer. 22:16; James 1:27). Rulers were warned not to take advantage of them (see v. 23; 10:2; Jer. 22:3). The nation was covered with the **scarlet** (v. 18) and **crimson** bloodstains of its victims, but if the people would repent, the Lord promised to make them **as white as snow**, a powerful figurative description of the result of forgiveness (see Ps. 51:7). The offer of forgiveness was conditioned on the people's reformation. Verses 19 – 20 vividly contrast the two options facing Judah. If they obeyed the Lord, they would **eat** (Hebrew, *akal*; v. 19) of the bounty of the land that the Lord would provide; if they persisted in their sinful ways, they would be **devoured** (from *akal*, "to eat"; v. 20) by the sword of their enemy.

1:21–26. Returning to the personification of Jerusalem as a young woman (see 1:8), the prophet charged that Jerusalem had been an unfaithful wife to the Lord (vv. 21–26). By following idols and foreign gods, she had become **a harlot** (v. 21; see 1:4; Jer. 3:6–14; Ezek. 16:25–26; 23:5–21). One of the important themes in Isaiah is the transformation of Zion (Jerusalem) from an unfaithful prostitute to the pure and holy wife of the Lord (see 54:4–8; 62:3–5). This transformation began with the Lord's judgment coming as a purifying fire to remove the sinful dross that has corrupted the once holy city (v. 25; see 4:4; 48:10). The goal is that Jerusalem would once again become a **faithful city** (v. 26; see Zech. 8:3).

1:27–31. Verses 27–28 contrast the redemption of **Zion** (v. 27) with the destruction of those individuals who refused to repent (see 65:8–16). Along with the religious hypocrisy and social injustice already condemned in this chapter, verses 29–30 focus on the practice of pagan idolatry in Jerusalem. The **oaks** (v. 29) and **gardens** allude to the sacrifices and sexual immorality associated with pagan worship that often occurred at such places, and the people's trust in pagan gods and idols would prove to be misplaced. God's judgment would also cause **the strong** to **be as tow** (v. 31). Self-reliant people would be consumed by God's judgment like tinder that quickly burns. The fire of God's judgment both refines and consumes (see 33:11–14; 34:9–10).

B. The Future Discipline and Glory of Judah and Jerusalem (chaps. 2–4)

1. Jerusalem's Future Blessings (2:1–4)

2:1–4. The second introduction, in verse 1 (see 1:1), contrasts the message of hope **concerning Judah and Jerusalem** (v. 1) that follows (vv. 2–4) with the preceding message of judgment (chap. 1). Verses 2–4 are almost identical to Micah 4:1–3 and focus on the future exaltation of Zion (Jerusalem) as the center of God's kingdom. The theme of **the mountain of the LORD's house** (Mount Zion; v. 2) is common in Isaiah and occurs most prominently in passages that depict the coming of both Jews and Gentiles to Jerusalem (Zion) in the last days to honor the Lord (see 11:9; 27:13; 56:7; 57:13; 65:25; Zech. 14:16). **The last days** (v. 2) can refer to the future generally (see Gen. 49:1) but usually seems to have in view the messianic era. In a real sense, "the last days" began with the first coming of Christ (see Acts 2:17; Heb. 1:1) and will reach their ultimate fulfillment at His second coming. In the kingdom era, the **nations** will come to Zion to learn **the law** (v. 3) of the Lord. There will be universal peace, and **swords** (v. 4) will be beaten **into plowshares**. There will be no need for weapons of war during Christ's kingdom reign.

2. The Coming Day of the Lord (2:5–22)

In contrast to the promised glories of the future, this section focuses on the coming judgment of "the day of the LORD" (v. 12). The phrase "in that day" occurs seven times in chapters 2–4 (2:11, 17, 20; 3:7, 18; 4:1–2), and "the day of the LORD" refers to a time of judgment and/or blessing when God intervenes decisively in the affairs of the nations (see Zeph. 1:14–2:3). Here "the day of the LORD" is the judgment that the Lord was about to unleash on the sinful nation of Judah but ultimately also has in view the judgment that the Lord will bring against the world of sinful humanity. A recurring refrain that refers to men hiding in the rocks and caves to avoid the wrath of God (vv. 10, 19, 21) highlights the horrific terror of the Lord's coming judgment. Kings in the ancient Near East often boasted of being able to defeat their enemies in a single day, and the idea behind the prophetic image of the day of the Lord is that the Lord's judgment against sinners will be swift and severe.

2:5–18. Judgment was about to fall on Judah because of its pagan worship practices (v. 6), its proud reliance on its **treasures** (v. 7) and military resources, and its idolatry (vv. 8–9). The Mosaic law specifically prohibited kings from accumulating gold, silver, and horses (Deut. 17:16–17) because they usually led to a failure to trust in God (see 31:1). The repeated theme in the warning of coming judgment is the humiliation of man and the exaltation of God (vv. 11–17). The prophet used numerous images as pictures of human pride—**the cedars of Lebanon** (v. 13), **the**

oaks of Bashan (a region east of the Jordan famous for its oaks and livestock), and **the ships of Tarshish** (large vessels Solomon and the Phoenicians used for commercial trading ventures; v. 16). Isaiah stressed that even these inanimate objects that humans stand in awe of would be brought **low** (v. 17) so that God alone would be **exalted**. Isaiah's theology was built on the foundation of his vision of the holy God who is "high and lifted up" (6:1), but Judah had committed the sin of exalting man to the level of God. Human pride is the root of all sin and is the attempt of humans to be their own god (see 14:13–14).

2:19–22. When God's judgment fell, the people would recognize the futility of their trust in **idols** (v. 20), as their gods would not be able to save them (vv. 19–20). Isaiah repeatedly noted the futility of worshiping idols (see 30:22; 31:7; 40:19–20; 44:9–20). The closing exhortation of this chapter calls for Judah to **Cease … from man** (v. 22), to stop putting their trust in man as their ultimate source of security. The human rulers that they were trusting for protection also would not be able to help them when God's judgment came. The verb "to cease" is also used elsewhere to describe the rejection of the Messiah ("he was despised," 53:3). Ironically, the one Man who should have been trusted was "forsaken," or "given up on," by men. He alone is worthy of the trust and esteem that has been wrongly given to frail leaders throughout history.

3. The Judgment of Judah and Its Leaders (3:1–15)

3:1–8. The leaders in whom Judah had wrongly trusted would be taken away by either death or deportation (vv. 1–3; see 2 Kings 24:14; 25:18–21). The Lord's judgment would take away the civil, spiritual, and military officials who held sanctioned positions of leadership but would also take away **the prudent** (v. 2) and **the eloquent orator** (v. 3), terms that in Hebrew refer to occult practitioners and snake charmers (see Deut. 18:10; Jer. 8:17), whose activities are condemned. Both legitimate and illegitimate kinds of assistance would be removed or deported (see 2 Kings 24:14–16; Hos. 3:4). There would be social and political chaos in Judah as young and inexperienced men

not qualified for leadership assumed positions of responsibility (v. 5). In the aftermath of God's judgment, there would be such extreme poverty that the one **brother** (v. 6) who had a cloak would be placed in a position of leadership. The end result would be the fall of Jerusalem and Judah (v. 8), a prophecy not completely fulfilled until almost 150 years later.

3:9–15. In spite of the warnings of judgment, Judah remained rebellious, and the defiant looks on the faces of the people showed their contempt for God. They were brashly open and public about their sin, like the wicked inhabitants of **Sodom** (v. 9) had been. In the midst of this defiant people, the Lord would preserve a **righteous** (v. 10) remnant but would bring judgment on the **wicked** (v. 11), especially on the leaders who practiced injustice and oppression (vv. 10–15). These leaders had consumed **the vineyard** (v. 14) of Israel (see 5:1) and were grinding the poor as men grind grain between two millstones (v. 15).

4. The Judgment of Judah's Wealthy Women (3:16–4:1)

3:16–4:1. Judah's contempt of the Lord was reflected in the attitude of the wealthy women of Jerusalem (**the daughters of Zion**; v. 16), who displayed their arrogance through their physical appearance and adornment. Their walk, with outstretched **necks** (v. 16) and flirting **eyes**, communicated their pride. They walked in short, **mincing** steps because of the ornaments on their ankles, which were symbols of their wealth. These women who were so concerned with outward beauty would have a different appearance when the judgment of the Lord fell upon them. The Lord would shame them by exposing their nakedness as they were led away as captives (v. 17). The Lord would take away their expensive jewelry and accessories, including the **cauls, and … round tires like the moon** (v. 18), round and crescent-shaped jewelry worn to indicate their veneration of the sun and the moon. Instead of wearing their fine clothing, the women of Zion would be taken away as captives and treated like cattle. They would be led away by ropes and branded (v. 24). These women would be led away as captives because their men would fall in battle (v. 25). Daughter Zion would observe this calamity, and the gates of the city would **lament** (v. 26) because the crowds that used to assemble there were gone. War would so decimate the male population that **seven women** (4:1) would all seek the same **man** to be their husband. The women, once so proud, would have to experience the double disgrace of widowhood and childlessness.

5. The Restoration of Zion (4:2-6)

4:2-6. After judgment comes salvation. The phrase **in that day** (v. 2; see 2:2, 11, 17, 20) refers to the time of the future kingdom, also portrayed in 2:2-4. Warnings of judgment and promises of salvation balance each other throughout chapters 1-12. The promise for the future is that **the branch of the Lord** will **be beautiful and glorious** (v. 2). Some interpreters view the "branch" (Hebrew, *tsemach*) as a messianic title related to the "rod" and "Branch" (Hebrew, *hoter*) in 11:1 (see Jer. 23:5-6). Others view the "branch" here as a metaphor for Israel's agricultural fertility during the kingdom era (see Joel 3:18; Amos 9:13-14), and the parallel reference to **the fruit of the earth** that follows appears to support this interpretation. The purifying fire of God's judgment will bring forgiveness and cleansing for Israel's past sins (v. 4; see 1:25; 48:10). The Lord's presence will bring peace and security to Jerusalem (v. 5). The references to **cloud ... fire ... and shadow** (vv. 5-6) recall Israel's wilderness wanderings, when the pillar of cloud and fire guided and protected the people (Exod. 13:21-22; 14:21-22). Isaiah often referred to the time of the exodus as a model of the deliverance from exile that God would provide in the future (see 11:15-16; 31:5; 51:10). These promises of peace for Jerusalem in the future would have reminded the people that the Lord had not abandoned His promises to protect and defend Zion from its enemies (see Psalms 46, 48, 76).

C. The Nation's Judgment and Exile (chap. 5)

1. The Parable of the Vineyard (5:1-7)

5:1-7. This parable of the **vineyard** (v. 1), in the form of a love song, portrays God's unique relationship with Israel. Israel is pictured as a vineyard elsewhere in the Old Testament (see 3:14; Ps. 80:8-16; Jer. 2:21), and this song is probably the basis of Jesus' parable of the tenants in the New Testament (Matt. 21:33-44; Mark 12:1-11; Luke 20:9-18; see also John 15:1-17). Like the covenant lawsuit in chapter 1, this song contrasts the Lord's faithfulness to Israel with Israel's unfaithfulness to the Lord. Isaiah was like the best man at a wedding, singing a song for the **wellbeloved** groom (the Lord) and His **vineyard** bride (Israel), with the ironic twist that the bride had been unfaithful to her loyal husband. The Lord had given His vineyard every advantage that was needed to produce fruit. He had planted it on fertile soil, removed **the stones** (v. 2) from the land, built a protective fence and watchtower, used the **choicest vine[s]**, and built **a winepress** to process the fruit, but He had received no return on the costly investment that He had made in His people. Several wordplays in this song bring out the idea that the Lord had received exactly the opposite from what He should have received from His people—**wild grapes** (*beushim*) instead of **grapes** (*anabim*), **oppression** (*mispach*) instead of **judgment** (justice, *mishpat*; v. 7), and **a cry** (*tse'aqah*) instead of **righteousness** (*tsedaqah*). A righteous and fruitful life is the only appropriate response to the investment of God's grace.

2. God's "Woe" Judgments against Judah (5:8-30)

This judgment speech elaborates the specific sins that Judah had committed in turning away from the Lord. In this speech, Isaiah pronounced a series of six woes (vv. 8; 11-12, 18-19, 20, 21, 22-23), followed by three judgment sections (vv. 9-10; 13-15, 24-30). The word "woe" was used in Israel to introduce a lament for the dead (see "Alas" in 1 Kings 13:30; "Ah" in Jer. 22:18; 34:5). By using this word, the prophet was, in effect, inviting Israel to listen in on their own funeral before it ever happened so that the people might repent and avert the coming judgment.

5:8-10. The first **Woe** (v. 8) focused on Judah's practice of accumulating large tracts of land and building large estates at the expense of their fellow countrymen. The greed of wealthy landowners had caused them to forget the basic tenet of the Mosaic law stating that land in Israel could only be leased, never sold, because parcels had been permanently assigned to individual families (see Num. 27:7–11; 1 Kings 21:1–3). God would judge their greed with a punishment that fit the crime. The wealthy land-owners would forfeit the **houses** (v. 9) and lands they had acquired through oppression and dishonesty. The lands they had stolen would produce only mea-ger crops—**one bath** (about six gallons; v. 10) of wine for every **ten acres**, and **a homer** (six bushels) of **seed** would produce only **an ephah** (one-tenth of a homer) of grain. Meager crops often accompanied national sin as a covenant curse (Deut. 28:38–39; Hag. 2:16–17).

5:11–17. The second **Woe** (v. 11) condemned Judah's extravagant lifestyle, characterized by drunk-enness and revelry (see Amos 4:1–3; 6:6–7). The people cared more about pleasure than they cared about the Lord or practicing justice toward their fel-low countrymen. These people with insatiable ap-petites would experience the judgment of hunger in **captivity** (v. 13) and would themselves be swallowed up by the grave. **Hell** (v. 14), from the Hebrew word *sheol*, refers to the grave or the abode of the dead (see Gen. 37:35), whose appetite is even greater than that of the drunkards of Judah (see Ps. 49:14; Hab. 2:5).

5:18–23. The third **Woe** (v. 18) condemned those who arrogantly practiced their **sin** and defied God to punish them. These sinners taunted God to **make speed** (v. 19) and **hasten his work** of judg-ment. These taunts correspond to the first and third elements of the name of Isaiah's son, Maher-shalal-hash-baz ("swift to the plunder, swift to the spoil"), in 8:1–3. When Isaiah named his son (8:3), he may have been responding to the sarcastic taunts of these sinners. These sinners failed to recognize that God would bring swift and sure judgment (see 5:26). The fourth through sixth woes (vv. 20–23) further con-demned the arrogance, excess, and injustice that the prophet mentioned in the first three woes.

5:24–30. This concluding announcement of judgment details how the Lord would respond to the sin and corruption of His people. When God takes action, even the mountains tremble (vv. 24–25; see 64:3; Jer. 4:24–26). The Lord would use the armies of foreign nations to carry out His judg-ment (vv. 26–30). The Lord would **lift up an ensign** (v. 26), a pole with a banner that was often placed on a hill as a signal for gathering troops, to call for the attack on Judah. In promising the reversal of this judgment, Isaiah later referred to the Lord lift-ing an ensign to call for the nations to bring Israel home from their exile (see 11:10, 12; 49:22; 62:10). **The nations from far** included the Assyrians, whose armies struck Israel and Judah in 722 and 701 BC, and Babylon, which began its invasions in 605 BC. These foreign armies would be swift and strong and would tear Israel and Judah apart like ferocious **lions** (v. 29). They would wipe out the land like the waves of **the sea** (v. 30) and would cover the land with **darkness** and gloom, like a thick cloud.

D. Isaiah's Unique Commission (chap. 6)

This chapter narrates Isaiah's call as a prophet of the Lord. Isaiah's commission probably preceded his preaching ministry, and the account was postponed to serve as a climax to the opening series of oracles and to provide warrant for the shocking announce-ments of judgment they contain. The people had mocked "the Holy One of Israel" (5:19), and He had commissioned Isaiah to call them to account.

6:1–2. Isaiah's call occurred in 740 BC, **the year that King Uzziah died** (v. 1). This was a time of na-tional crisis because Uzziah had been a godly and powerful king (792–740 BC). Uzziah, also known as Azariah, had been struck by leprosy as punish-ment for his presumptuous sin of burning incense in the temple and had remained leprous until his death (see 2 Chron. 26:16–21). The people needed to look beyond their frail and flawed human leaders to the Lord as their ultimate source of security. Isaiah's vi-sion reminded them that the Lord was the true King, who is **high and lifted up** above any human ruler. The Lord's greatness is such that the **train** of His robe filled the expanse of the **temple**. When individ-uals in the Old Testament saw God, they were never able to take in the fullness of His person (see Moses,

Exod. 33:17–23; and Ezekiel, Ezek. 1:26–28). The throne of God is surrounded by the **seraphims** (v. 2; 6:6), angelic beings not mentioned elsewhere. The Hebrew root underlying this word means "to burn," perhaps indicating their purity as God's ministers (the term refers to venomous snakes in 14:29; 30:6; see Num. 14:21–22). The seraphim correspond to the "four beasts" of Revelation 4:6–9, each of whom also had **six wings**. These creatures that surround the throne of God cover their faces because even they are unable to gaze directly at God's glory.

6:3–4. The seraphim cried out, **Holy, holy, holy** (v. 3), the repetition underscoring God's infinite holiness (see Jer. 7:4 and the triple use of "the temple of the LORD" to stress the security of Jerusalem). The threefold repetition here is not a Trinitarian formula or proof of the Trinity. God's **glory** and power caused the temple to shake and fill with **smoke** (v. 4). Similarly, the power of God's voice terrified the Israelites at Mount Sinai, and the mountain was covered with smoke (see Exod. 19:18–19; 20:18–19).

6:5–7. The vision of God's holiness and perfection filled Isaiah with an overwhelming sense of his own sinfulness and unworthiness (v. 5). Isaiah was dismayed because anyone who saw God expected to die immediately (see Gen. 16:13; 32:30; Exod. 33:20). Isaiah confronted the people's sin (chaps. 1–5) but also had to recognize his own moral corruption before a holy God. Isaiah's recognition of his sin brought cleansing and forgiveness from the Lord. A seraph flew to him with **a live coal** (v. 6), perhaps from **the altar** of burnt offering (see Lev. 6:12) or the altar of incense (see Exod. 30:1, 7–8). Coals of fire were also taken inside the Most Holy Place on the Day of Atonement (see Lev. 16:12), when sacrifices were made to atone for sin. The coal was placed on Isaiah's **mouth** to cleanse and purify his **unclean lips** (v. 5) so that he could speak for God. Similarly, when God commissioned Jeremiah, His hand touched the prophet's mouth (see Jer. 1:9). Isaiah's personal experience of cleansing modeled what Israel and Judah could experience if they would confess and turn from their sin. When sin is acknowledged, God purifies with grace and forgiveness; when there is no

confession or repentance, God can only purify with the purging fire of judgment (see 1:25).

6:8–13. Isaiah's mission was to speak for God to His sinful people (vv. 8–10). As the heavenly King in the divine assembly of angels, God inquired, **who will go for us?** (v. 8). As a true prophet, Isaiah was privy to the deliberations and decisions of that heavenly council (see 1 Kings 22:19–20; Jer. 23:18, 22) and obediently accepted the divine call upon his life: **Here am I; send me**. Isaiah's prophetic commission would have the ironic but justly deserved effect of hardening the callous hearts of rebellious Israel, and therefore rendering the warnings of judgment sure (vv. 9–10). The divine judgment for their refusal to hear was a spiritual hardening that would make it impossible for the nation to follow and obey the prophetic message that could save their lives. Israel's deafness and blindness are also mentioned in 29:2; 42:18; 43:8. The hardening of the nation, however, was to be temporary, because one day they will be able to see and hear (29:18; 35:5). In the parable of the sower, Jesus quoted from 6:9–10 to explain Israel's refusal to recognize Him as their Messiah (Matt. 13:14–15; Mark 4:12; Luke 8:10; see also John 12:40; Rom. 11:7–10, 25).

Israel's rebellious refusal to hear the word of the Lord would result in a devastating judgment that would leave their land **desolate** (v. 11) and their cities uninhabited (vv. 10–12). The judgment would leave **a tenth** (v. 13) of the people as a remnant, and even this tenth would be laid waste. Israel would be like a tall tree that was chopped down so that only a stump remained. Out of this stump, the faithful few would be a **holy seed** that would spring to new life in the age of Israel's restoration and renewal.

II. Prophecies Occasioned by the Aramean and Israelite Threat against Judah (chaps. 7–12)

Chapters 7–12 form the second section of Isaiah's prophecies, in which Isaiah once again alternated messages of judgment and salvation. Beginning with his own day and the judgment of unbelieving Ahaz and Judah, Isaiah progressed to songs of praise celebrating Israel's future salvation (chap. 12).

A. Ahaz Warned Not to Fear the Aramean and Israelite Alliance (chap. 7)

7:1–4. The invasion of Judah by **Rezin ... and Pekah** (probably in 735/734 BC; v. 1), known as the Syro-Ephraimite War, forms the historical setting for chapters 7–8. Aram (**Syria**) and **Israel** (Ephraim) were trying, unsuccessfully, to persuade **Ahaz** to join a coalition against Assyria, which had strong designs on lands to the west. Pekah, the king of Israel, ruled from 752–732 BC (see 2 Kings 15:27–31). Isaiah was trying to keep Ahaz from forming a counter-alliance with Assyria (see 2 Kings 16:5–8; 2 Chron. 28:16–21). When Ahaz heard of the impending attack on Jerusalem, he was fearful because he had been defeated by Aram and Israel earlier (v. 2; see 2 Chron. 25:5–8). Isaiah met Ahaz to encourage the king that the Lord would protect him from his enemies, a gracious promise in light of Ahaz's evil character and disregard for the Lord (see 2 Kings 16:2–4). Isaiah met the king at **the conduit of the upper pool** (v. 3), where Ahaz was probably inspecting the city's water supply to see if Jerusalem could survive a long siege. This location symbolizes the choice Ahaz faced: trusting in the Lord or trusting in his own political and military resources. Isaiah's son, **Shear-jashub**, whose name means "the remnant shall return," accompanied the prophet as a further reminder to the king of God's commitment to Jerusalem and the house of David. Isaiah's message to the king was to **Fear not** (v. 4), because the kings of Aram and Israel who threatened him were nothing more than **two tails of ... smoking firebrands**, that is, smoldering embers that were about to be snuffed out. Damascus, the capital of Aram, was crushed by Tiglath-pileser III in 732 BC, and Israel was soundly defeated that same year. Ahaz was foolish not to trust God because the enemies he feared were not going to be around much longer.

7:5–12. The kings of Aram and Israel attacked Jerusalem, intending to remove Ahaz from the throne and replace him with a puppet ruler (**the son of Tabeal**, meaning "a good for nothing"; v. 6) who would bring Judah into their anti-Assyrian coalition. Through Isaiah, the Lord assured Ahaz that the plans of his enemies to remove him from the throne would fail (v. 7). Ahaz, the son of David, was God's chosen ruler over His people, and these opposing leaders were mere men who had no right to attack the Lord's anointed (vv. 8–9). Isaiah further specified that Israel would not even be a people within sixty-five years. **Samaria** (v. 9), the capital of Israel, fell to Assyria in 722 BC.

The condition attached to this promise of deliverance was that Ahaz must **believe** (v. 9) and trust in the Lord for his security and protection and **be established**, a condition emphasized by the wordplay of these two verbs, which are from the same Hebrew word, giving the sense, "If you have a firm faith, your kingdom will be firmly established." The Lord even encouraged Ahaz to ask for a miraculous **sign** (v. 11) to confirm this promise of protection, which would strengthen his faith (vv. 10–11; see Exod. 3:12). Ahaz's protest that he would not **tempt the Lord** (v. 12) sounds pious but actually was a mask for his unwillingness to put his trust in the Lord.

7:13–14. Isaiah responded to the king's unbelief by stating that the Lord would give **a sign** (v. 14), but it would now connote judgment as well as ultimate deliverance for Israel and the house of David. The sign would involve the birth of a son named Immanuel to **a Virgin**. The identity of this child is a major source of controversy. Three primary options exist concerning the identity of this child **Immanuel**: (1) the prophecy refers to a child born during the time of Isaiah and Ahaz, whose birth served as a sign to the unbelieving king; (2) the prophecy is exclusively messianic and refers to the birth of Jesus to the Virgin Mary (see Matt. 1:18–25); (3) the prophecy has both a "near" (the child born in the time of Isaiah) and a "far" (the miraculous birth of Jesus to a virgin) fulfillment.

7:15–16. While this prophecy clearly is connected to the birth of Jesus, some insist the timing of the child's birth had significance for the political crisis that Ahaz was facing in his own day. Isaiah stated that the child would be raised during a time of national disaster, characterized by the eating of **Butter** (or curds, a kind of yogurt) **and honey** (v. 15). The implicit warning was that Ahaz's unbelief would bring about an Assyrian invasion that would devastate the countryside and make farming impossible (see 7:22–25). By the time this child was twelve or thirteen (the likely age of moral determination and responsibility under the law), the people would be eating the simple diet of curds and honey rather than agricultural products, due to the Assyrian invasion. Isaiah further added that by the time the **child** (v. 16) knew right from wrong, the two enemies that Ahaz feared—the **kings** of Aram and Israel—would already be plundered, an event that happened in 732 BC.

Attempts to identify the prophecy with a specific child in Isaiah's time, however, are difficult to reconcile with the obvious meaning of the term "virgin." The Hebrew word *'almah* for "virgin" specifies an unmarried young woman, and in Genesis 24:43, the same word refers to a woman who is about to be married (see Prov. 30:19). *Bethulah* is the more common Hebrew word for "virgin," but in at least two passages, it refers to a young widow (Deut. 22:19; Joel 1:8). While *bethulah* is a more common term, it is less precise, whereas *'almah* clearly means "virgin" and was so interpreted by the Septuagint, the Dead Sea Scrolls, and Matthew, Jesus' own disciple (see Hindson, *Isaiah's Immanuel*, pp. 64–80).

The birth of Jesus was the ultimate and final fulfillment of the prophecy in 7:14, for He was miraculously born of a virgin (see Matt. 1:18, 25) and was "God with us" (Matt. 1:23) in the fullest sense (see Isa. 9:6–7). The point of the New Testament quotation in Matthew 1:21–23 is that the birth of Jesus fulfilled the prophecy of 7:14. Through both His miraculous birth and His incarnate deity, Jesus fulfills this passage literally and specifically.

7:17–25. Isaiah employed the sign of the child Immanuel to highlight the tragic consequences of Ahaz's decision to appeal to Assyria for help against the Syro-Ephraimite coalition rather than put his trust in the Lord for deliverance and protection.

Ahaz's appeal to Assyria would bring temporary relief (see 2 Kings 16:8–9), but eventually Assyria would attack Judah (v. 17; see 8:7–8; 36:1). Verses 18–25 vividly describe what the Assyrian invasion of Judah would be like. The Lord would direct the Assyrian armies to accomplish His will, and their armies would be as numerous as swarms of flies and as vicious as stinging bees (v. 18; see Exod. 23:28). The Assyrians would occupy every part of the land, and escape would be impossible (v. 19). The mention of the Lord using Assyria as His hired **rasor** (v. 20) refers to the practice of forcibly shaving **the beard** of a defeated enemy, an act considered to be a great insult (see 2 Sam. 10:4–5). The Assyrian invasion would also bring destruction of the vineyards and farmlands (vv. 21–25), in fulfillment of the prophecy of judgment in 5:5–6.

B. Isaiah's Son and David's Son (8:1–9:7)

This section contrasts the prophecy of Isaiah's son as the sign of Judah's imminent judgment at the hands of Assyria in chapter 8 and the prophecy of the birth of Messiah and his coming kingdom as Israel's hope for its ultimate salvation in chapter 9. The birth of both children would demonstrate that God was with His people, first to judge and then to save.

8:1–4. These verses detail the birth of Isaiah's son. The recording of the name of **Maher-shalal-hash-baz** (v. 1) on a scroll and the presence of **witnesses** (v. 2) attesting the birth of the child indicate a legal transaction or symbolic deed associated with the child. Isaiah's marriage to **the prophetess** (v. 3) is the only known case of a prophetess marrying a prophet (see Exod. 15:20), but the young woman may be called a prophetess here simply because she had become the wife of a prophet. As in 7:15–16, the age of this child is connected to specific events that would transpire in the history of Judah as a nation, though the wording is somewhat different. **Samaria** (Israel; v. 4) would be plundered before the child knew how to say **father** or **mother** (around age two). The point, however, is essentially the same as in 7:15–16: the enemies that Ahaz feared would be defeated in the very near future. Verse 4 focuses on the first stage of the destruction of the northern kingdom (see 7:4), which was not completed until 722–721 BC.

8:5–6. Though Israel (and her ally, Syria) would be defeated, Ahaz and Judah would not enjoy the benefits of their defeat because of Ahaz's fateful decision to turn to Assyria for military assistance rather than trusting in the Lord. **The waters of Shiloah** (v. 6), flowing from the Gihon Spring (see 2 Chron. 32:30) to the Pool of Siloam in Jerusalem (see John 9:7), symbolize the sustaining and protective power of the Lord (see Ps. 46:4). Ahaz rejected this divine protection for his own political maneuvering. The people of Judah would **rejoice** over the collapse of Israel and the death of Pekah and Rezin (**Remaliah's son**), kings of Israel who both died in 732 BC (see 2 Kings 16:9; Isa. 7:1), not realizing that the fall and demise of Judah was also imminent.

8:7–10. Because Judah rejected "the waters of Shiloah" (the Lord's protection), they would experience the floodwaters of the mighty Assyrian army sweeping through their land (vv. 7–8; see 28:17–19). The mighty river of the Assyrian army would **reach even to the neck** (v. 8), a reference to Sennacherib's invasion in 701 BC, which overwhelmed all the cities of **Judah** except Jerusalem (see 1:7–9). In the middle of verse 8, the figure for the Assyrian army changes from a flooding river to a powerful bird of prey, perhaps the eagle, renowned for its speed, that would spread its **wings** over the entire **land**. All appeared lost in the face of this invading army, but Isaiah provided the reminder that **God is with us** (v. 10). The promise of Immanuel, not the power of the Assyrian army, was what truly mattered here, and the Lord would intervene to defeat the Assyrians after they had carried out His work of judgment against His disobedient people. The invading army of Assyria (and later Babylon) would be **broken in pieces** (v. 9). The foreign army planned to destroy Judah and Jerusalem, but only God's plans and purposes would stand (v. 10).

8:11–15. The Lord warned Isaiah not to be like Ahaz and the people of Judah who refused to put their trust in the Lord. These doubters viewed Isaiah's warnings against reliance on Assyria as trea-

son (as a **confederacy**, or "conspiracy"; v. 12). The prophet was to **fear** (v. 13) the Lord, not the people. For Isaiah and those who trusted the Lord, the Lord would be **a sanctuary** (v. 14), the cornerstone of their lives (see 28:16), but for those who refused to trust in Him, the Lord would become **a stone of stumbling**, over which they would fall. The New Testament uses the same imagery with reference to Christ (see Rom. 9:33; 1 Peter 2:6–8).

8:16–17. The Lord commanded Isaiah to **Bind up the testimony** (v. 16), perhaps a reference to the legal transaction connected with 8:1–2. **The law** refers to Isaiah's teaching, as this Hebrew term can also mean "teaching" or "instruction." The legal document containing Isaiah's warnings of the Assyrian invasion was to be tied, or sealed, and then given to the prophet's **disciples**, who were to preserve it until the time of its fulfillment (see Jer. 32:12–14, 44). By preserving Isaiah's teaching in written form, his disciples could later prove that his predictions had come true, and this scroll would serve to indict the nation of Judah for its failure to believe the word of the Lord.

8:18–22. In addition to the sealed scroll, the names of Isaiah's two sons, Shear-jashub and Maher-shalal-hash-baz, would serve as further **signs** (v. 18) that Isaiah had announced beforehand the Lord's plans and intentions concerning the Assyrian invasion. Instead of listening to the spokesman of the Lord, the people were turning to those who communicated with the spirits of **the dead** (necromancy; v. 19), to learn about the future (see 3:2–3). They would be judged for rejecting the truth and believing a lie. Only by heeding the Lord's word through Isaiah—reinforced by the signs and **wonders** (v. 18) that Isaiah and his sons represented—would the **light** (v. 20) dawn for Israel. Until then, the Assyrian invasion would bring deep distress on all Israel, distress that would cause them to **curse their king and their God** (v. 21), bringing them under a sentence of the even more severe punishment that faced anyone who cursed God or a ruler (see Exod. 22:28; Lev. 24:15–16).

9:1–5. The **darkness** (v. 2) of judgment announced in chapter 8 turns into the light of messianic deliverance in chapter 9. The **light** of blessing would especially fall on **Naphtali** (v. 1) and **Galilee**, areas in northern Israel that suffered greatly when the Assyrian Tiglath-pileser III attacked in 734 and 732 BC (see 2 Kings 15:29). The prophecy of special blessing on Galilee was partially fulfilled when Jesus lived and ministered there during His earthly ministry (see Matt. 4:13–15). The Lord would deliver Israel from their oppressors **as in the day of Midian** (v. 4), referring to when Gideon defeated the hordes of Midian (see Judg. 7:22–25). While the Messiah will provide Israel's final deliverance from all oppressors, the promise of the breaking of **the yoke … and the staff** also looked to the more immediate deliverance from Assyria, which was fulfilled in 701 BC (see 10:26–27; 37:36–38). The defeat of Assyria prefigures the Lord's final judgment of all nations who oppress God's people. **Garments rolled in blood** (v. 5) is symbolic of the violence that the enemy armies inflicted on Israel during the time of God's judgment. The future time of deliverance will bring a reversal, when military garb and equipment will no longer be needed (see 2:2–4).

9:6–7. The **child** (v. 6) and **Son** in these verses is the promised Messiah, who will rule over Israel in the future age of peace (see 2 Sam. 7:14; Ps. 2:7; Matt. 1:1; 3:17; Luke 1:32). This royal son of David is given four throne names, each consisting of two elements. The name **Wonderful, Counseller** ("Wonderful Counselor") points to the Messiah as a king who determines and carries out a program of action (see Ps. 20:4; Mic. 4:9). The royal program of the Messiah will cause the entire world to marvel. The title **mighty God**, used with reference to the Lord in 10:21, stresses His divine power as Warrior. **Everlasting Father** signifies that He will be the everlasting, compassionate provider and protector of His people (see 40:9–11). **Prince of Peace** is a designation indicating that the rule of the Messiah will bring wholeness and well-being to individuals and to society at large (see 11:6–9). Unlike "Immanuel" (see 7:14), these titles are not like normal Old Testament personal names and indicate the uniqueness and special character of the coming Messiah.

The coming Messiah will fulfill God's promise to David concerning the permanency of his dynasty and will enable the house of David to become all that God intended it to be. He will rule **with justice … for ever** (v. 7). In spite of the sins of kings like Ahaz, Christ is a descendant of David who will rule in righteousness forever (see 11:3–5; 2 Sam. 7:12–13, 16; Jer. 33:15, 20–22). These promises to David will be fulfilled because of God's **zeal** for Israel. God is like a jealous lover who will not abandon His people.

C. Judgment against Israel (9:8–10:4)

This section reverts back to warnings of the Lord's impending judgment on Israel.

9:8–17. **Israel** (v. 8) had experienced calamity but, in her prideful arrogance believed that she would be able to quickly rebound from this disaster and rebuild her cities to be stronger than ever before (vv. 9–10). Isaiah warned that judgment would fall on Israel through a succession of military invasions, beginning with **The Syrians … and the Philistines** (v. 12) and culminating with the Assyrians. In spite of the disaster already experienced, the Lord's **hand** would remain **stretched out** against His people (see v. 17, 9:21; 10:4) because **the people** (v. 13) refused to repent of their sin and return to the Lord. The Lord would **cut off** (v. 14) the leaders of Israel who had corrupted the nation (see 3:1–3). The word pairs of **head and tail** and **branch and rush** (vv 14–15) are also used with reference to the leaders of Egypt in 19:15. The Lord would not pity the **fatherless and widows** (v. 17) because even they had become wicked.

9:18–10:4. The people's wickedness would become **the fire** (v. 18) that would consume and destroy the nation as they experienced the natural consequences of their sinful choices (vv. 18–20). **Ephraim** (v. 21) and **Manasseh**, the two prominent tribes in the northern kingdom, descended from Joseph's two sons, are pictured as destroying each other, recalling the conflict that existed between these two tribes during the chaotic time of the judges (see Judg. 12:4). The message of judgment on Israel closes with a **Woe** (10:1) oracle (see the series of woes in 5:8–23) announcing a death sentence against Israel's corrupt leadership. They would face judgment from the Lord because they had deprived widows and orphans of justice (v. 2; see 1:17; 9:17). Their power and wealth would be of no help to them at the time of God's judgment, because they would become **the prisoners** (v. 4) and **the slain** who would be defeated in battle (see Jer. 39:6−7).

D. The Assyrian Empire and the Davidic Kingdom (10:5−12:6)

1. The Destruction of Assyria (10:5−34)

The "woe" against Israel's leaders becomes a message of doom for Assyria (vv. 5−19), continuing the interplay between judgment and salvation that characterizes chapters 1−12 as a whole. The Lord would judge the arrogance of Assyria, as well as the sinful pride of His own people.

10:5−11. Assyria was **the rod ... and the staff** (v. 5) of God's **anger**, sent to execute judgment against the **hypocritical nation** (v. 6) of Judah, who had abandoned the Lord (see 9:4; Jer. 50:23; 51:20; Hab. 1:6). Assyria's seizing of **spoil** and **prey** represented the last part of the fulfillment symbolized by Maher-shalal-hash-baz. "Spoil" is the translation of the Hebrew *shalal*, and "prey" is the translation of *baz*. In her pride, however, Assyria failed to recognize her role as God's instrument of judgment and instead attempted to destroy the people of Judah as an assertion of her own sovereign dominion (v. 7). To Assyria, Judah was just another conquered territory, like **Calno** (a region in northern Syria; v. 9), **Carchemish** (a great fortress on the Euphrates River, see Jer. 46:2); **Hamath** (a city on the Orontes River), and **Arpad** (a city near Hamath and Calno). The Lord was no different than the gods of other conquered peoples and would provide no more opposition than they had (vv. 10−11).

10:12−19. The Lord would judge the **stout** ("proud") **heart** (v. 12) of the Assyrian **king** as part of His judgment against all forms of human pride (see 2:11, 17). The Lord may use pagan nations and rulers to carry out His purposes, but He also holds them accountable for their cruel and wicked behavior. The Assyrian king's pride is reflected in his eight references to himself in verses 13−14 (see 14:13−14; Ezek. 28:2−5). The mighty warriors (**fat ones**; v. 16) of Assyria would be nothing against **the Lord of hosts**, who would **Send ... leanness** upon them. The **Holy One** (v. 17) would burn the Assyrian army like a **forest** (v. 18; see 10:33−34), a prophecy fulfilled with the fall of Nineveh in 612 BC and the defeat of the last vestiges of the Assyrian army at Carchemish in 605 BC.

10:20−23. The Lord promised that a **remnant of Israel** (v. 20) would survive the Assyrian invasion. "The remnant shall return" (Shear-jashub) was the name of Isaiah's first son (see 7:3). A faithful remnant led by Hezekiah survived the Assyrian invasion of 701 BC (see 37:4), and later, a remnant returned from Babylonian exile. God had promised Abraham that his descendants would be as numerous **as the sand of the sea** (v. 22; Gen. 13:16; 22:17), but the remnant would be small in number. This **consumption** (or defeat) of Israel would **overflow with righteousness** in the sense that God's judgment of His people was perfectly just.

10:24−34. Though the Lord would judge Israel, He appealed to her past history to assure His people of their ultimate deliverance (vv. 24−27). The king of Assyria was like the king of Egypt who oppressed Israel before the exodus, and the Lord would defeat him **after the manner of Egypt** (v. 24). This oppressive ruler will be like **Oreb** (v. 26) of the Midianites, whom Gideon defeated during the time of the judges (see Judg. 7:25). The Lord would enable Israel to break the yoke of Assyrian oppression. Verses 28−34 portray the promised defeat of the Assyrian army. As if seeing a vision, Isaiah described the approach of the Assyrian army to the outskirts of **Jerusalem** (v. 32) from about ten miles north of the city, mentioning the names of twelve specific locations (vv. 28−32). The Lord would cut down the Assyrian army like a lofty **forest** (v. 34) when it reached Jerusalem (see 10:17−19).

2. The Establishment of the Davidic King and His Kingdom (chap. 11)

11:1−5. In chapters 2−12, Isaiah used forest imagery to contrast the fates of Israel and Assyria. While the forest of Assyria would be cut down to never rise again, the hope for Israel was that the Messiah would grow as a shoot from the stump of David's dynasty (v. 1; see 11:10; 6:13). Verses 2–5 describe the qualities of the Messiah's person and rule. The Messiah, like David (1 Sam. 16:13), would be empowered by the Holy **Spirit** (v. 2). The Spirit would endow Him with the **wisdom** to undertake wise purposes and the power to carry them out. The Messiah will rule **in the fear of the** LORD (v. 3) and will rule over His kingdom with **righteousness** (v. 4) and **equity**, qualities sorely lacking in the rulers of Isaiah's day (see 1:17; 5:7). The rule of the Messiah will extend over all nations with absolute power (vv. 4b–5). Assyria was God's rod in 10:5, 24, but the Messiah will rule the nations **with the rod of his mouth** (v. 4; see Ps. 2:9; Rev. 19:15). The picture of **righteousness** (v. 5) and **faithfulness** as a **girdle** ("belt") stresses the centrality of these qualities in the Messiah's reign. When a man prepared for vigorous action, he tied up his loose, flowing garments with a belt (see 5:27), and commitment to justice will likewise be the stabilizing force in the rule of Messiah.

11:6–9. The Messiah's reign will bring peace and safety to the earth. In the future kingdom, little children will be unharmed as they play with formerly ferocious animals (vv. 6–8). The description is literal in that it portrays the transformation of nature that will occur through the removal of the Edenic curse in the kingdom era (see Gen. 3:16–19) and figurative in that it describes the conditions of world peace in a highly idealized and picturesque form. Similar descriptions of the peaceful conditions that will exist in the kingdom age are central to the eschatological hope of Isaiah and the Old Testament prophets (see 2:2–4; 35:9; 65:20–25; Ezek. 34:25–29). The reason for this peace is that **the earth** (v. 9) will be filled with **the knowledge of the** LORD (see 2:3; Hab. 2:14).

11:10–16. In the messianic age, the regathering of Israel from all over the world will be like a second exodus, only greater in scope than the first one (vv. 11–12). While Israel enjoyed an initial return from Assyrian and Babylonian exile, the language here points to the final return and restoration of Israel to occur at Christ's second coming. Promises of the future restoration and salvation of Israel are another key component of the Bible's eschatological message of hope (see 52:9–10; 54:6–8; Amos 9:1–15; Rom. 11:26–27). When restored, Israel will be a unified nation, with the conflict between **Ephraim** (Israel; v. 13) and **Judah** a thing of the past (see 9:21). Instead of suffering defeat and humiliation from enemy nations as in Isaiah's day, Israel will defeat and subjugate the peoples around them. The reference to the destruction of **the Egyptian sea** (v. 15) again recalls the exodus and God's powerful act of drying up the sea when delivering His people (see Exod. 14:21–22). After delivering His people from bondage, the Lord would provide a **highway** (v. 16), enabling Israel to return to their homeland. The removal of obstacles and the building of a highway leading to Jerusalem are also described in 35:8; 57:14; 62:10 (see also 40:3–4).

3. Songs of Joy for Deliverance (chap. 12)

This chapter contains two short psalms of praise for deliverance (vv. 1–3, 4–6) and provides the climax of chapters 7–11 and closes the first major section of the book of Isaiah with a message of hope. The hope and salvation that comes from the Lord would ultimately triumph over the judgment and despair that Israel and Judah had to face because of their unfaithfulness to the Lord.

12:1–3. In the first praise song, the nation is the collective **I** (v. 1), who praised the Lord for the deliverance He would surely bring. The Lord's anger against Israel was temporary and would be **turned away** (contrast 9:12, 17, 21). After God punished Israel, His anger would be directed against nations like Assyria and Babylon. While praising the Lord for this deliverance, the people recalled the Lord's great acts for Israel in the past. The last two lines of verse 2 are a quotation of Exodus 15:2, a verse commemorating the defeat of the Egyptians at the Red Sea (see Ps. 118:24). The reference to **wells of salvation** (v. 3) appears to allude to God's abundant provision of water for Israel during the wilderness wanderings (see Exod. 15:25, 27). But here God's saving act would itself be the "well" from which Israel would draw life-giving water (see Ps. 36:9; Jer. 2:13; John 4:10).

12:4–6. Exaltation is the theme of the second praise song, which contains repeated calls to praise the Lord. The imperatives **Cry out and shout** (v. 6) occur again in 54:1, where Zion rejoices over the restoration of her people. This praise song recognizes the greatness of **the Holy One of Israel**, who faithfully and powerfully acts on behalf of His covenant people.

III. Judgment against the Nations (chaps. 13–23)

Chapters 13–23 contain a series of prophecies against the nations (see similar collections of oracles against the nations in Jeremiah 46–51; Ezekiel 25–32; Amos 1–2; Zeph. 2:4–15). The prophecies begin with Babylon (13:1–14:23) and Assyria (14:24–27) before moving on to smaller nations. God's judgment on His people does not mean that the pagan nations will be spared (see Jer. 25:29). In fact, God's judgments on the nations are often a part of the ultimate deliverance of His people (see 10:12).

A. Against the King of Babylon (13:1–14:27)

13:1. The first oracle in this section was directed against **Babylon**, concerning Babylon during the Assyrian Empire rather than during the Neo-Babylonian Empire. Thus, the prophecy was actually against the Assyrian Empire, Babylon being its most important city. From 729 BC on, the kings of Assyria also assumed the title "king of Babylon." That there is no new "burden" heading at 14:24–27, where the prophet spoke of judgment against Assyria, indicates that 13:1–14:27 forms a unit.

The judgment of Babylon assumes an even larger importance because Babylon would later bring about the downfall of Judah and Jerusalem, between 605 and 586 BC. Babylon was conquered by Cyrus the Persian (see 45:1; 47:1) in 539 BC. Subsequently, Babylon came to symbolize the world powers arrayed against God's kingdom (see 1 Peter 5:13), and its final destruction is announced in Revelation 14:8; 16:19; 17:1–18:24.

These prophecies against the foreign nations are referred to as a **burden** (v. 1). The Hebrew word for this term is related to a verb meaning "to lift or carry." Thus, the prophet's message is to be understood as either lifting up one's voice or carrying a burden as the prophet delivered these oracles of judgment and doom. This section of Isaiah has a lasting significance that goes beyond the announcement of judgment on specific nations and peoples from past history. Each of these judgments is a reminder of God's final judgment on all peoples and every form of human wickedness that opposes God's rule in the world. God's judgments in the past are the sure guarantee of the full and final judgment to take place at the end of human history.

13:2–5. The Lord would assemble an unidentified army from a distant nation against Babylon in the same way that He earlier raised an ensign calling the nations to attack His own people (see 5:26–29). These troops would be God's **sanctified ones** (v. 3) because they would be set apart to do His will. As **The Lord of hosts** (v. 4), God is the head of the armies of Israel (1 Sam. 17:45), of angelic powers (1 Kings 22:19; Luke 2:13), and here of the army that would destroy Babylon. This army was God's weapon in the same way that Assyria was the club in God's hand in Isaiah's day and as Babylon would be in the near future (v. 5). God's **indignation** (v. 5) would no longer be turned against Israel (see 5:25; 9:12, 17, 21; 10:4) but against her enemies (see vv. 5; 13:9, 13; 30:27).

13:6–7. As with the judgment of Israel and Judah in chapter 2, this judgment is described as **the day of the Lord** (v. 6), the prophetic term for God's decisive intervention to judge His enemies. The day would come as **destruction** (*shod*) **from the Almighty** (*Shaddai*), a wordplay emphasizing the ferocious intensity of the judgment that was about to fall on Babylon. As the invading army attacked, **hands** (v. 7) would fall limp as courage failed and panic overtook the Babylonians, common responses when the Lord engages in holy war against His enemies (see Exod. 15:14–16; Judg. 7:21–22).

13:8–14. Isaiah employed various images and figures of speech to describe the suffering of war and judgment that Babylon would experience. Their suffering would be like the pains and anguish of childbirth (v. 8; see 26:17; Jer. 4:31; 6:24). The image of cosmic darkness also vividly pictures the devastation and destruction of the Lord's day of judgment (v. 10; see Joel 2:10, 31; Rev. 6:12 – 13). War would drastically reduce the male population of Babylon, so that one **man** (v. 12) would be as valuable as a **golden wedge of Ophir**, the place from which Solomon imported large quantities of gold. Thunderstorms, hail, and earthquakes accompany the powerful presence of the Lord (v. 13; see 30:30; 34:4; Exod. 19:16; Josh. 10:11). The Babylonians would be hunted down like **roe** (gazelle; v. 14) and **sheep**, which are easy prey.

13:15 – 18. These verses describe the actual horrors of siege warfare. Babylon would **fall by the sword** (v. 15), and **Their children** (v. 16) would be brutally slaughtered by the enemy. The army that would attack Babylon would be relentless and pitiless in their assault (vv. 17 – 18). The Medes, located in what is today northwestern Iran, joined the Babylonians in defeating Assyria in 612 – 609 BC but later united with Cyrus to conquer Babylon in 539 BC (see Jer. 51:11, 28; Dan. 5:31; 6:28).

13:19 – 22. The end result of God's judgment would be that the great city of **Babylon** (v. 19) would be reduced to ruins, as **Sodom and Gomorrah** had been. The Neo-Babylonian Empire was established by Nabopolassar in 626 BC, and his son, Nebuchadnezzar (605 – 562 BC), became its most powerful ruler. Babylon, with its temples and palaces, became a very beautiful city (see Dan. 4:29 – 30). The hanging gardens of Nebuchadnezzar were one of the seven wonders of the ancient world. The fall of the Babylonian Empire, however, was as meteoric as its rise to power. The great city is described as uninhabited and the haunt of demonic spirits (vv. 20 – 22). The word **satyrs** (v. 21) is connected with demons in Leviticus 17:7 ("goat idols") and 2 Chronicles 11:15 ("devils"; see also Rev. 18:2).

14:1 – 2. Babylon's fall would be linked with Israel's restoration. **Israel** (v. 1) would be returned to her **land**, and **strangers** ("foreigners") would join the Israelites as worshipers of the true God (see 11:10; 56:6 – 7; 60:3). After returning to their homeland, Israel would **rule** (v. 2) over the nations, like Babylon, that had oppressed them.

14:3 – 11. A mocking taunt against the fallen **king of Babylon** (v. 4) is given in 14:3 – 21. Similar taunts against the Babylonian king are found in Revelation 18. However exalted (and almost divine) the king of Babylon may have thought himself to be (see 14:12 – 14), he would go the way of all world rulers—down to the grave. The oppressed nations would celebrate as the Babylonian king went down into the underworld (vv. 3 – 8). Isaiah portrayed these nations as **fir trees** (v. 8) and **cedars of Lebanon** breaking into song, a fitting image in that the kings of Assyria and Babylon had hauled away these highly prized timbers for centuries. **Hell** (Hebrew, *sheol*; the Old Testament abode of the dead; v. 9) would be stirred in anticipation of the king's arrival, and deceased rulers would be surprised that the great king of Babylon had joined them (vv. 9 – 11). The **pomp** (v. 11) and music (**noise of thy viols**), symbols of the wealth and luxury the king enjoyed in life (see Amos 6:5 – 6), would accompany him to the grave and would be unable to keep him from his fate. The king of Babylon would become a rotting corpse covered with maggots. This description of existence after death is somewhat confusing to the modern reader in that it incorporates both the physical realities of the decomposition of the body and a highly figurative portrayal in which conditions among the dead are described in terms of their roles on earth.

14:12 – 15. Some believe that these verses provide a description of the fall of Satan. Such a view is perhaps supported by Luke 10:18, but Jesus there appears to be referring to an event contemporaneous with His earthly ministry. The name **Lucifer** (v. 12), found in the KJV, comes from the translation of the Latin Vulgate. The Hebrew for Lucifer actually means "shining one." The context of chapter 14 demands that these verses be connected to the continuing description of the fall and demise of the king of Babylon. While Satan is not specifically in view in chapter 14, the Bible teaches that evil world rulers are under satanic and demonic control (see Dan. 10:13, 20; Eph. 2:2;

6:12), and the king of Babylon is later also used as a type (prefiguration) of the Beast (the Antichrist) who will lead the Babylon of the last days (see Rev. 13:4; 17:3).

Highly exaggerated and mythical imagery describe the arrogance and pride of the Babylonian king. The name **Lucifer** (or "shining one"), **son of the morning** (v. 12), compares the Babylonian king to the morning star, Venus, which appears in the sky but is extinguished by the sun before reaching its zenith. The king of Babylon (like Satan in Luke 10:18) appeared to be great but would have a sudden fall. The king made pretentious claims to be godlike in his power. The king boasted that he would **ascend into heaven** (v. 13) and place his **throne** among the gods. The king's mention of **the mount of the congregation, in the sides of the north** most likely refers to Mount Zaphon, also called Mount Casius, located about twenty-five miles northeast of Ugarit in Syria. The Canaanites considered this mountain to be the home and meeting place of the gods, much like Mount Olympus for the Greeks. The king of Babylon committed the ultimate sin of thinking himself to **be like the most High** (v. 14; see Gen. 3:5). Despite this lofty estimation of himself, the king would be **brought down** (v. 15) to the grave like any other human.

14:16–21. Here the scene shifts to earth. The living would also express their amazement as they stared at the Babylonian king going down to the grave. The king, who had oppressed others and **opened not the house of his prisoners** (v. 17) in deporting large segments of defeated populations, would himself be a prisoner of death. Unlike other rulers, the Babylonian king would not even receive the honor of a proper **burial** (v. 20). A proper burial was considered important for an ordinary individual, and especially so for a king. To have one's body simply discarded was a terrible fate. The reference to the **abominable branch** (v. 19) serves to contrast the fate of the king of Babylon with the glory awaiting the messianic branch in 11:1 (see 4:2). The Babylonian king would be deprived of **children** (descendants; v. 21) to carry on a living memorial to his name.

14:22–23. The taunt against the king was extended to include all of Babylon. The people of the nation, as well as the king's family, would be **cut off** (v. 22), a prophecy fulfilled partially through Sennacherib's destruction of Babylon in 589 BC and ultimately fulfilled by the Medes and Persians after 539 BC. Israel would survive through a **remnant**, but Babylon would not. Babylon would be turned into a habitation for **bittern** (porcupines; v. 23) and reduced to swampland.

14:24–27. The prophet linked the overthrow of Assyria to the preceding destruction of Babylon. God's sovereign purposes concerning Assyria and Babylon would **stand** (v. 24). The Lord would destroy Assyria by stretching out **his hand** (v. 27), just as He had against Egypt at the Red Sea (see Exod. 15:12) and against His own people (9:12; 12:1).

B. Against Philistia (14:28–32)

14:28–32. Isaiah announced judgment against Israel's enemy the Philistines (**Palestina**; v. 29), as did other Old Testament prophets (see Jeremiah 47; Ezek. 25:15–17; Amos 1:6–8; Zeph. 2:4–7). The occasion of this prophecy appears to have been the Philistine revolt against Assyria in 715 BC, while King Sargon (see 20:1) was too preoccupied with serious revolts elsewhere to give much attention to Canaan. Philistine territory was vulnerable to attack by the great empires of Egypt and Assyria since it lay along the main route from Egypt to Mesopotamia. Along with announcing judgment on Philistia, this oracle served as a reminder to Judah of the dangerous consequences of joining political alliances against Assyria rather than trusting in the Lord for Judah's safety and deliverance.

The prophet warned Philistia not to **Rejoice** (v. 29) in Sargon's military troubles elsewhere because these distractions would not prevent him from becoming **the rod** that would inflict great destruction on Philistia. The Assyrian army would attack the Philistines like a "poisonous snake" (rather than **cockatrice**) and a cloud of **smoke** (v. 31). As this prophecy anticipated, Assyria defeated Ashdod in 711 BC and turned Philistia into an Assyrian province. The Lord promised deliverance and rescue for **Zion** (v. 32), unlike the fate awaiting Philistia.

C. Against Moab (chaps. 15–16)

15:1–9. The Lord's judgment would also fall on the Moabites, the descendants of Lot who lived east of the Dead Sea. **Moab** (v. 1) was a perpetual enemy of Israel (see 25:10; 2 Kings 13:20). The destruction of Moab was probably connected with an invasion by Sargon of Assyria in 715/713 BC. As a result of the invasion, the cities of **Ar** (location unknown) and **Kir** (perhaps the capital of Moab at this time) would be destroyed, which would lead to great mourning. The survivors in Moab would shave their **heads** (v. 2) and beards and put on **sackcloth** (v. 3) as signs of their grief. Refugees would flee from the land because the invading army had ruined the land and stopped up the major springs of Moab (vv. 5–9). The wordplay involving **waters of Dimon** (v. 9; referring to **Dibon**; v. 2) and **blood** (Hebrew, *dam*) highlighted the terrible fate awaiting Moab. Even the refugees fleeing from the land would be slain by the **lions** that had invaded the land.

16:1–5. The command **Send ye the lamb** (v. 1) was a call for Moab to submit to the king in Jerusalem. As King Mesha had sent 100,000 lambs to King Ahab of Israel each year (see 2 Kings 3:4), so now proud Moab, which had often oppressed Israel in the past, would have to turn to Judah for their survival. Moabite refugees were panicked like **wandering** (v. 2) birds thrown from the **nest** and pleaded for Judah to **Hide the outcasts** (v. 3). While their situation was desperate, the prophet assured Moab that **the spoiler** (v. 4) and **the extortioner** (i.e., the Assyrian king) were **at an end** and would be destroyed. The Lord would raise up a king in Judah, from the family of **David** (v. 5), who would reign with **judgment** (justice) and **righteousness**, and this king's reign would benefit Moab as well. While the initial fulfillment of this prophecy likely was Hezekiah, the ultimate fulfillment of this prophecy will occur when the Messiah comes to rule (see 11:2–4).

16:6–14. The reason for Moab's judgment was her **pride** (v. 6). Though a small nation, she was proud and defiant like Babylon and Assyria (see 10:12; 14:13; 25:11; Jer. 48:42). The people of Moab would mourn when their land became like a ruined vineyard (vv. 7–8). In verses 9–11, the Lord (and/or Isaiah) wept and lamented over the destruction brought on proud Moab to humble her. The Moabites would turn in prayer to their gods but would find no relief from the judgment that the Lord had decreed against her (v. 12). The Lord's sentence of judgment would be executed **Within three years** (v. 14). Other signs that had a three-year limit are given in 20:3; 37:30 (see also 7:14, 16). Moab's three years were over by circa 715 BC.

D. Against Aram and Israel (chap. 17)

17:1–2. Isaiah's next oracle of judgment was directed against **Damascus** (v. 1), the capital of Aram (Syria), located northeast of Mount Hermon on strategic trade routes between Mesopotamia, Egypt, and Arabia. Since the time of David, the Arameans of Damascus had been a frequent enemy of Israel (see 2 Sam. 8:5; 1 Kings 22:31). The threat was that Damascus would be reduced to **a ruinous heap** and that **Aroer** (v. 2), located some fourteen miles east of the Dead Sea at the southern boundary of Aram's sphere of control (see 2 Kings 10:32–33), would become a wasteland (vv. 1–2).

17:3–11. The fate of Aram was intertwined with that of **Ephraim**, the northern kingdom of Israel, because of their military alliance against Assyria (see chap. 7). Damascus would no longer provide a fortress of protection for Israel against Assyria. In 732 BC, Tiglath-pileser III captured Damascus and made it an Assyrian province; many of the cities of Israel were also captured (see 9:1). Israel would lose so many of its citizens that it would become like a harvested field, where only a few stalks of grain or **gleaning grapes** (v. 6) were left.

While the devastation would be severe, it would have the purifying effect of causing Israel to respect the Holy One of Israel as they repudiated trust in their idols (v. 8). The prophet reminded Israel that they had **forgotten** (v. 10) the Lord and had become a ruined vineyard through the planting of **strange** slips, most likely a figure for the worship of foreign gods. Because of their idolatry, Israel would not prosper, and the vineyard would be reduced to a heap (v. 11; for Israel as a vineyard, see 5:7; 18:5; 37:30–31).

17:12–14. The concluding message of this oracle was that the nations that roared against God's people like the raging sea would be destroyed. **Noise** (v. 12) and **rushing** are from the same Hebrew verb (*hamah*). A parallel is found in Psalm 46:3, 5, which states that Zion is secure even as the seas "roar" and the nations "rage." The churning sea represents the forces of evil and chaos that oppose God and His people. The underlying promise here is that the Lord has chosen Zion as His dwelling place (Ps. 132:13) and will protect the city and His people from their enemies. Assyria is also called "the waters of the river, strong and many" in 8:7. When circumstances appear to be hopeless, God's people must keep their focus on God's promises of ultimate triumph.

E. Against Cush (Ethiopia) (chap. 18)

18:1. The prophet next turned his attention to the land of Cush (also known as Nubia or ancient **Ethiopia**), which was south of Egypt. This land is not to be confused with modern Ethiopia, located farther to the southeast. In 715 BC, a Cushite named Shabako gained control of Egypt and founded the Twenty-Fifth Dynasty. The Ethiopian Tirhakah marched north to assist Hezekiah in his rebellion against Assyria in 701 BC. Thus, the oracle against Cush was a warning to Judah not to trust in an alliance with Cush rather than turning to the Lord for protection and deliverance.

18:2–7. Like the other nations, Cush would be judged for its pride. Their **ambassadors** (v. 2) came to Judah and other nations by lightweight boats made out of papyrus reeds to form alliances and coalitions. They were an impressive people described as **scattered and peeled** (lit., "tall and smooth"). Unlike the Semites, they were clean-shaven. The Cushites attempted to be players on the world scene, but the Lord was preparing to raise up His own army against them. The Lord would act thoughtfully and deliberately toward the nations, including Cush, that conspired against His people. Waiting for just the right moment, the Lord would destroy them when they were like **the bud** (v. 5) fully matured and ready for **harvest**. He would cut them down and leave their corpses for **the fowls** (v. 6) and **the beasts**. As defeated nations, the Cushites and other peoples would bring their tribute to the Lord at Jerusalem (v. 7). According to 2 Chronicles 32:23, gifts were brought to Hezekiah after Sennacherib's death.

F. Against Egypt and Cush (Ethiopia) (chaps. 19–20)

19:1–4. Like other Old Testament prophets, Isaiah delivered an extended oracle concerning the judgment of **Egypt** (v. 1; see Jeremiah 46; Ezekiel 29–32). Because of the history of the Egyptian bondage and exodus, Egypt serves as an archetype for all of the enemies of God and His people. After Assyria conquered the northern kingdom of Israel in 722–721 BC, King Hezekiah of Judah was under great pressure to make an alliance with Egypt, and Isaiah urgently warned against such a policy (see 30:1–2; 31:1).

To discourage an alliance with Egypt, Isaiah announced that Egypt would fall and that her **idols** (v. 1) would be unable to help her when the Lord attacked from His **cloud** chariot (see Pss. 68:4; 104:3; Matt. 26:64). God had previously judged Egypt's idols during the ten plagues (see Exod. 12:12) and would do so again. Civil war would turn **the Egyptians against the Egyptians** (v. 2). During the period of this prophecy, the Libyan dynasty clashed with the Cushites (see 19:1) and with the Saites of the Twenty-Fourth Dynasty. Though proud of its great wisdom traditions (see 1 Kings 4:30), Egypt would discover that their counselors and spiritists would be unable to thwart the Lord's plans. Weakened by internal division, Egypt would be given over to **a cruel lord** (v. 4)—Esarhaddon, the Assyrian king who conquered Egypt in 670 BC.

19:5–10. The Lord warned that He would dry up the Nile. The Nile was the lifeline of Egypt; its annual flooding provided essential water and produced the only fertile soil in the land. The river would become putrid; **they shall turn the rivers far away** (v. 6) should read "the rivers [or canals] will stink." The **fishers** (v. 8) and the **flax** (v. 9) producers, dependent on the Nile for their livelihood, would lament their fate.

19:11–15. The royal advisors would have no solution for Egypt's national dilemma. **Zoan** (v. 11), a city in the northeastern part of the Nile Delta would have been familiar to the Israelites enslaved in Egypt (see Num. 13:22; Ps. 78:12, 43). It was also the capital for the Twenty-Fifth Dynasty (see 18:1). **Noph** (v. 13) refers to Memphis, an important city fifteen miles south of the delta, which was the capital during the Old Kingdom. The prophets, priests, and political leaders in these prominent cities would give ineffective counsel to the Pharaoh because the Lord would cause them to stumble and stagger like drunks (v. 14; see 28:7–8, where Israel's leaders stagger).

19:16–25. In that day (vv. 16, 18–19, 21, 23–24) is a recurring phrase, referring to the coming day of the Lord (see 10:20, 27; 11:10–11). This section contains a chain of four announcements of coming events associated with "that day." Continuing the portrayal of Egypt's impending destruction, the first event announced was that God's judgment would cause Egypt to be in **terror** of **Judah** (v. 17). The next three events, however, would be more positive in nature. **Five** (i.e., many) **cities** (v. 18) in Egypt would **swear** an oath of loyalty to the Lord. Because of a divine act of deliverance and healing in Egypt, **an altar** (v. 19) would be erected in Egypt for offering sacrifices to the Lord. **Egypt** (v. 23), **Assyria**, and **Israel** (v. 24) would be joined into one people of the Lord. For centuries, the Egyptians and Assyrians had fought each other (20:4), but in the future they would be joined in a bond of friendship sealed by their common allegiance to the Lord (see 25:3).

The prophet looked well beyond the realities of his day, in which the world powers did not acknowledge the true God, proudly pursued their own destinies, and ran roughshod over the people of the Lord. He foresaw a series of divine acts that will bring about the conversion of the nations and the fulfillment of the promise that all peoples will be blessed through Abraham (see Gen. 12:3). The fact that this oracle focuses on Egypt, Israel's greatest historical enemy, and Assyria, the greatest threat to Judah in Isaiah's day, demonstrates the wideness of the Lord's mercy and grace.

20:1–6. These verses serve as an epilogue to the oracles in chapters 18–19. Isaiah received a message from the Lord **In the year** (probably 712 BC) **that Tartan** (referring to the Assyrian king Sargon II, who reigned from 721–705 BC; v. 1) captured the city of **Ashdod.** Ashdod was one of the five Philistine cities and was located near the Mediterranean Sea. The city had rebelled against Assyria in 713 BC under King Azuri. In 1963, three fragments of an Assyrian monument commemorating Sargon's victory were discovered at Ashdod.

Isaiah was to announce that Ashdod's fate prefigured what was about to happen to **Egypt and … Ethiopia** (v. 3). To make the message even more memorable, Isaiah performed, over a three-year period, the symbolic act of going about **naked** (probably wearing only a loincloth) **and barefoot** (v. 4) to depict the condition of Egyptian prisoners being taken away into captivity. Other prophets performed similar symbolic actions to impress their message upon their audiences (see Jeremiah 18–19; Ezek. 4:1–17; 5:1–4; Hosea 1–3). In light of Egypt's imminent demise, it made little sense for the leaders of Judah to think that an alliance with Egypt would protect them from the Assyrians. The prophet asked the people to consider **And how shall we escape?** (v. 6).

G. Against Babylon (21:1–10)

21:1–5. This oracle refers to Babylon as **the desert of the sea** (v. 1) because the coming judgment would turn Babylon into a wasteland (see 21:9; 13:20–22). "The sea" refers either to the Persian Gulf, which was just south of Babylon, or to the alluvial plain deposited by the Euprhates and Tigris rivers and their tributaries. Babylon was the **treacherous dealer** (v. 2) that had attacked and plundered other nations, but **Elam** and **Media** would inflict the same type of judgment on the Babylonians. The Elamites were a perpetual enemy of Assyria and Babylon.

Much later, they were part of the Persian army that conquered Babylon under Cyrus in 539 BC. The Medes also joined with Cyrus to conquer Babylon (see 13:11; Jer. 51:11, 28; Dan. 5:31; 6:28). Isaiah lamented the impending fall of Babylon (vv. 3 – 4), perhaps experiencing vicariously through his vision the horrors that the inhabitants of Babylon would endure or mourning for his countrymen who would make the mistake of believing that military assistance from Babylon would protect them from Assyria. The Babylonians would be eating and drinking when the enemy attacked unexpectedly (v. 5; see Daniel 5).

21:6 – 10. In the vision, the Lord commanded Isaiah to **set a watchman** (v. 6), probably on the walls of Jerusalem, to announce what occurred in the battle. The watchman observed chariots moving about until a messenger arrived to announce, **Babylon is fallen, is fallen** (v. 9). **O my threshing** (v. 10) refers to Judah, which, just like Babylon, would be punished by the Assyrians. Threshing was a common metaphor for judgment or destruction from war (see Amos 1:3). The phrase **corn of my floor** (lit., "son of my floor") compares Judah to threshed grain.

H. Against Dumah (21:11 – 12)

21:11 – 12. This oracle addressed **Dumah** (v. 11), an Arabian oasis (see Jer. 49:7 – 22; Ezek. 25:12 – 14; Amos 1:11 – 12). Refugees from Dumah apparently would flee to **Seir** (Edom; see Gen. 32:3), the homeland of Esau's descendants, and cry out for the **watchman** (see 21:6 – 9) to tell them what was about to happen. They would look for the **night** of catastrophe that had struck their homeland to pass. The prophet announced that **morning** (v. 12) was coming but then warned that **night** would return. Perhaps the meaning of this enigmatic oracle is that the long night of Assyrian oppression was almost over, but only a short "morning" would precede Babylonian domination.

I. Against Arabia (21:13 – 17)

21:13 – 17. The oracle concerning Arabia describes merchant caravans from **Dedanim** (v. 13; see Ezek. 27:20; 38:13) and the inhabitants of **Tema** (v. 14), an oasis in northern Arabia about four hundred miles southwest of Babylon (see Job 6:19; Jer. 25:23), fleeing from the enemy invader. The Assyrians began to attack the Arabs in 732 BC, and the Babylonians did the same under Nebuchadnezzar (see Jer. 25:17, 23 – 24). The simple bows of the Arabs would make it impossible for them to stand against the **swords** (v. 15) and composite **bow** of Assyria. **Kedar** (v. 16), the home of Bedouin tribes in the Arabian Desert known for their flocks (see 60:7; Ezek. 27:21), would be overtaken in less than **a year**. The Lord Himself announced and decreed this judgment.

J. Against the Valley of Vision (Jerusalem) (chap. 22)

Isaiah received a burden concerning Jerusalem. Its placement in a series of oracles against foreign nations is somewhat surprising and suggests that Judah was as guilty and as deserving of judgment as were the pagan peoples around them. The time reference of this prophecy is unclear but appears to encompass both the siege of Jerusalem by the Assyrian king Sennacherib in 701 BC and the final Babylonian siege of Jerusalem in 588 – 586 BC.

22:1 – 7. The valley of vision (v. 1) was a valley where God revealed Himself in visions, probably one of the valleys near Jerusalem. Jerusalem was a **tumultuous** (v. 2) and **joyous city**, behaving just like Babylon (see 21:5; see 23:7), and refused to acknowledge its impending doom. Because of the coming siege, many would die from disease and famine. Leaders would flee from the city (v. 3), only to be captured by the enemy. While the inhabitants of the city remained oblivious, the prophet grieved over the suffering Jerusalem would experience. The **day of trouble** (v. 5) Jerusalem faced was the day of the Lord, the time when He would come down to destroy His enemies (see 2:11, 12, 17, 20). Enemy soldiers from **Elam** (v. 6) and **Kir** would attack the city, and their **chariots** (v. 7) would fill the **valleys** around Jerusalem. The Elamites probably fought in the Babylonian army, and Kir is perhaps another name for Media, also an ally of Babylon (see 21:2).

22:8 – 14. The leaders of Judah fortified the city in preparation for the enemy assault. They removed

the armour (v. 8) from **the house of the forest**, which Solomon had built out of cedars from Lebanon (see 1 Kings 7:2–6; 10:17, 21), and repaired **the breaches** (v. 9) in the defensive walls. Hezekiah **gathered together the waters of the lower pool** by constructing a pool and tunnel to ensure that Jerusalem would have a sufficient water supply during Sennacherib's siege (see 2 Kings 20:20; see 7:3; 36:2). He also had **houses** (v. 10) torn down along the city **wall** so that the walls could be fortified (see 2 Chron. 32:5), likely resulting in injustices against the poor residents of the city, the ones most likely to lose their homes (see 28:15–19). The problem was that the leaders and people of Jerusalem trusted in their human efforts for protection rather than trusting in the Lord (**ye have not looked unto the Maker**; v. 11; see 31:1). Rather than **mourning** (v. 12) over their sins, the people were feasting and celebrating. In the context of national disaster, their actions reflect both deluded self-confidence and fatalistic resignation rather than a serious assessment of where they stood with God. If they refused to repent, certain death awaited them (v. 14).

22:15–25. The second half of this oracle contains a message directed against a governmental official named **Shebna** (v. 15), who would be judged for his selfish pride by having his office taken away from him. Shebna is representative of the leaders of Judah, who were singled out for judgment in the first half of this oracle because they "[had] not looked to" (22:11) the Lord as their source of security. Shebna was the official in charge of the royal house (**over the house**), a position second only to King Hezekiah (see 36:3; 1 Kings 4:6; 2 Kings 15:5). Rather than faithfully serving the people in a time of national crisis, Shebna had constructed an expensive tomb for himself (vv. 15–16). One's place of burial was considered very important, and Shebna coveted a tomb worthy of a king (see 2 Chron. 16:14). Shebna would receive a punishment fitting the crime; he would be taken away into **captivity** (v. 17) and would not be buried in his lavish tomb. The Lord would wad Shebna into **a ball** (v. 18) and throw him out of the city, where he would **die**, apparently without an honorable burial (see 14:19).

The Lord would replace Shebna with **Eliakim** (v. 20). By 701 BC, Eliakim had replaced Shebna, who was demoted to "scribe" (see 36:3). The promise of Eliakim's promotion to a position of authority (v. 22) is quoted in Revelation 3:14 with reference to the exaltation of Jesus as Messiah. The mention of **a father** (v. 21) and of the responsibility **upon his shoulder** (v. 22) recalls the words about the Messiah in 9:6. **The key of the house of David** refers to the authority delegated to Eliakim by the king, who belonged to David's dynasty—perhaps controlling entrance into the royal palace (see Matt. 16:19). Eliakim would be securely established in his position, like **a nail** (v. 23), or peg, that is driven into wood (see Ezek. 15:3), but unfortunately, Eliakim himself would eventually succumb to the temptations of power and be removed by the Lord.

K. Against Tyre (chap. 23)

23:1–13. The final oracle in this series of judgments against the nations focused on **Tyre** (v. 1), the main seaport along the Phoenician coast, about thirty-five miles north of Mount Carmel. Part of the city was built on two rocky islands about a half a mile from the shore. King Hiram of Tyre had supplied cedars and craftsmen for the temple (see 1 Kings 5:8–9) and sailors for Solomon's commercial fleet (1 Kings 9:27). Tyre's judgment was connected to pride over her status as a prosperous center of trade and commerce. **Zidon** (Sidon; vv. 2, 4, 12), another prominent Phoenician city, about twenty-five miles north of Tyre, would also be impacted by the destruction of Tyre (see Ezek. 28:20–26).

The trading **ships of Tarshish** (v. 1) that brought products to and from Tyre would mourn over the city's demise. The warning that Tyre would be **laid waste** was fulfilled through Assyria, Nebuchadnezzar, and Alexander. Nebuchadnezzar captured the mainland city in 572 BC (see Ezek. 26:7–11), but the island fortress was not taken until Alexander the Great destroyed it in 332 BC (see Ezek. 26:3–5).

The phrases and imagery in this oracle call attention to Tyre's wealth and prosperity. **Merchants** (v. 2) throughout the Mediterranean had been

replenished by Tyre's commercial ventures. Tyre had expanded its influence throughout the colonization of distant lands (**Her own feet shall carry her afar off**; v. 7). Carthage in North Africa was a colony of Tyre. Tarshish, perhaps Tartessus in Spain (see Jonah 1:3), may have been another. Tyre was **the crowning city** (v. 8) that appointed kings in her colonies. Her wealth and prominence, however, would disappear when the Lord stretched **his hand over the sea** (v. 11) to bring the judgment He had decreed against **the merchant city** (lit., "Canaan," here roughly equivalent to modern Lebanon). Sennacherib had destroyed Babylon (**the land of the Chaldeans**; v. 13) in 689 BC, and Phoenica would look like the ruined city of Babylon when **the Assyrian** executed the Lord's judgment on Tyre and Sidon (vv. 12–13).

23:14–18. Tyre would become a **forgotten** (v. 15) city for **seventy years**. This time period designates a full lifetime and was also the length of the Babylonian captivity (see Jer. 25:11; 29:10), as well as the length of time that Sennacherib decreed Babylon should remain devastated. After this time of desolation, Tyre would be restored as a prosperous center of commerce. Like a prostitute, she would gain **her hire** (v. 17) by committing **fornication** with other nations. A "harlot" nation was one that sought to make the highest profits regardless of the means. Self-gratification was the key (see Rev. 17:5). The merchants of Tyre, however, would not enjoy this wealth, as it would be devoted **to the LORD** (v. 18). The earnings of a prostitute could not be given to the Lord (see Deut. 23:18), but the silver and gold of a city devoted to destruction were placed in the Lord's treasury (see Deut. 2:34; Josh. 6:17, 19; Mic. 4:3). The prophet promised elsewhere that Israel would one day receive the wealth of the nations (see 18:7; 60:5–11; 61:6).

IV. "The Little Apocalypse" (chaps. 24–27)

The series of judgment oracles against the individual nations in chapters 13–23 naturally leads into this section on God's universal judgment of all nations, which will occur prior to the establishment of His earthly kingdom in the last days. This section is called "the Little Apocalypse" because of its eschatological focus on God's final victory over the forces of evil.

A. Universal Judgments for Universal Sin (chap. 24)

24:1–9. God's final judgment will bring devastation to all the **earth** (v. 1) and will include all peoples (vv. 1–4). Social distinctions will provide no escape from the judgment (see 3:1–3). The reason for the judgment is that the peoples of the earth **have transgressed the laws** (v. 5) and **broken the everlasting covenant.** "The laws" and "covenant" here most likely do not refer to the Mosaic covenant, which God made exclusively with Israel, but rather to the Noahic covenant, which God established with all humanity (see Gen. 9:8–17). This "everlasting" covenant demands the lives of those who are guilty of murder and thus condemns both individuals and nations guilty of violence and bloodshed. The Noahic covenant also appears to serve as the basis of the judgment of the nations surrounding Israel in Amos 1–2 (see Amos 1:9–10). Violation of the covenant brings the earth under God's **curse** (v. 6), which will burn up the earth's inhabitants and leave the earth ruined (vv. 6–9).

24:10–12. The world that will fall under judgment is represented by **The city of confusion** (v. 10). References to the ruined city also appear in 25:2; 26:5 (see also 17:1; 19:18), and this city stands in contrast to the "strong city" (Zion; 26:1) that will be established as the center of God's kingdom and the refuge of the righteous. The ruined city in view here is not a specific city but rather a composite of all cities and world centers opposed to God—such as Babylon, Tyre, and Rome.

24:13–23. God's judgment of the nations will leave only a small contingent of survivors, and these survivors will form a godly remnant (vv. 13–15). They will praise and worship the **majesty of the LORD** (v. 14). While the prophet anticipated the future kingdom age, in which the godly will worship the Lord in a world that has been purged of evil, he lamented the circumstances of his day, in which the godly community wasted away because of the villainy of the treacherous nations that sought to crush them (v. 16). Life in a fallen and corrupt world often suggests that evil is winning the battle, but while the wicked may temporarily have the upper hand, God will ultimately crush them when He shakes the earth and executes His final judgment (vv. 17–22). The opening of **the windows from on high** (v. 18) provides an echo of Noah's flood (Gen. 7:11; 8:20), an appropriate punishment in light of the cause for the judgment. Earthquakes and thunder will cause the earth to stagger **like a drunkard** (v. 20). The Lord's punishment will include not only **the kings of the earth** (v. 21) but also **the host of the high ones**, Satan and the fallen angels (see Eph. 6:11–12). After defeating His enemies, the Lord will **reign** (v. 23) from **Zion**. The **moon** and **sun** will not shine during divine judgment (see 13:10) or when the Lord is the "everlasting light" (60:19–20; Rev. 21:23).

B. Deliverance and Blessing (chap. 25)

25:1–5. The people of the Lord will sing a song celebrating the deliverance brought about by the judgments of chapter 24. The **city** (v. 2) that opposed God will be **a heap** of ruins, and the people of **the terrible nations** (e.g., Egypt, Assyria; v. 3) that occupied the city will acknowledge the Lord's sovereignty. The ultimate victory is not for the powerful and the mighty but for **the poor** (v. 4) and **the needy** who look to the Lord and recognize their need for Him.

25:6–8. The prophet lavishly described the eschatological feast of God that will occur on Mount Zion. **A feast** (v. 6) is associated with a coronation (1 Kings 1:25) or wedding (see Judg. 14:10; Rev. 19:9). The rich food and best **wines** (aged by being left on its dregs) are representative of both the spiritual and material blessings that God's people will enjoy in the future kingdom (see 55:2). The ultimate blessing of the future kingdom is that God will **destroy** (v. 7) death itself. There will be no need for the **covering** and the **vail** used to cover one's face when in mourning. The promise that the Lord will **swallow up death** (v. 8) relates to the portrayal of death in both the Old Testament and pagan mythology as having an insatiable appetite (see Pss. 49:14; 69:15; Prov. 30:15–16; Hab. 2:5). Death, the great swallower, will be swallowed.

25:9–12. With another brief song of praise, the godly will rejoice over having waited for the Lord and then experiencing His salvation. **Moab** (v. 10), symbolic of all the enemies of God (like Edom in 34:5–17), will be destroyed. Like **straw**, God's enemies will be trampled into the **dunghill**, from which they will not be able to escape even though they frantically **spread** (v. 11) their arms as if swimming. They believed themselves to be invulnerable because of their fortressed cities, but the Lord will destroy them and bring them down into **the dust** (v. 12).

C. Praise for the Lord's Sovereign Care (chap. 26)

26:1–7. In the future kingdom, the godly will praise the Lord for the salvation He has provided for them. He will make Zion **a strong city** (v. 1) and a place of refuge for the righteous. Those who have trusted in the Lord will have **perfect peace** (v. 3), while the arrogant wicked who trusted in their **lofty city** (v. 5) will be brought down. Throughout his ministry, the prophet encouraged exclusive trust in the Lord as the source of Israel's security (see 7:4–9; 10:24–27; 17:12–14; 28:16), and this passage demonstrates the ultimate and final reward for those who have put their trust in the Lord. The deliverance of Jerusalem from the Assyrians during the reign of Hezekiah (chaps. 36–37) anticipates the future salvation promised here.

26:8–15. Returning to the distress of his day, Isaiah longed for the Lord to reveal His power on behalf of His people (vv. 8–9; see Hos. 12:5–6) and appealed to God's justice. If the wicked enjoyed the blessings of the land, they would only act more **unjustly** (v. 10). The fate they deserved was to be destroyed **for their envy at the people** (lit., "jealousy of people"; v. 11), referring to God's zeal for His people Israel, which would cause him to act on their behalf. It was not right for **other lords** (i.e., the kings of Egypt and Assyria; v. 13) to rule over the land that God had given His people, and these rulers would be put to death when the Lord had **increased** (v. 15) the people of Israel by bringing them home from exile (see 14:9–10; 54:2–3).

26:16–21. The prophet spoke to the Lord on behalf of Israel (vv. 16–18) and then gave a word of reassurance to God's people (vv. 19–21). He asked the Lord to remember that Israel had suffered like **a woman** (v. 17) in labor at the hands of their enemies. In many ways, the suffering seemed senseless because it was as if Israel had given birth to the **wind** (v. 18). The Lord promised that **Thy dead men shall live ...** and **arise** (v. 19). While this promise certainly includes personal resurrection (see 26:7–8; Dan. 12:2), the primary focus is on the national restoration of Israel (see Ezek. 37:11–12). In the restoration, Israel would be like a nation that had risen from the grave. To make full restitution, the wicked would be destroyed when **the earth also shall disclose her blood** (v. 21). God would call the peoples of the earth to account for shedding blood and violating the Noahic covenant (see 24:5).

D. Israel's Enemies Punished but Israel's Remnant Restored (chap. 27)

27:1. This oracle provides the climactic word of judgment for this section. Employing imagery drawn from Canaanite myths, Isaiah identified the enemies that the Lord would destroy as **leviathan**, the name for one of the sea monsters defeated by Baal in his battle with the sea and the forces of chaos (see Job 3:8; 41:1; 74:14). This imagery served to stress that the Lord, not Baal, is the true king. "Leviathan" here represents the enemy nations that opposed God in Isaiah's day, such as Egypt and Assyria but, in an ultimate sense, also refers to Satan, the "dragon" (Rev. 12:4) or "serpent" (2 Cor. 11:3), who is the power behind the rulers and nations that stand against God and His people.

27:2–6. The Lord will defeat the enemy nations to preserve and protect Israel as His **vineyard** (v. 2). The vineyard song in these verses recalls the earlier parable describing Israel as an unfruitful vineyard worthy of destruction (5:1–7). In the future, the Lord will transform His vineyard. He will **burn** (v. 4) up **the briers and thorns** (i.e., the enemy nations) that have devastated Israel. Israel will be reconciled to the Lord and **make peace** (v. 5) with Him. Unlike

in the past, Israel will **blossom and bud** (v. 6) and its **fruit** will fill the earth.

27:7–13. Before the Lord could bless Israel, He first had to bring the purging judgment that would overtake Israel in Isaiah's day (vv. 7–11). If the people doubted the promise of future blessing (27:6), they needed to consider that the punishment they would receive from God would not be as severe as the one that He poured out on their pagan oppressors (see 10:24–26). Israel would have to atone for her guilt through this judgment, but the Lord would **measure** (v. 8) the punishment and **debate** ("contend") with Israel's enemies so that the punishment would not become too severe. Redemption lay beyond the judgment (vv. 12–13). The Lord will **beat** (v. 12), or "thresh," the nations into which Israel will be dispersed, and this threshing will separate Israel from the Gentiles. The boundaries of the Promised Land given here extend from **the river** Euphrates in the north to **the stream of Egypt** (probably the Wadi el-Arish) in the south.

V. Six Woes and the Promise of Israel's Restoration (chaps. 28–35)

This section contains a series of six woes (28:1; 29:1; 29:15; 30:1; 31:1; 33:1), with the first five focusing on Israel and the last on Assyria. Chapters 34–35 conclude these "woe" chapters and comprise an eschatological section corresponding to chapters 24–27, which conclude chapters 13–23. Chapter 34 describes "the day of the LORD's vengeance" (34:8) against the wicked, while chapter 35 portrays Israel's future salvation with vivid imagery and word pictures. The "woes" against Israel and Judah addressed the recurring themes of corrupt leadership and the danger of turning to political alliances for security rather than trusting in the Lord.

A. Woe to Ephraim (Samaria) (28:1–13)

28:1–6. Samaria, **the crown of pride** (v. 1), was the capital of the northern kingdom (**Ephraim**) and a beautiful city on a prominent hill. Isaiah characterized its leaders as **drunkards**, because in the eighth century BC, Samaria was a city of luxury and indulgence. Drunkenness was also a fitting image for the spiritual stupor of Israel's leaders, which kept them from hearing and obeying the word of the Lord. Despite its splendor, Samaria would be overthrown by **a mighty and strong one** (v. 2), the king of Assyria. The Assyrian army would be like a flood overwhelming Samaria (see 8:7–8), a prophecy fulfilled when the Assyrians captured the city in 722 BC. **The residue** (v. 5), or remnant, remaining from this judgment would realize their foolishness in trusting in the wealth and leadership of Samaria for their security and would instead recognize the Lord as their **crown of glory** and protection. New leadership would restore **judgment** (justice; v. 6) and military **strength** to Israel.

28:7–13. The religious leaders of Isaiah's day lacked wisdom and spiritual sensitivity because they were full of **wine, and … strong drink** (v. 7). In their drunken arrogance, they dismissed the words of Isaiah as the babbling sounds of a child. In Hebrew, **For precept … line upon line** (v. 10) reads, *Tsav latsav, tsav lasav, Kav lakav, kav lakav*, reflecting the leaders' mocking imitation of the prophet's encouragements to find **rest** (v. 12) in the Lord. The prophet's message of turning to the Lord seemed to them too simplistic when compared to their political and military solutions for Israel's problems. Since they had refused to listen to the straightforward message of the prophet, God would now speak to them **with stammering lips and another tongue** (v. 11), referring to the foreign language of the Assyrian soldiers that would invade their land (vv. 11–13). They dismissed the words of the prophet as childish nonsense, so the word of the Lord that he spoke would remain nonsense to them (see 6:9–10).

B. Woe to Jerusalem's Leaders (28:14–29)

28:14–16. In many ways, the leaders of Jerusalem were no better than those of Samaria. Judah's leaders were proud of their political alliance with Egypt, which they believed would protect them from the Assyrians (see 30:1–3; 31:1–3), but the prophet placed an ironic boast in the mouths of these leaders to show the ultimate consequence of their actions:

We have made a covenant with death (v. 15). Their covenant partner was not the Egyptians but death itself. They were in agreement with **hell** (Hebrew, *sheol*; the "grave"), which is where they would end up because they had trusted in men rather than in God. They believed that death had promised not to harm them, but death is a destroyer that can never be trusted as a covenant partner (see Prov. 30:15–16; Jer. 9:21–22).

Their **refuge** (v. 15) would collapse when the Assyrian (and later, Babylonian) armies invaded their land. The image of an **overflowing scourge** is a mixed metaphor picturing the invaders as both a flooding river (see 8:7–8) and a whip (see 10:26). Judah's real security was to be found in the **tried … and precious corner stone** (v. 16), a figure comparing the Lord's presence in Zion to the **foundation** of the Jerusalem temple. In the New Testament, Jesus Christ is identified as the "chief corner stone" (1 Peter 2:6) and "foundation" (1 Cor. 3:11) of the church.

28:17–22. Continuing the building imagery, the Lord declared that He would use **the line, and … the plummet** (v. 17) to test the stability of the refuge Jerusalem's leaders had built, with justice and **righteousness** as His standards of measurement (see 30:30; 32:19). In fortifying Jerusalem against enemy attack, the officials of Judah had torn down the houses of the poor (see 22:10), and the Lord would not overlook these abuses. The storm of enemy invasion would completely sweep away Jerusalem's poorly constructed **refuge** and nullify its **covenant with death** (v. 18). Judah would find itself unprepared both militarily and spiritually for the attack, like a man lying down on a **bed** (v. 20) that is too small. The Lord's judgment of Zion would be **his strange work** (v. 21) because He would fight against His people in the same way that He had fought for and with them in the past. The prophet encouraged the leaders to turn from their cynical unbelief and to take heed to his warnings of judgment (v. 22).

28:23–29. The chapter closes with a poetic parable in two stanzas (vv. 23–28), each ending with a verse that praises the Lord for His wisdom

(vv. 26, 29). The parable uses the image of **threshing** (vv. 27–28) grain to describe God's punishment of His people. The primary lesson of the parable is that God is like a wise farmer in carrying out His work of judgment. His work would be as measured and well-timed as the work of the farmer who knows precisely when to plant and harvest his various crops. God would judge but not destroy His people.

C. Woe to David's City, Jerusalem (29:1–14)

29:1–4. The condemnation of Judah's leaders led into a **Woe** (v. 1) oracle against Jerusalem itself. The name **Ariel**, used here for Jerusalem, sounds like the Hebrew *'ari'el*, or "altar hearth." The significance of this name is that the people of Jerusalem were going through the motions of offering their **sacrifices** to the Lord **year to year**, but Jerusalem itself was in danger of being sacrificed in judgment (for a similar use of sacrifice imagery with reference to Edom, see 34:5–7). In a series of **I will** (vv. 2–3) statements, the Lord expressed His intention to wage holy war against His own people. Jerusalem would be **brought down** (v. 4), and the people of Judah would **whisper** like a medium or spiritist (see 8:19) from the realm of the dead. Their "covenant with death" (see 28:15, 18) would not protect them from destruction.

29:5–8. After waging war against Jerusalem, the Lord, in His own time, would then deliver the city from its enemies (see 10:5–19). The description of the sudden destruction of the enemy resembles that of the Assyrian army in 701 BC. Israel's many enemies would be reduced to **dust, and ... chaff** (v. 5) when the Lord struck them down **with thunder, and with earthquake** (v. 6; see Judg. 5:4–5; Ps. 18:7–15; Hab. 3:3–7). The enemy armies who sought to destroy Jerusalem would be like **a hungry man** (v. 8) who dreamt that he was eating, only to wake up still hungry.

29:9–14. Isaiah spoke again of Israel's spiritual state and warned of the Lord's impending judgment. **Cry ye out, and cry** (v. 9) reads literally, "Blind yourself, and be blind." The prophet sarcastically commanded the people to remain in their blindness because they refused to hear the word of the Lord

spoken through the prophets. They were like drunk men who **stagger[ed]** about in their spiritual stupor (see 6:10; 28:1, 7). The totality of Isaiah's message (**the vision of all**; v. 11) is a closed book even to the educated. **Therefore** (v. 14), God needed to do **a marvellous work and a wonder** against His people. He who had shown them wonders in the exodus (see Exod. 15:11; Ps. 78:12) would now show them wonders in judgment. Their hypocritical devotion with the **mouth** (v. 13) but not the **heart** made them worthy of judgment. God referred to them as **this people** (v. 14), not "my people."

D. Woe to Those Who Trust in Human Wisdom and a Promise for the Future (29:15–24)

29:15–16. Isaiah again announced a **Woe** (v. 15) on the leaders of Judah who trusted in their own wisdom, rather than in God, to save their nation. They attempted to **hide their counsel** of making alliances with other nations **from the Lord**, but He knew what they were plotting and scheming in **the dark**. By trusting in themselves rather than in God as their ultimate security, they had reversed the way things should be and were like a **work** (v. 16) of pottery denying the potter as its maker.

29:17–24. While the series of "woe" messages cast a funeral tone over this section, verses 17–24 suddenly shift to the theme of redemption. The idea of reversal for Israel and her enemies predominates. **Lebanon** (v. 17), likely symbolic of Assyria, would be reduced from a great **forest** to only a **field** (see 2:13; 10:34). Israel, on the other hand, would be like a **deaf** (v. 18) person made able to **hear** and a **blind** man able to see. **The meek** (v. 19) and **the poor** would **rejoice** in the Lord, because **the terrible one** (Assyria; v. 20) and the wicked who perverted justice would be destroyed. The Lord promised to reverse Israel's shame by giving her many **children** (v. 23), just as He had **redeemed Abraham** (v. 22) from the shame of childlessness. While Isaiah's contemporaries showed little respect for the Lord, this future generation would **sanctify** (v. 23) and **fear** the Lord. The nation that had **erred in spirit** (v. 24) by not trusting and obeying the Lord would be transformed.

E. Woe to the Obstinate Nation (chap. 30)

30:1–7. The leaders and people of Judah were like **rebellious children** (v. 1) because of their political alliance with **Egypt** (v. 2). By turning to Egypt, they had not followed the leading of God's **Spirit** (v. 1) and were rejecting the Lord's sovereign prerogative to protect and defend His people. The phrase **cover with a covering** (lit., "pour out a drink offering") refers to the confirmation of their alliance through pagan ceremonies. After Shabako became pharaoh in 715 BC, the smaller nations in Aram (Syria) and Canaan sought his help against Assyria. Under Hezekiah's leadership, Judah apparently had joined them (see 20:5). While Judah had chosen to trust in Egypt's **shadow** (v. 2), a metaphor for a king's protection (see Judg. 9:15; Lam. 4:20), the Lord should have been Israel's "shadow" (see 49:2; 51:16; Ps. 91:1). Judah had turned to a people that could not help them, and had even braved the dangers of the wilderness to pay their tribute to the Egyptians. Israel's envoys going through the wilderness back to Egypt suggests a reversal of the exodus. The Hebrew term *rahab* is the word used for Egypt's **strength** (v. 7) and should probably be read as the proper name Rahab, comparing Egypt to the mythical sea monster by that name. Just as Rahab had been cut to pieces (see 51:9; see 27:1), Egypt would **sit still**, or "be destroyed."

30:8–11. The Lord instructed Isaiah to write down his prophecy concerning Egypt's destruction in a book so that the people would be reminded of its fulfillment when Egypt fell (v. 8). The Lord knew the tendency of His **rebellious people** (v. 9) to not listen to the prophets or to request that the prophets speak **smooth things** (v. 10), favorable messages like the ones they received from the false prophets (see 1 Kings 22:13; Jer. 6:14; 8:11; Mic. 2:6–11).

30:12–17. Judah refused to heed the prophetic warnings and turn from their sinful ways of **oppression** (domestic injustice; v. 12; see 1:15–17; 5:7; 29:21) and **perverseness** (guile and intrigue in foreign policy; see 30:1–2; 29:15). Thus, the Lord was about to **break** (v. 14) down the **wall** (v. 13) of security they had built for themselves through their corrupt practices. Their only true security would come through turning to God and resting in His promises (v. 15). The implication is not that faith is a life of passive inactivity, but Judah in this instance needed to cease from activity because their actions were counter to trusting in God. Rather than having quiet trust in God's promises, Judah trusted in **horses** (v. 16) and military strength (see Ps. 33:17). Because of their lack of faith, God would inflict on them the covenant curse of military defeat even when their troops outnumbered the enemy (v. 17; see Deut. 32:30).

30:18–33. The prophet's message took a positive turn as he anticipated Israel's future deliverance. After punishing Israel, God would once again be gracious and have mercy on them. He would save them because He is **a God of judgment** (justice; v. 18), and it is right for the Lord to deliver those who have trusted in His promises. The Lord would turn their weeping and **bread of adversity** (v. 20) into rejoicing (vv. 19–20a). True prophets would no longer have to hide in **a corner** (v. 20) for fear of persecution because the people would follow the ways of the Lord and renounce their idolatrous practices (vv. 20b–22). Because of their obedience, the Lord would bless them with agricultural and material prosperity (vv. 23–26). The darkness would be past; night would be like the day, and day would be illumined with **sevenfold ... light** (v. 26). The Lord would also repair **the breach** (see 30:13) caused by Judah's sin so that Israel would be safe and secure.

The language of theophany portrays the Lord coming as fire and storm to destroy His enemies as He rescued Israel (vv. 27–28). The image of a flood reaching to **the neck** (v. 28) of the enemy nations recalls a similar description of the Assyrian army overwhelming Judah (8:8). The prophet employed imagery associated with the exodus to portray Israel's deliverance (vv. 29–32). Israel would sing **a song** (v. 29) of rejoicing as they kept their holy feast, perhaps the Passover, which is alluded to in 31:5. After the Lord struck down the nations with His voice of thunder, Israel would celebrate **with tabrets and harps** (v. 32). After the deliverance at the Red Sea, the women rejoiced with singing and dancing (see Exod. 15:20–21). The references to the exodus contribute to the irony that Judah was trusting in a covenant with Egypt when they should have been looking to the One who had delivered them from Egypt.

The promise of deliverance closes with a final reference to **Tophet** (v. 33), a region outside Jerusalem where children were sacrificed in the **fire** to Molech (see 2 Kings 23:10; Jer. 7:31–32). Tophet would become the place where the Lord offered up **the king** (of Assyria) with fire. The Lord would act decisively to separate Israel from their pagan practices and to destroy the pagan rulers that had subjugated Israel.

F. Woe to Those Who Rely on Egypt (chap. 31)

31:1–3. This chapter recapitulates the preceding one in condemning Judah's alliance with **Egypt** (v. 1) and promising that the Lord would ultimately deliver Jerusalem after punishing His people. Judah trusted in Egypt because Egypt had large numbers of **horses** and **chariots** (see 1 Kings 10:28–29). The people found security in military might because they wanted to trust in something visible rather than exercise the faith necessary to **look** to the Lord. However, the Egyptians were only **men, and not God** (v. 3), who would **stretch out his hand** (see 5:25; 9:12, 17, 21) to judge both Judah and Egypt.

31:4–5. The Lord could deliver His people in ways that Egypt never could. He would destroy His enemies like a **lion** (v. 4) tearing apart his **prey**, and He would protect **Jerusalem** (v. 5) like a flock of hovering **birds**. The verb **passing over** is the technical word used of the destroying angel who "passed over" every house in Egypt that had blood on the doorposts (see Exod. 13:23). The prophet again recalled the exodus tradition to remind Judah that they were foolish to put their trust in the nation from which the Lord had delivered them long ago (see 30:29–32).

31:6–9. The prophet exhorted the people to **Turn** (v. 6) to the Lord because they would renounce their trust in **idols** (v. 7), another man-made source of security, when the Lord miraculously delivered them from their enemies. The Lord would use His

own **sword** (v. 8), not a weapon crafted by humans, to destroy the Assyrians. The fulfillment of this prophecy is described in 37:36, when the angel of the Lord struck down 185,000 soldiers. The king of Assyria would **pass over** (v. 9) and return to his own country but would not avoid judgment. Nineveh was destroyed by the Medes and Persians in 612 BC (see Nah. 3:7). The Assyrians would discover that the **fire** and **furnace** of the Lord's glory **is in Zion** and breaks out upon the wicked who oppose Him (see 10:17; 30:33; Lev. 10:2; Amos 1:2).

G. Israel's Ultimate Deliverance and the Promise of a King (chap. 32)

32:1–8. In these verses, the prophet looked forward to the messianic age, when **a king shall reign in righteousness** (v. 1) and his **princes** will promote justice. They will provide security and protection for the people, and the nation will thrive under their leadership (vv. 2–4). The promised leadership of the future sharply differs from the corrupt leaders of Isaiah's day, a point emphasized in the contrast between the **liberal** ("generous"; v. 5) and the **churl** ("fool") in verses 5–8. The generous leader cares for his people, while the fool disregards the needy and thinks only of carrying out **wicked devices** (v. 7) for his own gain.

32:9–14. Before Zion would know true security and blessing, the Lord would send the rich and pampered women of Jerusalem into exile (see 3:16–4:1). The word **careless** (v. 9–11) means "complacent," and this same Hebrew term is used in a positive sense for "quiet" in 32:18. Here it connotes the attitude of self-indulgence and a false sense of security that caused them to disregard the Lord. They would mourn when **the vintage ... fail[ed]** (v. 10) and the armies of Assyria brought widespread destruction on the land. They would lose everything they had lived for when their **houses of joy** (v. 13) and the city of Jerusalem were destroyed.

32:15–20. In the future Messianic age, the outpouring of the Holy Spirit upon the people of Israel would bring about the reversal of God's judgment (v. 15). The Old Testament prophets frequently pointed to the future outpouring of the Spirit as the source of Israel's spiritual transformation that would lead to physical blessing (see 44:3; 59:21; Ezek. 36:26–27; Joel 2:28). The land would be transformed from a **wilderness** (v. 15) to **a fruitful field**, and the **righteousness** (v. 17) of the nation would bring **peace** and security because there would be no need for the Lord to judge His people. The Assyrian invasion was about to flatten Judah like a **hail** (v. 19) storm, but that destruction would give way to the abundance of the covenant blessings from the Lord.

H. Woe to Assyria but Blessing for God's People (chap. 33)

33:1–9. The woes pronounced against Israel and Judah were next turned upon the nations that plundered Jerusalem, with Assyria being the prime example (v. 1). The prophet prayed for the Lord to bring about the promised destruction of the Assyrians. He expressed his confidence that the Lord would destroy His enemies and then establish Zion as a city of justice and **righteousness** (v. 5). The prophet further reminded the Lord of Judah's desperate situation as they waited for the Lord's deliverance. Judah's soldiers (**valiant ones;** v. 7) and **the ambassadors** attempting to negotiate a truce with the Assyrians mourned and lamented because their cause seemed hopeless. The Assyrian assault had made travel and trade impossible (v. 8), adding to Judah's economic hardship. The Assyrian king Sennacherib had **broken the covenant** by taking tribute from Hezekiah and then continuing to plunder the **cities** of Judah (see 2 Kings 18:14). The invaders had ruined farmland and pastures. Even the most fertile areas of **Lebanon ... Sharon ... Bashan and Carmel** (v. 9) had been laid waste.

33:10–24. The Lord responded to Isaiah's prayer in the first person (**Now will I rise;** v. 10) and promised to deliver His people. He would **be exalted** through the defeat of His enemies. The plan of these enemies to destroy Jerusalem would ultimately destroy only themselves. The **fire** (v. 11) of judgment would reduce them to **lime** (v. 12; see Amos 2:1) and consume them as if they were thorn branches (see 2 Sam. 23:6–7). The Lord's judgment of **fire** (v. 14)

would also devour **The sinners in Zion** so that only a righteous remnant remained (see 1:27–28). The righteous who practiced justice would **dwell on high** (v. 16) among the **rocks,** symbolic of the security found in God. Following their deliverance from Assyria, **the king** (v. 17) would reign over Israel in majesty (**beauty**) and would lead them into every blessing. This king is identified as the Lord Himself in verse 22, but comparison with 32:1 indicates that this promise also likely anticipates the future reign of the Messiah as the Lord's vice-regent. The prophet's oracle here blends promises concerning Israel's immediate deliverance from Assyria and the future eschatological kingdom.

In the restoration, the **terror** (v. 18) of the Assyrian invasion would only be a distant memory. There would be no **scribe** or **receiver** to collect tribute, and no foreign army speaking with a **stammering tongue** (v. 19) would invade their land. Several images convey the future peace and security that Zion will enjoy. **Zion** (v. 20) will be a **quiet habitation,** like a tent (**tabernacle**) that is firmly staked. The presence of the Lord will protect Zion like the **broad rivers and streams** (v. 21) that prevent enemies from having easy access, as in Tyre (23:1) or Thebes (see Nah. 3:8). Connected to this maritime image, it appears that Assyria is portrayed as a ship with its **tacklings ... loosed** (v. 23) and its **sail** unspread. Assyria will be incapable of going into battle because she has been destroyed by the Lord. With the Lord as King, Zion will be physically and spiritually whole.

I. The Destruction of the Nations and the Avenging of God's People (chap. 34)

34:1–4. The Lord will pour out His fierce anger on the nations. **Their armies** (v. 2) will be **utterly destroyed** (Hebrew, *herem;*), the verb referring to the irrevocable giving over of things and persons to the Lord and the type of destruction that God had intended for the Canaanites (see Deut. 7:2; Josh. 6:17). Cosmic disturbances will also characterize the future day of the Lord (v. 4; see 13:10, 13; Ezek. 32:7–8; Matt. 24:41; Rev. 6:13–14), but reference to **all the host of heaven** (v. 4) likely also pictures God warring

against Satan and the angelic powers who oppose His rule (see Eph. 6:12).

34:5 – 7. The Lord's **sword** (v. 5) will fall on **Idumea** (read as Edom), representative of all the enemies of God and His people (34:4 – 17; see Obadiah 8 – 9, 15 – 16). The Edomites were driven from their homeland by the Nabatean Arabs, perhaps as early as 500 BC. The enemies that will be killed by the Lord's sword are compared to sacrificial animals — **lambs and goats** (v. 6), **unicorns** ("wild oxen"; v. 7), and **bullocks**. The **fat** of these animals was considered the best part of the meat and was thus offered to the Lord (see Lev. 3:9 – 11). The prophets often compared battles to sacrifices (see Jer. 46:10; 50:27; Ezek. 39:17 – 19).

34:8 – 17. The destruction of Edom would be **the day of the LORD's vengeance** (v. 8). The Edomites were deserving of judgment because they had opposed Israel at every opportunity (see 2 Sam. 8:13 – 14) and later rejoiced when Jerusalem was destroyed (see Lam. 4:21; Ps. 137:7). But Edom's day was coming, and Edom's destruction would be permanent, the reference to **brimstone** (v. 9) recalling the overthrow of Sodom and Gomorrah (see Gen. 19:24; Jer. 49:17 – 18). Edom would be reduced to a smoldering heap of ruins that is the haunt of wild animals. After the destruction of Edom, people would read this prophecy **out of the book of the LORD** (v. 16). The fall of Edom is certain because of the Lord's decree. The severity of the language describing the judgment of Edom suggests that this judgment foreshadows God's final judgment of all peoples and nations. The image of smoke ascending forever (v. 10) is applied to Babylon, the final enemy of God (see Rev. 14:10 – 11; 19:3). Isaiah 63:1 – 4 describes the Lord's future judgment of the nations and depicts the Lord as a victorious warrior returning from Edom with bloodstained garments.

J. The Future Blessings of Restored Zion (chap. 35)

35:1 – 5. While chapter 34 focused on the judgment of the wicked, chapter 35 announces the salvation of the righteous who have trusted in the Lord. Israel will be like a **wilderness** (v. 1) that is transformed into a beautiful and fruitful land. **Lebanon** **... Carmel and Sharon** (v. 2) were all fertile areas renowned for their beautiful trees and foliage (see 33:9). **Be strong, fear not** (v. 4), God's words of encouragement to Joshua (see Josh. 1:6 – 7. 9, 18), are now spoken to Israel. Israel will take courage from knowing that **God will come** (v. 4) to bring **vengeance** and **recompense** on their enemies.

35:6 – 10. More images of reversal and transformation fill out the portrayal of Israel's future salvation. The **lame** (v. 6) will **leap**, and the **dumb** will **sing**. Returning to the imagery in 35:1 – 2, **the parched ground** (v. 7) of **the desert** (v. 6) will flow with **springs of water** (v. 7). There will also be a highway in the desert to make travel easier (see 11:16; 40:3). This highway will be called **The way of holiness** (v. 8) because it is the way set apart for those who are holy; only the redeemed can use it. In ancient times, certain roads were open only to those who were ceremonially pure. Travel on the road will be safe because no **lion** (v. 9) or **beast** will be near. Sometimes wild animals made travel dangerous (see Deut. 8:15; Judg. 14:5). **The ransomed** (v. 10) will **come to Zion with songs** of joy and celebration, just as the Israelites did when they returned from Babylonian exile (see Psalm 126).

VII. A Historical Transition from the Assyrian Threat to the Babylonian Exile (chaps. 36 – 39)

The Hezekiah narratives in chapters 36 – 39 provide an important literary hinge for the two major sections of the book of Isaiah. Chapters 36 – 37 conclude the first section of the book by narrating the deliverance of Jerusalem from the Assyrian threat, while chapters 38 – 39 warn of Judah's future subjugation to Babylon, which serves as the context for the message of hope and deliverance in chapters 40 – 66. The Hezekiah narratives in this section and the earlier account concerning Ahaz in chapters 7 – 8 are the only narrative portions in the book of Isaiah, and the parallels between these two narratives are vitally important to the rhetorical strategy of the book. The parallels include: (1) both kings were threatened by the attack of an enemy army (7:1; 36:2); (2) both kings were greatly concerned by this attack

(7:2; 37:1–4); (3) "the conduit of the upper pool," vital to Jerusalem's water supply in a time of siege, is prominent in both stories (7:3; 36:2); (4) both kings received a promising message from Isaiah, encouraging them to not be afraid of the approaching enemy (7:4–9; 37:6–7); and (5) both kings were offered "a sign" confirming the promise of deliverance (7:10–11; 37:30–31). These parallels highlight the contrast between the responses of these two kings to the Lord's promise of deliverance—Ahaz's unbelief, which led to a sentence of judgment (7:12–25; 8:5–8), and Hezekiah's faith, which led to Jerusalem's deliverance from the Assyrians (37:21–38).

Ultimately, the responses of Ahaz and Hezekiah represent the options facing the exilic community in the second half of the book as they chose how to respond to the Lord's call to "fear not" and trust in His promises of deliverance from Babylon (see 41:10; 43:1; 54:4). If they responded in faith, as Hezekiah had, they would experience the blessing of deliverance from exile and bondage. While Hezekiah's faith in the Lord when Jerusalem was surrounded by the Assyrian army was remarkably courageous, his faith in the Lord was not perfect. At another time, Hezekiah had sought an alliance with Babylon, which demonstrated a lack of trust in the Lord, and Isaiah warned him that this act of unbelief would lead to Judah's exile (see 39:1–10). Israel's full and final deliverance awaited the coming of the future Messiah. Much of chapters 36–39 is paralleled, sometimes verbatim, in 2 Kings 18:13–20:19. The compiler of 2 Kings may have used Isaiah 36–39 as one of his sources, or both may have drawn from a common source.

A. Jerusalem Preserved from the Assyrian Threat (chaps. 36–37)

1. The Siege of Jerusalem by Sennacherib and the Assyrian Army (chap. 36)

36:1–7. Sennacherib's siege of Jerusalem occurred in 701 BC, which was the fourteenth year (v. 1) of Hezekiah's sole reign of Judah. Hezekiah ruled as a sole king from 715 to 686 BC but was a coregent with his father Ahaz beginning in 729 BC (see 2 Kings 18:1). Sennacherib ruled over Assyria

from 705 to 681 BC and marched against Judah in response to Hezekiah's rebellion and captured all the defenced cities. In his annals, Sennacherib listed forty-six such cities (see 2 Kings 18:13). After capturing Lachish (v. 2), an important city about thirty miles southwest of Jerusalem that guarded the main approach to Judah's capital from that quarter, Sennacherib sent his Rabshakeh (or "field commander") and a great army to Jerusalem with his demands. The field commander met with three of Hezekiah's key officials and warned that Judah's rebellion against Assyria and refusal to pay tribute (see 2 Kings 17:4; 18:7) was a foolish and destructive policy (vv. 3–7). Egypt (v. 6) as a covenant partner was a broken reed that would provide no help or protection against the Assyrian onslaught. Hezekiah had been under pressure to make an alliance with Egypt since 715 BC, and Isaiah had also warned that a treaty with Egypt was not to be Judah's source of security (see 20:1; 30:1–3; 31:1). The Assyrian commander warned that even the Lord (v. 7) would not protect Jerusalem. Confusing the nature of Hezekiah's religious reforms, the commander argued that Hezekiah had forfeited the Lord's protection by destroying the high places and … altars devoted to the Lord. Hezekiah had in fact destroyed popular shrines that were devoted to Baal worship (see 2 Kings 18:4; 2 Chron. 31:1).

36:8–12. Sennacherib's first demand was that Hezekiah must send two thousand horses (v. 8), a sizable number for any army. The Assyrian claimed that the Lord had sent him to destroy Judah (vv. 9–10). The Lord had indeed used Assyria to punish Israel (see 10:5–6), but the king failed to see that it was now Assyria's turn to be judged. Hezekiah's officials encouraged the Assyrian officer to speak to them in the Syrian language (i.e., Aramaic, the diplomatic language of the day; v. 11), because they feared that the commander's speech might damage the people's morale. The commander refused, however, and stated that the people had the right to know the fate awaiting them if they continued their resistance (v. 12).

36:13–22. The Assyrian commander then specifically focused his message on the people. He warned them not to trust in Hezekiah or the Lord to deliver them from the Assyrian army (vv. 13–16). He demanded that they surrender Jerusalem and pay tribute to the Assyrian king: **Make an agreement with me by a present, and come out to me** (v. 16). Upon surrendering, they would be deported, as was the Assyrian policy toward rebellious peoples (see 2 Kings 15:29; 17:6), but they would at least have **corn and wine** (v. 17) rather than starving to death under siege conditions. Echoing the boasts of the arrogant Assyrians in 10:8–11, the commander claimed that the Lord was powerless to deliver Jerusalem even if He wanted to (vv. 18–20). No longer merely claiming that the Lord was angry with the people of Judah, this pagan official made the blasphemous assertion that the Assyrian gods and armies were more powerful than the Lord. Recognizing the severity of the situation, the Judean officials tore their garments as a sign of mourning when they came to report the Assyrian demands to Hezekiah (vv. 21–22).

2. The Lord's Deliverance of Jerusalem (chap. 37)

37:1–4. Hezekiah similarly recognized the urgency of the situation and **went into the house of the LORD** (v. 1) to pray. Hezekiah's faith was not always perfect, and he had previously given into the inclination to trust in alliances, political maneuvering, or building projects as his source of security. In his moment of greatest crisis, however, Hezekiah made the right choice and turned to the Lord. The Lord demanded that Judah trust in Him exclusively for deliverance and rewarded the faith of Hezekiah as the representative of the nation.

Hezekiah demonstrated his trust in the Lord by going to the temple to pray and sending messengers to Isaiah to plead for the Lord's help. The king described the **day of trouble** (v. 3) for Judah as a time when **the children are come to the birth, and there is not strength to bring forth**. The image of the child at the opening of the womb but unable to be born provides an even more vivid description of the pains of childbirth. The king expressed his hope that the Lord would defend His reputation by reproving the blasphemous words of the Assyrian field commander.

37:5–13. In response to Hezekiah's request, Isaiah sent a message calling on the king to **Be not afraid** (v. 6) and promising that Sennacherib would return to his homeland and not attack the city of Jerusalem. When the field commander returned to Sennacherib, the Assyrian king had moved a few miles from **Lachish** (v. 8) and was attacking **Libnah**. A report was heard **concerning Tirhakah king of Ethiopia** (v. 9) coming to aid Judah in the struggle with Assyria, but this was not the report that would cause the Assyrian king to return home, as promised in verse 7. Sennacherib continued to defy the Lord and repeated the warning that there was no escape for Judah (vv. 10–13). He claimed that the Lord was as powerless as the gods of the other peoples whom the Assyrians had captured.

37:14–20. Receiving this new message from Sennacherib in the form of a **letter** (v. 14), Hezekiah once again immediately turned to the Lord in prayer and spread the blasphemous letter **before the LORD** at the Jerusalem temple. The Lord is the great King who is enthroned **between the cherubims** (v. 16) and the Creator of the universe. The Assyrian king had dared to bring a **reproach** (v. 17) on the name of the Lord, who is not like the gods of the other peoples that Assyria had conquered. Thus, the Lord's reputation was at stake in how He responded to this threat.

37:21–29. Isaiah delivered the Lord's answer to Hezekiah's prayer with an extended promise of deliverance (37:21–35). Ironically, the tiny **daughter of Zion** (v. 22), a personification of Jerusalem and its inhabitants, mocked and taunted the proud and arrogant Assyrian king. With the Lord's protection, she had no reason to fear her more powerful enemy. In contrast, the Assyrian king viewed himself as invincible and made boasts that were almost a claim to deity (vv. 23–26; see 10:8–14). Nothing had stopped him from dominating other peoples. He had ascended **to the height of the mountains** (v. 24) in **Lebanon** and had chopped down its **tall cedars**. Desert lands could not hinder his army because he had dug wells and **drunk water** (v. 25) from them. He **dried up all the rivers** so that the branches of the Nile were no obstacle either. Sennacherib failed to recognize that his conquests were only possible because Assyria was God's tool of judgment against the nations (vv. 27 – 28). Because of his pride, the Assyrian king would be led away with the Lord's **hook in** his **nose** (v. 29) and His **bridle** in his mouth. The Assyrians often led away captives with hooks in their noses (see 2 Kings 19:28; Amos 4:2), and now they would experience the same humiliation they had inflicted on others.

37:30 – 35. With Assyria removed from the scene, the Lord would restore Judah's prosperity. The normal agricultural activities of sowing, reaping, planting, and eating would resume **in the third year** (v. 30; contrast 36:16). The remnant in Judah who had survived the Assyrian siege would also **take root ... and bear fruit** (v. 31). The Assyrian army would not capture Jerusalem, and Sennacherib would return home. The Lord protected Jerusalem to defend His reputation and to keep his covenant promise to David, to whom He had promised an enduring throne (v. 35; see 9:7; 55:3; 2 Sam. 7:16).

37:36 – 38. Recalling the death of the firstborn in Egypt (see Exod. 12:12), **the angel of the Lord ... smote** (v. 36) the Assyrian army, killing 185,000 soldiers. The Greek historian Herodotus attributed this destruction to a bubonic plague. In the biblical account, divine intervention caused the deaths of these soliders, fulfilling the prophecies of 10:33 – 34; 30:31; 31:8. Twenty years after returning to the Assyrian capital of **Nineveh** (in 681 BC; v. 37), **Sennacherib** went to the temple of his god and was assassinated by his sons. Hezekiah, however, had gone to the Lord's temple, gained strength, and found protection (37:1, 14).

B. The Lord's Extension of Hezekiah's Life (chap. 38)

38:1 – 4. This chapter describes Hezekiah's healing from a life-threatening disease. **In those days** (v. 1) refers to some time prior to Sennacherib's invasion in 701 BC (see 38:6); thus, the events in chapters 38 – 39 occurred prior to the deliverance of Jerusalem. The order of these events are reversed in Isaiah, so that chapters 36 – 37 provide the conclusion to the first section of the book, and chapters 38 – 39 conclude the introduction to the second section. Isaiah informed

Hezekiah of his impending death and instructed the king to make the proper arrangements for his successor to the throne. Hezekiah apparently had no son as natural successor to the throne at that time (see 39:7; 2 Kings 21:1), making his untimely death all the more tragic. Hezekiah fervently prayed for God to spare his life and appealed to the fact that he had served the Lord **with a perfect heart** (v. 3). The king was not claiming sinless perfection (see 38:17), but rather was reminding God of his faithfulness and fully devoted heart (see 38:7; 2 Kings 18:3 – 5).

38:5 – 8. The prophet returned and announced that **the Lord** (v. 5) had **heard** Hezekiah's **prayer** and had extended his life by **fifteen years**. The fervency of Hezekiah's prayers brought about a change in the Lord's decree. The Lord provided **a sign** (v. 7) to confirm this promise to Hezekiah: **the sun returned ten degrees** (v. 8). The receding of the shadow on the stairway was clearly a sign from the Lord (see 2 Kings 20:9 – 11; Josh. 10:12 – 14). As in 37:30, Hezekiah received a positive sign from the Lord because of his faith, unlike the sign announcing judgment that was given to the unbelieving Ahaz (7:11, 14).

38:9 – 20. Hezekiah delivered a hymn of thanksgiving in response to his deliverance from death and the Lord's answer to his prayer. Similar in structure to thanksgiving songs found in the Psalms, Hezekiah first voiced the complaint that he had expressed to God. Hezekiah pictured himself leaving the land of the living and going through the gates that lead into **the grave** (Hebrew, *sheol*; v. 10), or the land of the dead, and described his life ending suddenly like **a shepherd's tent** (v. 12) that was rolled up and put away, or like cloth that **a weaver** had **cut off** from his loom. The king used the image of aching or broken **bones** (v. 13) to describe the physical and spiritual distress caused by his life-threatening illness (see Pss. 6:2; 32:3). In his suffering, the king cried out with the mournful sounds of a bird (v. 14).

Following his complaint, the king offered praise for God's healing. The rhetorical question, **What shall I say?** (v. 15), expressed the awe and wonder that made it difficult for Hezekiah to put into words the greatness of God's deliverance. **These things**

(v. 16) refers to God's promises and gracious acts, which enable a person of faith to endure even the ordeals of sickness and peril. God had taken care of him and delivered him from death. The Lord delivered Hezekiah from **the pit of corruption** (v. 17), or the grave (see Ps. 55:23). Hezekiah was as good as dead until God reached down and rescued him from sheol itself. The Lord had also brought forgiveness of **sins**; physical and spiritual healing are often joined together (see 53:4–5). God not only removes sins from his sight; He also puts sin out of reach (see Mic. 7:19; Ps. 103:12), out of mind (see Jer. 31:34), and out of existence (see Isa. 43:25; Ps. 51:1, 9; Acts 3:19). Hezekiah's claims that **the grave cannot praise thee** (v. 18) or that the dead are without **hope** reflect the limited understanding of life after death in the Old Testament, while the New Testament provides a more complete understanding of the idea that death is the believer's ultimate deliverance because the gospel of Christ has "brought ... immortality to light" (2 Tim. 1:10). Hezekiah fulfilled his vow of **praise** (v. 19; see Ps. 66:13–14) by going to the temple and offering praise through singing and instrumental music. Hezekiah loved God's **house** (v. 20) and looked forward to spending all of his **days** there (see Ps. 23:6).

38:21–22. Isaiah instructed the court physicians to administer **a plaister** (v. 21) of **figs** as treatment for Hezekiah's illness. Figs were used for medicinal purposes in ancient Ugarit, and this passage demonstrates that praying for healing from God and receiving the best medical care possible are not inconsistent. **The sign** (v. 22) that Hezekiah asked about perhaps involved the healing of the boil as confirmation of the king's total healing from his disease.

C. The Babylonian Exile Predicted (chap. 39)

39:1–2. Merodach-baladan (v. 1), the **king of Babylon**, sent envoys to congratulate Hezekiah on his recovery from illness, but the real intent of their visit was to seek the support of Hezekiah and Judah in a military campaign against Assyria. Merodach-baladan reigned from 721–710 BC and again from 705–703 BC and staged several organized revolts against the hated Assyrians to the north. Hezekiah

responded favorably to the envoys and gave them **gold** (v. 2), **silver**, and other gifts from the royal treasuries to enlist Babylon's help against the Assyrian threat that Judah was experiencing at that time. Hezekiah made an unwise political decision because the tour of his palace and treasuries provided Merodach-baladan and his successors valuable information for exerting Babylonian control over Judah.

39:3–8. Isaiah confronted Hezekiah with his unwise decision to put his trust in man rather than in God for the protection of his kingdom. In contrast to the word of hope that Isaiah gave in 38:4–6, the prophet now issued a warning and a threat to Hezekiah. Isaiah's message to the king was that the people and wealth of Judah would be carried off to **Babylon** (v. 6) at a future time (vv. 5–7). This warning is the first mention of Babylon as Jerusalem's conqueror, though the Babylonian captivity is implied in 14:3–4. This prophecy must have taken Hezekiah by surprise in that Assyria, the dominant power of his day, was the threat he was most concerned with.

Hezekiah's recovery from illness in chapter 38 parallels Judah's fate in chapter 39. Hezekiah's life was extended by fifteen years, and Judah would not immediately experience the judgment of exile. The wickedness of Hezekiah's son Manasseh later became a major cause of the captivity (see 2 Kings 20:17; 21:11–15). Hezekiah's response of relief that the judgment would not fall in his lifetime seems somewhat self-centered, but it was also an acknowledgment of God's mercy in delaying the judgment that his foolish decision to seek help from Babylon deserved.

Part 2: The Book of Comfort (chaps. 40–66)

In chapters 1–35, Isaiah prophesied against the backdrop of the Assyrian threat against Judah and Jerusalem. The narratives in chapters 36–39 serve as a bridge between the first and second parts of the book, recording Assyria's failure and warning of the future rise of Babylon. The second part of the book focuses on the promise of Israel's deliverance from the Babylonian exile, and through divine inspiration, the prophet wrote as if Judah's Babylonian exile were almost over.

VIII. The Deliverance and Restoration of Israel (chap. 40–48)

A. The Coming of the Victorious God (chap. 40)

The Lord first called Isaiah to preach judgment until Judah was destroyed (see 6:1–11). He now commissioned Isaiah to announce a message of forgiveness and restoration to Israel (vv. 1–11). Through the prophet, the Lord proclaimed pardon for Israel's sin.

40:1–5. The Mosaic law had warned that Israel would have to pay for its sins through the experience of captivity (see Lev. 25:46), and Israel had in fact paid a **double** (or "full"; v. 2) punishment (see the "two things" of 51:19).

Three voices announced the coming salvation (v. 3, 40:6, 40:9), each showing how the comfort of 40:1 would come about. The unidentified first **voice** (v. 3) announced the coming of the Lord to Jerusalem as He brought Israel home from exile, and the language of verses 3–4 has in view the ancient Near Eastern custom of sending representatives ahead to prepare the way for the visit of a monarch. The voice commanded the preparation of a highway for the Lord's procession to Jerusalem, which involved removing obstacles in the path and making the road level and straight. The New Testament links this unidentified voice with John the Baptist (see Matt. 3:3; Mark 1:3; Luke 3:4; John 1:23), who called for Israel's repentance in preparation for the coming of their Messiah. God would reveal His **glory** (v. 5) for all nations to see by redeeming Israel from her Babylonian bondage. Ultimately, the glory of the redeeming God would be seen in Jesus Christ (see John 1:14; Heb. 1:3), especially at His return (see Matt. 16:27; 24:30; Rev. 1:7) and also in the lives of His redeemed people (see 1 Cor. 10:31; 2 Cor. 3:18).

40:6–8. A second **voice** (v. 6) called Isaiah to remind the people of the difference between humans and God. Human life is temporal, here today and gone tomorrow, like **grass** (v. 7) and flowers that wither in the hot sun (see 37:27; 51:12). Even the power of Assyria and Babylon, which seemed so permanent, would soon vanish. In contrast, **the word of God ... shall stand for ever** (v. 8). God's purposes would be carried out, and the plans of nations who opposed God would not prevail (see 8:10).

40:9–11. The third voice called for the announcement of **good tidings** (v. 9) that God was leading His people back to the land so that all could hear. The New Testament expands on this "good tidings" or "gospel" to refer to the salvation that God brings to all people (see 1 Cor. 15:1–4). The prophet announced, **Behold your God** as He returns to Jerusalem, words that apply to the return from exile (see 52:7–9), the first coming of Christ (see Matt. 21:5), and the second coming of Christ (see 62:11; Rev. 22:12). The deliverance of Israel from the Babylonian exile points to God's ultimate salvation of His people, and the prophet blended the immediate deliverance from exile with God's full and final salvation in the last days leading to His kingdom on earth. The Lord would return with both power (**his arm shall rule**; v. 10) and gentleness (He feeds, gathers, and carries **his flock**; v. 11).

40:12–31. Building on the previous section, this passage focuses on God's work as Creator of the universe and raises a series of rhetorical questions used to persuade the people to trust in the Lord, who has the ability to deliver, strengthen, and restore His people. The people needed to remember that Babylon was nothing compared to the Lord.

40:12–14. The prophet portrayed the Lord as a master craftsman sitting at His workbench, designing the creation (see Prov. 8:22–31). The images of the Lord measuring the waters in His palm, marking off the heavens with the **span** (v. 12) of His hand, and putting **the dust of the earth** in His basket are pictures of the immensity and greatness of God that served as reminders that God was fully capable of carrying out His promise to redeem Israel. Isaiah's portrayal of the Lord also reflects that no one can match God in skill or wisdom (v. 14). God needed no outside advice or counsel in carrying out the work of creation.

40:15–20. In contrast to God, man and **nations** (v. 15) are nothing more than **a drop of a bucket.** The forests of **Lebanon** (v. 16) could not provide enough wood and animals for the sacrifices needed to do justice to God's greatness. The Lord is also superior to the idols worshiped by the nations (vv. 18 – 20). More than any other prophet, Isaiah showed the utter folly of worshiping idols. His sarcastic caricature, satire, and denunciation of these false gods reach a peak in 44:9 – 20 (see also 41:7, 22 – 24; 42:17; 46:5 – 7; 48:5). He demonstrated the foolishness of idol worship by focusing on how an idol is made. The idolater worships an object made by human hands out of **gold** (v. 19) or **silver**. The person too poor to purchase gold or silver for the making of an idol must select a wood that **will not rot** (v. 20) away. The idol has to be properly constructed so that it will not topple over. While the Lord is Creator, the idols worshiped by the Babylonians were only lifeless objects made by man.

40:21 – 24. Beginning with these verses, Isaiah highlighted the distinctiveness of the Lord compared to these idols and continued the focus on God's work as Creator. The Lord is sovereign over His creation and sits above all **upon the circle** ("horizon," see Job 22:14) **of the earth** (v. 22). People are nothing more than **grasshoppers** in His sight. The Lord stretches out the earth like **a tent** (see Pss. 19:14; 104:2). **The princes** (v. 23) and **the judges of the earth**, who appear mighty, are reduced to **nothing** before God (see Jer. 25:17 – 26).

40:25 – 26. Apparently, some Israelite doubters were comparing their God with the gods of their captors and believed that the Lord was failing the test, as reflected in the rhetorical question, **To whom then will ye liken me?** (v. 25). The reality is that God has no equal. The Lord created even the stars that the nations worshiped as deities (v. 26).

40:27 – 31. After focusing on the greatness and majesty of God as Creator, the prophet stressed the goodness of God. Such a God was able to deliver and restore His distressed people if they would wait in faith for Him to act. The Lord never grows tired or weary, and He is willing to share this strength with His people (vv. 28 – 29). Israel's responsibility was to **wait upon the Lord** (v. 31), to trust God, and to look expectantly for Him to act (see 5:2; 49:23). Those

who trust in the Lord will **renew their strength**. The word "renew" denotes an exchange and is used for changing clothes (see Gen. 35:12; Judg. 14:12). Their weakness will give way to God's strength. They will become like **eagles**, which are known for their vigor (see Ps. 103:5) and speed (see Jer. 4:13; 48:40).

B. The Lord of History (chap. 41)

41:1 – 7. The call for the peoples to renew their strength (40:31) was a challenge for the nations and their gods to display the same power and wisdom as Israel's God. The nations had trusted in their idols, but only the Lord has the power to control and direct history. The Lord would raise up **the righteous man from the east** (v. 2), a reference to Cyrus, the Persian king who would conquer Babylon and make it possible for the Jews to return to their homeland (see 41:25; 44:28 – 45:5, 13; 46:11). Cyrus is called "righteous" because, like the Servant of the Lord in 42:6, he was chosen to carry out God's righteous purposes. The Lord is the one who **called him to his foot**, or who raised up and empowered Cyrus to rule. Since the Lord was present when the first **generations** (v. 4) were called and will be there with the **last** of them, He is the eternal Lord of history and the nations (see Heb. 13:8; Rev. 1:8, 17; 21:6; 22:13). The Lord demonstrated His sovereignty over history by predicting the rise of Cyrus before it occurred. Isaiah used sarcasm and satire to portray the futile attempt of the nations to withstand Cyrus and his armies by making more gods (vv. 5 – 7).

41:8 – 10. **Israel** (v. 8) has a special relationship with the Lord as His **servant** and therefore did not need to fear as the nations did. The title "servant" is a significant term in chapters 41 – 53, referring sometimes to the nation of Israel and other times to an individual, the future Messiah. The title does not indicate a person of lowly status but rather one who occupies a special position in the royal administration of God's kingdom, such as Moses (see Exod. 14:31; Num. 12:7), David (see 2 Sam. 7:5, 8), or the prophets (see 2 Kings 17:13; Jer. 7:25). **Israel** has this special standing with the Lord because they are the descendants of **Abraham**, who was God's **friend** (see Gen. 18;

2 Chron. 20:7; James 2:23). Israel was called as God's servant **from the ends of the earth** (v. 9), from Mesopotamia at the call of Abraham and from Egypt at the time of the exodus. The call to **Fear ... not** (v. 10) frequently introduces a message of hope and salvation (see 41:13–14; 35:4; 43:1, 5). The Lord promised He would **uphold** Israel and give them strength and help with His **right hand**, the hand of power and salvation (see Exod. 15:6, 12; Pss. 20:6; 89:13).

41:11–16. The Lord would act for Israel by defeating their enemies (vv. 11–12). The Lord would **hold** (v. 13) Israel by the **hand** to keep them from stumbling. Israel was like a **worm** (v. 14) in her feeble and despised condition (see Job 25:6), but the Lord would be her **redeemer**. The Hebrew word "redeemer" refers to an obligated family protector and thus portrays the Lord as the Family Protector of Israel. The Lord is related to Israel as Father (63:16; 64:8) and Husband (54:5). As the Family Protector, the Lord would redeem their property (by regathering them to the land, 54:1–8), guarantee their freedom (35:9; 43:1–4), avenge them against their tormentors (47:3; 49:25–26), and secure their posterity for the future (61:8–9). Through the Lord's strength, Israel would become like a **sharp threshing instrument** (v. 15), a wooden sledge with iron **teeth** used to thresh grain, which would reduce the enemy to **chaff**.

41:17–20. During Israel's return from Babylon, God would provide **water** (v. 17) for the returning exiles in the same way that He had provided water for Israel in **the wilderness** (v. 18) under Moses (see Exod. 17:1–7; Num. 20:2–11). Trees would beautify the wilderness, and God would bring about these fruitful conditions as part of His new creation on Israel's behalf (vv. 19–20; see 65:17–18).

41:21–29. The LORD called on the nations and their idols to present their case. He called on the idols to declare **the former things** (v. 22), their earlier predictions and accomplishments, to prove their divine power. The idols were **further challenged** to prove their deity by predicting **future events** before they unfolded. The Lord is **superior to the gods** of the nations in His ability to **predict the future**, as He did in announcing the rise of Cyrus (see 41:2–3;

24–26). The idols were unable to meet these challenges because they are mute (v. 24). Unlike these silent and impotent gods, the Lord controls the affairs of history and **raised up** (v. 25) Cyrus to accomplish His purposes.

Cyrus is described as being **from the north** (v. 25), but he actually came from the east. Cyrus conquered a number of kingdoms north of Babylon early in his reign. From the perspective of a writer in Jerusalem, the north was generally the point of origin for Israel's oppressors (see 14:31; Jer. 1:14; 6:1; 46:20; 50:3). Now Israel's deliverer would come from the north as well. Cyrus was one who called on the **name** of the Lord, which does not mean he was a true believer but only that he recognized the Lord in his decree allowing Israel to return to her homeland (Ezra 1:2) and acknowledged the Lord as one god among many.

C. The Role and the Mission of the Servant (42:1–9)

42:1–9. This is the first of four "servant songs," in which "servant" refers to the Messiah (see also 49:1–6; 50:4–9; 52:13–53:12). This passage is quoted in part in Matthew 12:18–21 with reference to Christ. This individual **servant** (v. 1) would be the ideal of what God had designed for the nation of Israel. The nation was to be a kingdom of priests (Exod. 19:6), but the Messiah would be the High Priest who would atone for the sins of the world (53:4–12). Cyrus was the deliverer who would rescue Israel militarily by conquering Babylon, which would allow Israel to return to the homeland. The Servant was the deliverer who would solve Israel's spiritual problem by atoning for the nation's sins. Cyrus would deliver Israel from Babylon, but the Servant would deliver Israel, and ultimately the world, from the prison of sin (see v. 7).

In the royal terminology of the ancient Near East, "servant" meant something like "trusted envoy" or "confidential representative." The Servant would be God's "elect" representative and, like the Branch (i.e., the Messiah) in 11:1–2, would be empowered by the Spirit of God. The primary role of the Servant would be to **bring forth judgment** (justice) **to the Gentiles** (v. 1). The Servant would not be a typical ruler who leads by loud proclamations (v. 2); instead, He would bring peace (see 9:6) and would mend broken lives. **A bruised reed** (v. 3) is figurative of someone who is weak (see Ps. 72:2, 4). He would not fail in his mission to bring justice to **the earth** (v. 4) and would proclaim God's law to the distant peoples as a new Moses (see Deut. 18:15–18; Acts 3:21–23, 26). The Servant-Messiah would ultimately become **a covenant of the people** (v. 6), or a mediator of the covenant for the nation of Israel. He would fulfill the Davidic covenant as King (see 9:7) and would institute the new covenant by His death (see Jer. 31:31–34; Heb. 8:6–13). The work of the Messiah would also become **a light of the Gentiles** and bring blessing to all nations, in fulfillment of the promise to Abraham in Genesis 12:3 (see Rom. 4:16–17; Gal. 3:8–14). The Servant would bring justice by opening spiritually **blind eyes** (v. 7) and rescuing **prisoners**, from bondage in Babylon and also from spiritual bondage to sin (see 61:1; Luke 4:18).

D. Praise and Exhortation (42:10–25)

42:10–17. Isaiah called all peoples to join in **a new song** (v. 10) of **praise** to the Lord, in celebration of the "new things" (42:9) that would be accomplished through the work of the Servant. The Lord is portrayed as **a mighty man** (v. 13), a Warrior who would go out to fight as He did at the Red Sea (Exod. 15:3). The Lord **refrained** (v. 14) Himself during Israel's humiliation and exile. "Refrained" is the same word used to describe Joseph's restraint in controlling his emotions while testing his brothers (Gen. 43:31; 45:1). Though the Lord had been long-suffering, He would cry out like a **woman** (v. 14) in labor in giving full vent to His fury. The Lord would destroy the **mountains and hills** (v. 15) and dry up the waters of the earth, the opposite of the fruitful conditions that He would bring in connection with Israel's restoration (see 35:1–2; 41:18). The Lord's judgment would bring humiliation to the nations that had trusted in idols (v. 17).

42:18–25. To experience the Lord's promised deliverance and blessing, the exiles would need to recognize their spiritual blindness and deafness. Israel

was the Lord's appointed **messenger** (like a prophet; v. 19; see 44:26; Hag. 1:13) to declare God's glory to the nations, but Israel had failed in her mission. Instead of leading the nations to God, Israel worshiped idols and false gods and became like the nations. Israel had failed to listen to the Lord (v. 20), even though the Lord had magnified His **law** (v. 21) by communicating the commandments to Moses and the people in the awesome setting of Mount Sinai (see Exod. 34:29). If Israel had kept the law, she would have demonstrated to the nations the blessings of living under God's righteous rule (see Deut. 4:4–8).

Because of her sin, Israel would become a plundered people, first by the Assyrians (see 10:6) and then the Babylonians (see 39:6). The Lord had given **Jacob for … spoil** (v. 24). Babylon would conquer Israel, not because their gods were stronger than the Lord but because the Lord was punishing Israel (see 40:17–18; 1 Kings 20:23). Israel would have a foretaste of the day of the Lord (see 5:25; 9:12; 34:2) when the Lord poured out His **anger** (v. 25) on them.

E. The Regathering and Renewal of Israel (43:1–44:5)

43:1–7. Though **Israel** (v. 1) would experience God's punishment for its sin, the people were encouraged to **Fear not** because God had created them and was committed to His promise to redeem them (vv. 1–7). God made the nation of Israel as surely as He made the first man (see Gen. 1:27; 43:7, 15, 21; 44:2, 24). The picture of passing through **waters** (v. 2) and **rivers** is probably an allusion to crossing the Red Sea (Exod. 14:21–22) and the Jordan River (Josh. 3:14–17). Isaiah portrayed Israel's deliverance from Babylon as a second exodus, even greater in scope than the first, which had given birth to Israel as a nation (see 43:16–17; 44:27; 50:2; 51:10).

The Lord (v. 3) is the **Saviour** who would give other nations as a **ransom** for Israel. The Persian conquest of peoples such as **Egypt … Ethiopia** (Cush) **and Seba** (perhaps Sheba in southern Arabia) was God's reward for Persia's kindness to Israel (see Ezek. 29:19–20). The Lord loved Israel so much that He would allow other nations to experience oppression in her place. While these nations would experience defeat and conquest, the Lord would return the exiles of Israel from all points of the compass (vv. 5–7). In addition to speaking of Israel's deliverance from exile, this promise looks to the ultimate salvation and restoration of Israel in the last days (see Rom. 11:25–26).

43:8–13. The Lord assembled the nations in a courtroom setting to consider His superiority to their gods. The Lord had predicted the rescue of His **blind** (v. 8) and **deaf** people Israel before it ever happened (vv. 8–9). God's work on behalf of His servant Israel is proof of His saving power (vv. 10–12). The gods of the nations could not match or duplicate the works of God on behalf of Israel, and these gods were also impotent to keep the Lord from carrying out His purposes and plans (v. 13).

43:14–28. The Lord would bring about Israel's redemption by turning **Babylon** (v. 14) from being the oppressor to being the oppressed. The glorious **ships** of Babylon (see 2:16), used for trading and commerce on the Persian Gulf and the Tigris and Euphrates rivers, would one day become their means of flight from their enemies (see Jer. 51:13). In contrast, the Lord would make **a way** (v. 16) through **the sea** for Israel, as He did when He destroyed the chariots and horsemen of the pharaoh (vv. 15–17; see Exod. 14:28; 15:4). In this second exodus, the Lord would take care of Israel and provide for them as they made their difficult and arduous journey through the barren desert on their way home from Babylon (vv. 19–21).

In spite of the Lord's covenant faithfulness to Israel, Israel had not been faithful to the Lord. Their future salvation would come to pass because of God's grace, not their righteousness. The prayers of the Israelites had been halfhearted (v. 22). They may have brought their sacrifices, but in effect, their sacrifices had not counted because their hearts were not right with God (vv. 23–24; see 1:10–15). Israel had given diluted devotion to the Lord in spite of the fact that He had not placed excessive demands on them. God had not **wearied** (v. 23) Israel, but Israel had **wearied** (v. 24) the Lord.

Israel had continuously sinned, but the Lord would blot out their sins (v. 25). In spite of the pun-

ishment that Israel would have to suffer, God was eager to forgive His people (see 1:18; 40:2; 44:22). In verses 26–27, the Lord took Israel to court (as He did the nations in vv. 21–22) to convince Israel that they were a sinful people who were deserving of judgment. Their sin extended back to their **first father** (v. 27), Abraham (see Gen. 12:18; 20:9), and included their **teachers** (the priests and the prophets). Because of their sin, Israel had been given over to the **curse** (v. 28) of total destruction, the punishment reserved for any town of Israel that harbored idolatry (see Deut. 13:12–15). The Lord was willing to forgive, but Israel first had to acknowledge her sinfulness.

44:1–5. The Lord spoke with tenderness to provide further assurance of the coming deliverance and salvation of Israel. The Lord would act on behalf of His **servant** (v. 1), also referred to as **Jeshurun** ("the upright one"; v. 2), an ironic title in a context that has just highlighted Israel's sinfulness. This name appears elsewhere in Deuteronomy 32:15; 33:5, 26, a passage that refers to Israel's rebellion and the Lord's promise to help His people, themes that are also prominent in this section of Isaiah. The Lord would pour the **water** (v. 3) of blessing on the parched and thirsty nation of Israel so that they would flourish (see 30:25; 32:2; 35:6–7). The Lord will also pour out His Spirit on His people, a blessing associated with the messianic age (see 32:15; Joel 2:28).

F. The Only God (44:6–23)

44:6–8. God would act with power as **the King of Israel** (v. 6), the **redeemer**, and **the LORD of hosts**. The Lord is the incomparable Creator, **the first** and **the last**, and was fully able to accomplish His promise of salvation. Israel had no need to **be afraid** (v. 8).

44:9–20. These verses contain a satire on the folly of idolatry (see 40:18–20), once again stressing the Lord's superiority to the gods of the nations. The words **vanity** (v. 9) and **nothing** (v. 10) describe both the idol maker and the idols he produces. Two idols are described: a metal one (v. 12) and a wooden one (vv. 13–20); the latter was more common (see 40:20). The craftsman who makes the idol becomes tired and weary (v. 12), but God never tires (see

40:28). The idol is even beneath the craftsman; the idol is made in **the figure of a man** (v. 13; see Deut. 4:16; Rom. 1:23), but the man who makes the idol is made in the image of God (see Gen. 1:26–27).

The idol maker plants a tree (v. 14) and then uses part of the wood to make an idol and part of the wood as fuel to cook his food (vv. 15–16). Wood is used for both common and sacred purposes, and the wood used for common purposes at least has a practical function. The idol can do nothing to help or assist its maker. The idolater prays to an idol that cannot hear his request for help, but the idol worshiper lacks the spiritual discernment to recognize the foolishness of his actions (vv. 17–18). The description of closed **eyes** (v. 18) and **hearts** characterizes both the idols and those who worship them. The idol worshiper cannot see that he might as well be praying to **the stock of a tree** (v. 19) used to cook his food because trusting in idols is nothing more than feeding **on ashes** (v. 20). For Isaiah, idol worship was not only irrational; it was also evil. Idol worship is **an abomination** (v. 19), something that the Lord hates and detests (see Deut. 27:15; 1 Kings 11:5, 7; 2 Kings 23:13). The prophet declared that those who worship idols are also "an abomination" (41:24).

44:21–23. This section closes with the Lord calling on **Israel** (v. 21) to put their trust in Him, remembering that their faith in God was not in vain, unlike the faith of those who put their trust in worthless idols. Forgiveness was available because the Lord had **blotted out** (v. 22) their sins. As in 40:2, the suffering of Israel would pave the way for the forgiveness and restoration of the nation. The Lord called out to Israel: **Return unto me**, because repentance was the condition for Israel receiving God's forgiveness and experiencing the promised restoration.

G. Cyrus and the Return of the Exiles (44:24–45:8)

This passage contains the second promise concerning the rise of Cyrus, which would enable the Jews to return to their homeland (see 41:2–3, 25–26), and even mentions him by name. While some dismiss the name of Cyrus as a later insertion or a prophecy written after the fact, the naming of Cyrus more than 150 years before his rise is central to the theology of this section of the book of Isaiah. The Lord's ability to announce the future before it happens is proof of His sovereignty and provides confirmation of the Lord's ability to fulfill His promises to the people of Israel. To deny that the naming of Cyrus is a supernatural prophecy strips away an important tenet of the message of Isaiah.

44:24–27. The Lord (v. 24) is the **redeemer** and Creator. Thus, pagan omen readers and soothsayers cannot use their mantic practices to thwart God's plans for the future (vv. 24–25). The Lord frustrates those who use **tokens** ("omens"; v. 25) to predict the future. God causes **diviners** (a term used for Balaam, Josh. 13:22; the witch of Endor, 1 Sam. 28:8; and false prophets, Jer. 27:9) to look foolish because their predictions do not come to pass. The Lord directs and controls history, and the predictions of His true prophets concerning the restoration of Israel will be fulfilled (vv. 26–27).

44:28–45:8. The Lord announced in advance that **Cyrus** (v. 28) would be His **shepherd**, a term often applied to rulers (see 2 Sam. 5:2; Jer. 23:2). Cyrus is also called the Lord's **anointed** (45:1), the Hebrew term from which the word "Messiah" comes. These titles were applied to Cyrus because the Lord would use this pagan ruler to carry out His sovereign purposes (see 10:5–6; Jer. 25:9; 27:6; 43:10). The decree of Cyrus (Ezra 1:2–4; 6:3–5) would authorize the rebuilding of the temple, which would lead to a restored Jerusalem (see 45:13). The Servant, Christ (see 42:1–4; called "the Messiah," i.e., "the Anointed One," in Dan. 9:25–26; see also Psalm 2) will bring about Israel's ultimate salvation and restoration. God called Cyrus **by … name** (v. 3), demonstrating His control over Cyrus's activities, and would use Cyrus to demonstrate His power. The Lord gave Cyrus the honor of being His servant even though the Persian ruler did not personally know the Lord (v. 4). Cyrus apparently worshiped the chief Babylonian deity, Marduk, whom he praised in his inscriptions. The Lord's use of Cyrus to accomplish His plans would cause all nations to acknowledge His sovereignty and incomparability (vv. 7–8).

H. A Call for the Nations to Recognize the Lord's Sovereignty (45:9–25)

This section returns to the theme of God's role in creation and calls for all people to recognize God's sovereignty.

45:9–13. For humans to resist God is like the clay attempting to resist the potter (v. 9; see 29:16; Jer. 18:6) or like a child attempting to resist **his father** (v. 10). As the Creator, the Lord has the power and authority to direct even a powerful ruler like Cyrus as His instrument (v. 13). Cyrus would do God's will without receiving **price** or **reward** (v. 13) since God would not receive payment when He sold the Israelites into bondage in Babylon (see 52:3).

45:14–19. Ultimately, the Lord will cause all nations to submit to Israel (v. 14). Israel's future domination over her former enemies and the nations' bringing tribute to Israel in acknowledgment of Israel's sovereignty are prominent themes in the book of Isaiah (see 11:14; 14:1–2; 49:23; 54:3; 60:11–14). The kingdom age will be like the ideal days of the past, during the Davidic and Solomonic empires, when surrounding nations gave their tribute to the Davidic ruler in Jerusalem (see 1 Kings 4:7–19; 10:14–15). The nations will also acknowledge Israel's God (see v. 23; 19:23–25; Zech. 8:20–23), and Israel will never again be put to shame by her enemies (vv. 16–17). The Lord's redemption and restoration of Israel will be like a new creation (v. 18). The Lord acted in creation to bring order out of chaos so that the earth would be inhabited. The Holy Land would be empty and chaotic because of the Babylonian exile (a return to the conditions of Gen. 1:2), but the land would soon have inhabitants (see 44:26, 28) and be orderly again.

45:20–25. Because of His incomparability, the Lord again appealed to the pagan nations to abandon their gods. Ultimately, all peoples will acknowledge the Lord's sovereignty and **bow** (v. 23) before Him, a passage Paul quoted in Romans 14:11 and Philippians 2:10–11 with reference to the exalted position of Christ. The Lord's call for the pagans to abandon their idols also served as a reminder for Israel to never return to her idolatrous ways, and one of the positive results of the Babylonian captivity would be that Israel would essentially be cured of her idolatrous tendencies.

I. The Lord's Sovereignty and the Fall of Babylon (chaps. 46–47)

1. The Lord's Superiority over Babylon's Gods (chap. 46)

Chapters 46–47 focus on the impending defeat and fall of Babylon. Chapter 46 stresses that Babylon would fall because the Lord is superior to the gods of the nations.

46:1–4. **Bel** (v. 1) is another name for Marduk, the chief deity of Babylon, and means "lord" (equivalent to the Canaanite "Baal"). **Nebo** refers to Nabu, the god of learning and writing who was the son of Marduk. These gods would stoop in defeat and would join their worshipers in **captivity** (v. 2). Unlike the helpless idols of Babylon, which were a heavy burden that had to be carried, the Lord would carry His people when He brought them home from exile. The Lord had sustained Israel **from the womb** (v. 3) and will sustain her until her **old age** (v. 4).

46:5–7. The gods made out of **gold** (v. 6) and **silver** cannot compare to the Lord. Idols have to be carried because they cannot move, they cannot answer in response to the prayers of their worshipers, and they cannot **save** or deliver out of **trouble** (v. 7). Isaiah repeatedly mocked the gods of the nations and the absurdity of making idols objects of faith and devotion (see 40:18–20; 44:9–20).

46:8–13. The Lord alone has the power to predict the future and to direct history to accomplish His purposes (vv. 8–10). The Lord would demonstrate this power by raising up Cyrus as **a ravenous bird from the east** (v. 11). Cyrus would swoop down on his enemies with the swiftness and power of a bird of prey (see 8:8; Dan. 8:4). The unrighteous and **stouthearted** ("stubborn"; v. 12) Babylonians would see the Lord bring His **righteousness** (salvation; v. 13) to Israel in demonstration of His **glory**.

2. The Fall of Babylon (chap. 47)

47:1–8. Babylon would fall because of her trust in inferior gods. The city of Babylon and its inhabitants are personified as the **virgin daughter**

of Babylon (v. 1), who would suffer shame and humiliation because of how she had treated the "virgin daughter" of Zion. The daughter of Babylon would sit in the dust as a sign of mourning after experiencing military defeat (see 3:26). Taken away in exile, this former queen would perform the menial task of grinding meal (v. 2a; see Exod. 15:11; Judg. 9:53). Her nakedness (v. 3) would be uncovered as she was reduced to nothing more than a slave girl or prostitute (vv. 2b–3). The Lord would carry out this judgment, and the warning that the Lord would not meet Babylon as a man (v. 3) literally means that He would befriend no one and extend no mercy to the Babylonians. As Israel's Redeemer, the Lord would take away Babylon's exalted position as queen (The lady of kingdoms; v. 5). The Lord would use Babylon to judge Israel because of His anger over Israel's sin (v. 6; see Isa. 10:5–6), and Israel's suffering was necessary to fulfill Moses' curse for covenant disobedience (see Deut. 28:49–50). Babylon, however, would carry God's punishment to excess with their cruel treatment of the ancient ("the elderly"; v. 6). Babylon arrogantly believed that she would never fall and boastfully claimed, I am, and none else besides me (v. 8), words that echo the Lord's assertions of incomparability in 43:11; 45:5–6, 18, 22. Babylon dwellest carelessly (see 32:9, 11), with a false sense of security, which the Lord was about to shatter.

47:9–15. The proud queen would become a childless widow because of her sorceries, and ... enchantments (v. 9), magical practices carried out to avoid danger and to inflict harm on the enemy (see 3:2–3). Babylon probably utilized the services of astrologers more than any other nation (see Dan. 2:2, 10), but their stargazing would do nothing to prevent the Lord's judgment from falling on them. Babylon would be consumed like stubble (v. 14) in a fire. The Babylonians would not be able to deliver themselves, but the mighty Savior of Israel was perfectly able to deliver His people (see 43:3).

J. The Lord's Exhortations to His People (chap. 48)

48:1–11. The prophet stressed that Israel had to turn from her sinful ways to experience the Lord's deliverance. The Lord reminded Israel of her heritage as His covenant people. In spite of her great privileges, Israel's devotion to the Lord had been tainted by hypocrisy (vv. 1–2). The people took oaths in the name of the Lord but were insincere in their commitments. The citizens of Jerusalem viewed themselves as residents of the holy city (v. 2), but their lifestyles were corrupt and sinful (see 1:21–23). They claimed to trust the Lord (stay themselves upon the God of Israel; v. 2), but their source of security was elsewhere (see 31:1; 36:6, 9).

Because of Israel's obstinate (v. 4) heart, the Lord announced their deliverance and future blessings in advance so that the people would not be tempted to attribute their salvation to the idols they had followed in the past (vv. 4–7). Israel needed to take these promises to heart and truly listen to the word of the Lord because her past history was one of stubborn refusal to hear and obey the Lord (v. 8). The Lord's purpose in judging Israel was not to destroy His people but rather to refine them (vv. 9–10). The use of refining and purifying fire is a common Old Testament image for God's judgment (see Deut. 4:20; Jer. 11:4; Jer. 9:7; Ezek. 22:18–22). The fall of Jerusalem and the Babylonian exile would provide a similar furnace of affliction (v. 10) for God's people. Though much of Israel's past history had been negative, the Lord would act in judgment to produce true faith and devotion in the hearts of His people. The Lord would deliver Israel to vindicate and glorify His own name (v. 11) by reversing the dishonor brought on His reputation by the fall of Jerusalem and the scattering of His people (see Ezek. 36:20–23).

48:12–22. The Lord called on Israel (v. 12) to hear His word and recognize His sovereignty. Here God's sovereignty is once again connected to His role as Creator (v. 13) and His work of raising up Cyrus to deliver Israel from exile. The Lord loved (v. 14) Cyrus by choosing him to carry out His special purposes and would cause Cyrus to prosper in every way. An unidentified speaker in verse 16 declared that Israel should be fully aware of God's plans for Cyrus because these predictions had not been made in secret.

The Lord warned Israel that she must not continue to disregard and ignore His word as she had in the past (vv. 17–19). The Lord had made His message clear, and Israel had no excuse for not paying attention to what He had told them. If Israel had obeyed the Lord's commands, they would have experienced **peace** like **a river, and … righteousness as the waves of the sea** (v. 18), images of abundant and overflowing blessing (see 45:8; Amos 5:24). Peace and righteousness are linked together throughout Isaiah (9:7; 32:17; 54:13–14; 60:17), and God's people could not experience the blessing of peace without practicing a lifestyle of righteousness. Israel had forfeited the blessing of numerous descendants, promised to Abraham, because of her past disobedience (v. 19; see Gen. 13:16; 22:17) and had to be careful not to miss out on the salvation that God had promised for the future.

As elsewhere in the book, Isaiah portrayed Israel's leaving **Babylon** (v. 20) as a second exodus. This exodus would surpass the first in that the Jews would not have to leave Babylon in haste as they had left Egypt (52:12). They were encouraged to depart quickly, however, because of the judgment that would soon fall on Babylon. This is the last mention of Babylon by name in Isaiah. In the book of Revelation, God's judgment of Babylon in the Old Testament prefigures God's final judgment on His enemies in the last days (see Revelation 18). When Israel left Babylon, the Lord would provide for them in **the deserts** (v. 21) as He had in the days of Moses (Exod. 17:6; Num. 20:11). On their way home from exile, God's people would have water in the wilderness.

IX. The Servant's Ministry and Israel's Restoration (chaps. 49–57)

A. The Servant's Mission to Israel and the Nations (49:1–13)

49:1–7. This is the second of the servant songs in Isaiah (see 42:1–4). The Servant announced that the Lord had given Him a mission to the Gentiles (**isles … people, from afar**; v. 1). He would be called to this mission **from the womb**, as were Jeremiah (Jer. 1:5) and Paul (Gal. 1:15), and He would declare and bring

about God's judgment on the wicked. The Servant's words are powerful, **like a sharp sword** (v. 2; see 11:4), and the Servant himself is **a polished shaft**, a special arrow kept in top condition until time for its use ("arrows" are used of God's judgment in Deut. 32:23, 42). The **servant** (v. 3) is called **Israel**, but "servant" here cannot refer literally to the nation of Israel, since in verse 5, the "servant" is said to have a mission to Israel. Rather, the "servant" here is the Messiah, the ideal Israel, through whom the Lord will be glorified. He will succeed where national Israel failed and will ultimately enable Israel to fulfill its servant role as God's messenger to the nations (compare 42:18–22).

Despite the power of His words, the Servant would claim to **have laboured in vain** (v. 4). Just as the nation of Israel had toiled in vain (see 65:23), so Christ would encounter strong opposition during His ministry and would temporarily suffer apparent failure. The suffering Servant theme is expanded on in the third and fourth servant songs (50:4–9; 52:13–53:12).

The Servant's mission would first be to **bring Jacob again to him** (v. 5), to release Israel from the Babylonian captivity (see 49:9–12, 22; 41:2) and from the greater captivity of sin (42:7) and would then extend to being **a light** (v. 6) to all nations. Along with Genesis 12:1–3 and Exodus 19:5–6, this verse is sometimes called "the great commission of the Old Testament" and was quoted in part by Paul and Barnabas with reference to their missionary outreach to the Gentiles (Acts 13:47). The fulfillment of this passage began with the church's efforts to proclaim the gospel to all nations and will climax with the submission of the nations to Christ in His future kingdom (see 2:1–4). Christ is the light of the world (Luke 2:30–32; John 8:12), and Christians are to reflect His light (Matt. 5:14). The end result of the Lord's deliverance of Israel is that former oppressors will bow before a restored Jerusalem in recognition of the Lord's power and sovereignty (see 52:15; 60:14).

49:8–13. The deliverance and restoration of Israel would be **a day of salvation** (v. 8). The background of this verse is probably the Year of Jubilee (see 61:1–2; Lev. 25:10). The return from exile would bring the same restoration of land for the people as that year of liberty did. The Servant would restore Israel's **desolate heritages**, acting as a new Joshua in dividing the land among the individual tribes and families (see Josh. 14:1–5). The Servant would also be a new Moses in leading the Jews through the wilderness as they returned home (vv. 9–10). Israel would enjoy the bounty of a fruitful land in her restoration (vv. 11–13).

B. The Repopulation of Zion (49:14–26)

49:14–16. The Lord would bring comfort to Israel because He is eternally committed to His people and His covenant promises. The exile would cause some to question God's love for Israel, but God's love for His people surpasses that of a mother for her children (vv. 14–15). The Lord had inscribed Israel on **the palms of** His **hands** (v. 16), just as the name of the tribes of Israel were engraved on stones and fastened to the ephod of the high priest as a memorial before the Lord (Exod. 28:9–12; see Song 8:6).

49:17–21. There would be a reversal when Israel's enemies departed from her and she returned to the homeland (v. 17). The beautiful clothes and jewels of **a bride** (v. 18) symbolize the strength and joy that God would bring His people. The exile would leave the land barren and desolate, but Israel's restoration would cause the city of Jerusalem to be too small for all of its **inhabitants** (v. 19). Jerusalem would no longer be a barren woman (see 54:1). This prophecy was partially fulfilled in the return from Babylon but will have its ultimate fulfillment when Christ returns to establish His kingdom on earth (see Zech. 2:1–5).

49:22–26. The theme of reversal continues. The Gentile nations would come to Jerusalem, not to attack the city but to acknowledge the Lord. The oppressors who would take Israel away in exile would become **nursing fathers, and ... mothers** (v. 23) who would bring the people home. The oppressors of Israel would eat their own children (v. 26), just as the inhabitants of Jerusalem had been reduced to cannibalism during the siege of the city (see Lam. 4:20). The Lord's deliverance would be full and complete.

C. Israel's Sin and the Servant's Obedience (chap. 50)

50:1–3. Israel's sin led the LORD (v. 1) to temporarily divorce His people. **The bill of ... divorcement** refers to the husband's obligation to provide a legal certificate to the wife he wished to divorce (see Deut. 24:1–3; Matt. 19:7; Mark 10:4). According to Jeremiah 3:8, God gave the northern kingdom her certificate of divorce, and Isaiah 54:6–7 indicates that God had also left Judah. Isaiah's point seems to be that God did not initiate the divorce; Judah broke her relationship with Him. Israel was also responsible for selling herself into slavery. If a man's debts were not paid, his children could be sold into slavery (see 1 Kings 4:1). But since God has no **creditors**, the Israelites had **sold** themselves. Israel had also failed to respond to the Lord's calls to return to Him and to put their trust in Him (vv. 2–3). Israel was deaf toward God (see 6:10; 66:4) and acted as if the Lord lacked the power to save His people, forgetting that God was the one who had brought Israel through the Red Sea (**I dry up the sea**; v. 2) and had caused the plagues that fell on Egypt (**fish stinketh**; see Exod. 7:18; **clothe the heavens with blackness**; v. 3; see Exod. 10:21).

50:4–9. The obedient Servant in the third servant song (see 42:1–9; 49:1–7) is the perfect contrast to sinful Israel. The faithful Servant would speak words of encouragement to the **weary** (v. 4) and be obedient to the Lord's word, unlike Israel. An open **ear** (v. 5) is a sign of obedience (see 1:19; Ps. 40:6). The Servant would willingly suffer to fulfill God's calling and mission (v. 6). He would endure beatings that were reserved for criminals or fools (see Prov. 10:13; 26:3; Matt. 27:26; John 19:1). Plucking a person's beard was a sign of disrespect and contempt (see 2 Sam. 10:4–5; Neh. 13:25). The Servant's enemies would spit on Him to show their hatred (see Job 30:10) and to insult Him (see Deut. 25:9; Job 17:6; Matt. 27:30). This treatment anticipates the Servant's ultimate suffering, described in 52:13–53:12.

In spite of the horrible suffering He would endure, the Servant would be firm in His confidence that the Lord was with Him and would **help** (v. 7) Him. Through the Lord's help, the Servant would ultimately be honored (see 49:7; 52:13; 53:10–12).

Confident that the Lord would ultimately vindicate Him, the Servant would serve with great determination (**I set my face like a flint**; v. 7), just as Jesus "stedfastly set his face to go to Jerusalem" (see Luke 9:51), knowing what awaited Him when He arrived. No one would be able to contend with the Servant or bring charges of wrongdoing against Him. While the Servant would ultimately triumph, His enemies would become like **old … garment[s]** (v. 9) consumed by moths (see 51:8).

50:10–11. The prophet called on Israel to trust in the Lord in the same way the Servant did. Isaiah also warned that those who **kindle[d] a fire** (v. 11) of wickedness would be consumed by their own evil actions.

D. The Remnant Comforted because of Their Glorious Prospect (51:1–52:12)

51:1–3. The righteous could look to the Lord as their **rock** (v. 1), confident and secure in His ability to redeem them. If the Lord was able to raise up a great nation from **Abraham** (v. 2) and **Sarah** when they could not even produce an heir, He surely would be able to make Israel a great nation in spite of their condition in exile. He would turn the ruins of **Zion** (v. 3) into a paradise **like Eden**.

51:4–8. In delivering Israel from exile, the Lord would execute justice on the nations (vv. 4–5). The Lord would fight against them with His powerful **arms** (v. 5), but then the nations would learn to **trust** in the Lord and to lean on His strong **arm**. Ultimately, salvation will come to all nations through Christ. The Lord's judgment will devastate the **earth** (v. 6) and destroy the wicked, but the Lord's **salvation** will last **for ever** for those who trust in Him (vv. 6–8).

51:9–11. With the double command **Awake, awake** (v. 9), the people called for God to carry out the salvation He had promised. They could not understand why God had powerfully defeated His enemies in the past but failed to act on their behalf in their day. The Lord's victory over Egypt at the Red Sea is depicted as the defeat of **Rahab** (v. 9), the sea monster from Canaanite mythology (see 27:1; 30:7; Job 26:12; Ps. 89:10). With this imagery, the people

asserted that the Lord is King and that no rival power can stand against Him. They longed for God to intervene so that they could **return** (v. 11) to **Zion** with joyful celebration.

51:12–23. The Lord responded that Israel's lack of faith was the reason for the delay of their deliverance (vv. 12–13). They feared the Babylonians, who were men, but had forgotten that the Lord is the Creator who possesses infinite power. The exiles would be set free when the Lord performed an exodus-like deliverance in bringing them out of Babylon (vv. 14–16). Zion was exhorted to **Awake, awake** (v. 17; see 51:9), because the people needed to respond in faith to the Lord's promise of salvation (vv. 17–23). Jerusalem would stagger like a drunken woman after drinking from the cup of God's wrath, but her time of judgment would come to an end. Experiencing God's judgment is often compared to becoming drunk on strong wine; it is the fate of wicked nations in particular (see 29:9; 63:6; Jer. 25:15–16; Ezek. 23:32–34). Jerusalem would have no one to care for her in her pathetic condition because her children would be taken away, but the Lord would act to remove **the cup of trembling** (vv. 17, 22) from Zion's hands. Judgment would then be transferred to the enemies of Zion that had mercilessly trampled the city.

52:1–6. The call **Awake, awake** (v. 1) repeats 51:9, 17 and announces that the Lord's deliverance was near. The drama of Zion's transformation, which is central to the book of Isaiah, is played out in this section as the drunken woman is called to become a beautifully adorned bride. Zion would arise **from the dust** (v. 2), a fate contrasting to the one prophesied for Babylon in 47:1. The Lord would redeem His people for the sake of His reputation (vv. 3–6). The captivity brought disrespect to God because it appeared that the gods of other nations were more powerful (see 36:20–23). Assyria itself had claimed to be more powerful than the Lord (37:23–24). The deliverance from exile would demonstrate, even to Israel, the greatness of the Lord's sovereign power to carry out what He has promised.

52:7–12. In prophetically proclaiming the **good tidings** (v. 7) of Israel's deliverance from exile, the prophet compared himself to a messenger running from the scene of battle to bring news of the outcome to a waiting king and people (see 2 Sam. 18:24–27). The **watchmen** (v. 8) of Jerusalem eagerly stood on the walls to receive this message of salvation (see 62:6–7). The messenger announced to Israel **Thy God reigneth!** (v. 7). The return of God's people to Jerusalem would emphasize His sovereign rule over the world and the infinite power of **his holy arm** (v. 10) to subjugate His enemies. In preparing to leave Babylon, the exiles would need to purify themselves from the pagan idols and influences they had encountered in Babylon (vv. 11–12). They were to be consecrated to the Lord because they would have the special privilege of returning to Jerusalem **the vessels** (v. 11) of the Lord's house, which Nebuchadnezzar would take to Babylon. The decree allowing the people to take back these articles of the temple would be issued by Cyrus (see Ezra 1:7–11). Israel's deliverance from exile would be superior even to the exodus from Egypt because there would be no need to hurry from their captors (see Exod. 12:39; 14:5–8). The Lord would both **go before** (v. 12) His people and be their **rearward** ("rear guard"; see Exod. 13:21; 14:29–30).

E. The Sufferings and Glories of the Lord's Righteous Servant (52:13–53:12)

This section represents the fourth and longest of the four servant songs (see 42:1–4). It constitutes the central and most important unit in chapters 40–66 as well as in chapters 49–57. This servant song is quoted in the New Testament more than any other Old Testament passage and is often referred to as "the gospel of Isaiah" because of its portrayal of the sufferings of the Servant-Messiah.

52:13–15. The Lord had promised to powerfully redeem His people Israel from bondage, but the manner in which the Lord would bring about this salvation contained a surprise element: it would involve the suffering of the Lord's **servant** (v. 13) on Israel's behalf. Though He would suffer greatly, the Servant would ultimately **be exalted and extolled**, words used to describe the Lord Himself in Isaiah's vision in 6:1. **The kings** (v. 15) of the nations would

be amazed (**shut their mouths**) at the transformation when the Lord exalted the Servant who had been **marred** (v. 14) by His enemies to the extent that He no longer appeared human.

53:1–6. The people of Israel expressed their own astonishment and initial unbelief concerning the servant. This passage looks forward to the time when Israel will recognize the Servant as their Messiah and Savior. **Who hath believed our report?** (v. 1) should be read, "Who has believed the report delivered to us?" The Lord promised to bare His **arm** and to act as the deliverer of His people, but here Israel confessed her initial failure in seeing how the Lord could bring salvation through a weak and pathetic figure like the Servant. He would be **a tender plant** (v. 2) with humble beginnings, unassuming in His appearance. He would be **despised and rejected of men** (v. 3), who would view His suffering as God's just punishment for His wickedness. What Israel would fail to see and here prophetically acknowledges is that the Servant suffered on Israel's behalf: **he was wounded for our transgressions, he was bruised for our iniquities** (v. 5). The Servant's suffering would bring healing to the sinful people of Israel, who had wandered from God like stray **sheep** (v. 6). The word **healed** (v. 5) is a figure for forgiveness and in this context does not imply that physical healing is one of the benefits of Christ's atonement (see 6:10; Jer. 30:17; 1 Peter 2:24).

This passage is often understood as providing a detailed and factual prediction or description of how Jesus would die on the cross as the suffering Servant. Certain details do remarkably correspond to what Jesus endured on the cross, but the primary intent of this song was to describe the Servant's suffering with highly figurative and emotional language to highlight the extent of His intense suffering. Four dominant images are joined together to provide a portrayal of the worst imaginable suffering a person can endure. The first image is that the Servant would suffer like a person afflicted with a terrible illness. The word **stricken** (v. 4) is associated with disease in Genesis 12:17 and 2 Kings 15:5. The second image is that the Servant would suffer like a criminal **bruised** (v. 5) by the physical beating He would receive for His crimes (see Deut. 25:3). The irony is that He would receive **the chastisement** for the crimes of others. The idea conveyed is that the Servant-Messiah would die a violent death, like that of a common criminal.

53:7–12. The third image compares the Servant to **a lamb** (v. 7) led away **to the slaughter**, a figure stressing the innocence and vulnerability of the Servant, as well as His willing compliance to the fate of dying on behalf of others. The Servant would **openeth not his mouth** (v. 7) before His accusers, just as Jesus remained silent before the chief priests and Pilate (see Matt. 27:12–14; Mark 14:60–61; 15:4–5; John 19:8–9). The fourth and most significant image is one of sacrifice and atonement, stressing the vicarious nature of the Servant's suffering and death. "The Lord hath laid on him the iniquity of us all" (53:6) recalls the Day of Atonement and how the priest laid his hands on the scapegoat and symbolically placed Israel's sins on it (see Lev. 16:21). The sacrifice of sheep was a prominent feature of Israel's sacrificial system, and John the Baptist would later declare Jesus to be "the Lamb of God" (John 1:29, 36). The mission of the Servant would entail suffering and death because the Lord would **make his soul an offering for sin** (v. 10).

After his death, the Servant would be buried **with the wicked** (v. 9). The manner of His death would indicate that as far as those who condemned Him were concerned, He was to be buried with other executed criminals, an obvious reference to Jesus being crucified with two thieves. The parallel idea of burial **with the rich** also refers to the dishonorable circumstances associated with the death of the Servant. He will be buried with the rich who had acquired their wealth by wicked means and/or had trusted in their wealth rather than in God (see Ps. 37:16; Prov. 18:23; Jer. 5:26–27). From a New Testament perspective, burial **with the rich** points to the honorable burial given to Jesus by the wealthy Joseph of Arimathea (see Matt. 27:57–60), who performed this act as an expression of his devotion to Christ. The Lord would be **pleased** (v. 10), however, that the Servant had fulfilled His

mission and given His life on behalf of others as "an offering for sin." The Lord promised to honor the Servant for His obedience by prolonging **his days** and blessing Him with **seed** and prosperity and to reward Him as a king sharing in **the spoil** (v. 12) of a great victory (see 52:15). This pictures that through His resurrection, Christ will live forever, He will have many spiritual descendants, and He will rule over a kingdom that has no end. This servant song begins and ends with a promise of the ultimate victory and exaltation of the suffering Servant.

F. The Future Glory of Zion and the Great Invitation (chaps. 54–55)

Chapters 54–55 celebrate the restoration that is made possible through the sacrifice of the Servant, described in the preceding section, and call on Israel to enjoy the blessings of restoration. This passage refers not only to Israel's restoration in Isaiah's day but also to her ultimate restoration in the messianic age.

54:1–4. Zion is again personified as a woman to represent all of Israel. The exile would leave Zion **barren** (v. 1), which was especially disgraceful for women in the ancient Near East (see 4:1). But here Zion was called to **Sing** and to **cry aloud** because she would have more **children** than **the married wife**. After being both barren and divorced (see 50:1), Israel would be a blessed mother. Jerusalem would in fact need to **Enlarge** (v. 2) her **tent** because of her many children. As an expanding nation, Israel would possess the land of the **Gentiles** (v. 3) and would also repopulate her **desolate cities**. **The shame of** Israel's **youth** (v. 4), probably the period of slavery in Egypt (see Jer. 31:19; Ezek. 16:60), and **the reproach of** her **widowhood**, most likely a reference to the exile, would come to an end.

54:5–17. The Lord would divorce Israel when He sent her away into exile, but this abandonment would be only for a moment (vv. 5–7). The Lord would have mercy on Israel because His covenant **kindness** (v. 8) and commitment to Israel is **everlasting**. The Lord's promises to Israel are as lasting as His promise to **Noah** (v. 9) that He would never again destroy **the earth** by flood (see Gen. 9:11). The Lord's **covenant**

of ... **peace** (v. 10) with Israel is even more permanent and stable than the **mountains** surrounding Israel. Ultimately, the Lord will not only rebuild Zion; He will rebuild her with jewels and precious stones (vv. 11–12). Israel will **be taught of the Lord** (v. 13) and become a righteous people so that they will never again come under the Lord's judgment. The Lord will never again send a nation against Israel as He did when He directed **the smith** (v. 16) to form weapons of war and sent nations like Assyria and Babylon to punish His people (vv. 15–17).

Israel's future blessing is their **heritage** (v. 17) as **the servants of the Lord**. Israel's restoration as the national "servant" is possible because of the work of the individual "servant" who would suffer for their sin (see 52:13–53:12). The plural "servants" are in a sense the seed of the singular "servant" (Jesus Christ; see 53:10). Because of the suffering of the Servant on her behalf, Israel will become all that God intended her to be, and the "servants" of the Lord will ultimately include all true believers, both Jew and Gentile (see 63:17; 65:8–9, 13–15; 66:14).

55:1–5. The prophet extended an invitation for Israel to receive the salvation that God had promised. Isaiah prophetically summoned the exiles to return and be restored. Though they would be thirsty, hungry, and poor, they were invited to a lavish banquet. **Wine and milk** (v. 1) are symbols of abundance, enjoyment, and nourishment and picture the rich blessings that God has in store for His people. Great spiritual blessings are compared to a banquet of rich foods elsewhere (see 25:6; Pss. 22:26; 34:8; Prov. 9:5; Jer. 31:14), and Christ similarly invited people to drink the water of life (John 4:14; 7:37). The people of Israel could come to this banquet **without money** because the death of the Servant (53:5–9) paid for the free gift of life (see Rom. 6:23).

The Lord **will make an everlasting covenant** (v. 3) with Israel that is also connected to **the sure mercies of David**. David had been promised an unending dynasty, one that would culminate in the Messiah (see 9:7; 54:10; 61:8; 2 Sam. 7:14–16). The Messiah will bring the blessings of the covenant to the whole nation, assuring the continuation of the

nation. The future Messiah will serve as a **witness** (v. 4) and **leader ... to the people**. In both instances of the phrase "to the people" in this verse, the Hebrew reads "to the peoples," referring to the impact of the Messiah's mission on all nations. Just as David exalted the Lord among the nations (Ps. 18:43, 49–50), so also will David's Son, the Messiah, be a light to the nations (42:6; 49:6) and a ruler over the nations. The rule of the Messiah will draw the **nations** (v. 5) to Zion, not to attack as in Isaiah's day, but rather to honor the Lord and His King.

55:6–11. If the people wished to experience the Lord's blessing, they had to seek Him while there was opportunity to do so (vv. 6–7). The Lord's promise demanded a response and needed to be appropriated through repentance and faith. The Lord would **abundantly pardon** (v. 7) those who turned to Him. Repentance was needed because the Lord's **ways** (v. 8) and **thoughts** were different from those of the people (vv. 8–9). Their plans and strategies for living often involved turning to idols or military strength for security and living a lifestyle that ignored God's commands. The people's plans had failed, but God always accomplishes what He intends through His word, and His promises always come true (vv. 10–11).

55:12–13. If the people would follow the ways of the Lord, they would know true life. The departure from Babylon provides the backdrop for the promise **ye shall go out with joy** (v. 12; see 35:10; 52:9–12). The personified images of **mountains ... singing** and **trees** clapping their **hands** express the fullness of Israel's celebration in leaving the land of exile. The natural world itself would seem to join in the celebration. The promise that Israel would become as fruitful as the **fir** (v. 13) and **myrtle tree** is a reversal of the earlier desolation (see 5:6; 32:13).

G. The Lord's Demand for Righteousness (56:1–8)

In the preceding chapter the Lord invited Israel to respond to His offer of salvation; here He exhorted Israel to obey the Lord as a necessary condition for experiencing the Lord's deliverance.

56:1–2. The Lord's **salvation** (v. 1) and His **righteousness** are related to one another here, for the Lord's salvation is reserved for those who do what is just and right. Keeping **the sabbath** (v. 2) is highlighted as behavior reflective of a desire to follow the law of God as a whole (v. 2, 56:4, 6). Just as the Sabbath had been instituted after the exodus from Egypt as a sign of the Mosaic covenant (see Exod. 20:8−11), so God's new deliverance would afford a new opportunity to obey Him.

56:3−8. Through the work of the Servant, the Lord's salvation would extend beyond Israel and would include the righteous from all nations. In the past, the **stranger** ("foreigner"; v. 3) who came to live among the Israelites as a resident alien had been excluded from worship for at least several generations (see Exod. 12:43; Deut. 23:3, 7−8), but the Servant's work would grant the alien inclusion in the worshiping community (see 49:19−20; 54:17; 60:10). **Eunuchs** (v. 4) were also excluded from the assembly of the Lord (Deut. 23:1), but in the future age of salvation, they would be given the right of access into God's presence if faithful to the Lord's commands. As part of God's offspring (see Acts 8:27, 38−40), they would receive **an everlasting name** (v. 5). **The sons of the stranger** (v. 6) would have as much right as the Israelite to identify themselves as the **servants** of the Lord (see 54:17). The Lord promised that His temple would become a place of worship and **prayer for all people** (v. 7). This passage anticipates the new-covenant era of the church, when the "wall of partition" would be torn down and the ethnic distinctions between Jew and Gentile would no longer matter (Eph. 2:11−16; Gal. 3:28−29).

H. The Condemnation of the Wicked in Israel (56:9−57:21)

The prophet moved from promises concerning Israel's glorious future to condemnation of Israel's present sinfulness. Israel's disobedience stood in the way of their experiencing the blessings that God had promised to them as His covenant people. Many verses in this section could apply to conditions before or during the Babylonian exile. Here again, Isaiah's message has an application both for the people of his day and for the future exilic community, who will continue to struggle with the same sins that the prophet observed in eighth-century Judah.

56:9−12. Judah's leadership was largely responsible for the corruption of the nation. The prophets called to be **watchmen** (v. 10) and warn the people of coming judgment had instead become mute **dogs** watching over the flock. Preaching only for personal gain and pleasure, they had failed to confront the people with their sinfulness and perpetrated the illusion that all was right between God and His people. They called the people to drink **wine** (v. 12) and to celebrate that **to morrow** would be even **more abundant** than **this day**.

57:1−7. As a result of this corrupt leadership, the people had abandoned the practice of justice, and the righteous were perishing (vv. 1−2). The people had turned to idols and pagan worship practices. The term **sorceress** (v. 3) refers to one who practices soothsaying or magic (see 3:2; 47:12; Deut. 18:10). In their arrogant defiance, they mocked (**sport ... make ye a wide mouth**; v. 4) the prophet for condemning them. They carried out pagan fertility rites **under every green tree** (v. 5; see 1 Kings 14:23) and had resorted to the practice of child sacrifice, associated with the worship of Molech or Baal, as a way of manipulating blessing from their gods (see 30:33; Ps. 106:37−38; Jer. 19:5). Using imagery found elsewhere in the Prophets, Isaiah portrayed the worship of idols as flagrant spiritual adultery, prostitution, and unfaithfulness to the Lord (vv. 5−7; 57:8; see Hos. 1−3; Jer. 3:6−10; Ezek. 16:15−20). The Lord was to be the "portion" (inheritance) of His people (Pss. 73:26; 142:5), but the people had instead made **the smooth stones of the stream** their **portion** (v. 6) by worshiping the creation rather than the Creator. The "stream" in view here is possibly the Hinnom Valley, southwest of Jerusalem, which was notorious as a place of Molech worship and child sacrifice.

57:8−14. The prophet charged that the people had set up their idols (**thy remembrance**; v. 8) in their homes, where they were supposed to have prominently displayed the Lord's commandments (see Deut. 6:9; 11:20). They gave lavish offerings of **ointment, and ... perfumes** (v. 9) to their gods (for

king, read the proper name Molech, which has the same spelling in Hebrew). They pursued these gods even to **hell** (*sheol*, the "grave"), which is precisely where these gods would lead them. The people had chosen the hopeless path of idolatry but refused to acknowledge the futility of their choice (v. 10). No matter how their idols had disappointed them, they still found strength to persist in their idolatry, when they could have found true strength by turning to the Lord (see 40:30–31). Fearing man more than the Lord, they had turned to the gods worshiped by the peoples around them (v. 11). The danger for those who worship idols is that God will give them over to their sinful desires and allow them to experience the consequences of their choices, and the consequence for Israel was that there would be no deliverance until they turned to the Lord (vv. 12–14).

57:15–21. Though Israel had been an unfaithful spouse in turning to many false gods, the Lord was willing to forgive and receive those who would turn from their sinful ways. He is **the high and lofty One** (v. 15), but He graciously allows the **contrite and humble** to dwell with Him. He would not persist in punishing Israel for their sins but would instead **heal** (v. 18) and forgive those who mourned their sin. Through His great act of salvation, the Lord would turn their mourning into praise. He provides true **peace** (v. 19) for those who turn to Him, a peace that the **wicked** (v. 20) can never know.

X. Everlasting Deliverance and Everlasting Judgment (chaps. 58–66)

A. False and True Worship (chap. 58)

In this oracle, Isaiah issued a call for repentance emphasizing the need for a lifestyle of justice rather than the mere performance of religious rituals. Israel would experience full restoration and renewal only when they were rightly related to the Lord. The hypocrisy that characterized Israel in Isaiah's day (see 1:1; 29:13) would carry over into the postexilic period.

58:1–7. The people persisted in their sinful ways while pretending to **seek** (v. 2) the Lord and to practice **righteousness**. They wanted to know why the Lord did not take notice of their fasting as a sign of their self-denial and devotion (see Mal. 3:14; Luke 18:12). The Lord explained that He had not responded because they continued to **exact** their **labours** (v. 3), or "oppress their workers." They worshiped God and exploited their workers on the same day. Their worship ended in fights and arguments with each other, which was not the kind of behavior that would cause their prayers to be answered (v. 4; see 1:15; 59:2). The fast that God desires is not one of going through the motions of bowing one's head or putting on **sackcloth and ashes** (v. 5), but of putting an end to the practices of wicked oppression (vv. 5–6). Taking care of **the hungry** (v. 7), **the poor**, and **the naked** is the outward expression of genuine righteousness (see Job 31:17–20; Ezek. 18:7, 16; Matt. 25:35–36).

58:8–14. When Israel became serious about practicing social justice, then they would enjoy the **light** (v. 8) of joy, prosperity, and salvation that comes from the Lord (vv. 8, 10–11; see 9:2; 60:1–3). Then the Lord would respond to their prayers and **answer** (v. 9) them with the reassuring **Here I am**. The Lord is quick to respond to a genuine cry of repentance and confession. Jerusalem would become like a watered garden (compare 1:30) when the Lord enabled the people to rebuild the ruined city (vv. 11–12). Israel's blessing was also conditioned on faithful observance of the **sabbath** (v. 13; see 56:2). Respect for the Lord and concern for one's fellow man are inseparable issues. Observing the Sabbath reflects the belief that business and personal gain are not the ultimate priorities in life, a perspective that is essential if one is going to practice fairness and generosity toward the poor and needy.

B. Zion's Confession and Redemption (chap. 59)

59:1–14. When the people complained that God lacked the power to save and restore them, they needed to remember that it was their sin that had **separated** (v. 2) them from God. Their **hands** (v. 3) were covered with **blood** because they had failed to practice justice, and this injustice poisoned their land. Their acts of injustice and violence, committed to make themselves prosperous and secure, were as worthless as garments made of spider **webs** (v. 6). They made **haste** (v. 7) to carry out the evil plans they devised against their victims. Paul quoted parts of verses 7–8 to show the universality of sin (Rom. 3:15–17). Identifying with the people, the prophet acknowledged that **judgment** (justice; v. 9) is **far from us**. Because of their sin, Israel would experience the covenant curse of darkness at **noonday** (v. 10; see Deut. 28:29; Job 5:14) rather than the **light** (v. 9) of God's favor and blessing (see 58:8, 10–11). In confessing the sins of the nations, the prophet employed a variety of synonyms for evil thoughts and deeds to assert that Israel was thoroughly wicked, and the most serious issue was that these sinful actions were committed **against the Lord** (v. 13). The personification of **judgment** (v. 14) and **truth** as individuals **turned away** and **fallen in the street** stresses the corruption of Israelite society.

59:15–21. Since **there was no intercessor** (v. 16) for the poor and needy in Israel, the Lord Himself would act in **righteousness** (vv. 16–17) to provide their salvation. He would go forth as a Warrior dressed in armor to execute **vengeance** (v. 17) on sinners who perverted justice (vv. 16–18). The Lord's judgment would extend beyond Israel to include even the distant islands so that all peoples would **fear the name of the Lord** (v. 19). In executing justice and destroying the wicked, He would redeem **Zion** (v. 20) and deliver those **that turn from transgression**, both in the return from exile and, more fully, through the person of Christ (see 35:4; 40:9; 52:7). The Lord would then establish a **covenant** (v. 21) with the redeemed, putting His **spirit** upon them so that they would obey His **words** and be His people **for ever**. This covenant matches the "new covenant" promised by the prophet Jeremiah (Jer. 31:31–34; see Ezek. 36:26–28).

C. Zion's Peace and Prosperity (chap. 60)

The restoration of Zion is the central theme in chapters 60–62.

60:1–12. The prophet described the **glory** (v. 1) that Zion will enjoy when the Lord comes as her "redeemer." The promised **light** of Israel's blessing and salvation (see 58:8, 10–11; 59:9) is here identified as the presence of **the Lord** Himself (vv. 1–2). The light will draw the **Gentiles** (v. 3) as all nations come together at Zion to worship the Lord, and Israel's exiles will return from distant lands (vv. 3–4). While the theme of Gentile inclusion in the future kingdom of God is a prominent theme in Isaiah, the nations generally assume a subservient role to Israel. The nations here bring their tribute to the Lord and enrich the wealth of Jerusalem (vv. 5–11; see also 18:7; 23:18; 45:14; 61:6; 66:12). The contribution of King Darius to Zerubbabel's temple may have been a partial fulfillment (see Ezra 6:8–9) of what will be fully realized in the messianic kingdom (see Hag. 2:7; Zech. 14:14; Rev. 21:26). Any nation refusing to honor the Lord with their tribute will be destroyed (v. 12).

60:13–22. The glories of the Solomonic era will return as the cedars of **Lebanon** (v. 13) are once again used to construct and adorn the temple of the Lord (see 1 Kings 5:10, 18). The exiles will return to a joyful and prosperous Jerusalem (vv. 14–17). They will **suck the milk of the Gentiles** (v. 16) as the wealth of the nations sustains them and provides them with an abundance of precious metals. **Violence shall no more be heard** (v. 18) because the Lord's presence will protect the land from enemy attack (vv. 18–20). The brilliant **light** (vv. 19–20) of the Lord's presence will surpass that of the **sun** and **moon** (see Rev. 21:23; 22:5), but the blessings of this future kingdom are reserved for the **righteous** (v. 21) whom the Lord has redeemed. The righteous will **inherit the land for ever** because God's "new covenant" with Israel will enable perfect obedience to the law (see 59:21; Jer. 31:31–34).

D. The Lord's Favor (chap. 61)

This chapter continues the themes of Zion's future restoration that are introduced in chapter 61, viewing the return from exile as prelude to the exaltation of Zion in the millennial kingdom.

61:1–3. The Spirit of … God (v. 1) empowered an anonymous messenger to proclaim the **good tidings** of liberation for the afflicted exiles. While the prophet Isaiah himself partially performed this role, this figure transcends the prophet and is ultimately to be identified as the messianic Servant (see 11:1; 42:1; 48:16). Jesus applied these verses to Himself in the synagogue at Nazareth (see Luke 4:16–21; see Matt.

11:5). In His quotation of this passage, Jesus omitted reference to **the day of vengeance** (v. 2), probably because that day will not occur until His second coming.

The **liberty** (v. 1) promised to the exiles is portrayed as the release and restoration that occurred in the Year of Jubilee (v. 2; see Lev. 25:10; see 49:8). Israel's restoration from exile prefigured the spiritual release from sin accomplished through the work of Christ. The wordplay involving **beauty** (Hebrew, *pe'er*; v. 3) and **ashes** (Hebrew, *eper*) highlights a series of contrasts between Israel's glorious future and its past degradation.

61:4-11. Israel will return home ultimately to rebuild her ruined **cities** (v. 4), and foreigners will serve her (vv. 4-5; see 56:3; 60:10). Righteous Israel will become **Priests of the LORD** (v. 6) among the Gentiles, fulfilling God's original design for the nation (see Exod. 19:3; compare 42:18-22). Instead of the "double" punishment (40:2) of her past, Israel will receive **double** (v. 7) honor. The blessings of the Lord's **everlasting covenant** (v. 8) will cause the **Gentiles** (v. 9) to acknowledge that Israel is **the seed which the LORD hath blessed**, recalling the Lord's promise to Abraham in Genesis 12:1-3. The oracle concludes with Zion rejoicing, as the **bride** (v. 10) of the Lord, over Israel's planting in the land (vv. 10-11).

E. Zion's Restoration and Glory (chap. 62)

62:1-5. The Lord promised to act on behalf of Zion (**will I not hold my peace**; v. 1) and to **not rest** until Zion's ultimate restoration is accomplished. When God's kingdom comes to earth, Zion will be exalted before the nations because she will become a city of **righteousness** (v. 2). The goal of the Lord's **salvation** (v. 1) is ultimately the spiritual transformation of His people, not merely their rescue from exile. The time of judgment when the Lord temporarily divorced His people will be reversed, and Zion will no longer be called **Forsaken** (v. 4) and **Desolate**. Her new names will be **Hephzi-bah** ("My delight is in her") and **Beulah** ("Married"). It is also stated that Zion's **sons** (inhabitants; v. 5) will **marry** her, but the imagery makes better sense if the Hebrew for "sons" is read as "Builder," referring to God.

62:6-12. The Lord will appoint **watchmen** (v. 6) to continually intercede on behalf of Zion and to pray for her deliverance (vv. 6-7). These verses demonstrate the harmony that exists between God's sovereignty and human responsibility. God has promised the restoration, but His people still are to pray for the realization of God's promises. There is an interesting contrast in Ezekiel 22:30, where the Lord stated that He had to destroy Jerusalem because there was no one to intercede for the city. The watchmen can pray with confidence, because the Lord has **sworn** (v. 8) to deliver His people from their enemies, and **the arm of his strength** will carry out this promise (vv. 8-9). There will never again be a time when enemy armies consume Israel's crops, but the people of Israel themselves will **eat** (v. 9) and **drink ... in the courts** of the temple at the festivals when they bring their tithes to the Lord (see Lev. 23:39-40; Deut. 14:22-26). The Lord called for the construction of a **highway** (v. 10) for the Jewish exiles returning to their homeland (vv. 10-12; see 40:3; 49:11). The way had to be prepared, because **the LORD** (v. 11) was about to perform His great work of **salvation**. Israel would once again become His **holy** (v. 12) and **redeemed** people.

F. Vengeance against the Lord's Enemies (63:1-6)

63:1-6. The Lord's deliverance of His people will also include the destruction of His enemies. The Lord is portrayed as a victorious Warrior returning from battle against **Edom** (v. 1). **Bozrah** was an important city in Edom (see 34:6). The Edomites had a long history of hostility toward Israel and here symbolize a world that hates God's people (see Obadiah). The Lord's **garments** (v. 2) will be stained **red** like one who has been treading grapes at the **winepress** (v. 3), but the stains will be from the blood of His enemies (see Lam 1:15; Joel 3:13; Rev. 14:17-20). While some would view this God of wrath and **vengeance** (v. 4) as incompatible with the God of love revealed in the person of Jesus in the New Testament, Revelation 19:13-21 provides a similar portrayal of Christ as He wages war against those who oppose Him at His second coming. The Lord's **fury** (vv. 3, 5-6) will prompt Him to act **alone** (v. 3) against

His enemies, but it is a holy anger against the wicked nations that have abused and mistreated His people (see the parallel passage in 59:16, where "righteousness" is substituted for "fury").

G. Prayer for Divine Deliverance (63:7–64:12)

63:7–14. The Lord's promises moved the prophet to prayer. As one of the "watchmen" the Lord has posted on the walls of Jerusalem (see 62:6), Isaiah asked the Lord to bring about the redemption He had promised. The prophet's prayer is similar to a national lament (see Psalm 44). The prayer begins with praise for the Lord's unfailing covenant love, demonstrated to Israel throughout her history (vv. 7–14). The Lord had **saved** (v. 9) and **redeemed** His people from their enemies. Israel, however, rewarded the Lord's love by rebelling against Him, necessitating judgment and the Lord fighting against Israel as an **enemy** (v. 10). Yet even when judging Israel, the Lord would remember His past saving acts on behalf of His people and refuse to completely destroy them. The exodus from Egypt stands as the greatest of the Lord's saving acts on behalf of Israel, and this rehearsal of His past faithfulness anticipates the new exodus that the Lord would perform in rescuing Israel from the bondage of exile.

63:15–19. The prophet next moved to petition, presenting the motivation for God to act on behalf of His people. This section demonstrates that genuine prayer involves dialogue with God, pleading one's case and expressing the reasons for God to act, while humbly submitting to His sovereign will and purposes. The prophet first appealed to God's compassion for His people. **The sounding of thy bowels** (v. 15) literally means "the stirring of your inward parts" and refers to God's deep emotional response to the desperate plight of His people. The Lord is Israel's **father** (v. 16; see 64:8; Deut. 32:6), which means He will not abandon them even if their human fathers, like **Abraham**, were to do so (see 49:14–15). Though the Lord would discipline the Israelites for their sin, they were His **people** (v. 18), to whom He had promised the land. The **adversaries** who would control the land while Israel was in exile **were not called by** His **name** (v. 19) and did not belong to Him (vv. 17–19).

It is important to recognize that in Isaiah's inquiry, **why hast thou made us to err from thy ways …?** (v. 17), he was not blaming the Lord for Israel's sin. Israel had chosen to go her own way, and the Lord would cause His people to experience the consequences of their choices. He hardened their hearts in the sense that He confirmed their choice to make their own hearts hard (see 6:10; Exod. 4:21; Ps. 95:8). The prophet was merely asking the Lord to graciously act so that the people would not remain in this hardened condition of unbelief and disobedience.

64:1–4. The petition proper in this prayer is that the Lord would **rend the heavens** (v. 1) and **come down** to rescue His people. Isaiah prayed that at the Lord's coming, the sky would be torn like a tent curtain, the earth would melt, and the seas would **boil** (v. 2; for similar descriptions of the cosmic effects of God's coming in judgment and redemption, see Judg. 5:4–5; Pss. 18:7–15; 144:5; Nah. 1:5; Hab. 3:3–7). The Lord's fame would spread throughout the **nations** because He would perform **terrible** ("awesome"; v. 3) deeds on behalf of Israel that had never been seen before.

64:5–7. God's blessing is conditioned on obedience, so the prophet acknowledged Israel's sinfulness. God's blessing is for those who live righteously, but Israel's **righteousnesses are as filthy rags** (v. 6), like the cloths a woman uses during her period, when she is ceremonially unclean (see Lev. 15:19–24; Ezek. 36:17). In confessing their lack of righteousness, the people would become open to God producing His righteousness within her. The difference between the old and new covenants is not a lessening of the demand for obedience; rather, in the new covenant, the enablement of grace makes obedience possible (see Jer. 31:31–34; 2 Cor. 3:6–9).

64:8–12. The prophet closed his petition with a final appeal for the Lord to cease being angry with His people (vv. 8–9). Isaiah lamented that the **holy cities** (v. 10) of the Promised Land were in ruins (vv. 10–11). The land was sacred because it was the Lord's dwelling place (see Ps. 78:54). Confident in the Lord's love and faithfulness, the prophet asked if He could refuse to act and reverse the suffering of His people (v. 12).

H. The Lord's Answer: Mercy and Judgment (chap. 65)

65:1–7. The Lord proceeded to answer Isaiah's prayer. The obstacle that stood in the way of the Lord blessing Israel was that they had not remained close to Him, and they continued to seek Him in only a superficial way (v. 1; see 55:6; 58:2). Rather than turning to the Lord, they provoked Him to anger by practicing idolatry (vv. 2–4). They burned **incense** (v. 3) as when worshiping "the queen of heaven" (Ishtar; see Jer. 7:18; 44:17–19), **remain[ed] among the graves** (v. 4) to consult the dead (see 8:19; 57:9; Deut. 18:11), and violated the Mosaic law by eating unclean **swine's flesh** (see 66:3, 17; Lev. 11:7–8). Rather than feeling remorse for their disobedience, those who engaged in pagan rituals believed themselves to be superior (**I am holier than thou**; v. 5). In response to Isaiah's question why the Lord held His peace (64:12), the Lord responded that He would **not keep silence** (v. 6). In His righteous anger, the Lord would judge those who had **blasphemed** (v. 7) His name through their idolatry. Before the Lord could save His people, He first needed to purge them of their sin.

65:8–10. While Israel was a vineyard that had produced bad grapes (see 5:2–7), the Lord promised that He would not completely destroy His people. Along with judging the sinners, **for** His **servants' sake** (v. 8) the Lord would also spare a faithful remnant (see 1:9). The **servants** (v. 9) would inherit the **mountains**, a figure for the whole of the Promised Land since so much of it was hills (see Judg. 1:9; Ezek. 6:2–3). **Sharon** (v. 10) and **the valley of Achor**, on the western and eastern edges of the land respectively, further point to Israel's full possession of the land. Even Israel's sin and rebellion could not abrogate the Lord's covenantal promises to Abraham and his descendants concerning the Promised Land (see Gen. 15:18; 17:8).

65:11–16. A different fate awaited the sinners who persisted in their pagan worship practices. The words **troop** (Hebrew, *gad*; v. 11) and **number** (Hebrew, *meni*) should probably be read here as the proper names Fortune and Fate, referring to two of the false gods worshiped by Israel. Those who worshiped these gods were destined for the **sword** (v. 12) of God's judgment. Alternating lines contrast the blessing of the **servants** (vv. 13–15) and the cursing of the wicked. In the future, the rebellious Israelites would be used as an example when curses were uttered (v. 15; see Jer. 29:22). The Lord would **call his servants by another name** (v. 15), perhaps referring to the "new name" of 62:2. Ultimately, the servants would rejoice that the Lord is **the God of truth** (v. 16), who keeps His promises. The Hebrew word for "truth" here is *amen* (see 1 Cor. 1:20; see Rev. 3:14).

65:17–25. The portrayal of the **new heavens and a new earth** (v. 17) is the climax of the "new things" (42:9; 48:6) that Isaiah had been promising. The prophet described the restoration of Jerusalem after the exile, and ultimately her restoration in the messianic kingdom, in the most expansive language possible: it would be as if God had created a new world. In the book of Revelation, John links the notion of a new heaven and a new earth with the "new Jerusalem" of the eternal state (Rev. 21:1–2). In the kingdom age, Jerusalem will be a city of joy, not a place of defeat and mourning. The effects of the Adamic curse will be reversed and physical longevity will be experienced, so that one who dies at the age of **an hundred years old** (v. 20) will be considered a **child**. This figurative language points to the complete destruction of death in the eternal state (see 1 Cor. 15:26; Rev. 21:4). The righteous will live in the land and enjoy its benefits to the fullest extent (vv. 21–23; compare Moses' curse for disobedience, Deut. 28:30). Completing the portrayal, the figure of **The wolf and the lamb ... and the lion** (v. 25) peacefully dwelling together points to the societal peace and harmony that will exist in the eschatological age and also describes the literal changes that will occur in nature through the reversal of the Edenic curse (see also 11:6–9).

I. Judgment for False Worshipers and Blessing for True Worshipers (chap. 66)

66:1–4. The contrast between the fate of the righteous and the fate of the wicked carries over into the final chapter of the book. The Lord is the Great King, to whom all must finally answer. Though the Lord's **throne** (v. 1) is in **heaven**, His grace is reserved for those who are **poor and of a contrite spirit** (v. 2). The Lord's judgment will fall on those who have offered Him insincere worship, and the prophet used extreme hyperbole to picture the wickedness of worship apart from the right attitude toward God (vv. 3-4). The sacrifice of a sinful person is no better than an act of murder in the eyes of God. Prescribed sacrifices and offerings presented by the wicked are no different than offering the Lord an unclean animal (dog or pig) or bowing to **an idol** (v. 3). It is delusion to think that going through the motions of worship can spare one from the wrath of Holy God.

66:5-14. In contrast to this warning of judgment, the Lord promised that the faithful remnant will enjoy the kingdom blessings associated with the restoration of Zion. Though they will have experienced the taunts of the wicked around them (**Let the Lord be glorified**; v. 5), they will not be disappointed for putting their trust in the Lord. They will rejoice as barren **Zion** (v. 8) is filled with inhabitants (see 54:1). In the future kingdom, it will be as if Israel is **born** in one day (see 49:19-20). In the book of Isaiah, the Lord's plan of salvation for Israel transformed Zion from "an unfaithful harlot" to the wife of the Lord, a blessed mother who has many children. Zion will be like a nursing mother providing milk for the children who inhabit her (see 60:16, where Zion is portrayed as drinking the milk of the nations).

Zion will enjoy **peace ... like a river** (v. 12), in contrast to the destructive flood of judgment that was experienced in Isaiah's day (vv. 12-14; see 8:7-8). Instead of attacking Jerusalem, the **Gentile** (v. 12) nations will bring their tribute. Lady Zion will carry her children in her arms (**borne upon her sides**). She will rejoice in them like a mother bouncing her newborn infant on her knees (**dandled upon her knees**), and all who love Zion will share in this joy and blessing.

66:15-20. Isaiah returned to the theme of judgment. The Lord will sweep down on His enemies in His war chariot, bringing the fire of destruction upon them (vv. 15-17). The Lord's wrath is for those who **sanctify ... and purify themselves** (v. 17) through their pagan rituals. Believing to have secured the protection of their gods, they have actually marked themselves out for destruction. The Lord will ultimately use the judgment of the wicked in Israel to bring Himself worldwide **glory** (v. 18). The survivors of this horrible judgment will be sent out among the **nations** (v. 19)—to **Tarshish** (perhaps in distant Spain; see 23:6), to **Pul** (the region west of Egypt, in **Libia**; see Nah. 3:9), to **Lud** (in west-central Asia Minor or Africa; see Gen. 10:13), to **Tubal** (the region southwest of the Black Sea; see Ezek. 27:13; 38:2-3; 39:1), and to **Javan** (Greece). They will proclaim God's **glory**, with the result that the Gentiles will bring back the Jewish exiles who have been scattered to the distant lands (see 11:11-12; 49:22; 60:4). Ironically, the Lord had designed Israel to be "a kingdom of priests" who would mediate the knowledge and blessing of the Lord to other nations (Exod. 19:5-6), but this blessing will ultimately become a reality only through Israel's final judgment.

66:21-24. While some apply the promise **I will also take of them for priests** (v. 21) to the Gentiles, indicating their full inclusion in the blessings of the new covenant, it more likely refers to the Jews who will experience God's salvation in the millennial kingdom. They will faithfully serve the Lord as all nations regularly **come to worship** (v. 23) the Lord at Jerusalem (vv. 22-23). The nations will be motivated to honor and worship the Lord as they see the corpses of those who rebelled against the Lord and were destroyed (v. 24). The graphic image of maggots feeding on decaying corpses that burn in a smoldering fire becomes a picture of hell in the New Testament (see Mark 9:48). The Valley of Hinnom (Hebrew, *gey hinnom*, from which the word "gehenna" comes), southwest of Jerusalem, contained a burning trash dump that provided a vivid reminder of the eternal torment awaiting the wicked. The prophecy of Isaiah closes with one final reminder of the differing fates awaiting the righteous and the wicked.

THE BOOK OF THE PROPHET JEREMIAH

INTRODUCTION

Author and Date

The book preserves an account of the prophetic ministry of Jeremiah, whose personal life and struggles are known in greater depth and detail than those of any other Old Testament prophet. The meaning of his name is uncertain. Suggestions include "the Lord exalts" and "the Lord establishes," but a more likely proposal is "the Lord throws," either in the sense of "hurling" the prophet into a hostile world or of "throwing down" the nations in divine judgment for their sins. Jeremiah's prophetic ministry began in 626 BC and ended sometime after 586 BC (see 1:2–3). His ministry was immediately preceded by that of Zephaniah. Habakkuk was a contemporary, and Obadiah may have been also. Since Ezekiel began his ministry in Babylon in 593 BC, he too was a late contemporary of the great prophet in Jerusalem. How and when Jeremiah died is not known; Jewish tradition, however, asserts that while living in Egypt, he was put to death by being stoned (see Heb. 11:37).

Jeremiah was a priest, a member of the household of Hilkiah. His hometown was Anathoth (1:1), so he may have been a descendant of Abiathar (see 1 Kings 2:26), a priest during the days of King Solomon. The Lord commanded Jeremiah not to marry and raise children because the impending divine judgment on Judah would sweep away the next generation (16:1–4). Primarily a prophet of doom, he attracted only a few friends, among whom were Ahikam (26:24), Gedaliah (Ahikam's son, 39:14), and Ebed-melech (38:7–13; 39:15–18). Jeremiah's closest companion was his faithful secretary, Baruch, who wrote down Jeremiah's words as the prophet dictated them (36:4–32). Jeremiah advised Baruch not to succumb to the temptations of ambition but to be content with his lot (chap. 45). He also received a deed of purchase from Jeremiah and deposited it for safekeeping (32:11–16) and accompanied the prophet on the long road to exile in Egypt (43:6–7). It is possible that Baruch was also responsible for the final compilation of the book of Jeremiah, since no event recorded in chapters 1–51 occurred after 580 BC (chap. 52 is an appendix added by a later hand).

Given to self-analysis and self-criticism (10:24), Jeremiah revealed a great deal about his character and personality. Although timid by nature (1:6), he received the Lord's assurance that he would become strong and courageous (1:18; 6:27; 15:20). In his "confessions"

(11:18–23; 12:1–4; 15:10–21; 17:12–18; 18:18–23; 20:7–18), he bared the deep struggles of his innermost being, sometimes making startlingly honest statements about his feelings toward God (12:1; 15:18). On occasion, he called for redress against his personal enemies (12:1–3; 15:15; 17:18; 18:19–23), a practice that explains the origin of the English word "jeremiad," referring to a denunciatory tirade or complaint. Jeremiah, so often characterized by anguish of spirit (4:19; 9:1; 10:19–20; 23:9), has often been called the Weeping Prophet. It should be pointed out that his "Book of Consolation" (chaps. 30–33) is placed in the middle of the book to emphasize his message of hope. It is also true that the memory of his divine call (1:17) and the Lord's frequent reaffirmations of his commissioning as a prophet (e.g., 3:12; 7:2, 27–28; 11:2, 6; 13:12–13; 17:19–20) made Jeremiah fearless in the service of his God (15:20).

Background

Jeremiah began prophesying in Judah halfway through the reign of Josiah (640–609 BC) and continued throughout the reigns of Jehoahaz (609 BC), Jehoiakim (609–598 BC), Jehoiachin (598–597 BC), and Zedekiah (597–586 BC). It was a period of storm and stress, when the doom of entire nations, including Judah itself, was being sealed. The smaller states of western Asia were often pawns in the power plays of such imperial giants as Egypt, Assyria, and Babylon, and the time of Jeremiah's ministry was no exception. Ashurbanipal, the last of the great Assyrian rulers, died in 627 BC. His successors were no match for Nabopolassar, the founder of the Neo-Babylonian Empire, who began his rule in 626 BC (the year of Jeremiah's call to prophesy). Soon after Assyria's capital city, Nineveh, fell under the onslaught of a coalition of Babylonians and Medes in 612 BC, Egypt (no friend of Babylon) marched northward in an attempt to rescue Assyria, which was near destruction. King Josiah of Judah made the mistake of trying to stop the Egyptian advance, and his untimely death near Megiddo in 609 BC at the hands of Pharaoh Neco II was the sad result (see 2 Chron. 35:20–24). Jeremiah, who had found a kindred spirit in the godly Josiah and had perhaps proclaimed the messages recorded in 11:1–8; 17:19–27 during the king's reformation movement, lamented Josiah's death (see 2 Chron. 35:25).

Josiah's son Jehoahaz (his throne name; see discussion on 22:10), also known as Shallum, is mentioned only briefly in the book of Jeremiah (22:10b–12), and then in an unfavorable way. Neco put Jehoahaz in chains and made Eliakim, another of Josiah's sons, king in his place, renaming him Jehoiakim. Jehoahaz had ruled for a scant three months (see 2 Chron. 36:2), and his reign marked the turning point in the court's attitude toward Jeremiah. Once the king's friend and confidant, the prophet then entered a dreary round of persecution and imprisonment, alternated with only brief periods of freedom (20:1–2; 26:8–9; 32:2–3; 33:1; 36:26; 37:12–21; 38:6–13, 28).

Jehoiakim was relentlessly hostile toward Jeremiah. On one occasion, when an early draft of the prophet's writings was being read to Jehoiakim (36:21), the king used a scribe's knife to cut the scroll apart, three or four columns at a time, and threw it piece by piece into the firepot in his winter apartment (36:22–23). At the Lord's command, however, Jeremiah simply dictated his prophecies to Baruch a second time, adding "many like words" to them (36:32).

Just prior to this episode in Jeremiah's life, an event of extraordinary importance took place that changed the course of history: in 605 BC, the Egyptians were crushed at Carchemish, on the Euphrates, by Nebuchadnezzar (46:2), the gifted general who succeeded his father, Nabopolassar, as ruler of Babylon that same year. Neco returned to Egypt with heavy losses, and Babylon was given a virtually free hand in western Asia for the next seventy years. Nebuchadnezzar besieged Jerusalem in 605 BC, humiliating Jehoiakim (see Dan. 1:1–2) and carrying off Daniel and his three companions to Babylon (see Dan. 1:3–6). Later, in 598–597 BC, Nebuchadnezzar attacked Jerusalem again, and the rebellious Jehoiakim was heard of no more. His son Jehoiachin ruled Judah for only three months (see 2 Chron. 36:9). Jeremiah foretold the captivity of Jehoiachin and his followers (22:24–30), a prediction that was later fulfilled (24:1; 29:1–2).

Mattaniah, Jehoiachin's uncle and a son of Josiah, was renamed Zedekiah and placed on Judah's throne by Nebuchadnezzar in 597 BC (37:1; see 2 Chron. 36:9–14). Zedekiah, a weak and vacillating ruler, sometimes befriended Jeremiah and sought his advice but at other times allowed the prophet's enemies to mistreat and imprison him. Near the end of Zedekiah's reign, Jeremiah entered into an agreement with him to reveal God's will to him in exchange for Jeremiah's own personal safety (38:15–27). Even then the prophet was under virtual house arrest until Jerusalem was captured in 586 BC (38:28).

While trying to flee the city, Zedekiah was overtaken by the pursuing Babylonians. In his presence, his sons were executed, after which he was blinded by Nebuchadnezzar (39:1–7). Nebuzaradan, commander of the imperial guard, advised Jeremiah to live with Gedaliah, whom Nebuchadnezzar had made governor over Judah (40:1–6). After a brief rule, Gedaliah was murdered by his opponents (chap. 41). Others in Judah feared Babylonian reprisal and fled to Egypt, taking Jeremiah and Baruch with them (43:4–7). By that time, the prophet was probably over seventy years old. His last recorded words are found in 44:24–30, the last verse of which is the only explicit reference in the Bible to Pharaoh Hophra, who ruled Egypt from 589 to 570 BC.

Theme and Theological Message

Referred to frequently as "Jeremiah the prophet" in the book that bears his name (20:2; 25:2; 28:5, 10–12, 15; 29:1, 29; 32:2; 34:6; 36:8, 26; 37:2–3, 6; 38:9–10, 14; 42:2, 4; 43:6; 45:1; 46:1, 13; 47:1; 49:34; 50:1) and elsewhere (2 Chron. 36:12; Dan. 9:2; Matt. 2:17; 27:9; see Matt. 16:14), Jeremiah was ever conscious of his call from the Lord (1:5; 15:19) to be a prophet. As such, he proclaimed words that were first spoken by God Himself (19:2) and were therefore certain to be fulfilled (28:9; 32:24). Jeremiah had only contempt for false prophets (14:13–18; 23:13–40; 27:14–18), such as Hananiah (chap. 28) and Shemaiah (29:24–32). Many of Jeremiah's predictions were fulfilled in the short term (e.g., 16:15; 20:4; 25:11–14; 27:19–22; 29:10; 34:4–5; 43:10–11; 44:30; 46:13), and others were—or will yet be—fulfilled in the long term (e.g., 23:5–6; 30:8–9; 31:31–34; 33:15–16).

As hinted earlier, an aura of conflict surrounded Jeremiah almost from the beginning. He lashed out against the sins of his countrymen (44:23), scoring them severely for their idolatry (16:10–13, 20; 22:9; 32:29; 44:2–3, 8, 17–19, 25), which sometimes even involved sacrificing their children to foreign gods (see 7:30–34 and discussions). But Jeremiah loved the people of Judah in spite of their sins, and he prayed for them (14:7, 20) even when the Lord told him not to (7:16; 11:14; 14:11).

Judgment is one of the all-pervasive themes in Jeremiah's writings, though he was careful to point out that repentance, if sincere, would postpone the inevitable. His counsel of submission to Babylon and his message of "life as usual" for the exiles of the early deportations branded him as a traitor in the eyes of many. Of course, his advice against rebellion actually marked him as a true patriot, a man who loved his countrymen too much to stand by silently and watch them destroy themselves. By warning them to submit and not rebel, Jeremiah was revealing God's will to them—always the most sensible prospect under any circumstances.

For Jeremiah, God was ultimate. The prophet's theology conceived of the Lord as the Creator of all that exists (10:12–16; 51:15–19), as all-powerful (32:27; 48:15; 51:57), and as everywhere present (23:24). Jeremiah ascribed the most elevated attributes to the God whom he served (32:17–25), viewing Him as the Lord not only of Judah but also of the nations (5:15; 18:7–10; 25:17–28; chaps. 46–51).

At the same time, Jeremiah saw God as being very much concerned about individual people and their accountability to Him. Jeremiah's emphasis in this regard (see, e.g., 31:29–30) is similar to that of Ezekiel (see Ezek. 18:2–4), and the two men have become known as the "prophets of individual responsibility." The undeniable relationship between sin and its consequences, so visible to Jeremiah as he watched his beloved Judah in her death throes, made him—in the pursuit of his divine vocation—a fiery preacher (5:14; 20:9; 23:29) of righteousness, and his oracles have lost none of their power with the passing of the centuries.

Called to the unhappy task of announcing the destruction of the kingdom of Judah, which had been thoroughly corrupted by the long and evil reign of Manasseh and only superficially affected by Josiah's efforts at reform, it was Jeremiah's commission to lodge God's indictment against His people and proclaim the end of an era. At long last, the Lord was about to inflict on the remnant of His people the ultimate covenant curse (see Lev. 26:31–33; Deut. 28:49–68). He would undo all that He had done for them since the day He brought them out of Egypt. It would then seem that the end had come, that Israel's stubborn and uncircumcised (unconsecrated) heart had sealed her final destiny, that God's chosen people had been cast off, that all the ancient promises and covenants had come to nothing.

But God's judgment of His people (and the nations), though terrible, was not to be the last word, God's final work in history. Mercy and covenant faithfulness would triumph over wrath. Beyond the judgment would come restoration and renewal. Israel would be restored, the nations that crushed her would be crushed, and the old covenants (with Israel, David, and the Levites) would be honored. God would make a new covenant with His people, in which He would write His law on their hearts (31:31–34) and thus consecrate them to His service. The house of David would rule them in righteousness, and faithful priests would serve them. God's commitment to Israel's redemption was as unfailing as the secure order of creation (chap. 33).

Jeremiah's message illumined the distant horizon as well as the near horizon. False prophets proclaimed peace to a rebellious nation, as though the God of Israel's peace was indifferent to her unfaithfulness. But the very God who compelled Jeremiah to denounce sin and pronounce judgment was the God who authorized him to announce that the divine wrath had its bounds, its seventy years. Afterward, forgiveness and cleansing would come, and a new day, in which all the old expectations, aroused by God's past acts and His promises and covenants, would yet be fulfilled in a manner transcending all God's mercies of old.

Literary Features

Jeremiah is the longest book in the Bible, containing more words than any other book. Although a number of chapters were written mainly in prose (chaps. 7; 11; 16; 19; 21; 24–29; 32–45), including the appendix (chap. 52), many sections are predominantly poetic in form. Jeremiah's poetry is as lofty and lyrical as any found elsewhere in Scripture. A creator of beautiful phrases, he has written an abundance of memorable passages (e.g., 2:13, 26–28; 7:4, 11, 34; 8:20, 22; 9:23–24; 10:6–7, 10, 12–13; 13:23; 15:20; 17:5–9; 20:13; 29:13; 30:7, 22; 31:3, 15, 29–30, 31–34; 33:3; 51:10).

Jeremiah used poetic repetition with particular skill (e.g., 4:23–26; 51:20–23). He understood the effectiveness of repeating a striking phrase over and over. For example, "by the sword, and by the famine, and by the pestilence" is found in fifteen separate verses (14:12; 21:7, 9; 24:10; 27:8, 13; 29:17–18; 32:24, 36; 34:17; 38:2; 42:17, 22; 44:13). He made use of cryptograms (see discussions on 25:26; 51:1, 41) on appropriate occasions. Alliteration and assonance were also a part of his literary style, examples being *zarim wezeruha* ("fanners, that shall fan her," 51:2) and *pahad wapahat wapah* ("Fear, and the pit, and the snare," 48:43; see *Zondervan KJV Study Bible* note on Isa. 24:17).

Like Ezekiel, Jeremiah was often instructed to use symbolic acts to highlight his message: a ruined and useless girdle (13:1–11), a smashed earthen jar (19:1–12), a yoke of straps and crossbars (chap. 27), large stones in a brick pavement (43:8–13). Symbolic value is also seen in the Lord's commands to Jeremiah not to marry and raise children (16:1–4), not to enter a house where a funeral meal or feasting was taking place (16:5–9), and to buy a field in his hometown, Anathoth (32:6–15). Similarly, the Lord used visual aids in conveying His message to Jeremiah: potter's clay (18:1–10) and two baskets of figs (chap. 24).

Unlike Ezekiel, the oracles in Jeremiah are not arranged in chronological order. Had they been so arranged, the sequence of sections within the book would have been approximately as follows: 1:1–7:15; chapter 26; 7:16–20:18; chapter 25; chapters 46–51; 36:1–8; chapter 45; 36:9–32; chapter 35; chapters 21–24; chapters 27–31; 34:1–7; 37:1–10; 34:8–22; 37:11–38:13; 39:15–18; chapters 32–33; 38:14–39:14; 52:1–30; chapters 40–44; 52:31–34. The outline below represents an analysis of the book of Jeremiah in its present canonical order.

Outline

    I. The Call of the Prophet (chap. 1)
    II. Warnings of the Judgment to Fall on Judah (chaps. 2–25)
        A. Earliest Discourses (chaps. 2–6)
           1. Judah's Faithlessness (2:1–3:5)

Bibliography

Brueggemann, W. *A Commentary on Jeremiah: Exile and Homecoming*. Grand Rapids, MI: Eerdmans, 1998.

Craigie, P., P. Kelley, and J. Drinkard. *Jeremiah 1-25*. Word Biblical Commentary 26. Waco, TX: Word, 1991.

Dearman, J. A. *Jeremiah/Lamentations*. The NIV Application Commentary. Grand Rapids, MI: Zondervan, 2002.

Feinberg, Charles. *Jeremiah: A Commentary*. Grand Rapids, MI: Zondervan, 1982.

Huey, F. B., Jr. *Jeremiah, Lamentations*. The New American Commentary 16. Nashville: Broadman & Holman, 1993.

Jones, D. R. *Jeremiah*. New Century Bible. Grand Rapids, MI: Eerdmans, 1992.

Keown, G., P. Scalise, and T. Smothers. *Jeremiah 26-52*. Word Biblical Commentary 27. Waco, TX: Word, 1994.

Thompson, J. A. *The Book of Jeremiah*. The New International Commentary on the Old Testament. Grand Rapids, MI: Eerdmans, 1980.

EXPOSITION

I. The Call of the Prophet (chap. 1)

The account of Jeremiah's call to the prophetic ministry consists of three major sections: the call proper (vv. 4-9), two prophetic visions (vv. 10-16), and some closing words of exhortation and encouragement (vv. 17-19).

1:1-9. Before I formed thee (v. 5), the opening of the Lord's calling of Jeremiah, was a reminder that God's creative act (see Gen. 2:7; Ps. 119:73) was the basis of His sovereign right to call Jeremiah into His service. **I knew thee** means that the Lord made Jeremiah the object of His choice. The Hebrew verb here could be rendered "chose" (see Gen. 18:19; Amos 3:2). The Lord had **ordained** Jeremiah to be **a prophet unto the nations**, not in the sense that he was to preach to other nations but in that his message would include these nations and reveal God's future intentions concerning these nations (see 25:8–38; chaps. 46–51).

Jeremiah's response, **I cannot speak: for I am a child** (v. 6), should not be understood as a reflection of a lack of faith but rather as an expression of proper humility in light of the awesome responsibility being entrusted to him. Moses, Gideon, Isaiah, and others expressed their personal inadequacies when commissioned by the Lord, and these protests of personal inability were improper only when they reflected a persistent lack of trust in God's promises of enablement and empowerment (as with Moses, Exod. 4:13–14).

The Lord immediately denied Jeremiah's objection (v. 7). Youth and inexperience do not disqualify someone whom God has called (see 1 Tim. 4:12). He equips and sustains those He commissions. Jeremiah's ability to **Be not afraid** (v. 8) was to come from the promise of God's abiding presence. The Lord did not promise Jeremiah exemption from persecution or imprisonment, but that no serious physical harm would come to him. To overcome Jeremiah's inability to speak, the Lord touched Jeremiah's mouth and gave the prophet the words to say. **I have put my words in thy mouth** (v. 9) provides a classic description of the relationship between the Lord and His prophet (see 5:15; Exod. 4:15; Num. 22:38; 23:5, 12, 16; Deut. 18:18; Isa. 51:16; 2 Peter 1:21).

1:10–16. Like the prophets before and after him, Jeremiah's message involved judgment and salvation. The words **to root out, and to pull down … to destroy, and to throw down … to build, and to plant** (v. 10) are used throughout the book to describe the dual nature of the prophet's mission (see 12:14–15, 17; 18:7–10; 24:6; 31:28; 42:10; 45:4). The first two pairs of verbs are negative, stressing the fact that Jeremiah was to be primarily a prophet of doom, while the last pair is positive, indicating that he was also to be a prophet of restoration—even if only secondarily. The first verb ("root out") is the opposite of the last ("plant"), and fully half of the verbs ("pull down," "destroy," and "throw down") are the opposite of "build."

In the prophetic visions in verses 10–16, Jeremiah first saw **a rod of an almond tree** (v. 11). This vision signified that the Lord would **hasten** (v. 12) to bring His judgment against Judah. The Hebrew for "hasten" sounds like the Hebrew for "almond tree." Just as the almond tree blooms first in the year (and therefore "wakes up" early; the Hebrew for "hasten" means to be wakeful), so the Lord is ever quick to ensure that His word is fulfilled.

The prophet then saw **a seething pot** (v. 13) that poured out from the **north**, which signified that **evil** (calamity; v. 14) would **break forth upon** Judah from the north. The Hebrew for "break forth" sounds like the Hebrew for "seething." This calamity referred to the kingdoms of the north that would invade the land of Judah. Since Assyria posed a minimal threat to Judah after the death of Ashurbanipal in 627 BC, the reference is most likely to Babylon and her allies. The fulfillment of the threat that these enemies would place their **throne** (v. 15) at the entrance to **Jerusalem** is found in 39:3. The Lord would bring these armies to invade Judah because they had abandoned Him and turned to other gods.

1:17–19. In the closing exhortation, the Lord commanded Jeremiah, **gird up thy loins** (v. 17), which means "get yourself ready" (see Exod. 12:11; 1 Kings 18:46; 2 Kings 4:29; 9:1; Job 38:3; 40:7). To counter the great opposition that Jeremiah would face, the Lord promised to make His prophet like **a defenced city, and an iron pillar, and brasen walls** (v. 18). Jeremiah would be able to withstand the abuse and persecution that his divine commission would evoke, even though his enemies themselves would be "brass and iron" (6:28). Jeremiah would need strength from the Lord because his opposition would come from **kings … princes … priests … people**. The whole nation would defy the prophet and his God.

II. Warnings of the Judgment to Fall on Judah (chaps. 2–25)

A. Earliest Discourses (chaps. 2–6)

It is generally agreed that these chapters are among Jeremiah's earliest discourses, delivered during the reign of Josiah (3:6). The basic theme is the virtually total apostasy of Judah (chaps. 2–5), leading inevitably to divine retribution through foreign invasion (chap. 6). Jeremiah issued frequent calls for Judah to return to the Lord before it was too late (3:1, 7–10, 14; 4:1–4), and such calls gradually diminish in the book as the people continued in their sin and judgment became an inevitable reality.

1. Judah's Faithlessness (2:1–3:5)

Jeremiah vividly portrayed the wickedness and backsliding of God's people with numerous colorful figures of speech designed to help the people see the foolishness of their rebellion against the Lord.

2:1–3. These verses recall Israel's devotion to the Lord in her early days as a nation. The Lord is often figuratively described as Israel's husband (see 3:14; 31:32; Isa. 54:5; Hos. 2:16), and the time of Israel's **youth** (v. 2) was one of betrothal to the Lord in the wilderness. Early in her history, Israel had enjoyed a close and cordial relationship with the Lord. But God's people later forsook Him and loved "strangers" (foreign gods; 2:25), tragically abandoning their first love (see Rev. 2:4). The Lord's people turned from Him in spite of the fact that they were **holiness unto the Lord** (v. 3), set apart to Him and His service (see Exod. 3:5; Lev. 11:44; Deut. 7:6).

2:4–8. Hear (v. 4) is a common divine imperative in the prophetic writings, summoning God's people—as well as the nations—into His courts to remind them of their legal obligations to Him and, when necessary, to pass judgment on them (see, e.g., 7:2; 17:20; 19:3; 21:11; 22:2, 29; 31:10; 42:15; 44:24, 26). Here the Lord reminded Israel of all that He had done for them as His covenant people and asked what more He could have done to win their love and faithfulness (vv. 4–8). He had redeemed them out of bondage in **Egypt** (v. 6) and **led** them like a shepherd in the wilderness, but His people had spurned His love. He had given them the Promised Land and its bounty as their **heritage** (inheritance; v. 7), but their sin had **defiled** the **land** (i.e., made it ceremonially unclean; see 3:1–2; 16:18; Lev. 4:12) and had turned it into **an abomination**. Even the Israel's spiritual

leaders had failed to consult the Lord. The prophets had spoken in the name of **Baal** (v. 8) rather than in the name of the Lord.

2:9–13. The Lord would **plead** (v. 9) with Judah because their rebellion against Him was incomprehensible. The Hebrew for "to plead" means to contend or bring charges against someone in the context of a lawsuit. The rhetorical question, **Hath a nation changed their gods …?** (v. 11), clearly expects a negative answer and emphasizes how incredible it was that Judah had substituted idolatry for the worship of the true God. The disloyalty of the Lord's people was not practiced even among the pagan nations. In addition, by her unfaithfulness, Judah had exchanged **the fountain of living waters** (v. 13) for **broken cisterns**. Watertight plaster was used to keep cisterns from losing water. Idols, like broken cisterns, will always fail their worshipers; by contrast, God provides life abundant and unfailing.

2:14–19. The Lord continued to rebuke Judah for her ingratitude. The rhetorical questions asking if Israel was a **slave** (v. 14) or **servant** again expect negative answers in light of God's redemptive acts during the exodus (see Exod. 6:6; 20:2). God had freed Israel from foreign bondage to serve Him, yet the people were **spoiled** for Egypt and Assyria. They preferred slavery over freedom. Foreigners had devastated their land, the **lions** (v. 15) symbolizing the armies of Assyria (see v. 18; 50:17; Isa. 15:9). Yet Judah turned to Egypt and Assyria as their source of security in times of trouble (v. 18). The tendency of Israel and Judah to seek help from these foreign powers was not restricted to Jeremiah's time (see, e.g., Hos. 7:11; 12:2; Isa. 30:1–5; 31:1–3). They chose to **drink the waters** (v. 18) provided by these nations rather than turning to the Lord for life.

2:20–21. Jeremiah used numerous figures of speech to vividly portray Judah's rebellion against Israel (2:20–3:5). Like a stubborn draft animal, Judah refused to obey the Lord's commands (v. 20). Judah had prostituted herself (**playing the harlot;** v. 20) in seeking other gods as her lovers rather than being faithful to the Lord as her Husband. **Every high hill and … every green tree** refers to the locale in which pagan fertility rites were carried out (see 1 Kings 14:23; 2 Kings 17:10; Ezek. 6:3). The Lord had planted Israel as **a noble vine** (v. 21; see Isa. 5:2), the Hebrew referring to a grape of exceptional quality (v. 21). Judah had become **a strange vine**, wording used to describe Israel's enemies in Deuteronomy 32:32.

2:22–28. Judah needed cleansing that went beyond the physical act of washing because she had been **polluted** (v. 23) by her worship of other gods (vv. 22–23). In pursuing other gods, Judah had been like **A wild ass** (v. 24) in heat, an unruly and intractable animal consumed by its passion. The feet of the people were **unshod** (v. 25) because they had worn out their sandals chasing after other lovers, instead of expressing the love for God that was expected under the terms of their covenant relationship with the Lord. Judah's idolatry was shameful and would ultimately not save her from the calamity that was about to befall her (vv. 25–28).

2:29–37. After the Lord had pleaded, or brought charges, against Judah, He asked if Judah had cause to **plead with** (v. 29) Him. The series of rhetorical questions asking if God had in any way mistreated His people were all to be answered in the negative; the exact opposite was true. The fault for the breach of covenant lay with the people, who were like **a bride** (v. 32) forgetting that her bridal jewelry and clothing symbolized commitment to her husband. Israel and Judah had **forgotten** the Lord. She was always to "remember" the Lord and all that He had done for her (Deut. 7:18; 8:18) and trust and worship Him alone, but she had often "forgotten" Him, put Him out of mind (see Judg. 2:10; Hos. 2:13). Though the wife protested her innocence, the Lord would severely punish her infidelity and cause her to be ashamed of her alliances with foreign nations and their gods (v. 36). The Lord warned Judah that she would **go forth** (v. 37) with **thine hands upon thine head**, a reference to the coming exile. Ancient reliefs depict captives with their wrists tied together above their heads.

3:1–5. Continuing the marriage motif, the Lord questioned whether Israel and Judah could return to the Lord as their husband if they had joined themselves to other lovers. The background for this passage is the divorce provision of the Mosaic law (Deut. 24:1–4), which states that a woman should not be reunited to her divorced husband if she marries another. The implication is that because Judah had **played the harlot** (v. 1) by worshiping other gods, the Lord might not allow His people to return to Him. The people had a brazen and shameless attitude (**a whore's forehead**; v. 3) toward their sin, which had made them oblivious to the judgment the Lord had brought by withholding rain from the land. Yet they referred to the Lord as **father** (v. 4) and **guide**, claiming to have an intimate association with Him as a faithful wife while persisting in their sinful ways.

2. The Need for Repentance and Return (3:6–4:4)

3:6–11. Jeremiah compared Israel and Judah to two sisters who had been unfaithful to the Lord as their husband (Samaria and Jerusalem are similarly compared to adulterous sisters in Ezekiel 23). In a sense, Judah was more guilty than the apostate northern kingdom. Judah had seen how the Lord had given Israel **a bill of divorce** (v. 8) by sending her into exile (722 BC), yet Judah persisted in her sinful ways. She refused to learn the obvious lesson from Israel's tragic experience, that the same fate awaited her. Despite the religious reforms and revival that had taken place in Judah during the reign of Josiah (640–609 BC), Judah had not turned to the Lord **with her whole heart** (v. 10). Judah had returned **but feignedly** in that the nation's response to Josiah's reform measures was superficial and hypocritical.

3:12–14. The Lord directed Jeremiah to turn to the Israelites in **the north** (v. 12), the Assyrian provinces to which many Israelites had been exiled, and call them to **Return** to the Lord. Though 3:1–5 raised the possibility that the Lord would not take back His sinful wife, she still was given the opportunity to turn back to the Lord, because He is **merciful** and would **not keep anger for ever**. Though the Lord had given Israel "a bill of divorce" (3:8), He spoke the assuring words, **I am married unto you** (v. 14).

The Hebrew root underlying the verb "married" is *ba'al*. Instead of allowing God to be their husband, His people had followed the Baals (see 2:23). If they would **Turn** to the Lord, He would bring them **to Zion** to worship as His people.

3:15–25. Looking ahead to Israel's future restoration in the messianic age, the Lord promised He will give them faithful leaders (v. 15) and to cause them to multiply and become numerous in **the land** (v. 16). **The ark of the covenant**, which formerly symbolized God's royal presence (see 1 Sam. 4:3), will be irrelevant when the Messiah comes as the embodiment of the Lord's sovereign reign over the earth. The reality of God's presence among His people will cause all of **Jerusalem** (v. 17) to become His **throne** rather than just the ark, over which the Lord sat enthroned "above the cherubim" (see 1 Sam. 4:4). In the messianic age, Israel and Judah, God's divided people, will again be reunited (v. 18).

The blessings described in verses 15–18 are what God intended His people to enjoy all along, but their unfaithfulness to Him as **father** (v. 19) and **husband** (v. 20) had necessitated their punishment instead. The image of God as both father and husband reflects the depth of intimacy in the relationship between the Lord and Israel. Because of the punishment they had experienced, the people were **weeping** (v. 21) and praying to the Lord, and the Lord once again encouraged them to **Return** (v. 22) from their backslidden condition. Anticipating Israel's return from exile, Jeremiah portrayed the people as acknowledging that their worship of other gods had been a shameful thing that had cost them dearly (vv. 23–25).

4:1–4. The prophet continued to stress the need for repentance (**return unto me**; v. 1), and his piling up of words such as **truth** (v. 2), **judgment** (justice), and **righteousness** underscored the need for repentance that was sincere and not perfunctory. If Israel would repent by putting away their idols and swearing absolute allegiance to the Lord, the Lord promised that **the nations shall bless themselves in him**, reflecting the language of God's covenant promise to Abraham (see Gen. 12:2–3). Israel's repentance

is a necessary precondition for the ultimate blessing of the nations. In verses 3–4, two images are used to picture true repentance. Turning to the Lord is compared to the breaking up of thorny unplowed ground in preparation for planting seed, and consecration to the Lord is compared to the physical act of circumcision. Both images reflect the need for a change of heart.

3. Judgment from the North (4:5–6:30)

Jeremiah had stressed the positive results that would occur if Judah returned to the Lord (3:15–18; 4:1–4). Here he emphasized the horrible consequences that would result from a failure to repent. Employing harsh and graphic imagery, the prophet described in vivid detail the horrors of invasion by the powerful army that the Lord would use to punish His disobedient people. The prophet sought to paint a picture of the realities of war to stir the people to seek the Lord so that judgment might be averted.

a. An Army Attacks (4:5–31)

Failure to repent would bring foreign invaders ("evil from the north"; v, 6) who would come as the human instruments of divine judgment.

4:5–9. The image of an army **from the north** (v. 6) is stereotypical language describing invasion by an enemy army (see 1:13–14; Isa. 14:31), because foreign armies normally invaded Israel and Judah from the north. **Blow ye the trumpet** (v. 5) was a call to sound the warning that the enemy army was approaching, and the people of Judah would **go into the defenced cities**. To avoid capture by hostile troops, people living in the countryside would take refuge in the nearest walled town (see 5:17; 8:14; 34:7; 48:18). The enemy from the north was a **lion** (v. 7) and **destroyer** who would attack Judah with ferocity, and the people of Judah would mourn and lament as they anticipated the coming national disaster.

4:10–18. Jeremiah's response to the coming disaster was to complain that God had **greatly deceived this people** (v. 10). It is difficult to understand why Jeremiah appears to blame God for the deception of the people, since it was the false prophets who had proclaimed, **Ye shall have peace** (see 6:13–14; 8:10–11; 14:23; 23:17). The Lord had sent prophets like Jeremiah to warn of the coming judgment, but the people had not listened. Jeremiah's words to the Lord recall the incident in 1 Kings 22:20–23, where God sent a "lying spirit" to deceive the prophets who counseled King Ahab. Because Ahab had rejected the true prophetic word, God punished his disobedience by causing him to believe a lie that brought about his death. In the same way, the Lord punished those who had rejected Jeremiah's words of judgment by causing them to believe a lie that would ultimately destroy them.

The judgment to fall on the people would be like **a dry wind** (the sirocco or khamsin; v. 11), bringing sand and dust that would sweep the people away (vv. 11–12; see Ps. 11:6; Jonah 4:8). Jeremiah described the attacking army as possessing supernatural strength: it would **come up as clouds** (v. 13), with **chariots** like **a whirlwind** and **horses … swifter than eagles**. Knowing that death was inevitable, the people would cry out, **Woe unto us!** The prophet exhorted the people to get right with God (**wash thine heart**; v. 14) because in the mind's eye of the prophet, the enemy was making fearfully rapid progress toward the Holy City, marching from **Dan** (v. 15), near the northern border of Israel, to **Ephraim**, only a few miles from Jerusalem.

4:19–26. These verses are a brief personal interlude, broken only by the divine complaint in verse 22. Jeremiah voiced his agony at the approaching destruction of his beloved land and its people. The verb **pained** (v. 19), used to describe the prophet's distress, is often associated with labor pains (see 6:24; 49:24; 50:43). When the Lord spoke, He reminded Jeremiah that the people had no one but themselves to blame for the disaster. They were **foolish** (v. 22), the Hebrew here referring to someone who is morally deficient. The leaders and the people had committed the ultimate sin because **they have not known** the Lord. They were like **sottish** (or "senseless") children.

In Jeremiah's response to the Lord (vv. 23–26), the striking repetition of **I beheld** at the beginning of each verse ties this poem together and underscores its visionary character, as the prophet saw his beloved land in ruins after the Babylonian onslaught. Creation, as it were, had been reversed. In Jeremiah's vision, the judgment was so severe that the conditions associated with the primeval chaos had returned. The earth was **without form, and void** (v. 23), a phrase that occurs elsewhere only in Genesis 1:2. There was **no light** (compare Gen. 1:3), and **there was no man** (v. 25; the Hebrew underlying this phrase occurs elsewhere only in Gen. 2:5). The Lord's anger had caused uncreation to replace creation.

4:27–31. Though the Lord would not completely destroy His people, He also would not **turn back** (v. 28) from His judgment because the people had not "returned" to Him. Feeling unsafe even in fortified towns, the inhabitants of Judah would seek to hide in **the rocks** (v. 29) when the Babylonians attacked. Personified as a woman, Jerusalem would, as a prostitute, attempt to seduce Babylon into not attacking her, but her plan would fail. Her **lovers** (v. 30), the foreign nations and their gods that Judah had lusted after, would attack and seek to put her to death. Under enemy attack, **the daughter of Zion** (v. 31) would spread out her hands in vain as she pleaded for God's help.

b. The Futile Search for an Upright Man (chap. 5)

5:1–11. The judgment against Jerusalem, representative of the nation of Judah, was necessary because corruption had pervaded the city. The Lord challenged anyone to find just one righteous person in Israel (v. 1; see Ps. 14:1–3; Isa. 64:6–7). The people were in this condition because they had **refused to receive correction** (v. 3). That both the **poor** (v. 4) and the **great** (v. 5) were spiritually corrupt demonstrates the depth of Judah's depravity. The enemy army who attacked Judah would be like **a lion … a wolf … a leopard** (v. 6) in its ferocity and destructive power. The Lord could not excuse Judah's spiritual adultery, and religious prostitution had led quite naturally to literal adultery, the breaking of God's moral laws (vv. 7–9). The Lord commanded the foreign enemy to attack (**Go**; v. 10) but not completely destroy His people (vv. 10–11).

5:12–19. Despite Jeremiah's warnings, the people of Judah did not believe that the Lord would judge them (vv. 12–15). Jeremiah used the characteristic triad of sword, famine, and pestilence fifteen times to describe the coming judgment against Judah (see, e.g., 14:12; 21:9; 24:10; see also Lev. 26:25–26), but the people had listened to the lies of the false prophets and did not believe that **sword** and **famine** (v. 12) would ever come to them. They failed to see that the words of the false prophets were full of **wind** (v. 13) and that these prophets themselves would be blown away in judgment (v. 15).

The "wind" of the false prophets contrasts to the **fire** (v. 14) of the word of the Lord spoken through Jeremiah, which would ultimately consume the people (vv. 16–19). This fire would take the form of a foreign army sweeping through and destroying the land (vv. 16–17). Rather than identifying the army by name (Babylon), the prophet created the image of a mysterious enemy **nation ... from far** (v. 15) that spoke an unknown language. **Their quiver is as an open sepulchre** (v. 16) conveys the idea that this enemy would have an insatiable desire to bring death and destruction upon Judah (see Ps. 5:9; Prov. 30:15–16). Though the Lord would **not make a full end** (v. 18) of Judah, the people would be taken away in exile to a foreign land. It was a fitting punishment that the nation who had **served strange gods** (v. 19) would be made to **serve strangers** in a foreign land.

5:20–31. Israel's and Judah's rebellion against the Lord demonstrated that they were a **foolish people** (v. 21) deserving of whatever judgment they received. Though **the sea ... cannot pass** (v. 22) its divinely appointed boundaries, God's people had violated the limits He had set for them. They disregarded that the Lord had blessed them with rains for their harvests (v. 24). Their sinful attitude toward the Lord had produced a corrupt culture in which violence and dishonesty were commonplace. The wealthy had gained their prosperity by setting **snares** (v. 26) and **a trap** to catch others in their dis-

honest schemes (vv. 26–27). In their prosperity, they had forgotten justice and saw no need to provide for **the fatherless** (v. 28) and **the needy**. Because they refused to punish wrongdoers, God would do their work for them by bringing **A wonderful and horrible** (v. 30) destruction upon the land.

c. Jerusalem under Siege (chap. 6)

This chapter records the prophet's vision of the future Babylonian attack on Jerusalem.

6:1–6. With the siege of Jerusalem imminent, Jeremiah's warfare imagery intensified. The Lord called for the trumpet to sound and the signal fires to be lit to warn of the approaching army. The people of **Benjamin** (v. 1), the tribal territory bordering Jerusalem to the north, and of **Tekoa**, a town near Jersualem, were told to flee for their lives. Wordplays in these verses (**blow** and **Tekoa** sound alike; **set up** and **sign** sound alike) were used to jar the people into realizing what was about to happen.

The invaders speak in verses 4–5. The call to **Prepare** (v. 4) for battle literally means "consecrate" (see Joel 3:9; Mic. 3:5). Since ancient battles had religious connotations, soldiers had to prepare themselves ritually as well as militarily (see Deut. 20:2–4; 1 Sam. 25:28). The invaders would prepare to attack **at noon** to take advantage of the element of surprise, since the usual time of attack was early in the morning. They would even continue their assault **by night** (v. 5). Since soldiers normally retired for the night and resumed the siege the following morning, the idea is that these enemy troops were eager and determined to carry out their mission. Reversing the holy war traditions of the Old Testament, the Lord would now fight for the enemies of Judah and would instruct them to cut down trees for a siege ramp and to mount their assault against the city (v. 6).

6:7–15. Jerusalem would be destroyed for her wickedness, which poured out like waters from **a fountain** (v. 7). The enemy army would **thoroughly glean** (v. 9) the city like a vineyard, stopping just short of complete destruction. Jeremiah expressed his frustration over Judah's refusal to hear his warnings of judgment and take them to heart

(vv. 10–11a). Because of the people's obstinacy, the prophet spoke a message **full of the fury of the Lord** (v. 11). With **I will pour it out**, the Lord resumed speaking and used a series of parallel images to convey the idea of complete destruction—from **the children** to **the aged**, from **their houses** (v. 12) to **their fields**, from **the least** (v. 13) to **the greatest**, and from **the prophet** to **the priest**. The spiritual leaders were especially culpable because they had misled the people with false promises of security (vv. 14–15). The message of **Peace, peace** (v. 14) was a common message of false and greedy prophets (see Ezek. 13:10; Mic. 3:5).

6:16–23. The Lord called His sinful people to **Stand** (v. 16) and **walk** in **the old paths**, the tried and true ways of Judah's godly ancestors, and He **set watchmen over** (v. 17) them, the true prophets who tried to warn them of the coming disaster. But the people would not listen and would not change their ways. **Therefore** (v. 18), the Lord would bring judgment on them, and all the **nations** would observe what happened to Judah because she had **rejected** (v. 19) God's law. Judah misunderstood God's intentions and believed that the rituals of **burnt offerings** (v. 20) and **sacrifices** were more important than a lifestyle of obedience. **Therefore** (v. 21), judgment would take the form of the Babylonian army, who would attack the land with vicious cruelty (vv. 21–23).

6:24–30. Speaking on behalf of Judah, Jeremiah expressed that the people were consumed by fear (vv. 24–26). **Fear is on every side** (v. 25) was a favorite expression of Jeremiah's (see 20:10; 46:5; 49:29). The Lord spoke to Jeremiah (vv. 27–30) and appointed him to test the people of Judah as a refiner tests metals (see 9:7; Isa. 1:25). The test of Judah's character would reflect nothing of value. In ancient times, lead was added to silver ore in the refining process. When the crucible was heated, the lead oxidized and acted as a flux to remove the alloys. The process would fail (**the lead is consumed**; v. 29; and **the founder melteth in vain**) because the ore was not pure enough (see Ezek. 24:11–13). Since Judah would prove to be nothing more than **Reprobate silver** (v. 30), the Lord would reject them.

B. Jeremiah's Temple Messages (chaps. 7–10)

This section contains a series of temple messages delivered by Jeremiah perhaps over a period of several years. Since 26:2–6, 12–15 is very similar in content to chapter 7, it seems likely that chapters 7–10 (or at least chap. 7) date to the reign of Jehoiakim. The account in chapter 7 focuses more on the prophet's message of warning; the account in chapter 26 focuses more on the response of various segments of the population to Jeremiah's message. It would appear that the sermon in chapter 7, delivered during the reign of Jehoiakim, marked a significant turning point in Jeremiah's ministry. From this point forward, the calls to repentance, found repeatedly in chapters 2–6, virtually disappear. It appears that because the people rejected God's offer of forgiveness at this very public moment in Jeremiah's ministry, accompanied by Jehoiakim's hostile rejection of the prophet's warnings, judgment became an inevitable certainty from this point forward.

1. Jeremiah's Warning concerning the Jerusalem Temple (7:1–8:3)

7:1–3. In the straightforward narrative of this section, Jeremiah asserted that Solomon's temple in Jerusalem would not escape the fate of the earlier sanctuary at Shiloh if the people of Judah persisted in worshiping false gods. The Lord sent Jeremiah to the temple to deliver the message, **Amend your ways** (v. 3), so that the people might continue living in the land that God had graciously given to them.

7:4–11. The Lord especially did not want the people to be deceived by the **lying words** (v. 4) of the prophets that viewed the Lord's presence at the temple as an absolute guarantee that Jerusalem would never fall to its enemies. The idea that God would not destroy Jerusalem simply because His presence was located there was a delusion, fostered in part by the miraculous deliverance of the city during the reign of Hezekiah (see 2 Kings 19:32–36; 2 Sam. 7:11b–13; Ps. 132:13–14). The only way that Judah could avoid judgment was to change their ways and turn back to the practices of justice established in the Mosaic law (vv. 5–7). The importance of obedience to the Mosaic law is reflected in verse 6; in this one verse, violations of fully half of the Ten Commandments are mentioned (see Hos. 4:2). By believing that God's presence protected them in spite of their sinful behavior, the people had turned the temple into **a den of robbers** (v. 11). As thieves hide in caves and think they are safe, so the people of Judah falsely trusted in the temple to protect them in spite of their sins.

7:12–15. The people did not think that God would destroy Jerusalem because it was their dwelling place, but they should have called to mind the fate of **Shiloh** (v. 12). The tabernacle had been set up in Shiloh after the conquest of Canaan (see Josh. 18:1) and was still there at the end of the period of the judges (see 1 Sam. 1:9). Modern Seilun, about eighteen miles north of Jerusalem, preserves the name of the ancient site. Archaeological excavations there indicate that Shiloh was destroyed by the Philistines circa 1050 BC. The tabernacle itself was not destroyed, since it was still at Gibeon during David's reign (see 1 Chron. 21:29). The city was likely destroyed sometime after the events described in 1 Samuel 4. The fate of Shiloh should have caused the inhabitants of Jerusalem to realize that the Lord was serious when He threatened, **I will cast you out of my sight** (v. 15).

7:16–34. The certainty that Judah had crossed the line and could not avoid judgment was demonstrated by the Lord's instruction to Jeremiah to **pray not thou for this people** (v. 16; see 11:14; 14:11). Intercession was a central function of the prophets (1 Sam. 12:23), and prophetic intercession had spared the people from catastrophic judgment at other times in Israel's history (see Exod. 32:31–32; 1 Sam 12:19; Amos 7:1–6). This prohibition against intercession did not mean that Jeremiah ceased to pray for his fellow countrymen (see 18:20), only that he would not pray for their deliverance from the Babylonians, the Lord's instrument of judgment. Jeremiah's ministry of intercession for Judah would resume after the fall of Jerusalem (see 42:2–4). At this point, however, there was virtually no hope for Judah because they persisted in their sinful ways (vv. 17–28). Their refusal to heed Jeremiah's warnings of judgment is reflective of their long-established pattern of refusing to listen to the Lord's prophetic messengers. For their refusal to believe, they would experience the covenant curses to the fullest extent.

8:1–3. Because the leadership of Judah (**kings … princes … priests … prophets**; v. 1) was especially guilty in leading the rest of the nation into sin, they would be subjected to the gross indignity and sacrilege of having their bones removed from the grave and exposed to the elements. Their bones would be spread **before the sun, and the moon, and all the host of heaven** (v. 2) to hasten their disintegration, and perhaps also to demonstrate that the heavenly bodies, which had been worshiped by some of Judah's kings (see 2 Kings 21:3, 5; 23:11), were powerless to help. They had given homage and devotion to the creation, which should have been reserved for the Creator alone.

2. The Punishment of Sinful Judah (8:4–9:26)

In contrast to 7:1–8:3, this section is almost completely in poetic form. Jeremiah resumed his extended commentary on the inevitability of divine judgment against sinners.

8:4–13. This is a standard judgment speech, with accusation (vv. 4–9) and announcement of the coming judgment (vv. 10–13). The words **turn away … return** (v. 4), **slidden back … backsliding … return** (v. 5) are all a form of the Hebrew verb *shub*. This fivefold repetition of the verb "to turn" stresses how the people had turned their backs on God but refused to "return" to Him. The rhetorical question, **What have I done?** (v. 6), reflects the Lord's amazement and anguish that the people could turn away from Him after all He had done for them. Migratory birds (**turtle** refers to the turtledove; v. 7) obey their God-given instincts, but God's rebellious people had not followed His laws. The announcement of judgment (vv. 10–12) repeated the warning of conquest and destruction found in 6:12–15. Jeremiah likely issued similar warnings in a variety of contexts and settings.

8:14–17. In response to the warning of judgment, Jeremiah envisioned what the Babylonian assault on Judah would be like (vv. 14–16). The people would flee for security into their **defenced cities** (v. 14). The catastrophe would be especially devastating because they had the false hope that disaster would not befall them. The Lord warned them that the Babylonian army would be like poisonous snakes (read "vipers" for **cockatrices**; v. 17) that would **bite** the people of Judah.

8:18–22. These verses contain a deeply emotional lament over the coming destruction of Judah. It is difficult to determine the speaker in these verses, but it appears that expressions like **my heart is faint in me** (v. 18) express the pain and anguish of both the Lord and the prophet over Judah's fate. Christian theology at times has muted the biblical teaching on the emotional aspect of God's nature, but here the Lord was deeply distressed, because He had entered into a love relationship with His people. The situation was even more disturbing because there truly was a **balm in Gilead** (v. 22) if the people would only accept it. The territory of Gilead was an important source of spices and medicinal herbs (see Gen. 37:25). The people's question, **Is not the LORD in Zion?** (v. 19), shows that they were still perplexed by their fate and wondered how God could permit the destruction of His land and temple (see 7:4). Rather than accepting responsibility for their actions, they continued to presume upon God's grace and mercy.

9:1–9. The Lord and His prophet dialogue, and the tone of grief and sorrow reflected in chapter 8 carries over into this chapter. Jeremiah took no pleasure in announcing the destruction of Judah (vv. 1–2). This passage reflects why Jeremiah is often referred to as the Weeping Prophet. He spoke of his fellow countrymen with tender sympathy and deep disgust, and his frustration was apparent. The Lord's response (vv. 3–9) focused on the deceitfulness of the people. Their tongues were like a **bow** (v. 3) shooting lies, and no one could be trusted to speak the truth. Because **deceit** (v. 8) had pervaded the very fabric of the nation, the Lord would **visit** (v. 9)

Judah with judgment so that He might **be avenged on such a nation as this**.

9:10–16. Jeremiah once again responded to this warning of judgment with **weeping and wailing** (v. 10). His grief led to a further exchange with the Lord. The Lord was determined to completely destroy Jerusalem (v. 11), and Jeremiah asked, **Who is the wise man?** (v. 12)—Who can discern God's purposes in destroying His own people? The Lord explained that judgment was necessary because the people had **forsaken** His **law** (v. 13) and turned to other gods (vv. 13–14). **Therefore** (v. 15) introduces the formal announcement of judgment, and this judgment would take the form of the covenant curses that Moses had warned the people about centuries earlier (vv. 15–16). The people would eat **wormwood** (v. 15) and drink **gall** (see Deut. 29:18), and the Lord would **scatter them** (v. 16) among the nations (see Deut. 28:64).

9:17–22. This devastating judgment would bring great mourning in the land. **The mourning women** (v. 17) refers to professionals who were paid to mourn at funerals and other sorrowful occasions (see 2 Chron. 35:25; Eccl. 12:5; Amos 5:16). The purpose of the professional mourners was to arouse the bereaved to weep and lament, and the sounds of **wailing** (v. 18) would emanate from **Zion** (v. 19). The wailing women would have to **teach** their **daughters** (v. 20) to lament, so great would be the need for their services. The mourners would lament that **death** (v. 21) had invaded their homes in the form of the enemy soldiers. Death is personified here (see Hab. 2:5). Canaanite mythology included a deity named Mot, the god of infertility and the netherworld. Because of death's invasion, corpses would fill the land of Judah.

9:23–26. In light of the coming judgment, no one had reason to boast in human **wisdom** (v. 23), **might**, or **riches**. The only ground for boasting was in knowledge of the Lord. Ultimately, only God and knowledge of Him and love for Him are worthwhile. Personal knowledge of God with a commitment to follow His ways was the only source of security for the days of coming judgment that were about to befall Judah. The time was coming when God would punish both the **circumcised** (v. 25) and the **uncircumcised** (vv. 25–26). Judah believed that they were exempt from the judgment that would fall on the uncircumcised nations that did not have a special covenant with the Lord, but the people failed to realize that they were just as deserving of judgment because they were uncircumcised in heart.

3. The Judgment of Judah's Idolatry (chap. 10)

Jeremiah concluded his series of temple messages with a poetic section that focused primarily on the vast differences between idols and the Lord (vv. 2–16). Idols and their worshipers are condemned in verses 2–5, 8–9, 11, 14–15, while the one true God is praised in the alternate passages (vv. 6–7, 10, 12–13, 16). Similar polemics against idols and idol worship are found in Isaiah 40:18–20; 41:7; 44:9–20; 46:5–7.

10:1–5. Rather than influencing the nations around them to know the true God, Israel and Judah had given their devotion to the false gods of the other nations. They had worshiped **the signs of heaven** (v. 2), like the pagans who looked to the stars for divine guidance and were **dismayed** by the unusual phenomena associated with the heavenly bodies, such as comets, meteors, and eclipses. The worship of the nations was **vain** (v. 3), because they worshiped man-made objects of wood that were covered **with silver and ... gold** (v. 4). Wood idols were plated with precious metals to beautify them (see Isa. 30:22; 40:19), but Jeremiah demonstrated the futility of idol worship by pointing out that the craftsman must **fasten** the idol **with nails** to keep it from toppling to the ground. The idol is immobile (**upright as the palm tree**; v. 5), unable to communicate, and impotent to do either **evil** or **good**.

10:6–16. In contrast, **there is none like ...** the **LORD** (v. 6) because He is the **King of nations** (v. 7; see Pss. 47:8–9; 96:10). Unlike the tribal deities, who were limited to their own territories, the Lord is King over all. The greatness of the Lord made Judah's worship of lifeless idols all the more incomprehensible (vv. 8–9). The Lord is everything that idols are not—**true** (v. 10), **living**, and **everlasting**. Judah was commanded to inform the nations that their gods would perish (v. 11), and the text of this verse is written in Aramaic. The other major Aramaic passages in the Old Testament are Ezra 4:8–6:18; 7:12–26; Daniel 2:4–7:28. Pagan idolaters would have been more likely to understand Aramaic (the language of diplomacy during this period) than Hebrew. The Lord is the true God because He is the Creator who spoke the universe into existence and stretched out the heavens like a tent or canopy (see Ps. 104:2; Isa. 40:22). Jeremiah described idol worshipers as **brutish** (lacking sense; v. 14), the same term he used to describe the idols themselves in verse 8. By turning to this same form of senseless worship, Judah had ignored their special privilege of having the creator God as their **portion** (v. 16) and of being the **inheritance** of the Lord as His chosen people.

10:17–25. Judgment would fall on Judah because of their idolatry. Destruction and exile were imminent; the Lord threatened that He would **sling** (v. 18) the people out of the land. On behalf of his countrymen, Jeremiah bemoaned their fate (vv. 19–21; see 4:19–21). The nation would lose its children because of the **brutish** (senseless; v. 21; see 10:8, 14) decisions of its corrupt leaders. **The noise** (v. 22) of the invaders would cause **a great commotion** as they came down from **the north country** to attack Judah. On behalf of the nation, Jeremiah prayed for divine justice to be worked out in the midst of this horrible situation. He pleaded with God not to bring Judah **to nothing** (v. 24) by completely destroying them and asked the Lord to **Pour out ... fury upon the heathen** (v. 25) who would invade and attack Judah. Jeremiah's prayer in verse 25 is repeated almost verbatim in Psalm 79:6–7, where the context (Ps. 79:1–5) shows that the prayer is not vengeful but an appeal for God's justice. Jews recite verse 25 annually during their Passover service.

C. Covenant and Conspiracy (chaps. 11–13)

Because of Judah's violations of its covenant obligations, the people would be exiled to Babylon. This section is perhaps to be dated to the reign of Josiah.

1. Judah Has Broken the Covenant (11:1–17)

11:1–10. The Lord called Jeremiah to announce that God's people had broken His **covenant** (v. 2) with them, specifically the covenant God established with Israel through Moses at Mount Sinai (see v. 4; Exod. 19–24). The prophet proclaimed, **Cursed be the man that obeyeth not** (v. 3). The phrase "Cursed be he" appears at the beginning of every verse in Deuteronomy 27:15–26. Blessings resulted from obedience to the covenant (see Deut. 28:1–14), and curses resulted from disobedience (see Deut. 28:15–68). The Lord had delivered Israel out of **Egypt** (v. 4) and brought them to the Promised Land with the intention of blessing them abundantly in **a land flowing with milk and honey** (v. 5). The people had walked **in the imagination of their evil heart** (v. 8), however, which required that the Lord bring the covenant curses upon them. **A conspiracy** (v. 9) had even been hatched among the people of Judah to resist the godly reforms of Josiah and to continue the idolatrous and ungodly practices of the past. Their sin was willful and deliberate; they had **refused** (v. 10) to walk in the ways of the Lord.

11:11–17. I will bring evil upon them (v. 11) was the Lord's warning that He would judge Judah, just as Israel had been judged earlier (see 2 Kings 17:18–23). Because of the people's rampant idolatry, the Lord once again commanded Jeremiah not to pray for Judah. Nothing could spare Judah because they had provoked the Lord to anger.

2. Jeremiah's Prayer for Vindication (11:18–23)

11:18–23. This is the first of Jeremiah's six "confessions" (see Introduction: "Author and Date"). In this confession, Jeremiah lamented his suffering as a prophet and prayed for his vindication and the judgment of his enemies. Jeremiah learned of a plot against his life, in which his enemies sought to treat him **like a lamb ... brought to the slaughter** (v. 19), and cried out to God for protection and ultimate vindication. The prophet prayed that he might see the working out of God's **vengeance** (v. 20) against his enemies. In response, the Lord promised to punish **the men of Anathoth** (Jeremiah's hometown;

v. 21) for plotting against Jeremiah. Those who conspired against Jeremiah, along with their families, would die so that **there shall be no remnant of them** (v. 23), a prophecy against the conspirators in Anathoth, not its entire population, since 128 men of Anathoth returned to their hometown after the exile (see Ezra 2:23).

For modern readers, the tone and language of Jeremiah's prayer here might be somewhat shocking. Jeremiah's questioning of God and expression of deeply negative emotions in his confessions parallel other model prayers in the Old Testament (see, e.g., Psalms 6, 22, 44). The negative tone of these prayers, rather than expressing self-pity or a lack of faith, reflects the freedom to be honest with God that comes from a deep personal relationship with the Lord. Jeremiah truly understood what it means to "pour out your heart" (Ps. 62:8) to the Lord. In praying for the destruction of his enemies, Jeremiah recognized that the enemies who opposed his message and mission were ultimately the enemies of the Lord. Rather than seeking personal revenge, the prophet prayed for the Lord to vindicate him and bring justice to an unjust situation.

3. Jeremiah's Prayer and God's Answer (chap. 12)

Jeremiah's second confession is closely related to and continues the thought of the first confession (11:18–23). Jeremiah spoke (vv. 1–4), and God responded (vv. 5–6).

12:1–4. Jeremiah opened his prayer with the affirmation, **Righteous art thou, O Lord** (v. 1). Because God is righteous, He is a dependable arbiter and judge. He is ready to listen to our questions and complaints. Because of his belief in God's righteousness, Jeremiah asked why **the wicked prosper**. The prophet prayed that his enemies would instead be destroyed like sheep for the slaughter, asking that his wicked countrymen receive the fate mentioned for himself in 11:19. His request arose out of a desire not so much for revenge as for the vindication of God's righteousness.

12:5–6. Before giving any words of reassurance to the prophet, the Lord first warned Jeremiah that his troubles would only increase in the future. His past difficulties, which had **wearied** (v. 5) him, had been like running with men, but the adversity awaiting him would be like running **with horses.** Jeremiah had experienced difficulty in open territory (**land of peace**), and he could expect even greater trouble in **the swelling of Jordan**, referring to dense brushland around the Jordan, which provided cover for lions (see 49:19; 50:44; Zech. 11:3). Jeremiah had also endured opposition from members of his own **house** (family; v. 6), who apparently were included in the "men of Anathoth" (11:21, 23) who wanted him dead, but he would face even greater tests.

12:7–13. In the midst of adversity, Jeremiah could trust in God's promise that the wicked in Judah would ultimately perish (vv. 7–13). Israel is God's **heritage** (v. 7) and His **beloved**, but He would withdraw His love (**I hated it**; v. 8) from Israel by giving her **into the hand of her enemies** (v. 7). The comparison of Israel to **a speckled bird** (v. 9) pictures Israel as a bird with distinctive markings that make her a target of attack by other nations. The leaders of the enemy nations were like "shepherds" (**pastors**; v. 10) who would come down to destroy the Lord's **vineyard** and turn it into a **desolate** wasteland. **The spoilers** (invaders; v. 12) who would attack would come bearing **the sword of the Lord** because they were the human instruments of divine judgment.

12:14–17. After the Lord judged Judah, He would extend His judgment to the nations and would destroy the wicked invaders who had destroyed Judah. These nations would be judged because they had dared to **touch** (v. 14) the Lord's **inheritance**. While God would use them to carry out His sovereign purposes in disciplining His disobedient people, these nations would themselves be held accountable for their murderous cruelty against the people of God. The Lord would **pluck** these nations out of the lands in which they lived, and the Lord would also **pluck out the house of Judah** from their places of exile to bring them back to their homeland.

The messianic age is in view in verses 16–17. While God will judge the nations, He will also show mercy to them. Like Israel, they will be recipients of the salvation of the Lord if they renounce their idols and give their loyalty to the Lord. God's grace will even extend to **Baal** (v. 16) worshipers who turn to the Lord, the very people that the Lord had commanded Israel to exterminate when coming into the Promised Land because of their evil influence (see Deut. 7:1–6). The wideness of God's love is demonstrated in the Old Testament by the fact that Israel's greatest enemies also become the recipients of God's mercy and salvation (see Isa. 19:17–25; Jonah 3–4). At the same time, the Lord will **pluck up** (v. 17) in judgment any nation that chooses not to follow Him.

4. Warnings of Coming Judgment (chap. 13)

This chapter contains a series of five warnings, the first two (vv. 1–11, 13:12–14) originally written in prose, and the last three (13:15–17, 18–19, 20–27) in poetry. The story of the ruined, useless girdle (i.e., belt) is the first major example of the Lord's commanding Jeremiah to perform symbolic acts to illustrate his message. These sign acts were an effective way of grabbing the attention of the complacent and apathetic audiences who did not take seriously Jeremiah's warnings of the coming judgment.

13:1–11. The **linen girdle** (v. 1) was made out of the same material as the priests' garments (see Ezek. 44:17–18) and was symbolic of Israel's holiness as a "kingdom of priests" (see Exod. 19:6). The use of a belt worn around the **loins** (waist) also symbolized the formerly intimate relationship between Israel and the Lord (see v. 11).

After wearing the belt, Jeremiah was commanded to **go to** the **Euphrates** (v. 4), a journey of several hundred miles, and bury the belt. The Euphrates serves as an appropriate symbol of the corrupting Assyrian and Babylonian influence on Judah that began during the days of Ahaz (see 2 Kings 16). This locale also pointed to Babylon as the place of Judah's future exile. Jeremiah returned after many days to retrieve the belt, and the belt was **marred** (v. 7) from being buried in the ground or silted over by the water of the river. As foreseen in Leviticus 26:39, God's people in exile would waste away because of their sins. The visual image of a ruined belt as a symbol of what Judah would become in exile was designed to counter **the great pride** (v. 9) that had kept Judah from properly responding to Jeremiah's warnings of judgment. Judah's vaunted pride would be a cause of her downfall and exile.

13:12–14. The Lord used the imagery of filled jars of **wine** (v. 12) to point toward the eventual destruction of Judah's leaders and people. Like jars that were full of wine, the leaders and people of Judah would become drunk as they were filled with the wine of God's wrath (see 25:15–29; Ps. 60:3; Isa. 51:17–20; Ezek. 23:32–34). The Lord would also smash the various factions in Judah like pottery jars (see 19:10–11) and would **not pity ... nor have mercy** (v. 14) on them.

13:15–17. The prophet warned the people that sinful pride carries the seed of its own destruction. Rather than exalting self, Judah needed to **Give glory to the LORD** (v. 16). If the nation failed to glorify the Lord, He would bring the **darkness** of judgment rather than the **light** of salvation and deliverance. The prophet would weep when he observed his fellow countrymen **carried away captive** (v. 17) because of their **pride.**

13:18–27. The threat of exile continued with the warning that exile was imminent (vv. 18–19). The prophet spoke (vv. 20–23), and the Lord responded (vv. 24–27), saying that Judah's willful rebellion had made exile inevitable. Because of her spiritual adulteries, Judah would be disgraced publicly, like a common prostitute (vv. 22, 26–27; see Isa. 47:3; Hos. 2:3, 10). Judah was so entrenched in her sinful and idolatrous ways that asking her to change was like having an **Ethiopian change his skin** (v. 23) color or a **leopard** remove its **spots.** Persistence in disobedience leads to bondage to sin, and Judah's spiritual bondage would ultimately be the cause of their physical bondage in exile.

D. Judah beyond Deliverance (chaps. 14–15)

This section contains messages Jeremiah delivered during an especially severe drought, the date of which is unknown. After an initial vivid description of the drought (14:2–6), Jeremiah alternatively prayed (14:7–9, 13, 17–22), and God responded (14:10–12, 14–16; 15:1–9). Drought was one of the curses threatened for disobedience to the covenant (see 23:10; Lev. 26:19–20; Deut. 28:22–24). The Lord sent these natural disasters as advanced warning of the greater judgment of invasion and exile (see Amos 4:6–9).

14:1–6. The Holy Land was especially dependent on adequate rainfall, so the effects of this severe **dearth** (drought; v. 1) had caused great mourning in Judah (14:2–6). Jeremiah compared Judah to a wild donkey panting for breath (**snuffed up**; v. 6) because of the drought brought on by their sin. This image of a wild donkey previously appeared in 2:24 to describe Jerusalem panting after its lovers in the heat of desire. Lust for sin had borne the fruit of struggle for physical survival.

14:7–12. The prophet prayed on behalf of the people that the Lord might send relief (vv. 7–9), but the Lord responded that He did not acknowledge **this people** (vv. 10–11) as His own. Jeremiah was not to pray for the **good** (v. 11) of this people because the Lord would not answer. The Lord also would not accept the sacrifices Judah offered to appease Him, because sacrifice is of no avail when unaccompanied by repentance. The Lord would send the covenant curses of **sword ... famine ... pestilence** (v. 12) against Judah (see Lev. 26:25–26). This triad of curses appears fifteen times in the book of Jeremiah.

14:13–16. Jeremiah reminded the Lord that the false prophets had deceived the people with empty promises of **peace** (v. 13). The people, however, had been willing partners in this deception, wanting to hear only promises of peace and security. The Lord responded that He would bring judgment against both the false prophets and the people who had followed them (vv. 14–16).

14:17–22. Jeremiah wept over the fate of Jerusalem, just as Jesus later did (Matt 23:37–38), and prayed once again on their behalf. The prophet confessed Judah's sin, anticipating the repentance that would lead to Israel's ultimate restoration (see Deut.

30:2–3). He pleaded on the basis of God's ancient **covenant** (v. 21) promises (see Lev. 26:44–45) that the Lord would not destroy His people. Jeremiah also acknowledged that the Lord, not Baal, is the one who can send the **showers** (v. 22) to end the drought.

15:1–9. The Lord responded as part of the ongoing dialogue with His prophet over Judah's imminent destruction. Jeremiah's intercession for Judah was useless, because the people did not share his repentant spirit. The people were so wicked that God refused to hear prayers offered on their behalf (see 7:16; 14:11–12). They were beyond divine help. Even if **Moses and Samuel** (v. 1), famed for their intercession for sinful Israel (see Exod. 32:11–14, 30–34; Num. 14:13–23; 1 Sam. 7:5–9; 12:19–25), were to pray for this people, God would not listen. The people of Judah would be subjected to **sword ... famine; ... and captivity** (v. 2), and the corpses of the dead would experience **four kinds** (v. 3) of desecration. The sentence of judgment against Judah had become irrevocable, in large part because of the wicked influence of **Manasseh** (v. 4). Manasseh, the grandfather of good King Josiah, was the most wicked king in Judah's long history (see 2 Kings 21:1–11, 16), and his sins were a primary cause of Judah's eventual destruction (see 2 Kings 21:12–15; 23:26–27; 24:3–4). Even with the reforms of Josiah and a final offer of repentance and the avoidance of judgment in the early days of Jeremiah's ministry, Judah had persisted in their sinful ways. The judgment of Judah would be severe, with even the mother of **seven** (v. 9) sons, the complete and ideal number of sons (see Ruth 4:15), grieving over the loss of her family.

15:10–21. The Lord's announcement of judgment prompted the third of Jeremiah's confessions (see Introduction: "Author and Date"), which contains the prophet's prayer and two further responses from the Lord (vv. 11–14, 15:19–21).

15:10–14. Jeremiah lamented that he faced opposition from **the whole earth** (or "all of the land"; v. 10). Jeremiah faced this severe opposition despite the fact that he had not been involved in either lending or borrowing money **on usury** (interest), mat-

ters likely to evoke dispute or differences of opinion. His only offense had been speaking the message that the Lord had communicated to Him. The Lord responded by encouraging Jeremiah and reminding the prophet of His protective presence. These words recall the Lord's original promise to Jeremiah at the time of his call (1:8–10, 17–19), and Jeremiah needed to hear them again in this time of great difficulty.

15:15–18. The prophet's words to the Lord become even more forceful and direct. Despite that Jeremiah had taken great delight in the word of the Lord, he had often had to stand **alone** (v. 17), having only a few friends, in carrying out his prophetic mission and had experienced extreme opposition that was like a **wound** (v. 18) that refused to heal. Jeremiah accused God of being undependable, like **a liar** or an intermittent stream that had become a dry brook (**waters that fail**; compare God's description of Himself as a "fountain of living waters," 2:13).

15:19–21. Much like Job in the midst of his great adversity, Jeremiah was dangerously close to speaking presumptuously about God, but the Lord responded to the prophet's complaint in an empathetic and understanding manner. The Lord commanded Jeremiah to repent, but then encouraged him and renewed his call. If Jeremiah would **return** (repent; v. 19), he would be allowed to **stand before** the Lord, the appropriate posture for an obedient servant (see Num. 16:9; Deut. 10:8). The people needed to **return** to Jeremiah by accepting his message, but Jeremiah was not to **return** to the people by capitulating to the pressure to soften his message. The Lord would continue to protect the prophet as he carried out his dangerous mission.

E. Disaster and Comfort (16:1–17:18)

The prophet delivered messages of disaster and comfort, with the note of disaster predominating (16:1–13, 16–18; 16:21–17:6; 17:9–13, 18). In the Hebrew, the first half of this section is prose (16:1–18), and the second half is poetry (16:19–17:18).

16:1–9. The prophet's personal life served as an object lesson of the disaster facing Judah as a nation.

The prophet was commanded not to marry, not to have children, and not to go into a **house of mourning** (v. 5) or **feasting** (v. 8). In the coming destruction, death would be such a common experience that there would be no time for mourning or feasting. A wedding celebration was pointless at this time because the joy of such an occasion would soon turn to grief.

Jeremiah's personal experiences are a reminder of the great sacrifices often required of those called to ministry. His ministry was such that he had to face life alone, without the comfort and support that a family could provide. The Lord similarly used the difficult family circumstances of the prophets Hosea (see Hosea 1–3) and Ezekiel (see Ezek. 24:16–17, 22–23) to teach important lessons to His people.

16:10–15. When the people asked Jeremiah why he had pronounced such a severe message of judgment against them, the prophet was to remind them of Judah's long history of disobedience and unfaithfulness to the Lord (vv. 10–13). The coming judgment could not be blamed on the sins of previous generations, because Jeremiah's contemporaries had **done worse** (v. 12) than their ancestors (see Ezek. 18:2–4). Despite the covenant unfaithfulness of Israel and Judah, the Lord promised that the restoration from exile would surpass even the original exodus in its scope and magnitude (vv. 14–15).

16:16–21. The invaders who would attack Judah would be like **fishers** (v. 16) and **hunters** (see Ezek. 12:13; 29:4; Amos 4:2), and there would be no place for the people to hide from God's judgment. The Lord would **recompense** (v. 18) Judah **double** (or "fully") for their sins. Their lifeless idols were like **the carcases** of dead animals that had made the Promised Land ceremonially unclean (see Lev. 4:12). The prophet concluded this section with a few brief words of hope. He confessed his trust in the Lord as **strength ... fortress, and ... refuge** (v. 19), images for God's dependability and protecting power that are common in the Psalms (see Pss. 18:1–2; 28:7–8; 59:16–17). God's judgment of Judah would ultimately cause even **the Gentiles** to acknowledge the futility of worshiping idols. As in 12:16, the prophet

envisioned the inclusion of the nations in the blessings of the kingdom.

17:1–4. The Lord responded to Jeremiah and continued His solemn warnings of judgment. **The sin of Judah** was **written with a pen of iron** (v. 1) that had **a diamond** (or "flint") **point**, an instrument used for inscribing permanent records (see Job 19:24). These sins were not only written on the people's hearts as a reflection of their internal corruption but were also indelibly engraved **upon the horns of** their **altars,** as a reminder to the Lord not to show mercy or to provide atonement (see Lev. 16:18). It was appropriate that their altars should signify judgment rather than mercy because these altars had become **high places for sin** (v. 3) where Judah carried out pagan rituals.

17:5–11. In a passage recalling Psalm 1, Jeremiah contrasted the **Cursed** (v. 5) and **Blessed** (v. 7) individuals. This contrast demonstrated the error of Judah's ways because they had trusted in human resources rather than putting their hope and trust in the Lord, who alone brings stability and security. Though the blessings of trusting in the Lord are obvious, the problem is that the human **heart** (v. 9) is wicked and prone to the choices that lead to cursing. The Lord knows the heart of each individual and will judge accordingly. Those who had gained wealth by unjust means are compared to a **partridge** (v. 11) that hatches **eggs** it did not lay, and the Lord would cause this dishonest wealth to disappear.

17:12–18. Jeremiah began his fourth confession (see Introduction: "Author and Date") with a recognition that God's sovereignty over the earth provides a **sanctuary** (v. 12) for the righteous and an expression of confidence that all who **forsake** (v. 13) the Lord will be put to shame. On the basis of this affirmation, Jeremiah prayed for the healing of vindication because of his opponents' accusation that he was a false prophet needlessly proclaiming judgment against Judah (see Deut. 18:21–22). This accusation must have been voiced before the first invasion of Judah by the Babylonians in 605 BC. Because of the unfair attacks against him, Jeremiah prayed for the **double** full **destruction** (v. 18) of his enemies.

F. Command to Keep the Sabbath Holy (17:19–27)

17:19–27. Jeremiah was commissioned to deliver to the people an extended commentary on **the sabbath day** (v. 22) commandment, probably the version recorded in Deuteronomy 5:12–15. Jeremiah warned the leaders and people of Judah not to be like their rebellious fathers, who had failed to keep the Sabbath laws. More than mere ritual, the Sabbath is the covenant sign of God's relationship with Israel (see Exod. 31:13–17; Ezek. 20:12), and adherence to the Sabbath laws demonstrates that God is valued above personal wealth and advancement. The Lord promised that if Judah obeyed, King David's dynasty would last forever (see 23:5–6; 30:9; 33:15; 2 Sam. 7:12–17), and **Jerusalem** (v. 25) would be inhabited for all time (see Zech. 2:2–12; 8:3; 14:11). The Lord would accept the worship and sacrifices of His obedient people. In contrast, failure to obey would bring disaster and would negate, at least temporarily, the promises of verses 24–26. **The gates** (v. 27) of Jerusalem, through which the people had carried their burdens in violation of the Sabbath, would be the first structures destroyed. Using common prophetic language for divine judgment against rebellious cities, Jeremiah also warned that the Lord would **kindle a fire** that would **devour the palaces of Jerusalem** (see 49:27; 50:32; Amos 1:4, 7, 10, 12, 14; 2:2, 5).

G. Lessons from the Potter (chaps. 18–20)

Chapters 18–20 focus on lessons the Lord taught Jeremiah at a potter's workshop, probably some time before 605 BC. On his first visit to the potter, Jeremiah learned of God's willingness to forgive Judah if they would repent of their sin. On the second visit, however, he learned of the inevitability of judgment because of Judah's refusal to turn from her evil ways.

1. The Parable of Potter and Clay (chaps. 18–19)

18:1–4. Jeremiah made two separate visits to the potter's workshop. In the first visit (v. 1–18:17), Jeremiah learned that as the potter controlled what he did with the clay, so the Lord was sovereign over the people of Judah. The potter shaped the clay on the wheels (lit., "two stones" v. 3). Both wheels were attached to a single upright shaft, one end of which was sunk permanently in the ground. The potter would spin the lower wheel with his foot and work the clay on the upper wheel. This process is described in the apocryphal book of Ecclesiasticus (38:29–30). As Jeremiah was observing the potter at work, the clay on the wheel became **marred** (v. 4). The same word appears in 13:7 with respect to the linen girdle that Jeremiah had hidden. Because the clay was flawed in some manner, the potter reshaped the clay **as seemed good** to him. The flaw was in the clay itself, not in the potter's skill.

18:5–12. The prophet then informed the people, **as the clay … so are ye** (v. 6). Biblical imagery often pictures mankind as made of clay by a potter (see 4:19). The point here is that Judah was like the soft clay that the potter was able to reshape. If Judah repented, there was still time to avoid the judgment that the Lord threatened to bring against them. A response of repentance can turn a threat of judgment into blessing, while promised blessing can be forfeited through disobedience (vv. 7–10). The Lord retains the right of limiting His own absolute sovereignty on the basis of human response to His offers of pardon and restoration and His threats of judgment and destruction. God's promises and threats are conditioned on man's actions. God, who Himself does not change (see Num. 23:19; Mal. 3:6; James 1:17), nevertheless will change His preannounced response to man, depending on what man does (see Joel 2;13; Jonah 3:8–4:2). The Lord sent Jeremiah to the people with the appeal to **return** (v. 11) to Him, because the people believed there was **no hope** (v. 12) and that they might as well continue in their sinful ways if the Lord had determined to bring catastrophe upon them. On the one hand, the unbelieving nation said that judgment would not come (see 6:14; 8:11), but on the other hand, they argued that there was nothing they could do to avoid the judgment if it did come.

18:13–17. Though the Lord offered Judah a genuine opportunity to return to Him and to avoid the coming judgment, He was not optimistic of a positive response to the prophet's message (vv. 13 – 14). Judah was fickle and unfaithful to the Lord, unlike **the snow of Lebanon** (v. 14), a constant and reliable source of water. They had repeatedly turned to other gods, which necessitated the Lord's judgment of driving them into exile (vv. 15 – 17).

18:18 – 23. This is the fifth of Jeremiah's confessions (see Introduction: "Author and Date"). Instead of turning to the Lord, Jeremiah's enemies continued to **devise devices** (v. 18) against the prophet. Jeremiah prayed for vindication and asked that he not be repaid **evil** (v. 20) for his faithfulness to the Lord's calling. The prophet also called down a curse on his enemies, praying that the Lord would put them and their children to death and not extend to them forgiveness for their sins. Though the language directed toward his enemies is extreme, it is important to remember that Jeremiah's petition is a prayer not for human vengeance but for divine vindication.

19:1 – 15. Jeremiah's second visit to the potter conveyed an entirely different message from that of the first visit. After delivering a verbal warning (vv. 1 – 9), Jeremiah deliberately broke a bottle (v. 10) to symbolize the forthcoming destruction of Judah and Jerusalem (vv. 11 – 15).

19:1 – 6. In chapter 18, the potter's clay was still moist and pliable, making it possible to reshape and rework it, but here the **earthen bottle** (clay jar; v. 1) was hard and could only be destroyed since it was unsuitable for the owner's use. Jeremiah performed the object lesson of smashing the clay jar in front of **the ancients** the elders **of the people, and … of the priests** to provide both a verbal and visual warning of the judgment to come.

Jeremiah performed this symbolic act at **the east gate** (v. 2) in **the valley of the son of Hinnom** (or Ben Hinnom), which was appropriate for two reasons. First, "the east gate" should be translated "the potsherd gate" because the Hebrew word underlying "east" is the same as that translated "earthern" in verse 1. The gate was given this name because it overlooked the main dump for broken pottery. Second, the Valley of Ben Hinnom was used as a place for sacrificing children to pagan gods (see 7:31).

Because of her violence and worship of other gods, Judah would be smashed to pieces like broken pottery, and the Valley of Ben Hinnom would become **The valley of slaughter** (v. 6).

19:7 – 9. Many of the inhabitants of Jerusalem would **fall by the sword** (v. 7) of the enemy, and the survivors would resort to eating their own children because of the scarcity of food. Cannabalism due to military siege is listed as one of the covenant curses in Leviticus 26:29 and Deuteronomy 28:53 – 57. When Jerusalem's food supply ran out during the Babylonian siege in 586 BC, cannibalism resulted (see Lam. 2:20; 4:10; Ezek. 5:10). Such shocking activity was not unprecedented in Israel (see 2 Kings 6:26 – 28) and would occur again in AD 70 during the Roman siege of Jerusalem. Josephus (*Jewish Wars*, 6.3.4) writes, "A woman … who … had fled to Jerusalem … killed her son, roasted him, and ate one half, concealing and saving the rest."

19:10 – 15. After pronouncing the warning of judgment, Jeremiah was to **break the bottle** (v. 10) in front of his audience to visualize the imminent destruction of Judah (vv. 10 – 13). Egyptians of the Twelfth Dynasty (1991 – 1786 BC) inscribed the names of their enemies on pottery bowls and then smashed them, hoping to break the power of their enemies by doing so. Though no magical power was ascribed to Jeremiah's act, the breaking of the pottery did signify that Judah had become the enemy of God. The Lord warned that Jerusalem would **be defiled** like **Tophet** (v. 13). Tophet was the sacred cemetery in the Valley of Hinnom that Josiah had already desecrated so that further pagan acts connected to child sacrifice would not occur there (see 2 Kings 23:10). Jerusalem and **all the towns** (v. 15) of Judah would be destroyed.

2. Jeremiah and Pashur (20:1 – 6)

20:1 – 6. These verses record Pashur's response to Jeremiah's symbolic act (vv. 1 – 2), and Jeremiah's rejoinder to him (vv. 3 – 6). Pashur was a **priest** (v. 1) and the **chief governor** of the temple, responsible for punishing troublemakers, real or imagined, in the temple courts (see 29:26). His position was second only to that of the chief priest himself (compare 29:25–26 with 52:24). Pashur most likely had Jeremiah beaten (**smote**; v. 2) in accordance with the Mosaic law of Deuteronomy 25:2–3 and then had him placed in **stocks** (lit., "restraint, confinement"; the word for "stocks" is translated "prison house" in 2 Chron. 16:10). Pashur's beating of Jeremiah was the first of many recorded acts of physical violence against Jeremiah.

In the announcement of judgment against Pashur for his mistreatment of Jeremiah, Pashur was given the new name **Magor-missabib** (v. 3), which means "terror on every side." His new name signified terror to himself and to all Judah, whose people would be exiled to **Babylon** (v. 4) or put to death. This prophecy was fulfilled in 597 BC (see 2 Kings 24:13) and 586 BC (see 52:17–23; 25:13–17).

3. Jeremiah Complains to the Lord (20:7–18)

20:7–13. Jeremiah's sixth and final confession (see Introduction: "Author and Date") was also his longest. In some respects, it was the most daring and bitter of them all. Jeremiah felt that when the Lord originally called him to be a prophet, He had overly persuaded him (see 1:7–8, 17–19). The word **deceived** (v. 7) literally means "seduced" (see Exod. 22:16) or "enticed" (see 1 Kings 22:20–22). The Lord had not fully revealed to Jeremiah all the sufferings that he would experience in fulfilling his prophetic calling. Jeremiah's statement that the word of the Lord was like **a burning fire** (v. 9) in his **heart** is a classic description of a prophet's reluctance overcome by divine compulsion (see 1:6–8; Amos 3:8; 1 Cor. 9:16). Despite the continual opposition of his enemies, Jeremiah declared, **the LORD is with me as a mighty terrible one** (v. 11). The Lord's strength produces dread in His opponents. Jeremiah prayed for divine vengeance to be carried out on his enemies and called for praise to the Lord because of his confidence in the Lord's deliverance.

20:14–18. From the heights of exultation, Jeremiah sunk to the depths of despair. The irreversibility of his divine call, the betrayal of his friends, and the negative and condemnatory nature of his mes-

sage had all combined to bring to his lips a startling expression of despondency and hopelessness. Echoing the words of Job, the prophet called for the day of his birth to be **Cursed** (v. 14; see Job 3:3). News of the birth of a son was normally a blessing in ancient times (see, e.g., Gen. 29:31–35), but Jeremiah saw it as a curse in his case. In his anguish, Jeremiah wished that his mother's womb, which had given him birth, had instead been his eternal tomb. Jeremiah's words here are a reminder that service for the Lord, while the source of great joy, can also bring hardship and difficulty that requires faithful endurance and perseverance.

H. Judgment on Judah's Corrupt Leaders (chap. 21–23)

Chapters 21–23 form a unit focusing on the judgment that would befall Judah's corrupt leaders. The rulers of Judah, who bore the primary responsibility for the nation's economic, social, and spiritual ills, were the first to be denounced by Jeremiah (21:1–23:7). Then Jeremiah turned his attention to the false prophets, who had led the people astray with their empty promises of peace and security (23:8–40).

1. Zedekiah's Prayer and God's Answer (chap. 21)

21:1–2. The incident in this passage occured sometime between 588 and 586 BC, when the Babylonians were besieging Judah (note **maketh war**; v. 2) because the brash Zedekiah had rebelled against Babylon (see 52:3). Zedekiah and his officials came to Jeremiah with a request: **Inquire ... of the LORD for us**. Their request reflects a desire for insider information concerning the future and divine assistance in carrying out their plans rather than a genuine willingness to seek the Lord and follow His will. Specifically, Zedekiah sought for the Lord to **deal with us according to all his wondrous works**, anticipating that the Lord would miraculously deliver Jerusalem from the enemy as He had in the days of Hezekiah (701 BC) when the Assyrian army had surrounded the city (see Isa. 37:36). Zedekiah made three similar inquiries of the prophet in chapter 38.

The king's request for the Lord's help apart from submission to the Lord's commands reflects how the belief in Jerusalem's inviolability to enemy attack had distorted the perspective of the leaders and people of Jerusalem. Despite Jeremiah's warnings not to trust in the temple as a sure sign of God's protection (see 7:4), Zedekiah held on to the false hope that the Lord would intervene at the eleventh hour to deliver Jerusalem from danger.

21:3–7. Jeremiah warned the king that the Lord would not deliver Jerusalem from the Babylonian army. The Lord would **turn back the weapons of war** (v. 4) used by the Judean army so that their defense of Jerusalem would fail. Instead of being the rescuer of Jerusalem, the Lord warned with a series of first-person verbs (**I will assemble,** v. 4; **I myself will fight,** v. 5; **I will smite,** v. 6; **I will deliver,** v. 7) that He would be the commander of the armies attacking Jerusalem. The Lord would fight against His own people **with an outstretched hand and with a strong arm** (v. 5; see 27:5; 32:17). A similar phrase was used to describe God's powerful redemption of Israel at the exodus (see 32:31; Deut. 4:34; 7:19; 26:8).

21:8–10. Because of the Lord's intention to destroy Jerusalem, Jeremiah encouraged Zedekiah and the people to give up their resistance efforts and surrender to the Babylonians. Jeremiah later again offered similar advice (38:2–3; 17–18). Those who continued the resistance would **die by the sword** (v. 9), while those who surrender would **live.** The advice in verse 9 is repeated almost verbatim in 38:2. Jeremiah's counsel of surrender branded him as a traitor in the eyes of many (see 37:13), but he was in fact a true patriot who wanted to stay in Judah even after Jerusalem was destroyed (see 37:14; 40:6; 42:7–22).

21:11–14. The Lord's judgment would fall on the **house of David** (v. 12) because of the failure of Zedekiah and other Davidic rulers to **Execute judgment** (i.e., "administer justice," see 5:28; 22:16; 1 Kings 3:28). Jerusalem would be the target of the Lord's judgment (vv. 13–14) because of the arrogant assumption of its inhabitants that no one was able to **come down against** (v. 13) them. They would fall in judgment because they believed themselves to be beyond the reach of God's justice.

2. A Burden about Evil Kings and the Promise of a True King (22:1–23:8)

22:1–9. The Lord commanded Jeremiah to go to the palace in Jerusalem and deliver a message of judgment to **the king of Judah** (v. 1), probably Zedekiah. Zedekiah's predecessors are mentioned in sequence later in the chapter (Josiah, 22:10a, 15b–16; Jehoahaz/Shallum, 22:10b–12; Jehoaikim, 22:13–15a, 17–19; Jehoiachin/Coniah, 22:24–30). These oracles condemning the ungodliness of Judah's final four rulers served to validate the Lord's judgment against the house of David and the removal of the Davidic ruler from the throne in Jerusalem. The Lord's covenant with David had unconditionally promised that David's line would continue "forever" (2 Sam. 7:13, 15–16; Ps. 89:29, 33–37), but had also warned that the Lord would reward or punish individual Davidic rulers based on the degree of their obedience to the Lord's commands (see 2 Sam. 7:14; Ps. 89:30–32). The disobedience of the Davidic rulers necessitated the ending of the Davidic dynasty within history, but the unconditional nature of the covenant promises to David guaranteed that God would raise up a new David (i.e., Messiah) at a future time (23:5–8; see also 33:15; Ezek. 34:23–24; Matt. 1:1). Though all the kings of the Davidic dynasty failed to a greater or lesser degree, the victorious Messiah would someday appear as the culmination of David's royal line.

Jeremiah warned Zedekiah that failure to administer **judgment** (justice) **and righteousness** (v. 3), the chief responsibilities of a king (see Ps. 72:1–4, 12–14), would result in severe judgment. The Lord would **prepare** (v. 7), or "consecrate," enemy armies to fight a holy war against the disobedient king (see 6:4). To capture the full sense of the warning that the enemy armies would **cut down** the **choice cedars** of Judah, see Psalm 74:3–6, an especially vivid description of the Babylonian troops smashing the carved paneling of the Jerusalem temple with their axes and hatchets.

22:10-12. Jeremiah delivered a message to **Shallum the son of Josiah** (v. 11), who briefly came to the throne following the death of Josiah in 609 BC. Shallum, whose throne name was Jehoahaz, ruled for three months before being taken to Egypt as a prisoner of Pharaoh Neco (see 2 Kings 23:29-34). While the people mourned the death of Josiah at the hands of the Egyptian army at Megiddo (see 2 Chron. 35:24-25), their real grief should have been for Shallum. Shallum would **return no more** (v. 10) to the homeland from his captivity, a prophecy confirmed by 2 Kings 23:34, which states that Shallum died in Egypt.

22:13-17. Jeremiah delivered a scathing denunciation of King Jehoiakim (609-598/597 BC). Jehoiakim is described in the third person in verses 13-14, rhetorically addressed in the first person in verses 15 and 17, and then identified by name in 22:18. Good King Josiah is referred to in verses 15b-16 by way of contrast.

Woe unto him that buildeth (v. 13) was a scathing denunciation of Jehoiakim for lavishly renovating his palace during a time of national crisis. Jehoiakim was concerned more for his personal residence than for the well-being of the nation. The king was guilty of using **his neighbour's service without wages.** The king had violated the Mosaic law by not paying the workers employed to renovate the palace (see Lev. 25:39; Deut. 24:14-15). Jehoiakim's refusal to pay them may have been due partly to inability, since Judah was under heavy tribute to Egypt during the early part of his reign (see 2 Kings 23:35). When the nation's resources were stretched to a breaking point, Jehoiakim had selfishly **cieled** (or paneled; v. 14) his palace with **cedar.** Haggai similarly deplored the postexilic community's use of paneling in their houses as an extravagant and unneeded luxury when construction of the temple remained unfinished (Hag. 1:4).

22:18-23. Because of Jehoiakim's selfish extravagance and failure to practice justice, Jehoiakim would not receive the honor due a king at the time of his death (vv. 18-23). The people would **not lament for him** (v. 18), honoring his memory. Rather, he would receive **the burial of an ass** (v. 19), which was tantamount to no burial at all (see 36:30). This fulfillment of this prophecy is found in 2 Kings 24:6, where no burial is described. Jehoiakim was like an **inhabitant of Lebanon** (v. 23) because of the cedar from Lebanon used to panel his palace (v. 23; see 1 Kings 7:2), but his luxurious accommodations would not be able to protect him (or the other inhabitants of Jerusalem) from the Lord's judgment.

22:24-30. Jeremiah delivered an oracle of judgment against King Jehoiachin (also known as Coniah), and the fulfillment of this prophecy is recorded in 24:1 and 29:2. Jehoiachin succeeded his father, Jehoiakim, to the throne in 598/597 BC and reigned for only three months before being taken to Babylon as an exile when Nebuchadnezzar captured Jerusalem (see 2 Kings 24:8-17). Jeremiah compared Jeconiah to a **signet** (v. 24) ring that the Lord would remove from His hand, signifying the removal of Jeconiah from the throne and the loss of his position as the Lord's anointed ruler over Judah. This curse against Jeconiah was later reversed by a promise of the future restoration of the Davidic dynasty (Hag. 2:23). Jeconiah would be taken into exile (**cast thee out … into another country,** v. 26), and 2 Kings 25:27-30 and Jeremiah 52:31-34 confirm that Jeconiah remained in Babylon for the remainder of his life. Babylonian administrative texts that mention Jeconiah by name also confirm his presence in Babylon. The Lord's announcement **Write ye this man childless** (v. 30) did not mean that Jeconiah would have no children (1 Chron. 3:17-18 indicates that he had at least seven), but that he would have none to sit on the throne of David in Judah. Jeconiah's grandson Zerubbabel (see 1 Chron. 3:17-19; Matt. 1:12) became the governor of Judah (see Hag. 1:1), but not king. Zedekiah was a son of Josiah (see 37:1), not of Jeconiah, and he and his sons died before Jeconiah (see 52:10-11). Thus, Jeconiah was Judah's last surviving Davidic king—until Christ.

23:1-8. This woe oracle provides a summary statement concerning God's judgment against the house of David, including both His warning that He intended to judge the wicked ruler and leaders of Judah (vv. 1–2) and His promise that He would bring His people back from exile (vv. 3–4, 7–8) and raise up an ideal Davidic king (vv. 5–6). Because **the pastors** (shepherds; v. 1) of Judah had not **visited** (attended to; v. 2) the people as their flock, God would **visit** calamity upon the shepherds.

When the Lord brought His people back from exile, they would then have shepherds (leaders) who would properly care for them (v. 4). The flock would fear no more, nor be dismayed. The absence of a concerned shepherd invites attacks by wild animals (see Ezek. 34:8), but the restored community would have no worries concerning their security. The Lord's promise to **raise unto David a righteous Branch** (v. 5; echoed in 33:15–16) is one of the most important messianic passages in the Old Testament prophets. The Messiah, unlike any previous descendant of David, would be the ideal King. He would sum up in Himself all the finest qualities of the best rulers, and infinitely more. "Branch" is also a messianic title in Zechariah 3:8; 6:12 (see "a rod out of the stem of Jesse," Isa. 11:1). "Righteous Branch" (v. 5) and **THE LORD OUR RIGHTEOUSNESS** (v. 6), both titles for the Messiah, reflect a play on the name Zedekiah, whose name means "the Lord is my righteousness." Although Zedekiah did not live up to the meaning of his name, Jesus the Messiah would bestow on His people the abundant blessings (see Ezek. 34:25–31) that come from the hands of a King who brings **judgment and justice** (v. 5).

3. Judgment on the False Prophets (23:9–40)

23:9–15. Along with Judah's rulers, the false prophets were also condemned for their failed leadership. In addition to this passage, Jeremiah also denounced the false prophets in 2:8; 4:9; 5:30–31; 6:13–15; 8:10–12; 14:13–15; 18:18–23; 26:8, 11, 16; 27–28. The false prophets, who refused to recognize that Judah's numerous covenant violations had brought the curse of drought upon the land, were deserving of judgment because they were as ungodly as the people were (vv. 10–12). The prophets of Judah who falsely spoke in the name of the Lord were no better than **the prophets of Samaria** (northern Israel;

v. 13) who had prophesied in the name of Baal. Their practice of adultery and other depraved behavior made them as wicked as the people of **Sodom** and **Gomorrah** (v. 14). As punishment for their perversity, the Lord would cause them to eat bitter (**wormwood**; v. 15) food and drink poisoned water (**gall**).

23:16–22. The essential problem with these prophets was that they preached a message that was **of their own heart** (v. 16) rather than one that came from God (vv. 16–22). **Ye shall have peace** (v. 17) was the essential message of the false prophets (see 6:14; 8:11; 14:13). While this message of peace was what the people wanted to hear, it offered no real security because it originated in **the imagination of** the prophet's **heart**. These false prophets were not like the true messengers of the Lord, who **stood in the counsel of the Lord** (v. 18) and were privy to the decisions made in the throne room of heaven (see 1 Kings 22:19–22; Job 1:6; 2:1). The false prophets were promising peace as God's wrath was about to fall upon the people as **a grievous whirlwind** (v. 19). If the Lord had **sent these prophets** (v. 21) and they had **stood in** His **counsel** (v. 22), they would have announced the Lord's true intentions so that the people would turn from their sinful ways.

23:23–32. The prophets could not hide their lies from the Lord, and He would hold them accountable for how they had deceived His people (vv. 23–32). By proclaiming these lies, the prophets had caused the people to **forget** (v. 27) the Lord and to worship **Baal**. As a contrast to the empty message of the prophets, the true word of God is symbolized in three figures of speech: **the wheat** (v. 28), **a fire** (v. 29), and **a hammer**. The difference between the words of the false prophets and the word of the Lord is like that of **chaff** (v. 28) and wheat. Of the two, only the wheat can feed and nourish (see 15:16). As "a fire", the word of the Lord ultimately tests the quality of each man's work (1 Cor. 3:13). As "a hammer," the divine word relentlessly works to judge "the thoughts and intents of the heart" (Heb. 4:12). The threefold repetition of **I am against** (vv. 30–32) expresses the Lord's determination to bring judgment against the false prophets.

23:33–40. Because the people had preferred the message of the prophets to the word of the Lord, a message (**burden,** or oracle; v. 33) from the Lord would not be available when they sought for one in their time of trouble. It would do no good for the people to ask, **What hath the LORD spoken?** (v. 35), because the Lord would abandon them. They had preferred the words of men to the words of God, so God would force them to get by as best they could on their own counsel (**burden;** v. 36). Hearing the word of the Lord brings accountability, and failure to carry through on God's commands brings judgment. Failure to obey the will of God is punished by the denial of access to the word of God and its life-giving blessings. The Lord would **forget** (a play on the word "burden"; v. 39) His people and would bring **reproach** (v. 40) and **shame** on them because of their disobedience.

I. The Sign of the Good and the Evil Figs (chap. 24)

Having denounced Judah's leaders (21:1–23:8) and false prophets (23:9–40), Jeremiah next described the division of Judah's people into good and bad (vv. 1–3) and summarized the Lord's determination to restore the good (v. 4–7) but destroy the bad.

24:1–4. Jeremiah's prophetic vision pictured the people of Judah as **two baskets of figs** (v. 1; see Amos 8:1–3 for similar imagery). Surprisingly, the basket of **good figs** (v. 2) represented the exiles that would be taken away with Jeconiah (Jehoiachin) in the exile of 597 BC, while the basket of **naughty figs** represented the Jews who would remain in the land. Those remaining in the land would view themselves as privileged and their countrymen taken to Babylon as the objects of divine wrath.

24:5–7. The Lord, however, declared that the hope for Israel's future lay with the exiles (v. 5). Just as good figs should be protected and preserved by their owner, so also the exiles would be watched over and cared for by the Lord (see 29:4–14). The Lord would **bring them again to** the **land** (v. 6) and **build them** as a nation, a promise that was partially fulfilled in the return from Babylonian exile in 538

BC and that will be ultimately fulfilled in the eschatological kingdom. In the future age of salvation, the Lord **will give them a heart to know** (v. 7) Him, a promise that is explained more fully in 31:31–34.

24:8–10. A much different fate awaited **the evil figs** (v. 8) that would remain in the land (vv. 8–10). As rotting fruit, they would be cast out and deported along with King Zedekiah to many nations. Though it would appear that they had avoided God's judgment by not being taken away to Babylon in 597 BC, they would eventually experience judgment in the form of **sword … famine, and … pestilence** (v. 10).

J. Judah's Coming Captivity (chap. 25)

25:1–10. In 605 BC (**the fourth year of Jehoiakim**; v. 1), Jeremiah announced that divine judgment would descend not only on **Judah** but on **all … nations round about** (v. 9). That was the year in which Nebuchadnezzar and Babylon defeated the Egyptian army at the Battle of Carchemish, allowing Babylon to become the dominant power in the ancient Near East. Babylon's rise to power was due to the Lord's plan to use the Babylonians as His instrument of judgment against His disobedient covenant people. Chapter 25 concludes the first major section of the book of Jeremiah by effectively summarizing all of the warnings of judgment found in chapters 1–24 and by identifying the Babylonians as the powerful and ruthless enemy from the north that Jeremiah had warned would attack Judah because of her covenant unfaithfulness toward the Lord (see 4:6–7; 5:15–17; 6:22–24).

Because the people of Judah had not responded to Jeremiah's warnings and turned from their sinful ways, the Lord would send Nebuchadnezzar against them as His **servant** (v. 9). The title "servant" is used here not in the sense of "worshiper" but of "vassal" or "agent of judgment," just as the pagan ruler Cyrus is called the Lord's "shepherd" in Isaiah 44:28 and His "anointed" in Isaiah 45:1. As the Lord's personal agent, Nebuchadnezzar would completely destroy Judah and the nations. The Hebrew term **utterly destroy** (*herem*) refers to the irrevocable giving over of things to the Lord in holy war (see 50:21, 26; 51:3; Deut. 2:34).

25:11-14. Judah and the nations would **serve the king of Babylon** for **seventy years** (v. 11). This round number (as in Ps. 90:10; Isa. 23:15) probably represents the period from 605 to 535 BC, which marked the beginning of Judah's return from exile (see 2 Chron. 36:20-23; Dan. 9:1-2). The seventy years of Zechariah 1:12 are not necessarily the same as those here and in 29:10. They probably represent the period from 586 BC (when Solomon's temple was destroyed) to 516 BC (when Zerubbabel's temple was completed). The seventy years indicates that the majority of those exiled to Babylon would die there before the return took place with a new generation. After the seventy years were over, the Lord would **punish the king of Babylon** (v. 12), a prophecy fulfilled when the city of Babylon was captured by the Persians in 539 BC. The statement that Babylon would become **perpetual desolations** is prophetic hyperbole for describing the downfall and demise of the Neo-Babylonian Empire, though it is interesting to note that the city of Babylon itself was completely deserted by the seventh century AD (see 50:12-13; 51:26; Isa. 13:20).

25:15-26. Jeremiah portrayed God's judgment as a **wine cup** (v. 15) from which all of the nations would drink (vv. 15-17; see 51:7; Isa. 51:17; Rev. 18:6). Like a drunk person, the nations would stagger (**they shall ... be moved, and be mad**; v. 16) under God's wrath. The stroke of **the sword** would cause them to fall, never to rise again. God's people (**Jerusalem, and ... Judah**; v. 18) were to be judged first and then the nations (vv. 15-26). As in chapters 46-51, which contain a series of oracles against foreign nations, the roster of nations in verses 19-26 begins with **Egypt** (v. 19) and ends with Babylon, but Damascus is omitted (see 49:23-27), and a few other regions are added. **Sheshach** (v. 26) is a cryptogram for Babylon. The cryptogram is formed by substituting the first consonant of the Hebrew alphabet for the last, the second for the next-to-last, and so on. Its purpose is not fully understood, but what is clear is that the Lord's agents of judgment would not be exempt from His judgment (see 51:48-49).

25:27-33. The Lord would compel all nations to **Drink** (v. 27) the wine of His judgment, and they would fall by **the sword**. If Jerusalem itself would not avoid judgment, no other nation could hope to escape God's wrath (v. 29). A series of images conveys the devastating nature of God's judgment (vv. 30-33). **The Lord** would **roar** (v. 30) like a lion. He would put the wicked to death with **the sword** (v. 31), and His judgment would be like **a great whirlwind** (v. 32) sweeping over the earth. Corpses would be littered over all the earth.

25:34-38. Jeremiah called for the leaders of the nations (**ye shepherds**; v. 34) to **Howl** and **wallow ... in the ashes** in mourning over the coming destruction (vv. 34-36). The leaders themselves would be put to death and would be shattered like expensive pottery (**like a pleasant vessel**). When the shepherds were removed, the nations would fall to the Lord, like prey to a stalking **lion** (v. 38).

III. The History of Judah's Refusal to Obey: The Suffering of Jeremiah and the Fall of Jerusalem (chaps. 26-45)

Whereas chapters 2-25 (predominantly poetry) consist primarily of Jeremiah's messages of judgment, chapters 26-45 (predominantly prose) contain a narrative record of events from the life of Jeremiah and the final days of Judah as a nation. Jeremiah had three major purposes in this section of the book. The first was to show that Judah was deserving of judgment because of Judah's unbelief and disobedience. Jeremiah's recurring charge in this section was that the leaders and people of Judah had not listened to and obeyed the word of the Lord (see 26:5; 29:19; 32:33; 34:14, 17; 35:14-15, 16, 17; 36:31; 37:14; 40:3; 42:13, 21; 43:7; 44:16, 23). This unbelief was particularly demonstrated in the way that various segments of the Judean population mistreated and persecuted Jeremiah for proclaiming the message that he had received from the Lord. The second purpose was to document the fulfillment of Jeremiah's warnings of judgment against Judah in the account of the fall of Jerusalem and the exile of Judah's king and people. The third purpose was to offer hope for Israel's future with the promise of a "new covenant" (31:31) that would erase Judah's past failures and enable Israel to follow the Lord at the time of the future renewal when Israel as a nation will be restored to the Promised Land.

A. Jeremiah Arrested and Released (chap. 26)

Jeremiah 26:1–19 appears to be a report of the temple message found in chapter 7. Whereas chapter 7 focuses on the content of the message, this account provides a brief summary of the message (vv. 2–6) but focuses primarily on how various groups responded to the prophetic warning concerning the impending destruction of the Jerusalem temple (vv. 7–19).

26:1–6. The Lord instructed Jeremiah to warn the people of coming judgment because if they would turn from their **evil way** (v. 3), the Lord might relent from sending **the evil** (calamity) that He intended for Judah and Jerusalem. The people had a genuine opportunity to repent and avoid the disaster that the Lord had planned for them. Jeremiah warned them that refusal to repent would result in God destroying the temple at Jerusalem in the same way that He destroyed the sanctuary at Shiloh at an earlier time in Israel's history (vv. 4–6; see 7:12).

26:7–9. The first groups to respond to the prophet's message were **the priests ... the prophets and all the people** (v. 7). Their response to Jeremiah was, **Thou shalt surely die** (v. 8). This same phrase occurs in Genesis 2:17, where the Lord warned Adam of the consequences of eating from the forbidden tree in the garden, and a similar phrase describes the ultimate penalty for gross violations of the law of Moses (see, e.g., Exod. 21:15–17; Lev. 24:16–17, 21). This response was perhaps because Jeremiah was viewed as a false prophet deserving of death because he had dared to proclaim the heretical message that God would destroy His own dwelling place (see Deut. 18:20).

26:10–15. The next group to become involved in the debate over Jeremiah's message were **the princes of Judah** (v. 10), those responsible for making legal decisions concerning disputes taking place in the temple precincts. They first listened to **the priests and the** false **prophets** (v. 11), who had a vested interest in Jerusalem and believed that Jeremiah should be put to death for predicting the destruction of the city and the Lord's house. The princes then heard Jeremiah's defense of his message, in which the prophet affirmed his divine calling and repeated the warning that repentance was the only way that Judah could avoid disaster (vv. 12–15).

26:16–19. After hearing this defense, the princes rendered their verdict concerning Jeremiah's message. The elders cited the precedent of Micah, who had lived a century earlier and who (together with Isaiah) had convinced King Hezekiah to pray for forgiveness on behalf of his people. The Lord answered the prayers of the king and the prophets, and in 701 BC, Jerusalem and the temple were spared (see Isa. 37:33–37). Though Micah's message that Zion would be **plowed like a field** (v. 18) was an absolute message of judgment, the repentance of the people led God to alter His sentence of doom. Rather than being a false prophet, Jeremiah was a prophet of judgment, just like Micah, who had also preached against Jerusalem. If the people and the king had listened to Micah in his day, the leaders and people of Judah needed to have the same respect for the message of Jeremiah. It is interesting that **all the people** (v. 16) had moved to side with those who defended Jeremiah rather than those who accused him (see 26:7–8). The people's recognition of Jeremiah as a true prophet made them even more culpable for their later unbelief and rejection of Jeremiah's prophetic counsel.

26:20–24. Appended to the story of Jeremiah's legal validation as a true prophet is an episode recounting King Jehoiakim's execution of the prophet Urijah for preaching a message of judgment against Jerusalem. An example of the right response to the prophetic word was recounted earlier (26:1–19); the wrong response is recounted here. Jehoiakim was the exact opposite of the Hezekiah, whose right response to the Lord had spared Judah from judgment. Hezekiah **besought the LORD** (v. 19), but Jehoiakim **sought** (v. 21) the prophet Urijah to put him to death when he escaped to Egypt. Hezekiah had feared the Lord, but the prophet Urijah feared the king who wanted him dead. Jehoiakim was able to have Urijah removed from Egypt and put to death because mutual rights of extradition were part of the treaty imposed on Judah when Jehoiakim became the vassal of Pharaoh Neco II (see 2 Kings 23:34–35). Jehoiakim's angry rejection of the prophetic word is also evidenced by his cutting up Jeremiah's scroll (chap. 36). In fact, the hostility between Jehoiakim and Jeremiah was so great that the two never have a face-to-face meeting in this book.

Apart from divine intervention, Jeremiah probably would have fallen victim to the same fate as Urijah. Jeremiah was also protected from the king's anger by a sympathetic royal official named Ahikam (v. 24). While the response to Jeremiah's message throughout his ministry was largely negative, a minority did respond favorably to the prophet and his message (see 36:11–19; 38:8–13; 45:1–5).

B. Jeremiah and the False Prophets (chaps. 27–29)

This section narrates Jeremiah's further attempts to counteract the teaching of false prophets, who claimed that Babylon's doom was near and that rebellion against Nebuchanezzar was therefore warranted and desirable.

1. Nebuchadnezzar's Victory (chap. 27)

Jeremiah told the nations (vv. 3–11), King Zedekiah (vv. 12–15), and the priests and people of Judah (vv. 16–22) to submit to the Babylonian yoke. The length of the third oracle in this chapter reflects that the people were the primary target of Jeremiah's message. The linking of the nations and Judah in this chapter reflects the idea that Judah had to come to grips with the fact that their status as the people of God did not exempt them from the need to submit to Babylonian rule as God's plan for the nations.

27:1–6. Verse 3 seems to indicate that the context of the messages in this chapter was a conference in Jerusalem at which leaders from the nations surrounding Judah had come to meet with Zedekiah

for the purpose of forming an organized rebellion against Nebuchadnezzar. These leaders may have counted on support from Egypt, where Psammetichus II had become pharaoh a year earlier (594 BC). Zedekiah went to Babylon in 593 BC (see 51:59), perhaps to be interrogated by Nebuchadnezzar, who had heard rumors of the coalition forming against him. In any case, Zedekiah ultimately made the fateful decision to rebel against Nebuchadnezzar, which led to the destruction of Jerusalem in 586 BC.

Jeremiah's reasons for declaring the subjugation of Judah and the nations to Babylon were theological rather than political. Jeremiah was not merely savvy enough to realize that rebellion against Babylon was futile; the prophet also asserted that the Lord had granted dominion over the nations to Nebuchadnezzar. The Lord again called Nebuchadnezzar **my servant** (v. 6; see 25:9); he would temporarily take from the house of David the position of the Lord's favored ruler because of the sin and disobedience that had characterized the house of David. Nebuchadnezzar was not merely a powerful ruler but was an Adam-like figure who even had power over **the beasts of the field** (see Gen. 2:20).

27:7–16. Jeremiah further described the false prophets who opposed his message as **diviners** (v. 9), **dreamers**, and **sorcerers**, activities that were forbidden in Israel (see Lev. 19:26; Deut. 18:10–11). These prophets provided theological legitimation for the politics of rebellion, affirming that Judah would **not serve the king of Babylon** (v. 14) and that **the vessels of the LORD's house** (v. 16), which had been taken to Babylon in 597 BC, would be shortly returned.

27:17–22. The conflict between Jeremiah and these false prophets centered around two fundamentally different understandings of the nature of God's covenant relationship with His people. Jeremiah's message was that privilege carries with it responsibility and that Judah was subject to judgment because they had failed to obey the Lord's covenant commandments. On the other hand, the false prophets based their message on the presumptuous belief that the covenant between God and His people was a guarantee of automatic blessing regardless of whether Judah was obedient or not. Jeremiah challenged his opponents to intercede for Judah if they were indeed true prophets so that their prophecies of deliverance from Babylon would come to pass (v. 18), but he himself would hold firm to his message of judgment (vv. 19–22). Though the events of 597 BC and the exile of Jehoiachin (**Jeconiah**, v. 20) had demonstrated the Lord's intent to judge Judah, the people still blindly held on to the false hope of deliverance from Nebuchadnezzar and the armies of Babylon.

2. Jeremiah Exposes Hananiah (chap. 28)

Chapters 28–29 narrates two specific instances of conflict between Jeremiah and the false prophets, who were promoting the empty expectation that the Babylonian domination of Judah would be short-lived.

28:1–5. Jeremiah confronted the false prophet Hananiah. Hananiah promised that the Lord would break the Babylonian **yoke** (v. 4) within two years and that the Lord would soon bring back the exiles of Judah and the temple articles that Nebuchadnezzar had taken to Babylon in 597 BC (vv. 2–3). Hananiah's message sought to overturn Jeremiah's symbolic act of wearing a yoke (see chap. 27) and directly contradicted the prophecy of Jeremiah (see 27:16–22).

28:6–11. In his response to Hananiah (vv. 6–9), Jeremiah stated that fulfillment was the sure indicator of the true prophet. While he was sympathetic with what Hananiah was predicting, Jeremiah reminded him that the majority of true prophets in the past had been prophets of doom. Hananiah's final overturning of Jeremiah's prophecy of extended exile involved breaking **the yoke from off the prophet Jeremiah's neck** (v. 10) and most likely represented an attempt to symbolically break the power of Jeremiah's earlier prophecy.

28:12–17. In his final response to Hananiah, Jeremiah reflected on the consequences of the false prophet's attempt to oppose the true word of the Lord. The national consequence was that Jeremiah's

wooden yoke would instead become **yokes of iron** (v. 13). The wooden yoke of submission would instead be exchanged for the iron yoke of servitude (v. 14; see 38:17–33). The personal consequence of Hananiah's deceptive message was that the Lord would **cast** him **from off the face of the earth** (v. 16). Since Hananiah was **not sent** (v. 15, using the same Hebrew root as the verb for "cast" in v. 16) by the Lord, the prophet would be sent away to his death. In fulfillment of Jeremiah's prophecy, Hananiah died two months later (v. 17). As a fitting act of justice, the prophet who had falsely prophesied restoration "within two full years" (28:3, 11) died two months later.

3. A Letter to the Captives (29:1–23)

Jeremiah's interaction with the false prophets among the exiles of 597 BC took on a dynamic similar to his conflict with Hananiah (chap. 28). Hananiah had attempted to overturn Jeremiah's symbolic act of wearing a yoke; Jeremiah and the false prophets in Babylon engaged in a war of dueling pens. The issue once again was the duration of the Babylonian exile and control over Judah. Jeremiah's letter encouraging the exiles to submit to their Babylonian captors (vv. 1–23) was countered by a letter from the false prophet Shemaiah, who became the object of God's judgment (see 29:24–32).

29:1–10. Jeremiah's letter to the exiles stated that they were to submit to their captors since ultimately God Himself had exiled His people (v. 4). The commands to **build … plant … Take ye wives** (vv. 5–6) instructed the exiles to prepare for a lengthy stay in Babylon. The exiles were even to seek the peace of Babylon, an unprecedented and unique concept in the ancient world: working toward and praying for the prosperity of one's captors. This concept would have been especially foreign to the people of Judah, who understood the peace of Jerusalem to be central to God's kingdom rule over the earth (see Ps. 122:6). Jeremiah warned the exiles not to listen to the false prophets predicting a speedy return to the homeland (vv. 8–9) and stated the return from Babylon would come after **seventy years** (v. 10), most likely a round number (see 25:10–11) that stressed that the generation going down to Babylon would not be the one that returned.

29:11–15. The prophet assured the exiles that in spite of appearances to the contrary, the Lord had not forgotten His people. Echoing Deuteronomy 4:29–30, the Lord promised to listen when the people prayed and to be found when the people chose to **search** (v. 13) and **seek** for Him. Summarizing Deuteronomy 30:3–5, the Lord promised to deliver His people from exile and return them to the Promised Land. The promise **I will turn away your captivity** (v. 14) becomes a dominant theme in the message of consolation in chapters 30–33 (see 30:3, 18, 21; 31:23; 32:44; 33:7, 11, 26; 48:47; 49:6, 39).

29:16–19. In contrast to the positive promise to the exiles in Babylon, Jeremiah warned that those who remained in the land would face destruction as the objects of divine judgment. As in his message concerning the good and bad figs (chap. 24), the prophet rejected the idea that continued existence in the land was a sign of God's favor and blessing. Those in the land were the **vile figs** (v. 17) that would be consumed. Their fate had been sealed by their continued failure to listen to the Lord, speaking through His prophets.

29:20–23. The final section of Jeremiah's letter to the exiles contained a word of judgment against two false prophets, **Ahab** (v. 21) and **Zedekiah**. These prophets would be delivered over to the Babylonians and be put to death by fire, a Babylonian form of execution attested in Daniel (see Dan. 3:6, 24) and the Code of Hammurapi (sections 25; 110; 157). Their sins were **villany** (v. 23) and **adultery**, referring to how they had caused the people to be unfaithful to the Lord as their covenant partner through the worship of other gods (see 23:10).

4. A Letter to Shemaiah (29:24–32)

29:24–30. Jeremiah's letter was countered by the letter-writing activity of another false prophet, **Shemaiah** (v. 24). Shemaiah wrote letters to the priests and officers in Jerusalem, seeking to have Jeremiah censured and put in prison. Jeremiah was castigated

as a madman, and prophetic behavior sometimes did appear deranged to the casual observer (see 2 Kings 9:11). Shemaiah was angered by Jeremiah's message that the exile would be of long duration.

29:31–32. Jeremiah's response was a warning of Shemaiah's impending death because of his presumption in speaking for the Lord when he had not been sent. The Lord's punishment of Shemaiah was similar to that of Hananiah (see 28:15–16). As a result of misleading the people, Shemaiah's family line would be cut off so that he would **not have a man to dwell among this people** (v. 32).

C. The Book of Consolation (chap. 30–33)

Chapters 30–33 are often called Jeremiah's "Book of Consolation." This section depicts the ultimate restoration of both Israel (the northern kingdom) and Judah (the southern kingdom) and is the longest sustained passage in Jeremiah concerned with the future hope of the people of God (for other and briefer passages on restoration, see 3:14–18; 16:14–15; 23:3–8; 24:4–7). This section stands at the very center of the book of Jeremiah to highlight its message of hope. The Book of Consolation is framed by the opening and closing promise that the restoration would "bring again" (30:3) or "return" (33:26), that is, reverse, the exile (see 30:18, 21; 31:23; 32:44; 33:7, 11).

1. The Restoration of Israel (chaps. 30–31)

The prophet looked forward to the time when God would redeem His people, and chapters 30–31, written almost entirely in poetry, are filled with optimism. These chapters refer both to the restoration from Babylonian exile and to the restoration that will be experienced in the messianic age.

30:1–11. The prophet was commanded to **Write** (v. 2) these prophecies to preserve for future generations the predictions of restoration. The oracle in these verses is typical of the messages of salvation in this section. The description of the horrors of exile gives way to images of restoration that directly reverse the experience of judgment. The **voice of trembling** (v. 5) portrays the sound of destruction, a battle that will reduce the nation to **a woman in travail** (v. 6). This time of judgment is the **day** (v. 7) of the Lord, a time that **is great, so that none is like it**. As in the Old Testament prophetic literature as a whole, "the day of the Lord" refers both to the foreseeable future of the prophet's day (see v. 8, 30:18) and to a more remote time, the messianic age (see Isa. 2:11, 17, 20; Amos 5:18; 8:9; Joel 1:15; 2:11; Zeph. 1:14).

In contrast to the turmoil of the day of the Lord, the future time of restoration will be one of **rest** (v. 10) and **none shall make him afraid**. Jeremiah's vision of the future also included the promise that a reunited Israel will be under the rule of David their king (i.e., the Messiah; see 23:5–6; 33:15–17).

30:12–24. The pattern of reversal continues in verses 12–17. The judgment of exile involves a **bruise** that **is incurable** (v. 12) and a **wound** that **is grievous**. The restoration, however, will be a time when God will **restore health** (v. 17) and **heal** the **wounds** of His people. The reversal will bring about the rebuilding of Israel's **tents, and ... dwelling places** (v. 18), the replacement of sorrow with **thanksgiving and the voice of them that make merry** (v. 19), and the reestablishment of Israel's leadership so that their **nobles** (v. 21) and **governor** will come from **of themselves**, not from the foreign power that rules over them. These terms for leaders probably referred to the rulers of Judah immediately after the exile, but ultimately, they refer to Jesus Christ, who fulfills this promise. It must be remembered, however, that this future restoration will not occur until **the whirlwind** (v. 23) and **The fierce anger of the Lord** (v. 24) have wrought their destruction on Israel.

31:1–40. Chapter 31 continues the theme of restoration begun in 30:1. Jeremiah recorded the words of the Lord to all the people of God (v. 1); to the restored northern kingdom of Israel (vv. 2–22); to the restored southern kingdom of Judah (vv. 23–26); and to Israel and Judah together (vv. 27–40).

31:1–9. As in chapter 30, images of reversal are predominant. The restoration will occur when the righteous remnant (**the people which were left of the sword**; v. 2) returns from captivity. Instead of the sorrow of exile, there will be music and rejoicing

(v. 7). There will be agricultural activity in **Samaria** (v. 5), which was conquered by Assyria in 722–721, and it will be common to enjoy the produce of this area because it will no longer be overrun by enemies. **The watchmen** (v. 6) will call for the people in both north and south to assemble together for worship in the rebuilt Jerusalem. Israel will even become **the chief of the nations** (v. 7; see Deut. 26:19; Amos 6:1). Israel was the greatest nation not because of its intrinsic merit but because of divine grace and appointment (see Deut. 7:6–8; 2 Sam. 7:23–24). Israel had become the "tail" among the nations for their disobedience but will be exalted to her rightful place as the "head" (see Deut. 28:13).

31:10–14. Israel will return to worship in Jerusalem and to enjoy the bounty of the land because the Lord will perform an act of redemption (**redeemed ... ransomed**; v. 11) on par with the exodus from Egypt. As the Lord had redeemed His people from Egyptian slavery (see Exod. 6:6; 15:13; Deut. 7:8; 9:26), so now He would redeem their descendants from Babylonian exile. The prophets often portrayed the return from Babylon as a new exodus, and the New Testament anticipates Jesus bringing the ultimate exodus, which will restore Israel from her spiritual bondage (see Isa. 4:5–6; 44:27–28; 51:9–11; 55:12–13; Luke 1:69–75).

31:15–19. Rahel (Rachel) **weeping for her children** (v. 15) refers to Israel's national grief over the exile. Rachel was the wife of Jacob and the grandmother of Ephraim and Manasseh (see Gen. 30:22–24; 48:1–2), the two most prominent and powerful tribes in the northern kingdom. Rachel thus represented all the women of Israel who watched their sons being carried away into exile. Matthew 2:15 refers to this passage being "fulfilled" in connection with Herod's orders to kill all the male infants in the vicinity of Bethlehem, in the sense that the mothers who lost their infant sons in Bethlehem shared the sorrow of the women in **Ramah** who lost their sons in the exile. Matthew presents Jesus as the promised Messiah, who will enable Israel to become all that God intended her to be, and thus, the life experiences of Jesus in His earthly ministry parallel the history of Israel that is unfolded in the Old Testament. Jeremiah promised that Israel's sorrow will turn to joy when they repent of their sinful ways (vv. 16–19).

31:20–26. The promise of restoration and return is certain because of God's love for Israel. The departing exiles are advised to set up markers (**Set thee up waymarks**; v. 21) along their path to exile so that in due time they will be able to find their way back to Judah. The Lord will do **a new thing** (v. 22) in order to create true intimacy with Israel as His people. In the past, Israel has been a **backsliding daughter**, but the Lord will transform Israel so that **a woman shall compass a man**. Israel will embrace the Lord with tender and unfailing love (see Ps. 32:7, 10) and will be devoted to Him without reservation. In this new relationship, Israel will be blessed and secure in the Promised Land. Jerusalem will become a **habitation of justice** (v. 23), the temple mount will become a place of **holiness**, the cities will be repopulated, and the Lord will meet the need of every **weary** (v. 25) and **sorrowful soul**.

31:27–40. These verses explain further concerning the new relationship between the Lord and Israel in the last days and how this relationship will be possible. The Lord's new work for Israel will remove the need for the people to repeat the proverb, **The fathers have eaten a sour grape, and the children's teeth are set on edge** (v. 29; repeated also in Ezek. 18:2). This apparently was a popular proverb that originated in a misunderstanding of such passages as Exodus 20:5 and Numbers 14:18, which teach that a man's sins can have a negative effect on his descendants. In the time of Jeremiah and Ezekiel, many people felt that God's hand of judgment against them was due not to their own sins but to the sins of their ancestors. Jeremiah reminded the people of God's justice and that **every one shall die for his own iniquity** (v. 30; see Deut. 24:16; Ezek. 18:3, 20; 33:7–18).

The new relationship will be possible because the Lord **will make a new covenant with … Israel** (v. 31). This covenant will not be like the one at Sinai; God will actually **write** (v. 33) His **law** upon **their hearts**. In other words, He will give them both the desire and capacity to follow the law so that it effectively governs their lives, in contrast to the ineffectiveness of merely presenting it in writing as at Sinai (see Exod. 24:4; 31:18; 32:15–16; 34:28–29; Deut. 4:13; 5:22; 10:4). There will no longer be a need to **teach** (v. 34) the law to one's **neighbour** because when the Lord has done His new work, there will no longer be among His people those who are ignorant of Him and His will for their lives. True knowledge of the Lord will be shared by **all**. The basis of the new covenant will be the Lord's forgiveness for all of Israel's past sins (see Heb. 10:14–17).

The new covenant does not abolish the old covenant but supercedes it in the sense that through the new covenant, the old covenant is fulfilled and its purpose is achieved. Verses 31–34 are the longest sequence of Old Testament verses to be quoted in its entirety in the New Testament (see Heb. 8:8–12; 10:16–17). Jeremiah stated that this new covenant is for Israel, but the New Testament teaches that the death of Christ has already actualized the new covenant and its blessings for the church (see Matt. 22:36–40; Luke 22:20; 2 Cor. 3:6; Heb. 8:13). There is a "now" and "not yet" element to the new covenant in that the church presently enjoys its benefits, but the full implementation of this covenant awaits the kingdom age, when "all Israel shall be saved" (Rom. 11:26).

The Lord's covenant with Israel guarantees that Israel is as permanent as the creation itself (**sun … moon … stars … sea**; v. 35). Just as God's creation order is established and secure, so also Israel will always have descendants. Even though a terrible judgment was about to sweep the kingdom of Judah away, Israel would continue to exist. Jerusalem would be rebuilt following the judgment and will be **holy unto the Lord … for ever** (v. 40).

2. Jeremiah Buys a Field (chap. 32)

32:1–16. This narrative records how Jeremiah, with some reluctance (see 32:25), obeyed the Lord's command to buy a field in Anathoth from his cousin (vv. 8–9). This purchase, **in the tenth year of Zedekiah** (587 BC; v. 1), provided a tangible expression of Jeremiah's trust in the message of hope presented in the poetic oracles of chapters 30–31. That Jeremiah bought the field even as the Babylonians were besieging Jerusalem (see v. 2, 32:24) showed his confidence that the Lord would bring Judah back from exile and that ownership of this property would return to his family.

While Jeremiah was in prison for preaching that Jerusalem would fall to the Babylonians (see 37:21; 38:13, 28; 39:14), his cousin **Hanameel** (v. 7) came and appealed to Jeremiah to purchase a piece of family property in **Anathoth** that he was being forced to sell. By acting in accordance with the ancient **right of redemption** (see Lev. 25:23–25; Ruth 2:20), Jeremiah could buy the field so that it would remain part of the family inheritance. In addition to paying the purchase price, Jeremiah had the transaction attested by witnesses and made two copies of the deed for the property. The first deed was **sealed** (v. 10) to guarantee the contents of the deed and to keep it from being tampered with (see Isa. 8:16; 29:11; Dan. 12:4; Rev. 15:1–5). The second deed remained **open** (v. 11) for ready reference, the authenticity of which would be guaranteed by the sealed copy if the unsealed deed was lost, damaged, or changed. Both deeds were then entrusted to Jeremiah's scribe, **Baruch** (v. 12), who placed them **in an earthen vessel** (v. 14) for safekeeping. Jeremiah's deed of purchase would enable him (or his heirs) to reclaim the field as soon as normal economic activity resumed after the exile. Documents found in clay jars at Elephantine (in southern Egypt) and Qumran (west of the Dead Sea) were preserved almost intact for more than two thousand years.

32:17–25. Jeremiah prayed for the Lord to fulfill His promise to restore Israel from exile, a promise that seemed almost too good to be true. Jeremiah began by praising God and grounded his confidence in the attributes of God. Creation demonstrates God's unlimited power, which means that **there is nothing too hard** (v. 17) for Him. The Lord is faithful to His covenant promises and just in all of His ways. He had demonstrated His power to rescue in the exodus from Egypt and would do the same

for the exiles in Babylon. While presenting his petition to the Lord, Jeremiah expressed both his faith in the Lord and his doubts concerning what must have seemed an unwise investment, the purchase of land that the enemy would soon take over (v. 25). Nevertheless, faith overcame doubt and Jeremiah remained an obedient servant (see 31:8–9).

32:26–36. The remainder of the chapter contains the Lord's response to Jeremiah's prayer. The Lord echoed Jeremiah's words, affirming that nothing is **too hard** (v. 27) for Him. The Lord would have no difficulty restoring Israel from exile because He is **the God of all flesh**. He has universal dominion and would use the Babylonians as the human instrument to carry out His judgment against sinful Judah (vv. 27–36). The Lord, not Babylon, would remain in control of all that happened to Judah.

32:37–40. After the judgment on the wicked was complete, there would be salvation for the righteous. The Lord would bring His people back to Jerusalem, where they would **dwell safely** (v. 37). Echoing the promises associated with the new covenant in 31:31–34, the Lord also declared that He will ultimately transform Israel by giving them **one heart** (v. 39) so that they will **fear** and obey Him forever. The new covenant is everlasting, and unlike the old covenant, it will never be broken (see 31:32; Isa. 24:5).

When Israel returned to the land, **fields** would **be bought** (v. 43) once again. The field purchased by Jeremiah was symbolic of the many fields that would be purchased in Judah after the Babylonian exile, when economic conditions returned to normal. **The land of Benjamin** (v. 44) is mentioned because it was the location of Anathoth, where Jeremiah had purchased the field. Jeremiah could be sure that his purchase was not in vain.

3. The Promise of Restoration (chap. 33)

Concluding Jeremiah's Book of Consolation, this chapter is divided into two roughly equal parts: (1) verses 1–13, which continue to build on chapter 32, and (2) verses 14–26, which summarize a wider range of earlier passages in Jeremiah and elsewhere.

Verses 14–26 are not found in the Septuagint (the Greek translation of the Old Testament).

33:1–5. While Jeremiah was in prison prior to the capture of Jerusalem in 586 BC, the word of the Lord came to him **the second time** (v. 1; chap. 32 comprises the first time), with an additional message of hope. The Lord invited Jeremiah to **Call unto me** (v. 3) and promised, **I will answer**. While Jeremiah found it difficult to understand how the Lord could bring about something as wonderful as the return from exile, the Lord invited the prophet to take Him at His word and to pray for Him to fulfill His promise. The Hebrew for the phrase **great and mighty** usually refers to the formidable cities of Canaan and is translated "great and walled up to heaven" in Deuteronomy 1:28. As the rest of chapter 33 demonstrates, the Lord would first judge His people (vv. 4–5) and would then restore them in ways that were nothing short of incredible (33:6–26).

33:6–13. The restoration that would bring Israel healing (v. 6) would involve four specific things: the rebuilding of Israel's cities (v. 7), the forgiveness of sins (v. 8), the renewal of joy (vv. 9–11), and the repopulation of the land (vv. 12–13). The forgiveness of Israel's sins would be the basis of the new covenant (31:34; see Ezek. 36:25–26). The joy experienced by the returnees would be like a wedding celebration, reversing the judgment proclaimed in 7:34; 16:9; 25:10.

33:14–26. Behold, the days come (v. 14) introduces this message, which expands on promises found elsewhere in the book of Jeremiah (see 23:5–6; 31:35–37) as a summary of Jeremiah's vision of the future. A new **David** (v. 15) would arise, **the Branch of righteousness**, who will rule over restored Israel (vv. 15–16). This prophecy is ultimately fulfilled in Jesus Christ, who is the Branch from David's tree (messianic line) and keeps the Davidic hope alive, despite the removal of Judah's kings by the Babylonian captivity. In the face of the impending judgment, in which the nation would be swept away and the Promised Land reduced to a desolate wasteland, all God's past covenants with His people — His covenants with Israel, with David, and with Phineas —

appeared to have been rendered null and void. The series of oracles found in verses 17–26, however, gave reassurance that the ancient covenants were not being repudiated; they are as secure as God's covenant concerning the creation order, and in the future restoration, they will all be fulfilled.

David shall never want a man (v. 17) promises that there will always be a descendant to carry on the Davidic dynasty (see 2 Sam. 7:12–16; 1 Kings 2:4; 8:25; 9:5; 2 Chron. 6:16; 7:18), and this passage is ultimately fulfilled in Jesus. The priests and Levites likewise will not **want a man** (v. 18). The priestly covenant with the Levites (see Num. 25:13), like the royal grant with David, was not a private grant to the priestly family, involving only that family and the Lord. Rather, it was an integral part of the Lord's dealings with His people and assured Israel of the ministry of a priesthood that was acceptable to the Lord and through whose mediation they could enjoy communion with Him. This ministry was and is being fulfilled by Jesus, who administers a higher and better priesthood. These covenants with the houses of David and Levi are as permanent as the **covenant of the day, and … the night** (v. 20), which may refer to God's sovereign establishment of the creation order in the beginning, or more likely to the covenant of Genesis 9:8–17, in which God promised Noah that He would not again send a flood to destroy His creation.

In words that echo the covenant promises to the patriarchs (Abraham, Gen. 22:17; Isaac, Gen. 26:4; Jacob, Gen. 32:12), the Lord assured Israel that the two mediatorial (royal and priestly) families would flourish and thus continue their ministry in the spiritual commonwealth He had established with His people (v. 22). The promise of a numerous progeny to both the royal and the priestly families will ultimately be fulfilled in that great throng who will reign with Christ (see Rom. 5:17; 8:17; 1 Cor. 6:3; 2 Tim. 2:12; Rev. 1:6; 5:10; 20:6). For emphasis, a second assurance was given that the covenant promises to David and Levi are as certain and secure as the creation itself (vv. 23–26). Nothing can prevent the Lord from fulfilling His promise to **return** (turn; v. 26) the **captivity** of His people.

D. Zedekiah's Broken Promise (chap. 34)

Zedekiah and the inhabitants of Jerusalem reneged on their promise to release their Hebrew slaves in accordance with the provisions of the Mosaic law, which was a blatant act of disobedience against the Lord and demonstrated that the king and the people would not take advantage of the opportunity to turn from their sinful ways and avoid the calamity that the Lord was about to bring upon them (see 26:3). Chronologically, the narrative in 34:8–22 is contemporary with the events described in 37:4–12.

34:1–7. Jeremiah warned the king that the Lord was going to **give** Jerusalem **into the hand of the king of Babylon** (v. 2), and Nebuchadnezzar and his armies had already captured all of the cities of Judah except Jerusalem, **Lachish, and ... Azekah** (v. 7). Lachish was important for Jerusalem's defense and had been besieged in 701 BC by the Assyrian king Sennacherib during the reign of Hezekiah (see 2 Chron. 32:9). The Lachish ostraca, military and administrative communiqués inscribed on pieces of broken pottery fragments discovered in 1935, contain a letter (Ostracon 4) written to the commander at Lachish shortly after the events described here. The letter ends: "We are watching for the signal fires of Lachish ... for we cannot see Azekah."

34:8–11. With increasing pressure from the Babylonian army and the fall of Jerusalem appearing imminent, Zedekiah and the people of Jerusalem entered into **a covenant** (v. 8) to grant freedom to their Hebrew slaves (vv. 8–10). The Mosaic law stipulated that the Israelites were not to permanently enslave each other (see Exod. 21:2–11; Lev. 25:39–55; Deut. 15:12–18), but the people had ignored this prohibition for their own financial benefit. They released their slaves as a way of manipulating God's blessing, also hoping that the freed slaves would be more willing to help defend Jerusalem. The insincerity of Zedekiah and the people is demonstrated by the fact that they took back their slaves **afterwards** (v. 11), when the Babylonian siege was temporarily lifted due to Egyptian intervention (see 34:21–22; 37:5, 11). They had no real intention of ordering their lives according to the precepts of the law; they had

only made a desperate attempt to save their own necks.

34:12–16. The Lord rebuked the people for their failure to keep the covenant that He had established with them at Sinai. The Mosaic law prescribed concern for the plight of servants and slaves because Israel had once been slaves in Egypt (see Exod. 13:3, 14; 20:2; Deut. 5:6; 6:12; 8:14; Josh. 24:17). Israelites forced to sell themselves into slavery because of debt were to be released every seventh year (v. 14; Exod. 21:2; Deut. 15:12), and the Israelites were to free their slaves because God had earlier freed the Israelites (see Deut. 15:15). Their failure to keep their word and to live by the covenant they had made to release their slaves was reflective of Israel's long history of failure to live according to the covenant commands. There is an ironic play on the verb "to turn" (or "repent") in verses 15–16. The people had **turned** (v. 15; as called for in 26:3) from their sinful practices by releasing their slaves, but then they **turned** (v. 16) and failed to carry through on their promise to do what was right. In other words, they had "repented" of their "repentance."

34:17–22. Therefore (v. 17) introduces the sentence of judgment against Judah for their disobedience. Because they failed to give "liberty" to their slaves (34:15), the Lord would now grant them **liberty** to die by **the sword ... the pestilence, and ... the famine**. The punishment fit the crime. In the ritual confirming their covenant, the people had solemnized their promise by cutting up a **calf** (v. 19) and walking between **the parts** of the animal, signifying that the same fate would befall anyone who did not abide by the terms of the covenant. In ancient times, making a covenant involved a self-maledictory oath ("May thus and so be done to me if I do not keep this covenant"). Thus, they had invited disaster upon themselves with their own words and actions. The Lord would give them over to their enemies and their corpses would become food for scavenging birds and animals (v. 20). The lifting of the Babylonian siege, which occurred in 588 BC because of the arrival of the Egyptians on the scene, would only be temporary (vv. 21–22). Zedekiah would be captured and Jerusalem would fall. Disobedience to the Lord's commands and failure to keep one's promises to Him have serious consequences.

E. The Promise to the Rechabites (chap. 35)

35:1–16. This narrative is a flashback to **the days of Jehoiakim** (609–598; v. 1), and the reference to **the army of the Chaldeans, and ... Syrians** (v. 11) dates the chapter to no earlier than the eighth year of Jehoiakim. During Jehoiakim's reign, Jerusalem was besieged by Nebuchadnezzar in 605 BC (see Dan. 1:1). Three or four years later, Jehoiakim rebelled against Nebuchadnezzar, an unwise act that led to raids on his territory by the Babylonians, the Syrians, and others (see 2 Kings 24:1–2). This chapter records an episode in which Jeremiah interacted with the Rechabite clan and promised that they would be spared from the destruction coming upon the land of Judah (35:18–19). The purpose behind the placement of this narrative here is twofold. First, the faithfulness of the Rechabite clan to their family customs (vv. 8–10) contrasts with the disobedience of the nation of Judah to the commandments of the Lord (vv. 14–15; see 34:16). Second, the promise of deliverance to the Rechabite tribe for their faithfulness (35:18–19) contrasts with the sentence of destruction against the nation of Judah as a whole (35:17; see 34:17–22). The Rechabites would enjoy the deliverance from judgment that all of Judah could have experienced if they had turned from their sinful ways and followed the Lord (see 26:3). That Jeremiah needed to use the tiny Rechabite tribe and their strange family customs as the model of faithfulness demonstrates how corrupt the society of Judah had become.

The Rechabites (v. 2) were a nomadic tribal group who appear to have descended from Jehonadab (**Jonadab the son of Rechab**; v. 6), who assisted Jehu in the removal of Baal worship from Israel (see 2 Kings 10:15–17). They were also related to the Kenites (see 1 Chron. 2:55), some of whom lived among or near the Israelites and were on friendly terms with them (see Judg. 1:16; 4:11; 1 Sam. 15:6; 30:26, 29). The distinctive feature of the Rechabites was their strict adherence to the family customs of not drinking wine (v. 6), of not living in permanent structures, of living in tents (v. 9), and of not planting vineyards and fields (v. 10). As an object lesson to the people of Judah, Jeremiah invited representatives of the clan to the temple and commanded them, **Drink ye wine** (v. 5). Ironically, when the Rechabites refused the prophet's instructions (as Judah had done), the prophet commended their faithfulness to the customs that Jonadab had established (v. 14).

The point of the object lesson was not that the Rechabites had followed a higher standard of righteousness in living by the customs of their forefathers. In fact, these practices had prevented them from fully enjoying the blessings of life in the land that God had promised to Israel as a reward for their obedience to him (see Deut. 6:11; 20:5–6). The point was that if the Rechabites had persevered for centuries in their obedience to their forefather Jonadab (v. 8), then Judah should have been all the more careful to follow the commandments that had come from God Himself (v. 16).

35:17–19. Therefore (v. 17) introduces the sentence against Judah. The Lord would bring calamity (**evil**) upon Judah because they had not obeyed. In contrast, the Lord would preserve and protect the Rechabite clan so that **Jonadab ... shall not want a man to stand before me** (v. 19). Various traditions in the Jewish Mishnah claim that the Rechabites were given special duties to perform in connection with the Jerusalem temple built after the return from Babylonian exile. The phrase "shall not want a man" also appears in 33:17 with reference to the promised continuity of the house of David and its rule over a restored reality. The sad reality was that Judah could have experienced this same protection and deliverance before the fall of Jerusalem if they had been obedient to the Lord's commands.

F. The Reading of the Scroll (chap. 36)

This account of Jehoiakim burning the scroll of Jeremiah's words of judgment parallels the episode in chapter 26 in a number of key ways. Both episodes took place at the Jerusalem temple and raised the possibility that repentance on the part of Judah might lead to the avoidance of judgment (see 26:3–4; 36:3, 7). The two accounts focus on the response of the leadership and "all the people" (v. 10) to the words of Jeremiah, and both culminate in an angry response on the part of King Jehoiakim to the prophetic message of judgment (see 26:20–24; 36:21–24). In each story, members of the family of Shaphan intervened to protect Jeremiah from Jehoiakim's anger (see 26:24; 36:10–16). As chapters 26–35 have already demonstrated, chapters 36–45 also show that Judah was deserving of exile because of their response of disobedience to the prophetic word. These chapters also document the fall of Judah and Jerusalem, which was prophesied in chapters 26–35.

36:1–3. **In the fourth year of Jehoiakim** (605 BC; v. 1), Jeremiah was commanded to **write** (v. 2) down on a scroll (**roll of a book**) the oracles of judgment that he had proclaimed against the nation of Judah. The time of judgment was drawing near, and recording these messages would preserve them for future generations and document that the Lord had warned His people beforehand that Jerusalem would be destroyed. Hearing these messages again would also provide Jeremiah's contemporaries with one more opportunity to turn from their sinful ways (v. 3). This "earliest edition" of Jeremiah's prophecies may have included all or most of chapters 1–25 and 46–51.

36:4–8. Baruch (v. 4), Jeremiah's faithful scribe, recorded the prophet's words of judgment and was then sent to read the scroll in front of all the people at the temple. Jeremiah himself could not read the messages because he was **shut up** (v. 5), restricted from the temple complex, perhaps because of his unpopular temple sermon (see 7:12–15; 26:2–6) or because of the incidents recorded in 19:1–20:6. Baruch read the scroll in the presence of all **the people** (v. 6) on **the fasting day**, proclaimed because of a national emergency (most likely the Babylonian attack of 605 BC; see Joel 2:15; Dan. 1:1). The timing of Baruch's reading would have certainly impressed upon the people the seriousness of the prophetic warnings of doom and destruction.

36:9–19. Jeremiah's words of judgment came to the attention of Jehoiakim's officials, who called for a private reading. As was proper, they feared the prophet's warnings (v. 16) and determined that Jehoiakim must be made aware of the prophet's message. Knowing Jehoiakim's violent disposition toward the prophets of judgment (see 26:20–24), however, the officials took steps to ensure that Jeremiah and Baruch would remain hidden and out of the king's reach.

36:20–26. Jehoiakim's response to the words in the scroll was the opposite of that of his officials. Jehoiakim was angered that a prophet had dared to speak against him and destroyed the scroll, perhaps in an attempt to thwart its warnings of judgment. While sitting in his **winterhouse** (v. 22) at the palace, Jehoiakim cut up the scroll with a **penknife** (v. 23) as it was read to him and had the strips thrown into **the fire that was on the hearth** (a depression or container in the middle of the floor where coals were kept burning to warm the room). Jehoiakim's response to the prophetic word provides a stark contrast to King Josiah's reaction to the message of a previously unknown scroll containing the word of the Lord (see 2 Kings 22, especially 22:11). Josiah had helped to spare the nation from threatened judgment because he tore his garments and repented of the nation's wrongdoing, but Jehoiakim did not fear (like the officials in 36:16) and did not rend his garments as a sign of mourning. The king wanted Jeremiah and Baruch arrested (and most likely executed) for their treasonous message, but **the Lord hid them** (v. 26).

36:27–32. Since the leaders and people of Judah would not repent, the Lord would not spare them from judgment. Jehoiakim's destruction of the scroll could not prevent the fulfillment of its message, because the Lord merely commissioned another scroll to be dictated. The king did not have the power to keep the word of the Lord from coming to pass. As for Jehoiakim, he would **have none to sit upon the throne** (v. 30) after him. His son Jehoiachin (see 2 Kings

24:6) ruled only three months (see 2 Kings 24:8) and was then captured and carried off to exile in Babylon (see 2 Kings 24:15), where he eventually died (see 52:33–34). As punishment for Jehoiakim casting the prophet's scroll into the fire (36:23), **his dead body** would **be cast out** into the cold without being given the honor of a proper burial (see 22:18–19).

G. Jeremiah Imprisoned (chap. 37–38)

Chapters 37–38 recount Jeremiah's imprisonment by the royal officials of Judah (see also 20:2) during the last two years of Zedekiah's reign (588–586 BC). A recurring phrase in these chapters is "Jeremiah remained in the court of the prison" (37:21; 38:13; see 37:16; 38:28), but despite every attempt to silence his message, the prophet's word of judgment from the Lord would come to pass with the fall of Jerusalem.

1. Jeremiah's Imprisonment (chap. 37)

37:1–11. The Babylonian army was threatening Judah, and King Zedekiah sent for Jeremiah and requested, **Pray now unto the LORD our God for us** (v. 3). The king likely sought the prophet to ask the Lord to make the temporary withdrawal of the Babylonians, in 588 BC (see 34:21–22), permanent. Zedekiah may have even been seeking a miraculous deliverance for Jerusalem, like that experienced by Hezekiah under the ministry of Isaiah (see 2 Kings 18–19; Isa. 36–38). Zedekiah lacked Hezekiah's faith, however, and Jeremiah was unable to respond positively to his request.

The troops of Pharaoh Hophra (**Pharaoh's army**; v. 5) had helped bring about the Babylonian withdrawal by marching up to help Zedekiah at his request. The Lachish ostraca (Ostracon 3) mention a visit to Egypt made by the commander of Judah's army. All of Zedekiah's military ploys to avoid God's judgment, however, would fail. Jeremiah warned that the Egyptian armies would return home (v. 7), which occurred when Hophra was defeated by Nebuchadnezzar (see Ezek. 30:21). Jeremiah warned that the Babylonian withdrawal was only a temporary respite and that Babylon would still destroy Jerusalem in spite of the serious handicap the Egyptian interference caused for their army (vv. 9–10).

37:12–16. Jeremiah's arrest occurred during the prophet's attempt to return to his hometown, Anathoth, during the time of the Babylonian retreat from Judah. Jeremiah returned to his hometown **to separate himself** (v. 12), or to buy land (see 1 Sam. 30:24). While there was a brief lull in the Babylonian invasion, Jeremiah wanted to settle matters of estate with other members of his family. Irijah, a royal official, had Jeremiah arrested and charged, **Thou fallest away to the Chaldeans** (v. 13). Irijah's fear was understandable, since Jeremiah recommended surrendering to the Babylonians (see 21:9; 38:2), and since many Judahites in fact defected (see 38:19; 39:9; 52:15). Jeremiah was imprisoned in a **dungeon** (lit., "house of the cistern"; v. 16), which was probably underground (see Exod. 12:29).

37:17–21. His imprisonment did not cower the prophet into changing his message. Zedekiah sent for Jeremiah **secretly** (v. 17), not wanting to do so in the presence of his officials, whom he apparently feared. Jeremiah had no fear of the king, however, and asked why he had been imprisoned when his only crime was telling the truth. The prophet warned that Zedekiah would **be delivered into the hand of the king of Babylon** if he continued his resistance. The king did not act on the prophet's words but did concede to have Jeremiah imprisoned at the court rather than returning him to **the house of Jonathan** (v. 20), apparently a place of grave danger for the prophet. Zedekiah's fearful refusal to obey Jeremiah's counsel would have grave consequences for the nation of Judah.

2. The Miry Dungeon (38:1–13)

The account of Jeremiah's conflict with the royal officials of Judah continues in chapter 38. Though he was confined to the courtyard of the guard (see 37:21), Jeremiah was allowed to have visitors and to speak freely with them. The charge of the royal officials was that Jeremiah's call for surrender to Babylon was discouraging the soldiers, who continued to hold out against the Babylonian assault.

38:1–13. Seeking to permanently silence Jeremiah, the officials had him cast into a **dungeon** (v. 6), or an underground cistern shaped like a bell with a narrow end at the top (see 37:16). Rather than taking the prophet's life with their own hands, the officials left him there to starve in the muck and the mire. Zedekiah respected Jeremiah but feared his officials and initially did nothing to stop their murderous intentions. A foreigner named **Ebed-melech** (meaning "king's servant"; v. 7) ultimately intervened on behalf of Jeremiah and persuaded the king to rescue the prophet from the cistern. It is telling that a foreigner had more respect for the prophet as a messenger of the Lord than did the leaders of Judah. The king sent **thirty men** (v. 10) to rescue Jeremiah from the cistern; the large number was probably needed to keep the officials and their friends from trying to prevent Jeremiah's rescue. Ebed-melech's kindness to Jeremiah was evidence that he trusted in the Lord, and the Lord rewarded him (see 39:15–18). Even in the midst of national judgment, the Lord rewards individuals who respond with faith and obedience to His word.

3. Jeremiah's Advice to Zedekiah (38:14–28)

38:14–23. Fear of man leads to disobedience to God. Zedekiah once again refused to obey Jeremiah's counsel to surrender to Babylon and spare the city of Jerusalem from total destruction. Zedekiah feared how he would be treated by Judean deserters after surrendering the city to the Babylonians (v. 19). If Zedekiah had trusted the Lord, he would not have had to fear either officials or deserters (see Prov. 29:25).

Jeremiah warned King Zedekiah of the dire consequences of failure to surrender to the Babylonians. The king's harem would become the property of his conquerors (v. 22; see 2 Sam. 16:21–22), the king and his family would be taken away as prisoners, and the city of Jerusalem would be burned with fire (v. 23). While Jeremiah was rescued from the mire of the dungeon (38:6), no one would deliver Zedekiah when his **feet** were **sunk in the mire** (v. 22).

38:24–28. Zedekiah instructed the prophet not to disclose the contents of their conversation to the

officials, and the prophet complied with this request. Jeremiah was not obliged to give the officials the information he had shared with the king, especially in light of their persistent rejection of his counsel. Because of the officials' unbelief, the Lord withdrew His word from them and did not give them the opportunity to hear a final warning of judgment.

H. The Fall of Jerusalem and Its Aftermath (chaps. 39–45)

1. The Fall of Jerusalem (chap. 39)

Chapters 39–45 provide the most detailed account in the Old Testament of the Babylonian conquest of Jerusalem and its aftermath. Chapter 39 offers a vivid summary of the siege and fall of Jerusalem and of the exile of its inhabitants (see also 52:4–27). The final Babylonian siege of Jerusalem began on the January 15, 588 BC and was concluded on July 18, 586 BC. The siege lasted just over two and a half years.

39:1–10. While paralleling other accounts of the fall of Jerusalem (see 2 Kings 25:1–26; Jeremiah 52), chapter 39 focuses especially on the fate of Zedekiah the king and Jeremiah the prophet. Zedekiah fled the city of Jerusalem but was captured at Riblah, on the Orontes River. Before having his eyes put out, Zedekiah's final sight was the execution of his sons and the nobles of Judah (vv. 6–7). The king's loss of the physical ability to "see" was due to his earlier failure to "hear" the word of the Lord (see 37:1–2). The king was carried away to Babylon, where he lived out the remainder of his life as a prisoner.

39:11–14. The tables were turned: Jeremiah was released from his imprisonment at the very time his persecutors were taken away into exile. The Babylonian commander **Nebuzar-adan** (v. 11) treated Jeremiah kindly and released him from his confinement at **the court of the prison** (v. 14). The commander further entrusted Jeremiah to the care of **Gedaliah**, whom the Babylonians appointed to serve as governor of Judah. An early sixth-century BC seal impression found at Lachish attests to the historicity of Gedaliah.

39:15–18. In addition to the release of Jeremiah, the Lord promised rescue and deliverance for

Ebed-melech (v. 16), who had persuaded Zedekiah to rescue Jeremiah from starvation in the cistern. God's deliverance is reserved for those who respond to His word with faith and obedience.

2. Jeremiah Released (40:1-6)

Chapters 40-44 contain a lively narrative of the aftermath of the fall of Jerusalem. Chronologically, the chapters are the latest in the book (although 52:31-34 is later, it is part of the appendix and not of the book proper). The relationship of 39:11-14 and 40:1-6 is somewhat confusing in that Jeremiah is once again being released from his imprisonment by the Babylonians. Most likely, 39:14 is a summary statement of Jeremiah's release from prison, with the specific details being given in 40:1-6.

40:1-6. When releasing Jeremiah from prison, Nebuzaradan reflected an awareness that God had brought about the fall of Jerusalem as an act of judgment (vv. 2-3). The commander doubtless knew the basic content of Jeremiah's prophetic message against Jerusalem, and as with the earlier example of Ebed-melech, it is ironic that once again a foreigner recognized Jeremiah as a true spokesman of God. If foreigners understood that Jeremiah spoke the truth, why did his own people reject his message? Nebuzaradan promised to carry out Nebuchadnezzar's wishes concerning Jeremiah (**I will look well unto thee**; v. 4). By choosing to remain with Gedaliah and the poor who were left in the land, Jeremiah made a selfless decision to minister to those who would experience constant hardships.

3. Gedaliah Slain by Ishmael (40:7-41:18)

40:7-12. Under Gedaliah, conditions in the land in the aftermath of the exile were initially favorable. Gedaliah espoused the same message as Jeremiah: **serve the king of Babylon, and it shall be well with you** (v. 9; see 27:6-7, 11-12). Gedaliah commanded the people, **gather ye wine, and summer fruits, and oil** (v. 10). Nebuzaradan had arrived in Jerusalem in August of 586 BC, and grapes, figs, and olives were harvested in August and September. Judeans returned from the various places to which they had been scattered by the Babylonian assault and began to serve Gedaliah (vv. 11-12). Gedaliah's leadership provided stability in the difficult days following the fall of Jerusalem.

40:13-16. This stability would not last, however, and Judah would once again experience disaster because of a failure to submit to the rule of Babylon, as Jeremiah counseled. Gedaliah refused to act when informed of a conspiracy brewing against him, instigated by **Baalis** (v. 14), the king of the Ammonites, and a Judean officer named **Ishmael**. King Baalis is attested by inscriptional evidence, and Ammon was among the nations that earlier had been allies against Babylon (see 27:3 and Ezek. 21:18-32). It appears that Baalis sought to remove Gedaliah to weaken Babylonian control over Syria-Palestine.

41:1-3. Ishmael was likely part of this plot, because he belonged to the family of David (**of the seed royal**; v. 1) and was one of **the princes** who had served Zedekiah. Ishmael considered Gedaliah to be a Babylonian puppet ruler and wished to restore Davidic control over Judah. By opposing God's purposes, Ishmael continued the pattern of Davidic disobedience, reflected in the final four rulers of Judah, that had necessitated the removal of the Davidic king from the throne.

Ishmael's assassination of Gedaliah, along with the killing spree that followed, is portrayed as particularly ruthless and brutal. Ishmael killed Gedaliah while sharing a meal with him (vv. 1-2). Ancient custom with respect to hospitality made Gedaliah assume that his guests would not harm him, much less kill him (see Judg. 4:21). Ishmael also murdered a contingent of Jews loyal to Gedaliah, who had accompanied him to the meal (v. 3).

41:4-9. Ishmael next brutally murdered a group of seventy worshipers who had come down from the north "in the seventh month" (41:1) to observe the Feast of Tabernacles at Jerusalem. After the northern kingdom was destroyed in 722-721 BC, many Israelites made periodic pilgrimages to Jerusalem, especially during the reform movements of Hezekiah (see 2 Chron. 30:11) and Josiah (see 2 Chron. 34:9). When these pilgrims came to worship as mourners (**beards shaven ... clothes rent, and having cut themselves**; v. 5), probably lamenting the destruction of Jerusalem, Ishmael pretended to share their sorrow and then killed them, sparing only **ten men** (v. 8) who offered him their provisions of food. It is shocking that a member of the house of David would act in such a brutal manner toward his own people, and the narrative implies that Judah was safer in the hands of a foreign conqueror like Nebuchadnezzar than under the control of the wicked members of David's family.

41:10–18. In a final desperate act, Ishmael took Jewish hostages at **Mizpah** (v. 10), most likely in an attempt to guarantee safe passage as he fled to the land of Ammon. His hostages included **the king's daughters**, women who had been members of King Zedekiah's court, not necessarily daughters of the king himself. **Johanan** (v. 11), the military commander who had earlier warned Gedaliah of Ishmael's murderous intentions (see 40:13), intervened to rescue the hostages. Ishmael was able to escape with eight of his men and made his way to Ammon. Ishmael was fearful of Babylonian reprisals for his attack on the governor whom they had appointed over the land.

The last image of the royal family in Jeremiah is the pathetic sight of Ishmael fleeing from the Promised Land. Disobedience had necessitated the judgment of the historical house of David, but God's faithfulness to His covenant promises guaranteed that a new David would one day arise (see 23:5–6; 30:9; 33:15–26).

4. The Flight to Egypt (chaps. 42–43)

42:1–6. Despite Ishmael's assassination of Gedaliah, the Judeans who remained in the land still had the opportunity to experience the Lord's blessing if they obeyed the Lord and heeded the Jeremiah's counsel. **Johanan** (v. 1) and his contingent sought out Jeremiah, who had been conspicuously absent in the midst of Ishmael's rampage, perhaps emphasizing Ishmael's disregard of the prophetic word. It appears that Johanan and the people, seeing no other option, were asking the Lord to confirm through Jer-

emiah their plan to flee to Egypt to escape Babylonian retaliation for the murder of Gedaliah (v. 3). Jeremiah agreed to seek the Lord and to relay His will to the people. Twice the people declared their desire to do God's will (**we will obey ... when we obey**, v. 6), but they soon demonstrated that they had already decided to follow their own inclinations.

42:7–22. After ten days (v. 7), Jeremiah returned with a message from the Lord: the people were not to fear **the king of Babylon** (v. 11) and were to remain in the land if they wished to experience God's blessing (vv. 10–12). Conversely, if they fled to Egypt, the Lord would bring **sword** (v. 17), **famine**, and **pestilence** against them, and they would die in the very place they thought would provide them with security (vv. 13–17). They would experience the same **anger and ... fury** (v. 18) that the Lord had poured out on Jerusalem if they chose to disobey (vv. 18–22).

43:1–7. Jeremiah's counsel angered **Johanan** (v. 2) and his men, and they accused the prophet of being a liar and traitor who only wished to betray them into the hands of the Babylonians, the same charge the royal officials had leveled against Jeremiah before the fall of Jerusalem (vv. 1–3; see 38:2–3). They accused Jeremiah's scribe, **Baruch** (v. 3), of inciting this message against them, deciding to put the blame on someone they considered less spiritually formidable than the prophet himself. In the end, Johanan and his men kidnapped Jeremiah and Baruch and took them to Egypt with the other refugees (vv. 4–7). The reason for their disobedience was the same as that of Zedekiah before the fall of Jerusalem. Fear led them to reject the counsel to submit to Babylonian authority, but the horrible consequences they feared were precisely what they would experience because of their decision to disobey the Lord.

43:8–13. In the city of **Tahpanhes** (v. 8), a city located in the eastern delta region of Egypt, Jeremiah performed a symbolic act outside the **Pharaoh's house** (v. 9) to warn of the fate that would befall the Judean refugees in Egypt (vv. 8–13). This house was probably not the pharaoh's main residence but rather a more modest dwelling for his use when visiting the area. The symbolic act involved burying **great stones** (v. 9) beneath the pavement outside the residence. The stones represented the foundation for the **throne** (v. 10) that Nebuchadnezzar would establish there when invading Egypt and defeating the Egyptian armies and their gods. Contrary to the thinking of Johanan and his men, Egypt would not provide a refuge from either Nebuchadnezzar or the Lord's judgment. While Nebuchadnezzar never fully conquered Egypt, a fragmentary text now owned by the British Museum states that Nebuchadnezzar carried out a punitive expedition against Egypt in his thirty-seventh year (568–567 BC) during the reign of Pharaoh Amasis (see Ezek. 29:17–20).

5. The Refugees Rebuked (chap. 44)

Chapter 44 contains the last of Jeremiah's recorded messages, an indictment of the Jewish community living in Egypt, where Jeremiah lived out the final years of his life. These Jews were living in Egypt as the result of previous deportations (see, e.g., 2 Kings 23:34) and/or the events surrounding Jeremiah's kidnapping in 43:5–7. Some time must have elapsed between chapters 43 and 44 to bring about the gathering of the "great multitude" (v. 15).

44:1–15. Jeremiah reminded the people of Israel's long history of covenant unfaithfulness, their disregard of the warnings of the prophets, and how God had poured out His **fury and ... anger** (v. 6) on Jerusalem (vv. 1–6). The prophet asked the Jews in Egypt how they could continue the pattern of disobedience and idolatry when they saw what had happened in previous generations and the recent past (vv. 7–10). The Lord intended to destroy the Jewish refugees in Egypt just as He had punished Jerusalem in 586 BC (vv. 10–14). The judgment would be so severe that only a small number would escape.

44:16–17. In the narratives of chapters 26–45, Jeremiah constantly leveled the charge that Judah had "not listened to" or "obeyed" the Lord; now the people had become so blatant in their rebellion that they openly admitted to Jeremiah, **we will not hearken unto thee** (v. 16). Instead, the men and women together took a vow to carry out their sacrifices and offerings to **the queen of heaven** (v. 17), or the Babylonian goddess Ishtar (see 7:18). Because Ishtar was a fertility goddess, this form of idolatry was especially enticing to Jewish women wanting to bear children. The one way in which the people were actually faithful was in their commitment to practice evil (compare the failure to keep the promise to obey in 34:14–16; 42:6).

44:18–19. The spiritual perception of the refugees in Egypt was so distorted that they believed the calamities of the Babylonian exile were the result of Josiah's reforms, which had brought an end to idolatrous practices in Judah. Judah had been relatively prosperous during King Manasseh's lengthy reign when idolatry was rampant, but the times following Josiah's reforms were especially difficult due to increasing pressure from Babylon.

44:20–30. The rebellion and idolatry of the Jewish community in Egypt demanded that God punish them in the same manner as He punished Jerusalem in 586 BC. By their own admission, the Jews in Egypt had severed their covenant relationship with the Lord, so the Lord would destroy them with **the sword and ... famine, until there be an end of them** (v. 27). Only a small remnant from Egypt would return to the Promised Land. Jeremiah promised a restoration for Israel (chaps. 30–33), but the community in Egypt would not participate in those blessings. This warning concerning the Jews in Egypt is consistent with the teaching in Jeremiah that the exiles in Babylon were the "good figs," with whom lay Israel's hopes for the future (see 29:5–7). The judgment of the Judahites in Egypt would take place in connection with the fall of **Pharaoh-hophra** (589–570 BC; v. 30), who would be assassinated by his rivals in a power struggle, and the subsequent Babylonian attacks on Egypt by **Nebuchadrezzar** (see 43:10–13).

6. Encouragement to Baruch (chap. 45)

45:1–5. The oracle of promise to **Baruch** following a statement of national judgment recalls the promise to Ebed-melech subsequent to the account of the fall of Jerusalem (39:16–18). While the Lord judged the nation for its disobedience to His word, He also rewarded His servants who had remained faithful to Him. Baruch had demonstrated his faithfulness to the Lord by delivering Jeremiah's oracles of judgment when Jeremiah himself was unable to (see 36:8–10) and by standing with the prophet in difficult circumstances (see 43:3, 6). Chronologically, the oracle in chapter 45 was given in 605 BC (**the fourth year of Jehoiakim**), occurring between 36:8 (when Baruch went to the temple to read Jeremiah's scroll) and 36:9.

Living in the midst of national judgment, Baruch had known great **sorrow** (v. 3), even being taken away, like Jeremiah, as a hostage to Egypt. Through Jeremiah, the Lord counseled Baruch not to seek **great things** (v. 5) for himself. Baruch's brother Seraiah would occupy an important position under King Zedekiah (see 32:12; 51:59), but Baruch's lot was not to enjoy such prestige. Instead, Baruch would escape from the fray of war and persecution with only his own **life … for a prey** (or as the spoils of war; see 21:9). Though not promised comfortable circumstances, God would protect Baruch and preserve his life in the midst of difficult circumstances. Standing in this position at the end of the narratives in chapters 26–45, this individual promise to Baruch became a word of hope for all the faithful who lived in the age of exile and awaited God's deliverance with confident expectation.

IV. Oracles against the Nations (chaps. 46–51)

Chapters 46–51 consist of a series of prophecies against the nations (see Isaiah 13–23; Ezekiel 25–32; Amos 1–2; Zeph. 2:4–15). They begin with Egypt (chap. 46) and end with Babylon (chaps. 50–51), the two powers that vied for control of Judah during Jeremiah's ministry. The arrangement of the prophecies is in a generally west-to-east direction.

A. The Prophecy about Egypt (chap. 46)

46:1–12. Jeremiah's message concerning Egypt parallels the extended prophetic oracles against Egypt found in Isaiah 19–20 and Ezekiel 29–32. The historical context of Jeremiah's oracle against Egypt was the impending battle of **Carchemish** (v. 2), in 605 BC. Egypt's defeat by **Nebuchadrezzar** and the Babylonians at Carchemish was one of the most decisive battles in the ancient world, ending Egypt's agelong claims and pretensions to power in Syria-Palestine. The prophet sarcastically called on the Egyptian army to assemble for battle and then prophesied their demise (vv. 3–6). Though the Egyptian army would rise up like the flood waters of the Nile, the Lord would have **a day of vengeance** (v. 10) and would avenge Egypt's cruelties toward Judah (vv. 7–10). The prophet applied the blood imagery from Israel's sacrificial ritual (**the sword … shall be satiate and made drunk with their blood**; v. 10) to portray the gruesome horror of Egypt's impending defeat. There would be no healing for Egypt (vv. 11–12), an ironic statement in light of Egypt's reputation for expertise in the healing arts.

46:13–28. In a second oracle, Jeremiah elaborated on Egypt's doom and prophesied that Nebuchadrezzar would **smite the land of Egypt** (v. 13), an event that occurred in 568–567 BC, long after the battle of Carchemish (see 43:11). Egypt's army consisted of **valiant men** (v. 15), a phrase used elsewhere to describe "stallions" (8:16; 47:3; 50:11) or "bulls" (Pss. 22:1; 50:13), but they would not stand because they had made others fall (vv. 15–16). The pharaoh would be exposed as **but a noise** (v. 17), and the Lord would reveal Himself as the true **King** (v. 18) as He fought together with the armies of heaven (vv. 17–18). While Egypt would experience defeat and death at the hands of the Babylonian army (vv. 19–26), the Lord also promised that **it shall be inhabited, as in the days of old** (v. 26). Egypt will be restored in the messianic age and is even portrayed in Isaiah 19:23–25 as one of the three peoples of God, along with Israel and Assyria. The inclusion of Israel's greatest enemies in the future blessings of the kingdom era reflect God's missionary concern for all peoples in the Old Testament and points to the fulfillment of the promise to Abraham that "in thee shall all families of the earth be blessed" (Gen. 12:3).

While the Lord vowed to defeat Egypt, He promised to save and deliver Israel, His **servant** (vv. 27–28). The call to fear not, in verses 27–28, is repeated almost verbatim from 30:10–11. Jeremiah's message called on the people to trust in a promise that must have seemed impossible at the time it was delivered. The Lord would reverse the defeat and exile of tiny Judah and would destroy the powerful nations of the day, who seemed to control their own destiny.

B. The Prophecy about the Philistines (chap. 47)

47:1–7. Jeremiah delivered this oracle against Philistia prior to the Egyptians' defeat of Gaza. It is uncertain whether Neco (see 46:2; 2 Kings 23:29) or Hophra (see 37:5; 44:30) is intended as the pharaoh who carried out this defeat. As with Judah (1:13–14) and Egypt (46:20), an enemy **out of the north** (v. 2) would attack Philistia. This defeat would include not only the Philistines but also the Phoenician cities of **Tyrus and Zidon** (Tyre and Sidon; v. 4) and the islands of **Caphtor** (Crete). Crete was one of the many islands in the Mediterranean believed to be the original homeland of the Philistines (see Gen. 10:14; Deut. 2:23). The prophecy of the defeat of the Philistine city of Ashkelon (vv. 5, 7) found its immediate fulfillment under Nebuchadnezzar in 604 BC.

C. The Prophecy about Moab (chap. 48)

Chapter 48 contains three extended oracles against Moab (vv. 1–13, 24–27, 28–47). Similar messages against Moab are found in Isaiah 15–16, Ezekiel 25:8–11; Amos 2:1–3; and Zephaniah 2:8–11. Josephus (*Antiquities*, 10.9.7) implied that Jeremiah's prophecy concerning the future destruction of Moab was fulfilled in the "twenty-third year of Nebuchadnezzar's reign" (582 BC; see 52:30).

48:1–13. The first oracle opened with a **Woe** (v. 1) against the city of **Nebo**, creating a funeral atmosphere for this entire message, fitting for a message of judgment that included even the **little ones** (v. 4) of Moab (vv. 1–5). Along with this message

of death, the prophet called for the people of Moab to **Flee, save your lives** (v. 6) as they came under enemy attack (vv. 5–10). They would discover that their trust in the god Chemosh (see 1 Kings 11:7, 33; 2 Kings 23:13) was futile when Chemosh accompanied them into exile (v. 7). Images of pagan deities were often carried about from place to place (see 43:12; Amos 5:26). The armies that would conquer Moab would be doing the Lord's work and are described as **Cursed** (v. 10) if they failed to accomplish their appointed task. The Lord's judgment would bring an end to the ease and security of Moab, which had become like wine **settled on his lees** (v. 11) to improve with age (see Isa. 25:6) but contained in vessels that would be shattered to pieces (vv. 11–13). This is apt imagery since Moab was noted for its vineyards (see 48:32–33; Isa. 16:8–10).

48:14–27. In the second oracle, the prophet affirmed the certainty of the fall of Moab. The defeat of the Moabites would demonstrate that the Lord, not Chemosh, is **King** (v. 15). Fitting with the woe announced in the first oracle was the call to **Howl and cry** (v. 20) in lament, as Moab wept for its dead. In verses 26–27, the Lord called on the Babylonian invaders to **Make ye him drunken** (v. 26) by causing Moab to drink the cup of God's wrath (see 13:13; 25:15–17, 28). Moab, in its strength, had mocked Judah (v. 27; see Zeph. 2:8, 10) but would now **wallow in his vomit** (v. 26) like a pathetic drunk.

48:28–47. In the third oracle, the language of lament and mourning continued. The prophet himself (vv. 31–32, 36), along with the people of Moab (38–39), wept over Moab's destruction. At the same time, the message also reflected a tone of mocking and scorning, as once proud Moab became an object of derision (vv. 29, 39, 42). The prophet grieved over Moab's destruction, while recognizing the justice of the Lord in her fall. In verses 45–46, the prophet echoed the oracles of Balaam against Moab (see Num. 21:28–29; 24:17). Hundreds of years of later, Balaam's oracles against Moab were about to be fulfilled. As in the oracle against Egypt (46:26), the Lord promised that Moab will be restored in the messianic era.

D. The Prophecy about Ammon, Edom, Kedar, and Elam (chap. 49)

49:1-6. Jeremiah's message against Ammon compares to similar oracles found in Ezekiel 25:1-7; Amos 1:13-15; Zephaniah 2:8-11. Ammon was east of the Jordan and north of Moab (see Gen. 19:36-38). Ammon's major crime was that they had taken possession of some of the territory belonging to the Israelite tribe of **Gad** (v. 1) in the aftermath of the Assyrian conquest of the Transjordan under Tiglath-pileser III in 734-732 BC. The Lord asked why **their king** had possession of this territory when it rightfully belonged to Israel by divine decree. "Their king" probably refers to Molech, the chief god of the Ammonites (see 1 Kings 11:5, 7, 33), also known as Milcom (see 1 Kings 11:5). According to Josephus (*Antiquities*, 10.9.7), Nebuchadnezzar destroyed Ammon in the twenty-third year of his reign (582 BC).

49:7-27. Jeremiah announced the coming judgment of **Edom** (v. 1; see Isa. 21:11-12; Ezek. 25:12-14; Amos 1:11-12; Obadiah 1-16). The hostilities between Israel and Edom extended back to the time of their respective ancestors, Jacob and Esau, and Edom is referred to as **Esau** (vv. 8, 10) in this oracle. The fact that Esau was Jacob's brother made Edom's enmity toward Israel all the more reprehensible (see Amos 1:11; Obad. 10). The punishment against Edom would be severe, and verses 7-22 share many memorable phrases and concepts with the book of Obadiah. Edom would be overthrown like **Sodom and Gomorrah** (v. 18), and the ground would shake at **the noise of their fall** (v. 21). Nebuchadnezzar would be like an **eagle** (or vulture; v. 22) that would spread his wings over the land of Edom. A more complete subjugation of the Edomites, however, was accomplished by the Nabatean Arabs beginning in 550 BC. Included in the oracle against Edom were messages against the Aramean cities of **Damascus ... Hamath ... and Arpad** (v. 23). Unlike other oracles in chapters 46-51, there is no promise of restoration here for Edom, for Philistia (47:1-7), for Kedar and Hazor (49:28-33), or for Babylon (50-51). It appears that the Lord's anger against these people was such that He offered them no hope for the future.

49:28-33. Kedar, and ... the kingdoms of **Hazor** (v. 28) may have included Dedan, Tema, Buz, and other Arab regions (see 25:23-24). This Hazor should not be confused with the Hazor north of the Sea of Galilee (see Josh. 11:1). Nebuchadnezzar would smite these kingdoms, a prophecy fulfilled in 599-598 BC. The wealth of the Arab kingdoms that made them a **wealthy nation ... without care** (v. 31) would be taken as plunder by the Babylonians (vv. 31-32). Hazor would become an uninhabited **dwelling for dragons** (undesirable creatures; v. 33; see 9:11).

49:34-39. The Lord as the leader of the heavenly armies would fight **against Elam** (v. 34), the land northeast of the lower Tigris Valley. The Elamites were skilled archers (v. 35; see Isa. 22:6) but would be unable to stand against the Lord. The Lord promised, however, that **in the latter days** (v. 39), He will restore Elam from her **captivity**.

E. The Prophecy about Babylon (chaps. 50-51)

Jeremiah's prophecy concerning Babylon (see Isa. 13:1-14:23; 21:1-9) was by far the longest of his oracles against foreign nations and expanded on his earlier and briefer statements (see 25:12-14, 26). Its date, in whole or in part, is 593 BC (see 51:59). The two chapters divide into three main sections (50:2-28; 50:29-51:26; 51:27-58), each of which begins with a summons concerning war against Babylon, Judah's mortal enemy (see 50:2-3; 50:29-32; 51:27-32).

50:1-12. In the first section (50:2-28), the Lord called for the defeat of Babylon to be published on **a standard** (v. 2) for all to read. A foe **out of the north** (Persia in 539 BC; v. 3) would attack Babylon. The tables were turned in that the foe from the north is almost always Babylon in the book of Jeremiah (see, e.g., 1:14-15). Babylon's enemy would become **an assembly of great nations** (v. 9). The defeat of Babylon and her gods would enable **Israel** (v. 4) and **Judah together** to return home **weeping** with tears of repentance over their past sins (see 3:21-22;

31:9). Judah would be **as the he goats before the flocks** (v. 8) in that they would be among the first of the captive peoples to be released from exile in Babylon.

50:13-28. In contrast, Babylon would be destroyed and would become an uninhabited ruin (v. 13). The Lord would lead the army that would surround and destroy Babylon (vv.14-16). The command to **Shout against her round about** (v. 15) recalls the armies surrounding Jericho prior to its fall (see Josh. 6:16). The Lord would defeat Babylon in the same way that He had destroyed the Assyrians so that Israel might return home to enjoy the blessing and prosperity of the Promised Land (vv. 17-20). Babylon was **the hammer of the whole earth** (v. 23) in carrying out the Lord's judgment against sinful Judah but now the Lord would use **the weapons of his indignation** (v. 25) against Babylon (vv. 21-28). Though Babylon carryied out God's sovereign purposes, she was culpable for the violence and bloodshed she had inflicted on other peoples (see Isa. 10:5).

50:29-43. The second section of the oracle against Babylon highlights the theme of divine retribution against Babylon (50:29-51:26). The armies attacking Babylon would return to her what she had done to other nations. In verses 35-37, the word **sword** is repeated five times, to emphasize the thoroughness of the military defeat that awaited Babylon. An oracle warning that **a people shall come from the north** (v. 41), originally delivered to Jerusalem (6:22-24), was now directed against Babylon (vv. 41-43).

50:44-46. These verses are repeated almost verbatim from 49:19-21. The oracle against Edom is here applied to Babylon. The Lord would bring about the defeat of Babylon, whose destruction was **the counsel of the Lord** (v. 45).

51:1-26. The phrase **them that dwell in the midst** in verse 1 literally reads "them that dwell in the Leb-Kamai." Leb-Kamai is a cryptogram for Chaldea, like "Sheshach" for Babylon in 25:26 and 51:41 (see discussion there). Babylon's judgment would be **the time of the Lord's vengeance** (v. 6; see

also v. 11), and the Lord is the one who **hath raised up the spirit of the kings of the Medes** (v. 11). The Lord's work in creation demonstrated His power to carry out His plans against Babylon (vv. 15-19). The Lord said to the armies of Cyrus, **Thou art my battle axe and weapons of war** (v. 20), and the twelvefold repetition of **will I** or **I will** in verses 20-25 stresses God's direct involvement in the defeat of Babylon. Babylon had been a **destroying mountain** (v. 25) but would become **a burnt mountain**, like an extinct volcano, after being judged by the Lord. Babylon would **be desolate for ever** (v. 26; see 25:12; 50:12-13).

51:27-33. The third section of the oracle against Babylon (51:27-58) continues the theme of military defeat with a variety of prophetic speech forms. The Lord issued a call to war for the nations that would attack Babylon. **The land shall tremble and sorrow** (v. 29), and the warriors of Babylon would become **as women** (v. 30) who refused to come out of their hiding places to fight.

51:34-40. These verses present a prophetic lawsuit explaining the reasons for Babylon's destruction. Nebuchadnezzar would be punished for his violence against Jerusalem. Because the king had consumed Zion **like a dragon** (or, "wild beast," v. 34), Babylon itself would become **a dwelling place for dragons** (v. 37). The prophet used the contrasting imagery of **lions** (v. 38) and **lambs** (v. 40) to portray Babylon's reversal of fortunes. Though in her past, Babylon had been like a ravenous lion devouring other nations, she would now be slaughtered like a helpless lamb.

51:41-44. The prophet delivered a taunt song mocking Babylon and gloating over its destruction. **Sheshach** (v. 41) is a cryptogram for Babylon (see 25:26). The Babylonians had been like the forces of chaos in devouring other nations, but now Babylon would be covered by **the waves** (v. 42) of **The sea.** The punishment of Babylon also involved the Lord's defeat of **Bel** (Marduk; v. 44), the chief god of the Babylonians. **The wall of Babylon shall fall**, an amazing statement of faith in the Lord's power because the protective wall surrounding Babylon was one of double construction. The outer wall (twelve feet thick) was separated from the inner wall (twenty-one feet thick) by a dry moat twenty-three feet wide. The famous Ishtar Gate, which was the primary entrance into the city of Babylon, stood almost forty feet high. Even these impressive barriers would not provide protection against the Lord's judgment.

51:45–58. The Lord issued one final statement of Judah's deliverance and Babylon's fall. The fall of Jerusalem in 586 BC had brought shame and humiliation to the people of Judah and had created a crisis of faith when Nebuchadnezzar defiled **the sanctuaries of the Lord's house** (v. 51), which symbolized God's presence with and protection of His people (vv. 45–50). This situation would be reversed, however, when God sent the **spoiler[s]** (vv. 48, 53, 56) to destroy Babylon and her gods. These prophecies asked God's people to live by faith, not by sight, as they waited for the Lord to fulfill His promises.

51:59–64. A prose narrative concludes the oracle against Babylon, with the prophet Jeremiah directing a court official named **Seraiah** (the brother of the scribe Baruch; v. 59) to carry out a symbolic act confirming the prophetic words against Babylon. In 593 BC, Seraiah went with Zedekiah to confer with Nebuchadnezzar in Babylon. Zedekiah may have been summoned to Babylon to be interrogated about his involvement in forming a coalition against Babylon (see 27:3). Jeremiah instructed Seraiah that when he arrived in Babylon, he was to read the prophet's message of judgment, **all these words that are written against Babylon** (v. 60; probably the words of 50:2–51:58). Seraiah was then to **bind a stone** (v. 63) to the scroll and cast it into the Euphrates River to symbolize Babylon's eventual fall. This act represented Jeremiah's confidence in his message. Before Jerusalem had even fallen to the Babylonians, Jeremiah was providing assurance of Babylon's ultimate defeat.

More than being a promise of the defeat of the historical enemy of Judah, the prophecies against Babylon in the Old Testament prophecies (see Isaiah 13–14) take on an eschatological significance in

that Babylon not only represents a specific geopolitical entity but also symbolizes human (and satanic) opposition to God. Babylon was the location where mankind built a city and tower in defiance of God (Genesis 11), and Babylon represents the forces of evil, led by the Antichrist, who will oppose God and His people in the last days (see the prophecy of the fall of Babylon in Revelation 18). In a sense, the church today lives in exile as "strangers and pilgrims" (1 Peter 2:11) in a world that is not their real home, and it often appears as if the enemy has the upper hand. The destruction of the oppressive empire of Babylon in the sixth century BC provides assurance that God will ultimately triumph over all evil in bringing His kingdom rule to earth.

V. The Downfall of Jerusalem and the Honor Given Jehoiachin (chap. 52)

52:1–34. The conclusion of the book of Jeremiah is an appendix added by a later hand, perhaps Baruch. The passages in 52:1–23, 31–34 are paralleled almost verbatim in 2 Kings 24:18–25:21, 27–30. The writer(s) of Kings and the writer of this appendix doubtless had access to the same sources. It is unlikely that either of the accounts copied from the other, since each has peculiarities characteristic of the larger work that it concludes. In a few passages, Jeremiah is fuller than Kings (compare especially Jer. 52:10–11 with 2 Kings 25:7; Jer. 52:15 with 2 Kings 25:11; Jer. 52:19–23 with 2 Kings 25:15–17; Jer. 52:31 with 2 Kings 25:27; and Jer. 52:34 with 2 Kings 25:30).

The prophet Jeremiah is not mentioned in this section, and the purpose of this appendix apparently was to provide a stark reminder of the reality of the fall of Jerusalem, the demise of the house of David under Zedekiah, and the bleak conditions of exile. Chapters 30–33 promise a glorious future for Israel in the time of restoration, and chapters 50–51 prophesy the ultimate demise and destruction of Babylon, but this closing chapter tempers those hopes by narrating the terrible experience of the fall of Jerusalem, which was God's judgment against His sinful people. The restoration would occur but not right away, and the people had to wait in faith for God to fulfill His promises.

The narrative of 52:4–27 is summarized in 39:1–10. This record of Jerusalem's fall especially focuses on Zedekiah, the final king of Judah, both as the individual responsible for the fall of Jerusalem, as punishment for his great sin (vv. 2–3), and as the personal object of God's judgment (vv. 8–10). In the summary of the destruction of Jerusalem, emphasis falls on the temple and the objects of the temple that were taken to Babylon.

The number of the exiles taken to Babylon in 586 BC is given as 3,323 (v. 28), and this figure most likely included only adult males, since the corresponding figures in 2 Kings 24:14, 16 are significantly higher. Verse 30 records a further deportation that occurred in 581 BC, when 745 Jews were taken to Babylon. This deportation was intended either to quell further rebellion (see v. 3) or to provide reprisal for the assassination of Gedaliah (see 41:1–3).

Like Kings (2 Kings 25:27–30), the book of Jeremiah (vv. 31–34) concludes with the news of Jehoiachin's release from prison in 561 BC. The statement of Jehoiachin's favorable treatment in Babylon provided a glimmer of hope in the midst of the disaster of exile. God still had a future for the house of David, though it appeared that the exile of Zedekiah and the execution of his sons had brought an end to any possible future for the Davidic dynasty. The honor given Jehoiachin **until the day of his death** (v. 34) contrasts with the fate of Zedekiah, who remained in prison **till the day of his death** (v. 11). The continuation of the house of David ultimately provided assurance that God had not abandoned His covenant promises and that there was a future for Israel as a people and a nation.

THE LAMENTATIONS
OF JEREMIAH

INTRODUCTION

Title

The Hebrew title of the book is 'ekah ("How …!"), the first word not only in 1:1 but also in 2:1 and 4:1. Because of its subject matter, the book is also referred to in Jewish tradition as *qinot*, "Lamentations" (the title given to it in the Greek Septuagint and Latin Vulgate).

Author and Date

Although Lamentations is anonymous and one cannot be certain who wrote it, ancient Jewish and Christian tradition ascribes it to Jeremiah. This is partly on the basis of 2 Chronicles 35:25 (though the "lamentations" are not to be identified with the Old Testament book of Lamentations), partly on the basis of such texts as Jeremiah 7:29; 8:21; 9:1, 10, 20, and partly because of the similarity of vocabulary and style between the books of Jeremiah and Lamentations. Also, since the prophet Jeremiah was an eyewitness to the divine judgment on Jerusalem in 586 BC, it is reasonable to assume that he was the author of the book that so vividly portrays the event. Lamentations poignantly shares the overwhelming sense of loss that accompanied the destruction of the city, temple, and ritual as well as the exile of Judah's inhabitants.

The earliest possible date for the book is 586 BC, and the latest is 516 BC (when the rebuilt Jerusalem temple was dedicated). The graphic immediacy of Lamentations argues for an earlier date, probably before 575 BC, during the life and ministry of Jeremiah.

Theme and Theological Message

Lamentations is not the only Old Testament book that contains individual or community laments. (A large number of the Psalms are lament poems, and every prophetic book except Haggai includes one or more examples of the lament genre.) However, Lamentations is the only book that consists solely of laments.

As a series of laments over the destruction of Jerusalem in 586 BC, it stands in a tradition with such ancient nonbiblical writings as the Sumerian "Lamentation over the Destruction of Ur," "Lamentation over the Destruction of Sumer and Ur," and "Lamentation over the Destruction of Nippur." Orthodox Jews customarily read Lamentations aloud in its entirety on the ninth day of Ab, the traditional date of the destruction of Solomon's temple in 586 BC as well as the date of the destruction of Herod's temple in AD 70. Many also read it each week at the Western Wall (known also as the "Wailing Wall") in the Old City of Jerusalem. In addition, the book is important in traditional Roman Catholic liturgy, in which it is read during the last three days of Holy Week.

This latter tradition recalls that the book of Lamentations describes Jerusalem's destruction not only for its own sake but also for the profound theological lessons to be learned from it. Of course, the horrors of 586 BC are not overlooked, which included: (1) wholesale devastation and the slaughter of kings (2:6, 9; 4:20), princes (1:6; 2:2, 9; 4:7–8; 5:12), elders (1:19; 2:10; 4:16; 5:12), priests (1:4, 19; 2:6, 20; 4:16), prophets (2:9, 20), and commoners (2:10–12; 3:48; 4:6) alike; (2) starving mothers were reduced to cannibalism (2:20; 4:10); (3) the flower of Judah's citizenry was dragged off into ignominious exile (1:3, 18); (4) an elaborate system of ceremony and worship came to an end (1:4, 10). Other matters, ultimately of far greater significance, are probed as well.

The author of Lamentations understands clearly that the Babylonians were merely the human agents of divine retribution and that God Himself has destroyed His city and temple (1:12–15; 2:1–8, 17, 22; 4:11). The Lord's action was not arbitrary; blatant, God-defying sin and covenant-breaking rebellion were the root causes of His people's woes (1:5, 8–9; 4:13; 5:7, 16). Although weeping (1:16; 2:11, 18; 3:48–51) is to be expected, and cries for redress against the enemy (1:22; 3:59–66) are understandable, the proper response in the wake of judgment is sincere, heartfelt contrition (3:40–42). The book that begins with lament (1:1–2) rightly ends in repentance (5:21–22).

In the middle of the book, the theological message of Lamentations reaches its apex as it focuses on the goodness of God. He is the Lord of hope (3:21, 24–25), of love (3:22), of faithfulness (3:23), of salvation (3:26). In spite of all evidence to the contrary, "His compassions fail not. They are new every morning: great is thy faithfulness" (3:22–23).

As a model for prayer, the book is a reminder that God desires for His people to "pour out" their hearts to Him (see Ps. 62:8). A deeply personal relationship with the Lord involves the ability to express even negative emotions and feelings to the Lord. Lamentations is a reminder that God's people are encouraged to come to Him with detailed expressions and descriptions of their troubles. Willingness to come to God with one's troubles opens the soul to a deeper experience of God's presence and allows for God's intervention to bring good out of even the worst of circumstances.

Literary Features

The entire book is poetic. Each of its five laments contains twenty-two verses (except the third, which has sixty-six verses—3 times 22), reflecting the number of letters in the Hebrew alphabet. Moreover, the first four laments are alphabetic acrostics (beginning in 1:1; 2:1; 3:1; 4:1). The first three laments are equal in length; in the first and second, each verse (except 1:7) has three Hebrew lines, while in the third, each of the sixty-six verses has one Hebrew line. The fourth is shorter (each of its twenty-two verses has two Hebrew lines), and the fifth is shorter still (each verse has one Hebrew line). Use of the alphabet as a formal structure indicates that, however passionate these laments are, they were composed with studied care. The rhetorical purpose of the acrostic format is that the poet wished to convey the totality of Jerusalem's suffering and the fullness of his lament and complaint to the Lord.

Outline

I. Jerusalem's Misery and Desolation (chap. 1)

II. The Lord's Anger against His People (chap. 2)

III. Judah's Complaint and Basis for Consolation (chap. 3)

IV. The Contrast between Zion's Past and Present (chap. 4)

V. Judah's Appeal for God's Mercy and Forgiveness (chap. 5)

Bibliography

Dearman, J. A. *Jeremiah/Lamentations*. NIV Application Commentary. Grand Rapids, MI: Zondervan, 2002.

Harrison, R. K. *Jeremiah and Lamentations: An Introduction and Commentary*. Tyndale Old Testament Commentaries 19. Downers Grove, IL: InterVarsity, 1973.

Heater, H. "Structure and Meaning in Lamentations." *Bibliotecha Sacra* 149 (1992): 304–15.

Huey, F. B., Jr. *Jeremiah, Lamentations*. New American Commentary 16. Nashville: Broadman & Holman, 1993.

Provan, Iain. *Lamentations*. New Century Bible. Grand Rapids, MI: Eerdmans, 1991.

Westermann, C. *Lamentations: Issues and Interpretation*. Translated by C. Muenchow. Minneapolis: Fortress, 1994.

EXPOSITION

I. Jerusalem's Misery and Desolation (chap. 1)

1:1–22. This lament divides into two sections — verses 1–11, where the main speaker is the poet, and verses 12–22, where the main speaker is Jerusalem personified. The personification of Jerusalem and its inhabitants as a woman ("widow" and "princess," v. 1; "daughter of Zion," v. 6) is the dominant image in this chapter, and two key themes lie behind the figure of Jerusalem as a woman. First, the portrayal of Jerusalem as a woman recalls the sin of spiritual adultery and prostitution that necessitated the destruction of the city. Jerusalem had pursued other "lovers" (gods and political allies; v. 2) and was deserving of the terrible punishment she had received (see vv. 2, 8–9, 19). Second, the image of Jerusalem as a desolate widow who has lost her children evokes sympathy for the inhabitants of the city and demonstrates the intensity of their suffering at the hand of the Babylonians (see vv. 16–18).

1:1–11. In the opening verses, the poet grieves over the desolate city of Jerusalem. **How … !** (v. 1) expresses a mixture of shock and despair (see 2:1; 4:1–2; Isa. 1:21; Jer. 48:17). Jerusalem is a woman who weeps all alone (**solitary**) because her **lovers** (v. 2) and **friends** have turned their back on her. She once was an exalted **princess** (v. 1) because of her status as "the city of the great King" (Ps. 48:3), but now she was relegated to the role of a slave because of her **captivity** (v. 3). The reason for her great suffering was that **the Lord hath afflicted her for … her transgressions** (v. 5).

Because of her infidelity toward the Lord, Jerusalem had become defiled (vv. 8–9). The Hebrew term for **removed** (v. 8) could also be translated "unclean," and appears to refer to the ceremonial uncleanness of a woman during her monthly period (see Lev. 12:2, 5; 15:19). This **filthiness** (v. 9) was caused by her willful sin, and therefore, she had been shamed by having her **nakedness** (v. 8) publicly exposed. The invading army had seized Jerusalem's treasures (**pleasant things**; v. 7), while the people of Jerusalem searched for food to stay alive (**relieve the soul**; v. 11). Food shortages were an ever-present problem during and after the siege of Jerusalem.

1:12–22. In these verses, Jerusalem speaks for herself to express the depths of her suffering. The **fire** (v. 13) of God's judgment had made her **desolate**, a term used to describe Absalom's defiled sister Tamar in 2 Samuel 13:20. Jerusalem had been **trodden ... as in a winepress** (v. 15), a common metaphor for divine judgment (see Isa. 63:2–3; Joel 3:13; Rev. 14:19–20; 19:15). The evidences of death and destruction were everywhere, and **Zion** (v. 17) found no **comfort**.

While mourning her desolation, Jerusalem pleaded for God's help and acknowledged her sinfulness (vv. 18–22). **The Lord is righteous** (v. 18) in bringing judgment because Zion had **rebelled against his commandment**. Zion admitted that the **lovers** (v. 19) she had turned to for blessing and security had failed her. Because her enemies had afflicted her and then rejoiced over her suffering, Jerusalem prayed for the Lord to turn the tables and destroy her enemies on **the day** (v. 21) of judgment that He had planned for the nations (see Jer. 25:15–38).

II. The Lord's Anger against His People (chap. 2)

2:1–22. The focus of this lament is the anger of the Lord, which had been expressed in the destruction of Jerusalem (vv. 1–10), and the grief of the poet over Jerusalem's fate (vv. 11–22).

Before Jerusalem had fallen to the Babylonians, the leaders and people of Judah had blindly trusted in the inviolability of Zion, due in part to the miraculous way the Lord had delivered the city from the attack of Sennacherib and the Assyrian army in 701 BC (see 2 Kings 18–29; Isaiah 36–37). The Zion psalms celebrated the Lord's protection of Jerusalem from its enemies (see Ps. 46:1–6; 48:3–8; 76:2–3), and Judah had believed that the Jerusalem temple provided a guarantee that the city would not be destroyed (see Jer. 7:4).

2:1–10. How ... ! (v. 1) once again introduces this second lament over the fall of Jerusalem. What the people had underestimated was the Lord's **anger** over Jerusalem's sin. Because of this divine wrath, the fact that Mount Zion (or perhaps the ark of the covenant; see 1 Chron. 28:2) was the Lord's **footstool** (see Ps. 99:5, 9) had meant nothing. In a reversal of Israel's past holy war traditions, the Lord was the Divine Warrior who **bent his bow** (v. 4) and fought against Jerusalem rather than against her enemies (see Deut. 32:42; Ps. 7:12–13; Zech. 9:13–14). Jerusalem herself had become the **enemy** of the Lord, and He had had no regard for the **tabernacle** (or temple), where He had met with His people (see Exod. 25:22; 29:42–43; Pss. 27:4–5; 74:4).

The Lord's destruction of Jerusalem was a deliberate and planned act. He **purposed to destroy** (v. 8) the city and **stretched out a line** for measuring so that He could destroy with the same standards of precision and propriety used in building (see Isa. 28:17; Amos 7:7–8). In addition to the physical destruction of Jerusalem, the Lord was punishing His people by no longer communicating to them through the prophets.

2:11–22. The poet shared Jerusalem's grief and was viscerally (**bowels ... liver**; v. 11) distressed by the suffering of the people. **The children** of Jerusalem were starving to death (vv. 11–12). The corrupt leaders of Jerusalem, especially the false prophets with their **foolish** (worthless; v. 14) promises of peace, had brought this **banishment** on the people. The enemies mocked the fact that Jerusalem, once **The joy of the whole earth** (v. 15; as in Ps. 48:2), was now in ruins (vv. 15–18). As in chapter 1, the closing verses of this lament are a prayer for God to turn from His excessive anger, which had resulted in mothers resorting to cannibalism and dead bodies being strewn through the city of Jerusalem (vv. 20–22). The poet sought to evoke the Lord's compassion and sympathy by portraying Jerusalem's suffering in the most graphic terms possible.

III. Judah's Complaint and Basis for Consolation (chap. 3)

3:1-66. The length (sixty-six verses consisting of three lines for every letter of the Hebrew alphabet) and central location (verse 1 is at the exact center of the book) of this chapter demonstrates that it is the focal point of the book. The chapter alternates between words of lament and hope. The confession that the Lord's mercies are "new every morning" (v. 22) and that He "is good unto them that wait for Him" (v. 25) gives hope in the midst of what appears to be the most hopeless situation imaginable.

3:1-20. In these verses, the poet speaks for himself, as a representative member of the community of which he is part, to lament his terrible suffering. His suffering represents the suffering of all the people. The Lord had **turned** (v. 3) against the poet and had attacked him (vv. 1-3). His **skin** (v. 4) had shriveled, his **bones** were broken, and there was no way to escape the relentless assault because the Lord would not even hear his prayers (vv. 4-9). The Lord was like **a bear** and **a lion** (v. 10) and like an armed warrior (vv. 10-13). Watching his people suffer had been for the poet like drinking poison and having his face slammed into the **gravel** (v. 16; see vv. 14-19).

3:21-26. The expression of hope in these verses is the theological high point of the book of Lamentations. **The Lord's mercies** (Hebrew, *hesed*; v. 22) denotes the Lord's loving faithfulness to His covenant promises (see Exod. 34:6-7; Deut. 7:7-9; Ps. 89:1), and the term for **compassions** (Hebrew, *racham*) is related to the Hebrew word for "womb," thus indicating parental kindness and tenderness. Despite the fact that the "anger" of the Lord is a dominant theme in this book, the Lord's basic disposition toward His people is one of mercy and love. These qualities of God are inexhaustible in that they come fresh every day. The **faithfulness** (v. 23) of the Lord is **great** beyond measure (see also 3:32; Ps. 36:5). Like the priests and Levites, the poet affirmed that the Lord is his **portion** (v. 24), or inheritance (see Num. 18:20).

The presence of God and the recognition that **the Lord is good** (v. 25) inspires hope even in the midst of the greatest of disasters.

3:27-39. Despite intense suffering, the poet acknowledged the benefits of God's discipline. It provided the opportunity to learn in **silence** (v. 28) and humility. The same Lord who disciplines also restores because of **the multitude of his mercies** (v. 32). God's intention is never **to crush** (v. 34) His people, as the Babylonians had done, and He never willingly causes humans to suffer for no reason (vv. 34-36). Though men might act unjustly, God will never **subvert a man in his cause** (v. 36). Judah had no right to **complain** (v. 39), as Israel had done in the wilderness (see Num. 11:1), because they had suffered as the **punishment** for their own **sins** (vv. 37-39).

3:40-54. The poet called for repentance (**Let us ... turn again to the Lord**; v. 40) and confessed on behalf of the people, **We have transgressed and have rebelled** (v. 42). Though the Lord had **not pitied** (v. 43) Judah and had refused to hear the prayers of His people in carrying out their destruction, this repentance opened the possibility that the Lord would **look down** (v. 50) and act on Judah's behalf (vv. 43-50). The poet waited in hope of the Lord's salvation even while continuing to bitterly mourn over Jerusalem's mistreatment at the hands of her enemies (vv. 50-54).

3:55-66. Even while praying for deliverance out of the **low dungeon** (v. 55), the poet spoke as if the Lord had already rescued him (**thou hast redeemed my life**; v. 58). He also prayed that the Lord would **Render** (v. 64) justice unto his enemies, who constantly taunted and mocked him (**I am their musick**; v. 63). Rather than merely a plea for personal vengeance, the poet's request for the Lord to **destroy** his enemies is a prayer for the working out of God's justice.

IV. The Contrast between Zion's Past and Present (chap. 4)

4:1-22. This fourth lament closely parallels chapter 2 in its focus on God's anger and the resulting conditions of siege and suffering for the city of

Jerusalem. The poet contrasts Zion's glorious past with its pathetic present.

4:1–11. The gold (v. 1) of Jerusalem, which had become dull, and **the stones of the sanctuary**, which had become like pottery jars, are symbolic of the weakened and fragile condition of God's chosen people (vv. 1–2). Their value and strength were no longer evident. Worse than "jackals" (instead of **sea monsters**; v. 3) and like **ostriches** who abandon their young, parents in Jerusalem were unable to feed their children (vv. 3–5). The punishment of Jerusalem was worse than that of **Sodom** (v. 6), which **was overthrown as in a moment** and was therefore spared the suffering of a lengthy siege. Those that were killed in the assault on Jerusalem were better off than the survivors, which included mothers forced to cook their children for food (vv. 9–10). Cannibalism was one of the curses that Moses had warned would come on Israel for disobedience to the covenant commands (see Deut. 28:53–57). Such intense suffering could only be the result of the Lord's **fury** and **fierce anger** (v. 11).

4:12–22. By stating that the kings of the nations considered Jerusalem invulnerable to attack, the poet appears to be subtly attacking Judah's own misguided belief that the city would never fall (v. 12). Jerusalem had fallen because of the corruption and injustice that had pervaded the city (vv. 13–15). The leaders of Judah were like lepers, who must go about crying **Depart ye; it is unclean** (v. 15), because the blood they had shed covered their garments and made them defiled.

The Lord's promises to protect and defend Zion from her enemies (see Psalms 46, 48, 76) only applied when the inhabitants of the city were living in a manner that allowed them to dwell in God's presence (see Pss. 15; 24:3–6). God's design was for Jerusalem to be a city of "justice" and "righteousness" (see Isa. 1:26–27). The prophet Ezekiel had seen a vision of the glory of the Lord leaving Jerusalem because of its wickedness (see Ezek. 11:23–25), meaning that His protective presence was also removed from the city.

Jerusalem also forfeited the Lord's protection because they had trusted in alliances with other na-

tions to be their source of security, and these nations had proven to be **vain help** (v. 17). The nations that Judah had turned to for protection turned out to be their **persecutors** (v. 19). King Zedekiah (**the anointed of the** Lord; v. 20) had himself been taken away as a prisoner by one of these nations (Babylon; see Jer. 39:4–7; 52:7–11). The Lord had the exclusive prerogative to protect and defend His royal city, and He demanded that His people put their trust in Him alone as their source of security (see Pss. 20:7–8; 33:13–17; 44:5–9).

This poem closes by anticipating a reversal of fortunes, in which Judah's enemy, **Edom** (v. 21) would become drunk with the wine of God's judgment (vv. 21–22). Edom was guilty of participating in and benefiting from the Babylonian assault on Jerusalem, and the Lord's promised destruction of this one nation serves as a guarantee that He will judge all of His enemies. In contrast to the promise of Zion's restoration from exile, the **daughter of Edom** (v. 22) could only look forward to future judgment.

V. Judah's Appeal for God's Mercy and Forgiveness (chap. 5)

5:1–22.

5:1–11. The poet pleaded for the Lord to **Remember** (v. 1) and **Consider** the **reproach** that had fallen on Jerusalem. Judah was under foreign oppression and struggled for even the basic necessities of life (vv. 2–6). The present generation suffered because of the sins of their **fathers** (v. 7), though the poet also later acknowledged that **we have sinned** (5:16). Fathers and sons alike were responsible for the calamity that had befallen Jerusalem (see Jer. 16:11–12; Ezek. 18:2–4).

5:8–20. That **Servants** (an ironic reference to the Babylonians; v. 8) now ruled over Jerusalem only added to the indignity of Judah's suffering. Jerusalem formerly was "princess among the provinces" (1:1), and Israel would have been blessed as "the head" of all nations if they had been obedient to the Lord (see Deut. 28:13). Marauding bandits made it perilous for Jerusalem's residents to gather food, and disease resulted from shortages of proper food (vv. 9–10). **Women** (v. 11) had been raped, leaders had been executed, and **young men** (v. 13) had been taken away to do the demeaning work of grinding grain (vv. 11–13). Young and old had died, and Jerusalem had been reduced to a **desolate** (v. 18) wasteland (vv. 14–18). The poet recited this litany of suffering so that the Lord might be moved to compassion and act on behalf of His people.

5:21–22. The closing petition of the book asks that the Lord would **Turn** (v. 21) to His people so that they might **be turned** back to Him (vv. 20–21). The Lord must take the sovereign initiative to restore His people to a right relationship with Him. **Renew our days as of old** (v. 21) is a petition for the return of Jerusalem's former glory. This prayer anticipates the reversal of what had happened to Jerusalem because of the Lord's anger toward Judah (v. 23).

THE BOOK OF THE PROPHET EZEKIEL

INTRODUCTION

Author

What is known of Ezekiel is derived solely from the book that bears his name. He was among the Jews exiled to Babylon by Nebuchadnezzar in 597 BC, and there among the exiles, he received his call to become a prophet (1:1–3). He was married (24:15–18), lived in a house of his own (3:24; 8:1), and along with his fellow exiles, had a relatively free existence.

He was of a priestly family (1:3) and therefore was eligible to serve as a priest. As a priest-prophet called to minister to the exiles (cut off from the temple of the Lord with its symbolism, sacrifices, priestly ministrations, and worship rituals), his message had much to do with the temple (see especially chaps. 8–11; 40–48) and its ceremonies.

Ezekiel was obviously a man of broad knowledge, not only of his own national traditions but also of international affairs and history. His acquaintance with general matters of culture, from shipbuilding to literature, is equally amazing. He was gifted with a powerful intellect and was capable of grasping large issues and of dealing with them in grand and compelling images. His style is often detached, but in places, it is passionate and earthy (see chaps. 16 and 23). More than any other prophet, he was directed to involve himself personally in the divine word by acting it out in prophetic symbolism.

Date

Since the book of Ezekiel contains more dates (see chart, *Zondervan KJV Study Bible*, p. 1148) than any other Old Testament prophetic book, its prophecies can be dated with considerable precision. In addition, modern scholarship, using archaeology (Babylonian annals on cuneiform tablets) and astronomy (accurate dating of eclipses referred to in ancient archives), provides precise modern calendar equivalents. Twelve of the thirteen dates specify times when Ezekiel received a divine message. The other date is that of the arrival of the messenger who reported the fall of Jerusalem (33:21).

Having received his call in July 593 BC, Ezekiel was active for twenty-two years, his last dated oracle being received in April 571 BC (see 29:17). If the "thirtieth year" of 1:1 refers to Ezekiel's age at the time of his call, his prophetic career exceeded a normal priestly term of service by two years (see Num. 4:3). His period of activity coincides with

Jerusalem's darkest hour, preceding the 586 BC destruction by seven years and following it by fifteen years.

Background

Ezekiel lived during a time of international upheaval. The Assyrian Empire, which had once conquered the Syro-Israelite area and destroyed the northern kingdom of Israel (which fell to the Assyrians in 722–721 BC), began to crumble under the blows of a resurgent Babylon. In 612 BC, the great Assyrian city of Nineveh fell to a combined force of Babylonians and Medes. Three years later, Pharaoh Neco II of Egypt marched north to assist the Assyrians and to try to reassert Egypt's age-old influence over Israel and Aram (Syria). At Megiddo, King Josiah of Judah, who may have been an ally of Babylon, as King Hezekiah had been, attempted to intercept the Egyptian forces but was crushed, losing his life in the battle (see 2 Kings 23:29–30; 2 Chron. 35:20–24).

Jehoahaz, a son of Josiah, ruled Judah for only three months, after which Neco installed Jehoiakim, another son of Josiah, as his royal vassal in Jerusalem (609 BC). In 605 BC, the Babylonians overwhelmed the Egyptian army at Carchemish (see Jer. 46:2), then pressed south as far as the Philistine plain. In the same year, Nebuchadnezzar was elevated to the Babylonian throne and Jehoiakim shifted allegiance to him. A few years later, the Egyptian and Babylonian forces met in a standoff battle in southwestern Judah, and Jehoiakim rebelled against his new overlord.

Nebuchadnezzar soon responded by sending a force against Jerusalem, subduing it in 597 BC. Jehoiakim's son Jehoiachin and about ten thousand Jews (see 2 Kings 24:14), including Ezekiel, were exiled to Babylon, where they joined those who had been exiled in Jehoiakim's "third year" (see Dan. 1:1 and discussion). Nebuchadnezzar placed Jehoiachin's uncle, Zedekiah, on the throne in Jerusalem, but within five or six years, he too rebelled. The Babylonians laid siege to Jerusalem in 588 BC, and in July 586 BC, the walls were breached and the city was plundered. On August 14, 586 BC, the city and temple were burned.

Under Nebuchadnezzar and his successors, Babylon dominated the international scene until it was crushed by Cyrus the Persian in 539 BC. Israel's monarchy was ended; the City of David and the Lord's temple no longer existed.

Theme

Though Ezekiel lived with his fellow exiles in Babylon, his divine call compelled him to suppress any natural expectations he may have had of an early return to an undamaged Jerusalem. For the first seven years of his ministry (593–586 BC), he faithfully relayed to his fellow Jews the harsh, heartrending, hope-crushing word of divine judgment: Jerusalem would fall (see chaps. 1–24). Though they were God's covenant people and Jerusalem was the city of His temple, that would not bring their early release from exile or prevent Jerusalem from being destroyed (see Jer. 29–30). The only hope the prophet was authorized to extend to his hearers was that of living at peace with themselves and with God during their exile.

After being informed by the Lord that Jerusalem was under siege and would surely fall (24:1–14), Ezekiel was told that his beloved wife would soon die. The delight of his eyes would be taken from him, just as the temple, the delight of Israel's eyes, would be taken from her. He was not to mourn openly for his wife, as a sign to his people not to mourn openly for Jerusalem (24:15–27). He was then directed to pronounce a series of judgments on the seven nations of Ammon, Moab, Edom, Philistia, Tyre, Sidon, and Egypt (chaps. 25–32). The day of God's wrath was soon to come, but not on Israel alone.

Once news was received that Jerusalem had fallen, Ezekiel's message turned to the Lord's consoling word of hope for His people: they would experience revival, restoration, and a glorious future as the redeemed and perfected kingdom of God in the world (chaps. 33–48).

Theological Message

The Old Testament in general and the Prophets in particular presuppose and teach God's sovereignty over all creation, people and nations, and the course of history. Nowhere in the Bible are God's initiative and control expressed more clearly and pervasively than in the book of Ezekiel. From the first chapter, which graphically describes the overwhelming invasion of the divine presence into Ezekiel's world, to the last phrase of Ezekiel's vision ("The LORD is there"; 48:35), the book sounds and echoes God's sovereignty.

This sovereign God resolved that He would be known and acknowledged. No less than sixty-five occurrences of the clause (or variations) "and they shall know that I am the LORD" testify to that divine desire and intention (see, e.g., 24:27). Chapters 1–24 teach that God would be revealed in the fall of Jerusalem and the destruction of the temple; chapters 25–32 teach that the nations likewise would know God through His judgments; and chapters 33–48 promise that God will be known through the restoration and spiritual renewal of Israel.

God is free to judge, and He is equally free to be gracious. His stern judgments on Israel ultimately reflect His grace. He allowed the total dismemberment of Israel's political and religious life so that her renewed life and His presence with her would be clearly seen as a gift from the Lord of the universe. Furthermore, as God's spokesman, Ezekiel's "Son of man" (2:1) status testifies to the sovereign God he was commissioned to serve.

Other prophets dealt largely with Israel's idolatry, with her moral corruption in public and private affairs, and with her international intrigues and alliances on which she relied instead of the Lord. They announced God's impending judgment on His rebellious nation but spoke also of a future redemption: a new exodus, a new covenant, a restored Jerusalem, a revived Davidic dynasty, a worldwide recognition of the Lord and His Messiah, and a paradise-like peace.

The contours and sweep of Ezekiel's message were similar, but he focused uniquely on Israel as the holy people of the holy temple, the Holy City, and the Holy Land. By defiling her worship, Israel had rendered herself unclean and had defiled temple, city, and land. From such defilement, God could only withdraw and judge His people with national destruction.

But God's faithfulness to His covenant and His desire to save His people were so great that He would revive them once more, shepherd them with compassion, cleanse them of all their defilement, reconstitute them as a perfect expression of His kingdom in the Promised Land under the hand of David, overwhelm all the forces and powers arrayed against them, display His glory among the nations, and restore the glory of His presence to the Holy City.

Ezekiel powerfully depicted the grandeur and glory of God's sovereign rule and His holiness, which He jealously safeguards. The book's theological center is the unfolding of God's saving purposes in the history of the world—from the time in which He must withdraw from the defilement of His covenant people to the culmination of His grand design of redemption. The message of Ezekiel, which is ultimately eschatological, anticipates and even demands God's future works in history as proclaimed in the New Testament.

Literary Features

Three major prophets (Isaiah, Jeremiah, Ezekiel) all delivered the same basic sequence of messages: (1) oracles against Israel, (2) oracles against the nations, and (3) consolation for Israel. In no other book is this pattern as clear as in Ezekiel (see "Outline," below).

Besides clarity of structure, the book of Ezekiel reveals symmetry. The vision of the desecrated temple fit for destruction (chaps. 8–11) is balanced by the vision of the restored and purified temple (chaps. 40–48). The God presented in agitated wrath (chap. 1) is also shown to be a God of comfort ("The Lord is there," 48:35). Ezekiel's call to be a watchman of divine judgment (chap. 3) is balanced by his call to be a watchman of the new age (chap. 33). In one place (chap. 6), the mountains of Israel receive a prophetic rebuke, but in another (chap. 36), they are consoled.

Prophetic books are usually largely poetic, the prophets apparently having spoken in imaginative and rhythmic styles. Most of Ezekiel, however, is prose, perhaps due to his priestly background. His repetitions have an unforgettable hammering effect, and his priestly orientation is also reflected in a case-law type of sentence (compare 3:19, "If thou warn the wicked ...," with Exod. 21:2, "If thou buy a Hebrew servant ...").

The book contains four visions (chaps. 1–3; 8–11; 37:1–14; 40–48) and twelve symbolic acts (3:22–26; 4:1–3; 4:4–8; 4:9–11; 4:12–14; 5:1–3; 12:1–16; 12:17–20; 21:6–7; 21:18–24; 24:15–24; 37:15–28). Five messages are in the form of parables (chaps. 15; 16; 17; 19; 23).

Outline

I. Oracles of Judgment against Israel (chaps. 1–24)
   A. Ezekiel's Opening Visions (chaps. 1–3)
      1. The Vision of the Four Creatures and Four Wheels (chap. 1)
      2. Ezekiel's Commissioning (2:1–3:15)
      3. Ezekiel as the Watchman (3:16–27)
   B. Symbolic Acts Portraying the Siege of Jerusalem (chaps. 4–5)
      1. Take Thee a Tile (4:1–3)
      2. Lie on Thy Side (4:4–8)
      3. Go on a Starvation Diet (4:9–17)
      4. Shave Your Hair (chap. 5)
   C. Oracles Explaining Divine Judgment (chaps. 6–7)
      1. Doom for the Mountains of Israel (chap. 6)
      2. The End (chap. 7)

Bibliography

Alexander, Ralph. *Ezekiel*. Everyman's Bible Commentary. Chicago: Moody, 1976.

Block, D. I. *The Book of Ezekiel*. 2 vols. New International Commentary on the Old Testament. Grand Rapids, MI: Eerdmans, 1998.

Craigie, Peter C. *Ezekiel*. Daily Study Bible. Philadelphia: Westminster, 1983.

Dyer, Charles H. "Ezekiel." In *The Bible Knowledge Commentary: Old Testament*, edited by John F. Walvoord and Roy B. Zuck. Wheaton, IL: Victor, 1985.

Feinberg, Charles L., *The Prophecy of Ezekiel*. Chicago: Moody, 1969.

Keil, C. F. *Ezekiel*. Vol. 9 of *Commentary on the Old Testament in Ten Volumes*. Translated by James Martin. 1866. Grand Rapids, MI: Eerdmans, 1982.

Pierson, Anton T. "Ezekiel" In *The Wycliffe Bible Commentary*, edited by Charles F. Pfeiffer and Everett F. Harrison. Chicago: Moody, 1962.

Taylor, John B. *Ezekiel: An Introduction and Commentary*. Tyndale Old Testament Commentaries 20. Downers Grove, IL: InterVarsity, 1969.

EXPOSITION

I. Oracles of Judgment against Israel (chaps. 1–24)

A. Ezekiel's Opening Visions (chaps. 1–3)

1. The Vision of the Four Creatures and Four Wheels (1:1–28)

1:1. Ezekiel began his prophecy with the setting. To the devout reader, it is truly a sad recounting. Instead of the banks of the River Jordan, a place of captivity formed the backdrop of the prophet's message from God. He was there with **the captives**. As the scene opens, their beloved city, Jerusalem, had been spared and there was great optimism that God would never allow it to be destroyed. Ezekiel's call was to prepare them for the unthinkable. Jerusalem would fall. Yet there was hope.

The reference to **the thirtieth year** (or "my thirtieth year") is probably Ezekiel's age. According to Numbers 4:3, a person entered the Levitical priesthood in his thirtieth year. Denied the priesthood in exile, Ezekiel received another commission—that of prophet. This was given on the banks of **the river of Chebar**, a canal of the Euphrates near the city of Nippur, south of Babylon in modern Iraq, and possibly a place of prayer for the exiles (see Ps. 137:1; Acts 16:13). On this occasion, the prophet saw **the heavens were opened**, and he experienced **visions of God**. This is a special term, always in the plural and always with the formal name: **God** (not with the more personal "Lord"). The expression precedes this and the two other major visions of the prophet (8:3; 40:2).

1:2–3. The time is given as **the fifth year of king Jehoiachin's captivity**. Verses 2–3 are written in the third person (the only third-person narrative in the book), clarifying the date given in 1:1. Jehoiachin had led an early group of exiles to Babylon in 597 BC. If Israel did not repent, she would be dealt with as God had dealt with Edom (see Isa. 34:5; Mal. 1:3–4).

The name **Ezekiel** (v. 3; see 24:24) means "God is strong" (see 3:14), "God strengthens" (see 30:25;

34:16), or "God makes hard" (see 3:8). Jehezekel (1 Chron. 24:16) is the same name in Hebrew but does not refer to the same person. The prophet was a member of a priestly family (**Ezekiel the priest, the son of Buzi** could be translated "Ezekiel the son of Buzi the priest"). Six times in this book it is said that **the hand of the Lord was . . . upon him** (see 3:14, 22; 8:1; 33:22; 37:1; 40:1), indicating an overpowering experience of divine revelation.

1:4. Twice the prophet said, **I looked** (here and "I beheld" in 1:15), and thereby introduced the two parts of this vision dealing with the four creatures and the four wheels. For the reference to **whirlwind**, see Psalm 18:10–12.

1:5–14. In Scripture, the number **four** (vv. 5–6, 8, 10) often stands for completeness (see the four directions in Gen. 13:14 and the four quarters of the earth in Isa. 11:12). Ezekiel used the number four often in this chapter and over forty times in the book. The living creatures, called "cherubims" in chapter 10, are throne attendants, here representing God's creation (see v. 10). Looking at them from four different directions, Ezekiel saw that their faces had **the likeness of a man** (v. 5), God's ordained ruler of creation (see Gen. 1:26–28; Psalm 8); **a lion** (v. 10), the strongest of the wild beasts; **an ox**, the most powerful of the domesticated animals; and **an eagle**, the mightiest of the birds. These four creatures appear again in Revelation 4:7 and are often seen in the paintings and sculpture of the Middle Ages, in which they were employed to represent the four Gospels. This may not be far off the mark, since the vision recounted the incarnation of God's message through the prophet to His people—fulfilled ultimately in the incarnation of God in Christ. The vision conveyed at once the attributes of holiness, omnipotence, omniscience, and transcendence. Such a vision should have caused the recipients to give serious attention to what was being said.

1:15–28. The second part of the vision further underscored the themes of God's majesty and glory, but more importantly, His presence among the captives. While they were far from home, they were still the "apple of His eye" (Deut. 32:10; see especially Lam. 2:18; Zech. 2:8). He knew where they were and how much they needed Him. The reference to **beryl** (v. 16) probably caused them to think of the priestly breastplate, again underscoring that God was with them. What the prophet saw must have been an amazing sight. He described it **as it were a wheel in the middle of a wheel**, probably two wheels intersecting at right angles in order to move in all four directions (see v. 17). The imagery, much as the previous one, symbolizes the omnipresence of God. In the midst of the wheels, the living creatures could be seen, **full of eyes** (v. 18), symbolizing God's all-seeing nature. The reference to **the firmament** (v. 22) seems to signify a covering above their heads. The same word occurs in Genesis 1:6–8, where its function is to separate the waters above from the waters below. Here it separated the creatures from the glory of the Lord.

As Ezekiel reported his vision of God, he carefully avoided saying that he had seen God directly (see Gen. 16:13; Exod. 3:6; Judg. 13:22). What he saw was a **likeness of the glory of the Lord** (v. 28). When God's glory was symbolically revealed, it took the form of brilliant light (see Exod. 40:34 and discussion; Isa. 6:3). What is remarkable about Ezekiel's experience is that God's glory had for centuries been associated exclusively with the temple in Jerusalem (see 1 Kings 8:11; Pss. 26:8; 63:2; 96:6; 102:16). Now God had left His temple and was appearing to His exiled people in Babylon—a major theme in the first half of Ezekiel's message (see 10:4; 11:23). In his later vision of the restored Jerusalem, the prophet would see the glory of the Lord returning (43:2).

2. Ezekiel's Commissioning (2:1–3:15)

2:1. It is no surprise that Ezekiel came away from his vision weak in the knees. So stunned was he that God's first admonition was, **stand upon thy feet**. God revealed His glory to the prophet not to impress him or to intimidate him, but to strengthen him. The prophet was but the **Son of man**, but the power observed in the vision would be in him. This expression

is used ninety-three times in Ezekiel, emphasizing the prophet's humanity as he was addressed by the transcendent God (see Ps. 8:4). Daniel 7:13 and 8:17 are the only other places where the phrase is used as a title in the Old Testament. Jesus' frequent use of the phrase in referring to Himself showed that He was the eschatological figure spoken of in Daniel 7:13 (see, e.g., *KJV Study Bible* note on Mark 8:31).

2:2. The prophet did not stand on his feet for God through his own strength, but instead said that **the spirit entered into me … and set me upon my feet**. The Spirit of God, who empowered the chariot wheels (1:12, 19; 10:16–17) and the creatures (1:20), now entered Ezekiel, symbolizing the Lord's empowering of the prophet's entire ministry. To whom much is given, much shall be required. Ezekiel was so empowered because his ministry would be an extremely difficult one, requiring God's enabling strength.

2:3–10. Ezekiel was called to **a rebellious nation** (v. 3), characterized as **briers and thorns … scorpions** (v. 6). These are vivid images of those who would make life difficult for the prophet. The **book** (v. 9) was thoroughly saturated (**within and without**; v. 10) with **lamentations, and mourning, and woe**. Although Ezekiel was later commanded to preach hope (see 33:1–48:35), his initial commission (until the fall of Jerusalem) was to declare God's displeasure and the certainty of His judgment on Jerusalem and all of Judah.

3:1–9. As with Jeremiah, Ezekiel's task was an unpleasant one. He declared that the message **was in my mouth as honey** (v. 3). What Jeremiah experienced emotionally (Jer. 15:16) was experienced by Ezekiel in a more sensory way: Words from God are sweet to the taste (see Pss. 19:10; 119:103), even when their content is bitter (see Rev. 10:9–10). Jesus later employed Ezekiel's words to describe the response of His generation to the message God gave Him to deliver (see Matt. 11:21). To perform the task, Ezekiel was made **harder than flint** (v. 9). Strength and courage were necessary equipment for this prophet, especially when preaching judgment. Jeremiah had been similarly equipped (see Jer. 1:18).

3:11–14. The prophet was to **go … to them of the captivity … the children of thy people** (v. 11). Ezekiel's ministry was to the exilic community, most of whom refused to believe that God would abandon Jerusalem and the temple. After the fall of Jerusalem, therefore, they were strongly inclined to despair. Ezekiel was taken away **in bitterness, in the heat of my spirit** (v. 14). The prophet, knowing the righteousness of God's anger, personally identified with the divine emotions. **The hand of the Lord was strong upon me**.

3:15. Tel-abib is the only mention of the specific place where the exiles lived. In Babylonian, the name meant "mound of the flood [i.e., destruction]," apparently referring to the ruined condition of the site. When used of the modern Israeli city, Tel Aviv, this name (*Abib* and *Aviv* are the same word in Hebrew) is understood to mean "hill of grain." Considering Ezekiel's priestly background, the period of **seven days** may have been a parallel to the time required for a priest's ordination (see Lev. 8:1–33).

3. Ezekiel as the Watchman (3:16–27)

3:16–25. I have made thee a watchman (v. 17). In ancient Israel, watchmen were stationed on the highest parts of the city wall to inform its inhabitants of the progress of a battle (see 1 Sam. 14:16) or of approaching messengers (see 2 Sam. 18:24–27; 2 Kings 9:17–20). The prophets were spiritual watchmen, relaying God's word to the people (see Jer. 6:17; Hos. 9:8; Hab. 2:1). Ezekiel's function as a watchman was not so much to warn the exiles of the impending doom of Jerusalem as to teach that God holds each one responsible for his own behavior. There was a dual responsibility: the obligation of the prophet to speak, and the obligation of those who are warned to heed the message. **The wicked … shalt surely die** (v. 18). If the prophet failed to speak, the **blood** of the wicked would God **require at his hand**. This commission, repeated in 33:7–9, is spelled out in chapter 18.

3:26–27. These verses indicate that the prophet would be unable to speak to reprove them. **I will make thy tongue cleave to the roof of thy mouth** (v. 26). Ezekiel would be **dumb** except when he had a direct word from the Lord. His enforced silence underscored Israel's stubborn refusal to take God's word seriously. It also would exacerbate their guilt before God. This condition was relieved only after the fall of Jerusalem (see 24:27; 33:22). From that time on, Ezekiel was given messages of hope, which he continually shared with his fellow exiles.

B. Symbolic Acts Portraying the Siege of Jerusalem (chaps. 4–5)

The Lord instructed the prophet to perform four symbolic acts. Each of these acts was to portray the reality of the coming judgment on the nation. No doubt the prophet would be subjected to much disdain and ridicule, but in time, the nation would come to appreciate that in the midst of this very difficult time in their history as a nation, at least one man could be counted on to tell them the truth.

1. Take Thee a Tile (4:1–3)

4:1. Thou also, son of man, take thee a tile. The first of several symbolic acts the prophet was to perform involved inscribing a likeness of the city of Jerusalem on a moist clay tablet, such as those commonly used in Babylon.

4:2–3. Ezekiel was to place around it models of siege works to represent the city under attack. He was then to place **an iron pan** (perhaps a baking griddle; v. 3) between himself and the symbolized city to indicate the unbreakable strength of the siege. Then God instructed the prophet, **and thou shalt lay siege against it**. Ezekiel's own presence in the scene signified that the siege would actually be laid by the Lord Himself.

2. Lie on Thy Side (4:4–8)

4:4–8. Lie thou also upon thy left side … lie again on thy right side (vv. 4, 6). In so doing, the prophet would **bear their iniquity** (v. 4). This act symbolized Israel's sins; it did not remove them. He was to lie on his left side for **three hundred and ninety days** (v. 5) to depict the number of years (**each day for a year**; v. 6) for **the iniquity of the**

house of Israel (v. 4). The 390 years may represent the period from the time of Solomon's unfaithfulness to the fall of Jerusalem. Correspondingly, the 40 years of verse 6 may represent the long reign of wicked Manasseh before his deathbed repentance (see 2 Kings 21:11–15; 23:26–27; 24:3–4; 2 Chron. 33:12–13). Lying on his "left side" (see v. 4) placed Ezekiel to the north of the symbolic city; lying on his "right side" (v. 6) placed him to the south—signifying the northern and southern kingdoms respectively.

3. Go on a Starvation Diet (4:9–17)

4:9–17. Take ... wheat, and barley, and beans, and lentiles, and millet, and fitches (v. 9). A scant, vegetarian diet, representing the meager provisions of a besieged city. Ezekiel was to prepare his bread with **cow's dung** (v. 15), which was commonly used in the Near East as a fuel for baking, even today. Ezekiel again showed his sensitivity to things ceremonially unclean (see 1:3), and God graciously responded to the prophet's objection by allowing this substitute for human excrement. The symbol represented a dire situation for the city.

4. Shave Your Hair (chap. 5)

5:1–4. Then God instructed Ezekiel, **son of man, take thee a sharp knife** (v. 1). What Isaiah had expressed in a metaphor (Isa. 7:20), Ezekiel acted out in prophetic symbolism. We need to recall that Ezekiel was forbidden to say anything. He was called to act out the catastrophe that would soon come upon Jerusalem. He was to cut off all his hair and beard and **divide the hair** into three equal parts. One part he was to **burn with fire** (v. 2). A second part he was to **smite ... with a knife.** And the third part he was to **scatter in the wind.** Any leftover scraps he was to **cast ... into the midst of the fire** (v. 4).

5:5. This is Jerusalem. After wordlessly acting out the symbols (beginning in 4:1), Ezekiel received and probably related the divine explanations. Israel was **in the midst of the nations.** She had a privileged position, which made her responsibility and judgment all the more severe (see 38:12).

5:6–11. I, even I, am against thee (v. 8). This is a short and effective phrase of judgment used often by Ezekiel (see 13:8; 21:3; 26:3; 28:22; 29:3, 10; 30:22; 34:10; 35:3; 38:3; 39:1; see also Jer. 23:30–32; 50:31; 51:25; Nah. 2:13; 3:5). Things got even worse for these people: **fathers shall eat the sons** (v. 10). Cannibalism, the most gruesome extremity of life under siege, was threatened as a consequence of breaking the covenant (Deut. 28:53; see Jer. 19:9; Lam. 2:20; Zech. 11:9).

5:12–17. The interpretive key to this section is verse 12. Each of the three sections of hair shorn from the prophet's head represented a section of the people. **A third ... shall die with the pestilence** (v. 12). A third would **fall by the sword.** And a third would be scattered **into all the winds.** God added, **I will draw out a sword after them.** God Himself would cause the judgment to fall upon them. In that day, **they shall know that I the LORD have spoken** (v. 13). This is the first of sixty-five occurrences in Ezekiel of this or similar declarations. God's acts of judgment and salvation reveal who He is. Since the people would not listen to God's words, they would be taught by His actions. A similar oft-repeated expression is, **when I have accomplished my fury in them** (see 6:12; 7:8; 13:15; 20:8, 21).

C. Oracles Explaining Divine Judgment (chaps. 6–7)

1. Doom for the Mountains of Israel (chap. 6)

6:1–7. That idolatry was commonplace throughout the land is indicated by the reference to **high places** (v. 3). These were open-air sanctuaries of Canaanite origin, condemned throughout the Old Testament. The high places, together with the **altars** (v. 4), **images,** and **idols,** make up a list of abominations against which God would take action. The "altars" were made of burnt clay, about two feet high, usually inscribed with animal figures and idols of Canaanite gods. The Hebrew for "idols" is a derisive term (lit., "dung pellets"), used especially by Ezekiel (thirty-eight times, as opposed to only nine times elsewhere in the Old Testament). These mountains and high places would be destroyed, and the dead bodies of those who served them would be caused to rot before them. All this God would do so that they would know, **I am the Lord** (v. 7).

6:8–10. Yet God did not leave them without hope. A remnant would survive. **They that escape …shall remember me** (v. 9). This was the corrective outcome God intended from the severe judgment to come (see v. 10). They would be **scattered** (v. 8) **among the nations** and would **lothe themselves** (v. 9) for their complicity in this disaster. The response would be one of repentance and sorrow for their sins. This allusion no doubt looked ahead to the promise of Zechariah that they "shall look upon me whom they have pierced" (12:10), and God would reconcile with His people.

6:11–14. God commanded Ezekiel to **Smite with thine hand** (v. 11), calling for his personal involvement in the tragedy. Israel's enemies had been condemned for the same practice (see 25:6) because, in that instance, it was an act of rejoicing in the calamity of God's people being trampled underfoot by their pagan enemies (see Isa. 10:5–12). Here it reflected God's utter astonishment at the judgment required for their sins. God added, **I will stretch out mine hand upon them** (v. 14), a common expression in Ezekiel (see 14:9, 13; 16:27; 25:7; 35:3). **Diblath.** Perhaps the Beth-diblathaim of Jeremiah 48:22, a city in Moab; or Riblah, a city north of Damascus on the Orontes River (a few Hebrew manuscripts read "Riblah" due to the confusion of the Hebrew *d* and *r*). This city was located at the northern frontier of the country (see Num. 34:11), and the reference would indicate the complete destruction of the land, all the way to the farthest borders.

2. The End (chap. 7)

7:1–9. The impact of God's chastisement of Israel would be felt in **the four corners of the land** (v. 2). The entire region would be affected by God's judgment on the land of Israel. The pronouncement was given in the ominous language of retribution rather than that of chastisement. God's judgment would be total. He declared, **I will … recompense upon thee all thine abominations** (v. 3). With the

ominous expression, **the day of trouble is near** (v. 7), the prophet introduced a final denouement that would spell disaster for the entire nation. None would be spared. It would be the day of the Lord. Beginning with Amos (Amos 5:18–20), all the prophets viewed that day as a day of great judgment, and often (though not here) as a judgment that sweeps away all the enemies threatening God's people, thereby bringing peace. The principle of this chapter underscores the finality of God's judgment. He was finished with this disobedient people. All that was left was the outpouring of certain judgment. When it came, there would be no mercy (see the repetition of the phrase "God gave them up" in Rom. 1:24, 26, 28). **Pour out my fury** (v. 8), an oft-repeated expression of God's wrath in the book of Ezekiel (see 9:8; 14:19; 20:8, 13, 21; 22:31; 30:15; 36:18), bespeaks not only God's retribution but also His anger. God was not isolated and detached from the sins of His people— nor yet was God unconcerned about the response required here of His holiness. He was emotionally involved to the point of furious anger.

7:10–15. The prophet described the horrible conditions that would prevail in the city when it was besieged by the enemy and all resolve and hope were lost. **The rod** (v. 10) is a symbol of the "sceptre to rule" (19:14); here it is a reference to the rule of Israel's enemies (see Isa. 10:5). The **rod of wickedness** (v. 11), on the other hand, speaks of the rule of wickedness that reigned throughout the land and that would bring with it more sorrow and suffering than their enemies would visit upon them. Conditions in the city would be such that neither **buyer** (v. 12) nor **seller** would rejoice. Gold would not buy what could not be had (see v. 19). **The sword is without, and the pestilence and the famine within** (v. 15) describes the condition of hopelessness and helplessness throughout the city.

7:16–22. Even those who escaped the city would not be able to escape the desolation and loss suffered by the people throughout the land. They would be **like doves of the valleys** (v. 16). Doves in their wild state build their nests in the clefts of the rocks. Perhaps there is a touch of irony here, as the prophet alluded to the image of the dove placed on the standards of the Assyrians and Babylonians in honor of Semiramis, a pagan deity. (See "the oppressing sword" in Jer. 46:16; Vulgate: "fierceness of the dove" in Jer. 50:16.) The **secret place** (v. 22) is the Jerusalem temple, where the turtledove was offered to the Lord. The temple would be polluted by **the robbers** who sacked the city.

7:23–27. Make a chain (v. 23) is a graphic depiction of the prisoners being taken into captivity. But it seems to introduce and link the calamities of the paragraph: **crimes** (v. 23), **possess** (v. 24), **Destruction** (v. 25), **Mischief** (v. 26), and **desolation** (v. 27). **The pomp of the strong** (v. 24) ridiculed those who took pride in the Jerusalem temple, described similarly in 24:21; 33:28. God would delight in bringing this pinnacle of pride to rubble.

The reference to the absence of **prophet … priest … the ancients** (v. 26) is particularly poignant. The people would receive no guidance from God and no direction from the elders (see 1 Sam. 28:6; Amos 8:11–12; Mic. 3:6–7). When their human schemes and devices were finally exhausted and they sought a word from God, none would be given.

D. The Vision of the Corrupted Temple (chaps. 8–11)

The vision contained in chapters 8–11 vividly depicts the departure of the divine glory from the corrupted temple (see 8:4; 9:3; 10:18–19; 11:23).

1. Wicked Abominations (chap. 8)

8:1. Ezekiel cited the date in the opening verse: **in the sixth year, in the sixth month, in the fifth day of the month**. It was September 17, 592 BC, the second of thirteen dates in Ezekiel. This date, like those in 1:2 and 40:1, introduces a vision. Ezekiel reported, **I sat in mine house**, together with **the elders**. The text is important both as a record of the vision and as a historical insight into the exiles' lives. Apparently, they were free to build houses (see Jer. 29:5). They also had freedom of movement, assembly, and worship. A year and two months after his first vision and preaching, the prophet commanded a hearing. Some

have seen here the beginnings of the synagogue form of worship. On this occasion, Ezekiel was suddenly aware of **the hand of the Lord God upon him**.

8:2. Ezekiel saw **a likeness as the appearance of fire … as the colour of amber**. The prophet saw an angel, similar in God's appearance in 1:26–27. The prophet's description of the blinding brightness of the divine messenger is similar to that seen elsewhere in Scripture where people saw a heavenly creature (see Matt. 28:3; see Acts 9:3).

8:3. Brought me … to Jerusalem. Ezekiel had been directed to prophesy stern judgments on Jerusalem (chaps. 1–7). Now he was transported to Jerusalem in visions of God (see 11:24) and shown the reason for the judgments. He specifically mentioned four idolatrous practices which had desecrated the temple. **The image … which provoketh to jealousy**. Any idol in the temple provoked the Lord to jealousy, but this one seems to have been a statue of Asherah, the Canaanite goddess of fertility, which Josiah had removed some thirty years previously (see 2 Kings 23:6).

8:4. The glory of the God of Israel was there contrasts with 8:12, where God showed the prophet what people "do in the dark … for they say, The Lord seeth us not." The irony is that God now showed to the prophet the secret sins of the people. God knew all along of their abominations. They alone lived with the perverse hope that "the Lord hath forsaken the earth" (8:12).

8:10–18. In the style of a legal brief, Ezekiel leveled the charges of idolatry against the people, those who had not been carried away into exile but had remained in Jerusalem. The abominable practices were carried out in the very temple built to worship Jehovah God. They were guilty of worshiping **every form of creeping things, and abominable beasts** (v. 10), probably reflecting Egyptian influence (see 2 Kings 23:31–35). These idols were specifically identified with the northern kingdom of Israel. The reference to **Tammuz** (v. 14) is the only biblical reference to this Assyro-Babylonian fertility god, the husband of Ishtar. The women of Jerusalem were bewailing his dying, which they felt caused the annual wilting of vegetation. Weeping was done in an attempt to resurrect the cycle of nature. Almost all ancient temples were oriented toward the east. Worshiping the sun as it arose required them to turn **with their backs toward the temple** (v. 16). Sun worship was particularly emphasized in Egypt in reference to the god Ra.

2. Destruction of the City (chap. 9)

9:1-3. God had pronounced His judgment. Now he commenced **with a loud voice** (v. 1) to call forth the guardian angels to execute His judgment against the wicked of the city. Responding to the thunderous voice of God (see Exod. 19:19 and Psalm 29), **six men came from the way of the higher gate** (v. 2). These six guardian angels of the city, plus the seventh **clothed with linen** (v. 3; see the seven angels of the judgment in Rev. 8:2, 6), came from the place where the idol stood that had provoked God to jealousy (see 8:3). In each of their hands was **a slaughter weapon**, probably a war club or a battle-axe. The seventh angel had **a writer's inkhorn**. Simultaneously, the prophet pictured the beginning of God's departure as **the glory ... was gone up** (v. 3). God began to vacate the temple, His glory moving to the door (see 8:1–11:25). Ezekiel depicted His sad departure in deliberate but reluctant stages. He departed to **the threshold**, then to the cherubim outside (10:18), then to the Mount of Olives (11:23), to which the glory will return again in the restoration (43:2–5).

9:4-7. The angels were to go through the city and "the man clothed with linen, which had the writer's inkhorn" (9:3) would **mark ... the men that sigh and that cry** (v. 4; see Rev. 7:2–4; 13:16; 14:9, 11; 20:4; 22:4). A *taw*, the last letter of the Hebrew alphabet, which originally looked like an X, was placed on the foreheads of those among the remnant who lamented the great wickedness in the city (see Exod. 12:23; 1 Kings 19:18). These people, like the Israelites of old who had blood on the doorposts and lintels of their home on Passover, would be spared. Then, without **pity** (v. 5) and sparing none, the angels were to **begin at** the **sanctuary** (v. 6) and **Slay utterly old and young**. The judgment began at the house of God

(see 1 Peter 4:17), and they were to **Defile the house** (v. 7) with the bodies of **the slain**.

9:8-11. The vision shown to the prophet was so horrible that he cried out in protest, **wilt thou destroy all the residue of Israel ...?** (v. 8). This was one of the few times Ezekiel questioned the Lord (see 11:13). God's response indicated that their abominations were **exceeding great**. He would **recompense their way upon their head** (v. 10).

3. God's Glory Leaves Jerusalem (chap. 10)

Chapter 10 echoes chapter 1, underscoring the identity of what Ezekiel saw at the river Chebar with what he saw in this vision (see 8:4).

10:1-7. I looked (v. 1). The creatures described in chapter 1 are here called **cherubims. And he spake** (the prophet is recording the voice of God; v. 2) to tell **the man clothed with linen** (who had marked the remnant with the inkhorn) to go **between the wheels ... under the cherub** and to **fill** his **hand with coals of fire**. While in 1:13 the living creatures looked like burning coals, here real coals were to be scattered **over the city**, depicting judgment by fire (see Gen. 19:24; Amos 7:4).

Meanwhile, **the glory of the LORD went ... and stood over the threshold** (v. 4). The glory of God awaited as it was departing. Though the "man clothed with linen" was initially commanded to get the coals himself (v. 2), he received them from the hand of one of the creatures (see 1:8). The sight and sound as the man approached the cherubim was like **the voice of the Almighty God when he speaketh** (v. 5). He **took it, and went out** (v. 7). One shudders to imagine the magnitude of the scene Ezekiel envisioned. In a culture that enjoys the palliative sound of the mention of God's love, the scene brings to mind only "the fear of the LORD" in the face of blatant sacrilege committed in the temple.

10:8-17. Once again the prophet was transfixed at the sight of the cherubim and the wheels. As in chapter 1, he again described what he saw. The description is much the same, with one exception: **the first face was the face of a cherub** (v. 14). While the faces of the **man**, the **lion**, and the **eagle** are identical with those in 1:10, the likeness of the "ox" (1:10) is here described as the likeness of "a cherub" (see Gen. 3:24). While one might be tempted to wonder if the writer made a mistake (here or in chapter one), one must allow him to record what he saw, not what the reader imagines it must have been like. Is it possible that these heavenly beings can appear in different forms? Does the face of a cherub have the appearance of an ox? Here is one of the places in Scripture where no clear answer is forthcoming to explain the difference between what Ezekiel saw in chapter 1 and what he saw here. One thing is clear; he recognized these beings as the same heavenly personages observed earlier (see 10:22).

10:18 – 22. As Ezekiel watched, no doubt with great sadness, he saw **the glory of the Lord** (v. 18) begin to move again from **the threshold ... over the cherubims.** The entire heavenly assembly was seen together **at the door of the east gate** (v. 19). Ezekiel saw another movement of the glory, again in an easterly direction (see 9:3; 10:4; see also 8:1 – 11:25). The glory of the Lord departed gradually and unnoticed by any but the prophet. With such promise and affection, God had come with glory to dwell between the cherubim over the mercy seat (Exod. 40:33 – 35) and later upon the completion of Solomon's grand temple (1 Kings 8:6 – 11). He now departed, and no one even saw Him go. When God sent His Son, they would reject Him as well (see Matt. 23:37 – 39; Luke 19:44). They would be scattered among the nations and will not be regathered until they receive Him as their King once again (43:1 – 12; see Zech. 12:10 – 13:1).

4. Conclusion of the Vision (chap. 11)

11:1 – 3. As the prophet turned his attention once again to the city of Jerusalem, the scene turned from glorious to gray. Ezekiel saw a cadre of twenty-five men who were stirring up **mischief** (v. 2) against the warning from Jeremiah (who was left behind and whose ministry was among those who were still in the city). These men put their own spin on what would happen. Using the metaphor of **the caldron** (v. 3), they suggested that a caldron could be used to protect what was inside, just as much as to cook

it. Here the vision pronounced God's judgment on these wicked counselors who were leading the people astray. The residents of Jerusalem who were not exiled in 597 BC felt smugly secure, thinking that nothing worse would befall them. These false counselors tickled their ears with the encouraging words, **It** (further calamity) **is not near; let us build houses.** As in chapter 24, Jerusalem is compared to a cooking pot. Those left behind boasted that they were the "meat," the choice portions, the inference being that the exiles in Babylon were the discarded bones (see 11:15).

11:4 – 13. God instructed Ezekiel, **Therefore prophesy against them, prophesy, O son of man** (v. 4). What followed was a solemn contradiction of all their comforting expectations of being protected and prospering within the gates of their city. The prophecy was to tell them that theirs was a false security and that they could expect to meet the same fate as those who had gone before them. **Your slain whom ye have laid ... are the flesh** (v. 7). The "meat," redefined by the prophet, was not those in power in Jerusalem (who would be driven out) but the innocent people they killed. **Ye shall know that I am the Lord: for ye have not walked in my statutes** (v. 12). They would meet their fate **in the border of Israel** (vv. 10 – 11). They would be overtaken at Riblah, Zedekiah's sons would be killed, and he himself would be blinded and bound (see 2 Kings 25:20 – 21; Jer. 52:9, 10). The prophet would also see **Pelatiah** (v. 13; one of the wicked counselors of 11:1) die. In response, Ezekiel cried out to the Lord in dismay at the sorrowful scene.

11:14 – 21. The first hopeful message was now given. The epithet used against the exiles by their seemingly fortunate counterparts in Jerusalem who had not been taken into exile was, **Get ye far from the Lord** (v. 15), as if these exiles had been taken out in an act of purification to cleanse the land. It was a cruel accusation to add insult to injury. Instead, God said, **Although I have cast them far off among the heathen** (v. 16), it will not be the case that I have abandoned them. Rather, I will **be to them as a little sanctuary.** This is a key verse in Ezekiel. Although the exiles had been driven from Jerusalem and its sanctuary (the symbol of God's presence among His people), God Himself became their sanctuary; that is, He was present among them. Later, Christ also became a substitute for the temple (see John 2:19–21). God would do a new thing while Israel was in captivity. His people would be separated from all their abominations, and He would **give them one heart, and … a new spirit** (v. 19). He was going to cause an inner spiritual and moral transformation that would result in single-minded commitment to the Lord and to His will (see 36:26). In that day, **they shall be my people, and I will be their God** (v. 20) — the heart of God's covenant promise (see Exod. 6:7).

11:22–25. The Lord showed the prophet the final departure of His glory from the temple. As Ezekiel watched, he saw **the cherubims lift up their wings** and the glory of Israel over them, **And the glory of the LORD went up** (v. 23). The final eastward movement of the glory (as the Lord left His temple), which stopped above **the mountain** (the Mount of Olives; see 9:3; 10:4, 19; see also 8:1–11:25), the highest point in the area. God is pictured, as it were, taking one sad and final searching look over the beloved city as He departed gradually and reluctantly. Perhaps He was still looking for evidence of their repentance. God's glory ascended back to heaven, from the same place where Jesus would lament (Matt. 23:37–39) and where He too would ascend (Acts 1:9–11), leaving the temple void of His presence. That God's glory moved eastward was probably not lost on those who first heard this vision recounted by Ezekiel. It was to the east that they had been taken, and it was there they most felt the pain of the distance from the temple in Jerusalem. It would seem that God was coming their way.

E. Symbolic Acts Portraying Jerusalem's Exile (chap. 12)

While this message was directed primarily to the exiles, it also involved what was going to happen to those still remaining in Jerusalem. They were connected in many ways, and the fate of the latter was inevitably bound up with how the exiles would in-ternalize their situation and God's timetable for their return to their homeland. It is important to put these events in the historical context. Daniel had been taken captive in 606 BC, more than a decade before the deportation that included Jehoiachin and Ezekiel, in 597 BC. The setting of this chapter is about four years into their exile, and people were beginning to doubt that Jeremiah and Ezekiel were warranted in their pessimistic predictions for the Holy City. God instructed the prophet to perform several symbolic acts ("signs," see vv. 6, 11) to communicate what was going to take place. The preceding section (chapters 4–11) emphasized the certainty of what would take place, and the next several chapters emphasize why this was so necessary to the completion of God's work in ultimately purging the nation of its idolatry and abominations and restoring it to Himself.

1. Escape through a Hole in the Wall (12:1–16)

12:1–13. The problem both Jeremiah and Ezekiel faced was one of spiritual blindness. On both sides of the exile, whether in Jerusalem or on the banks of the Chebar, there was a general reluctance to hear the word of the Lord or to see the clear evidence justifying God's judgment on the nation. The prospects of the certain destruction of Jerusalem, the ultimate death and/or captivity of those remaining there, and the expectation of spending the remainder of their lives in exile were not messages these people wanted to hear. The prophet was not in the business of creating truth to offer temporary comfort. He could only receive truth from God and communicate it as he received it. Concerning this obstinate people, the Lord said, they were **a rebellious house** (v. 2) with **eyes to see, and see not; they have ears to hear, and hear not**. This was the hardening about which the Lord had spoken to Isaiah (Isa. 6:9–10).

The prophet was instructed not to preach, but to act out what was going to happen to those still holed up in Jerusalem. He wanted them to see it so that when it came to pass, they would believe. It reflected the gracious heart of their God, still willing to lead them to repentance. **Prepare thee stuff for removing** (v. 3). As if he were to be preparing for an escape, Ezekiel packed a light bag. **Dig ... through the wall** (v. 5). Not the city wall, which was made of stone and was many feet thick, but the sun-dried brick wall of his house. This was to be **a sign unto the house of Israel** (v. 6; see 24:24, 27). Ezekiel did all that God commanded (v. 7), and **in the morning** (v. 8), the Lord instructed the prophet to give the inquisitive people an explanation of why he was doing this. This is the book's first indication of the people's response to the prophet's symbolic acts. Ezekiel was to explain that this was their **sign** (that is, a sign to the people; v. 11). It was to depict the effort of **the prince in Jerusalem** (King Zedekiah; vv. 10, 12) to escape from the city. The fulfillment of this prophecy is given in 2 Kings 25:1-11 and Jeremiah 52:1-11. God would see to it that he was captured. The king would **be taken in** His **snare** (v. 13). Zedekiah would be brought to **Babylon** and **yet shall he not see it, though he shall die there.** In fact, when Nebuchadnezzar caught up to Zedekiah at Riblah, his sons would be slain in front of him, and his eyes would be put out. He would be carried as a captive to Babylon, where he would die.

12:14-16. God would **scatter them ... and disperse them in the countries** (v. 15). He would do this, not in His mercy, but so that they might give testimony to **their abominations** (v. 16) and to the fact that He is **the LORD.**

2. Eat with Fear (12:17-20)

12:17-20. Eat ... with quaking (v. 18). Ezekiel was instructed to perform a second prophetic symbolic act. He was to make a meal of only **bread** and **water** and to do so with an attitude of severe anxiety, as if in fear of his life. Ezekiel's trembling must have been particularly violent, because the Hebrew word for "quake" is used elsewhere to describe an earthquake (see 1 Kings 19:11; Amos 1:1). Furtively looking about and with a trembling hand, the prophet depicted the coming siege and violence of Nebuchadnezzar. The land would be laid **waste** (v. 20), and **violence** (v. 19) would abound.

3. A Proverb to Ponder (12:21-28)

12:21-28. Son of man, what is that proverb ... The days are prolonged, and every vision faileth? (v. 22). This was a mocking proverb (probably coined by false prophets; see chap. 13; Jer. 23:9-40; 28:1-17) that had become a popular saying. It was used to call into question the warnings of the prophets concerning the impending doom of their nation and people. The Hebrew for "vision" is not the same as that used in 1:1 but rather is the term used in 7:26, referring to a message that could be written down (see Hab. 2:2), specifically, Ezekiel's oracles of judgment. Perhaps the popularity of the proverb had been encouraged by God's delay in bringing about the reality of the vision. Doubters took this as an occasion to mock the message of God. The Lord instructed His prophet that He would bring an end to this proverb when He brought **every vision** (v. 23) to pass. Nor would they be able to say that **the vision** (v. 27) was **for many days to come.** Sadly, the longsuffering of God, intended to lead the people to repentance (see 2 Peter 3:9), was instead used to induce skepticism and unbelief. They responded with **flattering** (lit., "smooth") **divination** (v. 24). The ominous message was, **the word which I have spoken shall be done, saith the Lord GOD** (v. 28).

F. Oracles Explaining Divine Judgment (chaps. 13-24)

1. False Prophets Denounced (chap. 13)

13:1-8. Much as Jeremiah did (see Jeremiah 23), Ezekiel had to endure the destructive influence of false messengers of God. The test of true prophecy is whether the prophet speaks the truth. The false prophets' pronouncements were not necessarily what the people wanted to hear (see Deut. 13:1-5; 18:21-22). They were known for their "smooth" sermons (see 12:24). To call them **prophets** (v. 2), of course, was to address them at the level of their own self-understanding. In fact, as the text bears out, they did not meet the necessary qualifications to be considered legitimate spokespersons of God. The Lord's message spoke with uncompromising language against the prophets of Israel who spoke **out of their own hearts** when in fact they had **seen nothing** (v. 3; see Jer. 23:21 – 22). They **follow[ed] their own spirit**, for they had received no revelation from God. Such persons are **foxes** (v. 4); the Hebrew word here may also be translated "jackals." Both are animals that travel in packs and feed on dead flesh — a powerfully negative image (see Ps. 63:10; Lam. 5:18). **Ye have not gone up into the gaps** (v. 5). The function of true prophets is described (see 22:30; Ps. 106:23). To stand in the gap is to take risks on behalf of the truth. **They have seen vanity** (v. 6). Whether the false prophets had actual visions is unknown, but they claimed to have received revelations from God when their messages actually proclaimed only what their hearers wanted to hear (see Isa. 30:10; Jer. 23:9 – 17; 2 Tim. 4:3). Of such prophets, God declared, **I am against you** (v. 8).

13:9 – 10. The expression **they shall not** (v. 9) introduces a threefold punishment, resulting in the false prophets' total exclusion from the community. They would not be included **in the assembly of my people.** They would not **be written in the writing of the house of Israel.** And they would not **enter into the land.** One thing, however, was certain: **ye shall know that I am the Lord God.** The false prophets were brought up for special censure because they had **seduced** God's **people, saying, Peace; and there was no peace** (v. 10; see 13:16; Jer. 6:14; 8:11). They had attempted to build a nation, like a building, **with untempered morter.** The Hebrew for this phrase is used only by Ezekiel (see 22:28). Ezekiel may have chosen the phrase because of its similarity to a similar-sounding Hebrew phrase meaning "unsatisfying things." One wonders if Paul was thinking of this passage when he wrote of building the church with precious things or with "wood, hay, [and] stubble" (1 Cor. 3:12; 3:10 – 15).

13:11 – 16. The edifice built by the false prophets would be brought to ruin when **there shall be an overflowing shower** (v. 11). The violent thunderstorm of God's judgment (imagery frequently used in the Old Testament, here anticipating the Babylonian **stormy wind** from the north) was about to sweep them away (see, e.g., Pss. 18:7 – 15; 77:17 – 18; 83:15; Isa. 28:17; 30:30; Jer. 23:19; 30:23). The violence of Iraqi wind and sandstorms are legendary even today. This is a graphic metaphor for the tragic judgment that was about to befall this disobedient people.

13:17 – 23. The prophet was then instructed to direct his message toward **the daughters of thy people, which prophesy out of their own heart** (v. 17). Women associated with the occult and with goddess worship were misleading the people in the same way the false prophets were. It is said that they **sew[ed] pillows to all armholes** (v. 18). Exactly what the women were doing is not known, but that it was some kind of black magic is clear. The Bible consistently avoids explicit descriptions of occult practices. The details of what they were doing are less important than why they were doing it. God said of them, **ye pollute me** (lit., "profane me") … **for handfuls of barley** (v. 19). Much as the money changers later condemned by Jesus (Matt. 21:12; Mark 11:15), it is evident that these corrupt religionists were merchandizing the Lord Himself for personal gain, and the price placed on a word from God was but a fistful of grain. Involvement in religious matters of any kind for mere gain is consistently condemned in the Bible (see, e.g., Jer. 6:13; 8:10; Mic. 3:5, 11; Acts 8:9 – 24; Titus 1:11; for the proper attitude and motivation, see 2 Cor. 11:7; 2 Thess. 3:8; 1 Tim. 3:3). These women were guilty of slaying **the souls that should not die** and saving **the souls alive that should not live.** That is, they protected the wicked and hurt the righteous **Because with lies** they had **made the heart of the righteous sad … and strengthened the hands of the wicked … by promising him life** (v. 22). The women were false prophets, speaking lies to the people to advance the cause of evil and to hinder the works of righteousness. God would **deliver** His **people** (v. 23) from these false prophets and their prophetic placebos. There is a perverse mercy in the false promises of those who would speak from "their own heart" instead of the heart of God (see Isa. 5:19 – 21). Such persons inevitably justify the wicked and condemn the good. The outcome enlarges the borders of the "wicked one" and brings great pain to the righteous.

2. The Penalty for Idolatry (14:1–11)

14:1–5. With false prophets and practitioners of black magic throughout the land, the people were given over to idols. The occasion for this prophecy was an inquiry made by **the elders of Israel** (v. 1), which is apparently interchangeable with "the elders of Judah." While the prophet's ministry was primarily to those in the exile, the message was intended for the entire nation. As these men sat before the prophet, the Lord spoke to him about the true condition of their hearts. While they may have presented themselves as being seriously concerned to hear from God, they had in fact **set up … idols in their heart** (v. 3). God knew this, so He raised the question before the prophet of whether He should **be inquired of at all by them**, a technical term for seeking an oracle from a prophet (see 2 Kings 1:16; 3:11; 8:8). In this form (Hebrew, *niphal*), the term is used only of God in the Old Testament in the sense "to allow oneself to be enquired of, or consulted." Since they had placed **the stumblingblock** (v. 4) of idolatry in their hearts, they were **estranged** (v. 5) from Him and undeserving of a word from the true God. Instead of turning them away, God told the prophet, "Very well, I will speak to **Every man** (v. 4), but it will not be what he is expecting." It would be out of the wellspring of each man's **own heart** (v. 5) and **according to the multitude of his idols** (v. 4). God would not respond to their inquiry (whether genuine or not). He would instead address their real need to repent of their idolatry. If they wanted to be saved, it would require their repentance. God would not play their games. The stakes were too high. Even now, in grace, God reached out to them and told them what they must do to be saved. The warning presents a chilling picture of how God responds to those who come to Him with hearts given over to idols. It is a warning to any who would offend the living God with misplaced spiritual affection.

14:6–11. Therefore say unto the house of Israel, Thus saith the Lord God (v. 6). These elders were prepared to hear a word of consolation, but God's message to them was not what they expected. In the

first of three calls for repentance (see 18:30; 33:11), the message began: **Repent, and turn … from your idols.** The promise was that everyone who came to inquire of the Lord through the prophet would instead hear directly from God, for **I the Lord will answer him by myself** (v. 7). Ezekiel's visitors must have been stunned. **I will set my face against that man** (v. 8). There would be no word of consolation. **And if the prophet be deceived** (v. 9), it could be accounted that the Lord Himself had deceived him and that he would fall under the same indictment as the rest of this wicked generation, to suffer the same **punishment** (v. 10).

3. Noah, Daniel, and Job (14:12–23)

14:12–23. God's determination to bring about the chastisement of the nation was fixed. Nothing would stop it from coming to pass. Perhaps it was with reference to Abraham's classic bargain with God (Gen. 18:32) that these elders (cited above) came to consider what chances they might have. God, however, declared that even **Noah, Daniel, and Job** (v. 14, see 14:20), individually or collectively, would not count for the wickedness of this people. While some have challenged whether the author of the book of Daniel (a contemporary of Ezekiel) could be included with the other two ancient men, Noah and Job, there seems no reason to question the appropriateness of the list here given. Noah and Job were known from their ancient Scriptures. Daniel was known by all the people, and indeed might have counted in this instance. It would not happen. **They should deliver but their own souls**, but Jerusalem would fall, and her people would be scattered. When God comes in judgment against a nation or people, no one can count on another's righteousness—**neither son nor daughter** (v. 20)—to deliver him.

When God was finished, even His **four sore judgments … the sword, and the famine, and the noisome beast, and the pestilence** (v. 21) would be seen as a source of **comfort** (v. 23) because the people would know that His judgment was just (see the "four horsemen of the Apocalypse," Rev. 6:1–8, especially 6:8).

4. Jerusalem as a Burnt Vine Branch (chap. 15)

The Lord presented Ezekiel with an analogy of a charred vine. Israel had been worthless before, "when it was whole" (v. 5); it was of far less value after it had been burned in the fire.

15:1–6. The vine (v. 2) was so worthless it cannot even be used as a peg (for Israel as a vine, see Ps. 80:8–13; Isa. 5:1–7; see also Luke 20:9–19; John 15:1–17). God asked the rhetorical question, **will men take a pin ... to hang any vessel thereon?** (v. 3; see Isa. 22:23–25). Indeed, **Is it meet for any work?** (v. 4). His point was that the vine had only one positive use: it was to bear fruit. Any other uses, those ordinarily appropriated from woody plants, such as for making tools or for building, was beyond what anyone could profitably do with a vine. Yet Israel had failed even to bear good fruit. Even as **fuel** (v. 6), the vine was far less efficient than other **trees**. The only value was that **when ... it is burned** (v. 5), it would be finally devoured and gone. Whereas Isaiah (5:1–7) and Jeremiah (2:21) expressed divine disappointment over Israel's failure to produce good fruit, Ezekiel typically lamented her total uselessness.

15:7–8. On the way to their end, **they shall go out from one fire, and another** (v. 7). This describes the siege of Jerusalem in 597 BC, which resulted in the exile of which Ezekiel was a part (see 1:2; 2 Kings 24:10–16). Ezekiel knew well what awaited the city the next time around. Indeed, the next time, **fire shall devour them.** This prophecy threatened an even more devastating siege—Ezekiel's main message before 586 BC (see 5:2, 4; 10:2, 7).

5. Jerusalem as a Wayward Foundling (16:1–43)

Chapter 16 depicts the ignominy of Israel among the nations. From the beginning, they brought nothing to be desired of the Lord. Yet they became the special objects of His tender love and affection. But in spite of God's loving-kindness, they abandoned Him for their idolatrous paramours. Time and again, they were delivered and cleansed; but again and again, they returned to their idols.

16:1–5. Thy birth and thy nativity (v. 3; see Deut. 26:5). Jerusalem had a centuries-old, pre-Israelite history (Gen. 14:18), and the city long resisted Israelite conquest (see Josh. 15:63). It became fully Israelite only after David's conquest (2 Sam. 5:6–9). **Thy father ... and thy mother.** This is not a reference to the pedigree of Abraham and Sarah but a reference to the city's non-Israelite origin generally. **Amorite.** Like the Canaanites, the Amorites were pre-Israelite, Semitic inhabitants of Canaan (see 16:45; Gen. 48:22; Josh. 5:1; 10:5; Judg. 1:34–36). **Hittite.** The Hittites were non-Semitic residents of Canaan who earlier had flourished in Asia Minor during the second millennium BC (see Gen. 23:10–20; 26:34; 1 Sam. 26:6; 2 Sam. 11:2–27; 1 Kings 11:1). They were, at best, low born. **Thou wast not salted at all** (v. 4) depicts neglect. The bodies of the newborn infants were rubbed with salt, a practice observed among Arab peasants in the Holy Land as late as AD 1918. To be **swaddled** (see Luke 2:7) speaks of tenderly wrapping the child but also of the careful rearing of a child (see Lam. 2:22). Instead, the city and its people were **cast out in the open field** (v. 5). They were abandoned to die. Exposure of infants, common in ancient pagan societies, was abhorrent to Israel. It seems God was saying that He had no investment in this city, as a city, or in its present inhabitants, who had in effect returned to their original abominable condition.

16:6–14. When His people were in their **blood** (v. 6), God declared that they should **Live.** The expression is of childbirth and God's desire from their very beginning. To live is God's basic desire for all people, summed up in one word (see 18:23, 32; 1 Tim. 2:4; 2 Peter 3:9). God nurtured Jerusalem to maturity, with **excellent ornaments** (v. 7). Changing the metaphor, Ezekiel bespoke God's tender love as a husband for his wife. God said of them, **I spread my skirt** (v. 8), symbolic of entering a marriage **covenant** (see Deut. 22:30; Ruth 3:9). Since the maiden symbolizes Jerusalem, this does not refer to the Sinai covenant but to a marriage covenant (see Mal. 2:14). Israel's finest hours were when she was in His care. No gift was too good for her. He clothed her **with broidered work, and shod** her **with badgers' skin ... fine linen, and ... silk** (v. 10). These represent the very best garments. "Broidered work" (see 27:16) was colored, variegated material fit for a queen (see Ps. 45:14). Badgers' skin was the same kind of leather used to cover the tabernacle (see Exod. 25:5; 26:14).

For **bracelets upon thine hands** (v. 11), see Genesis 24:22. The **jewel on thy forehead** (v. 12) did not pierce the nose but was worn on the outer portion of it (see Gen. 28:47). **Earrings** refers to circular ear ornaments worn by men (see Num. 31:50). The Hebrew for this word is not the same as that used in Genesis 35:4 and Exodus 32:2–3. The reference to the **crown** is probably to the wedding crown (see Song 3:11, where the groom wears it). Israel was bedecked **with gold and silver** (v. 13; see Hos. 2:8). The **fine flour**, used in offerings, was of high quality (see 6:19; 46:14). For the combination of **honey, and oil**, see Deuteronomy 32:13; Hosea 2:8. She **wast exceeding beautiful** (see Eph. 5:27). Her **renown went forth** (v. 14), especially in the time of David and Solomon.

16:15–34. But despite all the privilege granted to Israel, she **trust[ed] in** her **own beauty, and playedst the harlot** (v. 15). The accusation of prostitution referred both to spiritually turning away from the Lord and to physical involvement with the fertility rites of Canaanite paganism (see Jer. 3:1–5; Hos. 4:13–14; 9:1). **Fornications** were sexual favors. Verb and noun forms of the Hebrew for this word occur twenty-three times in this chapter. Jerusalem had used all of the Lord's previous gifts in prostituting herself to **every one that passed by** (see Gen. 38:14–16). **Garments** (v. 16). Cloths of some kind were needed in the Asherah cult practices (see 2 Kings 23:7), possibly for curtains or bedding (see Amos 2:7–8).

The litany of Israel's evils and vices is unimaginable considering her exalted position before God. **Images of men** (v. 17) refers to phallic symbols or pictures of naked men (see 23:14). **Thy sons and thy daughters … sacrificed** (v. 20; see 20:26, 31; 23:37; 2 Kings 21:6; 23:10; Jer. 7:31; 19:5; 32:35). Laws against child sacrifice are recorded in Leviticus 18:21; 20:2; Deuteronomy 12:31; 18:10. Cultic prostitution was moved from **the high places** (v. 16), which were outside the towns, into Jerusalem. Even

Israel's ancient enemies to the south are spoken of as **neighbours** (v. 26). Nowhere else in the Old Testament are the Egyptians called "neighbors." The expression **great of flesh** literally means "having oversized organs." The language reflects both God's and Ezekiel's disgust with Jerusalem's apostasy.

16:35–43. For these reasons and more, God would give Jerusalem over to her lovers. God would **judge** (v. 38) her. For this sin, the punishment was death (see Lev. 20:10; Deut. 22:22) by stoning (see v. 40; Deut. 22:21–24; John 8:5–7) or burning (see Gen. 38:24). The Lord declared, **I will also give thee into their hand**, and **they shall bring up a company against thee** (vv. 39–40). They would execute the prescribed punishment: **they shall stone thee** (v. 40; see 23:47), and **they shall burn thine houses** (v. 41), which was a common form of punishment (see Judg. 12:1; 15:6).

6. Jerusalem's Mother Was a Hittite (16:44–63)

Ezekiel's prophecy turned personal and anything but complimentary. If God was hurt and offended by Israel's immorality and idolatry, it would seem that this section was designed to shame her into repentance.

16:44–60. The prophet spit out an insulting proverb: **As is the mother, so is her daughter** (v. 44). What he specifically had in mind was her tendency to loathe **her husband and her children** (v. 45). This is an unmistakable reference to the sins committed against her God and the abominations inflicted on her own (Israelite) children. **Your mother was a Hittite, and your father an Amorite** is a reference to their pagan origins. **Thine elder sister is Samaria … thy younger sister … is Sodom** (v. 46) speaks of her contemporaries. Samaria was the result of intermarriage with pagans, and Sodom was a metaphor for the immoral practices Jerusalem had adopted. The Bible frequently compares a city or people to Sodom as the epitome of evil and degradation (see Deut. 29:23; 32:32; Isa. 1:9–10; 3:9; Jer. 23:14; Lam. 4:6; Matt. 10:15; 11:23–24; Jude 7), but here Sodom is referenced to say that the sins of Jerusalem were even worse than those of that wicked city.

Sodom's sins were mild in comparison with Jerusalem's (vv. 49–51). Sodom's destruction was fully justified in the face of her **haughty ... abomination** (v. 50). How much more would Jerusalem, who **judged thy sisters, bear thine own shame for thy sins** (v. 52). Before God stayed His hand, He would **bring again the captivity** (v. 53) of these wicked sisters (vv. 53–59). Jerusalem's arrogance and pride would only come back to condemn them when God visited them in His wrath. The reference to **the day of thy pride** (v. 56) probably refers to a time long before Ezekiel, when Jerusalem (as an Israelite city) was still relatively uncorrupted—as in the days of David and the early years of Solomon. In those days, the wickedness of Sodom was not even **mentioned by thy mouth**.

16:60–63. In spite of all that had been spoken, the prophecy concluded on a note of hope and reassurance. **I will remember my covenant** (v. 60), God declared. In that day, He would reestablish them with **an everlasting covenant** (see 37:26; Isa. 55:3; Jer. 32:40). When God was finished, they would never again mention this season of rebellion and its consequences. God contemplated a time when He would "forgive their iniquity, and ... remember their sin no more" (Jer. 31:34; see Isa. 40:2).

7. The Parable of the Tree and the Eagle (17:1–21)

The key events depicted in this chapter anticipated the destruction of Jerusalem—still two years away. When Nebuchadnezzar came the first time, he placed Zedekiah as his vassal in Jerusalem. Under oath, Zedekiah agreed to this arrangement. He broke his oath, however, and sought aid from Egypt. Even in God's eyes, this was considered treachery (2 Chron. 36:13) and worthy of severe consequences. Although the conquering king was a pagan, he was accomplishing God's work of purifying the nation. The interpretation of the chapter is clear since the prophet included it at the end of his message.

17:1–2. This message was given as both **a riddle, and ... a parable** (v. 2). It was "a riddle" because it required explanation. It was "a parable" because it was an allegorical depiction of international affairs

as they were about to impact Judah. The riddle/parable is in 17:3–10, and the explanation in 17:11–21.

17:3–4. In the opening section, the parable depicts the removal of King Jehoiachin to Babylon by **A great eagle** (Nebuchadnezzar; v. 3; see v. 12). This took place in the year 597 BC (see 2 Kings 24:8–16). **Lebanon** refers symbolically to Jerusalem (see 17:12). **The cedar** is David's dynasty, his royal family. **The top of his young twigs** (v. 4) references Jehoiachin. The **land of traffick** is the land of Canaan—the name applied to a trader (see 17:12; 16:29). Babylon is the **city of merchants**.

17:5–6. Nebuchadnezzar **took also of the seed of the land** (v. 5). Zedekiah son of Josiah was the brother of Jehoahaz and Jehoiakim and the uncle of Jehoiachin (see 2 Kings 23–24). Originally named Mattaniah, Zedekiah was the name given to him by Nebuchadnezzar (see 2 Kings 24:17; Jer. 37:1; see Dan. 1:6–7). He **planted it**; that is, Nebuchadnezzar made Zedekiah king and gave him the support he needed to succeed (2 Kings 24:17). He was to rule under the authority of Babylon as Nebuchadnezzar's vassal. No longer a tall cedar, the city was now depicted as **a spreading vine** (v. 6). The image of the vine reemerges as a pejorative (see 15:3). Thousands of Judah's leading citizens had been deported, and those left were lowly (see 2 Kings 24:15–16; see also Jer. 52:28).

17:7–8. Egypt, seen as **another great eagle** (v. 7), was viewed as an international paramour. The pharaoh referenced is either Psammetichus II (595–589 BC) or Pharaoh Hophra (589–570 BC). Pharaoh Hophra, mentioned in Jeremiah 44:30, is probably the pharaoh who offered help to Jerusalem in 586 BC (see Jer. 37:5). If the fact that chapter 17 is located between chapter 8 (dated 592 BC) and chapter 20 (dated 591 BC) is chronologically meaningful, Psammetichus is meant. The vine was said to **bend her roots toward him**. Zedekiah appealed to Egypt for military aid (17:15–19). This was an act of rebellion against Nebuchadnezzar (see 2 Kings 24:20), which would in turn evoke his severe response.

17:9–10. Finally, the parable predicted that Zedekiah would die in Babylon and that his forces would fall before Nebuchadnezzar, who would come as **the east wind** (v. 10), the hot, dry sandstorm that is known to wither vegetation (see v. 10; 19:12). Even today, these fierce Iraqi storms that sweep across the desert are well known. Here "the east wind" stands for the Babylonian forces who responded to Zedekiah's treachery. The parable continued with the metaphor of the plant that was planted by Nebuchadnezzar. **Without great power** (i.e., without much effort; v. 9), it would **wither in the furrows where it grew** (v. 10). Zedekiah would be brought down and his "house" (17:12) destroyed. The reference, of course, is not to a building but to the ruling family.

17:11–21. The exact time of the explanatory section is not clear. The implication, however, is that the prophet gave the interpretation at the same time as the parable. Here he made it clear that what was depicted in the previous parable/riddle was the certain fate of **the rebellious house** (v. 12) of Jerusalem and her remaining people. The rhetorical question, **shall he escape that doeth such things?** (v. 15), underscored the certainty of these events. **Egypt** would fail them (again), and this covenant-breaking people would not **be delivered**. There is a touch of irony here. The people had broken God's covenant again and again. They treated covenants with their neighbors in much the same way. God was disgusted with them. The vassal appointed by the Babylonian king would die **in the midst of Babylon** (v. 16; see 2 Kings 25:7), and he would **not escape** (v. 18). God went on to say that one of the reasons He would punish His people for breaking their agreement with the pagan empire was because they were, in effect, rejecting **mine oath ... my covenant** (v. 19). The king of Judah would have sworn faithfulness to the treaty in the name of the Lord. To swear such an oath and then violate it was to despise God. Beyond that, it was to scorn the gracious provision of God in staying His hand of total destruction when Nebuchadnezzar invaded the first time.

8. The Promise of Blessing (17:22–24)

17:22–24. Chapter 17 begins with reproof but ends with a promise of restoration. A beautiful messianic promise is given here, using the previous imagery in a totally new and unexpected way. **The highest branch** (v. 22) speaks of a member of David's family (see Isa. 11:1; Zech. 3:8; 6:12). No longer will it be a lowly bush, but it will be a **high cedar**. God Himself will **plant it upon a high mountain and eminent** — Jerusalem. In contrast to Zedekiah, one day a king will sit upon the throne of David (see Psalm 89) in fulfillment of God's promise to him that his house and his throne would be "forever" (see 2 Sam. 7:5–12).

9. Individual Accountability (chap. 18)

18:1–4. It seems that one of the ways Ezekiel's contemporaries deflected their personal guilt was to blame their situation on inherited guilt. Indeed, in doing so, they were ultimately blaming God, because it was He who was punishing them for the sins of previous generations. So commonplace was this attitude that they even had a **proverb** (v. 2) with which to express it. Jeremiah indicated that the proverb arose first in Jerusalem (see Jer. 31:29). The proverb said that the fathers had eaten **sour grapes** (poisonous fruit; i.e., they had adopted pagan ways), and their offspring had to pay the consequences. The Hebrew for **the children's teeth are set on edge** perhaps means "blunted" or "worn" (see Eccl. 10:10), but it probably refers to the sensation in the mouth when eating something bitter or sour. The proverb, though it expressed self-pity, fatalism, and despair, and though it mocked the justice of God, had its origin in the Israelite belief in corporate solidarity (see Exod. 20:5; 34:7 and Ezekiel's own words in chaps. 16 and 23). In Lamentations 5:7, the thought appears as a sincere confession. Jeremiah predicted the cessation of the proverb, and Ezekiel said its end had come. The expression **As I live** (v. 3) is a divine oath, revealing God's unalterable intention. It is used often in Ezekiel (5:11; 14:16, 18, 20; 16:48; 17:16, 19; 20:3, 31, 33; 33:11, 27; 34:8; 35:6, 11). God was not punishing Israel solely on the basis of her prior sins. The corrective here was not denying the principle of Exodus 20 but adding to it. Ezekiel declared that it was not merely the sins of the fathers that had brought them to the precipice of destruction but also their willing complicity—**the soul that sinneth, it shall die** (v. 4), or "only the soul that sinneth, it shall die." Soul here is used to speak of individual "persons."

18:5–9. Ezekiel expanded on his point by suggesting the scenario of a godly grandfather (vv. 5–9), an ungodly son (18:10–13), and a godly grandson (18:14–18). As some have suggested, these could well be allusions to godly King Hezekiah, wicked King Manasseh, and good King Josiah. If so, the prophecy would have been even more meaningful to his audience. Ezekiel's scenario represented three generations who broke the pattern of children having to inherit the sins of the father to the third and fourth generation.

The prophet's first example was of a **just** (v. 5) man, whose righteousness is measured by both positive and negative criteria. In the first instance, he is a person who keeps the laws of God. The fifteen commandments cited are partly ceremonial but are mostly moral injunctions (see the Ten Commandments in Exodus 20 and Deuteronomy 5; see also Pss. 15:2–5; 24:3–6; Isa. 33:15). In the second instance, he is a person who has not participated in forbidden practices. Eating **upon the mountains** (v. 6) alludes to eating meat sacrificed to idols on the high places (see 6:3; Hos. 4:13). **Lift up his eyes to** means "seek help from" (see 23:27; 33:25; Ps. 121:1), in this case, **idols**. To be **defiled** refers to committing adultery (condemned in Exod. 20:14; Deut. 22:22; Lev. 18:20; 20:10) and is here also associated with a menstrual prohibition (see Lev. 15:19–24; 18:19; 20:18), which is absent from the two listings that follow (see 18:11, 15). Not only is the godly man not given over to the abominations of idolatry, but he treats his neighbor justly (vv. 7–9). **Oppressed ... restored ... spoiled none** (v. 7) refers to the rich taking advantage of the poor (see Exod. 22:26; Deut. 24:12–13; Amos 2:8). **Spoiled none by violence**, or committed robbery (see the commandment against stealing in Exod. 20:15; Deut. 5:19), refers to violent ("armed") robbery rather than to secret theft or burglary (see Lev. 19:13). **Bread to the hungry.** See Deut. 15:7–11; Matt. 25:31–46. Such a man does not charge **usury**

(v. 8; see 22:12; Ps. 15:5; Prov. 28:8). What is forbidden in Exodus 22:25; Leviticus 25:35–37; Deuteronomy 23:19 is interest on loans to the needy. Deuteronomy 23:20 allows an Israelite to charge interest to a foreigner; Ezekiel condemned usury. (Interest on modern commercial loans is a different matter.)

Rather, this man **is just** (v. 9), and accordingly, **he shall surely live.** After the checklist of commandments has been gone over, the verdict is rendered (see Pss. 15:5; 24:5). The reference to "live" calls to mind God's gracious intention expressed in 16:6 (see Pss. 63:3; 73:27–28).

18:10–13. A godly man (such as Hezekiah), however, could well have a wicked son, **a son that is a robber** (v. 10), as was Manasseh. The second-generation son is described as having committed all the evils that the godly man eschewed. The prophet declared, **his blood shall be upon him** (v. 13). He is held responsible for his own sin (see Lev. 20:9, 11–12, 16, 27).

18:14–18. Finally, there is a third **son** (v. 14), who again rejects the ways of his father but does righteousness rather than evil. Again, the Judge of the earth will do what is right (Gen. 18:25). **As for his father** (v. 18), however, the evil deeds of the father will not be overlooked. This shows that the principle works both ways. The good will not be judged of God on the basis of the sins of his father, nor will the wicked be accepted of God on the merits of his father. The wicked one, **lo, even he shall die in his iniquity.**

18:19–30. In the concluding section of the chapter, the prophet responded to several hypothetical objections to his argument. The first objection seems to imply an attitude of self-righteousness. **When the son hath done that which is ... right** (v. 19), or "If what you say is true, why are we under the judgment of God?" His answer is: "I'll say it one more time— **The soul that sinneth, it shall die**" (v. 20). Then he goes on, **But if the wicked will turn ... and keep ... he shall surely live** (v. 21). As indicated in 18:1–20, the chain of inherited guilt can be broken, and verses 21–29 teach that the power of guilt accumulated within a person's life can be overcome. Manasseh, whom the prophet may have had in mind, would have been a supreme example of the principle (see 2 Chron. 33:11–20). **Therefore** (v. 30) gives a concluding challenge. **I will judge you ... every one**. While the house of Israel as a whole was guilty, God's judgment would be just and individual. Finally, Ezekiel issued his second call to **Repent** (see 14:6).

18:31–32. In conclusion, the prophet lamented, **why will ye die?** (v. 31). It was in the people's hands to live or die, why would they choose death? What had been promised unconditionally (11:19; 36:26) is here portrayed as attainable but not inevitable (see the same tension between Phil. 2:12 and 2:13). As for God, He appealed to Israel by once again exposing His heart: **I have no pleasure in the death of him that dieth** (v. 32). This final, grand summary, called by some the most important message in the whole book of Ezekiel (see 16:6), echoes 18:23. **Turn yourselves, and live ye**. One of the crucial tensions in Scripture, eminently seen in this prophecy, is the tension regarding God's sovereignty, which is so great that He turns even the hearts of wicked kings and nations to do His bidding. Yet he requires the obligation to "choose" whether one will live or die. As a lamentation, this final appeal forms a literary segue to the next chapter.

10. The Twofold Lament (chap. 19)

Although a lament, this chapter is an allegory, as is chapter 17, to which it is related in content. Chapter 17 gives an interpretation, but this one does not.

19:1–9. The opening is written in poetic form as **a lamentation** (v. 1), a metered (three beats plus two beats) chant usually composed for funerals of fallen leaders (as in 2 Sam. 1:17–27), but often used sarcastically by the Old Testament prophets to lament or to ironically predict the death of a nation (see Isa. 14:4–21; Amos 5:1–3; see also 2:10). The lament depicts the last of **the princes** (kings) of Judah.

The **lioness** (v. 2) may be a personification of Israel (see v. 1), Judah (see 4:6; 8:1, 17; 9:9), or Jerusalem (see 5:5), all of which may be considered mother to the kings (see 19:10–14). The context favors Jerusalem. In any case, the imagery is less than flattering. **She brought up one of her whelps** (v. 3),

Jehoahaz (see 2 Kings 23:31–34; Jer. 22:10–12), who reigned only three months. As a lion, he **devoured men**, a reference to his oppressive policies (see Jer. 22:13). He came to his end in **chains** (v. 4) when Pharoah Necho at Riblah led him in chains as an animal to his captivity in Egypt. She subsequently elevated **another of her whelps** (v. 5). This is possibly Jehoiachin (who reigned only three months, 2 Kings 24:8), but more probably Zedekiah (of whom v. 7 appears a more likely description). Both were taken to Babylon (v. 9). If the reference is to Jehoiachin (see 2 Kings 24:15), this was a true lament; if to Zedekiah, it was a prediction (see 2 Kings 25:7).

19:10–14. The final allegory parallels 17:5–8. The one previously pictured as a lioness (19:2) is here **a vine** (v. 10; see 15:2 and discussion; 17:7). Originally a fruitful vine, full of branches with **strong rods** (branches; v. 12) she was subjected to **the east wind** (v. 12), Nebuchadnezzar and his army (see 17:10). Her end was to be **planted in the wilderness**, in Babylon, which, to Israel, seemed like a wilderness (see 20:35). Zedekiah should have been a protector of the nation but instead became a **fire** (v. 14) and the instrument of her destruction (see 2 Kings 24:20). **This ... shall be for a lamentation**. Written in poetic form, this phrase indicates repeated use (see Ps. 137:1).

11. Israel Is a Repeat Offender (20:1–44)

20:1–4. Chapter 20 begins a series of oracles preceding the fall of Jerusalem. The time was **the seventh year ... the fifth month ... the tenth day of the month** (v. 1), or August 14, 591 BC. This is the third date in Ezekiel (see 1:2; 8:1), approximately a year since the last specified date (see 8:1). The elders had come once again to seek a word from God. The text does not state their specific inquiry. Regardless, God was not interested in their questions (see 20:3, 31). Instead, He subjected them to a long discourse on their national history. As the prophet began, it became abundantly clear that the story was different from how they likely understood their glorious history; it was the unvarnished version, with all Israel's failures in bold relief. The message Ezekiel delivered was that the nation God called had out of Egypt had disappointed Him again and again. On **the elders of Israel**, see discussions on 8:1; 14:1. The seriousness of the message was underscored by an oath, **As I live** (v. 3; see 18:3). For the expression **be inquired of**, see 14:3.

a. The Egyptian Generation (20:5-9)

20:5-9. Ezekiel presented Israel's history in several "acts," each of which had four scenes: (1) revelation, (2) rebellion, (3) wrath, and (4) reconsideration. In the opening act, Israel was in captivity in Egypt. At that time, God **chose** (v. 5) her and revealed Himself to her as **the LORD your God**. He further gave them the promise that He would bring them to **a land ... flowing with milk and honey** (v. 6; see Exod. 3:8). It would be **the glory of all lands** (for the land's natural beauty, see Deut. 8:7-10; Jer. 3:19). Its real beauty lay in being selected as God's dwelling place (Deut. 12:5, 11). Yet even at the outset, it became necessary to instruct them to cast away **the idols of Egypt** (v. 7; see also 6:4).

But they rebelled (v. 8; see 20:13, 21; Joshua 24:14). Because of Israel's spiritual perversity, God declared, **I will pour out my fury upon them**. This is an internal refrain seen elsewhere in the prophecy (see 20:13, 21; see also 7:8). Even before she was delivered from Egypt, God considered that He might **accomplish** His **anger against them** (see 5:13). God withheld His hand (see 20:14, 22, 44) only **for His name's sake** (v. 9). Name and person are closely connected in the Bible. God's name is His identity and reputation, that by which He is known. The phrase used here is equivalent to "for my own sake" (see Isa. 37:35; 43:25). God's acts of deliverance — past and future — identify Him, revealing His true nature (see 36:22; Ps. 23:3; Isa. 48:9). Lest His name be **polluted before the heathen**. God ultimately withheld His hand for His own sake, not for disobedient Israel's (see Num. 14:15-16).

b. The Exodus Generation (20:10-17)

20:10-17. The second act of Israel's history recalled the generation that God **caused ... to go forth out of the land of Egypt, and brought ... into the wilderness** (v. 10). He determined that those who lived in His **statutes ... shall even live in them** (v. 11; see v. 13, 20:21; compare 20:25; see also 16:6; 18:9; Lev. 18:5). He gave them the **sabbaths, to be a sign** (v. 12) so they would know that it was **the LORD that sanctif[ied] them**. Israel's observance of the Sabbath was to serve as a sign that she was the Lord's holy people (see Exod. 31:13-17). Ezekiel highlighted the Sabbath (see 22:8, 26; 23:38; 44:24; 45:17; 46:3), as did Jeremiah (Jer. 17:19-27; see Neh. 13:17-18). Jewish legalism later corrupted the Sabbath law (see Matt. 12:1-14). Rather than **live in them ... they greatly polluted** (v. 13) God's instructions (see 20:21; compare 20:25; see also 16:6; 18:9; Lev. 18:5). Because Israel did not observe the Sabbath rest (see Jer. 17:21-23) or did not observe it in the manner and spirit God intended (see Amos 8:5), God was required to once again lift up His **hand** (v. 15) against her. In mercy, God once again spared them and did not **make an end of them** (v. 17).

c. The Wilderness Generation (20:18-26)

20:18-26. I said unto their children (v. 18) is the opening of act three (see 20:5). God began anew with the second generation in the wilderness (see Num. 14:26-35). Again God came to them and declared that He was their **God** (v. 19) and challenged them to **hallow** His **sabbaths** (v. 20) as **a sign** between them. Nevertheless, they **rebelled** (v. 21) as their fathers had before them, and God was incited to **pour out** His **fury upon them**. And once again, He **withdrew** (v. 22) His hand of judgment. **Wherefore I gave them ... statutes that were not good ... and I polluted them in their own gifts, in that they caused to pass through the fire all that openeth the womb** (vv. 25-26; see 20:31; 16:20). The New Testament articulation of this principle of divine working is contained in Romans 1:24-32. The key to understanding what it means that the Lord "gave them statutes that were not good" is seen in the association with Molech worship (v. 26). They had so "polluted" the laws of God that Exodus 22:29 became a justification for the abomination of child sacrifice. Yet God gave them over to their idolatry so that they might become **desolate, to the end that they might know that I am the** LORD (v. 26). God will go to any lengths to get His people to acknowledge Him.

d. The Generations in the Land (20:27–32)

20:27–32. Israel had **blasphemed** (v. 27) the Lord. Act four in Ezekiel's history is not carried through with the same schematic consistency. Instead, God brought the people into the present. Again and again, He had withheld judgment and blessed them when He **had brought them into the land** (v. 28). **They saw every high hill, and all the thick trees**, where they should have given God their thanksgiving, and instead **offered ... their sacrifices** to false deities. **The name thereof is called Bamah** (v. 29) is introduced with the question, **What is the high place whereunto ye go?** This is a play on words. *Ba* ("go") and *mah* ("what") form *Bamah* ("high place"). The intent was to cause the hearers to consider the significance and folly of their idolatrous ways.

Are ye polluted ...? (v. 30). This question is pointedly directed to those who believed they were paying for the sins of their ancestors. His answer to this self-righteous attitude was, **Ye pollute yourselves ... even unto this day** (v. 31).

e. Future Judgment (20:33–39)

20:33–39. This message has two parts: a declaration of God's certain judgment (vv. 33–39) and a promise of final restoration (20:40–44). The fury of the Lord would fall like a hammer, **with a mighty hand, and with a stretched out arm** (v. 33). The terminology is reminiscent of the exodus (see Deut. 4:34; 5:15; 7:19; 11:2; 26:8), but then it was upon His enemies that His mighty strength was brought to bear. **As I live** contrasts the living God with the gods of wood and stone, referenced throughout this passage (see Jer. 10:1–10). Now He would use the same power to bring His people back **into the wilderness** (v. 35) to deal with them **face to face**. Exile among the nations would be for Israel like a return to the wilderness through which she had journeyed

on the way to the Promised Land (see Hos. 2:14). There God would cause them **to pass under the rod** (v. 37). In the way a shepherd counts or separates his flock (see Lev. 27:32; Jer. 33:13; Matt. 25:32–33), they would be examined and separated as sheep from the goats. God declared, **I will bring you into the bond of the covenant**. As He had in the Sinai wilderness (see 16:60, 62), God would **purge ... the rebels** (v. 38) from among them. As in the first wilderness experience, many were not allowed to enter the land (see Num. 14:26–35). God probably used irony as He concluded His rebuke, **Go ye, serve ye every one his idols** (v. 39). The opposite is meant (see 1 Kings 22:15; Amos 4:4). More than this is indicated, however. He would have them choose whether to serve Him or their idols, but He did not want them to pretend to worship Him with their words while in their hearts they still worshiped idols (see 14:3; 20:31).

f. Future Blessing (20:40–44)

20:40–44. God's **holy mountain** (v. 40), mentioned only here in Ezekiel, refers to Jerusalem or Zion (see Pss. 2:6; 3:4; 15:1; see also Isa. 11:9; 56:7; 57:13; 65:11; Obadiah 16; Zeph. 3:11). The vision referred to **all the house of Israel**. God said, **I will accept you** (v. 41). This included the northern kingdom, which fell in 722–721 BC (see 11:15; 36:10). In that day, God will **require** their **offerings, and ... oblations** (v. 40; see Deut. 23:21; Mic. 6:8). Those who did not deserve so much as an inquiry of the Lord (see 20:31) were caused to see a day when a generation would arise that would be accepted of Him as a **sweet savour** (v. 41). This expression is used either in a metaphorical sense (as in Eph. 5:2) or in a literal sense (as in 6:13). For **bring you out**, see 20:34. In that day **shall ye remember ... and ... lothe yourselves** (v. 43) describes a thorough repentance (see 6:9; 16:63; 36:31; Luke 15:17–19). The expression **for my name's sake** (v. 44) summarized and concluded the oracle. The final message was one of grace and hope. It was also a promise that when He was finished, God would ultimately bring glory to Himself.

12. Judgments of Fire and Sword (20:45–21:32)

20:45–49. The word of the LORD (v. 45) came once again to the prophet. It is not clear whether Ezekiel was still addressing the visitors who had come earlier to inquire of the Lord. The message turned abruptly from a brief promise of hope, with which he concluded the previous section, to a picture of pain and certain doom. The prophet also once again turned to allegory (**parables**; v. 49) to declare his message, signaling a change in his prophecy. The expression **set thy face** (v. 46) was a posture required eight times of Ezekiel (here; 13:17; 21:2; 25:2; 28:21; 29:2; 35:2; 38:2), always **against** the object of the prophecy. In this case, he was told to look **toward the south**, that is, toward Judah and Jerusalem, the object of all of Ezekiel's prophesying in these chapters. **The forest of the south field** would have seemed odd to his listeners. The Negeb area was desert land and had no trees. Perhaps this is why the prophet anticipated their ridicule (v. 49). Of course, his reference was not to the Negeb but to the southern kingdom, including Jerusalem. Any Babylonian invasion would traverse the Holy Land from north to south (see 26:7). Some translations read "toward Teman"; the Hebrew may be translated as a place-name (Teman) or as a point of the compass (south).

Kindle a fire (v. 47) is figurative language for invading forces (see Isa. 10:16–19; Jer. 15:14; 17:4, 27; 21:14; see also Ezek. 15:7). Using the imagery of a devastating forest fire, Ezekiel declared that all that was **green ... and every dry tree** would **be burnt**. Jesus used similar imagery to depict judgment (see 17:24; Luke 23:31). Everyone **from the south to the north** would experience the total destruction, and they would know that **the LORD** (v. 48) Himself had brought this to pass. In verse 47, it is understood that **the forest of the south** probably speaks of the people who would be destroyed in the ensuing conflagration (see Ps. 83:14; Isa. 9:18–19; 10:16–19; Jer. 21:14). History recounts the sad story of Nebuchadnezzar's destruction of the cities of Judah, which were utterly consumed. Letters discovered in the ruins of Lachish testify that the watchmen of Jerusalem looked to the signal fires of their city, evidence that it still

remained. In time, no lights could been seen, and all grew dark and silent. That his audience failed to heed and understand is noted in their response to the prophet. **Doth he not speak parables?** (v. 49).

21:1–7. The imagery changes here from fire to a sword. Some consider these verses to be the interpretation of the above parable. That could well be, because the message is the same. Again, the prophet remained in his house and spoke only when God spoke through him. God instructed him, **set thy face** (v. 2; see 20:46) and directed him **toward the holy places**, indicating that he was still looking **toward Jerusalem**. The Lord declared, **Behold, I am against thee** (see 5:8)**, and will draw forth my sword** (v. 3; for the sword of the Lord's judgment, see Isa. 31:8; 34:6; 66:16). This is the first of five sword oracles (see 21:8–17, 18–24, 25–27, 28–32). Here the sword refers to Babylon and Nebuchadnezzar (21:19). The prophecy included **the righteous and the wicked** (v. 4), indicating the completeness of the judgment that was about to come on Israel. No one would escape its devastating effects, not even the righteous in the land (contrast God's deliverance of Noah, Gen. 6:7–8, and Lot, Gen. 18:23; 19:12–13). The prophet was to **Sigh therefore ... with bitterness** (v. 6). **Breaking of thy loins** indicates deep emotion and fear (see Ps. 69:23; Nah. 2:10). Ezekiel's display of intense grief was also to serve as another prophetic sign and as an occasion for a new message of impending judgment, **and every heart shall melt** (v. 7; for the people's response to Ezekiel's behavior, see 12:9). This was Ezekiel's seventh symbolic act (see Introduction: "Literary Features").

21:8–11. The prophet continued with a song of **A sword** (v. 9). The song may possibly have been accompanied by dancing or symbolic actions. Such songs may have been sung by warriors about to go into battle (see 2 Sam. 1:18). Here God Himself is depicted as singing the war song. As He once drew the sword to defend His chosen, God now drew His sword against her (see Josh. 5:13). To think that the Babylonians would conquer every other country except Judah was a false hope. **The rod of my son** (v. 10). The rod represents rule, government, or kingdom. The most likely reference here is to Nebuchadnezzar, the ruler into whose hands the Lord had given His people (**every tree**; see 20:47, which refers to the people). As God spoke of Cyrus as His "anointed" (Isa. 45:1), He also called this conquering king **my son**, which should be understood as referring not to the familial relationship Israel enjoyed (as some suggest) but to God's "adoption" of him for this task as **slayer** (v. 11).

21:12 – 17. In this section, the prophet depicted both the totality of judgment and the fact that it would be from God Himself. **Cry and howl … smite … thy thigh** (v. 12). This was Ezekiel's eighth symbolic act (see Introduction: "Literary Features"). Smiting one's thigh was a sign of deep grief and despair. The prophet was to give a public demonstration of mourning to symbolize the impending calamity that would come upon the people — **a trial** (v. 13) of Judah and Jerusalem. The result would be that **even the rod** would be condemned; that is, those serving as her princes would fall (see 21:10). The question anticipated the final interruption of Davidic kingship, which occurred in 586 BC (see 21:25 – 27). **Smite thine hands together … smite mine hands together** (vv. 14, 17; see 6:11). God was acting in concert with His mortal agents. **Let the sword be doubled the third time** (v. 14) expressed the severity and totality of the judgment (see 2 Kings 13:18 – 19). God declared, **I will cause my fury to rest** (v. 17). The wrath of God is a terrible thing (see Heb. 10:31). The text here suggests that when so provoked, God's holiness must be satisfied (see Isa. 53:11). God's love was displayed in His longsuffering toward this wayward nation; His holy wrath was now required.

21:18 – 24. Here Ezekiel presented a new **word** (v. 18) from God, but he also extended the sword theme with further details, sketching the invasion of **the king of Babylon** (v. 19), Nebuchadnezzar. The prophet was instructed to **appoint … two ways.** The invading forces would come to a fork in the road, and Nebuchadnezzar would have to decide which road to take first — the one leading to **Rabbath** (modern Amman, capital of Jordan; v. 20) or the one leading to **Jerusalem**. To make this decision, he would use **divination** (v. 21). Not mentioned elsewhere in the Bible, divination was often used for the purpose of seeking good omens, in this case, for the coming campaign. The first divination practice Nebuchadnezzar used was belomancy. **Arrows** were labeled (e.g., "Rabbath," "Jerusalem"), placed into a quiver, shaken, and drawn out, one with each hand. A **right hand** (v. 22) selection was seen as a positive sign. Nebuchadnezzar also **consulted with images** (v. 21), or teraphim, which were household gods worshiped by the family or clan (see Gen. 31:19). Consulting teraphim is referred to in Hosea 3:4 and Zechariah 10:2. The household idols of Genesis 31:19 – 35 were small enough to be hidden in a saddle, but others were life-size (see 1 Sam. 19:13 – 16). Finally, **he looked in the liver.** The Babylonians considered the liver the seat of mental life. Hepatoscopy was the practice of looking at the color and configurations of the livers of sacrificed animals. It was believed that the thoughts of the god entered the animal's liver at the time he or she took hold of the sacrifice. Such was thought to foretell the future in ancient Babylonia and Rome, but the practice is not mentioned elsewhere in the Bible. While the result of Nebuchadnezzar's omen-seeking was initially considered **a false divination** (v. 23), when the king called **to remembrance** the treachery of Jerusalem's leaders against him, the divination only emboldened him to proceed against Jerusalem. The self-righteousness and hypocrisy of the people stands out in ironic contrast to the pagan ways of the invading king. As Ezekiel acted out this scenario, his audience no doubt grew increasingly anxious with suspense as they hung on every word; the fate of their friends and loved ones in Jerusalem was at stake. In the end, however, it would be their own **sins** (v. 24) that would cause them to **be taken with the hand**; that is, they would be brought down by the invading army.

21:25 – 27. The **profane wicked prince of Israel** (v. 25) refers to Zedekiah (see 7:27). His **day** had **come. The diadem** (v. 26), referenced only here as royal headwear, elsewhere is worn by priests (see Exod. 28:4, 37, 39; 29:6; 39:28, 31; Lev. 8:9; 16:4) or is a setting for **the crown** (see Exod. 28:36–37; 29:6; 39:31; Lev. 8:9). It was made of fine linen (Exod. 28:39; 39:28). By contrast, the king would experience a profound reversal of fortunes when the low were exalted and the exalted were brought low through the intervention of the Lord (see 17:24; 1 Sam. 2:7–8; Luke 1:52–53). The threefold **overturn, overturn, overturn** (v. 27) is for emphasis (see Isa. 6:3; Jer. 7:4). This condition would prevail **until he come whose right it is**, the Messiah (apparently an allusion to Gen. 49:10). Possibly the reference is to Nebuchadnezzar, translating "whose right it is" as "whose is the judgment" (see 2 Kings 25:6).

21:28–32. Finally, the Lord turned the prophet's attention to **the Ammonites** (v. 28; see 21:20). After God judged Jerusalem, the foreigners would be dealt with (see Isa. 10:5). Just as God judged the sins of Jerusalem, He would also remember the **reproach** of the invading forces (see 25:3, 6; also see 36:15). **The sword** was Nebuchadnezzar's (see 21:9, 19 and discussions). The sin of the Ammonites was that they saw **vanity** (v. 29) and **divine[d] a lie**. Apparently, Ammon also had false prophets of peace (see 13:10; Jer. 6:14; 8:11–12). Concerning the "sword" that Nebuchadnezzar had drawn, God asked, **Shall I cause it to return into his sheath?** (v. 30). Did they really think God would bless them for their blood deeds? Not on your life, answered the Lord. **I will judge thee … in the land of thy nativity.** While God's judgment on Israel was righteous, the arrogance of those He used to accomplish His purpose would ultimately bring them also to judgment. While the message to Israel ended with a promise of hope (see 17:22–24), the destiny of Babylon was that they would **be no more remembered** (v. 32).

13. Jerusalem, the City of Blood (chap. 22)

22:1–16. God presented a burning indictment against Jerusalem. Moving from the general to the specific, He detailed the crimes she had committed and for which she must be judged. Not only had the people offended their God; they had also lost their moral compass and, by all standards, had fallen to vice and wickedness. The Holy City had become

the bloody city (v. 2). The sacred and the secular, so often separated in modern culture, are shown to be intimately connected. Where violence is accepted in one sphere, it is practiced in the other. Jerusalem **sheddeth blood … and maketh idols** (v. 3; see 6:4). Due to their behavior, they had caused their **days to draw near** (v. 4), when the Lord would visit them with His wrath. In the practices of their abominable religions, they were guilty of shedding the blood of innocent children to Moloch. Likewise, in their courts, **the princes of Israel** (v. 6) used their power to further shed innocent blood. Taking advantage of the weak and helpless, **they vexed the fatherless and the widow** (v. 7; see Isa. 1:17). Through their profanation of God's **sabbaths** (v. 8) and through **lewdness** (v. 9), gross immorality (vv. 9–11), **extortion** (v. 12) of their **neighbours**, and **dishonest gain** (v. 13), they had created a situation in which God would bring dishonor to His holy name **in the sight of the heathen** (v. 16) if He did not bring an end to their abominations (see Lev. 18:7–20; 20:10–21; Deut. 22:22–23, 30; 27:22).

22:17–22. Earlier Ezekiel had likened Jerusalem to a fruitless vine (see 15:1–8), worthy only of being thrown in the fire and burned; now he likened her to **dross** (v. 18). As metal of special use or value is refined by smelting, so Jerusalem would be subjected to the fiery blast of God's wrath. She is not here viewed in terms of her value as the **silver** (v. 22); rather, she is pictured only as worthless dross that would be consumed and blown away. He would **gather** (vv. 19, 21) the city's inhabitants; that is, they would be removed. God would blow the hot breath of His fury on them as if in a smelting **furnace** (v. 22), and they would be **melted in the midst thereof**. The walls of the city were always seen as their protection. Here they are viewed as walls of containment, the place of their demise. Compare the rebuke of the Lord against the metaphor of "the caldron" (11:3–11) commonly used by Ezekiel's contemporaries (see also Isa. 1:21–26; Jer. 6:27–30). The metaphor was a vivid picture of the devastation that God would visit upon them.

22:23–31. In the concluding oracle of this chapter, the Lord declared that those who might have brought a fresh "rain" with which to "cleanse" the land had failed utterly. There appeared to be **a conspiracy** (v. 25) in the land. In particular, God called out the **prophets**, the **priests** (v. 26), the **princes** (v. 27), and as if to not miss anyone, He concluded with **The people** (v. 29). The prophets were like predatory animals **devour[ing] souls** (v. 25). The priests had **profaned ... holy things** (v. 26) so that there was no longer recognition of **the clean** and **unclean**, or the holy and the unholy. The princes, **like wolves** (v. 27), sought only **dishonest gain**, regardless of the cost in human suffering. The people had all collaborated in this world of sin, wickedness, and abomination. In the end, the Lord cried out, **I sought for a man** (v. 30) who might **stand in the gap before me** (see 13:5; Isa. 51:18; 59:16; 63:5). Even at this midnight hour, God lamented what He must do. The Lord **sought for a man**, only one person, to intercede effectually on behalf of the people, but He concluded, **I found none.** To intercede with God on behalf of the people was part of a prophet's task (see Gen. 20:7; 1 Sam. 12:23; Jer. 37:3; 42:2). Some interpret the task here as teaching, particularly calling the people to repentance (see the task of the prophetic "watchman," 3:17–21; 33:1–6). A similar message was given in 14:12–23, where the point was made that not even a few righteous among them would be able to stop the judgment. Here the point is that no righteous men were to be found, even if God were inclined to forgive the nation for the sake of one righteous person.

14. A Parable of Two Cities (chap. 23)

23:1–4. In the parable of **Aholah** (lit., "her tent"; v. 4) and **Aholibah** (lit., "My tent is in her"), little is left to speculation, or to the imagination for that matter. The **mother** (v. 2) is Israel, from which two capital cities were birthed when the kingdom divided into Israel to the north and Judah to the south. The symbolic significance of the two sisters is given at the opening of the prophecy: Aholah is **Samaria** (v. 4), and Aholibah is **Jerusalem** (on the "two sisters," see Jer. 3:6–12). At the time of the prophecy, Samaria had long since been judged and destroyed.

Now it was Jerusalem's turn. The root idea of the two names is "tent." This could stand for (1) Canaanite high places (see Gen. 36:2), (2) Israel's tent-dwelling origin, or (3) the Lord's tabernacle; although Ezekiel never used this word elsewhere for the legitimate shrine, it is used often for the "tent" covering of the tabernacle (see, e.g., Exod. 26:11–14, 36; 35:11). The first and third options seem best. "Her tent" (*Oholah*) compares to "My tent is in her" (*Oholibah*). Both names suggest places of cultic worship (see Jesus' reference to these two places of worship in John 4:20–24). Perhaps Ezekiel used "my tent" to ironically underscore that Jerusalem, where God had once dwelled ("tabernacled"), was now only an empty place; it was only a "tent" from which the glory had departed (see 9:1–11:25). Indeed, as Ezekiel's prophecies had shown, there was little difference between what happened in either tent. Oblations to false deities and abominations were commonplace in both centers.

Both of these sisters had **committed whoredoms in Egypt ... in their youth** (v. 3). The chronicle of their sins is detailed in chapter 20, beginning with their earliest days in Egypt. The sad reality concerning these sorry sisters was that they were given over to the gods of their oppressors and learned the ways of wickedness from the very people under whose heavy hand they sought relief.

23:5–10. The prophecy addressed the northern kingdom first. Israel, God declared, had **played the harlot** (v. 5). Here Israel's harlotry represents political dalliances with pagan powers, not idolatry, as in chapter 16 (see 16:15). The graphic language of the chapter underscores the Lord's disgust with Israel for playing the worldly game of international politics rather than relying on the Lord for her security—as clear a case of religious prostitution as idolatry. She had become enamored with the power and wealth of **the Assyrians** (see 2 Kings 15:19). But this was nothing new, for she had been dazzled with the gods and greatness of her enemies since the days when she was taken **from Egypt** (v. 8; see 20:5–8). Israel's entire history was marked by unfaithfulness (for her attachment to Egypt, see Exod. 17:3; Num. 11:5, 18,

20; 14:2–4; 21:5). Her judgment would be that those **upon whom she doted** (v. 9) would be the ones to expose **her nakedness** (v. 10). Aholah/Samaria fell to the Assyrians in 722–721 BC. Ezekiel's audience all knew the sad story that had taken place more than a century before this date. The Assyrians, to whom she had so willingly given herself, eventually took everything from her and cast her off as a spent prostitute.

23:11–21. The prophecy now turned to Aholibah—the capital city of the southern kingdom, Jerusalem. The indictment against the sister to the south was even greater. Her "affairs" were multiplied many times over. Moreover, she would eventually invite her paramours into her inner chambers (see 2 Kings 20:12–19). The Lord condemned Judah for her alliances with Assyria (Isa. 7:1–25), Babylon (2 Kings 24:1), and Egypt (Isaiah 30–31).

The reference to **men pourtrayed upon the wall ... with vermilion** (v. 14) suggests arousal through pictures (see 16:17; see also Jer. 22:14). **Girdles** (v. 15). For similar Assyrian military equipment, see Isaiah 5:27. The term **flesh** (v. 20) probably refers to genitals (see 16:26). The text drips with sexual innuendo to underscore the Lord's disgust for Judah's contemptible predilection for "strange flesh" (Jude 1:7). Yet Aholibah looked back at **the lewdness of** her **youth** (v. 21) with a sigh of regret, not that she had allowed herself to be given over to such debauchery but that she could no longer go back to it. Just as she had in the desert, she forgot the bondage of Egypt, from which she had been delivered, and recalled only the pleasures (see Num. 11:4–6; Luke 8:14; 2 Tim. 3:4; Titus 3:3; Heb. 11:25; but see also Ps. 16:11).

23:22–35. As with her sister to the north, Aholibah's international "lovers" would eventually be **alienated** (v. 22; see v. 28) and would come against her; only this time they would come from all sides. She still longed for the "good times" but would soon learn that the pleasures of sin had taken her farther than she had intended to go, kept her longer than she had intended to stay, and cost her more than she had intended to pay. In the end, the **desirable young men ... great lords ... chariots ... buckler and shield and helmet** (vv. 23–24) that she had so admired and

lusted after would **come against** (v. 24) her as instruments of destruction. It would be payback time.

The Babylonians, and ... Chaldeans (v. 23), ordinarily identified with one another (see 12:13), are here distinguished (as in 23:15), probably because the Chaldeans were relative newcomers. **Pekod** refers to Aramaic people located east of Babylon. **Shoa, and Koa** were Babylonian allies of uncertain origin and location. They would be dispatched **according to their judgments** (v. 24). These were cruel and gruesome (see v. 25) methods of terror and intimidation, known even today among the modern-day descendants of these nations (see David's words to Gad the prophet, 2 Sam. 24:14).

The **cup ... of astonishment** (vv. 31, 33) from which her **sister Samaria** (v. 33) had drunk would now be given to Jerusalem, and she would drink **deep and large** (v. 32). She would **drink it and suck it out** (v. 34). The cup was filled with the anger of the Lord. To drink it was to die. Aholibah would not only taste its contents; she would drink it dry. The reference emphasizes the totality of God's judgment on the people of this sinful city (for a development of the imagery, see Ps. 75:8; Isa. 51:17, 22; Jer. 25:15–29; 49:12; Lam. 4:21; Obadiah 16; Hab. 2:16; Matt. 20:22; 26:39; Rev. 14:10).

23:36–49. The prophet concluded with a summary of God's indictment against these two wicked sisters, including the specific nature of their spiritual adulteries and the just punishment, which had already begun and would be brought to completion. For the reference to **sons ... to pass for them through the fire** (v. 37), see 16:20. For **they have defiled my sanctuary** (v. 38; see chap. 8). For the profanation of God's **sabbaths**, see 22:8.

The historical note **ye have sent for men** (v. 40) is possibly a reference to the Jerusalem summit meeting in Zedekiah's time (see Jeremiah 27). As a harlot, Jerusalem had prepared herself **upon a stately bed, and a table prepared before it** (v. 41; see Isa. 21:5; Prov. 9:2). The outcome would be not as she expected. There was no longer anything desirable in these sisters, who were **old in adulteries** (v. 43). They would be used as **lewd women** (v. 44) and would then be judged by **righteous men ... after the manner of adulteresses** (v. 45). That is, the punishment prescribed in Deuteronomy 22:22–24 would be carried out: **the company shall stone them with stones** (v. 47). The reference to these pagan instruments of God's wrath as "righteous men" is ironic. They were hardly righteous in their own standing before God, and as had been shown, they would eventually "stand trial" for their own war crimes (see 21:28–32). For the moment, however, the prophet envisioned them as the instruments of God's righteous judgment.

15. The Final Fire: Jerusalem's End (24:1–14)

24:1–2. On the very day the siege of Jerusalem began, God came to Ezekiel with a "live" report (v. 1; see 2 Kings 25:1). It was **the ninth year ... the tenth month ... the tenth day of the month** (v. 1), or January 15, 588 BC, the fourth date in Ezekiel (see 1:2; 8:1; 20:1). The prophet was instructed to record **this same day** (v. 2), for it was on this momentous day that the king of Babylon inaugurated his terrible and final work against Jerusalem. It is dated relative to the time of Jehoiachin's exile, nine years after 597 BC, and does not depict future events but rather current events at a distance. When the official reports of this military campaign eventually reached Babylon, three hundred miles away, all would know that Ezekiel was a true prophet of God. Yet the news would prove to be as disheartening to the prophet as to the grief-stricken exiles.

24:3–6. The message was first given in the form of **a parable** (v. 3; see 17:2; 20:49) and then of "a sign" (24:24). Ezekiel began with the allegory of **a pot**, with which he depicted this **rebellious house**, the last occurrence of this condemning phrase in Ezekiel (see 2:5, 6, 8; 3:9, 26–27; 12:2–3, 9, 25; 17:12). Jerusalem's rebellion would soon be crushed. The Hebrew text of 24:3–13 is in poetic form (see the NIV and the NASB translations), which was commonly used by Ezekiel's contemporaries. Perhaps this was a song, and perhaps the prophet acted out the key events in the song for dramatic effect. The song typified a domestic scene repeated daily in the people's homes. A fire was lit, a pot was set on the fire, water

was added, and raw meat and bones were thrown in to make a stew. Everything went all wrong. The pot had rusty **scum** (v. 6), which leeched into the stew and ruined it for consumption. The spoiled pieces of meat were taken out **piece by piece** and exposed to the fire (see 24:10). Finally, even the worthless pot itself was thrown on the fire to be destroyed by the heat (see 24:11).

Ezekiel gave the people of the city the explicit interpretation of the allegory. **The pot** (v. 6) represented Jerusalem (see 11:3). The prophet was to take **every good piece** (v. 4). The people of Jerusalem thought they were spared from the exile of 597 BC because of their goodness (see 11:3). Nothing could have been further from the truth, as would be shown. **The choice** (vv. 4–5) pieces would all be taken out of the pot to be exposed to the fire in a special way.

Jerusalem was **the bloody city** (v. 6; see 22:3). The **scum** (in Hebrew, "rust") boiled to the surface, spoiling the stew. Appropriately, the "rust" would have been the color of blood. Jerusalem, like bilious stew, had been rendered irredeemable and would be thrown out. **Let no lot fall upon it** may recall the previous siege. After the siege of Jerusalem in 597 BC, perhaps the Babylonians had cast lots to determine those who would be taken away into exile and those who would stay. Now everyone would go.

24:7–8. Jerusalem had brazenly left **her blood ... upon the top of a rock** (v. 7), the blood she unjustly shed (see Isa. 3:9; for uncovered blood, see Gen. 4:10; Job 16:18; Isa. 26:21). Consequently, she would experience the **fury** (v. 8) of God's wrath. What Jerusalem had begun, God would finish (compare Exod. 8:32 with Exod. 9:12).

24:9–14. The prophet was told to **Heap on wood, kindle the fire, consume the flesh** (v. 10). **Then set it empty** (v. 11). The inhabitants of the city would be utterly destroyed or taken away. Then Jerusalem, emptied of inhabitants, would be set to the torch, in a final, futile act of purification. But even then, the Lord declared, **thou shalt not be purged** (v. 13). There would be no changing God's plan for these sinful people. They had crossed the final frontier of God's mercy.

16. The Death of Ezekiel's Wife and the Destruction of the Temple (24:15–27)

24:15–27. As Ezekiel came to the conclusion of this series of prophecies concerning Judah and Jerusalem, God's final word was the most personal word yet for the prophet. **The desire of thine eyes** (his wife; v. 16; see v. 18) would die, and as a sign to the exiles, he was commanded to refrain from publicly mourning her loss. She would die of **a stroke** (lit., "a blow"; see Exod. 9:14; Num. 14:37). The language suggests a sudden death. Whether she had been in ill health prior to this is not mentioned. At the very least, her death was unexpected, which certainly pictured well the optimism of the exiles toward their relatives in Jerusalem. In any event, the sign was not her death but the prophet's response. He was to display none of the ordinary gestures of sorrow. God made it clear that Ezekiel was not to **mourn nor weep**, shed **tears**, or engage in any of the customary practices for expressing one's grief (vv. 16–17).

The prophet did as he was commanded. The next day, he announced to the people that his wife had died and then he went about his business without any outward recognition of the tragic event. The people were stunned by his behavior and came to him for an explanation. He explained to them that his response was the same as theirs. Little did they know that their loved ones had died at the hand of Nebuchadnezzar, that very day. If they had known, they would all have gone about with signs of mourning. Indeed, when they heard of the death of their loved ones in Jerusalem, they would understand. Yet God's instruction was even more severe. They would **not mourn** (v. 23) but would **pine away for** their **iniquities**. When they heard of the sudden loss of all their **sons and** their **daughters** (v. 21) in Jerusalem, and the destruction of **the desire of** their **eyes**, God's **sanctuary**, they were to recognize this as God's doing and to mourn, not for their loved ones, but for their sins. Then, the Lord declared, they would certainly know that Ezekiel was **a sign unto them; and they shall know that I am the LORD** (v. 27). The news was coming; some would escape (v. 26; see 33:21–22) to verify what had happened. From that point forward, the

prophet would be **no more dumb** (v. 27). Ezekiel's wife died the same day the temple was burned (August 14, 586 BC; see discussions on 3:26; 33:21; see also 2 Kings 25:8–9). Ironically, "the desire of their eyes" was the sanctuary, the place of God's dwelling, not God Himself. For this, they would suffer dearly.

II. Oracles of Judgment against the Nations (chaps. 25–32)

Frequently in the Prophets, God's word of judgment on Israel is accompanied by oracles of judgment on the nations. These make it clear that while judgment would "begin at the house of God" (1 Peter 4:17), the pagan nations would not escape God's wrath. Often these judgments were implicit messages of salvation for Israel (see 28:25–26) since the Lord's victories over hostile powers removed an enemy of His people or punished them for their cruel attacks on His people. Ezekiel delivered seven oracles against the nations (the seventh of which has seven parts, each of which is introduced by the phrase, "the word of the LORD came unto me"; see Introduction: "Outline"). Beginning with Ammon to the east, the oracles followed a clockwise direction through Moab, Edom, Philistia, Tyre, Sidon, and Egypt, including the nations that formed the border around the nation Israel. It is possible that "seven" nations were selected because of number signifies a "whole"; that is, they represented the whole world against Israel. Even today it would seem that little has changed. Yet when God is finished with His work, these wicked nations will pay a severe price for their blasphemies and pride.

A. Against Ammon (25:1–7)

25:1–7. The prophecy against Ammon began with the common formula, **set thy face** (v. 2; see 20:46), which signaled a stern message from God against **the Ammonites**. Ammon (located in modern Jordan) was immediately east of Israel (see 21:20; see also Jer. 9:26; 49:1–6; Amos 1:13–15; Zeph. 2:8–11; for hostile Ammonite action during this time and later, see 2 Kings 24:2; Neh. 4:7). The Ammonites were guilty of malicious joy in the face of the collapse of Israel, their neighbor to the west. For **Aha** (v. 3), see 26:2; 36:2; Psalm 35:21–25. While it is not stated directly, the prophetic backdrop of this oracle is the judgment of God promised to Abraham upon those who would curse him, that is, his offspring (see Gen. 12:3).

Nomadic tribes of the desert, east of Ammon, might be indicated by the reference to **men of the east** (v. 4), though this is more likely a reference to Nebuchadnezzar and his army (see 21:31). If the latter is indicated, it suggests an attitude of complacency toward the invading armies. Little did they know (or care) that they might be next. **Rabbah** (v. 5) was the capital city (see 21:20). It too would become **a stable … a couching place**, a common Old Testament description for destroyed cities (see Isa. 34:13–15; Zeph. 2:13–15). The sites were returned to the conditions they were in before the cities were built, representing the undoing of human efforts.

I will stretch out mine hand (v. 7) is a common expression in Ezekiel (see 6:14; 14:9, 13; 16:27; 25:7; 35:3). Ammon would become **spoil to the heathen** (see 26:5; 34:28). God declared, **I will cut thee off from the people** (see 24:16). They would be removed from among the living. Later historians, such as Josephus, mark the end of Ammon with their destruction at this time. The Lord concluded His judgments by declaring to the Ammonites, **and thou shalt know that I am the LORD.**

B. Against Moab (25:8–11)

25:8–11. Ezekiel's second oracle against the nations was against **Moab** (v. 8), immediately south of Ammon, east of the Dead Sea (see Isaiah 15–16; Jeremiah 48; Amos 2:1–3; Zeph. 2:8–11). **Seir.** Edom, a country south of Moab and south of the Dead Sea (see chap. 35, especially 35:15; see also 36:5; Isa. 34:5–17; 63:1–6; Jer. 49:7–11; Amos 1:11–12). Israel wanted to be **like unto all the heathen** (see 20:32 and discussion), but when the nations saw Judah in her apparent vulnerability and lost their awe of her, they failed to take her God seriously (see Lam. 4:12). **The side of Moab** (v. 9) indicates the lower hills rising from the Dead Sea, visible from Jerusalem. **Beth-jeshimoth.** A town in the plains of Moab.

Baal-meon. A major Moabite town mentioned in an inscribed monument of Mesha, king of Moab. **Kiriathaim.** A city also mentioned in the Mesha inscription (see 2 Kings 3:4–5). Once again, the Lord concluded with, **and they shall know that I am the LORD** (v. 11; see 25:7).

C. Against Edom (25:12–14)

25:12–14. In the third oracle, as with the other neighboring powers, **Edom** (v. 12) was indicted for her offense against God's people in **taking vengeance**, in this case by not harboring Judah's refugees after the exile of 586 BC (see Obadiah 11–14). **Teman** (v. 13) was a district near Petra in central Edom (see Jer. 49:7, 20; Amos 1:12; Obadiah 9; Hab. 3:3). **Dedan** was a tribe and territory in southern Edom (see 27:20; 38:13; Isa. 21:13; Jer. 49:8). Of these peoples, God said, **they shall know my vengeance** (v. 14). This was just retribution for those who had taken their own vengeance out on those fleeing from the invading armies.

D. Against Philistia (25:15–17)

25:15–17. The fourth oracle was against **the Philistines** (v. 15). These inhabitants of the coastal plain along the Mediterranean west of Judah (see 1 Sam. 6:17) strove for control of Canaan until they were subdued by David. Their hostility to Israel continued, however (see Isa. 14:29–31; Jeremiah 47; Amos 1:6–8; Zeph. 2:4–7), until Nebuchadnezzar deported them. **Cherethims** (v. 16) were related to, if not identical with, the Philistines (see 1 Sam. 30:14 and discussion; 2 Sam. 8:18; 15:18; 20:7). **The sea coast** is that of the Mediterranean Sea. Again God ended His word to these people with, **and they shall know that I am the LORD** (v. 17). It is difficult not to call to mind the apostle Paul's warning to the Gentiles: "Behold therefore the goodness and severity of God: on them which fell, severity; but toward thee, goodness, if thou continue in his goodness: otherwise thou also shalt be cut off" (Rom. 11:22).

E. Against Tyre (26:1–28:19)

The fifth oracle was against Tyre and its king. In this oracle, Ezekiel's message was much more detailed and extensive. It was also more far-reaching than the others, extending even to the spiritual forces that had energized this ancient Phoenician city, located on the Mediterranean coast just north of Israel.

1. The End of the City (chap. 26)

26:1. The eleventh year ... the first day of the month (see discussion on 33:21). The number of the month is missing. The entire year dates from April 23, 587 BC, to April 13, 586 BC. The oracle likely dates from the end of that year, in the eleventh (February 13, 586 BC) or twelfth month (March 15, 586 BC). This is the fifth date in Ezekiel (see 1:2; 8:1; 20:1; 24:1).

26:2. Tyrus, or Tyre. The island capital of Phoenicia (present-day Lebanon) was involved in an anti-Assyrian coalition in 594 BC (see Jer. 27:3). Ezekiel, more than any other prophet, prophesied against Tyre (see chaps. 27–28; but see also Isaiah 23; Jer. 25:22; 47:4; Joel 3:4–5; Amos 1:9–10; Zech. 9:2–4). **Aha ... she is laid waste.** Divine judgment was leveled against Tyre because she thought she would be able to exploit the misfortune of Israel to her own advantage (see 25:3). **Gates of the people.** Because of Tyre's geographical location, its political importance, and the central role it played in international trade, the anti-Assyrian summit meeting was held there (see Jeremiah 27).

26:3–6. I am against thee (v. 3). See 5:8. **As the sea causeth his waves to come up ... a place for the spreading of nets in the midst of the sea** (vv. 3, 5). For invading armies likened to waves of the sea, see Isaiah 17:12–13. Since Tyre was an island, the metaphor is especially appropriate here. **Top of a rock** (v. 4) is a play on the name Tyre, which means "rock." The latter term (*sela*) signifies a "crag or cliff," over which God would **scrape her dust**. No longer would Tyre be a shining city; it would become **spoil to the nations** (v. 5; see 25:7; 34:28). **Daughters** (v. 6). The people of the inland towns who served under the rule of Tyre would come to **know that I am the Lord**.

26:7–14. This section depicts the campaign of **Nebuchadrezzar** (v. 7) against Tyre. This is the first of four references to Nebuchadrezzar in this proph-

ecy (see 29:18–19; 30:10). He ruled from 605 to 562 BC, and his name means "O [god] Nabu, protect my son" or "O [god] Nabu, protect my boundary." Jeremiah and Ezekiel both proclaimed that God would use this pagan king to do His work (see Jer. 25:9; 27:6). **I will bring.** A clear indication of God's sovereignty over the nations (see 28:7; 29:8). **North.** The direction from which Nebuchadrezzar would descend on Tyre after first marching his army up the Euphrates River valley rather than across the Arabian Desert (see Jer. 1:13). **Fort ... be built no more** (vv. 8, 14) Nebuchadrezzar's fifteen-year siege of Tyre began shortly after the fall of Jerusalem. There is no record that Tyre fell at this time (see 29:18). The eventual collapse of Tyre was fulfilled by Alexander's devastating siege in 332 BC (see Isa. 23:1).

26:15–21. There would be a great astonishment and mourning at the fall of Tyre. **Princes of the sea** (v. 16). Called kings in 27:35, they were probably trading partners with Tyre. **Lay away their robes.** Usually mourners tore their clothes (Job 2:12) and put on sackcloth, but the king of Nineveh also "laid his robe from him" (Jonah 3:6). **Clothe themselves with trembling.** Because of the political shock waves from the fall of such a powerful city, there would be international concern and fear (see 7:27; Pss. 35:26; 109:29). **Lamentation** (v. 17). See 19:1. **The deep** (v. 19) is the primeval, chaotic mass (as in Gen. 1:2). Ezekiel described Tyre's collapse into the sea in almost cosmic terms. At this point, he intensified the imagery with **the pit** (v. 20), which signifies the grave, "the earth below" (see Ps. 69:15). **People of old** refers to those long dead (see Ps. 143:3; Lam. 3:6). **I will make thee a terror, and thou shalt be no more** (v. 21). See 27:36; 28:19.

2. A Lament for Tyre (chap. 27)

This chapter expands on the final section of the previous chapter, in which the political fallout of Tyre's calamity is depicted. Chapter 27 contains three sections. The first (vv. 1–9) is written in poetry and is descriptive of Tyre's past glory. The second, written in both poetry and prose (vv. 10–25), details Tyre's many trading partners. The third (vv. 26–36) is again written in poetry and imagines Tyre's fall as a great shipwreck.

27:1 – 2. Lamentation for Tyrus (v. 2). The funeral dirge announced God's judgment on this ancient citadel of power even before she had come to her end (see 19:1). Her geographical location on the coast of the Mediterranean Sea, her political prowess, and her trade relations led Ezekiel to style Tyre as a beautiful ocean vessel that was doomed to be swallowed by the very sea upon which she rose to greatness.

27:3 – 9. Situate at the entry of the sea (lit., "entrances of the sea"; v. 3) seems to refer to the two main harbors of the city. **I am of perfect beauty** (see 28:12; for a similar prideful statement, see 28:2). In the following verses, Tyre's opulence is described in detail. The irony is that she was a ship bedecked for her funeral. **Thy builders have perfected thy beauty** (v. 4). See 27:11. The **ship boards** (v. 5) were from the famed **trees of Senir**. Senir is the Amorite name for Hermon (see Deut. 3:9), the Anti-Lebanon mountain (or range) famed for its cedar. Only the finest **cedars from Lebanon** were used to make her **masts** (see 1 Kings 4:33; 5:6; 1 Chron. 17:1 – 6; Ezek. 3:7; Isa. 2:13). Her **oars** (v. 6) were made from **the oaks of Bashan** (see 39:18; Isa. 2:13; Zech. 11:2). **The Ashurites have made thy benches of ivory** inlay from **Chittim** (Hebrew, *Kittim*). This was originally the name of a town in southern Cyprus colonized by Phoenicia. Her **sail** (v. 7) was of **Fine linen with broidered work from Egypt,** and the dye was from **Elishah,** a city on the east side of Cyprus and also the oldest name for Cyprus (but see Gen. 10:4). Those who served her were **wise men** (v. 8), seamen from **Zidon and Arvad,** famed from ancient times for their maritime skills and experience (see Gen. 10:15 – 19). Sidon was a harbor city twenty-five miles north of Tyre, which sometimes rivaled her in political and commercial importance (see 28:21). Arvad was another Phoenician island-city, off the Mediterranean coast and north of Sidon. As with **The ancients of Gebal** (v. 9), only the best were privileged to attend this "ship of beauty." Gebal, or Byblos, was an important ancient city on the coast between Sidon and

Arvad and was known for its craftsmen (see 1 Kings 5:18).

27:10 – 25. In this second section of the chapter, the prophet used both prose and poetry to describe the intricate network of Tyre's political partnerships, which literally spanned the civilized world of her day. **Lud** (v. 10). Lydia in Asia Minor. **Phut.** Libya, in North Africa, west of Egypt. **Men of war.** Ezekiel abandoned the ship image and described Tyre literally as a city (see **walls ... and ... towers**; v. 11), complete with a mercenary army gathered from the whole world. **Arvad.** See 27:8. **Gammadims** are men of Gammad, which was either (1) northern Asia Minor or (2) a coastal town near Arvad. It is not mentioned elsewhere in the Bible. **Tarshish** (v. 12) is traditionally thought to have been located on the coast of southern Spain, but the island of Sardinia has also been suggested. Passages such as 1 Kings 10:22 and Jonah 1:3 imply that it was a long distance from the Canaanite coast. The list of places in verses 12 – 23 generally follows a west-to-east direction. **Tubal, and Meshech** (v. 13) were both in Asia Minor. **The house of Togarmah** (v. 14), or Beth-Togarmah, was located in eastern Asia Minor, present-day Armenia (see 38:6). Asia Minor was known for its **horses** (see 1 Kings 10:28). For **Dedan** (v. 15), see 25:13. Since Damascus, the capital of Aram (**Syria;** v. 16), is mentioned in verse 18, perhaps Edom is meant here (some manuscripts read "Edom" instead of "Aram"; see 25:12 and discussion). **Israel ... thy merchants** (v. 17). In the past. Since 722 – 721 BC, Israel had ceased to exist as a political state. **Wheat of Minnith.** Minnith was an Ammonite town, apparently famous for its wheat; the phrase possibly denotes a superior quality of wheat. **Balm.** Gum or oil from one of several plants; a product of Gilead (see Gen. 37:25; Jer. 8:22; 46:11). **Damascus** (v. 18). The capital of Aram (see v. 16; see also Isa. 7:8). **Helbon.** A town north of Damascus, still in existence and still a wine-making center. The name occurs only here in the Bible. **Dan also** (v. 19) can be read as the place-name Vedan. Dan was a term that Homer used for Greeks (see Gen. 10:27; 1 Chron. 1:21) and perhaps here refers to Yemen or the area between Haran and the Tigris.

Cassia. Similar to the cinnamon tree. **Calamus**. An aromatic reed. For **Dedan** (v. 20), see 25:13. **Arabia, and all the princes of Kedar** (v. 21) is a general expression for the Bedouin tribes from Aram to the Arabian Desert (for Kedar, see Isa. 42:11; 60:7; Jer. 49:28). For **Sheba** (v. 22), see 23:42. **Raamah**. A city in southern Arabia. **Haran** (v. 23) was a city east of Carchemish, in present-day eastern Turkey. It was well-known in ancient times as a center both for trade and for the worship of the moon god Sin. From Haran, Abraham moved to Canaan (see Gen. 11:31; 12:4). **Canneh**. Of uncertain location, presumably in Mesopotamia. It is often identified with Calneh (see Amos 6:2; "Calno" in Isa. 10:9). **Eden**. A district south of Haran, mentioned in connection with Haran in 2 Kings 19:12. See Beth-eden in Amos 1:5. For **Sheba**, see 23:42. **Asshur**. Can mean the city, the country (Assyria), or the people (Assyrians). Here it probably refers to the city south of Nineveh, which gave its name to the country. **Chilmad**. If a town, it is yet unidentified, presumably in Mesopotamia. Some read "all Media." Ezekiel concluded with a reference to **The ships of Tarshish** (v. 25; see v. 12), resuming the ship image once again to focus on the impending doom of this great city (see discussion on 27:3). He described Tyre as a ship **made very glorious in the midst of the seas** (lit., "exceedingly heavy in the open sea"). In the end, the sheer weight of her riches would bring her down.

27:26-36. In the concluding section of this chapter, Ezekiel returned to the use of poetry to describe the catastrophic end of Tyre. She had been **brought ... into great waters** (v. 26) and was rowing against a battering **east wind**. Such a wind is disastrous at sea (see Ps. 48:7) as well as on land (see Jer. 18:17). It possibly symbolizes Nebuchadnezzar (as in 17:10; 19:12). In this treacherous situation, **all thy company which is in the midst of thee** (v. 27) would not only be of no help; they too would **fall into the midst of the seas in the day of thy ruin**, said the Lord through His prophet. **What city is like Tyrus?** (v. 32). In the end, all would lament the loss of this great icon of ancient power and might. This stands in contrast to 26:6, "they shall know that I am

the LORD." How like sinful humanity; in their pride, they would lament the loss of Tyre and overlook the Lord, whose hand of judgment was displayed with such power in Tyre's destruction. Those who served her would be **astonished** (v. 35) and filled with **terror** (v. 36) at the awesome power that brought her down, their fear induced by the reality that with Tyre gone, their own protection from the Babylonian "east wind" was removed (see 7:18; Isa. 15:2; 22:12).

3. Against the Prince of Tyre (28:1-10)

28:1-2. In his third and final **word** (v. 1) against Tyre, Ezekiel directed his prophecy specifically against **the prince of Tyrus** (v. 2). "Prince" may refer to the city of Tyre as ruler or to Ethbaal III, the king then ruling Tyre (see 28:12). The latter is more likely, given the nature of his condemnation (see 28:12-19), which best fits with an individual person rather than an entire city. His namesake, Ethbaal I, was the father of Jezebel (see 1 Kings 16:31), who advanced idolatry with such a devastating impact on Israel. **Lifted up** means lifted up in pride (see 27:3; Prov. 16:18; Acts 12:21-23). **Because ... thou hast said, I am a God**. This ruler of Tyre considered himself to be a god (see also 28:6, 9). God declared such claims false: **yet thou art a man, and not God** (see Ps. 82:1-8).

28:3. Ezekiel again cited **Daniel** (see 14:14, 20). To the proud prince of Tyre, he cited the already renowned prophet Daniel, whose wisdom and counsel were providentially influencing the policies of Nebuchadnezzar, the very man who would ultimately carry out the destruction prophesied against Tyre (see Dan. 1:19-20; 2:46-49). Daniel, by contrast, never arrogated to himself wisdom, which he acknowledged as only from God (see Dan. 2:27-28). **Thou art wiser**. Ezekiel was saying to this proud prince, "Are you wiser than Daniel? We shall see."

28:4-6. With cunning and skill, Ethbaal III had acquired **riches** (v. 4) and **gold and silver**. In the process, his **heart** was **lifted up** (v. 5) because of them. Unlike Daniel, he took all the glory to himself. The consequence would be the sure judgment of God (see 1 Chron. 16:24; Isa. 10:12; 42:8; 48:11).

28:7–10. Because of his pride and arrogance, Ethbaal would be brought down by **strangers** (v. 7). The Babylonians would be **the terrible of the nations** (Hebrew, *arits*; "terror" or "ruthless"). Ezekiel declared that "terrorists" would **defile** Ethbaal's **brightness**. They would **bring** him **down to the pit … in the midst of the seas** (v. 8; see 26:20; Job 33:22, 24). This one who considered himself to be a god would be brought to his end as one **uncircumcised** (v. 10). The Phoenicians, like the Israelites and the Egyptians, practiced circumcision (see 31:18; 32:19). Here the term is used in the sense of barbarian or uncouth.

4. Against the King of Tyre (28:11–19)

28:11–12. Lamentation (v. 12). See 19:1. The reference to **king** here is significant (*melek*; see "prince," *nagid*, in reference to Jehoiachin, 28:2). Ezekiel used the term only here and in 1:2. In the previous section, the prophecy was leveled against the local prince, but here the message seems to have been directed beyond him, to a much more powerful and significant personage, the true ruler of this pagan authority. **Sealest up the sum.** See Haggai 2:23, where Zerubbabel is called God's "signet" (ring). With cutting irony, Ezekiel likened this "god-prince" to the original fall in the garden of Eden (see 28:13 and discussion). The king is depicted as "having it all." He had all the wealth, power, and happiness this world can offer.

28:13–14. Thou hast been in Eden (v. 13). Ezekiel continued to use imagery of the creation and the fall to picture the career of the "king of Tyrus" (see 31:9, 16, 18). It is best to resist the suggestion of some that the prophet was drawing on local mythology. That this personage was not a mere human is also seen in the description of him: (1) he was in **Eden the garden of God**; (2) he was said to be **created** (not "born"); (3) he was an **anointed cherub** (v. 14) with access to **the holy mountain of God**; (4) created "perfect," he was later found with "iniquity" (28:15). While it is certain that this description was intended to depict (in metaphorical language) the pride and position of Ethbaal III, it has also long been under-

stood among biblical scholars that Ezekiel was drawing on the story of Adam in his original creation and fall, pointing ultimately to Satan and his complicity in that tragic event. This is generally argued from the manner in which this oracle seems to be paralleled or alluded to in other biblical texts which more clearly reference Satan (see Isa. 14:12–15; Dan. 10:13–21; 12:1; John 12:31; 14:30; 16:11; 1 John 5:19). The apostle Paul made a similar identification in 1 Corinthians 10:19–20: "in sacrifice to idols … they sacrifice to devils." **Every precious stone** (v. 13). The nine stones listed were among the twelve worn by the priest (Exod. 28:17–20); the Septuagint lists all twelve stones. The precious stones bespeak the "king's" glorious and exalted position.

Cherub that covereth (v. 14). See 28:16. The Genesis account has cherubim (plural) stationed at the border of the garden after the expulsion of Adam and Eve (see Gen. 3:24). **Holy mountain of God.** See 28:16. Here the prophet moved beyond the Genesis story. For the figure of God dwelling on a mountain, see Isaiah 14:13. **Stones of fire.** The association here with the description in 10:1–14 of the dwelling place of God is difficult to miss (see 28:16; Rev. 4:1–6; 21:15–21).

28:15. Thou wast perfect in thy ways … till. See 28:13. The parallel to Genesis 2–3 is interesting (see also Gen. 6:9; 17:1). As the fall of Satan led to the fall of Adam and Eve, the context here associates the satanic and human interplay. Perhaps the allusion to the earthly "king" reflects only how it seemed. He was so graced by his earthly benefits that it seemed "perfect," and furthermore, that he *deserved* all this. Such pride would inevitably bring him down.

28:16. The multitude of thy merchandise … filled … thee with violence. The reference is to the evil spiritual force behind him, but the reader must not miss the point that the "violence" was displayed by the human "prince," whose end was near (see 28:1–10).

28:17–19. I will cast thee to the ground (v. 17). As Satan, the "king" of Tyre was "cast out" (John 12:31), so the earthly "prince" of Tyre would experience a similar end for the same reason. "Because that, when they knew God, they glorified him not as God ... but became vain in their imaginations .... Wherefore God also gave them up" (Rom. 1:21, 24). **Never shalt thou be any more** (v. 19). This prince of Tyre would be destroyed without glory, just as the "king" he served will one day be removed, nevermore to work his evil upon the earth (Rev. 20:10).

F. Against Sidon (28:20-24)

28:20-21. **Again the word of the LORD came unto** (v. 20) Ezekiel, instructing him to **set thy face** (see 20:46) **against Zidon** (see 27:8 and discussion). This is the only time in the Old Testament that Sidon is mentioned apart from Tyre (see Isa. 23:1-4; Jer. 25:22; 47:4; Joel 3:4; Zech. 9:2; Luke 6:17; 10:13, 14). Due to her close ties with Tyre, it is likely that Sidon's condemnation also lay in her guilt by association and complicity with her wicked neighbors to the south. In the earliest biblical references to her, it is noted that Sidon was founded by Canaan's firstborn. She is also seen as a corrupting influence on God's people (see Judg. 10:6; 1 Kings 11:33).

28:22-23. I am against thee (v. 22). Possibly because of Sidon's involvement in the Jerusalem summit conference (see 5:8; Jer. 27:3). There would be two significant outcomes when God **executed judgments**. The first is seen in the words, **I will be glorified in the midst of thee ... they shall know that I am the LORD**. The Lord's glory would be recognized in Sidon's punishment. They would be forced to acknowledge God's supremacy (see Phil. 2:10-11).

28:24. The second outcome of this judgment would be that these people, who were **a pricking brier** ("a thorn in the side") of Israel due to their degraded worship practices, would be eliminated once and for all (see discussion on 28:1-2; see 1 Kings 16:31). For references to Israel's enemies as briers, see Numbers 33:55; Joshua 23:13.

G. A Note of Promise for Israel (28:25-26)

28:25. A frequent refrain in the Prophets is the reminder of God's ultimate promise to Abraham, Isaac, and Jacob, reiterated in the Palestinian covenant (Deuteronomy 28-30). Although God would

subject His people to judgment for their sin and would allow them to be scattered among the nations (see Deut. 28:15-68), the promise of their return still stood (see Deut. 30:1-14). So Ezekiel was directed to remind his readers, once again, of God's words of hope: **When I shall have gathered ... Israel** (see 11:17; 20:34, 41-42; 29:13; 34:13; 36:24; 37:21; 38:8; 39:27; Neh. 1:9; Zech. 10:8, 10). There would again be a day when they would **dwell in their land that I have given to my servant Jacob** (see 37:25; for the promise, see also Gen. 28:13; 35:12; Ps. 105:10-11).

28:26. In the day when God restored His people to their land, they would **dwell safely therein**. This perennial ideal had become an especially meaningful promise (see 34:28; 38:8, 11, 14; 39:26; Lev. 25:18-19; Jer. 23:6; 32:37; 33:16). The symbols of the "good life" in the promised kingdom are expressed with references to **houses ... vineyards ... confidence** (see Isa. 65:21; Jer. 29:5, 28; Amos 9:14). Most of all, they would then **know that I am the LORD their God**. It was not simply that they would come to know the reality of the "true" God (see 28:22-23); the prophet added the third-person plural for emphasis: "they shall know that I am the Lord *their* God."

H. Against Egypt (chaps. 29-32)

In the previous three chapters, Ezekiel addressed the sins and ultimate judgment of Tyre and its king. God now directed the prophet to turn toward the kingdom to the south, Egypt. Formerly a place of bondage, Ezekiel's contemporaries tended to think of Egypt as an important ally against their common enemies. In fact, at the time of this prophecy, the Egyptian forces were on their way to lift the siege against Jerusalem. Ezekiel's seven oracles against Egypt made it clear that the broken arm of Pharoah (30:21) would be no help to God's people in their hour of need (see Jer. 37:1-10 and discussions; see also Acts 13:17).

1. As a Doomed Dragon (29:1-16)

29:1. In the tenth year ... the tenth month ... the twelfth day of the month. January 7, 587 BC, is the sixth date in Ezekiel (see 1:2; 8:1; 20:1; 24:1;

26:1). This is the first of seven oracles against Egypt, all of which are dated except one (30:1). They represent divine and prophetic anger at Egypt's actions (or nonactions) at this time. With the exception of 29:17–21, all the prophecies dealing with Egypt are to be dated shortly before and after the fall of Jerusalem to Nebuchadnezzer in 586 BC. For a brief period extending a little more than a decade and a half, the Egyptians appeared to be useful allies. Throughout this time, the little nation of Israel was caught up in their more powerful neighbors' repeated efforts to consolidate their power in the region. For the moment, the pendulum was swinging toward Egypt for protection from the Babylonian juggernaut.

29:2–9. Set thy face (v. 2). See 20:46. **Pharaoh.** Pharaoh Hophra, 589–570 BC (see Jer. 44:30). In this section, Ezekiel's prophecy was directed particularly against the reigning pharaoh. **I am against thee.** (v. 3). See 5:8. **Great dragon.** Hebrew, *tannin*; "serpent," "sea monster," "venomous snake"; pictured as being in the Nile (see Exod. 4:3; see also Job 41:1 and discussion; Isa. 27:1). Throughout most of Egypt's history, the pharaoh wore a cobra on the front of his headdress. Ezekiel may have used the term "great dragon" here to play on this symbol, or quite possibly simply to highlight that this was not a friend but a dangerous enemy who lurked in **his rivers**, the Nile Delta and its canals (see Isa. 7:18; 19:6; 37:25). **Which hath said, My river is mine own, and I have made it for myself.** Boasts inscribed on Egyptian monuments (such as in Shelley's "Ozymandias") had become proverbial. The pharaoh was also considered to own the Nile River. **Hooks** (v. 4). See 19:4. **Fish of thy rivers.** Egypt's conquered territories or mercenaries would become as carnivorous fish "clinging" to his sides. Continuing the metaphor, Ezekiel said that Hophra would become as **meat to the beasts** (v. 5). To be given as carrion in the open fields was to deny the pharaoh's great hopes for an afterlife, as symbolized by the pyramids and expressed in *The Egyptian Book of the Dead*. When God was finished with His work, **all the inhabitants of Egypt shall know that I am the LORD, because they have been a staff of reed** (v. 6). A comparison made earlier (see

Isa. 36:6 and discussion). Pharaoh Hophra briefly but unsuccessfully diverted the Babylonians from laying siege to Jerusalem (see Jer. 37:1–10).

29:8–9. The **sword** (v. 8) is that of Nebuchadnezzar (see 21:3). For the entire expression, which is not found elsewhere in the Prophets, see 6:3; 11:8; 14:17; 33:2 (see also Lev. 26:25). God's judgment would be visited on **man and beast.** History records the brutal end of Hophra after his defeat at Cyrene. He was removed and strangled. **And the land of Egypt** (v. 9) segues from the pharaoh to the nation over which he presides. For the same reasons, pride and arrogance, it too would **be desolate and waste; and they shall know that I am the LORD.**

29:10–16. I am against thee, and against thy rivers (v. 10). If the Egyptians and their king believed that the river and the land were theirs, God was going to set the record straight. **From the tower of Syene** (see 30:6; Jer. 44:1; 46:14), or "From Migdol to Syene," probably indicated all Egypt, just as "from Dan to Beersheba" meant all Israel (see, e.g., Judg. 20:1; 1 Sam. 3:20). **Neither shall it be inhabited forty years** (v. 11). The number forty is sometimes used to signify a long and difficult period (see 4:4–8). Here it correctly predicted the forty years of Babylon's domination over Egypt from Nebuchadnezzar's conquest to Cyrus. **Scatter … disperse** (v. 12). While there is no evidence of Egypt ever being abandoned during this period, there is much evidence of their displacement under Nebuchadnezzar, against which time many fled to escape captivity. **Cause them to return** (lit., "cause them to inhabit") **… the basest of the kingdoms** (vv. 14–15). Again, while there are no inscriptions celebrating the fulfillment of this, there is no question that even down to the modern period, Egypt has never again been the international force it was before. **Pathros** (v. 14) is a reference to southern Egypt (see 30:14; Jer. 44:1, 15). The prophecy ended with what can only be understood as a rebuke to **the house of Israel** (v. 16), who would finally learn from the judgment on Egypt **when they shall look after them: but they shall know that I am the Lord GOD.** When God was finished, Israel would never again be inclined to look to this "broken reed."

2. As Payment to Nebuchadnezzar (29:17–21)

29:17. The second oracle against Egypt (see 29:1). **In the seven and twentieth year ... the first month ... the first day of the month**. April 26, 571 BC, is the seventh date in Ezekiel (see 29:1; 1:2; 8:1; 20:1; 24:1; 26:1) and the latest date given in the book—the last oracle known to be given to the prophet. Since the remaining dated oracles are in more or less chronological order, the date is mentioned here probably because of the subject matter (Egypt). The fulfillment of this prophecy is dated more than sixteen years after that given in 29:1–16. During the intervening years, Nebuchadnezzar was engaged in the conquest of Ammon, Moab, and Tyre. By the time he was free to turn his armies to the south, Egypt was particularly vulnerable. At this time, God revealed to Ezekiel that the fulfillment of the earlier prophecy was imminent (see also Jer. 43:10).

29:18. Nebuchadnezzar **caused his army to serve a great service.** He besieged Tyre for fifteen years, from 586 to 571 BC (see 26:7–14). Due to this long military campaign, the prophecy noted that **every head was made bald ... and every shoulder was peeled** from the leather helmets and heavy armor. History records that by the time Nebuchadnezzar took Tyre, its inhabitants had already smuggled their wealth out of the city. The conquering army received nothing for their labor. Unpaid and weary, they turned their frustration toward Egypt and its riches.

29:19–21. The Lord made it very clear that He is the sovereign over the nations, declaring, **Behold, I will give the land of Egypt unto Nebuchadrezzar** (v. 19). In time, it would be necessary to teach this same lesson to the king of Babylon (see Dan. 4:1–37). In 585–573 BC, Babylon conquered Egypt, bringing this prophecy to fulfillment. **Will I cause the horn ... to bud forth** (lit., "revive the strength of"; v. 21). Some have taken this as a messianic reference (see Luke 1:69), but such an interpretation would unduly strain the meaning in context. Rather, this promise looked ahead to the restoration of Israel's strength as a nation (see Pss. 92:10; 132:17). **And I will give thee the opening of the mouth.** Ezekiel's

muteness (see 3:26; 24:27) would be removed, and this word anticipates that of 33:22.

3. The Approaching Day (30:1–19)

30:1. The word of the LORD came again unto me. The third oracle against Egypt (see 29:1) has four divisions, each introduced with the words: "Thus saith the Lord GOD" (30:2, 6, 10, 13). No date is given, but it was probably between January and April of 587 BC. Compare 29:1 with 30:20. Jerusalem was under siege at this time. The prophecy revealed further details of God's impending judgment on Egypt.

30:2–3. Howl ye, Woe worth the day (v. 2) is literally, "Alas for the day." The terror of the coming destruction justified a dreadful response. **The day of the LORD** (v. 3). The day of God's coming in judgment (see 7:7 and discussion). Egypt's judgment is announced (see Isa. 13:6). **A cloudy day.** The metaphor depicts a stormy time for Egypt (see Joel 2:2; Zeph. 1:15; see also Exod. 19:9–18). The expression **the time** signifies "a time of judgment" that would be visited upon **the heathen** (see Ps. 79:6).

30:4. The sword was in the hand of Nebuchadnezzar (see 30:10; see also 21:3), yet he carried the sword in the fulfillment of God's judgment.

30:5. Ethiopia. Cush. **Libya.** Phut, in North Africa (see 27:10). **Lydia.** "Lud," the fourth listed son of Shem. Not in Asia Minor (see 27:10) but descendents of Shem somewhere in northern Africa. **All the mingled people** (see Jer. 25:20; 50:37) likely refers to the foreign mercenaries serving in the listed armies. **Chub.** Obscure, but probably from northern Africa in league with the others listed here. **Men of the land,** or "covenant men," apparently Jews living in Egypt (see Jeremiah 44). These would not be protected any more than Egypt's neighbors both in Africa and in Asia, for they would **fall with them.**

30:6–8. The desolation of the land and Egypt's allies is described with, **they shall fall in it by the sword, saith the LORD** (v. 6). For **from the tower of Syene,** see 29:10. Destruction would be throughout the land, for God would **set a fire in Egypt** (v. 8). This graphic image signified that God had declared war against this wicked nation. He further warned all others, **all her helpers shall be destroyed**.

30:9. Messengers … in ships. See Isaiah 18 for a similar oracle on Cush involving ships on the Nile. These will strike terror in the hearts of the **careless Ethiopians**. The irony of this moment is that all who once relied on Egypt for protection will now be those to whom the Egyptians shall flee in their desperation. Together they will all be brought to their end.

30:10–12. The multitude of the populous will be destroyed. **The terrible of the nations** (v. 11) is a common phrase for the Babylonians, who were known for their cruelty (see 2 Kings 25:7).

30:13–19d. Egypt's cities would be demolished. **I will cause their images to cease out of Noph** (Memphis; v. 13; see 6:4). Located fifteen miles south of Cairo, Memphis was a former capital of Egypt and one of her largest cities. The list of towns given here reveals no discernible pattern but is a literary device used to underscore the scope of the destruction (see Isa. 10:9–11, 27–32; Mic. 1:10–15; Zeph. 2:4). The places to be destroyed were also centers of worship and pagan ritual and power. God wanted it known that He is sovereign over all.

30:14. No area in the land would be exempt from the destruction. **Pathros**. See 29:14 and discussion. **Zoan**. A city in northeast Egypt in the delta region, also called Raamses (see Exod. 1:11), Avaris, and Tanis (see Isa. 19:11, 13; 30:4). **No**. Thebes, the capital of Upper Egypt; present-day Luxor and Karnak.

30:15. Sin. A fortress in the eastern delta region of the Nile.

30:17. Aven. Another name for On, called Heliopolis ("city of the sun") by the Greeks. Located six miles northeast of Cairo, Aven was a center for worship of the sun. **Pi-beseth** (Bubastis). The cat-headed goddess was Ubastet. Bubastis, at one time the capital of Lower (northern) Egypt, was located forty miles northeast of Cairo and was a place where sacred cats were mummified.

30:18–19. Tehaphnehes (v. 18). Tahpanhes, in extreme northeast Egypt, was named for the Egyptian queen Tahpenes and was a residence of the pharaohs. Johanan son of Kareah and his men fled there after the murder of Gedaliah (see Jer. 43:4–7). **Darkened**. A common biblical metaphor describing ruin, destruction, or death. **Cloud shall cover her**. See 30:3; 32:7. Once again the conclusion, as with all of these judgments, **they shall know that I am the LORD** (v. 19).

4. Pharaoh's Arms Are Broken (30:20–26)

30:20. The fourth oracle against Egypt (see 29:1). **In the eleventh year … the first month … the seventh day of the month**. April 29, 587 BC, the eighth date given in Ezekiel (see 1:2; 8:1; 20:1; 24:1; 26:1; 29:1, 17).

30:21. I have broken the arm of Pharaoh (see Pss. 10:15; 37:17; Job 38:15; Jer. 48:25). The "arm" is that which holds **the sword**. The military might of Egypt would be neutralized. This refers to Pharaoh Hophra's unsuccessful attempt to stop the invasion of Nebuchadnezzar the previous year (see 29:6; Jer. 37:5–8).

30:24. Put my sword in his hand (see 21:3). The prophet made it clear that the outcome of the battle would not be in the power of the political allies, but in the One who directed the battle. Nebuchadnezzar was a powerful king and military leader, but he was only the agent of the Lord, who commissioned him to do this work.

5. As a Felled Cedar (chap. 31)

31:1–2. The fifth oracle against Egypt (see 29:1). **In the eleventh year … the third month … the first day of the month** (v. 1). June 21, 587 BC, the ninth date in Ezekiel (see 1:2; 8:1; 20:1; 24:1; 26:1; 29:1, 17; 30:20). The Lord instructed Ezekiel to **speak unto Pharaoh … and to his multitude** (v. 2). In this chapter, the privileged status once enjoyed by Egypt is magnified, but that would soon be brought to an end. The prophecy proceeded as an extended metaphor, holding up the image of Assyria, whose greatness had surpassed that of Egypt under Pharaoh Hophra and whose leader had taken great pride in his superior status and was ultimately brought low.

31:3. Behold, the Assyrian. A great nation that had fallen. In 609 BC, Pharaoh Neco went to Carchemish to help the Assyrian Empire, which was reeling from Babylonian attacks. The effort failed, and Assyria passed from history. **Was a cedar**. The prophet again used the cedar tree as an allegory (see chap. 17; for other examples of the tree as a figure, see Daniel 4:10–15; Matt. 13:31–32). **Lebanon**. The allegory is entirely appropriate since this region was known for its cedars (see 31:15–18; Judg. 9:15; 1 Kings 4:33; 5:6; 2 Kings 14:9; Ezra 3:7; Pss. 29:5; 92:12; 104:16). **Shadowing shroud**. Just as Assyria's allies had looked to her for protection, Ezekiel's contemporaries believed Egypt offered them security from their enemies, but Egypt would come to the same end.

31:4–9. The waters made him great (v. 4). The Tigris and Euphrates rivers. **The deep**. See 26:19. As was Assyria, Egypt was blessed with a river (the Nile) by which its wealth and prosperity were nourished. The prophet began to show that the greatness that both Assyria and Egypt enjoyed was due not so much to their own prowess but to God's provision. All that could be said of their **beauty** (v. 8) pointed not to their achievements but to God's handiwork. This was, indeed, **the garden of God** (v. 9; see 31:10; 28:13). Rather than taking credit for all their benefits, they should have acknowledged that it was He who **made** them **fair**.

31:10–14. Therefore … Because thou hast lifted up thyself in height (v. 10). Egypt's greatness was to be credited to God, and her pride was a direct offense against the Almighty. He would deliver them to **the mighty one of the heathen** (v. 11). Probably Nabopolassar, or possibly Nebuchadnezzar. The Lord was therefore entirely justified in judging Egypt for her **wickedness** (see v. 10; Gen. 11:1–8).

31:15–18. In the concluding paragraph, God Himself began the official **mourning** (v. 15) for Egypt. He **made the nations to shake** (v. 16), as at Tyre's fall (see 27:35; 28:19). **Shall be comforted** (lit., "consoled") because the mightiest of trees had joined them in the grave (*sheol*). The Egyptians would be taken together with **them that be slain with the sword** (v. 17), that is, those who met a premature death. If they lived in glory, they would die as uncircumcised (see 28:10 and discussion). God concluded, **This is Pharaoh and all his multitude** (v. 18).

6. A Lament for Pharaoh (32:1–16)

32:1. The sixth oracle against Egypt (see 29:1). **In the twelfth year … the twelfth month … the first day of the month**. March 3, 585 BC, the tenth date in Ezekiel (see 1:2; 8:1; 20:1; 24:1; 26:1; 29:1, 17; 30:20; 31:1). If the Septuagint and Syriac are followed ("the eleventh year"), the chronological order of the Egypt oracles is preserved (and the date would be March 13, 586 BC; see 29:1; 30:20; 31:1; 32:17 and discussion).

32:2. Lamentation (see 19:1; Jer. 9:17–19; Amos 5:16). This chapter contains two lamentations. The first is over the fall of Egypt. The second (32:17–32) concerns the destruction and burial of the pharaoh and his people. Ezekiel first likened the king of Egypt to **a young lion of the nations**, a figure for royalty and grandeur (see 19:1–9), then to **a whale** (see 29:3 and discusssion), which was translated "dragon" in 29:3. Egypt was a predatory creature lying in wait in **the seas** and **rivers** (see 29:3), the tributaries and canals of the Nile. Egyptian influence and power was exercised over all who entered her waters. Her influence was a danger to all, a truth lost on many of Ezekiel's contemporaries. The pharaoh **troubledst the waters** and **fouledst their rivers**. As a crocodile plunging into a stream stirs up the mud, Egypt was involved in a foul business that ended only when Pharoah had devoured his prey. The judgment that follows was well earned.

32:3–4. Spread out my net (v. 3). Earlier it was Zedekiah over whom God's net was thrown (see 12:13; 17:20; 19:8). Here God's net was the snare in which Egypt would be taken captive. What follows is a graphic portrayal of the Egyptians' end. The Lord declared, **a company of many people … shall bring thee up**, and **I will cast thee forth upon the open field** (v. 4) as a fish out of water, for the **beasts** to take their fill of your corpses (see 29:3–5).

32:5–6. Mountains … water (vv. 5–6). The imagery of these verses suggests that neither the Egyptians' high places nor their places of military and commercial might would save them but would only serve to contain their dead. The original text for **height** (v. 5) is obscure but probably refers to their decaying bodies lying heaped up in the open fields where they fell by the sword. If they had lived in pomp and honor, they would die in disgrace.

32:7 – 8. I will cover the heaven (v. 7). The first of seven clauses threatening the darkness associated with the day of the Lord (see Joel 2:2, 10, 31; 3:15; Amos 5:18 – 20; Zeph. 1:15). Just as there would be no help from earth, there would be no response from the heavens when God visited them with His wrath.

32:9 – 10. Vex the hearts (v. 9). These verses reflect the anger and grief brought about whenever great world powers fall, reminding lesser nations that they were even more vulnerable (see the similar feelings aroused by Tyre's fall, 26:16 – 18; 27:35; 28:19). Christ predicted a similar dynamic (see Matthew 9 – 12). Great tribulation and calamity often brings out the worst of human nature, including anger, deceit, hatred, and evil of all kinds. The vassals of this once great nation would reel in their self-serving indignation that Egypt should fail them when they needed her most against the power from the north (Nebuchadnezzar).

32:11 – 16. The king of Babylon (Nebuchadnezzar; v. 11; see 21:19) is once again depicted as the one bearing God's sword of judgment and as **the terrible of the nations** (v. 12). Egypt's **pomp** was especially singled out as deserving of judgment. Where once her rivers teemed with life, the mud along her banks would no longer bear the imprint of **the foot of man ... nor the hoofs of beasts** (v. 13). God would **cause their rivers to run like oil** (v. 14). The rivers' surfaces undisturbed by any form of life is a surreal, lifeless image of the source of their national existence. This is the only place in the Bible where this eerie metaphor is used to describe desolation. **The daughters of the nations** (v. 16) would serve as a world chorus of professional wailers (see Jer. 9:17 – 18). **They shall lament for her, even for Egypt, and for all her multitude.**

7. As Consigned to the Pit among the Uncircumcised (32:17 – 32)

32:17. The seventh and last oracle against Egypt (see 29:1). **In the twelfth year ... the fifteenth day of the month.** This is the eleventh date in Ezekiel (see 1:2; 8:1; 20:1; 24:1; 26:1; 29:1, 17; 30:20; 31:1; 32:1).

No month is given (as in 26:1; 40:1). The whole year dates from April 13, 586 BC, to April 1, 585 BC. The Septuagint suggests the first month, the fifteenth day of which would be April 27, 586 BC.

32:18 – 32. The daughters of the famous nations (v. 18) would be **cast ... down** into **the nether parts of the earth**, which is "the grave" (*sheol*) in 31:15. The verb for "cast down" appears only here in the original text. **The pit** bespeaks the grave, the general place of all the dead. In this concluding prophecy regarding Egypt, the prophet was instructed to declare all those whose destiny was to be shared with **the multitude of Egypt.** Vain Egypt, obsessed with its **beauty** (v. 19), would instead be cast down **with the uncircumcised** (see 28:10). These include **Asshur ... and all her company ... which caused terror** (vv. 22 – 23); **Elam** (v. 24), a country east of Assyria, in present-day Iran; **Meshech, Tubal, and all her multitude** (v. 26), peoples and territories in Asia Minor; **Edom ... and all the Zidonians** (vv. 29 – 30), or Sidonians (see 28:21). From great to small, they would all be brought down to the pit together. That the prophet was told to trace the fate of these people beyond the grave to their final state serves as a warning to all who read. Existence does not end with the grave, nor can the destiny of those who enter it be changed.

III. Oracles of Consolation for Israel (chaps. 33 – 48)

The familiar pattern of the prophets is seen here (see Introduction, "Literary Features"). Ezekiel's delivered oracles against Israel (chapters 1 – 24), followed by oracles against the nations (chapters 25 – 32), and concluded with prophecies of consolation for Israel (chapters 33 – 48). Approximately five months after the fall of Jerusalem, a refugee arrived with the sad news. The Lord had already alerted Ezekiel that the messenger was coming (see 33:21, 22). So it was that the "hand of the LORD" (3:22) came upon Ezekiel, to open his mouth (see 3:26) and to give him a final message concerning God's loving-kindness and faithfulness. When it seemed all hope was lost, God would "sanctify [His] great name" (36:23) and bring His people together again. As "bone to his bone" (Ezek. 37:7), He would restore them to their rightful place among the nations. Ultimately, Israel will experience revival, restoration, and a glorious future as the redeemed and perfected kingdom of God on earth.

A. The Watchman (33:1-20)

Chapters 33–39 form a unit to depict this unusual work of God in bringing His errant nation back to Himself. With frequent words of warning (e.g., 33:23–29; 34:1–19; 35; 36:1–7), the prophet encouraged the Israelites to repentance and hope, with sermons and oracles of comfort following the fall of Jerusalem. God says, "I will take you from among the heathen, and gather you out of all countries, and will bring you into your own land ... A new heart also will I give you, and a new spirit will I put within you ... And ye shall dwell in the land that I gave to your fathers; and ye shall be my people, and I will be your God" (36:24, 26, 28).

The watchtower and the watchman, or sentry, who patrolled from a position high above (ninety feet) the walls that Nebuchadnezzar bragged were like "mountains," were a common sight in ancient Babylon. There were 360 such towers positioned around the inner wall of the great city of Israel's captivity to protect those inside from enemies intent on their destruction. Earlier (3:17) the prophet himself had been designated as the watchman. Here he used the image to indicate that while it was obligatory for the sentry to sound the alarm when needed, it was also incumbent on all who heard the alarm to act.

33:1–3. The word of the LORD (v. 1) was given to **the children of thy people** (v. 2), fellow Israelites in exile with Ezekiel. **When I bring the sword upon a land** (lit., "Suppose I bring ..."). God was raising a hypothetical situation: What if I send an invading army? What if **the people of the land** (full citizens who owned land and served in the army, see 7:27; 12:19; 45:16, 22; 46:3) appointed a **watchman** to patrol the wall for their protection? What if **he seeth the sword** (the enemy; v. 3) and **blow the trumpet, and warn the people**? The "trumpet" was

an instrument made from a ram's horn (see Josh. 6:4, 6, 13), used to warn of approaching danger (see Neh. 4:18–20; Jer. 4:19; Amos 3:6) and to announce the beginnings of religious periods (see, e.g., Day of Atonement, Lev. 25:9; new moon festival, Ps. 81:3).

33:4–5. In such an hypothetical situation, if someone **heareth the sound ... and taketh not warning; if the sword come ... his blood shall be upon his own head** (v. 4; see 18:13). On the other hand, he who heeded the **warning** (v. 5) would **deliver his soul**. The lesson was transparent. If the sentry did his job, the responsibility for the outcome was on the "head" of those to whom the warning had been delivered.

33:6. By the same token, if **the watchman** saw the threat and failed to warn the people, causing **the sword** to come upon someone, **his blood** ("his life," see Gen. 9:5; 42:22) **will I require at the watchman's hand**.

33:7. So thou, O son of man, I have set thee a watchman unto the house of Israel. The Lord now applied this principle (see discussions on 33:4–6) to the prophet and the people (see Jer. 6:17; Hab. 2:1). **Warn them from me**. The prophet spoke not his own words but the word of the living God.

33:8–9. When I say ... if thou dost not speak (v. 8). Calamity would come in the wake of the people's wickedness, but culpability would be assigned to the one who had been sent but failed to warn them. On the other hand, **if thou warn the wicked ... and he do not turn ... he shall die in his iniquity; but thou hast delivered thy soul** (v. 9). Even though the outcome would be the same, the responsibility was no longer that of the faithful messenger.

33:10–11. Thus ye speak, saying, If our transgressions and our sins (v. 10). The exiles had previously blamed their fathers (18:2) and even God (18:19, 25). Now the prophet was instructed to tell them, **As I live** (see 18:3) **... I have no pleasure** (v. 11). The question of 18:23 is now a statement. God's basic intention for His creation is life, not death (see 16:6). **Turn from his way** was Ezekiel's third call for repentance (see 14:6; 18:30). **Turn ye**

from your evil ways. The final punishment of the pagan nations about them, and even that which fell on Jerusalem, served only to remind the Israelites that sin brings judgment and death. This is not something God takes "pleasure" in; rather, it serves as an alarm. Thus, He asked them, **why will ye die, O house of Israel?** The choice was theirs.

33:12 – 20. This passage deals with the same subject as 18:21 – 29 — namely, that the individual, whether righteous or wicked, has a choice to live righteously each day.

33:15. Restore the pledge, give again that he had robbed. See 18:7. **Statutes of life**. Here is a wonderful expression for the law of God. The purpose of God's law is to foster and protect life (see 20:13, 21). **He shall surely live**. The entire section (vv. 12 – 20) was Ezekiel's answer to the despairing question of 33:10.

33:17 – 20. The way of the Lord is not equal (lit., "is not right"; v. 17; see 18:25, 29). The way of the wicked is to accuse God of injustice. God will, instead, **judge ... every one after his ways** (v. 20). That is to say, their own deeds will condemn them.

B. Jerusalem's Fall Reported and Explained (33:21 – 33)

33:21. And it came to pass ... The city is smitten. With this announcement, all of Ezekiel's previous prophecies were fulfilled and vindicated. The Lord now gave him a new mission of pastoral comfort. **In the twelfth year ... the tenth month ... the fifth day of the month,** the twelfth date in Ezekiel (see 1:2; 8:1; 20:1; 24:1; 26:1; 29:1, 17; 30:20; 31:1; 32:1; 32:17), is January 8, 585 BC, five months after the Jerusalem temple was burned (compare the date in 2 Kings 25:8, which in modern reckoning is August 14, 586 BC). The journey between Jerusalem and Babylon could be made in four months (see Ezra 7:9). **One that had escaped out of Jerusalem.** The first of the exiles of 586 BC (see "he that escapeth," 24:26).

33:22 – 23. After seven years of silence, during which time the prophet spoke only to utter God's judgment, he was now released to speak and to minister to the people. **My mouth was opened, and I**

was no more dumb (v. 22). The muteness that had come upon him at the beginning of his ministry was finally lifted (see 3:26 – 27). Immediately, **the word of the Lord came unto** (v. 23) him.

33:24. The message was first given to those who **inhabit[ed] those wastes of the land**. These were the residents of Jerusalem who were not exiled in 586 BC. Apparently, they had the idea that **Abraham was one ... but we are many; the land is given us for inheritance.** Giving no thought to their own sin, they thought that God had spared them from exile to bless them with the possession of the land. This boast by the unrepentant is similar to that of 11:15 (see also Luke 3:8). The problem with their boast was that whereas Abraham was righteous, they were wicked.

33:25. Wherefore say. The prophet was instructed to set the record straight. They too were guilty of serious violations of God's law. **Eat with the blood.** Forbidden in Genesis 9:4; Leviticus 7:26 – 27; 17:10; Deuteronomy 12:16, 23. **Lift up your eyes toward your idols.** See 18:6.

33:26. Ye stand upon your sword ... work abomination ... defile every one his neighbour's wife. With this threefold indictment, God asked ironically, **and shall ye possess the land?**

33:27. As I live. See 18:3. **Sword ... beasts ... pestilence.** These three judgments answer to the three indictments of 33:26. They also served to fulfill God's threat that He would cause their own works to condemn them (33:17; see the threefold threat in 5:12; 7:15; 12:16; and the fourfold threat in 14:12 – 21).

33:30 – 33. These words of assurance were meant for Ezekiel alone.

33:31. Sit before thee. As the elders had (see 8:1; 14:1). **Goeth after their covetousness.** The people were waiting for Ezekiel to tell them how they could personally profit from the situation rather than what God's larger designs were for them (see Matt. 20:20 – 28).

33:32 – 33. One that hath a pleasant voice (v. 32). This expression is taken by some to indicate that Ezekiel chanted his oracles (see 2 Kings 3:15; Isa. 5:1), but more likely, the prophet was using a metaphor. **They hear ... but they do them not** (see

Isa. 29:13; Matt. 21:28–32; James 1:22–25). When all these things came to pass, the people would **know that a prophet hath been among them** (v. 33). With certainty, the prophet added, **lo, it will come.**

C. The Lord as the Good Shepherd (chap. 34)

While Ezekiel's focus in this chapter was on the Good Shepherd, his opening message was against the present "shepherds" who served as leaders of Israel but whose leadership was characterized more by self-interest than by concern for the flock. He first detailed their sins (34:1–6) and then pronounced judgment on them (34:7–10).

34:1–3. Son of man, prophesy against the shepherds of Israel (v. 2), those who were responsible for providing leadership, especially the kings and their officials (see 2 Sam. 7:7; Jer. 25:18–19), but the prophecy also included the prophets and priests (see Isa. 56:11; Jer. 23:9–11). Ezekiel had earlier singled out the princes, priests, and prophets for special rebuke (chap. 22). To call a king a shepherd was common throughout the ancient Near East (for David's rise from shepherd to shepherd-king, see Ps. 78:70–71; for condemnation of the shepherds, see Jer. 23:1–4). **Woe be to the shepherds of Israel that do feed themselves! should not the shepherds feed the flocks?** The leaders were first cited for placing themselves ahead of the sheep. The text also indicates that they were using the misfortune of the people to increase their wealth. They **eat ... clothe ... kill them that are fed** (v. 3), but they **feed not the flock.** They exploited the flock and made no investment in its welfare.

34:4. The poor refugees are described as **diseased ... sick ... broken ... driven away ... lost.** Instead of ministering and caring for them, their shepherds **with force and with cruelty ... ruled them.** In the hour of their greatest need, their leaders had used them for personal advantage. Scripture makes much of this imagery elsewhere (see Jer. 50:6; Matt. 18:12–14; Luke 15:4; 19:10).

34:5. Once again Ezekiel described Israel's exile and dispersion with the term **scattered** (see 11:16–17; 12:15; 20:23, 34, 41; 22:15; 28:25). While he called the leaders "shepherds" in this prophetic

indictment, the reality was that **there** was **no shepherd** in the sense that God intended for the leaders of His flock. This picture is used often in the Bible (see, e.g., Mark 6:34).

34:6. And none did search or seek after them. See Luke 19:10. It is likely that Jesus also drew his language in John 10 from this chapter. His picture there is consistent with the kings of old who took the royal title "Shepherd." That title is used most often in a context in which the king provides for his flock and protects his flock from those who would harm it.

34:7–10. The conclusion of the matter begins with irony: **Therefore, ye shepherds** (v. 7) is followed by **there was no shepherd** (v. 8). Instead of being fed, the people **became meat to every beast of the field.** Because of the lack of courageous leaders to protect them, they were further exploited by those before whom they were driven. The prophet, however, would give them good news before he was finished (see 34:28). As for these **shepherds** (v. 9), God declared, **I am against the shepherds** (v. 10). The prophecy against the false leaders ended on a note of hope: **I will deliver my flock from their mouth.** The shepherds are viewed in the end as beasts (v. 8) together with all those depicted as the enemies of God's people throughout this prophecy (see 5:8).

In the concluding section of the chapter, the prophet declared God's intention to become Israel's personal Shepherd, to seek His people out, to bring them out, to restore His covenant relation with them, and to show them by His loving-kindness that they are the sheep of His pasture (34:11–31).

34:11. I, even I will ... search my sheep. Having dealt with the faithless shepherds (34:1–10), the Lord committed Himself to shepherding His flock (see Jer. 23:3–4).

34:12. Out of all places. Babylon was not the only place where the Israelites had gone (see Jer. 43:1–7). **Cloudy and dark day.** The day of the Lord that had come upon Israel when Jerusalem fell in August 586 BC (see 7:7 and discussion).

34:13. I will bring them out. The promises of restoration—begun in 11:17 and repeated in 20:34, 41–42; 28:25—find special emphasis in chapters

33–39 (see 36:24; 37:21; 38:8; 39:27). **Mountains of Israel**. Compare the tone of 6:3–7 with the judgment now past (see 34:12). The mountains perhaps represented the scene of salvation.

34:14–15. I will feed them (v. 14). See Isa. 40:11; John 10:11. **In a good pasture**. These images for leaders appear often in the ancient Near East. In a royal inscription, Tukulti-Ninurta I (ca. 1245–1208 BC) spoke of "the king" as the one who shepherded his land in green pastures with his beneficent staff, the one who subdued princes and all kings with his just scepter and fierce valor. Note the twin activities of providing and protecting.

34:16. The fat and the strong. Those with power who had fattened themselves by oppressing the other "sheep" (see 34:17–22).

34:17. I judge between cattle and cattle, between the rams and ... goats. People of power and influence were oppressing poorer Israelites. This prophetic word shows the same concern for social justice found elsewhere in the Prophets (see Isa. 3:13–15; 5:8; Amos 5:12; 6:1–7; Mic. 2:1–5). Compare the treatment of slaves that Jeremiah observed (Jer. 34:8–11). The language is remarkably close to that of Matthew 25:31–46, where Jesus spoke of the separation of the sheep and the goats at the inauguration of His kingdom.

34:23. My servant David. A ruler like David and from his line (see Ps. 89:4, 20, 29; Jer. 23:5–6). In John 10:24, the people asked, "If thou be the Christ, tell us plainly," to which Jesus responded, "I told you" (John 10:25). He was the Christ, the son of David.

34:24. Prince. The Lord announced a theocracy, a kingdom in which He would be King, and the earthly king a "prince" (see 37:25; 44:3; 45:7, 16–17, 22; 46:2–18; 48:21–22).

34:25. Covenant of peace. See 37:26. All of God's covenants aim at peace (see Gen. 26:28–31; Num. 25:12; Isa. 54:10; Mal. 2:5). This covenant (the "new covenant" spoken of by Jeremiah, Jer. 31:31–34) looks to the final peace, initiated by Christ (see Phil. 4:7) and still awaiting final fulfillment. "Peace" (Hebrew, *shalom*) is more than an absence of hostility; it is a fullness of life enjoyed in complete security.

They shall ... sleep in the woods, which was often dangerous (see Ps. 104:20–21; Jer. 5:6). The phrase "none shall make them afraid" is stock language for the shepherd sections of the Old Testament (Isa. 17:2; Jer. 30:9–10; Mic. 4:4) and, more important, in the merger of shepherd language and covenant language in Leviticus 26:6.

34:26. The shower ... in his season. Autumn rains, which signal the beginning of the rainy season, and spring rains, which come at the end (see Jer. 5:24). **Showers of blessing**. Blessing, the power of life promised to God's people through Abraham (Gen. 12:1–3), is beautifully symbolized in the life-giving effects of rain.

34:27. Bands of their yoke. These bands were bars or wooden pegs inserted through holes in the yoke and tied below the animal's neck with cords (see Isa. 58:6) to form a collar (see 30:18; Lev. 26:13; Jer. 27:2; 28:10–13). The entire picture represents foreign domination.

34:29. Shame of the heathen. See 22:4.

34:30. I the LORD their God am with them ... they ... are my people. Covenant language (see 11:20; Exod. 6:7; Hos. 1:9), though the exact wording of this verse has no parallel elsewhere in Ezekiel.

D. Oracles against Edom (chap. 35)

35:1. Earlier, Ezekiel had announced God's judgment against Edom, Israel's neighbor to the south (chap. 25). Now as the prophet was presenting God's message of hope and consolation to His chosen people, Ezekiel was instructed once again to speak **the word of the LORD** against these people who had time and again used their power and influence at Israel's expense. Here the specific offenses cited include Edom's aid to Babylon (35:5), her attempts to lay claim to territory belonging to Israel (35:10), and her sinister joy over Israel's misfortune (35:12). Just as God began with the judgment on the wicked leaders within the community of Israel, He would bring about the downfall of all who sought her destruction from without.

35:2–4. Set thy face against mount Seir (v. 2). Seir is the name for Edom that associates it with the mountain range south of the Dead Sea (35:15). Israel's relatives (Jacob and Esau being twins, Gen. 25:21–30) were her constant enemy, from whom brotherhood was sought but seldom found (see Amos 1:11). Edom (Seir) had to be dealt with before Israel could find peace (see Gen. 32–33). See 25:12 and discussion; Isa. 63:1–6.

35:5. Perpetual hatred. Beginning with Jacob's deception of Isaac to attain Esau's blessing (see Genesis 27; especially 27:41) and continuing later (see Num. 20:14–21; 2 Sam. 8:13–14; 1 Kings 9:26–28), Edom's enmity against Israel was proverbial. **Time of their calamity.** Edom looted Jerusalem in 586 BC (see Obadiah 11–14). This would earn them God's holy disfavor.

35:6. As I live. See 18:3. **Blood shall pursue thee.** God's response bespeaks retributive justice based on Genesis 9:6.

35:9. Perpetual desolations. Unlike Egypt, Edom would not experience restoration (see 29:13–16).

35:10. These two nations. It was Edom's plan that Israel and Judah **shall be mine.** The Edomites are depicted as lying in wait until the opportune moment when they could lay claim to that which was not their right to own.

35:11. As I live. See 18:3.

35:13. Ye have boasted against me (see Obadiah 12; Zeph. 2:8, 10; see also Ps. 35:26; Jer. 48:26, 42). Their boast was followed with the chilling words of an omniscient God, who declared, **I have heard them.** God Himself was witness to their evil plots.

E. Consolations for the Mountains of Israel (36:1–15)

36:1–15. Here is the comforting counterpart to chapter 6. Verses 1–7 announce punishment for the nations; verses 8–15 announce restoration for Israel.

36:2. The enemy hath said against you. See 25:3; 26:2. **Aha.** See 25:3. **Ancient high places.** The Promised Land, of which the elevated region between the Jordan Valley and the Mediterranean coast was the central core.

36:3. Residue of the heathen. All the nations that had in the past conquered parts of Israel, until finally they took full possession of her. Israel had been **taken up in the lips of talkers;** that is, she had become fodder for idle gossip and ridicule.

36:4. Mountains…hills…rivers…valleys. See 6:3 and 1:5.

36:5. Fire of my jealousy. The Lord was personally offended by the ridicule of the nations because it was His special land (**my land**) they were mocking and plundering. **Idumea,** or Edom, was singled out because of her long-standing hostility to Israel (see chap. 35, especially 35:2, 5 and discussions). For Edom in the day of the Lord, see Amos 9:12; see also Obadiah, where Edom is used as a catchword to connect the two books and their theme of the coming day.

36:7. I have lifted up mine hand. God raised His hand as if to take a vow and delivered a chilling declaration that Israel's enemies would **bear their shame.**

36:8. Branches, and…fruit represent signs of productivity (see 17:8, 23) and the Lord's restored favor (see Lev. 26:3–5), in contrast to Edom's desolation (see 35:3, 7, 15). **At hand.** As judgment neared (7:7; 12:23), a speedy return of the exiles was announced.

36:9. I will turn unto you (see Lev. 26:9 for the identical clause in a similar context). God was saying that He was on Israel's side. Not as in their earlier day of judgment; He now stood ready to help them.

36:10. All the house of Israel. In this chapter (as in 37:15–23), Ezekiel spoke of the restoration of all Israel.

36:11. Increase and bring fruit. This terminology is identical to the divine blessing at creation (Gen. 1:22, 28; 9:1; see also Gen. 8:17; 9:1, 7) and the subsequent covenant blessing (see Gen. 17:6; 35:11; 48:3–4; Exod. 1:7). **Your beginnings.** God's blessings would surpass those of the days of Abraham and Moses, when He called them by name and gave them His law and an inheritance. **Ye shall know that I am the Lord.** These words of recognition, used throughout the book to express God's revelation through judgment, here point to God's self-disclosure in salvation (see 5:13; see 34:30).

36:12. Walk upon you. The Lord was still addressing the mountains of Israel (beginning in 36:4).

Bereave them of men. The mountains are poetically pictured as having contributed to the depopulation brought about by the exile. This may refer to the fact that Canaan contained the Canaanites and their religious centers ("high places"), which had led Israel astray and so brought God's wrath down on His people (see 6:3).

F. Summary of Ezekiel's Theology (36:16–38)

36:16–38. This section summarizes all that Ezekiel prophesied concerning Israel. From this text, Ezekiel has sometimes been styled as "the first dogmatic theologian" (Feinberg, *The Prophecy of Ezekiel*, p. 205).

36:18. Wherefore I poured my fury upon them. See 7:8; 9:8; 14:19; 20:8–21; 22:22; 30:15. **Blood ... for their idols.** This forms a summary reference to Israel's social injustices and idolatrous religious practices (see 22:3 and discussion; for "idols," see 6:4). **Polluted it.** See Leviticus 18:28; Deuteronomy 21:23.

36:20. They profaned my holy name. Because Israel had been removed from her land, it seemed to the nations that her God was unable to protect and preserve His people (see Num. 14:15–16; 2 Kings 18:32–35; 19:10–12).

36:22. I do not this for your sakes. Not because God did not care for Israel but because they did not deserve what He was about to do (see Deut. 9:4–6). Statements like these made Ezekiel a preacher of pure grace. **For mine holy name's sake.** The reason given earlier for the withholding of divine punishment (see 20:9, 14, 22) is here given as a reason for divine restoration. What was at stake was not Israel's "right" to the blessing but God's integrity and reputation (see Gen. 12, 15, 17; Deut. 28–30).

36:23. The heathen shall know that I am the LORD. The ultimate purpose of God's plans for Israel is that through her the whole world may know the true God. It is difficult not to see allusions to the ultimate fulfillment of this in the work of the Messiah (see esp. Romans 9–11).

36:24–30. In this central passage, Ezekiel listed four stages of restoration: (1) return of the exiles (v. 24), (2) cleansing from sin (v. 25), (3) enablement by God's Spirit to live in God's way (vv. 26–27), and (4) prosperity in the land (vv. 28–30).

36:25. Will I sprinkle clean water. For sprinkling with water as a ritual act of cleansing, see Exodus 30:19–20; Leviticus 14:51; Numbers 19:18; see also Zechariah 13:1; Hebrews 10:22. **Idols.** See 6:4. **Will I cleanse.** See 36:33; 37:23; Jeremiah 33:8.

36:26–27. Contains new covenant terminology (see Jer. 31:33–34).

36:26. I will take away the stony heart. The "stone" was often associated with evil. In 1 Samuel 25:37, it is used to signify a stubborn heart. Here it signifies a heart that is dead to the things of God. Such a heart would be replaced with **A new heart** (see discussions on 11:19–20; 18:31). **A new spirit will I put within you.** God will transform the mind and heart. Here and in 11:19, God declared that He would bring about this change. In 18:31, He called on His people to effect the change. What He requires of His people He always provides. **Heart of flesh.** In the Old Testament, "flesh" is often a symbol for weakness and frailty (see Isa. 31:3); in the New Testament, it often stands for the sinful nature as a God-opposing force (as in Rom. 8:5–8). Here it stands for a pliable, teachable heart, as opposed to "the stony heart." What is in mind is a "new birth," regarding which Jesus told Nicodemus, "Art thou a master of Israel, and knowest not these things?" (John 3:10). From this text and that of Jeremiah, Nicodemus should have understood what Jesus was telling him.

36:27. My spirit. God bestows His Spirit to enable the human spirit to do His will. Psalm 51:7–11 closely parallels 36:25–27. The gift of the Spirit is often related to God's ultimate restoration of His chosen people. While this verse looks to the final day of restoration (see 39:29; Isa. 44:3; 59:21; Jer. 31:31–34; Joel 2:28–29; Acts 2:16), the coming of the Holy Spirit at Pentecost is properly understood as a foretaste of that future glory.

36:28. My people ... your God. This is covenant language (see 11:20; Exod. 6:7). That which God does is due not to the merit of His people but to His promise (see 36:22, 32).

36:29. From all your uncleannesses. God would deliver them from cultic and moral defilement (see 36:25; 37:23). **I will call.** As at the beginning when God called creation into being (see Gen. 1:5, 8, 10).

36:30. Reproach. See 36:15. The experience of Jonah is exemplary of such reproach. The calamity of the storm that threatened everyone on Jonah's ship was due to his disobedience. Here the judgment brought upon the nations was laid at the feet of this disobedient people, who had adopted the ways of the heathen rather than proclaim the majesty of their God. When Israel is finally restored, this reproach will be removed (see Isa. 66:23; Jer. 31:33, 34; Zech. 14:16).

36:31. Then shall ye remember. God's undeserved grace leads to recollection and repentance (see 6:9; 16:63; 20:43; Ps. 130:4).

36:33. In the day. Connects the promise of cleansing (36:24–32) and the promise of repopulation (36:33–36).

36:35. Garden of Eden. Primeval fertility is suggested (see 28:13; 31:9). **Are become fenced.** In contrast to 38:11, they would wall their villages and fence their dwellings in relative safety and peace.

36:36. Heathen ... shall know. See 36:23.

36:37. I will yet for this be inquired of by the house of Israel. Allowing petitions to come to Him again, God reversed His earlier refusals to hear (see 14:3; 20:3, 31).

36:38. Holy flock ... in her solemn feasts. See 1 Kings 8:63; 1 Chron. 29:21; 2 Chron. 35:7 for the appropriateness of the comparison. Feinberg notes that the "doctrines of Ezekiel are, indeed, those of Paul as well: forgiveness (36:25), regeneration (36:26), the indwelling and ruling Spirit of God (36:27), the spontaneous keeping of God's law (36:27; Rom 8:4), the inseparable connection of Israel's history with God's self-revelation to the nations (36:33–36; Romans 11), and the conversion of the nation Israel (36:24–31; Rom 11:25–27)" (Feinberg, *The Prophecy of Ezekiel*, p. 211).

G. Vision of National Restoration (chap. 37)

Chapter 37 contains one of Ezekiel's major visions. Surprisingly, no date is given (as in 1:2; 8:1; 40:1), but the event must have occurred sometime after 586 BC. In this vision, Ezekiel predicted the national and spiritual resurrection of Israel.

1. National Resurrection (37:1–14)

37:1. The hand of the LORD. See 1:3. **The spirit of the LORD.** Used elsewhere in Ezekiel only in 11:5, this phrase is usually simply translated "the Spirit," as in 8:3; 11:1, 24. **Valley.** The Hebrew for this word is the same as that translated "plain" in 3:22–23; 8:4. Ezekiel now received a message of hope, while he had previously heard only God's word of judgment. **Bones.** In 37:11, "bones" symbolizes Israel's apparently hopeless condition in exile.

37:2. There were very many. Symbolizing the whole community of exiles. **Very dry.** Long dead, far beyond the reach of resuscitation (see 1 Kings 17:17–24; 2 Kings 4:18–37; but see also 2 Kings 13:21). The story of Lazarus of Bethany, as John emphasized it (see, e.g., John 11:39), is a New Testament parallel. Lazarus was long past the time when Jesus might have done something about his sickness, yet he was raised to life.

37:4. Prophesy upon these bones. Ezekiel had previously prophesied to inanimate objects (mountains, 6:2; 36:1; forests, 20:47) and now prophesied to lifeless bones and the "wind" (37:9).

37:6. Sinews ... flesh ... skin ... breath. Lists of four items are common in Ezekiel (see 1:5). Here these items are symbols of the physical resurrection of the nation.

37:7. A shaking. Probably the sound of the bones coming together, but possibly recalling the sound accompanying God's presence, as in 3:12–13 ("a great rushing").

37:8. But there was no breath. This visionary recreation of God's people recalls the two-step creation of man (see Gen. 2:7), when man was first formed from the dust and then received the breath of life. Many also view this as a promise of physical regathering, followed by the spiritual rebirth of Israel.

37:9–10. Four (v. 9). See 1:5. **Breath.** The Hebrew (*ruach*) can also mean "wind" or "spirit." **Slain.** Ezekiel saw a battlefield strewn with the bones of the fallen (v. 10).

37:11. Our bones ... cut off. A sense of utter despair, to which the vision offers hope.

37:12–13. Graves. The imagery shifts from a scattering of bones on a battlefield (see 37:9) to a cemetery with sealed graves.

37:14. I shall place you in your own land. These words make it clear that here the Lord was not speaking of a resurrection from the dead but of the national restoration of Israel. Ezekiel foresaw a time when the nation of Israel would come back to life.

2. National Reunification (37:15–28)

37:15–16. Take ... one stick (v. 16). This is Ezekiel's last symbolic act involving a material object (see 4:1, 3, 9; 5:1). **Write upon it.** Zechariah 11:7 seems to be based on this passage in Ezekiel.

37:17. Join them one to another. The sticks may have been miraculously joined, or Ezekiel may have joined the sticks together in his hand to symbolize the future unification of Israel.

37:18. Wilt thou not shew us ...? Ezekiel's symbolic act successfully aroused the people's curiosity (see 12:9; 21:7; 24:19).

37:19–20. They shall be one in mine hand (v. 19). God would duplicate Ezekiel's symbolic act by uniting the two kingdoms, which had been separated since Solomon's death (see 1 Kings 12; for similar prophecies of the reunion of Israel, see 33:23, 29; Jer. 3:18; 23:5–6; Hos. 1:11; Amos 9:11).

37:21–22. Mountains of Israel (v. 22). See 6:2–3; 34:13; 36:1. **One king.** Only here and in 37:24 is the word "king" used of the future ruler. Usually "prince" is used (see 34:24), as in 37:25 (see 7:27 and discussion; see also 44:3; 45:7–9), and frequently in chapters 45–48, where the ruler in the ideal age is always referred to as "prince."

37:23. Idols. The old and basic offense (see 6:4). **Save them out of ... dwelling places.** Or "save them from their backslidings" (see Jer. 2:19; 3:22). **Cleanse.** See 36:25 for the same notion. **My people ... their God.** See 11:20.

37:24. David my servant. As in 34:23, the coming messianic ruler is called David because He would be a descendant of David and would achieve for Israel what David had, except more fully. **King.** See 37:22. **Shepherd.** As in 34:23, the coming ruler is likened to a shepherd who cares for his flock (see John 10, especially 10:16).

37:25. Jacob my servant. See 28:25 for this frequent reference to the nation Israel.

37:26–28. Covenant of peace (v. 26). See 34:25. **Everlasting covenant.** See 16:60. This phrase occurs sixteen times in the Old Testament, referring at times to the Noahic covenant (Gen. 9:16), the Abrahamic covenant (Gen. 17:7, 13, 19), the Davidic covenant (2 Sam. 23:5), and the new covenant (Jer. 32:40). Compare the covenant with Phinehas (Num. 25:12–13). Here the prophecy looks to that final day when Israel will be restored and their messianic King will rule and reign from His holy mountain (see chap. 38). **Set my sanctuary in the midst of them.** As in days past, God would establish His dwelling in the center of their national life (vv. 27–28). This word is further developed in Ezekiel's vision of the future age, in which the rebuilt sanctuary would have central position (chaps. 40–48).

H. The Final Battle (chaps. 38–39)

38:1. And the word of the LORD came unto me; repeated often when Ezekiel received God's word, this verse stands as an introduction to chapters 38–39, which are a unit. The future restoration of Israel under the reign of the house of David (chap. 37) will bring about a massive coalition of world powers to destroy God's kingdom. The vast host that will come against Jerusalem will end up as dead bodies strewn over the fields of the Promised Land. Israel will become the cemetery of the enemy hordes (see chap. 37). The events depicted here likely coincide with the eschatalogical events described in Matthew 24:9–31.

38:2–3. Son of man (v. 2). See 2:1. **Set thy face.** See 20:46. **Gog.** This is apparently a leader or king whose name appears only here and in Revelation 20:8. Several identifications have been attempted, notably Gyges, king of Lydia (ca. 660 BC). Possibly the name is purposely vague, standing for a mysterious, as yet undisclosed, enemy of God's people. **The**

land of Magog. Elsewhere (Gen. 10:2; 1 Chron. 1:5) Magog is one of the sons of Japheth, thus the name of a people. In Ezekiel 39:6, it appears to refer to a people. But since the Hebrew prefix *ma-* can mean "place of," here Magog may simply mean "land of Gog." Israel had long experienced the hostility of the Hamites and other Semitic peoples; the future coalition here envisioned will include, and in fact be led by, peoples descended from Japheth (see Genesis 10). **Chief prince**. Could refer to a military commander in chief. There is little grammatical evidence for translating this as "prince of Rosh." Of the 599 times this word appears, this would be the only case in which it is translated as a place-name. **Meshech and Tubal**. Probably located in eastern Asia Minor (see 27:13; 32:26), these sons of Japheth (see Gen. 10:2; 1 Chron. 1:5) are peoples and territories to the north of Israel (see 38:6, 15; 39:2). As in the days of the Assyrians and Babylonians, the major attack will come from the north.

38:4. I will turn thee back. Emphasis is on the fact that God is completely in control of all that is to follow. **Put hooks into thy jaws**. As was Pharaoh in 29:4, Gog is likened to a beast led around by its captor, here referring to God.

38:5. Ethiopia. Hebrew Cush, the upper (southern) Nile region. The invading forces from the north (see 38:2 and discussion) will be joined by armies from the south. **Libya**. In North Africa.

38:6. Gomer. Another of Gog's northern allies (see 38:2), mentioned elsewhere (Gen. 10:3; 1 Chron. 1:6) as one of the sons of Japheth. According to nonbiblical sources, these peoples originated north of the Black Sea. **House of Togarmah**. Or Beth-togarmah (see 27:14). According to Genesis 10:3 and 1 Chronicles 1:6, Togarmah was one of the children of Gomer. The force opposing the interests of Israel will be a coalition of seven nations, including nations to the north (Meshech, Tubal, Gomer, Beth-Togarmah), the southwest (Ethiopia, Put), and the east (Persia).

38:8. After many days ... in the latter years. After all the events of national restoration, the immigration and settlement in Israel (as described in

chapters 34–37) will be completed. Since no such invasion has yet occurred in Israel, many believe it will come in the future as part of the eschatological conflict of the last days. Some place this battle before the great tribulation, some during it, some after it (synonymous with Armageddon), and some place it at the end of the millennium (see Rev. 20:7–10).

38:9. Like a cloud. Jeremiah similarly described the invasion from the north (Jer. 4:13).

38:10. At the same time. A phrase common in other prophetic writings; here it refers to the day of Gog's invasion of Israel. **Shall things come into thy mind**. The divine initiative (38:4) is paralleled, as it often is in Scripture, by human action (see Deut. 31:3; Isa. 10:6–7). **Evil thought**. A raiding expedition (see 38:12).

38:11–12. Land of unwalled villages (v. 11). While the inhabitants of the land in this future time will imagine themselves to be secure, the enemy will come to **take a spoil, and to take a prey** (v. 12). The text implies that the people will be living under the illusion of peace while, in fact, the enemy is preparing for a slaughter. **Midst of the land**. The Hebrew for "midst" also means "navel," a graphic image for the belief that Israel was the vital link between God and the world (the idea occurs also in 5:5). The word occurs elsewhere in the Bible only in Judges 9:37. Since the Hebrew for "world" can also mean "land," theologically Jerusalem is both the center of the land of Israel and the center of the earth.

38:13. Sheba. Located in the southwest corner of the Arabian Peninsula (modern Yemen) and known for trading (Job 6:19; see 23:42; 27:22; 1 Kings 10:1–2). **Dedan**. See 25:13. **Tarshish**. See 27:12.

38:17–18. Art thou he of whom I have spoken ...? (v. 17). Probably a general reference to earlier prophecies of divine judgment on the nations arrayed against God and His people. When they **come against the land of Israel** (v. 18), God's **fury** will be aroused.

38:19–20. A great shaking (v. 19) will signal the mighty presence of God as He comes to overwhelm the great army invading His land. The fourfold listing of the animal world indicates the totality of nature (see 1:5; for similar listings, see Gen. 9:2; 1 Kings 4:33; Job 12:7–8).

38:21–23. I will call for a sword (v. 21); God's sword of judgment (see Isa. 34:5–6; Jer. 25:29). **Every man's sword shall be against his brother.** The coalition of Israel's enemies will turn on itself, as did the armies that attacked Judah in the time of Jehoshaphat (see 2 Chron. 20:22–23). The list of divine weapons suggests that God will intervene directly without the benefit of an earthly army.

39:1–8. In the ensuing battle, God will slaughter the enemy. Before they can fire a shot, they will be subdued by God Himself. **Gog, the chief prince of Meshech** (v. 1; see 38:2). While 39:1–16 adds new details, the same basic events as those in chapter 38 are described.

39:2. From the north parts. As in 38:6, 15.

39:3. Bow. See Jeremiah 6:23. The Lord will disarm Israel's enemies before they can shoot an arrow.

39:4. Give thee unto the ravenous birds. A theme expanded in 39:17–20.

39:6. I will send a fire. See 30:8 and discussion.

39:9–16. In the ensuing judgment of God upon the nations gathered against His people, the divine response will be as complete as the force of the opposition. **Seven** (v. 9). The number seven is symbolic of the finality of this great battle against God's people, as well as indicating the size of the invading armies. But those who come to seek to **spoil … and rob** (v. 10) will themselves be plundered. Their bodies will be buried where they fall, and the name of the valley will be changed to **The valley of Hamon-gog** (v. 11). It is further indicated that God will **cleanse the land** (v. 12). Ritual purity is a basic element in Ezekiel's theology (see 22:26; 24:13; 36:25, 33; 37:23). Corpses were considered especially unclean (see Lev. 5:2; 21:1, 11; 22:4; Num. 5:2; 6:6–12; 19:16; 31:19). **People of the land** (v. 13). See 7:27 and discussion, though here a special class may not be implied. **Sever out men of continual employment** (v. 14). After the seven-month burial period, observed by all the people, special squads will be hired full time to ensure total cleansing of the land, by marking for burial any human bones that may

have been missed. Total ritual purity is the aim. The **sign** (v. 15) is probably of stone, either a large one or a heap of smaller ones.

39:17–20. The carnage will create a feast for the birds and the beasts of the field. This again bespeaks the utter humiliation that will be visited upon those who would rise up against God's chosen ones. **Speak unto every feathered fowl … gather … to my sacrifice** (v. 17). Various interpretations are: (1) Since the enemies are all dead and buried, this section (vv. 17–20) is perhaps to be understood as poetic imagery. (2) If, however, the passage reverts back to 39:4, a more literal interpretation is possible; the dead bodies were not all buried at once. (3) These verses involve a restating of 39:9–16, employing a different figure (see Isa. 34:6; Jer. 46:10; Zeph. 1:7). The metaphor of sacrifice suggests a consecration to the Lord in judgment, as at Jericho (see Josh. 6:17 and discussion). **Ye shall eat the flesh of the mighty** (v. 18). A gory description of what birds of prey commonly do (see discussion on v. 17; and Rev. 19:17–21). The bodies of the victims are compared to animals commonly used for sacrifices. **Bashan.** Rich pastureland east of the Sea of Galilee, known for its sleek cattle (see Deut. 32:14; Ps. 22:12; Amos 4:1) and its oak trees (see 27:6; Isa. 2:13). The expression **eat fat … drink blood** (v. 19) further indicates that this is the Lord's sacrificial feast, in that fat and blood were normally reserved for God (see 44:15; Lev. 3:17). **My table** (v. 20) denotes a sacrificial altar (for descriptions of the tables in the new temple, see 40:38–43 and 41:22).

39:21–23. My glory (v. 21) represents God's visible presence in the world (see 1:28). Here that visibility is due to divine intervention in history. **The house of Israel shall know … the heathen shall know** (vv. 22–23). As God had made Himself known to Israel and the nations through His saving acts in Israel's behalf (see Exod. 6:7; 7:5, 17; 10:2; 14:18; 16:6–7, 12; Josh. 3:10; 4:24; see also Josh. 2:9–11; 5:1), so Israel and the nations will see Him again at work as He judges His people for their sin (see 39:27). **Hid I my face** (v. 23). For this expression of divine displeasure, see Psalm 30:7; Isaiah 54:8; 57:17.

39:24–26. Their uncleanness and ... their transgressions (v. 24). This condition is spelled out especially in chapter 22 but also throughout chapters 6–24. **Jacob** (v. 25). The nation of Israel, as in 20:5. The parallelism within the verse supports this identity. **My holy name.** See 20:9. **After that they have borne their shame** (v. 26). The remembrance of shame previously called for will be erased (6:9; 20:43; 36:31).

39:27–29. I ... am sanctified in them (v. 27). God will reveal Himself anew in a restored, holy people (see 20:41; 28:25; 36:23). **Then shall they know** (v. 28). See 39:22. **I have poured out my spirit** (v. 29) promises the gift of God's enabling Spirit (see 11:19; 36:26–27; 37:14). The end result of this great eschatological conflict will be the total vindication of God and His people.

I. Vision of Renewed Worship (chaps. 40–48)

The concluding section of Ezekiel's oracles of consolation for Israel forms a unit that in many ways has created a kind of "continental divide" (Feinberg, *The Prophecy of Ezekiel*, p. 233) among interpreters. Some emphasize the literal sense of the text to indicate a future when God will once again establish a temple in Jerusalem, to which all will come to worship. Others stress the spiritual character of the text to indicate a time when God's people will "worship him in spirit and in truth" (John 4:24). In the former approach, obviously the details are important, for they indicate a future temple in the millennial age. In the latter approach, the interpreter generally glances over the details to emphasize the symbolism relative to the church of the present era.

The previous section depicted the new life the believing nation would enjoy when finally reconciled to her God. In this section, the prophet was directed to tell the people about the new temple to be built (chaps. 40–43), their service of worship to be established in that day (chaps. 44–46), and finally, a sketch of the division of the land in the final kingdom (chaps. 47–48).

C. Dyer ("Ezekiel," p. 1304) asks the question, "Why did Ezekiel take so much space to describe the millennial temple?" He goes on to suggest two reasons. "(1) The sanctuary was the visible symbol of God's presence among His people. The prelude to Israel's judgment began when God's glory departed from Solomon's temple in Jerusalem (Ezek. 8–11). The climax to her restoration will come when God's glory reenters the new temple in Jerusalem (43:1–5). (2) The new temple will become the visible reminder of Israel's relationship to God through His New Covenant. Since God gave detailed instruction for building the tabernacle to accompany His inauguration of the Mosaic Covenant (see Exod. 25–40), it is not unusual that He would also supply detailed plans for His new center of worship, to accompany the implementation of the New Covenant."

1. Wall Around the Temple (40:1–47)

40:1. The vision came to Ezekiel **In the five and twentieth year ... the tenth day.** April 28, 573 BC, is the thirteenth date in Ezekiel (see 1:2; 8:1; 20:1; 24:1; 26:1; 29:1, 17; 30:20; 31:1; 32:1; 32:17; 33:21). **Of our captivity.** All the dates in the book of Ezekiel are reckoned from the 597 BC exile, but only here and in 33:21 is the exile specifically mentioned (see 1:2). **In the beginning of the year** marks the Hebrew Rosh Hashanah, the well-known Jewish New Year festival. It has long occurred in the fall (in either September or October), but since Ezekiel used a different and older religious calendar throughout the book, the spring date as given above is correct (see Lev. 23:24). **The hand of the LORD was upon me.** See 1:3. **And brought me thither.** That is, the Lord brought him to the land of Israel. See chapters 8–11 for a similar vision.

40:2. Visions of God. This phrase introduces all three of Ezekiel's major visions (see 1:1; 8:3). **Very high mountain.** Mount Zion, also seen as extraordinarily high in other prophetic visions (see 17:22; Isa. 2:2; Mic. 4:1; Zech. 14:10). Height here signifies importance, as the earthly seat of God's reign. **On the south.** With the city located on its southern slopes, the mountain was to the north (see Psalm 48; see Ps. 48:2).

40:3–4. There was a man (v. 3). The prophet was given a tour by a "man" who had **the appearance of**

brass. This indicates the man was other than human, probably an angel. **Line of flax**. Used for longer measurements, such as those in 47:3. **Measuring reed**. Used for shorter measurements, about ten feet and four inches long. **In the gate**. This is presumably of the outer court (see 40:17–19).

40:5. Wall on the outside of the house round about. Separating the sacred from the secular. **Six cubits**. In using the long cubit (seven handbreadths, or about twenty-one inches), which was older than the shorter cubit (six handbreadths, or about eighteen inches), Ezekiel was returning to more ancient standards for the new community (see 2 Chron. 3:3).

40:6–7. Gate which looketh toward the east (v. 6). This describes the gate of the outer court. The three gates (east, north, and south) of the outer court were similar to the three in the inner court (40:32), having six alcoves for the guards (three on each side) and a portico (40:8–9). Comparable gate plans have been discovered at Megiddo, Gezer, and Hazor, all dating from the time of Solomon (see 1 Kings 9:15). The guards kept out anyone who might profane the temple area (see Ezra 2:62). **Went up the stairs**. The first of three sets of stairs leading to the temple had seven steps (40:22); the next one (inner court), eight (40:31); and the last (temple), ten (40:49; based on the Septuagint reading of this verse)—possibly indicating increasing degrees of sacredness.

40:8–47. Porch of the gate was inward (v. 9). This reversed the position of the porticoes of the inner court gates, which faced away from the temple (v. 34). **Little chambers ... were three** (v. 10). These were alcoves for the guards, mentioned in 40:7. **Palm trees** (v. 16) decorated Solomon's temple (see 1 Kings 6:29, 32, 35). **Thirty chambers** (v. 17). The exact location of these rooms is not given. They were probably intended for the people's use (see Jer. 35:2, 4). **An hundred cubits** (v. 19). Over 170 feet separated the outer wall from the inner wall and was the width of the outer court. **Gate ... looked toward the north** (v. 20). Both it and the south gate (v. 24) were identical to the east gate. **Seven steps** (v. 22). See 40:6. **South gate** (v. 28). Of the inner wall, which is not described but must be assumed. **He measured ... according to these measures**. In both the outer walls. See discussion on 40:6. **By the posts of the gates** (v. 38). The porticoes of the inner gates were on the side of the outer court, facing away from the temple. **Washed**. The inner parts and the legs were washed (see Lev. 1:9). **Burnt offering** (v. 39). Probably one of the oldest kinds of sacrifice. The entire animal was burned in consecration to God (see Lev. 1). **Sin offering and the trespass offering**. See Leviticus 4–7. The peace offerings, which were more festive, are notable by their absence from this listing (see 43:27; 45:17; 46:2, 12). **Sons of Zadok** (v. 46). For the distinction between the sons of Zadok and the Levites, see discussion on 44:15–31. Upon entering **the inner court** (v. 44), Ezekiel saw two rooms, one by **the north gate** and the other toward **the south**. These rooms will no doubt serve the priests who attend **the altar** (v. 47). This is further described in 43:13–17.

2. Temple Exterior (40:48–41:26)

40:48. As if standing in the inner court, Ezekiel began to describe what he saw of the exterior of the temple building. **The porch** was similar to the portico in Solomon's temple, but the dimensions were slightly larger (see 1 Kings 6:3).

40:49. Pillars. Called Jachin and Boaz in Solomon's temple (see 1 Kings 7:21).

41:1–2. Temple (v. 1). The nave was the largest of the three rooms comprising the temple. This outer sanctuary was identical in size to Solomon's (see 1 Kings 6:17).

41:3–4. Went he inward (v. 3). Only the angel, not Ezekiel, entered the Most Holy Place. Leviticus 16 forbids anyone but the high priest to enter it, and then only once a year (see Heb. 9:7). **Six cubits**. Or "six cubits wide"; note the progressive narrowness of the door openings as one approaches the inner sanctuary (fourteen cubits, 40:48; ten cubits, 41:2).

41:5–11. Next the prophet described the areas surrounding the temple. **Thirty in order** (v. 6). These ninety side rooms were probably storerooms for the priests, possibly for the tithes (see Mal. 3:10).

41:12–26. The prophet went on to describe the dimensions of the temple proper and then its decorations. **An hundred cubits** (v. 13). The hundred-cubit symmetry stood for perfection. The temple was **cieled with wood round about** (v. 16), as in Solomon's temple (see 1 Kings 6:15). The **cherubims** (v. 18) are angelic beings who served as guards (see Gen. 3:24). These cherubim, as opposed to those mentioned in chapter 10, had only two faces—a man's and a lion's (see 1 Kings 6:29, 32, 35).

Ezekiel next mentioned **The altar ... of wood** (v. 22). As the great altar stood outside the temple proper (see 43:13–17), so a smaller altar (three feet five inches square by five feet high) stood outside the Most Holy Place. It served as a table, no doubt to hold the shewbread (see Exod. 25:30; Lev. 24:5–9; 1 Kings 7:48 and discussion). Ezekiel did not mention an altar of incense or of candlesticks, such as were found in Solomon's temple and in the tabernacle before it. Also not included were the "sea" (see 1 Kings 7:23) and the ark of the covenant. The **two doors** (v. 23) were folding doors, so that the entry could be made still narrower.

3. Temple Interior (chap. 42)

As the prophet continued to record the vision of the temple, he was careful to give every detail as God gave it. Crucial for the interpreter is to note how carefully God instructs the reader concerning the proper worship of Himself. Much of contemporary worship is characterized by cultural preference. Here there is no accommodation given over to the worshiper—only to Him to whom all glory is given.

Feinberg observes, "Sin makes a separation from Eden to the lake of fire. God must make a separation between the sacred and the profane, for He can never be worshiped or have fellowship with those who are unlike His holy character and nature" (*The Prophecy of Ezekiel*).

42:1–12. The chamber ... over against the separate place (v. 1). The chambers' function is described in 42:13–14. They have no parallel in Solomon's temple as described in 1 Kings 6.

42:13. Priests that approach unto the LORD. The sons of Zadok (see 40:6 and 44:15). **Eat the most holy things.** The priests normally received partial

maintenance by being allowed to eat certain sacrifices (see Lev. 2:3; 5:13; 6:16, 26, 29; 7:6, 10).

42:20. Measured it by the four sides. Perfect symmetry in the ideal temple's total area.

4. The Return of God's Glory (chap. 43)

43:1–12. If the lowest point of Ezekiel's prophecies was the vision of the glory departing (chap. 8–11), this passage was the high point. To begin, Ezekiel was brought **to the gate, even the gate that looketh toward the east** (v. 1). The prophet had seen the glory leave the city from this very gate (10:19). In a dramatic reversal of that dreadful vision, he now saw the glory return.

43:2. This verse signals the high point of chapters 40–48. The temple had been prepared for this moment, and all that followed flowed from this appearance. In what was no doubt a shout of acclamation, the prophet began, **And behold, the glory of the God of Israel came from the way of the east**, the direction in which Ezekiel had seen God leave (see 11:23). In the book of Ezekiel, God's glory is always active (see 43:4–5; 3:23; 9:3; 10:4, 18; 44:4). **And his voice was like a noise of many waters.** See 1:24; Rev. 1:15; 14:2; 19:6. Ezekiel experienced an audition as well as a vision. **And the earth shined with his glory.** God's visible glory is always described as being very bright (see 10:4; Luke 2:9; Rev. 21:11, 23).

43:3. According to ... the vision which I saw. Yet it was different, for no creatures or wheels are mentioned here. **When I came to destroy the city.** See chapter 9. **By the river Chebar.** See chapter 1. **I fell upon my face.** See 1:28; 3:23; 9:8; 11:13; 44:4.

43:4. By the ... gate whose prospect is ... east. See 43:2.

43:5. So the spirit took me up. With God being nearer, the function of the guiding angel was taken over by the Spirit of God. Ezekiel was transported into the inner court but not into the temple (see 3:14; 8:3; 11:1, 24). **Filled the house.** The Spirit of God filled the temple as at the consecration of Solomon's temple (see 1 Kings 8:11; see also Exod. 40:34–35; Isa. 6:4).

43:6. Him. God, but out of reverence, is not named here, preserving an air of awe and mystery.

43:7. Place of my throne. See Isaiah 6:1; Jeremiah 3:17. **Place of the soles of my feet**. See 1 Chronicles 28:2; Psalms 99:5; 132:7; Isaiah 60:13; Lamentations 2:1. **I will dwell in the midst of the children of Israel for ever**. Renewing the promise of 37:26–28 (see 43:9; 1 Kings 6:13; Zech. 2:11). **Whoredom**. The word can stand either for the sacred prostitution in the Canaanite religion (Baalism) or for spiritual apostasy from true worship of the Lord (see 16:15). **Carcases**. The reference is either to idols or to monuments or graves of past kings. Fourteen kings of Judah were buried in Jerusalem, possibly near (too near for Ezekiel) the temple area (see 2 Kings 21:18, 26; 23:30).

43:8. Their threshold by my thresholds. Solomon's temple was surrounded by many of his own private structures (see 1 Kings 7:1–12). The distinction between God's holy temple and the rest of the world is a central idea in the book of Ezekiel (see 43:12; 44:23). **I have consumed them**. As elsewhere in Ezekiel, the unstable practices of the people and their kings brought about their destruction (see 5:11; 18:10–12; and especially 22:1–15).

43:12. This is the law. Refers to the contents of chapters 40–42.

43:13–27. The remainder of the chapter describes **the altar** (v. 13). Alluded to in 40:47 and described in detail here. Although the material is not mentioned, dressed stones were probably used. Exodus 20:24–26 allowed an altar to be made of earth, but use of dressed stones for those altars was strictly forbidden (see *KJV Study Bible* notes on Exod. 20:24–25). Solomon's altar was bronze (see 1 Kings 8:64). Ezekiel's altar, much larger than Solomon's, was over twenty feet tall and was made of three slabs of decreasing size, like a pyramid or Babylonian ziggurat. The **lower settle** (v. 14) was two cubits high; the **greater settle**, four cubits high; and the **altar** (v. 15), or hearth, four cubits high.

43:15–16. Altar (hearth; v. 15–16). The Hebrew for this term appears only here in the Old Testament and may also mean "the mountain of God" or "the lion of God" (see the *KJV Study Bible* marginal note);

it is a variant of a term that appears in Isaiah 29:1–2. **Four horns**. Stone projections from each of the four corners of the altar hearth. On earlier altars, the horns afforded a refuge of last resort for an accused person (see Exod. 21:12–14; 1 Kings 1:50–51; 2:28–29).

43:17. His stairs. Forbidden in Exodus 20:26 but here required because of the size (see 43:13).

43:18. Burnt offerings. See 40:39. **Sprinkle blood**. See Exodus 29:16; Leviticus 4:6; 5:9.

43:19–20. Of the seed of Zadok (v. 19). See 44:15. **Sin offering**. To cleanse the altar from the pollution of human sin (see 40:39).

43:21. Without (i.e., "outside") **the sanctuary**. As prescribed in Exodus 29:14; Leviticus 4:12, 21; 8:17; 9:11; 16:27. This action foreshadows one aspect of Christ's sacrifice (see Heb. 13:11–13).

43:22. Cleanse. By the sprinkling of the blood (see 43:20).

43:27. Peace offerings. After the seven-day consecration by burnt offerings and sin offerings, the altar was ready for the celebration of the more festive peace offerings, in which the people partook of some of the meat (see Leviticus 3).

5. The Priesthood (chap. 44)

44:1–14. The first section of chapter 44 focuses on the closed gate. The regulation of the priesthood was crucial to life in the glorious kingdom. It was due to their faithlessness and spiritual treachery that the nation was led into the worship of false gods. God would close the gate on any such practices.

44:2. This gate shall be shut. The reason given is that God entered through the east gate (43:1–2), thus making it holy. Related reasons may be that God would never again leave as before (10:19; 11:23) and that sun worship would be made impossible (see 8:16). Today the east gate (called the Golden Gate) of the sacred Moslem area (*Haram esh-Sharif*) in Jerusalem is likewise sealed shut as a result of a later but possibly related tradition.

44:3. Prince. This is the first mention of the "prince" in chapters 40–48 (see 34:24 and discussion). **To eat**. Probably indicates his part of the peace offering (see Lev. 7:15; Deut. 12:7; see also Ezek. 43:27

and discussion). While this honor was accorded the prince, it is significant that he was given no other part in the ceremonial functions, reserved now solely for the priests (see 2 Chron. 26:16–20). **By the way of the porch.** Indicates from the inside of the outer court.

44:7. Uncircumcised in heart. Spiritually unfit.

44:9. No stranger, uncircumcised … shall enter into my sanctuary. Nehemiah enforced this restriction when he dismissed Tobiah (Neh. 13:8), an Ammonite (Neh. 2:10; see Deut. 23:3). Foreigners could, however, be a part of Israel (see 47:22).

44:10. Levites. Members of the tribe of Levi served as priests from the earliest days (see Deut. 33:8–11; Judg. 17:13). **When Israel went astray.** The reference is mainly to the period of the monarchy, especially to the last years, during which Ezekiel so often criticized the people's idolatry (see 6:3–6; 14:3–11; 16:18–21; 23:36–49; 36:17–18; 37:23).

44:11. Stand before them. The Levites still had an honorable position; see "they shall stand before [the Lord]," 44:15.

44:15–31. In the second section, the attention turned to **the priests** (v. 15) themselves. **Zadok** traced his Levitical lineage to Aaron through Aaron's son Eleazar (1 Chron. 6:50–53). He served as priest under David, along with Abiathar (see 2 Sam. 8:17 and discussion; 15:24–29; 20:25). He supported Solomon (as opposed to Abiathar, who pledged himself to Adonijah) and thus secured for himself and his descendants the privilege of serving in the Jerusalem temple (see 1 Kings 1). The Zadokites were later removed from office, but the Qumran (Dead Sea Scrolls) community remained loyal to them. **That kept the charge.** A distinction Ezekiel did not make in his oracles of judgment (see 7:26; 22:26 and the thrust of chap. 8). In chapters 40–48, however, the Zadokites received special consideration because of their faithfulness.

44:16. They shall enter. This elevation of the Zadokites and demotion of the Levites was part of the concern for ritual purity, a major theme of chapters 40–48. Only the fittest were to serve. **My table.** Either the table that held the bread (see 41:22 and discussion) or the large altar on which the Lord's food was presented (44:7).

44:17. Linen. This was cooler than wool (see 44:18).

44:18. Linen bonnets. Ezekiel wore one (see "the tire of thine head," 24:17).

44:19. Put off their garments. This was in the interest of ritual purity.

44:20. Neither shall they shave their heads. Because it was a mourning ritual (7:18) that rendered the mourner unclean (see Lev. 21:1–5). **Nor suffer their locks to grow long.** Because it implied the taking of a vow that might prevent the priest from serving (see Num. 6:5; Acts 21:23–26).

44:23. Difference between the holy and profane. This is one of Ezekiel's central concerns. The important task of declaring God's will on matters of clean and unclean food, the fitness of sacrificial animals, and ritual purity either had been done for pay (see Mic. 3:11) or had been neglected altogether (see Jer. 2:8; Ezek. 22:26; for a positive example, see Hag. 2:10–13).

44:24. They shall stand in judgment. This was one of their functions from the earliest days (see 1 Sam. 4:18 and discussion; 2 Chron. 19:8–11).

44:25. Dead person. Contact with the dead made a person ceremonially unclean (see Lev. 21:1–3; Hag. 2:13).

44:28. No possession. The statement that priests were not to own land agrees with Numbers 18:20, 23–24; Deuteronomy 10:9; Joshua 13:14, 33; 18:7.

44:31. Is dead of itself. That is, died a natural death, a restriction applied to all Israel according to Leviticus 7:24.

6. Land Allotment (chap. 45)

45:1–8. In the allotment of the land, God came first. **When ye shall divide by lot the land** (v. 1) envisioned a new acquisition and redistribution of the land. **Offer … unto the Lord.** The entire square area in the center of the land was to be set aside for the Lord. **Five and twenty thousand reeds.** With the five-thousand-cubit city area (v. 6), it was a perfect square. **Holy in all the borders.** Set apart for the Lord and owned by no tribe.

45:2. Five hundred … square round about. The temple area discussed in 42:16–20. **Suburbs.** Unoccupied strips of land that served as buffers between the more holy and the less holy, though the whole area was holy (see 42:20).

45:3. Shalt thou measure. The middle strip of the holy square was specifically for the temple.

45:4. Land ... for the priests. Not to own (see 44:28) but to live on.

45:5. Levites ... have for themselves. A section of equal size just to the north was for the Levites to dwell on, even though it was in the holy area. The Levites, as opposed to the Zadokite priests, could hold land as a possession.

45:6. City. The former Jerusalem contained the temple area. The new Holy City would not but would be adjacent to the temple. **Five thousand broad.** The southernmost section of the city completed the perfectly square area. **It shall be for the whole house of Israel**; not belonging to any one tribe or person, as in former days.

45:7. A portion shall be for the prince. A considerable portion of territory. In view of the next verse (see 46:18), the generous allotment should have kept the prince from greed like that of Ahab (see 1 Kings 21). The prince was also responsible for sizable offerings (45:17).

45:9–12. Exhortations for the people to practice justice and honesty in all their dealings with one another.

45:9. O princes of Israel. The language of this verse is reminiscent of the preaching Ezekiel did before 586 BC (see 22:6).

45:10. Ye shall have just balances. Israel was not to repeat the economic injustices of the past. The Old Testament often warns against cheating in weights and measures (see Lev. 19:35–36; Deut. 25:13–16; Mic. 6:10–12).

45:11. Shall be of one measure. A little more than half a bushel. **Homer.** About six bushels.

45:13–20. Instructions for the offerings of the people.

45:13. Oblation. Given to the prince as distinct from the gifts given to the priests (44:30). The prince was to use these gifts in part for the offerings to the Lord (see 45:16).

45:17. Drink offerings. Usually wine is meant (see Num. 15:5; Hos. 9:4); wine is not mentioned here, however, though oil is (45:14, 24).

45:18–46:24. This entire section involves so many variations from Pentateuchal law that the rabbis spent a great deal of effort trying to reconcile them. For example, the provision in 45:18 for an annual purification of the temple does not seem to take into consideration the Day of Atonement ritual, described in Leviticus 16.

45:21–25. Instructions concerning the celebration of Passover and the Feast of Tabernacles.

45:22. Sin offering. See 40:39.

45:25. In the seventh month ... the fifteenth day ... in the feast. In some respects, this is the most important of the festivals, called the Feast of Ingathering (see Exod. 23:16; 34:22) or the Feast of Tabernacles (see Deut. 16:16).

7. The Duties of the Prince (chap. 46)

46:1–10. Ezekiel gave instructions concerning the daily aspect of Israel's worship, specifically concerning the regulations for the Sabbath and new moon sacrifices.

46:1. Gate of the inner court. While the east gate of the outer court was permanently closed (44:2), the east gate of the inner court could be opened on festival days.

46:2. By the way of the porch of that gate. The portico of the gate of the inner court faced the outer court. **Stand by the post of the gate**, which had been ritually cleansed (45:19). From there, the prince could observe the sacrifices being performed on the great altar in the inner court, but he was not allowed into the inner court itself.

46:3. At the door of this gate. This was in the outer court.

46:4. Six lambs ... and a ram. Another example of a difference from Pentateuchal laws (see 45:18–46:24). Numbers 28:9 calls for two lambs and no ram on the Sabbath.

46:5. Ephah. Compare Numbers 28:9.

46:6. Day of the new moon. This was the first day of the month. Compare the requirement of Numbers 28:11.

46:7. A meat offering, an ephah. Compare Numbers 28:12.

46:9. He that entereth in ... the north gate. These appear to be crowd-control measures. If so, the new era will see masses of people thronging the sanctuary on the festival day.

46:11–15. The prince will have the prerogative to open the gate facing east when he desires to give a freewill offering to the Lord. For this one occasion, the prohibition from opening the gate is lifted.

46:12. Voluntary burnt offering. This was above and beyond what was required of the prince.

46:13. Every morning. Compare Numbers 28:3–8, where the daily sacrifice consists of one lamb in the morning and one in the evening (see 1 Chron. 16:40; 2 Chron. 13:11; 31:3). A different custom appears in 2 Kings 16:15, where a burnt offering was offered in the mornings and a grain offering in the evenings.

46:14. Sixth part of an ephah ... third part of a hin. Compare Numbers 28:5.

46:16–18. The Year of Jubilee will be observed.

46:16. His sons. Ezekiel pictured a hereditary rulership.

46:17. To the year of liberty. The Year of Jubilee—held, theoretically, every fiftieth year (see Lev. 25:8–15, especially 25:13).

46:18. The prince shall not take. See 45:7.

46:19–24. This passage fits well after 42:13–14, where other rooms for priests are described. The provisions here are a fitting conclusion to the sacrifice laws. The priests' area (vv. 19–20) was to be kept separate from the cooking areas of the Levites (vv. 21–24).

8. Life-Giving Water (47:1–12)

One of the central features of the future temple will be the life-giving river that flows out from the temple. While many seek only spiritual significance in this, the text presents little reason to consider it anything but a literal river.

47:1. He. The angelic guide (see 40:3), who here appears for the last time, concluded Ezekiel's visionary tour of the new temple. **Door of the house**. Ezekiel was standing in the inner court. **Waters**. The rest of

this section (47:1–12) makes it clear that healing, life-nurturing water is meant (see *KJV Study Bible* notes on Pss. 36:8; 46:4; see also Joel 3:18; Zech. 13:1; 14:8; Rev. 22:1–2). In the larger background was the river flowing from the Garden of Eden (see Gen. 2:10).

47:2. Brought he me out of the way of the gate northward, because the east gate was closed (44:2).

47:5. Measured a thousand, for a total of four measurings (see 1:5). **River that I could not pass over**. Amazing, in that a stream not fed by tributaries does not increase as it flows.

47:7. Very many trees. This is reminiscent of Eden (see Gen. 2:9).

47:8. Toward the east country. Compare Zechariah 14:8. **The desert**. Arabah. Here the waterless region between Jerusalem and the Dead Sea (i.e., part of the Jordan Valley). **The sea**. Usually means the Mediterranean Sea, but here obviously the Dead Sea is intended. **Shall be healed**. This is figurative for "become fresh." That this sea, the lowest (1,300 feet below sea level) and saltiest (25 percent) body of water in the world, should sustain such an abundance of life indicates the wonderful renewing power of this "river of water of life" (Rev. 22:1).

47:9. Every thing ... shall live. Overtones of Genesis 1:20–21, pointing to a new creation.

47:10. En-gedi. Means "spring of the goat"; a strong spring midway along the western side of the Dead Sea. **En-eglaim** means "spring of the two calves." It is possibly Ain Feshkha, at the northwestern corner of the Dead Sea, though some suggest a location on the east bank. **The great sea** is the Mediterranean Sea.

47:11. They shall be given to salt. Perhaps to provide the salt needed in the sacrifices (43:24).

47:12. New fruit according to his months is a marvelous extension of the promises in 34:27; 36:30 (see also Amos 9:13).

9. Land Allotment (47:13–48:35)

When God gave His promise to Abraham (Gen. 13:14–17; 15:17–21) and his descendants, He promised they would possess the land. Contrary to the claims of those who suggest this refers to some "spiritual realm," God specified to Abraham what that earthly territory looked like. Once again, attention is given to the precise boundaries of the land thus promised. Never rescinded, the Lord reiterated this promise so that His people would know that He keeps His word.

47:13. Joseph shall have two portions. Since the tribe of Levi received none (44:28), Ephraim and Manasseh (Joseph's two sons adopted by Jacob, Gen. 48:17–20) each received an allotment (see 48:4–5).

47:14. Which I lifted up my hand to give. This is a reference to the covenant made with Abram (Gen. 15:9–21; see Ezek. 20:5; 36:28).

47:15. This shall be the border. This approximates Israel's borders at the time of David and Solomon, except that the region across the Jordan is not included (see 47:18), which, in any event, was never within the boundaries of the Promised Land proper. The following specified boundaries closely resemble those in Numbers 34:1–12. **Way of Hethlon.** This is probably situated on the Mediterranean coast, somewhere in present-day Lebanon. **To Zedad.** Or "past Lebo Hamath to Zedad." Lebo probably does not mean "entrance" but should be identified with modern Lebweh, about fifteen miles northeast of Baalbek and twenty miles southwest of Kadesh on the Orontes River, near Riblah. At one time, Lebo must have served as a fortress guarding the southern route to Hamath. Perhaps the phrase should be translated "Lebo of Hamath." It is often referred to in Scripture as the northern limit of Israel (see 47:20; 48:1; Num. 13:21; 34:8; Josh. 13:5; 1 Kings 8:65; 2 Kings 14:25; Amos 6:14). Zedad is mentioned in Numbers 34:8 as one of the landmarks on the northern border of Israel, as promised by Moses and restated here.

47:16–17. Berothah. Probably to be identified with the Berothai of 2 Samuel 8:8 but otherwise unknown. **Sibraim.** Location unknown; probably the Sepharvaim of 2 Kings 17:24; 18:34. **Damascus.** Capital of Aram (Syria); according to 47:17, it was included in Israel. **Hamath.** A city about 120 miles north of Damascus on the Orontes River. **Hazar-hatticon.** Means "the middle enclosure." Its location

is unknown, but it is possibly the same as Hazar-enan (47:17).

47:18. East sea. The Dead Sea (see Joel 2:20; Zech. 14:8).

47:19. Waters of strife in Kadesh. Or "Meribath-kadesh," a district about fifty miles south of Beer-sheba, identified with Kadesh-barnea in Numbers 34:4. **The river.** The Wadi el-Arish, a deeply cut riverbed with seasonal flow that runs from the Sinai north-northwest until it enters the Mediterranean, fifty miles south of Gaza. It marked the southernmost extremity of Solomon's kingdom (see 1 Kings 8:65).

47:22. They shall be unto you as born in the country. This reflects a gracious inclusiveness that goes beyond the provision of 14:7. The same universalism is found in such prophecies as Isaiah 56:3–8.

48:1–29. The division of the land is further detailed. **Hethlon ... to the coast of Hamath** (v. 1). See 47:15. **Hazar-enan.** See 47:16. **Dan.** Occupies its historical location as the northernmost tribe (see the phrase "from Dan to Beersheba," giving northern and southern boundaries, in, e.g., Judg. 20:1; 1 Sam. 3:20). Dan was born to Rachel's maidservant Bilhah (see Gen. 35:25).

48:2. Asher was born to Leah's maidservant Zilpah (see Gen. 35:26). The tribes descended from maidservants were placed farthest from the sanctuary (see Dan, 48:1; Naphtali, 48:3; Gad, 48:27).

48:3. Naphtali. Born to Rachel's maidservant Bilhah (see 48:2).

48:4. Manasseh. See 47:13.

48:5. Ephraim. See 47:13.

48:6. Reuben. Leah's firstborn (see Gen. 29:31).

48:7. Judah. Son of Leah (see Gen. 35:23). He had the most prestigious place, bordering the central holy portion (48:8), because his tribe was given the messianic promise (see Gen. 49:8–12).

48:8–22. An expansion of 45:1–8.

48:9. Ten thousand in breadth. The width of the entire sacred district was twenty thousand cubits (see 45:1). This must refer to the width of either the priests' or the Levites' area. The Septuagint reads "twenty thousand."

48:11. Sons of Zadok; which have kept my charge. See 44:15.

48:14. Not sell of it, neither exchange. Since the land was the Lord's, it was not to be an object of commerce.

48:19. Out of all the tribes of Israel. The sacred district was national property, not the prince's private domain.

48:23. Benjamin. Rachel's son (see Gen. 35:24).

48:24. Simeon. Leah's son (see Gen. 35:23).

48:25. Issachar. Leah's son (see Gen. 35:23).

48:26. Zebulun. Leah's son (see Gen. 35:23).

48:27. Gad. Born to Leah's maidservant Zilpah (see 48:2).

48:28. Tamar. See 47:18. **Strife in Kadesh.** See 47:19. **The river.** See 47:19.

48:30–35. The gates of the city are described. This brings the reader back to the beginning of Ezekiel's prophecy concerning the city of Jerusalem, which began with the foreboding announcement of its destruction and ends with the promise of its final restoration to glory.

48:31. Reuben ... Judah ... Levi. The three most influential tribes—Reuben, the firstborn; Judah, the messianic tribe; Levi, the priestly tribe—had gates together on the north side. Since Levi was included in this list, Joseph (48:32) represented Ephraim and Manasseh (see 47:13) to keep the number at twelve. For the twelve gates, see Rev. 21:12–14.

48:35. The LORD is there. The great decisive word concerning the Holy City; the Hebrew is *Yahweh-Shammah*, possibly a wordplay on *Yerushalayim*, the Hebrew pronunciation of Jerusalem (for other names of Jerusalem, see 23:4; Isa. 1:26; 60:14; 62:2–4, 12; Jer. 3:17; 33:16; Zech. 8:3). Thus, the prophet's final prediction was that of a truly holy city when Jehovah Himself rules in Jerusalem.

THE BOOK OF DANIEL

INTRODUCTION

Author and Date

The book mentions Daniel as its author in several passages, such as 9:2 and 10:2. That Jesus concurred is clear from His reference to "the abomination of desolation, spoken of by Daniel the prophet" (Matt. 24:15), quoting 9:27; 11:31; 12:11. The book was probably completed circa 530 BC, shortly after the capture of Babylon by Cyrus in 539 BC.

Authenticity

The widely held view that the book of Daniel is largely fictional rests mainly on the modern philosophical assumption that long-range predictive prophecy is impossible. Therefore, all fulfilled predictions in Daniel, it is claimed, had to have been composed no earlier than the Maccabean period (second century BC), after the fulfillments had taken place. Objective evidence excludes this hypothesis on several counts.

(1) To avoid fulfillment of long-range predictive prophecy in the book, the adherents of the late-date view usually maintain that the four empires of chapters 2 and 7 are Babylon, Media, Persia, and Greece. In the mind of the author, "the Medes and Persians" (5:28) together constituted the second in the series of four kingdoms (2:36–43). Thus, it becomes clear that the four empires are the Babylonian, Medo-Persian, Greek, and Roman empires. See chart, *Zondervan KJV Study Bible*, p. 1226.

(2) The language itself argues for a date earlier than the second century. Linguistic evidence from the Dead Sea Scrolls (which furnish authentic samples of Hebrew and Aramaic writing from the second century BC; see "Dead Sea Scrolls," *KJV Study Bible*, p. 1345) demonstrates that the Hebrew and Aramaic chapters of Daniel must have been composed centuries earlier. Furthermore, as recently demonstrated, the Persian and Greek words in Daniel do not require a late date. Some of the technical terms appearing in chapter 3 were already so obsolete by the second century BC that translators of the Septuagint (the Greek translation of the Old Testament) translated them incorrectly.

(3) Several of the fulfillments of prophecies in Daniel could not have taken place by the second century anyway, so the prophetic element cannot be dismissed. The symbolism connected with the fourth kingdom makes it unmistakably predictive of the Roman

Empire (see 2:33; 7:7, 19), which did not take control of Syro-Palestine until 63 BC. Also, the prophecy concerning the coming of "the Messiah the Prince" 483 years after "the going forth of the commandment to restore and to build Jerusalem" (9:25) works out to the time of Jesus' ministry.

Objective evidence, therefore, appears to exclude the late-date hypothesis and indicates that there is insufficient reason to deny Daniel's authorship. The fact that Jesus Himself referred to "Daniel the prophet" (Matt. 24:15) is ample testimony of the Savior's belief that Daniel was the author of this book.

Theme and Theological Message

The theme of the book is God's sovereignty: "The most high God ruled in the kingdom of men" (5:21). Daniel's visions always show God as triumphant (7:11, 26–27; 8:25; 9:27; 11:45; 12:13). The climax of His sovereignty is described in Revelation: "The kingdoms of this world are become the kingdoms of our Lord, and of his Christ; and he shall reign forever and ever" (Rev. 11:15; compare Dan. 2:44; 7:27).

Literary Features

The book is made up primarily of historical narrative (found mainly in chaps. 1–6) and apocalyptic (revelatory) material (found mainly in chaps. 7–12). The latter may be defined as symbolic, visionary, prophetic literature, usually composed during oppressive conditions and being chiefly eschatological in theological content. Apocalyptic literature is primarily a literature of encouragement to the people of God (see Zechariah, Introduction: "Literary Features"; see also Revelation, Introduction: "Literary Features"). For the symbolic use of numbers in apocalyptic literature, see Revelation, Introduction: "Literary Features."

Outline

2. Prophecies concerning Persia and Greece (11:2–4)
3. Prophecies concerning Egypt and Syria (11:5–35)
4. Prophecies concerning the Antichrist (11:36–45)
5. Promise of the Resurrection (chap. 12)

Bibliography

Culver, Robert D. *Daniel and the Latter Days.* Chicago: Moody, 1977.

Kalafian, Michael. *The Prophecy of the Seventy Weeks of Daniel.* Lanham, MD: University Press of America, 1991.

Miller, Stephen R. *Daniel.* New American Commentary 18. Nashville: Broadman & Holman, 1994.

Walvoord, John F. *Daniel: The Key to Prophetic Revelation.* Chicago: Moody, 1971.

Whitcomb, John C. *Daniel.* Everyman's Bible Commentary. Chicago: Moody, 1985.

Wilson, Robert D. *Studies in the Book of Daniel.* 2 vols. Grand Rapids, MI: Baker, 1972.

Wood, Leon. *A Commentary on Daniel.* Grand Rapids, MI: Zondervan, 1973.

EXPOSITION

I. Prologue: The Setting (chap. 1; in Hebrew)

A. Historical Introduction (1:1–2)

Like most of the Old Testament prophets, Daniel began his account by stating who he was and the time in which he lived. The opening verses focus on the first Babylonian invasion of Jerusalem, led by Nebuchadnezzar in August 605 BC.

1:1. Third year. According to the Babylonian system of computing the years of a king's reign, the third year of Jehoiakim would have been 605 BC, since his first full year of kingship began on New Year's Day after his accession in 608 BC. But according to the Judahite system, which counted the year of accession as the first year of reign, this was the fourth year of Jehoiakim (Jer. 25:1; 46:2; see Whitcomb, *Daniel*, pp. 21–26).

1:2. Carried into. Judah was exiled to Babylonia because she had disobeyed God's word regarding keeping the covenant, observing the Sabbath years, and forsaking idolatry (see Lev. 25:1–7; 26:27–35; 2 Chron. 36:14–21). The first deportation (605 BC) included Daniel, and the second (597 BC) included

Ezekiel. A third deportation took place in 586 BC, when the Babylonians destroyed Jerusalem and the temple. **Vessels of the house of God** were the sacred items used for worship in the Jewish temple. **House of his god** probably refers to the temple of Marduk, a Babylonian deity.

B. Daniel and His Friends Are Taken Captive (1:3–7)

1:3. The king's seed were children from the royal family of Judah who were taken captive as "intellectual hostages" and forced to study in Babylon for three years (1:5) in preparation for government service under the new regime.

1:4. The learning and the tongue of the Chaldeans. Including the classical literature in Sumerian and Akkadian cuneiform, a complicated syllabic writing system. The language of normal communication in multiracial Babylon was Aramaic, written in an easily learned alphabetic script (see 2:4 and discussion). "Chaldean" is an ethnic term used for Babylonians, but it is also used to designate a special class of wise men who served as priests (Herodotus, *Persian Wars* 1.181–83).

1:6. Daniel means "God is [my] Judge." **Hananiah** means "the Lord shows grace." **Mishael** means "who is what God is?" **Azariah** means "the Lord helps."

1:7. In Babylonian, **Belteshazzar** probably means "Bel [i.e., Marduk], protect his life!" **Shadrach** probably means "command of Aku [the Sumerian moon god]." **Meshach** probably means "who is what Aku is?" **Abed-nego** means "servant of Nego/Nebo [i.e., Nabu]." In essence, their new Babylonian names were the equivalent of their Hebrew names with the exception of the names of deity. The purpose of the name change was to replace their Hebrew nationalism with a Babylonian identification in an attempt to assimilate them into the Babylonian system. Because of Daniel's longevity, he and his friends are generally considered to have been teenagers at the time of their abduction. Their names are the only names to have survived of all the captives because they alone stood for God in this unique time of testing.

C. The Young Men Are Faithful (1:8–21).

1:8. The king's meat ... wine. Israelites considered food from Nebuchadnezzar's table to be contaminated because the first portion of it was offered to idols. Likewise, a portion of the wine was poured out on a pagan altar. Ceremonially unclean animals were used, and they were neither slaughtered nor prepared according to the regulations of Jewish law. Whatever the problem was with the food and wine, they were considered by these Jewish teenagers to be "unclean" (not kosher). **But Daniel purposed in his heart** not to defile himself. This one statement is the key to the entire book in general and to Daniel's character in particular. Daniel demonstrated the courage of his convictions and set the example for his three friends to follow.

1:12. Prove thy servants. Daniel used good judgment and practical discernment by offering a creative alternative instead of rebelling against the command to eat at the king's table.

Pulse (Hebrew, *zeroim*) refers to "grain" or "vegetables." Daniel was not only refusing to eat the king's food but may have also refused to share a meal with pagans that involved ritual defilement.

1:14. Proved them ten days. The testing period was limited to ten days, but the successful outcome probably meant that Daniel and his friends continued this discipline for the entire three years of their training.

1:17. God gave them ... wisdom. With God's help, Daniel and his friends mastered the Babylonian literature on astrology and divination by dreams. In the crucial tests of interpretation and prediction (see 2:3–11; 4:7), all the pagan literature proved worthless. Only by God's special revelation (2:17–28) was Daniel able to interpret correctly.

1:19–20. The king communed with them (v. 19). Nebuchadnezzar himself conducted the "final exam" at the end of the training program. **Ten times better** (v. 20) may be hyperbole, but it certainly indicates the intellectual superiority of these faithful servants of God. **Magicians and astrologers** are specifically pointed out as being inferior to the God-given wisdom of the four Hebrew students. "Magician" (Hebrew, *hartom*) is also used of the Egyptian magicians in the times of Joseph (Gen. 41:8) and Moses (Exod. 7:11). They were religious scribes who employed sacred rituals to heal diseases, predict the future, or pronounce omens or curses (Miller, *Daniel*, p. 72). "Astrologers" (Hebrew, *assap*) were incantation priests who read the stars to interpret one's fate. These astrological "enchanters" were believed to be able to communicate with the spirit world and thus determine the future.

1:21. The first year of king Cyrus was 539 BC, which would have made Daniel eighty-five to ninety years old by that time. The point of this passage is that Daniel lived through the entire Babylonian captivity and was still alive when Cyrus the Persian conquered Babylon. The reference to the "first year" of Cyrus need not be regarded as contradicting 10:1, which is dated to the "third year" of Cyrus (537 BC). The emphasis in 1:21 is that Daniel lived at least until Cyrus's first year, when he conquered Babylon and set in motion the processes that would eventually lead to the Jews return from their exile to Babylon.

Miller (*Daniel*, p. 74) observes that Daniel "exemplifies active service in governmental affairs under divine leadership." The experiences of Daniel and his friends point to the proper balance between one's faithfulness to God and one's faithful service to society in general. Daniel is thus the epitome of a believer who succeeded at the highest levels of political and social involvement without compromising his biblical standards and personal convictions.

II. The Destinies of the Nations of the World (chaps. 2–7; in Aramaic, beginning at 2:4b)

A. Nebuchadnezzar's Dream of a Great Image (chap. 2)

2:1. The second year of … Nebuchadnezzar could refer to the second chronological year of his reign (604 BC) or to the second inclusive year (603 BC). Daniel and his friends were either still involved in the three-year training program or just about to complete it when the incident in this chapter occurred. Either way, as students, they were implicated in their teachers' failure.

2:3. To know the dream means to know the meaning of the dream. Nebuchadnezzar had not forgotten what he had dreamed (see discussion on 2:5). He simply wanted to know what it meant.

2:4. Syriack. Or "Aramaic." Since the astrologers were of various racial backgrounds, they communicated in Aramaic, the language everyone understood. From here to the end of chapter 7, the entire narrative is in Aramaic. These six chapters deal with matters of importance to the Gentile nations of the Near East and were written in a language understandable to all. The last five chapters (8–12) revert to Hebrew, since they deal with special concerns of the chosen people. Portions of Ezra (4:8–6:18 and 7:12–26) were also written in Aramaic.

2:5. The thing is gone from me. The KJV rendering has led many to assume that the "thing" is the dream and that, therefore, Nebuchadnezzar had forgotten what he had dreamed. However, the Aramaic term *millah* refers to the "word" or "command." The Aramaic *azda* (KJV, "gone from me") means "certain" or "assured." Thus, the proper translation should read: "The word [command] is certain." In

colloquial English, it might say, "I meant what I said." Whitcomb (*Daniel*, p. 40) comments: "Far from forgetting the dream … it was vivid in his memory as a measuring stick against which to determine the claims of his wise men."

2:6–9. The protests of the wise men expose the fraudulent claims of astrology, sorcery, and trickery. They hoped to gain **time** (v. 8) until the king told them the nature of the dream so they could make up an interpretation to go with it.

2:10–11. There is not a man upon the earth (v. 10). Only God in heaven could reveal such a secret. The Babylonian gods were distant and removed from the affairs of men. Thus, their **dwelling is not with flesh** (v. 11). This indicates that the astrologers believed the gods could not be bothered with such trivial matters. In reality, it was an admission of their failure to communicate with the divine.

2:12–13. Nebuchadnezzar responded angrily to the excuses of the wise men and ordered their immediate execution. The death sentence apparently affected the students as well. Thus, **they sought Daniel and his fellows** (v. 13) to be executed as well.

2:14–18. Daniel's character is revealed by the fact that he **answered with counsel and wisdom** (v. 14). The Aramaic text implies that he responded "tactfully" or "appropriately." Daniel asked his three friends, whose Hebrew names were **Hananiah, Mishael, and Azariah** (v. 17), to pray and **desire mercies** from **the God of heaven** (a common designation Hebrews used at that time to describe the God of the Bible; v. 18; see Ezra 1:2; 6:10; 7:12, 21; Neh. 1:5; 2:4).

2:19–23. The secret (Aramaic, *raz*; v. 19) is translated "mystery" (Greek, *mysterion*) in the Septuagint. It refers to the contents of the dream, which remained a "mystery" to the astrologers but was revealed to Daniel **in a night vision** (Aramaic, *hezu*). In response, Daniel praised **the name of God** (v. 20), which is synonymous with the person of God in Hebrew reasoning. The poetic beauty of this prayer forms a psalm of thanksgiving to God. It especially emphasizes the sovereignty of God over the **kings** (v. 21) of the earth and His superiority over the wise men of earth. In essence, Daniel acknowledged that divine **wisdom** (v. 23) was necessary in revealing the secret meaning of the king's dream.

2:24–28. I will shew unto the king the interpretation (Aramaic, *peshar*; "to explain"; v. 24). Daniel volunteered to tackle the king's request and promised to succeed where the astrologers had failed. **Belteshazzar** (v. 26) was Daniel's Babylonian name, so he is addressed as such by the Babylonian king. **There is a God in heaven** (v. 28) is Daniel's way of correcting the pagan king's theology about which God is indeed the true God. Daniel did not call Him the "God of Israel" but rather the "God in heaven," who is sovereign over all nations.

2:29–31. Daniel proceeded to explain to Nebuchadnezzar that he was about to show him **what shall come to pass** (v. 29). In other words, he was going to reveal the future regarding the prophetic symbolism contained in the king's vision of the **great image** (metallic statue; v. 31). Its appearance was **terrible** (Aramaic, *dehil*), or "awesome" or "frightful." Miller (*Daniel*, p. 91) notes, "The huge image would have stood like a dazzling colossus before the king."

2:32–35. The **head ... of fine gold** (v. 32) represents the Neo-Babylonian Empire (2:38; see Jer. 51:7); the **silver** chest of **arms**, the Medo-Persian Empire established by Cyrus in 539 BC (the date of the fall of Babylon); the **thighs of brass**, the Greek Empire established by Alexander the Great circa 330 BC; the **legs of iron** (v. 33), the Roman Empire. The "toes" (2:41) are understood by some to represent a later confederation of states occupying the territory formerly controlled by the Roman Empire. The diminishing value of the metals from gold to silver to brass to iron represents the decreasing power and grandeur (2:39) of the rulers of the successive empires, from the absolute despotism of Nebuchadnezzar to the democratic system of checks and balances that characterized the Roman senates and assemblies. Each successive empire lasted longer than the preceding one. The **feet ... of iron and clay** represent a final, weakened form of the Roman Empire in the last days. The **stone ... cut out without hands** (v. 34) represents the kingdom of God, which is of divine,

not human, origin. Notice that the stone fell on the **feet** of the statue, indicating that the final form of the kingdom of God will not replace human governments until they are catastrophically destroyed at the second coming of Christ. The **great mountain** (v. 35) is the millennial kingdom, which will fill **the whole earth** when Christ returns.

2:36–43. The interpretation (v. 36) was given by Daniel and his friends (see chart, *KJV Study Bible*, p. 1226). **Thou art this head of gold** (v. 38) applied to Nebuchadnezzar himself. After his death, the Babylonian Empire deteriorated rapidly and eventually fell to **another kingdom** (Media-Persia; v. 39). Then **a third kingdom** (Greece) would extend its rule **over all the earth**. **The fourth kingdom** (Rome; v. 40) remains unnamed in the book of Daniel since the Roman Empire did not actually exist at that time. The two legs of **iron** symbolize the obvious division of the empire into East (Constantinople) and West (Rome). The mixture of **iron, and ... clay** (v. 42) is weak and will cause the statue to become unstable. The weight of the metals make it too heavy. Thus, it will be easily crushed by the falling "stone" (the kingdom of God; v. 45).

2:44–45. In the days of these kings (v. 44) refers to the ten toes of the feet of the statue. Only then, during the final phase of human government, will God set up His kingdom on earth. Whitcomb (*Daniel*, p. 47) notes: "At the second coming of Christ, there will be no absorbing, adapting, modifying, merging or restructuring of previous kingdoms." As a result, every trace of humanistic influence will be removed from the kingdom of God on earth. Premillennialists believe this reality can only happen when Christ returns to set up His kingdom on earth (Revelation 19–20). Daniel finished his explanation of the dream by assuring the king that it was **certain** (Aramaic, *yattib*; "certain to occur"; v. 45) and **sure** (Aramaic, *yatstsib*; "true" or "trustworthy"). Miller (*Daniel*, p. 102) observes: "The prophecies of Daniel concerning past events (the four empires) have been accurately fulfilled, and his inspired messages concerning events yet future will just as assuredly occur."

2:46–49. Nebuchadnezzar responded with great adoration for Daniel and praise to his God, but his response fell far short of saving faith. In his pagan confusion, he **worshipped Daniel** (v. 46) and praised his God as **a God of gods** (v. 47). The king was impressed that Daniel's God could reveal such predictions and promoted Daniel and his friends **over the whole province of Babylon** (v. 48) and **over all the wise men of Babylon**. Thus, the students became greater than their teachers because they sought the Lord.

B. Daniel's Friends in the Furnace of Fire (chap. 3)

3:1. In arrogance and pride, Nebuchadnezzar apparently let the interpretation of the "head of gold" in his dream go to his head. Some time later, he built **an image of gold**. Large statues of this kind were not made of solid gold but were plated with gold. The **height was threescore cubits**, ninety feet, including the lofty pedestal on which it no doubt stood. **Dura.** Either the name of a place now marked by a series of mounds (located a few miles south of Babylon) or a common noun meaning "walled enclosure."

3:2. The seven classifications of government officials were to pledge full allegiance to the newly established empire as they stood before the image Nebuchadnezzar had built. The image probably represented the god Nabu, whose name formed the first element in Nebuchadnezzar's name (in Akkadian, *Nabu-kudurri-usur*, meaning "Nabu, protect my son!" or "Nabu, protect my boundary!").

3:5. The words for "harp," "psaltery," and "dulcimer" are the only Greek loanwords in Daniel. Greek musicians and instruments are mentioned in Assyrian inscriptions written before the time of Nebuchadnezzar. The Babylonian monarch seems to have imported the latest "band" from Europe (Greece) to play at the dedication of the statue. The constant repetition of terms in these verses is typical of Middle Eastern thought and expression.

3:6. Burning fiery furnace. Probably a brick kiln, used in ancient Iraq to fire clay bricks for construction of buildings, walls, and monuments, such

as the one described here. It is evident later that this "furnace" had both an opening in the top (3:19–23) and in the side (3:25–26).

3:8. Certain Chaldeans … accused the Jews. Everything about the details of this story implies anti-Semitism toward the Jewish minority which, despite their positions, were still living in captivity in a hostile land.

3:12. They serve not thy gods indicates that the statue was considered to be that of a deity. The refusal of the three Hebrews was viewed as both religious apostasy and civil disobedience.

3:15–18. If ye be ready … but if ye worship not (v. 15) represents both a threat and a challenge by the Babylonian king. He was apparently surprised by the resistance of his three trusted assistants and offered them a second chance to make amends. Notice, they responded with their own contrasting challenge: **If it be so, our God … is able to deliver us** (v. 17) … **But if not** (v. 18). They completely trusted God to deliver them, but even if He does not choose to do so, they were determined to remain faithful to Him.

3:19. The temperature was controlled by the number of bellows forcing air into the fire chamber. Therefore, sevenfold intensification was probably achieved by seven bellows pumping at the same time. The expression **seven times more** may have been figurative for "as hot as possible." Regardless, the fire was so hot, it slew the soldiers who threw them into it (3:22), presumably through the opening in the top, which was designed to release excess heat and smoke.

3:24–27. Nebuchadnezzar was able to look into the furnace from ground level, presumably through a side door, where the pallets of bricks would have been slid into the furnace by workmen. From there, he saw **four men … walking in the midst of the fire** (v. 25). His description of the fourth man is translated **the Son of God** but is rendered "Son of the gods" (*elhanin*) in Aramaic (see NIV). Miller (*Daniel*, p. 123) notes: "Nebuchadnezzar was polytheistic and had no conception of the Christian Trinity. Thus the pagan king only meant that the fourth figure in the fire was divine." In fact, he calls him an "angel" in 3:28. Whitcomb (*Daniel*, p. 60) observes: "In view of the fact that the pre-incarnate Christ had previously appeared in a burning bush (Exod. 3) and had ascended in a flame of fire (Judges 13), there is no biblical reason He could not have been the one who appeared in the furnace with these men."

3:28–30. The king addressed **Shadrach, Meshach, and Abed-nego** (v. 28) by their Babylonian names. Their survival and subsequent release was typical of the concept of "trial by ordeal" in ancient Babylonian law codes. According to their own laws and culture, Babylonians considered people to be innocent if they survived or escaped from punishment. Daniel's absence from this chapter may easily be explained by the fact that he was at times sent out of town (perhaps deliberately in this case) on official government business (see 8:2).

C. Nebuchadnezzar's Dream of an Enormous Tree (chap. 4)

4:1–3. These verses serve as an introduction to the testimony of Nebuchadnezzar, which follows in 4:4–18. The Septuagint rendering omits this introduction, but the Massoretic text retains it. Theologians have debated whether or not the king's experiences resulted in his personal conversion. Walvoord (*Daniel*, p. 95) calls it the "climax of Nebuchadnezzar's spiritual biography." The fourth chapter is written in the form of a decree, which records three elements: (1) Nebuchadnezzar's dream, (2) Daniel's interpretation, and (3) the king's subsequent response.

4:4–7. My palace (v. 4). Nebuchadnezzar himself is credited by historians as having been the great builder of Babylon, with its palaces, monuments, gates, hanging gardens, double-walled fortress, 360 battle towers, marble-paved procession way, and 288-foot ziggurat (stepped pyramid). **Dream which made me afraid** (v. 5). Unlike the previous dream, which had aroused his curiosity, this one frightened the aging monarch.

4:8. But at the last Daniel came in. It seems strange that Nebuchadnezzar would call in Daniel after consulting with the magicians and astrologers

(4:7). It may be that he was actually afraid to know the real meaning of the dream.

4:9. Belteshazzar, meaning "Bel [i.e., the god Marduk] protect his life," was Daniel's Babylonian name, by which he was officially addressed in the royal court. **Master of the magicians** simply means that Daniel was the "chief counselor" or "advisor" to the king and, therefore, was over the "university" (training program) of which he had previously been a student. **Spirit of the holy gods** may also be translated "spirit of the holy God." The context is unclear as to which Nebuchadnezzar meant in his yet unconverted state.

4:10–18. The king recounted the details of his dream about a **great ... tree** (v. 10), which he would later learn was the symbol of his kingdom, which was about to be cut down. Babylon is compared to a spreading tree in one of Nebuchadnezzar's building inscriptions. **A watcher and a holy one** (v. 13) refers to an angelic messenger. **Leave the stump** (v. 15) implies the tree would later be revived. **Seven times** (v. 16) refers to "seven years" during which the prophecy was fulfilled while Nebuchadnezzar was "cut down" by temporary insanity.

4:19–27. Daniel ... was astonished (v. 19). Despite being a Jewish captive, Daniel was very loyal to Nebuchadnezzar and was upset by the meaning of the dream. **The tree ... It is thou** (vv. 20, 22) refers to Nebuchadnezzar. **The interpretation** (v. 24) indicated that the king would be afflicted with insanity (generally believed to be a form of lycanthropy; "wolf man" disease). The monarch would actually believe that he was a wild animal, and this insane behavior would continue for seven years. This condition would persist until the king acknowledged that **the Most High** God **ruleth** (v. 25) over human kings and kingdoms. **Leave the stump** (v. 26) indicates that the kingdom would not be lost during this period of time. The appeal to **break off thy sins by righteousness** (v. 27) means to repent (Aramaic, *peruq*) of one's sins and renounce them.

4:28–33. Twelve months (v. 29) later, the king had not repented, and the prophesied judgment **came upon** (v. 28) him. **There fell a voice from heaven** (v. 31), or divine pronouncement. **Driven**

from men (v. 33) indicates that his behavior became so bizarre that he had to be locked up for his and their protection.

4:34–37. At the end of the days (v. 34) refers to the end of the "seven times" (4:25), or seven years. The king's sanity returned when he turned his **eyes unto heaven** and admitted that God alone ruled over the kingdoms of men. His repentance led to his restoration for the duration of his reign, which ended with his death in 562 BC.

D. Fall of Babylon (chap. 5)

5:1. Belshazzar the king. Nebuchadnezzar died in 562 BC after reigning for forty-three years. Ancient Babylonian records indicate that he was succeeded in order by Evil-Merodach, Neriglisar, Labashi-Marduk, and finally his son-in-law, Nabonidus, who had married Nebuchadnezzar's daughter Nitocris. This account focuses on their son, Belshazzar, who ruled as a coregent with his father, Nabonidus. Nebuchadnezzar is called his "father," but the Aramaic term is quite indefinite and can also mean "grandfather," "ancestor," or even "predecessor." See Walvoord (*Daniel*, pp. 70–74) for archaeological details (for example, the Nabonidus Chronicle) that verify the historicity of Belshazzar's reign.

5:2–4. Golden and silver vessels (v. 2) were the worship vessels from Solomon's temple, which Nebuchadnezzar destroyed in 586 BC. The orgy, revelry, and blasphemy that occurred on such occasions is confirmed by the ancient historians Herodotus and Xenophon. The date would have been October 12, 539 BC, some twenty years after the events of chapter 4. The description of false **gods of gold … silver … brass … iron** (v. 4), follows the pattern of the statue vision in chapter 2.

5:5. Fingers of a man's hand miraculously appeared during this drunken debauchery in response to the king's deliberate defiance of God and his desecration of the temple vessels. **The plaister of the wall** has been attested by archaeology. The throne room consisted of a huge chamber (170 by 56 feet) plastered with white gypsum. It was part of the royal residence, which covered 350 by 200 yards.

5:7. The third ruler in the kingdom. Belshazzar was technically the second ruler under his father, Nabonidus, who had already left Babylon and moved to Teima in Arabia. Thus, "third ruler" was the highest position he could offer anyone who could read the handwriting on the wall. This designation is significant in light of the absence of Belshazzar's name from ancient Babylonian king lists, which end with Nabonidus. However, Belshazzar is clearly attested in cuneiform documents known as the "Nabonidus Chronicle" and the "Persian Verse Account of Nabonidus," which clearly state that Nabonidus "entrusted the kingship" to Belshazzar.

5:10–13. The queen (v. 10) is unnamed but probably refers to the "queen mother," Amytis, Nebuchadnezzar's wife and, therefore, Belshazzar's grandmother. She had to remind the young ruler about Daniel's abilities. The king had to ask if he were **that Daniel** (v. 13) since apparently he had never met Daniel. Now an older man, Daniel was unimpressed by the king's offer to be the "third ruler" and refused his gifts.

5:18–23. Daniel reminded Belshazzar of the humiliation Nebuchadnezzar had experienced several years before and warned him of the consequences of his own rebellious attitude, even though **thou knewest all this** (v. 22). The story of Nebuchadnezzar's insanity evidently was well known among the royal family, even if it had been hidden from the general public.

5:25–28. MENE (v. 25) means "numbered." **TEKEL** means "weighed." **PERES** means "divided," as does the verbal form **UPHARSIN**. In other words, the message meant that his "number was up" and his kingdom was lacking on the scales of divine justice. The final word of the message was actually a prophecy predicting that Babylon would fall to the alliance of **the Medes and Persians** (v. 28), which it did that very night.

5:29–31. While Belshazzar drank the night away, the Medes and Persians attacked the city, surprising the guards, and great Babylon fell in one night without a fight (see Rev. 14:8). **Darius the Median** (v. 31) was a subordinate to Cyrus the Persian and may be the man referred to in ancient texts as *Gubaru*, "the governor of Babylon," who ruled Babylonia and Syria during the prolonged absence of Cyrus. For further details, see Whitcomb (*Daniel*, pp. 78–80) and Miller (*Daniel*, pp. 171–77).

E. Daniel's Deliverance from the Lion's Den (chap. 6)

6:1–3. Princes (*satraps*, "protectors"; v. 1) and **presidents** ("administrators"; v. 2). Daniel's elevation to the position of president by the Persians (ancient Iran) accords with the Iranian custom of respect and elevation of the aged. Daniel would now have been in his eighties. It also fits well with cuneiform records, which state that Gubaru appointed subordinates to help rule Babylon after Cyrus's conquest.

6:4–9. Daniel's integrity caused the other administrators great frustration, so they sought an **occasion** (well-planned conspiracy; v. 4) against him. Daniel was so honest, sincere, and genuine, they had only his devotion to **the law of his God** (v. 5) to attack. Knowing that he was a devout man of prayer, they tricked Darius into signing a law that forbade prayer **for thirty days** (v. 7) to anyone other than Darius himself. The conspirators lied in stating that **All** the royal administrators supported the proposed decree, knowing that Daniel was totally unaware of the proposal. Unfortunately, in the dual empire, **the law of the Medes and Persians** (v. 8) could not be changed, even by a king or royal governor.

6:10. Despite his loyal and faithful service, Daniel deliberately defied the law against public prayer and continued to pray at home, **his windows being open**. This reveals several things about the prayer life of the Jewish people during this time. Daniel prayed: (1) three times a day, (2) with his widows open, (3) facing Jerusalem, (4) kneeling down, (5) giving thanks. As far as Daniel was concerned, nothing had changed. His first obligation of obedience was to God, not the government.

6:11–17. Daniel's critics were quick to accuse him of breaking the newly signed law. Their attitude toward **That Daniel ... of the captivity of Judah** (v. 13) reflects deep anti-Semitism. Regardless, Darius sought **to deliver him** (v. 14) by sundown but could not. Thus, he reluctantly delivered Daniel to **the den of lions** (v. 16). Such beasts were normally half starved to incite them to kill and eat condemned victims. The king's **signet** (v. 17) was the sign of royal authority and prevented anyone from tampering with the seal to which it was affixed.

6:18–24. In the morning, Darius hurried to the lion's den to check on Daniel. He cried out **with a lamentable voice** (v. 20), fearing the worst but hoping for the best. His question, **is thy God ... able to deliver thee ...?** is reminiscent of the faith of the three Hebrews in the furnace in chapter 3. In response, Daniel announced that God's **angel** (v. 22) had **shut the lions' mouths**. The Septuagint renders the verse as though God Himself delivered Daniel. Again, the Babylonian concept of "trial by ordeal" vindicated Daniel's innocence. In response to Daniel's release, his accusers were **cast ... into the den of lions** (v. 24) and devoured in accordance with Persian custom.

6:25–28. The chapter ends with Darius's proclamation that all men should **tremble and fear before the God of Daniel** (v. 26) because He alone works **signs** (Aramaic, *atin*) **and wonders** (Aramaic, *timhin*; v. 27). The closing verse emphasizes that Daniel prospered in the reigns of Darius and Cyrus, indicating that he survived the entire Babylonian captivity.

F. Daniel's Dream of the Four Beasts (chap. 7)

7:1. The first year of Belshazzar, probably 553 BC, the first year of his coregency with Nabonidus (see chap. 5). Thus, the events in chapter 7 actually preceded those of chapter 5. This is the first of several visions that Daniel himself received in chapters 7–12.

7:3. Four great beasts represent four Gentile empires that would rule the known world in succession, each one controlling the fate of the Jewish people.

7:4–7. The **lion** (v. 4) with an eagle's wings symbolized the Neo-Babylonian Empire. The rest of verse 4 perhaps reflects the humbling experience of Nebuchadnezzar, as recorded in chapter 4. The **bear** (v. 5), raised up on one of its sides, refers to the superior status of the Persians in the Medo-Persian federation. The **three ribs** may represent the three principal conquests: Lydia (546 BC), Babylon (539 BC), and Egypt (525 BC). The **leopard** (v. 6) with **four wings** represents the speedy conquests of Alexander the Great (334–330 BC), and the **four heads** correspond to the four main divisions into which his empire fell after his untimely death in 323 BC (see 8:22): Macedon and Greece (under Antipater and Cassander), Thrace and Asia Minor (under Lysimachus), Syria (under Seleucus I), the Holy Land and Egypt (under Ptolemy I). The **fourth** unnamed **beast** (v. 7), with its irresistible power and surpassing all its predecessors, points to the Roman Empire. Its **ten horns** correspond to the ten toes of 2:41–42.

7:8. A **little horn** came **up among them** (the "ten horns," 7:7). Many commentators believe this to be the future Antichrist. That he is said to come up "among" the ten horns indicates that he will rise to power in the future along with these ten, **three** of whom he will subdue. His **eyes** refer to his intelligence, and his **mouth** refers to his persuasive nature.

7:9–10. Thrones were cast down (v. 9) refers to the collapse of human governments, as in 2:35. **The Ancient of days** is the eternal God, who gives the kingdom to the "Son of Man" in 7:13. The **fiery stream** (v. 10) represents the power, purity, and authority of God (see Ps. 97:3; Rev. 1:14–15). **The judgment** appears to be the great white throne judgment (see Rev. 20:11–15). **The books** are the record of human deeds by which judgment is determined. These books are not to be confused with the Book of Life, which records the names of all the saved (see Rev. 20:12–15).

7:11–12. The fate of the Antichrist is described as **the beast was slain** (v. 11) and cast into **the burning flame**. Revelation 19:20 describes this as "the beast" that was "cast alive into a lake of fire." These two statements may be harmonized by recognizing that the Antichrist will be defeated at the return of Christ and cast into the lake of fire without trial (i.e., prior to the great white throne judgment).

7:13–14. The Son of Man (v. 13) is Christ (see Rev. 1:13). This is the first reference to the Messiah as "the Son of Man," a title Jesus applied to Himself. He will be enthroned as Ruler over the whole earth, previously misruled by the four kingdoms of men. The extent of His earthly kingdom will include **all people, nations, and languages** (v. 14). His **everlasting dominion** speaks of His eternal kingdom, which begins on earth and extends into all eternity.

7:15–16. Daniel was grieved (v. 15) and **troubled**, seeking the **interpretation** (v. 16) of these things. From Daniel's perspective, he was realizing that it would be many centuries before the Messiah would eventually rule on earth—after the succession of the four kingdoms.

7:17–25. The **beasts** (v. 17) are clearly defined as human **kings. The saints of the most High** (v. 18) are the "holy ones" who will inherit **the kingdom**. Then Daniel inquired further about **the fourth beast** (v. 19), **the ten horns** (v. 20), and **the other** (eleventh) horn. The explanation given makes it clear that the "little horn" will arise **after** (v. 24) the ten and that the ten came out of the fourth beast, connecting each element to the Roman system. That the eleventh horn **made war with the saints** (v. 21) foreshadows the Antichrist's attack on the Jewish people. **Time and times and the dividing of time** (v. 25) refers to the three and a half years of the great tribulation (see Rev. 12:14; 13:1–10).

7:26–28. Whitcomb (*Daniel*, p. 105) notes: "The thoroughness of the Antichrist's destruction here parallels the effect of the crushing Stone of Daniel 2." Only when Christ returns in triumph will **the greatness of the kingdom** (v. 27) be fully realized on earth. The final assurance of this future vision is called **the end of the matter** (v. 28). Daniel was stunned, yet he **kept the matter in** his **heart**.

III. Destiny of the Nation of Israel (chaps. 8–12; in Hebrew)

A. Daniel's Vision of a Ram and a Goat (chap. 8)

8:1–2. At this point, the text of Daniel reverts back to Hebrew since the content of these visions deals specifically with the future of the nation of Israel and the Jewish people in particular. **The third year** (v. 1) of Belshazzar's reign (coregency) was 551 BC. These events preceded those of chapter 5. **Shushan** (or Susa; v. 2) was the main city in **the province of Elam**, near the Persian Gulf. It is the same place where events in the books of Esther and Nehemiah took place. The **Ulai** canal is now the Lower Karun River.

8:3-4. The **ram** (v. 3) represents the Medo-Persian Empire (8:20). The longer of its **two horns** reflects the predominant position of Persia. The ram is pictured as being in the east and **pushing westward** (v. 4). The Persians eventually encountered the Greeks as they moved west across Asia Minor.

8:5-7. The **he goat** (v. 5) represents Greece, which is depicted as coming **from the west**, headed east. That it **touched not the ground** implies the Greeks' rapid conquest of the Persians. The **notable horn** symbolizes Alexander the Great, the leader of the Greek armies, referred to as "the first king" (8:21). He conquered the known world from Greece to India in the ten years between 334 and 324 BC.

8:8. The great horn was broken refers to the untimely death of Alexander at the height of his power, in 323 BC. Interestingly, Alexander died in Babylon. The **four notable ones** refer to his four generals (Antigonus, Ptolemy, Cassander, and Lysimachus, known as the *Diadochoi*, "successors") who divided the empire after his death.

8:9. Antigonus eventually lost control of Babylon, Syria, and Israel to Seleucus I Nicator, the first of the "kings of the north" listed in chapter 11. Over a hundred years later, out of the Seleucid dynasty, came the **little horn**, Antiochus IV Epiphanes (175-164 BC). Whitcomb (*Daniel*, p. 111) notes: "He is the 'despicable person' of 11:21 and one of the greatest persecutors Israel has ever known."

8:10-12. The "little horn" (Antiochus IV) emerged, not from the ten horns belonging to the fourth kingdom (as in 7:8), but rather from one of the four horns belonging to the third kingdom. During the last few years of his reign (168-164 BC), Antiochus made a determined effort to destroy the

Jewish faith. He in turn served as a type of the even more ruthless beast of the last days, who is also referred to in 7:8 as "another little horn." Antiochus extended his power over Israel, "the pleasant land" (8:9; see Jer. 3:19), and defeated the godly believers there (referred to as **the host of heaven**; v. 10; see also v. 12), many of whom died for their faith. Then he set himself up to be the equal of God (**the prince of the host**; v. 11) and ordered the daily sacrifices to end. Eventually the army of Judas Maccabeus recaptured Jerusalem and rededicated the temple (8:14) to the Lord (December 165 BC), which is the origin of the Feast of Hanukkah (see John 10:22), still celebrated by Jewish people today (see also 1 Maccabees 1-4).

8:14. There were two daily sacrifices for the continual burnt offering (9:21; Exod. 29:38-42), representing the atonement required for Israel as a whole. The **two thousand and three hundred** evenings and mornings may refer to the number of sacrifices consecutively offered on 1,150 days, the interval between the desecration of the Lord's altar and its reconsecration by Judas Maccabeus on Kislev 25, 165 BC. Others believe the 2,300 days represent the six years (170-164 BC) from the beginning of Antiochus's intrusions into Jerusalem until he was finally expelled.

8:16-17. Gabriel (v. 16) is the messenger angel, first mentioned here in Scripture. He is also the revealer of the "seventy sevens" prophecy (chap. 9) and the angel who later announced the births of John the Baptist (Luke 1:19) and Jesus (Luke 1:26-38). The term **son of man** (v. 17) is used here of Daniel, as it was also of Ezekiel, to emphasize his humanity. **Time of the end** refers to the distant future.

8:18-22. Gabriel put Daniel into a **deep sleep** (Hebrew, *radam*; "trance"; v. 18) and gave him the explanation of the symbolism of the vision. **The ram** (v. 20) is **Media and Persia**. **The rough goat** (v. 21) is **Grecia** (Hebrew, *Yavan*). Thus, with this explanation, the reader knows the exact identity of the first three Gentile empires depicted in chapters 2 and 7.

8:23-27. Transgressors (Hebrew, *happoshe'im*; "rebels"; v. 23) may refer to Jews who have forsaken God. The **king of fierce countenance** refers to the merciless attitude of Antiochus. **Understanding dark sentences** refers to his being a "master of intrigue" (NIV). **The holy people** (v. 24) refers to devout Jews. **The Prince of princes** (v. 25) is God Himself. Miller (*Daniel*, p. 235) states: "Antiochus was a proud, self-exalting ruler (whose) ... coins were inscribed *theos epiphanies* ('God manifest')." But in the end, he would **be broken**. Antiochus died in 163 BC having lost control of Jerusalem and Judea.

B. Daniel's Prayer and His Vision of the Seventy "Weeks" (chap. 9)

9:1–2. Daniel's amazing prophecy of the future of Israel is introduced. **The first year of Darius** (v. 1), 539 BC, refers to the seventy years of the Babylonian captivity, predicted by **Jeremiah the prophet** (v. 2; Jer. 25:11). As Daniel was reading Jeremiah's prophecy, he realized the seventy years of exile were almost over, so he began praying fervently for Israel's deliverance.

9:3–9. Daniel's prayer contained humility (v. 3), worship (v. 4), confession (vv. 5–9; 9:10–15), and petition (9:16–19). It is one of the longest and most sincere prayers recorded in the Old Testament. Daniel's use of **fasting, and sackcloth, and ashes** (v. 3) emphasizes his deep humility and contrition. Miller (*Daniel*, p. 243) notes that the intensity of this prayer is expressed by frequent Hebrew cohortatives and emphatic imperatives. Daniel prayed, **We have sinned** (v. 5); he was personally expressing Israel's corporate guilt before God. He listed the nation's failures as sin, iniquity, wickedness, rebellion, and apostasy ("departing"). His confession included both **Judah** (v. 7) and Israel. Thus, **all Israel** was guilty before God.

9:10–19. Israel's sin had caused them to come under **the curse** (v. 11) of the law (see Deuteronomy 28). They had rejected God by failing to pray, repent, or understand (v. 13). **The LORD watched upon the evil** (v. 14) means that He held it in reserve for such a judgment as Judah had experienced. Daniel admitted that they deserved the judgment of God, but he prayed for God's anger to **be turned away**

from ... Jerusalem, thy holy mountain (Zion; v. 16) and for Him **to shine upon thy sanctuary that is desolate** (i.e., Solomon's temple; v. 17). Daniel concluded his prayer with a series of imperative pleas: **hear** (v. 18), see, **behold ... forgive** (v. 19), **hearken and do.**

9:20–23. The holy mountain (v. 20) refers to Mount Zion in Jerusalem. **Fly swiftly** (v. 21) is a rare reference to an angel actually flying (see Isa. 6:2). **Evening oblation** is a reference to the "evening sacrifice." Even though the temple had been destroyed years earlier, Daniel still recognized this time (usually around 4:00 p.m.) as the hour of prayer for the Jewish people. **Skill** (Hebrew, *sakal*, "insight") **and understanding** (Hebrew, *binah*; "clarity"; v. 22) indicate that the answer to Daniel's prayer would clarify the purposes of God in dealing with Israel, for whom he had prayed so fervently. **Greatly beloved** (Hebrew, *hamudot*; "counted precious") indicates God's favor toward Daniel, the recipient of this important revelation.

9:24. The prophecy of the **seventy weeks** is the most detailed chronological prophecy in the Old Testament. It indicates the exact amount of time that would pass until the coming of the Messiah. "Weeks" refer to "sevens" (Hebrew, *shavuah*), or seven-year periods of time, making a total of 490 years. Of the six purposes mentioned (all to be fulfilled through the Messiah), some believe that the last three were not achieved by the crucifixion and resurrection of Christ but await His further action: the establishment of everlasting righteousness (on earth), the complete fulfillment of vision and prophecy, and the anointing of **the most Holy** (either "the most holy place" or "the most holy One").

9:25–27. The time between **the commandment** (decree; v. 25) authorizing the rebuilding of Jerusalem and the coming of the Messiah ("the Anointed One") was to be sixty-nine (7 plus 62) "weeks," or 483 years (see discussion on Ezra 7:11). The **seven weeks** may refer to the period of the complete restoration of Jerusalem (partially narrated in Ezra and Nehemiah) and the **threescore and two weeks** (vv. 25–26) to the period between that restoration and the Messiah's coming to Israel. The final "week," the Seventieth Week, is not mentioned specifically until verse 27, following the prophecy of the destruction of Jerusalem by **the people of the prince that shall come** (the Romans, who destroyed the second temple in AD 70; v. 26). Therefore, while many hold that the Seventieth Week was fulfilled during Christ's earthly ministry and the years immediately following, others conclude that there is an indeterminate interval between the sixty-ninth week and the Seventieth Week—a period of **war** and **desolations** (see 11:31, 32; 12:11; Matt. 24:9–28). According to this latter opinion, in the Seventieth Week, the little horn, or the Beast (Antichrist), of the last days (referred to in **for the overspreading of abominations he shall make it desolate**; v. 27) will establish a covenant for seven years with the Jews but will violate the agreement halfway through that period. This latter view fits with the fact that the **Messiah** will be **cut off** (killed; v. 26) after sixty-nine sevens (483 years), leaving the final seven years (the Seventieth Week) to be fulfilled in the future. See Kalafian, Miller, Walvoord, and Whitcomb for various solutions to dating the 483 years, which ended with the crucifixion of Christ.

C. Daniel's Vision of Israel's Future (chaps. 10–12)

1. Revelation of Things to Come (10:1–11:1)

10:1. The third year of Cyrus refers to the third year after his conquest of Babylon, thus 536 BC. This is the last date to appear in Daniel's writing. The Babylonian captivity was about to end officially, and the Jews would be free to return home by 535 BC. **The time appointed was long** means that it would be a long time before all these events would unfold.

10:2. Three full weeks is literally "three weeks of days" in the Hebrew, to clarify that these are literal weeks, not symbolic weeks, as in chapter 9.

10:4. Hiddekel is the Tigris River. Nisan was **the first month** on the Jewish calendar. Passover was celebrated that month (March–April), commemorating Israel's deliverance from Egypt in the exodus. Daniel may have been moved to fast and pray in an-

ticipation of their return home from Babylon in a new "exodus."

10:5–6. A certain man clothed in linen (v. 5) is probably Christ Himself (a theophany). See the similar description of the risen Savior in Revelation 1:12–16. Miller (*Daniel*, p. 282) argues for a distinction between the theophany and the interpreting angel as two distinct messengers.

10:7–9. I Daniel alone (v. 7) is very emphatic in the Hebrew. While the other men felt a supernatural presence, only Daniel **saw the vision** (compare Paul's experience, Acts 9:1–7). **On my face** (v. 9; compare John's response, Rev. 1:17). Miller (*Daniel*, p. 282) adds: "Daniel's severe reaction to the presence of this person confirms that this being was no mere angel."

10:10–13. A hand touched me (v. 10), that of either the divine being or the interpreting angel. Daniel was again assured that he was **greatly beloved** (v. 11). **From the first day** (v. 12) indicates that God began to answer Daniel's prayer as soon as he began praying. **The prince of … Persia** (v. 13) apparently refers to a demon exercising influence over the king or realm of Persia in the interests of Satan (see also 10:20). His resistance was finally overcome by the archangel **Michael** ("who is like God?"), the angelic protector of Israel. This passage (like Job 1–2) certainly provides a glimpse into the reality of spiritual warfare, which goes on in the heavens and affects conditions on earth.

10:14–19. Thy people (v. 14) refers to the Jews throughout this section. **Latter days** (Hebrew, *be'aharit hayyamim*; "in the future") refers to the prophetic picture of Israel's future from Daniel's time until the consummation of the kingdom of God on earth, in which Daniel himself will participate at the "end of the days" (12:13). Thus, chapter 10 serves as an introduction to the details of the vision, which follow in chapters 11–12.

10:20–11:1. The prince of Grecia (v. 20) probably refers to a demon assigned to influence the king or realm of Greece. The context of this chapter clearly indicates that Satan was at work in the policies of both Persia and Greece in regard to their dealings with the Jewish people. God was at work as well, as testified in the books of Ezra, Nehemiah, and Esther. The conclusion of the angel's message is in 11:1.

2. Prophecies concerning Persia and Greece (11:2 – 4)

11:2. Yet three kings refers to Cambyses (530 – 522 BC), Smerdis (522 BC), and Darius I Hystaspes (522 – 486 BC). **The fourth** who is **far richer** refers to Xerxes I (486 – 465 BC), who married Esther (Esther 1 – 2). Xerxes also attempted to conquer Greece in 480 BC but was defeated and turned back.

11:3 – 4. A mighty king (v. 3) refers to Alexander the Great, the first ruler of the Greek Empire. He attacked Persia in 334 BC and conquered it by 331 BC. Afterward, he continued marching eastward to India before turning back. He died in Babylon in 323 BC. Upon his death, his empire was **divided toward the four winds** (v. 4), that is, among his four generals (see discussion on 8:8).

3. Prophecies concerning Egypt and Syria (11:5 – 35)

11:5 – 6. The king of the south (v. 5) refers to the rulers of Egypt, and **the king of the north** (v. 6) to the rulers of Syria during the Hellenistic period (323 – 140 BC). The intricate details of this prophecy have caused liberal scholars to object to its veracity. In reality, Daniel provided a detailed predictive overview of the conflicts within the Greek Empire between the rulers of Syria and Egypt, both of which directly affected Israel's future. "The king of the south" here refers to Ptolemy I Soter (323 – 285 BC) of Egypt. **One of his princes** (v. 5) was Seleucus I Nicator (312 – 280 BC), who served under Ptolemy I and later defeated Antigonus and took control of Babylon and Syria.

The king's daughter of the south (v. 6) refers to Berenice, daughter of Ptolemy II Philadelphus (285 – 246 BC) of Egypt. **King of the north.** Antiochus II Theos (261 – 246) of Syria. **An agreement.** A treaty cemented by the marriage of Berenice to Antiochus. **She shall not retain the power … neither shall he stand.** Antiochus's former wife, Laodice, conspired to have Berenice and Antiochus put to death. **That begat her.** Berenice's father, Ptolemy, died at about the same time.

11:7. Out of … her roots shall one stand up refers to Berenice's brother, Ptolemy III Euergetes (246 – 221 BC) of Egypt, who did away with Laodice. **Fortress** can be identified as either (1) Seleucia (see Acts 13:4), which was the port of Antioch, or (2) Antioch itself. **The king of the north** is Seleucus II Callinicus (246 – 226 BC) of Syria.

11:8. Their gods these were images of Syrian deities, and also of Egyptian gods that the Persian Cambyses had carried off after conquering Egypt in 525 BC.

11:10. His sons were Seleucus III Ceraunus (226 – 223 BC) and Antiochus III (the Great) (223 – 187), sons of Seleucus II. **His fortress** refers to Ptolemy's fortress at Raphia (southwest of Gaza). See chart, *KJV Study Bible*, pp. 1230 – 31.

11:11. The king of the south. Ptolemy IV Philopator (221 – 203 BC) of Egypt. **The king of the north.** Antiochus III. **Given into his hand.** At Raphia in 217.

11:12. Cast down many ten thousands. The historian Polybius records that Antiochus lost nearly ten thousand infantrymen at Raphia.

11:14. The king of the south. Ptolemy V Epiphanes (203 – 181 BC) of Egypt. **Robbers of thy people** are Jews who joined the forces of Antiochus. **They shall fall.** The Ptolemaic general Scopas crushed the Jewish rebellion but was later defeated at Sidon in 198 BC.

11:15. Most fenced cities refers to the Mediterranean port of Sidon.

11:16. He that cometh is Antiochus, who was in control of the Holy Land by 197 BC. **The glorious land** refers to Israel, which was now part of the Syrian Empire. Miller (*Daniel*, p. 296) notes that this "sets the stage for the reign of terror to follow under the Syrian Greek ruler Antiochus IV Epiphanes."

11:17. He shall give him the daughter of women. Antiochus gave his daughter Cleopatra I in marriage to Ptolemy V in 194 BC.

11:18. He. Antiochus. **Isles** refers to Asia Minor and perhaps also mainland Greece. **Prince.** The

Roman consul Lucius Cornelius Scipio Asiaticus, who defeated Antiochus at Magnesia in Asia Minor in 190 BC.

11:19. Stumble and fall. Antiochus died in 187 BC while attempting to plunder a temple in the province of Elymais.

11:20. In his estate. Seleucus IV Philopator (187–175 BC), son and successor of Antiochus the Great. **Raiser of taxes.** Seleucus's finance minister, Heliodorus. **He shall be destroyed.** Seleucus was the victim of a conspiracy engineered by Heliodorus.

11:21. Vile person. Seleucus's younger brother, Antiochus IV Epiphanes (175–164 BC). **They shall not give the honour of the kingdom.** Antiochus seized power while the rightful heir to the throne, the son of Seleucus (later to become Demetrius I), was still very young. **Kingdom.** Syro-Palestine.

11:22. The prince of the covenant. Either the high priest Onias III, who was murdered in 170 BC, or, if the Hebrew for this phrase is translated "confederate prince," Ptolemy VI Philometor (181–146) of Egypt.

11:23. He. Antiochus.

11:24. Fattest places. Either of the Holy Land or of Egypt. **Strong holds.** In Egypt.

11:25. The king of the south. Ptolemy VI.

11:26. His army. That of Ptolemy.

11:27. Both these kings. Antiochus and Ptolemy, who was living in Antiochus's custody.

11:28. Against the holy covenant. In 169 BC, Antiochus plundered the temple in Jerusalem, set up a garrison there, and massacred many Jews in the city.

11:30. Ships of Chittim. Roman vessels under the command of Popilius Laenas. **That forsake the holy covenant.** Apostate Jews (see also 11:32).

11:31. Abomination that maketh desolate (see 9:27; 12:11) refers to the altar to the pagan god Zeus Olympius, which was set up in 168 BC by Antiochus Epiphanes and which prefigures a similar abomination that Jesus predicted would be erected (see discussions on Matt. 24:15; Luke 21:20).

11:33. They that understand. The godly leaders of the Jewish resistance movement, also called the Hasidim. **Fall by sword, and by flame, by captivity, and by spoil.** See Hebrews 11:36–38.

11:34. A little help. The early successes of the guerrilla uprising (168 BC) that originated in Modein, seventeen miles northwest of Jerusalem, under the leadership of Mattathias and his son Judas Maccabeus. In December 165 BC, the altar of the temple was rededicated.

11:35. Time of the end. Here Daniel concludes his predictions about Antiochus Epiphanes and begins to prophesy about the more distant future.

4. Prophecies concerning the Antichrist (11:36–45)

11:36. The king … shall exalt himself. The details of this section do not fit with what is known of Antiochus Epiphanes. From here to the end of chapter 11, the Antichrist is in view (see discussions on 7:8; 9:27; *KJV Study Bible* notes on 2 Thess. 2:4; Rev. 13:5–8). Walvoord (*Daniel*, pp. 270–73) discusses various theories of the identification of this king, noting that Jerome and other church fathers were convinced it was the Antichrist. The indignation (Hebrew, *za'am*; "wrath" of God) describes the tribulation period (see Rev. 6:16–17; 16:1).

11:37. The desire of women may refer to the fact that he loves himself, which may preclude the love of women, although some commentators take this phrase to refer to the Messiah. **Magnify himself** indicates that the Antichrist will view himself as God. "He shall rule over many" (v. 39), presumably by force, is reminiscent of Rev. 13:4, "Who is like unto the beast? who is able to make war with him?"

11:40–45. The end-time wars of the Antichrist are in view here. **The time of the end** (v. 40) places these conflicts in the eschatological future. While various opinions have been expressed regarding the identity of those involved, several things are clearly predicted: (1) the final conflict will take place in the Middle East; (2) Israel, **the glorious land** (v. 41), will be attacked, (3) as will Egypt and North Africa; (4) the Antichrist will set up his headquarters in Jerusalem (**the glorious holy mountain**; v. 45); (5) he will be destroyed in Israel (v. 45); (6) his defeat will be followed by the resurrection of the saints (12:2);

(7) they will subsequently participate in the Messiah's earthly kingdom (12:13). See Revelation 19:11–20:6.

5. Promise of the Resurrection (chap. 12)

12:1. At that time refers to the period of the Antichrist's rule, which was described in 11:36–45. **Michael**, the archangel (see Jude 9). **Thy people**, the Jews. **Time of trouble** (Hebrew, *tsara*; "distress") translated *thlipsis* in the Septuagint, the same term used in the New Testament to describe the tribulation period. Jesus Himself quotes this event ("the tribulation of those days") as preceding His triumphal return (Matt. 24:29–30). Because **thy people** (the Jews) **shall be delivered** did not occur in AD 70, this prophecy obviously points to the eschatological future.

12:2–3. Shall awake (v. 2) is translated *anastesontai* ("will rise up") in the Septuagint. This is a clear reference to the resurrection of both the righteous and the wicked (see John 5:24–30). **Everlasting life** (Hebrew, *hayye 'olam*) appears only here in the Old Testament. Its Greek counterpart (*zoen aionion*), used in the Septuagint, is repeated in John 3:16. The resurrected wicked will face **everlasting contempt** (Hebrew, *harapot*), a plural intensive meaning "great shame," which is also of eternal duration. Thus, Daniel was told that there are two separate but eternal destinies for the saved and the lost.

12:4. Seal the book means to preserve the document until **the time of the end**, when the message of that book will be most needed. **Run to and fro** (Hebrew, *hesotetu*) means to search intensely to increase knowledge. Miller (*Daniel*, p. 321) states: "As the time of fulfillment draws nearer, the 'wise' will seek to comprehend these prophecies more precisely, and God will grant understanding ('knowledge') to them."

12:5–10. The question, **How long … to the end …?** (v. 6) is answered as **a time, times, and a half** (v. 7; see Rev. 12:14). This refers to three and a half years, or the last half of the seventieth seven (the Seventieth Week) of 9:24–27. This is the same as the 42 months and 1,260 days (Rev. 11:2–3; 12:6; 13:5) of the great tribulation.

12:11–13. A thousand two hundred and ninety days (1,290 days; v. 11) presumably includes a 30-day period of cleansing and purification of the temple in addition to the 1,260 days (see 2 Thess. 2:4; 2 Chron. 30:2–4). **The thousand three hundred and five and thirty days** (1,335 days; v. 12) includes another 45 days of preparation for the messianic kingdom to be inaugurated on earth. In the end, Daniel was promised that he would **stand in thy lot** (his allotted inheritance in the messianic kingdom; v. 13). This promise was especially significant since Daniel presumably would die in captivity in Babylon. Yet God promised that he would be resurrected to physically participate in Christ's rule on earth during the kingdom age.

THE BOOK OF HOSEA

INTRODUCTION

Author and Date

Hosea son of Beeri prophesied sometime around the middle of the eighth century BC, his ministry beginning during or shortly after that of Amos. Amos threatened God's judgment on Israel at the hands of an unnamed enemy; Hosea identified that enemy as Assyria (7:11; 8:9; 10:6; 11:11). Judging from the kings mentioned in 1:1, Hosea must have prophesied for at least thirty-eight years, though almost nothing is known about him from sources outside his book. He was the only one of the writing prophets to come from the northern kingdom (Israel), and his prophecy is primarily directed to that kingdom. Since his prophetic activity is dated by reference to kings of Judah, the book was probably written in Judah after the fall of the northern capital, Samaria (722–721 BC)—an idea suggested by references to Judah throughout the book (1:7, 11; 4:15; 5:5, 10, 13; 6:4, 11; 10:11; 11:12; 12:2). Whether Hosea himself authored the book that preserves his prophecies is not known. The book of Hosea stands first in the division of the Bible called the Book of the Twelve (in the Apocrypha, see Ecclesiasticus 49:10), or the Minor Prophets (a name referring to the brevity of these books as compared to Isaiah, Jeremiah, and Ezekiel).

Background

Hosea lived in the tragic final days of the northern kingdom, during which six kings (following Jeroboam II) reigned within twenty-five years (2 Kings 15:8–17:41). Four (Zechariah, Shallum, Pekahiah, Pekah) were murdered by their successors while in office, and one (Hoshea) was captured in battle; only one (Menahem) was succeeded on the throne by his son. These kings, given to Israel by God "in ... anger" and taken away "in ... wrath" (13:11), floated away "as the foam upon the water" (10:7). "Blood" followed "blood" (4:2). Assyria was expanding westward, and Menahem submitted to that world power as overlord and paid tribute (2 Kings 15:19–20). Shortly afterward, in 733 BC, Israel was dismembered by Assyria because of the intrigue of Pekah (who had gained Israel's throne by killing Pekahiah, Menahem's son and successor). Only the territories of Ephraim and western Manasseh were left to the king of Israel. Then, because of the

1100

disloyalty of Hoshea (Pekah's successor), Samaria was captured and its people were exiled in 722–721 BC, bringing the northern kingdom to an end.

Theme and Theological Message

The first part of the book (chaps. 1–3) narrates the family life of Hosea as a symbol (similar to the symbolism in the lives of Isaiah, Jeremiah, and Ezekiel) of the message the prophet had from the Lord for His people. God ordered Hosea to marry an adulterous wife, Gomer, and their three children were each given a symbolic name representing part of the ominous message. Chapter 2 alternates between Hosea's relation to Gomer and its symbolic representation of God's relationship with Israel. The children were told to drive the unfaithful mother out of the house, but it was her reform, not her riddance, that was sought. The prophet was ordered to continue loving her, and he took her back and kept her in isolation for awhile (chap. 3). The affair graphically represents the Lord's relationship with the Israelites (see 2:4, 9, 18), who had been disloyal to Him by worshiping Canaanite deities as the source of their abundance. Israel was to go through a period of exile (see 7:16; 8:14; 9:3, 6, 17; 11:5). The Lord still loved His covenant people, however, and longed to take them back, as Hosea took back Gomer. This return is described with imagery recalling the exodus from Egypt and the settlement in Canaan (see 1:11; 2:14–23; 3:5; 11:10–11; 14:4–7). Hosea saw Israel's past experiences with the Lord as the fundamental pattern, or type, of God's future dealings with His people.

The second part of the book (chaps. 4–14) gives the details of Israel's involvement in Canaanite religion, but a systematic outline of the material is difficult. Like other prophetic books, Hosea carries a call to repentance. Israel's alternative to destruction was to forsake her idols and return to the Lord (chaps. 6; 14). Information gleaned from materials discovered at Ugarit (dating from the fifteenth century BC) and from the writings of the early Christian historian Eusebius reveal more clearly the religious practices against which Hosea protested.

Hosea saw the failure to acknowledge God (4:6; 13:4) as Israel's basic problem. God's relation to Israel was that of love (2:19; 4:1; 6:6; 10:12; 12:6). The intimacy of the covenant relationship between God and Israel, illustrated in the first part of the book by the husband-wife relationship, is later amplified by the father-child relationship (11:1–4). Disloyalty to God was spiritual adultery (4:13–14; 5:4; 9:1; see Jeremiah 3). Israel had turned to Baal worship and had sacrificed at the pagan high places, which included associating with the sacred prostitutes at the sanctuaries (4:14) and worshiping the calf image at Samaria (8:5; 10:5–6; 13:2). There was also international intrigue (5:13; 7:8–11) and materialism. Yet despite God's condemnation and the harshness of language with which the unavoidable judgment was announced, the major purpose of the book is to proclaim God's compassion and love that cannot—finally—let Israel go.

Special Problems

The book of Hosea has at least two perplexing problems. The first concerns the nature of the summary told in chapters 1–3 and the character of Gomer. While some interpreters have thought the story is merely an allegory of the relationship between God and Israel, others claim, more plausibly, that the story is to be taken literally. Among the latter, some insist that Gomer was faithful at first and later became unfaithful; others believe she was unfaithful even before the marriage.

The second problem of the book is the relation of chapter 3 to chapter 1. Despite the fact that no children are mentioned in chapter 3, some interpreters claim that the two chapters are different accounts of the same episode. The traditional interpretation, however, is more likely, namely, that chapter 3 is a sequel to chapter 1 — that is, after Gomer proved unfaithful, Hosea was instructed to take her back.

Outline

I. The Unfaithful Wife and the Faithful Husband (1:1–3:5)
   A. Hosea's Wife and Children (1:2–2:1)
   B. The Unfaithful Wife (2:2–23)
      1. The Lord's Judgment of Israel (2:2–17)
      2. The Lord's Restoration of Israel (2:18–23)
   C. The Faithful Husband (chap. 3)
II. The Unfaithful Nation and the Faithful God (chaps. 4–14)
   A. Israel's Unfaithfulness (4:1–6:3)
      1. Israel's Immorality (chap. 4)
      2. God's Severity toward Israel (chap. 5)
      3. The Call to Repent (6:1–3)
   B. Israel's Punishment and God's Unending Mercy (6:4–11:11)
      1. Israel's Unfaithfulness (6:4–7:16)
      2. God's Sentence of Judgment (chap. 8)
      3. The Covenant Curses against an Unfaithful People (chap. 9)
      4. Sowing and Reaping: The Consequences of Sin (chap. 10)
      5. God's Compassion toward Israel (11:1–11)
   C. The Lord's Faithful Love to an Ungrateful People (11:12–14:9)
      1. Israel's Sin (11:12–12:14)
      2. Ephraim's Doom (chap. 13)
      3. Israel's Restoration after Repentance (chap. 14)

Bibliography

Davies, Graham I. *Hosea*. New Century Bible. Grand Rapids, MI: Eerdmans, 1992.

Feinberg, Charles. *The Minor Prophets*. Chicago: Moody, 1976.

King, P. J. *Amos, Hosea, Micah: An Archaeological Commentary*. Philadelphia: Westminster, 1988.

Mays, J. L. *Hosea*. Old Testament Library. Philadelphia: Westminster, 1969.

Wolff, H. W. *Hosea*. Translated by G. Stansell. Hermeneia. Philadelphia: Fortress, 1974.

Woods, Leon. "Hosea." In *The Expositor's Bible Commentary*, edited by Frank E. Gaebelein, vol. 7. Grand Rapids, MI: Zondervan, 1985.

EXPOSITION

I. The Unfaithful Wife and the Faithful Husband (1:1 – 3:5)

A. Hosea's Wife and Children (1:2 – 2:1)

1:1 – 2:1. The first section of the book unfolds the story of the marriage of Hosea and Gomer and the spiritual message behind this marriage for the nation of Israel. The prophets often use the image of adultery or prostitution to portray Israel's covenant infidelity to the Lord. Israel was like an unfaithful marriage partner, and the imagery of adultery is especially appropriate in that the pagan worship practices Israel engaged in often involved fertility rites of a sexual nature. Spiritual harlotry (unfaithfulness) is the one great sin of which the prophets speak.

1:1 – 2. The nature of the story told in chapters 1 – 3 and the character of Hosea presents a moral dilemma. Would God command a prophet to marry an immoral woman? While some interpreters have thought the story to be merely an allegory of the relationship between God and Israel, the story should more likely be taken literally. God often used a prophet's difficult family circumstances to teach the people valuable lessons (see Jer. 16:2; Ezek. 24:15 – 18), and this story certainly has more impact if it narrates actual events. If taken literally, it is possible that Gomer was unfaithful to Hosea before the marriage or that she was faithful at first and later became unfaithful. The latter option seems to parallel more closely Israel's experience of becoming unfaithful after entering into a covenant relationship with the Lord. It is further possible that the command **Go, take unto thee a wife of whoredoms** (v. 2) is Hosea's later understanding, after Gomer had been unfaithful to him, of God's initial command to marry her.

1:3 – 5. Three children are born to Gomer in chapter 1. The first son was given the name **Jezreel** (v. 4), which means "God scatters" and is used to reinforce the announcement of judgment on the reigning house of Israel. Jeroboam II was of the dynasty of Jehu (841 – 814 BC), and Jehu had established his dynasty by the bloody overthrow of Ahab's son Joram at Jezreel (2 Kings 9:14 – 37; see 1 Kings 19:16 – 17). The warning was that the house of Jehu would come to a similarly brutal end. Jehu's dynasty ultimately ended with the murder of Zechariah in 753 BC (2 Kings 15:8 – 10).

1:6 – 7. While Hosea clearly was the father of the first child, the text does not state that the second and third children were born to Hosea, which may indicate that Hosea was not their father. The second child was a daughter named **Lo-ruhamah** (v. 6), meaning "not loved." The name represents a reversal of the love (compassion) that God had earlier shown to Israel (Exod. 33:19; Deut. 7:6 – 8). God would not have compassion toward Israel when He acted in judgment and brought destruction on the land. In contrast to this warning concerning Israel, the Lord promised that He would **have mercy upon** (v. 7) and **save** Judah. The Lord saved Judah from Assyria in 722 – 721 BC and again in 701 BC (see 2 Kings 19:32 – 36).

1:8 – 9. The third child was a son named **Lo-ammi** (v. 9), whose name represents a break in the covenant relationship between the Lord and Israel (see Exod. 6:7; Jer. 7:23). The warnings became more severe in moving from the first child to the third child.

1:10 – 2:1. While the names of the three children pointed to future judgment for Israel, verses 10 – 11 contain a promise of the reversal of this judgment and a statement of God's perpetual commitment to Israel as His chosen people. The threatened judgment would be for only a limited time, and a period of blessing would follow. The prophet envisions both the more imminent return from exile and the final restoration of Israel in the Kingdom Age. The people of Israel will eventually become as numerous **as the sand of the sea** (v. 10), in fulfillment of God's promise to Abraham and Jacob (Gen. 22:17; 32:12; see Jer. 33:22; Heb. 11:12). Israel will become **sons of the living God**, in contrast to being the "children of whoredoms" (1:2) who worshiped idols "who were not God" (Deut. 32:17). In the future time of salvation, Israel and Judah will **be gathered together** (v. 11) as one nation. There will be a **day of Jezreel**, not when God judges His people but rather when He "scatters" them by sowing and planting them in the land. Israel will be known as **Ammi** (meaning, "My people"; 2:1) and **Ruhamah** ("having obtained mercy"), completely removing the negative connotations of the names given to the children of Gomer.

This promise that those who are not God's people would become his sons was later applied to the mission to the Gentiles under the new covenant (Rom. 9:26 and 1 Peter 2:10). While God's commitment to Israel remains intact, Gentiles also come under the blessings of the Abrahamic covenant (see Gen. 12:3; Rom. 4:12; Gal. 3:14).

B. The Unfaithful Wife (2:2–23)

1. The Lord's Judgment of Israel (2:2–17)

2:2–4. Though the marriage of Hosea was broken by unfaithfulness, reconciliation was sought, not divorce. The husband commanded his wife to put an end to her adulterous behavior and took disciplinary measures against her that were appropriate in the culture of ancient Israel. He threatened to **strip her naked** (v. 3). The husband supplied the wife's clothing (see Exod. 21:10; Ezek. 16:10), which shamed her and exposed her unfaithfulness (see Jer. 13:26; Ezek. 16:10). The woman would be reduced to poverty (v. 3), and the Lord would discipline Israel in the same way, returning the nation to the state she had been in when the Lord found her in Egypt—in slavery and with nothing (see Ezek. 16:4–8; Nah. 3:5).

2:5–13. The wife was chasing after other men (see Jer. 3:2; Ezek. 16;33), whom she credited with providing for her when her husband was the one who had actually taken care of her. Israel's **lovers** (vv. 7, 10) were the Canaanite deities (such as Baal) that they had worshiped in the hopes of receiving agricultural fertility. The Ugaritic texts portray **Baal** (v. 8) as the god who controls the weather and the fertility of the crops, animals, and man (see Judg. 2:13), and the Israelites had bought into this lie. Since Israel refused to acknowledge the Lord as their source of blessing, the Lord would **return, and take away** (v. 9) their crops. By withholding the fruits of field and flock, the Lord would make known the true source of those blessings. The Lord would expose Israel to public shame (**discover her lewdness**; v. 10; see Lam. 1:8; Ezek. 16:37; 23:39) and **cause all her mirth to cease** (v. 11). In exile, the joyous celebration of all their bounty would be only a memory. God would take away their crops because these gifts from Him had become **rewards** (harlot's pay; v. 12) in the eyes of the people; they had received these gifts by giving their love and devotion to the false gods.

2:14–17. After the time of judgment, the Lord would once again **allure** (v. 14) Israel and **bring her into the wilderness**. This time would be a second betrothal, as in the time of Israel's wilderness wanderings, before she had been tempted by the Baals in Canaan. Emphasizing the theme of reversal, the Lord promised to turn **the valley of Achor** (v. 15), the place near Jericho where God first punished Israel in the land (Josh. 7:1–26; 15:7; Isa. 65:10), into a place of **hope**. The Lord would also transform the people so that they no longer desired to follow the Baals. Using two words for "husband," the Lord promised that the people would call Him **Ishi** ("my husband"; v. 16) rather than **Baali** ("my lord"), because the latter term so closely resembles the name of Baal. There would be such a vigorous reaction against Baal worship that this Hebrew word for "lord" would no longer be used of the Lord.

2. The Lord's Restoration of Israel (2:18–23)

2:18–20. The Lord will bring peace to Israel by making a **covenant** (v. 18) with the animals (see 6:7; 8:1). Animals, the instruments of destruction in 2:12, will no longer threaten life. There will be no war; God will break **the bow and the sword**. Nature and history will combine in a picture of peace (see Isa. 11:6–9; 65:25). Israel will be married to the Lord forever and will never again have the desire to worship other gods (vv. 19–20). Rather than money, the five traits of **righteousness** (v. 19), **judgment** (justice), **lovingkindness**, **mercies**, and **faithfulness** (v. 20) will make up the bride-price (see Exod. 22:26–27; Deut. 22:23–29).

2:22–23. The closing verses of this section repeat the reversal of the threats behind the names of Gomer's children (vv. 22–23; see 1:11–2:1). **Jezreel** (v. 22) becomes a name for God's sowing Israel in the land to enjoy its agricultural bounty, the Lord **will have mercy** (v. 23) on Israel, and He will call Israel **my people.**

C. The Faithful Husband (chap. 3)

3:1. God commanded Hosea, **Go ... love a woman.** The relationship of chapter 3 to chapter 1 is somewhat problematic. Despite the fact that no children are mentioned in chapter 3, some interpreters claim that the two chapters are different accounts of the same episode. Others have argued that another woman is involved and that Hosea is taking another wife. It is Hosea's love for unfaithful Gomer, however, that illustrates God love for unfaithful Israel. Hosea loved his wife and restored the relationship that had been broken by her infidelity.

3:2–5. I bought her (v. 2) indicates that Gomer had become a slave and Hosea bought her back. The purchase price was paid half in money (**silver**) and half in produce (**barley**). Hosea instructed his wife to be faithful to him and pledged his faithfulness to her. Their reconciliation pictured what would happen to Israel in the exile and return. The exile would be a time of separation, but they could cling to the promise of return and restoration of Israel's relationship with the Lord. The term **return** (v. 5) was a basic word in Hosea's vocabulary as he looked forward to the future restoration (see 2:7; 5:4; 6;1; 7;10; 8:4; 13:10). The restoration would be a time when Israel would **seek the Lord** in true repentance (see 5:15). There is also the promise that Israel will follow **David their king,** referring to the future Messiah (see Jer. 30:9; Ezek. 34:24). Following the death of Solomon, Israel (the northern kingdom) had abandoned the Davidic kings. The return will occur **in the latter days.** The Hebrew for this phrase occurs thirteen times in the Old Testament, sometimes simply meaning the future ("the last day," Gen. 49:1), but most often, as no doubt here, referring to the messianic age ("afterward," Joel 2:28; see Acts 2:17; Heb. 1:2).

II. The Unfaithful Nation and the Faithful God (chaps. 4–14)

4:1–14:9. This section of the book contains the messages and oracles of the prophet Hosea and deals with Israel's involvement in Canaanite religion, her moral sins, and her international intrigues. These messages unfold in three cycles (4:1–6:3; 6:4–11:11; and 11:12–14:9) as a covenant lawsuit in which the Lord indicts the people for their unfaithfulness. Each cycle brings a formal charge: "the Lord hath a controversy" (4:1); "they like men have transgressed the covenant" (6:7); and "the Lord hath also a controversy with Judah" (12:2). Despite Israel's unfaithfulness, each cycle concludes with a promise of restoration (6:1–3; 11:1–11; 14:1–9). Though Israel had been unfaithful to Him, the Lord would not abandon His people and the covenant promises He had made to them.

A. Israel's Unfaithfulness (4:1–6:3)

1. Israel's Immorality (chap. 4)

4:1–3. The word **controversy** (v. 2) is a technical term in Hebrew for "lawsuit." As the Lord's spokesman, Hosea brought charges against unfaithful, covenant-breaking Israel (see v. 4; Isa. 3;13; Jer. 2:9; Mic. 6:2). The general charge was that Israel did not practice **truth** (loyalty to the covenant, Josh. 24:14) or **mercy** (right dealing with men, Prov. 3:3) and had no **knowledge of God.** This charge was validated in Israel's violation of the covenant commands, with the sins of **swearing** (v. 2), **lying, killing, stealing,** and **committing adultery** specifically transgressing the Ten Commandments, which summarize God's moral demands on Israel (see Exod. 20:13–16; Deut. 5:17–20). The accusation that **blood toucheth blood** refers to murder (see 6:8–9)—the assassinations following the death of Jeroboam II, when three kings reigned in one year (2 Kings 15:10–14)—and human sacrifice (Ps. 106:38; Ezek. 16:20–21; 21:37). When God is not acknowledged (v. 1), moral chaos prevails.

4:4–9. The prophet indicted the priests, whose duty it was to be the guardians of God's law and to furnish religious instruction (see Deut. 31:9–13;

2 Chron. 17:8–9; Ezra 7:6). Hosea warned the priests not to lodge charges against the people for bringing God's judgment down on the nation, for they themselves were guilty, and the people could also bring charges against them. The people were **destroyed for lack of knowledge** (v. 6) in part because the priests had failed to teach God's word to the people. Because they had **forgotten the law**, God would **forget** their descendants. The consequence of this failed leadership was that **like people, like priest** (v. 9), all would be punished for their sins.

4:10–13. Israel would be punished for their participation in pagan rites and festivals (vv. 10–19.) They were guilty of **whoredom** (vv. 10, 12; 4:18; see 2:4; 6:10; 9:1). Instead of giving themselves to the Lord, they had chosen the fertility rituals of Canaanite religion. They **sacrifice[d]** (v. 13) to these gods **upon the tops of the mountains**, places commonly chosen for pagan altars (see 10:8; Deut. 12:2; 1 Kings 14:23; 2 Kings 17:10; Jer. 2:20; 3:6). Clay tablets from Ugarit tell of fertility rites carried out by the Canaanites at the high places.

4:14. The fertility rites involved sexual activity, which led to a general erosion of morals in the land. The Lord stated that He would **not punish** the women involved in such activity. The men would punish the women for immorality, but God would have no part in their hypocrisy because the men were just as guilty. The pagan rites had reduced the women in the land to **whores**, or common prostitutes (see Gen. 34:31:l; Lev. 21:14), and to **harlots**, or women of the sanctuaries who served as partners for men in cultic sexual activity (see Gen. 38:21–22; Deut. 23:18).

4:15–18. The cult sites of **Gilgal** (near Jericho; v. 15) and Bethel were condemned because Israel had practiced syncretistic worship that combined worship of the Lord and worship of other gods. The Lord demands exclusive worship and devotion. Bethel ("house of God") is derisively referred to as **Beth-aven** ("house of wickedness"). Worship in the northern kingdom had been corrupted from the very beginning, when Jeroboam had established sanctuaries with golden calves at Dan and Bethel as rivals to the approved worship center in Jerusalem, where

the Lord had chosen to dwell among His people (see 1 Kings 12:27–30). Ephraim had been **joined to idols** (v. 17). This compromise under Jeroboam's leadership had created an environment conducive to the further apostasy of Baal worship, later promoted during the reign of King Ahab (see 1 Kings 16:31–33).

4:19. Ultimately, Israel **shall be ashamed because of their sacrifices**. Israel had hoped to flourish by means of their sacrifices, but God's punishment for their idolatry would bring them into disgrace among the nations as they were carried into exile.

2. God's Severity toward Israel (chap. 5)

5:1–7. This judgment speech was directed against the **priests** (v. 1), the **house of Israel**, and the **house of the king**. All three groups were responsible for maintaining justice, but it miscarried at their hands. They are portrayed as hunters with **snare** and **net**, the devices used for capturing animals and birds functioning as metaphors for the economic and legal maneuvers used to exploit innocent people (see Job 18:8–10; Prov. 29:5). While trapping others, the wicked had become so ensnared in their sin that they were unable **to turn unto their God** (v. 4; see 4:9; 7:2; 9:15; 12:2). Persistent sin can make repentance impossible (see Jer. 13:23; John 8:34). Both **Israel** (v. 5) and **Judah** would **fall** in judgment, and the Lord would not respond to their prayers for mercy when they came to Him with prayer and sacrifices (vv. 5–7). Offering sacrifices in their situation was useless. Israel would **not find** (v. 6) the Lord until she turned to Him with integrity of heart (see 3:15; 5:15; Deut. 4:29–31).

5:8–15. Blow ye the cornet ... and the trumpet (v. 8) is a call to war. The Syro-Ephraimite war fought in 734–732 BC appears to provide the backdrop for these verses (see 2 Kings 16:5–9; Isa. 7:1–9). The northern kingdom of Israel had allied with their Aramean (Syria) neighbors against the southern kingdom of Judah in an attempt to force Judah to join their anti-Assyrian coalition. Judah ultimately appealed to Assyria for military assistance, and as a result of this conflict, Israel and Judah both suffered great devastation and loss of life. These losses were a **sickness** (v. 13) and **wound** that God, as a roaring **lion** (v. 14), had inflicted on His people. The Lord might have used human agents (see Isa. 10:5–6), but He was ultimately responsible for this punishment, from which there was no escape (see Isa. 5:29; Amos 9:1–4). Instead of turning to the Lord in their time of crisis, Israel had turned to the king of Assyria (v. 13). Assyrian records tell of the tribute paid to Tiglath-pileser III by the Israelite kings Menahem and Hoshea (see 2 Kings 15:19–20). Israel had looked for a political solution for their spiritual problem, and their alliances were not able to **heal** (v. 13) or **rescue** (v. 14). Even the powerful Assyrian king was not able to protect them from the wrath of God. The Lord warned that He would withdraw from Israel (**return to my place**; v. 15) until they, in utter desperation, truly repented.

3. The Call to Repent (6:1–3)

6:1–3. Recognizing the futility of military and political solutions, the prophet called on Israel to **return unto the Lord** (v. 1). Some commentators view this section as reflecting a shallow and superficial attempt on the part of Israel to win the Lord's favor, that they took their sin so lightly they believed the Lord would restore them in three days (v. 2). However, shifts from judgment to salvation are a key component of the book's structure (see 1:9–2:2; 11:7–12; 14:1–9). There is a genuine recognition here that the Lord was the only one who could **heal** (v. 1) them because He was the one who had inflicted this judgment on Israel. The expression of hope for deliverance within three days is evidence of confidence and trust in the Lord rather than a display of arrogant presumption.

B. Israel's Punishment and God's Unending Mercy (6:4–11:11)

1. Israel's Unfaithfulness (6:4–7:16)

6:4–6. For the time being, the Israelites remained entrenched in their sinful ways. Their goodness was like **dew** (v. 4), which quickly evaporates, and they had not responded to the warnings of the prophets that the Lord had sent their way. The sum of what God requires of His servants is **mercy** (Hebrew, *hesed*; v. 6). This Hebrew word refers to cov-

enant loyalty and includes faithfulness to the Lord as well as right conduct toward one's fellow man. The Lord desires right character and not sacrifice. Sacrifice apart from faithfulness to the Lord's will is wholly unacceptable to Him (see 1 Sam. 15:22–23; Isa. 1:11–20; Jer. 7:21–22; Amos 5:21–24).

6:7–11. The precise meaning of the phrase **they like men have transgressed the covenant** (v. 7) is not clear. The Hebrew for "like men" can also be translated "like Adam," though Scripture records no specific covenant between God and Adam. More likely, "Adam" refers to a place (see Josh. 3:16), and some specific event that occurred there served as confirmation of Israel's unfaithfulness to the Lord. Acts of violence and immorality at **Gilead** (v. 8) and throughout the land provided similar confirmation (vv. 8–10). The Lord's judgment of this wickedness would include a **harvest** (v. 11) of judgment against Judah, who was just as guilty as Israel. (For the harvest as an image of judgment, see 8:7; 10:12–13; Jer. 51:13; Matt. 13:39; Rev. 14:15.)

7:1–7. Israel's sin prevented healing and reconciliation with the Lord (vv. 1–2). One glaring evidence of the pervasive evil in Israel were the political assassinations that occurred during this turbulent period of Israel's history (vv. 3–7). In the constant string of palace revolts, the king's attendants would get the king drunk and then put him to death. These conspirators were compared to hot ovens in their lust for power (vv. 4, 6, 7). Four **kings** (v. 7) were assassinated in twenty years, Zechariah and Shallum in a seven-month period (2 Kings 15:10–15).

7:8–12. In this context of political intrigue, Israel (**Ephraim**; v. 8) had become like **a cake not turned**, referring to a cake baked on hot stones (see 1 Kings 19:6) and burned on the bottom and raw on the top. With incompetent leaders who ruled with selfish motives, Israel had pursued foolish policies that would bring the nation to ruin. Israel was **like a silly dove** (v. 11), flitting about as they pursued alliances first with **Egypt** and then **Assyria** but never having the wisdom to seek the Lord. The Lord allowed Israel to choose her own way and to ultimately experience the consequences of her choices.

As a hunter, the Lord would spread His **net** (v. 12) to capture Israel. The Lord Himself was the hunter, not the nations, and Israel was certain to be caught. **7:13–16.** The Lord announced **Woe** (v. 13) on Israel, and the tragedy is that He would have to destroy the people that He had **redeemed** from Egypt (vv. 13–16). The people had feigned repentance with their tears but had not turned to the Lord with their hearts. Their insincerity made them **like a deceitful bow** (v. 16) that cannot be trusted on the day of battle. Despite their alliances, **Egypt** would fail to assist Israel and would then belittle God's power. Though verse 16 makes reference to exiles in Egypt, there is no record of a forced exile of large numbers to Egypt. Some captives were taken there (2 Kings 23:34; Jer. 22:11–14), and some fugitives voluntarily went there (2 Kings 25–26; Jeremiah 42–43). It seems that the reference to Egypt serves more as a symbol of foreign bondage (see Deut. 28:68) and serves to emphasize that the judgment of exile would bring about a reversal of Israel's salvation history.

2. God's Sentence of Judgment (chap. 8)

8:1–8. The call to war (**Set the trumpet;** v. 1) parallels 5:8 and warns of Israel's coming military defeat. Assyria would **come as an eagle,** or vulture, as the instrument of judgment for Israel's covenant unfaithfulness. Israel would protest, **My God, we know thee** (v. 2), but their actions showed otherwise. Politically, they had appointed **kings** (v. 4) without seeking the Lord. After Jeroboam II, five kings ruled over Israel in thirteen years (2 Kings 15:8–30), three of whom seized the throne by violence. Spiritually, their worship of the Lord had been thoroughly corrupted by pagan notions and practices. **The calf of Samaria** (v. 6), which the Lord would shatter, refers to the golden calves at the sanctuaries established by Jeroboam I (930–909 BC) at Bethel and Dan (1 Kings 12:28–33). Using a familiar proverb, Hosea declared that Israel had **sown the wind** (v. 7) and would **reap the whirlwind** (see 10:13; Job 4:8; Ps. 126:5–6; Prov. 11:18). Israel had sown the wind of idolatry and would reap the whirlwind of Assyria. Israel had been chosen to be God's own people and a witness to the nations (Exod. 19:5; Amos 3:2), but since she had conformed to other nations, she had lost her special identity and would be dispersed **among the Gentiles** (v. 8). She was as a worthless **vessel** to the Lord.

8:9–14. Israel had become like a prostitute who had **hired lovers** (v. 9). For the "prostitute fees" of Assyrian protection, Menahem (2 Kings 15:19) and Hoshea (2 Kings 17:3) had paid tribute to Assyria. Even though Israel had paid tribute to Assyria, that would not buy her security, for God would send judgment by the king of Assyria. Israel's real "enemy" was the Lord Himself (see 2:8–9, 13; 7:12). The Lord would not accept Israel's insincere sacrifices but would instead send them away to **Egypt** (v. 13; see discussion on 7:13–16). The cause for all of Israel's problems was that they had **forgotten** (v. 14) the Lord and were trusting instead in their **temples** and **fenced cities** to provide them security and protection.

3. The Covenant Curses against an Unfaithful People (chap. 9)

9:1–6. The imagery of prostitution, recalling the marriage of Hosea and Gomer, carries over into chapter 9. This message was probably spoken at a harvest festival, such as the Feast of Tabernacles (Lev. 23:33–43; Deut. 16:13–15). Israel had become like the prostitutes who frequented the threshing floors at harvesttime, selling their favors to the threshers who stayed there all night to protect the grain and who feasted at the end of the day's labors (see Ruth 3:2–3). Because of her prostitution, Israel would go into exile—to **Egypt** (v. 3) and to **Assyria,** the lands they had turned to for protection. Exile would cause the Israelites to live in a **polluted** (v. 4) land, where they would live in a continual condition of ceremonial uncleanness. Their sacrifices would become unclean, like bread in a house where there had been a death (v. 4; see Num. 19:14; Deut. 26:14). In exile, Israel would have no place where she could bring sacrifices to the Lord or celebrate her religious festivals (v. 5). The Israelites would return to Egypt and live as if the exodus had never occurred (v. 6).

9:7–9. The Lord had sent the prophets as watchmen to warn Israel of the coming judgment, but the people had abused and mistreated the prophets. Rather than reading **the prophet is a snare of a fowler** (v. 8), the Hebrew here should be understood to say that the prophet faced the dangers of constant opposition, which were like the traps of a hunter. The people were unable to receive the word of God because their corruption was like that **in the days of Gibeah** (v. 9), referring to the horrible events of Judges 19–21, which involved rape, murder, and civil war. The Lord would **remember** and would hold them accountable.

9:10–13. When the Lord established His covenant with Israel at Mount Sinai in the wilderness, Israel had been **like grapes** (v. 10) and the firstfruits (**firstripe**) of the fig tree, and the Lord had taken delight in His people. Their devotion to the Lord was short-lived, however, and turned to rebellion at **Baal-peor**, a reference to the events in Numbers 25, when Israel was seduced into worshiping Baal and engaging in acts of sexual immorality. This type of halfhearted devotion to the Lord characterized Israel's history throughout the Old Testament, and their covenant unfaithfulness would have devastating effects. **As for Ephraim, their glory** (v. 11), their large population, and the wealth enjoyed in the prosperous days of Jeroboam II's reign, would be lost. Their children would be handed over to the invading king (**the murderer**; v. 13) and killed or taken away into exile.

9:14–17. In these verses, the Lord and His prophet dialogue. Expressing a rather shocking sentiment, the prophet cried out for the Lord to bring His judgment to pass and to cause the women in the land to miscarry when giving birth. Hosea did not pray out of hateful vengeance against Israel but because he shared God's holy wrath against her sins. The Lord answered by saying that he would **drive them out of** His **house** (v. 15), just as an unfaithful wife is driven from the husband's house. Hearing the Lord's response, Hosea affirmed that the Lord would **cast ... away** (v. 17) Israel, and they would go into exile among the nations.

4. Sowing and Reaping: The Consequences of Sin (chap. 10)

10:1–10. This judgment speech contrasts Israel's past prosperity as a "fertile" vine (rather than **empty** vine as in KJV, v. 1; see Ps. 80:8–11) with its future humiliation and exile. When the Assyrian conqueror came, Israel would **have no king** (v. 3). The corrupt rulers who occupied the throne in Israel's last days were of no help to them anyway (v. 4). The golden-calf idol at Bethel and those who worshiped it would be taken out of the land (vv. 5–8). Hosea once again made reference to **Gibeah** (v. 9; see 9:9). The civil war resulting from the sin at Gibeah in Judges 19–21 had nearly resulted in the extermination of the tribe of Benjamin, but Israel had not learned from this past experience and would therefore once again experience national tragedy.

10:11–13. Up to this point, Israel had been as contented as a young cow (**heifer**; v. 11) that ate while threshing grain. Now God would cause Israel (**Ephraim**) and **Judah** to do the heavy work of plowing and harrowing under a yoke—a picture of the Assyrian and Babylonian captivities (vv. 10–13). Continuing with the agricultural imagery, the prophet warned that Israel could only avoid this fate if they learned to **Sow ... in righteousness** (v. 12) and **Reap in mercy** (Hebrew, *hesed*; see 6:6). If Israel would only do what was right, God would bless her. **Break up your fallow ground** was a call for Israel to make a radical beginning by repenting of their sin and becoming fruitful and productive for the Lord. In the past, Israel had only **plowed wickedness** (v. 13) and had lived a lie in pretending to be faithful.

10:14–15. The judgment against Israel would be as horrible as when **Shalman spoiled Beth-arbel** (v. 14). This event (and the names mentioned) is otherwise unknown but obviously involved atrocities against women and children, a common occurrence in ancient Near Eastern warfare (see 9:13; 13:16; 2 Kings 8:12–13; Ps. 137:8–9; Amos 1:13). The prophet painted a graphic picture of the coming judgment to motivate the people to change their ways.

5. God's Compassion toward Israel (11:1–11)

11:1–7. This positive message promises that the Lord will not abandon Israel as His covenant people because of His compassion for them. These verses focus on how Israel's unfaithfulness had necessitated judgment. Appealing to history (as in 9:10; 10:9), Hosea traced God's choice of Israel back to **Egypt** (v. 1), the exodus from that country having given birth to the nation (see 12:9; 13:4). Israel's response to the Lord is now illustrated by the wayward **son** rather than by the unfaithful wife (see chaps. 1–3; for Israel as a son, see Exod. 4:22–23; Isa. 1:2–4; for God as Father, see Deut. 32:6; Jer. 2:14). As a loving father, God had taught His people to walk and had **healed them** (v. 3) of their diseases. In verse 4, the imagery changes from family to farming to again stress God's loving care for Israel. The Lord had been like a farmer tending and taking care of his work animals. The Lord had done everything He possibly could for Israel, but His people had still rebelled against Him. Because of their ingratitude, they would be sent away into exile (vv. 5–7).

11:8–11. The stubborn son was subject to stoning (Deut. 21:18–21), but the Lord's compassion overcame His wrath, and He refused to destroy Ephraim (vv. 8–9). He would not treat them as **Admah** and **Zeboim** (v. 8), two cities of the plain that were destroyed with Sodom and Gomorrah (see Gen. 10:19; 14:2, 8; 19:24–25). The Lord is faithful to His covenant because He is **God, and not man** (v. 9). Although Israel had been as unreliable as man, God would not be untrue to the love He has shown Israel (see also 1 Sam. 15:29; Mal. 3:6). In the return from exile, Israel would **walk after the Lord** (v. 10) and no longer follow their sinful ways. The Lord would **roar like a lion**, this time not to destroy Israel (see 5:14; 13:7) but rather to save His people and to destroy their enemies. Israel would be like **a bird ... a dove** (v. 11), not with the negative connotation of 7:11, but in the positive sense that they would swiftly fly to the Lord (see Isa. 60:8).

C. The Lord's Faithful Love to an Ungrateful People (11:12–14:9)

1. Israel's Sin (11:12–12:14)

11:12–12:1. In the opening to this final series of judgment speeches, Israel is formally charged with covenant unfaithfulness (11:12–12:2). Israel had been deceitful as a covenant partner. Rather than allowing the Lord to exercise His divine prerogative to protect her, Israel had turned to foreign alliances (12:1). Israel's futile foreign policy, which vacillated between Egypt (2 Kings 17:4; Isa. 30:6–7) and Assyria (see 5:13; 7:11; 8:9; 2 Kings 17:3), was like chasing **after the east wind** (12:1) and would not deliver them from trouble.

12:2–6. In their history as a nation, Israel had relived the experiences of Jacob, who had taken **his brother by the heel** (v. 3) and was known for his deceit and treachery. Israel needed to return to God in the same way that Jacob had when he came to **Beth-el** (v. 4). In Hosea's time, Bethel was the most important royal sanctuary in the northern kingdom (see Amos 7:13), but the worship there had been corrupted by idolatry and insincerity. A true turning to the Lord also required a change of behavior, in which the people began to practice **mercy** (Hebrew, *hesed*) **and judgment** (or justice; v. 6) in their dealings with each other.

12:7–9. This change in behavior was needed because Israel had become a **merchant** (v. 7) who employed **the balances of deceit** to cheat others. The word "merchant" in Hebrew sounds like "Canaan," and the wordplay suggests that Israel was no better than the pagan Canaanites. Ephraim's riches brought a sense of self-sufficiency (see 10:13; Deut. 32:15–18), and like a dishonest merchant, **Ephraim** (Israel; v. 8) was confident that her deceitfulness would not be brought to light. The people did not take into consideration the fact that God would hold them accountable for how they had obtained their wealth. **I ... am the Lord thy God** (v. 9) was not a word of comfort but rather a warning that God would act to judge His covenant people. The Lord's judgment would force Israel **to dwell in tabernacles**, referring to the poverty of exile rather than to the feast of celebration in which Israel commemorated the wilderness journey (see Lev. 23:42–44).

12:10–14. The Lord had sent **the prophets** (v. 10) to warn the people, but the Israelites had refused to listen and continued in their sinful ways (vv. 10–11). If Israel believed that they would not be taken away into exile, they needed to again consider the example of **Jacob** (v. 12), who had been forced to leave the land and to serve Laban after fleeing from Esau. Israel had not returned to the land until after the exodus from Egypt (v. 13), so it is not beyond the realm of possibility for the Lord to remove Israel from the land once again. Israel had especially provoked the Lord to **anger** (v. 14) because of the **blood** of its violence, for which they would be held guilty.

2. Ephraim's Doom (chap. 13)

13:1–3. Ephraim (v. 1) had been exalted because of the blessing of Jacob (Gen. 48:10–20) and because of its rich history as a powerful tribe (Judg. 8:1–3; 12:1–7; 1 Sam. 1:1–4), from which came such prominent leaders as Joshua (Josh. 24:30) and Jeroboam I (1 Kings 11:26), but now faced death, as the end of the northern kingdom of Israel was at hand. They worshiped **molten images** (v. 2) and **kiss[ed] the calves** set up by Jeroboam to keep the northern tribes from going down to Jerusalem to worship (see 1 Kings 12:26–33). Hosea used the images of **the morning cloud** (v. 3), **the early dew**, and **the chaff** to speak of how Israel would vanish as a nation because of the coming judgment.

13:4–11. The Lord had delivered Israel from bondage in **Egypt** (v. 4) and had provided for Israel **in the wilderness** (v. 5), which made the fact that Israel had **forgotten** (v. 6) the Lord all the more unacceptable. The Lord, though previously pictured as a shepherd (4:16), would attack like **the wild beast** (v. 8) that often ravaged the flock (vv. 7–8). The Lord was Israel's **help** (v. 9) and **king** (v. 10), yet Israel had looked to human rulers as their source of security (vv. 9–11). Israel had rebelled against the Lord by asking for a king (see 1 Sam. 8:5–20), and the kings who ruled over them had in effect been the punishment for their sin. Now God was taking away even these rulers through the royal assassinations of the day and the coming exile, when the king would lose his throne.

13:12–16. Ephraim was like **a travailing woman** (v. 13). Their helpless situation is comparable to that of a woman in childbirth (see Isa. 13:8; 21:3; 26:17;

Jer. 4:31; Matt. 24:8) who cannot deliver the child (see 2 Kings 19:3; Isa. 37:3) and consequently dies (vv. 13–14). While verse 14 in the KJV and most English translations reads positively, it seems more likely in view of the negative message preceding and following this verse that the verse be read to say: "Will I ransom them, and will I redeem them from death?" The answer was no, as Israel needed to experience the full force of judgment before there could be deliverance. **Death** (v. 14) is here personified as the enemy that attacks and destroys Israel. It should be noted that Paul used this verse in a positive way with reference to the resurrection and the ultimate defeat of death (see 1 Cor. 15:55). The final image of judgment in this chapter is the comparison of Assyria to a drought-bringing **east wind** (v. 15; see Job 1:19; Isa. 27:8; Jer. 4:11) that would sweep through the land.

3. Israel's Restoration after Repentance (chap. 14)

14:1–3. This final section of promise begins with another appeal for repentance (see 10:12; 12:6). When Israel returned to the Lord, she needed to come with **words** (v. 2). None could come empty-handed (Exod. 23:15; 34:20), but animal sacrifices would not be enough. Only words of true repentance would be sufficient. The words that penitent Israel needed to speak follow: they needed to acknowledge their need for the Lord's forgiveness of **all iniquity**, and they needed to confess their misplaced trust in foreign alliances and idols.

14:4–9. When Israel returned to God in this manner, He would **heal** (v. 4) and **love** them. The Lord would be like refreshing **dew** (v. 5) that would cause Israel to flourish like the **lily**, the cedars of **Lebanon**, and the **olive tree** (v. 6). The Lord would be **like a green fir tree** (v. 8) that would provide shadow and protection for His people (vv. 7–8; see Ezek. 31:3–7; Dan. 4:12), a protection that could not be found when Israel looked to idols for their security. A concluding proverb (v. 9) contrasts the ways of the righteous and the wicked. Each individual must choose between walking or stumbling, the respective consequences of obedience and rebellion.

THE BOOK OF JOEL

INTRODUCTION

Author

The prophet Joel cannot be identified with any of the twelve other figures in the Old Testament who have the same name. He is not mentioned outside the books of Joel and Acts (Acts 2:16). The nonbiblical legends about him are unconvincing. His father, Pethuel (1:1), is also unknown. Judging from his concern with Judah and Jerusalem (see 2:32; 3:1, 6, 8, 16–20), it seems likely that Joel lived in that area.

Date

The book contains no references to datable historical events. Some have dated the book as early as the ninth century BC. However, three pieces of evidence support a postexilic date for the book: (1) the wording of 3:2–3 seems to view the exile as a past event, (2) the absence of any reference to a king reigning over the land, and (3) the reference to slave trade with the Greeks (3:6). Thus, Joel was most likely written in the sixth century BC, after Haggai and Zechariah. The message is not significantly affected by its dating, but a postexilic date would indicate the intransigence of the people in that they quickly turned away from the Lord and faced further judgment for continued sinfulness even after the nation had experienced the devastating judgment of the exile.

The book of Joel has striking linguistic parallels to those of Amos, Micah, Zephaniah, Jeremiah, and Ezekiel. The literary relationships of those books are determined by one's view of the date of Joel. If it was written earlier, the other prophets borrowed his phrases; if it was later, the reverse may have taken place. Some scholars maintain that all the prophets drew more or less from the religious literary traditions that they and their readers shared in common, liturgical and otherwise.

Theme and Theological Message

Joel sees the massive locust plague Judah had already experienced as a harbinger of "the great and the terrible day of the LORD" (2:31). The locusts are depicted as an army in chapter 1, and the image of the locust swarm becomes a figure for an approaching army in chapter 2. Confronted with this crisis, Joel called on everyone to repent: old and young (1:2–3), drunkards (1:5), farmers (1:11), and priests (1:13). Joel saw in the locusts a reminder and a warning that "the day of the LORD is at hand" (1:15). Unless the people repented, they would face further judgment from the Lord. Joel did not voice the popular notion that the day of the Lord will be one of judgment on the nations but deliverance and blessing for Israel. Instead—with Isaiah (2:10–21), Jeremiah (4:6), Amos (5:18–20), and Zephaniah (1:7–18)—he described the day as one of punishment for unfaithful Israel as well. Restoration and blessing will come but only after judgment and repentance.

Outline

I. The Locust Plague and the Coming Day of the Lord (1:3–2:17)
  A. A Call to Mourning and Prayer (1:2–12)
  B. The Day of the Lord Is Near (1:13–20)
  C. The Approaching Army from the North (2:1–11)
  D. A Call to Repentance and Prayer (2:12–17)
II. Judah Is Assured of Salvation in the Future Day of the Lord (2:18–3:21)
  A. The Lord's Restoration of Judah (2:18–27)
  B. The Lord's Renewal of His People and the Future Outpouring of the Spirit (2:28–32)
  C. The Nations Judged and Israel Restored (chap. 3)

Bibliography

Allen, Leslie C. *The Books of Joel, Obadiah, Jonah, and Micah.* New International Commentary on the Old Testament. Grand Rapids, MI: Eerdmans, 1976.

Finley, Thomas J. *Joel, Amos, Obadiah.* Wycliffe Exegetical Commentary. Chicago: Moody, 1990.

Garrett, Duane A. *Hosea, Joel.* New American Commentary 19A. Nashville: Broadman & Holman, 1996.

Hubbard, David A. *Joel and Amos: An Introduction and Commentary.* Tyndale Old Testament Commentaries 22B. Downers Grover, IL: InterVarsity, 1989.

Motyer, J. A. *The Message of Joel, Micah, and Habakkuk.* The Bible Speaks Today. Downers Grove, IL: InterVarsity, 1999.

Patterson, R. D. "Joel." In *The Expositor's Bible Commentary*, edited by Frank E. Gaebelein, vol. 7. Grand Rapids, MI: Zondervan, 1985.

EXPOSITION

I. The Locust Plague and the Coming Day of the Lord (1:2 – 2:17)

Chapter 1 contains a call for repentance consisting of two parts. Verses 2 – 12 calls for the elders and the people of the land to recognize a recent locust plague and drought as the Lord's hand of judgment. Verses 13 – 20 command a sacred assembly for the acknowledgment of national sin, with the warning that "the day of the LORD" is near. The prophet's message was that failure to repent would bring even further judgment from the Lord.

A. A Call to Mourning and Prayer (1:2 – 12)

1:2 – 12. In depicting the devastation of the locust plague, the prophet employed four different Hebrew words for **locust[s]** (v. 4), creating the image of wave after wave of insects swarming through the land. In verses 6 – 7, the locusts are compared to **a nation** (v. 6). Elsewhere, they are called the Lord's "army" (2:11, 25). The reverse comparison of armies to locusts is as old as Ugaritic literature (fifteenth century BC) and is common in the Old Testament (see Judg. 6:5; 7:12; Jer. 46:23; 51:14; Num. 3:15). The locusts who attack the land are **without number**, a phrase used to describe the locusts in the plague in Egypt (Ps. 105:34; see Exod. 10:4 – 6, 12 – 15). The judgment once inflicted on Egypt during Israel's formation as a nation was now turned against God's own sinful people.

The reference to **drunkards** (v. 5) and **drinkers of wine** highlights drunkenness as the only specific sin of Judah mentioned in this book. This sin suggests a self-indulgent lifestyle (see Isa. 28:7 – 8; Amos 4:1) pursued by those who value material things more than spiritual things. Fittingly, the destruction of the vines by the locusts (vv. 7 – 8) leaves the drunkards without a source of wine. The destruction caused by the locusts was intensified by drought (vv. 10 – 12), and the nation experienced severe agricultural deprivation. Locusts, drought, and famine were all specific manifestations of the covenant curses that Moses had warned that God would bring against Israel for violation of His commandments (see Lev. 26:19 – 20; Deut. 28:23 – 24, 38 – 42).

Joel called for the general population (v. 8), the farmers (v. 11), and the priests (v. 13) to mourn and fast over their sin instead of wallowing in their spiritual stupor. Fasting was required on the Day of Atonement (see Lev. 16:20) and was also practiced in times of calamity and national disaster (see Judg. 20:26; 2 Sam. 12:16; Jer. 14:12; John 3:4 – 5; Zech. 7:3) as a sign of penitent humility. The real issue, however, was not outward ritual but a genuine, inward change, which Joel pictured as a rending of the heart (2:13).

B. The Day of the Lord Is Near (1:13 – 20)

1:13 – 20. Joel's warning that **the day of the LORD is at hand** (v. 15) indicates that failure to repent would bring further and even more severe judgment from the Lord. The phrase "the day of the LORD" appears five times in Joel (see also 2:1, 11, 31; 3:14) and is the dominant theme of the book. Six other prophets also used this expression (Isaiah, 13:6, 9; Ezekiel, 13:5; 30:3; Amos, 5:18 – 20; Obadiah, 15; Zephaniah, 1:7, 14; Malachi, 4:5), and a similar expression occurs in Zechariah 14:1. This term refers to the decisive intervention of God in history during the time of the prophets, such as the locust invasion of Joel's day, the battle of Carchemish in 605 BC (Jer. 46:2, 10), and the Babylonian destruction of Jerusalem in 586 BC (Zeph. 1:7, 14). The day of the Lord also has reference to God's ultimate intervention in the final judgment at the coming of Christ to consummate history (see Joel 3:1 – 21; Mal. 4:5; Matt. 11:24; 1 Thess. 5:2; 2 Peter 3:10). It is important to recognize that the prophets often refer to the "near" and "far" elements of the day of the Lord without carefully distinguishing between the two. Each divine judgment from past history points to the final day of the Lord, when God will punish His enemies and bring security and blessing to His people.

The prophet lamented and cried out to God over the empty storehouses and starving animals, which the locust invasion and drought had caused (vv. 16–20). Judah had experienced the sweeping fire of God's judgment (see Jer. 4:4; 15:14; Ezek. 5:4; Hos. 8:14; Amos 1:4, 7, 10), but the judgment she had experienced in the past was nothing compared to the calamity that would come if the people persisted in their sin and rebellion.

C. The Approaching Army from the North (2:1–11)

2:1–11. This passage provides a second warning of the approaching day of the Lord. The command to **Blow … the trumpet in Zion** (v. 1) refers to the practice of using a ram's or bull's horn to signal approaching danger (Jer. 4:5; 6:1; Ezek. 33:3). The time of God's judgment would be a **day of darkness** (v. 2), a common metaphor for distress and suffering (see Isa. 5:30; 8:22; Jer. 2:6, 31; Ezek. 24:12). **As the morning spread upon the mountains** (v. 2b) suggests relief from the darkness but instead describes an enemy army crossing the land like the light of dawn that first illumines the eastern horizon and then spreads across the whole countryside.

The army that would invade the land (vv. 3–11) is once again a horde of locusts as in chapter 1, which raises an important interpretive issue. Perhaps this vision of the locust invasion is describing the same event as 1:6–7, but the warning of impending judgment argues against this option. Joel may be describing a coming locust plague even more severe than the one already experienced, but the ominous tone of this passage and the connection with the day of the Lord suggests more the idea that the locust swarm here is metaphorical of an invading army that would attack from the north. Just as the prophet compared the locust to an army in chapter 1, here he compared an army to a locust plague, suggesting both the size and swiftness of the army that would attack the land. The staccato character of the poetry in verses 3–11 is appropriate for the imagery of war.

Joel created a special effect by using the phrases **before them** (twice in v. 3, once in v. 10) and **behind them** (twice in v. 3) to portray the havoc and devastation wreaked by this enemy and the phrase **Before their face** (v. 6) with reference to the fear created by approach of this army. This army would destroy everything in its path. The land is like the garden of Eden before the fall as the army approaches and like a desert wasteland after they have marched through (v. 5). These attackers would have superhuman strength in carrying out their assault, and barriers such as mountains and walls would offer no protection against this locust-like army (vv. 6–9). The shaking of the earth (see Pss. 68:8; 77:18; Isa. 24:18–20), the trembling of the sky (see Isa. 13:13; Hag. 2:21; Heb. 12:26–28), and the darkening of the sun and moon links this judgment to the cosmic phenomena of God's theophany and the day of the Lord (v. 10). The rhetorical question, **who can abide it?** (v. 11), that closes this section suggests that this judgment would be so severe that there will be no escape except in turning to the Lord (see Nah. 1:6; Mal. 3:2; Rev. 6:17).

D. A Call to Repentance and Prayer (2:12–17)

2:12–17. The call to repentance stressed the importance of a genuine return to the Lord and a heartfelt repentance that went beyond the external sign of rending one's garment as a symbol of mourning and contrition (vv. 12–13). The motivation for repentance was that the Lord is **gracious and merciful, slow to anger, and of great kindness** (v. 13), recalling the great self-characterization of God in Exodus 34:6–7, which runs like a golden thread throughout the Old Testament (see Deut. 4:31; Mic. 7:18). The command to **Blow the trumpet in Zion** (v. 15) repeats 2:1 but here represents a call to religious assembly rather than an alarm (see Lev. 23:24; 25:9; Num. 10:10). This call for religious assembly was for the entire community, and no segment of the population, not even the nursing mother or **the bridegroom** (v. 16) in his chamber preparing to consummate his marriage, was exempt from participation. In their assembly, the people were to make petition by reminding the Lord that they were His **heritage** (v. 17), or special possession (see Exod. 15:17; 19:5; 34:9). Judah was to plead, not her innocence, but that God's honor was at stake before the world (see Exod. 32:12; Num. 14:13; Deut. 9:28).

II. Judah Is Assured of Salvation in the Future Day of the Lord (2:18–3:21)

A. The Lord's Restoration of Judah (2:18–27)

2:18–27. This section marks a dramatic change in tone as the prophet turned from the destruction caused by the locusts to the blessings God would give to a repentant people. The theme of the reversal of the Lord's judgment permeates this section. This change in tone suggests that the people had positively responded to Joel's calls for repentance and that the Lord at least temporarily relented from sending the judgment threatened in verses 1–11. In contrast to the recent agricultural deprivation, the Lord promised to send the blessings of **corn, … wine, and oil** (v. 19). The Lord also promised to drive away **the northern army** (v. 20) that would attack the land, further proof that the locusts in chapter 2 are figurative for a literal army in that military invasions into Palestine normally came from the north (see Isa. 14:31; 41:25; Jer. 1:14). As there was a threefold call to grief in the previous chapter (1:5, 8, 13), so now there was a threefold call to joy as the **land** (v. 21), the wild animals (v. 22), and the people (v. 23) were called on to rejoice in the Lord's bounty. The end result was that **Israel** (v. 27; used here without distinction between the northern and southern kingdoms, as in 3:2, 16) would know of the special covenant relationship that exists between the Lord and Israel. The expression **I am the Lord your God** recalls the covenant the Lord established with Israel at Sinai (see Exod. 20:2).

B. The Lord's Renewal of His People and the Future Outpouring of the Spirit (2:28–32)

2:28–32. The reference to **afterward** (v. 28) points to the messianic period, the eschatological last days, beyond the restoration portrayed in the previous verses. Up to this point, Joel had prophesied concerning the day of the Lord that was near; now the prophet turned his attention to the day of the Lord that was far. The Lord promises to **pour out my spirit**, and the promise of a future outpouring of the Spirit is a common theme in the Old Testament prophetic literature (see Isa. 32:15; Jer. 31:33–34; Ezek. 36:26–27; 39:29). The reference to **all flesh** means all Israelites, stressing that all will enjoy the blessing of the Spirit without regard to sex, age, or rank. This experience of the Spirit for the entire nation will bring the realization of Moses' wish in Numbers 11:29 and contrasts to the previous operation of the Spirit in the Old Testament, which focused primarily on empowerment of leaders and designated individuals within the nation.

This passage was quoted by Peter at Pentecost (Acts 2:16–21) with a few variations from both the Hebrew text and the Septuagint. The primary difficulty of Peter's quotation of Joel 2:28–32 is that all of the events prophesied here by Joel (especially the cosmic signs and full restoration of Israel envisioned in vv. 30–32) did not occur at Pentecost. Peter's quotation indicates that he understood the experience of Pentecost to be the initial fulfillment of Joel's promise concerning the outpouring of the Spirit. Peter extends the **all flesh** of verse 28 and the **whosoever** of verse 32 to include the Gentiles (see Acts 2:39), who are not excluded from the Spirit's outpouring or deliverance (see Rom. 11:11–24). The experience of the Spirit by believers today as Abraham's spiritual seed (see Gal. 3:28–29) points to the complete fulfillment of Joel 2 and the restoration of the nation of Israel when **whosoever shall call on the name of the Lord shall be delivered** (v. 32; see Rom. 11:25–27).

C. The Nations Judged and Israel Restored (chap. 3)

3:1. A common feature of the prophetic messages in the Old Testament is that the eschatological age of blessing is preceded by the nations of the earth descending on Jerusalem in a final battle against God and His people. The Zion tradition in the Old Testament celebrates God's protection of Jerusalem and His promise to defeat the enemy armies who attack Jersualem (see Pss. 46:4–5; 48:4–8; 76:2–3). The sin of Israel and Judah had necessitated a temporary setting aside of this protection as the Assyrians and the Babylonians wreaked havoc and destruction on Jerusalem. The Lord, however, will fulfill His promise to protect Jerusalem by reversing its former captivity, defeating the armies who make this final assault, and making the city secure for all time.

3:2 – 8. The Lord will gather all nations for this decisive battle at **the valley of Jehoshaphat** (v. 2; 3:12), also referred to as "the valley of decision" (3:14). The name Jehoshaphat means "the Lord judges," and thus "the valley of Jehoshaphat" seems to be a symbolic name for a valley near Jerusalem that is depicted here as the place of God's ultimate judgment on the nations gathered against Jerusalem. The name Jehoshaphat also recalls the Lord's historic victory over the nations during the reign of Jehoshaphat, which serves as a preview of God's great victory in the future (see 2 Chron. 20:1 – 30). Eight times in verses 2 – 5, God uses the pronoun **my** to emphasize His covenant relationship with Israel. The Lord promises to settle the score with the enemies who **cast lots** (v. 3) for Judah and treated God's people as mere chattel to be traded off for the pleasures of prostitution and wine. When God judges the nations, the punishment fits the crime. God promises to bring down on the nations what they have done to Israel and Judah (vv. 4 – 8).

3:9 – 21. This passage elaborates on the future battle when God will fight against the nations that attack Israel.

3:9 – 11. Here Joel is the speaker. The nations are to prepare for battle, for the Lord will come against them with His invincible heavenly army and bring them into judgment (see Ezekiel 38 – 39; Revelation 19). **Beat your plowshares into swords** (v. 10) is the reverse of Isaiah 2:4 and Micah 4:3, where the peaceful effect of God's reign is portrayed. Here God's enemies are summoned to their last great confrontation with Him, and this great battle of retribution and judgment must be carried out as the prelude to the kingdom of lasting peace.

3:12 – 13. The Lord speaks of the eschatological battle as a great **harvest** (v. 13). When the Lord's army had marched against Judah (2:3 – 11), there had been no harvest (2:3); that harvest was to be restored (2:19, 22, 24, 26). In the final great day of the Lord, there will also be a harvest — the har-

vest of God's judgment on the nations. Revelation 14:14 – 20 draws heavily on this picture of judgment from the book of Joel.

3:14 – 16. The prophet speaks of the Valley of Jehoshaphat as **the valley of decision** (v. 14), the word "decision" signifying the heavenly Judge's decision or judicial decree. This valley is viewed as the place where that decree will be executed. **The Lord … shall roar out of Zion** (v. 16); like a lion, He will destroy the nations. Just as God had thundered against Jerusalem (2:11), so He will thunder against Jerusalem's enemies (v. 16). After the time of judgment has passed, the Lord will fulfill His original promise of the Zion tradition to make Jerusalem a refuge (see Ps. 46:1) and to destroy the enemy armies who dare to attack His holy city.

3:17 – 21. The Lord speaks personally to assure the fulfillment of the promise to make Jerusalem a place of blessing and security. The final blessed state of the now unholy and vulnerable city will be God's abiding presence in **Zion** (v. 17; see 2:27; Ps. 46:4; Rev. 21:3). The future abundance of Jerusalem, described in terms of Edenic lushness (v. 18), stands in stark contrast to the conditions of drought and famine in 1:10. Flowing from God's presence at the Jerusalem temple, streams of blessing will refresh His people and make their place endlessly fruitful (see Pss. 36:8; 87:7; Ezek. 47:1 – 12; Rev. 22:1 – 2).

Verse 19 sets in sharp focus the contrasting destinies of God's people and the enemies of God's kingdom. In contrast to Israel's future blessing, **Egypt … and Edom** (v. 19), old enemies of Israel that are here representative of all nations hostile to God's people, will be reduced to desert wastelands. This picture of desolation recalls the earlier description of Judah's condition when under the sentence of God's judgment (see 2:3). When God's judgment and redemption are consummated, His kingdom will endure and will flourish eternally; Jerusalem shall dwell **from generation to generation** (v. 20). This book of judgment ends on a promising and encouraging note: **The Lord dwelleth in Zion** (v. 21), and therefore all is right with those who trust in God and live with Him.

THE BOOK OF AMOS

INTRODUCTION

Author

Amos was from Tekoa (1:1), a small town about six miles south of Bethlehem and eleven miles from Jerusalem. He was not a man of the court like Isaiah, nor a priest like Jeremiah. He earned his living from the flocks and the sycamore-fig grove (1:1; 7:14–15). Whether he owned the flocks or worked as a hired hand is not known. His skill with words and the striking broad range of his general knowledge of history and the world preclude his being an ignorant peasant. Though his home was in Judah, he was sent to announce God's judgment on the northern kingdom (Israel). He probably ministered for the most part at Bethel (7:10–13; see Gen. 12:8), Israel's main religious sanctuary, where the upper echelons of the northern kingdom worshiped. The book brings his prophecies together in a carefully organized form intended to be read as a unit. It offers few, if any, clues as to the chronological order of his spoken messages; he may have repeated them on many occasions to reach everyone who came to worship. The book is addressed also to the southern kingdom (hence the references to Judah and Jerusalem).

Date

According to the first verse, Amos prophesied during the reigns of Uzziah over Judah (792–740 BC) and Jeroboam II over Israel (793–753 BC). The main part of his ministry was probably carried out circa 760–750 BC.

Background

The northern and the southern kingdoms were both enjoying great prosperity and had reached new political and military heights (see 2 Kings 14:23–15:7; 2 Chronicles 26). It was also a time of idolatry, extravagant indulgence in luxurious living, immorality, corruption of judicial procedures, and oppression of the poor. As a consequence, God would soon bring about the Assyrian captivity of the northern kingdom (722–721 BC).

Israel at the time was politically secure and spiritually smug. About forty years earlier, at the end of his ministry, Elisha had prophesied the resurgence of Israel's power (2 Kings 13:17–19), and more recently, Jonah had prophesied her restoration to a glory not known since the days of Solomon (2 Kings 14:25). The nation felt sure, therefore, that she was in God's good graces. Prosperity increased Israel's religious and moral corruption. God's past punishments for unfaithfulness were forgotten, and His patience was at an end—which He sent Amos to announce.

The messages of the prophets, including Amos, began to be preserved in permanent form, being brought together in books that would accompany Israel through the coming debacle and beyond. (Since Amos was a contemporary of Hosea and Jonah, see Introductions to those books.)

Theme and Theological Message

The dominant theme is clearly stated in 5:24, which calls for social justice as the indispensable expression of true piety. Amos was a vigorous spokesman for God's justice and righteousness, whereas Hosea emphasized God's love, grace, mercy, and forgiveness. Amos declared that God was going to judge His unfaithful, disobedient, covenant-breaking people. Despite His special choice of Israel and His kindnesses to her during the exodus and the conquest and in the days of David and Solomon, His people continually failed to honor and obey Him. The shrines at Bethel and other places of worship were often paganized, and Israel had a worldly view of even the ritual that the Lord Himself had prescribed. They thought performance of the rites was all God required, and, with that done, they could do whatever they pleased—an essentially pagan notion. Without commitment to God's law, they had no basis for standards of conduct. Those who had acquired two splendid houses (3:15), expensive furniture, and richly furnished tables by cheating, perverting justice, and crushing the poor would lose everything they had.

God's imminent judgment on Israel would not be a mere punitive blow of warning but an almost total destruction. The unthinkable was about to happen: because they had not faithfully consecrated themselves to His lordship, God would uproot His chosen people by the hand of a pagan nation. Even so, if they would repent, there was hope that "the LORD God of hosts will be gracious unto the remnant" (5:15; see 5:4–6, 14). In fact, the Lord had a glorious future for His people, beyond the impending judgment. The house of David would again rule over Israel and would even extend its rule over many nations, and Israel would once more be secure in the Promised Land, feasting on wine and fruit (9:11–15). The God of Israel, the Lord of history, would not abandon His chosen people or His chosen program of redemption.

The God for whom Amos speaks is the God of more than merely Israel. He is the Great King who rules the whole universe (4:13; 5:8; 9:5–6). Because He is all-sovereign, the God of Israel holds the history and destiny of all peoples and of the world in His hands. Israel needed to know not only that He is the Lord of her future but also that He is Lord over all and that He has purposes and concerns that reach far beyond her borders. For that reason, Amos is the only prophet to open his book with oracles against the nations. As the first prophet to introduce the day of the Lord, he is the first to introduce the truth that God is no respecter of nations. Israel had a unique, but not an exclusive, claim on God. She needed to remember not only His covenant commitments to her but also her covenant obligations to Him.

Outline

I. Superscription (1:1)

II. Judgment on the Nations (chaps. 1–2)
  A. Introduction to Amos's Message (1:2)
  B. Judgment on Aram (1:3–5)
  C. Judgment on Philistia (1:6–8)
  D. Judgment on Phoenicia (1:9–10)
  E. Judgment on Edom (1:11–12)
  F. Judgment on Ammon (1:13–15)
  G. Judgment on Moab (2:1–3)
  H. Judgment on Judah (2:4–5)
  I. Judgment on Israel (2:6–16)

III. Oracles against Israel (3:1–5:17)
  A. Judgment on the Chosen People (chap. 3)
  B. Judgment on an Unrepentant People (chap. 4)
  C. Judgment on an Unjust People (5:1–17)

IV. Announcements of Exile (5:18–27)

V. Judgment of Israel's Sinful Pride (chap. 6)

VI. Visions of Divine Retribution (7:1–9:10)
  A. Visions of Judgment Relented (7:1–6)
  B. Visions of Judgments Unrelented (7:7–9:10)
    1. The Vision of the Plumbline (7:7–17)
    2. The Vision of the Basket of Summer Fruit (chap. 8)
    3. The Vision of the Lord by the Altar (9:1–10)

VII. Restored Israel's Blessed Future (9:11–15)

Bibliography

Finley, Thomas J. *Joel, Amos, Obadiah.* Wycliffe Exegetical Commentary. Chicago: Moody, 1990.

Hasel, G. F. *Understanding the Book of Amos.* Grand Rapids, MI: Baker, 1991.

Hubbard, David A. *Joel and Amos: An Introduction and Commentary.* Tyndale Old Testament Commentaries 22B. Downers Grove, IL: InterVarsity, 1989.

Motyer, J. A. *The Day of the Lion: The Message of Amos.* London: InterVarsity, 1974.

Smith, Billy K., and Frank S. Page. *Amos, Obadiah, Jonah.* New American Commentary 19B. Nashville: Broadman & Holman, 1995.

Smith, G. V. *Amos: A Commentary.* Grand Rapids, MI: Zondervan, 1989.

EXPOSITION

I. Superscription (1:1)

1:1. The name **Amos** is apparently a shortened form of a name like Amasiah (2 Chron. 17:16), meaning "the Lord carries" or "the Lord upholds." Before becoming a prophet to Israel, Amos was by vocation **among the herdmen**. The Hebrew for this word occurs elsewhere in the Old Testament only in reference to the king of Moab (see 2 Kings 3:4), where it is translated "sheepmaster." Perhaps Amos was not a simple shepherd but was in charge of the royal flocks (see 7:14, where a different Hebrew term is used). Amos was not a professional prophet who earned his living from his ministry; he stood outside religious institutions. Amos carried out his ministry in Israel two years before a devastating **earthquake**, which was evidently a major shock, long remembered, and also the one mentioned in Zechariah 14:5. Excavations have confirmed the damage caused by this earthquake in Samaria. Mention of the earthquake here suggests that the author viewed it as a kind of divine reinforcement of the words of judgment. Amos uses the verb form in 9:1 ("shake") to create an envelope effect between the past and coming quakes.

II. Judgment on the Nations (chaps. 1–2)

This opening section of the book of Amos contains a series of oracles against the nations that effectively demonstrates a rhetorical strategy of entrapment frequently found in the preaching of the prophets. After pronouncing judgments on Israel's neighbors for various atrocities—judgments that Israel would naturally applaud—Amos announced God's condemnation of His own two kingdoms for despising God's laws. After an apparently complete cycle of seven judgment speeches, Amos's eighth judgment speech focused on Israel, the real object of his prophetic indictment. His listing Israel's sins under the same form of indictment used against the other nations shockingly pictured Israel's sins alongside those of her pagan neighbors.

A. Introduction to Amos's Message (1:2)

1:2. This is a thematic verse, ominously announcing the main thrust of Amos's message. The Lord would **roar from Zion** like a lion. Amos, a shepherd, was sent to Israel to warn her that he had heard a lion roar and that the lion was none other than the Lord Himself, who had only wanted to be Israel's shepherd. "Roar" is also a link word connecting Joel and Amos (see Joel 3:16). Zion was where the Lord had established His earthly throne, in Jerusalem, among His special people, but now was the place from which He announced His judgment on them, as well as on the other nations. In addition to the picture of the Lord as a lion, Amos employed storm imagery to depict the ferocity of the Lord's wrath against sinners. Like a severe windstorm and drought, the Lord's judgment would bring devastation to all the land of Israel, even **the habitations of the shepherds** (i.e., pasturelands) and the lush forests on Mount **Carmel**. Lion and storm/drought imagery appear throughout the book with reference to the destruction that God would bring on the people of Israel (see 3:4, 12; 4:7; 5:19; 8:8; 9:5–6).

B. Judgment on Aram (1:3–5)

1:3–5. The opening **For three transgressions ... and for four** (v. 3) in each of these speeches is a poetic way of saying that the nations were guilty of many sins (see Prov. 6:16; 30:15, 18, 21, 29), but the one crime named was the particular focus of the prophet's indictment. **Damascus** was the capital of the Aramean state directly north of Israel and a constant enemy in that day. Her crime was brutality to the conquered people of Gilead, Israel's territory north of Galilee. This brutality is graphically pictured as **threshing** with **instruments of iron**. Heads of grain were threshed by driving a wooden sledge fitted with sharp teeth over the cut grain (see Ruth 1:22; 2 Kings 13:7; Job 41:30; Isa. 28:27; 41:15). Because of this atrocity, the **fire** (v. 4) of judgment would consume the city of Damascus and the palaces of the Aramean king, **Ben-hadad**, the son of **Hazael** who reigned circa 796–775 BC. Fire is a common figure for divine judgment, usually carried out by a devastating war that resulted in the burning of major cities and fortresses (see Jer. 17:27; 49:27; 50:32; Hos. 8:14).

C. Judgment on Philistia (1:6–8)

1:6–8. Gaza (v. 6) was one of the five Philistine cities, and it guarded the entry to Canaan from Egypt. The crime of the Philistines was that **they carried away captive the whole captivity**, most likely referring to the capture of villages in south Judah on the trade route and the selling of the people of these villages into slavery in **Edom**. The Philistines were guilty of trading the people of Judah like cattle to another country. The end of the book of Amos envisions a reversal of the situation of verse 8, with the promise that Israel would "possess Edom" (see 9:12). As in the previous oracle, the judgment would take the form of a devastating **fire** (v. 7) that would consume Gaza, as well as the Philistine cities **Ashdod, Ashkelon**, and **Ekron** (v. 8). The judgment would be swift and severe, with no **remnant** left for the Philistine people.

D. Judgment on Phoenicia (1:9–10)

1:9–10. Tyrus (v. 9), or Tyre, was the senior Phoenician merchant city, allied to Israel by a "brotherly covenant" in the days of David (1 Kings 5:1), later in the time of Solomon (1 Kings 12), and later still during the reign of Ahab, whose father-in-law ruled Tyre and Sidon (1 Kings 16:30–31). The crime of Tyre was like that of Philistia in that **they delivered up the whole captivity to Edom**, but even more heinous in that this abuse was committed against a covenant partner (**remembered not the brotherly covenant**). The Lord would again send **fire on the wall** (v. 10) of Tyre, which as an almost impregnable island fortress (see Ezek. 26:1–28:19), was boastful of her security.

E. Judgment on Edom (1:11–12)

1:11–12. Edom (v. 11) was the nation descended from Esau (Genesis 36; see Gen. 25:23–30;

27:39–40). Like Phoenicia, Edom violated their covenant commitments to Israel by engaging in persistent acts of hostility and violence against Israel (see Obadiah 8–10). For Edom's acts of aggression against Israel, the fire of judgment would fall on **Teman** (v. 12) and **Bozrah**, the major cities of Edom. With the destruction of these two cities, Edom would lose its capacity for continual warfare.

F. Judgment on Ammon (1:13–15)

1:13–15. The greed of **the children of Ammon** (v. 13) for land bred a brutal genocide against the inhabitants of Gilead (see 1:3 above). The announcement of judgment against Ammon centered on **Rabbah** (v. 14; see Deut. 3:11), modern Amman. Judgment in the form of Assyrian invasion would bring a tumult of men and nature, leaving the state without leaders to continue their violent policies. Amos used the word **captivity** (v. 15), here and later in 9:14, as an "envelope" term at the beginning and end of his prophecy to highlight the contrast between the permanent destruction of Israel's enemies and the ultimate reversal of Israel's captivity when God would restore His people.

G. Judgment on Moab (2:1–3)

2:1–3. Moab (v. 1) was guilty of war crimes against Edom. The burning of **the bones of the king of Edom** was particularly inhumane in that such an act deprived the king's spirit of the rest that was widely believed to result from decent burial. The name **Kerioth** (v. 2) is perhaps a plural noun meaning "cities" (thus "citadels of her cities") or the name of a major town (see Jer. 48:24) and shrine of Chemosh, the national god of Moab (see 1 Kings 11:7, 33).

Amos's oracles against these foreign nations reflect an outworking of God's promise to Abraham that "I will bless them that bless thee, and curse him that curseth thee" (Gen. 12:3). The prophet Zechariah declared that whoever oppressed Israel was in effect touching the "apple" (pupil) of God' eye (Zech. 2:8), and God promised that He will settle the score with those who have perpetrated acts of violence against Israel. At the same time, the judgment on Moab also demonstrates that the nations are responsible to God for the way in which they treat each other as well, a responsibility going back to the Noahic covenant in Genesis 9 and the prohibition against shedding blood (see Gen. 9:5–6). The prophet Isaiah also appears to base the judgment of the nations of the earth on "the everlasting covenant" established with Noah as a standard of conduct for all time (see Isa. 24:5). The words of Amos to these ancient nations from history also serve as a warning of coming judgment for nations guilty of crimes of inhumanity. Nations who practice genocide, war crimes, abortion, and racial injustice stand condemned before God, just as Israel's neighbors did in the eighth century BC.

H. Judgment on Judah (2:4–5)

2:4–5. Amos next condemned **Judah** (v. 4), Israel's bitter enemies to the south—the message that the prophet's audience might have applauded the most. The sin of Judah was that **they have despised the law of the LORD**. Judah's sins differed in kind from those of the other nations. Those nations had violated the generally recognized laws of humanity, but Judah had disobeyed the revealed law of God. These sins may be included in Amos's later indictment of Israel. Judah's punishment would be the same as that of Aram (1:4), Gaza (1:7), Tyre (1:10), Edom (1:12), Ammon (1:14), and Moab (2:2)—**fire** (v. 5) would destroy the physical defenses and the wealth in which they had trusted.

These oracles against the nations reveal Amos's incredible literary skill. Seven times "I will send fire" is followed by two triads, "on the wall" and "upon" (Teman), followed by seven times "it shall devour," followed by another triadic dual, "its palaces" and "the palaces of Jerusalem" and a final triad, "I will cut off." He was hardly a simple shepherd.

I. Judgment on Israel (2:6–16)

2:6–16. The length of the final oracle demonstrates that Israel was the real target of Amos's message. The long list of sins in the indictment stripped away Israel's sense of superiority over their pagan

neighbors and reflects the fact that Israel had a greater accountability because they were the recipients of God's special laws and commandments.

2:6–12. Israel was first guilty of ruthless oppression of the poor (vv. 6–7). Selling **the righteous** (v. 6) likely involved selling debtors into slavery and even selling those for whom there was no lawful reason to sell (see Lev. 25:39–43). Rather than helping the poor, as the law commanded (see Deut. 15:7–11), the Israelites enslaved the poor into debt slavery for failure to pay even a paltry debt, **a pair of shoes** referring to the sandals given as a pledge to pay back a loan (see 8:6). The phrase **pant after the dust … on the head of the poor** (v. 7) could also be translated "trample the head of the poor into the dust of the ground" or "tread upon the head of the poor as on the dust of the ground."

Mistreatment of the poor included sexual exploitation, in which **a man and his father will go in unto the same maid** (v. 7), likely referring to the treatment of a household servant as a prostitute. The law stated that a man who had sexual relations with an unbetrothed woman was obligated to marry her (see Exod. 22:16; Deut. 22:28–29). For a father and son to have sexual relations with the same woman was strictly forbidden (see Lev. 18:7–8, 15; 20:11–12).

Israel was also guilty of profaning her religious practices. The Israelites worshiped at their altars, lying down on **clothes laid to pledge** (v. 8). The law prohibited keeping a man's cloak overnight as a pledge (Exod. 22:26–27; Deut. 24:12–13) or taking a widow's cloak at all (Deut. 24:17). They also drank **the wine of the condemned**, fines paid as restitution for false charges of damage, at their sanctuaries. Israelites who had broken the laws that protected the powerless were brazenly using their wrongly gotten gains in places that were supposed to be holy.

Israel had committed these sins in spite of the divine privileges that she enjoyed over other nations (vv. 9–12). God had destroyed the **Amorite** (v. 9), a term used here for all the inhabitants of Canaan (see Gen. 10:16; 15:16; Deut. 7:1; Judg. 6:10), and had **brought up** (v. 10) Israel from **Egypt** in the exodus. These past blessings added to Israel's guilt and were a reminder that her status as the people of God was a position of responsibility and not a privilege that protected the Israelites from the demands of righteousness (see 3:1–2). In addition, they had showed disdain for God's choice servants (i.e., the **Nazirites** and **prophets**; v. 12) and thus betrayed their callous insensitivity to God's working among them (see 7:16).

2:13–16. After the lengthy accusation, Amos announced that Israel's system of oppressive social structures would perish. **I am pressed under you** (v. 13) sounds as if God is the one being pressed under and should be read "I will press you under," referring to how God's judgment would be like **a cart … that is full of sheaves** when it crushed Israel under its weight. No one who might be expected to stand his ground or escape — **the swift** (v. 14) and **the strong**, the warrior, the archer, the soldier, the horsemen, the bravest warriors — would be able to escape. The **day** (v. 16) of God's judgment against Israel would be the Assyrian invasion, which swept the northern kingdom away. Kings in the ancient Near East often boasted of their ability to defeat their enemies in a single day, and God's judgment against Israel would be just as swift and severe.

III. Oracles against Israel (3:1–5:17)

3:1–5:17. This section of the book contains oracles that underscore the certainty of God's judgment on Israel. It would seem that the rest of Amos's book is a continuation of his oracle against Israel. The call to "Hear this word" in 3:1; 4:1 and 5:1 introduce the individual messages as the Lord calls His people to account because of their sins.

A. Judgment on the Chosen People (chap. 3)

3:1–9. Here the Lord speaks in the first person to address His people more directly, reminding Israel of her special position as His covenant people. **You only have I known** (v. 2) conveys the idea of "You only have I entered covenant with," the verb "to know" denoting a personal and intimate relationship (see Gen. 4:1). Israel's present strength and prosperity had given rise to complacency about her privileged status as the Lord's chosen people. She was shockingly reminded of the long-forgotten responsibilities her privileges entailed.

In verses 3–6, Amos employs a series of rhetorical questions involving comparisons that each provide a picture of cause and effect, using images taken from daily life. These rhetorical questions build to the prophet's statements of judgment in verses 7–8 and explain why he was speaking such terrifying words. The first five questions in verses 3–5 expect an answer of no, and the last two questions in verse 6 call for an answer of yes. Amos wanted the people to see that his words of calamity were the effect, and God's intention to bring disaster on Israel was the cause of this message (v. 7). There was no avoiding the conclusion that the disaster planned for Israel would come directly from the Lord. The image of God in verse 8 recalls the opening statement about God in 1:2.

3:9–15. These verses provide a courtroom scene, which allows God to prosecute Israel and vindicate the disaster that he would bring on His people. As the scene opens, the rich and powerful of Philistia and Egypt are summoned to witness the Lord's indictment of those who had stored up ill-gotten riches in the fortress of Samaria (vv. 9–10). The nations are on the surrounding **mountains** (v. 9), witnessing Israel's behavior, which was scandalous even to the pagans. As in 1:2–2:16, Amos shattered Israel smug self-righteousness by placing them in a worse light than the pagan nations around them. Israel's sin was that she had stored up **violence and robbery** (v. 10), indicating that the prosperity of Israel's wealthy depended on oppression and robbery.

The punishment that Amos announced against Israel certainly fit the crime, because the estates that the wealthy of Samaria had greedily filled with plunder would **be spoiled** (v. 11). The wealth they had taken from others would now be taken from them by the **adversary** (Assyria). The hope for survivors was bleak, as Amos pictured the remnant of Israel after this attack as a sheep torn to pieces by a lion, with **two legs, or a piece of an ear** (v. 12) as the only remaining body parts. Only a mutilated remnant would survive. The nation as such would be more than wounded; it would be destroyed. The Lord would also bring judgment on **the altars of Beth-el** (v. 14), because Israel's sins were rooted in the false shrine built by Jeroboam I at Bethel (1 Kings 12:26–33). The judgment of Bethel would bring destruction of **the horns of the altar**, meaning that even the last refuge for a condemned man (see 1 Kings 1:50–53) would afford Israel no protection.

Amos effectively contrasted the prosperity that Samaria presently enjoyed with the calamity and disaster that was coming. The prophet pictured the idle luxury of those who reclined on **the corner of a bed** (v. 12; see 6:4), as well as the excess of those who enjoyed both **winter house** and **summer house** (v. 15; see 6:11) and houses that were decorated with ornate carvings and inlays of ivory (**houses of ivory**; see 6:4; 1 Kings 22:39). Excavations have confirmed the opulent wealth of Israel's capital city. The rich may have been proud of their possessions, but all of their symbols of prosperity would prove of no benefit on the day of God's judgment. This message in Amos 3 effectively demonstrates the Lord's hatred of a grasping materialism that values possessions over people.

B. Judgment on an Unrepentant People (chap. 4)

4:1–5. The opening words in verses 1–3 continue the condemnation of Israel's wealthy from the previous chapter, comparing the upper-class women of Samaria to the **kine of Bashan** (v. 1). The cattle of Bashan, raised in the pastures of the northern Transjordan, were the best breed of cattle in ancient Canaan (see Ps. 22:12; Ezek. 39:18). Whether intended as insult or ironic flattery, the point was that these pampered women and their families were about to experience the indignity of being taken away as captives, with **hooks** (v. 2) and **fishhooks**. According to Assyrian reliefs, prisoners of war were led away with a rope fastened to a hook that pierced the nose or lower lip (see 2 Kings 19:28; 2 Chron. 33:11; Ezek. 19:4, 9; Hab. 1:15).

The prophet speaks with sarcasm and irony in verses 4–5 to condemn Israel's perversion of reli-

gious life. The towns of **Beth-el** (v. 4) and **Gilgal** had historical importance as places where God's help was commemorated (see Gen. 35:1–15; Josh. 4:20–24), and both were popular places of worship in Amos's day (see 5:5; Hos. 4:15; 9:15; 12:11). Amos wanted the people to see that their perfunctory performance of rituals apart from the practice of personal justice and righteousness, served only to drive them further from God. Their acts of worship were in fact only further acts of sin. Israel loved the forms and rituals of religion but did not love what God loves—goodness, mercy, kindness, and justice (see 5:15; Isa. 5:7; 61:8; Hos. 6:6; Mic. 6:8).

4:6–11. These verses point further to Israel's spiritual insensitivity. Past disasters that God had inflicted on the people as punishment for their sins had brought no repentance. The Lord's statement **I also have given you** (v. 6) shows that these calamities were not simply natural disasters; they were direct acts of God (see 3:6). What is particularly remarkable is that Israel did not respond even though these disasters took the precise form of the covenant curses that Moses had warned would befall the nation if they were disobedient. The recurring phrase **Yet have ye not returned unto me** (vv. 6, 8–11) reflects Israel's stubborn refusal to turn from her sinful ways. These covenant curses included famine (v. 6; see Lev. 26:20; Deut. 28:17), lack of rain (vv. 7–8; see Lev. 26:19; Deut. 28:23–24), blight on crops and infestations of the palmerworm, or locust (v. 9; see Deut. 28:22, 38–39), pestilence (v. 10a; see Lev. 26:16; Deut. 28:21–22, 34–35, 60–61), and military defeat (v. 10b; see Lev. 26:17, 25; Deut. 28:25, 48–57). The specific disasters that Moses had warned of had now become a reality. The devastation that Israel was to experience if she persisted in her rebellion would be like that of **Sodom and Gomorrah** (v. 11), names that are proverbial for total destruction (see Deut. 23:19; Isa. 1:9; 13:19; Jer. 49:18; 50:40; Zeph. 2:9). Matching the image of the remnant as a mutilated lamb in chapter 3, Amos referred to the survivors of the Assyrian assault against Israel **as a firebrand plukt out of the burning**, saved only by the grace of God (see Zech. 3:2).

4:12–13. Amos concluded this message with a stern warning to **Prepare to meet thy God** (v. 12). Devastated Israel, brought to her knees by the Assyrians, would meet the God she had covenanted with at Sinai and had now so grievously offended. Verse 13 turns to God's work as Creator, not to encourage Israel of God's power to restore, as in the message of hope in the second half of Isaiah (see Isa. 40:12–17; 42:5–9), but rather to convince Israel that the God of such power and majesty could easily execute the judgment announced here (see 5:8–9).

C. Judgment on an Unjust People (5:1–17)

5:1–6. In his condemnation of Israel's practice of social injustice, Amos sorrowfully fashioned a lament, or funeral song, for Israel. Israel was like a **virgin** (v. 2) daughter struck down in the prime of her life (compare the similar imagery in 2 Kings 19:21; Isa. 23:12; Jer. 18:13; 31:4, 21). Israel was **forsaken upon her land** (v. 2), left like a dead body on the open field (see Jer. 9:22), and verse 3 envisions the populations of both large and small communities in Israel being reduced by 90 percent.

The funeral imagery in verses 1–3 was to provide the motivation for response to Amos's call to repentance in verses 5:4–17. The repeated command to **seek** (vv. 4, 6; 5:8, 14) emphasized the call for a response on the part of Israel. If Israel would seek the Lord, they (or at least a "remnant," 5:15) could yet escape the violent death anticipated in Amos's funeral song. While true repentance could save the nation, continuation of religious rituals and worship of idols at their religious centers in **Beth-el** (v. 5) and **Gilgal**, as well as pilgrimages to the religious center of **Beersheba** in the south, could not (see 4:4). The god that they worshiped in their pagan ceremonies would be powerless to save when the true God brought His judgment.

5:7–13. Amos specifically indicted Israel for her social abuses. They were guilty of turning **judgment** (justice) **to wormwood** (v. 7). "Wormwood" was a synonym for bitterness (see Prov. 5:4; Lam. 3:19), reflecting the effect of Israel's injustices on the lives of the oppressed. Turning God's order upside down

is inevitable in a society that ignores His law and despises true religion (see 6:12).

In the midst of this indictment, the prophet inserted a brief hymn (vv. 8–9, as in 4:13). Israel would only turn from her sinful ways when she comes to grips with the reality and character of the true God. Amos highlighted the contrast between those who turn good into bad (v. 7) and the One who changes night into day and governs the order of the universe (v. 8)—and whose power can smash the walls His people hide behind.

Following the hymn, Amos returned to the theme of injustice, introduced in verse 7, with both indictment and announcement of judgment (vv. 10–13). Israel's punishment was that God would take away their prized possessions acquired through wrongful gain. Their prosperity would be turned to grief (see Deut. 28:30, 38–30). The **prudent** (v. 13) in the land would recognize that they were unable to change the state of affairs and would only wait for the judgment that was coming.

5:14–15. Blending warning and exhortation, the prophet again called for Israel to **seek** (v. 14) what would bring them life (vv. 14–15). Seeking the Lord (5:4) is primarily to **Hate the evil, and love the good** (v. 15). The conditional statement **It may be** suggested that judgment might be averted if the people repent. It also emphasized the danger of presuming on God's grace. Even a widespread change of attitude would need the test of time to prove its genuineness. The mention of **the remnant** indicates that this offer of grace would only benefit the individual survivors of the disaster and not the nation as a whole. Even God's mercy has limits, and Israel as a nation has crossed the line of no return from disaster.

5:16–17. The message is tied together by a return to the theme of lament introduced in 5:1. The references to **streets** (v. 16), **highways, husbandman,** and **vineyards** (v. 17) depict the totality of the judgment that would befall Israel. All would be affected by God's judgment. Even farmers, usually too busy for such practices, would join the professional mourners in lament, and mourning would overflow from the cities to the countryside. Israel would experience a reversal of the exodus, as God would **pass through** (v. 17) Israel, just as He did in Egypt (see Exod. 12:12), this time bringing death rather than deliverance. It was as if the past history of Israel was being turned upside down.

IV. Announcement of Exile (5:18–27)

5:18–20. Continuing the relentless message of judgment, 5:18–27 is a **Woe** (v. 18) oracle warning of the coming day of the Lord. Like the funeral song in 5:1–17, the "woe" also connotes the idea of doom and death. **The day of the LORD** refers to God's decisive intervention in human affairs to bring both judgment and salvation (see 8:9; Isa. 2:11, 17, 20). The problem was that Israel expected to be exalted as God's people and were actually looking forward to the coming of the Lord's day. Amos shattered Israel's false expectations and warned that they were enemies of the Lord and would be destroyed in the day of judgment. It would be a day of **darkness, and not light**, because Israel had not been faithful to God. In this context, the day of the Lord refers primarily to an imminent and decisive judgment on Israel, not exclusively of the last day. This imminent judgment is a preview of the universal day of the Lord that will involve all peoples in the last days. The New Testament refers to this day with variations of "the day of our Lord Jesus Christ" (1 Cor. 1:8; 3:12–15; 5:5; 2 Cor. 1:14; Phil. 1:6, 10; 2:16), highlighting that the second coming of Christ and His judgment of all peoples will take center stage. This equation of the Old Testament "day of the Lord" and the New Testament "day of Christ" is also a strong affirmation of Christ's equality with the Lord (Yahweh) of the Old Testament.

5:21–27. The charge against Israel was unfaithfulness to the Lord, which was reflected in her corrupt religious practices. The point of verses 21–23 is not that the religious institutions were wrong in themselves; the problem was with the ways in which the people worshiped. The people had no basis on which to come to God because their conduct reflected disobedience to His law (see Isa. 1:10–15). The prerequisite for acceptance by God was the practice of **judgment** (justice; v. 24) and **righteousness**. The simile comparing social justice to **waters** and **a mighty stream** is particularly apt in that as plant and animal life flourishes where there is water, so human life flourishes where there is justice and righteousness.

The question concerning **sacrifices ... in the wilderness** (v. 25) presents some interpretive difficulties. It is not likely that Amos was saying that Israel never offered sacrifices during their wilderness wanderings, since commands concerning Israel's sacrifices and examples of Israel offering sacrifices are recorded from this period of Israel's history (see Exod. 20:5, 22–26; 32:6–8; 34:13–20; 40:29). Rather, the prophet was stressing that from the beginning, sacrifice had not been established as Israel's primary duty toward God. Israel's right relationship was based on obedience over sacrifice (see 1 Sam. 15:22–23; Rom. 1:15). The judgment that had led to Israel wandering in the wilderness for forty years (see Num. 14:32–35) had been the result of a failure to obey, not a failure to sacrifice. The language of verses 26 is somewhat obscure, but the proper names **Moloch** (v. 26) and **Chiun** (along with **the star of your god**) refer to idolatrous objects of worship that had also served to corrupt Israel's worship. This corrupt worship would result in the judgment of **captivity**, or exile (v. 27).

V. Judgment of Israel's Sinful Pride (chap. 6)

6:1–8. A second **woe** (v. 1) is presented in 6:1–14, with a message of doom directed against both **Zion** and **Samaria**. Although Amos spoke primarily to Israel, Judah (Zion) also deserved his rebuke (see 2:4–5), for Israel properly comprised all twelve tribes. Amos sarcastically punned Israel's self-inflated view of herself as the **chief of the nations**. The newly recovered power and prosperity in Israel and Judah in the eighth century BC had merely reinforced the arrogant complacency of these two nations. **Calneh** (v. 2) and **Hamath** had perhaps fallen to Israel during the campaigns of Jeroboam II, and the walls of **Gath** were broken down by Uzziah of

Judah (see 2 Chron. 26:6). Amos asked if Zion and Samaria were superior to these fallen cities and implied that the same fate awaited them. Unfortunately, the people's enjoyment of indulgent luxury had blinded them to the danger that lay ahead (vv. 3–6; see 3:15–4:2). The temporary prosperity of Israel and Judah was only the quiet before the storm. Yahweh swore an oath concerning the exile of Israel, demonstrating that this verdict against His people was final (vv. 7–8; see Gen. 22:16; Heb. 6:13–14).

6:9–11. These verses portray a fearfully realistic scene of what would happen to Israel in the coming Assyrian invasion. **Ten men** (v. 9) hiding in a house would die. A relative forbade a lone survivor cowering in the house to pray because of the severity of God's wrath against the city. Any **mention of the name of the** LORD (v. 10) could bring further disaster.

6:12–14. Israel was deserving of this crushing defeat because their perversion of justice flew in the face of even conventional human wisdom about the right order of things. Their conduct was as foolish as having **horses run upon the rock** (v. 12) or plowing the sea with oxen (a reading that arises from a slight textual change of the phrase **Will one plow there with oxen?**). Israel had become complacent because of her recent military success and expansion of her territories, but all such gains would be wiped away in the Assyrian invasion. The Hebrew for **a thing of nought** (v. 13) and **taken to us horns** may actually be the places-names Lodebar and Karnaim, referring to locales that had been regained from the Araemeans by Jehoash (2 Kings 10;32–33; 13:25) but that now would be forfeited to the Assyrians. The geographical reference to **from the entering in of Hemath unto the river of the wilderness** (v. 14) covers the area from the Orontes River in north Lebanon to the Dead Sea and signifies that the entire land would be impacted by the Assyrian assault.

VI. Visions of Divine Retribution (7:1–9:10)

7:1–9:10. The final major section of the book consists of a series of five visions, which are each introduced by the phrase "shewed unto me" (7:1, 4, 7; 8:1; see "I saw" in 9:1). These visions continue the theme of judgment and divine retribution by focusing on things seen as well as heard. God was giving Israel every opportunity to know of the judgment that was coming, but Israel's disobedience has rendered them deaf and blind to the divine warnings.

A. Visions of Judgment Relented (7:1–6)

7:1–6. Amos's first vision was of a swarm of **grasshoppers** (v. 1), or locusts (see 4:9; Joel 1:4), that would destroy **the latter growth**, or the growth that came up in the fields after the grains and early hay had been harvested. These grasses were important because the flocks and herds pastured on them until the summer drought stopped all growth (see 1 Kings 18:5). Amos pleaded for God's forgiveness by asking, **By whom shall Jacob arise?** (v. 2). The prophet reminded God that the locust plague would bring mass starvation, which would affect all the people, and that Israel was **small** and powerless to withstand the calamity. In response to Amos's intercession, God **repented** (lit., "changed his mind"; v. 3) and did not bring this calamity on Israel. God also relented from sending the judgment of a devastating **fire** (v. 4) against Israel.

Unlike God's unswerving oath concerning the exile in 6:8, God was willing to relent from the intended judgments of locusts and fire as a result of Amos's prayer. Without challenging God's attribute of omniscient foreknowledge, the Old Testament pictures God as "changing his mind" to affirm that prayer genuinely changes things because God is involved in give-and-take relationships with humans, who function as free moral agents. Intercession was an important aspect of the prophetic ministry in that the prayers of the prophets spared Israel from destruction throughout her history (see Exod. 32:10–14; Num. 14:11–20; 1 Sam. 12:18–23). Conversely, the greatest judgment God could bring against His people would be to cut them off from the benefit of prophetic intercession, as happened to Judah during the ministry of Jeremiah (see Jer. 7:11; 11:14; 14:11; 15:1).

B. Visions of Judgment Unrelented (7:7–9:10)

1. The Vision of the Plumbline (7:7–17)

7:7–9. Israel may have "dodged a bullet" as a result of Amos's prayers, but judgment became unavoidable as Israel persisted in her disobedience and rebellion. In the vision of the **plumbline** (v. 7), Israel was compared to a wall built true to plumb, God's standards of justice and righteousness. They were expected to be true to those standards, but were completely out of plumb when tested (see 2 Kings 21:13). The warning that **I will not again pass by them any more** (v. 8; repeated in 8:2) means that God was no longer open to the prophetic intercession that had spared Israel from the locusts and fire. In judgment, God would take away both their religious (**the high places** and **the sanctuaries**; v. 9) and political (**the house of Jeroboam**) pretensions, which had produced self-righteousness and a false sense of security.

7:10–17. These verses provide a narrative account of a dispute between Amos and **Amaziah the priest** (v. 10) concerning Amos's message of judgment. Amaziah reported to the palace Amos's message that **Jeroboam shall die by the sword** (v. 11) and that **Israel shall surely be led away captive.** The priest actually changed the words Amos had directed against "the house of Jeroboam" (7:9) into a direct prophecy against the king himself. Jeroboam died naturally (2 Kings 14:29), but his son and successor, Zechariah, was assassinated (2 Kings 15:10). Amaziah viewed Amos's message as traitorous because it was directed against **the king's chapel** (v. 13) and **the king's court.** The priest served the king in Samaria, not Israel's heavenly king, which is why he would not allow a prophetic word to be spoken against Jeroboam or his realm. Amaziah dismissed Amos as a **seer** (v. 12), that is, a prophet for hire who need not be taken seriously.

At first glance, Amos's response, **I was no prophet** (v. 14), seems to indicate a denial of his prophetic office. Actually, his words say exactly the opposite. What Amos denied was any previous connection with the prophets or their disciples (see

1 Kings 20:35). No one had hired him to come and announce judgment on Jeroboam and Israel. Amos was a **herdman** (see 1:1) and **a gatherer of sycamore fruit.** The sycamore is a large tree that yields a fig-like fruit and useful timber. The obscure term **gatherer** seems to refer here to the work of slitting the top of each fig, which was necessary to ensure good fruit. Amos's point was that only a divine commission from God could explain his presence in Israel or his message of judgment (v. 15).

Because Amaziah had opposed a message from God, Amos turned to condemn the priest personally. With the exile of Amaziah, the death of his children, and the loss of the family estate, his wife would be reduced to prostitution to survive. Amaziah's private estate would be divided up and given to others. Amaziah would **die in a polluted land** (v. 17), where his ceremonial purity as a priest would be defiled. In conclusion, Amos repeated (verbatim in Hebrew) the last two lines of Amaziah's earlier summary of Amos's message (v. 11), that Israel would **go into captivity** (v. 17).

2. The Vision of the Basket of Summer Fruit (chap. 8)

8:1–3. The vision concerning **a basket of summer fruit** (v. 1) is built around a wordplay based on **summer fruit** (Hebrew, *qayits*) and **The end** (Hebrew, *qets*; v. 2) that was announced for Israel. Israel was ready to be plucked in judgment. The dead bodies in Israel resulting from the judgment would bring **howlings** (v. 3) and **silence** at harvest time, rather than the expected songs of thanksgiving for agricultural bounty (compare Lev. 23:39–41).

8:4–6. The indictment now returned to the theme of the systemic social injustice that plagued Israelite society. Merchants in Israel could not wait for the end of official religious festivals (**the new moon** and **the sabbath**; v. 5), during which commerce ceased, so that they could return to **falsifying the balances**, a practice that the Lord prohibits and abhors (see Lev. 19:35–36; Deut. 25:13–16; Prov. 11:1; 16:11; 20:10, 23). While worshiping the Lord, they were planning how to cheat and steal from others.

8:7-14. This extended announcement of judgment contains several arresting images of doom. The disaster would be like **the flood of Egypt** (v. 8). Because of the heavy seasonal rains in Ethiopia, the Nile in Egypt annually rose by as much as twenty-five feet, flooding the whole valley except for the towns and villages standing above it. The judgment of **that day** (v. 9) would bring cosmic disturbances that will **darken the earth**, common imagery associated with the day of the Lord in other prophetic texts (see Isa. 13:10; 24:23; Ezek. 32:7-8; Joel 2:1031). Israel would mourn like a family that has lost its **only son** (v. 10), on whose life the future of the family depended (see 2 Sam. 18:18).

There would be a famine, not just of **bread** (v. 11) and **water**, but **of hearing the words of the LORD**. In times of great distress, Israel turned to the Lord for a prophetic word of guidance (see, e.g., 2 Kings 19:1-4, 14; 22:13-14; Jer. 21:2; Ezek. 14:3, 7), but in the coming judgment, the Lord would answer all such appeals with silence—a fitting judgment since Israel had refused to listen to the Lord's messengers, such as Amos. Through both physical and spiritual **thirst** (v. 13), even the lovely girls and strong boys of the nation would **faint** and fall useless. The gods of their various religious centers would not be able to protect them from the coming disaster (v. 14).

3. The Vision of the Lord by the Altar (9:1-10)

9:1-6. Amos's fifth vision was of **the Lord standing upon the altar** (lit., "beside the altar"; v. 1), poised on the earth and ready to bring judgment from the sanctuary. God was about to initiate the destruction from the very place from which the people expected to hear a word of peace and blessing (compare the "roar from Zion" in 1:2). God would shatter the temple completely, from the decorated capitals (**lintel**) down to the heavy stone thresholds (**posts**), so that the structure would crash down on the heads of those gathered to worship. It is disputed whether this vision shows the Lord at Jerusalem or Bethel, but the overall context of Amos would seem to indicate a preference for the destruction of the sanctuary of the golden calf at Bethel. Verses 2-4 emphasize the impossibility of escape from God's impending judgment. God's do-

main includes every place, from **heaven** (v. 2) to **the bottom of the sea** (v. 3; see Ps. 139:7-12), where the Israelites could possibly hide. Even those who went **into captivity** (v. 4) in other lands would not escape God's judgment.

The exposition of the vision begins with a hymnic reminder that Israel's God is the Creator and Sustainer of the universe, thus underlining the seriousness of the pronouncements of the preceding verses (vv. 5-6). His presence melts the earth and turns the solid land into **the flood of Egypt** (v. 5; see 8:8). The Lord is able to bring such devastation because He reigns from His storied palace (**stories**; v. 6) in heaven and established the earth as the foundation (**troop**) of His dwelling place. He has the power to unleash the **waters of the sea** (v. 6), which flood the land.

9:7-10. Amos refuted the idea that Israel could rely on God's blessing and protection regardless of their conduct simply because they are God's elect people. Speaking hyperbolically, Amos argued that Israel had no greater claim on God than the **children of the Ethiopians** (v. 7), a dark-skinned people who lived south of Egypt, far from Israel. Israel's stubborn rebelliousness had robbed the exodus of all special significance for her. Instead of being a great act of redemption, Israel's journey from Egypt was reduced to no more significance than the movements of other peoples, like the **Philistines from Caphtor** (see Jer. 47:4) or the **Syrians from Kir** (see 1:5). Israel, the chosen, was nothing more than a **sinful kingdom** (v. 8), whose disobedience was far worse than the sins of other nations (see 1:3-2:16; 3:1-2). God would **sift** (v. 9) the sinners of Israel **in a sieve**, which separated the wheat from the small stones and other refuse that were gathered with it when scooped up from the ground. Not one sinner would escape, and they would be put to death for their persistent rebellion.

VII. Restored Israel's Blessed Future (9:11-15)

9:11-15. It is remarkable that a book of such unrelenting judgment should close with a message of hope and salvation. In fact, many critical scholars view these verses as a secondary addition designed to soften the tone of Amos's original message, which viewed even the remnant surviving God's judgment as a mutilated sheep pulled from the mouth of a lion (see 3:12). Judgment is never the final word, however, in the preaching of the Old Testament prophets, and God's covenant commitment to Israel means that He will never abandon His people to destruction.

The promise to **raise up the tabernacle of David that is fallen** (v. 11) assured the future restoration of the Davidic dynasty and kingdom after the judgment of Israel was complete. The picture of the house of David as a "tabernacle" (lit., a "hut," see Isa. 1:8) and the reference to **the days of old** contrasts the pathetic state of the Davidic monarchy under judgment with the glorious empire enjoyed in the days of David and Solomon. The promise was that the former glories would be restored when the Lord repaired the broken **breaches** and **ruins** of the house of David.

The future David would possess the military power not only to subdue **the remnant of Edom** (v. 12), Israel's bitter enemy from the past (see 1:11), but also **all the heathen** (nations). This promise points to the fulfillment of the Davidic covenant, which guaranteed that a son of David would rule over the nations (see Pss. 2:8–9; 89:23–27; 110). Though Amos preached to the northern kingdom of Israel, this promise of a future Davidic ruler is significant, because the Messiah will rule over a unified Israel (see Hos. 3:5; Ezek. 37:15–22).

After all the forecasts of destruction, dearth, and death (see 5:9, 11, 27), Amos's final words in verses 13–15 picture a glorious Edenic prosperity, when the seasons will run together so that sowing and reaping are without interval. There will be a continuous supply of fresh produce, a reversal of the conditions portrayed in 4:6–11. God will make His people productive, fruitful, and secure in the Promised Land. **They shall no more be pulled up out of their land** (v. 15). When Israel is finally and fully restored, she will never again be destroyed.

THE BOOK OF OBADIAH

INTRODUCTION

Author

The author is Obadiah, whose name means "servant [or worshiper] of the Lord." His was a common name (see 1 Kings 18:3–16; 1 Chron. 3:21; 7:3; 8:38; 9:16; 12:9; 27:19; 2 Chron. 17:7; 34:12; Ezra 8:9; Neh. 10:5; 12:25). Neither his father's name nor the place of his birth is given.

Date

The date of composition is disputed. Dating the prophecy is mainly a matter of relating verses 11–14 to one of two specific events in Israel's history: (1) The invasion of Jerusalem by Philistines and Arabs during the reign of Jehoram (853–841 BC; see 2 Kings 8:20–22; 2 Chr 21:8–20). In this case, Obadiah would be a contemporary of Elisha. (2) The Babylonian attacks on Jerusalem (605–586). Obadiah would then be a contemporary of Jeremiah. This alternative seems more likely.

The parallels between Obadiah 1–9 and Jeremiah 49:7–22 have caused many to suggest some kind of interdependence between Obadiah and Jeremiah, but it may be that both prophets were drawing on a common source not otherwise known.

Theme

There is no compelling reason to doubt the unity of this brief prophecy. Its theme is that Edom, proud over her own security, had gloated over Israel's devastation by foreign powers. Edom's participation in that disaster, however, would bring on God's wrath. She herself would be destroyed, but Mount Zion and Israel would be delivered, and God's kingdom would triumph.

Edom's hostile activities spanned the centuries of Israel's existence. The following biblical references are helpful in understanding the relation of Israel and Edom: Genesis 27:41–45; 32:1–21; 33; 36; Exodus 15:15; Numbers 20:14–21; Deuteronomy 2:1–6; 23:7; 1 Samuel 22 with Psalm 52; 2 Samuel 8:13–14; 2 Kings 8:20–22; 14:7; Psalm 83; Ezekiel 35; Joel 3:18–19; Amos 1:11–12; 9:12.

Since the Edomites were related to the Israelites (v. 10), their hostility was all the more reprehensible. Edom was fully responsible for her failure to assist Israel and for her open aggression. That God rejected Esau (Gen. 25:23; Mal. 1:3; Rom. 9:13) in no way exonerated the Edomites. Edom, smug in her mountain strongholds, would be dislodged and sacked. Israel would again prosper because God was with her. It would seem that Obadiah's oracle against Edom and "day of the LORD" theme (v. 15) would explain its positioning after Amos.

Outline

 I. Title and Introduction (v. 1)
 II. Judgment on Edom (vv. 2–14)
    A. Edom's Destruction Announced (vv. 2–7)
       1. The Humbling of Edom's Pride (vv. 2–4)
       2. The Completeness of Edom's Destruction (vv. 5–7)
    B. Edom's Destruction Reaffirmed (vv. 8–14)
       1. Edom's Shame and Destruction (vv. 8–10)
       2. Edom's Crimes against Israel (vv. 11–14)
 III. The Day of the Lord (vv. 15–21)
    A. Judgment on the Nations (vv. 15–16)
    B. Deliverance for Zion (vv. 17–21)

Bibliography

Alexander, Desmond T., David W. Baker, and Bruce K. Waltke. *Obadiah, Jonah, Micah.* Tyndale Old Testament Commentaries 23A. Downers Grove, IL: InterVarsity, 1988.

Allen, Leslie C. *The Books of Joel, Obadiah, Jonah, and Micah.* New International Commentary on the Old Testament. Grand Rapids, MI: Eerdmans, 1976.

Baker, Walter L. "Obadiah." In *The Bible Knowledge Commentary: Old Testament,* edited by John F. Walvoord and Roy B. Zuck. Wheaton, IL: Victor, 1985.

Finley, Thomas J. *Joel, Amos, Obadiah.* Wycliffe Exegetical Commentary. Chicago: Moody, 1990.

Smith, Billy K., and Frank S. Page. *Amos, Obadiah, Jonah.* New American Commentary 19B. Nashville: Broadman & Holman, 1995.

Watts, John D. W. *Obadiah: A Critical Exegetical Commentary.* Grand Rapids, MI: Eerdmans, 1969.

EXPOSITION

I. Title and Introduction (v. 1)

Verse 1. Obadiah's **vision** from the Lord concerns an envoy sent to call the nations to battle against Edom, perhaps as part of a conspiracy between some of Edom's allies. Verse 1 sets the stage for Obadiah's prophetic message, which begins with verse 2.

II. Judgment on Edom (vv. 2–14)

A. Edom's Destruction Announced (vv. 2–7)

Although Edom felt secure, trusting in her mountain fortresses and her wise men (vv. 2–4, 8–9), Obadiah announced God's judgment on her for her hostility to Israel. The book illustrates the working out of God's original promise to Abraham to "bless them that bless thee; and curse him that curseth thee" (Gen. 12:3). Any nation attacking Israel attacks the apple of God's eye (see Zech. 2:9) and can expect to become the object of divine retribution.

1. The Humbling of Edom's Pride (vv. 2–4)

Verses 2–4. Edom, in her pride, believed herself to be immune from divine judgment, and thus the Lord declared that He would cut Edom down to size. The past tense of **I have made thee small** (v. 2) presents this judgment as if already accomplished. Edom's security came from dwelling **in the clefts of the rock** (v. 3), with its mountainous and rocky terrain providing protection from enemy attack. The city of Sela, the capital of Edom and perhaps the later Petra (both Sela and Petra mean "rock" or "cliff"), was a rugged site located some fifty miles south of the southern end of the Dead Sea (see 2 Kings 14:7). The prophet compared Edom to an **eagle** (v. 4), a proud and regal bird whose **nest** is found in the high and inaccessible recesses of the mountains, but Edom's confidence in her geographical advantage was misplaced, because the Lord promised to **bring** her **down**.

2. The Completeness of Edom's Destruction (vv. 5–7)

Verses 5–7. The armies that would come against Edom would bring total destruction. **Thieves** (v. 5) normally leave something behind when they rob a home, and **grape-gatherers** usually leave behind the sour fruit, but the plunderers of Edom would take everything, including **hid things** (v. 6), Edom's hidden treasures. The ancient Greek historian Diodorus Siculus indicates that the Edomites stored their wealth, accumulated from trade, in vaults in the rocks. Edom's plight would be especially bitter because they would be betrayed by their former allies (**They that eat thy bread**, v. 7; compare Ps. 41:9).

B. Edom's Destruction Reaffirmed (vv. 8–14)

1. Edom's Shame and Destruction (vv. 8–10)

Verses 8–10. Edom's judgment takes on larger significance than merely the destruction of this ancient people. The references to **in that day** (v. 8) not only point to the time of Edom's judgment but also have an eschatological ring. Since in Old Testament prophecy, Edom was often emblematic of all the world powers hostile to God and His kingdom (see Isa. 34:5–14; Ezekiel 35), her judgment anticipates God's ultimate removal of all such opposition. Every judgment that God has performed in the course of world history confirms the reality of the coming and final judgment that God will enforce on all nations.

Edom's **wise men** (v. 8) and their **mighty men** (v. 9), their warriors, would be ineffective in preventing their nation's defeat and destruction. **Shame** (v. 10) would cover Edom, and she would be **cut off for ever.**

2. Edom's Crimes against Israel (vv. 11–14)

Verses 11–14. Edom's violent crimes against Judah were all the more reprehensible in that they were committed against a brother nation. As the descendants of Esau, Edom had close ties to Israel but acted just like the Babylonians in their brutality and violence against Judah. The rebukes against Edom in verses 12–14 move from general to particular. Edom **rejoiced** (v. 12) over Jerusalem's misfortune, took plunder from the fallen city (v. 13), and turned over Judean refugees fleeing from Jerusalem to the

Babylonians (v. 14; for similar examples of Edom's reaction to Judah's misfortunes, see Ezek. 35:13 and Psalm 137). Judah's **day of distress** (v. 14) corresponds to "that day" (v. 8) of Edom's judgment, when God would settle the score with the Edomites.

III. The Day of the Lord (vv. 15–21)

A. Judgment on the Nations (vv. 15–16)

Verses 15–16. The eschatological glimmering of "in that day" (v. 8) becomes a strong ray here: **the day of the LORD is near upon all the heathen** (v. 15). The day of the Lord will bring judgment for the nations (including, but not limited to, Edom) and salvation for the house of Jacob. Edom was warned that her actions **shall return upon thine own head**. The situation for Judah and Edom would be reversed as retribution for Edom's hostility against God's people (detailed in verses 11–14). Ezekiel's denunciation of Edom (Ezekiel 35) reflects a similar "the punishment fits the crime" principle. The idea of exact retribution continues with the warning that the nations who oppose God's people will **drink** (v. 16) the bitter wine of God's judgment (see Jer. 25:15–16; 49:12), as the Edomites had **drunk** when they caroused on the temple mount after Jerusalem was destroyed. The nations will be compelled to keep on drinking until they are intoxicated and, ultimately, destroyed.

B. Deliverance for Zion (vv. 17–21)

Verses 17–20. These verses describe the eschatological blessings in store for the people of Israel and further contrast these blessings to the final judgment that will fall on God's enemies. The verbal root **possess** (v. 17) appears five times in this section to highlight Israel's owning her own land as well as the land of the Edomites. **The house of Jacob** (v. 18) would reduce Edom, **the house of Esau**, to **stubble**. Previously, it was stated that the Lord would destroy Edom, using other nations (v. 7); now it stated that God's people would carry out the destruction. The final word to Edom was that her house would be totally destroyed: **there shall not be any remaining** (v. 18; but see *Zondervan KJV Study Bible* note on Amos 9:12). With Edom annihilated, the remnant of Israel who would return from exile would take possession of the Edomite and Philistine territories (vv. 19–20).

Verse 21. The future leaders or kings of Judah who would take possession of these lands would be the **saviours** (v. 21) who would rule from **mount Zion**. Mount Zion would rule over the mountains of Esau, which were the source of Edom's pride and false sense of security (vv. 1–4). This passage also points to a future for the house of David beyond the exile, and the Messiah may ultimately be in view. The control of the future leader of Judah over the lands of Philistia and Edom is a microcosm of the universal reign that the Messiah will exercise over all nations (see Ps. 2:8–9). **The kingdom shall be the LORD's.** The conclusion of this prophecy is that this kingdom would belong to the Lord, as will all the nations in the final outcome of history. The last book of the Bible echoes this theme and promise (Rev. 11:15). Positioned before Jonah, this phrase effectively reminds the reader that God's kingdom includes even the Gentiles.

THE BOOK OF JONAH

INTRODUCTION

Title

The book is named after its principal character, Jonah, whose name means "dove." Compare the simile used of Ephraim in Hosea 7:11 to portray the northern kingdom as "without sense." See also *Zondervan KJV Study Bible* notes on Psalms 68:13; 74:19.

Author

Though the book does not identify its author, tradition has ascribed it to the prophet himself, Jonah son of Amittai (1:1), from Gath-hepher (see 2 Kings 14:25) in Zebulun (see Josh. 19:10, 13). In view of its many similarities with the narratives about Elijah and Elisha, however, it may come from the same prophetic circles that originally composed the accounts about those prophets, perhaps in the eighth century BC (see 1 Kings, Introduction: "Author, Date, and Sources").

Date

For a number of reasons, including Jonah's preaching to Gentiles, the book is often assigned a postexilic date. At least, it is said, the book must have been written after the destruction of Nineveh in 612 BC. These considerations, however, are not decisive. The similarity of this narrative to the Elijah-Elisha accounts has already been noted. One may also question whether mention of the repentance of Nineveh and the consequent averted destruction of the city would have had so much significance to the author after Nineveh's overthrow. To suppose that proclaiming God's word to Gentiles had no relevance in the eighth century BC is to overlook the fact that Elijah and Elisha had already extended their ministries to foreign lands in the previous century (1 Kings 17:7–24; 2 Kings 8:7–17). Moreover, the prophet Amos (ca. 760–750 BC) set God's redemptive work in behalf of Israel in the context of His dealings with the nations (Amos 1:3–2:16; 9:7, 12). Perhaps the third quarter of the eighth century is the most likely date for the book, after the public ministries of Amos and Hosea and before the fall of Samaria to Assyria in 722–721 BC.

Background

In the half-century during which the prophet Jonah ministered (800–750 BC), a significant event affected the northern kingdom of Israel: King Jeroboam II (793–753

BC) restored her traditional borders, ending almost a century of sporadic seesaw conflict between Israel and Damascus. Jeroboam, in God's good providence (2 Kings 14:26–27), capitalized on Assyria's defeat of Damascus (in the latter half of the ninth century), which temporarily crushed that center of Aramean power. Prior to that time, not only had Israel been considerably reduced in size, but the king of Damascus had even been able to control internal affairs in the northern kingdom (2 Kings 13:7). After the Assyrian campaign against Damascus in 797 BC, however, Jehoash, king of Israel, had been able to recover the territory lost to the king of Damascus (2 Kings 13:25). Internal troubles in Assyria subsequently allowed Jeroboam II to complete the restoration of Israel's northern borders. Nevertheless, Assyria remained the real threat from the north at this time.

The prophets of the Lord were speaking to Israel regarding these events. About 797 BC, Elisha spoke to the king of Israel concerning future victories over Damascus (2 Kings 13:14–19). A few years later, Jonah prophesied the restoration that Jeroboam II accomplished (2 Kings 14:25). Soon after Israel had triumphed, she began to gloat over her newfound power. Because she was relieved of foreign pressures — relief that had come in accordance with encouraging words from Elisha and Jonah — she felt jealously complacent about her favored status with God (Amos 6:1). She focused her religion on expectations of "the day of the LORD" (Amos 5:18–20), when God's darkness would engulf the other nations, leaving Israel to bask in His light.

It was in such a time that the Lord sent Amos and Hosea to announce to His people Israel that He would "not again pass by them any more" (Amos 7:8; 8:2) but would send them into exile "beyond Damascus" (Amos 5:27), that is, to Assyria (Hos. 9:3; 10:6; 11:5). During this time, the Lord also sent Jonah to Nineveh to warn it of the imminent danger of divine judgment.

Assyria's internal problems during this time of Israelite resurgence perhaps made the people of Nineveh more open to Jonah's warning of impending destruction. The reign of Asshur-dan III (771–754 BC) was an especially difficult period in Assyria, with recurring famines and other internal problems weakening the nation and limiting its imperial designs.

Since Jonah was a contemporary of Amos, see Amos, Introduction: "Date" and "Background" for additional details.

Interpretation

Many have questioned whether the book of Jonah is historical. The supposed legendary character of some of the events (e.g., the episode involving the great fish) has caused them to suggest alternatives to the traditional view that the book is historical, biographical narrative. Although their specific suggestions range from fictional short story to allegory to parable, they share the common assumption that the account sprang essentially from the author's imagination, despite its serious and gracious message.

Such interpretations, often based in part on doubt about the miraculous as such, too quickly dismiss (1) the similarities between the narrative of Jonah and other parts of the Old Testament and (2) the pervasive concern of the Old Testament writers, especially the prophets, for history. These interpretations also fail to acknowledge that Old Testament narrators had a keen ear for recognizing how certain past events in Israel's pilgrimage with God illumine (by way of analogy) later events. (For example, the events surrounding the birth of Moses illumine the exodus, those surrounding Samuel's birth illumine the series of events narrated in the books of Samuel, and the ministries of Moses and Joshua illumine those of Elijah and Elisha.) Similarly, the prophets recognized that the future events they announced could be illumined by reference to analogous events of the past. Overlooking these features in Old Testament narrative and prophecy, many have supposed that a story that too neatly fits the author's purpose must therefore be fictional.

On the other hand, it must be acknowledged that biblical narrators were more than historians. They interpretatively recounted the past with the unswerving purpose of bringing it to bear on the present and the future. In the portrayal of past events, they used their materials to achieve this purpose effectively. Nonetheless, the integrity with which they treated the past ought not to be questioned. The book of Jonah recounts real events in the life and ministry of the prophet himself. Further, Jesus certainly understood it as real history (Matt. 12:39–41), and His testimony alone ought to settle the matter of the historicity of the account.

Theme

The book of Jonah reveals a God of both absolute sovereignty and universal mercy. The Lord accomplishes His purposes despite the reluctance of Jonah to fulfill his divine commission. The Lord is the maker of "the sea and dry land" (1:8) who hurls the storm on the sea (1:4) and "appoints" the fish, the plant, the worm to work His will through His reluctant prophet (see 1:17; 4:6–8). Because He is the creator of all things, the Lord has a concern even for the wicked people of Ninevah that Jonah does not share or understand. The Lord shows mercy to even the most wicked of sinners. The Lord had appointed Israel to be a "Kingdom of priests" so that all nations would know Him (see Exod. 19:5–6). Unfortunately, Israel, like Jonah, often did not share God's missionary concern for the nations.

Literary Features

Unlike most other prophetic parts of the Old Testament, this book is a narrative account of a single prophetic mission. Its treatment of that mission is thus similar to the accounts of the ministries of Elijah and Elisha, found in 1–2 Kings, and to certain narrative sections of Isaiah, Jeremiah, and Ezekiel.

As is often the case in biblical narratives, the author has compressed much into a small space; forty verses tell the entire story (eight additional verses of poetry are devoted to Jonah's prayer of thanksgiving). In its scope (a single extended episode), compactness, vividness, and character delineation, it is much like the book of Ruth.

As in the book of Ruth, the author uses structural symmetry effectively. The story is developed in two parallel cycles that call attention to a series of comparisons and contrasts (see "Outline," below). The symmetry contrasts Jonah's initial disobedience (1:1–3) and eventual obedience (3:1–3) to the divine commission to preach to the Ninevites. Jonah's confession, "Salvation is of the LORD" (2:9) occupies a central position in the book, and the book focuses on three great acts of rescue performed by the Lord and the human response to these rescues: (1) the sailors were saved from the storm and feared the Lord

(1:16); (2) Jonah was saved from drowning in the sea and praised the Lord (2:2–9); and (3) Nineveh was spared from destruction, and Jonah became angry toward the Lord (4:1–8). Jonah's inappropriate response to the salvation of the Ninevites is the key to the story. Jonah rejoiced in his own salvation but did not want the Ninevites to experience the same divine mercy and grace that had been extended to him. The prophet's unresolved anger at the close of the book leaves the reader with the question of whether God's grace is for all peoples or only for Israel because of its favored nation status with God.

The author uses the art of representative roles in a straightforward manner. In this story of God's loving concern for all people, Nineveh, the great menace to Israel, is representative of the Gentiles. Correspondingly, stubbornly reluctant Jonah represents Israel's jealousy of her favored relationship with God and her unwillingness to share the Lord's compassion with the nations. The book depicts the larger scope of God's purpose for Israel: that she might rediscover the truth of His concern for the whole creation and that she might better understand her own role in carrying out that concern.

Outline

    I. Jonah Flees His Commission (chaps. 1–2)
        A. Jonah's Commission and Flight (1:1–3)
        B. The Endangered Sailors' Cry to Their Gods (1:4–6)
        C. Jonah's Disobedience Exposed (1:7–10)
        D. Jonah's Punishment and Deliverance (1:11–2:1; 2:10)
        E. Jonah's Prayer of Thanksgiving (2:2–9)
    II. Jonah Reluctantly Fulfills His Mission (chaps. 3–4)
        A. Jonah's Renewed Commission and Obedience (3:1–4)
        B. The Ninevites Repent and Turn to God (3:5–9)
        C. God's Compassion and Jonah's Anger (3:10–4:4)
        D. Jonah's Deliverance and Rebuke (4:5–11)

Bibliography

Allen, Leslie C. *Joel, Obadiah, Jonah, and Micah*. New International Commentary on the Old Testament. Grand Rapids, MI: Eerdmans, 1976.

Baker, David W., T. Desmond Alexander, and Bruce K. Waltke. *Obadiah, Jonah, Micah*. Tyndale Old Testament Commentaries 23A. Downers Grove, IL: InterVarsity, 1988.

Bruckner, James. *Jonah, Nahum, Habakkuk, Zephaniah*. NIV Application Commentary. Grand Rapids, MI: Zondervan, 2004.

Ogilvie, Lloyd J., and Charles K. Jordan. *Hosea, Joel, Amos, Obadiah, Jonah*. Mastering the Old Testament 20. Waco, TX: Word, 1993.

Stuart, Douglas. *Hosea–Jonah*. Word Biblical Commentary 31. Waco, TX: Word, 1987.

Walton, John H. "The Object Lesson of Jonah 4:5–7 and the Purpose of the Book of Jonah." *Bulletin for Biblical Research* 2 (1992): 47–57.

Wiseman, D. J. "Jonah's Nineveh." *Tyndale Bulletin* 30 (1979): 29–51.

EXPOSITION

I. Jonah Flees His Commission (chaps. 1–2)

A. Jonah's Commission and Flight (1:1–3)

1:1–2. God commanded Jonah to **Arise** and **go to Nineveh**. While other prophets preached messages directed toward the pagan nations (see Isa. 13–23; Jer. 46–51; Ezek. 25–32; Amos 1–2), Jonah's commission was unique in that he was called to actually go and preach to the people of Nineveh. Nineveh, the **great city** (see 3:2; 4:1), was first built by Nimrod, according to Genesis 10:11–12. About 700 BC, Sennacherib made it the capital of Assyria, which it remained until its fall in 612 BC (see Nahum, Introduction: "Background"). Nineveh was over five hundred miles from Gath-hepher, Jonah's hometown. Like Sodom and Gomorrah of old (see Gen. 18:20–21), the **wickedness** of Nineveh had **come up before** the Lord, necessitating the need for Jonah to go and announce the coming judgment. Except for the violence of Nineveh, her "evil way" (3:8) is not described in Jonah. Nahum later stated that Nineveh's sins included plotting evil against the Lord (Nah. 1:11), cruelty and plundering in war (Nah. 2:12–13; 3:1, 19), prostitution and witchcraft (Nah. 3:4), and commercial exploitation (Nah. 3:16).

1:3. Jonah responded to the Lord's command by rising up **to flee**. The reason for Jonah's flight, given in 4:2, was not fear of the Assyrians but rather Jonah's unwillingness to see God's mercy extended to the Assyrians, whom the prophet deemed unworthy of God's mercy. Jonah attempted to flee to **Tarshish**, perhaps the city of Tartessus in southwest Spain, a Phoenician mining colony near Gibraltar. By heading in the opposite direction from Nineveh, to what seemed like the end of the world, Jonah intended to escape his divinely appointed task. The drama is enhanced by the repetition of the divine call "Arise" (Hebrew, *qum*; 1:2) in the phrase **But Jonah rose up** (*qum*). The negative consequences of disobedience are highlighted by the repetition of the verb "to go down" (*yarad*); in chapter 1, Jonah **went down to Joppa**, he **went down into** (*yarad*) the ship, and he "was gone down" below the deck of the ship (1:5).

Sin initiated a downward descent that culminated with Jonah going down into the sea (see 1:15).

B. The Endangered Sailors' Cry to Their Gods (1:4–6)

1:4–6. In his flight, Jonah learned the futility of running from God (see Ps. 139:7, 9–10). **The LORD sent out** (lit., "hurled") **a great wind** (v. 4). God's sovereign working in bringing about the fulfillment of the reluctant prophet's mission is evident at several other points; the Lord sent a great fish (1:17), released Jonah from the fish (2:10), and sent the plant (4:6), the worm (4:7), and the wind (4:8). Jonah's flight from God brought him in contact with the pagan sailors on board the ship to Joppa. Although Jonah's mission was to bring God's warning to Nineveh, his refusal to go to Nineveh brought these sailors into peril. Furthermore, the pagan sailors were more spiritually sensitive than this Hebrew prophet in that they cried out to their gods for deliverance while the clueless prophet slept below deck (v. 5). **The shipmaster** (v. 6) came to wake Jonah, and the pagan captain's concern for everyone on board contrasts again with the believing prophet's refusal to carry God's warning to Nineveh.

C. Jonah's Disobedience Exposed (1:7–10)

1:7. Jonah's disobedience was exposed when the sailors decided to **cast lots** to determine who was guilty for bringing this calamity that had befallen them. The casting of lots was a custom widely practiced in the ancient Near East. The precise method used is unclear, though it appears that, for the most part, sticks or marked pebbles were drawn from a receptacle into which they had been "cast." By the lot of judgment, the Lord, not the gods of the sailors, exposed Jonah as the guilty party (see Josh. 7:14–26; 1 Sam. 14:38–44; Prov. 16:33).

1:9. Jonah made no attempt to hide his culpability and offered a thoroughly orthodox confession concerning the Lord's identity as the true God and the Maker of the heavens and the earth. The sailors would have understood Jonah's words as being descriptive of the highest divinity, and the storm at sea validated Jonah's claim in their minds since in the religions of the ancient Near East, the supreme god generally was the master of the seas (see Josh. 3:10). While fleeing from his commission to preaching to pagans in Nineveh, Jonah ended up preaching to pagans on the ship in spite of himself. As in 1:9, Jonah offered theologically correct confessions of God in 2:9c and 4:2, but unfortunately his orthodox beliefs were betrayed by his disobedient behavior. If Jonah affirmed that God is the Maker of the seas, why did he believe that he could flee via the sea from God's presence?

D. Jonah's Punishment and Deliverance (1:11–2:1; 2:10)

1:11–13. Jonah informed the terrified sailors that their only recourse for stopping the storm was to throw him overboard, **into the sea** (v. 12). The sailors **rowed hard** (the Hebrew verb "to dig" conveying the picture of strenuous effort; v. 13), attempting to evade the storm, but to no avail. The sailors once again appear superior to Jonah in that their reluctance to throw Jonah into the sea stands in sharp contrast to Jonah's reluctance to warn Nineveh of coming judgment.

1:16. When the storm ceased immediately after Jonah was thrown into the sea, the pagan sailors responded appropriately with fear and awe toward the Lord. There is no evidence here that the sailors renounced all other gods (compare Naaman, 2 Kings 5:15). Ancient pagans were ready to recognize the existence and power of many gods. At the least, however, the sailors acknowledged that the God of Israel was in control of the present events, that He was the one who both stirred up and calmed the storm, and that at this moment, He was the one to be recognized and worshiped. This was in marked contrast to Jonah, who seems to have had no fear of the Lord. That God responded to the pagan sailors' less than adequate acknowledgment of His power and sovereignty highlights His attributes of grace and mercy, qualities that were clearly lacking in the life of Jonah.

1:17. Despite Jonah's disobedience, **the LORD had prepared a great fish to swallow up Jonah** and to save the disobedient prophet from death by drowning. The verb "to prepare" occurs also in 4:6–8 and reflects the book's strong emphasis on the sovereignty of God. The Hebrew for "great fish" (and the Greek for "whale" in Matt. 12:40) refers in general to a large fish, not necessarily a whale. Jonah was inside this fish for **three days and three nights**. The New Testament uses this as a type, or foreshadowing, of the burial and resurrection of Jesus, who was entombed for "three days and three nights" (Matt. 12:40; see Matt. 16:4; Luke 11:29–32).

E. Jonah's Prayer of Thanksgiving (2:2–9)

2:1–6. Jonah responded to God's gracious deliverance from death in the sea with a psalm of thanksgiving. Jonah recalled his prayer for help as he was sinking into the depths. His gratitude was heightened by his knowledge that he deserved death but God had shown him extraordinary mercy. The language of this song indicates that Jonah was familiar with the praise literature of the Psalms.

Jonah used the imagery of death and going down into the underworld to describe his near-death experience in the sea (see Pss. 18:5; 30:3). The word **hell** (v. 2) should be translated "sheol," referring to the realm of the dead, the netherworld, where, it was thought, departed spirits lived on after death in some form of shadowy existence. Old Testament laments often speak of the person in danger or distress as already present in the abode of the dead (see Ps. 30:3). The imagery here should not be taken to infer that Jonah experienced physical death and resurrection but rather that Jonah was as good as dead until God rescued him from the sea. The imagery of death and sheol also appears as Jonah portrayed himself engulfed in **the waters** (v. 5) of the sea, sinking down to **the mountains** (v. 6), and being barred in the earth itself. When death was an inevitability, God intervened to rescue Jonah **from corruption** (i.e., the pit or the grave).

2:7–9. In expressing his thanks for the Lord's deliverance, Jonah recognized the folly of trusting in idols and promised to fulfill the vows that he had made to the Lord. In the book of Psalms, prayers were commonly accompanied by vows, usually involving thank offerings (e.g., Pss. 50:14; 56:12; 61:8; 116:12–19). The petitioner was not attempting to manipulate God by making the vow but rather was expressing confidence in the Lord's answer to prayer before the answer was received. The climax of Jonah's thanksgiving prayer is his confession that **Salvation is of the Lord** (v. 9). This is Jonah's second confessional statement (see 1:9) and stands at the literary midpoint of the book.

Ironically, Jonah recognized God as the source of salvation and rejoiced in his own undeserved deliverance from death but later was angry that the people of Nineveh experienced a similar undeserved deliverance (see 4:1–4). While Jonah's repudiation of idolatry in verse 8 is theologically precise, it perhaps reflects, in light of the overall message of the book, Jonah's arrogance in assuming that idol worshipers were not entitled to God's mercy in the same way as sinful Israelites. Jonah, perhaps representative of the nation of Israel as a whole, had a flawed understanding of the concept of grace.

II. Jonah Reluctantly Fulfills His Mission (chaps. 3–4)

A. Jonah's Renewed Commission and Obedience (3:1–4)

3:1–2. The repetition of **the word of the Lord came unto Jonah** (v. 1) and the command to **Arise, go unto Nineveh** (v. 2) from 1:1–2 introduces the second half of the book. Jonah got a second chance to obey the divine commission, and God accomplished His sovereign intent to send His messenger to Nineveh. Jonah's commission was to **preach** to the city of Nineveh concerning its impending judgment.

3:3–4. Jonah arose, and went unto Nineveh (v. 3), but he went reluctantly, still wanting the Ninevites to be destroyed. Nineveh is described as **an exceeding great city of three days' journey**. Jonah 4:11 states that the city had more than 120,000 inhabitants. Archaeological excavations indicate that the later imperial city of Nineveh was about eight miles around. That the city was a "three days' journey," however, may suggest a larger area, such as the five-city complex of Nineveh, Rehoboth, Ir, Calah, and Resen mentioned in Genesis 10:11–12. Greater Nineveh covered an area of some sixty miles in circumference. On the other hand, in ancient Near East-

ern idiom, "three days" represented a long journey (see Gen. 30:36; Exod. 3:18; Josh. 9:16–17). Another suggested interpretation is that "three days' journey" refers to the length of Jonah's ministry in Nineveh.

B. The Ninevites Repent and Turn to God (3:5–9)

3:5–8. The people of Nineveh responded to Jonah's message of impending judgment with **a fast ... sackcloth, and ... ashes** (vv. 5–6), the customary signs of humbling oneself in repentance (see 1 Kings 21:27; Neh. 9:1). Here it is reported that the Ninevites **believed God** (v. 5), which may mean that the Ninevites genuinely turned to the Lord (see Matt. 12:41). On the other hand, their belief in God may have gone no deeper than had the sailors' fear of God (see 1:16). It is not likely that the people of Nineveh here experienced a genuine conversion to exclusive faith in the Lord God of Israel, but at least they took the prophet's warning seriously and acted accordingly. Rather than an example of true revival, the repentance of Nineveh represents an example of God's willingness to extend forgiveness to the worst of sinners who respond to warnings of judgment with even minimal repentance. For example, Ahab and Manasseh are viewed as the worst kings of Israel and Judah respectively (see 1 Kings 16:30–31; 2 Kings 21:10–11), but God extended compassion toward both of these rulers even though it appears that their repentance was only sorrow over having to face the consequences of their sin (see 1 Kings 21:27–29; 2 Chron. 33:10–13). The sparing of Nineveh should have taught Israel not only about the wideness of God's mercy but also about the readiness of God to respond with forgiveness to even minimal repentance over sin.

The repentance of the Ninevites extended across the community and included the **king of Nineveh** (v. 6) himself, perhaps a reference to the Assyrian king or, more likely, a governor or important city official in light of the fact that Nineveh was not the royal capital at the time of Jonah's ministry. The king issued a proclamation that included even animals wearing **sackcloth** (v. 8). The inclusion of domestic animals was unusual and expressed the urgency with which the Ninevites sought mercy from God (see 4:11). The king recognized that God often responds in mercy to man's repentance by canceling threatened punishment. Jonah's message appears to be one of unavoidable judgment (3:4), but in the prophets' messages, even statements of absolute judgment carried an implied condition that repentance might lead to God's commuting the sentence of judgment (see Jer. 18:7–10; compare Jer. 26:17–19 with Mic. 3:9–12).

3:9. Who can tell if God will turn and repent …? The idea of God "turning" and "repenting" does not imply that God has limited foreknowledge of the future but merely recognizes that God is involved in true give-and-take relationships with humans and that there are times when His compassion overcomes His anger (see Joel 2:14).

C. God's Compassion and Jonah's Anger (3:10–4:4)

While God responded with compassion toward the Ninevites (v. 10), Jonah responded with anger toward God's compassion (4:1). Jonah was angry that God would show mercy to an enemy of Israel. He wanted God's goodness to be shown only to Israelites, not to the hated Assyrians.

4:2. Thou art a gracious God, and merciful. Jonah again used a fixed confessional statement in acknowledging God's grace and compassion (see Exod. 34:6–7), but his anger at God's mercy to the Assyrians represents the reversal of his confession. Just as God showed mercy to the willfully disobedient idolater in Exodus 33, now He would show mercy to the idolaters in Nineveh because it is part of His very nature to show such compassion. While God is **slow to anger**, Jonah became angry very quickly in this scene (vv. 1, 9).

4:3. Jonah was so angry that he wished **to die**, like the prophet Elijah in 1 Kings 19:4. To Jonah, God's mercy to the Ninevites meant an end to Israel's favored standing with Him. Jonah shortly before had rejoiced in his deliverance from death, but now that Nineveh lived, he preferred to die.

D. Jonah's Deliverance and Rebuke (4:5–11)

4:5–9. Jonah went outside the city to see what would transpire and apparently still hoped that Nineveh would be destroyed (v. 5). In verses 6–11, **God prepared** a plant (v. 6), a **worm** (v. 7), and a scorching **wind** (v. 8) to teach His prophet a valuable lesson. The **gourd** (v. 6) provided shade for Jonah as he sat outside the city. The word "gourd" here probably refers to a castor oil plant, a shrub that grows over twelve feet high and has large, shady leaves. God graciously increased the comfort of His stubbornly defiant prophet. As when Jonah slept in the boat while the sailors were crying out to God concerning the fierce storm (1:4–6), Jonah appears more concerned with himself than with the needs of those around him who were about to perish. He rejoiced in his deliverance from personal discomfort yet was angry that an entire city had been spared from divine destruction.

When the worm destroyed the vine, and the scorching wind and sun blazed down on Jonah, the prophet again expressed his desire **to die** (v. 8). Then God spoke, to teach the prophet about the reasons behind His divine compassion.

4:10–11. God has both the first word (see 1:1–2) and the last word in this book. The Lord's closing speech contrasted Jonah's concern for the vine, something of momentary and fleeting value, with God's concern for the people of Nineveh. God had a fatherly concern even for these pagans whom Jonah hated, because they were like small children who **cannot discern between their right hand and their left hand** (v. 11; see Deut. 1:39).

God's first word to Jonah, his commission, displayed God's mercy and compassion to the Ninevites, and His last word to Jonah emphatically proclaimed His concern for every creature, both people and animals. The Lord not only "preservest man and beast" (Ps. 36:6; see Neh. 9:6; Ps. 145:16), but He takes "no pleasure in the death of the wicked; but [desires] that the wicked turn from his way and live" (Ezek. 33:11; see Ezek. 18:21–23). Jonah and his countrymen traditionally rejoiced in God's special mercies to Israel but wished only His wrath on their enemies. God here rebukes such hardness and proclaims His own gracious benevolence.

THE BOOK OF MICAH

INTRODUCTION

Author

Little is known about the prophet Micah beyond what can be learned from the book itself and Jeremiah 26:18. Micah was from the town of Moresheth (1:1), probably Moresheth-gath (1:14) in southern Judah. Micah's prophecy attests to his deep sensitivity to the social ills of his day, especially as they affected the small towns and villages of his homeland.

Date

Micah prophesied sometime between 750 and 686 BC, during the reigns of Jotham, Ahaz, and Hezekiah, kings of Judah (1:1; Jer. 26:18). He was therefore a contemporary of Isaiah (see Isa. 1:1) and Hosea (see Hos. 1:1). Micah predicted the fall of Samaria (1:6), which took place in 722–721 BC. This would place his early ministry in the reigns of Jotham (750–732 BC) and Ahaz (735–715 BC; the reigns of Jotham and Ahaz overlapped). Micah's message reflects social conditions prior to the religious reforms under Hezekiah (715–686 BC). (The reigns of Ahaz and Hezekiah seem to have overlapped from about 729 to 715 BC; see 2 Kings 18:9 and Isa. 36:1.)

Background

The background of this book is the same as that found in the earlier portions of Isaiah, though Micah does not exhibit the same knowledge of Jerusalem's political life as Isaiah does. Perhaps this is because he, like Amos, was from a Judahite village.

Israel was in an apostate condition. Micah predicted the fall of her capital, Samaria (1:5–7), and also foretold the inevitable desolation of Judah (1:9–16).

Three significant historical events occurred during this period: (1) In 734–732 BC, Tiglath-pileser III of Assyria led a military campaign against Aram (Syria), Philistia, and parts of Israel and Judah. Ashkelon and Gaza were defeated. Judah, Ammon, Edom, and Moab paid tribute to the Assyrian king, but Israel did not fare as well. According to 2 Kings 15:29, the northern kingdom lost most of its territory, including all of Gilead and much of Galilee. Damascus fell in 732 BC and was annexed to the Assyrian empire. Significantly,

Tiglath-pileser III was the first Assyrian king to institute the policy of wholesale deportation. Thus, Israel was not only defeated in battle but was taken into exile as well. (2) In 722–721 BC, Samaria fell, and the northern kingdom of Israel was conquered by Assyria. (3) In 701 BC, Judah joined a revolt against Assyria and was overrun by King Sennacherib and his army, though Jerusalem was spared.

Theme and Theological Message

The theme of the book is judgment and deliverance by God. Micah's message alternated between oracles of doom and oracles of hope (see "Outline," below). Micah also stressed that God hates idolatry, injustice, rebellion, and empty ritualism, but He delights in pardoning the penitent. Finally, the prophet declared that Zion would have greater glory in the future than ever before. The Davidic kingdom, though it would seem to come to an end, would reach greater heights through the coming messianic deliverer.

Throughout the book of Micah, the promise of salvation directly overturns the effects of God's judgment. In 2:12–13, the promised return from exile reverses the threat of military defeat and captivity announced in 1:2–2:11. The judgment speech of chapter 3 warns that the temple mount will be reduced to a heap of ruins, but the message of hope in chapter 4 declares that Zion will be "exalted above the hills" (4:1). In the final chapter, the lament over God's judgment (7:1–7) turns into praise for His future salvation (7:15–20). Judgment is only temporary because the Lord will never abandon the covenant commitment that He has made to the nation of Israel.

Literary Features

Micah's style is similar to that of Isaiah. Both prophets used vigorous language and many figures of speech, and both showed great tenderness in threatening punishment and in promising justice. Micah made frequent use of wordplays, 1:10–16 being the classic example.

Outline

I. Judgment against Israel and Judah (1:1–3:12)
   A. The Predicted Destruction (1:2–9)
   B. The Assault on Jerusalem (1:10–16)
   C. The Wicked Deeds of the Rich (2:1–11)
   D. Hope in the Midst of Gloom (2:12–13)
   E. The Leaders Condemned (chap. 3)
II. Hope for Israel and Judah (4:1–5:15)
   A. The Coming of Law and Peace (4:1–5)
   B. The Lord Reigns in Zion (4:6–13)
   C. The Coming Ruler and His Reign (5:1–9)
   D. Idols and Weapons Destroyed (5:10–15)
III. The Lord's Case against Israel (chap. 6)
IV. Gloom Turns to Triumph (chap. 7)
   A. The Counsel of Despair (7:1–6)

B. Trust in God's Salvation (7:7–14)

C. God's Pardon and Love (7:15–20)

Bibliography

Allen, Leslie C. *Joel, Obadiah, Jonah, and Micah*. New International Commentary on the Old Testament. Grand Rapids, MI: Eerdmans, 1976.

Barker, Kenneth, and Waylon Baily. *Micah, Nahum, Habakkuk, Zephaniah*. New American Commentary 20. Nashville: Broadman & Holman, 1998.

Hannah, John D. "Jonah." In *The Bible Knowledge Commentary: Old Testament*, edited by John F. Walvoord and Roy B. Zuck. Wheaton, IL: Victor, 2000.

Hillers, D. R. *Micah*. Hermeneia. Philadelphia: Fortress, 1984.

Mays, J. L. *Micah: A Commentary*. Old Testament Library. Philadelphia: Westminster, 1976.

Waltke, Bruce. *A Commentary on Micah*. Grand Rapids, MI: Eerdmans, 2007.

Wolff, H. W. *Micah: A Commentary*. Translated by G. Stansell. Minneapolis: Augsburg, 1990.

EXPOSITION

I. Judgment against Israel and Judah (1:1–3:12)

A. The Predicted Destruction (1:2–9)

1:2–5. The call to **Hear** (v. 2; 3:1; 6:1) introduces the three major sections of the book of Micah (see also 3:9; 6:2). The prophet had an urgent message that required an obedient response from the people. In a masterful stroke of rhetoric, the prophet prepared his audience for the real focus of his message — the destruction of Jerusalem — by first focusing on God's judgment of the nations (vv. 2–4), then Samaria (v. 5a; 5:6–7), and finally Jerusalem (v. 5b; 5:8–9). Once the hearers had acknowledged that the Lord was just in His judgment of the nations and Samaria, they also had to acknowledge that Jerusalem was deserving of judgment because of its many sins. The focus on **all ye people** (v. 2) and the **earth** indicates an announcement that the day of the Lord was at hand, when God would call the nations to account. In view of that day, Micah spoke of the impending judgments of Israel and Judah. **The Lord cometh forth** (v. 3) is an Old Testament expression describing the Lord's intervention in history (see Pss.

18:9; 96:13; 144:5; Isa. 26:21; 31:4; 64:1–3), when God comes down to the earth as a warrior, and everything melts in the path of His destructive force (vv. 4–5).

1:6–7. The prophecy against Samaria would be fulfilled during Micah's lifetime, when Assyria destroyed Samaria in 722–721 BC (see 2 Kings 17:6). Samaria was to be destroyed because of its **graven images** (v. 7) and **idols**, which had turned the city into a **harlot**. Prostitution is often an Old Testament symbol for idolatry or spiritual unfaithfulness (Exod. 34:15–16; Judg. 2:17; Ezek. 23:29–30). The great wealth of the city was viewed as the **hire** (earnings) of a prostitute, and this wealth would be taken by the Assyrians and placed in their own temples to be used again in the worship of their idols.

1:8–9. Therefore (v. 8) introduces the prophet's response to this awful message of judgment. Rather than rejoicing over the destruction of ungodly Samaria, Micah vowed to **wail and howl** in lament over the terrible calamity about to befall the city. **I will go stript and naked** perhaps indicates that Micah actually walked stripped (clothed only in a loincloth) and barefoot through Jerusalem (see Isa. 20:2). The judgment to befall Samaria would be a **wound** (v. 9) that was **incurable** and that would eventually spread to the **gate of ... Jerusalem**. The gate was where the process of town government took place (see Gen. 19:1; Ruth 4:1–4).

B. The Assault on Jerusalem (1:10–16)

1:10–16. As if to visualize the coming assault on Jerusalem, Micah listed the cities of Judah that would fall to the Assyrians as they made their march to Jerusalem. The prophet engaged in a series of wordplays to highlight the danger facing the cities in the path of attack. The inhabitant of a town hearing his place of residence as a target of judgment would certainly have seen the urgency of responding to the prophet's warnings and turning to the Lord in repentance.

1:10–12. Declare ye it not in Gath (v. 10). Gath sounds like the Hebrew for "declare." This phrase also alludes to the tragedy when Saul and sons were killed in battle against the Philistines and points to a funeral lament over Judah. Micah did not want the pagan people in Gath to gloat over the downfall of God's people. **Aphrah roll thyself in the dust.** Aphrah sounds like the Hebrew for "dust," and the city would live up to its name by rolling in the dust as a sign of grief over the catastrophe befalling it (see Isa. 47:1). In **thou inhabitant of Saphir, having thy shame naked** (v. 11), there is a rhyme with "shame" and "inhabitant." The inhabitants of Saphir would suffer the shame of being taken away as prisoners to a foreign land (see Isa. 20:4). The town name **Zaanan** sounds like the Hebrew verb "to go out," but the people in this city would not dare to go out (**came not forth**) because of the coming invasion. The name **Beth-ezel** means "a place near," but the inhabitants of this city would receive no help from the neighboring towns. **Maroth** (v. 12) sounds like the noun "bitter," so this town would be disappointed when waiting for **good** and instead would experience only **evil** (calamity). The ultimate target of God's judgment would be **the gate of Jerusalem** and would reach even the city where God has placed His name and promised to protect His people from danger (see Psalms 46, 48, 76).

1:13. Lachish sounds like the Hebrew for "team" (of horses), and the inhabitants of the city were told to **bind the chariot**, not to fight against the enemy but rather to flee in fear. Lachish was one of the largest towns in Judah and an important military outpost protecting Jerusalem from attack (see Isa. 36:2). Later, Sennacherib was so proud of capturing it that he decorated his palace at Nineveh with a relief picturing his exploits.

1:14–16. Moresheth-gath (v. 14) sounds like the Hebrew for "dowry," and Jerusalem would have to **give presents**, or parting gifts, to this town when they went into exile, just as a father gave a dowry when his daughter married. Ironically, this town was the home of Micah, but the prophet was willing to proclaim judgment against even his own home in carrying out the Lord's calling to preach against the sins of Judah. The name **Achzib** rhymes with "lie" in Hebrew, and the imagined security of the city would prove deceptive when its houses fell. The **heir** (v. 15) to come to **Mareshah** and **Adullam** would not be a deliverer but rather a conqueror who would take the people captive. Micah predicted exile before deportation was actually practiced by the Assyrians, making his message all the more difficult to believe.

C. The Wicked Deeds of the Rich (2:1–11)

2:1–5. These verses contain a judgment speech directed primarily against the wealthy landowners who oppressed the poor. The rich, oppressing classes continued to get rich at the expense of the poor **because it is in the power of their hand** (v. 1), meaning that they controlled the power structures of their society. **They covet[ed]** (v. 2), in violation of the tenth command (see Exod. 20:17; Deut. 5:21), which led to their act of taking the land of the poor. Family property was a **heritage** from the Lord, which meant that the land was to be the permanent possession of a particular family (see Lev. 25:10, 13; Num. 27:1–11; 36:1–12; 1 Kings 21:1–19). The rich were taking this property **by violence**, not necessarily meaning murder and robbery but rather exploitation of the poor through the legal system. Corrupt judges rendered decisions in favor of wealthy landowners, at the expense of the poor. The rich used debt laws as an excuse to confiscate the lands of those who struggled to make a living.

Therefore (v. 3) announces the judgment to fall on Judah's exploitive rich. Because of their sins, the Lord would bring calamity (**evil**) on Judah in the form of the impending exile. The judgment was fitting in that the rich would lose the land they had stolen from others. It was also a fitting judgment of their pride. Because of their failure to "walk humbly" (see 6:8), they would not go **haughtily** as they were humiliated by their enemies.

2:4-11. Here the corruption in the society of Micah's day and the Lord's corresponding judgment is further described. When they were taken into exile, the rich landowners would cry out, **We be utterly spoiled** (v. 4). There is bitter irony in that they would lament their own situation but had felt no qualms about confiscating land from the poor. They would charge that the Lord **hath changed the portion of** His **people**, the very thing they had done in taking property given to the individual families in Israel as an inheritance from the Lord. Appropriately, the judgment of the oppressing classes was that there would be **none that shalt cast a cord by lot** (v. 5), meaning that they would be cut off from all the promises of the covenant people.

Judah's moral corruption was also due to the influence of its religious leaders, including the false prophets and corrupt priests. Verses 6-11 reflect a disputation between Micah and those who opposed his message. The false prophets said to Micah, **Prophecy ye not** (v. 6). They were not interested in hearing Micah's harsh words of judgment and did not believe that **the spirit of the Lord** (v. 7) was **straitened**, or impatient, with His people. Micah's opponents proclaimed that God's presence with Judah meant "None evil can come upon us" (3:11). They believed that Jerusalem, as the dwelling place of God, was invulnerable to attack.

Micah responded to this line of reasoning by pointing to the social injustice in Judah, which necessitated a response of judgment from the Lord (vv. 8-9). They had taken the clothes off the back of

the poor and had evicted widows and their children from their homes. The extreme plight of the poor and atrocities of the rich are a telling indictment of the failure of the kings, whose sacred task was to establish justice. Even pagan nations had a higher view of societal justice. The prophet commanded, **Arise ye, and depart** (v. 10). Since they had abused the gift of the Promised Land, they would go away into exile and not enjoy the **rest** (security) that God had offered to His people (see Deut. 25:19; Josh. 1:13-15; 21:43-44; 22:4). While the people had no desire to hear Micah's words of judgment, they were willing to give their allegiance to any prophet that would promise them **wine and ... strong drink** (v. 11). Their desire for pleasure dulled their spiritual sensibilities, resulting in an unwillingness to hear the warnings of the coming disaster.

D. Hope in the Midst of Gloom (2:12-13)

2:12-13. This is the first message of hope for Israel's future. **I will surely** (v. 12) is the Lord's oath affirming the promise given here, contrasting the true hope proclaimed by Micah with the empty hopes of the false prophets from the preceding section. The promise was that the Lord would **gather the remnant** from exile and that this remnant would become a multitude as God restored and blessed His people. The severity of the coming exile did not mean that God had abandoned His people or forgotten His covenant promises.

E. The Leaders Condemned (chap. 3)

3:1-12. Continuing the message of judgment, chapter 3 elaborates on the sins of the leaders of Israel (vv. 1-4), the false prophets (vv. 5-8), and the leaders, priests, and false prophets (vv. 9-12). Each judgment speech reflects the pattern of an indictment followed by an announcement of judgment. The privilege of leadership is a gift from God, and leaders are especially accountable to God because their actions have such a powerful influence on those under their leadership (see James 3:1).

3:1-4. This judgment speech contains some of the harshest language in the whole prophetic corpus. The leaders who practiced social injustice are compared to cannibals, who flay, cook, and **eat the flesh** (v. 3) of their victims. Because the leaders were insensitive to the poor and needy, the Lord would **not hear them** (v. 4) when they cried out to Him in their time of distress.

3:5–7. The false prophets predicted **Peace** (v. 5) for Judah, while Micah predicted destruction and captivity (see 3:12; 4:10). There would be darkness for both these prophets and their followers when God's judgment fell on them. As a true spokesman for God and one who was **full of power by the spirit of the Lord** (v. 8), Micah declared to Judah its full sin, no matter how unpopular that message might have been. The true prophets were Spirit-filled messengers (see Isa. 48:16), in contrast to the false prophets, who were "walking in the spirit and falsehood" (2:11).

3:9–12. Micah's final oracle focused on both the civil and spiritual leadership of Judah. The civil leaders **build up Zion with blood** (v. 10), with the image of murder graphically portraying their mistreatment of the people under their authority. Rather than practicing justice, they judged **for reward** (v. 11), or for bribes (see Isa. 1:23; 5:23). The priests and prophets also performed their ministries **for hire** and **money**, taking advantage of the people and proclaiming the popular message that judgment from God would not come. Their motto, **Is not the Lord among us?** reflects the presumptuous notion that God's presence was a guarantee of protection regardless of the nation's moral behavior. Micah warned that because of the sins of the leaders, Zion would be **plowed as a field** (v. 12) and would become a heap of ruins. The destruction of Jerusalem occurred in 586 BC. Verse 12 was quoted a century later, however, in Jeremiah 26:18–19, a passage that indicates that Micah's preaching may have been instrumental in the revival under King Hezekiah (see 2 Kings 18:1–6; 2 Chron. 29–31), which led to a temporary postponement of the judgment against Jerusalem. Even when warnings of judgment were expressed unconditionally, there was the possibility of the judgment being averted if the people responded with repentance. In His infinite mercy, the Lord provided every possible opportunity for the people to change their ways and experience blessing rather than destruction.

II. Hope for Israel and Judah (4:1–5:15)

A. The Coming of Law and Peace (4:1–5)

4:1–5. The salvation portrayal in verses 1–4 is almost identical to Isaiah 2:2–4, perhaps indicating a common source of tradition behind the preaching of these two contemporary prophets. These verses need to be understood as a perfect counterpart to 3:9–12. Zion would be reduced to a heap of ruins (3:12) but **in the last days** (v. 1) will **be exalted above the hills**. She was built in violence and bloodshed (3:10) and yet will be the place from which the Lord's word and teaching will go forth and the nations will be judged (v. 2). Only the Lord can effect such radical transformation. This passage portrays the prosperity and security of the future kingdom age, exalts Zion as the center of the Lord's earthly reign, and ultimately points to the blessedness of the heavenly Jerusalem, which will exist for all eternity (see Revelation 21).

B. The Lord Reigns in Zion (4:6–13)

4:6–8. **In that day** (v. 6) points to the messianic period and continues the portrayal of the blessings of the kingdom age. God will preserve **a remnant** (v. 7) of His people that will become the objects of His salvation (see Isa. 1:9). Zion, the capital city of David, will be the **tower of the flock** (v. 8). Micah used shepherd imagery to portray the security that the future messianic king will provide for Israel as the kingdom of David is restored (see 5:4–6).

4:9–13. Micah foresaw the collapse of the monarchy and the impending exile (586 BC) as well as the restoration (beginning in 538 BC). In judgment, Zion would become **as a woman in travail** (v. 9). The tables were turned, however, as judgment was prophesied against the gloating enemies of Jerusalem in verses 11–13. These enemies did not understand the Lord's plan to judge and then exalt Jerusalem. Using militaristic imagery, the prophet promised that Israel will **thresh** (v. 13) its enemies and **shalt beat in pieces many people**. The future kingdom will come by force, as the Lord will rule over the nations "with a rod of iron" (Ps. 2:9).

C. The Coming Ruler and His Reign (5:1–9)

5:1–9. Before the Messiah came, Jerusalem would be besieged, and her kings would be seized and taken to Babylon. After the judgment would come a new David, arising out of **Beth-lehem Eph-ratah** (v. 2). Verses 2–6 are clearly messianic, but less obvious is the relationship to the failed kingship of Micah's era. Mighty Jerusalem would bow to the village of Bethlehem, whose coming ruler would find his strength not in military power but **in the strength of the Lord** (v. 4). The future Messiah would be one **Whose goings forth have been from of old** (v. 2), reflecting his connection to the ancient dynasty of David but more fully pointing to the eternalness of the Christ and the fact that His beginnings were much earlier than His human birth. The Messiah arose within history as part of the family of David (see 2 Sam. 7:12–16; Isa. 9:6–7; Amos 9:11) but is also the eternal Son of God. The Messiah will shepherd and rule with **strength** and **majesty** (v. 4) and will bring **peace** (v. 5) to Israel as He delivers them from their enemies. **The Assyrian** (v. 6) is symbolic of all the enemies of God's people in every age. Rather than suffering under foreign oppression, Israel will become like a powerful **lion** (v. 8).

D. Idols and Weapons Destroyed (5:10–15)

5:10–15. These verses promise that in the messianic era, the people of God will not depend on weapons of war or pagan idols. The successes of God's people will always be achieved by dependence on Him. Much of Micah's language in this unit can be found in the curse section of Leviticus 26:21–33. Israel's idolatry would result in their experiencing the covenant curse of having their cities destroyed, but the Lord's judgment would purge the people of their militarism and heathenism, which caused them to trust in weapons and wealth rather than in the Lord as their ultimate source of security.

III. The Lord's Case against Israel (chap. 6)

6:1–16. This chapter depicts a courtroom scene in which the Lord lodged a legal complaint against Israel. In verses 1–2, the Lord summoned the people to listen to His accusation and to prepare their defense against His charges, which follow in verses 9–16. **The mountains** (v. 2) and **foundations of the earth** were called as third-party witnesses to the proceedings because of their enduring nature and because they had been witnesses to the establishment of the covenant (see Deut. 20:19; 31:28; 32:1). They had also silently observed Israel's disobedience to the Lord for generations.

6:1–5. The Lord poignantly reminded the people of His gracious acts in their behalf (vv. 3–5). The Lord called, **Testify against me** (v. 3), and challenged them to demonstrate in any way His unfaithfulness toward them. The Lord was frequently wearied with His people (see Isa. 1:14), but they had no reason to be wearied with Him.

6:6–7. Israel responded and inquired as to what they needed to do to please the Lord, asking if great sacrifices or even the giving of their **firstborn** (v. 7) children would satisfy His demands on their life. The speaker's words do not reflect a sincere inquiry about how to come to the Lord but rather reflect Israel's attempt at self-justification: "How can the Lord charge us with covenant unfaithfulness when we have been faithful in bringing our sacrifices and offerings?"

6:8. Micah answered for the Lord and declared that God is more interested in the character qualities of justice, **mercy**, and humility than in sacrifice and ritual. The same thought is expressed in 1 Samuel 15:22; Psalm 51:16; Hosea 6:6; Isaiah 1:11–15. Micah did not deny the desirability of sacrifice but showed that it does no good to offer sacrifices without obedience.

6:9–16. The prophet further elaborated on how the corruption of Israel demanded a response of judgment from the Lord. The Lord would bring **the rod** (v. 9) against Jerusalem because it was filled with **the treasures of wickedness** (v. 10). The rich oppressors were **full of violence** (v. 12) and practiced treachery and deceit. As a just judge, the Lord could not simply excuse their sin, so He would smite them by bringing on them the covenant curses of famine and infertility. The people of Judah no doubt believed that their worship at Jerusalem made them superior to the apostate northern kingdom of Israel, but the Lord charged that **the statutes of Omri ... and all the works of the house of Ahab** (v. 16) were observed in Judah as well. First Kings 16:25, 30 says that these two kings did more evil than did all the kings who preceded them. They practiced militarism, internationalism, and promoted the worship of Baal in Israel. In the eyes of the Lord, Judah was just as guilty as these wicked and apostate kings.

IV. Gloom Turns to Triumph (chap. 7)

7:1-20. The final section of the book begins with another indictment of Israel's sinfulness (vv. 1-6), moves to a call to trust in the Lord for deliverance, and concludes with a promise that the Lord would forgive Israel's transgressions because of His enduring love for His covenant people. The speakers in this chapter are Micah (vv. 1-7), Zion (vv. 8-10), Micah (vv. 11-13), Zion (v. 14), God (v. 15), and Micah (vv. 16-20).

A. The Counsel of Despair (7:1-6)

7:1-6. Looking for godly people in Jerusalem was like looking for **the summer fruits** (v. 1) when the harvest had ended (see also Jer. 8:20). Greed and selfishness had turned the inhabitants of the city into hunters who **lie in wait for blood** (v. 2) and who stalked with their nets until they captured their prey. As a result, **The day of thy watchmen** (v. 4), the time of judgment that the prophets warned about (see Jer. 6:17; Ezek. 3:17-21), was near. The family unit was disintegrating, and households turned on each other (v. 6). Poverty is harmful to any society, but poverty caused by oppressive leadership or rich land barons often causes a society to disintegrate into anarchy.

B. Trust in God's Salvation (7:7-14)

7:7-14. Micah affirmed his confidence in the Lord's **salvation** (v. 7), which awaited on the other side of judgment. The personified city of Jerusalem also expressed confidence that she would **arise** (v. 8) after she had fallen and that the **darkness** of judgment would be turned into the **light** of deliverance. Zion acknowledged her sin against the Lord but also declared that the enemies who taunted her would themselves be put to shame when God rebuilt her walls and restored her people (vv. 10-13). Zion prayed that the Lord would **feed** (v. 14) Israel and restore its past prosperity.

C. God's Pardon and Love (7:15-20)

7:15-20. Micah's prophecies conclude with a promise (or perhaps a prayer) that God will again show His wonders as in the exodus, that the nations will see and be ashamed and will turn to the Lord in fear. The passage anticipates both the return from Babylonian exile and the ultimate restoration of Israel when God's kingdom comes to earth. In the final restoration, the nations will be amazed at Israel's exaltation and will **lick the dust like a serpent** (v. 17), a picture of defeat and humiliation. This glorious future is possible because of the greatness of God's love and forgiveness. The prophet used powerful imagery to portray how God forgives, stressing that His grace is as strong as His wrath. Israel's sins are the enemy that the Lord will **subdue** (v. 19) and **cast ... into the depths of the sea**. This loving forgiveness reflects God's covenant commitment **to Jacob, and ... to Abraham** (v. 20). The transgression of Jacob (1:5) was the reason for the beginning of this book, but the faithfulness of God to His covenant is the answer to the question **Who is a God like unto thee ...?** (v. 18).

THE BOOK OF NAHUM

INTRODUCTION

Author

The book contains "the vision of Nahum" (1:1), whose name means "comfort" and is related to the name Nehemiah, meaning "the Lord comforts" or "comfort of the Lord." Nineveh's fall, which is Nahum's theme, would bring comfort to Judah. Nothing is known about Nahum except his hometown (Elkosh), and even its general location is uncertain.

Date

In 3:8–10, the author speaks of the fall of Thebes, which happened in 663 BC, as already having taken place. In all three chapters of the book, Nahum prophesied Nineveh's fall, which was fulfilled in 612 BC. Nahum therefore uttered this oracle between 663 and 612 BC, perhaps near the end of this period since he represented the fall of Nineveh as imminent (2:1; 3:14, 19). This would place Nahum during the reign of Josiah and make him a contemporary of Zephaniah and the young Jeremiah.

Background

Assyria (represented by Nineveh, 1:1) had already destroyed Samaria (722–721 BC), resulting in the captivity of the northern kingdom of Israel, and posed a threat to Judah. The Assyrians were brutally cruel; their kings were often depicted as gloating over the gruesome punishments inflicted on conquered peoples. They conducted their wars with shocking ferocity, uprooted whole populations as state policy, and deported them to other parts of the empire. The leaders of conquered cities were tortured and horribly mutilated before being executed (see 3:3). No wonder the dread of Assyria fell on all her neighbors!

About 700 BC, King Sennacherib made Nineveh the capital of the Assyrian Empire, and it remained the capital until it was destroyed in 612 BC. Jonah had earlier announced its destruction (Jonah 3:4), but the people had repented, and the destruction had been temporarily averted. Not long after that, however, Nineveh had reverted to its extreme wickedness, brutality, and pride. The brutality reached its peak under Ashurbanipal (669–627 BC), the last great ruler of the Assyrian Empire. After his death, Assyria's influence and power waned rapidly until 612 BC, when Nineveh was overthrown.

Theme and Theological Message

The focal point of the entire book is the Lord's judgment on Nineveh for her oppression, cruelty, idolatry, and wickedness. The book ends with the destruction of the city.

According to Romans 11:22, God is not only kind but also stern. In Nahum, God is "slow to anger" (1:3) and "a strong hold ... [for] them that trust in him" (1:7), but He "will not at all acquit the wicked" (1:3). God's righteous and just kingdom will ultimately triumph, for all kingdoms built on wickedness and tyranny must eventually fall, as Assyria did.

Nahum addressed some words to Judah (see 1:12–13, 15), but most were addressed to Nineveh (see 1:11, 14; 2:1, 13; 3:5–17, 19) or its king (3:18). The book, however, was meant for Judahite readers, to offer them hope of the removal of the Assyrian threat. In addition, Nahum declared the universal sovereignty of God. God is Lord of history and of all nations; as such, He controls their destinies.

Literary Features

The contents are primarily judicial (judgment oracles), with appropriate descriptions and vocabulary, as well as intense moods, sights, and sounds. The language is poetic, with frequent use of metaphors and similes, vivid word pictures, repetition, and many short — often staccato — phrases (see, e.g., 3:2–3). Rhetorical questions punctuate the flow of thought, which markedly stresses moral indignation toward injustice.

Outline

I. Nineveh's Judge (1:1–15)
   A. The Lord's Kindness and Sternness (1:2–8)
   B. Nineveh's Overthrow and Judah's Joy (1:9–15)
II. The Fall of Nineveh (2:1–13)
   A. Nineveh Besieged (2:1–10)
   B. Nineveh's Desolation Contrasted with Her Former Glory (2:11–13)
III. Nineveh's Total Destruction (3:1–19)
   A. Nineveh's Sins (3:1–4)
   B. Nineveh's Doom (3:5–19)

Bibliography

Bruckner, James. *Jonah, Nahum, Habakkuk, Zephaniah*. NIV Application Commentary. Grand Rapids, MI: Zondervan, 2004.

Johnston, G. H. "Nahum's Rhetorical Allusions to Neo-Assyrian Conquest Metaphors." *Bibliotheca Sacra* 159 (2002): 21–45.

Kohlenberger, J. R. *Jonah–Nahum*. Everyman's Bible Commentary. Chicago: Moody, 1984.

Maier, Walter. *The Book of Nahum*. Grand Rapids, MI: Baker, 1980.

Patterson, Richard D. *Nahum, Habakkuk, Zephaniah*. Wycliffe Exegetical Commentary. Chicago: Moody, 1991.

Roberts, J. J. M. *Nahum, Habakkuk, and Zephaniah: A Commentary*. Old Testament Library. Louisville: Westminster John Knox, 1991.

Robertson, O. Palmer. *The Books of Nahum, Habakkuk, and Zephaniah*. New International Commentary on the Old Testament. Grand Rapids, MI: Eerdmans, 1990.

EXPOSITION

I. Nineveh's Judge (1:1–15)

A. The Lord's Kindness and Sternness (1:1–8)

1:1–6. Nahum's opening oracle focused on the two sides of God's character—His wrath and His compassion—with emphasis on His wrath, to prepare his audience for the message of judgment against Nineveh and Assyria. **The Lord revengeth** (v. 2) and **will take vengeance**, stressing that God acts justly toward all who oppose Him and His kingdom. **The Lord is slow to anger** (v. 3) but must punish **the wicked**, such as Nineveh. God's compassion tempers His judgment of sin but not in such a way that He would allow Assyria's gross sin to go unpunished. Nahum compared the Lord's fury to **the whirlwind and … the storm** (see Pss. 18:7–15; 68:4; 77:16–19; 104:3–4). In history, the Lord unleashed His wrath against His enemies in the exodus (Exodus 14) and the conquest (Joshua 3), and these events serve as a preview of the judgment to come against the wicked in the future. **Bashan** (v. 4), **Carmel**, and **Lebanon** were places noted for their fertility, vineyards, and trees (see Song 7:5; Isa. 2:13; 33:9; 35:2; Amos 4:1), but at the Lord's word they would wither. The **mountains** (v. 5), **hills**, and **earth**, symbols of stability and permanence, would melt away when the Lord appeared to vent His anger. The rhetorical questions **Who can stand …?** (v. 6) and **who can abide …?** stress that no human can withstand the Lord's wrath. If mountains quake before the Lord, what human being can think he is not vulnerable? Even imperial Assyria, with all of its military and administrative might, was nothing compared to the Lord.

1:7–8. In contrast to the warnings of wrath and judgment, Nahum affirmed God's goodness and faithfulness toward **them that trust in him** (v. 7). The image of a **strong hold** pictures the security of Judah as they placed their faith in the Lord, contrasting the picture of the **overrunning flood** (v. 8), symbolic of an invading army (see Isa. 8:7–8), that would bring destruction upon Nineveh. In 612 BC,

that end came for Nineveh. Through the ministry of Jonah, Nineveh had formerly experienced the light of God. She later rejected it, and the result was the **darkness** of judgment.

B. Nineveh's Overthrow and Judah's Joy (1:9–15)

1:9–14. The Lord promised to make **an utter end** (v. 9) of Nineveh so that the Assyrians would no longer afflict the people of Judah. Judgment would come against the **wicked counseller** (v. 11), most likely Ashurbanipal, the last great Assyrian king (669–627 BC), whose western expeditions succeeded in subduing Egypt and to whom King Manasseh had to submit as vassal (see 2 Chron. 33:11–13). Contrasting images portray Assyria's reversal of fortunes. Their armies had been intoxicated like **drunkards** (v. 10) with the plunder of their enemies, but they would be consumed like dry **stubble**. Nineveh had been **quiet** (peaceful; v. 12) and populous, but they would be **cut down** when the Lord **pass[ed] through**. God had used the Assyrians as the rod of His anger against His covenant-breaking people (Isa. 10:5), but now the Lord would directly intervene to destroy the Assyrians, just as He had the Egyptians in the days of the exodus. Also as in the exodus, the Lord would **break his yoke** (v. 13) and deliver His people from foreign bondage and oppression. Because of Assyria's wickedness and idolatry, the Lord vowed to bring about Assyria's death as a nation (**I will make thy grave**; v. 14). God used the Babylonians, the Medes, and the Scythians to dig Nineveh's grave in 612 BC. For the fulfillment of this prophecy, see Ezekiel 32:22–23.

1:15. This verse focuses on the joy in Jerusalem at the news of Nineveh's defeat. **The feet of him that bringeth good tidings** refers to the messenger who would bring news of the fall of Assyria. In Romans 10:15, Paul applied similar imagery to those who proclaim the gospel and bring news of the even greater deliverance that comes through Jesus Christ. Judah was commanded to keep their **solemn**

feasts in celebration of the Lord's deliverance of His people. The promise that **the wicked shall no more pass through thee** means that the Assyrian invasion in the days of Manasseh would be the last. This deliverance from Assyria also anticipates the ultimate deliverance of Jerusalem from all enemies in the future kingdom of peace (see Isaiah 33, 35).

II. The Fall of Nineveh (2:1–13)

A. Nineveh Besieged (2:1–10)

2:1–2. Moving beyond the threat of judgment in chapter 1, this chapter portrays the assault on Nineveh that would occur in the near future. **He that dasheth in pieces** (v. 1) refers to the alliance of the Babylonians, the Medes, and the Scythians—particularly the Medes under Cyaxres and the Babylonians under Nabopolassar. With sarcasm, the prophet commanded the people of Nineveh to **keep the munition** and **watch the way**. They were to prepare for battle, but resisting the attacking army would be futile. Nineveh would fall because **the Lord hath turned away the excellency of Jacob** (v. 2); that is, Israel would be restored and united again.

2:3–5. To heighten the dread of what was to befall Nineveh, the prophet provided a graphic picture of the invading armies. They would be **mighty men** (v. 3) with shields **made red**, the result of the blood on them or the reflection of the sun shining on them. **The chariots** (v. 4) of the invaders would roar through the streets with the speed of **lightnings**. The attackers would **make haste to the wall** (v. 5). A moat 150 feet wide had to be filled in before the invaders could reach Nineveh's wall, which was almost eight miles long and had fifteen gates. Even these massive fortifications, however, would not provide protection for the inhabitants of Nineveh when the battering rams of the enemy were brought forward.

2:6–10. As part of the attack on the city, **The gates of the rivers shall be opened** (v. 6), perhaps a reference to the dams of the Khoser River, which ran through the city to the Tigris River. When the water was suddenly released, it would bring a flood that would damage the city walls. One ancient historian (the author of the *Babylonian Chronicles*) speaks of a flood that washed away some of the wall, making it easier for the invaders to enter the city.

As a result of the assault on Nineveh, **the palace** (v. 6) would fall, the armies (**Huzzab**, or "gallant ones"; v. 7) would be taken away as prisoners, the **maids** (possibly the temple prostitutes, whose places of business would be destroyed) would go out of the city mourning, and the people of Nineveh would flee like water draining from a **pool** (v. 8). The invaders would take vast amounts of plunder (v. 9), and Nineveh would be **empty, and void, and waste** (v. 10). The *Babylonian Chronicles* confirm the fact that a great quantity of plunder was carried off by the invaders. Assyria had terrorized the world, but now the powerful, insolent Ninevites would become helpless with fear: **the heart melteth, and the knees smite together**.

B. Nineveh's Desolation Contrasted with Her Former Glory (2:11–13)

2:11–13. Nahum ironically contrasted the devastated and desolate city of Nineveh with its former glory and power, expressed in figurative terms. He mentioned lions ten times, using four different Hebrew words (compare Isa. 5:29; Jer. 4:7; Mic. 5:8). The lion was an appropriate metaphor for Assyria because of the rapacious ways of the Assyrian monarchs and because Nineveh contained numerous lion sculptures. The lion hunt was also one of the ways that Assyrian kings demonstrated their courage and prowess; the message of Nahum was that the hunter was about to become the hunted.

In their days of power, the Assyrian lion tore its prey and **filled his holes** (v. 12) with the spoils of war from many nations. The glory days of Assyria would soon be over because the Lord was against them and would **burn** (v. 13) her weapons of war. Nineveh's fall would not be caused merely by natural forces or the superior power of her attackers; it would be an act of God. Nineveh had been put on trial, found guilty, and sentenced to destruction. History has confirmed this prediction.

III. Nineveh's Total Destruction (3:1–19)

A. Nineveh's Sins (3:1–4)

3:1–4. Woe (v. 1) announced a message of death against Nineveh because it was **the bloody city**. Nineveh's bloody massacres of her conquered rivals were well known. The Assyrians were noted for their ruthlessness, brutality, and terrible atrocities. Many of their victims were beheaded, impaled, burned, or skinned alive. Nineveh would now receive what it justly deserved. **A great number of carcases** (v. 3) were littered about the city. The Assyrian king Shalmaneser III boasted of erecting a pyramid of chopped-off heads in front of an enemy's cities. Other Assyrian kings stacked corpses like cordwood by the gates of defeated cities. The **well-favoured harlot** (v. 4) probably refers to the chief goddess of Nineveh, and by extension, to the city as a whole. The lure of luxury and wealth was a major motivation behind Assyria's cruelty toward other nations.

B. Nineveh's Doom (3:5–19)

3:5–9. Nineveh would receive the punishment of a prostitute. Her **nakedness** (v. 5) would be exposed to **the nations** that she had oppressed and mistreated. The rhetorical questions in verse 7 emphasize that Nineveh would receive no sympathy in her time of defeat. Assyria's military victories had given the nation a sense of invulnerability, but the prophet declared that Nineveh was no better than **No** (the Hebrew name for Thebes; v. 8), the great capital of Upper Egypt, which was destroyed by the Assyrians in 663 BC. Assyria would go into exile as had **Ethiopia ... Put and Lubim** (v. 9), Egypt's neighbors whom the Assyrians had defeated.

3:10–13. The people of Nineveh would be taken into captivity, and her young children would be brutally killed. The **great men** (v. 10) of Assyria would be **bound in chains**. Assyrian kings often did this to their enemies. King Ashurbanipal gave this description of his treatment of a captured leader: "I ... put a dog chain on him and made him occupy a kennel at the eastern gate of Nineveh." Now the leaders of Assyria would experience similar humiliation. Nineveh would **be drunken** (v. 11) from the cup of God's wrath. The attackers would eagerly gather the loot and plunder of Nineveh **like fig trees with the firstripe figs** (v. 12), and the people of Nineveh would become like **women** (v. 13), too weak and fearful to stand against the invading armies.

3:14–19. As in 2:1, Nahum again issued a sarcastic call for Nineveh to prepare for the coming **siege** (v. 14), the irony being that these preparations would do no good. Within their fortifications, the city would be destroyed by **fire** (v. 15). History and archaeology confirm that this prediction was fulfilled, and the king of Assyria died in the flames of his palace. Nineveh would be destroyed not only by the enemy armies but also by corrupt **merchants** (v. 16) and leaders who would exploit their people in this time of crisis. Their many merchants would become like the **cankerworm** and **locusts** (v. 17) as they stripped the land of its treasures. Their **shepherds** (v. 18) and **king** would **slumber** in death. There would be **no healing** (v. 19) for Nineveh. Nineveh was so totally destroyed that it was never rebuilt, and within a few centuries, it was covered with windblown sand. The "great city" (Jonah 1:2; see 3:2) fell in 612 BC, never to rise again—all in fulfillment of God's word through His prophet Nahum. It is significant that the last phrase in Nahum is **thy wickedness**. God will not leave such behavior unpunished.

THE BOOK OF HABAKKUK

INTRODUCTION

Author

Little is known about Habakkuk except that he was a contemporary of Jeremiah and a man of vigorous faith, rooted deeply in the religious traditions of Israel. The account of his ministering to the needs of Daniel in the lions' den in the apocryphal book *Bel and the Dragon* is legendary rather than historical.

Date

The prediction of the coming Babylonian invasion (1:6) indicates that Habakkuk lived in Judah toward the end of Josiah's reign (640–609 BC) or at the beginning of Jehoiakim's reign (609–598 BC). The prophecy is generally dated a little before or after the battle of Carchemish (605 BC), when Egyptian forces, who had earlier gone to the aid of the last Assyrian king, were routed by the Babylonians under Nabopolassar and Nebuchadnezzar and were pursued as far the Egyptian border (see Jeremiah 46). Habakkuk, like Jeremiah, probably lived to see the initial fulfillment of his prophecy, when Jerusalem was attacked by the Babylonians in 597 BC.

Theme and Theological Message

Among the prophetic writings, Habakkuk is somewhat unique in that it includes no oracle addressed to Israel. It contains, rather, a dialogue between the prophet and God (see "Outline," below). In the first two chapters, Habakkuk argues with God over His ways that appear unfathomable, if not unjust. Having received replies, Habakkuk responded with a beautiful confession of faith (chap. 3).

This account of wrestling with God is, however, just a fragment from a private journal that has somehow entered the public domain. It was composed for Israel. No doubt it represented the voice of the godly in Judah, struggling to comprehend the ways of God. God's answers, therefore, spoke to all who shared Habakkuk's troubled doubts. Habakkuk's confession became a public expression, as indicated by its liturgical notations (see discussion on 3:1).

Habakkuk was perplexed that wickedness, strife, and oppression were rampant in Judah but God seemingly did nothing. When told that the Lord was preparing to do something about it through the fierce Babylonians (1:6), his perplexity only intensified:

How could God, who is "of purer eyes than to behold evil [with approval]" (1:13), have "established them for correction" (1:12) "when the wicked devoureth the man that is more righteous than he" (1:13)? God makes it clear, however, that eventually the corrupt destroyer would itself be destroyed. In the end, Habakkuk learned to rest in God's appointments and await His working in a spirit of worship.

Habakkuk presents a model of prayer, also found elsewhere in the Old Testament, that encourages the faithful to come to God with their questions, doubts, and negative emotions. Abraham argued with God over the destruction of Sodom and Gomorrah (Gen 18:16–33). Moses pleaded with God not to destroy Israel following the golden-calf incident, and God relented in response to Moses' prayer (Exodus 32). The psalmist asked "How long?" when enduring times of suffering (Pss. 13:1–2; 89:46) and challenged the Lord to awake from sleeping and respond to the prayers of His people (Ps. 44:23–24). The Lord never condemns these honest expressions of the heart, and reflection on these model prayers from the Old Testament protect believers today from a sanitized view of prayer that keeps one from coming to God with one's needs and hurts.

Literary Features

The author wrote clearly and with great feeling and penned many memorable phrases (2:2, 4, 14–20; 3:2, 17–19). The book was popular during the intertestamental period; a complete commentary on its first two chapters has been found among the Dead Sea Scrolls.

Outline

I. Title (1:1)
II. Habakkuk's First Complaint: Why Does Evil in Judah Go Unpunished? (1:2–4)
III. God's Answer: The Babylonians Will Punish Judah (1:5–11)
IV. Habakkuk's Second Complaint: How Can a Just God Use Wicked Babylon to Punish a People More Righteous Than Themselves (1:12–2:1)
V. God's Answer: Babylon Will Be Punished, and Faith Will Be Rewarded (2:2–20)
VI. Habakkuk's Prayer: Confession of Trust and Joy in God (chap. 3)

Bibliography

Baker, David W. *Nahum, Habakkuk, and Zephaniah*. Tyndale Old Testament Commentaries 23B. Downers Grove, IL: InterVarsity, 1988.

Barker, Kenneth, and Waylon Baily. *Micah, Nahum, Habakkuk, Zephaniah*. New American Commentary 20. Nashville: Broadman & Holman, 1998.

Bruckner, James. *Jonah, Nahum, Habakkuk, Zephaniah*. NIV Application Commentary. Grand Rapids, MI: Zondervan, 2004.

Patterson, Richard D. *Nahum, Habakkuk, Zephaniah*. Wycliffe Exegetical Commentary. Chicago: Moody, 1991.

Robertson, O. Palmer. *Nahum, Habakkuk, and Zephaniah*. New International Commentary on the Old Testament. Grand Rapids, MI: Eerdmans, 1990.

Stoll, John H. *The Book of Habakkuk*. Grand Rapids, MI: Baker, 1972.

EXPOSITION

I. Title (1:1)

1:1. The word **burden** refers to the "oracles" received by the prophet, such as the ones found in 1:5–11 and 2:2–20. These oracles were frequently received in visions, and the Hebrew term for "burden" often refers to revelations containing warnings of impending doom (see Isa. 15:1; 19:1; 22:1; Nah. 1:1). The name Habakkuk is probably Babylonian and refers to a kind of garden plant.

II. Habakkuk's First Complaint: Why Does the Evil in Judah Go Unpunished? (1:2–4)

1:2–4. Here begins a dialogue (1:2–2:20) between the prophet and God, revolving around the age-old question of why evil seems to go unpunished. Like other persons of faith in the Old Testament, Habakkuk was bold in going to God with his complaints and felt the freedom to express negative thoughts and emotions to God. The psalmist asked, "Why sleepest thou, O Lord?" (Ps. 44:23), and Jeremiah inquired, "Wherefore doth the way of the wicked prosper?" (Jer. 12:1). The Lord's patient response to Habakkuk reflects that He welcomes hard questions, though He is not obligated to answer in a timely manner, or even to answer at all. Habakkuk's questions are not a reflection of skepticism and denial concerning God's fairness but are rather the heartfelt cry of a man of great faith longing for God to act in a way that is consistent with His character.

Habakkuk's first question was the familiar complaint **how long …?** (v. 2), which appears throughout the Psalms. The prophet did not understand why God failed to remedy or judge the **violence** done in the land of Judah. At that time, Judah was probably under King Jehoiakim, who was ambitious and cruel, and his corrupt leadership brought a social corruption and spiritual apostasy that permeated the nation of Judah. Habakkuk complained that the **law is slacked** (v. 4) and that **judgment doth never go forth** because wealthy landowners controlled the courts through bribery.

III. God's Answer: The Babylonians Will Punish Judah (1:5–11)

1:5–11. In response to Habakkuk's question, the Lord declared that He would **work a work** (v. 5) that involved the destruction of Judah at the hands of the **Chaldeans** (i.e., Babylonians; v. 6). The apostate nation of Judah was to be punished by an invasion of the Babylonians, a powerful people who regained their independence from Assyira in 626 BC, destroyed Assyrian power completely in 612–605 BC, and flourished until 539 BC. The speed with which Babylon conquered her enemies had become proverbial, an idea stressed by the vivid comparisons of their **horses** to **leopards** (v. 8) and their **horsemen** to **eagles**. When the Babylonian army attacked, they would **gather the captivity as sand** (v. 9), following the practice of their Assyrian predecessors in deporting conquered peoples as a matter of deliberate national policy (see 2:5). They would **heap dust** in building siege ramps and capturing the cities of Judah. The Babylonians would attribute their military successes to their gods, wrongly believing that their false gods were more powerful than the God of Judah.

IV. Habakkuk's Second Complaint: How Can a Just God Use Wicked Babylon to Punish a People More Righteous Than Themselves? (1:12–2:1)

1:12–17. God promised to act against the evil in Judah, but His response to Habakkuk's question raised a more serious issue. Habakkuk could not see the injustice in Judah's being punished by an even more wicked nation and thought that the Babylonians surely would not be allowed to conquer Judah completely. In verse 13, the prophet raises the classic statement of the problem of evil within the context of Israel's faith: Why does evil appear to flourish unchecked by a just and holy God?

The Babylonians are paragons of evil because of their brutality against other nations (vv. 14–17). Babylon's victims are compared to the **fishes of the sea**

(v. 14) caught with **angle** (i.e., hook; v. 15) and **net**. Mesopotamian reliefs portray, in symbolic fashion, conquering rulers capturing the enemy in fishnets. Just as a net captures many kinds of fish, so Babylon would conquer many nations. The repetition of "net" in verses 15–17 reflects the prophet's agitated state.

2:1. In conclusion to his question to the Lord, Habakkuk stated, **I will stand upon my watch**, using the figure of a guard looking out from a **tower** and expecting a response to his challenge. Having vented his frustration, he affirmed his belief in God and waited for any reproof that might come from questioning God's justice. This kind of affirmation in the Old Testament often springs forth from lament.

V. God's Answer: Babylon Will Be Punished, and Faith Will Be Rewarded (2:2–20)

2:2–5. Though Habakkuk would have to **wait for it** (v. 3), God promised to bring about the fall of Babylon, an event which occurred in 539 BC, about sixty-six years after Habakkuk's prophecy. The Lord told Habakkuk (and Judah) that fulfillment of this prophecy might **tarry** but that he and the people were to expect it (see 3:16). In contrast to the Babylonians, who were **lifted up** (v. 4) with their arrogant pride, the **just** person is the one who **shall live by his faith**, humbly waiting upon God to fulfill His promises to save and deliver. This clause is frequently quoted in the New Testament to support the teaching that people are saved by grace through faith (Rom. 1:17; Gal. 3:11; see Eph. 2:8) and should live by faith (Heb. 10:38–39). The same principle that was applicable in the area of national deliverance—trusting in the unseen promise of God—is also applicable in the area of spiritual deliverance (salvation). Babylon was the target of God's wrath, because **he enlargeth his desire as hell** (v. 5). The parallelism with **is as death, and cannot be satisfied** demonstrates that **hell** (Hebrew, *sheol*) here refers to the grave. The grave never says "enough" (Prov. 30:15–16), and Babylon as a nation had the same insatiable desire to destroy other peoples.

2:6–20. In a series of five "Woe" oracles in the form of a taunt song against Babylon (vv. 6–20; see

"Woe" in 2:6, 9, 12, 15, 19), the Lord declared that the destroyer was about to be destroyed.

2:6–8. The first **Woe** (v. 6) warned that the victims of Babylon's onslaught, especially Judah, would eventually taunt ruthless Babylon. Babylon would be destroyed **because of men's blood** (v. 8), in fulfillment of the Noahic mandate of Genesis 9:6 (see Hab. 2:17; Isa. 24:5; Amos 1–2).

2:9–11. The second **Woe** (v. 9) condemned Babylon's pride in building a **nest on high**. Like the eagle building an inaccessible nest, the Babylonians thought their empire to be unconquerable (see Obadiah 3–4; see Isa. 14:4, 13–15). The **stone[s]** (v. 11) and **beam[s]** in the Babylonian houses had been purchased with plunder taken from other peoples and testified against them.

2:12–14. The third **Woe** (v. 12) condemned Babylonian injustice. The cities built by the labors of the Babylonians would be burned. The Lord's destruction of Babylon and all her worldly glory would cause the whole world to be **filled with the knowledge of the glory of the** Lord (v. 14; see Exod. 14:4, 17–18; Isa. 11:9; Rev. 17:1–19:4). God uses even the wickedness of evil nations to magnify the reputation of His greatness.

2:15–18. The fourth **Woe** (v. 15) condemned Babylon's violence, using graphic sexual imagery. Babylon's rapacious treatment of her neighbors, which had stripped them of all their wealth (compare what she later did to Jerusalem, 2 Kings 25:8–21), is compared to one who makes his neighbor **drunken** so that he can take lewd pleasure from the man's **nakedness**. Babylon would receive just punishment, as he would drink the **cup of the** Lord's **right hand** (v. 16; see Jer. 25:15–17) and be shamefully exposed in front of his enemies.

Divine retribution would also fall on Babylon for their crimes against nature and the environment. **The violence of Lebanon** (v. 17) refers to how Babylon apparently had ravaged the cedar forests of Lebanon to adorn their temples and palaces (see Isa. 14:8). Babylon would be also held accountable for the **spoil of beasts**. Assyrian inscriptions record hunting expeditions in the Lebanon range, and such sport may have been indulged in by the invading Babylonians as well. Babylonian violence was destruction of all forms of life, not only of lands and cities. Verse 17 is a reminder of the seriousness of the creation mandate, in which God places upon humanity the responsibility to serve as His vice-regent over the creation (see Gen. 1:26-28).

2:19-20. The final **Woe** (v. 19) is a reminder of the futility of idolatry. Babylon would ultimately fall because of its misplaced trust in **dumb** idols. These worthless idols are contrasted to the Lord. The **wood** and **stone** idols of the nations are silent before people, but the people of the world are to be silent before the true God, who is about to judge (see Isa. 41:1; Zeph. 1:7; Zech. 2:13).

VI. Habakkuk's Prayer: Confession of Trust and Joy in God (chap. 3)

3:1-2. Chapter 3 contains Habakkuk's response of trust to the Lord's promise to destroy the wicked Babylonians. The prophet who had questioned God's justice now realized that God's justice would ultimately triumph. His prayer contained a petition for God to act and to remember His **mercy** (v. 2) toward His people but is primarily a recollection of God's mighty saving acts of old on Israel's behalf (vv. 3-15) and an expression of confidence and trust (3:16-19). Habakkuk's prayer appears to have been used as a psalm— note the psalm-like heading (v. 1) and the musical and/ or literary notations in verses 1-2 and 3:9, 13, 19.

3:3-10. The exodus is in view here, the time when God acted as the Divine Warrior to deliver His people from bondage and oppression. The Lord came down with His heavenly host and rode on the mighty thunderstorm as His chariot, with His arrows flying in all directions, a cloudburst of rain descending on the earth and the mountains quaking before Him (see Deut. 33:2; Judg. 5:4-5; Pss. 18:7-15; 68:4-10, 32-35; 77:16-19). When overwhelmed by the circumstances of the present or the prospects for the future, it is important to remember God's acts of the past, which is the prophet's focus in 3:3-15.

3:11-13. The focus here is the conquest and how God defeated the Canaanite peoples in giving Israel possession of the Promised Land. The reference to the **sun and moon** (v. 11) standing still recalls the victory at Gibeon (Josh. 10:12-13), indicating that God's triumph over His enemies would be just as complete as on that occasion. Due to the fact that the sun and moon were often worshiped in other religions, theophanic language in the Old Testament frequently portrays them in submission to the God of the universe. God acted to save Israel because they were His **people** (v. 13) and had been **anointed** as His "kingdom of priests" (Exod. 19:6) to all the nations.

3:14-15. The closing verses of Habakkuk's remembrance return to the theme of the exodus. God would vanquish His present foes in the way that He had destroyed the Egyptians in the Red Sea.

3:16-19. Habakkuk's confession contains one of the greatest statements of personal faith in all of Scripture. Hearing the hymnic recollection of God's mighty deeds of old on Israel's behalf had filled the prophet with an awe so profound that he felt physically weak. The mention of the disastrous harvests and decimation of Judah's **flock[s]** and **herd[s]** (v. 17) appears to anticipate the awful results of the imminent Babylonian invasion and devastation. Even in the midst of this deprivation, Habakkuk confessed that he would trust in the Lord (v. 18).

3:18-19. It is one thing to trust God when things are going well and one is prosperous, but quite another when the world is falling apart. Habakkuk had learned the lesson of faith (see 2:4)—to trust in God's providence regardless of circumstances. Habakkuk's struggle to trust in God reflects the spiritual odyssey of every true believer—consternation with the injustices of life, consideration of God as sovereign, and the conclusion that God can and must be trusted.

Habakkuk concluded by acknowledging **The Lord GOD is my strength** (v. 19). The Lord's enablement gave him sure-footed confidence (**he will make my feet like hinds' feet**) that he would be safe and secure. The prophet's psalm is dedicated to **the chief singer**, probably the conductor of the temple musicians. This chapter may have formed part of the temple prayers that were chanted with the accompaniment of instruments (see 1 Chron. 16:4-7).

THE BOOK OF ZEPHANIAH

INTRODUCTION

Author

The prophet Zephaniah was evidently a person of considerable social standing in Judah and was probably related to the royal line. The book opens with a statement of the author's ancestry (1:1), which in itself is an unusual feature in the prophetic books. Zephaniah was a fourth-generation descendant of Hezekiah, a notable king of Judah (715–686 BC). Apart from this statement, nothing more is said about Zephaniah's background. He was probably familiar with the writings of the prominent prophets of the eighth century BC, such as Isaiah and Amos, whose utterances he reflects, and he may also have been aware of the ministry of the young Jeremiah.

Date

According to 1:1, Zephaniah prophesied during the reign of King Josiah (640–609 BC), making him a contemporary of the prophets Jeremiah, Nahum, and perhaps Habakkuk. His prophecy is probably to be dated relatively early in Josiah's reign, before the king's attempt at reform (while conditions brought about by the wicked reigns of Manasseh and Amon still prevailed) and before the Assyrian king Ashurbanipal's death in 627 BC (while Assyria was still powerful, though threatened).

Background

See Jeremiah and Nahum, Introduction: "Background"; see also 2 Kings 22:1–23:30; 2 Chronicles 34–35 and discussions.

Theme and Theological Message

The intent of the author was to announce to Judah God's approaching judgment. A Scythian incursion into Canaan may have provided the immediate occasion. This fierce, horsemounted people originated in what is now southern Russia, but by the seventh century BC, they had migrated across the Caucasus and settled in and along the northern territories of the Assyrian Empire. Alternatively enemies and allies of Assyria, the Scythians seem to have thrust south along the Mediterranean sometime between 630 and 620 BC, destroying Ashkelon and Ashdod and halting at the Egyptian border only because of a payoff by Pharaoh Psamtik (Psammetichus). Ultimately, however, the destruction of Judah prophesied by Zephaniah came at the hands of the Babylonians, after they had overpowered Assyria and brought that ancient power to its end.

The book's main theme is the coming of the day of the Lord (see also Isa. 2:11, 17, 20; Joel 1:15; 2:2; Amos 5:18; 8:9), when God would severely punish the nations, including apostate Judah. Zephaniah portrayed the stark horror of that ordeal with the same graphic imagery found elsewhere in the Prophets. He also made it clear that God would yet be merciful toward His people; like many other prophets, he ended his pronouncements of doom on the positive note of Judah's restoration by the Lord, "the king of Israel" (3:15).

Outline

I. Introduction: The Prophet Identified (1:1)
II. The Day of the Lord Coming on Judah and the Nations (1:2–18)
    A. Judgment on Jerusalem (1:2–13)
    B. The Day of Wrath (1:14–18)
III. God's Judgment on the Nations (2:1–3:8)
    A. Call to Repentance (2:1–3)
    B. Judgment on Philistia (2:4–7)
    C. Judgment on Moab and Ammon (2:8–11)
    D. Judgment on Cush (Ethiopia) (2:12)
    E. Judgment on Assyria (2:13–15)
    F. Judgment on Jerusalem (3:1–8)
IV. Redemption of the Remnant (3:9–20)
    A. The Nations Purified, the Remnant Restored, Jerusalem Purged (3:9–13)
    B. Rejoicing in the City (3:14–17)
    C. The Nation Restored (3:18–20)

Bibliography

Bruckner, James. *Jonah, Nahum, Habakkuk, Zephaniah.* NIV Application Commentary. Grand Rapids, MI: Zondervan, 2004.

Hannah, John D. "Zephaniah." In *The Bible Knowledge Commentary: Old Testament*, edited by John F. Walvoord and Roy B. Zuck. Wheaton, IL: Victor, 2000.

Patterson, Richard D. *Nahum, Habakkuk, Zephaniah.* Wycliffe Exegetical Commentary. Chicago: Moody, 1991.

Roberts, J. J. M. *Nahum, Habakkuk, and Zephaniah: A Commentary.* Old Testament Library. Louisville: Westminster John Knox, 1991.

Robertson, O. Palmer. *The Books of Nahum, Habakkuk, and Zephaniah.* New International Commentary on the Old Testament. Grand Rapids, MI: Eerdmans, 1990.

EXPOSITION

I. Introduction: The Prophet Identified (1:1)

1:1. The name **Zephaniah** means "the Lord hides" or "the Lord protects," perhaps referring to God's protection of Zephaniah during the infamous reigns of Manasseh and **Amon**, the predecessors of good King **Josiah**. Based on his fourth-generation descent from **Hizkiah** (Hezekiah), it seems likely that Zephaniah began his ministry when he was in his early twenties. He is more closely identified with the ruling class than was Isaiah, although Isaiah also moved regularly in court circles and was perhaps of noble birth. God called the prophets as His spokesmen from diverse families, classes, and occupations.

II. The Day of the Lord Coming on Judah and the Nations (1:2–18)

A. Judgment on Jerusalem (1:2–13)

1:2–3. Zephaniah announced the coming judgment in catastrophic terms. The Lord spoke in the first person (**I will**; vv. 2–3, 1:4) to show His direct involvement in the coming disaster and to heighten the severity of the warning. In this judgment, the Lord **will utterly consume** (v. 2) the earth, language reminiscent of God's utterances prior to the flood (see Gen. 6:7), but this time, judgment would come in the form of God's fire (vv. 2–3; see 1:18; 3:8).

1:4–6. The reason for God's anger was Judah's rampant and gross idolatry, which included worship of **Baal** (v. 4), the participation of **Chemarims** ("pagan priests") in the rites of the Jerusalem temple, and the worship of **the host of heaven** (v. 5; see Deut. 4:15–10). That the Judahites swore oaths in the names of **the Lord, and ... Malcham** indicates that they were guilty of syncretism, blending the worship of the Lord with the worship of other gods, when the Lord had commanded exclusive loyalty and devotion from His people (see Deut. 13:1–4). Malcham (a variant of the god Molech) was worshiped by the Ammonites, and his rituals sometimes involved child sacrifice. This abhorrent practice was

forbidden for the Israelites (Lev. 18:21; 20:1–5). Despite this, Solomon had set up an altar to Molech on the Mount of Olives (1 Kings 11:7), and Manasseh had established these rituals in the valley of Ben-hinnom (2 Chron. 33:6; Jer. 7:31; 32:35).

This condemnation of idolatry seems to indicate that Zephaniah's main ministry took place before 621 BC, since the practices condemned here were abolished in Josiah's reforms (2 Kings 23:4–16). It would appear that Zephaniah's message was partly instrumental in motivating King Josiah and the people to undertake the reforms (see 2 Chron. 34:1–7). The effect of Zephaniah's preaching is a reminder that God uses His word to change lives and that heeding God's word brings life and spares from death (see Jer. 26:17–19).

1:7–13. The announcement of judgment introduces the main theme of Zephaniah's preaching: **the day of the Lord is at hand** (v. 7). This day of the Lord would be not a time of deliverance for Judah but of divine vengeance on the idolatrous nation. Zephaniah was referring to the impending Babylonian invasion of Judah, though Babylon is not identified here as the oppressor nation. The prophet compared the coming judgment to a **sacrifice**, in which Judah would be the victim. The slaughter of this sacrifice would bring wailing throughout the city (vv. 10–13; contrast the promise of 3:14–17). The Lord warned that He would bring thorough destruction, even searching the city **with candles** (v. 12) to make sure that every wicked person was put to death. The Babylonians later dragged people from houses, streets, sewers, and tombs, where they had hidden. The response of the wicked was to claim **The Lord will not do ... evil** (i.e., bring calamity), reflecting an arrogant refusal to acknowledge their accountability to the Lord (see Ps. 10:11; Mic. 3:11; and 2 Peter 3:4).

B. The Day of Wrath (1:14–18)

1:14–18. This dramatic passage of great lyrical power presents the Lord's description of the destruction that would sweep the earth in the day of God's wrath. The tenfold repetition of **day** (vv. 14–16) in these verses highlights the seriousness of the prophetic warning and the overwhelming nature of the devastation that was coming. The prophet warned that in this day of death and destruction, **Neither their silver nor their gold shall be able to deliver them** (v. 18). In the day of God's judgment, material wealth cannot buy deliverance from punishment.

III. God's Judgment on the Nations (2:1–3:8)

A. Call to Repentance (2:1–3)

2:1–3. The call to repentance following the warnings of total destruction in chapter 1 is a demonstration of the Lord's long-suffering mercy. The Lord offered the people of Judah yet another opportunity to change their ways and to avoid judgment, after hundreds of years of disobedience. The call to repentance and the indictment against Jerusalem in 3:1–8 frame this section on God's judgment of the nations in connection with the day of the Lord. This linking of the judgment of Judah and the pagan nations around them challenged the mistaken belief of the people of Judah that they were better than the pagans around them and that their status as God's elect nation exempted them from the coming destruction of the day of the Lord.

B. Judgment on Philistia (2:4–7)

2:4–7. The prophet announced that the day of the Lord would bring judgment on the Philistine cities of **Gaza** (v. 4), **Ashkelon, Ashdod,** and **Ekron.** The coming Babylonian invasion would reduce these once populous cities to pastureland. Looking beyond the immediate situation, the prophet anticipated a time when the Philistine territory **shall be for the remnant ... of Judah** (v. 7). The faithful remnant of Judah would occupy this land and grace it with their flocks. The Lord promised Judah a future restoration, when He would **turn away their captivity** (see 2:9, 11; 3:9–20). Judah would experience judgment and destruction like these other nations, but the Lord promised that Judah's judgment would not be final.

C. Judgment on Moab and Ammon (2:8–11)

2:8–11. Moab (v. 8) and **Ammon** would be judged for their hostility toward Israel and Judah (see Amos 1:13–15; 2:1–3). They had often threatened to occupy Israelite territory (see Judg. 11:12–13; Ezek. 25:3–6). This judgment, a working out of the original promise to Abraham to "curse him that curseth thee" (Gen. 12:3), would cause Moab and Ammon to become like **Sodom, and ... Gomorrah** (v. 9), cities used in the Old Testament to typify complete destruction at the hands of God (see Genesis 19; Deut. 29:23; Isa. 13:19; Jer. 49:18). Despite the ominous tone of this oracle, the ultimate outcome of God's judgment is that even these nations that are the objects of total destruction would turn from their false gods and would **worship** (v. 11) the Lord.

D. Judgment on Cush (Ethiopia) (2:12)

2:12. Without elaboration, the prophet simply announced God's purpose against Egypt. The Ethiopians (lit., "Cushites") were a people from the upper (southern) Nile region. A Cushite dynasty ruled Egypt from 715 to 663 BC. The Babylonians would become the Lord's **sword** in bringing death to the Cushites.

E. Judgment on Assyria (2:13–15)

2:13–15. The Lord promised to **destroy Assyria** (v. 13), the brutal and violent nation that had inflicted such pain and suffering on the kingdoms of Israel and Judah. Jonah's preaching had helped to delay the destruction of the Assyrian capital, **Nineveh,** but both Zephaniah and Nahum prophesied the destruction of this city, which was carried out by the Babylonians and the Medes in 612 BC. The great city of Nineveh would become **a desolation.** Even the site of Nineveh was later forgotten, until discovered through modern excavations. Nineveh would be judged for its proud boast **I am, and there is none beside me** (v. 15), a claim that properly belongs to God alone (see Isa. 45:5–6, 18, 21).

F. Judgment on Jerusalem (3:1–8)

3:1–5. In a shocking conclusion to these oracles of judgment, Zephaniah turned to the destruction of Jerusalem along with the pagan nations. Apostate Jerusalem was condemned as **the oppressing city** (v. 1; see Jer. 22:3), and all classes of Judah's leaders (**princes** and **judges**, v. 3; **prophets** and **priests**, v. 4) were castigated for indulging in conduct completely opposed to their vocations and their covenant-mandated responsibilities. The leaders were like **roaring lions** (v. 3) and **evening wolves,** rapacious in their use and abuse of power. The prophets were **treacherous persons** (v. 4), who claimed to speak for God but proclaimed only lies (see Jer. 5:31; 14:14; 23:16, 32). The priests did violence to the law when they should have been teachers of the law (see Deut. 31:9–13; 2 Chron. 17:8–9; Ezra 7:6).

3:6–8. The adage "like leaders, like people" is true; the inhabitants of Jerusalem were obstinate in their stubborn refusal to repent and turn from their sin. The Lord had **cut off** other **nations** (v. 6) to serve as a warning to wanton Judah, but to no avail. As a result, the Lord called on the nation to **wait ye upon me** (v. 8), a sarcastic statement for Judah to wait for the threatened catastrophe, which was surely coming.

IV. Redemption of the Remnant (3:9–20)

3:9–20. Judgment was not God's final word. This section looks beyond the events of the immediate future to the final day of the Lord, in which God's final judgment will purify a remnant from the nations and Israel. It contains a three-part oracle (vv. 9–13, 14–17, 18–20) announcing the redemption that will follow God's judgment.

A. The Nations Purified, the Remnant Restored, Jerusalem Purged (3:9–13)

3:9–10. The promise of 2:11 anticipated that the nations judged by the Lord will repudiate their idols and turn to God in worship; here the Lord promised to give the people of the nations **a pure language** (v. 9) so that **they may all call upon the name of the LORD.** God's fearful judgment of the nations will effect their purification so that they will call on His name and serve Him. Israel's God will be acknowledged by the nations, and God's people will be held in honor by them (see 3:19–20). This

verse represents nothing less than a divine promise to reverse the effects of the curse that God placed on the human race when He confounded the languages at Babel (see Gen. 11:1–9). The enablement of the apostles to communicate the gospel in other tongues at Pentecost (see Acts 2:1–11) provides a preview of the ultimate fulfillment of this promise.

3:11–13. Along with purifying the nations, the Lord will also purge Jerusalem and remove the wicked from the city. The statement that the Lord will leave **an afflicted and poor people** (v. 12) is not to be understood as a negative but rather as an assurance that the nation will no longer suffer from the pride and arrogance that plague the **haughty** (v. 11). The **poor** (v. 12) are those who humbly acknowledge their dependence on the Lord (see Ps. 9:9–12). The absence of sinners will mean the absence of judgment, and the people of Jerusalem **shall feed and lie down** (v. 13) under the absolute protection of the Lord as the Shepherd of His people.

B. Rejoicing in the City (3:14–17)

3:14–17. These verses portray the joy that will belong to the restored city. There will be no **enemy** (v. 15) to attack Israel, and the Lord will be **The king of Israel** (see Isa. 44:6). Toward the end of the Old Testament, there is a discernible shift away from the line of David. Earthly kingship had failed, and the kingship of God is highlighted. This kingship is fulfilled, of course, in Christ. Zechariah wrote that "the LORD shall be king over all the earth" (Zech. 14:9) and "all the nations ... shall ... go ... to worship the King, the LORD of hosts" (Zech. 14:16).

C. The Nation Restored (3:18–20)

3:18–20. These verses present a summary announcement of restoration and the Lord's final assurance to His people. The Lord promised to reverse the judgments of the past and to bring back the exiles (**turn back your captivity;** v. 20). In fulfillment of His promise to Abraham, the Lord **will make ... a name** for Israel among all the nations (see Gen. 12:2–3) as the nations observe the blessing and prosperity that God bestows on Israel.

HAGGAI

THE BOOK OF HAGGAI

INTRODUCTION

Author

Haggai (1:1) was a prophet who, along with Zechariah, encouraged the returned exiles to rebuild the temple (see Ezra 5:1–2; 6:14). The name Haggai means "festal," which may indicate that the prophet was born during one of the three pilgrimage feasts: the Feast of Unleavened Bread, the Feast of Weeks (or Pentecost), or the Feast of Tabernacles (see Deut. 16:16). Based on 2:3, Haggai may have witnessed the destruction of Solomon's temple. If so, he must have been in his early seventies during his ministry.

Date

The messages of Haggai were given during a four-month period in 520 BC, the second year of King Darius. The first message was delivered on the first day of the sixth month (August 29), and the last message on the twenty-fourth day of the ninth month (December 18).

Background

In 538 BC, the conqueror of Babylon, King Cyrus of Persia, issued a decree allowing the Jews to return to Jerusalem and rebuild the temple (see Ezra 1:2–4; 6:3–5). Led by Zerubbabel (but see discussion on Ezra 1:8, "Sheshbazzar"), about fifty thousand Jews journeyed home and began work on the temple. About two years later (536 BC), they completed the foundation amid great rejoicing (see Ezra 3:8–10). Their success aroused the Samaritans and other neighbors, who feared the political and religious implications of a rebuilt temple in a thriving Jewish state and who therefore opposed the project vigorously and managed to halt work until Darius the Great became king of Persia in 522 BC (see Ezra 4:1–5, 24).

Darius was interested in the religions of his empire, and Haggai and Zechariah began to preach in the second year of his reign, 520 BC (see 1:1; Zech. 1:1). The Jews were more to blame for their inactivity than were their opponents, and Haggai tried to arouse the Jews from their lethargy. When the governor of Trans-Euphrates and other officials tried to interfere with the rebuilding efforts, Darius fully supported the Jews (Ezra 5:3–6; 6:6–12). In 516 BC, the temple was finished and dedicated (see Ezra 6:15–18).

Theme and Theological Message

Next to Obadiah, Haggai is the shortest book in the Old Testament, but its teachings are nonetheless significant. Haggai clearly shows the consequences of disobedience (1:6, 11; 2:16–17) and obedience (2:7–9, 19). When the people give priority to God and His house, they are blessed rather than cursed (see Luke 12:31). Obedience brings the encouragement and strength of the Spirit of God (2:4–5).

Chapter 2 speaks of the coming of the Messiah, called "the desire of all nations" in verse 7. His coming would fill the rebuilt temple with glory (see 2:9 and discussion). The Lord made Zerubbabel His "signet [ring]" (2:23) as a guarantee that the Messiah would come. These passages are linked with the judgment of the nations at Christ's second coming, when the nations will be shaken and kingdoms overthrown (see 2:6–7, 21–22 and discussions; Heb. 12:25–29).

Literary Features

Like Malachi, Haggai used a number of questions to highlight key issues (see 1:4, 9; 2:3, 19). He also made effective use of repetition: "Consider your ways" occurs in 1:5, 7; 2:15, 18, and "I am with you" in 1:13; 2:4. "I will shake the heavens and the earth" is found in 2:6, 21. The major sections of the book are marked off by the date on which the word of the Lord came "to" (or "by," "through," or "unto") Haggai (1:1; 2:1, 10, 20).

Several times the prophet appears to echo other Scriptures (compare 1:6 with Deut. 28:38–39; and 2:17 with Deut. 28:22). The threefold use of "be strong" in 2:4 reflects the encouragement given in Joshua 1:6–7, 9, 18.

Outline

I. First Message: The Call to Rebuild the Temple (1:1–11)
    A. The People's Lame Excuse (1:1–4)
    B. The Poverty of the People and the Reason for God's Curse (1:5–11)
II. The Response of Zerubbabel and the People (1:12–15)
    A. The Leaders and the Remnant Obey (1:12)
    B. The Lord Strengthens the Workers (1:13–15)
III. Second Message: The Temple to Be Filled with Glory (2:1–9)
    A. The People Encouraged (2:1–5)
    B. The Promise of Glory and Peace (2:6–9)
IV. Third Message: A Defiled People Purified and Blessed (2:10–19)
    A. The Rapid Spread of Sin (2:10–14)
    B. Blessings to Come as the Temple Is Rebuilt (2:15–19)
V. Fourth Message: The Promise to Zerubbabel (2:20–23)
    A. The Judgment of the Nations (2:20–22)
    B. The Significance of Zerubbabel (2:23)

Bibliography

Baldwin, Joyce G. *Haggai, Zechariah, Malachi: An Introduction and Commentary*. Tyndale Old Testament Commentaries 24. Downers Grove, IL: InterVarsity, 1972.

Merrill, Eugene H. *Haggai, Zechariah, Malachi*. Wycliffe Exegetical Commentary. Chicago: Moody, 1994.

Verhoef, Pieter A. *The Books of Haggai and Malachi*. New International Commentary on the Old Testament. Grand Rapids, MI: Eerdmans, 1987.

Wolff, H. W. *Haggai: A Commentary*. Translated by M. Kohl. Minneapolis: Augsburg, 1988.

EXPOSITION

I. First Message: The Call to Rebuild the Temple (1:1–11)

A. The People's Lame Excuse (1:1–4)

1:1–4. Haggai's opening message was a challenge for the people of Judah to complete the task of rebuilding the temple, which had been destroyed by the Babylonians in 587 BC. This message is dated to August 29, 520 BC, in the reign of **Darius** (v. 1) Hystaspis (or Hystaspes), who ruled Persia from 522 to 486 BC. It was he who prepared the trilingual inscription on the Behistun cliff wall (located in modern Iran), through which cuneiform languages were deciphered. Two important leaders of Judah in the postexilic period were **Zerubbabel**, a descendant of David and the governor of Judah (see Ezra 1:8), and **Joshua**, the high priest.

Haggai presented the challenge to rebuild the temple as the messenger of **the LORD of hosts** (v. 2), or the Lord of the armies of heaven. Though Judah was only a Persian province, the Lord retained His sovereign power and authority. The Lord referred to Israel as **This people** rather than as "My people" because of their sin (see Isa. 6:9; 8:11–12; Jer. 14:10–11). The people protested that they had not rebuilt the temple because **The time is not come.** After the foundation of the temple had been laid in 536 BC (see Ezra 3:8–10), opposition hindered and then halted the work until 520 BC (see Ezra 4:1–5:24). The work had been dormant for more than twenty years, but the people had no incentive or spiritual motivation to finish the project of building God's house and establishing a place of worship.

The demonstration of their misplaced priorities was the fact that they lived in **cieled houses** (v. 4) while God's house remained unfinished. The term for "cieled houses" only appears six times in the Old Testament, and its meaning is obscure. It could also be translated as "paneled houses," since it normally appears in connection with royal dwellings, which had cedar paneling (see 1 Kings 7:3, 7; Jer. 22:14). The point is that the people were living in luxury, while giving no attention to God's house. They had been poor stewards of both time and resources in failing to take advantage of the opportunity to work for God in the same way that they had worked for themselves.

B. The Poverty of the People and the Reason for God's Curse (1:5–11)

1:5–7. The prophet challenges the people to consider how their disregard for God's house had brought them financial ruin. They **have sown much, and bring in little** (v. 6), one of the covenant curses set forth by Moses (see Lev. 26:20; Deut. 28:38–39). The people experienced futility in all of their activities, legitimate or illegitimate (see Hos. 4:10–11; Mic. 6:13–15). Their earnings were like coins put into a **bag with holes**, because famine had caused prices to rise sharply.

1:8–11. The Lord directly commanded His people to **bring wood, and build the house** (v. 8).

They were to gather wood from the hills surrounding Jerusalem to supplement the cedar wood that had already been purchased from Lebanon (see Ezra 3:7). The Lord promised that He would **take pleasure in it** and in the sacrifices that were offered there (contrast Isa. 1:11 before the exile). The Lord would **be glorified** as the nations surrounding Judah saw God's blessing poured out upon His obedient people (see Jer. 13:11). In contrast, the people had experienced only the covenant curses of lost crops, famine, and drought (vv. 9–11; see Deut. 28:23–24, 51).

II. The Response of Zerubbabel and the People (1:12–15)

A. The Leaders and the Remnant Obey (1:12)

1:12. The preaching of Haggai moved the people to action. They **did fear before the Lord**, showing respect and obedience to the prophet's message (see Deut. 31:12–13; Mal. 1:6; 3:5, 6), a remarkable response since most prophets were rejected.

B. The Lord Strengthens the Workers (1:13–15)

1:13. In response to their obedience, Haggai gave the people the Lord's assurance, **I am with you**, a sure indication of success (see 2:4; Gen. 26:3). With God's command comes God's enablement. God had, in the past, been "absent" for long periods of time (four hundred years in Egypt) and had seemed to be so for the two generations in exile. Both the curse they were experiencing and this timely reminder of God's presence assured them that His covenant was still in effect. Every new covenant believer has this same promise from Christ: "I am with you alway" (Matt. 28:20).

1:14–15. The Lord **stirred up the spirit** (v. 14) of Judah's leaders to take an active role in directing the people's efforts to rebuild the temple, in the same way that He had stirred many of these people to return to their homeland (see Ezra 1:5). Throughout Scripture, the vision, direction, and passion of godly leadership are essential for the accomplishment of any significant task for the Lord. The chronological notation in verse 15 is not an incidental detail but

demonstrates the people's immediate response to Haggai's preaching. Work on the temple commenced on September 21, 520 BC, just over three weeks after Haggai preached his first message.

III. Second Message: The Temple to Be Filled with Glory (2:1–9)

2:1–9. Haggai's second message was delivered on October 17, 520 BC. It was time to celebrate the summer harvest (see Lev. 23:34–43), though the crops were meager. In this time of somewhat muted celebration, the people needed encouragement concerning the temple they were building. Some of the older exiles (perhaps including Haggai himself) had seen Solomon's magnificent temple, which had been destroyed by the Babylonians sixty-six years earlier. By speaking of **this house in her first glory** (v. 3), Haggai was stressing that Zerubbabel's temple was a continuation of Solomon's. To the postexilic community, however, it seemed as if the temple they were building was **as nothing**, the same reaction noted in Ezra 3:12 when the foundation of the temple was completed.

A. The People Encouraged (2:1–5)

2:1–5. Haggai encouraged the leaders and people to **be strong** (v. 4), the same words used by David when he encouraged Solomon to build the temple (1 Chron. 28:20). As in 1:13, God again assured the people **I am with you**. In God's eyes, their building project was as important as Solomon's because God had promised, "mine eyes and mine heart shall be there perpetually" (2 Chron. 7:16). God was more concerned with the heart of His people than with the size and architectural impressiveness of the temple building.

B. The Promise of Glory and Peace (2:6–9)

2:6–9. While the province of Judah and their rebuilt temple may have appeared small and insignificant, the Lord promised a future time when He **will shake the heavens, and the earth, and … all nations** (vv. 6–7) in judgment. The fall of Persia to Alexander the Great (333–330 BC) would foreshadow the fall of all great world empires. Hebrews 12:26–27 relates this passage to the judgment of the nations at the second coming of Christ. This time of future judgment will also be when **the desire of all nations shall come** (v. 7). This could be understood as a reference to the future Messiah, because "desire" can refer to individuals (as in 1 Sam. 9:20; Dan. 9:23) and would be translated "greatly beloved." The term can also refer to objects of value, however, such as the contribution of King Darius to the temple in Ezra 6:8 (see also 2 Chron. 20:25; 32:27), and this option seems more likely. The prophet anticipated the nations bringing their tribute and offerings to Jerusalem, so that the **glory** (v. 9), or material splendor, of the new temple will eventually surpass that of the Solomonic temple (see Isa. 60:5–7, 13). The promise of the surpassing glory of the new temple also points to God's people experiencing His presence more fully (see Exod. 40:34–35; 1 Kings 8:10–11). When Christ came to the earthly temple, God's presence was evident as never before (see Luke 2:27, 32; John 1:14).

IV. Third Message: A Defiled People Purified and Blessed (2:10–19)

2:10–19. Haggai's third message, delivered on December 18, 520 BC, dealt with the issues of holiness and defilement.

A. The Rapid Spread of Sin (2:10–14)

2:10–12. Haggai dialogued with the priests and made the point that holiness is not transferable from one object or person to another, but defilement is. The prophet used two hypothetical scenarios to make his point. In the first scenario, meat (**flesh;** v. 12) that was consecrated to God made **holy** any **garment** that it touched (see Lev. 6:27). The holy garment, however, was not then able to sanctify any object that it came in contact with. Holiness is a personal issue and could not be transferred to the people simply by their participation in sacrifice and ritual.

2:13. In the second scenario, Haggai noted that a person who came in contact with **a dead body** became ceremonially unclean (see Num. 19:11) and

that the defilement was passed on to anyone or anything that the defiled person came in contact with (see Num. 19:22). The point here is that the corrupt lives of the people ultimately defiled the worship and sacrifices that the people offered to God.

2:14. Having established the principles of holiness, Haggai applied these principles to the postexilic community. Even though the people were back in the Holy Land, their works remained **unclean**. The holiness of the land did not make them pure. They needed to obey the Lord, particularly with regard to rebuilding the temple. Additionally, while rebuilding the temple was important, the restoration and renewal of Israel required more than simply reinstituting the rituals and sacrifices associated with the temple. The people themselves needed to truly return to God.

B. Blessings to Come as the Temple Is Rebuilt (2:15–19)

2:15–19. As the people began the process of rebuilding the temple, Haggai called on them to **consider from this day and upward** (v. 15, 18) and take note of the blessings that the Lord would bring to them as they took this important step of obedience. The past experience of the covenant curses would be replaced by the blessing of agricultural plenty. The Lord promised, **From this day will I bless you** (v. 19). This promise was especially significant because this message was delivered at the time when winter crops were planted.

V. Fourth Message: The Promise to Zerubbabel (2:20–23)

2:20–23. Haggai's fourth and final message, delivered on the same day as the preceding one, focused on Zerubbabel, the governor of Judah.

A. The Judgment of the Nations (2:20–22)

2:20–22. The Lord promised a future worldwide judgment that will **overthrow** (v. 22) the nations. The word "overthrow" recalls the destruction of Sodom and Gomorrah (see Gen. 19:25; Amos 4:1), and the mention of **chariots, horses,** and **riders**

brings to mind the defeat of Pharaoh's army at the Red Sea (see Exod. 15:1, 4, 9, 21).

B. The Significance of Zerubbabel (2:23)

2:23. The most problematic aspect of this oracle is how the defeat of the nations is connected to **Zerubbabel**. If the passage promised worldwide domination to Zerubbabel, then this prophecy failed miserably. Haggai was looking beyond the time of Zerubbabel to the eschatological day of the Lord (**In that day**; compare Isa. 2:11, 17, 20; Zech. 2:11). The promise that the Lord would make Zerubbabel a **signet** reversed the curse placed on King Jehoiachin in Jeremiah 22:24 in connection with the exile and the

removal of the Davidic king from the throne. The signet was a seal that functioned as a signature (see Est. 8:8) and was worn on one's finger as a symbol of authority (see Est. 3:3). Thus, the significance of the prophecy is that it reestablished the authority of the house of David, of which Zerubbabel was the contemporary representative. The passage is ultimately not about Zerubbabel but about the future Messiah who would come from the line of David and who will rule over the nations. This final oracle reminded the struggling postexilic community that the Lord's covenant promises remained in effect and encouraged them to look forward to the time when Israel will no longer be subject to the nations.

THE BOOK OF ZECHARIAH

INTRODUCTION

Author

Like Jeremiah (1:1) and Ezekiel (1:3), Zechariah was not only a prophet (1:1) but also a priest. He was born in Babylonia and was among those who returned to Judah in 538 BC under the leadership of Zerubbabel and Joshua (Iddo, Zechariah's grandfather, is named among the returnees in Neh. 12:4). At a later time, when Joiakim was high priest, Zechariah apparently succeeded Iddo (1:1, 7) as head of that priestly family (Neh. 12:10–16). Since the grandson succeeded the grandfather, it has been suggested that the father (Berechiah, 1:1, 7) died at an early age.

Zechariah was a contemporary of Haggai (Ezra 5:1; 6:14) but continued his ministry long after Haggai (compare 1:1 and 7:1 with Hag. 1:1; see also Neh. 12:1–16). Zechariah's young age (see 2:4) in the early period of his ministry makes it possible that he ministered even into the reign of Artaxerxes I (465–424 BC).

Most likely, Zechariah wrote the entire book that bears his name. Some have questioned his authorship of chapters 9–14, citing differences in style and other compositional features and giving historical and chronological references that allegedly require a different date and author from those of chapters 1–8. All of these objections, however, can be explained in other satisfactory ways, so there is no compelling reason to question the unity of the book.

Date

The dates of Zechariah's recorded messages are best correlated with those of Haggai and with other historical events as follows:

1. Haggai's first message (Hag. 1:1–11; Ezra 5:1)   Aug. 29, 520 BC
2. Resumption of the building of the temple (Hag. 1:12–15; Ezra 5:2)   Sept. 21, 520

    (The rebuilding seems to have been hindered from 536 to about 530 [Ezra 4:1–5], and the work ceased altogether from about 530 to 520 [Ezra 4:24].)
3. Haggai's second message (Hag. 2:1–9)   Oct. 17, 520

4. Beginning of Zechariah's preaching (1:1–6)   Oct./Nov. 520
5. Haggai's third message (Hag. 2:10–19)   Dec. 18, 520
6. Haggai's fourth message (Hag. 2:20–23)   Dec. 18, 520
7. Tatnai's letter to Darius concerning the rebuilding of
   the temple (Ezra 5:3–6:14)   519–518

(There must have been a lapse of time between the resumption of the building and Tatnai's appearance.)

8. Zechariah's eight night visions (1:7–6:8)   Feb. 15, 519
9. Joshua crowned (6:9–15)   Feb. 16 (?), 519
10. Repentance urged, blessings promised (chaps. 7–8)   Dec. 7, 518
11. Dedication of the temple (Ezra 6:15–18)   Mar. 12, 516
12. Zechariah's final prophecy (chaps. 9–14)   After 480 (?)

Background

Zechariah's prophetic ministry took place in the postexilic period, the time of the Jewish restoration from Babylonian captivity. For historical details, see Haggai, Introduction: "Background."

Theme

The theme is the same as that of the book of Haggai (see "Date" and "Background," above). The chief purpose of Zechariah (and Haggai) was to rebuke the people of Judah and to encourage and motivate them to complete the rebuilding of the temple (Zech. 4:8–10; Haggai 1–2), though both prophets were clearly interested in spiritual renewal as well. In addition, the purpose of the eight night visions (1:7–6:8) is explained in 1:3, 5–6: The Lord said that if Judah would return to Him, He would return to them. Furthermore, His word would continue to be fulfilled.

Theological Message

This book as a whole teaches the sovereignty of God in history, over people and nations, past, present, and future. The theological message of the book is related to its messianic as well as its apocalyptic and eschatological motifs. Regarding the messianic emphasis, Zechariah foretold Christ's coming in lowliness (6:12), His humanity (6:12; 13:7), His rejection and betrayal for thirty pieces of silver (11:12–13), His crucifixion (struck by the "sword" of the Lord; 13:7), His priesthood (6:13), His kingship (6:13; 9:9; 14:9, 16), His coming in glory (14:4), His building of the Lord's temple (6:12–13), His reign (9:10; 14), and His establishment of enduring peace and prosperity (3:10; 9:9–10). These messianic passages give added significance to Jesus' words in Luke 24:25–27, 44.

Regarding the apocalyptic and eschatological emphasis, Zechariah foretold the siege of Jerusalem (12:1–3; 14:1–2), the initial victory of Judah's enemies (14:2), the Lord's defense of Jerusalem (14:3–4), the judgment on the nations (12:9; 14:3), the topographical changes in Judah (14:4–5), the celebration of the Feast of Tabernacles in the messianic kingdom age (14:16–19), and the ultimate holiness of Jerusalem and her people (14:20–21).

The prophet's name, which means "the LORD [Yahweh] remembers," also has theological significance. "The LORD" is the personal, covenant name of God and is a perpetual testimony to His faithfulness to His promises (see discussion on Exod. 3:14). He "remembers" His covenant promises and takes action to fulfill them. In the book of Zechariah, God's promised deliverance of His people from Babylonian exile, including a restored kingdom community and a functioning temple (the earthly throne of the Divine King), leads into even grander pictures of the salvation and restoration to come through the Messiah.

Literary Features

The book is primarily a mixture of exhortation (call to repentance, 1:2–6), prophetic visions (1:7–6:8), and judgment and salvation oracles (chaps. 9–14). The prophetic visions of 1:7–6:8 are called apocalyptic (revelatory) literature, which is essentially a literature of encouragement to God's people. When the apocalyptic section is read along with the salvation (or deliverance) oracles of chapters 9–14, it becomes obvious that the dominant emphasis of the book is encouragement because of the glorious future that awaits the people of God.

Outline

Bibliography

Baldwin, Joyce G. *Haggai, Zechariah, Malachi: An Introduction and Commentary.* Tyndale Old Testament Commentaries 24. London: InterVarsity, 1972.

Boda, Mark J. *Haggai, Zechariah.* NIV Application Commentary. Grand Rapids, MI: Zondervan, 2004.

Duguid, I. "Messianic Themes in Zechariah 9–14." In *The Lord's Anointed: Interpretation of Old Testament Messianic Texts,* edited by P. E. Satterthwaite, R. S. Hess, and G. J. Wenham. Grand Rapids, MI: Baker, 1995.

Merrill, Eugene H. *Haggai, Zechariah, Malachi.* Wycliffe Exegetical Commentary. Chicago: Moody, 1994.

Redditt, Paul L. *Haggai, Zechariah, Malachi.* New Century Bible. Grand Rapids, MI: Eerdmans, 1995.

Unger, Merrill F. *Zechariah.* Grand Rapids, MI: Zondervan, 1963.

EXPOSITION

I. Vision of the Restoration of Jerusalem (chaps. 1–6)

A. Introduction: The Call for National Repentance (1:1–6)

1:1–6. Zechariah received a message from the Lord in October–November, 520 BC. Haggai also began his prophetic ministry in Darius's second year (August 29, 520 BC; see Hag. 1:1), and the Lord used the dual ministry of Zechariah and Haggai to challenge the postexilic community to complete the work of rebuilding the Jerusalem temple so that they might experience the fullness of God's blessing on their lives.

The book opens with a call for national repentance. The failure to rebuild the temple was merely symptomatic of Judah's broken relationship with the Lord. The prophet announced that the Lord had been **sore displeased with your fathers** (v. 2). The Lord had been angry because of the covenant-breaking sins of the Jews' preexilic forefathers, resulting in the destruction of Jerusalem and the temple in 536 BC, followed by exile to Babylon. Despite His past anger, the Lord called for repentance so that His relationship to Judah might be restored (**Turn ye unto me … I will turn unto you**; v. 3). If the people of Zechariah's day would change their course and go in

the opposite direction from that of their forefathers, the Lord would return to them with blessing instead of with a curse. They were not to be like their fathers, who had ignored the warnings of the **former prophets** (v. 4), such as Isaiah (see Isa. 45:22), Jeremiah (Jer. 18:11), and Ezekiel (see Ezek. 33:11). These prophets had not lived **for ever** (v. 5), but God's words through them had lived on and had come to fulfillment in the judgment of exile. The future of Israel as a nation depended on their faithful and obedient response to the word of the Lord.

B. A Series of Eight Night Visions (1:7–6:8)

1:7–6:8. On February 15, 519 BC, about three months after the date of 1:1, Zechariah received in one night a series of eight visions. These visions as a whole promised the Lord's intention to restore Israel and to bless the postexilic community in their rebuilding of the Jerusalem temple. The visions portrayed both the physical rebuilding of Israel as a nation and their spiritual restoration as the people of God.

1. The Horsemen among the Myrtle Trees (1:7–17)

1:7–17. Zechariah's first vision of four horsemen among some myrtle trees signified that although God's covenant people were troubled while the oppressing nations were at ease, God was jealous for His people and would restore them and their towns and their temple. The imagery of the first vision is also reflected in that of the eighth and final vision (6:1–8).

1:7–12. The **man riding upon a red horse** (v. 8) is identified as **the angel of the LORD** (v. 11). He must not be confused with the interpreting angel, who is mentioned in verse 9 and 1:13–14, 19; 2:3; 4:1, 4–5; 5:5, 10; 6:4–5. The horsemen on the **red … speckled, and white** (v. 8) horses also appear to be angelic messengers, whom the Lord sent to patrol **to and fro through the whole earth**. The text gives no indication of any special significance behind the different colors of these four horses (compare Rev. 6:1–8). These messengers observed that **all the earth sitteth still** (v. 11; see 6:8). The Persian Empire as a whole was secure and at ease by this time, while the Jews in Judah had been oppressed and under foreign domination for seventy years (see 7:5; Jer. 25:11–12; 29:10; 2 Chron. 36:21; Ezra 1:1; Dan. 9:2).

1:13–17. The Lord announced that the comfort of the nations and the oppression of Jerusalem was about to be reversed. Because of His **jealous** (v. 14) love for Israel, the Lord would act to vindicate Judah for the violations against her. God had been angry with Israel and had used the Assyrians (Isa. 10:5) and Babylonians (Isa. 47:6; Jer. 25:9) to punish her, but they had gone too far (**helped forward the affliction**; v. 15) by trying to destroy the Jews as a people. The Lord had **returned** (v. 16) to His people and was now ready to restore them. This restoration would include the rebuilding of **Jerusalem**, the temple, and the other **cities** (v. 17) of Israel.

2. The Four Horns and the Four Carpenters (1:18–21)

1:18–21. Zechariah's second vision promised that the nations that had devastated Israel would in turn be destroyed by other nations. The enemy nations that had attacked Israel are pictured as **four horns** (v. 18). If the number is to be taken literally, the reference is probably to Assyria, Egypt, Babylonia, and Medo-Persia. The horn is symbolic of strength in general (Ps. 18:2) or, as here, the military power or strength of a nation and its king (Ps. 89:17; Dan. 7:7–8; 8:20–21; Rev. 17:12). **The horns … scattered**

(v. 19) God's people, but the Lord was raising **four carpenters** (v. 20) to destroy the horns. If the number is to be taken literally, probably the reference is to Egypt, Babylonian, Persia, and Greece. The picture of "carpenters" (or craftsmen) as destroyers probably has reference to the weapons they designed for smashing the enemy (see Isa. 54:16–17). What is clear is that all of Judah's enemies would be destroyed.

3. A Man with a Measuring Line (chap. 2)

2:1–5. Zechariah's third vision announced that there would be full restoration for the covenant people, temple, and city. **A man** (possibly Zechariah) **with a measuring line** (v. 1) prepared to mark out the dimensions for the rebuilding of Jerusalem, but an **angel** (v. 3) announced that measurements were not necessary because **Jerusalem shall be inhabited as towns without walls** (v. 4). The city's population would overflow to the point that it would be as though it had no walls. The Lord would be a **wall of fire** (v. 5) in that His presence would provide protection and security for Jerusalem against its enemies (see Exod. 13:21; Isa. 4:5–6).

2:6–9. Because of this promise of restoration, the Lord called for His people to return from exile **as the four winds** (v. 6). The exiles would return from north, south, east, and west (see Isa. 43:5–6; 49:12). The Lord would punish the enemy nations, because in attacking Judah, they had dared to touch the **apple** (pupil) **of his eye** (v. 8; see Deut. 32:10). To attack God's people is to attack God Himself (see Acts 9:1, 4). These nations that had plundered Judah would themselves become **spoil to their servants** (v. 9).

2:10–13. Israel was to rejoice because God had promised to once again **dwell** (v. 10) among them (see Lev. 26:11–12). In fulfillment of the promise to Abraham (Gen. 12:3; see Isa. 2:2–4; 60:3; Zech. 8:20–23), **many nations** (v. 11) will come to Jerusalem to join with Israel as God's people in worshiping and serving Him. This passage looks beyond the restoration of Israel in the postexilic period to the eschatological age, when Israel and the nations will share in the kingdom blessings. The land of Judah is referred to as **the holy land** (v. 12). The Hebrew for this designation occurs only here in Scripture. The land was rendered holy chiefly because it was the site of the earthly throne and sanctuary of the Holy King, who dwelled there among His covenant people.

4. Clean Garments for the High Priest (chap. 3)

3:1–10. Zechariah's fourth vision declared that Israel would be cleansed and restored as a priestly nation. Israel's priestly mission was to mediate the knowledge and blessing of God to all other peoples and nations (see Exod. 19:5–6), but Israel had failed in this mission because of their unfaithfulness and disobedience to the Lord (see Isa. 42:18–25). Divine pardon would make it possible for Israel to once again become God's priestly people.

3:1–2. Joshua (v. 1), the high priest, here represents the sinful nation of Israel, and **Satan stood at his right hand to resist him.** The words "Satan" and "resist" come from the same Hebrew root and point to Satan's role as an adversary of God's people. Though Satan's actions are not specified here, he most likely presented the accusation that sinful Israel was not fit to serve as the Lord's priest, much in the same way that he accused Job (see Job 1:9–11; 2:4–5). Rather than giving credence to Satan's accusation, the Lord rebuked him (note the repetition of **rebuke,** v. 2, for emphasis) and reminded Satan that Judah was **a brand pluckt out of the fire.** The Jews had been retrieved from the fire of Babylonian exile to carry out God's future purpose for them.

3:3–6. The excrement-covered clothing of Joshua represents the sinfulness of the nation, but the Lord commanded His angels (**those that stood before him;** v. 4) to remove **the filthy garments** that would deprive Joshua of his priestly office. This act is symbolic of the removal of sin. The angels were also to **set a fair mitre upon his head** (i.e., "put a clean turban on his head"; v. 5), thus reinstating him to his high-priestly function so that Israel once again had a divinely authorized priestly mediator. On the front of the turban were the words: "HOLINESS TO THE LORD" (Exod. 28:36; 39:30).

3:7–10. If Joshua and his priestly associates were faithful, they would be coworkers with the angels in carrying out God's purposes for Zion and Israel. The Lord promised ultimately to bring forth Israel's Messiah, **the BRANCH** (v. 8). "Branch" is clearly a messianic title in Jeremiah 23:5; 33:15 (see Isa. 11:1 for the same imagery with a different term). This promise likely also refers to the contemporary leadership provided by the house of David in the person of Zerubbabel. **The stone** (v. 9) is probably another figure of the Messiah (see Ps. 118:22–23; 1 Peter 2:6–8). The **seven eyes** on this stone is perhaps symbolic of the infinite intelligence or wisdom with which this future king will rule. The Lord promised, **I will remove the iniquity of that land**, thus explaining the symbolic act of 3:4. In this vision, the individual cleansing of Joshua also represents the national restoration of Israel.

5. The Golden Candlesticks and the Two Olive Trees (chap. 4)

4:1–14. In Zechariah's fifth vision, the Jews were encouraged to rebuild the temple by being reminded of their divine resources. The light from the candlestick in the tabernacle/temple represents the reflection of God's glory in the consecration and holy service of God's people (see Exod. 25:31), made possible only by the power of God's Spirit (the oil, vv. 6, 12). This enabling power would equip and sustain Zerubbabel in the rebuilding of the temple (vv. 6–10). In the performance of their offices, Zerubbabel and Joshua (as representatives of the royal and priestly mediatorial offices) would channel the Spirit's enablement to God's people.

4:1–2. Seven lamps (v. 2) were arranged around a large **bowl** that served as a bountiful reservoir of oil. Each lamp had seven spouts or lips that held the wicks of the oil lamps, making a total of forty-nine flames. The large bowl represents an abundant supply of oil, symbolizing the fullness of God's power through His Spirit. The repetition of the number seven also represents the abundant light shining from the lamps.

4:3–14. The **two olive trees** (v. 3) represent the priestly and royal offices and symbolize a continuing supply of oil. The **two olive branches** (v. 12) stand for Joshua the priest (chap. 3) and Zerubbabel, who was from the royal house of David (chap. 4, see v. 14). These two leaders were to do God's work (e.g., on the temple and in the lives of the people) in the power of the Spirit. The combination of the royal and priestly lines and their functions points ultimately to the messianic King-Priest and His offices and functions (see 6:13).

6. The Flying Scroll (5:1–4)

5:1–4. Zechariah's sixth vision, of a flying scroll (**flying roll**; v. 1), provided a warning that lawbreakers would be condemned by the law they had broken and that sinners would be purged from the land. Israel had gone into exile because of their disobedience to God's commands, and continued disobedience would result in further judgment. The impressive feature of the scroll is its size (thirty feet long and fifteen feet wide). This unusually large scroll (especially in its width) was unrolled and waved like a banner for all to see. The purpose of this bold, clear message of judgment against sin was to spur the people on to repentance and righteousness.

The scroll warned of **the curse** (v. 3) on those who break the law (see Deut. 27:26), making specific reference to the eighth commandment against stealing (see Exod. 20:15) and the third commandment against swearing (i.e., taking God's name in vain, see v. 4 and Exod. 20:7). Although theft and falsely swearing by God's name may have been the most common forms of lawbreaking, they were probably mentioned here as representative sins. The first sin represents the broken relationships within the community, and the second sin, Israel's broken relationship with the Lord. The people of Judah had been guilty of infractions against the whole law (see James 2:10). **I will bring it forth** (v. 4) refers to the curse that God brings against lawbreakers. God's word, whether promise or warning, always accomplishes its purpose (see Ps. 147:15; Isa. 55:10–11; Heb. 4:12–13).

7. The Woman in the Basket (5:5–11)

5:5–11. In Zechariah's seventh vision, he saw **a woman** (v. 7) placed inside a sealed basket, which was carried away to Babylon by **two women** (v. 9), who

had **wings like ... stork[s]**. This vision, perhaps more than any of Zechariah's other visions, vividly illustrates the strange imagery that is often encountered in apocalyptic literature. The woman in the vision represents the **wickedness** (v. 8) of the land, and the people's sinfulness perhaps was personified as a woman because the Hebrew word for "wickedness" is feminine. She was placed inside an **ephah** (v. 6–7), a basket used for measuring. Since a normal ephah-sized container would not have been large enough to hold a person, this one undoubtedly was enlarged (like the flying scroll in 5:1–2). The basket was covered with a lid made from **lead** (v. 7) and was carried from the land by the two storklike women. The destination of the basket was **Shinar** (v. 11), or Babylonia (see Gen. 10:10; 11:2; Revelation 17–18). Babylonia, a land of idolatry, was an appropriate locale for wickedness, but not for Israel, where God chose to dwell with His people.

The message of this vision built on the warning associated with the flying scroll in 5:1–4. Not only would flagrant, persistent sinners be removed from the land; the whole sinful system would be removed, to the more fitting locale of Babylonia. Only after purging evil from its midst would the Promised Land truly become "the holy land" (2:12). Like the woman in the basket, sinners in the land would be sent back into exile in Babylon.

8. The Four Chariots of Divine Judgment (6:1–8)

6:1–8. Zechariah's eighth and last vision corresponded to the first vision (1:7–17), though there were differences in detail, such as the order and color of the horses. As in the first vision, the Lord was depicted as the One who controls the events of history. He would conquer the nations that oppress Israel.

The **four chariots** (v. 1) in the vision were angelic spirits sent out as agents of divine judgment on all the earth. The different colors of the horses in the vision may signify various divine judgments on the earth (see Rev. 6:1–8). The **two mountains** from which the chariots appeared are possibly Mount Zion and the Mount of Olives, with the Kidron Valley between them. The portrayal of the mountains as **brass**, or bronze, symbolizes either strength (see Jer. 1:18) or divine judgment (see Num. 21:9). The chariots with the black and the white horses went forth into **the north country** (v. 6), which signifies primarily Babylonia. North was also the direction from which most of Israel's foes invaded the nation (see 2:6). Their invasion of the north country served to quiet God's **spirit** (v. 8). The angelic beings dispatched to the north had triumphed over God's enemies and thus had pacified or appeased His anger (compare 1:15, where God's displeasure was aroused against the oppressive nations). The promise was that the Lord would reverse the effects of the exile by acting as the Divine Warrior and giving Israel victory over her enemies.

C. Conclusion: The Symbolic Crowning of Joshua, the High Priest (6:9–15)

6:9–12. Zechariah's fourth and fifth visions concerned the high priest, Joshua, and the civil governor belonging to the line of David, Zerubbabel. In this passage, **crowns** (v. 11) were placed on the head of **Joshua … the high priest**. The Hebrew word for "crowns," *keren*, is not the same as that used for the high priest's turban but rather refers to an ornate crown with many diadems (see Rev. 19:2). In connection with the coronation of Joshua, the prophet announced that **the man whose name is The BRANCH … shall grow up out of his place** (v. 12). As noted earlier in 3:1–10, "The BRANCH" is a messianic title, and the picture is of the royal line of David sprouting as a shoot from a dead tree stump.

6:13–15. The future Messiah will **rule upon his throne** (v. 13) and will **be a priest upon his throne**. The symbolic coronation of Joshua the high priest points to the crowning and reign of the future Messiah, because this future Davidic ruler will be both a priest and a king. Such a combination was not normally possible in Israel. For this reason, the sect of Qumran expected two messianic figures—a high-priest Messiah and a Davidic one. The two offices and functions would in fact be united in the one person of the Messiah (see Psalm 110; Hebrews 7). The crowning of Joshua also provided assurance that **the temple of the Lord** (v. 15) would be rebuilt and that Israel's worship of the Lord would be fully restored.

II. The Problem of Fasting and the Promise of the Future (chaps. 7–8)

7:1–8:23. This prophetic message was a response to the people's inquiry whether they should continue their customary fasts as a means of commemorating the destruction of Jerusalem by the Babylonians. The inquiry was directed to the prophet on December 7, 518 BC (7:1), not quite two years after the eight night visions.

A. True Fasting: The Call to Repentance (chap. 7)

7:1–4. The primary fast occurred in the **fifth month** (v. 3), when the temple had been burned by the Babylonians (v. 3; see 2 Kings 25:8–10; Jer. 52:12–14). As indicated in 8:19, additional fasts were held in the fourth month (lamenting the breach of the walls of Jerusalem by Nebuchadnezzar, see 2 Kings 25:3–4; Jer. 39:2; 52:6–7), the seventh month (marking the anniversary of Gedaliah's assassination, see 2 Kings 25:22–25; Jer. 41:1–3), and the tenth month (mourning the beginning of Nebuchadnezzar's siege of Jerusalem, see 2 Kings 25:1; Jer. 39:1; 52:4). Zechariah's response to the people's inquiry was that the Lord was not as concerned with the rituals of fasting and mourning as He was with the people living lives that reflected their repentance for the sins that had been the cause of the fall of Jerusalem and the exile (see Isa. 58:1–14).

7:5–14. The Lord asked, **When ye fasted … did ye at all fast unto me?** (v. 5). The people had practiced their rituals but had not truly sought the Lord. Covenant faithfulness to the Lord was not an issue of food and drink but rather of obedience to the Lord's commands (vv. 6–8). The four tests of faithful covenant living involved practicing **judgment** (justice; v. 9), showing **mercy and compassions**, refusing to **oppress** (v. 10) the needy, and refraining from planning **evil** against others. It was the refusal of the preexilic forefathers to follow the Lord's social, moral, and ethical laws that had caused God to scatter His people **among all the nations** (v. 14), one of the curses for covenant disobedience (see Deut. 28:36–37, 64–68).

B. The Promise of the Coming Peace and Prosperity of Zion (chap. 8)

8:1–23. The Lord ultimately desired to bless His people, and chapter 8 consists of a series of ten promises of blessing, each beginning with "Thus saith the LORD [of hosts]" (vv. 2, 3, 4, 7, 9, 14, 19, 20, 23).

8:1–2. The judgment of the past was reversed, and the Lord's plan of blessing was set in motion because He had been **jealous for Zion** (v. 2) and had dealt in **fury** with His enemies who had caused the destruction of Jerusalem. The Lord's defeat of Babylon, which allowed the Jews to return to their homeland, foreshadows the ultimate defeat of all of the enemies of the Lord and His people.

8:3–8. The Lord's blessing centered on the restoration and renewal of Zion. The Lord had **returned unto Zion, and will dwell** (v. 3) there among His people. The Lord would also transform Jerusalem so that it would become **a city of truth** that was worthy of His presence (see Isa. 1:26). The city would be filled with inhabitants, and young and old would enjoy the blessings of a peaceful and secure existence as the Lord brought His people home from exile (vv. 4–8). To **the remnant** (v. 6) returning to the land, this restoration would be **marvellous**, a term denoting something that is amazing and wondrous to behold (see Gen. 18:14; Jer. 32:17, 27). The promise that Jerusalem would be a populous and prosperous city must have been especially incredible to the small and struggling postexilic community. The promise that **they shall be my people, and I will be their God** (v. 8) is covenant terminology promising the restoration of intimate fellowship between Israel and the Lord (see 13:9; Gen. 17:7; Exod. 6:7; 29:45–46; Deut. 26:12; Jer. 31:33; Ezek. 34:30–31). This restoration of the relationship between God and Israel would be **in truth and in righteousness,** resting on the dependability of God and His faithfulness to the covenant promises.

8:9–13. The Lord encouraged the people to be **strong** (v. 9) in carrying out the command of the **prophets** Haggai and Zechariah to rebuild the temple. The Lord had withheld His blessing **before** the **days** (v. 10) in which the temple foundation was laid (see Hag. 1:6–11; 2:15–19), but the reasons for discouragement had passed. God would now provide the grounds for encouragement. The people would become **prosperous** (v. 12) and enjoy agricultural bounty as a reward for their obedience in turning to the Lord and rebuilding His house (see also Hag. 2:19). Fertility and bounty were part of the covenant blessings promised to Israel for obedience to the Mosaic law (see Lev. 26:3–10; Deut. 28:11–12). Just as Israel had become **a curse among the heathen** (v. 13) for their disobedience, as Moses had warned (see Deut. 28:37), the whole nation would now enjoy deliverance and blessing (see Jer. 31:1–31; Ezek. 37:15–28).

8:14–17. This promise specifies first God's part (vv. 14–15) and then the people's part (vv. 16–17) in their restoration to favor and blessing. The Lord had turned from His wrath and now intended **to do well** (v. 15) to His people. The people, however, had to respond to the Lord's offer of grace by speaking **truth** (v. 16) and practicing **judgment** (justice) toward one another. Such moral and ethical behavior sums up the character of those who are in covenant relationship with the Lord.

8:18–23. The prophet returned to the question of whether the people should fast to commemorate the destruction of Jerusalem, which had prompted this message of promised blessing in the first place. These fasts would become obsolete and would be turned into times of **cheerful feasts** (v. 19) as Israel celebrated the blessings of their renewal and restoration (see Isa. 65:18–19; Jer. 31:10–14). Because of the great blessing that Israel would experience, the Gentile nations would also come to Jerusalem **to seek the LORD** (vv. 22–23; see Isa. 2:2–4; Mic. 4:1–5) and to worship Him. This anticipates a fulfillment of the Abrahamic covenant's promise that Gentiles would be blessed (see Gen. 12:3; Isa. 56:6–7; Gal. 3:8, 26–29). The promise of **ten** (v. 23) Gentiles taking hold of one Jew and promising to worship the Lord at Jerusalem is one way of indicating a large or complete number (see Gen. 31:7; Lev. 26:26; Neh. 4:12). The Gentiles would come to worship because they had **heard** that the Lord was with the Jews. True godliness attracts others to the Lord, and Israel would finally fulfill its role as "a kingdom of priests" (Exod. 19:6) in leading the nations to know and worship the Lord.

III. Two Prophetic Oracles: The Great Messianic Future and the Full Realization of God's Kingdom (chaps. 9–14)

9:1–14:21. While chapters 1–8 focus more on the immediate restoration of Jerusalem in the postexilic period, the oracles in chapters 9–14 focus more on the ultimate restoration of Jerusalem in the eschatological age of the future kingdom. Promises concerning the future messianic ruler are especially prominent in this section. The Hebrew for "the burden of the word of the LORD" appears in 9:1 and 12:1, thus dividing this last section of the book of Zechariah into two halves. This phrase appears elsewhere in the Old Testament only in Malachi 1:1, making it likely that Zechariah 9–14 and Malachi were written during the same period.

A. The First Oracle: The Advent and Rejection of the King (chaps. 9–11)

1. The Coming of the King (chap. 9)

9:1–8. This section opens with a prophetic description of the Lord as Divine Warrior marching south to Jerusalem and destroying the traditional enemies of Israel, including the Arameans (v. 1), the Phoenicians (vv. 2–4), and the Philistines (vv. 5–7). As history shows, the agent of this divine judgment was Alexander the Great (332 BC), but this passage also looks forward to the full and final defeat of all of Israel's enemies in the last days prior to the establishment of God's kingdom on earth (see Ezekiel 38–39; Joel 3:1–17; Rev. 19:11–18). After defeating His enemies, the Lord will **encamp** (v. 8) around Jerusalem, keeping it safe so that **no oppressor shall pass through** the city ever again.

9:9. The Lord would also restore the Davidic line and provide a **King** for the people—the promised Messiah. This verse is quoted in the New Testament as messianic and as referring ultimately to the triumphal entry of Jesus into Jerusalem (see Matt. 21:5; John 12:15). This king would be **just**, a characteristic of the ideal king in the ancient Near East (see 2 Sam. 23:3–4; Ps. 72:1–3) and demanded especially of Israel's ruler in the moral and ethical standards set forth in the Mosaic legislation (see Deut. 17:14–20). The future Messiah would also be **lowly**, or humble (see Isa. 53:2–3, 7). The portrayal of the Messiah as **riding upon an ass** is appropriate since the donkey was a lowly animal of peace (contrast the warhorse of 9:10) as well as a princely mount before the horse came into common use (see 2 Sam. 18:19; 1 Kings 1:33). In his triumphal entry into Jerusalem, Jesus came riding on a donkey (see Matt. 11:29).

9:10. The reign of Messiah will bring an era of peace and disarmament (**cut off the chariot...horse ...battle bow**; see Isa. 2:4; 9:5–7; 11:1–10). In contrast to Alexander's empire, which was founded on bloodshed, the messianic King will establish a universal kingdom of peace as the ultimate fulfillment of the Abrahamic covenant (see 14:16; see Gen. 12:3; 18:18; 22:18). Nonetheless, Revelation also describes the great day of battle yet to come as the Divine Warrior comes riding on his war steed. The **dominion** of the Messiah will be universal (see Pss. 22:27–28; 72:8–11; Isa. 66:18).

9:11–17. In connection with the rule and reign of the Messiah, the Lord promised to fully release His people from their captivity and to return them to their homeland (vv. 11–17). The **prisoners** (v. 11) were perhaps those still in Babylon, the land of exile. The reference to **the blood of thy covenant** most likely has in view the blood sacrifices by which the Lord ratified His covenant with Israel at Sinai (see Exod. 24:8). The Lord will deliver Israel because of His covenant commitment to them as His chosen people. The Lord will provide a **double** (v. 12), or full, restoration that will involve the reunification of Israel and Judah (v. 13). The Lord compared Himself to a warrior who uses **Judah** as His **bow** and **Ephraim** (the northern kingdom of Israel) as His arrow. With the Lord's protection and empowerment, a renewed Israel will attack and defeat the **sons of Greece** (vv. 13). While the more immediate fulfillment of this prophecy was the defeat of the Seleucids of Syria (after the breakup of Alexander's empire) by the Maccabeans in the second century BC (see Dan. 11:34), it ultimately points to the eschatological age and Israel's final victory over its enemies. The apocryphal book of 1 Maccabees (3:16–24; 4:6–16; 7:40–50) records the historical events that provide a partial fulfillment of this prophecy.

2. The Redemption of God's People (10:1–11:3)

10:1–7. Because of the Lord's promise to deliver Israel, Zechariah encouraged the people of his day to seek the Lord and His provision of **rain** (v. 1) and bountiful crops. The Lord, not the Canaanite god Baal, is the one who controls the weather and the rain, giving life and fertility to the land (see Jer. 14:22; Amos 5:8). God's people are to pray and to trust in the Lord, rather than turning to pagan **idols** (v. 2) and **diviners** for guidance and direction. Because Israel had repeatedly turned to these pagan alternatives, spiritual leadership was missing (**there was no shepherd**), and the Lord had poured out His **anger** (v. 3a) on the shepherds who had misled Israel. As Israel's shepherd, the Lord will take the place of the faulty human leaders of the past and will turn Israel into a powerful warhorse as He goes out to fight against His enemies (v. 3b). The promise concerning the **corner** (cornerstone; v. 4), the **nail** (tent peg), and the **battle bow** is taken to be messianic in the Aramaic Targum, though the precise meaning of this verse is not clear. It appears that these images are symbols of Israel's future stability and strength rather than a direct reference to the Messiah. The Lord will reunite the people of **Judah** (v. 6) and **Ephraim** (v. 7).

10:8–17. Continuing the shepherd metaphor, the Lord promised that He will **hiss** (lit., "whistle" or "signal"; v. 8) for His people to redeem them from exile (vv. 8–12). The Lord will bring back His people from **Egypt** (v. 10) and **Assyria**, nations that were two of Israel's greatest enemies and that are representative of all the countries where the Israelites are dispersed. The promise that Israel **shall pass through the sea with affliction** (v. 11) portrays the restoration from exile as a second exodus (see Exod.

14:22). The Lord will bring down the **pride** and **sceptre** (power) of the enemy nations who afflict His people. That Zechariah, in the postexilic period, portrayed the deliverance of Israel as yet future demonstrates that the return of the Jews to their homeland in 538 BC does not represent the complete fulfillment of the prophetic promises of restoration and renewal for the nation of Israel.

11:1–3. These verses are most likely the conclusion to the preceding section rather than the introduction to a new oracle. These verses contain a taunt song related to the lament that will be sung over the destruction of the nations' power and arrogance, represented by the **cedar** (v. 2), the **fir**, and the **oaks**. Trees are used elsewhere in the Prophetic Books as symbols of human pride (see Isa. 2:13; 10:33–34; Ezek. 31:1–18). The **shepherds** (v. 3) and the **lions** are the kings of the doomed nations that will be consumed by the Lord's judgment.

3. Israel's Rejection of the King (11:4–17)

11:4–17. This passage is linked to the preceding one by the reference to "shepherds" (v. 5; see 11:3), but here the focus is on Israel rather than on the enemy nations that the Lord promised to destroy. The Lord promised to bless and restore the nation of Israel, but Zechariah warned that the people of his day were facing further judgment because they had rejected the Lord as their Shepherd and were once again turning to worthless human leaders like the ones that had led them astray in the past. The prophets often performed signs as a means of visual proclamation of their message (see Isaiah 20; Jer. 13:1–11; Ezekiel 4–5), and Zechariah appears to have acted out the allegory of the rejected shepherd to demonstrate how Israel had rejected the Lord.

11:4–6. The Lord commanded Zechariah to **Feed the flock** (v. 4) of Israel because they were being abused by the leaders that should have been protecting them and providing for them (**their own shepherds pity them not**; v. 5). In His anger over the people's continued wickedness, the Lord had allowed them to be abused by the surrounding peoples (**I will deliver the men … into his neighbour's**

hand; v. 6) and their corrupt leaders (**into the hand of his king**).

11:7-8. Zechariah, representing the Lord, promised to deliver Israel from their oppressors and to **feed the flock of the slaughter** (v. 7). The two **staves**, called **Beauty** and **Bands** (or "Unity"), reflect how the Lord's leadership would bring blessing and unity to the people of Israel. Acting as the Lord, the prophet removed **Three shepherds ... in one month** (v. 8). Although the three cannot be specifically identified, the prophet's action involved the removal of unfit leaders from their positions of authority.

11:9-14. Though the Lord desired to protect and bless Israel, the people ultimately rejected Zechariah (and the Lord) as their shepherd. The Lord refused to **feed** (v. 9) the flock, caused it to be **cut off**, and broke the staff of **Beauty** (v. 10) that represented His blessing of Israel. The Lord terminated the **covenant** that He had made **with all the people**, apparently a covenant of security and restraint, by which the Lord had been holding back the nations from His people (see Ezek. 34:25; Hos. 2:18). Now the nations (e.g., the Seleucids, Antiochus IV Epiphanes, and later the Romans) would be permitted to overrun Israel.

Acting out the drama of Israel's rejection of the Lord, Zechariah spoke on behalf of the Lord and asked the people to compensate him for his work as their shepherd-leader. The people responded by paying him the trifling amount of **thirty pieces of silver** (v. 12), the price of a slave among the Israelites in ancient times (see Exod. 21:32). Zechariah threw away the insulting amount he had been paid for his labor. **Cast it unto the potter** (v. 13) is an idiomatic proverbial expression similar to "throw it to the dogs." Matthew 27:3-10 indicates this was fulfilled when Christ was betrayed for thirty pieces of silver and Judas returned the money to the temple and the priests used it to buy the potter's field, where broken pottery could be discarded.

11:15-17. Zechariah took on the role of a **foolish shepherd** (v. 15). Since the people had rejected the Lord's leadership, a foolish and worthless shepherd would now take His place. This selfish, greedy, corrupt leader would arise and afflict the flock. This **idol** (counterfeit) **shepherd** (v. 17) found a partial historical fulfillment in the corrupt leadership of the Maccabean period and figures such as Simeon bar Kosiba, or Kokhba, who led the Jewish revolt against the Romans in AD 132-135 and who was hailed as the Messiah by Rabbi Akiba. The power of this false shepherd would ultimately be paralyzed (**His arm shall be clean dried up**) and his intelligence nullified (**his right eye shall be utterly darkened**) when the Lord removed him from power.

While this shepherd allegory refers to contemporary events at the time of Zechariah's ministry, the passage ultimately points to the drama of Israel's rejection of their Messiah and the judgment that would fall on the nation for this sinful refusal to recognize and acknowledge the Good Shepherd. In the New Testament, Judas's treacherous betrayal was a tangible expression of Israel's national rejection of Jesus as their Shepherd-Messiah (see Matt. 26:14-15; 27:3-10). While the prophecy of the "idol shepherd" appears to have a collective reference to Israel's corrupt leadership beginning with the time of Zechariah, it would seem that the final stage of the progressive fulfillment of the complete prophecy awaits the rise of the final Antichrist (see Ezek. 34:2-4; Dan. 11:36-39).

B. The Second Oracle: The Advent and Reception of the Messiah (chaps. 12-14)

12:1-14:21. The final section of this book revolves around two scenes: the final siege of Jerusalem and the Messiah's return to defeat Israel's enemies and establish His kingdom.

1. The Siege and Deliverance of Jerusalem (12:1-9)

12:1-9. This oracle looks forward to the final siege of Jerusalem when the Lord will purge His people and judge the nations in preparation for the establishment of His eschatological kingdom on earth. The recurring references to **that day** (vv. 3-4, 6, 8-9, 11; 13:1-2, 4; 14:4, 6, 8-9, 13, 20-21) in chapters 12-14 reflect the end-time focus of this section of the book.

In the final siege of Jerusalem, the Lord will cause His city to be **a cup of trembling** (v. 2) for its attackers. They will become drunk with the wine of God's wrath and stagger like drunken men under His judgment (see Isa. 51:17; Jer. 25:15–18). The enemy nations will also find Jerusalem to be **a burdensome stone** (v. 3) that will cut them to pieces. The Lord will inflict **astonishment ... madness ... blindness** (v. 4) on the troops attacking Jerusalem, maladies identified as Israel's curses for disobeying the stipulations of the covenant (see Deut. 28:28), which will be turned against Israel's enemies. In contrast to the corrupt leaders of the past, Israel's discerning leaders will consume their enemies like a **fire among the wood** (v. 6) or **in a sheaf** of grain. The Lord will save all of His people, not just **the house of David** (v. 7) or **the inhabitants of Jerusalem.** He will cause even the **feeble** (v. 8) to become great warriors **as David; and the house of David** will be empowered with the supernatural strength of **God** Himself. The Lord will completely rout the enemy **nations** (v. 9) that attack **Jerusalem** (v. 9).

2. The Lord's Compassion toward Jerusalem (12:10–13:9)

12:10. With the deliverance of Jerusalem, the Lord will act in **grace** to cause the people of Israel to turn to Him in repentance and faith. They will **mourn** over their past rebellion against the Lord. In context, **they shall look upon me whom they have pierced** is a direct prediction of the crucifixion of Jesus, as well as a metaphorical description of Israel's rejection of the Lord as their Shepherd (see 11:4–14). The Lord is the speaker in this passage and pictures Israel's rejection of His leadership as a piercing (fatal) wound. As in 11:12–13, the figurative expression of Israel's rejection of the Lord became literal in the experience of Jesus when He was pierced by the sword of the Roman soldier at the cross (see John 19:37) as the result of Israel's unbelief. The crucifixion of Jesus was the ultimate act of rejection of the Lord (see the similar prophecies of the crucifixion and death of Christ in Ps. 22:16; Isa. 53:4–9; Dan. 9:26).

12:11–14. When Israel recognizes that they have rejected the Lord through their piercing of the Messiah, their **mourning** (v. 11) will be like **the mourning of Hadadrimmon,** the place near Megiddo where the people mourned the tragic death of the godly King Josiah at the hands of the Egyptians (see 2 Chron. 35:20–27). This allusion to a past Davidic ruler suggests the idea of mourning for a future Davidic ruler (Jesus the Messiah) that becomes clear in the New Testament in connection with the death of Jesus. The repentance and mourning of Israel will be led by the nation's civil and religious leaders (vv. 12–14).

13:1–2. The Lord will provide **a fountain** (v. 1) that will bring cleansing and forgiveness for Israel's past **sin** (see 3:4–9). Cleansing from sin is one of the provisions of the new covenant (see Jer. 31:34; Ezek. 36:25). Israel will no longer worship idols, and the Lord will remove **the names of the idols** (v. 2), eradicating the influence, fame, and even the very existence of the idols.

13:3–6. There will no longer be false prophets to mislead the people. In obedience to Deuteronomy 13:6–9, the parents of any false prophet will carry out the execution of their disobedient child. The verb **thrust** (v. 3), used to describe the execution of the false prophet, is the same as the verb for "pierced" in 12:10, suggesting that the feelings and actions exhibited in the piercing of Messiah will now be directed toward the false prophets. Because of the stern measures to be taken, a false prophet will be reluctant to identify himself as such and will be evasive in his responses to interrogation. To help conceal his true identity, he will not wear a **rough garment** (like Elijah; v. 4; see 2 Kings 1:8). To avoid the death penalty, he will deny being a prophet and will claim to have been a farmer (**husbandman;** v. 5) since his **youth.** If a suspicious person notices marks on his body and inquires about them, he will claim he received them in a scuffle with **friends** (v. 6). Apparently, the accuser will suspect that the false prophet's wounds were self-inflicted to arouse his prophetic ecstasy in idolatrous rites (as in 1 Kings 18:28; see also Lev. 19:28; 21:5; Jer. 16:6; 41:5).

13:7–9. The Lord's purging judgment of His people is a necessary prelude to Israel's final deliverance and restoration. The Lord will **Smite** (v. 7) the worthless **shepherd** who leads Israel astray (see 11:15–17). In the New Testament, this verse is applied to the death of Jesus and the scattering of the apostles (see Matt. 26:31; Mark 14:27, 49–50). The context of Zechariah 13, however, has in view the final judgment of Israel. The flock of Israel will **be scattered** and will endure a refining process; only a **third** (v. 8) of the nation will remain. God will show His mercy in the midst of judgment by purifying the remnant so that they will **call on** (v. 9) the Lord and be rightly related to Him as His **people**.

3. The Coming of the Messiah and His Kingdom (chap. 14)

14:1–7. This prophetic oracle again views the day of the Lord in the last days as a time of first judgment and then deliverance for Jerusalem and Israel. In the final battle, the enemy nations will first plunder Jerusalem, leaving only a remnant (**residue**; v. 2) of the people. **Then** (v. 3) the Lord will fight for Israel and deliver them from their enemies as He did in the past **day of battle**, such as at the Red Sea (see Exod. 14:14). When appearing as Warrior, the Lord will **stand ... upon the mount of Olives** (v. 4; see Acts 1:11–12). The Lord's arrival will cause an earthquake, which will split the mountain in two and bring other cosmic and cataclysmic changes to the topography of the area surrounding Jerusalem (vv. 5–7). As the Lord destroys His enemies in the midst of this violent earthquake, there will be a way of escape for the surviving remnant. The Lord will appear to fight against Zion's enemies with His **saints** (v. 5), which appears to include both believers and angels who will accompany the Lord when He comes to earth (see Matt. 25:31; 1 Thess. 3;13; Rev. 19:14).

14:8–11. The Lord's victory will establish His sovereign dominion over all the earth. Life-giving **waters** (v. 8), perhaps both literal and symbolic (see Ps. 46:4; Isa. 8:6; Ezek. 47:1–12), will flow out of Jerusalem toward the Dead Sea (**the former sea** on the east) and the Mediterranean (**the hinder sea** on the west). The Lord's universal rule over the earth and all His creation is an eternal reality, but the full recognition and realization of His sovereignty over a fallen world awaits the final consummation. The inhabitants of Jerusalem will dwell securely and will never again experience **destruction** (v. 11) as at the time of the exile to Babylon.

14:12–15. These verses further portray the Lord's military victory over the enemy armies who will attack Jerusalem. The Lord will destroy these armies with a **plague** (v. 12) and will cause them to turn against each other, recalling past battles that the Lord fought for Israel (see Judg. 7:22; Isa. 37:36). Reversing the situation of 14:1, the people of Israel will take the plunder of battle (**gold, and silver, and apparel**; v. 14) from their enemies.

14:16–19. Just as there will be a remnant from Israel, however, there will also be a remnant (**every one that is left**; v. 16) from the **nations**, and they will become faithful worshipers of the Lord in the kingdom age (14:15–21). They will make a yearly pilgrimage to Jerusalem to celebrate **the feast of tabernacles** (v. 16). Of the three great pilgrimage festivals, perhaps the Feast of Tabernacles was selected as the one for the Gentile remnant because it was the last and greatest festival of the Hebrew calendar, culminating the year's worship (see Ezek. 45:25). It was to be a time of grateful rejoicing for the Lord's blessing (see Lev. 23:40; Deut. 16:13–15; Neh. 8:18) and thus seems to speak of the final, joyful regathering and restoration of Israel, as well as of the ingathering of the nations. Failure to observe the festival on the part of any nation will result in the covenant curse of **no rain** (v. 17; see Deut. 28:22–24).

14:20–21. The Jerusalem of the kingdom age will be a holy city that is completely devoted to the Lord. The holiness once attached to sacred utensils at the temple will be attached to even ordinary objects, like the **bells of the horses** (v. 20) and the **pots** used for cooking. Every taint of moral evil will be removed, and there will be no **Canaanite** (v. 21)—anyone who is morally or spiritually unclean—among the people of God (see Isa. 35:8; Ezek. 43:7; 44:9; Rev. 21:27).

THE BOOK OF MALACHI

INTRODUCTION

Author

The book is ascribed to Malachi, whose name means "my messenger." Since the term occurs in 3:1, and since both prophets and priests were called messengers of the Lord (see 2:7; Hag. 1:13), some have thought "Malachi" to be only a title that tradition has given the author. The view has been supported by appealing to the early Greek translation (the Septuagint), which translates the term in 1:1 as "His messenger" rather than as a proper noun. The matter, however, remains uncertain, and it is still very likely that Malachi was in fact the author's name.

Date

The similarity between the sins denounced in Nehemiah and those denounced in Malachi suggest that the two leaders were contemporaries. Malachi may have been written after Nehemiah returned to Persia in 433 BC or during his second period as governor. Since the governor mentioned in 1:8 probably was not Nehemiah, the first alternative may be more likely. Malachi was most likely the last prophet of the Old Testament era (though some place Joel later).

Background

Spurred on by the prophetic activity of Haggai and Zechariah, the returned exiles under the leadership of their governor Zerubbabel finished the temple in 516 BC. In 458 BC, the community was strengthened by the coming of Ezra the priest and several thousand more Jews. King Artaxerxes of Persia encouraged Ezra to develop the temple worship (Ezra 7:17) and to ensure the law of Moses was being obeyed (Ezra 7:25–26).

Thirteen years later (445 BC), the same Persian king permitted his cupbearer Nehemiah to return to Jerusalem and rebuild the walls (Neh. 6:15). As newly appointed governor, Nehemiah also spearheaded reforms to help the poor (Neh. 5:2–13), and he convinced the people to shun mixed marriages, to keep the Sabbath (Neh. 10:30–31), and to bring their tithes and offerings faithfully (Neh. 10:37–39).

In 433 BC, Nehemiah returned to the service of the Persian king, and during his absence, the Jews fell into sin once more. Later, however, Nehemiah came back to Jerusalem to discover that the tithes were being ignored, the Sabbath was being broken, the people had intermarried with foreigners, and the priests had become corrupt (Neh. 13:7–31). Several of these sins are condemned by Malachi (see 1:6–14; 2:14–16; 3:8–11).

Theme and Theological Message

Although the Jews had been allowed to return from exile and rebuild the temple, several discouraging factors brought about a general religious malaise: (1) their land remained but a small province in the backwaters of the Persian empire, (2) the glorious future announced by the prophets (including the other postexilic prophets, Haggai and Zechariah) had not (yet) been realized, and (3) their God had not (yet) come to His temple (3:1) with majesty and power (as celebrated in Psalm 68) to exalt His kingdom in the sight of the nations. Doubting God's covenant love (1:2) and no longer trusting His justice (2:17; 3:14–15), the Jews of the restored community began to lose hope. So their worship degenerated into a listless perpetuation of mere forms, and they no longer took the law seriously.

Malachi rebuked their doubt of God's love (1:2–5) and the faithlessness of both priests (1:6–2:9) and people (2:10–16). To their charge that God is unjust ("Where is the God of judgment?"; 2:17) because He had failed to come in judgment to exalt His people, Malachi answered with an announcement and a warning: The Lord they sought would come, but He would come "like a refiner's fire" (3:1–4). He would come to judge, but He would judge His people first (3:5).

Because the Lord does not change in His commitments and purpose, Israel had not been completely destroyed for her persistent unfaithfulness (3:6). Only through repentance and reformation would she again experience God's blessing (3:6–12). Those who honor the Lord will be spared when He comes to judge (3:16–18).

In conclusion, Malachi once more reassures and warns his readers that "the day ['the great and dreadful day of the LORD,' 4:5] cometh" and that it will "burn as an oven" (4:1). In that day, the righteous will rejoice, and "ye shall tread down the wicked" (4:1–3). So "remember ye the law of Moses my servant" (4:4). To prepare His people for that day, the Lord will send "Elijah the prophet" to call them back to the godly ways of their forefathers (4:5–6).

Literary Features

Malachi is called a "burden" (see 1:1), that is, an "oracle," and is written in what might be called lofty prose. The text features a series of questions asked by both God and the people. Along with Micah, this book reflects the "disputation" technique, in which the author and/or God disputes with his opponents, often in courtroom settings. Frequently, the Lord's statements are followed by sarcastic questions introduced by "Yet ye say" (1:2, 6–7; 2:14, 17; 3:7–8, 13; compare 1:13). In each case, the Lord's response is given.

Repetition is a key element in the book. The name "the LORD of hosts" occurs twenty times. The book begins with a description of the wasteland of Edom (1:3–4) and ends with a warning of Israel's destruction (4:6).

Several vivid figures are employed within the book of Malachi. The priests sniff contemptuously at the altar of the Lord (1:13), and the Lord spreads on their faces the offal from their sacrifices (2:3). As Judge, "He is like a refiner's fire, and like fullers' sope" (3:2), but for the righteous "shall the Sun of righteousness arise with healing in his wings" (4:2).

Outline

I. Introduction: God's Covenant Love for Israel Affirmed (1:1–5)

II. Israel's Unfaithfulness Rebuked (1:6–2:16)
   A. The Unfaithfulness of the Priests (1:6–2:9)
      1. They Dishonor God in Their Sacrifices (1:6–14)
      2. They Do Not Faithfully Teach the Law (2:1–9)
   B. The Unfaithfulness of the People (2:10–16)

III. The Lord's Coming Announced (2:17–4:6)
   A. The Lord Will Come to Purify the Priests and Judge the People (2:17–3:6)
   B. A Call to Repentance in View of the Lord's Coming (3:7–18)
      1. An Exhortation to Faithful Giving (3:7–12)
      2. An Exhortation to Faithful Service (3:13–18)
   C. The Day of the Lord Announced (4:1–6)

Bibliography

Baldwin, Joyce G. *Haggai, Zechariah, Malachi: An Introduction and Commentary*. Tyndale Old Testament Commentaries 24. Leicester: InterVarsity, 1972.

Feinberg, Charles. *The Minor Prophets*. Chicago: Moody, 1976.

Kaiser, W. C. *Malachi: God's Unchanging Love*. Grand Rapids, MI: Baker, 1984.

Merrill, Eugene H. *Haggai, Zechariah, Malachi*. Wycliffe Exegetical Commentary. Chicago: Moody, 1994.

Verhoef, Pieter A. *The Books of Haggai and Malachi*. New International Commentary on the Old Testament. Grand Rapids, MI: Eerdmans, 1987.

EXPOSITION

I. Introduction: God's Covenant Love for Israel Affirmed (1:1–5)

1:1–5. In his opening message, the prophet Malachi both confronts and comforts the people with a reminder of God's love for them. Because of the exile and their continuing struggles after returning to the land, the people had questioned God's love and His faithfulness to the covenant promises given to Israel. The first point of dispute in the book is that the people challenged the Lord's reassuring **I have loved you** (v. 2), saying **Wherein hast thou loved us?**

The proof of the Lord's love was the contrast between the Lord's ways with Israel (**I loved Jacob**; v. 2) and with Jacob's brother (**I hated Esau**; v. 3). Paul explains God's love for Jacob and hatred for Esau on the basis of election (Rom. 9:10–13). God chose Jacob but not Esau. "Love" and "hate" were used as covenant terms throughout the ancient Near East. The idea, then, is that God made a covenant with Jacob but refused to make one with Esau. **Edom** (v. 4), Israel's neighbor to the southeast, was the people descended from Esau. The demise of Edom, in contrast to Israel's preservation and return to the land, would be the confirmation of God's special commitment to Israel as a people. Edom was **laid ... waste** (v. 3) as the Nabatean Arabs gradually forced them from their homeland (circa 550–400 BC), resulting in the formation of the nation of Idumea in New Testament times (see Mark 3:8). Malachi's words about Edom echo those of the earlier prophets (see Isa. 34:5–15; Jer. 49:7–22; Ezek. 25:12–14; 35:1–15; Obadiah). When Israel observed the ultimate fate of Edom, the LORD would **be magnified** (v. 5) as Israel comes to acknowledge Him as the great Ruler over all the nations.

II. Israel's Unfaithfulness Rebuked (1:6–2:16)

A. The Unfaithfulness of the Priests (1:6–2:9)

1:6–2:9. In establishing Israel's guilt before the Lord, Malachi focused especially on the sins of the priests, who were supposed to teach by word and example the precepts of the Lord to the people. The second dispute of the book revolves around the issue of the priests dishonoring the Lord through the sacrifices that they offered (1:6–14). The Lord asked, **"where is mine honour?"** (v. 6), and the priests responded, **"Wherein have we despised thy name?"**

1. The Priests Dishonor God in Their Sacrifices (1:6–14)

1:6–9. By offering defiled sacrifices (**polluted bread**; v. 7), the priests had defiled the Lord Himself. The specific problem with their sacrifices was that they offered animals that were **blind** and **lame**. These animals with defects or serious flaws were unacceptable as sacrifices (see Deut. 15:21) and represented gifts that would not have been acceptable even to present to the Persian **governor** (see v. 14 and the payment of vows with defective animals, in violation of Lev. 22:18–23).

1:10–14. Israel was going through the motions of worship but was not honoring the Lord by giving their very best. The Lord wished that the priests would simply **shut the doors** (v. 10) of the temple and stop performing their empty rituals. Better no sacrifices than sacrifices offered with contempt (see

Isa. 1:11–15). God's rule is universal, **from the rising of the sun ... to the going down of the same** (v. 11; see 4:2; Pss. 50:1; 113:3; Isa. 41:25; 45:6), and His name would be **great among the Gentiles**, and they also would come to Jerusalem to worship. However, Israel had **profaned** (v. 12) and **polluted** the Lord's reputation with their corrupt worship. They were tired of honoring the Lord and treated the sacrifices in a contemptuous manner, reflecting the earlier behavior of Eli's sons (see 1 Sam. 2:15–17). The Lord is the **great King** (v. 14) and demands worship that is worthy of His character and reputation.

2. They Do Not Faithfully Teach the Law (2:1–9)

2:1–4. The Lord will discipline the priests for their failure to properly honor the Lord. He would **send a curse** (v. 2) upon the priests and that He would **curse your blessings**. It was the function of the priests to pronounce God's blessings on the people (see Num. 6:23–27), but their blessings would become curses so that their uniquely priestly function would be worse than useless. The Lord would spread the **dung** (i.e., entrails; v. 3) of the sacrificial animals over the faces of the priests to disgrace them. As gruesome as this is to a modern reader, it is simply the ancient legal concept of "an eye for an eye." The priests had dishonored the Lord, and the Lord would turn this dishonor upon the priests themselves.

2:5–9. Their actions violated the **covenant ... of life and peace** (v. 5) that the Lord had established with the tribe of Levi, which had the special privilege of serving as intermediaries between God and Israel (see Num. 3:12–13; Neh. 13:29). The covenant in view here is specifically the covenant made with Phineas, Aaron's grandson (Num. 25:10–13). Phineas defended God's honor by killing two offenders involved in the idolatry and immorality connected with Baal-peor (Nun 25:1–3). Because of the zeal of Phineas, the Lord promised that his descendants would serve perpetually as priests in Israel. The priests of Malachi's day had shown nothing of this zeal for the Lord. They had not fulfilled their roles as teachers of the law and messengers of the Lord (vv. 6–7; see Lev. 10:11; Zeph. 3:4; Hag. 2:11). In fact, the priests themselves had **corrupted the covenant** (v. 8), not only through unfaithful teaching but also by causing **many to stumble at the law** by promoting and practicing intermarriage with foreigners (v. 8; see Ezra 9:1; 10:18–22; Neh. 13:27–29). The Lord would dishonor these priests before the people because they had been **partial** (v. 9) in the administration of justice, something that is specifically forbidden in Leviticus 19:15. The priests were to be like the Lord in their fairness and justice (see Deut. 10:17), but through their actions, they had misrepresented the character of the Lord before the people of the Lord.

B. The Unfaithfulness of the People (2:10–16)

2:10–13. Malachi now turned from the unfaithfulness of the priests to the unfaithfulness of the people at large. Just as the priests had violated the "covenant ... of life and peace" (2:5), the people had violated the commands of the Mosaic **covenant of our fathers** (v. 10). Malachi rebukes the people in a passage framed by the verb "to deal treacherously" (vv. 10–11, 16; see v. 14). Two examples of their sin are specifically mentioned: marrying pagan women and divorce. The two sins are connected in that men were likely divorcing their wives to marry foreign women who belonged to families now in possession of land within Judah.

The question **Have we not all one father?** (v. 10) is not proof of the universal brotherhood of man but rather refers to Israel's special status as the chosen people of God (see Deut. 32:18; Isa. 63:16). Israel's sin was magnified by their disregard of their covenant relationship with God. The men of Judah had **married the daughter of a strange god** (v. 11). While marriage to a foreign woman is not specifically prohibited in the Old Testament law, marriage to those who worshiped pagan gods was strictly forbidden in the covenant law because it could lead to apostasy (see Exod. 34:15–16; Deut. 7:3–4; see Josh. 23:12–13). The story of Solomon is a prime example of how devotion to the Lord could be compromised by marriage to those who worshiped false gods (see 1 Kings 11:1–6). Ezra and Nehemiah both wrestled with this problem in the postexilic com-

munity (see Ezra 9:1–2; Neh. 13:23–29), and it was especially important during this time that Israel maintain its national identity as the people of God. The Lord would **cut off** (v. 12) those who married foreign women and would continue to disregard the empty worship offered by a disobedient people (vv. 12–13). The Lord would not respond to their prayers even when they came to Him **with weeping, and ... crying out** (v. 13).

2:14–15. Refusing to accept the prophetic rebuke, the people retorted, **Wherefore?** (v. 14), or why will the Lord not accept our worship? Elaborating on the issue of marriage, the prophet charged that the men of Judah had **dealt treacherously** with their wives by divorcing them and sending them away. The phrase **wife of thy covenant** reflects the idea that marriage is a covenant (see Prov. 2:17; Ezek. 16:8), and such covenants are affirmed before witnesses (see Deut. 30:19; 1 Sam. 20:23; Isa. 8:1–2).

The precise meaning of verse 15 is difficult to determine. It may refer to Abraham, who "married" the foreigner Hagar to have a son (**a godly seed**; v. 15; see Gen. 16:1–4) but did not divorce his wife Sarah in the process. This mention of Abraham prevented any appeal to Abraham's example as an excuse for divorcing one's wife to marry a foreign woman.

2:16. God's unchanging standard is that He **hateth putting away** (v. 16; see Isa. 50:1). The Lord allows for divorce in the Mosaic law as a concession to human sinfulness (Deut. 24:1–4), but God's design of one man and one woman for life, established with Adam and Eve (Gen. 2:21–25), remains the standard even in a fallen world (see Matt. 19:4–6). The equation of divorce with violence reflects the severity of God's displeasure with unfaithfulness to the marriage covenant. Even Scripture's allowance of divorce for violation of the marriage commitment (see Matt. 5:27–28) ultimately reflects the seriousness that God attaches to the permanence of marriage.

III. The Lord's Coming Announced (2:17–4:6)

2:17–4–6. The second half of Malachi's prophecy speaks of God's coming to His people. They had given up on God (see 2:17) and had grown religiously cynical and morally corrupt. So God's coming would mean judgment and purification as well as redemption. While continuing to warn the people that God would judge Israel's disobedience, the prophet pointed to a future restoration in which the Lord will decisively act to remove Israel's sin so that they will be forever blessed. The coming of the Messiah, in both His first and second comings, is central to this future hope.

A. The Lord Will Come to Purify the Priests and Judge the People (2:17–3:6)

2:17. The people disputed Malachi's charge that they had **wearied the Lord** (v. 17) with their words. The prophet explained that they had wearied the Lord with their challenge that He was unjust in His dealings. They asked, **Where is the God of judgment?** (or justice). The people were blaming the Lord for the exile and the pitiful living conditions of their own postexilic community, failing to recognize that Israel's sin and their continued unwillingness to obey the Lord were the real reasons for their circumstances.

3:1. The Lord promised to send **my messenger** prior to His own coming to His people. The New Testament explains that this promise was fulfilled in John the Baptist (see Matt 11:10; Mark 1:2; Luke 1:76). The role of the messenger was to **prepare the way** for the Lord Himself. When the Lord came, it would be to purify (v. 3) and to judge (v. 5), but He would mercifully send one before Him to prepare His people (see 4:5–6; Isa. 40:3). The work of "my messenger" was also connected to the coming of **the messenger of the covenant**, the Messiah, who as the Lord's representative would confirm and establish the covenant between God and Israel (see Isa. 42:6). The coming of the Lord portrayed in this passage was fulfilled in the accomplishments of the Messiah.

3:2–5. The future **day of his coming** (v. 2) is the eschatological "day of the Lord," when the Lord will come to complete His work in history. The question **who shall stand ...?** is a reminder that those who de-

sire the Lord's coming must know that clean hands and a pure heart are required (see Ps. 24:3–4; Isa. 33:14–15). The Lord's judgment will be like a **refiner's fire** (see Isa. 1:25; Zech. 13:8–9) and **fullers'** (i.e., launderers') **soap** (see Isa. 7:3) that purifies His sinful people (vv. 3–4). The Lord will also **purify the sons of Levi** (v. 3), the priests who were supposed to be the Lord's messengers and whose sins are the focus in 1:6–2:9. With the removal of their sin and the restoration of a right relationship, Israel's worship will once again become **pleasant** (or pleasing; v. 4) to the Lord. The warning in verse 5 is that this purging will involve the destruction of the wicked in Israel who persist in their sinful ways.

3:6. I change not is the Lord's response to the challenge of His justice in 2:17. Contrary to what many in Malachi's day were thinking, God remains faithful to His covenant. It is this covenant faithfulness that had kept Israel from being **consumed** (in contrast to Edom, see 1:3–5). Rather than blaming God, the people needed to face up to their own sinfulness as the cause of their plight.

B. A Call to Repentance in View of the Lord's Coming (3:7–18)

1. An Exhortation to Faithful Giving (3:7–12)

3:7–12. The promise/warning of the Lord's coming to purge sin demanded a response of repentance and changed behavior. Malachi issued the call to **Return** (v. 7) because the people had "robbed" God. When the people protested their innocence, the prophet pointed to the issue of **tithes and offerings** (v. 8; see 1:7–14). They were to bring their tithes to the **storehouse** (v. 10), the treasury rooms of the sanctuary (see 1 Kings 7:51; 2 Chron. 31:11–12; Neh. 13:12). In the ancient world, there were no banks. Temples were the places where wealth was stored. The Lord promised that in response to their faithful giving, He would open up **the windows of heaven**, an idiom that refers elsewhere to abundant provision of food (see 2 Kings 7:2, 19; Ps. 78:23–24). Their obedience would also bring removal of the covenant curses of famine and ruined crops (v. 11; see Deut. 28:39–40). Members of the postexilic community were claiming, "It is vain to serve God" (3:14), failing to recognize that their financial lack was due to their own covenant unfaithfulness.

Though never specifically commanded in the New Testament, tithing was an established practice before the giving of the Mosaic law (see Gen. 28:20; Heb. 7:1–4), and the tithe of 10 percent seems to reflect a general standard for giving to the Lord. The New Testament, however, commands the even higher standard of "grace giving" in proportion to the Lord's blessing on one's life (see 1 Cor. 16:2; 2 Cor. 8:7). Ultimately, the believer recognizes that all he possesses belongs to the Lord. While it is true that the Lord blesses those who give of their finances to Him (see Luke 6:38), financial reward is only one of the ways that the Lord blesses those who give. The specific details of God's covenant arrangement with Israel that promised prosperity in the land as a reward for obedience to the Mosaic law should not be directly applied to all peoples at all times.

It does not appear that the principle of "storehouse tithing," directing that the tithe be given exclusively to one's local church, can be directly inferred as a valid application of this passage from Malachi. At the same time, believers have a responsiblity to financially support those who faithfully minister the Word of God to them (see 1 Cor. 9:11), and so financial support of the local church should be a major focus of the believer's giving to the Lord.

2. An Exhortation to Faithful Service (3:13–18)

3:13–18. The Lord rebuked the people for their **stout** (i.e., harsh; v. 13) words against Him. Following the established pattern, the people protested that they did not understand how the Lord could bring such an accusation. The harsh words involved their claim that **It is vain to serve God** (v. 14) and that the wicked are **set up** (i.e., established; v. 15) and **delivered.** They believed that it was the wicked who are **happy** (or blessed). In their unbelief, the Jews called blessed those whom the godly knew to be cursed (see Ps. 119:21). The prosperity of the wicked is often a dilemma for the righteous (see Ps. 73:3, 9–12), but the people here, rather than genuinely seeking the

working out of God's justice, were merely blaming God for something that was their own fault.

The Lord will ultimately bless those who have **feared** (v. 16) Him and have encouraged one another to remain faithful in the face of widespread cynicism and complaining against God. Their names will be recorded in the Lord's **book of remembrance,** analogous to the records of notable deeds kept by earthy rulers (see Est. 6:1–3; Isa. 4:3; Dan. 7:10; 12:1). The Lord will honor the righteous as His **jewels** (v. 17; see Exod. 19:5) and will **spare them** in the day of judgment (see 4:1–2). When Israel is fully restored, they will recognize the distinction between how the Lord deals with **the righteous and the wicked** (v. 18).

C. The Day of the Lord Announced (chap. 4)

4:1. The day, the future day of the Lord, will be a time of fiery judgment against the **proud.** Hebrew has an extensive vocabulary for pride or arrogance. It is an issue of much greater proportional importance in the Bible than in contemporary culture. The expression **neither root nor branch** is an idiom picturing complete destruction (see Amos 2:9). The fire of God's judgment will consume the wicked.

4:2–4. In contrast, God's grace will be as a **Sun of righteousness** (v. 2) that brings **healing** to the godly. God and His glory are compared to the sun (Isa. 60:1, 19), just as Christ is the "Sunrise" from heaven (see Luke 1:78–79; Isa. 9:2). The metaphor of a king rising like the sun is ancient. The promised healing is a figure for the salvation and renewal bestowed on the righteous (see Isa. 45:8; 46:13; Jer. 30:17). The Lord also promised that the righteous **will tread down the wicked** (v. 3) as one treads the wine press (see Isa. 63:2–3). Malachi exhorted the faithful to **Remember ye the law of Moses** (v. 4) and to keep its commandments while waiting for this future salvation.

4:5–6. The Lord promised to send **Elijah the prophet** (v. 5) in connection with the future day of salvation. As Elijah came before Elisha, whose ministry was one of judgment and redemption, so a prophetic figure like Elijah would be sent to prepare

God's people for the Lord's coming. The New Testament explains that John the Baptist ministered "in the spirit and power of Elias [Elijah]" (Luke 1:17) as the messianic forerunner preparing the nation of Israel for their coming Messiah and the kingdom of God (see also Matt. 11:13–14; 17:12–13; Mark 9:11–13). Some also believe that Elijah may be one of the two witnesses in Revelation 11:3. Thus, the fulfillment of this passage began with the events associated with the first coming of Christ and will culminate with His second coming. The goal of this future Elijah's ministry will be to **turn the heart** (v. 6) of family members to one another as they are spiritually renewed in their relationship with the Lord (see Gen. 18:19; Deut. 7:9–11).

The book of Malachi closes with a warning. If Israel does not repent, then the Lord would **smite the land with a curse** (v. 6). There would be total destruction, and if Israel did not change her ways, she would be dealt with as God had dealt with Edom (see 1:3–4; Isa. 34:5). Thus, the Old Testament begins with the promise of creation and ends with the threat of the curse. It stands incomplete without the fulfillment of the New Testament. Only there does one find the Savior, Judge, Priest, Prophet, and King who fulfills all the types and prophecies of the Old Testament.

KING JAMES VERSION

BIBLE
COMMENTARY
——— *for* ———
TODAY

NEW TESTAMENT

KING JAMES VERSION

BIBLE
COMMENTARY
for
TODAY

NEW TESTAMENT

THE GOSPEL ACCORDING TO ST. MATTHEW

INTRODUCTION

Author

The early church fathers were unanimous in holding that Matthew, one of the twelve apostles, was the author of this gospel. In addition, every early manuscript of Matthew that has been preserved attributes the gospel to him. No one in the early church ever suggested that anyone else was the author. Matthew is quoted by Ignatius as early as AD 110 and is quoted by various church fathers more often than Mark or Luke.

The results of modern critical studies, however, in particular those that stress Matthew's alleged dependence on Mark for a substantial part of his gospel, have caused some biblical scholars to abandon Matthean authorship. Why, they ask, would Matthew, an eyewitness to the events of the Lord's life, depend so heavily on Mark's account? The best answer seems to be that he agreed with it and wanted to show that the apostolic testimony to Christ was not divided. In addition, writers often seek an outline to help them in their work, even when they are familiar with the subject. Mark offered a convenient and accurate framework for Matthew's work.

Matthew, whose name means "gift of the Lord," was a tax collector who left his work to follow Jesus (see 9:9–13). In Mark and Luke, he is called by his other name, Levi, and Mark also mentioned that he was "the son of Alpheus" (Mark 2:14). As a tax official, he had to be intelligent and literate, and thus capable of precisely recording the events of Jesus' life. Matthew frequently mentioned money and had an interest in large figures (see 18:24; 25:15).

Date and Place of Composition

The Jewish nature of Matthew's gospel may suggest that it was written in the Holy Land, though many think it may have originated in Syrian Antioch. Some have argued, on the basis of its Jewish characteristics, that it was written in the early church period, possibly the early part of AD 50, when the church was largely Jewish and the gospel was preached to Jews only (see Acts 11:19). Those who have concluded that both Matthew and Luke drew extensively from Mark's gospel, however, date it later—after the gospel of Mark had been in circulation for some time (see chart, *Zondervan KJV Study Bible*,

p. 1349). Accordingly, some feel that Matthew would have been written in the late 50s or in the 60s. Others, who assume that Mark was written between 65 and 70, place Matthew in the 70s or even later.

Recipients

Since his gospel was written in Greek, Matthew's readers were obviously Greek-speaking. They also seem to have been Jews. Many elements point to Jewish readership: Matthew's concern with the fulfillment of the Old Testament (his quotations from and allusions to the Old Testament are more numerous than that of any other gospel writer); his tracing of Jesus' descent from Abraham (1:1–17); his lack of explanation of Jewish customs (especially in contrast to Mark); his use of Jewish terminology (e.g., "the kingdom of heaven"; see discussion on 3:2) and "Father in heaven," in which "heaven" reveals the Jewish reverential reluctance to use the name of God); his emphasis on Jesus' role as the "Son of David" (1:1; 9:27; 12:23; 15:22; 20:30–31; 21:9, 15; 22:41–45). This does not mean, however, that Matthew restricted his gospel to Jews. He recorded the coming of the wise men (non-Jews) to worship the infant Jesus (2:1–12), as well as Jesus' statement that "the field is the world" (13:38). He also gave a full statement of the Great Commission (28:18–20). These passages show that, although Matthew's gospel is Jewish, it has a universal outlook.

Theme and Theological Message

Matthew's main purpose was to prove to his Jewish readers that Jesus was their Messiah. He did this primarily by showing how Jesus, in His life and ministry, fulfilled the Old Testament Scriptures. Although all the gospel writers quoted the Old Testament, Matthew included nine additional proof texts (1:22–23; 2:15; 2:17–18; 2:23; 4:14–16; 8:17; 12:17–21; 13:35; 27:9–10) to drive home his basic theme: Jesus is the fulfillment of the Old Testament predictions of the Messiah. Matthew even saw the history of God's people in the Old Testament recapitulated in some aspects of Jesus' life (see, e.g., his quotation of Hos. 11:1 in 2:15). To accomplish his purpose, Matthew also emphasized Jesus' Davidic lineage (see "Recipients," above).

Literary Features

The way the material is arranged reveals an artistic touch. The whole gospel is woven around six great discourses: (1) chapters 5–7; (2) chapter 10; (3) chapter 13; (4) chapter 18; (5) chapter 23; and (6) chapters 24–25. That this is deliberate is clear from the refrain that concludes each discourse: "When Jesus had ended these sayings," or a similar phrase (7:28; 11:1; 13:53; 19:1; 26:1). The narrative sections, in each case, appropriately lead up to the discourses. The gospel has a fitting prologue (chaps. 1–2) and a challenging epilogue (28:16–20).

Matthew begins as "The book of the generation of Jesus Christ" (1:1), much as Genesis begins each of its ten main sections with "the generations of …" (see discussion on Gen. 2:4). Jewish readers would have noticed the similarity immediately. Matthew cited Jesus' royal lineage and supernatural birth (chaps. 1–2), followed by His qualifications through His baptism and temptation (chaps. 3–4). Then he gave Jesus' basic message (chaps.

5–7), followed by a grouping of miracles (chaps. 8–10). After describing Christ's rejection (chaps. 11–12), Matthew recorded Jesus' parables that showed a different direction from the immediate kingdom He had been announcing for the Jews. The climax of Matthew is found in the passion story, which makes up much of the rest of the book.

Outline

E. Prophecy concerning Jerusalem (23:37–39)
F. Olivet Discourse (chaps. 24–25)
G. Jesus' Betrayal Plotted (26:1–16)
H. The Last Supper (26:17–35)
I. Garden of Gethsemane (26:36–56)
J. Trial before Caiaphas (26:57–68)
K. Peter's Denial (26:69–75)
L. Judas's Death (27:1–10)
M. Trial before Pilate (27:11–26)
N. The Soldiers Mock Jesus (27:27–32)
O. The Crucifixion (27:33–56)
P. The Burial (27:57–66)
VIII. The Risen Christ (chap. 28)
A. The Empty Tomb (28:1–10)
B. The Authorities Cover Up What Really Happened (28:11–15)
C. The Great Commission (28:16–20)

Bibliography

Blomberg, Craig L. *Matthew*. The New American Commentary 22. Nashville: Broadman & Holman, 1992.

Gundry, Robert H. *Matthew: A Commentary on His Literary and Theological Art*. Grand Rapids, MI: Eerdmans, 1982.

Hendriksen, William. *Gospel of Matthew*. Grand Rapids, MI: Baker Academic, 1974.

Hindson, Edward, and James Borland. *Matthew: God with Us*. Chattanooga: AMG, 2005.

MacArthur, John F. *Matthew*. 4 vols. The MacArthur New Testament Commentary. Chicago: Moody Press, 1985–89.

Walvoord, John F. *Matthew: Thy Kingdom Come*. Chicago: Moody Press, 1974.

EXPOSITION

I. The Birth and Early Years of Jesus (chaps. 1–2)

A. His Genealogy (1:1–17)

1:1–17. Matthew's gospel begins by connecting Jesus to the promised messianic line in the Old Testament. For a comparison of Matthew's genealogy with Luke's, see discussion on Luke 3:23–38. The types of people mentioned in this genealogy reveal the broad scope of those who make up the people of God as well as the genealogy of Jesus.

1:1. The son of David. A messianic title (see discussion on 9:27) found several times in this gospel (in 1:20, however, it is not a messianic title). **The son of Abraham.** Because Matthew was writing to Jews, it was important to identify Jesus in this way.

1:2–5. By including four women (contrary to custom) in his genealogy, Matthew may have been indicating, at the very outset of his gospel, that God's activity is not limited to men or to the people of Israel. The four women are: **Thamar** (v. 3; see Genesis 38), **Rachab** (v. 5; see Joshua 2), **Ruth**, and Bathsheba, "her that had been the wife of Urias" (1:6). At least three of these women were Gentiles (Tamar, Rahab, and Ruth). Bathsheba was probably an Israelite (see 1 Chron. 3:5) but was closely associated with the Hittites because of Uriah, her Hittite husband. **Aminadab** (v. 4). Aaron's father-in-law (see Exod. 6:23).

1:6. Because quite a long time had elapsed between Rahab and **David** (v. 6) and because of Matthew's desire for systematic organization (see discussion on 1:17), many of the generations between these two ancestors were assumed, but not listed, by Matthew.

1:7–15. Joram begat (v. 8). Matthew calls Joram the father of Ozias, but from 2 Chronicles 21:4–26:23 it is clear that, again (see discussion on 1:6), several generations were assumed (Ahaziah, Joash, and Amaziah) and that "begat" is used in the sense of "became the forefather of." **Josias begat** (v. 11). Similarly, Josias is presented as the father of Jechonias (i.e., Jehoiachin), whereas he was actually the father of Jehoiakim and the grandfather of Jehoiachin (see 2 Chron. 36:1–9). For **Salathiel begat** (v. 12), see discussion on 1 Chronicles 3:19.

1:16. Matthew did not say that **Joseph** was the father of Jesus, only that he was **the husband of Mary** and that Jesus was born of her. In this genealogy, Matthew showed that although Jesus was not the physical son of Joseph, He was his legal son and therefore a descendant of David. By not being Joseph's son, Jesus avoided the curse on Jechonias's descendants (see Jer. 22:30).

1:17. Fourteen generations … fourteen … fourteen. These divisions reflect two characteristics of Matthew's gospel: (1) an apparent fondness for numbers and (2) a concern for systematic arrangement. The number fourteen may have been chosen because it is twice seven (the number of completeness) and/or because it is the numerical value of the name David (see *KJV Study Bible* note on Rev. 13:17). For the practice of telescoping genealogies to achieve the desired number of names, see 1 Chronicles, Introduction: "Genealogies."

B. His Birth (1:18–2:12)

1:18. Mary was espoused to Joseph. There were no sexual relations during a Jewish betrothal period, but it was a much more binding relationship than a modern engagement and could be broken only by divorce (see 1:19). In Deuteronomy 22:24, a betrothed woman is called a "wife," though the preceding verse speaks of her as being "betrothed unto a husband." Matthew used the terms "husband" (1:19) and "wife" (1:24) of Joseph and Mary before their betrothal was consummated.

1:19. Just. To Jews, this meant being zealous in keeping the law. **Put her away privily.** Joseph was considering signing the necessary legal papers for a divorce but not having Mary judged publicly and stoned (see Deut. 22:23–24).

1:20. In a dream. This phrase occurs five times in the first two chapters of Matthew (here; 2:12–13, 19, 22) and indicates the means the Lord used for speaking to Joseph. **Thou Son of David** was perhaps a hint that the message of the angel related to the expected Messiah. **Take unto thee Mary thy wife.** Joseph and Mary were legally bound to each other but were not yet living together as husband and wife. **That which is conceived in her is of the Holy Ghost.** This agrees perfectly with the announcement to Mary (see Luke 1:35), except that the latter was more specific (see discussion on Luke 1:26–35).

1:21. JESUS … shall save. The name Jesus is the Greek form of Joshua, which means "the LORD saves."

1:22. That it might be fulfilled. Sixteen times (here; 2:15, 17, 23; 3:15; 4:14; 5:18; 8:17; 12:17; 13:14, 35; 21:4; 24:34; 26:56; 27:9, 35) Matthew spoke of the Old Testament being "fulfilled," that is, of events in New Testament times that were prophesied in the Old Testament—a powerful testimony to the divine origin of Scripture and its accuracy even in small details. In the fulfillments, we also see the writer's concern for linking the gospel with the Old Testament. Matthew, writing especially for the Jews, demonstrated how Jesus fulfilled numerous prophecies.

1:23. See discussion on Isaiah 7:14. This is the first of at least forty-seven quotations, most of them messianic, that Matthew cited from the Old Testament (see marginal notes throughout Matthew). **A virgin** refers to Mary, the mother of Jesus. Quoting

Isaiah 7:14, Matthew used the Greek *parthenos* to translate the Hebrew *'almah* precisely as a "virgin" in the technical sense. His usage of "fulfilled" in 1:22 clearly indicates that he believed the Isaiah passage prophesied the virginal conception of Jesus. **Emmanuel** means "God with us" and is used as a title of Jesus' divinity.

1:24–25. And knew her not till she brought forth her firstborn son (v. 25). Matthew and Luke both made it clear that Jesus was born of a virgin (see Luke 1:26–35). Although this doctrine is often ridiculed, it is an important part of the evangelical faith.

2:1. Bethlehem of Judea. A village about five miles south of Jerusalem. Matthew recorded nothing of the events in Nazareth (see Luke 1:26–56). Possibly wanting to emphasize Jesus' Davidic background, he began with the events that happened in David's city. It is called "Bethlehem of Judea," not to distinguish it from the town of the same name about seven miles northwest of Nazareth, but to emphasize that Jesus came from the tribe and territory that produced the line of Davidic kings. That Jews expected the Messiah to be born in Bethlehem and to be from David's family is clear from John 7:42. **Herod the king.** Herod the Great (37–4 BC), to be distinguished from the other Herods in the Bible (see chart, *KJV Study Bible*, p. 1355). Herod was a non-Jew, an Idumean, who was appointed king of Judea by the Roman senate in 40 BC and gained control only by military conquest by 37 BC. Like many other rulers of the day, he was ruthless. Herod murdered one of his wives, three of his sons, a mother-in-law, a brother-in-law, an uncle, and many others—not to mention the babies in Bethlehem (see 2:16). His reign was also noted for splendor, as seen in the many theaters, amphitheaters, monuments, pagan altars, fortresses, and other buildings he erected or refurbished—including the greatest work of all, the rebuilding of the temple in Jerusalem, begun in 19 BC and finished sixty-eight years after his death. **Wise men.** Perhaps they were from Persia or southern Arabia, both of which are east of the Holy Land. **Jerusalem.** Since they were looking for the "King of the Jews" (v. 2), they naturally came to the Jewish

capital city (see Map 10 at the end of the *KJV Study Bible*).

2:2. King of the Jews. Indicates the wise men were Gentiles. Matthew showed that people of all nations acknowledged Jesus as "King of the Jews" and came to worship Him as Lord. **Star.** Probably not an ordinary star, planet, or comet, though some scholars have identified it with the conjunction of Jupiter and Saturn. It must have been a supernatural object that looked like a star but that could actually move along and lead the wise men. It eventually led them to the proper house (see 2:9).

2:3–6. Chief priests (v. 4). Sadducees (see discussion on 3:7) who were in charge of worship at the temple in Jerusalem. The chief priests included the ruling high priest, Caiaphas; the former high priest, Annas; and the high priestly families. **Scribes.** The Jewish scholars of the day, professionally trained in the development, teaching, and application of Old Testament law. Their authority was strictly human and traditional. **Thou Bethlehem** (v. 6). This prophecy from Micah 5:2 had been given seven centuries earlier.

2:7–12. Child (v. 9). Contrary to tradition, the wise men did not visit Jesus at the manger on the night of His birth, as did the shepherds. They came some months later and visited Him in His **house** (v. 11). **The young child with Mary his mother.** Every time the child Jesus and His mother are mentioned together, He is mentioned first (here, 2:13–14, 20–21). **Gold, and frankincense, and myrrh** (for "myrrh," see discussion on Gen. 37:25). The three gifts perhaps gave rise to the legend that there were three wise men. The Bible does not indicate the number of the magi, however, and they were almost certainly not kings.

C. His Sojourn in Egypt (2:13–23)

2:13–15. Matthew saw the history of Israel (God's children) recapitulated in the life of Jesus (God's unique Son). **Into Egypt** (v. 13). Just as Israel as an infant nation went down into Egypt, so the child Jesus went there. **Out of Egypt have I called my son** (v. 15). As Israel was led by God out of Egypt, so also was Jesus. This quotation from Hosea 11:1 originally referred to God's calling the nation of Israel out of Egypt in the time of Moses, but Matthew, under the inspiration of the Spirit, applied it also to Jesus. How long Jesus and His parents were in Egypt is not known. **The death of Herod.** In 4 BC.

2:16. Slew all the children ... two years old and under. The number killed has often been exaggerated as being in the thousands. In so small a village as Bethlehem, however (even with the surrounding area included), the number was probably not large — though the act, of course, was no less brutal.

2:17-18. See discussion on Jeremiah 31:15.

2:19-23. Archelaus (v. 22). This son of Herod the Great ruled over Judea and Samaria for only ten years (4 BC-AD 6). He was unusually cruel and tyrannical and so was deposed by Rome. Judea then became part of the Roman province of Syria, administered by prefects appointed by the emperor. **Galilee.** The northern part of the Holy Land in Jesus' day.

Nazareth (v. 23). A rather obscure town, nowhere mentioned in the Old Testament. It was Jesus' hometown (see 21:11; 26:71; Luke 2:39; 4:16-24; John 1:45-46). **He shall be called a Nazarene.** These exact words are not found in the Old Testament and probably refer to several Old Testament prefigurations and prophecies (note the plural, **prophets**) that the Messiah would be despised (e.g., Ps. 22:6; Isa. 53:3), for in Jesus' day, "Nazarene" was virtually a synonym for "despised" (see John 1:45-46). Some hold that in speaking of Jesus as a "Nazarene," Matthew was referring primarily to the word "Branch" (Hebrew, *neṣer*) in Isaiah 11:1.

II. The Beginnings of Jesus' Ministry (3:1-4:11)

A. His Forerunner (3:1-12)

3:1. John the Baptist. The forerunner of Jesus, born circa 7 BC to Zacharias, a priest, and his wife Elisabeth (see Luke 1:5-80). **The wilderness of Judea.** An area that stretched some twenty miles from the Jerusalem-Bethlehem plateau down to the Jordan River and the Dead Sea, perhaps the same region where John lived (see Luke 1:80). The people of

Qumran (often associated with the Dead Sea Scrolls) lived in this area too.

3:2. Repent. Make a radical change in one's life as a whole. **The kingdom of heaven.** A phrase found only in Matthew, where it occurs thirty-two times (see Introduction: "Recipients"). Mark and Luke referred to "the kingdom of God," a term Matthew used only four times (see *KJV Study Bible* note on Mark 11:30). The kingdom of heaven is the rule of God and is both a present reality and a future hope. The idea of God's kingdom is central to Jesus' teaching and is mentioned fifty times in Matthew alone.

3:3. All three Synoptic Gospels quote Isaiah 40:3 (Luke quotes two additional verses) and apply it to John the Baptist. **Make his paths straight.** Equivalent to "Prepare ye the way of the Lord" (see discussion on Luke 3:4). The preparation was to be moral and spiritual.

3:4-6. A leathern girdle (v. 4). Used to bind up the loose outer garments. **Locusts and wild honey.** A man living in the wilderness did not hesitate to eat insects, and locusts were among the clean foods (see Lev. 11:21-22). John's simple food, clothing, and lifestyle were a visual protest against self-indulgence. For **Jordan** (v. 6), see discussion on Mark 1:5.

3:7. The Pharisees and Sadducees. The Pharisees (see discussions on Mark 2:16; Luke 5:17) were a legalistic and separatist group who strictly, but often hypocritically, kept the law of Moses and the unwritten "tradition of the elders" (Matt. 15:2). The Sadducees (see discussions on Mark 12:18; Luke 20:27; Acts 4:1) were more worldly and politically minded, and were theologically unorthodox — among other things denying the resurrection, angels, and spirits (see Acts 23:8). For **his baptism**, see discussion on Mark 1:4. **The wrath to come.** The arrival of the Messiah will bring repentance or judgment.

3:8-10. We have Abraham to our father (v. 9; see John 8:39). Salvation does not come as a birthright (even for the Jews) but through faith in Christ (see Rom. 2:28-29; Gal. 3:7, 9, 29). **These stones.** John may have pointed to the stones in the Jordan River. **Children unto Abraham.** The true people of God are not limited to the physical descendants of

Abraham (see Rom. 9:6). **The axe is laid unto the root of the trees** (v. 10). Judgment is near.

3:11. With water unto repentance. John's baptism presupposed repentance, and he would not baptize the Pharisees and Sadducees because they failed to give any evidence of repentance (see 3:7–8). **With the Holy Ghost, and with fire.** Demonstrated in a dramatic way at Pentecost (see Acts 1:5, 8; 2:1–13; 11:16), though here "fire" may refer to judgment to come (see 3:12). The outpouring of the Holy Spirit on all God's people was promised in Joel 2:28–29.

3:12. Fan. Or "winnowing fork" (for the process of winnowing, see discussion on Ruth 1:22). Here this implement is figurative for the day of judgment at Christ's second coming. The Old Testament prophets and the New Testament writers sometimes compressed the first and second comings of Christ so that they seem to be one event.

B. His Baptism (3:13–17)

3:13–15. This occasion marked the beginning of Christ's messianic ministry. There were several reasons for His baptism: (1) Jesus' baptism **fulfil[led] all righteousness** (v. 15), indicating that He was consecrated to God and officially approved by Him, as especially shown in the descent of the Holy Spirit (see 3:16) and the words of the Father (see 3:17; Ps. 2:7; Isa. 42:1). All God's righteous requirements for the Messiah were fully met in Jesus. (2) At Jesus' baptism, John publicly announced the arrival of the Messiah and the inception of His ministry (see John 1:31–34). (3) By His baptism, Jesus completely identified Himself with man's sin and failure (though He Himself needed no repentance or cleansing from sin) and became our substitute (see 2 Cor. 5:21). (4) His baptism was an example to His followers.

3:16–17. All three persons of the Trinity are clearly seen here. This alone is not a proof of the Trinity, but an intimation of it. We prove the Trinity by showing there are three eternal persons, each of whom has the attributes of deity, yet there is only one God.

The Spirit of God (v. 16). The Holy Spirit came upon Jesus, not to overcome sin (for He was sinless), but to equip Him (see discussion on Judg. 3:10) for His work as the divine-human Messiah. **Like a dove.** Either in the form of a dove or in a descent like a dove (see discussion on Mark 1:10).

A voice from heaven (v. 17). The voice (1) authenticated Jesus' unique sonship and echoes Psalm 2:7 ("Thou art my Son"), (2) identified Jesus with the suffering servant of Isaiah 42:1 ("whom I uphold"), and (3) offered the Father's support of Jesus in His mission (**in whom I am well pleased**). This word from the Father must have tremendously encouraged Jesus at the very outset of His earthly ministry. The idea of "I am well pleased" is not that the Father was well pleased with what Jesus had done. It was not an evaluation of Jesus' past performance. Similarly, it was not an evaluation of what the Father knew Jesus would do. Instead, it is a statement of God's eternal pleasure in the Son. He is at all times pleased with the Son simply because He is the Son.

C. His Temptation (4:1–11)

4:1–11. The significance of Jesus' temptations, especially because they occurred at the outset of His public ministry, seems best understood in terms of the kind of Messiah He was to be. He would not accomplish His mission by using His supernatural power for His own needs (first temptation), by using His power to win a large following with miracles or magic (second temptation), or by compromising with Satan (third temptation). Jesus had no inward desire or inclination to sin, for these in themselves are sin (see Matt. 5:22, 28). Because He was God, He did not sin in any way, whether by action, word, or inner desire (see 2 Cor. 5:21; Heb. 7:26; 1 Peter 2:22; 1 John 3:5); yet His temptation was real, not merely symbolic. Jesus "was in all points tempted like as we are, yet without sin" (Heb. 4:15). The Tempter confronted Him with a real opportunity to sin. Although Jesus was the Son of God, He defeated Satan by using a weapon that everyone has at his or her disposal: the sword of the Spirit, which is the Word of God (see Eph. 6:17). He met all three temptations with Scriptural truth (vv. 4, 7, 10) from Deuteronomy. Jesus was able to withstand temptation because He knew and relied on God's Word.

4:1. Led up of the Spirit ... to be tempted. This testing of Jesus (the Greek verb translated "tempted" can also be rendered "tested"), which was divinely intended, has as its primary background Deuteronomy 8:1–5, from which Jesus also quoted in His first reply to the Devil (see Matt. 4:4; Deut. 8:3). There Moses recalled how the Lord led the Israelites in the wilderness forty years "to humble thee, and to prove thee, to know what was in thine heart, whether thou wouldest keep his commandments, or no" (Deut. 8:2). Here at the beginning of His ministry, Jesus was subjected to a similar test and showed Himself to be the true Israelite who "live(s) by ... every word that proceedeth out of the mouth of the Lord" (Matt. 4:4; Deut. 8:3). Whereas Adam failed the great test and plunged the whole race into sin (see Genesis 3), Jesus was faithful and thus demonstrated His qualification to become the Savior of all who receive Him. It was, moreover, important that Jesus be tempted (tested) as are "His brethren," the Israelites and all of God's children, "that he might be a merciful and faithful high priest" (Heb. 2:17) and thus be "able to succour them that are tempted" (Heb. 2:18; see Heb. 4:15–16). Finally, as the one who remained faithful in temptation, He became the model for all believers when they are tempted. **Tempted of the devil**. God surely tests His people, but it is the Devil who tempts to evil (see discussion on Gen. 22:1; see also 1 John 3:8; Rev. 2:9–10; 12:9–10). Like the Hebrew for "Satan," the Greek for "devil" means "accuser" or "slanderer." The Devil is a personal being, not a mere force or influence. He is the leader of the hosts of darkness and is the great archenemy of God.

4:2. Forty days and forty nights. The number recalls the experiences of Moses (see Exod. 24:18; 34:28) and Elijah (see 1 Kings 19:8), as well as the forty years of Israel's temptation (testing) in the wilderness (see Deut. 8:2–3).

4:3. If thou be the Son of God. Meaning, "since you are." The Devil was not casting doubt on Jesus' divine sonship but was tempting Him to use His supernatural powers as the Son of God for His own ends.

4:4. Just as God gave the Israelites manna in a supernatural way (see Deut. 8:3), so also man must rely on God for spiritual feeding. Jesus relied on His Father, not on His own miracle-working power, for provision of food.

4:5–11. For **up into the holy city** (v. 5), see discussion on Luke 4:2. **A pinnacle of the temple** (see discussion on Luke 4:9). The temple, including the entire temple area, had been rebuilt by Herod the Great (see discussion on 2:1; see also John 2:20). The courtyard had been greatly enlarged, to about 330 by 500 yards. To accomplish this, a huge platform had been erected to compensate for the sharp falling off of the land to the southeast. An enormous retaining wall made of massive stones was built to support the platform. Today the drop from the pinnacle area is large. It was even more pronounced in Jesus' day. On the platform stood the temple, with its porches and courtyards flanked by beautiful colonnades. For **Satan** (v. 10), see discussion on 4:1.

III. Jesus' Ministry in Galilee (4:12–14:12)

A. The Beginning of the Galilean Campaign (4:12–25)

4:12. John was cast into prison. Jesus took this occasion to move to Galilee, there to begin His public preaching and teaching ministry (see Mark 1:14 and discussion on Luke 3:20). The reason for John's imprisonment is given in 14:3–4.

4:13. Capernaum. Although not mentioned in the Old Testament, Capernaum was evidently a sizable town in Jesus' day. Peter's house there became Jesus' base of operations during His extended ministry in Galilee (see Mark 2:1; 9:33). A fifth-century basilica now stands over the supposed site of Peter's house, and a fourth-century synagogue is located just several hundred feet from it.

4:14–16. Another messianic prophecy from Isaiah. **The people ... saw great light** (v. 16). Matthew never quoted Jesus saying, "I am the light of the world" (John 8:12), but clearly had this in mind here. The "great light" is Jesus Himself. To be in the presence of Jesus is to be in the presence of light, that is, the truth of God. Jesus is Himself the revelation of God and is the embodiment of truth. Of course, this is manifested best in His teachings and in His deeds, which reveal the character, will, and purposes of God. When Jesus came into an area, everyone saw and heard the truth about God. Jesus spent most of His public ministry in **the land of Zabulon, and the land of Nephthalim** (v. 15), which is north and west of the Sea of Galilee. Indeed, among these people, light had certainly **sprung up** (v. 16).

4:17. From that time. These words indicate an important turning point in the life of Jesus and occur three times in Matthew's gospel (see also 16:21; 26:16). Some think these words mark the three main sections of the book. **Repent.** Jesus began His public ministry with the same message as that of John the Baptist (see 3:2). The people were called to repent because God's reign was drawing near in the person and ministry of Jesus Christ. Repentance is more than a change of mind or feeling sorry for one's sins. It is a radical and deliberate change that affects not only one's mind and emotions but also the will. The Bible knows nothing of a repentance that does not bear fruit in deeds and words. Always be suspicious of a "repentance" that is nothing more than warm feelings or an acceptance of a new set of ideas. For **the kingdom of heaven**, see discussion on 3:2.

4:18. For **the sea of Galilee**, see discussion on Mark 1:16. **Net.** A circular casting net used either from a boat or while standing in shallow water.

4:19. Fishers of men. Evangelism was at the heart of Jesus' call to His disciples. As He came to "save his people from their sins" (1:21), so He calls others to the ministry of proclaiming His salvation. Evangelism was the business of Jesus and the business of His disciples. He called them so that they might bring the lost to Him, the only hope of a lost world.

4:20. See discussions on Mark 1:17–18.

4:21. Mending their nets. Washing, mending, and hanging the nets up to dry in preparation for the next day's work.

4:22. Left the ship and their father, and followed him. Some treat this passage as if Jesus were here giving us an object lesson on "leaving all to follow Him." While this is not likely, the parallel is certainly apt. As James and John left their preoccupation with making a living and the cares of this world to follow Jesus, so must every Christian make following Christ a priority. As these two left the entanglement of fishing nets, so must believers leave the entanglement of this world's cares to follow the Lord. This does not mean that secular employment is not part of God's plan for most believers. There is evidence that the disciples retained access to a boat and fishing equipment and used them on occasion even after the resurrection (see John 21:3–8). The question for believers today is one of priorities: are Jesus and His call first and foremost in one's life? Is the believer willing to be interrupted in the midst of life's cares to follow Him?

4:23. Teaching … preaching … and healing. Jesus' threefold ministry. The **synagogues** (see discussion on Mark 1:21) provided a place for Him to teach on the Sabbath. During the week, He preached to larger crowds in the open air. For **gospel**, see discussion on Mark 1:1.

4:24. Syria. The area north of Galilee and between Damascus and the Mediterranean Sea. **Lunatick.** In Greek, this word originally meant "moonstruck" and reflected the ancient idea that the moon could affect behavior. **Palsy.** The Greek word used here, *paralytikos*, has come directly into English, "paralytic." Greek physicians were among the best in ancient times, and many of our medical terms come from their language.

4:25. Decapolis. A league of free cities (Decapolis means "the ten cities") characterized by high Greek culture. All but one, Scythopolis (Beth Shan), were east of the Sea of Galilee and the Jordan River. The league stretched from a point northeast of the Sea of Galilee southward to Philadelphia (modern Amman).

B. The Sermon on the Mount (chaps. 5–7)

5:1–7:29. The Sermon on the Mount is the first of six great discourses in Matthew (chaps. 5–7; 10; 13; 18; 23; 24–25). It contains three types of material: (1) beatitudes, that is, declarations of blessedness (5:1–12), (2) ethical admonitions (5:13–20; 6:1–7:23), and (3) contrasts between Jesus' ethical teaching and Jewish legalistic traditions (5:21–48). The Sermon ends with a short parable stressing the importance of practicing what had just been taught (7:24–27) and the crowds' amazement at the authority with which Jesus spoke (7:28–29).

Opinion differs as to whether the Sermon on the Mount is a summary of what Jesus taught on one occasion or a compilation of teachings presented on numerous occasions. Matthew may have taken a single sermon and expanded it with other relevant teachings of Jesus. Thirty-four of the verses in Matthew's Sermon on the Mount occur in Luke in contexts other than the apparently parallel Sermon on the Plain (Luke 6:17–49; see discussion on Luke 6:20–49). Most likely, this account is a summary of what Jesus usually taught everywhere He went, with some variations due to time constraints and the situation.

Following the opening, the sermon develops one organizing theme: "Except your righteousness shall exceed the righteousness of the scribes and Pharisees, ye shall in no case enter into the kingdom of heaven" (5:20). Much of the sermon consists of examples of the traditional teaching of the Pharisees contrasted with a higher ethic, a righteousness exceeding that of the scribes and Pharisees. Jesus called His hearers to genuine faith in God, encouraging secret giving and private prayer rather than public demonstrations, as well as prayer made in simple faith that does not require "vain repetitions" and "much speaking" (6:3–7). In both cases, He challenged his hearers to believe that God really does hear prayer and that He rewards those who pray and who do good. Those who truly believe that God will reward them do not need to do these things publicly, thereby earning the praise of men as reward. Again, this points to a righteousness that "exceed(s) the righteousness of the scribes and Pharisees" (5:20) since it proceeds out of genuine faith in God Himself.

The Sermon on the Mount's call to moral and ethical living is so high that some have dismissed it as being completely unrealistic or have projected its fulfillment to the future kingdom. There is no doubt, however, that Jesus (and Matthew) gave the sermon as a standard for all Christians, realizing that its demands cannot be met in our own power. It is also true that Jesus occasionally used hyperbole to make His point (see, e.g., discussion on 5:29–30).

5:1. A mountain. The exact location is uncertain. It may have been the gently sloping hillside at the northwest corner of the Sea of Galilee, not far from Capernaum. Matthew may have recorded this incident with the giving of the Mosaic law on Mount Sinai in mind. The parallel may be incidental, but for Matthew's mostly Jewish audience, it may not have gone unnoticed. **When he was set.** It was the custom for Jewish rabbis to be seated while teaching (see Mark 4:1; 9:35; Luke 4:20; 5:3; John 8:2). **Disciples.** Literally, "learners." Since at the end of the sermon the crowd expressed amazement at Jesus' teaching (see 7:28), "disciples" may here be used in a broader sense than the Twelve. Or perhaps the sermon is addressed to the Twelve with the crowds also listening.

5:2–5. Blessed (v. 3). The word means more than "happy," because happiness is an emotion often dependent on outward circumstances. "Blessed" here refers to the ultimate well-being and distinctive spiritual joy of those who share in the salvation of the kingdom of God (see *KJV Study Bible* notes on Ps. 1:1; Rev. 1:3). **The poor in spirit.** In contrast to the spiritually proud and self-sufficient. **Theirs is the kingdom of heaven.** The kingdom is not something one earns. It is more a gift than a recompense. This beatitude should also be seen in light of Jesus' call to private prayer and private giving (see 6:3–7). The proud and self-sufficient do not pray because they need God, and they do not give because they care about the needs of others. Jesus was promising that "the poor in spirit," who know they need God and who are sensitive to the needs of others, will find grace in response to their faith. **Meek** (v. 5). This beatitude is taken from Psalm 37:11 and refers not so much to an attitude toward people as to a disposition before God, namely, humility. **The earth.** The new Promised Land (see Rev. 21:1). This is not a promise that "good people always win" in this age.

5:6–12. Heart (v. 8). The center of one's being, including mind, will, and emotions (see *KJV Study Bible* note on Ps. 4:7). **Peacemakers** (v. 9). Those who promote peace, as far as it depends on them (see Rom. 12:18). **They shall be called the children of God** because, in promoting peace, they reflect the character of their heavenly Father. **Theirs is the kingdom of heaven** (v. 10). A present reality as well as a future hope.

5:13–15. Salt (v. 13). Used for flavoring and preserving. **Lost his savour.** Most of the salt used in Israel came from the Dead Sea and was full of impurities, which caused it to lose some of its flavor. **Candle** (v. 15). In Jesus' day, people used small clay lamps that burned olive oil drawn up by a wick (see *KJV Study Bible* note on Exod. 25:37). **Bushel.** A basket that held about eight quarts of ground meal or flour.

5:16. Father which is in heaven. Matthew used the term "Father which is in heaven" or "heavenly Father" nineteen times, Mark twice, Luke once, and John not at all. Matthew apparently wanted to distinguish between God the Father and earthly fathers, something that may have been important to Jewish readers, as it was to those who heard Jesus originally.

5:17. The law. The first five books of the Jewish Scriptures (our Old Testament). **The prophets.** Not only the Latter Prophets—the Major Prophets (Isaiah, Jeremiah, and Ezekiel) and the twelve Minor Prophets (which the Jews grouped together as "the Book of the Twelve")—but also the so-called Former Prophets (Joshua, Judges, Samuel, and Kings). Taken together, "the law" and "the prophets" designates the entire Old Testament, including the Writings, the third section of the Hebrew Bible (see 13:35, where Matthew used "which was spoken by the prophet" to introduce a quotation from the Writings [Ps. 78:2]). **Fulfil.** Jesus fulfilled the law in the sense that He gave it its full meaning. He emphasized its deep, underlying principles and total commitment to it rather than mere external acknowledgment and obedience.

5:18–20. Jesus was speaking not against observing all the requirements of the law but against hypocritical, Pharisaical legalism. Such legalism was not the keeping of all details of the law but the hollow sham of keeping laws externally, to gain merit before God, while breaking them inwardly. It was following the letter of the law while ignoring its spirit. Here is the heart of the sermon. Jesus enjoined genuine, heartfelt obedience to the law and never called people to disobedience. The issue is not license versus legalism, but legalism versus righteousness arising from faith in God and His goodness. Here Jesus repudiated the Pharisees' interpretation of the law and their view of righteousness by works. He preached a righteousness that comes only through faith in Him and His work. In the verses that follow (5:18–37), He gave six examples of Pharisaical externalism.

Jot (v. 18). One word in Greek, *iōta*, which we use when we say, "It doesn't make one iota of difference." It is the nearest Greek equivalent to the Hebrew *yodh*, the smallest letter of the Hebrew alphabet (see Ps. 119:73 title). **Tittle.** The Greek word means "horn" and was used to designate the slight embellishment or extension of certain letters of the Hebrew alphabet (somewhat like the bottom of a *j*).

5:21. Ye have heard that it was said. The contrast that Jesus set up (here, 5:27, 31, 33, 38, 43) was not between the Old Testament and His teaching (He has just established the validity of the Old Testament law). Rather, it was between externalistic interpretation of the rabbinic tradition on the one hand and Jesus' correct interpretation of the law on the other. **Kill.** This word, used in Exodus 20:13, specifically means "murder."

5:22. Raca. This word may be related to the Aramaic word for "empty" and means "Empty-head!" For **council**, see discussion on Mark 14:55. **Hell.** The Greek word is *geenna*, which derives its name from a deep ravine south of Jerusalem, the "Valley of (the Sons of) Hinnom" (Hebrew, *ge hinnom*). During the reigns of the wicked Ahaz and Manasseh, human sacrifices to the Ammonite god Molech were offered there. Josiah desecrated the valley because of the pagan worship there (see 2 Kings 23:10; Jer. 7:31–32; 19:6). It became a sort of perpetually burning city dump and later became a figure for the place of final punishment.

5:23–26. Two illustrations of dealing with anger by means of reconciliation. **Farthing** (v. 26). The smallest Roman copper coin.

5:27–28. Looketh on a woman to lust after her (v. 28). Not a passing glance but a willful, calculated stare that arouses sexual desire. According to Jesus, this is a form of adultery even if it is only **in [one's] heart**. By extension, looking at any form of pornography violates this standard as well.

5:29–30. Here Jesus used hyperbole. He was not teaching self-mutilation, for even a blind man can lust. The point is that we should deal with sin as drastically as necessary. For **hell** (v. 30), see discussion on 5:22.

5:31–32. For **saving for the cause of fornication** (v. 32), see discussion on 19:3. Neither Mark 10:11–12 nor Luke 16:18 mentions this exception.

5:33–37. The Old Testament allowed oaths except those that profaned the name of God. Jesus would do away with all oaths, in favor of always speaking the truth.

5:38. For **an eye for an eye**, see *KJV Study Bible* notes on Exod. 21:23–25; Lev. 24:20.

5:39. Resist. Here it probably means in a court of law. **Smite.** The Greek verb used here means "slap with the back of the hand." It was more of an insult than an act of violence. The point is that it is better to be insulted, even twice, than to take the matter to court. This is an application of "Blessed are the meek" (5:5). One who responds with genuine meekness to an insult does so from the perspective that God is in control and will exact justice. This also is an application of "Blessed are the peacemakers" (5:9). Often one who insults another deliberately and repeatedly will give up if there is no response.

5:40. Coat. An undergarment. **Cloke.** A loose outer garment. Jesus wants His followers to be more eager to meet the needs of others than to hold on to worldly goods, which can be replaced. Believers should be to the world an example of sacrificial giving, of giving more than the minimum, and should give eagerly rather than grudgingly. Those who trust God to meet their needs can be eager and cheerful about meeting the needs of others.

5:41. Compel. The Greek verb comes from a Persian word meaning "press into service" and is used in 27:32, where the Roman soldiers pressed Simon into service to carry Jesus' cross. This is another application of the principle of eagerness to give, this time of one's time and energy rather than just material goods. Christians, of all people, should be the most accepting of interruptions in their plans, as another's need is an opportunity to minister and to show forth grace. The latter is why Jesus said, **go with him twain.** When Christians do more than is asked or compelled, they are an example of grace, of unmerited favor, in the way they relate to others. They are also an example of Paul's injunction that "each esteem other better than themselves" (Phil. 2:3).

5:42. This is probably not a general requirement to give to everyone who asks but rather a mandate to give to the poor (see Deut. 15:7–11; Ps. 112:5, 9).

5:43. Hate thine enemy. Words not found anywhere in the Old Testament. Hatred for one's enemies, however, was an accepted part of the Jewish ethic at that time (see *KJV Study Bible* note on Lev. 19:18).

5:44. Pray. Prayer is one of the practical ways love expresses itself (see Job 42:8–10). When we pray for our **enemies**, it forces us to focus on their benefit. The act becomes performative in our hearts in that as we seek the Lord for their good, our attitude toward them is transformed.

5:45. That ye may be the children of your Father which is in heaven. Loving one's enemy does not make one a son of the heavenly Father. It does make that relationship manifest in reality. **On the just and on the unjust.** God shows His love to people without distinction.

5:46–47. Publicans (v. 46). Or "tax collectors," local men employed to collect taxes for Roman tax contractors. Because they worked for Rome and often demanded unreasonable payments, the tax collectors gained a bad reputation and were generally hated and considered traitors.

5:48. Be ye therefore perfect. Christ set up the high ideal of perfect love (see 5:43–47). While we cannot fully attain this ideal in this life, it is, however, God's high standard for us.

6:1. Alms. Or "righteousness." This verse introduces the discussion of three acts of righteousness: (1) giving (6:2–4), (2) praying (6:5–15), and (3) fasting (6:16–18). **Reward of your Father.** Spiritual growth and maturity, or perhaps a heavenly reward of some kind. Jesus' point was that these good works are to be done out of faith in God and His goodness. If we seek earthly recognition or reward, it may be because we do not really have faith that God will reward us or that He really hears and sees what we do.

6:2–4. Sound a trumpet before thee (v. 2). Perhaps a reference to the noise that coins made as they were thrown into the temple treasury. Or the phrase may be used figuratively to mean "make a big show of it." **Hypocrites.** The Greek word means "playactor." Matthew used the word thirteen times (Mark, twice; Luke, three times). Here it refers to those who fake being pious. **They have their reward.** The honor they receive from people is all the reward they will get. **Let not thy left hand know what thy right hand doeth** (v. 3). Not to be taken literally but as a way of emphasizing that one should not call attention to one's giving. Self-glorification is always a present danger.

6:5–15. Closet (v. 6). The Greek word means "storeroom." Unlike most of the rooms in the house, it had a door that could be shut. **Use not vain repetitions, as the heathen do** (v. 7). Jesus was not necessarily condemning all long prayers but rather was condemning meaningless verbiage in prayer. God is not impressed when we ask for something in florid words, nor when we repeat ourselves over and over in the same prayer. He responds to faith, not performance. **Debts** (v. 12). Moral debts, that is, sins (see discussion on Luke 11:4).

6:16–18. For **fast** (v. 16), see discussions on Mark 2:18 and Luke 18:12. **Anoint thine head, and wash thy face** (v. 17). Jews put ashes on their heads when they fasted, but Jesus told them to maintain their regular appearance. Fasting should not be done in an ostentatious way. One should fast to seek God, not to be thought "spiritual" by others.

6:19–21. The dangers of riches are often mentioned in the New Testament (e.g., 6:24; 13:22;

19:22; Mark 10:17–30; Luke 12:16–21; 1 Tim. 6:9–10, 17–19; Heb. 13:5), but nowhere are riches condemned in and of themselves. What Jesus condemned here was greed and hoarding of money. There are more important things than wealth, and believers ought to seek spiritual treasures over worldly riches. Greed betrays a heart attitude that says this world's riches are of ultimate importance, and hoarding demonstrates a lack of faith that God will provide. None of this is to be taken to mean that Christians should not plan for retirement or save for "a rainy day." Believers are to be wise in financial affairs but focus their hearts' attention on the things of God and trust Him to take care of their needs, both for today and for the future.

Moth and rust (v. 19). Representative of all agents and processes that destroy worldly possessions. **Break through and steal.** Houses in the Holy Land had walls made of mud bricks and could be broken into easily.

Treasures in heaven (v. 20). Anything done in this life that has eternal value. The phrase is the equivalent of being "rich towards God" (Luke 12:21). In this context, it probably more specifically refers to using one's material wealth for good causes.

6:22–23. See discussions on Luke 11:33–36.

6:24–34. See discussion on Luke 12:27–28. **Lilies** (v. 28). Here represents flowers generally. **Cast into the oven** (v. 30). Grass was commonly used to heat the clay ovens of the Holy Land.

7:1–2. The Christian is not to judge hypocritically or self-righteously, as can be seen from the context (7:5). The same thought is expressed in 23:13–39 (see also Rom. 2:1). This is not meant to be a prohibition against discerning persons' characters and motives. The standard, however, is God and His Word, not ourselves, and we must not set ourselves up as the final arbiter but rather point to God's Word as the "judge" in every case. In fact, to obey Christ's commands in this chapter, we must first evaluate a person's character — whether he is a "dog" (see 7:6) or a false prophet (see 7:15), or whether his life shows fruit (see 7:16). Scripture repeatedly exhorts believers to evaluate carefully and choose between good and bad people and things (whether they are sexually immoral, 1 Cor. 5:9; "dogs," Phil. 3:2; "false prophets," 1 John 4:1; or masquerading as "an angel of light," 2 Cor. 11:14). The Christian is to "prove all things" (1 Thess. 5:21).

7:3–6. Mote ... beam (v. 3). An example of Jesus' use of hyperbole in His teachings (see 19:24, where Jesus spoke of a camel going through the eye of a needle). Its purpose is to drive home a point. Everyone has known people who talk about the sins of others, when bigger sins, often of similar kind, may be found in their own lives. Jesus here warned His followers to be aware of this possibility and to examine themselves first. A believer's words will have more credibility when he has first dealt with the issue in his own life and can share out of his own struggles. Then he can **see clearly** (v. 5) in ways that one who is still in the sin cannot. **Dogs** (v. 6). The unclean dogs of the street were held in low esteem. Teaching should be given in accordance with the spiritual capacity of the learners.

7:7–12. Asketh ... seeketh ... knocketh (v. 8). Greek present imperatives are used here, indicating constant asking, seeking, and knocking. Persistent prayer is being emphasized.

Whatsoever ye would that men should do to you, do ye even so to them (v. 12). The so-called Golden Rule is found in negative form in rabbinic Judaism and also in Hinduism, Buddhism, and Confucianism. It occurred in various forms in Greek and Roman ethical teaching. Jesus stated it in positive form. It summarizes the sermon's theme of loving others in every possible way (see 5:7, 9, 23–24, 40–48), in faith that God will take care of our own needs if we trust Him. A believer can consider others' needs and preferences as much as she would want her own considered because she has confidence that God is considering her as much or more than she is considering others. For **the law and the prophets**, see discussion on 5:17.

7:13–14. The strait gate (v. 13). The gate that leads into the kingdom of heaven. It is synonymous with **life** (v. 14). **Destruction** (v. 13). Separation from God in hell. Jesus left no room here for any

such foolishness as the ideas that all religions lead to heaven or that one need only be sincere to enter the kingdom. God has made the way **narrow** (v. 14). Only Christ can save. There is no other way, and believers are not necessarily arrogant when they bear witness to that fact.

7:15. False prophets. People who have not been sent by God but claim that they have been (see 24:24; Jer. 23:16–22 and discussions). This verse is an apt warning in light of 7:13–14. Believers are to beware of anyone who preaches another gospel or who offers salvation by any means other than by grace through faith in Jesus Christ (see Gal. 1:8–9).

7:16–20. Here the Lord used an analogy. A tree is known by its fruit, by what it produces. Likewise, whether a prophet is true or false can be known by the results he produces. As men do not gather fruit from trees that produce **thorns, or ... thistles** (v. 16), so also we should not seek truth from those who preach false doctrine. This passage also emphasizes that God's main concern is with truth. False doctrine very often comes couched in attractive packages. Even Satan quoted the Bible when he sought to lead Christ away from His mission (see 4:3–11). Today, false teaching may come with glitzy packaging or point to numbers and dollars as an indicator of "God's blessing." Here Jesus reminded believers not to be fooled by externals. The same Lord who prayed that His followers "might be sanctified through the truth" (John 17:19) here warned His followers to discern whether a teaching is true or false, by examining the fruit it produces.

7:21–27. This is the invitation section of the Sermon on the Mount. Jesus invited His hearers to apply to their lives the truths He had taught.

7:21–23. Lord (v. 21). A title that sometimes means only "sir" or "master." Here, however, it seems to mean more than that, since Jesus is the one who makes the final decision about a person's eternal destiny. For **the kingdom of heaven**, see discussion on 3:2.

That day (v. 22). The day of judgment (see Mal. 3:17–18). **Prophesied**. In the New Testament, this verb primarily means to give a message from God, not necessarily to predict. **Devils.** Or "demons" (see discussion on Mark 1:23).

I never knew you (v. 23). Jesus made it clear that the issue was not what they had done but whom they knew. The one who does not know Christ, or whom Christ does not know, has no hope regardless of good works, even good works done in His name. Conversely, the implication is that the one who does know Christ, or whom Christ knows, has assurance of salvation apart from works. Jesus said that the one **that doeth the will of my Father** (v. 21) will enter the kingdom of heaven, but this is not a commendation of works salvation. The whole thrust of the Sermon on the Mount is that believers should put their faith in God. It is faith, not works, that saves. Faith, then, is "the will" of God the Father.

7:24 – 27. Jesus again used analogy to make a teaching vivid. Some who hear His words will act on them — that is, live a life of faith in God and His goodness and care, which will show forth in their attitudes and actions — and some will not. Those who act on Christ's words are like the **wise man, which built his house upon a rock** (v. 24), and those who do not act on His words are like the **foolish man, which built his house upon the sand** (v. 26). The "rock" here is God's Word, what Jesus revealed in this sermon. He who builds on that foundation will withstand the storms. It is not pushing the analogy too far to see these storms as the trials that life sends, the temptations to sin and to trust in men rather than in God. The one who builds on a foundation of "sand" will face the same trials but will not be able to stand up against them.

7:28 – 29. The people were astonished (v. 28). The reaction of the people came because they had never heard teaching that was so direct. They were used to teaching that quoted different rabbis and often seemed to "referee" between them. Jesus' teaching went straight to the Scripture and was given with divine **authority** (v. 29; see discussion on 2:4).

C. A Collection of Miracles (chaps. 8 – 9)

8:1 – 2. Leper (v. 2). The Greek word was used for various diseases affecting the skin, not necessar-ily leprosy (see Leviticus 13 – 14 and *KJV Study Bible* note on Lev. 13:2). For **Lord**, see discussion on 7:21. **Make me clean.** Leprosy made a person ceremonially unclean as well as physically afflicted (see discussion on Luke 5:12 – 16).

8:3 – 4. Tell no man (v. 4; see 9:30; 12:16; Mark 1:44; 5:43; 7:36; Luke 8:56). Perhaps for several reasons: (1) Jesus did not want to be considered just a miracle worker, (2) He did not want His teaching ministry hindered by too much publicity being given to His healing miracles, and (3) He did not want His death to come prematurely, that is, before He had finished His ministry. For **shew thyself to the priest**, see discussion on Luke 5:14. **Them.** Refers to the priests.

8:5 – 13. Although the incident in John 4:43 – 54 is similar, it probably is a separate episode in the life of Jesus.

8:5 – 8. For **Capernaum** (v. 5), see discussion on 4:13. **Centurion.** A Roman military officer in charge of a hundred soldiers. In Luke's account (Luke 7:1 – 5), Jewish elders and friends of the centurion came to Jesus on his behalf, but Matthew did not mention these intermediaries. He may have had in mind his intention to show the universality of the gospel to his Jewish readers. Since the centurion's faith is in view here, and since he caused the meeting between his friends and Jesus, it is proper to say that the centurion came to Him. A parallel situation is the flogging of Jesus by Pilate. Pilate himself obviously did not carry out the act but ordered the Roman soldiers under him; "he had Jesus scourged" (27:26; lit., "he flogged Jesus").

I am not worthy that thou shouldest come under my roof (v. 8). In Greek, the words "I am not worthy" are the same as those used by John the Baptist in 3:11 ("I am not worthy"). The entire statement reveals how highly the centurion regarded Jesus. Or perhaps his response reflects his sense of moral guilt in the presence of Jesus. Clearly, Jesus had become known to this man as someone who lived an exemplary life, in line with the principles He set forth in the Sermon on the Mount (chaps. 5 – 7). Apparently, the purity of Jesus' life was well known from early on, which may help explain why no one was able to bring charges of any substance against Him at His trial (see Mark 14:55–59).

8:11–12. The universality of the gospel is one of Matthew's themes (see Introduction: "Recipients"). In these verses, Jesus was saying that many will be in the kingdom who are not of Israel, while many others will be left out who thought they were in. **Many shall … sit down … in the kingdom of heaven** (v. 11). This may be a reference to the eschatological messianic banquet, which symbolizes the blessings of an intimate relationship with God (see Isa. 25:6–9). **The children of the kingdom** (v. 12). Jews who thought their Judaism was an inherited passport for entrance into the kingdom (see 3:9–10 and discussion on 3:9). **Outer darkness** is a reference to judgment. **Weeping and gnashing of teeth** indicates that the "outer darkness" will be a place of conscious sorrow, not a matter of annihilation for those who are condemned.

8:13. In this instance, Jesus healed without going into the presence of the one who was sick. Jesus healed by the power of God. He did not need spells or incantations or potions. He responded to the centurion's faith, **and his servant was healed.** So also one need only trust Him for salvation and for daily needs. Believers are in His care, and His power sustains them and fulfills His promises to them.

8:14–17. This act of healing took place, not in public, but in the intimacy of the home of a disciple. It was followed by a public service in the evening, during which many more people were healed and evil spirits were cast out. Perhaps the leper Jesus had healed earlier (see 8:1–4) had not followed His injunction not to tell anyone. Clearly, Jesus had by this time developed a reputation as one who could heal, and many of the sick were coming to Him.

His wife's mother (v. 14). Peter was married (see 1 Cor. 9:5; Mark 1:30; Luke 4:38). **Bare our sicknesses** (v. 17). The quote is from Isaiah 53:4.

8:18–22. The other side (v. 18). The east side. The Sea of Galilee is about twelve miles long and eight miles wide. Two men came to Jesus, wanting to follow Him, but were turned away. The first, a **scribe**

(v. 19; see discussion on 2:4), was unwilling to make the necessary sacrifices and risks involved in a life of faith. The second man placed family obligations ahead of discipleship. The parallel account in Luke 9:57–62 states that a third would-be disciple also approached Jesus. For reasons unknown, Matthew chose to describe only two men. For **the Son of man** (v. 20), see discussion on Mark 2:10.

Let the dead bury their dead (v. 22). Let the spiritually dead bury the physically dead. The time of Jesus' ministry was short and demanded full attention and commitment. This statement stresses the radical demands of Jesus' discipleship, since Jews placed great importance on the duty of children to bury their parents. In no way does Jesus place low priority on the family, and no one should treat their family shabbily. A Christian life involves new priorities, however, and those who would live a life of faith must put Jesus first in all things and let Him work out every other circumstance of life.

8:23–9:38. This section shows different reactions to Jesus. First there are reactions that sprang from a lack of faith. The disciples panicked in the storm on the lake and marveled that nature obeys Christ (8:23–27). The Gerasenes, rather than marveling that God was in their midst, demonstrated by His power over the demons, invited Him to leave (8:28–34). Then the scribes who witnessed a demonstration of His deity, accused Him of blasphemy rather than believing His claim to be God (9:1–8). The Pharisees' expectations were overturned when Jesus dined with sinners (9:9–13). Next there are a series of healings in response to the faith of the persons involved (9:18–31). The contrast between the lack of faith or refusal to believe on the part of so many and the eager, expectant faith of a few is hard to miss. In addition, Jesus overturned the expectations of the established rulers by His behavior and claims. It is not the job of the Lord, or of His church, to maintain the status quo or to confirm people in their current situations. Rather, it is to meet human needs in the context of calling people to repentance and faith and to a lifestyle that is consistent with the revealed will of God. This long section is well seen in light of that mission. The different reactions to Jesus ranged from outright rejection, surprise, accusations, all the way to overcoming faith. These reactions to the gospel are typical of those one may expect in any age.

8:23–27. For **great tempest** (v. 24), see discussion on Mark 4:37. **But he was asleep.** This is a picture of exhaustion. If the events immediately preceding this section were typical of Jesus' ministry, well might He have been tired. It causes one to note the humanity of the Lord. Being fully man, He was capable of tiredness and other weaknesses of the body, such as hunger (see Matt 4:2) and thirst (see John 19:28), yet being fully God, He was able to command the forces of nature. **Even the winds and the sea obey him** (v. 27; see discussion on Mark 4:38). Early in His ministry, Jesus revealed His true identity to the disciples little by little. They had seen Him heal people as He commanded sickness to leave, and they had seen Him cast out demons (see 8:6). Now they saw great forces of nature obey His word. God is the Creator, and He is in command of His creation. These incidents reveal the deity of Christ, but the disciples at this point could still **marvelled [at] What manner of man** He was.

8:28. The country of the Gergesenes. The region around the city of Gergesa, in the hills to the east of the Sea of Galilee. Mark and Luke identify the region by the city of Gadara, located about six miles southeast of the sea. **Two possessed with devils.** Mark and Luke mention only one Gadarene/Gergesene demoniac (see Mark 5:2; Luke 8:27 and discussion).

8:29. The time. The time of their judgment. The demons were fearful of being sent into eternal punishment, that is, "into the deep" (see discussions on Mark 5:10; Luke 8:31).

8:30. A herd of many swine. Large numbers of Gentiles lived in Galilee. Normally, Jews did not raise pigs, since they were considered the most "unclean" of all animals.

8:31–32. Though Jesus seemingly consented to the demons' request, the pigs carried the demons into the depths of the sea—perhaps symbolic of the Abyss (see Luke 8:31 and discussion). The biblical accounts here and in Mark and Luke make it clear that Jesus was encountering a supernatural spiritual reality. This was not merely a man with emotional problems, whom Jesus healed while accommodating the superstitions of the people. Nor was this a case of the man's screams scaring the pigs. They had heard him, no doubt, for many days. The demonic spirits were quite real. Too often Christians today explain away matters in the Bible that challenge modern secularistic assumptions. The call from God is to "repent and believe," not "ignore and explain away."

8:33–34. They besought him that he would depart (v. 34). The townspeople may have been more concerned about their financial loss than about the deliverance of the miserable demon-possessed man. Certainly, they valued their peace and prosperity over the meeting of real human needs. Jesus has a way of upsetting expectations, of opening unexpected doors, and of challenging people beyond their comfort zones. As long as He remains the meek and mild moral philosopher whom all can admire, He is welcomed. When the Lord gets down to the serious business of changing lives and overturning expectations, He is too often shunned and pushed away. So it was here.

9:1. Passed over. The northern end of the Sea of Galilee. **His own city.** Capernaum (see discussion on 4:13).

9:2. Their faith. The faith of the men who carried him as well as the faith of the paralytic. Jesus focused first on the man's deepest need: forgiveness of sins. He also had in mind the lesson for His disciples and for the Pharisees who were present. By forgiving the man's sins, Jesus implicitly claimed to be God. It is often His implicit claims, the ones in which He assumes He is God and acts on that assumption, that are the most startling. In other places, He made explicit claims, such as, "I and my Father are one" (John 10:30). However, these implicit claims, coming as they did in the course of ministry and as teaching opportunities, are also worthy of study. Here the implication to deity lies in the fact that He did what only God can do: forgive sins. Once again Jesus upset the expectations of the religious establishment, in the course of meeting someone's need. The reaction, which Jesus surely expected, was swift in coming.

9:3. The Pharisees who were present recognized Jesus' implicit claim at once. They might have acknowledged that here indeed was "God with us," but instead they rejected His claim and accused Him "in [their] hearts" (v. 4). Here the term **blasphemeth** includes usurping God's prerogative to forgive sins (see discussion on Mark 2:7). The Pharisees' charge again stemmed from Jesus' implicit claim to be God. The Pharisees assumed that Jesus was only a man, and a man's claims to be God diminish God, making Him out to be something less than He is.

9:4–8. Jesus had read their thoughts, and He replied. Of course it is **easier, to say** (v. 5) that someone's sins are forgiven than it is to heal someone, and Jesus acknowledged this (see *KJV Study Bible* notes on Mark 2:9–10; 14:64). Jesus healed the paralytic to prove that He could also do the harder work, forgiving sins. Through His power to heal, He showed that He has also the power to forgive sins. Once again, Jesus met a physical need, but as always, His focus remained on the deeper spiritual need. The man's healing demonstrated that his spiritual need had been met, and even more important for the Lord's teaching and revealing purpose, it demonstrated that Jesus is God and has the authority that God alone has. For **the Son of man** (v. 6), see discussion on Mark 2:10.

9:9–13. Here is an instance of Jesus acting in a way that overturned the expectations of social respectability. He ate with those whom most people avoided. This passage challenges one to take the gospel to those who are not respectable. Some people do this more easily than others. It is often society's outcasts who are the most eager for grace, for a second chance. Those who have known rejection and scorn respond most joyfully to acceptance and love. They are more likely than others to see their need and the value of being accepted unconditionally in the love of God.

9:9. One would do well to study all of the times Jesus said **Follow me** in the Gospels (here; 4:19; 9:9; 16:24; 19:21; the parallels in the other gospels and

additional occurrences recorded in them). **Matthew.** This disciple is called Levi in the parallel accounts in Mark and Luke (but see also Mark 3:18; Luke 6:15; Acts 1:13). For **the receipt of custom**, see discussion on Mark 2:14. For **he arose, and followed him**, see discussion on Luke 5:28.

9:10–12. For **publicans** (v. 10), see discussions on 5:46 and Mark 2:16. For **sinners**, see discussion on Mark 2:15. For **Pharisees** (v. 11), see discussion on Mark 2:16. Jesus was not saying here that the Pharisees were spiritually healthy; far from it. They, however, did not see their need.

9:13. I am not come to call the righteous, but sinners to repentance. Jesus knew the Pharisees had a false righteousness, and it would not be wrong to see a touch of irony in His words here. In addition, Jesus knew that it is difficult to call to repentance those who see themselves as having no need of it (see discussion on Mark 2:17). One cannot preach repentance to those who do not see themselves as sinners. The Pharisees would have to wait for another time to be called to repentance.

9:14–17. For **the disciples of John** (v. 14), see discussions on Mark 2:18 and Luke 5:33. For **fast**, see discussions on Mark 2:18 and Luke 5:33. For **the bridegroom** (v. 15), see discussions on Mark 2:19–20.

New bottles (v. 17). Or "new wineskins." In ancient times, goatskins were used to hold wine. As the fresh grape juice fermented, the wine would expand, and the new wineskin would stretch. A used skin, already stretched, would break. Jesus brings a newness that cannot be confined within the old forms. New ways of understanding the Messiah's role and the power and purposes of God are required. It is well to note, however, that Jesus did not preach new doctrines or the abandonment of God's moral teachings. Jesus left no room for such an option. He had already said that the Law will not pass away and that He had not come to destroy it (see 5:17–18). Jesus' statements about **new wine** and "new wineskins" have to do with fulfilling truth, not replacing it, and with deepening people's understanding of God's plan, not changing it utterly.

9:18. A certain ruler. From Mark and Luke, we know that the official was Jairus (see *KJV Study Bible* note on Mark 5:22). The amazing thing here is that the man expressed full confidence that Jesus could raise his daughter to life. That confidence was well placed, a contrast with the disciples' amazement that the forces of nature obey Jesus (see 8:27).

9:20–22. An issue of blood twelve years (v. 20; see *KJV Study Bible* notes on Lev. 15:25; Mark 5:25, 28). This woman demonstrated great faith and great humility. Unlike Jairus, she could not approach boldly, but she did approach. This account, embedded in the account of the healing of Jairus's daughter, demonstrates the extent to which faith alone is all one needs to approach the Lord. Whether bold faith or timid faith, it is sufficient. The Lord responds to faith, not to public demonstrations of righteousness. Both Jairus and this woman would have their needs met, for both demonstrated faith in the Lord Jesus Christ, though in very different ways.

For **Daughter** (v. 22), see discussion on Luke 8:48. **Made thee whole** (see discussion on Mark 5:34). Her faith, born of desperation, was honored by the Lord. While she sought anonymity, the Lord called her out of the crowd, not to embarrass her, but to commend her faith. It is never the intention of God to minister impersonally. His power is not like the power of an electrical battery or the force of gravity. It is the outworking of His personal intention to do good and meet needs. Rather than let her be healed with no personal attention, Jesus offered her a word of comfort and encouragement, along with physical healing. He also desired that her healing would be a testimony, that all would know that it had come by God's power and was no accident.

9:23–26. Minstrels (v. 23). Musicians hired to play in mourning ceremonies. **People making a noise**. Mourners hired to wail and lament. For **not dead, but sleepeth** (v. 24), see discussion on Luke 8:52.

The people were put forth (v. 25). Jesus had often healed in public places, along roadsides and in the midst of crowds. Here He had the people put out of the room, possibly so that the child would not wake up in a room full of official mourners, which might have been traumatic. Once again this is a demonstration of the Lord's sensitivity to people's needs and His pastoral concern for them.

9:27. Blind men. Isaiah prophesied the healing of the blind in the messianic age (see Isa. 35:5). **Son of David**. A popular Jewish title for the coming Messiah (see, e.g., 12:23; 20:30; 21:9; 22:41–45; see also discussion on 1:1). Again people are expressing their faith in Jesus. These men recognized who Jesus was, based on what He had just done for the woman with an issue of blood and for Jairus's daughter (8:18–26).

9:28. When he was come into the house. Why, in this instance, Jesus waited until they were in the house is unknown. He questioned whether the men's faith was genuine, and it may be that He wanted them to examine their faith before He healed them. Often the Lord will delay His answer to prayers so that one's faith may be tested and strengthened.

9:29. Jesus rewarded the men's faith by healing them. They had faith that He would heal them, and He did so **According to [their] faith**, that is, in line with their faith and what they sought. Their faith was rewarded specifically, as they had come to Him with a specific need and request. The Lord will bless according to one's faith, that is, in line with what one believes and as specifically as one believes. Christians should learn to ask God for specific things, not for "blessings" in general. He will reward "according to" the faith that one brings Him.

9:30–31. Here again Jesus charged the men not to tell anyone, but they disobeyed and **spread abroad** (v. 31) the news of their healing (see discussions on 8:4 and 16:20).

9:32. Dumb man. Isaiah prophesied that the mute would talk in the messianic age (see Isa. 35:6).

9:33–34. In this case, the man's infirmity was caused not by a physical problem but by an evil spirit that specialized in making people unable to speak. When Jesus had **cast out** (v. 33) this spirit, **the dumb spake**.

While **the multitudes marvelled** (v. 33), the Pharisees charged that Jesus' power over demons came from **the prince of the devils** (see discussion on 10:25). Here is the beginnings of tension between the public acceptance of Jesus and the official rejection of His ministry. While this tension is implied earlier in Matthew's gospel, here the multitude's reaction is directly contrasted with the Pharisees' "official" rejection. Later on, the Pharisees would be delayed in their plans to arrest Him because "they feared the multitude" (21:46; see Mark 12:12, Luke 20:19).

9:35. For **synagogues**, see discussion on Mark 1:21. For **the gospel**, see discussion on Mark 1:1.

9:36–38. When he saw the multitudes (v. 36), Jesus felt **compassion** for those seeking help and direction in life. As "the good shepherd" (John 10:11), He cared for the **sheep** and wanted to bring them under His care and protection. Even here, His focus was on the condition of their souls. In verses 37–38, Jesus used an agricultural metaphor to make the point that evangelism is a priority. Here the people are the grain or the fruit ready to be taken in, and the need for laborers to work the harvest is great. He had promised His disciples earlier that they would be "fishers of men" (4:19), and His heartbeat for evangelism remained undiminished. The need was not physical care, but spiritual care. Compassion led Jesus to evangelism and to His prayer for more evangelists.

D. The Commissioning of the Twelve Apostles (chap. 10)

10:1–42. In this chapter, Jesus sent the Twelve out on their first preaching mission. Before doing so, He instructed them on some practical matters related to ministry. Some of the instructions related to the apostles' immediate mission, but others were clearly intended for their extended ministry after His death and resurrection. All of His instructions should be seen in light of the call to live a life of faith and to trust God in all circumstances.

The heart of the chapter (v. 16–23) is a discussion of the opposition that the disciples would face from three sources: difficult people they might witness to (vv. 14–16), official governmental sources (vv. 17–20), and family members (v. 21). Jesus'

admonitions, while different for each of the three situations, were in line with His exhortations to live by faith, in obedience to His teachings, putting Him first always.

10:1. In preparation for their preaching mission, the Lord gave His apostles certain powers that, up to this point, He had been exercising. They had seen Him preach, teach, heal, and cast out unclean spirits. They had gained a clear idea of how these things fit into the overall ministry. Jesus never did anything as a stunt, nor to draw a crowd. He always sought to respond to people's faith, meet their needs, and point them to repentance and righteousness through faith. His disciples, now aware of His priorities, were ready to minister in His name. In ministry, one must do God's work, in God's way, with His priorities in mind, or it is not legitimate ministry. As with the disciples, believers' preparation for ministry comes from getting to know God and His Word, until they have His priorities and heartbeat within themselves.

10:2–4. See discussions on Luke 6:14–16. **Apostles** (v. 2). This is the only occurrence of this word in Matthew's gospel. The word is in fact rare in the Gospels and more common in the Epistles. Its basic meaning is "one who is sent" as a representative or ambassador. It can denote a messenger or a missionary of the church (as in 2 Cor. 8:23) but is usually used as a title for the Twelve and for Paul (see discussion on Mark 6:30).

10:5–7. Go not (v. 5). The good news about the kingdom was first to be proclaimed to Jews only. After His death and resurrection, Jesus commanded that the message be taken to all nations (see 28:19; 21:43). Also, the apostles may yet have lacked the maturity, and certainly the experience, to minister effectively in different cultures. It may have been best to start them out "close to home" in a sense, until they had built up confidence and had learned a few things that come only with direct experience. **Samaritans.** A mixed-blood race resulting from the intermarriage of Israelites left behind when the people of the northern kingdom were exiled and Gentiles brought into the land by the Assyrians (see 2 Kings 17:24). Bitter hostility existed between Jews and Samaritans in Jesus' day (see John 4:9). For **The kingdom of heaven** (v. 7), see discussion on 3:2.

10:8–13. Lepers (v. 8). The Greek word for "leprosy" was used for various diseases affecting the skin, not necessarily leprosy (see *KJV Study Bible* note on Lev. 13:2). The last half of verse 8 belongs with verses 9 and 10. The gospel is given freely, and the disciples had received their calling freely from the Lord. If they had charged a fee, it would have detracted from their message. They were to take no provisions, trusting God to supply for them. This way their faith in God would be evident. They were working for the Lord, and **the workman is worthy of his meat** (v. 10). The Lord pays for what He orders and would supply their needs. God's people are often eager to give when they see a godly minister doing God's work in God's way. Jesus challenged the apostles to live such a life and see God work (see discussions on Mark 6:8–9). They were to trust God for a **worthy** (v. 11) person who would give them lodging and food. **Salute it** (v. 12). The Jews' greeting then, even as now, was *shalom*, meaning "peace."

10:14–16. Here is Jesus' first advice on how to handle opposition. The first type of opposition He addressed was opposition from difficult people. **Shake off the dust of your feet.** A symbolic act that the Pharisees practiced when they left an "unclean" Gentile area. Here it represented an act of solemn warning to those who rejected God's message (see discussions on Luke 9:5; Acts 13:51; see also Acts 18:6).

10:15. Those who rejected the preaching of the gospel would fare worse than **Sodom and Gomorrha** (see Gen. 19:23–29). This is quite a warning. Truly, when people are given additional light, refusing it brings additional judgment. This is a warning to all who have heard the gospel of God's grace and refused it.

10:16. As sheep in the midst of wolves. It is interesting that Jesus used this analogy in the context of their doing ministry in Israel. The spiritual condition of the nation must have been poor, even after the revival under John the Baptist's preaching.

Jesus used another unusual analogy: **be…wise as serpents.** The comparison to serpents may seem odd at first, as serpents are usually associated with evil. The context, however, governs the comparison here. Consider that a serpent will slither away to avoid conflict if at all possible. Rarely does a snake bite unless it is cornered. Jesus was telling them to avoid conflict, to depart as a serpent would to avoid conflict, and to be **harmless as doves.** Jesus was encouraging an attitude that would result in their being wise for their own protection, without being combative. This fits with His teaching to turn the other cheek (5:39) and is in the same context as the admonition to let their peace return to them if they were rejected (10:13). In other words, they were not to force the message on anyone, and if they met with active and possibly violent rejection, they were to move on rather than start an argument or a fight.

10:17–20. The second type of opposition the Lord addressed was that from official governmental sources. Here the context broadens. It is unlikely that the apostles faced much of this type of opposition on their first preaching tour, but later as opposition arose, especially after Christ's resurrection and ascension, this increasingly became the situation the apostles faced. Jesus told them to beware of officials who might cause them trouble. **Councils** (v. 17). The lower courts, connected with local synagogues, that tried less serious cases and flogged those found guilty. For **synagogues**, see discussions on Mark 1:21 and Luke 21:12.

Ye shall be brought before governors and kings (v. 18). It was unlikely that this would happen on the disciples' first preaching tour, but Jesus took advantage of a teachable moment to warn them of future persecution and what to expect and what to do.

Take no thought how or what ye shall speak (v. 19; see Luke 21:14–15). This is not to be used by preachers as an excuse for lack of sermon preparation. The context is that of a courtroom situation, in which the disciples might be tried for the preaching of the gospel, not a church service. One cannot change the context without violating the intent of the Scriptures. In a courtroom setting, where the Christian is not in charge and may not know what questions will be asked, a special level of dependence on the Spirit is necessary, and here Jesus promised that such faith will not go unrewarded. An example of this in action might be Acts 6:8–7:60. When Stephen was arrested and asked to testify, he delivered a brilliant sermon apparently spontaneously, as the Spirit led him.

10:21. The third type of opposition Jesus addressed was opposition from family members. The governing context here is not limited to this particular preaching mission; Jesus was speaking of the apostles' ministry in general. The apostles were being sent out "as sheep in the midst of wolves" (10:16) and could expect persecution of all three types in the course of their ministry.

10:22. For **he that endureth to the end shall be saved**, see *KJV Study Bible* note on Mark 13:13.

10:23. This is a more direct statement of the admonition to "be … wise as serpents" (10:16), that is, to flee from places where they were rejected. Here Jesus explicitly told them to go to **another** city in such cases. Jesus' statement about all **the cities of Israel** is best seen, in light of the wider context of His remarks here, as a promise that there will always be places to minister. The gospel being rejected in one place does not mean there is nowhere to keep on preaching. One should just move on and find another place.

10:24–25. Jesus, again thinking in terms of their total ministry, reminded the apostles that the servant is no greater than the master. If the **master** (v. 24) suffers something, **the servant** can expect no less. These words would have more meaning for the Twelve after the crucifixion of Christ, when they would face persecution, which happened rather quickly in Jerusalem (see Acts 4:1–22; 5:17–41). **Beelzebub** (v. 25). Satan, the ruler of demons (see 12:24). The Hebrew epithet Baal-Zebub ("lord of flies") is a parody on and mockery of the Hebrew name Baal-Zebul ("Exalted Baal" or "Prince Baal"; see discussion on Judg. 10:6).

10:26–33. Here Jesus offered the apostles words of comfort. They were not to fear what anyone might do to their bodies but were to speak boldly what He had taught them. In other words, they should withdraw in situations where oppositions arose, but not

out of fear. Rather than engaging in useless fights, they were to move on quickly to more fertile ground. They were not to be fearful, however, for men can **kill the body, but are not able to kill the soul** (v. 28), the true self. Body and soul are closely related in this life but are separated at death and then reunited at the resurrection (see 2 Cor. 5:1–10; Phil. 1:23–24). **Fear him**. God. He alone determines the final destiny of us all. For **hell**, see discussion on 5:22.

10:34–37. Jesus again addressed opposition from family members. Sometimes this is more difficult for believers than official persecution. **I came not to send peace, but a sword** (v. 34). At first glance, this saying seems like a contradiction of Isaiah 9:6 ("Prince of Peace"), Luke 2:14 ("on earth peace among men"), and John 14:27 ("Peace I leave with you"). It is true that Christ came to bring peace — peace between the believer and God, and peace among men. Yet the inevitable result of Christ's coming is conflict — between Christ and the Antichrist, between light and darkness, between God's children and the Devil's children. This conflict can occur even between members of the same family (vv. 35–36). Believers must always be aware that their highest loyalty is to Jesus Christ. They cannot allow opposition from family to turn them away from their task any more than they allow official opposition to do so.

10:38. His cross. The first mention of the cross in Matthew's gospel. The cross was an instrument of death and here symbolizes the necessity of total commitment, even unto death, on the part of Jesus' disciples (see discussion on Mark 8:34).

10:39. Jesus made this statement in the context of sacrificing all for Him. Many people try to "find their lives" by seeking what will make them happy or fulfilled in this world. Jesus turned this upside down. The life that does not focus on the self is the most satisfying. It is in a life of service that one finds the greatest happiness, and thus **findeth his life**. The highest and greatest service is that rendered to Christ, and therefore the way to find one's life is to **lose it** in service to Him. Jesus was telling the apostles that the loss of their "life" in terms of reputation, relationships, personal freedom, and even physical well-being, was worth it, for no believer ever truly regrets the time, energy, and sacrifice expended for the glory of the Lord.

10:40–42. During times of persecution, hospitality is especially important, and providing help to God's people during such times can be dangerous. Jesus indicated that those who provide it and show kindness to God's people will receive a reward.

E. Ministry throughout Galilee (chaps. 11–12)

11:1. While the twelve apostles were carrying out their first mission, Jesus continued His ministry in Galilee. This verse actually ends the material in chapter 10. Often the chapter divisions in the Bible do not follow the real divisions in the narrative. Verse 1 ends the account of Jesus sending out the Twelve. Verse 2 begins a new narrative.

11:2–3. John had heard ... [of] the works of Christ (v. 2), the works of teaching and healing recounted in the previous chapters. John apparently had some doubts, even though he had heard of what Christ was doing. One would think that the works would have confirmed John's knowledge of who Jesus was, something John had borne witness to at Jesus' baptism (see John 1:29). Perhaps these doubts arose because Jesus had not freed him from prison (see Gundry, *Matthew*, p. 182). So often one sees God's works only in terms of personal need or advantage. John was in prison, and the one miracle Jesus had not worked, was freeing him. God has His own plans and purposes, and rescuing one believer may or may not fit that plan. He may have a higher purpose that one does not see. **He that should come** (v. 3). The Messiah. For **look for another**, see discussion on Luke 7:19–20.

11:4–5. Shew John again those things (v. 4). Jesus' reference to the **blind ... lame ... lepers** (v. 5; see discussion on 8:2) are allusions to the signs that Isaiah said would point to the Messiah (see Isa. 29:18–21; 35:5–6; 61:1). Jesus was reminding John that He was indeed the Messiah because He was doing what Isaiah prophesied the Messiah would do. John was encouraged to believe because of this. Christians' task today is to continue to believe, for

He is still at work in the world. One need only to see again the things that He is doing and rejoice in them. **The poor have the gospel preached to them** (see discussion on Luke 7:22). Jesus' ministry to the poor was also evidence of His divine mission. He was concerned about those most in need of God's grace.

11:6. Whosoever shall not be offended (see discussion on Luke 7:23). This may have been directed at John himself. God had left John in prison, while Jesus' ministry increased. Jesus may have been implying that the success of another's ministry should not cause John to be jealous. Nor should John claim any special point of privilege with Jesus; that is, he should not be offended if Jesus' ministry did not include rescuing him. It may also be a more general statement. All who rejoice in what Christ is doing shall be blessed, but those who reject Him and are offended by His offer of salvation (and they are many, even to this day) shall miss the blessing.

11:7–30. Jesus preached this sermon in several cities right after the encounter with two of John's disciples. Jesus introduced the ministry of John the Baptist and reminded the hearers that they had all gone out to hear him (vv. 7–15). He then stated the point of the message, that just hearing the Word preached is not enough (vv. 16–19). The hearer must do something with what he has heard. The tone is one of anger with people who heard the message but only criticized or ignored it. Reinforcing the main point, Jesus called for judgment upon the cities that had heard the Word preached and had not repented (vv. 21–24). He concluded with a public prayer and an invitation (vv. 25–30). Overall, this sermon is reminiscent of the prophetic messages in the Old Testament, where the prophet called down woe and judgment on the people for their sins but ended with a promise of restoration and grace (see, e.g., Isaiah, Ezekiel, Amos, Obadiah).

11:7–10. This passage introduces the sermon. The formula **What went ye out into the wilderness to see?** (vv. 7–9) is repeated three times. Each time Jesus answered His own question, each time more specifically and pointedly, thereby building his hearers' interest in the message. One imagines His voice rising each time He repeated the question and His hearers leaning forward with just a little more expectation. His first response to the question was, **A reed shaken with the wind?** (v. 7), but of course the people would not go into the wilderness for that, as it would hardly be worth the trip. His second response was, **A man clothed in soft raiment?** (v. 8). Everyone knew, as Jesus pointed out, that such people are found not in wilderness areas but in palaces. In His third response, Jesus got to the real answer: **A prophet? yea ... and more than a prophet** (v. 9). The people had gone out to hear John the Baptist preach, for there had not been a prophet in Israel for many years. In this sermon, Jesus would upbraid the people for not repenting upon hearing the preaching of John (and later of Jesus), and here He set the stage. They had gone out to hear a prophet but had not done what the prophet said to do. Jesus explained what He meant when He called John "more than a prophet." John was the **messenger** (v. 10) sent to **prepare** (the) **way** for the Messiah. The people had not repented upon hearing John's preaching and were not ready for the preaching of Jesus. He could offer them the kingdom, but it would fall on deaf ears, dulled by the effects of sin and by the effect of rejecting the message.

11:11. He that is least in the kingdom ... is greater than he (John the Baptist). Given John's influence and notoriety, Jesus' statement must have seemed surprising. After all, John was a noted prophet who had influenced thousands. The key to the meaning of this is found in 18:4: "Whosoever ... shall humble himself as this little child." Such a person, though "least," is regarded by God as even greater than John the Baptist. This should also be seen in light of Jesus' statement that "he that is greatest among you shall be your servant" (23:11).

11:12. Suffereth violence. The Greek here carries a passive sense. In this context, the passive meaning is "suffers violent attacks." The verse emphasizes the ongoing persecution of God's people and opposition to God's Word.

11:13. The prophets and the law. The entire Old Testament **prophesied** the coming of the kingdom.

These prophecies were available for all the people to hear. John's message had not been new, but was one prophets had given time and again. Their message had been rejected and in John's preaching found rejection one more time, before the coming of Christ. John represented the end of the old economy.

11:14. This is Elias. A reference to Malachi 4:5, which prophesied the reappearance of Elijah before the day of the Lord. Some of the people remembered the prophecy and asked John the Baptist, "Art thou Elias?" He answered, "I am not" (John 1:21). John was not literally the reincarnation of Elijah, but he did fulfill the function and role of the prophet (see Matt. 17:10–13; discussion on Luke 1:17). In other words, Elijah was a prophetic type of John.

11:15. He that hath ears to hear, let him hear. Jesus used this oratorical device to alert the listener that He was saying something important. He used the same device elsewhere (see 13:9, 43, Luke 14:35), always to warn the listener that what He is saying was important.

11:16–19. These verses present Jesus' main point: the people had heard the prophecies, both in the reading of Scripture and in the preaching of John, and it had fallen on deaf ears.

11:16–17. Drawing an analogy, Jesus said the people were **like unto children sitting in the markets** (v. 16; see discussion on Luke 7:31–34). In the markets, children would call to one another with little set rhymes or calls. Those who had heard John and Jesus preach had not responded to the message. **Piped** (v. 17). As if providing music at a wedding. **Mourned.** As if providing music at a funeral. Here Jesus was perhaps likening the latter to John's ministry and the former to His own ministry. In any case, the people of Jesus' **generation** (v. 16) were like children who did not respond to the music in that they did not respond to the preaching of God's Word.

11:18–19. Instead of repenting, the people griped about the lifestyles of both men. **John came neither eating nor drinking** (v. 18), and the people did not like it, saying he had a devil. **The Son of man** (see discussion on Mark 2:10) **came eating and drinking** (v. 19), and they did not like that either.

Rather than responding to the message, people found fault with the messenger. This may stand as a warning to believers today. One may not like the preacher's hairstyle or clothing, and his delivery may not be as entertaining as the former pastor's, but the important matter is the content of the message. Believers should never let the incidentals get in the way of the main point, which is to take the message to heart and live it out in their lives. **Wisdom is justified of her children**. This apparently means that God (wisdom) had sent both John and Jesus in specific roles and that this would be vindicated by the lasting works of both men (see discussion on Luke 7:35).

11:20. Then began he to upbraid the cities. This is a turning point in the message. Jesus here made the point very specific, mentioning by name the cities where He had preached, and perhaps even where He was preaching at this time. In each case, He emphasized that they should have repented at the preaching of the Word but had not.

11:21 – 22. Chorazin (v. 21). Mentioned in the Bible only twice (here and in Luke 10:13), Chorazin was near the Sea of Galilee, probably about two miles north of Capernaum. **Bethsaida**. On the northeast shore of the Sea of Galilee. Philip the tetrarch rebuilt Bethsaida and named it "Julias," after Julia, daughter of Caesar Augustus. **Tyre and Sidon** (v. 22). Cities on the Phoenician coast north of the Holy Land. **Sackcloth** (v. 21). Here a sign of repentance (see discussion on Gen. 37:34; Rev. 6:12). **Ashes**. Also a sign of repentance. Jesus' point was that these cities would have repented had they seen the signs that Jesus had performed in Chorazin and Bethsaida. How much more would these cities be held accountable, if Tyre and Sidon had already met judgment. Truly, all are accountable for the light they are given. If we are given more, we are more liable to judgment if we do not repent.

11:23 – 24. The mighty works that Jesus had done in **Capernaum** (v. 23; see discussion on Luke 10:15) would have brought **Sodom** to repentance, and God would have spared the city. It is interesting to note that God knows not only what will happen

but also what would have happened. One cannot say, however, that God did not give Sodom adequate warning. Paul indicates (Rom. 1:18 – 32) that sinners have sufficient knowledge of God to lead them to repentance, if they do not deliberately refuse it.

11:25 – 30. Jesus ended the sermon with a prayer and an invitation.

11:25 – 26. These verses give the content of the prayer. **These things** (v. 25). Probably including an understanding of Jesus' mission and certainly including the matters Jesus had just preached on (11:7 – 24), the need for repentance and faith in response to the preaching of God's Word. In this context, **the wise and prudent** are the teachers of the law and the Pharisees, and **babes** are the humble followers of Jesus, those who responded with childlike faith to the call to repentance and faith. This echoes Paul's statement in 1 Corinthians 1:26 – 27 that "not many wise men after the flesh … are called" to faith, for "God hath chosen the foolish things of the world to confound the wise; and God hath chosen the weak things of the world to confound the things which are mighty." Jesus was thankful perhaps because God's way of salvation does not demand that people have great learning or intelligence. No one is disqualified. Knowing every point of doctrine is not a requirement for salvation. All that is needed is simple faith, to trust God and what He has said in His Word. No one has to pass a test to "qualify" for salvation. There is no secret wisdom that only the initiates can have. The truth is available to whosoever will believe it. Therefore, those cities that had not repented could not plead doctrinal ignorance or a lack of qualified rabbis to interpret the message for them.

11:27. No man knoweth the Son, but the Father; neither knoweth any man the Father, save the Son. Here Jesus used "knoweth" in the sense of knowing who He is and what His secret counsels are. Only the Son knows the Father this intimately and vice versa.

11:28. This is the sermon's invitation. Jesus ended His message with a word of comfort and an offer of grace. **Come unto me** is a call to repentance. Many had rejected Him, questioning His teaching and lifestyle (see 11:19). Others had rejected His preaching, as they had rejected John's. Here Jesus called them to a change of mind and heart. Instead of setting themselves up against Jesus and criticizing His message, they could respond to His call and come to Him in simple faith as a child, in humble dependence on Him. **All ye that labour and are heavy laden** here means all those who sought to make themselves righteous on their own, as the Pharisees had taught. Though the Lord certainly offers encouragement and comfort to those who are discouraged in the Lord's work or who have lost their zeal, here He was offering salvation to those who had labored under legalism.

11:29–30. Take my yoke upon you (v. 29) is in contrast to the yoke of the law, or legalism, which is a theme found elsewhere in the New Testament (see Acts 15:10; Gal. 5:1). **For my yoke is easy, and my burden is light** (v. 30). Jesus contrasted His offer of free grace with the yoke of legalism. This invitation may be seen as a stark contrast to the message it accompanies. The reason is clear, however, upon reflection. The message of repentance is a harsh message, promising judgment on those who turn their backs on God. At the same time, however, the message offers hope to those who do repent.

12:1–50. In chapter 12, the conflict between Jesus and the Pharisees begins to come to a head. Jesus' Sabbath-breaking activities raised their ire, and they began to accuse Him falsely and question Him while seeking an opportunity to destroy Him. Their opposition at this point begins to show signs of an organized effort, which would lead to their official rejection of Jesus as the Messiah.

12:1–14. This section contains two accounts in which the Pharisees challenged Jesus about activities He and the disciples did on the Sabbath. In the first account (vv. 1–8), the disciples picked grain and ate it as they walked through a field. In the second account (vv. 9–14), Jesus healed a man on the Sabbath. The reason the Pharisees challenged Him on this matter becomes clearer in light of Middle Eastern history at that time. The Greeks had conquered the area over three hundred years earlier and had imported Greek culture, language, and architecture

into the area. Some Jewish people had adopted Greek ways, much to the chagrin of those who sought to preserve tradition. The Pharisees were among those who sought to purify Israel from Greek influence. One thing that distinguished the Jewish people from the surrounding cultures was their observance of the Sabbath. Keeping the Sabbath was a very public expression of one's Jewishness and commitment to the law of Moses. When Jesus or His disciples even seemed to break the Sabbath, it upset the Pharisees, for they saw it as a compromise of Jewish culture. In His remarks, Jesus revealed their lack of understanding of the Scriptures in the first account and their hypocrisy in the second, and in both instances, He showed that the main point was not Sabbath-keeping but rather doing the will of God from the heart.

12:1–8. This is the chapter's first account of the Pharisees' reaction to a seeming violation of the Sabbath.

12:1–2. The corn (i.e., "kernel"; v. 1). "Corn" does not mean what most people think of as corn today, which was unknown in Israel. These were fields of wheat or barley; the latter was eaten by poorer people. **Pluck the ears of corn.** They pulled off some of the wheat. This was not illegal, even though the disciples did not own the field; the Old Testament law specifically stated that people passing a field were allowed to do this (see Deut. 23:25). The problem was that they were doing it on the Sabbath. To the **Pharisees** (v. 2; see discussion on Mark 2:16), that was harvesting, which is a work activity. For **that which is not lawful to do upon the sabbath**, see discussion on Mark 2:24.

12:3–4. Jesus' reply seems at first to be unrelated to the Pharisees' reaction. He directed their attention to **what David did** (v. 3; see discussions on Mark 2:25–26). David and his men on one occasion **did eat the shewbread** (v. 4). Each Sabbath, twelve fresh loaves of bread were to be set on a table in the Holy Place (see Exod. 25:30; Lev. 24:5–9). The old loaves were eaten by the priests. The "hot bread" replaced the old bread every Sabbath day (see 1 Sam. 21:6). David was not breaking the Sabbath by doing this, but Jesus' remarks had an underlying point: David's men were hungry, and meeting their need took precedence over the strict letter of the law. It would not have been God's will for the bread to sit there, while hungry men looked on, unable to touch it due to a ritual restriction. In the same way, Jesus' disciples were hungry, and the Sabbath should not interfere with their meeting their need for food.

12:5. Jesus offered another example, one more directly related to the Pharisees' concern. Without guilt, **the priests in the temple profane the Sabbath** by doing work associated with the sacrifices on the Sabbath day.

12:6. Jesus' point seems to be that He is **greater than the temple**, and in His presence, His disciples may do as He wills without blame. Jesus was thus bearing witness to His deity. People sometimes raise the question whether Jesus ever claimed to be God. He did so explicitly in many places (see Matt. 22:44–45; 24:30–31; 26:63–66; Mark 14:61–64; Luke 22:67–71; John 8:58; 10:30–33; 11:25–26; 14:1–6; 17:4–5; 18:37), but perhaps more convincing are His claims that are based on the assumption that He is God. This was one of those occasions. Jesus' statement makes no sense at all unless He really is God. He made no effort here, or anywhere else, to prove that He is God but rather assumed it and made the statement on that basis. By doing so, He once again challenged the Pharisees to accept Him for who He is. As in the previous chapter (11:20–24), this was an invitation to repentance, but the Pharisees rejected it.

12:7. Jesus alluded to several Old Testament passages where the Lord makes it clear that matters of the heart (compassion and **mercy**) are more important than the ritual of the law. His point was that God wants the hungry to eat and will not forbid it on the basis of adherence to ritual and that service to God is more important than adherence to ritual. This verse makes clear an area where repentance on the part of the Pharisees was necessary.

12:8. The Son of man is Lord even of the sabbath day (see discussion on Luke 6:5). This is a summary statement that points up especially the application of Jesus' second example.

12:9–14. This is the chapter's second account of "Sabbath-breaking." Jesus had developed a reputation as someone who could heal the sick. The Pharisees were aware of this but were more focused on the matter of working on the Sabbath than on meeting the man's need or on the fact that Jesus' healings were miracles. They challenged Him, not on whether He could perform miracles. At this point, they assumed that He could. Their challenge was strictly related to whether He would heal on the Sabbath. That they could ask Him this question and not recognize that these healings were miraculous and pointed to Jesus' deity shows how spiritually dull these men were.

12:9. For **synagogue**, see discussion on Mark 1:21.

12:10. Is it lawful to heal on the sabbath days? The rabbis prohibited healing on the Sabbath, unless it was feared that the victim would die before the next day. Obviously, the man with the withered hand was in no danger of this.

12:11–12. Jesus challenged the Pharisees on a point that showed their hypocrisy. That **a man** (v. 12) is worth more than **a sheep** is obvious, and to do good to a man is better than to do good to a sheep. If it is lawful to do good to a sheep on the Sabbath, then it must be lawful to do good to a man on the Sabbath. Jesus was saying that nothing in the will of God should ever prohibit someone from doing good. One is never excused on the basis of ritual from doing what is right.

12:13. Stretch forth thine hand. And he stretched it forth. That the man did what Jesus asked shows a connection between faith and Jesus' healing power. The man did not say, "I can't; I'm paralyzed." He stretched out his hand by faith and was healed.

12:14. The Pharisees reacted to the healing, not by marveling over the miracle, though they had seen it, nor by recognizing the deity of Christ and submitting to Him, but by redoubling their resolve to **destroy him**. Such is the power of sin in one's life; it blinds people to God's truth.

12:15. Jesus **withdrew** because His time had not yet come. He needed to continue to minister until the time was right.

12:16. For **not make him known,** see discussions on 8:4; 16:20.

12:17–21. Another fulfillment passage (see discussion on 1:22). This one is from Isaiah's first servant song (42:1–4) and is the longest Old Testament quotation in Matthew's gospel. It summarizes the quiet ministry of the Lord's servant, who will bring justice and hope to the nations.

12:17–18. My servant (v. 18). Jesus is called God's servant only here and in Acts 3:13 (see discussion there), 26; 4:27, 30. **My beloved, in whom my soul is well pleased** echoes the statement made at Jesus' baptism (see discussion on 3:17).

12:19. He shall not strive, nor cry specifically points out that Jesus' ministry was carried out without fanfare, though multitudes followed Him. More than once, including in 12:16, Jesus is seen forbidding people to whom He ministered to speak about Him. This is in contrast to His words in Matthew 28:19–20, which are in a different context.

12:20. Jesus mends broken lives (see 12:15; John 4:4–42; 8:3–11). Here is shown the extraordinary tenderness and care of the Lord, with imagery of **bruised** plants and **smoking flax** lamp wicks making the picture more vivid in the reader's mind.

12:21. In his name shall the Gentiles trust. Here again Matthew quoted a verse showing his original readers that the significance of the gospel goes beyond just the nation of Israel.

12:22–37. This section begins with an account of Jesus casting out a demon spirit, for which the Pharisees criticized Him more sharply than ever. Chapter 12 steps up the tension between Jesus and the Pharisees, something seen in each incident recorded. This section concludes with Jesus refuting the claims of the Pharisees and setting forth the issue of genuine faith.

12:22–23. Is not this the son of David? (v. 23; see discussion on 9:27). The people now began to recognize that Jesus was the Messiah. This is in sharp contrast to the Pharisees' reaction (see 12:24).

12:24. The Pharisees attributed Jesus' power to **cast out devils,** or demons, to Satan. This was the most serious charge they had brought against Him

so far. Jesus' response (12:25–37) left no room for doubt as to where He saw these Pharisees standing. For **Beelzebub,** see discussion on 10:25.

12:25–27. Jesus began by giving the general principle by which He would refute them. A **kingdom** (or "household") **divided against itself shall not stand** (v. 25). He then made the direct application. He could not be working by the power of **Satan** (v. 26), for He was working against Satan. If He was doing a work that led the people to recognize His messiahship (see "the son of David," 12:23), then He could not be doing a work empowered by Satan.

Jesus then turned the tables on the Pharisees. Apparently, some of them had been involved in a ministry of casting out demons. If Jesus cast out demons by the power of Satan, **by whom [did they] cast them out?** (v. 27). They had to either say they were in league with Satan or repudiate their own criticism of Jesus. Of course, they did neither one.

12:28–29. Jesus made it clear that He **cast out devils by the Spirit of God** (v. 28). This becomes important in 12:32. For **the kingdom of God,** see discussion on 3:2. The Pharisees were in the position of having the kingdom in their midst in the person and work of the Messiah, and they did not recognize it. Having attributed the power of the kingdom to Satan, they were now under even greater condemnation. Jesus had to **first bind the strong man** (v. 29) by the power of the Spirit of God. That is, He had to break the power Satan had gained in people's lives before they could be taken back from him and brought unto the Lord.

12:30. Here Jesus offered a significant statement related to one's attitude and actions toward Him. The first part of the verse deals with attitude: **He that is not with me is against me.** Either one identifies with Jesus or one opposes Him. Obviously, these Pharisees were against Him. This verse has significance for the matter of the exclusivity of Christ, the truth that there is only one way to heaven, and in no way can one say that "all religions lead to God." Also, nothing in the context bars the use of this verse in an evangelistic context. It leaves no room for fence-sitters. One is either with Jesus or against Him. There is no middle ground. In this context, the Pharisees were definitely against Him, but then so is the person who makes no decision or who believes he will "decide later." This passage makes it very clear that anyone who hears the gospel walks away either "with Jesus" or "against Him."

The second part of the verse deals with actions: **he that gathereth not with me scattereth abroad**. This relates directly to evangelism. Jesus had earlier used fishing as a paradigm, calling His disciples to be "fishers of men" (4:19). Here the idea of harvest is in view, an analogy Jesus also used elsewhere for evangelism (see John 4:35). Jesus reminded His hearers that one is either bringing people to the kingdom of heaven or one is sending them away from it. Again, there is no neutral ground. This applies to evangelism today. Either one is winning souls for Christ or one is sending people away from the gospel.

12:31–32. These two verses have caused much trouble in the hearts of believers. This is because they are so often taken out of context. Jesus here pronounced a specific condemnation on these Pharisees. Since His power to cast out demons comes from the Holy Spirit, and they had said it comes from Satan, they had spoken, not against Jesus, but against the Spirit.

12:31. Blasphemy against the Holy Ghost shall not be forgiven. The context (see 12:24, 28, 32) suggests that the "unpardonable sin" was attributing to Satan Christ's authenticating miracles done in the power of the Holy Spirit (see discussion on Mark 3:29).

12:32. To avoid any misunderstanding, Jesus restated the matter in slightly different words, but to the same effect. It was one thing to accuse Jesus of being a Sabbath-breaker, but quite another to attribute to Satan the work of the Spirit.

12:33–37. This section is a general commentary on the fact that an evil heart will produce evil words. The application to what the Pharisees had just said (see 12:24) is clear. They had spoken evil words because their hearts were evil. In fact, they had seen Jesus do a number of miracles, and they had heard His teaching. The multitudes had begun to sense who Jesus really was. The Pharisees had re-

jected Him, thus showing how far from God they really were, even though outwardly they looked like godly men.

12:33. To further his point, Jesus made a comparison between people and trees. This is one of a number of instances in the New Testament where what a person's life produces is likened to **fruit**. Fruit is what a **tree** produces. By implication, evil words are what evil people produce, and good words are what good people produce. It is not enough just to look at the tree; one must try the fruit. In the same way, it is not enough just to see a man saying prayers and keeping the outward forms of the law. One must examine what his life produces. As an evil tree produces evil fruit, so an evil heart produces evil words, and by implication, evil deeds as well. All of this is based on much of what Jesus said in the Sermon on the Mount about the nature of genuine righteousness. His statement here presupposed that the hearers understood that teaching and would interpret His words in light of it.

12:34. Jesus compared the Pharisees to **vipers**, poisonous snakes. As the viper uses its mouth to inject poison, so these Pharisees had used their mouths to inject spiritual poison into their hearers. How could they, **being evil**, do otherwise? They could only produce what was in their hearts. As a viper produces poison, so the Pharisees produced evil words.

12:35–37. Jesus made the application clearly in these verses. Verse 35 states the point of 11:33–34. Verse 36 contains a warning. Words should be spoken carefully, with attention to the motive. Verse 37 makes it clear that one's **words** reveal the content of one's heart. Judgment will be based on one's words, for they reveal what is inside.

12:38. The Pharisees wanted to see a spectacular miracle, preferably in the sky (see Luke 11:16), as **a sign** that Jesus was the Messiah. Instead, Jesus cited them a "sign" from history (see discussion on Luke 11:29).

12:39. Adulterous. Referring to spiritual, not physical, adultery, in the sense that their generation had become unfaithful to its spiritual husband

(God). Jesus promised only **the sign of the prophet Jonas**. What He meant is made clear in 12:40–42.

12:40. Three days and three nights (see discussion on Luke 24:46). Including at least part of the first day and part of the third day, a common Jewish reckoning of time. **The whale's belly.** The Greek word means "sea creature," that is, a huge fish or marine mammal (see discussion on Jonah 1:17). Jesus drew an analogy between Jonah's time inside the fish and His own coming death and resurrection. The sign, the indicator that Jesus is who He says He is, would be the resurrection. It would vindicate His ministry and point unmistakably to God's acceptance of His death on the cross as payment for sins.

12:41–42. The men of Nineveh shall rise in judgment (v. 41). They repented of their sins (see Jonah 3:5–10), and who better to condemn those who did not repent? Jesus is the one who is **a greater than Jonas** (v. 41) and **a greater than Solomon** (v. 42; see discussion on Luke 11:31–32). Those who had heard Jesus preach had even more reason to repent than Nineveh, for they had heard the message directly from God. **The queen of the south.** In 1 Kings 10:1, she is called "the queen of Sheba," a country in southwest Arabia, now called Yemen.

12:43–50. This passage appears at first glance to be unconnected to the context of the preceding passage, but actually it fits well. Jesus' disciples are His "family" in the sense that they are "with Him" as the Pharisees were not.

12:43–45. See discussion on Luke 11:24.

12:46–49. For **his mother and his brethren**, see discussion on Luke 8:19–20.

12:50. For **whosoever shall do the will of my Father**, see discussion on Mark 3:35.

F. The Parables of the Kingdom (chap. 13)

13:1–58. The first twelve chapters of Matthew emphasize Jesus' presentation of Himself as the King of the Jews. Chapter 13 represents a major shift. It now became apparent that the Jewish leaders would reject the kingdom. The parables in this chapter serve to explain and illustrate the events of chapters 9–12. The disciples had seen a variety of reactions to

Jesus' message. The Pharisees had moved from vague dislike to open opposition (12:14). Some among the multitudes had begun to realize that Jesus was more than just a prophet (9:27; 12:22–23). Some of the cities, however, had rejected Him completely (12:41–42). To His disciples, it must have seemed incomprehensible that anyone would reject Jesus and His message, which they had come to love. The parable of the sower demonstrates that people will have different reactions to the Word of God, and the parable of the wheat and the tares demonstrates that some will not respond to God's Word.

13:1. The same day connects these parables to the material in chapter 12. The parables should be interpreted in light of those events.

13:2. And sat. Sitting was the usual position for Jewish teachers (see 5:1; Luke 5:3; John 8:2).

13:3–9. For the interpretation of this parable, see 13:18–23.

13:3. Parables. The word "parable" comes from the Greek *parabolē*, which means "a placing beside," thus a comparison or an illustration. Its most common use in the New Testament is for the illustrative stories that Jesus drew from nature and human life. The Synoptic Gospels contain about thirty of these stories (see discussions on Mark 4:2; Luke 8:4). John's gospel contains no parables but uses other figures of speech. For **to sow**, see discussion on Luke 8:5. It is reasonable to assume that Jesus spoke other parables on this occasion as well, but the ones Matthew chose to reproduce here are illustrative both of Jesus' teaching and of the reactions to the word His disciples had witnessed among the people. Parables of the Kingdom — Matthew 13

1. Sower and Seed 13:3–9; 18–23
2. Wheat and Tares 13:24–30; 36–43
3. Mustard Seed 13:31–32
4. Leaven (Yeast) 13:33
5. Hidden Treasure 13:44
6. Pearl of Great Price 13:45–46
7. Net 13:47–50

13:4. Each of the places where the **seeds** (v. 4) fell represents a different type of hearer of God's Word (see discussion on Mark 4:3–9), as Jesus explained in 13:18–23. For the seed that **fell by the way side**, see 13:19 and discussion.

13:5–6. Stony places (v. 5). Not ground covered with small stones, but shallow soil on top of solid rock (see discussion on Luke 8:6). Seed in such a situation will spring up quickly, as will seed in other places, but the plants cannot take **root** (v. 6). Jesus' hearers lived close to the soil. They knew well the loss that a failed crop meant and the importance of prepared soil for success. Their lives depended directly on proper planting of each year's crop.

13:7. Some fell among thorns. The seed fell on a place where seeds of thorny plants were already in the soil. The thorny plants grew along with the good plants and won out, as weeds often will.

13:8–9. An hundredfold (v. 8). Again, an agricultural people knew well that one part of a field might yield more than another and that well-prepared soil, **good ground**, was the best guarantee of any harvest at all (see discussion on Luke 8:8). For **Who hath ears to hear, let him hear** (v. 9), see discussion on 11:15.

13:10. Why speakest thou unto them in parables? Since they themselves understood only some of the parables, **the disciples** (see discussion on Luke 8:9) knew that the people, who were less familiar with Jesus' teaching, might not understand. Jesus' answer confirmed their suspicion and explained it.

13:11. The mysteries of the kingdom of heaven (see discussions on Mark 4:11; Luke 8:10). These "mysteries," or "secrets," were not revealed in the Old Testament. They are unique to the New Testament and reveal new information about Christ's earthly rule.

13:12. Whosoever hath refers to those who have faith in Christ, as opposed to those who do not believe, **whosoever hath not**. Those who believe live by faith and gain even more, whereas those who do not believe miss out on God's blessings altogether. **From him shall be taken away** refers to those who refuse to believe in Jesus as the Messiah. By rejecting the King, they reject the blessings of His kingdom.

13:13–14. These verses expand on what Jesus said in 13:12 and apply it to His teaching session of

that day. Jesus spoke **in parables** (v. 13) because of the spiritual dullness of the people (see discussion on Luke 8:4). For **they seeing see not**, see *KJV Study Bible* note on Mark 4:12; discussion on Luke 8:10. Once again Matthew pointed to an Old Testament **prophecy** (v. 14) that was fulfilled here (see Isa. 6:9–10). Jesus' life and ministry, for Matthew, was a matter of fulfilling prophecy, which confirmed His Messiahship.

13:15. Lest at any time they should see … and hear … and should be converted means that many had closed their eyes and ears to avoid being converted. The idea here is not that God does not want people to hear and understand. God wills that all men should repent (see Acts 17:30), but when people refuse the truth, "lest at any time they should see … and hear …," God will not force them. Jesus used parables so that those eager for the truth will explore and discover it, while those who want to avoid it can do so.

13:16–17. Jesus affirmed the rightness of seeking spiritual truth. The disciples were receiving the fuller revelation that the prophets had not received.

13:18. Hear ye therefore the parable of the sower. Jesus seldom interpreted His parables, but here He did.

13:19. Jesus explained that the soil is the hearer. **The wicked one** is the Devil, who snatches away spiritual truth that is not understood. This is why the Word of God never penetrates so many people who hear it. The Devil takes it away by distracting the hearer with the pleasures of sin or by reminding the hearer of other priorities. If the Devil gets us focused on immediate wants, we will not be thinking about eternal truths. **The way side** refers to the walking path beside the field. In other words, when the **seed** of God's Word falls on a hard heart, that person has no response or receptivity to it, so the Devil snatches it away, as though the person never heard it in the first place.

13:20–21. Stony places (v. 20) refers to shallow or rocky ground that has insufficient soil. **Anon with joy** refers to shallow and emotional responses to the gospel that do not last but wither away. **Persecution** (v. 21) causes those whose profession of faith is not real to turn away from following Christ. Some people believe that coming to Christ means all of their problems go away. When this does not happen, they become disappointed and drop out. This verse may be used as a reminder to believers that even after they have received the Word of God, that is, after they have been saved, troubles may still come.

13:22. The seed that falls "by the way side" (13:19) never takes root. Such a person hears the truth but never believes it, having other priorities in life. The seed that falls "into stony places" (13:20) produces much joy in the listener, but it is only a temporary emotional response. The seed that falls **among the thorns** is soon choked out by **the care**(s) **of this world**. The person hears and receives **the word** and claims to believe the gospel but is soon distracted with worldly matters and material goods.

13:23. Regarding the seed that falls into **good ground**, Jesus described a threefold process: the person **heareth the word**, he **understandeth it**, and it **beareth fruit**. These three responses must all be present for one to be a genuine disciple. Hearing the Word includes reading it. In Jesus' day, most people could not read, and the Word of God was most often heard in the synagogues and memorized. Understanding God's Word involves meditating on it, asking questions and finding answers, memorizing it, and imagining it lived out in one's life. The Word bears fruit when it is applied to one's life. In the New Testament, the word "fruit" is used in various ways. Usually it involves living the Christian life, in the sense of obedience to God's Word. In Galatians 5:22–23, however, Paul used it to describe the kinds of virtues the Spirit produces in one's life. Theologians debate which of these responses to the gospel actually produces saving faith, but only the final one produces spiritual fruit.

13:24–30. This is the parable of the wheat and tares. Jesus again wanted His disciples to see that while some people respond to the preaching of God's Word, not all will. Since much of the opposition in the preceding chapter came from the Pharisees, Jesus may have had them in mind here. As tares look like the wheat during the growing season and are hard to

separate out, so also the Pharisees "looked" spiritual even though theirs was only a surface spirituality, not a matter of the heart. For the interpretation of this parable, see 13:36–43.

13:24. The kingdom of heaven is likened unto. This phrase introduces six of the seven parables in this chapter (all but the parable of the sower).

13:25–30. Tares (v. 25). Probably darnel, which looks very much like wheat while it is young but can later be distinguished. The **field** (v. 27) is "the world" (13:38). Thus, the people of the kingdom live side by side with the people of the Evil One. It is wise not to press the analogy too far. While a farmer might have trouble distinguishing wheat from darnel, God does not have any trouble distinguishing His own from the lost people of the world. As the wheat and the tares were mixed together, so also God's people live in the world with the lost. God does not separate them out, until the time for harvest. The point of this parable is that some people will initially profess to be believers, but later it will be clear that they are not.

13:31–33. These two short parables, that of the mustard seed (vv. 31–32) and the leaven (v. 33), are meant to counterbalance the parables of the sower and of the wheat and tares. The disciples could have easily become discouraged. They had just seen evidence that there would be opposition to the message they loved so well, and Jesus had just related two parables confirming that not everyone will respond to the Word of God. If not everyone will respond to the Word positively, why bother with preaching at all? Sometimes we have an all-or-nothing attitude about things we care about. When Christians witness and meet with opposition or indifference, it is easy to give up in discouragement. Jesus therefore wanted the disciples to realize that while God's plan in this world may have a small beginning, it will be influential in significant ways. The mustard seed and the leaven, though small and easily overlooked, do make a difference. God's Word may produce little fruit among a group of hearers, but that fruit will have a lasting effect. Preaching impacts eternity.

13:31–32. Although the kingdom will seem to have an insignificant beginning, it will eventually spread throughout the world. **The least of all seeds … the greatest among herbs** (v. 32). The **mustard seed** (v. 31) is not the smallest seed known today, but it was the smallest seed used by farmers and gardeners in the Holy Land, and under favorable conditions, the plant could reach some ten feet in height. **A tree … the branches thereof** (v. 32). This could be an allusion to Daniel 4:21, suggesting that the kingdom of heaven will expand to world dominion and that people from all nations will find rest in it (see Dan. 2:35, 44–45; 7:27; Rev. 11:15), or it could picture evil coming into the kingdom, since "the fowls" in 13:4 is interpreted as "the wicked one" in 13:19.

13:33. In the Bible, **leaven** usually symbolizes that which is evil or unclean (see discussion on Mark 8:15). Here it could picture evil, or possibly it is a symbol for growth. As leaven permeates a batch of dough, so **The kingdom of heaven** spreads through a person's life. Alternatively, the leaven may signify the growth of the kingdom by the inner working of the Holy Spirit (using God's Word).

13:34. This summary statement introduces a bridge to Jesus' interpretation of the parable of the tares.

13:35. Spoken by the prophet. The quotation is from Psalm 78, a psalm ascribed to Asaph, who, according to 2 Chronicles 29:30, was a "seer" (prophet). Matthew's determination to show that the ministry of Jesus fulfilled Old Testament prophecy is again seen here. This statement could have been left out without changing the sense of this chapter. One can only imagine that Matthew included it because of his emphasis on fulfilled prophecy.

13:36. Here is an example of what Jesus meant by "good ground" (13:23). The disciples remembered what Jesus said and now they sought to understand it. One reasonably expects that they intended to apply it in their lives and ministry as well. All believers should do the same and should not become discouraged if people do not respond to their witness for Christ.

13:37–39. For **the Son of man** (v. 37), see discussion on Mark 2:10. Jesus answered their request and interpreted the parable of the tares. The parable is something of an allegory, in which each element is a symbol of something else. Readers of the Gospels should be careful, however; not every parable may be interpreted in this way. That Jesus offered an interpretation of this parable and that of the sower should alert readers to the fact that these two are different from most of His parables.

In the parable of the tares, **the reapers are the angels** (v. 39). They are the ones who will **harvest** the crop; that is, they will gather those who have been saved. Jesus said essentially the same thing in Matthew 24:31, where he said that angels will gather believers at the end of the age. **The enemy** is Satan, who seeks to pervert the Word and work of God in our lives.

13:40–43. Here we see a promise of judgment. **A furnace of fire** (v. 42) is often mentioned in connection with the final judgment in apocalyptic literature (see Rev. 19:20; 20:14). Notice that the fire of the parable (see 13:30) is clearly said to be **fire** (v. 40) in Christ's interpretation. **Wailing and gnashing of teeth** (v. 42) occurs six times in Matthew's gospel (8:12; here; 13:50; 22:13; 24:51; 25:30) and nowhere else in the New Testament. It is important to note that it is in the furnace that there will be the wailing and gnashing of teeth. In no way may this be seen as annihilation of the wicked. This is conscious and continuous punishment for sin. Hell is always treated in Scripture as a reality and as a place of continual punishment, not a place of cessation.

13:44–46. These two parables, that of the hidden treasure (v. 44) and the pearl of great price (v. 45–46), teach the same truth: The kingdom is of such great value that one should be willing to give up all he has to gain it. Jesus was not implying that one can purchase the kingdom with money or good deeds. He was emphasizing that those who had rejected His preaching had missed something very valuable, something that would have been worth giving up anything else, including worldly goods or prestige, to have.

13:44. Treasure hid in a field (v. 44). In ancient times, it was common to hide treasure in the ground since there was no widespread equivalent of modern bank vaults for the safekeeping of funds, though there were "exchangers" (see 25:27 and discussion). Sometimes one unexpectedly stumbles across the gospel message, without searching for it, as with the treasure in this parable.

13:45–46. Seeking goodly pearls (v. 45). The pearl was found after a diligent search, in contrast to the treasure. Either way, whether one stumbles across the gospel or discovers it after a long search for truth, it is of inestimable value.

13:47–51. The parable of the **net** (v. 47) teaches the same general lesson as the parable of the tares: There will be a final separation of the righteous and the wicked. The parable of the tares also emphasizes that we are not to try to make such a separation now and that this is entirely the Lord's business (see 13:28–30, 41–42). The Lord used this fishing analogy to illustrate the same truth, perhaps because some of the disciples were fishermen. This demonstrates His intention to make His teaching interesting and relevant to the audience, without compromising the message. At the end of this, Jesus confirmed that His disciples had **understood** (v. 51) the parable.

13:52. Every scribe. This verse may seem odd, but Jesus was speaking to His disciples, not to scribes. The key may be that the disciples had understood the parables. Having been instructed in spiritual matters, they had an abundance to share.

13:53. This verse concludes a teaching section and introduces a narrative section (compare 7:28–29).

13:54–57. In a sense, this passage returns to the theme of some not receiving the Word in their hearts. The key is that He was in **his own country**, Galilee, and Nazareth (v. 54; see discussion on 2:23), the town He called home, where He grew up. For **he taught them in their synagogue**, see discussion on Mark 1:21. Those who have done it know that some of the most difficult preaching comes when a preacher returns to the church of his childhood.

The carpenter's son (v. 55). The word translated "carpenter" could mean "stonemason" (see discussion on Mark 6:3). Joseph may or may not have been living at the time of this incident. **Brethren.** Sons born to Joseph and Mary after the virgin birth of

Jesus (see discussion on Luke 8:19–20). Essentially, the people were saying, "Hey, we know this man. He is nothing special." It is part of human nature to regard someone from out of town as an automatic "expert" while overlooking or not taking seriously the local person. Many in Jesus' audience probably remembered Him as a child. It is difficult to see someone you knew as a child behaving as one with authority. The Lord understands human nature on this matter, which is why He calls some to be evangelists or missionaries. The "expert" from out of town can preach the same message the local pastor has preached for years and get results where before there were none, simply because he is from out of town.

13:58. Unbelief. The close relationship between faith and miracles is stressed in Matthew's gospel (see 8:10, 13; 9:2, 22, 28–29).

G. Herod's Reaction to Jesus' Ministry (14:1–12)

14:1. Tetrarch. The ruler of a fourth part of a region. **Herod** (Herod Antipas) was one of several sons of Herod the Great. When Herod the Great died, his kingdom was divided among three of his sons (see charts, *KJV Study Bible*, pp. 1355, 1451). Herod Antipas ruled over Galilee and Perea (4 BC–AD 39). Matthew correctly referred to him as "tetrarch" here, as Luke regularly did (Luke 3:19; 9:7; Acts 13:1). In 14:9, however, Matthew called him "king," as Mark also did (Mark 6:14), because that was his popular title among the Galileans as well as in Rome.

14:2. John the Baptist ... is risen from the dead (see discussion on Mark 6:16). This curious assumption on Herod's part is explained in the parenthetical section that follows (14:3–12). Matthew gave much attention to this incident, most likely in light of his Jewish readers (see Introduction, "Recipients"). John the Baptist's ministry had a long-lasting impact on all of Judea and beyond. Many years after his beheading, Paul found some disciples of John the Baptist at Ephesus (see Acts 19:1–7). Matthew apparently believed it was necessary to explain to his readers what had happened to John and why he was not active in the church in the years following the day of Pentecost.

This incident also displays yet another reaction to Jesus' ministry. That Herod would come up with this explanation shows human depravity and credulity. How often have we encountered people who are ready to believe anything rather than humble themselves and repent before the Lord. Herod would believe in the resurrection of John the Baptist before he would believe the message of Christ. Haunted by his sin and guilt, he would believe a fantasy before he would bow before a gracious and loving God.

14:3. Herodias was a granddaughter of Herod the Great. Her first husband was her uncle Herod Philip I (Herod the Great had two sons named Philip), who lived in Rome. While a guest in their home, Herod Antipas had persuaded Herodias to leave her husband for him. Marriage to one's brother's wife while the brother was still living was forbidden by the Mosaic law (see Lev. 18:16). Philip I was the son of Herod the Great and Mariamne, the daughter of Simon the high priest, and was thus a half-brother of Herod Antipas, born to Malthace (see chart, *Zondervan KJV Study Bible*, p. 1355).

14:4–5. John the Baptist was a man of conviction unintimidated by worldly authority and willing to preach the truth, even if it is unpopular with his audience. John held up Herod's life to the unfailing plumb line of God's Word and found Herod wanting. Would that more of God's people would confront the world with the truth of God. Compromise, for the sake of one's life or for the sake of respectability, is displeasing to the Lord. The contrast between the fearless man of God and the fearful sinner is hard to miss in these two verses. Herod was a man who **feared the multitude** (v. 5) and could not act because he feared the opinion of men. This had kept him from doing a greater evil, until the events in 14:6–12, and he should have been as fearless in doing good as he was fearful in doing evil.

14:6–7. The daughter of Herodias (v. 6). Salome, according to Josephus. She later married her grand-uncle Philip II (a son of Herod the Great), who ruled the northern territories (see Luke 3:1). At this time, Salome was a young woman of marriageable age. Her dance was undoubtedly lascivious, and the performance pleased both Herod and his guests. Under the influence of her charms, Herod made a rash promise. Perhaps he underestimated her, thinking that as a mere child, she would ask for trinkets or for wealth, which he had in abundance. He never anticipated that she would ask what he feared to do most.

14:8. Charger. A flat wooden dish on which meat was served. Salome was **instructed [by] her mother** to request **John Baptist's head**. Perhaps her mother, knowing Herod's probable reaction, also goaded her to dance. Her mother may have expressed her hatred for John in the past and told Salome that if she ever got the chance, she should make this request. It is interesting that Salome requested John's head; surely she would have wanted other things more. Perhaps her mother had threatened her if, given the opportunity, she requested something else.

14:9. Herod, a man driven by his lusts and by guilt and fear, nevertheless could be morally scrupulous at certain points, which is why he granted her request, **for the oath's sake.** The Bible presents fallen humanity in all of its complexity. People can commit serious sins and yet be scrupulous regarding other sins. In addition, this verse shows again how Herod was driven by public opinion. He granted her request also because of **them which sat with him at meat,** that is, his guests. He would not go back on his word for fear of what those around him would think. Both his having spared John previously and his decision to behead him were thus driven, in part, by fear of what people would think. Would that we all would heed this warning and be driven by what God thinks rather than by the opinions of others.

14:10–11. Herod fulfilled her request immediately.

14:12. Jesus was told of John's beheading. This verse connects the section to what follows.

IV. Jesus' Withdrawals from Galilee (14:13–17:20)

A. To the Eastern Shore of the Sea of Galilee (14:13–15:20)

14:13–21. This incident, the feeding of the five thousand, is recorded in all four gospels (see Mark 6:33–44; Luke 9:10–17; John 6:1–15 and discussions). It must have made quite an impression on the disciples. In all four accounts, the event is recorded as a miracle, leaving no room to see it as anything else. Some have tried to say that the people were shamed into sharing their food and that this is how everyone got fed, but if that had been the case, the story would have been recorded that way somewhere, and the accounts we have would vary far more widely than they do. As it is, the variations between the four accounts can be harmonized and in no way indicate that the Bible is in error in any detail. Nor do the variations justify the notion that this account is fabricated in any way. What is recorded is what happened. A noteworthy miracle took place, one that the disciples never forgot.

14:13–14. Jesus **departed** (v. 13) because of the beheading of John. Jesus' ministry was not yet complete, and He did not want to be in danger at this time. He thus went to a remote location, yet even there, He attracted crowds. That they were far from the city, and therefore from food supplies, sets the scene for the miracle that follows.

14:15–16. Jesus wanted to test the faith of the disciples. He prompted them to do what He knew they could not do on their own. They needed to trust Him for what was to follow. Many times God will ask of believers what may seem impossible, and which, in their own resources, is impossible. We should remember that when He leads us into a ministry, He will provide the resources for success. All we need to do is obey Him.

14:17–19. Here the lack of resources on the part of the disciples is made clear, as well as their obedience to the Lord. With no fanfare, Jesus accepted the little food they had and used it to bless the people. He gave the food to the disciples, who gave it to **the multitude**. Other gospels reveal that the source of what food the disciples did have was a small boy's lunch, but that detail did not concern Matthew. It is hard to read this passage without seeing a parallel to ministry in general. We offer to God what we have. He blesses it and commands us to share of our spiritual resources with the people to whom He calls us to minister. This is not an allegory, as it is a historical

incident, but the parallel is clear and is at least a part of the significance of this passage.

14:20–21. There was more than enough food for everyone. God is not limited by personal resources. All He asks for is availability and obedience, and He will take care of the rest. **Beside women and children** (v. 21). Matthew alone noted this. He was writing to the Jews, who did not permit women and children to eat with men in public. The women and children were thus in a place by themselves.

14:22. Constrained. The Greek word used here is strong. It means "to compel" and suggests a crisis. John recorded that after the miracle of the loaves and fish, the crowds "would come and take him by force, to make him a king" (John 6:15). This involved a complete misunderstanding of Jesus' mission. The disciples may have been caught up in the enthusiasm and needed to be removed from the area quickly (see 16:5–12). Also, Jesus may have wanted to set the scene for the miracle of His walking on water. Jesus **sent the multitudes away** after He sent the disciples away. Apparently, He had more in mind than just telling the people goodbye and leaving immediately. He probably preached to them one more time and left them with words of encouragement and exhortation. Perhaps He spoke to them in small groups according to where they lived, with specific exhortations, before dismissing them.

14:23. To pray. Matthew recorded Jesus praying fewer times than Luke recorded, who emphasized Jesus' humanity. Besides here, Matthew showed Jesus praying in Gethsemane (cf. 26:36–46) and on the cross (27:46). Jesus also thanked the Father for the provision both for the five thousand (14:19) and for the four thousand (15:36). Jesus certainly needed spiritual strength at this time; He had just completed a strenous time of ministry, and many needs had been brought to Him during the course of the day.

14:24. This verse sets the scene for the miracle of Jesus walking on the sea. The disciples were in a stormy sea, in the night. It was perhaps frightening even for the skilled boatmen among them, and well might they have thought they saw "a spirit" (14:36) coming to them on the water.

14:25. The fourth watch. 3:00–6:00 a.m. According to Roman reckoning, the night was divided into four watches: (1) 6:00–9:00 p.m., (2) 9:00 p.m.–midnight, (3) midnight–3:00 a.m., and (4) 3:00–6:00 a.m. (see *KJV Study Bible* note on Mark 13:35). The Jews had only three watches during the night: (1) sunset–10:00 p.m., (2) 10:00 p.m.–2:00 a.m., and (3) 2:00 a.m.–sunrise (see Judg. 7:19; 1 Sam. 11:11). For **walking on the sea**, see discussion on Mark 6:48.

14:26–27. As noted in 14:24, it was a dark, stormy night. The disciples did not recognize Jesus immediately and would not have expected to have seen Him coming in that way in any case. Jesus **spake unto them** (v. 27) a word of comfort.

14:28–31. This passage describes Peter walking on the water. It is a favorite passage for preaching, as it is a vivid example of genuine faith and of faith that yet falls short. Apparently, Peter either did not recognize Jesus' face due to the darkness or was not sure it was really Him, for he said, **Lord, if it be thou** (v. 28). His request to come out onto the water is startling. It is often, and perhaps rightly, seen as an example of Peter's impetuosity, his tendency to speak before thinking. Having made the challenge, Peter had no choice but to step out of the boat at the Lord's bidding. Peter was fine until **he saw the wind boysterous** (v. 30), then, shifting his focus away from the Lord, he suddenly and naturally became **afraid** and began **to sink**. It is no misuse of this passage to point out that Peter looked at the circumstances rather than at the Savior, and thus his faith failed. He prayed the shortest prayer in all of the Bible, **Lord, save me**, and Jesus did so. They returned to the boat together. One should be careful when preaching this passage, however. Matthew's purpose was to show that Jesus is the Messiah, not to give an illustration of faith. The passage can be used in that way, as long as one keeps in mind Matthew's real purpose, which is made clear in the next two verses.

14:32–33. When Peter and Jesus returned to the ship, **the wind ceased** (v. 32), meaning that the storm ended immediately. The disciples had witnessed, in a fairly short period of time, several miracles. Jesus had healed the people (14:14), had fed five thousand of them miraculously, had walked on water, and had enabled Peter to do the same. Then He stilled the storm. He had shown power over nature and power to supernaturally meet needs. The disciples **worshipped him** (v. 33), recognizing that He is **the Son of God**. This was Matthew's point. Only God could do the things Jesus had done in the space of the last twenty-four hours.

14:34–36. These verses briefly explain what Jesus did once on the other side of the sea and demonstrate His growing popularity. He had been healing since early in His ministry, and the leaders of the community quickly spread the word of His arrival. People were healed merely by **touch[ing] the hem of his garment** (v. 36; see discussion on Mark 5:28), which was symbolic of their faith in Him. Jesus often challenged those whom He healed about their faith (see, e.g., Matt. 9:22; 15:28), and there is no warrant to assume that faith was not central here as well. Jesus' healing ministry made clear that His power came from God. He was no conjurer or caster of spells. His power came from God, and He needed no aids to heal.

Gennesaret (v. 34). Either the narrow plain, about four miles long and less than two miles wide, on the west side of the Sea of Galilee near the north end (north of Magdala), or a town in the plain. The plain, fertile and well watered, was considered a garden spot of the Holy Land.

15:1–20. This passage illustrates a familiar pattern. An incident raised a particular question, and Jesus took the opportunity to teach on the matter. Here Matthew recorded another instance of opposition to Christ on the part of the Pharisees, along with some scribes (vv. 1–2). Jesus answered them with a specific challenge on the matter they had brought up (vv. 3–9), and then He called the multitudes to Himself and taught them a more general principle based on the same incident (vv. 10–20).

15:1–2. These **scribes and Pharisees … were of Jerusalem** (v. 1). Matthew noted this since he was beginning to point the narrative toward the showdown in Jerusalem, at the trial of Jesus. His ministry had now attracted attention as far away as Jerusalem, and opposition to Him from official sources came from there as well. **The tradition of the elders** (v. 2). After the Babylonian captivity, the Jewish rabbis began to make meticulous rules and regulations governing the daily life of the people. These were interpretations and applications of the law of Moses, handed down from generation to generation. In Jesus' day, this "tradition of the elders" was in oral form. It was not until circa AD 200 that it was put into writing in the Mishnah. The Pharisees complained that the disciples **wash not their hands** (see Mark 7:1–4). Their objection had to do with an outward observance. By eating with unwashed hands, the disciples were possibly putting into themselves something that was not pure. This became the touchstone of Jesus' teaching to the multitude (see 15:10–11).

15:3–6. In responding to their objection, Jesus began by issuing the Pharisees and scribes a counterchallenge, asking why they had substituted for the written law a man-made **tradition** (v. 3), one that many had taken advantage of to the detriment of their parents. Jesus was admittedly answering a question with a question, but in doing so, He revealed the hypocrisy of His questioners. He cited the commandment about honoring one's parents (v. 4) and then their tradition that set aside the clear commandment (vv. 5–6; see discussions on Mark 7:10–11, 13). The Pharisees had no answer. They had raised a point of strict observance to ceremonial law, and Jesus countered with a point on which they were setting aside a law that involved important family relationships. No one could argue that the point on which they had challenged Jesus was more important than taking care of family, and clearly these leaders were making an issue of something that was small in comparison to their own teaching, which also violated the strict letter of the law.

15:7–9. Jesus then condemned the Pharisees as **hypocrites** (v. 7) and cited Isaiah's prophecy against those who honor the Lord outwardly **with their lips; but their heart is far from me** (v. 8; Isa. 29:13). Their worship was **vain** (v. 9); that is, it was empty of any value and did neither them nor the Lord any

good. This condemnation relates to Jesus' teaching to the multitude (see 15:10–11). God is concerned not with what is on the outside but with what is in the heart. Going through the motions of worship or obeying laws that relate only to the physical side of life does not mean much if one's heart is not in it.

15:10–11. Jesus **called the multitude** (v. 10) and told them that what **cometh out of the mouth** (v. 11), or out of one's heart, is what **defileth a man**. What goes in does not defile. In other words, what a person has in her heart, not what she eats, determines her character. Outward observance of the ceremonial law is easy and proves nothing about the heart. The heart attitude, which comes out in the way one treats others, demonstrates whether one is righteous or defiled. This harks back to the Sermon on the Mount, in which Jesus pointed out in different ways how the heart attitude, not the actions, demonstrate true righteousness. Here again the people were challenged to seek a righteousness that "shall exceed the righteousness of the scribes and Pharisees" (Matt. 5:20).

15:12–14. Jesus' disciples were concerned that Jesus had **offended** (v. 12) the authorities, perhaps because this incident occurred so soon after the beheading of John. Jesus' reply seems not to relate directly to their concern, but He was showing them that the Pharisees were on the wrong side of the question. God would take care of the problem in His own time. **Every plant, which my heavenly Father hath not planted** (v. 13) may be understood in two ways. (1) It may refer to the false teaching of the Pharisees, harking back to the parable of the sower. In this case, Jesus was saying that the false teaching would not take root in the people's hearts. (2) It may refer to the Pharisees themselves, harking back to the parable of the tares. In this case, Jesus was saying that the scribes and Pharisees, as false teachers, would be rooted out by God. Either way, Jesus wanted His disciples to know that the truth He preached would prevail and that they should not be concerned that some opposed it. Jesus did not deal specifically with the possible consequences to Himself for upsetting the Pharisees, but His teaching made it clear that His mission was to teach the truth and let God take care of error, in whatever form.

15:15 – 20. Jesus, in response to Peter's request, explained to the disciples clearly that what is in the heart is most important. Outward things do not defile. He used the example of eating food. Even "unclean" food is eliminated by the body. To make sure He was understood concerning what comes out of the heart, Jesus presented a sin list. The list, which includes not only things forbidden in the Ten Commandments but also **evil thoughts** (v. 19), harks back to matters He discussed in the Sermon on the Mount. His point was that the outward keeping of the commandments is no good if the heart is not right.

B. To Phoenicia (15:21 – 28)

15:21. For **Tyre,** see discussion on Mark 7:24. **Sidon.** About twenty-five miles north of Tyre. Matthew did not say why Jesus went to minister in this region.

15:22. A woman of Canaan. This term is found many times in the Old Testament but only here in the New Testament. In New Testament times, there was no country known as Canaan. Some think this was the Semitic manner of referring to the people of Phoenicia at the time. Mark wrote, "The woman was a Greek, a Syrophenician" (Mark 7:26). This woman knew that Jesus was the **Son of David** and apparently knew why that was important. She also was aware that Jesus cast out demons.

15:23. Jesus' response appears cold, but He wanted to test the woman's faith. The disciples wanted Him to **Send her away.**

15:24. Here Jesus gave an answer that Matthew's Jewish readers would have readily understood. Jesus told the woman that His mission was to the Jewish people, **the lost sheep of the house of Israel.** Jesus had every intention of meeting her need, but His focus in ministry at this time was the Jewish people. Matthew used this incident, however, to remind his readers that the gospel has a universal aspect as well. By contrasting Jesus' statement regarding the focus of His mission with His subsequent action, Matthew

was able both to confirm his readers' understanding of Israel's position as the chosen people of God and to challenge them with the wider ministry of the church as it would develop over time.

15:25 – 26. The children's bread (v. 26). That belonging to "the lost sheep of the house of Israel" (15:24). **Dogs.** The Greek says "little dogs," meaning a pet dog in the home. Jesus' point was that the gospel was to be given first to Jews.

15:27 – 28. Truth, Lord (v. 27; see *KJV Study Bible* note on Mark 7:28). The woman understood Jesus' implication and was willing to settle for **crumbs.** Twice she called Him "Lord" in this passage. The Greek for this title can mean something close to "sir," but in light of the nature of her request and the fact that she called Him "Son of David" (15:22), it is not unreasonable to assume that she understood at least His messianic role, though not necessarily His deity.

Jesus left the region immediately after this event, and it is reasonable to suppose that He believed that His work there was now finished. This incident could have been left out of Matthew's account with no loss of continuity. That he recorded it was most likely due to his desire to show his readers the universal nature of the gospel.

C. To the Decapolis (15:29 – 16:12)

15:29 – 39. See Mark 7:31 – 8:10 and discussions.

15:29 – 31. Jesus **departed** (v. 29) and ministered near **the sea of Galilee.** The **multitudes came** (v. 30), bringing the sick, **and he healed them.** Because of the healings, **they glorifed the God of Israel** (v. 31). Jesus' miracles always pointed to God. They were never done just for their own sake. Jesus taught many things just by doing these miracles of healing: the compassion of God, the grace of God, the need for faith, and the perfect will of God, among others.

15:32 – 38. The feeding of the five thousand is recorded in all four gospels, but the feeding of the four thousand is only found in Matthew and Mark. In the feeding of the five thousand, twelve baskets were filled with leftovers, which Jesus possibly gave to the twelve apostles, though some think He gave them to the little boy. The **seven baskets** (v. 37) mentioned here were possibly larger baskets.

15:39. Magdala. The home of Mary Magdalene. Mark 8:10 has "Dalmanutha."

16:1–4. This incident marks a turning point in Jesus' interaction with the Pharisees. For one thing, the Saducees joined in the effort to trap Jesus. The Pharisees and Saducees were rivals over some matters of Old Testament interpretation relating to the supernatural, but they were now working together to discredit Jesus. Another mark of a turning point is how they sought to trap Jesus. Whereas previously the Pharisees had asked for a sign (see 12:38), now they asked for **a sign from heaven** (v. 1). They sought something spectacular and more directly supernatural, a heavenly affirmation of His ministry (see discussion on Mark 8:11). It is hardly credible that they actually believed Jesus could or would do this. They wanted to expose Him as a fraud when He either refused or failed. Apparently, they were aware that the multitudes recognized Jesus as the Messiah. In the past, the Pharisees had challenged Jesus on matters related to Sabbath-breaking and the interpretation of the law; now they challenged the central point of His ministry at this stage: His messiahship. Jesus did not provide them with "a sign from heaven" but instead rebuked them for being able to forecast the weather but unable to **discern the signs of the times** (v. 3). He also rebuked them for seeking a sign at all and promised them only **the sign of the prophet Jonas** (v. 4). This is the second time that Jesus pointed to Jonah in reply to a request for a sign (see 12:39–40). He offered no explanation, unlike the previous occasion, but one may assume that He had the same point in mind. The sign that He would give would be His own resurrection (see discussion on Luke 11:30). That would be proof and vindication of His ministry, His messiahship, and His right to rule on the throne of David forever.

16:5–6. This is another situation in which Jesus took advantage of a teaching opportunity. The disciples **had forgotten to take bread** (v. 5) with them for the journey. For **the leaven of the Pharisees and of the Saducees**, see 16:12; see also discussions on 3:7; Mark 2:16; 8:15; 12:18.

16:7–12. The disciples' discussion reveals that they were clueless as to what Jesus meant (v. 7). He explained the matter directly, pointing to the feeding of **the five thousand** (v. 9) and the feeding of **the four thousand** (v. 10) and reminding them of the abundance of the leftovers. When they were with Jesus, they had no need to worry about food, for He could supply all they needed. Jesus had something much more important in mind here, however. Matthew ended with a short commentary on what the disciples now **understood** (v. 12), that Jesus was warning them about **the doctrine of the Pharisees and the Saducees**. Matthew often explained the meaning of Jesus' words (see 17:13).

Christians today might well heed this warning. So often believers are led astray because they like the personality of the minister or they enjoy the music program of a church. All of these things are good, but believers must be careful that they do not sacrifice truth on the altar of entertainment and good feelings. Christian faith is faith in the truth about Jesus Christ — His life, death, and resurrection — and its significance for salvation. It is faith in the truths revealed in God's Word. Considerations other than truth should not guide one's choices in matters of faith and practice.

D. To Caesarea Philippi (16:13–17:21)

16:13. Cesarea Philippi. To be distinguished from the magnificent city of Caesarea Maritima, which Herod the Great built on the coast of the Mediterranean. Caesarea Philippi, rebuilt by Herod's son Philip (who named it after Tiberius Caesar and himself), was twenty-five miles north of the Sea of Galilee, near the slopes of Mount Hermon. Originally it was called Paneas (the ancient name survives today as Banias) in honor of the Greek god Pan, whose shrine was located there. The region was especially pagan. It is interesting to note that Jesus took His Jewish disciples to this very Gentile place to announce the establishment of His church, which would include both Jews and Gentiles.

Jesus asked His disciples about the peoples' understanding of His identity. For **the Son of man**, see discussion on Mark 2:10. His purpose was to set up the revelation of the truth concerning who He is. Sometimes one must clear up misconceptions before stating the truth.

16:14 – 15. Perhaps in the moment of stating out loud, for the first time, some of what they had heard, the disciples saw that none of these answers made any sense, but His messiahship did. The answers the disciples gave included the one that Herod had earlier believed, that Jesus was John the Baptist resurrected from the dead. Jesus followed up with a question that required them to make a decision. Good preaching and teaching should always aim for a decision. The disciples could have debated the relative merits of different theories all day long, but it was time for them to recognize and state the truth.

16:16. It was Peter who spoke, but his confession may be understood as reflecting the understanding of all the disciples. **Christ**, or "Messiah" (also in 16:20). Both mean "the Anointed One." The Old Testament equivalent ("Messiah") is used of anyone who was anointed with the holy oil, such as the priests and kings of Israel (see, e.g., Exod. 29:7, 21; 1 Sam. 10:1, 6; 16:13; 2 Sam. 1:14, 16). The word carries the idea of being chosen by God, consecrated to His service, and endued with His power to accomplish the assigned task. Toward the end of the Old Testament period, the word assumed a special meaning. It denoted the ideal king anointed and empowered by God to rescue His people from their enemies and establish His righteous kingdom (see Dan. 9:25 – 26). The ideas that clustered around the title "Messiah" tended to be political and national in nature. Probably for that reason, Jesus seldom used the term. He did, however, on occasion acknowledge Himself as Messiah (see Mark 8:27 – 30; 14:61 – 63; John 4:25 – 26).

16:17. Jesus pointed out that Peter had come to this knowledge not by human means but by revelation. Others had come up with answers to His identity that made no sense, such as that he was John the Baptist or Elijah. This is because human reasoning cannot get to divine truth. Christians today might well recognize that it is by submitting to the teaching of God's Word, illumined by the Spirit, that one will come to the knowledge of the truth. Human wisdom leads to a dead end. Submission to God's Word under the teaching of God's Spirit leads to life.

16:18. Peter … rock … church. In the Greek, "Peter" is *Petros* ("detached stone") and "rock" is *petra* ("bedrock"). Several interpretations have been given to these words. The "bedrock" on which the church is built is (1) Christ; (2) Peter's confession of faith in Jesus as the Messiah (16:16); (3) Christ's teachings — one of the great emphases of Matthew's gospel; (4) Peter himself, understood in terms of his role on the day of Pentecost (see Acts 2) and in the Cornelius incident (see Acts 10) and his leadership among the apostles. The best answer is that it refers to Peter's confession, which is expressive of the disciples' faith and hence the apostles' doctrine. The rock on which the church is built is the confession that Jesus Christ is Lord, that He is the "chosen one," chosen to die for the sins of the world and chosen to reign. Ephesians 2:20 indicates that the church is "built upon the foundation of the apostles and prophets." This perhaps means that it is built on the foundation of the Old Testament and the preaching of the apostles, that is, on the Word of God in the Old and New Testaments. In the Gospels, the word **church** (Greek, *ekklēsia*; "called out" or "assembly") is used only by Matthew (here and twice in 18:17). In the Septuagint, it is used for the congregation of Israel. In Greek circles of Jesus' day, it indicated the assembly of a city's free, voting citizens (see Acts 19:32, 39, 41). Matthew's use of "church" need not be understood as a later addition. Jesus could very well have used the word here, or an Aramaic word that could well be translated this way. Jesus meant that He would gather His people, "assemble" them, around the truth of His identity and mission. **Hell.** The English word here translates the Greek name for the place of departed spirits, Hades, generally equivalent to the Hebrew *sheol* (see discussion on Gen. 37:35). **The gates of hell** refers to the kingdom of Satan (i.e., all forces opposed to Christ and His kingdom). It has been noted, however, that gates are not an offensive weapon; they are for defense. Believers need to take the initiative. Too often Christians lament that the forces of evil seem to be winning in the world, when they should be on the offensive, presenting truth and bringing people to Christ.

16:19. Keys. Perhaps Peter used these keys on the day of Pentecost (see Acts 2), when he announced that the door of the kingdom was unlocked to Jews and proselytes, and later when he acknowledged that it was also opened to Gentiles (see Acts 10). **Bind … loose.** Not authority to determine, but rather to announce guilt or innocence (see 18:18 and the context there; see also Acts 5:3, 9). In other words, Peter could carry on his ministry of evangelism because God had already opened doors of mercy in heaven.

16:20. That they should tell no man. Because of the false concepts of the Jews, who looked for an exclusively national and political Messiah, Jesus told His disciples not to publicize Peter's confession, lest it precipitate a revolution against Rome (see discussion on 8:4).

16:21–22. Began … to shew unto his disciples (v. 21). The beginning of a new emphasis in Jesus' ministry. Instead of teaching the crowds in parables, He concentrated on preparing the disciples for His coming suffering and death. The disciples' recognition of His identity certainly was the factor in opening this chapter in His ministry. **That he must … be killed.** This was Jesus' first prophecy of His death. Peter understandably sought to stop Him from making these comments. No one likes to hear that a loved one will have to suffer, and it is natural to always hope for and expect the best.

16:23. Satan is a loanword from Hebrew, meaning "adversary" or "accuser," and Jesus may have meant it only in that sense, rather than accusing Peter of being in league with the Devil. Peter's offense was that he was looking at the matter from a purely human standpoint. He was Jesus' "adversary" in that the cross was the plan of God, and Peter should not oppose what God had ordained. It may be that Peter's opposition went beyond merely private words with Jesus and that he had been laying plans with the other disciples to keep Jesus away from Jerusalem.

16:24. Take up his cross (see discussion on 10:38; *KJV Study Bible* note on Mark 8:34). Coming right on the heels of His statements regarding His coming death, these words had real significance. Jesus was pointing out to His disciples that they had to be ready to suffer if they were to follow one who was ordained to suffer.

16:25. This verse lays out a general principle. **Save his life** implies someone seeking ways to make his own life comfortable, good, and pleasant. Everyone wants a pleasant and happy life, one that is fulfilling. Unfortunately, most people seek it directly by trying to make themselves happy. The principle here is that such an effort will fail. The proof is seen by looking around at most Americans today. America has been defined as 305 million people desperately trying to make themselves happy. A better route is for one to **lose his life** for the sake of the Lord; then he **shall find it.** That is, if someone sacrifices their own goals, dreams, and happiness for the sake of following Christ, the end result will be a happier, more fulfilling life. In general, a life lived unselfishly will be happier than a life lived for oneself. Specifically, in this context, Jesus was pointing out that someone who dies for Christ and the gospel has lost nothing. He or she will find blessing in eternity. Jesus was making an extreme application of the general principle here, one that Matthew may have felt a need to record for the encouragement of his readers who may have faced just such a possibility.

16:26. Jesus reiterated the reason for the principle. What good is it to **gain the whole world,** that is, every physical pleasure, if in the end it means one will **lose his own soul?**

16:27. For **the Son of man,** see discussion on Mark 2:10. **Shall come.** Refers to the parousia, the eschatological coming of Christ. When Christ returns, those who have suffered for Him will be rewarded. Those who sought this world's pleasures will receive no reward and will know then that they traded away what was truly worthwhile for something worthless.

16:28. There are two main interpretations of this verse: (1) It is a prophecy of the transfiguration, which happened a week later (see 17:1) and which demonstrated that Jesus will return in His Father's glory (see 16:27; discussion on 2 Peter 1:16). (2) It refers to the Son of Man's authority and kingly reign in His post-resurrection church. Some of His disciples would witness and even participate in this, as described in the book of Acts. The context seems to favor the first view.

17:1–9. The transfiguration was: (1) a revelation of the glory of the Son of God, a glory now hidden but to be fully revealed when He returns; (2) a confirmation of the difficult teaching given to the disciples at Caesarea Philippi (see 16:13–20); and (3) a beneficial experience for the disciples, who were discouraged after having been reminded so recently of Jesus' impending suffering and death (see 16:21). See discussions on Mark 9:2–13; Luke 9:28–36.

17:1. After six days. Mark also has "after six days" (Mark 9:2), counting just the days between Peter's confession and the transfiguration, whereas Luke, counting all the days involved, wrote, "about an eight days after" (Luke 9:28). **Peter, James, and John.** These three disciples had an especially close relationship with Jesus (see 26:37; Mark 5:37). **High mountain.** Its identity is unknown, although the reference to Caesarea Philippi (16:13) may suggest that it was Mount Hermon, which was just northeast of Caesarea Philippi (see discussion on Luke 9:28). **Apart.** Luke added "to pray" (Luke 9:28).

17:2. Was transfigured. His appearance changed. The three disciples saw Jesus in His glorified state (see John 17:5; 2 Peter 1:17).

17:3. Moses and Elias (i.e., "Elijah"; see discussion on Luke 9:30). Moses appeared as the representative of the old covenant (the law) and the promise of salvation, which was soon to be fulfilled in the death of Jesus. Elijah appeared as the appointed restorer of all things and as the representative of the prophets (see Mal. 4:5–6; Mark 9:11–13). Luke 9:31 says that they talked about Christ's death.

17:4. Peter was not thinking but rather was speaking out of his excitement. For **three tabernacles,** see *KJV Study Bible* note on Mark 9:5; discussion on Luke 9:33.

17:5. Them. Jesus, Moses, and Elijah. **This is my beloved Son, in whom I am well pleased.** The same words spoken from heaven at Jesus' baptism (3:17). No mere man, but the very Son of God, was transfigured.

17:6. Sore afraid. Primarily with a sense of awe at the presence and majesty of God.

17:7–9. They came down from the mountain (v. 9), the disciples certainly being excited and perhaps a little shaken by the experience. Jesus forbade them to speak of the incident, however, until after the resurrection.

17:10–11. The traditional eschatology of the teachers of the law, based on Malachi 4:5–6, held that Elijah must appear before the coming of the Messiah. The disciples reasoned that if Jesus really was the Messiah, as the transfiguration proved Him to be, why had not Elijah appeared?

17:12. Elias is come already. John the Baptist was Elias in the sense that he prophesied in the spirit and manner of Elijah, against great wickedness. **Likewise.** As John the Baptist was not recognized but was killed, so Jesus would be rejected and killed.

17:13. The disciples understood what Jesus meant (see discussion on 16:12). This also echoed the teaching He had given them in chapter 16 about His coming suffering and death.

17:14–18. The child was possessed by a demon, and the disciples were unable to deal with it. The man seemed to be unaware that the child's lunacy was caused by a demon, since he sought only a **cure** (v. 16) rather than to have it "cast out." Oftentimes we do not know what we really need, but when we come to our Lord with our petitions, He answers our real need, not our specific request.

How long …? (v. 17). Here Jesus was rebuking not the child's father but rather His disciples. It may be understood as a gentle rebuke for their lack of faith (see 17:20). Jesus cast out the demon, **and the child was cured** (v. 18). Where the disciples had struggled, Jesus accomplished the task easily.

17:19–21. The ease with which Jesus dealt with the demon impressed the disciples, and they asked Him, **Why could not we cast him out?** (v. 19). Jesus' answer pointed to their need for faith. For **mustard seed** (v. 20), see discussion on 13:31–32. **Say unto**

this mountain, **Remove hence to yonder place**. A proverbial statement meaning to remove great difficulties (see Isa. 54:10; 1 Cor. 13:2). Jesus ended with the statement that **this kind goeth not out but by prayer and fasting** (v. 21). Two things may be learned from this. (1) Prayer and fasting increase faith. It was the disciples' lack of faith that hindered them, and prayer and fasting would have given them success, so faith increases with prayer and fasting. (2) There are different kinds of demons. One should not make too much of this, but the inference from this Scripture is at least interesting. It should also serve as a warning to Christians who think the area of demons and exorcism is one they want to explore. It is more complex than one can imagine and requires more faith than most Christians have. It is best left alone.

V. Jesus' Last Ministry in Galilee (17:22–18:35)

A. Jesus Foretells His Death (17:22–23)

17:22–23. For the second time, Jesus tells His disciples of His coming death, the first time having been in 16:21. Jesus, however, at least alluded to it when He mentioned the Son of Man being raised from the dead in 17:9. Here He was much more explicit: **The Son of Man shall be betrayed** (v. 22), **they shall kill him** (v. 23), and on **the third day he shall be raised again**. Earlier the disciples had reacted with fear and rejection of this message, probably under the leadership of Peter. Now, perhaps because of the transfiguration and Jesus' rebuke, Peter made no move. The disciples **were exceeding sorry**. It may be that the specificity of Jesus' words account for the different reaction.

B. Temple Tax (17:24–27)

17:24. Tribute money. The annual temple tax was required of every male twenty years of age and older (see Exod. 30:13; 2 Chron. 24:9; Neh. 10:32). It was literally a double drachma, worth approximately two days' wages, and was used for the upkeep of the temple. Perhaps the leaders were again trying to find some way to accuse Jesus.

17:25. Peter, being loyal, answered **Yes** and then went to Jesus. Jesus gently pointed out that He did not owe the tax. He is the Son. He was exempt from the tax, as one of the **kings ... children**.

17:26–27. Then are the children free (v. 26). Jesus would pay the tax, not because He owed it, but because it would prevent offense. Likewise, Christians should never use their standing with the Lord to offend others. They should be willing to make any sacrifice, to give up any "right," if doing so will prevent them from being a stumbling block to the gospel. Jesus might have asserted His privilege as the Son, but such an assertion would have looked egotistical and like an effort just to avoid making a minor tax payment. How much better to simply pay the tax, offend no one, and gain a hearing for the message. Jesus' manner of paying the tax, however, involved a miraculous event. Peter was to go fishing, and **the fish that first cometh up** (v. 27) would have in its mouth enough money to pay the tax for both of them.

C. Discourse on Life in the Kingdom (chap. 18)

18:1. The disciples brought a question to Jesus: **Who is the greatest in the kingdom ...?** (see discussion on Luke 9:46). This was not a proper question, as the kingdom is not about self-exaltation. Their question showed a positive note as well, however. The disciples, under the influence of Jesus' teaching, were taking the kingdom of God seriously, as a reality on which they were now willing to plan. This question opens a section of teaching that extends into chapter 20. Jesus used a variety of means to teach that the kingdom is not about self-exaltation but rather about humility, service, and sacrifice. Rewards in the kingdom are not given out on the same basis as in this world, and the "path to the top" is very different from the self-centered, backbiting world that the disciples knew in their day and that still prevails in our time.

18:2–4. Jesus did not upbraid the disciples for their poor understanding but instead used the opportunity to teach them further about the nature of the kingdom. He told them that they must be **as little children** (v. 3). They must trust God, as a child trusts adult authorities, and they must be humble rather than exalted. The kingdom is not about exalting oneself but rather about humbling oneself. Jesus had taught them in the Sermon on the Mount to turn the other cheek and to go beyond whatever someone might request of them. These actions require an attitude of humility as well as trust in the sovereignty of God. One who trusts God to care for his needs can give his coat to another, and one who trusts God to bring about justice in His own time can turn the other cheek. Jesus reinforced His prior teaching with the illustration of being childlike. He called the one who **shall humble himself ... the greatest in the kingdom of heaven** (v. 4). This is hyperbole and reinforces the point that Christ's followers are to value humility as much as the world values self-exaltation.

18:5–6. Jesus said that to **receive [a] child in [His] name** (v. 5) is to receive Him. This is an affirmation of children's ministry but also a promise that Jesus notes and blesses kindnesses bestowed in His name. He followed this promise, however, with a warning about **offend[ing] one of these little ones which believe in me** (v. 6). "Offend" is contrasted with "receive" in this context. The idea is that one who points a child away from Jesus and toward sin will suffer grave consequences, whereas one who receives a child "in [Jesus'] name," that is, pointing the child toward Christ and His teaching, will be blessed. In His warning, Jesus again, as He often did, used a vivid image drawn from agriculture to make His point. **A millstone** is literally "a millstone of a donkey," that is, a millstone turned by a donkey. This type of millstone was far larger and heavier than the small millstones (see 24:41) that women used each morning in their homes.

18:7. This is a general statement about **offences**, bridging between what Jesus had just said about offending children (18:5–6) and the comments about the one who offends in verses 8–9.

18:8–9. "That man by whom the offence cometh" (18:7) is here **thy hand or thy foot** (v. 8)

or **thine eye** (v. 9). If it is so bad for a whole man who brings an offense that it were better if "he were drowned" (18:6), then losing one part of the body should seem small by comparison. Jesus was not being literal but wanted to impress on His disciples the need to be serious about repentance of sin (see discussion on 5:29–30).

18:10. Their angels. Guardian angels are not exclusively for children but are for God's people in general (see Ps. 34:7; 91:11; Heb. 1:14). **Do always behold** means that they have constant access to God.

18:11. Here Jesus' statement appears to refer specifically to saving children, following immediately upon the context of 18:1–10. "Little ones" (v. 10) may have application to any child of God, however, making the application of this verse universal. His mission is to save lost people in general. It ties in to 18:14 because Jesus does the will of His Father. Put together, this whole passage means that God does not want His children to stumble or perish, and Jesus wants to save them. "Their angels" (18:10) are thus always in the presence of God in heaven, ready to do His will on their behalf. Anyone who hinders their spiritual life is therefore justly condemned.

18:12–14. The parable of the lost sheep is also found in Luke 15:3–7. There it applies to unbelievers, here to believers. Jesus used the same parable to teach different truths in different situations. On **sheep** (vv. 12–13), see discussion on Luke 15:4.

18:15–20. This is the well-known "Matthew 18 passage" on church discipline. It outlines specific steps to take when one is offended by a Christian brother. This passage deals specifically with an offense between church members. Often it is applied to a believer who is caught in sin generally. It may certainly be applied that way, as the steps outlined here are workable for that situation as well, but the context is of an offense between two people. The larger context includes the preceding passage, where Jesus condemned those who might offend the "little ones" of the kingdom.

18:15–17. Here **brother** (v. 15) refers not to a biological brother but to a fellow believer. When dealing with an offense between believers, the first step is to approach the brother privately. This is important in case there has been a misunderstanding. In fact, people rarely offend others deliberately. If the misunderstanding can be cleared up privately, often no one is embarrassed. **Hear thee** means simply to agree to reconcile.

The second step is to approach the brother with a small group. This allows for **witnesses** (v. 16) that the offense has taken place. It also underlines for the errant brother the seriousness with which the grieved party takes the matter. A larger group would be intimidating and would expand too greatly the circle of those who know about the offense.

The third and final step is to **tell it unto the church** (v. 17), meaning the local congregation. Here and 16:18 are the only two places where the Gospels speak of the "church." If the offending brother does not listen to the church on the matter, he is to be shunned as **a heathen**, which to the Jews meant any non-Jewish person, **and a publican**, whom they saw as something of a traitor to Israel (see discussion on 5:46). This verse establishes one basis for excommunication.

18:18. In context, the idea here is that someone who rejects the church's verdict and is shunned by the church will forfeit any blessing from God until he repents (see discussion on 16:19).

18:19–20. These verses teach that when the church is assembled, the mind of Christ is available to them. It affirms that believers together can seek the will of God confidently. Specifically, they can move on matters of church discipline with confidence, assuming that they really **are gathered together in [Jesus'] name** (v. 20). This does not sanction actions taken by divisive factions in the church or by those who seek to impose their own will on the congregation. If, however, the church is assembled with a clear sense that they are on the Lord's business and sincerely pray, seeking His will, they can be confident of His guidance.

18:21. Peter came to Jesus with this question in light of the teaching He had just given. Peter may have been wondering whether he should go through the steps Jesus had just outlined (18:15–17) if the

same brother repeated the same offense. When Peter asked about forgiving **seven times**, he was using the number of perfection. In other words, "Should I forgive him as many times as he sins against me, if he repents?"

18:22. Seventy times seven, or "seventy-seven times." In either case, the sense is "times without number" or "as many times as necessary." Jesus was agreeing with Peter but intensifying it so that there would be no question that grace and forgiveness are to be extended to the repentant brother as often as necessary.

18:23–35. This parable explains why forgiveness should be so freely extended. In **the kingdom of heaven** (v. 23; see discussion on 3:2), forgiveness has been freely received and should be just as freely given. Believers have been forgiven much. In light of how much we have offended God, any offense done to us is a small matter. Jesus was not teaching here that an unforgiving heart leads to loss of salvation. With parables, it does not pay to push the analogy too far. Jesus intended only to teach that those who have been forgiven much should, in turn, forgive much. (For the practice of selling into slavery, see Exod. 21:2; Lev. 25:39; 2 Kings 4:1; Neh. 5:5; Isa. 50:1.)

From your hearts forgive (v. 35) is the one main teaching of the parable. One who does not have a forgiving heart will not enjoy fellowship with God. The one who lets bitterness and a hard heart spring up within may be saved but will not enjoy the benefits and blessings thereof, being instead in bondage once again to the power of sin. "From your hearts forgive" is another allusion to the Sermon on the Mount, in which Jesus taught that true obedience is more than just outward actions. It comes from the heart, if one's righteousness is to "exceed the righteousness of the scribes and Pharisees" (5:20).

VI. Jesus' Ministry in Judea and Perea (chaps. 19–20)

A. Teaching concerning Divorce (19:1–12)

19:1–2. Jesus had finished these sayings (v. 1) is one of Matthew's markers of a transition (see Introduction, "Literary Features"). Jesus went to **the**

coasts of Judea beyond Jordan, which is the east side (known later as Transjordan or Perea and today simply as Jordan), and began ministering there (see discussion on Luke 13:22).

19:3. For **Pharisees**, see discussion on Mark 2:16. **For every cause**. This last part of the Pharisees' question is not in the parallel passage in Mark (Mark 10:2). Matthew included it possibly because he was writing to the Jews, who were aware of the dispute between the schools of Shammai and Hillel over the interpretation of Deuteronomy 24:1–4. Shammai held that "some uncleanness" (Deut. 24:1) meant "immorality" (see Matt. 19:9), the only allowable cause for divorce. Hillel (ca. 60 BC–AD 20) emphasized the preceding clause, "she find no favour in his eyes" (Deut. 24:1). He would allow a man to divorce his wife if she did anything he disliked, even if she burned his food while cooking it. Jesus clearly took the side of Shammai (see Matt. 19:9), but only after first pointing back to God's original ideal for marriage in Genesis 1:27; 2:24.

19:4–9. This is the famous passage in Matthew that lays out the prohibition on divorce except in cases of infidelity (v. 9). The Pharisees again sought to test Jesus, trying to find fault with His teaching so that He might be condemned as a heretic, and Jesus once again confounded their efforts. He did this by going beyond the law of Moses to the creation and showing that God's plan from the beginning did not include divorce.

19:5–6. Jesus quoted from the creation account in the book of Genesis. One inference one can draw from this is that the Genesis account of creation is to be treated seriously. It is not an allegory, nor is it a myth. Here Jesus treated it as truth, something that was to be taken seriously in His day and something on which to base one's life decisions. Would that the Old Testament were treated in that way today.

19:7–8. The Pharisees questioned Jesus about the law of Moses' permission for divorce. Jesus' answer reveals an important point about interpreting the Old Testament law. The law was adapted to a sinful world and its conditions. Divorce was permitted because people's hearts were hardened. God's original plan for marriage should guide us, not a loophole

created by conditions of the fall. One may infer that other regulations were treated similarly. For example, the regulation that requires one to return someone's ox if he sees it out running loose (Exod. 23:4) was not permission to allow one's ox to run loose, knowing it would be returned. It was a concession to a less than ideal situation. In the same way, Moses' prescription for divorce was not permission to divorce for any reason whatever. It was a concession to reality. Jesus affirmed this and upheld the ideal.

19:9. Here is the specific statement on divorce. Marriage is a permanent relationship and not severable, **except it be for fornication**. The marriage relationship has been severed already in cases of infidelity, and divorce is permitted. Jesus did not say that divorce is required. In light of the ideal that Jesus had already emphasized, it is best if the marriage can be reconciled and the relationship restored.

19:10–12. See 1 Corinthians 7:7–8, 26, 32–35. The disciples came to a conclusion: **it is not good to marry** (v. 10). Not everyone can accept this teaching, **this saying** (v. 11), because it is not meant for everyone. Jesus then gave three examples of persons for whom it is meant. **Made themselves eunuchs for the kingdom of heaven's sake** (v. 12). Those who have voluntarily adopted a celibate lifestyle to give themselves more completely to God's work. Under certain circumstances, celibacy is recommended in Scripture (see 1 Cor. 7:25–38), but it is never presented as superior to marriage.

B. Teaching concerning Little Children (19:13–15)

19:13–15. Jesus is once again associated with **little children** (vv. 13–14). He reiterated the teaching given in 8:1–14, saying **For of such is** (see discussions on Mark 10:14–15) **the kingdom of heaven** (v. 14; see discussion on 3:2).

C. The Rich Young Man (19:16–30)

19:16–22. This is the story of the rich young man who came to Jesus, wanting eternal life. Jesus used the opportunity to challenge him to live out the meaning of grace. He rejected the challenge.

19:16. For **one came**, see discussion on Mark 10:17. **What good thing shall I do …?** The rich man was thinking in terms of righteousness by works. Jesus had to correct this misunderstanding before answering the question more fully. **Eternal life**. This is the first use of this expression in Matthew's gospel (see 19:29; 25:46). In John, it occurs much more frequently, often taking the place of the term "the kingdom of God [or heaven]," used in the Synoptics, which treat the following three expressions as synonymous: (1) "eternal life" (here; Mark 10:17; Luke 18:18), (2) "enter into the kingdom of heaven [or God]" (Matt. 19:23; Mark 10:24; Luke 18:24), and (3) "be saved" (Matt. 19:25; Mark 10:26; Luke 18:26).

19:17–19. If thou wilt enter into life, keep the commandments (v. 17). To "enter into life" is the same as to "have eternal life" (9:16). One should "keep the commandments," not to establish one's merit before God, but as an expression of true faith. The Bible always teaches that salvation is a gift of God's grace received through faith (see Eph. 2:8). **There is none good but one**. Jesus was not denying His own deity. He may have been challenging the man to see Him as more than just a "Good Master" (19:16). He was also teaching him a lesson about the source of goodness. This man wanted to be "good" so as to qualify for heaven. The only goodness that will count is that which comes from God. The good is not something to be done as meritorious in itself. God alone is good, and all other goodness derives from Him—even the keeping of the commandments, which Jesus proceeded to enumerate (vv. 18–20).

19:20. All these things have I kept (see discussion on Mark 10:20). On the basis of performance, this man had been exemplary.

19:21. Perfect (Greek, *teleios*; "goal," "end"). His goal was eternal life, but wealth and lack of commitment stood in his way. **Go and sell that thou hast**. Jesus was not prescribing a salvation by works. This young man had much wealth, and it is likely that he or his family had earned it. Now he wanted to earn eternal life as well. It may be that Jesus saw an opportunity here to teach him something about grace

by immersing him in it. Eternal life comes by grace, not by works. It is unmerited; it is not a reward for good performance. Jesus challenged the young man to do something that would involve grace. If he gave to the poor what they had not earned, perhaps he would see that God is gracious and gives eternal life to those who have not earned it. As long as he saw blessing and reward as something earned, not something that one receives by grace, he could not see the truth about eternal life. There is no "right" to God's blessing, no "right" to eternal life. God is gracious and gives it to us, not as a reward for doing the right things, but out of His own mercy toward us as sinners. It may be also that Jesus wanted to see the fruits of repentance in the man. He had done "good works" in the sense of keeping the commandments. Now he needed to show forth righteousness from the heart.

19:22. The young man did not accept Jesus' challenge. For **he went away sorrowful**, see discussion on Mark 10:22.

19:23. Jesus offered a commentary for His disciples on what had just taken place, as He had done previously. He was not saying that it is impossible for rich people to be saved, nor that every rich person must sell all that they have. The problem is one of self-reliance. The young man with whom Jesus had just spoken was used to relying on his own resources rather than on God. Rich people often see less need for faith on a daily basis. This is why it is hard for them to **enter into the kingdom of heaven** (see discussion on 3:2).

19:24–25. A camel to go through the eye of a needle (v. 24; see discussion on Mark 10:25). This may well be an example of humor or sarcasm. Obviously, it is hyperbole. The disciples responded as we might, not seeing the hyperbole, and asked the obvious question: **Who then can be saved?** (v. 25).

19:26. Jesus' answer leaves open the possibility that rich people can indeed be saved. It is **impossible** for anyone to save themselves, but God can save anyone (see discussion on Mark 10:27). No one is beyond the reach of God's grace; one need only repent and turn to Christ in simple faith.

19:27–28. Peter spoke up, as was his habit. He pointed out that the disciples had **forsaken all, and followed thee** (v. 27), just what Jesus had commanded the rich young man to do (see 19:21), and asked about their reward. For **Verily I say unto you** (v. 28), see discussion on Mark 3:28. For **the Son of man**, see discussion on Mark 2:10. **Judging**. Governing or ruling. The twelve disciples will someday rule with Christ in His literal millennial kingdom on this earth (see Acts 1:6; compare the Old Testament "judge"; see Judges, Introduction: "Title").

19:29. Jesus then gave a promise for all who follow Christ. They shall not suffer loss in the long run, but of all they give up, they **shall receive an hundredfold**. Mark added, along "with persecutions" (Mark 10:30; see discussion there). In addition, they **shall inherit everlasting life**.

19:30. Here Jesus referred back to His teaching about the kingdom in chapter 18. It is not those who are powerful in the worldly sense who will be great in the kingdom. Earthly fame and wealth are no indication of God's eternal blessing. Just as one must "become as little children" (18:3), so also it is important to remember that many who are unknown in this world will be great in the kingdom. There will be Sunday school teachers who are first because of their faithfulness through many years, while noted preachers and evangelists may find themselves at the back of the line. Jesus was not saying to turn down a significant ministry if the doors open. Accept whatever opportunities God gives you to be an influence for Christ, but recognize that greatness is not measured by earthly success. His statement is meant to encourage humility, regardless of position, not to artificially minimize one's influence for the Lord.

D. The Parable of the Laborers in the Vineyard (20:1–16)

20:1–16. This parable is unique to Matthew. It may emphasize the sovereign graciousness and generosity of God extended to "latecomers" (the poor and the outcasts of society) into God's kingdom. It is not wrong to see this also as referring to those who

trust Christ late in life. Deathbed conversions can be legitimate, and those people are just as saved as the ones who trusted Christ as a small child and served Him for a lifetime. Jesus offered this parable in answer to Peter's question about rewards (see 19:27). Believers are simply to serve and leave the rewards to God. Finally, it points out that all who enter the kingdom do so by grace and are rewarded by God's grace, not on the basis of merit.

20:1–7. A penny (v. 2). This coin, the denarius, was the usual daily wage of a common laborer. A Roman soldier also received one denarius a day. This was not a large wage, but neither was the **householder** (v. 1) taking unfair advantage of the workers. **The third hour** (v. 3). 9:00 a.m. The householder offered the same wage to those hired at this time. **The sixth and ninth hour** (v. 5). Noon and 3:00 p.m. respectively. **The eleventh hour** (v. 6). 5:00 p.m.

20:8–10. When even was come (v. 8). Because farmworkers were poor, the law of Moses required that they be paid at the end of each day (see Lev. 19:13; Deut. 24:14–15). They were all paid a full day's wages, even those who served a short while. In this respect, the householder was generous.

20:11–14. Those who had agreed to the wage that morning supposed they would get more, but it was not to be so. They had agreed to a set wage and could expect no more.

20:15. Is thine eye evil …? The evil eye apparently was associated with jealousy and envy (see 1 Sam. 18:9). Sometimes this parable, especially this verse, is used to justify employers who are stingy with wages. The parable is not about that and should not be used in this way. In fact, the householder was generous, paying those who had worked little the same wage as those who had worked much. If anything, the parable might be seen as justifying generosity, but again the point has nothing to do with economics, labor relations, and wages. The parable should not be put to service in that way.

20:16. This is the summary statement. In this parable, **the last** were **first** in that they got the same reward as the others. So shall it be in the kingdom of heaven.

E. Jesus Prophesies His Coming Death Again (20:17–19)

20:17–19. Once again Jesus emphasized that when they reached **Jerusalem** (v. 18), He would be **condemn[ed] ... to death**. This is the third time Matthew recorded Jesus saying this (see 16:21; 17:22–23; see also Mark 10:32–34; Luke 18:31–33 and discussions). It may be that Matthew used this as a literary device to build the dramatic tension. One may suppose that Jesus may have emphasized this prophecy on numerous occasions. Matthew recorded those that fit his needs, or perhaps the ones that stood out for him most vividly.

And shall deliver him to the Gentiles to mock, and to scourge, and to crucify him (v. 19). This is an additional statement in this third prophecy of the passion. Jesus would not be killed by the Jews, which would have been by stoning, but would be crucified by the Romans. All three instances when Jesus foretold His death included the resurrection on **the third day** (see 16:21; 17:23).

F. A Mother's Request (20:20–28)

20:20. The mother of Zebedee's children. In Mark, "James and John, the sons of Zebedee" (Mark 10:35), asked the question, yet there is no contradiction. The three joined in making the petition. She was a typical mother, wanting the best for her sons.

20:21. For **What wilt thou?** see discussion on Mark 10:35. For **sit, the one on thy right hand, and the other on the left**, see discussion on Mark 10:37. The mother certainly asked for something big, on their behalf and apparently with their approval. This demonstrates that the disciples, or at least these two, did not fully grasp Jesus' teachings in the previous two chapters. Jesus had emphasized over and over that humility is a virtue, that the last shall be first, that the least in the kingdom will be the greatest, that His disciples must become as little children — and now He was faced with this. Jesus betrayed no impatience, though His answer was certainly pointed.

20:22. Jesus pointed out that He would have to suffer (see 26:39). Could they be honored with Him if they did not go through what He would? He

called it **to drink of the cup** (see discussion on Mark 10:38), a figure of speech meaning "to undergo" or "to experience" (the same figure of speech is used for divine wrath or judgment in Jer. 25:15; Ezek. 23:32; Hab. 2:16; Rev. 14:10; 16:19; 18:6). The two disciples answered, **We are able**.

20:23. Jesus promised that they would indeed suffer but said that, even so, the place of honor **is not mine to give** (see discussion on Mark 10:40). His **Father** alone has the right to make that determination. It may be thought that Jesus had gotten them to make the commitment, "to drink of the cup that I shall drink of" (v. 22), with the implication of the reward for it, and then had withdrawn the reward. Actually, His point was that those who are not willing to suffer cannot expect rewards, but that is the minimum requirement. The Father still is the one who determines what and how much each believer will be rewarded. There is no possibility of "striking a deal" for a specific reward for a specific sacrifice. Still, there will be degrees of reward in heaven. The servant is not greater than his Master, and those who avoid the tough commitment of discipleship can expect less than those who give up all to follow the Master.

20:24. The reaction of the other disciples was normal, but the jealousy was still sin (see discussion on Mark 10:41).

20:25–27. It shall not be so among you (v. 26; see discussions on Mark 10:42–45). Jesus contrasted the way the world promotes and rewards people with the way it will be in the kingdom. Again, this is the same principle Jesus had been at some pains to teach in the preceding chapters.

20:28. Jesus pointed to Himself as an example of what He had tried to teach the disciples. He **came not to be ministered unto, but to minister**, as a servant of our need, not to exalt Himself over us. His disciples needed to take the same attitude toward one another and toward life, as servants, not "climbers." Jesus came to **give his life a ransom**. The word "ransom" was often used for the price paid to redeem a slave. Similarly, Christ paid the ransom price of His own life to free us from the slavery of sin.

The preposition **for** emphasizes the substitutionary nature of Christ's death. **Many.** Christ "gave himself a ransom for all" (1 Tim. 2:6). Salvation is offered to all, but only the "many," those who receive Christ, obtain it (see discussion on Mark 10:45).

G. Restoration of Sight at Jericho (20:29–34)

20:29. For **Jericho**, see discussion on Mark 10:46. Jesus was nearing Jerusalem, heading toward His passion.

20:30. Two blind men. The other Synoptics mention only one (see discussion on Luke 18:35). **Son of David** is a messianic title (see discussion on 9:27).

20:31–34. Jesus healed them. This incident looks like a parenthesis. It does not obviously tie in to Jesus' statement in verses 25–28. A closer look, however, reveals that Jesus was illustrating with His actions what He had just said. He "came not to be ministered unto, but to minister" (20:28). A seemingly chance meeting on the roadway provided an opportunity for Him to allow an interruption in His schedule to become a priority. The disciples saw their Lord and Master putting the needs of two strangers ahead of His itinerary toward Jerusalem, reinforcing the teaching that His kingdom is not about privilege and position but about service and humility.

VII. Passion Week (chaps. 21–27)

A. The Triumphal Entry (21:1–11)

21:1–11. This is Christ's triumphal entry into Jerusalem. It had been prophesied in Daniel (Dan. 9:25), something Matthew did not mention. The striking feature is the extent to which Jesus' fame had spread among the multitudes. Matthew indicated at numerous points that the multitudes had begun to recognize Jesus' true identity and referred to Him in messianic terms. Here it all came together as crowds thronged the roads into Jerusalem, calling Him the Son of David.

21:1. Bethphage means "house of figs." Bethphage is not mentioned in the Old Testament, and in the New Testament only in connection with the triumphal entry. In the Talmud, it is spoken of as being near Jerusalem. For **the mount of Olives**, see discussion on Mark 11:1.

21:2. An ass. The donkey was symbolic of humility, peace, and Davidic royalty (see discussions on Zech. 9:9; Luke 19:30). For **colt**, see discussions on Mark 11:2–3 and Luke 19:30.

21:3. For **Lord**, see discussion on Luke 19:31. Perhaps Jesus had made a prior arrangement. More likely, His words were prophetic. Jesus knew supernaturally that a donkey would be there.

21:4–5. Here Matthew cited a prophetic passage, Zechariah 9:9, that was fulfilled in this incident.

21:6–7. Brought the ass, and the colt (v. 7). Mark 11:2 and Luke 19:30 records that Jesus rode the colt. Typically, a mother donkey follows her offspring closely. Matthew mentions two animals, while the other gospels have only one (see discussion on Luke 19:30). This is a matter of detail, and since the other gospels do not deny that there was a colt as well, there is no contradiction.

21:8. The **great multitude spread their garments in the way.** This was an act of royal homage (see 2 Kings 9:13). The people recognized Jesus as the messianic successor to David. It may be that this incident helped to seal the Pharisees' resolve to remove Him. Their power and position was so much tied to the approval of Rome that any seeming challenger to Roman authority could not be tolerated. It is ironic that the Pharisees, wanting to preserve "pure" Judaism, felt so dependent on Rome for the right to do so.

Anytime Jesus and His Word invade the world, things will be upset. He is in the business of challenging assumptions about life, about what is important, and about one's own self-importance. Anytime following Christ seems to get in the way of one's own agenda, that believer needs to check whether he has gotten away from God's will. The teachings of Christ are meant to challenge one's assumptions. The Pharisees were not willing to have their world upset in any way. Christians should be more open than the Pharisees were. Believers should read God's Word expecting to be challenged and should be ready to change their lives to conform to what it says.

21:9. These are three separate quotations, not necessarily spoken at the same time. **Hosanna** (see

KJV Study Bible note on Jer. 31:7) means both prayer and praise. For **Son of David**, see discussion on 9:27. **Hosanna in the highest**, that is, "May those in heaven sing 'Hosanna'" (see Ps. 148:1–2; Luke 2:14).

21:10–11. Jesus' entry into the city set matters astir. Many in the city apparently did not know who He was, but the multitudes who had come to Jerusalem for Passover knew and spread the word.

B. The Cleansing of the Temple (21:12–17)

21:12–17. In the Synoptic Gospels, the cleansing of the temple occurs during the last week of Jesus' ministry; in John, it takes place during the first few months (see John 2:12–16). Two explanations are possible: (1) there were two cleansings, one at the beginning and the other at the end of Jesus' public ministry; (2) there was only one cleansing, which took place during Passion Week but which John placed at the beginning of his account for theological reasons—to show that God's judgment was operative through the Messiah from the outset of His ministry. Different details are present in the two accounts (the selling of cattle and sheep in John 2:14, the whip in John 2:15, and the statements of Jesus in Matt. 21:13; John 2:16). From Matthew's and Luke's accounts, one might assume that the cleansing of the temple took place on Sunday, following the so-called triumphal entry (21:1–11). But Mark 11:15–19 clearly indicates that it was on Monday. Matthew often compressed narratives. This does not violate biblical inerrancy and is a literary device to save space. It is much as one might say, "We were in Canada on the fifth, doing some fishing early this month." They may have been in Canada two or three days before they actually started fishing, on the seventh, but they arrived on the fifth. No one would say that the abbreviated statement is false. In the same way, no one should say that Matthew contradicts the other Synoptic Gospels.

The temple (v. 12). The buying and selling took place in the large outer court of the Gentiles, which covered several acres (see discussions on Mark 11:15 and Luke 19:45). For **the house of prayer** (v. 13), see discussion on Mark 11:17. **Bethany** (v. 17). A village on the eastern slope of the Mount of Olives, about

two miles from Jerusalem and the final station on the road from Jericho to Jerusalem.

C. The Last Controversies with the Jewish Leaders (21:18–22:46)

21:18–22. This is another example of a compressed narrative (see discussion on 21:12–17). Mark 11:12–14, 20–25 places the cursing of the fig tree on Monday morning and the disciples' finding it withered on Tuesday morning. In Matthew's account, the tree withered as soon as Jesus cursed it, emphasizing the immediacy of judgment. For the theological meaning of this event, see discussions on Mark 11:12–14; 20–26.

21:18. City. Jerusalem.

21:19–20. Jesus often used "visual aids" in His teaching. Recall that earlier He had called a child into the midst of the disciples to make a point about the kingdom of heaven (see 18:1–6). Here coming upon **a fig tree** (v. 19) provided a teachable moment regarding the judgment that was to come for Israel's rejection of Christ.

21:21. For **say unto this mountain, Be thou removed**, see discussion on 17:20.

21:22. Jesus' point was about prayer. He does not want people to literally move mountains around, but He does want people to pray boldly for things that will glorify God.

21:23. The **chief priests** (see discussions on 2:4; Luke 19:47) and elders asked Jesus, **By what authority doest thou these things?** (see discussions on Mark 11:28 and Luke 20:2).

21:24–27. Jesus answered their question with a question: **from heaven, or of men?** (v. 25; see *KJV Study Bible* note on Mark 11:30; discussion on Luke 20:4). Jesus was not being evasive. He wanted them to see that His ministry, like John's, called into question the assumptions on which they had built their lives and teaching. If they were not willing to accept John's ministry as valid, they would not accept His. It was the chief priests, in fact, who were evasive here. They attempted to "not decide" on the question. Under the circumstances, Jesus was under no obligation to answer their question.

Well might one take warning from this passage. Jesus always calls people to a decision about Him. No one can say, "I don't want to decide." Not to decide is to decide. You can either choose to embrace Christ and trust Him or choose not to. **We cannot tell** (v. 27) was not an answer that put off a decision until later; it was a rejection of Christ and His authority (the matter they were challenging Him on in the first place). Once they had rejected His authority, there was no point in Him telling them where His authority came from.

21:28–32. This parable, that of the **two sons** (v. 28), points to the fact that those who do not repent can expect nothing from God. The less desirable elements of society had repented upon hearing John's preaching, but the more "respectable" elements had not. The former had thus done the will of the Father, while the latter, who "looked" more spiritual, were in reality out of God's will. Christian faith is about turning from sin, whether it is notorious sin or "respectable" sin. One cannot look to his position in the community or how others regard him and derive from that that he is in right relationship with God. The issue is whether one has repented and turned to Christ. **The publicans and the harlots** (v. 31) who had repented had more favor in God's sight than hard-working, respectable people who had not, and so it is today.

21:33–46. See discussions on Mark 12:1–12 and Luke 20:9–18.

21:33–44. This is the parable of the husbandmen. It illustrated how Israel repeatedly rejected the word of God and the prophets who preached it. Now the Son Himself is in their midst and He too is being rejected by them. **Tower** (v. 33). For guarding the vineyard, especially when the grapes ripened, and for shelter. The rabbis specified that it was to be a raised wooden platform, fifteen feet high and six feet square. The **husbandmen** (v. 33) represent the Jews, or their leaders. The **servants** (v. 34) represent the Old Testament prophets, many of whom were killed. The **son** (v. 37) represents Christ, whom the religious leaders condemned to death. **They will reverence my son.** The **householder** (v. 33) represents

God. He sent His Son to the world, and the Son also was rejected by Israel.

21:38–40. Let us seize on his inheritance (v. 38). Here is another case in which one must not push the analogy too far in interpreting the parables. Of course, the Jewish leaders could not have taken Christ's position in heaven much less over the church. In purely earthly terms, however, they believed that eliminating Jesus Christ would protect their position over the people and with Rome. Verse 40 may thus be seen as a warning to these leaders that God was still in control, and they should see things from heaven's perspective, something they were too shortsighted to do.

21:41. Other husbandmen. These are the Gentiles, to whom Paul turned when the Jews, for the most part, rejected the gospel (see Acts 13:46; 18:6). By the second century, the church was composed almost entirely of Gentiles.

21:42–43. Jesus pointed to Himself as **The stone which the builders rejected** (v. 42). This image is used elsewhere in the New Testament. Mark and Luke both recorded this saying of Jesus (see Mark 12:10; Luke 20:17). Peter used it in Acts and again in his first epistle (see Acts 4:11; 1 Peter 2:7). It must have made an impression on him when he heard it on this occasion, especially in light of the events that followed.

21:44. For **shall be broken**, see discussion on Luke 20:18.

21:45. Chief priests. Once again the leadership had been shown as in a mirror their own inner selves. Rather than repent, however, they became even more determined to destroy Jesus (see discussions on 2:4; Luke 19:47). For **Pharisees**, see discussions on 3:7; Mark 2:16; Luke 5:17. For **parables**, see discussions on 13:3; Mark 4:2; Luke 8:4.

22:1–14. The main point of this parable, that of the marriage dinner, relates to the Jews' rejection of the kingdom and the opening of God's grace to the Gentiles. Secondarily, it may refer to Jesus' teaching that the harlots and publicans would enter the kingdom before the chief priests (see 21:31–32).

22:1–2. It is not wrong to see the **king** (v. 2) as God the Father and Jesus as **his son**. In light of the overall point of the parable, it is probably reading too much into it to see **the wedding** as an allusion to the marriage of Christ to His bride, the church. That image is found in Scripture but is not intended here.

22:3–5. The refusal of the invited guests to come to the wedding symbolizes the Jews' rejection of the kingdom.

22:6. This is where the analogy between a wedding and the kingdom of God breaks down. The reaction of the invited guests, **the remnant**, would be rather harsh if this were a literal wedding. The allusion is to the Jews' rejection of Jesus and His message. The identity of the remnant is merely internal to the parable. They are the ones who had not gone off to work their fields or run their businesses (see 22:5). Jesus was not making a distinction between different members of the Jewish community, though it is tempting to see the remnant as a reference to the chief priests and Pharisees. Nothing in this parable or in history warrants that identification, however.

22:7. Burnt up their city. This was a common military practice; here it is possibly an allusion to the coming destruction of Jerusalem in AD 70. In terms of the parable, the king's reaction seems rather severe. Again, Jesus was looking beyond the parable itself, most likely to events that would take place in a few decades.

22:8–12. Had not on a wedding garment (v. 11). It has been conjectured that it may have been the custom for the host to provide the guests with wedding garments. This would have been necessary for the guests at this feast in particular, for they were brought in directly from the streets (vv. 9–10). The man's failure to avail himself of a wedding garment was therefore an insult to the host, who had provided the garments.

Jesus was not saying that some will get into the kingdom unworthily and will be later cast out. He was merely taking the opportunity to teach another truth, that those who are truly admitted to the kingdom of heaven will be there not by virtue of their own righteousness but by virtue of another. Here the garments represent righteousness. The wedding guests had on clothes that were not their usual every-

day wear; so also the redeemed will have a righteousness that is not their own. The man at the wedding without a wedding garment just serves to point out that no one gets into heaven on the basis of their own righteousness.

22:13. Gnashing of teeth (see discussion on 13:42) again goes beyond the scope of the parable. It is hardly credible that merely not being at a wedding that no one cared to attend anyway would be the occasion of much sorrow. Obviously, Jesus was looking beyond the bounds of the parable and alluding to final judgment.

Two images of hell are found in Scripture: fire and **outer darkness**. These are not contradictory. Darkness emphasizes exclusion from the presence of God, and fire emphasizes pain. Both, however, point to conscious experience of judgment rather than to annihilation. In addition, both types of imagery should be given equal weight in formulating a doctrine of hell. One should not use the outer darkness imagery here as an excuse to minimize the fact that judgment will involve real pain and suffering.

22:14. This is a proverbial summary of the parable's meaning. God invites **many** (likely "all" in view of the Semitic usage of "many") to be part of His kingdom, but only a **few are chosen** by Him, that is, those who wear the proper garment of Christ's righteousness.

22:15–17. The Pharisees were ardent nationalists, opposed to Roman rule, while **the Herodians** (v. 16), as their name indicates, supported the Roman rule of the Herods. At this point, however, the Pharisees enlisted the help of the Herodians to trap Jesus in His words. After trying to put Him off guard with flattery, they sprang their question: **Is it lawful to give tribute unto Caesar, or not?** (v. 17). If He said no, the Herodians would report Him to the Roman governor, and He would be executed for treason. If He said yes, the Pharisees would denounce Him to the people as disloyal to His nation.

22:18–19. Jesus perceived their wickedness (v. 18). Their attempted trap did not fool Him at all. Jesus called them what they were, **hypocrites**. They had said that He taught "the way of God in truth"

(22:16), which indeed He did. They did not believe it, however. They were hypocrites for pretending to. Their question was an intended trap, but Jesus turned it into a teachable moment. **Penny** (v. 19). The denarius, the common Roman coin of that day (see discussion on 20:2). On one side was a portrait of Emperor Tiberius, and on the other was the Latin inscription, "Tiberius Caesar Augustus, son of the divine Augustus." The coin was issued by Tiberius and was used for paying tax to him.

22:20–22. Jesus answered the Pharisees' question with a question: **Whose is this image and superscription?** (v. 20). The question forced them to admit that, whatever their opinion of Roman rule, the nation was under Caesar's jurisdiction. The fact could not be denied. Then Jesus gave a wise answer: **Render therefore unto Caesar the things which are Caesar's; and unto God the things that are God's** (v. 21). Jesus accomplished more than one thing with this statement. First, He threw the ball back into their court. It is a principle of Old Testament law that it is proper to render to everyone what they are due. The law knew nothing of cheating anyone out of what was rightfully theirs. Jesus underscored this principle. In the existing situation, they were under Roman governance and should render to the authorities what was properly due them, while being obedient to God. Doing so was in no way a contradiction of the law but rather a requirement. The matter was altogether separate from the matter of whether Rome *should* rule over Palestine. Second, Jesus underscored the proper role of civil government. There is a realm in which government, apart from religious authorities, plays a proper role. Israel had known nothing of this in its history until Rome conquered them. Even the Babylonians had not separated religious and civil authority. Jesus here opened a door to a new way for God's people to conceive of their relationship to government. Third, Jesus distinguished clearly between Caesar and God, implicitly protesting against the false and idolatrous claims made on the coins (see discussions on 22:19; Mark 12:17). Only God should receive worship, not the emperor; but the emperor should receive what is actually due him. Finally, Jesus handed his question-

ers the dilemma of determining exactly what they should "render ... unto Caesar." He did not say exactly how much or what was proper. He thus pointed them back to the law and to their own consciences for the real answer to their question. In all, it was a brilliant answer, which seemed to commit Jesus to nothing either way but which actually placed Him squarely in line with the law and with His own teaching in the Sermon on the Mount that true righteousness comes from one's heart, not just from following a set of rules and precepts. In light of all of this, it is little wonder that **they marvelled, and left him** (v. 22).

22:23. The Sadducees, which say that there is no resurrection. The Sadducees were a group committed only to the Pentateuch as the Word of God. They also rejected the supernatural as an active force in the world. Like skeptics today, they loved to come up with "Bible difficulties" to taunt believers. Here they believed that they had found one that Jesus could not answer, but they were shortly proven wrong. The context of their question about the practice of levirate marriage was purely hypothetical and was intended to undermine the doctrine of the resurrection.

22:24–28. Moses said. The Pentateuch had special authority for the Sadducees (see discussion on Mark 12:18). The reference (Deut. 25:5–6) is to the levirate law (from Latin *levir*, "brother-in-law"), which was given to protect the widow and guarantee continuance of the family line.

22:29–30. Biblical questions can often be resolved when one looks at a Scripture in context. The levirate law was given not to create confusion in heaven but to guarantee that widows' needs would be met on earth. Jesus pointed out that **the resurrection** (v. 30) will offer a different context for life than what is experienced on earth. Laws that apply now may not in that age. Their question was irrelevant.

22:31–32. Jesus turned to the Sadducees' real problem. They had asked a question about the resurrection when they did not believe in the resurrection. Jesus wanted to get to the root of their unbelief and deal with that, not with the details that flowed from it. When a skeptic raises a question, often something more basic is behind it. The important thing is to get to the foundational matter with which the skeptic has a problem.

These verses demonstrate the importance of good, careful exegesis. Jesus quoted, **I am the God of Abraham ... Issac, and ... Jacob** (v. 32; Exod. 3:6). His comment on this quote pointed to the present tense of the verb: **God is not God of the dead, but of the living**. It is important that one examine each word of Scripture carefully, including verb tenses. One must not build doctrine on "pretty close" to what Scripture says but must rather follow the Lord's example and build on *exactly* what the Scripture says. This has implications for inspiration as well. God did not simply inspire the general ideas He wanted to communicate and leave the words up to the authors. Every word and every tense and case is inspired and must be taken seriously as one ponders the meaning of Scripture.

22:33. Now **the multitude**, rather than the leadership (see 22:22), **were astonished at his doctrine**. Matthew continued to subtly emphasize the idea presented at the beginning of this chapter, that the "less respectable" elements of society were more open to His teaching than the religious establishment.

22:34. Here **the Pharisees** (see discussions on 3:7, Mark 2:16; Luke 5:17) made one more attempt to trap Jesus.

22:35–36. The Pharisees' question was, as far as it goes, a fair one, but it had a trap. If Jesus chose any one commandment, He could be accused of diminishing the others.

22:37–39. Jesus' answer is brilliant. In one statement, He managed to quote the Old Testament while showing that the two commandments He cited cover "all the law and the prophets" (22:40). The key word in both commandments is **love** (vv. 37, 39). The Greek verb is not *phileō*, which expresses friendly affection, but *agapaō*, the commitment of devotion that is directed by the will. **With all thy heart ... soul, and ... mind** (v. 37) means with one's whole being. The Hebrew of Deuteronomy 6:5 has "heart ... soul, and ... might," but some manuscripts of the Septuagint (the Greek translation of the Old Testament) add "mind." Jesus combined all four terms in Mark 12:30. Jesus was again pointing to the inner attitude.

True obedience comes from one's heart, soul, and mind. It is not strictly an outward show.

22:40. All the law and the prophets. The entire Old Testament (see discussion on 5:17). Note that Jesus mentioned both the Law and the Prophets here. He was speaking to Pharisees, who accepted all of the Old Testament as inspired.

22:41–46. See discussions on Mark 12:35–37; Luke 20:44–47. Here Jesus became the questioner. His goal was not to "tempt" the Pharisees, as they had tried to do to Him (see 22:35). He wanted not want to trap them but to teach them. He did so by presenting them with a conundrum.

22:41–42. Jesus began by asking an easy question about the Messiah: **whose son is he?** (v. 42). This was easy enough for the Pharisees to answer: **The Son of David**.

22:43–45. Then Jesus quoted from the Psalms, where David called Christ **Lord** (v. 44; Ps. 110:1). Jesus' question pointed out that the Messiah is both a descendant of David and yet recognized as divine. By implication, the Pharisees were in the wrong for not recognizing that Jesus is both the son of David and the Son of God. He should thus be recognized as Messiah but revered as Lord. His authority should not be questioned, as the priests, the Pharisees, and the Sadducees did throughout this chapter and the previous one.

22:46. The Pharisees missed the point completely, but they recognized that they had met their match in matters of understanding Scripture, and **neither durst any man from that day forth ask him any more questions**. People who will not recognize Jesus as Lord and yet cannot disprove His claim, often just give up all together and walk away from Him. No man can be Jesus' master, in that no man can argue against His authority on spiritual matters. In the end, one must trust Him as Lord or walk away. There is no middle ground.

D. The Denunciation of the Scribes and Pharisees (23:1–36)

23:1–2. Jesus spoke to **the multitude** (v. 1), most likely those who had just marveled at His response to the Pharisees (see 22:33), and to **his disciples**, who had heard it as well, since the substance of His teaching was a warning to them not to do as **the scribes and the Pharisees** (v. 2) did. **Sit in Moses' seat**. They were the authorized successors of Moses as teachers of the law.

23:3. Jesus warned His listeners to do as the scribes and the Pharisees said, for they were in authority. To the extent that they taught the law of Moses rightly, they were to be followed. Jesus never said that it was good to break the law, though ever since the Sermon on the Mount, He had been trying to get the people to see that the law must be rightly understood and followed from the heart, not just as an outward show.

23:4–5. Jesus' major contention with the scribes and the Pharisees was that they were hypocrites, teaching what they themselves did not obey. Jesus did not want His followers doing the same thing. Jesus said also that the Pharisees **make broad their phylacteries** (v. 5). These small boxes, worn on forehead and arm, contained four Old Testament passages (Exod. 13:1–10; 13:11–16; Deut. 6:4–9; 11:13–21). Jesus would have had them live up to these passages rather than just wear them. They also **enlarge the borders of their garments**. Both of these actions had to do with making themselves look religious and moral before men, while their hearts were far from God.

23:6–7. The chief seats in the synagogues (v. 6; see discussion on Mark 12:39). Whereas 22:4–5 dealt with actions the scribes and Pharisees performed to make themselves look religious and moral, these verses point to the consequences they sought from those actions, that is, public honor.

23:8–9. Jesus here applies this to His hearers. What He had just described the scribes and Pharisees were doing was exactly what the people should not do. They should not seek to be honored as holy and wise. They should be content to actually be holy and wise. The warning is against seeking titles of honor to foster pride. Obviously, one should avoid unreasonable literalism in applying such commands. A title should be regarded as just that. One can be

proud of refusing to use a title just as much as one can be proud of having one. The heart attitude again is what is important here.

23:10–12. Jesus returned to a theme He had touched on before. The disciples were not to exalt themselves. They had one **Master** (v. 10) and were under His authority. It is important to note something that the disciples did not see at the time but that became clear to them later. Jesus, as God, humbled Himself when He became a man (see Phil. 2:5–11). He took a lower spot than the one to which He was entitled, so that our great need might be met. If we call Him Lord, can we exalt ourselves higher than He who went to the cross, who suffered and died, who gave His own life for us? Are we greater than He? Why then should we jockey for position when we are under one who humbled Himself so thoroughly?

23:13–39. This is a long sermon. It actually ends at verse 33, but verses 34–39 form something of an epilogue. The sermon is structured around the sevenfold repetition of the phrase **woe unto you, scribes and Pharisees, hypocrites!** (vv. 13, 14, 15, 23, 25, 27, 29). Each time, Jesus followed this phrase with an indictment of sins they had committed, usually related to hypocrisy.

23:13. This is the first **woe**. Here Jesus pronounced a general statement of what was wrong with the scribes and Pharisees spiritually. They were not right with God; that is, they did not **go in**, nor did they **suffer … them that are entering to go in** to the kingdom of heaven. Examples of these errors are given in 23:14–15. They were spiritually wrong, and they led others astray.

23:14. This is the second **Woe**. Here their spiritual condition is laid out. They were greedy, taking **widow's houses** (i.e., their livelihood) in offerings, and they were hypocrites, **for a pretence mak[ing] long prayer**. God is not impressed with prayers that are not sincere. In the Sermon on the Mount, Jesus had warned His disciples that they should not pray long prayers, expecting to be heard for their many words, and He had warned them not to make prayer a public show (see 6:5–8). The condemnation here is in line with that teaching. Jesus promised these hypocrites a **greater damnation** (than the unrighteous, apparently, who were not so public in trying to appear righteous).

23:15. This is the third **Woe.** It is the second part of the spiritual problem Jesus raised in 23:13. The scribes and Pharisees led others astray. Jesus did not criticize them for their evangelistic zeal; He objected to its results. The converts wound up "out-Phariseeing" the Pharisees, and that meant the converts became even **more the child[ren] of hell** (i.e., bound for hell) than their teachers were (for "hell," see discussions on 5:22; Luke 12:5).

23:16–22. Here the word **Woe** (v. 16) does not follow the sermon's formula but is merely for emphasis, as this is a longer section. In this passage, Jesus gave a lengthy example of how the scribes and Pharisees were leading their converts astray. They made **the gold of the temple** more valuable than **the temple** (v. 17) itself, and **the gift** (v. 19) of more value than **the altar that sanctifieth the gift.** In both cases, Jesus was upset that they had perverted the truth. A sacrifice is just an animal until it is put on the altar, that is, given to God. That makes the animal something more. The altar sets apart (**sanctifieth**) what is placed on it and thus is more valuable. Similarly, gold is valuable, but the temple that it gilds is more valuable. The reason gold was used on the temple at all was a measure of the temple's value and the value of the One who dwelt there. The point is that God is of more value than any earthly thing, and thus what is given to God gains value. This may be applied, in a distant way, to believers today in that they should not focus on incidentals in church life. The color of the carpet or the brand of microphone is not as important as the God who is worshiped by means of them.

23:23. This is the fourth **Woe.** Jesus did not criticize the observance of the minutiae of the law (He said, **these ought ye to have done**), but He did criticize the hypocrisy often involved (see discussion on 5:18–20). It is wrong to do little things and leave big things undone. Jesus wanted the Pharisees to know that they should not think they were spiritual because they did little outward things, because true spiritual life must come from within. Jesus contrasted outward activity with **judgment, mercy, and faith.** The scribes and Pharisees had an outward righteousness, but for the kingdom, it is necessary that "your righteousness shall exceed the righteousness of the scribes and Pharisees" (5:20), as Jesus had said in the Sermon on the Mount.

23:24. Strain at a gnat. A strict Pharisee would carefully strain his drinking water through a cloth to be sure he did not swallow a gnat, the smallest of unclean animals. Figuratively, however, he would swallow a camel—one of the largest animals. This exaggeration is not meant to be taken literally. The Pharisees had done what was not important and left off what was important.

23:25. This is the fifth **Woe.** Once again Jesus issued a general statement of what the scribes and Pharisees did, focusing on their pretense to religiosity.

23:26. Here Jesus turned to application, once again pointing out that the scribes and Pharisees needed to focus on their inner life and motivation rather than on outward appearance. It amounts to a call for them to practice a righteousness that "exceed[s] the righteousness of the scribes and Pharisees" (5:20).

23:27. This is the sixth **Woe.** Here Jesus used a different analogy. Instead of likening the scribes and Pharisees to unclean cups (see 23:25–26), He likened them to tombs or **whited sepulchres.** A person who stepped on a grave became ceremonially unclean (see Num. 19:16), so graves were whitewashed to make them easily visible, especially at night. They appeared clean and beautiful on the outside, but they were dirty and rotten on the inside. Jesus may have wanted to emphasize their spiritual deadness.

23:28. Here Jesus made the meaning of 23:27 clear.

23:29. This is the seventh and last **Woe.** The scribes and Pharisees were guilty of honoring spiritual leaders of the past and yet not following their teachings. This relates to the theme of doing little things while ignoring the weightier matters.

23:30–32. Their claim that they would have honored the prophets who were stoned in their fathers' day confirmed the hypocrisy of the scribes and Pharisees. They were guilty of the same sins as their fathers, who had stoned the prophets. Their own sins confirmed that they were children of these men. Jesus may have even been looking toward the cross at this point. These men were the ones who would turn Him over for condemnation.

23:33. This verse ends the sermon proper. Jesus pronounced judgment on the scribes and Pharisees: **how can ye escape the damnation of hell?** (see discussions on 5:22; Luke 12:5). Calling them **serpents** and **vipers** is a colorful way of saying that they were evil, as the serpent in the garden had been, and dangerous, as vipers injecting spiritual poison into those whom they taught. It was better to shun them than to admire them.

23:34–38. This passage forms something of an epilogue to the sermon. Here Jesus apparently was addressing the city of Jerusalem and its people. The reference to their killing the ones He had sent to them, however, harks back to the accusations against the scribes and Pharisees and their fathers. It is important to remember that the previous woes were spoken to the multitude and to His disciples (23:1), not directly to a group of scribes and Pharisees. It was altogether appropriate for Jesus to end His sermon with a personal word for His listeners, having just given them quite a negative bombast about their teachers. They had been led astray by the false teachings of the Jewish leaders and were the object of Jesus' concern here for that reason.

23:35. Abel unto … Zacharias (i.e., Zechariah). The murder of Abel is recorded in Genesis 4:8 and that of Zechariah, son (probably grandson) of Jehoiada, in 2 Chronicles 24:20–22. Chronicles is placed at the end of the Old Testament in the Hebrew arrangement of the books. The expression is similar to the Christian saying "from Genesis to Revelation." Jesus was summing up the history of martyrdom in the Old Testament.

23:36. This may be a reference to the coming siege and destruction of Jerusalem in AD 70. Jesus prophesied here that the city would suffer what prophets had suffered in the past.

E. Prophecy concerning Jerusalem (23:37–39)

23:37–39. See discussions on Luke 13:34–35. Jesus expressed tender emotions for the people and expressed His sorrow over their rejection of Him. He knew that His time was drawing near and that He would soon face death and resurrection, and the city would face a harsh judgment not many decades hence. This passage is a window into the tender heart of God, who loves His people even in the face of rejection.

F. Olivet Discourse (chaps. 24–25)

24:1–25:46. These two chapters present the Olivet Discourse, which is the sixth and last of the great discourses in Matthew's gospel (see Introduction, "Literary Features"; discussions on 5:1–7:29; Mark 13:1–37). Jesus in these chapters discussed with his disciples signs of the end of this age (chap. 24), gave them parables of the kingdom (25:1–30), and told them about the judgment that will take place when He returns (25:31–46).

24:1–51. Chapters 24 and 25 are the Olivet Discourse. This relates the second coming of Christ and the Great Tribulation which precedes it. 24:4–14, however, relate to the church age. It tells of how even in "apocalyptic times," times of war and famine and earthquakes (vv. 6–8), the end is not yet. Jesus warns his disciples not to be deceived by these "signs," for no one knows the day or the hour (24:42) of His coming. Even the events surrounding the destruction of the temple (24:15–16), about which the disciples asked in 24:3, are not yet a sign of the end, which will not happen until the gospel is preached in all the world (24:14). Then follows a series of signs and events directly related to the coming of Christ (24:15–41) and a call to be ready (24:42–51). Chapter 25 continues the appeal to be ready for His coming (25:1–30) and also contains a statement about the judgment of the nations (25:31–46).

24:1. Jesus went out, and departed from the temple. Jesus' denunciation of the Scribes and Pharisees apparently had taken place within the temple complex. His disciples now wanted to **shew him the buildings of the temple.** This temple, built by Herod the Great, was a much more elaborate structure than the one built by Solomon. The disciples were rather in awe of it. They would soon discover, however, that Jesus was far less impressed with the works of men than they were and that He knew these buildings would not last for long.

24:2. There shall not be left here one stone upon another (see discussion on Mark 13:1). Fulfilled literally in AD 70, when the Romans under Titus completely destroyed Jerusalem and the temple buildings. Stones were even pried apart to collect the gold leaf that melted from the roof when the temple was set on fire. **Thrown down.** Excavations in 1968 uncovered large numbers of these stones, toppled from the walls by the invaders. Jesus was piquing their interest with this statement. He knew that they would be provoked into asking questions about it and was ready to answer.

24:3. The mount of Olives. A ridge a little more than a mile long, beyond the Kidron Valley east of Jerusalem and rising about two hundred feet above the city (see discussion on Mark 11:1). Here the disciples **came unto him privately** to ask about His statement that the temple would be destroyed (see 24:2). Well did they know that such matters were best not discussed within the city, nor in the presence of others generally. They asked Jesus three questions: **when shall these things be? and what shall be the sign of thy coming, and of the end of the world?** Jesus dealt with these three questions but did not distinguish them sharply. It appears, however, that the description of the end of the age is discussed in 24:4–14, the destruction of Jerusalem in 24:15–22 (see Luke 21:20), and Christ's second coming in 24:23–31.

24:4–5. Jesus warned His disciples, **Take heed that no man deceive you** (v. 4). Jesus knew that much confusion would reign on matters related to the end times. His first concern was the coming of false messiahs. He meant people claiming to be the Messiah, not even necessarily people claiming to be Jesus Himself. Such messianic claims may be understood as claiming to be the Savior sent from God. For **Christ** (v. 5), see discussion on 16:16.

24:6–8. Wars (v. 6), **famines ... and earthquakes** (v. 7) are apocalyptic events, especially when they come together. Jesus said that when these things

occur, **the end is not yet** (v. 6). They are merely signs that the end is coming.

Jesus repeated the point, calling these events **the beginning of sorrows** (v. 8). The rabbis, as well as the prophets, spoke of "birth pangs," that is, sufferings, that would precede the coming of the Messiah and lead into "the time of Jacob's trouble" (Jer. 30:7).

24:9. Jesus prophesied that His followers will suffer persecution and that it will increase as the end draws near. The persecution of Christians around the world has increased dramatically in the last century. This will apparently continue as the time of the end draws near.

24:10. Here Jesus was not focusing on the disciples' relationships with one another or with the world. Instead, He was speaking of a general societal breakdown as family, business, and social relationships come apart. There has been a dramatic increase in this in the West over the past generation.

24:11. False religions and heresies will increase in the last days.

24:12. Iniquity and a lack of love are linked here, as they are in life. People who are given over to sin cannot love sacrificially and purely. When the focus is on satisfying the lower urges, one cannot express the higher emotions. People who love their own bellies cannot love their neighbors.

24:13. Jesus ended the depressing picture of the end times with a word of encouragement: **He that shall endure unto the end ... shall be saved.** He was not saying that one must survive the end times or be lost. He meant that anyone who is saved can endure whatever troubles the world goes through at that time. All of Jesus' words in 24:4–13 describe events that will characterize the world prior to the rapture of the church.

24:14. This is a promise. It looks forward to the Great Commission (28:19–20) and to its fulfillment before the end of the age. The **gospel of the kingdom** is the gospel of the death, burial, and resurrection of Christ (see Mark 16:15; Acts 20:24; 1 Cor. 1:17; 15:1–4; Eph. 1:13; Col. 1:5).

24:15. Here Jesus began to answer the disciples' question regarding the destruction of the temple.

His answer has apocalyptic implications as well. **The abomination of desolation** is the detestable thing causing the desolation of the Holy Place. The primary reference in Daniel (9:27; 11:31; 12:11) was to 168 BC, when Antiochus Epiphanes erected a pagan altar to Zeus on the sacred altar in the temple of Jerusalem. There are two more stages in the progressive fulfillment of the prophecies in Daniel and Matthew: (1) the Roman destruction of the temple in AD 70 and (2) the setting up of an image of the Antichrist in Jerusalem (see 2 Thess. 2:4; Rev. 13:14–15; see also discussions on Dan. 9:25–27; 11:31). This is not, then, a single event but a series of similar events. Jesus thus answered their specific question about the destruction of the temple while discussing their other questions regarding His second coming and the end of the world.

24:16. The mountains. The Transjordan mountains, where Pella was located. Christians in Jerusalem fled to that area during the Roman siege shortly before AD 70. A similar fleeing will occur during the future great tribulation period (identified with Daniel's Seventieth Week, see Dan. 9:27; discussion on Rev. 12:6, 14).

24:17–18. Take his clothes (v. 18). This is not to be understood as saying that it will be all right to return for other things. The point is that events will happen quickly, and it will be time to flee, leaving behind everything.

24:19. Jesus again emphasized that life will be difficult when these events occur and that being able to move quickly will be important (see discussion on Mark 13:17).

24:20. For **in the winter**, see discussion on Mark 13:18. **Neither on the sabbath.** Matthew alone included this, because he was writing to Jews, who were forbidden to travel more than about half a mile on the Sabbath. Verses 15–19 of this chapter paint a picture of a time of trouble and hardship in which people will need to have their wits about them and be very mobile to survive. Indeed, when Jerusalem was besieged in AD 70, it was a very difficult time for those who had not already left the city. So will it be in the time of the end.

24:21–22. Great tribulation (v. 21). Josephus, the Jewish historian who was there, described the destruction of Jerusalem in almost identical language. The phrase **no nor ever shall be**, however, places this reference in the distant future. The Holocaust during World War II was far more devastating for the Jewish people than the event of AD 70, yet ultimately their greatest suffering will come during the great tribulation of the future (see Dan. 12:1). This statement thus marks the transition to Jesus' second coming, which He took up in 24:23. Verse 22 anticipates that subject, speaking of the level of disaster the people will experience. **Except those days should be shortened** (v. 22) speaks directly of the days of the destruction of Jerusalem, and **no flesh** means none of the Jewish people living there. The statement looks forward to the future great tribulation, however, when it will be fulfilled ultimately. Some hold that this means that the tribulation will be of such intensity that if allowed to continue, everyone would be destroyed. These days will be shortened **for the elect's sake**, that is, for the people of God, including some Jews and Gentiles. "The elect" are not the same as the "flesh" mentioned. Jesus' point was that it is better for the people of God if the entire human race is not wiped out.

24:23–31. Jesus here focuses on the specific question about His second coming posed by the disciples in verse 3. He has treated it in verses 4–22, along with other issues. From here to the end of chapter 25, only the second coming is in view.

24:23–26. Jesus warned His disciples, and by extension, those who have come after, not to believe anyone who says that He, or another messiah, is in a certain place. Even if someone is able to do miracles, it does not establish their claim. This implies that there will always be miracle workers, especially at the end of the age. God's people should not be led astray by such events. Jesus performed miracles but emphasized His teaching ministry. Believers are to be set apart by the truth (see John 17:17), believing it and looking for His coming, rather than following any miracle worker who comes along.

24:27. As the lightning cometh out of the east, and shineth even unto the west; so shall also the

coming of the Son of man be. Jesus was not saying that His coming will be accompanied by flashes of light, though it may well be. His point was that just as lightning is obvious and easily observed, so also will His coming be obvious and easily observed. This refers to His triumphal return to earth at the end of the great tribulation. People will have no need to say, "Look, He is here" or "He is over there." His coming will be so obvious that it will be hard to ignore—like a flash of lightning.

24:28. There will the eagles be gathered together. The coming of Christ will be as obvious as the gathering of vultures around a carcass (see discussion on Luke 17:37, where the saying is used in a slightly different sense).

24:29. See discussion on Mark 13:25. This is a reference to the end of **the tribulation**, when Christ will appear (see Rev. 19:11). Disturbances in the heavens are often used in apocalyptic literature to describe the magnitude and significance of this event, which will bring an end to history.

24:30. For **Son of man**, see discussion on Mark 2:10. This verse describes the Christ's second coming. **Then shall all the tribes of the earth mourn**. The second coming is usually associated with fear or with rejoicing. Many will mourn, for they will see that they have wasted their lives in sin and debauchery and now face judgment. There will be more mourning than rejoicing on that day for those who have rejected Christ as their Messiah and King.

24:31. This description ends with the gathering of God's people to Himself, which will begin the millennial reign of Christ on earth (see Rev. 20:1–6).

24:32–33. Here Jesus called His disciples to apply the message. As they could tell the times and seasons by what was happening in nature, so also they should be able to discern the time of His return. The natural disasters and persecutions that will increase just before the tribulation should not be a cause of concern for believers. They should read the signs and know that God is in control of events and will win in the end.

24:34. For **Verily I say unto you**, see discussion on Mark 3:28. For **This generation**, see discussions on Mark 13:30; Luke 21:32.

24:35. Jesus' **words** will last until all these things have happened, and even then, they will still be true. The events preceding and during the tribulation will not eradicate His Word. Even in those dark days, people will come to faith, having heard the Word of Christ preached.

24:36. Knoweth no man (see discussion on Mark 13:32). Having told His disciples to watch for the signs of His return, Jesus saw the need to warn them about date setting. They could see the signs, but guessing the date was foolish. He was saying, to put it simply, "Do not waste your time guessing the time, because I could come at any time!"

24:37–39. These verses are often misunderstood. Jesus was not saying here that the wickedness of the world will be as bad as in Noah's day, though other Scriptures teach that it certainly will be that bad or worse (see 1 Tim. 3:1–5). His point was that the coming of the Lord will be sudden and unexpected. In Noah's day, people were **eating and drinking** (v. 38); that is, they were going about their daily lives, and **marrying and giving in marriage**, that is, planning for the future. Then **the flood came, and took them all away** (v. 39). They were in the midst of life's business, and then the end came. Likewise, no believer can say, "I know Jesus is not coming soon, for I am getting married next year. He would not lead us to get married and plan a life together if He were coming back." Jesus was saying that this is precisely what will happen. His return will cut across all the business of life as it is happening and will stop everything.

24:40–42. Jesus gave two examples of people going about their business, working side by side; **the one shall be taken, and the other left** (vv. 40–41). Scripture knows nothing of the idea of people gathering at some place to await the Lord's coming. He will come in the midst of life's activities, and He will come suddenly and dramatically.

24:43–44. Jesus used an illustration to reiterate His point. This may be the source of Paul's saying that the Lord will come "as a thief in the night" (1 Thess 5:2). Although Paul was not present on this occasion, he surely heard the teaching. Peter used the same phrase (2 Peter 3:10), undoubtedly thinking back to this incident, and had likely shared the allusion with Paul.

24:45–51. Jesus used a parable to warn His disciples to be alert and faithful. The ending of this parable is perhaps to be understood as a warning to the scribes and Pharisees and to all false teachers. Jesus was not saying here that His people will be lost forever if they are not looking for the Lord's return at the exact moment when it happens. **There shall be weeping and gnashing of teeth** (v. 51; see discussion on 13:42). That these people are not among the saved is made clear in 25:1–13.

25:1–30. Here Jesus told His disciples two parables, that of the ten virgins (25:1–13) and the talents (25:14–30), to further instruct them about the kingdom of God.

25:1–13. This is the parable of the ten virgins. The point of the parable is that some people will be ready when Christ returns, and others will not. Some will be admitted to the kingdom, and others will not. The Bible knows nothing of universalism, the belief that all people will ultimately be saved. Throughout Scripture, there is a sharp division between those who belong to God and those who do not.

25:1. Jesus said that at that time, the rapture, **the kingdom of heaven [will] be likened unto ten virgins.** These virgins were bridesmaids, responsible for preparing the bride to meet the bridegroom. Notice, there was only one bride. The ten virgins were the attendants at the wedding; they were not the bride. Many commentators therefore view them as survivors of the tribulation, of whom some were saved and some were not. The **lamps** refers to torches that consisted of long poles with oil-drenched rags at the top. (Small clay lamps would have been of little use in an outdoor procession.)

25:2. The division is between **wise** and **foolish** virgins. Jesus would not say that wisdom gets people into heaven; that happens by faith. For His purposes in the parable, however, wisdom and foolishness separates them, and His point is about separation, not about wisdom and foolishness.

25:3. Took no oil. Olive oil would have been used. In that day, other kinds of lamp oil were un-

available or very expensive. The oil seems to represent the Holy Spirit.

25:4–5. The **wise** (v. 4) virgins brought additional oil for their lamps. All slept, awaiting **the bridegroom** (v. 5).

25:6. At midnight came **a cry** announcing the arrival of **the bridegroom.** Here is the parallel to the second coming of Christ, or more specifically, the rapture. Jesus' point was that it will happen suddenly. No one should delay trusting Christ, for He might come at any time. Only a foolish person would "plan" a deathbed conversion, hoping to enjoy the pleasures of sin and then repent at the end of life. The Lord may return before that time, and all should be ready.

25:7. Trimmed their lamps. The charred ends of the rags were cut off, and oil was added.

25:8. The **foolish** virgins requested oil from the others. They wanted to join the wedding party on the basis of what others had, not on the basis of what they themselves had. Likewise, some people think they can be numbered among the people of God without faith in their own hearts. Many people depend on their parents' faith, or their cultural heritage, or perhaps their membership in an exciting dynamic church. The Lord will not accept any of this. One cannot be saved on the faith of others. It will not help him in that day. One's faith must be his own. Even if this parable is interpreted in ways that see the oil as representative of the Holy Spirit, a common understanding in the Old Testament, the point remains that only those who, by faith, have become Christians (and thus received the Spirit) are saved, not those who are merely associated with people who have faith.

25:9. There be not enough. Torches required large amounts of oil to keep burning, and the oil had to be replenished about every fifteen minutes. Jesus was not teaching selfishness here, only that one must have one's own faith to be saved. As with previous parables, it is best not to push the parable beyond what Jesus intended.

25:10–12. It is not likely that the bridesmaids would have been shut out at a real wedding, but this illustrated Jesus' point that some will not be admitted into heaven.

25:13. Watch. This is the application of the parable. Christians are to be alert for His coming. Ones does not know **the day nor the hour** of His return. Christ's coming is always imminent; therefore, one must be ready.

25:14–30. This is the parable of the talents. Having just related a parable showing that one must be saved to enter the kingdom, Jesus directed this parable toward those who are saved. The point of the parable is that there will be degrees of reward in the kingdom.

25:14. The **man travelling into a far country** is Jesus Christ Himself. He was soon to leave His disciples but will return one day. He does not leave believers empty-handed but equips them for ministry. This is represented by the man giving **his own servants ... his goods**.

25:15. The term **talents** was first used for a unit of weight (about seventy-five pounds), then for a unit of coinage (see discussion on Luke 19:13). The present-day use of "talent" to indicate an ability or gift is derived from this parable, since the servants received five, two, or just one talent, **to every man according to his several ability**. This is a reminder that not every Christian is gifted in the same way or to the same degree. Some have more, and others less. Believers are not to try to outdo one another in ministry. Jesus had earlier forbidden any competition, calling believers to serve one another rather than seek position. Each believer, however, is called to use whatever he or she is given to the Lord's glory (represented in this parable by the profits derived from the talents).

25:16–18. Each servant did something different with what he was given. The first two servants were able to double what they were given, while the third simply **hid** (v. 18) his talent and did nothing with it.

25:19–23. After a long time the lord of those servants cometh (v. 19). This is one of the few biblical references to the fact that a long time will elapse before Christ returns. The first two servants received a reward for what they had produced. The reward appears to involve greater responsibility (25:21, 23), but one should not push the analogy too far. There may be work in heaven, though the Bible indicates that it will be a place of worship and celebration. The servants perhaps receive a promotion rather than are wearied with a heavier load.

25:24–28. This passage deals with the servant who hid his talent. He explained that he had hidden his talent because he **was afraid** (v. 25). Again, one should not push the analogy too far. Jesus is not unjust, and believers' service should come from love and loyalty, not from fear and despair. The story demands that the servant have a motive, and one should leave his motive there in the story. It is incidental to Jesus' main point, that His servants will be rewarded on the basis of the quality of their service. This servant was not commended and in fact lost what he had been given. Jesus was not saying that those who are poor servants will lose their salvation. Again, the story has a direction of its own. He was saying that poor servants will lose what reward they might have had.

25:27. The Greek for **the exchangers** comes from *trapeza* ("table"), a word seen on the front of banks in Greece today. Bankers sat at small tables and changed money (see 21:12). The Greek for **usury** was first used in the sense of offspring, interest being the "offspring" of invested money. Even a minimal service would have been more acceptable than nothing at all. It would not be wrong to see this parable in terms of earthly service and earthly reward. Jesus' point was about heavenly rewards, but in fact, faithful preachers or teachers of God's Word will often see their ministry grow and become a wider blessing. A ministry that remains small is no indication of a lack of God's blessing, however, since the main point is about rewards that will be given when Jesus returns. Jesus wants all to be faithful in service, whether one's ministry is large or small. The real rewards will be given out when Christ returns.

25:28. In an earthly sense, if a believer is unfaithful to the ministry God has given him, it may well be given to another.

25:29–30. This is the main point of the parable. Being ready for Christ's coming involves more than playing it safe and doing little or nothing. It demands the kind of service that will bring glory to God regardless of the size of one's ministry. The principle that from the one who **hath not shall be taken away even that which he hath** relates to service and usefulness in ministry, not to salvation. Jesus was not saying that some Christians will be cast into hell.

25:31–46. This section describes the judgment that will take place when Christ returns. Just when the judgment will take place is difficult to determine, as much of chapters 23–24 deal with various parts of the end times but not always chronologically. The two most widely accepted interpretations of this judgment are: (1) It will occur at the beginning of Christ's earthly millennial kingdom (vv. 31, 34), and its purpose will be to determine who will be allowed to enter the kingdom (v. 34). The criterion for judgment will be the kind of treatment shown to the Jewish people ("these my brethren," v. 40) during the preceding great tribulation period (vv. 35–40, 42–45). Ultimately, how a person treats the Jewish people will reveal whether or not he is saved (vv. 41, 46). (2) The judgment will occur at the great white throne at the end of the age (see Rev. 20:11–15), and its purpose will be to determine who will be allowed to enter Christ's eternal kingdom and who will be consigned to eternal punishment in hell (vv. 34, 46). The basis for judgment will be whether love is shown to God's people—true believers of every type (see 1 John 3:14–15).

25:31–33. Before him shall be gathered all nations (v. 32). The word "nations" is *ethnē* and here properly means ethnic groups. All people will be judged as individuals. Entrance to God's kingdom is based not on one's relationship with a certain country but rather on one's relationship with Jesus Christ.

25:34–40. Rewards in the kingdom of heaven will be given to those who serve without thought of reward. There is no hint of merit here, for God gives out of grace, not debt.

25:41–46. Clearly, the division in this judgment is between the saved and the unsaved. This is not a judgment for reward, as in the parable of the talents. Again, the Bible makes it clear that punishment of the wicked is real and conscious and permanent. **Everlasting punishment** (v. 46) implies that it is a punishment that never ends. It must therefore be conscious and more than mere annihilation.

G. Jesus' Betrayal Plotted (26:1–16)

26:1–16. In this passage, Matthew did something that is often seen on television, but he did it with words. Many times, a few short scenes will set the mood and establish a framework for what is coming. The scenes, in different places but happening one close upon another, will treat one aspect of the story from different angles, showing the viewer how events taking place perhaps simultaneously relate to one theme. Similarly, here Matthew presented four scenes of events related to the death of Christ, which is the major concern of the next few chapters. In scene 1, Jesus tells His disciples of His coming death (vv. 1–2). Scene 2 takes place in the palace of the high priest, where the decision is finally made to kill Him (vv. 3–5). This fades into scene 3: in Bethany, where Jesus is anointed with expensive ointment in anticipation of His burial (vv. 6–13). Scene 4 apparently takes place back in Jerusalem: Judas agrees to betray Jesus to the chief priests for thirty pieces of silver (vv. 14–16). These four quick scenes set the stage for the narrative of Christ's crucifixion. The reader is brought back from concerns about the end times and the judgment (see chaps. 24–25) to the present reality from the perspective of the narrative, that Jesus' crucifixion was just about to happen, and is prepared emotionally for the drama to follow. The rapid succession of these four scenes, unusual in Matthew, serves to quicken the pace and builds anticipation and concern in the reader's mind.

26:1–2. Scene 1: Jesus prepared His disciples for His death. **Ye know** (v. 2). For some time, Jesus had been speaking of His death. The time had now come. For **passover**, see discussion on Mark 14:1. For **Son of man**, see discussion on Mark 2:10.

26:3–5. Scene 2: in the high priest's palace. The decision to kill Jesus, which had been discussed on previous occasions, was made. **The chief priests, and the scribes, and the elders of the people** (v. 3) refers to the clerical and lay leadership of the Sanhedrin (see discussion on 2:4). **Caiaphas** was the high priest in AD 18–36 and the son-in-law of Annas (see John 18:13), a former high priest, who served AD 6–15. **And consulted that they might take Jesus …and kill him** (v. 4). They were no longer considering whether they would do it; they were merely determining the details. The passage might be read that they "consulted in order that they might take Jesus."

An uproar among the people (v. 5). Hundreds of thousands of Jewish pilgrims came to Jerusalem for Passover, and riots were not unknown. The religious leaders (see 26:3) knew that many people admired Jesus. They thus decided to avoid doing the deed on the **feast day** itself. Doing it during that week, however, did not pose a problem for them.

26:6–13. Scene 3: in Bethany. A seemingly celebratory fellowship occasion turned into a teachable moment for Jesus to again emphasize His coming death (see discussion on John 12:1–11).

26:6. For **Bethany**, see discussion on 21:17. **Simon the leper** is mentioned elsewhere only in Mark 14:3, though Simon was a common Jewish name in the first century. He was probably a well-known victim of leprosy who had been healed by Jesus.

26:7. Alabaster box. Most "alabaster" of ancient times was actually marble (see *KJV Study Bible* note on Mark 14:3). The anointing of Jesus happened during dinner, which likely was a festive occasion. Simon probably did not often have so many or so notable guests.

26:8–9. The disciples reacted with **indignation, saying, To what purpose is this waste?** (v. 8). Their concern was that the ointment might have been sold and the money given to the poor. This was certainly true, but something more important was going on.

26:10. Jesus rebuked the disciples and described the woman's actions as **good**. In Greek, the word has an aesthetic as well as an ethical meaning.

26:11. Ye have the poor always with you is often cited as an excuse for doing nothing for them. Jesus was not teaching that poverty is an eternal problem and thus no efforts should be made to alleviate it. His point was one of priority. It is good to help the poor, and one should do so at every opportunity. Jesus is more important, however, because He is God. Sometimes doing good works can get in the way of glorifying Jesus. Many churches have lost their focus on Jesus because a particular cause, however noble and good, took over. There are those who would rather save the whales than save the lost. This verse should serve as a reminder that good works gain their value only in relationship to glorifying Jesus Christ.

26:12–13. Jesus used the occasion to point to His death. The woman's motive is not known or what she knew of what was about to happen to Him. **She did it for my burial** (v. 12). Jesus was not saying that this was her intention, only that it had that effect. He had been anointed and would soon be buried, and Jesus connected the two events. His statement in verse 13 has been fulfilled in that the story is recorded in Scripture and is thus told wherever the gospel is preached. One can only wonder what effect His remarks had on the occasion. The disciples never really grasped what His talk of death, burial, and resurrection really meant until the events took place. They must have wondered why He now mentioned the matter again. One can imagine a puzzled and perhaps troubled silence, followed by a slow resumption of conversation. The reader is not privy to this, however, as Matthew portrayed one more quick scene before beginning his narrative proper.

26:14–16. Scene 4: the setting is most likely in Jerusalem, perhaps only hours later, or the next day. For **Judas Iscariot** (v. 14), see discussion on Mark 3:19. Judas agreed to betray Jesus **for thirty pieces of silver** (v. 15). Equivalent to 120 denarii, this was quite a sum of money. Laborers customarily received one denarius for a day's work (see 20:1–16). Judas then began to seek an **opportunity to betray him** (v. 16). At this point, Judas did not know enough of the schedule for the next few days to be sure of just when and where he would have such an opportunity. This sets up the background and atmosphere for what lies ahead. The reader's attention, riveted on the future in chapters 24–25, is now focused on the dramatic events about to unfold.

H. The Last Supper (26:17–35)

26:17. The first day of the feast of unleavened bread. The fourteenth of Nisan (March–April), it was also called the preparation of the Passover. The Passover meal was eaten the evening of the fourteenth after sunset, and therefore technically on the fifteenth, since the Jewish day ended at sunset. The Feast of Unleavened Bread lasted seven days, Nisan 15–21 (see Lev. 23:5–6), but in the time of Christ, the entire period, Nisan 14–21, was referred to under that name (see discussion on Mark 14:12).

26:18–30. These verses clearly indicate that Jesus ate the Passover meal with His disciples the night before His crucifixion. For more information on the Lord's Supper, see discussions on Mark 14:22–24.

26:18. My time is a reference to Jesus' crucifixion.

26:19. For **Made ready the passover**, see discussion on Mark 14:15.

26:20. For **sat down**, see discussion on Mark 14:18.

26:21. Verily I say unto you (see discussion on Mark 3:28). Jesus knew who would betray Him.

26:22–23. Naturally, the disciples were startled that one of their own would betray Jesus and were **exceeding sorrowful** (v. 22). The idea is not so much that they grieved but that they were distressed. Jesus answered their question indirectly, saying that it was **He that dippeth his hand with me in the dish** (v. 23). It was the custom, still practiced by some in the Middle East, to take a piece of bread or a piece of meat wrapped in bread and dip it into a bowl of sauce (made of stewed fruit) on the table. **Shall betray me.** In that culture, as among Arabs today, to eat with a person was tantamount to saying, "I am your friend and will not hurt you." This fact made Judas's deed all the more despicable (see Ps. 41:9). The disciples did not turn on Judas to stop him during the meal, and it is possible that more than one of them actually used the same dish of fruit sauce as Jesus. It could be that He simply meant, "It is one of you here at this table." Either way, the disciples were still unclear as to who exactly Jesus meant. This was necessary, for they might have tried to stop Judas, thus interfering with the plan of God.

26:24. Jesus pronounced a particularly sad evaluation of Judas's life at this point. He acknowledged that, in accordance with God's plan, He would be killed but still recognized that Judas would be held responsible for his deed. This verse serves notice that even though God directs the affairs of men, one is still responsible for one's actions. For **as it is written of him**, see discussion on Mark 14:21. For **Son of man**, see discussion on Mark 2:10.

26:25. Master, is it I? Judas's question is pointed out especially. He had already made plans to betray Jesus and was covering his tracks by asking the same question as the other disciples (see 26:22). Jesus replied, **Thou hast said**, letting Judas know that He knew what he was about to.

26:26. Jesus took bread. This would have been flat bread (unleavened), something like today's matzoh or perhaps pita bread. **And blessed it** here most likely means that He gave thanks for it (see discussions on Mark 14:22–24). Afterward, He **brake it, and gave it to the disciples, and said, Take, eat; this is my body.** The context makes it clear that He meant the bread represents His body. As bread, broken and consumed, gives physical life, so also His body, broken on the cross, gives spiritual life everlasting. He wanted the disciples to remember the source of their spiritual life as they consumed the source of physical life.

26:27–28. Jesus gave thanks for **the cup** (v. 27) and passed it to the disciples as well. The red color of wine is reminiscent of blood. He wanted them to remember that their sins are forgiven because His **blood** (v. 28) was shed. **The new testament** is a reference to the promise in Jeremiah 31:31–33, where the Lord promised a new covenant with His people. As Old Testament covenants were often sealed with a sacrifice, so the new covenant was sealed by the sacrifice of Jesus Christ on the cross.

26:29. This is a reference to the coming wedding supper of the Lamb, when Jesus and His church will celebrate together in the kingdom.

26:30. Hymn. The Passover fellowship concluded with the second half of the Hallel Psalms (Psalms 115–118).

26:31. All ye shall be offended. Not Peter only, but all the eleven (Judas had previously withdrawn, see John 13:30). The meaning of the words "be offended" is seen in Peter's denial (see 26:69–75) and in the terrified flight of the other disciples (see 26:56). For **I will smite the shepherd,** see discussion on Zechariah 13:7.

26:32. Jesus knew that the resurrection would happen and, based on that knowledge, discussed a future meeting with the disciples. One of Jesus' strongest claims to deity lies not so much in His specific claims as in statements He made based on the assumption that He is God. This was one of those occasions. For **into Galilee,** see 28:10, 16–20; Mark 16:7; John 21:1–23.

26:33. Peter, always quick to speak rather than to reflect, here denied that he would ever be offended. It is odd that Peter, who had confessed earlier that Jesus is "the Son of the living God" (16:16) would find himself, in effect, disagreeing with God. Often the Word of God will challenge believers' assumptions about themselves and their commitments. Rather than spasmodically disagree, as Peter did here, it would be better to reflect on what God has said and see what faults may lie within. This verse is a reminder that God's Word should challenge believers to examine their values and the depth of their commitment.

26:34–35. Before the cock crow (v. 34) may refer to the third of the Roman watches into which the night was divided (see discussion on 14:25; see also Mark 13:35), or it may simply refer to early morning, when the rooster crows. Jesus prophesied that Peter would deny Him, but Peter remained adamant that he would not, and the disciples joined him in this. They were to find that their hasty words, spoken in the relative safety of the upper room, would soon be tested in real life. Often God will test a believer's commitments and convictions in real-life situations, and often one fails. As Peter discovered (John 21:16–17), the mercy of God provides forgiveness and a fresh chance. Sometimes the testing comes on a small scale. How often have believers prayed saying, "Lord, I will go anywhere, suffer any hardship for you!" only to make excuses later in the week when asked to help in the nursery or to teach a class.

I. Garden of Gethsemane (26:36–56)

26:36. Gethsemane means "oil press," a place for squeezing the oil from olives. A garden or orchard on the lower slopes of the Mount of Olives, Gethsemane was one of Jesus' favorite places (see Luke 22:39; John 18:2).

26:37. Peter and the two sons of Zebedee. The latter were James and John. These three disciples seem to have been especially close to Jesus (see Mark 5:37; discussion on Acts 3:1). They were the only disciples to accompany Jesus into Jairus's house and to the Mount of Transfiguration.

26:38–39. Jesus did not die serenely, as many martyrs have. He was no mere martyr; He was the Lamb of God bearing the penalty of the sins of the entire human race. The wrath of God was turned loose on Him. Only this can adequately explain what took place at Gethsemane. **This cup** (v. 39) is a symbol of deep sorrow and suffering. Here it refers to His Father's face being turned away from Him when He who had no sin was made sin (i.e., a sin offering) for us (see 27:46; 2 Cor. 5:21).

26:40–41. The disciples still had no clue as to what was about to happen. They had just had a meal, and in the cool of the night, they fell asleep. Jesus' words were not so much a rebuke as encouragement (see discussion on Mark 14:38).

26:42–44. Jesus prayed a second time, again found the disciples asleep, then prayed a third time. His Father's answer apparently was no, for the events proceeded.

26:45. For **Son of man,** see discussion on Mark 2:10.

26:46. It seems odd that Jesus would say **Rise, let us be going** right after telling the disciples to "Sleep on" (25:45). It may be that He almost immediately saw the party coming to arrest Him.

26:47. For **a great multitude with swords and staves,** see *KJV Study Bible* note on Mark 14:43. For **The chief priests and elders,** see discussions on 2:4; 26:3. The party apparently was much larger than was needed, but those who oppose God's people often overreact.

26:48. For **Whomsoever I shall kiss,** see discussion on Luke 22:47.

26:49. Master is the Hebrew word for "(my) teacher." **Kissed him**. The same word is used of the father's kissing of the prodigal son, indicating affection. **He** refers to Judas (see discussions on Mark 14:45 and Luke 22:47).

26:50. It is a mark of God's mercy that even in the moment of betrayal, Jesus called Judas **Friend**.

26:51. One of them which were with Jesus refers to Peter (see John 18:10). **A servant of the high priest's** refers to Malchus (see John 18:10).

26:52. Here Jesus applied what He had said in the Sermon on the Mount about turning the other cheek. In this situation, it was proper to submit to the authorities. Jesus was not giving a general condemnation of war at all times in all places but rather was teaching personal submission to authority and turning the other cheek when opposed.

26:53. Legions. A Roman legion had six thousand soldiers. One is struck by the fact that Jesus, though arrested, tried, and convicted, seems never to have been out of control of the situation. They did not take His life; He gave it up. He was not killed; He died. He was not taken; He gave Himself up.

26:54. The scriptures be fulfilled. In view of 26:56, this is probably a reference to Zechariah 13:7.

26:55–56. Jesus pointed out to those who had come to arrest Him that they could have taken Him at any time. Again, His attitude was one of submission, not resistance. It was not so much that they took Him as it was that he went. **Then all the disciples forsook him, and fled** (v. 56). In the upper room, Jesus had told the disciples, "All ye shall be offended because of me this night" (26:31), and here they flee in terror.

J. Trial before Caiaphas (26:57–68)

26:57–68. Jesus' trial consisted of two stages: the religious trial held under Caiaphas (here) and the civil trial held under Pontius Pilate (27:1–2, 11–26). For a summary of the two stages, see *KJV Study Bible* note on Mark 14:53–15:15.

26:57–58. The disciples were scattered, but **Peter followed** (v. 58) from a distance **to see the end**. This was not idle curiosity on his part, nor was it morbid.

It was a measure of the devotion with which he held his Lord. He would soon be tested and found wanting. This is not to say, however, that Peter had no love, devotion, or commitment, only that the Lord knew better than he did the level to which he possessed these traits.

26:59. The council (see discussion on Mark 14:55). It is interesting that in carrying out a trial that they knew was a sham, they were meticulous in matters of procedure. How often when one is guilty of major sin that one focuses on minor points of scruple.

26:60–61. I am able to destroy the temple of God (v. 61) evidently was an intentional distortion of Jesus' words (see John 2:19).

26:62. Jesus answered not His accusers. Again, He was "turning the other cheek" as He had taught His disciples. It would not do for Him to get into a verbal battle with His accusers.

26:63. Jesus held his peace. He refused to answer the question of 26:62. **I adjure thee**. When the high priest used this form, however, Jesus was legally obliged to reply. For **Christ**, see discussion on 16:16.

26:64. Jesus obeyed the law in the matter and replied with the truth. He described His second coming as well, emphasizing that though He was in their hands now, His power would be manifest at the right time.

26:65. Rent his clothes. Ordinarily the high priest was forbidden by law to do this (see Lev. 10:6; 21:10), but this was considered a highly unusual circumstance. The high priest interpreted Jesus' answer in 26:64 as blasphemy (see discussion on Mark 14:64).

26:66. The verdict was given: **He is guilty of death**.

26:67–68. Mark reported that they blindfolded Jesus (Mark 14:65), which explains the mocking command, **Prophesy . . . Who is he that smote thee?** (v. 68).

K. Peter's Denial (26:69–75)

26:69–72. Peter, being outside, was questioned, and his association with Jesus was pointed out. Twice he denied it.

26:73. A third time Peter was approached and questioned. **Thy speech be[t]rayeth thee.** Peter had a decidedly Galilean accent, which was conspicuous in Jerusalem.

26:74. Curse ... and swear. We are not told what Peter said, but the third time when he denied knowing Jesus, **the cock crew.** There is no indication that these people were threatening in any way. The authorities had the one they wanted, Jesus, and would have taken little interest even if the crowd had pointed Peter out to them. The women certainly could have offered no threat. Peter was in no apparent danger if he had admitted his relationship with Jesus. His denials only piqued the interest of the group, who were sure he was one of them. Perhaps they only wanted an insider's details of life and ministry with Jesus. Peter, blinded by fear, could not see past his own perception of danger.

26:75. And Peter remembered the word of Jesus, who had prophesied this very event. Peter, now confronted with the reality of his lack of commitment and of the rashness of his words the night before, **went out, and wept bitterly.**

L. Judas's Death (27:1–10)

Chapter 27 deals primarily with Jesus' trial before Pilate and the crucifixion. After setting the scene for the trial (vv. 1–2), however, Matthew reported what happened to Judas after he had betrayed Jesus (vv. 3–10).

27:1–2. When the morning was come (v. 1). The Sanhedrin could not have a legal session at night, so at daybreak, a special meeting was held to make the death sentence (see 26:66) official (see discussion on Mark 15:1). **Delivered him to Pontius Pilate** (v. 2). The Roman government had deprived the Sanhedrin of the right to carry out capital punishment, except in the case of a foreigner who invaded the sacred precincts of the temple. Jesus therefore had to be handed over to Pilate for execution. For additional information about Pilate, see discussion on Mark 15:1.

27:3–10. See Acts 1:16–19. This is a parenthesis in the narrative, but an important one. Judas had

disappeared except for a brief scene in the garden of Gethsemane, after his meeting with the chief priests earlier in the week. Matthew tied up the loose end by telling what happened to Judas, preventing the reader from wondering about this rather than focusing on the narrative. Also, it appears that Judas approached the chief priests and elders sometime on the morning of the crucifixion, so the incident happened at this point chronologically.

27:4. The callousness of these leaders is shown in that Judas admitted his sin, and they offered him no counsel or solace, only scorn.

27:5. For **hanged himself,** see discussion on Acts 1:18.

27:6–10. The potter's field (vv. 7, 10) may have been purchased some days later, but since Matthew's purpose was to tie up the story, he related it here. **The field of blood** (v. 8). Compare "The valley of slaughter" in Jeremiah 19:6. **Jeremie** (v. 9). The quotation seems to be a combination of Zechariah 11:12–13 and Jeremiah 19:1–13 (or perhaps Jer. 18:2–12 or 32:6–9), but Matthew attributed it to the major prophet Jeremiah, just as Mark (1:2–3) quoted a combination of Malachi 3:1 and Isaiah 40:3 but attributed it to the major prophet Isaiah.

M. Trial before Pilate (27:11–26)

27:11–12. Thou sayest (v. 11). Jesus answered Pilate's direct question but **answered nothing** (v. 12) to the charges brought by His accusers.

27:13–14. Pilate **marvelled** (v. 14), probably because Jesus was calm in the face of false accusations and that He did not get into a shouting match with them. A guilty man will often rant against his accusers. Pilate was astute enough to recognize an innocent man when one appeared in his court.

27:15. The governor was wont to release unto the people a prisoner. A custom of which nothing is known outside the Gospels. It was probably never mentioned because it was incidental to the activities of the Passover week. The Jewish leaders normally did not ask for a notorious or dangerous prisoner to be released, which also minimized the importance of the custom. On this occasion, it was quite different.

27:16–18. A notable prisoner, called Barabbas (v. 16). Barabbas had taken part in a rebellion (see Luke 23:19; John 18:40), presumably against the Romans, and would have been a folk hero among the Jews. Why Pilate offered the choice of him or Jesus is unclear. Was he the only prisoner Pilate had? This is unlikely. Was he unpopular? If so, Pilate may have hoped that the contrast would lead the people to ask for Jesus, whom he by now surely knew was popular with the multitudes.

27:19. This incident is found only in Matthew's gospel. It forms something of an interruption of the narrative, but it heightens the drama and emphasizes that Pilate knew that Jesus was innocent.

27:20–23. If manipulating the situation was Pilate's intent, it failed. **The chief priests and elders persuaded the multitude that they should ask Barabbas** (v. 20). Apparently, the same crowd that had hailed Jesus on the first day of the week now called for His crucifixion. It may be that the crowd was "handpicked" by the chief priests and elders and was not representative of the majority. Certainly, all the people could not have been in one place at this time.

27:24. This is the origin of the saying "I wash my hands of the situation."

27:25. His blood be on us. The bloodthirsty crowd gave a chilling response, which has often been used to justify the persecution of the Jewish people. It should be noted, however, that it was not God but the people themselves who uttered these words. There is no evidence here that God granted their request. In addition, this crowd was certainly not all the Jewish people alive at the time. Had Jesus' fate been submitted to a vote across all of Judea and Galilee, it is doubtful that He would have been convicted.

27:26. Scourged. Roman floggings were so brutal that sometimes the victim died before crucifixion (see discussion on Mark 15:15).

N. The Soldiers Mock Jesus (27:27–32)

27:27. The common hall. The governor's official residence in Jerusalem was the "Pretorium" (Mark 15:16; see discussion there).

27:28–31. A scarlet robe (v. 28). The outer cloak of a Roman soldier. For **a crown of thorns** (v. 29), see discussion on Mark 15:17. **Reed** (v. 29). A mock scepter. None of this was likely an official part of the sentence. The soldiers apparently took advantage of the time it took for the preparations for the crucifixion to mistreat Him.

27:32. Cyrene. A city in North Africa on the Mediterranean Sea about seven hundred miles west of Jerusalem. For **Simon ... to bear his cross**, see discussion on Mark 15:21.

O. The Crucifixion (27:33–56)

27:33. For **Golgotha**, see discussion on Mark 15:22.

27:34. Mingled with gall. Tradition says that the women of Jerusalem customarily furnished this painkilling narcotic to prisoners who were crucified. Jesus refused to drink it because He wanted to be fully conscious until His death (see 27:50).

27:35. For **crucified**, see *KJV Study Bible* note on Mark 15:24. **Casting lots** is explained more precisely in John 19:23–24.

27:36–37. See discussion on Mark 15:26.

27:38. For **two thieves**, see discussion on Mark 15:27.

27:39–43. It is ironic that the people called Him to **save** (v. 40) Himself, when it was by being there that He saved us. The leaders also mocked Him, saying **let him now come down from the cross, and we will believe him** (v. 42). In fact, had He not gone to the cross, believing in Him would have done no good.

27:44. Luke recorded that one of these thieves repented. Matthew omitted this detail, but the two accounts are easily harmonized.

27:45. From the sixth hour ... unto the ninth hour. From noon until 3:00 p.m.

27:46–49. ELI, ELI, LAMA SABACHTHANI? (v. 46) is a mixture of Aramaic and Hebrew, translated by Matthew for his readers (see discussion on Mark 15:34). Some mistook this for a call to **Elias** (Elijah; v. 49). It may be that the crowd knew little of Aramaic, one of the languages commonly spoken in the Holy Land in Jesus' day, as many were visiting Jerusalem for the feast and may have spoken mostly Greek (see discussion on Mark 15:35).

27:50–51. The vail is the inner curtain that separated the Holy Place from the Most Holy Place. The tearing of the curtain signified Christ's making it possible for believers to go directly into God's presence (see Heb. 9:1–14; 10:14–22).

27:52–53. This incident is found only in Matthew's gospel. These **saints** (v. 52) were a witness to Christ's victory over death.

27:54. The Son of God. It cannot be determined whether **the centurion** (see discussion on 8:5) made a fully Christian confession or was only acknowledging that, since the gods had so obviously acted to vindicate this judicial victim, Jesus must have been one especially favored by them (the Greek can also be translated "a son"). In view of the ridicule voiced by "they that passed by" (27:39–40), however, it seems probable that Matthew intended the former (see discussion on Luke 23:47).

27:55–56. These women were involved in Jesus' burial, and among them were the witnesses to the risen Christ on Sunday morning (see discussion on Mark 15:40).

P. The Burial (27:57–66)

27:57. Arimathea. A village in the hill country of Ephraim, about twenty miles northwest of Jerusalem.

27:58. For **begged the body of Jesus**, see discussion on Luke 23:52.

27:59–60. Others helped Joseph with the burial. He caused it to happen but did not do the preparations alone (see discussion on Mark 15:46).

27:61. These women probably helped with the burial and certainly knew exactly where the tomb was. No one can assert with any credibility that these women went to the wrong tomb on Easter Sunday.

27:62–64. This meeting indicates that Jesus' opponents had a good idea of what He had taught His disciples. They knew that He had not spoken of the literal temple when He said "in three days I will build it again" (16:21), yet this was the statement that provided motivation for the trial against Him.

27:65–66. Ye have a watch (v. 65), most likely made up of Roman soldiers (see 28:4, 11–12).

VIII. The Risen Christ (chap. 28)

A. The Empty Tomb (28:1–10)

28:1. For **the first day of the week**, see discussion on Luke 24:1. **The other Mary**. The wife of Clopas (see 27:56; John 19:25).

28:2. A great earthquake. Only Matthew recorded this earthquake and the one at Jesus' death (27:51, 54). It is clear from the parallel accounts (Mark 16:2–6; Luke 24:1–7; John 20:1) that the events of 28:2–4 occurred before the women arrived at the tomb. The earthquakes, at His death and at the tomb, may have served to emphasize the apolcalyptic aspect of these events. Jesus was, in His death, opening up heaven to all who believe. His death set in motion the events that will culminate in the great tribulation and the millennium and was thus accompanied by apocalyptic signs.

28:3–4. His countenance was like lightning (v. 3) describes the angel that rolled away the stone (see 28:2) and is most likely a reference to brightness. The angel probably had a glow from within. Well might **the keepers ... shake** (v. 4) in the presence of such a creature. **Became as dead men** may mean that they fainted or were so afraid that they were unable to move.

28:5–7. The angel announced the risen Christ and reminded the women of His words when He told the disciples He would meet them in **Galilee** (v. 7) after the resurrection (see 26:32).

28:8–10. Fear and great joy (v. 8). These two emotions can certainly go together. The women were fearful most likely because of the unexpectedness of the events and joyful because their Lord was alive. **As they went to tell his disciples ... Jesus met them** (v. 9). They **worshipped him**, now recognizing His deity. Jesus reminded them again that He would meet the disciples in **Galilee** (v. 10).

B. The Authorities Cover Up What Really Happened (28:11–15)

28:11–15. Only Matthew related the posting of the guard (see 27:62–66), and here he followed up by telling of their report. The chief priests and elders bribed the soldiers and gave them a false story to report. Apparently, the story still circulated when Matthew wrote this account, which is why he took time to treat its origin here.

C. The Great Commission (28:16–20)

28:16–17. The eleven (v. 16). Judas had committed suicide (see 27:5). For **had appointed**, see 28:10. Meeting Jesus in Galilee as He had instructed them (see 26:32), the disciples **worshipped him**. This is the second time in a few verses that Jesus was worshiped. It stands as a proof of His deity, for when others in the Bible are worshiped (Paul in Acts 14:11–15 and an angel in Rev. 19:10; 22:8), they refuse it and point to the true God. The counterexample is Herod in Acts 12:22, and he was killed for taking to himself the honor due to God. **But some doubted**. They saw the risen Christ, but even with all He had taught them concerning His death and resurrection, it was so miraculous that some were still hesitant to believe, though the record in Acts clearly indicates that they eventually did.

28:18–20. This is the Great Commission. It forms the biblical basis for missions and evangelism.

28:18. Here is the power of missions: Jesus has **All power . . . in heaven and in earth**. Missions is not a human endeavor; it takes place under the anointing and empowerment of God Himself.

28:19. The goal of missions is to **teach all nations**. The idea is to make disciples. The commission of Christ's followers is not just to tell the story

and move on but to create faith communities— churches—where living out the Christian life becomes the basis of the evangelization of the world. Here also is the universal scope of missions: "all nations." No one is to be excluded from hearing the gospel. Matthew's readers needed the reminder that the gospel was to be taken to the Gentiles (compare 10:5–6). Also, the scope of Christ's Great Commission shows that although it was spoken to the eleven, it was meant for the entire church, in all ages, until He returns. **Baptizing them**. This is the proper activity of the ministry: to build the church, by "baptizing them" (the new disciples) and forming them into communities of faith that worship and study together to evangelize the world with the gospel. This baptism is a sign of their identification with and commitment to Christ (see discussions on Acts 2:38; Rom. 6:3–4). **In the name of the Father, and of the Son, and of the Holy Ghost**. Christ is associated with the other persons of deity in the Trinity. Christians are to baptize new disciples "in the name of the Father, and of the Son, and of the Holy [Spirit]." The elliptical clause in the Greek text clearly distinguishes each member of the Trinity. There is only one God whom we are to worship, and it is this God, the Three in One, and no other.

28:20. I am with you alway. Matthew ended his gospel with the reassuring and empowering words of the One who came to earth to be "God with us" (1:23). **Even unto the end of the world**. Again, this demonstrates that the Great Commission applies to the church at all times until Christ returns.

THE GOSPEL ACCORDING TO ST. MARK

INTRODUCTION

Author

A title "According to Mark" appears with the second gospel in the oldest manuscripts of the New Testament, which originate from the end of the first century, many years after the gospel of Mark had been written. Since there is no direct internal evidence of authorship for the second gospel, the title represents early and valuable external evidence regarding the identity of the writer. The information that the title furnishes is highly reliable since an early Christian author writing a gospel under an assumed name (pseudonymously) would likely have chosen a more prominent name (such as that of an apostle). Mark is, therefore, the probable author. The title "The Gospel according to St. Mark" in the KJV reflects that certainty.

The unanimous testimony of the early church is that the Mark of this gospel is John Mark of the New Testament. The first mention of him is in connection with his mother, who had a house in Jerusalem that served as a meeting place for believers (see Acts 12:12). This house was also thought to be the upper room (see Mark 14:12–15). When Paul and Barnabas returned to Antioch from Jerusalem after the famine visit, Mark accompanied them (see Acts 12:25). Mark next appears as a helper to Paul and Barnabas on their first missionary journey (see Acts 13:5), but he deserted them at Perga, in Pamphylia, to return to Jerusalem (see Acts 13:13). Paul must have been deeply disappointed with Mark's actions on this occasion, because when Barnabas proposed taking Mark on the second journey, Paul flatly refused—a refusal that broke up their working relationship (see Acts 15:36–39). Barnabas took Mark, who was his cousin, and departed for Cyprus. No further mention is made of either of them in the book of Acts. Mark reappears in Paul's letter to the Colossians, written from Rome. Paul sent a greeting from Mark and added: "touching whom ye received commandments: if he come unto you, receive him" (Col. 4:10; see Philemon 24, written about the same time). At that point, Mark apparently had begun to win his way back into Paul's confidence. By the end of Paul's life, Mark had fully regained his favor; the apostle now considered Mark "profitable to me for the ministry" (2 Tim. 4:11). It is also thought that the one Peter mentioned as "Marcus my son" (1 Peter 5:13) was this same Mark. He was Peter's son in the faith.

The most important evidence regarding John Mark and the authorship of the second gospel comes from Papias (ca. AD 140), who quoted an even earlier source as saying:

(1) John Mark was a close associate of Peter, from whom he received the tradition of the things the Lord said and did; (2) this tradition did not come to Mark as a finished, sequential account of the life of Jesus but rather as the preaching of Peter, which was directed to the needs of the early Christian communities; (3) Mark accurately preserved this material. Thus, the gospel of Mark largely consists of the preaching of Peter, arranged and shaped by John Mark. In composing his gospel, Mark drew from Peter's preaching those reminiscences that especially contributed to his own distinctive theological purposes.

Since the gospel contains eyewitness accounts of the life of Jesus—accounts of the apostle Peter himself—it stands as weighty historical evidence that attests to the life and deeds of Jesus. Those eyewitness accounts in which Peter himself appears represent words and events that must have had special significance for him as a disciple of Jesus. Peter's successes (see 8:29) and failures (see 14:66–72) serve as examples for other disciples. John Mark, recognizing the value of these personal disclosures in Peter's preaching, related them to his own audience as he sought to build them up in the ways of discipleship.

Date

Precise dating of the gospel of Mark is virtually impossible. Some have proposed dates in the mid- to late-40s or in the 50s. Others have suggested that Mark wrote in the early to mid-60s before Peter's death, which occurred circa AD 64–67. Still others believe that the content of the gospel and statements made about Mark by the early church fathers indicate that the book was written shortly after Peter's death in Rome but before the destruction of Jerusalem in AD 70. The date for Mark in this view is therefore circa AD 67–70.

Regardless of the difficulty in precise dating, a good case can be made for a date sometime before AD 70, even before 64. According to the two-source hypothesis, Matthew and Luke both utilized Mark and a hypothetical document called Quelle (German for "source"), or Q, in the composition of their gospels. If this hypothesis is true, Mark must predate Matthew and Luke-Acts (Luke's two-volume work). Paul was under house arrest in Rome at the end of Acts, and since neither the outcome of Paul's trial nor his martyrdom (ca. AD 64–67) are mentioned in Acts, Luke-Acts (and Mark's gospel, which was used by Luke) was most likely written sometime before AD 64.

Some recent scholars have suggested that the date of Mark is as late as circa AD 70–73. The saying of Jesus about "the abomination of desolation" (13:14) enters the discussion at this point. Mark's editorial comment in 13:14 ("let him that readeth understand") infers that Jesus' words in that verse have relevance for his contemporary audience, not just for readers in the distant future. Luke understood the saying to refer to the siege and conquest of Jerusalem by the Romans in the war of AD 66–70 (see Luke 21:20), and one may assume that Mark had the same understanding. Mark recalled for his audience Jesus' prophecies of events that were some forty years distant when the Lord spoke. The fulfillment of Jesus' prophecy regarding Jerusalem's fate was still future for Mark, but that fulfillment could be seen on the horizon as he wrote.

Place of Composition

According to early church tradition, Mark was written "in the regions of Italy" (Anti-Marcionite prologue) or, more specifically, in Rome (as stated by Irenaeus and Clement of Alexandria). These same authors closely associate Mark's writing of the gospel with the apostle Peter. The above evidence is consistent with (1) the historical probability that Peter was in Rome during the last days of his life and was martyred there and (2) the biblical evidence that Mark also was in Rome about the same time and was closely associated with Peter (see 2 Tim. 4:11; 1 Peter 5:13, where the word "Babylon" is possibly a cryptogram for Rome).

Further evidence that points to Rome as the place of composition is an incidental reference in 15:21, which describes the Roman soldiers compelling Simon, a Cyrenian, to carry Jesus' cross. Mark noted that Simon was "the father of Alexander and Rufus," a detail that evidently was unimportant for Matthew and Luke (they omitted it from their versions of Jesus' passion) but was important for Mark. He assumed that his readers knew and appreciated the identity of these sons of Simon. But who were Alexander and Rufus? Since Alexander was, in all likelihood, not the same person as any of the other men of that name in the New Testament, nothing can be known about him. An identification of Rufus is more promising, however. In Romans 16, Paul instructed the believers in Rome to greet various members of the church there, including a person named Rufus ("Salute Rufus chosen in the Lord," Rom. 16:13). Since no other Rufus besides the one whom Mark mentioned appears in the New Testament, the Rufus of Mark 15:21 and of Romans 16:13 are probably the same man. If so, the gospel of Mark is closely linked to Rome by the name Rufus. Mark mentioned Rufus in his gospel as one whom the Roman Christians would know; he was one of them. Although some interpreters have suggested other places of composition (Alexandria, Antioch, Galilee), a Roman provenance is most likely.

Recipients

The evidence indicates that Mark's audience was the church at Rome, or at least to Gentile readers there. Mark explained Jewish customs (7:2–4; 15:42) and translated Aramaic words (3:17; 5:41; 7:11, 34; 15:22, 34). Aramaic was one of the languages of the Holy Land in the first century AD, and probably the language Jesus and His disciples ordinarily spoke (though they probably also spoke Hebrew and Greek). Mark's use of Latin technical terms does not absolutely prove that he wrote in the imperial capital and for the believers there, but it does allow for that possibility. In two instances, Mark explained common Greek words by Latin terms. The first instance is in 12:42. In the temple, a poor widow came to the treasury and "threw in two mites [Greek, *lepta duo*], which make a farthing [Greek, *kodrantēs*; Latin, *quadrans*]." In the second instance, at 15:16, Jesus had been delivered over to be crucified, "And the soldiers led him away into the hall [Greek, *aulē*], called Pretorium [Greek, *praitōrion*; Latin, *praetorium*]." These explanations agree with the view that this gospel was written in Rome for the church there. Furthermore, Mark also seems to have had a special interest in persecution and martyrdom (8:34–38; 13:9–13), subjects perhaps of special concern to Roman believers. A Roman origin and audience would explain the almost immediate acceptance of this gospel and its rapid dissemination. In short, Mark's original readers and hearers were quite likely Christians within the city of Rome.

Theme and Theological Message

Throughout Mark, Jesus is consistently portrayed as a person of stature and honor. He receives popular approval in His exchanges with religious leaders, subdues forces of nature, exorcizes demons, and teaches with authority. Even Jesus' opponents must grudgingly withdraw in their attempts to discredit Him. They are finally able to force a trial and condemnation of Jesus, but even in the legal proceedings and execution, Jesus is seen as a person of honor. The shame of the cross is counteracted throughout the gospel. Mark's intention, therefore, may have been to convince unbelievers, and to encourage believers, that Jesus ultimately has honor despite the shame of crucifixion.

Since Mark's gospel is traditionally associated with Rome, it may have been occasioned by the persecutions of the Roman church in the period circa AD 64–67. The famous fire of Rome in 64, probably set by Nero himself but blamed on Christians, resulted in the severe persecution, even martyrdom, of the Roman believers. Whatever the precise circumstances, the gospel of Mark addresses a community or communities under distress. Mark may have wanted to prepare his readers for this suffering by placing before them the life of the Lord, as his gospel contains many references, both explicit and veiled, to suffering and discipleship (see 1:12–13; 3:22, 30; 8:34–38; 10:30, 33–34, 45; 13:8, 11–13). Mark's audience needed a refresher course reviewing the honorable identity of Jesus, the one who inaugurated the kingdom of God in His life and ministry. The confusion of the disciples in the gospel narrative parallels that of Mark's audience. The narrative reminded them that Jesus has glory and honor as the Christ, the Son of God. The anguished disciples in Mark's audience could therefore count it an honor to follow Him.

Mark particularly emphasized several themes in his gospel. (1) *The cross.* Both the human cause (12:12; 14:1–2; 15:10) and the divine necessity (8:31; 9:31; 10:33) of the cross are emphasized. (2) *Discipleship.* Special attention should be paid to the passages on discipleship that arose from Jesus' prophesy of His passion (8:34–9:1; 9:35–10:31; 10:42–45). (3) *The teachings of Jesus.* Although Mark recorded far fewer actual teachings of Jesus than did the other gospel writers, he placed a remarkable emphasis on Jesus as teacher. The words "teacher," "teach" or "teaching," and "Master" are applied to Jesus nearly forty times in Mark. (4) *The messianic secret.* On several occasions, Jesus warned His disciples or the person for whom He had worked a miracle to keep silent about His true identity as the Messiah or what He had done (1:34, 44; 3:12; 5:43; 7:36–37; 8:26, 30; 9:9). Some scholars theorize that Mark invented the messianic secret to remove an embarrassing failure of Jesus to proclaim Himself as Messiah. Words are put into Jesus' mouth that prohibit demons and people from talking about Him and His mighty deeds. According to this theory, Jesus' privately teaching some that He is the Messiah is a fiction. There is no reason to assume, however, that Jesus did not indeed instruct people against revealing His messianic characteristics. He did not want to encourage the masses to follow Him merely as a political liberator who would lead them in revolt against the Roman occupation. The early Christian belief in Jesus as the Messiah and Son of God could have originated only as a result of Jesus' own statement about this. (5) *The Son of God.* Although Mark emphasized the humanity of Jesus (see 3:5; 6:6, 31, 34; 7:34; 8:12, 33; 10:14; 11:12), he did not neglect His deity (see 1:1, 11; 3:11; 5:7; 9:7; 12:1–11; 13:32; 15:39).

Literary Features

Mark's gospel is a simple, succinct, unadorned, yet vivid account of Jesus' ministry, emphasizing more what Jesus did than what He said. Mark moves quickly from one episode in Jesus' life and ministry to another, with frequent use of the adverb translated "immediately." The book as a whole is characterized as "The beginning of the gospel" (1:1). The life, death, and resurrection of Christ comprise the "beginning," of which the apostolic preaching in Acts is the continuation. In recent scholarly study of the second gospel, its literary features (narration, setting, plot, and character) have been a focus. The craftsmanship of Mark as a skilled storyteller has justly been recognized.

Outline

I. The Beginnings of Jesus' Ministry (1:1–13)
   A. His Forerunner (1:1–8)
   B. His Baptism (1:9–11)
   C. His Temptation (1:12–13)
II. Jesus' Ministry in Galilee (1:14–6:29)
   A. Early Galilean Ministry (1:14–3:12)
      1. Call of the First Disciples (1:14–20)
      2. Miracles in Capernaum (1:21–34)
      3. A Tour of Galilee (1:35–45)
      4. Ministry in Capernaum (2:1–22)
      5. Sabbath Controversy (2:23–3:12)
   B. Later Galilean Ministry (3:13–6:29)
      1. Selection of the Twelve Apostles (3:13–19)
      2. Teachings in Capernaum (3:20–35)
      3. Parables of the Kingdom (4:1–34)
         a. The Parable of the Sower (4:1–20)
         b. The Parable of the Candle under a Bushel (4:21–23)
         c. The Saying about Measure (4:24–25)
         d. The Parable of the Growing Seed (4:26–29)
         e. The Parable of the Mustard Seed (4:30–34)
      4. Trip across the Sea of Galilee (4:35–5:20)
      5. More Galilean Miracles (5:21–43)
      6. Unbelief in Jesus' Hometown (6:1–6)
      7. Six Apostolic Teams Tour Galilee (6:7–13)
      8. King Herod's Reaction to Jesus' Ministry (6:14–29)
III. Withdrawals from Galilee (6:30–9:32)
   A. To the Eastern Shore of the Sea of Galilee (6:30–52)
   B. To the Western Shore of the Sea of Galilee (6:53–7:23)
   C. To Phoenicia (7:24–30)
   D. To the Region of the Decapolis: More Miracles (7:31–8:10)
   E. To the Vicinity of Caesarea Philippi (8:11–9:32)
      1. The Pharisees' Demand for a Sign and the Danger of Yeast (8:11–21)
      2. The Healing of a Blind Man at Bethsaida (8:22–26)
      3. Peter's Confession and Jesus' Prophesy of His Death and Resurrection (8:27–9:1)
      4. The Transfiguration (9:2–13)

8. The Soldiers Mock Jesus (15:16–20)
9. The Crucifixion and Death of Jesus (15:21–39)
10. The Burial of Jesus (15:40–47)
VII. The Resurrection of Jesus (chap. 16)
   A. The Empty Tomb (16:1–8)
   B. The Longer Ending of Mark (16:9–20)

Select Bibliography

Cole, R. Alan. *The Gospel according to Mark: An Introduction and Commentary*. 2nd ed. Tyndale New Testament Commentaries 2. Grand Rapids, MI: Eerdmans, 1989.

Edwards, James R. *The Gospel according to Mark*. Pillar New Testament Commentary. Grand Rapids, MI: Eerdmans, 2001.

France, R. T. *The Gospel of Mark: A Commentary on the Greek Text*. New International Greek Testament Commentary. Grand Rapids, MI: Eerdmans, 2002.

Guelich, Robert A. *Mark 1–8:26*. Word Biblical Commentary 34A. Dallas, TX: Word, 1989.

Gundry, Robert H. *Mark: A Commentary on His Apology for the Cross*. Grand Rapids, MI: Eerdmans, 1993.

Hurtado, Larry W. *Mark*. A Good News Commentary. San Francisco, CA: Harper & Row, 1983.

Lane, William L. *The Gospel according to Mark*. The New International Commentary on the New Testament. Grand Rapids, MI: Eerdmans, 1974.

Taylor, Vincent. *The Gospel according to St. Mark*. New York: St. Martin's Press, 1963.

Witherington, Ben. *The Gospel of Mark: A Socio-Rhetorical Commentary*. Grand Rapids, MI: Eerdmans, 2001.

EXPOSITION

I. The Beginnings of Jesus' Ministry (1:1–13)

A. His Forerunner (1:1–8)

1:1–8. In the opening section, Jesus' activity is linked with God's activity and Old Testament prophecy.

1:1. The beginning (Greek, *archē*) suggests the opening verse of Genesis (see John 1:1). The word **gospel** is from the Old English *godspel*, "good story" or "good news"; the latter term accurately translates the Greek. The good news is that God has provided salvation through the life, death, and resurrection of **Jesus Christ, the Son of God.** "Gospel" could refer to Mark's gospel or to the good news whose story and unfolding begins in 1:2. The significance of **Christ**

and **Son of God** for Mark become clear in the unfolding of his gospel. In brief, however, "Christ" designates the divinely anointed and commissioned Messiah, the deliverer of God's people. For Mark, the title "Son of God" complements "Son of man" (see discussion on 2:10) and refers to the One who has power over the natural and supernatural realms, the authority to bring salvation and judgment, the right to declare the meaning of the Scriptures, and a unique relationship with God the Father. The reader knows from the outset who Jesus is and takes His side against His antagonists.

1:2–3. The prophets (v. 2) should read "Isaiah the prophet" (NIV), the most accurate reading of the manuscripts. Since the quotation of these verses is a combination of texts (v. 2 is from Mal. 3:1; v. 3 is from Isa. 40:3), Mark simply attributed the entire formula to the more prominent prophet, Isaiah. The passages cited speak of the **messenger** (v. 2), **the wilderness** (v. 3), and **the Lord**, each of which is stressed in 1:4–8.

1:4. Mark, like John, has no nativity narrative but begins with the ministry of **John** the Baptist. The name John means "the Lord is gracious." John's practice of baptizing those who came to him in repentance was so characteristic of his ministry that he became known as "the Baptist" or "the Baptizer." **The wilderness** refers to the unpopulated region near the Jordan River. The wilderness setting reminds the reader of the exodus; the One whom John announced would duplicate God's salvation of His people in the wilderness. John's travels may have taken him into the arid region west of the Dead Sea, whose inhabitants included those who wrote and preserved the Dead Sea Scrolls. No evidence exists to connect John conclusively with the settlement of Qumran, near the caves where the scrolls were found. **The baptism** that he preached, however, is similar to the washings practiced at Qumran. John was preaching repentance-baptism, baptism that was preceded or accompanied by **repentance**. The word "repentance" (Greek, *metanoia*) involves turning one's entire person to God, not just feeling sorrow for sin. As did the community at Qumran, John taught that forgiveness (**the remission of sins**) is based on repentance, not baptism. God always grants forgiveness when one has truly repented. John's emphasis on repentance recalls the preaching of the prophets (e.g., Hos. 3:4–5); his stress on forgiveness pointed to the salvation bestowed by the coming One.

1:5. All the land of Judaea and **were all baptized** are obvious hyperboles, indicating the high interest John's preaching created. For centuries, Israel had had no prophet. John created intense excitement throughout Judea: at last God was at work to fulfill His promises and reveal the kingdom of God! Even though **the river of Jordan** is the principal river in the Holy Land, it is located in the rift valley, away from the population centers. It begins from the snows of Mount Hermon and ends at the Dead Sea. Its closest point to Jerusalem is about twenty miles.

1:6. John was a man of simple means: he **was clothed with camel's hair, and with a girdle of a skin** (clothing worn by Elijah and other prophets, see 2 Kings 1:8; Zech. 13:4), and his diet was **locusts and wild honey**. "Locusts" could refer to the insects (allowed as food in Lev. 11:22–23) or to the carob bean or nut.

1:7. Mark's account of John's message is brief (see Matt. 3:7–12; Luke 3:7–17). He **preached** with a focus on the coming of the mighty One. The reader's interest is aroused by this message. Who is **mightier than** the honored prophet John? Whoever he is, he must be a person of great honor since even John was **not worthy to stoop down and unloose** the thongs of His sandals. As great as John's ministry was, the ministry of the coming One would be greater.

1:8. John **baptized … with water: but [Christ] shall baptize you with the Holy Ghost**. An eschatological outpouring of the Holy Spirit, the coming of the Holy Spirit upon God's people in the last days, is an Old Testament expectation (see Isa. 32:15; Ezek. 36:27; Joel 2:28–32). The baptism carries two aspects: salvation conveyed by the Holy Spirit and the fire of judgment (see Matt. 3:11; Luke 3:16).

B. His Baptism (1:9–11)

1:9–11. In those days (v. 9), when Jesus began His public ministry, He was approximately thirty years old (see Luke 3:23), probably circa AD 27. As far as can be known, He had spent most of His earlier years in **Nazareth**. When Jesus **was baptized of John in Jordan**, all three persons of the Trinity were involved (vv. 10–11): (1) the Father spoke, (2) the Son was baptized, and (3) the Holy Spirit descended on the Son. All three persons are characters in Mark's drama. Although distinct, they act in complete and divine harmony with one another. Jesus is shown, at the beginning of His ministry, to be a person with the highest honor and approval. Throughout the gospel, the opponents' slanders and schemes are therefore unjustified and fail to cast Jesus in a negative light for the alert reader. **The Spirit like a dove descending upon him** (v. 10) is Mark's way of describing Jesus' anointing for ministry. The simile of a dove represents the gentleness, purity, and guilelessness of the Holy Spirit (see Matt. 10:16). In certain Jewish literature, the dove symbolizes the Holy Spirit as well as Israel itself. The picture in Mark may convey the idea that the One on whom the Spirit rested would recreate Israel. **Thou art my beloved Son** (v. 11) alludes to Psalm 2:7, and **in whom I am well pleased** alludes to Isaiah 42:1. The allusions bring together the tradition of David's royal descendant and the suffering Servant of the Lord, respectively. The degrading treatment of Jesus in the gospel does not determine Jesus' true status of honor.

C. His Temptation (1:12–13)

1:12–13. A distinctive characteristic of Mark's style is his use (some forty-seven times) of the Greek word *euthys*, "immediately," also translated as "just then," "straightway," "forthwith," and "anon." Rapidity of movement in Mark's narrative lends urgency to the drama. The reader senses the urgency of the mission and message (see 1:14–15) of Jesus, the protagonist in the drama.

Upon Jesus' baptism and anointing for ministry, **immediately the Spirit driveth him into the wilderness** (v. 12). A preferable translation is, "Immediately the Holy Spirit compelled Jesus to go into the wilderness" (NLT). One might think that the next event in the narrative would involve some miraculous deed or victory, but not so. The Father's will was that Jesus be **tempted of Satan** (v. 13) for a time. Nevertheless, divine resources were adequate for the divine plan: **the angels ministered unto him** as they had attended Israel in the wilderness (see Exod. 23:20, 23; 32:34). Jesus' followers today can also face temptations with confidence that God will supply what is necessary for those temptations to be endured (see 1 Cor. 10:13).

The setting (**in the wilderness**; v. 13) and the duration (**forty days**) of Jesus' time there recall the theophany that Moses experienced (Exod. 24:18) and the forty-year wandering of God's people when He led and protected them (see Deut. 8:1–5). A new exodus was beginning, with Jesus as the new Moses. The severity of Jesus' testing is emphasized by the reference to **the wild beasts**. In Jesus' day, there were many more wild animals, including lions, in Israel than there are today. Only Mark reported their presence in this connection, emphasizing that God kept Jesus safe in the wilderness.

II. Jesus' Ministry in Galilee (1:14–6:29)

A. Early Galilean Ministry (1:14–3:12)

1. Call of the First Disciples (1:14–20)

1:14. Mark did not explain why **John was put in prison**, arousing the reader's curiosity. The details of John's imprisonment are not given until chapter 6. The message of Jesus' preaching at this time was **the gospel of the kingdom of God** (some manuscripts have "the gospel of God"). The kingdom of God is God's rule in which His perfect will for righteousness, justice, and peace is revealed and experienced. In Jesus' life and ministry, the reign of God had come into earthly history and, unexpectedly, overlapped for a time with the present age. In the future, the rule of God will be fully revealed in the final judgment of the wicked and the salvation of the righteous. Now the kingdom is God's saving activity; in the future, the kingdom will be an actual place or realm. In the New Testament, the kingdom of God has both an "already" and a "not yet" aspect.

1:15. Jesus' proclamation that **The time is fulfilled** relates to the hope of the Old Testament and Judaism for God's redemptive purpose to be accomplished. That hope was realized with Jesus' coming, which is why the good news (the gospel) announces that **the kingdom of God is at hand**. Scholars debate the proper translation of the Greek verb *ēngiken*; varying translations are "at hand," "is near" (NIV), "has come near" (NRSV), and "has come." One may conclude that, at least, the powers of the age to come were at work in Jesus and His ministry even if the kingdom was not yet present.

Jesus' announcement of the kingdom demanded a response: **repent ye** (see discussion on 1:4), **and believe the gospel**. In light of the drawing near of God's dominion, one must make a total commitment of oneself to God, trusting God to work out His gracious purposes of that reign. The verbs "repent" and "believe" are plural; Jesus called for a corporate response from the Jewish people, but an individual response was necessary as well.

1:16–20. These verses illustrate what repentance and belief are all about. Mark included the story of the calling of the first disciples to inform his audience what true discipleship entails. Discipleship is a major concern of Mark's gospel, and this is a crucial passage on that topic. The call-and-response pattern and the fishing imagery are powerful literary devices in Mark's theology of discipleship.

1:16–18. The sea of Galilee (v. 16) is a beautiful lake, almost 700 feet below sea level, 14 miles long and 6 miles wide, fed by the waters of the upper Jordan River. It was also called "the lake of Gennesaret" (Luke 5:1) and "the sea of Tiberias" (John 6:1; 21:1). In Old Testament times, it was known as "the sea of Chinnereth" (Num. 34:11, e.g.). The metaphor of fishing for people is striking, seizing the attention of **Simon and Andrew his brother** as they were **casting a net into the sea**. The name Simon is probably a contraction of the Old Testament name Simeon. Jesus later gave Simon the name Peter (see 3:16; Matt. 16:18; John 1:42).

Jesus called Simon and Andrew in the midst of their daily lives, speaking to the fishermen in their own language. He called them to a task for which they had preparation and capability; He would supply all that was yet needed (**I will make you to become fishers of men**, v. 17). This was not Jesus' first encounter with Simon and Andrew (see John 1:35–42). John 2–3 states that they were with Jesus at the wedding at Cana and at the Passover in Jerusalem, where they encountered Nicodemus. They had been with Jesus on a part-time basis; now Jesus called them to follow Him full-time. **Come ye after me** demanded a response of total comittment.

By Jesus' own words, He is an honorable person of unusual authority: He calls individuals of His own choosing to be His disciples (unlike the rabbis, who were chosen by their followers), and He promises to transform the lives of those who follow Him. The immediacy of the brothers' response conveys to the reader that there is urgency in the call of discipleship: **and straightway they forsook their nets, and followed him** (v. 18).

1:19–20. The call and response of another pair of brothers, James and John, was also urgent: **he called them: and they left** (v. 20), not only their fishing business (which was evidently thriving, since **hired servants** are mentioned) but also their family (**their father Zebedee**). Discipleship is costly, but those whom Jesus calls are called according to their capabilities and are given even greater resources—the transforming power of Christ Himself.

2. Miracles in Capernaum (1:21–34)

1:21–34. This section serves as an introduction to Jesus' ministry. He is a person of great honor in that He has authority in His teaching, over supernatural forces of evil, and over oppressive powers of nature. Once again Mark created urgency in the narrative by using the word *euthys* four times in this section ("straightway," v. 21; "Just then," v. 23 [NASB; omitted in KJV]; "forthwith," 1:29; "anon," 1:30). The action is fast-paced and intense.

1:21. The village **Capernaum**, on the northwest shore of the Sea of Galilee, was the nearest Galilean settlement to the Jordan River. A fishing village of not more than one thousand people in the first century, it served as Jesus' ministry headquarters (see Matt. 4:13; Mark 2:1). Recent archaeological discoveries have identified the traditional house of Peter as part of a church that incorporated it. A splendid fourth-century **synagogue** has been excavated, perhaps on the site of the synagogue where Jesus ministered. The synagogue was a very important religious institution among the Jews of that day. Originating during the exile, it provided a place where Jews could study the Scriptures and worship God. A synagogue could be established in any town that had at least ten married Jewish men. Jesus, like Paul (see Acts 13:15; 14:1; 17:2; 18:4), took advantage of the custom that allowed visiting teachers to participate in the worship service by invitation of the synagogue leaders.

1:22. Mark frequently reported the amazement that Jesus' teaching and actions produced (see 2:12; 5:20, 42; 6:2, 51; 7:37; 10:26; 11:18; see also 15:5). In these instances, it was Christ's inherent authority that amazed the people. **They were astonished at his doctrine** since He did not quote human authorities, as did **the scribes** ("the teachers of the law," NIV). His authority was directly from God. The scribes had a threefold function: (1) the preservation of the law (i.e., oral legal applications of the Mosaic law); (2) the instruction of pupils who would pass on their teaching without alteration; and (3) to serve as judges in the Sanhedrin (the national Jewish legal council). The scribes' work often tended toward legalism.

1:23–24. A man with an unclean spirit (v. 23) was present in the synagogue, **and he cried out**. It was actually the demon who cried out. Demonic possession intends to torment and destroy those who are created in God's image, but the demon recognized that Jesus is a powerful adversary, capable of destroying the forces of Satan. The title **the Holy One of God** (v. 24) is used elsewhere in the New Testament only in the parallel passage in Luke 4:34 and points to Christ's divine origin rather than to His Messiahship (see Luke 1:35). The demon's use of this name was perhaps in accordance with the occult belief that the precise use of a person's name gave certain control over him. One of the ironies of Mark's gospel is that religious leaders, who should have been in the know, failed to recognize Jesus' identity, but the demons recognized it.

1:25–28. With the commands, **Hold thy peace** (lit., "Be muzzled!"), **and come out of him** (v. 25), Jesus' superior power silenced the shrieks of the demon-possessed man. In the synagogue episode, Jesus is shown to be a person of the highest honor and authority—authority demonstrated in His teaching and in His confrontation with demonic forces. Jesus' **fame** ("news about him," NIV; v. 28) thus spread throughout Galilee.

1:29–31. The intensity extended beyond the synagogue and **into the house of Simon and Andrew** (v. 29). Jesus and the disciples probably went there for a meal, since the main Sabbath meal was served im-

mediately following the synagogue service. **Simon's wife's mother lay sick of a fever** (v. 30), but she was cured by the power of Jesus. Simon's mother-in-law demonstrated a lesson of discipleship: life in the kingdom of God demands a response of thanksgiving and obedience. Upon being raised up, **she ministered unto them** (i.e., Jesus and His disciples; v. 31).

1:32–34. The news of the day's events prompted others to seek Jesus' help for neighbors and loved ones. They waited until the Sabbath was over (after sunset) before carrying the sick to Him (see Jer. 17:21–22). Those who were brought to Jesus were healed of **divers diseases** ("various diseases," NKJV; v. 34), and Jesus **cast out many devils**. Jesus' authority over the demons is seen in the prohibition He gave them: they were not to speak about Him. Jesus probably wanted first to show by word and deed the kind of Messiah He was (in contrast to popular notions) before He clearly declared Himself, and He would not let the demons frustrate this intent. Mark showed that Jesus is able and willing to heal people. His ability and willingness are still available today for those who need His healing touch.

3. A Tour of Galilee (1:35–45)

1:35. A great while before day, he went ... into a solitary place, and ... prayed. Jesus' prayer life was effective because it was planned, private, and prolonged. He got up early enough, went far away enough, and stayed long enough to commune with the Father. The Greek word for "solitary place" is *erēmos*, meaning "wilderness" (see 1:3–4, 12–13), and reminds the reader of the wilderness wanderings where God gave His people guidance and rest through the Spirit (Isa. 63:11, 14). Jesus initiated a new exodus, a new age of deliverance, and His source of power is His relationship with the Father. Guidance (see 1:38), preaching (see 1:39), power over the forces of evil (see 1:39), and miraculous healing (see 1:40–41) all emerge from the center that is His communion with God.

"How can God pray to God?" is a question that arises for some here and at the other passages in Mark that describe Jesus praying (e.g., 6:46; 14:32–39).

Mark apparently did not see a problem with Jesus' act of praying; he offered no explanation or rationale. For Mark, Jesus is the Son of God, who exercises the very prerogatives of God the Father. Jesus shares the divine power and authority of God the Father, with whom He, the Son, is in the most intimate communion. No doctrine of the Trinity is present in Mark, but the basis of its later development is present.

1:36–39. Simon and others **followed after him** (lit., "hunted him down"; v. 36). Despite the prayerful interlude, urgency surrounded Jesus. He decided to leave the area of Capernaum and **go into the next towns** (v. 38). Neither Jesus nor His followers could meet all the requests made of them. The same is true for believers today, but prayerfully seeking God's guidance helps one distinguish between what is good and what is better. Jesus now embarked upon the first of what seem to be three tours of Galilee (second tour, Luke 8:1; third tour, Mark 6:6 and Matt. 11:1).

1:40–45. The story of the leper's cleansing is a masterful piece of storytelling. The action is vivid and fast-paced. In this section, Mark used the "historical present" tense of certain verbs; the dramatic nature of past action is described as if it were happening right now. The KJV preserves this tense with **saith** in verses 41 and 44. Mark's details in verse 41 create suspense as the reader awaits Jesus' answer to the leper's request: **I will; be thou clean**. The conclusion is full of irony: instead of obeying Jesus' fourfold command (v. 44), the cured leper **began to publish it much, and to blaze abroad the matter** (v. 45). One would expect this person of faith to be as obedient as the demons (see 1:25, 34), but he was not.

The characters in the story are well developed. The **leper** suffered from some sort of skin disease; "leper" or "leprosy" refer not only to leprosy proper but also to other maladies. Leprosy rendered one ceremonially unclean (see Lev. 13–14), and lepers were quarantined to prevent the spread of disease. They were thus completely cut off from religious and social life, and those who had the more severe forms of the illness experienced a living death. Often the leper was thought to be a person under divine judgment. In this story, the leper is a person of exemplary

faith. His faith is shown in his coming to Jesus, **beseeching him, and kneeling down to him** (an act of submission and worship; v. 40), and in his words: **If thou wilt, thou canst make me clean**. He did not doubt Jesus' power but left room in his request for Jesus' will to be done (see Mark 14:36).

Jesus' actions reveal not only that He indeed has power over destructive forces of nature (leprosy) but also that He loves. The Lord, **moved with compassion** (some manuscripts, e.g., NRSV marginal note, have "moved with anger"—probably toward the devastation of disease), **put forth his hand, and touched him** (v. 41). According to Mosaic law, touching a leper was an act that brought defilement (see Leviticus 13, especially vv. 45–46; see also Lev. 5:2). Jesus' compassion for the man superseded ceremonial considerations. A similar act today would be touching an AIDS sufferer. Jesus' followers become His hands of compassion and healing as they reach out to suffering outcasts.

The sacrifices **which Moses commanded** (v. 44) were to be evidence to the priests and the people that the cure was real and that Jesus respected the law. The healing was also a **testimony** to Jesus' divine power, since Jews believed that only God could cure leprosy (see 2 Kings 5:1–14). Although Jesus had allowed Himself to become ritually unclean, He commanded the leper to observe legal regulations. For Jesus, the requirement of the law to love one's neighbor (see Lev. 19:18) sometimes superseded a ritual ordinance. Only by following Jesus' instructions could the healed man be fully integrated back into Jewish society. The kingdom of God involves the total restoration of persons, including spiritual, physical, and social restoration.

Jesus' growing popularity with the people finally made it necessary for Him to withdraw into **desert places** (v. 45). The people were still determined to find Him, however, and they did.

4. Ministry in Capernaum (2:1–22)

2:1–12. The "pronouncement story" in these verses, the healing of the paralytic, introduces a set of five pericopes (2:1–12, 15–17, 18–22, 23–28;

3:1–6) in which Mark further established Jesus' honor as the Son of God. Each of the five brief narratives describes a contest for honor between Jesus and His opponents. In ancient Mediterranean society (and in many cultures today), virtually every social exchange outside one's family was such a contest. Honor was the highest cultural value. By contrast, money, possessions, and rank tend to be the prime cultural values in North American society. In honor cultures, the honor contest follows the challenge-riposte pattern, in which one person issues a *challenge* to the honor of another person, who answers with a counterchallenge, or *riposte*. The exchange may take several turns. Finally, honor is publicly ascribed (the *verdict*) to the party that most effectively responds to challenge or counterchallenge. Positive expressions (e.g., gifts) and negative challenges (e.g., insults) must both be answered appropriately; otherwise, one loses face.

2:1–5. When Jesus returned to **Capernaum** (v. 1), news quickly spread that He was in a certain **house.** So many people gathered to see Him that there was **no room** (v. 2) for all of them. **One sick of the palsy** (v. 3). Nothing definite can be said about the nature of the man's affliction beyond the fact that he could not walk. The determination of the **four** men to reach Jesus suggests that his condition was desperate. **They uncovered the roof** (v. 4). A typical Palestinian house had a flat roof accessible by means of an outside staircase. The roof was often made of a thick layer of clay (packed with a stone roller), supported by mats of branches across wood beams. **Jesus saw their faith** (v. 5). The bold action of the paralyzed man and his friends was evidence of their faith. Jesus' pronouncement, **Son, thy sins be forgiven thee,** signifies that He first met the man's deepest need: forgiveness.

2:6–12. With His pronouncement, "Son, thy sins be forgiven thee" (2:5), Jesus had issued a challenge (for challenge and riposte, see discussion on 2:1–12) to the religious perceptions and security of **certain of the scribes sitting there** (v. 6), in the house. According to their understanding, Jesus spoke **blasphemies** (v. 7). After all, **who can forgive sins but God only?**

Jesus knew that they **so reasoned within themselves** (v. 8), that they were silently issuing a riposte to Him. Jesus had extraordinary perception, in fact omniscience, and before the scribes could even speak their riposte, He began to issue His second challenge: **Why reason ye these things in your hearts?** Jesus' challenge continued in verses 9–10 with a rhetorical question. Of course, the answer is that it is **easier to say ... Thy sins be forgiven thee** (v. 9), since the effectiveness of that statement cannot be verified, whereas a pronouncement of healing can be. The effective command for the sick man to **Arise, and take up thy bed, and go thy way into thine house** (v. 11) continued the challenge and demonstrated that Jesus indeed has power to forgive sins. Mark recorded the verdict of the observers: **they were all amazed, and glorified God, saying, We never saw it on this fashion** (v. 12). Jesus won the contest in that the scribes could not effectively answer his second challenge. His honor was upheld despite the opposition from certain religious leaders.

Who can forgive sins ...? (v. 7). In Jewish theology, even the Messiah could not forgive sins, and Jesus' forgiveness of sin was a claim to deity, a claim that certain scribes considered to be blasphemous. Here Mark used irony. The scribes uttered something the importance and truth of which escaped them. Yes, only God can forgive sins. Since Jesus forgives sins, He is God incarnate who brings the kingdom of God. The scribes, however, did not recognize Jesus' true identity. The reader, however, knows who Jesus is and thus is in tension with these opponents. The reader begins to ask, "Will the antagonists ever see the truth?" and "What will happen to Jesus if the opponents continue in their ignorance?"

The Son of man (v. 10). This is Jesus' most common title for Himself, used eighty-four times in the Gospels and never used by anyone but Jesus. Whereas in the Old Testament, the term may be used in the sense of "human being" or "mortal" (see, e.g., Ps. 8:4; Ezek. 2:1), Jesus' usage of it requires a different sense. In Daniel 7:13–14, the Son of Man is pictured as a heavenly figure who in the end times is entrusted by God with absolute authority, divine glory, and sovereign power. That Jesus used "Son of man" as a messianic title is evident by His use of it (see 8:31) in juxtaposition to Peter's use of "Christ" (8:29). When Jesus referred to Himself as "the Son of man" before the Sanhedrin, they called it blasphemy, understanding it to be a claim of deity (see Mark 14:62–64). In Mark, the association of "Son of man" with the authority to forgive sins (v. 7) and with the power of judgment and salvation (see 8:38; 13:26–27) requires the term to be understood in light of Daniel 7.

2:13–17. The dramatic calling of Levi is another pronouncement story. Jesus was once again **by the sea** of Galilee (v. 13), where He had first called disciples (see 1:14–20). In scene 1 of the story, **he saw Levi the son of Alphaeus** (v. 14), also known as Matthew (see Matt. 9:9; 10:3), and He called to him, **Follow me.** Levi was probably his given name, and Matthew ("gift of the Lord") his apostolic name. **The receipt of custom** ("the tax collector's booth," NIV) was probably a tollbooth on the major international road that went from Damascus through Capernaum to the Mediterranean coast and on to Egypt. Levi was a tax collector under Herod Antipas, tetrarch of Galilee. The immediacy of Levi's positive response (**he arose and followed him**) demonstrates Mark's view that the call to discipleship is urgent and to be answered without hesitation.

In scene 2 of the short drama, **as Jesus sat at meat in his [Levi's] house** (v. 15), a large number of people who were considered disreputable joined those gathered for the meal. Jewish tax collectors (**publicans;** v. 15; see discussion on Matt. 5:46) were regarded as outcasts. They could not serve as witnesses or judges and were expelled from the synagogue. In the eyes of the Jewish community, their disgrace extended to their families. Popular disdain of them may have been more for the widespread dishonesty in their profession than for anything else. The term **sinners** (v. 15) refers to notoriously evil people as well as to those who refused to follow the Mosaic law as interpreted by the scribes. The term was commonly used of tax collectors, adulterers, robbers, and the like. To eat with a person was a sign

of friendship, and Jesus extended that honor to those considered to be sinful people. Levi opened his home so that such people could meet Jesus—still a good evangelistic method.

Jesus' response to the challenge of **the scribes and Pharisees** (v. 16) was effective and maintained His honor. Not all scribes were Pharisees—successors of the Hasidim, pious Jews who had joined forces with the Maccabees during the struggle for freedom from Syrian oppression (166–142 BC). They first appeared under the name Pharisees during the reign of John Hyrcanus (135–105). Although some Pharisees, no doubt, were godly, most of those who came into conflict with Jesus were hypocritical, envious, rigid, and formalistic. According to Pharisaism, God's grace extended only to those who kept His law.

The pronouncement saying ends the story: **They that are whole have no need of the physician, but they that are sick: I came not to call the righteous, but sinners to repentance** (v. 17). The statement does not mean that some people do not need salvation, whereas others do. Jesus' point was that self-righteous people do not realize their need for salvation; as long as they think that they are okay, a Savior cannot help them. Those who admit that they are sinners, however, find that Jesus offers them healing. Jesus brings salvation for all who recognize their need.

2:18–20. In the following text (another pronouncement story), the question of fasting and Jesus' view on the topic arose. **The disciples of John** (v. 18) were those of John the Baptist, who may have been fasting because he was in prison (see 1:14), or fasting may have been a practice among them as an expression of repentance, intended to hasten the coming of the redemption announced by John. The **disciples ... of the Pharisees** may refer to people influenced by the Pharisees and thus may be a nontechnical expression. In Jesus' time, the Pharisees fasted twice a week (see Luke 18:12). These two groups came to Jesus and asked, **Why do [we] fast, but thy disciples fast not?** In the Mosaic law, only the fast of the Day of Atonement was required (see Lev. 16:29, 31; 23:27–32; Num. 29:7). After the Babylonian exile, the Jews observed four other yearly fasts (see Zech. 7:5; 8:19).

In His question, **Can the children of the bride-chamber fast, while the bridegroom is with them?** (v. 19), Jesus compared His disciples with the guests of a bridegroom. A Jewish wedding was a particularly joyous occasion, and the celebration associated with it often lasted a week. It was unthinkable to fast during such festivities, because fasting was associated with sorrow. Jesus is the "bridegroom"; when He would be **taken away from them** (v. 20) by death, fasting would then be in order. In the life of the kingdom, joy is the controlling element. Those religious observances that gave expression to sorrow and penitence could now give way to celebration of the kingdom's presence in Jesus' life and ministry.

Jesus upheld His honor in effectively answering the objectors of verse 18. He also prophesied His death, although in a cryptic manner. Jesus' predictions of His death in the gospel (see, e.g., 8:31) minimize the shamefulness of it: His execution was something for which He had come and which He accepted.

The value of this story for the early church was that it gave Jesus' view on what evidently was a controversial subject: fasting. The practice is valuable as a spiritual discipline in which one can seek and find God's strength and guidance. While the church awaits the fullness of the kingdom of God to come, this exercise of self-denial has value. One's voluntary abstinence for a period of time from certain foods (or from food altogether), from a particular practice, or from a daily comfort can sharpen one's focus on God. Certain Christian traditions advocate abstention in such areas during Lent as a spiritual preparation for Holy Week. The New Testament has little to say about fasting; Jesus assumed that His followers would follow the practice (see v. 20; Matt. 6:16–18), but He did not clearly command it.

2:21–22. Two parables supplement the discussion of fasting. Their common element, the relationship of the new and the old, continues an idea introduced in 2:18–20. Both parables contain folk wisdom. The parable of **new cloth on an old gar-** ment (v. 21) teaches that the new way of life in the kingdom of God is incompatible with the old legalistic observances of the scribes and Pharisees regarding ritual purity and fasting. Such practices were overly restrictive applications of ceremonial laws of the Old Testament, and the result was arrogance and the exclusion of those who had need. The life of the kingdom cannot simply be superimposed on old legalism (whose lack is signified by the tear that must be covered). Without an abandonment of the old scribal interpretations of the law, the tension of the new and the old cannot be eased (**the rent is made worse**; "making the tear worse," NIV; v. 21).

A completely new expression of the new life of the kingdom is necessary—that of joy and a joyous welcome of those in need—otherwise that new life will not be preserved. That is the point of the parable of **new wine** (v. 22) in old **bottles**, or "wineskins" (NIV). Old wineskins have already reached their limits of expansion, which occurs when the wine that they hold ferments. If new wine is poured into them, therefore, they will burst. New wineskins, which provide greater elasticity, are necessary for new wine that has not yet completed its fermentation process. **No man putteth new wine into old bottles,** Jesus said.

5. Sabbath Controversy (2:23–3:12)

2:23–28. The incident recorded in these verses is the fourth of five controversies of Jesus with scribes and/or Pharisees. Following the pattern of a pronouncement story, the account reveals Jesus' attitude to the Sabbath (and the law generally), which was a controlling principle for His actions throughout the gospel. There was nothing wrong in the action itself **to pluck the ears of corn** (v. 23), which comes under the provision of Deuteronomy 23:25.

According to Jewish tradition (in the Mishnah), however, harvesting (which is what Jesus' disciples technically were doing) was doing **on the sabbath day that which is not lawful** (v. 24; see Exod. 34:21). **What David did** (v. 25) in regard to the **shewbread** ("the consecrated bread," NIV; v. 26; see Exod. 25:30; Lev. 24:5–9) is related in 1 Samuel 21:1–6. Although

Ahimelech, Abiathar's father, was then high priest, the general time frame is the tenure of **Abiathar the high priest**, son of Ahimelech. The relationship between the Old Testament incident and the apparent infringement of the Sabbath by the disciples lies in the fact that on both occasions godly men did something forbidden. Since, however, it is always "lawful" to do good and to save life (even on the Sabbath), both David and the disciples were within the spirit of the law (see Isa. 58:6–7; Luke 6:6–11; 13:10–17; 14:1–6).

The pronouncement saying that concludes the story completely frees a person from the chains of legalism: **The sabbath was made for man, and not man for the sabbath** (v. 27). Jewish tradition had so multiplied the requirements and restrictions for keeping the Sabbath that the burden had become intolerable. Jesus cut across these traditions and emphasized the God-given purpose of the Sabbath, a day intended for man (for spiritual, mental, and physical restoration; see Exod. 20:8–11). Whatever contributes to that restoration on the Christian's day of worship and rest ought to be undertaken with joy and thanksgiving. Sports, games, movies, television, computers, and other so-called secular pursuits may contribute significantly to the refreshment of the Christian soul on the Lord's Day. The individual must decide in her or his own conscience the suitability of these things. In any case, worship and devotion ought not to be replaced by such things but rather augmented by them.

Jesus claimed that, as **the Son of man** (v. 28), He had the authority to define, regulate, and overrule the Sabbath and its restrictions because it is His by right. The astounding assertion that He is **Lord also of the sabbath** was put to the test by His opponents in the following story.

3:1–6. In the account of Jesus' healing of the man with the **withered hand** (v. 1), the challenge-riposte pattern is again evident (see discussion on 2:1–12). Jesus issued the challenge regarding the appropriate actions on the Sabbath: is that which effects wholesomeness or destruction to be permitted? Since the riposte was not forthcoming (**they held their peace**; v. 4), Jesus' honor was upheld. The healing of the man was a further challenge that could not be answered. The verdict is not explicit but may be inferred (see 2:12). **The Pharisees** (v. 6) then consulted with **the Herodians** on **how they might destroy** Jesus. "The Herodians" evidently were influential Jews who favored the Herodian dynasty, meaning they were supporters of Rome, from which the Herods received their authority. They joined the Pharisees in opposing Jesus because they feared He might have an unsettling political influence on the people. The plotting of the Pharisees and the Herodians is seen again on Tuesday of Passion Week (see 12:13). Their antagonism toward Jesus from 3:6 on is seen by the reader in light of the honor contest: Jesus had bested His opponents, and their malice resulted from their refusal to ascribe to Him the honor that He deserves.

Whether he would heal him on the sabbath day (v. 2) is an indication that the Pharisees believed in Jesus' power to perform miracles. The question was not "Could he?" but "Would he?" Jewish tradition prescribed that aid could be given the sick on the Sabbath only when the person's life was threatened, which obviously was not the case here. Jesus' presence demanded a decision about His preaching, His acts, and His person. The hostility of the religious establishment, first seen in 2:6–7, continued to spread.

Jesus asked, **Is it lawful to do good on the sabbath days, or to do evil? to save life, or to kill?** (v. 4). Which is better, to preserve life by healing or to destroy life by refusing to heal? The question is ironic since, whereas Jesus healed a man, the Pharisees were plotting to put Him to death. It is obvious who was guilty of breaking the Sabbath.

Mark's language in the short account of the man with the withered hand is graphic and intense. He employed the historical present to create for the reader a sense of actually hearing Jesus' words as He spoke them (**saith**; vv. 3, 4, 5). In the last instance, Jesus spoke only after **he had looked round about on them with anger** (v. 5), thus creating tension and suspense in the narrative. The narrator reveals the inner Jesus: He was righteously angry, and He was **grieved for the hardness of their hearts**. The Lord has compassion even for those who are hard-hearted; He is "grieved to find them so obstinate" (NJB). Once again the Greek *euthys* (**straightway**; v. 6) conveys urgency, this time of the danger beginning to confront Jesus.

3:7–12. In a scene reminiscent of John the Baptist's ministry (see 1:5), Jesus attracted large crowds for His ministry. The reach of Jesus' notoriety was greater than John's, however, thus denoting that Jesus is a figure of even greater honor than John. The geographical list in verses 7–8 indicates that the crowds came not only from areas in the vicinity of Capernaum but also from considerable distances. The regions mentioned included virtually all of Israel and its surrounding neighbors. Mark wrote of Jesus' work in all these regions except **Idumea** (v. 8). "Idumaea" is the Greek form of the Hebrew "Edom" but here refers to an area south of Judea, not to earlier Edomite territory. For Jesus' entry into the other regions, see 1:14 for **Galilee** (v. 7); 10:1 for **Judea**; 5:1 and 10:1 for the region across the **Jordan** (v. 8); 7:24, 31 for **Tyre and Sidon**; 11:11 for **Jerusalem**.

Jesus' honor is evident from his widespread reputation, His extraordinary power to heal (even by **touch**; v. 10), and the submissive recognition of the **unclean spirits** (v. 11) that He is **the Son of God**. The time for revealing Jesus' identity had not yet come (see 1:34), and since demons were hardly the proper channel for such disclosure, He **straitly charged them that they should not make him known** (v. 12).

B. Later Galilean Ministry (3:13–6:29)

1. Selection of the Twelve Apostles (3:13–19)

3:13–15. According to Mark, Jesus' custom was to withdraw for solitude after having encountered the demands of the crowds, after meeting opposition, or before crucial decisions. Quiet seclusion afforded Him time for prayer and for His Father's guidance and strength for what lay ahead (see 1:35; 6:46; 8:10; 9:2; 14:32–42). Although Mark did not mention that Jesus was praying on the **mountain** (v. 13), Luke stated that He was (see Luke 6:12). Jesus'

choice of those whom He wanted to be particularly close to Him was a result of prayer. He **ordained twelve** [some witnesses add "whom he also named apostles" (NRSV)], **that they should be with him, and that he might send them forth to preach, and to have power to heal sicknesses, and to cast out devils** (vv. 14–15).

This appointment, of twelve individuals from a larger number of disciples (see Luke 6:13), was to four responsibilities. Primarily, and often overlooked by students of the subject of discipleship/leadership in the Gospels, was (1) "that they should be with him"(v. 14), or as translated elsewhere, "to be his regular companions" (NLT). The training of the Twelve included not only instruction and practice in various forms of ministry but also continuous association and intimate fellowship with Jesus Himself. Jesus wants fellowship and friendship before He wants service. Some ministers of the gospel are so busy "doing" for Jesus that they neglect "being" with Jesus. Just as Jesus' ministry often grew out of His time with God, so Christ's workers must allow service to arise out of their intimacy with the Lord. After being with Jesus, the Twelve were then sent out with (2) the responsibility "to preach," to announce the kingdom of God and its blessings, (3) "to have the power to heal sicknesses" (v. 15), and (4) to have the authority "to cast out devils." (The words "and to have power to heal sicknesses" are not found in some witnesses.)

3:16–19. The Twelve are known from this list and from the other lists in the New Testament (see Matt. 10:2–4; Luke 6:14–16; Acts 1:13 [eleven at that point]). The name **Boanerges** (v. 17), or **sons of thunder**, was probably descriptive of the dispositions of James and John (see 10:37; Luke 9:54–55). **Thaddaeus** (v. 18) is apparently the same as "Judas the brother of James" (Luke 6:16; Acts 1:13). **Simon the Canaanite** (see Matt. 10:4) is Simon Zelotes in Luke 6:15 and Acts 1:13. The best manuscripts have "Cananaean" rather than "Canaanite." The former is Aramaic for "zealot." A fanatical Jewish nationalistic party named "the Zealots," pledged to oppose the Roman occupation of Israel to the extreme of murder if necessary, may be indicated by the term. Some scholars contend, however, that the Zealots did not emerge as an identifiable movement until the war of AD 66–70. The title may still characterize Simon as a fervent nationalist.

Judas (v. 19) has the additional name **Iscariot**, which probably means "the man from Kerioth," the town Kerioth-hezron (see Josh. 15:25), twelve miles south of Hebron (see Jer. 48:24). For Judas's betrayal of Jesus, see 14:10–11, 43–46. The **house** was probably the home of Peter and Andrew (see 1:29; 2:1).

2. Teachings in Capernaum (3:20–35)

3:20–21. Here the scene is set once again for a controversy narrative that puts Jesus in debate with the scribes. In the passage, even those closest to Jesus do not recognize who He is or understand His mission. **His friends** (v. 21) could refer instead to "His own people" (NKJV) or "his family" (NRSV). Christians commonly share this experience of Jesus: a believer's own family members or close friends fail to comprehend his or her faith. In Jesus' case, the misunderstanding was so severe that His loved ones attempted to seize Him, **for they said, He is beside himself** ("out of His mind," NKJV). No doubt they had come all the way to Capernaum from Nazareth, some thirty miles away (**they went out**; see 3:31). The only course to take in the face of resistance from others is to endure in faith in company with God's people (see 3:34–35).

3:22–27. The controversy concerned **Beelzebub** (v. 22) and the source of Jesus' miraculous power of exorcism. Jesus' opponents did not deny His miracles but rather denied that they were from a divine source. The name "Beelzebub" (alternate spelling "Beelzebul," NRSV) is not found among extrabiblical Jewish writings. The name could refer to an entity who was believed to have prominence in a hierarchy of demons. The charge that Jesus was a sorcerer is attested in early Jewish and Christian texts. Jesus used **parables** (v. 23) to answer the charge of collusion with Satan. (In this context, the word "parables" is used in the general sense of comparisons.) Unity and division can coexist neither within a **kingdom**

(v. 24) nor within a **house** (v. 25). Neither is it possible, Jesus said, for Satan to oppose his own purposes. Jesus' exorcisms, therefore, were not the work of Satan. Jesus had bound **the strong man** (Satan; v. 27), entered his house, and plundered **his goods** (released through exorcism his captives).

When did this binding of Satan take place? Was it during the temptation in the wilderness (see 1:12–13)? Mark did not say, but the parable makes it clear that the eschatological defeat of Satan, his final defeat and judgment at the end of history, had already occurred. Jesus' victory was already being experienced in lives that had been freed from the Devil's malignant power.

3:28–30. Jesus then uttered a solemn affirmation, **Verily I say unto you** (v. 28) — an expression that He often used to strengthen His assertions (see 8:12; 9:1, 41; 10:15, 29; 11:23; 12:43; 13:30; 14:9, 18, 25, 30). Anyone who has been in ministry for even a few years has probably been asked by a worried Christian, "Have I committed the unpardonable sin of blasphemy against the Holy Spirit?" The very fact that someone is agitated about this sin is evidence that he or she has not committed it. Just what, then, did Jesus mean when He spoke about a person who **shall blaspheme against the Holy Ghost** (v. 29)? The context furnishes the answer: the teachers of the law attributed Jesus' healing to Satan's power (**an unclean spirit**; v. 30) rather than to the Holy Spirit (see 3:22). When a person refuses obstinately and finally to give reverence and worship to Jesus and instead attributes His power to satanic influence, that person has made a grim and irrevocable choice. Such a one **hath never forgiveness, but is in danger of** ("subject to," NKJV) **eternal damnation** ("but is guilty of an eternal sin," NASB). A person who does not accept the evidence of Jesus' miracles (now attested in the Gospels) has not necessarily come to the point where salvation is impossible. That point may be reached, however, if he or she continues in willful unbelief.

3:31–35. After their special appointment (see 3:14–15), the Twelve viewed nothing but opposition to Jesus. His friends had said that He was "beside himself" (3:21), and His opponents went so far as to say that He was in league with "the prince of the devils" (3:22) and that Jesus had "an unclean spirit" (3:30). Now **his brethren and his mother** (v. 31) summoned Him. Jesus' question (**Who is my mother, or my brethren?** v. 33) and answer (**For whosoever shall do the will of God, the same is my brother, and my sister, and mother;** v. 35) emphasize three facts. (1) His relationship with His followers is precious to Him. They are His family. (2) His followers enjoy intimacy with Him that transcends the closeness that they have with their own family members. Membership in God's spiritual family, evidenced by obedience to Him, is more important than membership in human families. (3) Jesus' disciples have one another as spiritual siblings and are able to find with one another the closeness that they may have missed within their own biological family. The story does not indicate that Jesus excluded His family members from the circle of people around Him; they were simply unable to approach Him because of the crowd.

3. Parables of the Kingdom (4:1–34)

a. The Parable of the Sower (4:1–20)

4:1–2. Mark carefully set the scene for the reader before presenting the first, and lengthiest, of several parables to appear in his gospel. The details in these verses are sharp; readers can imagine themselves actually present. Jesus **entered into a ship, and sat** (v. 1). He is described not just as teaching while sitting (sitting was the usual position for Jewish teachers; see Matt. 5:1; Luke 5:3; John 8:2); He was in the unusual position of sitting in a boat on the lake.

The imperfect tense of the verbs **taught** (v. 2) and **said** demonstrate these actions as actually going on. Jesus "was teaching" **many things by parables.** "Parables" (lit., "something thrown alongside") are stories or illustrations from everyday life or nature that are used to illustrate spiritual or moral truths. Sometimes parables are in the form of brief similes, comparisons, analogies, or proverbial sayings. Ordinarily they have a single main point, and not every detail is necessarily meant to have significance. Jesus' parables are striking and vivid, intended to

startle people and help them think in new ways. If one includes illustrative sayings among "parables," as many as sixty-five parables are found in the Synoptic Gospels. About one third of Jesus' teaching in those gospels is therefore in parables.

4:3–9. The parable of the sower serves as a key to the other parables in Mark's gospel (see 4:13). It highlights the various possible responses to the message of the kingdom of God and is one of only two parables (see 7:14–23) in Mark for which Jesus gave detailed explanations (for Jesus' interpretation of this parable, see 4:14–20). The other parables describe, expand, or bring about the ideas of this parable.

The parable describes common first-century agricultural practices in Israel for the production of barley, wheat, and other grains. Arable land in Galilee was divided into strips separated by narrow footpaths. Each person cultivated his own strip of land, scattering seed as he walked along. In that day, seed was broadcast by hand, and therefore some seed would naturally fall on unproductive ground. Seed that happened to fall on the path, **the way side** (v. 4), would not penetrate the earth and **the fowls of the air** found it ready food. **Stony ground** (v. 5) refers not to earth with rocks in it but rather to a limestone shelf with a veneer of soil. Seed that fell on such ground had no chance of taking firm root and developing. Neither was there hope for the seed to thrive when it **fell among thorns** (v. 7). Only the **good ground** (v. 8), earth that was soft, deep, and clean, gave seed any hope of survival.

4:10–12. Before giving His detailed explanation of the parable of the sower, Jesus gave His reason for speaking in parables. In answer to a question from His followers (including **the twelve;** v. 10), Jesus affirmed that they had been given the privilege of understanding **the mystery of the kingdom of God** (v. 11). In the New Testament, "mystery" refers to something God has revealed to His people. The mystery (that which was previously unknown) is proclaimed to all, but only those who have faith understand. In this context, "the mystery" seems to be that the kingdom of God had drawn near in the coming of Jesus Christ. For those who harden themselves to Jesus and His message, the parables have the effect of causing misunderstanding and further hardening. The perplexing phrase **seeing they may see, and not perceive; and hearing they may hear, and not understand** (v. 12; see Isa. 6:9) is helpfully rendered in the NLT as, "They see what I do, but they don't perceive its meaning. They hear my words, but they don't understand." Of course, the possibility of repentance is open to those who harden themselves: **lest at any time they should be converted, and their sins should be forgiven them.** Many do not repent, however, and thus remain outside the circle of faith and the kingdom ("So they will not turn from their sins and be forgiven," NLT). The parables of Jesus are invitations to investigate and pursue the way of the kingdom of God. If one refuses the invitations, however, one cannot expect to understand spiritual realities.

4:13-20. The interpretation that Jesus gave of the parable of the sower reveals that it is an allegory, an extended comparison in which something on one level points to another reality altogether. Each detail in the narrative corresponds to a detail in the alternate reality. Some interpreters argue that this passage constitutes a secondary interpretation that did not originate with Jesus, but there is no reason to believe that Jesus could not have given such an allegorical interpretation of one of His own parables.

The parable balances three negative responses and three positive responses. The conditions upon which the seed falls represent typified responses to the good news of the kingdom. The seed that fell on the path, or **way side** (v. 15), represents those who stubbornly resist the message of the kingdom. "The fowls of the air" (4:4) represent **Satan,** who **cometh immediately, and taketh away the word that was sown in their hearts.** The seed on **stony ground** (v. 16) represents those who **receive [the Word] with gladness** but, at the first sign of trouble, abandon their promising start in the way of the kingdom, being **immediately ... offended** ("they quickly fall away," NIV; v. 17). Their experience is comparable to that of the newly sprouted plant that lacks sufficient roots to survive in the rocky soil. The seed

that fell **among thorns** (v. 18) represents those who **becometh unfruitful** (v. 19) because of **the cares of this world, and the deceitfulness of riches, and the lusts of other things entering in.** Such things **choke the word,** just as thorny weeds spring up and choke young grain plants. Prosperity tends to give a false sense of self-sufficiency, security, and well-being (see 10:17-25; Deut. 8:17-18; 32:15; Eccl. 2:4-11; James 5:1-6). People under duress, as Mark's readers were, often turn to material pursuits in an attempt to find relief from the pressure. Finally, there appear three degrees of good harvest that come from **good ground ... some thirtyfold, some sixty, and some an hundred** (v. 20). Those who respond to Jesus' message bear fruit; that is, they manifest in their lives the very saving power of God. Jesus' promise of the harvest is striking: in His day, normally only a five-fold increase of grain would have been expected in reaping (today, with the aid of modern fertilizers and technology, it is thirty- or fortyfold). The abundance of the harvest highlights the miraculous nature of the kingdom and its effects.

The conclusion of the parable stresses the continual hearing and receiving of the Word plus the continual bearing of fruit that the proper response produces (the verb "hear/heard" [Greek, *akouō*] is in the aorist tense in vv. 15, 16, 18 and in the present tense in v. 20). The disciples may have already become disillusioned about the fledgling Jesus movement: although Jesus had been popularly acclaimed, He had met resistance from the religious establishment and even from His own family (see chaps. 2-3). This kind of opposition threatened to squelch widespread recognition of Jesus as the bringer of the kingdom. The parable of the sower served to encourage Jesus' disciples that despite opposition or lack of response to the good news of the kingdom, good fruit would nevertheless certainly come forth. Mark's readers, who were also suffering persecution and opposition, could take comfort that their witness would bring results. Jesus' recognition that positive and negative responses to the Word occur neutralizes the shame of the cross that some might attach to the Christian message.

b. The Parable of the Candle under a Bushel (4:21-23)

4:21 - 23. The parable about the **candle ... under a bushel** (v. 21) relates to the fact that the kingdom of God is presently hidden from the understanding of outsiders (see 4:10-12). The purpose of its coming, however, is that it might be manifested to the world. The comparison to a practice from ancient Palestinian life makes that purpose clear. The "candle" (Greek, *lychnos*) is the small clay lamp that, burning olive oil, gave light to the single living area of the home. No one lit the lamp only to hide its light "under a bushel" ("basket," NKJV) or under the couch on which people reclined at mealtime. Rather, it was **to be set on a candlestick** ("the lampstand," NASB).

The ministry of Jesus will one day emerge from the shadows of obscurity and be vindicated as the coming of the very reign of God. That which is now **secret** (v. 22) will **come abroad**. Jesus' followers can expect the same for their ministry in the kingdom as well. God will honor their service to Him even when they are apparently unsuccessful. The Lord emphasized His point with His call to urgent attention: **If any man have ears to hear, let him hear** (v. 23).

c. The Saying about Measure (4:24-25)

4:24 - 25. This saying underscores the necessity for one who hears Jesus' preaching to continue thoughtfully contemplating its meaning. The one who does so **shall more be given** (v. 24). The one who is inattentive, however, shall begin to be confused and lose his grasp on whatever degree of truth regarding the kingdom of God that he had attained. Paradoxically, Jesus said, **And he that hath not, from him shall be taken even that which he hath** (v. 25). Inattentiveness to Jesus' message means that the hearer has virtually nothing, and even that will soon disappear. The saying, therefore, has this warning, but a promise as well: **For he that hath, to him shall be given.** The teaching on measure serves as an effective introduction to the seed parables of 4:26-32: their instruction on the kingdom must be heeded. An application today is that, the more truth is appropriate now, the more it will be received in the future;

and if one does not respond to what little truth one may know already, one will not profit even from that.

d. The Parable of the Growing Seed (4:26-29)

4:26 - 29. Only Mark recorded this parable. Whereas the parable of the sower stresses the importance of proper soil for the growth of seed and the success of the harvest, here the mysterious power of the seed itself is emphasized. **The kingdom of God** (v. 26), sown as a mere seed in the ministry of Jesus, contains its own power. One day, a harvest will come. Humans cannot do anything but sow the seed of the kingdom. They cannot bring the reign of God themselves, and the New Testament never speaks of the kingdom being "built" by anyone. This parable takes the pressure off the disciple of Jesus to feel that he or she must "do" anything to establish the kingdom. Its success is God's work; people can only act for the sake of the kingdom (see Matt. 19:12; Luke 18:29-30) and preach about it (see Matt. 10:7; Luke 10:9). Only God, however, can give the kingdom to people (see Luke 12:32). The phrase **immediately he putteth in the sickle, because the harvest is come** (v. 29) is a possible allusion to Joel 3:13, where harvest is a figure for the consummation of God's kingdom.

e. The Parable of the Mustard Seed (4:30-34)

4:30 - 32. This parable, unlike the parable of the growing seed (4:26-29), is also in Matthew and Luke (see Matt. 13:31-32; Luke 13:18-19). Like that parable, however, the parable of the mustard seed emphasizes the paradoxical nature of the kingdom: its manifestation has insignificant beginnings, but that manifestation will spread and become great. What a comfort to Jesus' disciples, who were discouraged by opposition and lack of response to His message.

The kingdom of God (v. 30), Jesus said, **is like a grain of mustard seed** (v. 31), or more precisely, "like a mustard seed" (NKJV). Jesus was perhaps referring to the black mustard, a plant that was cultivated for its seeds, which were used for oil and for cooking. Proverbially, the mustard seed was the smallest of all things. In the parable, the seed becomes **greater than all herbs** ("larger than all the garden plants," NASB;

v. 32). The mustard plant can grow to a height of more than fifteen feet but is usually much smaller.

Mustard also grew wild, and farmers tried to eradicate it from their fields. Here is a further paradox: mustard is, on the one hand, something to cultivate and nurture; on the other hand, it is a nuisance and must be controlled. The mustard, therefore, is perfectly suited for a comparison to the kingdom of God. Hearers would have asked themselves, "How can the kingdom of God be small and yet large?" "If the kingdom is desirable, why is it also like a big, intrusive weed?" Jesus' parables are designed to provoke just these kinds of thought so that people will be drawn in to His message.

Birds are attracted to the mustard plant; they love the seeds, which they pick out of the pods. In the parable, **the fowls of the air** (v. 32) find refuge in the shade of the mustard bush. One interpretation of the parable identifies the birds as evil influences within a monstrous plant that is Christendom. Birds correspond to Satan in the parable of the sower (see 4:4, 15), but the same correspondence need not occur in another parable. Jesus' hearers would not have imagined "Christendom," in which the presence of the kingdom of God coexists with evil. They would have understood what the reign of God is (the subject of the comparison, see v. 30), however. And they would have understood the Old Testament allusions to Israel (see Ezek. 17:22–24) and Assyria (see Ezek. 31:3–9) as great trees in which the nations (birds) roost. The kingdom of God is not exclusive; all the nations are welcome to its shelter. Jesus concluded this parable with a missionary interest that contradicted the nationalistic dreams prevalent in the Judaism of His day.

The way of the kingdom of God is one of small beginnings that become great. Such is the presence of the kingdom in a Christian's life: anything that one does for God usually has a small beginning that takes time to progress (a ministry, an education, a job, a new habit). A person must be patient with oneself and others during the initial stages of growth.

The kingdom of God is also inclusive. Believers should ask themselves, "Is there a particular person against whom I hold a grudge that keeps me from extending the welcome of the kingdom?" "Do I hold a judgmental attitude against a kind of people so that I reject them as equals in the kingdom?"

4:33–34. These verses indicate that Jesus habitually used parables to teach the disciples. He spoke to their level of understanding while **he expounded all things** (v. 34) to them. When alone with His disciples, Jesus taught more specifically than He did to the crowds, but even the disciples usually needed to have things explained.

4. Trip across the Sea of Galilee (4:35–5:20)

4:35–5:20. The two stories in this section establish Jesus' honor in contests that were not against human foes but against the forces of nature (4:35–41) and against supernatural foes (5:1–20). Previous contests with human foes (see 2:1–3:6) had revealed that Jesus could maintain His honor in the face of opposition. Jesus showed that He is a person of honor in His handling of all three kinds of challengers. His exalted status argues against the shame of the cross in Mark's gospel. Not only was His honor that of a human, but in all these contests, He claimed and exercised the very authority of God.

4:35–41. An apparently serene trip across the Sea of Galilee was threatened with danger when **there arose a great storm of wind** (v. 37) so fierce that **the waves beat into the ship, so that it was now full.** Situated in a basin surrounded by mountains, the Sea of Galilee is particularly susceptible to sudden, violent storms. Cool air from the mountains, including nearby Mount Hermon, the highest point in all the Middle East, descends rapidly and clashes with the hot, humid air lying over the lake, which is 700 feet below sea level. The picture of Jesus, tranquilly **asleep on a pillow** (the cushion customarily kept under the coxswain's seat; v. 38) in the stern of the boat, is in sharp contrast with the panicked disciples. After they had awakened Jesus, they protested to him, **Master, carest thou not that we perish?** They should not have been afraid but rather should have believed in His present power to protect them.

The main point of the story, however, is the almighty power of Jesus over the destructive forces of nature. The sea typified for the Jewish mind the chaos of the primeval ocean, to which God brought order (see Gen. 1:1 – 10). Jesus **rebuked the wind** (v. 39) and, with a terse command, brought an immediate and absolute calm to the lake: **and there was a great calm**. Because Jesus exercises the very sovereignty of God over wind and sea, His disciples may entrust themselves to His protection.

Jesus' disciples exclaimed, **What manner of man is this …?** (v. 41). In view of what Jesus had just done, the only answer to this rhetorical question was, He is the very Son of God. God's presence, as well as His power, was demonstrated (see Pss. 65:7; 107:25 – 30; Prov. 30:4). Mark indicated his answer to this question in the opening line of his gospel (1:1). By such miracles, Jesus sought to establish and increase the disciples' faith in His deity. The disciples **feared exceedingly** in the presence of Jesus' power. The motif of fearful awe runs throughout Mark and reveals that, rather than seeing Jesus as a disreputable person, very frequently people regard Him with a reverent, though at times a perplexed, amazement— even terror (see 1:27; 2:12; 4:41; 5:15, 20, 42; 16:8).

5:1 – 20. The second story of the section is the healing of the demoniac in **the country of the Gadarenes** (v. 1). Some witnesses read "Gerasenes" (see NASB, NRSV); others "Gadarenes" (as in the KJV), probably due to a later harmonization with Matthew 8:28. "Gergesenes" is yet another reading found in some manuscripts. "Gerasenes" is the best reading, although the site of the city of Gerasa (modern Jerash) is thirty-seven miles southeast of the Sea of Galilee. Gadara is five miles in that direction. If Mark associated a wide region around the Sea of Galilee with Gerasa, no geographical inaccuracy is present. The proximity of the sea in Mark's account suggests a location near the Sea of Galilee for the exorcism, and the environs of the town of Gergesa are possible settings. Apparently, in Mark's thinking, the town was within a region that might be associated with Gerasa, one of the Ten Cities (Decapolis) to the east of the Sea of Galilee. The territory was largely inhabited by Gentiles, as indicated by the presence of the large herd of pigs, animals that Jews considered "unclean" and therefore unfit to eat.

5:1 – 5. Mark's account of the demon-possessed man is vivid, colorful, and full of suspense. The urgency of the situation confronting Jesus is underscored by Mark's use once again of **immediately** (Greek, *euthys*; v. 2). No sooner had Jesus emerged from the boat than a terrifying figure encountered Him: **a man with an unclean spirit**, of whom, Mark said, **no man could bind him** (v. 3) … **neither could any man tame him** (v. 4). He had been chained hand and foot, but he broke his shackles apart. Though the villagers no doubt chained him partly for their own protection, this harsh treatment added to his humiliation.

The shameful and desperate condition of the demoniac is evident: **and always, night and day, he was in the mountains, and in the tombs, crying, and cutting himself with stones** (v. 5). He was continuously isolated from the society of the living— alone in the mountains and among the tombs of the dead—all the while "howling" (NRSV) in agony and "gashing" (NASB) himself with stones. It was not unusual for the same cave to provide burial for the dead and shelter for the living. Very poor people often lived in such caves.

5:6 – 9. The superior strength that the demoniac exhibited toward others who attempted to subdue him completely vanished when he saw Jesus. Jesus' presence completely changed a situation that appeared desperate. The tormented man, after having seen Jesus from **afar … ran and worshipped him** (v. 6). Although the second verb is at times translated "worshipped" (Greek, *proskyneō*), as it is here in the KJV (see Matt. 28:9, 17: Luke 24:52), the idea is not that the demons gave devotion and homage to Jesus but that they recognized His absolute authority to command them. A better translation is "bowed down before him" (NASB). **What have I to do with thee …?** (v. 7) is a way of saying, "What do we have in common?" Similar expressions are found in the Old Testament (see, e.g., 2 Sam. 16:10; 19:22), where they mean, "Mind your own business!" The demoniac feared that Jesus would **torment** him (that is, the demons within) when He commanded the demons to **Come out of the man** (v. 8). The man's statement is ironic since he was already immeasurably tormented in his present state. When Jesus demanded that the demons identify themselves, they answered, **My name is Legion: for we are many** (v. 9). A legion of Roman infantry was six thousand men. A common supposition in Jesus' day was that if one named the demon in a ritual of exorcism, one could exercise control over it. Jesus' question and the demons' answer publicly demonstrated the reality of Jesus' power over evil supernatural forces.

5:10–13. The complete possession of the man by the "Legion" (5:9) is evident in Mark's language: the reader is unclear whether the man or the demons are speaking: **he besought him much that he would not send them away out of the country** (v. 10). The demons knew that they must go wherever Jesus commanded them and were fearful of being sent into eternal punishment, "into the deep" (Luke 8:31). Evidently, the evil spirits longed for habitable bodies and/or residence in a particular locality. The only bodies readily available were those of the **swine feeding** (v. 11) nearby. Jesus allowed the demons to enter them and, consistent with the destructive intention of the demons, the pigs were drowned in the lake after running over the cliff into the water (v. 13).

5:14–20. Mark then profiled two distinct witnesses to Jesus' power and authority over the demons. Their testimony was to the power of the kingdom of God and the salvation that it brings. The first witness was that of the swineherds, who **fled, and told it in the city, and in the country** (v. 14). Their testimony was widespread and initially effective: many came to see for themselves what had happened. When the residents of the area came in response to the swineherds' testimony, they found an astounding sight: the demoniac **sitting, and clothed, and in his right mind** (v. 15), completely transformed from his previous possessed state. The Gerasenes were confronted with a paradox: how could this calm and tranquil person be the same lunatic who had roamed among the dead? Here is

good Markan irony: the reader knows that the power of Jesus had everything to do with the transformation that had occurred, but the onlookers did not. Rather, in their misunderstanding, **they were afraid**. Not even the explanation of the herdsmen sufficed to convince them that here was something powerful but good: **And they began to pray him to depart out of their coasts** (v. 17). Faithful and accurate testimony for Jesus does not always bring about a good response. The drowning of the pigs seemed to be a major concern, no doubt because it was so dramatic and brought considerable financial loss to the owners (although the text is unclear whether monetary damages were an issue here). Jesus had effectively answered the challenge to His honor brought by supernatural forces of evil. His honor remained to be established through the witness of the demoniac, however. According to their request, Jesus prepared to take leave of the Gerasenes.

The second witness was that of the former demoniac himself. When Jesus was about to depart from the Gerasene country, the man **prayed him that he might be with him** (v. 18). Jesus did not permit this but rather gave him a command that continues to be a recipe for evangelism for anyone who has encountered the saving power of Jesus: **Go home to thy friends, and tell them how great things the Lord hath done for thee, and hath had compassion on thee** (v. 19). This is in marked contrast to Jesus' exhortation to silence in the case of the man cleansed of leprosy (1:44; see 1:34; 3:12; 8:30), perhaps because the healing of the demoniac occurred in Gentile territory, where there was little danger that erroneous messianic ideas about Jesus might be circulated. The Gerasene man is an example of faithful obedience: going away, he **began to publish** ("proclaim," NKJV; v. 20) all that Jesus had done for him. He is a foil (contrast) to the women in Mark 16:7–8, who were silent despite being commanded to announce the resurrection and Jesus' plan to meet with the disciples in Galilee. The former madman complied with Jesus' command and preached widely (in the Ten Cities, or **Decapolis**; v. 20) and effectively. Jesus, although abruptly and rudely rejected at the scene of the miracle, received honor through the faithful testimony about Him: **and all men did marvel**.

5. More Galilean Miracles (5:21–43)

5:21–43. In this section, Mark related two more astounding miracles exhibiting Jesus' power over natural forces of destruction: disease and death. The construction is interesting; the raising of Jairus's daughter is related in two "acts" (vv. 21–24; vv. 35–43) that are "sandwiched" around the healing of the woman who touched Jesus' clothes (vv. 25–34). Other "Markan sandwiches" occur in the gospel (see 11:12–24, the fig tree around the cleansing of the temple; 14:1–11, plots on Jesus' life around His anointing at Bethany; 14:53–72, Peter's denial around Jesus' hearing before the high priest). Such a framing of one story around another provides suspense. When the action shifts to another scene, the reader wonders what will happen next. Sandwiching also provides internal commentary: two stories clarify the meaning of one another by comparison and contrast. Both stories in the Markan sandwich of chapter 5 follow the general pattern of healing stories in the Gospels: the setting, the miracle, and the effect or confirmation of the miracle. In both stories, the hopeless situation of each supplicant is emphasized.

5:21–24. Jesus crossed over the sea westward to Galilee (v. 21). **Jairus** (v. 22), who was **one of the rulers of the synagogue**, approached Jesus and **fell at his feet**. "Rulers of the synagogue" were laymen whose responsibilities were administrative and included such things as looking after the building and supervising the worship. Though there were exceptions (see Acts 13:15), most synagogues had only one ruler. Sometimes the title was honorary, with no administrative responsibilities assigned. Jairus's **daughter** (v. 23) was dying, but he had faith that if Jesus would only **lay ... hands on her ... she shall live**. A crowd followed as Jesus and Jairus began making their way to his house.

5:25–34. It was while Jesus was on his way to Jairus's house that a seeming interruption occurred, which was not an interruption at all but a divine appointment, one which revealed even more clearly the uniqueness of Christ. The woman who **had an issue of blood twelve years** (v. 25) **... was nothing bettered, but rather grew worse** (v. 26) after she **had spent all that she had** on doctors' failed efforts. The Jewish Talmud preserves a record of medicines and treatments prescribed for illnesses of this sort. Her condition, probably continuous vaginal bleeding, rendered her unclean spiritually and socially (see Lev. 12:1–8; 15:19–30). The woman could be restored to ritual cleanliness only when her bleeding stopped and the appropriate sacrifice had been made. Those who came in contact with her or articles she had touched would be unclean as well. If married, her husband would be unclean if he had sexual intercourse with her. The woman had faith that Jesus could heal her: **If I may touch but his clothes, I shall be whole** (v. 28). Although it needed to be bolstered by physical contact, her faith was rewarded. She came to Jesus out of the most extreme desperation and found that, when nothing else had worked, Jesus' power healed her because of her belief. Jesus was aware that **virtue** ("healing power," NLT) **had gone out of him** (v. 30), that God had graciously determined to heal the desperate woman through the power then active in Jesus.

Jesus **looked round about to see her that had done this thing** (v. 32). Jesus would not allow the woman to recede into the crowd without publicly commending her faith and assuring her that she was permanently healed. Her healing, to be complete, involved the restoration of her social relationships by His recognition. He assured her, **thy faith hath made thee whole** (lit., "has saved you"; Greek, *sōzō*; v. 34). The woman could therefore **go in peace, and be whole of thy plague**. Here both physical healing ("be whole of thy plague") and spiritual salvation ("go in peace") are meant. Jesus' healing "saved" her in the sense of complete restoration and wholeness, with God, within herself, and with others. The idea of peace in the Bible is the notion of reconciliation and peace in all one's relationships. Mark's use of the word *sōzō* in this context may have signified for his audience salvation from sin and all its effects. The story is still a lesson for today: Jesus saves from the most desperate crises of life.

5:35–43. Faith was also the basis of the restoration of Jairus's daughter to life. Although his daughter was reported to be already **dead** (v. 35), Jesus did not consider His continued involvement in the father's crisis as troublesome. **Be not afraid, only believe** was the Master's response (v. 36). Then followed the miracle that is the summit of the miracles related in Mark's gospel to this point: a dead girl was raised to life. At Jesus' command, **Damsel (I say unto thee) arise** (v. 41) **... straightway the damsel arose, and walked** (v. 42). Was the girl genuinely dead or just in a coma or a similar state, a kind of deep sleep? According to the text, the bystanders believed that the girl had died; they mocked Jesus' words that she was only sleeping (vv. 39–40). Mark's language also emphasizes that she was "dead" (vv. 35). If those who **wept and wailed greatly** (v. 38) were hired mourners, their presence in the house signifies that the girl's death had been confirmed. In this case, however, it is not certain that enough time had elapsed for professional mourners to have been secured. The people in grief may have been friends and family members. Jesus, knowing that He would raise the girl to life, could say that **the damsel is not dead, but sleepeth** (v. 39). From His perspective, her death, being a temporary state, was but a "sleep." Although the girl's recovery was more of a resuscitation than a resurrection, the event foreshadows Jesus' own resurrection and that of those who are united to Him in faith. The story also stresses the necessity of faith and that Jesus is willing and able to save us from life's most extreme crises.

Mark is the only gospel writer who preserved the original Aramaic TALITHA CUMI (v. 41; "Damsel [I say unto thee] arise"), a feature that indicates Mark was in touch with eyewitness material in his gospel. Only the few chosen especially by Jesus (the girl's parents, Peter, James, and John) witnessed this extraordinary miracle. Those who were outsiders (v. 40; see 4:11–12) remained in their skeptical unbelief, although they may have been among those who were **astonished with a great astonishment** (v. 42).

6. Unbelief in Jesus' Hometown (6:1–6)

6:1–6. Though Mark did not specifically mention Nazareth, it is obviously implied by the words **his own country** (v. 1). The setting of Jesus' hometown is significantly ironic. One would expect greater recognition of the native son, but not so here. Jesus' proverbial statement underlined the irony: **A prophet is not without honour, but in his own country, and among his own kin, and in his own house** (v. 4). Mark's point is that any dishonor that Jesus experienced from His own people did not negate His honorable status. The fact that **he could there do no mighty work** (v. 5) besides a few healings was not because Jesus did not have power to perform miracles at Nazareth but because He chose not to in such a climate of unbelief. His honor was intact.

Despite their astonishment, Jesus' own townspeople and family **were offended at him** ("They were deeply offended and refused to believe in him," NLT; v. 3). **Is not this the carpenter ...?** While Matthew reports that Jesus was called "the carpenter's son" (Matt. 13:55), only in Mark is Jesus Himself referred to as a carpenter. The Greek word can also apply to a mason, wood-worker, or builder in general. The question is derogatory, meaning, "Is He not a common worker with His hands like the rest of us?" They saw no reason to believe that He was different from them, much less that He was specially anointed by God.

7. Six Apostolic Teams Tour Galilee (6:7–13)

6:7–13. Jesus had already chosen the Twelve, "that they should be with him, and that he might send them forth to preach, and to have power to heal sicknesses, and to cast out devils" (3:14–15). Now that they had been with Jesus and had seen His power, the Twelve were sent out **two** (by) **two** (v. 7) to fulfill the other purposes of their calling. Sending them in pairs may have been to bolster credibility by having the testimony of more than one witness (see Deut. 17:6), as well as to provide mutual support during this training period. Jesus instructed the Twelve to take **no scrip** (a scrip was a small bag; we might call it a knapsack), **no bread, no money in their purse** (v. 8). Their clothing was to be extremely simple: **be shod with sandals; and not put on two coats** (v. 9). An extra tunic was helpful as a covering to protect from the cold night air, and the implication here is that the disciples were to trust in God to provide lodging each night. Jesus' instructions regarding meager provisions and clothing may seem strange, but the point was for the disciples to depend on the hospitality of the villages that they entered on their itinerant ministry.

Jesus knew that the honor contest would occur every time that a commissioned pair entered a settlement. The preachers would enter a town, and because of their lack of provisions for travel, whatever household they approached was, in an honor culture, required to extend hospitality. That involved lodging, food, and provisions for further journeying. Those who refused to offer such hospitality dishonored themselves, and in the Mediterranean world, an adequate response to the refusal was necessary to maintain one's honor. To **shake off the dust under your feet for a testimony against them** (v. 11) was a public challenge to the mistreatment that the messengers of the kingdom of God had received. Such an act was a vehement insult and rejection; shaking the dust off one's feet conveyed the idea of being unwilling to touch anything that the villagers had touched since it was common or unclean. In the judgment, the messengers will be vindicated: **Verily I say unto you, It shall be more tolerable for Sodom and Gomorrha in the day of judgment, than for that city**. This mission marks the beginning of the disciples' own ministry in Jesus' name, and their message was precisely the same as His (1:15). Evidently, the Twelve received a welcome in some places that they visited: the tense of the verbs **cast out** (v. 13), **anointed**, and **healed** is imperfect. The disciples were continually doing these things.

8. King Herod's Reaction to Jesus' Ministry (6:14–29)

6:14–29. Having recorded Jesus' announcement of the kingdom of God (see 1:14–15), as well as that of the Twelve whom He had commissioned to preach the same message (see 6:12), Mark addressed the reader's interest in the fate of John the Baptist. What happened to John after his imprisonment (see 1:14)? Mark's flashback in this section satisfies the reader's curiosity.

Here Mark may have used the title **king** (v. 14) with a bit of sarcasm (since Herod was actually a tetrarch), or perhaps he simply used Herod's popular title. At any rate, **king Herod** is Herod Antipas, one of the sons of Herod the Great. The region over which Herod Antipas ruled was Galilee and Perea, but his reign was under the auspices of Roman overlords. Disturbed by an uneasy conscience and disposed to superstition, Herod feared that Jesus was **John ... risen from the dead** (vv. 14, 16) and come back to haunt him. Herod, who **feared John** (v. 20) and willingly listened to him, had arrested John only **for Herodias' sake, his brother Philip's wife** (v. 17). Herodias resented John's preaching against her adulterous marriage with Herod, **for John had said unto Herod, It is not lawful for thee to have thy brother's wife** (v. 18). Josephus says that John was imprisoned at Machaerus, the fortress in Perea on the eastern side of the Dead Sea. Herodias's daughter danced at Herod's birthday party, something which prostitutes normally did. Her stepfather was so pleased with her that he made a foolish vow: **Whatsoever thou shalt ask of me, I will give it thee, unto the half of my kingdom** (v. 23), a proverbial reference to generosity, not to be taken literally (see Est. 5:3, 6). Generosity suited the occasion and would win the approval of the guests. The hasty nature of his vow is reminiscent of Jephthah's vow (see Judg. 11:29–40); in both cases, the one who vowed later regretted that to which he had committed himself.

John was **beheaded ... in the prison** (v. 27). His death was by no means a just sentence, however. Instead, the Baptist's death was brought about by Herodias's hostility toward John in response to his righteous preaching against her adulterous affair with Herod. Herod's shameless arrogance led him to fulfill the heinous request for John's execution. Justice had been trodden into the ground by the dysfunction of the royal house. This dysfunction was so terrible and perverse that a mother and stepfather, after permitting a questionable dancing display by their daughter for their dinner guests, honored her gruesome request for John's beheading (v. 25)—a request encouraged by the girl's mother.

The flashback not only answers the reader's question about John's fate; it also foreshadows Jesus' fate. If John was so abused, what would happen to Jesus, who also announced the kingdom? Moreover, Jesus was greater than John and posed more of a threat. Mark again emphasized that a person who dies ignominiously is not necessarily a person without honor. A travesty of justice may be the reason for a seemingly dishonorable death. Such a travesty had occurred in John's case, as it would in Jesus' case also. All the while, Mark's readers, who faced opposition for their faith in Jesus, had this sober warning: commitment to the righteousness of the kingdom of God entails suffering. The realization of this fact is to be prepared to face the onslaught of hostility when it arrives. Any distress that Mark's audience might have been undergoing, however, was itself for an honorable cause since it was on behalf of the One who has honor despite the shame of the cross.

III. Withdrawals from Galilee (6:30–9:32)

A. To the Eastern Shore of the Sea of Galilee (6:30–52)

6:30–44. The story of the feeding of the five thousand is masterful storytelling. Suspense builds and draws the reader into the tale, from the introduction of the crowds' hunger by the disciples' request (vv. 35–36); through Jesus' command (v. 37a), the disciples' incredulous reply (v. 37b), the period of waiting until the disciples returned with the disheartening disclosure of insufficient resources (v. 38), Jesus' apparently hopeless measure of seating the crowd in groups (vv. 39–40), and the prayer for the utterly impossible supply of food for all (v. 41); to the unbelievable provision underscored by Mark's terse climactic statement, "And they did all eat, and were filled" (v. 42).

6:30. Here Mark picks up his story from 6:13 and focused once again on **the apostles** and their minis-

try. The Twelve were returning from a third preaching tour in Galilee and reported to Jesus **both what they had done, and what they had taught**. In Mark's gospel, the word "apostles" occurs only here and in 3:14 (in some manuscripts). The apostles were Jesus' authorized agents or representatives. In the New Testament, the word is sometimes used quite generally (see John 13:16, where the Greek *apostolos* is translated "he that is sent"). In the technical sense, it is used (1) of the Twelve, in which sense it is also applied to Paul (see Rom. 1:1), and (2) of a larger group including Barnabas (see Acts 14:14), possibly James the Lord's brother (see Gal. 1:19), and less probably Andronicus and Junias (see Rom. 16:7).

6:31–34. So that they could get some rest, Jesus instructed the disciples to **Come ye yourselves apart into a desert place** (v. 31). Being a disciple of Jesus does not mean one must work to exhaustion and deny oneself rest and recreation. It is still true that if the Christian worker does not "come apart," he or she will "come apart." So **they departed** (v. 32). John reports that they went to the other side of the Sea of Galilee (see John 6:1). Luke, more specifically, says that they went to Bethsaida (see Luke 9:10), which locates the feeding of the five thousand on the northeast shore. **The people saw them departing** (v. 33), however, and outran them on foot. Perhaps a strong headwind slowed the boat so that the people had time to go around the lake and arrive before the boat. Jesus **saw much people, and was moved with compassion toward them** (v. 34). Despite His intention and desire to retire with His disciples, Jesus had time for the crowd and their needs. Interestingly, Jesus Himself preached and did not delegate this task to His weary disciples.

6:35–41. Two hundred pennyworth (v. 37). The usual pay for a day's work was one penny or denarius (see Matt. 20:2), meaning that about two hundred denarii would take about eight months to earn. **Green grass** (v. 39). Grass is green around the Sea of Galilee after the late winter or early spring rains. **In ranks, by hundreds, and by fifties** (v. 40) recalls the order of the Mosaic camp in the wilderness (e.g., Exod. 18:21). The word translated "ranks" means "garden plots," a picturesque figure.

6:42–44. And they did all eat, and were filled (v. 42). Attempts to explain away this miracle (e.g., by suggesting that Jesus and His disciples shared their lunch, and the crowd followed their good example) are inadequate. If Jesus was, as He claimed to be, God incarnate, the miracle presents no difficulties. God had promised that when the true Shepherd came, the wilderness would become rich pasture where the sheep would be gathered and fed (Ezek. 34:23–31), and here the Messiah feasts with followers in the desert (see Isa. 25:6–9). Jesus is the Shepherd who provides for all needs so that there is no lack (see Ps. 23:1).

Twelve baskets full of the fragments, and of the fishes (v. 43). The Jews regarded bread as a gift of God, and it was required that scraps that fell on the ground during a meal be picked up. The fragments were collected in small wicker baskets that were carried as part of daily attire.

Five thousand men (v. 44). The size of the crowd is amazing in light of the fact that the neighboring towns of Capernaum and Bethsaida probably had populations of only 2,000–3,000 each. "Men" are literally "males," as in all four gospels. Matthew further emphasized the point by adding "beside women and children" (Matt. 14:21).

6:45–52. Linking the feeding of the five thousand to the story of Jesus walking on the water, Mark emphasized the disciples' failure to appreciate Jesus' power and compassion, which He had just demonstrated so clearly. **For they considered not the miracle of the loaves: for their heart was hardened** (v. 52). Here was a lesson of discipleship for Mark's readers, who could see their own weaknesses in those of the Twelve. The failure to learn from demonstrations of God's compassion, provision, and power means that future distress will appear overwhelming. If the Twelve had remembered that their Lord was sympathetic to their needs and could provide for their needs just as He had in the immediate past, they would not have responded with terror when Jesus was **walking upon the sea** (v. 49). Even though **they supposed it had been a spirit** ("ghost," NRSV), if the disciples had truly believed in Jesus' sufficient

power, fear would not have overtaken them as it did (note that Jesus said, **Be of good cheer: it is I; be not afraid**; v. 50).

The sight of Jesus walking on the sea must have been initially fearsome. It occurred deep in the night, during **the fourth watch** (i.e., 3:00–6:00 a.m.; v. 48), and popular Jewish superstition held that the appearance of spirits during the night brought disaster. The disciples' terror was prompted by what they may have thought was a water spirit. Jesus meant to reveal His divine glory as He walked in front of them, however, and the disciples' "heart was hardened" (v. 52). Their failure to recognize the divinity of Jesus, revealed in the miracle of the loaves and fish, precluded them from believing that the strange sight that they saw from the boat could be Jesus Himself. If they had understood the feeding of the five thousand, they would not have been amazed at Jesus' walking on the water or His calming the waves, which were special displays of the majestic presence and power of the transcendent Lord, who rules over the sea. Jesus' closest followers were showing themselves to be similar to Jesus' opponents, who also exhibited hardness of heart (see 3:5). The disciples' lack of faith thus prevented them from apprehending yet another theophany of Jesus. Incidentally, this significant event in Jesus' ministry followed a period when He devoted Himself to prayer (see v. 46; see also 1:35; 3:13).

B. To the Western Shore of the Sea of Galilee (6:53–7:23)

6:53–56. This section is a hinge in Mark's gospel. It serves as a climactic summary of Jesus' ministry up to this point, but it also introduces the next rounds of activity, back on the western side of the Sea of Galilee (**Genessaret** [v. 53], either the fertile plain along the northwest shore of the sea or the town of that name). In language reminiscent of the healing of the woman in 5:25–34, many **besought him that they might touch if it were but the border of his garment: and as many as touched him were made whole** (v. 56). The Greek word used for "made whole" is *sōzō* ("to save"). Mark may have chosen this word rather than the word *therapeuō* ("to heal") so that he might point to Jesus' power to save spiritually, socially, and physically. The verb is in the imperfect tense: His healing ministry was continuous and widespread.

7:1-23. The significance of the controversy between Jesus, **the Pharisees, and ... the scribes** (v. 1) cannot be overestimated. Jesus' teaching in this section established a precedent regarding the Jewish legal tradition, a precedent that was reiterated and developed in the earliest days of the church (see Acts 10:9-16, 28, 34-35; Gal. 2:11-21). The statement in verse 19 about **purging all meats** probably should be considered an editorial comment by Mark (as the NRSV does by enclosing it in parentheses). Thus, the participial construction "purging all meats" ("Thus he declared all foods clean," NRSV; v. 19) modifies Jesus' entire saying in vv. 18-19, not just the phrase **goeth out into the draught** ("goes out into the sewer," NRSV; v. 19). Cole's helpful paraphrase catches the meaning: "by saying this, He was abolishing all distinction between ceremonially clean and unclean foods" (Cole, *The Gospel according to Mark*, p. 186). Mark's editorial addition possibly extends all the way through verse 23. The point of the passage for Gentile Christians at Rome and everywhere in the Mediterranean world would have been of great relevance, assuring them that they had been absolved from the requirement of strict obedience to Jewish purity laws.

In this passage, Jesus convincingly set forth the danger of legalism. By focusing on the minutiae of human standards and traditions, the Pharisees and scribes whom Jesus addressed had missed the actual intention of the Old Testament law. The rabbinic standards involving the washing of hands and utensils were very rigorous; even contact in **the market** (v. 4) with Gentiles, or with Jews who did not observe the ceremonial law, rendered one ceremonially unclean. Jesus denounced such legalism in no uncertain terms: **This people honoureth me with their lips, but their heart is far from me** (v. 6; see Isa. 29:13); **in vain do they worship me, teaching for doctrines the commandments of men** (v. 7); **laying aside the commandment of God** (v. 8); **Full well ye reject the commandment of God, that ye may keep your own tradition** (v. 9); and **making the word of God of none effect through your tradition** (v. 13). This accumulation of condemnations highlights the extreme to which the hypocrisy of the legalists had gone (see v. 6).

Jesus' denunciation targeted a particularly outrageous practice among the Pharisees that illustrates their legalistic hypocrisy: the practice of **Corban, that is to say, a gift** (v. 11). "Corban" is the transliteration of a Hebrew word meaning "offering." That Mark explained this Hebrew word reveals that he was addressing Gentile readers, probably Romans primarily. An irresponsible Jewish son, by using this word in a religious vow, could formally dedicate to God (i.e., to the temple) his earnings that otherwise would have gone for the support of his parents. The money, however, did not necessarily have to go for religious purposes. The Corban formula was simply a means of circumventing the clear responsibility of children toward their parents as prescribed in the law. (**Honour thy father and thy mother; and, Whoso curseth father or mother, let him die the death**; v. 10; see Exod. 20:12; Deut. 5:16; and Exod. 21:17; Lev. 20:9). The teachers of the law held that the Corban oath was binding, even when uttered rashly. The practice was one of many traditions that adhered to the letter of the law while ignoring its spirit.

The teachers of the law appealed to Numbers 30:1-2 in support of the Corban vow, but Jesus categorically rejected the practice of using one biblical teaching to nullify another. They were "making the word of God of none effect through your tradition" (v. 13). The scribal interpretation of Numbers 30:1-2 satisfied the letter of the passage but missed the meaning of the law as a whole. God never intended obedience to one command to nullify another.

The teaching of verses 21-23 replaced the normal Jewish understandings of defilement with the truth that defilement comes from an impure heart, not from the violation of external rules. Fellowship with God is not interrupted by unclean hands or food, but by sin. Perhaps the strangest member of the vice list is **an evil eye** (v. 22). During the first century (and in some cultures today), many people feared that certain persons, gods, demons, or even animals could cast a spell or cause misfortune for humans by looking at them. Although the evil eye is associated with envy or jealousy (the NRSV has "envy" here), demonic power is elsewhere recognized in Mark's gospel, and that power may well be involved in a given practice of the evil eye. The attempt to jealously harm others with occult power compounds the sin of envy (**covetousness**), also condemned in Mark's list.

Two very important principles for the church today emerge from this section. First, Jesus affirmed the commandment to honor one's parents. This command continues to be obligatory for Christians. During their minority, children show their honor by obedience to their parents; during their majority, honor is still to be demonstrated. Grown sons and daughters who regularly and willingly visit or contact their parents fulfill this commandment. Expressions of appreciation and thanks for parental care are never overly repetitive. When aged parents can no longer take care of themselves, children give them honor by opening their home to the parents or by doing what they can to help their parents acquire appropriate residential care.

Second, Jesus focused on a person's inner life instead of on legalistic rules. Christians often set up their own human standards of righteousness and neglect the habits of the heart that replace the sins enumerated in verses 21–22 with the fruit of the Spirit (Gal. 5:22–23). Christian leaders are especially prone to legalism: an increase in church attendance, the size of church buildings, the number of decisions for Christ, a workweek of sixty to eighty hours, all can too easily become false benchmarks for spiritual success. The passage at hand is an effective antidote to legalism.

C. To Phoenicia (7:24–30)

7:24–30. What does this remarkable story of a Greek woman's faith convey? Does it teach that Jesus' assistance is available only to those who are quick-witted enough to come back at the Master with a snappy and effective retort? Was Jesus outmatched in verbal exchange by this woman? Does it teach that certain people are second-class citizens ("dogs," vv. 27–28)? Is it possible that Luke omitted this story because he found it potentially offensive to Gentile readers?

Mark's placement of this event is also important: it comes immediately after Jesus' definition of what is pure and impure. The woman who came to Jesus was **a Greek** (v. 26), more specifically, **a Syrophenician by nation.** "Greek" here has general reference to a Gentile who has Hellenism as a cultural background. At the time, Phoenicia belonged administratively to Syria. Mark possibly used the term to distinguish this woman from the Libyan-Phoenicians of North Africa. Her home was **the borders** ("region," NKJV) **of Tyre and Sidon** (v. 24). Tyre was a Gentile city located in Phoenicia (modern Lebanon), which bordered Galilee to the northwest. A journey of about thirty miles from Capernaum would have brought Jesus to the vicinity of Tyre. Ever since the feeding of the five thousand (see 6:30–44), Jesus and His disciples had been, for the most part, skirting the region of Galilee. In Tyre, His purpose was to remain secluded for a time, but to no avail. Despite her status as "unclean" regarding Jewish purity laws, the woman was exemplary in her faith, which demonstrates again that old distinctions of clean and unclean are no longer valid in the kingdom of God.

The woman is one of the "little people" of Mark's gospel who are examples of faith, often in contrast to the disciples. Her request was **that he would cast forth the devil** ("the demon," NASB) **out of her daughter** (v. 26). Her belief in Jesus was demonstrated by her immediate and urgent plea ("as soon as she heard about him," NIV; v. 25), her desperate reverence, and her respectful persistence in her entreaty despite an apparent rebuff by Jesus. His initial response has the ring of a proverb: **Let the children first be filled: for it is not meet** ("fair," NRSV) **to take the children's bread, and to cast it unto the dogs** (v. 27). Indeed, for a Jew to call a Gentile a "dog" was an insult (although the Greek word used for "dog," *kynarion*, is diminutive). The idea behind the metaphor of the table is that the Gentiles have second claim on the blessings of God enjoyed by Israel. Jesus may have been testing the woman's faith: did she believe that Jesus' concern and power could transcend ethnic distinctions and boundaries? Her answer proves that she did so believe: **Yes, Lord: yet the dogs under the table eat of the children's crumbs** (v. 28). This is the only time in Mark's gospel that Jesus is addressed as "Lord." In this context, however, it may have the sense only of "Sir," or "Master." Because of the woman's unshakable and persistent faith expressed through her retort, Jesus cast **the devil** ("the demon," NASB; vv. 29–30) out of her daughter.

The challenge-riposte pattern (see discussion on 2:1–12) is once again evident in this story, but with a twist. The woman issued the initial challenge to Jesus when He entered her social space (v. 26). His riposte was that "the dogs" have no equal claim on "the children's bread" (v. 27). The woman continued the contest with yet another challenge: even "the crumbs" may be eaten by "the dogs" (v. 28). She had the last say, and gained the honor in this debate with Jesus. Still, the Master retained His honor through the exorcism of the demon. Faith brings with it its own honor from the Lord.

D. To the Region of the Decapolis: More Miracles (7:31–8:10)

7:31–37. The challenge-riposte pattern (see discussion on 2:1–12) is evident yet again in the healing of the deaf-mute. This time, however, the miracle occurred when Jesus directly and physically contacted the person in need, not by means of His powerful word spoken at a distance (see 7:29–30). The itinerary (**departing from the coasts of Tyre and Sidon, he came unto the sea of Galilee;** v. 31) suggests that Jesus went north from Tyre to Sidon (about twenty-five miles) and then southeast through the territory of Herod Philip to the east side of the Sea of Galilee. The route was circuitous possibly to avoid entering Galilee, where Herod Antipas was in power (see 6:17–29).

In Galilee, many people wanted to take Jesus by force and make Him king (see John 6:14–15). Herod had intimated a hostile interest in Jesus.

The description of the healing sounds somewhat bizarre. Having drawn the deaf-mute away privately, Jesus **put his fingers into his ears, and he spit, and touched his tongue** (v. 33). Then, **he sighed** (as He looked to Heaven in dependence on the power of the Father) and commanded the deaf man's ears to **Be opened** (v. 34). Mark's typical **straightway** (Greek, *eytheōs*; v. 35) emphasizes the overwhelmingly great power of Jesus over physical impediments and disease. The man's **ears were opened, and the string of his tongue was loosed, and he spake plain** (see Isa. 35:5–6). Why did Jesus not merely say the word and permit the healing to take place? Why the rigmarole?

In ancient acts of healing, the very words spoken were thought to have power. Mark preserved the Aramaic form of Jesus' command, Ephphatha ("Be opened"; v. 34), out of this assumption. Healers (not professional physicians) touched their clients, and spittle was believed to ward off evil. Jesus adopted commonly accepted healing gestures as an accommodation to folk understanding and expectation of what genuine healers would do. Of course, His power is from His own divine person and not from magical or occult sources.

8:1–10. Although there are striking similarities between the accounts in 8:1–10 and 6:34–44, they are two distinct incidents, as indicated by the fact that Jesus Himself referred to two feedings (see 8:18–20). The differences in details are as definite as the similarities.

Since the feeding of the four thousand took place in the region of the Decapolis (see 7:31), **the multitude being very great** (v. 1) probably was made up of both Jews and Gentiles. As Jesus had compassion formerly because the people were like sheep without a shepherd (see 6:34), He now had **compassion** (v. 2) because they had been so long without food. The outreach that neglects human need for food, clothing, and shelter is not following the model of Jesus. He was moved with pity at others' physical pain and discomfort and enlisted His disciples to meet that need.

The disciples' question, **From whence can a man satisfy these men with bread here in the wilderness?** (v. 4), displays an astonishing dullness in the face of the need as it was defined by Jesus. How could these same disciples who witnessed the feeding of five thousand not even imagine that their Lord could meet the need of the hour? The lesson of discipleship for any age is embarrassingly clear: the believer's forgetfulness of the Lord's provision in the past dooms that believer to fret over and try to muddle through new challenges. Believers often encounter challenges that are simply tests of their willingness to recall God's blessing in the past. The Twelve would soon be faced with the inadequacy of their recollection of His past blessing. As they and Jesus proceeded to the area of **Dalmanutha** (v. 10), the stage was set. The place was south of the plain of Gennesaret. A cave has been found bearing the name "Talmanutha," perhaps the spot where Jesus landed. Matthew says Jesus went to the vicinity of Magdala (see Matt. 15:39). Dalmanutha and Magdala, located on the western shore of the Sea of Galilee, may be names for the same place or for two places located close to each other.

E. To the Vicinity of Caesarea Philippi (8:11–9:32)

1. The Pharisees' Demand for a Sign and the Danger of Yeast (8:11–21)

8:11–13. The unwillingness to believe the obvious manifestations of the kingdom of God in Jesus' life and ministry had led some of **the Pharisees** (v. 11) to demand yet further proof of the origin of His work. Mark reported that they were **tempting** ("testing," NKJV) **him**. Their motive was not sincere but rather one of putting Jesus into a corner by demanding a **sign** that He could not produce. Of course, Jesus **sighed deeply in his spirit** (v. 12) at this stubbornness. Because the request came from disbelief, He refused their demand, although He was capable of meeting it: **There shall no sign be given unto this generation.** Even today, resistance to the gospel is often rooted in a refusal to accept the clear testimony of the New Testament and its requirements

of faith and obedience. With a satisfactory answer to each objection comes yet another one. Eventually, a decision of faith must be made regarding the overwhelming evidence of the truthfulness of the biblical record. Sometimes what seems like determined resistance is simply ignorance of the witness of the biblical documents. An open and inquiring reading of the texts may very well dispel such a lack of knowledge and lead to faith. All believers need do initially with skeptics is to challenge them to read the New Testament for themselves. Sincere doubts are one thing, hardness of unbelief another.

8:14–21. The disciples' failure to remember bread for the journey across the lake gave Jesus an opportunity to teach the disciples about the dangers of unbelief. **Take heed, beware of the leaven of the Pharisees, and of the leaven of Herod** (v. 15) was a warning for them not to miss the significance of the miraculous deeds that they observed Him do. These deeds, like the miraculous provision of loaves for the five thousand and then the four thousand (19–20), were ample testimony to Jesus' power, compassion, and honor. "Leaven" ("yeast," NIV) often has a negative connotation in the New Testament; it is a symbol of evil or corruption (Matt. 16:6, 11; Luke 12:1; 1 Cor. 5:6–8; Gal. 5:9; but see Matt. 13:33 and Luke 13:20–21, where the kingdom of God is compared to leaven). The idea of the metaphor is that a tiny amount of leaven is able to ferment a large amount of dough. In Mark's context, it refers to the evil disposition of the Pharisees who called for Jesus to produce a sign (i.e., a proof of His divine authority); the leaven represents their stubborn refusal to believe. The disciples were already slipping into this sin, so Jesus questioned them as if they were outsiders, **Having eyes, see ye not? and having ears, hear ye not? and do ye not remember?** (v. 18; see v. 21; 4:12).

2. The Healing of a Blind Man at Bethsaida (8:22–26)

8:22–26. The context of the healing of the blind man is important in appreciating the significance of this story for Mark. The link between the myopia of the disciples in 8:18 and the blindness of the man at **Bethsaida** (on the northeast shore of the

Sea of Galilee; v. 22) is no coincidence. The disciples were like the blind man after Jesus' first touch upon him: they could see, but not clearly. They were not completely blind, like the outsiders in Mark (the scribes, 3:22–23; Pharisees and Herod, 8:10–13; those outside, 4:11–12). The Twelve had been specially taught by Jesus (4:10–13, 33–34), but they had failed to understand Jesus' status (see 8:17–18, 21). They needed a second touch from Jesus, just as the blind man did, to clearly see Jesus' true identity. That perception would not come for them until after the resurrection. At that time, the disciples would clearly see (the verbs in v. 25 denote complete restoration of sight: "Then his eyes were opened, his sight was restored, and he saw everything clearly," NIV). Meanwhile, they were like the unsighted man who, before Jesus' second touch, stated, **I see men as trees, walking** (v. 24).

This second laying on of hands is unique in Jesus' healing ministry, but as in God's original creation over six days, He can choose to do things in stages. Giving sight to the blind was another indication that Jesus was doing what God had promised to do when He came to bring salvation (see Isa. 35:5). Note the similarities of this text with 7:31–37. Once healed, the formerly blind man was to **neither go into the town, nor tell it to any in the town** (v. 26) so as not to broadcast what Jesus had done for him and precipitate a crisis before Jesus had completed His ministry.

3. Peter's Confession and Jesus' Prophecy of His Death and Resurrection (8:27–9:1)

8:27–33. While traveling near or among the villages of **Caesarea Philippi** (v. 27), Jesus asked His disciples, **Whom do men say that I am?** Popular opinions of Jesus were somewhat strange; many people viewed Jesus as some sort of reincarnation of prophetic figures from the past. Then Jesus posed the question that every reader of Mark's gospel since its composition must ask of himself or herself: **But whom say ye that I am?** (v. 29). All objections, arguments, and smokescreens aside, this is the bottom line, and all Christian witness and apologetics must

ultimately arrive at it. Of all the disciples, Peter alone answered as the reader knows is correct. The fisherman appears finally to have begun to believe the evidence about Jesus. His great confession, **Thou art the Christ**, is a high point of Peter's career as a disciple, and the confession to which Mark's gospel is intended to lead the reader. Because popular Jewish ideas associated with the term "Christ" were largely political and national, Jesus seldom used it. Of its seven occurrences in Mark, only three appear in the sayings of Jesus (9:41; 12:35; 13:21), and in none of these did He use the title of Himself (with the possible exception of 9:41). Mark identified Jesus as the Christ in 1:1. Jesus answered affirmatively the high priest's question whether He is the Christ (14:62) but defined His identity as Messiah in terms of the Son of Man.

With Peter's confession, the reader senses that perhaps, finally, the entire group of the Twelve might begin to understand Jesus' power, compassion, and identity. But even Peter's insight broke down immediately after Jesus prophesied His coming death and resurrection. The second touch signified by the healing of the blind man (see 8:22–26) still awaited.

Verse 31 represents the first of three prophecies of Jesus' death in Mark (here; 9:31; 10:33–34). It also indicates a geographical shift from Galilee, where most of Jesus' public ministry reported by Mark took place, to Jerusalem and the closing days of Jesus' life on earth. Jesus would now define the true meaning of "Christ" as the title applies to Him. Some scholars discount Jesus' prophecy regarding His own passion. They maintain that it was impossible for Jesus to foresee that He **must suffer many things, and be rejected … and be killed, and after three days rise again** (v. 31) and that these words were put into Jesus' mouth by the early church as a way to explain His death as something that He willed and ordained. Since His death and resurrection were foretold in Scripture, however, Jesus, as the Son of God, knew His destiny and acquiesced accordingly in the dire events that occurred around Him. If one accepts Mark's testimony from the outset, that he wrote of "Jesus Christ, the Son of God" (1:1), Jesus' foresight is not problematic. If one's worldview disallows the possibility of God incarnate and of miraculous deeds wrought by Jesus as God-man, then there is no room for Jesus' prophecy. Such a worldview is certainly not that of Mark, however.

Suffering and rejection had no place in Peter's conception of the Messiah, which left no room for God to do the unexpected. Therefore, **Peter took him, and began to rebuke him** (v. 32). Peter's own rebuke was rebuked by Jesus, however: **Get thee behind me, Satan**. Peter insisted that Jesus play a role fitting for the Messiah, one that did not allow suffering. By this insistence, Peter ended up playing the part of the adversary (the basic meaning of "Satan") and even allied himself with the Devil at this point. Peter's refusal to allow his Master's suffering (perhaps because of what it might have meant for himself) led Jesus to say to him, **thou savourest not the things that be of God, but the things that be of men** ("you are setting your mind not on divine things but on human things," NRSV).

8:34–38. Jesus now spelled out for the crowd the call, the cost, and the conditions of discipleship. The Twelve needed to grasp this instruction to be able to receive the second touch that was signified in the healing of the blind man (see 8:22–26). **Whosoever will come after** (Greek, *erchomai opisō*) **me** (v. 34) has, in effect, received the call to follow Jesus. The implication is that a person has a choice in the matter of discipleship (and salvation). God's sovereignty and human freedom intersect. The phrase "come after" is typical Markan language for following Jesus in discipleship. Jesus bluntly stated the cost for the potential disciple: **let him deny himself, and take up his cross, and follow** (Greek, *akoloutheō*) **me**. Self-denial is not rigorous asceticism that believes that any pleasure in life is sinful. Rather, it means saying no to one's inclination to self-preservation, comfort, self-justification, and protection of reputation and status. The readiness to share abuse, and even the same ignominious death, with Jesus is also part of discipleship; in this way, the disciple bears his or her cross. This kind of sacrifice, however, is a daily commitment to walk with Jesus; a one-time decision for

martyrdom can come out of only daily discipleship. Luke therefore wrote, "let him ... take up his cross daily" (9:23).

The church must not evade the rigorous conditions of discipleship either in its own corporate life or in its proclamation to the world. Otherwise, the church is guilty of fostering "cheap grace." As Dietrich Bonhoeffer wrote, "Cheap grace is the preaching of forgiveness without requiring repentance, baptism without church discipline, Communion without confession, absolution without personal confession. Cheap grace is grace without discipleship, grace without the cross, grace without Jesus Christ, living and incarnate." Rather, he said, the grace of God is costly: "Such grace is *costly* because it calls us to follow, and it is *grace* because it calls us to follow *Jesus Christ*. It is costly because it costs a man his life, and it is grace because it gives a man the only true life" (*The Cost of Discipleship*, rev. ed., trans. R. H. Fuller and Irmgard Booth [New York: Macmillan, 1959], p. 47). Bonhoeffer, the great German theologian and martyr, echoes the Markan Jesus: **For whosoever will save his life shall lose it; but whosoever shall lose his life for my sake and the gospel's, the same shall save it** (v. 35). The great paradox of life is that one can find life only when one gives it up for Jesus and for His service.

Whosoever ... shall be ashamed of me and of my words (v. 38) refers to that person who is concerned more about fitting into and pleasing his own "adulterous and sinful generation" than about following and pleasing Christ. That person will have no part in God's kingdom. To "be ashamed of" someone also means refusing to acknowledge his honor and claims to honor. To preserve one's own status and honor, one dissociates oneself from the claimant. Since Jesus claims, maintains, and deserves honor, to be ashamed of Him places oneself in a dishonorable position. One's refusal to acknowledge Jesus and His honor as Son of God means that Jesus will dissociate Himself from that person **when he cometh in the glory of his Father with the holy angels** (see 2 Thess. 1:6–10). The situation in which Jesus was rejected, humiliated, and put to death will be reversed when

He returns in glory as the Judge of all people. The way to honor for Mark's harassed community was not to compromise with the world around them, nor was it to dissociate itself from Jesus and be "anonymous Christians." The way to honor, for all believers, is to live for Christ and to proclaim Him before an **adulterous and sinful** society.

9:1. Jesus' prophecy that **some ... shall not taste of death, till they have seen the kingdom of God come with power** links Jesus' prophecy of His death, resurrection, and second coming in 8:31–38 with the transfiguration (see 9:2–13). The transfiguration not only shows that God's rule and power for salvation are centered and revealed in Jesus; it also demonstrated Jesus' power to prophesy His own future. Since the transfiguration fulfilled Jesus' prophecy in this verse, the fulfillment of His prophecy in 8:31–38 became more certain. Jesus' ability accurately to prophesy His destiny mitigates the shame of the cross.

4. The Transfiguration (9:2–13)

9:2–4. In the Bible, a **mountain** (v. 2) is typically the setting for theophanies (see Exod. 19:16–23; 20:18–21; 1 Kings 19:8–13), and the transfiguration (9:2–13) is one of those appearances, here of the Father and the divine Son of God. The imagery in Mark's account is stunning and thus vividly conveys that the transcendent reality of heaven intersected earthly and ordinary reality. Jesus' garments **became shining, exceeding white as snow** ("dazzling white," NRSV)**; so as no fuller** ("launderer," NKJV) **on earth can white them** (v. 3). **Elias** (i.e., Elijah; v. 4) may signify the time of eschatological fulfillment (see Mal. 4:5); **Moses** (v. 4) signifies that Jesus is the Prophet whose coming he prophesied (see Deut. 18:15).

9:5–10. The **cloud that overshadowed** (v. 7) Jesus, Elijah, and Moses sufficed as a shelter, rather than the **three tabernacles** (v. 5) that Peter suggested that the disciples build. He may have been thinking of the booths used at the Feast of Tabernacles (see Lev. 23:42). His plan arose out of confusion and awe at the theophany: **For he wist not what to say; for**

they were sore afraid ("because he did not know what to say, for they were greatly afraid," NKJV; v. 6). **A cloud** (v. 7) is frequently a symbol of God's presence to protect and guide (e.g., Exod. 16:10; 19:9; 24:15–18; 33:9–10). The Father's **voice came out of the cloud, saying, This is my beloved Son: hear him**, an echo of Psalm 2:7.

The Father's command to "hear" (v. 7) the Son was especially relevant in light of Jesus' command that the disciples not say anything about what they had seen on the mountain until **the Son of man were risen from the dead** (v. 9). A report of the glorious event would have detracted from the suffering that was Jesus' purpose. So the "messianic secret" here is explainable as something that really happened in Jesus' life: He was Messiah, and He revealed His messianic glory. At this time, however, that glory had to be downplayed. Nevertheless, the disciples still did not understand the notion of **rising from the dead** (v. 10). As Jews, they were familiar with the doctrine of the resurrection; it was the resurrection of the Son of Man that baffled them, because their theology had no place for a suffering and dying Messiah.

9:11–13. Jesus' destiny of suffering was tied to the coming of **Elias** (i.e., Elijah; vv. 11–13). John the Baptist, as a second Elijah, **cometh first, and restoreth all things** (v. 12). His suffering foreshadowed that of the Son of Man. No prophecy of suffering is associated with Elijah's ministry in the end times. What happened to Elijah under the threats of Jezebel (see 1 Kings 19:1–10), however, foreshadowed what would happen to John the Baptist. The order of events suggested in Mark 9:11–13 is as follows: (1) Elijah ministered in the days of wicked Jezebel; (2) Elijah was a type of John the Baptist, who in turn suffered at the hands of Herodias; (3) **the Son of man** (v. 12) suffered and was rejected a short time after John was beheaded.

5. The Healing of a Boy with an Unclean Spirit (9:14–29)

9:14–26. This story of the boy **which hath a dumb spirit** ("possessed with a spirit which makes him mute," NASB; v. 17) is one of the most colorful and dramatic in Mark's narrative. The story displays Jesus' power and honor in challenges from a desperate supplicant and from demons, features dominical instruction on faith with an example of true faith by the boy's father, and teaches a valuable lesson for discipleship through a failure of Jesus' followers. Mark's characteristic **straightway** (Greek, *euthys*) appears three times in this section (vv. 15, 20, 24) and propels the narrative forward. The severity of the boy's affliction is highlighted by Mark's vivid descriptions of the demonic torment, made even more striking by the rare and graphic vocabulary in the following list (some terms are accompanied by the number of times the particular Greek word appears in the New Testament and/or with an alternative translation): **taketh** (v. 18; thirteen times; "seizes," NASB), **teareth** (seven times; "throws him violently to the ground," NLT), **foameth** (two times, both in Mark; "foams at the mouth," NIV), **gnasheth with his teeth** (one time), **pineth away** ("and becomes rigid," NKJV), **the spirit tare him** (v. 20; two times; "it convulsed the boy," ESV), **fell on the ground, and wallowed** (one time; "lay writhing," NJB), **foaming** ("foaming at the mouth," NRSV), **ofttimes it hath cast him into the fire, and into the waters, to destroy him** (v. 22), **the spirit cried** (v. 26; "shrieked aloud," REB), and **rent him sore** (three times; "throwing him into terrible convulsions," NASB).

9:27–29. Although the boy appeared dead after the exorcism, **Jesus took him by the hand, and lifted him up; and he arose** (v. 27). Despite the power of the spirit that had oppressed the boy, Jesus met the challenge and further established His honor as one who cannot be thwarted by demonic opponents.

Jesus' instruction on faith surprisingly came in the form of a rebuke to what appears to be a genuine and believing prayer. The pleading parent begged Jesus, **but if thou canst do any thing, have compassion on us, and help us** (v. 22). Jesus' retort, **If thou canst believe, all things are possible to him that believeth** (v. 23) picked up the supplicant's own language "thou canst" and turned the tables on him. The question was not whether Jesus had the power to heal the boy but whether the father had faith to

believe it. A person who truly believes will set no limits on what God can do. He is able to do whatever one asks. Some New Testament manuscripts read, "Jesus said to him, "If you are able!—All things can be done for the one who believes'" (NRSV). The lesson is the same whichever reading one adopts.

Jesus demanded not perfect trust but genuine trust. He honored the man's desperate (**with tears;** v. 24), honest, and genuine prayer for his son and for his own faith (**I believe; help thou mine unbelief**). The miracle itself assisted his unbelief. Since faith is never perfect, belief and unbelief are often mixed. **When Jesus saw that the people came running together, he rebuked the foul spirit** (v. 25). Jesus wanted to avoid further publicity, as much as possible, and therefore answered the father's plea without further delay.

Next came the disciples' lesson in the matter of the failed exorcism. The construction **His disciples asked him privately, Why could not we cast him out?** (v. 28) reflects an intensive questioning since the verb "asked" is in the imperfect tense. "His disciples kept on asking him privately" (Wuest) is the sense here. The exact wording of Jesus' reply, **This kind can come forth by nothing, but by prayer and fasting** (v. 29), is uncertain because of differences among the New Testament manuscripts. The words "and fasting" are not in some of the oldest and best manuscripts. As time went on, fasting received increased emphasis in the church. "And fasting" is therefore probably a gloss to the text of Mark that reflects this emphasis.

The expression "This kind" (v. 29) seems to suggest that there are different kinds of demons. The disciples apparently had taken for granted the power given to them or had come to believe that it was inherent in them. Their lack of prayer indicates they had forgotten that their power over the demonic spirits was from Jesus. A prayerless approach to the challenges of spiritual warfare is bound to end in frustration for the church, just as it did for the Twelve. When people are demonically oppressed or possessed, urgent and protracted times of corporate prayer by the church are most critical. Sometimes fasting is also required. It demonstrates to God one's determination and perseverance, one's willingness to sacrifice to see His will accomplished. All things, including release from spiritual bondage, are possible to the believing church (see 3:15; 6:7, 13).

6. Jesus Again Foretells His Death and Resurrection (9:30-32)

9:30-32. Jesus and the disciples **departed thence, and passed through Galilee** (v. 30) quietly and privately. Jesus' public ministry in and around Galilee was completed, and He was now on His way to Jerusalem to suffer and die (see 10:32-34). Once again Jesus discussed His passion and resurrection. As He had been doing for several months, Jesus continued to focus His teaching ministry on the Twelve, **But they understood not** (v. 32; see v. 10; 8:32-33). The significant difference between this prophecy and that in 8:31 is that Jesus now spoke of the process of His suffering as having already begun: **The Son of man is delivered** (present tense) **into the hands of men** (v. 31). The outcome of this deliverance would be that **they shall kill him** and that **he shall rise the third day** (both future tense). Jesus knew His destiny and allowed the gruesome injustices of it to come upon Him. This means that His suffering was voluntary, and He thus maintained His honor in the face of it.

IV. Final Ministry in Galilee (9:33-50)

A. True Greatness (9:33-37)

9:33-37. The disciples' obtuseness regarding Jesus' prophecy that He would suffer at the hand of men is highlighted by His instruction on true greatness. As often happens in Mark's gospel, Jesus instructed His disciples privately (see 4:34; 6:31-32; 9:28; 13:3; see also 9:2), now **in the house** (v. 33; probably the one belonging to Peter and Andrew; see 1:29) at **Capernaum**. That Jesus asked, **What was it that ye disputed among yourselves by the way?** does not imply that Jesus was unaware of the subject of the dispute among the Twelve. He intentionally put them in the awkward position of having to face their ambitiousness and confess it, for the disciples

had argued about **who should be the greatest** ("who was the greatest," NIV; v. 34). Their silence (no doubt due to embarrassment) gave Jesus the perfect opening for teaching about true greatness.

In this passage, Jesus was not forbidding a desire for leadership but rather defining leadership in the kingdom of God as being **last of all, and servant of all** (v. 35), two synonymous descriptions in which the emphasis is on others, not on self (the Greek is literally, "of all last and of all servant"). Jesus' teaching is still relevant for today's Christian leader. Oftentimes a believer thinks that the way to influence others for Christ is to give them orders, that the believer always know what's best, and that to listen to advice or criticism is weakness. Many leaders never admit mistakes, nor extend appreciation to others for their achievements, out of an erroneous belief that the leader must do it all and do it right all the time. Jesus instead demonstrated servant-leadership in the object lesson of the **child** (v. 36) whom he took up **in his arms**. To **receive one of such children in my name** (v. 37) is to receive Jesus and the Father Himself. The emphasis should be on not "who should be the greatest" but rather on humble service to the point of welcoming a child. This passage affirms the necessity of ministry to children as people who are just as worthy of adults' attention as other adults are. Working in the church nursery, teaching preschool and elementary children, and leading teens are just as important in the kingdom as ministry to adult learners.

B. Jesus Forbids an Exclusive Attitude (9:38-41)

9:38-41. Not only does humble service involve service to children; it also has no room for an exclusive attitude that refuses to recognize others outside its own circle of ministry. John (representing the Twelve) is portrayed in this text as zealous for the maintenance of discipleship boundaries. In his opinion, only those immediately around Jesus were legitimately to be identified as His followers. **We forbad** (v. 38), John said, an exorcist outside the circle of the Twelve **because he followeth not us**. "We forbad" may mean either "We tried to forbid him" or "We were forbidding him." In any case, Jesus said, **Forbid him not** (v. 39). Ironically, the Twelve were trying to stop someone who was successfully carrying on the very work (casting out demons) that they themselves had failed in doing (see 9:17–18). Rather than being something noble, John's zealous action may have been jealous action.

Jesus' explanation, **For he that is not against us is on our part** (v. 40), serves as a warning to all His disciples against exclusivity. Just because a person belongs to another church or denomination, or differs on some points of doctrine, or worships differently than another does not invalidate that person's service for Christ. The litmus test is, **For whosoever shall give you a cup of water to drink in my name, because ye belong to Christ, verily I say unto you, he shall not lose his reward** (v. 41). The "outsider" who extends even the smallest service to others within another circle of disciples reveals herself to be identified with and included within Jesus' larger circle of citizens of the kingdom.

C. Teaching on Temptation and Sin (9:42–50)

9:42. Jesus' teaching on welcoming children (9:36–37) led to a prohibition on exclusivity (9:38–41) and here to a further consideration of children. To **offend one of these little ones that believe in me** means to cause "one of these little ones who believe in me to sin" (NIV). This is a heinous injustice. Jesus focused on the adult who, by example, deed, or persuasion, takes advantage of a child who, being weaker, is incapable of resistance to the stronger adult. These words contain a dire warning for those who abuse children physically or emotionally and for leaders who are careless about the role model that they present. The "little ones" may also be adults who are either innocent or relatively immature in faith. Nevertheless, the principle still holds true: a believer's influence on others is to be carefully considered. The hyperbole **it is better for him that a millstone were hanged about his neck, and he were cast into the sea** effectively conveys the seriousness of leading children astray. The "millstone" to which

Jesus referred was a heavy circular stone slab laid on its side and turned by a donkey in grinding grain.

9:43–48. The hyperbole of the "millstone" (9:42) is the first of several hyperbolic warnings. In these verses, the warnings concern the need for one to radically eliminate sin in one's life. The treatment of sin should be so decisive that it is as if one cuts off the very member of the body associated with a particular sin. The phrase **if thy hand offend thee, cut it off** ("If your hand causes you to sin, cut it off," NLT; v. 43) is paralleled in **if thy foot offend thee, cut it off** (v. 45) and in **if thine eye offend thee, pluck it out** (v. 47). In each case, the member of the body is closely associated with the sin it practices and so is used in place of it in Jesus' command to expunge sin from one's life. Jesus therefore employed not only hyperbole (exaggeration) but also metonymy (association) in His shocking instructions. The element of shock conveys the seriousness of dealing radically with sin in one's life. **To enter into life** (v. 43, 45), that is, **the kingdom of God** (v. 47), with loss (being **maimed**, v. 43; **halt** ["lame," NKJV], v. 45; **with one eye,** v. 47) is better than to go into **hell** without loss of those things that ultimately destroy anyway and prevent one from entering the kingdom.

The repetitions in this text emphasize the gravity of the situation: every kind of sin is considered, and the terrible destiny of those who practice sin in these ways comes up again and again in Jesus' speech. **Hell** appears three times (vv. 43, 45, 47); **worm** three times (vv. 44, 46, 48); **dieth not** three times (vv. 44, 46, 48); **fire** six times (vv. 43, 44, 45, 46, 47, 48); and the negated **quenched** five times (vv. 43, 44, 45, 46, 48). The repetition of so many words lends intensity and urgency to Jesus' warnings. (Such an effect does not arise in some more recent translations, such the NIV and the NRSV, which omit verses 44 and 46. Although these two verses are in the majority of manuscripts, major early witnesses to the original reading of Mark 9 do not include these verses. They are included by several early church fathers, however.)

"Hell" (vv. 43, 45, 47) is *geenna,* Gehenna ("the valley of the sons of Hinnom"; see discussion on Matt. 5:22). This valley near Jerusalem was once the site of abhorrent sacrifices of children by fire to Molech (see 2 Kings 23:10; 2 Chron. 28:3; 33:6; Jer. 7:31; 32:35). Later, the area was a smoldering dump, where fires and worms perpetually consumed the garbage and offal of the city. It thus had become an apt image for the place of eternal punishment by the time of Jesus. Isaiah 66:24 speaks of sinners who have perished, whose "worm shall not die, neither shall their fire be quenched"—the punishment for rebellion against God. As the final word of Isaiah's message, the passage became familiar as a picture of endless destruction. The Bible clearly teaches the reality of eternal judgment for those who practice sin and refuse to repent in faith. Jesus' words are a warning, however, not a condemnation. The person who hesitates to follow Christ because of his or her disinclination to forsake a particular sin should hear these words. Likewise for a Christian who refuses to deal with a sinful habit.

9:49–50. The saying about **salt** (vv. 49–50) corresponds to the discussion of judgment in 9:43–48. The saying may mean that everyone who enters hell will suffer its fire, or (if only loosely connected with the preceding passage) it may mean that every Christian in this life can expect to undergo the fire of suffering and purification. **For every one shall be salted with fire** (v. 49) is metaphorical: the fire as judgment (see 1 Cor. 3:13) will thoroughly test every person and their work, as if they were permeated with fire just as food is permeated with salt. In other words, **every sacrifice shall be salted with salt**.

Jesus affirmed the disciples to be salt and the possibility of that salt going bad. Matthew wrote, "Ye are the salt of the earth: but if the salt have lost his savour, wherewith shall it be salted?" (Matt. 5:13). The idea of salt becoming insipid is the same here in Mark. Jesus is warning His disciples against the power of sin to corrupt one's spiritual life, thus infecting the whole community. Such corrupting influences are to be "cut off" (see 9:43–48), drastically removed from the community. Such extreme measures are not unknown in the New Testament (see Matt. 18:15–17; 1 Cor. 5:1–13; 2 Thess. 3:14–15). To **Have salt in yourselves** (v. 50) points to the main-

tenance of the positive influence that Jesus' disciples exerted toward one another and toward the "little ones." Only by guarding against contaminating influences can citizens of the kingdom **have peace one with another.** A disciple of Jesus is marked by his or her diligence to maintain harmonious relationships with others through extending and seeking forgiveness, showing honor and appreciation, praying for others, and developing nondefensive openness to advice and criticism.

V. Jesus' Ministry in Judea and Perea (chap. 10)

A. Teaching concerning Divorce (10:1–12)

10:1–12. In this passage, the discussion involving three parties (Jesus, the Pharisees, and the disciples) may follow an early threefold pattern of Jewish debate: (1) a question from an opponent (v. 2); (2) a public response that answers the opponent only partially (vv. 3–9); and (3) a private elaboration to one's followers (vv. 10–12).

10:1. Jesus' travels now took Him **into the coasts of Judea by the farther side of Jordan** (v. 1). "Judea" is the Greek and Roman equivalent to the Old Testament land of Judah, essentially the southern part of the Holy Land (now exclusive of Idumea), which formerly had been the southern kingdom. Jesus' journey took Him south from Capernaum, over the mountains of Samaria into Judea, and then east across the Jordan into Perea, where He was in the territory of Herod Antipas.

10:2. Stage 1 of the debate (see discussion on 10:1–12) consists of the question posed by Jesus' opponents. **The Pharisees came to him, and asked him** about divorce: **Is it lawful for a man to put away** ("divorce," NKJV) **his wife?** Their intention was hostile, however; they were once again attempting to trap Him. It was for unlawful divorce and remarriage that John the Baptist denounced Herod Antipas and Herodias (see 6:17–18), and this rebuke cost him first imprisonment and then his life. Jesus was now within Herod's jurisdiction, and the Pharisees may have hoped that Jesus' reply would cause the tetrarch to seize Him as he had John. Jews of that day generally agreed that divorce was lawful, the only debated issue was the proper grounds for it.

10:3–9. Stage 2 of the debate consists of Jesus' public answer. He immediately turned the tables and put His questioners on the defensive with a question of His own. His honor was upheld in that Jesus effectively parried the challenge and had the last word that could not be successfully countered. The Lord inquired, **What did Moses command you?** (v. 3). The opponents were correct in their answer that Moses permitted a woman to be given **a bill of divorcement** (v. 4). However, the Mosaic legislation (see Deut. 24:1) was not a license for people simply to bail out of a difficult marriage; it was meant to release a woman from an irremediably oppressive situation. The bill was a means of grace that allowed women, socially unequal to men in Israel, to be free to marry again. Divorce was an accommodation to human weakness and was used to bring order in a society that had disregarded God's will. The purpose of Deuteronomy 24:1 was not to make divorce acceptable but to reduce the hardship of its consequences. **For the hardness of your heart** (a husband's callousness) **he wrote you this precept** (v. 5), Jesus said. God's original intention in the creation of **male and female** (v. 6) is that **they twain** ("the two," NKJV) **shall be one flesh** (v. 8). The marital union, especially signified by sexual intercourse, is to be permanent (**let not man put asunder**; v. 9).

10:10–12. Stage 3 of the debate consists of Jesus' instruction to the disciples in private. If this is the elaboration stage of traditional Jewish debate, we must understand verses 11–12 to be explanatory. **Whosoever shall put away his wife, and marry another, committeth adultery against her** (v. 11) would thus pinpoint the specific circumstances to which Jesus was referring in His public response. If 10:9 is restricted to those marriages formed under the special guidance of the Holy Spirit, who works within citizens of the kingdom, verses 11–12 apply only to disciples. If 10:9 refers to the institution of marriage in general, however, then these verses impose universal obligation. Jesus may have been addressing the practice of divorce with the purpose of remarriage

to another. He did not nullify the Mosaic permission to divorce but did disallow subsequent remarriage. Hence, according to the Markan text, one who divorces his or her spouse must remain single. (For Jesus' exception to this rule, see discussions on Matt. 5:32; 19:9. Another exception may be 1 Cor. 7:15.)

In Jewish culture, only the man traditionally was allowed to initiate divorce proceedings. By Jesus' day, however, Jewish women in Israel may have occasionally exercised the right of writing a bill of divorce and pronouncing the standard divorce formula. Jesus' instructions therefore concern a divorce initiated by either spouse: **And if a woman shall put away her husband, and be married to another, she committeth adultery** (v. 12). In this historical and geographical context, Jesus' pronouncements confirmed John the Baptist's bold denunciation of Herod Antipas and Herodias (see 6:17–19) and equally condemned them. The society of Mark's Roman audience allowed either husband or wife to file for legal divorce. Jesus forbade either husband or wife from divorcing in order to remarry. In verse 11, the words "against her" could also be translated "with her." In the first case, Jesus indicated adultery *against* the wife who is divorced; in the second, the man commits adultery *with* the new partner.

Pastors and counselors too often overlook the permission of divorce that Jesus recognized in this text and advise a woman to remain in an abusive marriage in which her health or life (and that of her children) are in danger. Divorce, according to Jesus, is clearly not in God's original plan for marriage. In a fallen world, however, it may have to occur as a recognition of human callousness and of the irredeemable nature of the marital breakdown. Only as a last resort should divorce be counseled or contemplated. Although Mark did not envisage a situation in which remarriage is legitimate, the text may leave open that possibility if the remarriage is not the purpose of the divorce in the first place. At any rate, Jesus' other teaching on divorce (see Matt. 5:32; 19:9) must be considered also.

Anglican and Episcopal churches around the world are debating the consequences of the consecration of an openly gay American bishop. Any such debate must consider the words of Jesus on marriage in Mark 10–12. Although the passage does not directly address the issue of homosexual bishops or gay/lesbian unions, marriage as monogamous, heterosexual, and permanent is the paradigm of Jesus, one that affirms the divinely intended order in creation (Gen. 1:27; 2:24; 5:2).

B. Teaching concerning Children (10:13–16)

10:13–16. Mark's narrative proceeds from the sanctity of marriage to the privileged status and example of children in the kingdom of God. The brief story in these verses constitutes an honor contest (see discussion on 2:1–12). When children were brought to Jesus for Him to touch (as a blessing, see v. 16), the disciples perceived some kind of threat to the apostolic company and the Master's ministry. They judged these children to be unworthy of Jesus' attention. The disciples issued a challenge: **his disciples rebuked those that brought them** (v. 13). The antecedent of "them" is not clear in some very early witnesses; later scribes apparently replaced "them" (see NASB, NIV) with "those that brought them." Jesus **was much displeased** (v. 14) with this action and came to the defense of the children. He answered with the riposte **Suffer** ("Permit," NASB) **the little children to come unto me, and forbid them not**. No one could answer His riposte in this story; He upheld the honor of the parents and/or children and shamed the disciples for their harshness. Jesus gave a specific reason for His command: **for of such is the kingdom of God**. The kingdom belongs to people who have the same utter sense of dependence upon God (**receive the kingdom of God as a little child**; v. 15) as children have upon their parents. The kingdom may be entered only by those who know they are helpless, without claim or merit.

This text is a complete endorsement by Jesus of the importance of ministry to children. Many in the church regard "real" ministry as involving adults. Since adults pay the bulk of tithes and offerings to support the church, children are often regarded as having little to contribute. The honored place of children in the kingdom of God means, however,

that they have much to teach the church about faith. Children are not just "the church of tomorrow"; they are of inestimable value to Jesus today and deserve every opportunity to be taught the ways of the kingdom. Parenting, teaching of children, and caregiving of youngsters should be valued as ways to "suffer the little children to come" to Jesus.

C. The Rich Young Ruler and Teaching on Wealth (10:17–31)

10:17–22. Discussion of wealth in two separate units comprise this section. First, Jesus engaged in discussion with one who **came ... running, and kneeled** (v. 17). Mark does not identify the man, but Luke 18:18 calls him a "ruler," meaning he was probably a member of an official council or court, and Matthew 19:20 says he was "young." The acquisition of eternal life was his concern (**Good Master, what shall I do that I may inherit eternal life?**). With Jesus' objection, **Why callest thou me good? there is none good but one, that is, God** (v. 18), He was not denying His own goodness but was forcing the man to recognize that his only hope was in total reliance on God, who alone can give eternal life. Jesus may also have been encouraging the young man to consider the full identity and nature of the one he was addressing.

In verse 19–21, Jesus did not invalidate the Decalogue (the Ten Commandments). Rather, by forcing the inquirer to choose between treasure on earth and **treasure in heaven** (v. 21), He defined the condition of eternal life to be a matter of the heart and its affections. **Come, take up the cross, and follow me** (elsewhere defined as faith in the New Testament) becomes the condition for eternal life; the fulfillment of the commands is its solid evidence in a person's life. The prohibition of fraud may have represented the tenth commandment (against covetousness). If so, Jesus here mentioned all six commandments that prohibit wrong actions and attitudes against one's fellowman (see Exod. 20:12–16; Deut. 5:16–21). **All these have I observed** (v. 20). The inquirer probably spoke sincerely, because for him keeping the law was a matter of external conformity. That the law also required inner obedience, which no one can fully satisfy, apparently escaped him completely. Paul spoke of having had a similar outlook before his conversion (see Phil. 3:6). The rich man's observance of the commandments **from my youth** (v. 20) is probably a reference to the age of thirteen, when a Jewish boy assumed personal responsibility for obeying the commandments.

Jesus' command to **sell whatsoever thou hast, and give to the poor** (v. 21) originated in His love for the seeker. It was obligatory upon the rich man only (**One thing thou lackest**). The injunction would apply to others only if their riches are the focus of their lives to the point that they would not part with them even if their souls were at stake. The story has a tragic outcome: the rich man was **sad** (v. 22) at Jesus' demands and **went away grieved** since he was unwilling to part with his many **possessions**. "Sad" and "grieved" are both strong terms to describe the man's response. The first term is used in Matthew 16:3 to describe an "overcast" (NIV) sky, and can be used of a gloomy appearance ("the man's face clouded at these words," TCNT Mark 10:22). The Greek word for "grieved" (*lypoumenos*) could be translated to be "in heaviness" (1 Peter 1:6) or to be "with a heavy heart" (NEB). The tragic decision to turn away reflected the man's greater love for his possessions than for eternal life ("treasure in heaven"; v. 21).

Money (and the comfort, possessions, and prestige that it can acquire) keeps many from coming to Christ initially or from continuing in the way of discipleship. A good test of one's attitude toward wealth is the degree to which one is actively sharing it to meet needs. Regular financial support of one's church and of outreach to the poor demonstrates that wealth has not gained mastery over a person, but that he or she has mastery over it.

10:23–25. The necessity and difficulty of coming to terms with riches was Jesus' point in these verse. The urgency of this matter is apparent in Jesus' repetition of the point: **How hardly** ("hard," NKJV) **shall they that have riches enter into the kingdom of God!** (v. 23; with variations in v. 24) and in His hyperbole, **It is easier for a camel to go through the eye of a needle, than for a rich man to enter into the kingdom of God** (v. 25). The camel was the largest animal found in the Holy Land. The vivid contrast between the largest animal and the smallest opening represents what, humanly speaking, is impossible.

10:26–27. Who then can be saved? (v. 26), exclaimed the disciples. Jesus' rejoinder was, **With men it is impossible, but not with God** (v. 27). Salvation is totally the work of God. Every attempt to enter the kingdom on the basis of human achievement or merit is futile. Apart from the grace of God, no one can be saved. Through Jesus' life and ministry, the kingdom of God broke into human history and can now reach even the most unreachable. As demonstrated in the story of the rich ruler (10:17–22), a willingness to be reached must be present, however, for the kingdom to manifest itself in an individual's life.

10:28–31. Peter's claim, **Lo, we have left all, and have followed thee** (v. 28), was not disputed by Jesus. It accurately expressed the sacrifice that the Twelve had made in behalf of their Lord. The claim, since it contains Mark's characteristic term of discipleship ("follow"; Greek *akoloutheō*), contains an indispensable condition for life in the kingdom of God. Jesus' list of sacrifices for His **sake, and the gospel's** (v. 29), whether **house, or brethren, or sisters, or father, or mother, or wife, or children, or lands**, is not exhaustive, nor is it in every case obligatory (Peter maintained his family after deciding to follow Jesus; see Mark 1:29–30). The call of Jesus upon a person might temporarily or permanently involve a separation from family, home, and present livelihood. In such cases, the disciple receives more than enough to make up for any loss incurred: **an hundredfold now in this time** (v. 30). With this provision, however, the disciple must be ready for **persecutions**. The life of discipleship is a combination of promise and persecution, blessing and suffering. God takes nothing from a Christian without making multiplied restoration in a new and glorious form.

The maxim with which Jesus concluded this section on wealth could be a warning against pride in sacrificial accomplishments (an attitude that Peter may have manifested, see v. 28). More likely, the saying speaks of the reversal of honorable status that the kingdom of God effects. Those who presently are honored and enjoy the benefits of this life (**first**; v. 31) will find themselves in a place of disadvantage (**last**). Jesus' followers now appear to have nothing, having forsaken whatever advantages they had in this present world to follow Jesus. They are **last**, but they shall be **first**.

D. Prophecy of Jesus' Death (10:32–34)

10:32–34. The importance of this brief section is the link it provides between the preceding discussion of discipleship and wealth (10:13–31) and the following discussion of discipleship and humble service (10:35–45). This last journey **in the way going up to Jerusalem** (v. 32) began in a city called Ephraim (see John 11:54) and took Jesus into Galilee (see Luke 17:11), south through Perea to Jericho (see Luke 18:35), then to Bethany (see Luke 19:29), and finally to Jerusalem (see Luke 19:41). Those who **followed**, probably pilgrims on their way to observe the Passover in Jerusalem, **were amazed** and **afraid**. The note of fearful wonder runs throughout Mark's gospel.

In the hearing of the Twelve, Jesus foretold His suffering, His cross, and His resurrection—a third forecast of His destiny (see 8:31; 9:9–13). The threefold prophecy shows that Jesus was in control of His fate and was not robbed of His honor by others. The word "crucify" does not occur in any of the passion prophecies in Mark's gospel, but the statement that Jesus would be handed over to Gentiles to be killed by them suggests crucifixion, since this was the usual means of Roman execution of non-Romans. The absolute control that Jesus had over His destiny is demonstrated by Mark's threefold witness to it: the Old Testament law maintains that "A matter must be established by the testimony of two or three witnesses" (Deut. 19:15 NIV). Jesus' death and resurrection were an incontrovertible element of God's plan for the salvation of humanity.

E. A Request of Two Brothers (10:35–45)

10:35–45. This passage and 9:33–37 both deal with true greatness, and both follow a prophecy of Jesus' suffering and death. Both also show how spiritually undiscerning the disciples were. The irony in this section is stunning: immediately after Jesus foretold His own gruesome fate, James and John (the sons of Zebedee; see 1:19; 3:17) came with a request to be co-rulers with Him in His **glory** (v. 37). Their request was not only audacious (**Master, we would that thou shouldest do for us whatsoever we shall desire**; v. 35); it also showed their complete unwillingness to hear and share Jesus' suffering (see 10:32–34). One might have expected the disciples to be more attuned to the necessity of self-denial by this time (see 8:34), but not so. The brothers' petition did not express confidence in Jesus' future triumph after suffering; it revealed their abject greed for positions of prestige and power (to sit at His **right hand** and **left hand**; v. 37) above others. Mark recorded that **when the ten heard it, they began to be much displeased** ("began to feel indignant," NASB) **with James and John** (v. 41), not merely because James and John were so unspiritual, but possibly because they desired the positions of prestige and power for themselves. Apparently, all the disciples sorely lacked even a basic grasp of true leadership in the kingdom.

To **drink of the cup that I drink of** (v. 38) is a Jewish expression that means to share someone's fate. In the Old Testament, the cup of wine was a common metaphor for God's wrath against human sin and rebellion (see Ps. 75:8; Isa. 51:17–23; Jer. 25:15–28; 49:12; 51:7). Accordingly, the cup Jesus had to drink refers to divine punishment of sins that He bore in place of sinful humankind (see 10:45; 14:36). In the words **be baptized with the baptism that I am baptized with**, the image of baptism is parallel to that of the cup; thus Jesus was referring to His suffering and death as a baptism (see Luke 12:50). The brothers were ambitious (**We can**; v. 39), and Jesus affirmed that they would share a fate similar to His. He could not promise them, however, that their request for positions of honor would be granted (**is not mine to give**; v. 40). Jesus would not usurp His Father's authority.

Here Jesus defined greatness, not in terms of power but in terms of service. His own life was the model for leadership that the disciples were to imitate; they were not to imitate those **accounted to rule over the Gentiles** (v. 42). In relationship to those who are led, such rulers **exercise lordship over them; and ... exercise authority upon them** (lit., "lord it down" and "use power down" on their subjects; v. 42). Contrary to such tyranny, Jesus said, **Whosoever will be great** (chiefest) **among you, shall be** (the) **minister** (v. 43) and **servant** ("slave," NIV) **of all** (v. 44). Since Jesus as the **Son of man came not to be ministered unto, but to minister** ("did not come to be served, but to serve," NKJV), **and to give his life a ransom for many** (v. 45), His followers should do likewise. The Christian leader serves others by tolerating others' imperfections, by readily forgiving and seeking forgiveness of others, by desiring and seeking to recognize others before being recognized, by using persuasion and not coercion, and by listening to criticism in a spirit of openness.

"Ransom" (Greek, *lytron*; v. 45) is a word that refers to the purchase of a slave's freedom. In this case, the ransom "for ['instead of,' 'in place of'] many" means freedom for the many from the guilt, penalty, and power of sin. One should not press the metaphor too far so that the Devil is seen as the one to whom the ransom is paid. The idea is that God's justice is fully satisfied by Jesus' willing sacrifice on behalf of sinful humanity. Verse 45 is a key verse in Mark's gospel. Jesus came to this world as a servant — indeed, the Servant — who would suffer and die for humanity's redemption, as Isaiah clearly prophesied (see Isa. 52:13 – 53:12).

F. Restoration of Bartimeus's Sight (10:46 – 52)

10:46 – 52. Jericho (v. 46) is a very ancient city located five miles west of the Jordan River and about fifteen miles northeast of Jerusalem, but down a decline of 3,700 feet to more than 1,000 below sea level. In Jesus' time, Old Testament Jericho was largely abandoned, but a new city, south of the old one, had been built by Herod the Great. In contrast to Mark (**as he went out of Jericho**) and Matthew ("as they departed from Jericho; Matt. 20:29), Luke reported that Jesus "was come nigh unto Jericho" (Luke

18:35). He may have been referring to the new Jericho, while Matthew and Mark may have meant the old city. The presence of a blind beggar just outside the city gates, on a road pilgrims followed on the way to Jerusalem, was a common sight in that day and is not unknown in Israel today.

This section could well be entitled "A Model Disciple" (Edwards, *The Gospel according to Mark*, p. 328) because **Bartimeus** (v. 46; of all those healed in this gospel, his is the only name that Mark recorded) exhibited the qualities of discipleship that none of the Twelve possessed. The story of the healing of this blind beggar is a climax to chapter ten and its numerous references to discipleship (10:10, 13, 23 – 24, 27 – 28, 32, 35 – 36, 46, 52). Three characteristics of Bartimaeus in this story make him an example of discipleship.

(1) The blind beggar had faith. Twice he cried out, **Thou Son of David, have mercy on me** (vv. 47 – 48). The request expressed the belief that, through Jesus, God shows His covenant love to His people. Bartimaeus was convinced that Jesus could save Him, and the beggar persisted in his urgent cries despite the opposition of the bystanders. **Many charged him that he should hold his peace** ("'Be quiet!' some of the people yelled at him," NLT), **but he cried the more a great deal** (v. 48). The beggar's example would have inspired Mark's Roman audience, who were undergoing opposition and ridicule to their worship and witness.

(2) Bartimaeus also had insight that other disciples have not displayed in this chapter. He confessed Jesus to be "the Son of David." By using this address, the beggar confessed Jesus as Messiah, He who fulfills God's ancient promises to David of the coming One who would sit on David's throne forever (see 2 Sam. 7:11 – 16; see Isa. 11:1 – 3; Jer. 23:5 – 6; Ezek. 34:23 – 24). Jesus affirmed to the beggar that **thy faith hath made thee whole** (lit., "has saved you"; Greek, *sōzō*). **And immediately he received his sight** (v. 52). The healing demonstrates Jesus' powerful status as God's anointed one. In this passage, the title **Lord** (ascribed to Jesus; v. 51) translates the Hebrew word *Rabboni*, which means literally "(my) teacher."

(3) Once he was "saved" from his blindness, Bartimaeus **followed Jesus in the way** (v. 52). In Mark, the verb "follow" characterizes true discipleship, and so the formerly blind man demonstrated that being a disciple of Jesus means to associate with Jesus continually (the verb is in the imperfect tense, "and was following") and publicly, even on a path that leads to suffering and death. The decision was intentional and final for Bartimaeus. Mark conveyed with vivid details the suspense and seriousness of the moment when Jesus **called** (v. 49): **And he, casting away his garment, rose, and came to Jesus** (v. 50).

VI. The Passion of Jesus (chaps. 11–15)

A. The Triumphal Entry (11:1–11)

11:1–11. The reader now enters Mark's passion narrative, all of which must be seen against the backdrop of this opening scene. In His triumphal entry into Jerusalem, Jesus received the public honor that is His due, despite the outrageously brutal suffering that lay ahead of Him. The theme of discipleship, so prominent in chapter 10, carries over into this new major section of the gospel. In the vicinity of Jericho, Bartimaeus had chosen to "[follow] Jesus in the way" (10:52), and following Jesus continues to be a theme in the environs (Bethphage and Bethany; v. 1) of Jerusalem. Discipleship involves both the fulfillment of Jesus' commands (vv. 1–7) and the worship of the One in whose person the kingdom of God is present (vv. 8–11).

11:1–7. Jesus arrived in **Jerusalem** (v. 1), and the rest of his ministry took place within the confines of the Holy City. The triumphal entry, which inaugurated Passion Week, was a deliberate messianic action, and the clue to its understanding is found in Zechariah 9:9 (quoted in Matt. 21:5; John 12:15). Jesus purposefully offered Himself as the Messiah, knowing that this would provoke Jewish leaders to take action against Him. **The mount of Olives** is directly east of Jerusalem, where it rises to a height of about 2,700 feet (some 200 feet higher than Mount Zion). Its summit commands a magnificent view of the city and especially of the temple. Olive trees still grow on this mount, and the garden of Gethsemane,

with its ancient olive trees, is at the base of its western slope.

The task of the two disciples whom Jesus **sendeth forth** (Greek, *apostellō*, related to the word "apostle"; v. 1) was to **find a colt tied, whereon never man sat; loose him, and bring him** (v. 2). The Greek word for "colt" can mean the young of any animal, but here it means the colt of a donkey. If questioned about their task, the disciples were simply to say that **the Lord hath need of** (v. 3) the colt. The task might seem mundane, but since unused animals (**whereon never man sat**) were regarded as especially suitable for religious purposes (see Num. 19:2; Deut. 21:3; 1 Sam. 6:7), the responsibility was sacred. The Lord's purpose of proclaiming the kingdom was served by the finding of the colt. Any commission from the Lord that a disciple undertakes is a sacred duty.

11:8–11. Jesus entered Jerusalem amid much fanfare and jubilation. As in the feast of Sukkoth, the Jewish festival when celebrants dwelt outside in "booths," the **branches off the trees** (v. 8) were used, but now for a new and higher purpose. The triumphal entry was the eschatological celebration of Sukkoth that Zechariah foretold (see Zech. 14:16–19). King Jesus' riding on the colt over branches and **garments** enacted Zechariah's prophecy, which said that the horses in Jerusalem would bear the inscription "HOLINESS UNTO THE LORD" (Zech. 14:20) as the Lord was recognized as King. Among those celebrating were **they that went before, and they that followed** (Greek, *akoloutheō*; v. 9), the latter verb designating disciples in Mark. The cry of **Hosanna** has the sense of "Save now." This word and the following line (**Blessed is he that cometh in the name of the Lord**) echo Psalm 118 (vv. 25–26), one of the Hallel ("Praise") psalms sung at Passover and especially fitting for this occasion. The disciples' worship of Jesus was a recognition that in Jesus is salvation, since He is the one who comes with the authority ("name") of Yahweh. All the promises to **David** (v. 10) for a perpetual **kingdom** are fulfilled in Him as Messiah (see Bartimaeus' confession in 10:47–48). Throughout Mark, faith is that trust which stems from a confession of Jesus' person and character. Faith without accurate knowledge, and belief without proper theology, are not to be found in the gospel. Faith never has exhaustive understanding, but it does have true understanding. The description of Jesus' victory parade ends with a foreshadow of activity in the temple soon to come: **when he had looked round about upon all things ... he went out unto Bethany with the twelve** (v. 11).

B. The Fig Tree and the Cleansing of the Temple (11:12–26)

11:12–26. This segment of the gospel of Mark, comprising two distinct pericopes, must be read as a whole. The entire construction is an example of a "Markan sandwich" (see discussion on 5:21–43) in which the story of the fig tree (vv. 12–14; 20–26) is a commentary on the cleansing of the temple (vv. 15–19).

11:12–14. The incident involving the fig tree was perhaps a parable of judgment, an acted prophecy in the vein of certain Old Testament prophecies of Isaiah, Jeremiah, Ezekiel, and Hosea. In the Old Testament, the **fig tree** (v. 13) represents Israel's relationship to God (see Jer. 8:13; 29:17; Hos. 9:10, 16; Joel 1:7; Mic. 7:1–6; Nah. 3:12). A tree full of leaves normally should have fruit, but this one was cursed because it had none. That the cleansing of the temple (11:15–19) is sandwiched between the two parts of the account of the fig tree (here and 11:20–26) may underscore the theme of judgment. If this suggestion is correct, Jesus' malediction against the tree (**No man eat fruit of thee hereafter for ever**; v. 14) was not a selfish, uncontrolled outburst because He was denied breakfast. It was a pronouncement against Israel's religious establishment, represented by the temple that He cleansed (see 11:15–19). When the disciples later saw "the fig tree dried up from the roots" (11:20), they beheld the corrupted condition of Israel that already existed. That condition would reach its culmination in the destruction of the temple in AD 70.

11:15–19. The temple (v. 15) refers to the court of the Gentiles, the only part of the temple in which Gentiles could worship God and gather for prayer (see v. 17). Pilgrims coming to the Passover feast needed animals that met the ritual requirements for sacrifice, and the vendors set up their animal pens and money tables in the court of the Gentiles. There they **sold and bought** (v. 15). That pilgrims needed their money changed into the local currency because the annual temple tax had to be paid in that currency explains the presence of **the tables of the money-changers**. The Mishnah required Tyrian currency for some offerings. **Doves** were required for the purification of women (see Lev. 12:6; Luke 2:22–24), the cleansing of those with certain skin diseases (see Lev. 14:22), and other purposes (see Lev. 15:14, 29). They were also the usual offering of the poor (see Lev. 5:7). Apparently, the temple area was being used as a shortcut between the city and the Mount of Olives. Jesus thus forbade anyone to **carry any vessel through the temple** (v. 16), a detail found only in Mark. Jesus acted against the commercialization of the temple and the careless use of it. It had become **a den of thieves** (v. 17) and was no longer of **all nations the house of prayer**. Isaiah 56:7 assured godly non-Jews that they would be allowed to worship God in the temple. By allowing the court of the Gentiles to become a noisy, smelly marketplace, the Jewish religious leaders were interfering with God's provision. The religious leaders' response to Jesus was hostile, but fearfully so: they **sought how they might destroy him** (v. 18).

11:20–26. Jesus had yet another purpose in the incident of the fig tree. The entire occurrence, according to this passage, is a fivefold lesson on believing prayer. (1) Any formidable task or obstacle (**this mountain**; v. 23) can be completely altered (**Be thou removed, and be thou cast into the sea**) through prayer. Jesus' language is metaphorical; although in the comparison, the mountain itself is addressed, the context makes clear that He was referring to prayer to God (vv. 22, 25–26). In other words, (2) anything that one desires (**what things soever ye desire**; v. 24) may be requested, but one must (3) **believe that ye receive them** (24) and (4) without **doubt** (v. 23) (5) one must **forgive** (v. 25–26) so that he or she may be forgiven by God. This condition is true whether the "mountain" for which one prays is the forgiveness (removal) of sins or not. Since some very early and reliable witnesses omit verse 26, it is relegated to the margin (NIV, NRSV) or is bracketed (NASB) in certain English translations. A later scribe probably added the verse to Mark's text to harmonize the passage with Matthew 6:15.

C. Concluding Controversies with Jewish Leaders (11:27–12:44)

11:27–12:44. Mark's passion narrative includes a series of controversies between Jesus and the religious leaders. These controversies include important teachings of Jesus, but they also show the reader how Jesus had maintained His honor despite numerous challenges to it. Ultimately, the opponents' attempts to trap Jesus in debate failed, and they had to resort to even more desperate measures to fulfill their murderous intent (see 11:18).

1. Jesus' Authority and the Question regarding John's Baptism (11:27–33)

11:27–33. Jesus skillfully turned the tables in His favor when He was questioned about His **authority** (v. 28). The Sanhedrin was asking why Jesus performed what appeared to be an official act if He possessed no official status. His riposte to the challenge (see discussion on 2:1–12) was to ask **the chief priests, and the scribes, and the elders** (v. 27) whether **The baptism of John** (v. 30) had a divine commission or a purely human impulse behind it. Mark provided the reader with insight into the aptness of this question, insight that Jesus Himself had. His opponents were now in jeopardy of falling into their own trap. Because they did not believe John, they could not maintain a divine origin for his prophetic work, but since the people counted John **a prophet** (v. 32), they dared not attribute a purely human inspiration to his prophetic activity. Hence, the opponents were stymied and could not give an answer. Jesus won the debate. Since they could not respond to His counterchallenge, Jesus maintained honor. He did not need to continue the debate: **Neither do I tell you by what authority I do these things** (v. 33).

2. The Parable of the Husbandmen (12:1–12)

12:1–12. The details of the parable of the husbandmen fit the social situation in Jewish Galilee in the first century. Large estates, owned by absentee landlords, were put in the hands of local peasants who cultivated the land as tenant farmers (**husbandmen**; v. 1). The key in interpreting this parable is given by the narrator: **for they knew that he had spoken the parable against them** (v. 12; i.e., the chief priests, scribes and elders of 11:27). The parable exposed the planned attempt on Jesus' life and God's judgment on the planners. The details of the parable correspond to the elements of the dispute between the religious leaders and Jesus. The correspondence is in three notable ways: (1) by this story, Jesus condemned those who maliciously sought His life, (2) He prophesied His own death at their hands (**they took him, and killed him, and cast him out of the vineyard**; v. 8), and (3) He identified Himself as the beloved **son** (v. 6), **the heir** (v. 7). One shows reverence or disregard for the owner by how one treats his agents, especially the son. A citation of Psalm 118:22–23 affirms Jesus' honor despite the infamy of His suffering: He is **The stone** (v. 10) that, although **rejected**, has the honored prominence of the cornerstone. Parallel versions of this parable are found in Matthew 21:33–46 and Luke 20:9–19.

3. The Question regarding Payment of Taxes to Caesar (12:13–17)

12:13–17. In an attempt to trap Jesus, some **Pharisees** (v. 13) and **Herodians** (for their alliance, see 3:6) questioned Jesus about the payment of a poll tax: **Is it lawful to give tribute to Caesar, or not?** (v. 14). Their question was out of **hypocrisy** (v. 15) but was clever. Would Jesus effectively maintain His honor in the face of a challenge that potentially could lead to a charge of either idolatry or rebellion against Rome? Jews in Judea were required to pay tribute money to the emperor. The tax was highly unpopular, and some Jews flatly refused to pay it, believing that payment was an admission of Roman right to rule.

Jesus effectively parried the challenge and took the offensive. The request for the **penny** (v. 15) itself slows the narrative and takes the momentum away from the questioners. The coin, a "denarius" (NASB), was a common coin worth the daily wage of a laborer (see Matt. 20:1–16). Jesus' question, **Whose is this image and superscription?** (v. 16), relates to the image of Tiberius Caesar on the obverse of the coin; the inscription read, "Tiberius Caesar Augustus, Son of the Divine Augustus." The inscription was considered by some to be a blasphemous claim of Caesar to deity. The opponents were now on the defensive, and their answer became the very basis for Jesus' concluding saying in this pronouncement story: **Render to Caesar the things that are Caesar's, and to God the things that are God's** (v. 17).

Jesus' honor was maintained: the opponents could not retort with a counterchallenge; they only **marvelled at him** (v. 17). Jesus recognized the state and its right to govern but affirmed the necessity of humans and human institutions to give God His due. The earthly power may not usurp God's sovereignty since the human ruler is only a created individual who bears His image (see Gen. 1:27). This story would have encouraged Mark's audience to remain loyal to the state insofar as it did not exceed its legitimate demands. (See Acts 4:29 and Dan. 3:16–18, where, for religious reasons, one must be ready to respectfully obey God rather than men, if the occasion clearly warrants it.)

4. The Question regarding the Resurrection (12:18–27)

12:18–27. The next controversy was initiated by **the Sadducees** (v. 18), a Jewish party that represented the wealthy and sophisticated classes. They were located largely in Jerusalem and made the temple and its administration their primary interest. Though they were small in number, in Jesus' time, they exerted powerful political and religious influence. The Sadducees said **there is no resurrection**. They denied the resurrection, accepted only the five books of Moses as authoritative, and flatly rejected the oral tradition. These beliefs set them against the Pharisees and common Jewish piety.

Of course, the question was a trap. For the Sadducees, one of the difficulties of the doctrine of the

resurrection arose in the light of levirate marriage. A dead brother who died without an heir could still perpetuate his lineage and inheritance through a living brother. The latter married the widow of the former, and children from their union were legally considered the offspring of the dead brother. The Sadducees correctly cited Genesis 38:8 and Deuteronomy 25:5 for this practice, but they implied that it made resurrection impossible. Seven brothers cannot have one wife, nor can one woman have seven husbands! **Whose wife shall she be of them? for the seven had her to wife** (v. 23), they asked. The questioners anticipated an answer that would be invalidated by their denial of resurrection since any solution would obviously be unjust to six of the brothers (polyandry was not practiced by the Jews).

The Sadducees' denial of the resurrection revealed an ignorance of **the scriptures** (and) **the power of God** (v. 24). Jesus affirmed that resurrection life is of a different order: people **neither marry, nor are given in marriage** (v. 25). Furthermore, the fact of the resurrection is established by the incident at the burning bush. There, God claimed to Moses, **I am the God of Abraham, and the God of Isaac, and the God of Jacob** (v. 26; see Exod. 3:6). Jesus took that to mean that **He is not the God of the dead, but the God of the living** (v. 27). But was that interpretation a misapplication of the original divine utterance in Exodus (**the book of Moses;** v. 26)? Did God mean that the patriarchs were alive in a resurrected state when He spoke with Moses, or did God mean that He was the God whom these Old Testament heroes worshiped as their own God before their deaths? The answer may be both/and: God's faithfulness to His covenant people continues even after their deaths. Once again Jesus' answer could not be contradicted, and His honor was maintained.

5. The Question regarding the Greatest Commandment (12:28–34)

12:28–34. In response to the question **one of the scribes**, Jesus identified, **the first commandment of all** (v. 28), the heart of the Old Testament law: **thou shalt love the Lord thy God** (v. 30). Love for God is a complete response of devotion, trust, and obedience in each dimension of the human person and the entirety (**all thy**) of each dimension. The reason for complete dedication is that **The Lord our God is one Lord** (v. 29). One loves God with the **heart** (v. 30; the seat of one's affections and will; "passion," MSG), with the **soul** (one's entire life activities and pursuits), the **understanding** (the intellect in a pursuit of truth, or mind; v. 33), and **strength** (all one's energies are focused on service to God; v. 30).

Jewish rabbis counted 613 individual statutes in the Law and attempted to differentiate between "heavy" (or "great") and "light" (or "little") commands. **Hear, O Israel** (v. 29), came to be known as "the Shema," named after the first word of Deuteronomy 6:4 in Hebrew, which means "hear." The Shema became the Jewish confession of faith, which was recited by pious Jews every morning and evening. To this day, it begins every synagogue service.

Jesus added, **And the second is like, namely this** ("And the second, like it, is this," NKJV), **Thou shalt love thy neighbour as thyself** (v. 31). Love for God and neighbor summarize all that the Old Testament law intended to accomplish for Israel (Jesus cited Deut. 6:4-5 and Lev. 19:18). The scribe therefore **answered discreetly** ("wisely," NIV; v. 34) in affirming that love for God and neighbor are **more than all whole burnt offerings and sacrifices** (v. 33). With such insight, he was **not far from the kingdom of God** (v. 34). Since a member of the opposition, a scribe (see 11:27), had come to recognize that Jesus spoke **the truth** (v. 32), Jesus' honor in the controversies was upheld. The series of five controversies from 11:27-12:34 begins with scribal opposition to Jesus and ends with scribal affirmation of Jesus. Mark commented, **And no man after that durst ask him any question** ("And after that, no one dared to ask him any more questions," NLT; v. 34). The controversies that occurred from this point on were at Jesus' own instigation.

6. The Question regarding the Son of David (12:35-37)

12:35-37. In recording Jesus' question, Mark did not intend to deny **that Christ is the Son of David**

(v. 35). After all, he endorsed both titles in his gospel (e.g., 8:29; 10:47-48). Rather, Jesus' question indicates that His Davidic ancestry does not mean that He is only a human descendant of the great king. Jesus is also Lord; David himself called him such by the inspiration of the Holy Spirit (in Ps. 110:1). Although in Greek, the word *kyrios* is used for both instances of "Lord" (**The LORD said to my Lord**; v. 36), the KJV capitalizes entirely the first instance and only the initial letter of the second. The KJV thus indicates the distinctions in the Hebrew text: "YHWH said to my *'ādōn*" (see Ps. 110:1). Thus, the Messiah was more than a descendant of David; He was David's Lord. Jesus' honor was once again affirmed: **And the common people heard him gladly** (v. 37).

7. The Scribes Are Denounced (12:38-40)

12:38-40. In this denunciation of **the scribes** (v. 38), Jesus redefined the honor code for His hearers. The characteristics of the scribes, which they held to be badges of honor, were actually badges of shame. Rather than being indicative of God's favor, they brought **greater damnation** (v. 40) since the scribes sought them out of wicked motives. The list results in the climactic **devour widows' houses, and for a pretence make long prayers**, two practices that revealed the scribes' self-interest, as did their **love** (v. 38) of going around **in long clothing** and other practices mentioned. The scribes wore long, white linen robes that were fringed and almost reached to the ground. The **chief seats in the synagogues** (v. 39) refer to the bench in front of the "ark" that contained the sacred scrolls. Those who sat there could be seen by all the worshipers in the synagogue. The hyperbolic "devour" (lit., "eat down"; "shamelessly cheat widows out of their property," NLT; v. 40) expresses abusive greed that preys on the powerless. Since the scribes were not paid a regular salary, they were dependent on the generosity of patrons for their livelihood. Such a system was open to abuses, and widows were especially vulnerable to exploitation. A spiritual leader may appear successful, and even win the admiring praise of people, but without love for God and neighbor (see 12:30-31), religious achievements are worthy of condemnation. They are deceptive, destructive, and dishonorable.

8. The Widow's Offering (12:41–44)

12:41–44. In immediate and stark contrast to the greed of the scribes, who exploited widows, is the widow who exhibited a selfless and sacrificial love for God in the giving of her offering. **The treasury** (v. 41) was located in the court of the women. Both men and women were allowed in this court, but women could go no farther into the temple buildings. It contained thirteen trumpet-shaped receptacles for the worshipers' contributions. The **poor widow** (v. 42) was a contrast not only to the scribes but also to the **rich** (v. 41). The rich members of the synagogue **cast in [out] of their abundance, but she ... cast in all that she had** (v. 44). They **cast in much** (v. 41); **she threw in two mites** (i.e., a farthing; "two very small copper coins," NIV v. 42). The *lepton* was the smallest coin then in circulation in the Holy Land, worth less than one hundredth of a denarius (the daily wage of a laborer). Jesus commended the widow for her sacrificial devotion to the work of the temple (she gave up **all her living**). The heart of the giver, not the amount of the gift, is what pleases God. What the world considers as spiritually successful is not necessarily what brings honor from God. This passage does not constitute a condemnation of wealth, but it does serve as a warning about the proper motivation in giving. It should cause twenty-first-century Christians in the West, all of whom are wealthy by the standards of the world, to question whether their giving is merely perfunctory or truly sacrificial.

D. The Olivet Discourse concerning the End of the Age (chap. 13)

13:1–37. The Olivet Discourse, as this chapter of Mark is commonly called, falls into five sections: (1) Jesus' prophecy of the destruction of the temple and the disciples' questions (vv. 1–4); (2) events surrounding the fall of Jerusalem and the destruction of the temple (vv. 5–23); (3) the coming of the Son of Man (vv. 24–27); (4) the lesson of the fig tree

(vv. 28–31); and (5) an exhortation to watchfulness (vv. 32–37).

The Olivet Discourse is obviously a prophetic text, but precisely which future events it describes is debated. Three views that surface are the following. (1) Jesus' discourse exclusively forecasts the end of history. This view is unlikely in light of the Markan context: Jesus was responding to the disciples' questions about the destruction of the temple, and certain events in the discourse are definitely localized (vv. 14–18). (2) The entire discourse is a description of events that took place in Israel during the war of AD 66–70. The coming of the Son of Man (vv. 24–27) refers to God's vindication of Jesus and the overthrow of the temple and the sacrificial system. An obstacle to this view is the gathering of the elect from the ends of the earth in verse 27—a strongly eschatological image. (3) Jesus prophesied both the fall of Jerusalem and the last days. According to this view, Jesus was describing events surrounding the fall of Jerusalem (vv. 5–23) and His second coming (vv. 24–37). Some who hold to this view see some of the events in verses 5–23 as happening in the future as well.

1. Jesus' Prophecy and the Disciples' Questions (13:1–4)

13:1–4. Mark's "Little Apocalypse" is a discourse of Jesus in response to the questions of certain disciples about the destruction of the magnificent edifices of the temple complex, for Jesus had told them, **there shall not be left one stone upon another, that shall not be thrown down** (v. 2). The **manner of stones** (v. 1), according to Josephus (*Antiquities* 15.11.3), was impressive: they were white, and some of them were 37 feet long, 12 feet high, and 18 feet wide. The remains of some of these stones may be seen today in the tunnel of the western wall and in the excavation of the temple stones at the corner of the western and southern walls beneath the temple mount. When Jesus was on **the mount of Olives** (v. 3), a vantage point east of the temple mount across the Kidron Valley, **Peter and James and John and Andrew asked Him privately** about the catastrophe to befall the temple. The four asked Jesus about the time (**when;** v. 4) and the accompanying circumstances (**the sign**) for the event.

2. Events Surrounding the Fall of Jerusalem and the Destruction of the Temple (13:5–23)

a. Hardships (13:5–8)

13:5–8. Jesus foretold the coming of false Christs who shall **deceive many** (v. 6) and issued the appropriate warning: **Take heed** (v. 5). It is clear from such words as "take heed" (both here and in 13:9), "But take ye heed" (13:23), "Take ye heed, watch and pray" (13:33), "Watch ye therefore" (13:35), and "Watch" (13:37) that one of the main purposes of the Olivet Discourse was to alert the disciples to the danger of deception. **Wars and rumours of wars** (v. 7) are not to cause excessive alarm. Such things have already been foreseen by God and do not indicate that the end is at hand. Jesus did not minimize the gravity of warfare, nor the misery it brings. Christians should always strive to be peacemakers. His point here was to fortify the disciples to endure during times of conflict since **the end** was still some distance in the future. **Nation** (v. 8) and **kingdom** shall fight one another, a reference to the ongoing conflict of the nations. **Earthquakes in divers** ("various," NKJV) **places ... famines and troubles** are only **the beginnings of sorrows**. The "earthquakes" (Greek, *seismoi*) may be a metaphor for the violent upheavals that nations experience during combat. The word has a figurative meaning in the Septuagint (see Isa. 29:6; Jer. 10:22; Ezek. 38:19). "Famines," tragic accompaniments to war throughout the ages, were to be expected in the coming war in Jerusalem. The word "troubles" does not appear in some Greek manuscripts; therefore it is absent from English translations such as the NASB, NIV, and NRSV. The woes that Jesus mentions are harbingers of agonies yet to come.

b. Mistreatment of the Disciples (13:9–13)

13:9. The company of Jesus' followers would experience the distress of the general populace but also the sufferings that came with their relationship to Christ. These troubles necessitated Jesus' command of watchfulness: **take heed to yourselves**. The troubles would be threefold: arrests on local charges, beatings, and formal hearings before imperial rulers. **They shall deliver you up to councils** probably refers to arraignments before local Jewish law courts (perhaps connected with synagogues). In Israel, the synagogue had the authority to adjudicate on matters relating to Jewish law and to administer corporal punishment (**ye shall be beaten**). Infraction of Jewish regulations was punishable by flogging, the maximum penalty being thirty-nine strokes with the whip (see 2 Cor. 11:23–24). Roman officials (**rulers**) might hear more serious charges; a Christian's case might even go to the emperor (**kings**), as Paul's case did (see Acts 25:10–11). A formidable legal proceeding has redeeming merit, Jesus said, when it is **for my sake, for a testimony against them** ("as a testimony to them," NRSV).

13:10. This verse has the character of a parenthesis since v. 9 and v. 11 seem to represent unbroken thought. Verse 10, then, could be an editorial comment by Mark or an insertion of a saying of Jesus that Mark imported from another context. In any case, the statement reminds the readers that they too have a responsibility to see that the good news **first be published** ("preached," NIV) **among all nations**. This has been the task of the church through world evangelism since the time of Pentecost. Many believe that its final completion will not come until the preaching of the gospel during the tribulation period.

13:11. Jesus did not forbid the disciples to prepare thoughtfully before legal proceedings when they would give testimony for Jesus. The single Greek word that the KJV translates **take no thought beforehand** is *promerimnaō* and has the sense of "do not worry beforehand" (Phillips). A. T. Robertson suggests "not to be stricken with fright beforehand" as an English equivalent. Since Jesus was referring not to preaching but to legal defenses, Robertson adds, "There is no excuse here for the lazy preacher who fails to prepare his sermon out of the mistaken reliance upon the Holy Spirit" (*Word Pictures in* the New Testament, vol. 1, *The Gospel according to Matthew, The Gospel according to Mark* [Nashville: Broadman, 1930], p. 376). The disciple may rely on the Holy Spirit to give the right word for the right occasion when he or she is called to account.

13:12–13. The opposition that Christ's followers can expect is seriously tragic since it may come even from one's own immediate family. One's **brother** (v. 12), **father**, and even one's **children** may **betray** one **to death**. Jesus stated that His disciples will **be hated of all men for my name's sake** (v. 13). To what does **endure unto the end** refer? It could be the culmination of the catastrophic events to which this section points. The expression **shall be saved** would thus have the sense of "shall be preserved from destruction" (Wuest). If "unto the end" has the sense of "forever" or "for as long as it takes," however, eschatological salvation may be in view here.

Christian discipleship does not mean immunity from the world's suffering. Warfare, political turmoil, and economic hardship affect Christians just as they do all people. Furthermore, God's people are subject to suffering for His name's sake. This section of the Olivet Discourse is a serious warning for believers of any age to "take heed to yourselves" (13:9). In the midst of sorrows and opposition, however, the mandate still stands to preach the gospel "among all nations" (13:10). The Holy Spirit assists God's people in this task (see 13:11).

c. The Abomination of Desolation (13:14–23)

13:14. Perhaps no single image in Mark 13 is as controversial as **the abomination of desolation**. The translation of the phrase poses problems enough. Other renderings of the Greek *to bdelygma tēs erēmōseōs* are "the desolating sacrilege" (NRSV), "the abomination that causes desolation" (NIV), "the sacrilegious object that causes desecration" (NLT). The phrase comes from **Daniel the prophet** (see Dan. 9:27; 11:31; 12:11 Septuagint). The image originally referred to Antiochus Epiphanes who, by installing a statue in the temple and offering swine's flesh on the altar, profaned the temple. In AD 70, the temple was overrun by the Romans, whose standards were

placed over the ruined temple. This abomination reached its ultimate heinousness for the Jew when, after the revolt of AD 135, the Romans placed Zeus's statue in a shrine dedicated to him on the site of the Jewish temple that had been destroyed some sixty-five years earlier. Later, the site was further profaned in the Jewish mind by the erection of the Moslem shrine, the Dome of the Rock, on this site in AD 638.

At this point in the narrative, Mark interjected an editorial comment: (**let him that readeth understand**). The KJV's parentheses note the editorial nature of the phrase. Mark may have intended for his readers to consider some phenomenon with which they were familiar, to give evidence that the tragic events of this verse were already unfolding. Luke understood the "desolation" to be near whenever Jerusalem was surrounded by Roman armies (see Luke 21:20). Luke's paraphrase of Mark's expression is strong evidence that Jesus was referring to the events of AD 66–70, and Mark wanted his readers not to miss the reference. Though Jesus' prophesied in this verse has a first-century reference, it also provides an eschatological warning of an even greater "desolation" by the Antichrist in the future.

The command **let them that be in Judaea flee to the mountains** indicates that the abomination would be in Jerusalem. The subsequent instructions that Jesus gave are obviously intended for residents of Israel. The immediate referent of the prophecy was a warning to first-century believers to flee Jerusalem before the destruction of the temple, but many believe it also provides a warning for those who will be living there in the end times. Jesus' warnings thus foreshadow a final fulfillment just prior to His second advent.

13:15–18. The **housetop** (v. 15) refers to the living and sleeping areas atop typical first-century Jewish homes in the area. The flat roof was also used for midday prayer. Escape from the coming disaster could only be made if one left in extreme haste; individuals were not even to go down into the **house** to retrieve anything. Everyday business activity—the one **in the field** (v. 16) represents a typical worker in the agrarian economy of Israel—should be abandoned. One was not to go back even for the outer coat that had been cast aside during working hours. **Them that are with child** (v. 17) represents anyone forced to flee under especially difficult circumstances, which might cause them to perish. **Winter** (v. 18) would be a difficult time for anyone in Israel, particularly pregnant or nursing women. The season would bring discomforting rain and cold. Rivers and fords would be impassable, making escape perilous, if not impossible.

13:19-20. The **affliction** (v. 19) of the Jewish War of AD 66-70 would bring with it unprecedented catastrophe. In fine prophetic fashion, Jesus employed hyperbole to emphasize the severity of the woes ahead: **such as was not from the beginning of the creation**. One could argue that distress of greater intensity and duration has been seen in human history. From the perspective of the hearers, however, Jesus' words proved true. A similar hyperbolic expression is that **no flesh should be saved** (v. 20). For the sake of those **whom he hath chosen**, the Lord cut short the period of suffering. The notions of an **elect** and of a predetermined amount of time for the affliction (**he hath shortened the days**) should be appreciated for their intended function in the discourse. Those who faced the grim prospect of seeing their homeland devastated could take courage from knowing that God was watching out for them as His people and that an end of suffering lay beyond the devastation.

13:21-23. Jesus' prophecy of the catastrophe to come to Judea concluded as it began (see 13:5-6), with a warning about **false Christs and false prophets** (v. 22). The same command **But take ye heed** (v. 23) is reiterated. The intention of the pretenders would be to **seduce** ("to lead astray," NRSV; v. 22) even those who are the **elect**, if that were possible (arguably it is not!). To be forewarned is to be forearmed, and the disciples now had no excuse to be deceived by bogus messiahs or prophets in the days ahead when they longed for deliverance from the distress that Jesus had prophesied.

Although the first part of the discourse relates specifically to the period leading up to the devastation of the temple and the city (ca. AD 66-70), its warnings also speak in at least four ways to Christians who live in the time after this event. (1) The believer is not immune from the fallout of political and military turbulence in the world. Troubles of this kind should not cause the believer to think that God has failed, or that he or she has sinned and lost God's favor. A certain amount of human suffering is common to all people. For the Christian, God is powerfully present to help and guide during times of distress. (2) Vigilance is needed so that one does not succumb to the seductions of false teachers. Jesus' words throughout Mark's gospel are themselves a solid foundation for Christian stability. (3) The Holy Spirit gives the words to all who are called on to give a testimony for their Lord before unbelievers. Preparation in the way of study, knowing an outline of the facts of the gospel, or the rehearsal of one's personal conversion experience are not forbidden by Jesus. Worry about the outcome of witnessing for Christ is forbidden, however. (4) Every Christian must determine to live a life of endurance. Persecution will come, but Jesus guarantees that the Lord Himself has determined our destiny for the sake of the elect.

3. The Coming of the Son of Man (13:24-27)

13:24-25. In those days (v. 24) must not be taken as a reference to the time under discussion in the immediately preceding section (13:14-23). The prepositional phrase is a common Old Testament expression having to do with the end time (see Jer. 3:16, 18; 31:29; 33:15-16; Joel 3:1; Zech. 8:23). Jesus identified the time more precisely as **after that tribulation** (i.e., "after those horrible days end" [NLT], the days of the battle for Jerusalem). Jesus, in genuine prophetic fashion, now blended the near view with the far view. That is, the events near to the prophet's time blend with events that are distant from his perspective. The upheavals of the siege of Jerusalem are similar, albeit on a smaller scale, to the cosmic upheavals that the coming of the Son of Man will inaugurate. The events at the end of history will come after an unspecified amount of time.

The language that Jesus used to describe His second coming reflects the poetry and symbolism of

Old Testament apocalyptic language. The intensity of the eschatological events is conveyed through two synonymously parallel constructions (typical of Hebrew poetry):

First Parallelism (v. 24)

(a) **the sun shall be darkened,**
(b) **and the moon shall not give her light,**

Second Parallelism (v. 25)

(a) **and the stars of heaven shall fall,**
(b) **and the powers that are in heaven shall be shaken.**

The failure and disintegration of heavenly bodies are common in Old Testament language regarding the Day of the Lord. When God acts in judgment, both historically and eschatologically, life's predictability and routine comes to an end. Sin is requited; righteousness is vindicated (see Isa. 13:10; 24:21–23; 34:4; Ezek. 32:7–8; Joel 2:10, 31; 3:15; Amos 8:9; see Rev. 6:12–14; 8:12). Jesus' words are not to be taken literally, but as a poetic description of the power, scope, and finality of the judgment that He brings at His coming.

"The powers" (v. 25) could designate angelic beings (good and/or evil) since "stars" (with which "powers" is synonymous in this passage) in ancient Jewish literature sometimes signify angels (see Rev. 1:20; 9:1; 12:4). The stars/powers, however, may simply represent planetary or stellar objects that will be transformed or destroyed. These conditions may also refer to severe judgments on the earth that will shake the planet and thus appear to be shaking the heavens.

13:26–27. Although the expression **the Son of man** (v. 26) can point to a human being (see Ezek. 2:1), the details surrounding the term in Mark unmistakably recall the description of "one like the Son of man" in Daniel 7:13–14: he comes with **the clouds,** attended by **glory.** The Son of Man in Mark is given universal right of judgment in that He dispatches **his angels** (to) **gather together his elect** (v. 27) from every place they inhabit (hyperbolically **from the uttermost part of the earth to the uttermost part of heaven**). Daniel's Son of Man likewise has "an everlasting dominion" (Dan. 7:14) and represents His people in exercising sovereignty (see Dan. 7:22). In both cases, "the Son of man" refers to Jesus Christ, who will return in power and great glory to gather His own.

4. The Lesson of the Fig Tree (13:28–31)

13:28–31. As Jesus often did, here he used a common everyday image (**the fig tree;** v. 28) as an illustration of a spiritual reality. A sure sign that **summer** is close at hand is the profusion of **leaves** from **tender** shoots or branches on the tree. Certain events are also the sign of the nearness of a new season — in this case, a season that will involve upheaval in the present cosmic order for judgment and salvation. Four questions arise upon which the interpretation of this **parable** hinge: (1) What are **these things** (v. 29), and (2) what is **it** that will be **nigh** upon their occurrence? (3) What is **this generation** (v. 30), and (4) what are **all these things** whose accomplishment must precede its passing?

This part of the prophecy points to the distant eschatological future since it involves the triumphal return of Jesus Christ, which did not occur in AD 70. Remember, Jesus was answering questions regarding two things: (1) the destruction of the temple and (2) the sign of His second coming. In 13:24, Jesus used the word "But" (Greek, *alla*) to designate a contrast between the appearance of false messiahs and the coming of the true messiah in "that day" ("those days," NASB; 13:32).

The reference to the "fig tree" is for illustrative purposes. It is not likely a symbolic reference to Israel, as some have claimed. The cross-reference in Luke 21:29 refers to "the fig tree, and all the trees," indicating that Jesus was simply saying that one can determine the seasons by the budding of the trees. So it is that one can determine the prophetic time by the "signs" of the times. **See these things come to pass** (v. 29) refers to the events of the tribulation (see 13:24). **This generation** (v. 30) refers to the generation of the tribulation period, which will live to "see these things come to pass" (v. 29). There is no way this can be limited to the generation of Jesus' time, since He did not (1) come in power and great glory (see 13:26), (2) gather his elect (see 13:27), (3) come at a time when no one expected him (see 13:32).

5. Exhortation to Watchfulness (13:32–37)

13:32. But of that day and that hour knoweth no man, no, not the angels which are in heaven, neither the Son, but the Father is an unusual expression, found only in Mark, because it seems to rob Jesus of the omniscience that one associates with this figure who acts and speaks with the authority of God Himself. The saying ought to be understood as an indication that in the divine economy, Jesus Christ the Son is subordinate to the will and purpose of His Father. This was part of Jesus' voluntary self-emptying. He chose not to use some of His divine attributes at certain times, so that He could function fully as a man. The certainty with which He spoke of His return in Revelation 22:20 indicates that the risen, glorified Christ fully knows the time of His return. The verse emphasizes that the time of Jesus' coming in power and glory (see 13:24–27) is completely unknown to human reckoning. A map of the future would be a hindrance, not a help, to faith. Certain signs have been given, but not for the purpose of making detailed, sequential prophecy. "That day" is an Old Testament expression for the day of the Lord's appearance (see Amos 8:3, 9, 13; 9:11; Mic. 4:6; 5:10; 7:11). Here it refers specifically to the coming of the Son of Man (see 13:26). The "day" and "hour" refer to the coming of the Son of Man in glory (see 13:24–27), the time "when the master of the house cometh" (13:35).

13:33–37. Here Jesus cited a familiar occurrence in Israel: the owner of an estate would leave on business for an undisclosed period of time and delegate responsibilities to his slaves during his absence. Lack of diligence in their assigned tasks would result in the master's displeasure when he suddenly returned, which could be **at even, or at midnight, or at the cockcrowing, or in the morning** (the four watches of the night used by the Romans; v. 35). The obvious meaning is that Jesus could return at any time.

Three distinct commands for Jesus' servants appear in this passage: **Take ye heed** (Greek, *blepete*; "stay alert," NLT), **watch** (*agrypneite*; "keep awake," ESV) **and pray** (v. 33). The final admonition is widely attested in the manuscripts and witnesses. Since it is missing in some witnesses (including some early Latin manuscripts), however, the term is omitted in several recent English translations (e.g., ESV, NASB, NIV, NLT). The emphasis in these commands reinforces the concept of the imminent coming of Christ. Believers are told to watch for the coming of the Lord, who could potentially return at any time (see discussion on Matt. 24:40–42).

All too often Christians become obsessed with fixing the dates for the events surrounding Jesus' second coming. Jesus Himself said that no one knows the time, so we can be sure that any calculation that claims to have figured out the precise time is erroneous. Of far greater importance than date-setting is the necessity of watchfulness. Since His followers cannot know the precise time of His return, the proper conduct in anticipation of the Lord's return is wakeful alertness. Laziness and inattentiveness to responsibilities at hand are how *not* to wait for Jesus' coming!

E. The Anointing of Jesus (14:1–11)

14:1–11. The story of Jesus' anointing is a stunning study in contrasts: the extravagance of devotion for Jesus that the anonymous woman displayed is offset by the revulsion that the bystanders felt for what they believed was a monumental squandering of an invaluable commodity. Between the two parties in this picture of devotion and the lack of it is Jesus. He was honored by the woman in the anointing, and He honored her in His commendation of her. Once again Mark portrayed Jesus as a person of honor. Not only was He given an honorable anointing with ointment of almost incalculable worth, but He associated the anointing with His burial. The prediction of His death reveals that He willingly underwent it for purposes that have already been mentioned.

14:1–2. The chief priests and the scribes (v. 1) determined to seize Jesus before **the feast of the**

passover, and of unleavened bread. The leaders feared **an uproar of the people** (v. 2) if their murderous plot was effected during the holy days. The Jewish festival of Passover commemorates the time when the angel of the Lord passed over the homes of the Hebrews rather than killing their firstborn sons as He did in the Egyptian homes (see Exod. 12:13, 23, 27). The lambs or kids used in the feast were killed on the fourteenth of Nisan (March-April), and the meal was eaten the same evening between sundown and midnight. Since the Jewish day began at sundown, the Passover feast took place on the fifteenth of Nisan. The Feast of Unleavened Bread followed Passover and lasted seven days (see Exod. 12:15–20; 23:15; 34:18; Deut. 16:1–8).

14:3. In Bethany, Jesus **sat at meat**. The usual posture for eating a banquet meal was to recline. **Ointment of spikenard** was an unguent made from an herb that was imported from northern India. It was popular among the Hebrews and Romans in the anointing of the dead. Balms like the one in this story were preserved most effectively in **an alabaster box** ("jar," NRSV) since the container contributed to an aging process that made the ointments of great value after a number of years. Mark thus said that the oil was **very precious** ("very costly perfume, pure oil of nard," NEB).

14:4–5. The violence of the bystanders' reaction was in inverse proportion to the devotion of the woman. Her devotion was exorbitant: the value of the ointment she poured on Jesus was **more than three hundred pence** (v. 5). The monetary unit denoted is the denarius, a day's wage for a common laborer (see Matt. 20:1–15). Almost a year's pay was invested in this expression of love for Jesus! The bystanders' response was **indignation** (v. 4). In other words, **they murmured against her** (v. 5).

14:6–9. The protesters seem to have had a valid criticism: the ointment could have been sold, and the proceeds of the sale could have been given to the poor. Instead, the oil was used up in one action that apparently did no one any good. On the contrary, said Jesus. The pouring was **a good work on me** (v. 6). The expense of the ointment spoke of the honor Jesus would have even in death. The woman's work was of the utmost importance since the opportunity to anoint Jesus before burial was rare and fleeting. Jesus certainly advocates care of the poor (**whensoever ye will ye may do them good**; v. 7), but never to the extent that His honor is overlooked. Since what the woman had done has become **a memorial of her** (v. 9), she is honored as she honored Jesus.

Costly expressions of devotion to Jesus still draw responses of contempt and derision. Those who labor in ministries or missions in which responses to the gospel are few and far between are sometimes seen as wasting their time and resources. Christian work with the derelict and despondent is viewed by many as poor stewardship. Jesus could be better served in more strategic and important ministries, according to the critics. In this story, however, Jesus affirmed the one who gave extravagantly and "wastefully" for Him. Good stewardship should always be a consideration, but that may involve a costly expression of devotion that others may disapprove.

14:10–11. The treachery of **Judas** (v. 10) is another contrast to the devotion of the woman in Simon's house. **The chief priests** offered him **money** (v. 11), but not nearly as much as the 300 denarii that the spikenard would have brought had it been sold. The lack of specificity by Mark regarding the betrayal price shows that the repudiation of Jesus ultimately brings nothing of value to the one who rejects Him (see 8:36–37).

F. The Arrest, Trial, and Death of Jesus (14:12–15:47)

1. Jesus and the Disciples Celebrate Passover (14:12–17)

14:12–17. This passage sets the scene for the climactic events that occurred at the Passover table. **The first day of unleavened bread** would ordinarily mean the fifteenth of Nisan, the day after Passover. However, the added phrase, **when they killed the passover**, makes it clear that the fourteenth of Nisan is meant because Passover lambs were killed on that day (see Exod. 12:6). The entire eight-day celebration was sometimes referred to as the Feast of Unleavened Bread, and there is evidence that the fourteenth of Nisan may have been loosely referred to as the "first day of unleavened bread."

The preparations for the feast were carried out by two disciples according to Jesus' prearrangement of **a large upper room furnished and prepared** (v. 15). The disciples' encounter with **a man bearing a pitcher of water** (v. 13) is unusual in itself (women fetched the household water from the well or spring) but even more remarkable because Jesus knew that the disciples would encounter the man in a crowded city teeming with pilgrims. Jesus' honor continues to be upheld in this section: He is a person of divine foresight.

The question **Where is the guestchamber ...?** (v. 14) infers the Jewish custom that anyone in Jerusalem who had a room available would give it upon request to a pilgrim to celebrate the Passover. It appears that Jesus had made previous arrangements with the owner of the house. To **make ready** (v. 15) would have included preparation of food for the meal: unleavened bread, wine, bitter herbs, sauce, and the lamb. **And in the evening he cometh with the twelve** (v. 17) is full of suspense and tension in light of the plots against Jesus that were being formed.

2. The Last Supper (14:18–26)

14:18–21. They sat and did eat the Passover meal (v. 18). Originally, the meal was eaten standing (Exod. 12:11), but in Jesus' time, it was customary to eat it while reclining. **Verily I say unto you**. The disciples finally comprehended the grim reality of Jesus' prophecy of His death (unlike earlier prophesies that were met with miscomprehension; see 8:32; 9:10; 10:35–45). Jesus stated that **One of you which eateth with me shall betray me**. Although they are **sorrowful** (v. 19), their concern was not so much for the fate awaiting Jesus as it was for their own self-defense: **one by one** the Twelve asked, **Is it I? and another said, Is it I?** Jesus affirmed that the betrayer was indeed of their number, one **that dippeth with me in the dish** (v. 20). The predetermined

plan of God required that **The Son of man indeed goeth** (i.e., to death)**, as it is written of him** (v. 21); the Scripture prophesies such. Jesus no doubt had the suffering Servant passage of Isaiah 53 in mind. Despite the Son's predestined fate, however, the delivery of Him was not something forced upon the individual who would betray Him. Verse 21, reveals the mysterious mixture of God's predestined will that cannot fail to be accomplished and the free choice of individuals. In their freedom, they ultimately serve the purposes of the Lord of history. **Woe to that man by whom the Son of man is betrayed!**

During the first course of the Passover meal, the participants all shared from a common bowl that contained a mixture of bitter herbs and stewed fruit. Jesus did not specifically identify the betrayer but merely affirmed three times (vv. 18, 20, 21) that it was one of the Twelve. His threefold affirmation corresponds to the certainty of a threefold witness in Jewish legal contexts (see Deut. 17:6; 19:15). Jesus affirmed the veracity of His prophecy also by the formula, "Verily I say unto you" (v. 18). The foreknowledge of Jesus contrasts with the ignorance of the disciples regarding the traitor's identity.

14:22–26. The New Testament gives four accounts of the Lord's Supper (Matt. 26:26–28; Mark 14:22–24; Luke 22:19–20; 1 Cor. 11:23–25). Matthew's account is very much like Mark's, while Luke's and Paul's have similarities. All the accounts include the taking of the bread, the thanksgiving or blessing, the breaking of the bread, the saying "this is my body," the taking of the cup, and the explanation of the relation of blood to the covenant. Only Paul and Luke recorded Jesus' command to continue to celebrate the Supper. The **bread** (v. 22) that Jesus distributed during the meal may represent the *afikoman* of the Passover celebration—the bread that comes after the meal proper and that represents the Passover lamb's flesh. Jesus thus inaugurated a new Passover, a deliverance for the entire world, by His own flesh. **Take, eat: this is my body** constitutes a metaphor: the bread represents Jesus' body.

Similarly, **the cup** (v. 23) represents **my blood of the new testament** (v. 24). In the Jewish Passover

Seder, the cup of Elijah follows the *afikoman*. That may be the cup for which Jesus gave **thanks** (v. 23) and distributed to the Twelve. The word "Eucharist" is derived from the Greek term that is here translated "had given thanks." Some manuscripts do not have the word "new" (*kainos*), but the meaning is clear even without it: Jesus' blood ratified the new covenant and put it into effect (see Heb. 9:15-22). The redemptive value of the blood is evident since it is that **which is shed for many** (v. 24). The word "for" (Greek, *hyper*) has the idea of substitution. Jesus foretold His own death and claimed that it has atoning significance. Any interpretation of Jesus' death must begin here with His own statement regarding its significance (see Mark 10:45).

There is finality in Jesus' assertion that the meal was His last (**I will drink no more of the fruit of the vine**; v. 25), but it is counterbalanced with the affirmation of a future vindication and victory on **that day that I drink it new in the kingdom of God**. The church's own celebration of the Lord's Supper from the earliest time has included this same affirmation of the glorious future that was opened by Jesus' death (see 1 Cor. 11:26). The **hymn** (v. 26) that Jesus and His disciples sang before going out to **the mount of Olives** may have been the second part of the Hallel (Psalms 115-118).

3. Peter's Denial Foretold (14:27-31)

14:27-31. The abandonment of Jesus by His followers now shifted from the one who would betray Him (see 14:18) to the wholesale scattering of the entire flock (**the sheep shall be scattered**; v. 27). Jesus spoke as a prophet in this passage (probably while en route to the Mount of Olives), thus further highlighting that His death was not a deserved result of dishonorable conduct. Rather, it was part of the foreordained will of God and undeserved. The words of prophecy are a quotation of Zechariah 13:7. At the same time, Jesus prophesied, **after that I am risen, I will go before you into Galilee**.

Peter then spoke up, claiming, **Although all shall be offended** (see v. 27), **yet will not I** (v. 29). The verb "be offended" (Greek, *skandalizō*) is related to

the word for bait in a trap. The verb can have the sense of "to entrap," "to trip up," "to fall away." Jesus' response to this boast was, **in this night, before the cock** ("rooster," NKJV) **crow twice, thou shalt deny me thrice** (v. 30). Protesting, Peter vowed in the strongest terms possible that he would not deny Jesus: the phrase **more vehemently** ("emphatically," NIV; v. 31) is the double-negative *ou mē* paired with the verb: **I will not deny thee in any wise**. Peter's rejection of the possibility of denying Jesus was picked up by all the Twelve at this point (**Likewise also said they all**).

Peter's exhibited brave intentions here, but they outran his capacities for loyalty and faithfulness in the face of danger. Whenever the Christian becomes confident in his or her own strength and refuses to face one's own weakness and inclinations to sin, a catastrophe looms ahead. Perhaps Peter's threefold denial might have been avoided if he had heeded Jesus' prophecy as a warning of his own weakness.

4. In the Garden of Gethsemane (14:32-52)

14:32-34. Jesus and the disciples reached their destination: the lower slopes of the Mount of Olives, specifically, **a place which was named Gethsemane** (v. 32). This was one of Jesus' favorite places (see Luke 22:39; John 18:2). The name is Hebrew and means "oil press," that is, a place for squeezing the oil from olives. East of the old city of Jerusalem, one can still see extremely old olive trees in this place that may be described as "a garden" (John 18:1), "a grove of olive trees" (John 18:1 NLT), or an orchard. Jesus intended to **pray** in the solitude of the place and separated Himself from the larger company of disciples, taking only **Peter and James and John** (v. 33) with Him. These three were to **tarry ye here, and watch** (v. 34), instructions that probably involved serious and concentrated prayer for Jesus in His time of need. The word "watch" has the idea of alert vigilance (see Mark 13:34-35, 37) in the face of impending danger or stress. Mark's descriptions of Jesus signify His extreme anguish before the events that He knew awaited Him. He **began to be sore amazed, and to be very heavy** ("And he began to feel terror and anguish," NJB; v. 33), and Jesus' soul was **exceeding sorrowful** (v. 34). The adverbial **unto death** could indicate either the basis of Jesus' overwhelming dread or the intensity of His distress (see "my heart is ready to break with grief," REB).

14:35. Mark emphasized that private prayer was Jesus' practice during critical points of His life (1:35–39; 6:46), and He continued that habit at this most extreme crisis. Mark further highlighted the duress of the occasion in that Jesus **fell on the ground** (v. 35) and then **prayed that ... the hour might pass from him**.

14:36. Mark recorded the very words of Jesus' prayer, indicating their importance as a model for His followers who face crises in their lives of discipleship. Four elements of Jesus' crisis prayer are evident.

(1) He addressed God as **Abba** (v. 36). (Mark provided his Greek readers with the translation, **Father**, of the Aramaic word). This term of familiar endearment is equivalent to "Daddy" or "Dad." Little children as well as grown sons and daughters used it to address their fathers. Jesus' use of it in this anguished situation shows His union with the Father and His willingness to do the will of God. As Christ's disciples, believers also have an intimate relationship with God, by which they can and should cry in prayer, "Abba, Father" (see Rom. 8:15; Gal. 4:6).

(2) Jesus recognized God's omnipotence when He exclaimed, **all things are possible unto thee** (v. 36). Biblical affirmations of God's power to accomplish anything exclude those absurdities that the skeptic often raises, such as, "Can God make a stone so big that He can't lift it?" God's power is consistent with His wisdom and nature. Ludicrous phenomena are excluded by the reality of God and of the universe that He has created. A believer's prayer, like that of Jesus, must be founded on the recognition of God's limitless might in order for it to qualify as a prayer of faith to a loving Father.

(3) An urgent and agonized plea, **take away this cup from me** (v. 36), followed Jesus' recognition of God's power to do anything that might be asked of Him. The word "cup" (Greek, *potērion*) echoes 10:38–39 (where the cup represents Christ's bear-

ing the divine punishment of sins on behalf of others) and 14:23–24 (where the cup represents Christ's blood). The Son prayed to be spared the sufferings that lay ahead. His followers also may pray to be spared trials, temptations, and persecutions. The granting of such a request, however, is not guaranteed. The fourth element of Jesus' crisis prayer makes that clear.

(4) The proviso for Jesus' prayer and for any prayer of His followers must be **nevertheless not what I will, but what thou wilt** (v. 36). One must not presume that one will receive an answer to prayer as it has been prayed. Although God is able to do everything, He may not will to do what one has asked. Our individual wills must thus bend to His. If Jesus prayed with subordination of His will to that of His Father, how much more must one pray in this fashion? God always answers prayers, but not always in the way that one would like.

14:37–42. The perfect example of what prayer should *not* be like is Peter's and the other disciples' sleepy prayerlessness. Rather than **watch** (v. 37) but **one hour**, Peter and the disciples failed three times (see v. 41) to fulfill Jesus' instruction to **Watch ye and pray, lest ye enter into temptation** (v. 38). The threefold failure emphasizes the laxity of the Twelve in the face of danger and foreshadows Peter's imminent threefold denial (see 14:66–72). The present tense of the two verbs lends them special emphasis in this context ("Be constantly watching and praying," Wuest).

Jesus' word "temptation" (v. 38) refers not just to an enticement to evil but also to the testing that any challenge to faith brings. Here the temptation was to be unfaithful in face of the threatening circumstances confronting the disciples. The failure to meet the test is to sin, to fall into temptation (see 1 Tim. 6:9). The testing of the disciples, and especially Peter, in this context becomes a lesson on temptation for the disciple today. The testing may come by way of an attraction to sin, persecution for one's testimony to Christ, illness, depression, fatigue, financial hardship, loss of a loved one, or demands of work and life's responsibilities. Regardless of its source, the time to prepare for challenges is not after they have sprung and are overwhelming, but beforehand. The strength and direction that God grants through vigilant prayer then enable us to withstand the evil onslaught, or allow one to be spared it altogether. The proverbial statement of Jesus, **The spirit truly is ready, but the flesh is weak** (v. 38), provides a basis for the approach to prayer that is presented in the Gethsemane story.

When Jesus found His followers sleeping **the third time** (v. 41), He said, **Sleep on now, and take your rest: it is enough**. This was not a command to keep on in their indolence; the statement rather conceded that the disciples had been asleep and has the notion of, "Are you going to sleep all night? No— you've slept long enough. Time's up" (MSG). Jesus summoned His disciples to alertly witness the events about to unfold around them when **the Son of man is betrayed into the hands of sinners**. The enormity of these events is underscored by the phrase **he that betrayeth me is at hand** (v. 42). The phrase "is at hand" is the second of two instances of this form in the gospel. In Mark 1:15, Jesus announced that "the kingdom of God is at hand." The kingdom of God was now about to be manifested in an ultimate sense. The events of Jesus' passion make it possible for the rule of God to come into the lives of people. Jesus' death is "a ransom for many" (Mark 10:45), the fact of which is demonstrated by His resurrection from the dead. In this sense, the kingdom of God was also "at hand" in Gethsemane.

14:43–52. To this point, the Twelve had not known who the betrayer was. Jesus had known, and His foreknowledge means that the course of events was completely and divinely predetermined. His death occurred not because of dishonorable conduct but because He willed it. **Judas, one of the twelve** (v. 43) led Jesus' foes to Him. These foes were auxiliary police or servants of the court assigned to the task of maintaining public order beyond the precincts of the temple. They carried **swords and staves** ("clubs," NRSV), weapons that the reader knows are completely unnecessary because of Jesus' intention to go to His death (see 10:32–34). By the prearranged

token ("signal," NKJV; v. 44) of a **kiss**, Judas identified the one whom those **from the chief priests and the scribes and the elders** were to seize (v. 43). Jesus was taken into custody after Judas **kissed him** (v. 45). The kiss was a token of respect with which disciples customarily greeted their teacher. A kiss as a greeting in Mediterranean culture, then and now, represents friendship and esteem (without sexual connotations). Jesus' statement that **the scriptures must be fulfilled** (v. 49) is perhaps a reference to Isaiah 53, or more particularly to Zechariah 13:7, which Jesus quoted in 14:27 and which was fulfilled (at least in part) at this time. In fulfillment of 14:27–31, **they all** (i.e., the disciples) **forsook him** (v. 50).

Two questions arise at this point in the narrative. (1) Why did Judas instruct those arresting Jesus to **lead him away safely** (v. 44)? Did Judas not realize what was in store for Jesus if He fell into the hands of the Jewish authorities, or did he have second thoughts and now wanted Jesus to be given protection? (2) If those seeking Him had been with Jesus **daily** (v. 49) while He was **in the Temple teaching**, why would they have needed Judas to distinguish the Master from His disciples? Would those who had come to arrest Jesus not have known who He was? The answer to the first question is that the word translated "safely" (v. 44) should be understood in the sense of "securely" (NAB) or "under guard" (NIV, NRSV). Judas did not want Jesus to escape, nor did he want His followers to stage a rescue. The second difficulty is cleared up when one understands that those seizing Jesus were not the religious authorities themselves but police sent by them to capture Jesus. The opponents who arrived in Gethsemane were "a great multitude" (14:43) sent by Jewish leaders.

Among the minor characters or character groups in Mark's gospel, four of the most intriguing appear in Gethsemane. They are (1) an unnamed **servant of the high priest** (v. 47) whose ear was cut off; (2) an anonymous bystander, presumably one of the Twelve, who **drew a sword, and smote [the] servant ... and cut off his ear**; (3) **a certain young man** (v. 51) who **left the linen cloth** (v. 52) with which he had been clothed when (4) **the young men laid**

hold on him (v. 51). The young man **fled from them naked** (v. 52). These characters stand in opposition to one another and reveal the only two positions that could be taken regarding Jesus at this crucial hour. One was either for Jesus (the bystander and the young man) or against Him (the servant and the young men).

In his superb storytelling, Mark even presented the bystander and the young man as foils to one another: the former took his loyalty to an unnecessarily bold and violent extreme, while the latter shows the other extreme in his panicky and timid flight. In their contrasting responses to the situation, both characters were ineffective allies for Jesus at this fatal moment. Mark's treatment of these minor characters clearly presents the only two alternatives between which the reader may choose regarding Jesus. If one chooses the way of discipleship, one must then avoid the two undesirable extremes (fight or flight), and that can be done only by watchful prayer (see 14:38).

The exact identities of these minor characters is left tantalizingly obscure by Mark. John recorded that Simon Peter drew the sword and struck the servant. It was his right ear that was cut off and that the servant's name was Malchus (see John 18:10). Malchus may have ducked his head to avoid having his entire head severed. Perhaps Peter, whose sermons Mark had collected, according to Papias, was ashamed to identify himself as the recklessly bold wielder of the sword. "The young men" (v. 51) may have been the police sent from the religious authorities (see 14:43). The "certain young man" (v. 51) also is not specifically identified, but his anonymity may suggest that this was John Mark, the writer of this gospel. If the upper room were indeed at his mother's house (see Acts 12:12), he may have followed Jesus and the others to the garden after the supper. The young man had **a linen cloth cast about his naked body.** Ordinarily, the outer garment was made of wool. The fine linen garment left behind in the hand of a guard indicates that the youth was from a wealthy family. The absence of an undergarment (he "fled from them naked"; v. 52) suggests that he had dressed hastily to follow Jesus. This was

an embarrassing fact. Who would have known of this incident, since all of Jesus' disciples had fled, and why place this in the gospel unless to indicate that the author was there also? Whoever he was, the young man is evidently a disciple of Jesus who fled in terror and shameful nakedness. In the narrator's mind, the linen cloth may have been an association with the death of Jesus. The Greek word for "linen cloth" (*sindōn*) also appears in 15:46, where Jesus was wrapped in a linen cloth and laid in a tomb. Abandoning Jesus at the hour of His death (represented by the forsaken linen), the young man displayed an imperfect and cowardly discipleship.

5. Jesus before the Sanhedrin (14:53–65)

14:53–59. Here the scene shifts to the residence of **the high priest** (v. 54), but the motif of timid discipleship continues, only now with Peter as one who **followed him afar off.** The word "followed" is Mark's usual word (Greek, *akoloutheō*) for following Jesus in discipleship, but here it is modified with the adverbial "afar off." Peter may not have fled completely (see 14:52), but his coming after Jesus was now more out of fearful curiosity than out of an intention to give testimony on behalf of his Lord. Peter's failure of nerve is especially lamentable in light of the fact that, while he **warmed himself at the fire** (v. 54) … **many bare false witness against** (v. 56) Jesus. Their contradictory testimonies perhaps could have been silenced by a bold and truthful defense by Peter.

The council (v. 55) refers to the entire Sanhedrin, the high court of the Jews. In New Testament times, it was made up of three kinds of members: chief priests, elders, and scribes. Its total membership numbered seventy-one, including the high priest, who was presiding officer. At this time, he was Caiaphas, son-in-law of Annas, the former high priest. Under Roman jurisdiction, this council was given a great deal of authority, but it could not impose capital punishment. This Sanhedrin **sought for witness against Jesus to put him to death; and found none.** In Jewish judicial procedure, witnesses functioned as the prosecution. According to Deuteronomy 19:15, a person could not be convicted unless two or more witnesses gave testimony, which assumes that their testimonies had to agree. The **false witnesses** (v. 56) given included the erroneous accusation that Jesus said, **I will destroy this temple that is made with hands, and within three days I will build another made without hands** (v. 58). Jesus, according to John, did indeed make a claim like this. His accusers, however, had misconstrued His words (see John 2:19–21). Their stories did not **agree** (vv. 56, 59).

14:60–61. The drama in the high priest's residence now reaches its climax. Jesus, as the suffering Servant who does not open his mouth in his affliction (see Isa. 53:7), **held his peace, and answered nothing** (v. 61) during the inquest. To answer the accusations would have elevated baseless and treacherous lies to the status of legitimate charges. When questioned by the high priest, however, Jesus did respond. **Art thou the Christ, the Son of the Blessed?** The high priest used "the Blessed" as an epithet for "God" out of respect for the very name of God, which was not uttered in Jewish piety. The question concerned not a charge of false identity but Jesus' true identity as "the Christ" (the Anointed One) who is the Son of God. In this context, "the Son of the Blessed" might be understood to refer not to deity but to royal messiahship (since in popular Jewish belief, the Messiah [Christ] was to be a man, not God).

14:62. Jesus' answer is stunning, because in three ways He asserted His divine nature and prerogatives. (1) His affirmation **I am** (Greek, *Egō eimi*) echoes the language of Exodus 3:14. The identical phraseology appears there (in the Septuagint) as well as here. The association that the statement has with the high priest's reaction (14:63–64) makes it an unmistakable claim to Jesus' identification with Yahweh. (2) Jesus' claim to be **the Son of man** recollects Daniel 7:13 where "one like the Son of man came with the clouds of heaven, and came to the Ancient of days." The Son of Man, granted an everlasting dominion, is worshiped by all (see Dan. 7:14). (3) Jesus added to this description an affirmation that He is the Messiah, who shall be seen **sitting on the right hand of power**—a reference to Psalm 110:1 (a passage that Jesus had already identified as messianic,

see Mark 12:35–37). "The right hand of power" is an anthropomorphic epithet that signifies a position of absolute authority in the universe. The threefold claim of Jesus—"I am," the Son of Man, the Christ—is the most significant proclamation that Jesus made of Himself in the gospel. His possession of divine nature and power cannot be any more clearly or forcefully stated.

14:63–64. That Jesus made claims to share in divine authority and power was recognized in the high priest's response to Jesus' words. After he **rent** ("tore," NIV) **his clothes** (v. 63; an impassioned show of protest, outrage, grief, or shock [see Gen. 37:29; 2 Kings 18:37; 19:1]), the high priest addressed the Sanhedrin: **Ye have heard the blasphemy: what think ye?** (v. 64). The answer was a unanimous condemnation: **they all condemned him to be guilty of death**, or "deserving death" (NRSV). The sin of blasphemy not only involved reviling the name of God (see Lev. 24:10–16) but also included any affront to His majesty or authority (see Mark 2:7; 3:28–29; John 5:18; 10:33). Jesus' claim to be the Messiah and, in fact, to have majesty and authority belonging only to God, was therefore regarded by Caiaphas as blasphemy. For blasphemy, the Mosaic law prescribed death by stoning (see Lev. 24:16). "They all condemned him" may refer to a unanimous or nearly unanimous vote. Certainly it did not include the commendable Joseph of Arimathaea, who obtained Jesus' body from Pilate after the crucifixion to give Him a proper burial (see 15:43). Joseph was probably not present when the council met, nor was Nicodemus likely present. He accompanied Joseph in the burial procedures, according to John 19:39. Perhaps any council member who was sympathetic to Jesus was not invited to the sham trial, or perhaps such a member refused to attend out of protest.

14:65. Rather than receiving the honor that is His due as the Son of Man, Jesus underwent treatment that was outrageously brutal. The severity of the abuse is emphasized by the present tense of the verbs in Mark's description: **to spit on him, and to cover his face, and to buffet him.** Furthermore, **the servants did strike him with the palms of their**

hands. The NASB has "the officers received Him with slaps in the face." "Slaps" translates the Greek *rhapisma*, a word that, in a sixth-century AD papyrus, has the sense of a facial scar resulting from a blow. The violence of the word's later usage might have been in Mark's mind as he wrote. The word appears in the Septuagint of Isaiah 50:6 ("I gave my cheeks to slaps of the hand"). The indignity of the entire scene is highlighted in the tormentors' mocking call for Jesus to **Prophesy,** that is, to identify the one who stuck Him while He was unable to see (His face was covered). An old interpretation of Isaiah 11:2–4 held that the Messiah could judge by smell without the aid of sight.

6. Peter's Denial of Jesus (14:66–72)

14:66–72. What little hope, humanly speaking, there might have been for even a faint voice to be raised in Jesus' defense dissolved with Peter's threefold denial of Jesus. The way was now clear for His own prophecies to be fulfilled regarding His death (8:31; 10:33–34). Peter denied Jesus exactly as the Lord had foretold—three times before the rooster crowed twice (see 14:30). Some manuscripts omit certain words that are in the Greek text that is the basis for the KJV: **and the cock crew** (v. 72), **the second time,** and **twice.** Nevertheless, the meaning is clear: Peter succumbed to fear and denied association with Jesus the accused.

While Jesus was being beaten in an upstairs room of Caiaphas's house, **Peter was beneath in the palace** (i.e., below in the courtyard; v. 66). The resoluteness with which Peter denied Jesus is evident in that the denial was threefold ("on the evidence of two or three witnesses a matter shall be confirmed," Deut. 19:15 NASB). Ironically, Peter the disciple furnished the testimony-in-agreement that was being sought in Jesus' own trial before the high priest. Mark also emphasized Peter's resolute denial in recording that Peter **began to curse and to swear, saying, I know not this man of whom ye speak** (v. 71). "To curse" is *anathematizō*. Since the object of the cursing is unclear, the meaning may be that Peter was invoking a curse on himself ("He began to call down curses on himself," NIV) if what he said was untrue. "To swear" is to add gravity to the curse and may have the sense of "May God do such and such to me if I am not telling the truth." The object of the curse may, however, have been Jesus. If so, Peter—the disciple of the great confession that Jesus is the Christ—was guilty of the very sin that true Christians can never commit: cursing Jesus (see 1 Cor. 12:3). Peter would then be the blasphemer, not Jesus (see 14:64)—more Markan irony. Peter had regressed from saying, **I know not, neither understand I what thou sayest** (common in Jewish law for a formal, legal denial; v. 68) to saying, **I know not this man of whom ye speak** (v. 71). This is further irony in that such an absolute denial is not what one would have expected of Peter.

Peter could not easily escape or deny his association with Jesus since he was readily marked as **a Galilean** (v. 70). Galileans were easily identified by their dialect. Peter's speech showed him to be a Galilean, and his presence among the Judeans in the courtyard suggested he was a follower of Jesus. When the apostle realized that he had denied his Lord—at the crowing of the rooster (v. 72; see 14:30)—**he wept** ("and he went out, and wept bitterly," Matt. 26:75; Luke 22:62).

William Barclay's comment on Peter's denial is striking: "Peter's failure was the kind of failure that could have happened only to a brave man. He alone was in a position to fail; the others had fled long ago. Again, it must always be remembered that this tragic story of Peter's denial must go back to none other than Peter himself. If Mark consists of the preaching material of Peter, then one of Peter's favorite sermons must have been on how he had failed and how Christ had forgiven" (*The Master's Men* [Nashville: Abingdon, 1959], pp. 23–24).

7. Jesus before Pilate (15:1–15)

15:1–5. The Jewish authorities **delivered [Jesus] to Pilate** (v. 1) because only the Roman governor had the authority in Judea to issue a capital sentence. Such a sentence had already been determined by the Sanhedrin to be appropriate in Jesus' case (see 14:64). The scene before Pilate occurred **straightway in the morning** ("Early in the morning," NASB). The working day of a Roman official began at daylight. It was now Friday of Passion Week.

Pilate was the Roman governor (prefect) of Judea from AD 26 to 36, whose official residence was in Caesarea on the Mediterranean coast. (In 1961, archaeologists working at Caesarea unearthed a stone contemporary with Pilate and inscribed with his name.) When he came to Jerusalem, he stayed in the magnificent palace built by Herod the Great, located west and a little south of the temple area. Mark used the Latin word "Pretorium" to indicate this palace in 15:16, and it was here that the Roman trial of Jesus took place.

Pilate's question, **Art thou the King of the Jews?** (v. 2) probably reflects the accusation that councilors made against Jesus before Pilate when they came to him with Jesus. The charge of blasphemy (see 14:64) was a Jewish concern, not a Roman one. A charge of treason against the emperor, however, was definitely a Roman concern, and a claim to kingship would be deemed a challenge to the supreme imperial authority in territory occupied by Rome, such as Judea was.

The Greek (*Sy ei*) of Pilate's question contains the emphatic personal pronoun: "Are you, a man like you, the King of the Jews?" Pilate's question was thus one of incredulity. Jesus immediately turned the tables, however. His answer, **Thou sayest it** (v. 2), also contains the emphatic pronoun *sy*; "you yourself are the one who says so" is the idea. The dynamic of reversal in the exchange is captured in Wuest's translation of verse 2: "And Pilate asked Him, 'As for you, are you the King of the Jews?' And answering him He says, 'As for you, you are saying it.'" Once again Jesus responded to questions about His own identity, **but he answered nothing** to false accusations (v. 3; see v. 5; 14:61). Pilate then became quite insistent and **asked him again, saying, Answerest thou nothing? behold how many things they witness against thee**. If Jesus made no defense, then according to Roman law, Pilate would have to pronounce against Him. Pilate was left with his own words to consider as he **marvelled** at Jesus and His refusal to answer the accusers. Did the governor consider Jesus to be the King of the Jews? Pilate was now the one on trial.

What would he do with Jesus? It is the question that every reader of Mark's gospel must also answer.

15:6 – 8. Beside what little about it is in the New Testament accounts (see Matt. 27:15; Luke 23:17; John 18:39), nothing specific is known about the **prisoner** (v. 6) release that Mark reported was a custom at the time of the Passover feast. Such a practice, however, is hinted at in the Mishnah, the ancient collection of rabbinic teaching. **Barabbas** (v. 7), in custody for the crime of insurrection and murder along with others charged with the same crimes, nevertheless was released by Pilate (see 15:15). Barabbas may have been a member of the Zealots, a revolutionary Jewish group. This group, however, may not have existed as an identifiable group until the period of the Jewish War, AD 66 – 70. Nothing from other sources is known about this insurrection, or uprising, though Mark wrote of it as if it were well known. Under the Roman prefects, however, such revolts were common.

Barabbas's presence in the narrative has a twofold function in Mark's narrative. (1) Barabbas is an ironic foil for Jesus. Despite the fact that Barabbas was guilty of insurrection and murder (Mark, as the narrator, did not say that he and the others were merely accused), the criminal was released — effectively pronounced innocent of the charges for which he was guilty. Jesus, on the other hand, was condemned on the charge of treason despite being innocent of hostility to Rome (see Mark 12:13 – 17). Jesus maintained His honor, however, since "the chief priests had delivered him for envy" (15:10) and Pilate was "willing to content the people" ("anxious to please the crowd," NLT; 15:15). All legal proceedings against Jesus were a corruption of justice.

(2) The second function of Barabbas's presence in the narrative is a theological one. Mark's audience could see a dramatization of their own release from sin when Barabbas went free and Jesus took his place. Jesus' death was a substitutionary ransom (see 10:45) for their sins, and the Barabbas story vividly demonstrated the practical benefits of that ransom.

15:9 – 15. Sadly and tragically, Pilate's shifting of the decision that he had to make about Jesus onto the crowd ended in the death of the Son of God. The feeble **Will ye ...?** (v. 9), **What will ye ...?** (v. 12), and **Why, what evil ...?** (v. 14) all introduce questions of Pilate that sought to shirk his responsibility for deciding what to do with Jesus. Ultimately, not to decide about Jesus is to decide against Him. Pilate's threefold evasion is equivalent to Peter's outright threefold denial since the result was the same. The call of the multitude to **Crucify him** (vv. 13–14) was certainly not a verdict by a reasonable and impartial jury. The crowd had been moved by the envious **chief priests** (vv. 10–11). So, at the behest of the pliable crowd, the jealous priests, and the ingratiating Pilate, Barabbas was **released** (v. 15). Jesus was **delivered** to His executioners to be **scourged** and **crucified**.

The scourging that preceded the crucifixion of Jesus was the Roman practice of flogging. The Romans used a whip made of several strips of leather into which were embedded (near the ends) pieces of bone and lead. Such a whip could flay the victim's flesh so that bones and organs were exposed. The Jews, in their whippings, limited the maximum number of stripes to forty (in practice, to thirty-nine in case of a miscount), but no such limitation was recognized by the Romans, and victims of Roman floggings often did not survive. Mel Gibson's cinematic presentation *The Passion of the Christ* portrays accurately the gruesomeness of the torture of Roman scourging. It was this scourging that Jesus received.

8. The Soldiers Mock Jesus (15:16–20)

15:16. This section is one of the best examples of Markan irony. Jesus, whom the reader knows to be the Christ, the Son of God, and the Son of Man — a figure of supreme honor — was now ridiculed shamefully by Roman soldiers. They were not aware, as is the reader, that their crude and malicious jesting of Jesus as a pretender to kingship was in reality a recognition of that kingship. **The whole band** is "the whole cohort" (NRSV) of Roman soldiers attached to the governor and the palace that was his headquarters, the **Praetorium**. The word "Pretorium" was used originally of a general's tent or of the head-

quarters in a military camp. The soldiers quartered in the Pretorium were recruited from non-Jewish inhabitants of the Holy Land and assigned to the military governor. A cohort was a tenth part of a Roman legion — about six hundred men (but the number could vary). A great number of soldiers took part in the mockery of Jesus.

15:17. The derision was vicious and continual, and Mark presented it graphically. Jesus was given a robe of **purple**, and after the soldiers had **platted** ("twisted," NKJV) **a crown of thorns**, they **put it about his head**. Purple robes signified power; they were often an element of the insignia of field commanders, magistrates, and kings. Although Jesus' crown was undoubtedly painful, it mainly served to mock Him as a clown-king. The acanthus shrub would have been readily available for the crude wreath. Its spikes would have been a parody of ancient images that show monarchs with crowns whose points symbolically radiate their glory.

15:18–20. After mocking Jesus with the salutation, **Hail, King of the Jews!** (v. 18; a mocking salutation that corresponded to "Hail, Caesar!"), the soldiers inflicted continual abuse on Him: **And they smote him on the head with a reed, and did spit upon him, and bowing their knees worshipped him** (v. 19). The NASB captures well the torrential nature of the indignities (the verbs in v. 19 are in the imperfect tense): "They kept beating His head with a reed, and spitting on Him, and kneeling and bowing before Him." The spitting was probably a parody on the kiss of homage that was customary in the Near East when in the presence of royalty. When the mockery had ceased, the soldiers **took off the purple from him, and put his own clothes on him, and led him out to crucify him** (v. 20). A crucifixion detail was normally comprised of four soldiers and a commanding officer for each prisoner.

9. The Crucifixion and Death of Jesus (15:21–39)

15:21. Simon a Cyrenian (Cyrene was an important city of Libya in North Africa that had a large Jewish population) was compelled by the Roman soldiers to carry Jesus' cross. Men condemned to death were usually forced to carry a beam of the cross, often weighing thirty or forty pounds, to the place of crucifixion. Jesus started out by carrying His cross (see John 19:17), but He had been so weakened by flogging that Simon was pressed into service. Simon becomes an example of discipleship in Mark's account. The words **to bear his cross** recall Jesus' words regarding those who would follow Him: "let him … take up his cross" (8:34). The same Greek construction (*airō ton stauron*) appears in both places. To bear one's cross is to publicly identify with Jesus in the shamefulness of His death. Simon proves to be a foil, however unwilling he might have been in carrying the cross, to those who had already forsaken Jesus in the hour of His suffering. Mark's Roman audience would have taken courage in their suffering from Simon's example. Apparently, they were acquainted with his sons since Simon is identified as **the father of Alexander and Rufus**. Only Mark mentioned these men, and he referred to them in a way that suggests they were known by Mark's readers. Rufus may be the same person spoken of in Romans 16:13. Otherwise, who would care to know the names of this man's children? When Simon took up Jesus' cross, he dignified the suffering Jesus (His cross is worth bearing) and dignified himself as an ideal disciple.

15:22. Jesus was brought to **Golgotha, which is, being interpreted, The place of a skull**. The actual location of Golgotha is uncertain. One suggested site, known as Gordon's Calvary, is a rocky knoll pockmarked with caves, atop which has been a Muslim cemetery for centuries. Its perennial association with death, its situation outside the old city walls of Jerusalem (see Heb. 13:12), and its proximity to a tomb like that described in the Gospels has persuaded some that it was the execution site of Jesus. But one cannot be certain. Whatever the location of Jesus' execution, it was outside the city walls, was in a conspicuous place (perhaps near a highway and a city gate), and may have been a place that the Romans habitually used for crucifixions.

15:23–25. They crucified him (v. 25) by means of the execution that the Romans reserved for slaves,

people of the provinces, and dangerous criminals. Roman citizens were exempt from it, except in extreme instances like high treason. Its ghastliness made crucifixion generally effective as a deterrent to rebellion against Roman authority in Judea. Death typically came torturously slowly, through shock and asphyxiation, sometimes days after the victim had been bound or nailed to a cross, stake, or tree. The public disgrace of the victim was compounded by the executioners if they left the body on the cross to rot and/or to feed carrion birds. First-century authors vividly describe the agony and disgrace of being crucified. In Mark's account, however, the shame of Jesus' crucifixion is mitigated by several factors. The notation of crucifixion at **the third hour** (i.e., "nine o'clock in the morning," NLT) suggests that Mark wanted his audience to know the time at which Jesus' crucifixion began and ended (see discussion on 15:34). The brevity of Jesus' time on the cross reduces the shame associated with His death; the time that Jesus was exposed to public disgrace was short.

Jesus was fully alert to the pain and shame of His crucifixion. He refused the **wine mingled with myrrh** (v. 23), a concoction whose narcotic effects would have lessened the pain to some degree. The Talmud gives evidence that incense was mixed with wine to deaden pain. Myrrh is a spice derived from plants native to the Arabian deserts and parts of Africa. Jesus died wakeful and strong, not in any kind of undignified stupor.

When the soldiers of the crucifixion detail **parted** ("divided," NKJV) **his garments, casting lots upon them, what every man should take** ("They gambled for his clothes, throwing dice to decide who would get them," NLT; v. 24), they demonstrated that Jesus' garments were desirable. Hence, the wearer of them is dignified in the narrative. Mark's intention may have been to highlight that fact as much as to show that the gambling fulfilled Old Testament prophecy (see Ps. 22:18). It was the accepted right of the executioner's squad to claim the minor possessions of the victim. Jesus' clothing probably consisted of an undergarment, an outer garment, a belt, sandals, and possibly a head covering.

15:26 – 28. Further Markan irony lies in his identification of **the superscription of his accusation** ("The written notice of the charge against him," NIV; v. 26) affixed to the cross: **THE KING OF THE JEWS**. It was customary to write the charge on a wooden board that was carried before the victim as he walked to the place of execution, after which the board was affixed to the cross above his head. Although Jesus' judges had not ascribed the title "the King of the Jews" to Him, their identification on the basis of His condemnation (a political challenge to imperial sovereignty) unwittingly substantiated Jesus' claims.

Mark's term (Greek, *lēstēs*) to describe the **two thieves** (v. 27) could simply designate them as robbers or bandits. However, Josephus used the term to designate Jewish resistance fighters against Roman domination. Since according to Roman law, robbery was not a capital offense, Mark's term must signify men guilty of insurrection, crucified for high treason. The thieves might have been revolutionaries whose activities against the Romans involved banditry. Perhaps they were accomplices of Barabbas and others who at this time were in custody for sedition (see 15:7). Whatever their identity, the thieves' presence was a fulfillment of prophecy: **And he was numbered with the transgressors** (v. 28). Mark did not include many Old Testament quotations in his gospel, writing as he was for a non-Jewish audience, but these words are from Isaiah 53:12. The contents of verse 28 were almost certainly added to the original wording of Mark. Nevertheless, though the verse does not appear in older witnesses to the text of Mark's gospel, the hand responsible for it rightly appreciated Jesus' position between thieves as a symbol of His death for sinners.

15:29 – 32. Yet more irony is embedded in the mockery that Jesus' opponents hurled at Him as He hung on the cross. **He saved others; himself he cannot save** (v. 31), exclaimed **the chief priests** together **with the scribes**. Their statement was true; they unwittingly ascribed to Jesus' death an atoning quality (see 10:45; 14:24). For this reason, He could not save Himself. To do so would have meant that the ransom would not be paid. Mark thus portrayed Jesus' death to be His own willing self-sacrifice—a death of inestimable worth and honor, not of dishonor. Passersby **railed on him** ("were hurling abuse at Him," NASB), **wagging their heads** ("shaking their heads in mockery," NLT; v. 29). They also rehearsed the accusation that Jesus would destroy **the temple** only to rebuild it **in three days**, a charge that Mark already showed to be false (see 14:57 – 59). The readers of Mark's crucifixion account know Jesus' honor to be intact despite His apparently ignominious death. Whatever slander Mark's readers might experience because they are Christians is parallel to the suffering of their Lord. Their honor too remains intact.

15:33 – 34. Mark's careful chronology designates a time of **darkness over the whole land** (v. 33) from **the sixth** up to **the ninth hour** (i.e., from noon until 3:00 p.m.; see NRSV). In the Bible, darkness connotes judgment and death, particularly the eschatological day of the Lord (see 13:24). Darkness at the crucifixion scene symbolizes God's judgment on sin. The judgment on the sin of all men was focused on the Son of Man hanging on the cross since His death was "a ransom for many" (10:45). **At the ninth hour** (v. 34), Jesus therefore cried, **My God, my God, why hast thou forsaken me?** These words were so important to Mark's concept of salvation that he preserved their Aramaic form along with his Greek translation. The words from Psalm 22:1 indicate that Jesus is the ultimate righteous sufferer who cried to God in His distress. For Jesus to quote the initial verse of this psalm was to declare its fulfillment in His own life. Jesus' cry further signifies that He had entered human "godforsakenness." Humans may therefore now have Jesus' Father as their Father too. Through the cross, Jesus is the one present with humanity in its estrangement from God and in its sense of abandonment and loneliness, whatever the cause. In Mark, Jesus is both one's representative in this sense and one's ransom who died as one's substitute (see 10:45; 14:24).

Readers may ask, but how can God forsake God? How can He be separated from Himself? German theologian Jürgen Moltmann says, "To understand what happened between Jesus and his God and Father on the cross, it is necessary to talk in trinitarian terms. The Son suffers dying, the Father suffers the death of the Son. The grief of the Father here is just as important as the death of the Son. The Fatherlessness of the Son is matched by the Sonlessness of the Father, and if God has constituted himself as the Father of Jesus Christ, then he also suffers the death of his Fatherhood in the death of the Son" (*The Crucified God: The Cross of Christ as the Foundation and Criticism of Christian Theology*, trans. R. A. Wilson and John Bowden [New York: Harper & Row, 1974], p. 243).

15:35–37. Some of the bystanders misunderstood Jesus' cry and thought that He had called for **Elias** ("Elijah," NASB; v. 35). It was commonly believed that Elijah would come in times of critical need to protect the innocent and rescue the righteous. The mockers sarcastically urged one another to await the great prophet's rescue of Jesus. At the same time, a **spunge full of vinegar** (a type of wine used by laborers and soldiers; v. 36) was offered to Jesus to drink.

It may have quenched Jesus' thirst, but it did not deaden His pain. He may well have refused it altogether (see 15:23). **Jesus cried with a loud voice, and gave up the ghost** ("Jesus breathed his last," NIV; v. 37). The strength of His cry indicates that Jesus did not die the ordinary death of those crucified, who normally suffered long periods of complete agony, exhaustion, and then unconsciousness before dying. The shame of the cross is counteracted by Jesus' sturdiness at this point.

15:38. The effect of Jesus' expiration was that **the vail of the temple was rent in twain** ("torn in two," NJB) **from the top to the bottom.** This is a curious statement and appears somewhat out of place in the narrative, which has focused so precisely on the suffering of Jesus, but the tearing of the veil was important for Mark as another symbol of the meaning of Jesus' death. "The vail" (Greek, *katapetasma*) may refer to the "curtain" (NRSV) that separated the Holy of Holies from the Holy Place in the temple, or it may refer to the curtain that hung at the entrance from the courtyard into the Holy Place, the place where incense was burned. Both curtains were

enormous (perhaps 60 feet by 30 feet and about 5 inches thick). If Mark identified the former curtain, the theological meaning is clear: the way to God's presence (localized in the Holy of Holies and accessible only to the high priest) is now open to all by the death of Jesus (see Heb. 6:19; 9:3; 10:19–20). If the latter veil is Mark's reference, however, the tearing was more of a public event and vindicated Jesus in terms of the slanderous mockery that He had endured (v. 29). In Jesus' death, God had begun the destruction and replacement of the temple. In either case, the tearing of the curtain symbolizes a new era that began with Jesus' death. This new era could have been inaugurated only by the work of God ("from the top to the bottom"). Jesus' crucifixion has inestimable importance and great honor attached to it. His was not the execution of a common criminal but a death for the sins of the world.

15:39. The confession of **the centurion** who witnessed the crucifixion and observed Jesus' death is the climax of Mark's gospel. In the Roman army, a centurion was a commander of one hundred men. The centurion at the cross was in a Roman auxiliary unit that was attached to a legion and that had the same number (six thousand) of soldiers. This officer of an infantry cohort was perhaps a Roman citizen. His utterance, **Truly this man was the Son of God**, forms a parallel between the end of the narrative and Mark's opening statement, "The beginning of the gospel of Jesus Christ, the Son of God" (1:1). In His death, Jesus was given the highest ascription of honor that a man can receive. Rather than being inglorious and demeaning, Jesus' death established and revealed His glory in an ultimate way. Although the phrase "the Son of God" could be translated "a son of God" (Goodspeed), the parallel with 1:1 suggests that the reader ought to understand the title in the way Mark has repeatedly portrayed Jesus' sonship in his gospel: Jesus Christ is uniquely *the* divine Son of God.

10. The Burial of Jesus (15:40–47)

15:40–41. Mark's mention of **women looking on afar off** (v. 40) is important to his narrative for three reasons. (1) Women who observed Jesus' death and burial were the ones who came to the tomb to anoint His body (see 16:1). They could not have mistakenly visited the wrong tomb on Easter morning since two of the three women whom Mark named in 16:1 "beheld where he was laid" (15:47). Any skepticism of the Resurrection that says the women went to the wrong tomb is thus effectively silenced.

(2) Mark specifically named some of the many women who observed Jesus' death: **Mary Magdalene, and Mary the mother of James the less and of Joses, and Salome** (v. 40). Mark 16:9 and Luke 8:2, reveal that Jesus had driven seven demons from Mary Magdalene. Salome was probably the wife of Zebedee and the mother of James and John (see Matt. 27:56). The author thus furnished the names of three eyewitnesses to Jesus' death and of the empty tomb (see also 16:1 – 8), two of whom witnessed His burial also (see 15:47). Their individual testimonies about the events of Good Friday and Easter morning could have been independently corroborated. The fact that theirs is *female* testimony further validates the historical reliability of the account since a woman's testimony was legally inadmissible in official Judaism. No one concocting the series of events Mark describes would invent witnesses who were women.

(3) Within the wider circle of disciples (beyond the Twelve) were women who **followed him** (Greek, *akoloutheō*; Mark's usual term for designating disciples; v. 41). They also **ministered unto him**, which indicates that they were women of means who shared their wealth with Jesus and His apostolic band. Their commitment was solid, for they "were accustomed to follow with Him and minister to Him the necessities of life" (Wuest). Even while Jesus was alive, a group of women counterpart to the Twelve were disciples and had a distinct and important ministry.

15:42 – 47. Jesus' burial was handled by **Joseph of Arimathaea** (v. 43). Mark described him as **an honourable counsellor** ("a prominent member of the council," NASB) whose sympathies lay with the Jesus movement since he awaited **the kingdom of God.** He **went in boldly unto Pilate, and craved the body of Jesus** ("asked for the body of Jesus,"

NRSV). Since victims of crucifixion normally suffered much longer, sometimes for days, before dying, **Pilate marvelled if he were already dead** ("Pilate couldn't believe that Jesus was already dead," NLT; v. 44). The Roman centurion officially verified the death of Jesus, a fact that should not be missed lest one is inclined to think that Jesus did not really die but merely swooned only to revive later. It was the "corpse" (ASV; v. 45) that Pilate gave to Joseph. Joseph then took Jesus' body and **wrapped him in the linen** (v. 46) that he had bought for the occasion. The release of the body of one condemned for high treason, and especially to one who was not an immediate relative, was quite unusual.

Joseph placed Jesus' body **in a sepulchre which was hewn out of a rock.** There is archaeological evidence that the traditional site of the burial of Jesus (the Church of the Holy Sepulchre in Jerusalem) was a cemetery during the first century AD. There is also good evidence, however, that the site known as the "Garden Tomb" was also used in the first century and that an early church was once constructed over that site as well. Before the **door** was **rolled a stone**, a large, disc-shaped boulder that rolled in a sloped channel. The placement of the stone was Joseph's responsibility but almost certainly occurred with assistance. Jesus' burial was completed **before the Sabbath** (v. 42), on **the preparation** (Friday). Since it was now late in the afternoon, there was an urgency to get Jesus' body down from the cross before sundown, when the Sabbath began.

In Mark's account of Jesus' burial, the shame of the cross is counteracted in several ways: (1) Jesus was buried after hanging on the cross but a short time; (2) a pious and noble person attended to Jesus' burial; (3) Jesus did not suffer the indignity of hanging on a cross overnight and into the Sabbath day, as the burial was complete before the Sabbath (when these procedures were prohibited); (4) Pilate allowed the burial to proceed although the Romans forbade such a burial to those who were put to death under the charge of high treason, as Jesus was; (5) Jesus received the dignity of a new burial shroud of fine linen; (6) He was placed in a tomb that allowed a dignified and careful placement of the corpse within it; and (7) the blocking of the tomb with a stone shielded Jesus' remains from predatory animals and public exposure. Mark, as he did throughout the gospel, established Jesus as a figure who received honor in life and death. The shame of His cross and the travesty of justice that led Him to it are effectively counteracted. When Mark's readers were abused for their association with Jesus the crucified, they would have been encouraged that their Lord is honorable and to be honored as the Son of God.

VII. The Resurrection of Jesus (chap. 16)

A. The Empty Tomb (16:1–8)

16:1–2. Now that **the sabbath was past** (v. 1), the women could attend to the body of Jesus in such a way that the haste of Friday's burial had not allowed. The same three women mentioned in 15:40 **had bought sweet spices**, which they now brought to the tomb of Jesus that they might **anoint him**. The women probably bought the spices during the brief interval after sundown on Saturday (about 6:00 p.m. Saturday evening) when the shops opened for business at the conclusion of the Sabbath. There would have been no time, however, to visit the tomb then. Therefore, **very early in the morning** (v. 2) on Sunday they came to pay Jesus one last act of devotion and honor. "Anoint" is probably used here in the sense of "to apply to the body," not specifically "to pour over the head." The stench of decomposition was lessened by the application of spices. In light of Jesus' prophcies of His resurrection (8:31; 9:9–10; 10:34), suspense builds for the reader: what will the women find when they arrive at the tomb? How will they react to what they find? In captivating irony, the reader knows that Jesus will rise, but the actors in the story do not expect that event. The women certainly did not since they came expecting to find a corpse to anoint.

16:3–4. The stone (v. 3) now becomes the focus of the narrative. Setting the large stone in place was a relatively easy task, but once it had slipped into the groove cut in bedrock in front of the entrance, it was very difficult to remove. Boulders that covered entrances of tombs like the tomb of Jesus were from five to six feet in diameter, and although of varying thicknesses, their average weight was hundreds of pounds. Mark's description of the stone as **very great** (v. 4) might have been his way of saying that its removal was a supernatural event.

16:5. Inside the large opening of the facade of the tomb was a forechamber, at the back of which a low rectangular opening led to the burial chamber. **Entering** (v. 5) the forechamber, the women encountered **a young man**. He is not identified, and he is described only as **clothed in a long white garment**. Could this be the young man who fled from Gethsemane, leaving his garment behind (14:51–52)? Had he now been reinstated by the Lord, had his nakedness covered, and had been entrusted by the Lord Himself with a message for the band of Jesus' followers whom he had previously forsaken? The word "young man" (Greek, *neaniskos*) is the same word in both accounts, as is the word "clothed" (Greek, *periballō*). Almost certainly, however, here the "young man" is an angelic figure and is to be distinguished from the mere youth in 14:51–52. The same term could describe both. The word for garment here (Greek, *stolē*) is different from that in 14:51–52 (Greek, *sindōn*) and is described as "white," suggesting a supernatural origin. The women would not have been **affrighted** ("alarmed," NRSV), so distressed, at the sight of a mere youth in the tomb, although they would have undoubtedly been surprised. Matthew understood him to be an angel (see Matt. 28:2–4; see also Luke 24:4–5).

16:6. The announcement of this alarming figure was that **Jesus of Nazareth, which was crucified**, whom the women seek, **is risen**. The proof of His resurrection was the absence of a corpse on the shelf within the tomb where the body would have been laid. The use of the passive verb here (lit., "was raised") indicates that the resurrection was accomplished by the power of God. Jesus was not merely resuscitated; He, though dead, was raised up to a totally new plane of existence: **he is not here**. The stranger's announcement is the early Christian preaching in a nutshell: Jesus, who was crucified, had risen from the dead by the power of God.

16:7. The women were to carry the astounding message of Jesus' resurrection to **his disciples**. In **Galilee**, they would see Him once again, just as His promise (unrecorded by Mark) had guaranteed. The two words **and Peter**, found in no other gospel, powerfully express the forgiveness of any sin. "How that message must have cheered Peter's heart when he received it! He must have been tortured with the memory of his disloyalty, and suddenly there came a special message for him. It was characteristic of Jesus that he was concerned not so much because of him, but due to the remorse he was undergoing. Jesus was far more eager to comfort the penitent sinner than to punish the sin" (William Barclay, *The Gospel of Mark*, rev. ed. [Philadelphia: Westminster, 1975], p. 369).

16:8. The women did not heed the young man's command not to be afraid (see 16:6). Rather, they **fled from the sepulchre; for they trembled and were amazed** ("because they were frightened out of their wits," JB; they were "beside themselves with terror," NEB). The women said nothing to anyone, **for they were afraid**. The reader would expect these faithful disciples (see discussion on 15:41) to deliver the message that they had been enjoined to deliver by the angelic stranger in the tomb. That message had Christ's own authority behind it. Here is more Markan irony: the women at the tomb, who were commanded to speak, did not. The leper, who had been commanded to silence, nevertheless spoke out (see 1:44–45). Only the formerly demon-possessed man (see 5:19–20) and the evil spirits themselves were obedient in this matter (see 1:27; 3:12; see also 9:10, where the disciples' silence stemmed from confusion, not obedience).

B. The Longer Ending of Mark (16:9–20)

16:9–20. Some textual critics, even some conservative scholars, have serious doubts as to whether these verses belong to the gospel of Mark. They point out that Mark 16:9–20 is absent from important early manuscripts and displays certain peculiarities of vocabulary, style, and theological content that are unlike the rest of Mark, noting that his gospel probably ended at 16:8 or that its original ending has been lost.

In modern translations of the New Testament (e.g., NASB, NIV, NRSV), this passage is distinguished from the rest of Mark 16 by brackets and/or marginal notes. Since the seventeenth century, when the KJV was translated, older and more reliable manuscripts have become available. The textual tradition of these manuscripts does not have verse 9–20, whereas the textual tradition of more recent manuscripts includes them. One witness (an Old Latin manuscript) concludes Mark with an unnumbered "shorter ending." Furthermore, some manuscripts not only have the so-called longer ending of Mark but also have the shorter ending as well. One manuscript contains verses 9–20 with an expansion of verse 14.

Various positions have been taken regarding the ending of Mark in light of the different readings among the witnesses (Greek New Testament manuscripts, early versions of the New Testament in other languages, lectionaries, and citations among the early church fathers). Among the views regarding Mark 16:9–20 are the following: (1) Mark's gospel originally included the longer ending of Mark. Verses 9–20 should therefore be considered genuine. (2) The ending of the gospel was lost. The various readings that follow verse 8, including the longer ending of verses 9–20, represent attempts to complete the gospel. (3) Mark intended his gospel to end with verse 8. The ending, therefore, is not lost.

An argument in favor of the first view is that the majority of witnesses to the text of the gospel of Mark include verses 9–20 and, therefore, the longer ending should be accepted as the original closing to the book. Only a small handful of manuscripts omit these verses, and the arguments for seeing them as original are equally compelling to some. The number of witnesses, however, does not in itself constitute a conclusive argument.

For the second view to be a viable theory, one must establish that Mark was virtually unnoticed after the practically immediate publication of two other, more popular gospels, Matthew and Luke. Mark, however, undoubtedly enjoyed a substantial circulation before Matthew and Luke drew from it for their gospels, and no reason exists to doubt widespread recognition of Mark after these gospels were composed. There never was a time when a lost ending could not have been retrieved.

Finally, in favor of the third view is that the tone of fearful amazement by the women at the tomb is consistent with responses to Jesus elsewhere in Mark. According to this view, the author intended to leave the reader in a state of awe. One must decide for oneself what to do in response to the empty tomb. Will one take the challenge and proclaim the risen Jesus or fall into fearful silence? Nevertheless, the third view may be challenged by the fact that, in Mark, Jesus' prophecies always come true. One would expect the prophecy of a Galilean appearance (see 16:7) to be followed with a record of its fulfillment.

If Mark intended his gospel to end with verse 8, the reader is thus left with the decision whether to be a bold witness of the resurrected Lord or not. The element of alarm and terror with which the gospel ends is an effective literary device and reinforces the motif of awe that has already emerged in the narrative (see 4:41; 5:15, 33; 6:20, 50; 9:15, 32; 10:32; 11:18, 32; 12:12). The fulfillment of Jesus' prophecy in 14:28 of meeting them in Galilee, which is mentioned and reinforced by the angel in 16:7, is unrecorded because Mark wanted to leave the reader in a place where he or she must decide whether to go on with Jesus in obedient discipleship or not.

How is one to regard verses 9–20? Whether integral to the gospel or not, they represent old tradition — historically reliable — and ought to be considered carefully in any study of Mark. The material offers insight into early understandings of Jesus and the apostolic mission. It ought to be used with reserve, however, in teaching and preaching. No doctrine or practice should be based exclusively on Mark 16:9–20.

16:9–11. Jesus **appeared first to Mary Magdalene, out of whom he had cast seven devils** ("demons," NASB; v. 9). This information is also given in Luke 8:2 and represents a motif in the gospel of Mark: Jesus is sovereign over the powers of darkness (see 1:21–28, 34; 3:22–28; 5:1–20; 7:24–30; 9:14–29), and He delegates His sovereignty to His

followers so that they may be victorious in their encounters with demonic foes (see 3:15; 9:29; 16:17). Mary **went and told** (v. 10) the disciples as they **mourned and wept** that Jesus had risen from the tomb. But they **believed not** (v. 11).

16:12–13. The disciples persisted in their unbelief even when Jesus **appeared in another form unto two of them** (v. 12) as they were in the countryside. The NLT expands the translation to include the effect of the metamorphosis: "but they didn't recognize him at first because he had changed his appearance." The phenomenon is recorded in Luke 24:13–35 but in a much expanded form. When these two disciples reported to the others that they had seen Jesus, **neither believed they them** (v. 13). Throughout the narrative, the disciples display fear and unbelief. The reader does not condemn them, for they are not outright enemies, but the reader criticizes their obtuseness and disbelief. By evoking such responses, the narrator enables the reader to judge the quality of his or her own discipleship. "Would I have been willing to believe in the miraculous and have acted on it, or would I have let only what I could have seen for myself determine my faith?'

16:14–15. Later, **as they sat at meat** ("as they sat at the table," NKJV; v. 14), Jesus **appeared unto the eleven** (the original group now missing Judas Iscariot). He **upbraided** ("reproached," NASB) **them with** ("for," NASB) **their unbelief and hardness of heart**. The testimony of those **which had seen him after he was risen** is sufficient as a basis for faith, according to Jesus. That testimony is preserved in the New Testament. The seeker should investigate the evidence firsthand in the gospels in order to decide whether belief in a risen Jesus is reasonable. In Mark's gospel, it most certainly is!

Faith in Jesus is lived out in a commitment to **preach the gospel to every creature** (v. 15; the word "go" is grammatically subordinate to "preach": "having gone into the whole world, preach!"). The one who believes what is preached — the good news of Christ's death as a ransom and His resurrection from the dead — will be saved. The Great Commission is found here, in the other three gospels (see Matt.

28:19–20; Luke 24:47–48; John 20:21), and in Acts 1:8. Jesus' final words are our "marching orders."

16:16. According to Mark, **he that believeth and is baptized shall be saved**. One cannot teach that baptism is necessary for salvation from this doubtful text. In the New Testament, as important as baptism is (see Matt. 28:19), it is the public demonstration of salvation, which takes place inwardly through faith in Christ. Faith in the New Testament has a public dimension to it (see Mark 8:34–38), and baptism is an integral feature of that public quality. Baptism does not save, nor is it required for salvation. Notice that to **be damned** one has only not to believe. Nothing is said about not being baptized.

16:17–18. Accompanying **signs** (v. 17) should probably be understood as miraculous phenomena that serve to confirm the truthfulness of the gospel and the reality of the faith that believers have placed in Christ (see 16:16). Jesus mentioned five such phenomena. Those who believe shall (1) **cast out devils**; (2) **speak with new tongues** (not necessarily in the sense of languages that were previously unspoken, but perhaps "new" in the sense of unknown to the speaker; see Acts 2:1–12); (3) **take up serpents** (v. 18; see Acts 28:3–6); (4) not be **hurt** if they happen to **drink** something poisonous (an accidental ingestion of poison, not an intentional act of proving one's faith by doing something foolish); and (5) **lay hands on the sick**, effectively being God's agents of healing (see James 5:14–15).

A word of caution is in order here. One is ill-advised to base a practice on this text. Any doctrine or practice derived from this section of Scripture ought to have a basis in passages of the New Testament whose genuineness is certain. Furthermore, simply because a practice is mentioned in Scripture does not mean that it is normative for every believer. Because a biblical passage is *descriptive* does not mean that it is *prescriptive*. Hence, unless the author clearly indicated that he intended to establish a phenomenon as a precedent, the reader must not conclude that its presence is equivalent to a command for him or her. This text does not require the reader to consider anything in it as prescriptive rather than simply descriptive.

16:19–20. Jesus' authority was confirmed in His ascension to **heaven** (v. 19), where He sits at **the right hand of God** (both ideas, that of Jesus sitting in one place and that of God having a physical hand, are examples of anthropomorphism). Jesus is seen in this concluding passage as the Lord who accompanied the obedient disciples in their ministry wherever they might go: He was **working with them** (v. 20) and **confirming the word with [the] signs** that He promised in 16:17–18. Whatever the specific task in Christian service, the disciple has the very power of Jesus working with him or her. One's ministry is Jesus' ministry, and He will energize His servants and bring through them the results that He wills, and when He wills. **Amen.**

THE GOSPEL ACCORDING TO ST. LUKE

INTRODUCTION

Author

The author's name does not appear in the book, but much unmistakable evidence points to Luke. This gospel is a companion volume to the book of Acts, and the language and structure of these two books indicate that both were written by the same person. They are addressed to the same individual, Theophilus, and the second volume refers to the first (see Acts 1:1). The author was not present in Palestine during the ministry of Christ but relied on testimony gathered later (see Luke 1:2–4). He was present during at least part of Paul's ministry, however, as certain sections in Acts use the pronoun "we" (Acts 16:10–17; 20:5–15; 21:1–18; 27:1–28:16), indicating that the author was with Paul at that time. Paul mentioned Luke in the epistles as one of his companions, further strengthening the association and thus the authorship of this gospel as well as Acts.

By process of elimination, "Luke, the beloved physician" (Col. 4:14) and Paul's "fellowlabourer" (Philemon 24), becomes the best possible candidate for authorship. This is supported by the uniform testimony of early Christian writings (e.g., the Muratorian Canon, AD 170, and the works of Irenaeus, ca. 180). Other early church writers allude to Luke as the author of this gospel as well, including Clement and Justin Martyr (see *Dictionary of Jesus and the Gospels*, s.v. "Luke, Gospel of").

Luke was probably a Gentile by birth, well educated in Greek culture, a physician by profession, a companion of Paul at various times from his second missionary journey to his first imprisonment in Rome, and a loyal friend who remained with the apostle after others had deserted him (see 2 Tim. 4:11). Some, citing Luke's knowledge of the Old Testament, have argued that he was a Hellenistic Jew who had become a Christian, but this has not gained much popularity. Antioch (of Syria) and Philippi are among the places suggested as his hometown, though it is not certain.

Although Luke acknowledged that many others had written of Jesus' life (1:1), he did not indicate that he relied on these reports for his own writing. He used personal investigation and arrangement, based on testimony from "eyewitnesses and ministers of the word" (1:2), including the preaching and oral accounts of the apostles. His language differences from the other Synoptics and his blocks of distinctive material (e.g., 10:1–18:14;

19:1–28) indicate independent work, though he obviously used some of the same sources. While Paul was imprisoned at Caesarea, Luke would have had ample time to research Jesus' life and to talk with many eyewitnesses then living in Israel.

Date and Place of Composition

The two most commonly suggested periods for the composition of the gospel of Luke are: (1) AD 59–63 and (2) the 70s or the 80s (see chart, *Zondervan KJV Study Bible*, p. 1349). Luke's gospel was written before the Acts of the Apostles and is referred to as Luke's "former treatise" (Acts 1:1). Since the book of Acts closes with Paul in Rome awaiting trial, about AD 62, some assume that Luke was written while Paul was imprisoned in Caesarea awaiting the appeal of his trial before the Roman emperor. That would date the gospel's publication at about AD 60.

The place of writing was probably Rome, though Achaia, Ephesus, and Caesarea also have been suggested. The place to which it was sent would, of course, depend on the residence of Theophilus. By its detailed designations of places in the Holy Land, the gospel seems to be intended for readers who were unfamiliar with that land. Antioch, Achaia, and Ephesus are possible destinations.

Recipient

The gospel is specifically directed to Theophilus (1:3), whose name means "one who loves God" and almost certainly refers to a particular person rather than to lovers of God in general. The use of "most excellent" (1:3) with the name further indicates that this was an individual and supports the idea that he was a Roman official or at least someone of high position and wealth. He was possibly Luke's patron, responsible for seeing that the writings were copied and distributed. Such a dedication to the publisher was common at that time. Theophilus, however, was more than a publisher. The message of this gospel was intended for his instruction (1:4) as well as for the instruction of those among whom the book would be circulated.

Theme and Theological Message

The third gospel presents the works and teachings of Jesus that are especially important for understanding the way of salvation. Its scope is complete from the birth of Christ to His ascension, and it appeals to both Jews and Gentiles. That the gospel was initially directed to Theophilus does not narrow or limit its purpose. It was written to inform and undergird the faith of believers and to displace disconnected and ill-founded reports about Jesus. Luke wanted to show that the place of the Gentile Christian in God's kingdom is based on the teaching of Jesus; he wanted to commend the preaching of the gospel to the whole world.

Since the Synoptic Gospels (Matthew, Mark, and Luke) report many of the same episodes in Jesus' life, one would expect much similarity in their accounts. The dissimilarities reveal the distinctive emphases of the separate writers. Luke's characteristic themes include: (1) universality, recognition of Gentiles as well as Jews in God's plan; (2) emphasis on prayer, especially on Jesus' praying before important occasions (see discussion on 3:21); (3) joy over the announcement of the gospel or "good news" (see discussion on

1:14); (4) special concern for the role of women; (5) special interest in the poor (some of the rich were included among Jesus' followers, but He seemed closest to the poor); (6) concern for sinners (Jesus was a friend to those deep in sin); (7) stress on the family circle (Jesus' activity included men, women, and children, with the setting frequently in the home); (8) repeated use of the title "Son of man" (e.g., 19:10); (9) emphasis on the Holy Spirit (see discussion on 4:1). The main theme of this gospel, however, is the nature of Jesus' messiahship and mission, and the key verse is 19:10.

Literary Features

Luke had outstanding command of the Greek language. His vocabulary is extensive and rich, and his style at times approaches that of classical Greek (as in the preface, 1:1–4), while at other times it shows Semitic influences (1:5–2:52), much like the Septuagint Greek translation of the Old Testament. His vocabulary reveals geographical and cultural sensitivity in that it varies with the particular land or people being described. When Luke referred to Peter in a Jewish setting, he used more Semitic language than when he referred to Paul in a Hellenistic setting.

The writing is characterized by literary excellence, historical detail, and warm, sensitive understanding of Jesus and those around Him. The arrangement of Luke's gospel is orderly, and his account of Jesus' ministry can be divided into three major parts: (1) the events that occurred in and around Galilee (4:14–9:50), (2) those that took place in Judea and Perea (9:51–19:27), and (3) those of the final week in Jerusalem (19:28–24:53). Luke's uniqueness is especially seen in the amount of material devoted to Jesus' closing ministry in Judea and Perea. This material is predominantly made up of accounts of Jesus' discourses. Sixteen of the twenty-three parables that occur in Luke are found there (9:51–18:14; 19:1–28). Of the twenty miracles recorded in Luke, only four appear in these sections. Already in the ninth chapter, Jesus is seen anticipating His final appearance in Jerusalem and His crucifixion (see discussions on 9:51; 13:22).

Outline

I. The Preface (1:1–4)
II. The Coming of Jesus (1:5–2:52)
  A. The Annunciations (1:5–56)
  B. The Birth of John the Baptist (1:57–80)
  C. The Birth and Childhood of Jesus (chap. 2)
III. The Preparation of Jesus for His Public Ministry (3:1–4:13)
  A. His Forerunner (3:1–20)
  B. His Baptism (3:21–22)
  C. His Genealogy (3:23–38)
  D. His Temptation (4:1–13)
IV. Jesus' Ministry in Galilee (4:14–9:9)
  A. The Beginning of the Ministry in Galilee (4:14–41)
  B. The First Tour of Galilee (4:42–5:39)
  C. A Sabbath Controversy (6:1–11)
  D. The Choice of the Twelve Disciples (6:12–16)

G. Jesus' Arrest (22:47–65)

H. Jesus on Trial (22:66–23:25)

I. The Crucifixion (23:26–56)

J. The Resurrection (24:1–12)

K. The Post-Resurrection Ministry (24:13–53)

Bibliography

Bock, Darrell L. *Luke 1:1–9:50.* Baker Exegetical Commentary on the New Testament. Grand Rapids, MI: Baker Academic, 1994.

———. *Luke.* The IVP New Testament Commentary. Downers Grove, IL: InterVarsity Press, 1994.

Godet, Frederick Louis. *Commentary on Luke.* Grand Rapids, MI: Kregel, 1982.

Liefeld, Walter L. "Luke." In *The Expositor's Bible Commentary,* edited by Frank E. Gaebelein, vol 8. Grand Rapids, MI: Zondervan, 1995.

Marshall, I. Howard. *The Gospel of Luke.* The New International Greek Testament Commentary. Grand Rapids, MI: Eerdmans, 1978.

Morris, Leon. *Luke: An Introduction and Commentary.* Tyndale New Testament Commentaries 3. Grand Rapids, MI: Eerdmans, 1988.

Robertson, A. T. *A Harmony of the Gospels.* San Francisco: HarperOne, 1932.

Stein, Robert H. *Luke.* The New American Commentary 24. Nashville: Broadman & Holman, 1992.

EXPOSITION

I. The Preface (1:1–4)

1:1–4. Using language similar to classical Greek, Luke began his gospel with a formal preface, common to historical works of that time, in which he stated his purpose for writing and identified the recipient. He acknowledged other reports on the subject, showed the need for this new work, and stated his method of approach and sources of information.

1:1. Things which are most surely believed among us. Things prophesied in the Old Testament and now fully accomplished.

1:2. Delivered them unto us. A technical term for passing on information as authoritative tradition. **Eyewitnesses, and ministers of the word.** Luke, though not an eyewitness himself, received testimony from those who were eyewitnesses and were dedicated to spreading the gospel. Apostolic preaching and interviews with other individuals associated with Jesus' ministry were available to him.

1:3. Having had perfect understanding of all things. Luke's account is exact in historical detail, having been checked in every way. Inspiration by the Holy Spirit does not rule out human effort. The account is complete, extending back to the very beginning of Jesus' earthly life. It has an orderly, meaningful arrangement that is generally chronological. **Most excellent.** Paul used this respectful term for governors Felix (Acts 24:3) and Festus (Acts 26:25). **Theophilus.** See Introduction: "Recipient."

1:4. That thou mightest know the certainty of those things. While John focused on a personal outcome, that his readers might know Christ (see John

20:31), Luke focused on a more informational outcome: that Theophilus might know about the events that happened.

II. The Coming of Jesus (1:5–2:52)

A. The Annunciation (1:5–56)

1:5. Herod, the king of Judea. Herod the Great reigned 37–4 BC, and his kingdom included Samaria, Galilee, much of Perea, and Coele-Syria (see discussion on Matt. 2:1). The time referred to here is probably circa 7–6 BC. **Zacharias … Elisabeth**. Both were of priestly descent from the line of Aaron. **The course of Abia**. From the time of David, the priests were organized into twenty-four divisions, and Abia (Abijah) was one of the "priests, the chief of the fathers" (Neh. 12:12, 17; see 1 Chron. 24:10).

1:6. Righteous … blameless. Zacharias and Elisabeth were not sinless but were faithful and sincere in keeping God's commandments. Simeon (see 2:25) and Joseph (see Matt. 1:19) were given similar praise.

1:7. For **no child**, see discussion on 1:25.

1:9. To burn incense. One of the priest's duties was to keep the incense burning on the altar in front of the Most Holy Place. He supplied it with fresh incense before the morning sacrifice and again after the evening sacrifice (see Exod. 30:6–8). **His lot was**. Ordinarily, a priest would have this privilege very infrequently, and sometimes never, since duty assignments were determined by lot (see discussions on Neh. 11:1; Prov. 16:33; Jonah 1:7; Acts 1:26).

1:11. An angel of the Lord (see 1:19). In this story, the angel appears to make an announcement of tremendous importance (the coming birth of John as forerunner to Christ). Whenever angels appear in Scripture, they are always on very important business related to God's overall plan for His people. We should remember that angelic appearances in Scripture are rare, sometimes separated by hundreds of years. We should not expect to see angels appearing before us, nor should we expect to see them on trivial business, such as giving moral advice (we have God's Word for that) or "helping out" in little ways, though Hollywood often treats angels in this way. Jesus' statement in Matthew that little chil-

dren receive the attention of angels is no exception, for Jesus said that "in heaven their angels do always behold the face of my Father" (Matt. 18:1), not that they make appearances on earth. **The right side of the altar**. The south side, since the altar faced east.

1:12. Fear fell upon him. A common reaction to the appearance of an angel, as with Gideon (see Judg. 6:22–23) and Manoah (see Judg. 13:22). Readers are told nothing of the angel's physical appearance or whether that was what evoked fear in Zacharias. The angel may have resembled the living creatures that Ezekiel saw, but more likely, it had a more human appearance. Zacharias's fear may have stemmed simply from the angel's sudden and supernatural appearance.

1:13. Fear not. This word of reassurance is given many times in both the Old Testament and the New Testament (see, e.g., 1:30; 2:10 and discussion; 5:10; 8:50; 12:7, 32; Gen. 15:1; 21:17; 26:24; Deut. 1:21; Josh. 8:1). Often it accompanies a commission for an important task or an assurance of success. Here it simply means that the angel posed no threat to Zacharias. **John**. The name (derived from Hebrew) means "The Lord is gracious."

1:14. Joy. A keynote of the opening chapters (see 1:44, 47, 58; 2:10).

1:15–16. These verses describing John's life begin with a general statement that is then further explained. **He shall be great in the sight of the Lord** (v. 15), not in terms of human greatness but in terms of the spiritual influence that his life would have on others. First, his greatness would be seen in his high level of moral purity; he would take neither **wine nor strong drink**. It appears likely that John was subject to the Nazarite vow of abstinence from alcoholic drinks (see Num. 6:1–4). If so, he was a lifelong Nazarite, as were Samson (see Judg. 13:4–7) and Samuel (see 1 Sam. 1:11). Second, he would be great in that **he shall be filled with the Holy Ghost**. This is often a reference to one's anointing for a speaking ministry. In the book of Acts, someone is said to be "filled with the Holy Ghost" (e.g., Acts 4:8, 31; 13:9) just before preaching, and Paul linked this phrase with singing and worship (see Eph. 5:18–19).

John would have a preaching ministry that the Lord would anoint with power and effectiveness. Third, he would be great in the sight of the Lord because of the influence of his ministry. **Many** (v. 16) would **turn to the Lord** through him.

1:17. Elias. John was not Elijah returning in the flesh (see John 1:21), but he would function like that Old Testament preacher of repentance and would therefore be a contingent fulfillment of Malachi 4:5–6 (see Matt. 11:14; 17:10–13). Three results would flow from the revival that John's preaching would engender. (1) John's ministry would **turn the hearts of the fathers to the children** (see discussion on Mal. 4:6). When revival comes, it should turn people who are absorbed with themselves and their own needs toward the future and the needs of others. It should also emphasize family. A sure sign that revival is more than just emotions is when fathers take responsibility for their families. (2) John's ministry would turn **the disobedient to the wisdom of the just.** Revival always brings about true repentance. Disobedience here is contrasted with wisdom. No matter how much people may know, until they humble themselves before the Lord in obedience, they lack wisdom. (3) John's ministry would create **a people prepared for the Lord.** John would help fulfill Isaiah's prophecy (see Isa. 40:3–5; Luke 3:4–6). He would spiritually prepare the people to receive the message Christ preached and to receive Him as Lord.

1:18. Whereby shall I know this? Like Abraham (see Gen. 15:8), Gideon (see Judg. 6:17), and Hezekiah (see 2 Kings 20:8), Zacharias asked for a sign (see 1 Cor. 1:22).

1:19. Gabriel. The name can mean "God is my hero" or "mighty man of God." Only two angels are identified by name in Scripture: Gabriel (see Dan. 8:16; 9:21) and Michael (see Dan. 10:13, 21; Jude 9; Rev. 12:7).

1:20. Thou shalt be dumb, and not able to speak. The punishment fit the crime. The angel sentenced Zacharias to months of silence, unable to form words, **because thou believest not my words,** that is, the angel's message regarding John's birth and ministry (see 1:13–17).

1:21. And the people waited for Zacharias. They were waiting for him to come out of the Holy Place and pronounce the Aaronic blessing (see Num. 6:24–26).

1:22. He could not speak. Luke begins with a priest who cannot speak to bless the people and ends with Christ, our High Priest, being lifted up into heaven as He dispenses a final blessing. The people **perceived that he had seen a vision,** probably because he indicated with gestures something of what had happened.

1:23. The days of his ministration. Each priest was responsible for a week's service at the temple once every six months. For **his own house,** see 1:39.

1:24. Elisabeth … hid herself. Perhaps in joy, devotion, and gratitude that the Lord had taken away her childlessness.

1:25. The Lord … looked on me, to take away my reproach. Not only did lack of children deprive the parents of personal happiness, but it was generally considered an indication of divine disfavor and often brought social reproach (see Gen. 16:2, Sarai; 25:21, Rebekah; 30:23, Rachel; 1 Sam. 1:1–18, Hannah; see also Lev. 20:20–21; Ps. 128:3; Jer. 22:30).

1:26–35. This section speaks clearly of the virginal conception of Jesus (vv. 27, 34–35; see Matt. 1:18–25). The conception was the work of the Holy Spirit; in this act, the eternal second person of the Trinity, while remaining God, was also "made flesh" (John 1:14). From conception, Jesus was fully God and fully man.

1:26. In the sixth month. That is, from the time of John's conception. For **Nazareth,** see discussion on Matthew 2:23.

1:27. For espoused, see discussion on Matthew 1:18.

1:28–30. Hail. "Ave" in the Latin Vulgate (from which comes "Ave Maria"). **Thou that art highly favoured, the Lord is with thee.** The Lord found in Mary a special quality of servanthood. She was willing to serve God in whatever way He wanted. God resists the proud but gives grace to the humble (see James 4:6). It is interesting that the angel had to say to Mary, "Fear not" (v. 30), just as Zacharias was told the same. Angelic appearances must have been quite frightening.

1:31. JESUS. The name Jesus is the Greek form of Joshua, which means "the LORD saves."

1:32–33. He shall be great (v. 32), but His greatness would differ from that of John the Baptist. Jesus would change not just Israel for a time but the world for all time. **The Son of the Highest.** This title has two senses: (1) the divine Son of God and (2) the Messiah born in time. The context makes it clear that Jesus' messiahship is referred to in these verses. "The Highest" is a title frequently used of God in both the Old Testament and the New Testament (see 1:35, 76; 6:35; 8:28; Gen. 14:19 and discussion; 2 Sam. 22:14). After His resurrection, Jesus would be given **the throne** that was promised in the Old Testament to the Messiah descended from David (see 2 Sam. 7:13, 16; Pss. 2:6–7; 89:26–27; Isa. 9:6–7). Jesus promised His disciples that they would sit upon twelve thrones, ruling over the twelve tribes of Israel, in conjunction with His own reign (see Matt. 19:28). **His father David.** Mary was a descendant of David, as was Joseph (see Matt. 1:16), so Jesus could rightly be called a "son" of David.

He shall reign ... for ever (see Ps. 45:6; Rev. 11:15); **and of his kingdom there shall be no end** (v. 33). Although Christ's role as mediator will one day be finished (see 1 Cor. 15:24–28), the kingdom of the Father and Son, as one, will never end. David's lineage, of which, humanly speaking, Jesus is a part, will thus never cease to rule over Israel.

1:34. How shall this be ...? Mary did not ask in disbelief, as Zacharias had (see 1:20, 45). She sought information rather than expressing doubt. Rather than centering on how it could be that her Son would be so great, her question centered on her virginity: how could she be with child, **seeing I know not a man.**

1:35. Holy thing. Jesus never sinned (see 2 Cor. 5:21; Heb. 4:15; 7:26; 1 Peter 2:22; 1 John 3:5). He was born sinless because the supernatural overshadowing of the Holy Spirit prevented sin from being passed to Him from His mother. The virgin birth (conception) was necessary for three prominent

reasons: (1) to fulfill prophecy (see Isa. 7:14); (2) to be a sign; (3) to avoid the curse on Coniah (see Jer. 22:30).

1:36. Thy cousin Elisabeth. It is not known whether Elisabeth was Mary's cousin, aunt, or other relation. The Greek word has a breadth of meaning, suggesting simply a "relative." Given the likely age difference between the two women, it is not wrong to suppose that another relationship is in view here.

1:37. With God nothing shall be unpossible. This verse is often quoted out of context. All things are indeed possible to Him who has all power and all knowledge. Believers must not presume, however, that God will always smooth the way for them or give them success in whatever schemes they cook up. The reality is that since all things are possible to Him, believers can be confident that His plans will be worked out. No barrier is too great for God to overcome in the fulfillment of His plan for the ages. The believer's task is not to invoke His aid for one's personal plans but rather to submit to Him and be a part of His plan.

1:38. Be it unto me. Mary submitted to God's will for her life. The context reveals that sometimes God's plan may not always be the easiest for us. A pregnancy would certainly cause problems for Mary, who was not yet married. She would also be taking on the responsibilities of motherhood right on the heels of marriage and would have no time to adjust to her new circumstances before starting a family. Truly, God's plan may not be the easiest or most comfortable path. God loves us and wants to bless our lives, but living according to His will sometimes means moving out of one's comfort zone and change one's plans in response to His. Mary could react to the announcement in this way because of how well she knew God, through knowing His Word. This becomes clearer in light of her words in 1:46–55. Knowing God as she did, Mary fortunately had no false illusions about God wanting to always make her happy. She instead saw herself as His servant and humbly accepted His will.

1:39–40. Saluted Elisabeth (v. 40). This simply means that Mary greeted Elisabeth in the usual respectful manner of a younger person toward her elders in that day and setting.

1:41–43. Elisabeth, **filled with the Holy Ghost** (v. 41), spoke under divine inspiration. Being filled with the Spirit is here again associated with speaking (see discussion on 1:15). Elisabeth recognized that Mary was **the mother of my Lord** (v. 43). It is unclear whether she had already heard of the angel Gabriel's announcement to Mary or whether she received a revelation from the Lord at that moment. In either case, she recognized the lordship of Jesus Christ as a reality that touched her life personally, even before He was born.

1:44. Leaped … for joy. In some mysterious way, the Holy Spirit produced this remarkable response in the unborn baby.

1:45. Elisabeth recognized that Mary had been singled out for the work of bearing Jesus because she was submitted to the Lord. It is noteworthy that Luke cast Mary's role in all of this as humble rather than exalted. Mary was the humble servant of God and was willing to be an instrument of His plan. She saw herself not as exalted in any sense but merely as a humble servant of God (see 1:46–55).

1:46–55. This is the first of four hymns preserved in Luke 1–2 (see 1:68–79; 2:14; 2:29–32 and discussions). This hymn of praise is known as the "Magnificat" (meaning, "exalts"), from its opening word in the Latin Vulgate Bible. This song is like a psalm and should also be compared with the song of Hannah (see 1 Sam. 2:1–10 and discussions). It was not at all unusual for young girls of that day to write poetry; thus, it is not surprising that Mary handled the astounding news that she would be the virgin mother of the Christ child by writing poetry about it, nor that she shared her poem with an older relative whom she respected. Mary had something unique to write poetry about, and her poem reveals a deep understanding of who God is and what He does.

1:46–47. The poem opens with Mary's heart reaction to what God had said. **My soul doth magnify the Lord** (v. 46). This means she sought to make Him great in the world as well as to give Him a bigger

place in her life. She wished to give Him the glory for what was happening to her.

1:48–49. Mary then wrote what God had done for her: **He hath regarded the lowly estate of his handmaiden** (v. 48). He had noticed her even though her place in the world was small. Note that she again called herself "handmaiden" (see 1:38), which in this context means a very humble and lowly servant (*Holman Bible Dictionary*, s.v. "Maid"). **All generations shall call me blessed.** God had done something great for her, and she recognized this. It had not changed her estimation of herself, however, which is rather surprising. When God uses one in a great way, the temptation to become proud is very real. Mary is an example and encouragement to remain humble even when great things happen through one's life and ministry. Believers must remember that when God does great things for a person, it reveals not so much how wonderful that person is as how wonderful He is.

1:50–55. This section reveals how Mary found it in her heart to accept from God's hand such a blessing as this, to be His instrument for bringing God's Messiah into the world. She could accept God's surprising will for her life because she knew something of His character. The Old Testament had given her clues as to how God works in the world. She revealed her understanding of these things in this part of her poem.

1:50. His mercy is on them that fear him. God is merciful. Mary recognized that people need mercy; they deserve wrath, but God is a God of grace. If people fear Him, that is, revere Him and live in harmony with His will, He will show them mercy.

1:51–53. He hath shewed strength with his arm (v. 51). God is powerful. He is able to accomplish what He intends. Mary knew that God had acted powerfully in the past. These verses explain how God is powerful. **He hath scattered the proud.** Mary knew her Bible well. God had done this for Israel many times, and she had heard in the synagogue how God had overthrown the mighty Assyrian Empire and how He had swept away the Egyptian army in the Red Sea. Mary knew how God treated the proud, and she would have expected Him to do the same again. God never changes.

Put down the mighty ... exalted them of low degree (v. 52). One cannot help but think of Saul and David here, and perhaps Mary did too. Mighty Saul was removed from the throne of Israel, and lowly David, the little shepherd boy and the youngest of his family, was raised by the appointment of God to be king.

He hath filled the hungry with good things (v. 53). Elijah was fed by ravens in the wilderness. The Israelites received the manna. Mary knew these things and knew that God would take care of those in need. He has regard for "them of low degree" (v. 52), that is, the poor.

1:54 – 55. In remembrance of his mercy (v. 54). The song ends with an assurance that God will be true to His promises to His people. Mary's faith was in a God who puts down the proud, exalts the humble, shows mercy to those who fear Him, and fulfills His promises to His people. Mary knew the Old Testament stories of what God had done in the past. She knew that a Messiah was promised to Israel, and she expected God to fulfill that promise. It did not surprise her one bit that God would choose someone like her, someone of a lowly background, to bear Christ. A God who puts down the proud and exalts the humble would do that. Mary could humbly accept what God intended for her because she knew God so well.

B. The Birth of John the Baptist (1:57 – 80)

1:56 – 63. Three months (v. 56). Mary evidently remained with Elisabeth until John's birth and then returned to her home in Nazareth. **Called him ... after the name of his father** (v. 59). An accepted practice in that day, as seen in Josephus (*Life* 1). **They made signs to his father** (v. 62). Apparently assuming that since he was mute, he was also deaf. **A writing table** (v. 63). Probably a small wooden board covered with wax.

1:64 – 67. Filled with the Holy Ghost, and prophesied (v. 67). Prophecy not only but also proclaims God's word. Both Zacharias and Elisabeth

(see 1:41 – 45) were enabled by the Holy Spirit to express what they otherwise could not have formulated.

1:68 – 79. This is the second of four hymns preserved in Luke 1 – 2 (see 1:46 – 55; 2:14; 2:29 – 32 and discussions). This hymn is called the "Benedictus" (meaning, "Blessed be"; v. 68), from its opening word in the Latin Vulgate. Whereas the Magnificat (see discussion on 1:46 – 55) is similar to a psalm, the Benedictus is more like a prophecy. Here we have the content of Zacharias's words of praise to God mentioned in 1:64.

1:68. He hath visited and redeemed his people. Not limited to national security (see 1:71) but including moral and spiritual salvation (see 1:75, 77). "Visited" may simply mean that God had made His power known among them in the way that John was born, and "redeemed" here means that He would bring people to repentance through John's ministry. This prophetic hymn needs to be seen in light of what the angel had told Zacharias months before. Zacharias, certainly being aware of the circumstances of his wife's relative, Mary, may have had Jesus Christ in mind as well (see 1:69).

1:69. Horn. Here symbolizes strength, as in the horn of an animal (see Deut. 33:17; Ps. 22:21; Mic. 4:13). Jesus, the Messiah from **the house of ... David**, has the power to save.

1:70 – 73. Zacharias saw what was happening in his family and in his community as evidence that God was about to fulfill the promises made to Abraham and to his descendants. Jesus embodied that fulfillment in His earthly life and ministry and will complete it when He returns.

1:74. We being delivered. No doubt including liberation from all kinds of oppression and bondage as well as deliverance from sin. **Might serve him without fear.** Perfect love casts out all fear, and Zacharias foresaw a time when, according to the promises of God, serving Him would be a response of love to a loving God rather than a response of fear of God's judgment. That judgment was surely accomplished at the cross, that all who are in Christ may serve without fear, knowing God's mercy.

1:75. In holiness and righteousness. This carries forward the theme of service after Christ's had accomplished redemption for all sinners. Servants of Christ are set apart by Christ and justified by the Father. Believers therefore not only are free of fear but are secure in their position in Christ.

1:76. John would be **called the prophet of the Highest**, whereas Jesus would be called "the Son of the Highest" (see 1:32 and discussion). **To prepare his ways** (see discussion on 3:4). The angel had told Zacharias that his son would go before the Lord to ready the people for His coming (see 1:16–17). Well might he have remembered those words in this moment, for it was right after hearing them that he had expressed the doubts that had caused his voice to cease.

1:77. John's ministry would be characterized by evangelism, something else Zacharias had learned from the angel (see 1:16–17).

1:78. The dayspring. A reference to the coming of the Messiah (see also similar figures in Num. 24:17; Isa. 9:2; 60:1; Mal. 4:2). Zacharias not only praised his own son, "the prophet of the Highest" (1:76), but also gave honor to the coming Messiah (see 1:79).

1:79. This verse describes the ministry of Jesus. Under divine inspiration, Zacharias said, He will **give light to them that sit in darkness**, that is, to the lost, those who are separated from God (see Isa. 9:1–2; Matt. 4:16). "Light" here means truth, and "darkness" means error. This imagery is common in Scripture and is one of the keys to John's gospel. **To guide our feet into the way of peace** (see discussion on 2:14). Here is the idea of the reversal of the fall, which will be fully accomplished when Christ returns. The fall put man at enmity with God, with others, and with himself. Jesus reconciles us to God so that "we have peace with God through our Lord Jesus Christ" (Rom. 5:1), just as He reconciles each to one another so that all might "live peaceably with all men," and to oneself so that one might have His peace, "which passeth all understanding" (Phil. 4:7).

1:80. Was in the deserts. John's parents, old at his birth, probably died while he was young, and he apparently grew up in the desert of Judea, which lies between Jerusalem and the Dead Sea. **Till ... his shewing unto Israel.** John's preaching and announcing the coming of the Messiah marked his public appearance. He was about thirty years old when he began his ministry (see discussion on 3:23).

C. The Birth and Childhood of Jesus (chap. 2)

2:1. Luke is the only gospel writer who related his narrative to dates of world history. **Cesar Augustus.** The first and, according to many, greatest Roman emperor (31 BC–AD 14). Having replaced the republic with an imperial form of government, Augustus expanded the empire to include the entire Mediterranean world, established the famed *Pax Romana* ("Roman Peace"), and ushered in the golden age of Roman literature and architecture. Augustus (which means "exalted") was a title voted to him by the Roman senate in 27 BC. **The world.** That is, the Roman Empire. **Taxed.** This was a type of census or enrollment used for military service and taxation. Jews, however, were exempt from Roman military service. God used the decree of a pagan emperor to fulfill the prophecy of Micah 5:2.

2:2. Cyrenius. This official was possibly in office for two terms, first in 6–4 BC and then in AD 6–9. A census is associated with each term. This verse refers to the first term; Acts 5:37 refers to the second.

2:3. Every one into his own city. Probably the city of their ancestral origin.

2:4. God not only used the decree of a pagan emperor; He also provided Joseph and Mary with an opportunity to demonstrate submission to earthly authority, for **Joseph also went up** in obedience to the command. Joseph may not have been aware of the prophecy of the Messiah coming from Bethlehem, and how obedience to a Roman decree would bring about the will of God. One must be wary of assuming that God cannot work His will through those who do not acknowledge Him. The Romans, due to their tendency for meticulous record-keeping, ensured that this prophesy would be fulfilled. **Nazareth ... Bethlehem.** Bethlehem, the town where David was born (see 1 Sam 17:12; 20:6), was at least a three-day trip from Nazareth. **Judea**. The Greco-Roman designation for the southern part of the Holy Land. Judea had earlier been included in the kingdom of Judah.

2:5. With Mary. Mary too was of the house of David and probably was required to enroll. In Syria, the Roman province in which the Holy Land was located, women twelve years of age and older were required to pay a poll tax and therefore to register. For **espoused**, see discussion on Matthew 1:18.

2:6–7. How long Joseph and Mary stayed in Bethlehem is not known. Mary may have been near to term when they arrived, or perhaps they could not leave because of her condition once they had registered. **Swaddling clothes** (v. 7). Strips of cloth were regularly used to wrap a newborn infant. **Manger**. The feeding trough of animals. This is the only indication in the Bible that Christ was born in a stable. Very early tradition suggests that Christ was born in a cave, perhaps used as a stable.

2:8. Shepherds abiding in the field. This does not necessarily mean that it was summer, the dry season. The flocks reserved for temple sacrifice were kept in the fields near Bethlehem throughout the year. **Keeping watch**. Against thieves and predatory animals.

2:9. The angel of the Lord. A designation used throughout the birth narratives (see 1:11; Matt. 1:20, 24; 2:13, 19). The angel of 1:11 is identified as Gabriel (1:19; see 1:26). **The glory of the Lord shone**. This was the Shekinah glory, which had once rested upon the temple (see 1 Kings 8:11).

2:10. Fear not. Fear was the common reaction to angelic appearances (see discussion on 1:13), and encouragement was needed. The angel's message was one of good news, over which the shepherds should rejoice. In addition, the universal implication of the gospel is emphasized: **which shall be to all people**. Luke was writing to a Gentile audience and emphasized early that the coming of Christ was an event with worldwide consequences, not just local ones.

2:11. City of David. Bethlehem. **Saviour**. Many Jews were looking for a political leader to deliver them from Roman rule, while others were hoping for a savior to deliver them from sickness and physical hardship, but this announcement concerns the Savior who would deliver from sin and death (see Matt. 1:21; John 4:42). **Christ**. Or "Messiah." "The Christ" (Greek) and "the Messiah" (Hebrew) both mean "the Anointed One." **The Lord**. A designation originally reserved for God but later applied to the Messiah as well (see Acts 2:36; Phil. 2:11).

2:14. This is the third hymn preserved in Luke 1–2 (see 1:46–55; 1:68–79; 2:29–32 and discussions). This brief hymn is called the "Gloria in Excelsis Deo," from its opening words in the Latin Vulgate Bible (meaning, **Glory to God in the Highest**). The angels recognized the glory and majesty of God by praising Him. "In the highest" is a reference to heaven, where God dwells (see Matt. 6:9). **Peace, Good will**. Peace is assured not to all but only to those who are pleasing to God, the objects of His good pleasure (see Luke's use of the words "well pleased," 3:22; "good," 10:21; and "good pleasure," 12:32). The Roman world was experiencing the *Pax Romana* ("Roman Peace"), which was marked by external tranquillity, but the angels proclaimed a deeper, more lasting peace than that, a peace of mind and soul made possible by the Savior (see 2:11). Peace with God is received by faith in Christ (see Rom. 5:1), and it is believers who, through faith, are pleasing to God (Heb. 11:6). The Davidic Messiah was called "The Prince of Peace" (Isa. 9:6), and Christ promised peace to His disciples (see John 14:27). Christ also brought conflict (the "sword," Matt. 10:34–36; see also Luke 12:49), however, for peace with God involves opposition to Satan and his work (see James 4:4).

2:15–18. The shepherds had heard the word of God, and now they sought to see for themselves what God was doing. These shepherds dropped every other priority to be involved personally with what God was doing. **With haste** (v. 16) can literally mean, "jumping fences."

2:19. Mary's life at this time was a whirlwind of new experiences, many of which were overwhelming. Being a new mother is a major turning point in itself, but when the shepherds showed up with their story, confirming what she had heard from the angel, from Joseph no doubt, and from Elisabeth, her store of **all these things** grew. Certainly she had much to ponder **in her heart**. It may be that Mary was still alive when Luke wrote his gospel, and if so, she certainly would have been among the people that he talked with during his preparation and research (see Luke 1:2–3).

2:20. Glorifying and praising God. Terms of praise and giving glory to God often used by Luke (see 1:64; 2:13, 28; 5:25–26; 7:16; 13:13; 17:15, 18; 18:43; 19:37; 23:47; 24:53).

2:21–28. Her purification (v. 22). Following the birth of a son, the mother had to wait forty days before going to the temple to offer sacrifices for her purification. If she could not afford a lamb and a pigeon (or dove), then two pigeons (or doves) were acceptable (see Lev. 12:2–8; 5:11). **To Jerusalem**. The distance from Bethlehem to Jerusalem was only about six miles. **To present him to the Lord**. The firstborn of both man and animal were to be dedicated to the Lord (see 2:23; Exod. 13:12–13). The animals were sacrificed, but the human beings were to serve God throughout their lives. The Levites served in the place of all the firstborn males in Israel (see Num 3:11–13; 8:17–18).

The consolation of Israel (v. 25). Refers to the comfort the Messiah would bring to His people at His coming (see 2:26, 38; 23:51; 24:21; Isa. 40:1–2; Matt. 5:4). **The Holy Ghost was upon him**. Not in the way common to all believers after Pentecost. Simeon was given special insight by the Spirit so that he would recognize the Christ.

2:29–32. This is the fourth hymn preserved in Luke 1–2 (see 1:46–55; 1:68–79; 2:14 and discussions). This hymn of Simeon has been called the "Nunc Dimittis" (meaning, "Now…You are releasing"), from its opening words in the Latin Vulgate Bible.

2:29–30. Simeon had seen the means by which God would bring salvation to the world. He could die in peace knowing that the promises of God were being fulfilled. It is not that he had doubted but rather that he wanted to see the Savior, so great was his devotion to God and to his people.

2:31–32. All people (v. 31). Simeon recognized, as had some of the Old Testament prophets (see, e.g., Isa. 11:1; 42:6; Mal. 1:11), that God's plan would include the Gentiles. As a Gentile himself, Luke was careful to emphasize the truth that salvation would now be offered to **the Gentiles** (v. 32) as well as to Jews. This may be why he recorded Simeon's hymn. It does not advance the narrative significantly, although it does point out that spiritually sensitive people recognized Jesus for who He is.

2:33. Joseph. Luke, aware of the virgin birth of Jesus (see 1:26–35), never referred to Joseph as Jesus' human father. He was, however, Jesus' legal father. Mary and Joseph **marvelled at those things which were spoken of him**. This seems strange at first, as both Mary and Joseph had been given supernatural revelation regarding this child (see 1:26–38; Matt. 1:20). They were wise to expose themselves to people who were spiritually sensitive. Often when God does something significant in one's life, He will confirm it among those who are spiritually sensitive.

2:34. Fall and rising again of many in Israel. Christ raises up those who believe in Him but is a stumbling block for those who disbelieve (see 20:17–18; 1 Cor. 1:23; 1 Peter 2:6–8). **A sign which shall be spoken against**. In the years ahead, Jesus would be spoken against by the Pharisees, later on by the Romans, and afterward by yet others. The church has suffered persecution through the centuries, no less in current time than in earlier ones.

2:35. A sword shall pierce through thy own soul also. The word "also" indicates that Mary, as well as Jesus, would suffer deep anguish. This is the first reference in this gospel to Christ's suffering and death.

2:36. Anna. The same name as the Old Testament's Hannah (see 1 Sam. 1:2), which means "gracious." Anna praised God for the child Jesus, as Hannah had praised God for the child Samuel (see 1 Sam. 2:1–10). **Prophetess**. Other prophetesses were Miriam (see Exod. 15:20), Deborah (see Judg. 4:4), Huldah (see 2 Kings 22:14), and the daughters of Philip (see Acts 21:9).

2:37. Departed not from the temple. Herod's temple was quite large and included rooms for various uses, and Anna may have been allowed to live in one of them. This statement, however, probably means that she spent her waking hours worshiping in the temple. Both Anna and Simeon are presented as quite elderly.

2:38. Jerusalem. This is the holy city of God's chosen people (see Isa. 40:2; 52:9). Naturally, people would have looked there, the center of Jewish worship, for Israel's **redemption.**

2:39. They returned into Galilee. Luke did not record the coming of the wise men, the danger from Herod, or the flight to and return from Egypt (see Matt. 2:1–23). Harmonizations of the Gospels, however, often place those events between verses 38 and 39 (see Robertson, *Harmony*, 12–13). Luke's omission of these events is no error. His audience would hardly have cared about these details in the way that Matthew's certainly did. Luke's birth narrative was already long, and he included material that was relevant for his Gentile audience (such as the hymn of Simeon) and left out other matters that would not be as relevant.

2:40. Jesus laid aside certain attributes of His deity when He took on flesh. It is no denial of His deity to recognize that He **grew** and changed in the days of His flesh. He was not, as medieval painters often depicted Him, a child-sized adult.

2:41. The feast of the passover. The law commanded that all adult males (normally accompanied by their families) annually attend three feasts: Passover, Pentecost, and Tabernacles (see discussions on Exod. 23:14–17; Deut. 16:16). Distance prevented many from attending all three, but most Jews tried to be at Passover.

2:42–46. Twelve years old (v. 42). At age twelve, Jewish boys began preparing to take their places in the religious community the following year. **Three days** (v. 46). One day traveling away from Jerusalem, a second traveling back, and a third looking for Him. **The doctors.** The rabbis, experts in Judaism.

2:47–52. I must be about my Father's business (v. 49). Jesus pointed to His personal duty to His Father in heaven. He contrasted His "my Father" with Mary's **thy father** (v. 48). At twelve years of age, He

was aware of His unique relationship to God, but He was also obedient to His earthly parents (v. 51).

And Jesus increased ... in favour with God and man (v. 52). Here Luke appears to have borrowed the words of 1 Samuel 2:26. Although Jesus was God, there is no indication that He had all knowledge and wisdom from birth. He seems to have matured like any other boy as to the regular elements of His human nature.

III. The Preparation of Jesus for His Public Ministry (3:1–4:13)

3:1–4:13. This section describes the events that led to Jesus beginning His public ministry. Luke described the ministry of John the Baptist (3:1–20) in terms that echo statements made in chapters 1–2, showing that he fulfilled the ministry that had been ordained for him as Christ's forerunner. After recording John's baptism of Jesus (3:21–22), Luke offered his genealogy of Christ (3:23–38), followed by his account of the temptation of Jesus (4:1–13).

A. His Forerunner (3:1–20)

3:1. The fifteenth year of the reign of Tiberius Cesar. Historians frequently dated an event by giving the year of the ruler's reign in which the event happened. Several possible dates could be indicated by this description, but the date AD 25–26 (Tiberius had authority in the provinces beginning in AD 11) best fits the chronology of the life of Christ. The other rulers named do not help pinpoint the beginning of John's ministry but only serve to indicate the general historical period. **Pontius Pilate.** The Roman prefect who then ruled in Judea, Samaria, and Idumea. **Herod being tetrarch of Galilee.** At the death of Herod the Great (4 BC), his sons—Archelaus, Herod Antipas, and Herod Philip—were given jurisdiction over his divided kingdom. Herod Antipas became the tetrarch of Galilee and Perea (see discussion on Matt. 14:1). **Lysanias the tetrarch of Abilene.** Nothing more is known of this Lysanias than that his name has been found in certain inscriptions.

3:2. Annas and Caiaphas being the high priests. Annas was high priest from AD 6 until the Roman official Gratus deposed him in AD 15. He was followed by his son Eleazar, his son-in-law Caiaphas, and then four more sons. Even though Rome had replaced Annas, the Jews continued to recognize his authority (see John 18:13; Acts 4:6), so Luke included his name as well as that of the Roman appointee, Caiaphas. **The word of God.** The source of John's preaching and authority for his baptizing. God's message came to John as it came to the Old Testament prophets (see Jer. 1:2; Ezek. 1:3; Hos. 1:1; Joel 1:1). **Wilderness.** Refers to a desolate, uninhabited area.

3:3. Baptism of repentance (see discussion on Matt. 3:11). John's baptism represented a change of heart, which includes sorrow for sin and a determination to lead a holy life. **Remission of sins.** Christ would deliver the repentant person from sin's penalty by dying on the cross.

3:4. Prepare ye the way. Before a king made a journey to a distant country, the roads he would travel were improved. Similarly, preparation for the Messiah was made in a moral and spiritual way through John's ministry, which focused on repentance, forgiveness of sin, and the need for a Savior. The words in 3:4–6 are a quotation of Isaiah 40:3–5.

3:5. While it is tempting to find allegorical meaning in **every valley ... every mountain and hill ... and the crooked** ways, this verse is a literal description of the way a road might be prepared. At most, the verse simply means that as the preparation for the king should be thorough, so also should be the spiritual preparation for the Messiah. It does, however, point to the need for full rather than partial repentance.

3:6. All flesh. God's salvation was to be made known to both Jews and Gentiles — a major theme of Luke's gospel (see discussion on 2:31–32).

3:7. The wrath to come. A reference to both the destruction of Jerusalem (see 21:20–23), which occurred in AD 70, and the final judgment (see John 3:36; but see also discussions on 1 Thess 1:10; 5:9). John was not forbidding the people to repent; he was attempting to shock them into recognizing that his ministry was more than just an entertainment, more than just a wonder. He had come to do serious busi-

ness with God's people and was questioning whether they had come to do serious business with God.

3:8. Bring forth ... fruits worthy of repentance. John exhorted the people to show a lifestyle of repentance. Works do not save, but salvation is shown by works. Fruit, that is, good works, is the inevitable result of a genuine change of heart. **Children unto Abraham.** John reminded the people that their background, heritage, and ancestry did not matter. God looks upon the heart. Only by faith and a genuine repentance toward God, which show forth in one's actions, can one claim that they are truly made new in Christ.

3:9. The axe is laid unto the root. A symbolic way of saying that judgment is near for those who give no evidence of repentance. **Fire.** A symbol of judgment (see Matt. 7:19; 13:40–42).

3:10. What shall we do then? Luke presented this general question, followed by specific examples of what genuine repentance looks like.

3:11. Two coats. The coat, or tunic, was something like a long undershirt. Since two such garments were not needed, the second should be given to a person in need of one (see 9:3).

3:12–13. Publicans (v. 12). Taxes were collected for the Roman government by Jewish agents, who were especially detested for helping the pagan conqueror and for frequently defrauding their own people. John said the best way they could show that they had repented was to treat people fairly in matters of taxation.

3:14. Soldiers. Limited military forces were allowed for certain Jewish leaders and institutions (such as those of Herod Antipas, the police guard of the temple, and escorts for tax collectors). The professions of tax collector and soldier were not condemned, but the common unethical practices associated with them were. **Do violence to no man.** Obviously, as soldiers, they might find themselves in conflict. To mistreat the people and take by force what one wanted, however, was a violation of the power given to a military force. **Neither accuse any falsely.** Those who have been given a little power may be tempted to abuse it, either to get back at someone or simply to show that they have power over others. John said people should be treated fairly, even if one has the power to mistreat them. **Be content with your wages**. Again, the soldiers had the power to take things from people but not the right to do so. Officials expected corruption among soldiers and did little about it. John's applications are good advice for anyone in any age. If one seeks to live peaceably, to tell the truth, and to live simply on what God supplies, one shows forth the fruits of repentance, whatever one's occupation or circumstances.

3:15. Luke apparently included this statement simply as a way of demonstrating how influential John's ministry was. Many thought he might be the Christ, something John squelched as soon as he heard it (see 3:16).

3:16. One mightier than I cometh. John knew that his ministry was not about himself but pointed to another. This is something all believers would do well to remember. Christians serve not themsevles but one who is mightier and who has the real power. **He shall baptize you with the Holy Ghost**. Fulfilled at Pentecost (see Acts 1:5; 2:4, 38). **And with fire**. Here fire is associated with judgment (see 3:17; compare the fire of Pentecost in Acts 2:3 and the fire of testing in 1 Cor. 3:13).

3:17. Whose fan. Or "winnowing fork" (see discussion on Ruth 1:22). **The chaff** represents the unrepentant, and **the wheat** represents the righteous. Many Jews thought that only pagans would be judged and punished when the Messiah came, but John declared that judgment would come to all who did not repent, including Jews.

3:18. And many other things. This is a summary statement indicating that Luke did not record all that John preached but rather gave a representative sampling of the kinds of things he preached.

3:19–20. These verses carry the story forward before returning in 3:21 to the baptism of Jesus. That is, they summarize what happened some months later before returning to the most important event in John's ministry. **Herod … being reproved … for Herodias** (v. 19). Herod Antipas had married the daughter of Aretas IV of Arabia but divorced her to marry his own niece, Herodias, who was already his brother's (Herod Philip's) wife (see Matt. 14:3; Mark 6:17). Aretas is mentioned in 2 Corinthians 11:32.

He shut up John in prison (v. 20; see Matt. 4:12; Mark 1:14). According to Josephus (*Antiquities* 18.5.2), John was imprisoned in Machaerus, east of the Dead Sea. This did not occur until sometime after the beginning of Jesus' ministry (see John 3:22–24), but Luke mentioned it here to conclude his section on John's ministry before beginning his account of the beginning of Jesus' ministry (4:14–41). He later briefly alluded to John's death (see 9:7–9).

B. His Baptism (3:21–22)

3:21. For **being baptized**, see discussion on Matthew 3:15. **And praying**. Only Luke noted Jesus' praying at the time of His baptism. Jesus in prayer is one of the special themes of Luke's gospel (see 5:16; 6:12; 9:18, 28–29; 11:1; 22:32, 41; 23:34, 46).

3:22. The Holy Ghost descended. Luke specified that the Holy Spirit descended **in a bodily shape**. To John, the Spirit's descent was a sign (see John 1:32–34; see also discussion on Mark 1:10). **Thou art my beloved Son** (see Ps. 2:7; Isa. 42:1; Heb. 1:5). The gospel writers recorded the declarations of a voice from heaven addressing Jesus on two other occasions: (1) on the Mount of Transfiguration (see 9:35) and (2) in the temple area during Jesus' final week (see John 12:28).

C. His Genealogy (3:23–38)

3:23–38. There are several differences between Luke's genealogy and Matthew's (see Matt. 1:2–16). Matthew began with Abraham (the father of the Jewish people), while Luke traced the line in reverse order, going all the way back to Adam and showing Jesus' relationship to the whole human race (see discussion on 2:31). From Abraham to David, the genealogies of Matthew and Luke are almost the same, but from David on, they are different. Some scholars suggest this is because Matthew traced the legal descent of the house of David, using only heirs to the throne, while Luke traced the complete line of Joseph to David. A more likely explanation, however, is that Matthew followed the line of Joseph (Jesus' legal father), while Luke emphasized that of Mary (Jesus' blood relative). Although tracing a genealogy through the mother's side was unusual, so was the virgin birth. Luke's explanation here that Jesus was the son of Joseph, "as was supposed" (v. 23), brings to mind his explicit virgin birth statement (see 1:34–35) and suggests the importance of Mary's role in the genealogy of Jesus.

3:23. About thirty years of age. Luke, a historian, related the beginning of Jesus' public ministry both to world history (see 3:1–2) and to the rest of Jesus' life. Thirty was the age when a Levite undertook his service (see Num. 4:47) and when a man was considered mature. **As was supposed.** Luke had already affirmed the virgin birth (see 1:34–35) and here again made it clear that Joseph was not Jesus' physical father.

3:24–38. Cainan (v. 36). The mention of Cainan here, and not in Genesis 10:24, demonstrates that the earlier genealogy was not meant to be complete. Thus, not too much should be made of adding up all the years given in the earlier genealogies, although extremely long gaps in them are probably not to be found either. **Adam, which was the son of God** (v. 38). Luke was not saying that Adam was a biological son of God, nor that he held sonship in the same sense as Jesus Christ. In the original, "the son" does not appear. The idea is that while the others owed their origins and family identities to their fathers, Adam owed his to God, being a direct creation of God.

D. His Temptation (4:1–13)

4:1. Full of the Holy Ghost. Luke emphasized the Holy Spirit not only in his gospel (see 1:35, 41, 67; 2:25–27; 3:16, 22; 4:14, 18; 10:21; 11:13; 12:10, 12) but also in Acts, where the Holy Spirit is mentioned fifty-five times. **Returned from Jordan** puts the reader back into the time frame that Luke had been describing before the genealogy. This is a necessary help to the reader, a matter of which Luke, a master at literary craftsmanship, was well aware. **Into the wilderness.** The desert of Judea (see discussion on 1:80; Matt. 3:1).

4:2. Being forty days tempted (see discussions on Matt. 4:1–11; Heb. 2:18; 4:15). Luke stated that Jesus was tempted for the forty days He was fasting, and the three specific temptations recounted in Matthew and Luke seem to have occurred at the close of this period, when Jesus' hunger was greatest and His resistance lowest. The sequence of the second and third temptations differs in Matthew and Luke. Matthew probably followed the chronological order, since at the end of the mountain temptation (Matthew's third), Jesus told Satan to leave (see Matt. 4:10). To emphasize a certain point, the gospel writers often brought various events together, not intending to give chronological sequence. Perhaps Luke's focus here was geographical, as he concluded with Jesus in Jerusalem (see 4:9).

4:3. For **If thou be the Son of God,** see discussion on Matthew 4:3. **Command this stone that it be made bread.** The Devil always makes his temptations seem attractive. In fact, error will often look good to us. It rarely comes in an unpleasing package.

4:4. It is written. Three times Jesus met Satan's temptations with Scripture. Only God's Word can provide the strength needed to overcome Satan's wiles. All of Jesus' quotes were from Deuteronomy. Note that Jesus did not challenge Satan's assertion that He *could* turn the stone to bread if He wished. His reply pointed to a higher value than the one to which Satan was appealing. Satan sought to induce Him to satisfy His physical need. Jesus pointed out that something more important than the physical would guide Him, and should guide believers as well.

4:5–6. The Devil's control of this world is asserted here, and Jesus did not contest the fact. Satan rules in this world, a fact believers would do well to remember when they are tempted to put this world's pleasures and this world's offer of power and prestige ahead of their calling to love God and to serve Him.

4:7. Worship me. The Devil was tempting Jesus to avoid the sufferings of the cross, which He came specifically to endure (see Mark 10:45). The temptation offered an easy shortcut to world dominion.

4:8. Jesus' answer, from Deuteronomy 6:13, again pointed to a higher value. There is no power, no glory, no prestige, and no dominion in this world that is worth more than just being God's servant. No pursuit in this world is more glorious than that of worshiping the Lord. Let Christians be diligent to put the Lord first in all things and let nothing stand in the way of loving Him and serving Him with all that they have and are.

4:9. A pinnacle of the temple. Either the southeast corner of the temple colonnade, from which there was a drop of some 100 feet to the Kidron Valley below, or the pinnacle of the temple proper. For **If thou be the Son of God**, see discussion on Matthew 4:3. **Cast thyself down.** Satan was tempting Jesus to test God's faithfulness and to attract public attention dramatically.

4:10–11. For it is written (v. 10). This time Satan also quoted Scripture, though he misused Psalm 91:11–12.

4:12. Jesus answered with Scripture from Deuteronomy (Deut. 6:16), as He did in the first (Deut. 8:3) and second (Deut. 6:13) temptations.

4:13. The devil … departed from him for a season. Satan continued his testing of Jesus throughout His ministry (see Mark 8:33), culminating in the supreme test at Gethsemane.

IV. Jesus' Ministry in Galilee (4:14–9:9)

A. The Beginning of the Ministry in Galilee (4:14–41)

4:14. For **in the power of the Spirit**, see discussion on 4:1. **There went out a fame of him.** Jesus' ministry was accompanied by early success in Galilee.

4:15. For **He taught in their synagogues**, see discussion on Mark 1:21. **Being glorified of all.** This means that everyone spoke well of him.

4:16. He came to Nazareth. Not at the start of His ministry but perhaps almost a year later (4:23 presupposes that Jesus had already been ministering). All the events described in John 1:19–4:42 probably occurred between Luke 4:13 and 4:14. **As his custom was.** Jesus' custom of regular worship sets an example for all His followers. **To read.** Jesus probably read from Isaiah in Hebrew, and then He or someone else paraphrased it in Aramaic, one of the other common languages of the day.

4:17. The book of the prophet Esaias. The books of the Old Testament were written on scrolls, which were kept in a special place in the synagogue and handed to the reader by a special attendant. The passage Jesus read about the Messiah (Isa. 61:1–2) may have been one He chose to read, or it may have been the assigned passage for the day.

4:18. This verse tells of the Messiah's ministry of preaching and healing, to meet every human need. **He hath anointed me.** Not with literal oil (see Exod. 30:22–31) but with the Holy Spirit. **To preach the gospel to the poor.** Both the financially poor and the spiritually poor. The financially poor know they need to depend on God, for so much in this life is clearly uncertain. The spiritually poor have no less need but may have a harder time accepting the message. **To heal the broken-hearted.** The fall changed the world so that life is full of disappointments, but in His mercy, Jesus Christ will heal the broken-hearted, whatever the cause. **To preach deliverance to the captives.** Those caught in sin as well as victims of injustice. **And recovering of sight to the blind.** Spiritual as well as physical blindness. Christ healed many physically blind people, but His greater work was to remove spiritual blindness that people might see their sin and God's gracious offer of salvation. **To set at liberty them that are bruised.** Again, this includes a spiritual dimension. Everyone has been bruised by this world; sin has left its mark, but in Christ, one can find healing for the heart.

4:19. The acceptable year of the Lord. Not a calendar year but the period when salvation would be proclaimed—the messianic age. This quotation from Isaiah 61:1–2 alludes to the Year of Jubilee (see Lev. 25:8–55), which occurred every fifty years and during which slaves were freed, debts were canceled, and ancestral property was returned to the original family. Isaiah prophesied primarily the liberation of Israel from the Babylonian captivity, but Jesus proclaimed liberation from sin and all its consequences.

4:20. Sat down. It was customary to stand while reading Scripture (see 4:16) but to sit while teaching (see Matt. 5:1; 26:55; John 8:2; Acts 16:13).

4:21. Today is this scripture fulfilled. Jesus, by His presence and His teaching, fulfilled the prophecy before them, for He was proclaiming these things and had been doing them in His ministry.

4:22. The people were surprised. They had all known Jesus from childhood. Too often people fail to see the extraordinary in the familiar.

4:23. For **Capernaum**, see discussion on Matthew 4:13. **Thy country.** Nazareth. Although Jesus was born in Bethlehem, He was brought up in Nazareth, in Galilee (see 1:26; 2:39, 51; Matt. 2:23).

4:24. No prophet is accepted in his own country This has become a proverb in the English language, and there is some truth to it. Jesus went on, however, to point out that it is not wise to reject the message simply because the messenger is familiar.

4:25–27. Jesus here began to show examples from Scripture in which a prophet went outside Israel to minister to needs. The idea seems to be that if Israel, or here specifically Nazareth, rejected His message, God would open it to the Gentiles. Mention of Jesus' reference to God's helping two non-Israelites (see 1 Kings 17:1–15; 2 Kings 5:1–14) also reflects Luke's special concern for the Gentiles. Jesus' point was that when Israel rejected God's messenger of redemption, God sent him to the Gentiles, and so it would be again if Israel refused to accept Jesus (see 10:13–15; Rom. 9–11). **Sidon** (v. 26). One of the oldest Phoenician cities, twenty miles north of Tyre. Jesus later healed a Gentile woman's daughter in this region (see Matt. 15:21–28). **Naaman** (v. 27) was not an Israelite but found healing though the ministry of Elisha.

4:28–29. Filled with wrath (v. 28). Because of Jesus' inclusion of Gentiles as recipients of God's blessings, the people took Him up a **hill** (v. 29), intending to kill Him. This may seem extreme, but apparently the crowd was quite upset.

4:30. Passing through the midst of them. Luke did not explain whether the escape was miraculous or simply the result of Jesus' commanding presence. In any case, His time to die had not yet come (see John 7:30).

4:31–32. Jesus did what anyone who encounters resistance to the gospel should do. He went to another place and began to teach the Word of God there. God always has a place where people are prepared to hear the Word. Here, rather than being indifferent or angry, the people **were astonished at his doctrine: for his word was with power** (v. 32; see discussion on Mark 1:22).

4:33. A spirit of an unclean devil. This was an evil spirit. Such a demon could cause mental disorder (see John 10:20), violent action (see Luke 8:26–29), bodily disease (see 13:11, 16), and rebellion against God (see Rev. 16:14).

4:34. The Holy One of God (see discussion on Mark 1:24). This title is used in the Gospels only here and in Mark 1:24 and John 6:69. It emphasizes that Jesus was set apart for a special mission (see Morris, *Luke*, p. 109). As such, it was a confession of the truth about Jesus, but was offered in a spirit that indicates the demon was not expressing faith but rather seeking to blunt the effect of Jesus' ministry simply by describing it. Perhaps he wanted to see if he could catch Jesus off guard.

4:35. Jesus was not ruffled in the slightest by the words of the demon but spoke authoritatively to it and made it **come out of** the man.

4:36–37. The people **were all amazed** (v. 36) that Jesus could do this. That **he commandeth the unclean spirits, and they come out** demonstrated His power over the forces of darkness in the world. **The fame of him went out into every place** (v. 37). Jesus used this type of ministry as a way to meet spiritual needs and to demonstrate who He is, but He may not have wanted to gain a reputation as a sorcerer.

4:38. Simon's wife's mother. Peter was married (see 1 Cor. 9:5). **A great fever.** All three Synoptics tell of this miracle (see Matt. 8:14–15; Mark 1:29–31), but only Luke, the doctor, used the more specific phrase "a great [i.e., 'high'] fever."

4:39. Immediately she arose and ministered unto them. A genuine supernatural healing is a complete healing. Simon's mother-in-law was restored fully and immediately. She did not need rest in the aftermath of her fever breaking.

4:40. When the sun was setting. The Sabbath (see 4:31) was over at sundown (about 6:00 p.m.).

Until then, according to the tradition of the elders, Jews could not travel more than about two-thirds of a mile or carry a burden. Only after sundown could they carry the sick to Jesus, and their eagerness is seen in that they set out while the sun was still setting.

4:41. Jesus rebuked the demons and ordered them **not to speak**, perhaps due to His experience with the unclean spirit who had proclaimed His true identity (see 4:33–37), **for they knew that he was Christ** (see discussion on Mark 1:34). Jesus certainly wanted time to teach and to demonstrate who He is before He gained too much publicity. He would not let events prevent Him from going to the cross or from doing so at the right time.

B. The First Tour of Galilee (4:42–5:39)

4:42. Jesus **went into a desert place**. Mark included the words "and there prayed" (Mark 1:35).

4:43. The kingdom of God (see discussion on Matt. 3:2). This is Luke's first use of this phrase; it occurs over thirty times in his gospel. Some of its different meanings in the Bible are (1) the eternal kingship of God, (2) the presence of the kingdom in the person of Jesus, the King, (3) the approaching spiritual form of the kingdom, (4) the future kingdom.

4:44. This summary statement includes not only the beginning of Jesus' ministry (4:14–43) but also what lay ahead in His ministry. No express mention is made in the Synoptics of the early Judean ministry recorded in John 2:13–4:3, though it may be reflected in Matthew 23:37 and Luke 13:34.

5:1. The lake of Gennesaret. Luke is the only gospel writer who called it a lake. Josephus always used this term. The other gospel writers called it the Sea of Galilee, and John twice called it "the sea of Tiberias" (John 6:1; 21:1). It is the largest fresh water lake in Israel. Capernaum, which was a major center for Jesus' Galilean ministry, was a major fishing center.

5:2. Washing their nets. After each period of fishing, the nets were washed, stretched, and prepared for use again.

5:3. He sat down. The usual position for teaching (see discussion on 4:20). The boat provided an ideal arrangement, removed from the press of the crowd but near enough to be seen and heard. Sound carries well over water, and Jesus was better able to be heard by the crowd spread out on the shore than He would have been on land.

5:4–6. Jesus was not only interested in helping **Simon** (Peter; vv. 4–5) catch fish. He wanted to demonstrate His power to him and to make a point (see 5:10). **Their net brake** (v. 6). Work prospers as God wills. Not only did they catch fish; they caught way too many fish.

5:7. For **their partners**, see 5:10.

5:8–9. Depart from me (v. 8). Simon Peter got the message that this was no ordinary man and that He had supernatural power. The nearer one comes to God, the more he feels his own sinfulness and unworthiness, as did Abraham (Gen. 18:27), Job (42:6), and Isaiah (6:5). Sometimes when one encounters God, one's own unworthiness comes to the forefront, as happened here.

5:10. Jesus issued the call to **James, John**, and **Simon** to leave fishing and **catch men** instead. At least part of what Jesus was trying to communicate to them was that their success in life was in His hands. He could make them successful and prosperous fishermen if He chose, or He could call them to another occupation. If God could care for them by blessing their fishing efforts, so also could He care for them if they left their profession. All honorable work is service to God if it is done at His call and for His glory, but no work is more important than spiritual service to Him.

5:11. They forsook all, and followed him. This was not the first time these men had been with Jesus (see John 1:40–42; 2:1–2). Their periodic and loose association now became a closely knit fellowship as they followed the Master. The scene is the same as Matthew 4:18–22 and Mark 1:16–20, but the accounts relate events from different hours of the morning.

5:12–16. The healing of the man with leprosy is described in all three of the Synoptic Gospels (see Matt. 8:1–4; Mark 1:40–45), but the setting is different in each. In Matthew, it is part of a collection of miracles; in Mark and Luke, it is probably one incident that occurred on the first tour of Galilee.

5:12. A man full of leprosy. Luke alone noted the extent of this man's disease. The Greek term for "leprosy" could refer to other skin diseases as well as leprosy and was not used for leprosy in medical literature (see *KJV Study Bible* note on Lev. 13:2). The man expressed faith. His **if thou wilt** was not doubt but rather allowance for God's sovereignty in the matter.

5:13. Jesus replied, **I will**, and healed the man.

5:14. For **tell no man**, see discussions on Matthew 8:4; 16:20. **But go, and shew thyself to the priest.** By this command, Jesus urged the man to keep the law, to provide further proof for the actual healing, to testify to the authorities concerning His ministry, and to supply ritual certification of cleansing so the man could be reinstated into society. For **a testimony unto them**, see discussion on Mark 1:44.

5:15–16. The more went there a fame abroad of him (v. 15). The man could not keep the matter quiet. Jesus may well have known that this would be the case and that, at least among the man's family and friends, the matter would cause quite a stir. It may be that the man himself could not help but tell the miracle to all who would listen. In any case, Jesus' increased reknown forced Him to withdraw **into the wilderness** (v. 16), where He **prayed**. The press of responsibility must not take precedence over prayer and dependence on God.

5:17–26. In Luke's gospel, this incident, the healing of a paralyzed man, begins the active confrontation between Jesus and the religious leaders. They recognized that Jesus' claim to be able to forgive sins was tantamount to a claim to deity. Jesus proved His ability to do the higher work of forgiving sins by doing the lower work of healing. While healing is not as difficult as forgiving sins, at least not for God, anyone can *say* that sins are forgiven. To say "Arise" (v. 24) to a paralyzed man and have the power to make it happen requires more than mere words. It demonstrates divine power, the power that can also forgive sins.

5:17. Pharisees and doctors of the law (see discussions on Matt. 2:4; 3:7; Mark 2:16). Opposition was rising in Galilee from these religious leaders. "Pharisees," meaning "separated ones," are mentioned here for the first time in Luke. They numbered about six thousand and were spread over the whole of the Holy Land. They were teachers in the synagogues, religious examples in the eyes of the people, and self-appointed guardians of the law and its proper observance. They considered the interpretations and regulations handed down by tradition to be virtually as authoritative as Scripture (see Mark 7:8–13). "Doctors of the law" refers to scribes, who studied, interpreted, and taught the law (both written and oral). The majority of these teachers belonged to the party of the Pharisees. Already Jesus had run counter to the Jewish leaders in Jerusalem (see John 5:16–18). Now they came to a home in Capernaum (see Mark 2:1–6) to hear and watch Him.

5:18–19. These men brought their friend who could not come on his own. Their great desire to see him healed was evident in their zealously lowering him through the roof. For **housetop** (v. 19), see discussion on Mark 2:4. **Tiling.** Probably ceiling tiles. How long the man had been in this condition or whether it was due to disease or accident is not known. He had probably not been born this way, however. That he had a network of friends willing to do so much for him indicates that he had probably once been vigorous.

5:20. Man, thy sins are forgiven thee. Jesus met the man's spiritual need first. He did not always do this. Here He wanted to make a point to the Pharisees and scribes in the crowd. By forgiving the man's sins, which cannot be demonstrated and which only God could do, Jesus implicitly claimed to be deity.

5:21. Who is this which speaketh blasphemies? (see discussion on Mark 2:7). The Pharisees considered blasphemy to be the most serious sin a man could commit (see discussion on Mark 14:64). If Jesus were saying that the man's sins were forgiven when they were not, not only was He claiming to be God but He was promising what only God could do. If He were not God, He was making a false promise in God's name. All of this was included in the Pharisees' charge of blasphemy.

5:22-23. Jesus perceived their thoughts (v. 22), but then He had created the situation under which they would raise questions in their minds as to His motive and identity. **Whether is easier, to say ...?** (v. 23; see *KJV Study Bible* note on Mark 2:9-10). In asking this question, Jesus showed that it is easier to promise what cannot be proven than to promise what can be proven.

5:24. That ye may know. Jesus had every intention of doing what could be seen by all, however. His power to heal was a visible affirmation of His power to forgive sins. Both are things only God can do.

5:25-26. The man was healed **immediately** (v. 25) and was able to leave on his own. It is ironic that his friends could not get him in due to the crowd, but he was able to get out. The people must have backed away from him in wonder.

5:27. For **A publican,** see discussion on 3:12-13. **The receipt of custom** (see discussion on Mark 2:14). The place where customs were collected. **Levi.** This was Matthew.

5:28. He left all, rose up, and followed him. Since Jesus had been ministering in Capernaum for some time, Levi probably had known Him previously (see discussion on 5:11).

5:29. A great feast. When Levi began to follow Jesus, he did not do it secretly. He sponsored a public dinner to introduce people to Jesus personally.

5:30. Their scribes and Pharisees murmured. They may have stood outside and registered their complaints from a distance, or perhaps some of them had been invited to the party. **Why do ye eat with and drink with publicans and sinners?** (see discussion on Mark 2:15). They assumed guilt by association, but it was instead ministry opportunity by association. Christians can never reach the lost if they never get involved with them. As a new believer, Levi knew many lost people and wanted to help them meet the Lord.

5:31-32. They that are whole need not a physician; but they that are sick (v. 31). Implies not that the Pharisees were "They that are whole" but that a person must recognize himself as a sinner before he can be spiritually healed (see discussion on Mark

2:17). The people Levi had invited to his dinner had no illusions about their righteousness. The Pharisees had only illusions about theirs.

5:33. The disciples of John fast often, and make prayers. John the Baptist had grown up in the wilderness and learned to subsist on a meager, austere diet of locusts and wild honey. His ministry was characterized by a sober message and a strenuous schedule. (For a contrast between Jesus' ministry and John the Baptist's, see 7:24-28; Matthew 11:1-19.) The Pharisees also had rigorous lifestyles (see discussion on 18:12). Jesus, however, went to banquets, and His disciples enjoyed a freedom not known by the Pharisees. **Fast** (see discussion on Mark 2:18). While Jesus rejected fasting legalistically for display (see Isa. 58:3-11), He Himself fasted privately and permitted its voluntary use for spiritual benefit (see Matt. 4:2; 6:16-18).

5:34-35. This is more of an analogy than a parable, though the function is the same. Jesus here is the bridegroom. **The days will come** (v. 35), after His resurrection and ascension, **when the bridegroom shall be taken away from them, and then shall they fast** (see discussions on Mark 2:19-20). This was a time of celebration, for Jesus was with them. The time for fasting would come later.

5:36. This again is more like an analogy but is specifically called **a parable** (see discussions on Matt. 13:3; Mark 4:2). The point is that God was doing something new and different, something that would not fit the old mold. The **new garment** was the offer of grace to the Gentiles, something Luke was eager to emphasize for his audience.

5:37-39. For **old bottles** (v. 37), see discussion on Matthew 9:17. **The old is better** (v. 39). Jesus was indicating the reluctance of some people to change from their traditional religious ways and try the gospel.

C. A Sabbath Controversy (6:1-11)

6:1-11. This passage presents two incidents in which Jesus (or His disciples) seemingly violated Sabbath laws. In both cases, Jesus defended the action as consistent with what God has revealed. In the first case (6:1-5), the disciples were plucking grain to eat on the Sabbath. Jesus' point was that Sabbath-keeping is not a ritual that should violate meeting needs. As David and his men had eaten what was technically not lawful, because taking care of hunger is more important than following a rule, so Jesus' disciples were doing nothing wrong by taking care of their hunger on the Sabbath. In the second case (6:6–11), Jesus healed a man on the Sabbath. The need in this case was that of another, not that of Jesus or the disciples.

6:1. He went through the corn fields; and his disciples plucked the ears of corn, and did eat (see discussion on Mark 2:23). "Corn" refers not to the yellow grain that grows on stalks but more likely to wheat. Corn as commonly known was found only in the Western Hemisphere at that time. When the King James Bible was translated, "corn" referred to any kind of grain. In much of the world today, what Americans refer to as "corn" is called "maize."

6:2. The Pharisees had sought to keep the Sabbath very strictly because of the cultural changes brought about by Alexander the Great's conquest of the area three centuries earlier. One clear way to distinguish between those Jews who were "pure" and those who had been "tainted" by Greek culture was their strict observance of the Sabbath. The Pharisees' contention with Jesus over Sabbath-keeping was motivated, in part, by a fear that He was being a traitor to pure Judaism.

6:3. What David did (see discussion on Mark 2:25). Jesus invoked the Old Testament here, demonstrating by the Jewish Scriptures that what His disciples were doing was not out of line with God's Word.

6:4. For **shewbread**, see discussion on Matthew 12:4.

6:5. For **the Son of man**, see discussion on Mark 2:10. **Lord also of the sabbath.** Jesus has the authority to overrule laws concerning the Sabbath, particularly as interpreted by the Pharisees (see Matt. 12:8; Mark 2:27). Jesus never broke the Mosaic law, and since meeting one's genuine needs is more important than a ritual observance, this was not a genuine case of breaking the law.

6:6–7. By now, **the scribes and Pharisees** (v. 7) were watching Jesus and His disciples for occasions of Sabbath-breaking, looking for an opportunity to make **an accusation against him**.

6:8. Stand forth. So there would be no question about the healing.

6:9. Is it lawful ... to do good ...? (see discussion on Mark 3:4). Jesus had been enduring questions and attacks from the Pharisees and now took the initiative by putting the questions to everyone in the synagogue. Here He was invoking not a specific Old Testament law or incident but rather a general principle. His question was rhetorical; the answer is obvious.

6:10. Looking round about upon them all. Jesus wanted to see whether anyone objected to His question or to the implied answer, but no one was bold enough to do so. By their silence, the people agreed with Him.

6:11. They were filled with madness because they could not withstand Jesus' reasoning. Instead of humbly admitting they were wrong, they became enraged. Already the Pharisees were plotting to take His life (see John 5:18; see *KJV Study Bible* note on Mark 3:6). Their reaction is typical of human nature. When people are proven wrong, they often become angrier rather than repenting of their error.

D. The Choice of the Twelve Disciples (6:12–16)

6:12. Characteristically, Jesus spent the **night in prayer** before the important work of selecting His twelve apostles. Perhaps he had names in mind and spent time laying each name before His Father, meditating on their strengths and potential. Luke does not indicate how many people He considered before settling on the twelve He would call when day came.

6:13. He called unto him his disciples. Among those who came to hear Jesus was a group that regularly followed Him and who were committed to His teachings. At least seventy men were included, since this many disciples were sent out on an evangelistic campaign (see 10:1, 17). Later, 120 believers waited and worshiped in Jerusalem following His ascension (see Acts 1:15). From such disciples, Jesus at this time chose **twelve** to be His **apostles**, meaning "ones sent with a special commission" (see discussions on Mark 6:30; 1 Cor. 1:1; Heb. 3:1).

6:14–16. Lists of the apostles appear also in Matthew 10:2–4; Mark 3:16–19; Acts 1:13. Although the order of the names varies, Peter is always first and Judas Iscariot last. The same disciples are always listed in each of the same three groupings of four each.

6:14. Bartholomew. Seems to be (in the Synoptics) the same as Nathanael (in John). Nathanael is associated with Philip in John 1:45.

6:15. Matthew. Another name for Levi. **James the son of Alpheus.** Probably the same as James the Less (see Mark 15:40).

6:16. Judas the brother of James. Another name for Thaddeus (see Matt. 10:3; Mark 3:18). **Judas Iscariot** (see discussion on Mark 3:19). Probably the only one from Judea; the rest likely came from Galilee.

E. The Sermon on the Plain (6:17–49)

6:17. Stood in the plain. Perhaps a plateau, which would satisfy both this context and that in Matthew 5:1. The crowd that gathered here **came to hear him, and to be healed of their diseases.**

6:18–19. Jesus met the people's need for healing before preaching to them. Often, when one meets a person's felt needs, he or she is then ready to hear the Word of God.

6:20–49. Luke's Sermon on the Plain is apparently parallel to Matthew's Sermon on the Mount (Matt. 5–7). Although this sermon is much shorter than the one in Matthew, they both begin with the Beatitudes and end with the lesson of the builders. Some of Matthew's sermon is found in other portions of Luke (e.g., 11:2–4; 12:22–31, 33–34), suggesting that Jesus may have presented the material on various occasions. It is not unusual for itinerant preachers to have one basic sermon that they give on different occasions and that they vary according to circumstances and time constraints.

6:20–23. The Beatitudes (see Matt. 5:3–12) go deeper than material poverty (v. 20) and physical **hunger** (v. 21). Matthew's account indicates that Jesus spoke of poverty "in spirit" (Matt. 5:3) and hunger "[for] righteousness" (Matt. 5:6).

6:24–26. This section is a point-by-point negative counterpart of 6:20–22.

6:24. Woe unto you that are rich contrasts with "Blessed be ye poor" (6:20). **Ye have received your consolation** means that the rich have their reward in this life. This is not a blanket condemnation of all rich people. Jesus' point seems to be that those who look for rewards only in this life will find them only in this life. Those who set their hearts on things above will find their reward there.

6:25. Woe unto you that are full contrasts with "Blessed are ye that hunger" (6:21). Jesus pointed out how transitory the goods of this world are. Hunger and plenty are both temporary. One should look beyond the temporary to what is permanent. The same is true of laughter and weeping. Those who **laugh … shall mourn and weep**, as those who "weep … shall laugh" (6:21). When life is good, one should remember that temporal goods will pass. When life is bitter, one should take comfort in knowing that even that is temporary.

6:26. Woe unto you, when all men shall speak well of you contrasts with "Blessed are ye, when men shall hate you" (6:22). Another parallel is that the prophets were hated in olden times (6:23), while **the false prophets** were well spoken of in those days. The contrast warns one that others speaking well of them is not an indication that one is blessed of God.

6:27–28. Love your enemies (v. 27). The heart of Jesus' teaching is love. While the Golden Rule (6:31) is sometimes expressed in negative form outside the Bible, Jesus not only forbade treating others spitefully but also commanded that believers love everyone, even one's enemies. This can be done only when one has faith that God is in control and that He will work justice in the end. Hatred for an enemy arises when he has frustrated one's goals, when one fears he will do so, or when he has taken what is rightfully another's. That is how one's enemies **curse** (v. 28) or **despitefully use** one. In such cases, people can love the person more easily if they are seeking something higher than this world's goods, as Jesus encouraged in 6:22–23, or if one believes that God will bring about justice in the end. Loving one's enemies, then, is an act of faith in God.

6:29. Offer also the other. Believers are not to have a retaliatory attitude but rather are to trust that God will right all wrongs and that one need not do so oneself (see Rom. 12:9).

6:30. Give to every man that asketh of thee again requires faith that God is in control. This can be done only by those who believe that God will take care of their needs. Jesus was not saying that one is obligated to honor every request. In certain circumstances, honoring another's request may do more harm than good. His point was that one should not regard one's possessions as sacrosanct when another has a genuine need.

6:31. This general principle is often called the "Golden Rule." People should treat others as they wish to be treated. Fundamental to this is a belief in basic human equality: I will treat others' needs as being as important as my own, because others are as important as I am. In the hierarchical society of the Greco-Roman world of that day, this was a radical idea, and it still is today in many non-Christian societies.

6:32–34. Here Jesus elaborated on the reasoning behind the Golden Rule as well as His other instructions in 6:27–30. He was not saying that we should do good to others in hope of recognition. **What thank have ye?** (vv. 32, 33, 34) simply means "what have you really accomplished?" Loving those who love us is easy. Loving those who are difficult or demanding is the hard part.

6:35–36. These two verses summarize what Jesus said in 6:27–34. If everyone followed these three commands, **love ye your enemies, and do good, and lend, hoping for nothing again** (v. 35), the world would certainly be better for it. Not only would one's **reward … be great** in heaven but blessings on earth would abound to all. Finally, Jesus summed up the matter in terms of mercy: **Be ye therefore merciful, as your Father also is merciful** (v. 36). God's perfection should be the example and goal (see Matt. 5:48). Mercy is important because it is goodness given to the undeserving. Enemies, difficult people, and those who borrow have no claim. They do not "deserve" kindness and have not earned it, but as God gives kindness to those who do not deserve it, including Christians, so believers should give kindness to those around them who do not deserve it.

6:37. Judge not. Jesus did not relieve His followers of the need for discerning right and wrong (see 6:43–45), but He condemned unjust and hypocritical judging of others. In addition, He recognized that human nature is such that the person who criticizes will draw criticism. In the same way, the one who forgives **shall be forgiven**. It is easy to forgive a good-hearted person who has made a mistake. One recognizes such people by the way they treat others. It is hard to believe that the man who forgives others easily really means to do wrong, and thus one can more easily forgive and understand him.

6:38. Jesus extended the principle of 6:37 to the area of giving. As the one who forgives will be forgiven, someone who is generous will receive generosity. This is also the case in ministry. This passage clearly teaches that one cannot outgive God. **Give into your bosom**. Probably refers to the way the outer garment was worn, with a fold over the belt that could be used as a large pocket to hold a measure of wheat.

6:39–40. Can the blind lead the blind? (v. 39). This has become a proverb in the English language. In light of verse 40, Jesus was enjoining His disciples to heed His words. Until the light of God's truth shines, people are blind. One should therefore look to the source of light for truth and turn to God, not worldly sources, for the true meaning of life. This passage serves as a reminder that one should look to godly teachers, who know the truth, rather than to those who are not spiritually qualified to give advice. Likewise, one should examine one's own qualifications before presuming to teach others (see 6:41–42).

6:41–42. Mote … beam (v. 41). Jesus used hyperbole (a figure of speech that uses exaggeration for emphasis) to emphasize how foolish and hypocritical it is to criticize someone for a fault while remaining blind to one's own considerable faults. Jesus did not say that one cannot advise others. One should in fact do so, but one must **cast out first the beam** (v. 42) that hinders one's vision. This relates to Jesus' question, "Can the blind lead the blind?" (6:39). Jesus' point was not about whether one has the right to advise another, though that is how this passage is often taken. His point was that one must be qualified, one must **see clearly**, if one presumes to do so. The warning is against attempting to counsel others if one is unqualified to do so because of one's own spiritual inadequacy.

6:43-44. For **every tree is known by his own fruit**, see discussion on Matthew 7:16-20.

6:45. Jesus emphasized the importance of the **heart**. Believers should guard their heart's condition, that is, pay attention to their spiritual life. Those who are given over to evil desires can speak only evil. Those who seek what is good and are oriented toward the things of the Lord will show this in what they say.

6:46. Jesus here raised the central question that every Christian must ask: **Why call ye me, Lord, Lord, and do not the things which I say?** All who profess that Jesus is Lord must check their obedience in light of that profession and try to bring the two into line. If one calls Him Lord and does not act like He is Lord, one becomes hypocritical.

6:47-49. Jesus drew an analogy between responses to His words and building a house. The one who obeys what Jesus says builds a house **on a rock** (v. 48), while the one who does not heed His words builds **upon the earth** (v. 49). The house on the rock stands, and the other falls. Everyone builds their life on some foundation. No other foundation will stand the tests of life as well as Jesus Christ.

F. Miracles in Capernaum and Nain (7:1-18)

7:1. Jesus returned to **Capernaum**, where His ministry was headquartered. There He performed two healings.

7:2. The first healing was due to the faith of a Gentile. Luke's concern was always to show that Gentiles were a part of God's plan. The person healed was a **centurion's servant**. The centurion was probably a member of Herod Antipas's forces, which were organized in Roman fashion, ordinarily in companies of one hundred men. Many Roman centurions referred to in the New Testament showed characteristics to be admired (see, e.g., Acts 10:2; 23:17-18; 27:43). This centurion showed genuine concern for his slave, **who was dear unto him**, and he was admired by the Jews, who spoke favorably of him even though he was a Gentile (see 7:5, 9).

7:3. The elders of the Jews. These were highly respected Jews of the community, though not necessarily rulers of the synagogue (see discussion on 8:41). They were willing to come and plead for the centurion. In Matthew's account, the centurion spoke with Jesus Himself (see Matt. 8:5-13), while in Luke's account, he spoke with Jesus through his friends. Either way, the centurion was the originator and cause of the communication. There is no contradiction between the two accounts (see discussion on Matt. 8:5).

7:4-5. The elders of the Jews approached Jesus on the basis of the man's worthiness, though he had sent them because he believed himself to be unworthy (see 7:7). **He loveth our nation, and he hath built us a synagogue** (v. 5). He certainly had impressive credentials, but one must not suspect that Jesus went to him because he had done these things. There was no sense of obligation that Jesus should perform this healing in return for what the man had done for the people. In all likelihood, the elders mentioned the centurion's good deeds at their own behest, not at his. Had he approached Jesus on his own behalf with these words, he might have been dismissed. God will not make deals.

7:6. As Jesus neared, the man again spoke through intermediaries, sending a humble message: **I am not worthy that thou shouldest enter under my roof** (see discussion on Matt. 8:8).

7:7-8. But say in a word, and my servant shall be healed (v. 7). The centurion showed genuine faith in Jesus' ability to heal. In verse 8, he used an analogy to show that he believed that Jesus has authority over diseases. As a leader, the centurion was used to giving orders and seeing them obeyed. As evidenced by his sending others on his behalf to Jesus, he was used to his word being carried out even when he was not present. Likewise, he believed that Jesus could "say in a word" and it would be done.

7:9. Jesus ... marvelled. The Greek word (*ethaumasen*) for "marvel" is used of Jesus only twice. Here He "marvelled" at faith, while in Mark 6:6, He "marvelled" at a lack of faith. Jesus marveled not that the centurion had built a synagogue but that he had faith. Christians do well to remember this when they are inclined to view their works as a sign of spiritual life. God looks at one's faith. While one may admire those who do mighty works, God admires the one who has a mighty faith.

7:10. Found the servant whole that had been sick. Jesus' word, without His physical presence, was enough to heal the man.

7:11. The second work of healing that Jesus did upon returning to Capernaum was done at **Nain**, not Capernaum itself. The two towns were probably in close proximity, however, since **many of his disciples ... and much people** accompanied Him there.

7:12. There was a dead man carried out who was the sole support of his mother, for **she was a widow**. Death is normal in the course of life in this fallen world. Jesus rarely raised the dead, though He did so at times (see discussion on 7:14–15). This miracle was on a different order than most of the healings He did.

7:13. He had compassion on her. Jesus was motivated by the widow's need as well as by the desire to show His glory.

7:14–15. Bier (v. 14). The man was probably carried in an open coffin, suggested by Jewish custom and by the fact that he **sat up** (v. 15) in response to Jesus' command. This is the first of three instances of Jesus' raising someone from the dead, the others being Jairus's daughter (see 8:40–56) and Lazarus (see John 11:38–44).

7:16–18. Besides compassion for the widow, Jesus may have had two additional purposes in performing this exceptional miracle. The people who accompanied Jesus said **That God hath visited his people** (v. 16). Jesus' miracles were designed to show that He was God.

The second reason for performing this miracle may have been to attract the attention of **the disciples of John** (v. 18). They went to John and **shewed him of all these things**. Despite John the Baptist's

imprisonment, his disciples kept in contact with him and continued his ministry. Jesus may have wanted word of this miracle to reach John for purposes of encouraging him in his imprisonment or so that he would face some of his own doubts.

G. The Inquiry of John the Baptist (7:19–29)

7:19–21. Look we for another? (v. 19). John had announced the coming of the Christ, but now John had been languishing in prison for months, and the work of Jesus had not brought the results that John apparently expected. His disappointment was natural. He wanted reassurance, and perhaps he also wanted to urge Jesus to further action. John's disciples came to Jesus on a day when He performed many miracles of healing (v. 21). This gave shape to Jesus' answer (see 7:22–23).

7:22. Tell John what things ye have seen and heard. Jesus pointed to the healing and life-restoring miracles that He performed, such as those that John's disciples had just witnessed. He gave not promises but clearly observable evidence—evidence that reflected the prophesied ministry of the Messiah. **To the poor the gospel is preached.** In Jesus' review of His works, He used an ascending scale of impressive deeds, ending with the dead being raised and the gospel being preached to the poor. Jesus thus reminded John that these were the things prophesied of the Messiah in the Scriptures (see Isa. 29:18–21; 35:5–6; 61:1; see also Luke 4:18).

7:23. Whosoever shall not be offended in me. Jesus did not want discouragement and doubt to ensnare John. John's doubts may well have been engendered by his imprisonment. Often believers expect God to bless their ministry by smoothing the path and bringing them success. This had not happened in John's situation. His early high-profile ministry had been replaced by a time of waiting in prison day after day, not knowing his fate, possibly having only limited contact with his disciples and others. Jesus' answer showed that God's work was being done, and that without John's active involvement at this point. It is believers who need God, not the other way around, as John should have known.

7:24–29. Jesus always recognized a teachable moment. The people certainly knew who John's disciples were and that they had been consulting with Jesus. What better moment than this to preach on John and his message?

7:24–27. Jesus structured the first part of the message around the phrase **What went ye out ... to see?** (vv. 24, 25, 26). Jesus proposed answers to His question each time He asked it.

A reed shaken with the wind? (v. 24). A reed shaken by the wind is a small thing, not something that would draw a crowd. It might make a little noise, as John certainly made noise, but that alone would not draw a crowd either. John was not a weak messenger, swayed by the pressures of human opinion. On the contrary, he was a true prophet. Jesus' point was that the people went out to hear John because he had something worthwhile to say.

A man clothed in soft raiment? (v. 25). The answer to this one is obvious. Such people are not found in the wilderness where John preached but rather **in kings' courts**. John's raiment was much rougher than this. The people certainly were not attracted to John's ministry by the clothing he wore.

A prophet? ... and much more than a prophet (v. 26). John was the unique prophet sent to prepare the way for the Messiah. Jesus' answers to the question moved from the lesser to the greater: a reed, a man in nice clothing, and a prophet. Jesus implied that the last answer was the only worthy reason to have gone out into the wilderness: to hear the words of a prophet.

7:28. For **he that is least in the kingdom of God**, see discussion on Matthew 11:11.

7:29. Justified God. Jesus meant that their response to John's ministry demonstrated that God had anointed him and was using him greatly. It showed that God was truly at work in John's ministry. The people saw the righteousness of God because of the preaching of John and responded by being baptized.

H. Jesus and the Pharisees (7:30–50)

7:30. Lawyers. A designation used by Luke (see 10:25; 11:45–46, 52; 14:3; see also Matt. 22:35) for the scribes (the teachers of the law), most of whom were **Pharisees** (see discussion on 5:17). **Rejected the counsel of God**. Tax collectors had shown their willingness to repent by accepting John's baptism, whereas the Pharisees had shown their rejection of God's message by refusing to be baptized. The contrast is between the ones who knew they were sinners and those who thought they were righteous (see Luke 5:31–32).

7:31–34. Jesus said that the people of His day were **like unto children sitting in the marketplace** (v. 32). They had rejected both John and Jesus, but for different reasons—like children who refuse to play either a joyful game or a mournful one. They would not associate with John when he followed the strictest of rules, nor with Jesus when He freely associated with all kinds of people.

7:34. A friend of publicans and sinners. Jesus ate and talked with people who were religious and social outcasts. He even called a publican to be an apostle (see 5:27–32).

7:35. Wisdom is justified of all her children (see discussion on Matt. 11:19). In contrast to the foolish critics who rejected the ministries of John and Jesus, spiritually wise persons could see that both ministries were godly, despite their differences.

7:36. One of the Pharisees (see discussion on 5:17). Jesus, who was "a friend of publicans and sinners" (7:34), would also give time to a Pharisee who wanted it. Jesus did not reject the self-righteous in favor of the lowly but rather opened Himself to all and accepted those who came to Him. The motive of this Pharisee may have been to entrap Jesus rather than to learn from Him, but Jesus used the situation as a teaching opportunity anyway.

7:37. A woman ... which was a sinner. A prostitute. She must have heard Jesus preach, and in repentance, she determined to lead a new life. She came to Jesus out of love and gratitude, in the understanding that she could be forgiven. **An alabaster box.** A long-necked, globular bottle. **Ointment.** A perfumed ointment.

7:38. Stood at his feet behind him. Jesus reclined on a couch with His feet extended away from the table, which made it possible for the woman to wipe **his feet** with her hair and still not disturb His eating. **Anointed them with the ointment**. The anointing, perhaps originally intended for Jesus' head, was instead applied to His feet. A similar act was performed by Mary of Bethany the week before the crucifixion (see John 12:3).

7:39–40. What manner of woman this is ... for she is a sinner (v. 39). It is odd that the Pharisee apparently invited the woman into his home but believed that Jesus should have rejected her attention. The Pharisee, **Simon** (v. 40), may have been looking for an opportunity to discredit Jesus and may have thought he had found it here. If so, Jesus proceeded to prove him wrong.

7:41–42. Five hundred pence (v. 41). Pence is the plural of penny, the denarius, a coin worth about a day's wages. This amount was thus over a year's wages. **The other fifty**. This was about six weeks' wages. The contrast was to make the point that the one forgiven the most would love the most.

7:43. When Simon answered that the creditor would be most loved by the one **whom he forgave most**, Jesus replied, **Thou hast rightly judged**. The more sin one has in one's life, ironically, the less willing one is to approach the Lord. This is why younger people are more easily reached for Christ than older people. Once one who has a major burden of sin finds forgiveness, however, the love is greater. This is not to say that believers should go out and sin more so that they may be forgiven more and thus be more grateful (see Rom. 6:1–16).

7:44–46. The Pharisee had gotten the point, and thus Jesus moved on to apply it to his situation by contrasting his treatment of Him with that of the woman. Simon had given **no water for my feet** (v. 44), which was the minimal gesture of hospitality. She, however, **hath washed my feet with tears**. He had given Jesus **no kiss** (v. 45), again a Middle Eastern custom that the Pharisee had ignored. He had not provided oil for anointing Jesus' head, but she **hath anointed my feet** (v. 46). Jesus, then, had been shown much more honor by her than by His host.

7:47–50. For she loved much (v. 47). The woman's love was evidence of her forgiveness but not the basis for it (see Eph. 1:7). **Thy faith hath saved thee** (v. 50) clearly states that she was saved by faith. She had done no wrong in anointing Him, and Jesus had already made it clear that He would associate with sinners, not to participate in sin but to open the gates of God's mercy to those who would repent. Her sins were forgiven and she could experience God's **peace** (see 1:79; discussion on 2:14).

I. The Second Tour of Galilee (8:1–3)

8:1. He went throughout every city and village. Jesus' ministry had been centered in Capernaum, and much of His preaching was in synagogues, but now He traveled again from town to town on a second tour of the Galilean countryside (for the first tour, see 4:43–44; Matt. 4:23–25; Mark 1:38–39; for the third tour, see discussion on 9:1–6.) For **the kingdom of God**, see discussion on 4:43.

8:2. Mary called Magdalene. Her hometown was Magdala. She is not to be confused with the sinful woman of chapter 7 or Mary of Bethany (see John 11:1).

8:3. Susanna. Nothing more is known of her. **Ministered unto him of their substance**. Jesus and His disciples did not provide for themselves by miracles but were supported by the service and means of grateful people, such as these women. Miracles were the exception rather than the norm. Jesus could have fed Himself and His disciples as He did the five thousand. God, however, most often uses people to accomplish His work by normal means. These women were blessed through their giving, as they were a blessing through their gifts. Jesus depended on the donations of faithful disciples, and so His work does today.

J. Parables of the Kingdom (8:4–21)

8:4. Parable. From this point on, Jesus used parables (see discussions on Matt. 13:3; Mark 4:2) more extensively as a means of teaching. They were particularly effective and easy to remember because He used familiar scenes. Although parables clarified

Jesus' teaching, they also included hidden meanings that needed further explanation. These hidden meanings challenged those who were sincerely interested to inquire further and taught truths that Jesus wanted to conceal from unbelievers (see 8:10). From His parables, Jesus' enemies could find no direct statements to use against Him. The parable of the sower is one of three parables recorded in each of the Synoptic Gospels (8:5–8; Matt. 13:1–23; Mark 4:1–20). The others are those of the mustard seed (13:19; Matt. 13:31–32; Mark 4:30–32) and of the vineyard (20:9–19; Matt. 21:33–46; Mark 12:1–12).

8:5–8. In the parable of the sower, almost every element has an allegorical meaning. This is not always true of parables, and a wise interpreter ensures that the point of the parable governs the interpretation of its various elements. The point of the parable of the sower is that people respond differently to the Word of God (for Jesus' interpretation of the parable, see 8:11–15).

8:5. To sow his seed. In Eastern practice, the seed was sometimes sown first and the field plowed afterward. **Some fell by the way side.** Roads and pathways went directly through many fields, and the traffic made much of the surface too hard for seed to take root in.

8:6. Some fell upon a rock. On a thin layer of soil that covered solid rock. In such conditions, moisture quickly evaporates, and germinating seeds soon wither and die (see Matt. 13:5–6).

8:7. Some fell among thorns. Or plants that grow thorns, that is, weeds and useless plants.

8:8. And other fell on good ground ... and bare fruit an hundredfold. Luke's description of the harvest is more abbreviated than Matthew's and Mark's (see Matt. 13:8; Mark 4:8), but the point is the same: the quantity of increase depends on the quality of soil. **He that hath ears to hear, let him hear.** A challenge for listeners to understand the message and appropriate it for themselves.

8:9. His disciples. This included "they that were about Him with the twelve" (Mark 4:10).

8:10. The mysteries of the kingdom of God (see discussion on Mark 4:11). These are truths that can

be known only by revelation from God (see Eph. 3:2–5; 1 Peter 1:10–12). **That seeing they might not see** (see discussion on Mark 4:12). This quotation of Isaiah 6:9 does not express a desire that some would not understand but simply states the sad truth that those who are not willing to receive Jesus' message will find the truth hidden from them. Their ultimate fate is implied in the fuller quotation in Matthew 13:14–15.

8:11–15. In this passage, Luke recorded Jesus' interpretation of the parable.

8:11. The word of God. The message that comes from God. Jesus had in mind the specific messages He had been preaching, but it may be extended to include all of the Bible, for truly, people respond differently to the whole of God's Word.

8:12. Lest they should believe and be saved. The Devil's purpose is that people will not hear with understanding and therefore will not appropriate the message and be saved. Often the Devil uses various distractions to ensure that God's Word will not take root within a person.

8:13. For a while believe. This kind of belief is superficial and does not save. It is similar to what James calls "dead" faith (James 2:17, 20, 26). Faith is more than emotions. It is a decision made with one's will to trust God and what He has said.

8:14. These people hear and believe the word but are distracted by three things: **cares**, the sheer busyness of life, making a living, caring for family and self, contributing to the community, and so on; **riches**, either the pursuit of them or the enjoyment and contemplation of them; and **pleasures**, entertainment and fun. None of these things are bad in themselves, but any of them can distract Christians from letting God's Word bear fruit in their lives.

8:15. Here, in one verse, is a manual for making the most of God's Word. The first requirement is **an honest and good heart**. This means one must come to God's Word ready to receive it, not predetermining what it says, nor seeking to misuse it. **Having heard the word.** This means exposure to it. Too often Christians hear or read the Bible only on Sundays and wonder why they never grow. Believers should seek regular exposure to God's Word. **Keep it**. This means doing what God's Word says, applying it to life and shaping one's beliefs according to what it says. **And bring forth fruit**. Hearing the Word of God with a receptive heart brings about results in life, for the glory of God. **With patience**. Christians must persevere. If they are to bring forth fruit consistently, hearing and keeping the Word for a few weeks is not enough. Rather, one must be dedicated to a lifestyle of regularly hearing the Word of God with a receptive heart and applying it to life.

8:16. Lighted a candle (see discussion on 11:33). Although Jesus couched much of His message in parables, He intended for the disciples to make the truths known as widely as possible. For **setteth it on a candlestick**, see discussion on Matthew 5:15.

8:17. This verse explains 8:16. The destiny of the truth is that it will be made known (see 12:2). The disciples were to begin a proclamation that would become universal.

8:18. Take heed therefore how ye hear (see Mark 4:24; James 1:19–22). The disciples heard not only for themselves but also for those to whom they would minister. Truth that is not understood and appropriated will be lost (see 19:26), but truth that is used will be multiplied.

8:19–20. Then came to him his mother and his brethren (v. 19; see discussion on Mark 3:21). More is known about their motive from Mark 3:21, 31–32. The family, thinking "He is beside himself" (Mark 3:21), probably wanted to get Him away from His heavy schedule. Jesus' brethren did not believe in Him at this time (see John 7:5). Various interpretations concerning their relationship to Jesus arose in the early church: they were sons of Joseph by a previous marriage (according to Epiphanius) or were cousins (said Jerome). The most natural conclusion (suggested by Helvidius) is that they were the sons of Joseph and Mary, younger half brothers of Jesus. Four of these brothers are named in Mark 6:3, where it also says that Jesus had sisters. Since Joseph is not mentioned here, it is possible that he had died, or perhaps he was home taking care of the carpenter's shop.

8:21. Jesus' reply was not meant to reject His natural family but to emphasize the higher priority of His spiritual relationship to those who believed in Him. The Bible presents reality as interconnected. Jesus shares a connection with those who **hear the word of God, and do it**.

K. The Trip across the Sea of Galilee (8:22–39)

8:22–23. Jesus said to the disciples, **Let us go over unto the other side of the lake** (v. 22), and then **he fell asleep** (v. 23). For **a storm of wind**, see discussion on Mark 4:37. **They … were in jeopardy** only apparently as the boat was swamped, but Jesus had said they would go to the other side. When God says you will go to the other side, circumstances cannot prevent that from happening. The discples were being tested, and they did not pass the test (see 8:25).

8:24. We perish. The disciples had their own ideas about how this would turn out. In the midst of the storm, however, the disciples did turn to Jesus, which was the right thing to do. The parallel to how one should behave in the storms of life is apt, but one should not push the analogy too far. Believers may apply these verses to the storms of life, but they must remember that this is not the meaning of the passage. The passage is not an allegory. It is an account of what really happened.

8:25. Where is your faith? The disciples certainly did not have faith that they would make it to the other side of the lake, as Jesus had said (see 8:22).

8:26. The country of the Gadarenes. The Gospels describe the location of this event in two ways: (1) the region of the Gergesenes (see discussion on Matt. 8:28) and (2) the region of the Gadarenes (see discussion on Mark 5:1–20). Some manuscripts of Mark and Luke read "Gergesenes," but this spelling may have been introduced in an attempt to resolve the differences with Matthew. The significance of this region was that is was Gentile territory and was thus considered unclean by Orthodox Jews.

8:27. A certain man, which had devils (see discussion on 4:33). Matthew recorded that there were two demon-possessed men, but Mark and Luke mentioned only one, probably the one who was prominent because he did the talking (see Matt. 8:28; Mark 5:2). **Tombs.** An isolated burial ground avoided by most people (but see discussion on Mark 5:5). Graveyards were considered unclean by many Jews.

8:28. Son of God most high (see 1:32; 4:34). The title "God most high" was commonly used by Gentiles (see Gen. 14:19 and discussion; Acts 16:17); its use here perhaps indicates that this man was not a Jew (but see discussion on Mark 1:24).

8:30. What is thy name? Jesus asked the man his name, but it was the demons who replied, thus showing they were in control. For **Legion**, see discussion on Mark 5:9.

8:31. The deep. Or "the Abyss," a place of confinement for evil spirits and for Satan (see *KJV Study Bible* note on Rev. 9:1).

8:32. Swine. Pigs were unclean to Jews, and eating them was forbidden (see Lev. 11:7–8), but this was the Decapolis, a predominantly Gentile territory. For **he suffered them**, see discussion on Matthew 8:31–32. The point of this passage, from a Jewish perspective, is that Jesus went to an unclean place to minister to an unclean man.

8:33. The Scriptures always present demon possession as a real, supernatural happening, not just a form of mental illness. **The herd ran violently down a steep place into the lake.** It will not do to explain this away on the basis that the man's screams scared the pigs. The biblical account emphasizes the demonic influence throughout the entire incident.

8:34–37. Such an incident caused a stir in the town. **They were afraid** (v. 35). A major supernatural event had happened, and the people were afraid due to the unfamiliar nature of it and due to the power that Jesus had demonstrated in this event. They thus **besought him to depart from them** (v. 37). Jesus did so.

8:38. Jesus sent him away. Jesus had another call on this man's life. When God does a work in a life, often one wants to sit and contemplate His goodness. That is not usually God's plan, however.

8:39. Return to thine own house, and shew how great things God hath done unto thee. Jesus directed the man to make the miracle known in his native territory. The testimonies of those to whom Jesus ministered were incredible evidences of His divine power.

L. The Third Tour of Galilee (8:40–9:9)

8:40. Even though Jesus' ministry in the Gadarenes was rejected, **when Jesus was returned** to Galilee, **the people gladly received him**. There will always be a place where God's Word is accepted with joy, just as there will always be places where it is rejected. Believers should never be discouraged if the Word is rejected but rather should move on until they find people who are prepared to receive it.

8:41–56. In this section, Jesus performed two healings. Here is proof that "the people gladly received him" (8:40). Two people made their way through the crowd to come to Jesus with their needs, knowing that He could heal them. These were people with faith, people who knew the value of Jesus' ministry. What a contrast to those across the lake, in the Gadarenes, who had just rejected Him (see 8:26–39).

8:41. A ruler of the synagogue (see discussion on Mark 5:22). The "ruler of the synagogue" was responsible for conducting services, selecting participants, and maintaining order. **He fell down at Jesus' feet.** This man humbled himself before the Lord. No one can demand anything of God, but if one asks, He is eager to bless His children.

8:42. The people thronged Him. Jesus was at the height of His popularity in His Galilean ministry.

8:43. An issue of blood. This woman's hemorrhage had made her ceremonially unclean for **twelve years** (see Lev. 15:19–30). **Neither could be healed of any.** Comparison with Mark 5:26 shows the restraint of Luke, the physician, in describing the failure of doctors to help her.

8:44. Immediately. The woman was healed instantly by the power of God. When all human efforts fail, one must turn to God in faith. No one should wait twelve years, as this woman did, but here there is no condemnation. This may have been her first opportunity.

8:45. Who touched me? Jesus was not asking for information but rather, for the woman's good and for a testimony to the crowd, He was insisting that the miracle be made known.

8:46. Virtue is gone out of me (see discussion on Mark 5:30). To the Greeks, "virtue" had the idea of fulfilling something's purpose, involving the power to do what it was intended to do. Jesus' purpose was to meet needs by His power. Healing power, the power to meet the woman's need, had gone out of Him. As God, Jesus' power was unlimited and this was no weakening thereof but was a matter of His power being used effectually.

8:47. The woman **came trembling** and **declared unto him before all the people**. Believers should never let fear keep them from giving testimony to what God has done in their lives. This woman's faith was honored even though her voice may have quavered and her words may have been hesitant and unsure.

8:48. Daughter. This woman is the only individual Jesus addressed with this tender term (see 23:28). **Thy faith hath made thee whole.** The woman was healed not by the touch of His garment but by faith. This was not magic; the garment was not a talisman or charm. Instead, her faith in Christ was the key. For **go in peace,** see 7:50.

8:49. Thy daughter is dead. Seemingly, the delay had led to disaster. The man's daughter had died before Jesus could heal her. God is not limited by circumstances, however, as the crowd would soon see.

8:50. She shall be made whole (see discussion on Mark 5:34). Jesus offered a word of comfort. This is another situation in which Jesus, while not directly claiming to be God, said something that makes sense only on the assumption that He is God.

8:51. Jesus wanted only His closest disciples and the girl's parents with Him.

8:52. For **all wept, and bewailed her,** see discussion on Mark 5:38. **She is not dead, but sleepeth.** Jesus meant that she was not permanently dead (for a similar statement about Lazarus, see John 11:11–14).

8:53. They laughed him to scorn. Their lack of faith is in sharp contrast to the faith of the woman who had just been healed by touching Jesus' garment (see 8:43–48).

8:54–55. Jesus raised the girl with no fanfare. Jesus was not a "miracle worker"; rather, He did miracles. He was not a magician or charmer; rather, He showed the power of God while meeting genuine human needs. Jesus never engaged in stunts or used dramatic effects for the sake of showmanship or publicity. His simple words to the child here are just the opposite of what one would expect of a charlatan. His quiet confidence and the fact that the girl returned to life were further evidence of the truth of His claim to deity.

8:56. He charged them that they should tell no man (see discussion on Matt. 8:4; *KJV Study Bible* note on Mark 5:43). Further publicity at this time concerning someone being raised from the dead would have been counterproductive to Jesus' ministry.

9:1–6. A new phase of Jesus' ministry began when He sent out the apostles to do the type of preaching, teaching, and healing that they had observed Him doing (see Matt. 9:35). This was the third tour of Galilee by Jesus and His disciples (see discussion on 8:1). On the first tour, Jesus traveled with the four fishermen; on the second tour, all twelve were with Him; on the third tour, Jesus traveled alone after sending out the Twelve two by two.

9:1–2. His twelve disciples (v. 1). The apostles (see 6:13). **Power and authority.** Special power to heal (see 5:17; 8:46), authority in teaching, and control over evil spirits. **Devils.** Evil spirits (see discussion on 4:33). Jesus sent His disciples out **to preach the kingdom ... and to heal the sick**.

9:3. Take nothing. The disciples were to take no excess baggage that would encumber travel, not even the usual provisions. They were to be entirely dependent on God's provision through the people with whom they were staying (see discussions on Mark 6:8–9). Such dependence led them to exercise faith every day and demonstrated God's faithfulness. This leant further authenticity to the message they were bringing.

9:4. There abide. They were not to move from house to house, seeking better lodging, but rather were to use only one home as their headquarters while preaching in a particular community. This kept them from being distracted from their ministry by thinking about themselves and their needs and wants. It also made it easy for people to find them, as everyone would quickly learn where they were staying.

9:5. Shake off the very dust from your feet. A sign of repudiation for a community's rejection of God's message and a gesture showing separation from everything associated with the place (see 10:11; see also discussions on Matt. 10:14; Acts 13:51).

9:6. The disciples were obedient. Christians today would do well to cultivate a habit of obedience to the promptings of the Lord.

9:7. For **Herod the tetrarch**, see discussion on Matthew 14:1. **John was risen from the dead** (see discussion on Mark 6:14, 16). Luke did not record details about John's death (see Matt. 14:1–12; Mark 6:17–29), which occurred about this time, but simply noted that it had taken place (see 9:9).

9:8. For **Elias had appeared**, see discussions on 1:17; Mark 9:11–13.

9:9. He desired to see him. Herod's desire to see Jesus was not fulfilled until Jesus' trial (see 23:8–12).

V. Jesus' Withdrawal to Regions around Galilee (9:10–50)

A. To the Eastern Shore of the Sea of Galilee (9:10–17)

9:10–17. The feeding of the five thousand is the only miracle besides Jesus' resurrection that is reported in all four gospels (see discussions on Mark 6:30–44; John 6:1–14).

9:10. The disciples reported to Jesus the results of their ministry. In doing so, they also reported to one another. The stories of the others encouraged the disciples and motivated them to further ministry. Surely a time of rejoicing followed. **Bethsaida** (see discussion on Matt. 11:21). Jesus and the disciples must have retired to a remote area near the town (see 9:12).

9:11. Although He sought time alone, Jesus welcomed the crowds. People who interrupt may not always be aware that they are doing so, and a minister should at times make allowances for such interruptions, seeing them as opportunities rather than distractions.

9:12. The day began to wear away. After the preaching and healing, the question of food and lodging was raised because they were in an isolated place. Jesus may have introduced the question (see John 6:5), but the Synoptics indicate that the disciples were also concerned.

9:13. Jesus challenged the disciples, knowing that their resources were not adequate but knowing also what He was about to do. When God calls Christians to a ministry, often they do not see the provision until they have begun the work. God is faithful, however, and will provide the resources when believers are committed to doing His will for His glory.

9:14. For **Make them sit down by fifties in a company**, see discussion on Mark 6:40.

9:15–16. And they did so. The disciples obeyed the Lord, even though they did not know where the food would come from. Christians today also should simply be obedient, trusting Him to provide. The disciples distributed the food at His direction. Apparently, the food was multiplied as they distributed it, and not before.

9:17. There was taken up of fragments ... twelve baskets. This act served as an example of avoiding wastefulness and as a demonstration that everyone had been adequately fed (see discussion on Mark 6:43).

B. To Caesarea Philippi (9:18–50)

9:18–19. Whom say the people that I am? (v. 18). The disciples' report was the same as the one that had reached Herod (see 9:7–8). This event occurred to the north, outside Herod's territory, in the vicinity of Caesarea Philippi (see Matt. 16:13 and discussion; see also discussion on Mark 7:24).

9:20. Peter answering said. He was the spokesman for the disciples. **The Christ of God** (see discussion on 2:11). This predicted Deliverer (the Messiah) had been awaited for centuries (see John 4:25; see also discussions on Matt. 16:16; Mark 8:29).

9:21. He straitly charged them ... to tell no man. The people had false notions about the Messiah and needed to be taught further before Jesus identified Himself explicitly to the public. He had a crucial schedule to keep and could not be interrupted by premature reactions (see discussions on Matt. 8:4; 16:20; Mark 1:34).

9:22. For **The Son of man**, see discussion on Mark 2:10. **Must suffer**. This was Jesus' first explicit prophecy of His death (for later references, see 9:44; 12:50; 17:25; 18:31–33; see also 24:7, 25–27). The disciples did not really understand what He said. Perhaps they thought He was using figurative language or speaking a mystery. This passage should remind one that God means what He says, and unless the context demands otherwise, one should take God's Word literally.

9:23. Take up his cross daily. To follow Jesus requires self-denial, complete dedication, and willing obedience. Luke emphasized continued action; "daily" is not explicitly mentioned in the parallel accounts (Matt. 16:24–26; Mark 8:34). Disciples from Galilee knew what the cross meant, for hundreds of men had been executed by this means in their region.

9:24. Whosoever will lose his life for my sake. This saying of Jesus is found in all four gospels and in two gospels more than once (Matt. 10:38–39; 16:24–25; Mark 8:34–35; Luke 14:26–27; 17:33; and, in slightly different form, John 12:25). No other saying of Jesus is given such emphasis. Jesus, in this context, is emphasizing self-sacrifice. Most people want to "save" their lives; that is, they want to live for themselves and make themselves happy. The one who loses his life, that is, gives up personal aggrandizement to live for Christ, giving his life to Him, will find his life. In other words, true happiness and satisfaction will be the result of a life lived not for true happiness and satisfaction but for the sake of Jesus Christ and the gospel.

9:25. This verse is an example of hyperbole. If to **gain the whole world** is worth less than the soul, then certainly any lesser material goal one might set is worth far less than the soul. People should be far more concerned with their spiritual condition than with the things they own. Jesus' words should be a corrective when one begins to measure their quality

of life by what one owns rather than by identifying with Christ.

9:26. Whosoever shall be ashamed of me (see 12:9; see also discussion on Mark 8:38). In this context, there are three kinds of errors people make. Some focus on themselves and their own happiness, others seek material goods, and some trust Christ but keep that fact hidden because they fear what people will think. None of these paths lead to real satisfaction in life. Only open, committed discipleship will lead to true happiness.

9:27. See discussion on Matthew 16:28. For **the kingdom of God**, see discussion on Matthew 3:2.

9:28–36. The transfiguration. This is a turning point in Jesus' ministry. He soon after sends out the seventy (10:1–24), and the level of conflict with His opponents increases (11:14–28; 37–54).

9:28. An eight days. Frequently used to indicate a week (see John 20:26; discussion on Matt. 17:1). **Peter and John and James**. These three were also with Jesus when He healed Jairus's daughter (see 8:51) and during His last visit to Gethsemane (see Mark 14:33). **Into a mountain**. Although Mount Tabor is the traditional site of the Mount of Transfiguration, its distance from Caesarea Philippi (the vicinity of the last scene), its height (about 1,800 feet), and its occupation by a fortress make it an unlikely location. Mount Hermon fits the context much better by being both closer and higher (over 9,000 feet; see Mark 9:2). **To pray**. Luke again pointed out the importance of prayer to Jesus, especially before special occasions.

9:29. The fashion of his countenance was altered. The change in Jesus' appearance is not specified, but the brightness of His clothing is described as "white and glistening." It may have been due to the brightness of the light that shone on Him or due to a physical change.

9:30. Moses and Elias. Moses was the great Old Testament deliverer and lawgiver, and Elijah was the representative of the prophets. Moses' work was finished by Joshua, Elijah's by Elisha (another form of the name Joshua). Moses and Elijah now spoke with Jesus (whose Hebrew name was Joshua) about the new exodus He was about to accomplish, by which He would deliver His people from the bondage of sin and bring to fulfillment the work of both Moses and Elijah (see discussion on 1 Kings 19:16).

9:31. Decease. Greek *exodos*, a euphemism for Jesus' approaching death. It may also link Jesus' saving death and resurrection with God's saving of His people out of Egypt.

9:32. Heavy with sleep. Perhaps the event was at night. For **they saw his glory**, see *KJV Study Bible* note on Exodus 33:18.

9:33. Three tabernacles. Temporary structures to prolong the visit of the three important persons: lawgiver, prophet, and Messiah. The idea was not appropriate, however, because Moses and Elijah were outshone by Jesus' glory.

9:34–35. My beloved Son (v. 35). Or "my Chosen One," related to a Jewish title found in Dead Sea Scrolls literature and possibly echoing Isaiah 42:1 (see Luke 23:35). God the Father spoke in such a manner to emphasize the priority of Jesus over the two greatest figures of the Old Testament.

9:36. The event ended with **the voice**. The disciples well knew that any attempt to describe this event would be met with disbelief, until after Jesus' resurrection. Then it became one more sign of His messiahship.

9:37–38. Much people met him (v. 37). As so often happened, a crowd was waiting to hear Jesus, and someone had a desperate need to call His attention to.

9:39–40. A spirit taketh him (v. 39). This evil spirit was causing seizures (see Matt. 17:15) and a speechless condition (see Mark 9:17). Evil spirits were responsible for many kinds of affliction (see discussion on 4:33). The disciples were unable to drive out this spirit (v. 40).

9:41. Jesus' concern was not with the man who wanted his son to be delivered. This man had come to His disciples, and to Him, in faith. Perhaps Jesus was frustrated with His disciples, who lacked the faith needed for the situation and had failed miserably. Also, He may have been frustrated with the crowd, who may have been more interested in wit-

nessing a spectacle than in seeing the boy healed. Jesus' ministry was designed to point to Himself as Messiah and as God. The people did not perceive this (see Morris, *Luke*, p. 174).

9:42–43. Jesus easily **rebuked the unclean spirit** (v. 42), even as it was tormenting the boy.

9:44. Another prophecy of Jesus' coming death (see discussion on 9:22), with an indication of how it would be brought about (see 22:21).

9:45. Once again, the disciples **understood not** what He meant. **It was hid from them**. Here it is made clear that God was keeping the true import of Jesus' words from them. This may have been because they would have sought to engineer events to prevent His death. Some will wonder why Jesus foretold His death, knowing that the disciples would not understand. It may have been that He knew they would remember after the events took place, thus confirming and strengthening their faith in Him.

9:46. Which of them should be greatest. This subject arose on a number of occasions (see 22:24; see also Mark 10:35–45). The question revealed, as in 9:45, their lack of full understanding of what Jesus' mission and message were all about. Their lack of understanding may have been due to the pride revealed in this incident (see Morris, *Luke*, p. 175).

9:47–48. Jesus ... took a child (v. 47). Children had no status at that time and were certainly not treated with the type of consideration they receive in modern times. A child thus served as a perfect example of what Jesus wanted to teach about humility. **Receive this child in my name**. Here Jesus was teaching that service given in Christ's name to those who are not important, those who cannot help themselves, is accepted as service to Him. People who exalt themselves will not want to take note of the least important members of society. No one who believes they have attained a place in society will want much to do with those who have not earned their place. Children have not earned anything. Everything they receive is by grace. Jesus' point was that as His grace is given to those who have not earned it and cannot help themselves, so His followers should willingly give grace to those in like condition. **He that is least ... shall**

be great. A person will become great as he or she sincerely and unpretentiously looks away from self to revere God. One who serves the lowest in society (as modeled by the child) must esteem oneself even lower. The key to greatness in God's sight is humility.

9:49. This did not immediately follow from what Jesus said in 9:46–48. Luke apparently moved on to another topic. For **he followeth not with us,** see *KJV Study Bible* note on Mark 9:38.

9:50. He that is not against us is for us. Spoken in the context of opposition to the disciples' work (see 11:23, set in a different context). Jesus wanted the disciples to see that service rendered in His name is acceptable to God. Nothing in the context would lead to religious pluralism, nor does it mean that any ministry that uses the name of Jesus Christ is automatically above question on matters of doctrine and practice.

VI. Jesus' Ministry in Judea (9:51–13:21)

A. Journey through Samaria to Judea (9:51–62)

9:51. He stedfastly set his face to go to Jerusalem. Luke emphasized Jesus' determination to complete His mission (see discussion on 13:22; Isa. 50:7). This journey to Jerusalem, however, was not the one that led to His crucifixion but marked the beginning of a period of ministry in Judea, of which Jerusalem was the central city. Mark 10:1 notes this departure for Judea, which John more specifically describes as a journey to Jerusalem during the Feast of Tabernacles (see John 7:1–10). The Judean ministry is recounted in 9:51–13:21 and John 7:10–10:39.

9:52. A village of the Samaritans. Samaritans were particularly hostile to Jews who were on their way to observe religious festivals in Jerusalem. It was at least a three-day journey from Galilee to Jerusalem through Samaria, and Samaritans refused overnight shelter for the pilgrims. Because of this antipathy, Jews traveling between Galilee and Jerusalem frequently traveled on the east side of the Jordan River.

9:53. His face was as though. The words "his face" appear three times in 9:51–53 and once again in 10:1. In each case, it simply means that Jesus had

set His intention to go in that direction. Since it involved movement in a certain direction, He naturally would be looking in the direction He was going, and so He "set his face" (9:51). With this passage, Luke emphasized the turning point in Jesus' ministry. From this point on, His teaching and activities would be determined by the need to prepare His disciples for the rising opposition from the leadership and for the time after His ascension.

9:54. Command fire to come down from heaven. As Elijah had (see 2 Kings 1:9–16). James and John were known as "The sons of thunder" (Mark 3:17). The Samaritans had rejected Jesus and His disciples. While their anger was understandable, they needed to recognize the purposes of God.

9:55–56. Jesus **rebuked them** (v. 55; see discussion on 2 Kings 1:10). Jesus' purpose was to save lives, not to bring judgment. This should not be treated as applying to all times and places. Scripture makes it clear that, in His own time, God will come in judgment.

9:57–62. In this passage, three people indicated their desire to follow Christ. Each of them had conditions under which he would fulfill that commitment. Jesus made it clear, however, that this commitment must be absolute. One cannot place conditions on God. He must come first, and all other considerations in life must be placed in the background.

9:57–58. As they went in the way (v. 57). Continuing their journey through Samaria to Jerusalem. **I will follow thee whithersoever thou goest.** This man indicated that he would make any sacrifice in order to be Christ's disciple, but Jesus' reply revealed the shallowness of his commitment. **The Son of Man hath not where to lay his head** (v. 58). The man was unwilling to suffer personal discomfort for the glory of the Lord. Jesus spoke of the lack of sleeping accommodations, and that was enough to cool his ardor. When a specific sacrifice was called for, his commitment withered away.

9:59. The second man made his condition clear at the outset. He wished **first to go and bury my father.** If his father had already died, the man would have been occupied with the burial then, so evidently he wanted to wait until after his father's death, which might have been years away. Jesus told him that the spiritually dead could bury the physically dead and that the spiritually alive should be busy proclaiming the kingdom of God. Jesus did not believe that family is unimportant, only that one's priorities must be right.

9:61-62. The third man laid down another condition: **let me first go bid them farewell, which are at home** (v. 61). This seems to be a proper request. Jesus would never have counseled rudeness. His reply to this man indicates that He discerned a deeper problem than a mere desire to say goodbye. **Having put his hand to the plough and looking back** (v. 62). This man was too attached to home and to familiar surroundings. His ministry would have been hindered by constantly looking back to an earlier day. A plowman who constantly looks over his shoulder does not have his eyes on the goal and tends to plow crooked rows.

Jesus' reply does not mean that anyone who lapses in their service to the Lord has thus lost their salvation. Nor does it mean that there is no second chance for a Christian who is active in church work and then backslides. If "all have sinned, and come short of the glory of God" (Rom. 3:23), then none **is fit for the kingdom of God**. Jesus here was speaking in terms of service, not salvation. His words mean that as long as someone is looking back to a previous time of bliss, his service is hindered. Such a person should repent and turn to the task at hand and to his commitments. Once the focus is on the present demands of the ministry, the problem will cease to exist.

B. The Mission of the Seventy (10:1-24)

10:1. The Lord appointed other seventy also. Recorded only in Luke, though similar instructions were given to the Twelve (see 9:3-5; Matt. 9:37-38; 10:7-16; Mark 6:7-11). Jesus covered Judea with His message (see discussion on 9:51) as thoroughly as He had Galilee. **Sent them two and two.** During His ministry in Galilee, Jesus had also sent out the Twelve in pairs (see 9:1-6; Mark 6:7 and discus-

sions), a practice continued in the early church (see Acts 13:2; 15:27, 39-40; 17:14; 19:22).

10:2. The harvest. Souls as "fruit" is the idea here. Jesus was encouraging His disciples with the promise of results in their ministry. Evangelism and missions are surely in view here. We should pray for workers and should be willing to go ourselves. Jesus urged believers to pray for those who are going as **labourers into his harvest**.

10:3. As lambs among wolves. As with so many metaphors, this one has layers of meaning. (1) It points out the physical danger they might face. Fallen humanity does not like to hear the message of repentance. (2) It implies that their message might be "devoured" by those who would twist it into something else. In like manner, Christians today should expect to meet opposition to the message of the gospel. Increasingly, such opposition is not a matter of friendly disagreement. (3) It indicates the manner in which opposition to the message will come. (4) It indicates the manner in which the gospel is to be shared. Lambs are a symbol of meekness and gentleness. (5) It indicates the nature of the message as well. The call to repentance, that is, to give up one's pride for humility, selfishness for servanthood, bitterness for forgiveness, and anger for gentleness, is a call that must be demonstrated in the life of the witness. A witness who goes forth as a wolf rather than as a lamb will hinder the message rather than help it.

10:4. Carry neither purse, nor scrip, nor shoes. The seventy disciples were to travel light, without a money bag, luggage, or extra sandals. **Salute no man by the way.** They were not to stop along the way to visit and exchange customary lengthy greetings. The mission was urgent.

10:5-7. Jesus here simply meant that the disciples should not stay where they were not welcome. They were not to go **from house to house** (v. 7) but were to find permanent lodging in a place fairly quickly (see discussion on 9:4).

10:8. Here Jesus gave a final word about accepting hospitality: **Eat such things as are set before you**. This is proper for several reasons. For one thing, it is polite. No one likes a picky eater, and no one appreciates having to make special accommodations for one person. Graciously accepting what is offered creates an atmosphere of friendliness that can hasten the acceptance of the message. When people eat together in harmony and fellowship, it creates a sense of common participation and bonding. In addition, pickiness can expose selfishness and a demanding spirit that is antithetical to the Lord's message of repentance and humility. Finally, food choices and standards vary from place to place, and even from family to family. Believers should not treat certain foods or presentations as being beneath them. Again, that is a kind of pride that is counterproductive to preaching and teaching about humility before the Lord. Humble acceptance of whatever food is offered is more in line with a life of faith in the sovereignty of God and His care for His people.

10:9. The kingdom of God is come nigh (see discussions on 4:43; Matt. 3:2). This was the heart of Jesus' message.

10:11. For **the very dust … we do wipe off**, see discussion on 9:5.

10:12. More tolerable in that day for Sodom. Although Sodom was so sinful that God destroyed it (see Gen. 19:24–28; Jude 7), the people who heard the message of Jesus and His disciples were even more accountable, because they had the gospel of the kingdom preached to them. This passage clearly teaches degrees of punishment. Some sins are worse than others and bring more judgment. "That day" is a reference to the judgment day.

10:13. Chorazin … Bethsaida (see discussion on Matt. 11:21). Jesus here turned on the fulcrum of judgment to discuss various cities where He had already preached the gospel. These cities faced judgment.

10:14. Tyre and Sidon were Gentile cities in Phoenicia, north of Galilee, which had not had opportunity to witness Jesus' miracles and hear His preaching as the people had in most of Galilee (see discussion on 10:12).

10:15. Capernaum. Jesus' headquarters on the north shore of the Sea of Galilee (see Matt. 4:13 and discussion), whose inhabitants had many opportu-

nities to see and hear Jesus. The condemnation for their rejection was therefore greater.

10:16. Jesus here offered His disciples some encouragement. They were to preach in His name and to consider opposition to their message as opposition to Jesus, not to them. As "lambs among wolves" (10:3), they would face opposition, but it was opposition to Christ. A believer's responsibility is simply to bear witness to the message of the truth.

10:17–18. The seventy disciples returned and reported the results of their ministry, with great joy. Jesus replied, confirming their experience, **I beheld Satan as lightning fall from heaven** (v. 18). Even the demons were driven out by the disciples (v. 17), which meant that Satan was suffering defeat. This could also refer to Satan's original fall from glory (see 2 Peter 2:4; Jude 6; Rev. 12:9). In any case, Jesus was offering affirmation, confirmation of what they had seen, and encouragement to continue preaching the truth, for God's power was with them.

10:19. Serpents and scorpions … the power of the enemy. In this context, the snakes and scorpions most likely represent evil spirits (see 10:20); the enemy is Satan himself. Jesus was not saying that Christians do not need to be careful of natural evils in the world. People should avoid things that are dangerous. Someone has said that Christians, the same as everyone else, should look both ways before crossing the street. Not to do so is a presumptuous test of the sovereignty of God.

10:20. Man's salvation is more important than power to overcome the Evil One or escape his harm. **Your names are written in heaven.** Salvation is recorded in heaven (see Ps. 69:28; Dan. 12:1; Phil. 4:3; Heb. 12:23; Rev. 3:5). The focus of believers' lives and preaching should be "God is merciful and will save," not "We have power; look at us." Christians should focus their ministries on the gospel of salvation, on God's great work on the cross, and not get sidetracked with other matters, especially those that would draw attention to themselves and how God may be using them.

10:21–22. This is one of Jesus' prayers of thanksgiving. **Thou hast hid these things from the wise**

and prudent, and hast revealed them unto babes (v. 21). This should be seen in context of Jesus' statement elsewhere that one should become "as a little child" (18:17) to enter the kingdom. God reveals truth to those who come in childlike faith, not to those who are wise in their own eyes. This is not to say that education is useless; it certainly has an important place in God's plan. Rather, it is to say that attitude is important. Jesus commends simplicity, trust, and humility. He never commends ignorance.

10:23-24. Jesus followed up His prayer with a word of commendation and encouragement for His disciples. They had seen things that the **prophets and kings** (v. 24) of old would have wanted to see, that is, the power of God at work in their ministries, and numbers coming to faith. How many of the Old Testament prophets never saw the kinds of numbers that Jesus and His disciples saw coming in repentance and faith.

C. The Lawyer and the Parable of the Good Samaritan (10:25-37)

10:25. Lawyer (see discussions on 5:17; 7:30). A scholar well versed in Scripture asked a common question (see 18:18; Matt. 22:36), either to take issue with Jesus or simply to see what kind of teacher He was. **What shall I do to inherit eternal life?** There was nothing wrong with this question. In context of what Jesus had just told the disciples in 10:24, it was quite proper. People were coming with spiritual needs wanting them met, which the prophets and kings had longed to see.

10:26. Jesus answered the question with a question. He was not trying to put the man off but was pushing him to work through the answer. Sometimes people will learn more if they are led to discover the truth rather than merely told the truth. Jesus, the master teacher, knew this and sought to offer the man a lesson he would not forget.

10:27-28. Love ... God ... and thy neighbour (v. 27). Elsewhere Jesus used these words in reply to another question (see Matt. 22:35-40; Mark 12:28-32), putting the same two Scriptures together (Deut. 6:5; Lev. 19:18). Whether a fourfold

love (heart, soul, strength, and mind, as here and in Mark 12:30) or a threefold love (as in Deut. 6:5; Matt. 22:37; Mark 12:33), the significance is that total devotion is demanded. **This do, and thou shalt live** (v. 28). Jesus was not teaching salvation by works. He was leading the man to see how high the demands of the law are. Believers must help people understand the nature of righteousness before they can see the depth of sin. The high demands of the law will lead people to despair and to seeking reconciliation with a God who is holy. People repent lightly, and serve God poorly because they have not been challenged to look beyond the surface. God's requirements are high, and the sin that separates people from Him creates a vast chasm.

10:29. Willing to justify himself. The answer to the lawyer's first question was obviously one he knew, so to gain credibility, he asked for an interpretation. In effect he said, "But the real question is, Who is my neighbor?" This was the right question to ask. Obviously, the easy answer would be, whoever you see around you. Sometimes, though, one fails to see certain people. Those who are significant, those with whom one identifies, can be easy to love. Jesus, wanting to challenge this man with an even higher demand, offered a parable (see 10:30-37), specifically to challenge him to a higher requirement for love than he had known in the past.

10:30-37. The parable of the good Samaritan. As with so many of Jesus' parables, this one should be carefully interpreted with its context in view. There is so much temptation to allegorize the parables. The context offers no warrant to see this as an allegory of sin (the thieves), Jesus (the Samaritan), and the church (the inn). In fact, such an approach would take away from the meaning that Jesus intended. The parable contains a message of grace (see note on v. 37), which should not be ignored, but Jesus mainly wanted the lawyer to see that genuine love demands much more than he had been willing to do in the past. The parable was designed to convict him of not loving God or his neighbor with all his heart.

10:30. Jerusalem to Jericho. A distance of seventeen miles and a descent from about 2,500 feet above sea level to about 800 feet below sea level. The road ran through rocky, desolate country, which provided the perfect setting for robbers to waylay defenseless travelers.

10:31–34. Priest (v. 31) … **Levite** (v. 32) … **Samaritan** (v. 33). It is significant, and a completely shocking reversal, that the person Jesus commended was neither the religious leader nor the lay associate but rather a hated foreigner. Jews viewed Samaritans as half-breeds, both physically (see discussion on Matt. 10:5) and spiritually (see discussions on John 4:20, 22). Samaritans and Jews practiced open hostility (see discussion on 9:52), but Jesus asserted that love knows no national boundaries. He wanted the lawyer to see that loving your neighbor includes loving the one who is unlovely, the one whom society rejects. Christians do not have the luxury of choosing their neighbors, only the responsibility to meet their needs. Nor does one have the luxury of choosing the time and occasion for practicing love. Their need creates the time and occasion. Finally, one does not have the luxury of determining what resources will be used. The Samaritan used resources that he had planned for other uses, and he left the matter of the final bill open-ended.

10:35. Two pence. Two days' wages. This was a demonstration of grace. Jesus may have intended, as a subtheme, to demonstrate that God's love is given to those who have not earned it and who do not deserve it, that grace is given to sinful people who have no resources within themselves and who need grace and mercy. If so, it is not the main theme of the parable, which should be kept in mind. It does, however, fit in with the lawyer's question (see 10:25). Eternal life is impossible with one's own resources. All need the help of Christ, who comes in genuine love and mercy and meets the need.

10:36. Which … was neighbour unto him …? (v. 36). The question now became, who proved he was the good neighbor by his actions? Notice, the self-righteous theologian could not bring himself to say "the Samaritan." He begrudgingly said, **He that shewed mercy** (v. 36), or kindness. Jesus replied, **Go, and do thou likewise** (v. 37). The call to live out the

gospel of grace, to humbly demonstrate to others that grace and mercy are realities, is the essence of love.

D. Jesus at Bethany with Mary and Martha (10:38–42)

10:38–40. A certain village (v. 38). Bethany, about two miles from Jerusalem, was the home of Mary and Martha (see John 12:1–3). These two women demonstrated two different approaches to the Christian life. While it is not a deliberate allegory, the comparison is too apt to miss and may have been intended by Luke. Martha may be likened to busy Christians who are always serving. Many saintly women through the years have served on church committees and done over and above in their work for God's glory. Mary may be likened to the contemplative Christian who adores her Lord. Martha complained to Jesus that Mary was not helping enough, which demonstrates that wherever He went, He was "in charge." His authority was recognized even above the normal authority structure of the household, so much so that Martha appealed to Him rather than directly to her sister or to their brother Lazarus.

10:41–42. Jesus' answer reveals that too much service may be a distraction. **Thou art careful and troubled about many things** (v. 41). Martha may have become busy for busyness' sake. Jesus did not question the quality of Martha's faith or her heart. An important person had come into the household, and Martha wanted to mark the occasion properly. In her preparations, however, she forgot the one for whom they were being done. **One thing is needful** (v. 42). Jesus did not need a lavish feast or everything laid out perfectly; He needed only the devotion of those who loved Him. Devotion should lead to service, not be a replacement for it, and vice versa. Jesus said that **Mary hath chosen that good part**, not that Martha had chosen something bad.

E. Teachings in Judea (11:1–13:21)

11:1. He was praying. Jesus prayed not only on special occasions (e.g., His baptism, 3:21; choosing the Twelve, 6:12; at Gethsemane, 22:41) but also as a regular practice (see 5:16; Matt. 14:23; Mark 1:35).

Teach us to pray. The disciples' request was met with a model prayer and some teaching on prayer. At this point, Jesus was headed toward Jerusalem, and His teaching was increasingly aimed at preparing the disciples for the time when He would no longer be with them. The Lord's model prayer given here is similar to Matthew 6:9–13, where it is a part of the Sermon on the Mount. Matthew included six petitions in the prayer in the Sermon on the Mount (combining the last two petitions into one), whereas Luke included five petitions.

11:2. Our Father. Jesus was addressing a group of disciples here, not a lone individual. He was teaching them about praying together. Much of the Bible is directed at groups. The address to "our Father" rather than to "my Father" should be a reminder that the church is to pray together, express its needs and dependence on God together, and find strength for prayer in lifting up concerns together.

Thy kingdom come. Thy will be done. The first part of the prayer concerns the will of God. The church should be concerned first and foremost that God's will be done. This concern cannot honestly be expressed if church members are not seeking the will of God in all that they do. During prayer, it is wise to always do some soul-searching to be certain that one can honestly pray, "Thy will be done."

11:3. Our daily bread. It is interesting that physical needs are mentioned ahead of forgiveness. It is a measure of God's love and of one's confidence in His love that believers pray for their physical needs.

11:4. Forgive us our sins. Matthew 6:12 has "debts," but the meaning is the same as "sins." Jesus taught this truth on other occasions as well (see Matt. 18:35; Mark 11:25). The prayer is a pattern for believers, who have already been forgiven for their sins. Jesus spoke here of daily forgiveness, which is necessary to restore broken communion with God.

11:5–13. Jesus next urged persistence in prayer (vv. 5–8) and gave assurance that God answers prayer (vv. 9–13). The argument is from the lesser to the greater (see v. 13). If some humans will grant one's petitions, "how much more" (v. 13) will God help His dear children.

11:5–8. The parable of a friend in need. This parable encourages persistence in prayer. Having just given the model prayer, Jesus wanted the disciples to understand that merely praying it as a rote prayer and then forgetting it would not do. One must be persistent in prayer. As with so many parables, the analogy should not be pushed too far. The man got out of bed and gave to his friend because he was annoyed and wanted his rest. God answers prayers not out of annoyance but out of love. The analogy is to the good result of persistence, not to the attitude with which the petition is granted. Believers should pray persistently, in confidence that God loves them and wants to answer their prayers.

11:9–10. Ask … seek … knock (v. 9). These verses are a commentary on the parable in 11:5–8. As the man persisted with his friend, so should one persist with God. Again, interpreters should not push the analogies here too far. The asking, seeking, and knocking are different ways of saying the same thing: be persistent. Jesus used this formula as a mnemonic device to make His oral teaching more memorable.

11:11–12. Having discussed the need for persistence, Jesus turned to the need for faith and confidence in God's goodness. The analogy is to the father-son relationship. The rhetorical questions assume the answer will be, "No, of course not!"

11:13. To make sure the analogy was not missed, Jesus made it explicit here. If even **evil** men (here Jesus assumed that His listeners knew that "all have sinned" Rom. 3:23) give good gifts to their children, God, who is good, will not give evil things to His children who pray. Instead, He will **give the Holy Spirit**. Matthew 7:11 has "give good gifts," probably referring to spiritual gifts. Luke emphasized the work of the Spirit, however, the greatest of God's gifts. Jesus was not saying that believers should pray only for the Holy Spirit. Nor was He saying that believers do not have the Spirit and must pray for Him to come into their lives. Rather, He was saying that Christians should pray for things that are in accord with the working of the Spirit, in their lives and churches.

11:14. A devil, and it was dumb (see discussion on 4:33). This evil spirit caused muteness. The probable parallel passage in Matthew 12:22–30 (see also Mark 3:20–27) indicates that the man was also blind.

11:15. Beelzebub the chief of the devils (see discussion on Matt. 10:25). Satan (see 11:18).

11:16. A sign from heaven. Jesus had just healed a mute (see 11:14). That was the sign, but the Pharisees would not recognize it.

11:17–18. Kingdom divided against itself (v. 17). If Satan gave power to Jesus, who opposed Him in every way, Satan would be supporting an attack on himself.

11:19. By whom do your sons cast them out? Jesus did not say whether the followers of the Pharisees (see Matt. 12:24) actually drove out demons (see discussion on 11:24), but they claimed to drive them out by the power of God, and Jesus claimed the same. To accuse Jesus of using Satanic power was implicitly to condemn their own followers as well. **Your judges.** The Pharisees would be condemned by those whom they had taught, because their accusation against Jesus would apply also to their followers (sons).

11:20. The kingdom of God is come. In the sense that the King was present in the person of Jesus (see discussion on 4:43) and that the powers of evil were being overthrown.

11:21. Here Jesus introduced an analogy to what He was doing. The devil is the **strong man. His goods are in peace.** This means not that those in Satan's dominion have peace but that the Devil is not worried about them, until one stronger comes along.

11:22. A stronger than he shall overcome him. Jesus was stronger than Beelzebub, and by His exorcism of demons, He demonstrated that He had overpowered Satan and disarmed him. It was therefore foolish to suggest that Jesus cast out demons by Satan's power.

11:23. The one who does not intentionally support Jesus opposes Him, making neutrality impossible. Even the worker of whom the disciples said "he followeth not with us" (9:49) was apparently a believer, acting in Jesus' name (see *KJV Study Bible* on Mark 9:38), and Jesus did not condemn him.

11:24–28. The unclean spirit is gone out (v. 24; see Matt. 12:43–45, where Jesus makes a similar comment about the Jewish nation of that day). Jesus was perhaps referring to the work of Jewish exorcists, who claimed to cast out demons (see 11:19) but who rejected the kingdom of God and whose exorcisms were therefore ineffective. **He findeth it swept** (v. 25). The place had been cleaned up but left unoccupied. A life reformed but lacking God's presence is open to reoccupancy by evil.

11:29. They seek a sign (v. 29). On several occasions, Jews asked Jesus for miraculous signs (see 11:16; Matt. 12:38; Mark 8:11), but He rejected their requests because they had wrong motives.

11:30. As Jonas was a sign. Jonah spent three days "buried" in the huge fish, just as Jesus would be buried for three days before His resurrection (see discussion on Matt. 12:40).

11:31–32. A greater than Solomon (v. 31) … **a greater than Jonas** (v. 32). Jesus argued from the lesser to the greater. If the **queen of the south** (the queen of Sheba; v. 31) responded positively to the wisdom of Solomon (see 1 Kings 10:1–13 and discussions), and the men of Nineveh to the preaching of Jonas, how much more should the people of Jesus' day have responded positively to the ministry of Jesus, who is infinitely greater than Solomon or Jonas!

11:33. A bushel. A container holding about one peck. **May see the light.** A lamp is meant to give light to those who are near it (see 11:36). Jesus had publicly exhibited the light of the gospel for all to see, but "an evil generation" (11:29) requested more spectacular signs. The problem was not with any failure on Jesus' part in giving light; it was with the faulty vision of His audience.

11:34. Thine eye is single. Those asking for a sign do not need more light; they need clear eyes to allow the light to enter.

11:35. This warning flows from 11:34. Obviously, **light** cannot be literal **darkness.** Figuratively speaking, however, darkness can look like light to fallen minds. Jesus was warning His detractors that they might not recognize truth when they saw it. Evil can keep one from knowing what is good. Christians today should indeed **Take heed** of this warning. They often reject the truth simply because it is uncomfortable. This could be a result of sin in the heart that resists or rejects God's truth.

11:36. Here is a word of encouragement. If Jesus' detractors repented of all sin, then they would see the truth more clearly. One sure sign that sin is present in one's life is an inability to take in spiritual truth and apply it. Sometimes a stagnant spiritual life is nothing more than a result of unconfessed sin.

11:37–38. He had not first washed before dinner (v. 38). Not commanded in the law but added in the tradition of the Pharisees (see Mark 7:3; see also Matt. 15:9).

11:39. Clean the outside. Engage in ceremonial washings of the body. **Ravening and wickedness.** These Pharisees were more concerned about keeping ceremonies than about being moral (see Mark 7:20–23). God is concerned with the heart. Here Jesus used another analogy. **The cup and the platter** represent outward deeds.

11:40. Did not he ... make that which is within also? The inside of man (the "heart" and inner righteousness) is more important than the outside (ceremonial cleansing). God made them both, and to give attention to one without the other is an error.

11:41–42. Jesus continued His warning and exhortation here but changed His focus. The statement **rather give alms** (v. 41) does not fit the previous context. It becomes clear in verse 42 where Jesus was going with this. He was using almsgiving as an example of an outward act. Jesus was not saying that inward attitudes are all that matter. The outward deed is important, but the heart must be right as well. **All things are clean** (v. 41). Jesus may have been referring to the dietary regulations of the law. The Pharisees needed not only to do the outward action of giving but also to observe the law outwardly too. Jesus issued a **woe unto you, Pharisees!** (v. 42) because they were doing the outward things, even being fastidious to **tithe mint and rue**, but were ignoring the inward matters of **judgment and the love of God.** Jesus said they should continue to do the one and not fail to do the other.

Too many Christians today are lax about obedience and justify it on the basis that the heart attitude is all that matters. Jesus here made it clear that obedience is both inward and outward. He was rebuking the Pharisees not for tithing but for tithing without a heart for the things of God. Believers should ensure that their hearts are right and then live daily for God's glory in everything they do.

11:43. Ye love the uppermost seat ... and greetings. The Pharisees loved the outward trappings of respectability but not the substance of it. There is nothing wrong with being well known or locally prominent, but they should not pursue these things; nor should Christians deceive themselves that they are spiritual merely because the religious community thinks they are. God looks upon the heart.

11:44. Graves which appear not. The Jews whitewashed their tombs so that no one would accidentally touch them and be defiled (see Num 19:16; Matt. 23:27). Just as touching a grave resulted in ceremonial uncleanness, being influenced by these corrupt religious leaders could lead to moral uncleanness. They were "graves which appear not," in that they looked respectable and thus spiritual, but in truth, they were corrupt. People should be on the inside what they appear to be to others.

11:45. One of the lawyers (see discussions on 5:17; 7:30). This man recognized that Jesus' words had a broader application than just to the Pharisees: **thus saying thou reproachest us also.**

11:46. Ye lade men with burdens. By adding rules and regulations to the authentic law of Moses (see discussion on Matt. 15:2) and doing nothing to help others keep them (see Matt. 23:4), while inventing ways for themselves to evade them, these lawyers had been guilty of the same sin as the Pharisees. That is, they had made themselves look respectable or spiritual, while their hearts remained unchanged.

11:47. Ye build the sepulchers of the prophets. Outwardly, these "lawyers" (11:46) appeared to honor the prophets by building or rebuilding memorials, but inwardly, they rejected the Christ the prophets announced. They lived in opposition to the teachings of the prophets, just as their forefathers had done.

11:48. Ye allow the deeds of your fathers. This means that the lawyers approved of their fathers' deeds. They honored the prophets by building their tombs but not by doing what the prophets said. They did outward deeds that looked good to the public but missed what is most important. By not following the teachings of the prophets, they wound up approving their fathers' deeds in killing the prophets. The connection between their deeds and their fathers' deeds is that neither did what God wants, and both had some connection to the prophets' deaths.

11:49–50. Said the wisdom of God (v. 49). The saying in these verses is not a quotation from the Old Testament or any other known book. It may refer to God speaking through Jesus, or it may refer in quotation form to God's decision to send prophets and apostles even though He knew they would be rejected. Jesus was saying that those who hear His teaching and have the teaching of all the prophets found in the Old Testament as well have an even greater burden of sin and will be judged more harshly, for their sin comes with greater knowledge.

11:51. The blood of Abel unto ... Zacharias (see discussion on Matt. 23:35). Jesus was reenforcing what He said in 11:49–50 by emphasizing the specific prophets.

11:52. The key of knowledge. The lawyers, the very ones who should have opened the people's minds concerning the law, instead obscured their understanding with faulty interpretation and an erroneous system of theology. They kept themselves and the people in ignorance of the way of salvation, or as Matthew's account puts it, they "shut up the kingdom of heaven against men" (Matt. 23:13).

11:53. The Pharisees began to urge him vehemently simply means that the Pharisees began to question Him intently. Their motive, as the next verse reveals, was not a thirst for knowledge or a desire for righteousness, however.

11:54. Laying wait ... to catch something. The determination of the religious leaders to trap Jesus is evident throughout Luke (see 6:11; 19:47–48; 20:19–20; 22:2).

12:1–12. Jesus here offered words of exhortation and encouragement to His disciples. After issuing a warning against hypocrisy (vv. 1–3), He gave them advice on dealing with persecution (vv. 4–12), telling them (1) not to fear, (2) not to deny Christ, and (3) to trust God in the hour of persecution.

12:1. Jesus wanted the disciples to **Beware ... of the leaven of the Pharisees** (see discussion on Mark 8:15). By this, he meant **hypocrisy**. In the previous chapter, Jesus condemned the Pharisees and the lawyers for doing outward deeds while ignoring matters of the heart and for teaching laws that they themselves did not follow. Now He warned His disciples against doing the same things.

12:2. There is nothing covered, that shall not be revealed. In this context, the meaning is that nothing hidden through hypocrisy will fail to be made known. It is not clear whether Jesus meant that one's hypocrisy will be exposed and proclaimed at the judgment seat of Christ or that it will become evident in the natural course of life. Most likely, He meant the latter.

12:3. In closets. Storerooms were surrounded by other rooms so that no one could dig in from outside. Even things that were said that deeply in the house would become known. One's hidden motives are usually clearer to others than one might think. Jesus' words should challenge believers to examine their lives and the extent to which they live consistently with their testimony. Believers' lives should be transparent, especially to one another within the church; indeed, one's life is more transparent than one might think.

12:4–7. Jesus moved on to exhort and encourage His disciples regarding persecution. This passage has no direct relationship to the previous context. Again, however, Jesus was headed toward Jerusalem and was preparing His disciples in a variety of ways for the ministry they would perform after He was gone.

12:4. Them that kill the body, and after that have no more that they can do. Encouragement in the face of persecution (see Matt. 10:28). Persecution can bring about death, but the soul cannot be killed by any man. In the hour of trial, disciples of Jesus Christ should remember this and face whatever comes with a confidence that will be a testimony of the reality of their eternal relationship with God.

12:5. Hath power to cast into hell. God alone has this power. The Greek word for "hell" is *geenna* ("gehenna"; see discussion on Matt. 5:22), not to be confused with Hades, the general name for the place of the dead. In the New Testament, *geenna* is used only in Matthew, Mark, James 3:6, and here. **Fear him.** Respect His authority, stand in awe of His majesty, and trust in Him. When the disciples faced persecution, they would be standing between the men who would kill them and the God who has ultimate power over all men. As believers, they themselves did not face hell but were to be aware that their persecutors would have to deal with the one who would one day judge them. That knowledge would give the disciples a measure of courage and trust.

12:6–7. Five sparrows sold for two farthings (v. 6). God cares even for little birds, which were sold cheaply for food. God cares even more for His children, and even when the situation is bad, God is aware of them and will preserve their souls. Three Greek words used for Roman coins are *dēnarion* (denarius; Matt. 18:28), *assariōn* (Matt. 10:29), and *kodrantēs* (Matt. 5:26), very loosely related to each other as are a fifty-cent piece, a nickel, and a penny. The word for "farthings" is *assariōn*, so the transaction would be something like five birds for two nickels.

12:8–12. These verses deal with the matter of confessing or denying Jesus. Jesus was encouraging the disciples in the face of future persecution.

12:8. Confess me. When a person acknowledges that Jesus is the Messiah, the Son of God (see Matt. 16:16; 1 John 2:22), Jesus acknowledges that individual as His loyal follower (see Matt. 7:21). When the disciples faced persecution, they would be tempted not to confess their faith. Jesus wanted them to recognize their responsibility.

12:9. Shall be denied (see 9:26; 2 Tim. 2:12; Matt. 7:21; 25:41–46). The same word is used for Peter's denial (see 22:34, 61). This is not to say that such

people will lose their salvation. Rather, they will be embarrassed before heaven.

12:10. In this context, Jesus may have had in mind those who persecute believers. If someone who has spoken against Jesus Christ repents, forgiveness is available. Luke may have had in mind Paul's conversion as he recorded Jesus' words here, and Jesus Himself may have looked ahead to that important event and to other occasions when the church would need to admit to their number those who had persecuted them in the past. **Blasphemeth against the Holy Ghost** (see discussion on Matt. 12:31; Mark 3:28–29). Jesus here contrasted those who spoke against the Son of Man with those who go beyond that to blasphemy against the Spirit Himself. Such people have hardened their hearts to the point that they will never repent.

12:11–12. These verses are often misused. They are not teaching that it is wrong to prepare before going into the pulpit. Jesus was not endorsing laziness in sermon preparation. Rather, the context is the persecution of believers. Jesus was telling the disciples that **in the same hour** (v. 12) that they were brought before the authorities, the Holy Spirit would inform them what to say. They were not to worry that their faith would fail in the last moment and that they would deny Christ. Nor were they to plan ahead as to what they might say if they were to face persecution. If the disciples were active in ministering to God's people, building churches, and evangelizing, they would do well. If persecution arose, the Spirit would be with them to help them at that time.

12:13–21. The parable of the rich fool. This well-known parable arose from a question raised by "one of the company" (v. 13). Presumably, this was one of Jesus' disciples.

12:13. Divide the inheritance. Deuteronomy 21:17 gave the general rule that an elder son was to receive double a younger one's portion. Rabbis normally settled disputes over such matters. This man's request of Jesus was selfish and materialistic. There is no indication that the man had been listening seriously to what Jesus had been saying (see 12:1–11).

Jesus replied with a parable about the consequences of greed.

12:14. Jesus is indeed **judge** over all men. In this specific situation, however, He was asserting that He would not get involved in such a minor matter. His ministry was to point people to spiritual realities. Any rabbi could have helped this man if he had a legitimate claim.

12:15. In speaking to the assembled group about the evil of covetousness and materialism, Jesus mildly rebuked the man. It is possible that the group did not overhear the private conversation between Him and the man. In any case, Jesus saw a teachable moment and a lesson that the disciples needed to remember, as do believers today.

12:16. For **parable**, see discussion on 8:4. **The ground ... brought forth plentifully**. The man likely prospered due to rich soil, good farming methods, and careful management. None of these things are sins in themselves, nor is prospering from them. The man's sin was not that he prospered but that he believed prosperity counted for more than spiritual matters (see 12:21).

12:17-19. The man, looking only to this life, planned to store up his wealth and retire early and live for himself.

12:20-21. Fool (v. 20). A strong word (see 11:40; Eph. 5:17). The man would die that very night. None of his wealth would do him any good. This parable is not teaching that it is wrong to be wealthy, nor that it is wrong to plan for the future. Life is more than the wealth one can accumulate, however. One's heart should be focused on eternal matters, even if one prospers in temporal ones. Even early retirement is not a sin, as long as one sees it as an opportunity for service to the Lord and for focusing on more than making oneself happy. This was the man's sin. He thought only of his own happiness in this life and gave no thought to eternity. Eternity came for him quickly, and he was unprepared.

12:22-30. In these verses, Jesus explained the application of the parable for His disciples. If they focused on spiritual riches rather than material riches, it would have important implications for

their behavior and for their faith. These verses need to be examined closely to avoid misunderstanding them.

12:22. Jesus instructed the disciples to **Take no thought** for two things: **your life** and **the body**. In other words, they should not worry about whether they would eat or whether they would have anything to wear. These are concerns for all people at different levels. The poor worry about whether they will have *anything* to eat or to wear. Wealthier people are too often concerned about having the *best* food and the *most stylish* clothes. Jesus was saying that these things, at either end of the spectrum, are of no consequence. He did not mean that there is any virtue in dressing poorly or eating meager fare. The disciple who endeavors to have the poorest and the worst of these things, thinking that this is the path to a truly spiritual life, is just as guilty of "taking thought" for these things as is the one who is obsessed with having the best. Similarly, these verses cannot be used to say that there is any virtue in not looking one's best. Jesus' point was that His disciples should accept what God provides, trust Him to provide it, and then focus on more important things.

12:23. This verse explains why food and clothing are of little importance and echoes the point of the parable Jesus had just told (see 12:16-21). One's life and body have uses far more important than mere feeding and adornment. These are means to an end, not an end in themselves.

12:24-28. Here Jesus began a series of examples. The example of the ravens (v. 24) relates to God's provision of food, and the example of the lilies (vv. 27-28) relates to God's provision of clothing. Between these is the matter of stature (vv. 25-26), which relates to trusting God.

12:24. In the first example, Jesus focused on **the ravens**. They do not toil for their food. Rather, **God feedeth them**. People are more important than birds, and God, who feeds the birds, will feed His people as well.

12:25-26. In the second example, Jesus spoke of one's **stature** (v. 25), pointing out that no one can change height. People can do nothing about it since it is determined apart from a willing of it. Jesus' point was that since one cannot change **that thing which is least** (v. 26), why should one worry about **the rest**? All should accept God's provision of food and clothing in the same way that one accepts His will for one's height.

12:27–28. Finally, in the third example, Jesus considered **the lilies** (v. 27). They are more beautiful than even **Solomon in all his glory**, yet they do not worry about their raiment. God takes care of plants, and He will take care of His children.

12:29–31. These verses sum up Jesus' teaching in 12:16–28. Disciples should not seek food and clothing; that is, they should not worry about these matters but rather should accept them as God gives them, trusting and not doubting that He will provide. **Rather seek ye the kingdom** (v. 31) is a word of exhortation. Since 12:32 suggests that Jesus was speaking to believers, who already possess the kingdom, this command probably means that Christians should seek the spiritual benefits of the kingdom rather than the material goods of the world (see Matt. 6:33).

12:32. Jesus ended this teaching with a word of comfort: **Fear not.** That is, do not be afraid about food or clothes. **Give you the kingdom.** God had given them the kingdom; providing for their physical needs was a small thing. It would be inconsistent for the disciples to say that God had given them the kingdom and yet worry over whether they would eat the next day. It would betray the kind of hypocrisy that Jesus had just warned them against (see 12:1–3).

12:33–34. Give alms (v. 33). The danger of riches and the need for giving are characteristic themes in Luke (see 3:11; 6:30; 11:41; 14:13–14; 16:9; 18:22; 19:8). Jesus, having exhorted His disciples not to worry, now told them to sell their goods and give to the poor. He tied this to the idea that caring for the poor will result in **treasure in the heavens**. He was not saying that this is like an economic transaction. That is, one cannot "buy shares" in heaven by giving to the poor here. It is not the outward action but rather the heart that is important. Those who care nothing for this world's goods but who are

concerned, in the Lord, to meet the needs of others care more about the things of heaven than the things of this world. They exhibit grace, by giving to those who have not earned it, and thus show forth the grace that is a living reality in their hearts. Being focused on God's riches, they are free to share what they have of this world's riches with those in need. They thus have treasure in heaven, not because of an "investment" in this world but because that is where their hearts are (v. 34).

12:35–40. The parable of the watchful servants. This parable points to the need to be busy about serving the Lord at all times, for He may return at any time.

12:35. This is an exhortation to busy oneself with the work of the Lord.

12:36. His disciples were to be like servants awaiting their master's return so that **they may open unto him immediately**, that is, servants who are ready to serve. By analogy, Jesus was going to leave, but when He returns, He wants to find His people busy doing His work.

12:37. He shall gird himself. In this parable, the master reversed the normal roles and served the slaves (see 22:27; Mark 10:45; John 13:4–5, 12–16). So also, when Christ returns, He will bring blessings and joy to His people, not a heavier burden.

12:38. If he shall come in the second watch, or come in the third (see discussion on Matt. 14:25). Night was divided into four watches by the Romans (see Mark 13:35) and three by the Jews (see Judg. 7:19). These were probably the last two of the Jewish watches. The feast would have begun in the first watch.

12:39. Jesus, still thinking of His second coming, changed to another analogy here, that of His coming "as a thief in the night" (1 Thess. 5:2; 2 Peter 3:10).

12:40. Christ's return is certain, but the time is not known (see Matt. 24:36).

12:41. Jesus taught the people in parables but usually used a more direct approach with the disciples. Peter's question, then, was proper. In context, it appears that Jesus was aiming this teaching directly at the disciples. Jesus, still keeping to the analogy of earthly servants and their master, emphasized the duty to fulfill one's responsibilities (see 12:42–28).

12:42–44. Wise steward (v. 42). An outstanding slave was sometimes left in charge of an estate (see 16:1). This had happened to Joseph, whom the Pharaoh put in charge of all of Egypt (see Gen. 41:37–46). By analogy, Jesus was saying that those who serve Him faithfully will be rewarded.

12:45. By contrast, Jesus warned of a disciple who takes advantage of any delay in the Lord's coming, using God's gifts to him for his own pleasure rather than in God's service. If God has given certain gifts and responsibilities, then one must see them as tools to be used in His service. Those who do not will not be rewarded.

12:46–48. Will cut him in sunder (v. 46) ... **shall be beaten with many stripes** (v. 47) ... **shall be beaten with few stripes** (v. 48). Three grades of punishment meted out, in proportion to both the privileges each person enjoyed and his response to those privileges (see Rom. 2:12–16). Those who have much to offer in service to the Lord will be called to do more, and those who have less will not be burdened with ministries for which they are unsuited. Jesus was not threatening His disciples with literal punishment, for He would take care of that at the cross. His point was that there is no room for laziness or self-serving in God's ministry.

12:49–59. Jesus wanted His disciples to understand the seriousness of the ministry and mission to which He was calling them. It was not a ministry of "being nice." It would involve conflict, and they needed to be prepared.

12:49. Fire. Applied figuratively in different ways in the New Testament (see discussion on 3:16). Here it is associated with judgment and division (see 12:51). Judgment falls on the wicked, who are separated from the righteous.

12:50. Baptism. The suffering that Jesus was to endure on the cross (see discussion on Mark 10:38). **Till it be accomplished.** Christ's words on the cross would pronounce the completion of redemption and the end of His suffering on humanity's behalf (see John 19:28, 30). Jesus wished that His hour of suffering were already past.

12:51. Division (see discussion on Matt. 10:34). Jesus brought division, for He would not compro-

mise on the truth. His followers should not compromise on matters of truth for the sake of unity. Division is inevitable as long as people insist on believing things contrary to what God has revealed in His word. Jesus wants His disciples to stand squarely on the truth regardless of the consequences.

12:52–53. Division will happen even within households, but disciples of Jesus Christ should stand firm, even if their families oppose their faith.

12:54–56. Wind from **the west** (v. 54) was from the Mediterranean Sea; wind from **the south** (v. 55) was from the desert. Although people could use such indicators to forecast the weather, they could not recognize the signs of spiritual crisis, the coming of the Messiah, the threat of His death, the coming confrontation with Rome, and the eternal consequences these events would have for their own lives.

12:57. Of yourselves judge. Despite the insistence of the Pharisees, despite the Roman system, and even despite the pressure of one's family, the people needed to accept God on His terms. The signs of the times called for immediate decision, before judgment came on the Jewish nation.

12:58–59. Here Jesus began a new subject related to His teaching in 12:49–53. As an earthly judge will judge a case strictly according to the law, God will do no less. **Give diligence that thou mayest be delivered from him** (v. 58). Settle accounts before it is too late. This is only sensible if one wants to avoid judgment. In the same way, Jesus' disciples were to preach repentance and not waver on this. People should settle with God now rather than later. The disciples were to stand firm on the reality of judgment and the need for repentance before that day comes. **Last mite** (v. 59). If a *kodrantēs* corresponds to a penny (see discussion on 12:6–7), a mite (Greek, *lepton*) corresponds to half a penny.

13:1. There were present at that season is a clue that what follows happened at about the same time as the events of chapter 12. The teaching in chapter 13 did not necessarily happen the same day. In the Bible, the setting often changes with only the barest of clues. The events of 11:1–13:35 all could have taken place on the same day (13:31), though not necessarily so. The events of 13:20–30 and of 13:31–35 certainly did happen on the same day (13:31). (It is possible that 12:1 indicates a break, but the context does not demand it, as Jesus continued to teach on the same theme.) **The Galileans**. This incident is otherwise unknown, but having people killed while offering sacrifices in the temple fits Pilate's reputation. These Galileans may have broken an important Roman regulation, which led to their bloody punishment.

13:2–3. Sinners above all … because they suffered such things? (v. 2). In ancient times, it was often assumed that a calamity would befall only those who were extremely sinful (see John 9:1–2; see also Job 4:7; 22:5, where Eliphaz falsely accused Job). Jesus, however, pointed out that all are sinners who must repent or face a fearful end. This should stand as a warning for believers today. It is easy for those who know Jesus Christ and who live for Him to begin to think of themselves as morally superior to others. Nothing in the Bible gives warrant for this. Christians are sinners who have admitted it and who have cast themselves on the mercy of God through faith in Jesus Christ. Believers seek to live lives that are pure before the Lord and before the world, with the help of the Spirit. They are not "less bad sinners" in any sense, only sinners who have found, in Christ, the remedy.

13:4–5. Those eighteen (v. 4). Another unknown incident. **The tower in Siloam**. Built inside the southeast section of Jerusalem's wall. Jesus Himself mentioned this incident, perhaps anticipating what the people would ask next or perhaps taking advantage of the teachable moment. He was nearing Jerusalem, and some in the crowd may have seen the fallen tower and perhaps knew some of those who had been killed. His point was the same as in verses 1–3: accidents happen. They are not necessarily the result of divine judgment. All have sinned, and all must repent. An unfortunate demise is not a sign of greater sinfulness. The misfortune of others should not lead to spiritual complacency. Misfortunes happen in this world, and one must therefore be ready to meet God at any moment.

13:6–9. The parable of the fig tree. As with other parables, one should not look for an allegorical meaning for every element of this parable. Many of the elements simply reflect how fig trees were cultivated. Jesus' point was simply that God could judge all men quickly, but He is merciful and gives further time to repent.

13:6. A fig tree. Possibly refers to the Jewish nation (see discussion on Mark 11:12–14) but most likely applies to the individual soul.

13:7. These three years. A period of ample opportunity. The three-year delay relates to the fig tree. This is not an opportunity to look for hidden meanings as to when God's judgment will occur, nor for some sign as to how much sin God will tolerate before He judges.

13:8–9. The implication is that the man allowed the fig tree more time to produce, though the account does not say so. Likewise, God is patient and gives people ample opportunity to repent.

13:10. This is a transition sentence. As Jesus traveled to Jerusalem, apparently at a leisurely pace, He often stopped to teach in the towns and synagogues.

13:11. A spirit of infirmity. Evil spirits caused various disorders (see discussion on 4:33). The description of this woman's infirmity suggests that the bones of her spine were rigidly fused together.

13:12–13. Woman, thou art loosed (v. 12). The spirit had been cast out, and the woman was freed from the bond of Satan and from her physical handicap.

13:14. For **the ruler of the synagogue,** see discussion on 8:41. **Jesus had healed on the sabbath**. A focal point of the Jewish leaders' attacks against Jesus was His conduct on the Sabbath (see 6:6–11; 14:1–6; Matt. 12:1–8, 11–12; John 5:1–18; see also Exod. 20:9–10). For Jews who felt threatened by the inroads of Greco-Roman culture, observing the Sabbath was an important way of maintaining the distinction between Jews and Gentiles. This is why it was elevated to such a position of importance in the first century. Jesus' healings on the Sabbath was disturbing to these leaders, who saw it as a challenge to the very heart of Jewish life and culture. Still, it is surprising that the ruler of the synagogue reacted as he did. His words indicate that he was aware that a miracle had taken place; he exhorted the people to come on other days of the week for healing miracles.

13:15–16. Loose his ox (v. 15). The Jewish leaders had more regard for the needs of an animal than for the far greater need of a person. Jesus exposed what must have been a common exception among many people who were otherwise strict observers of the Sabbath. In healing the woman, Jesus also made an exception, but with much greater warrant. **Thou hypocrite.** Jesus called His critics hypocrites because they pretended zeal for the law, but their motive was to attack Him and His ministry of healing. Believers should take warning from this. It is easy to speak in terms of spiritual ideals and yet make exceptions personally.

13:17. It was altogether right that **his adversaries were ashamed.** He had left them with no credibility. The Lord did this not as a matter of playing intellectual games. He knew that the issue was deadly serious. He sought to goad them into repentance, not just to win points. **And all the people rejoiced,** not that their leaders' pretensions had been punctured but that good things had happened.

13:18–21. Jesus offered two short parables, that of the mustard seed (vv. 18–19) and the leaven (v. 20–21), to describe the kingdom of God.

13:18. With an introductory statement, Jesus alerted His hearers that He was about to make an analogy (also in 13:20).

13:19. Mustard seed (see discussions on Matthew 13:31–32; Mark 4:31). Its growth symbolizes that the kingdom will grow not through military conquest but as people repent and come into it. **A great tree.** In Scripture, trees are sometimes symbols of nations (see Ezek. 17:23; 31:6; Dan. 4:12, 21). **The fowls of the air** nesting in the tree symbolize that the kingdom of God brings blessings and benefits to those who are within it.

13:20. Jesus varied the introductory statement, using one question here, where He had used two in verse 18. Nothing should be made of this, as it was most likely simply an oratorical device to prevent too much repetition. Jesus was a master teacher who knew when to repeat Himself for emphasis and when to vary His words to add interest.

13:21. Jesus emphasized the permeating quality of **leaven** (see discussion on Matt. 13:33); it works from the inside to affect all the dough. This parable could speak of the powerful influence of God's kingdom to change things, or it could represent how evil can pervade and grow even in God's institutions. **Three measures.** About one-half bushel, or twenty quarts (twenty-two liters); Sarah used the same amount in Genesis 18:6.

VII. Jesus' Ministry in and around Perea (13:22–19:27)

A. The Narrow Gate (13:22–30)

13:22–19:27. Somewhere between the events of 11:1 and 13:21, Jesus left Judea and began His work in and around Perea, which is recorded here and in Matthew 19:1–20:28; Mark 10; John 10:40–42. During the last part of the Perean ministry, it appears that Jesus went north to Galilee and then traveled south again through Perea to Jericho and to Jerusalem. Some of Jesus' sayings that Luke attributes to the period of ministry in Perea are found in different settings in Matthew (see Matt. 7:13–14, 22–23). Perhaps He repeated various sayings on different occasions.

13:22. He went through the cities and villages. Jesus was **journeying towards Jerusalem,** where He would die. Although Jesus was ministering throughout Perea, His eyes were constantly set on the Holy City and His ultimate destiny.

13:23. Are there few that be saved? Perhaps the questioner had observed that in spite of the very large crowds that came to hear Jesus' preaching and to be healed, only a few followers were loyal. Jesus did not answer directly but warned that many would try to enter the kingdom after it was too late.

13:24. Some have seen this verse as teaching works salvation, but it instead teaches exclusivity. Jesus' use of the term **the strait gate** is a reference not to morals but to the exclusive means of salvation. There is no salvation apart from Jesus Christ. **Many ... will seek to enter in,** that is, by means other than by repentance and faith in Christ, **and shall not be able**. This passage should be seen in light of Jesus' words "except ye repent" (13:3, 5). In this context, Jesus may have been warning the people not to depend on mere exposure to the gospel. Merely having heard the message of Jesus, and even rejoicing in it, will not be enough.

13:25. Jesus told a parable to illustrate the problem. **The master of the house** is Jesus. Those who **knock** are the ones who did not repent when they had the chance.

13:26. Those outside will protest that they **have eaten and drunk in thy presence, and thou hast taught in our streets.** They were exposed to the message of repentance and faith.

13:27. I know you not whence you are (see Matt. 7:23; 25:12). Jesus called these people **workers of iniquity**, demonstrating that the problem was that they had not repented. People should take warning from these words today as well. Merely being a church member does not guarantee salvation. Jesus indicated that such protests will fall on deaf ears.

13:28. Weeping and gnashing of teeth is often used to describe those who are in hell or those who are excluded from heaven, as here. It indicates that those who are not allowed to enter heaven will be conscious of their exclusion, and they will sorrow and suffer because of it.

13:29. They shall come from the east, and from the west, and from the north, and from the south. From the four corners of the world (see Ps. 107:3) and from among all people, including Gentiles.

13:30. A theme in Jesus' teaching has been that God values humility (see Luke 14:11; 18:14). This is rooted in the Old Testament (2 Chron. 7:14; Prov. 16:19; Isa. 57:15). Jesus gives it creative expression here. **Last which shall be first, and … first which shall be last.** Earthly greatness has little to do with greatness in God's sight. In this context, Jesus was telling His hearers not to look to their standing in the community as an indicator of standing with God. Today many who are "pillars" of the church will be less than others who are unknown but who serve faithfully wherever God has put them.

B. Warning concerning Herod (13:31–35)

13:31. Herod will kill thee (see discussion on Matt. 14:1). Jesus was probably in Perea, which was under Herod's jurisdiction (see discussion on 3:1). The Pharisees may have wanted to frighten Jesus into leaving this area and going to Judea. On the other hand, these Pharisees may have viewed His ministry positively and wanted to protect Him. Some Pharisees had such a view, as evidenced by Nicodemus (see John 3).

13:32. Jesus called Herod a **fox**, a crafty animal. The reference is to Herod's tendency to trickery and slyness. **To day and to morrow.** In Semitic usage, this phrase could refer to an indefinite but limited period of time. Jesus, then, was not being literal. He meant that His ministry would continue for a while longer. **I shall be perfected.** Jesus' life had a predetermined plan that would be carried out, and no harm could come to Him until His purpose was accomplished (see 4:43; 9:22). He did not mean that He would move from a state of imperfection to a state of perfection. Jesus never sinned. The Greek word for "perfected" carries the idea of completion. Jesus would complete His ministry, no matter what others might attempt to do.

13:33. Out of Jerusalem. Jesus' hour had not yet come (John 7:30; 8:20; see also John 8:59; 10:39; 11:54). He would die in Jerusalem, as had numerous prophets before Him. This, then, is yet another prophecy of His death. It led Him to lament over the city that had killed so many of the prophets (see 13:34–35).

13:34–35. How often …? (v. 34). This lament over Jerusalem may suggest that Jesus was in Jerusalem more often than the Synoptics indicate (see John 2:13; 4:45; 5:1; 7:10; 10:22). The statement in these verses may have been uttered some distance from Jerusalem, however, possibly in Perea. According to Matthew 23:37–38, the same utterance was spoken on Tuesday of Passion Week. Jesus repeated many of His teachings and sayings. Perhaps He had said this on many occasions when the subject of Jerusalem came up.

Your house is left unto you desolate (v. 35). God would abandon His temple and His city (see

21:20, 24; Jer. 12:7; 22:5). For **Ye shall not see me, until the time come**, see Zechariah 12:10; Revelation 1:7 (see also Isa. 45:23; Rom. 14:11; Phil. 2:10–11). **Blessed is he that cometh in the name of the Lord**. The crowds spoke like this upon his triumphal entry (see Luke 19:38), but here Jesus was referring to His second coming.

C. At a Pharisee's House (14:1–24)

14:1. On the sabbath. Of the seven recorded miracles that Jesus performed on the Sabbath, Luke recorded five (4:31, 38; 6:6; 13:14; 14:1); the other two are John 5:10; 9:14. For the importance of the Sabbath to the Pharisees, see discussion on 13:14. Sabbath meals were prepared the day before. The Pharisees were seeking an opportunity to trap Jesus. He sought an opportunity to challenge them. They both found it in the same incident. Jesus did not avoid the controversy but rather met it head-on (see 14:3–4).

14:2. Dropsy. An accumulation of fluid that would indicate illness affecting other parts of the body. The Greek for this word is a medical term, *hydrōpikos*, found only here in the New Testament (see Introduction: "Author").

14:3–4. Lawyers (see discussions on 5:17; 7:30). By questioning them before the miracle, Jesus made it difficult for them to protest afterward.

14:5. Have an ass or an ox fallen into a pit. In Deuteronomy 5:14, the law says that even animals were not to work on the Sabbath, but it was never wrong to help an animal that was in need. Jesus' action was unlawful only according to rabbinic interpretations, not according to the Mosaic law itself.

14:6. By meeting the controversy head-on, Jesus had left these Jewish leaders unable to raise any objections: **they could not answer him**. Jesus had appealed to them before healing the man (see 14:3) and instructed them afterward, pointing out how their own behavior was consistent with Jesus' practice (see 14:5). Sometimes more trouble brews by avoiding controversy until it boils over. If one is in the right, then it is appropriate to meet one's opponents and challenge them, not in a way that antagonizes them but merely to show the rightness of one's position.

14:7. This incident took place at the same dinner party (see 14:1). **The chief rooms**. Maneuvering for better seats may have caused trouble at the Last Supper also (see 22:24). Jesus seized the opportunity for a teachable moment as a result of this incident.

14:8–10. Jesus' words here are a bit of practical advice, but they illustrate a spiritual truth.

14:8. Sit not down in the highest room. Jesus was telling the lawyers and Pharisees to do something contrary to normal expectations. God's Word will often startle the reader and challenge one's assumptions. Many times the right thing to do is not what human nature would indicate. Everyone wants to have a place of honor. Jesus said not to seek it, however, contrary to normal human desires.

14:9. Thou begin with shame to take the lowest room. Following Jesus' advice will prevent embarrassment. In Roman times, honored guests at a meal often were given better treatment than the normal guests, for example, a better seat and better food. No one thought this was unusual. It would be embarrassing, however, if one assumed he was honored when he was not.

14:10. Here is a further reason for taking the **lowest place**. One may find oneself called up to the head table, in a sense, and thus honored before the whole assembly.

14:11. Jesus applied the lesson of 14:7–10 in spiritual terms: **he that humbleth himself shall be exalted**. This is a basic principle repeated often in the Bible (see 11:43; 18:14; 20:46; 2 Chron. 7:14–15; Prov. 3:34; 25:6–7; Matt. 18:4; 23:12; James 4:10; 1 Peter 5:6). This principle played out in Jesus' own experience as well. He humbled Himself when He became a man in order to die for humanity's sins, and God highly exalted Him (see Phil. 2:5–11). He is the ultimate example of what He was teaching here.

14:12–13. Jesus, speaking to His host, taught another lesson: **when thou makest a feast, call the poor** (v. 13). By inviting those who cannot return the favor, disciples become an example of grace in action. Again, what one can do on a small scale, God did on a large scale in the work of the cross. God gives grace to sinners who have nothing to offer.

There is no way we can ever pay Him back for what He has done. Those who have been given grace can demonstrate grace, and that is what Jesus was encouraging here.

14:14. The resurrection of the just. All will be resurrected (see Dan. 12:2; John 5:28–29; Acts 24:15). The resurrection of the righteous (see 1 Cor. 15:23; 1 Thess. 4:16; Rev. 20:4–6) is distinct from the resurrection of the unrighteous. There is no "general resurrection" (see 1 Cor. 15:12, 21; Heb. 6:2; Rev. 20:11–15). "The just" are those whom God has pronounced so on the basis of Christ's atonement and whose actions have evidenced their faith (see Matt. 25:34–40).

14:15. Eat bread in the kingdom. The great messianic banquet to come. The association of the future kingdom with a feast was common (see 13:29; Isa. 25:6; Matt. 8:11; 25:1–10; 26:29; Rev. 19:9).

14:16–24. The parable of the great supper, which warns that not everyone will enter the kingdom.

14:16. Then said he unto him. Jesus used the man's remark as the occasion for the parable. In this parable, the **certain man** represents God. The **great supper** is the kingdom of God.

14:17–20. I have bought a piece of ground (v. 18). The initial invitation must have been accepted, but when the final invitation came (by Jewish custom, the announcement that came when the dinner was ready), other interests took priority. None of the reasons given was genuine. For example, one did not buy a field without first seeing it, nor oxen without first trying them out (v. 19).

14:21–23. The master sent the servant out to bring in those who had not originally been invited and who would not normally have been invited to a rich man's feast. These guests most likely represent the Gentiles, to whom the gospel would be taken after Israel rejected it.

14:24. Those men which were bidden. Without explicitly mentioning them, Jesus warned "the lawyers and Pharisees" (14:3) that those who refused the invitation to his messianic banquet would not get one taste of it, but others would (see 20:9–19). Luke wrote to a Gentile audience, who would have found assur-

ance of their position in Christ in this parable, which emphasizes the calling of those who were not part of the original guest list (see discussion on Matt. 21:41).

D. The Cost of Discipleship (14:25–35)

14:25–35. In this section, Jesus challenged those who were following Him whether they really had the commitment to be His disciples. Things would get rough once He was in Jerusalem, and tougher times lay ahead for them all. Those whose discipleship was nothing more than a lark would not be prepared for persecution, opposition, and hardships.

14:25. This is a transition statement, moving the reader from the context of the dinner party to that of Jesus teaching in a town or on the roadside.

14:26. If any man … hate not his father. Vivid hyperbole. Jesus' point was that one must love Him even more than one's immediate family (see Matt. 10:37). The word "hate" in the Bible does not always carry the emotional connotation that it does today. (Remember that God "loved Jacob" but "hated Esau" [Mal. 1:2–3; Rom. 9:13], meaning simply that Jacob received favor from God, whereas Esau, and his descendants, did not. This had nothing to do with God's emotional feelings about them but rather indicated His choice of one over the other.) Jesus was saying that those who follow Him must choose Him over family if a conflict arises from their commitment to Christ.

14:27. Bear his cross (see 9:23; Matt. 10:38 and discussions). One must be willing to follow Jesus before one knows where the journey will lead.

14:28–32. Jesus used two analogies to make His point clear. The cost of discipleship is like that of building a tower (vv. 28–30) or going to war (vv. 31–32). In both cases, one must consider what the commitment will cost before starting out.

14:28–30. Counteth the cost (v. 28). Jesus did not want a blind, naive commitment that expected only blessings. **Build a tower**. As a builder estimates costs, so a person must consider what Jesus expects of His followers. Being a disciple is like building a building; it is a long-term project that demands one's full attention, not something done quickly or in one's spare time. Jesus was looking for long-term commitment.

14:31–32. Going to make war (v. 31). This is like being a disciple in that it requires the expenditure of one's resources. When someone trusts Christ, their money is no longer their own, nor are their time and talent. It is all given over to the cause of Christ, much like when a nation goes to war and wartime realities determine its policies and the use of its resources and time.

14:33. Whosoever … forsaketh not all that he hath. The cost of being a disciple, Jesus warned, is complete surrender to Him.

14:34–35. Salt is good (see *KJV Study Bible* note on Mark 9:50). This ties into Jesus' analogies in 14:28–32. Salt that has lost its flavor is like someone who starts to build a tower and cannot finish or like someone who goes to war without adequate resources. Such salt does not complete its purpose, and it lacks the resource, the saltiness, to do the job it was intended for. A disciple who does not maintain his commitment is like such salt. Believers must determine never to be "useless Christians," like salt that has **lost his savour**.

E. The Parables of the Lost Sheep, the Lost Piece of Silver, and the Lost Son (chap. 15)

15:1. This is a transition sentence. Jesus was still teaching either in a town or along the roadside (see 14:25). He had a new audience, however: **publicans and sinners** (see discussions on 3:12; Mark 2:15).

15:2. The Pharisees and scribes murmured. They complained among themselves but not openly. **Eateth with them**. More than simple association, eating with a person indicated acceptance and recognition (see Acts 11:3; 1 Cor. 5:11; Gal. 2:12). Jesus came to save sinners, and that required identifying with them. This is in line with His teaching that His followers must humble themselves (see 14:1). He cared not about being "respectable" but rather about being identified with the spiritually needy, whatever the cost. Because He humbled Himself, the Father has exalted Him.

15:3–32. In this section, Jesus told three parables intended to explain the importance of His mission to bring sinful people to repentance. "That which is lost" (v. 4) sets the tone for these three parables, each an illustration of being spiritually lost: the lost sheep (vv. 4–7), the lost piece of silver (vv. 8–10), and the lost son (vv. 11–32). The theme throughout is that when something that was lost is found, one rejoices. The lesson is that God seeks lost sinners to reclaim them, and there is great rejoicing in heaven when one of them repents.

15:3. This parable. Of the three parables in chapter 15, the word "parable" appears only here. Some see these parables as one parable with three parts. The subject matter of each is different, though the point is the same, and thus it is best to see these as three parables that teach the same lesson.

15:4–7. The parable of the lost sheep. This parable contrasts the love of God with the exclusiveness of the Pharisees.

15:4. Sheep. The shepherd theme was familiar (see Psalm 23; Isa. 40:11; Ezek. 34:11–16) to Jesus' audience. As Israelites, it was easy to identify themselves as God's sheep.

15:5. The image here points to the idea that God loves His people and treats them with gentleness and kindness.

15:6. The shepherd rejoices more over one lost sheep that was found than over the ones that were never lost.

15:7. To ensure that the people did not miss the lesson of the parable, Jesus spelled it out for them. **Joy shall be in heaven**. God's concern and joy over the sinner's repentance are set in stark contrast to the attitude of the Pharisees and the scribes (see 15:2). **Just persons which need no repentance** is probably irony. Jesus was referring to those who think they are righteous (such as the Pharisees and the scribes) and feel no need to repent. The parable reveals the value God places on each individual. Like the shepherd who valued a single sheep, so God loves each individual person. It also explains why Jesus spent time with sinners (see 15:2). As the shepherd in the parable sought the lost sheep, so also Jesus pursued sinners, seeking to bring them to repentance and faith.

15:8–10. The parable of the lost coin. The coin lost represents the sinner whom God seeks and values.

15:8. Ten pieces of silver. Ten drachmas. A drachma was a Greek coin approximately equivalent to the Roman denarius and worth about an average day's wages (see Matt. 20:2). **Seek diligently.** Near Eastern houses frequently had earthen floors and no windows, making the search for a single coin difficult. Sweeping would move the coin in the midst of the dust.

15:9–10. Rejoice with me. Again there is celebration and rejoicing, and again Jesus explained the lesson.

15:11–32. This parable is popularly known as "the prodigal son," though modern translations have begun calling it "the lost son" to parallel "the lost sheep" and "the lost coin."

15:11–12. The portion of goods (v. 12). The father might divide the inheritance (the older son received a double portion; see discussion on 12:13; Deut. 21:17) but retain the income from it until his death. To give a younger son his portion of the inheritance upon request was highly unusual, however. **He divided unto them.** The son's request is strange enough, but that the father met his request is even more startling. The story is implausible, but not so completely as to be beyond the bounds of believability. Jesus, like any storyteller, took certain liberties and assumed a certain suspension of belief for the sake of the story. This is not intended to deceive the listener but to spark his interest and curiosity.

15:13. The younger son gathered all together. The son's motive became apparent when he departed, taking with him all his possessions and leaving nothing behind. He wanted to be free of parental restraint and to spend his share of the family wealth as he pleased. **Wasted his substance with riotous living.** More details are provided in 15:30, though the older brother may have exaggerated because of his bitter attitude.

15:14. The younger son failed to plan for the future and instead lived only for the moment. When problems arose, he was unprepared. While this is not the main point of the parable, one can certainly see here a lesson on the wisdom of restraint and foresight. Fulfilling every sensual desire just because one wants to and has the means to is never wise. Living just for the moment, not worrying about tomorrow, is never wise. This young man had done both and was thus doubly foolish. Worse, he had squandered his father's hard-earned money.

15:15. To feed swine. The ultimate indignity for a Jew. Not only was the work distasteful, but pigs were considered unclean animals (see Lev. 11:7).

15:16. Husks. Or "pods," seeds of the carob tree.

15:17. He came to himself. He came to his senses and realized how much worse his condition was than even that of his father's servants. The flow of the story indicates that he truly repented.

15:18. The young man made plans for his return, even as to what he would say. When one has wronged someone, as this young man had done to his father, it is only proper to seek reconciliation. This should be done with all the seriousness the situation requires. **I have sinned against heaven, and before thee.** The young man recognized that his sin was against God as well as against his father.

15:19. He had left home as an arrogant, self-willed young man. He returned as a willing servant. He left wanting to serve himself. He returned ready to serve his father. He left as one unwilling to be a son to his father. He returned as one knowing he was unworthy to be a son to his father. There is much to be learned about the nature of repentance here. No one can come to God as one who has a "right" to salvation.

15:20. In his eagerness, the father **ran** to meet his returning son. So also, God eagerly accepts the repentant sinner. God is eager to save, certainly, but that gives people no warrant to demand it of Him.

15:21. The young man's speech appears to have been cut short by the father's warm welcome. Jesus may have assumed that people would know that he would have given the entire speech he had planned and so did not repeat it, or He may have wanted to emphasize the father's eagerness to forgive.

15:22–23. Bring forth the best robe (v. 22) … **ring … shoes … fatted calf** (v. 23). Each was a sign of position and acceptance (see Gen. 41:42; Zech. 3:4): a long robe of distinction, a signet ring of authority, sandals as a son wore (slaves went barefoot), and the fattened calf for a special occasion.

15:24. Again, the picture is one of rejoicing: **they began to be merry.** In each of these parables, rejoicing is the result of recovering what was lost. Jesus wanted to emphasize that God is eager for sinners to repent, which is why Jesus spent so much time with them.

15:25-27. The **elder son** (v. 25) discovered what had happened.

15:28. The older brother's resentment represents the attitude of the Pharisees and teachers of the law who opposed Jesus, whereas the forgiving love of the father symbolizes the divine mercy of God. The older son resented that much was made of his brother's return. His sense of justice required that his brother be punished or rejected. So also was the Pharisees' attitude toward those to whom Jesus ministered.

15:29. A kid. Cheaper food than a fattened calf. The older brother was not really worried about having a party for himself, only that his younger brother got one. Given his father's demonstrated generosity, he certainly could have thrown a party whenever he wanted. He brought this up as a ploy, to shame his father, as people will often do. Children often use such tactics to try to manipulate their parents. Jesus' stories are very much in touch with human nature, which is why they have such appeal.

15:30. This thy son. The older brother would not even recognize him as his brother, so bitter was his hatred. Like the Pharisees and others that Jesus dealt with, this son did not understand grace at all.

15:31. All that I have is thine. He did not allow the son to manipulate him into guilt. The father's love included both brothers. The parable might better be called the parable of "the father's love" rather than "the prodigal son." It shows a contrast between the self-centered exclusiveness of the Pharisees, who failed to understand God's love, and the concern and joy of God over the repentance of sinners.

15:32. Thy brother was dead, and is alive again. A beautiful picture of the return of the younger son,

which also pictures Christian conversion (see Rom. 6:13; Eph. 2:1, 5). The words **lost, and is found** are often used to mean "perished, but is saved" (see 19:10; Matt. 10:6; 18:10-14). Jesus did not reiterate the lesson at the end of this parable. He had done so twice already (see 15:7, 10), and this parable is so clear that He may have believed it was not necessary.

F. The Parable of the Unrighteous Steward (16:1-18)

16:1. After addressing the Pharisees who had criticized His association with sinful people, Jesus turned to **his disciples.** Perhaps this was more than just the Twelve (see 6:13; 10:1). The Pharisees were still nearby and heard His words, however (see 16:14). **A steward** was one who handled all the business affairs of his master. **Wasted.** The steward had squandered his master's possessions, just as the prodigal (or "wasteful") son had squandered his inheritance (see 15:13).

16:2. The steward was put into a difficult situation. He now had to give **an account** of his management of his boss's financial affairs. Apparently, the master did not ask for an immediate accounting. His holdings must have been vast enough that the steward was given time to get the books into order.

16:3. What shall I do? The steward was unable to do physical work and was ashamed to become a beggar. Under the circumstances, merely finding another household to manage would have been impossible, as his current boss would give him a poor reference.

16:4. I am resolved is analogous to "Aha!" or "I've got it!" as in getting a sudden inspiration (see Morris, *Luke,* p. 247).

16:5-7. The unjust steward had no scruples about using his position for his own benefit, even if it meant cheating his master. Knowing he would lose his job, the steward planned for his future by discounting the debts owed to his master to obligate the **debtors** (v. 5) to himself. Interpreters disagree as to whether his procedure of discounting was in itself dishonest. Was he giving away what really belonged to his master, or was he forgoing interest payments his master did not have a right to charge? The steward may have originally overcharged the debtors, a common way of circumventing the Mosaic law that prohibited taking interest from fellow Jews (see Deut. 23:19). To reduce the debts, he may have therefore returned the figures to their initial amounts, which would both satisfy the steward and gain the good favor of the debtors. In any event, the point remains the same: the steward was shrewd enough to use the means at his disposal to plan for his future well-being. A sinner also must take extraordinary measures if he would plan for the future time when God will cast him out. He must obtain salvation.

16:6. An hundred measures of oil. The yield of about 450 olive trees.

16:7. An hundred measures of wheat. The approximate yield of about 100 acres.

16:8. The man was **commended** by his boss, not for being unjust — he was being fired for that — but for acting wisely under the circumstances. Here Jesus began to make the point of the parable: lost people are often wiser with material things than God's people, **the children of light** (see John 12:36; Eph. 5:8; 1 Thess. 5:5), are with spiritual things.

16:9. This continues the spiritual lesson of the parable by pointing out an application: **Make to yourselves friends**. By helping those in need, who in the future will show their gratitude when they welcome their benefactors into heaven (**everlasting habitations**). In this way, worldly wealth may be wisely used to gain eternal benefit. **The mammon of unrighteousness**. Or "worldly wealth." God's people should make use of what God has given them.

16:10. Faithful also in much (see 19:17; Matt. 25:21). Faithfulness is determined not by the amount entrusted but by the character of the person who uses it. He who is faithful in little things will also be faithful in big things. When choosing leaders in the church, we should seek those who are faithful in minor details and unimportant matters. The person who handles this world's goods poorly because they are not worthy of bother will not handle eternal matters well either. Faithfulness is learned by practicing it every day. People naturally spend more time on lit-

tle things than on things of eternal value. That is the way life is. These little things are given as exercises so that one might learn to handle them well and thus develop the habit of faithfulness. One should learn to manage the small details of life well so that when eternal matters come into one's area of concern, one will be well practiced in good management.

16:11 – 12. True riches (v. 11). The things of highest value, ultimately matters of the spirit, the eternal. If one is not faithful in the little things, one cannot expect to be trusted with these important matters.

16:13. No one **can serve two masters** (see Matt. 6:24; James 4:4). Jesus was stating something that is obvious when one thinks about it, yet so many people try to do just this. Christians should determine that they will serve God only and that all other relationships and obligations will be subsumed under that. Doing so will resolve much of the conflict so many face in their lives as they try to serve their own desires and God at the same time.

16:14. Jesus was telling the truth. He was stating things that were self-evident, that should have been obvious, but which needed stating due to spiritual blindness and foolishness. It is a measure of the spiritual blindness and foolishness of these Pharisees that **they derided him**. Could they not see that He was telling the plain truth in plain language? Did they believe that faithfulness in little things had nothing to do with faithfulness in the things that really mattered and that one could indeed serve God and mammon? Surely not. They were so set on opposing Him that even when He stated the obvious, truths that were self-evident, they still found fault with Him. Believers should remember this when they encounter opposition to the gospel. People who oppose the gospel and Christianity will do so even when confronted with clear evidence of the goodness and truth of the gospel and of the gentleness and humility of Christian people. This is not to say that one should not be gentle and humble, thinking that it does not matter. Disciples should practice these virtues because they are right, not because they will make the gospel attractive. One should not be surprised, however, when one's good life does not convert those who oppose the truth.

16:15. Jesus confronted the Pharisees directly in His reply to their derision. The Pharisees justified themselves before men. One is reminded of Jesus' condemnation of those who pray in the public squares and who love greetings in the marketplace. **God knoweth your hearts**. This refers back to Jesus' teaching that denounced the Pharisees for doing outward deeds but having no inward spiritual life to go with it (see 11:27–44).

16:16. Until John. The ministry of John the Baptist, which prepared the way for Jesus the Messiah, was the dividing line between the Old Testament (**the law and the prophets**) and the New Testament (see *KJV Study Bible* note on Jer. 31:31–34; discussions on Heb. 8:6–12). **Every man presseth into it**. The meaning of this is disputed, but it probably speaks of the fierce earnestness with which people were responding to the gospel of the kingdom. Multitudes were coming to hear Jesus and to receive His message.

16:17. The ministry of Jesus (introducing the new covenant era) was a fulfillment of the law (defining the old covenant era) in the most minute detail (see 21:33; discussion Matt. 5:17). For **one tittle**, see discussions on Matthew 5:18.

16:18. Putteth away his wife (see Matt. 5:31–32; 19:9; Mark 10:11–12; 1 Cor. 7:10–11). Jesus affirmed the continuing authority of the law. For example, adultery was still adultery, still unlawful and still sinful. Matthew's treatment is fuller in that (1) it shows that the law was given because of man's hardened heart in regard to divorce, and (2) it includes one exception as permissible grounds for divorce: marital unfaithfulness (see Matt. 19:9).

G. The Parable of the Rich Man and Lazarus (16:19–31)

16:19–31. Longer than most of Jesus' parables, the parable of the rich man and Lazarus condemned the Pharisees for their attitude toward society's outcasts and for their focus on this world's goods at the expense of spiritual matters. The parable begins as does that of the unrighteous steward (see 16:1–8).

It appears to be the real history of two individuals, yet like a parable, it has one basic lesson: once death comes, one cannot change his eternal destiny.

16:19. A certain rich man. Sometimes given the name Dives (from the Latin for "rich man"). **Purple and fine linen**. Characteristic of costly garments.

16:20. Lazarus. Not the Lazarus whom Jesus raised from the dead (see John 11:43–44). **Full of sores**. The Greek for this phrase is a common medical term found only here in the New Testament.

16:21. Lazarus did not ask for much. He humbly accepted his position and sought only **the crumbs which fell from the rich man's table**. Jesus, on many occasions, taught that God honors humility.

16:22. Abraham's bosom. Both Abraham's bosom and paradise (see 23:43) are mentioned in the Talmud as the home of the righteous. "Abraham's bosom" refers to the place of blessedness to which the righteous dead go to await future vindication. Its bliss is the quality of blessedness reserved for people like Abraham. Simply put, it is being with Abraham.

16:23. Hell. The place to which the wicked dead go to await the final judgment. That torment begins in Hades is evident from the plight of the rich man. The location of Abraham's bosom is not specified, but it is separated from Hades by an impassable chasm. It could be the distance that separates heaven from hell. Hades includes the torment that characterizes hell (fire, Rev. 20:10; agony, Rev. 14:11; separation, Matt. 8:12). Some understand Jesus' description of Abraham's side and Hades in a less literal way, but the passage gives no direct warrant for this.

16:24. Here the positions of the rich man and Lazarus are reversed. On earth, Lazarus had desired "crumbs … from the rich man's table" (16:21); now the rich man desired that Lazarus be sent to give him just a few drops of **water**. This is in line with Jesus' statement that the first shall be last and vice versa (see 13:30). This is a spiritual principle that those who are not honored in this world will be honored in the kingdom and those who "had it made" in this life will have no place in the kingdom.

16:25–26. The rich man's request was refused on two grounds: (1) justice: he had already received his

good things (v. 25) in life and now received his just punishment; (2) opportunity: even if helping him were just, it was impossible. The lesson, then, is that people should take care of spiritual matters in this life, for it will be too late in the next.

16:27-28. I have five brethren (v. 28). For the first time, the rich man showed concern for others. He wanted them to be warned.

16:29. Moses and the prophets. A way of designating the whole Old Testament. The rich man had failed to pay attention to Scripture and its teaching and feared his brothers would do the same. People are responsible for what spiritual truth they have received. In the next world, they will have no warrant to plead ignorance.

16:30-31. If one went unto them from the dead (v. 30). The parable may suggest that Lazarus was intended here, but Luke's account seems to imply that Jesus was speaking also of His own resurrection (see v. 31; 9:22). If a person's mind is closed and Scripture is rejected, no evidence, not even a resurrection, will change his mind. It is human nature, however, to believe that somehow a miracle or a spectacle of some kind will change people's hearts, and one often wishes that this would happen. Congregations sometimes use special events of various kinds in their churches, thinking that they will lead people to the gospel. These events may draw a crowd and thus may be useful, but the preaching of God's Word is what will bring about true repentance and faith. **If they hear not Moses and the prophets** (v. 31), they will not be impressed by anything else.

H. Miscellaneous Teachings (17:1-10)

17:1. Jesus again turned His attention to the disciples but began a new subject. He laid down a general truth: people will hinder the spread of the gospel. Their lives and words will be **offences** in that they will turn people away from the truth. Jesus recognized that this is inevitable. Those who do so, however, will still bear responsibility.

17:2. A millstone. A heavy stone for grinding grain. **One of these little ones.** Either young in the faith or young in age (see 10:21; Matt. 18:6; Mark 10:24).

17:3. Since it is inevitable that offenses will occur, believers must learn to forgive **thy brother** (see Matt. 18:15-17; see also Matt. 12:50).

17:4. Seven times. That is, forgiveness is to be unlimited (see Ps. 119:164; Matt. 18:21-22). Here seven is not a limitation; it is the number of perfection. Jesus meant that as many times as one is offended, one must forgive. If not, the problem is compounded.

17:5. Increase our faith. The disciples felt incapable of measuring up to the standards set forth in 17:1-4. They wanted greater faith so that they might have the power to live up to Jesus' standards.

17:6. Faith as a grain of mustard seed (see Matt. 17:20; Mark 11:23; see also discussions on Matt. 13:31-32; Mark 4:31). Jesus was in no way commending miracles done as a stunt or for amusement. He was simply saying that great things may be accomplished with very little faith if that faith is applied in a godly direction.

17:7-8. A servant (v. 7). A slave is used to illustrate performance of duty (see 12:37). Naturally, the servant serves the master first, not the other way around.

17:9. Does he thank that servant ...? Jesus was not commending ingratitude. Naturally, when one does what is expected and routine, one does not expect thanks.

17:10. This is the application of verses 7-9. Believers should never expect special commendation from God for being obedient to His will. They should never be proud of their record of service in the church or of their spiritual activities. Were believers perfect in every way, which is impossible, they still would have done only what the Lord commanded.

I. Ten Healed of Leprosy (17:11-19)

17:11. He passed through the midst of Samaria and Galilee. From this point, Jesus seems to have journeyed to Perea, where He ministered on His way south to Jerusalem (see discussions on 9:51; 13:22).

17:12-13. The **ten ... lepers** recognized Jesus as Lord, for they addressed Him as **Master** (v. 13). They also knew that they did not deserve to be cured. They had no "right" to be healthy, for they said to Him,

have mercy on us. Mercy is always undeserved favor. These men were asking for grace, something God is eager to give. Perhaps they knew they were sinners and saw their illness as a part of God's judgment on their sin. In any case, they were not demanding a right but rather were asking for something above and beyond that.

17:14. Shew yourselves unto the priests. This was normal procedure after a cure (see Lev. 13:2–3; 14:2–32). In this case, it was an act of faith. The only way the men could carry out this command was to do so in faith that they were healed, and **as they went, they were cleansed**. The best way to demonstrate repentance and faith is to be obedient to Jesus Christ. These men did what Jesus said, thus showing their willingness to submit to Him as Lord and their faith that He would heal them. God moved in response to their faith.

17:15–16. One of them (v. 15). Only one of the men returned to thank Jesus for healing him. **Samaritan** (v. 16; see discussion on 10:31–33). Jews did not normally associate with Samaritans (see John 4:9), but it appears that leprosy broke down some social barriers while erecting others.

17:17–18. Jesus was not ungrateful to this man who showed such dedication. Rather, He was making an observation about human nature. People often turn to God in a crisis, see Him move in response to their faith, and then forget Him when their situation improves. This passage should be a reminder that God notices this and is not pleased. One's gratitude and faith should be constant, not something given only in time of need.

17:19. Thy faith hath made thee whole (see Matt. 9:22). The phrase may also be rendered "thy faith hath saved thee" (7:50). That the Samaritan returned to thank Jesus may indicate that he had received salvation in addition to the physical healing all ten had received (see 7:50; 8:48, 50).

J. The Coming of the Kingdom (17:20–37)

17:20. Jesus was now questioned by **the Pharisees**. They wanted to know when the kingdom of God will come. Either they were looking for a way to trick Him or they misunderstood completely the nature of the kingdom. Jesus assumed the latter and offered them a theologically rich and truthful answer. He began, **The kingdom of God cometh not with observation**. They were to look not for an earthly kingdom at that time with all of its trappings but rather for a spiritual reality.

17:21. Again, the kingdom cannot be pointed out, as one would point out the temple or a city. **The kingdom of God is within you** (see discussion on 4:43). Probably indicating that the kingdom is present in the person of its King, Jesus (see 19:11; 21:7; Acts 1:6). "Within you" could mean that the kingdom is spiritual and internal (see Matt. 23:26), rather than physical and external (see John 18:36). If this is the correct view, the pronoun "you" in the phrase "within you" is to be taken in a general sense rather than as referring to the unbelieving Pharisees personally. The kingdom certainly was not within them. If "you" is specific rather than general, it argues for an interpretation of "in your midst." Thus, the reality of the kingdom was present in the person of the King.

17:22. Jesus turned to His disciples, and His teaching moved to a deeper level than that given to the Pharisees. **Ye shall desire to see.** In time of trouble, believers will desire to experience the day when Jesus returns in His glory and delivers His people from their distress. One should be aware that in prosperous and peaceful times, it is easy to forget the Lord's second coming. Those who suffer persecution and distress understand far more the need for His return.

17:23. Go not after them, nor follow them. Do not leave your work to pursue predictions of Christ's second advent. Many in history, and even these days, would have been spared a lot of trouble by heeding this admonition.

17:24. As the lightning. His coming will be sudden, unexpected, and public (see 12:40).

17:25. First must he suffer. Jesus repeatedly foretold His coming death (see 5:35; 9:22, 43–45; 12:50; 13:32–33; 18:32; 24:7; see also Matt. 16:21), which had to occur before His glorious return.

17:26 – 27. As it was in the days of Noe, so shall it be also in the days of the Son of man (v. 26). Much misunderstanding often accompanies this passage. Many see it as a statement that the sin in this world during the end times will be like that in Noah's day. Certainly, Scripture teaches that sin will abound before Christ's coming, but that is not the meaning here. Jesus was reinforcing the idea that His coming will be sudden and unexpected. The activities Jesus mentioned are the normal activities of life, **they did eat, they drank** (v. 27), and normal plans for the future, **they married wives, they were given in marriage**. These people were not shutting down their lives in anticipation of the flood. When Christ returns, people will likewise be engaging in normal daily life and planning for the future. His coming will cut across all of that.

17:28 – 29. Also as it was in the days of Lot (v. 28; see Gen. 18:16 – 19:28). Again, in Lot's day, the people were engaging in the normal activities of life until Sodom was suddenly destroyed. Neither here nor in 17:26 – 27 was Jesus saying that these activities are wrong. Both situations saw God's judgment because of sin, not because of normal life. In both cases, however, the judgment came without warning. So also, when Christ returns, there will be no warning, no time to arrange one's affairs, no diminution in the hum of daily activity, until His coming breaks into history and changes everything.

17:30. When the Son of man is revealed. At Jesus' second coming, He will be plainly visible to all (see 1 Cor. 1:7; 2 Thess. 1:7; 1 Peter 1:7, 13; 4:13). His coming will be sudden and unexpected.

17:31. Upon the housetop. In Jesus' day, it was customary to relax on the flat rooftop. When the final hour comes, however, the individual there should not even think of going into the house to retrieve some material objects. Matthew and Mark referred similarly to flight at the fall of Jerusalem, and indirectly to the end time (see Matt. 24:17 – 18; Mark 13:15), but here the reference is explicitly to Jesus' return (see 17:30; see also 21:21).

17:32. This short verse recalls when **Lot's wife** looked back (see Gen. 19:26) and was turned into a pillar of salt. Whoever looks back on this world's goods, on what God will judge, shows that their heart is not perfect toward God. When Christ returns, nothing else will matter.

17:33. Whosoever shall seek to save his life shall lose it (see discussion on 9:24; Matt. 10:39). Seeking to save one's life, in this context, refers to seeking to hold on to the material goods of this life, to make one's life as comfortable and pleasurable as possible. A person seeking to "save his life" in this way will find himself uncomfortable and miserable. The pleasures of this world do not last, nor, in the end, do they really satisfy. **Whosoever shall lose his life shall preserve it**. That is, the one who lets go of what this world offers will find real satisfaction in the things of the Lord. He may seem to have less of a "good life" in this world's terms but will, in reality, find true happiness and satisfaction. He will thus "preserve" his life. In the context of the second coming of Christ, believers hearts should be so filled with the riches of heaven that they are ready to leave this world behind. If one is attached to any material pleasures in this world, one is not truly ready for His coming. This teaching harks back to the parable of the rich fool (see 12:13 – 21) who sought to "save his life" by building bigger barns but lost it all when his soul was required.

17:34 – 35. Taken (v. 34). Could refer to being "taken to/from destruction" or "taken into the kingdom." What is clear is that no matter how close two people may be in life, they have no guarantee of the same eternal destiny. One may go to judgment and condemnation, the other to salvation, reward, and blessing. The reference here seems to be about judgment, however. The context talks about the people in the days of Noah (see 17:26 – 27) and of Lot (see 17:28 – 29) being swept away to destruction. At Christ's return, a similar separation will occur.

17:36. The one shall be taken, and the other left. This probably refers not to being taken in the rapture but rather being taken away to judgment, as the next verse seems to indicate.

17:37. Wheresoever the body is, thither will the eagles be gathered together (see discussion on

Matt. 24:28). A proverb. Those taken away will become a feast for eagles and other birds of prey (see Rev. 19:17–18).

K. The Parable of the Persistent Widow (18:1–8)

18:1. Luke introduced the parable of the persistent widow with an explanation of its purpose: to teach the disciples that **men ought always to pray, and not to faint.** Jesus had just been describing things related to judgment and the end times (see 26–37). He may have believed that the disciples needed some encouragement. As was often the case, Jesus chose to offer it with a parable so that the point would be more memorable.

18:2. The story concerns **a judge, which feared not God, neither regarded man.** He did not recognize the law of God and was unconcerned about the needs of others or about their opinion of him. As a judge, he was in a position to judge legal matters, but his moral and spiritual character made him unable to do so well. Jesus emphasized this point, because He wanted the disciples to see that even the unjust can be made to behave justly. How much more could they, then, expect good things from God, who is just? Persistence is the key.

18:3. A widow. This woman was particularly helpless and vulnerable because she had no family to uphold her cause. Only justice and her own persistence were in her favor, and the judge cared little for justice.

18:4–5. The judge granted her justice, not because he cared but because he wanted to be left alone.

18:6–7. What the unjust judge saith (v. 6). Jesus was referring not so much to the judge's literal words but rather to what the story about him says about the value of persistence. **Shall not God avenge his own elect…?** (v. 7). If an unworthy judge who feels no constraint of right or wrong can be compelled by persistence to deal justly with a helpless individual, how much more will God answer persistent prayer? **Though he bear long with them.** Although God may delay coming to the aid of His chosen ones, His intention to do so is certain because He is just. He

is not like the unjust judge, who had to be badgered until he wearied and gave in.

18:8. He will avenge them speedily. This does not contradict the previous verse. Jesus simply meant that when God's judgment happens, it will be swift and certain. Those who have suffered wrong should exercise faith, then, and not waver, for to do so would be to doubt God. In fact, Jesus asked whether when He returns, **shall he find faith on the earth?** Particularly, will He find faith that perseveres in prayer and loyalty (see Matt. 24:12–13)? Here Christ made a second application that looks forward to the time of His second coming. A period of spiritual decline and persecution is assumed, a time that will require perseverance such as the widow demonstrated.

L. The Parable of the Pharisee and the Publican (18:9–14)

18:9. Jesus offered another parable, **unto certain which trusted in themselves that they were righteous.** Apparently not the Twelve but perhaps other disciples who had not completely understood repentance, faith, and grace. **And despised others.** One of the worst things about self-righteousness is that it leads to contempt for those who seem to be less righteous than oneself. Christians should remember that "all have sinned" (Rom. 3:23) and none of us has a corner on righteousness. Many Christians, unfortunately, see themselves as people who have grown beyond major sins. It is well not to commit such sins, but one should all remember that, in the end, none are really superior to the worst of sinners.

18:10. A Pharisee, and … a publican. These two men represent the "best" and "worst" of Jewish society of that day. One was a pillar of the community, and the other an outcast. Jesus chose these two figures to ensure that the contrast was not missed. **To pray.** Periods for prayer were scheduled daily in connection with the morning and evening sacrifices. People could also go to the temple at any time for private prayer.

18:11. The Pharisee … prayed thus with himself. Standing for prayer was normal in that day, but the fact that he prayed "with himself" says that his prayer was uttered in a spirit of self-praise and was more for his own edification than to make contact with God. When engaging in public prayer, Christians today should be careful that they are seeking God rather than merely hoping to sound spiritual. **Extortioners, unjust, adulterers.** The man offered a list of sins he had not committed. Would that he had considered the sin of pride. It would have stopped his prayer in its tracks. **Even as this publican.** The Pharisee's insensitivity is astonishing. He used the presence of the publican as an occasion for self-praise, and that in a prayer to God.

18:12. In his prayer, the Pharisee mentioned two things he did that were spiritual. **I fast twice in the week.** Fasting was not commanded in the Mosaic law except for the fast on the Day of Atonement, but the Pharisees fasted also on Mondays and Thursdays (see 5:33; Matt. 6:16; 9:14; Mark 2:18; Acts 27:9). **I give tithes of all that I possess.** As a typical first-century Pharisee, he tithed all that he acquired, not merely what he earned. Again, as in some of His earlier parables and sayings, Jesus condemned spiritual life that is merely a matter of outward actions. Luke emphasized these teachings more than the other gospel writers did. Being influenced by Greek thought and culture, his Gentile audience may have been receptive to these teachings. The Greeks emphasized the mind over the body, and Luke's readers would have readily agreed that what is in the heart is more essential than outward actions. By the second century, however, this led to Gnosticism, which saw the body as evil and as a trap for the mind. This heresy is never in view in Luke, nor anywhere in Jesus' teachings. The emphasis is not that the mind (or heart) is more important than the body but rather that both the inner heart and the outward actions are essential to a healthy spiritual life. Luke made this point clear in 11:42, where Jesus said, "these ought ye to have done, and not to leave the other [outward actions] undone." Here He said nothing to indicate that the Pharisee's outward actions were wrong. He had done good, even commendable, things. His heart was wrong, however, for he trusted in his own righteousness, unlike the publican whose prayer is presented in 18:13–14.

18:13. Be merciful to me. The verb used here means "to be propitiated" (see discussion on 1 John 2:2). The tax collector did not plead his good works but rather the mercy of God in forgiving his sin. He had nothing to offer God, but then, neither did the Pharisee. The difference was that he knew it and the Pharisee did not.

18:14. Justified. God reckoned him to be righteous; that is, his sins were forgiven and he was credited with righteousness, not his own (see 18:9) but that which comes from God. This passage is one of the clearest presentations of righteousness through faith and not by works that is to be found anywhere in the Gospels.

M. Jesus and the Children (18:15–17)

18:15–16. The disciples here were diligently ensuring that their Master's time was well spent. Their sense of priorities, however, was quite different from that of Jesus. He made this clear in His gentle rebuke.

18:17. As with so much in Jesus' ministry, His receiving the children illustrated a spiritual truth: people should **receive the kingdom of God as a little child**, that is, with total dependence, full trust, frank openness, and complete sincerity (see Matt. 18:3; 19:14; Mark 10:15 and discussion; 1 Peter 2:2). For Jesus, the visual imagery of little children coming to Him and being received and welcomed would impact people's minds as they considered their own approach to God.

N. The Rich Young Ruler (18:18–30)

18:18–27. For this event, see also discussions on Mark 10:17–27. Jesus' point to the man was that he needed grace and should live so as to demonstrate grace as well.

18:18. Eternal life (see discussion on Matt. 19:16). This man asked a legitimate question.

18:19. Why callest thou me good? This may seem like a diversion at first, but Jesus wanted the man to acknowledge that he himself needed grace to have eternal life, pointing out that God alone is good. He used the man's address to Him ("Good Master," 18:18) as a touchstone to gently suggest the truth.

18:20–21. Jesus cited some of the Ten Commandments, and the young ruler asserted, **these have I kept** (v. 21). He had not grasped the import of Jesus' words in 18:19. He still, like the Pharisee in the parable Jesus had just related (see 18:9–14), believed that he was righteous.

18:22. Yet lackest thou one thing. Jesus knew that the one thing this man needed was to recognize that grace was what he needed. He told the man to do three things. (1) **Sell all that thou hast,** that is, rid himself of every encumbrance that tied him to this world. Like the rich fool in the parable related in 12:16–21, this man had "much goods" (12:19) and may have been in danger of relying too much on them. (2) **Distribute unto the poor.** Here was the crux of the matter. The poor had not earned any wealth. Jesus wanted him to go and be an example of grace, giving people what they had not earned and did not deserve. He would have thus learned something about grace and prepared his heart to receive it. In Luke 14:13 Jesus taught about being an example of grace (see 14:13) and perhaps saw this as a key to living the Christian life before the world. Disciples could all stand to learn ways to be an example of God's grace in their dealings with the lost world. (3) **Come, follow me;** that is, He invited the man into the open-ended adventure of faith. Unencumbered by worldly goods, living a life of grace, he would be ready to hear the message of repentance and faith and thus would find eternal life. This kind of commitment cannot be made halfway or with reservations. Jesus had already sent away others who had placed conditions on their discipleship (see 9:57–62). Following Jesus will lead one to places they know not and into situations they cannot have predicted. It was true then and still is true today. Such a commitment requires faith in the goodness and sovereignty of God and a willingness to suffer any hardship. It is to abandon oneself to the belief that God is good and that His will is better than anything one could accomplish without Him.

18:23. The man was not equal to the challenge. It is interesting, and certainly an insight into the darkness of human nature after the fall, that this man left.

He had asked about eternal life but then refused to do what Jesus said, knowing that it meant he would not inherit eternal life. He loved the riches of this world so much more that he was willing to give up eternity, knowing he was doing so, to enjoy the pleasures of this life for a short time.

18:24–25. Jesus, sorrowing, offered a commentary on the situation. He did not say that no rich people will ever be saved. He only said that people in such circumstances see little need to depend on God. Those who have made a financial fortune may have trouble understanding grace. In any case, they see little need to depend on God or anyone else, having the means to live physically with little expenditure of effort. They experience this world as a pleasant place to live and thus have trouble longing for a better world to come.

18:26. Who then can be saved? Those who heard Jesus' commentary asked the right question, considering the culture of the day. Wealth was often seen as a sign of God's favor. If even the rich, the favored of God, would have trouble being saved, then who had any hope of it at all?

18:27. Jesus' reply brought the discussion right back to grace. It is possible for the rich, as well as the poor, to be saved. Neither can depend on themselves, for salvation is **unpossible with men.** But salvation does not depend on men, on their striving and effort. It depends on God and His grace and power; thus, salvation is **possible with God** for anyone who repents, rich or poor.

18:28–29. Peter's words were not a matter of pride. He was stating the fact that they had done what Jesus counseled the rich young ruler to do: they had **left all, and followed thee** (v. 28). Jesus' reply was a word of assurance for those who had made sacrifices. His words are as true today as they were then, and Christians should not be afraid to leave behind **house, or parents, or brethren, or wife, or children** (v. 29), for Jesus promised that it will be worth it (see 18:30).

18:30. Who shall not receive manifold more. Jesus was not saying those who leave something behind to follow Him will receive the same things, houses and family, but that what they receive will be of greater value. Among them is the joy of knowing they have lived a life of service to God, that they have made the very best of what God has given them, and that their life and work will count for eternity. Notice that Jesus did not say that anyone who follows Him must leave their families, only that if one must do so, the reward will be worth it. Nor did He say that one may not care about family. He did not teach that Christians should not love those dearest to them. In fact, His words recognize that family and possessions have a legitimate value, which is why it is hard to leave them and why God rewards those who do so for His sake; He understood the sacrifice involved. No one should use this verse as a basis for saying that they should not care about their families. The verse says only that the call to follow Jesus may involve leaving behind things and people one legitimately cares about. It will always be worth it to do His will, however, both **in this present time, and in the world to come**. In that future day, eternal rewards will be given out at the judgment seat of Christ.

O. Christ Foretells His Death (18:31–34)

18:31–33. All things that are written by the prophets (v. 31). Sometimes referred to as the third prophecy of Jesus' death, though the total number is more than three (see discussion on 17:25). The first distinct prophecy is in 9:22, and the second is in 9:43–45. The Messiah's death had been prophesied and/or prefigured centuries before (see, e.g., Psalm 22; Isaiah 53; Zech. 13:7; see also Luke 24:27; Matt. 26:24, 31, 54). For **the Son of man**, see discussion on Mark 2:10.

18:34. The disciples **understood none of these things** that Jesus said regarding His death. Perhaps Jesus' use of the third person made it difficult for them, or perhaps it was the natural inclination to take something obscure and out of one's experience and try to spiritualize it. This passage is an example that God's Word is best taken literally unless the context demands that it be seen in an allegorical or figurative sense. Also, God may have worked supernaturally, for the import of these words **was hid from them**.

P. A Blind Beggar Given His Sight (18:35–43)

18:35. For **as he was come nigh unto Jericho**, see discussion on Mark 10:46. **A certain blind man**. Bartimeus (see Mark 10:46). Matthew recorded that two blind men were healed (see Matt. 20:30). Probably since one was the spokesman and thus more outstanding, Mark and Luke did not record the presence of the other.

18:36–37. The man was probably well known to the crowd.

18:38–39. Son of David (v. 38). A Messianic title (see Matt. 22:41–45; Mark 12:35; John 7:42; see also 2 Sam. 7:12–13; Ps. 89:3–4; Amos 9:11; Matt. 12:23; 21:15–16).

18:40. Jesus apparently stopped to deal with the man. This brought the entire procession to a halt. It is testimony to the Lord's commitment to meet people's needs. He could have sent one of the disciples to tell the man where He would be stopping to rest and to meet Him there. Instead, He halted everything to meet the man's need.

18:41–42. Thy faith (v. 42; see discussion on 17:19). Jesus healed the man when he told Him what he wanted. Surely Jesus could see that the man was blind but wanted him to confess his need and thus express his faith. That faith was what made it possible for him to be healed. God knows human needs before they are expressed but often waits until one comes to Him, expressing a need and faith in His ability and willingness to act, before He meets the need. God loves to hear the prayers of His people, and faith opens doors for His mercy to be shown in one's life.

18:43. Having **received his sight**, the man followed Jesus, **glorifying God**, as did **all the people**. When God answers prayer, it is an opportunity for us to give Him glory, and we should be sure to do so.

Q. Jesus and Zaccheus (19:1–10)

19:1. Earlier Jesus had "come nigh unto Jericho" (18:35). Here He **entered and passed through Jericho** (see discussion on Mark 10:46). This is a transition sentence. It establishes that the events of 19:1–10 happened just shortly after the healing of the blind man (see 18:35 – 43). It also serves to quicken the pace of Jesus' journey toward Jerusalem. Luke wanted to increase the tension as he drew close to Jesus' trial and passion. Earlier in the narrative, events that took place on the same day might not have these kinds of markers.

19:2. The chief among the publicans. A position referred to only here in the Bible, probably designating one in charge of a district, with other tax collectors under him (see discussions on 3:12; Mark 2:14 – 15). The region was prosperous at this time, so it is no wonder that **Zaccheus … was rich**.

19:3. For the press means the press of the crowd. Zaccheus could not see Jesus because the people would not let him through. It is ironic that their interest in Jesus, the teacher of humility and servanthood (in this gospel especially), led them to be inconsiderate of others.

19:4. A sycamore tree (see discussion on Amos 7:14). A sturdy tree from thirty to forty feet high, with a short trunk and spreading branches, capable of holding a grown man.

19:5. I must abide at thy house implies a divine necessity.

19:6. Zaccheus **made haste** and obeyed what Jesus said. He was already interested in being a disciple of Jesus, for he sought Him and he obeyed Him. However, Luke did not intend to provide a paradigm for discipleship here; he was simply telling the story as it happened. One can take this lesson from it, however, as long as we keep Luke's intention in mind.

19:7. When they saw it. Just who "they" are is not made clear here. Was it the crowd? They were usually supportive of Jesus. Was it the Pharisees? This is the most likely possibility, for they had raised this very issue before.

19:8. If I have taken any thing. Zaccheus was not holding back in the sense of saying, "I don't think I have done so, but *if* I have …" Instead, he meant, "Wherever I have …" **Fourfold**. Almost the extreme repayment required under the law in case of theft (see Exod. 22:1; 2 Sam. 12:6; see also Prov. 6:31).

19:9. A son of Abraham. A true Jew, one not only of the lineage of Abraham but who also walked "in the steps of [Abraham's] faith" (Rom. 4:12). Jesus recognized the tax collector as such, though Jewish society excluded him. His faith was demonstrated by his repentance. He genuinely repented of what he had stolen, because he was willing to make restoration.

19:10. This is the key verse in Luke's gospel (see Introduction: "Theme and Theological Message"). In his gospel, Luke showed over and over that Jesus spent time with sinners, and he recorded Jesus' parables (the lost sheep, the lost coin, and the lost son) that reveal His heart for seeking the lost. **The Son of man** (see discussion on Mark 2:10). This Messianic title (see Dan. 7:13) was used only by Jesus in the four gospels, by Stephen (see Acts 7:56), and in John's vision (see Rev. 1:13). **To seek and to save** (see discussion on 15:32). This was an important summary of Jesus' purpose: to bring salvation, meaning eternal life (see 18:18), and the kingdom of God (see 18:25).

R. The Parable of the Pounds (19:11 – 27)

19:11. He was nigh to Jerusalem. Here again is a geographical reminder, serving to build tension because of what would soon happen there. Jesus chose to tell the parable of the pounds (see 19:12 – 27) because of the proximity of Jerusalem, the location of His coming trial and death. The reader presumably knows this, something Jesus' hearers did not. Also, Jesus told this parable because His disciples **thought that the kingdom of God should immediately appear.** They expected the Messiah to appear in power and glory and to set up His earthly kingdom, defeating all their political and military enemies. Events would soon dash that hope, something that must have been in Jesus' mind at this time.

19:12 – 27. The parable of the pounds. This parable is again one in which some elements do not parallel to the real situation, and it is best not to push the analogies too far. For example, the ruler in the parable is hardly a picture of the loving, gracious, and just Savior that Jesus is. Many elements of the parable do illustrate spiritual truths, however, specifically the ones Jesus wanted to emphasize at this point. The ruler left to receive a kingdom and returned much later to give rewards to those who had served him well and to bring judgment on the people. This is what Jesus Himself would do.

19:12. To receive for himself a kingdom. A rather unusual procedure, but the Herods did just that when they went to Rome to be appointed rulers over the Jews. Similarly, Jesus would soon depart and in the future will return as King. During His absence, His servants are entrusted with their Master's affairs (for a similar parable, see Matt. 25:14–30).

19:13. Ten pounds. Each pound, or mina, was about three months' wages. One talent equaled sixty minas (see Matt. 25:15), and a mina equaled one hundred drachmas, each drachma being worth about a day's wages (see discussion on 15:8). The total amount thus equaled between two and three years' average wages, and a tenth would be about three months' wages. This was small, however, compared with the amounts mentioned in Matthew's version of the parable (see Matt. 25:14–30). Here all **ten servants** were given the same amount and had equal responsibility to use what they were given.

19:14. Sent a message. Such an incident had occurred over thirty years earlier in the case of Archelaus (Josephus *Wars* 2.6.1; *Antiquities* 17.9.3), when the Jews complained to Rome of his cruelty, as well as in a number of other instances. This aspect of the story may have been included to warn the Jews against rejecting Jesus as King.

19:15. He commanded these servants to be called unto him. It may be pressing the point to see this as an allusion to the rapture of the church, prior to the Lord's return to judge the world, but it certainly seems to fit.

19:16–17. The first servant was rewarded in accordance with what he had done.

19:18–19. The second servant, who had produced less, was nevertheless commended but given less reward. There will be degrees of reward in heaven.

19:20–21. The third servant had done nothing with what he was given. This illustrates primarily a lack of faith on his part. He assumed the worst of his

master and yet did not do even the minimum to attempt to please him. His action stemmed from fear, and fear is the opposite of faith.

19:22–23. Thou knewest that I was an austere man …? (v. 22). The master did not admit to the statement of the servant but repeated it in a question. If this was the servant's opinion, he should have acted accordingly. The master pointed out to the servant the safest and easiest kind of investment he could have made (v. 23). God will accept even the most meager service from one who, for whatever reason, can do no more. Again, however, that is not central to Jesus' point but may be inferred from it. Of course, one should not use this inference as an excuse to do little for the Lord but should instead make the most of every opportunity for service that He provides.

19:24–25. What the servant had was taken from him and was given to the one who had the most, in spite of the surprised reaction of those who wondered why one who had so much would be given more.

19:26. Jesus explained the actions of the ruler and drew a spiritual parallel. To the one who has much, more **shall be given,** and to the one who has little, **even that he hath shall be taken away** (see 8:18; 17:33; Matt. 13:12). Those who seek spiritual gain in the gospel, for themselves and others, will become richer, and those who neglect or squander what is given them will become impoverished, losing even what they have.

19:27. Those mine enemies … slay them. Perhaps a reference to Jerusalem's destruction in AD 70. The punishment for those who rebelled and actively opposed the king (see 19:14) was much more severe than that of the negligent servant.

VIII. Jesus' Last Days: Sacrifice and Triumph (19:28–24:53)

A. The Triumphal Entry (19:28–44)

19:28–44. The triumphal entry occurred on Sunday of Passion Week.

19:28. He went before, ascending up to Jerusalem. Here Luke finished the chronology of the journey to Jerusalem. Having built up to this moment, he summed it up in a single sentence. Beginning with the next verse, he went back and filled in the details of Jesus' entry into the city. It is well to remember that Jerusalem sat on a hill. Going to Jerusalem meant to "ascend," for the journey was uphill.

19:29. Bethphage. A village near the road going from Jericho to Jerusalem. **Bethany.** A village about two miles southeast of Jerusalem (see John 11:18) and the home of Mary, Martha, and Lazarus. **The mount called the mount of Olives.** A ridge a little more than a mile long, separated from Jerusalem by the Kidron Valley, east of the city (see *KJV Study Bible* note on Zech. 14:4; discussion on Mark 11:1). **Two of his disciples.** Not named here or in the parallel passages (Matt. 21:1; Mark 11:1; see also John 12:14).

19:30. The village. Probably Bethphage. **A colt.** Other accounts specify a donkey colt (see John 12:15) and that the disciples were to take the mother of the colt also (see Matt. 21:2, 7). Luke used a Greek word that the Septuagint frequently employed to translate the Hebrew word for "donkey." Jesus chose to enter Jerusalem mounted on a donkey to claim publicly that He was the son of David chosen to sit on David's throne (see 1 Kings 1:33, 44), the one of whom the prophets had spoken (see Zech. 9:9). **Whereon yet never man sat.** One that had not been put to secular use (see Num. 19:2; 1 Sam. 6:7). Perhaps He wanted to demonstrate His lordship over nature by riding a donkey that would normally balk at being ridden.

19:31. The Lord. Either God or, more likely, Jesus Himself, here claiming His unique status as Israel's Lord.

19:32–34. The two disciples whom Jesus sent to get the colt found the situation as He had described. He thus showed His disciples that He knew the future and could make accurate predictions even of details. This was important because they would soon lose Him; they needed reminders and assurances of His deity.

19:35. They cast their garments upon the colt. They made a more comfortable seat for Jesus than the colt's spine would have been. In verses 30–35,

Luke combines inferences of His deity and His humanity. This is because Jesus could describe a situation he could not see, humanly speaking, yet He would have been uncomfortable, like any man, riding bareback. The Bible moves easily between His divine and human attributes. We should note these inferences, however, so that we may never forget that He was fully human and fully divine, not half of one and half of the other.

19:36. They spread their clothes in the way. This prevented dust from being kicked up by the colt or by those surrounding Him in the procession. It would not do for the Lord to arrive in Jerusalem covered with dust. It was a practical way to honor Him.

19:37. All the mighty works. The raising of Lazarus (John 11) and the healing of blind Bartimeus (Mark 10:46; Luke 18:39–43) were recent examples but included also were the works that John recorded of various occasions in Jerusalem, as well as the whole of His ministry in Galilee (see Matt. 21:14; John 12:17).

19:38. The disciples quoted from Psalm 118:26 and used words similar to ones used at His birth (Luke 2:14). One wonders if they had heard the story of the shepherds and the angels and were alluding to that event. It is impossible to know for sure.

19:39–40. The Pharisees told Jesus, **rebuke thy disciples** (v. 39). They may have wanted to see whether He would claim the kingship, which would give them a basis for accusing Him, or refuse it. He did neither specifically. His reply indicated that what the disciples were saying about Him was true, but He did not give them much basis for a serious charge that He was set to challenge Rome.

19:41–42. Jesus **wept** (v. 41) when He saw the city. Once again we see the compassion and tenderness of God and yet the very human emotions of the Lord.

19:43. Thine enemies shall cast a trench (see 21:20). Fulfilled when the Romans took Jerusalem in AD 70, using an embankment to besiege the city. The description is reminiscent of Old Testament prophecies (see Isa. 29:3; 37:33; Ezek. 4:1–3). Having just accurately foretold small details about the disciples finding and taking the colt, His prophecy here must have made quite an impression on their minds. Surely they knew by now that His prophecies were not to be taken lightly. Little wonder that this one was remembered in detail and reported to Luke.

19:44. The time of thy visitation. God came to the Jews in the person of Jesus the Messiah, but they failed to recognize Him and rejected Him (see John 1:10–11; see also Luke 20:13–16).

B. The Cleansing of the Temple (19:45–48)

19:45. Mark 11:11–17 makes it clear that this cleansing occurred the day after the triumphal entry, that is, on Monday of Passion Week. **The temple**. The outer court (the court of the Gentiles), was where animals for sacrifice were sold at unfair prices. John recorded a cleansing of the temple at the beginning of Jesus' ministry (see John 2:13–25), but the Synoptics (see Matt. 21:12–13; Mark 11:15–17) speak only of a cleansing at the close of His ministry (see discussions on Matt. 21:12–17; John 2:14–17).

19:46. Jesus quoted from Isaiah 56:7 and Jeremiah 7:11. The entire incident must have been dramatic, but it demonstrated to His disciples that holiness in worship was important to Him and that He is Lord over matters related to worship. By His actions, He claimed the authority over the temple to determine what was proper behavior and to enforce it. This must have made an impression on them, as had His prophecy concerning Jerusalem (see 19:43–44).

19:47. Having cleansed the temple, Jesus **taught daily** there, again demonstrating His lordship and authority in that place. It is interesting that Jesus taught there openly, considering the controversy caused by His cleansing the temple on Monday. His authority and presence must have been obvious and overwhelming. **The chief priests** (see 3:2; 22:52; 23:4; 24:20). They were part of the Sanhedrin, the ruling Jewish council (see discussion on Mark 14:55). For **sought to destroy him**, see 20:19–20; John 7:1; 11:53–57.

19:48. The people supported Jesus and heard Him eagerly. This prevented the chief priests from

being able to act. The people had no authority over them, but they were attentive to public opinion. It would not do for them to act in ways that would discredit them before the people. In their challenge of Jesus' authority (see 20:1–8), however, the leadership demonstrated that they both recognized His authority and yet were spiritually blind as to its source.

C. The Last Controversies with the Jewish Leaders (chap. 20)

20:1. The events of this chapter and the next all occurred on Tuesday of Passion Week, a long day of controversy. **One of those days**. The day is not specified, but Mark's parallel accounts (Mark 11:19–20, 27–33) indicate that this day (Tuesday) followed the cleansing of the temple (Monday), which followed the triumphal entry (Sunday). For **chief priests**, see 19:47 and discussion on Matthew 2:4; **scribes**, see 5:30; discussions on 5:17; 7:30; Matthew 2:4; **elders**, see discussion on Matthew 15:2. Each of these groups was represented in the Jewish council, the Sanhedrin (see 22:66).

20:2. Who … gave thee this authority? The religious leaders had asked this of John the Baptist (see John 1:19–25) and of Jesus early in His ministry (see John 2:18–22). Here the reference is to the cleansing of the temple, which not only defied the authority of the Jewish leaders but also hurt their monetary profits. The leaders may also have been looking for a way to discredit Jesus in the eyes of the people or raise suspicion of Him as a threat to the authority of Rome. In asking this question, they implicitly recognized that Jesus' actions and the confidence and presence with which He did them betrayed a certain level of authority. It also showed that they were clueless as to His deity and messiahship.

20:3. As He often did, Jesus answered a question with a question. There is no hint that He hesitated or that He was not prepared to challenge the leaders.

20:4–6. The baptism of John, was it from heaven, or of men? (v. 4). For **From heaven** (v. 5), see *KJV Study Bible* note on Mark 11:30. By replying with a question, Jesus put the burden on His opponents, indicating only two alternatives: the work of John was either God-inspired or man-devised. **They reasoned with themselves.** The leaders recognized that they were in a spot. They saw that either answer would be trouble for them. It is interesting that they could not harm Jesus during these days, for fear of the people (see 19:48), and here they could not honestly answer this question, in part due to **all the people.** By refusing to answer, they placed themselves in an awkward position anyway.

20:7-8. Jesus was not required to answer since they would not. The obvious answer was that His authority, as that of John, had come from God. Their refusal to answer in this way was because they had not recognized God's authority in the preaching of John. If they had not recognized God's authority in John (which would have been shown by being baptized), they would not recognize God's authority in Jesus. He therefore had no reason to tell them where His authority came from, as they would have rejected it anyway.

20:9-18. The parable of the husbandmen. This parable was aimed directly at the Jewish nation. As they had rejected the prophets, so now they rejected God's own Son. The parable foretells what, in fact, did happen a few years later. The nation was destroyed, and the gospel went to the Gentiles. The parable does not say this, but nothing here gives warrant to assume that God will not fulfill His promises to Israel. Jesus' parables teach what they have to teach and one should not try to impose more on them than is legitimately there.

20:9. Planted a vineyard. This parable is best seen in light of Isaiah 5:1-7. There, the Lord describes Israel as His vineyard, which has disappointed Him. The idea of comparing Israel to a vineyard would have been familiar to Jesus' audience. In Jesus' parable, those who are in charge of the vineyard are the ones who disappoint. The **certain man** represents God, and the **husbandmen** may be seen as the chief priests and Pharisees.

20:10-12. He sent a servant (v. 10). Those who were sent to the husbandmen represent the prophets God sent in former times who were rejected (see Neh. 9:26; Jer. 7:25-26; 25:4-7; Matt. 23:34; Acts 7:52; Heb. 11:36-38). **Give him of the fruit.** In accordance with a kind of sharecropping agreement, a fixed amount was due the landowner. At the proper time, he would expect to receive his share.

20:13. My beloved son. The specific reference to the "beloved son" clarifies that the intended application of the son in this parable is to the Son, Jesus Christ (see 3:22; Matt. 17:5).

20:14. That the inheritance may be ours (see *KJV Study Bible* note on Mark 12:7). It is chilling to know that, in just a few days, these leaders would have Jesus arrested and tried, for fear that the Romans would "take away both our place and our nation" (John 11:48). They wanted to maintain their role and not give spiritual leadership over to another (Jesus), just as the husbandmen wanted to keep the vineyard for themselves.

20:15-16. Give the vineyard to others (v. 16; see discussion on Matt. 21:41). This means that God would cease to work through Israel (for a time), and the center stage of His activity in the world would move to the Gentiles. **When they heard it, they said, God forbid.** The crowd's reaction indicates either that they were very caught up in the story or that they at some level understood the meaning.

20:17. Jesus felt the need to make the point even more clearly, however well the people may have understood it. He made an analogy: **The stone which the builders rejected, the same is become the head of the corner** (see *KJV Study Bible* note on Psalm 118:22). "The stone" is Jesus; "the builders" are the Pharisees and chief priests.

20:18. It will grind him to powder. As a pot dashed against a stone is broken, and as one lying beneath a falling stone is crushed, so those who reject Jesus the Messiah will be doomed (see Isa. 8:14; see also Dan. 2:34-35, 44; Luke 2:34).

20:19-44. In this passage, two different groups challenged Jesus. He answered their questions in ways that affirmed the authority of Scripture and the teachings they already accepted as true. They thus had no basis for their opposition to Him. Then He offered a challenge of His own, designed to help them see that the Messiah must be the Son of God.

20:19. The chief priests and the scribes. For their opposition to Jesus, see 5:30; 9:22; 19:47; 22:2; 23:10. For the third time, Luke reported that **they feared the people** (see also Luke 22:2). These leaders were "men pleasers." It delayed, in this case, their doing evil, but it still indicates a character flaw. No one who regards the opinions of others is free, whether they seek to do right or wrong, and they may even be unable to distinguish between them.

20:20. They . . . sent forth spies. They apparently sent people whom Jesus had not spoken with before, hoping to trap Him. These people pretended to be righteous so that they could catch Him in His words, which shows just how dark the human heart can be. These men pretended to be good in order to do evil, by trapping one who really was good, pretending that He was evil. **Authority of the governor**. Fearing to take action themselves, the Jewish religious leaders hoped to draw from Jesus some statement that would bring action from the Roman officials and remove Him from His contact with the people.

20:21. The spies' words reek with insincerity. What they said was technically true, but the reader knows that the spies themselves did not believe it. It makes the wickedness and hypocrisy of these men all the more apparent.

20:22. To give tribute unto Cesar. The questioners hoped to trap Jesus with this dilemma. If He agreed to the taxes demanded by Caesar, it would disappoint the people; if He advised no payment, it would disturb the Roman officials.

20:23. Jesus **perceived their craftiness**. He was not fooled for a moment. Those who seek to flatter often overstate their case and make themselves obvious.

20:24. A penny (see discussion on Matt. 22:19). The denarius, a Roman coin, was worth about a day's wages. **Whose image . . . hath it?** In answering Jesus' question, the spies answered their own.

20:25 – 26. Render . . . unto God the things which be God's (v. 25; see discussion on Matt. 22:21). Jesus avoided the dilemma of seeming either to support or to oppose an invading power, but at the same time, He put the question back into their laps. In doing so,

He turned the situation into a teachable moment. Human government is a legitimate institution, set up by God (see Rom. 13:1 – 7). At the same time, one owes God one's ultimate allegiance. One is to render to each whatever is proper. **They marvelled at his answer** (v. 26). None of Jesus' listeners, whatever their motive, could disagree with His statement. It did not commit Him to the legitimacy or the illegitimacy of the Roman government. That question was left to the listener to decide. As long as that government coined the money, however, they had some legitimate claim to it.

20:27. The second group seeking to trap Jesus now approached. The challenges in this chapter may have happened in immediate succession or at different times during the day. This group was **the Sadducees** (see discussions on Matt. 2:4; 3:7; Mark 12:18; Acts 4:1), an aristocratic, politically minded group willing to compromise with secular and pagan leaders. They controlled the high priesthood at this time and held the majority of the seats in the Sanhedrin. They did not believe in the resurrection or an afterlife, and they rejected the oral tradition taught by the Pharisees (Josephus *Antiquities* 13.10.6).

20:28. His brother should take his wife. The levirate law (see Gen. 38:8; discussion on Matt. 22:24 – 28).

20:29 – 32. This passage sets up the dilemma. The woman's husband had brothers, and each married her in turn as the one before him died.

20:33. Now the Sadducees attempted to spring the trap. Not believing in **the resurrection**, they saw their question as the kind of argument that would reduce belief in a bodily resurrection to absurdity. They thus sought to prove the Pharisees wrong and, at the same time, to trap Jesus in a contradiction. Either, they believed, He must deny the resurrection or He must assert that a woman would have seven husbands.

20:34 – 36. This world (v. 34) **. . . that world** (v. 35; see discussion on 18:30). Jesus did not fall into the trap. He pointed out that the world to come will be different in quality from this one. Marriage is an institution of the present creation. It will not be of the next. An indicator of that change in quality is the lack of death in that world; rather than having a mortal life span, people will be **equal unto the angels** (v. 36). The resurrection order cannot be assumed to follow present earthly lines. In the new age, there will be no marriage, no procreation, and no death. **The children of the resurrection.** Those who are to take part in the resurrection of the righteous (see Matt. 22:23–33; Mark 12:18–27; Acts 4:1–2; 23:6–10).

20:37–38. Jesus turned to the Old Testament Scriptures to demonstrate a point. The Saducees accepted only the first five books of the Old Testament. Jesus thus referred them to the book of Exodus: **Moses shewed at the bush** (v. 37). Since Scripture chapters and verses were not used at the time of Christ, the passage was identified in this way, referring to Moses' experience with the burning bush (see Exod. 3:2). There, God had called Himself **the God of Abraham, and the God of Isaac, and the God of Jacob.** The use of the present tense here indicates that these men lived on after the grave. The Saducees' insistence that this life is all there is was thus discredited by the Scriptures they themselves accepted as true.

20:39–40. Master, thou hast well said (v. 39). Even though they had great animosity against Jesus, **the scribes** (who were Pharisees) sided with Jesus against the Saducees on the matter of resurrection. **And after that they durst not ask him any question at all** (v. 40). Again, Jesus left His opponents speechless.

20:41–43. Jesus threw out a challenge of His own. The dilemma He presented was that the Messiah is the son of David and yet David called Him **Lord** (v. 42; Ps. 110:1).

20:44. David therefore calleth him Lord (see *KJV Study Bible* note on Psalm 110:1). If the Messiah was a descendant of David, how could this honored king refer to his offspring as Lord? Unless Jesus' opponents were ready to admit that the Messiah was also the divine Son of God, they could not answer His question.

20:45–46. Jesus turned to **his disciples** (v. 45) but addressed them **in the audience of all the people.**

He wanted His words to be heard by the people and by **the scribes** (v. 46), whom He was chastising. Luke recorded this teaching because it once again sounds a theme that is important in this gospel: the need for inner righteousness, not just the outward appearance of it. **Long robes ... chief rooms** (see discussions on Mark 12:38–39). The scribes liked to be recognized, honored, and treated as leading members of the community.

20:47. These scribes had only the outward show of respectability, however. They did not hesitate to **devour widows' houses.** They took advantage of this defenseless group by fraud and schemes for selfish gain. **And for a shew, make long prayers.** Their religious practices were only to show off to the people. **Receive greater damnation** (see 12:47–48). The higher the esteem of men, the more severe the demands of true justice, and the more hypocrisy (see Matt. 23:1–36), the greater the condemnation. Jesus wanted the people to see that the external appearance is not as important as the heart. If these scribes were worthy of the honor they received, they would have lived lives that were morally different: they would have used their power to do good rather than to take advantage of the people, and they would have prayed to communicate with God rather than for show.

D. The Olivet Discourse (chap. 21)

21:1. And he looked up. This incident happened right after the teaching given just previously (Luke 20:45–47) and served as an illustration of the principle that making a show of religion has no value in the sight of God. **Rich men** were **casting their gifts into the treasury.** In the court of women, thirteen boxes, shaped like inverted megaphones, were positioned to receive the donations of the worshipers.

21:2. A certain poor widow casting in thither two mites. Mites were Jewish coins worth very little.

21:3–4. Naturally, people would have thought well of the generous gifts of the rich. They saw the outer reality of the large amounts of money they placed into the treasury. The poor widow's money seemed insignificant. From God's perspective, however, she was worthy of more honor than the rich were. She could well have justified giving nothing at all. Such was her heart for God, however, that she gave **all … that she had** (v. 4; see *KJV Study Bible* note on 2 Cor. 8:12; discussion on Mark 12:41–44) counting His glory as worth more than her comfort. The rich had given what had cost them little in terms of comfort but had gained them much in terms of public recognition. She had given what had cost her much but gained her little in the sight of men. The connection to what Jesus had just taught in Luke 20:45–47 is that He had just warned His hearers not to look at the outward appearance. Public recognition and esteem count for less than what is in the heart. The widow valued the things of God highly, from her heart, and this was worth much to God.

21:5–36. This passage is known as the Olivet Discourse (see discussion on Mark 13:1–37.)

21:5. Some of Jesus' disciples were impressed with the outward appearance of **the temple**, remarking on **how it was adorned**. One stone at the southwest corner was some thirty-six feet long. "Whatever was not overlaid with gold was purest white" (Josephus *Jewish Wars* 5.5.6). Herod had given a golden vine for one of the temple's decorations. Its grape clusters were as tall as a man. The full magnificence of the temple as elaborated and adorned by Herod has only recently come to light through archaeological investigations on the temple hill. It was indeed a magnificent building.

21:6. Jesus took advantage of the teachable moment that the disciples' comments offered. Outward adornment is not impressive to God. This temple would in fact be destroyed, Jesus said, so thoroughly that **there shall not be left one stone upon another** (see discussion on Matt. 24:2). This was fulfilled in AD 70 when the Romans took Jerusalem and burned the temple.

21:7. When shall these things be? Jesus' statement must have startled the disciples, even in light of the teaching they had just heard (Luke 21:34). This, certainly, was the effect Jesus intended. Like any good teacher, He wanted to reinforce the lessons He taught, and He used opportunities to evoke

questions from His disciples. He knew that people would pay attention to the answers to questions that the disciples asked. Had Jesus merely launched into a lecture on the destruction of Jerusalem and on the end times, they might have been bored. Mark reported that this question was asked by four disciples: Peter, James, John, and Andrew (see Mark 13:3). Matthew gave the question in a fuller form, including an inquiry for the sign of Jesus' coming and the end of the age (see Matt. 24:3). **What sign will there be …?** What signs would announce the imminence of these events?

21:8. I am Christ, or I am Jesus the Messiah (having come a second time). **The time** refers to the end time. False messiahs would come, and the disciples were not to be deceived by them.

21:9–10. The end is not by and by (v. 9). Refers to the end of the age (see Matt. 24:3, 6). All the events listed in 21:8–18 are characteristic not only of the end of the age but also of the entire present age.

21:11. Great signs shall there be from heaven (see 21:25). For prophetic descriptions of celestial signs accompanying the day of the Lord, see discussion on Mark 13:24–25.

21:12. Delivering you up to the synagogues. Synagogues were used not only for worship and school but also for community administration and confinement of those awaiting trial. **Brought before kings and rulers.** The disciples would face official governmental persecution.

21:13–15. The disciples were to see times of persecution as opportunities **for a testimony** (v. 13), but they were not to make a prepared speech. The context rules the proper understanding of this passage. Jesus was not saying that preachers should not prepare a sermon. He was saying that before people in authority or in a trial setting, a prepared, "canned" testimony would not be the best thing. The disciples were instead to depend on God for a testimony at the time. This would, Jesus said, be effective so that **your adversaries shall not be able to gainsay nor resist** (v. 15; see Acts 6:9–10).

21:16–17. The disciples would face opposition from unofficial sources as well, including family.

21:18–19. Although the disciples would face persecution and possibly even death, God was in control, and the ultimate outcome would be eternal victory. **There shall not a hair of your head perish** (v. 18). In view of 21:16, this cannot refer to physical safety. The figure indicates that there will be no real, that is, spiritual, loss. For **In your patience possess ye your souls** (v. 19), see *KJV Study Bible* note on Mark 13:13.

21:20–24. This section deals with the destruction of Jerusalem in AD 70.

21:20. Jerusalem compassed with armies (see 19:43). The sign that the end was near (see 21:7) would be the surrounding of Jerusalem with armies. Associated with this event would be "the abomination of desolation" (Matt. 24:15). This has three stages of fulfillment. The first was when Antiochus Epiphanes desecrated the temple. The second was when Rome destroyed the temple in AD 70. The third will be during the Great Tribulation.

21:21. Flee to the mountains (see discussion on Matt. 24:16). When an army surrounds a city, one's natural inclination would be to seek protection inside the city walls, but Jesus directed His followers to seek the safety of the mountains because the city was doomed to destruction.

21:22. The days of vengeance. God's retributive justice was the consequence of faithlessness (see Isa. 63:4; Jer. 5:29; Hos. 9:7).

21:23. Bearing children and nursing children is difficult during times of siege and while traveling, when food is hard to get.

21:24. Jerusalem shall be trodden down of the Gentiles. Except for brief revolts in AD 66–70 and AD 132, Jerusalem remained under Gentile rule until June 1967. Since that time, the Jews have retaken their city, signaling that God's time clock for the Jews perhaps is now set in motion once again. **The times of the Gentiles.** The Gentiles would have both spiritual opportunities (see 20:16; Mark 13:10; Rom. 11:25) and domination of Jerusalem.

21:25–28. Jesus returned to the theme of His second coming. These **signs** (v. 25) are associated with the time of the great tribulation. **Then shall they see the Son of man coming** (v. 27). The time of

Christ's second coming (see Dan. 7:13). **Lift up your heads** (v. 28). Do not be downcast at the appearance of these signs, but look up in joy, hope, and trust. **Redemption.** Final, completed redemption.

21:29–31. The parable of the fig tree. Jesus offered this parable as part of His response to the disciples' question regarding signs (see 21:7). **Behold the fig tree** (v. 29; see Matt. 24:32–35; Mark 13:28–31). The coming of summer is announced by the greening of the trees. Likewise, one can anticipate the coming of the kingdom when certain signs are seen.

21:32. This generation. If the reference is to the destruction of Jerusalem, which occurred about forty years after Jesus spoke these words, "generation" is used in its ordinary sense of a normal life span. All these things were fulfilled in a preliminary sense in the AD 70 destruction of Jerusalem. If the reference is to the second coming of Christ, "generation" might indicate the Jewish people as a nation, who were promised existence to the very end, or it might refer to the future generation who will be alive at the beginning of these things. It does not mean that Jesus had a mistaken notion that He would return immediately. The context indicates that He was referring to a future generation that would experience "all these things" (21:36), that is, the signs of the end of time.

21:33. This verse seems to be something of an aside to Jesus' main point. **My words shall not pass away.** He used the words "pass away" as an opportunity to reiterate the permanence of His word, in contrast with the physical universe, **Heaven and earth**, which is not permanent (see Morris, *Luke*, p. 301).

21:34. That day come upon you unawares. This does not mean that Christ's second coming will be completely unannounced, since there will be introductory signs (see 21:28, 31). Those caught up in the affairs of this life will miss the signs, however. As the rich fool was unprepared for his death because he was caught up in the affairs of this life (see 12:13–21), so Christians may be unprepared when Christ returns.

21:35. The whole earth. The second coming of Christ will involve the whole of mankind, whereas the fall of Jerusalem did not.

21:36. Jesus ended with an exhortation to **Watch ... and pray**. In telling His disciples to pray that they **may be accounted worthy to escape all these things that shall come to pass**, He was not telling them to pray that they might be worthy of salvation. Remember that part of this chapter has dealt with the events surrounding the siege of Jerusalem as well. Other portions have dealt with things that will happen around the time when Christ returns ("wars and commotions ... but the end is not by and by," 21:9). It would be well to escape any kind of hardship at any time, but the Lord was warning that the siege of Jerusalem and the tribulation in the distant future would be especially dire.

21:37 – 38. Luke ended his account of the Olivet Discourse with a summary statement: **in the day time he was teaching** (v. 37). Each day during the final week of His life, from His triumphal entry to the time of the Passover (Sunday to Thursday), Jesus was teaching the kinds of things Luke recorded here. Nights He spent at **the mount that is called the mount of Olives** (see discussions on 19:29; Matt. 21:17). He may have been camping there with His disciples, or He may have gone there to be alone. **All the people** (v. 38). Right up to the end, Jesus drew large crowds.

E. The Last Supper (22:1 – 38)

22:1. The feast of unleavened bread ... Passover. The word "Passover" denotes two things: (1) a specific meal that began at twilight on the fourteenth of Nisan (see Lev. 23:4 – 5) and (2) the week following the Passover meal (see Ezek. 45:21), otherwise known as the Feast of Unleavened Bread, a week in which no leaven was allowed (see Exod. 12:15 – 20; 13:3 – 7). By New Testament times, the two names for the weeklong festival were virtually interchangeable.

22:2. The chief priests and scribes (see 20:1 and discussion). They **sought how they might kill him; for they feared the people.** The Jewish leaders were in a quandary. They needed some way to accomplish their aim either without public knowledge or with public approval.

22:3. Then entered Satan into Judas. In the Gospels, this expression is used on two occasions: (1) before Judas went to the chief priests and offered to betray Jesus (here) and (2) during the Last Supper (see John 13:27). The gospel writers thus depicted Satan's control over Judas, who had never displayed a high motive of service or commitment to Jesus.

22:4. Captains. These men were Jews selected mostly from the Levites. Judas' motive is not known, though many have speculated on it.

22:5 – 6. Judas offered the leaders the one thing they wanted: an opportunity to capture Jesus without the multitude, whom, as Luke repeatedly pointed out, "they feared" (20:19; 22:2).

22:7. When the passover must be killed. The Passover lamb had to be sacrificed on the fourteenth of Nisan according to the Jewish calendar, between 2:30 and 5:30 p.m. in the court of the priests — Thursday of Passion Week.

22:8 – 9. Jesus delegated this matter to **Peter and John**, who asked for instructions on carrying out His command.

22:10. A man ... bearing a pitcher of water. It was extraordinary to see a man carrying a pitcher of water, since this was normally women's work. Perhaps Jesus had somehow arranged this earlier as a way for the two to identify him.

22:11. The Master saith. This form of address may have been chosen because the owner was a follower already known to Jesus.

22:12. A large upper room furnished. Jesus basically had them rent a banquet hall. They continued to use this place for at least several weeks after the events of this week (see Acts 1 – 6).

22:13. As he had said unto them. It may be that Jesus had made previous arrangements with the man to ensure that the Passover meal would not be interrupted. Since Jesus did not identify ahead of time just where He would observe Passover, Judas was unable to inform the enemy, who might have interrupted this important occasion.

22:14 – 30. Apparently, Luke did not attempt to be strictly chronological in his account of the Last Supper. He recorded the most important part of the occasion first, the sharing of the bread and the cup. Then he recorded Jesus' comments about His betrayer and about the argument over who would be greatest, though both of these subjects seem to have been introduced earlier. John's gospel, for example, indicates that Judas had already left the room before the bread and cup of the Lord's Supper were shared (see John 13:26–30), but Luke did not say when Judas left.

22:14. He sat down. The usual posture for eating a banquet meal was to recline. It is significant that **the twelve apostles** are mentioned specifically here. It is likely that they alone observed the Passover meal with Jesus. The other disciples in and near Jerusalem were most likely at their own homes (the apostles had come with Him from Galilee, remember), and the room most likely would not have accommodated more people anyway. The identification of the Twelve as the specific group is important in that it identifies "the disciple whom Jesus loved" (John 21:7, 20) as one of the apostles. This has helped scholars to defend the apostle John as the author of the gospel that bears his name since the identity of this disciple is limited to the Twelve.

22:15–16. Until it be fulfilled (v. 16). Jesus yearned to keep this Passover with His disciples because it was the last occasion before He would be slain as the perfect Passover lamb (see 1 Cor 5:7) and thus fulfill this sacrifice for all time. Jesus said He would eat no more Passover meals until the coming of the future kingdom. After this, He will renew fellowship with those who through the ages have commemorated the Lord's Supper. Finally, the fellowship will be consummated in the great messianic "marriage supper" (Rev. 19:9) to come.

22:17. He took the cup. Either the first or the third of the four cups shared during regular observance of the Passover meal.

22:18. Until the kingdom of God shall come (see discussions on 22:16; 4:43). A reference to Jesus' second coming.

22:19–20. These two verses comprise Luke's account of the institution of the Lord's Supper. Perhaps Luke made little of it because his readers, being

Christians, were already very familiar with what happened since they were regular celebrants of the Supper.

22:19. This is my body. Jesus meant it represents or signifies His body. **Given for you.** He was anticipating His substitutionary sacrifice on the cross, where His body would be given as a sacrifice. **This do in remembrance of me.** The purpose of the Lord's Supper is to remember what Jesus Christ did on the cross. Just as the Passover was a constant reminder and proclamation of God's redemption of Israel from bondage in Egypt, so the keeping of Christ's command would be a remembrance and a proclamation of the deliverance of believers from the bondage of sin through Christ's atoning work on the cross.

22:20. For **also the cup,** see *KJV Study Bible* note on Mark 14:24. **After supper.** This fact is mentioned only here and in 1 Corinthians 11:25 (see *KJV Study Bible* note on 1 Cor. 11:23–26). **This cup is the new testament in my blood** (see *KJV Study Bible* note on 1 Cor. 11:25). This refers to the new covenant promised through the prophet Jeremiah (see Jer. 31:31–34); it is the fuller administration of God's saving grace, founded on and sealed by the death of Jesus ("in my blood"). **Which is shed for you.** Here again is the truth that the blood of Jesus was shed for the salvation of others. He did not die for His own sins, for He had no sin. He died for our sins.

22:21–22. Jesus foretold His betrayal. He also indicated that the one who would betray Him was present. One wonders what Judas must have thought at that point.

22:23. The disciples had no clue as to which of them it would be. At Jesus' words, the disciples did not all immediately turn and look at Judas. Sometimes, in paintings, Judas is portrayed as a somewhat sinister-looking figure. Such could not have been the case. Anyone who has been betrayed by someone they trusted will understand that. When one is betrayed, one should take comfort in knowing that the disciples were similarly deceived about the character of one among them. At this point, Judas must have done a first-rate acting job, as he drew no suspicion to himself.

22:24. Strife among them, which of them should be accounted the greatest. This was not the first time this issue came up (see 9:46).

22:25. Benefactors. A title assumed by or voted for rulers in Egypt, Syria, and Rome as a display of honor. Frequently, however, it did not represent actual service rendered.

22:26. As he that doth serve. Jesus urged and exemplified servant leadership, a trait that was as uncommon then as it is now.

22:27. I am among you as he that serveth. Jesus used Himself as an example. He recognized that the disciples had some idea of His greatness. If He was in the position of a servant, they could aspire no higher.

22:28. In my temptations. Including temptations (see 4:13), hardships (see 9:58), and rejection (see John 1:11).

22:29. I appoint unto you a kingdom. The following context (see 22:30) indicates that this refers to the future form of the kingdom (see discussions on 4:43; Matt. 3:2).

22:30. Sit on thrones. As the disciples shared in Jesus' trials, so they will share in His rule (see 2 Tim. 2:12). **Judging** here is meant in the Hebrew sense of leading or ruling **the twelve tribes of Israel** (see Matt. 19:28).

22:31. Sift you. The Greek for "you" is plural. Satan wanted to test the disciples, hoping to bring them to spiritual ruin.

22:32. Jesus' comments here apparently were directed at Peter, who would have a ministry of encouragement and exhortation after his failure. Jesus, even before Peter sinned, already had his reconciliation and recommissioning for ministry in mind.

22:33. Peter, with his usual impetuosity, made a rash statement of the extent of his commitment to Christ. When one looks at how Peter failed, in light of his desire to be the best servant of Christ he could be, one should never be too surprised at one's own failures. However sincere the heart, sin is always waiting to catch people unaware. God, in His grace, gives people a second chance, and more.

22:34. Jesus specifically foretold of Peter's denial. **This day.** The Jewish day began at sundown. When the cock crowed in the early morning hours, it would still be the same day by Jewish reckoning.

22:35. Jesus reminded the Twelve of how He had sent them out to preach, trusting for their every physical need (see Matt. 10:9).

22:36. Purse ... scrip. Compare Jesus' previous instructions in 9:3; 10:4. Until now, the disciples had been dependent on generous hospitality, but future opposition would require them to be prepared to pay their own way. This is a warning and reminder not to absolutize any one form of missions support. Jesus gave different instructions to the disciples, and thus different circumstances may demand different means of support. **He that hath no sword, let him ... buy one.** Jesus did not mean that they would stop on the way to the garden to buy weapons right then. Rather, Jesus used this extreme figure of speech to warn them of the perilous times that would soon come. They would need defense and protection, as Paul did when he appealed to Caesar (see Acts 25:11) as the one who "beareth not the sword in vain" (Rom. 13:4).

22:37. He was reckoned among the transgressors. Jesus would soon be arrested as a criminal, in fulfillment of prophetic Scripture, and His disciples also would be in danger for being His followers.

22:38. Here are two swords ... It is enough. Sensing that the disciples had taken Him too literally, Jesus ironically closed the discussion with a curt "That's plenty!" Not long after this, He rebuked Peter for using a sword (see 22:50).

F. Jesus Praying in Gethsemane (22:39–46)

22:39. The mount of Olives (see 21:37; John 18:2). Matthew specified Gethsemane (see Matt. 26:36), and John specified an olive grove (see John 18:1). The place apparently was located on the lower slopes of the Mount of Olives.

22:40. Temptation. This refers to severe trial of the kind referred to in 22:28–38, which might lead to a faltering of the disciples' faith.

22:41. A stone's cast. Jesus would have been about forty or fifty feet away from the disciples. He wanted to pray alone but was not far away from them.

22:42. Remove this cup (see *KJV Bible Study* note on Mark 14:36). The cup of suffering (see Matt. 20:22–23; see also Isa. 51:17; Ezek. 23:33). One should recognize that sometimes God's answer to prayer will be no and that this is just as legitimate and real an answer as yes. Christians are no greater than their Master and Lord. If His Father could refuse His request, how much more might He refuse them. Jesus qualified His prayer with **nevertheless, not my will, but thine, be done**. Disciples too should find, through prayer, the grace to accept their Father's will, even if it is not the same as their own.

22:43. An angel. Matthew and Mark reported that angels ministered to Jesus at the close of His fasting and temptations (see Matt. 4:11; Mark 1:13), but Luke did not. Here, however, Luke reported the strengthening presence of an angel, but the other gospel writers did not.

22:44. Drops of blood. Probably hematidrosis, the actual mingling of blood and sweat, as occurs in cases of extreme anguish, strain, or sensitivity.

22:45–46. Jesus offered comfort and encouragement to His disciples. He exhorted them to pray, knowing better than they the trials and stress they would soon face.

G. Jesus' Arrest (22:47–65)

22:47. A multitude. These people were sent by the chief priests, elders (see Matt. 26:47), and teachers of the law (see Mark 14:43), and they carried swords and clubs. Included was a detachment of soldiers with officials of the Jews (see 22:52; John 18:3). **To kiss him.** This signal had been prearranged to identify Jesus to the authorities (see Matt. 26:48). It was unnecessary because Jesus identified Himself (see John 18:5), but Judas acted out his plan anyway.

22:48. Jesus was aware of the irony of betrayal carried out with a sign of friendship and affection.

22:49–50. The disciples were ready to fight. True to their commitment, they, at this point, feared no foe in the service of their Lord. Peter was especially eager, something to remember when reading of the following hours, when he denied Jesus. **The servant of the high priest**. Malchus by name; Simon Peter struck the blow to his ear (see John 18:10).

22:51. Healed him. Jesus rectified the wrong done by His follower. No faith on the part of Malchus was involved, but to allow such action would have been contrary to Jesus' teaching.

22:52–53. This is your hour (v. 53). It was the time appointed for Jesus' enemies to apprehend Him, the time when the forces of darkness (the powers of evil) would do their worst in their attempt to defeat God's plan. Jesus was an example of submission to authority here, in contrast with His disciples.

22:54. The high priest's house. Caiaphas, the son-in-law of Annas, the former high priest (see discussion on 3:2).

22:55. Peter sat down among them. Peter was certainly concerned but did not want to be identified, yet he could not stay away.

22:56. A certain maid. She may have seen Peter with Jesus as He taught in the temple or along the roadsides. She too may have been seeking to hide her association with Him by deflecting attention onto Peter. This is uncertain; but certainly she had seen Peter with Jesus at some point and recognized him.

22:57. Woman, I know him not. Peter's first denial of Jesus.

22:58. Another saw him. If deflection had been the maid's motive, it worked. **I am not.** Peter's second denial of Jesus.

22:59. He is a Galilean. Peter was recognized by his speech (see Matt. 26:73) and identified by a relative of Malchus, the high priest's slave (see John 18:26).

22:60. I know not what thou sayest. Peter's third denial of Jesus. **And immediately, while he yet spake, the cock crew**. Lest anyone think that Jesus merely made a guess based on the probability that Peter would deny Him before dawn and on His knowledge of Peter's character, one should look at the specifics of the matter. Jesus had foretold that Peter would deny Him, that it would happen three times, and that it would happen before the cock crowed. Consider that, to have made a "best guess," Jesus would have had to guess the maid's tendency to ask questions and to remember faces, Peter's tendency to buckle when things got uncomfortable, the tendency of the rest of the crowd to ask follow-up questions, not to mention the tendency of the high priest's cook to decide not to make chicken soup on cold nights when the high priest had been up late. It truly is one of the more remarkable prophecies found anywhere in Scripture.

22:61. The Lord ... looked upon Peter. Peter was outside in the enclosed courtyard, and perhaps Jesus was being taken from the trial before Caiaphas to the Sanhedrin when Jesus caught Peter's eye. **Peter remembered the word** Jesus had spoken (see 22:34).

22:62. Peter ... wept bitterly. He had acted contrary to his own profession of loyalty, had been shamed before the one who meant most to him, and had failed to live up to his own ideal of zeal for the Lord. It is difficult to imagine the depth of despair he felt in that hour. He may have drawn little comfort from Jesus' promise that he would be "converted" and His call for Peter to "strengthen thy brethren" (22:32).

22:63–65. Jesus was treated with contempt and suffered great pain even before being brought before the Sanhedrin. One can only wonder at the motivation of these men.

H. Jesus on Trial (22:66–23:25)

22:66. As soon as it was day. Only after daylight could a legal trial take place for the whole council (the Sanhedrin) to pass the death sentence. Considering that the trial was based on trumped-up charges, their zeal for minor points of legality seems odd, except that human nature often is to "major on the minors" when someone wants to avoid the real issue.

22:67–68. Art thou the Christ? tell us (v. 67). This demand is related to a question asked later: "Art thou then the Son of God?" (v. 70). Jesus' answer was not direct but rather was designed to point to their spiritual blindness.

22:69. Jesus foretold His ascension in these words. The assembly could not have understood what He meant at the time.

22:70. They asked Him again directly, **Art thou then the Son of God?** This time Jesus' reply was

more direct. He apparently was saying that although He would not have put it in those words, He would not deny what the leaders were asserting by them (see Morris, *Luke*, pp. 318–19).

22:71. We ourselves have heard. The reaction to Jesus' reply shows that the leaders understood it as a strong affirmative. Mark has simply, "I am" (Mark 14:62). It was blasphemy to claim to be the Messiah and the Son of God (see discussion on Mark 14:64)—unless, of course, the claim was true.

23:1. The whole multitude of them. The multitude of the Sanhedrin (see Matt. 26:59; 27:1), who had met at the earliest hint of dawn (see 22:66). **Led him unto Pilate** (see discussions on Matt. 27:2; Mark 15:1). The Roman governor had his main headquarters in Caesarea, but he was in Jerusalem during Passover to prevent trouble from the large number of Jews assembled for the occasion.

23:2. Perverting the nation. Large crowds followed Jesus, but He was not misleading them or turning them against Rome. **Forbidding to give tribute to Cesar.** Another untrue charge (see 20:25). **Saying that he himself is Christ a King.** Jesus claimed to be the Messiah but not a political or military king, the kind Rome would have been anxious to eliminate.

23:3. Thou sayest it. Jesus affirmed that He is a king but then explained that His kingdom is not the kind that characterizes this world (see John 18:33–38).

23:4. Pilate could find no basis in Roman law to convict Jesus. The Romans, at their best, believed in the rule of law over the rule of men and especially of mobs. Pilate could not be easily moved to execute an innocent man.

23:5. Throughout all Jewry. This phrase may here refer to the whole of the land of the Jews (including Galilee) or to the southern section only, where the region of Judea proper was governed by Pilate.

23:6–7. Herod's jurisdiction (v. 7; see discussion on 3:1). Although Pilate and Herod were rivals, Pilate did not want to handle this case, so **he sent him to Herod** (see 23:12). Pilate could have freed Him but knew that doing so would be politically risky and may have believed that the issues could be better sorted out in a Jewish court. **At Jerusalem**. Herod's main headquarters was in Tiberias on the Sea of Galilee, but like Pilate, he had come to Jerusalem because of the crowds at Passover.

23:8. He was desirous to see him. Herod was worried about Jesus' identity (see 9:7–9) and had desired to kill Him (see 13:31), though the two had never met. There is no record that Jesus ever preached in Tiberias, where Herod's residence was located.

23:9. Jesus did not answer either Herod or His accusers, but this was not due to defiance on His part. Perhaps He knew that no answer would satisfy them, and certainly He knew that the events must take their course according to His Father's will.

23:10. Jesus' accusers were fervent. Often, the less merit to one's words, the more fervently one asserts them; the less grounds one has, the more vehemently one defends the matter. Luke was very much aware, here as elsewhere, of human nature.

23:11–12. A gorgeous robe (v. 11; see *KJV Study Bible* note on Mark 15:17). Herod found no basis in the charges brought against Jesus **and sent him again to Pilate**. This incident forged a new friendship between the two men (v. 12). Again, human nature is such that sin loves company, something Luke did not fail to note.

23:13–15. Pilate's speech reveals that he honestly believed in Jesus' innocence.

23:16. I will therefore chastise him. Although Pilate found Jesus "not guilty" as charged, he was willing to have Him illegally beaten to satisfy the chief priests and the people and to warn against any possible trouble in the future. Scourging, though not intended to kill, was sometimes fatal (see discussion on Mark 15:15). Pilate was attempting a compromise. Rather than release Jesus, as the law would require, or crucify Him, as the chief priests wanted, Pilate offered a halfway measure. The problem is that, in doing so, he revealed a willingness to punish Jesus even though he knew He was innocent. Once you have given ground on your opponent's main point, it is difficult not to go the whole way. It is like pulling an unraveling thread from a sweater. Soon the sweater is gone. Once Pilate gave in on the main point, there was no going back.

23:17–18. Pilate wanted to release Jesus, but now he could not. Another, any other, would be accepted in this charged atmosphere. **Barabbas** (v. 18). Means "son of Abba." Pilate offered a choice between Jesus and an obviously evil, dangerous criminal (see Matt. 27:15–20; Mark 15:6–11; John 18:39–40), in an effort to manipulate the situation. It only made matters worse, for it solidified their desire to see Jesus crucified. Once the chief priests and rulers had begun on that path, any movement Pilate made toward them only strengthened their resolve.

23:19. Sedition … murder. This particular uprising is otherwise unknown but, coupled with murder, it shows the gravity of Barabbas's deeds (see John 18:40).

23:20. Pilate was by now desperate. Having agreed to punish Jesus at all, and having offered them a choice as to whom to release, he found himself maneuvered into a corner from which there was no way out. All of this reveals Pilate was a weak-willed man and a poor politician.

23:21. But they cried … Crucify him. Reading Luke's short sentences describing these events, one can sense the intensity of the situation increasing and the rising fervor of the people who called for Jesus' death.

23:22–23. The third time (v. 22; see 23:4, 14). Pilate made one last futile attempt to release Jesus. Had Pilate been a better student of human nature, he would have known that his position was by now impossible. **And the voices of them and of the chief priests prevailed**, as they inevitably would under such circumstances.

23:24. Pilate gave sentence … as they required. What else could he do? This is not to absolve Pilate of any guilt in this matter; he condemned someone he knew to be innocent. His choice of strategy in the matter, however, made the outcome inevitable.

23:25. He delivered Jesus to their will. Luke's account is abbreviated. Pilate had already handed Jesus over to the soldiers for scourging before He was convicted (see John 19:1–5). He now handed Him over for crucifixion.

I. The Crucifixion (23:26–56)

23:26. Simon. His sons, Rufus and Alexander (see Mark 15:21), must have been known in Christian circles at a later time and perhaps were associated with the church at Rome (see Rom. 16:13). **Cyrenian**. Cyrene was a leading city of Libya, west of Egypt. For **on him they laid the cross**, see discussion on Mark 15:21.

23:27–28. Weep for yourselves, and for your children (v. 28). Because of the terrible suffering to befall Jerusalem some forty years later, when the Romans would besiege the city and utterly destroy the temple. Jesus chose this time to bring these matters up because this devastation would come as punishment for Jerusalem's rejection of the Messiah. He was on His way to crucifixion, and many people **bewailed and lamented** because He had been rejected. It is a measure of His love that He expressed concern for the welfare of His followers even in the midst of His own pain and anguish.

23:29. Blessed are the barren (see Jer. 16:1–4; 1 Cor. 7:25–35). It would be better not to have children than to have them experience such suffering.

23:30. Fall on us. People would seek escape through death rather than endure continuing suffering and judgment (see Hos. 10:8; Rev. 6:16).

23:31. In a green tree … in the dry. If the people of Jerusalem treated the Messiah this way when the "tree" was well-watered and green, what would their plight be when He withdrew from them and they suffered, in the dry period, for their rejection of Him?

23:32. Malefactors (see discussion on 23:18). Luke mentioned them here, because he intended to deal with them in some detail a few verses later (23:39–43), and as a master literary craftsman, he wanted his readers to have them in mind as the crucifixion scene is described. It is better to set the scene or its essential elements early than to introduce a new factor later on that will surprise the reader.

23:33. Calvary (see *KJV Study Bible* note on Mark 15:22). The Latin word for skull is *calvaria*,

hence the name "Calvary." For **they crucified him**, see *KJV Study Bible* note on Mark 15:24.

23:34. They parted his raiment. Any possessions an executed person had with him were taken by the executioners. The soldiers (see John 19:23–24) were unwittingly fulfilling the words of Psalm 22:18 (but see introduction to Psalm 22; *KJV Study Bible* notes on Ps. 22:17, 20–21).

23:35. The chosen of God (see discussion on 9:35). The words of the Jewish leaders and people made clear their rejection of Jesus as Messiah.

23:36–37. Vinegar (v. 36). Or wine vinegar, a sour drink the soldiers carried. Jesus refused a sedative drink (see Matt. 27:34; Mark 15:23) but later was given the vinegar drink when He cried out in thirst (see John 19:28–30). These verses show that it was offered in mockery.

23:38. A superscription. Indicated the crime for which a person was dying. This was Pilate's way of mocking the Jewish leaders as well as announcing the crime for which Jesus had been accused. For **THIS IS THE KING OF THE JEWS**, see discussion on Mark 15:26.

23:39–40. One of the malefactors (v. 39; see Mark 15:32). Ungodly men, even in the hour of death, will sometimes hurl abuse at God. This man died bitter. **But the other** (v. 40). These two men are a study in contrasts. Both were evil, and both deserved the sentence they received, most likely. Luke never indicated that they were other than "malefactors." One had faith, however, while the other did not. One of the thieves wanted proof, **If thou be the Christ** (v. 39), while the other believed without proof.

23:41. The first thief was unrepentant. He wanted to avoid the punishment for his crime but would not admit the evil he had done. The second thief recognized himself as a sinner: **we receive the due reward of our deeds**. In addition, the first thief taunted Jesus for His claim to be the Christ. The second believed in Him and in His innocence: **this man hath done nothing amiss**.

23:42–43. Finally, the second thief acknowledged Jesus as Lord: **Lord, remember me when thou comest into thy kingdom** (v. 42). It is true that the

Greek word here rendered "Lord" can mean nothing more than "sir," but in this context, more than that is demanded. This man knew that Jesus was innocent of any wrongdoing. He also knew, as this verse reveals, that Jesus would live after the crucifixion, that He will return, and that He will usher in a new kingdom. Notice that he made this request of Jesus while He was dying on a cross; this man must have believed that Jesus had a future beyond the cross and that He would have a kingdom, otherwise the request makes no sense. The man also believed in his own immortality. Otherwise, he would not have asked anything for himself; he too was dying at that moment. He also must have had faith that God is merciful to sinners. If he had believed that there was no hope for him because of his sins, his request would have made no sense.

When a sinful person approaches Jesus, acknowledges his or her sinfulness, expresses faith in Him as Lord, and believes that He is merciful and will pardon a sinner, this is the kind of answer such a person will receive: **To day shalt thou be with me in paradise** (v. 43). In the Septuagint (the Greek translation of the Old Testament), the word "paradise" designated a garden (as in Gen. 2:8–10) or a forest (as in Neh. 2:8), but in the New Testament (used only here and in 2 Cor. 12:4; Rev. 2:7), it refers to the place of bliss and rest between death and resurrection (see Luke 16:22; 2 Cor. 12:2), which is apparently in the very presence of God. The salvation of the repentant thief proves the reality of deathbed conversions. Luke recorded as the heart of his gospel Jesus' statement that He had "come to seek and to save that which was lost" (Luke 19:10). Little wonder that he alone recorded this remarkable incident.

23:44. About the sixth hour ... until the ninth hour. From noon to three in the afternoon, by the Jewish method of designating time. Jesus had been put on the cross at the third hour (9:00 a.m.; see Mark 15:25). "The sixth hour" of John 19:14 (see discussion there) may be Roman time (6:00 a.m.), when Pilate gave his decision.

23:45. The vail of the temple. The curtain between the Holy Place and the Most Holy Place. Its tearing symbolized Christ's opening the way directly to God (see Heb. 9:3, 8; 10:19–22).

23:46. Jesus died, having given up His life. His life was not taken but was given up willingly, for the sins of the world. At the end, He commended His spirit into the hands of His Father, having completed the work of redemption on the cross.

23:47. The centurion ... glorified God. Either for having seen God publicly vindicate Jesus by mighty signs from heaven or, out of fear (see Matt. 27:54), to appease the heavenly Judge and thus ward off a divine penalty for having carried out an unjust judgment. **Certainly this was a righteous man.** The centurion realized that Jesus was completely innocent. Matthew and Mark report the centurion's words as "Truly this was the Son [or son] of God" (Matt. 27:54; Mark 15:39). "The Righteous One" and "the Son of God" would have been essentially equivalent terms. Similarly, "the son of God" and "a righteous man" would have been virtual equivalents. Which one the centurion intended is difficult to determine (see discussion on Matt. 27:54). It is likely that the centurion spoke in Latin and that his words had a wide enough range that Greek translations could encompass both possibilities. It seems clear, however, that the gospel writers saw in his declaration a vindication of Jesus, and since the centurion was the Roman official in charge of the crucifixion, his testimony was viewed as significant (see also the declarations of Pilate, 23:4, 14–15, 22; Matt. 27:23–24).

23:48. Smote their breasts. A sign of anguish, grief, or contrition (see 18:13).

23:49. All his acquaintance, and the women ... from Galilee (see 24:10; Matt. 27:55–56; Mark 15:40–41; John 19:25). One often assumes Jesus was abandoned by the disciples after His arrest. This apparently was not the case. They were watching from a distance, but given their emotional ties to Him, that may be understandable. In addition, their emotional anguish may have caused the Roman officials to bar them from the site for fear of what they might do.

23:50. Joseph, a counseller. Either Joseph was not present at the meeting of the Sanhedrin (see 22:66), or he did not support the vote to have Jesus killed (see 23:51). Mark's account suggests Joseph was not present, for the decision was supported by "all" (Mark 14:64).

23:51. Arimathea. A village in the hill country of Ephraim, about twenty miles northwest of Jerusalem. For **waited for the kingdom of God**, see 2:25.

23:52. The remains of an executed criminal often were left unburied or, at best, were put in a dishonored place in a pauper's field. A near relative, such as a mother, might ask for the body, but it was a courageous gesture for Joseph, a member of the Sanhedrin, to ask for **the body of Jesus**.

23:53. Wherein never man before was laid (see discussion on 19:30; *KJV Study Bible* note on Mark 15:46). Rock-hewn tombs were usually made to accommodate several bodies. This one, though finished, had not yet been used.

23:54. That day was the preparation. Friday, the day before the Sabbath, was when preparation was made for keeping the Sabbath. This phrase could be used for Passover preparation, but since in this instance it is followed by the Sabbath, it indicates Friday.

23:55. The women (see 23:49; 24:10; see also 8:2–3). They **beheld the sepulchre** where Jesus was buried and would not have mistaken the location when they returned (see 24:1–8).

23:56. Spices and ointments. Yards of cloth and large quantities of spices were used in preparing a body for burial. About a hundred pounds of myrrh and aloes (see John 19:39) were used on that first evening. More was purchased for the women's return to the tomb after the Sabbath. **According to the commandment**. This phrase makes it clear that the Sabbath in question was Saturday, the day the fourth commandment enjoins to be kept holy. That Christ died on Friday seems beyond question.

J. The Resurrection (24:1–12)

24:1. The first day of the week. According to Jewish time, Sunday began at sundown on Saturday. Spices could then be bought (see Mark 16:1), and the women were ready to set out early the next day. When they started out, it was dark (see John 20:1),

and by the time they arrived at the tomb, it was still early dawn (see Matt. 28:1; Mark 16:2).

24:2. They found the stone rolled away. A tomb's entrance was ordinarily sealed to keep vandals and animals from disturbing the bodies. This stone, however, had been sealed by Roman authority for a different reason (see Matt. 27:62–66).

24:3–4. They ... found not the body of the Lord Jesus (v. 3). The women were **much perplexed** when they found the tomb empty. **Two men** (v. 4). They looked like men, but their clothes were remarkable (see 9:29; Acts 1:10; 10:30). Other reports call them angels (see 24:23; John 20:12). Although Matthew speaks of one angel (not two, see Matt. 28:2) and Mark of a young man in white (see Mark 16:5), this is not strange because frequently only the spokesman was noted and an accompanying figure was not. Another difference in the accounts is the posture of these two figures (standing, here; seated, John 20:12), but since one's posture often changes during the course of a conversation, these variations are not necessarily contradictory but are merely evidence of independent accounts. Angels are connected with Christ's birth and temptation, as well as His agony, resurrection, and ascension.

24:5. Why seek ye the living among the dead? The angels' question contains irony. They were waiting there because they knew that the women would come looking for Jesus. This was a way of announcing to them that Jesus was alive.

24:6–7. When he was yet in Galilee (v. 6). Jesus had His death and resurrection on a number of occasions (see 9:22), but the disciples failed to comprehend or accept what He was saying.

24:8–9. Unto the eleven, and to all the rest (v. 9). "The eleven" is sometimes used to refer to the group of apostles after the betrayal by Judas (see Acts 1:26; 2:14). Judas was dead when the apostles first met the risen Christ, but the group was still called the Twelve (see John 20:24). "The rest" included disciples who, for the most part, came from Galilee.

24:10. Mary Magdalene (see discussion on 8:2). She is named first in most of the lists of the women (see Matt. 27:56; Mark 15:40; but see John 19:25) and was the first to see the risen Christ (see John 20:13–18). **Joanna** (see 8:3). Only Luke listed Joanna as present at this time (and only Mark listed Salome as being present, see Mark 16:1). **Mary the mother of James** (see Mark 16:1). She is "the other Mary" of Matthew 28:1. The absence of the mother of Jesus is significant. She was probably with John (see John 19:27).

24:11. It is surprising that the apostles **believed them not**, considering that Jesus had prophesied that He would rise on the third day. That they did not believe the women helps establish that the resurrection appearances were not a matter of mass hallucinations, which happen only if there is a clear expectation of seeing something. The disciples, however, had no expectation of seeing Jesus alive again.

24:12. Peter … ran unto the sepulchre. John 20:3–9 says that Peter went to the tomb with another disciple: John himself.

K. The Post-Resurrection Ministry (24:13–53)

24:13–14. Two of them (v. 13). One was named Cleopas (see 24:18). Many have surmised that the other was Cleopas's wife. Obviously, the events of that morning would have been a major topic of conversation between them.

24:15–16. Jesus himself drew near (v. 15). He appeared to them, without revealing His identity. **But their eyes were holden** (v. 16). By special divine intervention, they could not recognize Jesus.

24:17. Jesus knew what they were discussing. He wanted to begin a conversation with them and to help them put together in their minds the order of events. He wanted to help them understand what was happening.

24:18. Cleopas's words indicate that the trial and crucifixion of Christ had attracted quite a bit of attention. This would be expected, considering His triumphal entry a week earlier and the crowds He had drawn while teaching in the temple. Details like this give Luke's account a ring of authenticity. Cleopas's response to the Lord is just what someone would say, given the events Luke recorded earlier, yet the reader does not get the feeling that Luke was justifying his account by making up the words. They seem quite natural, a part of the total event. Verses like this one are helpful in establishing the authenticity of the gospel accounts.

24:19–20. A prophet (v. 19). They had respect for Jesus as a man of God, but after His death, they apparently were reluctant to call Him the Messiah.

24:21. We trusted. The verb tense indicates that they used to be trusting. Their hopes had been dashed, however. **He which should have redeemed Israel.** To set the Jewish nation free from bondage to Rome and usher in the kingdom of God (see 1:68; 2:38; 21:28, 31; Titus 2:14; 1 Peter 1:18–19). It is ironic that Cleopas used these words since it was this very death that brought about true redemption to all who will believe. **The third day.** A reference either to the Jewish belief that after the third day, the soul left the body or to Jesus' remark that He would be resurrected on the third day (see 9:22). In any event, this time reference indicates that Jesus was crucified on a Friday, since Jews counted the day on which the event occurred as day one. They would have said it was the fifth day, for example, if Christ had been crucified on Wednesday.

24:22–23. Certain women (v. 22) … **had also seen a vision of angels, which said that he was alive** (v. 23; see discussion on 24:4). Cleopas's account shows that he did not believe the women.

24:24. For **Certain of them … with us**, see 24:12 and discussion. **But him they saw not.** Cleopas had not made the connection between these events and Jesus' words in Galilee.

24:25–27. Jesus gently chastised them for their lack of understanding. **All that the prophets have spoken** (v. 25). Here Jesus provided a hermeneutical key to the Old Testament. It all points to Him and to the redemption He wrought. **Moses and all the prophets** (v. 27). A way of designating the whole of the Old Testament Scriptures. **The things concerning himself.** Everything in the Old Testament ultimately refers back to Jesus. While one should be careful not to force an interpretation onto a passage, one should read the entire Old Testament with an eye to how it points ahead to Jesus Christ.

24:28. As though he would have gone further. He knew that they would invite Him in. He could not politely assume He was invited but had to act as if He would continue His journey until He was asked. This was not deception in any sense. He was only doing what a normal traveler would do, until invited to join the couple for dinner.

24:29. Abide with us. Cleopas and his fellow traveler did invite Jesus to stay with them.

24:30–31. Their eyes were opened (v. 31; see 24:16). This indicates that they had been supernaturally prevented from seeing who He was. Perhaps also, as they took the bread from His hands, they saw the nail marks, but this is not indicated. **He vanished out of their sight.** Apparently, He just disappeared.

24:32. Did not our heart burn within us ...? They realized that their engagement with Him in conversation and the emotions they had felt were a result of His "teaching as one having authority" (Matt. 7:29), as had happened during His pre-resurrection ministry. They realized that they should have recognized who was teaching them.

24:33. For **the eleven gathered together, and them that were with them,** see discussion on 24:9.

24:34–35. The two disciples related the account of what had happened. It is possible that Luke spoke with these two in the preparation of his gospel. At the beginning of his gospel, he indicated that he had spoken with "eyewitnesses" (1:2).

24:36. As they thus spake, Jesus himself stood in the midst of them. Behind locked doors (see John 20:19), indicating that His body was of a different order. It was the glorified body of the resurrection (see Mark 16:12).

24:37–38. Jesus' appearance frightened the disciples. This is understandable. People do not normally suddenly materialize in a room. Nothing Jesus could have said would have prevented the panic that ensued. It is safe to infer that the two disciples who had seen Him on the road to Emmaus were there and may have been somewhat less frightened than the others.

24:39. Behold my hands and my feet (see John 20:20, 27). Indicating that Jesus' feet as well as His hands were nailed to the cross (see KJV Study Bible

note on Mark 15:24). **A spirit hath not flesh and bones, as ye see me have.** Jesus retained His physical body, yet it had other powers as well. All ideas such as that Jesus was raised "spiritually" or that the disciples used "resurrection language" to account for their sense of God's presence with them after the death of Christ must be utterly rejected in light of Jesus' words here.

24:40–41. The disciples were still reluctant to believe. This fact contradicts those who attempt to show that the disciples were credulous, eager to believe in a miracle, and looking for the risen Christ.

24:42–43. A piece of a broiled fish (v. 42). Jesus ate, thus demonstrating that He had a physical body that could consume food.

24:44. In the law of Moses, and in the prophets, and in the psalms. The three parts of the Hebrew Old Testament (Psalms was the first book of the third section, called "the Writings"), indicating that Christ (the Messiah) was foretold in the whole Old Testament.

24:45. Opened he their understanding. Jesus again taught regarding the Old Testament Scriptures that teach about Him (24:27).

24:46. To suffer, and to rise from the dead the third day. The Old Testament depicts the Messiah as one who would suffer (see Psalm 22; Isaiah 53) and rise from the dead on the third day (see Ps. 16:9–11; Isa. 53:10–11; compare Jonah 1:17 with Matt. 12:40).

24:47. Repentance and remission of sins (see Acts 5:31; 10:43; 13:38; 26:18). The prophecy of His death and resurrection (see 24:46) is joined with the essence of man's response (repentance) and the resulting benefit (forgiveness; see Isa. 49:6; Acts 13:47; 26:22–23). **Beginning at Jerusalem** (see Acts 1:8). This is very much like the Great Commission (see Matt. 28:18–20). The difference in wording is easily understood. The setting is different (the upper room rather than outdoors), and the timing is different (the evening of the same day He rose, not several weeks later). Surely, Jesus gave them this all-important commission to go and preach the gospel to all the world on more than one occasion.

24:48. Ye are witnesses of these things. They were witnesses of the "repentance and remission of sins" (24:47) through Jesus Christ, that would be preached in all the world.

24:49. The promise of my Father (see Joel 2:28–29). The reference is to the coming power of the Spirit, fulfilled in Acts 2:4.

24:50. Bethany (see discussions on 19:29; Matt. 21:17). A village on the Mount of Olives. This is a transition sentence, moving the action to a time forty days later.

24:51. While he blessed them. Luke's gospel begins with a priest who had no blessing to impart (Zacharias) and ends with the great High Priest giving a blessing as He was departing from His disciples. **Carried up into heaven.** Different from His previous disappearances (see 4:30; 24:3; John 8:59). They saw Him ascend into a cloud (see Acts 1:9).

24:52. They worshipped Him. By this time, the disciples understood Christ's deity. Worship is a proper response to deity.

24:53. Continually in the temple. During the period immediately following Christ's ascension, the believers met continually in the temple (see Acts 2:46; 3:1; 5:21, 42), where many rooms were available for meetings (see discussion on 2:37). Luke ended his account with the disciples meeting there. The context is Jewish, and the gospel ends with a small group of disciples, in Jerusalem, worshiping Jesus within that context. In the book of Acts, which is a sequel to this gospel, Luke recorded how the gospel spread far beyond Jerusalem to encounter the Gentile world, bringing in many converts as churches began in Asia and eastern Europe and as far away as Rome.

THE GOSPEL ACCORDING
TO ST. JOHN

INTRODUCTION

Author

The author is the apostle John, the disciple "whom Jesus loved" (13:23; 19:26; 20:2; 21:7, 20, 24). John was prominent in the early church but is not mentioned by name in this gospel, which would be natural if he wrote it but is hard to explain otherwise. The author knew Jewish life well, as seen from references to popular messianic speculations (e.g., 1:20–21; 7:40–42), to the hostility between Jews and Samaritans (4:9), and to Jewish customs, such as the duty of circumcision on the eighth day taking precedence over the prohibition of working on the Sabbath (see discussion on 7:22). He knew the geography of the Holy Land, locating Bethany about fifteen furlongs (about two miles) from Jerusalem (11:18) and mentioning Cana (2:1; 21:2), a village not referred to in any earlier writing known to us. The gospel of John has many touches that were obviously based on the recollections of an eyewitness, such as the house at Bethany being filled with the fragrance of the broken perfume jar (12:3; see Matt. 14:3). Early writers such as Irenaeus and Tertullian say that John wrote this gospel, and all other evidence agrees (see 1 John, Introduction: "Author"). The earliest manuscripts have as their title, "The Gospel According to John."

The internal evidence makes it clear that the author was Jewish. He had a thorough knowledge of Jewish feasts and customs, including weddings (2:1–12), ceremonial purification (3:25), religious feasts (2:13; 6:4; 13:1; 18:28), and burial customs (11:38; 19:40). It also indicates he was (or had been) a resident of Israel. He knew the exact distance from Bethany to Jerusalem (11:18) and that Jacob's well is deep (4:11). He also provided several details that indicate he was one of the twelve disciple and an eyewitness of Jesus' earthly ministry. He knew the number and size of the waterpots used in Cana (2:6), the distance from the shore to the apostles' boat (21:8), the number of fish they caught (21:11), and the details of the private conversations that occurred at the Last Supper (chaps. 13–17). The accumulative weight of all these factors favors John the apostle as the author.

Date

The traditional view dates this gospel toward the end of the first century, circa AD 85 or later (see 1 John, Introduction: "Date"). John has always been known as "the fourth gospel." The early church fathers believed it was written toward the end of John's life, between AD 85–95. Those who hold this view maintain that John 21:18, 23 requires a later date, with Peter becoming old and John outliving him. This view may be supported by the statement of Clement of Alexandria that John wrote to supplement the accounts found in the other gospels (Eusebius *Ecclesiastical History* 6.14.7), and thus his gospel is later than the first three. It has also been argued that the seemingly more developed theology of the fourth gospel indicates that it originated later.

An earlier date has been suggested, between AD 50–70, because it has been thought more recently that John wrote independently of the other gospels. This does not contradict the statement of Clement referred to above. Also, those who hold this view point out that developed theology does not necessarily argue for a late origin. The theology of Romans (written ca. AD 57) is every bit as developed as that in John. Further, the statement in 5:2 that there "is" (rather than "was") a pool "by the sheep market" may suggest a time before AD 70, when Jerusalem was destroyed. Others, however, observe that elsewhere John sometimes used the present tense when speaking of the past.

Most liberal scholars advocate a late date, sometime in the second century (ca. AD 150). They agree that this gospel's developed Christology, with an emphasis on the deity of Christ, must have come later than the first century. However, archaeological discoveries of fragments of John's gospel (namely, p52, which contains parts of John 18) predate the supposed late date. This fragment is conservatively dated no later than AD 125, and accounting for circulation pushes its origin no later than AD 100.

Theme and Theological Message

Some interpreters believe that John's aim was to set forth a version of the Christian message that would appeal to Greek thinkers, but his gospel is so thoroughly steeped in Jewish and Old Testament thought that this could hardly have been his main goal. Others have seen a desire to supplement (or correct) the Synoptic Gospels, to combat some form of heresy, to oppose the continuing followers of John the Baptist, or to achieve a similar goal. The writer himself, however, stated his main purpose clearly: "But these are written, that ye might believe that Jesus is the Christ, the Son of God; and that believing ye might have life through his name" (20:31). John may have had in mind mainly Jews and proselytes to Judaism, especially those of the Diaspora (see Carson, *The Gospel According to John*, pp. 91–92), but his primary intention was evangelistic. It is possible to understand "might believe" in the sense of "may continue to believe," in which case, John's intention was to build up believers as well as to win new converts.

John was the only gospel writer to mention more than one Passover. In fact, he listed three (2:13; 6:4; 13:1) and hinted at a fourth (5:1). This enumeration allows one to reconstruct a full three-year ministry for Christ on earth. It also helps to demonstrate that John was familiar with the other three gospels and consciously supplemented as necessary. Fully 92 percent of John's gospel is unique, that is, not contained in any of the other accounts. For the main themes of this gospel, see discussions on 1:4, 7, 9, 14, 19, 49; 2:4, 11; 3:27; 4:34; 6:35; 13:1–17:26; 13:31; 17:1–2, 5; 20:31. A convenient picture of some of the important themes in the gospel of John can be created by comparing vocabulary:

	Matthew	Mark	Luke	John
Love (*agapē*)	9	5	14	44
Truth (*alētheia*)	2	4	4	46
Know (*ginoskō*)	20	4	4	56
Scripture (*graphē*)	0	1	1	11
I am (*eimi*)	14	4	16	54
Work (*ergō*, ergon)	9	3	18	35
Life (*zoē*)	7	4	5	36
World (*kosmos*)	8	2	3	78
Judge (*krinō*)	6	0	6	19
Witness (*martyreō*)	4	6	5	47
Remain (*menō*)	3	2	7	39
Father (*patēr*, used of God)	44	4	16	118
Send (*pempō*)	4	1	10	32
Send (*apostellō*)	22	20	26	28
Send (Jesus, object of)	2	1	4	42
Manifest (*phaneroō*)	0	1	0	9
Light (*phōs*)	7	1	6	23

Adapted from C. K. Barrett, *The Gospel according to St. John*, 5–6.

Perhaps the most prominent theme in John's gospel, however, is that the Father sent the Son to earth as His representative. Not only is it said that "God sent ... his Son into the world" (3:17), but Jesus routinely identified God as "the Father which hath sent me" (e.g., 5:30, 37; 6:44; 8:18; 12:49) or "him that sent me" (e.g., 4:34; 5:24; 6:38, 40). Opposed to other backgrounds to explain this emphasis, Jewish ideas of sending a representative in one's place are conventional in John (13:16; 1:19–24) and best explain the character of Jesus' representation of the Father. The cardinal tenet in Jewish agency, that the one sent is equivalent to the one who sends him, presumes the fidelity of the representative to the will and purpose of the sender, whose authority is resident in the representative. The human institution is the starting point for apprehending the Father's supernatural sending of Jesus and accounts for the otherwise perplexing tension between Jesus' humble subordination to the Father and Jesus' exalted authority.

Gauged by just the verbs used for "to send," the gospel of John contains no less than forty direct references to the fact that Jesus was sent by the Father. A cursory survey of these references leads to a distinct picture of Jesus as *the* representative of the Father. The coming of Jesus is conveyed as a representation commissioned by the Father: "I proceeded forth and came from God; neither came I of myself, but he sent me" (8:42; see 7:28–29; 10:36). To the one whom the Father sent to represent Him, He "hath given all things into his hand" (3:35; 13:3), authorizing Jesus to act on behalf of "the Father which hath sent him" (5:24; see 5:22–24, 27). Accordingly, Jesus stated, "I am come in my Father's name" (5:43) and that the works that He did, He did "in my Father's name" (10:25). The Father gave these works, which Jesus called "the works of him that sent me" (9:4), to Jesus to accomplish during His earthly ministry (5:36; 4:34; 17:4).

Jesus' will, therefore, was to do the will and command of the one who sent Him (3:34; 5:30; 6:38–39; 10:18, 12:49–50; 14:31); He sought not His own glory but the glory of the one who sent Him (7:18; 8:50; 17:4; see also 5:41; 8:54): "he that sent me is with me … I do always those things that please him" (8:29). Jesus did "nothing of himself" (5:19; see 5:30; 7:16–18; 28–29; 8:26–28, 42; 12:49). His "doctrine" (7:16), His "word" (14:24), what He "[spoke] to the world" (8:26), was not His own but what He had "heard" from (8:26) or been "taught" by (8:28) the Father to speak: "the Father which sent me … gave me a commandment, what I should say, and what I should speak … whatsoever I speak therefore, even as the Father said unto me, so I speak" (12:49–50). Consequently, "the word which you hear is not mine, but the Father's which sent me" (14:24), and "he whom God hath sent speaketh the words of God" (3:34; see 17:8).

In the gospel of John, Jesus' representation of the Father, who commissioned and authorized Him, serves as the basis for His legally validated authority (5:36, 38; 6:29, 57; 10:36; 11:42; 17:3, 8, 18). Accordingly, to "honour the Son" is to "honour the Father … which hath sent him" (5:23; see 8:49), to receive Jesus is to "receiveth him that sent me" (13:20), to believe in Jesus is to "believeth … on him that sent me" (12:44; see 14:1), to behold Jesus is to "seeth him that sent me" (12:45).

After completing His commission, Jesus was to return to the one who sent Him (7:33; 13:1, 3; 14:28; 16:5, 17, 27–28). In anticipation of His return, Jesus reported to the Father what He had accomplished (chap. 17). That Jesus had faithfully represented the Father in all that He was sent to do is summed up most clearly in the refrain that punctuated His report to the Father: "that the world may believe [or 'know'] that thou hast sent me" (17:21, 23; also 17:3, 8, 25; see 6:29; 11:42).

Outline

I. Prologue (1:1–18)
II. Beginnings of Jesus' Ministry (1:19–51)
   A. The Ministry of His Forerunner (1:19–34)
   B. Jesus' Introduction to Some Future Disciples (1:35–51)
III. Jesus' Public Ministry: Signs and Discourses (chaps. 2–11)
   A. Changing Water into Wine (2:1–11)
   B. Cleansing the Temple (2:12–25)
   C. Interview with Nicodemus (3:1–21)
   D. Parallel Ministry with John the Baptist (3:22–4:3)
   E. Journey through Samaria: The Woman at the Well (4:4–42)
   F. Healing of the Nobleman's Son (4:43–54)
   G. Trip to Jerusalem for an Annual Feast (chap. 5)
   H. The Feeding of the Five Thousand and the Sermon on the Bread of Life (chap. 6)
   I. Jesus at the Feast of Tabernacles (chaps. 7–8)

Bibliography

Barrett, C. K. *The Gospel According to St. John: An Introduction with Commentary and Notes on the Greek Text.* 2nd ed. Philadelphia: Westminster John Knox, 1978.

Beasley-Murray, George R. *John.* Word Biblical Commentary 36. Waco, TX: Word, 1987.

Borchert, Gerald L. *John 1–11.* The New American Commentary 25A. Nashville: Broadman & Holman, 1996.

Brown, Raymond, E. *The Gospel According to John.* 2 vols. The Anchor Bible 29–29A. Garden City, New York: Doubleday, 1966–70.

Bruce, F. F. *The Gospel of John: Introduction, Exposition, and Notes.* Grand Rapids, MI: Eerdmans, 1983.

Carson, D. A. *The Gospel According to John.* Pillar New Testament Commentary. Grand Rapids, MI: Eerdmans, 1991.

Danby, Herbert. *The Mishnah.* Oxford: Oxford University Press, 1933.

Dodd, C. H. *Studies in the Fourth Gospel.* Ed. F. L. Cross. London: A. R. Mowbray, 1957.

Hendriksen, William. *A Commentary on the Gospel of John.* Grand Rapids, MI: Eerdmans, 1953.

Morris, Leon. *The Gospel According to John.* The New International Commentary on the New Testament. Grand Rapids, MI: Eerdmans, 1971.

Smalley, Stephen S. *John: Evangelist and Interpreter.* Exeter, UK: Paternoster, 1978.

Talbert, Charles H. *Reading John: A Literary and Theological Commentary on the Fourth Gospel and the Johannine Epistles.* New York: Crossroad Publishing, 1992.

Westcott, B. F. *The Gospel According to St. John.* 1881. Reprint, Grand Rapids, MI: Eerdmans, 1975.

EXPOSITION

I. Prologue (1:1–18)

1:1–18. The gospel of John opens with the most towering vista of Jesus as the Word (Greek, *logos*) found in all of the New Testament. Perched on the horizon between heaven and earth, the reader is granted an omniscient perspective of Jesus that holds within its scope the creation of the cosmos and the redemptive history of the world. Colossians 1:15–20, Philippians 2:5–11, and Hebrews 1:1–13 offer this vista, but none matches the scope of Jesus' celestial and terrestrial significance, nor the glory, majesty, and intimacy of Jesus' sonship, as presented in John's prologue. As one reads John's gospel, the omniscient knowledge of the prologue will return again and again to inform the reader of the true identity of Jesus.

1:1–2. John's gospel and Genesis begin alike. The connection is strong. John's opening words are the Greek translation of the very first word of Genesis 1:1 in Hebrew: *bereshith*. If one were to open the old Greek Bible, the Septuagint, one would find that the opening words of Genesis are the same as John's opening. As those familiar with the Genesis account of creation will recognize, John featured the agency of the Creator and revealed the preeminent role of the Word, or Logos (Jesus), in the action of creation.

In the beginning (v. 1) is not only the Greek translation of the very first word of the Bible in Hebrew but is also the Hebrew title of the book of Genesis (Hebrew, *bereshith*). The English title "Genesis" (Greek, *genesis*; "source," "origin") comes from the Septuagint, the old Greek translation of the Hebrew Bible.

In the beginning was the Word (v. 1) was a powerful and pregnant expression for both Greeks and Jews. Greeks used the term "Word" (Greek, *logos*) not only of the spoken word but also of the unspoken word, the word still in the mind, the reason. When they applied it to the universe, they meant the rational principle that governs all things. Jews, on the other hand, were acquainted with its near equivalent in Hebrew (*davar*). "The word of the LORD" was a common expression linked to God's action in both revelation and creation. These associations with "the Word" were already in place when a Greek or Jewish listener heard the opening words of John's gospel. Using this one term, meaningful to both Jews and Gentiles, John joined two hemispheres to communicate a new and unique fact (see Dodd, *Studies*, p. 12).

The words **was with God** (v. 1) make it clear that the Logos is distinct from God. In John 1:14 (also 1:18), the relationship of the Logos to God is clarified as the relationship of the Son and Father. **The Word was God** clearly identifies the Logos (Jesus) as God in the fullest sense (see discussion on Rom. 9:5). Perhaps the best alternative translation to capture the full sense is that of the New English Bible: "what God was, the Word was." The opening and closing of John's prologue (1:1, 18) present a ringing affirmation of Jesus' deity (see discussion on 1:18).

The verb "was" functions uniformly in each of the four clauses of this passage, to predicate or assert something about the Logos. Different nuances of meaning are suggested by the complete predicate and not by the verb "was" alone: (1) "In the beginning was," preexistence; (2) "was with God," relationship; (3) "was God," identity. The combination of these clauses climaxes into one indissoluble burst of thought: **The same** (lit., 'this one') **was in the beginning with God** (v. 2). This is the crown of the clauses in that it is the sum of its parts. John opened his gospel with a concise and concentrated command of the language to communicate that the Logos, Jesus, is uniquely qualified to reveal God.

1:3. All things were made by him (see Col. 1:16–18). Jesus was the agent of creation. John's pattern of speech is exclusive; "all or nothing" becomes "all and nothing," with the final addendum **that was made** sealing the circle: (1) all through Him came, and (2) without Him came nothing. The parallel (positive and negative) statements are an antiphonal chorus of one truth: everything, without exception, is the work of the Logos.

1:4. Life is always eternal life in this gospel and 1 John (see 1:1–2). One of the great concepts of this gospel, "life" (Greek, *zōē*) is found thirty-six times in John, while no other New Testament book uses it more than seventeen times. Life is Christ's gift (see 10:28), and He, in fact, is "the life" (14:6). **The life was the light of men** specifies the relation of the Life to men as light. As eternal Life (see 1 John 5:11), the Logos (Jesus) is the source of natural life (see 1:3), but only as eternal Life is the Logos "the light" (1:5) and "the light of men." In John's gospel, eternal life is more than endless natural life. It is a quality of life defined by the life of God. The revelation of the Logos (see discussion on 1:14) thus gives eternal life to "men" (or "the world"). "Light" features the spiritual illumination that the Logos presents to the world. Jesus is "the "light of the world" (8:12), who holds out wonderful hope for the world. For an Old Testament link between "life" and "light," see Psalm 36:9.

1:5. The stark contrast between **light** and **darkness** is a striking theme in this gospel (see, e.g., 12:35). "Darkness" connotes not only the absence of light and the spiritual ignorance of the heart but also the evil that breeds in its retreat from the light (see 3:19–21). As "light" cannot be disassociated from the scope of the Life, so "darkness" cannot be disassociated from the specter of death. In this gospel, judgment belongs to sphere of the revelatory nature of light (see 3:18–19; 12:44–47).

1:6–7. In this gospel, the name **John** (v. 6) always refers to John the Baptist, and he is never called "the Baptist." His role as witness is emphasized in this gospel. If there is a model witness, it is John (see 1:19–37). His singular ministry was to testify to Jesus (see 10:41), and the first disciples were introduced to Jesus through the testimony of John.

That all men through him might believe (v. 7) identifies the Baptist's important role as a witness to Jesus. People were to believe not "in" John the Baptist but "through" him. Similarly, the author's purpose was to draw them to belief in Christ (20:31); he used the verb "believe" (Greek, *pisteuō*) ninety-eight times. **Witness** is an important concept in this gospel. The Greek noun for "witness" or "testimony" is used fourteen times (in Matthew not at all, in Mark

three times, in Luke once), and the verb ("testify") thirty-three times (found once each in Matthew and Luke, not at all in Mark)—in both cases, more often than anywhere else in the New Testament. John (the author) thereby emphasized that the facts about Jesus are amply attested.

1:9–10. As the light coming into the world, Jesus **lighteth every man** (v. 9). Although the punctuation of the KJV suggests that "every man" is the subject of **cometh into the world**, the Greek grammar and the clear allusion to the technical epithet for Jesus as the "Coming One" make clear that it is the Light coming into the world that illumines every man. John was referring to the incarnation of Christ, not to a prenatal illumination. Jesus is He who "cometh into the world," and He is "the light of the world" (8:12; 9:5; see 3:19; 6:14; 11:27; 16:28; 12:46). Here John introduced the grand truth that Jesus is the Light of the World (see 8:12; 9:5). Jesus is the **true Light** (v. 9). The adjective "true" (Greek, *alēthinos*) denotes that which is genuine, real, and authentic. **World** (Greek, *kosmos*; vv. 9, 10) is a common word in John's writings, found seventy-eight times in this gospel and twenty-four times in his letters (only forty-seven times in all of Paul's writings). It can mean the universe, the earth, the people on earth, most people, people opposed to God, or the human system opposed to God's purposes. John emphasized the word by repetition and moved without explanation from one meaning to another (see, e.g., 17:5, 14–15 and discussions). Here "the world" clearly denotes "humankind," for the reader is told that **the world knew him not**; that is, it did not recognize or acknowledge its Creator.

1:11. Here the meaning of "the world" (1:9–10) is narrowed by the words **his own** (Greek, *idios*; see 19:27). The notion of Israel as "a peculiar treasure unto me above all people" (Exod. 19:5) may be in view here: the "framework of life to which as Messiah he belonged" (Barrett, *The Gospel According to St. John*, p. 163). The second occurrence of **his own** (a different gender from the first) refers to those who belong to "his own" (perhaps meaning Israel). They **received** (or "accepted") **him not**.

1:12–13. By birth, people are not **the sons** (Greek, *tekna*; "children") **of God** (v. 12). Unlike the Stoic or the Hermetic systems that taught one's divine origin needs only to be realized or exercised, the revelation of God in Jesus Christ is redemptive and calls one to receive Jesus through a trust relationship of faith. Membership in God's family is by grace alone; it is a gift of God (see Eph. 2:8–9). It is never a human achievement (**gave he**; v. 12), yet the imparting of the gift is dependent on man's reception of it, as the words **received** and **believe** make clear. **Power** (Greek, *exousia*) denotes an "authority" or "status" granted through Jesus (see 14:6). The status of the children of God is thus associated with **his name**, the name of Jesus.

1:14. The Word, the Logos (Jesus), existed before He became man, as indicated by the words **was made**. To state that God (the Logos) had become frail and transitory flesh (see Isa. 40:6) was poignant, if not scandalous. **Flesh** is a strong, almost crude, word that stresses the reality of Christ's manhood. The Greek for **dwelt** is connected with the word for "tent" or "tabernacle." The verse would have reminded John's Jewish readers of the tabernacle, which was filled by the glory of God (see Exod. 40:34–35). This is an important clue to the background of John's thought regarding the glory of the Son. **His glory** points to the unique character qualities of God revealed to Moses in answer to his request to see God's glory (see Exod. 33:18): "I will make all my goodness pass before thee" (Exod. 33:19); "While my glory passeth by … I will put thee in a clift of the rock" (Exod. 33:22); "And the LORD passed by before him, and proclaimed, The LORD, The LORD God, merciful and gracious, longsuffering, and abundant in goodness and truth" (Exod. 34:6).

Significantly, God's character qualities are synonymously associated with, if not synonymous with, the revelation of His glory. The crowning qualities, "abundant in goodness and truth" (Exod. 34:6), are the Hebrew equivalent to John's Greek wording, **full of grace and truth** (see 1:17; *Zondervan KJV Study Bible* note on Ps. 26:3; discussion on Prov. 16:6). These qualities are the glory of **the only begotten of the Father**. One expects the Son to bear the unique stamp of the Father, but the resemblance is the glory of grace and truth. Now too the relationship of the Logos with God (see 1:1) is viewed through a new lens of intimacy, that of Father and Son.

1:15. John again placed the testimony of the Baptist (the chief historical witness in the prologue) strategically. Here the Greek is in the present tense, even though when John wrote it, the action was in the past. The present tense suggests that John the Baptist's message still sounded in people's ears beyond his death. John characteristically used present-tense verbs in his writing. The Baptist's testimony corroborates 1:14 and the eternal existence of the Logos. This is supported by the closing words of his witness: **He that cometh after me is preferred before me: for he was before me**. In ancient times, the older person was given respect and regarded as greater than the younger. People would normally have ranked Jesus lower in respect than John, who was older. John the Baptist explained that this was only apparent, since Jesus, as Logos, existed before He was born on earth. Westcott (*The Gospel According to St. John*, p. 13) maintains it was a reference not merely to relative priority but to absolute priority: the Logos was not just "former" (prior to the Baptist) but was "first" in an absolute sense. It may be understood as, "He who comes after me has precedence over me, because he was (existed) prior to me (and all else)."

1:16–17. Of his fulness (v. 16; see 1:14) points to the full complement of grace and truth in Jesus Christ. The scope of grace experienced (**have all we received**) is defined by the words **grace for grace**, or "grace upon grace," which suggests the continuous disbursement of grace from His fullness. In view of John the Baptist's testimony ("he was before me," 1:15) and the preexistent Logos "made flesh" (1:14), John's clarification that **grace and truth came by Jesus Christ** (v. 17), makes it clear that there is only one mediator of God's grace, just as there was only one agent of creation (see 1:3), and both are none other than Jesus Christ. Sinai and Moses give a telltale historical vantage point to the range of His mediation. The highly esteemed role of Moses as mediator of God's Law and his exclusive witness to God's glory on Sinai (see Exod. 34:29–35; 2 Cor. 8:7–18) offer a historical comparison by which to measure the superior mediation of Jesus Christ, who mediates grace and truth, the very glory of God (see discussion of 1:14). John will go on to express the unparalleled and exclusive role of Jesus as mediator and revealer of God in v. 18.

1:18. The only begotten Son is an explicit declaration of Jesus' uniqueness (see 1:1, 14 and discussions; 3:16). The "Son" (other Greek manuscripts read "God") is clearly implied by the repetition of "the only begotten" (see 1:14), and the word **bosom** indicates the intimacy of the relationship of the Father and Son. The manuscript support for either reading ("Son" or "God") is strong and cannot be decided on the manuscript support alone. Both readings make sense based on the teaching of John's prologue (1:1–18). "Son" fits well the immediate sense by complementing "Father" and echoes "the only begotten of the Father" of 1:14. "God" strikes one as awkward but would round out the prologue by echoing the opening (1:1) at the end and tying the prologue together with a literary inclusion. In either case, this verse forms a climax to the prologue and clarifies the peerless status of Jesus as the one uniquely qualified to reveal the Father: **he hath declared him**. Indeed, **No man hath seen God at any time**. In the Old Testament, people are sometimes said to have seen God (see, e.g., Exod. 24:9–11), but they are also told that no one can see God and live (see Exod. 33:20). Therefore, since no human being can see God as He really is, those who saw God saw Him in a form He took on Himself temporarily for the occasion. Those events are termed "Christophanies," Old Testament appearances of Christ in human form. It seems John was saying that they saw none other than Jesus preincarnate (see discussion on 12:41). Now, however, Christ "hath declared him," or "has made him known."

II. Beginnings of Jesus' Ministry (1:19–51)

A. The Ministry of His Forerunner (1:19–34)

1:19. And this is the record of John points to the Baptist's role as witness (see 1:6–7). "Record"

(Greek, *martyria*) is literally "testimony." Here the testimony of John was given a formal venue with the inquest of the delegation that **the Jews sent ... from Jerusalem**. The phrase "the Jews" occurs about seventy times in this gospel. It is used in a favorable sense (see, e.g., 4:22) and in a neutral sense (see, e.g., 2:6), but generally John used it of the Jewish leaders who were hostile to Jesus (see, e.g., 8:48). Here it refers to the delegation sent by the Sanhedrin to look into the activities of an unauthorized teacher. **Levites** are descendants of the tribe of Levi, who were assigned to specific duties in connection with the tabernacle and temple (see Num. 3:17–37). They also had teaching responsibilities (see 2 Chron. 35:3; Neh. 8:7–9), and it was probably in this role that they were sent with the **priests** to John the Baptist.

1:20. The Baptist used the emphatic "I" to establish a stark contrast. His disavowal, **I am not the Christ** implies the question "Are you the Christ?" according to the pattern of the questions and answers that follow. It may be, however, that the unique introduction of **And he confessed, and denied not; but confessed** suggests the leading question was more benign, such as, "Who are you?" to which the Baptist assumed a proactive posture ("I am not the Christ"). If so, that triggered the follow-up questions (all associated with messianic expectations). The Baptist's emphatic use of "I" implies the avowal that another was the Christ. Throughout the following verses, this emphatic "I" occurs frequently, and almost invariably implies a contrast with Jesus, who is always given the higher place.

1:21. Art thou Elias? ... I am not. The Jews remembered that Elijah had not died (see 2 Kings 2:11) and believed that the same prophet would come back to earth to announce the end time. In this sense, John properly denied that he was Elijah. When Jesus later said the Baptist was Elijah (see Matt. 11:14; 17:10–13), He meant it in the sense that John was a fulfillment of the prophecy of Malachi 4:5 (see Luke 1:17). **That prophet** refers to the prophet of Deuteronomy 18:15, 18. The Jewish people expected a variety of persons to be associated with the coming of the Messiah. The Baptist emphatically denied being "that prophet." He had come to testify about Jesus, yet they kept asking him about himself. His answers became progressively more terse.

1:22–23. The voice of one crying in the wilderness (v. 23). The Baptist applied the prophecy of Isaiah 40:3 to his ministry of calling people to repent in preparation for the coming of the Messiah. The men of Qumran (the community that produced the Dead Sea Scrolls) applied the same words to themselves, but they prepared for the Lord's coming by isolating themselves from the world to secure their own salvation. John concentrated on helping people come to the Messiah (the Christ). In 1:31, the Baptist expressly stated that the objective of his baptism was to reveal to Israel the Coming One.

1:24. Within Judaism, **the Pharisees** (see discussions on Matt. 3:7; Mark 2:16; Luke 5:17) were the conservative religious party and most influential among the people. Here they probed deeper than the rest of the delegation (see 1:19).

1:25. Christ (Greek) and "Messiah" (Hebrew) both mean "Anointed One." In Old Testament times, anointing signified being set apart for service, particularly as king (see 1 Sam. 16:1, 13; 26:11) or priest (see Exod. 40:13–15; Lev. 4:3). People were looking for not just an anointed one, however, but the Anointed One, the Messiah. The Pharisees appear to have associated baptism with initiation, an activity appropriate to one with a title. The Baptist, who refused all titles, saw his baptism as an anticipation of and preparation for the Messiah.

1:26–27. The Baptist responded to the question "Why baptizeth thou …?" (1:25) with a twofold answer that compared what he did and who he was with the one whom his ministry anticipated. First, the Baptist defined what he did: **I baptize with water** (v. 26). The Baptist was not just stating the obvious; he was inviting a comparison of his water ministry with a ministry greater than water (see Mark 1:7–8; Luke 3:16; Matt. 3:11). This impending ministry, which would supercede the Baptist's, belonged to none other than the Messiah. The Baptist alluded to this with the words **there standeth one among you, whom ye know not**, echoing a popular belief that

the Messiah would remain hidden until He was suddenly revealed (see 1:33). Second, the Baptist defined who he was with the description of a slave. How much greater was the Unknown One if the Baptist, who commanded the attention of the religious authorities, was no more important that His slave? Disciples would perform all sorts of service for their rabbis (teachers), but loosing their **shoe's latchet** (sandal thongs; v. 27) was expressly excluded. This was a menial and lowly task. Unloosing another's shoe's latchet was a prelude to footwashing (compare Peter's reaction to his Master, 13:4–8). The Baptist describes the greatness of Jesus by defining his worthiness as beneath that of a slave.

1:28. The site of **Bethabara** ("house of the ford," or crossing point) is not known, except that it was located on the east side of the Jordan.

1:29–30. The next day (v. 29). For the sequence of days enumerated by John, see discussion on 2:1. It would seem that the baptism of Jesus had already taken place. In 1:32–35, the Baptist recounted the event and the Spirit's revelation, which now allowed him to identify Jesus as **the Lamb of God**. Was the occasion of the Baptist's questioning also the occasion of Jesus' baptism (see 1:26)? In verse 30, John linked the events of the previous day with the Baptist's testimony ("bare record," 1:32, 34) to Jesus, who now approached. "Lamb of God" (v. 29) is an expression found in the Bible only here and in 1:36. Many suggestions have been made as to its precise meaning (e.g., the lamb offered at Passover, or the lamb of Isa. 53:7, of Jer. 11:19, or of Gen. 22:8). The expression seems to be a general reference to sacrifice, however, not the name for a particular offering. The Baptist was saying that Jesus would be the sacrifice that would atone for **the sin of the world**. A sacrifice was offered first for the individual (see Genesis 4), then for a family at Passover (see Exodus 12), and then for the nation on the Day of Atonement (see Leviticus 16). With Jesus' death, it would be broadened: He would be a sacrifice for the entire world.

1:31. I knew him not suggests that the Baptist was unable to identify the Messiah by appearance alone. John the Baptist, who lived "in the deserts till the day of his shewing unto Israel" (Luke 1:80), may not have known Jesus in a familiar sense. The words probably mean only that he did not know that Jesus was the Messiah until he saw the sign mentioned in 1:32–33.

1:32–33. The baptism of Jesus is not recorded in John, only recounted (for Jesus' baptism, see discussions on Matt. 3:15–17). The descent of the Spirit upon Jesus (v. 32) took place at His baptism according to all four gospels (see Matt. 3:16; Mark 1:10; Luke 3:22). The perfect tense "I have seen" is not apparent in the KJV's **I saw**, but it underscores the Baptist's testimony to the dwelling of the Spirit upon Jesus (**it abode upon him**), which John witnessed and which characterized Jesus' ministry. John baptized **with water** (v. 33), but Jesus would baptize **with the Holy Ghost**. If a specific event is intended by these words, the fulfillment was the sending of the Holy Spirit on the day of Pentecost (see Acts 2).

1:34. This is the Son of God (see 1:14, 18; 3:16; 20:31). Here the Baptist definitively bore witness to Jesus as the Son of God with a capstone statement that additionally pointed to the very purpose of this gospel (see 20:31).

B. Jesus' Introduction to Some Future Disciples (1:35–51)

1:35–37. Again the next day (v. 35) reveals an unfolding sequence of days (see 1:29, 35, 43; 2:1; for the possible importance of the pattern, see discussion on 2:1). The Baptist was **Again** there (**stood**) with **two of his disciples**. One was Andrew (see 1:40). The other is not named, but from early times, it has been thought that he was John, the author of this gospel. The two were his disciples in the sense that they had been baptized by John the Baptist and looked to him as their religious teacher. The Baptist again identified Jesus as **the Lamb of God** (v. 36; see discussion on 1:29) with the call to **Behold**, an interjection intended to draw the listeners' attention to what the speaker was about to say. From the disciples' response, the Baptist's intent seems to have been understood as a call to heed and not just ob-

serve, for the two **followed Jesus** (v. 37). Because "to follow" means to move behind someone in the same direction, it is also used figuratively of discipleship (see 1:43; 8:12; 10:4–5, 27; 12:26; 21:19–21). Here not only did the two disciples walk after Jesus, but their steps led to a shift in allegiance from the Baptist to Jesus.

1:38–40. Jesus asked the two, **What seek ye?** (v. 38), or "What are you searching for?" The question appears innocent enough, but more was at work here. The two deferentially called Him **Rabbi** (lit., "my lord" or "my master"), which John translated as **Master** (or "Teacher"), bringing together two important qualities of discipleship: devotion and instruction. One may infer that the two understood that Jesus was expressing more than a benign curiosity in the reason they were walking after Him. The invitation to **Come and see … where he dwelt** (v. 39; Greek, *menō*; also used for **dwellest** [v. 38] and **abode** [v. 39]) would gain deeper significance in Jesus' teaching on discipleship (see 12:26; chap. 15) and is anticipated here. Their stay with Jesus gave the two deeper insight into Him and caused **Andrew** (v. 40) to bring his brother Peter to Jesus (see 1:41–42). For **that day** (v. 39), see discussion on 2:1.

1:41–42. Andrew (see 6:8; 12:22) brought his brother Peter to Jesus based on insight he had gained from his stay with Jesus (see 1:39). Jesus' question, "What seek ye?" (1:38) is here answered: **We have found the Messias** (see discussion on 1:25). Both **Cephas** (Aramaic; v. 42) and Peter (Greek, *Petros*) mean "rock." In the Gospels, Peter was anything but a rock; he was impulsive and unstable. In Acts, he was a pillar of the early church. Jesus named him not for what he was but for what, by God's grace, he would become.

1:43–44. Jesus made His way **into Galilee** (v. 43) and called to **Philip … Follow me. Bethsaida** (v. 44; see discussion on Matt. 11:21) was **the city of Andrew and Peter** and Philip. Had Andrew, now joined by his brother Peter, influenced Jesus to travel to their hometown? The Greek does not specify the subject of what literally reads, "he decided to leave for Galilee." Carson (*The Gospel According to John*, pp. 157–58) argues that it was Andrew who made the decision. If so, this would reinforce a chain of witness and belief, showing that everyone who came to Jesus in 1:35–42 did so because of someone else's witness. On the other hand, the chain of witness (Baptist, Andrew, Peter, Philip, Nathanael), if broken by Jesus' intention to find Philip, does show Jesus to always be the common denominator of the faith that resulted. Each person in the chain had an encounter with Jesus.

1:45–46. Philip findeth Nathanael (v. 45) and said, **We have found him, of whom Moses in the law, and the prophets, did write** points notably to Deuteronomy 18:15–19 and a store of other references in what the prophets wrote. "The law, and the prophets" at that time denoted the Torah, the Jewish Bible. **Nazareth, son of Joseph** is a stock reference to a man in first-century Palestine by his village and lineage (see Carson, *The Gospel According to John*, p. 159) and is not a denial of the virgin birth of Christ (see Matt. 1:18, 20, 23, 25; Luke 1:35). Joseph was Jesus' legal, though not His natural, father. **Can … any good thing come out of Nazareth?** (for "Nazareth," see 7:52; discussion on Matt. 2:23). Since Nathanael was from Cana (see 21:2), it has been suggested (see Brown, *The Gospel According to John*, p. 83; Carson, *The Gospel According to John*, p. 160) that the fault-finding question reflected a local rivalry between the nearby towns. Certainly Philip's testimony had created an expectation of Jesus that did not match His village and lineage.

1:47–49. Nathanael asked, **Whence knowest thou me?** (v. 48), and Jesus answered with a knowledge that showed His greater-than-human ability and fulfilled Philip's advanced billing of Jesus. A **fig tree** (v. 48) was known for its shade and was a favorite place for study and prayer in hot weather. In view of Nathanael's confession, Jesus' identification of Nathanael as **an Israelite indeed** (v. 47), or "truly an Israelite," becomes important. Athough "indeed" or "truly" is explained by the words **in whom is no guile** (or deceit), there appears to be an added significance. As the "true Israelite," Nathanael confesseed, **Rabbi, thou art the Son of God; thou art the King**

of Israel (v. 49). The confession not only formed a faith acknowledgment of Jesus but harkened back (a literary inclusion) to the Baptist, whose testimony revealed to Israel that this was the Son of God (see 1:31, 34). Nathanael's confession thus provided John's readers a dependable confirming testimony that Jesus is the Son of God, the King of Israel, and served as a climax to the chain of witness starting with the Baptist. The title "the Son of God" (see 1:14, 18, 34; 3:16; 20:31) was later used in mockery (see 19:7; Matt. 27:40). "The King of Israel" (see 12:13) and "Christ" are equated in Mark 15:32.

1:50–51. Only the gospel of John records Jesus' use of the double **Verily, verily** (v. 51), which appears exactly twenty-five times in the book. This phrase signifies important sayings and carries the sense of firm or solemn conviction. Jesus addressed not only Nathanael (**saith unto him**) but also the other disciples present (**ye** is plural). **Ye shall see … the angels … ascending and descending upon the Son of man** alludes to a definitive moment in Israel's history when it was similarly revealed that Jacob was God's elect one and would be the progenitor of God's people (see Gen. 28:12 and discussion). Here the symbolism of angelic traffic between heaven and earth marked Jesus, the Son of Man, as God's elect one through whom redemption would come to the world, perhaps identifying Jesus as the true Israelite (see 1:47). Carson (*The Gospel According to John*, p. 164) puts it well: "Every Jew honoured Jacob/ Israel, the father of the twelve tribes; now everyone must recognize that this same God has appointed Jesus as his Messiah." In Jesus' ministry, the disciples would see heaven's (God's) testimony to Jesus as plainly as audibly hearing an announcement from heaven concerning Him. "The Son of man" was Jesus' favorite self-designation (see discussions on Mark 2:10; Luke 19:10).

III. Jesus' Public Ministry: Signs and Discourses (chaps. 2–11)

A. Changing Water into Wine (2:1–11)

2:1–2. And the third day (v. 1) probably should be understood as the third day after the last event,

Jesus' meeting with Nathanael, placing the wedding and Jesus' first miracle on the seventh day. This accounting, based on the pattern of days numbered from the opening day at 1:19, is widely acknowledged, although opinions as to its significance vary. At minimum, the days of testimony to Jesus now culminated in a most important event: "This beginning of miracles did Jesus in Cana of Galilee, and manifested forth his glory; and his disciples believed on him" (2:11).

Cana (v. 1) is mentioned only in John's gospel (see 2:11; 4:46; 21:2). It was west of the Sea of Galilee, but the exact location is unknown. John expressly paired this first miracle, the wedding at Cana, with the second miracle (or "sign"; see discussion on 2:11) of Jesus in his gospel (compare 2:1, 11 with 4:46, 54).

Little is known of how a wedding was performed in the Holy Land in the first century, but clearly the feast was very important and might go on for a week. To fail in proper hospitality was a serious offense. Whether the invitation to **Jesus … and his disciples** (v. 2; meaning the disciples of chap. 1) came from Jesus' mother or Nathanael, who lived in Cana (see 21:2), is not plain. It is more likely that it came from Mary, given her initiative in 2:3, and with it the sense of responsibility for the shortage of wine when Jesus and His disciples arrived. Whether the wedding was that of a relative is no more than a hunch, albeit not an inconceivable one.

2:3. When they wanted wine is more exactly translated, "when the wine was gone," indicating a shortage of what was required. The shortage was more than a minor social embarrassment, since the family had an obligation to provide a feast of the socially required standard. There was no great variety in beverages in that day, and people normally drank water or wine.

2:4–5. To address your mother as **Woman** (v. 4) sounds impersonal and rude to the modern ear. In that day, however, it was a polite form of address, and Jesus used it to address his mother (19:26), the Samaritan (4:21), the adulteress (8:10), and Mary Magdalene (20:13, 15). Even so, the address does not match what one would expect of a son to his mother. In a mother-child relationship, the distance

"woman" implies matches Jesus' question to Mary: **what have I to do with thee?** or literally, "what to me and to you?" This expression was not uncommon (see Mark 1:24; 5:7; Luke 8:28; Judg. 11:12; 1 Kings 17:18; 2 Kings 3:13; 2 Chron. 35:21) and could serve either to rebuke or to contest an obligation. Here Jesus introduced a higher obligation, that of His **hour**, which in this gospel pictures Jesus moving inevitably toward the destiny for which He had come: the time of His sacrificial death on the cross (see 7:6, 8, 30; 8:20). In this gospel, Jesus' use of the word "hour" (Greek, *hōra*; v. 4; also in 4:21, 23; 5:25, 28, 29; 7:30; 8:20; 12:23, 27; 13:1; 16:25, 32; 17:1) refers to more than a division of time as an hour of the day. Its meaning is shaped by the critical events of Jesus' death and resurrection, an incumbent period of Jesus' life when He was to leave this world and return to the Father (see 13:1), the hour when the Son of Man would be glorified (see 17:1).

In His reply to Mary, Jesus altered and redefined the normal expectations of a mother-child obligation. Mary's instruction to the servants reflect her acceptance: **Whatsoever he saith unto you, do it** (v. 5). Mary left the matter to Jesus. Did she expect a miracle? It is unlikely in view of 2:11. This was Jesus' first miracle.

2:6–7. Jews became ceremonially defiled during the normal circumstances of daily life and were cleansed by pouring water over the hands. For a lengthy feast with many guests, a large amount of water was required for this purpose. The word **containing** (v. 6) refers to capacity, not to actual content. These **waterpots of stone** could contain **two or three firkins apiece**, about twenty to thirty gallons each. The presence of these emblems of religious practice even in Galilee (**after the manner of the purifying of the Jews**) attests to the prominence of outward purification far and wide. Here the emblems were literally empty, and they would be transformed in value by Jesus, who appropriated them to provide an abundance of wine for the joyous occasion of a wedding.

2:8–10. Following Jesus' instructions, the waterpots were filled with water, and out of them a sampling was drawn for the approval of **the governor of the feast** (v. 8), or **the ruler of the feast** (v. 9; the same Greek word), identifying the one in charge of the banquet. His qualified evaluation was not only discriminating but impartial; he **knew not whence it was**. Had he known he was drinking from purification jars, he would never have tasted it. The sampling produced a call to the bridegroom, the one presumed responsible for the wine.

When men have well drunk (v. 10) is an indication not of drunkenness but simply of having consumed a lot of the particular beverage that was served. His remark attests to the clever custom of serving the superior wine before the inferior. Moreover, and without knowing it, he attested that the superior wine had been served last. Indeed, a new standard had been established, with implications for the transcending work of God in Jesus (see 2:11).

2:11. This beginning of miracles. Unlike the other gospel writers (Matthew, Mark, and Luke), John always used the Greek word for "signs" (Greek, *sēmeion*) to refer to Jesus' miracles, emphasizing the significance of the action rather than the marvel (see, e.g., 4:54; 6:14; 9:16; 11:47). Elsewhere (e.g., 2:18; 6:14, 30; 10:41), people emphasized the miraculous feature of a *sēmeion* when it signified and revealed insight to Jesus. These signs revealed Jesus' glory (see 1:14). The first sign, changing water into wine, thus had the same purpose that all the following signs would have: revelation about the true stature and person of Jesus.

Seven "signs" are listed in John's gospel: (1) changing water into wine (2:1–11), (2) healing an official's son (4:46–54), (3) healing the invalid at Bethesda (5:1–18), (4) feeding the five thousand (6:5–14), (5) walking on the water (6:16–21), (6) healing a blind man (9:1–7), and (7) raising Lazarus from the dead (11:1–45). A final miracle, though not specified as a "sign," involved the miraculous catch of fish (21:6–11).

B. Cleansing the Temple (2:12–25)

2:12. The city of **Capernaum** was on the shore of the Sea of Galilee (below sea level) and geographically at a lower level than Cana, which was in the hill country to the west. This cameo of Jesus with His mother, brothers, and disciples features an interval of **not many days** in which Jesus and His disciples enjoyed the company of His family. This historical detail brings before the reader the very human and very divine features of Jesus. This interlude links the events at the marriage in Cana and at the temple in Jerusalem and places side by side, almost at once, Jesus the son of His earthly mother and Jesus the Son of His heavenly Father. Jesus' **brethren** most likely were the children of Joseph and Mary, His half brothers (see discussion on Luke 8:19).

2:13. Passover (see *KJV Study Bible* notes on Exod. 12:11–23; discussions on Matt. 26:17, 18–30; Mark 14:1–2, 12; Luke 22:1; chart, *KJV Study Bible*, p. 92) was one of the annual feasts that all Jewish men were required to celebrate in Jerusalem (see Deut. 16:16). This is the first of at least three (and possibly four) Passovers noted in John's gospel (see 5:1 and discussion; 6:4; 11:55; 12:1; 13:1; 18:28, 39; 19:14). The chronology of Jesus' three-year ministry is based on the gospel of John and its attention to the Passovers. The other gospels only narrate one Passover in the life of Jesus.

2:14–17. Matthew, Mark, and Luke recorded a cleansing of the temple toward the end of Jesus' ministry (see discussion on Matt. 21:12–17). Jesus also began His ministry with such a cleansing.

Oxen and sheep and doves (v. 14) were required for sacrifices. Jews who came great distances had to be able to buy sacrificial animals near the temple. The merchants, however, were selling them in the outer court of the temple itself, the one place where Gentiles could come to pray. **Changers of money** were necessary (see discussion on Mark 11:15) because many coins had to be changed into currency acceptable to the temple authorities. They should not have been working in the temple itself, however.

From strands of rope lying about, Jesus fashioned a whip and drove out the merchants and livestock. He could not very well drive out the **doves** (v. 16), so He reproached the vendors. **House of merchandise** (Greek, *emporion*; "market," "emporium") identifies a marketplace and the moneymaking (buying and selling of goods) that had eclipsed the purpose of sacrificial offering and the sanctity of the temple. The disciples connected the authority of Jesus' action with Zechariah 69:9: **The zeal of thine house hath eaten me up** (v. 17).

2:18. The Jews (see discussion on 1:19), probably temple authorities of the Sanhedrin, **answered** Jesus' action with a request for a **sign** (Greek, *sēmeion*) to authorize His action in the temple. Jesus resisted such demands (see 6:30; Matt. 16:1). The authorities were looking for miraculous credentials to match the authority one presumed with such an act in the temple. There is probably a note of irony here, for John's use of the word *sēmeion* ("sign"), in contrast with the request, emphasizes the significance of a sign over the miracle itself, which is what Jesus gave them in His response (see 2:19). Jesus' answer alluded to a future miracle, His resurrection (see 2:19, 22), and to His ultimate authority over life and death (see 5:24–29).

2:19. The Jews thought Jesus was referring to the literal temple, but John made it clear that He was not (see 2:21). Just a few years later, Jesus was accused of saying that He would **Destroy** (the) **temple, and … raise it up** again (see Matt. 26:60–61; Mark 14:57–59). Mockers repeated the charge as He hung on the cross (see Matt. 27:40; Mark 15:29). The same misunderstanding may have been behind the charge against Stephen (see Acts 6:14).

2:20–22. When therefore he was risen … his disciples remembered (v. 22; see 14:26). Like the temple authorities, Jesus' disciples were thinking only in material terms at this point. The temple was not finally completed until AD 64. Work had been going on for **Forty … six years** (v. 20). Since it had begun in 20 BC, the event recorded here occurred in AD 26 or 27.

2:23–25. This summary of Jesus' actions and the people's response during **the passover** (v. 23) feast (see discussion on 2:13), is closely connected with what follows. Jesus performed **miracles** ("signs," Greek, *sēmeion*), and people **believed in his name** (see 1:12; 3:18). In ancient times, an individual's

"name" summed up his whole person, and here John used the characteristic expression "believed in" (or "on"), which is elsewhere used in the most positive sense of moving into a believing relationship with Jesus. Only with verses 23–24 does one become aware of some inadequacy in the people's belief and seek an explanation for Jesus' reservation to **commit himself**, or "entrust himself," to them. The reason is found in what Jesus knew. **He knew all men** (lit., "all" in the masculine gender), signifying His knowledge of the human heart. Initial "belief in" Jesus at this stage in His ministry may have been uninformed fascination, as the story of Nicodemus, who sincerely sought Jesus, illustrates (see 3:1–21). One should thus probably understand Jesus' response as "a general reference to having no confidence in their enthusiasm" (Brown, *The Gospel According to John*, p. 127) and read the conversation of Jesus with Nicodemus as an illustration (see 3:1–21). Nevertheless, just as the disciples had grown in their belief, Nicodemus appears to have grown in his (see 7:50; 19:39).

C. Interview with Nicodemus (3:1–21)

3:1–2. A man of the Pharisees (see discussions on Matt. 3:7; Mark 2:16; Luke 5:17), **named Nicodemus** (v. 1), probably witnessed the signs of Jesus during Passover (see 3:23), for he said, **for no man can do … that thou doest, except God be with him** (v. 2). Nicodemus may have connected the miraculous actions of Jesus with the expected kingdom of God (see 3:3, 5; discussion on Matt. 3:2). He visited Jesus **by night** because he was afraid to come by day, or perhaps because he wanted a long talk, which would have been difficult in the daytime with the crowds around Jesus. Each time John introduced Nicodemus, he is identified by his night visit (see 7:50; 19:39).

3:3–4. Born again (v. 3) also means "born from above." The Greek word *anōthen* (here and in 3:7), with its double meaning of "again" and "from above," is important to the conversation between Jesus and Nicodemus. English translations must choose one or the other, but both meanings are in play. Nicodemus obviously understood Jesus in the first sense and quite literally, but he is presented as misunderstanding Jesus and failing to comprehend the second sense, the origin of this birth "from above." No one can **see** (or "enter"; see 3:5) **the kingdom of God** without this birth from above. The question of Nicodemus implies not only his incomprehension but also his sense of disqualification and disappointment: **How can a man be born when he is old?** (v. 4).

3:5–6. The phrase **born of water** (v. 5) has been understood in various ways: (1) It means much the same as "born of the Spirit" (3:8; see Titus 3:5). (2) "Water" here refers to purification (see 2:6). (3) "Water" refers to baptism, that of John (see 1:31) or that of Jesus and His disciples (see 3:22; 4:1–2). (4) "Water" refers to natural birth. Even as one is born of water, he must experience a second birth, a spiritual birth. Option 1 has much to commend it. "Born of water" must not be separated from **and of the Spirit**. On the strength of Jesus' parallel wording in 3:3 and the grammatical bond of the words "water" and "Spirit" (the Greek preposition "of" binds them together), "born from above" is the counterpart of "born of water and … Spirit" here. Only one birth is in view, not two. Moreover, the water-spirit bond has an Old Testament connection. If Jesus expected Nicodemus, a religious teacher (see 3:10), to understand His amplification and explanation in verse 5, one may look to the Old Testament, where water and spirit come together most forcefully in Ezkeiel 36:25–27 to denote the work from above that God does in people's hearts (see Carson, *The Gospel According to John*, pp. 191–96). Jesus went on to confirm this with His distinction between **flesh** (v. 6) and **Spirit**, a contrast of origin (human and superhuman).

3:7. Ye must be born again. This assertion applies to everyone, not just to Nicodemus (the Greek for "Ye" is plural here). "Must" makes it clear there are no exceptions. For **born again**, see discussion on 3:3.

3:8–10. The work of the Holy Spirit, superhuman and sovereign, is as real and as mysterious as **The wind** (v. 8) in the renewal of the human heart. Again there is a play on words or dual meaning at work. The word "wind" (Greek, *pneuma*; like English "pneuma-tic") is also the word for "Spirit" (*pneuma*).

As with the wind, one cannot fathom or control the Spirit, yet the effects are undeniable. The incomprehension of Nicodemus (**How can these things be?** v. 9) points to the very truth of Jesus: **so is every one that is born of the Spirit** (v. 8). Nicodemus had to be born from above to understand, for these truths are spiritually appraised. In chiding Nicodemus, Jesus made a case in point out of the **master** ("teacher") **of Israel** (v. 10).

3:11–13. The plural **We** (v. 11), on the face of it, associated others, perhaps the disciples, with Jesus. It may also be the case, and likely is, that Jesus was employing "we" as Nicodemus used it in 3:2, representatively. In saying, **ye receive not our witness** (for "witness," see discussion on 1:7), Jesus further strengthened the contrast between the earthly (elementary), which the teacher of Israel could not comprehend, and the heavenly, which he longed to understand. **No man hath ascended … but he that came down from heaven** (v. 13) points to Jesus' unique and unparalleled qualification to speak of heavenly things. In other words, no one has been up but He who came down: Jesus. Jesus is the heavenly man, **even the Son of man which is** ("dwells") **in heaven**, whom the Jews associated with residence in heaven. "The Son of man" was Jesus' favorite self-designation (see discussions on Mark 2:10; Luke 19:10), and in the gospel of John, it emphasizes Jesus as the heavenly one who descended and revealed the Father (see 1:18).

3:14–15. As Jesus had just identified Himself with the heavenly Son of Man, He now revealed that He must **be lifted up** (v. 14; see discussions on 12:31–32), even **as Moses lifted up the serpent** (see Num. 21:4–9). Jesus was alluding to His crucifixion and being lifted up on the cross. The primary connection to the action of Moses and the bronze serpent on a pole is that of being lifted up for the sake of salvation. Just as the people looked in faith to that serpent, so must they look to Jesus or perish. **Eternal life** (v. 15) is an infinitely high quality of life in living fellowship with God, both now and forever. By contrast, **perish** suggests eternal death and the specter of being forever cut off from God.

It may be that verse 15 concludes the conversation between Jesus and Nicodemus and the words of John begin again.

3:16–17. God so loved the world (v. 16) is the great truth that motivated God's plan of salvation (see 1 John 4:9–10). In English, "so" can suggest quality ("in this way") and quantity ("so much"). Although the Greek word emphasizes "in this way," the way in which God loved suggests "so much." "World" identifies all people on earth, or perhaps all creation (see discussion on 1:9–10). For **only begotten Son**, see 1:14, 18 (see also Gen. 22:2, 16; Rom. 8:32). Although believers are also called "sons of God" (see 1:12; 2 Cor. 6:18; Rev. 21:7), Jesus is God's Son in a unique sense; sons by adoption do not become members of the Godhead. The divine purpose of God's love in sending His Son (**that whosoever believeth … have everlasting life**) is restated (**that the world through him might be saved**; v. 17). A comparison of the wording brings to the forefront the importance of belief in Jesus and His agency.

3:18–21. Here John was not speaking of momentary beliefs and doubts but of continuing, settled attitudes. The person who refuses to believe in Jesus stands **condemned already** (v. 18) by virtue of his or her refusal. **Darkness** (v. 19) is John's expression for the condition of a perishing world in which evil is compounded by self-rule and rejection of God. The **light** of God, Jesus Christ, **is come into the world** to intervene and offer deliverance. People who cling to the darkness and to that which is condemned (see 3:17) reject the light and will perish (see 3:16). Conversely, what is **wrought in God** (v. 21) shows its origin in the truth that operates in the light and demonstrates its difference from the darkness by gravitating to the light.

D. Parallel Ministry with John the Baptist (3:22–4:3)

3:22. And baptized. According to 4:2, only the disciples baptized; Jesus did not.

3:23. The location of **Aenon** is unclear. Possibly, it was about eight miles south of Scythopolis (Bethshan), west of the Jordan.

3:24. John offered a brief explanation of the presence of John the Baptist. For the reason the Baptist was imprisoned, see Luke 3:19–20.

3:25. Purifying. Many viewed baptism as a ceremonial purification, and proper purification was a matter of great concern to some Jews (see, e.g., Mark 7:1–5). The religious authorities had questioned John about his baptism (see 1:25), and such differences of opinion may have led to that interrogation.

3:26. The Baptist's disciples knew that he had testified about Jesus, but they loved their master and were envious of Jesus' success. For **barest witness**, see discussion on 1:7.

3:27. Except it be given. These words were true of both Jesus and John (and of everyone). Both had what God had given them, so there was no place for envy. The Greek for "to give" is used frequently in this gospel (seventy-five times), especially of the things the Father has granted or entrusted to the Son. **Heaven** is frequently a respectful substitute for "God."

3:28–30. The bridegroom (v. 29) is the most important man at a wedding. It refers here to Jesus, **the Christ** (v. 28), and alludes to the Baptist's testimony that he was not the bridegroom but rather the best man. It is the function of **the friend** (the best man; v. 29) to handle the marriage arrangements and to help the bridegroom, which describes the role of John the Baptist. Customary was the joyous delight of the best man, enough so that the Baptist could compare his disposition toward Jesus to the wedding experiences of his disciples. The best man was known to **rejoiceth greatly** at the arrival of the groom and would then turn **the bride** over to the him. At that point, the friend would **decrease** and the groom would **increase**. Similarly, John the Baptist had been sent to prepare the way for the Messiah, and here he reaffirmed his subordinate position and joy in the role that God had granted him.

3:31–36. Here John (the author) apparently reflected on Jesus' distinguishing characteristics, with comparisons to John the Baptist and themes from the entire chapter as background.

3:31. Jesus **cometh from above** (Greek, *anōthen*; see discussion on 3:3) and is of heavenly origin, which puts Him above people and things of earth. **Earth** (Greek, *gē*) and **earthly** emphasize finite limitation; unlike *kosmos* ("the world"; see discussion on 1:10), these words lack John's insinuation of sinfulness. They could apply to anyone, but here they particularly refer to John the Baptist.

3:32–33. Jesus spoke from divine experience **what he hath seen and heard** (v. 32; see 3:11–13). **No man** means not that no person accepted what Jesus said (see v. 33) but rather that people in general refused His teaching (see 3:11). Those who **received** (accepted) **his testimony hath set to his seal** (v. 33), or "certified," the truth that Jesus came from heaven and that God was acting in Him for the world's salvation. That reception thereby certified not only that Jesus is truthful but also that God is truthful. John repeatedly stated that to believe in Jesus is to believe in God because Jesus reveals the Father, and nothing but what the Father has shown Him and told Him (see 5:19–30; 6:37–40; 8:29).

3:34–36. He **whom God hath sent speaketh the words of God** (v. 34). Communication in the ancient Mediterranean world depended on reliable messengers. Jesus was more than a messenger, however; He was an authorized agent, able to transact business as well as to deliver messages. In the Jewish institution of agency, the authority of the agent is defined this way: the one sent is as the one who sends. Moreover, Jesus is a unique agent in that He is the Son of the one who sent Him (similar to the householder's son in Matt. 21:33–39). John set out the credentials of Jesus' agency: (1) He has been given the Spirit without **measure**. (2) He is the beloved **Son** (v. 35). (3) **The Father ... hath given all things into his hand**, which in Jewish law indicated right of ownership to legally transact business (see also 13:3). In view of these credentials, the offer of eternal life is guaranteed. Jesus is fully authorized to speak for God and act for God. **Everlasting life** (v. 36) is a present possession, not something the believer will obtain only later (see discussion on 3:15). Conversely, **the wrath of God** also is guaranteed. This is a strong expression meaning that God is actively opposed to everything evil. The word "wrath" occurs only here in John's gospel (see discussion on Rom. 1:18). The offer of life is held out in Jesus, and for one who rejects it, the wrath of God **abideth on him**. One may put God out of mind, but John made it clear that God's wrath does not eventually fade away. His opposition to evil is both total and permanent.

4:1–3. The gospel record of partisan Jewish views about ceremonial purity and baptism (see 1:25; 3:22–23, 24–26) offers a hint as to why the baptisms conducted by Jesus' disciples attracted the interest of **the Pharisees** (v. 1). The religious leaders took a close interest in John the Baptist (see discussion on 1:24) and then also in Jesus. The disciples did not baptize without Jesus' approval (see 3:22) and quite possibly baptized in Jesus' name (under His authority). Success in baptizing many disciples (which aroused opposition; see 7:1), as well as God's timetable (see 4:4), was why Jesus **left Judea** (v. 3) and went **again into Galilee**. It was in Galilee that most of Jesus' work was done.

E. Journey through Samaria: The Woman at the Well (4:4–42)

4:4. Must needs go through Samaria expresses a necessity that lay in Jesus' mission, not in the geography. Jews often avoided Samaria by crossing the Jordan and traveling on its east side (see discussions on Matt. 10:5; Luke 9:52). To proceed through Samaria was the direct route to Galilee, but Jesus' necessity to travel through this region apparently was due to spiritual opportunities that demanded His presence. According to Josephus (*Life* 52§269), it took three days to travel from Jerusalem (in Judea) to Galilee by way of Samaria.

4:5. Sychar was a small village near Shechem (see Map 11, p. 2149). Jacob bought some land in the vicinity of Shechem (see Gen. 33:18–19), not far from Mount Gerizim, and it was apparently this land that he gave to Joseph (see Gen. 48:21–22).

4:6. At **about the sixth hour** (reckoned from sunup), or about 12:00 noon, Jesus, fatigued from the journey and the midday heat, **sat thus on the**

well, a detail suggesting that the shaft of the well was protected by stone blocks. For all of Jesus' divinity, John was equally at ease with recording His humanity. **Jacob's well** is mentioned nowhere else in Scripture, but modern identification of the well agrees with John's detail. Its depth of approximately one hundred feet corresponds to the words of the Samaritan woman in 4:11.

4:7–9. A woman of Samaria (the region and not the city, which was further north; v. 7) came to **draw water** at noon (see 4:6). People normally drew water earlier or later in the day to avoid the midday heat (see Gen. 24:11 and discussion), but the practice of drawing water at midday is attested by Josephus, who says that the young ladies whom Moses helped (see Exod. 2:15–17) came to draw water at noon. Even so, the Samaritan woman came alone rather than with other women, as was common. Her solitary presence may reflect a loss of social acceptance owing to her many alliances with men; even her current one was not her husband (see 4:16–18).

Give me to drink (v. 7). A weary traveler asking for a drink was not unusual. What surprised the woman was that Jesus, being a Jew (see v. 9), was not deterred by the social and religious liabilities, so obvious to her, of His association with "a woman of Samaria" (v. 7). Issues of hereditary pedigree and theological purity divided the two peoples and resulted in deep-seated historical prejudice. Jesus broke the mold, and His uncharacteristic request intrigued her. The woman knew well that the Jews viewed all Samaritans as unclean. The Greek words translated **have no dealings with** imply "do not use dishes Samaritans have used." A Jew would become ceremonially unclean if he used a drinking vessel handled by a Samaritan. This meaning squares with verse 8 and the "dealings" of the disciples with the Samaritans to purchase food.

4:10. Jesus implied that the woman lacked knowledge of **the gift of God** and the identity of **who it is that saith to thee, Give me to drink**. Otherwise, she would have been the one asking for water, **living water.** "The gift of God" (only here in the gospel of John) has been variously understood. Two strong possibilities

are (1) Jesus Himself (see 3:16) and (2) the Torah (the Pentateuch, revered by both Jews and Samaritans). Knowing the identity of Jesus functions a little differently in each case, however. If, on the one hand, Jesus is the gift, then knowing His identity functions as a repetition tying His very presence to the wonderment of God's gift and an expectancy of things divine. If, on the other, Torah is "the gift of God" (a description used in Judaism), then knowing the identity of Jesus (Messiah) would be an additional piece of knowledge. In other words, if she had the combined knowledge of the Torah and the identity of Jesus as Messiah, she would have asked Him for a drink of living water, for together, Torah and the presence of Messiah points to the fulfillment of Deuteronomy 18:18. Both have much to commend them, but the latter has the advantage of addressing the Samaritan expectation of a prophet like Moses (see Deut. 18:15–18), and that expectation of prophet and Messiah surfaced later in the conversation (see 4:19, 24–25).

The "living water" (or "flowing water," a dual meaning) that springs from a fountain is preferable to the standing water of a cistern. Jesus would make it clear that He is the fountain, the source of water far superior to that of a cistern like Jacob's well (see 4:12–14). In 7:38–39, "living water" is explained as meaning the Holy Spirit, but here it refers to eternal life (see 4:14).

How dramatic is the contrast between the status of this woman, whom Jesus met at midday, and that of Nicodemus (see 3:1–21), whom Jesus met at night. The two are polar opposites, and almost back-to-back in John's account, they together show the inner reality of human need and the truth that Jesus knows the inner person (see 2:25).

4:11. In the arid setting, the woman could only entertain one source of water, **the well,** in the midst of her conversation with Jesus. Christian pilgrim sources as early as the fourth century mention a well in this area that was about 100 feet deep. When the well was cleaned out in 1935, it was found to be 138 feet deep.

4:12–13. Art thou greater than our father Jacob? (v. 12) is a question that in Greek expects a negative answer. Respect for the past and the prized provision of the patriarch prevented the woman from seeing the great opportunity of the present. For her to conceive of Jesus as greater than their founding father, He would have to produce a water unlike that upon which they had depended since the time of Jacob himself. Her response led Jesus to underscore her point: she had to depend on that water, because as often as she came to the well, she would always **thirst again** (v. 13; see 4:15).

4:14-15. Jesus offered the Samaritan woman a water that perpetually satisfies one's thirst. This variety of water quenches the imbiber because it produces an internal and eternal fountain **springing up** (v. 14) that never runs dry. The expression is a vigorous one, with a meaning like "leaping up." Jesus was speaking of vigorous, abundant life (see 10:10). Compare her misunderstanding with that of Nicodemus (see 3:4). In both cases, the way was opened for further instruction.

4:16-18. Jesus had already bridged gaping social and religious divisions to offer this woman "living water" (4:10). Now He needed to cross the personal barriers she had erected to guard her heart and conceal her shame. The woman could not, however, protect her past from Jesus, who knows what is in a person (see 2:25), and His knowledge of her would lead to her recognition of Him (see 4:29). When Jesus touched on the subject of her marital status with His invitation **Go, call thy husband** (v. 16), her response was preemptory: **I have no husband** (v. 17). Her truth was not the whole truth. What she concealed, Jesus revealed: **For thou hast had five husbands** (v. 18). The Jews held that a woman might be divorced twice or at the most three times. If the Samaritans had the same standard, at best the woman's past had certainly been marked by unquestionable troubles and questionable morality.

4:19-20. In calling Jesus **a prophet** (v. 19), the woman acknowledged His special insight. The reason she diverted the focus from her personal life to a long-standing and divisive religious debate over the proper place **to worship** (v. 20) was mixed. She may have wished only to change the subject, but she may

have also wanted to test His prophetic power and status (see 4:25). Samaritans held that **this mountain** (Mount Gerizim; see Map 11) was especially sacred. Abraham and Jacob had built altars in the general vicinity (see Gen. 12:7; 33:20), and the people had been blessed from this mountain (see Deut. 11:29; 27:12). In the Samaritan Scriptures, Mount Gerizim (rather than Mount Ebal) was the mountain on which Moses had commanded an altar to be built (see Deut. 27:4-6). The Samaritans had built a temple on Mount Gerizim circa 400 BC, which the Jews destroyed circa 128 BC. Both actions, of course, increased hostility between the two groups.

4:21. Woman (see discussion on 2:4) was a polite form of address and was in no way disrespectful. Jesus asserted that her question, although not irrelevant, was shortsighted. Jesus pointed her beyond the present to a time when worship would not be enhanced nor thought proper by virtue of its location. For the Samaritan woman, the word **hour** would have conveyed little more than an indication of a time in the future. The reader of John's gospel, however, knows that it bore a special meaning for Jesus and signified the world-altering events of His death, resurrection, and exaltation (see discussion on 2:4), which would inaugurate that time. Jesus characteristically called God **Father**, and strikingly so in the gospel of John. Whereas the Old Testament identifies God as Father only rarely (15 times), in the gospel of John, God is called Father 119 times, and 96 of them in the words of Jesus Himself.

4:22. The Samaritan Bible contained only the Pentateuch. Although Samaritans worshiped the true God, their failure to accept much of His revelation meant that they knew little of Him. They were therefore ignorant not only of the rich fund of prophetic revelation heralding God's promised salvation but also that the Messiah would be a Jew. Accordingly, **salvation is of the Jews**, for "unto them were committed the oracles of God" (Rom. 3:2).

4:23-24. The hour cometh (v. 23) recalls Jesus' earlier declaration that "ye shall neither in this mountain, nor yet at Jerusalem, worship the Father" (4:21). Standing logically on this declaration, Jesus now emphasized the reality that would come into effect when that hour arrived and its present impetus (**and now is**): the Father desires **worship ... in spirit and in truth** from **true worshippers**. True worship must be in keeping with God's nature, which is spirit. The KJV mars the Greek emphasis on God's nature or essence as spirit. The grammatical construction is qualitative and should be translated "God is spirit" rather than **God is a spirit** (v. 24). The KJV's "in spirit and in truth" (vv. 23, 24) suggests two elements to true worship, but the Greek has one preposition ("in") governing the two nouns (as in 3:5) and is equivalent to "the Spirit of truth" (14:17, 15:26; 16:13). This serves as a clue to the nature of true worship; it corresponds not only to the nature of God, who is spirit, but also to the coming of the Spirit, the endowment of God whose coming belonged to the hour of Jesus' death, resurrection, and exaltation (see 7:37–39; 14:26; 15:26, see also 3:6, 34).

4:25. The Samaritan woman's last attempt to evade the issue came with an appeal to the **Messias** (see discussion on 1:25) **... he will tell us all things**. The matter was too important, she reasoned, for people like Jesus and herself to work out. Understanding would have to await the coming of the Messiah. The Samaritans expected a Messiah, but their rejection of all the inspired writings after the Pentateuch meant that they knew little about Him. They thought of Him mainly as a teacher.

4:26. With the words **I ... am he**, Jesus told the Samaritan woman that the Messiah to whom she would defer the issue was none other than the one to whom she was talking. Now she knew the identity of Jesus and "who it is that saith to thee, Give me to drink" (4:10), the very one who could supply her with "living water" (4:10). This was the only occasion before His trial on which Jesus specifically said that He was the Messiah (but see Mark 9:41). The term "Messiah" did not have the political overtones in Samaria that it had in Judea, which may be part of the reason Jesus used the designation here, although He was also speaking to the woman privately.

4:27. His disciples ... marvelled that he talked with the woman. Jewish religious teachers rarely spoke with women in public, and with the continuous tense (Greek imperfect), John reported the sustained surprise of the disciples. The questions the disciples swallowed and never voiced illustrate the need-centered love of Jesus that looks beyond custom, culture, race, and gender.

4:28–30. Upon hearing Jesus say that He was the Messiah, **the woman left her waterpot, and went ... into the city** (v. 28) to tell others. Why did John report this small detail? Brown (*The Gospel According to John*, p. 173) suggests it was John's way of emphasizing the waterpot's uselessness for the living water that interested her. Also, leaving her waterpot is reminiscent of the disciples leaving their nets to follow Jesus (see Matt. 4:20; Mark 1:18). What had preoccupied them lost its commanding interest upon their recognition of Jesus. Her haste corresponds to her eager interest in broadcasting her discovery. The woman's testimony (**all things that ever I did**) was an exaggeration, but it shows the impression Jesus made on her. **Is not this the Christ?** Her question seems full of longing, as though she did not expect the people to say yes, but she could not say no.

4:31–33. This misunderstanding is similar to that of the woman (see 4:15). The disciples, presumably sent by Jesus to buy food (see 4:8), now returned to the once weary and thirsty Jesus (see 4:6–7). Jesus had been energized by provisions they could only assume were like those that they went to purchase. Once again, the theme of heavenly versus earthly determined the disciples' mindset and confusion.

4:34. My meat (Greek, *brōma*; "food," "that which is eaten") **is to do the will of him that sent me** (see Matt. 4:4). John often mentioned that Jesus depended on the Father and did the work that the Father sent Him to do (see, e.g., 5:30; 6:38; 8:26; 9:4; 10:37–38; 12:49–50; 14:31; 15:10; 17:4).

4:35. There are yet four months, and then cometh harvest apparently was a proverb that meant something like, "Harvest cannot be rushed." Crops take time to ripen, but in **the fields** to which Jesus referred, the harvest was already ripe (see Matt. 9:38).

4:36. Receiveth wages implies that the work, or at least part of it, had been done, and others were working hard. The disciples were not to think that the harvest was far off. Jesus was speaking not of grain but of **fruit unto life eternal**. There was urgency, for the crop would not wait. Joint effort brings joint rejoicing. There is no competition among Christ's faithful servants, and sower and reaper share in the joy of the crop.

4:37. For **One soweth, and another reapeth**, see 1 Corinthians 3:6–9.

4:38. Other men may refer to John the Baptist and his supporters, on whose work the apostles would build. Perhaps Jesus was looking further back, to the prophets and other godly men of old. Either way, He expected the apostles to be reapers as well as sowers.

4:39–42. The Samaritan woman's testimony brought many to belief in Jesus, and **his own word** (v. 41) brought **many mo[r]e**. Although this contrast records the unequal strength of their respective "words" and the superiority of a direct encounter with Jesus, it would be a mistake to overlook the confirmation of the woman's testimony to Jesus: **this is indeed the Christ** (v. 42). What the people found in Jesus was a confirmation of her testimony to Jesus. In the New Testament, the expression **the Saviour of the world** occurs only here and in 1 John 4:14. It points to the facts (1) that Jesus not only teaches but also saves and (2) that His salvation extends to the world (see discussion on 3:16).

F. Healing of the Nobleman's Son (4:43–54)

4:43–45. After two days (v. 43) in Samaria, Jesus resumed His journey north to Galilee (see 4:1–3). John clarified that Jesus did not go to Galilee for honor. Indeed, Jesus testified that **a prophet hath no honour in his own country** (v. 44). Nonetheless, Jesus went to Galilee, because He came to die for our salvation (see 1:29).

4:45–47. The welcome of **the Galileans** (v. 45) actually was a kind of rejection, for they were interested only in his miracles (see 4:48). They were welcoming not the Messiah who could save them but only a miracle worker who could amaze them. Nevertheless, news of the arrival of this miracle worker, known to those from Galilee who had seen what Jesus **did at Jerusalem** over Passover, piqued the interest of **a certain nobleman** (v. 46) whose little boy (Greek, *paidion*) was very sick. The "nobleman," or royal official (Greek, *basilikos*; "of the king"), was evidently an officer or advisor in Herod's service.

4:48. Except ye see signs and wonders, ye will not believe reveals the general attitude of the Galileans who had flocked to Jesus, not that of the official. "Signs [Greek, *sēmeion*] and wonders [Greek, *teras*]" connoted authenticating miracles associated with God's great deliverance of the Jews out of Egypt (see, e.g., Deut. 6:22; Neh. 9:10; Jer. 32:20) and were expected to be met with belief. Jesus looked for belief that was not conditioned on a steady diet of the miraculous.

4:49–50. The nobleman **believed the word** (v. 50) of Jesus in advance of seeing its miraculous fulfillment. **Thy son liveth** was not simply a prophecy but a powerful pronouncement. Jesus was healing the little boy with these words, not forecasting a happy ending (see 4:51, 53). The man believed; he took Jesus at His word, believed what Jesus said about his little boy, and turned to go home.

4:51–53. It was no happy coincidence that the boy's **fever left him** (v. 52). The effect and the cause corresponded to the time of Jesus' pronouncement: **the seventh hour,** or 1:00 p.m. Not only did the nobleman rightly attribute the break in the little boy's fever to Jesus, but his household did too. That he **believed** (v. 53) implies that he believed Jesus was more than a miracle worker (see the aim of this gospel in 20:31).

4:54. The second miracle was hardly the second of only two. There had, of course, already been many such miracles (see 2:23; 3:2), but this was the second time Jesus performed a miracle after coming from **Judea into Galilee.** The numbering of this miracle as a "sign" (see discussion on 2:11) also shows John's focus on the purpose of such miracles: to bring about belief in the person of Jesus.

G. Trip to Jerusalem for an Annual Feast (chap. 5)

5:1. After this (lit., "after these things") is an indefinite expression (see 6:1; 7:1), and given the context, it suggests "some time later." In 4:46, Jesus was in Cana of Galilee. Now **a feast of the Jews** had brought Jesus to Jerusalem. One can only surmise the passage of some time. "A feast of the Jews" probably refers to one of the three pilgrimage feasts to which all Jewish males were expected to go: Passover, Pentecost, and Tabernacles. The identity of this feast is significant for the attempt to ascertain the number of Passovers included in Jesus' ministry and thus the number of years His ministry lasted. John explicitly mentioned at least three different Passovers: the first in 2:13, 23 (see discussion on 2:13), the second in 6:4, and the third several times (e.g., in 11:55; 12:1). If three Passovers are accepted, the length of Jesus' ministry was between two and three years. If, however, the feast of 5:1 was a fourth Passover or assumes that a fourth Passover had come and gone, Jesus' ministry would have lasted between three and four years.

5:2. Note the wording **there is** rather than "there was." This may mean that the **pool** was still in existence at the time this was written, that is, that John wrote before the destruction of Jerusalem (AD 66–70). This falls short of proving the time of writing, however (see Introduction: "Date"). More likely, John used the present tense as a literary expression to vividly recount past events. The manuscripts have a variety of names for **Bethesda** (e.g., Bethzatha and Bethsaida), but one of the Dead Sea Scrolls seems to show that Bethesda is the right name. **By the Sheep Gate** (rather than **sheep market**) likely indicates the narrow entrance where sheep were brought to the temple for sacrifice. The site is generally identified with the twin pools excavated near the present-day Saint Anne's Church, where colonnades correspond to the five porches (v. 2).

5:3–4. Waiting for the moving of the water (v. 3). Some manuscripts do not have this phrase or verse 4, but these verses explain why people waited by the pool in large numbers: **For an angel went down ... into the pool** (v. 4). This picture of desperate hope underscores the dire condition of those who waited, many without success (see 5:7). While others were preoccupied with the feast, Jesus was

preoccupied with people not far from the festivities but forgotten and lying in a pathetic state.

5:5–7. John did not record what the man's **infirmity** (v. 5) was, but judging from Jesus' command, "Rise ... and walk" (5:8), it was a form of paralysis or at least lameness. That **Jesus saw ... and knew** (v. 6; see 2:23) matched His extraordinary offer: **Wilt thou be made whole?** He who has the power to heal also has the power to see and know what others do not. The question was important. The man had no means of getting to the water, and his answer to Jesus may have harbored the hope that, if He truly cared as His question implied, Jesus Himself would help him to the water. Clearly, the man did not see Jesus as his healer, and the question led his mind only to the water and the supposed place of God's power to cure. In healing the man, Jesus demonstrated where the power of God is truly located.

5:8–9. Rise, take up thy bed, and walk (v. 8; see Mark 2:11) is the evidence of the man's healing (**immediately the man was made whole**; v. 9). Without uttering a word in reply, a man debilitated thirty-eight years (see 5:5) by physical malady and discouraged hope was made whole; he needed only to "stand up ... and walk around" (as the Greek conveys). Ordinarily, faith in Jesus was essential to the cure (see, e.g., Mark 5:34), but this man did not even know who Jesus was (see 5:13). One can see the man's faith, however, in his obedience to Jesus' command. For at the word of Jesus, he attempted to do what on so many occasions he had surely tried and failed to do at the moving of the water: "Rise." The man "was made whole," not only sound but also robust. No physical therapy was necessary for his muscles and limbs withered by atrophy. The healing was complete. John, however, added a retrospective and repercussive note: **and on the same day was the sabbath** (v. 9).

5:10–11. Jesus had run afoul of the Sabbath law and up against **The Jews** (the religious authorities; v. 10; see discussion on 1:19) in performing this act of healing on **the sabbath** (see 5:9, 16, 18). They declared to the healed man, **it is not lawful for thee to carry thy bed,** and Jesus had commanded the man to do just that (see 5:8). The gravity of the violation was clear to the man, and he shifted responsibility to the one who had cured him. The Jews had very strict regulations on keeping the Sabbath. To "carry thy bed" belonged to the last of the thirty-nine classes of work prohibited on the Sabbath ("taking out aught from one domain to another," Mishnah, Shabbat 7:2). The Jews contested such a violation, however, not specifically by the law of Moses (see Exod. 20:8–11) but by application of the law that prohibited carrying loads of any kind on the Sabbath (see Jer. 17:21).

5:12–13. Then asked they him, What man is that …? (v. 12). The Jews were contrasting the authority of the law of God, which in their view prohibited the action, and that of a mere man (as they considered Jesus to be) who promoted it. Sadly, the marvelous and glorious healing of the disabled man was completely ignored. The violation and "What man" had endorsed it were all that occupied the attention of the religious authorities. Jesus was unknown to the man by name, and as suddenly as Jesus had come to the man, He **conveyed himself away** (v. 13) as the man walked around among the crowd that had assembled in the precincts of the temple for the feast of the Jews (see 5:1).

5:14–15. Later, in the temple area, **Jesus findeth** (present tense; v. 14) the man. The tense implies that Jesus was deliberately looking for him. More important than the man's physical need was his spiritual need. The sequence of what Jesus told him, **thou art made whole: sin no more, lest a worse thing come unto thee,** makes it clear that the spiritual well-being of the man was more important than the physical. A number of interpreters connect the man's infirmity to sin because of Jesus' command. There is not enough in the text to assure this conclusion, however. Certainly, Jesus did not accept this conclusion in the case of the blind man (see 9:2–3 and discussions; see also Luke 13:1–5). Although suffering (physical or emotional) ultimately may be traced to sin and the broken condition of a fallen world, here Jesus' command is in the present imperative, "stop sinning," pointing to a continuous issue of

the man's life and outlook toward God that had not been arrested or exhausted by either his infirmity or his healing. What Jesus was addressing in the man's life is not known. "A worse thing" points to the judgment of God rather than men (e.g., the Pharisees), and just as the man obeyed Jesus when he was told to "Rise" (5:8), there is no reason to believe he did not obey Jesus' additional command. Just as the man promptly obeyed Jesus at His command to rise (v. 8), the man now directly professed Jesus; he went away and **told** (Greek, *anangellō;* "proclaimed"; always positive in John; see 4:25; 16:13–15) the Pharisees **that it was Jesus, which had made him whole** (v. 15). One may infer that because of Jesus' command, God's authority over his life was given its rightful place, an authority mediated by "He that made me whole" (5:11), whom the man now proclaimed by name.

5:16. The authority of Jesus had been displayed to the man in his miraculous healing, in Jesus' command that trumped the Sabbath prohibition, and in His admonition to sin no more. In identifying Jesus to the religious authorities, this was the very authority the man claimed for carrying his bed on the Sabbath (see Talbert, *Reading John,* p. 123). Apart from any motive one may discern in the man, however, the religious authorities were now armed with the information they needed to prosecute Jesus. It should be noted that the word **persecute** (Greek, *diōkō*) may in this context mean "prosecute." John did not report what form the action took, but the continuous action of the Greek verb, **he had done,** points to more than one incident, and the Jews apparently discerned a pattern.

5:17. Without a shift in setting, John conveyed a verbal exchange between the authorities and Jesus over the Sabbath violation in which Jesus defended Himself. Not evident in English translation, the word **answered** (Greek, *apokrinomai;* middle voice; only here and 5:19), indicates a formal reply with legal overtones. Such a reply matches the implication of "prosecution" in 5:16. With this reply, Jesus offered a formal defense against the charge of questionable Sabbath activity by identifying His actions with the actions of His Father: **My Father worketh hitherto.** The Jews did not refer to God as "My Father," regarding the term as too intimate, though they might have used "Our Father" or, in prayer, "My Father in heaven." Jesus also exemplified the way the Sabbath should be observed. God does not stop His deeds of compassion on that day, and neither did Jesus.

5:18. The authorities understood well the implications of Jesus' defense: **he not only had broken the sabbath, but said also that God was his Father, making himself equal with God.** The Jews did not object to the idea that God is the Father of all, but they strongly objected to Jesus' claim that He stood in a special relationship to the Father, a relationship so close as to "mak[e] Himself equal with God." This indictment is ominous and was later formally called "blasphemy" (10:33) when Jesus was condemned to stoning, and it eventually fueled the punishment of crucifixion sought from Pilate (see 19:7).

5:19. Jesus again formally replied (see 5:17) and began an extended and uninterrupted defense against the leaders' charges, which now included blasphemy. **The Son can do nothing of himself.** Because of who and what He was, it was not possible for Jesus to act except in dependence on the Father who sent Him. Such dependence (see 5:30) and Jesus' emphasis that the Father had sent Him (5:23, 24, 30, 33, 36, 37, 38) pointed to His role not only as the Son but also as the agent of the Father's will. As Jesus' defense in this chapter reveals, because He is the beloved Son, He is the familial choice to act as the Father's agent, a legal form of representation. In the Jewish institution of agency, the one sent is as the one who sends, and the validity of Jesus' authority to act and transact business on behalf of the sender (the Father) rests on the fidelity of the agent (Jesus) to the will of the one who sent Him (see Introduction: "Theme and Theological Message"). The Jews charged Jesus with "making himself equal with God" (5:18). In Jesus' extended defense, again and again He emphasized that the "making" came from the Father and that the equality was not the maverick action of a man who would be equal with God, but was that of a beloved and fully authorized Son who

dutifully and dependently represented the will of the Father who sent Him.

5:20. Because **the Father loveth the Son**, He revealed to the Son His plans and purposes, and the Son obediently carried them out. Even **greater works** belong to the Father's purposes than have been attested to in the Sabbath healing of the lame man that brought the charges of the religious authorities to which Jesus now defends His actions (see vv. 14–18). As Brown (*John*, p. 2114) aptly puts it, "Physical healing ('life') is merely a sign of the power to give eternal life" (see, e.g., the Son's activities in raising the dead and judging in 5:21–29). The word "loveth" is the Greek word *phileō* (only here in the gospel of John), capturing the affection of any father for his son but here used of the divine relationship between God and Jesus.

5:21. That **the Father raiseth up the dead** was a firm belief among the Jews. They also held that He did not give this privilege to anyone else. Jesus claimed a prerogative that, according to His opponents, belonged only to God. **The Son quickeneth** probably refers to Christ's gift of abundant life here and now, though possibly also to the future resurrection (see 11:25–26).

5:22. Not only has the Father given Jesus the right of giving life (see 5:21); He **hath committed all judgment unto the Son.** The Jews believed that the Father is Judge of the world, so this teaching seemed heretical to them.

5:23. In legal terms, Jesus had claimed the right to act as the Father acts (5:17), not only because of His relationship as Son (see 5:19–20) but also because the Father has "given" (5:26–27; 3:35; 13:3) to Him God's quintessential rights as Life-giver and Judge (see 5:22–23, 26–27). As a defense, this not only explained but also justified Jesus' unity of action with the Father and Jesus' right to intervene between God and His creation. It brought to the forefront the importance of Jesus' obedience to the Father who sent Him, for He acted not alone but in concert with the Father's will. The honor that God deserves is therefore the honor that His Son deserves; the Son is His duly authorized representative.

5:24–25. Because Jesus possesses God's divine prerogatives (power and rights), not least of which are the rights of Life-giver and Judge (see 5:21–23), to hear His word and believe the one who sent Him is to pass from under judgment into eternal life. **Heareth** (v. 24) and **believeth** are not separate but rather twin actions because the word of Jesus is the word of the Father who sent Him (see 5:38). **Everlasting life** is a present possession (see discussion on 3:15). The decisive action (**is passed**) has taken place, and the believer no longer belongs to **death**. The words **is coming, and now is** (v. 25) clearly underscore that Christ gives life now. The spiritually dead who hear Him receive life from Him and do not come into judgment. There is no undoing of this action, and Jesus solemnized this promise with the words **Verily, verily.**

5:26–27. These two verses reiterate the authority of the Son in terms of the special prerogatives of God (Life-giver and Judge) He has been given (see 5:21–23). **Hath life in himself** (v. 26) must be understood against the background of the Old Testament, where life is spoken of as belonging to God and as being His gift (see, e.g., Deut. 30:20; Job 10:12; 33:4; Pss. 16:11; 27:1; 36:9). The Son has been given the same kind of life that the Father possesses (for the benefit to man, see 1 John 5:11). Here the Son is identified as **the Son of man** (v. 27; see discussion on 1:51).

5:28–29. Do not marvel at this (v. 28) refers to Jesus' claims of authority as life-giver and judge. The present exercise of His rights will have a corresponding and irreversible impact on the future raising of the dead. Existing Jewish notions of the final judgment and resurrection of the dead are subject to the **voice** of Him whom they now heard (see 5:24–25). As always in Scripture, judgment is on the basis of works, though salvation, of course, is a gift from God in response to faith (see 5:24).

5:30. In saying, **I can of mine own self do nothing,** Jesus again stressed His dependence on the Father (see discussions on 5:19, 23). He judges only as He hears from the Father, which makes His judgment not only fair but also a proof that His representation

as the Father's agent is valid and intact. Jesus had in no way violated the trust of His responsibility to act on the behalf of His Father. Again, in legal terms, He had not "[made] himself equal to God" (5:18) but rather had acted on the behalf of and in accordance with the representation of the Father's making. Jesus' representation was an equality of agency established by the will of the Father.

The correspondence of this verse and 5:19, the opening and closing of the first part of Jesus'defense, has been noted by numerous scholars. This is called an *inclusio* and serves to highlight the main line of Jesus' defense against the indictment of 5:18.

5:31–47. If Jesus' representation of the Father was disputed on the grounds that He had overreached the authority of His commission, the testimony of the Father, the one who sent Him, became vital to His defense. His testimony could not stand alone. This section stresses the testimonies (see discussion on 1:7) of John the Baptist (v. 33), of the works of Jesus (v. 36), of God the Father (v. 37), of the Scriptures (v. 39), and of Moses (v. 46). A close reading reveals that the testimony of the Father who sent Jesus was most important; He above all could verify that Jesus had been duly authorized to act on His behalf.

5:31–32. Another (v. 32) points to a greater testimony than that of Jesus (see 5:36), the testimony of the Father who sent Him. The Jews might not have accepted this testimony, but it was the testimony that mattered most.

5:33–34. Ye sent unto John (v. 33) refers to the delegation of representatives that the Jewish leaders sent to John the Baptist (see 1:19). The leaders therefore understood the tenets of representation. The representatives had acted under strict orders to question John and return with his testimony, and the leaders had received that testimony (see 1:19–23). The testimony of John was important, though not, of course, equal to the testimony of the Father. Had the Jews believed John, however, they would have believed Jesus and recognized His authority and the offer of salvation.

5:35. The past tense **he was** may indicate that John the Baptist was dead or at least imprisoned. In any case, his work was done. John himself was sent from the Father (see 1:6) and **was a burning and a shining** that the Jews themselves enjoyed **for a season**. John's giving light was costly to him. The Jewish leaders never came to grips with John's message, and their responses to him were always at best tentative and superficial.

5:36. The works refers to the authorized actions of Jesus, which testified to His true identity and to His divine mission (see 10:25). Since the actual testimony of the Father has been ambiguous to interpreters, proposals have pointed to (1) the Scriptures, (2) direct internal testimony, (3) the Torah, and (4) the word of the Father which He has given to Jesus and which Jesus gives to the world. In view of the agency of Jesus, the testimony of God can be nothing other than "the works" that Jesus performed, which testified that He had been commissioned and authorized as God's representative agent and Son (see 10:25, 36–38). Jesus' works, His words and deeds, realized what God the Father had commissioned Him to do. Because Jesus did not deviate from the will of His Father, nor act on His own, His works testified to their origin and source in the commission of God. Since the legal validity of Jesus' agency stood open to challenge, and the very fact of agency presumed that the Father was not accessible to offer direct testimony to the commission in question, the only way to demonstrate its validity was to argue on the presumptions of agency: because Jesus was faithfully executing His commission, the commission of the Father in fact remained valid. In this sense, the works themselves offered the direct testimony of the Father.

5:37–40. The Jews had never heard the very voice of God, but it found concrete expression in Jesus' works, which **hath borne witness of me** (v. 37; see 5:36) that **the Father … hath sent me**. That they had **neither heard his voice at any time, nor seen his shape** underscored the history of God's representation upon which the Jews had depended for knowing God. Even that had failed. If they had **His word** (v. 38) in them, the correspondence between the Father's word from earlier representatives in Scrip-

ture and the word of Jesus would have led to belief. **Search[ing] the Scriptures** (v. 39) is not an end in itself. The Jewish leaders studied Scripture in minute detail. Despite their reverence for the very letter of Scripture (see discussions on Matt. 5:18–21), they did not recognize the one to whom Scripture bears supreme testimony.

5:41–44. In these verses, the ongoing issue of Jesus' valid representation of the Father is picked up in the opening disavowal, **I receive not honour from men** (v. 41). The word "honour" (Greek, *doxa*; "glory") points to the question of motive. The implication is that Jesus' enemies may have imagined He sought His own advantage or benefit, but Jesus' disavowal again pointed to His faithful pursuit of someone else's honor (advantage or benefit): that of the Father who sent Him (see 7:18). They did not have love for God in them because they dishonored (see 5:23) the one God had sent, the one who came **in [the] Father's name** (v. 43). To come in the name of someone is to function under the authority of the one named. A person's name is the quintessential token of his personal identity, his status, and his character. Jesus not only executed His commission in the Father's name but also shares the identity, status, and character of the name because He is not only the agent of God but also the Son of God ("I am," 8:58). When Jesus said, **if another shall come in his own name, him ye will receive**, He was stating that His opponents would accept anyone who came in his own authority because that one would function as their peer and not as their superior. In Jesus, God had a claim on them that they rejected. The question Jesus asked is rhetorical. The answer was clear already. They did not want to submit to God. They therefore rejected the one who came in His name. Their self-seeking honor (advantage and benefit) showed that they did not accept the one who came from God, and therefore they missed the advantage and benefit that comes from God.

5:45–47. Jesus' opponents prided themselves on their attachment to **Moses** (v. 45), their great lawgiver. It was thus an unexpected thrust for Jesus to say that Moses himself **accuseth** them before

God. Jesus came back to the testimony of Scripture (5:39): it is Moses, who wrote of Jesus, who will be the accuser of the Jews who reject Him. All the New Testament writers stressed or assumed that the Old Testament, rightly read, points to Christ (see Luke 24:25-27, 44). Jesus applied this truth specifically to the writings of Moses (see, e.g., discussion on Gen. 49:10; *KJV Study Bible* notes on Exod. 12:21; Lev. 16:5; Num. 24:17; Deut. 18:15).

What began with the accusation of Jesus, an indictment of blasphemy in 5:18, closes with the indictment of His accusers. Those who would prosecute Jesus on the basis of the law of Moses and the witness of the Scriptures found their star witnesses condemning them.

H. The Feeding of the Five Thousand and the Sermon on the Bread of Life (chap. 6)

6:1-14. The feeding of the five thousand is the one miracle, apart from the resurrection, found in all four gospels. It shows Jesus as the supplier of human need and sets the stage for His testimony that He is the bread of life (see 6:35). This was perhaps Jesus' greatest miracle, and it was witnessed by the largest number of people.

6:1. After these things (see 5:1 and discussion) is John's general notation indicating the elapse of time and events between what precedes and what follows. John drew a geographical connection between **the sea of Tiberias**, probably the official Roman name, and **the sea of Galilee**, the popular name. The name came from the town of Tiberias (named after the emperor), the capital city of Galilee founded circa AD 20.

6:2. The crowd **followed him** (vividly depicted in the present tense in the Greek), **because they saw** more than once (imperfect active tense) **his miracles.** Here John again used *sēmeion*, "signs," to refer to Jesus' miracles (see discussion on 2:11). Indeed, the picture is one of a crowd eager to see more of the miraculous, but John's use of the word "signs" alerts readers to a deeper significance that the crowd was missing.

6:3. The **mountain** cannot be located with certainty, and its identity is of no importance in and of itself. The parallels that Jesus drew between Moses and Himself (see 6:31-32) and the reference to Passover (see 6:4) have prompted a symbolic allusion to Sinai as a constituent piece of the overall motif.

6:4. This is the second **Passover** expressly identified by John (for the chronological significance of this Passover, see discussion on 2:13). Here significance is attached to its nearness and Jesus' comparisons with Moses; the people's yearning for a new Moses and a new exodus was seasonally high.

6:5-7. Since **Philip** (v. 5) came from nearby Bethsaida (see 1:44), it was appropriate for Jesus to ask him, **Whence shall we buy bread ...?** Brown (*The Gospel According to John*, p. 233) points out that the **great company** hardly could have been made up of pilgrims to the Passover feast since the Sea of Galilee was en route to Jerusalem and pilgrims would have carried their own provisions. There are subtle comparisons and contrasts between Numbers 11 and the actions of Jesus in this chapter, not least of which is the question Jesus posed here (compare Num. 11:13). Practically, the question begged for a supernatural solution to a human impossibility (clarified in 6:7-9). Jesus **knew what he would do** (v. 6) and used the question to draw out the impossibility of human ingenuity to meet the need. Philip quickly sized up the challenge. Not even **Two hundred pennyworth** (v. 7; the equivalent of as many days' wages), or denarii, could meet the demand, assuming that much bread was available. John reported that Jesus was testing (**prove**; v. 6; Greek, *peirazō*; "test" in a good sense, "tempt" in a negative sense) Philip to expose what he thought or how he would behave. Perhaps Jesus was not only looking for Philip to prove the impossibility of feeding the crowd but was also providing an opportunity for Philip to look to Him in faith.

6:8-9. Andrew (v. 8) explored the crowd for resources and located the equivalent of one lunch. The lunch of one person, and that of a child, was hilariously insufficient, **What are they among so many?** (v. 9), for Philip had just established the minimum bid of eight months' wages to provide food for the crowd (see 6:7). **Barley loaves** refers to cheap bread, the food of the poor. The **two small fishes** were probably dried and pickled for eating with bread.

6:10. The note that **there was much grass** indicates it was springtime. **About five thousand** does not include the women and children. Only the men were numbered, as Matthew made clear (Matt. 14:21). Consequently, one may easily imagine a number twice that.

6:11–13. Jesus gave **thanks** (Greek, *eucharisteō*; "praise," "thanks," "bless"; v. 11), acknowledging God; His focus was on praising the Father rather than on blessing the food. Jesus Himself **distributed to the disciples,** who then distributed the food to the people. **As much as they would** indicates there was more than enough bread and fish to satisfy their desire; **they were filled** (v. 12). **Gather up the fragments that remain** (see discussion on Mark 6:43) and the **twelve baskets** (v. 13) indicate not only that the surplus was ample but that more remained than was available at the start.

6:14. Once again, **the miracle** (Greek, *sēmeion*) was for John a "sign" (see discussion on 2:11). It pointed people to the Son of Man and the food for eternal life that He gives (see 6:27), but those who witnessed it thought of Him only as **that prophet** (see 1:21 and discussion), that is, the prophet of Deuteronomy 18:15 who would be like Moses. Through Moses, God had provided food and water for the people in the wilderness. They saw in Jesus a similar leader and provider.

6:15. Emboldened by Jesus' display of power, the crowd saw in Jesus the attributes necessary to displace the rule of Rome and its client king Herod. Convinced of this opportunity, the people had a mind to **take him by force, to make him a king.** Jesus wanted no part of such rebellion or such kingship. He rejected the world's version of kingship (see discussion on 18:36) as a temptation of the Devil (see Matt. 4:8–10). Jesus was sent by the Father to achieve not a political and temporal victory but a spiritual and eternal one. Jesus therefore went in another direction, going up **a mountain ... alone.**

6:16–19. As the sun was setting, the disciples made their way **down unto the sea** (v. 16). Mark 6:46 reports that Jesus left the disciples to pray. Perhaps as Brown (*The Gospel According to John*, p. 251) suggests, the disciples were initially making their way to Capernaum, not far off the shore, hoping to spot Jesus. As darkness fell and the weather changed, however, they pushed on. The distance of **five and twenty or thirty furlongs** (v. 19) would have been about three or four miles. Mark reported that they were "in the midst of the sea" (Mark 6:47). Fighting the winds and making little progress, they saw a figure coming toward them, **walking on the sea.** John summed up the situation with the words **they were afraid.** All together, it was a very ominous state: the storm, the foreboding darkness, and an approaching figure that Matthew said the disciples thought was a ghost (see Matt. 14:26).

6:20–21. What sweet relief to hear the words of Jesus, **It is I; be not afraid** (v. 20). To know that Jesus was there was enough, but this natural form of self-identification has added meaning: "I am" (see 8:58; Exod. 3:14). When the disciples **received him into the ship** (v. 21), it was **immediately ... at the land,** pointing to the presence of the Lord who commands the sea and all creation.

6:22–24. Here John narrated details bridging the events of the previous day and the setting of a significant discourse by Jesus on the Bread of Life. John made it clear that a number of people, enough to occupy a small flotilla, had remained the night in the vicinity of the feeding of the five thousand in the hope that Jesus would return. In the morning, unable to locate Him or figure out what had happened to Him, they boarded their small boats, crossed the lake, and looked for Him in the most likely place, **Capernaum** (v. 24). They found Him in the synagogue (see 6:59).

6:25–27. When camest thou hither? (v. 25). The question the people posed expressed more than curiosity about when and how Jesus had arrived. It implied that they thought Jesus was beholden to them. Indeed, His answer pointed to their demanding spirit. If the "signs" (**miracles**; v. 26; see discussion on 2:11), which revealed who it was that performed them, had motivated the people, they would have sought Jesus for who He was and not for what He could do for them. Rather, they wanted Jesus to satisfy their hunger over and over again. He is more than that. He is the giver of **everlasting life** (v. 27), **the Son of man** (see Mark 8:31), approved (**sealed;** see 3:33) by none other than **the Father.**

Labour (v. 27) implies the toil and unending endeavor that goes into acquiring daily bread, something the people believed Jesus could ease, if not eliminate. Like the contrast between well water and living water (see 4:10–15), Jesus was contrasting bread that must be earned and eaten over and over with the bread that He offers and that satisfies (**endureth;** Greek, *menō;* "stay," "remain") once and for all (compare 4:14). Therefore, eternal life is something not to be achieved but to be received by faith in Christ (see 6:28–29; discussion on 3:15).

6:28–29. What shall we do ...? (v. 28). The people missed the point that eternal life is Christ's gift and instead thought in terms of achieving it by pious works. They asked for a listing of specific **works** to perform (**work**), but Jesus said the **work of God** (v. 29) is singular in focus: to **believe on him whom he hath sent.** Believing in Jesus Christ is the indispensable "work" God calls for, the one that leads to eternal life. John's use of "believe" is dynamic and emphasizes an ongoing trust and dependence on the one whom the Father sent. John used the verb ("believe") ninety-eight times and never the noun ("faith") in his gospel. Notable is the verb "believe" used with the preposition "in" or "on" to emphasize this dynamic trust in Jesus (thirty-four times in John, three times in 1 John; all other New Testament uses of this expression total five uses, once each in Matthew, Mark, and Acts and twice in Romans).

6:30–31. What sign shewest thou ...? (v. 30). The people sought from Jesus a sign greater than the gift of **manna** (v. 31) that had accompanied Moses' ministry. A popular Jewish expectation was that when the Messiah came, He would renew the sending of manna. The crowd probably reasoned that Jesus had done little compared to Moses. He had fed five thousand people; Moses had fed a nation. He did it once; Moses did it for forty years. He gave ordinary bread; Moses gave **bread from heaven.**

6:32–33. Jesus corrected them, pointing out that the manna in the wilderness came not from Moses but from God and that the Father still **giveth** (the present tense is important) **... the true bread from heaven** (life through the Son; v. 32). **The bread of God** (v. 33), Jesus alluded, is the one the Father sent (see 6:29), **he which cometh down from heaven, and giveth life unto the world.** Jesus moved the discussion to something (and someone) much more important than manna.

6:34–35. Lord (v. 34) is closer to "sir" here. The people had not made the connection between Jesus and the "bread from heaven" (6:32). Their misunderstanding, like that of the woman at the well (see 4:15; see also Nicodemus, 3:4), ran along materialistic lines, as seen in their request: **give us this bread.** Jesus replied, **I am the bread of life** (v. 35). What Jesus offers can never be separated from who He is; they are inextricably united in a way that is unique and unparalleled in the history of world religion and philosophy. "The bread of life" may mean "the bread that is living" and/or "the bread that gives life." What Jesus implied in 6:33 He now made explicit and repeated with minor variations in 6:41, 48, 51.

This "I am" saying is the first of seven self-descriptions: (1) "I am the bread of life" (here), (2) "I am the light of the world" (8:12), (3) "I am the door" (10:7), (4) "I am the good shepherd" (10:11), (5) "I am the resurrection, and the life" (11:25), (6) "I am the way, the truth, and the life" (14:6), (7) "I am the true vine" (15:1). In the Greek, the words are solemnly emphatic and echo Exodus 3:14, where God identified Himself as the "I AM."

6:36. Earlier the people had asked, "What sign shewest thou then, that we may see, and believe thee?" (6:30). As the "bread from heaven" (6:32), Jesus was the sign, the manna from God greater than that given through Moses. Everything Jesus had said pointed out that He was what the people ostensibly sought, yet they did not believe (compare 20:29).

6:37–40. Jesus put His declaration of the people's unbelief into perspective. Here Jesus made it plain that He was the authorized agent and representative of God. The people had not believed Him or responded to Him as such, and their unbelief was a rejection of God's own purposes expressed in sending Jesus (see 6:27; 3:33; 5:23–24). Jesus now outlined the implications of such unbelief. In Jewish thought, "to give" means to put into one's control and responsibility. "Giving" falls into two parts: transfer and custody. From 3:35 and 13:3, we know of the transfer: the Father has put all things into Jesus' hands. Here Jesus emphasized the second part, the custody of all that comes under His control. He will not cast out those who come to Him (believe) but rather will safeguard all whom His mission brings under His control. Jesus was saying that the people's unbelief had grave implications. Despite the good will of God expressed in Jesus' mission to gain custody of those who believe in Jesus (vv. 39–40), their unbelief did not dismiss His sovereign authority. In fact, they were rejecting it and the protection of His custody that brings eternal life.

6:38. I came down from heaven occurs six times in this context (6:33, 38, 41, 50, 51, 58) and emphasizes the divine origin of Jesus and His mission: **the will of him that sent me** (see 4:34).

6:39. I should lose nothing points to the believer who perseveres because of Christ's firm hold on him (see Phil. 1:6). **The last day** is an expression found only in John in the New Testament (see 6:40, 44, 54).

6:40. For **everlasting life**, see discussion on 3:15. The one who puts his or her trust in Jesus will be **raise[d] ... up at the last day**. The life that Christ gives cannot be destroyed.

6:41–42. The Jews (v. 41; see discussion on 1:19) were murmuring because they did not acknowledge the origin or the heavenly credentials of Jesus and therefore did not acknowledge the invitation of the Father expressed in Jesus' mission. Rather, they dismissed Him as the "bread from heaven" (6:32); they could not see past His earthly rearing. How often is it that one fails to see the extraordinary work of God in what is for all appearances ordinary and familiar? Yet the words of Jesus as to who He is and what He came to do were far from ordinary.

6:43–45. Jesus admonished the Jews to **murmur not** (v. 43). Such murmuring characterized the Isra-

elites during the exodus (see Exod. 16:2, 7–8). Shared faultfinding, such as was expressed in their murmuring to one another, is harmful. It reinforces resistance to what God is doing in the heart of the individual. People do not come to Christ strictly on their own initiative; the Father draws them. Murmuring reinforces human negativity and rehearses human answers to divine queries. Group negativity can create a democratic din that makes it harder to hear the voice of God and easier to resist it. One must beware of inhibiting the tutoring of God. Only those who learn from God come to salvation, and all who learn from Him are saved. The quotation from the Old Testament drawn from that division known as **the prophets** (v. 45) corresponds to a free quotation of Isaiah 54:13.

6:46. Jesus asserted in yet another way His credentials as the one uniquely qualified to represent and reveal God the Father. No one has **seen the Father** (v. 46; see 1:18; 5:37; 14:7; 1 John 4:12). No one has such privileged knowledge of the Father, **save he which is of God, he hath seen the Father**. The word "of" is the Greek preposition *para*, denoting "from the side of" or "originating from" God. If the people took this to heart and responded to the one who stood before them, they would know eternal life (see 5:24, 26).

6:47–51. As is profoundly expressed in 1 John 5:11–12, **everlasting life** (v. 47), eternal life, is not a possession but a person. Life eternal cannot be separated from the Life-giver. The metaphor of bread to denote Jesus Himself illustrates this truth: **I am that bread of life** (v. 48). The image of ingesting the Bread of Life is powerful and graphic. The comparison of eating the **manna in the wilderness** (v. 49) brings a certain literalness to eating the Bread of Life and creates a strong impression that the appetite for life must be satisfied by the true **bread ... from heaven** (v. 50), not the manna, but Jesus. In contrast to that which could neither give nor sustain spiritual life, Jesus is the bread that brings eternal life. To **eat of this bread** (v. 51) is to appropriate Jesus as the sustenance of one's life. **My flesh** looks to the cross. Providing eternal life was won at great cost by the one who conquered death.

6:52. The literal character of Jesus' language led to a literalness on the part of His listeners. Language that emphasized the necessity of Jesus Himself over temporal and earthly substitutes had led the materially minded to a gory misconception rather than spiritual insight.

6:53–58. Jesus' absolute statement that **Except ye eat … ye have no life in you** (v. 53) precludes a direct reference to the Lord's Supper. He clearly did not teach that receiving that sacrament is the one requirement for eternal life or that it is the only ordinance through which Christ and His saving benefits are received. In this very discourse, Jesus emphasized the commitment of faith in response to His testimony (see vv. 35, 40, 47, 51). Now, Jesus mandates faith acceptance in the alarming language of wholly ingesting Him as a sacrifice, eating and drinking Jesus' **Flesh** and **blood** (cf. "life," v. 53, resurrection, v. 54), a foreshadowing of His sacrificial death on the cross. Furthermore, the deepest mutual bond between Jesus and the partaker is expressed by the words **dwelleth in me, and I in him** (v. 56 "dwelleth" is Greek *meno*, "bide," "remain"). It should be noted that "flesh and blood" carries Old Testament relevance as an idiom for the whole person (Brown, *The Gospel According to John*, p. 282). Here it points to the totality of Jesus and His cross as the object of faith.

In these verses, Jesus ostensibly responded to the query of His listeners (see 6:52), but what He elaborated did nothing to ease or civilize their literal comprehension. Nevertheless, the graphic wording of verse 54 conceptually corresponds to the wording of 6:40, where looking to Jesus and believing in Him brings eternal life and the assurance of being raised on the last day. Carson (*The Gospel According to John*, p. 297) cites Augustine of Hippo (In Tract. Ev. Jo. xxvi.1): "Believe, and you have eaten." As graphic as it is ("eateth" in Greek is *trōgō*; "chew"), Jesus was talking about a graphic belief that comes to grips with the exclusiveness of the life He offers by virtue of His flesh-and-blood death.

As in 6:49, the value of the **manna** (v. 58) is limited and is contrasted with the heavenly food that Christ gives. **Came down from heaven.** This is the tenth reference in this chapter to Jesus' coming down from heaven or to the bread from heaven.

6:59. John made it clear that the entire exchange between Jesus and the people took place **in the synagogue … in Capernaum** (see 6:24).

6:60. The thought of eating the "flesh" of the Son of Man and drinking His "blood" (see 6:53–58) was doubtless shocking to most of Jesus' Jewish hearers (taboos and purity laws notwithstanding). Even some who considered themselves **disciples** (clearly not the Twelve but a wider circle of followers; see 6:22–24; discussion on 6:67) found these words harsh. **Hard** (Greek, *sklēros*) is an adjective derived from a Greek verb meaning to be dry or parched. These words were very unpleasant. After **they had heard this** saying, they said, **who can hear it?** The same Greek word is used for both instances of "hear." It is similar to the saying, "I can't swallow what you're saying."

6:61. Jesus knew in himself implies supernatural discernment. **Offend you** is quite literally "cause you to stumble."

6:62. In the Greek, this is an "if-then" sentence that lacks a "then" statement. To resolve this, translators supply the word **What** to stand in the place of the "then" statement. One may presume that Jesus expected His listeners to supply the "then" themselves. Earlier Jesus said He "came down from heaven" (6:38). Now He asked what they would conclude **if** they saw **the Son of man ascend up where he was before**. Judging from 6:61, the offense they experienced at Jesus' words would be either heightened or lessened by this sight. Such a sight would vindicate Jesus' claim of heavenly origin. For "the Son of man," see discussions on 1:51; 3:13.

6:63. Jesus now put the literal misunderstanding of His hearers into perspective. His words were of the **spirit** that generates **life;** the **flesh**, or the human, does not profit. What He had been telling them had a dimension that transcended the natural, and if they would hear it as such, it would be transforming, indeed life-giving, because it was of the Spirit (see 3:5–6, 8).

6:64. This verse is another evidence of Jesus' supernatural knowledge and is reminiscent of 2:25.

From the beginning refers to the beginning of Jesus' ministry (see 16:4).

6:65. Coming to Christ for salvation is never a merely human achievement (see 6:37, 39, 44–45).

6:66. Jesus had already made it clear what discipleship meant, and many were not ready to receive life in the way He taught. His words brought His hearers to a threshold that their lack of faith prevented them from crossing, and they turned away.

6:67–68. The twelve (v. 67) were now singled out and distinguished from the broader category of disciples identified in 6:60. This is the first use of "the twelve" in the gospel of John. **Will ye also go away?** The wording of the question in Greek (interrogative *mē*) implies the expectation of a negative answer: "You do not wish to go away also, do you?" This rhetorical element in the question may have had Judas in view (see 6:64, 70–71). As in the Synoptic Gospels, Peter acted as spokesman. The expression **words of eternal life** (v. 68) is general. Peter perceived the truth of 6:63 and was speaking not of a formula but of the thrust of Jesus' teaching.

6:69. We believe and are sure. The Greek verbs are in the perfect tense and convey the meaning, "We have entered a state of belief and knowledge that has continued until the present time." **Thou art that Christ, the Son of the living God** (as in Matt. 16:16). A well-attested alternative reading is, "You are the Holy One of God." If the former reading entered the stream of manuscript copies through a scribe's inadvertent harmonization of Peter's answer to his well-known confession in Matthew, the harder reading of "Holy One of God" is preferred. It too has messianic implications and squares with the disciples' incomplete but firm grasp of Jesus' mission and consecration to the Father. In Peter's later speeches, recorded in Acts 3:14; 4:27, 30, he called Jesus "holy" (see Brown, *The Gospel According to John*, p. 298).

6:70–71. A devil (v. 70) alludes to **Judas** (v. 71), who would oppose Christ with the very desires of the Devil (see 8:44). **Iscariot** means "a man from Kerioth" (in Judea; see Josh. 15:25) and would apply equally to the father and the son (see 12:4). Judas seems to have been the only non-Galilean among the

Twelve. Judas was **one of the twelve** and therefore one of the last persons likely to betray Jesus. Carson (*The Gospel According to John*, p. 304) puts it well: "The supreme adversary … of God so operates behind failing human beings that his malice becomes theirs. Jesus can discern the source, and labels it appropriately."

I. Jesus at the Feast of Tabernacles (chaps. 7–8)

7:1–8:59. In chapters 7–8, John recorded strong opposition to Jesus, including repeated references to threats on His life (see 7:1, 13, 19, 25, 30, 32, 44; 8:37, 40, 59). The apostle seems to have gathered the major arguments against the messiahship of Jesus and here answered them.

7:1. After these things. As in 5:1 and 6:1, the time is indefinite. Since, however, 6:4 refers to the Passover feast and 7:2 to the Feast of Tabernacles, the interval was about six months.

7:2. Feast of tabernacles. The great feast in the Jewish year, celebrating the completion of the harvest and commemorating God's goodness to the people during the wilderness wanderings (see Lev. 23:33–43; Deut. 16:13–15; Zech. 14:16–19). The name came from the leafy shelters in which people lived throughout the seven days of the feast.

7:3–5. His brethren (vv. 3, 5), the sons of Mary and Joseph, His half brothers (see discussion on Luke 8:19). **Disciples** may refer here to a broad number of followers (see 6:60) who now were in Judea for the feast. It is not clear whether the brothers claimed some knowledge of Jesus' miracles (lit., **works**) that other people did not have or were suggesting that any claim to messiahship must be decided in Jerusalem. Their advice was not given sincerely, for they did not yet **believe in him** (v. 5).

7:6. My time (Greek, *kairos*; "right time," "proper time") **is not yet come.** Unlike His brothers, whose time was **alway ready** ("right"), Jesus moved in accordance with the will of God (see discussion on 2:4).

7:7. The world is either (1) people opposed to God or (2) the human system opposed to God's purposes (see discussion on 1:9–10). Jesus' brothers belonged to the world and therefore could not be the objects of its hatred. Jesus, however, rebuked the world and was hated accordingly.

7:8–9. I go not up yet (v. 8). Jesus was not refusing to go to the feast but rather refusing to go in the way the brothers suggested, as a pilgrim. When He went, it would be to deliver a prophetic message from God, for which He awaited His "time" (7:6).

7:10. Not openly, but as it were in secret (see 7:4) suggests that Jesus went privately and not among the crowds or pilgrims. In this way, He rejected His brothers' suggestion to show Himself (see 7:4).

7:11–13. The Jews (v. 11; see discussion on 1:19), or religious authorities of Jerusalem, are contrasted with **the people** (v. 12; lit., "the crowds," plural only in John). **Where is he?** (v. 11) is literally, "Where is that man?" and typifies the misunderstanding of Jesus echoed among the people. **Murmuring** (v. 12), the same Greek expression used in 6:41, 46, characterizes the significant disagreement about who Jesus was. **A good man** is obviously an inadequate appraisal of Jesus, but it clearly conveys a perception of His pure intentions, a view contested by others who argued His intentions were impure and aimed at deception (**deceiveth**; Greek, *planaō*; "cause to go astray," see English "planet"). **Openly** (v. 13; Greek, *parrēsia*; "frankly," "boldly"; see 7:4, 25) contrasted with **fear** suggests a "gag order" discouraging any mention of Jesus.

7:14. The midst of the feast, or the middle of the weeklong feast, connotes a time when the crowds would be at their maximum. Teaching in the temple courts at such a time would reach many.

7:15. The Jews (see discussion on 1:19), distinct from "the people" (7:12), who were also Jews, were especially observant of Jesus as He taught in the temple precincts. **Having never learned**, Jesus' knowledge of **letters** (Greek, *grammata*; lit., "letters"; fig., "knowledge") points not to literacy but to recognized schooling. Jesus had never been schooled under a rabbi or recognized Jewish teacher.

7:16. If Jesus' knowledge was not the studied knowledge of a recognized rabbi, where had He acquired such learning? Jesus answered the query

directly. **My doctrine** (lit., "teaching) **is not mine, but his that sent me** (see discussion on 4:34). "The Father which hath sent me" (5:30, 37; 6:44) had been His "rabbi."

7:17. Will do his will reflects a disposition or attitude of open and receptive willingness to hear and obey God. A person sincerely set on doing God's will welcomes Jesus' teaching and believes in Him (see 6:29). Commenting on the words **he shall know,** Augustine said, "Understanding is the reward of faith … What is 'If any man be willing to do his will'? It is the same thing as to believe."

7:18. Jesus truly represented and revealed the will of the Father because, as He argued, He sought not **his own glory** (or "benefit"; see 5:41–44): **but … his glory that sent him**. As so often in the gospel of John, the credibility of Jesus' representation of the Father is cast in the language of Jewish agency: the one sent is as the one who sends. His righteousness verified His faithfulness (**true**). In this gospel, no one is spoken of as being "true" except God the Father (3:33; 8:26) and Jesus (here). Once again, John ranked Jesus with God.

7:19. The Jews congratulated themselves on being the chosen recipients of **the law** (see Rom. 2:17), but Jesus told them that they all broke the law of which they were so proud. **Keepeth the law** is literally "doing the law," and Jesus charged each of them (**none of you**) with the failure (see 3:10–11).

7:20. The people probably refers to the pilgrims who had come up to Jerusalem for the feast, different from "the Jews" who were trying to kill Jesus (see 7:1) and the Jerusalem mob that knew of the plot (see 7:25). **Thou hast a devil** is an accusation of demon possession made elsewhere in John (see, e.g., 8:48–52; 10:20–21; see also Matt. 12:24–32; Mark 3:22–30). This was an unfortunate but typical human response to discredit the person (ad hominem) when one cannot discredit the word of the person. Such a response is atypical of a person with a "will [to] do his will" (7:17).

7:21. One work apparently refers to the healing of the lame man (see 5:1–9), as the discussion about the Sabbath shows (see 7:22–23).

7:22–23. The requirement of **circumcision** (v. 22) was included in the law Moses gave (see Exod. 12:44, 48; Lev. 12:3), yet it originated not with Moses but rather with Abraham (see Gen. 17:9–14). The Jews took such regulations as that in Leviticus 12:3 to mean that circumcision must be performed on the eighth day even if it was **the sabbath day**, a day on which no work should be done. This exception is of critical importance in understanding the controversy. Jesus was not saying that the Sabbath should not be observed or that the Jewish regulations were too harsh. He was saying that His opponents did not understand what the Sabbath meant. The command to circumcise showed that sometimes work not only might be done on the Sabbath but must be done then. Deeds of mercy were in this category. **Whole** (v. 23) is a direct reference to the healing of chapter 5; the word is found only here and there (in 5:6, 9, 11, 14–15) in John.

7:24. Judge not is a command to "stop judging" superficially. On the contrary, Jesus admonished them to **judge [the] righteous judgment**, which is equivalent to the whole truth or "the one true and complete decision of which the case admits" (Westcott, *The Gospel According to St. John*, p. 120). The Old Testament (see Deut. 16:18; Isa. 11:3; Zech. 7:9) is an ally to Jesus' admonition.

7:25. Them of Jerusalem is an expression found only here and in Mark 1:5 in the New Testament, probably referring to the Jerusalem mob (see discussion on 7:20). They did not originate the plot against Jesus, but they knew of it.

7:26. That Jesus could **speaketh boldly** in a climate where fear (see 7:13) and plots (7:24) abounded was matched by an equally peculiar silence on the part of the rulers. This strange juxtaposition led to an uneasy suspicion: **Do the rulers know indeed…?** In Greek, the question is in a form that expects a negative answer. The people thought it unlikely, but what else could such silence mean but that Jesus **is the very Christ?** (see discussion on 1:25).

7:27. Howbeit we know proved to be another instance of superficial judgment (see 7:24). What first presented itself caused them to stumble over the whole truth. At face value, He was Jesus of Nazareth. **No man knoweth whence he is.** Some Jews held that the Old Testament gave the origin of the Messiah (see 7:42; Matt. 2:4–6), but others believed that it did not.

7:28–29. Ye … know me (v. 28). Irony, because in a sense they knew Jesus and that He came from Nazareth, but in a deeper sense, they did not know Jesus or the Father (see 8:19) who sent Him. Jesus mentioned again His dependence on the Father (see 4:34) and went on to declare that He had real knowledge of God and that they did not. Both His origin and mission were from God. **He hath sent me** (v. 29) is the confirmation of Jesus' knowledge of the Father and another bold declaration that the people were dealing with the authorized representative of God.

7:30. They sought to take him. Jesus' enemies were powerless against Him until His "time" (7:8) or "hour" (2:4) came (see discussion on 2:4).

7:31. Many of the people, the pilgrims (see discussion on 7:20), **believed on him** and accepted His miraculous signs (**miracles**; see discussion on 2:11) as a peerless credential that the Christ (the Messiah) was before them (compare 6:26).

7:32. The Pharisees (see discussions on Matt. 3:7; Mark 2:16; Luke 5:17) confirmed earlier expressed fears (see 7:12–13), and the **murmured** acclamation of Jesus prompted them to seek a warrant from **the chief priests**. There was only one ruling chief priest, but the Romans had deposed a number of chief priests, and these retained the title by courtesy.

7:33–34. Yet a little while … then I go (v. 33). Jesus changed the topic from His miracles to His death, to which He referred enigmatically (v. 34). Even as the warrant for His arrest directed the temple guards to apprehend Jesus and take Him away, Jesus spoke of leaving. He would return to **him that sent me**. His departure was not in the hands of human authority but was dictated by the commission of the Father who sent Him. In agency, every sending is completed with the fulfillment of the commission and the return and report of the one who was sent. As Passover and the cross loomed, Jesus saw at hand the completion of His commission and return to the Father. Since His commission was of divine origin, His return was also divine and beyond human parallel.

7:35–36. The dispersed among the Gentiles (or "Greeks"; v. 35) points to what is commonly referred to as "the dispersion." From the time of the exile, many Jews lived outside the Holy Land, and Jews were found in most cities throughout the Roman Empire. Without a grasp of Jesus' heavenly origin, human explanations of Jesus' enigmatic talk of departure led to distant locations and realms outside of Judea.

7:37–38. The last day … of the feast (v. 37). The Feast of Tabernacles lasted seven days (see Lev. 23:34; Deut. 16:13, 15) but had a "holy convocation" on the eighth day (see Lev. 23:36). Each morning of the feast, the Jews attended a ceremony in which a priest drew water from the Pool of Siloam as the words of Isaiah 12:3 were recited. Upon drawing the water, the joyful procession set out for the temple, singing from the Hallel Psalms (Psalms 113–118). With the priest carrying the water in a golden pitcher and each participant carrying a *lulab* (myrtle and twigs tied with a palm, symbolizing the construction of a tabernacle hut) and an *ethrog* (a lemon, symbolizing harvest), the procession approached the temple. Upon reaching the Water Gate, the procession was greeted with three blasts of the ram's horn (*shofar*) as the procession made its way to the altar of sacrifice, where it circled the altar, singing the Hallel (Psalm 118:25) and waving its *lulabs*. On the seventh day, the procession would circle the altar seven times before the priest would commence with the pouring of the water, which the rabbis associated with the blessing of rain. It was on this final day of the festivities that Jesus stood up in the temple court and proclaimed that He was the source of **living water** (v. 38). John recorded that Jesus **stood and cried, saying** (v. 37). Teachers usually sat, so Jesus drew special attention to His message. **Thirst** refers to a basic human need that was a feature of the water ceremony associated with the feast. Here Jesus pointed beyond physical demands to spiritual necessities, even as He did with

the woman at the well (see discussion on 4:10). Jesus is the true source of abundant water, and it is obtained by placing one's trust and belief in Him.

7:39. Explaining the "living water" (7:38), John commented that Jesus was referring to **the Spirit**. He further clarified that the Spirit **was not yet given** in the manner in which He would be given at Pentecost (see Acts 2). **Glorified** refers to Jesus' crucifixion, resurrection, and exaltation (see discussion on 13:31). The fullness of the Spirit's work depends on Jesus' work of salvation. Associations of the Spirit with water or liquid imagery are found in the Old Testament (see, e.g., Isa. 44:3; Joel 2:28–32). Luke spoke of the Spirit poured out (see Acts 2:17, 18, 2:33; 10:45), and Paul spoke of being filled with the Spirit (see Eph. 5:18).

7:40–42. The people (v. 40; see discussion on 7:20) identified Jesus as **the Prophet**, probably the one who would be like Moses (see Deut. 18:18). Even as Jesus' miraculous feeding of the five thousand (see 6:1–14) linked Jesus to Moses and the manna (see 6:14), Jesus' water pronouncement may have evoked images of the water Moses provided the people at the rock of Horeb (see Exod. 17:6). **Others** deemed Jesus **the Christ** (v. 41), or Messiah, but this was met with skepticism because Jesus hailed from **Galilee** (Nazareth) and not from **Bethlehem** (v. 42). There is irony here. Just as the people did not know His heavenly origin (see 3:8; 8:14, 23), they did not know His nativity. Nonetheless, there were different ideas about the Messiah's place of origin (see 7:27).

7:43–46. The officers (v. 45) knew they would be in trouble for failing to arrest Jesus but did not mention the hostility of part of the crowd, which would have given them something of an excuse before the Pharisees. **Never man spake like this man** (v. 46). The officers were favorably impressed by the teaching of Jesus and were not inclined to cause Him trouble.

7:47–48. Then answered them the Pharisees (v. 47). The Pharisees must have been greatly irritated. Ordinarily, the chief priests would have rebuked the temple guards. For the position that Jesus **deceived** the people, see 7:12. The wording of both questions expects a negative answer. The first question (v. 47) appears genuinely inquiring, if not hopeful. The second question (v. 48) appears rhetorically bolstering and reassuring; it led to a comparison of opinions. When it came to assessing Jesus, the opinion of the religious authorities, the elite, mattered most, not the religious inferiors or common people.

7:49. This people refers to commoners, the Am HaAretz, or people of the land. The elitist view of the pilgrim crowd (see discussion on 7:20) was that they were ignorant, or **knoweth not**. The Pharisees exaggerated the people's ignorance of Scripture (see 7:42), but the average Jew paid little attention to the minutiae that mattered so much to the Pharisees. The traditions of the elders were too great a burden for people who earned their living by hard physical work, and consequently, these regulations were widely disregarded.

7:50–51. There is irony here. The Pharisees implied that no leader believed in Jesus, yet **Nicodemus** (v. 50), "a ruler of the Jews" (3:1), spoke up. They called for people to observe the law, but Nicodemus pointed to their own disregard of the law in this instance.

7:52. Out of Galilee ariseth no prophet (see 1:46). The Pharisees were angry, and wrong. Jonah came from Galilee, and perhaps other prophets as well. Moreover, the Pharisees overlooked the right of God to raise up prophets from wherever He chooses.

7:53–8:11. This story is absent from some early manuscripts, and of those that have it, some place it elsewhere (e.g., after Luke 21:38). This passage is contained in more than 1,700 New Testament Greek manuscripts, however. Although the location of the story is debated, it is largely regarded as authentic.

7:53–8:2. Jesus went to the **mount of Olives** (v. 1; see discussion on Mark 11:1). This is the only time that the Mount of Olives is mentioned in John. Luke recorded, however, that Jesus spent the day teaching in the temple and the night on the Mount of Olives, as He did during His final days in Jerusalem (see Luke 21:37).

8:3. Scribes (see discussions on Matt. 2:4; Luke 5:17) **and Pharisees** are a frequent couplet found in the other gospels, but only here in John. The expression **a woman taken in adultery** points to sin that cannot be committed alone. Consequently, the question arises as to why only one offender was brought before Jesus. The incident was staged to trap Jesus (see 8:6), and provision had been made for the man to escape. The woman's accusers must have been especially eager to humiliate her, since they could have kept her in private custody while they spoke to Jesus. Her position **in the midst**, or in front of everyone, is indicative of a formal and legal inquiry.

8:4. Taken … in the very act reflects the fact that compromising circumstances were not sufficient evidence, as Jewish law required witnesses who had seen the act.

8:5. Such should be stoned. Death was prescribed (in Lev. 20:10 and Deut. 22:22) for an unfaithful wife and the male counterpart, but the method was not. Stoning was not prescribed unless the woman was a betrothed virgin (see Deut. 22:23–24). This distinct prescription has lead some to suppose the woman was betrothed and not married. Ezekiel 16:38–40, however, shows that stoning was the typical method of execution for all types of adultery (see Brown, *The Gospel According to John*, p. 333). At any rate, that the paramour was not standing beside the woman indicates an uneven application of the law.

8:6. This they said, tempting him. The Romans did not allow the Jews to carry out death sentences (see 18:31), so if Jesus had said to stone her, He would have been in conflict with the Romans. If He had said not to stone her, He could have been accused of being unsupportive of the law. What was it that Jesus **wrote on the ground**? Educated guesses have ranged from a portion of Jeremiah 17:13, to successive portions of Exodus 23:1 (here) and 23:7 (in 8:8). Others have suggested that any content was incidental and that the act of writing was parabolic or a tactic of delay and suspense. Whatever the case, no one knows.

8:7. The phrase **without sin** is quite general and means "without any sin," not "without this sin." Jesus' answer disarmed them. Since He spoke of throwing a stone, He could not be accused of failure to uphold the law. The qualification for throwing it, however, prevented anyone from acting.

8:8–9. After His pronouncement, Jesus **again ... wrote on the ground** (see discussion on 8:6). The people **went out one by one** (v. 9) because they were not "without sin" (8:7). **The eldest** were the first to realize what was involved, but all the people were either conscience-stricken or afraid, and in the end, only Jesus and the woman remained.

8:10. Woman is not a harsh form of address (see discussion on 2:4; 19:26).

8:11. Go, and sin no more. Jesus did not condone what the woman had done. The ostensible purpose of the law is to sin no more. Even as her accusers had failed, so had she. The grace of God now compelled her to go and live out the law. Her accusers left because they lacked the moral validation to impose the penalty of the law. She was compelled to go for a different reason: the compelling power of grace.

8:12. I am the light of the world (see discussion on 6:35). It is also true that "God is light" (1 John 1:5). As Jesus' followers reflect the light that comes from Him, they too are "the light of the world" (Matt. 5:14; see Phil. 2:15). **Darkness** connotes both the darkness of this world and that of Satan. **The light of life** points not only to Jesus as "the light of men" (see 1:4 and discussion; 9:5; 12:46) but also to the grand truth that "God is light" (1 John 1:5). Jesus is also the light from God that lights the way for life, as the pillar of fire lighted the way for the Israelites (see Exod. 13:21; Neh. 9:12).

The pronouncement of Jesus was magnified by its timing against the background of the Feast of Tabernacles. The Feast of Tabernacles, which lasted seven days (see 7:37), was inaugurated with a grand opening ceremony that featured the lighting of specially prepared beacons of light. Pillars of light, branched candlesticks or candelabras 50 cubits (about 75 feet) high according to the Jewish Talmud, were set up in the temple courtyard. Each pillar was affixed with four basins holding fifteen gallons of oil, with wicks fashioned from the garments of the priests. When these were lit, the Mishnah (Mishnah, Sukkah 5:3) records, "there was not a courtyard in Jerusalem that

did not reflect the light." As a highpoint of the opening festivities, these words were repeated: "We are the Lord's and our eyes are turned to the Lord." With the rich symbolism of the Feast of Tabernacles in view, Jesus declared, "I am the light of the world."

8:13. The Pharisees (see discussions on Matt. 3:7; Mark 2:16; Luke 5:17) opposed Jesus on the basis that He offered unsupported attestation. Jesus was well aware of the legal objection (see 5:31) and the position was later codified in the Mishnah: "No man can give witness for himself" (Mishnah, Ketuboth 2:9). Jesus had already answered such an objection with additional witnesses, citing the testimony of the Baptist, His works, the Father, the Scriptures, and Moses (see 5:32–47). Jesus, however, never conceded that He alone testified to Himself. His testimony was not His alone but also that of the Father who sent Him (see 5:32; 8:16, 18).

8:14. Jesus made two points in reply to His opponents' objection that He bore witness to Himself (see 8:13). The first is here, and the second is in 8:16–18. He based both points on the fact that He was the commissioned representative of the Father. Just as a human agent representing a potentate from a foreign land might arrive to transact official business, so now He stood before them. They were challenging the authority of Jesus without knowing **whence I come, and whither I go.** Even if He were to bear witness (**record**) to Himself, but He was not, His testimony **is true** (verifiable). **I know whence I came, and whither I go** is a direct reference to the fact that Jesus operated under the authority of a commission that remained intact; He was not a rogue operating on His own, as the reference to His return makes clear. In short, the argument of the Pharisees showed their ignorance of His official representation.

8:15. The judgment of the Pharisees was limited and worldly. **After the flesh** is literally "according to the flesh," or human standards. As Jesus would make clear, His judgments are not His own but those of the one who sent Him (see 8:16).

8:16–18. Jesus' second point in replying to His opponents' objection that He bore witness to Himself (see 8:13) was that His testimony was not unsupported. The Father was behind Jesus' testimony (see 5:31–39). In legal terms, He and the Father were the two witnesses required by the law (see Deut. 17:6; 19:15). Jesus was always aware of His mission (see discussion on 4:34). **The Father that sent me** (v. 16) drew the argument against Jesus' testimony into the larger question of the authority of the one Jesus represented.

8:19. If ye had known me. John made it clear that "the Word [Jesus] was with God, and ... was God" (1:1) and revealed God (see 1:18). Jesus here stressed that the Father is known through the Son and that to know the one is to know the other. Of course, Jesus' opponents were thinking in terms of a human father. **Where is thy Father?** Their question may express some rhetorical sarcasm, as if to bring Him down to earth. They were confident they knew who they were dealing with and where He was from (see 6:42; 7:27). Jesus' answer contested that hidden supposition.

8:20. The treasury identifies the precinct within the temple where Jesus was teaching and where this verbal exchange took place. The location appears to correspond to the setting of Mark 12:41–43. Significant is the point that hostility toward Jesus remained high, and one would expect His presence in the temple to result in His arrest, but **no man laid hands on him**, because the Father who sent Him determined **his hour** (see discussion on 2:4).

8:21–24. I go my way (v. 21) was Jesus' manner of speaking about His death and return to the Father (see 7:33–34). Despite His indirect language, **the Jews** (v. 22; see discussion on 1:19) suspected that Jesus spoke of His death. Ostensibly, the death of Jesus would please His opponents, but Jesus exposed them to the grave jeopardy attached to such a hostile disposition: **ye ... shall die in your sins** (vv. 21, 24). **And ye shall seek me** (v. 21) pointed to their ongoing quest for the Messiah (see Carson, *The Gospel According to John*, p. 341), a search that would continue in vain unless they came to believe **that I am he** (v. 24), the Messiah and more (see 8:58; discussion on 6:35; *KJV Study Bible* note on Exod. 3:14). Two realms, one characterized by that which is be-neath ... **of this world** (v. 23) and sin, is contrasted with its opposite, that which is **above ... not of this world** and, by inference, salvation. In rejecting Jesus, the Jews were turning from the very one they sought.

8:25. The question **Who art thou?** confirms the ambiguity of "I am he" (8:24), for its sense is subject to more than one interpretation. The Jewish leaders were disinclined to automatically attach a higher meaning to it. Its range of meaning is reflected in the distance between the two realms that characterized the difference between Jesus and His opponents ("not of this world" and "of this world," 8:23). Here the leaders' question itself implies that they suspected Jesus meant something higher than any of the denotations to be found in a conversational dictionary. **Even the same that I said unto you from the beginning.** Jesus' answer is a notoriously difficult sentence in the Greek. It may read as a question or an affirmation. Presuming it is an affirmation, Jesus was saying one of two related things: either (1) "You have the answer in what I have just told you" or (2) "You have the answer in what I have been telling you from the beginning of my ministry."

8:26–27. Jesus refused to give the Jewish authorities any explanation beyond what He had already told them (see 8:25). Here He put His refusal into perspective. Notice how Jesus turned their original question ("Who art thou?"; 8:25) into an appraisal of His opinion of them (**I have many things to say and to judge of you: but ...**; v. 26). In saying this, Jesus implied that the answer they sought would have hinged on His opinion of them rather than on the testimony He brought from the one who sent Him. That testimony was as true as its source, and it was the same for the whole **world**. Once again, Jesus' reply focused on the fact that He was the representative of the one who sent Him, and **he that sent me is true**. Two implications, therefore, may apply: (1) the message the Father deemed clear enough for the whole world must suffice for them; and (2) their lack of spiritual discernment had to do more with them than with the message, whose source was true. As if to confirm this, John added, **They understood not that he spake to them of the Father** (v. 27).

8:28–29. Jesus' mission and message would be vindicated and verified in the death that He had spoken about (see 8:21–24). **Lift up** (v. 28) is normally used in the New Testament in the sense of "exalt," and in Acts 2:33, the word is used of the ascension of Jesus, but John used it of the crucifixion (see 3:14; 12:32–33). The certainty of Jesus' claim ("then shall ye know") is based on the fidelity (**I do nothing of myself**) of Jesus to the mission and message of His commission. All that He said and did was prescribed by the will of the Father who sent Him. His ability to carry out what the Father had set before Him was fortified by the faithfulness of God. For **I am he**, see discussions on 8:24, 58.

8:30–31. John left **many** (v. 30) unqualified, and one may presume that it included a considerable number of those who had observed the exchange between Jesus and His more hardened opponents (see 8:22, 25, 27). What is clear is that they had responded to the Jesus' compelling prescriptions to believe in Him or die in their sin (see 8:21–24). **Believed on him** is the same positive expression John used elsewhere to characterize authentic belief (2:11; 4:39; 7:31; 10:42; 11:45; 12:42; see 20:31).

It is notoriously difficult to reconcile the characterization of those who believed on Jesus in these verses with those characterized in 8:33, 37. John's description of their belief in 8:30 is used elsewhere of authentic faith. It may be that John's narrative does not adequately partition two different groups within one crowd, or perhaps he intended the description of their belief to point up the issue at hand: they made some discernible expression of faith ("many believed in him," v. 30) but did not **continue** (Greek, *menō;* "abide"; v. 31) as Jesus prescribed. In that case, they were professors. If we are to take "the many that believed" as possessors, John's description of their belief in verse 30 stands as a bold anomaly in his otherwise consistent pattern of language used to describe authentic faith.

8:32. The truth is closely connected with Jesus (see 8:36; 14:6). The truth that belongs to the disciple who abides in Christ's word (see 8:31) is not philosophical truth but the truth that leads to salvation, the revelation of the Father that comes in Jesus Himself (see 8:36). **Free** thus means freedom from the slavery of sin, not from ignorance (see 8:34–36). Given the following context, one may understand "an implicit contrast between the power of Jesus' revelation and that of the Law" (Brown, *The Gospel According to John,* p. 355).

8:33. Abraham's seed. The word "seed" is singular and refers collectively to the descendants of Abraham. For Paul, the singular "seed" was a significant pointer to Jesus, the true descendant of Abraham (see Gal. 3:16). If John chose the singular for the same reason, there is irony in this protest. On a physical plane, **We … were never in bondage to any man** presented an amazing disregard of their Roman overlords. The words, however, are probably to be taken on a spiritual plane, as suggested by the topics of "truth" (8:32) and "sin" (8:34).

8:34–36. Jesus spoke of **the servant of sin** (v. 34) because the sinner cannot break free by his own strength. The consequences of sin are grave, as underscored by Jesus' use of **Verily, verily.** Jesus illustrated the consequences with a metaphor drawn from the household of a landowner. In the master's household are servants and heirs. A servant's affiliation with the household is conditional and temporary, whereas an heir is a son who belongs to the household without limit or condition. The way Jesus developed the metaphor, the Jewish leaders, who thought they belonged to the household were, as are all sinners, no more than servants, temporarily and conditionally affiliated, unless the Son intervened and set them free. Paul used this metaphor of the household to argue that in Christ believers are no longer servants but are sons and heirs through adoption (see Gal. 4:4–7).

8:37. Ye seek to kill me (see discussion on 7:1–8:59). Biological paternity is not the same as spiritual paternity. Harboring murderous intentions was an evidence that His opponents were servants to sin and had not been freed by the word of Jesus, which liberates true disciples (see 8:31–32).

8:38. Note the contrasts: **I … my Father** and **ye … your father.** Not until later (8:44) did Jesus say who their father was, but it was clear even at this point that it was neither God nor Abraham, as they claimed (see 8:39).

8:39–41. The **deeds** (v. 41) of Jesus' opponents revealed their parentage. Today, paternity may be confirmed by blood or DNA tests. Yet even today, parents rear their children to share their values and cherish what they cherish. To hear that your child is a "chip off the old block" points to signs of parenting more highly prized than the genetics of paternity. For Jesus, the test of paternity was the desire of one's father detectable in the behavior of the child (see 8:38–39; 44; Luke 6:35–36; Mark 3:33–35). **Born of fornication** may have been a slander aimed at the circumstances surrounding Jesus' birth.

8:42. I proceeded forth and came from God specified Jesus' commission and mission (**He sent me**) and was itself an evidence of Jesus' desire to fulfill the will the Father. **Neither came I of myself** shows Jesus' subordination to the will of the Father. Animosity rather than love for Jesus was evidence that His opponents' desires were not from God.

8:43. Jesus said His opponents could not **understand** (lit., "know") **my speech**, His vocalized words, because they were not able to **hear** (accept and therefore obey) **my word**. These descendants of Abraham (see 8:33) were so convinced of their own preconceptions that they did not really hear what Jesus was saying (see 8:47).

8:44–45. Your father the devil (v. 44) specifies explicitly the Jewish leaders' relationship to Satan by virtue of common desires and the common influence of falsehood. Jesus performed a spiritual autopsy to expose inner motives that were inconsistent with outward appearances and their professions of allegiance to Abraham. Mimicking the "right" things may fool others, but not Jesus. **Ye will do** points to the determination of the will. Their problem was basically spiritual, not intellectual. Being oriented toward Satan, they were bent on seeing Jesus put to death (see 8:37) and eventually would (see 8:28). **Truth** is foreign to Satan, and those who are his (see 14:6) do not believe Jesus because He speaks **the truth** (v. 45).

8:46. Which of you convinceth me of sin? That Jesus asked this question was more significant than the Jews' failure to answer in that it showed He had a perfectly clear conscience. Jesus knew no one could prove Him guilty of sin.

8:47. Heareth God's words (compare 8:43; see 10:3–4; 1 John 4:6). Jesus represented the Father as His agent and messenger. Therefore, Jesus' opponents could not **hear** His word (see 8:43), nor could they "hear" God's word because the word of Jesus is the word of God. Those who oppose Jesus are **not of God**.

8:48. The Jews, Jesus' opponents (see discussion on 1:19), took up personal slurs in an attempt to disqualify what they could not refute on the strength of theological argument. *Ad hominem* aspersions were calculated to dismiss any accountability or responsibility for what Jesus had said. Such aspersions attacked Jesus' character rather than answered His contentions. They could not "hear" His word (see 8:43, 47), so they characterized the word of Jesus, and thus of God, as the ravings of an unqualified and demonically controlled unworthy. Since Samaritans did not recognize the exclusive claim of the Jews to Abraham, calling Jesus **a Samaritan** demeaned Him as an adherent of false and unorthodox beliefs, "no better than a Samaritan." **Thou … hast a devil** (see 10:20; discussion on 7:20), or literally, "a demon." Their accusation was that Jesus was not in control of Himself and was the tool of an ungodly force. The opponents of Jesus thought that they could dismiss the message by "killing" the messenger.

8:49–50. I have not a devil; but I honour my Father (v. 49) points to the mistreatment of God Himself in the dishonoring treatment of His representative (see 5:23). In Jewish agency, the one sent is as the one who sends, and the dishonor shown to Jesus was dishonor shown to the Father who sent Him. If Jesus had glorified Himself or sought His own benefit, He would have been representing Himself and not the Father who sent Him. If Jesus had acted on His own ("If I honour myself" 8:54), slurs such as His opponents had thrown at Him in 8:48 would have been against Him alone (see v. 54). Jesus did not glorify Himself, however. In saying that He honored the Father, Jesus confirmed that He represented the Father faithfully. Jesus certified this fact by deferring to **one that seeketh and judgeth** (v. 50). In other words, Jesus sought the Father's glory (implied in **I seek not my own glory**), and it was the Father who would judge the Jesus' faithfulness and therefore His opponents' dishonor and rejection of Him.

8:51. My saying refers to the whole of Jesus' message, which when accepted, brings deliverance from death.

8:52-53. Never taste of death (v. 52) expresses the experience of physical death, as even **Abraham ... and the prophets** experienced. Jesus, however, was speaking of spiritual death. **Art thou greater ...?** (v. 53). The question was framed to expect the answer no. This is ironic, since Jesus was indeed far greater than Abraham, even as He was greater than Moses (see 6:30-35 and discussions).

8:54-55. Jesus answered the Jewish leaders' question, "whom makest thou thyself?" (8:53), in terms of His agency as the representative of the Father who had sent Him. His opponents claimed as their own the God that sent Him, yet they accused Jesus of seeking His own **honour** (lit., "glory"; v. 54) and failed to recognize that God's honor was at stake in the way they treated Jesus, because God honored Him. Knowing God is confirmed by **keep[ing] his saying** (v. 55), or word; they could not "hear" (8:43, 47) God's word because they did not know Him. Jesus was so faithful to God's word that to say He did not know God would have been as much a lie as them saying they knew God. All in all, Jesus was answering their question by declaring that it was not so much what He made of Himself (see 8:53) as what God made of Him by virtue of His faithful representation of the Father. The honor of God was vested in Jesus in that the Father conferred on Jesus His quintessential rights of life and judgment (see 5:21-27) and put "all things into his hand" (3:35; 13:3). Jesus stood before His opponents as the supreme plenipotentiary of God.

8:56. Abraham rejoiced to see my day. "My day" probably refers to all that was involved in the incar-

nation. It is unlikely that Jesus was referring to any one occasion but rather to Abraham's general joy in the fulfilling of the purposes of God in Christ, by which all nations on earth would receive blessing (see Gen. 18:18). **He saw it** in faith, from afar (see Heb. 11:1, 9-13).

8:57. Not yet fifty years old was a generous allowance for Jesus' maximum possible age. Jesus was "about thirty" (Luke 3:23) when He began His ministry.

8:58. I am. A solemnly emphatic declaration echoing God's great affirmation in Exodus 3:14 (see 8:24, 28; see also discussion on 6:35). Jesus said not "I was" but "I am," expressing the eternity of His being and His oneness with the Father (see 1:1). With this climactic statement, Jesus concluded His speech that had begun with the related claim, "I am the light of the world" (8:12).

8:59. Stones to cast at him. The Jews could not interpret Jesus' claim as other than blasphemy, for which stoning was the proper penalty (see Lev. 24:16).

J. Healing of the Man Born Blind (chap. 9)

9:1-12. Jesus performed more miracles of restoring sight than of any other. Giving sight to the blind was prophesied as a messianic activity (see Isa. 29:18; 35:5; 42:7). These miracles were thus additional evidence that Jesus was the Messiah (see 20:31).

9:1-2. The question of the disciples, **who did sin ...?** (v. 2), presupposed the wide influence of a common theological and cultural view of suffering (see 9:34). The rabbis had developed the principle that there is no death without sin, and there is no suffering without iniquity. They were even capable of thinking that a child could sin in the womb or that its soul might have sinned in a preexistent state. They also held that terrible punishments came on certain people because of the sin of their parents. Jesus plainly contradicted these beliefs.

9:3-5. The disciples also looked at the man's blindness in the way that most Jews and the Pharisees did; they sought to know whose sin had caused the man's blindness, who was responsible (see 9:2).

Jesus wanted them to look at the man the way He did, as an opportunity for doing the work of God as expressed in Jesus' mission (see 9:4−5). He objected to the presupposition of responsibility and turned the question of cause into one of opportunity. He addressed no ostensible cause, only the purpose **that the works of God should be made manifest in him** (v. 3). The KJV properly renders this phrase as the Greek reads. In English, one must supply a main sentence, as do other translations by adding the words, "this happened" (NIV) or "it was" (NASB). It is not necessary to suppose the wording of the main sentence, however, since it is supplied in verse 4. The passage should read, "but, that the works of God should be made manifest in him, I [we] must work the works of him that sent me, while it is day" (vv. 3b−4a). Although this grammatical construction is hard to see in English as opposed to Greek, it is found elsewhere in John (1:31; 13:18; 14:31; 15:25).

Jesus connected the opportunity that this man's blindness provided and His mission as the Father's representative. There is good manuscript evidence that **I must** (v. 4) should read "we must." If so, the disciples were included in this work. **Day** and **night** signify the open-and-closed cycle of a regular workday and the occasion and cessation of work. That daytime alone provides an opportunity suitable for work is proverbial. Jesus' higher meaning was that the works of His mission and its opportunity belonged to the day, the period before the cross and Jesus' return to the Father. Just as there are natural time constraints in a normal workday, Jesus was under the constraints of His impending death. Accordingly, the word "night" (see 13:30) has an ominous quality. Both the proverbial and the higher significance of "day" and "night" are evident in 11:9−10. Nonetheless, there is no reason to think this an allegory. It is unlikely that Jesus was saying work could not be conducted after He died, only that there was urgency for Him to do the work of God, an urgency He called His disciples to share.

The healing of the blind man and the following irony and interplay of physical and spiritual vision and blindness must not be separated from Jesus' self-declaration, **I am the light of the world** (v. 5; see discussion on 8:12). Surely the man heard this pronouncement as Jesus and the disciples stood over him. Its meaning for the man, as for the reader, gains dimension as the chapter unfolds. Initially, it meant physical sight. What more it meant emerged as the man opened his physical eyes to discover he was not among the seeing but rather among the blind.

9:6−7. He spat ... and made clay (v. 6). Jesus used variety in His cures. Such mediums were not necessary, as the healing of 5:8−9 attests. Later, the procedure Jesus chose was directly linked to the violation of sabbath law (see 9:14). **Siloam** (v. 7), already an ancient name (see discussions on 2 Kings 20:20; Neh. 2:14; Isa. 8:6; *KJV Study Bible* note on Job 28:10), was a rock pool on the southern end of the main ridge on which Jerusalem was built. It served as part of the major water system developed by King Hezekiah. For its significance during the Feast of Tabernacles, see 7:37. John drew out the meaning of Siloam (**Sent**), alluding to the true source of the healing, Jesus, the one whom the Father sent as His representative.

9:8−12. John now revealed that **neighbours** (v. 8) and acquaintances had known the man as a beggar. Begging was about the only way a blind person of that day could support himself. His transformation was dramatic, and the questions about his identity are a reminder that people seldom look intently at beggars. His new mobility and manner of bearing caused people to question not only whether it was truly the same man they had known as a beggar but also how such a transformation had taken place. The man identified his healer, whom he knew by name although not by sight, and detailed step by step what Jesus had done and what He had instructed him to do. This would prove significant. The neighbors who wished to know the whereabouts of Jesus and who took the man to the Pharisees proved to be the only source of the detail that Jesus made clay and instructed him to wash in the Pool of Siloam. The man himself never disclosed these details to his official interrogators (see discussion on 9:13−16).

9:13–16. John disclosed that **it was the Sabbath day when Jesus made the clay, and opened his eyes** (v. 14). Both of these activities were violations of the Sabbath. "Kneading," involved in making clay, is one of the thirty-nine works prohibited on the Sabbath by Jewish law, according to Mishnah, Shabbat 7:2. "Opening eyes" was not necessary on the Sabbath, because there are six other days on which to heal a person whose life is not in jeopardy (see Luke 13:14). Notably, the man omitted these details in his testimony to the Pharisees: **He put clay upon mine eyes, and I washed, and do see** (v. 15). Although he apparently was protecting Jesus, the Pharisees nonetheless concluded that **This man** (Jesus) **is not of God** (v. 16) and that the Sabbath had been violated. Beside the man himself, only the neighbors who brought him to the Pharisees were in a position to convey such detail. The Pharisees were divided. Three questions occupied the investigation. (1) Had a miracle happened? This question would not be resolved until the man's parents testified (see 9:18–23). (2) How had it happened? This question focused on the specifics of whether or not Sabbath prohibitions had been violated. (3) Who had performed this miracle? This question focused not only on the identity of the healer but also on His culpability. Until the first question was confirmed, the Pharisees debated the second and third questions as theological lawyers. **There was a division among them**. The first group (v. 16a) started from the position that Jesus had violated the Sabbath and ruled out the possibility of His being from God. The second group (v. 16b) started from the fact of the miraculous sign and ruled out the possibility of His being a sinner (see 9:31–33).

9:17. What sayest thou of him …? It is curious that the Pharisees would pose this question to a man of inferior learning; it indicates their perplexity. At this point, the man identified Jesus as **a prophet**, probably the highest rank appropriate. There is, however, a notable progression to be seen in the man's understanding. His conception of Jesus grew and gained dimension, moving from "A man" (9:11), to "a prophet" (here) who might be followed by "disciples" (9:27), to one who was "of God" (9:33), to one

who was properly to be worshiped (9:38). Ironically, the interrogators' questions, and even their misrepresentations of Jesus, pushed the man to see more and more clearly the unique character of Jesus.

9:18–23. The man's parents confirmed that he was their son and that **he was born blind** (v. 20). This dual confirmation corresponds to the dual question of identity, **Is this your son, who ye say was born blind?** (v. 19). The parents were only as specific as the questions. They stuck to what they knew (**We know**; v. 20). When they came to what they did not know (**we know not**; v. 21), they actually went beyond the Pharisees' question of **how … doth he now see?** (v. 19; **by what means**; v. 21) to the unexpressed question of **who hath opened his eyes**. It may be that the question was asked and John omitted it. From the sequence of questions and answers, however, it appears their additional answer was intended to circumscribe all they knew and did not know to end the interrogation as quickly as possible. There was much to which the parents could not testify, but their emphasis on the son's responsibility, **he is of age** (vv. 21, 23), showed their fear of getting involved. It dramatically illustrates a climate of fear and the high stakes of being associated with Jesus. Excommunication is reported as early as the time of Ezra (see 10:8), but there is practically no information about the way it was practiced in New Testament times. The synagogue was the center of Jewish community life, so excommunication cut a person off from many social relationships (although in some of its forms, at least in later times, not from worship).

9:24. This begins the second interrogation of the man whose sight Jesus had restored. **Give God the praise**, or "glory," was a solemn admonition charging the man to tell the truth (see Josh. 7:19) under oath. There is irony here. The man's testimony would give glory to God, but it would not be the truth that his interrogators want to hear. **We** is emphatic in the Greek, showing the consensus that had emerged among the authorities.

9:25–27. The man refused to alter his previous testimony even when his interrogators prompted him as to what they wanted to hear. How eloquent and powerful is the truth of what he knew, all the more so against the background of what John recorded had frightened his parents (see 9:22).

What the authorities had professed to know ("we know that this man is a sinner"; 9:24) proved to be more an opinion than substantiated fact. They had yet to acquire any incriminating evidence from the man himself, apart from the evidence of a healing, which he himself represented. They lacked firsthand testimony as to how this miracle substantiated a violation of the Sabbath. They therefore resumed an earlier line of questioning (see 9:15), but the man refused to review it all again, saying only, **I have told you already, and ye did not hear: wherefore would ye hear it again?** (v. 27). In effect, the man said, "My testimony will not change, and hearing it again will not produce what you want to hear." His rhetorical question, **Will ye also be his disciples?** shows that he already counted himself a disciple.

9:28–29. The authorities **reviled** (v. 28) the man. In all likelihood, they had contempt for him from the outset. They would have viewed him as an inferior not only because he was a beggar but because they believed his blindness from birth was evidence of sin (see 9:2); this underlying prejudice is expressed openly in 9:34. That such a man as this should insult their dignity by suggesting they would give their allegiance to his healer (Jesus), a man they had declared a sinner (see 9:24), was more than they could tolerate. With a condescending attitude, evidenced by their expressed allegiance to Moses, they belittled the man. In declaring that **God spake unto Moses** (v. 29), they elevated Moses above the healer they knew nothing about, implying that Moses was not a sinner (see 9:31).

9:30–33. In these verses, the exceptional reasoning of a man, presumably unschooled, is revealed, especially when compared to the training of his interrogators. With a dash of sarcasm, the man chided the learned ones for missing the obvious: **Why herein is a marvellous thing, that ye know not from whence he is, and yet he hath opened mine eyes** (v. 30). In other words, how could anyone who

had performed such a miraculous work as opening his eyes go unrecognized as coming from God? The man then proceeded to adduce proof of his healer's higher origin. The first part of his proof he based on the premise that God answers only the prayers of the godly man who **doeth his will** (v. 31). This starting point built on what his interrogators had already expressed with their description of Moses (see 9:29). The second part of his proof he based on the extraordinary character of his healing (v. 32). The implication was clear. Only God could effect such a healing. The third and final part of his proof brought the deduction: **If this man were not of God, he could do nothing** (v. 33), yet his prayers had been answered in a way no other man's prayers had ever been answered. The conclusion is clear: Jesus must be from God. It may be remembered that earlier some of the Pharisees had followed this same line of reasoning (see 9:16b).

9:34. They cast him out may mean they expelled him physically from their assembly, but judging from 9:22, it is more likely that they excommunicated him.

9:35. John's wording sets the scene for the question Jesus posed to the man. The specifics of this man's life portray what is characteristic of John's gospel: no outcast is beyond the love of Jesus. Hearing how the man had been treated, Jesus sought him and **found him**. The question Jesus posed to the man, **Dost thou believe on the Son of God?** is a question more of trust than of whether the man acknowledged the existence of the Son of God. Strong manuscript evidence and the widest scholarly support suggest that "the Son of God" should read "the Son of man." It is certainly easier to explain why copyists might have inadvertently introduced the more common "Son of God" than the rarer "Son of Man." Where "Son of man" occurs in John, it is rich in meaning (1:51; 3:13, 14; 6:27, 53, 62; 8:28; 12:23, 34; 13:31). Jesus invited the man to put his trust in the one who is the revelation of God to man (see Carson, *The Gospel According to John*, p. 376).

9:36. The man was ready to follow any suggestion from his benefactor. Certainly he had become disenchanted, if not exasperated, with the traditional religion that had rejected him and with the authorities that had no place in their theology for the one who had restored his sight. He asked only that Jesus identify the one in whom he had been asked to put his trust: **that I might believe on him**. At this point, **Lord** is probably closer to "sir," but it is appropriately rendered "Lord" in 9:38.

9:37. With the words **Thou hast both seen him, and it is he that talketh with thee,** Jesus revealed His identity to the man, as He had to the Samaritan woman (see 4:26). What the man's heart was eager to embrace, he now realized stood before him. He had already come to see Jesus as more than a man, even before he set eyes on Him; now his physical eyes behold much more: the Son of Man.

9:38. Lord, I believe (see discussions on 1:7; 20:31). **And he worshipped him**. The man expressed his belief and worshiped Jesus, giving Him the reverence due to the very revelation of God.

9:39. Although 9:39-41 may have occurred a little later, it is possible the conversation of 9:35-38 occurred in a public place, where the intimate words of a personal conversation could have been overheard by the Pharisees. Jesus turned the occasion of restoring the man's sight into an opportunity to speak of spiritual realities. **For judgment I am come into this world** points to a function of Jesus' commission. Jesus defined specifically the nature of what He meant by "judgment" (Greek, *krima*): **that they which see not might see; and that they which see might be made blind**. The mission and ministry of Jesus is a catalyst. The foundational condition of humankind is that all people are in darkness, and Jesus is the light. John 3:17-19 states that Jesus came not to "condemn" (or "judge"; Greek, *krinō*) but to save (see 12:47), yet belief (coming to the light) and unbelief (retreating to the darkness) is defined by Jesus' mission in terms of being condemned (or "judged"; Greek, *krinō*): "He that believeth on him is not condemned: but he that believeth not is condemned already" (3:18; see 12:47). Here the same reality applies (see "your sin remaineth," 9:41), and Jesus emphasized the outcome of His ministry and not the intent (see 3:17; 12:47).

9:40-41. The Pharisees found it incredible that anyone would consider them spiritually blind. Their claim to sight showed their complete unawareness of their spiritual blindness and need. **If ye were blind, ye should have no sin** (v. 41). These words of Jesus are striking in view of 9:2-3. As at the beginning of chapter 9 with physical blindness, so here at the end of chapter 9 with spiritual blindness: blindness is an opportunity to manifest the work of God. **But now ye say, We see; therefore your sin** (your blindness) **remaineth**.

K. Parable of the Good Shepherd (10:1-21)

10:1-30. The parable of the good shepherd should be understood in light of the Old Testament (and ancient Near Eastern) concept of a "shepherd," symbolizing a royal caretaker of God's people. God Himself was called the "Shepherd of Israel" (Ps. 80:1; see Ps. 23:1; Isa. 40:10-11; Ezek. 34:11-16), and He had given great responsibility to the leaders ("shepherds") of Israel, which they failed to respect. God denounced these false shepherds (see Isa. 56:9-12; Ezekiel 34) and promised to provide the true Shepherd, the Messiah, to care for the sheep (see Ezek. 34:23).

10:1-3. The sheepfold (v. 1) was a court surrounded by stone walls but open to the sky and with only one entrance. The walls kept the sheep from wandering and no doubt protected them from certain wild animals. The twofold description **a thief and a robber** conveys not only theft but also a note of violent force with the addition of Greek *lēstēs* ("robber," "bandit," "insurrectionist"). Access had to be gained by stealth and force unless one was **the shepherd** (v. 2), whom **the porter** (lit., "doorkeeper"; v. 3) recognized as authorized to enter. The porter functioned as a watchman, especially at night, when the flocks were in the fold. Apparently, a large fold might house several flocks belonging to different shepherds yet be monitored by a joint porter. The porter recognized a shepherd, but the sheep responded to **his voice**. Sheep recognized the voice of their own shepherd and responded only to him. The shepherd did not call sheep randomly but only those that belonged to him (**his own sheep**). Commentators cite the shepherding practice of giving names to individual sheep.

10:4–5. He goeth before them (v. 4). The Palestinian shepherd led his sheep (he did not drive them), and the sheep followed because they knew **his voice**. Recognition of their shepherd's voice was how the sheep distinguished their shepherd from a stranger ("a thief and a robber"; 10:1). The well-being and safety of the sheep depended on this bond.

10:6. A **parable** (Greek, *paroimia*; "proverb," "figure of speech," John's equivalent to the Greek *parabolē* found in Matthew, Mark, and Luke) is a similitude with a primary and generally single point of emphasis. Jesus' hearers were familiar with the practices described in the parable **but they understood not** its meaning.

10:7–10. To make the moral of the parable plain, Jesus gave a fuller explanation. In the parable, Jesus is not only the shepherd (see 10:11), the authorized and recognized caregiver of the sheep, who enters and leads His sheep through the door; He is **the door** (or "entrance"; vv. 7, 9) itself. There is no legitimate access to the blessings of the fold's protection (v. 9a) or the pasture's forage (v. 9b) without Jesus. It appears, however, that Jesus was attributing to His role as the true Shepherd the exclusive attributes of "the door" to metaphorically magnify the exclusive rights of the true Shepherd (see 10:11–18). Consequently, **All ... before me** (v. 8) were "false shepherds," or **thieves and robbers**, like the Pharisees and the chief priests (but not the true Old Testament prophets; see discussion on 10:1–30). As "the door," Jesus is the one way to salvation. Inside the fold is safety, and one is able to **go ... out, and find pasture** (v. 9), the supply of all needs. Conversely, **the thief** (v. 10) has only one interest, himself. Christ's interest is in His sheep, which He enables to **have life** to the full (see discussion on 1:4). For Jesus' use of **I am** (vv. 7, 9), see discussion on 6:35.

10:11. Jesus declared, **I am** (see discussion on 6:35) **the good** (Greek, *kalos*; "beautiful," "praise-worthy") **shepherd**, probably in the sense of the ideal shepherd who puts his sheep ahead of himself.

Jesus **giveth his life for the sheep**. A shepherd might risk danger for his sheep (see Gen. 31:39; 1 Sam. 17:34–37), but he expected to come through alive. Jesus, however, said that the Good Shepherd would die for His sheep.

10:12–13. A **hireling** (v. 12) is interested in wages, not sheep. In time of danger, he runs away because of what he is (v. 13) and abandons the flock to predators.

10:14–15. I ... know my sheep, and am known of mine (v. 14) expresses a deep mutual knowledge, like that of the Father and the Son. **I lay down my life** (v. 15; see 10:11) reiterates a fact of central importance. Jesus is unlike any other shepherd because He is willing to set His sheep above Himself. His knowledge of the Father makes this possible.

10:16. Other sheep already belonged to Christ, though they had not yet been brought to Him. **Not of this fold** refers to those outside Judaism. Here Jesus gave a glimpse of the future worldwide scope of the church. There is **one fold** because all God's people have the same Shepherd (see 17:20–23).

10:17–18. That Christ would die for His people runs through 10:11–18. Both the love and the plan of the Father were involved, as well as the authority He gave to the Son. Christ obediently chose to die; otherwise, no one would have had the power to kill Him. **I have power to take it again** (v. 18). Jesus effected His own resurrection, though the Father and the Holy Spirit were also involved (see Rom. 8:11 and 1 Peter 3:18).

10:19–21. Division (v. 19; see 7:43; 9:16), or divided opinions, about Jesus was voiced **again among the Jews**. Some attributed His words to **a devil** (lit., "a demon"; v. 20; see 7:20) or to madness, as of one who is out of control and not in his right mind. **Others** (v. 21), however, protested these opinions. How could one who was under the control of a demon or not in control of himself **open the eyes of the blind?** (see 9:16). The assumption was that even if Jesus was not under His own control, it was a benevolent and good power His opponents were ignoring. Psalm 146:8 reminds us that "the LORD openeth the eyes of the blind."

L. Debating at the Feast of Dedication (10:22–39)

10:22. The feast of the dedication. The commemoration of the dedication of the temple by Judas Maccabeus in December, 165 BC, after it had been profaned by Antiochus Epiphanes (see discussions on Ezra 6:16; Dan. 8:9–12). This was the last great deliverance the Jews had experienced. This is what modern Jews celebrate at Hanukkah. Its origination antedates Christmas. **It was winter.** A description for those unfamiliar with the Jewish calendar.

10:23. Solomon's porch (see Acts 3:11; 5:12) was a roofed structure, somewhat similar to a Greek stoa, commonly but erroneously thought to date back to Solomon's time.

10:24. If thou be the Christ (see discussion on 1:25; 20:31). This was the critical question, but it was not easy to answer because of the different ideas of messiahship then in vogue. **Plainly** (see 7:13, 26 and discussions), or "openly," as His brothers had requested in 7:4.

10:25. I told you. Jesus had not specifically affirmed His messiahship except to the Samaritan woman (see 4:26). **The works that I do in my Father's name, they bear witness of me** points again to Jesus' authorization as the Father's agent and representative (see 5:36). Jesus' messiahship was contained within His faithful representation of the Father and the works He performed as a part of that commission. He may have meant here that the general thrust of His teaching made His claim clear or that such statements as that in 8:58 were sufficient. Or He may have been referring to the evidence of His whole manner of life (including the miracles), all He had done in the Father's name (for "name," see discussion on 2:23).

10:26–27. Jesus said that His opponents' failure to **believe** (v. 26) confirmed that they were **not of my sheep.** This not only was the topic of His parable but may have indeed classified them as wolves (see 10:12). If they were sheep, they would have known His **voice** (v. 27; see 10:3–5), Jesus would **know them** (see 10:14), and they would **follow** Him (see 10:4–5).

10:28. The sheep of the ideal shepherd (see 10:11) are safe in His care. Jesus now turned the metaphor into spiritual certainties. **Eternal life** (see discussion on 3:15) is the positive assurance, and **never perish** is a restatement in opposite terminology. The Greek construction here is a strong denial that the sheep will ever perish. The sheep's security is in the power of the Shepherd, who will let no one take them from Him.

10:29. My Father (see discussion on 5:17) **is able.** The Father's power (**hand**) is greater than that of any enemy, making the sheep completely secure.

10:30. I and my Father are one. The Greek for "one" is neuter: "one thing," not "one person." Jesus and the Father are one in essence or nature (see 17:21–22), but they are not identical persons. This great truth is what warranted Jesus' "I am" declarations (see discussion on 6:35; see also 8:24, 28, 58).

10:31. The Jews (see discussion on 1:19) **took up stones again to stone him.** They took Jesus' words as blasphemy and therefore prepared to carry out the law (see Lev. 24:16), though without due process. This reaction to Jesus' statement of "oneness" with His Father (see 10:30) was evidence that they perceived Jesus to be claiming equal authority with God (see 5:18).

10:32. Good works, as in 10:25, are the works that the Father had authorized Jesus and entrusted Him to carry out in the Father's authority ("name"; 10:25). The underlying Greek words refer in general to works that are fine and noble in character. Here Jesus defined their character as being **from my Father** (see 5:36, 43; 10:38 and discussions). Jesus turned His opponents' raised stones into an appraisal of the Father since He acted on the Father's behalf. Obviously, they vehemently disliked the claims of Jesus, but no work that He had performed had been carried out on His own (see 5:19, 30; 7:16–18, 19–20).

10:33. The clarification that the Jewish leaders would stone Jesus **for blasphemy** shows that they correctly understood the thrust of Jesus' words, but their preconceptions and unbelief prevented them from accepting His claim as true. **Makest thyself God.** To the Jews, Jesus was guilty of "making"

Himself God; they clearly understood Jesus to be claiming that He was God.

10:34–36. In its strictest sense, the term **law** (v. 34) meant the Pentateuch, but it was often used, as here, of the whole Old Testament, as evidenced by Jesus' reference to the Psalms. **Ye are gods** echoes Psalm 82:6 and refers to the judges (or other leaders or rulers), whose tasks were divinely appointed (see Exod. 7:1; 22:28 and *KJV Study Bible* note; Deut. 1:17; 16:18; 2 Chron. 19:6). The judges of Psalm 82 were unfaithful to their office, and God, who had **called them gods** (v. 35; see Ps. 82:6) because they were His representatives, judged them for their failure to faithfully represent Him (see Ps. 82:7). This figured prominently in Jesus' defense against the religious leaders who had challenged His claims as God's representative.

Since the religious leaders were taking the law into their own hands (10:31), Jesus challenged them on legal grounds. Unlike the judges, whom God called "gods," Jesus had been faithful to represent the Father who sent Him. The evidence Jesus presented was His faithful execution of the works the Father sent Him to do on His behalf (see 10:32; 5:36 and discussion). Since the religious leaders admitted that they had no grounds to stone Him for His "good work[s]" (10:33), Jesus took up their charge of blasphemy ("thou … maketh thyself God," 10:33).

As the crux of His defense, Jesus used their own judicial standard to legally demonstrate the contradiction of their indictment. If **in your law** (v. 34), He said, other representatives were called "gods," albeit unfaithful ones, how much more legitimate was it for a faithful representative to be so identified? Jesus argued, however, that He was more than a peer. Whereas the **word of God came** (v. 35) to them and they were legally (**the scripture cannot be broken**) called "gods," how much more did "God" befit the one **whom the Father hath sanctified, and sent into the world** (v. 36).

10:37–38. Here Jesus turned from a defendant into a plaintiff, from defense to prosecution. His accusers now had to defend themselves against the claims of His authoritative representation of the Fa-

ther. **The works of my Father** (v. 37; see discussion on 10:32) demonstrated the claims and validated the obligations imposed by Jesus' representation: **that the Father is in me, and I in him** (v. 38).

10:39. They sought again to take him. It is not clear if this was to arrest Him for trial or to take Him out for stoning. **But he escaped** (see Luke 4:30). John did not record why they failed, but he often made it clear that Jesus could not be killed before the appointed time (see discussion on 2:4).

M. Ministry in Perea (10:40–42)

10:40–42. Jesus left Jerusalem and crossed the Jordan to the east and the vicinity where John the Baptist had begun his ministry. The narrative's focus here on the ministry of the Baptist, who had prepared the way for Jesus' public ministry, is thematically the fitting echo to the closing of Jesus' public ministry. The raising of Lazarus (see 11:1–44) would initiate a sequence of events that thematically climb toward the cross and resurrection. Using the words of the people, John (the author) confirmed the Baptist's success in what Carson (*The Gospel According to John*, p. 400) calls a fitting epitaph: **all things that John spake of this man were true** (v. 41). The Baptist's testimony is highlighted once again (see 1:6, 15, 19–34; 3:27–30; 5:33–34). Here it is favored by two garlands. First, the Baptist **did no miracle** (v. 41), a point which magnified the praise of his testimony. Second, the Baptist's testimony bore fruit in the people's response to Jesus: **many believed on him there** (v. 42).

N. The Raising of Lazarus (chap. 11)

11:1–3. Lazarus (v. 1) is mentioned only in chapters 11–12 of John's gospel (the name is found also in the parable of Luke 16:19–31, but it is not the same Lazarus). **His sisters** (v. 3) are mentioned in Luke 10:38–42. **Bethany** (v. 1) was near Jerusalem, not quite two miles to the east (see 11:18 and discussion). John introduced Lazarus (**a certain man**) by linking him to his sisters, **Mary and … Martha**, with a tone of implied familiarity that prepares even the uninformed reader to recognize that an exceptionally close relationship existed between Jesus, these two sisters, and Lazarus, **he whom thou lovest** (v. 3). Yet despite such mutual affection (see 11:5), Jesus would wholly conduct Himself, not according to the constraints of human pressure (see 2:3–4; 7:8–9), but according to the will and leading of God (see Talbert, *Reading John*, p. 172). For **Mary … anointed the Lord**, see 12:1–8.

11:4. This sickness is not unto death anticipates the raising of Lazarus (see 11:44), since Jesus already knew his death would occur (see 11:14). In fact, Lazarus must have died shortly after the messengers left Bethany, accounting for the "four days" of 11:17, 39: one day for the journey of the messengers, the two days when Jesus remained where He was (see 11:6; 10:40), and a day for Jesus' journey to Bethany (but see discussion on 11:17). **The glory of God** (see 9:3) and the glorification of Jesus (see discussions on 7:39; 12:41; 13:31–32) are linked by Jesus' agency and representation of the Father (see discussion on 5:41–44). **The Son of God [would] be glorified** through what happened to Lazarus, partly because the miracle would display the glory of God (who alone can raise the dead; see 5:21) in Jesus (see 11:40) and partly because it would help initiate events leading to the cross (see 11:46–53).

11:5–6. Jesus loved (v. 5) this family (see discussion on 11:1–3). As John thus underscored, it was not indifference that led Jesus when **he abode … where he was** (v. 6). Jesus moved as the Father directed, not as people (here Mary and Martha) wished (see 2:3–4).

11:7–8. Then (v. 7) clarifies the divine will and timetable (see 11:4) according to which Jesus acted, despite His personal relationships (see 11:5) or safety. To **go into Judea again** clearly presented danger, for **the Jews** (see discussion on 1:19) **… sought to stone thee** (v. 8; see discussion on 10:31).

11:9–10. Twelve hours in the day (v. 9) specifies daylight hours allotted each person to accomplish what is obligated. Jesus was under obligation to the Father, which transcended the danger of returning to Judea (see 11:8). There was enough time for what needed to be done, but no time for waste. To help

the disciples to grasp this, Jesus placed Himself in the metaphor: He was their daylight, and they must trust Him (see 8:12; 9:5; 12:35–36, 46).

11:11–13. Sleepeth (Greek, *koimaomai*; v. 11) is a euphemism for death, used by the unbelieving world as well as by Christians (see 1 Thess. 4:14–15). The disciples took Jesus literally, thereby assuming that Lazarus would recover, which would obviate any need to go to Judea.

11:14–16. Jesus dispelled the disciples' confusion and their hope of staying out of Judea with a blunt clarification of Lazarus's condition: **Lazarus is dead** (v. 14). Jesus' obligation had become their obligation (see 11:9–10 and discussion), and they could learn to trust Him (**believe**; v. 15) through this trip into Judea with its attendant danger (see 11:7–8). The Hebrew word from which **Thomas** is derived (v. 16) and the Greek word **Didymus** both mean "twin." Thomas is usually remembered for his doubting, but he was also capable of devotion and courage. Knowing the danger Jesus faced in Judea, Thomas said, **Let us also go, that we may die with him**.

11:17. Four days (see discussion on 11:4) confirmed what Jesus had already revealed, that Lazarus was unquestionably dead (see 11:14). Many Jews believed that the soul remained near the body for three days after death in the hope of returning to it. If this idea was in the minds of these people, they obviously thought all hope was gone; Lazarus was irrevocably dead.

11:18–19. It was usual for friends to visit the family **to comfort them** (v. 19). John's details of the distance of Bethany from Jerusalem implies that many who came to comfort the family traveled from Jerusalem. **Fifteen furlongs** (v. 18) was just less than two miles. A "furlong" identifies the Greek *stadiōn* (compare English "stadium"), which measures 606 feet 9 inches, or an eighth of a Roman mile. Jewish custom provided for three days of very heavy mourning, then four days of heavy mourning, followed by lighter mourning for the remainder of thirty days.

11:20. Martha … went and met him, perhaps because as the elder, she was hostess and was alerted to Jesus' near arrival (see 11:30). **Mary sat ... in the house**, mourning (see 11:31) with those who had gathered (for Martha and Mary, see Luke 10:38–42). It is possible that Mary was unaware of Jesus' arrival (see 11:28–30; note "secretly," 11:28).

11:21. When Martha saw Jesus, she said, **If thou hadst been here, my brother had not died**. Mary repeated this statement in 11:32. Perhaps the sisters had said this to one another often as they awaited Jesus' arrival. Clearly, they had every confidence in Jesus' power to heal their brother, and with the window of opportunity closed by Lazarus's death, their grief spilled forth in a contrary-to-fact wish: "If you had been here, but you were not; my brother would not have died, but he did."

11:22. Whatsoever thou wilt ask. This comment seems to indicate that Martha hoped for an immediate resurrection in spite of the fact that Lazarus's body had already begun to decay. Nothing is too difficult for God to do.

11:23–24. On the surface, it appears that Jesus assented to fulfill Martha's request: **Thy brother shall rise again** (v. 23). Martha's answer, however, makes it clear that she received this apparent assent as holding no more promise than a pious consolation to the grieving, expressing confidence in the final **resurrection** (v. 24). Martha heard **at the last day** (v. 24) and not "today." Strictly worded, Jesus expressed nothing more than the Pharisaic belief in the resurrection (see Acts 23:8; Josephus *War* 2.8.14; Mishnah, Sanhedrin 10:1), which was the more widely held view of life after death than that of the Sadducees (see Mark 12:18–27).

11:25–26. Martha wanted Jesus to petition God (see 11:22). Jesus wanted Martha to understand that the Father had "given all things into his hands" (3:35; 13:3) and that the resurrection and the life she sought were not only His to bestow (5:21, 24–29) but were resident in Him and realized through personal faith in Him. What she abstractly attributed to God is to be identified with the person of Jesus: **I am the resurrection, and the life** (v. 25; see discussion on 6:35). Jesus is life (see 1:4; 14:6; Acts 3:15; Heb. 7:16; 1 John 5:11–12). **He that believeth ... shall**

he live is the confirming confidence that death will never triumph over the one who finds the resurrection and the life in Jesus (see 1 Cor. 15:54–57).

11:27. Yea, Lord; I believe. Martha is often remembered for her shortcoming recorded in Luke 10:40–41, but she was a woman of faith, as this magnificent declaration shows. It succinctly embodies the highest tenets of personal belief in the person and work of Jesus in John's gospel (see 20:31). Indeed, it closes Martha's concern with an assent of trust marked by her departure (see 11:28).

11:28–30. The Master (v. 28), or literally, "the Teacher," a significant description to be given by a woman. The rabbis would not teach women (see 4:27), but Jesus taught them frequently. **Secretly**, or without others being aware, either privately or with whispers, Martha alerted Mary to the arrival and whereabouts of Jesus. Carson (*The Gospel According to John*, p. 414) has suggested that Jesus remained outside the village for the purpose of separate private time with the sisters, an impossibility in a house full of mourners and a better explanation in light of 11:11 than that of protection or anonymity.

11:31. Wailing at a tomb was common, and **the Jews** (see discussion on 1:19) immediately thought Mary had in mind **to weep there**. Jesus may have requested a private meeting with Mary, but her hasty departure caught the attention of the mourners. Because they followed her, Jesus got maximum publicity.

11:32–34. Lord, if thou hadst been here (v. 32). Mary repeated Martha's statement (see 11:21). The two occurrences of the word **weeping** (v. 33) both denote a loud expression of grief, that is, "wailing." Jesus was deeply and internally moved: **he groaned in the spirit** is matched by "groaning in himself" in 11:38. In both places, the word "groaned" (Greek, *embrimaomai*) is closer to an "an articulate expression of anger" (Brown, *The Gospel According to John*, p. 425) and implies a sense of indignation or emotional vexation within Jesus (see Matt. 9:30; Mark 1:43). It was more than empathy or grief and closer to ire welling up within Him. For **troubled** (Greek, *tarassō*; "agitated") see 12:27; 13:21; discussion on

14:1. Jesus' strong inner reaction is probably best understood as His reaction to the despoiling effects of sin and its most potent outcome: death, with its wake of anguish and grief. Before this triumph of death, with its victory trumpeted in wailing, stood Jesus, "the resurrection, and the life" (11:25), and the scene brought forth not only His guttural indignation but also His intervention: **Where have ye laid him?** (v. 34.)

11:35–37. Jesus wept (v. 35). The Greek word used here for "wept" is not the one for loud grief, as in 11:33, but one that denotes quiet weeping, that is, "shed tears." Observing the tears of Jesus, perhaps more authentic than some of the mourning at that point, others noted Jesus' love for Lazarus (v. 36, see 11:5). Their position, **Could not this man ...?** (v. 37), echoes that of Martha (see 11:21) and Mary (see 11:32): there could have been a different outcome if Jesus had arrived prior to Lazarus's death. Although Jesus **opened the eyes of the blind** (see chap. 9), the reality of the power of death prevailed in the beliefs of those who had yet to realize that Jesus is "the resurrection, and the life" (11:25).

11:38–39. Again groaning in himself (v. 38; see 11:33). John clarified that **the grave**, or tomb, **was a cave** with an horizontal approach rather than a vertical shaft. The **stone** prevented the approach of animals. Martha's objection proves how startling was the command of Jesus to remove the stone. It also confirms that she did not expect Jesus to raise her brother that very day and that she had more to fathom from her earlier conversation with Jesus (see 11:23–27 and discussions). For **four days**, see discussions on 11:4, 17.

11:40. Jesus had used the expression **the glory of God** with the disciples (see discussion on 11:4) but not expressly with Martha. Carson (*The Gospel According to John*, p. 418) deems His use of this expression a summary of what was promised in 11:23–26.

11:41–42. The prayerful acknowledgment of the Father accorded with Jesus' purpose here, as elsewhere: to glorify God (see 11:4, 40). As in 11:4, the glory of God was inextricably linked with the glorification and acknowledgment of His representative,

the one whom God had sent, who acted on God's behalf and for His benefit.

11:43–44. He cried with a loud voice (v. 43) is proleptic of that day when the dead shall hear the voice of the Son of God (see 5:25, 28–29). No one present could mistake that it was the voice of Jesus to whom Lazarus **came forth** (v. 44). **Graveclothes** were narrow strips of cloth, like bandages. Sometimes a shroud was used (see discussion on 19:40). **A napkin** was a separate item (see 20:7). **Loose him, and let him go** signaled that Lazarus was alive.

11:45–46. Many of the Jews (see discussion on 1:19) **... believed on him** (v. 45; see 20:31) implies that perhaps some who had been opposed to Jesus now came to believe in Him. On the other hand, **some** (v. 46) could only defer what they had seen with their own eyes to the opinion of **the Pharisees**. The actions of these people may not have been hostile. The Pharisees believed in the resurrection (see discussion on 11:23–24), and those who **told them what ... Jesus had done** may have had an agreeable intent. The consequent action of the Pharisees (see 11:47), however, underscored their opposition to Jesus.

11:47. The chief priests and the Pharisees. In all four gospels, the Pharisees appear as Jesus' principal opponents throughout His public ministry. They lacked political power, however, and it was the chief priests who were prominent in the events that led to Jesus' crucifixion. Here both groups associated in a meeting of the Sanhedrin (see discussion on Mark 14:55). They did not deny that Jesus did **many miracles** ("signs"; see discussion on 2:11), but they did not understand their meaning, for they failed to believe.

11:48. Our place most likely refers to the temple (see Acts 6:13–14; 21:28), though sometimes the Jews used the expression to denote Jerusalem.

11:49. Caiaphas, the high priest circa AD 18–36, was the son-in-law of Annas (see 18:13), who had been deposed from the high priesthood by the Romans in AD 15. **The high priest that same year** means "the high priest at that time." The high priesthood was not an annual office but one supposed to be held for life. **Ye know nothing at all** is a remark typical of Sadducean rudeness (Caiaphas, as high priest, was a Sadducee). Josephus (*Jewish War* 2.17.14) says that the Sadducees "in their intercourse with their peers are as rude as to aliens." (For the Sadducees, see discussions on Matt. 2:4; 3:7; Mark 12:18; Luke 20:27; Acts 4:1.)

11:50. It is expedient for us. Caiaphas was concerned with political expediency, not with guilt and innocence. He believed that **one man**, no matter how innocent, should perish rather than that **the whole nation** be put in jeopardy. Ironically, the Jews went ahead with their execution of Jesus, and in AD 70, the nation perished nonetheless.

11:51. Being high priest, Caiaphas was not a private citizen but God's high priest, and God ruled over what he said. For **that year**, see discussion on 11:49. Caiaphas **prophesied** in that his words were true in a way he could not imagine. Prophecy in Scripture is the impartation of divinely revealed truth. In reality, Caiaphas's words meant that Jesus' death would be **for [the] nation**, not by removing political trouble but by taking away the sins of those who believed in Him.

11:52. The children of God ... scattered abroad makes it clear that Jesus' death would have effects far beyond the nation (see, e.g., 1:29; 3:16; 4:42; 10:16).

11:53–54. Jesus' opponents now sought to **put him to death** (v. 53), but **went thence** (v. 54) again shows that Jesus was not to die before His "hour" (see discussion on 2:4). He did not act imprudently, however. Knowing the attitude of His opponents, He withdrew. He would die for others, but in His own time, not that of His enemies. If **Ephraim** was the city known as Ophrah, it was about fifteen miles north of Jerusalem.

11:55. For passover, see discussions on 2:13; 5:1. It was especially important for the Jews **to purify themselves** at a time like Passover, because otherwise they could not keep the feast (see 18:28; see discussion on 2:6–7).

IV. The Passion Week (chaps. 12–19)

A. The Anointing of Jesus' Feet (12:1–11)

12:1–11. All four gospels present an account of a woman anointing Jesus. John's account seems to tell of the same incident recorded in Matthew 26:6–13 and Mark 14:3–9, while that in Luke 7:36–50 is different.

12:1–2. Key words such as **Bethany** (see discussion on Matt. 21:17) and **Lazarus** easily set the scene, connecting Jesus' demonstration of His identity as "the resurrection, and the life" (11:25) in the events of chapter 11 with Mary's anointing of Him, which presaged His own death (see 12:7) at Passover, six days away. For **Martha served**, see Luke 10:38–42. The note that **Lazarus ... sat at the table with him** shows the normal life to which Lazarus had been restored with being raised from the dead by Jesus.

12:3. Spikenard denotes both a plant and the fragrant oil it yielded. Since it was **very costly** (Greek, *polytimos*; "very precious," "very valuable"), Mary's act of devotion was costly. It was also an unusual act, both because she poured the oil on Jesus' **feet** (normally it was poured on the head) and because she used **her hair** to wipe them (a respectable woman did not unbind her hair in public). Further, it showed her humility, for it was a servant's work to attend to the feet (see discussions on 1:27; 13:5).

12:4–5. What Jesus saw as a costly and humble act of devotion worthy of His death (see 12:7), **Judas Iscariot** (v. 4; see discussion on 6:71) saw as an extravagant and prodigal waste. Judas estimated the value of the costly ointment at **three hundred pence** (v. 5), or denarii. One denarius was a day's wage (see Matt. 20:2), and thus Mary's anointing equaled the annual wage of a laborer and could have fed many who were without food (see 6:7).

12:6. Perhaps a gauge of Mary's extravagance is to be discerned in what John's readers might have thought, for John was quick to clarify and separate the motives of Judas from those of the observer, with the revelation that **he was a thief**. This is the one passage from which we learn that Judas was dishonest. He must have been thought to be a man of some reliability, however, for he was the keeper of the money bag.

12:7–8. Jesus defended Mary's action by exposing an intention entirely foreign to the mindset of Judas. The meaning of **kept** (v. 7) is probably "saved for this purpose." Perfume was normally associated with festivity, but it was also used in burials (see 19:39–40), and Jesus linked it with His burial, which Mary's anointing unwittingly anticipated. It is not that **the poor** (v. 8) are unimportant, but unlike the priority of Jesus, the precedence of the poor is limitless (see Deut. 15:11; see Matt. 26:11; Mark 14:7).

12:9–11. The crowd that came to see not only Jesus but **Lazarus also, whom he had raised from the dead** (v. 9), heightened the resolve of the Jewish leaders to eliminate the threat (see v. 11). The Jewish leaders previously had spoken of the death of Jesus (see 11:50–53), but now they conspired to **put Lazarus also to death** (v. 10). Sin grows.

B. The Triumphal Entry (12:12–19)

12:12. Much people identifies the pilgrims who had come up from the country for the Passover feast. Many of the pilgrims had doubtless seen and heard Jesus in Galilee, and they welcomed the opportunity to proclaim Him as Messiah.

12:13. Branches of palm trees were used in celebration of victory. Later in his life, John saw a multitude with palm branches in heaven (see Rev. 7:9). **Hosanna** was a Hebrew expression meaning "Save!" that became an exclamation of praise (see *KJV Study Bible* note on Jer. 31:7). The people added an acclamation, **the King of Israel**, to the words of the psalm (see Ps. 118:25–26), which John alone recorded. It reflects his special interest in Jesus' royalty, which he brought out throughout the passion narrative. **In the name of the Lord** carries a notable significance in John, for Jesus was the unique one sent in the Father's divine name (see 5:43; 10:25; 17:11–12).

12:14–15. A young ass (v. 14; see Matt. 21:2, 7; Mark 11:2; Luke 19:30) has messianic overtones in light of Zechariah 9:9. The political and nationalistic aspirations of the crowd implied in the acclamation "King of Israel" (12:13) were different from those of the humble King who fulfilled Zechariah 9:9.

12:16. Only after the crucifixion and the coming of the Holy Spirit did the disciples appreciate the meaning of the prophecy of Zechariah 9:9 and its fulfillment. The later illumination of the disciples is

an example of the meaning of 16:13. For **glorified**, see discussions on 12:41; 11:4; 13:31.

12:17–19. Two crowds are described in John's account of the triumphal entry. The crowd that had witnessed the raising of **Lazarus** (v. 17) came with Jesus and was met by the crowd of 12:12–13, which had come out of Jerusalem to see Him. The one bore witness to what they had seen as it met the second, which had heard the news and had come from Jerusalem. This general enthusiasm was loaded with political implications, and the ramifications were not lost on the frustrated **Pharisees** (v. 19; see 11:46–50).

C. The Coming of the Greeks (12:20–36)

12:20–22. The **Greeks** (or Gentiles; v. 20) who sought an audience with Jesus represent "the whole world" (Carson, *The Gospel According to John*, p. 435). They belonged to the ranks of "God-fearers," people attracted to Judaism by its monotheism and morality but repelled by its nationalism and requirements such as circumcision. They worshiped in the synagogues but did not become proselytes. As Brown (*The Gospel According to John*, p. 466) insists, "only the understanding that the first Gentiles have come to Jesus explains his exclamation that the hour has come" (see 12:23).

Philip (v. 21) is a Greek name, which may be why the Greeks came to this disciple (though he was not the only one of the Twelve to have a Greek name). **See** means "to have an interview with." The roundabout approach to Jesus is left unexplained but may underscore the novelty and therefore the uncertainty of how Jesus would receive Gentiles (see Carson, *The Gospel According to John*, p. 427). After verse 22, John recorded no more about these Greeks (but see discussion on 12:32). He regarded their coming as important but not their conversation with Jesus. Jesus came to die for the world, and the coming of these Gentiles indicated the scope of the effectiveness of His approaching crucifixion.

12:23–24. The hour is come (v. 23). The hour to which Jesus' whole ministry had led (see discussions on 2:4; 12:20). **Glorified.** Jesus was speaking about

His death on the cross and His subsequent resurrection and exaltation (see discussions on 11:4; 12:41; 13:31). Jesus used the metaphor of **a corn of wheat** (v. 24) to convey the necessity of His death: **if it die, it bringeth forth**. The principle of life through death is seen in the plant world. The kernel must perish as a kernel if there is to be a plant.

12:25-26. He that hateth his life ... shall keep it (v. 25; see Matt. 16:24-25; Mark 8:34-35; Luke 9:23-24). To love one's life here and now—to concentrate on one's own success—is to lose what matters. Supremely, of course, the principle is seen in the cross of Jesus and the implications of His hour, with its glorification for those that follow and serve Jesus. "Hateth" is a Semitic expression that implies "loves less." One's love for God must be such that all other loves are, by comparison, hatred. For **life eternal**, see discussion on 3:15.

12:27. Now is my soul troubled (Greek, *tarassō*) is John's equivalent to the agony in Gethsemane described in the other gospels. **This hour** (see 12:23-24) held for Jesus the prospect of becoming sin (or a sin offering) for sinful people (see 2 Cor. 5:21). He considered praying for God to save Him from this death but refused to pray it because the very reason He had come was to die.

12:28. Father, glorify thy name. Jesus' prayer was not for deliverance but for the Father to be glorified. **A voice from heaven** gave the answer. For "name," see discussions on 2:23; 5:43; see also 10:25; 17:11-12.

12:29-30. Jesus heard distinctly what the crowd mistook for thunder or the voice of an **angel** (v. 29). Although our knowledge of what **This voice** (v. 30) said must have been mediated by Jesus, who presumably revealed it to the disciples, in the language of exaggerated contrast, Jesus explained it was more for their sake than for His. This point is confirmed by the existing record.

12:31. Of this world. The cross was God's judgment on the world. **The prince of this world** identifies Satan (see 16:11). The cross would seem to be his triumph, but in fact, it was his defeat. Out of it would flow the greatest good ever to come to the world.

12:32-33. Lifted up (v. 32; see discussion on 3:14) alludes to the cross, the supreme exaltation of Jesus (see discussions on 12:41; 13:31). It is significant that Greek Gentiles were present on this occasion (see 12:20). Through His death and resurrection, Christ would **draw all** people to Himself, without regard for nationality, ethnic affiliation, or status. "Draw" renders a form of legal Jewish acquisition. Through the cross, Jesus acquired, or took legal possession of, "all" by drawing to Himself that which rightfully belongs to God and thereby divested (evicted) the ruler of this world from his hold on God's possession. **Signifying what death** (v. 33) refers to the manner of His death ("lifted up") and its purpose (to "draw all").

12:34. The law here seems to mean Old Testament Scripture in general (see discussion on 10:34), the reference being to passages such as Psalms 89:36; 110:4; Isaiah 9:7; Daniel 7:14. No particular Scripture says the **Christ abideth for ever**, but Psalm 89:36 is a close possibility (see Brown, *The Gospel According to John*, p. 469). For "Christ" (or "Messiah"), see discussion on 1:25. In Aramaic, **the Son of man** is the equivalent of "I" (12:32), but in context, it could have messianic overtones. The people sensed the "more" in what Jesus was saying and inquired how what He was saying related to their understanding of the Messiah. Here is the only place in the Gospels where anyone other than Jesus used the expression "the Son of man," and even here Jesus was being quoted (see discussion on Mark 2:10).

12:35-36. The light (v. 35) is closely identified with Jesus, as seen from the call to **believe in the light** (v. 36; see discussions on 1:4; 8:12). **Lest darkness come upon you** (v. 35) is literally, "lest darkness overcome you," as in "the darkness comprehended it not" (1:5), or "the darkness did not overtake it (the light)." Jesus did not debate but, as "the light of men" (1:4; see 8:12), challenged them to acknowledge the light (Jesus), that is, to believe and walk in it. **Children** (or "sons") **of** is a Semitic idiom. The hereditary meaning led to the figurative "characterized by" (see, e.g., "Barnabas ... The son of consolation," Acts 4:36).

D. Continued Jewish Unbelief (12:37–50)

12:37–40. They believed not on him (v. 37). God's ancient people should have responded when He sent His Messiah. They should have seen the significance of the signs Jesus did. John related this hardened unbelief to the fulfillment of Isaiah 53:1 (see Rom. 10:16). The idea of seeing and not believing is also prominent in God's judgment in verses 39–40 (compare 9:39–41 and the sign of healing the blind man). The words **could not believe** (v. 39) mean not that the people in question had no choice. They purposely rejected God and chose evil, therefore **He hath blinded their eyes, and hardened their heart** (v. 40). These words from Isaiah 6:10 were quoted by Jesus (see Matt. 13:14–15; Mark 4:12; Luke 8:10) and by Paul (see Acts 28:26–27). Many Jewish leaders did believe in Jesus as the Messiah, however (see 12:42).

12:41. Saw his glory. Isaiah spoke primarily of the glory of God (see Isa. 6:3). John spoke of the glory of Jesus and made no basic distinction between the two, attesting Jesus' oneness with God. Thus, if "his" refers to Jesus (preincarnate), the judicial hardening (see 12:40) belongs to Him as well (see Carson, *The Gospel According to John*, p. 450). The thought of "glory" here is complex and includes majesty and the idea (which meant so much to John) that Jesus' death on the cross and His subsequent resurrection and exaltation showed His real glory. Isaiah foresaw the rejection of Christ, as the passages (Isa. 53:1; 6:10) quoted in 12:38–40 show. He spoke of the Messiah in the words both about blind eyes and hard hearts, on the one hand, and about healing, on the other. This is the cross and this is glory, for the cross and resurrection and exaltation portrayed both suffering and healing, rejection and triumph, humiliation and glory.

12:42–43. Among the chief rulers ... believed (v. 42; see discussion on 1:7). John did not give a picture of unrelieved gloom. Many Jewish leaders believed, though they remained secret believers for fear of excommunication (see discussion on 9:18–23). **They loved the praise** (lit., "glory") **of men more than the praise of God** (v. 43; see 5:44).

12:44–45. Words that are said to have been **cried** (v. 44) or spoken in a loud voice give what was uttered a special emphasis. **Believeth on me**. John ended his story of Jesus' public ministry with an appeal for belief. He did not say when Jesus spoke these words (they may have been uttered earlier), but they are a fitting close to this part of his account. Belief in Jesus is ultimately belief in **him that sent me** (see 1:18). Jesus' mission and representation of the Father, as well as the inseparability of the Father and the Son, are stressed throughout this gospel and given summary emphasis here.

12:46. The words **I am come ... into the world** point to both Jesus' preexistence and His mission. For **light**, summarized here, see discussions on 1:4; 8:12.

12:47–49. To judge (v. 47) was not the purpose of Jesus' coming. Judgment, however, is the other side of salvation. It is not the purpose of the sun's shining to cast shadows, but when the sun shines, shadows are inevitable. The theme of judgment is tied to Jesus' mission and representation of the Father's will (see 5:30; 7:42; 8:15–16, 26; see also 9:39–41). **The Father ... gave me a commandment, what I should say** (v. 49). Because Jesus is the authorized representative of the Father, Jesus' hearers have a great responsibility. His **word** (v. 48) is that which the Father commanded Him to say. To reject it, therefore, is to reject God.

12:50. Life everlasting (see discussion on 3:15) is the content of the Father's command and the purpose of His sending Jesus to the world. Jesus **therefore** said what He did to fulfill the will of the Father, a wonderful note on which to end the account of Jesus' public ministry.

E. Farewell Discourses (chaps. 13–17)

1. Discourse at the Last Supper (chaps. 13–14)

13:1–17:26. John has by far the longest account of the upper room, though curiously, he recorded nothing about the institution of the Lord's Supper. Nonetheless, John records the most detail about what the Lord said to His disciples on that night. One feature of the discourse is Jesus' emphasis on love. The Greek noun (*agapē*) and verb (*agapaō*) for "love" occur only eight times in chapters 1–12 but thirty-one times in chapters 13–17.

13:1. Before the feast of the Passover (see discussions on 2:13; 5:1) suggests to some that this feast was a fellowship meal or "supper" (13:2) eaten sometime before the Passover feast. This would mean that the Last Supper could not have been the Passover meal as the Synoptic Gospels clearly indicate. However, this was probably intended to be a Passover-like meal and celebrated as a substitute in significance. In the gospel of John, Jesus is crucified at the time the Passover lambs were being slaughtered for the Passover feast (see 19:14; compare Dabny, *Mishnah*, Pesa 5.1, 3). **His hour** (see discussion on 2:4) would demonstrate the extent of Jesus' love. **He loved them unto the end** (Greek, *eis telos*) may express adverbally the extent of His love as "fully" or "utterly."

13:2. The desires of **the devil** (Greek, *diabolos*; "slanderer"; see 6:70; 8:44; see 13:27) had already influenced a plan in **the heart of Judas Iscariot** (see discussion on 6:71). John emphasized this influence with a play on words. In accordance with his name, the Devil had "cast deception" and **put** (lit., "cast"; Greek, *ballō*) into Judas's heart the plan **to betray** Jesus. And Judas received it.

13:3. The Father had given all things into his hands (see 3:35). The Father vested the Son with all authority and control in carrying out His will. His death was by no means outside of the Father's purpose for sending His Son. John again emphasized the fulfillment of God's plan and Jesus' control of the situation.

13:4–5. Began to wash the disciples' feet (v. 5). Sandaled feet become grimy with travel. It was customary hospitality to provide water for a guest to wash his own feet (see Luke 7:44). To wash another's feet was viewed as such a menial task (see discussion on 1:27; see 1 Sam. 24:41) that even Jewish slaves should not be required to perform it (Midrash, Mekilta 82a on Exodus 21:2). On this occasion, Jesus deliberately washed His disciples' feet during the meal (v. 4) rather than upon their arrival to emphasize a point. It was a lesson in humility, but it also set forth

the principle of selfless service that would so soon be exemplified in the cross. John alone recorded this incident, but Luke reported that in rebuking the disciples over a quarrel concerning who would be the greatest, Jesus said, "I am among you as he that serveth" (Luke 22:27). Jesus' life of service would culminate on the cross (see Phil. 2:5–8 and discussions).

13:6–9. Never (v. 8). Characteristically, Peter objected, though apparently no one else did. Jesus' reply, **If I wash thee not, thou hast no part with me**, shows that a crucial lesson was being taught and Peter had to learn it if he was to have anything to do with Jesus. Peter then realized what was at stake and thus asked Jesus to wash every part of him that might need to be cleaned (because of exposure), including **my hands and my head** (v. 9). What was the crucial lesson? Peter, like all disciples, had to accept the reversal of roles that the Master and Lord willingly accepts in order to love. What was menial service for any person, none other than the Lord and Master Himself assumed to exemplify what the cross would epitomize. As Jesus later taught (see 13:12–15), and as every disciple must learn, no title is too majestic and no service is too menial for such sacrificial love. It is a most profound lesson that every disciple must learn to be identified with Jesus; such is the thrust of much of this chapter.

13:9–11. Peter first refused Jesus' humble service, then, still not understanding, connected the washing to cleanliness. Wanting to "have a part with Jesus" (see 13:8), Peter asked for more washing, dramatically reversing his initial refusal. He did not need more, however, **save to wash his feet** (v. 10). A man would bathe himself before going to a feast. When he arrived, he needed to wash only his feet to be entirely clean again. Although Jesus corrected Peter's request for an extended washing, He then pivoted from the physical to the spiritual, by exempting one (Judas) from the declaration **ye are clean**. John immediately explained Jesus' shift. **He knew** (v. 11), as the others did not, that Judas, whose feet Jesus had washed, would **betray Him**.

13:12–13. After washing the feet of each disciple, Jesus fully interpreted His actions and explained the lesson shown to be so crucial at Peter's initial refusal (see 13:8). He who is **Master and Lord** (v. 13) became lower than a servant to wash their feet (see discussion on 13:4–5). Such a reversal of roles by none other than the Master and Lord demonstrated the obligation of love for those who call Him Master and Lord. An instructor would normally be called "master," or "teacher," but "Lord" referred to one occupying the supreme place. Jesus accepted both titles. Some Christians believe that Christ intended to institute a footwashing ordinance to be practiced regularly. More than an ordinance, however, Jesus was exemplifying a lowly and humble attitude that comes from sacrificial love, is epitomized in the cross, and is identified with His own character.

13:14–15. To wash one another's feet (v. 14) is symbolic (**an example**; v. 15), as was Jesus' action, and not limited by its literal wording. Disciples must be willing to perform the most menial services for one another. **Do as I have done to you** is tantamount to saying, "Let not your status or a menial task get in the way of serving one another with the love I have shown you."

13:16. Jesus used easily recognizable social institutions to illustrate clearly demarcated roles of obligation: the **servant** ("slave") and the **lord**; the representative (**he that is sent**) and the sender. A little later, Jesus would personalize the connections made here between His disciples and both the "servant" (see 15:15, 20) and the representative (see 13:20; 20:21). For now, the implication was clear: no servant has any right to judge a task menial which his master has already performed, and no representative is excluded from undertaking what his sender has deemed worthy of doing. With minor variations, this saying, which Jesus used often, is found in 15:20; Matthew 10:24; Luke 6:40 (see also Luke 22:27).

13:17. Happy points to a spiritual reality that defied the social judgments of Jesus' day, as it does still today. It can be affirmed only by doing; obedience is the path to knowing and understanding.

13:18. I speak not of you all. Jesus was leading up to His impending betrayal (see 13:21). **Eateth bread with me**. To eat bread together was a mark of close fellowship (see *KJV Study Bible* note on Ps.

41:9). **Hath lifted up his heel against me** is perhaps derived from a horse's preparing to kick or from shaking off the dust from one's feet (see Luke 9:5; 10:11); both are signs of contempt.

13:19. That, when it come to pass, ye may believe (see 20:31) shows Jesus' concern for the disciples, not Himself. **I am he** is an emphatic form of speech, such as that in 8:58 (see discussion there).

13:20. Whomsoever I send receiveth me; and … him that sent me. Jesus' mission as the representative of the Father is a major theme of this gospel (see Introduction: "Theme and Theological Message"). Jesus now linked the mission of His followers with His own mission (see 20:21).

13:21. For troubled, see 11:33 and discussion on 14:1. Though Jesus knew long before it happened that a friend would betray Him, He was nonetheless grieved.

13:22. Doubting of whom he spake. The disciples' astonishment shows that Judas had concealed his collaboration with Jewish authorities to betray Jesus. No one suspected him (see 13:28), but all seem to have thought that the betrayal would be involuntary (see Mark 14:19).

13:23. At a dinner, guests reclined on couches, **leaning** on the left elbow with the head toward the table. **One of his disciples, whom Jesus loved** is usually thought to be John, the author of this gospel (see 19:26; 20:2; 21:7, 20). The expression does not, of course, mean that Jesus did not love the others but rather that there was a special bond with this man.

13:24–26. He it is, to whom I shall give a sop, when I have dipped it (v. 26). Evidently Judas was near Jesus, possibly in the seat of honor. In the Mediterranean with its code of honor and shame, it was a gesture of intimacy to allow a guest to dip his "sop," or "piece of bread," in one's bowl. The intimacy of Jesus' act starkly contrasted the act of betrayal it identified. Reciprocity to such intimacy was expected. Ironically, in the other gospels, Judas met it with the kiss of betrayal (see Matt. 26:48; Mark 14:44; Luke 22:47), but John did not report it or what happened to Judas following the betrayal, which Matthew reported in his gospel (Matt. 27:3–10).

John used Judas's full name (see discussion on 6:71) in recording this solemn moment.

13:27–29. After the sop (v. 27) identifies the critical moment. If giving bread to Judas was a mark of honor, it also seems to have been a final appeal, which Judas did not accept. Rather than reciprocity, the hardness of Judas's resistance is seen in the expression **Satan entered into him** (compare the language of possession in Mark 5:12; Luke 8:30). The name Satan (Hebrew, *ûâṭân;* "adversary") is used only here in John (see 13:2). Jesus' words, **Do quickly**, once more indicate His control. He would die as He directed, not as His opponents determined.

For what intent (v. 28) Jesus said this to Judas was not clear to the disciples. John, who was reporting, excluded himself (see 13:25–26) and reported only what the others surmised. Some thought Jesus intended Judas to purchase food for **the feast** (v. 29; see discussion on 13:1), perhaps the Feast of Unleavened Bread, which follows Passover; others thought He intended Judas to care for **the poor** (see 12:5).

13:30. In light of John's emphasis on the conflict between light and darkness, **night** may here be more than a time note, picturing also the darkness of Judas's soul.

13:31–32. The Son of man (v. 31; see discussion on Mark 2:10) and **glorified** (see discussion on 7:39) are connected here with the inevitability of the cross (see 3:13–14; 6:62; 8:28; 12:34 see 13:23), which was now impending. As inglorious as crucifixion was meant to be, Jesus' sacrificial death on the cross was far from inglorious. It manifested the glorious salvation that the Father sent His Son to achieve. Therefore, **God is glorified in him** (v. 32). The glory of the Father is closely bound to the attainment of what the Father sent the Son to do.

13:33–34. In a sense, **a new commandment** (v. 34) was an old one (see Lev. 19:18), but for Jesus' disciples it was new because it was the mark of their brotherhood, created by His great love for them (see Matt. 22:37–39; Mark 12:30–31; Luke 10:27). The standard is Christ's love for us: **as I have loved you**.

13:35. Love is the distinguishing mark of Jesus' followers (see 1 John 3:23; 4:7–8, 11–12, 19–21).

13:36. Whither goest thou? Peter seems to have ignored Jesus' words about love and was more concerned about his Master's departure. In Jesus' reply, **thou** is singular and thus personal to Peter, whereas in 13:33, "ye" is plural.

13:37. The words **I will lay down my life** are similar to those of the good shepherd in 10:11. Peter was characteristically sure of himself, when in fact he would not at this time lay down his life for Jesus. Exactly the opposite would be true.

13:38. Denied me thrice. Peter's denial of Jesus is prophesied in all four gospels (see Matt. 26:33–35; Mark 14:29–31; Luke 22:31–34).

14:1. Jesus' talk of death and departure distressed the disciples, and He offered them words of confident encouragement: **Let not your heart be troubled**. "Troubled" (Greek, *tarassō*) is a vivid word that can mean "agitated" or "disturbed." John used it of the water that was "troubled" in 5:7. Jesus Himself knew what it was to be troubled (see 11:33; 12:27; 13:21). "Your" is plural. All the disciples needed comfort. The "heart" is the seat of the emotional, intellectual, and volitional life. In this sense, all of life is lived out of the heart. In speaking of the heart, Jesus was speaking not only to their feelings but also to their faith: **ye believe in God, believe also in me**. This is Jesus' antidote for a troubled heart. The KJV translates this as a statement (indicative mood) followed by a command (imperative mood). The grammar permits this, but it also permits other combinations. The strongest option is two imperatives: "Believe in God; believe also in me." This corresponds not only to "Let not your heart be troubled" (imperative) but also to the underlying need of a troubled heart: faith in God. The heart of God is known through Jesus. The certainty of His word, the basis of the peace He offers the troubled heart, is that His word is as God's word; His heart is as God's heart.

14:2–3. My Father's house (v. 2) refers to heaven, the abode of **many mansions**. "Mansions" is literally "dwellings," or places to abide (Greek, *monē*, from the verb *menō*; "remain," "abide"). In the Father's house, there is ample room for permanent living. There is no rival in all Scripture to the tender picture that these verses present of God the Father's household filled with rooms and, by extension, alive with His children. They need not fear the future. **I go to prepare a place for you.** The Father's house already exists. Jesus was saying not that He must go to build it but rather that He must go because His departure and return to the Father (the cross and resurrection) was the means of enabling believers to inhabit the house of the Father. In addition to preparing the way, however, He is also preparing a dwelling place for them in the Father's house. The terminology is reminiscent of the Jewish wedding custom in which the betrothed groom (Christ) prepares a place for his bride (the church) in his father's house (heaven). **I will come again** (v. 3) refers to the rapture, when Jesus will return to take the believers home to the Father's house (see 1 Thess. 4:13–17).

14:4. The emphasis here is on **the way**, which anticipates Jesus' statement, "I am the way" (14:6). Peter's question of 13:36 had been answered (see 14:2–3), and the disciples now knew not only "whither goest thou?" (13:36) but "the way" (Jesus), even though they continued to think geographically.

14:5. Thomas was candid and plainly told the Lord that he and the others (**we**) did not understand the answer to Peter's original question (see 13:36). If **whither thou goest** remained unclear, **the way** was all the more unclear. In the gospel of John, Thomas is portrayed as a loyal disciple with a penchant for the concrete and tangible (see discussion on 11:16; 20:24–25): what he could not see, he could not accept. One may discern here a desire on the part of Thomas to become familiar with the topography of getting from one place to another, as if the disciples should be able to visualize the turns and the milestones that would incrementally mark a successful journey. Jesus had already confirmed that He would return to get them (see 14:3). It appears characteristic of Thomas's loyalty and bent for the observable to push for a backup plan to follow Jesus (see 13:37). Note that although Thomas spoke for the other disciples, Jesus directed His answer to Thomas ("him," 14:6).

14:6. I am the way (see discussion on 6:35) expressly answered the question of Thomas. The coordinate and additional words, **truth** and **life**, expand and confirm the virtue of why Jesus is "the way." In other words, "I am the way (to the Father) in that I am the truth and the life." **No man cometh unto the Father, but by me** is an exclusive truth that is general in scope, and it certainly envelops any thought on the part of the disciples that they could go on their own to where Jesus was going. He was going to God the Father (see 13:1), the "Father's house" (14:2), and His death and resurrection was the only way. Jesus is not one way among many, but the only way (see Acts 4:12; Heb. 10:19–20). In the early church, Christianity was sometimes called the "way" (see, e.g., Acts 9:2; 19:9, 23). Jesus is **the truth** because He is the genuine revelation of God: "he hath declared him" (1:18; see 1:1, 14). Jesus is **the life** because He is the source of life (see 1:3–4; 5:26), the resurrection and life eternal (see 11:25; 1 John 5:20).

14:7. Me … my Father. Jesus once again stressed the intimate connection between the Father and Himself. Jesus brought a full revelation of the Father (see 1:18), so the apostles had real knowledge of Him.

14:8–10. Philip (v. 8) discerned that the Father could indeed be seen in Jesus. It was not the Father's physicality, however, but rather His nature and character that was present in Jesus. Jesus therefore oriented Philip's thinking toward "knowing" Him (v. 9). As the Son of the Father, Jesus was the fitting representative and revealed the Father not only in His person but also in His faithful expression of the Father's will through His words and works.

14:11. Believe … that I am in the Father, and the Father in me. Saving faith is trust in a person, Jesus, but it must also have factual content. Faith includes believing that Jesus is the expression of the Father as apprehended in Jesus' words and works.

14:12–14. Works … greater works (v. 12) point to the actions, even the miraculous ones, that Jesus performed on behalf of the Father in representing the Father's will (see 4:34; 5:20, 36; 9:4; 17:4). Just as Jesus did these works not of His own accord but in the name of the Father (see 5:43; 10:25; 12:28; 17:6, 12, 26), the greater works of the disciples would represent Jesus and be carried out in His name (see 20:21). The glory of the Father is the mutual end of such works. **In my name** (vv. 13, 14) is a reference not to prayer that merely utters Jesus' name but to prayer in accordance with all that the person who bears the name is (see discussion on 2:23). It is prayer aimed at carrying forward the work that Jesus did, prayer that He Himself will answer. The works that the disciples would do depended on Jesus' going to the Father, because they would be done in the strength of the Holy Spirit, whom Jesus would send from the Father (15:26; 16:7; see 14:16–17).

14:15. Love ... keep. Love, like faith (see James 2:14–26), cannot be separated from obedience (see 14:21, 23–24).

14:16. The Father ... shall give you. The first of a series of important passages about the Holy Spirit (14:26; 15:26; 16:7–15), the gift of the Father. After Jesus' departure, the Father would send **another**, besides Jesus, whom Jesus identified as the **Comforter**, or "Counselor" (Greek, *parakletos*; one who acts on another's behalf, "advocate," "intercessor," "helper"). This was a legal term but had a broader meaning than "counsel for the defense" (see 1 John 2:1). It referred to any person who helped someone in trouble with the law. The Spirit will always stand by believers; **he [will] abide with you for ever** (see 14:18).

14:17. The Spirit of truth. In essence and in action, the Spirit is characterized by truth. He brings people to the truth of God. All three persons of the Trinity are linked with truth (for the Father, see 4:23–24; Ps. 31:5; Isa. 65:16; for the Son, see 14:6). The Spirit of God, **whom the world cannot receive**, or apprehend (see 1 Cor. 2:14), would be **with** Jesus' disciples and **in** them. Some believe the latter relationship (indwelling) specifically anticipated the coming of the Holy Spirit on the day of Pentecost (see Acts 2; Rom. 8:9).

14:18. I will come to you relates to the coming of the Spirit, but Jesus was also speaking of His own appearances after the resurrection and at His second coming (see 14:3, 19, 28; 16:22). **Comfortless**, or "as orphans" (Greek, *orphanos*), suggests helplessness, those who must fend for themselves.

14:19. The world ... but ye. The cross separated the world (who would not see Jesus thereafter) from the disciples (who would see Him). **Because I live, ye shall live also.** The life of the Christian always depends on the life of Christ (see 1:4; 3:15).

14:20. At that day ye shall know. The resurrection would radically change the disciples' thinking.

14:21. Keepeth ... loveth. Love for Christ and keeping His commands cannot be separated (see discussion on 14:15). "Keepeth" means to observe and fulfill the will of Jesus as expressed in His commands. **Shall be loved of my Father, and I will love him** points once again to the oneness of the Father and the Son. Love that is genuine enough to obey Jesus is not only love for Jesus but love for the Father. In turn, not only Jesus but also the Father loves the believer who obeys Jesus' will. The love of the Father cannot be separated from that of the Son.

14:22. How is it ...? Judas (and for that matter, the others) probably looked for Jesus to fulfill popular messianic expectations. It was not easy therefore to understand how that would mean showing Himself to the disciples but not to the world.

14:23–24. Love ... keep ... love (v. 23) forms an unbroken chain. The links of love and obedience are of one piece in an authentic relationship with Jesus and the Father (see 14:15, 21). In answering the question of Judas, Jesus made it clear that no one is excluded, but there is a condition: love must issue in **keep[ing] my words** (v. 24; see 14:21; 1 John 2:3–5). Once more the close relationship between Jesus' words and the Father's is stressed (see 14:10; 7:16).

14:26. The Comforter (see discussion on 14:16) **... is the Holy Ghost**, which is His normal title in the New Testament (though only here and in 1:33; 20:22 in this gospel), emphasizing His holiness rather than His power or greatness. **Whom the Father will send.** Both the Father and the Son would be involved in the sending (see 15:26). **In my name** (see discussions on 2:23; 14:13) points to the Spirit's operation on Jesus' behalf (see 15:26; 16:13–15) in the lives of His disciples. One of the Spirit's functions is to **bring all things to your remembrance, whatsoever I have said unto you.** The sending of the Spirit thus was crucial for the life of the church, as it was for the writing of the New Testament.

14:27. Peace … my peace is a common Hebrew greeting (see 20:19, 21, 26), which Jesus used here in an unusual way. The Old Testament word for peace (Hebrew, *shalom*) speaks of wholeness, as in altogether well, particularly in relation to God. The way Jesus used the word "peace" incorporated the salvation that His redemptive work would achieve for His disciples: total well-being and inner rest of spirit, in fellowship with God. All true peace is His gift, which the repetition emphasizes. His peace is given **not as the world giveth**. In its greetings of peace, the world can only express a longing or wish, but Jesus' peace is real and present. For **troubled**, see discussion on 14:1.

14:28–29. Heard how I said (v. 28) echoes the explanation of 14:3. **Ye would rejoice** defines the outlook of the disciple that loves Jesus and appreciates His mission, which necessarily involved returning to the one who sent Him. **My Father is greater than I** attests once again to the subordinate role Jesus accepted as a necessary part not only of the incarnation but also of His fidelity to fulfilling the Father's will as His representative (see Introduction: "Theme and Theological Message"). The statement must be understood in the light of the unity between the Father and the Son (see 10:30).

14:30. For **prince of this world**, see discussion on 12:31. **Hath nothing in me.** Satan has a hold on people because of their fallen state. Since Christ was sinless, Satan could have no hold on Him.

14:31. As the Father gave me commandment, even so I do. Jesus had stressed the importance of His followers being obedient (see 14:15, 21, 23), and He set the example. With these words, He went to fulfill His mission (see chaps. 18–19).

2. Discourse on the Way to Gethsemane (chaps. 15–16)

15:1. I am the true vine (see discussion on 6:35). The vine is frequently used in the Old Testament as a symbol of Israel (see, e.g., Ps. 80:8–16; Isa. 5:1–7; Jer. 2:21). When this imagery is used, Israel is often shown as lacking in some way. Jesus, however, is "the true vine." For this sense of "true," see discussion on 1:9.

15:2. Taketh away speaks of removal of deadwood and implies judgment (see discussion on 15:6). God, "the husbandman" (15:1), **purgeth** (i.e., prunes) the fruitful branch to increase fruitfulness. In the New Testament, good fruit symbolizes the product of a godly life (see Matt. 3:8; 7:16–20) or virtues of character (see Gal. 5:22–23; Eph. 5:9; Phil. 1:11).

15:3. The word, or message, of Jesus is the pruning instrument that corresponds to the work of the husbandman (see 15:2). It may also be that because of Jesus' word, these branches emerge **clean** and fruitful. The Greek for "clean," however, is the same root word as "purgeth" (15:2). Christ wants to use the Word to cleanse us, but He may use other more severe measures if believers will not allow the Word to do its work in them.

15:4. Abide in me emphasizes the vitality of the vine as the source of fruitfulness. The believer has no fruitfulness apart from his or her union and fellowship with Christ. A branch out of contact with the vine is lifeless.

15:5. For **I am the vine**, see discussion on 15:1. The repetition gives emphasis. **Abideth in me, and I in him** speaks of a living union with Christ, the vine, that is as necessary for the believer as it is for the branch; without that vital connection, there is **nothing**.

15:6. The branches that are not connected to the vine do not bear fruit and are **cast … into the fire, and they are burned** (see Ezek. 15:1–8). Apart from Christ, there is no life, and the outcome is destruction, a picture of judgment (see discussion on 15:2). In light of such passages as 6:39 and 10:27–28, these branches probably do not represent true believers. Genuine salvation is evidenced by a life of fruitfulness (see discussions on 15:2, 4; see also 15:10; Matt. 7:19–23; Heb. 6:9, "things that accompany salvation").

15:7. The evidence of this vital union, Jesus said, is whether **My words abide in you**. The words of Jesus are like the sap of the vine that brings life to every branch. It is impossible to pray correctly apart from knowing and believing the teachings of Christ. For **ask what ye will**, see 14:13–14 and discussion.

15:8–9. My Father [is] glorified (v. 8) in the work of the Son (see 13:31–32), and He is also glorified in the fruit-bearing of His disciples (see Matt. 7:20; Luke 6:43–45). A failure to bear fruit results not from any deficiency in the vine; Jesus loves with the same love that the Father has given Him. The admonition **continue** (or "abide") **ye in my love** points to the sufficiency of Jesus' (and the Father's) love for all manner of fruitfulness.

15:10. Keep … as I have kept stresses once again the importance of obedience (see 14:15, 21, 23) to the character of love and the example of Christ (see 14:31). **My love … his love** (see 15:12, 14) shows not only that obedience and love go together (see 1 John 2:5; 5:2–3) but also that love, as Jesus defined it, is more than a sentiment or emotion (see 15:12, 13).

15:11. Joy is mentioned previously only in 3:29 but is one of the characteristic notes of the Upper Room Discourse (see 16:20–22, 24; 17:13). The Christian way is never dreary, for Jesus desires His disciples' joy to be complete (see 1 John 1:3–4).

15:12–13. Christ's love was revealed not only in words but also in His sacrificial death. How selfless is such love? The extent of its depth is immolation of the self for another.

15:14–15. I call you not servants … but I have called you friends (v. 15). With the emphasis that Jesus put on obedience, one might think He described the servile obedience of a servant or slave, but voluntary obedience inspired by shared purpose points to a different status: friends. Jesus takes His friends into His confidence: **all things … I have made known unto you**. From 16:12, one learns that though Jesus had let His disciples know as much as they were able to absorb of the Father's plan, the revelation was not yet complete. The Spirit would make other things known in due course.

15:16. I have chosen you … bring forth fruit … ask. Disciples normally chose the particular rabbi to whom they wanted to be attached, but it was not so with Jesus' disciples. He chose them, and for a purpose: the bearing of fruit. Believers usually desire a strong prayer life so that they may be fruitful, but in this passage, it is the other way around. Jesus enables believers to bear fruit, and then the Father will hear their prayers. Normally, prayer is addressed to **the Father in [Christ's] name** (see discussions on 2:23; 14:13–14), meaning on the basis of His access to the Father, and with the help of the Holy Spirit.

15:17. Now that Jesus has detailed their status and privileges, He commences to speak of their obligations. **These things** refers to what follows, notably the obligation to **love one another**.

15:18–19. The world (vv. 18) refers to the human system that opposes God's purpose (see discussion on 1:9–10). **Ye are not of the world** (v. 19), because the believer's essential being, his new life, comes specially from God, and therefore he is not the same as those who oppose God.

15:20–21. Disciples, even with their status of friends of the Master (see 15:14–15), are not exempt from the world's hatred that association with Jesus will attract. **The servant is not greater than his lord** (v. 20). Here Jesus underscored the point with the pithy, almost proverbial saying He used in 13:16. **All these things will they do unto you** (v. 21). Persecution from the world is inevitable because those who identify with Jesus (for **for my name's sake**, see discussion on 2:23) give their allegiance to Him and not to the world. Jesus explained that the basic reason for such persecution is the world's ignorance and rejection of the Father (see 16:3) who sent Him.

15:22–24. Jesus came to the world as the Father's representative, and one's response to Jesus is likewise one's response to God (see 5:23). Because Jesus **had … come and spoken unto them** (v. 22), those who rejected Him had **no cloke**, or "excuse" (see KJV marginal note). The Jews had the great privilege of having the Son of God among them, in addition to having received God's special revelation in the Old Testament. Privilege and responsibility go together. Their rejection of Jesus left them totally guilty and without excuse. Had He not come to them, they would still have been sinners, but they would not have been guilty of rejecting Him directly (v. 24).

15:25. That the word might be fulfilled that is written. In the end, God's purpose is always accomplished, despite the belief of sinful men that they have successfully opposed it. The **law** (see discussions on 10:34; 12:34), the very revelation of God that the Jews jealously guarded as their own, condemned them.

15:26. Testimony to Jesus and His coming would continue after He returned to the Father. **The Comforter** (see discussions on 14:16, 26), whom Jesus said He **will send unto you from the Father** (see discussion on 14:26), would bear witness to Jesus. Thus, **the Spirit of truth** (see discussion on 14:17) would equip the disciples of Jesus. **Proceedeth from the Father** parallels or equivocates what Jesus said about sending the Spirit but emphasizes that the Spirit is the Father's special endowment.

15:27. Ye also shall bear witness is emphatic and accentuates that believers bear their testimony to Christ in the power of the Spirit. It is their testimony, however, and they are responsible for bearing it. **From the beginning** qualifies the witness of the apostles as the definitive testimony, for they were uniquely chosen and taught by Christ and were eyewitnesses of His glory (see Luke 24:48; Acts 10:39, 41).

16:1–2. They shall put you out of the synagogues (v. 2) echoes 9:22 and the jeopardy of identifying with Jesus. **Think that he doeth God service** alerts one to the mindset of religious people who persecute others in the strong conviction that they are honoring God (see Acts 26:9–11; Gal. 1:13–14).

16:3. The service supposedly rendered to God in 16:2 is here shown to be defined by one's relationship to Jesus. Abstract notions of God are supplanted by Jesus' revelation of God as **the Father** (see discussion on 5:17). With the words **nor me**, Jesus again linked the Father and the Son. Not to know Christ is to be ignorant of the Father.

16:4–5. None of you asketh me, Whither goest thou? (v. 5). Peter had asked such a question (see 13:36) but quickly turned his attention to another subject. His concern had been what would happen to himself and the others and not where Jesus was going.

16:6. Jesus again perceived the condition of His disciples' hearts because of His announced departure. Earlier their hearts had been "troubled" (14:1; see discussion there); now that agitation was followed or compounded by sadness (Greek, *lypē*; "pain," often of mind or spirit): **sorrow hath filled your heart**.

16:7. If I go not away. Jesus did not say why the Spirit would not come until He went away, but He clearly taught that His saving work on the cross was necessary before the sending of the Spirit. The Spirit is again identified as **the Comforter** (see discussions on 14:16, 26), and His title was appropriate to the disciples' "sorrow" (16:6). **I will send him** (see discussion on 14:26) assured the disciples that Jesus' departure, or return to the Father (see 13:1), was **expedient** (Greek, *sympherō*), to their "advantage" or "benefit."

16:8–11. In this passage, Jesus amplified the benefit of the Comforter. The New Testament normally speaks of the Spirit's work in believers, but here a wider arena of activity is in view. The dimensions of the Spirit's convicting work are elaborated in verses 9–11.

16:8. One of the Spirit's operations is the threefold work of spiritual prosecution: **He will reprove the world of sin … righteousness … judgment**. To "reprove" means to "expose the guilt of."

16:9. Through the Spirit's convicting work, people are brought to a recognition of their sin. **Of sin, because they believe not** may mean either that their sin is their failure to believe or that their unbelief is a classic example of sin. Typically, John may have had both of these in mind. In either case, it is willful unbelief and not ignorance.

16:10. Unbelief involves a rejection of who Jesus is and that He was sent from God. Jesus' return to the Father would ratify that God sent Him and would show God's approval of Him through the glorifying work of His death and resurrection. This is seen in the words **because I go to my Father**, commonly referred to as the ascension. As part of Christ's exaltation, the ascension placed God's seal of approval on Christ's redemptive act. **Of righteousness** points to the Spirit's work of confirming Jesus' righteousness and, with it, the righteousness brought about by His sacrificial death (see Rom. 1:17; 3:21–22). No one but the Holy Spirit can reveal to a person that a righteous status before God does not depend on good works but on Christ's death on the cross.

16:11. In referring to the Comforter's work **Of judgment**, Jesus was speaking of the defeat of Satan, which was a form of judgment, not simply a victory. More than power is in question. God acts with justice. Satan is referred to as **the prince of this world** (see discussion on 12:31), conveying the power that Satan exercises over this domain.

16:12. Ye cannot bear them now. This may mean "more than you can understand now" or "more than you can perform without the Spirit's help" (to live out Christ's teaching requires the enabling presence of the Spirit).

16:13. For **the Spirit of truth**, see discussion on 14:17. Jesus said the Spirit would speak **whatsoever he shall hear**, but it is unclear whether He hears from the Father or the Son. It obviously does not matter, however, for the verse stresses the close relationship among the three. **Things to come** probably means the whole Christian way or revelation (presented and preserved in the apostolic writings), still future at the time Jesus spoke.

16:14–15. The Spirit draws no attention to Himself but promotes the glory of Christ. For **glorify me** (v. 14), see discussion on 1:14. The Spirit exalts and gives expression to the character, reputation, and presence of Christ, for **All things that the Father hath are mine** (v. 15; see 3:35; 13:3; see 17:10). The three persons are closely related.

16:16. A little while … a little while. Few doubt that the first phrase refers to the interval before the crucifixion, but interpretations differ as to whether the second refers to the interval preceding the resurrection, or the coming of the Spirit, or the second coming of Christ. It seems that the language best fits the resurrection.

16:17–19. Jesus had not linked the words **I go to the Father** (v. 17; see 16:10) with **a little while** (see 16:16), but the apostles saw them as connected.

Apart from their confusion, Jesus had addressed His death and the resurrection, which correspond to **ye shall not see me** and **ye shall see me**. The disciples were speaking to one another, but Jesus clarified the pattern in His question of verse 19.

16:20–21. Weep (v. 20) is the same verb for loud wailing used in 11:33, which carries the idea of deep sorrow and its outward expression. Weeping and **joy** correspond to the sequence of death and resurrection, "ye shall not see me" and "ye shall see me" (16:16). Jesus related this to **A woman when she is in travail** (v. 21). Giving birth usually causes both pain and joy (see Isa. 26:17–19; 66:7–14; Hos. 13:13–14).

16:22. As in 16:16, **I will see you again** is probably a reference to Jesus' appearances after His resurrection. **Your joy no man taketh from you** speaks of the resurrection, which would change things permanently, bringing a joy that the world's assaults cannot remove.

16:23. Ye shall ask me nothing seems to mean asking for information (rather than asking in prayer), which would not be necessary after the resurrection. Jesus then moved on to the subject of prayer. He may have been saying that His disciples previously had been praying to Christ, but after His death and resurrection they were to go directly to the Father and pray in Christ's **name** (see 16:24, 26–27; see also 2:23; 14:13–14 and discussions).

16:24. Hitherto (previously) the disciples had asked the Father or Christ, but they had not asked the Father in Christ's name. **Ask** implies "keep on asking," involving the disciples in persistence when petitioning. For **your joy**, see discussion on 15:11.

16:25. Have I spoken unto you in proverbs points to figures of speech Jesus used throughout the discourse (chaps. 15–16), not just in the immediately preceding words. **The time cometh**, after the resurrection, when Jesus would speak **plainly** (Greek, *parrēsia*; "frankly," "boldly"; see 7:4, 25).

16:26. I say not unto you, that I will pray the Father for you. This is not a contradiction of Romans 8:34; Hebrews 7:25; 1 John 2:1. Those passages mean that Christ's presence in heaven as the crucified and risen Lord is itself an intercession. Here the teaching is that there will be no need for Him to make petitions on believers' behalf.

16:27–29. The Father himself loveth you (v. 27). Christ explained why the disciples could come directly to the Father in prayer. Because they had loved and trusted in Jesus, God would hear their requests in Jesus' name. Jesus' mission, His being sent by the Father and His return to the Father, is crucial to properly apprehending His unique authority to reveal the Father and achieve salvation. The disciples needed to grasp this, and they did (see 16:30).

16:29. For no proverb, see 16:25 and discussion.

16:30–31. We believe that thou camest forth from God (v. 30). This statement reflects two recurring themes of this gospel: believing (see discussion on 1:7) and Jesus' coming from God (see 16:27–28; discussion on 4:34).

16:32. Ye shall be scattered. The disciples had faith but not enough to stand firm in the face of disaster. Jesus knew they would fail; however, His church is built not on people's strength but on God's ability to use people even after they have failed.

16:33. Notice the contrasts: between **in me** and **In the world** (see discussion on 1:9–10) and between **peace** and **tribulation**. Just before His death, Jesus encouraged His disciples with an affirmation of His final victory: **I have overcome**.

3. Jesus' Prayer of Intercession (chap. 17)

17:1–26. Jesus' longest recorded prayer is found here in the gospel of John. It is truly deserving of the title "the Lord's Prayer." Jesus devoted this prayer to the primary concerns and issues of His mission (His sending), which was all but completed. The pattern of Jewish agency, which illumines one's understanding of the sending of Jesus (see Introduction: "Theme and Theological Message"), is evident here too, with one significant change. Every human agent returned and reported to his sender. Here Jesus, the divine agent and representative of the Father, took up the concerns and accomplishments of His mission in anticipation of His return. As the Son who was sent (see Mark 12:5; Matt. 21:37), endowed with

the Father's supreme authority, Jesus entailed in His prayer both the intimacy of such an extraordinary relationship as well as the deference of one who had officially and faithfully acted on the Father's behalf.

17:1. Lifted up his eyes to heaven was the customary attitude in prayer (see 11:41; Ps. 123:1; Mark 7:34), though sometimes the person prostrated himself (see Matt. 26:39). **Father** is used of God in John's gospel 119 times, and 96 of them are in the words of Jesus (see discussion on 4:21). **The hour** (see discussion on 2:4) upon which Jesus had focused throughout His ministry was at hand (see 13:1). Glory (**glorify … glorify**) was mutual because the character and will of both the Father and the Son were bound together in what had to be accomplished in this hour (see discussions on 1:14; 7:39; 13:31–32). Glorification involves a benefit that belongs also to believers: the death by which Jesus would glorify God would lead to eternal life for all who believe (see 17:2).

17:2. Thou hast given him all power (see 3:35; 13:1) is elaborated throughout the prayer in references to what the Father had given, or entrusted, to Jesus (see 17:4, 6–9, 11–12, 14, 22, 24; discussion on 3:27). **That he should give eternal life** expresses the purpose the Father had in granting Jesus such vast authority (see discussions on 3:15; 5:21–27). **As many as thou hast given him**, or entrusted to Jesus, shows again God's initiative in salvation.

17:3. Eternal life is the believer's endowment, but as the word **sent** indicates, it is the achievement of Jesus' mission and brings before believers the role of Jesus' agency in the divine plan, mission, and salvation that He achieved.

17:4. I have glorified thee. Christ's mission was not self-centered but on behalf of the Father. **The work which thou gavest me to do** expresses the supreme aegis of the Father in Jesus' mission.

17:5. Glorify thou me … with the glory which I had with thee. Jesus asked the Father to reinstate Him to His previous position of glory, to exchange humiliation for glorification. This occurred at Christ's resurrection and exaltation to God's right hand. The Greek for **world** occurs eighteen times in this prayer. Here it identifies the universe (see discussions on 1:9–10; 17:14).

17:6. I have manifested thy name (see 1:18) is another way of saying "I have glorified you" (17:4), for the "name" stands for the person (see discussions on 2:23; 14:13). **The men which thou gavest me** again points to the divine initiative (see 6:44).

17:7. All things ... are of thee expresses the aegis of the Father in His sending Jesus to the world and the fulfillment of Jesus' revelation of the Father: "he hath declared him" (1:18). Throughout John's gospel, Jesus never varied from His faithful dependence on and devotion to the Father's will, expressed in Jesus' words and works. Only as people see the Father at work in Jesus do they have a proper concept of God. The disciples had at last reached this understanding.

17:8. Three things about the disciples are mentioned: (1) They accepted Jesus' teaching (unlike the Pharisees and others who heard it but did not receive it). (2) They knew with certainty Jesus' divine origin. Acceptance of the revelation led them further into truth. (3) They believed (see discussion on 1:7; see 1:12; 20:31).

17:9–10. I pray not for the world (v. 9). The only prayer Jesus could pray for the world was that it cease to be worldly (i.e., opposed to God), and this He did pray (see 17:21, 23).

17:11. Holy Father is a form of address found only here in the New Testament (but see 1 Peter 1:15–16; Rev. 4:8; 6:10). The title suggests both remoteness and nearness; God is both awe-inspiring and loving. To **keep through thine own name** suggests the aegis of the Father, which earmarked Jesus' mission and on which He was totally dependent (see 17:6–7, 12). It was instrumental to the unity of the Father and the Son and was now featured in Jesus' prayer for those entrusted to Him and to whom He had manifested the Father (see 17:6). **That they may be one** summarizes the focus of the latter part of the prayer, which strongly emphasizes unity. The unity was already given, not something to be achieved. The meaning is "that they continually be one" rather than "that they become one." The unity of believers is to be like that of the Father and the

Son. While it is much more than unity of organization, the church's present divisions are the result of the failures of Christians.

17:12. I kept ... I have kept makes it clear that Christ's power is adequate for every need. Jesus Himself had kept the disciples safe ("I kept"; Greek, *tēreō*) and guardedly watched over ("I have kept"; Greek, *phylassō*) them. **The son of perdition** means "the son of destruction," that is, one belonging to the sphere of damnation and destined for destruction (but predestination is not here in view). The reference is to Judas Iscariot.

17:13. From the features of Jesus' prayer to this point, it may be inferred that **My joy** (see discussion on 15:11) refers to Jesus' enjoyment of the Father's all-sufficient provision, protection, direction, and authority (aegis) for His mission. His delight was in the Father. Now Jesus prayed that this joy might be replicated in His disciples.

17:14. The world is the domain that is hostile to God and God's people (see discussions on 1:9; 17:5). The disciples were **not of the world**, or having the mindset of the world (i.e., hostility to God), for they had been "born of the Spirit" (3:8) and were "sons of God" (1:12).

17:15–16. Jesus prayed not that God would **take them out of the world** (v. 15) but rather that they would be "in the world but not of the world" (see 1 Cor. 5:9–10; 2 Cor. 10:3). He prayed that the disciples would be resistant to the world's influence. The world is where Jesus' disciples were to do their work; He did not wish them to be taken from it until that work was done (see 17:18). **The evil,** or the Evil One (see 1 John 2.13–14; 3:12; 5:18–19), Satan, who is especially active in the world, makes God's protection indispensable.

17:17. Sanctify means "to set apart for sacred use" or "to make holy" (also in 17:19). **Thy truth: thy word** indicates that sanctification and revelation (as recorded in God's Word) go together. For the connection of Christ's teaching with truth, see 8:31–32.

17:18. Jesus' mission is one of the dominant themes of this gospel, and **As thou hast sent me ... even so have I also sent them** shows that the Father's sending of Jesus is the pattern for His followers. **Into the world** (see 17:14–15) is the arena where the disciples would carry on Jesus' commission. One may long for heaven, but it is on earth that one's work is done.

17:19. I sanctify myself is a statement that appears to be unparalleled. In the Septuagint (the Greek translation of the Old Testament), the verb is used of consecrating priests (Exod. 28:41) and sacrifices (Exod. 28:38; Num. 18:9). Jesus solemnly "set himself apart to do God's will," which at this point meant His death. **That they also might be sanctified** (see discussion on 17:17). Jesus died on the cross not only to save all humanity but also to consecrate them to God's service.

17:20. Them also which shall believe on me points beyond those that "have believed" (17:8) to future disciples. Jesus had just spoken of the mission and the sanctification of His followers (see 17:18–19). He was confident that they would spread the gospel, and He prayed for those who would believe as a result. All future believers are included in this prayer.

17:21. For **that they also may be one**, see discussion on 17:11. For **Father**, see discussion on 17:1. **That the world may believe**. The unity of believers should have an effect on outsiders, to convince them of the mission of Christ. Jesus' prayer is a rebuke of the groundless and often bitter divisions among believers.

17:22. The glory (see discussion on 17:1). Believers are to be characterized by humility and service, just as Christ was, and it is on them that God's glory rests. Jesus' repeated emphasis on unity, **that they may be one, even as we are one**, shows the importance of unity among His followers, and again the standard is the unity of the Father and the Son.

17:23. I in them, and thou in me. This refers to two indwellings: that of the Son in believers and that of the Father in the Son. It is because the latter is a reality that the former can take place. **Made perfect in one**. The emphasis on unity again has an evangelistic aim. This time it is connected not only with the mission of Jesus but also with God's love for people and for Christ.

17:24. Father (see discussion on 17:1), as so often and so appropriate to prayer, is in direct address here, as throughout this prayer. Jesus said, **I will**, His last will and testament for His followers. "I will" (Greek, *thelō*) expresses His "desire." Where He Himself was concerned, He prayed, "not that I will, but what thou wilt" (Mark 14:36). **Be with me** (see 14:3) is the Christian's greatest blessing. **My glory** is perhaps used here to refer to Jesus' eternal splendor (see 1 John 3:2). Or Jesus' prayer may have been that in the life to come they might fully appreciate the glory of His lowly service (see Eph. 2:7).

17:25. Righteous Father is a form of address found only here in the New Testament (see "Holy Father," 17:11). The disciples did not know God directly and personally, but **these have known** that God had sent Christ. To recognize God in Christ's mission is a great advance over anything **the world** can know.

F. Jesus' Betrayal and Arrest (18:1–12)

18:1. The brook Cedron lies east of Jerusalem and remains dry except during the rainy season. "Brook" translates a Greek word that compounds "winter" and "flowing" and literally reads as "winter-flowing Cedron." The disciples may have expected to spend the night in the **garden** since the city was crowded with pilgrims for Passover. Judas knew the place (see 18:2).

18:2–3. Judas (v. 2; see discussion on 6:71) led **a band** (v. 3), or "cohort" (the Greek translates the Latin *cohors*), **and officers from the chief priests and Pharisees**. A "cohort" (Greek, *speira*; also in 18:12) always refers to Roman soldiers in the New Testament and need not denote a full detachment of 600 men, nor even a full maniple of 200, which *speira* usually connotes. "Officers" is equivalent to the temple guard sent by the Sanhedrin. **Lanterns** were terra-cotta holders into which household lamps could be inserted, and **torches** were resinous pieces of wood fastened together.

18:4–9. Jesus was not taken by surprise, **knowing all things that should come upon him** (v. 4). Taking the initiative, Jesus controlled the encounter and went out of the garden to meet the advancing company. **Whom seek ye?** One may infer from Jesus' question that Judas, who had guided them, receded behind the officials vested with the responsibility of arresting Jesus. As John parenthetically explained, however, the one **which betrayed him, stood with them** (v. 5). In John, the kiss of Judas is overshadowed (and perhaps for that reason omitted) by the formal exchange: the warrant for **Jesus of Nazareth** answered with the consequential **I am he** (see discussions on 6:35; 8:58). At that, **they went backward, and fell to the ground**. They came to arrest a meek peasant and instead were met in the dim light by a majestic person.

The formal question and answer occurred twice, but John's threefold repetition of **I am he** (vv. 5, 6, 8) emphasizes these solemn words. Twice Jesus made the arresting party say plainly that He was the one they wanted (18:4–5, 7). His petition, **let these go their way** (v. 8), verbalized His concern for the disciples even as He was going to His death. **That the saying might be fulfilled** conveys the authority of Jesus and His words. Carson (*The Gospel According to John*, p. 579) puts it well: "Just as events fulfill the authoritative and prophetic words of Scripture, so this event fulfills Jesus' own words, which cannot be less authoritative (cf. Mark 13:31)." John also bears witness to the certification of Jesus' prayer in 17:12; see also 6:39 and 10:28.

18:10. It is John to whom is owed the information that the man with the **sword** (the Greek for this word refers to a short sword) was **Simon Peter** and that the man he wounded was named **Malchus**.

18:11. The cup often points to suffering (see Ps. 75:8; Ezek. 23:31–34) and the wrath of God (see Isa. 51:17, 22; Jer. 25:15; Rev. 14:10; 16:19). **My Father hath given me** reveals once again that God was in control, but Peter needed to be reminded. The Synoptic Gospels also speak of "the cup" at the time of Jesus' prayer at Gethsemane (see Matt. 26:39; Mark 14:36; Luke 22:42), and John said it came from the Father.

18:12. For **band**, see 18:3 and discussion. The **captain** (Greek, *chiliarchos*) is literally a "leader of a thousand soldiers" but is used of a military tribune

or commander of a cohort. It may be that "band" (or "cohort") here designates the Roman soldiers under this tribune and not a full detachment. The reason they **bound him** is not clear. Perhaps it was standard procedure, much like the modern use of handcuffs.

G. The Trials of Jesus (18:13–19:15)

18:13. Annas had been deposed from the high priesthood by the Romans in AD 15 but was probably still regarded by many as the true high priest. In Jewish law, a man could not be sentenced on the day his trial was held. The two examinations, this one (mentioned only by John) and that before Caiaphas, may have been conducted to give some form of legitimacy to what was done. For **the high priest that same year**, see discussion on 11:49.

18:14. Caiaphas ... gave counsel to the Jews is a reference to 11:49–50. For John, it was this unconscious prophecy, **that one man should die for the people**, that mattered most about Caiaphas. John may also have been hinting that a fair trial could not be expected from a man who had already said that putting Jesus to death was **expedient** (see 11:50).

18:15–16. Another disciple (v. 15) perhaps refers to John himself. **Known unto the high priest** refers to more than casual acquaintance; this disciple had entrée to the high priest's house and **brought in Peter** (v. 16) as well.

18:17. The damsel that kept the door, a maidservant, is mentioned in all the accounts of Peter's denial (see Matt. 26:69–75; Mark 14:77–72; Luke 22:54–62). Peter's first challenge came from a slave girl, the most unimportant person imaginable. The form of the girl's question implied a negative answer, and Peter capitalized on her expectation by saying, **I am not**. The other gospels seem to indicate that the other denials followed immediately, but it is likely that they were separated by intervals during which other things happened (see Luke 22:58–59).

18:18. Peter stood with them, for on a cold night, he would have been conspicuous if he had stayed away from the fire.

18:19. Asked Jesus refers not to legal questioning, since witnesses were supposed to be brought in first to establish guilt. The accused was not required to prove his innocence. Perhaps Annas (see 18:13) regarded this as a preliminary inquiry, not a trial, since Caiaphas apparently was not present at this inquiry (see 18:24).

18:20–21. I spake openly (v. 20). It should not have been difficult to find witnesses; **them which heard me ... know what I said** (v. 21). When Jesus asserted, **In secret have I said nothing** (v. 20), He was denying not that He taught the disciples privately but that He had secretly taught them subversive teaching different from His public message.

18:22. The **stroke**, or "blow," was one of many indignities and another illegality that Jesus suffered. The word apparently means a blow with the open hand, a slap.

18:23–24. Bear witness (v. 23) is a legal term, indicating an invitation to act according to proper legal form. John stressed the importance of testimony throughout his gospel (see discussion on 1:7). The audience proved to be unproductive, and Annas failed to solicit any information from Jesus that might be used to incriminate Him. This and Jesus' request for witnesses (see 18:21) called for a more formal hearing, and Jesus was sent to **Caiaphas** (v. 24), the presiding **high priest**.

18:25. Some find a difficulty in that Matthew 26:71 says another girl asked this question, whereas Mark 14:69 says it was the same girl, and Luke 22:58 that it was a man. With a group of servants talking around a fire, however, several doubtless would have taken up and repeated such a question, which could be the meaning of John's **They said therefore unto him**. As on the first occasion (see 18:17), the question anticipated the answer no. The servants probably did not really expect to find a follower of Jesus in the high priest's courtyard, but the question seemed worth asking. Again Peter answered, **I am not**, his second denial of Christ.

18:26. Being his kinsman whose ear Peter cut off is another piece of information readers owe to John. A relative would have a deeper interest in the swordsman than other people had. The light **in the garden** would have been dim, however, as it was in

the courtyard ("a fire of coals" [18:18] glows but does not have flames). In Greek, the question **Did not I see thee ...?** expects the answer yes.

18:27. Peter then denied again, his third denial of Christ. **Immediately the cock crew**, and Jesus' prophecy in 13:38 found fulfillment.

18:28. The hall of judgment (Greek, *praitōrion*; a Latin loanword for *praetorium*) was the palace of the Roman governor, Pilate (see Mark 15:16). John recorded little about the Jewish phase of Jesus' trial but much about the Roman trial. It is possible that John was in the Praetorium, the governor's official residence, for this trial. **It was early**. Evidently, the chief priests held a second session of the Sanhedrin after daybreak to give some appearance of legality to what they did (see Mark 15:1). This occasion would have been immediately after that, perhaps between 6:00 a.m. and 7:00 a.m. Ironically, in order to eat the Passover and avoid being **defiled**, a result of entering a Gentile residence, the Jewish authorities remained outside, yet their hands were sullied with manipulated justice to secure the death of Jesus, the true Passover (Carson, *The Gospel According to John*, p. 589). **Eat the passover** does not mean that the time of the Passover meal had not yet come, for this would contradict the Synoptic Gospels, which have Jesus eating the Passover meal the night before. The term "passover" was used to refer to the whole festival of Passover and Unleavened Bread, which lasted seven days and included a number of meals.

18:29–30. Pilate (v. 29; see discussion on Mark 15:1), the Roman governor, showed himself tolerant of Jewish ways. **What accusation ...?** was a normal question at the opening of a formal trial, but it was difficult to answer because the Jews had no charge that would stand up in a Roman court of law. Since Roman soldiers were party to the arrest of Jesus, Pilate likely had been briefed of the apprehension of **a malefactor** (v. 30), or one who had violated the law. Now specific violation of Roman law was required.

18:31–32. Without an opening accusation, Pilate remanded Jesus to **the Jews** (v. 31; see discussion on 1:19) with the words, **Take ye him**. In other words, no Roman charge, no Roman trial.

The retort, **It is not lawful for us to put any man to death**, shows they were looking for an execution, not a fair trial. The restriction was important, for otherwise Rome's supporters could be quietly removed by local legal executions. The Romans seem to have sometimes condoned local executions (e.g., of Stephen; see Acts 7), but normally they retained the right to inflict the death penalty. With **what death he should die**, John recalled the words of Jesus and the necessity of crucifixion (see 12:32–33 and "must" in 12:34). Jewish execution was by stoning, but Jesus' death was to be by crucifixion, whereby He would bear the curse (see Deut. 21:22–23). The Romans, not the Jews, had to put Jesus to death. God was ruling over the whole process.

18:33. Pilate's first words to Jesus, identical in all four gospels, were, **Art thou the King of the Jews?** Since a capital sentence was required for capital punishment (crucifixion), a political charge had to be found, and thus the question. "Thou," or "you," is emphatic and Brown (*The Gospel According to John*, p. 851) suggests that Pilate's question bears a tone of incredulity. If so, Jesus did not meet Pilate's expectation (see 18:34).

18:34–35. Jesus answered Pilate with a question: **Sayest thou this thing of thyself …?** (v. 34). If so, Pilate's question (see 18:33) had meant, "Are you a rebel?" If the question had originated with the Jews, it meant, "Are you the messianic King?" Pilate's retort makes it clear that (1) he was unacquainted with Jesus apart from what he had been told, and (2) he harbored reservations about the Sanhedrin's charges.

18:36. My kingdom. Jesus agreed that He has a kingdom but asserted that it is not the kind of kingdom that has soldiers to **fight** for it. It was not built, nor is it maintained, by military might.

18:37. Jesus admitted to being a king and having a kingdom, but he defined its rule and domain as truth and its subjects as those who hear the truth. It is therefore a kingdom of truth, and Jesus came to **bear witness unto the truth**, two of this gospel's important themes (see 1:7; 1:14; 14:6 and discussions).

18:38. What is truth? Pilate may have been jesting and meant, "What does truth matter?" Or he may

have been serious and meant, "It is not easy to find truth. What is it?" Because John specified the immediacy with which Pilate departed, the former is the more likely. Either way, it was clear to him that Jesus was no rebel: **I find in him no fault**, or "cause" ("crime") for which He was worthy of punishment. Teaching the truth was not a criminal offense.

18:39. Ye have a custom. In antiquity, prisoners are known to have been released on special occasions in other places. Pilate's direct appeal to the people may indicate an effort on his part to circumvent the Sanhedrin. Although Pilate had pronounced Jesus innocent of any political crime, his use of the title **King of the Jews** may have been meant to influence the people toward the way he wanted them to decide. At any rate, the note of royalty is a prominent emphasis in John's account.

18:40. Barabbas was a **robber**, a rebel, and a murderer (see Luke 23:19). The name is Aramaic and means "son of Abba," that is, "son of the father." In place of this man, the Son of the Father died.

19:1. Pilate hoped a flogging would satisfy the Jews and enable him to release Jesus (see discussion on Mark 15:15). Brown (*The Gospel According to John*, p. 874) suggests that here and in 19:3, John's selection of vocabulary to describe the treatment of Jesus may have been drawn from Isaiah 50:6.

19:2–3. Thorns (v. 2) is a general term relating to any thorny plant, but fashioned into a wreath, those thorns became a mockery of Jesus and the opposite of the laurel wreath that adorned the emperor. **Purple** was associated with royalty because purple dye was hard to obtain and expensive. John's record of the soldier's mistreatment of Jesus is graphic and brutal. Again and again, one after another, the soldiers humiliated Jesus emotionally and physically with their mocking words and blows. The earthly symbols of power mocked the King whose reign is not of this world.

19:4–5. A second time, Pilate pronounced the innocence of Jesus and, as if to draw attention to it, called out, **Behold the man** (v. 5). This time Pilate did not use the title "King of the Jews" (18:39). Pilate's words were meant not to pour scorn on Jesus but to demonstrate to the Jews the ridiculous nature of their charge that He was a royal claimant. Thus, he said, "Look at this man!" Before them stood a pitiable figure; should they not grant amnesty to such a beaten and broken, bruised and bleeding man?

19:6. Any spark the crowd may have had to grant Jesus amnesty was quickly quenched by the ready and repeated chant of the Jewish officials: **Crucify him**. The exasperated Pilate petulantly replied, **Take ye him, and crucify him**. It was a sarcastic suggestion, not only because Jewish authorities could not carry out this form of execution but because Pilate did not concur with their indictment. **I find no fault**. For the third time, Pilate proclaimed Jesus' innocence (see 18:38; 19:4). Luke also recorded this threefold proclamation (see Luke 23:4, 14, 22).

19:7–8. We have a law ... he ought to die (v. 7) refers to the penalty for blasphemy (see Lev. 24:16). **The Jews** (see discussion on 1:19) countered Pilate with their own law, which Pilate would not have known, and the content of the allegation, **he made himself the Son of God**, raising the stakes and a new level of fear for Pilate. That **he was the more afraid** (v. 8) may have had a dual source: (1) Pilate was likely superstitious, and this charge, akin to a claim of divinity, frightened him (see 19:9 and 8:36–37). (2) As a Roman governor, Pilate was responsible for upholding local laws, and the depth of the Jews' resolve and motivation suggested a new level of political jeopardy.

19:9. Whence art thou? Pilate's question belongs to a theme of puzzlement throughout John's gospel (see, e.g., 7:27–28; 8:14; 9:29–30). The answer, of course, is "from above" (19:11), with all that it entails (see 1:1–18), but **Jesus gave him no answer**. The reason is not clear since Jesus had answered other questions readily. Perhaps Pilate would not have understood the answer or would not have believed it.

19:10. I have power. Pilate was incredulous and very conscious of his authority. Ironically, he touted his authority to none other than the one given supreme authority, Jesus (see 3:35; 13:3; 5:24–27). Pilate's second question indicates his personal responsibility for crucifying Jesus.

19:11. These were Jesus' last words to Pilate. The answer to Pilate's earlier question (see 19:9) is embedded in the words **from above**. Jesus, sent to earth as the Father's representative, had come from the realm of all authority, a kingdom not of this world (see 18:36–37). All earthly authority comes ultimately from God. **The greater sin** belonged to Caiaphas (not Judas, who was only a means), but "greater" implies that there was a lesser sin, so Pilate's sin was also real.

19:12. Not Caesar's friend. Some people had official status as "Friends of Caesar," but the term seems to be used here in the general sense. There was an implied threat that if Pilate released Jesus, he would be accused before Caesar. His record was such that he could not face such a prospect without concern. Ties of patronage between Pilate and the Praetorian prefect Lucius Aelius Sejanus, who had recently been executed (AD 31) by Tiberius Caesar on suspicion of plotting against the emperor, magnified the dangers of such a charge: **whosoever maketh himself a king speaketh against Caesar**.

19:13. The judgment seat, or "bench" (Greek, *bēma*), was a platform outside the palace (see 18:28; see also Acts 18:12, 16, 17; 25:6, 10, 17). **The Pavement** is not a translation of **Gabbatha**, which seems to mean "the hill of the house," but a different name for the same place.

19:14. The preparation. Normally, Friday was the day people prepared for the Sabbath. Here the meaning is Friday of Passover week. **About the sixth hour**, or about noon. Mark 15:25 says that Jesus was crucified at "the third hour." It is possible that Mark's gospel contains a copyist's error, for the Greek numerals for three and six could be easily confused. Or it may be that John was using Roman time, in which case the appearance before Pilate would have been at 6:00 a.m. and the crucifixion at 9:00 a.m. (the third hour according to Jewish reckoning; see Mark 15:33; for other time references, see Matt. 27:45–46; Mark 15: 33–34; Luke 23:44). **Behold your King**. John does not let his readers forget the sovereignty of Jesus. Pilate did not mean the expression seriously, but John did.

19:15. The chief priests answered, We have no king but Caesar. More irony. They rejected any suggestion that they were rebels against Rome but expressed the truth of their spiritual condition.

H. The Crucifixion and Burial (19:16–42)

19:16–17. Bearing his cross (v. 17). A cross might be shaped like a T, an X, a Y, or an I, as well as the traditional form. A condemned man would normally carry the crossbeam (Latin, *patibulum*) to the place of execution. Somewhere along the way, Simon of Cyrene took Jesus' cross (see Mark 15:21), probably because Jesus was weakened by the flogging. **Golgotha** is Aramaic for "the skull" (see discussion on Mark 15:22). The name of the site is given in both Greek and Aramaic ("Calvary" is from the Latin, with the same meaning).

19:18. They crucified him (see discussion on Mark 15:25). As with the scourging, John described this horror with one Greek word. None of the gospel writers dwelt on the physical sufferings of Jesus. The positioning of **two others ... on either side** of Jesus may have been meant as a final insult, but it brings out the important truth that in His death, Jesus was identified with sinners.

19:19–20. A title (v. 19), or placard, stating the crime for which a man was executed was often fastened to his cross. The full title, **JESUS OF NAZARETH THE KING OF THE JEWS**, and John's detail that Pilate caused it to be written corresponds to the formal criminal charge of sedition. Only John mentioned the languages in which the title was written. **Hebrew** (v. 20) was one of the languages of the Jewish people at that time (along with Aramaic). **Greek** was the common language of communication throughout the empire. **Latin** was the legal and official language of Rome. The threefold inscription may account for the slight differences in wording in the four gospels.

19:21–22. The chief priests of the Jews (v. 21) protested the implications of the charge itself. Pilate needed sufficient reason for the execution, and he was not above mocking the Jews, but for John, Pilate's insistence on the wording may also have served to underscore that Jesus' kingship is final and unalterable. As Carson (*The Gospel According to John*, p. 611) puts it, "Pilate's malice serves God's ends."

19:23–24. Jesus' **coat** (Greek, *chitōn*; "tunic"; v. 23), a type of shirt that reached from the neck to the knees or ankles, **was without seam** and therefore too valuable to be cut up. Rather than mar the coat, the soldiers **cast lots** (v. 24) for the final division of Jesus' clothing and thus fulfilled **the Scripture** (see introduction to Psalm 22 and discussions on Ps. 22:17–18, 20–21).

19:25. Although the number of women that **stood by the cross** is unclear (two, three, or four), it remains simplest to understand four women, two unnamed and two named. **Cleophas** is mentioned only here in the New Testament. **Mary Magdalene** appears in the crucifixion and resurrection story in all four gospels, but apart from that, one reads of her only in Luke 8:2–3.

19:26–27. The disciple standing by, whom he loved (v. 26) most likely was John (see discussion on 13:23). According to Barrett (*The Gospel According to St. John*, p. 552), the words of Jesus, **behold thy son** (v. 26) ... **Behold thy mother** (v. 27), recall the wording of legal adoption formulas. Jesus demonstrated a dying concern for His mother and made provision for her care. **Woman** (see discussion on 2:4), as His concern showed, was not a term of disrespect. The **disciple took her unto his own home** and so took responsibility for her. It may be that Jesus' brothers still did not believe in Him (see 7:5).

19:28–29. I thirst (v. 28; see Ps. 22:15) is a detail of Jesus' agony; dehydration was a cruelty of crucifixion. This detail, however, belonged to the completion of a larger plan now nearing perfection, His sacrificial death, and probably refers to Psalm 69:21. **Vinegar** (v. 29), equivalent to cheap wine, was the drink of ordinary people. **A spunge** was a useful way of giving a drink to one on a cross and may indicate forethought and compassion on someone's part. Affixed to a **hyssop** branch (the name given to a number of plants), the sponge was lifted up to Jesus.

19:30. Jesus ... said, It is finished, apparently with the loud cry of Matthew 27:50; Mark 15:37.

Gave up the ghost, or "handed over" His Spirit, is an unusual way of describing death and suggests an act of will (see 19:29). Jesus died as a victor and had completed what He came to do.

19:31–33. The Jews (v. 31; see discussion on 1:19) did not want the Romans to follow the practice of leaving the bodies hanging on the cross since the following day was **a high day**, the Sabbath that fell at Passover time. The Passover meal had been eaten on Thursday evening, the day of preparation was Friday, and the Sabbath came on Saturday, commencing at sunset on Friday. These arrangements may have been discussed earlier (see 19:21) and now came into play. To hasten death, **legs might be broken** (v. 31) so that the victim could not put any weight on his legs and breathing would be difficult. At the time this was implemented, Jesus **was dead already** (v. 33). John elaborated the significance of this in 19:36.

19:34. To be sure Jesus was dead, a soldier **pierced his side** (see 19:37; Isa. 53:5; Zech. 12:10; see also Ps. 22:16). This action was more than a prodding; it was a brutal thrust issuing in **blood and water**, the result of the spear piercing the pericardium (the sac that surrounds the heart) and the heart itself.

19:35. He that saw it points to the significant eyewitness testimony of the Beloved Apostle, who was present at the cross (see 19:25–27; 21:24). The incident proved important because it underscored not only the incarnation but also the additional fulfillment of Scripture (see 19:36–37).

19:36–37. Scripture (v. 36). John again observed God's overruling in the fulfillment of Scripture. It was extraordinary that Jesus was the only one of the three whose legs were not broken and that He suffered an unusual spear thrust that did not break a bone (see Zech. 12:10). The law dictated that no bone of the Passover lamb be broken (see Exod. 12:46; Num. 9:12). Jesus, as "the Lamb of God" (1:29) and "our passover" (1 Cor. 5:7; see 1 Peter 1:18–19), thus fulfilled the Scripture that **A bone of him shall not be broken** (see Ps. 34:20).

19:38. Joseph was a wealthy disciple (see Matt. 27:57) and a member of the Sanhedrin who had not agreed to Jesus' condemnation (see Luke 23:51).

The place-name **Arimathea** (see discussion on Matt. 27:57) points to Joseph's hometown or place of birth. It is likely that he resided in Jerusalem. His allegiance to Jesus had been expressed only **secretly**. It would have been hard for a member of the Sanhedrin to support Jesus' cause openly (see 12:42–43; 3:1). Joseph now expressed courage (see Mark 15:43) when Jesus' closest followers had all run away (see Mark 14:50); it was left to Joseph and Nicodemus to provide for His burial. Permission was required to take the body, **and Pilate gave him leave**. Otherwise, people could take away their crucified friends before they died and revive them.

19:39. John alone reported that **Nicodemus** (see 3:1) joined Joseph in the burial. John characteristically identified Nicodemus as he that **came to Jesus by night** (see 7:50). John's emphasis **at the first** may indicate his perception of a man whose faith had grown. **An hundred pound weight** was a very large amount, such as was used in royal burials (see 2 Chron. 16:14). A "pound" (Greek, *litra*) was about twelve ounces, and thus a "hundred pound weight" was about seventy-five pounds by current standards.

19:40. Linen clothes denotes thin strips like bandages. A shroud, a large sheet, was also used (see Matt. 27:59; Mark 15:46; Luke 23:53).

19:41–42. Jesus' body was placed in **a new sepulchre** (v. 41), a tomb that had never been occupied, hewn out of the rock (see Mark 15:46; Matt. 27:60; Luke 23:53) and situated in **a garden** near Golgotha (see 19:17). It was Joseph's own tomb (Matt. 27:60), and its proximity—**nigh at hand**—was important since labor must cease at sunset, the beginning of the Sabbath. That it was "new" would also readily prove that it was empty upon the resurrection of Jesus. For **preparation**, see discussion on v. 14.

V. The Resurrection (20:1–29)

20:1. Mary Magdalene (see discussion on 19:25; Mark 16:9) went to the garden early, **when it was yet dark**. Mark says it was "at the rising of the sun" (Mark 16:2). Perhaps the women came in groups, with Mary Magdalene coming very early. Or John may have referred to the time of leaving home, and

Mark to that of arriving at the tomb. John's account of the open tomb and Mary's discovery presumes the details of Mark 15:46–47: Joseph "rolled a stone unto the door of the sepulchre. And Mary Magdalene and Mary the mother of Joses beheld where he was laid."

20:2. Despite his denials of Jesus (see 18:15–27), **Simon Peter** was still the leading figure among the disciples. Peter and **the ... disciple, whom Jesus loved** (John; see discussion on 13:23) were the prominent disciples and likely had remained in the vicinity. Unlike the disciples who had fled (see Mark 14:50; Matt. 26:56), Peter and John were around during the interrogations (18:15). The word **we** indicates that others were with Mary (see Matt. 28:1; Mark 16:1; Luke 24:10), though John did not identify them. **They have taken away the Lord ... we know not where they have laid him.** Mary had no thought of resurrection. It was not uncommon for graves to be robbed, as Mary's immediate suspicion confirms.

20:3–7. To describe the exigent concern over the empty tomb, John recorded the running of Mary (see 20:2), then of **Peter** (v. 4) and **the other disciple.** Speculation over John's report that one **did outrun** the other, such as allusions to age, should not lose sight of the individual haste and concern that this detail portrays. Mary's words were troubling and suggested tomb robbery, but John's report emphasizes the short time and the chain of evidence between Mary's finding and the finding of what the disciples closely inspected. The detailed description of the location of the **linen clothes** in vv. 5–7 and the **napkin that was about his head** (v. 7) portrays an evacuation of the bindings, as though passing through them rather than evidence of being humanly removed (compare Lazarus wrapped in grave clothes and his face bound with a napkin, 11:44); see discussion of Carson, *The Gospel According to John*, p. 637.

20:8. He saw, and believed (see 20:29). John did not say what he believed, but it must have been that Jesus was resurrected.

20:9. Peter and John first came to know of the resurrection through what they saw in the tomb; only later did they see it in **scripture**. It is obvious they did not make up a story of resurrection to fit a preconceived understanding of scriptural prophecy. **Must rise** conveys that Scripture and the will of God coincided. John's placement of this note may explain why "that other disciple ... [who] saw, and believed" (20:8) did not relate what was in his heart as a certainty. As Luke 24:12 tells us, "Peter ... departed, wondering in himself at that which was come to pass."

20:10–11. Nothing in John's account confirms that **Mary** (v. 11) and the two disciples met at the tomb. The word **But** contrasts not only that **the disciples went away** (v. 10) and **Mary stood** (v. 11) but also two perspectives: hers (see 20:2; 20:13), leading to tears, and theirs (see 20:6–8), leading to home. Mary's **weeping** means "wailing" (as in 11:33), a loud expression of grief. Perhaps Jesus appeared first to Mary (see 20:14) because she needed Him most at that time.

20:12–13. When Mary ventured to peer into the tomb, the findings of the disciples were eclipsed by the presence of **two angels** (v. 12; see discussion on Luke 24:4). Matthew has one angel (see Matt. 28:2), Mark a young man (see Mark 16:5), and Luke two men who were angels (see Luke 24:4, 23). The presence of these angels, garmented **in white**, "make clear that the empty tomb cannot be explained by appealing to grave robbers; this is nothing other than the invasion of God's power" (Carson, *The Gospel According to John*, p. 640).

20:14–15. Presumably alerted by the approach of a stranger, Mary turned to see who was there but **knew not that it was Jesus** (v. 14). A number of times the risen Jesus was not recognized (see 21:4; Matt. 28:17; Luke 24:16, 37). He may have looked different, or He may have intentionally prevented recognition. If the disciples who had heard Jesus speak of His resurrection had trouble absorbing the hope of it, how difficult would it have been for Mary to think of any reason for the empty tomb but a robbery? She thus asked **the gardner** (v. 15) if he was responsible.

20:16. Perhaps the familiar tone and that He addressed her by name caused Mary to recognize that the one speaking to her was none other than

Jesus (see 10:3–4). **Rabboni** is a strengthened form of "Rabbi" and in the New Testament is found elsewhere only in Mark 10:51 (in the Greek). Although the word means "(my) teacher," there are few if any examples of its use in ancient Judaism as a form of address other than in calling on God in prayer. However, John's own interpretation of the expression as "teacher" (Greek *didaskalos*, JKV: "Master") casts doubt on any thought that Mary intended to address Jesus as God here.

20:17. The grammar of **Touch me not** suggests that it is to be understood as "Stop clinging to me." The picture of Mary immediately embracing Jesus is altogether in keeping with this unexpected answer to her grief: the appearance of Jesus. Taken with the words **for I am not yet ascended**, Jesus was assuring Mary that she would have opportunity to see Him again, so she need not cling to Him. Conversely, Mary was to go and alert the **brethren** with an important message. Here "brethren" refers to the disciples (see 20:18; Matt. 12:50), and its use coincides with the message Mary was to deliver: **I ascend unto my Father, and your Father**. By virtue of what Jesus accomplished in His death and resurrection, His disciples are able to enjoy the full-fledged status of being a child of God. Jesus succinctly expressed its realization in the message Mary was given.

20:18–19. The disciples (v. 18) probably includes others besides the apostles, "the twelve" (20:24). On the heels of her exciting news **that she had seen the Lord**, Mary delivered His message. The danger remained real, however, and the doors were locked **for fear of the Jews** (v. 19; see discussion on 1:19). That the doors were locked also accentuates the miraculous appearance of the resurrected Jesus **in the midst** of the disciples (see Luke 24:36). **Peace be unto you** (see discussion on 14:27) was the normal Hebrew greeting (see Dan. 10:19). Because of their behavior the previous Friday, they may have expected rebuke and censure, but Jesus calmed their fears.

20:20. In keeping with His greeting of peace, Jesus showed the disciples **his hands and his side**, where the wounds were (John did not refer to the wounds in the feet). According to Luke 24:37, the disciples thought they were seeing a ghost. Jesus was clearly identifying Himself.

20:21. It is unlikely that this second **Peace be unto you** (see discussion on 20:19) indicates a need for added assurance, given John's description of the disciples' joy in 20:20. Rather, the repetition prepares for Jesus' solemn commissioning of the disciples: **as my Father hath sent me, even so send I you** (see discussion on 17:18). Different Greek verbs are used for "sent" and "send," but the order is consistent with John's use throughout his gospel. The first verb (Greek, *apostellō*) is used of the commissioning of Jesus, and the second verb (Greek, *pempō*) is used to identify the Father as the sender. Here Jesus mediated the continuation of His commission to His disciples. Jesus' commission stemmed not from His own authority but from that of the Father, and Jesus now transferred this commission to His disciples in anticipation of His departure.

20:22. John clarified that in the continuation of Jesus' commission and authority (17:8, 22), only the Resurrected One was able to pass on the Spirit to those who would carry on His commission. **Receive ye the Holy Ghost** anticipates what happened fifty days later on the day of Pentecost (see Acts 2). The disciples needed God's help to carry out the commission they had just been given.

20:23. This verse reads literally, "Those whose sins you forgive have already been forgiven; those whose sins you do not forgive have not been forgiven." God does not forgive people's sins because believers do so, nor does He withhold forgiveness because Christians do. Rather, those who proclaim the gospel are in effect forgiving or not forgiving sins, depending on whether the hearers accept or reject Jesus Christ.

20:24–25. Thomas (v. 24; see discussion on 11:16) was not present when Jesus first appeared to the disciples (see 20:19–23), so he met the excited announcement of the disciples with skepticism: **Except I shall see … and put … I will not believe.** Hardheaded skepticism can scarcely go further than this.

20:26–28. A week had passed. Jesus appeared again to the disciples, and this time **Thomas** (v. 26) was present. For **Peace**, see discussions on 14:27; 20:19. Jesus addressed Thomas's unbelief with specific attention to the points of his skepticism. For believers today, Thomas may serve as a model of doubts that can be avoided. **Be not faithless, but believing** (v. 27) is a poignant flip of the Greek adjective *pistos* (here rendered "believing"): "Be not an 'unbeliever' [*a-pistos*, or dis-believer], but [be] a 'believer' [*pistos*]." Although the verb "to believe" occurs frequently in John (100 times), the adjective occurs only here. It appears that "seeing was believing" for Thomas, and rather than resort to touching the Lord, he answered Him with a confession of belief: **My Lord and my God** (v. 28). To acknowledge Jesus as one's Lord and God is the high point of faith (see discussion on 1:1).

20:29. They that have not seen, and yet have believed would have applied to very few at this time. All whom John mentioned had "seen" in some sense. The words, of course, apply to future believers as well. **Blessed** (Greek, *makarios*; "happy," "fortunate"; see Matt. 5:3–11) tells one not only something about those who have not seen yet believe as Thomas did (see 20:28); it tells one something about the regard of the Lord Jesus. In short, Jesus assured future generations of believers that they are in no way at a disadvantage in His eyes because they were not present to touch or see Him.

VI. The Statement of Purpose (20:30–31)

20:30. Signs (Greek, *sēmeion*; see discussion on 2:11) refers to the miraculous actions of Jesus that revealed His significance. John had selected from among many the signs that he recorded in his gospel. **In the presence of his disciples** points to those who could testify to what He had done and who He revealed Himself to be. John again stressed testimony (see discussion on 1:7).

20:31. These signs were chosen for a purpose: **that ye might believe** (see discussion on 1:7). John's purpose in writing his gospel was evangelistic. Faith has content. The signs revealed that **Jesus is the Christ** (see discussion on 1:25), **the Son of God**. This whole gospel was written to show the truth of Jesus' mes-

siahship and to present Him as the Son of God, so that the readers may believe in Him. **That believing ye might have life** expresses another purpose: to bring about faith that leads to life (see discussions on 1:4; 3:15). **Through his name** represents all that Jesus is and stands for (see discussion on 2:23) and points to the authority or credentials of the one who gives life.

VII. Epilogue (chap. 21)

21:1. After these things merely puts the following episode later in the sequence of John's record. **Jesus shewed himself** (lit., "revealed himself") **again**, this time **at the sea of Tiberias** (the Sea of Galilee; see discussion on 6:1). The Greek for **on this wise** means "as follows."

21:2. John identified the disciples that were present, those known to the readers and two not known. For **Simon Peter**, see discussion on Mark 1:16–18. For **Thomas**, see discussion on 11:16. For **the sons of Zebedee**, not mentioned by name in this gospel, see Matthew 4:21, which names them as James and John.

21:3. The outline of an unsuccessful night of fishing provides a prequel to the appearance of Jesus. Nighttime was favored by fishermen in ancient times (as Aristotle, e.g., informs us). One must be cautious about assuming that the disciples had abandoned their charge because they engaged in a night of fishing. Peter's eager reaction to the recognition that it was the Lord who addressed them (see 21:7) is not the response of a man that has knowingly displeased his Master.

21:4–6. The disciples **knew not that it was Jesus** (v. 4; as with Mary Magdalene; see discussion on 20:14). Dim light and distance may have been factors in their not recognizing the Lord. Jesus' question, **have ye any meat?** (v. 5), expected an answer of no even before the disciples confirmed it. "Meat," or "fish," translates a word found only here in the New Testament. Literally, the word refers to "a relish" of whatever sort to go with bread (see 21:9). When the Lord's instruction to **Cast the net on the right side** (v. 6) was met with a great catch (see Luke 5:6), it awakened the recognition that the stranger was none other than Jesus (see 21:7).

21:7. The disciple whom Jesus loved, John (see discussion on 13:23; 21:20), characteristically exhibited quick insight, and Peter quick action (see Carson, *The Gospel According to John*, p. 671). It is curious that Peter put on **his fisher's coat**, or "outer garment" (the word appears only here in the New Testament), before jumping into the water, but Jews regarded a greeting as a religious act that could be done only when one was clothed. Peter may have been preparing himself to greet the Lord.

21:8. Peter recklessly abandoned the others and swam to shore, leaving the rest to labor with the huge catch of fish. **Two hundred cubits** is a distance of about one hundred yards.

21:9–10. Jesus had already prepared a breakfast for them of **fish … and bread** (v. 9), to which they could add from their catch. Both supplies were provided by the Lord.

21:11. Peter … drew the net to land apparently means that Peter headed up the effort, for the whole group had not been able previously to haul the net into the boat (see 21:6). One would expect that the size of the catch would cause the net to tear, **yet was not the net broken** (compare Luke 5:6). The number of fish, 153, has triggered not a little speculation over its symbolic importance, but John's emphasis on the net being intact suggests that the number was intended to stress the size of the catch.

21:12–13. Come and dine (v. 12), or literally "eat breakfast." The disciples did not ask for confirmation, for they knew **it was the Lord**. In view of 20:28, "master" is an inadequate lexical option here.

21:14. The third time. This was Jesus' third appearance to a group of disciples (see 20:19–23, 24–29), though He had appeared to individuals (e.g., Mary Magdalene; see 20:14–18). John's repetition of **shewed himself** (see 21:1) forms a literary inclusion. An inclusion is an author's device to begin and end a discussion with the same or closely related words (see 1:18). This verse closes the account of Jesus' appearing to the disciples and transitions to His intimate discussion with Peter, which followed breakfast (see 21:15). The setting remains the same, and one can imagine Jesus and Peter strolling beside

the Sea of Tiberias (see 21:1), with the Beloved Disciple (and the others) just behind them (see 21:20).

21:15–17. The Greek word for "lovest" in Jesus' first two questions (Greek, *agapaō*; vv. 15, 16) is different from the word for "lovest" in His third question (Greek, *phileō*; v. 17), which is the same word Peter used for "love" in all three verses. It is uncertain whether a distinction in meaning is intended since John often made slight word variations, apparently for stylistic reasons. No distinction is made between these two words elsewhere in this gospel. In this passage, however, they occur together, and the variations seem too deliberate to be explained on stylistic grounds. *Agapaō* refers to a love in which the entire personality, including the will, is involved, whereas *phileō* refers to spontaneous natural affection or fondness in which emotion plays a more prominent role than will. Whatever interpretation is adopted, the important thing is that in so serious a matter as the reinstatement of Peter, the great question was whether he loved Jesus. Peter had been restored privately and personally (see Luke 24:34; 1 Cor. 15:5), but now it was to be a public matter. Peter had disowned Christ in public three times. Now he needed to own Christ three times in front of the other disciples.

Intriguing variations are also seen in Jesus' repeated command to Peter.

Verse 15	Feed (*boskō*) my lambs (*arnion*)
Verse 16	Feed (*poimainō*) my sheep (*probaton*)
Verse 17	Feed (*boskō*) my sheep (*probaton*)

Boskō means to "feed as a herdsman," "graze." *Poimainō* means to "tend" or "shepherd" and involves the shepherd's responsibilities of caring, feeding, and protecting (see 1 Peter 5:2). In the end, the distinctions are slight, and the overall emphasis appears to fall on Jesus' thrice-repeated call to fulfill the responsibilities of a shepherd who fully cares for a flock that belongs not to him but to Jesus (see 10:12–13).

21:15. Son of Jonas. The name of Peter's father is mentioned only in John's gospel (see 1:42). That Jesus addressed Peter as He had when they first met (see 1:42) may indicate that He was treating Peter less familiarly and questioning his friendship (see Brown, *The Gospel According to John*, p. 1102). **More than these** may mean "more than you love these men," "more than these men love me," or "more than you love these things" (i.e., the fishing gear). Perhaps the second is best, for Peter had claimed a devotion above that of the others (see 13:37; Matt. 26:33; Mark 14:29). Peter did not take up the comparison, and Jesus did not explain it.

21:16-17. The third time (v. 17) matches Peter's threefold denial (see 13:38; 18:17, 25, 27), and Peter's "grief" (see Mark 14:72) expresses a sad remorse that corresponds to the cumulative toll of Jesus' probing questions. The combined effect of Jesus' command amounted to a call for Peter to be more than "a hireling" (see 10:12-13). He was to be a true shepherd of Jesus' flock. **Thou knowest all things.** Peter's replies stressed Christ's knowledge, not his own grasp of the situation.

21:18-19. Stretch forth thy hands (v. 18). The early church understood this as a prophecy of crucifixion. **By what death** (v. 19). Peter would be a martyr. Tradition indicates that he was crucified upside down.

21:20. The disciple whom Jesus loved (see discussion on 13:23) is pictured as **following** Jesus and

Peter. He was doing what Peter was twice told to do (see 21:19, 22). For **leaned on his breast at supper**, see 13:23-25.

21:21-23. The Lord censured Peter for entertaining comparisons. What mattered was Peter's faithfulness in what the Lord had called him to do: **follow thou me** (v. 22; see 21:19). **Till I come** (vv. 22, 23) is a clear declaration of the second coming. John repeated Jesus' statement to dispel the rumor of verse 23.

21:24. The disciple which testifieth. Testimony is important throughout this gospel (see discussion on 1:7). The Beloved Disciple was the witness behind this account. **These things** must refer to the whole book. **And wrote these things** makes it clear that the Beloved Disciple was not only the witness but also the author of this gospel. **We know** evidently includes some of John's contemporaries in a position to know the truth.

21:25. Many other things. As in 20:30, one is assured that the author has been selective. **Even the world itself could not contain** is probably a case of hyperbole, exaggeration to stress a point, but our historical knowledge of Jesus is at best partial. Nevertheless, readers have been given all they need to know.

THE ACTS OF THE APOSTLES

INTRODUCTION

Author

Although the author does not name himself, evidence outside the Scriptures and inferences from the book itself lead to the conclusion that the author was Luke.

The earliest of the external testimonies appears in the Muratorian Canon (ca. AD 170), which explicitly states that Luke was the author of both the third gospel and the "Acts of All the Apostles." Eusebius (ca. 325) lists information from numerous sources to identify Luke as the author of these two books (*Ecclesiastical History* 3.4).

The book itself presents some clues as to who the author was:

(1) *Luke, the companion of Paul.* In the description of events in Acts, certain passages use the pronoun "we." At these points, the author includes himself as one of Paul's companions in his travels (16:10–17; 20:5–21:18; 27:1–28:16). A historian as careful with details as this author proves to be would have had good reason for choosing to use "we" in some places and "they" elsewhere. The author was therefore probably present with Paul during events described in the "we" sections.

These "we" passages include the period of Paul's two-year imprisonment at Rome (chap. 28). During this time, Paul wrote several letters, including Colossians and Philemon. In these letters, he sent greetings from his companions, and Luke was included among them (see Col. 4:14; Philem. 24). In fact, after eliminating those who, for one reason or another, would not fit the requirements for the author of Acts, Luke is left as the most likely candidate.

(2) *Luke, the physician.* Although it cannot be proved that the author of Acts was a physician simply from his vocabulary, the words he used and the traits and education reflected in his writings fit well his role as a physician (see, e.g., discussion on 28:6). It is true that doctors of the first century did not have as specialized a vocabulary as that of doctors today, but some terms in Luke and Acts suggest that a physician was the author of these books. Paul himself used the term "physician" in describing Luke (Col. 4:14).

1511

Date

Two dates are possible for the writing of this book: (1) circa AD 63, soon after the last event recorded in the book, and (2) circa AD 70 or even later.

Two arguments support the earlier date. (1) Silence about later events. While arguments from silence are not conclusive, it is perhaps significant that the book contains no allusion to events that happened after the close of Paul's two-year imprisonment in Rome: for example, the burning of Rome and the persecution of the Christians there (AD 64), the martyrdom of Peter and Paul (possibly AD 67), and the destruction of Jerusalem (AD 70). (2) No outcome of Paul's trial. If Luke knew the outcome of the trial Paul was waiting for (28:30), why did he not record it at the close of Acts? Apparently, at the time that Luke wrote, the outcome was still in the future.

Those who prefer the later date hold that 1:8 reveals one of Luke's purposes for writing his historical account and that this purpose influenced the way he ended the book. Luke wanted to show how the church penetrated the world of his day in ever-widening circles (Jerusalem, Judea, Samaria, the ends of the earth; see 1:8) until it reached Rome, the world's political and cultural center. Based on this understanding, mention of the martyrdom of Paul (ca. AD 67) and of the destruction of Jerusalem (AD 70) was not pertinent. This would allow for the writing of Acts circa AD 70 or even later. The evidence for this is so thin, however, that the earlier date is much to be preferred.

Recipient

The recipient of the book, Theophilus, is the same person addressed in the first volume, the gospel of Luke (see Luke, Introduction: "Recipient").

Theme and Theological Message

The book of Acts, as a second volume to Luke's gospel, joins what "Jesus began both to do and teach" (1:1), as told in the Gospels, with what He continued to do and teach through the apostles' preaching and the establishment of the church. It unites the writings of the New Testament by providing a bridge between the Gospels and the Epistles. Without Acts, there would be a gap between Jesus' giving the Great Commission, and a series of letters to already established churches, and no context through which to understand them. In addition, Acts supplies an account of the life of Paul, the author of so many of these letters. Geographically, its story spans the lands between Jerusalem, where the church began, and Rome, the political center of the empire. Historically, it recounts the first thirty years of the church. It also ties the church in its beginning to each succeeding age. This book may be studied to gain an understanding of the principles that ought to govern the church of any age.

The major theme of Acts is best summarized in 1:8. It was ordinary procedure for a historian at this time to begin a second volume by summarizing the first volume and indicating the contents anticipated in his second volume. Luke summarized his first volume in 1:1–3; the theme of his second volume is presented in the words of Jesus: "ye shall be witnesses unto me both in Jerusalem, and in all Judea, and in Samaria, and unto the uttermost part of the earth" (1:8). This is, in effect, an outline of the book of Acts (see "Outline," below).

Luke seems to have written Acts with several themes in mind. His theological and exhortation-encouragement themes are especially prominent, however.

(1) *Historical.* The significance of Acts as a historical account of Christian origins cannot be overestimated. It tells of the founding of the church, the spread of the gospel, the beginnings of congregations, and evangelistic efforts in the apostolic pattern. One of the unique aspects of Christianity is its firm historical foundation. The life and teachings of Jesus Christ are established in the four Gospel narratives, and the book of Acts provides a coordinated account of the beginnings of the church and its geographical spread over the first three decades of its existence (see Ger, *The Book of Acts*, p. 8).

(2) *Apologetic.* One finds embedded in Acts a record of Christian defenses made to both Jews (e.g., 4:8–12) and Gentiles (e.g., 25:8–11), with the underlying purpose of conversion. It shows how the early church coped with pagan and Jewish thought, the Roman government, and Hellenistic society.

(3) *Legal.* Luke probably wrote Acts while Paul awaited trial in Rome. It has been suggested that he wrote with the purpose of helping in Paul's defense before the emperor. If Paul's case came to court, what better court brief could he have had than Luke's account of the life of Jesus, history of the beginnings of the church (including the activity of Paul), and early collection of Paul's letters? Advocates of this view point out that Roman officials always vindicate Paul in Acts.

(4) *Prescriptive.* Luke had no way of knowing how long the church would continue on this earth, but he may have wanted to provide guidance to congregations facing common problems. Indeed, as long as the church pursues its course, the book of Acts will be one of its major guides. In Acts, basic principles are applied to specific situations in the context of problems and persecutions. These same principles will continue to be applicable until Christ returns.

(5) *Theological.* Since Acts is the second volume of the work that Luke began in his gospel, these two books are best viewed together. A major theme in the gospel of Luke is that the grace of God is available to Gentiles as well as to Jews (see Ger, *The Book of Acts*, p. 8). Acts highlights the spread of the gospel to the Gentile world in a manner consistent with the theological theme so prominent in Luke's earlier work: the universality of the gospel. This explains Luke's emphasis on Paul's missionary work, as well as why so much attention is given to the conversion of Cornelius and why the Jerusalem church receives comparatively little attention after the early chapters of the book (see Marshall, *Acts of the Apostles*, pp. 18–20).

(6) *Exhortation and encouragement.* Churches in the second half of the first century faced increased persecution in various places. Isolated groups of Christians might easily become discouraged. Despair often results from persecution as the vision wanes and as success continually eludes those seeking to evangelize. The success of the church in carrying the gospel from Jerusalem to Rome and in planting local churches across the Roman Empire demonstrated that Christianity was not a mere work of man; God was in it (5:35–39). Churches could read Luke's account and be strengthened to endure the trials they faced while being emboldened to tell the good news of Jesus Christ to their communities.

Literary Features

The book of Acts is a delight to read. Luke was a master of good style and knew how to tell a story well. Several features are evident to the reader who pays attention to matters of style.

(1) *Accurate historical detail.* Every page of Acts abounds with sharp, precise details, to the delight of the historian. The account covers a period of about thirty years and reaches across the lands from Jerusalem to Rome. Luke's description of these times and places is filled with all kinds of people and cultures, a variety of governmental administrations, court scenes in Caesarea, and dramatic events involving such centers as Antioch, Ephesus, Athens, Corinth, and Rome. Barbarian country districts and Jewish centers are included as well. Yet in each instance, archaeological findings reveal that Luke used the proper terms for the time and place being described. Hostile criticism has not succeeded in disproving the detailed accuracy of Luke's political and geographical designations.

(2) *Literary excellence.* Luke not only had a large vocabulary compared with other New Testament writers, but he also used these words in literary styles that fit the cultural settings of the events he was recording. At times, he employed good, classical Greek; at other times, the Palestinian Aramaic of the first century shows through his expressions. This is an indication of Luke's careful practice of using language appropriate to the time and place being described. Aramaisms are found in Luke's descriptions of events in the Holy Land (chaps. 1–12). These cease, however, in his descriptions of events in the Hellenistic lands beyond the territories where Aramaic-speaking people lived.

(3) *Dramatic description.* Luke's skillful use of speeches contributes to the drama of his narrative. Not only are they carefully spaced and well balanced between Peter and Paul, but the speeches of a number of other individuals add variety and vividness to the account. Luke's use of details brings the action to life. Nowhere in ancient literature is there an account of a shipwreck superior to Luke's with its nautical details (chap. 27). The book is vivid and fast-moving throughout.

(4) *Objective account.* Luke's careful arrangement of material need not detract from the accuracy of his record. He demonstrated the objectivity of his account by recording the failures as well as the successes, the bad as well as the good, in the early church. Luke recorded not only the discontent between the Grecian Jews and the Hebraic Jews (6:1) but also the discord between Paul and Barnabas (15:39). He recognized the divisions and differences within the early church (15:2; 21:20–21).

Outline

Luke wove together different interests and emphases as he related the beginnings and the expansion of the church. The design of his book revolves around (1) key persons: Peter and Paul; (2) important topics and events: the role of the Holy Spirit, pioneer missionary outreach to new fields, conversions, the growth of the church, and life in the Christian community; (3) significant problems: conflict between Jews and Gentiles, persecution of the church by some Jewish elements, trials before Jews and Romans, confrontations with Gentiles, and other hardships in the ministry; (4) geographical advances: five significant expansions of the gospel (see the quotations in the outline; see also map, *Zondervan KJV Study Bible*, p. 1582).

Bibliography

Bruce, F. F. *The Book of Acts*. Rev. edition. The New International Commentary on the New Testament. Grand Rapids, MI: Eerdmans, 1988.

Ger, Steven. *The Book of Acts: Witnesses to the World*. Twenty-first Century Biblical Commentary. Chattanooga, TN: AMG, 2005.

Larkin, William J. *Acts*. The IVP New Testament Commentary. Downers Grove, IL: InterVarsity, 1995.

Longenecker, Richard N. "Acts." In *The Expositor's Bible Commentary*, edited by Frank E. Gaebelein, vol 9. Grand Rapids, MI: Zondervan, 2002.

Macaulay, Joseph C. *Expository Commentary on Acts*. Chicago: Moody Press, 1978.

Marshall, I. Howard. *The Acts of the Apostles: An Introduction and Commentary*. Tyndale New Testament Commentaries 5. Grand Rapids, MI: Eerdmans, 1980.

Polhill, John B. *Acts*. The New American Commentary 26. Nashville: Broadman & Holman, 1992.

Talbert, Charles H. *Reading Acts: A Literary and Theological Commentary on the Acts of the Apostles*. New York: Crossroad, 1997.

EXPOSITION

I. Peter and the Beginnings of the Church in Palestine (chaps. 1–12)

A. First Geographical Expansion of the Church: "Throughout all Judea and Galilee and Samaria" (1:1–9:31; see 9:31)

1. Introduction (1:1–2)

1:1. The former treatise. The gospel of Luke. Luke and Acts are addressed to the same patron, **Theophilus** (see Luke, Introduction: "Recipient"). **All that Jesus began both to do and teach**. An apt summation of Luke's gospel, implying that Jesus' work continued in Acts through His own personal interventions and the ministry of the Holy Spirit.

1:2. Taken up. The last scene of Luke's gospel (see Luke 24:50–52) and the opening scene of this second volume (see 1:6–11). The ascension occurred forty days after the resurrection (see 1:3). **Through the Holy Ghost**. Jesus' postresurrection instruction of His apostles was carried on through the Holy Spirit, and succeeding statements make it clear that what the apostles were to accomplish was likewise to be done through the Spirit (see 1:4–5, 8; Luke 24:49;

John 20:22; see also Judges, Introduction: "Theme and Theological Message"). Luke characteristically stressed the Holy Spirit's work and enabling power (see, e.g., 1:8; 2:4, 17; 4:8, 31; 5:3; 6:3, 5; 7:55; 8:16; 9:17, 31; 10:44; 13:2, 4; 15:28; 16:6; 19:2, 6; see discussion on Luke 4:1).

2. Christ's Postresurrection Ministry (1:3–11)

1:3. For many infallible proofs, see the resurrection appearances in Matthew 28:1–20; Mark 16:1–20; Luke 24:1–53; John 20:1–29; 1 Corinthians 15:3–8. **The kingdom of God**. The heart of Jesus' preaching (see discussions on Matt. 3:2; Luke 4:43).

1:4. The promise of the Father. The Holy Spirit (see John 14:26; 15:26–27; 16:12–13).

1:5. For John truly baptized with water, see Luke 3:16. **Not many days hence**. The day of Pentecost came ten days later, when the baptism with the Holy Spirit occurred (see 2:1–4).

1:6. Restore again the kingdom to Israel. Like their fellow countrymen, the apostles were looking for the deliverance of the people of Israel from foreign domination and for the establishment of an earthly kingdom. The reference to the coming of the Spirit (see 1:4–5) had caused them to wonder if the new age was about to dawn.

1:7. The times or the seasons. The elapsing time or the character of coming events (see 1 Thess. 5:1).

1:8. Ye shall be witnesses unto me. An important theme throughout Acts (see 2:32; 3:15; 5:32; 10:39; 13:31; 22:15). This verse is a virtual outline of Acts: the apostles were to be witnesses **in Jerusalem** (see chaps. 1–7), **and in all Judea, and in Samaria** (see chaps. 8–9), **and unto the uttermost part of the earth,** including Caesarea, Antioch, Asia Minor, Greece, and Rome (see chaps. 10–28). They were not to begin this staggering task, however, until they had been equipped with the **power [of] the Holy Ghost** (see 1:4–5). Judea was the region in which Jerusalem was located. Samaria was the adjoining region to the north.

1:9. He was taken up. This is the fullest description of the ascension of Jesus Christ is recorded in Scripture. Jesus was not continually with the disciples during the forty days leading up to this incident, and one may suppose that He was already in the heavenly places with His Father. The uniqueness of this disappearance of the Lord lies in the fact that He ascended from the ground, was received into a cloud, and did not appear on earth again to the disciples. (The Lord's appearance to Stephen in chap. 7 was an altogether different matter.) His reception into **a cloud** brings to mind His words to the disciples that He would return again some day in the clouds (see Mark 13:26; 14:62 and Bruce, *The Book of Acts,* p. 38). The cloud here thus marked the fact that this time they would not see Him again until His return.

1:10. Two men ... in white apparel. A common description of angels.

1:11. Men of Galilee. The Twelve were all from Galilee except Judas, and he was no longer present. **In like manner.** In the same resurrection body and "in the clouds ... with power and great glory" (Matt. 24:30). This also was an indication to the disciples that they should expect no more appearances of the risen Christ but should begin waiting for the promise of the Spirit (see 1:8).

3. The Period of Waiting for the Holy Spirit (1:12–26)

1:12. The mount called Olivet (see Luke 19:28–29, 37; discussions on Zech. 14:4; Mark 11:1; Luke 19:29). The ascension occurred on the eastern slope of the mount between Jerusalem and Bethany. **A sabbath day's journey.** About three-quarters of a mile (1,100 meters). This distance was drawn from rabbinical reasoning based on several Old Testament passages (Exod. 16:29; Num. 35:5; Josh. 3:4). A faithful Jew was to travel no farther on the Sabbath. This is not an indication that the ascension took place on a Sabbath; in fact, it would not have since it occurred forty days after the resurrection. The resurrection happened on a Sunday. The ascension happened on a Friday. The Sabbath would not have begun until sundown.

1:13. An upper room. Probably a room on the upper floor of a large house, such as the one where the Last Supper was held (see Mark 14:15) or that of Mary, mother of Mark (see discussion on 12:12). **Bartholomew.** Apparently, John called him Nathanael (see John 1:45–49; 21:2). **James the son of Alpheus.** The same as James the younger (see Mark 15:40). For **Simon Zelotes,** the same as Simon the Canaanite, see discussion on Matthew 10:4. **Judas the brother of James.** Not Judas Iscariot, but the same as Thaddeus (see Matt. 10:3; Mark 3:18).

1:14. With the women. Possibly wives of the apostles (see 1 Cor. 9:5) and those listed as ministering to Jesus (see Matt. 27:55; Luke 8:2–3; 24:22). **Mary the mother of Jesus.** Last mentioned here in Scripture. **Brethren** (see discussion on Luke 8:19). These brothers would have included James, who later became important in the church (see 12:17; 15:13; Gal. 2:9).

1:15–16. About an hundred and twenty (v. 15). The first of a series of progress reports given periodically throughout the book of Acts (here; 2:41; 4:4; 5:14; 6:7; 9:31; 12:24; 16:5; 19:20; 28:31). Luke often used these reports, which frequently point to a period of growth in numbers for the church, to indicate that he was concluding one topic and moving on to another. **This scripture must needs have been fulfilled** (v. 16; see 1:20). Peter was referring to Psalms 69:25; 109:8. Both before and after Christ came, numerous psalms were viewed as messianic. The psalmist's experiences were typical of the Messiah's experiences. No doubt Jesus' teaching in Luke 24:27, 45–47 included these Scriptures.

1:17–18. This man purchased a field (v. 18). Judas bought the field indirectly: the money he returned to the priests (see Matt. 27:3) was used to purchase the potter's field (see Matt. 27:7). **Falling headlong**. Matthew 27:5 reports that Judas "hanged himself." It appears that when the body finally fell, either because of decay or because someone cut it down, it was in a decomposed condition and so broke open in the middle. Another possibility is that "hanged" in Matthew 27:5 means "impaled" (the Hebrew of Est. 2:23 can be translated "impaled"; see discussion there) and that the gruesome results of Judas's suicide are described here.

1:19. Aceldama … The field of blood. An Aramaic term, no doubt adopted by people who knew the circumstances, for the field was purchased with Judas's blood money (see Matt. 27:3–8).

1:20. It is written (see 1:16). Two passages of Scripture (Pss. 69:25; 109:8) were put together to suggest that Judas had left a vacancy that had to be filled. **His bishoprick** would not have designated a church office. The word means literally "superintendence" or more literally "overseership."

1:21. All the time that the Lord Jesus went in and out among us. The first requirement for the person selected to replace Judas was that he be someone who had been with Jesus during the entire time He ministered publicly.

1:22. A witness with us of his resurrection. The second requirement was that he be someone who had seen the risen Christ. Apparently, several met this requirement. On this occasion, however, the believers were selecting someone to become an official witness to the resurrection, a twelfth apostle (see 1:25). The number twelve here has no mystical significance; it is the number of the tribes of Israel, which Jesus had promised the apostles would judge, sitting on twelve thrones (see Matt. 19:28). It would not do if one of the thrones was vacant.

1:23. Barsabas. Means "son of [the] Sabbath." This patronymic was used for two early Jewish Christians, possibly brothers. One was Joseph (here); the other was Judas, a prophet in Jerusalem who was sent to Antioch with Silas (see 15:22, 32). **Justus**. Joseph's Hellenistic name. Nothing more is known of him.

1:24. Once two qualified men were chosen, the disciples prayed. Their prayer was directed to God but included a relevant fact about God. Since God **knowest the hearts of all men,** He would know who was best suited to the office of apostle.

1:25. Judas by transgression fell. That is, Judas fell from a position of authority and inclusion among the apostles. Some want to determine from this or from **that he might go to his own place** that Judas was unsaved and went to hell. This is reading more into this verse than is warranted. The euphemism "go to his own place" in those days meant one's final destiny and could be either heaven or hell (see Marshall, *Acts of the Apostles*, p. 66). It may be that Luke himself was unsure and deliberately left the matter ambiguous. All that Scripture clearly reveals here is that Judas lost his apostleship. Anything else is a matter of inference, whether from here or from other passages that mention Judas.

1:26. They gave forth their lots. By casting lots, the disciples were able to allow God the right of choice. The use of rocks or sticks to designate the choice was common (see 1 Chron. 26:13–16; see also discussions on Neh. 11:1; Prov. 16:33; Jonah 1:7). This is the Bible's last mention of casting lots. This, at least by implication, indicates that after the coming of the Holy Spirit, such a device was no longer necessary. Again, that is inference as well as argument from silence, but there is no indication that the early church continued the practice, nor was it a part of later practice. **And the lot fell upon Matthias.** One should not make too much of the fact that Matthias plays no major role in the book of Acts. Most of the other apostles do not either. Luke's purpose was not to trace the ministry of each apostle but to focus on Peter and later Paul and the spread of the gospel to the Gentiles.

4. *The Filling with the Spirit (chap. 2)*

2:1. The day of Pentecost. The fiftieth day after the Sabbath of Passover week (see Lev. 23:15–16), thus the first day of the week. Pentecost is also called "the feast of weeks" (Deut. 16:10), "the feast of harvest" (Exod. 23:16), and "the day of the firstfruits" (Num. 28:26). **They were all with one accord.** The nearest antecedent of "they" is "the eleven apostles" (plus Matthias; 1:26), but the reference is probably to all those mentioned in 1:13–15. **In one place.** Evidently not the upstairs room where they were staying (see 1:13) but perhaps somewhere in the temple precincts, for the apostles "were continually in the temple" (Luke 24:53; see discussion there) when it was open.

2:2. A rushing mighty wind. "Wind" (Greek, *pnoē*), or "breath," is a symbol of the Spirit of God (see Ezek. 37:9, 14; John 3:8). The coming of the Spirit was marked by audible (wind) and visible (fire) signs. **The house.** Some say this may refer to the temple (see 7:47), but that is hardly possible. It would not be referred to as a "house" in this context, and **they were sitting**, which may indicate that they were together in a smaller room, not in the much larger space of the temple.

2:3. Tongues. A descriptive metaphor appropriate to the context, in which several languages were soon to be spoken. In the Old Testament, when the Spirit came upon someone, they would prophesy (declare the message of God; see 2:11; 1 Sam. 19:20–23). This seems to be what happened here. **Fire.** A symbol of the divine presence (see *KJV Study Bible* note on Exod. 3:2), it is also associated with judgment (see Matt. 3:12).

2:4. All could refer either to the Twelve or to the 120 disciples mentioned in 1:15. Those holding that the 120 are meant point to the fulfillment of Joel's prophecy (see 2:16–18) as involving more than the twelve apostles. The nearest reference, however, is to the apostles (see discussion on 2:1), and the narrative continues with "Peter, standing up with the eleven" (2:14) to address the crowd. In addition, the tongues speakers are referred to as Galileans in 2:7, which points to the apostles (see Ger, *The Book of*

Acts, p. 38). **Filled with the Holy Ghost.** A fulfillment of 1:5, 8; see also Jesus' promise in Luke 24:49. Their spirits were completely under the control of the Spirit; their words were His words. **With other tongues.** The Spirit enabled them to speak in languages they had not previously learned (the Greek can mean "tongues" or "languages"; also in 2:11). Two other examples of speaking in tongues are found in Acts (10:46; 19:6). One extended New Testament passage deals with this spiritual gift (1 Cor. 12–14). Not all agree, however, that these other passages refer to speaking in known languages. The gift had particular relevance here since people of different nationalities and languages were gathered.

2:5. Jews, devout men. Devout Jews from different parts of the world were assembled in Jerusalem either as visitors or as current residents (see Luke 2:25).

2:6. Every man heard them speak in his own language. Jews from different parts of the world would have understood the Aramaic of their homeland as well as the Greek language, which was common to all parts of the world. More than this was occurring, however; they heard the apostles speak in languages native to the different places represented.

2:7. Are not all these which speak Galileans? This must refer to the apostles (see 2:4), for surely some among the 120 disciples (see 1:15) were Judeans.

2:8. How hear we every man in our own tongue …? This was, however, a miracle not of hearing but of speaking, since the apostles are referred to as speaking in "other tongues" (2:4).

2:9. Parthians. Inhabitants of the territory from the Tigris to India. **Medes.** Media lay east of Mesopotamia, northwest of Persia, and south-southwest of the Caspian Sea. **Elamites.** Elam was north of the Persian Gulf, bounded on the west by the Tigris. **Mesopotamia.** Between the Euphrates and Tigris rivers. **Judea.** The homeland of the Jews, perhaps used here in the Old Testament sense of "from the river of Egypt unto the … Euphrates" (Gen. 15:18), including Galilee. **Cappadocia, in Pontus, and Asia.** Districts in Asia Minor.

2:10. Phrygia, and Pamphylia. Districts in Asia Minor. **Egypt.** Contained a great number of Jews. Two out of the five districts of Alexandria were Jewish. **Libya.** A region west of Egypt. **Cyrene.** The capital of a district of Libya called Cyrenaica. **Rome.** Thousands of Jews lived in Rome. **Proselytes.** Gentiles who undertook the full observance of the Mosaic law were received into full fellowship with the Jews.

2:11. Cretes. Represented an island lying south-southeast of Greece. **Arabians.** From a region to the east. The kingdom of the Nabatean Arabs lay between the Red Sea and the Euphrates, with Petra as its capital. **We do hear them speak in our tongues.** A miracle not of hearing but of speaking. The believers were declaring God's wonders (prophesying) in the native languages of the various visiting Jews.

2:12–13. They were all amazed (v. 12). Everyone was surprised at what they heard. Apparently, it was unusual for fishermen and workmen such as these to be fluent in foreign languages. **Others mocking** (v. 13). Some people will scorn even the most evident work of God. **Full of new wine.** They accused the disciples of being undisciplined and sensual, the opposite of what they were.

2:14–40. The pattern and themes of Peter's Pentecostal sermon became common in the early church: (1) an explanation of events (vv. 14–21); (2) the gospel of Jesus Christ—His death, resurrection, and exaltation (vv. 22–36); (3) an exhortation to repentance and baptism (vv. 37–40). The outline of this sermon is similar to those in 3:12–26; 10:34–43; 13:16–41.

2:14. With the eleven. The apostles had been baptized with the Holy Spirit and had spoken in other languages to various groups. Now they stood with **Peter,** who served as their spokesman.

2:15. The third hour of the day. On a festival day such as Pentecost, a Jew would not break his fast until at least 10:00 a.m. It was therefore extremely unlikely that this group of Jewish men would have been drunk at such an early hour.

2:16–18. Upon all flesh: your sons and your daughters ... your young men ... and your old men (v. 17) **... on my servants and on my handmaidens**

(v. 18). The Spirit is bestowed on all, irrespective of sex, age, and rank (see Gal. 3:26–4:7).

2:16. The prophet Joel. Peter quoted from Joel 2:28–32, an apocalyptic passage. **This is that which was spoken.** Peter meant not that this event was the final fulfillment of Joel's prophecy, for obviously there had been no changes in the sun and moon (see 2:19–20), but rather that this was the kind of event Joel had in mind, and it inaugurated a new dispensation in God's dealings with His people, just as will happen at the end.

2:17. In the last days (see Isa. 2:2; Hos. 3:5; Mic. 4:1; Heb. 1:2; discussions on 1 Tim. 4:1; 2 Tim. 3:1; 1 Peter 1:20; 1 John 2:18). In Joel 2:28, the Hebrew has "after this," and the Septuagint has "after these things." Peter interpreted the passage as referring specifically to the latter days of the new covenant (see Jer. 31:33–34; Ezek. 36:26–27; 39:29) in contrast to the former days of the old covenant. The age of messianic fulfillment had arrived. For **my Spirit,** see discussion on 1:2.

2:19–20. Certain apocalyptic signs are described here, quoted from Joel 2:30–31. Peter was not asserting that these things were happening. He was giving the fuller context of the prophecy and linking the event that had just happened to God's overall plan for His people, which includes the **day of the Lord** (v. 20).

2:21. Whosoever shall call (see 2:39) means faith and response rather than merely using words (see Matt. 7:21). Luke would not have meant that one could merely say the words. In his gospel, he highlighted Jesus' emphasis on the need for genuine faith, faith from the heart, not just outward actions.

2:22. This begins the second theme of Peter's sermon: the presentation of the gospel. He first commended Jesus to his audience in terms of what they had already seen and heard: **as ye yourselves also know.** Even those who were in town just for the feast would likely have heard of the events surrounding the ministry of Jesus. He thus had been **approved ... by miracles and wonders and signs.** The mighty works that Jesus did were signs that the Messiah had come.

2:23. Having attested to who Jesus is, Peter next focused on His work on the cross. Peter pointed out that Jesus' crucifixion was not an accident but was done **by the determinate counsel and foreknowledge of God**. The cross was not a tragic end or even a tragic interlude; it was the plan of God to accomplish the work of redemption. **Wicked hands**. The Greek has "those not having the law," that is, Gentiles. The reference is to the Romans involved in the trial and crucifixion of Christ. These Gentiles had acted in an evil ("wicked") way. The counsel of God and His eternal purposes may thus take into account the wickedness of men, without excusing their responsibility for their deeds.

2:24. Peter turned to the resurrection. **Whom God hath raised up**. Once again, this was a work of God. **It was not possible he should be holden of it**. That is, it was not possible for Jesus to be kept in the grave.

2:25–28. In explaining why it was impossible for Jesus to remain in the grave, Peter quoted Psalm 16:8–11. David was prophesying, but even though he used the first person, his words refer not to himself but, Peter asserted, to Jesus. These verses, then, say that Jesus could not be kept in the grave because God had promised not to leave Him there. Peter began with the prophecy's assertion that God is always before Him and God is on His **right hand** (v. 25). Again, as Peter went on to point out (see 2:29–31, 34), David was not speaking of himself here, though it would appear that way on the surface.

My flesh shall rest in hope (v. 26). Jesus went to His death knowing that He would not remain there (see Luke 23:43, where Jesus made a promise to one of the thieves that assumed that they both would live beyond their physical deaths: "To day shalt thou be with me in paradise"). **Thou wilt not leave my soul in hell** (v. 27). David referred ultimately to the Messiah (see 2:31). God would not allow His physical body to decompose in the grave (Hades).

Since God had made known to David **the ways of life** (v. 28), he could face the future with **joy**, and by extension, so could the Messiah, the real first-person narrator here.

2:29. To emphasize that David did not have himself in view in this psalm, Peter pointed to a fact his hearers knew well: **his sepulchre is with us**. The sepulchre of David could be seen in Jerusalem. It still contained the remains of David's body. The words of Psalm 16:8–11 thus did not fully apply to him.

2:30–31. Peter made the point of 2:29 explicit as he began to turn toward a consideration of the exalted Christ in heaven.

2:32. Jesus hath God raised up. Peter again pointed out that the resurrection was a work of God (see 2:23–24).

2:33. The promise of the Holy Ghost refers to "the promise of the Father" in 1:4. **He hath shed forth this** (see 2:17; Joel 2:28). Peter tied his words regarding the work of Christ to the events of that morning, the coming of the Holy Spirit.

2:34–35. The LORD said unto my Lord (v. 34; see discussion on Ps. 110:1). Meaning, "The Lord [God] said unto my Lord [the Son of David, the Messiah]." According to Peter, David addressed his descendant with uncommon respect because he, through the inspiration of the Spirit, recognized how great and divine He would be (see Matt. 22:41–45). Not only was He to be resurrected (see 2:31–32); He was to be exalted to God's **right hand**. His presence there was now being demonstrated by the sending of the Holy Spirit (see 2:33; John 16:7).

2:36. Peter began the final part of his sermon: the call for a response. **Let all the house of Israel know**. Peter called for a response based on knowledge. Faith is always tied to what we know of the truth that is in Christ. **God hath made**. Peter again emphasized that this was the work of God. God allowed the death of Christ, God raised Him up, and God exalted Him to heaven. Peter's audience would have found this a persuasive argument for repentance and faith. Throughout the Old Testament, the Jewish people were blessed when they responded in faith to the mighty acts of God. Peter was letting his Jewish audience know that they were now being confronted with a new mighty act of God, for which they were accountable to respond in faith.

2:37. They were pricked in their heart. Reflects both belief in Jesus and regret over their former rejection of Him.

2:38. Repent, and be baptized. Repentance was important in the message of the forerunner, John the Baptist (see Mark 1:4; Luke 3:3), in the preaching of Jesus (see Mark 1:15; Luke 13:3), and in the directions Jesus gave His disciples just before His ascension (see Luke 24:47). Baptism also was important in the work of John the Baptist (see Mark 1:4), in Jesus' instructions to His disciples (see Matt. 28:18–19), and in the preaching recorded in Acts. In Acts, baptism is associated with belief (see 8:12; 18:8), acceptance of the Word (see 2:41), and repentance (here). **In the name of Jesus Christ.** Not a contradiction to the fuller formula given in Matthew 28:19. The abbreviated form emphasizes the distinctive quality of this baptism, for Jesus was now included in a way that He was not in John's baptism (see 19:4–5). **For the remission of sins.** Not that baptism effects remission (forgiveness); rather, forgiveness comes through that which is symbolized by baptism (see Rom. 6:3–4 and discussion). **The Holy Ghost.** Two gifts had now been given: the forgiveness of sins (see also 22:16) and the Holy Spirit. The promise of the indwelling gift of the Holy Spirit is given to all Christians (see Rom. 8:9–11; 1 Cor. 12:13).

2:39. The promise is unto you, and to your children, and to all that … God shall call. Peter here acknowledged that this new work of God, the gift of the Holy Spirit, was not temporary. Those who had witnessed the coming of the Spirit could not pass it off as something merely temporary or local. This was therefore a call to respond in faith, in that moment, to the call of God.

2:40. This verse indicates that Luke did not record all of Peter's message here. The systematic treatment given here, however, shows that readers have the gist and outline of it. This verse may also indicate that Peter (and presumably the disciples with him) followed up the message with personal evangelism.

2:41. They that gladly received his word. Many, but apparently not all, believed. **There were added unto them.** Added to the number of believers. **About three thousand souls** (see discussion on 1:15). It is possible that all three thousand might have heard Peter's sermon. Equally likely, however, is that the entire day was spent in witnessing to the truth of Christ and making converts. The commotion surely attracted latecomers, who then heard the Word expounded or heard the testimonies of new believers. One mark of genuine faith is an eagerness to testify to the Lord's grace. The initial band of hearers thus became a force for evangelism that same day.

2:42. The apostles' doctrine. Included all that Jesus Himself taught (see Matt. 28:20), especially the gospel, which centers on His death, burial, and resurrection (see 2:23–24; 3:15; 4:10; 1 Cor. 15:1–4). Luke used the term here to emphasize that what "Jesus began both to do and teach" (1:1) He was now doing through His Spirit-anointed apostles. Their doctrine was a unique teaching in that it came from God and was clothed with the authority conferred on the apostles (see 2 Cor. 13:10; 1 Thess. 4:2). Today, this same teaching is available in the books of the New Testament. **Fellowship.** The corporate fellowship of believers in worship. **Breaking of bread.** Although this phrase is used of an ordinary meal in 2:46 (see Luke 24:30, 35), the Lord's Supper seems to be indicated here (see discussion on 20:7; see 1 Cor. 10:16; 11:20). **Prayers.** Acts emphasizes the importance of prayer, private as well as public, in the Christian life (see 1:14; 3:1; 6:4; 10:4, 31; 12:5; 16:13, 16).

2:43. Fear came upon every soul. This was not the fear that comes from a lack of faith or assurance. Everyone took the things of God seriously and were in awe of what God had done and was doing. **Many wonders and signs were done by the apostles.** It is well to note here that these "wonders and signs were done by the apostles," not by believers generally. Later, Stephen would perform "wonders and miracles" (6:8) and then Phillip (see 8:6), but nowhere do these things happen generally by all believers, nor even by all leaders in the church.

2:44. All that believed were together. This expresses the unity of the early church. They were together in their sense of purpose and common life. Obviously, all three thousand (see 2:41) could not have lived in one household. **Had all things common** (see 4:34–35). This was a voluntary sharing to provide for those who did not have enough for the essentials of living (for examples of good and bad sharing, see 4:36–5:10).

2:45. Parted them to all men. The disciples sold off surplus goods and gave to the needy. That Luke mentioned this here indicates that a communal lifestyle was not common in the churches of the first century. If it had been, he would not have felt the need to mention this as an unusual thing.

2:46. Breaking bread from house to house. Here the daily life of Christians is described, distinguishing their activity **in the temple** from that in their homes, where they ate their meals—not the Lord's Supper (see discussion on 2:42)—with gladness and generosity. **With gladness and singleness of heart**. The fellowship, oneness, and sharing enjoyed in the early church are fruits of the Spirit. Joy is to be the mood of the believer (see discussions on 8:39; 16:34).

5. Conflict between the New Church and Jewish Authorities (3:1–4:31)

3:1–4:31. These chapters deal with conflict between the new church and the Jewish authorities. Luke's report of it sets up Paul's later conflict with them in Jerusalem, which led to his arrest (see 21:27–36). Luke seems eager to point out that the authorities did not understand the gospel and opposed it on wrong grounds. Since the Jews had hardened their hearts to the gospel, it was to be taken to the Gentiles, and Luke was demonstrating that fact here.

3:1. Peter and John. Among the foremost apostles (see Gal. 2:9). Along with John's brother, James, they had been especially close to Jesus (see Mark 9:2; 13:3; 14:33; Luke 22:8). They may have been going to the temple together because of the pattern that Jesus had established of traveling in twos for ministry (see Marshall, *Acts of the Apostles*, p. 86). They appear together in Acts on several occasions; they were arrested together (see 4:3), and they were together in Samaria (see 8:14). **The hour of prayer**. The three stated times of prayer for later Judaism are midmorning (the third hour, 9:00 a.m.), the time of the evening sacrifice (**the ninth hour**, 3:00 p.m.), and sunset. Most likely, they were at the temple in late afternoon.

3:2. A certain man lame. It is likely that this man had been at the gate daily. Perhaps Peter and John had given him alms in the past. **The gate … called Beautiful**. The favorite entrance to the temple court, it was probably the bronze-sheathed gate that led from the court of the Gentiles to the court of women, on the east wall of the temple proper, though other possibilities have been suggested (see Marshall, *Acts of the Apostles*, p. 87).

3:3. Asked an alms. The man sought financial support from them but may have done so mechanically, without paying much attention to who was walking by (see Marshall, *Acts of the Apostles*, p. 88). That Peter had to ask for his attention (see 3:4–5) indicates this was the case.

3:4–5. Fastening his eyes upon him (v. 4) … **and he gave heed unto them** (v. 5). The encounter moved from an impersonal request of strangers to a personal encounter between one who had great need and the representatives of the One who gives life abundantly (see Marshall, *Acts of the Apostles*, p. 88).

3:6. In the name of Jesus Christ. Not by the apostles' own power, but by the authority of the Messiah. This reinforces that Luke's account records the continuing acts of Jesus through His church.

3:7. And lift him up. Here Peter did a miracle through the power of Jesus Christ, but that is not the whole story. To be healed, the man had to have faith (see 3:16). Perhaps he had heard of Jesus but had not been present to hear Him teach. Perhaps he knew of others who had found healing, and he despaired, knowing that Jesus had been crucified. When Peter evoked His name, however, the man realized that the power of God through Christ was still available, and in that moment, the faith he had not had opportunity to exercise during Christ's earthly ministry was again aroused, and he found the Lord still faithful.

3:8. Entered … the temple. Assuming that this was the bronze-sheathed gate mentioned in 3:2, the man entered from the outer court (for Gentiles also) into the court of women, which contained the treasury (see Mark 12:41–44), and then into the court of Israel. From the outer court, nine gates led into the inner courts.

3:9–10. Many people were present in the temple at this time. **And they were filled with wonder and amazement** (v. 10). This harks back to 2:43, where everyone was amazed as the apostles performed "wonders and signs." The context there seems to require that "every soul" means "everyone in the church," though it is not impossible that Luke had in mind something like "everyone in town." Here it is clear that the witnesses of the miracle were the general population.

3:11. The porch that is called Solomon's (see discussion on John 10:23). A porch along the inner side of the wall enclosing the outer court, with rows of 27-foot-high stone columns and a roof of cedar.

3:12–26. For the pattern and themes common in the sermons of the early church, see discussion on 2:14–40. Once again, as on the day of Pentecost, Peter explained a miracle to the resultant crowd, which provided him an opportunity to preach the gospel. He combined the explanation of the miracle with the fact that Jesus was killed by their action and decision but was raised by God (vv. 13–15). Verse 16 is the hinge of the message, as Peter pointed out that it was faith in Jesus Christ that had made the man well. Verses 17–26 constitute Peter's appeal to the crowd to repent and trust in Jesus, whose coming Moses had promised.

3:12–13. Peter's explanation of the miracle moved quickly to Jesus Christ. God the Father, whom Peter here tied to the people's religious understanding, **hath glorified his Son Jesus** (v. 13; see Matt. 12:18; Acts 4:27, 30), or "his servant," a reminder of the suffering Servant prophesied in Isaiah 52:13–53:12. **Whom ye ... denied.** They had voted against Jesus, spurned Him, denied Him, and refused to acknowledge Him as the true Messiah. For **Pilate ... was determined to let him go**, see John 19:12.

3:14. The Holy One and the Just. Blameless in relation to God and man. Peter provided a bit of theology here. Jesus was blameless, just as He was the Son of God. Later in this sermon, Peter stated that He is "the Prince of life" (3:15) and the Christ (see 3:20). All of this pointed to His deity, His special mission, and thus to the people's responsibility to own Him as their Lord.

3:15. Killed ... God hath raised ... we are witnesses. A recurring theme in the speeches of Acts (see 2:23–24; 4:10; 5:30–32; 10:39–41; 13:28–29; see also 1 Cor. 15:1–4).

3:16. Through faith in his name. Here Peter came to the point. Faith in Jesus brings blessing and life. Conversely, by implication, rejection of Jesus brings misfortune. Peter's words up to this point demonstrated that his hearers had been rejecting Jesus, the source of true life.

3:17. I wot (know) **that through ignorance ye did it.** Here Peter turned pastoral. He wanted his audience to repent. Having shown them that they were sinners and had rejected God's grace, he now wanted to make it clear that God still had a door of pardon open for them.

3:18. God before had shewed by ... all his prophets. This echoes what Jesus said (see Luke 24:25–27). **That Christ should suffer** was prophesied (compare Isa. 53:7–8 with Acts 8:32–33; Ps. 2:1–2 with Acts 4:25–26; Ps. 22:1 with Matt. 27:46; see also 1 Peter 1:11). In saying these things, Peter was also showing the crowd that their rejection of Jesus had played a part in God's overall plan.

3:19–21. Peter issued his invitation. **Repent** (v. 19). Repentance is a change of mind and will that arises from sorrow for sin and leads to a transformation of one's life (see discussion on 2:38). **Be converted.** Subsequent to repentance and not completely identical with it (see 11:21, "believed, and turned"; 26:20, "repent and turn"; see also 9:35; 14:15; 15:19; 26:18; 28:27). In the strictest sense, repentance is turning from sin, and faith is turning to God. The word "turn," however, is not always used with such precision. **Your sins ... blotted out.** One's sins are forgiven as a result of repentance. If the people would repent and trust in Jesus Christ, their former rejection of Him would no longer count against them. God's grace is freely offered to any sinner who repents and turns to Jesus Christ, no matter what one has done in the past. **When.** The Greek for this word normally means "so that." **Until the times of restitution** (v. 21). This refers to the time after the return of Jesus Christ from heaven.

3:22–26. Peter offered his listeners further proof that they should repent. The Old Testament points to Jesus Christ and offers a warning to those who do not accept Him. Christ is the fulfillment of prophecies made relative to Moses, David, and Abraham. He was the prophet like unto Moses (vv. 22–23), He was foretold in Samuel's declarations concerning David (v. 24), and He was to bring blessing to all people, as promised to Abraham (vv. 25–26).

3:22. Him shall ye hear in all things whatsoever he shall say unto you. Moses wrote about Jesus and warned the people that they should believe Him. Peter was appealing to them to do so, and thus this continues the invitation to repentance and faith offered in 3:19–21.

3:23. Peter followed the appeal with a warning for those who refuse to heed Jesus Christ.

3:24. All the prophets from Samuel and those that follow after. Samuel anointed David to be king and spoke of the establishment of David's kingdom (see 1 Sam. 16:13; 13:14; 15:28; 28:17). Nathan's prophecy (see 2 Sam. 7:12–16) was ultimately messianic (see Acts 13:22–23, 34; Heb. 1:5). Peter here provided a hermeneutical principle. All of the prophets point forward to Jesus, and they should be read and understood in that light. Peter's main concern, however, was to link the people's faith in the prophets with the need to believe in Jesus.

3:25. Peter made the invitation personal: **Ye are the children of the prophets.** His hearers owed the prophets their allegiance. If the prophets pointed toward Jesus, they as their "children" should believe in Him. The Bible often presents past and present as intimately interconnected. The Jews recognized genuine obligations to the past, especially to their ancestors. These days, alas, Westerners no longer honor their ancestors by practicing the values and upholding the beliefs they did, and they are the worse off for it. These Jews, however, took the matter seriously. Knowing this, Peter used terminology that would drive home to them their obligation to uphold the values and beliefs passed down to them, which, Peter said, pointed directly to exercising faith in Jesus Christ. **Seed.** The word is singular, ultimately signifying Christ (see Gal. 3:16).

3:26. Peter continued the personal note: **Unto you first God … sent him to bless you.** Peter was appealing to the people to trust Christ because God had opened a door of blessing through Him. This sermon, then, made it clear that repentance and faith in Jesus were what the people needed, that they were in line with the Old Testament teaching they had believed, and that the doors of God's mercy were open to them. In his invitation, Peter thus issued four different appeals to the people (3:19, 23, 25, and 26). We don't know what else Peter might have said. Either Luke did not record it, or as 4:1 seems to indicate, the message was interrupted.

4:1. And as they spake unto the people. The sermon was interrupted by officials who intervened and arrested Peter and John. **The priests.** Those who were serving that week in the temple precincts (see discussion on Luke 1:23). **The captain of the temple.** A member of one of the leading priestly families, next in rank to the high priest (see 5:24, 26; Luke 22:4, 52). He was head of the temple police and responsible for maintaining order (see Bruce, *The Book of Acts*, p. 89). His concern here perhaps lay in the fact that a crowd had gathered for an "unauthorized" meeting. **The Sadducees** (see discussions on Matt. 3:7; Mark 12:18; Luke 20:27). A Jewish sect whose members came from the priestly line and controlled the temple. They did not believe in the resurrection or a personal Messiah but held that the messianic age, an ideal time, was then present and needed to be preserved. They were thus concerned about the content of the disciples' preaching. The high priest, one of their number, presided over the Sanhedrin (see 5:17; 23:6–8; Matt. 22:23–33).

4:2. Being grieved that they … preached through Jesus the resurrection from the dead. In the Greek, this immediately follows the word "Sadducees," and this doctrine of the resurrection is one they did not like. Luke thus may have meant that they were the ones with the specific grievance and that the ones "grieved" did not include the whole company.

4:3. Eventide. The evening sacrifices ended about 4:00 p.m., and the temple gates were closed at that time. Any judgments involving life and death were required to begin and end during daylight hours.

4:4. Many … believed. Peter's sermon must have been effective, though it must be remembered that the Lord was adding "daily" (2:47) to their number. Perhaps only a few hundred more were converted here. **Men.** Literally, "males." **Five thousand** (see discussion on 1:15). A growth from the three thousand converted at Pentecost (see 2:41; for later growth, see 5:14; 6:7). In all likelihood, the entire company of believers did not worship at the temple, at least not at the same time.

4:5. The trial was held off until the next day. Then there came together the **rulers, and elders, and scribes.** These three groups made up the Sanhedrin, Israel's supreme court (see Luke 22:66; see also discussions on Matt. 2:4; 15:2; Mark 14:55; Luke 5:17).

4:6. Annas the high priest. Annas was high priest in AD 6–15 but was deposed by the Romans and succeeded by his son Eleazar (AD 16–17), then by his son-in-law, **Caiaphas** (AD 18–36), who was also called Joseph. The Jews, however, still recognized Annas as high priest (see Luke 3:2; John 18:13, 24). **John.** This may refer to Annas's son Jonathan, who was appointed high priest in AD 36. Others suggest it refers to Johanan ben Zaccai, who became the president of the Great Synagogue after the fall of Jerusalem. **Alexander** is named here but is not further identified. Luke may have been using material gained while in Jerusalem. He could not expect Theophilus or his other readers to know who this Alexander was, yet it had become so much a part of the story that Luke did not see fit to omit it.

4:7. By what power, or by what name, have ye done this? The question holds a note of scorn. In the Greek, "ye" is emphatic, which may offer a clue regarding the word "this." The problem may have been that laypeople, those who were not officially rabbis, had presumed to teach. The question "By what power, or by what name …?" implies that the Sanhedrin wanted to know what authority the apostles had to teach. At this point, the interrogators had not yet identified Peter and John as disciples of Jesus, though they were about to do so (see 4:13).

4:8. Peter, filled with the Holy Ghost (see discussion on 2:4). Here there seems to be a causal link between being filled with the Spirit and the message Peter gave. One might render the idea as "Peter, because he was filled with the Holy Ghost." When Luke wrote of someone, often Peter, being filled with the Spirit, it usually was in the context of public speaking (see 4:31; 13:9). Paul linked being "filled with the Spirit" to "speaking to [one another] in psalms and hymns" (Eph. 5:18–19). Being filled with the Spirit, then, is closely linked to giving a bold witness for Christ and glorifying Him.

4:9. If we this day be examined for the good deed done to the impotent man. Peter, for whatever reason, took the "this" in the question (see 4:7) as a reference to the healing of the lame man. He may have known that there was nothing inherently wrong with healing a man. By focusing on that, he perhaps sought to prevent further trouble for himself and John and effect a quick release.

4:10. By the name of Jesus Christ. Peter went quickly to his main purpose in speaking: to glorify Christ. Their teaching and healing were both done in the name of Jesus, so he gave a correct answer to the question.

4:11. The stone … set at nought. Jesus also used this quotation from Psalm 118:22 (see Matt. 21:42; see also 1 Peter 2:7; Rom. 9:33; Isa. 28:16). Fulfillment of prophecy was an important element in early Christian sermons and defenses. Peter wanted again to point out that the rulers were culpable for their lack of belief. It is as if he picked up the thread of the previous day's message (see 3:19–26) and once again began to preach. His text was a messianic one, which he here applied to the Jewish rulers. They had "set at nought" Jesus, who **is become the head of the corner.** Thus far Peter's sermon followed the format of his sermons in 2:14–40 and 3:12–26, though this one was briefer. He explained what had happened, then pointed to Jesus as the Messiah, whom Peter's listeners had rejected.

4:12. Peter next proclaimed the exalted Christ as the answer to their spiritual needs. **None other name** (see 10:43; John 14:6; 1 Tim. 2:5; see also discussion on Matt. 1:21). This passage is used by those who seek to defend the exclusivity of Christ. This was not Peter's concern here; he did not fear that his hearers might believe that all religions bring salvation. He wanted only to exhort the rulers to faith in Christ as opposed to expecting a future Messiah. In the context of his previous day's preaching (see 3:12–26), Peter was aware that rejecting Jesus meant missing God's blessing and favor.

4:13. Boldness. The apostles' boldness was characterized by assurance, authority, and forthrightness (see 2:29; 4:29; 28:31) and was shared by the believers (see 4:31). **They were unlearned and ignorant men**. Meaning only that Peter and John had not been trained in the rabbinic schools, nor did they hold official positions in recognized religious circles. This may have been the precipitating cause of their arrest. Peter's words left them no doubt that he and John were disciples of Jesus Christ. This did not help their case, but Peter was more concerned to bear witness to Christ than he was to avoid prison.

4:14. The man which was healed. The evidence that the apostles had some kind of spiritual authority could not be denied.

4:15–16. In private conference, the Sanhedrin admitted that the **miracle** (v. 16) was so **notable** and so public that they could not **deny it** or its significance.

4:17. But that it spread no further. Apparently, the council's concern had shifted to the fact that the apostles' healing and teaching were done in the name of Jesus. The Sanhedrin had recently dealt with Jesus as a problem for them politically and morally, or so they had thought. The problem now confronted them again. It is interesting that they did not deny the miracle but were still, as during Jesus' earthly ministry, more concerned with their power and position than they were with doctrinal truth. Truly, the church was continuing the work "that Jesus began both to do and teach" (1:1), often with the same results in people's hearts.

4:18. They called them, and commanded them not to speak at all ... in the name of Jesus. Clearly, Jesus was the problem for the Sanhedrin now,

though it had not been at the time of the Peter and John's arrest.

4:19. To hearken unto you more than unto God. The apostles did not retreat an inch on the matter of truth. The Sanhedrin was on the wrong side of truth, and the apostles boldly proclaimed themselves to be on God's side in the matter. There is no hint in their response that they were willing to accept a compromise or that they were willing to agree that truth may be seen from different perspectives. To oppose the message of the gospel is to oppose God, and that is the end of the matter.

4:20. We cannot but speak (see 5:29; Jer. 20:9). Peter and John were accountable for telling the truth about what God had done in Jesus Christ. This involved much more than just relating their own experiences. The apostles were not merely telling of their personal experiences; they were reporting what God had done. **The things which we have seen and heard**, not their inner experiences, were the focus of their preaching.

4:21. The Sanhedrin could not punish Peter and John, partly because, as during the ministry of Jesus, the Jewish leaders feared the people. It seems strange that men who were so concerned to hold on to power were so powerless before the public will.

4:22. One reason the miracle caused so much public comment was the man's age, **above forty years old** (v. 22), which means he was known to many in the city, since he had been lame from birth and sat daily at the gate of the temple (see 3:2, 10). Though this information, picked up in Luke's investigation, would have held little interest for his hearers, it points to the truthfulness of the account. Made-up stories rarely have such extraneous details in them.

4:23. Being let go, they went to their own company. Probably where the apostles had met before (see 1:13) and where they may have continued to meet (see 12:12). This would not have been the place where all the believers gathered. They had been three thousand in number (see 2:41) and growing and were now up to five thousand or more (see 4:4). They either met in smaller groups or met in the temple at different times. **And reported all that the chief priests and elders had said.** The other disciples may not have known the cause of Peter and John's disappearance. They had been held overnight and may not have been able to get a message out to the others. Some certainly must have heard of the healing of the lame man by now, but they may not have known that Peter and John were involved.

4:24. In response to Peter and John's report, the believers offered a prayer to God. Luke emphasized that the prayer was offered **with one accord.** More than once he emphasized the unity of the early church in Jerusalem (see, e.g., 2:44–47; 4:32–35). The believers began their prayer with a confession of God's greatness: **Thou art God, which hast made heaven, and earth, and the sea.** Such a confession was appropriate since human authorities were opposing them, yet the one who is greater than man upheld them in their testimony.

4:25–26. Following their initial confession, the believers quoted Scripture applying to the situation they faced. They cited Psalm 2:1–2 as evidence that those in power often oppose the work of God. The message was that this had gone on for centuries and was to be expected; it in fact confirmed their calling as witnesses to the work of God.

4:27. Here the believers made a specific application: **Herod** (Herod Antipas, tetrarch of Galilee and Perea; see Luke 23:7–15), **Pontius Pilate** (Roman procurator of Judea; see Luke 23:1–24), **the Gentiles, and the people of Israel** had all opposed Jesus.

4:28. Though these parties had acted in their own perceived interest, they brought about that which God had **determined.** Not that God had compelled them to act as they did, but He willed to use them and their freely chosen acts to accomplish His saving purpose. Thus, even their opposition to Christ was part of God's overall plan. By extension, the opposition to the work that Christ was continuing to do through the apostles was a part of God's plan too and confirmed that they were in the will of God.

4:29. Only after confessing their faith in God and appling His truth to their specific situation, did the believers offer a petition. They prayed that **with all boldness they may speak thy word.** That they prayed for boldness shows that they were faced with the temptation to fear. Being afraid to witness is not a reason to avoid it but is rather a reason to pray.

4:30. Holy child. Or "holy servant" (see discussion on 3:13). The believers would be emboldened as they saw God continue **to heal** and to work **signs and wonders,** thus vindicating their testimony.

4:31. The place was shaken. An immediate sign that the believers' prayer had been heard (see 16:26). **They spake the word of God.** They continued preaching the gospel despite the warnings of the council (see discussion on 4:18). Again, being **filled with the Holy Ghost** (see discussion on 2:4) is linked to speaking the word of God (see discussion on 4:8). Luke did not mean that they immediately quoted additional Scripture to one another. Instead, in the weeks that followed, they had renewed **boldness** to proclaim the gospel.

6. The Community of Goods (4:32–5:11)

4:32–37. Luke, as a literary master, knew how to bring facts to the table almost casually or incidentally so that they become part of the reader's mindset before they become important. In this passage, Luke related information intricately linked with later events. He again emphasized the extraordinary unity of the disciples and reported that they collected funds to feed the poor among them (vv. 32–35; see 2:44–45). This sets the scene for the situation in 6:1–7, when the apostles had to deal with the issue of the daily distribution of food, an issue that threatened their unity. Here Luke also introduced Barnabas (vv. 36–37), whose example of giving contrasts that of Ananias and Sapphira (see 5:1–11). Barnabas went on to become a companion of Paul (see chap. 13). The alert reader thus will not be completely unfamiliar with these characters and situations when they again take the stage.

4:32. Of one heart and of one soul. In complete accord, extending to their attitude toward personal possessions: **they had all things common** (see 2:44).

4:33. Witness of the resurrection. As significant as the death of Christ was, the most compelling event was the resurrection, an event about which the disciples could not keep silent. No one in Jerusalem at that time sought to refute their testimony on this point. Apparently everyone, at least those in authority, knew of the empty tomb and that a body could not be produced to discredit the apostles.

4:34–35. As many as were possessors of lands or houses sold them (v. 34; see discussion on 2:44). That this was not a forced selling and that everyone was free to do as they were led is made clear by Peter's question "was it not in thine own power?" (5:4).

4:36. Barnabas. Presented as a good example of giving. In this way, Luke introduced the one who would become an important companion of Paul (see 13:1–4; for other significant contributions of this great-hearted leader to the life and ministry of the early church, see 9:27; 11:22, 25; 15:37–39). **The son of consolation.** The name Barnabas means "son of encouragement." "Son" in Jewish thought could mean something like "essential nature" (Ger, *The Book of Acts*, p. 82). **A Levite, and of the country of Cyprus.** Although Levites did not own inherited land in the Holy Land, these regulations may not have applied to the Levites in other countries. Jews had settled in Cyprus, an island in the eastern part of the Mediterranean Sea, since Maccabean times. Perhaps Barnabas sold land he owned in Cyprus and brought the proceeds to the apostles (see 4:37), or perhaps he was married, and the land was his wife's property. It is also possible that the prohibition against Levite ownership of land in the Holy Land was no longer observed.

4:37. Brought the money, and laid it at the apostles' feet. Barnabas's money was given to the apostles for charity.

5:1–11. Having presented Barnabas as a good example of giving (see discussions on 4:36–37), Luke recorded the story of Ananias and Sapphira as a bad example of giving. These two have not been previously introduced to the reader. Luke may have intended to bring them onstage suddenly and without introduction for their one scene. The reader thus has no previous experience of them and no sympathy for them. The sudden deaths of these two strangers to

the reader stand out all the more as a result. Again, Luke was very much aware of the literary qualities needed for effective narrative. In the case of these two, love of praise for (pretended) generosity and love of money led to the first recorded sin in the life of the church. It is a warning to the reader that "God is not mocked" (Gal. 6:7). Compare this divine judgment at the beginning of the church era with God's judgments on Nadab and Abihu (Lev. 10:2), on Achan (Josh. 7:25), and on Uzzah (2 Sam. 6:7).

5:1–2. Ananias, with Sapphira … sold a possession, and kept back part. They had a right to keep whatever they chose. The sin was to make it appear that they had given all when they actually had not. Peter made it clear in 5:3–4 that giving was not compulsory. Ananias could well have said, "Here is part of the money; the rest we will use to meet our needs." No one would have thought the worse of them for it, and no sin would have been committed.

5:3. Satan filled thine heart. The continuing activity of Satan is noted (see Luke 22:3; John 13:2, 27; 1 Peter 5:8). **To lie to the Holy Ghost.** A comparison with 5:4 shows that the Holy Spirit is regarded as God Himself present with His people.

5:4. Was it not thine own … in thine own power? Ananias sinned only in that he **lied … unto God.**

5:5. Ananias died immediately. **And great fear came on all.** That apparently was God's purpose in Ananias's sudden death: that the new church should take sin and obedience seriously.

5:6. It appears that no funeral service was held for Ananias. They simply **wound him up, carried him out, and buried him.** They wrapped him in the manner that a body would be wrapped at that time, with strips of linen, and placed him in a tomb.

5:7. It is peculiar that no one was sent to inform Ananias's widow. Perhaps the apostles forbade it, knowing that she might have had a part in the sin. Peter apparently wanted to give her the opportunity to repent or to fill up the measure of sin, as she chose. She chose wrongly.

5:8. Peter asked Sapphira a leading question. Still, she had the option of saying, "No, it was for more than that, but that is the amount of our gift."

Had she done so, things would have been different for her. Peter did not tell her of her husband's death until after she answered. Her decision to repent or to participate in the deceit was thus free of outside influence.

5:9. To tempt the Spirit of the Lord. If no dire consequences had followed this act of sin, the results among the believers would have been serious when the deceit became known. Not only would dishonesty have appeared profitable, but the conclusion that the Spirit could be deceived would have followed. It was important to set the course properly at the outset to leave no doubt that God will not tolerate such hypocrisy and deceit.

5:11. Great fear came upon all. Bruce (*The Book of Acts*, p. 107) suggests that one reason for this fear is that many of the members "had reason to tremble and think." He thereby suggests that many others were guilty of similar sins. This may be true, but it is not the most likely interpretation. Fear will grip anyone confronted with the stark realities of God's judgment on sin. **The church**. This is the first use of the term in Acts. It can denote either the local congregation (see 8:1; 11:22; 13:1) or the universal church (see 20:28). The Greek word for "church" (*ekklēsia*) was already being used for political and other assemblies (see 19:32, 40) and, in the Septuagint (the Greek translation of the Old Testament), for Israel when gathered in religious assembly.

7. The Arrest of the Twelve Apostles (5:12–42)

5:12. For the third time, Luke mentioned that **by the hands of the apostles were many signs and wonders wrought** (see 2:43; 5:12; 6:8). This was in answer to the prayer of the church (see 4:30). For **Solomon's porch**, see discussion on 3:11.

5:13. Of the rest durst no man join himself to them. Because of the fate of Ananias and his wife, no pretenders or halfhearted followers risked identification with the believers. Luke could not have meant that no one joined the Christian community, since 5:14 indicates that many were coming to Christ. **But the people magnified them**. This does not mean that people made more of the apostles' significance than

was warranted, only that people had a high level of awareness of the church. Today, one would say that the church had a "high profile."

5:14. Added … multitudes both of men and women (see discussion on 1:15). This is the first specific mention of women believing (compare 4:4; see 8:3, 12; 9:2; 13:50; 16:1, 13–14; 17:4, 12, 34; 18:2; 21:5; but see also 1:14).

5:15–16. Luke often made a general statement and then gave examples of it. Here, having said that the apostles performed "many signs and wonders" (5:12) and having described the results, he went back and offered examples.

5:15. The shadow of Peter. This parallels such items as Paul's handkerchiefs (see 19:12) and the edge of Jesus' cloak (see Matt. 9:20). Not that any of these material objects had magical qualities, but the least article or shadow represented a direct means of contact with Jesus or His apostles. Luke thus again linked the works done by the apostles to those of Jesus, in line with his desire to present in Acts the continuation of all that "Jesus began both to do and to teach" (1:1) during His earthly ministry.

5:16. Out of the cities round about unto Jerusalem. This is testimony not only to the "signs and wonders" (5:12) that the apostles performed but also to the fact that "the people magnified" (5:13) the disciples.

5:17. Then indicates that the reaction of the leadership was in response to the healings the apostles performed and to their teaching. The incident involving Peter and John was most likely still fresh in the minds of the leaders. Possibly, the crowds the apostles were drawing raised fears among the temple authorities that the Romans would crack down on them. More likely, they feared that their credibility and standing with the people would be affected. The crowds being drawn by the miracles were hearing daily that the Jewish leaders had delivered up Jesus to be crucified. It could not have helped their standing (see discussion on 5:28). **High priest**. The official high priest recognized by Rome was Caiaphas, but the Jews considered Annas, Caiaphas's father-in-law, to be the actual high priest since the high priesthood was to be held for life (see discussion on 4:6). **All they that were with him**. His family members. For **the sect of the Sadducees**, see discussion on 4:1.

5:18. Put them in the common prison. To await trial the next day. Apparently, all of the apostles were arrested this time, not just two.

5:19–20. The angel of the Lord (v. 19; see Matt. 1:20–24; 2:13, 19; 28:2; Luke 1:11–38; 2:9; discussions on Gen. 16:7; 2 Kings 1:3; Zech. 1:11). This phrase is used four other times in Acts: (1) Stephen spoke of him (7:30–38); (2) he guided Philip (8:26); (3) he liberated Peter (12:7–10); and (4) he struck down Herod (12:23). **Go, stand and speak** (v. 20). The angel commanded the apostles to preach **all the words of this life**. This may have served as an affirmation to the apostles that they were indeed obeying God rather than men in the matter of preaching. The angel commanded them to preach rather than to perform signs. Perhaps too much attention had been focused on the healing miracles. Crowds were drawn by these, but it is likely that the Lord wanted to keep the focus on the gospel itself.

5:21. The apostles began to teach in the temple in response to the angel's command. Meanwhile, **the high priest … called the council** (see discussion on Mark 14:55) **together** for a meeting. This was the Sanhedrin, the supreme Jewish court, consisting of seventy to one hundred men (seventy-one being the proper number). They sat in a semicircle, backed by three rows of disciples of the "learned men," with the clerks of the court standing in front. The council, unaware that the apostles had been freed, **sent to the prison to have them brought**.

5:22–23. The officers (v. 22) found the prison still **shut** (v. 23) and the guards outside, but the apostles were gone. It seems the officers saw this as a miracle.

5:24. For **the captain of the temple**, see discussion on 4:1. **They doubted of them whereunto this would grow**. The leaders were unsure how all of this would turn out.

5:25. Then came one and told them. The apostles made no effort to hide their activities. It is testimony to the size of the temple complex that the council was able to convene for a meeting without noting the apostles' presence in the temple precincts.

5:26. Brought them without violence: for they feared the people. Luke again pointed out the extent to which the people and the leadership were at odds. Their fear of the people constrained the leaders' actions. In his gospel, Luke mentioned this twice in relation to their desire to take Jesus (Luke 20:19; 22:2). In Acts, Luke again mentioned twice that the leaders could not act aggressively against the apostles because of their popularity with the people (here and 4:21).

5:27–28. Did we not straightly command you that ye should not teach in this name? (v. 28) The leaders had issued a clear command "not to speak at all nor teach in the name of Jesus" (4:18). Their problem was the apostles' teaching in the name of Jesus. **Bring this man's blood upon us**. Probably a reference to the apostles' repeated declaration that some of the Jews and some of their leaders had killed Jesus (see 2:23; 3:13–15; 4:10–11; Matt. 27:25). The leaders feared the people, and the apostles' teaching was casting doubt on their spiritual knowledge, morals, and credibility in the people's eyes.

5:29. We ought to obey God rather than men. Having been encouraged by the angel of the Lord in the rightness of their calling, the apostles boldly asserted their intention.

5:30–32. Peter's message here is similar to his preaching in Acts 2:14–40 (see discussion there) and elsewhere, though much shortened.

5:30. Peter went right to the heart of the authorities' problem. **Jesus … ye slew and hanged on a tree**. "Tree" here is used to describe the cross (see 1 Peter 2:24; Deut. 21:22–23). Like its Hebrew counterpart, the Greek for this word could refer to a tree, a pole, a wooden beam, or some similar object. **God … raised up** the one whom the Jewish leaders had slain.

5:31. Jesus is **exalted** and is now in a position to **give repentance … and forgiveness**. Peter could assume that they had heard this message, and thus he shortened it. This was not a change from the gospel he had preached but rather a summary. The council could not have failed to hear the implicit call for them to repent and turn to Christ.

5:32. Peter finished with a statement about the apostles' calling as Jesus' **witnesses**. They were not alone in this, however, for **so is also the Holy Ghost, whom God hath given to them that obey him** (see John 15:26–27). The disciples' testimony was directed and confirmed by the Holy Spirit, who convicts the world through the Word (see John 16:8–11) and is given to those who respond to God with "obedience to the faith" (Rom. 1:5; see discussion on 6:7).

5:33. They were cut to the heart. Apparently, Peter's words stung sharply. At this point, the council considered killing the apostles. Bruce (*The Book of Acts*, p. 114) indicates that the Sadducean party might have done this, except that the Pharisees, a minority on the council, would not have gone along. Because the Pharisees were more popular with the people, who were supportive of the apostles, the Sadducees' hands were tied in the matter.

5:34. A Pharisee, named Gamaliel. The most famous Jewish teacher of his time and traditionally listed among the heads of the schools of Jewish thought. Possibly he was the grandson of Hillel. Like Hillel (see discussion on Matt. 19:3), he was moderate in his views, a characteristic that is apparent in his cautious recommendation on this occasion. Saul (Paul) was one of his students (see 22:3).

5:35. Take heed. Gamaliel's counsel was to adopt a wait-and-see attitude. He did not want the council to act in haste and went on to provide several reasons for waiting (see 3:36–39).

5:36. Theudas. We know of him from no other historical source. Gamaliel asserted that after Theudas's death, his followers **were scattered**, and his movement came to nothing. The analogy that Gamaliel drew, however, is false. Theudas was **boasting himself to be somebody**; Jesus, who really was somebody, had carried on His ministry humbly. Theudas **was slain** and apparently was still in his grave; Jesus had risen, and the apostles, who were on trial here, were witnesses to that resurrection. Movements often end when their founders die. The "movement" begun by the living Christ has never died, nor ever will, for He lives and reigns in His church. Seen from an unbeliever's perspective, Ga-

maliel's analogy makes sense, but as history has shown, it fails.

5:37. Gamaliel offered a second and similar analogy: **Judas of Galilee**, whom the Jewish historian Josephus refers to as a man from Gamala in Gaulanitis who refused to give tribute to Caesar. His revolt was crushed, but a movement started in his time may have lived on in the party of the Zealots. **The days of the taxing**. Refers to a census for the purpose of taxing, not the first census of Cyrenius (see discussion on Luke 2:2) but the second one, in AD 6. **As many as obeyed him, were dispersed**. The analogy fails here as well. The "movement" that Jesus founded was not dispersed; it was growing and spreading. This was a work of God, energized by the Spirit, not a movement that was running out of steam.

5:38–39. And now I say unto you, Refrain from these men (v. 38). Gamaliel drew this application from his analogies (see 5:36–37). That Gamaliel was wrong about what would happen is a fortunate thing for the church. He ended, however, with a final reason for not persecuting the apostles: **if this counsel or this work be of men, it will come to nought**, as had happened with the two incidents he cited, **But if it be of God, ye cannot overthrow it** (v. 39). Here Gamaliel was absolutely right. The works "of men" that he cited have disappeared, but the church, which is "of God," has never been overthrown.

5:40. To him they agreed, sort of. The council agreed that it would come to nothing if it were not of God, but they did not agree to "Refrain from these men, and let them alone" (5:38). Still apparently insecure about their credibility before the people, they had the apostles **beaten**, that is, flogged with the Jewish penalty of thirty-nine lashes (see 2 Cor. 11:24). Then **they commanded that they should not speak in the name of Jesus, and let them go**. That they could issue this command while agreeing that this work could not be stopped if it was of God is testimony to the ability of fallen and lost men to think and act contrary to even their own counsel in their opposition to God.

5:41. The apostles left **rejoicing that they were counted worthy to suffer shame for his name**. They are an example of the advice given in James 1:2. They rejoiced in the midst of trials. Their rejoicing did not come from suffering in itself. The Bible never teaches that there is any virtue in pain for its own sake; rather, the virtue comes because of some other benefit. Pain and suffering become valuable when these things are a test of faith, or they come because of faith. The cause of the apostles' suffering, the name of Jesus, made it worthwhile. It assured them that they were faithfully following their Lord, who had Himself suffered shame at the hands of these same leaders.

5:42. This verse stands as testimony that the apostles did not obey the council's command. **Daily in the temple,** the disciples were able **to teach and preach Jesus Christ** despite the command they had been given to cease. Perhaps the punishment inflicted was a result of the council's frustration, but their ongoing policy became to adopt Gamaliel's advice to leave them alone (see 5:38–39).

8. The Choice of the Seven (6:1–7)

6:1. The number of the disciples was multiplied. A considerable length of time may have transpired since the end of chapter 5. The church continued to grow (see 5:14), but this gave rise to inevitable problems, both from within (see 6:1–7) and from without (see 6:8–7:60). At this stage of its development, the church was entirely Jewish in its composition, but two groups of Jews existed within the fellowship: (1) **Grecians.** Hellenists, those born in lands other than the Holy Land who spoke the Greek language and were more Grecian than Hebraic in their attitudes and outlook. (2) **Hebrews.** Native Hebrews who spoke the Aramaic and/or Hebrew language(s) of the Holy Land and preserved Jewish culture and customs. **The daily ministration.** Daily funds were given to widows who had no one to care for them and so became the church's responsibility (see 4:35; 11:28–29; see also 1 Tim. 5:3–16).

6:2. The twelve. At this early stage, the apostles were responsible for church life in general, including the ministry of **the word of God** and the care of the needy. The early church was concerned about a spir-

itual ministry ("prayer, and … the ministry of the word," 6:4) and a material ministry (**serve tables**).

6:3. Look ye out … seven men. The number most likely was determined by the size of the task and has no other significance. The men were to have certain qualifications. **Of honest report.** Since they would be handling money and perhaps material goods in the name of the church, it was important not only that they be honest but also that they be known to be honest. **Full of the Holy Ghost** (see discussion on 2:4) **and wisdom.** This presents two sides of good decision making, an ability the men would need since they would be handling funds and making financial decisions. "Full of the Holy Ghost" means that they would need God's wisdom and direction in these matters. "Wisdom" means that they should also possess good sense. Christians should never ignore the importance of having plain wisdom simply because they are led by the Spirit. The early church recognized that human wisdom is not enough by itself, for it is limited. They did not, however, toss it aside on the grounds that being filled with the Spirit was enough. Certainly, the church should not be served by those who have quenched the Spirit in their lives, but these early Christians recognized that it is not a matter of choosing one over the other; both are required for effective ministry. The church elected seven men for the task (see 6:5), and the apostles ordained them (see 6:6). In this way, they were appointed to their work.

6:4. We will give ourselves continually to prayer and the ministry of the word. The apostles were making the point that some things had priority. Meeting physical needs was important, but other believers could do this ministry well, and the apostles had a specific calling as official witnesses of the resurrection. The church had grown to the point that the apostles could no longer do all of the work themselves. That the complaints about the distribution were directed at the apostles was another reason that others needed to be involved in the ministry, so that a misunderstanding on administrative matters might not reflect on them.

6:5. They chose Stephen … Nicolas. The seven men chosen all had Greek names. The murmuring had come from the Greek-speaking segment of the church (see 6:1), so those elected to oversee the work came from their number to ensure that their interests were represented fairly. Of the seven, only Stephen and Philip receive further notice (for Stephen, see 6:8–7:60; for Philip, see 8:5–40; 21:8–9). **A proselyte of Antioch**. It is significant that a proselyte was chosen and that Luke pointed out his place of origin as Antioch, the city to which the gospel would soon be taken and which would become the headquarters for the forthcoming Gentile missionary effort. That the grace of God was available to the Gentiles is a major theme in both the gospel of Luke and Acts. Here Luke again introduced the names of people and places that become important later on (see discussion on 4:32–37).

6:6. They laid their hands on them. In the Old Testament period, laying on of hands was used to confer blessing (see Gen. 48:13–20), to transfer guilt from sinner to sacrifice (see Lev. 1:4), and to commission a person for a new responsibility (see Num. 27:23). In the New Testament period, laying on of hands was used in healing (see 28:8; Mark 1:41), blessing (see Mark 10:16), ordaining or commissioning (see 6:6; 13:3; 1 Tim. 5:22), and imparting of spiritual gifts (see 8:17; 19:6; 1 Tim. 4:14; 2 Tim. 1:6). These seven men were appointed to responsibilities turned over to them by the twelve apostles. The Greek verb used to describe their responsibility (*diakoneō;* "serve," 6:2) is the root of the noun "deacon" (see Phil. 1:1; 1 Tim. 3:8–13), which can also be translated "minister" or "servant." The men appointed on this occasion were simply called "the seven" (21:8), just as the apostles were called "the twelve" (6:2). It is disputed whether these seven were the first deacons or were later replaced by deacons (see discussion on 1 Tim. 3:8). In actual function, they apparently formed a benevolence committee.

6:7. The number of the disciples multiplied (see discussion on 1:15). Luke apparently saw the division of labor and the settlement of the dispute as the cause of the growth that followed. Freed from administrative duties, the apostles were able to fully devote themselves to preaching. **A great company**

of the priests. Though involved by lineage and life service in the priestly observances of the old covenant, they accepted the preaching of the apostles, which proclaimed a sacrifice that made the old sacrifices unnecessary (see Heb. 8:13; 10:1–4, 11–14). **Were obedient to the faith**. That is, they responded to the gospel. "Faith" here carries the same sense as in Jude 3, where it refers to the body of doctrinal truths revealed concerning the gospel. The priests were obedient to the truth that Christ died for their sins and to the call to repentance inherent in that truth. Exercising faith in Christ is obedience, but faith also produces obedience (see Rom. 1:5; Eph. 2:8–10; James 2:14–26).

9. Stephen's Arrest and Martyrdom (6:8–7:60)

6:8. Stephen … did great wonders and miracles. Up to this point, Luke reported only the apostles working miracles (see 2:43; 3:4–8; 5:12). Now Stephen worked miraculous signs, and Philip would soon do the same (see 8:6).

6:9. There arose certain of the synagogue … Libertines. Persons who had been freed from slavery. They came from different Hellenistic areas. **Cyrenians**. Halfway between Alexandria and Carthage, Cyrene was the chief city in Libya and north Africa (see discussion on 2:10). One of its population groups was Jewish (see 11:19–21). **Alexandrians**. Alexandria was the capital of Egypt and second only to Rome in the empire. Two out of five districts in Alexandria were Jewish. **Cilicia**. A Roman province in southeastern Asia Minor, adjoining Syria. Tarsus, the birthplace of Paul, was one of its principal towns. **Asia**. A Roman province in western Asia Minor. Ephesus, where Paul later ministered for a few years, was its major city. **Disputing with Stephen**. Since Saul was from Tarsus, this may have been the synagogue he attended, and he may have been among those who argued with Stephen. He was present when Stephen was stoned (see 7:58).

6:10. They were not able to resist. This means not that they believed what Stephen said but that they were unable to come up with counterarguments to the truths he was defending.

6:11. Since they could not refute Stephen, their reaction was to discredit him falsely. Again, this shows how far fallen men may go in their rejection of the truth. They found men who would accuse him of speaking **blasphemous words against Moses, and against God**. Since Stephen declared that the worship of God was no longer to be restricted to the temple (see 7:48–49), his opponents twisted these words to trump up an accusation that Stephen was attacking the temple, the law, Moses, and ultimately, God.

6:12. With their misrepresentation of what Stephen had said, **they stirred up the people, and the elders, and the scribes** (see discussions on Matt. 2:4; 15:2; Luke 5:17) against Stephen. Nowhere, however, did Luke report that Stephen's preaching itself caused opposition from the people. They opposed Stephen due to what was reported to them, not due to what Stephen had actually said. For **the council**, see discussion on 5:21.

6:13–14. Against this holy place, and the law (v. 13). This is similar to the charges brought against Christ (see Matt. 26:61). The next charge is similar but refers directly to Jesus: **this Jesus of Nazareth shall destroy this place, and shall change the customs which Moses delivered us** (v. 14). Stephen may have referred to Jesus' statement in John 2:19, and his words may have been misunderstood or purposely misinterpreted, as at the trial of Jesus.

6:15. His face as it had been the face of an angel. The meaning of this is unclear. It may simply mean that Stephen faced this tense situation with a supernatural peace that showed on his countenance. Many Christians have reported experiencing supernatural peace in a moment of trial. Or it may mean that Stephen's face glowed supernaturally, as Moses' had, but this is unlikely.

7:1. The high priest. Probably Caiaphas (see Matt. 26:57–66; but see discussion on 4:6; John 18:13, 24). **Are these things so?** "These things" refers to the charges that Stephen had spoken against the law and sought to harm the temple (see discussions on 6:11, 13).

7:2–53. Stephen, in his defense, sought to turn the charges back on the Jewish leaders. It was they,

not he, who had spoken against the law, not directly but by missing its true meaning and intent. In an attempt to show them that they were in a long line of people in Israel's history who had resisted the plan and people of God, Stephen reviewed the history of the patriarchs (vv. 2–16) and the story of Moses and the exodus (vv. 17–43). Then, because he had been accused of speaking against the "holy place" (6:13), he spoke briefly about the sanctuary (vv. 44–50) before issuing his counteraccusations (vv. 51–53).

7:2–16. Stephen began with Abraham and related Israel's patriarchal history up to the time of Jacob's death.

7:2. Abraham … in Mesopotamia, before he dwelt in Charran. "Charran" is the Greek spelling for "Haran." Abraham's call came in Ur, not Haran (see Gen. 15:7; Neh. 9:7). Or perhaps his call came first in Ur and was later renewed in Haran (see discussion on Jer. 15:19–21).

7:3–4. The land of the Chaldeans (v. 4). A district in southern Babylonia, the name was later applied to a region that included all Babylonia. **When his father was dead**. Genesis 11:26 does not mean that all three sons—Abraham, Nahor, and Haran—were born to Terah in the same year when he was 70 years old (see Gen. 11:26–12:1). It may be that Haran was Terah's firstborn and that Abraham was born 60 years later. The death of Terah at 205 years of age thus could have occurred just before Abraham, at 75, left Haran.

7:5. Here Stephen's point was that Abraham believed the promise of God, though he never owned the land that was promised. Stephen's accusers were, by contrast, guilty of a lack of faith in the promises of God fulfilled in Jesus Christ.

7:6. Four hundred years. A round number for the length of Israel's stay in Egypt (Exod. 12:40–41 has 430 years). That four generations would represent considerably less than four hundred years is not a necessary conclusion (see discussion on Gen. 15:16). Exodus 6:16–20 lists Moses as the great-grandson of Levi (son of Jacob and brother of Joseph). This would make four generations from Levi to Moses. In 1 Chron. 7:22–27, however, a list of ten names represents the generations between Ephraim (son of Joseph) and Joshua. The ten generations at forty years each would equal four hundred years, the same period of time noted as four generations in Exodus. The list in Chronicles gives a full genealogy, however, while that in Exodus is abbreviated.

7:7. The nation to whom they shall be in bondage will I judge. Those who oppose the work of God will face judgment. Stephen later accused the Jewish leaders of spurning the work of God in Christ (see 7:51–53).

7:8. The covenant of circumcision (see discussions on Gen. 17:10–11). The essential conditions for the religion of Israel were already fulfilled long before the temple was built and their present religious customs began. For **the twelve patriarchs**, see Genesis 35:23–26.

7:9. The patriarchs ... sold Joseph. Israel consistently rejected God's favored individuals. Stephen built his case about Jesus' rejection by noting Joseph's rejection by his brothers (see Gen. 37:12–36).

7:10–12. These verses describe Joseph's rise to power and the famine in Canaan. Stephen's point was that Joseph's situation was part of God's plan to rescue His people and preserve them.

7:13. The second time (see Genesis 43). God used the circumstances and Pharaoh's esteem for Joseph to effect His plan.

7:14. Jacob ... and all his kindred, threescore and fifteen souls. Seventy-five people. Although the Hebrew Bible uses the number seventy (see Gen. 46:27; Exod. 1:5; Deut. 10:22), the Greek translation of the Old Testament (the Septuagint) adds at Genesis 46:20 the names of one son of Manasseh, two sons of Ephraim, and one grandson of each. This makes the number seventy-five and was the number that Stephen used.

7:15–16. Jacob went down into Egypt, and died (v. 15), but he was buried in the land God had promised. **He, and our fathers** (v. 16). Stephen greatly compressed Old Testament accounts of two land purchases (by Abraham and Jacob) and two burial places (at Hebron and Shechem). According to the Old Testament, Abraham purchased land at Hebron

(see Gen. 23:17–18), where he (see Gen. 25:9–11), Isaac (see Gen. 35:29), and Jacob (see Gen. 50:13) were buried. Jacob bought land at Shechem (see Gen. 33:19), where Joseph was later buried (see Josh. 24:32). Josephus preserves a tradition that Joseph's brothers were buried at Hebron. Stephen's rhetorical device (by which he recalled that Jacob and the twelve patriarchs were buried not in Egypt but in Canaan) is strange to modern ears but would have been well understood by his hearers. His point was that they were buried in Canaan because God had promised that land to Israel. Canaan, not Egypt, was the homeland of their fathers, and to it they would surely return.

7:17–43. Here Stephen turned to the story of Moses and the exodus, including his time in Egypt (vv. 17–29), his experience at the burning bush (vv. 30–34), the exodus (vv. 35–36), his prophecy that God would send "A prophet ... like unto me" (v. 37), and the apostasy of the people in the wilderness (vv. 38–43).

7:17–19. The time of the promise drew nigh. In his review of Israel's patriarchal history (7:2–16), Stephen had been leading up to this point. For **another king arose, which knew not Joseph** (v. 18), see discussion on Exodus 1:8.

7:20–21. Stephen introduced Moses, saying he **was exceeding fair** (v. 20). This, to Stephen's hearers, would have denoted God's favor upon Moses. Stephen was aware that his hearers knew this story well. Their familiarity with the Old Testament accounts allowed him to greatly compress the narrative. His purpose was to show them that God had been at work in all of this, through people who had faith.

7:22. Moses was learned in all the wisdom of the Egyptians. Not explicitly stated in the Old Testament but to be expected if he grew up in the household of Pharaoh's daughter. Both Philo and Josephus speak of Moses' great learning.

7:23. When he was ... forty. Moses was 80 years old when he was sent to speak before Pharaoh (see Exod. 7:7) and 120 years old when he died (see Deut. 34:7). Stephen's words agree with a tradition that Moses was 40 years old when he first departed from Egypt.

7:24–25. Moses had avenged a wronged Israelite. Stephen commented that Moses **supposed his bretheren would have understood how that God by his hand would deliver them** (v. 25). Moses had reason to believe that the people would see God at work and trust Him, **but they understood not**. Stephen here introduced the idea that the Jewish people, by their hardness of heart, had failed to discern the work of God. He was leading up to his indictment of his hearers.

7:26–28. Who made thee a ruler and a judge over us? (v. 27). Stephen offered this incident as an example of the Israelites' lack of understanding. It was key to how the Israelites, up to Stephen's own day, responded to God's plan. This is why he devoted so much attention to the incident, though he had just narrated several hundred years in a few verses.

7:29. Madian. Commonly known as Midian. Rejected by his own people, Moses feared that they would inform the Egyptians, and this led to his flight to Midian (see Exod. 2:15), the land flanking both sides of the Gulf of Aqaba. **He begat two sons.** Gershom and Eliezer (see Exod. 2:22; 18:3–4; 1 Chron. 23:15).

7:30–34. When forty years were expired (v. 30). Plus the forty years of 7:23 totals the eighty years of Exodus 7:7. **Mount Sina.** That is, Mount Sinai, which is called Mount Horeb in Exodus 3:1 (see discussion there). In relating Moses' experience at the burning bush, Stephen was contrasting the Israelites' initial rejection of Moses' leadership (see 7:24–29) with God's plan **to deliver them** (v. 34). God had plans for His people, but they lacked faith, which was exactly the situation that Stephen and the church faced with respect to his opponents in the court.

7:35–36. This Moses whom they refused ... did God send to be a ruler and a deliverer (v. 35). Israel had rejected Moses, their deliverer, just as the Jews of Stephen's day were rejecting Jesus, their deliverer. Yet both had been sent by God. God did great things for and through Moses. With **wonders and signs,** Moses **brought them out** of Egypt and led them **in the wilderness forty years** (v. 36).

7:37. Here Stephen's narrative took a turn. For the first time, he brought in a reference to Jesus, in a prophecy delivered by Moses: **A prophet ... like unto me** (see 3:22–23; discussion on Deut. 18:15). **Him shall ye hear**. This prophet had arisen, His name was Jesus, and the Jewish leaders were not willing to hear His teaching and thus were disobeying God.

7:38. The church in the wilderness. Though the Greek word *ekklēsia* ("church") takes on a technical, theological sense in the New Testament, its more common sense of "assembly" is used here (see discussion on 5:11). **The angel which spake to him**. According to Jewish interpretation at that time, the law was given to Moses through the mediation of an angel, after the manner of Moses' original call (see Exod. 3:2; see also 7:53; Gal. 3:19; Heb. 2:2). **Who received the lively oracles to give unto us**. Moses was the mediator between God and man on Mount Sinai.

7:39. Whom our fathers would not obey. The Israelites again rejected God's representative and His commands. As Stephen neared the conclusion of his speech, he began to heighten the tension in his narrative. The reader can almost sense the air crackling in the court.

7:40–43. Make us gods (v. 40). While Moses was on Sinai receiving the law, the people **made a [golden] calf** (v. 41), rejecting God and His representative (see Exod. 32:1). The people had not traveled far from the idolatry of Egypt. **God ... gave them up** (v. 42; see discussion on Rom. 1:24). Stephen compressed the idolatry of the Israelites in the wilderness and their later idolatry, which were essentially different parts of one long act of betrayal on the part of the people. His point was that the Israelites had a history of turning their backs on God and what He had done for them. In these verses, Stephen quoted from Amos 5:25–27 as translated in the Septuagint, except that he replaced "Damascus" with **Babylon** (v. 43) since the Babylonians had carried out Israel's final exile from the Promised Land (Amos was speaking first of the Assyrian exile of the northern kingdom).

7:44–50. Because he had been accused of speaking against the "holy place" (6:13), Stephen concluded his recital with a word about the sanctuary. Presumably, he had been preaching that the risen

Christ had now replaced the temple as the mediation of God's saving presence among His people and as the one ("the place," v. 49) through whom they (and "all nations," Mark 11:17) could come to God in prayer (see discussion on 6:13–14).

7:44. The tabernacle of Witness, or "the tabernacle of the Testimony." Stephen used this term because the primary contents of the wilderness tabernacle were the ark of the covenant and the two covenant tablets it contained, which were called "the Testimony" (see *KJV Study Bible* notes on Exod. 25:16, 22).

7:45–46. Stephen speeded up the narrative, carrying the story up to the time of David. His point was that God had continued to work His purpose even though the people may have turned away from Him.

7:47. Solomon built him a house. Solomon built the first temple.

7:48. Here Stephen addressed the matter that may have been the touchstone of the accusations against him: **the most High dwelleth not in temples made with hands.**

7:49–50. Stephen quickly cited Scripture to prove his point, quoting from Isaiah 66:1–2, where Isaiah reminded Israel that all creation is the temple that God Himself made. Stephen thus reminded his hearers that ultimately God builds His own temple.

7:51–53. Having traced the history of Israel and her faithlessness, even in the face of God's mighty deeds on her behalf, Stephen made the application to his hearers and issued counteraccusations to their charges against him. **Ye stiffnecked and uncircumcised in heart and ears** (v. 51). Though physically circumcised, these Jews were acting like the uncircumcised pagan nations around them. They were not truly consecrated to the Lord. Their faith was not in God and what He was doing through Jesus Christ. Stephen drew an analogy. As their fathers had persecuted the prophets, who foretold the coming of Jesus Christ, so also his hearers were **now betrayers and murderers** (v. 52) of this same Jesus. For **the law by the disposition of angels** (v. 53), see discussion on 7:38. **And have not kept it.** In that they had not

believed God and had spurned the grace offered in Jesus Christ.

7:54. Stephen's speech affected his hearers: **they were cut to the heart.** Rather than repent, however, they became angry.

7:55. For **full of the Holy Ghost,** see discussion on 2:4; see also 6:5. **And saw the glory of God, and Jesus standing on the right hand of God.** Luke wanted his readers to know that Stephen received affirmation that he had borne true testimony to his Lord.

7:56. Stephen described what he saw as he looked to heaven. **The Son of man** (see discussion on Mark 2:10). Jesus used this title of Himself (see Mark 2:10) to emphasize His relationship to messianic prophecy (see Matt. 25:31; Dan. 7:13–14). It is unusual for someone other than Jesus to apply this term to Him (see also Rev. 1:13).

7:57. They cried out … stopped their ears, and ran upon him. They refused to listen further. The picture is of an irrational mob.

7:58. Cast him out of the city, and stoned him. Luke made a general statement here of what happened and gave details in 7:59–60. **Laid down their clothes at a young man's feet … Saul.** Some have thought that this marked Saul as being in charge of the execution. In any case, it was Luke's way of introducing the main character of the second part of the book (see discussion on 4:32–37).

7:59. They stoned Stephen, calling upon God. At first glance, it is hard to tell who was calling upon God. The rest of the verse makes it clear this was Stephen. The idea is that they stoned Stephen, "who was calling upon God," or, "while he was calling upon God."

7:60. Lord, lay not this sin to their charge. This is similar to Jesus' words seeking forgiveness for His executioners (see Luke 23:34).

10. The Scattering of the Jerusalem Believers (8:1–4)

8:1. Saul was consenting unto [Stephen's] death (see 22:20). Luke recorded this to present Saul as a zealous persecutor of the church. This marks the beginning of persecution in Jerusalem. As a result, the disciples **were all scattered abroad throughout**

... Judea and Samaria. This was the beginning of the fulfillment of the commission in 1:8, not by the church's plan but by events beyond the believers' control. **Except the apostles**. The apostles' presence in Jerusalem would encourage those in prison and provide a center point of communication for those scattered. The church now went underground.

8:2. Luke returned to Stephen one more time, to briefly describe **his burial**. This verse indicates that Stephen was well loved in the church, in contrast to the official condemnation that led to his execution (see Bruce, *The Book of Acts*, p. 162). By first reporting the scattering of the church through persecution and then returning to Stephen, Luke slowed the pace of the narrative and made the transition easier. Rather than finishing with Stephen and then dealing with persecution, he introduced persecution and then finished the account of Stephen on a tender note, thus making both the death of Stephen and the persecution of the church a little easier on the reader's psyche.

8:3. Saul ... made havock of the church (see 22:4). The Greek underlying this phrase sometimes describes the ravages of wild animals. Saul was, "concerning zeal, persecuting the church" (Phil. 3:6), and this in no uncertain terms.

8:4. Preaching the word. Many witnesses to the gospel **went every where**, proclaiming the good news. The number of witnesses multiplied, and the territory covered was expanded greatly (see 11:19–20). Persecution often causes the church to grow, further confounding the wishes of those who would crush it.

11. Philip's Ministry (8:5–40)

a. In Samaria (8:5–25)

8:5. Philip. One of the seven men elected in the Jerusalem church to oversee the care of the needy (see 6:3, 5; discussion on 6:6), Philip now became an evangelist, proclaiming Christ (see 21:8). Philip is an example of one of those who had been scattered (see 8:1). **The city of Samaria**. A reference to the old capital Samaria, renamed Sebaste or Neapolis (modern Nablus).

8:6–8. Luke recounted the success of Philip's preaching in the city of Samaria to show that the gospel was to spread to all the world. Early success in Samaria confirmed Jesus' will in this matter (see 1:8) and must have encouraged the scattered disciples that their activities were not outside the blessing of God even though their circumstances had changed.

8:9. Simon. In early Christian literature, Simon the sorcerer (Simon Magus) is described as the archheretic of the church and the father of Gnostic teaching (see 1 John, Introduction: "Gnosticism").

8:10. This man is the great power of God. The people were saying either that Simon was God Himself or, more likely, that he was His chief representative.

8:11. Simon had deceived many for a **long time**.

8:12. Here Luke provided a hint of the content of Philip's preaching. **The things concerning the kingdom of God**. Philip taught much like what Jesus had taught on these matters. **And the name of Jesus Christ**. This was the specific teaching that there is life in His name for all who repent and believe.

8:13. Simon himself believed ... was baptized. It is difficult to know whether Simon's faith was genuine. Though this verse says Simon believed, Peter's statement that Simon had no part in the apostles' ministry because his heart was "not right in the sight of God" (8:21) casts some doubt on the depth of his belief.

8:14. Samaria had received the word of God. The people were obedient to the gospel proclaimed by Philip. **The apostles ... sent unto them Peter and John**. The Jerusalem church assumed the responsibility of inspecting new evangelistic efforts and the communities of believers they produced (see 11:22). The apostles had responsibility for proper doctrine. In the absence of the New Testament, they were the guarantors of this. Today, the Bible performs that function.

8:15. Prayed for them, that they might receve the Holy Ghost. The apostles may have laid hands on believers individually or at a joint service much like a large ordination service today.

8:16. Was fallen upon none of them. Since the day of Pentecost, those who belong to Christ (see

Rom. 8:9) also have the Holy Spirit. In Samaria, however, the Spirit had not yet been made manifest to the Christians by the usual signs. This deficiency was now graciously supplied (see 8:17).

8:17. For **laid ... their hands on them**, see discussion on 6:6; see also 8:18; 19:1–7; 2 Tim. 1:6.

8:18–19. He offered them money (v. 18). Simon had boasted of having great powers (see 8:9, discussion on 8:10), and now he tried to buy the magical power he believed that the apostles possessed.

8:20–21. Luke recorded in detail Peter's rebuke of Simon. These verses show Peter's integrity; he was unwilling to profit from the gospel. They also show that the apostles' ability could not, and would not, be sold and that Simon's desire to purchase it was itself sinful.

8:22. Peter exhorted Simon to **Repent therefore of this thy wickedness and pray God**. He called Simon to prayer, but **if perhaps** left some doubt whether God would answer. The doubt most likely stemmed from the question of whether Simon would actually exercise the faith necessary to trust God to forgive him.

8:23. In the gall of bitterness (see Deut. 29:18). At this point, the state of Simon's heart was such that he could neither receive God's forgiveness nor offer a prayer in faith. If he set his heart in that direction, however, it could result in faith being generated. When one is far from God and has no heart for prayer, one ought the more to pray, that God may soften one's heart and bring one back to Him.

8:24. Pray ye to the Lord for me. It is unclear whether Simon genuinely repented. He asked only for prayer that he not suffer the consequences of his actions.

8:25. Luke used this summary statement to indicate he was finishing one topic and moving on to another. Apparently, **they ... preached the gospel in many villages of the Samaritans** on their way back to Jerusalem. "They" here seems to mean Peter and John since they were the ones who had come from Jerusalem to see what was happening (see 8:14). It is possible, however, that at least Philip returned with them (see 8:26).

b. To the Ethiopian Eunuch (8:26–40)

8:26. For **the angel of the Lord**, see 8:29; discussion on 5:19. **From Jerusalem unto Gaza**. A distance of about fifty miles. Philip most likely was in Jerusalem at this time. Perhaps the persecution that had sent all but the apostles out of the city had eased somewhat (but see 9:1–2). **The way ... unto Gaza, which is desert**. A road through the wilderness, a largely uninhabited area.

8:27–28. A man of Ethopia, an eunuch (v. 27). In this period, Ethiopia corresponded to Nubia, from the upper Nile region at the first cataract (Aswan) to Khartoum. **Candace**. The traditional title of the queen mother, who was responsible for performing the secular duties of the reigning king. The king was thought to be too sacred for such activities. **Had come to Jerusalem for to worship**. If not a full-fledged proselyte (see Deut. 23:1), the Ethiopian was a Gentile God-fearer. **Read Isaiah the prophet** (v. 28). Perhaps he had purchased the scroll while in Jerusalem.

8:29. The Spirit said unto Phillip. This is the first time Luke indicated that certain leaders were led of the Spirit toward a ministry direction. It was not the last time, however (see 10:19, 11:12, 16:7, 21:4). Most likely, the Spirit spoke to Philip's heart rather than in an audible voice.

8:30. Heard him read. It was customary to read aloud. **Understandest thou what thou readest?** Philip's question was the obvious opening and began a conversation that would inevitably lead the eunuch to Christ.

8:31. The Ethiopian's reply, followed with an invitation to **sit with him** in the chariot, was an implicit request for Philip to interpret for him.

8:32–33. The Ethiopian was reading Isaiah 53:7–8, which is a poetic passage. Thus, **as a sheep** (v. 32) and **like a lamb** are parallelisms. **Opened he not his mouth**. The reference to Jesus is clear to readers today, and certainly was to Philip, but it would not have been clear to someone unfamiliar with the details of the trial and crucifixion of Christ.

8:34. Of whom speaketh the prophet this? of himself ...? It was more common in biblical times for writers to refer to themselves in the third person. Paul may have done this in 2 Corinthians 12:2.

8:35. Philip ... preached unto him Jesus. Philip proclaimed the way of salvation through Jesus Christ. Beginning with Isaiah 53, Philip may have identified the suffering Servant with the Davidic Messiah of Isaiah 11 or other suffering Servant passages. Depending on the Ethiopian's familiarity with Scripture, Philip may have referred to many other passages as well.

8:36. They came unto a certain water. This could be (1) a brook in the valley of Elah (which David crossed to meet Goliath, see 1 Sam. 17:40), (2) the Wadi el-Hasi just north of Gaza, or (3) water from a spring or one of the many pools in the area. **What doth hinder me to be baptized?** indicates that Philip had explained to him doctrinal matters besides the person of Jesus Christ.

8:37. Philip's reply, **If thou believest with all thine heart, thou mayest**, indicates that the only condition was faith. **I believe that Jesus Christ is the Son of God** indicates the proper content of faith. The Ethiopian had by this time come to more than a general faith in God and a desire to be "a better person."

8:39. Rejoicing (see discussion on 16:34). Joy is associated with salvation in Acts. New believers often radiate joy, with the realization of sins forgiven and burdens lifted.

8:40. Azotus. Old Testament Ashdod (see 1 Sam. 5:1), one of the five Philistine cities. It was about nineteen miles from Gaza and sixty miles from Caesarea. **Cesarea**. Rebuilt by Herod, the city had an excellent harbor and served as the headquarters of the Roman procurators. The account leaves Philip in Caesarea at this time; his next appearance is twenty years later, and he is still located in the same place (see 21:8).

12. Saul's Conversion (9:1–31)

9:1. Saul. Introduced at the stoning of Stephen (see 7:58), Saul was born in Tarsus and trained under Gamaliel (see 22:3; see discussions on Phil. 3:4–14). **Yet breathing out threatenings and slaughter**. It is

not known whether Saul was directly involved in the death of anyone other than Stephen (see 8:1), but there appear to have been similar cases (see 22:4; 26:10). **The high priest**. Probably Caiaphas (see discussion on 4:6) and the members of the Sanhedrin, who had authority over Jews both in Judea and elsewhere.

9:2. Desired of him letters. These would have been writs of authority granting him power of arrest. **To Damascus**. Located in the Roman province of Syria, Damascus was the nearest important city outside the Holy Land. It also had a large Jewish population. The distance from Jerusalem to Damascus was about 150 miles, four to six days' travel. **Any of this way** (see discussion on 19:23). "The way" was an early name for Christianity and occurs a number of times in Acts (16:17; 18:25–26; 19:9, 23; 22:4; 24:14, 22; see 2 Peter 2:2). Jesus called Himself "the way" (John 14:6). **He might bring them bound unto Jerusalem**. Where the full authority of the council could be exercised in trial for either acquittal or death. This was in reaction to the fact that persecution at Jerusalem had led to the spread of the gospel elsewhere.

9:3. There shined round about him a light from heaven. This occurred "at midday" and was "above the brightness of the sun" (26:13). The bright (literal) light not only got Saul's attention but also indicated to him that he was in contact with a heavenly reality. Jesus called Himself "the light of the world" (John 8:12).

9:4. Saul, Saul, why persecutest thou me? To persecute the church is to persecute Christ, for the church is His body (see 1 Cor. 12:27; Eph. 1:22–23).

9:5. Who art thou, Lord? In rabbinic tradition, such a voice from heaven would have been understood as the voice of God Himself. The solemn repetition of Saul's name and the bright light suggested to him that he was in the presence of deity. He asked the question because he believed he was serving the God of Israel with his actions; now he was no longer certain. The answer came directly: **I am Jesus whom thou persecutest**. The next statement, **it is hard for thee to kick against the pricks**, has led some to speculate that Saul might have been experiencing guilt over the death of Stephen, and his rabid zeal for persecution was a cover for an uneasy conscience. This is not impossible, but it is more likely that Saul was at this point resisting the grace offered to him. In that case, the phrase expresses Jesus' compassionate understanding of Saul's situation along with an appeal to repent.

9:6. Lord, what wilt thou have me to do? Here is an expression of submission to Christ. Most people assume that Saul's conversion took place here, though some insist that it did not come until Ananias spoke with him (see 9:17–18). The Lord told Saul to **go into the city** and await instructions.

9:7. Hearing a voice. "Heard not" in 22:9 perhaps means that those with Saul did not understand what the voice was saying (see Dan. 10:7). The voice of God from heaven is sometimes described as sounding like thunder (see John 12:29). That may have been the case here.

9:8–9. Saul was blind when he opened his eyes. Perhaps God wanted to symbolize for him the spiritual darkness in which he had been living, but the text neither supports nor denies this. He was **led ... by the hand** to Damascus, where he apparently had living quarters already arranged. **Neither did eat nor drink** (v. 9). Saul's fasting was most likely for spiritual enlightenment, not a result of trauma. Bruce (*The Book of Acts*, p. 185) points out that there is nothing to warrant the idea that Saul was engaging in the practice of fasting prior to baptism. That practice came later in the life of the church.

9:10. Ananias. This Ananias is mentioned elsewhere only in 22:12. His was a common name (see 5:1; 23:2). The Greek form is derived from the Hebrew name Hananiah, meaning "The Lord shows grace" (see Dan. 1:6).

9:11. The street which is called Straight. This street probably followed the same route as the long, straight street that today runs through Damascus from east to west. It is a decided contrast to the numerous crooked streets of the city. For **Tarsus**, see discussion on 22:3. **Prayeth.** Prayer is often associated with visions in Luke and Acts (see 10:9–11; Luke 1:10; 3:21; 9:28).

9:12. And hath seen in a vision. This must have reassured Ananias. A believer who ministers as God leads often finds that God has prepared the way for him or her.

9:13. Saints (see discussions on Rom. 1:7; Phil. 1:1). This is the first use of "saints" to describe believers in the book of Acts.

9:14. Apparently, word of Saul's intentions had reached Damascus ahead of him.

9:15. The Lord cut short Ananias's protest. His implied, "I can't go down there!" remained unexpressed. **He is a chosen vessel unto me.** God had called Saul to be a missionary. The image of a person as a "vessel," or container (in this case, a container of the gospel), is common in Scripture. Paul himself made a similar comparison in 2 Corinthians 4:6–7, where he wrote that believers have the treasure of "the light of the knowledge of the glory of God ... in earthen vessels." Isaiah said that God is the potter and we are the clay (see Isa. 64:8). **To bear my name before the Gentiles** (see Rom. 1:13–14). The spread of the gospel to the Gentiles is the major theme of Acts. That fact, as much as any other, most likely determined Luke's decision to devote much of the book to Paul's ministry. **Kings.** Agrippa (see 26:1) and Caesar at Rome (see 25:11–12; 28:19). **And the children of Israel.** Paul's ministry was not confined to the Gentiles, though that was his primary focus.

9:16. Great things he must suffer. The things Paul suffered for Christ's name were the product of the times and situations in which he ministered. They happened in the sovereignty of God and for His purposes. In no way, however, is Paul's suffering to be seen as any kind of payback for his persecution of the church. When Saul trusted Christ, all his sins were paid for on the cross. God's grace is sufficient and complete. No Christian pays for his or her sins by increased suffering after salvation (Bruce [*The Book of Acts*, p. 187] is wrong on this point).

9:17. Brother Saul. This form of address indicates just how much Ananias's feelings toward Saul had changed as a result of the Lord's word to him. **Jesus, that appeared unto thee.** Saul's experience on the Damascus road was not merely a vision. The resurrected Christ actually appeared to him, and on this fact Saul based his qualification to be an apostle (see 1 Cor. 9:1; 15:8).

9:18–19. There fell from his eyes as it had been scales (v. 18). This is unique in Scripture. In every case in which Jesus healed a blind man, sight was restored, but no physical barrier to sight fell away. The incident most similar to this is when He put clay on a blind man's eyes (see John 9:6), but that is not really a true analogy. **Was baptized**. Saul's baptism most likely was performed by Ananias.

9:20. Straightway. Following his baptism. **He preached Christ in the synagogues**. It became Saul's regular practice to preach at every opportunity in the synagogues (see 13:5; 14:1; 17:1–2, 10; 18:4, 19; 19:8). For Saul, it really was, "to the Jew first, and also to the Greek" (Rom. 1:16). **He is the Son of God**. Saul's message was a declaration of what he had become convinced of on the Damascus road: Christ's deity and messiahship (see 9:22; discussion on Luke 2:11). Notice that Saul "preached Christ" and gave content to that message ("He is the Son of God"). He apparently did not focus on his own conversion experience, though he was not averse to relating it; rather, he focused on Christ Himself and who He is.

9:21. All that heard him were amazed. This may perhaps be seen as the first "celebrity conversion" in the history of the church. Many came to hear Saul simply because of who he was and what he had done in the past.

9:22. Proving that this is very Christ. Saul, due to his already vast store of Old Testament knowledge, was quickly able to offer proofs of Jesus' messiahship. Luke thus offered here an early example of apologetics in service to the church's evangelistic efforts.

9:23. After that many days were fulfilled. Three years (see Gal. 1:18). It is probable that Saul spent the major part of this period in Arabia (see Gal. 1:17), away from Damascus, though the borders of Arabia extended to the environs of Damascus. That Luke did not discuss Saul's Arabian visit should not trouble readers. It simply played no part in the story he was telling (see Bruce, *The Book of Acts*, p. 191).

The Jews took counsel to kill him. Upon Saul's return to Damascus, the governor under Aretas gave orders for his arrest (see 2 Cor. 11:32). The absence of Roman coins struck in Damascus between AD 34 and 62 may indicate that Aretas was in control during that period.

9:24. Saul was aware that the Jewish leaders were **laying await** for him and likely was careful to stay out of public view. He was now fully identified with the Christians he had sought to persecute, hiding with them from those who would persecute him. **They watched the gates day and night**. This most likely happened in shifts.

9:25. Let him down by the wall in a basket (see 2 Cor. 11:33; Josh. 2:15; 1 Sam. 19:12). Those watching by night did so at the gates of the city. The disciples chose a place on the wall far from any gate. It must be remembered that there were no streetlights in that day. On a moonless night, it would have been extremely dark.

9:26. When Saul was come to Jerusalem. Galatians 1:18–19 relates that the only apostles in Jerusalem at that time were Peter and James, the Lord's brother. James was not one of the Twelve, but he held a position in Jerusalem comparable to that of an apostle. **They were all afraid of him**. The disciples in Jerusalem either had not heard of his conversion, a thing not impossible in those days, or they did not believe the reports they had heard.

9:27. Barnabas (see discussion on 4:36). Barnabas apparently knew details of Saul's conversion, or perhaps he took the opportunity to visit Saul and heard the story from him. In either case, he came to believe in Saul's sincerity and became his advocate.

9:28. He was with them. After Barnabas vouched for Saul, he was admitted to the company of the disciples at Jerusalem and was able to be seen in public with them. Apparently, by this time, persecution in Jerusalem had died down. Perhaps the Sanhedrin felt more secure, since years had passed and there had been no public uprising against them. By this time, there was certainly new leadership in the Sanhedrin as well. In any case, the church must have seemed less of a threat.

9:29. He spake boldly. Formerly Saul had argued against Christ; now he forcefully presented Jesus as the Messiah.

9:30. For **Cesarea**, see discussion on 8:40. **Tarsus** (see discussion on 22:3). Saul's birthplace.

9:31. The churches ... throughout all Judea and Galilee and Samaria. The whole Christian body, including Christians in these three districts. **Walking ... in the comfort of the Holy Ghost.** The work of the Spirit is particularly noted in the book of Acts (see 13:2; discussion on 1:2), which is why it is sometimes called "The Acts of the Holy Spirit." This verse constitutes one of Luke's progress reports (see discussion on 1:15).

B. Second Geographical Expansion of the Gospel: "As far as Phenice, and Cyprus, and Antioch" (9:32–12:25; see 11:19)

1. Peter's Ministry on the Mediterranean Coast (9:32–11:18)

a. To Aeneas and Dorcas (9:32–43)

9:32–43. Without Luke's summary statement in 9:31, his shift back to Peter might be jarring. In this section, Luke's account of Peter's activity explains how he came to be in Joppa, where he was called on to take the gospel to Cornelius, a Gentile (see chap. 10). Peter performed miracles of healing at least twice while traveling. Luke wanted to show that the church had spread beyond Jerusalem in preparation for portraying its reception by the Gentiles.

Peter probably did much else besides travel and heal people during the time of Saul's conversion and early ministry. Luke chose these incidents because they reestablish in the reader's mind that the apostles were performing "many wonders and signs" (2:43) and that Peter was a significant leader in the church. An alert reader would not have forgotten these matters entirely, but a good writer knows it is helpful to reestablish things after a significant diversion.

9:32. Lydda. A town two or three miles north of the road connecting Joppa and Jerusalem. Lydda was about twelve miles from Joppa.

9:33. Aeneas. Since Peter was in Lydda to visit the believers, Aeneas was probably one of the Christians.

9:34. Peter put his statement in the present tense: **Jesus Christ maketh thee whole.** This indicates that faith operates when Christians trust as a present reality what God wants to do; "faith is the substance of things hoped for" (Heb. 11:1). Aeneas was called on to believe not that Jesus *could* heal him or *should* heal him but that his healing was present reality. One may wonder, since Aeneas was a Christian, why he had not trusted Christ for healing sooner. Miracles are not common, however, and at no time have Christians been able simply to "claim" healing and have it become reality. God's intention here was to affirm Peter's apostleship before the people and to establish his credibility in preaching the gospel. Aeneas was called on to trust Christ for healing in that very moment, but that moment did not happen until Peter was present and God's purpose could be worked out.

9:35. Saron. The Greek spelling of "Sharon." The fertile plain of Sharon runs about fifty miles along the Mediterranean coast, roughly from Joppa to Caesarea. The reference here, however, may be to a village in the neighborhood of Lydda instead of to a district (an Egyptian papyrus refers to a town by that name in the Holy Land).

9:36. Joppa. About thirty-eight miles from Jerusalem, the main seaport of Judea. Today it is known as Jaffa and is a suburb of Tel Aviv.

9:37. Washed. In preparation for burial, a custom common to both Jews (purification of the dead) and Greeks. **An upper chamber.** If burial was delayed, it was customary to lay the body in an upper room. In Jerusalem, the body had to be buried the day the person died, but outside Jerusalem, up to three days might be allowed for burial.

9:38. For **nigh to Joppa**, see discussion on 9:32. **Would not delay to come.** Whether for consolation or for a miracle, Peter was urged to hurry in order to arrive before the burial.

9:39. Shewing the coats and garment which Dorcas made. Dorcas apparently was a talented and giving woman who was much loved in the community. When loved ones pass on, it is natural to focus on the things they loved and handled and worked on, as these are indicators of why they were loved so much.

9:40. Put them all forth (see 1 Kings 17:23; 2 Kings 4:33). Peter had been present on all three occasions recorded in Scripture when Jesus raised individuals from the dead (see Matt. 9:25; Luke 7:11–17; John 11:1–44). Like Jesus when he raised Jairus's daughter, Peter told the crowd in the room to leave. Unlike Jesus, however, Peter **kneeled down, and prayed.**

9:41. Presented her alive. Peter's prayer was answered, much to the wonder of the assembled people.

9:42. Many believed (see John 12:11). Peter's miracle was an act of compassion, but it also led more people to the church. While works of compassion should never be done with evangelism as the sole motive, nothing is wrong with using the occasion afforded to bear witness to Christ. In fact, it would be wrong not to do so.

9:43. Simon a tanner. Occupations were frequently used with personal names to identify individuals further (see 16:14; 18:3; 19:24; 2 Tim. 4:14), but in this case, it is especially significant. Tanners treated the skins of dead animals, thus contacting the unclean according to Jewish law, so many people would have despised Simon. Peter's decision to stay with him shows his willingness to reject Jewish prejudice and prepares the way for his coming vision and the mission to the Gentiles.

b. To Cornelius (10:1–11:18)

10:1. Cesarea. Located thirty miles north of Joppa and named in honor of Augustus Caesar, it was the headquarters for the Roman forces of occupation (see discussion on 8:40). **Cornelius.** A Latin name made popular when Cornelius Sulla liberated some ten thousand slaves over one hundred years earlier. The freed slaves had all taken his family name, Cornelius. **A centurion.** The commander of a military unit that normally numbered at least one hundred men (see discussion on Luke 7:2). A Roman legion (about six thousand men) was divided into ten regiments, each of which had a designation. This was **the Italian band** (another was the "Augustan," or "Imperial," band; see 27:1). A centurion commanded

about a sixth of a regiment. Centurions were carefully selected; all of the centurions mentioned in the New Testament appear to have had noble qualities (see, e.g., Luke 7:5). The Roman centurions provided necessary stability to the entire Roman system.

10:2. A devout man. In spite of all his good deeds, Cornelius needed to hear the way of salvation from a human messenger. The role of the angel (see 10:3) was to bring Cornelius and Peter together (see 8:26; 9:10). **One that feared God.** The term used of one who was not a full Jewish proselyte but who believed in one God and respected the moral and ethical teachings of the Jews.

10:3. A vision. This was not a dream or trance but rather a revelation, through an angel, given to Cornelius while at prayer (see 10:30; discussion on 9:11). **About the ninth hour.** About 3:00 p.m. This is another indication that Cornelius followed Jewish religious practices; three in the afternoon was a Jewish hour of prayer (see 3:1), the hour of the evening incense.

10:4. A memorial. A portion of the grain offering burned on the altar was called a "memorial" (Lev. 2:2). Cornelius's salvation, however, must not in any sense be seen as a reward for his prayers and generosity. The angel was simply saying that Cornelius's **prayers … and alms** had not gone unnoticed. Had these in any way paid for his salvation, there would have been no need to send for Peter, or anyone else.

10:5–6. Joppa (v. 5; see discussion on 9:36) … **Simon a tanner** (v. 6; see discussion on 9:43). The angel told Cornelius exactly where to find Peter.

10:7–8. The three men Cornelius sent to Joppa included a **soldier** (v. 7), possibly for their protection in traveling.

10:9. Upon the house. Eastern houses customarily had flat roofs with outside stairways. The roof was often used for relaxation and privacy. Peter used it as a place for prayer, perhaps regularly.

10:10. He fell into a trance. God produced this state of mind in Peter to communicate with him. It was not merely his imagination or a dream. Peter's consciousness was heightened to receive the vision from God.

10:11–12. All manner of fourfooted beasts (v. 12). Including animals both clean and unclean according to Leviticus 11.

10:13. Rise, Peter; kill, and eat. The command was not literal, as the rest of the story demonstrates, for the "great sheet" (10:11) was taken back up into heaven before Peter could actually kill and eat one of the animals. Peter was meant to learn an important spiritual point from this: God was not restricting the gospel to the Jewish people. It was not necessary for him to actually kill one of the animals; in a sense, God was leading Peter in a role-playing scenario. Killing and eating an unclean animal is something a Gentile would do. Peter, as a Christian, had always seen himself as a "Jewish Christian" and could not imagine any other kind. Even the Samaritans who were saved were at least partially Jewish. Now God was asking him to do something a Jewish person would not do. As a Christian, Peter wanted to obey God; as a Jew, he wanted to avoid unclean foods. He was being asked to obey God in doing something only a Gentile, and therefore a Gentile Christian, could do. God thus put Peter in the role of imagining himself as a Christian and a Gentile, a startling new idea for Peter.

10:14. Not so, Lord. So deeply ingrained was the observance of the laws of clean and unclean that Peter refused to obey immediately. **Common or unclean.** Eating anything common (impure) was forbidden by the law.

10:15. What God hath cleansed. Jesus had already laid the groundwork for setting aside the laws of clean and unclean food (see Matt. 15:11; 1 Tim. 4:3–5). Here the central point was the spiritual truth that Gentiles were now to be accepted in Christ.

10:16. Thrice. To make a due impression on Peter.

10:17. While Peter doubted in himself what this vision which he had seen should mean. Apparently, Peter did not immediately understand the full meaning of the vision. Sometimes one comes to understand God's truth more fully in the midst of service for Him. Peter would soon be called on to preach the gospel to Cornelius, a Gentile, and the vision would then become clear. Even now, the men that Cornelius had sent **stood before the gate**.

10:18. The three men that Cornelius had sent (see 10:5–8) asked either Simon the tanner or a servant whether Peter was staying there.

10:19–20. The Spirit gave Peter direction concerning those who had come. Since Peter had not yet come to an understanding of the vision, he would have had trouble going to Cornelius's home without assurance that this was God's will.

10:21. I am he whom ye seek. Peter spoke thus based on what the Spirit had said to him upstairs.

10:22. Three phrases describe Cornelius. He was **a just man**, meaning that he lived a morally upright life, both personally and in his dealings with others; he was **one that feareth God**, a Gentile who recognized one God and respected the Jewish law; and he was **of good report among all the nation of the Jews.** Preaching to a Gentile was outside of Peter's comfort zone. That Cornelius was an honorable man who feared God made it less of a stretch for Peter. It would have been more difficult for him if he had been called to preach to a sensual and evil Gentile who mocked God.

10:23. Called he them in. By providing lodging for them, Peter was already taking the first step toward accepting Gentiles. Such intimate relationship with Gentiles was contrary to prescribed Jewish practice. Having heard their story, Peter must have realized what God was doing. **On the morrow.** It was too late in the day to start out on the long journey to Caesarea (see discussion on 10:1). **Certain brethren.** Six in number (see 11:12), these men were Jewish in background (see 10:45).

10:24. Had called together his kinsmen and near friends. Cornelius well knew that the message Peter would deliver was important. He eagerly invited all those close to him to be present to hear the word of God.

10:25. Fell down at his feet, and worshipped him. Perhaps Cornelius intended only to honor Peter as one having a rank superior to his own, since he was God's messenger. Even so, this went beyond what would normally be expected in a greeting.

10:26. I myself also am a man. Peter allowed no chance for misunderstanding: he was not to be worshiped because he was not God.

10:27. He went in. Apparently, Cornelius had met Peter outside the house.

10:28. God hath shewed me. Peter recognized that his vision had deeper significance than declaring invalid the distinction between clean and unclean meat; he saw that the barrier between Jew and Gentile had been removed (see Eph. 2:11–22).

10:29. Gainsaying simply means "denying." Peter did not deny the truth that God had shown him, and based on that truth, he had accepted Cornelius's invitation. **I ask therefore for what intent ye have sent for me?** Peter surely knew by now that he had been sent to preach the gospel to Cornelius, but he wanted Cornelius to give testimony to the fact. This would also provide Peter with an opening to broach the subject. He did not want to walk into the house and immediately begin preaching. After all, he was a guest. Cornelius telling his story not only constituted an invitation for Peter to begin preaching; it also allowed Cornelius's assembled family and friends to hear once again what had happened and to establish in their hearts an expectation of hearing the truth of God.

10:30. Four days ago. The Jews counted a part of a day as a day: (1) the day the angel appeared to Cornelius, (2) the day the messengers came to Joppa and Peter received a vision, (3) the day the group set out from Joppa, and (4) the day they arrived at Cornelius's house. **Until this hour**. Exactly what Cornelius meant here is unclear. Had he been praying ever since the incident? Did he simply mean that he normally prayed at this time every day? The latter is the best understanding of the text and is inferred in the KJV's translation (see Marshall, *Acts of the Apostles*, p. 188). **A man … in bright clothing**. Common language to describe an angel when appearing in the form of a man.

10:31–32. Luke summarized these details of the story since the reader already knows them. That he repeated them rather than simply saying, "And Cornelius described all that had happened," was

probably due to his great concern that his readers understand that the admission of the Gentiles into the grace of God was a genuine and supernatural act of God.

10:33. We are all here present before God. When people come together to hear the preaching of God's word, God is present with them. This is the only place in the New Testament where this phrase is used in this way, however (see Marshall, *Acts of the Apostles*, p. 189).

Once again, Peter is called upon to speak a word for Christ in light of a miraculous event (see discussion at 2:14–40 and 3:12–26). In this case the event was the appearance of an angel to Cornelius, seen in light of Peter's vision in Acts 10:9–16. Peter recognizes that the gospel sent to Israel (Acts 10:26) is meant for the Gentiles as well. Peter's message emphasizes the universal aspect of the gospel that everyone who believes is forgiven (Acts 10:43).

10:34–35. God is no respecter of persons (v. 34; see discussion on James 2:1). God does not favor an individual because of his station in life, his nationality, or his material possessions. He does, however, respect his character and judge his work. This is evident because **in every nation he that feareth him, and worketh righteousness, is accepted with him** (v. 35). Cornelius already worshiped the true God, but this was not enough; he lacked faith in Christ (see 10:36). Peter was not saying here that God accepts people apart from faith in Jesus Christ. All who come to Him in a true spirit of repentance and faith, however, are accepted. That may be implied in the phrase "feareth him [repentance], and worketh righteousness [faith]." Righteous deeds are an act of faith when they are done not to earn salvation but because, in faith, one believes that they are what God wants done. This happens in the context of Christian discipleship, and thus Peter may be seen as meaning that God accepts all, people from every nation, who repent and have faith in Jesus Christ. He did not explain all of this to Cornelius and his guests, probably because he had not yet preached Christ to them, so it would have been confusing since they did not know yet *how* God accepts people to Himself. Cornelius was about to learn, however.

10:36. Peace. Between God and man (reconciliation). **Lord of all.** Lord of both Jew and Gentile (see 10:34–35).

10:37. After the baptism which John preached. Similar to the outline of Mark's gospel, Peter's presentation of the gospel begins with John's baptism and continues to the resurrection of Jesus (for Peter's preaching, see 2:14–40; 3:12–26; 4:8–12; 5:29–32; discussion on 2:14–40). This is significant since the early church fathers viewed Mark as the "interpreter" of Peter (see Mark, Introduction: "Author"). Peter assumed that Cornelius was aware of John the Baptist. John's ministry, which had ended some years earlier, certainly had made a wide impact (see Acts 18:25; 19:3).

10:38. How God anointed Jesus (see Isa. 61:1–3; Luke 4:18–21). Peter assumed that Cornelius also knew the basic story of the ministry of Jesus. His ministry had attracted much attention, especially after His trial and crucifixion at the hands of Pilate, which would have been known among Roman officials throughout the region.

10:39. Both in the land of the Jews, and in Jerusalem. It may seem that Peter was making a false distinction between the two, but he was not. One might say today, "throughout all the land of the Jews, as well as in Jerusalem itself, the major city there." For **hanged on a tree,** see discussion on 5:30.

10:40. Him God raised up the third day. Peter presented the resurrection as an act of God and therefore something to be reckoned with. It was not something that just happened, nor just another event. When God acts, people must respond, either with faith or with rejection. No one can be neutral in the presence of God's mighty deeds.

10:41. Who did eat and drink with him. Those who ate with Jesus after He rose from the dead received unmistakable evidence of His bodily resurrection (see Luke 24:42–43; John 21:12–15).

10:42. For he commanded us to preach, see 1:8; Matthew 28:18–20.

10:43. To him give all the prophets witness. Luke took every occasion to point out that the Old Testament testifies to Jesus (see Luke 18:31; 24:27, 44; Acts 3:18; 10:43; 13:27). It is thus to be read christologically, that is, with reference to its testimony to Jesus Christ. This was not uppermost in Luke's mind; he was relating what happened historically, but he certainly may have been aware of the hermeneutical and spiritual import of what he was recording.

10:44. For the Holy Ghost fell on all them, see 8:16 and discussion.

10:45. Astonished … because that on the Gentiles also was poured … the Holy Ghost. Apparently, Peter's associates failed to understand that the gospel was for the Gentiles as well as for the Jews and that they would share alike in the benefits of redemption. Gentile proselytes to Judaism, however, were accepted (see 6:5). Peter himself was still just coming to understand it fully, and his companions may have been skeptical despite his testimony concerning what had happened on the roof in Joppa.

10:46. They heard them speak with tongues. This was, to the Jewish believers, a sign that these Gentiles had received the Holy Spirit. Tongues speaking is rare in the book of Acts and normally happened when a new ethnic group was admitted into the church: the inauguration of the church among the Jews (see 2:3–13); the inauguration of the church among the Samaritans, with no mention of tongues, but it is implied that they had received the Holy Spirit (see 8:14–17); the inauguration of the church among the Gentiles (here); the inauguration of the church among the Ephesians (see 19:6). No other accounts of tongues speaking are found in Acts, though there are many conversions to Christ.

10:47–48. Can any man forbid water, that these should not be baptized …? (v. 47). The Gentiles had received the same gift as the Jewish believers (see 11:17); they spoke in tongues as the Jewish Christians had on the day of Pentecost. This was unavoidable evidence that the invitation to the kingdom was open to Gentiles as well as to Jews. **He commanded them to be baptized in the name of the Lord** (v. 48), in obedience to Matthew 28:19–20.

11:1. The apostles and brethren. "Brethren" sometimes refers to those of common Jewish lineage (see 2:29; 7:2), but in Christian contexts, it denotes those united in Christ (see 6:3; 10:23). In matters of deep concern, the apostles did not act alone. The divine will gave guidance, and the apostles interpreted and exhorted, but the consent of the whole church was sought ("the whole multitude," 6:5; "apostles and brethren," here; "the church," 11:22; "the church, and … the apostles and elders," 15:4; "the apostles and elders, with the whole church," 15:22).

11:2. They … of the circumcision. Jewish Christians.

11:3. Men uncircumcised. Gentiles, who did not observe the laws of clean and unclean food and violated Jewish regulations concerning food preparation. The church in Jerusalem was rather startled that their leaders **wentest in … and didst eat with them.**

11:4–17. This section repeats, in summary form, the material from 10:1–46 (see discussions there), including Peter's vision (vv. 4–6), his conversation with God concerning the vision (vv. 7–10), his agreeing to journey to Caesarea (vv. 11–12), his encounter with Cornelius (vv. 13–14), the results of his preaching (vv. 15–17). That Luke repeated these details further indicates the importance of this event to the whole book. Readers have now read of Cornelius's encounter with the angel three times, of his encounter with Peter twice, and of Peter's vision on the rooftop three times. Much of the rest of Acts focuses on the reception of the gospel among the Gentiles.

Thou and all thy house (v. 14; see discussion on Gen. 6:18). Not only Cornelius's family but also the slaves and employees under his authority. **Withstand God** (v. 17). Peter could not deny the Gentiles the invitation to be baptized (see 10:47) and to enjoy full fellowship in Christ with all believers. The Jewish believers were compelled to recognize that God was going to save Gentiles on equal terms with Jews. By divine action rather than by human choice, the door was being opened to Gentiles.

11:18. Then hath God also to the Gentiles granted repentance unto life. God had opened the door for the Gentiles to experience repentance, the change of one's attitude toward sin, which leads to a turning from sin to God and results in eternal life

(see discussion on 2:38). What had been happening among the Jews and the Samaritans was undeniably happening among the Gentiles also. A result of the gospel coming to the Gentiles was that Gentile churches began to appear.

2. The New Gentile Church in Antioch (11:19–30)

11:19–30. Here Luke returned to the scattering of the disciples after the martyrdom of Stephen (see 8:1). The intervening material has been something of a parenthesis. It has, however, explained how and why the gospel spread beyond Jerusalem and demonstrated clearly that God intended for Gentile churches to be planted. Luke began with a catalogue of several places where new churches were started (v. 19). Barnabas, who comes into this section, was sent to Antioch to provide leadership to a new church plant that was growing there (vv. 22–23).

11:19. Phenice. Commonly called Phoenicia, a country about 15 miles wide and 120 miles long, stretching along the northeastern Mediterranean coast (modern Lebanon). Its important cities were Tyre and Sidon. **Cyprus.** An island in the northeastern Mediterranean; the home of Barnabas (see 4:36). **Antioch.** The third city of the Roman Empire (after Rome and Alexandria). It was 15 miles inland from the northeast corner of the Mediterranean. The first largely Gentile church was located in Antioch, and it was from this church that Paul's three missionary journeys were launched (see 13:1–4; 15:40; 18:23). **Preaching the word to none but unto the Jews only.** Remember that these disciples had scattered abroad before Peter met Cornelius and would not have heard of the incident until their return to Jerusalem.

11:20. Some of them. Perhaps these disciples had gone out to preach later and knew of Cornelius's conversion, but this is not explicitly stated. For **Cyrene,** see discussion on 2:10. **Grecians.** Not Greek-speaking Jews, but Gentiles. This is the first instance of disciples besides Peter preaching to truly non-Jewish people.

11:21. The hand of the Lord (see 4:30; 13:11; Luke 1:66). Indicates divine approval and blessing, sometimes evidenced by signs and wonders (see

Exod. 8:19). The disciples saw results among the Gentiles perhaps to a greater degree than they had expected.

11:22. They sent forth Barnabas (see discussions on 4:36; 9:27) **... as far as Antioch** (see discussion on 11:19). This apparently was in keeping with the Jerusalem church's policy of sending leaders to check on new ministries that came to their attention (see 8:14). Barnabas would later depart from Antioch to accompany Paul on his first missionary journey (see 13:2–3).

11:23. Was glad. Barnabas was pleased with what he saw. He was originally from Cyprus and may have been more comfortable in a non-Jewish setting than other church leaders at Jerusalem were. He was thus the logical choice to go and investigate and to bring words of exhortation to them.

11:24. He was a good man, and full of the Holy Ghost and of faith. Luke's description of Barnabas resembles his description of Stephen (6:5). That Luke commended Barnabas is important in light of his role in the church at Antioch and especially in light of the division that later arose between him and Paul (see 15:36–39).

11:25. For Tarsus, see 9:11, 30; discussion on 22:3.

11:26. Barnabas brought Saul back from Tarsus, an event that would affect the whole future of Christianity, for it was at Antioch that the major missions thrust of the church began. **A whole year.** Luke noted definite periods of time (see 18:11; 19:8, 10; 24:27; 8:30). **Christians.** Whether adopted by believers or invented by enemies as a term of reproach, this is an apt title for those "belonging to Christ" (the meaning of the term).

11:27. Prophets. The first mention of the gift of prophecy in Acts. Prophets preach, exhort, explain, or as in this case, foretell (see 13:1; 15:32; 19:6; 21:9–10; Rom. 12:6; 1 Cor. 12:10; 13:2, 8; 14:3, 6, 29–37; see also *KJV Study Bible* notes on Jonah 3:2; Zech. 1:1; discussion on Eph. 4:11).

11:28. Agabus. Agabus later foretold Paul's imprisonment (see 21:10). In Acts, prophets engaged in foretelling (see 11:27; 21:9–10) at least as often as in "exhortation" (see 15:32).

11:29. Every man according to his ability. Apparently, some gave more and others less, but no one was forced to give a set amount. **To send relief.** This is the first instance in Acts of one congregation reaching out to help another in a time of physical need. This incident must have made a deep impression on Paul, since he later led the churches of Asia and Greece in a larger offering for the church in Jerusalem (see 1 Cor 16:1–4). No word is given regarding any motive here, other than the need itself. Paul's later offering, however, may have been an act of gratitude to the Jerusalem church as the place from which the blessing of the gospel had come to the other congregations (see Rom. 15:27).

11:30. To the elders. This is the first reference to "elders" in Acts (see discussions on 1 Tim. 3:1; 5:17, 19). That the offering was not presented "to the apostles" is at first surprising. Since the Jerusalem church had elected seven men to oversee the ministry of physical needs (see 6:1–7), it may be that they were the ones who officially received the offering. Perhaps they were now referred to as "elders" by virtue of their long service, Christian example, and leadership abilities (see Marshall, *Acts of the Apostles*, p. 205).

3. Herod's Persecution of the Church and His Subsequent Death (chap. 12)

12:1. About that time. There are two views regarding the time frame of chapter 12. (1) Some hold that it groups together matters concerning Herod, and the events may not be in strict chronological order. For example, the arrival of Barnabas and Saul in Jerusalem (see 11:30) may have followed Herod's persecution of Christians and Peter's release from prison. Since Herod died in AD 44, these events probably occurred in 43. According to this view, the famine of 11:28 occurred circa 46, following Herod's death (see 12:23). The famine visit of 11:30; 12:25 was the Jerusalem visit recorded in Galatians 2:1–10. (2) Others hold that such juggling of events is not necessary. According to this view, the relief gift of 11:30 was delivered before Herod's death in 44, and Barnabas and Saul returned from Jerusalem (see 12:25) after Herod's death. The Jerusalem council visit of 15:1–29 was the Jerusalem visit recorded in Galatians 2:1–10. **Herod the king**. Agrippa I, grandson of Herod the Great (see discussions on Matt. 2:1; 14:1) and son of Aristobulus. He was a nephew of Herod Antipas, who had beheaded John the Baptist (see Matt. 14:3–12) and had tried Jesus (see Luke 23:8–12). When Antipas was exiled, Agrippa received his tetrarchy as well as those of Philip and Lysanias (see Luke 3:1). In AD 41, Judea and Samaria were added to his realm.

12:2. Killed … with the sword. Beheaded, like John the Baptist. **James**. Brother of John the apostle and son of Zebedee (see Matt. 4:21). This event took place about ten years after Jesus' death and resurrection. Jesus had warned the disciples of coming suffering (see Matt. 20:23).

12:3–5. The days of unleavened bread (v. 3; see discussion on Luke 22:1). Because of this feast, Peter was imprisoned rather than killed immediately (see Marshall, *Acts of the Apostles*, p. 208). **Four quaternions** (v. 4). One company of four soldiers for each of the four watches of the night. **Easter**. The New Testament word is "Passover," which was often used to refer to the whole week of the festival (see discussion on Luke 22:1). **Prayer … without ceasing of the church unto God for him** (v. 5). Perhaps the church held regular prayer sessions or, more likely, around-the-clock home prayer meetings to which people would come and go. Under the circumstances, it probably was best not to have the disciples gather in large groups.

12:6. The same night. For Jews, the day began at sunset. Peter thus was freed the night before he would have been brought before Herod.

12:7. A light shined. The glory of the Lord (see Luke 2:9). The angel awakened Peter, **And his chains fell off from his hands**, apparently miraculously.

12:8–9. The angel allowed Peter time to get dressed. Apparently, those who might have prevented Peter's escape (see 12:6) were asleep, which perhaps had been supernaturally enduced. **He went out** (v. 9). Out of the prison, probably the tower of Antonia, located at the northwest corner of the temple—the "castle" where Paul was later held (see

21:34). **Thought he saw a vision**. The circumstances were so unusual that Peter assumed it was a dream of some kind. James had recently been killed, and Peter had no reason to expect supernatural intervention.

12:10. The iron gate … which opened to them of his own accord. Again, this occurred supernaturally. Normally, Peter never would have gotten out of the tower without being spotted and without having to open barred doors and gates.

12:11. Peter spoke to himself of his assurance of the reality of what had happened. Why Luke recorded this in such detail is unclear. Perhaps he wanted to set the scene for the disciples' disbelief when Rhoda claimed that Peter was free and at the door (see 12:13–14).

12:12. Mary. The aunt of Barnabas (see Col. 4:10). Apparently, her home was a gathering place for Christians. It may have been the location of the upper room where the Last Supper was held (see Mark 14:13–15; see also Acts 1:13) and the place of prayer in 4:31. For **John … Mark**, see discussion on 12:25.

12:13. Rhoda. A hired servant who sympathized with the family and the church.

12:14. Told how Peter stood before the gate. In her excitement, Rhoda forgot to let Peter in but instead **ran in** to tell the others.

12:15. It is his angel. Perhaps this reflects the belief that everyone has a personal angel who ministers to him or her (see Matt. 18:10; Heb. 1:14), but this is unlikely. The word "angel" in the Greek means only "messenger," not necessarily a supernatural being (which may explain why so often in the Bible the term is qualified with "of the Lord" to make it clear that no human messenger is meant). The disciples likely assumed that Peter had sent the church some word of encouragement on the eve of his trial and that Rhoda had heard through the gate the words "a message from Peter" but had latched on to just the word "Peter." Their assumption was reasonable, given that James had recently been killed (see 12:2). They probably had been praying that Herod would relent, not for a supernatural release for Peter. Even in those days, miraculous events were rare, and no one in the church presumed that they would happen.

12:16. They were astonished. Though "prayer was made without ceasing of the church unto God for him" (12:5). God often answers prayers in ways that go beyond what one imagines or thinks.

12:17. James. The Lord's brother, a leader in the Jerusalem church (see Gal. 1:19). James the brother of John had been killed (see 12:2).

12:18. No small stir among the soldiers. The soldiers had been responsible for keeping Peter and feared that they would be held accountable for his escape.

12:19. Cesarea (see discussions on 8:40; 10:1). Not only the headquarters for Roman procurators but also Agrippa's capital when no procurators were assigned to Judea.

12:20. Herod was highly displeased with them of Tyre and Sidon, the leading cities of Phoenicia (Lebanon today). **They came with one accord to him**. Apparently, they sought reconciliation and goodwill. They were dependent on the grain fields of Galilee for their food. **Blastus the king's chamberlain**. The treasurer. Blastus is otherwise unknown.

12:21–22. Upon a set day (v. 21). The historian Josephus (*Antiquities* 19.8.2) provides additional details about this event, a festival that Herod was celebrating in honor of Claudius Caesar. **Royal apparel**. Josephus describes that Herod wore a dazzling silver robe that day. When the people acclaimed him **a god** (v. 22), he did not deny it. This was an error on the part of the people but a much worse error on his part to accept such worship.

12:23. Immediately the angel of the Lord (see discussion on 12:15) **smote him**. Josephus (*Antiquities* 19.8.2) reports that Herod was seized with violent pains, was carried out, and died five days later. **Eaten of worms**. A miserable death associated with Herod's acceptance of acclaim to be divine, but it may also be seen as divine retribution for his persecution of the church. The phrase is often used to describe the deaths of evil men (see Marshall, *Acts of the Apostles*, p. 212). It emphasizes that the one who has died no longer exists in this world and is analogous to today's "and good riddance!"

12:24. The word of God grew and multiplied. One of Luke's progress reports (see discussion on 6:7).

12:25. Here Luke returned to the story of **Barnabas and Saul** in preparation for the account of their mission activity, which begins in chapter 13. **John ... Mark** (see 12:12). The author of the second gospel (see Mark, Introduction: "Author") and a companion of Barnabas and Saul on the first part of their missionary journey (see 13:5, 13; discussions on 15:37–39). He was perhaps the young man who fled on the night of Jesus' arrest (see Mark 14:51–52).

II. Paul and the Expansion of the Church from Antioch to Rome (chaps. 13–28)

A. Third Geographical Expansion of the Gospel: "Throughout Phrygia and the region of Galatia" (13:1–15:35; see 16:6)

1. Paul's First Missionary Journey (chaps. 13–14)

13:1. There were in the church that was at Antioch certain prophets (see discussion on 11:27). These believers had the special gift of inspiration experienced by Old Testament prophets (see Deut. 18:18–20; 2 Peter 1:21) but known also in the New Testament (see 2:17–18; 1 Cor. 14:29–32; Eph. 3:5). Prophets are second to apostles in Paul's lists (see 1 Cor. 12:28–29; Eph. 2:20; 4:11; but see Luke 11:49; Rom. 12:6; 1 Cor. 12:10). For **teachers**, see 11:26; 15:35; 18:11; 20:20; 28:31; 1 Cor. 12:28–29; Eph. 4:11. **Barnabas** (see discussion on 4:36) **... Saul**. These are the church leaders at Antioch, perhaps listed in the order of their importance. Barnabas was originally sent to Antioch by the church in Jerusalem (see 11:22), had recently returned from taking alms to Jerusalem (see 12:25), and was a recognized leader in the church at Antioch. **Simeon that was called Niger**. "Simeon" suggests a Jewish background, and "Niger" is Latin for "dark-complexioned" (see Marshall, *Acts of the Apostles*, p. 214). **Lucius of Cyrene**. Lucius is a Latin name. In the second group of preachers coming to Antioch, some were from Cyrene (see 11:20), the capital of Libya (see discussion on 6:9). **Manaen**. In Hebrew, Menahem. Since he was the foster brother of Herod Antipas, he would have been able to tell of Herod's thoughts and actions (see Luke 9:7–9).

13:2. They refers to the prophets and teachers listed in 13:1. **Ministered to the Lord, and fasted.** Paul's first missionary journey did not result from a planning session but from the Spirit's initiative as the leaders worshiped (see 13:4). **Separate me Barnabas and Saul for the work whereunto I have called them.** The communication from the Holy Spirit may have come through the prophets. "Separate" here means "to set aside" and "to give them exclusive responsibility for." This may have included the idea that the church would support them financially so that they could devote themselves to the work.

13:3. Laid their hands on them. This was a means of appointing Barnabas and Saul and of recognizing the church's participation in their mission. Fasting and prayer accompanied this appointment (see 14:23; Luke 2:37).

13:4. Seleucia. The seaport of Antioch (sixteen miles to the west and five miles upstream from the mouth of the Orontes River). **Cyprus** (see discussion on 11:19). Many Jews lived there, and the gospel had already been preached there (see 11:19–20).

13:5. Salamis. A town on the east coast of the central plain of Cyprus, near modern Famagusta. **John.** John Mark, a cousin of Barnabas (see Col. 4:10; discussion on 12:25).

13:6. Paphos. At the western end of Cyprus, nearly one hundred miles from Salamis, Paphos was the headquarters for Roman rule. **Bar-jesus.** "Bar" is Aramaic for "son of"; "Jesus" is derived from the Greek for "Joshua" (see discussion on Matt. 1:21).

13:7. Deputy. Since Cyprus was a Roman senatorial province, a proconsul was assigned to it.

13:8. Elymas. A Semitic name meaning "sorcerer," "magician," or "wise man" (probably a self-assumed designation).

13:9. Saul, (who also is called Paul,). The names mean "asked [of God]" and "little" respectively. It was customary to have a given name, in this case Saul (Hebrew, Jewish background), and a later name, in this case Paul (Roman, Hellenistic background). From this point on, Saul is called Paul in Acts. This may be because he was now entering the Gentile phase of his ministry. The order in which the names

are mentioned now changes from "Barnabas and Saul" (13:2, 7) to "Paul and Barnabas" (13:43, 46). Upon their return to the Jerusalem church, however, the order reverts to "Barnabas and Paul" (15:12). **Filled with the Holy Ghost** (see discussions on 2:4; 4:8). Here again is an instance in which a disciple's being filled with the Spirit accompanied a speaking ministry.

13:10. Paul's address to Elymas begins with three descriptive names: **O full of all subtilty and all mischief** ("one who is" is understood here to preface this), **thou child of the devil,** and **thou enemy of all righteousness.** By calling him these names, Paul made explicit Elymas's character. Exactly what this man was in his heart was not at all hidden from Paul. Each of these names points to some aspect, and each is more explicit in describing Elymas's motives. A sinful man does not want to have his sin exposed. The one who exposes it will certainly get that man's attention. **Wilt thou not cease to pervert the right ways of the Lord?** In one sense, Paul's question was a plea for Elymas to repent. In another, it gave moral justification for the judgment that came upon him with Paul's next words.

13:11. Thou shalt be blind. Elymas's spiritual blindness is signified by his physical blindness. Sorcery is about having power and being independent, even of the normal laws of nature. Elymas's judgment caused him to depend on **some to lead him by the hand.** What he had treasured most, his power and independence, was thus removed by the One who humbles the proud and exalts the humble.

13:12. The deputy (see discussion on 13:7) … **believed.** He was convinced by the miracle and the message.

13:13. Perga in Pamphylia. Perga was the capital of Pamphylia, a coastal province of Asia Minor between the provinces of Lycia and Cilicia, and was five miles inland and twelve miles east of the important seaport Attalia. **John departing from them.** Homesickness to get back to Jerusalem, an illness of Paul necessitating a change in plans and a trip to Galatia, and a change in leadership from Barnabas to Paul have all been suggested as reasons for John Mark's return. Paul's dissatisfaction with his departure is noted later (see 15:37–39).

13:14. Antioch in Pisidia (see discussion on 14:24). This is a different Antioch, not the one from which Paul and his companions had departed. Named after Antiochus, king of Syria after the death of Alexander the Great. It was 110 miles from Perga and was at the hub of good roads and trade. The city had a large Jewish population. It was a Roman colony, which meant that a contingent of retired military men was settled there. They were given free land and were made citizens of the city of Rome, with all the accompanying privileges. **Synagogue.** Paul's regular practice was to begin his preaching in the synagogue. He would preach there regularly for as long as the Jews would allow it (see 13:5; 14:1; 17:1, 10, 17; 18:4, 19; 19:8). His reason for doing so was grounded in his understanding of God's redemptive plan: to the Jew first (see 13:46; Rom. 1:16; 2:9–10; see also Romans 9–11). Paul was not neglecting his Gentile mission, for the God-fearers (Gentiles committed to worshiping the one true God) were part of the audience. Moreover, the synagogue provided a ready-made preaching situation with a building, regularly scheduled meetings, and a people who knew the Old Testament Scriptures. It was customary to invite visitors, and especially visiting rabbis (such as Paul), to address the gathering.

13:15. The law and the prophets. Sections from the Old Testament were read, followed by exposition and exhortation. **The rulers of the synagogue.** Those who were responsible for calling readers and preachers, arranging the service, and maintaining order.

13:16–41. This is Paul's first extended speech in Acts. His presentation of the gospel is fairly similar to that of Stephen (see 7:2–53) but with a milder tone. Stephen's speech must have made quite an impression on him. Like Stephen, he rehearsed the history of Israel (vv. 16–22), announced Jesus as the promised Messiah (vv. 23–26), accused the Jews of having Him killed (vv. 27–28), and proclaimed that God had raised Him from the dead (vv. 29–31). In conclusion, he presented Jesus as the fulfillment of the promises of God to the patriarchs (vv. 32–35) and issued an appeal to faith (vv. 36–41).

13:16–22. Paul recounted the history of Israel from the patriarchs through David. This is a quicker recitation than Stephen's, but Luke may have been summarizing Paul's words. Paul presented the history as something God did, not as something that "happened." He wanted to link God's activity in establishing the nation with His activity in sending Jesus Christ and raising Him from the dead.

13:16. For ye that fear God, see discussion on 10:2.

13:17–18. The God of this people of Israel chose our fathers (v. 17). The establishment of the nation was a mighty act of God, which the people held to by faith. Paul was laying the groundwork for calling them to faith in another mighty act of God: raising Jesus from the dead.

13:19–20. He divided their land to them (v. 19). Paul's audience knew that God gave them the land; he would go on to tell them that God gave them Jesus Christ also. **About the space of four hundred and fifty years** (v. 20). The Greek manuscripts create some uncertainty whether this phrase identifies the time of the events in verse 19 or 20. If verse 19, then it refers to the four hundred years of the stay "in the land of Egypt" (13:17; see discussion on 7:6) plus the forty years in the wilderness and the time between the crossing of the Jordan and the distribution of the land (see Josh. 14–19).

13:21–22. God gave unto them Saul (v. 21) ... **[and] raised up unto them David** (v. 22). Jesus, as Paul would point out, was of the lineage of David (see 13:23) and thus was also one whom God had anointed and chosen.

13:23–25. Paul next moved to contemporary events, connecting them with Israel's past and God's mighty actions on her behalf, and proclaimed that Jesus was the promised Messiah.

13:23. Of this man's (David's) **seed hath God according to his promise** (see, e.g., Isa. 11:1–16) **raised unto Israel a Saviour, Jesus.** This was Paul's main point. God, who had done mighty acts in creating, establishing, and leading the nation, was now doing another mighty act. Just as the Israelites had faith that God was in the previous deeds, so also they were responsible for believing God in this latest deed.

13:24–25. Paul then turned to a recent matter that his hearers all knew of, the ministry of John the Baptist. That a prophet had arisen in Israel after centuries of silence from heaven had certainly been the occasion of much discussion among Jews around the Mediterranean world. The impact of this event is difficult to fathom today. Christians today recognize John as the forerunner of Christ and focus on Christ. Jewish people of that time recognized John as a true prophet and focused on his ministry itself. Paul could legitimately use this fact to turn their focus toward Christ. His audience recognized John as one who had announced the will of God, and he had testified of Christ, as One greater than he, **whose shoes of his feet I am not worthy to loose** (v. 25). Paul now had a reasonable expectation that his audience was ready to hear of what God had done in Jesus Christ, whom even John had testified was greater than he, and this at a time when God was again actively dealing with His people, evidenced by the fact that He had sent John at all.

13:26–31. Here Paul told of the death and resurrection of Jesus Christ.

13:26. Paul desired that his hearers would come to faith in Jesus Christ. He thus prefaced the story of Jesus' death and resurrection with an appeal: **to you is the word of this salvation sent**. They were the recipients of the word of God, who had created their nation and led them and had now sent Jesus Christ. Paul understood that it was not enough just to tell people to believe in Jesus; they needed to know why they should believe in Him and what He had done that made faith in Him necessary.

13:27–28. Paul made it clear that the rulers in Jerusalem were culpable in Jesus' death. He apparently did this more mildly than Stephen had done. The point held, however. **Because they knew him not, nor yet the voices of the prophets** (v. 27), they became accomplices in accomplishing the will of God. Paul assumed that his hearers would not categorize themselves as ones who did not know the prophets. If the prophets foretold Jesus' coming and His death, then surely they would believe it rather than reject it.

13:29. The death of Christ **fulfilled all that was written of him**. It therefore fulfilled the purposes of God, and Paul's hearers should believe this.

13:30. But God raised him from the dead. Just as God "chose our fathers" (13:17), "divided their land to them" (13:19), "gave unto them judges" (13:20), "gave unto them Saul" (13:21), and "raised up unto them David" (13:22). Paul presented each of these as an act of God, and equally to be accepted on faith by Israel. The parallel between "raised him from the dead" and "raised up unto them David" may not have been accidental on Paul's part, as Jesus' right to reign was humanly established by His being in the lineage of David.

13:31. Eyewitnesses, Paul said, had seen the risen Christ and even now bore testimony to Him. **Many days.** Forty days (see 1:3).

13:32–35. Paul presented Jesus as the fulfillment of God's promises to the patriarchs.

13:32–33. We declare unto you glad tidings (v. 32). Paul had good news to bring: God had fulfilled His promises to Israel in the ministry of Jesus Christ, whom they should trust. To demonstrate the truth of what he preached, Paul quoted from the Old Testament: **Thou art my Son, this day have I begotten thee** (v. 33; Ps. 2:7). Jesus is the Son of God.

13:34. I will give you the sure mercies of David. This, Paul said, was God's promise to Jesus. In Him, the promise to David that his line would rule Israel forever is fulfilled.

13:35. Not suffer thine Holy One to see corruption. This passage from Psalm 16:10, quoted also in Peter's sermon at Pentecost (see discussion on 2:27), testifies to the permanent nature of the resurrection. Jesus lives forever to save His people.

13:36–41. Paul concluded his sermon with an appeal to his audience to exercise faith in Jesus Christ.

13:36–37. David himself did not see the fulfillment of the promise; he died **and saw corruption**

(v. 36). Jesus, as the fulfillment of the promise, was the one they should trust, for he **saw no corruption** (v. 37).

13:38. That through this man is preached unto you the forgiveness of sins. Since Jesus' resurrection was an act of God, just as the establishment of Israel was, and since God had given Jesus the throne of David, then Israel should trust in Him for whatever they needed; and their greatest need was for forgiveness of sins.

13:39. All that believe are justified from all things. Justification combines two aspects: (1) the forgiveness of sins (here) and (2) the gift of righteousness (see Rom. 3:21–22).

13:40–41. Paul's appeal included a warning not to be like those who disbelieved in the mighty acts of God, including and especially His most recent act in sending Jesus Christ and raising Him from the dead.

13:42. After the worship time, the Jews left the synagogue, but **the Gentiles**, those "that fear[ed] God" (13:16), remained and invited Paul to speak to them again **the next Sabbath**.

13:43. That **many of the Jews** also wanted to hear Paul does not contradict 13:42, which speaks of the time right after the service. **When the congregation was broken up** could well imply later that same day, or even during the week. **Continue in the grace of God**. Apparently, Paul and Barnabas saw from that first meeting some converts of both Jews and **proselytes**, God-fearing Gentiles.

13:44. Those who had heard Paul must have spread the word, including the fact that grace was offered to non-Jews as well, for **the next Sabbath day came almost the whole city together to hear the word of God**.

13:45. The Jews ... were filled with envy. The idea that Gentiles also might be shown grace did not set well with many of the Jews. It had been difficult even for Peter and the Jerusalem church to accept this idea.

13:46. It was necessary that the word [be] first ... spoken to you (see discussion on 13:14). This was necessary because the gospel came from and was for the Jews first and because Paul was himself a Jew with great compassion for his people (see Rom. 9:1–5; 10:1–3).

13:47. The Lord commanded us ... to be a light of the Gentiles ... for salvation unto the ends of the earth. Luke again emphasized that the grace of God was available to the Gentiles. This is a major theme in both the gospel of Luke and Acts.

13:48. As many as were ordained to eternal life believed. Possession of eternal life involves both human faith and divine appointment.

13:49. Though this appears to be one of Luke's summary statements, it is not, for the verses that follow continue the same story. Luke simply wanted to show that Paul and Barnabas had a successful ministry in the district.

13:50. The Jews ... expelled them. Paul and Barnabas were exiled from the city. While most of the people in the city had heard the gospel and many had believed, still more had not. Rarely does the gospel penetrate to the point that the majority of people in an area are saved.

13:51. They shook off the dust of their feet (see discussion on Luke 9:5). To show the severance of responsibility and the repudiation of those who had rejected their message and had brought suffering to the servants of the Lord. **Iconium**. Modern Konya. It was an important crossroads and agricultural center in the central plain of the province of Galatia.

13:52. Filled ... with the Holy Ghost (see discussion on 2:4). Luke wanted to emphasize that rejection did not daunt the disciples in their mission. This is one of the rare times that Luke mentioned disciples being filled with the Spirit without a direct reference to speaking.

14:1. Their mixed results at Antioch of Pisidia did not discourage Paul and Barnabas. It was time to move on, as a growing body of disciples had been established there. They went on to **Iconium** (see discussion on 13:51), where they preached to many and **a great multitude ... believed**. Paul continued his practice of going to **the synagogue** first.

14:2. Following their initial success, Paul and Barnabas faced bitter opposition from **the unbelieving Jews**. They evidently failed in this attempt to cause trouble, for Paul and Barnabas remained in Iconium a considerable time (see 14:3). A second wave of persecution was planned, however, involving violence (see 14:5).

14:3. Gave testimony ... and granted signs and wonders. A major purpose of miracles in Acts was to confirm the truth of the words and the approval of God.

14:4. The apostles. Paul and Barnabas are both called "apostles" (see 14:14; see also discussion on Mark 6:30). The term is used here not of the Twelve but in its broader sense of persons sent on a mission, that is, missionaries (see 13:2–3).

14:5. Stone them. Stoning was a Jewish mode of execution for blasphemy. Mob action probably was planned.

14:6. Lystra. A Roman colony (see discussion on 13:14) and probable home of Timothy (though he was known in Iconium as well), Lystra was about 20 miles from Iconium and 130 miles from Antioch. **Derbe** (see discussion on 14:20). About 60 miles from Lystra, Derbe was the home of Gaius (see 20:4). **Cities of Lycaonia.** Lycaonia was a district east of Pisidia, north of the Taurus Mountains. It was part of the Roman province of Galatia.

14:7. And there they preached the gospel. Most likely, Paul and Barnabas preached in all of the cities in this region as well as the surrounding areas. Wherever they found success, they stayed a while and taught. Otherwise, they moved on more quickly.

14:8–10. In Paul's time, **Lystra** (v. 8) was a minor place, a "small country town" (Polhill, *Acts*, p. 312). There, Paul saw a man crippled and healed him supernaturally. There is no mention of Paul having gone to a synagogue there, and it is possible that this was a wholly Greek city. In Judea and Samaria, the "signs and wonders" (2:43; 5:12) the apostles performed had validated their message. In Lystra, however, Paul's miracle was completely misunderstood (see 14:11–13).

14:11. In the speech of Lycaonia (see discussion on 14:6). The main language of these people apparently was not Greek, though certainly they knew it. Since Lystra had no Jewish population of any size,

the people had no knowledge of a religion in which miracles validated the message of God rather than indicating that the miracle worker was himself a god.

14:12. Jupiter ... Mercurius. The Latin names for the Greek gods Zeus and Hermes, respectively. Zeus was the patron god of the city, and his temple was there. People who had come to bring sacrifices to Zeus apparently decided to make an offering to Paul and Barnabas instead. That Barnabas was identified as the god Zeus may indicate that his appearance was more imposing, and Paul was identified as the god Hermes **because he was the chief speaker** (see 28:6). This incident may have occurred because of an ancient legend that told of a visit of Zeus and Hermes to the same general area. The gods, however, were not recognized by anyone except an old couple. The people of Lystra thus were determined not to allow such an oversight to happen again.

14:13. Gates. The Greek can refer to the temple gates, the city gates, or house gates.

14:14. They rent their clothes. A Jewish way of expressing great anguish (see Gen. 37:29, 34).

14:15. Vanities. Used in the Old Testament to denote false gods (see 1 Sam. 12:21).

14:16–17. In bearing testimony to the living God, Paul did not cite Scripture because these people would not have recognized it. He turned instead to natural revelation.

14:18. Scarce restrained they the people, that they had not done sacrifice unto them. Paul and Barnabas barely prevented the people from offering a sacrifice to them.

14:19. Apparently, some of Paul's opponents now began to follow him. **Stoned Paul.** This was done inside the city rather than at the usual place of execution outside the city walls. This incident may have happened several days or several weeks after the people's initial encounter with Paul and Barnabas. Enough time had passed for a body of disciples to have been established (see 14:20).

14:20. The disciples stood round about him. Young Timothy may have been present (see 2 Tim. 3:10–11). **Derbe.** A border town in the southeastern part of the Lycaonian region of Galatia (see discussion on 14:6). An inscription naming the city has been discovered about thirty miles east of what was previously thought to be the city site.

14:21–22. Paul and Barnabas returned to the cities they had preached in, **confirming the souls of the disciples** (v. 22), that is, helping them grow in the faith and in assurance and knowledge. **We must through much tribulation enter into the kingdom of God.** This has always been the case, though among Western Christians of the past two centuries, there has been little real tribulation. These circumstances, however, are an aberration for which believers should be thankful. Even today, tribulation is not the usual experience of the church in other parts of the world.

14:23. Ordained. The Greek for this word (used also in 2 Cor. 8:19) can mean (1) to stretch out the hand, (2) to appoint by show of hands, or (3) to appoint or elect without regard to the method. In 6:6, the appointment of the seven included selection by the church and presentation to the apostles, who prayed and laid their hands on them. **Elders in every church.** Because these were new churches, at least partly pagan in background, Paul and Barnabas may have both selected and appointed the elders.

14:24. Pisidia. A district about 120 miles long and 50 miles wide, north of Pamphylia (13:13–14). Bandits frequented the region (see perhaps 2 Cor. 11:26). **Pamphylia.** A district 80 miles long and 20 miles wide, on the southern coast of Asia Minor. After AD 74, Pisidia was included in the Roman province of Pamphylia (see 13:13).

14:25. For **Perga**, see discussion on 13:13. **Attalia.** The best harbor on the coast of Pamphylia (see 13:13).

14:26. For **Antioch**, see 11:20; discussion on 11:19.

14:27. Opened the door of faith. God had brought Gentiles to faith. He had, as it were, opened the door for them to believe (see 11:18).

14:28. Long time. Possibly more than a year.

2. The Jerusalem Council (15:1–35)

15:1. Certain men … came down from Judea. To Antioch. These men, probably from "the sect of the

Pharisees which believed" (15:5), were believers who insisted that to become a true Christian, one must first keep the law of Moses, and the test of such compliance was circumcision. They in no way correctly represented the apostles and elders of Jerusalem (see 15:24). The content of their preaching was that circumcision was necessary for salvation. This added a work to simple faith. Circumcision was the rite of initiation into the covenant God had made with Abraham, which was renewed in the law of Moses. In other words, these Judaizers maintained that the Gentile Christians had to become Jewish to be true Christians. This violated the doctrine of salvation by faith alone.

15:2. Paul and Barnabas had no small dissension and disputation with them. The argument went on apparently for weeks and was rancorous. Perhaps these Judaizers argued that Christ had come to the Jews and that while all are admitted to God's grace, so were all admitted into Judaism if they would be circumcised. Gentiles wishing to become Christians therefore needed first to become Jews, the people to whom Christ came. Cast this way, the argument is not completely unplausible. These men were not arguing mere nonsense. They were, however, arguing contrary to the truth of the gospel, which is that God saves by grace through faith, and no works of any kind are required. **Go up to Jerusalem** (see discussions on 12:1; Gal. 2:1). It was decided that these Judaizers (or legalists) would be given a hearing by the church in Jerusalem. Those who hold that Galatians 2:1–10 refers to the famine visit of 11:27–30; 12:25 argue that since Galatians 2:2 says that the visit mentioned there was occasioned by a revelation, it must refer to Agabus's prediction of the coming famine (see 11:27–28). Those who believe that Galatians 2:1–10 refers to the Jerusalem council visit of 15:1–22 assert that the famine visit occurred at the time of Herod Agrippa's death in AD 44 (see 11:27–30; 12:25).

15:3. Being brought on their way by the church. The Antioch church paid their travel expenses. **Declaring the conversion of the Gentiles.** In those days, when news traveled slowly, many of the churches had not heard about the missionary journey of Paul and Barnabas, nor about the conversion of Cornelius. This was completely new information for them, and it understandably **caused great joy unto all the brethren**. Hearing reports from missionaries encourages local churches in their own outreach and brings joy in knowing that God's word is going forth with power.

15:4–22. The sequence of meetings described in this section is: (1) a general meeting of welcome and report (vv. 4–5); (2) a meeting of the apostles and elders (perhaps to one side) while the church was still assembled (vv. 6–11); (3) a meeting of the apostles, the elders, and the whole assembly (vv. 12–22).

15:4. The first meeting was a report, cordially received, about the work done among the Gentiles.

15:5. Certain of the sect of the Pharisees which believed. Some Pharisees became Christians and brought their Judaic beliefs with them. They believed that Gentiles must first become converts to Judaism and be circumcised (see 15:1), and then they would be eligible to be saved by faith. Perhaps some of them had gone to Antioch and now returned to present their case.

15:6. The apostles and elders came together for to consider of this matter. The idea is that this was an official meeting. Since all the believers in the Jerusalem church were Jewish, the issue had not arisen, other than theoretically. If Cornelius had moved to Jerusalem and sought admission to the church there, the matter might have come up much sooner.

15:7. Peter rose up. After the apostles and elders had discussed the matter for a considerable period, Peter addressed them. **Gentiles by my mouth should hear**. Peter's argument was his own experience: God had sent him to preach to the Gentiles (see 10:28–29).

15:8. Giving them the Holy Ghost. This for Peter was the irrefutable proof of God's acceptance (see 10:44, 47; 11:17–18). Since Cornelius had received the Spirit without circumcision, then circumcision was not necessary.

15:9. Purifying their hearts by faith. This was Peter's way of saying what Paul affirmed (see Rom.

5:1; Gal. 2:15–16). Peter recognized that, as Jesus had taught, faith is a matter of the heart, not of outward acts. Genuine faith results in moral behavior, but mere outward behavior of any kind cannot be substituted for faith.

15:10. A yoke. The law (see Gal. 5:1; Matt. 11:28–29). No one had been able to keep the law, and in fact, it served mainly to demonstrate how far short of perfection one fell. It was assumed that when anyone was circumcised, they thereby agreed to abide by the law of Moses.

15:11. Through the grace of the Lord. Circumcision was not required. **We shall be saved, even as they** (see Rom. 3:9). Peter could have said, "They shall be saved, even as we." He said it this way to emphasize that Gentiles were saved by faith but that circumcision offered no barrier to the Jews' salvation, which was also by faith.

15:12. The multitude kept silence (see discussion on 15:4–22). Apparently, the people had remained in place while the apostles and elders met. The assembly had not remained quiet during that time but now became silent to listen to the leaders. **Barnabas and Paul**. Here Barnabas is mentioned first, perhaps reflecting his importance in Jerusalem, whereas in the account of the missionary journey the order was "Paul and Barnabas" after the events on the island of Cyprus (see 13:7, 9, 13, 42, 46). **Miracles and wonders** (see 8:19–20; 14:3). Barnabas and Paul had ministered more extensively among the Gentiles than had Peter or any of the others. They therefore had the greatest store of anecdotal evidence of God's grace at work among them.

15:13. James. The brother of the Lord. His argument added proof from Scripture (see 15:15–18).

15:14. Simeon. Peter (see 15:7). James used Peter's Hebrew name in its Hebrew form (Simeon is a variant of Simon). **A people for his name**. A new community largely made up of Gentiles but including Jews as well (see John 10:16; 1 Peter 2:9–10).

15:15. James invoked Scripture. **The prophets**. Specifically, Amos 9:11–12. Anecdotal evidence is good and must not be totally dismissed, but the controlling factor in determining truth is what God's

Word says. It provides the authoritative interpretation of human experience and thus was used to validate what Barnabas and Paul reported.

15:16–18. After this I will return (v. 16). This quotation from Amos 9:11–12 may set forth a sequence of the end times, including (1) the church age ("God … did visit the Gentiles, to take out of them a people for his name," 15:14), (2) the restoration of Israel as a nation (**build again the tabernacle of David**), and (3) the inclusion of the Gentiles (**all the Gentiles, upon whom my name is called**; v. 17).

15:19–20. Trouble not them (v. 19). Circumcision was not required, but four stipulations were laid down (see discussion on 15:20) regarding areas where the Gentiles had specific weaknesses and where the Jews were especially repulsed by Gentile violations. **Abstain from pollutions of idols** (v. 20; see 15:29; 1 Cor. 8:7–13; Rev. 2:14, 20); **from fornication**, a sin taken too lightly by the Greeks and also associated with certain pagan religious festivals; **from things strangled**, which thus retained the blood that was forbidden to be eaten (see Gen. 9:4); **from blood**, expressly forbidden in Jewish law (see Lev. 17:10–12). Reference here may be to consuming blood apart from meat. If these stipulations were observed, it would help both the individual Gentile and the relationship between Gentile and Jew. These were things that the foreigner residing in Israel would be expected to do according to Leviticus 17 and 18 (see Talbert, *Reading Acts*, p. 142).

15:21. Moses of old time hath in every city them that preach him. These four stipulations were not put upon the Gentiles as conditions for salvation. Instead, the concern most likely was that the Gentiles in the churches should behave in ways that would not offend Jewish believers or potential converts. The church at Antioch and in most of the places Paul had preached had mixed memberships of Jewish and Gentile believers, and the law was **read in the synagogues every Sabbath day**. The stipulations were intended to promote unity and to prevent barriers to outreach, not to secure salvation, which as James had made clear, was evidently by grace through faith alone.

15:22. The apostles and elders, with the whole church. Apparently, there was unanimous agreement on the choice of messengers and the content of the letter (see 15:23–29). **Judas surnamed Barsabas**. The same surname as that of Joseph Barsabas (see discussion on 1:23). The two may have been brothers. **Silas**. A leader in the Jerusalem church, a prophet (see 15:32), and a Roman citizen (see 16:37).

15:23. Here begins the content of the letter. Most likely, many copies were made, to be kept by the churches the delegation visited (see 16:4). Luke surely would have had access to these copies in his research for this book. **In Antioch and Syria and Cilicia**. Antioch was the leading city of the combined provinces of Syria and Cilicia.

15:24. To whom we gave no such commandment. The early church was already facing the problem of maintaining doctrinal purity and of separating themselves from those who preached falsely in the church's name. This problem has plagued the church throughout its history. Separating from false teachers has sometimes caused sharp division and hurt feelings, but the protection of the truth must always be uppermost (see John 17:17).

15:25. Being assembled with one accord emphasized that the church was unified in this matter, **to send chosen men unto you**. The delegation members had been chosen for the task; they were not acting on their own authority. This may have set a precedent. Official declarations on doctrinal matters coming from the Jerusalem church would have certification, while preachers claiming such authority but unable to produce written credentials might be suspect.

15:26. Men that have hazarded their lives. This refers to the hardships Paul and Barnabas had endured on their first missionary journey (see chaps. 13–14). Their testimony was the more credible because they had suffered for it.

15:27. Shall also tell you the same things. Perhaps the letter was read to the congregations and then explained in more detail by the delegation.

15:28. It seemed good to the Holy Ghost, and to us. Prior authority was given to the Spirit (whose working in the assembly was thus claimed), but "the apostles and elders and brethren" (15:23) also agreed on the matter.

15:29. For **abstain from … fornication**, see discussion on 15:20.

15:30. Luke skipped over details of other congregations the delegation might have visited along the way. Antioch was the main church in the region that was being disturbed and the home church of Barnabas and Paul.

15:32. Prophets. One of the primary functions of prophets in the early church was to encourage and strengthen the believers.

15:33. In peace. Apparently, the letter and the testimony of Judas and Silas ended the dispute. The church had wisely chosen the right people to carry the letter and to add their verbal testimony to its authority (see Talbert, *Reading Acts*, p. 143).

15:34. Silas decided to stay in Antioch. He became an associate of Paul in his later missionary work.

15:35. The church at Antioch was blessed with a multitude of knowledgeable and talented teachers and preachers.

B. Fourth Geographical Expansion of the Gospel: "Over into Macedonia" (15:36 – 21:16; see 16:9)

1. Paul's Second Missionary Journey (15:36 – 18:22)

15:36. In every city where we have preached the word. In the towns of Paul's first missionary journey (see 13:4 – 14:26).

15:37. Barnabas determined to take with them John, whose surname was Mark (see discussion on 12:25). Barnabas was perhaps more willing than Paul to offer a second chance to Mark, who now had another year or more of maturity.

15:38. Who departed from them (see discussion on 13:13). Mark had turned back at Perga and did not go to Antioch, Iconium, Lystra, and Derbe.

15:39. They departed asunder. That Paul and Barnabas would come to such a division is startling. It demonstrates that unity among believers has always been difficult, no matter how desirable it may

be. Barnabas and Mark do not appear again in Acts. In 1 Corinthians 9:6, however, Paul named Barnabas as setting a noble example in working to support himself. Galatians 2:11 – 13 describes another scene in Antioch that includes Barnabas. Mark evidently returned from his missionary work with Barnabas and became associated with Peter (see 1 Peter 5:13). During Paul's first imprisonment, Mark was included in Paul's group (see Col. 4:10; Philem. 24). By the end of his life, Paul came to admire Mark so much that he requested Mark to come to be with him during his final days (see 2 Tim. 4:11; Mark, Introduction: "Author"). **Cyprus.** The birthplace of Barnabas (see discussion on 4:36).

15:40. And Paul chose Silas. Apparently, Paul and Silas had become friends, beginning with the journey from Jerusalem to Antioch (see 15:22, 30 – 35). Luke's statement that Paul and Silas were **recommended by the bretheren unto the grace of God** is in no way meant to take away from whatever ministry Barnabas and Mark might have had. Luke's purpose now was to trace Paul's journeys.

15:41. Confirming the churches. Paul and Silas may have used the opportunity not only to deliver news of the Jerusalem council's letter but also to check up on doctrinal matters and to encourage the churches in their outreach and service to the Lord.

16:1. Derbe (see discussions on 14:6, 20). Paul had approached Derbe on the first trip from the opposite direction, so the order of towns is reversed here. For **Lystra**, see discussion on 14:6. **Timotheus.** Since Paul addressed him as a young man some fifteen years later (see 1 Tim. 4:12), Timothy must have been in his teens at this time. **His father was a Greek.** Statements concerning his mother's faith (here and in 2 Tim. 1:5) and silence concerning any faith on his father's part suggest that his father was neither a convert to Judaism nor a believer in Christ.

16:2. Which was well reported of by the bretheren. "Which" refers back to "Timotheus" not to "his father" (16:1), which might appear to be the immediate antecedent.

16:3. Circumcised him. Timothy's circumcision was a matter of expediency so that his work among the Jews might be more effective. This was different from Titus's case (see Gal. 2:3), in which circumcision was refused because some were demanding it as necessary for salvation. Timothy's standing among the Jews could have been problematic given his mixed Jewish-Gentile parentage.

16:4. They delivered them the decrees. Paul, Silas, and Timothy circulated among the churches copies of the letter written at Jerusalem. These may have been some of the copies produced there, or perhaps additional copies were made at Antioch. Silas, having been part of the Jerusalem church, would have been able to authenticate their contents.

16:5. The churches … increased in number daily. Luke used this progress report (see discussion on 1:15) to set the scene for the gospel's spread into Europe.

16:6. They. Paul, Silas, and Timothy. **Phrygia.** The district was formerly the Hellenistic territory of Phrygia, but it had more recently been divided between the Roman provinces of Asia and Galatia. Iconium and Antioch were in Galatian Phrygia. **The region of Galatia.** The name had been used to denote the Hellenistic kingdom, but in 25 BC, it had been expanded considerably to become the Roman province of that name. **Asia.** This also had been a smaller region but now was a Roman province including the Hellenistic districts of Mysia, Lydia, Caria, and parts of Phrygia.

16:7. Mysia. In the northwest part of the province of Asia. Luke used these old Hellenistic names, but Paul preferred the provincial (Roman) names. **Bithynia.** A senatorial province formed after 74 BC, Bithynia was east of Mysia. **The Spirit suffered them not.** The Spirit may have led Paul and Timothy in any of a number of ways: vision, circumstances, good sense, or the gift of prophecy.

16:8. Troas. Located ten miles from ancient Troy, Alexandria Troas (its full name) was a Roman colony and an important seaport for connections between Macedonia and Greece on the one hand and Asia Minor on the other. Paul returned to Troas following his work in Ephesus on his third journey (see 2 Cor. 2:12). On Paul's second or third journey, a church

was started in Troas. Later, Paul ministered to believers there, following his work in Ephesus and again when he returned from his third journey on his way to Jerusalem (see 20:5–12).

16:9. A vision. One of the ways God gave direction (see 10:3). **A man of Macedonia.** Macedonia had become a Roman province in 148 BC. There is no indication that the man of the vision was Luke, as some have suggested, but he did join the group at this point.

16:10. We endeavoured to go. This is where the "we" passages of Acts begin (see Introduction: "Author"), indicating that Luke had joined the party at Troas.

16:11. Samothracia. An island in the northeastern Aegean Sea. It was a convenient place for boats to anchor rather than risk sailing at night. **Neapolis.** Known today as Kavalla, Neapolis was the seaport for Philippi, which was ten miles away.

16:12. Philippi. A city in eastern Macedonia named after Philip II, father of Alexander the Great. Since it was a Roman colony, it was independent of provincial administration and had a governmental organization modeled after that of Rome (see discussion on 13:14). Many retired legionnaires from the Roman army settled there but few Jews (see Philippians, Introduction: "The City of Philippi"). **The chief city.** Thessalonica was the capital of Macedonia. Macedonia had four districts, however, and Philippi was in the first of these.

16:13. By a river side, where prayer was wont to be made. So few Jews lived in Philippi that it had no synagogue, so the Jews who were there met for prayer along the banks of the Gangites River (see Bruce, *The Book of Acts*, p. 311). It was customary for such places of prayer to be located outdoors near running water. Paul chose this place because it was as near to being a synagogue as he could find. Wanting to proclaim religious truth, he naturally went to a location where religious concerns, especially connected to the one true God, were expressed.

16:14. Lydia. A businesswoman. Her name may be associated with her place of origin, the Hellenistic district of Lydia. **Thyatira** (see Rev. 1:11; *KJV Study*

Bible note on Rev. 2:18). In the Roman province of Asia, twenty miles southeast of Pergamum (in the Hellenistic kingdom of Lydia). It was famous for its dyeing works, especially royal **purple** (crimson). **Worshipped God.** Lydia was a Gentile who, like Cornelius (see 10:2), believed in the true God and followed the moral teachings of Scripture. She had not, however, become a full convert to Judaism. **Whose heart the Lord opened.** After the resurrection, the minds of the disciples were opened to understand the Scriptures (see Luke 24:45); similarly, Lydia's heart was opened to respond to Paul's gospel message.

16:15. If ye have judged me to be faithful to the Lord. In other words, if the disciples believed that her conversion was genuine. She had not been saved long enough, nor had they known her long enough, for "faithful to the Lord" to mean what it usually does for people today. She offered them the hospitality of her home, which may have been large, as she was active in a prosperous business.

16:16. A spirit of divination. A "python" spirit, a demonic spirit. The python was a mythical snake worshiped at Delphi and associated with the Delphic oracle. The term "python" came to be used of the persons through whom the python spirit supposedly spoke. Since such persons spoke involuntarily, the term "ventriloquist" was used to describe them. To what extent the woman actually predicted the future is not known.

16:17. Us. The "we" section (see discussion on 16:10) ends here and begins again in 20:5. Perhaps Luke was not traveling with Paul on that day, as he was not arrested with Paul and Silas (see 16:19–24). Apparently, Timothy also was not with them on this day. It is pure speculation, but it is possible that Luke stayed at Philippi after Paul and Silas left, to help establish the new church there, or even that he returned to Troas. He may have intended to go with them only as far as Philippi. **The most high God.** The man possessed by an evil spirit in Mark 5:7 also used this title. It was a common title among both Jews (see Num. 24:16; Isa. 14:14; Dan. 3:26) and Greeks (found in inscriptions), but in the New Testament, the title is not used of God by Christians or Jews (see 7:48).

16:18. And this she did many days. It is surprising that Paul did not act sooner to deal with this problem. He either was very patient or believed that his preaching alone might deliver the woman or drive her off.

16:19. The motivation of **her masters** was simply financial. When **their gains** were taken away, they found reason to arrest Paul and Silas.

16:20. Magistrates. The Greek term *stratēgos* (Latin, *praetor*) is not the usual word for magistrates but rather a term of courtesy used in some Roman colonies, such as Philippi. **These men, being Jews, do exceedingly trouble our city.** The woman's masters knew that magistrates want, above all else, to maintain order. Such a charge would be hard to disprove and would motivate them to act.

16:21. Customs … not lawful. If a religion failed to receive Roman approval, it was considered *religio illicita*. Judaism had legal recognition, but Christianity did not. Since Paul and Silas were not preaching "normal" Judaism, they could be seen as troublemakers by the magistrates.

16:22–23. Beat them (v. 22). With rods. **Cast them into prison** (v. 23). Apparently, all of this was done in haste, without checking the facts.

16:24. Inner prison … stocks. Used not only for extra security but also for torture.

16:25. Paul and Silas prayed, and sang praises unto God. They knew joy in the midst of hardship. **And the prisoners heard them.** The disciples used the opportunity to give testimony to God's goodness, in spite of less than good circumstances, and their testimony seems to have made an impact on those near them.

16:26. All the doors were opened, and every one's bands were loosed. Apparently, not just Paul and Silas but all the prisoners were freed, a fitting picture of the spiritual freedom found in Christ (see Gal. 5:1). This incident recalls Isaiah 61:1 (which Jesus quoted in Luke 4:18), which states that the Messiah would "proclaim liberty to the captives, and the opening of the prison to them that are bound."

16:27. The keeper ... would have killed himself.
If a prisoner escaped, the life of the guard was demanded in his place (see 12:19). The guard would have taken his own life to shorten his shame and distress.

16:28–29. We are all here (v. 28). No one had actually escaped, though their chains were off. The other prisoners may have found the situation so startling that they did not take advantage of the opportunity to escape.

16:30. What must I do to be saved? The jailer had heard that Paul and Silas were preachers of a way of salvation (see 16:17). He had heard them singing and praying, and it had certainly worked on his heart.

16:31. Believe on the Lord Jesus Christ. A concise statement of the way of salvation (see 10:43). The word "believe" here means more than mental assent; it means to actively trust in or rely on Jesus.

16:32–33. The word of the Lord (v. 32; see 10:36). Paul and Silas explained the gospel more thoroughly to the jailer and the members of his household, and they all believed in Christ and were saved (see 16:34).

16:34. They enjoyed a meal together, in fellowship. **Rejoiced.** The consistent consequence of conversion, regardless of circumstances (see discussion on 8:39).

16:35. For **magistrates**, see discussion on 16:20. **Let those men go.** Cooler heads prevailed after the initial excitement. The magistrates knew they had no grounds to hold Paul and Silas under Roman law.

16:36. The jailer probably saw this as good news for Paul and Silas. Paul did not see it this way; there was a legal matter still to settle.

16:37. Beaten us ... uncondemned, being Romans. Public beating as punishment for Roman citizens would have been illegal (see 16:38), let alone beating them without a trial. **Let them come themselves.** There is no sin in asserting one's legal rights, if it is done in the right spirit. In this case, the gospel and its credibility were at stake. Paul and Silas were not asking for an escort to salve their injured pride as much as they were establishing their innocence for

the sake of the church in Philippi and its future. They wanted a public declaration of their innocence and, by extension, the legitimacy of the new church there.

16:38–39. The magistrates ... feared (v. 38), but they need not have. As Christians, Paul and Silas had no intention of pressing the legal point out of spite.

16:40. Rather than leave the city, they went back to Lydia's house. **Comforted them.** Paul and Silas, having been beaten and imprisoned, were more concerned for the comfort of the new believers than for their own circumstances.

17:1. Amphipolis ... Thessalonica. The Egnatian Way crossed the whole of present-day northern Greece east to west and included Philippi, Amphipolis, Apollonia, and Thessalonica on its route. At several locations, such as Kavalla (Neapolis), Philippi, and Apollonia, the road is still visible today. If a person traveled about thirty miles a day, each city could be reached after one day's journey. Located about a hundred miles from Philippi, Thessalonica was the capital of the province of Macedonia and had a population of more than 200,000, including a colony of Jews (and **a synagogue**). These factors contributed to Paul's decision to preach there (see 1 Thessalonians, Introduction: "Thessalonica: The City and the Church").

17:2. Paul ... went in unto them. To the synagogue (see 17:1; discussion on 13:14). **Three sabbath days.** These two weeks represent the time spent in the synagogue reasoning with the Jews, not Paul's total time in Thessalonica. An analysis of the Thessalonian letters reveals that Paul had taught them much more doctrine than would have been possible in two or three weeks.

17:3. Paul's message was that it was necessary for the Messiah to suffer and be resurrected and that Jesus, who suffered, died, and rose again, is the Messiah. This was a message tailored for a Jewish audience.

17:4. For **the devout Greeks**, see discussions on 10:2; 16:14. **The chief women.** These women were perhaps the wives of the leading men of the city but also deserved notice and position in their own right (see 17:12).

17:5. Moved with envy. Because of the large number of people (including some Jews, many God-fearing Gentiles, and many prominent women) who responded to Paul's ministry (see 13:45). **The house of Jason**. Paul had probably been staying there.

17:6. The rulers of the city. The Greek term *politarchēs* (lit., "city ruler"), used here and in 17:8, is found nowhere else in Greek literature, but it was discovered in 1835 in a Greek inscription on an arch that had spanned the Egnatian Way on the west side of Thessalonica. (The arch was destroyed in 1867, but the block with the inscription was rescued and is now in the British Museum in London.) The term has since been found in sixteen other inscriptions in surrounding towns of Macedonia and elsewhere.

17:7–8. Do contrary to the decrees of Caesar (v. 7). Blasphemy was the gravest accusation for a Jew, but treason—to support a rival king above Caesar—was the worst accusation for a Roman. **And they troubled the people and the rulers of the city** (v. 8). Once again, the local leaders were motivated as much by a desire to prevent civil disorder as they were to enforce specific laws.

17:9. Taken security of. Jason was forced to guarantee a peaceful, quiet community, or he would face the confiscation of his properties and perhaps even death.

17:10. Paul and Silas. It has been suggested that Timothy was left at Philippi and rejoined Paul and Silas at Berea (see 17:14). **By night unto Berea**. Modern Verria, located fifty miles from Thessalonica in another district of Macedonia. For **synagogue**, see discussion on 13:14.

17:11. These were more noble. It may be that Luke was not so much complaining about the Thessalonians as merely reporting that the Bereans received the word more openly. **Searched the scriptures daily**. This is the best reaction one can make to any new religious ideas one encounters, to see what the Scriptures say on the matter (see Bruce, *The Book of Acts*, p. 327).

17:12. Therefore, because they had searched the Scriptures, **many of them believed**. There is a direct connection between exposure to the Word of God and the moving of faith in the heart ("Faith cometh by hearing, and hearing by the word of God," Rom. 10:17).

17:13. The Jews of Thessalonica. Sometimes when people are emotionally engaged, they cannot leave a matter alone, and that seems to have been the case here. The Thessalonians had no rational reason to go to Berea, but uncontrolled emotions can cause people to do many things. Apparently, they came to Berea and told stories which upset the populace against Paul. We have no idea what they said, but it may have been charges similar to ones found elsewhere in Acts (13:45, 50; 16:19–21).

17:14. To go as it were to the sea. One might conclude that Paul went by boat to Athens. The road to Athens was a coastal road, however, and Paul may have walked the distance after having been escorted to the coast (some twenty miles). In any event, Christian companions stayed with him until they reached Athens.

17:15. Athens. Five centuries before Paul, Athens had been at the height of its glory in art, philosophy, and literature. She had retained her reputation in philosophy through the years and still maintained a leading university in Paul's day. **Silas and Timotheus** were called to join Paul there. They may have been in different locations. Paul could have expected a wait of more than just a few days.

17:16. His spirit was stirred in him. Paul was unable to see the level of idolatry in Athens without being disturbed. Much of the prophetic writings, not to mention the law of Moses, forbids idolatry. As a Christian, Paul knew even better that such activity diminished God and misrepresented Him.

17:17. For disputed he in the synagogue, see discussion on 13:14. **Devout persons**. God-fearing Gentiles (see discussions on 10:2; 16:14). Paul was not simply being combative; he was using Scripture and reason to point the Athenians to Christ. His method probably was much like the one he used in Antioch of Pisidia (see 13:14–44), perhaps with a more pointed defense of the truth since the synagogue was located in an idolatrous city. **In the market daily**. Paul engaged in what today would be called "street witnessing." The circumstances in Athens encouraged this approach; people gathered in the marketplace for conversation as well as to buy and sell, and there may have been something of a festival atmosphere on certain days.

17:18. Philosophers of the Epicureans. Originally, these philosophers taught that the supreme good is happiness, but not mere momentary pleasure or temporary gratification. By Paul's time, however, this philosophy had degenerated into a more sensual system of thought. **Stoicks**. The Stoics taught that people should live in accord with nature, recognize their own self-sufficiency and independence, and suppress their desires. At its best, Stoicism had some admirable qualities, but like Epicureanism, by Paul's time, it had degenerated into a system of pride. The two systems were at opposite poles, with the Epicureans emphasizing physical pleasures as the chief end in life, and the Stoics emphasizing moral duty as the chief end. **Babbler**. The Greek word originally meant "seed picker," a bird picking up seeds here and there. Then it came to refer to the loafer in the marketplace who picked up whatever scraps of learning he could find and paraded them without digesting them. **A setter forth of strange gods**. Some of the philosophers at least dimly understood the religious nature of Paul's message, though unclearly.

17:19. Areopagus means "hill of Ares." Ares was the Greek god of thunder and war (the Roman equivalent was Mars). The Areopagus was located just west of the acropolis and south of the agora and had once been the site of the meeting of the court or council of the Areopagus. Earlier the council had governed a Greek city-state, but by New Testament times, it retained authority only in the areas of religion and morals and met in the Royal Portico at the northwest corner of the agora. The council members considered themselves the custodians of teachings that introduced new religions and foreign gods. Paul thus had an opportunity to present the gospel to the people who had some authority in religious matters in Athens. If he could win this group to Christ, or even gain their sympathetic approval, the way would be cleared for many in Athens to believe.

17:20. Certain strange things. To the Greeks, the ideas that there is only one God and that people are morally responsible to Him would have been odd indeed. It was certainly encouraging to Paul that the group wanted to know more.

17:21. Luke seems to have dismissed as mere curiosity the Athenians' motive for wanting to hear more. Even if that were so, Paul did not waste the opportunity to tell them the truth about God. Luke here presented a picture of Paul as knowledgeable on matters of Greek thought, something he did nowhere else in Acts (see Ger, *The Book of Acts*, p. 237).

17:22. Too superstitious. The Greek for "superstitious" could be used to congratulate a person or to criticize him, depending on whether the person using it included himself in the circle of individuals he was describing. The Athenians would not know which meaning to take until Paul continued. In this context, it is clear that Paul wanted to be complimentary in order to gain a hearing. Paul, because he was not speaking to a Jewish-oriented audience, did not begin with a recounting of God's mighty acts in history, as that would have meant nothing to these people. He tailored his presentation to the awareness level of the audience. Here he had to begin with theology, not with history, as he did with Jewish audiences. Jews would have already known the theology Paul presented here.

17:23. TO THE UNKNOWN GOD. The Greeks were fearful of offending any god by failing to give him attention, so they felt they could cover any omissions with the label "the unknown god." Other Greek writers confirm that such altars could be seen in Athens. This was a striking point of contact for Paul. **Him declare I**. Paul could claim that the God he preached was this "unknown god," because God really is unknown apart from His self-revelation in Scripture and especially in Jesus Christ. He may be known partially from the evidences in nature and the human heart that He has put there, but men have rejected this revelation and turned away from the truth.

17:24. God that made the world. A personal Creator, in contrast with the views of pantheistic

Stoicism. **Lord of heaven and earth**. God is in authority and must be believed. With the Jews, Paul had pointed out that God was to be believed because of His mighty acts in history. With the Athenians, Paul took a more philosophical approach. **Dwelleth not in temples made with hands**. Paul thus invalidated all of the temples of Athens. He saw no need to accommodate the truth to their understanding but instead challenged their beliefs. He accommodated their lack of understanding by beginning with theology rather than history, but he never accommodated their beliefs by compromising the truth.

17:25. Neither is worshipped with men's hands. That is, sacrifices do no good, in the sense of appeasing God or buying His favor, for He needs nothing. In fact, it is the other way around: **he giveth to all life, and breath, and all things**.

17:26. Hath made of one blood all nations. All people are of one family (whether Athenians or Romans, Greeks or barbarians, Jews or Gentiles). All are descended from Adam (had Paul been able to finish this address, he might have discussed universal sin). **Determined the times before appointed**. God planned the exact times when nations should emerge and decline. **The bounds of their habitation**. He also planned the specific area to be occupied by each nation. He is God, the Designer (things are not left to chance, as the Epicureans thought).

17:27. God set the nations in place to **seek the Lord**, which they had not done.

17:28. Certain also of your own poets. Paul alluded to two Greek poems here: (1) "In him we live and move and have our being," from the Cretan poet Epimenides (ca. 600 BC) in his *Cretica*, and (2) "For we are also his offspring," from the Cilician poet Aratus (ca. 315–240 BC) in his *Phaenomena*, as well as from Cleanthes (331–233 BC) in his *Hymn to Zeus*. Paul quoted Greek poets elsewhere as well (see *KJV Study Bible* note on 1 Cor. 15:33; discussion on Titus 1:12). Here he used truth familiar to the Athenians as a bridge to introduce them to truth they had not yet heard.

17:29. Paul here used logic: **we are the offspring of God**, and therefore God cannot be **like unto gold, or silver, or stone**. No effect can be greater than its cause. God is not an idol, because God created humans, and humans are greater than man-made idols.

17:30. The times of this ignorance God winked at. God had not judged them for worshiping false gods in their ignorance (see 17:31). **But now commandeth all men every where to repent**. Paul was calling the Athenians to repudiate false gods and to acknowledge the one true living God who had created them.

17:31. That man whom he hath ordained. Jesus, the Son of Man (see 10:42; Matt. 25:31–46; Dan. 7:13). **He hath raised him from the dead**. Here is the point of contact with Paul's preaching to the Jews. Paul moved from the philosophical theology of the previous verses to historical reality. God will judge (something the Jews knew), and He will do it through Jesus Christ, whom He raised from the dead. It was at this point that Paul hit a roadblock.

17:32–34. The resurrection of the dead (v. 32). The Greeks accepted immortality of the soul but not resurrection of a dead body. Paul's speech produced three reactions: (1) **Some mocked**. They were unwilling to engage in an idea so new to them. (2) **Others said, We will hear thee again of this matter**. They delayed making a decision but were at least open to the possibility. (3) **Certain men clave unto him, and believed** (v. 34). These men had faith. "Clave" here means "attached themselves," with the idea of separating themselves from their prior beliefs. **Dionysius**. Later tradition states that he became the bishop of Athens, though it cannot be proved. **Damaris**. Some have suggested that she must have been a foreign, educated woman to have been present at a public meeting such as the Areopagus. It is also possible that she was a God-fearing Gentile who had heard Paul at the synagogue (see 17:17).

18:1. Came to Corinth. Either by land along the isthmus (a distance of about fifty miles) or by sea from Piraeus, the port of Athens, to Cenchrea, on the eastern shore of the Isthmus of Corinth (see 1 Corinthians, Introduction: "The City of Corinth").

18:2. Pontus. In the northeastern region of Asia Minor, a province lying along the Black Sea between

Bithynia and Armenia (see 2:9). **Aquila ... Priscilla** (the diminutive form of Prisca). Since no mention is made of a conversion and since a work partnership was established (see 18:3), it may be that they were already Christians. They may have been converted in Rome by those returning from Pentecost or by others at a later time. **Claudius**. Emperor of Rome (AD 41–54). **Commanded all Jews to depart from Rome**. Recorded by the Roman historian Suetonius (*Claudius* 25). The expulsion order was given, Suetonius writes, because of "their [the Jews'] continual tumults instigated by Chrestus" (a common misspelling of "Christ"). If "Chrestus" refers to Christ, the riots obviously were "about" Him rather than led "by" Him.

18:3. Tentmakers. Paul would have been taught this trade as a youth. It was the Jewish custom to provide manual training for sons, whether rich or poor. Tents were provided to the Roman army and to people who wanted shade for outdoor events or other reasons.

18:4. He reasoned in the synagogue (see discussion on 13:14). Here again Paul used reason to defend the truth of Christ. One may infer from Paul's earlier speeches that he used Scripture as a basis and then reasoned from that to the truth that Jesus is the Messiah. **And persuaded the Jews and the Greeks**. Among the Greeks, Paul may have used tactics similar to those he used in Athens (see 17:19–31). Luke did not say, but it would seem logical. In any case, Paul found ways to present the truth concerning Christ logically to whomever he encountered.

18:5. When Silas and Timotheus were come from Macedonia. Paul had instructed these two to come to him at Athens (see 17:15). Evidently they did (see 1 Thess. 3:1), but they may have been sent back to Macedonia almost immediately to check on the churches, perhaps Silas to Philippi and Timothy to Thessalonica. **Paul was pressed in spirit**. This means that Paul sensed the Lord leading him strongly to devote himself to preaching the gospel. He may have given up tentmaking to preach full time. **And testified to the Jews that Jesus was Christ**. Apparently, Paul pressed the claim with more emotional fervor than he had previously.

18:6. When they opposed themselves. That is, to Paul. **And blasphemed**. The Jews spoke evilly against Christ. **I am clean**. Paul had done his part in sharing the gospel with them. He bore no responsibility for their reaction. A faithful witness for Christ has only to tell the truth and call people to repentance and faith. The results are in God's hands. **From henceforth I will go unto the Gentiles**. Paul indeed did this during his long stay in Corinth (but see 18:19, where Paul went straight to the synagogue in Ephesus). Truly, Paul's fervent "desire and prayer to God for Israel is, that they might be saved" (Rom. 10:1).

18:7. Paul's desire to see his Jewish brethren saved may be why he moved into a house next door to **the synagogue**. It may have been coincidence, but one cannot be sure.

18:8. Crispus. Paul baptized him (see 1 Cor. 1:14). For **ruler of the synagogue**, see discussion on 13:15. **Believed, and were baptized**. The tense of the Greek verbs indicates that this response to this gospel was an ongoing, daily process.

18:9–10. By a vision (v. 9). Paul had seen the Lord in His resurrection body at his conversion (see 9:4–6; 1 Cor. 15:8) and in the temple at Jerusalem while in a trance (see 22:17–18). Now he saw Him in a vision (see 23:11). **Be not afraid, but speak**. Apparently, Paul felt some fear. It should comfort Christians today to know that even the apostles experienced fear about witnessing. Jesus' words of encouragement to him should speak to every Christian in every time; the Great Commission is not suspended due to local opposition. **For I am with thee** (v. 10). There is no fear in the presence of Christ for those who know Him and serve Him. "With thee" may also mean that Jesus was in favor of what Paul sought to do in Corinth. When Christians are doing His will, He is "on our side" or "with us," and one has no reason to fear.

18:11. A year and six months. During this time, Paul may have taken the gospel also to the neighboring districts of Achaia (see 2 Cor. 1:1).

18:12. Gallio. The brother of Seneca, the philosopher, who was the tutor of Nero. Gallio was admired as a man of exceptional fairness and calmness.

From an inscription found at Delphi, it is known that Gallio was proconsul of Achaia in AD 51–52. This information helps to date Paul's visit to Corinth on his second journey as well as his writing of the Thessalonian letters.

18:13. Contrary to the law. The Jews were claiming that Paul was advocating a religion not recognized by Roman law, as Judaism was. If he had been given the opportunity to speak, he could have argued that the gospel he was preaching was the faith of his fathers (see 24:14–15; 26:6–7) and thus was authorized by Roman law.

18:14. If it were a matter of wrong. According to Roman law, or local ordinance. Since Paul had committed no such crime, Gallio had no reason to punish him.

8:15. If it be a question of words and names, and of your law. Gallio saw the problem as an internal one among Jewish people about religious beliefs and the roles and identities of various persons and beings. Gallio was very fair, having only a passing familiarity with either Judaism or Christianity, and recognized at least that his government had nothing to say in a dispute involving the matter.

18:16. He drave them. That is, Gallio dismissed the case and moved on to other matters. To modern imaginations, the image of "drave them" is probably stronger than what actually happened.

18:17. The Greeks took Sosthenes ... and beat him. It is not clear whether the Greeks beat Sosthenes to vent their feelings against the Jews or beat him, their own synagogue ruler, because he was unsuccessful in presenting their case, but probably the former. A Sosthenes is included with Paul in the writing of 1 Corinthians (see 1 Cor.1:1). Perhaps he was the second ruler of the synagogue at Corinth to become a Christian in response to Paul's preaching (see 18:8).

18:18. Priscilla and Aquila. The order of the names used here (but see 18:2) may indicate Priscilla's prominent role or her higher social position (see Rom. 16:3; 2 Tim. 4:19). **He had a vow.** Grammatically, this could refer to Aquila, but the emphasis on Paul and his activity makes Paul more probable.

It was probably a temporary Nazarite vow (see Num. 6:1–21). Different vows were frequently taken to express thanks for deliverance from grave dangers. Shaving one's head marked the end of a vow.

18:19. Ephesus (see Ephesians, Introduction: "The City of Ephesus"; see also map, *KJV Study Bible*, p. 1694). The leading commercial city of Asia Minor, the capital of provincial Asia, and the warden of the temple of Artemis (Diana). **Left them there.** Priscilla and Aquila would give valuable aid upon Paul's return, providing advice about where and how the work in Ephesus could be started. For **synagogue**, see discussion on 13:14.

18:20–21. He consented not (v. 20) to tarry with Priscilla and Aquila in Ephesus, wanting to continue his church-planting activities. Paul always was focused more on planting new churches than on staying with one church for a time. This was a matter of his calling and ministry.

18:22. Saluted the church. This could refer to a congregation in Caesarea, but the explanation that Paul went **up** makes it more likely that it was the church in Jerusalem, some 2,500 feet above sea level. **Down to Antioch,** his home church. He did not stay long there either (see 18:23).

2. Paul's Third Missionary Journey (18:23–21:16)

18:23. The country of Galatia and Phrygia. The same route Paul had taken when starting on his second missionary journey but in the reverse order (see 16:6). The use of the phrase may indicate the southern part of Galatia in the Phrygian area (see discussion on 16:6).

18:24. Alexandria. Alexandria, in Egypt, was the second most important city in the Roman Empire and had a large Jewish population. **Apollos ... an eloquent man.** This means that Apollos knew much and perhaps had a large vocabulary. **Mighty in the scriptures.** Education is no barrier to faith, especially if one is well educated in matters related to Scripture. Apollos knew the Scriptures well and knew how to present scriptural truths persuasively.

18:25. The baptism of John. It was not in the name of Jesus (see also 19:2–4). Apollos knew something about Jesus, but basically he, like John, was still looking forward to the coming of the Messiah. John's baptism was based on repentance rather than on faith in the finished work of Christ.

18:26. Expounded unto him the way of God more perfectly. Apollos's heart was prepared due to his knowledge of Scripture. He was ready to receive Jesus Christ as soon as he heard the truth concerning Him.

18:27. Achaia. The Roman province of which Corinth was the capital. **The bretheren wrote, exhorting the disciples to receive him**. It may be that the letter from the Jerusalem church (see chap. 15) established a precedent that traveling speakers carried letters of commendation to certify their credentials. Apollos's ministry in Achaia was effective, for he **helped them much which had believed through grace**. The word "grace" is used ten times in Acts. The nearest parallel to this occurrence is 15:11, "But we believe that through the grace of the Lord Jesus Christ we shall be saved, even as they."

18:28. He mightily convinced the Jews … that Jesus was Christ. Because Apollos was "mighty in the scriptures" (18:24), he was able to show the Jews that Jesus was the Messiah promised in the Old Testament.

19:1. Apollos was at Corinth. Apollos was introduced at Ephesus (see 18:24) in the absence of Paul and moved to Corinth before Paul returned to Ephesus. Apollos later came back to Ephesus during Paul's ministry there (see 1 Cor. 16:12). **Through the upper coasts**. Not the lower direct route down the Lycus and Meander valleys but the upper Phrygian route approaching Ephesus from a more northerly direction. If Paul got to northern Galatia, which is unlikely, it must have been on one of these trips through the interior (see 16:6; 18:23). For **Ephesus**, see discussion on 18:19. **Certain disciples**. These twelve men (see 19:7) seem to have been followers of Jesus, but indirectly, through John the Baptist or some of his followers. Or perhaps they had received their teaching from Apollos himself in his earlier state of partial understanding (see 18:26). Like Apollos, they had a limited understanding of the gospel (see discussion on 18:25).

19:2. Have ye received the Holy Ghost …? The men's response to Paul's question was that they had **not so much as heard** of the Holy Spirit. Since they knew the Old Testament and John's preaching, they probably did know of the Holy Spirit. What they apparently did not know was the fulfillment of John's preaching that occurred on the day of Pentecost with the coming of the Holy Spirit. That they were rebaptized (see 19:5) clearly indicates the uniqueness of Christian baptism.

19:3. Unto what then were ye baptized? … Unto John's baptism. Apparently, these disciples preached about baptism, for Paul knew that they had received some kind of baptism, and hence his question.

19:4. John verily baptized with the baptism of repentance (see discussions on Matt. 3:11, 15; Mark 1:4). A summation of John's teaching. It was preparatory and provisional, stressing man's sinfulness and thus creating a sense of need for the gospel. John's baptism looked forward to Jesus, who by His death would make possible the forgiveness of sins.

19:5. The mark of true discipleship is willing obedience to the truth. These disciples did not argue that their previous baptism was "good enough," nor that baptism was unimportant. They had not had Christian baptism, and they needed to do things properly. Their willingness to do so is a mark of God's grace at work within them.

19:6. For **laid his hands upon them**, see discussion on 6:6. **The Holy Ghost came on them; and they spake with tongues, and prophesied**. The same experience that the disciples had at Pentecost (see 2:4, 11) and the Gentiles had in Caesarea (see 10:46).

19:7. One should not make too much of the fact that there were **about twelve** of these disciples. It is not a parallel to the apostles but only a passing fact that Luke recorded because he had it in his records.

19:8. Three months. Much longer than the "three sabbath days" (17:2) that Paul spent in Thessalonica, but he used the same approach: Jews first, then Greeks (see discussion on 13:14).

19:9. For **that way**, see discussions on 9:2; 19:23. **The school of one Tyrannus**. Probably a school used regularly by Tyrannus, a philosopher or rhetorician.

Instruction at the school was probably given in the cooler, morning hours. One Greek manuscript adds that Paul did his instructing from 11:00 a.m. to 4:00 p.m. This would have been the hot time of the day, but the hall was available then and the people were not at their regular work.

19:10. Two years. Paul's stay in Ephesus, totaling two years and three months (see 19:8), was the longest stay in one missionary location that Luke recorded. By Jewish reckoning, any part of a year is considered a year, so this period can be spoken of as "three years" (20:31). **All they which dwelt in Asia heard the word**. One of the elements of Paul's missionary strategy is seen here. Many of the cities where Paul planted churches were strategic centers that, when evangelized, served as focal points from which the gospel radiated out to the surrounding areas. Other examples are Antioch in Pisidia (see 13:14), Thessalonica (see 17:1), Athens (see 17:15), and Corinth (see 18:1).

19:11. God wrought special miracles by the hand of Paul. Luke mentioned this also in 14:3. It may be that such miracles were intermittent. One certainly does not get the impression from reading Acts that Paul constantly did miracles everywhere he went, though they did happen at times.

19:12. Handkerchiefs or aprons. Probably used by Paul in his trade of tentmaking (see discussion on 18:3): one for tying around his head, the other around his waist. Luke recorded this as something unusual; it was not an everyday occurrence in Paul's ministry. A similar phenomenon occurred in Peter's ministry (see 5:15).

19:13. By Jesus whom Paul preacheth. The name of Jesus cannot be used as a talisman or incantation. That these Jews referred to Jesus in this way also indicates that they had no personal knowledge of Him. It was thirdhand knowledge, and their efforts came to nothing. One cannot rely on the faith of another.

19:14. Sceva, a Jew, and chief of the priests. Sceva may have been related to the high-priestly family of Jerusalem, but more likely, he took this title himself to make a greater impression with his magical wiles. Drawn by Paul's ability to drive out evil spirits, Jewish exorcists wanted to copy his work (see 13:6; 19:13), but the genuine power of God cannot be successfully copied.

19:15. The evil spirit asked, **but who are ye?** The men had no spiritual standing of their own.

19:16. Overcame them. The power of the evil spirit was such that the man was able to defeat seven others and send them fleeing (for another example of supernatural strength coming from an evil spirit, see Mark 5:3–4).

19:17. And the name of the Lord Jesus was magnified. This incident impressed upon people that the name of Jesus was not to be taken lightly or misused. That Jesus was the Messiah became well known to many people as a result of Paul's ministry, the outreach of the church, and the incident with the sons of Sceva.

19:18. Confessed, and shewed their deeds. One mark of a genuine revival or awakening is that people will openly confess their sins.

19:19. Books. Such documents bearing alleged magical formulas and secret information have been unearthed. Ephesus was a center for magical incantations. **And burned them before all men**. By publicly repudiating magical arts, they glorified the Lord and gave public testimony to the lordship of Jesus Christ over all matters of spiritual life and truth. **Fifty thousand pieces of silver**. The high price was not due to the quality of the books but to the supposed power gained by their secret rigmarole of words and names.

19:20. Mightily grew the word of God. This progress report (see discussion on 1:15) concludes Luke's account of the significant events at Ephesus.

19:21. Paul purposed in the spirit. Paul made the determination to go through Greece, then to Jerusalem, and on to Rome from there. Luke did not say so, but part of Paul's purpose in this itinerary was to collect an offering for the church in Jerusalem to be distributed to the poor (see 1 Cor. 16:1).

19:22. Erastus (see discussion on Rom. 16:23). An important figure at Corinth, the city treasurer at one time (see Rom. 16:23). Here Erastus returned to Corinth by way of Macedonia with Timothy. He is also located later at Corinth (see 2 Tim. 4:20).

19:23–41. The success of the preaching of the gospel caused a major upheaval in Ephesus. This indicates that as widespread as the gospel was, a sizable majority in the area had not believed in Jesus Christ. The Christian minority had, however, made an impact on at least one segment of the local economy (see 19:24–27), and it was economic hardship more than religion that drove the opposition.

19:23. No small stir. One wonders if this is a bit of understatement on Luke's part. What happened was a near riot. **That way.** Luke first used this phrase in 9:2 to describe Christianity. It recalls Jesus' statement "I am the way" (John 14:6). It also implies that faith in Christ is more than a onetime event; it is a way of life radically different from the way most people live. Paul had once opposed people who followed "this way" (9:2); here local merchants opposed "that way." In both cases, the emphasis is on how different living for Christ is from living like other people. If the Christians had been indistinguishable by their lifestyles from the respectable people around them, there would have been no opposition. Christians in all ages are called to follow a different "way."

19:24. Demetrius, a silversmith. Each trade had its guild, and Demetrius was probably a responsible leader of the guild for the manufacture of **silver shrines** and images. **Diana.** The Greek name for the Roman goddess Diana is Artemis, which is found in the Greek New Testament. The Ephesian Artemis, however, was very different from the Greco-Roman goddess. She had taken on the characteristics of Cybele, the mother goddess of fertility worshiped in Asia Minor and served by many prostitute-priestesses. A meteorite may be the basis of the many-breasted image of heavenly workmanship claimed for Artemis (see 19:35; some have identified the objects that cover the torso of the image as ostrich eggs). Reproductions of the original image from the time of the emperor Domitian (AD 81–96) have been found in Ephesus.

19:25. Wealth. Since the temple of Diana (Artemis) was one of the seven wonders of the ancient world, people came from far and wide to view it. Their purchase of silver shrines and images produced a lucrative business for the craftsmen.

19:26. Saying that they be no gods, which are made with hands. Paul was right on this point, but it is interesting that Demetrius mentioned this second. His main concern was financial, but religion was useful in inspiring others to action.

19:27. The temple of the great goddess. This temple was the glory of Ephesus. It was 425 feet long and 220 feet wide, having 127 white marble columns 62 feet high and less than 4 feet apart. In the inner sanctuary was the many-breasted image that supposedly dropped from heaven. **Her magnificence should be destroyed.** Demetrius used inflammatory language here. There was no evidence that anyone in Ephesus wanted to destroy the building itself. He implied, however, that should the craftsmen's trade be hindered, destruction of the building would soon follow. **Whom all Asia and the world worshippeth.** This was exaggeration on his part. Many people worshiped at the temple of Diana certainly, but not everyone. This is an example of the "bandwagon" fallacy. Worshiping Artemis was something, Demetrius said, that everyone did. Therefore, it was right, and such worship should not be interfered with. He implied that this interference came from a small minority who opposed what "everyone" believed and did. Demetrius shaped the argument in ways that were inaccurate and that isolated the Christian minority, making them appear more of a threat to society than a help. Unbelievers in every age do this, and no less so today, in which those who have the public "megaphone" often use inflammatory language and inaccuracies to shape people's perceptions of Christians as people whose existence threatens the fabric of society.

19:28. They were full of wrath. The inflammatory speech Demetrius had given had the intended effect. **Great is Diana of the Ephesians.** The angry crowd reacted with fervor in upholding the religious concept that both shaped their worldview and filled their pocketbooks.

19:29. Aristarchus. He later traveled with Paul from Corinth to Jerusalem (see 20:3–4) and also accompanied Paul on the voyage from Jerusalem to Rome (see 27:1–2; Col. 4:10).

19:30. Paul would have entered in. Paul's motivation was to speak to the people, not to run away. Under the circumstances, he might not have wanted to present the gospel, but he certainly would have wanted to correct misperceptions about Christians and to defend their right to live in Ephesus. Had the crowd calmed down at this, surely Paul would then have seized the opportunity to present Christ as the true God, in contrast to idols made with human hands (at least that part of Demetrius's speech was accurate).

19:31. The chief of Asia (Greek, *Asiarchēs*). Members of a council of men of wealth and influence elected to promote the worship of the emperor. Paul had **friends** in this high circle. Their primary concern here may have been maintaining order and preventing a murder from taking place.

19:32. The assembly was confused. Demetrius's words were not accurate, and the efforts of some to correct them led to further confusion. **Knew not wherefore they were come together**. Many in the assembly had gathered simply because a crowd was gathering and had no idea what the issue was but did not want to miss it. "Wherefore" simply means "why."

19:33. Alexander. Why he was pushed forward by the Jews is unclear. It may have been to make clear the disassociation of the Jews from the Christians or perhaps to accuse the Christians further of an offense against the Greeks. **Would have made his defense** indicates that Alexander may have sought to defend the Christians, since the Jews agreed with the Christians that idolatry is wrong. It may be that he was a better choice for this than Paul, who was new in town and was the center of controversy. In any case, the crowd did not even give him the chance to speak (see 19:34).

19:34. When they knew that he was a Jew. The crowd recognized that the Jews were not worshipers of Diana any more than the Christians were. Alexander's presence only fanned the flames further.

19:35–40. "The townclerk" (v. 35) was the secretary of the city who published the decisions of the civic assembly. He was the most important local official and the chief executive officer of the assembly,

acting as go-between for Ephesus and the Roman authorities. In contrast to Demetrius's rhetoric, the clerk made a speech offering common sense and truth.

19:35–36. When the townclerk had appeased the people (v. 35), he made his first point: everyone knew **that the city of the Ephesians is a worshipper of … Diana**. The city's position as the center for that kind of worship had not been threatened, and thus the people had overreacted. **These things cannot be spoken against** (v. 36). In other words, no one could bring any evidence that the city's position was threatened. Demetrius had claimed that Paul had "persuaded and turned away much people" (19:26), and while this was true, there were still many who practiced pagan ways. In that first century, the church had not completely demolished the pagan worldview. It was not until the fifth century, after the fall of Rome, that paganism ceased to be the majority worldview in that part of the world. At that time, Augustine devoted a major portion of his *City of God* to refuting paganism as a false and illogical understanding of reality.

19:37. The clerk's second point focused on the Christians themselves. They had not done anything wrong before the law. **Robbers of churches**. Literally, he meant that the Christians had not broken into any pagan temples and stolen anything. They were not guilty of sacrilege (see Bruce, *The Book of Acts*, p. 377). **Nor yet blasphemers of your goddess**. The Christians had said that idolatry is wrong and that a god made with human hands is not real. They had not, however, launched a deliberate attack against a specific deity, or so the clerk claimed. He may or may not have been correct in this. His goal was to prevent a riot and to restore order.

19:38–39. The town clerk next offered a legal remedy for Demetrius and the craftsmen. **The law is open, and there are deputies**. Any real problem could be brought before the courts. Apparently, the clerk understood that the only real complaint they had was that their business had been hurt. The government could not do anything about the law of supply and demand. Since the Christians had not prevented anyone from worshiping wherever they chose, any harm to the craftsmen's trade was a result of the wholly legal success of the Christians' preaching, not due to a violation of the law.

19:40. We are in danger to be called in question. This was the clerk's main concern. Rome wanted order and peace, and a riot over a point of conflict between religious perspectives would only make the leadership at Ephesus look bad in the eyes of Rome. By implication, the town clerk had upheld some principles that are recognizable today: (1) people have the right to preach their religious views without hindrance by government or society; (2) people have the right to believe as they choose, without hindrance; (3) that some people do not like the religious views of others is not sufficient reason for the government to step in; (4) genuine complaints about actual behavior should be brought before the proper authorities, in the courts, not made fodder for public approbation. Would that certain people and organizations today recognized these principles when Christians assert their right to meet and preach the gospel in the public square.

19:41. He dismissed the assembly. By the time the town clerk finished speaking, the crowd had quieted. Truth won out over inflammatory rhetoric in the end, and a riot was averted.

20:1. Departed … into Macedonia. Paul wanted to (1) leave Ephesus, (2) preach in Troas on his way to Macedonia, (3) meet Titus at Troas with a report from Corinth (see 2 Cor. 2:12–13), and (4) continue collecting the offering for Judea (see 1 Cor. 16:1–4; 2 Cor. 8:1–9:15; Rom. 15:25–28).

20:2. He had gone over those parts. This may cover a considerable period of time. Paul may have gone as far as Illyricum (see Rom. 15:19) at this time.

20:3. There abode three months. Probably a reference to the stay in Corinth, the capital of Achaia. These would have been the winter months, when ships did not sail regularly. Paul probably wrote Romans at this time (see Romans, Introduction: "Background"). **The Jews laid wait for him.** The Jews were determined to take Paul's life. Since he was carrying the offering for the Christians in Judea, there would have been a temptation for theft as well. The port at

Cenchrea would have provided a convenient place for Paul's enemies to detect him as he entered a ship **to sail into Syria.**

20:4. The men listed in this verse seem to be the delegates appointed to accompany Paul and the money given for the needy in Judea (see *KJV Study Bible* note on 2 Cor. 8:23). Three were from Macedonia, two from Galatia, and two from Asia. Luke may have joined them at Philippi ("we sailed," 20:6; see discussion on 16:10). **Sopater.** May be the same as Sosipater (see Rom. 16:21). For **Aristarchus**, see discussion on 19:29. **Secundus.** Not mentioned elsewhere. His name means "second," as Tertius (see Rom. 16:22) means "third" and Quartus (see Rom. 16:23) means "fourth." **Gaius of Derbe.** A Gaius from Macedonia was associated with Aristarchus (see 19:29), but the grouping of the names in pairs (after the reference to Sopater) indicates that this Gaius was associated with Roman Galatia and is different from the Macedonian Gaius. **Timotheus.** May have represented more than one congregation. He was from Lystra but had been responsible for working in other churches (see 1 Cor. 16:10–11; Phil. 2:19–23). He had been sent to Macedonia before Paul left Ephesus (see 19:22). **Tychicus.** A constant help to Paul, especially in association with the churches of Asia (see Eph. 6:21–22; Col. 4:7–9; 2 Tim. 4:12; Titus 3:12). **Trophimus** (see 2 Tim. 4:20). Appears again in 21:29. He was an Ephesian, and it is implied that he was a Gentile.

20:5. Troas. Was to be the rendezvous for Paul and those who went on ahead by sea from Neapolis, the seaport of Philippi (see 16:11). Paul and his immediate companions stayed in Philippi before sailing a week later. This is the beginning of the "we" passages in Acts (20:5–15; 27:1–29; 28:2–16), passages written in first-person plural, indicating that the author was a participant in the events recorded.

20:6. From Philippi. From the seaport, Neapolis, about ten miles away. **The days of unleavened bread.** Began with Passover and lasted a week. Paul spent the period in Philippi. He had initially hoped to reach Jerusalem sooner (see 19:21), but now he hoped to arrive there for Pentecost (see 20:16). The voyage from Neapolis to Troas took **five days**. It had taken about two days going the other direction (see 16:11). Although Paul was in a hurry to arrive at Jerusalem by Pentecost, he remained **seven days** at Troas. This might have been because of a ship schedule, but more likely, Paul wanted to meet with the believers on the first day of the week to break bread.

20:7. The first day of the week. Sunday. Although some maintain that they met on Saturday evening since the Jewish day began at six o'clock the previous evening, there is little indication that Luke was using the Jewish method of reporting time to tell of happenings in this Hellenistic city (but see 20:8, 11). **To break bread**. Here refers to the Lord's Supper, since breaking bread was the expressed purpose for this formal gathering. The Lord's Supper had been commanded (see Luke 22:19), and it was observed regularly (see 2:42).

20:8. Many lights. The disciples were meeting at night (see 20:11). It may have been Saturday night, by modern reckoning, or Sunday night. It is interesting that Luke recorded this small detail. He may have been an eyewitness.

20:9. Eutychus. A name common among the freedman class (see discussion on 6:9). **Paul was long preaching**. This tendency has not died out in the life of the church.

20:10. His life is in him. As Peter had raised Tabitha (9:40), so Paul raised Eutychus. It may be that life returned when Paul embraced him (see Bruce, *The Book of Acts*, p. 385).

20:11–12. Were not a little comforted (v. 12). Everyone rejoiced that Eutychus was alive. Verse 12 did not happen chronologically later than verse 11. Luke was summing up Paul's ministry that night before finishing his account of Eutychus.

20:13. Assos. On the opposite side of the peninsula from Troas, about twenty miles away by land. The coastline, however, was about forty miles. Paul thus was not far behind the ship that sailed around the peninsula.

20:14. Mitylene. After the first day of sailing, the ship put into this harbor on the southeast shore of the island of Lesbos.

20:15. Chios. Paul and his companions spent the second night off the shore of this larger island, which lay along the west coast of Asia Minor. **Samos**. Crossing the mouth of the bay that leads to Ephesus, they came on the third day to Samos, one of the most important islands in the Aegean. **Miletus**. Thirty miles south of Ephesus, Miletus was the destination of the ship Paul was on. He would have had to change ships to go to Ephesus, which would have cost him time (see 20:16). If he had gone to Ephesus, he would have had to visit a number of families, which would have taken more time. If trouble arose, such as the riot of a year ago (see 19:23–41), even more time would be lost. A delay could not be risked.

20:16. The day of Pentecost. Fifty days after Passover. Five days plus seven days (see 20:6) plus four days (see 20:13–15) had already gone by, leaving only about two-thirds of the time for the remainder of the trip.

20:17. The elders of the church. The importance of the leadership of elders was evident throughout Paul's ministry. He delivered the famine gift from the church at Antioch to the elders of the Jerusalem church (see 11:30). He appointed elders on his first missionary journey (see 14:23) and addressed elders later in Philippi (see Phil. 1:1, where they are called "bishops"). He requested the Ephesian elders to meet with him on this solemn occasion (see 20:28). Some years later, he wrote instructions regarding the qualifications for elders (see 1 Tim. 3:1–7; Titus 1:5–9).

20:18–35. Paul's speech has more in common with his letters than with any of his addresses in Acts (see Polhill, *Acts*, p. 422). This may be because Paul would soon be absent from the Ephesians and because of his concern for their doctrinal purity, a matter he addressed often in his letters.

20:18–21. Paul began his speech by laying out his philosophy of ministry, describing his manner of conducting his ministry (vv. 18–19), the scope of his ministry (v. 20), and the content of his ministry (v. 21).

20:18–19. What manner I have been with you at all seasons (v. 18). Paul could point to a life of consistency, both in terms of ethics and in terms of performing his ministry. This involved two factors: **humility of mind, and with many tears** (v. 19; see 20:31). There is no inconsistency between standing up for truth and being humble. Paul had proclaimed the gospel without compromise and yet with humility. "Humility" indicates Paul's attitude as a servant of God, and "tears" indicate his burden that people would come to know Christ. Both are necessary if one is to fulfill the call to ministry. Paul's ministry at Ephesus was conducted with emotional fervency and a sense of urgency.

20:20. Paul turned to the scope of his ministry: **I kept back nothing that was profitable**. Paul preached the whole truth of God. **Shewed you, and ... taught you**. Paul's ministry included living out the truths of the gospel as well as teaching them. Both are essential for a fully effective ministry. Paul's ministry among the Ephesians, then, was characterized by humility and genuine caring, and it included both living out and teaching the truth.

20:21. Paul concluded this section with the content of his ministry: **repentance toward God, and faith toward our Lord Jesus Christ**. This is the gospel in a sentence. "Repentance" is turning from evil and sin and toward God and His will. "Faith" is directed toward the Lord Jesus Christ, that is, toward His work on the cross. Anyone who comes to God in genuine repentance of sin and who trusts in the finished work of Christ will be saved. Thus, repentance and faith, properly understood, constitute the essence of the gospel.

20:22. Paul then moved on to matters related to his travel plans. **I go bound in the spirit unto Jerusalem**. Paul did not go to Jerusalem against the guidance of the Spirit, as some have suggested, but because of the guidance of the Spirit. People pleaded with him not to go (see 21:4, 12), not because the Spirit prohibited his going but because the Spirit revealed the capture that awaited him there (see 21:11–12).

20:23. Witnesseth in every city. Perhaps Paul was hearing in all of the churches warnings that he should not go to Jerusalem, similar to what Luke recorded in 21:12. **Bonds and afflictions abide me.**

Paul was aware of what awaited him but was also convinced that God wanted him to go. Sometimes God's will is the path of joy, peace, and comfort. Other times, it is a path of hardship and opposition. One must not let such matters be a hindrance us from doing the will of God.

20:24. None of these things move me, neither count I my life dear unto myself. Paul would rather die because he had done God's will than live for many more years outside of His will.

20:25. Shall see my face no more. This was not a message from God but rather what Paul anticipated. He had been mistaken before in his plans: he had intended to stay in Ephesus until Pentecost, but he had to leave earlier (see 20:1; 1 Cor. 16:8–9). His prophetic power was not used to foresee his own future, just as his healing power was not used to heal his own disease (see 2 Cor. 12:7–9). As it turned out, it seems Paul did revisit Ephesus (see 1 Tim. 1:3).

25:26–27. I am pure from the blood of all men (v. 26). Paul meant not that he had not committed murder during his ministry (his supporters were certainly well aware of that) but that he had faithfully preached the gospel. Perhaps Paul had in mind the passage in Ezekiel 3:18–19, which says that one must warn the wicked man or be guilty of his blood. Paul had preached "repentance toward God" (25:21) and had done it "both publickly, and from house to house" (25:20) and thus was not guilty before God of failing to warn the wicked.

20:28. Overseers. "Elders" (20:17) were called "overseers" and were told to pastor ("shepherd") the flock, demonstrating that they could be called "elders," "overseers," or "pastors." **His own blood**. Literally, "the blood of his own one," a term of endearment (such as "his own dear one," referring to His own Son).

20:29. Shall grievous wolves enter in among you. Paul had seen what had happened in the churches in Galatia and Corinth when certain men posing as apostles or their representatives came and preached a "works" salvation. They had avoided Ephesus, probably because of the presence of Paul and his associates. Paul did not need a prophet's vision to see that his absence would mean these false teachers would attempt to influence this large and important church.

20:30. Of your own selves. That is, men who would preach false doctrine would arise among the Ephesians, not just come in from the outside. Paul well knew the reality of fallen human nature. Humans need little help to be led astray into heresy. Christians need much help from God if they are to stay true to His Word.

20:31. Three years (see discussion on 19:10). Paul's ministry in and around Ephesus had been long and influential. Even though he had traveled from Ephesus to other places, his ministry had been headquartered there for some time, and his associates—Timothy, Titus, and perhaps Luke himself—had carried on his work even when he was away.

20:32. I commend you to God. That is, Paul left the Ephesians in God's care **and to the word of his grace.** Paul left them under the authority of God's Word. They would face doctrinal heresy from outside and from within (see 20:29–30), but their protection would be from God and from His Word. Paul was especially concerned that they would depart from the truth of salvation by grace through faith, as this had so often been the point of departure for other churches, to salvation by works. That Paul was primarily concerned about the church's doctrinal purity is a reminder of its importance in the life of the church today. Paul was not worried about their relevance to the culture, nor about their external unity or number of programs, so long as they remained true to the gospel and to God's Word. **Are sanctified.** Positional sanctification (see 26:18; see *KJV Study Bible* note on 1 Cor. 1:2).

20:33. Paul then turned to the matter of financing his ministry. **I have coveted no man's silver, or gold, or apparel.** Paul had not charged a fee for preaching the gospel. He may have been contrasting his behavior with that of those who had disturbed the Corinthian church (see 1 Corinthians 9). Paul had asserted to the Corinthians that he had the right to charge for the gospel but had not done so (1 Cor. 9:14, 18). He hinted that others, perhaps the false

teachers at Corinth, had charged a fee for their ministries (1 Cor. 9:11–12). None of these Scriptures are to be used to justify not paying ministers today. Paul even asserted that it is right to pay the minister (see 1 Cor. 9:3–11). A minister should be paid so that he can devote himself to the work of the ministry, not having to be concerned for physical needs. Paul, believing God had called him to ministry in a special way, believed that he should not charge for ministry, perhaps to contrast himself with the false teachers of his time.

20:34. Ministered unto my necessities. Paul had worked in Thessalonica (see 1 Thess. 2:9) and Corinth (see Acts 18:3).

20:35. Remember the words of the Lord Jesus. A formula regularly used in the early church to introduce a quotation from Jesus (see 1 Clement 46:7). This is a rare instance of a saying of Jesus that is not found in the canonical Gospels.

20:36–38. Paul ended the meeting with prayer and goodbyes. Many tears were shed, especially over the possibility that the Ephesians would not see him again. Nothing is wrong with Christians bidding tearful goodbyes to one another. Believers will see each other in heaven, but especially among close family and friends, leave-taking in this world is always tearful, yet sometimes necessary, in answer to God's call.

21:1. A straight course unto Cos. Favorable winds took Paul and his fellow travelers to a stopping place at this island. **Rhodes.** The leading city on the island of Rhodes, once noted for its harbor colossus, one of the seven wonders of the ancient world (but demolished over two centuries before Paul arrived there). It took them a day to get to Rhodes. **Patara.** On the southern coast of Lycia.

21:2. Paul changed ships from a vessel that hugged the shore of Asia Minor to one going directly to Tyre and Phoenicia.

21:3. For **Cyprus,** see 13:4. **Tyre.** Paul had passed through this Phoenician area at least once before (see 15:3; Mark 7:24).

21:4. Seven days. These, added to the twenty-nine days since the Passover in Philippi, would leave only two weeks until Pentecost. **Finding disciples.** Apparently, Paul and his associates did not know of these Christians, at least not directly. **Who said to Paul through the Spirit, that he should not go up to Jerusalem.** The Spirit warned of the coming trials in store for Paul at Jerusalem. Because of these warnings, Paul's brothers urged him not to go on, knowing that trials lay ahead, but Paul felt "bound in the spirit" (20:22) to go.

21:5-6. We kneeled down on the shore, and prayed (v. 5). This was much like Paul had done with the Ephesian elders (see 20:36). Luke did not record what Paul said to the disciples, but most likely, it was a less personal and tearful goodbye due to the different circumstances. Praying together on the occasion of a departure may have already become a common practice among Christians. **And they returned home again** (v. 6). This again is a detail Luke did not need to supply but indicates he was with Paul during this "we" section.

21:7. Ptolemais. The modern city of Acco, north of and across the bay from Mount Carmel. It was one day's journey from Tyre on the north and another thirty-five miles to Caesarea on the south.

21:8. Cesarea. A Gentile city, the capital of Roman Judea (see discussions on 8:40; 10:1). **Philip the evangelist.** Philip's evangelistic work may have focused on Caesarea for almost twenty-five years (see discussion on 8:40). "Evangelist" is a title used only here and in Ephesians 4:11; 2 Timothy 4:5.

21:9. Four daughters, virgins. They may have been dedicated in a special way to serving the Lord. For **which did prophesy,** see 1 Cor. 11:5; 12:8-10; see Luke 2:36. For Old Testament prophetesses, see Exodus 15:20; Judges 4:4; 2 Kings 22:14; Nehemiah 6:14.

21:10. A certain prophet, named Agabus. Evidently he held the office of prophet, as Philip held the office of "evangelist" (21:8). This is the same prophet who, some fifteen years earlier, had been in Antioch prophesying the coming famine in Jerusalem (see 11:27-29).

21:11. He took Paul's girdle. That is, Paul's belt. Agabus acted out the prophecy, as Jeremiah had done centuries earlier when he shattered a clay pot

and said, "Thus saith the LORD of hosts; Even so will I break this people and this city, as one breaketh a potter's vessel" (Jer. 19:11). Ezekiel also had acted out his prophecy of the siege of Jerusalem by laying siege to a model of the city (see Ezek. 4:1-4). The use of visual aids or object lessons was thus an old tradition among prophets. Agabus was not just being dramatic; he was prophesying in a manner that Jewish people would recognize as valid. The content of his prophecy was that Paul would be bound and that his captors would **deliver him into the hands of Gentiles.** Indeed, this is exactly what happened.

21:12. We, and they of that place. Luke, in the company of travelers with Paul, joined in urging him not to go to Jerusalem. Agabus did not say that Paul should not go, only that these things would happen if he did. Naturally, Paul's friends did not want him to endanger himself.

21:13. Paul, however, was willing **not to be bound only, but also to die at Jerusalem for the name of the Lord Jesus.** This was not mere bravado on his part. If Paul had any doubt whether going to Jerusalem was God's will, he would not have gone.

21:14. The will of the Lord be done. This may mean that Paul's companions finally recognized that it was the Lord's will for him to go to Jerusalem. Or it could mean that they simply cast the situation into God's hands and prayed for Paul's protection.

21:15. We took up our carriages. The idea is that they prepared for the trip. The expression could imply that they were provided with horses (see Bruce, *The Book of Acts*, p. 402, who translates this rather freely as "got ready for the road"). **Went up to Jerusalem.** Jerusalem was one of the highest elevations in the region.

21:16. Mnason. He must have been a disciple of some means to be able to accommodate Paul and a group of about nine men traveling with him.

C. Paul in Jerusalem and Caesarea (21:17-26:32)

1. Paul Arrested in Jerusalem (21:17-23:35)

21:17. We were come to Jerusalem. No more than a day or two before Pentecost. **The brethren**

received us gladly. May indicate the grateful reception of the offering as well.

21:18. James. The brother of the Lord, author of the letter of James, and leader of the church in Jerusalem (see Gal. 1:19; 2:9). He is called an apostle but was not one of the Twelve.

21:19. He declared particularly what things God had wrought among the Gentiles by his ministry. When Paul had last departed from Jerusalem, he had taken the letter to the Gentile churches with him (see chap. 15). Since then, churches had been planted in many places in Asia and had spread to Europe through Macedonia and Achaia. Paul had much to tell the Jerusalem church.

21:20. They glorified the Lord. The believers gave credit to God for the things that had happened in Paul's ministry. **Thousands of Jews there are that believe**. These were disciples in and around Jerusalem. Apparently, this was a time of relative peace and freedom from the persecution experienced earlier (see chaps. 3–4, 6–7). **And they are all zealous of the law**. James and the elders apparently meant that many of the Christians among the Jews still believed that circumcision was necessary for salvation (see Bruce, *The Book of Acts*, p. 405).

21:21. Thou teachest all the Jews ... to forsake Moses. The leadership of the church did not believe this, but they were quite aware that many of the laity did. How tragic it is that once an ugly rumor gets started in a church, it is often impossible to squelch it. The very people who most need to believe the truth often refuse to accept it and cause much heartbreak for God's noblest servants, often damaging their ministries for years to come.

21:22. The multitude. That is, the entire body of believers in and around Jerusalem would come together once they knew that Paul was there.

21:23. The leadership proposed a plan that would demonstrate publicly that Paul had not repudiated Moses. **Four men which have a vow on them**. They were evidently under the temporary Nazarite vow (see Num. 6:2–12) and became unclean before the completion time of the vow (perhaps from contact with a dead body). Apparently, the Jewish practice

of this vow continued among those who believed in Christ.

21:24. Purify thyself. In some instances, the purification rites included the offering of sacrifices. Some Jewish Christians observed such rites by choice, but they were not required of Christians, whether Jew or Gentile. **Be at charges with them**. Paul's part in sponsoring these men would include (1) paying part or all of the expenses of the sacrifices (in this case, eight pigeons and four lambs; see Num. 6:9–12) and (2) going to the temple to notify the priest when their days of purification would be fulfilled so that the priests would be prepared to sacrifice their offerings (see 21:26). **Keepest the law**. Paul had earlier taken a vow himself (see 18:18), he had been a Jew to the Jews (see 1 Cor. 9:20–21), and Timothy had been circumcised (see 16:3). Paul was very careful, however, not to sacrifice Christian principle in any act of obedience to the law (he would not compel Titus to be circumcised; see Gal. 2:3).

21:25. The leadership assured Paul that they still abided by the Jerusalem council's decree that the Gentiles were not under the law of Moses in any way, only that they should observe the four restrictions set forth in the letter to the Gentile churches, for the sake of unity and peace (see chap. 15).

21:26. Paul complied with the church's request that he sponsor the men who were taking vows. It involved nothing that would compromise his own convictions regarding Christ, and the public testimony it would provide would only further the spread of the gospel and the credibility of his own ministry.

21:27. Seven days (see Num. 6:9). These were the days required for the men's purification, shaving their heads at the altar, the sacrifice of a sin offering and a burnt offering for each, and announcing the completion to the priests. **Jews which were of Asia**. Paul had already suffered at the hands of Asian Jews (see 20:19).

21:28. Brought Greeks also into the temple. Explicitly forbidden according to inscribed stone markers (still in existence). Any Gentiles found within the bounds of the court of Israel would be killed. There was no evidence, however, that Paul had brought anyone other than Jews into the area. Paul's willingness to comply with the request of the church leaders in the matter of the vow indicates that he was sensitive to the situation and would not, in any case, have violated the custom and beliefs of the Jews.

21:29. Trophimus. Paul probably would not have taken him into the forbidden area. If he had, they should have attacked Trophimus rather than Paul.

21:30. The doors were shut. By order of the temple officer to prevent further trouble inside the sacred precincts.

21:31. The chief captain (Greek, *chiliarchos*). A commander of one thousand men (a regiment). This captain was named Claudius Lysias (see 23:26) and was stationed at the Fortress of Antonia (see discussion on 21:37).

21:32. Centurions. Since the plural is used, it is likely that at least two centurions and two hundred **soldiers** were involved.

21:33. Two chains. Paul's hands probably were chained to a soldier on either side. At this point, Agabus's prophecy (see 21:11) was fulfilled.

21:34–36. Since there was confusion as to exactly what Paul had done, the chief captain had him taken away until he could sort out the problem. **The multitude** (v. 36) may have included Jewish believers as well as members of the general populace, as there was a serious misunderstanding among the believers about Paul's preaching and activities (see 21:21–22).

21:37. Castle. The Fortress of Antonia, which was connected to the northern end of the temple area by two flights of steps. The towers overlooked the temple area.

21:38. That Egyptian, which ... madest an uproar. Josephus tells of an Egyptian false prophet who some years earlier had led four thousand Jews (Josephus, through a misreading of a Greek capital letter, says thirty thousand) out to the Mount of Olives. These Jews were Zealots, members of a party that sought to overthrow Rome and achieve independence for Israel. Roman soldiers killed hundreds, but the leader escaped. **Men that were murderers.** The Greek here is a loanword from Latin *sicarii*, mean-

ing "dagger-men," who were violent assassins. One might almost think that the chief captain was disappointed that he had not captured so notorious and wanted a criminal.

21:39. No mean city. The Greek means that Tarsus was not an obscure or insignificant city (see discussion on 22:3). Paul asked to be allowed to speak to the multitude still gathered outside. He certainly had confidence in his persuasive powers. It may have been warranted, given the amount of speaking he had done in his travels. He had earlier sought to speak to the Ephesians when they were on the verge of a riot (see 19:30), and those with him had dissuaded him. Here he was allowed the opportunity to speak.

21:40. The Hebrew tongue. More likely Aramaic than Hebrew, since Aramaic was the most commonly used language among Palestinian Jews.

22:1–21. Paul's defense before the Jews. Here Paul once again recounts his conversion on the Damascus Road, emphasizing how he had once opposed Christians. He also tells of God's call to him to preach to the Gentiles since the Jews were rejecting his message. His purpose was to convince the crowd to repent of their opposition to what was clearly the will of God.

22:1. Paul began his speech with the following address: **Men, brethren** (see discussion on 11:1)**, and fathers.** He thus identified with the people. The accusation was that he had betrayed Jewish law and tradition. He wanted to begin in a way that said he was one of them. The word "fathers" especially acknowledged that he saw them as people to be respected and treated as authorities. Someone who wanted to challenge rather than affirm would not have addressed them in this way.

22:2. The Hebrew tongue (see discussion on 21:40). Luke meant the tongue used by the Hebrews (Aramaic), not the Hebrew language.

22:3. Verily. Means "truly," "certainly." **Born in Tarsus.** Paul was a citizen of Tarsus (see 21:39) as well as of Rome. "No mean city" (21:39) was used by Plato to describe Ephesus (in the dialogue *Ion*), and the term may have been in common use up until Paul's day. Tarsus was ten miles inland on the Cydnus River and thirty miles from the mountains, which were cut by a deep, narrow gorge called the Cilician Gates. It was an important commercial center, university city, and crossroads of travel. **Brought up in this city at the feet of Gamaliel**. Paul must have come to Jerusalem at an early age. Another translation ("brought up in this city, being educated under Gamaliel, strictly according to the law of our fathers" NASB) suggests that Paul came to Jerusalem when he was old enough to begin training under Gamaliel. Gamaliel was the most honored rabbi of the first century. Possibly he was the grandson of Hillel (see 5:34–40). By pointing out his association with Gamaliel, Paul again emphasized his knowledge of and respect for Jewish law and traditions. **Was zealous towards God, as ye all are**. Paul meant that his training was effective, and he was not an enemy of God and His revelation.

22:4. I persecuted this way (see 9:1–4). Remember that Paul was speaking to an audience of both Christians and unbelievers who were all zealous for the law, with many from both groups convinced that he opposed the law of Moses and sought to commit sacrilege in the temple. With this statement, he said to the unbelievers that he had stood with them in opposition to Christianity before his conversion; to the believers, he emphasized how much his life had changed after he trusted Christ. To both groups, he wanted to emphasize that he was not an impious or unholy man who would speak or behave in ways that would denigrate Moses and the law.

22:5. The high priest. Caiaphas, the high priest over twenty years earlier, was now dead, and Ananias was high priest (see 23:2). The records of the high priest, however, would show Paul's testimony to be true.

22:6–21. Paul related his encounter with Christ on the road to Damascus. To unbelievers, he wanted to emphasize that what had happened to him was from God. To believers, he wanted to emphasize that his conversion was genuine. One may wonder why Paul spoke of this incident now, so many years later, and how it related to the specific problem the crowd

had with him. Because it had happened so long ago, many in the crowd, both believers and unbelievers, would not have heard the story or would have heard it only secondhand. In addition, his personal testimony of his encounter with Christ established his credentials as a man who was called of God and thus was not an enemy of God and His truth. The basic charge against him here was that he was living and teaching in opposition to God.

22:6. About noon. A detail not included in the earlier account (see 9:1–22).

22:7–8. Why persecutest thou me? (v. 7; see discussions on 9:4–5). By persecuting the church, Paul was persecuting Jesus. For **Who art thou, Lord?** (v. 8), see discussion on 9:5.

22:9. They heard not the voice. They heard the sound (see 9:7) but did not understand what was said.

22:10. Paul was told to **go into Damascus** and there receive instructions. **Appointed for thee to do**. God had a specific call and plan for Paul.

22:11. I could not see for the glory of that light. Paul's attributed his blindness to the light itself, which left him temporarily unable to see.

22:12–13. Ananias, a devout man according to the law (v. 12; see discussion on Luke 1:6). This fact would have been important to Paul's audience. The crowd was upset that he was overturning the law. Affirmation of him from one who followed the law would make this charge more difficult to sustain.

22:14. See that Just One (see 3:14). Seeing the resurrected Jesus was all-important to Paul (see 26:16; 1 Cor. 9:1; 15:8). It was that experience that had convinced him of the truth of the gospel and became the foundation of his theology.

22:15. Thou shalt be his witness unto all men. Paul made no distinction between Jew and Greek here, nor mentioned his desire to carry to gospel to the Gentiles. He would mention this later in the speech (see 22:21).

22:16. Be baptized, and wash away thy sins (see discussion on Rom. 6:3–4). Baptism is the outward sign of an inward work of grace. The reality and the symbol are closely associated in the New Testament (see 2:38; Titus 3:5; 1 Peter 3:21). The outward rite, however, does not produce the inward grace (see Rom. 2:28–29; Eph. 2:8–9; Phil. 3:4–9).

22:17. When I was come again to Jerusalem. Refers to the visit described in 9:26 (see also Gal. 1:17–18). **While I prayed in the temple, I was in a trance** (see 10:10; 11:5; see also 2 Cor. 12:3). Paul was not a blasphemer of the temple but continued to hold it in high honor. Paul saw the temple as a proper place for prayer, which would ameliorate the charge that he wished to defile it.

22:18. They will not receive thy testimony concerning me. Paul's audience knew that the preaching of Christ was controversial. He had no need to hide it.

22:19–20. Paul's reply indicates that he believed he would gain a hearing as a former persecutor of the church. God, however, had other plans for him (see 22:21). **Standing by, and consenting** (v.20). This does not necessarily mean that Paul had been a member of the Sanhedrin, though some believe he was (see discussion on 26:10). He could have shown his approval by allowing them to put their cloaks at his feet.

22:21. Jesus told Paul, **I will send thee far hence unto the Gentiles**. Paul was coming to the point of contention between him and the crowd. He presented this as a call from God that was given to him while he was praying in the temple (see 22:17). In other words, his ministry to the Gentiles was something God had given him, not something by which he sought to oppose the things of God.

22:22–23. Paul's effort to clarify these matters did not work. At this point, the crowd became upset. Paul had sought to present himself as a loyal Jew who had a call from God to present Christ to the Gentiles, but the people's assumptions about his ministry activities got in the way of what he was actually saying.

22:24. For **The chief captain**, see discussion on 21:31. For **castle**, see discussion on 21:37. **Scourging**. Not with the rod, as at Philippi (see 16:22–24), but with the scourge, a merciless instrument of torture. It was legal to use it to force a confession from a slave or alien but never from a Roman citizen. The

scourge consisted of a whip of leather thongs with pieces of bone or metal attached to the ends.

22:25. They bound him with thongs. The Greek implies tying a person to a post for whipping. For **centurion**, see discussion on 10:1. **A Roman, and uncondemned**. Roman citizenship did not mean that one lived within the city of Rome, nor even that one lived in the empire. Citizenship was a special privilege not extended to all and gave certain rights not shared by all who lived under Roman rule. According to Roman law, all Roman citizens were assured exclusion from all degrading forms of punishment, including beating with rods, scourging, and crucifixion. See 16:37.

22:26–27. This man is a Roman (v. 26). Luke did not record whether or how the officers verified Paul's claim. Perhaps falsifying the claim would have brought worse punishment, or perhaps Paul carried documents authenticating his Roman citizenship.

22:28. With a great sum obtained. There were three ways to obtain Roman citizenship: (1) receive it as a reward for some outstanding service to Rome; (2) buy it at a considerable price; (3) be born into a family of Roman citizens. How Paul's father or an earlier ancestor had gained citizenship, no one knows. By 171 BC, a large number of Jews were citizens of Tarsus, and in the time of Pompey (106–48 BC), some of these could have received Roman citizenship as well.

22:29. They departed from him which should have examined him. Paul's Roman citizenship made a great difference. "Should have examined him" does not mean that they were supposed to do so and changed their minds but rather that they "would have examined him" had he not been a Roman citizen. As it was, they had no authority to do so. **The chief captain also was afraid … because he had bound him**. This could have gotten him into trouble if Paul had sought to pursue the matter out of spite. The captain should have ascertained Paul's status before acting. Paul did not take action against the captain, however. It is no part of a Christian's calling to act out of spite or revenge or to be petty toward others, even if he or she has a legal right to do so.

22:30. He loosed him. Paul was no longer bound, and presumably he would have been free completely if the council had not wished to detain him. **The chief priests**. Those of the high-priestly line of descent (mainly Sadducees), but the council now included a considerable number of Pharisees. These men constituted the ruling body of the Jews. The Jewish court was respected by the Roman governor, whose approval had to be obtained before sentencing someone to capital punishment.

23:1. For the council, see discussion on 5:21. **Brethren**. Fellow Jews (see discussions on 11:1; 22:1). **Good conscience**. A consistent claim of Paul (see 24:16).

23:2. Ananias. High priest AD 47–59, son of Nebedaeus. He is not to be confused with the high priest Annas (AD 6–15; see discussion on Luke 3:2). Ananias was noted for cruelty and violence. When the revolt against Rome broke out, he was assassinated by his own people. **Them that stood by him**. Apparently a guard detachment, whether of Romans or Jews is not clear. Most likely, they were Jews, since they were under Ananias's authority. That Paul's defense was interrupted and in such a manner indicates that the chances of his getting a fair hearing before this group were impossible.

23:3. Thou whited wall. Whitewashed, having an attractive exterior but filled with unclean contents, such as tombs holding dead bodies (see Matt. 23:27), or walls that look substantial but fall before the winds (see Ezek. 13:10–12). It is a metaphor for a hypocrite. Paul certainly showed courage here. He pointed out that he was being judged under Jewish law but that the command to hit him was contrary to that law. He pointed out both the injustice of the proceeding and the inconsistency between their profession and practice. He also demonstrated his knowledge of and commitment to the law, the very matter under contention.

23:4–5. I wist not (did not realize), **brethren, that he was the high priest** (v. 5). Paul's failure to recognize the high priest is explained in different ways: (1) He had poor eyesight (suggested by such passages as Gal. 4:15; 6:11) and failed to see that the one who presided was the high priest. (2) He failed to discern that the one who presided was the high priest because on some occasions others had sat in his place. (3) He was using pure irony: a true high priest would not have given such an order. (4) Having been away from Jerusalem for many years, Paul did not recognize him on sight. Pictures of people were rare in those days, even of public officials other than the emperor.

23:6. Sadducees (v. 6; see discussions on 4:1; Matt. 3:7; Mark 12:18; Luke 20:27). The Sadducees denied the resurrection and angels and spirits (see 23:8). For **Pharisees**, see discussions on Matt. 3:7; Mark 2:16; Luke 5:17. **Of the hope and resurrection of the dead I am called in question**. Since these two groups disagreed on the resurrection, Paul was able to shape the proceedings to his advantage by creating division and confusion among them, getting one group to sympathize with him. That several stories had been told about the specific charge against Paul (see 21:34) only added to the confusion. Paul was not being untruthful in this matter for the sake of his own legal advantage. The resurrection is a central doctrine of Christianity, and the basis on which Christians have this hope is faith in Jesus Christ, not works of the law. To the extent that Paul was on trial because he preached a gospel of grace rather than law, he was there because of the hope of the resurrection from the dead. Paul's strategy worked: the assembly **was divided** (v. 7).

23:8. Luke felt the need to explain to his readers the nature of the disagreement between the Pharisees and the Sadducees. He was writing to a Gentile audience, who would not have been familiar with the distinctions between the Jewish groups.

23:9. Paul was also successful in getting the Pharisees on his side.

23:10. The chief captain (see discussion on 21:31) once again rescued Paul from what threatened to become a mob. Luke often presented the Roman officials as enlightened, sympathetic, and just. To the extent that Luke wanted to commend the gospel to a Gentile audience, the circumstances Paul found himself in were often helpful, as the Gentiles were usually more open to the message and the messenger than the Jews. For **castle**, see discussion on 21:37.

23:11. The Lord stood by him. In times of crisis and need for strength, Paul was given help (see 18:9; 22:18; 27:23). **Jerusalem ... Rome**. One was the spiritual capital of Judaism; the other was the political capital of the Mediterranean world. That the Lord would call Paul to bear testimony in both places affirmed the universality of the gospel. It was for all the world, not just for the Jews. It also points out how God's concerns span both the sacred and the secular. Both realms are under his reign, both realms need to be brought to an awareness of the truth, and both realms evidence the same spiritual needs.

23:12–13. Bound themselves under a curse (v. 12). Under an oath. Probably these Jews were Zealots (see discussion on 21:38), who were later responsible for a revolt against Rome. This was a large group, **more than forty** (v. 13), and was a force to be reckoned with.

23:14–15. The Jews who had vowed to kill Paul did not hide their plot from **the chief priests and elders** (v. 14), who would have been sympathetic to this plan. Their goal was to get rid of Paul, and Roman authority must have seemed an impediment. Bureaucratic procedure can be slow and ponderous, but it protects innocent people from the whims of those who would use power in corrupt ways.

23:16. Paul's sister's son. This is the first time Luke mentioned that Paul had relatives in Jerusalem, but until now, it was not important to his story. How Paul's nephew heard of the plot and how he gained access to Paul is unknown. Perhaps family members were allowed to visit prisoners.

23:17. For **centurions**, see discussion on 10:1. For **the chief captain**, see discussion on 21:31.

23:18–19. By now, **the chief captain** (vv. 18–19) apparently was sympathetic to Paul and more than willing to hear **privately** (v. 19) a message from him. The commander had seen the proceedings before the high priest and could not have been impressed from a legal standpoint.

23:20–21. Paul's nephew provided a succinct account of what was to happen. Once again, this Roman official is shown to be committed to truth and justice and determined to prevent an injustice from happening under his watch.

23:22. Tell no man. For the boy's own safety and because of the commander's plans to transfer Paul under cover of night (see 23:23).

23:23–24. Soldiers ... horsemen ... spearmen. Heavily armed infantry, cavalry, and lightly armed soldiers. The commander assigned 470 men to protect Paul, the Roman citizen (see 22:25–29). The Greek for "spearmen," however, is an obscure word and could perhaps be translated "additional mounts and pack animals." The numbers indicate that the commander took the threat seriously. The assassination of a Roman citizen in his custody would have been a blot on his record (see Bruce, *The Book of Acts*, p. 433), something that must have been on his mind as well as his desire to see justice done.

23:25. He wrote a letter after this manner. Luke apparently did not quote the letter verbatim but gave the substance of it.

23:26. Cladius Lysias unto. This is the way first-century letters normally began. Whereas today the sender's name is at the bottom of the letter, at that time, the letter began with it.

23:27. Having understood that he was a Roman. The commander inserted this to gain favor with Rome. It was not a true statement, however, because the commander did not learn of Paul's citizenship until he was about to scourge him to gain information.

23:28–29. This is a true statement of what happened. **Accused of questions of their law** (v. 29). This had been the Roman perception of charges against Paul earlier in his ministry (see 18:14–15). **Nothing ... worthy of death or of bonds**. The chief captain pronounced Paul innocent of any charge under Roman law.

23:30. If Paul was not guilty, the captain had to explain why he was holding him and, further, why he was sending him to Caesarea. He apparently believed that the exact accusations against Paul could be better set forth outside the emotionally charged atmosphere of Jerusalem. Many of his less credibile accusers would not want to make the trip, and a fairer hearing would result.

23:31. Antipatris. Rebuilt by Herod the Great and named for his father. It was a military post between Samaria and Judea, thirty miles from Jerusalem.

23:32–33. The soldiers did not complete the journey, returning from Antipatris and letting **the horsemen** (v. 32) take him the rest of the way. The main danger was past; they were away from Jerusalem, and Paul's enemies had not yet learned of his departure. Also, the chief captain may have wanted to emphasize that Paul was not at this point charged with any specific crime under Roman law and thus was not a prisoner but rather one under protection. **Cesarea** (v. 33; see discussions on 8:40; 10:1). Twenty-eight miles from Antipatris, Caesarea was the headquarters of Roman rule for Samaria and Judea.

23:34. The governor. Antonius Felix (see 23:26). The emperor Claudius had appointed him governor of Judea circa AD 52, when Felix's brother was the emperor's favorite minister. The brothers had formerly been slaves, then freedmen, then high officials in government. The historian Tacitus said of Felix, "He held the power of a tyrant with the disposition of a slave." Felix married three queens in succession, one of whom was Drusilla (see discussion on 24:24). **Of Cilicia.** If Paul had come from a nearby province, Felix might have turned him over for trial under another's jurisdiction.

23:35. Herod's judgment hall. Erected as a royal residence by Herod the Great but now used as a Roman government center (a praetorium), where official business of the emperor was conducted and/or personnel directly responsible to the emperor was housed. Praetoria were located in Rome (see Phil. 1:13), Ephesus, Jerusalem (see John 18:28), Caesarea, and other parts of the empire.

2. Paul's Defense in Caesarea (chaps. 24–26)

a. Paul before Felix (chap. 24)

24:1. After five days. After the departure from Jerusalem. This would have allowed just enough time for a messenger to go from Caesarea to Jerusalem, the council to appoint their representatives,

and the appointees to journey to Caesarea. **Ananias** (see discussion on 23:2). The high priest made the sixty-mile journey to supervise the case personally. **The elders.** The council was made up of seventy-one elders. The designation was used of both the religious and the political councils (see discussions on Exod. 3:16; 2 Sam. 3:17; Matt. 15:2; *KJV Study Bible* note on Joel 1:2). **Orator.** In a court trial, one trained in forensic rhetoric would serve as an attorney-at-law. **Tertullus.** A common variant of the name Tertius. He possibly was a Roman but more likely was a Hellenistic Jew familiar with the procedures of the Roman court.

24:2–3. Great quietness (v. 2) **…with all thankfulness** (v. 3). The expected eulogy with which to introduce a speech before a judge. In his six years in office, Felix had eliminated bands of robbers, thwarted organized assassins, and crushed a movement led by an Egyptian (see discussion on 21:38). In general, however, his record was not good. He was recalled by Rome two years later because of misrule. His reforms and improvements are hard to identify historically.

24:4–5. A pestilent fellow … a ringleader of the sect of the Nazarenes (v. 5). In other words, a troublemaker. To excite dissension in the empire was treason against Caesar. To be a leader of a religious sect that did not have Roman approval was contrary to law. "The sect of the Nazarenes" was a term for Christianity.

24:6. Hath gone about to profane the temple. The charge against Paul was now qualified by "an attempt" rather than the former claim (see discussion on 21:28).

24:7. Lysias … with great violence took him away out of our hands. Note the contrast between this account and the one Lysias sent in his letter (see 23:27). Tertullus presented the Jews as having been ready to judge Paul fairly "according to our law" (24:6) and Lysias presented them as having been violent and too swift to act. Felix had Lysias's letter before him, which Tertullus would not have known. The reader has seen both accounts, plus Luke's own account in 21:27–36. The significant and perhaps self-serving differences in these accounts could not have been lost on Luke. He intended for his readers to note them as well, surely.

24:8. Commanding his accusers to come unto thee. Tertullus treated it as if Lysias's intent was from the first to send this case to Felix for trial. In fact, the case was sent to Felix only because the Jews were plotting to assassinate Paul, a fact that Tertullus neglected to mention but that Felix knew (see 23:30).

24:9. The Jews also assented. The group, in all likelihood, had gotten their story straight with Tertullus before the proceedings began. When everyone in a group agrees to all the details of a story, one may be certain that it is just that: a story.

24:10. Paul's reserved introduction lacks the flattery that Tertullus employed (see 24:2–4).

24:11. Yet but twelve days. Paul answered each accusation. He was not a troublemaker, and he had not been involved in disturbances. He had but recently arrived in Jerusalem. He had spent five days in Caesarea and nearly seven in Jerusalem.

24:14–15. After the way … so worship I … God (v. 14). Paul admitted to his part in "the way," (see discussion on 19:23) but he still believed **the law and the prophets**. He shared the same hope as the Jews: resurrection and judgment.

24:16. For **a conscience void of offence**, see discussion on 23:1.

24:17. To bring alms to my nation. This is the only explicit reference in Acts to the collection that was so important to Paul (see discussion on 20:4). **Offerings**. May refer to Paul's help in sponsoring those who were fulfilling their vows (see 21:24). He also may have intended to present offerings for himself. In any case, this was the kind of thing a devout Jew would do and thus helped refute the case made by Paul's accusers (see Talbert, *Reading Acts*, p. 207).

24:18–19. Jews from Asia (see 21:27–29). Paul is careful to point out that the absence of these Asian Jews suggests that they could not substantiate their accusations. The trial was stacked against him. Paul was not accusing Felix, who would not have known this fact. It did provide a basis for Felix delaying a decision, however (see 24:22).

24:20. Paul was so certain that no solid evidence could be brought against him that he was willing to forgo having his associates brought to testify. He believed that even his accusers could prove nothing that would stand up in court.

24:21. Touching the resurrection. Paul again introduced the point of contention between the Pharisees and Sadducees. His accusers knew that Paul had said this, and he did not dispute it. This issue was of no concern under Roman law.

24:22. Having more perfect knowledge of that way (see discussion on 19:23). Felix could not have governed Judea and Samaria for six years without becoming somewhat familiar with the beliefs and activities of the Christians. Felix intended to question Lysias. Apparently, he considered Lysias's letter a more accurate account of events than Tertullus's but wanted Lysias's testimony officially entered before he rendered a decision.

24:23. Let him have liberty. Perhaps Paul was under house arrest (as he later was while awaiting trial in Rome, see 28:30–31), in recognition of the fact that he was a Roman citizen who had not been found guilty of any crime.

24:24. Drusilla. Felix's third wife, daughter of Herod Agrippa I. At age fifteen, she married Azizus, king of Emesa, but deserted him for Felix a year later. Her son, also named Agrippa, died in the eruption of Vesuvius (AD 79). **Heard him concerning the faith in Christ**. Felix had knowledge about Christianity but probably had not heard firsthand about the faith. Having Paul at hand, Felix did not pass up the opportunity to learn more about Christianity.

24:25. He reasoned of righteousness, temperance, and judgment. Paul is again shown as an apologist for the truth. He did not merely quote Scripture, nor did he merely tell of his own and others' experiences. He sought to show why the doctrines of the faith were true and reasonable. **Felix trembled**. Hearing Paul speak of righteousness, self-control, and the judgment, Felix looked at his past life and was filled with fear. He had a spark of sincerity and concern. Paul was persuasive. He did not merely give dry lectures on doctrine. He sought, even as a prisoner, to lead this man to make a personal commitment to Christ. Paul's example should encourage believers today. No one, no matter how high their position, is above the need for the gospel. Nor is anyone so far from God that the word of the truth, persuasively presented, cannot have some effect. **When I have a convenient season**. Lust, pride, greed, and selfish ambition made it continually inconvenient to change.

24:26. Money should have been given him. Felix supposed that Paul had access to considerable funds. He had heard of his bringing an offering to the Jewish Christians in Jerusalem (see 24:17). He wanted Paul to give him money to secure his release. Paul no longer had that money, nor would he have offered a bribe if he did have it.

24:27. Festus came into Felix' room. Festus succeeded Felix. Readers who forget which of these men is first and which is second should remember that they served in this office in alphabetical order. Felix comes before Festus. Felix was recalled to Rome in AD 59/60 to answer for disturbances and irregularities in his rule, such as his handling of riots between Jewish and Syrian inhabitants. Festus is not mentioned in existing historical records before his arrival in Judea. He died in office after two years, but his record for that time shows wisdom and honesty superior to both his predecessor, Felix, and his successor, Albinus. **Willing to shew the Jews a pleasure**. To do them a favor. Felix did not want to incite more anger among the Jews, whom he shortly would be facing in Roman court. To release Paul from prison would have done just that.

b. Paul before Festus (25:1–12)

25:1. From Cesarea to Jerusalem. Sixty miles, a two-day trip. Festus was anxious to go immediately to the center of Jewish rule and worship.

25:2. The high priest and the chief of the Jews. The council (see discussions on 5:21; Mark 14:55). This group was aware that Festus would not have had time for much, if any, briefing on Paul's case. They took advantage of the opportunity to shape his perceptions before he had seen a legal document on the case.

25:3. Laying wait. To ambush Paul. Probably the same group that had earlier made a vow to take Paul's life (see discussion on 23:12).

25:4. Festus wisely discerned that these men had more interest in the case than merely wanting justice done. He decided to do nothing until he had further knowledge of the matter. Once again, Luke took the opportunity to show a Roman official being fair-minded in judging between Christians and their accusers.

25:5. Festus was willing to hear the council's accusations against Paul, but only in a proper setting.

25:6. Sitting in the judgment seat. To make his decision binding as a formal ruling.

25:7. Which they could not prove. Again, as in the first hearing, Paul's adversaries produced no witnesses or evidence of any kind.

25:8. Neither against the law of the Jews … have I offended. Paul had respect for the law (see Rom. 7:12; 8:3–4; 1 Cor. 9:20). **Against the temple** (see discussions on 21:28–29). Paul had not defied temple customs by taking Trophimus into forbidden areas (see 21:29). Jesus had prophesied the temple's destruction, but He was not responsible for its plight (see Luke 21:5–6). **Against Caesar**. Paul proclaimed the kingdom of God, but not as a political rival of Rome (see 17:6–7). He advocated respect for law and order (see Rom. 13:1–7) and prayer for civil rulers (see 1 Tim. 2:2).

25:9–10. Wilt thou go up to Jerusalem …? (v. 9). Obviously not. Festus had said that the trial would be before him, so Paul insisted that he was standing in the Roman civil court, where his case should be tried. He wanted to keep his trial there rather than suffer at the hands of a Jewish religious court. As a Roman citizen, he could refuse to go to a local provincial court.

25:11. I refuse not to die. Paul was willing to accept the penalty for any crime he had committed, but he had committed no crime. **I appeal unto Caesar**. Nero had become the emperor by this time. It was the right of every Roman citizen to have his case heard before Caesar himself (or his representative) in Rome. This was the highest court of appeal, and winning such a case could have led to more than just Paul's acquittal; it could have resulted in official recognition of Christianity as distinct from Judaism.

25:12. The council. The officials and legal experts who made up the advisory council for the Roman governor. Since Paul's appeal to Caesar was valid and legal, it was granted.

c. Paul before Agrippa (25:13–26:32)

25:13. King Agrippa. Herod Agrippa II. He was seventeen years old at the death of his father in AD 44 (see 12:23). Being too young to succeed his father, he was replaced by Roman procurators. Eight years later, however, a gradual extension of territorial authority began. Ultimately, he ruled over territory north and northeast of the Sea of Galilee, over several cities in Galilee, and over some cities in Perea. During the Jewish revolt, when Jerusalem fell, he was on the side of the Romans. He died circa AD 100, the last of the Herods. **Bernice**. The oldest daughter of Agrippa I, she was sixteen years old at his death. When only thirteen, she married her uncle, Herod of Chalcis, and had two sons. When Herod died, she lived with her brother, Agrippa II. To silence rumors that she was living in incest with her brother, she married Polemon, king of Cilicia, but soon left him to return to Agrippa. She became the mistress of the emperor Vespasian's son Titus but was later ignored by him. **To salute Festus**. To pay their respects. It was customary for rulers to pay a complimentary visit to a new ruler at the time of his assignment. It was advantageous to each that they get along (see Luke 23:6–12, which led to a friendship between Herod Antipas and Pilate).

25:14. Many days. Apparently, Agrippa and Festus spent several days celebrating and consulting on matters of mutual concern, perhaps cutting some deals for their mutual benefit. Once the major business had been conducted, Festus wanted to present Paul, perhaps as a kind of entertainment. He was not seeking advice except in the matter of how to word his statement to Nero (see discussion on 25:26). That Paul would be sent to Caesar had already been decided (see 25:12).

25:15–18. Festus gave an accurate account of what had happened, pointing out that Paul was guilty of no crime against Rome.

25:19. The only problem Festus could find, like Felix and Gallio (see 18:12–16) before him, lay in the matter of religious claims, not Roman law. **Superstition**. Or "religion," the same word used by Paul in 17:22 (see discussion there).

25:20–21. Paul would have been foolish to go back to Jerusalem. His appeal to Caesar not only was strategically sound, but it also ended a stalemate situation.

25:22. I would also hear. Agrippa had been wishing to hear Paul (as Antipas had wanted to see Jesus; see Luke 9:9; 23:8).

25:23. The place of hearing. Not the judgment hall, for this was not a court trial. The hearing took place in an auditorium appropriate for the **great pomp** of the occasion, with the king, his sister, the Roman governor, and the outstanding leaders of both the Jews and the Roman government present. **The chief captains** (see discussion on 21:31). Five regiments were stationed at Caesarea, so their five commanders would have been in attendance.

25:24–25. Festus made the opening remarks, perhaps introducing Paul to the group. **Nothing worthy of death** (v. 25). Festus mentioned this again, possibly because Jewish officials were present, and he wanted to keep matters crystal clear with them.

25:26. I have no certain thing to write. Festus was required to send Caesar an explicit report on a case when an appeal was made. He hoped for some help from Agrippa in this matter. This was not an official trial but a special hearing to satisfy the curiosity of Agrippa and to provide an assessment for Festus. **Specially before thee, O king Agrippa**. Agrippa would have been sensitive to differences between Pharisees and Sadducees, expectations of the Messiah, differences between Jews and Christians, and Jewish customs pertinent to these problems.

25:27. Unreasonable to send a prisoner, and not … to signify the crimes. Festus wanted to protect his own credibility before Roman officialdom.

26:1. Thou art permitted to speak. Agrippa gave permission for Paul to speak because Festus allowed the king to have charge of the hearing.

26:2. Paul began with the usual courtesies required of one who is speaking to a superior in an official setting.

26:3. Expert in all customs and questions … among the Jews. As king, Agrippa controlled the temple treasury and the investments of the high priest and could appoint the high priest. The Romans consulted him on religious matters. This was one of the reasons Festus wanted him to assess Paul.

26:4. All the Jews. Paul's assertion here, that all of them knew of his life and religious commitments, seems designed to imply that his accusers had knowingly fabricated the charges against him.

26:5. I lived a Pharisee (see Gal. 1:14). Paul again emphasized this fact, as he had on a previous occasion when it helped his case (see 23:6). Pharisees were zealous in keeping the law, and since Paul was identified with them, it made no sense that he would teach Jewish people to scorn and disobey the law.

26:6. The hope of the promise made of God. Including God's kingdom, the Messiah, and the resurrection (see 26:8). Paul wanted to show that the religious beliefs he now preached were in line with traditional Old Testament teaching. He also may have been harking back to his statement in 23:6, for that had divided the Pharisee and Sadducee camps and gained the support of the Pharisees at that time.

26:7. Paul said that he was **accused of the Jews** for the hope of the promise given to Israel. Once again, Paul presented himself as being on trial for opposing the Jewish faith, yet his teachings were the fulfillment of that faith's promises and teachings.

26:8. Paul had been speaking to Agrippa but at this point must have addressed others as well, such as Festus and the chief captains (see discussions on 21:31; 25:23), who did not believe in the resurrection. Agrippa was allied with the Sadducees, whom he appointed high priests, and was likely to reject both the resurrection of Christ and resurrection in general.

26:9. Paul presented himself as someone who had sincerely believed that opposing Jesus was the

right way to uphold Jewish beliefs, just as his accusers believed now. Since Paul had been wrong on this point, so must they be wrong and should see that Paul was the true defender of the hope and promises God gave to Israel, which were fulfilled in Jesus Christ.

26:10. I gave my voice against them. Meaning "I cast my vote against them," since the Greek word translated "voice" literally means "pebble," which was used to vote. This does not necessarily mean that Paul was a member of the Sanhedrin (see discussion on 22:20). He may have been appointed to a special commission to carry out the prosecution of the Jerusalem Christians (see 26:12), where his vote was given.

26:11. Compelled them to blaspheme. Paul tried to force them either to curse Jesus or to confess publicly that Jesus is the Son of God, in which case they could be condemned for blasphemy, a sufficient cause for death (see Matt. 26:63–66).

26:12. As I went to Damascus. Once again, Paul gave an account of his conversion (see 9:1–19; 22:4–21 and discussions).

26:13. At midday. Once again, Paul said his conversion happened around noon (see 22:6).

26:14. For **I heard a voice**, see discussions on 9:7; 22:9. **To kick against the pricks**. A Greek proverb for useless resistance: in kicking the pricks on the goad, the ox succeeds only in hurting itself.

26:15–16. Paul reported that Jesus had called him to be **a minister and a witness** (v. 16) of what he had seen that day on the Damascus road and of things which he would soon learn. In giving this testimony, Paul was fulfilling that calling.

26:17. Unto whom now I send thee. Not only to the Jews but also to the Gentiles (see 22:21; Gal. 1:15–16). Paul's mission was from God (see Gal. 1:1).

26:18. From darkness to light. A figure especially characteristic of Paul (see Rom. 13:12; 2 Cor. 4:6; Eph. 5:8–14; Col. 1:13; 1 Thess. 5:5). **Are sanctified**. Positional sanctification (see *KJV Study Bible* note on 1 Cor. 1:2). This is the most extensive account of what Jesus said to Paul. It differs from previous accounts in Acts. Most likely, Luke, as a master of literary style, knew that this book would include several accounts of this incident. With each retelling, he intentionally provided certain details not given previously, both to maintain the reader's interest and to emphasize different facts that were important at that point in his narrative. Here, because Paul was speaking before a mostly Gentile audience, the details of his call to preach to them were of major importance for his evangelistic purpose, as well as for his defense of his ministry. Bruce (*The Book of Acts*, p. 491) proposes that Paul may have brought together some things the Lord said to him on the road, through Ananias, and later in Jerusalem at the temple. This is not likely, however. Paul heard from Ananias things in line with this passage, but the text indicates that Paul heard this directly from Jesus. Luke was not so much of a literary stylist that he would have changed facts to fit his literary needs.

26:19-20. Here Paul's account of his ministry, except for beginning in **Damascus** (v. 20), echo Jesus' words in Acts 1:8: Paul had indeed taken the gospel to **Jerusalem ... the coasts of Judaea, and then to the Gentiles**. His ministry had involved taking the gospel outward from Jerusalem to the Gentiles. His goal was to go "unto the ends of the earth" (13:47), that is, to Spain (see Rom. 15:24, 28, which he had written before coming to Jerusalem). In his overall ministry, Paul had gone "to the Jew first, and also to the Greek" (Rom. 1:16), just as he did in each town he visited. **Repent and turn to God**. Paul knew that his accusers believed, in theory at least, that God's people should obey Him. Paul was pointing out that his preaching was in line with that belief, not contrary to it.

26:21. It was Paul's preaching of Christ that caused the Jews to want to kill him, he said, not desecration of the temple or teaching Jewish believers to denigrate the law. Paul was not trying to confuse matters here. He was looking beyond the false charges against him, to the motivation behind them. Those who had spread false rumors about his preaching opposed Christ, as he once did. His accusers included some believers, but surely they had been led astray by the false accusations of those who opposed Christ. Paul had seen a spiritual truth that is

important to remember today. People may and often do oppose Christianity for a multitude of reasons that hold no water. The real problem is spiritual; they oppose the preaching of Christ as the answer to sin. Truly, "men loved darkness rather than light" (John 3:19), and still do to this day.

26:22. The prophets and Moses. The Old Testament Scriptures (see Luke 24:27, 44). Paul reiterated his main defense: he preached only what God Himself had promised Israel, and he pointed people toward these truths rather than away from them.

26:23. The Gentiles (see Isa. 49:6). The prophets and Moses pointed directly to Christ, whom Paul preached, and for which he was on trial. Luke used every opportunity to emphasize that the gospel was intended, even from the days of the prophets, to be preached to the Gentiles as well as the Jews. Luke's purpose, at least in part, was to present Jesus and the gospel as the answer to the spiritual needs not just of the Jews but of the whole world. This guided his selection of material in both his gospel and Acts.

26:24. Thou art beside thyself ... mad (see John 10:20; 1 Cor. 14:23). In other words, "You are out of your mind!" The governor felt that Paul's education and reading of the sacred Scriptures had led him to a mania about prophecy and resurrection.

26:25. Truth and soberness. Paul's assertion, made so clearly, in itself testified that he was not insane or manic.

26:26. Was not done in a corner. The gospel that Paul proclaimed was based on actual events, lived out in historical times and places. The king himself had to attest to the truth of what Paul had affirmed.

26:27. Believest thou the prophets? Paul's question presented King Agrippa with a dilemma. If he said yes, Paul would press him to recognize that their words were fulfilled in Jesus; if he said no, he would be in trouble with the devout Jews, who accepted the message of the prophets as the very word of God. It is altogether proper to press people to make a decision about Christ. Paul was defending himself, but he could not resist such a great opportunity to present Christ as the answer to Agrippa's need as well.

26:28. Almost thou persuadest me to be a Christian. The Greek phrase has the sense of, "You will persuade me to become a Christian by few words" or "in a short time." Agrippa's answer was an evasion of Paul's question and an answer to what he anticipated Paul's next question to be. His point was that he would not be persuaded by such a brief statement. Aggrippa was no different from many today, for whom no amount of proof is enough. Their problem is not intellectual, but spiritual.

26:29. These bonds. Paul was still bound as a prisoner. Paul revealed his heart's desire here. Preaching Christ was more important than his own defense, and he spoke in hope of bringing his audience to faith.

D. Fifth Geographical Expansion of the Gospel: "Into Italy" (chaps. 27–28; see 27:1)

1. Sea Voyage and Shipwreck (chap. 27)

27:1. We should sail. The "we" narrative (see discussion on 16:10) begins again (the last such reference appeared in 21:18). Luke probably had spent the two years of Paul's Caesarean imprisonment nearby, perhaps researching material for his gospel, and now he joined those ready to sail. **Julius, a centurion**. Otherwise unknown. Perhaps he was given the specific duties of an imperial courier, which included delivering prisoners for trial. **Augustus' band**. A Roman band, or cohort, was a military unit composed of 300–600 men. The Roman legions were designated by number, and each of the regiments also had designations (see discussion on 10:1). The identification "Augustan," or "Imperial" (belonging to the empire), was common.

27:2. Adramyttium. A harbor on the west coast of the province of Asia, Adramyttium was southeast of Troas and east of Assos. **By the coasts**. At one of these stops, Julius would have planned to transfer to a ship going to Rome. **Aristarchus** (see 19:29; 20:4). Other New Testament passages (Col. 4:10; Philem. 24) indicate that he was in Rome with Paul later.

27:3. Sidon. About seventy miles north of Caesarea.

27:4. We sailed under Cyprus. They sought the protecting shelter of the island by sailing north on the eastern side of the island, then west along the northern side. **The winds were contrary**. The prevailing winds in summer were westerly.

27:5. Cilicia and Pamphylia. Adjoining provinces on the southern shore of Asia Minor. From Sidon to Myra along this coast would normally be a voyage of ten to fifteen days. **Myra ... of Lycia**. The growing importance of the city of Myra was associated with the development of navigation. Instead of hugging the coast from point to point, more ships were daring to run directly from Alexandria in Egypt to harbors like Myra on the southern coast of Asia Minor. Myra was considerably out of the way on the trip to Rome from Egypt, but the prevailing westerly wind would not allow a direct voyage toward the west. Myra became an important grain-storage city as well.

27:6. A ship of Alexandria. A ship from Egypt (with grain cargo; see 27:38) bound for Rome. Paul and the others could have remained on the first ship and continued up the coast to Macedonia, then taken the land route over the Egnatian Way across Greece and on to Rome, entering Italy at the port of Brundisium. Julius instead chose to change ships, accepting the opportunity of a voyage direct to Rome. Some suggest that Aristarchus from Macedonia stayed with the first ship and went to his home area to tell of Paul's coming imprisonment in Rome. If so, he later joined Paul in Rome (see discussion on 27:2).

27:7. Cnidus. From Myra to Cnidus, at the southwest point of Asia Minor, was about 170 miles. The trip probably took another ten to fifteen days. **Crete**. An island 160 miles long. Rather than cross the open sea to Greece, the ship was forced to bear south, seeking to sail west with the protection of the island of Crete on the north ("under the shelter of Crete"). **Salmone**. A promontory on the northeast point of Crete.

27:8. The fair havens. A port about midway on the southern coast of Crete. **Lasea**. A city about five miles away.

27:9. The fast. The Jewish Day of Atonement fell in the latter part of September or in October. The usual sailing season by Jewish calculation lasted from Pentecost (May – June) to the Feast of Tabernacles, which was five days after the fast. The Romans considered sailing after September 15 doubtful and after November 11 suicidal.

27:10 – 11. Sirs, I perceive (v. 10). Paul was not engaging in predictive prophecy here (in fact, he suggested that their lives were in danger, though all survived the shipwreck that came; see 27:44). He was making an educated guess as an experienced traveler. Those who stood to profit from the voyage rejected his counsel, and the centurion chose to believe them. One who has no personal or financial incentive often can see the truth more clearly than those who are biased due to the possibility of some benefit to themselves.

27:12. Phenice. Also known as Phoenix, a major city of Crete that served as a wintering place, having a harbor with protection against the storms.

27:13. Supposing that they had obtained their purpose. The wind seemed to be good for sailing. Their decision may not have been foolish based on the evidence of the moment.

27:14. Euroclydon. A typhoon-like, east-northeast wind (a "northeaster"), which drove the ship away from their destination.

27:15. We let her drive. Sometimes the safest thing to do, especially in open water, is to allow the ship to go where it will. Fighting a strong wind puts a strain on the rigging and perhaps even on the ship's structure.

27:16. Clauda. An island about twenty-three miles from Crete. This island provided enough shelter to make preparations for the storm. **To come by the boat**. A small boat was being towed behind the ship, and it was interfering with the progress of the ship and with the steering. It may also have been in danger of being crushed against the ship in the wind and the waves. It had to be taken aboard (see 27:17).

27:17. They used helps, undergirding the ship. They used cables, probably placed crosswise, to keep the ship from being broken apart by the storm. **Fall into the quicksands**. A long stretch of desolate banks of quicksand (called Syrtis) along northern Africa off the coast of Tunis and Tripoli. It was still far away,

but in such a storm, the ship could be driven a great distance.

27:18. They lightened the ship. By dumping the cargo. They kept some bags of grain, however (see 27:38).

27:19. The tackling of the ship. Spars, planks, and perhaps the yardarm with the mainsail attached. At times, these were dragged behind the ship, serving as a brake.

27:20. All hope that we should be saved was then taken away. Luke meant that they had given up hope. Of course, they were saved in short order (see 27:44), but that was contrary to hope.

27:21. Ye should have hearkened unto me. The crew had lost the cargo from which they had hoped to profit. Paul was not engaging in triumphalism here. The situation hardly warranted such an attitude. He wanted to establish his credibility before making the next statement. They should have listened to Paul's warning (see 27:10). Although they had not done so, Paul had good news for everyone, to which they now should certainly give ear (see 27:22 – 26).

27:22. There shall be no loss of any man's life. Paul's first statement was one of reassurance.

27:23. The angel of God. Paul had received a supernatural visitor from God. **Whose I am, and whom I serve**. The antecedent is "God." Paul belonged to God, and therefore his life was in His hands. If God had a plan for Paul, it would not be derailed by a storm.

27:24. Thou must be brought before Caesar. God had called Paul to go to Rome. Paul was not making this journey because of the legal system or happenstance. God had used the legal system and circumstances, but these served His will. **God hath given thee all them that sail with thee**. God had granted Paul that all those on board would survive also.

27:25. I believe God, that it shall be even as it was told me. Paul most likely was giving testimony to a mixed group of believers and unbelievers. In these circumstances, he was testifying to his faith that God would keep His word. The pagans on board, having given up hope, were ready to believe anyone who could give a confident word from any deity who might help them. Paul, by giving credit to God for their rescue from these circumstances, was engaging in preevangelism here, showing that God rules in all the affairs of life and is to be believed. Those who came through this experience would certainly be more open to hearing the gospel message later on.

27:26. Paul predicted that they would wash ashore **upon a certain island**. It is likely that the angel had told him this as well.

27:27. The fourteenth night. After leaving "The fair havens" (27:8). **In Adria**. That is, in the Adriatic Sea, which lies between Italy, Malta, Crete, and Greece. In ancient times, the Adriatic Sea extended as far south as Sicily and Crete (some think that it included all the area between Greece, Italy, and Africa and that it was known as the Adrian, not the Adriatic, Sea.) Today its extent is considerably reduced. **Deemed that they drew near**. By now, the men were looking for land, as Paul had gained much credibility with them by what he had said. They may have seen birds or noticed a change in the water color, indicating that land was near.

27:28. Sounded. Measured the depth of the sea by letting down a weighted line. The water, they discovered, was getting shallower.

27:29. Fallen upon rocks. With land close, rocks could wreck the ship and drown all of them, only a few feet from land. They could not take that risk.

27:30. The shipmen were about to flee out of the ship. Without a port for the ship, the sailors felt their chance for survival was better in the single lifeboat, unencumbered by the many passengers.

27:31. Except these abide in the ship. If the sailors had been allowed to desert the ship in seeking to save themselves, the passengers would have been unable to beach the ship the following day.

27:32. The soldiers cut off the ropes. Paul's word was heeded, and the soldiers took charge. Most likely, these were the soldiers guarding Paul.

27:33–34. Having taken nothing (v. 33). No provisions had been distributed, nor regular meals eaten, since the storm began. It may have been difficult to hold food down in the midst of the storm.

Now they could think about food, and they would need the strength for swimming ashore soon.

27:35. He took bread, and gave thanks to God. Paul gave two good examples: he ate food for physical nourishment and gave thanks to God. To give thanks before a meal was common practice among God's people (see Luke 9:16; 24:30; 1 Tim. 4:4–5). Paul did this in the presence of unbelievers as a testimony of God's provision and protection.

27:36. Then were they all of good cheer. Eating lifted everyone's spirits.

27:37. Two hundred threescore and sixteen souls. Noting the number on board may have been necessary in preparation for the distribution of food or perhaps for the coming attempt to get ashore. The number is not extraordinary for the time. Josephus (*Life* 3[15]) refers to a ship that had six hundred aboard. Luke may have noted the number in preparation for the account of all being saved (see 27:44).

27:38. They lightened the ship. They threw overboard the remaining bags of wheat (see 27:18), which had probably been kept for food supply. The lighter the ship, the farther it could sail in to shore.

27:39. Creek … shore. These details are further evidence that Luke was an eyewitness. The experience must have made quite an impression on him.

27:40. Loosed the rudder bands. They loosed the ropes of the rudder to lower the stern rudders into place so the ship could be steered toward the sandy shore. Ancient ships had a steering oar on either side of the stern.

27:41. A place where two seas met. That is, two currents came together, perhaps near the mouth of the creek. A sandbar normally forms at such locations, as each current deposits whatever it is carrying. **They ran the ship aground; and the forepart stuck fast**. Again, all of these details indicate that Luke was an eyewitness.

27:42. The soldiers' counsel was to kill the prisoners. If a prisoner escaped, the life of his guard was taken in his place. The soldiers did not want to risk having a prisoner escape.

27:43. The centurion. Once more, the centurion is to be admired for stopping this plan and trusting the prisoners. Perhaps Paul's testimony had made an impression on him. Also, he may have been aware that no charge under Roman law could be sustained against Paul and that Paul was thus trustworthy.

27:44. They escaped all safe to land. Since the ship was breaking up, remaining on it was not an option. They made their way to shore as best they could. The ship most likely was quite close to land, not more than a hundred feet or so.

2. Ministry in Malta (28:1–10)

28:1. Melita. Also known as Malta. It was included in the province of Sicily and is located fifty-eight miles south of that large island.

28:2. Barbarous people. The Greeks called all non-Greek-speaking people "barbarians." Far from being uncivilized tribesmen, the islanders were Phoenician in ancestry and used a Phoenician dialect but were thoroughly Romanized. **Rain, and ... cold**. It was the end of October or the beginning of November.

28:3. A viper. This snake must have been known to the islanders to be poisonous. That no poisonous snakes live on the island today is not an objection. In two thousand years, the native animals living in a place that is populated but isolated can easily change (see Bruce, *The Book of Acts*, pp. 521–22).

28:4. Vengeance suffereth not to live. The islanders assumed that Paul was getting the justice due him that had not come by way of the sea. The Greeks had a strong understanding of fate.

28:5. Paul, knowing that God had called him to appear before Caesar, was not concerned. This account, however, in no way supports the idea that any Christian can be bitten by a poisonous snake and survive. God would not allow happenstance to short-circuit his special calling for Paul.

28:6. He should have swollen. The usual medical term for inflammation; in the New Testament, it is used only by Luke (see Acts, Introduction: "Author"). **Said that he was a god**. Parallel to the Lystrans' attempt to worship Paul and Barnabas (see 14:11–18).

28:7. The chief man. The "first man" of Melita, a technical term for the top authority. Luke's designation is accurate here, as elsewhere, even though the Greek term used is not a common one. Other terms Luke used for authorities include "the deputy of the country," or proconsul (Greek, *anthypatos*; 13:7); "magistrates" (Greek, *stratēgos*; 16:20); "the rulers of the city" (Greek, *politarchēs*; 17:6); "the chief of Asia," or Asiarchs (Greek, *Asiarchēs*; 19:31). **Publius**. A Roman name, but his first name rather than his family name. It must have been what the islanders called him.

28:8–9. Publius's father most likely had gastric fever and dysentery (see Bruce, *The Book of Acts*, p. 499). Paul healed him, which opened the door for further healing ministry. Surely this opened the door for preaching the gospel, though Luke did not say so here. It is likely that no church had been planted on the island and that this was the islanders' first exposure to the gospel. This is conjecture, as Luke is silent on these points, but it seems reasonable. The healings authenticated Paul's preaching.

28:10. Many honours. The islanders honored Paul and his companions greatly, out of gratitude for the healings and perhaps for Paul's preaching.

3. Voyage to Rome and Ministry There (28:11–31)

28:11. After three months. Paul and his fellow travelers had to remain on the island until the sailing season opened in late February or early March. Another ship had wisely wintered there and was able to take them on to Rome. **Castor and Pollux**. The two "sons of Zeus" (Greek, *Dioskouroi*), the guardian deities of sailors. Considering the size of the entire party, it may be that only the soldiers and Paul's party made this portion of the journey, their business in Rome being official, and that the rest waited or took other ships.

28:12. Syracuse. The leading city on the island of Sicily, situated on the east coast.

28:13. Rhegium. A town on the coast of Italy, near the southwestern tip and close to the narrowest point of the strait separating that country from Sicily, opposite Messina. Around the promontory north of the town was the whirlpool of Charybdis and the rock of Scylla. Coming from his triumph in Judea, the general Titus landed here on his way to Rome. **Puteoli**. Modern Pozzuoli, almost two hundred miles from Rhegium. It was situated in the northern part of the Bay of Naples and was the chief port of Rome, though seventy-five miles away. The population included Jews as well as Christians.

28:14. To tarry with them seven days. As at Troas (see 20:6) and Tyre (see 21:4), Paul stayed with the believers for one or perhaps two Sundays to observe the keeping of the Lord's Supper and to teach and preach. Either the centurion had business to care for or he was free to delay the journey at Paul's request (see 27:42–43; see also 27:3).

28:15. Appii forum. The market of Appius, which was a small town forty-three miles from Rome and noted for its wickedness. Some Roman Christians came this far to meet Paul. Beyond this point, they could not be certain of the way he would come. **The three taverns**. Or "The Three Inns," a town thirty-three miles from Rome. Other Roman believers met Paul there. The term "inn" was used to designate any kind of shop.

28:16. To dwell by himself. "In his own hired house" (28:30). Paul had committed no flagrant crime and was not a politically dangerous rival, so he was allowed to have his own living quarters. A guard was with him at all times, however, perhaps chained to him (see Eph. 6:20; Phil. 1:13–14, 17; Col. 4:3, 18; Philem. 10, 13).

28:17–19. The chief of the Jews (v. 17). This refers not to one person but rather to all the leading Jews of Rome. The decree of the emperor Claudius (see 18:2) had been allowed to lapse, and Jews had returned to Rome with their leaders. **Brethren**. An epithet that recognized the common Jewish blood Paul shared with them (but see discussion on 11:1). Paul offered a defense of himself and his presence in Rome on two fronts. First, he had not violated Jewish law: **I have committed nothing against the people, or customs of our fathers**. Paul wisely wanted to make this clear to them, in case they had heard otherwise, which as it turned out, they had not (see 28:21). Second, Paul had committed no crime against Rome (v. 18). The unreasonableness of the Jewish authorities had led to his being **constrained to appeal unto Caesar** (v. 19), which explained his presence in Rome.

28:20. The hope of Israel (see discussion on 26:6). For Paul, the hope of Israel was Jesus Christ, something he would make clear to the Jews in Rome at the appropriate time (see 28:23).

28:21. We neither received letters out of Judea … neither any of the brethren that came shewed or spake any harm of thee. Perhaps Paul's opponents had not traveled to Rome, or they had not considered the matter worth mentioning since it was now a governmental affair. His opponents had been irrationally enraged, and as is human nature, they may have forgotten their rage since the cause was no longer present. Paul had been away from Jerusalem for some time and had not been actively preaching around the Mediterranean world for over two years. Passions had cooled, and no one thought to mention the matter.

28:22. We desire to hear … what thou thinkest. The Jews in Rome were well aware of the dispute over whether Jesus was the Messiah. There were certainly Jewish Christians in Rome at this time, and these leaders had heard them. The opportunity to hear expert testimony from an apostle was not to be passed up, however. They wanted to hear Paul's presentation of the gospel, and he was eager to present it before the arrival of adverse opinions from the Jewish leaders of Jerusalem.

28:23. Persuading them concerning Jesus, both out of the law of Moses, and … the prophets. The Old Testament Scriptures (see Luke 24:27, 44). Here Paul was once again engaged in apologetics. As he had done previously, he reasoned from the Scriptures, showing them what the Old Testament said about the Messiah and that these things point to Christ.

28:24. As so often happens, **some believed … and some believed not**. No evangelist is ever 100 percent effective.

28:25–26. Paul quoted Isaiah 6:9–10 to show that the Jews did not hear the truth concerning Christ, even as it was presented to them.

28:28. The salvation of God is sent unto the Gentiles. The major theme of the book of Acts. The gospel is meant for all. Paul was a chosen vessel to carry the message to Gentiles as well as to Jews. He had such a heart for his Jewish bretheren that he often had to remind himself of his call.

28:29. Paul's words created some controversy among the Jews, as well they might. Paul at least had done his duty before God, to bring the gospel to them.

28:30. Two whole years. Paul served the Lord (see 28:31) during the full period of waiting for his accusers to press the trial in Rome.

28:31. Preaching the kingdom of God, and teaching those things which concern the Lord Jesus Christ. This may be related to what Paul told the Ephesian elders. "Preaching the kingdom of God" may be related to "repentance toward God" (20:21). God rules, and sinful men must acknowledge this and repent, submitting themselves to the truth of God. "Teaching those things which concern the Lord Jesus Christ" may be related to "faith toward the Lord Jesus Christ" (20:21). Paul's ministry was consistent. He preached and taught as he always had, that humankind should repent and put their faith in Jesus Christ as their only hope.

Acts ends here, with no word of Paul's fate. There are a number of indications, however, that Paul was released from this imprisonment: (1) Acts abruptly stops here. (2) Paul wrote to churches of his plans to visit them soon, so he must have anticipated a release (see Phil. 2:24; Philem. 22). (3) A number of the details in the Pastoral Epistles do not fit into the historical setting given in the book of Acts. These details indicate that Paul later returned to Asia Minor, Crete, and Greece. (4) Tradition indicates that Paul went to Spain. Even if he did not go, the very fact that a tradition arose suggests a time when he could have taken that journey.

The ending of Acts is not so abrupt as it might seem, however. Luke closed with a summary of Paul's activities during his two years in Rome, and if the trial had not yet taken place, Luke may have thought this was the best stopping point. He had achieved his objective. He had shown, both in doctrine and in history, that salvation by grace alone, through faith alone, is for everyone. The apostles certified this fact in Jerusalem (see chap. 15), and Paul's ministry demonstrated the truth of it as he established churches among the Gentiles. Luke, like any good writer, knew when to stop. The book of Acts, lying between the Gospels and the Epistles, forms a bridge between the historical and doctrinal aspects of this great truth.

THE EPISTLE OF PAUL THE APOSTLE TO THE ROMANS

INTRODUCTION

Author

The writer of this letter was the apostle Paul (see 1:1). No voice from the early church was ever raised against his authorship. The letter contains a number of historical references that agree with known facts of Paul's life. The doctrinal content of the book is typical of Paul, which is evident from a comparison with other letters he wrote.

Date and Place of Composition

The book was probably written in the early spring of AD 57. Very likely, Paul was on his third missionary journey, ready to return to Jerusalem with the offering from the mission churches for poverty-stricken believers in Jerusalem (see 15:25–27). In 15:26, it is suggested that Paul had already received contributions from the churches of Macedonia and Achaia, so he either was at Corinth or had already been there. Since he had not yet been at Corinth (on his third missionary journey) when he wrote 1 Corinthians (see 1 Cor. 16:1–4) and the collection issue had still not been resolved when he wrote 2 Corinthians (2 Cor. 8–9), the writing of Romans must have followed that of 1–2 Corinthians (dated ca. AD 55).

The most likely place of composition is either Corinth or Cenchrea (about six miles away) because of references to Phebe of Cenchrea (16:1) and to Gaius, Paul's host (16:23), who was probably a Corinthian (see 1 Cor. 1:14). Erastus (16:23) may also have been a Corinthian (see 2 Tim. 4:20).

Recipients

The original recipients of the letter were the people of the church at Rome (1:7), who were predominantly Gentile. Jews, however, must have constituted a substantial minority of the congregation (see 4:1; chaps. 9–11; see also discussion on 1:13). Perhaps Paul originally sent the entire letter to the Roman church, after which he or someone else used a shorter form (chaps. 1–14 or 1–15) for more general distribution (see discussion on 2 Peter 3:15).

Background

When Paul wrote this letter, he was probably at Corinth (see Acts 20:2–3) on his third missionary journey. His work in the eastern Mediterranean was almost finished (see 15:18–23), and he greatly desired to visit the Roman church (see 1:11–12; 15:23–24). At this time, however, he could not go to Rome because he felt he must personally deliver the collection taken among the Gentile churches for the poverty-stricken Christians of Jerusalem (see 15:25–28). So instead of going to Rome, he sent a letter to prepare the Christians there for his intended visit in connection with a mission to Spain (see 15:23–24). For many years, Paul had wanted to visit Rome to minister there (see 1:13–15), and this letter served as a careful and systematic theological introduction to that hoped-for personal ministry. Since he was not acquainted directly with the Roman church, he said little about its problems (but see 14:1–15:13; see also 13:1–7; 16:17–18).

Paul's purposes for writing this letter were varied. (1) He wrote to prepare the way for his coming visit to Rome and his proposed mission to Spain (see 1:10–15; 15:22–29). (2) He wrote to present the basic system of salvation to a church that had not received the teaching of an apostle before. (3) He sought to explain the relationship between Jew and Gentile in God's overall plan of redemption. The Jewish Christians were being rejected by the larger Gentile group in the church (see 14:1) because the Jewish believers still felt constrained to observe dietary laws and sacred days (see 14:2–6).

Theme and Theological Message

Paul's primary theme in Romans is the basic gospel, God's plan of salvation and righteousness for all mankind, Jew and Gentile alike (see 1:16–17). Although some have suggested justification by faith as the theme, it would seem that a broader theme states the message of the book more adequately. "The Righteousness of God" (1:17) includes justification by faith but also embraces such related ideas as guilt, sanctification, and security.

Paul began the letter by surveying the spiritual condition of all mankind. He found Jews and Gentiles alike to be sinners and in need of salvation. That salvation has been provided by God through Jesus Christ and His redemptive work on the cross. It is a provision, however, that must be received by faith—a principle by which God has always dealt with mankind, as the example of Abraham shows. Since salvation is only the beginning of Christian experience, Paul moved on to show how the believer is freed from sin, the law, and death—a provision made possible by his union with Christ in both death and resurrection and by the indwelling presence and power of the Holy Spirit. Paul then showed that Israel too, though presently in a state of unbelief, has a place in God's sovereign redemptive plan. Now she consists of only a remnant, allowing for the conversion of the Gentiles, but the time will come when "all Israel shall be saved" (11:26). The letter concludes with an appeal to the readers to work out their Christian faith in practical ways, both in the church and in the world. None of Paul's other letters states so profoundly the content of the gospel and its implications for both the present and the future.

Literary Features

The letter displays several notable literary features. (1) It is the most systematic of Paul's letters, reading more like an elaborate theological essay than a letter. (2) The emphasis is on Christian doctrine. The number and importance of the theological themes Paul touched on are impressive: sin, salvation, grace, faith, righteousness, justification, sanctification, redemption, death, resurrection, and glorification. (3) Paul used a large number of Old Testament quotations. Although he regularly quoted from the Old Testament in his letters, in Romans, the argument is sometimes carried along by the quotations (see especially chaps. 9–11). (4) The letter displays Paul's deep concern for Israel. He wrote about her present status, her relationship to the Gentiles, and her final salvation.

Outline

Bibliography

Barrett, C. K. *A Commentary on the Epistle to the Romans.* New York: Harper & Row, 1957.

Black, Matthew. *Romans.* New Century Bible. Grand Rapids, MI: Eerdmans, 1981.

Bruce, F. F. *The Epistle of Paul to the Romans.* Tyndale New Testament Commentaries 6. Grand Rapids, MI: Eerdmans, 1963.

Cranfield, C. E. B. *A Critical and Exegetical Commentary on the Epistle to the Romans.* 2 vols. Edinburgh: T&T Clark, 1979.

Luther, Martin. *Luther: Lectures on Romans.* Edited and translated by Wilhelm Pauck. Philadelphia: Westminster, 1961.

Moo, Douglas J. *Romans.* The NIV Application Commentary. Grand Rapids, MI: Zondervan, 2000.

Morris, Leon. *The Epistle to the Romans.* Pillar New Testament Commentary. Grand Rapids, MI: Eerdmans, 1988.

Mounce, Robert H. *Romans.* The New American Commentary 27. Nashville: Broadman & Holman, 1995.

Murray, John. *The Epistle to the Romans.* The New International Commentary on the New Testament. Grand Rapids, MI: Eerdmans, 1965.

Stott, John. *Romans.* Downers Grove, IL: InterVarsity Press, 1994.

EXPOSITION

I. Introduction (1:1–15)

1:1. Paul. In ancient times, writers put their names at the beginning of letters. For more information on Paul, see discussions on Acts 9:1; Philippians 3:4–14. The Greek for **servant** means (1) a "slave," who completely belongs to his owner and has no freedom to leave, and (2) a "servant," who willingly chooses to serve his master (see discussions on Psalm 18 superscription; Isa. 41:8–9; 42:1; *Zondervan KJV Study Bible* note on Exod. 14:31). **An apostle** is one specially commissioned by Christ (see discussions on Mark 6:30; 1 Cor. 1:1; Heb. 3:1). **Gospel** (Greek, *euangelion*), in general, refers to "good news" as proclamation. Here its content concerns God's Son (see 1:3, 9; see also 15:16, 19). "Gospel" occurs sixty times in Paul's writings (see discussion on Mark 1:1).

1:2. His prophets are not just the writers of the prophetic books, for the whole Old Testament prophesied about Jesus (see Luke 24:27, 44). **Holy scriptures** refers to the Old Testament.

1:3–4. God's promised gospel (see 1:1–2) proclaims **his Son** (v. 3). Christ's supernatural status as God's Son is given historical dimension with the addition of two balanced clauses that correspond to and amplify His title, **Jesus Christ our Lord.** As "Christ" (Messiah), He was descended from David (**the seed of David**). As "Lord," He was **declared to be the Son of God with power** (v. 4). The one is **according to the flesh** (v. 3), which reveals His title "Christ" through His messianic birth. The other is **according to the Spirit of holiness** (v. 4), which ratifies His title to "Lord" through His **resurrection from the dead.** Both belong to history and both redound to His proclamation in the gospel of God. The continuum of these two verses and these two historical touchstones not only spans the birth, ministry, death, and resurrection of Jesus but, through His sonship, reaches back into eternity past and ahead into the eternal present and the glorious reign of Christ our Lord.

1:5–6. By whom (v. 5) refers to the Son, who now, in view of 1:2–3 and especially His resurrection, mediates **grace and apostleship**. These two words summarize Paul's mission and authority. As an apostle (see 1:1), Paul belonged to the grand scope of the gospel of God (see 1:1–4) and its objective, **obedience to the faith**, which is both global (**all nations**) and local (**ye also**; v. 6).

1:7. According to the conventional salutation of a first-century letter, Paul, after a digression on the gospel of God (1:2–4) and its relation to him and the recipients (1:5–6), completed the normal X-to-Y salutation, begun in 1:1, by naming the recipients with a greeting. **All that be in Rome,** (who are) **beloved of God** specifies the Christians of the imperial city. The basic idea of the Greek word for **saints** is "holiness." All Christians are saints in that they are positionally "set apart" to God and are experientially being made increasingly "holy" by the Holy Spirit (see *KJV Study Bible* note on 1 Cor. 1:2). For **Grace,** see discussions on Jonah 4:2; Galatians 1:3; Ephesians 1:2. For **peace,** see discussions on John 14:27; 20:19; Galatians 1:3; Ephesians 1:2.

1:8. I thank my God characteristically opens the "thanksgiving" with which Paul regularly began his letters (see 1 Cor. 1:4; Eph. 1:16; Phil. 1:3; Col. 1:3; 1 Thess. 1:2; 2 Thess. 1:3; 2 Tim. 1:3; Philemon 4), following his salutation and greeting. **Through Jesus Christ** points to the New Testament theology of prayer. Christians must go through Christ not only for requests to God (see John 15:16) but also to give thanks. **Throughout the whole world** refers to every place where the gospel had been preached.

1:9–10. The word for **serve** (Greek, *latreuō*; v. 9) has a rich background in sacred and priestly service (see Heb. 9:9; 10:2). For Paul, such dutiful service was spiritual (**with my spirit**); that is, he carried out his service not in a physical temple but in his heart, wherever he went. **The gospel of his Son** is the same as "the gospel of God" (1:1; see 15:16, 19). Paul alluded to God's watchful eye and His ability to bear witness to Paul's service on behalf of the Christians in Rome, for whom he interceded through prayer, just as a priest serves before God on behalf of His people. The extension of Paul's prayerful service was to serve the Roman Christians in person (**to come unto you**; v. 10).

1:11–12. Paul stated that he wished to visit the church in Rome, **that I may impart ... some spiritual gift** (v. 11); that is, he wished "to share" some of his gifts of the Spirit. Paul was an apostle, but more important, he saw himself as an instrument of the Holy Spirit. "Spiritual gift" occurs only here in Paul's letters and was probably used here because he had not yet visited the Romans in person and did not want them to misunderstand the "gift" that he intended to bring them. In chapter 12, Paul taught about "spiritual gifts." Here he states what is fundamental to all of his teaching on the gifts of the Spirit: their purpose is that **you may be established,** to "strengthen" the church. **Together** (v. 12) points out that the work of the Spirit and the mutual exercise of the Spirit's gifts can be anticipated among God's people even when the gifts have yet to be labeled and taught as such. Paul's genuine humility is seen in his desire to be ministered to by the believers at Rome as well as to minister to them.

1:13. Fruit refers to new converts as well as the spiritual growth of those already converted. **Among you ... among other Gentiles** suggests that the church at Rome was predominantly Gentile.

1:14. The Greeks identifies those Gentiles who spoke Greek or followed the Greek way of life, even though they may have been Latin-speaking citizens of the Roman Empire. A further specification of the Gentiles to whom Paul ministered is found in the word **barbarians**. The word is onomatopoeic; it sounds out the bar-bar-bar of non-Greek languages that was unintelligible to Greek ears.

II. Theme: The Righteousness of God (1:16–17)

1:16–17. The theme of the entire book of Romans is found in these two verses.

1:16. Paul was **not ashamed of the gospel** anywhere or at anytime, not even in the capital city of the Roman Empire (see 1:15; for "gospel," see 1:1 and discussion on Mark 1:1). Paul knew of a power to deliver that eclipsed that of Rome. **The power** (Greek, *dynamis*) **of God** (see 1 Cor. 1:18 for the same expression) effects **salvation** for those who believe and reveals "the righteousness of God" (1:17). The Jews come **first** not only in time but also in privilege. "Salvation is of the Jews" (John 4:22), and the Messiah was a Jew. "The oracles of God" (3:2), the covenants, law, temple worship, revelation of the divine glory, and messianic prophecies came to them (see 9:3–5). These privileges, however, were not extended to the Jews because of their superior merit or because of God's partiality toward them. It was necessary that the invasion of this world by the gospel begin at a particular point with a particular people, who in turn were responsible for carrying that gospel to the other nations.

1:17. The righteousness of God points to "a righteousness from God," the state of being "in the right" in relation to God (see discussions on 2:13; 3:21, 24) as well as to "the righteousness of God" (see 3:5, 25–26; 10:3), which is foundational in Romans. The gift must not be separated from the Giver of the gift. Paul's understanding of God's righteousness is informed by the Old Testament, in which God's righteousness is related to His covenant faithfulness and demonstrated in His acts to deliver and save. The words **from faith to faith** and the citation of Habakkuk 2:4 (**The just shall live by faith**; see discussion on Gal. 3:11) point to the two dimensions—righteousness of God and righteousness from God—revealed in the gospel.

III. The Unrighteousness of All Mankind (1:18–3:20)

1:18–3:20. In developing the theme of righteousness from God (see 1:17; 3:21–5:21), Paul set the stage by showing that all have sinned and therefore need the righteousness that only God can provide. He discussed the sin of the Gentiles (1:18–32) and the sin of the Jews (2:1–3:8) and then summarized the sin of all, Gentile and Jew alike (3:9–20).

A. Gentiles (1:18–32)

1:18–20. No one, not even one who has not heard of the Bible or of Christ, has an excuse for not honoring God, because the whole created world reveals Him.

1:18. The wrath of God is not a petulant, irrational burst of anger, such as humans often exhibit, but a holy, just revulsion of what opposes and is contrary to His holy nature and will. God's wrath is not limited to the end-time judgment of the wicked (see 1 Thess. 1:10; Rev. 19:15; 20:11–15), as the words **is revealed** make clear. Here the wrath of God is His abandonment of the wicked to their sins (see 1:24–32). **The truth** is the truth about God that is revealed in the creation order.

1:19–21. God can be acknowledged and known through general revelation, that is, from seeing His revelation in creation (vv. 19–20), as Paul attested with the words **they knew God** (v. 21). Since general revelation is not redemptive, as is God's special revelation distinguished in Scripture, what people know of God through creation is **his eternal power and Godhead** ("deity"; v. 20). **Understood** implies not only the perception but its inference or conclusion. Thus, all people **are without excuse** before the witness of creation if they have not **glorified him** (v. 21) as God. In other words, they had not suitably and properly honored and extolled the divine benefactor for what was understood through creation as divine benefaction. That these people were idolaters (see 1:23) and knew God only through the creation order indicates that they were Gentiles. **Thankful** expresses recognition and gratitude for earthly blessings, such as sun, rain, and crops (see Matt. 5:45; Acts 14:17).

1:22–23. Professing themselves to be wise (v. 22), those who fail to acknowledge God assert their own superiority. When God is the rival, the folly is most calamitous. **Glory** (v. 23) refers to God's unique majesty (see Isa. 48:11), which fallen mankind lost sight of and for which the idolators had substituted deities of their own devising, patterned after various creatures.

1:24. Wherefore, or "For this reason," connects God's reaction to the base behavior described in 1:22–23. Like a bell toll, the refrain **God … gave them up** (see 1:26), or "God gave them over" (1:28), declares that God allowed sin to run its course as an act of judgment. Here God gave them over **to uncleanness,** with the consequence that **through**

the lusts of their own hearts ... they dishonoured **their own bodies between themselves.** Inasmuch as God was not glorified (see 1:21) but dishonored (see 1:23), Paul portrayed their consequential and commensurate dishonoring of one another. This perversion is spelled out in 1:25–27.

1:25. The idolaters' "exchange" of 1:23 is here fathomed succinctly. **Who** has the sense of "They actually" (Cranfield, *Epistle to the Romans*, p. 123). **The truth of God** refers not only to the truth about God and His self-revelation but to the truth about all things. The **lie,** the worship of creation, is a perversion of the truth, an absurdity of idolatry. **Amen** can mean either "Yes indeed, it is so" or "So be it" (see 9:5; 11:36; 15:33; 16:27; see also *KJV Study Bible* note on Deut. 27:15; 1 Kings 1:36).

1:26–27. For the refrain **God ... gave them up** (v. 26), see discussion on 1:24. **Their women** is a gender reference that refers to females generally, not necessarily their wives, even as **men** (v. 27) refers to males. Interpreters have suggested that the order of Paul's treatment, females before males, was for emphasis on the male perversion. **Likewise** makes it clear that the unnatural sexual relations of the males applied also to the females. Homosexual practice is sinful in God's eyes. The Old Testament condemns the practice (see Lev. 18:22). **Receiving in themselves that recompence of their error** explains that the punishment matched the offense.

1:28–31. Not ... retain God in their knowledge (v. 28; see 1:19, 21) is tantamount to a restatement of 1:22–23, 25, and here summarizes human rejection of God and refusal to acknowledge God. **God gave them over** is the third time (see 1:24, 26, 28) God's response is described as the judgment of abandonment. Paul made the correlation clear through a wordplay. They did not "retain God," or "find Him fit" (Greek, *dokimazō*), so God "gave them over" to **a reprobate** ("an unfit"; Greek, *adokimos*) **mind.** The intent preceded the act (see 1:21; Mark 7:20–23).

The "reprobate mind" that has rejected the knowledge of God has engaged in an exchange (see 1:23, 25). Empty of the knowledge of God, the reprobate mind is filled with **things which are not con-**

venient (v. 28), or "unfitting," meaning "not proper" or "morally wrong." The word has a rich history as a technical ethical term among the Stoics. For people with such a mind, Paul grammatically divides the list of their vices into three categories: (1) they are **filled with all unrighteousness, fornication, wickedness, covetousness, maliciousness** (v. 29); (2) they are **full of envy, murder, debate, deceit, malignity, whisperers;** (3) they are **backbiters, haters of God, despiteful, proud, boasters, inventors of evil things, disobedient to parents** (v. 30), **without understanding, covenantbreakers, without natural affection, implacable, unmerciful** (v. 31). This is the fullest and most detailed list of vices of all of Paul's "sin lists" (see Rom. 13:13; 1 Cor. 5:10–11; 6:9–10; 2 Cor. 12:20–21; Gal. 5:19–21; Eph. 4:31; 5:3–5; Col. 3:5–8; 1 Tim. 1:9–10; 2 Tim. 3:2–6; Titus 3:3).

1:32. Although they rejected the knowledge of God, the people described in 1:28–31 were not void of **knowing.** Their outrageous conduct was not due to total ignorance of what God required but rather due to self-will and rebellion. **Have pleasure in them that do them** points to a culture and pattern of attitude and action that glories not in God but in what is shameful. The extreme of sin is applauding, rather than regretting, the sins of others.

B. Jews (2:1–3:8)

2:1–16. In this section, Paul set forth principles that govern God's judgment. God judges (1) "according to truth" (v. 2), (2) "according to ... deeds" (v. 6–11), and (3) according to the light a person has (vv. 12–15). These principles laid the groundwork for Paul's discussion of the guilt of the Jews (2:17–29).

2:1. Inexcusable. Paul's teaching about judging agrees with that of Jesus (see discussion on Matt. 7:1), who did not condemn judging as such, but hypocritical judging. **Whosoever ... that judgest** posed a warning that had relevance for any moralist but special relevance for Jews. They were inclined to look down on Gentiles because of their ignorance of God's revelation in the Old Testament and because of their immoral lives.

2:2. Paul frequently used the expression **We are sure** (lit., "We know"), which assumed the persons addressed agreed with the statement that followed (see 3:19; 7:14; 8:22, 28; 1 Cor. 8:1, 4; 2 Cor. 5:1; 1 Tim. 1:8). **According to truth** means that justice is impartial and that God is no respecter of persons (see 2:11), either outward appearance or national origin. This theme is spelled out in 2:3–11.

2:3. Jesus also condemned this attitude (see Matt. 7:3; see Luke 18:9). It is the height of perverted miscalculation to presume on the judgment of God.

2:4. The purpose of God's kindness is to give opportunity for **repentance** (see 2 Peter 3:9). The Jews had misconstrued His patience to be a lack of intent to judge. **Despisest** conveys the sense of looking down with contempt, but the Greek word can also convey disregard and presumption. In this context, **not knowing** comes closer to the sense of "ignoring" rather than "ignorant."

2:5. The day of wrath, or judgment, at the end of time stands in contrast to the judgment discussed in 1:18–32.

2:6–8. God is impartial in His judgment (see 2:2, 11) and **will render to every man according to his deeds** (v. 6; see Ps. 62:12; Prov. 24:1). Paul was not contradicting his continual emphasis in all his writings, including Romans, that a person is saved not by what he does but by faith in what Christ does for him. Rather, he was discussing the principle of judgment "according to … deeds" (see discussion on 2:1–16). If anyone persists in doing good deeds (i.e., lives a perfect life), he will receive eternal life. No one can do this (see 3:10–12), but if anyone could, God would give him life, because God judges according to what a person does.

2:9. Every soul … that doeth evil makes it clear that there is no exemption (see 3:9–10), although there is an order: **the Jew first**. With spiritual privilege comes spiritual responsibility (see Amos 3:2; Luke 12:48).

2:11. There is no respect of persons with God is a basic teaching of both the Old Testament and the New Testament (see Deut. 1:17; 10:17; 16:19; 2 Chron. 19:7; Prov. 24:23; 28:21; Eph. 6:9; Col. 3:25;

James 2:1; Acts 10:34). "Respect of persons," or partiality (Greek, *prosōpolēmpsia*; "accept face"), is defined quite literally in Galatians 2:6: "God accepteth no man's person [face]." The Lord does not evaluate any person on the basis of "face" (one's pedigree or credentials).

2:12. For as many as have sinned without law refers to Gentiles ("law" refers to the Mosaic law). God judges according to the light available to people. Gentiles will not be condemned for not obeying a law they did not possess. Their judgment will be on other grounds (see 1:18–20; 2:15; Amos 1:3–2:3).

2:13. In a courtroom, the word **justified**, or "declared righteous," represents the verdict of a judge over the accused. **The doers of the law** are vindicated. Knowledge alone (**the hearers of the law**) is not enough. Paul was setting forth a general principle that Roman hearers, with their sense of justice, could readily appreciate. This principle is the basis of God's pronouncement of acquittal on judgment day (see discussion on 3:24).

2:14–15. By nature (v. 14) suggests an inner moral code, **written in their hearts** (v. 15), ratified by **their conscience**, and reflected in **their thoughts**, apart from the external constraint of the law written on tablets, the Mosaic law revealed specifically to Israel. It must be kept in view, however, that **things contained in the law** (v. 14) does not mean that pagans fulfilled the requirements of the Mosaic law. Rather, it refers to practices in pagan society that agreed with the law, such as caring for the sick and elderly, honoring parents, and condemning adultery. **A law unto themselves** also speaks of the moral nature of pagans, enlightened by "their conscience" (v. 15), which functioned for them as the Mosaic law did for the Jews.

2:16. God shall judge all people by the standard of **Jesus Christ**. This verse picks up Paul's thought from 2:12; the material in 2:13–15 is parenthetical in Paul's argument.

2:17–24. Here the presentation takes the form of a dialogue. Paul knew how a self-righteous Jew thought, for he had been one himself. He cited one advantage after another that Jews considered to be unqualified assets. Those assets became liabilities, however, when profession and practice did not correspond. Paul applied to the Jew the principles of judgment set forth in 2:1–16 (see discussion there).

2:19–20. The blind (v. 19) and **babes** (v. 20) are descriptives of a superior to an inferior. Although Paul sought to chagrin the elitist, not shame the insulted, one may see the Jewish outlook on the Gentiles, to whom Jews regarded themselves as vastly superior because they (the Jews) possessed the Mosaic law.

2:21–24. These verses present several pictures of hypocrisy, double standards, and partiality. **Dost thou commit sacrilege?** (v. 22) is literally, "Dost thou rob temples?" (see Acts 19:37). Large amounts of wealth were often stored in pagan temples. **Makest thy boast** (v. 23) is a case of bragging about the law and at the same time bringing the Giver of the law into disrepute by breaking the law. As Paul's quotation in verse 24 (from Ezek. 36:20, 22; Isa. 52:5) suggests, it would not be the first time that the Jews had given the Gentiles cause to blaspheme God.

2:25. Circumcision was a sign of the covenant that God made with Israel (see Lev. 12:3) and a pledge of the covenant blessing (see Genesis 17 and discussions on Gen. 17:10–11). The Jews had come to regard circumcision as a guarantee of God's favor.

2:26–27. If a Gentile's deeds excelled those of a Jew in righteousness, that very fact condemned the Jew, who had an immeasurably better set of standards in the law of Moses.

2:28–29. That which is **inwardly ... in the spirit ... of God** (v. 29), in contrast to that which is **outwardly** (v. 28), points to the authenticity of what is subject to God alone as opposed to the partiality of human standards. The true sign of belonging to God is not an outward mark on the physical body but the regenerating power of the Holy Spirit within, which is what Paul meant by **circumcision ... of the heart** (v. 29; see Deut. 30:6).

3:1–2. Paul raised two rhetorical questions. He knew the answers and wanted to explain the advantage of the Jew (see 1:16; 2:9–10) more fully in view of what he had just written about them (see

2:17–29). **Chiefly** (v. 2). Paul did not discuss the other advantages of being a Jew until 9:4–5. He used the word **committed** because the advantage of having the very words of God involves a duty. Indeed, the Jews were guilty of infidelity to their greatest treasure, **the oracles of God**, that is, the Word of God, with particular emphasis on His promises. Overall, Paul was arguing that God had been faithful to the oracles, whereas the Jews had not.

3:3. Here **the faith of God** means "faithfulness." The Greek word means either "faith" or "faithfulness." God is faithful to His promises and would punish Israel for its unbelief (see 3:5; 2 Tim. 2:13). Also, although not at this point, Paul will argue in 3:31 that God's faithfulness is preeminently demonstrated in the gospel, in the deliverance of His Son, Jesus Christ.

3:4. God's punishment of sin exhibits His faithfulness to His righteous character.

3:5. By contrast, human **unrighteousness [can] commend the righteousness of God**, in showing it up against the dark background of man's sin. **I speak as a man** was Paul's way of saying, "I am using a human argument," implying its weakness and absurdity.

3:6. God will **judge the world** on judgment day. Here "the world" identifies all moral creatures (also in 3:19) and is a more limited reference than in 1:20.

C. Summary: All People (3:9–20)

3:7–8. Again, although not expressly labeled as a "human argument" (3:5), Paul posed a monstrous proposition in the form of a question to further address God's just condemnation of sin.

3:9. Are we better than they? Are Jews better than Gentiles in the sight of God? Paul's answer was inclusive: **all [are] under sin**, its power and condemnation. Nine times in four verses (3:9–12), Paul declared the universality of sin ("all," twice; "none," four times; "not even one," twice; "together," once).

3:10–18. Paul used this collection of Old Testament quotations to underscore his charge that both Jews and Gentiles are under the power of sin. Several factors explain why the citations are not always verbatim: (1) New Testament quotations sometimes gave the general sense and were not meant to be word for word. (2) Quotation marks were not used in Greek. (3) The quotations were often taken from the Greek translation (the Septuagint) of the Hebrew Old Testament, because Greek readers were not familiar with the Hebrew Bible. (4) Sometimes the New Testament writer, under the inspiration of the Holy Spirit, would purposely adapt an Old Testament passage or combine two or more passages to drive home a point.

3:10–12. In these three verses, Paul set forth the universal indictment of humanity. In logic, the statements are comprehensive, with a universal affirmative, **all** (the totality; v. 12), punctuating a series of universal negatives, "none." **None that understandeth** (v. 11) refers to the failed equation of the perception and that which is perceived, here of God and what is right. **They are all gone out of the way** (v. 12) speaks of "turning away" from seeking God's interests (v. 11) and, as a result, becoming depraved or morally **unprofitable** ("corrupted" or "broken"; v. 12).

3:13–18. In these verses, the depth of human depravity is described in terms of human anatomy: **throat** (v. 13), **tongues, lips, mouth** (v. 14), **feet** (v. 15), and **eyes** (v. 18). **Their throat is an open sepulcher** (v. 13) expresses the corruption of the heart. **Before their eyes** is a cipher for mental and spiritual understanding in which **There is no fear of God** (v. 18). This important Old Testament expression refers to an awesome reverence for God, who is the source of all godliness (see discussion on Gen. 20:11). Fundamentally, what people fear, aside from the emotional associations that predominate contemporary understanding, is that which people give priority. What one fears is what commands one's attention and respect. In the Old Testament, the "fear of God" denotes the positive preeminence that His lordship should receive.

3:19–20. The issue of the advantage of the Jew, which Paul raised at the outset of this chapter, here comes back into focus. In short, **the law** (and circumcision, which binds one to the law; v. 19) does not deliver the Jew from sin. The law ratifies the existence of sin by identifying it and condemning its presence. Here "the law" refers to the Old Testament (as in John 10:34; 15:25; 1 Cor. 14:21). For **we know**, see discussion on 2:2. **Them who are under the law** are the Jews. **Every mouth ... and all the world** is profound, because if the Jews are not vindicated by the law but are in fact indicted by it, Jews as well as Gentiles are guilty. For **justified**, see discussions on 3:24; 2:13. To conclude his argument, Paul drew on Psalm 143:2: "For in thy sight shall no man living be justified." Interestingly, in the preceding verse, the psalmist prayed for and anticipated deliverance, by appealing to God's "faithfulness" and "righteousness" (Ps. 143:1). That is, although the psalmist did not deserve it, he appealed to God's covenant virtues, believing that God would do what he did not warrant. Although not expressly stated by Paul, the twin virtues of God's character and subjects of dispute in 3:3, 7, come forward in 3:21–22 as Paul addresses "the righteousness of God" and "faith ['faithfulness,' as in 3:3] of Jesus Christ" (3:22) expressing apart from the law a deliverance through Christ that is unwarranted by human unrighteousness.

IV. Righteousness Imputed: Justification (3:21–5:21)

A. Through Christ (3:21–26)

3:21–5:21. Having shown that all (both Gentiles and Jews) are unrighteous (1:18–3:20), Paul went on to show that God has provided a righteousness for mankind.

3:21. The words **But now** offer two possible meanings: (1) temporal—all of time is divided into two periods, and in the "now" period, **the righteousness of God** has been made known; (2) logical—the contrast is between the righteousness gained by observing the law (which is impossible; see 3:20) and the righteousness provided by God. For **witnessed by the law and the prophets**, see Genesis 15:6; Psalm 32:1–2; Habbakuk 2:4.

3:22–23. For there is no difference (v. 22) ... **all have sinned, and come short of the glory of God** (v. 23) is a parenthetical thought. Thus, **all them that believe** (v. 22) are "justified freely" (3:24), not "all have sinned" (v. 23) are "justified freely" (3:24); "justified" goes with "believe," not with "sinned." "No difference" (v. 22) targets the equal standing of Jews and Gentiles (see 10:12). "All have sinned" (v. 23) is literally defined in the words "come short of." The Greek word that Paul used for "sinned" (a form of the verb *hamartanō*) is the same word that the Greek historian Xenophon (*Anabasis* 1.v.12) used in a scene in which an axe was hurled and missed its target. In other words, it fell short. "The glory of God" includes what God intended man to be. The glory that man had before the fall (see Gen. 1:26–28; Ps. 8:5–6; Eph. 4:24; Col. 3:10) the believer will again have through Christ (see Heb. 2:5–9).

3:24. Justified was a significant term for Paul. He used the Greek verb for "justified" twenty-seven times in his letters, mostly in Romans and Galatians. The term describes what happens when someone believes in Christ as his Savior: from the negative viewpoint, God declares the person to be not guilty; from the positive viewpoint, He declares him to be righteous. He cancels the guilt of the person's sin and credits righteousness to him. Paul emphasized two points in this regard: (1) No one lives a perfectly good, holy, righteous life. On the contrary, "There is none righteous" (3:10), and "all have sinned, and come short of the glory of God" (3:23). "By the deeds of the law there shall no flesh be justified in his sight" (3:20). (2) Even though all are sinners and not sons, God will declare everyone who puts his trust in Jesus righteous rather than guilty. This legal declaration is valid because Christ died to pay the penalty for sin and lived a life of perfect righteousness, which can in turn be imputed to all humans. This is the central theme of Romans and is stated in the theme verse, 1:17 ("the righteousness of God"). Christ's righteousness (His obedience to God's law and His sacrificial death) will be credited to believers as their own. Paul used one Greek word meaning "reckoned," "imputed," or "counted" eleven times in chapter 4 alone. **Freely by his grace** is God's unmerited provision that finds expression in justification. The central thought in justification is that, although man clearly and totally deserves to be declared guilty (3:9–19),

God declares him righteous because of his trust in Christ. This is stated in several ways here: (1) "freely" (for nothing), (2) "by his grace," (3) **through the redemption that is in Christ Jesus,** and (4) "through faith" (3:25). "Redemption" is a word taken from the slave market; the basic idea is that of obtaining release by payment of a ransom. Paul used this word to refer to release from guilt, with its liability for judgment, and to deliverance from slavery to sin, because through His death, Christ paid the ransom for all humanity.

3:25a. To be a propitiation points to an atoning sacrifice and defines Jesus' sacrificial death "as the One who would turn aside God's wrath, taking away sin." The Greek for this phrase speaks of a sacrifice that satisfies the righteous wrath of God; without this appeasement, all people are justly destined for eternal punishment (see discussion on 1 John 2:2). **Through faith in his blood** makes it clear that saving faith looks to Jesus Christ in His sacrificial death for us.

3:25b–26. The sins of God's people, punished symbolically in the animal sacrifices of the Old Testament period, were totally punished in the once-for-all sacrifice of Christ on the cross.

B. Received by Faith (3:27–4:25)

1. The Principle Established (3:27–31)

3:27–28. There can be no **boasting** (v. 27) whatsoever; the grounds for boasting have been **excluded,** or literally "shut out." In short, **works** or merits of any kind are eliminated as a ground for justification. Only what God has done through the sacrificial death of Christ offers justification, which can be claimed only **by the law of faith.** When Luther translated this passage, he added the word "alone," which, though not in the Greek, accurately reflects the meaning (see discussion on James 2:14–26). Verse 28 states in positive terms what 3:20 stated in negative terms.

3:29. If justification were by the "works of the Law" (3:28), then God would indeed be **the God of the Jews only.** But such is not the case. Thankfully, God is the **God of the Gentiles also.**

3:30. Seeing it is one God refers to the first article of Jewish faith ("the LORD our God is one," Deut. 6:4). With this appeal, Paul argued that there is only one way of salvation for both Jew and Gentile, namely, faith in Christ.

3:31. Do we then make void the law through faith? Paul anticipated being charged with antinomianism ("against law"): If justification comes by faith alone, then is not the law rejected? He gave a more complete answer in chaps. 6–7 and reasserted the validity of the law in 13:8–10 (see also 1 Tim. 1:8–10).

2. The Principle Illustrated (chap. 4)

4:1. The great patriarch of the Jewish nation and the true example of a justified person (see James 2:21–23) is **Abraham our father.** The Jews of Jesus' time used Abraham as an example of justification by works, but Paul held him up as a shining example of righteousness by faith (see Gal. 3:6–9).

4:2. Paul raised the question of whether Abraham was **justified by works** but stopped short of saying that Abraham had no works worthy of **glory** (human respect). Indeed, he was a great man, but Paul made it clear that he had no grounds for glory **before God.**

4:3. What saith the scripture? The reference is to Genesis 15:6, where nothing is mentioned about works. Abraham's faith, not his works, was **counted unto him** (or "credited") **for righteousness.** Abraham had kept no law, rendered no service, and performed no ritual that earned credit to his account before God. His belief in God, who had made promises to him, was credited to him as righteousness.

4:4–5. Paul explained in general workday terms the difference between works and grace. **Him that justifieth the ungodly** (v. 5) is truly a remarkable description of God and His grace. In a court of law, such as a Roman one, a reputable human judge vindicates or justifies only the innocent person, one who has been proven righteous and innocent of the charge that landed him before the court. Here, then, is the grace of God and the heart of the gospel, for God justifies the ungodly, the unrighteous, those who are guilty and not innocent.

4:6–8. God does not continue to impute unrighteousness to the sinner who repents but forgives him when he confesses (see Ps. 32:3–5; Ezek. 18:23, 27–28, 32; 33:14–16).

4:9–10. For the Jews, **circumcision** (v. 9) represented the fulfillment of the covenant between God and Abraham (see Gen. 17:10–14), the first divine command of the Pentateuch, that every male child shall be circumcised. By contrast, **uncircumcision** identified the Gentiles. Paul was developing his argument (see 4:1–2) that the covenant between God and Abraham was based on faith, not works. **Not in circumcision, but in uncircumcision** (v. 10) points to the fact that Abraham was declared righteous (see Genesis 15) some fourteen years before he was circumcised (see Genesis 17; for a similar statement, see Gal. 3:17).

4:11–12. Circumcision was, among other things, the outward **sign ... of the righteousness** (v. 11) that God had credited to Abraham for his faith. For this reason, Paul showed that Abraham became **the father of all ... not circumcised** (v. 11) **... and the father of circumcision** (v. 12). Abraham is the father of believing Gentiles (the uncircumcised), because he believed and was justified before the rite of circumcision (the mark of Jews) was instituted. Abraham is also the father of believing Jews. His story thus shows that, for Jew and Gentile alike, there is only one way of justification: the way of faith. All believers (Jews and Gentiles), therefore, are called his spiritual children (v. 12) and referred to as the "seed" or "descendants" of Abraham (see, e.g., Gal. 3:16; Heb. 2:16).

4:13. Paul drew a significant inference here in his argument that the towering figure of Abraham is a model of righteousness by faith, or justification by faith. In 4:9–12, Paul established that the righteousness imputed to Abraham was based on faith apart from and before circumcision. Here Paul made it clear that what was before circumcision was also before and apart from the law, namely, the blessing or divine promise that Abraham would become the father of all, **the heir of the world.** "World" here refers to the creation, as in 1:20. No express mention of this heirship is made in the Genesis account of Abraham. He was promised "seed as the dust of the earth" (Gen. 13:16), possession of the land of Canaan (see Gen. 12:7; 13:14–15; 15:7, 18–21; 17:8), and that all peoples of the earth will be blessed through him (Gen. 12:3; 18:18) or his offspring (Gen. 22:18). Genesis makes it clear, however, that God purposed to work out the destiny of the whole world through Abraham and his offspring; it was therefore implicit in God's promises to Abraham that he and his offspring would "inherit the earth" (see Ps. 37:9, 11, 22, 29, 34; Matt. 5:5). The full realization of this awaits the consummation of the messianic kingdom at Christ's return. **Not … through the law** means that the promise to Abraham was not conditioned on its being merited by works of the law. **His seed** refers to all those of whom Abraham is said to be father (see 4:11–12).

4:14. They which are of the law specifies those whose claim to the inheritance is based on the fulfillment of the law. For **the promise**, see discussion on 4:13.

4:15. Paul could say **the law worketh wrath** because the law reveals sin and even stimulates it (see 7:7–11); it produces wrath, not promise. **Transgression** (Greek, *parabasis*) is an act of crossing, deviating from, or overstepping a clearly defined line. **Where no law is**, there is still sin, but it does not have the character of transgression or violation.

4:16. Here Paul summarized the thought of 4:11–12. For the close correlation between **faith** and **grace**, see 3:24–25; Ephesians 2:8. **Which is of the law** identifies Jewish Christians. **Which is of the faith of Abraham** identifies Gentile Christians, who share Abraham's faith but who, like Abraham, do not possess the law.

4:17. Before him refers to God and here accentuates the importance of God's verdict over that of human opinion or tradition. God considers Abraham to be the **father** of Jews and believing Gentiles alike, no matter how others (especially the Jews) may see him. The specific honorific, **God, who quickeneth the dead**, is primarily a reference to the birth of Isaac through Abraham and Sarah, both of whom were far past the age of childbearing (see 4:19; Gen. 18:11). Secondarily, Paul was alluding also to the resurrection of Christ (see 4:24–25). **Calleth … as though they were** is an expanded description of God, who has the ability to create out of nothing, as He demonstrated in the birth of Isaac. Together, these characterizations of God give focus to the exercise of His divine power in the fulfillment of His promise to Abraham.

4:18. Abraham **against hope believed in hope**. When all hope, as a human possibility, failed, Abraham placed his hope in God. It was not the ambition or gumption of Abraham that generated such hopeful belief, but rather the One who promised (see Heb. 11:11).

4:19–21. Being not weak in faith (v. 19) is a statement that points to the triumph of Abraham's conviction that God would be true to His promise. Abraham had some anxious moments (see Gen. 17:17–18), but God did not count those against him. The words **considered not** illustrate the wisdom of a proper focus. Faith does not refuse to face reality but looks beyond all difficulties to God and His promises. The twin descriptions **his own body now dead** and **the deadness of Sara's womb** underscore the impossibility of human potency as a ground of hope (see 4:18). Sarah was ten years younger than Abraham (see Gen. 17:17) but well past the age of childbearing. Only the power of God (see 4:17), devoted with a promise, can explain such faith and sustain such hope. Because Abraham had faith to believe that God would do **what he had promised** (v. 21), he is characterized as **giving glory to God** (v. 20). Whereas works are man's attempt to establish a claim on God, faith brings glory to Him.

4:22. Therefore means "as a consequence" or "for this reason" and here introduces Paul's quotation of Genesis 15:6. Abraham's faith **was imputed to him for righteousness** because it was true faith, that is, complete confidence in God's promise.

4:23–24. Abraham's experience was not private or individual, **not written for his sake alone** (v. 23), but had broad implications. If justification by faith was true for him, it is universally true, as confirmed in the words **for us also** (v. 24). As Abraham was justified because he believed in a God who brought life from the dead (see 4:19), so Christians will be justified by believing **on him that raised up Jesus our Lord from the dead**.

C. The Fruits of Righteousness (5:1–11)

5:1. Peace with God means more than a subjective feeling (peace of mind); it primarily refers to an objective status, a new relationship with God: once humans were His enemies, but now they are His friends (see 5:10; Eph. 2:16; Col. 1:21–22).

5:2. We have access describes the believer's introduction or entrance to grace. Paul said the believer now stands on the inside, as in an estate that one can admire and enjoy as a resident. Jesus ushers believers into the presence of God. The heavy curtain (of the temple) that separated man from God and God from man has been removed (see discussion on Matt. 27:51). For the Christian, **hope of the glory of God** carries the confidence that the purpose for which God created him will be ultimately realized (see discussion on 3:23).

5:3. The believer can **glory in tribulations**—not "because of" them but "in the midst of" them—because of God's unveiled grace and glorious purpose for the Christian. Paul was advocating, not a morbid view of life, but a joyous and triumphant one.

5:4. A Christian can rejoice in suffering because he knows that it is not meaningless. Part of God's purpose is to produce character in His children.

5:5. Hope maketh not ashamed because hope placed in God is not disappointed. The believer's hope is not to be equated with unfounded optimism. On the contrary, it is the blessed assurance of believers' future destiny and is based on God's love, which is revealed to them by the Holy Spirit and objectively demonstrated to them in the death of Christ. Paul moved from faith (5:1) to hope (5:2, 4–5) to **love** (see 1 Cor. 13:13; see also discussion on 1 Thess. 1:3). **Is shed abroad** is literally, "has been poured out." From this, it may be inferred that God has not held some back but has poured out all there is to pour. The verb indicates a present status resulting from a past action. When we first believed in Christ, the Holy Spirit poured out His love **in our hearts**, and His love for us continues to dwell in us.

5:6. In due time denotes the appointed moment in God's redemptive plan (see Mark 1:15; Gal. 4:4). Compare the words **Christ died for the ungodly** with "justifieth the ungodly" in 4:5 (see discussion there). Christ's love is grounded in God's free grace and is not the result of any inherent worthiness found in its objects (mankind). In fact, it is lavished on believers in spite of their our undesirable character.

5:7–8. The difference of **a righteous man** (v. 7) and **a good man** is one of relationship to the reader. Whereas the former may be thought worthy because of his justness, the latter evokes sympathy because of his benefaction. Paul's point is clear. In the realm of human affairs, what men may aspire to do for the most worthy, God has done for all, even the most unworthy. Christ made the ultimate sacrifice: giving one's life to redeem another. Moreover, we were neither righteous nor good, but **sinners** (v. 8), when **Christ died for us** (see 3:10–12). How profound is the sacrificial love of Christ, a love that acts on our behalf before any "I'm sorry," before any repentance, before any amends—in short, not because of us, but for us. Christ indeed loved His enemies (see 5:10; see Luke 6:27, 34–35).

5:9. By his blood is a reference to Christ's death for humanity's sins (see 3:25), by laying down His life as a sacrifice. **Wrath** refers to the final judgment, as the verb **shall be saved** makes clear (see 1 Thess. 1:9–10).

5:10. Enemies is a word that sums up the status of all for whom Christ died (see 5:7–10). Man is the enemy of God, not the reverse. Thus, the hostility must be removed from man if reconciliation is to be accomplished. God took the initiative in bringing this about through **the death of his Son** (see 5:11; Col. 1:21–22). **Reconciled** points back to 5:1. To "reconcile" is to "put an end to hostility" and is closely related to the term "justify," as the parallelism in 5:9–10 indicates:

5:9	5:10
justified	reconciled
by his blood	by the death of his Son
we shall be saved	we shall be saved

We shall be saved by his life is a reference to the unending life and ministry of the resurrected Christ for His people (see Heb. 7:25). Since believers were reconciled when they were God's enemies, they will be saved because Christ lives to keep them.

5:11. Atonement is the noun form of the verb used twice in 5:10, "reconciled." The noun is translated with the sense of "reconciliation" elsewhere in the New Testament (see 2 Cor. 5:18–19). Reconciliation, like justification (see 5:1), is a present reality for Christians and is something to rejoice about.

D. Summary: Man's Unrighteousness Contrasted with God's Gift of Righteousness (5:12–21)

5:12–21. This passage presents a contrast between Adam and Christ. Adam introduced sin and death into the world; Christ brought righteousness and life. The comparison begun in verse 12 is completed in verse 18. These two verses summarize the whole passage, and these two men, Adam and Christ, sum up the message of the book up to this point. Adam stands for man's condemnation (see 1:18–3:20); Christ stands for the believer's justification (see 3:21–5:11).

5:12. Death, referring to physical death, is the penalty for **sin.** It is also the symbol of spiritual death, man's ultimate separation from God. Although the wording may suggest it, **for that all have sinned** is not a repetition of 3:23. The context shows that Adam's sin involved the rest of mankind in condemnation (see 5:18–19) and death (see 5:15). Humans do not start life with even the possibility of living it sinlessly; humans begin it with a sinful nature (see Gen. 8:21; Pss. 51:5; 58:3; Eph. 2:3).

5:13. Sin is not imputed means that sin is not credited to a person. In other words, God did not lay responsibility or blame. In the period **when there [was] no [Mosaic] law,** sin was not charged against man (see 4:15). Death, however, continued to occur (see 5:14). Since death is the penalty for sin, people between Adam and Moses were involved in the sin of someone else, namely, Adam (see discussion on 5:12).

5:14. A figure is an image or type (Greek, *typos*), and **similitude** is a likeness or analogy. The analogy here is one of contrast. Through his sin, Adam brought universal ruin on the human race. In this act, he is the prototype of Christ, who, through one righteous act (see 5:18), brought universal blessing.

5:15. Many is the same as "all men" in 5:12 (see Isa. 53:11; Mark 10:45). **Much more** describes a degree of difference and is a theme that runs through this section. **The grace of God** is infinitely greater for good than is Adam's sin for evil.

5:16. The gift equals salvation. **Many offences** encompasses the sins of the succeeding generations.

5:17. Shall reign in life points to the future reign of believers with Jesus Christ (see 2 Tim. 2:12; Rev. 22:5).

5:18. The free gift came upon all men does not mean that everyone eventually will be saved. Rather, Paul was saying that salvation is available to all. To be effective, God's gracious gift must be received (see 5:17).

5:19. Made righteous refers to a standing (status) before God (see 2 Cor. 5:21), not to a change in character. The latter (the doctrine of sanctification) is developed in chapters 6–8.

5:20–21. The law entered (v. 20) not to bring about redemption but to point up the need for it. The law made sin even more sinful by revealing what sin is in stark contrast to God's holiness.

V. Righteousness Imparted: Sanctification (chaps. 6–8)

A. Freedom from Sin's Tyranny (chap. 6)

6:1–8:39. After explaining how God has provided for redemption and justification (3:21–5:21), Paul proceeded to explain the doctrine of sanctification, the process by which believers grow to maturity in Christ. He treated this subject in three parts: (1) freedom from sin's tyranny (chap. 6), (2) freedom from the law's condemnation (chap. 7), and (3) life in the power of the Holy Spirit (chap. 8).

6:1. Shall we continue in sin, that grace may abound? This question arose out of what Paul said in 5:20: "where sin abounded, grace did much more abound." Such a question expresses an antinomian ("against law") viewpoint. Apparently, some objected to Paul's teaching of justification by faith alone because they thought it would lead to moral irresponsibility.

6:2. Dead to sin refers to a past event and is explained in 6:3.

6:3–4. Here Paul explained the when and how of the Christian's death to sin. In New Testament times, baptism so closely followed conversion that the two were considered part of one event (see Acts 2:38 and discussion). So although baptism is not a means by which one enters into a vital faith relationship with Jesus Christ, it is closely associated with faith. Baptism depicts graphically what happens as a result of the Christian's union with Christ, which comes with faith. Believers are united with Christ through faith, just as they are united with Adam through their natural birth. As they fell into sin and became subject to death in father Adam, so they now have died and been raised again with Christ, which baptism symbolizes. It is noteworthy that although Paul had yet to visit the Christians in Rome, he expected that they shared the church's understanding of baptism and that its enactment corresponded with burial and resurrection.

Buried with him by baptism into death (v. 4) is amplified in 6:5–7. **By the glory of the Father** means "by the power of God." God's glory is His divine excellence, His perfection. Any one of His attributes is a manifestation of His excellence. Thus, His power is a manifestation of His glory, as is His righteousness (see 3:23). Glory and power are often closely related in the Bible (see Ps. 145:11; Col. 1:11; 1 Peter 4:11; Rev. 1:6; 4:11; 5:12–13; 7:12; 19:1). **Walk in newness of life** is amplified in 6:8–10.

6:5–6. Our old man (v. 6) refers to the unregenerate self, what believers once were. **The body of sin** connotes the self in its pre-Christian state, dominated by sin. This is a figurative expression in which the old self is personified. It is a "body" that can be put to death. For the believer, this old self has been rendered powerless so that it can no longer enslave him to sin, whatever lingering vitality it may yet exert in its death throes.

6:7. Is dead describes the believer's death with Christ to sin's ruling power. **Freed from sin** visualizes the believer's emancipation and release from sin's confines; the believer is set free from its shackles and power.

6:8–9. As resurrection followed death in the experience of Christ, so the believer who dies with Christ is raised to a new quality of moral life here and now. Resurrection in the sense of a new birth is already a fact, and it increasingly exerts itself in the believer's life. Assurance of this comes from Jesus Christ and His total victory over death and sin (see 6:10).

6:10. He died unto sin once shows the efficacy (power) of Christ's death; once was thoroughly effective. In His death, Christ, for the sake of sinners, submitted to the reign of sin (see 5:21), but His death broke the judicial link between sin and death, and He passed forever from the sphere of sin's reign. Having been raised from the dead, He now lives forever to glorify God. **Unto God** means "for the glory of God."

6:11. In contemporary language, **reckon … yourselves** is like saying, "Do the math." When one adds up what Christ has done for the believer, the sum is a new way of seeing oneself. Such reevaluation is the first step toward victory over sin (for the succeeding steps, see discussion on 6:12–13). Believers are **dead indeed unto to sin** and **alive unto God**, and by faith, they are to live in the light of this truth.

6:12–13. These verses are a call for the Christian to become in experience what he already is in position: dead to sin (see 6:5–7, 11) and alive to God (see 6:8–11). The second step toward the Christian's victory over sin is a determination to **Let not sin … reign** (v. 12) in his life. The third step is to **yield … unto God** (v. 13). "Yield" denotes putting oneself in the service of another. It may also echo the language of sacrifice, in which supplicants "present" or "bring" a sacrifice. In either case, sin is an unworthy overlord (see 6:14, 16). **Your members** refers to all the separate capacities of one's being (also in 6:19).

6:14. Sin shall not have dominion over you. Paul conceived of sin as a power that enslaves and therefore personified it. It would be a misunderstanding to take **ye are not under the law** to mean that the

Christian has been freed from all moral authority. Rather, the Christian has been freed from the law in the manner in which God's people were under the law in the Old Testament era. The law does not enable one to resist the power of sin; it only condemns the sinner. Conversely, the believer is **under grace**, and grace enables rather than condemns. For the disciplinary aspect of grace, see Titus 2:11–12.

6:15–23. The question raised in verse 15 seems to have come from those who were afraid that the doctrine of justification by faith alone would remove all moral restraint. Paul rejected such a suggestion and showed that a Christian does not throw morality to the wind. To the contrary, he exchanges sin for righteousness as his master.

6:16–17. The contrast between **sin** (v. 16) and **obedience** suggests that sin is by nature disobedience to God. Conversely, faith entails obedience, a willing submission to God that welcomes His loving will and truth (see 1:5, "obedience of faith"). Accordingly, Paul could speak of believers that **have obeyed from the heart** (v. 17). Christian obedience is not forced or legalistic, but willing. **That form of doctrine** probably refers to a summary of the moral and ethical teachings of Christ that was given to new converts in the early church.

6:18. A Christian has changed masters and is numbered among **the servants of righteousness**. Whereas he was formerly a slave to sin, he has become a slave (a willing servant) to righteousness.

6:19–22. I speak after the manner of men (v. 19) was Paul's way of apologizing for using an imperfect analogy. The word **servants** (v. 19–20), when applied to Christians, who are free in Christ, naturally presents problems. As implied in 6:16–17, "obedience unto righteousness" involves a willing heart, not enslavement. Paul argued that serving righteousness is better than any freedom enjoyed under sin (**free from righteousness**; v. 20). He secured this point by asking his readers to survey the **fruit** (v. 21) of their former service to unrighteousness. Indeed, **the end** (or "harvest") ... **is death**.

The contrast of fruit in verses 21–22 juxtaposes death and eternal life, the opposing trajectories of unrighteousness and righteousness (see 6:18–21). For **made free from sin** (v. 22), see discussion on 6:6. **Holiness** refers to sanctification (for other uses of various forms of the word "sanctification," see 6:19; 1 Cor. 1:30; 1 Thess. 4:3–4, 7; 2 Thess. 2:13; 1 Tim. 2:15; Heb. 12:14; 1 Peter 1:2) and corresponds to the **fruit** of righteousness. Slavery to God produces holiness (or sanctification), and **the end** of the process is **everlasting life** (viewed not in its present sense but in its final, future sense). Without holiness, one cannot receive eternal life (see Heb. 12:14). Anyone who has been justified will surely give evidence of that fact by the presence of holiness in his life.

6:23. Two kinds of servitude are contrasted here. One brings **death** as its **wages**; the other results in **eternal life**, not as wages earned or merited, but as a **gift of God** (for the contrast between wages and gift, see 4:4).

B. Freedom from the Law's Condemnation (chap. 7)

7:1. The law. Although Paul may have had in mind the Mosaic law, his concern here was with the fundamental character of law as such.

7:2–3. These verses illustrate the principle set down in 7:1. Death decisively changes a person's relationship to the law.

7:4. Wherefore ("For this reason") signifies a direct logical relationship between the principle Paul stated in 7:1 and illustrated in 7:2–3 and the conclusion he drew here. By virtue of the bodily death of Jesus Christ, Christians have been made **dead to the law**. The law's power to condemn no longer threatens the Christian, whose "death" here is to be understood in terms of 6:2–7. There, however, he is "dead to sin" (6:2); here he is "dead to the law." The result is that the law has no more hold on him. **By the body of Christ** underscores the personal and physical death He died, the body (self) crucified. The words **married to another** pick up the theme of freedom from the law, illustrated in 7:3, which now finds expression in new life through the resurrected Christ (see 6:5). The purpose of this union is to produce in the believer the **fruit** of holiness.

7:5. In the flesh identifies the control of the sinful nature, a condition, so far as Christians are concerned, that belongs to the past—the unregenerate state. **The motions of sin, which were by the law** shows the law's instrumental power; it not only reveals sin but also stimulates sin. The natural tendency in man is to desire the forbidden thing. **Death** means physical death and, beyond that, spiritual death—final separation from God—which were the **fruit** of our "union" with the law.

7:6. Christians **are delivered from the law** in the sense of its condemnation (see discussion on 7:4). **Wherein we were held** pictures the law as a captor restraining or checking the captives' freedom (see 7:4, 6). **Newness of spirit** relates to the believer's new condition, also signified by the word **now** at the beginning of this verse (see discussion on 8:4). **The oldness of the letter** points to life under the Old Testament law (see 2 Cor. 3:6).

7:7. Is the law sin? This question was occasioned by the remarks about the law in 7:4–6. Paul's use of the first-person pronoun **I** in 7:7–25 is a topic of considerable interest. He seems to have used the first-person pronoun of himself but also as representative of mankind in general (7:7–12) and of Christians in particular (7:13–25). **I had not known sin** points to the important function that the law fulfilled, that of revealing the presence and reality of sin.

7:8. To better appreciate the words **sin, taking occasion by the commandment**, see discussion on 7:5. **Sin was dead** does not mean that it was nonexistent but that it was not fully perceived.

7:9. I was alive without the law once. Here Paul was reviewing his own experience from the vantage point of his present understanding. He was alive before he realized that the law condemned him to death, meaning either before his bar mitzvah or before his conversion, when the true rigor of the law became clear to him (see Luke 18:20–21; Phil. 3:6). **When the commandment came,** or when Paul came to the realization that he stood guilty before the law, again is a reference either to his bar mitzvah, when he (at age thirteen) assumed full responsibility for the law, or to his conversion, when he became aware

of the full force of the law. With the realization that he was condemned to death, Paul could say **I died**, because law reveals sin, and "the wages of sin is death" (6:23).

7:10. For **ordained to life**, see Leviticus 18:5. As it worked out, the law became the avenue through which sin entered, both in Paul's experience and in that of mankind. Instead of giving life, the law brought condemnation; instead of producing holiness, it stimulated sin.

7:12. The law comes from God and reflects His character. **The law is holy.** Despite the despicable use that sin made of the law, the law was not to blame. The law is God's, and as such, it is **holy, and just, and good** (see 7:13–14).

7:13–25. Whether Paul was describing a Christian or non-Christian experience here has been hotly debated through the centuries. That he was speaking of the non-Christian life is suggested by (1) the use of phrases such as "sold under sin" (v. 14), "I know that in me ... dwelleth no good thing" (v. 18), and "wretched man that I am!" (v. 24)—which do not seem to describe Christian experience; (2) the contrast between chapters 7 and 8, which makes it difficult for the other view to be credible; (3) the problem of the value of conversion if one ends up in spiritual misery. In favor of the view that Paul was describing Christian experience are (1) the use of the present tense throughout the passage; (2) Paul's humble opinion of himself (v. 18); (3) his high regard for God's law (vv. 14, 16); (4) the location of this passage in a section dealing with sanctification, the Christian's growth in holiness.

7:13. Sin used a holy thing (the law) for an unholy end (death), which reveals the contemptible nature of sin.

7:14. The law can be called **spiritual** because it had its origin in God. Paul's use of **I am**, the personal pronoun and the verb taken together, suggests that he was describing his present (Christian) experience. **Carnal** ("fleshly") stands in contrast to "spiritual" and describes humanness that cannot rise above a disappointing level of conduct and character. Even a believer has the seeds of rebellion in his heart. Paul's description **sold under sin** is a phrase so strong that many refuse to accept it as descriptive of a Christian. It may graphically point out, however, the failure of even Christians to meet the radical ethical and moral demands of the gospel. It also points up the persistent nature of sin, which in 7:13–25, Paul nearly personified as a tyrannical and irresistible power (see, e.g., 7:17). It must be remembered, however, that sin is resident within all people, part of human nature (see 7:17, 20).

7:15. I allow not renders the Greek for "I do not understand [or 'recognize']." What a person wants to do and what a person does often fail to match. The struggle within creates tension, ambivalence, and confusion.

7:16. I consent unto the law that it is good. Even when Paul was rebellious and disobedient, the Holy Spirit revealed to him the essential goodness of the law.

7:17. It is no more I that do it, but sin is a clear concession to the power of sin; this is in no way an attempt on Paul's part to escape moral responsibility but is a statement of the insidious influence that sin can have over a Christian's life.

7:18–21. In these verses, one can perceive the depth of sin. Humanly, sin is uncontrollable. **In me ... dwelleth no good thing** (v. 18) is a reference to man's fallen nature, as the last phrase of the sentence indicates. Paul was not saying that no goodness at all exists in Christians, but certainly aspirations and coordinate actions are flawed by sin. For **sin ... in me** (v. 20), see discussion on 7:17.

7:22–23. I delight in the law of God (v. 22) refers to the Mosaic law or to God's law generally. It is difficult to see how a non-Christian could say this (see discussion on 7:13–25). Paul's "delight in" (lit., "experience joy in connection with") the law is assigned to **the inward** (inner) **man**, the "I" of Paul as concerns the aspirations of his **mind** (v. 23). This is contrasted with **another law**, a principle or force at work in Paul preventing him from giving obedience to God's law. **The law of my mind**, Paul's desire to obey God's law, was confounded by **the law ... in my members**. By this, Paul meant a power, an au-

thority, or a control exercised in his members, which he revealed is **the law of sin**. Essentially the same as "another law," it opposes and usurps the prerogative of God's law (see Cranfield, *Epistle to the Romans*, p. 364).

7:24. Paul's description **the body of this death** is figurative for "the body of sin" (6:6), which hung on him like a corpse and from which he could not gain freedom.

7:25. The first half of this verse is the answer to the question stated in 7:24: deliverance comes, not through legalistic effort, but through Christ. The second half is a summary of 7:13–24. **I myself** connotes the real self, the inner being that delights in God's law (see 7:22).

C. Life in the Power of the Holy Spirit (chap. 8)

8:1. Therefore now connects the victory sounded in 7:25 to the Spirit-enabled life presented in chapter 8. The law brings **condemnation** because it points out, stimulates, and condemns sin. The Christian, however, is no longer "under the law" (6:14) because the Christian is **in Christ Jesus**, that is, united with Him (see 6:1–10; discussion on 6:11).

8:2. In Christ, there is a different law, **the law of the Spirit of life**. Here "the law" speaks of "the controlling power" (as in 7:22–23) of the Holy Spirit, who is life-giving. Accordingly, **the law of sin and death** refers to the controlling power of sin, which ultimately produces death. Paul used the word "law" in several different ways in Romans, for example, to mean a controlling power (here), God's law (2:17–20; 9:31; 10:3–5), the Pentateuch (3:21b), the Old Testament as a whole (3:19), and a principle (3:27).

8:3. For all of the law's authority, it suffered a power shortage. **What the law could not do** (lit., "the impossibility of the law") is possible, Paul went on to explain, through the power of the Spirit. **The flesh**, which weakened the law, is countered by the Spirit, who comes to believers through **God sending his own Son in the likeness of sinful flesh**. Christ in His incarnation became truly a man but, unlike all other men, was sinless. The final expression **in the flesh** may refer either to man's flesh or to Christ's. If the latter, it states where God condemned sin, namely, in Christ's human (but not sinful) nature. This interpretation seems more consistent with Paul's teaching.

8:4. The righteousness of the law cannot be thought of here without an echo of chapter 7. The law still plays a role in the life of a believer—not, however, as a means of salvation but as a moral and ethical guide, obeyed out of love for God and by the power that the Spirit provides. This is the fulfillment of Jeremiah 31:33–34 (a prophecy of the new covenant). **Fulfilled in us** recognizes that God's aim in sending His Son was that believers might be enabled to embody the true and full intentions of the law. **Walk ... after the Spirit** is equivalent to living according to the influence and power of the Spirit, which is how the law's righteous requirements can be fully met—by no longer letting the sinful nature hold sway but instead yielding to the directing and empowering ministry of the Holy Spirit.

8:5–8. Two mindsets are described here, that of the sinful nature and that of the Spirit. The former leads to **death** (v. 6), and the latter to **life and peace**. The sinful nature is bound up with death (v. 6), hostility to God (v. 7), insubordination (v. 7), and unacceptability to God (v. 8).

8:9. To every Christian belongs the indwelling presence and power of the Holy Spirit. **If any man have not the Spirit of Christ, he is none of his.** If a person does not possess the indwelling Holy Spirit, he does not possess Christ either. The Spirit indwells the Christian as a result of his justification. There is a practical identification of the Spirit of God and the Spirit of Christ in Paul's letters. Paul identified the indwelling of the Spirit as "the Spirit of God" (here, 1 Cor. 3:16), "the Spirit of Christ" (here), "the Spirit of his Son" (Gal. 4:6), "the Holy Ghost" (1 Cor. 6:19; 2 Tim. 1:14), as well as writing of Christ's indwelling the believer (Gal. 2:20; Eph. 3:17; Col. 1:27, 29).

8:10–11. The body is dead because of sin (v. 10), even as a Christian's body is subject to physical death, the consequence of sin, **but the** (Holy)

Spirit is life because of righteousness. This is a compact way of saying that the indwelling and life-giving Spirit is an evidence of the believer's justification through Christ, and, Paul continued, it is an evidence, even a guarantee of, the resurrection: **he ... shall also quicken your mortal bodies** (v 11). The life of the Spirit is evidenced by a Spirit-controlled life (see 8:4–9), which in turn provides assurance that one's resurrection is certain even now (for the close connection between the resurrection of Christ and that of believers, see 1 Cor. 6:14; 15:20, 23; 2 Cor. 4:14; Phil. 3:21; 1 Thess. 4:14).

8:12–14. In these verses, Paul very plainly and practically illustrated that the indwelling Spirit can be deduced from the manifestation of the Spirit's life. There are no **debtors ... to the flesh** (v. 12) among those possessing the Spirit. Character and conduct correspond to the rule of the Spirit. **The sons of God** (v. 14) points in the same direction. The "biological" features that distinguish God's children are not physical, but spiritual, as evidenced by a growing likeness in character and conduct. It must be remembered, however, that although God is the Father of all in the sense that He created all and His love and providential care are extended to all (see Matt. 5:45), not all are His children. Jesus said to the unbelieving Jews of His day, "Ye are of your father the devil" (John 8:44). People become children of God through faith in God's unique Son (see John 1:12–13), and the hallmark of this relationship is one's being led by God's Spirit.

8:15. Paul drew on his readers' familiarity with the practices of **adoption** to communicate a spiritual truth greater than its analogy. The underlying Greek term for "adoption" occurs four other times in the New Testament and only in Paul's letters (8:23; 9:4; Gal. 4:5; Eph. 1:5; see discussion on Gal. 4:5). Common among the Greeks and Romans, adoption granted the adopted son all the privileges of a natural-born son, including inheritance rights. Paul, however, went further. In the Mediterranean world, such legal rights were no guarantee of familial affection, whereas the Spirit of God's family assures it. Paul therefore complemented the legal privileges of the child adopted into God's family with a picture of familial affection: God's children greet their Father with the cry, **Abba, Father**. "Abba" (Aramaic for "Father") is expressive of an especially close relationship to God. It is akin in intimacy to "Papa." Through adoption, God's love for His own Son now welcomes His adopted children. Christians are adopted sons by grace; Christ, however, is God's Son by nature.

8:16. Beareth witness with our spirit expresses the inner testimony of the Holy Spirit to believers' relationship to Christ. **The children of God** and "the sons of God" (7:14) are synonymous terms in Paul's letters.

8:17–18. Heirs (v. 17) are those who have already entered, at least partially, into the possession of their inheritance. Adopted sons are **joint-heirs with Christ**. Everything really belongs to Christ, but by grace, Christians share in what is His. The Greek construction of **if so be that we suffer with him** does not set forth a condition but states a fact. The meaning, then, is not that there is some doubt about sharing Christ's glory; rather, despite the fact that Christians presently suffer, they are assured a future entrance into their inheritance. **The glory which shall be revealed in us** (v. 18) most certainly includes a personal glorification, "the recovery of the divine image or glory originally lost at the Fall, but restored in Christ" (Black, *Romans*, p. 120; see discussion on 3:23).

8:19. The creature here means "that which is created," "the creation," and refers to God's creation both animate and inanimate exclusive of human beings (see 8:22–23, where "the whole creation" and "ourselves" are contrasted). **The manifestation of the sons of God** points to the full manifestation of all that this means (see 1 John 3:1–2). Christians are already sons of God, but the full manifestation will not come until Christ returns (see 1 John 3:1–2).

8:20. Was made subject to vanity is a reference to Genesis 3:17–19. In the Bible, "vanity," or that which is "futile," means "without use" or "without result." **In hope** is possibly an allusion to the promise of Genesis 3:15.

8:21. Shall be delivered from the bondage of corruption. The physical universe is destined, not for destruction (annihilation), but for renewal (see 2 Peter 3:13; Rev. 21:1). Living things will no longer be subject to death and decay, as they are today.

8:22. The Greek words for **groaneth and travaileth** occur in the New Testament only here. Futility (see 8:20) compounds the hardships of existence and endurance (see 8:19). Some interpreters surmise that here creation is personified as a woman in labor waiting for the birth of her child. If so, the **now** painfully endures the "not yet" in full expectancy, unable to produce what God alone can deliver.

8:23. The firstfruits of the Spirit is an expression drawn from the imagery of harvest. In general, the firstfruits forecast the quality and delivery of the whole harvest. Similarly, the Christian's possession of the Holy Spirit is not only evidence of his present salvation (8:14, 16) but also a pledge of his future inheritance, and not only a pledge but also the down payment on that inheritance (see 2 Cor. 1:22; 5:5; Eph. 1:14). Christians are already God's children; **the adoption** (see discussion on 8:15) is a reference to the full realization of our inheritance in Christ. **The redemption of our body** points to the resurrection as the final stage of one's adoption (for the Spirit's vital role in this stage, see 8:11; 2 Cor. 1:22; 5:4–5; Eph. 1:13–14; 4:30). The first stage was God's predestination of one's adoption (see Eph. 1:5); the second is one's present inclusion as children of God (see 8:14; Gal. 3:26).

8:24–25. We are saved (v. 24) by faith (see Eph. 2:8), not **by hope**, but hope accompanies salvation. Hope, as Paul alluded, is a close ally of faith, for it appreciates what it cannot see, just as faith does. Real hope brings patient endurance.

8:26. Likewise means "similarly" or "in the same way." As hope sustains the believer in suffering, so the Holy Spirit helps him in prayer. **With groanings which cannot be uttered** suggests "groanings" that are inaudible yet deeply felt. In 8:23, it is the believer who groans; here it is the Holy Spirit. Whether Paul meant words that are unspoken or words that cannot be expressed in human language is not clear — probably the former, though 8:27 seems to suggest the latter. As Barrett (*Epistle to the Romans*, p. 168) put it, "communion between Spirit[-filled worshipper] and God is immediate and needs no spoken word."

8:27. The relationship between the Holy Spirit and God the Father is so close that the Holy Spirit's prayers need not be audible. God knows His every thought.

8:28. Good can best be understood as that which conforms one "to the image of His Son" (8:29). **Called** connotes an effectual calling, the call of God to which there is invariably a positive response.

8:29. Some insist that the knowledge referred to in **did foreknow** is not abstract but is couched in love and mixed with purpose. They hold that God not only knew believers before they had any knowledge of Him but that He also knew them, in the sense of choosing them by His grace, before the foundation of the world (see Eph. 1:4; 2 Tim. 1:9 and discussions). Others believe that Paul was referring to the fact that in eternity past God knew those who by faith would become His people. As it is used here, **predestinate** connotes moral conformity to the likeness of His Son. **That he might be the firstborn amongst many brethren**. God foreknew, predestined, and conformed believers to Christ's likeness so that the Son might hold the position of highest honor in the great family of God.

8:30. Predestinate … glorified outlines the sequence by which God carries out predestination. The word **glorified** should not be separated from, but rather magnified by, Paul's other references to glory in this chapter (8:17–18, 21). Since this final stage is firmly grounded in God's set purpose, it is as certain as if it had already happened.

8:31. In Greek, **If God be for us** expresses no question mark in Paul's mind. The form of the condition makes it clear that there is no doubt about it.

8:32. The argument (from the greater to the lesser) here is similar to that in 5:9–10. If God gave the supreme gift of **his own Son** to save humanity, He will certainly also give whatever is necessary to bring to fulfillment the work begun at the cross (see discussion on Gen. 22:16).

8:33–34. A court of law is in view here. No charge can be brought against the Christian because God has already pronounced a verdict of not guilty.

8:34. Paul gave three reasons why no one can condemn God's elect: (1) Christ died for them; (2) He is alive and seated **at the right hand of God**, the position of power; and (3) He is interceding for them.

8:35–39. Paul wanted to show his readers that suffering does not separate believers from Christ but actually carries them along toward their ultimate goal.

8:36. Paul quoted Psalm 44:22 to show that suffering has always been part of the experience of God's people.

8:37. Through him that loved us refers especially to Christ's death on the cross.

8:38–39. Nor height, nor depth (v. 38) shows that it is impossible to get beyond God's loving reach. **Nor any other creature** includes all created things. Only God is not included, and He is the one who has justified believers (see 8:33).

VI. God's Righteousness Vindicated: The Problem of the Apparent Rejection of Israel (chaps. 9–11)

A. The Justice of the Rejection (9:1–29)

9:1–2. Paul offered solemn testimony to **the truth** (v. 1) with a triple confirmation: (1) **in Christ**; (2) **I lie not**; (3) **my conscience … in the Holy Ghost**. The conscience is a reliable guide only when enlightened by the Holy Spirit. Paul wanted his readers to know, and know without reservation, the heartache that accompanied his knowledge of the truth about his own people, the Jews of his own heritage who had rejected Jesus Christ. Their fate without Christ was not something Paul spoke about with indifference or superiority, only with great pain.

9:3. The Greek word for **accursed** is *anathema* and means "delivered over to the wrath of God for eternal destruction" (see 1 Cor. 12:3; 16:22; Gal. 1:8–9). Such was Paul's great love for his fellow Jews that he would have forfeited his own salvation if such a substitutionary action could have benefited them (for a similar expression of love, see Exod. 32:32). That bespeaks the depth of Paul's heartfelt love and longing to see his people accept God's provision, the substitutionary sacrifice of Jesus Christ. Christ alone, however, could make the necessary sacrifice (see Gal. 3:10, 13).

9:4. Israelites denotes the descendants of Jacob (who was renamed Israel by God; see Gen. 32:28). The name was used of the entire nation (see Judg. 5:7), then of the northern kingdom after the nation was divided (see 1 Kings 12), the southern kingdom being called Judah. During the intertestamental period and in New Testament times, Palestinian Jews used the title to indicate that they were the chosen people of God. Its use here is especially relevant because Paul was about to show that, despite Israel's unbelief and disobedience, God's promises to her are still valid. By **adoption**, Israel had been accepted as God's son (see Exod. 4:22–23; Jer. 31:9; Hos. 11:1). Because of Israel's special relationship with God, **glory**, by association, involves the evidence of the presence of God among His people (see Exod. 16:7, 10; Lev. 9:6, 23; Num. 16:19). Israel's unique relationship with God is marked by its **covenants** with God, for example, the Abrahamic (Gen. 15:17–21; 17:1–8); the Mosaic (Exod. 19:5; 24:1–4), renewed on the plains of Moab (Deut. 29:1–15), at Mounts Ebal and Gerizim (Josh. 8:30–35), and at Shechem (Joshua 24); the Levitical (Num. 25:12–13; Jer. 33:21; Mal. 2:4–5); the Davidic (2 Samuel 7; 23:5; Ps. 89:3–4, 28–29; 132:11–12); and the new (prophesied in Jer. 31:31–40). **The promises** refer especially to those made to Abraham (Gen. 12:7; 13:14–17; 17:4–8; 22:16–18) but also include the many Old Testament messianic promises (e.g., 2 Sam. 7:12, 16; Isa. 9:6–7; Jer. 23:5; 31:31–34; Ezek. 34:23–24; 37:24–28).

9:5. The fathers are the patriarchs Abraham, Isaac, Jacob, and his sons. **Christ ... who is over all, God** sets forth one of the clearest statements of the deity of Jesus Christ found in the entire New Testament, assuming that "God" refers to "Christ" (see 1:4; Matt. 1:23; 28:19; Luke 1:35; 5:20–21; John 1:1, 3, 10, 14, 18; 5:18; 20:28; 2 Cor. 13:14; Phil. 2:6; Col. 1:15–20; 2:9; Titus 2:13; Heb. 1:3, 8; 2 Peter 1:1; Rev. 1:13–18; 22:13).

9:6. The word of God includes His clearly stated purpose, which has not failed, because **they are not all Israel, which are of Israel**. Paul was not denying the election of all Israel (as a nation) but rather stating that there is a separation within Israel, that of unbelieving Israel and believing Israel. Physical descent is no guarantee of a place in God's family.

9:7–8. The seed (v. 7) refers to physical descendants (e.g., Ishmael and his offspring), as Paul made clear in the expression **children of the flesh** (v. 8), those merely biologically descended from Abraham. By contrast, **children of God** refers to the Israel of faith (see 9:4). Not all Israelites were God's children.

9:9–13. Paul makes clear that God's promise was given prior to birth and prior to any good or bad behavior in order to dismiss a challenge to his point on the ground that his distinction belonged not to promise but to a difference between Isaac and Ismael.

9:11. Neither having done any good or evil shows that God's choice of Jacob was based on sovereign freedom, not on the fulfillment of any prior conditions. **The purpose of God according to election** means God's purpose is embodied in His election (see discussion on Eph. 1:4). A further proof is presented in the words **not of works, but of him that calleth** (for "calleth," see 8:28 and discussion). Before Rebekah's children were even born, God made a choice; obviously, that choice was not based on works.

9:13. Jacob have I loved, but Esau have I hated sounds very harsh but is the Semitic equivalent of "Jacob I chose, but Esau I rejected" (see Mal. 1:2–3). In 9:6–13, Paul dealt with national election and portrayed the nation Israel (Jacob) over the nation Edom (Esau). His intention is evident in light of the problem he was addressing: How can God's promise stand when so many who comprise Israel (in the Old Testament collective sense) are unbelieving and therefore cut off?

9:14. Is there unrighteousness with God? God forbid. Is He unjust to elect on the basis of His sovereign freedom, as with Jacob and Esau?

9:15. Quoting Exodus 33:19, Paul denied injustice in God's dealing with Isaac and Ishmael, and Jacob and Esau, by appealing to God's sovereign right to dispense mercy as He chooses.

9:16. It refers to God's choice, which is not controlled in any way by man. Paul made it clear, however, that the basis for Israel's rejection was her unbelief (see 9:30–32).

9:17. Pharaoh is the pharaoh of the exodus. **Raised thee up** means "made you ruler of Egypt." God's **purpose** was exercised through Pharaoh, **that I might shew my power ... and that my name might be declared** ("published"). "My name" represents the character of God (see Exod. 34:6–7), particularly as revealed in the exodus (see Exod. 15:13–18; Josh. 2:10–11; 9:9; 1 Sam. 4:8).

9:18. The first part of this verse again echoes Exodus 33:19 (see Rom. 9:15), and the last part echoes such texts as Exodus 7:3; 9:12; 14:4, 17, in which God is said to have hardened the hearts of Pharaoh and the Egyptians. **Whom he will** cannot mean that God is arbitrary in His **mercy**, because Paul ultimately based God's rejection of Israel on her unbelief (see 9:30–32).

9:19. This objection could be phrased, "If God determines whose heart is hardened and whose is not, how can God blame anyone for hardening his heart?"

9:20. Who art thou that repliest against God? Paul was not silencing all of man's questioning of God but was speaking to those with an impenitent, God-defying attitude who wanted to make God answerable to man for what He does and who defamed God's character with their questions.

9:21. The analogy between God and **the potter** and between man and **the vessel** (the pot) should not be pressed to the extreme. The main point is the sovereign freedom of God in dealing with man.

9:22–24. These verses are an illustration of the principle stated in 9:21. The emphasis is on God's mercy, not His wrath, as verse 24 makes clear. No one can call God to account for what He does, but He does not exercise His freedom of choice arbitrarily, and He shows great patience toward even the objects of His wrath. In light of 2:4, the purpose of such patience is to bring about repentance. Both God's judgment and His saving power are magnified and intensified with His continued restraint. For **glory** (v. 23), see

discussion on 3:23. Because of God's forbearance in the service of His purpose, "the children of the promise" (9:8–9), **the vessels of mercy**, are called **not of the Jews only, but also of the Gentiles** (v. 24) .

9:25–26. In the original context, these passages from Hosea (the two quotes are from Hos. 2:23 and 1:10 respectively) refer to the spiritual restoration of Israel. Paul, however, found in them the principle that God is a saving, forgiving, restoring God who delights to take those **which were not my people** (v. 25) and make them **my people**. Paul then applied this principle to Gentiles, whom God made His people by sovereignly grafting them into a covenant relationship (see chap. 11); they are **children of the living God** (v. 26).

9:27–29. The two passages from Isaiah indicate that only a small **remnant** (v. 27) will survive from the great multitude of Israelites. For Paul, the remnant and the **seed** (v. 29) were reduced to one: Jesus Christ (see Gal. 3:16). God's calling includes both Jews and Gentiles (see 9:24), but the vast majority are Gentiles, as 9:30 suggests.

B. The Cause of the Rejection (9:30–10:21)

9:30–32. Here Paul took a new step in his argument: the reason for Israel's rejection lay in the nature of her disobedience; she failed to obey her own God-given law, which in reality was pointing to Christ. She pursued the law, yet not by faith but by works. Thus, the real cause of Israel's rejection was that she failed to believe.

The law of righteousness (v. 31) should be understood as "the law that prescribed the way to righteousness," as is made very clear in verse 32. Paul did not reject obedience to the law but rather rejected righteousness by works, the attempt to use the law to put God in one's debt.

Israel's pursuit of righteousness was **not by faith** (v. 32). The failure of Israel was not that she pursued the wrong thing (i.e., righteous standing before God) but that she pursued righteousness by works in a futile effort to merit God's favor rather than pursuing it by faith. **That stumblingstone** refers to Jesus, the Messiah. God's rejection of Israel was not arbitrary but was based on Israel's rejection of God's way of gaining righteousness: faith.

9:33. Apparently, early Christians commonly used these two passages from Isaiah (Isa. 8:14; 28:16), which are here combined, in defense of Jesus' messiahship (see 1 Peter 2:4, 6–8; see also Ps. 118:22; Luke 20:17–18).

10:1. Paul often prayed for the churches (see Eph. 1:15–23; Col. 1:3; 1 Thess. 1:2–3; 2 Thess. 1:3). Here his **prayer to God for Israel** was for the salvation of his fellow countrymen.

10:2. A zeal of God should be understood as zeal "for" God rather than "from" God. The Jews' zeal for God (see Acts 21:20; 22:3; Gal. 1:14) was commendable in that God was its object, but it was flawed because it was not based on right knowledge about God's way of salvation. Paul, before his conversion, had been an example of such zeal (see Gal. 1:14).

10:3. Their own refers to a righteous standing based on mere human effort. **Being ignorant of God's righteousness** led the Jews to **establish their own righteousness** ("establish" means to "set up" or "put into force") and also caused them to resist and not submit to **the righteousness of God**. Paul probably had in mind their rejection of the Messiah, as 9:33 would suggest. Righteous standing based on faith in Jesus Christ (see 1:17) comes from God as a gift and cannot be earned by man's works.

10:4. Christ is the end of the law. Although the Greek word for "end" (*telos*) can mean either (1) "termination," "cessation," or (2) "goal," "culmination," "fulfillment," it seems best here to understand it in the latter sense. Christ is the fulfillment of the law (see Matt. 5:17) in the sense that He brought it to completion by obeying perfectly its demands and by fulfilling its types and prophecies. The Christian is no longer "under the law" (6:15) since Christ has freed him from its condemnation, but the law still plays a role in his life. He is liberated by the Holy Spirit to fulfill the law's moral demands (see 8:4). **For righteousness**, or "So that there may be righteousness," speaks of the righteous standing before God that Christ makes available **to every one that believeth** (see discussions on 1:17; 3:24).

10:5. The man which doeth those things shall live by them is a quotation of Leviticus 18:5, which speaks of the righteousness to which Israel was called under the Sinai covenant (see *KJV Study Bible* note on Lev. 18:5; see also Deut. 6:25). Some understand Paul's purpose in quoting this text as describing the way of obtaining righteousness ("shall live") by keeping the law (see 2:6–10). Others think that the reference is to Christ, who perfectly fulfilled the law's demands and thus makes salvation available to all who believe (see Heb. 5:9).

10:6–8. In these verses, **the righteousness which is of faith** (v. 6) is personified (**speaketh**), a vivid way of letting the Old Testament speak for itself. Paul's purpose in this quotation was to explain the nature of the righteousness that is by faith. It does not require heroic feats such as bringing Christ down from heaven or up from the grave. In its original context, Deuteronomy 30:12–13 refers to the law, and Paul here applied the basic principle to Christ.

"The righteousness which is of faith speaketh" (v. 6) continues to communicate in verse 8, **But what saith it?** The answer is from Deuteronomy 30:14: **The word is nigh thee.** In the Old Testament passage, "the word" is God's word as found in the law. Paul applied the passage to the gospel, **the word of faith**, the main point being the accessibility of the gospel. Righteousness is gained by faith, not by deeds, and is readily available to anyone who will receive it freely from God through Christ. **Even in thy mouth, and in thy heart** corresponds to "shalt confess ... and shalt believe" in 10:9.

10:9–11. Confess with thy mouth the Lord Jesus (v. 9) echoes the earliest Christian confession of faith (see 1 Cor. 12:3), probably used at baptisms. Since "Lord" (Greek, *kyrios*) is used over six thousand times in the Septuagint (the Greek translation of the Old Testament) to translate the name of Israel's God (Yahweh), it is clear that Paul, when using this word of Jesus, was ascribing deity to Him. What one is to "confess with thy mouth" is his genuine inner belief, which is **in thine heart**. In biblical terms, the heart is the seat not merely of the emotions and affections but also of the intellect and will. **God hath raised him from the dead** is the bedrock truth of Christian doctrine (see 1 Cor. 15:4, 14, 17) and the central thrust of apostolic preaching (see, e.g., Acts 2:31–32; 3:15; 4:10; 10:40). Christians believe not only that Jesus lived but also that He still lives. The future tense in **shalt be saved** brings into focus the certainty of final salvation— salvation at the last day. Salvation involves inward belief (**with the heart**; v. 10) as well as outward confession (**with the mouth**); the two cannot be separated, although the order no longer follows Deuteronomy 30:14 but instead corresponds to experience. Here righteousness and salvation are not separate stages but one and the same. A confirmation of this is Paul's citation of Isaiah 28:16: **Shall not be ashamed** (v. 11), which is a proof of both righteousness and salvation.

10:12. There is no difference between the Jew and the Greek in the sense that both are on the same footing as far as salvation is concerned (see 10:13).

10:13. Peter cited this same passage (Joel 2:32) on the day of Pentecost (see Acts 2:21).

10:14–16. Since it might be argued that Jews had never had a fair opportunity to hear and respond to the gospel, Paul, through a series of rhetorical questions, stated (in reverse order) the conditions necessary to call on Christ and be saved: (1) a preacher sent from God, (2) proclamation of the message, (3) hearing the message, (4) believing the message.

How beautiful are the feet of them that preach the gospel of peace (v. 15). This is a quotation from Isaiah 52:7, which refers to those who brought the exiles the good news of their imminent release from captivity in Babylon. Paul applied it to gospel preachers, who bring the good news of release from captivity to sin. For **obeyed the gospel** (v. 16), see 1:5. Faith not only apprehends the content of the gospel but responds submissively to the Lord of the gospel. **Not all** presents a contrast to the "Whosoever" of 10:11. The testimony of Isaiah verifies that resistance and rejection is based not on the message but on the absence of faith (see Isa. 53:1). What was true in Isaiah's day was relevant in Paul's day and is still relevant today.

10:17. The word of God refers either to the gospel concerning Christ or to Christ speaking His message through His messengers.

10:18. Their sound belongs to Paul's citation of Psalm 19:4 (from the Septuagint), where it is paralleled with "their words" and refers to the testimony of the heavens to the glory of God. Here Paul applied "their sound" to gospel preachers and used it to show that Israel could not offer the excuse that she had not had the opportunity to hear. "Their sound" (originally used to describe God's revelation in nature) aptly describes the widespread preaching of the gospel, showing that Jews had ample opportunity to hear the message of redemption.

10:19. Did not Israel know? The quotation that follows (from Deut. 32:21) answers this question by suggesting that the Gentiles, whom the Jews considered to be spiritually unenlightened, understood. If the Gentiles understood the message, surely the Jews could have. **Them that are no people** refers to the Gentiles, who were not a nation of God's forming in the sense that Israel was.

10:20–21. Isaiah (Isa. 65:1–2) added a second witness to that of Moses (see 10:19). The opportunity that was open-ended (**All day long**) for Israel had been opened to others. The responsibility for Israel's rejection as a nation rested with Israel herself. She had failed to meet God's requirement, namely, faith. Incidentally, Paul himself followed a similar course in his ministry: first to the Jew and then to the Gentile (see Acts 13:46–47).

C. Facts That Lessen the Difficulty (chap. 11)

1. The Rejection Is Not Total (11:1–10)

11:1. Cast away implies total rejection. The expression comes from 1 Samuel 12:22 and Psalm 94:14, where God promises to never forsake Israel (see also Jer. 31:37). In Greek, the question Paul asked clearly expects a negative answer: "God has not cast away His people, has He?" Paul added to what is already explicit in the Greek: an emphatic **God forbid**. Indeed, Paul himself was proof that God had not totally rejected the Jews.

11:2–4. Paul reiterated the impossibility that God should "cast away" (11:1) His people but added the words **which he foreknew** (v. 2). As in 8:29 (see discussion there), God's foreknowledge is associated with His election. Since they are God's chosen people, a faithful remnant has always existed among the Jewish people (see 11:5). Paul made this point by quoting the exasperated pleading of Elijah against Israel (see 1 Kings 19:10, 14, 18). In the face of Israel's apostasy, Elijah lamented that he alone believed in God and that his life was in danger. **I have reserved** (v. 4) points to God's faithfulness, which 11:5 says is "according to [God's] election of grace."

11:5–6. If God had "cast away" (11:1) His people, no **remnant** (v. 5) would have remained. As it was in Elijah's day, so it was in Paul's day (**Even so**). Despite widespread apostasy, a faithful remnant of Jews remained. **According to the election of grace** means the remnant existed because of God's grace, not because of their good works.

11:7. What then? indicates that Paul was drawing a conclusion from 11:1–6. **Israel … seeketh** refers to a righteous standing before God, which eluded the greater part of Israel. **The election hath obtained it.** In other words, the faithful remnant within Israel obtained righteousness through faith in response to the gracious choice of God. **The rest were blinded** because they refused the way of faith (see 9:31–32). God made them impervious to spiritual truth (see discussion on Isa. 6:8–13) — a judicial hardening of Israel.

11:8. Scripture (Isa. 29:10; see Deut. 29:4) accounts for Israel's condition and remains relevant **unto this day.** The spiritual dullness of the Jews had continued from Isaiah's day to Paul's day.

11:9–10. This passage from Psalm 69:22–23 was probably originally spoken by David concerning his enemies. Paul used it to describe the results of the divine hardening of Israel.

2. The Rejection Is Not Final (11:11–24)

11:11. The form of Paul's question corresponds to the pattern of the question in 11:1; it explicitly expects a negative answer, to which Paul again added an emphatic **God forbid** (see 11:1). **Have they stumbled that they should fall?** "They" corresponds to "the rest" in 11:7, and "should fall" (Greek, *piptō*; "fall down") is distinguished from the word "stumbled" (Greek, *ptaiō*; "trip") in a way that suggests a dire fall resulting in destruction. **Their fall** (here and in 11:12) uses yet a different word in Greek (*paraptōma*), denoting a "trespass" or a "transgression," and refers to the Jews' rejection of the gospel. In accordance with Deuteronomy 32:21, God's purpose for "their fall" is **to provoke them to jealousy** (see 11:14; 10:19). Gentiles enjoying the privileges of God's salvation through faith will prod "the rest [who] were blinded" (11:7) to accept what they have hitherto rejected.

11:12. The riches of the world is equivalent to **the riches of the Gentiles** and refers to the abundant benefits of salvation that believing Gentiles already enjoyed, which had come about because of the Jews' rejection of the gospel. That rejection had caused the apostles to turn to the Gentiles (see Acts 13:46–48; 18:6). **The diminishing of them** is equivalent to "their transgression" (see discussion on 11:11) but focuses on the loss that this transgression entailed. **How much more** indicates a correlation based on a pattern of lesser to greater or light to heavy (for more on this correlation, see discussion on 11:15. **Their fulness** speaks of the salvation of Israel (see 11:26–27; see also "the fulness of the Gentiles," 11:25).

11:13–14. Paul positioned his own ministry and his Gentile hearers within God's purpose to provoke **them which are my flesh** (v. 14) to jealousy (see 11:11) and salvation. As **the apostle of the Gentiles** (v. 13; see 1:5; Acts 9:15; Gal. 1:16; 2:7, 9), Paul's ministry was an end in itself, worthy of his greatest endeavor: **I magnify mine office.** Yet in turning to the Gentiles, he could hardly be accused of turning away from unbelieving Jews, for in God's purpose, the ministry to the one is a ministry to the other. **Provoke to emulation** (v. 14) means "provoke to jealousy" (see 11:11)

11:15. As in 11:12, here Paul's train of thought runs from lesser to greater. **Casting away** is here used of God's temporary and partial exclusion of the Jews. **The reconciling of the world** is similar to "the riches of the world" (11:12; see discussion there). **Life from the dead** is equivalent to "how much more" in 11:12. The sequence of redemptive events, each of which leads to the next, is: (1) the "fall" and "diminishing" (11:12) of Israel; (2) the salvation of the Gentiles; (3) the jealousy of Israel; (4) the "fulness" (11:12) of Israel when the hardening is removed; (5) even more riches for the Gentiles. To what, however, does the "how much more" (11:12) for the Gentiles refer, which Paul described here as "life from the dead"? Three views may be suggested: (1) an unprecedented spiritual awakening in the world; (2) the consummation of redemption at the resurrection of the dead; (3) a figurative expression describing the conversion of the Jews as a joyful and glorious event (like resurrection), which will result in even greater blessing for the world. Of these three views, the first seems least likely, since before Israel's spiritual rebirth, the fullness of the Gentiles will have already come in (see 11:25). Since the Gentile mission will then be complete, a period of unprecedented spiritual awakening seems to have no place. The second view also seems unlikely, since the context suggests nothing of bodily resurrection.

11:16. The first half of this verse is a reference to Numbers 15:17–21. Part of the dough made from the first of the harvested grain (the firstfruit) was offered to the Lord, which consecrated the whole batch. **The firstfruit** and **the root** refer to the patriarchs, and **the lump** and **the branches** refer to the Jewish people. In this analogy of the firstfruit, **holy** means "consecrated to God." Paul was saying, not that all Jews are righteous (i.e., saved), but that God will be true to His promises concerning them (see 3:3–4) because of the patriarchs, which involves God's election of grace. Paul foresaw a future for Israel, even though she is for a time set aside.

11:17. In 11:17–24, Paul used the metaphor of a tree to vividly explain what he had taught so far in chapter 11. As he established in 11:16, "the branches" refers to the Jewish people. Even as Paul drew a distinction between the "remnant" (11:5) and "the rest [who] were blinded" (11:7), **some of the branches**

... broken off is a new word picture corresponding to their "fall" (11:11–12), their "diminishing" (11:12), and "the casting away of them" (11:15). **A wild olive tree** refers to Gentile Christians. What Paul earlier described as "the riches of the Gentiles" (11:12) and "the reconciling of the world" (11:15) belongs to the wild olive that was **graffed in**. The usual grafting procedure is to insert a shoot or slip of a cultivated tree into a common or wild one. In Paul's metaphor, however, the grafting procedure is "contrary to nature" (11:24): a wild olive branch (the Gentiles) is grafted into a cultivated olive tree. Such a procedure is unnatural, which is precisely the point. Normally, such a graft would be unfruitful. **The root and fatness** points to the patriarchs. The whole olive tree, the old olive tree with its graft from a wild start, represents the people of God.

11:18–19. Paul warned the graft (the Gentiles) against an attitude of superiority: **thou bearest not the root, but the root thee** (v. 18). The salvation of Gentile Christians is dependent on the Jews, especially the patriarchs (e.g., the Abrahamic covenant; see John 4:22). For **The branches were broken off** (v. 19), see 11:17.

11:20–21. With the word **Well** (v. 20), Paul granted the correctness of the hypothetical rebuttal in 11:19 (compare the same Greek word in John 4:17: "Thou hast well said"). He went on, however, to warn his readers against the attitude behind the statement. Behind **unbelief** is arrogance. The graft that **standest by faith** must remember that pride comes before a fall (see Prov. 16:8; 3:34; 1 Peter 5:5). Better is humility that brings grace, and **fear** that acknowledges God (on "the fear of God," see discussion on Gen. 20:11; see also Prov. 3:7; Phil. 2:12–13; Heb. 4:1; 1 Peter 1:17).

11:22. Any adequate doctrine of God must include **the goodness and severity of God**. These two elements should not be separated. When one ignores His goodness, God seems a ruthless tyrant; when one ignores His sternness, He seems a doting Father.

11:23. God is able to graff them in again. Paul held out hope for the Jews. God is able to restore them (see Matt. 19:26; Mark 10:27; Luke 18:27).

11:24. Paul cautioned the Gentiles against limiting God with the "impossible." What is possible with God (**how much more**) could be seen in their own salvation experience: **contrary to nature**, God had grafted the Gentiles into the family of God (see Eph. 2:12–13). Paul recognized that such a grafting procedure was not commonly practiced (see discussion on 11:17). Obviously, the reasoning in this verse is more theological than horticultural. It would be difficult horticulturally to graft broken branches back into the parent tree, but the Jews really belong (historically and theologically) to the parent tree. Thus, they will "much more" **be graffed into their own olive tree**.

3. God's Ultimate Purpose Is Mercy (11:25–36)

11:25. Paul's teaching on Israel and the Gentiles belongs to God's **mystery**: a divine truth hidden from God's people in the past but now revealed in the gospel. The so-called mystery religions of Paul's day used the Greek word *mystērion* to refer to something that was to be revealed only to the initiated. Paul, however, used it to refer to truth formerly hidden in God's eternal plans but now revealed by God for all to know and understand (see 16:25; 1 Cor. 2:7; 4:1; 13:2; 14:2; 15:51; Eph. 1:9; 3:3–4, 9; 5:32; 6:19; Col. 1:26–27; 2:2; 4:3; 2 Thess. 2:7; 1 Tim. 3:9, 16). Paul used the word "mystery" to refer to (1) the incarnation (1 Tim. 3:16; see discussion there), (2) the death of Christ (1 Cor. 2:7, "the wisdom of God in a mystery"), (3) God's purpose to sum up all things in Christ (Eph. 1:9) and especially to include both Jews and Gentiles in the New Testament church (Eph. 3:3–6), (4) the change that will take place at the resurrection (1 Cor. 15:51), and (5) God's plan by which both Jew and Gentile, after a period of disobedience by both, will by His mercy be included in His kingdom (here). **Lest ye should be wise in your own conceits**, Gentiles must understand their place in the mystery. God's merciful plan to include the Gentiles in His great salvation plan should humble them, not fill them with arrogance. **In part** means that Israel's hardening is partial, not total. Indeed, Israel's hardening

is not final and permanent but temporary and effective, as the word "until" clearly indicates. **The fulness of the Gentiles** refers to the total number of the elect Gentiles.

11:26. And so introduces an emphatic statement that this is the way all Israel will be saved. What did Paul mean by **all Israel?** Three main interpretations of this phrase are: (1) the total number of elect Jews of every generation, or the "fulness" (11:12) of Israel, which is analogous to "the fulness ['full number'] of the Gentiles" (11:25); (2) the total number of the elect, both Jews and Gentiles, of every generation; (3) the great majority of Jews of the final generation. Given Paul's discussion in this chapter, there is no basis for taking the words **shall be saved** in any sense other than that of 11:14. The salvation of the Jews will, of course, be on the same basis as anyone's salvation: personal faith in Jesus Christ, crucified and risen from the dead. **There shall come out of Sion the Deliverer** is a quotation from Isaiah 59:20, where "the redeemer" ("the Deliverer") seems to refer to God. The Talmud understood the text to be a reference to the Messiah, and Paul appears to have used it in this way. For "Sion," see discussion on Galatians 4:26.

11:27. Covenant refers to the "new covenant" of Jeremiah 31:31–34. **When I shall take away their sins** (see Jer. 31:34; Zech. 13:1). Just as salvation for Gentiles involves God's merciful forgiveness of sins, so it is for the Jews. For Jew and Gentile alike, God's forgiveness is based on only repentance and faith (see 11:23; Zech. 12:10–13:1).

11:28. They (the Jews) **are enemies** only temporarily and **for your sakes**, as explained in 11:11. With respect to God's election, **they are beloved for the fathers' sakes**, not because any merit was passed on from the patriarchs to the Jewish people as a whole but because God, out of love, chose Israel, and that choice is irrevocable.

11:29. The gifts and calling of God are without repentance means that God does not change His mind with reference to His call. Even though Israel is presently in a state of unbelief, God's purpose will be fulfilled in her.

11:30 – 31. In this carefully balanced sentence, Paul articulated the relationship of God's grace to Gentile Christians and to the Jews.

Gentile Christians (v. 30)	Jews (v. 31)
For as ye	Even so have these
in times past	also now
have not believed	not believed
yet now have obtained mercy	that … they also may obtain mercy
through their unbelief	through your mercy

Through your mercy means "Through the mercy that God has shown to you, the Gentiles."

11:32. So that God may have mercy on **them all**, meaning both groups under discussion, Jews and Gentiles have each undergone a period of disobedience. Paul was in no way teaching universal salvation.

11:33 – 36. The doxology that ends this section is the natural outpouring of Paul's praise to God, whose **wisdom and knowledge** (v. 33) brought about His great plan for the salvation of both Jews and Gentiles.

VII. Righteousness Practiced (12:1 – 15:13)

12:1 – 15:13. Here Paul turned to the practical application of all he had written up to this point. This does not mean that he had not yet said anything about Christian living. Chapters 6 – 8 touched on this, but now Paul went into detail to show that Jesus Christ is to be Lord of every area of one's life. This section is not a postscript to the great theological discussions in chapters 1 – 11. In a real sense, Paul directed the entire letter toward the goal of showing that God demands one's action as well as one's believing and thinking. Faith expresses itself in obedience.

A. In the Body, the Church (chap. 12)

12:1. Paul called every believer to total sacrifice. His exhortation was not without leverage: (1) **I beseech you therefore** makes it clear that total sacrifice is an important inference drawn from and compelled by the truth set forth in chapters 1 – 11. (2) Total sacrifice is warranted **by the mercies of God**; it is the fitting response to His gracious action in Christ. Much of the letter has been concerned with demonstrating this. **Present** is a technical term for offering a sacrifice. **Your bodies** (see 6:13 and discussion) is suited to the imagery of sacrifice and is a concrete expression tantamount to "yourselves," as the words **a living sacrifice** confirm. The altars of daily life are concrete occasions to present oneself to God as "a living sacrifice," in contrast to dead animal sacrifices. The words **reasonable service** also belong to the imagery of sacrifice. "Service" in particular alludes to temple duties and the kind of service a priest renders. Here Paul extolled the presentation of living sacrifices as worship that befits what God has achieved in Christ. Accordingly, "reasonable service" is not merely ritual activity in a place such as the temple; it takes place in the heart, mind, and will (see 1 Cor. 3:16; 6:19).

12:2. This world in Greek is the word "age" (*aiōn*), as in Gal. 1:4 and Eph. 2:2. Christians are to resist the shaping and molding forces and philosophies of this world. Instead of being **conformed**, believers are to be **transformed**. Transformation is not attributed to this world. This world conforms, but God's truth (His will) transforms. **Be ye transformed** denotes a process, not a single event. Interestingly, the same word is used in the transfiguration narratives (Matt. 17:2 – 8; Mark 9:2 – 8) and in 2 Corinthians 3:18. The **mind** — thought and will as they relate to morality (see 1:28) — must be renewed by God's revealed truth, His will. God's truth renews and transforms. Through faith, God's truth is rooted in the mind and heart, and its transforming action has an outcome: **that you may prove** (or ascertain) **what is … [the] will of God. Good** is that which leads to the spiritual and moral growth of the Christian. **Acceptable** means what is acceptable to God, not necessarily to humans. God's will is **perfect**; no improvement can be made on His will.

12:3. To think soberly, or in a clearheaded, sensible way, calls for seeing oneself accurately. The touchstone is God's grace, or as Paul put it, **according as God hath dealt**. Since the power comes from

God, there can be no basis for a superior attitude or self-righteousness. All believers are on equal footing because any distinctions belong to God's grace and not to anyone's superiority. Accordingly, **the measure of faith** belongs to the power that God gives to each believer to fulfill various ministries in the church (see 12:4–8).

12:4–8. Here Paul likened Christians to members of a human body. There are **many members** (v. 4), and each has a different function, but all are needed for the health of the body. The emphasis is on unity within diversity (see 1 Cor. 12:12–31).

12:5. The key to Paul's concept of Christian unity is found in the words **in Christ** (see discussions on 6:11; Eph. 1:1). Only in Jesus Christ is any unity in the church possible. True unity is spiritually based.

12:6. The Greek word for **gifts** is *charismata*, which refers to special gifts of grace (Greek, *charis*). God freely gives these gifts to His people to meet the needs of the body (see *KJV Study Bible* notes on 1 Cor. 1:7; 12:4). **Prophecy** (Greek, *prophēteia*) is the ability to interpret and communicate in clear speech God's direct and relevant will or purpose for His people (see *KJV Study Bible* note on 1 Cor. 12:10). From 1 Corinthians 14, it is clear that prophesying delivers a message addressed to the church's understanding and comprehension. Its purpose is "edification, and exhortation, and comfort" (1 Cor. 14:3), instruction so "that all may learn" (1 Cor. 14:31). The exercise of this gift, however, must be **according to the proportion of faith**, meaning "according to the standard." The word "proportion" (Greek, *analogia*) is similar to yet different from "the measure of faith" in 12:3 (see discussion there). The "standard" acts as a safeguard and suggests that the exercise of this gift will conform to faith. On the one hand, it suggests that prophecy will not contradict faith in and knowledge of Jesus Christ. On the other hand, it suggests that the one who prophesies is equally subject to the prophecy.

12:7. Ministry (Greek, *diakonia*) connotes any kind of service needed by the body of Christ or by any of its members. For **teacheth** (Greek, *didaskalia*), see discussion on Ephesians 4:11; *KJV Study Bible* note on 1 Corinthians 12:28.

12:8. Paul used the verb **exhorteth** (Greek, *parakaleō*) and the noun **exhortation** (Greek, *paraklēsis*) frequently in his letters—the verb fifty-four times, and the noun twenty times. Judging from his use of these words and his practice of instilling others with courage or encouragement, the gift of exhortation involves an uplifting, cheerful call to worthwhile accomplishment. The teacher often carried out this function. In teaching, the believer is shown what he must do; in encouraging, he is helped to do it. **Giveth** (Greek, *metadidōmi*) connotes giving what is one's own, contributing material resources to the work of God and the needs of others or possibly distributing what has been given by others. **Simplicity** is to accompany giving, suggesting that the hallmarks of the gift of giving are generosity and sincerity. **Ruleth** (Greek, *proistēmi*) suggests leading, modeling, motivating, and inspiring others to accomplish the work of the ministry. "He that ruleth" is possibly a reference to an elder; it clearly alludes to a qualification for church leaders (see Paul's use of *proistēmi* in 1 Thess. 5:12; 1 Tim. 5:17; 3:4–5, 12). The gift of leadership is to be complemented with **diligence**. In Greco-Roman literature and inscriptions, "diligence" characterized extraordinary commitment to civic and religious responsibilities. In relationships, diligence is expressed as devotion and goodwill toward others—an important quality for leaders if others are to follow. **Sheweth mercy** (Greek, *eleeō*) speaks of tenderly and empathetically caring for people who are suffering, certainly the sick, the poor, and the aged. Mercy is to be exercised **with cheerfulness**, a spirit and countenance that dispels gloom.

12:9–21. With short brushstrokes, Paul painted a truly extraordinary and altogether beautiful figure of the transformed and renewed life (see 12:1–2) of the believer. He connected Christ's transformation of one's inner life to the outer application of that life within the community of believers and the concrete world and was thus addressing, not individual believers, but the community.

12:9. Love, the Christian's love for fellow Christians and perhaps here also for his fellow man, must be **without dissimulation**, that is, genuine, true love, not pretense. In view of 12:6–8, with its emphasis on social concern, the love Paul was speaking of here is not mere emotion but active love. **Abhor ... cleave** speaks of a disposition that finds evil repugnant and good attractive.

12:10. Brotherly love (Greek, *philadelphia*) denotes family affection and devotion, love within the family of God. **In honour preferring one another** was once translated, "compete in honoring one another." Paul pictured a noble competition for the privilege of putting others first. Only one whose mind has been renewed by the Holy Spirit (see 12:2) would participate in such a competition (see Phil. 2:3).

12:11. Not slothful in business is literally "not indolent in diligence" (see "diligence" in 12:8), meaning that believers are to exhibit wholehearted devotion and goodwill toward others. If **fervent in spirit** means "fervent in the Holy Spirit," the reference would be to the fervor the Holy Spirit provides. The same expression is used of Apollos in Acts 18:25. Since the Greek word for "fervent" (*zeō*) means "to boil," effervescence, liveliness, and exhilaration befit the spirit of one serving the Lord.

12:12. Rejoicing in hope shows that the certainty of the Christian's hope is a cause for joy (see 5:5; see also 8:16–25; 1 Peter 1:3–9) and implicitly expresses the importance of a forward focus and expectancy that regularly looks to a future grounded in God's favor. Hope makes one **patient in tribulation** (see Rom. 8:25; 1 Thess. 1:3). Patience maintains its belief and its course of action in the face of opposition and affliction. The patience to endure triumphantly is necessary for a Christian, because affliction is the believer's inevitable experience (see John 16:33). As Paul's sequence of thought (hope, patience) suggests, **continuing instant in prayer** calls one not only to pray in hard times but also to maintain communion with God through prayer at all times (see Luke 18:1; 1 Thess. 5:17).

12:13. The Christian has social responsibility to all people, but **distributing to the ... saints** calls the Christian to the necessary responsibility of caring for other believers (see Gal. 6:10). **Given to hospitality** is literally "pursuing" or "aspiring" to hospitality.

Hospitality (Greek, *philoxenia*) is to strangers what brotherly love (Greek, *philadelphia*) is to family.

12:14. Bless them which persecute you. Here Paul echoed Jesus' teaching in Matthew 5:44 and Luke 6:28.

12:15. Identification with others in their joys and in their sorrows is a Christian's privilege and responsibility.

12:16. Be of the same mind. Paul prayed for this in 15:5 and beseeched it in 1 Corinthians 1:10 and Philippians 4:2. It made his joy complete in Philippians 2:2 (see discussion there). What unifies Christians into one mindset is the mind of Christ: "Let this mind be in you, which was also in Christ Jesus" (Phil. 2:5).

12:17. For **Recompense to no man evil for evil**, see Matthew 5:39–42, 44–45; 1 Thessalonians 5:15; 1 Peter 3:9. **Provide things honest in the sight of all men**. Paul's exhortation is quite possibly a reflection of Proverbs 3:4 in the Septuagint (the Greek translation of the Old Testament). Christian conduct should never betray the high moral standards of the gospel, or it will provoke the disdain of unbelievers and bring the gospel into disrepute (see 2 Cor. 8:21; 1 Tim. 3:7).

12:18. If it be possible ... live peaceably. Jesus pronounced a blessing on peacemakers (see Matt. 5:9), and to the extent that it depends on them, believers are to cultivate peace with everyone.

12:19–21. Heap coals of fire on his head. Doing **good** (v. 21) to one's enemy, instead of trying to take revenge, may bring about his repentance (see discussion on Prov. 25:22).

B. In the World (chap. 13)

13:1–7. The question of responsibility and obligation to the state is an important issue for the Christian, whose allegiance and true citizenship belong to the rule of Christ. The question had an added dimension for believers in Rome, the seat of imperial, even world, power. At the time, currents of political unrest over taxes within Rome and winds of religious resistance to human rule within the empire may have prompted Paul to safeguard a proper outlook and attitude toward government and its authority (see Moo, *Romans*, p. 426). Paul called all believers to recognize that they stand under government in God's instituted order for ruling the world.

13:1. Be subject is a significant phrase in 13:1–7. In scripture, to "be subject" is to be volitionally subordinate, not abject. The Greek word *hypotassō* ("to submit," "be subject") is not fully explained by the word "obey." Within the heart of the word is an attitude of willingness; as Paul made clear here, its virtue is deference to the ultimate authority of God. **Higher powers** refers to civil rulers and governing officials (see Titus 3:1), all of whom were probably pagans when Paul wrote this letter. Christians may have been tempted not to submit to them and to claim allegiance only to Christ. **Ordained of God** means that God puts in place the structures of authority. Even the possibility of a persecuting state did not shake Paul's conviction that civil government is ordained by God.

13:2. The word **damnation** concerns either divine judgment or, more likely, punishment by the governing authorities, since 13:3 ("For") explains this verse (see also 13:4).

13:3. Do that which is good, and thou shalt have praise. Paul was not stating that this will always be true but was describing the proper, ideal function of rulers. When civil rulers overstep their proper function, the Christian is to obey God rather than man (see Acts 4:19; 5:29).

13:4. He is the minister of God. In the order of divine providence, the ruler is God's servant (see Isa. 45:1). **Good** means "advantage," "benefit," "well-being" in a general sense. Rulers exist for the benefit of society, to protect the public by maintaining good order. Cranfield, however, giving full weight to the words "a minister of God to thee [the Christian] for good," suggests that "good" should be taken in the sense of 8:28 (*Epistle to the Romans*, pp. 665–66). **The sword** was the symbol of Roman authority on both the national and the international levels. It represented Rome's power of life and death over its citizens (Tacitus, *History* 3.68). This verse illustrates the biblical principle of using force for the maintenance of good order.

13:5. This statement summarizes 13:1–7. The necessity (**must needs**) to **be subject** is **not only for wrath**, fear of the law and punishment (see 13:3–4), **but also for conscience sake** (see 13:1–2). "For conscience sake" points to the deference the Christian owes to the authority of God. He ordains civil authorities, and to maintain a good conscience, Christians must duly honor them.

13:6–7. Pay you tribute (v. 6) refers to "taxes" (see Luke 20:22 for the same word), and **custom** (v. 7) refers to "revenues" (see Matt. 17:25). The pairing of monetary obligations leads to a pairing of obligations concerning deferential recognition: **fear** and **honour**. Paul made the most of similar sounding words to make his point: in Greek, "tribute," "custom," "fear," and "honour" are, in order, *phoron, telos, phobon, timēn*. The spectrum and variation of these pairings appears to have been an effort on Paul's part to open and close loopholes and to ask and answer questions of exception, as if an exemption might apply to something he did not specifically address. Paul's point was that the Christian with a proper attitude of submission to God's authority will in turn exercise a proper attitude of submission to civil authorities, whom God has ordained, and to the various obligations that entails.

13:8. A connection to 13:1–7 comes in the word **Owe**, which can designate a duty or a debt. All debts may be paid and all duties discharged except for the duty **to love**. To love is the one debt that is never paid off, the one duty that is never done. No matter how much one has loved, he is obligated to keep on loving. **One another** includes not only fellow Christians but all people. **The law**, as becomes clear from 13:9, refers to the Mosaic law, which lays down both moral and social responsibilities.

13:9. Here Paul further explained the last statement of 13:8, namely, that love of neighbor encompasses all one's social responsibilities. **Thy neighbour**, as Jesus taught, is anyone in need (see Luke 10:25–37), which is probably the idea that Paul had in mind here. **As thyself** reflects the Golden Rule (see Matt. 7:12; Luke 6:31). This is not a command to love oneself but a recognition of the fact that one naturally does so and knows how one wants to be treated.

13:10. Whereas love has been defined actively with "thyself" as the standard (13:9), here love is defined passively with one's **neighbour** as the standard: **Love worketh no ill**. The word "ill" connotes "harm" or "wrongdoing" of any kind. This so-called negative definition of love corrects a view of love that rests on sentiment and strong emotion. Love is a quality of action that is courteous of God's best for another.

13:11–14. In this section, as in other New Testament passages, the certain coming of the end of the present age is used to provide motivation for godly living (see, e.g., Matt. 25:31–46; Mark 13:33–37; James 5:7–11; 2 Peter 3:11–14).

13:11. The time refers to the time of salvation, the closing period of the present age, before the consummation of the kingdom. **It is high time to awake** means it is time for action. **Salvation** entails the full realization of salvation at the second coming of Jesus Christ (see 8:23; Heb. 9:28; 1 Peter 1:5). **Nearer than** is even nearer today. Every day brings closer the second advent of Christ.

13:12–13. Darkness (v. 12; see 1 Thess. 5:5) belongs to **The night**, a metaphor for the present evil age; **light** belongs to **the day**. With the words **The night is far spent, the day is at hand**, Paul evoked a picture of the dawning of a new day. His image presents a clear example of the New Testament teaching of the "nearness" of the end times (see Matt. 24:33; 1 Cor. 7:29; Phil. 4:5; James 5:8–9; 1 Peter 4:7; 1 John 2:18). These texts do not mean that the early Christians believed that Jesus would return within a few years (and thus were mistaken); rather, they regarded the death and resurrection of Christ as the crucial events of history that began the last days. Since the next great event in God's redemptive plan is the second coming of Jesus Christ, "the night," no matter how long it may last chronologically, is almost gone. "The day" denotes the appearing of Jesus Christ, which will usher in the consummation of the kingdom. Daytime conduct (**as in the day**; v. 13) is to characterize the believer since he belongs to the coming day and not to the passing night.

13:14. Put ye on the Lord Jesus Christ. "Put on" is an expression that Paul used frequently. Even as one "dresses" for the day, the believer is to "put on," or "clothe himself in," the garment of Christ (see Col. 3:10; Eph. 4:24; see also Gal. 3:27, where the metaphor pertains to baptism). Paul exhorted believers to display outwardly what has already taken place inwardly and to practice all the virtues associated with Christ.

C. Among Weak and Strong Christians (14:1–15:13)

14:1. Him that is weak in the faith probably refers to Jewish Christians in Rome who were unwilling to give up the observance of certain requirements of the law, such as dietary restrictions and observing the Sabbath and other special days. Their concern was not quite the same as that of the Judaizers of Galatia. The Judaizers thought they could put God in their debt by works of righteousness and were trying to force this heretical teaching on the Galatian churches, but the "weak" Roman Christians did neither. They were not yet clear as to the status of Old Testament regulations under the new covenant inaugurated by the coming of Christ. Believers are not to receive or succumb to **doubtful disputations**. Fellowship among Christians is not to be based on everyone's agreement on disputable questions. Christians do not agree on all matters pertaining to the Christian life, nor do they need to do so.

14:2. In contrast to "him that is weak in the faith" (14:1), here Paul described the "strong" Christian. **One believeth** denotes assurance or confidence. The strong Christian's understanding of the gospel allows him to recognize that one's diet has no spiritual significance.

14:3–4. For **despise** and **judge** (v. 3), see 14:10. Scruples of conscience, pro or con, must not be allowed to justify disdain or condemnation, **for God hath received him**. How can a fellow believer reject one whom God has received? Paul pursued this train of thought in his question about **another man's servant** (v. 4), which is a thinly veiled reference to God. A Christian must not reject a fellow Christian, who is also a servant of God. **To his own master he stan-**

deth or falleth, meaning the "weak" Christian is not the master of his "strong" brother, nor is the "strong" the master of the "weak." God is Master, and to Him alone all believers are responsible.

14:5. Questions of preference are not limited to food. Paul expanded the range of possibilities by touching on differing views of calendar observance. Some feel that **one day above another** refers primarily to the Sabbath, but it is probably a reference to all the special days of the Old Testament ceremonial law. One who **esteemeth every day alike** is of the conviction that all days are to be dedicated to God through holy living and godly service. Paul was fully aware that powerful personal convictions were at work, as is clear from his words **fully persuaded in his own mind**. The importance of personal conviction in disputable matters of conduct runs through this passage (see 14:14, 16, 22–23).

14:6. The motivation behind the actions of both the strong Christian and the weak Christian is to be the same: both should want to serve the Lord and give thanks for His provision.

14:7–9. None of us liveth to himself (v. 7). "Us" refers to Christians, who live to please the Lord rather than themselves. **No man dieth to himself**. Even in death, the important thing is one's relationship to the Lord. Paul repeated these truths in verse 8 to emphasize that Christians do not live for themselves or for their own gratification but instead live for Him who is greater to them than even life or death, the **Lord** (v. 9; see discussion on 10:9). Christ's lordship over **both … the dead and [the] living** arises out of His death and resurrection.

14:10–12. Paul asked the weak Christians, **Why dost thou judge thy brother?** (v. 10). To "judge" is stronger than to "consider" or "have an opinion about." Here, as in 14:3, it carries the sense of "criticize," "find fault with," or "condemn," as the context confirms. Paul then asked the strong Christians, **Why dost thou set at nought thy brother?** "Set at nought" means to treat with disdain or as if lacking merit or worth (the same word as "despise" in 14:3). **We shall all**, each and every Christian, whether weak or strong, give an account at **the judgment seat of Christ**. In

the New Testament, "judgment seat" (Greek, *bēma*) refers to the platform or raised place that designates the official seat of a judge, usually the governor or emperor (see, e.g., Acts 25:10) but also Christ (here and in 2 Cor. 5:10). Paul cited Isaiah 45:23, **every knee … and every tongue** (v. 11; see Phil. 2:10–11), to certify that no one is exempt from accountability to the Lord. **Every one … shall give account of himself** (v. 12), a formal account or "reckoning" (Greek, *logos*; see Heb. 13:17; Matt. 12:36), especially of one's actions. The problem for the Roman Christians was just the opposite. The "weak" and "strong" were engaged in giving an account of others. Paul therefore urged them to think of giving an account of themselves, for all will be judged, and the judgment will be based on works (see discussion on 2:6–8; 2 Cor. 5:10; 1 Cor. 3:10–15).

14:13. In light of what Paul wrote in 14:10–12, judging one's brother would smack of taking the very "seat" (Greek, *bēma*) of the Lord Jesus Christ, even as Paul questioned the propriety of displacing the Master by judging His servant (see 14:4). **But judge this rather** pointed Paul's readers to self-examination (see "give account of himself," 14:12) and a better use of judgment. The rest of the verse addressed the strong Christians. **A stumblingblock** is anything that causes one to fall into sin. A comparison of 4:13–14 and 15:1 with 1 Corinthians 8:4–9 shows that Paul's own position belonged to that of the strong Christian, but he made it clear that sympathy for those who have understanding must be matched with sensitivity for those who lack understanding.

14:14. I know, and am persuaded by the Lord Jesus. Now that Paul was a Christian, the old food taboos no longer applied (see Matt. 15:10–11, 16–20; Mark 7:14–23). For Paul's teaching **that there is nothing unclean of itself**, see 1 Timothy 4:4; Titus 1:15. **To him that esteemeth any thing to be unclean, to him it is unclean**. Paul's words must not to be generalized to mean that sin is only a matter of subjective opinion or conscience. He was not discussing conduct that is clearly sinful in the light of Scripture but discussing conduct concerning which Christians may legitimately differ (in this case, food regulations). With regard to such matters, a believer's decisions should be guided by his conscience.

14:15. Walkest thou not charitably means that choices and decisions of conduct are not being governed or guided by love. Love is the key to proper settlement of disputes. **For whom Christ died**, the supreme act of love, is a reminder that Christ so valued the weak brother that He died for him. Surely the strong Christian ought to be willing to make adjustments in his own behavior for the sake of such brothers.

14:16. Your good refers to a legitimate good as gauged by one's own understanding of Christian liberty. If, however, one engages in that "good" apart from the guidance of love (see 14:15), it may **be evil spoken of**. To exercise freedom without responsibility may lead to evil results.

14:17–18. The kingdom of God (v. 17; see discussions on Matt. 3:2; Luke 4:43) invites a change of perspective on matters that concern largely the economy and culture of this world. To be concerned with such trivial matters as **meat and drink** is to miss completely the essence of Christian living. **Righteousness** refers to righteous living. Paul's concern for the moral and ethical dimension of the Christian life stands out in all his letters. For **peace**, see 5:1 and discussion. **Joy in the Holy Ghost** identifies joy given by the Holy Spirit. **In these things serveth Christ** (v. 18) includes the aforementioned qualities belonging to the Spirit.

14:19. Edify another refers to the spiritual building up of individual Christians and of the church (see 1:11–12).

14:20–21. The work of God (v. 20) is here not an abstract program but the weak Christian brother, who as a redeemed person is God's work and in whom God continues to work (see Eph. 2:10). Paul recognized a strong Christian's right to certain freedoms but qualified it with the principle of regard for a weak brother's scruples. **With offence**, like the "stumblingblock" of 14:13, speaks of the inconsiderate exercise of freedom that is detrimental to the spiritual growth of those who are weak in faith. It would be wiser to forgo one's freedom than to exercise it and thereby hinder the advance of God's work.

14:22–23. Have it to thyself before God (v. 22) means that a believer should be secure within himself that before God his faith is valid (see 14:14). The strong Christian is not required to go against his convictions or change his standards, yet he is not to flaunt his Christian freedom but to keep it a private matter. **Which he alloweth** is probably a reference to the eating of certain foods. For **eateth not of faith** (v. 23) and the issue of certainty and uncertainty, see 14:14. **Whatsoever** pertains to the matters discussed in 14:20–21, namely, conduct about which Christians may have legitimate differences of opinion.

15:1–2. With the words **we then that are strong** (v. 1), Paul identified himself with the strong Christians, those whose personal convictions allow them more freedom than the weak. **To bear** means not merely to tolerate or put up with but to uphold lovingly. **Infirmities** are not sins, since Scripture gives no clear guidance on the matters under discussion. **Not to please ourselves** does not mean that a Christian should never please himself but that he should not insist on doing what he wants without regard to the scruples of other Christians.

15:3. Christ pleased not himself. Christ came to do, not His own will, but the will of His Father, which involved suffering and even death (see Matt. 20:28; Mark 10:45; 1 Cor. 10:33–11:1; 2 Cor. 8:9; Phil. 2:5–8). **The reproaches of them that reproached thee fell on me.** In this quotation from Psalm 69:9, "thee" refers to God, and "me" refers to the righteous sufferer, whom Paul identified with Christ. The quotation serves to show that Christ did not please Himself but voluntarily bore man's hostility toward God.

15:4. Here Paul defended his application of Psalm 69:9 to Christ. In so doing, he stated a great truth concerning the purpose of Scripture: it was written for instruction, so that as one patiently endures, one might be encouraged to hold fast one's **hope** in Christ (see 1 Cor. 10:6, 11).

15:5–6. To be likeminded (v. 5) does not mean that believers should all come to the same conclusions on matters of conscience but rather means that believers should agree to disagree in love. What unifies and harmonizes discordant opinions is the greater and higher agreement found in Jesus Christ (see 15:7), which enables believers to glorify God.

15:7. As Christ also received us (see 14:3–4, 15) introduces grace and thus restores humility to both sides of an opinion.

15:8. Jesus Christ was a minister of the circumcision should be understood as "… to the circumcision," the Jews, as clearly revealed in His earthly ministry. Christ was sent to the Jewish people and largely limited His ministry to them (see Matt. 15:24). God gave a special priority, so far as the gospel is concerned, to the Jews (see 3:1–8). **Promises made unto the fathers** refers to the covenant promises made to Abraham (Gen. 12:1–3; 17:7; 18:19; 22:18), Isaac (Gen. 26:3–4), and Jacob (Gen. 28:13–15; 46:2–4).

15:9–12. The purpose God's redemptive work in and for Israel was **that the Gentiles might glorify God** (v. 9). From the beginning, He had in view the redemption of the Gentiles (see Gen. 12:3). Both the Jews and the Gentiles would see God's mighty and gracious acts for His people and hear their praises as they celebrated what God had done for them (a common theme in the Psalms; see discussion on Ps. 9:1; see also Paul's quotations in these verses, from Deut. 32:43; Ps. 117:1; Isa. 15:12). Thus, they would come to know the true God and glorify Him for His mercy (see discussions on Pss. 46:10; 47:9). God's greatest and climactic act for Israel's salvation was sending the Messiah to fulfill the promises made to the patriarchs and thus to gather in the great harvest of the Gentiles. **A root of Jesse** (v. 12) refers to David, whose father was Jesse (see 1 Sam. 16:5–13; Matt. 1:6); the Messiah was "the Son of David" (Matt. 21:9; see Isa. 11:1; Rev. 5:5). **In him shall the Gentiles trust.** The early church's mission to the Gentiles was a fulfillment of this prophecy, as is the continuing evangelization of the nations.

15:13. God is **the God of hope.** Any hope the Christian has comes from God (see discussion on 5:5). Hope comes **through the power of the Holy Ghost.** Hope cannot be conjured up by man's effort; it is God's gift by His Spirit (see 8:24–25).

VIII. Conclusion (15:14–33)

15:14–15. Paul began the close of his letter with an expression of high praise. In case anyone had taken offense after reading the topics of this letter (**I have written the more boldly;** v. 15), the apostle took steps to assure the Roman Christians of his high regard. **I myself also am persuaded of you** (v. 14) indicates that the following opinion was not that of others only: "I am convinced; yes, indeed, I am" (Black, *Romans*, p. 174). **Full of goodness** is tantamount to saying that the Roman Christians were thoroughly characterized by interest in the welfare of others. **Filled with all knowledge** probably pertains to Christian knowledge, certainly a measure of such sufficiency that Paul could commend their fitness **to admonish one another** (elsewhere the word "admonish" [Greek, *noutheteō*] presumes Christian maturity and is associated with teaching; see 1 Thess. 5:12; Col. 1:28; 3:16). **As putting you in mind** (v. 15) means "as a reminder," inasmuch as the topics of Paul's letter were broadly relevant to all the churches and not at every point directed to specific problems in the church at Rome. Since Paul had never preached or taught in Rome, he referred to generally known Christian doctrines of which the Romans needed to be reminded. **The grace that is given to me of God** alludes to Paul's apostleship (see 1:5, 15:16). Paul validated his ministry (particularly in 15:16–19), a ministry he hoped the Roman Christians would support in its expansion to the west and Spain (see 15:24).

15:16. The minister of Jesus Christ to the Gentiles emphasizes Paul's "administrative" role as "the apostle to the Gentiles" (11:13; see discussion there). The word "minister," used one other time in Romans of civil leaders ordained by God (13:6), is here associated with priestly ministry (see Heb. 8:2), as the words **ministering the gospel** confirm. The Greek word that Paul used for "ministering" (only here in the New Testament) refers to "ministering as a priest." Paul's priestly function was different from that of the Levitical priests. They were involved with the rituals of the temple, whereas he preached the gospel. **That the offering ... might be acceptable, being sanctified by the Holy Ghost**. The offering that Paul brought to God was the Gentile church.

15:17-18. With the words **I have therefore whereof I may glory** (v. 17), Paul was boasting, not of his own achievements, but of what Christ had accomplished through him.

15:19. Paul's ministry had been credentialed, so to speak, by the power of the Spirit, one evidence of which was **signs and wonders** (see Acts 14:8-10; 16:16-18, 25-26; 20:9-12; 28:8-9; 2 Cor. 12:12; Heb. 2:3-4). The breadth of Paul's ministry ran **from Jerusalem**, the home of the mother church, where the gospel originated and its dissemination began (see Acts 1:8), to **Illyricum**, a Roman province north of Macedonia (present-day Albania and Yugoslavia). Acts mentions nothing of Paul's ministry there, and perhaps he meant only that he had reached the border. **I have fully preached the gospel** does not mean that everyone in the eastern Mediterranean had heard the gospel. Rather, Paul believed that his work there had been completed and that it was time to move on to other places.

15:20-21. Paul elucidated a guiding principle or policy of his ministry: to preach in territories where Christ had yet to be named and where no other preacher had yet laid a **foundation** (v. 20; see 1 Cor. 3:10-12). In this effort, Paul was conscious of and inspired by Isaiah 52:15.

15:22-23. For which cause (v. 22) refers to Paul's great desire to complete the missionary task in the eastern Mediterranean. Completing that task **much hindered** or prevented him from making a trip to Rome. His **having no more place in these parts** (v. 23) can be attributed to the principle stated in 15:20. Paul's **great desire these many years to come unto you** was also expressed at the outset of the letter (see 1:11-15).

15:24. To be brought on my way thitherward by you. Paul wanted to use the Roman church as a base of operations for a mission to Spain. **Be somewhat filled with your company** pictures a visit to Rome of some length; more than a quick stop was contemplated (see 1:11-12).

15:25-26. Before Paul's desired visit to Rome could take place, he first had to fulfill a responsibility to the church **at Jerusalem** (v. 26; see 15:28) and there **minister unto the saints** (v. 25). "Saints" refers generally to believers in Jesus Christ (see discussion on 1:7). Paul wanted to present a gift, **a certain contribution** (v. 26), personally to the Jerusalem church. The gift needed interpretation. It was not merely money; it represented the love and concern of the Gentile churches in **Macedonia and Achaia** for their Jewish brothers and sisters. Paul called the gift "a certain contribution" (Greek, *koinōnia*; as in 2 Cor. 8:4; 9:13; see 1 Cor. 16:1-4; 2 Corinthians 8-9) because this was its first mention to the Romans.

15:27. Their spiritual things refers especially to Christ and the gospel.

15:28-29. This fruit (v. 28) symbolizes the contribution collected from the Gentile churches. Paul assured the Roman Christians that the delay would not diminish his visit but rather cause it to come **in the fulness of the blessing of the gospel of Christ** (v. 29).

15:30-31. Paul invited the Roman church to begin supporting him through prayer, **that I may be delivered from them that do not believe in Judea** (v. 31). Paul wanted to go to Jerusalem. The delivery of the collection was important to him (see 15:25-28), but he had received warnings about what might happen to him there (see Acts 20:22-23). **May be accepted** is perhaps a reference to the way in which the money was to be distributed—often a delicate and difficult task.

15:32. Paul believed that the prayers he requested in 15:30 would accelerate his visit to Rome. For **be refreshed**, see 1:11-12.

15:33. This verse is a provisional close to the letter. For **the God of peace**, see discussions on 5:1; 1 Thessalonians 5:23.

IX. Commendation and Greetings (chap. 16)

16:1-2. Phebe (v. 1) was quite possibly one of the carriers of the letter to Rome. She was **our sister** in the sense of being a fellow believer. **A servant** (Greek, *diakonos*) is one who serves or ministers in any way. Regarding women serving in the early church, see discussions on 1 Timothy 3:8–11. **Cenchrea** was a port located about six miles east of Corinth on the Saronic Gulf. **Assist her** (v. 2) suggests the same kind of help that she had provided Paul and others at Cenchrea. Judging from the word **succourer** (Greek, *prostatis*), Phebe was a benefactor or patron to many Christians.

16:3–5. Greet (v. 3, 5) occurs five times in chapter 16. **Priscilla and Aquila** (v. 3) were close friends of Paul who were tentmakers, as he was (see Acts 18:2–3). The two had risked their lives for Paul; they had **laid down their own necks** (v. 4). There is no other record of this in the New Testament or elsewhere, but it must have been widely known, as the last part of the verse indicates. **The church that is in their house** (v. 5) clearly shows that the word "church" denoted an assembly of believers that congregated in a residence or home, the people of God and not a building.

16:6–7. Six persons in the New Testament are known by the name **Mary** (v. 6). This one is unknown apart from this reference. **Andronicus and Junia, my kinsmen** (v. 7) probably refers to fellow countrymen (as in 16:11, 21), possibly Jews by birth. They were **apostles** in the sense of being "missionaries" or "messengers" (as in 2 Cor. 8:23; Phil. 2:25).

16:8–10. Amplias (v. 8), **Urban … Stachys** (v.9), and **Apelles** (v. 10) were all common slave names found in the imperial household. **Aristobulus** may refer to the grandson of Herod the Great and brother of Herod Agrippa I.

16:11. Herodion my kinsman is perhaps a reference to Herodion's being a Jew (see 16:7). **Narcissus** is sometimes identified with Tiberius Claudius Narcissus, a wealthy freedman of the Roman emperor Tiberius.

16:12. Tryphena and Tryphosa were perhaps sisters, even twins, because it was common for siblings and especially twins to be given names from the same root. **Persis** means "Persian woman."

16:14–15. None of these persons can be further identified, except that they were slaves or freedmen in the Roman church.

16:16. Justin Martyr (AD 150) tells us that **a holy kiss** (see 1 Cor. 16:20; 2 Cor. 13:12; 1 Thess. 5:26; 1 Peter 5:14) was a regular part of the worship service in his day. It is still a practice in some churches.

16:17–20. These verses present a theological application of the story of man's fall (see Genesis 3). We cannot tell who **them which cause divisions and offences** (v. 17) were, but some of their characteristics are mentioned in verse 18. **Wise unto that which is good** (v. 19) shows that Christians are to be experts in doing good. For **the God of peace** (v. 20), see 15:33. **Shall bruise Satan** is a reference to Satan's final doom (see Gen. 3:15). For **shortly**, see discussion on 13:12.

16:21. Jason is possibly the Jason mentioned in Acts 17:5–9. **Sosipater** was probably Sopater son of Pyrrhus from Berea (see Acts 20:4).

16:22. I Tertius, who wrote this epistle. Tertius is not mentioned elsewhere in the New Testament. In writing this letter, he functioned as Paul's secretary (for clues to Paul's use of an amanuensis, or secretary, see 1 Cor. 16:21; 2 Cor. 10:1; Gal. 6:11; 2 Thess. 3:17; Col. 4:18).

16:23. Gaius is usually identified as Titius Justus, a God-fearer, in whose house Paul stayed while in Corinth (see Acts 18:7; 1 Cor. 1:14). His full name was Gaius Titius Justus. **The whole church** refers to the church in Corinth (see Introduction: "Date and Place of Composition"). The name **Erastus** has been identified on an inscription at Corinth. Archaeologists have discovered a reused block of stone in a paved square, with the Latin inscription: "Erastus, commissioner of public works, bore the expense of this pavement." This may refer to the Erastus mentioned here. If it does, it is the earliest reference to a Christian by name outside the New Testament. He may also be the same person referred to in Acts 19:22 and 2 Timothy 4:20, though it is difficult to be certain because the name was fairly common. **Quartus** means "fourth (son)."

16:25–27. Paul concluded his letter with a grand doxology. **My gospel** (v. 25) refers not to a gospel different from that preached by others but to a gospel Paul received by direct revelation (see Gal. 1:12). **The preaching of Jesus Christ** is a description of the gospel; it is about Jesus Christ, who is its content. For **mystery**, see 11:25 and discussion.

THE FIRST EPISTLE OF PAUL THE APOSTLE TO THE CORINTHIANS

INTRODUCTION

Author and Date

Paul is acknowledged as the author both by the letter itself (1:1–2; 16:21) and by the early church fathers. His authorship was attested by Clement of Rome as early as AD 96, and today practically all New Testament scholars concur. The letter was written circa 55, toward the close of Paul's three-year residency in Ephesus (see 16:5–9; Acts 20:31). It is clear from his reference to staying at Ephesus until Pentecost (16:8) that he intended to remain there somewhat less than a year when he wrote 1 Corinthians.

The City of Corinth

It has been estimated that in Paul's day Corinth had a population of about 250,000 free persons, plus as many as 400,000 slaves. In a number of ways, it was the chief city of Greece. (See map, *Zondervan KJV Study Bible*, p. 1641.)

Its commerce. Located just off the Corinthian isthmus, Corinth was a crossroads for travelers and traders. It had two harbors: (1) Cenchrea, six miles to the east on the Saronic Gulf, and (2) Lechaion, a mile and a half to the west on the Corinthian Gulf. Goods flowed across the isthmus on the Diolkos, a road by which smaller ships could be hauled fully loaded across the isthmus, and by which cargoes of larger ships could be transported by wagons from one side to the other. Goods flowed through the city from Italy and Spain to the west and from Asia Minor, Phoenicia, and Egypt to the east.

Its culture. Although Corinth was not a university town like Athens, it was characterized nevertheless by typical Greek culture. Its people were interested in Greek philosophy and placed a high premium on wisdom.

Its religion. Corinth contained at least twelve temples. Whether they were all in use during Paul's time is not known. One of the most infamous was the temple dedicated to Aphrodite, the goddess of love, whose worshipers practiced religious prostitution. About a fourth of a mile north of the theater stood the temple of Asclepius, the god of healing, and in the middle of the city the sixth-century BC temple of Apollo was located. In addition, the Jews had established a synagogue; the inscribed lintel of it has been found and placed in the museum at old Corinth.

Its immorality. Like any large commercial city, Corinth was a center for open and unbridled immorality. The worship of Aphrodite fostered prostitution in the name of religion. At one time, one thousand sacred prostitutes served her temple. So widely known did the immorality of Corinth become that the Greek verb "to Corinthianize" came to mean "to practice sexual immorality." In a setting like this, it is no wonder that the Corinthian church was plagued with numerous problems.

Background

Paul had received information from several sources concerning the conditions existing in the church at Corinth. Some members of the household of Chloe had informed him of the factions that had developed in the church (1:11). Three individuals—Stephanas, Fortunatus, and Achaicus—had come to Paul in Ephesus to make some contribution to his ministry (16:17), but whether they were the ones from Chloe's household is not known.

Some of those who had come had brought Paul disturbing information concerning moral irregularities in the church (chaps. 5–6). Immorality had plagued the Corinthian assembly almost from the beginning. From 5:9–10, it is apparent that Paul had written previously concerning moral laxness. He had urged believers "not to company with fornicators" (5:9). Because of misunderstanding, he now found it necessary to clarify his instruction (5:10–11) and to urge immediate and drastic action (5:3–5, 13).

Other Corinthian visitors had brought a letter from the church that requested counsel on several subjects (7:1; see also 8:1; 12:1; 16:1).

It is clear that, although the church was gifted (1:4–7), it was immature and unspiritual (3:1–4). Paul's purposes for writing were: (1) to instruct and restore the church in its areas of weakness, correcting erroneous practices such as divisions (1:10–4:21), immorality (chap. 5; 6:12–20), litigation in pagan courts (6:1–8), and abuse of the Lord's supper (11:17–34); (2) to correct false teaching concerning the resurrection (chap. 15); and (3) to give instruction concerning the offering for poverty-stricken believers in Jerusalem (16:1–4).

Theme and Theological Message

The letter revolves around the theme of problems in Christian conduct in the church. It thus has to do with progressive sanctification, the continuing development of holiness of character. Obviously Paul was personally concerned with the Corinthians' problems, revealing a true pastor's (shepherd's) heart.

This letter is timely for the church today, both to instruct and to inspire. Most of the questions and problems that confronted the church at Corinth are still very much current—problems like immaturity, instability, divisions, jealousy and envy, lawsuits, marital difficulties, sexual immorality, and misuse of spiritual gifts. Yet in spite of this concentration on problems, the book contains some of the most familiar and beloved chapters in the entire Bible—for example, chap. 13 (on love) and chap. 15 (on resurrection).

Outline

I. Introduction (1:1–9)
   A. Greetings (1:1–3)

Bibliography

Barrett, C. K. *The First Epistle to the Corinthians*. Black's New Testament Commentaries. Peabody, MA: Hendrickson, 1996.

Hodge, Charles. *An Exposition of the First Epistle to the Corinthians*. Grand Rapids, MI: Eerdmans, 1956.

Hunter, Jack. "1 Corinthians." In *What the Bible Teaches*, vol. 4. Ritchie New Testament Commentaries. Edited by Tom Wilson and Keith Stapley. Kilmarnock, Scotland: John Ritchie Ltd., 1986.

Kistemaker, Simon J. *1 Corinthians*. Grand Rapids, MI: Baker, 1993.

Lenski, R. C. H. *The Interpretation of 1 and 2 Corinthians*. Minneapolis: Augsburg, 1963.

Lowery, David, K. "First Corinthians." In *The Bible Knowledge Commentary: New Testament*, edited by John F. Walvoord and Roy B. Zuck. Wheaton, IL: Victor, 1983.

MacArthur, John. *1 Corinthians*. MacArthur New Testament Commentary. Chicago: Moody, 1984.

Mitchell, Dan. *The Book of First Corinthians: Christianity in a Hostile Culture*. Twenty-First Century Biblical Commentary. Chattanooga: AMG, 2004.

Vine, W. E. *The Collected Writings of W. E. Vine*. 5 vols. Nashville: Nelson, 1996.

EXPOSITION

I. Introduction (1:1–9)

The letters of the apostle Paul have common introductory remarks. He generally identified himself, addressed his audience, and then added a courteous greeting to the readers that always brought forth his love for the Lord Jesus and for God the Father. As a chief apostle, Paul was compelled to include a loving greeting from both the Father and the Son.

A. Greetings (1:1–3)

1:1. The apostle wanted to make certain the church understood that his authority was imparted by Christ. Paul was **called to be an apostle** ("one sent with a message"), to carry the good news of the glorious work of Christ on the cross for sinners. From chapter 9, it seems that some believers within the church challenged his apostolic role and ministry. Paul made it clear that he bore witness to the truth **through the will of God**. Many scholars believe **Sosthenes** ("of safe strength") was one of the rulers of the Corinthian synagogue who was beaten when an attempt to prosecute Paul failed (see Acts 18:8).

This beating may have driven him to Christ, and he became a devoted helper of the apostle. God sometimes uses persecution to drive people to the Lord.

1:2. The apostle here addressed the issue of the larger church and the local church. The believers in the church in Corinth positionally were **sanctified in Christ Jesus**, but they belonged to the larger body of Christians, **all that in every place call upon the name of Jesus Christ our Lord**. He is the same Lord, **both theirs and ours**. By faith, every child of God is placed "in Christ." Paul was addressing the setting aside that is the result of union with Christ. Believers are "sanctified," or "made holy," by their relationship to Him. The problem of the Corinthian church was that many were not experiencing daily sanctification and were therefore living carnally (see 3:3). Their walk was out of sorts with their position.

1:3. While "grace and peace" was a common greeting in Paul's day, he did not use it in a perfunctory manner. **Grace** (Greek, *charis*) has the idea of undeserved kindness, while **peace** (Greek, *eirēnē*) is the calmness and inner serenity that comes only from God and the Lord Jesus Christ. The grace and peace that humans give are limited, but true satisfaction and blessing come when these qualities are of a spiritual nature.

B. Thanksgiving to God (1:4–9)

Though Paul took the Corinthian church to task for its sins, he also complimented the church. Here he wanted to make certain these believers understood how blessed they were. While setting out to reform them in their carnality, he reminded them how much God was still at work in their midst. The Lord does not throw away even the most sinful believer. This church had an opportunity to change its ways. It had a wide influence throughout the region for the sake of the gospel and had much work to do.

1:4. Despite the many problems in the Corinthian church, Paul still thanked God for this body of believers. Christ benefited this assembly by **the grace of God**. In Greek, **is given** is an aorist passive particle and may better be translated "was given." Paul may have been thinking of the salvation "grace" that is imparted through Jesus Christ. Perhaps concerned that the Corinthians were puffed up in their self-esteem, Paul reminded them that they were saved by the grace of God, not by their goodness.

1:5. In every way and **in every thing**, the Corinthians were **enriched by** Christ. **Utterance** and **knowledge** could refer to the speaking and knowledge gifts, such as prophecies, tongues, and knowledge (see 13:8). The apostle again reminded them of how blessed they were to have these gifts operating in the assembly. He later chided them for their misuse of these impartations of the Holy Spirit (see chaps. 12–14).

1:6. The spiritual gifts mentioned in 1:5 seem to clearly confirm **the testimony of Christ** in their lives. The Christians in Corinth were not fakes, but they did have tremendous problems with carnality. Though Paul considered himself a feeble speaker (see 2:4), the word of salvation in Christ and the message of the cross was delivered "in the power of God" (2:5).

1:7–8. The apostle pointed out that the Corinthians possessed spiritual gifts and did not **come behind** (v. 7) in the exercise of those gifts. He wanted the believers to have full use of what the Holy Spirit imparted to them (see 12:7–11). **Waiting** (Greek, *apekdechomenous*; see 1 Peter 3:20) is here "waiting patiently," with expectation and longing, **for the coming of our Lord Jesus Christ**. The Greek for "the coming" (*apokalypsin*; "the revelation") is not the term one would expect here. Since Paul and the Corinthians were waiting for this to happen, more than likely he was referring to the revelation of Christ in the rapture of the church. Potentially, this could have happened in Paul's day because no one knows God's timetable for this glorious event.

The Lord would **also confirm** (Greek, *bebaiōsei*; v. 8) the believers, meaning He would make them steadfast and preserve them from falling. **Unto the end** of their lives, the believers would be prevented from falling away, kept steadfast in their belief and in obedience to the truth (see 2 Cor. 1:21). They would be kept **blameless** and would not be charged with apostasy. This does not mean that they would live absolutely perfect lives but that they would be kept from walking away from their faith in Christ (see 1 Thess. 5:23).

1:9. In Greek, **God is faithful** has no verb. It simply says "faithful God." God had **called** the Corinthians into fellowship with his Son, and whom the Lord calls to such a relationship, He also justifies and even glorifies (see Rom. 8:30). Being "called" is the effectual calling of the Holy Spirit, by which the soul is renewed and given an eternal inheritance in glory. **The fellowship** (Greek, *koinōnia*) has to do with the personal communication with which the believer is blessed to enjoy his Savior intimately. Believers are also "conformed to the image of [the] Son" (Rom. 8:29), participate in "the blood of Christ" (1 Cor. 10:16), and participate in "the communion of the Holy Ghost" (2 Cor. 13:14).

II. Schisms and Divisions in the Church (1:10–4:21)

In this lengthy section of the book, Paul spelled out the many problems the Corinthian church faced. The apostle pulled no punches. He was specific about the things that were destroying this body of believers and ruining their testimony before the lost. One of the most compelling objects of this letter was to correct the evils that had come to the surface. Human wisdom had brought about divisions and contentions, and from this came all kinds of sinful practices that were hindering the gospel. The apostle set forth a long list of problems he wanted this assembly to contemplate spiritually.

A. Specific Contentions and Divisions (1:10–17)

1:10. Paul pleaded with these brothers in Christ (**I beseech you**), not in his own name, but **by the name of the Lord Jesus Christ**. The final authority was not the apostle but Christ. Paul wanted them to **all speak the same thing**, stressing their spiritual and biblical unity. Their common moral and spiritual thoughts were to come from God, not simply from their own ideas about the Christian walk. He urged the congregation to stop its **divisions** (*schisma*) and **be perfectly joined together**. "Joined" (Greek, *katartizō*) means "cauterized" (meaning to heal), "restored" (as in healing) or "made fit or complete" (as sometimes used to describe the mending of fishing nets; see Matt. 4:21; Mark 1:19). In Galatians 6:9, Paul used the same Greek word to refer to the restoration of a brother who had been caught in a trespass.

The union Paul had in mind has to do with being of **the same mind** and possessing **the same judgment**. "Mind" has to do with the faculty by which truth is grasped, and "judgment" is the opinion formed in regard to truth, not by insistence upon uniformity (Vine, *Collected Writings*, p.). The believers were to move forward in spiritual unity rooted in truth.

1:11. The house of Chloe had reported to Paul what was going on in the Corinthian church. Chloe (meaning "verdant") is mentioned only here in the New Testament. It is not known whether she was a widow or had a husband who was not a Christian. Her "house" could have been her believing children who informed Paul of the **contentions** (Greek, *er-*

ides; "strifes," "wranglings") **among you**. The following verses seem to indicate that these "wranglings" had to do with the religious teachers among the congregation. Jealousies had sprung up.

1:12. The divisions in the church seem to have been sharp and apparently placed members in different camps: **every one of you saith, I am of Paul; and I of Apollos; and I of Cephas; and I of Christ**. Since Paul was an apostle of the Gentiles, and Peter of the Jews (see Gal. 2:8), more than likely the Gentile converts were in a struggle with the followers of Peter (see Hodge, *First Epistle to the Corinthians*, p. 13). These contentions were driven by false teachers who were Jews (see 2 Cor. 11:13, 22). They worked hard to undermine Paul, possibly not realizing that he also was Jewish.

Apollos was a Jew from Alexandria who was well known for his eloquence, education, and literary culture. The more highly educated Corinthians followed his teachings. The name Apollos comes from the Greek god and means "the destroyer." Early on, Priscilla and Aquila had given him instruction in the faith (see Acts 18:26), and he had grown to become one who greatly strengthened the believers by using the Word of God to show that Jesus was the promised Christ (see Acts 18:28). Apollos was last mentioned in Acts 19:1.

1:13. These three questions are rhetorical and demand a clear no. Christ did not die just for certain people. Paul was certainly not the crucified Savior, nor were the Corinthians **baptized** in Paul's **name**. There is only one redeemer, one Savior, and one expression of baptism. Christians worship Christ alone and are committed and consecrated to Him only. Christianity is not a man-centered religion but one that focuses on the Savior Himself (see Hodge, *First Epistle to the Corinthians*, p. 15).

1:14–15. Paul made it clear that he had gone to Corinth, not to make a huge issue of baptism, but to preach the gospel. He initially recalled that he had baptized no one **but Crispus and Gaius** (v. 14; see 1:16). He mentioned this because he suspected that others would want him to baptize them so they could claim some form of religious fame: "I was baptized by the apostle Paul!" (see v. 15). Crispus ("curly") was a leader in the synagogue (see Acts 18:8) and one of the few whom Paul personally baptized. Tradition says Crispus became the bishop of Aegina. Gaius (Latin, Caius; "I rejoice") was Paul's host in Corinth (see Rom. 16:23). The positions of these two men may indicate why the apostle remembered them.

1:16. As Paul wrote, he then recalled that he had also baptized **the household of Stephanas** ("crown"). "The household" indicates that this man's family and maybe even some of his servants had accepted Christ. Stephanas apparently was one of the first converts Paul made in Achaia and may have been the Stephanas who delivered a letter from the Corinthians when Paul was in Ephesus (see 16:17), though this may not be the same individual.

1:17. Paul made an important point about the relation between baptism and the gospel. While baptism is important as a witness of the believer's cleansing through the work of Christ on the cross, it is not part of the gospel message, nor does it save. Paul separated baptism from the gospel by saying, **Christ sent me not to baptize, but to preach the gospel**. The implication of this is important: baptism is not necessary for salvation (see Mitchell, *First Corinthians*, p. 27), which is not to say baptism is not important. It was commanded by Jesus (see Matt. 28:19) and practiced by the early church (see Acts 2:41), and along with the Lord's Supper, it is a symbol of the sacrifice of Christ and His redemption.

Paul focused on the Corinthian believers' attempt to solve their spiritual problems **with wisdom words of** rather than with spiritual and biblical principles. The apostle was not about to ascribe to the simple gospel its power to save by using poetic oratory (see Mitchell, *First Corinthians*, p. 27). He was repudiating, not godly wisdom, but human reason that attempts to justify one's actions and motives. Such self-effort nullifies **the cross of Christ**. Paul was not talking about a loss of salvation. He was saying that the redemptive work of Christ was having no effect in the Corinthians' daily walk. Whatever obscures the cross deprives the gospel of its power (see Hodge, *First Epistle to the Corinthians*, p. 18).

B. The Various Causes of Divisions (1:18–4:5)

In this section, the apostle went to great lengths to spell out the problems the Corinthian Christians were having. The message to them regarding these problems is certainly applicable to congregations today. Paul cited carnality as a major cause of what was happening in the church and addressed the assembly with strong language. Some have noted that he did not address any elders in his correction and therefore surmise that none in the congregation were qualified for the office. If this was the case, Paul was acting as the elder-apostle, governing the believers and chiding them for having allowed divisions to take hold in the church.

1. A Wrong View of the Christian Message (1:18–3:4)

Without a doubt, the Corinthian church was attempting to live the Christian life by unsanctified ways rather than by focusing on Christ. Such self-serving behavior is ultimately self-destructive (see Luke 9:24–25).

1:18. The preaching of the gospel (see 1:17) and **the preaching of the cross** are virtually the same thing. Actually, Paul said "the word [Greek, *ho logos*] of the cross." Hodge (*First Epistle to the Corinthians*, p. 19) sees this as "the doctrine of the cross." It is the cross that brings salvation; otherwise, there is no redemption. To the world and those who are perishing, the cross is **foolishness** (Greek, *mōria*, from which the word "moronic" comes). What Paul wrote here still stands today. Christ made a similar statement in Matthew 7:13–14: "broad is the way [that leads] to destruction … and narrow is the way [that leads] unto life, and few there be that find it." For the saved, the cross is **the power of God**. For the world, the doctrine of salvation through a crucified Savior is absurd. "The Death of Christ seems, to natural wisdom, unfit to attain its end, and therefore foolishness" (Vine, *Collected Writings*, p. 11).

1:19. Paul quoted Isaiah 29:14: **I will destroy the wisdom of the wise, and will bring to nothing the understanding of the prudent**. "Prudent" (Greek, *synesis*) carries the thought of a quickness of comprehension, a mental alertness that precedes action. It is a human quality admired by the world but useless for salvation. Humanity boasts in such attributes, but God says He will destroy such frail and limited thinking. The context of Isaiah 29:14 has to do with Sennacherib's invasion, when Judah sought the assistance of Egypt. Human political wisdom rendered Judah helpless. The nation of Judah was to depend on God.

1:20–21. Here Paul mocked those who relied on natural wisdom. One would think **the wise** (Greek, *sophos*; v. 20), **the scribe**, and **the disputer** (Greek, *syzētētēs*; "debater") would have the answers to spiritual questions. Instead, **God made foolish the wisdom of this world**. The apostle put this last thought in the form of a question as a challenge to every class of people admired by the world. Neither the esteemed Jewish rabbi and scholar nor the Greek philosopher could ever attain to God's thinking.

The world (Greek, *kosmos*; v. 21) has to do with not simply the "globe" but also the worldly system of humanity. This system is controlled by Lucifer, or Satan, who is the god "of this world" (see also Luke 16:8). This is the realm of spiritual darkness and natural thinking that in no way can please God (see Eph. 2:1–3). Satan is described as "the prince of the power of the air, the spirit that now worketh in the children of disobedience" (Eph. 2:2).

The world could not know God **by wisdom** but only by the **preaching to save them that believe**. This encompasses all that is included in the gospel about who Jesus is, what He did at the cross, and what He accomplished through His resurrection, without which there is no salvation (see 15:17).

1:22–23. Further explaining 1:18–21, Paul pointed out that **the Jews require a sign, and the Greeks seek after wisdom** (v. 22). Both Jew and Gentile found it difficult to rely on God's authoritative word about spiritual and eternal issues, especially in regard to the crucifixion. "Both found it equally difficult to accept a dead man on a cross as an eternal Savior" (Mitchell, *First Corinthians*, p. 31). That Christ was **a stumblingblock** (v. 23) to the Jews is made quite clear in the Gospels. They rejected Him outright as a malefactor and refused to see Him as

their Messiah. Christ became a rock of offense (see Rom. 9:33; 1 Peter 2:8). Whether Jew or Gentile, nothing was more absurd than saying that the blood of the cross could remove sin and secure salvation (see Hodge, *First Epistle to the Corinthians*, p. 23).

1:24–25. Unto them which are called (Greek, *klētos*; v. 24) of God in a sovereign way, whether **Jews and Greeks**, the preaching of Christ crucified (and Christ Himself) is **the power of God, and the wisdom of God**. The Lord calls people by opening their eyes to faith and belief in the gospel. The initiative belongs to God, not man. The doctrine of Christ crucified produces effects on those who are saved, effects that only divine power can accomplish (see Hodge, *First Epistle to the Corinthians*, p. 23).

Paul used hyperbole to explain why human wisdom is not enough: if God acted with **foolishness** (v. 25) and **weakness**, this would still be greater, or **stronger**, than anything man could do. Of course, God is neither foolish nor weak. The Corinthians got the point.

1:26–31. In these verses, the apostle's summary furthered his point about human wisdom and God's divine way of doing things. God uses **the foolish things of the world** (v. 27), things the world would consider foolish, **to confound** those who think they are **wise**. He also uses **the weak things … to confound** those who think they are **mighty**. The wise are operating from the **flesh** (v. 29), from their own wisdom, human nature. The hierarchy of "wise" men includes the **mighty** (Greek, *dynatoi*; "the powerful" who have authority; v. 26) and the **noble**, those who are "well-born." "The things which elevate man in the world, knowledge, influence, rank, are not the things which lead to God and salvation" (Hodge, *First Epistle to the Corinthians*, p. 25). "Paul's readers were not the recipients of the grace of God because of their social status" (Mitchell, *First Corinthians*, p. 31). God is not impressed with what impresses men.

God turns around the things that people think are important. He chooses the **base things** (Greek, *ta agenē*; v. 28), the "ignoble," things that are in contrast to what is "wise." "Base things" refers to those who are not well-bred and who do not come from the nobility. He also chooses the **things which are despised**, the lowly, and **things which are not**, meaning "the things that do not even exist." In other words, the Lord uses things that people do not even think about to accomplish His purposes, that is, **to bring to nought things that are**. This proves that man's thoughts are not God's thoughts and that human beings do not counsel Him (see Isa. 55:8; Rom. 11:34).

God rejects human "things" so **That no flesh should glory in his presence** (v. 29). No one can stand before the Lord Almighty and claim that his conversion or his redemption came about through his own wisdom, birth, station in life, or education. Men may use such means to differentiate themselves, but God does not. The glory belongs to God, not man (see v. 31).

Believers are placed **in Christ Jesus** (v. 30), whom God **made unto us wisdom ... righteousness ... sanctification, and redemption**. God's "wisdom" initiates salvation through certain doctrinal accomplishments that He renders through Christ. "Righteousness" (Greek, *dikaiosynē*) has to do with the "applied" righteousness, or the justification that comes through the infinite merit of Christ (see Rom. 3:21–22; 2 Cor. 5:21). Believers share in His attribute of perfection, or perfect righteousness, which is imputed to them (see Rom. 4:1–10). "Sanctification" (Greek, *hagiasmos*) here is positional sanctification, which credits Christ's holiness to the believer's account because of the union with Him (see 2 Thess. 2:13; 1 Peter 1:2). "Redemption" (Greek, *lytrōsis*) is here also used in a positional sense (see Titus 2:14; Heb. 9:12; 1 Peter 1:18) and pictures one being redeemed from the slave market of sin and freed by the payment of the Redeemer. Christ paid the price by taking our place at the cross. All believers will experience the final redemption of their bodies, "the redemption of the purchased possession, unto the praise of his glory" (Eph. 1:14).

As a conclusion of 1:18–30, Paul quoted Jeremiah 9:23: **He that glorieth, let him glory in the Lord** (repeated in 2 Cor. 10:17). The citation is an abridged combination of Jeremiah and 1 Samuel 2:10. **In the Lord** is the Septuagint's condensed rendering of "Jehovah." "All that is significant in that title is demonstrated in the New Testament to be true of Christ. To glory in the Father is to glory in the Son (cf. John 14:13)" (Vine, *Collected Writings*, p. 15).

2:1–5. Despite the Corinthians' problems, Paul still called them **brethren** (v. 1). He reminded them that he had not come to them with flattery or **excellency of speech or of wisdom**. These things he repudiated. The word "excellency" (Greek, *hyperochē*) denotes that which "overhangs" with preeminence, that which is superior. It is used in 1 Timothy 2:2 to mean "a high place," a place of "authority." Paul had apostolic authority (see 2 Cor. 11), but he did not like to wield that power unless it was necessary to silence those who rebelled against the Word of the Lord.

Paul had gone to the Corinthians declaring the **testimony of God** (v. 1), or "the witness [Greek, *martyrion*] of God," probably referring either to God's own testimony about the gospel or to Paul's testimony about God, that is, what the Lord revealed and testified to be true. What Paul had testified among the Corinthians was **Jesus Christ, and him crucified** (v. 2). Salvation does not come about by believing that Christ was simply a good teacher, a blessed prophet. The cross of Christ cannot be excluded from who He is and what He came to do. Salvation comes about only by Christ's substitution under the wrath of God and His death for sinners. The apostle already stated that such a message is, from the human standpoint, foolishness to those who are perishing (see 1:18).

Paul had not witnessed to the Corinthians with a pompous demeanor but with **weakness ... fear, and ... much trembling** (v. 3). Again, he was probably using hyperbole here. He came to them with simplicity, though he may have had some anxiousness of mind because of what he perceived as his insufficiency. He realized how important his task was (see 2 Cor. 7:15; Phil. 2:12; Eph. 6:5). "He had a work to do which he felt to be entirely above his powers" (Hodge, *First Epistle to the Corinthians*, p. 31).

Paul's **speech** (Greek, *logos*) **and ... preaching** (Greek, *kērygma*) **was not with enticing words of**

man's wisdom (v. 4) but in the work of the Holy Spirit. His ability did not come from his talent and oratory skills. Without the dynamic work and power of God's Spirit in the heart of the hearer, the wisdom and eloquence of the human preacher is not effective. In the New Testament, **demonstration** (Greek, *apodeixis*) means a "showing forth" or "proving by force." This "demonstration" manifests the sovereign work **of the Spirit and of power**, the power He wields in working salvation in the chosen. Contrasting the Holy Spirit with the spiritually impotent human spirit, Paul said that the Corinthians' **faith should not stand in the wisdom of men, but in the power of God** (v. 5). The preposition "in" (Greek, *en*) indicates the sphere in which their faith had its roots. "It has been well said that what depends upon a clever argument is at the mercy of a cleverer argument" (Vine, *Collected Writings*, p. 17). "Those who put their faith in God's power to save them, their faith ... 'has found a resting place'" (Mitchell, *First Corinthians*, p. 39).

2:6. The Lord puts a premium on ignorance and rejects human wisdom of all sorts, but there is a place for divine wisdom, the **wisdom** of God that is spoken **among them that are perfect** (Greek, *tois teleiois*). "Perfect" refers to believers who are mature, complete, whole, spiritually competent. God's wisdom does not originate with the **world**, nor from **the princes of this world**. All such human wisdom will **come to nought** (Greek, *katargeō*). Human wisdom will be rendered inactive, and the policies of human potentates are destined to become ineffective (see Vine, *Collected Writings*, p. 18).

2:7. The apostle put forth God's secret wisdom, known only to the Lord and made known to humankind only through His revelation (see Matt. 11:25): **the wisdom of God ... a mystery ... the hidden wisdom, which God ordained**. "Mystery" refers to God's work or purpose that was once "kept secret" (Rom. 16:25–26) but has now been revealed to His people (see Mitchell, *First Corinthians*, p. 41). Such wisdom was **ordained before the world unto our glory** (Greek, *doxa*). "Glory" refers not to the self-glory of the believer but to God's blessing of those

who are in Christ and the working of His glory for their benefit. "The word *glory* is often used for all the benefits of salvation" (Hodge, *First Epistle to the Corinthians*, p. 35). "Ordained" is *proorizō*, which means "predetermined" in reference to human glory. "The idea that the scheme of redemption, which the apostle here calls the wisdom of God, was from eternity formed in the divine mind" (ibid.).

2:8. As did the apostle John (see John 17:1), Paul linked **glory** with the crucified Savior. This was a total paradox for both the Jews and the Gentiles (see 1 Cor. 1:23), who, though not knowing it, were to a degree witnesses of God's great plan for the redemption of His lost creatures (see Luke 23:24). If they had **known it** (the plan), **they would not have crucified the Lord of glory**. "The Lord of glory" literally means "the Lord whose attribute was glory."

2:9–12. The magnificent blessings of redemption were planned by God the Father, carried out by the Son, and then directed toward those who were chosen (see Eph. 1:3–4), those who love God (see 1 John 4:19). This great truth about redemption cannot be known apart from **his Spirit** (v. 10), who **searcheth ... the deep things of God** and gives it to His children. This "searching" demonstrates the personality of the Spirit; intelligent activity is ascribed to Him. His divinity is omniscient; He knows all that God knows and progressively shares this with the believers—an activity referred to as "the doctrine of illumination." That which is beyond human knowledge (see 1 Cor. 2:9) is revealed to those who have received the Spirit, who is **not the spirit of the world, but the Spirit which is of God** (v. 12). Besides the knowledge of salvation, the Holy Spirit conveys to the believer "the deep things of God," or "the depths of God," the inmost recesses of His being, His "perfections and purposes" (Hodge, *First Epistle to the Corinthians*, p. 39).

People can know **the things of a man** (v. 11) only through **the spirit of man** by which they are able to communicate with another human being. Likewise, a Christian can know the things of God only through **the Spirit of God**. The Lord's Spirit is given to us so that we can know God the Father. What believers

have received (v. 12) is not the spirit of the world but **the Spirit which is of God**, who helps us better understand what God has **freely given** to us. **That we might know** (Greek, *oida*) stands in contrast to *ginōskō* (used earlier in v. 11), which suggests an understanding of the relation and meaning of things. *Oida* is knowledge, while *ginōskō* is comprehension.

2:13. Which things also we speak probably refers to the apostles and all who were ministering and setting forth the truth. The source was not **man's wisdom** but what **the Holy Ghost teacheth**. The evangelist or teacher, then, is speaking words "taught by the Spirit," **comparing**, or better "combining" (Greek, *synkrinō*; "together judging, evaluating"), spiritual thoughts with spiritual words. In classical Greek, *synkrinō* is always used in the sense of "to compound" or "to interpret" (cf. Gen. 40:8 Septuagint) (Mitchell, *First Corinthians*, p. 43).

2:14. The natural man cannot receive **the things of the Spirit of God** because such things **are foolishness unto him**. He cannot even **know them** because they have to be **spiritually discerned**, and he, in the natural sense, is incapable of this. This verse stresses the depravity of humanity in that the lost are cut off from God and cannot "reason" up to Him (see Rom. 1:18–32). Also, as Paul explained in 2:11–12, one must have the Holy Spirit to know the things of God, which certainly includes the truth about salvation. "The natural man" (Greek, *psychikos*) operates from the center of himself. He cannot reason spiritually from his inner self. James 3:15 renders *psychikos* "sensual," with the idea of "natural" or "animal-like" (see also Jude 19). Spiritual things are therefore distasteful and unintelligible to the lost.

2:15–16. Here Paul drew a conclusion, stating that the one who **is spiritual judgeth all things** (v. 15). "Spiritual" is *pneumatikos* and is in contrast to *psychikos* (2:14), the "natural" man who has no relationship with God and receives no spiritual enlightenment from the Holy Spirit. The spiritual man is able to comprehend spiritual issues and live the life God desires of him because he "judgeth," or "discerns," all things. Because of this, he receives but limited criticism and condemnation and **is judged of**

no man. "The spiritual man is a riddle to the merely natural. This does not mean that he stands above [all] criticism" (Vine, *Collected Writings*, p. 21). Much of what Paul described here happens progressively. No believer is "born again" with perfect spiritual knowledge.

If the Holy Spirit, who dwells within the believer, gives spiritual discernment, the child of God knows **the mind of the Lord** (v. 16) because he has **the mind of Christ**. When the Spirit of God gives inner spiritual instruction, the Christian knows the mind of God the Father and the mind of His Son, Jesus Christ. "That the phrase 'the mind of Christ' is used as the equivalent of 'the mind of the Lord' (Jehovah, in the Old Testament), is a testimony to the Deity of Christ (cf. Gal. 4:6)" (Vine, *Collected Writings*, p. 21). "We have the mind of Christ because we have the words and thoughts stirred up in our minds through the indwelling Holy Spirit (see Col. 3:16–17; cf. also Eph. 3:17; James 4:5)" (Mitchell, *First Corinthians*, p. 46).

3:1–4. Concluding his discussion of the Corinthians' wrong view of the Christian message, Paul aimed his thoughts even more directly at the problems of the Corinthian church. He again called the believers **brethren** (v. 1; see 1:10; 2:1) but said he could speak to them not **as unto spiritual** but rather **as unto carnal** (Greek, *sarkinos*), or "fleshly," believers. Being "carnal" in spiritual maturity, the Corinthians were **babes** (Greek, *nēpiois*; "non-speakers," or "infants") **in Christ**. The apostle put forward the three types of humanity: (1) "the natural man," who operates only from his own soul and "receiveth not the things of … God" (2:14), (2) the "spiritual" man (2:15; 3:1), who listens to the Spirit of God, and (3) immature, or "carnal" (3:1), believers, who are characterized as "babes in Christ" in contrast to the mature believers mentioned in 2:6.

Paul had to feed this body of Corinthian believers with **milk** (v. 2), which means he could not give them the **meat** of the Word of God to help them grow and mature in the Lord. Previously they **were not able to bear it**, and **neither yet now are ye able**, Paul said. "As newborn babes this condition would be natural and to be expected (1 Pet. 2:2). But, at this state in their development, it is embarrassing. They still are acting like spiritual babes" (Mitchell, *First Corinthians*, p. 49). The proof of their immaturity was their **envying ... strife, and divisions** (v. 3), which clearly demonstrated that they were **carnal, and walk[ed] as men**. "'Are you not on a purely human level,' lacking spiritual discernment?" (Vine, *Collected Writings*, p. 23). The division continued as it had begun, over baptism (see 1:12). The church was divided into the camps of Paul and Apollos. Some were claiming, **I am of Paul** (v. 4), and others claimed, **I am of Apollos**. Paul pointed to this as final proof that the Corinthians were still **carnal**. They had focused on men, forgetting that God alone is the true source of blessing (see 3:5–9).

2. A Wrong View of the Christian Ministry (3:5–4:5)

3:5–9. Paul explained that there are no divisions with God. In the pioneering ministry of the gospel, **Paul, and ... Apollos** (v. 5) were but human instruments used of the Lord, **ministers by whom ye believed**. These two men were means God used for bringing people to salvation; they were not the first cause. They were only servants who had to give an account to God the Father (see 3:10–17). Each man had his own ministry and his own particular place in God's plan. Paul said, **I have planted, Apollos watered; but God gave the increase** (v. 6).

Again, Paul stressed God's sovereignty over His servants, saying, **So then neither is he that planteth** (Paul) **any thing, neither he that watereth** (Apollos)**; but God that giveth the increase** (v. 7). Three principles are seen here. Paul and Apollos were practicing (1) *faithfulness*. Since they differed somewhat in ministry, there was (2) *diversity*. The (3) *ownership*, however, belonged to God (see Mitchell, *First Corinthians*, p. 50). The work is God's, and so is the harvest. "Ministers are nothing. They are the instruments in the hands of God" (Hodge, *First Epistle to the Corinthians*, p. 52). Despite the fact that the servants of the Lord are but carrying out His purposes, He will still reward each one **according to his own labour** (v. 8). "Paul does not develop the thought of the *pay*, or reward (*misthos*), received by God's

gardeners, and it is not clear whether he refers to recompense in heaven, or a return for his labours in the growth of his plants" (Barrett, *First Epistle to the Corinthians*, p. 86). In God's providence, Christians are but **labourers together with God** (v. 9). "Labourers" are but **God's husbandry**, or "farm," producing the yield that He has planned. Believers are also called **God's building**, which is being constructed for His purposes.

3:10–17. It is interesting to note the various analogies Paul used to get across his point about the ministry: earlier he spoke of planting and watering; here he spoke of laying a foundation and constructing a building. In this building process, the apostle was not reluctant to share the ministry and the rewards. **The grace of God** (v. 10) was given to Paul to make him **a wise masterbuilder**. He **laid the foundation**, but Apollos **buildeth thereupon**. In the Christian life, no **other foundation** (v. 11) can be laid except that **which is Jesus Christ**. Salvation and the entire spiritual life are held up by Him. Once faith establishes Jesus as the foundation, the believer is constructing his spiritual life, his existence, upon Him. The quality of that construction is important. Will it be of precious materials, such as **gold, silver, precious stones** (v. 12), or flimsy building elements, such as **wood, hay, [and] stubble**? "'Gold, silver, precious stones refer to the apostle's teaching, also that of Apollos and other good men, whereas the 'wood, hay, and stubble' refer to teaching that was divisive, marked by the wisdom of this world" (Hunter, *1 Corinthians*, p. 37).

There will be an answering, or a **day** (v. 13) of reckoning, that **shall declare** what kind of work it is. That work **shall be revealed by fire**, and that **fire shall try every man's work of what sort it is**. These verses and others (see, e.g., 2 Cor. 5:9–11) describe what is called the *bēma*, or "the judgment seat of Christ," where "every one [will] receive the things done in his body ... whether it be good or bad" (2 Cor. 5:10). This judgment, mentioned in both letters to the Corinthians, is not meant to determine the believer's eternal destiny but rather his ministry reward. If the works done in this life, based on the foundation of Jesus Christ, were for His sake, the believer **shall receive a reward** (v. 14).

Some have mistakenly argued that this passage refers to a judgment in which the believer's life will be tested by fire to determine whether he will be admitted into heaven. The believer's eternal destiny, however, was completely and fully settled at the cross. Salvation is assured because of the faithfulness of Christ, not because of human efforts to stay saved. It is one's works that will be tested as by fire, to determine their durability. **If any man's work shall be burnt, he shall suffer loss: but he himself shall be saved; yet so as** if he had passed through **fire.** "If the person's work remains undamaged by the fire, he or she receives rewards (*misthos*, "wages"; cf. v. 8). Of course, it goes without saying that even the wages mentioned here are entirely a gift of grace (cf. Dan. 12:3; 1 Cor. 9:19; 2 John 1:8; Rev. 4:4; 11:18)" (Mitchell, *First Corinthians*, pp. 54–55).

As important as rewards may be, Paul reached for a higher incentive. He reminded the Corinthians that they were collectively **the temple of God** (v. 16) in which **the Spirit of God dwelleth**. If someone comes against the temple, **him shall God destroy** (v. 17). The apostle was describing the church as a group, a body of believers with whom God fellowships and resides. He does not want the church to suffer tampering. "The prospect of such people [harming the church] is a fearful one. They will fall under the condemnation of God" (Mitchell, *First Corinthians*, p. 55). "The verb *phtheirō* signifies to destroy by corrupting; here it is used, firstly, of the marring of an assembly by unprofitable teaching and by producing a party spirit thereby, or by leading it away by any means" (Vine, *Collected Writings*, p. 26). God takes this seriously because despite the imperfections of how believers may walk at any specific moment, they are still seen positionally as **holy** because they belong to Christ.

3:18–23. The apostle continued to drive home the issue that human wisdom does not bring one to God. In a twist in his argument, he said one needs to put away what the world calls wisdom and **let him become a fool, that he may be wise** (v. 18). He again

said that **the wisdom of this world is foolishness with God** (v. 19; see 1:18). The apostle then quoted Job 5:13, **it is written, He taketh the wise in their own craftiness**, and Psalm 94:11, **the thoughts of the wise … are vain** (v. 20). **Therefore,** Paul said, one should not **glory in men** (v. 21). He then made what seems to be a strange statement: **For all things are yours.** The answer appears to be, "Only as we belong to Him do things belong to us. Since we are members of Christ, and all things are under His authority and control (Matt. 28:18; Rom. 14:9; 1 Cor. 15:27), they are *ipso facto* subservient to our real welfare" (Vine, *Collected Writings*, p. 27).

Because "all things" (v. 21) belong to believers, the child of God has access to all, **whether Paul, or Apollos, or Cephas** (Peter), **or the world, or life, or death, or things present, or things to come** (v. 22). Paul concluded this section by saying, **ye are Christ's; and Christ is God's** (v. 23). The church belongs to the Lord Jesus, and He is subject to God the Father. Since the church is the possession of Christ, both the church and Christ are in subordination to the Father. The Son and Father are of the same substance, yet the *economic* submission of the Son to the Father exists within the Godhead. This is beyond human comprehension, yet it stands as a solid doctrine in Scripture (see Phil. 2:6–11; Heb. 1:3).

4:1. In view of the previous passage, it is clear that all who serve the Lord Jesus Christ are responsible as **ministers** to Him and are **stewards** (Greek, *oikonomos*; "household managers") **of the mysteries of God.** Because the word "mystery" (Greek, *mystērion*) is in the plural, Paul's meaning is openended. "Mystery" means "something not before revealed," and the New Testament speaks about many subjects as a mystery: (1) "the mystery of the kingdom of God" (Mark 4:11); (2) the mystery of the unification of Jews and Gentiles into one body, the church (Ephesians 2–3); (3) "the mystery of the gospel" (Eph. 6:19); (4) "the mystery of the faith" (1 Tim. 3:9); and (5) the mystery of the rapture of the church (1 Cor. 15:51), among others.

4:2. Because such great truths are revealed to God's **stewards**, it is imperative that they be **found**

faithful. They must be ready to give their Master an account of their loyalty. The Lord certainly sees one's faithfulness, but others also witness it.

4:3. Paul considered himself a faithful servant of Christ. He made it clear, however, that he was not to **be judged** by the Corinthian church or by any other **man's judgment**, adding even, **I judge not mine own self**. The Lord alone was his judge. One of the problems Paul had to contend with in this body of "carnal" (3:3-4) believers was their criticism of him and his apostleship. In 4:6-21 and in 2 Corinthians 10-11, he forcefully answered their criticisms. Though an apostle, Paul still could not judge his own motives or the quality of his service. How could others decide such issues?

4:4-5. In writing, **I know nothing by myself** (v. 4), Paul was not repudiating his apostolic and prophetic offices, nor the revelations that were given to him exclusively. Likewise, **I [am] not hereby justified** does not refer to salvation and justification by faith. In this passage, Paul was discussing motives and actions. He was responsible to God: **he that judgeth me is the Lord**. "'My judgment of myself is not final... Paul felt himself accountable to Christ" (Hodge, *First Epistle to the Corinthians*, pp. 66-67).

Paul stated that judgment needs to be held off **until the Lord come** (v. 5), who will then **bring to light** what is **hidden** and make clear **the counsels of the hearts**, so that all will **have praise of God**. Apparently, this judgment of believers will occur at the rapture of the church. James seems to have had this in mind when he wrote, "The coming of the Lord draweth nigh. Grudge not one against another, brethren, lest ye be condemned: behold, the judge standeth before the door" (James 5:8-9).

C. Overcoming Divisions (4:6-21)

The apostle came out swinging to rebuke those within the Corinthian church who were attempting to discredit his ministry to the church. Having set forth the guidelines that should govern this assembly, he went on to discuss their divisions. With strong appeals against this state of things (vv. 7-8), he maintained that he ministered to them in full in-

tegrity and openness, even foregoing any help from them (v. 12) and abiding their defamation of his work and his character (v. 13).

4:6. To make a point, he wrote **in a figure transferred** what he was writing about to himself and Apollos for the sake of the Corinthian believers. "Transferred" is the Greek word *metaschēmatizō*, which means to "change in appearance or form." It is translated "change" in Philippians 3:21, where it refers to the fashioning anew of the believer's body in the rapture of the church. Paul used himself and Apollos to illustrate the principle underlying his instruction. "Paul avoided singling out guilty persons by name. Instead he applied the problem cases to Apollos and himself (and Peter and Christ; cf. 1:12; 3:4-6, 22:33)" (Lowery, "First Corinthians," p. 512). Paul desired for the Corinthians to **learn** (Greek, *manthanō*; "to learn by practice or doing") so that they would not be **puffed up ... one against another** in spiritual competition.

4:7. People **differ from** each other because they **receive** unique talents or characteristics from God. Paul therefore asked the Corinthians, **why doest thou glory, as if thou hadst not received** such differences from the Lord? The word "differ" (Greek, *diakrinō*) means to "make a distinction." With those distinctions, however, many in the church were saying that such abilities were self-generated and not divinely imparted. This was bringing about self-conceit.

4:8. Because of God's gifts given to the Corinthian believers, they were **rich**, or **as kings**, but they were taking these blessings and **reign[ing] as kings** over the apostles and their guidance. They were **full** (Greek, *korennymi*; "satiated") with assumed spiritual fullness. They believed they had reached the goal of perfection very quickly, and that **without us**, the apostle added. "Paul represents the Corinthians as thinking that they had already attained the full blessedness of the Messiah's reign ... and were already perfect" (Hodge, *First Epistle to the Corinthians*, pp. 71-72).

4:9-13. Using irony and sarcasm, Paul mocked the Corinthians' sense of superiority in the realm of

Christian service and maturity. He said, **God hath set forth us the apostles last** (v. 9), as if destined for **death**. They had been **made a spectacle unto the world**, and even **to angels, and to men**. The apostles were **fools** (v. 10) for the sake of Jesus, but the Corinthians were **wise**; Paul and others were **weak**, but the Corinthians were **strong**. The apostles were **despised**, but the Corinthians were **honourable**.

The apostles were hungry, thirsty, naked, buffeted about, with **no certain dwellingplace** (v. 11). They worked hard with their **own hands** (v. 12) but were **reviled**. They **bless[ed]** but were **persecuted** and **suffer[ed]** it. The apostles were **defamed** (v. 13) and were seen as **the filth** ("refuse," "scum," "rubbish") of humanity. Even **unto this day**, the apostles continued to be treated as **offscouring** (Greek, *peripsēma*; "filth," "that which is wiped off").

4:14–17. While Paul could have written **these things to shame** (v. 14) his critics, he did not. Instead, he wrote to them **as my beloved sons to warn** them. While they could have had **ten thousand instructers in Christ** (v. 15) in place of the apostles, they had **not many fathers** who really cared for their spiritual growth. **In Christ Jesus** and **through the gospel**, Paul had **begotten** them. "Instructors" (Greek, *paidagōgos*) means "child leaders." Such an instructor was often a slave that gave supervision over the pedagogical learning of the master's son. For Paul, "a spiritual relationship had been established between him and the saints through the Gospel which he brought to them" (Vine, *Collected Writings*, p. 33). Because of this, Paul said, **I beseech you, be ye followers of me** (v. 16). "Followers" (Greek, *mimētēs*) refers to those who imitate or attempt to emulate a teacher, or in this case the father, in how he thinks and acts (see Eph. 5:1; Phil. 3:17).

For this cause (v. 17), that the Corinthians might become true "followers," Paul had sent **Timotheus** (Timothy), his **beloved son** who was **faithful in the Lord**, to refresh the Corinthians in his **ways ... in Christ**. Paul said that these "ways" were the same spiritual principles he taught **in every church**. This is an important statement because it shows that in the church dispensation, spiritual principles are the same in every local assembly. While some issues each congregation may face, generally problems are the same, and biblical and spiritual answers are for everyone in the body of Christ. Paul sent Timothy because he could trust him, and he gave Paul much comfort. Elsewhere Paul said, "I have no man likeminded" as Timothy (Phil. 2:19–20).

4:18–21. Some members of the congregation in Corinth disregarded Paul, were **puffed up** (v. 18), and argued that he would not give his time to come and visit their church. Paul, however, said that **if the Lord will** (v. 19) allow it, **I will come to you shortly**. He reminded them that **the kingdom of God** (v. 20) is not simply about speaking a **word**; it is about **power**, the power of God. By speaking of "the kingdom of God," Paul was not referring to the millennial reign of Christ, which is yet to come on earth. The ultimate destiny of all things, even believers in Christ in this present dispensation of grace, is the one-thousand-year rule of Christ in Jerusalem. Paul may have had this in mind, but it is also possible that he had in view "the Kingdom of God is as a general term, the realm of His [present] rule. As, however, the earth [now] is the scene of rebellion against Him" (Vine, *Collected Writings*, p. 34).

Paul asked, How **shall I come unto you[?] with a rod, or in love, and in the spirit of meekness?** (v. 21). The "rod" of discipline is a metaphor for the rebuke administered by a pedagogue or teacher. "Love" emphasizes parental patience and concern. "The spirit of meekness" is in contrast with stern discipline. "The question implies that the choice of the alternatives, in his mode of dealing with them, lay with themselves" (Vine, *Collected Writings*, p. 34).

III. Immorality in the Church (chaps. 5–6)

A. The Fruit of a Lack of Discipline in the Church (chap. 5)

Besides the divisions in the Corinthian church, another evil caught Paul's attention. The church had allowed a man guilty of incest to stay within the fellowship; it was reported that fornication was generally tolerated among them, without any punishment or discipline (v. 1). Incest was not allowed even among the pagan Gentiles. With apostolic anger, Paul reproved the Corinthians for being so insensitive and spiritually inflated. They did not have a sense of humility and penance, nor had they excommunicated the one who was engaging in incest (v. 2).

5:1. The incest apparently had to do with a Corinthian Christian who was carrying on with his stepmother, a relationship that is forbidden in the Old Testament (see Lev. 18:8; Deut. 22:22, 30). Such a relationship was forbidden even in Roman law (see Cicero *Cluentes* 6; Gaius *Instutitis* 1.63; Lowery, "First Corinthians," p. 514). That Paul said nothing about the woman may suggest that she was not a believer in the Lord. The incestuous affair was not hidden from the assembly but was engaged in openly and **reported commonly**. The whole community knew about it.

5:2. Instead of feeling shame that one of their members was involved in incest, the congregation was **puffed up**, apparently gloating over their Christian liberty, which was a distortion of the doctrine of grace. The church had not **mourned** before God or others, that this man might be removed from the fellowship. Evidently, no one was doing anything or saying anything to correct the situation.

5:3–5. These verses make up one long sentence, which shows how disturbed Paul was about the matter; he could not stop writing until he had completed his thoughts (see Hodge, *First Epistle to the Corinthians*, p. 83). Though Paul was **absent in body** (v. 3), he was still **present in spirit** and had **judged already** the matter **concerning him that hath so done this deed**. Paul did not have to come to the Corinthian church to determine whether the relationship was right or wrong. In both the Old Testament and the New Testament, God has spelled out His eternal moral principles.

In the name of our Lord Jesus Christ (v. 4), with the church **gathered together**, and **with the power of ... Christ**, the offending brother was to be delivered **unto Satan for the destruction of the flesh** (v. 5). The reason: so that his **spirit may be saved in the day of the Lord Jesus**. Since "the whole world lieth in wickedness" (1 John 5:19), the idea is

that the man would get a taste of what Satan does in his own realm. He brings on the human race severe retribution and affliction, even physical destruction. Satan the "adversary is ever seeking to tempt the children of God to turn aside from the right ways of the Lord, and is occupied in laying snares for them (1 Tim. 3:7)" (Vine, *Collected Writings*, p. 37). The man might have to suffer physically in a terrible way to cause him to drop his sinful ways and thus not be castigated so intensely "in the day of the Lord Jesus," more than likely referring to the *bēma* judgment. The issue was not the man's eternal destiny but rather the sins he was practicing openly in his Christian walk. "It thus became a painful example of the price of self-centered indifference and a powerful reminder of the demand for holiness in God's temple (1 Cor. 3:17; 6:19)" (Lowery, "First Corinthians," p. 514). The man would still be saved, "yet so as by fire" (3:15).

5:6. Having chided them for being "puffed up" (5:2) over this issue, Paul added that they were **glorying** (Greek, *kauchēma*; "boasting") and that such glorying **is not good**. He reminded them of the principle of the **leaven** and **the whole lump** of dough. As does leaven, sin spreads throughout the entire loaf of dough (see discussion on Mark 8:15). The whole congregation was morally polluted because of this issue. "It is no less true of any community, that any [toleration of] evil deteriorates its whole moral sense" (Hodge, *First Epistle to the Corinthians*, p. 86).

5:7–8. Paul commanded the church to **purge out ... the old leaven** (v. 7) that they might **be a new lump**. His next statement may seem contradictory at first: **ye are unleavened** because Christ **our passover ... is sacrificed for us**. Walking and living as "a new lump" has to do with believers' daily experience in Christ. The Corinthians were not to be a polluted lump of dough; they were to be dough without leaven. Christ was "sacrificed for us" and yet was without sin. Because He offered a pure sacrificial body, believers are to live in their bodies in a pure and holy way. Jesus fulfilled the true meaning of the Old Testament sacrifice. He was the Passover Lamb of God (see Isa. 53:7; John 1:29). He was crucified on Passover day, a time of celebration that began the evening before the Passover supper was consumed (see Exod. 12:8).

Paul used the Passover feast as an analogy, encouraging the Corinthians to partake of **the feast** (v. 8), not with sinful **old leaven**, satiated with **malice and wickedness; but with the unleavened bread of sincerity and truth**. The apostle was saying, "Let your entire life be as a sacred festival, that is, as a consecration to the Lord." This was to be done in "sincerity" (Greek, *eilikrineia*; "purity," "transparent clarity") and living subjective "truth" that can be seen by all.

5:9–10. Paul had previously written to the Corinthians about not keeping **company with fornicators** (v. 9), but in the providence of the Lord, that letter was not kept as part of the New Testament canon. The church was not to mix with **the fornicators of this world** (v. 10). Moreover, the church was not to associate or have fellowship **with the covetous, or extortioners, or with idolaters**. The covetous defraud, the extortioners exact what is not justly theirs, and the idolaters worship false gods. These descriptions are but the tip of the iceberg of sin and evil in the world. If the Corinthian believers associated regularly with such people, **then must ye needs go out of the world**. Believers would "have to seek another world to live in" (Hodge, *First Epistle to the Corinthians*, p. 90). The believers' "future role should have radically affected their practice in the present (cf. 1 John 3:3)" (Lowery, "First Corinthians," p. 516).

5:11–13. Paul did not want the believers **to keep company** (v. 11) with such people. Here he added in these lines **a railer, or a drunkard** to the list in 5:9–10. The "railer," or "reviler," is one who uses abusive and violent language against someone else. This could also be a "slanderer." The "extortioner" (Greek, *haparx*) is one who robs or takes as spoil another's goods. The believer is **not to eat** with such people.

The apostle made it clear that believers are not to **judge** (v. 12) the lost, those who **are without**. Instead, those in the church should **judge them that are within**. God will take care of those who are with-

out (v. 13). The responsibility of the local church is to **put away** from the body **that wicked person**.

B. Strife from a Lack of Discipline in the Church (6:1–11)

In this section, Paul addressed an issue that must have been a persistent problem, that of fellow Christians taking each other before secular judges to solve disputes. He questioned why believers should settle issues this way. Why could they not solve their problems in an amicable way? Even if they couldn't, they were not to go before pagan arbitrators but rather to take their cases before qualified Christians.

6:1. Paul spoke his mind on the matter and even called the secular judges **the unjust**. This may indicate that most Gentile judges in the government courts were prejudiced or could be bribed. When a believer has **a matter against another** brother, why does he not go **before the saints** to settle the problem?

6:2–4. Six times in this chapter, Paul said, **Do ye not know** or **Know ye not** (vv. 2, 3, 9, 15, 16, 19). He appears to have been provoking them to their senses in realizing how foolish they were being over certain problems. Did the Corinthian church not realize that someday (probably in the millennium) **the saints shall judge the world** (v. 2) and even **angels** (v. 3)? If believers are someday going to have such responsibility, why can they not now judge **the smallest matters** (v. 2) and **things that pertain to this life** (v. 3) in a proper manner without rumblings? To Paul, something appeared to be out of order. The problems in this church were petty, and the believers had their noses too close to small issues and minor grievances. In their Christian relationships, they had lost their perspective. The peace in the assembly was broken because these problems were taking place **in the church** (v. 4). Some feel Paul was using irony when he instructed the Corinthians to set the **least esteemed** to judge. He could have meant, "Set your least esteemed members to decide such matters" or "Do you set as judges those least esteemed in the church?" (Hodge, *First Epistle to the Corinthians*, p. 96).

6:5–6. I speak to your shame (v. 5) indicates Paul was disgusted with their practice of taking each other before secular courts. He questioned whether there was **not a wise man**, meaning one with spiritual wisdom, among them, **not one that shall be able to judge between his brethren**. He could not understand why **brother goeth to law with brother, and that before the unbelievers** (v. 6). "Such lawsuits certainly did not glorify God (10:31–33)" (Lowery, "First Corinthians," p. 515). When those who claim to be Christians wrangle before the lost, it casts doubt on the effect of the gospel.

6:7–8. Paul said that their practice of **go[ing] to law one with another** was **utterly a fault**. It was a **wrong**, and they **suffer … to be defrauded**. It appears that the main motive for such actions was personal gratification rather than redressing wrongs. Under the Mosaic law, God appointed judges to administer justice among the people, but He did not do so under the dispensation of the church. Believers are to solve issues among themselves, operating from a sense of grace and not from a heart of carnality. In view of this passage, one might question Paul's appeal to Caesar when he was accused of teaching things against the Jewish law, against the temple, and even against Caesar (see Acts 25:8). Did the apostle not wish to be tried by Caesar Augustus (see Acts 25:25)? Being a citizen of the Roman Empire, Paul had the right to such an appeal. The Jews accused him of civil disturbance and even with insurrection against the name of Caesar. Paul was willing to "stand at Cesar's judgment seat" (Acts 25:10) because he had done no wrong against the Jews. The Jews were Paul's natural brethren in the flesh, but since they had not trusted Christ, they were not his spiritual brethren.

6:9–10. Why have a relationship with **the unrighteousness** (v. 9), who **shall not inherit the kingdom of God**? Here Paul used the term "unrighteousness" to describe those who are "unjust," the spiritual state of the lost, in contrast to those who have trusted Christ as their Savior. While believers can do unrighteous acts, they are categorized as "saints" because of their position in Christ. It is only natural for the lost to freely and without conscience practice unrighteousness. The apostle again added to his list of sins (see 5:9–11) that are common to those

without Christ: **adulterers … effeminate … abusers of themselves with mankind**. "Adulterers" implies those who have relations with another's wife. "Effeminate" means "soft" and refers to the male who plays the female role in a homosexual relationship. "Abusers" (Greek, *arsenokoitēs*; "man-bed") seems to refer to homosexual acts.

6:11. Even the vilest person can be saved by the grace of Christ, for, Paul said, **such were some of you**. Now, however, they were **washed … sanctified**, and **justified in the name of the Lord Jesus, and by the Spirit of our God**. "Washing" refers to the baptism of the Holy Spirit, whereby believers are placed into the spiritual body of Christ (see 12:12). "Sanctified" refers to the spiritual sanctification whereby the believer united to Christ is "set aside," or "made holy" (made a "saint"), by his new relation to the Lord (see 1:2; 2 Thess. 2:13; Titus 3:5). Some in the Corinthian church, in fact all of them before their conversion, had been as Paul described in 6:9–10. Now, however, they had a new position in Christ.

C. Failure to Judge Immorality in the Church (6:12–20)

Paul has already written about all the moral failures of the Corinthian church. "All things are lawful" (v. 12) introduces the idea of liberty in Christ. The context, however, makes it clear that this does not include immoral acts. Believers are not free to practice sin without impunity; freedom in Christ does not remove the need for self-governance. If one has been made holy because of his relationship to Christ, it would be foolish to argue that he now has open season to sin as he wishes. In this section, Paul continued to hammer away at the sins this church apparently was practicing without compunction.

6:12. All things are lawful … but all things are not expedient (Greek, *sympherō*). "Not expedient" means "not to be brought together," "not profitable." "All use of Christian liberty must be beneficial" (Vine, *Collected Writings*, p. 45). No matter that there is some freedom in some things, Paul refused to **be brought under the power of any**. Wisdom and self-discipline are the rule in Christian life.

6:13–14. Meats (food; v. 13) and **the belly** are legitimate connections; the Lord designed them to function together. The time will come, however, when **God shall destroy both**, and men will no longer be sustained by this natural order. The human body is not made **for fornication**. The body is for the Lord's use, and the Lord will use the body for His own purposes. "The body was never designed for promiscuous" use (Hodge, *First Epistle to the Corinthians*, p. 103).

By his own power (v. 14), God will **raise up us** as He **raised up the Lord** Jesus from the grave. The intensive form of "raise up us" is "perhaps suggesting that the future act will be no less sure than the past. The same power which wrought in the resurrection of Christ will be put forth in the resurrection of believers" (Vine, *Collected Writings*, p. 45).

6:15–17. Believers' bodies belong to Christ and not to **a harlot** (v. 15). **God forbid.** The believer's union with the Lord Jesus affects both him and the Savior. One cannot act without affecting the other. To prove his point, Paul quoted Genesis 2:24 (and Matthew 19:5), where the Lord said the **two** (v. 16), man and woman, **shall be one flesh.** One of the key doctrines of the Bible is that the union of the believer with Christ creates a community of life. The Bible clearly teaches that this life pertains to the body as well as the soul (see Rom. 8:6–11; Eph. 2:6–7; 5:30).

He that is joined unto the Lord is one spirit (v. 17). In the Upper Room Discourse (John 13–17), Christ expressed this spiritual union to the disciples (see John 14:20; 15:4–5). He mentioned it again in His prayer to the heavenly Father (John 17:21–23). This vital spiritual union with the Lord is kept in place and maintained by the indwelling Holy Spirit of God. This profound truth is all too often simply forgotten. The Christian does not walk through this life alone; he has a new and unbroken relationship with Christ that gives comfort.

6:18. Paul commanded the Corinthians to **Flee fornication.** This indicates that some in this church were flirting with the worst of sins. Most sins are those that go outward, that is, outside, **without the body.** Fornication, however, is more specific and

personal. For the Christian, it is sinning **against his own body.**

6:19–20. Paul asked a rhetorical question, something they should have already known: **know ye not that your body is the temple of the Holy Ghost ...?** (v. 19). He had earlier told them, "Ye are the temple of God, and ... the Spirit of God dwelleth in you" (3:16). This indwelling is made clear in Scripture (see, e.g., 12:13; 1 John 3:24). Because of His indwelling, the Spirit can be grieved (see Eph. 4:30) and quenched (see 1 Thess. 5:19). The believer has been **bought with a price** (v. 20; see Acts 20:28; Gal. 3:13); **ye are not your own** (v. 19). The purchase was made "with the precious blood of Christ" (1 Peter 1:19). The child of God, then, is to **glorify God in your body, and in your spirit** (v. 20), which belong to the Lord.

IV. Various Problems in the Church (chaps. 7–14)

A. Directives concerning Marriage (chap. 7)

The Corinthians had written to the apostle about some troubling issues in their church. Paul wanted to make sure they understood that marriage was not expedient. He wrote that every man should have his own wife, and every wife should have her own husband. The obligation is mutual for both parties; neither has the right to desert the other. Temporary separation for devotional reasons is permissible. What Paul wrote here seems to be only advice (see v. 6). He could only tell them what was expedient under the circumstances; each one must act according to the grace given him (see vv. 6–9). Ideally, divorce was not an option for any Christian, though if an unbelieving spouse left, they would not be judged for their decision. Paul's discussion of marriage logically follows his words about honoring the body (chap. 6).

1. Concerning Celibacy (7:1–9)

7:1. Now concerning shows that Paul knew there was some inappropriate intimacy in Corinth because the Christians there had written him regarding this matter. Because of the dangers of lust, **it is good for a**

man not to touch a woman. While many take this to mean that it is good for a man to remain unmarried, it may refer to actual touching.

7:2. Paul apparently was concerned about fraternization between single (or married) men and women, which could lead to sexual problems. Thus, to avoid fornication ... every man should have his own wife, and ... every woman should have her own husband.

7:3–4. No one can accuse Paul of being against marriage. He commanded the husband (v. 3) and the wife to render ... due benevolence in the marriage relationship. "Render" means that this is an obligation, not simply the granting of a favor. "The recognition of the conjugal rights of marital intercourse is to be regulated by mutual consideration" (Vine, *Collected Writings*, p. 48). Paul stressed the equality and reciprocity of the husband and wife's sexual relationship by emphasizing the "responsibilities of each to satisfy the other" (Lowery, "First Corinthians," p. 517).

7:5–7. Defraud (v. 5) not each other, Paul said, although it is permissible with consent to abstain for a time, that ye may give yourselves to fasting and prayer. The couple is then to come together again so that Satan might not win over for your incontinency. He told them that his advice was that of permission, and not of commandment (v. 6). In general, the apostle's advice seems to have been that he desired that the married couple work these issues out by mutual agreement and with no hard feelings or resentments.

These verses show that the Christian community, even in the carnal Corinthian church, was very serious about their appeals to God. Fasting was practiced, and devoting oneself to intense prayer during a period of isolation seems to have been common. That there is no hint of any special adherence to seasonal prayers or specific times of the year to carry out these spiritual dedications shows that the early church did not observe set ceremonial feasts and holidays, which came about later in church history.

For the sake of the ministry, Paul wanted the church to be even as I myself (v. 7). It seems clear

that Paul was unmarried or possibly widowed. He urged celibacy because of the encumbrance that marriage can be when serving the Lord (see Acts 26:29). Paul saw the act of celibacy as a proper gift that not all can carry forward in their lives. He added that the gift is not the same for everyone, but instead, one after this manner, and another after that. The gift ultimately for celibacy comes from God.

7:8–9. Widows (v. 8) are particularly mentioned here to avoid any thought that Paul was leaving them out of this discussion. The unmarried, however, refers not only to widows but also to women who are young and unmarried. Specific issues regarding virgins are addressed in 7:25–28. "As to the apostle himself, there is no indication that he was a widower" (Vine, *Collected Writings*, p. 49). There has been much speculation on Paul's marital state. If he was previously married, either his wife (more than likely Jewish) left him because of his dedication to Christ or she was deceased. In any case, he was free to crisscross the Roman world, carrying the gospel. "Paul affirmed the suitability of remaining single, if they had the appropriate enablement from God" (Lowery, "First Corinthians," p. 518).

2. Concerning Divorce (7:10–24)

7:10–11. The apostle next tackled the difficult issue of divorce. The mixed marriages of believers in Christ and nonbelievers make this a complicated issue. To the married (v. 10), Paul said, I command, yet not I, but the Lord, Let not the wife depart from her husband. He was drawing on what Christ said regarding divorce (see Matt. 5:32; 19:3–9; Mark 10:2–12). If the wife leaves the marriage, and the marriage is not broken, she is to remain unmarried, or be reconciled to her husband (v. 11). The husband is not to put away his wife as in divorce. It seems clear in these two verses that the apostle was working to hold marriages together, even mixed marriages. "If the covenant [of marriage] be annulled, it can only be by the sinful act of one of the parties" (Hodge, *First Epistle to the Corinthians*, p. 113). That Paul addressed divorce in this letter indicates that it was rampant within the church.

7:12–14. Here Paul gave his own opinion about divorce, beginning with the issue of mixed marriages between believers and unbelievers. **To the rest** (v. 12) addressed those in the congregation who were married to nonbelievers. More than likely, the unsaved partner was antagonistic to the saved partner. The tension in such circumstances can certainly be appreciated in modern times. A spiritually divided marriage is torn at every corner: spiritually, emotionally, sexually, and domestically.

If either partner **be pleased to dwell with** (vv. 12–13) the other, the marriage should be held together. Paul gave a powerful spiritual reason for this: **the unbelieving** (v. 14) wife or husband **is sanctified** by the believing partner, and in the intact family, even the **children** are kept from being **unclean** and remain **holy**. The words "sanctified" (Greek, *hagiazō*) and "holy" (*hagios*) both come from the same root word. Here Paul used these words in an unusual way. He was saying that the unbelieving partner and the children are especially "blessed" by the Christian husband or wife. Also, keeping the family together means that the unsaved spouse and the children may come to Christ, though Paul did not say this directly.

Paul's statement that the children would be "unclean" (v. 14) if one parent were not a believer means they would no longer have the sanctifying power or influence of that parent. He was convinced of this influence, which comes through the believing spouse. His statement, however, must not be taken too far, as if some kind of sacramental force is at work. All he was saying is that the believing spouse has a strong witness and influence in the family unit.

7:15–16. **If the unbelieving depart** (v. 15), the Christian **brother or … sister is not under bondage**. This means not only that the believing spouse is not held culpable but also that he or she is not held to the marriage. Though he did not say so here, Paul may have been intimating that such a marriage is in continual strife because one in the union is a believer and the other is not. He added, **but God hath called us to peace**. "There were exceptions to the rule of no divorce" (Lowery, "First Corinthians," p. 518). The Christian was not in "bondage" to stay in a marriage

that was truly broken but was free to marry again (see also 7:39). "The point is that the divine standard cannot be imposed upon the unregenerate" (Mitchell, *First Corinthians*, p. 111).

Paul then presented a counterargument. If, for example, the believing wife remains in the marriage, she may **save thy husband** (v. 16). Likewise, the apostle said to the man that he could not know **whether thou shalt save thy wife**. This is certainly a compelling argument for any man or woman who loves his or her spouse. What a blessing if, through perseverance and prayer, the lost companion comes to saving faith in Christ. "We have here, therefore, an additional reason for avoiding separation" (Hodge, *First Epistle to the Corinthians*, p. 119).

7:17. God gives believers the ability to persevere in tough situations. In this verse, Paul was saying that whatever lot in life God has assigned, so the believer must remain. "Accordingly, the believing partner must not take any step to bring about a separation" (Vine, *Collected Writings*, p. 51). Believers must live contentedly where God has placed them. **As the Lord hath called every one, so let him walk**. Paul placed his apostolic authority behind this command and made his a broad rule applicable to all the churches: **so ordain I in all churches**. "Ordain" (Greek, *diatassō*) has the idea to "thoroughly order," "prescribe," "appoint." He was not laying upon the Corinthians undue commands. This was an order that applied to all the congregations.

7:18–19. To pick up on the idea of social status among Christians, Paul shifted the subject to the issue of circumcision and the believers' handling of this "legal" problem. He wanted to make sure the believers knew that **Circumcision is nothing** (v. 19); the important thing is the **keeping of the commandments of God**. Paul was not placing the Corinthian church under the dispensation of law. There are legitimate moral commandments that are eternal in their application to both the period of the Mosaic covenant and the church age. Jewish circumcision or Gentile uncircumcision has nothing to do with being obedient to the Lord. Paul addressed this issue because many Jews were saying, "Yes, you have accepted Christ as your Savior, but now you must also be circumcised." Paul was putting this issue to rest.

7:20–24. Every believer must **abide in the same calling** (v. 20) in which God has called him. Paul was addressing the social status of new believers, but he had a twist in mind: a new Christian was to remain in the social status he held when he was called, whether **servant** (v. 21) or **freeman** (v. 22). If one's position changed, well and good, but a Christian **called in the Lord, being a servant, is the Lord's freeman: likewise also he that is called, being free, is Christ's servant.** "What matters is that every Christian should realize he is Christ's slave and needs to render obedience to Him" (Lowery, "First Corinthians," p. 519). Since the children of God have been **bought with a price** (v. 23), the sacrifice of Christ (see 1 Peter 1:18–19), they are not **the servants of men.** In this calling, what is most important is to **abide with God** (v. 24), that is, "near him, perpetually mindful of his presence and favour. This would secure their contentment and happiness" (Hodge, *First Epistle to the Corinthians,* p. 125).

3. Concerning Marriage and Ministry (7:25–38)

7:25. Young Christian women faced particular problems in the early church. **Virgins** were unmarried and sexually inexperienced. Here the word is used as an adjective to refer to both sexes (see Hodge, *First Epistle to the Corinthians,* p. 126). The natural desire for companionship made marrying an unbeliever a great temptation. Paul was concerned about this issue, but he was also concerned about the marrying of the young in general because of the persecutions he saw coming against Christians. He stated that what he was writing was not a **commandment of the Lord** but his own **judgment.** "Here, Paul means that he is one whose advice can be trusted ... even when he has no direct command of the Lord to quote" (Barrett, *First Epistle to the Corinthians,* p. 174).

7:26–28. Paul was concerned about what he called **the present distress** (v. 26), "the impending crises," "the distress standing near" (Greek, *enestōsan anankēn*), that he saw coming against the communities of the faithful. No one knows for certain what

this "distress" was. Persecution seems to be most likely, but some have surmised that Paul was referring to the social upheaval that was taking place in the mixed marriages of the saved with the unsaved. Paul saw persecutions coming upon the church and apparently believed that someone who was single could better handle its onslaught. For those responsible for a spouse and children, martyrdom (see 13:3) would be terrible. Paul was not saying that marriage is wrong; he was simply saying that it would be more prudent not to be married.

7:29–31. Because **the time is short ... they that have wives [should] be as though they had none** (v. 29). Likewise, **they that weep ... rejoice ... buy** (v. 30) or **use this world** (v. 31), should live above these things, because **the fashion of this world passeth away.** This list consists of normal things that make up life. Normal life, however, will be stopped by what is coming. The apostle "was calling for a commitment to eternal matters and a corresponding detachment from the institutions, values, and substance of this world which was passing away (v. 31)" (Lowery, "First Corinthians," p. 519).

7:32–35. A man who remains **unmarried** (v. 32) can take care of **the things that belong to the Lord** and **how he may please the Lord.** A **married** (v. 33) man must care for **the things ... of the world** and provide for and **please his wife.** Here Paul did not use the concept of "the world" in the evil sense as the word *kosmos* is usually used. He simply meant that the married man must look after his wife in the provision of living and existing. He must provide food, shelter, comfort, and companionship.

In the same sense, the **virgin** (v. 34), or **unmarried woman,** can care for **the things of the Lord.** She can be a missionary of sorts and totally give herself to Him. She can **be holy both in body and in spirit.** The woman who is **married** must also care for the worldly needs of her husband and **how she may please** him. "The situation illustrates Paul's point that the single life with its greater simplicity in obligations allows a potentially greater commitment of time" (Lowery, "First Corinthians," p. 520). Paul said these things for the Corinthians' **profit** (v. 35).

He was not trying to **snare** them in some kind of spiritual trap. He was saying these things so that they could **attend** to the things of the Lord **without distraction**. "Everywhere the apostle is careful to show that celibacy was preferred merely on the grounds of expediency, and not on the ground of its being a higher state of virtue" (Hodge, *First Epistle to the Corinthians*, p. 132).

7:36–38. There is some question whether **he [who] behaveth himself uncomely** (v. 36) refers to a father or to a potential bridegroom. The point seems to be whether the father (or bridgegroom) is disgracing himself by not allowing this young woman to marry. What **if she pass the flower of her age** and she wants children? What should happen? Paul instructed the father to **do what he will**. He would not be sinning to **let them marry**. If, however, the father **standeth stedfast in his heart** (v. 37), has **power over his own will**, and is determined **in his heart that he will keep** his daughter a **virgin**, he **doeth well**. He who allows her to marry **doeth well, but he that giveth her not in marriage doeth better** (v. 38). It is better if she not marry. The father needs to act with all human and godly wisdom. Paul's twists and turns in this matter show the seriousness of the events that continued to swirl around such problems in the early church. It "is not a case of what is morally right or wrong but of what is expedient or advantageous" (Vine, *Collected Writings*, p. 55).

4. Concerning Remarriage (7:39–40)

7:39–40. Here Paul again addressed the issue of marriage and divorce. **The wife is bound by the law as long as her husband liveth; but if her husband be dead, she is at liberty** (v. 39) to marry again, but **only in the Lord**. Most commentators take these last words to mean she is to marry only a Christian. Paul repeated the advice given throughout the chapter, returned to the issue of remaining unmarried, and said she will **be happier** (v. 40) if she remains unmarried. The apostle stated that this was **after [his] judgment** but added that he thought he had **the Spirit of God** in such a decision. Remarriage is permitted, though not encouraged.

B. Directives concerning Christian Liberty (chaps. 8–11)

1. Eating Meat Offered to Idols (chap. 8)

Paul hit home in regard to a sore issue, that of eating meat offered to idols. Meat was placed on the altars of all the pagan temples in Corinth. When it began to spoil, the meat was taken from the altars and offered in the bazaars for food. Whether Christians could or should eat meat that had been offered to pagan gods became a huge contention among the believers.

8:1. In writing **we all have knowledge**, Paul may have been saying that all the churches knew that this meat, though offered to idols, meant nothing in a spiritual sense. Such knowledge, however, could bring about insensitivity and cause some to **puffeth up** and be short on the **charity** that **edifieth** the brother. Paul may have mentioned the issue of knowledge because of the growing Gnostic religion, which pandered to secretive, hidden "spiritual" knowledge. Christians were continually exposed to some form of idolatrous homage without knowing it. The apostle wanted the believers to focus on "charity," or love, which builds up the brother. In saying "we all have knowledge," he was also reminding the Corinthians that Christians have been given the open truth of God and Christ, and the basics of faith are well-known.

8:2–3. With a twist of argument, Paul then said that the man who boasts **he knoweth any thing** (v. 2) is presumptuous and a spiritual braggart. When one is blessed with understanding spiritual truth, humility should follow, not pride. "He whose knowledge is superficial often displays a readiness to impart instruction. His very readiness betrays his ignorance (3:18)" (Vine, *Collected Writings*, p. 57).

What counts is that **if any man love God, the same is known of him** (v. 3). Some commentators feel the sense of this is not certain. It could mean, "If any man loves God, he has been brought by Him to the true knowledge," which appears to fit the context. Or it could mean, "If a man is without love, he has not true knowledge; but if he love God, he has the right kind of knowledge" (Hodge, *First Epistle to the*

Corinthians, p. 141). The apostle John wrote something similar: "Beloved, let us love one another: for love is of God; and every one that loveth is born of God, and knoweth God. He that loveth not, knoweth not God; for God is love" (1 John 4:7–8).

8:4. Paul then leapt into one of the burning issues that was dividing the Corinthian assembly—the issue of eating meat offered to idols. Some believers had no problem eating meat **offered in sacrifice unto idols**. Paul said, **an idol is nothing ... there is none other God but one**. The idol (Greek, *eidōlon*) is but a wooden or stone image of the false deities of the pagans. There is no Jupiter, Juno, or Mars. In the whole of **the world**, the idols mean nothing.

8:5–6. It is true, however, that the pagan world believes in the pantheon of the many **gods** (v. 5) and **lords**, as they **are called**, which are supposed to dwell **in heaven or in earth. ... But to us** (v. 6), to believers, **there is but one God**, and He is **the Father**, to whom belongs **all things, and we [are] in him**. There is also only **one Lord Jesus Christ, by whom are all things, and we** too came into existence **by him**. In these short phrases and clauses, the apostle assigned all deity to the person of God the Father and to His Son Jesus Christ. Both the Father and Jesus Christ created everything and own everything.

"The Father is the source of all (Gen. 1:1) and the One for whom the Corinthians should live (1 Cor. 10:31). The Lord Jesus Christ was the agent of Creation (Col. 1:16) and the One through whom the Corinthians lived (1 Cor. 12:27; Eph. 1:23)" (Lowery, "First Corinthians," p. 521).

8:7–8. Some believers in the congregation still did not have full **knowledge** (v. 7) about the falsehood of the pantheon of the gods. They had a **conscience of the idol unto this hour**, even up to that day. If they ate that which was offered to idols, **their conscience being weak is defiled**. These Christians could not indifferently eat meat offered on the pagan altars. Besides, Paul argued, eating such **meat commendeth us not to God** (v. 8). "Commendeth" carries the idea of "approval." Eating or not eating meat sacrificed to idols had no bearing on whether a believer was **better** or **worse**.

8:9–10. Paul issued a caveat for those who were strong in their faith: they should not exercise their **liberty** (v. 9) to eat such meat if it **become[s] a stumblingblock to them that are weak** in this matter. Apparently, "idol meat" restaurants were located near the temples of the gods and served leftover meat that had been previously sacrificed to the deities. The one who had **knowledge** (v. 10) and freedom concerning the issue was to consider carefully whether to **sit at meat in the idol's temple**. The example of the stronger Christian might strike **the conscience** of the **weak** brother, who would therefore **be emboldened to eat** the same food. Unfortunately, "many repeat the mistake of the Corinthians by assuming that liberality in matters of personal conduct is a sign of spiritual maturity and strength, while scrupulosity is a sign of weakness" (Mitchell, *First Corinthians*, p. 127).

8:11–12. Seeing stronger Christians eat meat sacrificed to the idols might lead a weak Christian to eat the same food even if he believed it was wrong. If this happened, his conscience would be "seared" (1 Tim. 4:2), and his ability to distinguish right from wrong would be lost (Titus 1:15), leading to his spiritual ruin, whereby **the weak brother [would] perish** (v. 11). "Perish" often has to do with physical death (see Matt. 2:13; Acts 5:37), but here it is probable that Paul meant the weak brother's spiritual life would be destroyed. The apostle warned the brother who had proper **knowledge** and spiritual understanding about the meat offered to idols that exercising his freedom to eat such meat might cause him to **sin ... against the brethren** (v. 12) by harming the **weak conscience** of the one who had stumbled over this issue. Moreover, Paul said, **ye sin against Christ**, because exercising one's freedom to eat the meat caused spiritual confusion for the weaker brother, who also belongs to the body of Christ. Since Jesus died for this soul, the strong should be able to give up eating the meat offered to idols to keep from destroying his brother's conscience.

8:13. Wherefore indicates Paul's conclusion and summary statement on this subject: if eating such meat might cause a weaker brother **to offend**, Paul would never eat it again **while the world standeth**. Paul did not say that a knowledgeable Christian had to set aside his freedom. It was unlikely that Paul saw this weak brother as permanently shackling the freedom of the knowledgeable Christian (Lowery, "First Corinthians," p. 522). The weak brother needed to be properly taught so that he could enjoy his spiritual freedom (see Gal. 5:1).

2. Paul's Apostleship and Authority (chap. 9)

There were rumblings of doubt about Paul's authority. Here Paul set forth his defense against those who questioned whether he had any right to presribe the moral and spiritual behavior of the Corinthian church. He later defended his calling as an apostle in more detail (see 2 Cor. 11–13). Also at issue "was his steadfast refusal to derive material support from those to whom he was ministering, so no one could say he was motivated by money (cf. 2 Cor. 2:17)" (Barrett, *First Epistle to the Corinthians*, p. 522).

9:1. With a staccato of quick and direct questions, Paul asked the Corinthian believers, **Am I not an apostle? am I not free? have I not seen Jesus Christ our Lord? are not you my work in the Lord?** The apostle pulled no punches. He got to the point and attacked their criticisms, which were seething just below the surface. Paul seems especially direct in the Corinthian letters. Some have suggested this was because no men in this assembly were qualified to act as elders, and carnality in the congregation was rampant. Paul made it clear that his authority came from Christ. In 9:1–13, he hammered his readers with sixteen questions, forcing them to think twice about their objections to his ministry.

9:2–6. Paul said that even if he was **not an apostle unto others, yet doubtless I am to you** (v. 2). **The seal of [his] apostleship** was over the Corinthian church. He had birthed this church and was now correcting their spiritual and moral waywardness. He had an **answer** (Greek, *apologia*; v. 3) for those who wished to **examine** (Greek, *anakrinō*) him. "Answer" and "examine" are forensic terms, showing that his opponents felt they had the right to judicially scrutinize his authority. Paul was answering

in so many words, "I have seen the Lord Jesus, and He has set His seal to my calling by the success with which He has crowned my work." This answer satisfied Peter, James, and John, who gave to Paul "the right hands of fellowship" (Gal. 2:9).

In asking whether he had the **power to eat and to drink** (v. 4), Paul probably had in mind whether he had the "right" to do so. Many believe he meant that he had some authority to be helped along the way by the churches in his ministry. He had the right to be supported by the various congregations, but having said that, Paul went on to show that he had not availed himself of that right. On the other hand, he may have meant that he could live as he wished as an apostolic leader. This argument, however, is doubtful (see v. 6; 9:13–14).

Paul said he had the right **to lead about a sister, a wife** (v. 5). Some believe this should be read as "a sister, [who is my] wife" and that it indicates Paul was married. The New Testament and the writings of the church fathers, however, are silent about Paul's marital status. This right to "lead about … a wife" belonged also to **other apostles**, including Christ's **brethren** (who would have been His half-brothers, the children of Joseph and Mary; see Matt. 12:46; 13:55) and **Cephas**, or Peter.

Further pushing the issue, Paul asked, **Or I only and Barnabas, have not we power to forbear working?** (v. 8), that is, "Do Barnabas and I not have the power, the right, to forbear working?" While Paul at times refused to accept remuneration in order to silence criticism, he argued that those working in a teaching ministry should be compensated by those who are blessed. "Let him that is taught in the word communicate unto him that teacheth in all good things" (Gal. 6:6). Paul seems to have been saying, "Are Barnabas and I the only exceptions to the rule that ministers should be supported by their respective churches?" At the beginning of his ministry in Corinth, the apostle had supported himself. When financial aid did come, it did not come from the Corinthian assembly.

9:7–9. Does a soldier go into **warfare** (v. 7) and pay for it himself? **Who planteth a vineyard, and**

eateth not of the fruit ... **or who feedeth a flock, and eateth not of the milk?** I can say **these things as a man** (v. 8), but **saith not the law the same also?** Paul spoke from the position of a human being who had to find sustenance while he labored. Reminding them that this is **the law of Moses** (v. 9), Paul cites Deuteronomy 25:4 to support his case: **Thou shalt not muzzle ... the ox that treadeth out the corn.** Since God takes care of the oxen and even feeds the young ravens when they cry (see Job 38:41), He certainly will take care of His gospel ministers.

9:10–12. Paul maintained that the words of Moses were written not only for those in the past but also **for our sakes, no doubt** (v. 10). If the farmer **should plow** and thresh his grain **in hope** and also **be partaker of his hope,** how much more so for those who plow, plant, and thresh the Word of God to reap a spiritual harvest? The ministers of the gospel had **sown unto** (v. 11) the Corinthian church **spiritual things;** was it not only right that these same ministers should be able to **reap ... carnal things?** If others had the right to benefit from and **be partakers of** (v. 12) blessing, should Paul and his fellow workers not also have that right? Still, Paul said, **we have not used this power** or authority but instead **suffer all things** so as not to **hinder the gospel of Christ.** Paul was saying that he would do anything that did not violate his allegiance to Christ or forgo anything so that no one could criticize and thus besmirch the gospel of the Lord Jesus Christ.

9:13–14. Paul asked the Corinthians, Is it not true that **they which minister ... holy things live of the things of the temple** (v. 13) and **are partakers** of the meat placed on the altar, just as the farmer partakes of that which he sows? **Even so hath the Lord ordained that they which preach the gospel should live of the gospel** (v. 14). Paul likely had in mind the temple service in Jerusalem and portion given to the priests from the food taken for offerings (see Lev. 7:31–34), but the Corinthians certainly would have been aware that even the pagan priests lived off of their service at the pagan temples and altars.

9:15–17. Paul reminded his readers that he had taken nothing from this church, nor had he **writ**-ten these things, that it should be so done unto me (v. 15). He would have preferred to die rather than be deprived of his ground for glorying in their salvation. Paul was not a braggart, but he was genuinely joyful and proud as a parent of the spiritual birth of this congregation. He was not in it for himself. He then reversed that thought and said, **I have nothing to glory** (v. 16) about, because **necessity is laid upon me** to proclaim the truth of Christ. **Woe is unto me, if I preach not the gospel!** Because he did **this thing willingly** (v. 17), he had **a reward.** The apostle was driven because the **dispensation of the gospel [was] committed** to him. Paul made it clear that he was fully committed to the ministry of the gospel. The English word "economy" comes from the Greek word for "dispensation" (*oikonomia*). The gospel dispensation is what governs the church age, the age of grace. This is in contrast to the older dispensation of the Mosaic law. The word is used four times in the New Testament to refer to the church age (1 Cor. 9:17; Eph. 1:10; 3:2; Col. 1:25). This dispensation was especially "committed" to Paul (see Gal. 2:7; Col. 1:25). The word "dispensation" can be translated "stewardship." Paul was given a "stewardship" to preach. That was enough (see 4:1–2; Luke 17:10). A steward received no pay. "Such a one was merely a slave doing an assigned task" (Mitchell, *First Corinthians,* p. 134).

9:18. How, then, was Paul rewarded for his service? He preached **the gospel of Christ without charge** so that he would not **abuse** his **power** (i.e., "right") **in the gospel.** No one could deny this claim (see 2 Cor. 11:9–10), and Paul could see the gospel at work in those to whom he ministered (see 7:3–4). His reward was to sacrifice himself for others. Any satisfaction gained would be made void if there was self-glorification before the Lord.

9:19–23. While Paul was **free from all men** (v. 19) and their authority, he still made himself a **servant unto all, that [he] might gain the more.** The apostle did not have to conform to the opinions of others, especially that of his critics. By serving all, however, he could do them good and bring a greater number to the cross of Christ. To prove his point

Paul made a long list of those to whom he ministered in order to gain their confidence for the gospel's sake.

To **the Jews** (v. 20) and others **under the law,** Paul **became as a Jew** and lived **as under the law, that [he] might gain them that are under the law.** By "gain," he meant to win them to the gospel, though their spiritual orientation was the law. He did the same with those who were **without law** (v. 21), more than likely referring to the Gentiles. He related to the religious or ethnic situation of those he was trying to reach. He wanted to make sure, however, that the Corinthians did not think he was antinomian, a rebel against law and reason, **being not without law to [before] God.** Yet he lived as one governed by Christ, **under the law to Christ.** He did this to **gain them that are without law.** He did the same with **the weak** (v. 22) to **gain the weak.** His main purpose was **that I might by all means save some.**

The apostle worked hard to identify with others in situations different from his own. This he did **for the gospel's sake** (v. 23). He did the same thing with the Corinthians; he became a **partaker** ("joint partaker") with them to win them to the Lord. Paul's focus was on great eternal issues over and above temporal issues. It can be said that he went about reaping the joyful harvest of many won to Christ (see John 4:36).

9:24-25. Paul saw himself **in a race** (v. 24) to receive **the prize.** He wanted the same spirit of achieving for the sake of Christ to be in the Corinthian believers. **So run, that ye may obtain.** Being an athlete and running the race means that one must **striveth for the mastery** (v. 25). Discipline is required, and one must be **temperate in all things.** The world expends energy for glory **to obtain a corruptible crown,** but the believer is to serve diligently to receive **an incorruptible** reward. In the Olympic games, the prize was a perishable wreath, a garland of leaves that faded quickly after the contest was over. The Lord will reward the believer in Christ, however, a crown given that is incorruptible and lasting (see 2 Tim. 4:8; James 1:12; 1 Peter 5:4; Rev. 2:10; 3:11; 4:10).

9:26-27. Paul had explained himself, his motives, and his actions to the congregation at Corinth. **I ... run, not as uncertainly** (v. 26). He fought as a boxer, not without purpose, as one that simply **beateth the air.** He brought the needs and wants of his **body ... into subjection** (v. 27) so that when he **preached to others,** he **should be a castaway.** "Castaway" (*adokimos*) should better be translated "disqualified," "unapproved." While the word in other contexts is applied to the lost (see Rom. 1:28; Titus 1:16), here the apostle was not addressing salvation but rather faithfulness in the Christian walk. He wanted it to be said of him, "I have fought a good fight, I have finished my course, I have kept the faith: Henceforth there is laid up for me a crown of righteousness, which the Lord, the righteous judge, shall give me at that day: and not to me only, but unto all them also that love his appearing" (2 Tim. 4:7-8).

3. Temptations (10:1-13)

The apostle Paul next turned to the issue of various temptations: lust, drunkenness, fornication, even complaining and doubt. He used the history of the Israelites in the wilderness because they were "our examples" (v. 6), and they were "overthrown in the wilderness" (v. 5). In all of these experiences, the Jews were a warning to every Christian. Therefore, the one who thinks he is secure from such temptations should "take heed lest he fall" (v. 12).

10:1. Lest the Corinthians **should be ignorant** of how God works, it was appropriate to look back at the story of the Exodus. God gave the children of Israel supernatural guidance (see Exod. 13:21) and protection (see Exod. 14:19-20) by leading them **under the cloud** of blessing. All of the Israelites experienced a miraculous deliverance from the Egyptians: God led them **through the sea,** the Red Sea (Exod. 14:21-29). This blessing of their liberation, however, was not enough. It is not enough to begin well; one must also finish well.

10:2-5. Coming out of Egypt, the Jews **were all baptized unto Moses in the cloud and in the sea** (v. 2). Moses was their spiritual head and God's servant. He was the object of their trust (Exod. 14:31). In a similar manner, the Corinthians had been baptized into the body of Christ (1 Cor. 12:13). Christ is the Head (see Eph. 1:22), in whom believers have faith (see Matt.

12:21; Eph. 1:12). What did Paul mean when he said the Jews "were all baptized unto Moses"? He was not using this expression about baptism in a technical sense, though he will discuss spiritual baptism as a distinct New Testament doctrine in 12:12–18. Paul meant that the children of Israel "were immersed into Moses' authority." Thus, the expression speaks of divine leadership (see Exod. 14:31).

The Jews were also said to have eaten **the same spiritual meat** (v. 3). This could refer to the Passover meal, which consisted of slaying a lamb and eating unleavened bread (see Exod. 12:43–51). Passover, though a meal of physical food, was a prophetic event that pointed to the Lord Jesus, who became the spiritual Passover (see Luke 22:19–21; 1 Cor. 5:7). Many believe, however, that the "spiritual meat" is the *manna* (Hebrew; meaning, "What is it?") that miraculously sustained the Jews in the desert. The manna was spiritual in that it was supernatural in origin (see Ps. 78:25). Christ Himself is the Bread of Life (see John 6:31–32).

In addition to the "spiritual meat," Paul referred to the **spiritual drink** (v. 4) that came forth from the **spiritual Rock that followed them: and that Rock was Christ**. The apostle used real historic events that took place when Israel came out of Egypt as symbolic figures representing the supernatural subsistence the Lord used to preserve the Jewish people in the desert (Exod. 16:2–36; 17:1–7; Num. 20:2–11; 21:16). The manna, the water, and the rock all represent the saving work of Christ for His people. Because of the disobedience and doubt of many of the people, however, **God was not well pleased** (v. 5), and **they were overthrown in the wilderness** (see Num. 14:22–24, 28–35; Josh. 1:1–2). Caleb and Joshua, however, were allowed to enter the Promised Land of Canaan because they trusted God.

10:6. These wilderness events became **examples** so that believers today **should not lust after evil things** as that generation did. Though the church is not under the Old Testament economy, it still receives tremendous spiritual blessings that should act as warnings for the child of God. The Corinthian complacency corresponded to what happened to ancient Israel. Christian liberty should not lead to self-indulgence and spiritual compromise.

10:7–10. In these verses, Paul set forth a list of warnings. Each verse begins with "Neither," indicating that the Christian should not act as the Jews did under the leadership of Moses. **Neither be ye idolaters** (v. 7) as the Jews were when they **sat down to eat and drink**. Moses recorded that the people rose up early and made offerings to a molten calf, which was one of the gods they said had brought them out of bondage (see Exod. 32:4–5). Their "eating and drinking" more than likely was a drunken orgy. When they **rose up to play** is an expression of the sexual carousing that followed.

Neither let us commit fornication (v. 8). This specifies what the Jews were doing, and because of their actions, God slew **in one day** 23,000 people (see 32:6; Ps. 106:29). At first, Paul's figure seems to contradict his account of what happened. Some of the Jews had committed whoredom with the pagan daughters of Moab and had also bowed down to the gods of these people. God instructed Moses' judges to slay all who had participated in this idolatry (see Num. 25:1–5). A plague also came upon the congregation. It was the final judgment that wiped out 24,000 (see Num. 25:9). Paul probably did not include those who were killed by the judges (see Num. 25:5). Though Paul says they **fell in one day**, he could have meant that they were judged in one day, but the carrying out of God's sentence took longer. Another view is that Paul was counting only those who fell in one day, while the others followed in death a short time later. Some surmise that the apostle was only rounding down the number. This entire warning is strong and hints that some in the church at Corinth continually practiced fornication and possibly flirted with idolatry also.

Neither let us tempt Christ as some of them also tempted, and were destroyed of serpents (v. 9). A vivid account of this event is found in Numbers 21:6–9. The children of Israel had forgotten God's liberation of them from Egypt and blamed both God and Moses for bringing them into the wilderness to die. They complained, "our soul loatheth this light bread" (Num. 21:5), the manna. As God had authority over Israel in the wilderness, so Christ has authority over the church. For a Christian to resist Christ is the same as when the Jews resisted God. Christians must not "tempt" Him to overlook their spiritual failures, because He will not do so.

Neither murmur ye (v. 10). The Jews in the desert **were destroyed** (see Num. 14:37) by the same death angel that came to the Egyptians and took their first-born sons (see Exod. 12:13, 23). **The destroyer** was "an angel commissioned by God to use the pestilence as an instrument of destruction" (Hodge, *First Epistle to the Corinthians*, p. 180). "The destroyer here mentioned is not Satan, but the destroying angel" of Exodus (Vine, *Collected Writings*, p. 69).

10:11–13. The historical events recorded in the Old Testament became lessons, or **ensamples** (v. 11), for the church. They **are written for our admonition**, both to encourage and to warn. These lessons have an impact on all those who go to **the ends of the world,** by which Paul meant the successive periods of God's entire dealing with mankind. **Are come** (Greek, *katantaō*) signifies arrival at a certain period, to come upon or reach certain persons. The events recorded in the Old Testament will stand as spiritual lessons until the end. Paul warned his audience to avoid moral pride and thinking they would not be judged for their open sins. **Let him that thinketh he standeth take heed lest he fall** (v. 12). Self-satisfaction leads to arrogance, which in turn leads to a downfall.

No one can escape **temptation** (v. 13) because it is **common to man**. The most spiritual person can trip up, but God **will not suffer** (allow) the believer **to be tempted above that ye are able**. When a believer is tempted, God will **make a way to escape, that ye may be able to bear it.** He is **faithful** in doing this. The Lord is aware of the temptations His children face; He is not detached from the events that come upon His own. Through His Holy Spirit, believers can overcome whatever comes against them.

4. Fleeing from Idolatry (10:14–22)

10:14–15. Wherefore (Greek, *dioper*; v. 14) is a strong word for the summary introduction. To show that he was not simply judging the Corinthians, Paul

addressed them as **my dearly beloved**. After moving from a serious admonition to terms of affection, he summarized the admonition very simply: **flee from idolatry**. Idolatry seems to be the central problem from which the other heinous sins originated. "The only safety is keeping at a distance. This includes two things; first, avoiding what is questionable; that is, every thing which lies upon the border of what is allowable" (Hodge, *First Epistle to the Corinthians*, pp. 184–85). Those who heard and heeded Paul's words were the **wise** (Greek, *phronimos*; v. 15), those who are wise practically and who are prudent. He wanted the Corinthians to judge for themselves: **judge ye what I say.**

10:16–18. Some in the church may have been looking at the Lord's Supper as something similar to the idol feasts. **The cup of blessing** (v. 16) is **the communion** (Greek, *koinōnia*), the "fellowship" that centers around **the blood of Christ**. The high churches that believe there is some efficaciousness in the communion service misread this passage. "The cup" and **the bread** presented to those in the fellowship *are* the communion. Together the church centers itself around the **one bread** (v. 17). They **all** become **partakers of that one bread**. Here the unity of the local assembly is emphasized. Paul probably stressed this because the Corinthians had been so divided. This occasion of mutual partaking symbolizes the unity they should have around the body of Christ. In fact, Paul later went further in his description of the new unity: believers, though "being many, are one body: so also is Christ" (12:12).

Returning to what happened to Israel, Paul asked, Did they not become as one **after the flesh** (v. 18) because of what they had experienced together in the wilderness and also when they came into the Land of Promise? And were not the priests who ate **of the sacrifices partakers of the altar?** After a part of the sacrifice had been burned on the altar, the priests partook together of a portion of the animal offerings (see Lev. 7:15–21; Deut. 12:5–7; 18:18). These happenings are types and pictures of how the church is to unite around the remembrance of the death, burial, and resurrection of Christ.

10:19–22. Verse 19 may show how mixed up this church was. Is **the idol … any thing** (v. 19), or are the **sacrifice[s] to idols … any thing?** But the Gentiles (v. 20–21) were making such sacrifices, **sacrifice[s] to devils, and not to God.** Paul added, I do not want you to **have fellowship with devils. Ye cannot drink the cup of the Lord, and the cup of devils** (v. 21); you cannot come to both **the Lord's table, and … the table of devils.** In the pagan Greek world, the words *daimōn* and *daimonion* were both used to describe the gods, the deities and spirits of the underworld. Interestingly, here the word Paul used, *daimoniōn*, is the plural. The pagan feasts were in honor of more than one demonic spirit. In no way could the Christian have fellowship both with Christ and with these evil beings. Paul asked, **Do we provoke the Lord to jealousy** (v. 22) in this matter? Did some in the assembly in Corinth think they could worship devils and God? Concerning the worship of other gods, the Lord said in the Old Testament: "They have moved me to jealousy with that which is not God; they have provoked me to anger with their vanities" (Deut. 32:21). Paul asked, **Are we stronger than** God? The answer to this question brings a warning. The child of God cannot arouse the Lord to anger with impunity. Fear of and respect for God should cause believers to do what is right (see Eccl. 6:10; Isa. 10:15; 45:9; Ezek. 22:14).

5. Lawful Things and Maturity (10:23–11:1)

10:23–24. Paul again asserted, **All things are lawful for me** (v. 23; see 6:12), though not everything is **expedient** (Greek, *sympherei*), meaning "right to do," "useful for others." While believers have a wide range of liberty in their Christian walk, wisdom must play a part in what one does. While all things may be **lawful … all things edify not.** "Edify" has the idea of "strengthen," "build up another." The "principle for us all toward others is that we might be a means of edifying" (Vine, *Collected Writings*, p. 72).

A believer is not to simply **seek his own** (v. 24) but is instead to pursue **another's wealth**, or "welfare," "benefit," "gain." Only in this way can a believer really be helpful to others. Self is not to be the object of the actions of the Christian.

10:25–28. Paul here gave permission to **eat** (v. 25) that which was purchased **in the shambles** (v. 25), meaning the public marketplace. In a large city like Corinth, it was difficult to determine what had been slaughtered for general food and what had been offered in sacrifice to the gods. **No question** (v. 27) needed to be asked **for conscience sake.** "For a Christian who bought meat at a market with the intent of eating it at home, Paul recommended that selections be made without reservation. No one could contaminate what God had made clean" (Lowery, "First Corinthians," p. 528). **The earth is the Lord's** (vv. 26, 28), and all that is in it, **the fulness thereof.**

Paul advised his readers that if an unbeliever asked them to dine with him, and they wished to go, **whatsoever is set before you, eat, asking no question for conscience sake.** By this, Paul meant that the believer did not have to worry about what is unclean everywhere he went. It was alright to partake in what was served. If the host told believers, however, that the meat had been **sacrifice[d] unto idols** (v. 28), they were not to eat the meat. Such a refusal would be a witness to him **that shewed it.** The believer needed to be careful that the unbeliever did not get the idea that he might be willing to partake of idolatrous food. As well, if another Christian was present, the refusal would not cause him to sin in regard to meat offered to idols (Rom. 14:14–23). A weak brother might act against his conscience and thus be harmed (see 8:11).

10:29–33. The believer needed to be concerned about others' **conscience** (v. 29) and aware of how exercising one's personal **liberty** in these matters might affect someone else. If **by grace** (v. 30) one partook of meat offered to idols, he might be **evil spoken of,** even if he gave **thanks** for that food. Therefore, whether eating or drinking, all must be done for **the glory of God** (v. 31). "Paul's message is cohesive from start to finish, and each chapter plays a crucial role in demonstrating why and how to correct misconceptions about the practice of Christian liberty" (Mitchell, *First Corinthians*, p. 149). One's actions could offend **Jews … Gentiles … the church of God** (v. 32). To do all to His glory is to manifest

Him in all respects. In these debatable matters, the Christian must **please all men in all things** (v. 33), not being self-serving but profiting others, the **many, that they may be saved**. If they are to be saved, a stumbling block must not be placed before them. To possibly bring the lost to conversion to Christ, good must be done to them.

11:1. The apostle concluded, **Be ye followers of me, even as I also am of Christ**. Paul was perhaps saying that this church was not yet mature enough to follow Christ in a direct manner, in which case, they were to imitate Paul, as he did Christ, who is the ultimate standard of the Christian life.

6. The Veiling of Women (11:2–16)

This section has cultural overtones, but eternal doctrinal principles are established here. Some things Paul said may not be fully clear because observors today do not fully understand the cultural and historical setting, but the conclusions are doctrinally sure. The apostle addressed issues that must have been great concerns in the Corinthian church. Paul's discussion of whether women should wear veils was possibly unsolicited by the congregation. This discussion has to do with behavior in the worship service and with gender leadership.

11:2–9. Paul began by praising the Corinthians that they had **remember[ed]** (v. 2) what he taught previously and that they had kept **the ordinances** he gave to them. The word "ordinances" (Greek, *paradosis*) could best be translated "traditions." Godly traditions should not be cast off lightly.

Paul then established a gender order based on the order of how God relates people to Christ, in relation to prophesying and other matters. Christ is the **head** (v. 3) of every man, the man is the **head** of the woman, and the head of Christ **is God**. The idea of headship does not mean that women are inferior to men or that they have a lesser status before God. It is about an order, an arrangement, in the spiritual "social" order of how the Lord wants to relate to men and women in a church setting.

Because there should be "an openness" between Christ and a man who is **praying or prophesying**

(v. 4), the man is to have his head uncovered or he **dishonoureth his head**. "Prophesying" here is more than likely a teaching ministry not prophesying into the future, as only a few did apart from the other apostles and Paul (such as Abagus, Acts 11:28). The **woman that prayeth or prophesieth with her head uncovered dishonoureth her head** (v. 5). It is as if her hair is **shaven**. Paul instructed, **Let her be covered** (v. 6). Some think he was referring to a face covering, but a veil is more than likely a head shawl.

Notice here how Paul permitted and even encouraged women to pray and to have their own teaching ministry. Since the apostle forbade women to teach a mixed audience (see 1 Tim. 2:11–15), this means women were to be spiritual instructors for other women.

Since Adam was created first, he was to reflect **the image and glory of God** (v. 7; see Gen. 2:26; Ps. 8:4–6). Adam was created first and then **the woman for the man** (v. 9; see Gen. 2:18, 21–22). The woman is the **glory of the man** (v. 7). She is not, however, in his image (see Vine, *Collected Writings*, p. 77). She is his "help meet" (Gen. 2:18). Paul wanted to maintain this gender order even in the affairs of the church. He challenged men to be leaders in the churches. Again, this does not imply that women are inferior or have less intelligence; it simply reflects a proper order for the congregations. The creation order is to be maintained. "God could, indeed, have created both man and woman, Adam and Eve, in one undivided act" (Lenski, *1 and 2 Corinthians*, p. 443), but He did not. What the apostle instructed "is not merely a perfunctory observance … It is obligatory upon the woman as *agent* to exercise her will in a free demonstration of godly submission" (Mitchell, *First Corinthians*, p. 162).

11:10–16. Paul's continuation of this discussion indicates that it must have been a very contentious issue in the assembly. A woman's hair is her **glory** (v. 15) and it is her **power** (Greek, *exousia*; "authority"; v. 10). This is so on account of **the angels**. This "implies that God's good angels are present when God's people come together to pray" (Lenski, *1 and 2 Corinthians*, p. 445). On "power," Barrett (*First Epis-*

tle to the Corinthians, p. 255) suggests the covering "represents the new authority given to the woman under the new dispensation to do things which formerly had not been permitted her." Still, the man is not **without the woman, neither the woman without the man, in the Lord** (v. 11). The authority of the man does not make him independent of the woman, and the subordination of the woman does not make her dispensable. They are not independent of each other (Hunter, *1 Corinthians*, p. 127).

Paul again used the example of the order of creation. The man and the woman are interdependent. The woman comes from the man, and the man is given birth by the woman. This shows that **all things (are) of God** (v. 12). "Man and woman, everything that pertains to birth, relationships, and married life—all come from God" (Kistemaker, *1 Corinthians*, p. 378).

Paul provoked his readers, asking, **Judge in yourselves: is it comely** (right) **that a woman pray unto God uncovered?** (v. 13). With all that he had said and with what was clearly traditional, and even logical, the answer was no. **Even nature** (Greek, *physis*; "the natural world") shows that **if a man have long hair, it is a shame unto him** (v. 14). **But if a woman have long hair, it is a glory to her** (v. 15). In fact, it is given to her by God **for a covering**.

Paul completed his long argument on this issue and reminded the Corinthians not **to be contentious** (v. 16), because there was no other **custom, neither [in] the churches of God**. No assembly among the new churches being formed across the Roman Empire had any other view on the subject. Long hair was considered a woman's glory because it gave visible expression to the differentiation of the sexes.

7. Practice of the Lord's Supper (11:17–34)

Paul was given a report that factions were also developing over the Lord's Supper, which involved practices that dishonored the remembrance of Christ's death for the believer. Possibly some believers were taking the elements of the Lord's Supper in a fashion that echoed the pagans' bacchanalian and debauched practices in the feasts to their gods. Paul needed to continue his criticisms of this church to set doctrinal and practical things in order.

11:17–22. The apostle began by saying, **I praise you not** (v. 17), because the church was coming together at the Lord's table **not for the better, but for the worse**. "Better" (Greek, *kreisson*) refers to that which is advantageous, and "worse" (Greek, *hēsson*) refers to something deteriorating, referring to the spiritual effect and the contentious fallout in the congregation. Paul had heard that the Corinthians still came together with their schisms and spiritual **divisions** (v. 18). This he could **partly believe**. While what was taking place was deplorable, it exposed and **made manifest** (v. 19) the **heresies** among them. This celebration, meant to show unity, instead expressed conflict. "Heresy" (Greek, *hairesis*) means an act or choice, an opinion that is different from that of the whole church or a doctrine that is contrary to Scripture.

Paul knew that their main motive when they came together was **not to eat the Lord's supper** (v. 20). Instead, they came to eat and to get drunk. They were dishonest in their motives, and they dishonored the memory of the Lord's sacrifice on the cross. When they came together, apparently the wealthy brought full meals and became intoxicated, while the poor, **them that have not** (v. 22), could bring nothing. They gave the appearance of having a common meal, but this was not the case. Did they not have homes in which to eat their ordinary meals? Were they not despising the church? Regarding this matter, Paul said, "I praise you not" (v. 17).

11:23–25. The apostle does not say how he received the revelation about the Lord's Supper. Generally, he received revelation two ways: by direct revelation and maybe also by the instruction of the disciples. The bread represented the body of Christ given unselfishly for the benefit of the lost. It is a constant reminder of why he died (v. 26).

This cup ... my blood (v. 25) points to the sacrifice of Christ for the forgiveness of sins (see Heb. 9:22). This is a **new testament** ("contract," "agreement"), the new covenant, made by God (see Heb. 9:14–15). The word "testament" has to do with a relationship and contrasts with the old Mosaic covenant of the law (see Exod. 20; 24:1–8). The new covenant (see Jer. 31:31–32) while first promised to Israel spills over to benefit the church, but it will not be "fulfilled" with the Jews until the kingdom. The new covenant represents Christ the Living Word (see John 1:14–18). Jesus meant for this **cup** representing His **blood** to be taken in **remembrance of** Him (v. 25; Luke 22:19).

11:26–28. The Lord's table is to **shew the Lord's death till he come** (v. 26). "Shew" (Greek, *katangellō*) means "exhibit," "show forth," "proclaim," even "preach" (as in Acts 4:2; 13:5, 38; 15:36). The communion meal expresses believers' confidence in the death and resurrection of Christ as well as their confident expectation of His second coming.

To **drink ... unworthily** (v. 27) means to come with an attitude of irreverence. It is a privilege to represent the Lord's sacrifice and partake in the communion of the saints remembering His work on the cross. To be **guilty** (Greek, *enochos*) means being liable to the penal effect of committing a misdeed. Each one in the church was to **examine himself** (Greek, *dokimazetō*) to test or even judge, his actions and then eat and drink the meal with a good conscience. "This is defined in verse 29 as 'not judg[ing] the body rightly.' In other words, an irreverent and careless attitude is displayed at the Lord's Table" (Mitchell, *First Corinthians*, p. 168).

11:29–32. The one who eats and drinks **unworthily** (v. 29) brings **damnation to himself**. "Damnation" (Greek, *krima*) carries the idea of "judgment" in a special sense. While all believers will stand before the Lord for what is done in this life (see Rom. 14:10; 2 Cor. 5:10), this damnation is a special judgment, though not a loss of salvation. The judgment is temporal and has physical consequences. Because of it, **many are weak and sickly** (v. 30) in the congregation, **and many sleep**; that is, they are taken away to the Lord by death. This is a special penalty the Lord has imposed so that the sacrifice of Christ would not be besmirched among Christians and even among the lost in Corinth. Other sins can be equally evil and carry a temporal penalty for the believer. John the apostle adds, "There is a sin unto death: I do not say

that he shall pray for it. All unrighteousness is sin: and there is a sin not unto death" (1 John 5:16b–17).

Believers can escape such a harsh penalty by coming to their senses and **judg[ing] ourselves** (v. 31), and if this is done, **we should not be judged**. If this is not done, however, when the Lord judges, **we are chastened** (v. 32) so that believers will not be **condemned with the world**. "God disciplines us, so that we may turn to him in full penitence. By repenting of our sinful ways, we experience God's forgiveness, grace, mercy, and love (II Cor. 7:10)" (Kistemaker, *1 Corinthians*, p. 404).

11:33–34. Paul concluded this discussion with warmth and conciliation. **Wherefore, my brethren** (v. 33). By addressing the Corinthians as "brethren," he still spoke to them as part of the family of the children of God. He advised them to be considerate **when ye come together to eat**, even to **tarry** and wait for each other. If one was hungry, **let him eat at home** (v. 34) so that he would not bring upon himself **condemnation**. The Lord's Supper is to be more than food and drink. It has a spiritual purpose of reminding all the Christians of what Christ did at the cross. "Paul's primary interest is not reprobation, but restoration" (Mitchell, *First Corinthians*, p. 169). **And the rest**, other issues he was concerned about, he would **set in order** when he came to them. The apostle was hoping he could come to minister to them (see 4:19; 16:5–9). If he was able to come, he would arrive with the full authority of all of the apostles that the Lord had commissioned.

C. The Use of Spiritual Gifts (chaps. 12–14)

The Corinthian church also had problems regarding, and some cases of abuse of, the special spiritual gifts that the Holy Spirit imparts for the edification of the church. Having a gift did not ensure that it would not be used improperly. Many in the church had an inflated idea of their gifts and ostentatiously displayed their extraordinary abilities. Paul put the gifts into a proper balance in the Christian experience. In the midst of this discussion, he wrote that love, and all of its ramifications, is far more important than exercising spiritual gifts.

1. The Varieties of Spiritual Gifts (12:1–11)

In Paul's day, the issue of spiritual gifts was controversial in churches, as is often the case today. The Corinthian believers had spiritual gifts but were abusing them. Paul wanted to show that the gifts are given by the Holy Spirit, they are to help the churches minister, they do not replace love, they are primarily for ministry and not for show, and—especially regarding the gift of tongues—they have guidelines for their use.

12:1–3. That Paul started out with **concerning spiritual gifts** (v. 1), indicates that he was aware of some confusion or that the Corinthians had inquired about spiritual gifts. He did not want this church to be **ignorant** about the subject. He wanted to address the issue clearly so that none in the congregation would have an opportunity to contradict his message (see 14:37). He reminded them that they had practiced a false mysticism when, as **Gentiles**, they had been misled by **dumb idols** (v. 2). Misusing the miracle of the spiritual gifts could cause the church to fall into strange practices that they had all previously experienced as pagans. Paul was concerned both about their attitude on the subject and about the misconceptions taught by false teachers. The test of a lying apostle was that no one with **the Spirit of God** (v. 3) could **calleth Jesus accursed**, nor could one **say that Jesus is the Lord, but by the Holy Ghost**. The false prophets claimed special visions, revelations, and messages (see 2 Cor. 12:1) as if these has been given to them by the Lord, but apparently they were denying the humanity of Christ, as with the words "Jesus accursed."

12:4–6. Paul wanted the Corinthians to understand that there are **diversities** (Greek, *diaireseis*) **of gifts** (v. 4), though it is **the same Spirit** giving them, **And there are differences of administrations, but the same Lord** (v. 5). Both the Holy Spirit and the Lord Jesus Christ are involved in the working of the spiritual gifts. "Administrations" (Greek, *diakonia*) means "service" or "ministry," for each believer has his particular service to render and each has a gift to exercise for Christ's glory. There are **diversities of operations** (Greek, *energēma*), **but it is the same**

God at work in every believer: (1) the Spirit grants the gift, (2) the Lord Jesus administers it, and (3) the heavenly Father energizes it, or makes it work, for His purposes. Taken all together, these verses "suggest that for each there is a specific *gift* that correlates with a specific *place* and a specific *work*. As he proceeds, Paul weaves these three ideas in and out of his teaching on the subject" (Mitchell, *First Corinthians*, p. 176).

12:7–10. Every man (v. 7) is given **the manifestation of the Spirit** so that he may **profit withal**. The Holy Spirit imparts a gift to each Christian. The gifts come from the same source but are uniquely expressed (see 14:4; 1 Peter 4:10). "Profit" (Greek, *sympherō*) means "bring together." Most gifts are for the edifying of the believers in the body of Christ. Paul noted individuality in his comment, **For to one … to another** (v. 8). **The same Spirit** is at work here, not simply human energy. Spiritual gifts are not simply talents or skills; they are placements and activities that have a distinct purpose in God's plan.

The gift of **the word of wisdom** (v. 8) means that certain believers have a Spirit-given ability to share common sense and wisdom in specific situations, while others may not have this ability to discern. **The word of knowledge** is given to some to comprehend and process spiritual information that is not fully understood by all. This might have been confined to the early apostles and prophets, because it seems to be identified here as a revelatory gift for the apostles.

The **working of miracles** (v. 10), **prophecy**, and **discerning of spirits** were also important gifts. "It was … of importance to have a class of men with the gift of discernment, who could determine whether a man was really inspired, or spoke only from the impulse of his own mind, or from the dictation of some evil spirit" (Hodge, *First Epistle to the Corinthians*, p. 248). On prophecy, "After the canon of the New Testament was completed, the special needs for this gift was substantially diminished" (Mitchell, *First Corinthians*, p. 176).

Divers kinds of tongues (v. 10) and **the interpretation of tongues** work in tandem. They were probably the most exotic and controversial gifts in the early church. Today there are three views as to what "tongues" are about: (1) an ecstatic utterance or an "unknown" (14:2) language, (2) a language spoken by angels (13:1), (3) a foreign language that communicated the message of the gospel to one who could not understand the language being used. Those who hold that it is an ecstatic language argue that when tongues were spoken in Acts (2:4; 10:46; 19:6), they were certainly foreign languages because the text in Acts 2 clearly says that every man at Pentecost heard the disciples speak in "his own language" (Acts 2:6–8) or dialect. It is argued, however, in 1 Corinthians 12 and 14, that tongues are an ecstatic utterance or angelic languages, different from what was recorded in Acts. The Greek expression "other tongues" (Greek, *hetera glōssa*) is used in both Acts 2:4 and 1 Corinthians 14:21, which indicates that what happened in Acts 2 was the same as in 1 Corinthians 12 and 14. It would thus be a foreign language that the speaker would not know except by the Holy Spirit working a miracle in the speaker.

12:11. The Spirit of God is required to make **all these worketh**, giving to each believer **severally** (differently) **as he will**. Gifts are sovereignly initiated and divided for God's purposes in the body of believers. "The Spirit chooses what gift shall be given to each Christian, so that none have occasion for boasting, or for a sense of inferiority" (Barrett, *First Epistle to the Corinthians*, p. 286). It is not for the believer to dictate to the Holy Spirit what gifts they, or anyone else, should have.

2. Spiritual Gifts and the Body of Christ (12:12–31)

12:12–17. Here Paul explained the spiritual body of Christ, how the Spirit places the **many members** (v. 12) into Christ. There is but **one body: so also is Christ**. All believers are **baptized into** (v. 13) this one spiritual body, **whether … Jews or Gentiles … bond or free**. All classes who trust Christ are united to Him by spiritual baptism and are **made to drink into one Spirit** (see Rom. 12:4–5; Eph. 4:4–5). Since Paul said there is only "one baptism" (Eph. 4:5), he was not here referring simply to water baptism. It is the baptism of the Holy Spirit that actually brings

about salvation by uniting the believer with Christ. "The baptism of the Spirit is experienced by all who believe, at the moment of salvation (cf. Rom. 8:9). In that baptism, believers,… are identified with Christ … and are indwelt by the Spirit …" (Lowery, "First Corinthians," pp. 533–34). Jesus prophesied that believers would "drink into one Spirit" (v. 13) in John 4:14; 7:38–39.

Since each believer is a member of the body, and each is given a specific gift for a distinct task, **the foot … the hand** (v. 15), **the ear … the eye** (v. 16), **the hearing … the smelling** (v. 17) cannot say, **I am not of the body** (v. 16). It would be ridiculous for the foot or hand to claim that they were **the whole body** (v. 17). Each member is different and unique and is carrying out its function as given by the Lord. As the members cooperate together, they increase the effectiveness of the ministry of the local church.

12:18–22. God set the members … in the body, as it hath pleased him (v. 18). No one can request a specific gift, not even the gift of tongues. Nor can the members laud their gifts over other members as if the others' gifts are not as important. Even **those members … which seem to be more feeble, are necessary** (v. 22). The physical body has small organs and larger members that appear more essential, but all together, they make up the body. If any member is missing or is sickly, the body does not function properly.

12:23–27. The member of the body that is "ill" needs a compensation, another member to bring him strength. Upon the **less honourable** (v. 23) the **more abundant honour** is **bestow[ed]**, and the **uncomely parts** are given more abundance. **We bestow** (Greek, *peritithemen*) means "we clothe." This is like giving someone a coat that bestows honor upon the one who was previously not so blessed. In like manner God is bestowing gifts to the individual "to secure the result that more abundant honor should be given to those which lacked. By making the uncomely parts essential to the well being of the rest …" (Hodge, *First Corinthians*, p. 260). In this way, **there should be no schism** (v. 25) or competition. Each should **care one for another**. In a healthy body, when **one member suffer, all the members suffer with it; or one member be honoured, all the members rejoice with it** (v. 26). Paul did not single out the weaker members but laid down a principle that all should heed and abide by. Elsewhere the apostle said, "Let us therefore follow after the things which make for peace, and the things wherewith one may edify another" (Rom. 14:19).

12:28–31. To make sure the Corinthians did not suddenly feel they were high and mighty, Paul emphasized that there is an order to how God works in the church. He has **set some in the church, first apostles, secondarily prophets, thirdly teachers, after that miracles, then gifts of healing, helps, governments, diversities of tongues** (v. 28). Here Paul put forth an order of authority when he wrote of the apostles, prophets, and teachers. These were the teaching and writing disciples and included Paul himself.

Paul then asked a rhetorical question: does everyone in the church have the same gifts? (see vv. 28–29). The answer is no. In fact, his list does not include all of the gifts that he could have listed. He concluded that believers should **covet earnestly the best gifts** (v. 31). He had more to say, however. He would show them **a more excellent way**. When he says "covet earnestly" ("desire earnestly"), he was looking forward to chapter 14, where he said that it is good to want to promote the gifts, but only if one is driven by love (see chap. 13). Paul was not trying to arouse a spirit of competition among the believers. The "more excellent way" (or road) leads right into Paul's discussion of being driven by love in all things, rather than being driven by jealousy, as many of the Corinthians had been. Demonstrating the love of God is more important than seeking gifts.

3. The Primacy of Love over Gifts (chap. 13)

All of Paul's great authority and influence, his high and holy office, were because of God's love. The apostle laid open his whole heart for the Corinthians in this chapter. Paul stopped the flow of his discussion on spiritual gifts to point the church to something higher. He had experienced the love and grace of God when he was mercifully knocked down on the road to Damascus (see Acts 9:1–17). Whatever service the Corinthians had through their gifts needed to be tempered with charity that "never faileth" (1 Cor. 13:8).

13:1–3. Even having the gift of **tongues** (v. 1) of **angels**, if there was no **charity** (love) in what was said it would all sound like gonging **brass** or the gentle sound of a small, bell-like **tinkling cymbal**. Angels do communicate with each other, and in some cases the Lord allows them to speak with humans (see Matt. 28:5), but Paul's point was that it would be a miraculous gift to actually know the vocabulary of the angelic realm. He was not saying he had such a gift. And even if one had **the gift of prophecy** (v. 2), and comprehended **all mysteries, and all knowledge**, and had complete **faith** in order to be able to **remove mountains**, and yet had **no charity**, it would be as if one had **nothing**. Paul here used hyperbole and exaggeration to contrast the extremes of being able to do almost anything and yet be devoid of love—such power would be useless. By referring to prophecy, mysteries, and knowledge, he hit upon spiritual abilities that would be attractive to someone religiously ambitious. But such gifts the Lord would discount. When he mentioned the moving of the mountains by faith, he may have been referring to the words of Christ when He said that the faith of a grain of mustard seed could "remove [it] to yonder place" (Matt. 17:20). Some of the Corinthians may have hoped for such authority, but if it was without charity, it would be a spiritually useless gesture.

What if one gave away **all [his] goods to feed the poor** (v. 3), or gave his body as a sacrifice to **be burned**? Without **charity, it profiteth … nothing**. Great acts of charity or the giving of oneself in martyrdom would be wasted without love. "The exercise of the gifts accomplishes something in each case, but without love he who exercises them is himself of no value" (Vine, *Collected Writings*, p. 93).

13:4–7. In poetic fashion, the apostle made a long list of the blessedness of **Charity** (love; v. 4). The list is nearly exhaustive because he wanted the

Corinthians to become a model church. Charity **suffereth long** (v. 4), does not retaliate; **is kind**, outgoing with goodness; **envieth not**, will not show jealousy; **vaunteth not itself**, refuses to exalt oneself; **is not puffed up**, is not conceited; **doth not behave itself unseemly** (v. 5), does not act improperly; **seeketh not her own**, is never selfish; **is not easily provoked**, is not short-tempered; **thinketh no evil**, does not plot to do wrong; **rejoiceth not in iniquity** (v. 6), does not rejoice over wrong; **rejoiceth in the truth**, embraces what is right; **beareth all things** (v. 7), endures quietly even when suffering; **believeth all things**, anticipates what is good; **hopeth all things**, knows no pessimism; **endureth all things**, bears up under trials.

The Christian who exercises such godly love is showing forth the nature of Christ. Love always expects that grace will conquer and win its way in the struggles of the human drama. Exercising love raises the believer into the heights of the spiritual life. Paul would not allow the Corinthians to fall below this standard, which they had not been living and practicing among themselves.

13:8-10. Charity never faileth (v. 8). Some of the more miraculous gifts may cease, but love will not. The grammatical construction of "never faileth" means "does not fall." **Prophecies** will in the future be made inoperative, and the gifts of **tongues** and of **knowledge** will one day **cease**. These three gifts can be called "the communication gifts"; that is, they were used to transmit spiritual truth in the churches where the people spoke different languages. Also, a special source for revealed truth was needed because the New Testament books had not been finally written under the inspiration of the Holy Spirit. There had to be those who could "move the message" and explain doctrine, though revelation had not been finalized. "Perhaps what is most significant is that these gifts *will* stop. Some have agued that tongues are the language of heaven. If that were true, Paul could hardly have said that they will stop" (Mitchell, *First Corinthians*, p. 190).

The gifts of knowledge and prophecy are useful only in an imperfect state of existence. They have a purpose for the present but are limited in vision and scope; they do not tell the believer all there is to know. **In part** (v. 9) means that **we know** partially, or with limitation, but a change will come **when [the] perfect is come** (v. 10). The "perfect" (Greek, *teleion;* "complete," "mature," "finished") apparently does not refer to the coming of Christ because the word is in the neuter gender, not masculine. There are three views on what it means: (1) the completion of the New Testament canon (as suggested in the preceding paragraph), (2) the state of perfection of the new heavens and new earth, and (3) the state of the church when God's program for it is consummated at the coming of Christ.

13:11-12. Paul used two illustrations to get his point across. The first is that of the immaturity of **a child** (v. 11), who has limited speech, understanding, and thinking skills. In saying **I thought** (Greek, *elogizomēn*) **as a child**, the apostle may have been speaking of the church and "hinting that it was childishness that led the Corinthians to overvalue tongues and to undervalue love" (Barrett, *First Epistle to the Corinthians*, p. 306). When Paul **became a man, [he] put away childish things**.

Paul's second illustration argues that Christians can see only as **through a glass, darkly** (v. 12), or dimly. His reference is to a polished bronze mirror, which distorts a reflection and shows it with imperfection. The Christian now only **know[s] in part**, or partially, but someday will know as if seeing the Lord **face to face**. Only when the believer sees God face-to-face will partial knowledge (see 8:1-3) be displaced by the perfect knowledge of God. Elsewhere Paul added, "While we look not at the things which are seen, but at the things which are not seen: for the things which are seen are temporal; but the things which are not seen are eternal" (2 Cor. 4:18).

4. The Primacy of Prophecy over Tongues (14:1-25)

Tongues must have been extremely divisive issue in the Corinthian church. Apparently, when the Spirit imparted such a gift, the receiver could use this miraculous phenomenon on a continual basis. This became a contentious issue because pride set in.

The Corinthians must have had a fascination with this gift and quickly perverted its use. In this chapter, Paul spelled out the guidelines for its manifestation in the assembly.

14:1. Both this verse and 13:13 seem to set the stage for Paul's answer about tongues. The Corinthians were to **Follow after charity** but also **desire spiritual gifts**; the better gift, however, was **that ye may prophesy**. Paul was not saying that everyone should prophesy, for he had already said that not everyone has the same gifts (12:28-30). His point was that prophecy, or teaching, is preferable over the gift of tongues.

14:2-4. Verse 2 may seem confusing. In the Greek, Paul used what is known as "a dative of reference." The verse best reads: "He that speaketh in an unknown tongue speaketh not *in reference to the things* of men, but *in reference to the things* of God." In other words, he speaks of spiritual matters, not simply human matters. The word **unknown** (v. 2, 4) was added to the text for clarification. This **tongue** (v. 2, 4) would not have been understood by most in the company, yet **in the spirit he speaketh mysteries** (v. 2). The "mysteries" were "truths requiring a supernatural disclosure which God had not provided the Corinthians" (Barrett, *First Epistle to the Corinthians*, p. 538). As a result, for the church as a whole, tongues were a futile exercise that few could benefit from, except the speaker, who **edifieth himself** (v. 4) in his own spirit. Because all of the gifts were to edify **the church**, what the "Corinthians are experiencing fails this litmus test and should be laid aside in preference to those gifts" that benefit the church (Mitchell, *First Corinthians*, p. 197). **He that prophesieth speaketh [for] edification, and exhortation, and comfort** (v. 3). Preaching in a known tongue brings greater edification than preaching in an unknown tongue.

14:5-6. When Paul wrote that he wished **all spake with tongues** (v. 5), he was using hyperbole, because he already said that not everyone has the same gifts. He was contrasting this wish with **but rather that ye prophesied** and explained that **except he interpret** (tongues), prophesying was the greater

gift because it edifies **the church**. To understand Paul's statements here, one must consider the context. His point was that if the gift of tongues is used, it must be interpreted by one who has this gift (see 12:30). He probably was not saying that the one who speaks in tongues must then interpret what he has just said.

Paul was not deprecating the gift of tongues, which is a gift the Holy Spirit imparts. He was trying to ensure that the gift was used properly and that the extremes that the Corinthians fell into were avoided. What would **tongues ... profit** (v. 6) them unless it came with some deep spiritual substance, such as with special **revelation ... knowledge ... prophesying, or ... doctrine**? While the apostle mentioned his own gifted abilities here, he was trying to communicate to them that unless tongues were used in a way that had meaning, it was simply for show.

14:7-12. Here Paul presented a long illustration. He needed to use object lessons to communicate to this very immature congregation. He pointed out that different sounds are made by the **pipe ... harp** (v. 7), and **trumpet** (v. 8), and these sounds have different purposes, such as the trumpet calling the soldier **to the battle**. **So likewise** (v. 9), **what is spoken** in the general assembly must be **easy to be understood**. Otherwise, **ye ... speak into the air**. In this world, **There are ... many voices** (sounds) (v. 10), but they have a purpose; they are not **without signification**. So it is with the gift of tongues if not used properly. It must have a spiritual purpose, or one **speaketh [as] a barbarian** (v. 11). A "barbarian" was one who did not speak Greek or one who was simply a foreigner. To illustrate his point, Paul used what was happening in the metropolis of Corinth. The city was a melting pot of races and languages. It was teeming with sailors and traders from all points in the known world. This may be one of the reasons that the Holy Spirit activated the gift of tongues there, so that those who spoke other languages could miraculously hear the gospel and then take it back to their homeland.

Paul came to his point. Because this church was **zealous [for] spiritual gifts** (v. 12), it was best to excel to the edifying of the church, which meant that the gift of prophecy (teaching) was the most beneficial. Paul wanted the Corinthians to "seek after gifts that will benefit the church. Note that where Paul gives direction to his argument, it moves toward Acts 2 as the normative experience" (Mitchell, *First Corinthians*, p. 198).

14:13–17. This is the second time Paul said that an unknown tongue (v. 13) should be interpreted (see 14:5). In fact, Paul exhorted the one who spoke in tongues to pray that it may be interpreted. "This is always the case when the ability is lacking" (Lenski, *1 and 2 Corinthians*, p. 591). He urged this because the tongue (v. 14) given without interpretation is unfruitful and will not benefit those who do not know that language. Interpreted tongues, like prophecy, could edify the congregation (see Acts 19:6). If no one present was able to interpret, the tongues speaker was to keep silent (see 1 Cor. 14:28).

If one miraculously spoke in another tongue or language and did not comprehend what he said, the experience had no value. One could pray (v. 15) or even sing in tongues, but if it was done without understanding, the process was no better than the babbling of the heathen demon worshipers who put themselves into ecstatic trances. The speaker was to use tongues with the understanding also. Otherwise, one coming into the assembly or one who is unlearned (v. 16) and does not know what is going on would not know what thou sayest. Without a lucid understanding of what the Lord is revealing through these gifts the speaker was giving thanks well enough, but others were not edified. What was said may have been good, but no one spiritually benefited from it. Thanks (v. 17) and other spiritual expressions may go forth, but the other is not edified. "In short, anyone who gives leadership in worship service [including the tongues speaker] must speak intelligently to enlighten and instruct his fellow man" (Kistemaker, *1 Corinthians*, p. 494).

14:18–21. Paul had the gift of tongues and used it often: I speak with tongues more than ye all (v. 18). Yet in the church (v. 19), he preferred to speak clearly, with my understanding (v. 19), that he might teach others also, rather than speak ten thousand words in a tongue that most could not comprehend. The apostle was chipping away at the abuse and the arrogance displayed at Corinth. He was rebuking the Corinthians, not for speaking in tongues, which is a gift of the Holy Spirit, but for their irresponsible flaunting of the practice, which brought about more confusion than light.

In the midst of correcting the Corinthians' practice of tongues, Paul called them Brethren (v. 20) and told them to no longer be children in this matter but rather men who acted as spiritual adults. Their infatuation with tongues was another manifestation of their immaturity.

The apostle quoted the law (v. 21), a broad reference that included even the Prophets, such as Isaiah. The Lord said through Isaiah that Israel will be reached "with stammering lips and another tongue" (Isa. 28:11). Because of their hardness of heart, God will use Gentiles to speak to His people. With a foreign tongue unintelligible to Israel, this stiff-necked people will hear the truth of God's judgment on them.

14:22–25. Wherefore tongues are for a sign (v. 22), not for believers, but for unbelievers. Prophesying, or teaching, however, was for them which believe. Since the church is mainly for the spiritual nourishment of believers, prophecy is the more appropriate gift. If the skeptic, the doubter, the unlearned, and the unbeliever were to come into the assembly and hear what seems but a rambling of tongues, will they not say that ye are mad? (v. 23). The word "unlearned" ("idiots") refers to the uninitiated regarding tongues. Upon hearing what to them would be gibberish, they and the unbelievers would regard the congregation as a company of lunatics, whereas God's purpose in ministry, whether for the saved or unsaved, is to reach the understanding and appeal to the conscience.

If prophecy or teaching was being practiced, however, the unbeliever or the unlearned (v. 24) could be taught and convinced of all, and even convicted or judged [by] all. The secrets of his heart (v. 25), of the one who is so convicted, would cause him to fall down on his face and worship God. Then he would testify that in this assembly, **God is in you of a truth**. The unbeliever will only come to faith as a result of clearly hearing and understanding God's Word.

5. Regulating Spiritual Gifts (14:26-40)

Paul continued on the subject about tongues and prophecy, but here he laid down certain principles for regulating the use of these gifts. Prophecy has the highest value because it edifies all of those in the body of Christ and even works to bring unbelievers to repentance. Having established the theological and doctrinal issues regarding the gifts of tongues and prophecy, Paul set biblical parameters to eliminate abusive practices.

14:26-28. In the assembly, how should the services be conducted? **When ye come together** (v. 26), whether one brings **a psalm** to sing, gives **a doctrine**, speaks in **a tongue**, gives **a revelation**, or has **an interpretation ... Let all things be done unto edifying**. Paul's point was that it must all be done to edify the congregation. If one spoke **in an unknown tongue** (v. 27), it was to be done **by two, or at the most by three ... by course** (in turn); **and let one interpret**. The phenomenon of tongues was a gift of the Spirit of God, but carnality could set in, and the person speaking could be simply uttering his own thoughts. If this happened, it could lead to heresy. That is why the presence of one who had the gift of interpretation was necessary, to assure that this was a word from God, not man. **If there be no interpreter** (v. 28), the tongues speaker was to **keep silence in the church**. Paul added, **let him speak to himself, and to God**, meaning that he should keep his thoughts to himself and to God rather than speak in tongues without the counterbalance of an interpreter.

14:29-33. Turning to prophecy, the apostle applied the same principle and said that those prophesying may speak by **two or three** (v. 29), with others judging what was said. Again, this proves that while these gifts are from God, the flesh can intervene and spoil the message. Therefore, the message must be judged by the wisdom of others to ensure that it fits within the full scope of previous revelation. "When a person who receives such a revelation makes it known to fellow believers, they in turn must subject this revelation to the authoritative teaching of the Scriptures" (Kistemaker, *1 Corinthians*, p. 509).

Teaching and receiving prophecy must "be done decently and in order" (14:40). If a revelation was given **to another**, Paul instructed, **let the first hold his peace** (v. 30). Prophecy was to be given in an orderly fashion, **one by one [so] that all may learn, and all may be comforted** (v. 31). In human terms, **the spirits of the prophets are subject to the prophets**; that is, a consensus must be reached to confirm a teaching or a doctrine. No one could prophesy independently. Paul said that if there was confusion in the church while prophecy was being given, it was not from God, **For God is not the author of confusion** (v. 33); He is the author **of peace**. The obvious conclusion, then, is that confusion comes from the flesh and from believers' carnality and pride. Paul wanted peace to prevail **in all the churches of the saints**. "Saints" refers to those who are spiritually and positionally sanctified in Christ. The church is to be a unified body of believers, not a forum for self-promotion.

14:34-35. Scholars have differing opinions on these verses. Some say that Paul was referring to women who have the gift of tongues. Others believe Paul was simply continuing his argument about order and peace in the church. He was concerned that the women might disrupt the service. If Paul's context was prophecy, it ties into 11:5, where he permitted women to prophesy. Paul's main concern can be found in 1 Timothy 2:12, where he stated that he wanted the women "to be in silence." "Silence" is the Greek word *hēsychia*, which carries the idea "to not be excitable," or "to remain unemotional." Again, his concern was about the decorum and emotional state during the gathering of the congregation. He wanted the wives **to be under obedience** (v. 34), as is stated in **the law**. In a broad sense, it appears he was referring to the demeanor of Jewish women in the synagogues. Peter mentioned this and wrote that wives should be "in subjection unto their own husbands: even as Sara obeyed Abraham, calling him lord: whose daughters ye are, as long as ye do well, and are not afraid" (1 Peter 3:5b-6).

When Paul wrote, **Let your women keep silence** (v. 34), he used the Greek word verb *sigaō*, which comes from the noun *siagōn*, meaning the "jaw." Some have reasoned that, with a bit of humor, he was saying he did not want the woman "to move the mouth" or "flap the jaw" in a disruptive and emotional display. He instead wanted the women to **ask their husbands at home** (v. 35). "This contrasts with a disturbance caused by their talking to their husbands during the service" (Barrett, *First Epistle to the Corinthians*, p. 541). Paul was saying not that women should not speak at all but that they should not disturb the public services.

14:36–40. The church at Corinth was not an exclusive group of believers, acting independently as interpreters or as those handed down **the word of God** (v. 36). They, like all assemblies (see 14:33), were to obey the Lord's Word and truth by obeying its standards of conduct and even the traditions that come from His Word. If anyone claimed **to be a prophet, or spiritual** (v. 37), he must **acknowledge that the things** Paul wrote **are the commandments of the Lord**. This supports the doctrine of the inspiration of Scripture. What the apostle wrote came from the Lord and was not to be ignored or challenged. Whoever wanted to remain **ignorant** (v. 38) about this matter, however, **let him** do so. Paul may have been saying some will remain unconvinced.

The church should **covet** (in the good sense of "earnestly desire") **to prophesy** (v. 39) but **forbid not to speak with tongues**. Paul here emphasized the teaching ministry and held a neutral position on tongues, only because that gift was abused in the Corinthian church. He summarized the discussion with the desire that **all … be done decently and in order** (v. 40). Harmony and order should characterize public church services.

V. The Importance of the Doctrine of the Resurrection (chap. 15)

This entire chapter focuses on one of the most significant doctrines of Christianity, the resurrection, a doctrine which sets it apart from other religions. Without the resurrection, those who profess faith in Christ have no hope. If He did not come forth from the grave, Christians' belief is in vain, and there is certainly no guarantee of being resurrected. Paul also touched on the fulfillment or summing up of all things in the messianic kingdom. The resurrection was an historical event, was witnessed by a large company of the disciples and others, and was even attested to by many others who saw the Lord for themselves. Paul apparently was answering some skeptics who denied the resurrection of Christ and therefore were also repudiating the resurrection of believers. He seems to have been saying that a strong belief "in it would help solve many of the Corinthians' problems. Certainly if the message of Christ crucified were foolishness to the Greek mind (1:23), the corollary doctrine of the Resurrection was no less so (cf. Acts 17:31–32)" (Lowery, "First Corinthians," p. 542).

A. The Historical Fact of the Resurrection (15:1–11)

15:1–2. The essence of **the gospel** (v. 1) is the doctrine of the resurrection. **I declare** (Greek, *gnōrizō*) actually means "I make plain," "I cause [you] to know." Paul was reminding the Corinthians of what they ought never to have forgotten. He spells this out in verse 3 on. **I preached** the gospel and the resurrection, which **ye have received**, and now **ye stand** in it. By this **ye are saved, if ye keep in memory what I preached unto you, unless ye have believed in vain** (v. 2). In writing "keep in memory," Paul was putting forth the idea that if they did not keep in their memory what he had preached to them, it was possible they did not ever have saving faith. Judas Iscariot, for example, showed by his denial of the Lord Jesus that he was never a true believer.

15:3–7. When Paul said he had delivered **first** (v. 3) what the Corinthians believed, he used the Greek word *prōtois*, meaning "among the first things," or the things of primary importance (see Kistemaker, *1 Corinthians*, p. 535). This he had **received** from the Old Testament (see Ps. 16:8–11; Isa. 53:5–6, 11) and from eyewitnesses, the apostles and others (see Acts 1:21–22). These facts, **that Christ**

died (v. 3) and **was buried, and ... rose again** (v. 4) are all confirmed and prophesied in the Old Testament, that is, **according to the scriptures**. The Word of God is the first line of defense for all truth.

After His resurrection, Jesus was first seen by one of the most respected disciples, **Cephas** (Peter; v. 5; see Luke 24:34), then by the other apostles, **the twelve**. "The twelve" became a symbolic description of the inner circle of the disciples as a group. Judas had already killed himself when Christ revealed Himself to Peter and the others. In other places in the Gospels, they are often called "the eleven" (Matt. 28:16; Mark 16:14; Luke 24:9; Acts 1:26).

Even more astounding is that others beside the twelve saw Christ. More than **five hundred brethren** (v. 6), or believers, saw Him at the same time (**at once**), many of whom were still alive when Paul was writing, though some had already died, or **fallen asleep** (an often used expression of the death of believers, see Acts 7:60). Paul then mentioned one of the most respected elder leaders of the disciples, **James** (v. 7), and a wider circle of believers, **all the apostles**, who saw the living Jesus. This James is probably the Lord's brother (see Matt. 13:55), since the apostle James was included in "the twelve" (v. 5). The brother James earlier had been an unbeliever (see John 7:5), though he later joined the assembly of disciples (see Acts 1:14; Mitchell, *First Corinthians*, p. 213). Paul could not have mentioned these facts if they were not true. Any skeptic could have searched for eyewitnesses and asked pertinent questions. This was too large of a crowd of eyewitnesses to refute.

15:8–11. Next the apostle added his own firsthand witness. The resurrected Christ **was seen of me also** (v. 8) but as **one born out of due time**, meaning Paul was not saved when the Lord appeared to him (see Acts 9:3–9) and commissioned him as "a chosen vessel unto me, to bear my name before the Gentiles, and kings, and the children of Israel" (Acts 9:15). Paul considered himself **the least of the apostles** (v. 9) because he tormented the early believers in Jerusalem, placing them in chains, using "threatenings and slaughter against the disciples of the Lord" (Acts 9:1). He considered himself the chief of sinners (see 1 Tim. 1:15) and "the least of all saints" (Eph. 3:8). "This recollection of a sinful past is set as an example to all in whom the grace of God has so wrought" (Vine, *Collected Writings*, p. 107). This grace was not **bestowed ... in vain** (v. 10) because it brought on a greater appreciation of the gospel, causing Paul to labor **more abundantly than they all**, possibly meaning the other apostles. The apostle shows how personal his ministry was when said, **the grace of God ... was with me**. Regardless of who was preaching and teaching, however, **I or they** (v. 11), the message was going forth, **and so ye believed**.

B. No Salvation without the Resurrection (15:12–19)

15:12–14. Paul asked, **If Christ be preached that he rose from the dead, how say some among you that there is no resurrection of the dead?** (v. 12). If there is no promise of resurrection anywhere in God's Word, **then is Christ not risen** (v. 13). In seed form, Job prophesied, "For I know that my Redeemer liveth, and that he shall stand at the latter day upon the earth: and though after my skin worms destroy this body, yet in my flesh shall I see God" (Job 19:25–26). David also echoed the words of the Messiah, "My flesh also shall rest in hope. For thou wilt not leave my soul in hell [the grave]; neither will thou suffer thine Holy One to see corruption" (Ps. 16:9b–10). Ezekiel spoke of the resurrection (Ezekiel 37), and so did Daniel (Dan. 12:1–3). The doctrine of the resurrection was well established and certain for all believing Jews during the time of Christ. Martha said to Jesus, "I know that he [Lazarus] shall rise again in the resurrection at the last day" (John 11:24). Jesus answered with these famous words: "I am the resurrection, and the life: he that believeth in me, though he were dead, yet shall he live" (John 11:25). Christ is the epitome and the embodiment of this doctrine.

15:15–19. All of the great company, including Paul, were **false witnesses of God** (v. 15) if they **testified** that God **raised up Christ** and it was not so. The principle would have been destroyed; there would never be such a thing as the resurrection. If the dead cannot be raised, neither can Christ (v. 16). Here Paul may have been referring to Lazarus, whose resurrection had to be well known among the believers of the church. If there is no resurrection, then **faith is vain** (v. 17) and the Corinthians and all Christians **are yet in your sins**. "Vain" (Greek, *mataios*) means "lacking in result." "Since the resurrection of Christ is essential to our justification (Rom. 4:25), the denial of it vitiates the forgiveness of our sins" (Mitchell, *First Corinthians*, p. 216). Therefore, all who have died, those **fallen asleep in Christ are perished** (v. 18). If there is no hope in this life for a future resurrection, then Christians are among **all men most miserable** (v. 19).

C. All in Christ Shall Be Made Alive (15:20-34)

15:20-24. Here Paul focused on the central truth of Christ's resurrection from the dead. By Christ's resurrection, He led the way for others to follow, like the first of the spring crops from the field, **the firstfruits of them that slept** (v. 20). Because He came forth from the grave, believers are certain to follow. Christ was the first to be resurrected, **the firstfruits** (Greek, *aparchē*; v. 23). "Paul (in dependence on the Old Testament) takes the word to mean the first installment of the crop which foreshadows and pledges the ultimate offering of the whole" (Barrett, *First Epistle to the Corinthians*, p. 350). This is similar to Him being also called "the beginning, the firstborn from the dead" (Col. 1:18).

By one **man** (Adam) **came death** (v. 21), and by another **man** (Jesus) **came ... the resurrection of the dead** (see Rom. 5:12-18). Adam brought upon all judgment, but Christ brought upon all the free gift of "righteousness" (see Rom. 5:18). Some have mistakenly seen this as a form of universalism. In verse 21-22 and in 15:45, however, Paul made it clear that **in Adam all die, even so in Christ shall all be made alive** (v. 22), and the only way to be "in Christ" is to trust Him as Savior. "Union with Adam is the cause of death; union with Christ is the cause of life" (Hodge, *First Epistle to the Corinthians*, p. 324). There is an order for every man: (1) **Christ**

the firstfruits (v. 23), then (2) they who belong to Him **at his coming**. Paul's nearest reference would be the rapture, which he described in some detail in 15:51-54 and 1 Thessalonians 4:13-18.

Paul carried his eschatological thought on to the end of history as described in Scripture. **The end** (v. 24) will arrive when Christ has **delivered up the kingdom to God, even the Father.** At that time, Christ **shall have put down all [human] rule and all authority and power.** This is when "every knee shall bow" (Isa. 45:23; Rom. 11:4; 14:11; Phil. 2:10 but "should") and Christ will be a root of His distant fathers David and Jesse and be "an ensign [flag] of the people; to it shall the Gentiles seek: and his rest shall be glorious" (Isa. 11:10). As for putting down "all rule and all authority," the Messiah, the Son of God, shall have the nations as an inheritance and shall "break them with a rod of iron ... shalt dash them in pieces like a potter's vessel" (Ps. 2:9). Then begins His kingdom that will last one thousand years (see Rev. 20:1-6).

15:25-28. For he must reign (v. 25) was Paul's prevailing conclusive statement. At that time, as a conquering king of days gone by, Christ shall place His foot on the neck of His foes, subduing them **under his feet**. As God's Son, the Lord "madest him to have dominion over the works of thy hands" (Ps. 8:6). Meanwhile, in heaven, seated at the right hand of the Father, He waits until His enemies become His footstool (see Ps. 110:1). He will reign from Zion in Israel (see Ps. 110:2a) but will reign over the world. The Father will say to Him: "Rule thou in the midst of thine enemies" (Ps. 110:2b). When God is **all in all** (v. 28; see Rom. 11:36), the new creation will be consummated, and the church will share in Christ's resurrection. At that time, even the Son of God will be **subject unto him,** the God of the universe. Though equal in essence to the Father, the Son remains submissive in carrying out His will.

15:29-34. These cryptic verses have generated over two hundred explanations. "It is clear from the context, however, that Paul distinguishes his own practice and teaching from that described here" (Lowery, "First Corinthians," p. 542). The baptism **for the dead** (v. 29) initially raises problems, but considering what Paul may have meant and what he certainly could not have meant sheds light on the passage. The rules of Bible interpretation dictate that one should not hold a doctrine based on an obscure passage, and an obscure passage must be interpreted in light of the more clear verses that contradict what the obscure passage seems to be saying.

Some have tried to explain this passage by saying that Paul was refuting a pagan practice of ritual and religious washings. Mormons try to explain the passage by saying that one can be a substitute in baptism for those who have died, thus "making" them saved by the waters of baptism. Another view is that the Corinthians had distorted water baptism, as they apparently did in chapter 1, and as they had distorted the Lord's Supper (see 11:17–34). Yet another view is that Paul was talking about those who come along as believers, are baptized, and replace those who have fallen asleep in Christ.

The best explanation, which seems similar to the last suggestion, is put forth by Mitchell (*First Corinthians*, p. 221): "The logic of the passage would thus connect to the import of resurrection. People (now dead) have proclaimed the message and have led others to faith in the same gospel promising life and participation with Christ at His coming. What will we do if we now say that there is no resurrection and that the dead are simply gone?" In asking **why stand we in jeopardy** (v. 30), Paul could have meant, "Why do we continue to risk ourselves, giving our lives for the gospel, if all of this is not true?"

By your rejoicing (v. 31) means "By my boasting concerning you." Paul added, **I die daily**, meaning that he was continually exposed to death for the sake of Christ (see 2 Cor. 4:10). In fact, he had even fought with **beasts at Ephesus** (v. 32), probably referring to how he nearly lost his life when the mob tried to kill him (see Acts 19). Paul asked why he would struggle so and **what advantageth it me, if the dead rise not?** If this were the case, **let us eat and drink; for to morrow we die**, as cited by the Epicurean philosophers. Paul advised his readers to be careful what they listen to: **Be not deceived** (v. 33). Do not be fooled by what others say. Hang on to what is right and good.

Awake to righteousness (v. 34), in this case, what is right, and **sin not** by being led into doing what is wrong. Paul reminded the Corinthians that **some have not the knowledge of God**. They are but pretenders. Because some of the Corinthians had thus been led astray, Paul said, **I speak this to your shame**. "False doctrine never aids true moral conduct but works to corrupt that conduct" (Lenski, *1 and 2 Corinthians*, p. 701).

D. The Promise of the Resurrection (15:35–49)

Having proved the authenticity of the resurrection, Paul next focused on the promise of the resurrection. Here he wanted to illustrate its nature and show what kind of bodies the dead are to be raised in. Apparently, the overwhelming objection that Paul was aware of was, How can the future body be different from the one believers now have? The future body will definitely be material and identical to the present one, though it will be "organized" in a very different way. A seed is planted, yet it does not come out of the ground like a seed but like a flower. So it is with the eternal resurrected body.

15:35–38. Some would question, **How are the dead raised up? and … what [kind of] body** (v. 35) will they have when **they come** out of the place of the dead? With a tinge of anger, Paul said, **Thou fool** (Greek, *aphrōn;* "without reasoning intelligence"; v. 36), a seed does not come alive, **is not quickened**, unless it dies. This is the great mystery of the ground bearing fruit. So it is with the miracle of the resurrection. The body placed in the ground is **not that body that shall be** (v. 37), yet it will not come forth as some other kind, **some other grain**. Every seed has its own essence, its **own body** (v. 38), and that is given, is created, as God has made it **as it hath pleased him**. God has created us, and we shall come forth from the dead as is pleasing to Him, God's "choice not being determined by man's act of sowing … God himself appoints and chooses [the seed and the body] for various purposes" (Barrett, *First Epistle to the Corinthians*, pp. 370–71). God is in charge of the resurrection.

15:39–45. Paul's main purpose in these verses has to do with the resurrection, yet they provide an excellent explanation of how God created biological kinds and how He specifically created the bodies in space for distinct purposes. Creation and nature are fully in His design and operate by His power and authority.

When God created **men, beasts, fishes,** and **birds** (v. 39), He gave to each **kind** a distinct makeup, or **flesh.** The discovery and workings of the chromosomes of living cells shows that they do not cross over between kinds. They do not have **the same flesh.** The same is true of the **celestial** (v. 40) and **terrestrial** bodies. "As to the stars, their differences in luster and brilliance are endless, and in this they testify to the infinite wisdom and inexhaustible power of God their Creator" (Vine, *Collected Writings*, p. 113). These bodies each have a distinct glory (Greek, *doxa*) that sets them apart, **for one star differeth from another star in glory** (v. 41).

Paul explained, **So also is the resurrection of the dead** (v. 42). The human body is **sown in corruption** and **raised in incorruption.** "Corruption" (Greek, *phthora*) is the state of creation because of the entrance of sin into the universe (see Rom. 8:21; 2 Peter 2:12); because of the resurrection of Christ, however, the very body of the believer is to be raised and redeemed (see Rom. 8:23), with "the redemption of the purchased possession, unto the praise of his glory" (Eph. 1:14). As well, the body **is sown in dishonour** (v. 43) and **weakness** as **a natural body** (v. 44), but it is **raised in glory [and] power** (v. 43) as **a spiritual body** (v. 44). The reader must not assume that the resurrected saint's receiving "a spiritual body" means he is resurrected simply as a nonmaterial being, a floating wisp without form or corporality. By "a spiritual body," the apostle meant that the resurrection is accomplished through the supernatural operation of God the Spirit. God is going to change everything around. Nothing will be the same, and sin will be forever eradicated. Paul drew this conclusion partly from Genesis 2:7, which states that **Adam was made a living soul** (v. 45) that failed the test and succumbed to the temptation placed

before him by Satan, who was embodied in the serpent (see Genesis 3). Because of his disobedience to God's instructions, Adam would die, and the Lord added, "unto dust shalt thou return" (Gen. 3:19). Christ, **the last Adam,** is **a quickening** (life-giving) **spirit,** however, who has given those of Adam's race eternal life. Apart from the coming of the rapture, when the saints who are alive will be taken from the earth, Christians "still face the effect of death, even though we know that its power has been abrogated" (Kistemaker, *1 Corinthians,* p. 572).

15:46–49. The first Adam and his children were from the **earth, earthy.** The second man, the Lord, is from **heaven.** So those who trust in Him will be of the **heavenly.** Redeemed human beings are not meant to be earthbound but are instead bound for heaven. As believers **have borne the image of the earthy** (v. 49), likewise they will **also bear the image of the heavenly.** "*The heavenly* is Christ; *they that are heavenly* are his risen people. The descendants of Adam derive from him an earthly body like his. Those who are Christ's are to have a body fashioned like unto his glorious body, Phil. 3, 21" (Hodge, *First Epistle to the Corinthians,* p. 352).

E. Christ's Victory over Death (15:50–58)

15:50–54. Paul reminded his readers that simple **flesh and blood** (v. 50), humans residing in the same spiritual and physical mold as Adam, as sinful beings, **cannot inherit the kingdom of God** because this is comparable to **corruption inherit[ing] incorruption.** The thousand-year reign of Christ in the millennial kingdom will be the first stage in the eternal state of the new heavens and the new earth (see Rev. 21:1–7) "wherein dwelleth righteousness" (2 Peter 3:13). It is possible that many believers of this present church age may not die (**We shall not all sleep**; v. 51). If the rapture transformation took place today, **we** (the living) **shall all be changed** (see 1 Thess. 4:15; Phil. 3:21). The rapture **trumpet shall sound** (v. 52), and believers who have died **shall be raised incorruptible,** and those believers who are left **shall be changed.** This trumpet is called **the last trump,** meaning the trumpet that ends the church dispensation. This trumpet should not be confused with the seventh trumpet of Revelation (see Rev. 11:15–18). That trumpet is a war trumpet signaling the wrath to come upon the world before the kingdom of Christ is established (see Rev. 11:15). The rapture trumpet will be sounded to call the workers home from the fields of Christian labor. It is a trumpet of blessing, not a trumpet of terror.

The resurrection of those that are asleep will come just before the change that will take place for the living (see v. 52). The living will receive new and eternal bodies like those of the dead in Christ, who will be "raised incorruptible" (v. 52). This entire rapture process is called **a mystery** (v. 51) because it is not revealed in the Old Testament. Paul had written of this earlier in his first letter to the Thessalonians (1 Thess. 4:13–18). Those who are the dead in Christ shall be resurrected, and then "we which are alive and remain shall be caught up together with them in the clouds, to meet the Lord in the air: and so shall we ever be with the Lord" (1 Thess. 4:17). All of this will happen because **this mortal** (that which is dying) **must put on immortality** (v. 53), the state in which dying is eliminated. This fulfills Isaiah 25:8, which states that **Death is swallowed up in victory** (v. 54).

15:55–56. Death's **sting** (v. 55) is gone, and so is the triumph of the **grave** (see Hos. 13:14). John the apostle summarized this when he wrote, "And God shall wipe away all tears from their eyes; and there shall be no more death, neither sorrow, nor crying, neither shall there be any more pain: for the former things are passed away" (Rev. 21:4).

The sting of death (v. 56) came about as a result of the penalty for **sin**. The power and **strength of sin** is administered by the force of God's righteous demands, as laid down in **the law**. The main purpose of the law was to bring conviction about sin, so that "all the world may become guilty before God" (Rom. 3:19). Therefore "by the deeds of the law there shall no flesh be justified in his sight: for by the law is the knowledge of sin" (Rom. 3:20). Justification comes only through faith in Christ (see Rom. 3:26–28).

15:57–58. Because of these wonderful revelations, the apostle concluded with this triumphant message:

But thanks be to God, which giveth us the victory through our Lord Jesus Christ (v. 57). The only way out of the judgment laid upon humanity is to trust in Christ as one's Savior. These facts should make an impact on the **beloved brethren** (v. 58). They should live out the Christian life in a steady and **unmoveable** manner. They should be **always abounding in the work of the Lord**, knowing that their **labour is not in vain in the Lord**. The Christian life has purpose; it is not an empty existence. For Paul, this purpose was found in the sure conviction that he would one day share in the glory of the resurrection.

VI. Practical and Personal Exhortations (chap. 16)

As was his usual custom, Paul closed his letter with words of encouragement. The flow of the last chapter here concludes with an exhortation about very practical matters, focusing on the needs of the persecuted church in Jerusalem and a collection that would be made for them. In this chapter, Paul also cited the work of many who were laboring, sometimes under terrible circumstances, in various places.

A. The Collection for the Needy Saints (16:1–4)

16:1. God's people, **the saints** (see 1:2), needed help. Paul gave the same order to all **the churches of Galatia** that they too should put together a **collection**, probably meaning monies to relieve the lack of temporal things needed for survival. Paul wanted to go to Jerusalem to help (see Rom. 15:25) and had written to the Roman church, "For it hath pleased them of Macedonia and Achaia to make a certain contribution for the poor saints which are at Jerusalem" (Rom. 15:26). These Gentile churches wished to help their Jewish brothers who were suffering. Paul added, "For if the Gentiles have been made partakers of their spiritual things, their duty is also to minister unto them in carnal things" (Rom. 15:27), or temporal things. The apostle continued this reminder in 2 Corinthians 8:1; 9:1–4. The Galatian churches were contributing, and Paul instructed the Corinthian church, **even so do ye.**

16:2–4. The collection was to be taken **Upon the first day of the week** (v. 2), or compiled on a Sunday, when the churches were meeting for teaching and fellowship. The principle was that during the week they were putting aside, laying up **in store**, their money and even possibly some goods to be transported. They were to do this from a spiritual perspective: **as God has prospered.** Paul was always careful about money matters, avoiding solicitations for himself (see 9:12, 15), "but also when he acted to meet the needs of others he avoided direct involvement in handling the gift" (Lowery, "First Corinthians," p. 546). The believer was to do this not out of compulsion but in relation to what the Lord had done for him. Paul wanted the gift to be steadily collected so that there would **be no gatherings when I come.** The church would **approve by [their] letters** (v. 3) whom they chose to deliver their **liberality** (bounty) **unto Jerusalem.** If possible, **if it be meet** (v. 4), Paul would go with this envoy of believers to make the delivery. He may have had other missionary business to accomplish also.

B. Paul's Desire to Visit Corinth (16:5–9)

16:5–9. Paul had travel plans to **pass through Macedonia** (v. 5) and then possibly to **winter** (v. 6) in Corinth. With prayer support and possibly also with supplies, the church could help him on his way: **ye may bring me on my journey whithersoever I go.** This may mean that he wanted to journey straight to Macedonia, but the plans needed to be fluid as circumstances dictated. Though he could not come to Corinth at that time, he still wanted **to tarry a while with you** (v. 7). It is interesting to observe that after having been so "heavy" regarding the situations in the Corinthian church, Paul could now come along side of them and speak with such kind thoughts of intimate fellowship and concern. Paul knew that nothing would happen unless **the Lord permit.** There is human responsibility in the ministry, yet it is God who directs His work for His own purposes. Along his route of evangelization and teaching, Paul wanted to **tarry at Ephesus until Pentecost** (v. 8). Though the Corinth congregation was

mainly a Gentile church, they knew of the Jewish festivals that had their origins in the Old Testament. Paul said, though **there are many adversaries** (v. 9) in Ephesus, still **a great door and effectual is opened unto me.**

C. Personal Exhortations and Encouragements (16:10–18)

16:10–11. Timothy (**Timotheus**; v. 10) was well-known as Paul's traveling companion and ambassador who carried messages and even ministered on behalf of the great apostle. If Timothy went to Corinth, Paul wanted to make sure he labored with them **without fear.** Timothy and Erastus had gone into Macedonia (see Acts 19:22), but then Timothy was to go on to Corinth (see 1 Cor. 4:17). Paul did not want Timothy intimidated by harsh treatment in Corinth, because Timothy, as Paul, **worketh the work of the Lord.** Some argue that the issue was not "fear" but simply that Timothy appeared to be somewhat timid (see 1 Tim. 4:12; 2 Tim. 1:7). The apostle did not want him to be **despise[d]** (v. 11) but rather to come **in peace** and then be able to go back to Paul. Paul wanted him to be a part of the congregations, **for I look for him with the brethren.** Mitchell (*First Corinthians*, p. 230) suggests that Timothy "appears as a man of character, courage, and resourcefulness under whose leadership many crisis situations in the fledgling New Testament churches were confronted (cf. Acts 16–20; Phil. 2:19–24; 1 Thess. 3:1–6)."

16:12. Paul also **greatly desired** for **Apollos** to visit the assembly in Corinth. Apollos, however, had some legitimate reasons not to go. He desired **not at all to come at this time**, but he would come later, at a more **convenient time.** This may indicate that Apollos was operating independently of Paul, though there was no conflict between them.

16:13–16. Here Paul began a short series of pithy commands and encouragements. He wanted the Corinthian church to examine carefully what they were doing spiritually. He said, **Watch ye, stand fast in the faith** (v. 13). They were to look around, be aware of what was going on, and stand firm in their trust in the Lord. Barrett notes that "Watch ye" (Greek, *grēgorein*) is a present infinitive with the idea "to be continually watching" (*First Epistle to the Corinthians*, p. 393). This expression is often used not of purely general events but of eschatological happenings, or signs that may signal the coming of Christ (see 15:51–54). **Quit you like men** (Greek, *andrizesthe*; "play the man") refers to "manliness," which was a virtue recognized in the ancient world. Paul wanted the Corinthian assembly to shape up spiritually and **be strong** for the Lord's sake, yet all things were to **be done with charity** (v. 14), or love.

Paul issued another command that seems to have come from deep personal conviction. Apparently, **the house of Stephanas** (v. 15), whom Paul had baptized in Corinth (see 1:16), had originally come from **Achaia** (Greece), were some of the first converts there, and were viewed as among **the firstfruits** of that region. **They have addicted themselves** means "they have set themselves" to ministering to the believers, **the saints**. The entire household of Stephanas was serving the Lord. The larger body of believers in Corinth needed to **submit** to this family. They had helped Paul and were now laboring for and with him. "Stephanas and his household are not the only members of the church whose lead must be valued, respected, and followed" (Barrett, *First Epistle to the Corinthians*, p. 394).

16:17–18. Stephanas and Fortunatus and Achaicus (v. 17) were coming to Paul to help him with what the whole church had not **supplied**. This could mean that they made up for the absence of the Corinthians as a whole or that they had done what the Corinthians had failed to do. **For** (v. 18) introduces the reason these men were so important to Paul: **they have refreshed my spirit and yours**. Because of this, they were to be **acknowledge[d]**, "recognized" and "appreciated."

D. Final Greetings and Benedictions (16:19–24)

16:19–20. There must have been a great "telegraphing" of communication between the churches of Greece (Achaia) and all the churches **of Asia** (v. 19). Asia was a Roman province that is today western Turkey, including Ephesus and the surround-

ing cities (see Acts 19:10). The churches of Colosse, Laodicea, and Hierapolis were on the border of the province of Asia (see Col. 4:13–16; Rev. 1:11). These churches **salute[d]** (greeted) the Corinthian believers. Paul specifically mentioned **Aquila and Priscilla**, the couple who had helped found the Corinthian church (see Acts 18:1–4) but who had since gone to Ephesus (see Acts 18:18–19). **Much** (Greek, *polla*) means that their greetings were enthusiastic, carrying much delight and fond memories of the church. They sent their greetings **in the Lord**, with His blessing and for His purposes. The salute was also from the house church of Aquila and Priscilla. In fact, the Corinthians were urged to **Greet … one another with an holy kiss** (v. 20), an expression of the day that indicated camaraderie and friendship. "This was the conventional token of Christian affection. In the East, the kiss was a sign either of friendship among equals, or of reverence and submission on the part of an inferior" (Hodge, *First Epistle to the Corinthians*, p. 372).

16:21–24. Paul wrote the **salutation** (v. 21) **with mine own hand**. He generally used the services of an amanuensis or a secretary when writing his letters but often concluded with his own writing as an authentication of his letters (see Col. 4:18; 2 Thess. 3:17). He mentioned in Galatians 6:11 that he had written the entire epistle with his own hand, as something that was unusual (see Hodge, *First Epistle to the Corinthians*, p. 372).

Paul wanted to weed out those in the Corinthian assembly who did not love **the Lord Jesus Christ** (v. 22). Note that he used the full title of the Lord, wanting to ensure undying love and honor for the entire person and all that He represents to the world. The one who did not so love Christ, **let him be Anathema**, or "cursed." These are strong words, but Paul was concerned that the local assembly might become spiritually polluted through the efforts of those who were pretenders to the faith. In a sudden burst of expression, he added, **Maran-atha**, an Aramaic word meaning "the Lord comes." It is both a solemn warning of judgment for those who are false believers and a statement of blessed hope for genuine believers. It is suggested that "the warning is against those whose lack of love proves their lostness. The gracious affection is expressed to those who, with Paul, *do* love the Lord and each other" (MacArthur, *1 Corinthians*, p. 488). **The grace of our Lord ... be with you** was a common greeting of the day, but for Paul, it was not a meaningless pious platitude. He really wanted to see this church increasingly graced and blessed by the Lord.

The last thing Paul wanted the Corinthian congregation to read in this letter was that he loved them all **in Christ Jesus**. Christianity is about Christ from start to finish. By closing with **Amen**, Paul was saying "surely," "absolutely," "verily." The epistle ends on a positive note, but the challenges for this church remained, as is evident in the second letter to the Corinthians.

THE SECOND EPISTLE OF PAUL THE APOSTLE TO THE CORINTHIANS

INTRODUCTION

Author, Date, and Place of Composition

Paul is the author of this letter (see 1:1; 10:1). It is stamped with his style and contains more autobiographical material than any of his other writings. The available evidence indicates that AD 55 is a reasonable estimate for the writing of this letter. From 1 Corinthians 16:5–8, we conclude that 1 Corinthians was written from Ephesus before Pentecost (in the spring) and that 2 Corinthians was written later that same year before the onset of winter. Second Corinthians 2:13; 7:5 indicate that it was written from Macedonia.

Recipients

The opening salutation addresses the letter to the church in Corinth and to the Christians throughout Achaia (the Roman province comprising all the territory of Greece south of Macedonia).

Theme

The Corinthian church had been infiltrated by false teachers who were challenging both Paul's personal integrity and his authority as an apostle. Because he had announced a change in his itinerary, with the result that he would pay the Corinthians one (long) visit instead of two (short) visits, these adversaries were asserting that his word was not to be trusted. They were also saying that he was not a genuine apostle and that he was putting into his own pocket the money they had collected for the poverty-stricken believers in Jerusalem. Paul asked the Corinthians to consider that his personal life in their midst was always honorable and that his life-transforming message of salvation was true. He urged them to prepare for his impending visit by completing the collection they had started a year previously and by dealing with the troublemakers in their midst. He warned them that he meant what he wrote.

Literary Features

The structure of the letter relates primarily to Paul's impending third visit to Corinth. The letter falls naturally into three sections: (1) Paul explained the reason for the change in his itinerary (chaps. 1–7); (2) he encouraged the Corinthians to complete the collection in preparation for his arrival (chaps. 8–9); (3) he stressed the certainty of his coming, his authenticity as an apostle, and his readiness as an apostle to exercise discipline if necessary (chaps. 10–13).

Some have questioned the unity of this letter (see discussion on 2:3–4), but it forms a coherent whole, as the structure shows. Tradition has been unanimous in affirming its unity (the early church fathers, e.g., knew the letter only in its present form). Furthermore, none of the early Greek manuscripts breaks up the book.

Outline

I. Paul's Defense of His Apostolic Ministry and Calling (chaps. 1–7)
   A. Salutation and Introduction (1:1–2)
   B. Thanking God for Comfort in Troubled Times (1:3–11)
   C. Paul's Motives and Plans in the Ministry (1:12–2:4)
   D. Forgiveness for the Offender (2:5–11)
   E. The Lord's Leading in the Ministry (2:12–17)
   F. The Corinthians Are a Letter from Christ (3:1–11)
   G. Unveiled Faces Seeing the Glory of God (3:12–4:6)
   H. Treasures in Earthen Vessels (4:7–16a)
   I. Death and Its Meaning for the Christian (4:16b–5:10)
   J. The Ministry of Reconciliation (5:11–6:10)
      1. Reconciliation Accomplished (5:11–21)
      2. The Cost of Reconciliation (6:1–10)
   K. Appealing to Spiritual Children (6:11–7:4)
   L. Comfort from Titus (7:5–16)
II. The Collection for the Jerusalem Christians (chaps. 8–9)
   A. The Blessing of Generosity (8:1–15)
   B. Titus and Companions Sent to Corinth (8:16–9:5)
   C. The Results of Generosity (9:6–15)
III. Paul's Strong Defense of His Ministry Calling and Apostleship (chaps. 10–12)
   A. Paul's Authority Granted by the Lord (chap. 10)
   B. Paul's Service to Christ (chaps. 11–12)
      1. Warning of False Teachers (11:1–15)
      2. Paul's Rightful Claims (11:16–33)
      3. Paul's Testimony of His Vision (12:1–21)
IV. Closing (chap. 13)
   A. Spiritual Concerns (13:1–10)
   B. Farewell and Benediction (13:11–14)

Bibliography

Barrett, C. K. *The Second Epistle to the Corinthians.* Peabody, MA: Hendrickson, 1997.

Hodge, Charles. *An Exposition of the Second Epistle to the Corinthians.* Grand Rapids, MI: Eerdmans, 1956.

Hughes, Philip E. *Paul's Second Epistle to the Corinthians.* The New International Commentary on the New Testament. Grand Rapids, MI: Eerdmans, 1972.

Kistemaker, Simon J. *2 Corinthians.* New Testament Commentary. Grand Rapids, MI: Baker, 1997.

Lenski, R. C. H. *The Interpretation of 1 and 2 Corinthians.* Minneapolis: Augsburg, 1963.

Lowery, David. "2 Corinthians." In *The Bible Knowledge Commentary,* edited by John R. Walvoord and Roy B. Zuck. Wheaton, IL: Victor, 1983.

Stanley, Arthur P. *The Epistle of St. Paul to the Corinthians.* Minneapolis: Klock & Klock, 1981.

EXPOSITION

I. Paul's Defense of His Apostolic Ministry and Calling (chaps. 1–7)

As he did in 1 Corinthians, Paul dealt with moral and spiritual issues in his second epistle. In his second letter, however, he spent many more pages defending his apostolic authority. His first letter must have stirred debate and resistance from the many members of the Corinthian congregation who challenged Paul's leadership. He made it clear to them that he was not speaking from within himself but had been commissioned by Christ Himself to teach the Word and defend the truth.

A. Salutation and Introduction (1:1–2)

1:1. Paul immediately made it clear that he was **an apostle of Jesus Christ** not by his own will but **by the will of God.** God's "will" (*thelēmatos*) implies His sovereign calling and appointment. It was no accident that Paul was an apostle ("one sent forth"). **Timothy** (meaning, "honoring God") also joined Paul in the Corinthian endeavor; he was Paul's spiritual **brother.** Timothy came from a godly family (see 2 Tim. 1:5; 3:15), was converted by Paul possibly on his first missionary journey (see Acts 14:6–23), was referred to by Paul as "my own son in the faith" (1 Tim. 1:2; see 1 Cor. 4:17; 2 Tim. 1:2), and was well-respected by the believing community (see Acts 16:1–2). His father was Greek and his mother was Jewish. He not only accompanied the apostle on many trips but also was his courier and ambassador to various churches. When Paul saw his end coming,

he challenged Timothy to remain true to his calling (see 1 Tim. 1:18), and he asked this younger leader to be with him until the end (see 2 Tim. 4:9). It is believed that Timothy had been imprisoned but was finally released (see Heb. 13:23).

While this letter focuses on the problems of the Corinthian church, it also had application to **all the saints,** mainly, though not exclusively, Greeks who lived throughout the region of **Achaia.** This area was distinct from the northern territory of Macedonia.

1:2. For Paul, **Grace ... and peace** were not polite but empty words. The Corinthians desperately needed to experience these spiritual and emotional qualities because their source was **from God.** God, however, is not seen in the abstract; He is **our Father.** "God's essence consists in mercy, and also that He is the Father and source of mercies" (Stanley, *Corinthians,* p. 370). Since the Lord Jesus is very God, grace and peace originate from Him also.

B. Thanking God for Comfort in Troubled Times (1:3–11)

With all the problems in the Corinthian church, it is interesting that Paul moved quickly to the issue of comfort in times of tribulation. Believers will suffer for Christ's sake but will also experience abounding consolation. The persecutions in Corinth must have been accelerating because these were the apostle's first thoughts as he penned this second epistle.

1:3–4. Despite any persecution or suffering that believers face, God is still **blessed** (Greek, *eulogētos;*

"good-worded"; v. 3). He is not only our Father but also the **Father of our Lord Jesus Christ**. As a loving Father, He showers His children with **mercies** and **all comfort** (Greek, *paraklēseōs*). God is the Author of comfort. At the root of the word "comfort" is the idea of calling one alongside to help. When people fail and even Christians offer no help, God can always be relied on to soothe and repair the soul that is lonely.

Verse 4 has an interesting twist. Paul wrote that God **comforteth us in all our tribulation** (Greek, *thlipsei*; "pressure," "trouble," "distress"), **[so] that we may be able to comfort them which are in any trouble** (v. 4). Christians are to do this with the same **comfort** God uses to aid them. God's purpose in afflicting and consoling Paul was to qualify him for the office of a consoler of the afflicted. In this design, Paul acquiesced; he was willing to be thus afflicted in order to be the bearer of comfort to others.

1:5 – 7. The sufferings (v. 5) that Christ went through **abound in us**, so that our comfort **also aboundeth by Christ**. As union with Christ Jesus was the cause of the affliction that Paul experienced, so it was the source of the comfort that he enjoyed. That Paul and the other servants of Christ were afflicted turned out to be a benefit of comfort for even the Corinthians. **Our hope of you is stedfast** (v. 7) probably carries the thought, "Whenever we are afflicted, it is for your benefit; whenever we are given consolation, it is for your good. It is passed on to you!" No matter what happened, Paul told them, **it is for your consolation and salvation** (v. 6). Hodge explains: "Whether we be afflicted, (it is) for your consolation and salvation, which is effectual in enduring the same sufferings which we also suffer" (Hodge, *2 Corinthians*, p. 7). As **partakers of the sufferings** (v. 7), they likewise received **the consolation**, or comforting. Affliction and comfort are experienced simultaneously, though this does not exclude the thought of future deliverance. Paul's sufferings were a source of strength for those he led to the Lord. He had no motive for concealing his sufferings.

1:8 – 11. Paul did not hold back on informing the Corinthians of the persecution he had experi-

enced. He did not want them to be **ignorant** ("unknowing"; v. 8) of the **trouble** (Greek, *thlipseōs*; see discussion on 1:4) he had faced **in Asia**, probably broadly referring to Asia Minor, Mysia, Lydia, Caria, and parts of Phrygia. Some have assumed he also included Ephesus (see Acts 19:23 – 41), but this may not be so. The "trouble" may have been sufferings inflicted on Paul by his many enemies, like the Jews and many pagans who thirsted for his blood. Another suggestion is what happened in Lycus Valley, where he was possibly beaten by the Jews (see 2 Cor. 11:24). Whatever Paul was talking about must have been terrible because he wrote, **we were pressed out of measure**, beyond our strength, so that **we despaired even of life**.

With **the sentence of death** (v. 9) hanging over his head, Paul could in no way **trust in** himself but had to have faith in **God which raiseth the dead**. The apostle may have meant that if he died, the Lord would someday give him resurrection life, but more than likely he meant that God, who has such power, could deliver him from experiencing death. Paul confirmed this by saying, God **delivered us from so great a death** (v. 10). In fact, He **doth deliver**; that is, He delivers believers from the martyrdom of physical death, and He will continue to deliver us: **he will yet deliver us**. God would deliver Paul from impending or immediate threat of death (see 4:8 – 14) until his course was finished (see 2 Tim. 4:7), and even at that time, Paul would be certain of the final deliverance from death at the resurrection (see 1 Cor. 15:55; 2 Cor. 4:14).

Paul was being helped by the **prayer** (v. 11) of the Corinthians, along with that of **many persons**, and these prayers were the **thanks** given on Paul's **behalf**. Joint prayers were offered as a cooperation in the work of intercession with other churches, rather than with the apostle himself. The design of God in thus uniting His people in praying for each other when in affliction and danger results in common congratulation and praise. **The gift** could refer to their intercession before God but probably refers to the gift of a deliverance. It does not refer to the past deliverance of Paul and of Timothy; most likely, it refers to a future deliverence, to God's wonderful, gracious help in response to the prayers of the many readers.

C. Paul's Motives and Plans in the Ministry (1:12 – 2:4)

While the apostle reserved confrontational words for those questioning him in Corinth, he was more conciliatory in these verses. Although he was more positive here, a mild polemic pervades even these early chapters. Here he laid out his activities and itinerary of ministry.

1:12. With **the testimony** of a good **conscience**, and **in simplicity and godly sincerity**, yet without human **fleshly wisdom**, Paul and Timothy had served the Lord. Their ministry was blessed **by the grace of God**. The word "simplicity" (Greek, *haplotēti*) speaks for itself. Paul's ministry was not complicated but to the point: to give the gospel to as many people as he could, in as many places as he could. "Paul performs his work as a minister of the gospel for everyone to see. In this setting, he demonstrates his love for God's people [also] in Corinth" (Kistemaker, *2 Corinthians*, p. 54). Paul's **conversation** (Greek, *anestraphēmen*; "to move about") **in the world** (Greek, *kosmos*) shows how he conducted himself, but this expression also "includes all the manifestations of his inward life" (Hodge, *Second Epistle to the Corinthians*, p. 15). This spilled over to the Corinthians also; they knew how Paul operated, and they should have known what motivated him. That is, the evidence of his sincerity was **more abundantly** (more especially) **to you-ward** in regard to his ministry as an apostle.

1:13 – 14. Paul wrote to the Corinthians what he did and what drove him, and they **read or acknowledge[d]** (v. 13) what he wrote. "Acknowledge" (Greek, *epiginōskō*) is in the present tense and "is used with the signification of the present … [It] combines the sense of 'recognition' with that of 'complete knowledge'" (Stanley, *Corinthians*, p. 379). Paul did not want the Corinthians to deny what he informed them about; he **trust[ed]** they would agree to the same **even to the end**. Here Paul may have

been trapping some who wanted to "rewrite" what he was doing for the sake of Christ. He must have known that a clique in Corinth despised him.

Grudgingly, the Corinthians had **acknowledged … in part** (v. 14) the truth about Paul's ministry, yet even with this, Paul said, **we are your rejoicing**, and in turn, **ye also are ours in the day of the Lord Jesus**, that is, when He returns. The Corinthians should acknowledge Paul and his coworkers, and in like manner, Paul wished to boast about that congregation. Believers should never boast about themselves.

1:15 – 16. With all of this in mind and **in this confidence** (v. 15), Paul wanted to come to them earlier so that they could have **a second benefit** (Greek, *charis*), or "kindness," "blessing," "gifting," "favor." By "second" blessing, Paul meant the act of helping twice. "'Gift' would be a good rendering if not taken in too concrete a sense; a 'second mark of his esteem'" (Barrett, *Second Epistle to the Corinthians*, p. 74). After staying a while in Corinth, he would travel on to **Macedonia** (v. 16), then return back to Corinth on his way **toward Judaea** and Jerusalem. Paul eventually met up with Titus in Macedonia and picked up the collection from the churches (see 8:1 – 7) for the poor believers in Jerusalem. Perhaps Luke and Titus were the couriers whom the assembly in Corinth had chosen to deliver the monetary gifts to the Jerusalem saints (see 8:16 – 19).

1:17 – 18. While Paul was thinking about his itinerary, he used the word **lightness** (Greek, *elaphria*; v. 17), which may refer to the fact that some had accused him of being thoughtless and inconsiderate. Had he planned all of this **according to the flesh**, or for fleshly and selfish reasons? Or was he wishy-washy, going back and forth with **yea yea, and nay nay**? This may be an Aramaic expression like, "Again and again yes and again and again no" (Kistemaker, *2 Corinthians*, p. 59). With the pledge **as God is true** (v. 18), Paul wrote that he did not go back and forth and **was not yea and nay**. God is faithful, and his proclamation of the truth was not uncertain. The gospel is true and trustworthy. Notice **our word**. Paul, Timothy, and their associates were equally involved in this ministry of the Lord.

1:19 – 22. For (Greek, *gar*; v. 19) gives the reason for all that Paul had previously preached concerning the Son of God. **The Son of God, Jesus Christ**, had been preached among the Corinthians by Paul, **Silvanus** (Silas) **and Timotheus** (Timothy) in the synagogue at Corinth (see Acts 18:5). There had been no **yea and nay**, back and forth, yes and no. God is firm and sure in the work of His Son. It is first mentioned in Psalm 2 that God has a Son who will someday rule over the nations. All are warned in prophecy that someday they will have to "Kiss [honor] the Son, lest he be angry, and ye perish from the way" (Ps. 2:12). About this matter and about **all the promises of God … are yea, and in him Amen** (v. 20), or "absolutely," "verily," "certainly." The promises of God concerning Christ were **unto the glory of God** by proclamation of the gospel by Paul and his cohorts. Here Paul was hinting at the providence of God as He works in the lives of those who serve Him. There are no accidents in the work of the gospel. Paul stated in his letter to the Philippians, "For it is God which worketh in you both to will and to do of his good pleasure" (Phil. 2:13).

God has both **stablishe[ed]** (v. 21) and **anointed** all believers **in Christ**. He has also **sealed us, and given the earnest of the Spirit in our hearts** (v. 22). "Stablisheth" (Greek, *bebaiōn*) means "to give a guarantee" and "to make firm." "Anointed" (Greek, *chrisas*) means a special marking that is given for the benefit of all in the body of Christ (see 1 John 2:20, 27) so that they have spiritual comprehension. Paul mentioned the "sealing" of ownership in several places in his writings (Eph. 1:13 – 14; 4:30). All who believe in the gospel are sealed "until the redemption of the purchased possession, unto the praise of his glory" (Eph. 1:14). The work of the Spirit of God at salvation is His conformation that what the Lord has begun, He will certainly finish. Present redemption is only a foretaste of what eternal glory holds for the child of God (see Rom. 8:23).

1:23 – 24. Apparently, Paul's change of plans had caused problems in Corinth. This is why, in a strong statement, Paul said **I call God for a record** (v. 23), or "as a witness" (see Rom. 1:9; Phil. 1:8; 1 Thess. 2:5, 10). The apostle staked his life, his very **soul** (Greek,

psychēn), his inner being, **that to spare** the Corinthians, he **came not as yet unto Corinth**. "To spare" (Greek, *pheidomenos*) carries the idea, "that I might not have occasion to exert my power to the full and take vengeance on your sins." Because of the incident of incest in the church (1 Corinthians 5), he had decided to go first to Macedonia, then to Corinth, and then on to Jerusalem (see 1 Cor. 16:5 – 8). Having been charged by those who hated him (see 2 Cor. 1:17) and accused of being afraid to come to Corinth (see 1 Cor. 4:18), he explained why he had altered his plans.

Not for that we have dominion over your faith (v. 24) means, "We do not lord it over your faith." By "we," Paul included his partners in the ministry. He wanted the Corinthians to realize that what he was doing was not simply his own idea but the consensus of others also. "All are free in the Lord but are obligated to help one another. So Paul writes that he and his partners do not lord it over the faith of the Corinthians but instead minister to the believers" (Kistemaker, *2 Corinthians*, p. 70). They wanted to be **helpers of your joy: for by faith ye stand**. The Corinthians were independent and stood before the Lord by their own trust. Paul truly desired their spiritual good.

2:1 – 2. Paul did not want to return to this congregation with **heaviness** (Greek, *lypē*; v. 1), being pulled down with "grief." This would be his third visit; nothing is known about his second trip except that he was there (see 12:14; 13:1), but it seems apparent that it did not go as the apostle would have hoped. If he visited Corinth and a moral quarrel occurred, he would be making them **sorry** (v. 2), and if that happened, who then could bless him and make him **glad**? The **I** (Greek, *egō*) is the personal pronoun, indicating that whether they liked it or not, he was personally involved with all of the mess in Corinth. On one of his past visits, some painful event had transpired that grieved the Corinthians and Paul. To spare grief for them both, Paul postponed his visit.

2:3 – 4. Paul wished to avoid a terrible confrontation again with this church, which is why he decided to write them a letter. He wrote **out of much afflic-**

tion and anguish of heart ... with many tears (v. 4), not so they would **be grieved** but so they **might know the love** he had for them. These verses show the heart of the apostle Paul. While he could at times be tough and straightforward, in cases like this, he poured his heart out. He really cared for this flock. Such grief robbed him of the **joy** (v. 3) that he should have had, joy which should have been theirs also, as well as their great comfort.

D. Forgiveness for the Offender (2:5–11)

Here Paul returned to the issue of the incest offender (see 1 Cor. 5:1). The assembly had brought tremendous shame upon itself because of their casual attitude about the problem. The church had become "puffed up" and had "not rather mourned" (1 Cor. 5:2) over this sin, that a man would have intercourse with "his father's wife" (1 Cor. 5:1). Paul had therefore instructed that the man "be delivered to Satan for the destruction of the flesh" (1 Cor. 5:5). With repentance, however, restoration should follow.

2:5. The apostle certainly may **have caused grief** for the man guilty of incest, but Paul was not offended himself **but in part**. As an apostle, he had a duty to chide the church, and in some sense, he did not apologize. Some have questioned whether this incident is the incident described in 1 Corinthians 5, but all evidence indicates that it is identical. Many commentators seem to repudiate the connection, but compare what Paul wrote here with 1 Corinthians 5:5. While Kistemaker (*2 Corinthians*, pp. 82–83) admits there may not be absolute proof that the two incidences are related to the same offender, he gives five reasons that seem to support such a view: (1) Both accounts mention only one offender. (2) The Corinthians had reason to be ashamed of the affair (see 1 Cor. 5:2, 6; 2 Cor. 2:5). (3) In the first account, Paul insisted that the church punish the wrongdoer, and in the second account, the majority of the church followed through (1 Cor. 5:5, 13; 2 Cor. 2:6). (4) The apostle referred to Jesus Christ in both accounts (1 Cor. 5:4; 2 Cor. 2:10). (5) Finally, Satan can advance his cause either with evil and diabolical force or with deliberate deceit.

2:6–8. The **punishment** (Greek, *epitimia*; v. 6), better translated "censure," that the church had placed upon the offender was enough and had been dished out by **many**. They had done their duty to bring conviction and stop this sin so that it would not destroy the church. Thus, **contrariwise** (v. 7), to bring the pendulum back in place, it was now time **to forgive him, and comfort him**. Paul was not suggesting that they should coddle the offender, but lest he become discouraged and be overwhelmed with **overmuch sorrow**, they needed to **confirm** (Greek, *kyrōsai*; General: *kyroō* v. 8), or "ratify," their **love toward him**. When one is truly repentant, restoration then needs to take place, as the apostle so pointedly urged in Galatians 6:1–2. With this, Paul drew to a conclusion: **Wherefore** (Greek, *dio*; a strong word of summary) **I beseech** (Greek, *parakalō*; "call alongside," "counsel") **you** to restore your brother and **confirm your love toward him**.

2:9–11. The apostle tested their resolve, their sensitivity in such spiritual and moral matters. He wanted to **know the proof** (v. 9) of the Corinthians, whether they were **obedient**. "If you forgive, I forgive, and if I forgive, you should forgive." This was to be done **for your sakes ... in the person of Christ** (v. 10). The Devil hates forgiveness and wants to hold people in bitterness. Paul taught the Corinthians to forgive one another in love just as Christ had forgiven them (see Eph. 4:32).

E. The Lord's Leading in the Ministry (2:12–17)

Paul again turned to some of his travel issues. He not only wrote positively of how God was at work to bring people to salvation but also described the open door for the gospel he had encountered, as well as the diabolical opposition to the Word of God. Many who opposed the truth had set out to corrupt the message of grace.

2:12–13. Paul apparently had journeyed from Ephesus to Troas, a city on the Aegean coast, where he hoped to find Titus and get from him any news he might have about the Corinthian church. No matter where Paul was, he seemed to place this congregation at the forefront of his interest and concern, possibly because of the size of the assembly or its vital influence in the Greek world. The city was a cosmopolitan hub teeming with people of mixed races, languages, and cultures. Traders crisscrossed through the Corinthian canal, going into Asia, Europe, and even into Africa. Paul wanted the truth, moral and spiritual, to go forth from Corinth with integrity.

When Paul arrived in **Troas** (v. 12), he had an open door from the providence **of the Lord**. He was troubled **in [his] spirit** (v. 13), however, because he could not find his **brother** in the Lord, **Titus**. Leaving his other companions, Paul traveled on **into Macedonia**.

2:14–16. Though he had "no rest in [his] spirit" (2:13), Paul did not want his readers to think he was losing heart. God causes believers **to triumph in Christ, and maketh manifest the savour** (v. 14), as that of votive incense. Here Paul used the imagery of the Roman victory triumph that honored the victorious general. The general rode ahead of the troops and was showered with laurels by the crowds. Christ is the one who is victorious over death (see 1 Cor. 15:57). This truth of the gospel is going forth **by us**, and it is **his knowledge** of salvation **in every place**. While there is opposition and persecution, the gospel still goes forth and brings to the lost the knowledge of Christ. But not everyone hearing receives the message. The manifestation of the knowledge of God does not mean that everyone is saved by it.

Those who witness are **a sweet savour of Christ** (v. 15) to God. Believers are "a savour" both to **them that are saved** and to **them that perish**. Barrett (*Second Epistle to the Corinthians*, p. 99) introduces the word "sacrifice" because Paul seems to have been portraying himself and those with him as the fragrance emanating from the Lord's personal sacrifice, which ascended to honor God. Here is another parallel to the Roman triumph. The enemies of the conquering general were slain following the triumph. In writing "them that perish," Paul was referring to those who reject the gospel and spurn the salvation being offered, as indicated by, **to the one we are the savour of death … and to the other the savour of**

life (v. 16). Paul was saying, "We are to the latter a smell of death to death and to the former an aroma of life to life" (Kistemaker, *2 Corinthians*, p. 91). "We bring both death and life to our hearers."

With emotion, Paul asked, **Who is sufficient for these things?** (v. 16). In other words, "These facts are too overwhelming to comprehend." Paul's own life, which gave forth the knowledge of God, was a "sweet savour" (v. 15) rising up before Him, as described in the Old Testament (see Lev. 1:9; Stanley, *Corinthians*, p. 394).

2:17. Apparently, scores of false prophets and apostles were spreading lies and distorting the gospel (see 2 Peter 2:1). Paul had addressed this in some of his earlier letters (e.g., 1 Thess. 2:1–5). These **many** false teachers set out to **corrupt** (Greek, *kapēleuontes*) **the word of God**, to "hawk" or "peddle," as dishonest merchants, a diluted or poisoned gospel. In contrast, Paul and his fellow workers came **as of God** and with **sincerity**, and **in the sight of God speak we in Christ**, meaning they stood before God in connection with the Lord Jesus Christ. Paul was warning the Corinthians to be careful of false messengers. He himself had been commissioned from the Lord. "Here is the source of the sincerity that fills his soul, the impossibility of his dealing with that Word like a haggling, dickering huckster" (Lenski, *1 and 2 Corinthians*, p. 906).

F. The Corinthians Are a Letter from Christ (3:1–11)

The apostle again wrote with frankness, asking the Corinthians whether he had to start all over with them again in proving himself in order to gain their confidence. This section shows that many were attempting to discredit him in the eyes of this church.

3:1–2. Well aware of the strategies of his critics, Paul knew that his criticism of the false apostles and defense of his own ministry might be turned against him. He therefore asked the Corinthians, **Do we** (need to) **begin again to commend ourselves? or need we** give or receive **letters of commendation …?** (v. 1). "Commendatory" (*systatikos*) letters were common in biblical days. Letters of recommendation were widely used among the churches to vouch for someone's truthfulness and integrity. **Some others** (v. 1) indicates that travelers with questionable credentials were moving about. **Ye are our epistle written in our hearts, known and read of all men** (v. 2). Everyone could see the effect that Paul's ministry had had on them, and they were placed permanently in the "hearts" (Greek, *kardia*) of Paul and his companions.

3:3–6. The Corinthians were as an **epistle of Christ** (v. 3), penned **not with ink, but with the Spirit of the living God**. Paul added a comparison with the Old Testament law: **not in tables** (tablets) **of stone, but in fleshly** (flesh-and-blood) **tables of the heart**. He was pointing out that the church dispensation benefits from the new covenant ("the new testament," 3:6), though it does not fulfill it. The new covenant will be fulfilled for Israel when the Jews return to the land for the millennial reign of Christ. The new covenant, in contrast with the old covenant, the Mosaic covenant written in stone (see Exod. 24:12), is first mentioned in Jeremiah 31:31–34, where it was prophesied that the new covenant would be penned upon human hearts (see also Ezek. 11:19; 36:26). The characteristics of the new covenant include: (1) God's law principles being written within the heart (Jer. 31:33), (2) an intimate relationship with God (Jer. 31:33), (3) a permanent forgiveness of sin (Jer. 31:34), (4) an inner cleansing and the Spirit placed within the heart (Ezek. 36:25–27), (5) and the new birth ("my spirit in you, and ye shall live") (Ezek. 37:14; see Titus 3:5). Besides these spiritual elements, the nation of Israel will have its land restored ("I shall place you in your own land," Ezek. 37:14). The promise of a territorial land is not given to the church.

Paul's **trust** (v. 4) was his conviction that the truth of the gospel of Christ had been entrusted to him and that his vocation as an apostle was given to him by the Lord. The ministry's **sufficiency** (v. 5) came from God; it was not self-driven. Paul said that he and his fellow workers could not **think any thing as of ourselves**. God **hath made us** (v. 6), he continued, **able ministers** (Greek, *diakonos*) **of the new testament; not of the letter** (as of the Old Tes-

tament law), **but of the spirit … [who] giveth life**. Again, the comparison is obvious. Paul was writing virtually the same as the prophet Jeremiah wrote concerning Israel in 31:31–32: God would make a new covenant, not like the covenant He made when He brought the Jews out of the land of Egypt, the Mosaic covenant, which they broke. That the church now benefits from the new covenant does not mean that the church has replaced Israel in God's plans. "The physical and national aspects of the New Covenant which pertain to Israel have not been appropriated to the church. Those are yet to be fulfilled in the Millennium. The church today shares in the soteriological aspects of that covenant, established by Christ's blood for all believers [cf. Heb. 8:7–13]" (Lowery, "2 Corinthians," pp. 560–61).

3:7. **The ministration of death**, the law (see Rom. 3:20; Gal. 3:10), was carved **in stones** (tablets; see Exod. 32:15–18; 34:1; Deut. 10:1), and it **was glorious** because it was the law from God, and it came directly from Him to Moses. When Moses returned from Mount Sinai with the two tablets of the law, his "face shone while he talked with [God]" (Exod. 34:29). "And when Aaron and all the children of Israel saw Moses, behold, the skin of his face shone; and they were afraid to come nigh him" (Exod. 34:30). In time, the glow on Moses' face **was to be done away**.

3:8–11. How much greater is the work of the Spirit, how much more **glorious** (v. 8) than even the "glorious" (3:7) law. This new work of the Spirit in the new covenant brings **righteousness** (v. 9) and even **exceed[s] in glory**. If the law, which was **done away** (v. 11) with, was **glorious** (v. 10), how much more will be **the glory** and blessing of the new covenant? The old covenant condemns (see Rom. 7:11), but **the ministration** (v. 8) of the new covenant, by means of **the spirit**, leads men to faith in Christ and the imputation of His righteousness (see Rom. 3:21–22; 4:24).

G. Unveiled Faces Seeing the Glory of God (3:12–4:6)

To focus on the age of grace and the blessings that believers now have under the gospel, Paul presented an illustration referring to Moses and the giving of the law on Mount Sinai as a contrast to the new dispensation of grace. Some in the Corinthian assembly may have had a wrong view about the dispensation of the Mosaic law.

3:12–15. Paul gloried in the new **hope** (v. 12) of the cross and wanted to speak with **great plainness of speech**. "Plainness" (Greek, *parrēsia*) means "outspokenness," "boldness." Here he made his case. It was his firm conviction of his divine mission and of the truth of the gospel, which he preached without regard to the consequences. With the giving of the law, Moses had to cover his face with **a vail** (v. 13), a cloth covering, because **the children of Israel could not stedfastly look** upon his face (see Exod. 34:33–35) after he returned from the mountain with "the two table[t]s of Testimony" (Exod. 34:29). They were overwhelmed by the shining of his face, and he had to cover it until he again went to speak with God (Exod. 34:35).

Did Moses cover his face because the Jews would be less inclined to obey God if they saw a diminishing of this awesome radiance? Or did he believe they were unworthy to see the display of God's glory and so veiled his face as a commentary on the hardness of their hearts? We may never know.

More than their eyes were blinded, however; **their minds were blinded** (v. 14) as well, and it **remaineth the same** now when **the old testament** is read. The **vail** must now be **done away in Christ**; otherwise, Israel will remain in darkness. **But even unto this day, when Moses** (the law) **is read, the vail is upon their heart** (v. 15). They hear the words of Moses, but they cannot look upon the glory of God. "Paul preaches the new covenant of God's justifying righteousness and of the Spirit. This carries with it the abolition of the law … The law is done away in Christ" (Barrett, *Second Epistle to the Corinthians*, p. 121). Stanley sees "the vail" as a metaphor in that the Jews in the synagogue prayed and read with "veils upon their heads — the Tallith, or four-cornered white scarf, still seen in the Jewish … worship" (*Corinthians*, p. 407).

3:16–18. There is still hope for Israel: if the Jews **turn to the Lord, the vail shall be taken away** (v. 16).

This will be the work of **the Lord** (v. 17), and He **is that Spirit: and where the Spirit of the Lord is, there is liberty** from the law. The apostle was describing regeneration that only the Spirit can accomplish (see Titus 3:5). Paul made this clear to the Galatians when he wrote that "no man is justified by the law in the sight of God," because "the law is not of faith: but, the man that doeth them shall live in them. Christ hath redeemed us from the curse of the law, being made a curse for us … Wherefore the law was our schoolmaster to bring us unto Christ, that we might be justified by faith" (Gal. 3:11–13, 24), and not by the law.

Now with an unveiled face, an **open face** (v. 18), and looking **as in a glass** (a polished bronze mirror), we behold **the glory of the Lord**. Believers **are changed into the same image from glory to glory**, as is accomplished **by the Spirit of the Lord**. The glory in Moses' face finally faded away, but the believer in this age of grace is promised ever-increasing glory, "from glory into glory"; that is, this glory just keeps building and will not diminish. The believer's glory is a mirror reflection of the Lord's glory. The indwelling Holy **Spirit** (v. 17) enhances the believer's glory, which is therefore unlimited. Believers are progressively being transformed (**changed**; see Rom. 12:2) into His **image** (Greek, *eikona*; "likeness"). "Christlikeness is the goal of the Christian walk (Eph. 4:23–24; Col. 3:10)" (Lowery, "First Corinthians," p. 562).

4:1–2. Paul and his associates had **this ministry** (Greek, *diakonia*; "task," "service"; v. 1) because they **received mercy**, and therefore they could not stop serving the Lord: **we faint** (Greek, *enkakeō*; "grow weary," "despondent") **not**. "This ministry" has broad meaning and includes the gospel of salvation in Christ, which contrasts the law and includes the work of the Holy Spirit in the life of the individual. Paul said, **we have renounced** once for all (aorist tense, middle voice) **the hidden things of dishonesty** ("shame"; v. 2), refusing to walk **in craftiness, not handling the word of God deceitfully**, that is, not "adulterating" God's Word. Here Paul may have used words that his opponents had used against him.

Unspiritual conduct is paired with adulterating the Word of God. Paul and his friends, however, practiced the opposite. They **manifest[ed] … the truth** (v. 2), showing themselves **to every man's conscience** (see 1:12), not only before the Corinthian congregation and other believers but also **in the sight of God** (see 2:17). "Manifest" (Greek, *phanerōsis*) means to "shed light on," "publish." "Conscience" carries the thought of collective knowledge. Though the conscience may be seared, branded with an iron (see 1 Tim. 4:2), so that it no longer accepts truth, it may also be "deceived so that it thinks truth is falsehood and falsehood truth" (Lenski, *1 and 2 Corinthians*, p. 957). Many despise truth simply because it is truth (see John 8:45), and they hate the light because their works are evil and they want darkness (see John 3:19–21).

4:3–6. Those who do not accept the **gospel … are lost** (v. 3); they are without God and without Christ in this world (see Eph. 2:12). In fact, Satan, **the god of this world** (v. 4), has **hid** (v. 3) the gospel and **blinded the minds** (v. 4) of the lost, those who refuse to believe. He has done this because he hates the truth of Christ. He wants to bring darkness so that **the light of the glorious gospel of Christ, who is the image of God**, does not **shine unto them**. Here Paul's language is similar to the language he used about the law and the veiling of Moses' face (see 3:7–18), but in reverse. The gospel of Christ is glorious and it is light, though Satan tries to extinguish or hide it. Those who serve Christ do not **preach** themselves **but Christ Jesus the Lord**. To the Corinthians, Paul and his companions were but **servants for Jesus' sake** (v. 5). "Paul proclaims Jesus Christ as Lord (Rom. 10:9; 1 Cor. 12:3; Phil. 2:10–11) and thus indicates he and his associates are Christ's servants … Jesus is Lord and the apostles are servants" (Kistemaker, *2 Corinthians*, p. 142).

God … commanded the light of salvation to give **the knowledge of the glory of God in the face of Jesus Christ** (v. 6). At the beginning of creation, God ordered physical light (see Gen. 1:3). Now He commands light to be **shined in our hearts** for salvation. In the face of Christ, the glory of God is made known. God illumines for salvation but then continues the illumination, through the Holy Spirit, so that the believer "might know the things that are freely given to us of God" (1 Cor. 2:13). With Paul, God caused the light to shine both into his heart and into his eyes (see Acts 9:3–9). "Paul recognized the parallel of creation and re-creation, the material and the spiritual domains" (Kistemaker, *2 Corinthians*, p. 143).

H. Treasures in Earthen Vessels (4:7–16a)

Moving to a metaphor of the treasure of the gospel (see 4:6) and clay vessels, or pots, that have no value, Paul continued his contrast between the old covenant and the new covenant. In many places in Israel, the ground is littered with potsherds, or broken pottery. In ancient days, clay vessels were expendable; if they had the slightest crack, they were thrown out on the ground, where they were trampled into broken pieces and dust. Human beings are sinful and frail, but God has elected to use such objects for His design.

4:7–12. The **treasure** (v. 7) of the gospel has been stored away **in earthen vessels**, but **the power** is not in the earthen vessels; it comes from God. The vessels have little resilience and can break easily. Because of God's power, however, believers can be **troubled … yet not distressed … perplexed, but not in despair; persecuted, but not forsaken; cast down, but not destroyed** (vv. 8–9). With great poetry, the apostle listed all the things that had come upon him, things which can also come against all believers in Christ. Believers are given no guarantees of absolute protection in the Christian life, though through it all, the child of God is able to rise above and have the final victory.

As Christ lived and went to the cross to die, so believers carry about a death sentence, so that His life **might be made manifest in our body** (v. 10). Not every believer in every generation faces such pain and even martyrdom, but in the early church, thousands did. This persecution began with the apostles and then came upon average Christians. Living often means facing **death for Jesus' sake**, showing forth Christ **in our mortal flesh**. The early Christians realized that, to a lesser or greater degree, they would be persecuted, and many would face even death.

By speaking of himself first in these verses, Paul was preparing the church at large for troubled times. The apostle and his coworkers would suffer terribly in the future. Paul often mentioned the sufferings of Christ as related to him (see Rom. 8:17; 1 Cor. 15:31; Gal. 6:17; Col. 1:24). Though our souls "hold the priceless treasure, our bodies are nothing but 'earthern vessels' that are liable to be broken at any time (v. 7)" (Lenski, *1 and 2 Corinthians*, p. 981).

Paul's suffering had a distinct purpose. It was placed upon him and his coworkers, even possibly unto **death** (v. 12), but **in you**, the Corinthians, it was **life**. At any moment, the authorities could seize Paul and his companions and deliver them to the door of death; they had no sureties as they traveled about.

4:13–15. The same spirit of faith (v. 13) that was within Paul kept him going. He trusted his Savior and his God. To make his point, he quoted Psalm 116:10, where David said, "I believed, therefore have I spoken: I was greatly afflicted." Paul latched hold of this verse and added, **we also believe, and therefore speak.** In other words, "What is inside us, by faith, we are compelled to set forth in words. We cannot hold back!" Paul was specific about the gospel: **that he which raised up the Lord Jesus shall raise up us also by Jesus, and shall present us with you** (v. 14). Whether through death or the resurrection, all believers will be together and shall stand before the Lord. No single event in history is better authenticated than that the Lord Jesus Christ rose from the dead. Believers too have the same ground for assurance of the resurrection of those who are Christ's when He returns.

4:16a. For which cause, the cause of seeing the Lord someday, **we faint not**, Paul said. The apostle was driven; he could not stop or grow weary. The truth spurred him on. Because of his faith that God will raise us up with Jesus, he could not neglect his duty.

I. Death and Its Meaning for the Christian (4:16b–5:10)

It seems as if verse 16 should be broken at this point. Paul moved from saying that in ministry "we faint not" (4:16a) to discussing heavenly and eternal matters. Here His words seem to transcend his previous discussions; he now looked heavenward.

4:16b–18. The physical body, **our outward man** (v. 16b), is limited in years. It will someday **perish**, though a change awaits all believers. The spiritual soul, **the inward man[,] is renewed** every day. The spiritual nature receives new life and vigor each day. The anticipation for the believer becomes more real as time and age advances. **Day by day** is a Hebrew expression that comes from Genesis 39:10 and Psalm 68:19. This continual renewal of strength is the opposite of weakness and despair.

Light affliction ... which is but for a moment (v. 17). Life is but a wisp, and we are all but grass, here today and gone tomorrow (see Ps. 90:5–6; 103:15–16; Isa. 40:6–8), and life is "soon cut off, and we fly way" (Ps. 90:10b). Working for the believer also is an **eternal weight** (Greek, *baros;* "load") **of glory.** "Weight," or "load," carries the thought of "abundance," and Paul probably chose this word as a suitable contrast with his earlier description of tribulations suffered for Christ's sake (see 4:7–12). What the apostle said here is applicable only to the believer, because he alone has an inner, spiritual, renewable life and the expectation of glorious eternal life in the presence of God.

The child of God looks at **the things which are seen** (v. 18), but he must look not simply at these visible things but also at **the things which are not seen**, the spiritual issues that are **eternal** and not just **temporal** and tangible. Through the prophetic promises in Scripture, the Christian has hope and a clear sense that life consists of much more than that which is visible. This is not the same for the unbeliever (see 1 Cor. 15:19). Paul touched on this subject in his first letter to the Corinthians (1 Cor. 15:46–49). Christians will bear the heavenly and will not simply remain in the earthly.

5:1–4. Here Paul explained the change that is the great expectation of the believers in Christ. **Our earthly house of this tabernacle** (Greek, *skēnous;* "tent"; v. 1) will be **dissolved** ("taken down," "folded up"); of that, there is no doubt. Believers, however, will one day reside in **a building of God, a house**

not constructed with physical **hand[s]**. This "house" will be **eternal** and **in the heavens**. A tent is flimsy and temporary, but this "house," "a building," will be eternal and heavenly and eternal.

Now believers **groan** (v. 2) because of persecution and because of the diminishing of the physical faculties. "Groaning" has a positive value because it means Christians are longing for something to happen; it creates within them an anticipation for heaven, a longing for the time of fulfillment, when the Lord will bring to an end the course of this age and establish the eternal glory. Believers want **to be clothed upon with our house which is from heaven** so that they might **not be found naked** (v. 3). The "house which is from heaven" is the resurrected body. In eternity, believers will not be floating spirits, as if "naked" without a corporal body. A new, eternal body will be given at the resurrection.

In this tabernacle (v. 4), we **groan** and are **burdened**, but the new body will be like that of Christ's. **Mortality [will] be swallowed up [with] life** that is eternal, immortal, and pure, without sin. This temporary "tentlike" existence, which is something that will fade away, shall soon be taken down and no longer used.

5:5–7. God **hath wrought** (v. 5) this transaction for believers, and as assurance that this will take place, He has given the Spirit as **the earnest** (Greek, *arrabōn*; "surety," "pledge," "guarantee"). In Romans 6:5, 8, Paul wrote: "For if we have been planted together in the likeness of his death, we shall be also in the likeness of his resurrection … we believe that we shall also live with him."

This assurance should make the believer **always confident** (v. 6), knowing that no matter what, he will always be with the Lord. "Always" (Greek, *pantote*) signifies "on all occasions," "under all circumstances," even in the midst of dangers, discouragements, and despair. To be **at home** (Greek, *endēmeo*) means to be "in the house," "among one's people," while to be **absent** (Greek, *ekdēmeo*) means "out of the house." Even now, the Christian's conversation, or citizenship, is not here on earth. "For our conversation is in heaven; from whence also we look for the Saviour, the Lord Jesus Christ: Who shall change our vile body, that it may be fashioned like unto his glorious body, according to the working whereby he is able even to subdue all things unto himself" (Phil. 3:20; see also Heb. 11:13; 13:14).

Looking forward to this day of liberation means that **we walk by faith, not by sight** (v. 7). Believers do not see heaven now, nor do they understand what the new body will be like. The day-by-day experience is waiting for the final redemption, that is, the redemption into the final stated of "the purchased possession, unto the praise of his glory" (Eph. 1:14).

5:8. Believers, then, **are confident** (Greek, *tharroumen*; "of good courage") because they are **willing** to wait and, for a time, **to be absent from the body**. They are ready, however, and long "to be absent from the body" so that they can **be present with the Lord** in the glorious state. This shows that there is no intermediate state. The believer passes from this physical life directly into the presence of Christ. This simple but straightforward verse has comforted thousands, if not millions, through the ages as, trusting in the Lord Jesus, they faced eternity in death.

5:9–10. Whether present or absent (v. 9), the believer continues his **labour, that … we may be accepted of him**. The believer is not working for his salvation but is living out his free servitude of gratitude to Christ for eternal life. Whether in this world or the next, the Christian strives to be pleasing to the Lord.

We must all appear (Greek, *phaneroō*) **before the judgment seat of Christ** (v. 10) carries the idea, "We will all be made manifest before Him" or "the light will shine on us in His presence." **The judgment seat** (Greek, *bēma*) is, according to Hodge, "the step," "raised platform," or "seat," used by the Roman magistrate for judgment but also for handing out civil rewards (*Second Epistle to the Corinthians*, p. 125). Paul discussed this in his first letter to the Corinthians (1 Cor. 3:11–15), but here he added some additional thoughts. This appearance is to evaluate what has been **done in** ("by means of") [the] **body, whether it be good or bad**. To **receive** (Greek, *komizō*) means "to take for one's life," "to receive what is entitled."

One will have to give an account of what he did while in his earthly body. "Bad" (Greek, *phaulon*) can mean "foul," "worthless," "of no account," and in some cases, "wicked." This corresponds to the "wood, hay, stubble" of Paul's previous letter (1 Cor. 3:12).

J. The Ministry of Reconciliation (5:11–6:10)

The apostle wanted the Corinthians to understand how important his ministry was in reaching the world. He had a deep, solemn sense of his great responsibility to the Lord his God. Christ's love constrained him to live not for himself but for Christ, who gave His life for him and came forth from the grave to redeem humankind (5:14–15). God had wrought the great transformation that Paul had experienced; it was not a self-willed act. God is the author of the entire work of redemption. Paul's new task was to present Christ, who reconciles the world to the almighty God. The apostle was God's ambassador, exhorting men to accept His offer of reconciliation so that they "might be made the righteousness of God in him" (5:20–21). For his ministry, Paul's paid a high price of pain and suffering (6:1–10), and yet through it all, he saw himself as "yet possessing all things" (6:10).

1. Reconciliation Accomplished (5:11–21)

5:11. Paul began this section with a grammatical perfect participle: **Knowing therefore,** or "having become aware then." He was saying that he had come to realize that he must **persuade men** of **the terror** (Greek, *phobos*; "fear") **of the Lord.** Spiritual issues are serious matters. Paul persuaded the Jews and endeavored to convince them of the truth and bring them to Christ (see Acts 28:23). He was tireless in this effort and did the same thing with the Corinthians. God saw his efforts, he was **made manifest unto God,** but he wanted to be equally manifest to this church. "Manifest" (Greek, *phaneroō*) means Paul wanted to "appear as with a light," transparent to their **consciences.**

While Paul was misunderstood and rejected by so many, he still wanted the Corinthian Christians, as a circle of believers, to have a deep conviction about his integrity. He had won many over with his arguments, but apparently, many still did not trust his motives.

5:12–15. The apostle reminded his readers that he did not again **commend** (v. 12) himself, as if he had to prove himself all over again, as some said he had done before. (He returned to this issue in 12:11–12). Self-laudation was not his style. He did not intend to **give [them] occasion** that would cause them **to glory** over him. Some in the assembly must have sought self-glorification, as did some traveling ministers. Concerning himself, he wanted the Corinthians to have an **answer** for those who sought **glory in** outward and superficial **appearance, and not in heart.** This seems to show that great religious pride was being promoted in Christian circles. Paul vehemently rejected that he could be accused of this.

Whether Paul and his companions were **besides [them]selves** (Greek, *existēmi*; v. 13), "outside of their minds," or whether they were mentally **sober,** they served **God** and the **cause** of the Corinthians. Whether they were crazy or sane did not matter; their service to both God and the Christian community was what mattered. **The love of Christ constraineth us** (v. 14), Paul wrote, **because we thus judge,** make a ruling, a determination, **that if [Jesus] died for all, then were all dead.** By "constraineth" (Greek, *synechō*), he meant that Christ's love, which sent Him to the cross, pressed on Paul, coercing and impelling him to serve. "If one died for all, then were all dead" has four possibilities meanings: (1) all died to themselves and sin, (2) then all *ought* to die, (3) if one died for all, all were subject to death, (4) if one died for all, they all died (Hodge, *Second Epistle to the Corinthians*, p. 136). The word "died" (Greek, *apethanon*) is in the aorist tense and means that this action is completed. The Word of God seems to show that the relationship Christ now has with those for whom He died is analogous to that of Adam and his offspring (see Rom. 5:12–21; 1 Cor. 15:21–22). The fall of Adam affected all humanity, all who were united with him. Christ's death on the cross was for all of those who would be united with Him by faith. All who were in Adam died; all who are in Christ are made alive.

Because Christ **died for all** (v. 15) who would be related to Him in salvation, the same **should not ... live unto themselves, but unto Him which died for them, and rose again**. Paul could not get away from the truth of the death, burial, and resurrection of the Lord Jesus Christ. Christianity was founded on these great doctrines. They are central to living faith and absolutely essential for guaranteeing the promise of eternal life. Quoting and applying Psalm 68:18 in Ephesians 4:8, Paul said, "When he ascended up on high, he led captivity captive, and gave gifts unto men." Paul applied this passage to the spiritual powers and enemies that Christ defeated at the cross.

5:16–19. Here Paul further explained 5:15. **To wit** (Greek, *hōs hoti*; v. 19) means "seeing that," "because," as a clarification to what he has just said. **God was** working within **Christ, reconciling the world unto himself**. "Reconciling" (Greek, *katallassōn*) carries the thought of bringing two parties together, thus making peace. Through the death of His Son, God made the salvation of the world possible. Because of Christ, God was **not imputing their trespasses unto** believers. Here the doctrine of imputation comes into play. The Greek for "impute" (*logizomai*) means to "put something to one's account." Paul addressed imputation at some length in Romans 4:1–25; 5:12–20, using Abraham as an illustration. Abraham's faith "was imputed to him for righteousness. Now it was not written for his sake alone, that it was imputed to him" (Rom. 4:22–23). Here in verse 19, the verb is a present participle in the Greek, meaning that this imputation is a continuous action. God will no longer continuously impute sin to the sinner who comes to Christ for salvation. The Lord has **committed** to all His servants **the word of reconciliation**, who are to declare that God is ready to grant forgiveness and be reconciled to all and that whoever has faith in Christ will live.

5:20–21. Because Paul and his fellow laborers in Christ had been so blessed, they were now **ambassadors for Christ** (v. 20). As they appealed to the Corinthians and others, it was **as though God did beseech** them through Paul and those with him. Those who share the gospel make the appeal as if

they are the very voice of the Lord. Christians are acting for God, in His name, when they go out as His ambassadors.

In Christ's stead (v. 20), for His name's sake, **be ye reconciled** to God. Was this an appeal to some in the Corinthian assembly who had not trusted Christ as Savior or an appeal to the converted to daily avail themselves of the continual offer of peace with the Lord? Kistemaker believes it was both and says, "The imperative *be reconciled* is directed to both the Corinthians and the world" (*2 Corinthians*, p. 200).

Here God's divine "exchange" program is seen: Christ, who **knew no sin** (v. 21), was **made ... to be sin** in behalf of the believer, and in turn, the child of God was **made the righteousness of God** because of being related to Him. The Lord Jesus was without sin, but in the divine transaction, God saw Him bearing the sins of the world. The sins of the human race were "imputed" (see 5:19) to Him, and His righteousness was imputed to the believer. This is a judicial reckoning in the mind of God in order to accomplish redemption. Jesus became the substitute for sinners by taking the place before God of those under condemnation. He is the Lamb of God who removed the sin of the world by His sacrificial death on the cross (see John 1:29; 3:14–15). The prophet Isaiah prophesied, "All we like sheep have gone astray; we have turned every one to his own way; and the LORD hath laid on him the iniquity of us all" (Isa. 53:6).

2. The Cost of Reconciliation (6:1–10)

Paul demonstrated his patient endurance as a minister of God through all kinds of trials and tribulations. In every adverse circumstance, brought against him by the unbelieving world and often even by other brothers, Paul suffered. His list of sufferings is long but so is his list of positives, through which he even received kindnesses "by the Holy Ghost" (v. 6b).

6:1–3. Paul saw the Corinthians **as workers together with** Christ (v. 1). He pleaded that they would **not receive ... the grace of God in vain**. Some think this refers to: (1) salvation grace, (2) a warning of "falling from grace," (3) or spurning grace to live by.

The key could be in the word "vain" (Greek, *kenon*), which means "empty," "without content," "useless." While they were redeemed through saving faith in Christ, their belief was having little effect on their Christian walk. When the Corinthians responded to the gospel, Paul had **succoured** (v. 2) them, giving them encouragement and support. He quoted Isaiah 49:8, where the Lord said through the prophet, "In a day of salvation have I helped thee." This **day of salvation** had come to Israel in the work of Christ at the cross. There may have been some in the Corinthian congregation who spurned grace and were turning to Jewish legalism (see 3:12–16; Gal. 3:1–6). If so, they may have been living out their salvation in a twisted and legalistic way. Paul therefore warned them to give **no offence** (v. 3) so **that the ministry be not blamed.** In the following verses, he illustrated the price one must pay for being true to truth. Suffering will follow, but so will reward.

6:4–10. In all things (v. 4), Paul and his companions were **approving [them]selves as … ministers of God,** before the Corinthians and before the world. With poetic flare, Paul made a long list of what was happening to him for the sake of the gospel. Much that he listed here can be found in his other writings, as well as in the recorded events of his ministry (see the cross-references). In verses 4b–5, he listed words describing negative events and happenings: **in much patience** (v. 4b; see Rom. 12:12); **afflictions** (see 5:3); **necessities** ("needs"; see 1 Cor. 9:16); **distresses** ("anguishes"; see Rom. 8:35); **stripes** (v. 5; see Acts 16:23); **imprisonments** (see 6:24); **tumults** ("uproar"; see 20:1); **labours** ("deeds"; see 2 Cor. 10:11); **watchings** ("absence of sleep"; see 11:27); **fastings** (see Acts 13:2–3). In verses 6–7, he listed positive spiritual qualities: **pureness** (v. 6; see 1 Tim. 5:22); **knowledge** (see 2 Cor. 8:7); **longsuffering** (see Col. 1:11); **kindness** ("gentleness," "goodness"; see Col. 3:12); **by the Holy Ghost** ("by His work within"; see Gal. 5:16); **love unfeigned** ("unprejudiced love"; see Rom. 12:9); **the word of truth** (v. 7; see Eph. 1:13); **the power of God** (see 2 Cor. 13:4); **the armour of righteousness** ("the instruments of righteousness"; see Rom. 6:13). And in verses 8–10, he compared the negative with the positive: **honour and dishonour** (v. 8; Greek, *doxa*, "honour"; *atimia*, "despise"; see Gal. 1:24; 1 Cor. 4:10); **evil report and good report** (defamed report; good report; see 4:13); **deceivers, and yet** (we speak what is) **true** (see 1 Thess. 2:3); **unknown, and yet well known** (see 1 Cor. 4:9–13); **dying, and behold, we live** (see 2 Cor. 1:9–10), **chastened, and not killed** (see Acts 23:11–24); **sorrowful, yet always rejoicing** (see Phil. 1:18); **poor, yet making many rich** (see 1 Tim. 6:18); **having nothing, and yet possessing all things** (see Rom. 9:23).

Paul's list of descriptives about the Christian walk is unmatched. In comparison to what the world offers, in an eternal perspective, believers have everything that is of permanent and lasting value. Even if the child of God has nothing in this world, he has everlasting life in the presence of the God of the universe. What this physical life offers cannot be compared with eternity with Christ.

K. Appealing to Spiritual Children (6:11–7:4)

Here Paul challenged the Corinthian church regarding other moral issues they were facing. What he wrote makes it clear that many in the congregation were compromising their faith and were flirting with evil company among the unsaved. The Christians were being polluted spiritually. They were practicing immorality with those outside of Christ. They were walking in the world "as men" who were lost (1 Cor. 3:3).

6:11–15. With a strong plea from his heart, Paul cried out, **O ye Corinthians, our mouth is open … our heart is enlarged** (v. 11), meaning, we are large-hearted, generous, and warm in our affections. He added, You Corinthians **are not straitened** (restricted, blocked) **in us, but you are straitened in your own bowels** (v. 12). The Greek word for "bowels" (*splanchnon*) means "intestines." For the ancient peoples, the bowels were the seat of affection, compassion, sympathy, and mercy. Paul was saying that there was plenty of room for the Corinthian believers in his affections because he loves them all. He did not hold back his love. Even if the church had some reservations about the apostle, he was wide-open to them.

Paul continued to write to them as his **children** (v. 13) and wanted them to have an **enlarged** heart, to be open to him and to his instructions. Without giving details, he hit them head-on with that which was bothering him, commanding them, **Be ye not unequally yoked together with unbelievers** (v. 14). Believers are in the world, yet they must live morally and spiritually above the world. Addressing the issue of **fellowship** with unbelievers, the apostle focused on the differences: **righteousness** versus **unrighteousness**, **light** versus **darkness**. He elaborated on this in the following verses.

6:16–17. The believer's body is **the temple of the living God** (v. 16), and in this "temple," the heavenly Father dwells. In a spiritual sense, the church is like ancient Israel when the Lord told the Jews of His special relationship with them: **I will be their God, and they shall be my people** (see Exod. 29:45). In the Exodus passage, God said He would dwell "amongst" the children of Israel, whereas now with the church, He takes up residence **in them** personally. How can believers cohabit in a spiritual sense **with idols**? The problem this congregation had seems so elementary, but it escaped the Corinthians, or they simply lived in denial of the facts of their Christianity.

Paul then commanded the Corinthians to depart from idol worshipers: **Come out from among them, and be ye separate** (v. 17). He added that this was not simply an imperative from him; it was God's command (**saith the Lord**). The apostle loosely quoted Isaiah 52:11–12, where the nation of Israel heard the **word** calling forth salvation but also warning His people to "Depart ye" from sinners, and **touch not the unclean thing**. Believers are not to be monkish, to be isolated from sinners, but they are to be "separate" from sin and sinful things. Believers rub shoulders with the lost, but they are not to succumb to the world's sinful ways. Their testimony of purity becomes a witness to the grace of God to deliver from sin.

6:18. While the child of God has a relationship with the heavenly Father that is based on the work of Christ and that positionally cleanses from sin, daily fellowship is based on confession of sin and is conditional. John wrote, "If we say that we have fellowship with him, and walk in darkness, we lie, and do not the truth … If we confess our sins, he is faithful and just to forgive us our sins, and to cleanse us from all unrighteousness" (1 John 1:6, 9). By walking in a close and transparent fellowship with the **Father**, believers are His **sons and daughters**. This is a promise, **saith the Lord Almighty**. While this is an issue for the believers in the church age, Paul may have drawn the illustration from Isaiah 43:6: "I will … bring my sons from far, and my daughters from the ends of the earth."

7:1. In his summary, Paul spoke with affection for the Corinthian Christians, calling them **dearly beloved**. His comments in 6:18 are **promises**, but in similar words to 1 John 1, he urged that all those in Christ, including even himself, should **cleanse ourselves from all filthiness of the flesh and** even of the **spirit**. Doing so brings about a **perfecting holiness** with respect and **fear** of the Lord. Sinning can be both external and internal, of the body and the inner person, the spirit. The word "perfecting" (Greek, *epiteleō*) means "completely finishing," "carrying out," "discharging," or "completely carrying forth" holiness, living separate from sin.

7:2–4. The apostle continued his rapprochement with the Corinthian assembly. He urged the readers to **Receive us** (v. 2), because in no way had the apostle and his ministry companions **wronged** (Greek, *ēdikēsamen*; "treated unjustly"), **corrupted** (Greek *phtheirō*; "injured," "destroyed"), or **defrauded** (Greek, *pleonekteō*; "took advantage of," "made gain of") anyone. The apostle walked carefully to avoid every possibility of suspicion that he was defrauding with monies, fooling the believers spiritually, or bringing them harm in any other way. Therefore, he was to be accepted and not rejected. He did not, however, want to **condemn** (v. 3) them. He told them, **you are in our hearts to die and live with you.** With an exuberant burst of emotion and accolades, Paul spoke positively, with **boldness** (v. 4), in **glorifying** the Corinthians, saying he was **filled with comfort** and was **exceeding joyful,** even when suffering **tribulation.**

In 2:13, Paul said he "had no rest in [his] spirit," because he had hurried to Troas to meet Titus to find out how the Corinthians were doing. His soul was no longer troubled about them, his mind was at rest, and he was full of warm consolations. The favorable account of what was happening in that church had relieved his anxieties and turmoil.

L. Comfort from Titus (7:5-16)

Titus was able to help Paul understand the changes that were taking place in the Corinthian church, which gave the apostle much comfort. Paul did not apologize, however, for his heavy-handedness when dealing with blatant sin. In this section, Paul focused on explaining himself and getting his relationship with the church back on track.

7:5-7. Picking up the discussion from 2:12-14, Paul gave additional details about his side of the story and how he had received from Titus the positive message he had been longing to hear. When he had reached Macedonia, he was in great consternation over the Corinthian assembly with all of its problems. He knew that the news of their sins could affect the entire family of new churches spread throughout the region. Disappointed that he did not find his helper Titus in Troas but having received his report, Paul pressed on into Macedonia. There, he found Titus and was comforted. Before that, however, he **had no rest** (v. 5), was **troubled**, was having **conflicts** without and within, and was full of **fears**. **Nevertheless** (Greek, *alla*; "in contrast") **God, that comforteth** (Greek, *ho parakalōn*, present participle; v. 6), "the One who is continually comforting, "the **cast down** comforted Paul through Titus.

Titus' arrival in Corinth had brought **consolation** (v. 7) and **comforted** the believers. He reported to Paul the repentance of the Corinthian congregation, who, after being reprimanded, had mourned over their sins and focused their **fervent mind** (Greek *zēlos*), or "zeal," "enthusiasm," **toward** Paul. In other words, the church got on the same page with him both morally and spiritually. Titus reported to Paul (see Acts 14:27; 16:38) all that had happened. Their **mourning** (Greek, *odyrmos*; "wailing," "lam-

entation"; see Matt. 2:18), was certainly because of their sins but also possibly because they had so grieved the apostle Paul. Hearing this good report, Paul **rejoiced the more**, that is, beyond the fact that he was glad to see Titus again. These verses show that Paul was not simply a good, theologically oriented apostle; he felt deeply about the human drama going on with the believers he had led to Christ.

7:8-11. Paul knew that he had made the Corinthians **sorry with a letter** (v. 8), 1 Corinthians, in which he had scolded them. On one hand, he **did repent** for hurting them; on the other hand, he said, **I do not repent**, because the letter had caused them to change their ways. Their sorrow was but for **a season**; they would get over it. He had been heavy-handed in the letter so that they might be **sorrowed to repentance** (v. 9), **after a godly manner**, so that in the future, they might not have to **receive damage** (hurt) again. Paul had known that the church in Corinth would be torn up with his comments but that the sorrow he brought would be only temporary, and in the final analysis, he did not regret his judgments.

In the world, **the sorrow** (v. 10) imposed by stern punishment **worketh death**; that is, it destroys and gives no opportunity for forgiveness or hope. **Godly sorrow**, however, brings forth **repentance to salvation** that does not have to be continually **repented of**. Scholars are divided as to how Paul was using "salvation" in this verse. Some believe he was referring to the repentance that causes one to turn to Christ and receive Him for deliverance. Others believe he was using the idea of salvation in the broader sense of a moral deliverance from evils that "destroy," meaning being rescued from the penalty of the wrongs done as Christians (see 1:6). Either way, a true principle is cited here: godly sorrow brings about a repentance that leads to salvation.

Verse 11 had a powerful rhetorical sense. **For behold** (Greek, *idou*; emphatic; v. 11), "For look!" True sorrow is **after a godly sort**. If repentance and sorrow are carefully initiated, they bring forth a **clearing of yourselves**, a certain feeling of **indignation**, even **fear**, but also a **vehement desire**, a zealousness (**zeal**), and possibly a sense of **revenge**. The Corinthians had **approved** themselves and were **clear[ed]** of allowing the incestuous relationship to fester in the church. Some suggest that the Corinthians had not fully understood the seriousness of the matter of the incest until they had received Paul's letter. They had argued with him about the fact that they had not given him proper respect over the matter. They had even shown a desire for revenge to clear themselves of the charge and had issued a countercharge. The people repented not for the wrong they had committed but for their error in not dealing with it.

7:12-14. The apostle clarified himself by noting that he had written the first epistle not simply for the one who had done wrong, nor for his suffering, but to show his **care** (v. 12) for the congregation, which he wanted them to know about, **in the sight of God**. These words seem somewhat exaggerated or extreme, but they show that Paul had a larger principle in view. He wanted the Corinthian assembly, in the greater sense, to know that there was an overall concern for this body of believers, before the eyes of the Lord.

At this point, all seems to be turning out well. Paul and his friends were **comforted** (v. 13) in the Corinthians' **comfort**. Because Titus was joyful and **his spirit was refreshed** by what was happening in the church, Paul and the others could be **exceedingly the more joyed**. He was pleased and **not ashamed** (v. 14) that he had **boasted** of the church in Corinth. Paul's **boasting** to Titus was discovered to be **truth**. "Boasted" (Greek, *kauchaomai*) as used here does not mean Paul had "bragged" about the Corinthians but rather that he had shared news of them with positive conviction, commendation, and pleasantness.

One of the members of the assembly had committed a sin (see 2:5-11). The entire congregation apparently had repented. The church had shown godly sorrow, which was felt and shared by all. Since the believers are one body in the Lord Jesus, and all belong to each other as members of that body, when one suffers, all suffer. The experience is shared among all the members (see 1:6-7).

7:15-16. Because of what he had observed in the church at Corinth, Titus had greater **inward af-** fection (v. 15) toward the assembly. He **remembereth the obedience** the Corinthians had shown, **how with fear and trembling you received him**. This caused Paul to **rejoice** (v. 16) and **have confidence** in the church **in all things**.

With these two verses, the entire issue was concluded. The first seven chapters of this letter are tightly connected and seem to revolve around the great all-pervasive sin of the incident of incest. These same chapters can be said to relate to the spiritual and moral state of the church with which Paul was so concerned. Here the problematic issue was put to rest, with a full restoration of confidence.

II. The Collection for the Jerusalem Christians (chaps. 8-9)

In these two chapters, Paul digressed to an issue that weighed heavy on his heart: the collection of funds to help the distressed believers in the church at Jerusalem. The Corinthians had started a relief fund but had not completed it. He reminded the Corinthian congregation of the generosity of the churches in the Macedonian region. Liberality to the poor was only a part of their devotion to the Lord. The conduct of the Macedonians caused Paul to urge Titus, since he had begun the task, to carry it to completion in Corinth (8:6).

Paul did not want to arrive in Corinth to receive the collected funds and find them unprepared to give their pledge. God had commanded that they give, and He would supply their needs. In these chapters, the apostle was not so much concerned about the temporal needs of the poor (though he certainly was); he was more concerned about the mutual love and care that Christians should have for each other. Gifts to the poor cannot be compared to the gift of Christ, given by the heavenly Father (9:15).

A. The Blessing of Generosity (8:1-15)

Give oneself to the Lord is the first principle of sharing with others. The Macedonian believers stood out as a great example for the Corinthian assembly. The ultimate example for believers, however, is the grace of the Lord Jesus Christ in giving of Himself over to the cross. While rich in glory as the Son of God, He became poor on earth for others. Regarding giving, Paul was looking first for "a willing mind" (v. 12).

8:1–5. The Greek word **Moreover** (Greek, *de*; v. 1) begins the transition to the new subject. Paul started this section by reminding the Corinthians of **the grace of God bestowed on the churches of Macedonia. To wit** (Greek, *gnōrizomen*) means "cause you to know." Though the Macedonian churches were under **affliction** (v. 2), they still carried on with a great **abundance of … joy**. They experienced **deep poverty** (Greek, *bathous ptōcheia*), "poverty down to the depths," though this **abounded** forth to **the riches of their liberality**. While facing trials, they still had joy and dug deeper into their purses to exercise generosity ("liberality").

The apostle spoke often of God's "riches" (v. 2), His "fullness" (*ploutos*). He spoke of "the riches of his goodness" (Rom. 2:4), "the riches of his grace" (Eph. 1:7), and "the riches of the glory of his inheritance" (Eph. 1:18). He used this word over and over in the sense of God's great abundance. Because of what God was doing with the Macedonian Christians, they were operating in **power** (v. 3), to which Paul bore **record**, and from this **power**, or ability (Greek, *dynamis*), they became **willing of themselves** to give. Furthermore, the Macedonians were **praying … with much intreaty** (v. 4) that Paul would take their **gift** of funds, and thus share even more in **fellowship**, to **the ministering to the saints**. In essence, "They gave far beyond their ability, without any further urging by me." They were giving of **their own selves to the Lord** (v. 5) but also **unto us by the will of God**.

The enthusiasm of the Macedonians far surpassed Paul's expectations. Their liberality was in their gift of money but also in the gift of themselves. Some commentators think that "unto us" in verse 5 means they had offered themselves to go to Corinth or elsewhere, for Paul, to collect more money for the Jerusalem poor.

8:6–7. Paul urged Titus to continue **as he had begun** (v. 6) and to **finish** in the Corinthian church

with the **same grace** of God's riches as seen with the Macedonian believers. Paul had instructed the Corinthians (1 Cor. 16:1) to take a collection for the poor who were suffering in Jerusalem. Titus probably visited Corinth after that epistle had been written and made a start with this endeavor. When Paul discovered how giving the Macedonian congregations were, he then urged Titus to return to Corinth and finish what he had so successfully started. Paul exhorted Titus to go back for a renewed visit. Titus would **finish**, or bring the work to completion.

As the church at Corinth was **abound[ing] … in faith, and utterance, and knowledge, and in all diligence, and in your love to us** (v. 7), they should likewise **abound in this grace also** that the Macedonian congregations were blessed with. With "faith, and utterance [speech], and knowledge," Paul was reminding the church of the spiritual gifts of 1 Corinthians 12:8–10. "Utterance" and "knowledge," however, are also used in the same combination in 1 Corinthians 1:5. "Utterance" (Greek, *logō*) may refer to the teaching of doctrine (see Hodge, *Second Epistle to the Corinthians*, p. 198). The Greek word *spoudē* ("diligence") is used five times in this letter (7:11, 12; 8:7, 8, 16) and twice in Romans 12:8, 11. It could be translated "to be careful," "to be business-like."

8:8–10. The apostle was continually concerned with the charge that he had dominated unreasonably the churches he had begun (see 1:24). He trusted, however, that their spiritual motivation was not simply externally driven (see 8:7b) or driven **by [his] commandment** (v. 8). He preferred that their motivation be internal devotion, **the sincerity of your love**, and wanted that love to be focused on the **Lord Jesus Christ** (v. 9), who had lavished upon them His **grace**. By grace, they were now **rich**, though for them and all who are saved, **he became poor**. From the glory of the heavenlies, Christ came to earth to die for the sins of condemned humanity.

Paul gave his **advice**, urging the Corinthians to finish their financial pledge begun **a year ago** (v. 10). This material offering for the church in Jerusalem was really for the Lord (see Matt. 25:34–40). Was this too much to ask? "If we have sown unto you spiritual things, is it a great thing if we shall reap your carnal things?" (1 Cor. 9:11). Therefore, it was only **expedient** for the Corinthians to carry forward their promise and pledge they **have begun before**.

8:11–14. Therefore, the church was to carry on to **perform the doing of it** (v. 11), or literally, "complete ye also the doing of what you promised." **There was a readiness to will**, and that needed to be put into **performance**, coming from what they had. **For if there be first** (Greek, *prokeitai*; better translated, "If there be present") **a willing mind** (v. 12). Was this congregation mentally prepared to follow through? That willingness was to be **according to [what] a man hath, and not according to [what] he hath not**. The Lord Jesus taught the same principle (see Mark 12:42). The issue was the "readiness" (Greek, *prothymia*), or "disposition," of the mind. God looks at the disposition ("readiness") of the mind and heart, which will be judged based on the individual's resources, related somewhat to ability. Paul did not intend, however, to bring about a church **burdened** (v. 13) in their giving while other congregations went free, being **eased** in their contribution. He argued for **an equality** (v. 14) among the assemblies **now at this time**. Those who can give to the needs of other Christians should, and if the situation is reversed and they have a need, a **want**, some other church can **supply** what is required so **that there may be equality**.

Some have thought Paul was teaching a form of early church communism. The same claim is leveled at the story of the punishment Peter placed upon Ananias and his wife Sapphira (see Acts 4:32–5:1–11). In the case of that event, the couple sold possessions to help many who were without, but they lied about how much they had taken in, claiming that they were giving funds from the entire sale. Yet they were not! This is not communism, and neither is what Paul taught here. In communism, every possession belongs to the state. In Christianity, every possession belongs to the individual, though whatever one has really comes from God. The Christian is to share out of the resources he is blessed with. All

of one's material goods do not belong to the group. However, from the heart, the one who "soweth bountifully shall reap also bountifully" (9:6).

8:15. To make his point, the apostle quoted Exodus 16:18, about the children of Israel who had to collect the Lord's supply of manna each morning as they traveled through the wilderness. Whether they collected a lot or a little, everyone had plenty. They "gathered every man according to his eating." But if they gathered too much out of selfishness, and could not even eat it all, the manna spoiled and rotted before their eyes (see Exod.16:19–20). Paul used this story to tell the church that they need not hoard their possessions. As with the children of Israel wandering in the wilderness, every blessing of food and even clothing came from the Lord. Too much could be a curse. Trusting God's supply is a blessing.

B. Titus and Companions Sent to Corinth (8:16–9:5)

In this section, Paul provided some details for how to collect the funds in a judicial manner, so that no one can complain or accuse a brother of stealing. He wanted fail-safe conditions put into place for integrity's sake. The same should be practiced today where money is concerned. It is wise to have a check-and-balance of several eyes when accounting for finances in the congregation.

8:16–19. But thanks be to God (v. 16), He had placed **into the heart of Titus** a distinct consideration for this church. While he had accepted Paul's **exhortation** (v. 17) to serve the Corinthian congregation, he did it not out of the apostle's urging but had responded (**being more forward**) on his own account and went to Corinth. This younger man was genuinely "concerned about the welfare of those he served" (Lowery, "First Corinthians," p. 574).

Along with Titus, Paul sent to the Corinthians another **brother, whose praise** (v. 18) in his work **in the gospel** was well-known **throughout all the churches**. This servant of Christ must have been fervent in his presentation of the cross of Christ for sinners. Commentators are undecided about his identity and cannot be dogmatic. The suggestions are Luke, Mark, Barnabas, or Trophimus. Whoever the brother was, he had a zeal and labored hard to promote the gospel.

Because this unnamed servant was **chosen of the churches to travel** (v. 19) with Paul and his fellow workers, many scholars point to the sending forth of Paul and Barnabas to Antioch, and beyond, which is referred to here (see Acts 15:22-35). They were "chosen," "called out," "selected" (Greek, *cheirotoneō*) by the Jerusalem congregation, the elders, and the other apostles for their journey (see Acts 15:22, 25). Other congregations may have joined in approval of the choice of these two men. Whoever this anonymous servant was, he traveled **with this grace, which is administered** through Paul **to the glory** of God. The gospel is being spread through human means, but the God's providence is active to bring about His glory and His purposes.

8:20-22. The reason several other respected disciples would be in charge of the collected offerings for the Jerusalem church was **avoiding** (v. 20) any **blame** over **this abundance which is administered by us**. Every transaction and handling of money must be kept **honest ... not only in the sight of the Lord, but also in the sight of men** (v. 21). Apparently, this unnamed brother was not only to accompany Titus but also to help in the distribution of the alms to the churches in Judea, so that there could be no misrepresentation of what was happening. The accounting of two is better than that of one. Paul did not want his or anyone else's integrity questioned. This brother had **proved diligent** (v. 22) in his service to Christ, and the apostle placed **great confidence** in him, as he did also with the saints in the Corinthian church. Paul did not explain how large these funds were, but that was not his point. Whether the collection was large or small, he wanted it handled in an above-board manner so that no one could complain.

8:23-24. If any held doubts about Titus, they should not, Paul said, because **he is my partner and fellowhelper** (v. 23) for the Corinthian church. The **brethren** with him were **messengers of the churches**, and they served for **the glory of Christ**.

Paul urged the Corinthians to show to this entire retinue of traveling servants **the proof of [their] love**. He desires others to see all that he had said about the kindnesses of the Corinthians, to prove his **boasting** (v. 24) about them. He wanted this church to exhibit the evidence of their love in the presence of other congregations. This entire chapter shows how intimately the early churches were bound together. Their influence, sympathy, and love obviously was shown forth and shared from assembly to assembly.

9:1-4. Paul said it was not necessary (**superfluous**; Greek, *perisson*; v. 1) to write concerning the importance of **ministering**, or better, "concerning the ministering," to the believers. This "ministering" was unto **the saints** (Greek, *hoi hagioi*; "the sacred ones"), believers, who are "sanctified" in a positional sense in Christ (see 1:1). In their daily experience, however, believers may "be carnal, and walk as men" (1 Cor. 3:3). In the good sense, the Corinthians had **forwardness** ("readiness"; v. 2) of mind, as he had boasted to those in **Macedonia**, that is, that this church was ready to do its duty in the alms collection. Paul's mention of **Achaia** has caused some scholars to believe that all the Christians of that region belonged to the assembly in Corinth, but this cannot be proven. Since Achaia was the Roman province of southern Greece, with its capital in Corinth, it may be that this congregation was the mother church for the region. It might be noted that Cenchrea, a seaport six miles east of Corinth, had an established church (see Rom. 16:1). It certainly was influenced by the larger Corinthian assembly.

So that Paul's rightful pride (**boasting**; v. 3) in the Corinthian church should not fall short and **be in vain**, he had already **sent the brethren** and urged the Corinthians to **be ready**. This was important lest any from **Macedonia** (v. 4) came with Paul and found this church not prepared with their offering. He did not want anyone to be **ashamed** after all of the **confident boasting** about how generous this church was.

9:5. Though Paul said he was coming to Corinth, he thought it best to send Titus and the other companions first to prepare, **make up beforehand**, the collection of their **bounty** so that that there would be no **covetousness**. He wanted their gift to be genuine, not something extracted from them by compulsion, deceit, or some kind of moral blackmail. Some commentators think Paul wanted to avoid causing some to react by stinginess, but this may not be what he had in mind. It must be noticed again how delicate this matter was emotionally and spiritually. Issues of money can often separate brothers in Christ.

C. The Results of Generosity (9:6 – 15)

In this section, Paul turned the discussion of the collection for Jerusalem into a positive spiritual lesson by focusing on inner motives for giving. He set the pattern for charity and giving for all of the churches, for all generations to come. Here he takes believers to the heights, into heaven itself, in understanding how giving bountifully is not simply a material matter but a spiritual issue.

9:6. Here Paul laid out the great principle for Christian giving. Unreserved sharing of one's assets brings a blessing and a return from the Lord. Care must be taken with this verse, however. How much one gave was not Paul's major concern; he cared more about one's motive and openness before God as guiding principles. Many believe this verse was a known proverb. Though it is not found in Scripture, it seems to allude to Proverbs 11:24: "There is that scattereth, and yet increaseth; and there is that withholdeth more than is meet, but it tendeth to poverty." The righteous who sow bountifully will always be taken care of by the Lord. The righteous will not be without. **But this I say** means, "You know this is true" (Barrett, *Second Epistle to the Corinthians*, p. 235).

9:7 – 9. God looks at the **heart** (v. 7), where every man **purposeth**. One is to **give** from the heart, **not grudgingly, or of necessity: for God loveth a cheerful giver**. No one can be forced to give, and the Lord would not want it that way. "Grudgingly" (Greek, *ek lypēs*) means "out of being pulled down," out of sorrow or from a reluctant state of mind, grieving about what is given as something that is lost. "A cheerful giver" (Greek, *hilaron dotēn*) is one whose sharing is a delight, done with "hilarity."

God will not allow His saints to starve. **God is able to make all grace** (v. 8) overflow, so that the giver has **all sufficiency** in everything and may be able to go beyond in **every good work**. God does not prosper His saints simply so they can enjoy material things; He does it so they can share with others, in a ministry of charity or a ministry of promoting the gospel.

The one who generously **hath dispersed** (v. 9) the seed abroad and **hath given to the poor** in charity, **his righteousness** can be seen by all; it **remaineth for ever**. Here Paul was quoting Psalm 112:9, which is full of words such as "righteousness" and "the righteous." Of the righteous man it is said, "He is gracious, and full of compassion, and righteous" (Ps. 112:4).

9:10 – 14. God is the one who **ministereth seed to the sower** (v. 10). This then **minister[s] bread for ... food**, multiples the seed, and in turn, brings an **increase [in] the fruits of your righteousness**. Every farmer can understand Paul's analogy about the seed. Seed has life in itself; it is meant to grow, flourish, feed, and produce more seed so that the process can continue. Giving must come from a spiritual motive, not simply for an economic purpose. God is the one who, by His providence, multiplies generous giving for His unfolding plan. This brings about "enrichment," to **all bountifulness** (v. 11), which then results in **thanksgiving to God**. This is an **administration** (Greek, *diakonia*; v. 12) of **service** (Greek, *leitourgias*; "liturgy") that blesses the public nature of the body of Christ; that is, it spreads and benefits the whole church of the Lord, which God causes to happen and again brings **many thanksgivings unto God**. That this happens, **the experiment** (v. 13), causes many to **glorify God** because the church shows forth a **professed subjection unto the glory of Christ**.

This process set forth the **liberal distribution** (v. 13) to the Macedonians, as it does for all others who receive such bounty. Many give thanks to the Lord because of the shown by the givers. Through the Corinthians' service to their needy brothers, their obedience and fellowship with all the saints in other places was demonstrated (see Hodge, *Second Epistle to the Corinthians*, p. 225). It may have surprised the Corinthian church to know that the recipients of their generosity offered **prayer** (v. 14) for them, **long[ed]** to be with them, and thanked God for **the exceeding grace of God** that could be seen flourishing in them.

9:15. The apostle concluded with a poetic anthem that has blessed believers throughout the ages. It is simple and to the point and gives God the glory. The word **gift** (Greek, *dōrea*) is only used here in 2 Corinthians and is in the singular. Some have assumed it refers to "the gift" of alms the Corinthians were to collect, but more likely, it refers to the gift of the Savior and His wonderful salvation. **Unspeakable** (Greek, *anekdiēgētō*) carries the thought of "unable to recount," "not able to describe fully." Calvin and others believe the gift bestowed on the Corinthians has to do with their generosity. Others apply it to God's unspeakable gift of salvation in His Son, Christ, who was rich but became poor in order to grant spiritual riches (see 8:9).

III. Paul's Strong Defense of His Ministry Calling and Apostleship (chaps. 10–12)

The apostle now turned back to more serious issues concerning his authority and apostleship. He strongly defended his ministry and his calling by the Lord Jesus Christ. He answered criticism about his "weighty" (10:10) letters and showed that it was the Lord who had commended him for service. Reminding his readers that false teachers were stalking the churches, he said their criticisms are motivated by Satan, who is transformed into an angel of light and has followers who appear to be "apostles of Christ" (11:13). Paul gave them the sign of a true apostle (12:11–12).

A. Paul's Authority Granted by the Lord (chap. 10)

The tone and style of this letter drastically changes here. The contrast and differences between chapters 10–13 and some of the preceding chapters are extreme, to say the least. Some have conjectured that this should be a separate letter or that possibly

Paul wrote this part of the letter after he heard additional information from the Corinthian church. Such theories are not necessary, however. It is quite reasonable that Paul's tone would change as he took on the evil false prophets and teachers and their followers, about whom he had written earlier. They were falsifying the gospel, and the apostle stepped forth to defend his position as an apostle. He very naturally wrote with a tone of apostolic authority, with firmness and severity.

10:1. Paul began this verse with a strong authoritative attitude: **I Paul myself.** He used the first-person plural often in this letter, to make his words inclusive of the junior apostles traveling with him, but here, he spoke as an individual so that the Corinthians could sense that he alone was dealing with the problems he addressed here.

Paul pleaded with the Corinthian assembly **by the meekness and gentleness of Christ.** He claimed the meek and gentle virtues of the Lord Jesus yet coupled these attributes with a certain boldness and righteous indignation in what he had to say. When with them, he was **base** (Greek, *tapeinos*), meaning "lowly," "humble," but he was **bold** (Greek, *tharreō*), or "confident," "assertive," in what he had to say when away from the church.

10:2–4. This was the second time Paul said, **I beseech you** (Greek, *deomai*; v. 2; see 10:1), which means to "exhort" or "implore." This shows that he did not wish to use force; he wanted to avoid severity in his expression. He preferred persuasion and reason in what he had to write. With the majority of those in Corinth, he wanted to work from the position of **confidence** and not compulsion, though he would **be bold against some, which think of us as if we walk according to the flesh.** In other words, they refused to listen to him. They thought he was simply blowing up and giving commands from his own fleshly desires rather than from the order of the Lord. Those he was referring to considered Paul just an ordinary man and not an apostle. They said he was acting under the guidance of his own corrupt nature and was but following his selfish or malicious emotions, relying simply on himself.

Showing how his enemies were mistaken, Paul made a clarification. All the apostles **walk[ed] in the flesh** (v. 3), he said, yet the war they were involved in was not simply a fleshly conflict but was instead a spiritual battle, a battle waged not only against evil men but also against unseen spiritual forces lurking in spiritual darkness. Paul amplified this thought in Ephesians 6:12: "We wrestle not against flesh and blood, but against principalities, against powers, against the rulers of the darkness of this world, against spiritual wickedness in high places."

Believers do not fight with the handmade **weapons** (v. 4) of flesh (**carnal**), but the struggle (**warfare**) is waged **through God**, and by His power, **strong holds** ("secure towers," "walls") are **pull[ed] down**. Some have paraphrased verse 4 as, "Our weapons are mighty, in that we pull down strong holds."

10:5 – 6. Continuing the analogy of war in this spiritual struggle, Paul wrote that, like pulling down the walls of a fortress, we are to be **casting down imaginations, and every high thing that exalteth itself** (v. 5) against what the Lord has revealed about Himself, that is, **the knowledge of God**. "Imaginations" (Greek, *logismous*) has the idea of "opinions," "convictions," "thoughts," referring to human self-reasoning that is contrary to the truth of God. "Every high thing" again refers to the towers and fortresses, the human pride and reasoning that exalts itself against God's revelation of Himself and against the gospel He has given by grace to lost humanity. Human beings will use human logic, philosophy, and wisdom in attempting to defeat what the Lord has said. "A rationalistic Christian, a philosophizing theologian, therefore, lays aside the divine for the human, the wisdom of God for the wisdom of men, the infinite and infallible for the finite and fallible" (Hodge, *Second Epistle to the Corinthians*, pp. 235 – 36).

Verse 6 is difficult. The word **revenge** means "punishment" and conveys, "We are ready to punish every disobedience." Using military language, the apostle spoke of bringing defeat upon enemies who must suffer the consequences of their actions. When their **obedience** was complete (**fulfilled**), the Lord

Jesus would act to control the unstable situation in Corinth. When the time arrived, and using Paul as His instrument, Christ would bring about a judgment on the false teachers. Some scholars believe Paul was talking about the collection for the Judean saints, but that issue is not mentioned here. It is better to take his statement as looking forward to 11:4. Paul was referring to "another Jesus" and "another gospel" proclaimed by the false apostles. The congregation had to excise the heretical teachers and false prophets and obey the gospel of Christ. The church is responsible for carrying out such discipline to stabilize the church with purity in ministry to which it is called.

10:7. Paul asked how the Corinthian congregation judged issues, by **the outward appearance** or by something more substantive? If those criticizing the apostle trusted Christ and were sure that they belonged to Him, then in this same way, they should look at Paul and his companions, because **so are we Christ's**. Paul's adversaries continually tried to place a division between him and the Corinthian church. They tried to concoct reasons for not trusting his leadership and apostleship. **Let him … think this again**, let him realize that Christians are all in this together; believers belong to the Lord Jesus. From the general drift, it appears that a whole class of persons stood firmly against Paul's authority.

10:8 – 11. While Paul could **boast** (v. 8) in his **authority**, which was given by the **Lord … for edification**, this power was not given to him for the **destruction** of the Corinthian church. As in 7:14, **boast[ing]** does not mean bragging, but simply stating what was fact. "Edification" means the building up of the church in holiness, spirituality, and peace. Power in the church does not come from civil authority or from the talents of the people but from the Lord Jesus only.

Paul assured his readers that his purpose was not to **terrify** (v. 9) them with the seemingly harsh words in his **letters**. His opponents argued that **his letters … are weighty and powerful** (v. 10). They also criticized him physically, however, claiming, **his bodily presence is weak**. They criticized his speaking abilities, saying, **his speech [is] contemptible**. That Paul cited what his critics said about him shows his great confidence in his appointment as an apostle by the Lord. Whether the claims are true or not, for an ordinary mortal, such comments bring pain to the soul, but apparently not for Paul. Some scholars have an opposite take on these verses. "Weighty" (Greek, *bareiai*) could have the idea of "impressive" in a positive sense, while "powerful" (Greek, *ischyrai*) carries the thought of "vigor," "authority." This could be a way of saying that he was convincing in his speech, though his detractors still disagreed with his claims. Verse 11 may confirm that theory. As truth was given in his **letters** (v. 11) when he was **absent** from the Corinthian church, so it would be **in deed** when he was in their presence. His letters are full of force and energy, and so it would be when he was present. His deeds would correspond to his written words. Because he said **such a one**, some commentators believe that only one person was opposing Paul. But most believe this is a figure of speech, and more than likely, a larger group opposed his ministry.

10:12. Paul assured his readers that he was not playing the comparison game. He and his companions were not looking at the number of those who opposed them, nor did they **measure themselves by themselves**, as their opponents did. Paul was not in a competitive race, nor was he counting heads. This is what the false teachers were doing, and they were **not wise**. The opponents had a faulty standard by which to test themselves; they used their own human standard rather than God's standard. The divine standard was exemplified by Christ. This is what Paul used.

10:13–15. In proclaiming the truth, and in ascertaining whether one is sent by God or man, the **measure** (v. 13) must be of the **rule** of **God**. God had **distributed** to Paul and his companions the right **measure** based on truth. This **measure** reached even to the Corinthians and blessed them. Paul did not go beyond his commission from Christ. He and his followers did not **stretch** (v. 14) beyond the authority God meted out. Paul, not the opposition, was designated "the apostle to the Gentiles" (see Gal. 2:8).

The Lord authenticated him by producing a bounty among the Corinthians; he came **in preaching the gospel of Christ** (see 1 Cor. 3:6). The false teachers had gone beyond that limit.

Paul did not ride on the back of others, **of other men's labours** (v. 15). As he preached the gospel to the Corinthians, he had **hope**. And when the fruit came forth, when the **faith** of the Corinthians was **increased**, he and his cohorts were **enlarged by** the **rule** they had followed.

10:16–18. As the Corinthian church matured and grew, the believers could help expand his work of evangelizing other Gentiles in the **regions beyond** them, even as far away as Spain (see Rom. 15:23–24). They could help by praying for Paul and his traveling companions (see Eph. 6:19–20) and by giving monetary support (see 1 Cor. 16:6; Phil. 4:15–17). First, however, this congregation needed to get things straight spiritually (see 2 Cor. 10:6). Paul did not want to take the easy route and follow after someone else's efforts, **in another man's line of things** (v. 16). He did not want to minister where it would be easy, where things were **made ready to our hand**. The apostle was a pioneer; he was not a follower. In this, **he that glorieth** would do so **in the Lord**, and not by man. Self-glory goes nowhere and is invalid by all standards. To **glory in the Lord** (v. 17) is to ascribe all good to Him and to realize that by His grace spiritual battles have been won. Final approval comes from the Lord, not from **he that commendeth himself** (v. 18). Paul never commended himself; his claims were founded not on conceit but on the clear calling and appointing of the Lord Himself. If God gave him favor, being judged by puny human judgment would be a small thing (see 1 Cor. 4:3).

B. Paul's Service to Christ (chaps. 11–12)

To prove his servitude to the Lord Jesus, the apostle was forced to do what appeared to be some kind of self-glorification. While he condemned all such personal boasting, he told the Corinthians it was necessary in order to clarify his role as an apostle. The Corinthians appeared to be in jeopardy of turning away from Christ because their respect of

Paul was being undermined by the false accusations of his opponents. It was thus necessary to present the basis on which he had claimed his authority from Christ. He had to support his miraculous calling from the Lord. This was a repugnant task to his sensibilities. Time after time, when he presented his claims, he quickly turned away to some other issue. These chapters were painful for the apostle Paul, though necessary for the sake of the gospel.

1. Warning of False Teachers (11:1–15)

In these verses, Paul begged the Corinthians to bear with him while he appeared to praise himself, though his motive was pure. He spoke this way because he was seen on the same level as the other apostles, who were highly esteemed.

11:1–3. Paul asked that the Corinthians **bear** (v. 1) with him, in his **folly**, in the words to come. He was **jealous over** (v. 2) this church because he had **espoused** (engaged) them to **one husband**, that is, **as a chaste virgin to Christ**. He was zealous for this congregation of believers because he had acted as a matchmaker in bringing them, as a new bride, to the Lord for salvation. In writing **godly jealousy** (Greek, *theou zēlō*), the apostle communicated that the emotions he had arose from his zealous desire to promote the honor of God the Father. **Fear** (v. 3) came upon the apostle because they were being **beguiled** by Satan, **the serpent**, who was attempting to **corrupt** them **from the simplicity** that is found in **Christ**. Satan did the same to **Eve** in the temptation in the garden (see Gen. 3:4). His work was to corrupt their **minds**. "Beguile" (Greek, *exēpatēsen*) means to "thoroughly deceive," "seduce by means of deception." Their "minds" (Greek, *noēmata*) has to do with their "thoughts" and "understanding" of what is right. Satan attempts to sidetrack the thinking of believers to derail them from what God intends for them. "Simplicity" (Greek, *haplotētos*) has to do with single-mindedness for the things of Christ, the undivided devotion to Him that is like the loyalty of a bride to her spouse (see Hodge, *Second Epistle to the Corinthians*, p. 253).

11:4–6. Verse 4 is one of the strongest verses in this section. Paul hit the church head-on, warning them not to accept the words from one who **preacheth ... another gospel** (v. 4), a gospel **not preached** by Paul. If they **receive[d] another spirit**, which they had not previously, that was **not accepted**, they were **bear[ing] with** the messenger, or with his message. In the Greek text, **ye might well bear** (Greek, *kalōs anechesthe*) is in the imperfect tense, and seems to infer that they would be tolerating or accepting this message. At the least, they would be giving it some credence, which would be terribly confusing for the doctrinal stability of the church. The congregation had come close to forsaking their commitment to Christ, choosing a form of doctrinal liberty, and departing from the truth. It is interesting that Paul spoke of this "new" message as receiving "another spirit." Ideas have a "spirit" about them, a driving philosophy that can mislead the spirit of the hearer. To keep out error, vigilance always must be maintained in the assemblies.

Paul then brought himself forward in the right sense, saying that he **was not a whit behind the very chiefest apostles** (v. 5). He was saying something like, "I want you to put up with me, and my bringing forth my position, because I am not in any way less that the chief apostles." He wanted to make certain that they did not think of him as any less in gifts, labors, or success than the other apostolic leaders. He was clearly authenticated as a servant of Christ and was completely entitled to all the deference and authority that was due them.

While he seemed to have to be **rude in speech** (v. 6), he did not fall short **in knowledge** of Christ and the gospel. And he knew what the Lord Jesus Christ had called him to do, and he had **been throughly made manifest** (Greek, *phaneroō*; "to shed light on") before them in everything he did, **in all things**. Paul's motives and his work were carried out not in the dark but in the light, and the Corinthians knew this well. At every point, in every respect, "in all things," he was clearly known; he stood revealed before them in every way as an apostle of Jesus Christ.

11:7–9. No one could claim **an offence** (v. 7) with Paul when he **abas[ed]** himself so that the Corinthians **might be exalted**. He did this when he **preached … the gospel of God** to them **freely.** He was not under compulsion, nor was he seeking monetary compensation. Paul gave them the gospel to raise them up spiritually; he had no other motive.

With tongue in cheek, with hyperbole, and with a figurative sense, Paul said he had **robbed other churches** (v. 8) by **taking wages** from them so that he could be of **service** to the Corinthians. Though Paul was a traveling evangelist and teacher, the principle still stands in what he wrote to Timothy: "For the scripture saith, Thou shalt not muzzle the ox that treadeth out the corn. And, The labourer is worthy of his reward" (1 Tim. 5:18).

When Paul had been with the Corinthians, probably during his first visit, he had **wanted** (v. 9), that is, had been "reduced to want" since he had run out of the support that came from the Macedonian churches. He was **chargeable** to no one, literally, "I pressed as a dead weight upon no one" or "I was a burden to no one." **The brethren** of the Macedonian churches **supplied** (Greek, *prosaneplērōsan;* "supplied in addition") what he needed so that he was not **burdensome** to anyone. This is reminiscent of what he wrote to the Ephesians: "I have coveted no man's silver, or gold, or apparel. Yea, ye yourselves know, that these hands have ministered unto my necessities, and to them that were with me" (Acts 20:33–34). The "hands" that ministered to him probably refers to the generosity of the Thessalonian church to help him along the way.

11:10–14. The truth of Christ (Greek, *alētheia;* v. 10), or the "veracity" or "truthfulness" that Christ produces, **is in me,** Paul said, and **this boasting** shall not be stopped. In all the **regions of Achaia,** he was not willing to accept help, though he did from the churches in Macedonia. The attitudes of the Corinthians seem to have had a negative impact on the Achaians. Paul did not love the Corinthians any less than those in other congregations **God knoweth** (v. 11). It seems clear from what he wrote in 1 Corinthians 9:15–18 that His "boasting" was that he shared the gospel of Christ gratuitously and not for gain. The number of verses given over to this issue clearly show that the issue of money and compensa-

tion was huge in the eyes and minds of the Corinthian church.

Paul's opponents (**false apostles;** v. 13) fueled this issue and infected the entire congregation with suspicion about Paul. They were **deceitful workers, transforming themselves into the apostles of Christ.** The Devil is behind those who oppose the gospel. **Satan himself is transformed** (Greek, *metaschēmatizō;* v. 14) literally means that he is able to "change the schematics" or "alter the configurations." Satan then appears as **an angel of light,** making people think that his lies are the truth. He is "the spirit that now worketh in the children of disobedience" (Eph. 2:2).

11:15. Satan's lackeys, **his ministers,** are capable of doing what he does; they can **be transformed** as workers of **righteousness.** Their **end,** however, will come about because of their self-righteous **works.** Revelation 20:11–15 vividly describes the judgment of the lost: books are opened that describe their evil sins, by which they are to be judged, because they have not trusted the only one who gives a way of escape—the Lord Jesus Christ. These who are unsaved are resurrected for this great white throne judgment (Rev. 20:11), before which they will be judged "out of those things which were written in the books, according to their works" (Rev. 20:12). Without trusting in Christ, men will have no recourse, and they must face "the second death" (Rev. 20:14). They then will be "cast into the lake of fire" (Rev. 20:15).

2. Paul's Rightful Claims (11:16–33)

In these verses, Paul gave his strongest attestation to his calling and authority as an apostle. This was not his first desire, but it was necessary in order to put down once and for all the criticisms that were continually being hurled at his character, his calling, and his motives. He reaffirmed his calling but also showed that he was no less than the other twelve apostles of Christ. He had the same authority and the same miraculous demonstrations of the power of the Spirit to prove it.

11:16–20. Paul repeated some of the thoughts he had previously shared. He was not **a fool** (v. 16). Even if he were, however, he should still be accepted so that he could **boast** about himself **a little**. Here he again used exaggeration to get his point across. He was speaking **not after the Lord, but ... foolishly** (v. 17), with a certain **confidence of boasting**. In other words, "If you have to, then accept me as if I was a fool. Give me a little slack, let me boast a little!" His readers would have noticed that he was spoofing them somewhat, but his comments would have caused them to think twice about the opinions of those attacking him. The Corinthians ought to take him as a apostle of Christ, even though he ironically let himself be called a fool. With irony, Paul said that if he was a fool, and others who had gloried in their **flesh**, should allow him **glory also** (v. 18). Since the Corinthians saw themselves as wise and yet they put up with fools (v. 19), the Corinthians in their wisdom should bear with the apostle.

Verse 20 is a hypothetical thought. What if **ye suffer** (v. 20) because you are put in chains, **devour[ed]**, taken captive, **exalt[ed]** over, and smitten **on the face**? What if the Corinthians were so abused? All of this had been done to Paul, yet he said, "I still love you" (see 1 Cor. 4:21). If they had been fooled by false teachers, it was time to admit they were blinded and were wrong. They needed to take action to get rid of the "invaders" who so mistreated and misled them. As with many Christians even today, the Corinthians were slow to realize the truth that what God says is different from what the world says. Paul had tried to put forth the message of the cross and that the wisdom of God is foolishness to the world (see 1:18–25). Yet if the Corinthians continued to look at things from the world's vantage point, he would accommodate himself to their thinking.

11:21–27. This is a long list of all that Paul had suffered for the sake of Christ. He mentioned this punishment to prove to the Corinthians how he had suffered for truth. Because most of this torment came from the Jews who hounded Paul because of the gospel, this passage may be proof that the false prophets who spiritually poisoned the Corinthians were also Jewish.

Paul mentioned his **reproach** (Greek, *atimian*; "shame"; v. 21) and admitted, with a bit of irony,

that he had been ministering somewhat as a weakling (**weak**). Those who hated him marked him in this way (see 10:10; 1 Cor. 2:3). While he had tried to be gentle, his foes used force. So what they had said about him must have been true. Yet Paul came right back and asserted that if they had been **bold** or brash, he would be **bold also**.

Were his enemies Jews (**Hebrews**; v. 22)? Paul answered, **so am I**. Were they **Israelites ... the seed of Abraham? so am I**. The word "Hebrew" was one of the first designations for Abraham (see Gen. 14:13). Most scholars believe the word comes from *eber*, meaning "from the other side." This could be a reference to the fact that Abraham had crossed over the Euphrates River to enter the land of Canaan. Israel (which means "He strives [with God]") is the name given to Jacob after he wrestled with the angel of Jehovah (see Gen. 32:28). "The seed [descendants] of Abraham" encompasses the entire nation of the Jewish people. Paul used all of these expressions and names in a synonymous sense. He was proud of his Jewish heritage, but to his grief, the Jews were vehemently against the message of the gospel (see Rom. 9:2–5; 10:1–3, 16–21).

With tongue in cheek, Paul asked, **Are they ministers of Christ? (I speak as a fool)** (v. 23). He hoped this question would cause the Corinthian church to think. If they were ministers of Christ, he was even **more**. Actually, they were opposing the gospel; Paul was proclaiming it. He listed all that he had suffered at the hands of the Jews, or from their influence, for the sake of the truth. He **labour[ed] more abundant[ly]** (see 1 Cor. 15:10), suffered **stripes above measure** (see Acts 9:16), was **in prisons more frequent[ly]** (see Acts 16:23; 23:10; 24:27; 28:16), was left for dead, **in deaths oft** (see Acts 14:19; 1 Cor. 15:30), was beaten **five times** (v. 24) by the Jews with **forty stripes save one**, was **beaten with rods** (v. 25; see Acts 16:22), was **once ... stoned** (see Acts 14:19), **suffered shipwreck** three times (see Acts 27:41), spent **a night and a day** in the sea, **in the deep**.

In all of his **journeyings** (v. 26), he had often been **in perils of waters ... of robbers ... by [his] own countrymen ... by the heathen** (Gentiles) **... in** the city ... in the wilderness ... in the sea ... among **false brethren**. He had suffered **in weariness and painfulness, in watchings often** (sleepless nights), **in hunger and thirst, in fastings often, in cold and nakedness** (v. 27).

While it may seem that Paul was seeking sympathy, this is not the case. He simply wanted the Corinthians to be aware of what he had gone through for the sake of Christ. While the believers in other churches may have known of Paul's ordeals for the gospel, this congregation needed some historical perspective on what he had endured. Everything that he experienced is not recorded in Scripture, but the truthfulness of these experiences was certainly well known by his traveling companions.

11:28. Paul added that **Besides those things that ... cometh upon me daily** (see 11:21–27), he still had the **care of all of the churches**. The many letters Paul wrote to the widely scattered congregations throughout the Roman and Greek world certainly verify this and that he had great personal care and interest in the many believers whose names he mentioned in his writings. Most scholars believe that the apostle wrote many more letters, letters that the Holy Spirit deemed not to include in the canon of Scripture (Christians have just the epistles He wanted them to possess). Paul was an amazing apostle. He traveled thousands of miles by land and by sea, wrote probably dozens of letters, counseled and taught night and day—all for the love of his Savior, Jesus Christ.

11:29–31. Paul had sympathy for his believing brothers in Christ, who were his children in the faith. Their sorrows were his also. In the best sense, this was the blessed result of the fellowship of the saints. Paul had earlier written, "And whether one member suffer, all the members suffer with it; or one member be honoured, all the members rejoice with it" (1 Cor. 12:26). If one was **weak** (v. 29), so also was Paul. If one was **offended** (Greek, *skandalizō*; "caused to stumble"), so also was Paul **burn[ed]**, that is, left "indignant" or moved with concern. He was never indifferent about what was happening with the believers. He was filled with grief when the weak fell or when someone stumbled.

The apostle never gloated over the weaknesses of other brothers in Christ. Rather, his own weaknesses and deficiencies made him **glory** (v. 30) over only the things that had to do with his own **infirmities**, that is, that God's grace and strength carried him through such experiences. This testimony was confirmed by **The God and Father of our Lord Jesus Christ, which is blessed for evermore** (v. 31). He knew that Paul **lie[d] not**. Because Paul knew that the Corinthians were not trusting him (see 1:12–18), he cited this witness that he was not a liar.

11:32–33. To illustrate how he began his ministry with his life in jeopardy, Paul briefly related the story of his early witnessing of the Lord Jesus Christ (see Acts 9:20–31). When **Aretas** (v. 32) was **the king** of **Damascus**, his **governor** tried to capture Paul because he was boldly endangering his life by proclaiming in the synagogue the message that Jesus was the Son of God (Acts 9:20), and that He was the Christ, the promised Messiah (Acts 9:22). The Jews in Damascus tried to kill him (Acts 9:23) and placed watches at the gates to capture him (Acts 9:24). The disciples had lowered him down the wall in a basket, and he had escaped to Jerusalem (Acts 9:25–26). Paul "had preached boldly at Damascus in the name of Jesus" (Acts 9:27). Was this not proof enough that his ministry had been genuine from the very beginning? The genuineness of Paul was witnessed by those who saved his life even though he continued to preach the Lord Jesus before the hostility of the Jews. God confirmed that what he had said was true. What more could this apostle add in regard to his genuineness?

3. Paul's Testimony of His Vision (12:1–21)

In this chapter, Paul did give additional testimony to his calling as an apostle. This calling was not simply that he would be a New Testament prophet but that he would be given equal status with the twelve apostles. To show God's revelations to him, Paul spoke of being "caught up to the third heaven" (v. 2) and given visions that no one had seen before. In spite of this great proof of the Lord's divine favor, Paul was still left with painful bodily afflictions that would not be removed. This was to demonstrate further God's grace but also to keep him humble.

12:1–5. Paul did not have to **glory** (v. 1) before the Corinthians about his reputation. "Glorying," or "boasting," was **not expedient** or necessary. It did not become him, was not profitable, and was not the proper thing to do. He had a better way of demonstrating his divine mission and calling. To boast in the fleshly sense would be foolish, derogatory, and painful. The better way was to give testimony to the **visions and revelations** he had received from **the Lord**. The visions were what he saw, and the revelations were the content of those visions.

Paul began by speaking about himself in the third person: **I knew a man in Christ** (v. 2), one who was a believer and part of the body of Christ. This man had been saved **above fourteen years**. He did not know whether this one was physically carried away **in the body** or not when he was **caught up to the third heaven** (the very presence of God). The ancients considered the sky and clouds as the first heaven, the starry heavens as the second heaven, and the presence of the Lord as the third heaven. Only **God knoweth** the true state of this experience and whether the man (Paul) was simply transported in spirit into this vision or was caught up physically. The word translated "caught up" (Greek, *harpazō*) means to "snatch away suddenly" and is used to describe the miracle of the rapture of the church (see 1 Thess. 4:17).

This man had been elevated **into paradise, and heard unspeakable words, which it is not lawful** (right) **for a man to utter** (v. 4). The word "paradise" (Greek, *paradeisos*) is from a Sanskrit word meaning "park" or "garden." To the Jews, it was the designation for heaven, or the abode of those who have died believing in the Lord. Christ told the repentant thief that he would be with Him "in paradise" upon his death (Luke 23:43). The word is used in the same sense of "heaven" in Revelation 2:7. Other verses add to this understanding of what Paul saw and where the Lord now resides. When He ascended, He passed "into the heavens" (Heb. 4:14), to be exalted and "ascended up far above all heavens" (Eph. 4:10), to be

"made higher than the heavens" (Heb. 7:26). Believers who have passed away are now "at home with the Lord" (2 Cor. 5:8; "with Christ" in Phil. 1:23).

Paul could not **glory** (v. 5) in a personal way that this miracle had happened to him, but he could glory because it indeed had taken place. His greatest **glory**, however, was in his **infirmities**. Why did Paul wish to deny self-glory? He probably was saying, "This event is just grounds for giving glory, but not to me personally." He did not want to take on any personal superiority that would cause boasting about his particular qualities, entitling him to religious admiration. One of the proofs that God was using him, however, is seen in his personal infirmities, which he explained in 12:9.

12:6–9. Humanly speaking, Paul wanted **to glory** (v. 6), but this would have been **foolish[ish]**. He said, **now I forbear** ("hold back"), yet he desired to speak only **the truth**. He did not want anyone to think wrongly of him based on what they saw in him or heard about him. He did not want to be judged by what he said about himself or of his experiences. His focus was on Christ. What mattered most were not his achievements for the Lord but how God was working through his ministry of proclaiming the gospel message.

Because he was being so used, and to keep him from being **exalted** (v. 7), because of the many **revelations** he was given, God gave him **a thorn in the flesh**. Paul called this "thorn" **the messenger of Satan**. Its purpose was to **buffet** him, as he said, **Lest I should be exalted above measure**. Paul's use of the present tense of "buffet" means that this is a permanent, ongoing affliction to ensure he kept the proper perspective about his service for the Lord. The role of Satan is uncertain. Did Paul mean that Satan had direct influence on the physical problem, or was he saying that the problem was as painful as if Satan were administering the ailment? Scholars disagree on this.

"Buffet" (v. 7) is a boxing term, again indicating that this "thorn" (Greek, *skolops*) was continually beating up on him. A thorn is an object that pierces the flesh and injures. Most scholars believe that this is to be taken in a physical sense, that it was some kind of malady he had to painfully endure. Many suggestions are given as to what this affliction might have been: neuralgia, hysteria, malaria, epilepsy, leprosy, rheumatism, or eye difficulties. Paul wrote about "my temptation … in my flesh" (Gal. 4:14). He also spoke of having to write with large letters, which might mean he had eye problems (ophthalmia; see 6:11). When the Lord struck him down on the road to Damascus, a bright light "shined round about him … from heaven" (Acts 9:3), which was followed by blindness (Acts 9:7 – 8). Paul's blindness was removed by God's righteous messenger, Ananias, who put his hands on him, by which the Lord restored his sight (Acts 9:17). "Scales," or scabs, fell from his eyes (Acts 9:18). While he could then see again, his eyesight may have suffered permanent damage.

Paul **besought the Lord thrice** (v. 8) to remove this affliction, but He had answered: **My grace is sufficient for thee: for my strength is made perfect in weakness**. The apostle **Most gladly** accepted the **infirmities** so that he would receive no personal **glory**. He would carry out his calling by **the power of Christ**. God always answers prayer: "yes," "no," or "later!" This was a case of "no" because the Lord had spiritual purposes beyond simply giving Paul physical relief from a painful situation. The Lord's power is sometimes best displayed against the backdrop of human frailties so that He alone receives the praise. Rather than removing the problem, He supplies the believer with grace to allow one to endure with contentment (see Lowery, "First Corinthians," p. 583).

12:10. **For Christ's sake**, Paul was able to **take pleasure** (joy) in his **infirmities**, and even **in reproaches, in necessities, in persecutions, in distresses**. He added other difficulties to what he may have been experiencing for the name of the Lord. He embraced these problems because of the principle that when he was **weak**, then he was **strong** in the strength of Jesus Christ. It would have been natural for Paul to abhor such experiences in his ministry and in his personal life, but he welcomed them from the supernatural point of view because Christ's power was made evident through these adversities.

When Paul arrived at the end of himself, the Lord Jesus alone could be manifested.

12:11 – 13. With a twist of irony, Paul added that he had **become a fool** (v. 11) with his **glorying**. He had not wanted to get into all that had happened to him, but the Corinthians' doubts had **compelled** him to do so. The Corinthian church should have **commended** him because they should have recognized who he was. For in no way, **in nothing**, was he less than (**behind**) the **chiefest apostles**, while in another sense he said, **I be nothing**.

To prove that he was no less than the recognized apostles, Paul said, **the signs of an apostle were wrought among you in all patience, in signs, and wonders, and mighty deeds** (v. 12). Paul must have been performed such signs among the Corinthians, but apparently they had refused to acknowledge them. Hodge believes these nouns are different designations for the same thing (*Second Epistle to the Corinthians*, p. 292). They could have been miracles of healings and of speaking in tongues (see 1 Cor. 12:29 – 30). Paul knew that he was equal with the Twelve (see 11:5), as illustrated by the long list of abilities he had just put forth. It was foolish to argue about this, however, because ultimately his credentials came from God; they were not his own. It is interesting to note that Paul included "patience" (probably with the believing sheep) as a sign that verified apostleship.

The Corinthian congregation may have felt they **were inferior to other churches** (v. 13) because Paul did not want to be **burdensome** to them. He had founded many assemblies that were replete with gifts and graces. This demonstrates that he was equal to the other disciples. At one time in the past, however, he had not wanted to ask for their help because they had not trusted him. What God did through Peter with the Jews was done in like manner through Paul with the Gentiles: "For he [God] that wrought effectually in Peter to the apostleship of the circumcision, the same was mighty in me towards the Gentiles" (Gal. 2:8). The apostolic pillars, James, Cephas (Peter), and John, also "perceived the grace that was given unto me," Paul added, and he and Barnabas had received "the right hands of fellowship," with all the apostles, "that we should go unto the heathen" (Gal. 2:9).

12:14 – 16. Paul must have made two other visits to Corinth, as indicated in 2:1 and 13:1 – 2. On this **third** visit, he would act on the same principles as before in that he would take for himself nothing from this church, though their alms for the Judean church would be received by Titus and others. Paul was their spiritual parent and believed he should not receive anything from the children he spiritually birthed. Since he was their spiritual father, he would **gladly spend** ("give out"; v. 15) himself, though **the more abundantly I love you, the less I [am] loved**.

Paul was saying he forfeited their love by doing what love forced him to do. This is the strongest statement of disinterested love. He was willing to give his possessions and himself, his life and strength, not only without pay but at the cost of their love. He repeated that he did not want to place a **burden** (v. 16) on them, though he thought it important to guard against unfounded insinuations from the antagonists who doubted the purity of his motives. He **caught** them **with guile** (Greek, *dolō*), as an animal is fooled by a camouflaged trap.

12:17 – 18. Paul pointedly asked, **Did I make a gain of you by any of them whom I sent unto you?** (v. 17). The critics and the naysayers, if they were honest, could only answer no. With this, he appealed to facts they could not deny. The mention of **Titus** (v. 18) visiting Corinth is not the visit discussed in chapter 8, which had not yet been accomplished, but rather that discussed in chapter 7. Titus and another **brother** (see 8:18) had been sent earlier. Had Titus sought personal **gain**? Was not everyone walking **in the same spirit** and **in the same steps**? By "same spirit," Paul meant with the same inward thinking or walking in the same Holy Spirit. The believers were to be imbued and led by the same divine agent who controls the conduct of all believers.

12:19 – 21. Paul did not **excuse** (Greek, *apologeomai*; v. 19) himself and his fellow workers, meaning "apologize," "talk to oneself," "answer for oneself." The problems were with the Corinthians, not with

Paul and his companions. **We speak before God in Christ**; God was their witness. **All things** were done for the **dearly beloved** for their **edifying**, for their benefit. Paul's aim was to build them up, **For** (v. 20), he said, he **fear[ed]** their spiritual state of mind was not what he wanted it to be. He was concerned that they would not be acceptable to him and he would not be in favor with them. He was afraid that the evil contentions that had been going on still existed among the Corinthians. These evils were **debates** (Greek, *eris*; "contentions"), **envyings** (*zēlos*; "feelings of jealousy"), **wraths** (*thymoi*; "outbreaks of anger"), **strifes** (*eritheiai*; "partisan factions"), **backbitings** (*katalaliai*; "evil speakings"), **whisperings** (*psithyrismoi*; "gossip"), **swellings** (*physiōseis*; "full of pride and insolence"), **tumults** (*akatastasiai*; "taking a stand with disorder"). The explanation for all of this uproar was that part of the assembly was penitent and humble, while the others were just the opposite. It must be remembered that most at this church were Gentiles who were ignorant of Christian sensibilities and ways of doing things. In Paul's writings, there are abundant examples of such behavior among them. The first part of 1 Corinthians is full of the strongest words of praise, but what follows speaks of contentions that could have ripped the church apart.

When he arrived in Corinth, Paul did not want to be **humble[d]** again in the presence of the church by those who had sinned and not repented (v. 21). He would also **bewail many which have sinned** and continue in that state. They had **not repented of the uncleanness and fornication and lasciviousness which have committed.** "Lasciviousness" (Greek, *aselgeia*) is a common word for "filth." Most of these words hint at sexual sins, open debauchery, and possibly even orgies. With this, Paul reached the bottom of his accusations. They could not escape or deny that this was going on in the church, not that many who had participated had not "repented" (Greek, *metanoeō*), "changed their minds."

To turn around a sinful church in the midst of heathenism was virtually impossible without the sanctifying work of the Holy Spirit. The transformation of these Christians would not be instant, for God's omnipotent power often works gradually. These early believers were but babes in the Lord Jesus.

IV. Closing (chap. 13)

Paul closed with positive words for this church, saying that he desired to speak to them with kind words and not with words that are sharp in nature.

A. Spiritual Concerns (13:1–10)

Having given strong warnings in the previous chapters, Paul intended to exercise his apostolic authority in punishing the heretical offenders (vv. 1–2). They had questioned him about his apostleship; he would now show that although he was weak in his own power, he was invested with the supernatural authority and power of the Lord Jesus. As Christ seemed to be weak in His death yet nonetheless was imbued with divine power, as proved by His resurrection, so the apostle Paul in some ways was weak but in other ways was strong in the Lord (vv. 3–4). By giving the church warning before his impending visit to Corinth, he hoped to avoid judging them as an apostle, as he had been invested by Christ.

13:1–3. Paul's second trip to the Corinthian church (see 2:1) must have been a spiritual disaster and a humiliating experience (see 12:21). Many challenged his person and his right to be an apostle (see 2:5–11), and they were living out their Christian walk in defiance of God's desire and will (see 12:21). The apostle had given ample warning about their sins, and did so again in this epistle. As Christ used Deuteronomy 19:15 against sinners (see Matt. 18:16), so Paul promised harsh discipline aimed at those walking in carnality without repentance. They would be wise to avoid his apostolic authority (see 1 Cor. 5:5).

Paul reminded the Corinthians that when he came **the third time** (v. 1), he would seek out **two or three witnesses** to verify their sinful, errant ways. As he had told them on **the second** visit, for all who **have sinned**, and sinned grievously, that when he

returned, he would **not spare**. The **proof of Christ speaking in me** (v. 3) would not come in weakness, which they had been counting on, but would come **mighty in you**.

13:4–6. As the Lord Jesus **was crucified** (v. 4) because of what seemed **weakness, yet he liveth by the power of God**, likewise Paul and his followers were **weak in him** yet would **live with him by the power of God** through the Corinthians. The apostle was proclaiming that the Lord Jesus is not dead but alive. "Liveth" (Greek, *zaō*) is present tense in the Greek text. "He is right now, presently alive!"

The Corinthians needed to look at themselves carefully. Paul urged them to **examine** (v. 5) and **prove** themselves, whether they were in **the faith**. While it appears he was concerned about their salvation, this may not be the case. Many commentators believe Paul had some doubts about the salvation of some of the Corinthians. "Those therefore in whom Christ does not dwell cannot stand the test, and are proved to be Christians, if at all, only in name" (Hodge, *First Corinthians*, p. 306). He may have been saying, "If you are saved, do you not know that Jesus Christ is in you?" And, "if He is not in you," **ye be reprobates?** Hodge thinks Paul was trying to goad the Corinthians to look at the issue of sanctification in the daily experience (see *Second Epistle to the Corinthians*, p. 306). Paul appealed directly to the consciences of his readers: "Do you not recognize in yourselves, that is, in your consciences, that Christ is in you?" The thought that **Christ is in you** does not mean "Christ is among you as a people" but refers to an indwelling of Christ in the child of God, as the apostle said, "Christ liveth in me" (Gal. 2:20; 4:19; see also Rom. 8:11). Paul **trust[ed]** (v. 6) that the Corinthians were well aware that he and his companions were **not reprobates**. "Reprobates" refers to the lost who are judicially condemned.

13:7–9. Paul did not want the Corinthians to practice **evil** (v. 7). He did not have to stand **approved** (Greek, *dokimos*). "The good state of the Corinthian church was therefore an evidence that he was approved, i.e. could stand the test" (Hodge, *First Corinthians*, p. 308) like someone concerning whom there was not a shadow of a doubt that Christ was dwelling in him. He had many verifications and proofs that he was a believer, a child of God, and that he was an apostle called to a special mission by Christ. Even if Paul and his companions were **reprobates**, the Corinthians needed to do the moral and **honest** thing. Because the spotlight was on him and on his many ministry workers, he could **do nothing against the truth, but [only] for the truth** (v. 8). He was delighted and **glad** (v. 9) to be **weak** (limited and human), for then the Corinthians had to look at what was right, and not simply at Paul. Then they would be **strong**, resulting in their **perfection** (Greek, *katartisis*), their "being put in order," "being made complete." This would liberate them from carnality, confusion, contention, and evil.

13:10. Paul concluded this section (**Therefore**) by reminding the Corinthians that he wrote while **being absent, lest being present** with them, he **should use** (Greek, *chraomai*; "to necessarily act") **sharpness**. This "sharpness" came not from his own carnality and meanness but from **the power** (Greek, *exousian*; "ability," "authority," "right") **the Lord** had given to him for **edification, and not [for] destruction** (see 1 Cor. 4:21).

B. Farewell and Benediction (13:11–14)

13:11–13. This letter is unusual in that Paul did not address anyone personally, as he did in most of his epistles. In writing **farewell** (Greek, *chairete*, present imperative; v. 11), he meant "you be rejoicing" or "may joy be continually coming to you." **Be perfect** (Greek, *katartizō*; present imperative) means "be sound," "be complete," "be put in order," "be mended," as in fixing a torn fishing net. The Corinthians were also to walk in **good comfort**, and with **one mind**. If they were to do these things and **live in peace ... the God of love and peace shall be with you.** If they had claimed the Lord Jesus as Savior, the God of love was already dwelling within them (see John 14:23; 1 John 4:12–13). Paul meant that they would have fellowship established with the Father for their daily Christian walk (see 1:6–7). God's fellowship presence gives perfect peace and inner contentment.

To **greet one another with a holy kiss** (v. 12) was an expression of communion and love within the early church. This practice did not go out of usage in the Western churches until about the thirteenth century, though it is still carried on in the Eastern Orthodox churches. It is not a command or a required ordinance for fellowship. It is a practice that some are comfortable with, and some are not. **All the saints** (v. 13) with Paul, and possibly from other churches as well, **salute[d]** their Corinthian brothers. The "salute" (Greek, *aspazomai*) was a slight gesture, a hand motion, even an embrace and a kiss. Here it is a verbal greeting, used to wish the other brothers in Corinth well.

13:14. This verse is a Trinitarian benediction that has remained as a traditional Christian farewell. All three persons of the Trinity are included and are attributed as passing on to the believers some aspect of love and communion. To **be with you all,** Paul mentioned **the grace of the Lord Jesus Christ, and the love of God [the Father], and the communion** (Greek, *koinōnia*; "sharing") **of the Holy Ghost**. It is obvious that the personality and divinity of each person in the Trinity is addressed here. Each person in the Godhead, with their particular work in salvation, is mentioned separately. This passage is recognition of the doctrine of the Trinity, which is basic to Christianity. Paul could not have written a better ending for this important letter.

THE EPISTLE OF PAUL THE APOSTLE TO THE GALATIANS

INTRODUCTION

Author

The opening verse identifies the author of Galatians as the apostle Paul. Apart from a few nineteenth-century scholars, no one has seriously questioned his authorship. The author calls himself Paul both in the opening verse and in the body of the letter (5:2). Most of the first two chapters are autobiographical and harmonize with the events in Paul's life as recorded in the book of Acts.

Date

The date of Galatians depends to a great extent on the destination of the letter. There are two main views: (1) The older North Galatian theory holds that the letter was addressed to churches located in north-central Asia Minor (Pessinus, Ancyra, and Tavium), where the Gauls had settled when they invaded the area in the third century BC. Paul visited this area on his second missionary journey, though Acts contains no reference to such a visit. This view maintains that Galatians was written between AD 53 and 57 from Ephesus or Macedonia. (2) According to the South Galatian theory, Galatians was written to churches in the southern area of the Roman province of Galatia (Antioch, Iconium, Lystra, and Derbe) that Paul founded on his first missionary journey. Some believe that Galatians was written from Syrian Antioch in AD 48–49 after Paul's first journey and before the Jerusalem council meeting (see Acts 15). Others say that Galatians was written in Syrian Antioch or Corinth between AD 51 and 53.

Background

"Judaizers" were Jewish Christians who believed, among other things, that a number of the ceremonial practices of the Old Testament were still binding on the New Testament church. Their "gospel" proclaimed not only the Messiah, Jesus, as God's fulfillment of His promises to His people the Jews but also the covenant made to their father Abraham and the law given to Moses. In some sense, then, the special status of the Jews was folded into the messianic privileges of believing in Jesus, the Messiah. In short, the Judaizers insisted on Jesus plus Judaism. For Gentiles, that meant Jesus plus becoming a Jew through circumcision (the sign of the covenant with Abraham/Jesus) and the law (which binds the covenant). Consequently, after Paul's successful campaign in Galatia, they insisted that Gentile converts to Christianity become circumcised and abide by observations of the law (see, e.g., 5:2–4; 4:21; 6:12–13). Other motives apparently heightened their opposition to the preaching of Paul. The Judaizers argued that Paul was not an authentic apostle and that, desiring to make the message more appealing to Gentiles, he had removed from the gospel certain legal requirements. The Judaizers may have been motivated also by a desire to avoid the persecution of Zealot Jews, who objected to their fraternizing with Gentiles (see 6:12).

Paul responded by clearly establishing his apostolic authority and thereby substantiating the gospel he preached. By introducing additional requirements for justification (e.g., works of the law), his adversaries had perverted the gospel of grace and, unless prevented, would have brought Paul's converts into the bondage of legalism. It is by grace through faith alone that man is justified, and it is by faith alone that he is to live out his new life in the freedom of the Spirit.

Theme and Theological Message

For Paul, the acknowledgment of the crucified Jesus as God's Messiah logically implied the nullification of the law (see 3:15–26), and with it circumcision. "I do not frustrate [lit., "nullify"] the grace of God: for if righteousness come by the law, then Christ is dead in vain" (2:21). Therefore, Galatians stands as an eloquent and vigorous apologetic for the essential New Testament truth that man is justified by faith in Jesus Christ—by nothing less and nothing more—and that he is sanctified not by legalistic works but by the obedience that comes from faith in God's work for him, in him, and through him by the grace and power of Christ and the Holy Spirit. It was the rediscovery of the basic message of Galatians that brought about the Reformation. Galatians is often referred to as "Luther's book," because Martin Luther relied so strongly on this letter in his writings and arguments against the prevailing theology of his day. A key verse is 2:16 (see discussion there).

Outline

I. Introduction (1:1–9)
   A. Salutation (1:1–5)
   B. Denunciation (1:6–9)
II. Personal: Authentication of the Apostle of Liberty and Faith (1:10–2:21)
   A. Paul's Gospel Was Received by Special Revelation (1:10–12)
   B. Paul's Gospel Was Independent of the Jerusalem Apostles and the Judean Churches (1:13–2:21)
      1. Evidenced by His Early Activities as a Christian (1:13–17)
      2. Evidenced by His First Post-Christian Visit to Jerusalem (1:18–24)
      3. Evidenced by His Second Post-Christian Visit to Jerusalem (2:1–10)
      4. Evidenced by His Rebuke of Peter at Antioch (2:11–21)
III. Doctrinal: Justification of the Doctrine of Liberty and Faith (chaps. 3–4)
   A. The Galatians' Experience of the Gospel (3:1–5)
   B. The Experience of Abraham (3:6–9)

C. The Curse of the Law (3:10–14)
D. The Priority of the Promise (3:15–18)
E. The Purpose of the Law (3:19–25)
F. Sons, Not Slaves (3:26–4:11)
G. Appeal to Enter into Freedom from Law (4:12–20)
H. The Allegory of Hagar and Sarah (4:21–31)
IV. Practical: Practice of the Life of Liberty and Faith (5:1–6:10)
A. Exhortation to Freedom (5:1–12)
B. Life by the Spirit, Not by the Flesh (5:13–26)
C. Call for Mutual Help (6:1–10)
V. Conclusion (6:11–18)

Bibliography

Barclay, William. *The Letters to the Galatians and Ephesians*. Daily Study Bible. Rev. ed. Philadelphia: Westminster, 1976.

Bruce, F. F. *Commentary on Galatians*. Grand Rapids, MI: Zondervan, 1982.

George, Timothy. *Galatians*. The New American Commentary 30. Nashville: Broadman & Holman, 1994.

Guthrie, Donald. *Galatians*. Grand Rapids, MI: Zondervan,1973.

Lightfoot, Joseph Barber. *The Epistle of St. Paul to the Galatians*. 1865. Reprint, Grand Rapids, MI: Zondervan, 1957.

McKnight, Scot. *Galatians*. Grand Rapids, MI: Zondervan, 1995.

Witherington, Ben, III. *Grace in Galatia: A Commentary on Paul's Letters to the Galatians*. Grand Rapids, MI: Eerdmans, 1998.

EXPOSITION

I. Introduction (1:1–9)

A. Salutation (1:1–5)

1:1. Paul, as was customary and conventional in letters of the time, put his name at the beginning of his letters (for more information on Paul, see discussions on Acts 9:1; Phil. 3:4–14). **An apostle**, Paul was sent on a mission with full authority of representation, as an ambassador (see *Zondervan KJV Study Bible* note on 1 Cor. 1:1). Given the Judaizers' opposition to his apostleship (see Introduction: "Background"), Paul opened his letter with the credentials of his apostleship and its character, defined by its origin through Christ. With the words **raised him from the dead**, Paul gave principal emphasis to the resurrection, the central affirmation of the Christian

faith (see Acts 17:18; Rom. 1:4; 1 Cor. 15:20; 1 Peter 1:3), for two reasons: (1) because it validated the message of his apostleship, the gospel, and (2) because he had seen the risen Christ, Paul was qualified to be an apostle (see Acts 1:22 and discussion; 2:32; 1 Cor. 15:8).

1:2. Brethren, or fellow Christians (see 3:15; 4:12; 5:11; 6:18), in this case probably coworkers in spreading the gospel and planting churches (see Phil. 4:21). The plural **churches** makes it clear that this letter was a circular letter, intended to be read to several congregations. The term **Galatia** occurs four times in the New Testament. In 2 Timothy 4:10, the reference is uncertain. In 1 Peter 1:1, it refers to the northern area of Asia Minor occupied by the Gauls.

Here and in 1 Corinthians 16:1, Paul probably used the term to refer to the Roman province of Galatia and an additional area to the south, through which he traveled on his first missionary journey (see Introduction: "Date"; see also Acts 13:14–14:23).

1:3. Grace be to you and peace is characteristic of the opening of Paul's epistles (see Rom. 1:7; 1 Cor. 1:3; 2 Cor. 1:2; Gal. 1:3; Eph. 1:2; Phil. 1:2; Col. 1:2; 1 Thess. 1:1; 2 Thess. 1:2; Philem. 1:3). "Grace" is a Christian adaptation of a common Greek form of greeting (see discussions on John 4:1–3; Eph. 1:2). "Peace" is the common Hebrew form of greeting (see discussions on John 14:27; 20:19; Eph. 1:2). The meaning of both is informed by the added words, **from God the Father, and from our Lord Jesus Christ.**

1:4. For our sins. See Matthew 1:21; John 1:29; 1 Corinthians 15:3; 1 Peter 2:24. **This present evil world,** or "age," refers to the present period of the world's history (see *KJV Study Bible* note on 2 Cor. 4:4; discussion on Eph. 1:21), which stands in stark contrast with the "age" to come (the climax of the messianic age). This present age is characterized by wickedness (Eph. 2:2; 6:12), and its influence is to be countered with new thinking, God's revealed truth (Rom. 12:2).

1:5. For other doxologies, see Romans 9:5; 11:36; 16:27; Ephesians 3:21; 1 Timothy 1:17.

B. Denunciation (1:6–9)

1:6–7. So soon (v. 6) likely refers to the shortness of time between the Galatians' conversion (Paul's founding visit) and the coming of the Judaizers. The gospel they brought (see Introduction: "Background") swayed some to defect (**removed**) from the true gospel to **another gospel.** Paul impressed on them not only his surprise but something that may have surprised them. Contrary to claims, "another gospel" did not move them toward God but away **from Him that called you into the grace of Christ.** The call of God comes by virtue of the grace of Christ. Grace is the "good" in the "good news" of the gospel. The grace of Christ is the core of the true, unadulterated gospel and the chief characteristic by

which one appreciates its difference ("another," v. 6) and its uniqueness ("not another," v. 7) from other so-called gospels. **Some that trouble you** (v. 7) specifies the Judaizers (see Introduction: "Background"). Their message, the un-gospel, had done two things among the Galatian churches: (1) unsettled the Galatian believers and (2) perverted the true gospel. As the word **pervert** implies, the Judaizers had contorted the gospel to such a degree that it could no longer be called the gospel; it had been disfigured and no longer resembled "good news."

1:8–9. Paul made it clear that the messenger, whether earthly or heavenly, was not what mattered most. The message, **that which we have preached unto you** (v. 8), was what mattered most. For, as Paul wrote to the church at Rome, the gospel "is the power of God unto salvation" (Rom. 1:16). Since salvation itself was at stake, it was not too strong for Paul to call **accursed** (v. 8–9) the one who preaches **any other gospel.** The Greek word for "accursed" (*anathema*) originally referred to a pagan temple offering in payment for a vow and devoted to sacred destruction. Later it came to represent a curse (see v. 9; 1 Cor. 12:3; 16:22; Rom. 9:3).

II. Personal: Authentication of the Apostle of Liberty and Faith (1:10–2:21)

A. Paul's Gospel Was Received by Special Revelation (1:10–12)

1:10. Paul was in the business of persuading men, not God, and pleasing God, not men. If matters had been the other way around, as evidently some had charged, then Paul would have not been a **servant of Christ.** Paul once wore "the yoke of bondage" (5:1), but having been set free from sin by the redemption that is in Christ, he became a slave of righteousness, a slave of God (see Rom. 6:18, 22).

1:11–12. I certify you, brethren (v. 11). A similar phrase is found in 1 Corinthians 15:1, where Paul sets forth the gospel he received. **The gospel ... preached of me,** Paul called "my gospel" in Romans 2:16; 16:25. As F. F. Bruce (*Commentary on Galatians,* p. 88) aptly pointed out, Paul also called his gospel "the gospel of God" (1 Thess. 2:8, 9; 2 Cor. 11:7) because God authored it and "the gospel of Christ" (1 Thess. 3:2; 2 Cor. 2:12; Rom. 15:9) because Christ is its content (see Rom. 1:1–3). The words **not after man** make it plain that Paul's gospel, in nature and character, was not of human ingenuity or authority, nor was he indebted to any human for its reception or instruction. The validity of Paul's gospel was ensured by none other than **the revelation of Jesus Christ** (v. 12; see Eph. 3:2–6).

B. Paul's Gospel Was Independent of the Jerusalem Apostles and the Judean Churches (1:13–2:21)

In defense of his gospel, Paul opened with an autobiography of his changed life, a powerful witness to the genuine gospel over against the Judaizers' gospel (see Introduction, "Background"). Paul's opening point and evolving case is clear: Why would one who was so completely committed to the values of Jewish faith and practice turn to embrace that which he persecuted as wrong? One would not, Paul argued, unless God Himself intervened and revealed to him his error, calling him to what is right and therefore bringing about a conversion so radical it owed nothing to his once beloved life with its law and its circumcision but only to the risen Christ. The very gospel he had once persecuted he now preached, and it was this very gospel that Jerusalem approved when it was later compared with that of the apostles before him. Indeed, even Peter had to accede and submit to this very gospel. In the end, the implicit question to the Galatians became, by what means do the Judaizers leverage your faith with another gospel?

1. Evidenced by His Early Activities as a Christian (1:13–17)

1:13–14. Paul's **conversation** (v. 13), or "manner of life," **in the Jews' religion** ("Judaism") attested to his piety in the Jewish faith and way of life to the degree that he was a **zealous** (v. 14; see Phil. 3:6) champion of every effort to annihilate the church of God (see 1:23). Further attestation came from none other than the ruling Sanhedrin, which had deemed him fit and granted him formal authoriza-

tion to arrest and imprison Christians (Acts 9:1–2; 22:4–5; 26:10–11). **Ye have heard** (v. 13) may point to Paul's own testimony among the Galatians, but his reputation for piety and persecution was evident to both peers and opponents (see v. 14, 1:23). **The traditions of my fathers** (v. 14) were authoritative ancestral doctrines and customs that regulated religious and social life. These traditions, which may be described as complementary explanation and illustration of the law, were orally transmitted from previous generations and contrasted with the written law of Moses (see the "tradition of the elders," Matt. 15:2 and discussion).

1:15–17. When Paul wrote of how God **separated me from my mother's womb** (v. 15), he declared his calling and apostleship (see Rom. 1:1) to be rooted in the foreordained purposes of God, even as God's servant (Isa. 49:1) and prophet (Jer. 1:5). His professed role in the economy of God's salvation plan was not the consequence of Paul's claim to it but God's calling to it.

Paul's point in 1:15–2:10, that the apostles of Jerusalem recognize (2:6–10) his God-given commission to preach to the Gentiles, begins here with the declaration that God had **called** (v. 15) him and had **reveal[ed] his Son in [him]** (v. 16), which initiated Paul's preaching to the Gentiles and not any conference with human authorities, not even in Jerusalem. **Heathen** (lit., "nations" or "peoples") is the term commonly designated "foreigners," hence pagans, or the non-Jewish world. **Jerusalem** (v. 17) was important because it was not only the religious center of Judaism but the birthplace of Christianity and the recognized capital of apostolic rule. Paul had not been led there but to **Arabia**, the Nabatean kingdom in Transjordan stretching from Damascus southwest to the Suez, and to **Damascus**, the ancient capital of Syria (Aram in the Old Testament). Paul had been converted en route from Jerusalem to Damascus (Acts 9:1–9). That Paul received his message from God and did not confer with **flesh and blood** (v. 16) contested any notion that his gospel omitted crucial tenets (e.g., circumcision) of the gospel that the Judaizers (see Introduction, "Background") asserted came from Jerusalem and the apostles. Remember, it was by grace, Paul asserted, that he had been called (v. 15). In the New Testament, "flesh and blood" always carries the implication of human impotence or imperfection (see Matt. 16:17; 1 Cor. 15:50; Eph. 6:12).

2. Evidenced by His First Post-Christian Visit to Jerusalem (1:18–24)

1:18. Then after three years, or from the time of his departure into Arabia (see 1:16–17). The text does not say he spent the three years in Arabia. **I went up to Jerusalem** probably refers to the visit recorded in Acts 9:26–30, though some equate it with the visit recorded in Acts 11:30. **Peter**, from the Greek word for "stone," is the Aramaic equivalent to "Cephas" (see Matt. 16:18 and discussion). The name designates a like quality in the bearer (see discussion on John 1:42). Paul went **to see**, or "to make the acquaintance of" (Greek, *historeō*; to know by inquiry), Peter. This meeting followed Barnabas's endorsement of Paul (see Acts 9:26–27).

1:19. The only other apostle Paul **saw**, that is, set eyes upon, a verb different from the word "see" in 1:18, was **James** (see James, Introduction: "Author") **the Lord's brother** (see discussion on Luke 8:19). Whether Paul viewed James as numbered among the "other apostles" pivots on the question of whether the word **save** introduces an exception to the whole statement or just the verb "see." Like Paul, James was converted by an appearance of Jesus (see 1 Cor. 15:7). Although not among the original twelve, James rose to prominence in the Jerusalem church (see Acts 12:17; 15:13; 21:18–19).

1:20. Here Paul inserted a solemn oath (**before God**) to underscore his central and vital point: his gospel was not derived from any source save the "revelation of Jesus Christ" (1:12). In other words, it did not come from Jerusalem, despite his visit with Peter and his "sighting" of James.

1:21. Afterwards, or "then," introduces the second of three instances (1:18, 21; 2:1) in which Paul used the same adverb to produce an unbroken account of his missionary movements, independent of Jerusalem, as he was led from the reception of his gospel and calling (see 1:12) to the conference and formal presentation of his gospel in Jerusalem (2:1–10). **Syria and Cilicia** were provinces in Asia Minor. Specifically, Paul went to Tarsus (see Acts 9:30), his hometown.

1:22–24. As a further testimony to Paul's independent missionary work, the churches of Judea didn't even know what Paul looked like, although they **had heard** (lit., "kept hearing"; v. 23) of his preaching. Their response was a tacit confirmation of Paul's gospel apart from any recognition out of Jerusalem. That recognition, as Paul recounted in 2:1–10, came next in Paul's argument. For the moment, as it were, the Galatian readers were standing at the doorstep of the Jerusalem meeting and proceeded to it with these words from the Judean churches ringing in their ears: **they glorified God in me** (v. 24).

3. Evidenced by His Second Post-Christian Visit to Jerusalem (2:1–10)

2:1. Then fourteen years after is probably to be reckoned from the date of Paul's conversion, or "call" (see 1:15–16 and "immediately," 1:16). This probability is strengthened by Paul's use of the same Greek adverb, *epeita* ("Then," or "thereupon"; 1:18, 21; 2:1), that he used to show he was omitting nothing from the succession of events stemming from God's call and revelation of His Son. **I went up again to Jerusalem.** According to some, this refers to the visit mentioned in Acts 11:30; according to others, the one in Acts 15:1–4 (see discussions on Acts 12:1; 15:2). "Went up" is consistently used with reference to Jerusalem in the New Testament, not only because of its elevation but because of its prestige. **Barnabas** means "one who encourages." His given name was Joseph, and he was a Levite from the island of Cyprus (see Acts 4:36 and discussion). Barnabas endorsed Paul in Jerusalem (see Acts 9:26–27) and was Paul's companion on the first missionary journey (see Acts 13:1–14:28). **Titus** was a Gentile Christian who served as Paul's delegate to Corinth and later was left in Crete to oversee the church there (see Titus 1:5). It is likely that Titus was a convert of Paul's early ministry ("mine own son after the common faith," Titus 1:4) and accompanied Paul as a prime example of the gospel Paul preached.

2:2. I went up by revelation. Paul disclosed that the impetus for visiting Jerusalem this time came not from a felt need on his part but from the prompting of God. To whom this revelation came, Paul did not specify (as in 2:12, 16); whether it came to Paul himself, to Barnabas, to fellow believers as at Antioch (Acts 11:27–30), or in some other way, Paul did not make clear. What is clear is that it was not Paul's idea but God's. **Them which were of reputation** points to men of acknowledged authority and refers to James, Peter, and John (see 2:6, 9). To them, Paul had communicated **that gospel which I preach**. Why them? Paul had not been summoned by them. Paul had taken pains to establish that the validity of his gospel was subject not to them but only to Christ. In part, an answer has already been supplied: Paul had been compelled by God ("by revelation"), which accounts for Paul's humility on a matter of such importance. The further answer comes in Paul's use of an athletic metaphor picturing a race than cannot be won but is **run** nonetheless (see 1 Cor. 15:58; Phil. 2:16). Paul did not want to run such a race if there was any possibility (**by any means**) its victory can be assured. The prize to be won was a more unified church and the recognition of the one gospel. That is what was won (see 2:2–10). The words "that gospel which I preach" (present tense) made clear to Paul's Galatian readers that the same gospel he had always preached, and had preached to them, was the very gospel that those "of reputation" heard and recognized. It was "that gospel which I preach" that some Galatians were abandoning at the time of his letter.

2:3–5. In different words, Paul stated that the subject of circumcision, so prominent among the Judaizers (see Introduction: "Background"), was not even raised by "them … of reputation" (2:2), let alone any insistence of it being a necessity, and **Titus** (v. 3) had been right there. On the contrary, the matter was introduced by others, by **false brethren** (v. 4), the Judaizers, who imposed on Gentile converts cir-

cumcision and adherence to the law of Moses (see Acts 15:5; 2 Cor. 11:26). This Paul called **bondage**. The **liberty which we have in Christ Jesus** (see 5:1, 13; Rom. 6:18, 20, 22; 8:2) they sought only to detect and **spy out**. The Greek word *kataskopeō* can carry a tone of treachery and is used in the Septuagint (the Greek translation of the Old Testament) in 2 Samuel 10:3 and 1 Chronicles 19:3 to refer to spying out a territory. Paul not only describes the manner of their admission, but his vocabulary decries their motives: they were clandestinely smuggled in **that they might bring us into bondage**. It should not be missed that Paul saw a parallel between their earlier actions in Jerusalem and their present actions in Galatia. Paul fixed the connection between the two situations when he addressed his readers directly (**with you;** v. 5). His Galatian readers may have fairly imagined that as Paul had given the Judaizers and their gospel of bondage no quarter then, nothing now had changed.

2:6. These who seemed to be somewhat (see discussion on 2:2) refers to James, Peter, and John (see 2:9). Paul's use of the present tense here (as well as in 2:2, 9) points to the issue: they were "being reputed" (see 2:2) at the time of his writing by the Judaizers in what had become among the Galatians a contest over the right gospel. Paul stated that it did not matter what he or anyone else thought about them. What mattered was what God thought. **God accepteth no man's person** (see Deut. 10:17; 1 Sam. 16:7; Luke 20:21; James 2:1). Literally, the Greek reads, "God does not accept the face of man" (or a human being), an expression that is common in the New Testament (see Luke 20:21; Acts 10:34; Rom. 2:11; Eph. 6:9; Col. 3:25; 1 Tim. 5:21; James 2:1, 9). In a Mediterranean culture that valued the giving and accepting of honor, Paul asserted quite powerfully that God has a different outlook on outward human evaluations of honor or status: they matter not at all. In short, Paul was saying that those who were esteemed—and it did not matter what they were because it was irrelevant to God—**added nothing to me**. They neither added nor subtracted anything with respect to the gospel that he preached, nor to his honor or status as an apostle. Paul's tone, although not one of disrespect (as 2:2, 9, make clear; see "pillars," 2:9), may well have been agitated by the echo of reported appeals to just such reputation by the Judaizers who had attacked the gospel he had preached among the Galatian churches.

2:7–9. But contrariwise (v. 7), or just the opposite of any recommended alteration, there was only recognition of (**saw**, v. 7; and **perceived**, v. 9) Paul's calling from God to the **gospel of the uncircumcision** (v. 7). Paul's ministry was not exclusively to the Gentiles. In fact, he regularly went first to the synagogue when arriving in a new location (see discussion on Acts 13:14). He did, however, consider himself to be foremost an apostle to the Gentiles (see Rom. 11:13 and discussion). Paul acknowledged **James** (see discussion on 1:19), **Cephas** (see discussion on 1:18), **and John** (v. 9) as the ascribed church **pillars,** a common metaphor for those who represent and strongly support an institution. **The right hands of fellowship** they had extended, a common practice among both Hebrews and Greeks, indicating a pledge of friendship and cooperation, was a proof of their recognition of Paul. The message to Paul's readers was clear: any claim from the Judaizers that the Jerusalem leadership disapproved of Paul's ministry is patently false and contrary to the divine approval they duly recognized.

2:10. One thing James, Peter, and John asked was that Paul encourage Gentile churches to **remember the poor.** Even that was not novel to Paul's attitude or practice. It may have fallen into line with an impetus for coming to Jerusalem in the first place if, as some have suggested, the revelation of 2:2 was in any way connected to the events of Acts 11:27–30.

4. Evidenced by His Rebuke of Peter at Antioch (2:11–21)

2:11. Antioch was the leading city of Syria and third-leading city of the Roman Empire (after Rome and Alexandria). From there, Paul had been sent out on his missionary journeys (see Acts 13:1–3; 14:26). Peter **was to be blamed** for yielding to the pressure of the circumcision party (the Judaizers; see Introduction: "Background") and thus going against what

he knew to be right. The seriousness of Paul's action was due to the seriousness of Peter's. God stands behind the passive "was to be blamed," which is more accurately rendered "stands condemned" (perfect tense). "God condemns what Peter has done" (Witherington, *Grace in Galatia*, pp. 151–52; see Bruce, *Commentary on Galatians*, p. 159).

2:12–13. Paul set forth the reason for Peter's condemnation and opposition and indirectly painted a picture of the early church at Antioch, that influential church where the disciples were first called Christians (Acts 11:26). Peter was there, as were Barnabas and other Jews. Like Peter, they were comfortable living after the manner of Gentiles (2:14). **He did eat with the Gentiles** (v. 12) summarizes the regular and unrestricted fellowship Peter and others enjoyed. This was as it should be, as Peter well knew from his rooftop vision in Joppa and subsequent fellowship with Cornelius (see Acts 10:9–11:18). Such was the atmosphere before the arrival of certain men of James. After their arrival, Paul described Peter's actions as a contagious reduction of and final withdrawal from fellowship with the Gentile Christians. **Other Jews** (v. 13) and even **Barnabas,** Paul's ally in the evangelism of the Gentiles, followed Peter's lead out of fear of **them which were of the circumcision** (v. 12). These were not them who **came from James,** nor were they Jewish Christians, but Zealot Jews (see Introduction: "Background") who persecuted (see 6:12) Jews and Jewish Christians for fraternizing with Gentiles. It is probable that James and the others thought the mission of bringing the gospel to the Jews, of which Peter was the apostle to the Jews (see 2:7–8), was in jeopardy because of Peter's open fellowship with Gentiles in flagrant violation of Jewish purity and dietary laws.

2:14. Paul publicly and directly challenged Peter, addressing him as one who **livest after the manner of Gentiles.** In other words, Paul told Peter: You do not observe Jewish customs, especially dietary restrictions (see 2:12). For Peter to now resume Jewish practices was to **compellest ... the Gentiles to live as do the Jews.** Peter's actions amounted to imposing Jewish purity and dietary laws as a condition for fellowship with Peter and other like-minded Jewish Christians.

Such conditions for acceptance struck at the heart of the gospel. "To live as do the Jews" translates the Greek verb *Ioudaizō*, from which comes the expressions "Judaize" and "Judaizer." It is a significant word that Paul used here only, and it occurs nowhere else in the New Testament. It means to adopt Jewish customs and practices, including Sabbath observance, laws concerning purity and diet, and circumcision. In effect, Peter's actions were not "Christianizing" but "Judaizing" the Gentiles. Paul made clear to Peter that his actions were promoting a unity of believers found, not in Christ, but in Judaism.

2:15–16. Paul made it plain that Jews and Gentiles alike are justified by faith and not by works of the law. Verse 16 is a key verse in Galatians (see Introduction: "Theme and Theological Message"). Three times it tells us that no one is justified by observing the law, and three times it underscores the indispensable requirement of placing one's faith in Christ. **Justified by ... the faith of Jesus Christ** (v. 16) is the essence of the gospel message (see Rom. 3:20, 28; Phil. 3:9; see also discussions on Rom. 3:24, 28). Faith is the means by which justification is received, not its basis. On the other hand, no one is justified **by the works of the law**. Paul was not depreciating the law itself, for he clearly maintained that God's "law is holy ... and just, and good" (Rom. 7:12). He was arguing against an illegitimate use of the Old Testament law that made the observance of that law the grounds for God's acceptance.

2:17–18. We ourselves also (v. 17) underscores the perspective of the Jewish Christians (see 2:15–16) or Jews who sought justification in Christ (2:15–16) and not in the law. As such, they came to justification just as "sinners of the Gentiles" (2:15); seeking justification in Christ and not in the law implies the recognition of sin and the ineffectiveness of the law to justify. Of course, Paul quickly clarified that justification apart from the law did not mean that Jesus promotes or services immorality (v. 17b). It means that Jesus does what the law cannot: justify. Then Paul addressed in principle what Peter, Barnabas, and other Jews had done by resuming Jewish practices: **If** (v. 18) as a Jewish Christian

I build again what I effectively destroyed (i.e., the law) when I accepted justification by faith in Jesus, **I make myself a transgressor** of that which cannot justify. Moreover, such a rebuilding of the law communicates that justification in Christ is ineffective.

2:19–20. Paul had rhetorically identified himself with Jews who sought justification through Christ. Now the "I" became most personal as he distanced himself from any notion of the law's vitality in justification: there could be no transgression of the law because he was **dead to the law** (v. 19; see discussion on Rom. 7:4). Where did Paul die to the law? He died at the cross. Every believer who identifies with the accomplished work of Christ recognizes that he or she has been **crucified with Christ** (v. 20; see 5:24; 6:14; Rom. 6:8–10; 7:6; see also discussion on Rom. 6:7). The only life that has ever followed crucifixion is the resurrected life of Jesus Christ. That was the life Paul now enjoyed. The words **gave himself for me** (see 1:4; 1 Tim. 2:6; Titus 2:14) tenderly and personally summarizes the profound truth that the death of Jesus abolished the law's indictment by sacrificially settling the debt that the law emphatically points out is owed to God's holiness. Now there is no indictment for those in Christ and therefore no law with power to inhibit the life God wants believers to live through Jesus Christ. Such life and its power can only be gained through a lively relationship with God made possible by Jesus Christ.

2:21. However, Paul said, to empower the law by making it the means of righteousness is to **frustrate** (or nullify) **the grace of God**. When that is done, one nullifies the power and effect of Christ's death: **Christ is dead in vain**. In short, to mingle legalism with grace distorts grace and makes a mockery of the cross.

III. Doctrinal: Justification of the Doctrine of Liberty and Faith (chaps. 3–4)

A. The Galatians' Experience of the Gospel (3:1–5)

3:1. Paul's use of the word **foolish** (see Luke 24:25; Rom. 1:14; 1 Tim. 6:9; Titus 3:3) to vocalize the absurdity of the Galatian defection, corresponds to his use of **bewitched**. The Galatians were not mentally deficient, but their powers of perception had been so sorely altered, it was if they had been put under a spell. The question, **who hath ...?** (see 5:7), although rhetorical since Paul knew the answer, prodded the Galatians into picturing the legalistic Judaizers (see Introduction, "Background") that had been among them pedaling "another gospel" (1:6). Rhetorical questions, however, prod one into looking beyond the obvious answers in the mind to the deeper issues in the heart. **Evidently set forth, crucified** (see 1 Cor. 1:23; 2:2) translates the Greek verb meaning "to publicly portray or placard as crucified." With this expression, Paul was recalling not only the portrayal but also the purpose of Jesus' death on the cross. In other words, Paul was asking how the importance of Jesus' crucifixion and death could be ignored or overlooked; it is the crux of the gospel. How could they get around something so obvious? Yet some of them were acting as though they had never seen the cross, by embracing the legalism of the Judaizers' gospel.

3:2. Paul knew the answer. Works of the law were not the substance of the gospel he preached or the basis for **the Spirit** they received. Their experience of the Spirit (see 3:5; 4:6) could not be denied, and the admission was a concession they owed not to works of the law but to **the hearing of faith** (see 3:5). It was also an admission to Paul's argument against the Judaizers' **works of the law**. The work of the Spirit could in no way be attributed to "works," and from this point on in Galatians, Paul refers to the Holy Spirit sixteen times.

3:3–4. Begun in the Spirit ... made perfect (v. 3). The Spirit is the hallmark of life in Christ (Eph. 1:13–14; Rom. 8:9). Both salvation and sanctification are the work of the Holy Spirit. To try to perfect **by the flesh** what only God can do through the power of the Spirit is folly (**foolish**). "Flesh" is a reference to human nature in its unregenerate weakness. All attempts to achieve righteousness by works, including circumcision, belong not to faith but to the "flesh." Paul hoped that by leading his Galatian converts through a course of right thinking, those who had been misled would return to the true gospel (v. 4).

3:5. Paul reiterated the contrast between **the works of the law** and **the hearing of faith**, (as in 3:2). Although the Spirit's **miracles**, or "mighty deeds" (Greek, *dynamis*), belonged to the marks of an apostle (2 Cor. 12:12), there is no grammatical or theological reason in Paul's teaching on the Spirit to exclude from his meaning here the whole range of the Spirit's ministry, both **among you** and "in you" (see 4:6; 5:16–25). Paul's use of the Greek word *epichorēgeō*, here translated **ministereth**, suggests (as in 2 Cor. 9:10 and Col. 2:19) the provision or supply of a necessity. Accordingly, Paul conveyed that God's provision of the Spirit supplies to faith what is necessary for a relationship with God. The Spirit belongs to God's grace and the reception of faith; its provision is not a payoff for works, performance, or earnings.

B. The Experience of Abraham (3:6–9)

3:6–7. Abraham provides a crucial example. **Even as** (v. 6) "the hearing of faith" (3:5), not works, was operative in God's supply of the Spirit, Abraham was justified (accounted righteous) by faith, not works. Abraham's example was pivotal to Paul's argument with the Judaizers. If, for all intents and purposes, the Judaizers required Gentiles like the Galatians to become Jews to be justified in Christ, one might ask how Abraham was justified and became the father of the Jews. Was it by works of the law and circumcision, as required by the Judaizers, or by faith alone? Paul's answer came in a declaration: it is through faith that a person belongs to **the children of Abraham** (v. 7). Abraham was the physical and spiritual father of the Jewish race (see John 8:33, 39, 53; Acts 7:2; Rom. 4:12). Here all believers (Jews and Gentiles) are called his spiritual children (see discussions on Rom. 4:11–12). They are also referred to as the "seed" (3:16; Heb. 2:16), or "descendants," of Abraham.

3:8. The scripture, foreseeing is a personification of the Scripture that calls attention to its divine origin (see 1 Tim. 5:18). By virtue of the Scripture, the testimony of Abraham's example is unimpeachable. This very same Scripture provided the divine and advance testimony to the gospel preached to the Galatians, not by the Judaizers, but by Paul. At the very inception of all that became Jewish, Abraham, the Gentile who became the father of the Jews, was justified by faith. Thus, the blessing of **all nations** ("Gentiles") in Abraham was conceived with Abraham and consummated with Christ (see 3:14–15).

3:9. The expression **faithful Abraham** again highlights and underscores the role of faith; Paul uses the adjective (*pistos*) of the verb "believed" (*pisteō*) in 3:6. Paul develops this theme at length in Romans 4 (see also Heb. 11:8–19).

C. The Curse of the Law (3:10–14)

3:10. Are of the works of the law is Paul's shorthand to describe those who insist on pursuing righteousness through works. Seeking to fulfill the demands of the law serves only to confirm **the curse** because no one under the law ever perfectly keeps the law. God's blessing has never been earned but has always been freely given. **All things ... do them** (Deut. 27:26) defines the scope of the demand and also the potential for failing to keep the law (see James 2:10).

3:11. That no man is justified by the law ... is evident. Not only is it plain and clear, but Abraham's justification by faith was not an exception or a special case. In his argument, Paul moved from the principle in particular (Abraham, 3:6) to the principle in general, citing Habakkuk 2:4 to show that the law was never God's method for justification. Paul's citation comes from the Septuagint, the Greek translation of the Old Testament. The wording in Greek reads, "The just on the basis of faith shall live." The curse of the law (3:10) is contrasted with life that comes "on the basis of [by] faith." **Just** (or "righteous") is the noun and **justified** its verb; thus, the sense becomes clear: "the one justified on the basis of faith shall live." F. F. Bruce (*Commentary on Galatians*, p. 161) rendered it, "It is the one that is righteous (justified) by faith [not by law] that will live (find life)" and therefore not come under the curse.

3:12. Paul cited Leviticus 18:5 (see Luke 10:28) to demonstrate that the law has to do with only works (**doeth them**; see 3:10), not faith. Anticipating 3:13

and comparing Romans 10:5, one may infer that only one, Jesus Christ, has fulfilled the demands of the law.

3:13. Christ hath redeemed us from the curse of the law (see 4:5; Rom. 8:3). **Tree** is used in classical Greek of stocks and poles on which bodies were impaled. Here it is used of the cross (see Acts 5:30; 10:39; 1 Peter 2:24). The **curse** (see 3:10), or penalty of death, that must be met or suffered because of the law's demand has been met and suffered by Christ. To capture the sense of what Christ has done for us, Paul used the word **redeemed**, a metaphor familiar to his contemporaries from the formal emancipation of a slave. At the price of His own life, Jesus has satisfied the debt demanded (see 1 Cor. 7:23). To the same realm of thought belong Paul's associations of bondage (slavery) under the law (see 4:9; 4:24; 5:1).

3:14. Two promises stated as purposes (Greek, *hina*; "that") are realized through the redeeming death of Jesus Christ. First, **the blessing of Abraham** (see 3:8; Rom. 4:1–5) to the Gentiles is fulfilled through "his seed" (see 3:16), and second, **the promise of the Spirit** is supplied (see 3:5; Ezek. 36:26; 37:14; 39:29; John 14:16; Eph. 1:13).

D. The Priority of the Promise (3:15–18)

3:15. Brethren (see discussion on 1:2) solicited not only the Galatians' attention but also their identification with Paul and the human comparison he was about to draw between earthly and heavenly covenants. **After the manner of men**, or "drawn from our common human experience," established the vantage point of Paul's argument as he moved from the lesser to the greater. The Greek word for **covenant** (*diathēkē*) normally indicates a last will or testament, which is the legal instrument Paul was referring to here. In the Septuagint (the Greek translation of the Old Testament), it had been widely used of God's covenant with His people (see Matt. 26:28; Luke 1:72; Acts 3:25; 7:8; 2 Cor. 3:14; Heb. 8:9), so Paul's choice of analogy was apt for his purpose. Paul's point was that everybody acknowledges and counts on the inviolable and irrevocable character of a man's last will and testament. Paul argued that if a covenant a man sets up is binding, how much more so when God sets up a covenant?

3:16-18. The promises (v. 16; see discussions on Rom. 4:13; 9:4) of which Paul wrote were made in a covenant with **Abraham and his seed**, which is Jesus Christ. This covenant, Paul argued, God set up apart from and before the law given much later to Moses. That law cannot change or amend the covenant previously made by God. **Four hundred and thirty years** (v. 17; see Exod. 12:40-41) is the period of time the children of Israel dwelt in Egypt. The law was given to Moses after they left. The period in Egypt is designated in round numbers as "four hundred years" in Genesis 15:13; Acts 7:6.

E. The Purpose of the Law (3:19-25)

3:19. From the time of Abraham, the promise covenanted to him (Gen. 12:2-3, 7; 15:18-20; 17:4-8) had stood at the center of God's relationship with His people. After the exodus, the law contained in the Sinaitic covenant (Exod. 19-24) became an additional element in that relationship—what Jeremiah by implication called the "old covenant" when he brought God's promise of a "new covenant" (Jer. 31:31-34). Paul posed and answered an obvious question. If the law does not change or amend the covenant with Abraham, why was it introduced or **added**? Paul expounded a twofold answer: (1) to make evident the **transgressions** (v. 19) being committed (see Rom. 5:13, 20) and (2) to "conclude [or confine] all under sin" (3:22, see Rom. 11:32). Thus, the law was added **till the seed should come**. After God promised to regenerate the nations through Abraham's seed (Jesus Christ), He added the Mosaic law to reveal and restrain sin until Christ should come and provide righteousness to all who believe (Rom. 10:4). The purpose of the law has been fulfilled within those who have obtained righteousness and sonship in Christ (see 3:24-25). **By angels** (see Deut. 33:2; Acts 7:38, 53; Heb. 2:2) **in the hand of a mediator** (Moses) serves to describe the mediation involved in God's giving of the law. Paul's argument capitalized on contemporary rabbinic views of the law's mediation to contrast the superiority of the promise given directly by God (see 3:20).

3:20. The Mosaic covenant was a formal arrangement of mutual commitments between God and Israel, with Moses as the mediator. Since the promise God covenanted with Abraham involved commitment only from God's side (and God is one; see *KJV Study Bible* note on Deut. 6:4), no mediator was involved.

3:21. The reason the law is not opposed to God's promise to Abraham is that, although in itself it cannot save, it serves to reveal sin, which alienates God from man, and to show the need for the salvation that the promise offers.

3:22. The Greek word translated **concluded** means "to catch by enclosing," as when a shoal of fish is netted on every side. The same word is translated "shut up" in 3:23. No one can escape the confining and imprisoning effect of the Scripture, which is here equivalent to the written law.

3:23. Faith, or faith in Christ (see 3:22), is the only key that liberates one confined or **kept under the law**. Paul's terminology was consistent with the Roman practice of using prisons primarily for holding prisoners until the disposition of their cases. To be a prisoner of sin (see 3:22) and a prisoner of the law amounts to much the same, because law reveals and stimulates sin (see 4:3; Rom. 7:8; Col. 2:20).

3:24-25. Was our schoolmaster (v. 24) translates the Greek *paidagōgos* (from which "pedagogue" is derived). It refers to the personal slave-attendant who supervised a freeborn boy wherever he went and had charge over the child's rearing and behavior. Contrary to the English use of the word pedagogue, the *paidagōgos* was not the teacher but was responsible for getting the child to the teacher for his education. After this analogy from daily life, Paul portrayed the law as the *paidagōgos* that leads one to the teacher, Jesus Christ. Once the child is in the hands of the teacher, the *paidagōgos* steps back and does not interfere with the teacher. In Roman culture, the duties of the *paidagōgos* were concluded when the boy assumed the toga of adulthood.

F. Sons, Not Slaves (3:26-4:11)

3:26-27. By adoption, the justified believer enters a relationship with God the Father as a full-fledged heir in God's family, with all the attendant rights and privileges (see 4:1–7; Rom. 8:14–17). Since Paul was writing to Christians, some of whom were struggling with their identity and privileges because of the misinformation of the Judaizers, he stressed that they were the full-fledged children of God through faith. The act of being **baptized into Christ** (v. 27; see Rom. 6:3–11; 1 Cor. 12:13) was outward proof of their inward faith and commensurate adoption. To **put on Christ** is to be clothed in His identity and cloaked in the privileges of His sonship.

3:28–29. Unity in Christ transcends ethnic, social, and sexual distinctions (see Rom. 10:12; 1 Cor. 12:13; Eph. 2:15–16). These earthly distinctions and roles remain, but all who are in **Christ** (v. 28) are positioned as full and equal sons and heirs of God. **Free** (see 5:1, 13; Rom. 6:18, 20, 22; 8:2) and "freedom" are key words in Galatians, occurring ten times (here; 4:22–23, 26, 30–31; 5:1, 13; see "liberty" in 2:4). All who are "in Christ," or Christians, regardless of ethnic heredity or pedigree, are Abraham's true, spiritual descendants (v. 29).

4:1. In the ancient Mediterranean world, customs connected to a child's status and advance to adulthood were more uniformly observed than are customary today. Once again, these human customs helped to make plain the spiritual truths of the gospel as Paul communicated them to the Galatians. A minor, or **a child** (compare "men" in 1 Cor. 14:20; "perfect" in Phil. 3:15), regardless of pedigree or inheritance, has no decision-making authority; the heir has no more freedom in this regard than a slave does.

4:2. In Roman and Greek law, **tutors and governors**, or guardians and trustees, have distinct legal responsibilities in the charge of a minor. Here, like the *paidagōgos*, they represent the role of the law governing the child until he comes of age, or **until the time appointed of the father**. Paul's wording has a double duty, strategically drawing on the meaning of familiar customs while anticipating new spiritual meanings. In this case, the "time appointed" is echoed in "the fulness of the time" in 4:4.

4:3. Even so we are the words Paul used to draw a spiritual comparison to the human customs surrounding the custody of a minor (4:1–2). **In bondage**, as defined by the restricted status of a minor (4:1), goes back also to 3:23 (see discussion there). The Greek term used for **elements** meant essentially "things placed side by side in a row" (as the ABCs) and then came to mean fundamental principles or basic elements of various kinds. The context here suggests that it refers to the elemental forms of religion, whether those of the Jews ("under the law," 4:5) or those of the Gentiles (under their old religious bondage, 4:8).

4:4. The fulness of the time was come. "The time appointed" (4:2) by God for His children to become adult sons and heirs. In Paul's immediate argument, the words **God sent forth his Son** (see John 1:14; 3:16; Rom. 1:1–6; 1 John 4:14) are descriptive not only of the divine initiative but also the full authority of an heir (see 4:2) as He undertakes His representation of the Father who sent Him. **Made of a woman** shows that Christ was truly human. **Made under the law** shows that Christ was subject to the Jewish law.

4:5. The adoption of sons not only incorporates a child into the family but invests the child with all the rights of sonship (see Rom. 8:15, where "the Spirit of adoption" is contrasted with "the spirit of bondage"; see also Eph. 1:5). God takes into His family as fully recognized sons and heirs both Jews (those who had been under law) and Gentiles who believe in Christ. Adoption is linked with "redemption" (see 3:13; 1:10), the emancipation from slavery, leading to a startling reversal of status, with the slave becoming a son with full rights and an inheritance.

4:6–7. The Spirit of his Son (v. 6), the selfsame "Spirit of God" in Romans 8:9 (see Rom. 8:2; Eph. 1:13–14), identifies the believer as belonging to God and being His child, just like His Son, Jesus. "Of His Son" profiles the Christlike character and quality of the believer's experience of the Spirit. Through the Spirit, a Christian's character and relationship with God is patterned on Jesus and shaped by the image of Christ. Thus, the Spirit is a new "tutor" (4:2). The Greek for **crying** is a vivid verb expressing deep emotion, often used of an inarticulate cry. In Matthew 27:50, it is used of Jesus' final cry. **Abba, Father**, is the instinctive and intimate cry of the Spirit, here given expression first in Aramaic (*abba*) and then in Greek (*patēr*). "Abba" (see Mark 14:36; Luke 11:2), expressive of an especially tender relationship with God as Father, is likened to the affectionate use of "Papa." All in all, the Spirit **sent forth** initiates the kind of spontaneous recognition that accompanies a homecoming, the spiritual reunion with one's father experienced at the core of one's being, the heart. Such a cry belongs not to a slave but to a son, a son who is an heir to all the Father's benevolent love.

4:8. When ye knew not God, that is, before being liberated ("redeem[ed]," 4:5) and adopted to sonship (4:7), the Galatians were slaves or in bondage to masters (see 1 Cor. 12:2; 1 Thess. 4:5) that **are no gods**. When the Galatians were pagans, they thought that the beings they worshiped were gods, but when they became Christians, they learned better.

4:9 – 10. As with the questions of 3:1 – 3, Paul appealed to the Galatians' experience when they became Christians (see 4:6 – 7). In verses 8 – 10, the question, **how turn ye again …?** (v. 9), drew a comparison between their former allegiance to the feasts and observances of the pagan calendar of public emperor worship and their acceptance of the Jewish calendar of the Mosaic covenant. **The weak and beggarly elements** (see discussion on 4:3), regardless of whether they belonged to pagan or Jewish religion, demanded the observance of sacred dates and rites. Paul declared that they were impotent and impoverished because they had no power to liberate, only to enslave: **ye desire again … bondage**. Legalistic trust in rituals, moral achievement, law, good works, or even cold, dead orthodoxy may invigorate a personal sense of achievement, but these achievements fall under the curse of the law and far short of sonship. **Days** (v. 10), such as the Sabbath and the Day of Atonement (the tenth day of Tishri; see Lev. 16:29 – 34), **months, and times**, such as new moons (see Num. 28:11 – 15; Isa. 1:13 – 14), Passover (Exod. 12:18) and the Feast of Firstfruits (Lev. 23:10), **and years**, such as the Sabbath year (see Lev. 25:4), had never been, and can never be, in themselves means of salvation or sanctification. The

Pharisees meticulously observed all these to gain merit before God.

4:11. In vain characterizes primarily the failed potential of Paul's labor invested in those who returned to the old covenant law but secondarily characterizes the equivocal failure of pagan and Jewish religion. In Paul's argument, changing from one to the other is merely a shift in the duties of a slave and is empty of the emancipating sonship Christ won on the cross and confirmed through His Spirit.

G. Appeal to Enter into Freedom from Law (4:12 – 20)

4:12. Paul adjured the **brethren** (see discussion on 1:2) with a real, not a rhetorical, request: **be as I am**, which implies "not as I was" (see 1:13 – 14). Some of the Galatians were moving to that which Paul had been in Judaism, not to what he had become in Christ (2:19 – 21). When Paul was with them, he was like them; they enjoyed harmonious Christian fellowship apart from any observance of the Mosaic law. With the coming of the Judaizers with their introduction of the Mosaic law and animosity toward Paul had brought discord to the Galatians and their relations with Paul. In favor of returning to better times (see 4:13), Paul easily dismissed any notion of personal injury.

4:13. On the basis of 4:15 and 6:11, a strong suggestion for Paul's **infirmity of the flesh** is recurring or chronic eye trouble. Others have suggested malaria or epilepsy. **I preached … at the first** refers to the occasion when Paul visited Galatia on his first missionary journey (see Acts 13:14 – 14:23).

4:14. Received me implies that under the influence of Judaizers, the Galatians had changed their attitude toward him. In the Mediterranean world, superstition and corollary social conventions were attached to encounters with illness and disease. For example, the Greek word for **rejected** is literally "spit out." Although a gesture of disrespect, it was a convention of defense in the presence of disease, averting a demon or warding off the "evil eye." The Galatians treated Paul just the opposite; they received him as a messenger (**an angel**) of God, even the representation of Jesus Christ. Paul's argument is clear: if they had at first seen Paul as God's agent, indeed, as the very representation of Christ, they should now have no problem imitating Paul and becoming more Christlike (Witherington, *Grace in Galatia*, p. 312).

4:15. Where is then the blessedness you spake of? Because of the restraints of legalistic Judaism, the Galatians had lost their blessing and joy. **Plucked out your own eyes** may legitimately gain significance if Paul's infirmity was situated in his eyes, but even so, the hyperbole stressed the Galatians' willingness, for his benefit, to part with that which was most precious to them (see Mark 2:4, where the same verb is used of digging through a roof).

4:16–18. Your enemy (v. 16) marks the dramatic shift that had come to pass. **They** (v. 17), the Judaizers (see 2:4, 12), **zealously affect you.** The language of zeal, often associated with the law, alludes to the exclusionary not inclusive effect of the law. As the law shut out Gentiles, it made Gentiles zealous for inclusion. The exclusion may have made Paul and some of the Galatians "enemies," for it put them on opposite sides of the law.

4:19–20. My little children (v. 19), although more affectionate, is in keeping with Paul's tenderhearted use of "brethren" and his frequent use of "we." Given the distance that had come between him and some of the Galatians, this expression of affection is a remarkable testament to Paul's selfless, pastoral heart. It is akin to a parent's affirming love in the face of a child's hasty "I hate you!" (for Paul's affectionate relationship to his converts, see Acts 20:37–38; Phil. 4:1; 1 Thess. 2:7–8). The expression occurs only here in Paul's writings but is common in John's (see, e.g., John 13:33; 1 John 2:1; 3:7). Paul expressed the goal of his ministry with **until Christ be formed in you** (see Rom. 8:29; Eph. 4:13, 15; Col. 1:27). That goal was real to Paul's own experience (see 2:19–20) and explains the eclipse of his own ego in the way he handled relationships of great personal interest.

H. The Allegory of Hagar and Sarah (4:21–31)

4:21–23. Here Paul was teaching all the Galatians, but he wanted the special attention of those among them who were near to embracing the law. Abraham had **two sons** (v. 22). Ishmael was born to the slave woman, Hagar (Gen. 16:1–16), and Isaac to the free woman, Sarah (Gen. 21:2–5). In the allegory to follow, Hagar and Sarah illustrate law and grace, with their sons corresponding to bondage and freedom in as much as they contrast that which is born after the flesh and after the promise (the Spirit; see 4:24–26, 28).

4:24. Which things are an allegory, or literally "allegorized" (Greek, *allēgoreō*). This is the only place in Scripture where this word occurs. The Sarah-Hagar account is not an allegory in the sense that it was nonhistorical but in the sense that Paul used the events to illustrate a theological truth. For the word **covenants,** see discussion on 3:15. **Mount Sinai** is where the old covenant was established, with its law governing Israel's life (see Exod. 19:2; 20:1–17).

4:25. Answereth to Jerusalem which now is. Jerusalem could be equated with Mount Sinai because it represented the center of Judaism, which was still under bondage to the law issued at Mount Sinai.

4:26. Jerusalem which is above represents the opposite of Jerusalem below. This contrast between heavenly and earthly Jerusalem is not unique to Paul. Rabbinical teaching held that the Jerusalem above was the heavenly archetype that would be let down to earth in the messianic period (see Rev. 21:2). Here it refers to the heavenly city of God in contrast to the "Jerusalem which now is" (4:25). Elsewhere in the New Testament, it symbolizes the place of Christ's reign and the realm of Christian citizenship. Thus, **the mother of us all** identifies Jerusalem as the spiritual complement to Sarah and as the mother of the freeborn citizens of the heavenly Jerusalem; Christians are her children.

4:27. Paul applied Isaiah's (54:1) joyful promise to exiled Jerusalem (in her exile **barren** of children) to the ingathering of believers through the gospel, by which "Jerusalem's" children have become many.

4:28. Even **as Isaac was,** Christians are now **children of promise** by virtue of God's promise (see 3:29; Rom. 9:8).

4:29. Persecuted him that was born after the Spirit is most likely suggested by Genesis 21:9 (see

Ps. 83:5–6). **So it is now** points to the opposition and persecution suffered for the gospel (see Acts 13:50; 14:2–5, 19; 1 Thess. 2:14–16).

4:30. Cast out the bondwoman. Paul used Sarah's words in Genesis 21:10 as the scriptural basis for teaching the Galatians to put the Judaizers out of the church.

4:31. We are not children of the bondwoman. The believer is not enslaved to the law but is a child of promise and lives by faith (see 3:7, 29).

IV. Practical: Practice of the Life of Liberty and Faith (5:1–6:10)

A. Exhortation to Freedom (5:1–12)

5:1. Made us free is emphasized by its position in the Greek sentence. Paul also prominently underscored its thematic importance by opening the sentence with "the freedom believers enjoy in Christ." The freedom spoken of here is freedom from the entangling bonds of the law. In classical Greek, the verb **entangled** means "to be held, caught or entangled in." **The yoke of bondage** points to the burden of the rigorous demands of the law as the means for gaining God's favor—an intolerable burden for sinful man (see Acts 15:10–11).

5:2–4. To be **circumcised** (v. 2) as a condition for God's acceptance represented a grave choice in two ways. First, Paul said, **Christ shall profit you nothing**, for such a condition nullified the work of Christ on the cross, the very grace of God (see 2:21). Second, one who accepted such a condition would become **a debtor to do the whole law** (v. 3; see 3:10; James 2:10); its demand cannot be satisfied through selective submission nor tokens of compliance (circumcision). The Galatians were **fallen from grace** (v. 4) because they no longer relied on it and no longer put their **faith** (believed) in it. Accepting circumcision and the was tantamount to saying that the cross of Jesus Christ was inadequate and grace was insufficient. Gaining God's favor by observing the law and receiving it by grace are mutually exclusive (see 2 Peter 3:17).

5:5. The hope of righteousness refers to God's final verdict of "not guilty," assured presently to the believer by faith and by the sanctifying work of the Holy Spirit. This is one of the few eschatological statements in Galatians (see Rom. 5:1–5; 8:10–21; 2 Cor. 5:5; Eph. 1:13–14).

5:6. Neither circumcision availeth any thing, nor uncircumcision (see 5:2; 2:21; 6:15; 1 Cor. 7:19), for they are external and irrelevant to the expression of faith. Faith works from the inside out. The operation of faith is not invisible; it shows itself at work in love. Therefore, **faith which worketh by love** speaks not of a faith that is mere intellectual assent (see James 2:18–19) but of a living trust in God's grace that expresses itself in acts of love (see 1 Thess. 1:3).

5:7–8. Ye did run well (v. 7), before the Judaizers (see Introduction: "Background") hindered them. Paul was fond of depicting the Christian life as a race (see, e.g., 2:2; Phil. 2:16). The picture of a race preempted by onlookers who obstruct the progress of those running is vividly contrasted with God, **him that calleth you** (v. 8). The metaphor pictures God inspiring them to run and run well. **Persuasion** refers to the Judaizers' coaxing to abandon the race; Paul was coaching them to continue the race.

5:9. Here Paul used a proverb to stress the pervasive effect of Judaism. When the word **leaven** is used as a symbol in the Bible, it indicates evil or false teaching (see discussion on Mark 8:15), except in Matthew 13:33.

5:10. Through the Lord expresses the source of Paul's optimism even as it alludes to the unseen work of God in the Galatians' hearts through the Spirit and the truth (see 5:7). **Whosoever he be** is here probably generic, ruling out any exception. Elsewhere, Paul used the plural to identify the agitators (the Judaizers), as in 1:7; 5:12.

5:11. Brethren (see discussion on 1:2) is here an alert to capture the Galatians' attention as Paul took up an allegation, presumably the false charge that he preached circumcision. If such were the case, Paul asked, why the persecution and why were his opponents offended by the cross? In short, Paul asked, would not **the offence of the cross** (see Rom. 9:32–33; 1 Cor. 1:23) disappear if he preached circumcision?

5:12. The allegation that Paul himself preached circumcision was so outrageous that he could imagine only one form of circumcision that he would preach: **I would they were even cut off**. The Greek word "to cut off" or "to castrate" connotes that the agitators should go even further and make themselves eunuchs. F. F. Bruce (*Commentary on Galatians*, p. 238) points out the term identifies eunuchs in Deuteronomy 23:1 (Septuagint), where they are debarred from the congregation of the Lord. The Galatians would be better off if these Judaizers who were preaching circumcision were themselves "cut off." In Philippians 3:2, Paul used a related word to describe the same sort of people as "the false circumcision." His sarcasm is evident.

B. Life by the Spirit, Not by the Flesh (5:13–26)

5:13. Use not liberty for an occasion to the flesh (see Rom. 6:1; 1 Peter 2:16). Liberty is not license but rather freedom to serve God and each other in love.

5:14. All the law is fulfilled. Doing to others what you would have them do to you expresses the spirit and intention of "the law and the prophets" (Matt. 7:12; see Mark 12:31). The words **as thyself** are not a condition but a standard. The meaning of "as thyself" is explained by the Golden Rule (Luke 6:31): treat others the way you would have them treat you. This is the great doctrine that must not be diminished under the banner of defending either the law or some other doctrine in the service of God. Jesus significantly linked the application of this doctrine to the first great commandment, "Thou shalt love the Lord thy God" (Luke 10:27).

5:15. Paul represented those involved in quarrels and controversy as wild animals that **bite and devour one another**. Here, in contrast to 5:13–14, Paul addressed the potential harm of partisan strife, presumably incited by doctrinal disputes among the Galatians over the teachings of the Judaizers (see Introduction: "Background"). Untempered by love, such acrimony is fueled by the flesh, not by the Spirit (see 5:16, 18). Seeking to attain status with God and man by mere observance of the law breeds a self-righteous, critical spirit.

5:16. Walk is a meaningful Jewish metaphor that Paul frequently used to express the way one conducts oneself or lives. The present tense, "go on living," prescribes a pattern of habitual conduct. Living by the promptings and power of the Spirit is the key to conquering sinful desires (see 5:25; Rom. 8:2–4). Paul used various metaphors to communicate the necessity of submitting to the Spirit's control (see 5:18, "be led"). In addition to "Walk in the Spirit" (see Rom. 8:4), Paul admonished Christians to "mind [set the mind on] … the things of the Spirit" (Rom. 8:5) and to "be filled with the Spirit" (Eph. 5:18). All these expressions underscore the occupying and controlling influence of the Holy Spirit as the defining reality of the Christian life.

5:17. Are contrary the one to the other. See Romans 7:15–23; 1 Peter 2:11.

5:18. Led of the Spirit expresses the guidance and direction the Spirit gives to those who follow or willingly submit to the Spirit's supervision (see 5:16; Rom. 8:14). Under the supervision of the Spirit, one is **not under the law**, not under the bondage of trying to please God by minute observance of the law for salvation or sanctification (see Rom. 8:4; discussion on Rom. 6:14).

5:19–21. For other lists of vices, see 1 Corinthians 6:9–10; Ephesians 5:5; Revelation 22:15.

5:22–23. For other lists of virtues, see 2 Corinthians 6:6; Ephesians 4:2; 5:9; Colossians 3:12–15. Christian character is produced by the Holy Spirit, not by the mere moral discipline of trying to live by law. Paul made it clear that justification by faith does not result in libertinism. The indwelling Holy Spirit produces Christian virtues in the believer's life.

5:22. Fruit of the Spirit. Compare the singular "fruit" with the plural "works" (5:19).

5:23. No law. See 1 Timothy 1:9.

5:24. Crucified the flesh. See 2:20; 6:14.

5:25. Walk in (Greek, *sticheō*) is a military term meaning "to keep in step with" or "to walk in line with." A different Greek word for "walk" (*peripateō*) was used in 5:16, meaning "to walk" or "to live" and involving one's conduct. Interestingly, Paul used the noun (*stoicheia*) translated "elements" in 4:3, 9, to refer to elementary principles of religion (pagan and Jewish). Paul purposely used the verb (*stoicheō*) here to suggest that the Galatians did not have to align themselves with any elementary principles when they aligned themselves with the Spirit of God.

C. Call for Mutual Help (6:1–10)

6:1. In addition to expressing the affection of familial brotherly love, **Brethren** (see discussion on 1:2), as often in this letter, marks the opening of a new thought or section. For a contrast that further defines **ye which are spiritual**, see 1 Corinthians 3:1–3. **Restore** (Greek, *katartizō*; see Matt. 4:21) is used elsewhere for setting bones, mending nets, or bringing factions together.

6:2. Bear ye one another's burdens. The translation "burden" here and in 6:5 represents two different Greek nouns. In 6:5, the term requires that each one is to bear their own normal load. Believers are to help others, however, when they have an overload or are overburdened. The emphasis here is on moral burdens (see 6:1; Rom. 15:1–3). **The law of Christ** (see *KJV Study Bible* note on 1 Cor. 9:21) cannot be legislated but is articulated by the Spirit, the Spirit of His Son (4:5–6; Rom. 8:2), that engenders the character of what Christ would do, or the measure of Christlikeness in one's daily walk.

6:4. Let every man prove his own work. The emphasis here is on personal responsibility (see 1 Cor. 11:28; 2 Cor. 13:5). The alternative is to "prove" (Greek "test" or "examine") the work of others, which can lead to comparison, fault-finding, and **rejoicing** by subtraction. Here the word "rejoicing" points to a proper "pride" that is grounded in the substance of one's own work. Paul may also have been implying that one should keep his "rejoicing" to himself and not direct it toward others. In 6:14, Paul featured the sure ground of his pride, or "glory," in the work of Jesus Christ and the cross and nothing other.

6:5. Bear his own burden. The **For** at the beginning of this verse connects it with 6:4. Each of us is responsible before God. The reference may be to the future judgment (the verb is in the future tense),

when every person will give an account to God (see Rom. 14:12; 2 Cor. 5:10).

6:6. Communicate unto him that teacheth in all good things elucidates a general principle (see Luke 10:7; Matt. 10:10; 1 Tim. 5:18) calling those that are taught to support the teacher (see Phil. 4:14–19).

6:7–9. Mocked (v. 7) translates a Greek word that visualizes a gesture of contempt: "to thumb the nose at." Paul warned that God will not ignore such disdain. **Whatsoever a man soweth, that shall he also reap** (see 2 Cor. 9:6). As verses 8–9 show, the principle applies not only negatively but also positively (see Rom. 8:13). On the negative side, sowing to the flesh reaps **corruption** (v. 8; see 5:19–21). On the positive side, sowing to the Spirit reaps **life everlasting**. In 5:21, Paul wrote of inheriting "the kingdom of God," here of reaping "life everlasting." The first focuses on the realm (sphere, context) that will be inherited (as Israel inherited the Promised Land); the second focuses on the blessed life that will be enjoyed in that realm. **Weary in well doing** speaks of losing one's motivation when the payoffs ("harvest") for doing what is right are not timely. Keep doing what is good and right, Paul said; do not lose heart when you cannot see the results. A harvest will come in due season.

6:10. Especially unto them who are of the household of faith (see 1 Tim. 5:8). Sow good without discrimination, but make sure to sow within the household of faith, the fellowship of believers.

V. Conclusion (6:11–18)

6:11. The words **how large a letter** may have been used for emphasis or, as some have suggested, because Paul had poor eyesight (see discussion on 4:13). **With mine own hand** indicates that the letter up to this point had probably been dictated to a scribe, after which Paul took the pen in his own hand and finished the letter (see Rom. 16:22; 1 Cor. 1:1; 16:21; 2 Thess. 3:17; Col. 4:18).

6:12–13. Constrain you to be circumcised (v. 12) points to not only the pressure but the conditional necessity that must be met before acceptance and inclusion may be experienced (see 2:3).

Lest they should suffer persecution. By advocating circumcision (see 5:11), the Judaizers (see Introduction: "Background") were less apt to experience opposition from the Jewish opponents of Christianity and were thinking only of themselves.

6:14. Glory, save in the cross. See 1 Corinthians 1:31; 2:2. **The world**. All that is against God. **Crucified unto me, and I unto the world**. See 2:19–20; 5:24; see also discussions on James 4:4; 1 John 2:15.

6:15. In Christ, a person undergoes a transformation and becomes **a new creature**, an entirely new being. Creation again takes place (see 2 Cor. 5:17).

6:16. This rule. See 6:14–15. **Peace … and mercy**. See Psalms 125:5; 128:6. **The Israel of God**, or the Christian Jews. If the conjunction is translated

"even" instead of "and," the phrase stands in contrast to "Israel after the flesh" (1 Cor. 10:18; a literal rendering of the Greek for "national Israel"). The New Testament church, made up of believing Jews and Gentiles, is included in the seed of Abraham and is an heir according to the promise (3:29; see Rom. 9:6; Phil. 3:3).

6:17. In ancient times, the Greek word **marks** (*stigma*) was used of the brand marks that identified slaves or animals. Paul's suffering (stoning, Acts 14:19; beatings, Acts 16:22; 2 Cor. 11:25; illness, 2 Cor. 12:7; Gal. 4:13–14) marked him as a "servant of Christ" (1:10; see 2 Cor. 4:10).

6:18. Amen. A word of confirmation often used at the close of a doxology or benediction.

THE EPISTLE OF PAUL THE APOSTLE TO THE EPHESIANS

INTRODUCTION

Author, Date, and Place of Composition

The author identifies himself as Paul (1:1; 3:1; see also 3:7, 13; 4:1; 6:19–20). Some have taken the absence of Paul's usual personal greetings and the verbal similarity of many parts to Colossians, among other reasons, as grounds for doubting Paul's authorship. This was probably a circular letter, however, intended for other churches in addition to the one in Ephesus (see discussions on 1:1, 15; 6:21–23). Paul may have written Ephesians about the same time as Colossians, circa AD 60, while he was in prison in Rome (see 3:1; 4:1; 6:20).

The City of Ephesus

Ephesus was the most important city in western Asia Minor (modern-day Turkey). It had a harbor that, at that time, opened into the Cayster River, which in turn emptied into the Aegean Sea (see map, *Zondervan KJV Study Bible*, p. 1694). Because it was also at an intersection of major trade routes, Ephesus became a commercial center. It boasted a pagan temple dedicated to the Roman goddess Diana (Greek Artemis; see Acts 19:23–31). Paul made Ephesus a center for evangelism for two years and three months (see discussion on Acts 19:10), and the church there apparently flourished for some time but later needed the warning of Revelation 2:1–7.

Theme and Theological Message

Unlike several of Paul's other letters, Ephesians does not address any particular error or heresy. Paul wrote to expand the horizons of his readers, so that they might better understand the dimensions of God's eternal purpose and grace and come to appreciate the high goals God has for the church. Indeed, Ephesians may well be called Paul's chief theology of the church. To view the church as God does, one must appreciate the message of this grand epistle.

The letter opens with a sequence of statements about God's blessings, which are interspersed with a remarkable variety of expressions drawing attention to God's wisdom, forethought, and purpose. Paul emphasized that believers have been saved not only for their personal benefit but also to bring praise and glory to God. The climax of God's purpose, in "the fulness of times" (1:10), is to bring all things in the universe together under Christ. It is crucially important that Christians realize this, so in 1:15–23, Paul prayed for their understanding (a second prayer occurs in 3:14–21).

Having explained God's great goals for the church, Paul proceeded to show the steps toward their fulfillment. First, God has reconciled individuals to Himself as an act of grace (see 2:1–10). Second, God has reconciled these saved individuals to each other, Christ having broken down the barriers through His own death (2:11–22). God has done something beyond even that: He has united these reconciled individuals in one body, the church. This is a "mystery" not fully known until it was revealed to Paul (see 3:1–6). Paul was then able to state even more clearly what God has intended for the church, namely, that it be the means by which He displays His "manifold wisdom" (3:10) to "the principalities and powers in heavenly places" (3:10; see 3:7–13). The repetition of "heavenly places" (1:3, 20; 2:6; 3:10; 6:12) makes it clear that Christian existence is not merely on an earthly plane. It receives its meaning and significance from heaven, where Christ is exalted at the right hand of God (see 1:20).

Nevertheless, Christian life is lived out on earth, where the practical daily life of the believer continues to work out the purposes of God. The ascended Lord gave gifts to the members of His church to enable them to minister to one another and so promote unity and maturity (see 4:1–16). The unity of the church under the headship of Christ foreshadows the uniting of "all things … in heaven, and … on earth" (1:10) under Christ. The new life of purity and mutual deference stands in contrast to the old way of life without Christ (see 4:17–6:9). Those who are "strong in the Lord" (6:10) have victory over the Evil One in the great spiritual conflict, especially through the power of prayer (see 6:10–20).

Outline

I. Greetings (1:1–2)
II. The Divine Purpose: The Glory and Headship of Christ (1:3–14)
III. Prayer That Christians May Realize God's Purpose and Power (1:15–23)
IV. Steps toward the Fulfillment of God's Purpose (chaps. 2–3)
    A. Salvation of Individuals by Grace (2:1–10)
    B. Reconciliation of Jew and Gentile through the Cross (2:11–18)
    C. Uniting of Jew and Gentile in One Household (2:19–22)
    D. Revelation of God's Wisdom through the Church (3:1–13)
    E. Prayer for a Deeper Experience of God's Fullness (3:14–21)
V. Practical Ways to Fulfill God's Purpose in the Church (4:1–6:20)
    A. Unity (4:1–6)
    B. Maturity (4:7–16)
    C. Renewal of Personal Life (4:17–5:20)
    D. Deference in Personal Relationships (5:21–6:9)
        1. The Principle (5:21)
        2. Husbands and Wives (5:22–33)
        3. Children and Parents (6:1–4)
        4. Slaves and Masters (6:5–9)
    E. Strength in the Spiritual Conflict (6:10–20)
VI. Conclusion, Final Greetings, and Benediction (6:21–24)

Bibliography

Barclay, William. *The Letters to the Galatians and Ephesians*. Daily Study Bible. Rev. ed. Philadelphia: Westminster, 1976.

Barth, Marcus. *Ephesians*. The Anchor Bible. 2 vols. Garden City, NY: Doubleday, 1974.

Bruce, F. F. *The Epistles to the Colossians, Philemon, and the Ephesians*. The New International Commentary on the New Testament. Grand Rapids, MI: Eerdmans, 1984.

Hendricksen, William. *Galatians, Ephesians, Philippians, Colossians, and Philemon*. New Testament Commentary. Grand Rapids, MI: Baker, 1995.

Martin, Ralph. *Ephesians, Colossians, and Philemon. Interpretation: A Bible Commentary for Teaching and Preaching*. Edited by James L. Mays. Louisville: John Knox, 1991.

Snodgrass, Klyne. *Ephesians*. Grand Rapids, MI: Zondervan, 1996.

EXPOSITION

I. Greetings (1:1–2)

1:1. An apostle is one specially commissioned by Christ (see discussions on Mark 6:30; 1 Cor. 1:1; Heb. 3:1). **By the will of God** stresses not only Paul's authority under God but also anticipates the strong emphasis on God's sovereign plan and purpose that Paul made later in this chapter and the book. The destination, **at Ephesus**, is not found in the oldest available Greek manuscripts, which adds to the opinion that the letter may have been intended as a circular letter to several churches, in particular the chief city in the vicinity, Ephesus (see discussions on 1:15; 6:21–23; Acts 19:10). Interestingly, the oldest Greek manuscripts retain the prescript, "to the Ephesians." This phrase **in Christ Jesus** (or a similar one) occurs eleven times in 1:1–13. It refers to the spiritual union of Christ with believers, which Paul often symbolized with the metaphor "body [of Christ]" (see, e.g., 1:23; 2:16; 4:4, 12, 16; 5:23, 30).

1:2. Grace be to you, and peace are words that were commonly used in the greetings of secular letters. The words that follow show that Paul intended a spiritual dimension. Paul used the word "grace" twelve times and "peace" eight times in Ephesians.

II. The Divine Purpose: The Glory and Headship of Christ (1:3–14)

1:3–14. All one sentence in Greek, this section is often called a "doxology" because it recites what God has done and is an expression of worship to honor Him. Paul spoke first of the blessings through the Father (v. 3), then of those through the Son (vv. 4–13a), and finally of those through the Holy Spirit (1:13b–14). Strikingly, such a long sentence (unparalleled in Paul's letters) is not only typical of doxologies, but its advance, clause by clause, is marked by repeated reference to God's action or decision in, through, or by Christ (or an equivalent).

1:3 in Christ	**1:10** in Christ
1:4 in him	**1:10** in him
1:5 by Jesus Christ	**1:11** In whom
1:6 in the beloved	**1:12** in Christ
1:7 In whom	**1:13** In whom
1:7 through his blood	**1:13** in whom
1:9 in himself (Greek, "in him")	

Clearly, the scope of all of God the Father's (v. 3) redemptive will and work, from beginning to end, in heaven and on earth (compare vv. 3–4 and v. 10) is focused on and featured in the person of Jesus Christ.

1:3. God is worthy of blessing. Moreover, God is hailed as **Blessed** at the opening of the doxology (1:3–14), because He has become expressly recognized and honored as Father: the **Father of our Lord Jesus Christ** (see John 20:17 and discussion) and, therefore, the Father of those who know sonship by virtue of the Son (see 1:5). The sequence of "Blessed" and **blessings ... in Christ** fathoms God as Father through the privileged and redemptive (**spiritual**) blessings met in the Son (the Christ). Jewish people used the word "bless" to express both God's kindness to believers and their thanks or praise to Him. Appropriately, the doxology to God's glorious redemptive work in the Son ends with "the praise of his glory" (1:14). **Heavenly places** occurs five times in Ephesians, emphasizing Paul's perception that in the exaltation of Christ (His resurrection and enthronement at God's right hand) and in the Christian's union with the exalted Christ, ultimate issues are involved—issues that pertain to the divine realm and that, in the final analysis, are worked out in and from that realm. At stake are God's eternal eschatological purpose (see 3:11) and the titanic conflict between God and the powerful spiritual forces arrayed against Him—a purpose and a conflict that come to focus in the history of redemption.

Here Paul asserted that through their union with the exalted Christ, Christians have already been made beneficiaries of every spiritual blessing that belongs to and comes from the heavenly places. Paul proclaimed Christ's exaltation to that realm and His elevation over all other powers and titles so that He rules over all for the sake of His church (1:20–22). According to 2:6, those who have been made alive with Christ (2:5) share in Christ's exaltation and enthronement in heaven. Thus, by gathering Gentiles and Jews into one body of Christ (the church), God triumphantly displays His "manifold wisdom" (3:10) to "the principalities and powers in heavenly places" (3:10). As a result, the spiritual struggle of the saints here and now is not so much against "flesh and blood" (6:12) as against the great spiritual forces that war against God in heaven.

1:4. The word **chosen** points to God's elective decision implemented in Christ. Divine election is a constant theme in Paul's letters (see Rom. 8:29–33; 9:6–26; 11:5, 7, 28; 16:13; Col. 3:12; 1 Thess. 1:4; 2 Thess. 2:13; Titus 1:1). In this chapter, it is emphasized in the following ways: (1) **He hath chosen us in him**; (2) "predestined us ... by Jesus Christ" (1:5); (3) "In whom also we have obtained an inheritance" (1:11); (4) "being predestined according to [His] purpose" (1:11). God's elective decision was fixed in Christ **before the foundation of the world** (see John 17:24). **Holy and without blame** (see 5:27 for the same pair of words) is used of the church, the bride of Christ. Holiness is the result, not the basis, of God's choosing. It refers both to the holiness imparted to the believer because of Christ and to the believer's personal sanctification (see discussion on 1 Cor. 1:2). Grammatically, the words **in love** (or "by love") may be construed with either what follows (1:5) or with what precedes (in v. 4). Elsewhere (3:17; 4:2, 15–16), "in love" stands at the end of a sentence. Accordingly, here it probably is to qualify both God's elective decision in Christ and the appearance of those whom God has chosen (Barth, *Ephsians*, vol. 1, pp. 79–80).

1:5. Adoption was common among the Greeks and Romans, who granted the adopted son all the privileges of a natural son, including inheritance rights. On God's part, our adoption to such privileged sonship was not an afterthought but a decision predetermined, or **predestined** (Greek, *proorizō*; "to decide upon beforehand"), to become effective for us **by**, or "through," **Jesus Christ**. Christ is the means of God's election ("in him," 1:4) and adoption ("by Jesus Christ"). Christians are adopted sons by grace (**adoption ... by Jesus Christ to himself, according to the good pleasure of his will**; compare 1:6); Christ, however, is God's Son by nature. The Greek term for "adoption" occurs four other times in the New Testament (Rom. 8:15, 23; 9:4; Gal. 4:5).

1:6. All the aforementioned benevolence of God is the glory of His grace and is worthy of **praise** (see 1:14; 4:30; Rom. 3:24; Titus 2:14). **Hath made us accepted** translates the verb form of the noun **grace**.

The sense may be rendered, "grace by which he favored [graced] us in the beloved."

1:7–8. Redemption (v. 7) was familiar to the Ephesians. In the Greco-Roman practice of redemption, slaves were freed by the payment of a ransom. Similarly, the ransom necessary to free sinners from the bondage of sin and the resulting curse imposed by the law (see Gal. 3:13) was the death of Christ (**through his blood**; see 2:13; 1 Peter 1:18–19). The word "redemption" is linked and further explained by the words "the forgiveness of sins" (the cancellation of debt) through the vast resources of God's grace. God exercised His lavish and extravagant disbursement of such riches (**abounded toward us; v. 8**) **in all wisdom and prudence.** Far from foolish, the objective and outcome of God's action, as seen in 1:9–12, verifies God's wisdom and prudence.

1:9–11. The mystery (v. 9; see discussions on Rom. 11:25; Col. 1:26) of God's own counsel (**his will**), previously unknown, has been revealed. It accords with His benevolent purpose in Christ: **That in the dispensation of the fulness of times … in Christ** (lit., "in him"; v. 10). Paul used a significant term (**the fulness of times … in Christ**) here that not only has the idea of leadership but also was often used of adding up a column of figures. A contemporary way of putting it might be to say that in a world of confusion, where things do not "add up" or make sense, one looks forward to the time when everything will be brought into meaningful relationship under the headship of Christ. With the words **in him** comes the reverberation that Christ is the center of God's plan. This point is amplified in verse 11 (**In whom**). Whether the universe or the individual Christian is in view, it is only in relationship to Christ that there is a meaningful future destiny. Paul went on to speak not of the world as a whole but of those who respond to God's call.

1:12. Who first trusted in Christ is probably a reference to those Jews who, like Paul, had become believers before many Gentiles had. For **to the praise of his glory,** see 1:6.

1:13–14. Ye also probably refers to the majority of the Ephesians, who were Gentiles. **Sealed** in those days was a mark of identification and denoted ownership. **The earnest** (v. 14; Greek, *arrabōn*; "deposit," "down payment," "pledge") is an assurance of what is promised or yet to come (see discussion on Rom. 8:23). The same word is used today in modern Greek of the wedding ring, the symbol of matrimonial pledges. The Holy Spirit is God's "earnest" that identifies and marks ("sealed") the believer as belonging to God.

III. Prayer That Christians May Realize God's Purpose and Power (1:15–23)

1:15–16. Wherefore (v. 15), or "therefore," points back to the doxology and sets Paul's apostolic and pastoral care squarely within the grand scope of God's salvation. What God has accomplished in Christ inspired Paul's intercession (see 1:17–22) and prayers for his readers to grow in their personal understanding of what God has done for them. Coming from one who had spent several years in Ephesus, **after I heard** seems strange. Paul may have been referring either to a greatly enlarged church there, many of whose members he did not know, or, if Ephesians was intended as a circular letter (see discussion on 1:1), to news from the whole area, only a part of which he had visited.

1:17. The God of our Lord Jesus Christ (see discussion on 1:3) **… knowledge of him** is the object of knowledge but not, as Paul made clear, in isolation from "our Lord Jesus Christ." **The spirit** points to a disposition or attitude (see Col. 1:9), not to the "giving" of the Holy Spirit (see 1:13–14). Nonetheless, it is the Spirit of God that generates the new person (4:23) and enables a deeper understanding of God (see 1 Cor. 2:7, 10). With the doxology of 1:3–14 close at hand, **the spirit of wisdom and [of] revelation** points to the believer's acquisition and expression of true understanding and insight into God's mystery made known. The practical side of such a disposition may be implied in Paul's indirect questions that follow: "what is the hope of his calling" (1:18), "what [are] the riches … of his inheritance" (1:18), and "what is the … greatness of his power" (1:19).

1:18. The eyes of your understanding is tantamount to "your mind" or "your inner awareness." **Hope** has an objective quality of certainty (see Rom. 8:25). It is the assurance of eternal life guaranteed by the present possession of the Holy Spirit (see 1:14; for **calling**, see Phil. 3:14; 2 Tim. 1:9; Heb. 3:1). **The glory of his inheritance in the saints** refers to either the inheritance the saints have from God (see 1:14; Col. 1:12) or the inheritance God receives, that is, the saints themselves. **Saints** identifies those whom God has called to be His own people, that is, all Christians (see 1:1, 15). The word carried the idea of dedication to a deity.

1:19 – 20. In verse 19, Paul piled term upon term to emphasize that the extraordinary divine force by which Jesus Christ was **raised** (v. 20) is the same power at work in and through believers (see 3:20). The expression **right hand** is symbolic for the place of highest honor and authority.

1:21. All principality ... every name that is named is inclusive. Paul deliberately calculated his wording here to draw within the scope of Christ's supremacy every conceivable power, natural or supernatural, whatever his contemporaries might imagine. In Paul's day, many people believed not only in the existence of angels and demons but also in that of other beings. Christ is above them all. **This world ... that which is to come.** Like the rabbinic teachers of his day, Paul distinguished between the present age, which is evil, and the future age when the Messiah will consummate His kingdom and there will be a completely righteous society on earth.

1:22. Under his feet further expresses the supremacy of Christ's authority (see Ps. 110:1). Psalm 8:5 – 6 emphasizes the destiny of man, and Hebrews 2:6 – 9 shows that ultimately it is the Son of Man who rules over everything (see Heb. 10:13). This is a certainty for the church. Christ, who is **head** of the church, is head over everything (see discussion on 1:10).

1:23. His body (see 2:16; 4:4, 12, 16; 5:23, 30) is Paul's metaphor for the church, all believers incorporated by and under the Head. In addition to the theological implication, an anatomical implication may be connected to 1:22: what is under His feet is

beneath His body. **Fulness ... filleth** explains that the church is the fullness of Christ, probably in the sense that it is filled by Him who fills all things.

IV. Steps toward the Fulfillment of God's Purpose (chaps. 2 – 3)

A. Salvation of Individuals by Grace (2:1 – 10)

2:1 – 10. In chapter 1, Paul wrote of the great purposes and plan of God, culminating in the universal headship of Christ (1:10), all of which is to be for "the praise of his glory" (1:14). He next proceeded to explain the steps by which God will accomplish His purposes, beginning with the salvation of individuals.

2:1 – 3. These verses describe the Ephesians' past moral and spiritual condition, separated from the life of God. Clearly, this is a condition of being spiritually dead, as they **walked according to the course** (lit., "age") **of this world** (v. 2; see "present evil age," Gal. 1:4) and its ruling **prince**. Satan is "the prince of this world" (see John 14:30). As prince of **the power** (lit., "dominion" or "authority") **of the air**, Satan is no mere earthbound enemy (see 6:12). Satan is a created, but not a human, being (see Job 1:6; Ezek. 28:15; discussion on Isa. 14:12 – 15). He is **spirit**, in contrast to human, or "flesh and blood" (6:12), and he operates (**worketh**) in ways discernible **in the children of disobedience.** The expression "children of" is a Semitic way of saying "characterized by." Paul used the expression twice, first of disobedience, then of wrath. The first summarizes human culpability in terms of cosmic opposition to God as it is marshaled and organized by the operation of the prince of "the course of this world." The second summarizes human culpability under the penalty of God's wrath. **We all** (v. 3), both Jews and Gentiles, **fulfilling the desires of the flesh and of the mind,** were rebellious and **were by nature the children of wrath** (see Rom. 1:18 – 20; 2:5; 9:22). In short, Paul wanted to show that the natural bent ("by nature") of the human condition aligns all humanity against God and warrants the penalty of His wrath.

2:4 – 5. But God (vv. 1 – 4); our condition that warrants God's anger is, by contrast, met with mercy from His great love, offered not because of any human merit but because of God's divine character. **Quickened us together with Christ** (v. 5) is literally, "made us alive together with Christ," and refers to the joint resurrection of both Jew and Gentile in the resurrection of Christ. This truth is expanded in Romans 6:1–10. **By grace ye are saved** summarizes these two verses. The scope of God's action to deliver children of disobedience and children of wrath is all of God's mercy and love through Jesus Christ, His grace.

2:6. Raised us up ... and made us sit together ... in Christ Jesus gives corroborating meaning to the words "quickened us together with Christ" (2:5). Here is a picture of full participation in the life of Christ through union with Christ. **Heavenly places** (see discussion on 1:3) is best defined by 1:19–21, a position of honor and authority at the right hand of God with Jesus. Paul pictures complete deliverance from "the prince of the power of the air" (2:2) through our union with Christ.

2:7. The word **That** indicates God's purpose. **In the ages to come** (see 1:21), probably referring to the future of eternal blessing with Christ, God will **shew** ("exhibit" or "prove") **the exceeding riches of his grace ... through Christ Jesus**. In view of 1:23 and 3:8–11, the church, "quickened," "raised," and seated "in heavenly places" (2:5–6), is the emblem of God's grace and belongs to God's demonstration to all men and all principalities and powers.

2:8. This verse is a major passage for understanding God's grace, that is, His kindness, unmerited favor, and forgiving love. **Are ye saved**. "Saved" has a wide range of meanings, including salvation from God's wrath, which all had incurred through sinfulness. The tense of the verb (also in 2:5) suggests a completed action, with emphasis on its present effect. **Through faith** (see Rom. 3:21–31 and discussions) establishes the necessity of faith in Christ as the only means of being made right with God. **And that not of yourselves** refers to God's act of saving. No human effort can contribute to salvation; it is the gift of God.

2:9. Not of works. One cannot earn salvation by "the deeds of the law" (Rom. 3:20, 28). Such a le-

galistic approach to salvation (or sanctification) is consistently condemned in Scripture. **Lest any man should boast**. No one can take credit for his or her salvation.

2:10. The Greek for the word **workmanship** (Greek, *poiēma*; "that which is made," see the English word *poem*, which is derived from the Greek word Paul uses here) sometimes has the connotation of a "work of art." **Before ordained** carries forward the theme of God's sovereign purpose and planning, seen in chapter 1.

B. Reconciliation of Jew and Gentile through the Cross (2:11–18)

2:11–22. From the salvation of individuals, Paul moved to another aspect of salvation in which God reconciles Jews and Gentiles, previously hostile peoples, not only to Himself but also to each other through Christ (vv. 11–16). Even more than that, God unites these now reconciled people in one body, a truth introduced in verses 19–22 and explained in chapter 3.

2:11. Wherefore refers to the state of those without Christ, described in 2:1–10. **Ye ... Gentiles in the flesh** addressed most of the Ephesians (see "ye also," 1:13). **Uncircumcision ... Circumcision** demarcates Gentiles and Jews. The rite of circumcision was applied to all Jewish male babies, so this physical act (**in the flesh made by hands**) was a clear distinction between Jew and Gentile. These distinctions "in the flesh"—the Gentile in the flesh ("birth") and the circumcision in the flesh ("body")—have been superceded by a new act of God: Jesus' death "in the flesh" made peace with God for both Jew and Gentile and therefore abolished distinctions between them (see 2:14).

2:12. At that time, or before salvation, stands in stark contrast to "But now" (2:13). **Without Christ ... without God** are expressions emphasizing the distance of unbelieving Gentiles from Israel, as well as from Christ. Paul did not diminish the inherent advantages of the Jews. **The covenants** point to God's blessings promised to and through the Jewish people (see discussion on Rom. 9:4).

2:13. The words **But now** not only pose a contrast with "at that time" (2:12) but also introduce the contrast between "without Christ" (2:12) and **in Christ. The blood of Christ** expresses the violent death of Christ as He poured out His lifeblood as a sacrifice (see 1:7).

2:14. He is our peace, who hath made both one means that believing Jews and believing Gentiles enter peace with God through Jesus Christ. If Gentile and Jews have peace with God on the same basis, the blood of Jesus Christ, there are no advantages (for Jews) or disadvantages (for Gentiles) "in the flesh" (2:11). Distinctions have been abolished "in his flesh" (2:15; or "by His death"). **The middle wall of partition** is a vivid description of the total religious isolation that Jews and Gentiles experienced from each other even in the temple.

2:15. Abolished ... the law is an advantage to obtaining peace with God. Since Matthew 5:17 and Romans 3:31 teach that God's moral standard expressed in the Old Testament law was not changed by the coming of Christ, what was abolished here was the effect of the specific **commandments contained in ordinances** in approaching God, on the one hand, and separating Jews from Gentiles, on the other. Observance of the Jewish law (circumcision, ritual cleanness, keeping the festivals) is not the basis of peace with God. The blood of Jesus reconciles (see 2:16; "our peace," 2:14) Gentile and Jew with God. Therefore, all distinctions (advantages or disadvantages) owing to "the flesh" (2:11) are abolished **in himself**, referring to the death of Christ. This makes possible the **one new man**: the united body of believers, the church.

2:16. One body. While this could possibly mean the body of Christ offered on the cross (see "in his flesh," 2:15), it refers to the "one new man" just mentioned, the body of believers.

2:17–18. Afar off ... nigh (v. 17) denotes Gentiles and Jews respectively. Paul made it clear that the Jew has no advantage over the Gentile if nearness or farness is judged "in the flesh" (2:11). Distance from God is bridged not by human effort but by the peace extended through Jesus Christ. The "one new man"

(2:15) has "one body" (2:16) with one Spirit. As the KJV rightly recognizes, the word "spirit" is here not the human spirit or an *esprit de corps*; it is the Holy Spirit (see 2:22; see also "one body, and one Spirit," 4:4).

C. Uniting of Jew and Gentile in One Household (2:19–22)

2:19. With the words **Now therefore,** Paul introduced a comprehensive conclusion to the whole passage. He indicated that the unity described in 2:19–22 is based on what Christ did through His death, described in 2:14–18. **Ye** indicates that Paul had the Gentiles at Ephesus particularly in mind here. **Fellowcitizens ... the household of God** are two powerful metaphors Paul used to communicate the dramatic shift in status and privilege that "outsiders" acquire through Christ. In the first metaphor, the contrast of **strangers and foreigners** with "fellowcitizens" pictures an entire class of disparate people who are not enfranchised with the rights and privileges belonging to the enviable class of equal citizens. "Outsiders" are now "insiders" through Jesus Christ. In the second metaphor, Paul's teaching on "reception" is more intimate. Outsiders are accepted into the family of God. The "household" (Greek, *oikeios*; "belonging to a family or house") in ancient times was what today might be called an extended family. Paul later extended this metaphor of belonging in the direction of a building, turning the inhabitants of God's household into constituent parts of God's house, His temple (see 2:21). It is not by accident that Paul appropriated Greek words formed from the root of "household" (*-oik-*): "built on the foundation" (*epoikodomeō*, 2:20), "building" (*oikodomē*, 2:21), "built together" (*sunoikodomeō*, 2:22), and "habitation" or "dwelling" (*katoikētērion*, 2:22). His readers would not have missed the connections.

2:20–21. The word **foundation** (v. 20) offers further metaphorical language to convey the idea of a solid, integrated structure. **The apostles and prophets** probably refers to the founding work of the early Christian apostles and prophets as they preached and taught God's word (see 1 Cor. 3:10–11). The **corner stone** (see 1 Peter 2:6) as in Isaiah 28:16, which uses the same term in its pre-Christian Greek translation (the Septuagint), refers to a foundation with a "tested" stone at the corner. Such a stone is foundational to the entire structure as the load-bearing stone that forms the plumb of the entire edifice. Christ is the cornerstone, and **In [Him] all the building[is] fitly framed together** (for "fitly framed together," see 4:16). This passage and 4:16 speak of the close relationship between believers. **Groweth** gives a description of a building under construction and conveys the sense of the dynamic growth of the church. Paul used the metaphor of **a holy temple**, thereby indicating the purpose ("to become") for which God has established His church. This is the temple that is a worthy "habitation" (2:22) for God.

2:22. A habitation of God describes the church. The church is to be a people or community in whom the Holy Spirit dwells.

D. Revelation of God's Wisdom through the Church (3:1–13)

3:1–13. Having saved people individually by His grace (2:1–10) and having reconciled them to each other as well as to Himself through the sacrificial death of Christ (2:11–22), God unites them on an equal basis in one body, the church. This step in God's eternal plan was not fully revealed in previous times. Paul calls it a "mystery" (vv. 3–4).

3:1. For this cause reaches back to all that Paul explained in the preceding chapter about what God has done, notably the inclusion of the Gentiles. Indeed, it was for this cause that Paul was called to be an apostle to the Gentiles (see 3:2; Rom. 15:15–16; Gal. 2:7–9; Acts 9:15), a **prisoner ... for you Gentiles**. Paul was under house arrest at this time (see Acts 28:16, 30). **Of Jesus Christ** is shorthand for the fact that Paul was imprisoned because of his obedience to Christ's calling (see Acts 9:15–16) to this great cause. This verse was probably meant to begin an intercessory prayer (see 3:14), but Paul paused to further explain his ministry (see 2:7; "dispensation

of grace," 3:2) as it belongs to "the mystery" (3:4). He resumed his initial thought in 3:14.

3:2. The expression **If ye have heard** contains a Greek conjunction used to introduce a justifiable assumption and may be rendered, "Surely you have heard" (Barth, *Ephesians*, vol. 1, p. 328). Most of the Ephesians would have heard of Paul's ministry because of his long stay there earlier. If this was a circular letter (see discussion on 1:1), however, the other churches may not have known much about it from Paul himself. **Dispensation** (Greek, *oikonomia*; "administration," "stewardship," "plan") was used in 1:10 of God's plan consummated and executed in Jesus Christ. With God's administrative plan for the church and for the universe (see especially 1:3–12) as background, Paul now defined his own ministry with the word "dispensation," explaining that he had been given a significant responsibility in the execution of this plan in the dispensation of the church age.

3:3–4. The mystery (v. 3) is a truth known only by divine revelation (see 3:5; Rom. 16:25; discussions on Rom. 11:25; Col. 1:26). Here the word "mystery" refers to the eternal and wise plan of God, once hidden in God but now revealed and proclaimed to the world (see 3:9–10). In Ephesians, "mystery" points to the unification of believing Jews and Gentiles in the new body, the church (see 3:6). **As I wrote afore in few words** (v. 3) may refer to 1:9–10. Paul's **knowledge** (v. 4), or comprehension, of the "mystery" was not a boast but belonged to the special dispensation (see v. 2) of his ministry from God.

3:5. For **not made known unto the sons of men**, see discussion on 3:6. **Holy** means set apart for God's service. **Apostles and prophets** is best defined by Paul's use of the expression in 2:20. Although Paul was the chief recipient of this revelation, others received it also. **By the Spirit** indicates the agency of the Spirit in revealing God's truth (for the role of the Spirit, see 1 Peter 1:10–12).

3:6. The words **fellowheirs** (see discussion on 1:18) **... same body ... partakers** indicate the unique aspect of the mystery that was not previously known: the equality and mutuality that Gentiles had with Jews in the church, the one body.

That Gentiles would turn to the God of Israel and be saved was prophesied in the Old Testament (see Rom. 15:9–12); that they would come into an organic unity with believing Jews on an equal footing was unexpected.

3:7–8. Paul understood his strategic role as apostle to the Gentiles as being entirely God's calling through His grace (see 3:2, Rom. 11:32; 15:15–16; Gal. 2:7–9; Acts 9:15) and not of any personal merit. As a result, Paul saw himself as **less than the least** (v. 8; see 1 Tim. 1:15). Paul never ceased to be amazed that one so unworthy as he should have been chosen for so high a task. His modesty was genuine, even though one may disagree with his self-evaluation. **Grace** (v. 7), in this case, was a special endowment that brought responsibility for service (see Rom. 12:6). The **riches of Christ** (v. 8; see 1:3) are **unsearchable**, far beyond what can be known but not beyond appreciation, at least in part (see Rom. 11:33).

3:9–10. Now (v. 10) stands in contrast to the previous "ages." **Fellowship** (v. 9) translates the Greek word *oikonomia* ("administration," "stewardship," "plan"), used also in 3:2. This grand plan of God, the mystery now unfolding, is being executed in Christ (see 1:10), and the incorporation of both the Jews and the Gentiles into the church is manifesting the manifold wisdom of God to all men and no less to **the principalities and powers in heavenly places** (v. 10; see 1:20–21, discussion on 1:3). It is a staggering thought that the church on earth is observed, so to speak, by these spiritual powers and that, to the degree the church is spiritually united, it portrays to them the wisdom of God. This thought may be essential in understanding the meaning of "vocation" in 4:1. What is manifested is demonstrated and known **by the church**. That God has done the seemingly impossible—reconciling and organically uniting Jews and Gentiles in the church—makes the church the perfect means of displaying God's wisdom. **Manifold** means "variegated" or "multifaceted" (in the way that the many facets of a diamond reflect and enhance its beauty).

3:11. In all of Scripture, there is no theology of the church more profound or focused than is given in Ephesians. Human characterizations of "the church" must be elevated and transformed by Paul's majestic illumination of the church according to God's **eternal purpose**. The effective headship of Christ over a united church is in preparation for His ultimate assumption of headship over the universe (see 1:10).

3:12–13. Note well the believer's prerogative in Christ (**In whom**; v. 12). The believer's **boldness and access [to God] with confidence** is a privilege attributed to the manifold wisdom of God made known in the church and observed by the "loftiest" principalities and powers in the heavenly places (see 3:10). By virtue of Jesus Christ and faith in Him, the "lowliest" enjoys prerogatives with God that belong only to the loftiest of the lofty, the exalted status of Jesus Christ (see 1:17–21). "Boldness" (Greek, *parrēsia*; "frank speech," "open expression," "fearlessness"), a word that had a rich history in the Greek *demos*, referring to a citizen's right to speak openly, was also used to "signify the right to stand with uplifted head before a potentate (Luke 21:28)" (Barth, *Ephesians*, vol. 1, p. 348). The latter fits the picture Paul painted here of the believer's comfortable access to and audience with God (see Heb. 4:16). Paul enjoyed this too, even in prison, and therefore assured his readers and encouraged them. His tribulations belonged to the glory of what God is doing in the church according to His eternal purpose in Christ.

E. Prayer for a Deeper Experience of God's Fullness (3:14–21)

3:14–21. Here Paul expressed a prayer that grew out of his awareness of all that God is doing in believers. God's key gifts are "might" (vv. 16, 20) and "love" (vv. 17–19).

3:14–15. For this cause resumes the thought of 3:1. **I bow my knees** expressed Paul's deep emotion and reverence, as people in his day usually stood to pray.

In Greek, **family** (v. 15) is similar to the word for "father," so it can be said that the "family" derives its name (and being) from the father. God's universal preeminence and power as Sovereign Creator is reflected in this absolute use of **Father** (v. 14). Nevertheless, God is our Father, and Christians can commit their prayers to Him in confidence (see 3:12–13).

3:16–19. According to the riches of his glory (v. 16) points to the inexhaustible fund of God's vast resources aligned with the purpose of Paul's prayer for the Ephesians. Three objectives occupy Paul's prayer: (1) inner strength (vv. 16–17), (2) comprehension (v. 18), and (3) fullness (v. 19). The key to inner strength is Christ, who inwardly **dwell[s] in your hearts** (v. 17). When Christ is completely at home in the believer, He is free to exercise power through His effective presence. Christ was already present in the Ephesian believers' lives (see Rom. 8:9). Through faith, however, the believer must rest in the strength of Christ rather than wrest control from Him through independent human effort. "Heart" denotes the whole inner being. **Passeth knowledge** (v. 19) does not mean that the love of Christ is unknowable but that His love is so great that it cannot be completely known (compare God's peace "which passeth all understanding," Phil. 4:7). **Filled with all the fulness of God** conveys the idea of such inconceivable scope and incalculable measure that its conception becomes nearly imponderable. The stature of God's perfection ("fulness"), however, must not obscure the dynamic and qualitative emphasis here on "filling." Believers are to be permeated by God, absorbing His person and His provisions more and more. God, who is infinite in all His attributes, allows one to draw on His resources—in this case, His love.

3:20. Exceeding abundantly above refers specifically to the matters presented in this section of Ephesians but is not limited to these. **Power that worketh in us** (see 1:19–21) refers to the operative presence of the Holy Spirit, the power of **him that is able** to **worketh** in the believer. In Greek, the word "power" (*dynamis*) takes up the verb *dynamai* of "him that is able."

3:21. Unto him be glory expresses the ultimate goal of human existence (see 1:6 and discussion). **In the church by Christ Jesus** poses a remarkable parallel. God has called the church to an extraordinary position and vocation (see 3:10; 4:1).

V. Practical Ways to Fulfill God's Purpose in the Church (4:1–6:20)

4:1–32. The chapter begins (v. 2) and ends (v. 32) with exhortations to love and forgive one another.

4:1–16. Earlier in Ephesians, Paul taught that God brought Jew and Gentile into a new relationship with each other in the church and that He called the church to display His wisdom. Paul now showed how God made provision for those in the church to live and work together in unity and to grow together into maturity.

A. Unity (4:1–6)

4:1. Paul retained the self-designation **prisoner**, introduced in 3:1 (see discussion there). With its repetition, he called not for pity (see 3:13) but carried forward the example of his calling (see 3:1–2, 8–10) on behalf of the Lord as he exhorted the Ephesians to **walk worthy of** (their) **vocation**. Indeed, they now belonged to the same grand vocation (see 3:10, 21 and discussions).

4:2–3. Keep the unity (v. 3) points to the peace that God produced through the reconciling death of Christ (see 2:14–22). **The bond** has already been established by "our peace" (2:14), Jesus Christ, and its unity is maintained in the Spirit. Christians have the heavy responsibility of keeping that unity from being disturbed, a responsibility that is given specific expression in the self-effacing attitude believers are to have toward each other: **lowliness and meekness, with longsuffering, forbearing one another in love**. In Greek, the word **endeavouring** as Paul used it here means to be especially conscientious in discharging an obligation. This responsibility belongs to the very foundation of the church's existence and identity, its oneness (see 4:4–6).

4:4. One body is the church, the union of believers incorporated in Christ (see, e.g., 1:22–23; 2:16; 3:6; 5:30). **One Spirit** is the Holy Spirit (see 1:13; 2:18, 22). **One hope** has different aspects (e.g., 1:5, 10; 2:7), but it is still one hope; its substance is the calling of God in Jesus Christ (1:18) and the glorious future of Christ, in which all believers share.

4:5-6. One Lord (v. 5) is Jesus Christ, who is the Head of the church, His body (see 1:2-3, 22; 3:11; 4:15). **One baptism** refers not to the baptism of the Spirit (see 1 Cor. 12:13), which is inward and therefore invisible, but to water baptism (see discussion on Rom. 6:3-4). Since Paul apparently had in mind that which identifies all believers as belonging together, he would have naturally referred to the church ordinance in which every new convert participated publicly. At that time, it was a more obvious, common identification mark of Christians than it is now, when it is observed differently and is often seen by only those in the church. **One God, and Father of all** (v. 6) is "the God of our Lord Jesus Christ, the Father of glory" (1:17), and the foundation of the church is God's universal rule. His sovereign presence is exemplified by the description of His care for the church in what follows (see Barth, *Ephesians*, vol. 2, p. 429).

B. Maturity (4:7-16)

4:7. Grace (see 3:7-8) is given **according to the measure of [God's] gift**, the Christ (Messiah). Jesus is the measure (see Rom. 8:32) and, as expressed in what follows, the donor (see 4:11).

4:8. Psalm 68:18 (see *KJV Study Bible* note) speaks of God's triumphant ascension to His throne in the temple at Jerusalem (symbol of His heavenly throne). Paul applied this to Christ's triumphal ascension into heaven. Where Psalm 68:18 states that God "received gifts among men," Paul apparently took his cue from certain rabbinic interpretations current in his day that read the Hebrew preposition "among" in the sense of "unto" (a meaning it often has) and the verb for "received" in the sense of "take and give" (a meaning it sometimes has, but with a different preposition; see Gen. 15:9; 18:5; 27:13; Exod. 25:2; 1 Kings 17:10-11). **Captivity** probably refers to the spiritual enemies that Christ defeated at the cross.

4:9-10. Ascended ... descended (v. 9) belongs to Paul's elaboration and explanation. Although Paul quoted from the psalm to introduce the idea of the "gifts unto men" (4:8), he took the opportunity to remind his readers of Christ's coming to earth, His incarnation ("descended"), and His subsequent resurrection and ascension ("ascended"). This passage probably does not teach, as some think and as some translations suggest, that Christ descended into hell.

4:11. He gave picks up the leading thought in 4:7, that Jesus is the measure or gold standard of God's grace. His qualifications as donor were established in 4:8-10. Consequently, the quotation of Psalm 68:18 has its ultimate meaning when applied to Christ as the ascended Lord, who Himself has given gifts. **Apostles** are mentioned here because of their role in establishing the church (see 2:20; for qualifications of the initial group of apostles, see Acts 1:21-22; see also discussions on Mark 6:30; Rom. 1:1; 1 Cor. 1:1; Heb. 3:1). In a broader sense, Paul was also an apostle (see 1:1). **Prophets** are men or women (Acts 21:9; Rev. 2:20; 1 Cor 11:15) who spoke of God's revelation to the particular need or situation of the church (see 1 Cor. 14:3-4; see also note on 1 Cor. 12:10). True prophetic utterance for the church adhered to and upheld the apostles' testimony to Jesus. For **evangelists**, see Acts 21:8; 1 Corinthians 1:17. While other gifted people help the church grow through edification, evangelists help the church grow by augmentation. Since the objective mentioned in 4:12 is "for the perfecting of the saints for the work of the ministry," one may assume that evangelists, among their various ministries, help other Christians in their testimony. As Paul's wording indicates, **pastors and teachers** belong closer together than do apostles and prophets or prophets and evangelists; the Greek grammatical construction (also, the word **some** introduces both words together) suggests these gifted people are closely related. Those who have pastoral care for God's people (the image is that of shepherding) will naturally provide "food" from the Scriptures (teaching). They will be especially gifted as teachers (see 1 Tim. 3:2).

4:12. People are given (see 4:11) as gifts for a twofold function: First, they are given **For the perfecting of the saints for the work of the ministry.** Those mentioned in 4:11 were not to do all the work for the people but were to train the people to do the work themselves. "Perfecting" (Greek, *katartismos*) occurs only here. Outside the New Testament the word is used in association with actions taken to make something fit for its intended use. Accordingly, the saints are "trained" or "equipped." All believers are to be enlisted in the work of the ministry. The second function develops and expands the first: **for the edifying of the body of Christ** (see 4:16). Spiritual gifts are for the body, the church, and are not to be exercised individualistically (see 1 Peter 4:10). "Edifying" or "building up" reflects the imagery of 2:19–22. These concepts, body and building, occurring together emphasize the key idea of growth.

4:13. **Till** (or "until") expresses not merely duration but also purpose. **Unity** carries forward the ideal of 4:1–6. **Of the faith** here refers to the Christians' common conviction about Christ and the doctrines concerning Him, as the following words (e.g., **knowledge**) make clear (see also "the apostles' doctrine" in Acts 2:42). The word **unity** makes it clear that **the knowledge of the Son of God** is not a private or an individual "familiarity." Unity is a matter not just of a loving attitude or religious feeling but of truth and a common understanding about God's Son. The final goal, the **perfect man … the fulness of Christ**, is conceived not as an individual achievement but as the collective attainment of the church. There is no room in this picture for competition, only for mutual and cooperative fellow ministry that cherishes the words **till we all** (see 4:15–16). More than the maturity of doctrinal conviction referred to by "of the faith" or a personal maturity that includes the ability to relate well to other people (see 4:23), the "perfect man" is the maturity of the perfectly balanced character of Christ.

4:14. For the sense of the word **children**, contrast the maturity described in 4:13. The nautical imagery of **tossed to and fro** and **wind of doctrine** pictures the instability of those who are not strong Christians. Then, as now, there were many distorted teachings and heresies that could easily throw the immature off course. For this reason, the church must be intentional and deliberate about its responsibility (see 4:12–13). Additionally, it must withstand the very

intentional and deliberate nature of its opposition: **sleight … craftiness … deceive**. Those who try to draw people away from the Christian faith are not innocently misguided but deliberately deceitful and evil (see 1 Tim. 4:1–2).

4:15. Speaking the truth in love is contrasted with the deceiving practices of those who oppose the truth (4:14). A truthful and loving manner of life is implied. **Grow up into him … the head** is a slightly different restatement of 4:13, based here on the imagery of Christ as the Head of the body, which is the church. Paul thus was speaking primarily of corporate maturity: "the body of Christ" needs to be edified or built up (4:12); "we all" are to become "a perfect man," or mature (4:13).

4:16. Paul further detailed the body growing under the Head's direction with the anatomical imagery of interconnected parts functioning in a vital and essential design. The parts of the body help each other in the growing process, picturing the mutual ministries of God's people spoken of in 4:11–13. All believers, each and every one, have a vital and essential role and place in the healthy growth of the church. In the physical body, the mechanics are anatomical; in the spiritual body of Christ, the motive is love. **Love** is instrumental, for maturity and unity are impossible without it (see 4:2, 15).

C. Renewal of Personal Life (4:17–5:20)

4:17–5:20. In the preceding section, Paul discussed unity and maturity as twin goals for the church, which God brought into existence through the death of Christ. Here he went on to show that purity is also essential among those who belong to Him.

4:17–19. Christians from a Gentile background were to eschew their former way of life. **The vanity of their mind** (v. 17) points to the empty and futile reasoning of a mind devoid of revealed truth and moral clarity. Accordingly, life without God is intellectually frustrating, useless, and meaningless (see, e.g., Eccl. 1:2; Rom. 1:21). Paul further described the "vanity" of the Gentile mind as **understanding darkened** (clouded judgment; v. 18) and **ignorance** (lacking knowledge, namely, revealed truth), conditions of a heart that is increasingly hardened and calloused (**past feeling**; v. 19). In this kind of internal environment, impurities and immorality thrive. The Ephesians were instructed to **walk not as other Gentiles walk** (v. 17), who **have given themselves over** (v. 19). Just as Pharaoh's heart was hardened reciprocally by himself and by God (see Exod. 7–11), so here the Gentiles had given themselves over to a sinful kind of life, while Romans 1:24, 26, 28 says that God gave them over to that life. The wording of verses 17–19 is comparable to that of Romans 1:21, 24.

4:20–21. Ye (v. 20) is emphatic and complements the strong contrast of the vain ways of "other Gentiles" (4:17) with the way Paul's readers **learned Christ**. This is shorthand for being taught and learning the will of God as it is embodied in Christ. **The truth is in Jesus** (v. 21). The wording and the use of the name Jesus (rather than Christ) suggest that Paul was referring to the embodiment of truth in Jesus' earthly life. The internal benefits of "learning Christ" can be imagined by contrasting the internal degeneration described in 4:17–19, which was associated with "being alienated from the life of God through … ignorance" (4:18). The contrast is summarized in 4:22–23.

4:22–23. The old man (v. 22) refers to everything humans are naturally, by birth, being part of the fallen human race. It includes the old lifestyle, resulting from natural deceitful desires. **The spirit of your mind** (v. 23) and its renewal is directly contrasted here with "the old man" and the degeneration associated with the vanity of one's mind (see 4:17–18). Romans 12:2 is helpful here. Revealed truth (see 4:20–21) is the medium of transformation and the disposition or spirit of the mind.

4:24. The new man refers to everything believers are in Christ through rebirth (see Rom. 6:6–11; 2 Cor. 5:17; Gal. 2:20; Col. 3:9–10).

4:25. Inner **truth**, such as Christ embodies (see 4:20–21), when it takes root and renews the spirit of the mind, is necessarily matched by truth that graces one's speech (see 4:15). **Neighbour** probably means fellow Christians in this context. **We are members**

one of another, as anatomically illustrated in 4:16, integral to and interconnected in one body, the church.

4:26. Be ye angry. Christians do not lose their emotions at conversion, but their emotions should be purified. Some anger is sinful; some is not. Anger is a God-given emotion that can serve the righteous purposes of God if expressed constructively and not destructively. Anger that does not serve sin must serve the higher demands of God's love. **Let not the sun go down.** No anger is to outlast the day. The sooner it is dealt with, the better.

4:27. Personal sin is usually due to personal evil desires (see James 1:14) rather than to direct tempting by the Devil. However, **the devil** can, as his very name, "Slanderer," indicates, use our sins—especially those, like anger, that are against others—to bring about greater evil, such as divisions among Christians.

4:28. Steal no more … labour … give to him that needeth. It is not enough to cease from sin; one must reverse the practice and replace wrongdoing with what is right. The former thief must now help those in need.

4:29. But that … edifying is an exhortation parallel to the previous one (4:28). The Christian not only stops saying unwholesome things; he also begins to say things that will help build up others.

4:30. Grieve is used of actions that vex, irritate, offend, or insult, actions that cause severe mental or emotional distress. The verb also demonstrates that the Holy Spirit is a person, not just an influence, for only a person can be grieved. "Corrupt communication" (4:29) and the sins mentioned in 4:31 belong to the kinds of sinful actions that "grieve" the heart of God. **Sealed** (see discussion on 1:13) reminds one of the abiding personal presence of God in the person of the Holy Spirit, identifying believers as His **unto the day of redemption** (see 1:14; *KJV Study Bible* note on 1 Peter 1:5).

4:31. Bitterness … malice are among the things that grieve the Holy Spirit. **Put away** does not mean to put away for safekeeping but to "remove" and so "renounce" such things (see 22). This continues the instruction concerning one's speech (4:29), which ought to correspond to the truth within (see 4:20–21, 25).

4:32. Kind ... tenderhearted are opposites of the negative qualities of 4:31. These are the outward expressions of "the new man" (see 4:21–24), the Christlike person being forged by the presence of the Spirit (see 4:30). **Forgiving** is the basic Christian attitude, which is a result of being forgiven in Christ, and along with being kind and compassionate, it brings to others what Christians have received from God.

5:1. Be ... followers of God. One way of imitating God is to have a forgiving spirit (see 4:32). The way one imitates the Lord is to act "even as" (4:32) He did. The sacrificial way Jesus expressed His love is not only the means of salvation (as seen in chap. 2) but is also an example of the way to live, for the sake of others.

5:2. With the imagery of **an offering ... a sweet-smelling savour**, Paul's assigned the highest rank to the imitation of Jesus' sacrificial love in attitude and action. In the Old Testament, the offering of a sacrifice pleased the Lord so much that it was described as "a sweet savour" (Gen. 8:21; Exod. 29:18, 25, 41; Lev. 1:9, 13, 17).

5:3. With the sequence of **all uncleanness, or covetousness**, Paul moved from specifically sexual sins to more general sins, such as greed. These sins include sexual lust but refer to other kinds of excessive desire as well. **Not be once named** (see 5:12) adds the perspective of outsiders who observe the relevance of Christ through the lens of His **saints** (lit., "holy ones"). Believers are also "a holy temple" (2:21; see 2 Cor. 6:16; 1 Peter 2:5, 9).

5:4. The context and the word **filthiness** indicate that **foolish talking** and **jesting** refer not to humor as such but to dirty jokes, caustic sarcasm, and the like, which are out of place. Always appropriate and worthy of God's generosity is the **giving of thanks**. By being grateful for all that God has given, one can displace evil thoughts and words.

5:5. The behaviors and attitudes profiled in 5:3–4 belong to the culture of the **whoremonger**

... covetous man and not to the character of those ruled by Christ and God's reign (see 5:3). Paul appealed to what his readers already knew (**For this ye know**), probably alluding to a realization attested by their own conversion as well as his teaching (see 2:1–3; "children of disobedience," 5:6). **An idolater** (see Col. 3:5) is a greedy person who wants things more than he wants God and puts things in place of God, thereby committing idolatry. **Inheritance** literally refers to the property or possessions of a bequest and identifies the spiritual belongings that are bequeathed in salvation to those who belong to God, his heirs (see 1:14, 18; Col. 1:12; 1 Peter 1:4). The person who persists in sexual and other kinds of greed has excluded God, who therefore excludes him from the kingdom (but see discussions on 1 Cor. 6:9, 11).

5:6–7. Paul instructed the Ephesians to withstand any and all efforts to **deceive** (v. 6) them into being drawn aside or led astray from what they knew (see 5:5). Believers will always be confronted with plausible and attractive justifications and rationalizations of worldly ungodliness, but such words are **vain words**. "Vain" may refer to the content of the words (lit., "empty") as being devoid of truth or to the outcome or effect of the words as having no clout or impact. **These things** summarizes not the "vain words" but the ungodly ways represented in the previous verses. **Partakers** (v. 7) refers to taking part in or experiencing something with others. The foundation of this prohibition is laid in 5:8–14. Although Christians live in normal social relationships with others, as did the Lord Jesus (Luke 5:30–32; 15:1–2), they are not to participate in the sinful lifestyle of unbelievers.

5:8. Darkness and **light** are metaphors that convey moral opposites. Behind this polarization lies the contrast of revelation and the illumination of God's truth (see 4:18). The contrast between light and darkness in 4:8–14 shows that those who belong to Him who is "light" (1 John 1:5), that is, pure and true, not only have their lives illumined by Him but also are the means of introducing that light into the dark areas of human conduct (see Matt. 5:14).

5:9–10. Walking in the light (see 5:8; 1 John 1:7) is demonstrable, showing the effects of the light, **the fruit of the Spirit** (v. 9; see Gal. 5:22–23), and what pleases the Lord (see Rom. 12:2).

5:11. Have no fellowship with (see 5:7), or mutual partnership with, **unfruitful works of darkness.** The "fruit" of the light, "goodness and righteousness and truth" (5:9), is contrasted with "unfruitful works": evil and wickedness and falsehood. **Reprove** means "convict, refute, and confute." Light, by nature, exposes what is in darkness, and the contrast shows sin for what it really is.

5:12. Paul wrote with a tone of disdain of the disgraceful things, "the deeds of darkness" done in secret. So disgraceful are they, **it is a shame even to speak of those things.** How unthinkable must it be for the believer to associate with and participate in such darkness as children of the light? Moreover, Christians should not dwell on the evils that their lives expose in others.

5:13–14. All things ... made manifest ... for whatsoever doth make manifest is light (v. 13). The repetition of these words indicates that Paul was stressing the all-pervasive nature of the light of God and its inevitable effect. **He saith** (v. 14) is the opening of what may well be a hymn used by the early Christians (see discussion on Col. 3:16). **Sleepest ... dead** are two images that describe a sinner (see 2:1). **Christ shall give thee light.** As the sun and its dawn arouse and awaken one from physical slumber, Christ and His life-giving light awaken one from spiritual slumber.

5:15–17. Paul challenged his readers to **walk circumspectly** (v. 15), to watch their step, or conduct. With the word **Wherefore** (v. 17), the contrast between light and darkness turns to the contrast between wisdom and foolishness. Walking circumspectly requires wisdom. Paul's method for walking wisely entailed **redeeming the time** (v. 16; see Col. 4:5). The commercial associations of the verb "buy, buy up" makes time the valued commodity to be bought up. "Time" (Greek, *kairos*) connotes opportunity. The present is a precious opportunity to do **the will of the Lord** (v. 17). Perspective on *kairos*

is gained from a different word for time, *chronos*, found elsewhere in the New Testament, which connotes the elapse and measure of time. **Days** (v. 16) are increments of *chronos* that Paul characterized as "evil," not because they are intrinsically so but because people exhaust time with their evil, largely because they are foolish. Christians, on the other hand, are to "buy up" the time, the present, as an opportunity to walk wisely, doing the will of God in an environment of evil, even as light in an environment of darkness reproves the darkness.

5:18. Paul stated that the means of walking wisely as children of the light is the power of the Holy Spirit (see 5:10). Christians are to operate under the influence, or control, of God, His will (4:17), and His power: **be not drunk ... but be filled with the Spirit.** Paul used the Greek present tense to indicate that the filling of the Spirit is not a onetime experience. Repeatedly, as the occasion requires, the Spirit empowers for worship, service, and testimony. The contrast between being filled with wine and being filled with the Spirit is obvious. The two have something in common, which enabled Paul to make the contrast, namely, that one can be under an influence that affects him, whether of wine or of the Spirit. Since Colossians 3:15–4:1 is very similar to Ephesians 5:18–6:9, one may assume that Paul intended to convey a similar thought in the introductory sentences of each passage. When he wrote here of being filled with the Spirit and when he wrote in Colossians of being under the rule of the peace of Christ and indwelt by the "word of Christ" (Col. 3:16), he meant that believers are to be under God's control. The effect of this control is essentially the same in both passages: a happy, mutual encouragement to praise God and a healthy, mutual relationship with people.

5:19–20. Paul encouraged the Ephesians to sing every kind of appropriate song, whether **psalms** like those of the Old Testament, **hymns** directed to God, or other **spiritual songs** Christians were accustomed to singing. Such songs provide a means for **giving thanks** (v. 20) and praise to God. Actually, however, all three terms may refer to different types of psalms (see discussion on Col. 3:16). All in all, music fills the heart when it is filled with God's Spirit.

D. Deference in Personal Relationships (5:21–6:9)

5:21–6:9. In chapters 2–4, Paul showed how God brought believing Jews and Gentiles together into a new relationship in Christ. In 4:1–6, he stressed the importance of unity. In this section, he showed in a practical way how believers, filled with the Spirit, can live together in various human relationships. This list of mutual responsibilities is similar to the pattern found in Colossians 3:18–4:1 and 1 Peter 2:13–3:12 (see also Rom. 13:1–10).

1. The Principle (5:21)

5:21. Submitting yourselves one to another is basic to the following paragraphs. Paul showed how, in each relationship discussed, the partners can have a conciliatory attitude that will help that relationship. The grammar indicates that this submission is associated with the filling of the Spirit in 5:18. The command "be filled" (5:18) is followed by a series of participles in the Greek: speaking, singing, making melody (5:19), giving thanks (5:20), and submitting (v. 21). **In the fear of God** denotes the positive posture of submitting to the rightful priority of God. Honoring God with priority of place over oneself by giving Him rightful power over one's will and wishes makes submitting to one another an easy step (see Col. 3:18). Alternatively, submission owed to another person should never exceed the submission owed to God.

2. Husbands and Wives (5:22–33)

5:22. Wives, submit yourselves is an aspect of the submission taught in 5:21. To be subject to another meant to yield one's own rights. Biblical submission is not to be confused with passivity but rather is a noble act of the will that places another ahead of oneself. If the relationship calls for it, as in the military, the term can connote obedience, but that meaning is not called for here. In fact, the word "obey" does not appear in Scripture with respect to

wives, though it does with respect to children (6:1) and servants (6:5). **As unto the Lord** does not put a woman's husband in the place of the Lord but rather shows that a woman ought to submit to her husband as an act of submission to the Lord (see 1 Peter 3:1–6, especially 3:6).

5:23–33. Throughout this crucial and very practical text, Paul instructed wives and husbands that the husband is to take his cues from Christ and the wife is to take hers from the church. This insight is important both for the marriage partners and for the church (see v. 32).

5:23–24. The husband is the head of the wife (v. 23; see *KJV Study Bible* note on 1 Cor. 11:3) only and in the same way **as Christ is the head of the church**. The words "as Christ" are the control. The analogy between the relationship of Christ to the church and that of the husband to the wife is basic to the entire passage. **He is the saviour of the body** (see 2:16; 4:4, 12, 16) makes it clear that Christ earned, so to speak, the right to His special relationship to the church. As to Christ, the wife is to submit to her husband.

5:25. Paul proceeded to show that this is not a one-sided submission but a reciprocal relationship. The command **Husbands, love your wives** is also a command showing that the husband's headship is under the authority of Christ and subject to His command, even as the wife's submission is. "Love" (Greek, *agapaō*) generally means "the attitude and acts of unselfish giving" (Barth, *Ephesians*, vol. 2, p. 621). Here it is given its supreme example and definition. **Gave himself for it** not only points to the expression of the Lord's love but exemplifies how the husband ought to devote himself to his wife's good. To give oneself up to death for the beloved is a more extreme expression of devotion than the wife is called on to make.

5:26. Many attempts have been made to see marriage customs or liturgical symbolism in the words **the washing of water by the word**. One thing is clear: the Lord Jesus died not only to bring forgiveness but also to effect a new life of holiness in the church, which is His "bride." A study of the concepts of washing, water, and the Word should include John 3:5; 15:3; Titus 3:5; James 1:18; 1 Peter 1:23; 3:21.

5:27. Holy and without blemish (see 1:4) expresses the beauty and splendor of the bride at her presentation. This objective, albeit on a spiritual plane, finds its corollary and application for the husband and his bride in the following verses.

5:28–29. As their own bodies ... loveth himself (v. 28) **... his own flesh** (v. 29). The basis for such expressions and for the teaching of these verses is the quotation from Genesis 2:24 in 5:31. If the husband and wife become "one flesh" (5:31), then for the man to love his wife is to love one who has become part of himself.

5:30. We are members of his body ties the thought of 5:28–29 into the experience of the church and its reception of Christ's love: believers ought to love as they have been loved.

5:31. See Genesis 2:24.

5:32. Mystery. See discussion on Rom. 11:25. The profound truth of the union of Christ and his "bride," the church, is beyond unaided human understanding. It is not that the relationship of husband and wife provides an illustration of the union of **Christ and the church**; rather, the basic reality is the latter, and marriage is a human echo of that relationship.

5:33. Love ... reverence is a rephrasing and summary of the whole passage.

3. Children and Parents (6:1–4)

6:1–2. Children, obey your parents in the Lord (v. 1). The words "in the Lord," or "because of the Lord," are the motivation to obey whether parents are Christians or not. This is borne out by the other pairs of social relationships. In both the preceding example (wives and husbands) and the latter example (slaves and masters), the subordinate is addressed first. In all three cases, the traditional social duty is now configured in relation to Christ. **First commandment** (v. 2) refers here to the "basic" or "primary" command for children. **With a promise** refers to the promise of 6:3, the fifth commandment (Exod. 20:12), and apparently the second commandment with a promise (see Exod. 20:6).

6:3. Note the words **on the earth.** In Deuteronomy 5:16, where this commandment occurs (see also Exod. 20:12), the "promise" (6:2) was expressed in terms of the anticipated occupation of the "land," that is, Canaan. That specific application was, of course, not appropriate for the Ephesians, so Paul made a more general application here.

6:4. Fathers as the governing heads of families are addressed with an obligation to control the spirit of discipline: **provoke not.** Fathers must surrender any right they may feel they have to act unreasonably toward their children.

4. Slaves and Masters (6:5–9)

6:5–7. Servants (v. 5) are to view their responsibilities to their earthly **masters according to the flesh** as they would their service to Christ. Both the Old Testament and the New Testament included regulations for societal situations such as slavery and divorce (see Deut. 24:1–4), which were the results of the hardness of hearts (see Matt. 19:8). Such regulations did not encourage or condone such situations but were divinely given, practical ways of dealing with the realities of the day. **Fear and trembling** was a fairly stock expression for Paul (see 2 Cor. 7:15; Eph. 6:5; Phil. 2:12; 1 Cor. 2:3) and expresses respect. **Singleness of your heart** speaks of "wholeheartedness" or "complete sincerity." The heartfelt service with which one serves Christ is introduced in verse 5 and is amplified in verses 6–7.

6:8. Knowing ... whether he be bond or free points to the general principle and encouragement that properly motivated actions or service to the Lord (see 6:5–7) do not go unrecognized by the Lord (see Rom. 2:6; Ps. 62:12; Prov. 24:12; 1 Peter 1:17).

6:9. Likewise, **masters** are to treat slaves according to the treatment of their **Master ... in heaven.** Once again, Paul stressed reciprocal attitudes (see 5:21–6:4; see discussion on Titus 2:9). **Neither is there respect** (or "partiality"; Greek, *prosōpolēmpsia*; "accept face") **of persons with him** is defined quite literally in Galatians 2:6: "God accepteth no man's person." The Lord does not evaluate any person on the basis of "face" (one's status and credentials). One may be a "master" by earthly standards but not by heavenly ones.

E. Strength in the Spiritual Conflict (6:10–20)

6:10–20. Paul's scope in Ephesians was cosmic. From the very beginning, he drew attention to the unseen world (see discussion on 1:3; see also 1:10, 20–23; 2:6; 6:10); now he described the spiritual battle that takes place against evil "in high places" (v. 12).

6:10–11. Strong ... might (v. 10) implies that human effort is inadequate, but God's power is invincible. Such strength, the Lord's might, is found in **the whole armour of God** (v. 11; repeated in 6:13), and its inventory given in 6:14–17. The ready purpose of the Lord's might and armor is to withstand **the wiles of the devil**. "Wiles," or "methods" (Greek, *methodeia*), are the schemes of Satan, which may be encountered and administered by the forces of darkness identified in 6:12 (see Satan's "devices," 2 Cor. 2:11; Greek, *noēma*; meaning "design" or "intention," as the product of an intellectual process).

6:12. Not against flesh and blood is a caution against lashing out against human opponents as though they were the real enemy and also against assuming that the battle can be fought using merely human resources. Compare **principalities ... spiritual wickedness** with Paul's earlier allusions to powerful beings in the unseen world (see discussions on 1:21; 3:10). The Greek phrase for **high places** is the same as in 1:3 and is better translated "heavenly places" (see discussion on 1:3).

6:13–14. In this context, the imagery of **withstand** (v. 13) and **Stand therefore** (v. 14) is not that of a massive invasion of the domain of evil but of individual soldiers withstanding assault. **Loins girt about with truth** (see the symbolic clothing of the Messiah in Isa. 11:5). Character, not brute force, wins

the battle, just as in the case of the Messiah. **Breastplate of righteousness** is a metaphor Paul used to show that Christians are to put on righteousness to protect their hearts as a soldier puts on a breastplate to protect himself.

6:15. Feet shod with the preparation of the gospel. Whereas the description of the messenger's feet in Isaiah 52:7 reflects the custom of running barefooted, here the message of the gospel is picturesquely connected with the protective and supportive footgear of the Roman soldier.

6:16. Taking the shield of faith ... to quench all the fiery darts is an description pointing to the large Roman shield covered with leather, which could be soaked in water and used to put out flame-tipped arrows.

6:17–18. The sword of the Spirit (v. 17) and **Praying ... in the Spirit** (v. 18) are reminders that the battle is spiritual and must be fought in God's strength, depending on the Word and on God through prayer. Isaiah 59:17 has similar language, along with the breastplate imagery (see discussion on 6:14). As a helmet both protects a soldier and provides a striking symbol of military victory, **the helmet of salvation** (v. 17) caps the spiritual armor and victory of the Lord's might.

VI. Conclusion, Final Greetings, and Benediction (6:21–24)

6:21–23. Paul concluded with greetings that lack personal references, such as are usually found in his letters. This is understandable if Ephesians was a circular letter (see discussion on 1:1). **Tychicus** (v. 21) was an associate of Paul who traveled as his representative (see Col. 4:7; 2 Tim. 4:12; Titus 3:12). Thus, Paul closed with practical advice and personal concern for the believers at Ephesus.

THE EPISTLE OF PAUL THE APOSTLE TO THE PHILIPPIANS

INTRODUCTION

Author, Date, and Place of Composition

The early church was unanimous in its testimony that Philippians was written by the apostle Paul (see 1:1). Internally, the letter reveals the stamp of genuineness. The many personal references of the author fit what is known of Paul from other New Testament books.

It is evident that Paul wrote this letter from prison (see 1:13–14). Some have argued that this imprisonment took place in Ephesus, perhaps circa AD 53–55; others put it in Caesarea, circa AD 57–59. The best evidence, however, favors Rome as the place of composition and the date as circa AD 61. This fits well with the account of Paul's house arrest in Acts 28:14–31. When Paul wrote Philippians, he was not in the Mamertine dungeon as he was when he wrote 2 Timothy. He was in his own rented house, where for two years he was free to impart the gospel to all who came to him. Silva (pp. 5–8) discusses these options in detail, providing a thorough defense of the Roman imprisonment, reconciling the time elements involved.

The City of Philippi

The city of Philippi was named after King Philip II of Macedon, father of Alexander the Great. It was a prosperous Roman colony, which meant that the citizens of Philippi were also citizens of the city of Rome itself. They prided themselves on being Romans (see Acts 16:21), dressed like Romans, and often spoke Latin. No doubt this was the background for Paul's reference to the believer's heavenly citizenship (see 3:20–21). Many of the Philippians were retired military men who had been given land in the vicinity and who in turn served as a military presence in this frontier city. That Philippi was a Roman colony may explain why there were not enough Jews there to permit the establishment of a synagogue and why Paul did not quote the Old Testament in the Philippian letter.

Theme and Theological Message

Paul's primary purpose in writing this letter was to thank the Philippians for the gift they had sent him upon learning of his detention at Rome (1:5; 4:10–19). However, he made use of this occasion to fulfill several other desires: (1) to report on his own circumstances (1:12–26; 4:10–19); (2) to encourage the Philippians to stand firm in the face of persecution and rejoice regardless of circumstances (1:27–30; 4:4); (3) to exhort them to humility and unity (2:1–11; 4:2–5); (4) to commend Timothy and Epaphroditus to the Philippian church (2:19–30); and (5) to warn the Philippians against the Judaizers (legalists) and antinomians (libertines) among them (chap. 3).

Literary Features

Philippians is a missionary thank-you letter in which the missionary reports on the progress of his work and contains no Old Testament quotations (but see discussion on Job 13:16). It manifests a particularly vigorous type of Christian living: (1) a self-humbling attitude (2:1–4); (2) pressing toward the goal (3:13–14); (3) a lack of anxiety (4:6); (4) an ability to do all things (4:13). It is outstanding as the New Testament letter of joy; the word "joy" (Greek, *chara*) in its various forms occurs some fourteen times. Other distinctive terms in Philippians include the word "think" (Greek, *phroneō*), used ten times; "consider" (Greek, *hēgeomai*), used six times; and "bond," used four times. Philippians contains one of the most profound christological passages in the New Testament (2:5–11). Yet, profound as it is, Paul included this passage mainly for illustrative purposes. In general, Philippians has a warm, practical, and personal tone, with an emphasis on rejoicing. Thus, it has often been called the "Epistle of Joy."

Outline

   I. Salutation (1:1–2)
  II. Thanksgiving and Prayer for the Philippians (1:3–11)
 III. Paul's Personal Circumstances (1:12–26)
 IV. Exhortations (1:27–2:18)
     A. Living a Life Worthy of the Gospel (1:27–30)
     B. Following the Servant Attitude of Christ (2:1–18)
  V. Paul's Associates in the Gospel (2:19–30)
     A. Timothy (2:19–24)
     B. Epaphroditus (2:25–30)
 VI. Warnings against Judaizers and Antinomians (3:1–4:1)
     A. Against Judaizers, or Legalists (3:1–16)
     B. Against Antinomians, or Libertines (3:17–4:1)
VII. Final Exhortations, Thanks, and Conclusion (4:2–23)
     A. Exhortations concerning Various Aspects of the Christian Life (4:2–9)
     B. Concluding Testimony and Repeated Thanks (4:10–20)
     C. Greetings and Benediction (4:21–23)

Bibliography

Fee, Gordon D. *Paul's Letter to the Philippians*. Grand Rapids, MI: Eerdmans, 1995.
Gromacki, Robert. *Philippians and Colossians*. Twenty-First Century Biblical Commentary. Chattanooga, TN: AMG, 2003.

Lightfoot, J. B. *St. Paul's Epistle to the Philippians.* 1913. Reprint, Grand Rapids, MI: Zondervan, 1953.

Martin, Ralph, P. *The Epistle of Paul to the Philippians.* Grand Rapids, MI: Eerdmans, 1959.

O'Brien, Peter T. *The Epistle to the Philippians: A Commentary on the Greek Text.* The New International Greek Testament Commentary. Edited by I. Howard Marshall and W. Ward Gasque. Grand Rapids, MI: Eerdmans, 1991.

Silva, Moises. *Philippians.* Wycliffe Exegetical Commentary. Chicago: Moody Press, 1988.

EXPOSITION

I. Salutation (1:1–2)

1:1–2. As in all his letters, Paul followed the conventional letter format of his day, with its three elements: (1) identification of the sender, (2) identification of the recipients, (3) greeting.

1:1. For **Timotheus**, see 1 Timothy, Introduction: "Recipient." The contents of the letter identify Timothy as Paul's associate but not as coauthor. Here Paul identified himself not as an apostle but as among **the servants of Christ Jesus** (see Rom. 1:1; Titus 1:1; Philemon 1). In Paul's case, this designation brings out an essential aspect of the more usual identification of himself as "an apostle." **Saints** is a common designation that Paul used to address and identify believers. The expression, derived from "holy ones," is descriptive not of individual moral purity but of the believer's status and spiritual union with Christ, as the following **in Christ Jesus** shows (see Rom. 1:7; 1 Cor. 1:2 and discussions). **Philippi.** See Introduction: "The City of Philippi." **Bishops and deacons.** This is the only place in Paul's writings where he singled out church officers as a group as recipients of a letter. "Bishops" (Greek, *episkopos*; "overseer") are equivalent to "elders" (Greek, *presbyteros*) and "pastors" (Greek, *poimēn*), judging from a comparison of Acts 20:17, 28 with 1 Peter 5:1–2 (see discussion on 1 Tim. 3:1). For "deacons," see discussion on 1 Timothy 3:8.

1:2. The opening greeting is not merely a matter of polite custom but has a distinctively Christian tone and content.

II. Thanksgiving and Prayer for the Philippians (1:3–11)

1:3–4. I thank my God (v. 3) **... in every prayer of mine** (v. 4) **... with joy.** Prayers of joyful thanksgiving for his readers' response to the gospel are a hallmark of the opening sentences of Paul's letters (see Rom. 1:8; 1 Cor. 1:4; Col. 1:3; 1 Thess. 1:2; 2 Thess. 1:3; 2 Tim. 1:3; Philemon 4). Here Paul modeled what he later advised the Philippians to practice in their own prayer life (see 4:6–7). Throughout his "thank-you" (1:3–11), the sanctuary doors to Paul's personal prayer life stand wide open, which allowed the Philippians to see not only the vital role that prayer plays in the work of the gospel but also the scope of their partnership in the greater work of God. For God to shape a partnership that is bigger than its partners, it begins with partners mutually dependent on God through prayer.

1:5. Your fellowship in the gospel. The basis of Paul's prayerful thanksgiving was not only their reception of the gospel but also their active support of his ministry (see 4:15). **From the first day.** When Paul first came to Philippi (see Acts 16:12). **Until now.** Toward the close (see 2:24) of Paul's first Roman imprisonment (see Acts 28:16–31).

1:6. The basis of Paul's confidence was God's divine **work in you**. Paul was confident not only of what God had done "for" the readers in forgiving their sins but also of what He had done "in" them (see 1:11). "Work" refers to God's activity in saving them and the dynamic impact of God's presence, "For it is God which worketh in you both to will and to do of his good pleasure" (2:13). **The day of Jesus Christ** specifies the time of His return, when their salvation will be brought to completion (see 1:10; 2:16; 1 Cor. 1:8; 5:5; 2 Cor. 1:14). It is God who initiates salvation, who continues it, and who will one day bring it to its consummation.

1:7. Paul emphasized his partnership with the Philippians by calling them "mutual partners," or **partakers of my grace**, the grace God had extended to Paul in his imprisonment for the gospel. Even in Paul's imprisonment, they willingly identified themselves with Paul by sending Epaphroditus and their financial gifts. They had become one with Paul in his persecution.

1:8. Bowels of Jesus Christ denotes "the affection of Jesus Christ," the deep yearning and intense, compassionate love exhibited by Jesus Himself and now fostered in Paul by his union with Christ. The term "bowels" (Greek, *splagchnon*; pronounced "splanknon") identifies the viscera, where deep emotion is experienced. Although this affection reaches out to all impartially and without exception, here Paul's heart is a human locus of the divine affection. Paul called God as his witness since God alone could verify the emotion of His Son's affection that Paul professed to feel for the Philippians.

1:9. A focal point and petition of Paul's prayer is that the love of the Philippians would **abound yet more and more**. Real love requires growth and maturation (see 1 Thess. 3:12; 4:10; 2 Thess. 1:3). Love grows in two ways: **in knowledge** of God, the source of love, as evidenced by what love approves (see 1:10–11; Col. 1:9), and in **judgment**, or practical discernment and sensitivity. Christian love is not mere sentiment; it is rooted in knowledge and understanding.

1:10. Love operating with the tandem qualities of knowledge and judgment (see 1:9) enables the be-liever to **approve things that are excellent**. The word "approve" (Greek, *dokimazō*) carries the sense of "put to the test, examine" and then its consequence of "accept as proved, approve." In view of 1:9, the latter sense is prominent here. Christians are to approve (and practice) what is morally and ethically superior. **Sincere and without offence** portrays the outcome and goal of love. A life molded and shaped by love is a life formed without any mixture of evil. Indeed, God's love is the vital and effective power in leading a moral and ethical life. If holiness may be described as the absence of evil, it is the operation of God's love that functionally occupies its space and evacuates it (see 1:11). **Till the day of Christ** points to the occasion when the goal will be perfectly realized (see discussion on 1:6), and then Christians will have to give an account (see 2 Cor. 5:10).

1:11. Filled with the fruits of righteousness may be thought of as the continuous springtime of a flourishing fruit tree, only here it is a flourishing life planted in the heart of God. A life nourished by God's love yields on every limb fruit with the quality of God's character: righteousness. Such character is expected of all Christians (see Matt. 5:20–48; Heb. 12:11; James 3:18; see also Amos 6:12; Gal. 5:22). **By Jesus Christ** means "produced by Christ" (in union with Him) through the work of the Holy Spirit (see John 15:5; Eph. 2:10). **Unto the glory and praise of God** speaks of the ultimate goal of all that God does in believers (see Eph. 1:6, 12, 14).

III. Paul's Personal Circumstances (1:12–26)

1:12. Things which happened unto me, or "my circumstances," pertains to Paul's detainment in prison. **Have fallen out** (lit., "have come moreover" or "have come rather") implies a standard of comparison that has been exceeded. Here the standard, which, as it often is, is unexpressed, was the expectation of the Philippians. Instead of confining the gospel, Paul's imprisonment had served to "advance," or bring about, **the furtherance of the gospel**. Paul's shackles proved strategic to the release of the gospel (see "manifest in all the palace," 1:13).

1:13. The conditions under which Paul had been imprisoned are explained by the words **bonds in Christ**. "Bonds," or "restraints," may refer either to actual chains ("fetters") or broadly to his sufferings and imprisonment (see 1:14). They were **manifest**, or apparent, to all who knew of Paul's situation that he was imprisoned not because he was guilty of some crime but because of his stand for the gospel. **All the palace** (lit., "the whole praetorian"; Greek, *praitōrion*) refers to the imperial guard, a contingent of soldiers numbering several thousand. Many would have had personal contact with Paul or would have been individually assigned to guard him during the course of his imprisonment (see Acts 28:16, 30).

1:14. Not only had the gospel for which Paul was imprisoned circulated in unexpected ways, but timid brethren were **much more bold**. Encouraged by Paul's example, other believers were forcefully proclaiming the gospel. Since **brethren in the Lord** is redundant and occurs nowhere else, the sense and punctuation should read, "many of the brethren, having become more confident in the Lord due to my bonds, dare much more to speak the word without fear."

1:15. **Even of envy and strife ... of good will**. The preaching of the gospel that Paul's imprisonment had stimulated stemmed from either one of these two sharply opposed motives. These divisions (1:15–17) are grammatically and most naturally categories of the "many" (lit., the "majority") mentioned in 1:14. Paul scrutinized the motive, not the content, of the proclamation.

1:16. **The one preach Christ of contention**. Those who preached with wrong, insincere motives did so out of a sense of competition with Paul and so thought they were making his imprisonment more difficult to bear. Paul described their motive as insincere (**not sincerely**), or not with "pure" (Greek, *hagnōs*; "purely") intentions. Not all preaching of the gospel is based on proper motives.

1:17. **The other of love**. Those who preached with a right motive recognized the true reason for Paul's imprisonment (see 1:13) and were encouraged to take the same bold stand that he had taken. The

contrast of motives, "[out] of love" (Greek, *agapē*) and "not sincerely" (Greek, *hagnōs*; "purely"; 1:16), reminds the reader that love is pure.

1:18. **Whether in pretence, or in truth, Christ is preached**. The insincere preachers were not to be viewed as being heretical. Their message was true, even though their motives were not pure. The gospel has its objectivity and validity apart from those who proclaim it; the message is more than the medium. **I ... rejoice ... and will rejoice** characterizes Paul's hearty and buoyant confidence in Jesus, despite his surrounding circumstances. Although Paul was under arrest and fellow Christians sought, by their preaching, to add to his difficulties, he kept on rejoicing, because his emotional life was ever inspired by an effervescent perspective encouraged by Christ.

1:19. **Salvation**, or "deliverance," speaks either of Paul's release from prison (see 1:25; 2:24) or, in view of the immediately following verses, of the deliverance brought to the believer by death (see Rom. 8:28). The former interpretation, however, seems to be indicated in 1:25. **Spirit of Jesus Christ** denotes not only the Holy Spirit, the Spirit of God the Father (see Rom. 8:9, 14; 1 Cor. 2:10–11, 14), but also the Spirit of Christ, the second person of the Trinity (see Acts 16:7; Rom. 8:9; Gal. 4:6). He is sent by the Father (see John 14:16–17, 26; Gal. 4:6) and by the Son (see John 15:26; 16:7).

1:20. For the sense of **earnest expectation**, or "eager expectation," see Romans 8:9 for the one other New Testament example of this poignant word of expectancy. The words **hope** and **boldness** aptly attend the expectation expressed by this word (Greek, *apokaradokian*). Rather than **be ashamed**, Paul wanted to magnify **with all boldness** and elevate the reputation of Christ through the actions and attitudes of his life. The circumstances of imprisonment, with all its attendant suffering and oppression, constituted a real temptation for Paul to abandon the gospel and his resolute service for Christ. **My body** is the instrument of human activity and, from this perspective, refers to Paul himself. Accordingly, the body is where the exalted Christ dwells by His Spirit and is at work (see Rom. 8:9–10), and Christ was therefore exalted by what Paul did. **Whether it be by life, or by death**. Whether his service for Christ continued in life or ended in death.

1:21. To live is Christ. Christ was the source and secret of Paul's continual joy (even in prison), for Paul's life found all its meaning in Christ. **Gain** specifies that the gain brought by death is "be[ing] with Christ" (1:23), so that here Paul was saying that his ultimate concern and most precious possession, both now and forever, was Christ and his relationship with Him.

1:22. Fruit of my labour. The spread of the gospel and the upbuilding of the church. **I wot not**, or as some translations word it, "I know not," fails to bring out the sense of this word found elsewhere in the New Testament. Elsewhere (e.g., Luke 2:15; Rom. 9:22; Eph. 6:19) it means "to make known," "to reveal." There is no reason to give it a meaning here other than its usual meaning, which here may be rendered, "What I would choose, I am not going to declare." Why? As 1:23–24 shows, Paul was torn between two positives: his desire to be present with his beloved Christ and his desire to be present with his beloved Philippians.

1:23–24. Depart, and to be with Christ (v. 23) **... abide in the flesh** (v. 24). Either alternative was a good one. While mysteries remain, this passage clearly teaches that when believers die, they are with Christ, apart from the body. The word "depart" has a background of colorful usage, which includes references to weighing anchor (and putting out to sea), breaking camp, and, euphemistically, death.

1:23. Far better, or beyond compare, leaves no room for doubt about the advantages of death for the Christian: to face death is to face Christ. Being with Christ after death must involve some kind of conscious presence and fellowship (see 2 Cor. 5:6, 8).

1:24. More needful for you expresses the pull of Paul's concern and love for the Philippians. Paul put the needs of those he ministered to ahead of his personal preference.

1:25. I shall abide. It is entirely possible that Paul was later released from prison (see map, *Zondervan KJV Study Bible*, pp. 1738–39). Certain unknowns, however, make a definitive conclusion impossible. **Furtherance and joy of faith** indirectly make it clear that the Christian life is to be one of joyful growth and advance (see discussion on 1:9).

IV. Exhortations (1:27–2:18)

A. Living a Life Worthy of the Gospel (1:27–30)

1:27. Conversation, or "manner of life," translates the Greek word *politeuomai*, "live [behave] as citizens." Given the Philippian pride of Roman citizenship (see Introduction: "The City of Philippi"), Paul was calling them to a healthier pride of conduct, one that **becometh the gospel** and their true citizenship "in heaven" (3:20). Therefore, Paul said the one important thing (**Only**) is to live as citizens "worthy" of the gospel. In other words, live in a way that is appropriate to the privileges, standards, and goals given with the gospel. **In one spirit** speaks of having a common disposition and purpose. Citizens of heaven are to be united **with one mind striving together**. This is particularly necessary when the gospel is under attack. Christians need each other and must stand together.

1:28. The word **token** (Greek, *endeixis*) as a law term denoted "'proof' obtained by appeal to the facts" and connoted a sure sign or clear omen (O'Brien, *The Epistle to the Philippians*, p. 155). In the face of opposition, the Philippians could gain courage from the fact that the demonstration of their heavenly citizenship (1:27–28a) functioned as a proof or "evident token" of their salvation and their opponents' destruction. Persistent opposition to the church and the gospel is a sure sign of eventual destruction since it involves rejection of the only way of salvation. By the same token, when Christians are persecuted for their faith, it is a sign of the genuineness of their salvation (see 2 Thess. 1:5).

1:29. With the words **given** (Greek, *charizomai*) **... to suffer**, Paul expressed suffering **in the behalf of Christ** as a gift or privilege. Through Christ, God had graciously given the Philippians not only the privilege of salvation (**not only to believe on him**) but also the privilege of suffering **for His sake**. Both expressions of God's privilege in Christ (believing and suffering) are balanced by one Greek expression, translated here as "in the behalf of Christ" and "for His sake." Christian suffering, as well as faith, is a blessing (see Matt. 5:11–12; Acts 5:41; James 1:2; 1 Peter 4:14) and is in no way a proof (see 1:28) of anything but salvation and God's privilege in Christ. The Christian life is to be a "not only … but also" proposition: not only believing but also suffering.

1:30. Paul assured the Philippians that the opposition engaging them was not unique; overall, it belonged to the **same conflict**, or "struggle," engaging Paul. They had witnessed it (**Ye saw**) when Paul and Silas first visited Philippi and were imprisoned (see Acts 16:19–40), and now they heard about it (1:12–26). All in all, in 1:27–30, Paul dissuaded the Philippians from any discouragement or any deduction of defeat that they might have drawn from the opposition they faced to their faith in the gospel of Jesus Christ. They needed to stand fast in one Spirit (1:27), strive with one soul for the faith of the gospel (1:27), and do so boldly, in nothing terrified by their adversaries.

B. Following the Servant Attitude of Christ (2:1–18)

2:1. In Paul's teaching, the words **in Christ** refer to the believer's personal union with Christ, the basic reality of salvation. To be in Christ is to be saved. It is to be in intimate personal relationship with Christ the Savior. From this relationship flow all the particular benefits and fruits of salvation, such as encouragement (see, e.g., 3:8–10; Rom. 8:1; 2 Cor. 5:17; Gal. 2:20). **Comfort of love** speaks of the comforting knowledge and assurance that come from God's love in Christ, demonstrated especially in Christ's death for the forgiveness of sins and eternal life (see John 3:16; Rom. 5:8; 8:38–39; 1 John 3:16; 4:9–10, 16). **Fellowship of the Spirit** denotes the fellowship among believers produced by the Spirit, who indwells each of them (see 2 Cor. 13:14). **Bowels and mercies** expresses the experience of intense care and deep sympathy that Christians have for each other (see 1:8; Col. 3:12). Paul viewed all these benefits—encouragement, comfort, fellow-

ship, tenderness, and compassion—as present realities for the Philippians.

Paul's repeated use of **If** with each of these notable Christian benefits served to heighten his readers' awareness of not only their personal experience but also their obligation as beneficiaries. Laced together, these spiritual incentives offered the Philippians a powerful motivation to welcome and fulfill Paul's appeal in 2:2.

2:2. Paul's string of incentives (2:1) is adorned with a cluster of synonymous or matching phrases that reflect one glowing idea: harmonious devotion. The words **likeminded … same love … one accord … one mind** emphasize the unity that should exist among Christians. Rather than uniformity in thought, "one mind" denotes the common disposition to work together and serve one another—the "attitude" of Christ (see 2:5; 4:2; Rom. 12:16; 15:5; 2 Cor. 13:11).

2:3. The mortal enemies of unity and harmony in the church (see 1:17; see also Gal. 5:20, where the Greek for "selfishness" is rendered "disputes" and listed among the "works of the flesh," Gal. 5:19–21) are **strife or vainglory**. Strife, on the one hand, beats one's rival down; vainglory, on the other hand, boosts one's ego up. Both are self-centered and devoted to personal advancement. By contrast, the source of Christian unity is **lowliness of mind**, or humility. Humility is not inferiority. The divine definition given here shows that humility involves a noble and strong act of the will, a decision to put others above oneself, a disposition modeled on Christ (2:5). The key to humility is to put God first (see 2:8). Therefore, Paul's admonition to **esteem other better than themselves** should not be taken to mean that everyone else is superior or more talented but that Christian love sees others as worthy of preferential treatment (see Rom. 12:10; Gal. 5:13; Eph. 5:21; 1 Peter 5:5).

2:4. A person's concern for **his own things** is certainly proper, but only if there is equal concern for the interests of others (see Rom. 15:1).

2:5. Let this mind be in you, which was also in Christ Jesus. In spite of all that is unique and radically different about the person and work of Christ (see 2:6–11), Christians are to have His attitude of self-sacrificing humility and love for others (see 2:2–4; Matt. 11:29; John 13:12–17).

2:6–11. The poetic, even lyric, character of these verses is apparent. Many scholars view them as an early Christian hymn (see discussion on Col. 3:16), taken over and perhaps modified by Paul. If so, they nonetheless express his convictions. The passage treats Christ's humiliation (2:6–8) and exaltation (2:9–11). This kenotic pattern of suffering, followed by glory, became an important one for Paul, who applied it to himself (see 3:7–14) and his readers (see 2:5; 3:15–16; Rom. 8:17–19).

2:6. In the form of God affirms that Jesus is fully God (see discussion on Rom. 9:5). "Form" (only here and in 2:7 in the New Testament) is taken to mean essential form, "the specific character" (Lightfoot, *St. Paul's Epistle to the Philippians*, p. 129) or sum of those qualities that make God specifically God. **Equal with God** points to the status and privileges that inevitably follow from being in very nature God. In Jesus' mind (see "Let this mind be in you," 2:5), this divine equality was not regarded as **robbery**, something to be seized or used for His own advantage. He did not consider that high position to be something He could not give up.

2:7. Made himself of no reputation. He did this not by giving up deity but by laying aside His glory (see John 17:5) and submitting to the humiliation of becoming man (see 2 Cor. 8:9). Jesus is truly God and truly man. Another view is that He emptied Himself, not of deity itself but of its prerogatives— the high position and glory of deity. In either case, the words "made himself of no reputation" should be explained by addition and not subtraction: "He made himself of no reputation by taking the form of a servant and being made in the likeness of men." **The form of a servant** emphasizes the full reality of His servant identity (see Matt. 20:28). As a servant, He was always submissive to the will of the Father.

2:8. Fashion as a man shows not only that Jesus was "like" a human being (2:7) but also that He took on the actual outward characteristics of a man (see

John 1:14; Rom. 8:3; Heb. 2:17). **Humbled** (see 2:7; 2 Cor. 8:9) is the same word Paul used in 2:3, here the verb and there the noun. How Jesus humbled himself and how one can likewise humble oneself is revealed in the word **obedient** (see Heb. 5:7–8). Obedience to God properly enthrones Him above all and puts Him first. A "servant" (2:7) obeys, and Jesus willingly accepted the position of a servant. **Death** stresses both the totality and the climax of Jesus' obedience. **Of the cross** heightens Jesus' humiliation; He died as someone cursed (see Gal. 3:13; Heb. 12:2). Crucifixion was the most degrading kind of execution that could be inflicted on a person.

2:9. With **Wherefore**, the description of Jesus' sacrificial humiliation is matched by a description of His supreme exaltation from on high (2:9–11). Regal imagery abounds, but the servant (2:7) is **exalted** (see Matt. 28:18; Acts 2:33; Isa. 52:13) far above any earthly king. The regal inauguration and reign of Jesus is hailed with the **name ... above every name**. Reference doubtless is to the office or rank conferred on Jesus—His glorious position, not His proper name (see Eph. 1:21; Heb. 1:4–5). That name would be God's own name, Yahweh (see "Lord," 2:11; and His attendant worship, 2:10; compare the Septuagint, where "Lord" stands for Yahweh). Thus, "Lord" forms an inclusion with "God" in 2:6, only now all creation is bound to Jesus' glory in an obligatory way because of His redemptive work.

2:10–11. Bow (v. 10) **... confess** (v. 11; see Isa. 45:23) describes the visible posture and vocal profession of every living creature before the supremacy of Jesus. God's design is that all people everywhere should worship and serve Jesus as Lord. Ultimately, all will acknowledge Him as Lord (see Rom. 14:9), whether willingly or not.

2:12. With **Wherefore**, Paul tied two motivations together as he exhorted the Philippians, **work out your own salvation**. One looks back to the incomparable example of Jesus and His obedience (2:5–11); the other looks to the history of obedience on the part of the Philippians. Both were an encouragement to the Philippians. **Obeyed** identifies the commands of God as passed on to the Philippians by Paul (see

Rom. 1:5; 15:18; 2 Cor. 10:5–6). **My presence** refers to the times Paul was with them during the course of his second (see Acts 16:12–40) and third (see Acts 20:1–3, 6) missionary journeys. In saying "work out your own salvation," Paul compelled them to work it out to the finish. He was referring not to an attempt to earn their salvation by works but to the expression of their salvation in spiritual growth and development. Salvation is not merely a gift received once for all; it expresses itself in an ongoing process in which the believer is strenuously involved (see Matt. 24:13; 1 Cor. 9:24–27; Heb. 3:14; 6:9–11; 2 Peter 1:5–8)—the process of perseverance, spiritual growth, and maturation. Rather than expressing doubt or anxiety, **fear and trembling** measures the importance of an active reverence and a singleness of purpose in response to God's grace.

2:13. Imitation depends on incarnation: God is at work **in you**, so work out what He is working within. **To will and to do** speaks of both God's intention and His inner operation to effect **his good pleasure**—what God enables in a believer's life as one obediently works out one's salvation. Faith and obedience cannot be separated (see Gal. 5:6; James 2:18, 20, 22).

2:14–17. These verses list some things involved in working out our salvation.

2:14. Murmurings and disputings, or grumbling and arguing, model not the mind of Jesus Christ (2:5) but the mind of a world preoccupied with its own good pleasure. "Murmurings," or being discontented with God's will, is an expression of unbelief that prevents one from doing what pleases God (see 2:13; 1 Cor. 10:10). "Disputings" are the arguments that erupt and divide people over conflicting points of view. Debatable points that do not need to be settled for the good of the church (see 2 Tim. 2:23; Titus 3:9) are in view. Such will be far from the one who puts the interests of others (see 2:3–4) ahead of his own, because that person's mind is occupied by the mind of Christ (see 2:5).

2:15. Blameless and harmless ... without rebuke speaks not of absolute, sinless perfection but of wholehearted, unmixed devotion to doing God's will. The objective is to have a character distinctive of God's children, contrasted with the character of **a crooked and perverse nation**, a description of the unbelieving world (see Acts 2:40; Eph. 2:1–3; Matt. 17:17). Children of God should **shine as lights**, standing out like eye-catching stars, all the brighter in darkness; Christians are to shine brighter in the world around them (see Matt. 5:15–16).

2:16. In exhorting the Philippians, Paul added a personal motive to the preceding divine incentives that have dominated the chapter. As if in a race, Paul imagined the finish line drawn by **the day of Christ** (see discussion on 1:6). He pictured a day of joy over a race run well, in part because of what God had done through Paul (see 1 Thess. 2:19), in part because the Philippians had held forth (like a torch) or clutched (like a baton) **the word of life**, as had others in his apostolic work. **In vain** (see 1 Cor. 9:24–27) speaks of running in futility or without effect.

2:17–18. The all too real and near possibility of Paul's martyrdom (see 1:19–26) was surely in Paul's mind as he spoke of his life, a slowly poured drink offering, pictured as being drained in service. Paul assured the Philippians that his service, like the spirit of a drink offering, was offered unreservedly with joy, a joy that is best appreciated with mutual joy: **I** (v. 17) **... rejoice ... also do ye** (v. 18) **... rejoice.** Christian joy ought always to be mutual. **I be offered** (v. 17) portrays Paul's life as a drink offering that accompanies other sacrifices. **Upon the sacrifice** is informed by the Old Testament background of the daily sacrifices described in Exodus 29:38–41. From the first to the last, Paul offered his life with joy.

V. Paul's Associates in the Gospel (2:19–30)

2:19–30. Judging from verses 23–24, Paul had every intention of coming to Philippi, should the Lord grant him his desire. In the meantime, he sent two associates in the gospel. Paul wrote first of his plan to send Timothy (vv. 19–24), "so soon as I shall see how it will go with me" (v. 23), but in advance, it was "necessary to send ... Epaphroditus" (v. 25; vv. 25–30), who carried Paul's letter to the Philippians. Thus, verses 19–30 set forth Paul's travel plans, conveying his apostolic attention and care as outlined in the sending of the letter bearer, Epaphroditus, to be followed by the visit of Timothy, to be followed by the arrival of Paul himself, should he be released from prison as hoped.

A. Timothy (2:19–24)

2:19–23. Paul planned to send Timothy, who was with him in Rome (see 1:1), to discover and report on conditions in the Philippian church.

2:20–21. Likeminded (Greek, *isopsychos*; lit., "of equal soul"; v. 20) is a rare expression, occurring only here in the New Testament. No one could best or equal Timothy's genuine concern (**who will naturally care**) for the best interests of the Philippians. Since all others sought their own interests, Timothy was a good example of the kind of person envisioned in the exhortation of 2:4. There was a wide divide and sharp contrast between Timothy and Paul's other associates—an outstanding commendation for one so young.

2:22. The proof (Greek, *dokimē*; a test with attention to the result, "standing a test," "character") of Timothy's worth had already been demonstrated and so was known to the Philippians. What the Philippians knew of Timothy's character, Paul explained as the outcome of an ongoing devotion to the work of the gospel, which had united Timothy and Paul **as a son with the father**. Paul's own commendation of Timothy could hardly reach higher than this tender description of their ministry partnership. The relationship between Timothy and Paul is developed at length in 1-2 Timothy. The words **served with me** show that Timothy, like Jesus and Paul, had a servant attitude.

2:23–24. Given Paul's regard (see 2:20–23), sending Timothy to the Philippians was like sending an apostolic letter, the closest substitute for Paul's own presence. Paul anticipated his release and arrival in the near future (see 1:25).

B. Epaphroditus (2:25–30)

2:25–30. Epaphroditus, too, after a close brush with death (vv. 27, 30), was being sent home to Philippi.

2:25. Paul commended **Epaphroditus**, and thus the Philippians, by describing what their **messenger**, who had **ministered to** Paul, had become to him: **my brother, and companion in labour, and fellow-soldier**. These five phrases characterize the role of Epaphroditus, the first three describing what he became on Paul's behalf, and the last two explaining why he came on the behalf of the Philippians. "Messenger" (Greek, *apostolos*) is a broader use of the Greek word often translated "apostle," applied here to Epaphroditus as a commissioned representative of the Philippian church (see 2 Cor. 8:23). "Ministered" (Greek, *leitourgos*), with its rich connections to the performance of priestly duties, suggests that Epaphroditus as a "priestly minister" had earnestly and fittingly served Paul's need in prison (see "service"; Greek, *leitourgia*; 2:30). Clearly, what Epaphroditus became to Paul fulfilled, if not exceeded, what the Philippians had intended (see 2:30).

2:26–28. Having clarified Epaphroditus's value to Paul and the gospel ministry (2:25), Paul further qualified his mutual value, explaining that his return not only brought this letter but safeguarded him who came near to **death** (v. 27; see 1:21–26) in their mutual service. **Sorrowful** (v. 28) implies the legitimate cares and concerns that come with the Christian life and the gospel ministry (see discussion on 4:6; see also 2 Cor. 4:8; 11:28).

2:29–30. To supply your lack of service toward me (v. 30) refers not to a standard of expectation on Paul's part but to the expectation of what the church wanted to accomplish and fulfill. In other words, a "lack" the Philippians wanted to fulfill, yet unable to do so themselves, they sent Epaphroditus to fulfill it on their behalf. In this pursuit, Epaphroditus nearly gave his life. For that, the Philippians were to have a sense of "mission accomplished" and commensurately honor the man who had acted on their behalf. Paul spoke of this "service" as a priestly service in the most positive terms and imagery (see 2:25; 4:18).

VI. Warnings against Judaizers and Antinomians (3:1–4:1)

A. Against Judaizers, or Legalists (3:1–16)

3:1. Finally marks a transition to a new section as Paul moved toward his conclusion; this does not mark the close of the letter, however (see 4:8). With the injunction to **rejoice in the Lord** (see 4:4), Paul set the tone both theologically ("in the Lord") and experientially ("rejoice," "express gladness"; Greek, *chairō*) for the reminders that follow on a subject matter that could otherwise be **grievous** or disturbing. Paul stated it was not grievous for him, so the Philippians should not let it be grievous for them. **The same things** refers to matters in the following verses that Paul had previously dealt with either orally when he was in Philippi or perhaps in an earlier letter. For the Philippians, there was a benefit: **it is safe**. Where serious error is present, there is safety in repetition.

3:2. The threefold repetition of **beware** ("watch out"), one with each epithet, underscores how important it was to Paul that his opponents did not overtake the Philippians. **Dogs** is pejorative and a harsh fault-finding word for Paul's opponents. The image portrays not only their aggressive opposition to the gospel but the seriousness of their error and its destructive, "devour[ing]" (Gal. 5:15) results. Their teaching probably was similar to what Paul had to oppose in the Galatian churches (see Galatians, Introduction: "Background"). **Concision**, or "mutilation," is a strong, painfully vivid term; the false teachers had so distorted the meaning of circumcision (see 3:3) that it had become nothing more than a useless cutting of the body.

3:3. The true, inner meaning of **circumcision** is realized only in believers, who worship God with genuine spiritual worship and who glory in Christ as their Savior rather than trusting in their own human effort (see Rom. 2:28–29; Col. 2:12–13; see also Deut. 30:6; Ezek. 36:26). **Rejoice ... no confidence**. Unlike in 3:1, here the word "rejoice" translates the Greek word *kauchaomai*; "boast," "glory," "take pride"). Everyone is a "boaster," either in Christ or in himself. The medium of **the flesh** (weak human nature) is the antithesis of **in** ("by means of") **the spirit**. Although the term "flesh" in Paul's letters often refers to sinful human nature, here it speaks of the frailty of human nature: it is not worthy of our confidence; it cannot save.

3:4–14. Paul's personal testimony, a model for every believer. This is one of the most significant autobiographical sections in his letters (see Gal. 1:13–24; 1 Tim. 1:12–16; Acts 22:1–21; 26:1–23).

3:4–6. Paul's pre-Christian confidence, rooted in his Jewish pedigree, privileges, and attainments, he eschewed in 3:7–8 and thus brought full circle his personal endorsement of "we" in 3:3.

3:5. Circumcised the eighth day (see Gen. 17:12) alludes to the Jewish piety of Paul's family. Paul was born a Jew, **of the stock of Israel**, and was not a proselyte. Paul's family traced its genealogy to **the tribe of Benjamin**, the tribe of Saul—Paul's name. His Jewish roots were deep and unambiguous. Jerusalem, the Holy City, lay on the border of the tribal territory of Benjamin. Narrower than "Israelite" or "descendant of Abraham," **a Hebrew of the Hebrews** draws a distinction located in language, attitudes, and lifestyle (see Acts 22:2–3; Gal. 1:14; 2 Cor. 11:22). **Pharisee** points to the strictness of Paul's allegiance to and observance of the Torah (the Law) and all the authoritative ancestral doctrines and customs that regulated religious and social life (see Acts 22:3; 23:6; 26:5).

3:6. Concerning zeal (see Gal. 1:13–14), Paul's fervor in persecuting the church could be gauged by reference to the zeal of Phinehas (see Num. 25:11; Ps. 106:30–31), who became a prototype and emblem of righteous zeal in Jewish tradition. **Righteousness ... in the law** refers to righteousness produced by using the law as an attempt to merit God's approval and blessing (see 3:9)—a use of the law that Paul strongly opposed as being contrary to the gospel itself (see Rom. 3:27–28; 4:1–5; Gal. 2:16; 3:10–12). Finally, Paul's "confidence" (3:3–4) had come from his legal disposition of being **blameless**. In terms of legalistic standards of scrupulous external conformity to the law, Paul was above reproach.

3:7–14. Paul contrasted his confidence in Christ with his pre-Christian confidence (3:4–6), a confidence he now designated as having belonged to the flesh and its standards (3:3).

3:7. What things, or the things mentioned in 3:5–6, are given an accounting in terms of the bottom line: **gain ... loss**, which refers to the great reversal in Paul, begun on the road to Damascus (see Acts 9:3–16), from being self-centered to being centered in Christ.

3:8. The knowledge of Christ Jesus is not only a knowledge of facts but a knowledge gained through experience that, in its surpassing greatness, transforms the entire person. The following verses spell this out. **Dung** (Greek, *skubalon*) may refer to refuse, such as the excrement of animals, kitchen scraps, or foul-smelling garbage. Although its etymology remains uncertain, its origin has been reasoned from the expression "to fling to the dogs," which if valid, may here have been a knock on Paul's opponents ("dogs," 3:2). What Paul now had as a Christian was not merely preferable or a better alternative; his former way of life was worthless and despicable. **Win** means to gain or acquire by effort or investment.

3:9. Be found in him expresses the premium of Paul's investment (to gain or "win Christ," 3:8) in terms of his union with Christ (see discussion on 2:1; 1 Cor. 1:30)—not simply an experience in the past but a present, continuing relationship. **Righteousness ... of the law** (see discussion on 3:6) is contrasted with its diametrical and polar opposite, righteousness **through the faith**. The latter, a principal benefit of union with Christ (see Rom. 3:21–22; 1 Cor. 1:30; Gal. 2:16), sets forth plainly why Paul radically revised his principles of accounting and how gain became loss on the revised balance sheet.

3:10. Know him, as in 3:8, is not merely factual; it includes the experience of the power of Christ's resurrection (see Eph. 1:17–20), of fellowship in His sufferings (see Acts 9:16), and of being like Him in His death (see 2 Cor. 4:7–12; 12:9–10). Believers already share positionally in Christ's death and resurrection (see Rom. 6:2–13; Gal. 2:20; 5:24; 6:14; Eph. 2:6; Col. 2:12–13; 3:1). Here, however, Paul was speaking of the actual experience of Christ's resurrection power and of suffering with and for Him, even to the point of death. Paul already knew this world and its power; what he wanted to know fully was Christ.

3:11. I might attain does not convey any indication of doubt or uncertainty on Paul's part but

rather his intense yearning to advance his experience of **the resurrection**, the great personal anticipation of every believer (see Dan. 12:2; John 5:29; Acts 24:15; 1 Cor. 15:23; 1 Thess. 4:16). Paul so longed for Christ (see 1:20–23) that if he had his druthers, he would have already been resurrected.

3:12–14. The Christian life is like a race; elsewhere Paul used athletic imagery in a similar way (1 Cor. 9:24–27; 1 Tim. 6:12; 2 Tim. 4:7–8; see also Matt. 24:13; Heb. 12:1). Here Paul describes the athlete's attitude (v. 12), aim (v. 13), and award (v. 14).

3:12. Apprehend ... I am apprehended. Paul's goal was Christ's goal for him, and Christ supplied the resources for him to "press toward the mark" (3:14; see 2:12–13). In light of 3:10–11, the "mark" (3:14, 17), or "goal," may be imagined as the apprehension of Christ Himself (see 1:21).

3:13. Forgetting speaks not of losing all memory of a sinful past (see 3:4–6) but of leaving it behind as something done with and settled.

3:14. The prize denotes an award for exceptional accomplishment. The winner of the Greek races received a wreath of leaves and sometimes a cash award; the Christian receives an award of everlasting glory. The locus of **the high calling of God** is in Christ Jesus (see 3:12), the focus of God's invitation. Paul's ultimate aspirations were found not in this life but in heaven, because Christ is there (see 3:20; Col. 3:1–2).

3:15. Perfect should be set in quotations as follows: "Those of us who are 'perfect' should think this." In view of his own example (**thus minded**; see 3:12–14), Paul recommended an adjustment in the mindset of any among the Philippians who thought of themselves as "perfect." Paul was certainly not dismissing reasonable progress in spiritual growth and stability (see 1 Cor. 2:6; 3:1–3; Heb. 5:14). He was saying that there were heights yet to be scaled; no one should become complacent. **Otherwise minded** was Paul's way of anticipating an opposing view of what he had just written. If the readers accepted the view set forth in 3:12–14 and yet failed to agree in some lesser point, God would clarify the matter for them.

3:16. Let us walk by the same rule, meaning, "Let's agree to conduct ourselves by the same standards," in particular, practicing the truth the Philippians had already comprehended. One is responsible for the truth one currently possesses.

B. Against Antinomians, or Libertines (3:17–4:1)

3:17. Be followers ... of me, or "join with others in following my example" (lit., "be a fellow imitator"), as Paul followed the example of Christ (see 1 Cor. 11.1). **Mark them** (from the Greek verb *skopeō*; "to pay careful attention to") here carries a strong allusion to the related noun in 3:14, "mark" or "goal" (Greek, *skopos*). The lifestyles Christians lead ought to be models worth following. Indeed, believers should run with those who have their eyes on the ultimate goal, Jesus Christ. The writer of Hebrews wrote from the same perspective in Hebrews 12:1–2.

3:18–19. These two verses form an explanation (**For;** v. 18) that served as a supporting incentive to Paul's urging them to join in following him (3:17). **Told you often** (see 3:1) calls to mind Paul's repeated warnings. **Weeping** (see Acts 20:19, 31) reveals the lament that beset Paul's heart; he was not emotionally detached from the pitiable tragedy of those who **are the enemies of the cross.** Such enemies stand in glaring contrast to Paul's conduct (see 3:17) and to the truth of the gospel. The tragedy of their status is described in one poignant word: **destruction** (Greek, *apōleia*; "utter ruin," "annihilation"; v. 19), the opposite of salvation (see 3:20–21). **Whose God is their belly** depicts a deep self-centeredness; their appetites and desires come first. Such people **mind earthly things,** the opposite of heavenly things (see 3:20; Col. 3:1, 3). They set their minds on the things of this life; they are antinomians (libertines), the opposite of the legalists of 3:2.

3:20. The word **conversation** (lit., "citizenship") picks up the theme of 1:27. As a colony of Rome, Philippians were citizens of Rome and governed as if they lived in Italy; their civic life mirrored Rome in every way possible. Now the Philippian believers existed and functioned as a colony of heaven. The Christian has a new citizenship **in heaven,** where Christ is and where believers are, in union with Him

(contrast the "earthly things" of 3:19; see Eph. 2:6; Col. 3:1–4). **From whence ... look** points to the different focus that heavenly citizenship brings (see Rom. 8:19; 1 Cor. 1:7; 1 Thess. 1:9–10; 2 Tim. 4:8). In this world, Christians are aliens, fully involved in it yet not of it (see John 17:14–16; 1 Cor. 7:29–31; 1 Peter 2:11).

3:21. Shall change means to transform, referring to a supernatural and radical alteration by the Holy Spirit at the resurrection (see Rom. 8:11; 1 Cor. 6:14; 15:50–53). **Our vile body** is more literally "lowly" and characterizes the human body's weakness, decay, and death, due to sin (see Rom. 8:10, 20–23; 1 Cor. 15:42–44). **Fashioned like unto his glorious body** (see Rom 8:29; 1 John 3:2). The resurrection body, received already by Christ, who is the "firstfruits," will be received by believers in the future resurrection "harvest" (see 1 Cor. 15:20, 49). It is "spiritual," that is, transformed by the power of the Holy Spirit (see 1 Cor. 15:44, 46). **According to the working ... to subdue** explains the power that is able to effect such a transformation, a power measured by Christ's ability to subject all things to Himself. Christ's present power, earned by His obedience unto death (see 2:8) and received in His resurrection and ascension, is universal and absolute (see Matt. 28:18; 1 Cor. 15:27; Eph. 1:20–22).

4:1. Paul's sincere affection for his "brethren" is expressed in two pairings of four modifiers: **beloved and longed for** (see discussions on 1:8; 2:1), **my joy and crown.** Among Paul's letters, nothing quite equals the tender sentiments expressed in this chain of endearing terms. The word "crown" adds dimension and scope to them all: his outlook on the Philippians was not only true at that time but envisioned the return of Christ (see 1 Thess. 2:19). **So** refers to the closing statements of chapter 3. In the face of libertine practices (3:18–19), the Philippians were to follow Paul's example (3:17), having their minds set on heavenly things (3:20–21), and **stand fast** in the midst of their struggles for the sake of the gospel (see 1:27–30; 1 Cor. 15:58). Paul hallowed the sincerity of his affectionate admonition with a repetition of "beloved."

VII. Final Exhortations, Thanks, and Conclusion (4:2-23)

A. Exhortations concerning Various Aspects of the Christian Life (4:2-9)

4:2-3. The disagreement between **Euodias, and ... Syntyche** (v. 2) was serious enough to be mentioned in a letter to be read publicly, but it seems Paul was confident that **those women** (v. 3) would be reconciled. His handling of the situation is a model of tact; he did not take sides but encouraged others closer to the situation to promote reconciliation (see 2:2). How realistic and true to life that even in this letter of such joy, differences do arise between devoted Christian workers. Paul already prescribed the remedy to differences of the heart in 2:1-5. Here is a reminder that harmony of heart is found "in the Lord" (3:1; 4:4).

Laboured with me ... my fellowlabourers (v. 3) identifies those associated with the apostle in the cause of the gospel (women as well as men) as his equals, not as his subordinates (see 2:25; Rom. 16:3, 9, 21; Philemon 24). **Clement** is not mentioned elsewhere in the New Testament. "My fellowlabourers" refers to coworkers not mentioned but nonetheless known to God, for their names are entered **in the book of life**, the heavenly register of the elect (see *KJV Study Bible* note on Rev. 3:5).

4:4. Rejoice in the Lord (see 3:1) **always**, in all circumstances, including suffering (see Hab. 3:17-18; James 1:2; 1 Peter 4:13). This appeal for uninterrupted rejoicing is repeated for emphasis and the sake of its importance. "In the Lord" is the ground of our rejoicing.

4:5. Moderation refers to Christlike consideration for others (see 2 Cor. 10:1), which is especially essential in church leaders (see 1 Tim. 3:3; "shewing all meekness," Titus 3:2). **At hand** (see Rom. 13:11; James 5:8-9; Rev. 22:7, 12, 20) expresses the imminence of the next great event in God's prophetic schedule, the return of Christ (see 3:20). The whole period from Christ's first coming to the consummation of the kingdom is viewed in the New Testament as "the last time" (1 John 2:18). From God's vantage point, a thousand years are as a day. Thus, there is a sense in which the Lord's coming is near for every generation.

4:6. Be careful (i.e., "anxious") **for nothing** (lit., "not one thing"). Here Paul was speaking of self-centered, counterproductive worry, not legitimate cares and concerns for the spread of the gospel (see 2:28 and discussion; 2 Cor. 11:28; Matt. 6:25-31; 1 Peter 5:7). Note well Paul's alternative: **in every thing by prayer**. Anxiety and prayer are two great opposing forces in Christian experience. **With thanksgiving** is the antidote to worry (along with prayer and petition). To give thanks with prayer and supplication—at the outset, not just at the outcome—honors God's perspective and recognizes that His attentive provision is far above one's ability to care for oneself.

4:7. The peace of God is more than a psychological state of mind; it's an inner tranquility based on peace with God—the peaceful state of those whose sins are forgiven (see John 14:27; Rom. 5:1). The opposite of anxiety, it is the tranquility that comes when the believer commits every care to God in prayer and worries about them no more. Such peace **passeth all understanding**; it achieves "more than our clever forethought and ingenious plans can accomplish" (Martin, *The Epistle of Paul to the Philippians*, p. 170). The full dimensions of God's love and care are beyond human comprehension (see Eph. 3:18-20). **Keep your hearts and minds** draws on a military metaphor to portray God's peace as a sentry guarding or maintaining watch over the heart and mind. God's "protective custody" of those who are in Christ Jesus extends to the core of their beings and to their deepest intentions (see 1 Peter 1:5).

4:8-9. For Paul's use of **finally** (v. 8), see discussion on 3:1. **Whatsoever things** denotes anything of the caliber or quality of what follows: **true ... praise**. Paul understood the influence of one's thoughts on one's life. What a person allows to occupy his mind will sooner or later determine his speech and his action. Paul's exhortation to **think on these things** is followed by a second exhortation: **those things ... do** (v. 9). The combination of virtues listed in verses 8-9 is sure to produce a wholesome thought pattern, which in turn will result in a life of moral and spiritual excellence.

Together the verbs **learned, and received, and heard, and seen** (v. 9) offer a profile of Paul's pastoral care of and personal familiarity with the Philippians. How worthy an example was Paul's own life when he could invite attention to and imitation of both his teaching and the pattern of his conduct (see 3:17). What Paul knew from the pattern of his devotion would be the blessing of their imitation: **the God of peace shall be with you** (see discussion on 1 Thess. 5:23; see also "the peace of God," 4:7).

B. Concluding Testimony and Repeated Thanks (4:10–20)

4:10–20. In this section of the letter, Paul confirmed that it is the thought that counts (v. 10), that happiness is in the heart, not in the circumstances (vv. 11–12), that a "can do" spirit belongs to the inner power of Christ (v. 13), that the Philippians' gift to Paul was first a gift to God (v. 18), who is the true source of ongoing generosity (vv. 15–17).

4:10. Paul targeted the thoughtful concern behind the Philippians' gifts rather than the gifts themselves (see 4:15–18). **At the last ... lacked opportunity** expresses his awareness that the thought was there all the time; only the opportunity was lacking. It is likely that the gifts carried by Epaphroditus came with apologies voiced on behalf of the congregation. Paul took pains to let them know that he found no fault in them for the delay, nor did he imagine any lack of concern for him (see 2 Cor. 11:9). Perhaps Paul's uncertain itinerary prior to his arrival at Rome or the lack of an available messenger had prevented the Philippians from showing their concern.

4:11–12. Paul genuinely appreciated the gifts from Philippi (see 3:14, 18), but he was not ultimately dependent on them (see 1 Tim. 6:6–8). **Whatsoever state ... to be content** (v. 11) was for Paul a secret (v. 12) to living independently through dependency on Christ. Paul revealed that contentment, or "self-sufficiency" (Greek, *autarkēs*), is actually a sufficiency found not in the self but in Christ

(see 4:13). For all intents and purposes, Paul redefined the meaning of this favorite Stoic expression by converting the highly prized virtue of "self-sufficiency" into "Christ-sufficiency" (Fee, *Paul's Letter to the Philippians*, p. 427). **I know ... abased ... abound** (v. 12) means in every situation, in all things (see 4:6–7). Paul knew that true contentment is a matter of inner sufficiency that neither poverty can abash nor prosperity can assure. Prosperity too can be a source of discontent.

4:13. All things refers to any and all situations that Paul faced (see 4:11–12). **Through** (lit., "in") **Christ which strengtheneth me** expresses Paul's vital union with the living, exalted Christ—the inner power effecting Paul's strength. The secret of Paul's being content (see 4:11–12) and the source of his abiding strength (see especially 2 Cor. 12:9–10; see also John 15:5; Eph. 3:16–17; Col. 1:11) was a Christ-centered life, powered by the inner presence of Christ.

4:14. The verb **communicate** means to share, participate, or partake in something. Compare the noun "partakers" in 1:7. The Philippians' gifts were a means of involving them in Paul's troubles (see Heb. 10:33).

4:15. Paul appreciated the significant help of his Philippian partners by identifying the strategic importance of their participation (**communicated**) in the travelogue of his second missionary journey (4:15–16). **Beginning** refers to Paul's initial work in the region, when he first preached in Philippi (see Acts 16:12–40). When Paul **departed**, or set out, for the south (Achaia), where Athens and Corinth were located (see Acts 17:14–16; 18:1–4), he left **Macedonia**, the northern part of modern-day Greece, where Berea and Thessalonica, as well as Philippi, were located, and only the church of Philippi helped Paul on his way. **But ye only** expresses the unique and unmatched generosity of the Philippian church (see 2 Cor. 8:1–5). Paul used commercial language to describe **giving and receiving** (credit and debit) between the Philippians and himself (see "abound to your account," 4:17). Yet this commercial imagery clearly was transcended by the mutual concern and self-sacrifice of their relationship.

4:16. Even in Thessalonica, or while Paul ministered there (see Acts 17:1–9), the partnership of the Philippians was evident. The word "even" calls the reader's attention to an unexpressed but implied comparison. Thessalonica was the capital and largest city of Macedonia. Far greater was its influence and prestige than that of Philippi. Even there, in the biggest of the cities, Paul said, it was the church of smaller Philippi that had the bigger partnership in the ministry. **Sent once and again** enumerates two and alludes to three occasions. Clearly, the gifts sent to Rome through Epaphroditus were the latest in a long and consistent pattern of generosity (see 2 Cor. 8:1–5).

4:17. For the commercial character of the words **abound to your account,** see discussion on 4:15. The "investment value" of the Philippians' gift was not primarily what Paul received, but the "spiritual dividends" they received.

4:18. The phrase **a sweet smell, a sacrifice acceptable** is drawn from the language and imagery of Old Testament sacrifice, not of atonement for sin but of thanksgiving and praise (see Lev. 7:12–15; Rom. 12:1; Eph. 5:2; Heb. 13:15–16). Paul had already associated their gifts, involving Epaphroditus, with priestly service (see 2:25, 30); now he spoke of its outcome, the offering **acceptable, well pleasing to God.** For this wording, compare also the language and imagery of Christ's work for believers (see 1 Peter 2:5) and God's work in believers (see Phil. 2:13).

4:19. Paul's use of **my God** added not only a personal touch (see "my God," 1:3) but also a tone of personal testimony to his note of assurance. **Shall supply** is a promise that was given to a church that had sacrificially given to meet Paul's need. **Your need** made it clear that Paul was concerned about not only his own situation but also that of the Philippians. Paul assured them that God has more than enough to cover their need: **his riches in glory by Christ Jesus** sets forth the measure of God's supply (see Eph. 1:18; 3:16–20).

4:20. Paul could not hold back a doxology, especially as he considered the truth of 4:19.

C. Greetings and Benediction (4:21–23)

4:21–22. Final greetings are a typical feature of Paul's letters (see, e.g., Rom. 16:3–16, 21–23; 1 Cor. 16:19–20; 2 Cor. 13:12–13; Col. 4:10–12, 14–15, 18).

4:21. For **every saint,** see discussion on 1:1. **Brethren which are with me** is a reference to Paul's fellow workers at Rome, especially Timothy (see 1:1, 14, 16).

4:22. Cesar's household refers not to blood relatives of the emperor but to those employed (slaves or freemen) in or around the palace area (see "palace," 1:13).

THE EPISTLE OF PAUL THE APOSTLE TO THE COLOSSIANS

INTRODUCTION

Author, Date, and Place of Composition

That Colossians is a genuine letter of Paul is not usually disputed. In the early church, all who spoke on the subject of authorship ascribed it to Paul. In the nineteenth century, however, some thought that the heresy refuted in chapter 2 was second-century Gnosticism. A careful analysis of chapter 2, however, shows that the heresy referred to there is noticeably less developed than the Gnosticism of leading Gnostic teachers of the second and third centuries. Also, the seeds of what later became the full-blown Gnosticism of the second century were present in the first century and already making inroads into the churches. Consequently, it is not necessary to date Colossians in the second century, at a time too late for Paul to have written the letter.

Instead, the letter is to be dated during Paul's first imprisonment in Rome, where he spent at least two years under house arrest (see Acts 28:16–31). Some have argued that Paul wrote Colossians from Ephesus or Caesarea, but most of the evidence favors Rome as the place where Paul penned all the Prison Letters (Ephesians, Colossians, Philippians, and Philemon). Colossians should be dated circa AD 60, the same year Ephesians and Philemon were written.

Colosse: The Town and the Church

Several hundred years before Paul's day, Colosse had been a leading city in Asia Minor (present-day Turkey). It was located on the Lycus River and on the great east-west trade route leading from Ephesus on the Aegean Sea to the Euphrates River. By the first century AD, Colosse was diminished to a second-rate market town, which had long ago been surpassed in power and importance by the neighboring towns of Laodicea and Hierapolis (see 4:13).

What gave Colosse New Testament importance, however, was the fact that Epaphras had been converted during Paul's three-year ministry in Ephesus and had carried the gospel to Colosse (see 1:7–8; Acts 19:10). The young church that resulted then became the target of heretical attack, which led to Epaphras's visit to Paul in Rome and ultimately to the penning of the Colossian letter.

Perhaps as a result of the efforts of Epaphras or other converts of Paul, Christian churches had also been established in Laodicea and Hierapolis. Some of them were house churches (see 4:15; Philemon 2). Most likely, all of them were primarily Gentile.

The Colossian Heresy

Paul never explicitly described the false teaching he opposed in the Colossian letter. The nature of the heresy must be inferred from statements he made in opposition to the false teachers. An analysis of his refutation suggests that the heresy was diverse in nature. Some of the elements of its teachings were:

1. Ceremonialism. It held to strict rules about permissible food and drink, religious festivals (2:16–17), and circumcision (2:11; 3:11).
2. Asceticism. "Touch not; taste not; handle not" (2:21; see 2:23).
3. Angel worship (see 2:18).
4. Depreciation of Christ. This is implied in Paul's stress on the supremacy of Christ (1:15–20; 2:2–3, 9).
5. Secret knowledge. The Gnostics boasted of this (see 2:18 and Paul's emphasis in 2:2–3 on Christ, "in whom are hid all the treasures of wisdom and knowledge").
6. Reliance on human wisdom and tradition (see 2:4, 8).

These elements seem to fall into two categories, Jewish and Gnostic. It is likely, therefore, that the Colossian heresy was a mixture of an extreme form of Judaism and an early stage of Gnosticism (see 1 John, Introduction: "Gnosticism"; see also discussion on 2:23).

Theme and Theological Message

Paul's purpose was to refute the Colossian heresy. To accomplish this goal, he exalted Christ as the very image of God (1:15), the Creator (1:16), the preexistent Sustainer of all things (1:17), the Head of the church (1:18), the first to be resurrected (1:18), the fullness of Deity in bodily form (1:19; 2:9), and the Reconciler (1:20–22). Thus, Christ is completely adequate. Believers "are complete in [Christ]" (2:10). On the other hand, the Colossian heresy was altogether inadequate. It was a hollow and deceptive philosophy (2:8), lacking any ability to restrain the old sinful nature (2:23). The theme of Colossians is the complete adequacy of Christ as contrasted with the emptiness of mere human philosophy.

Outline

I. Introduction (1:1–14)
  A. Greetings (1:1–2)
  B. Thanksgiving (1:3–8)
  C. Prayer (1:9–14)
II. The Supremacy of Christ (1:15–23)
III. Paul's Labor for the Church (1:24–2:7)
  A. A Ministry for the Sake of the Church (1:24–29)
  B. A Concern for the Spiritual Welfare of His Readers (2:1–7)
IV. Freedom from Human Regulations through Life with Christ (2:8–23)
  A. Warning to Guard against the False Teachers (2:8–15)

Bibliography

Bruce, F. F. *Epistles to the Colossians, Philemon, and Ephesians.* The New International Commentary on the New Testament. Grand Rapids, MI: Eerdmans, 1984.

Gromacki, Robert. *Philippians and Colossians.* Twenty-First Century Biblical Commentary. Chattanooga, TN: AMG, 2003.

Lightfoot, J. B. *Saint Paul's Epistles to the Colossians and Philemon.* 1879. Reprint, Grand Rapids, MI: Zondervan, 1959.

Martin, Ralph P. *Colossians and Philemon.* Grand Rapids, MI: Eerdmans, 1981.

O'Brien, Peter T. *Colossians–Philemon.* Word Biblical Commentary 44. Waco, TX: Word, 1982.

EXPOSITION

I. Introduction (1:1–14)

A. Greetings (1:1–2)

1:1. Paul identified himself at the beginning of the letter as was customary in ancient letter writing. It was conventional to follow a pattern of address that listed the letter writer and the recipients (from A, to B) followed by a greeting (1:1–2). Paul described himself as **an apostle of Jesus Christ** because he was not known in person to the church in Colosse (see 2:1), and he was writing this letter as Christ's emissary to the church (for more information on Paul, see discussions on Acts 9:1; Phil. 3:4–14). Paul was very Christ-centered, as seen by this short letter, in which he used the title "Christ" twenty-five times and the title "Lord" (alone) nine times. **Timotheus** is mentioned as being present with Paul (see "we," 1:3, 4, 28; and "us," 1:8; 4:3), and as Paul's coworker, he concurred with the message of Paul's letter. Paul also mentioned Timothy in 2 Corinthians, Philippians, 1–2 Thessalonians, and Philemon, but Paul is really the sole author, as seen by the constant use of "I" (see especially 4:18).

1:2. Although Paul did not use the word church (Greek, *ekklēsia*), he did use the word **saints** (Greek, *hagios*; as in Rom. 1:7; Phil. 1:1; and Eph. 1:1) of those who were consecrated by God and to God through Christ. For **faithful**, see 1:7; 4:7, 9. Because of Christ's substitutionary death for the Colossian believers, they were declared holy in the sight of God, and because of the Holy Spirit's work, they were continuing to be made holy in their lives. **In Christ** points to the believer's spiritual union with Christ, mentioned by Paul eleven times in Colossians (see discussion on Eph. 1:1). The greeting proper comes with the words **Grace ... and peace** (see discussions on John 14:27; 20:19; Gal. 1:3; Eph. 1:2).

B. Thanksgiving (1:3–8)

1:3. We (Paul and Timothy) **give thanks to God**. Every one of Paul's letters, except Galatians, begins with thanks or praise (see discussion on Phil. 1:3–4). In Colossians, thanks is an important theme (see 1:12; 2:7; 3:15–17; 4:2). The Bible never thanks man for his faith and love, but rather thanks God, who is the source of these virtues.

1:4. Faith in Christ (see 1:2) recognizes not only the Colossians' identifiable trust but their mutual bond of belief that united them together in Christ. They had a living and dynamic faith, as is detected by their **love** for one another and **all the saints** (see John 13:35).

1:5. The three great Christian virtues of faith, love, and hope appear elsewhere also (Rom. 5:2–5; 1 Cor. 13:13; Gal. 5:5–6; 1 Thess. 1:3; 5:8; Heb. 10:22–24). Everywhere, the church should exhibit this triune profile; it is a healthy hallmark of Christ-centered fellowship. **Hope** is not wishful thinking but a firm assurance. The disposition of hope comes from the content of hope (**the word of the truth of the gospel**); the compelling truth of the gospel ("hope") orients one's entire outlook on the present, encouraging faith and love. For this thought of faith and love coming from hope, see Titus 1:2.

1:6. In all the world is an example of hyperbole, the literary technique of dramatic emphasis. Here Paul used this phrase to summarize the rapid and dynamic (**fruit** bearing) spread of the gospel, which, in three decades of Pentecost (see 1:23; Rom. 1:8; 10:18; 16:19), was growing in every quarter of the Roman Empire. In refutation of the charge of the false teachers, Paul insisted that the Christian faith is not merely local or regional but worldwide.

1:7. Epaphras was a native of Colosse (4:12) and probably founded the Colossian church. **Learned** (Greek, *manthanō*) gives the clear impression of guided instruction in the gospel at the hands of Epaphras, a picture that resonates with his evangelistic labors in nearby Laodicea and Hierapolis (4:13). Paul loved and admired Epaphras, calling him a "fellowprisoner" (Philemon 23), his dear fellow servant and a faithful minister of Christ. Given the threat of heretical teaching, Paul clearly endorsed the gospel the Colossians had "learned" from Epaphras. It was he who told Paul at Rome about the Colossian church problem and thereby stimulated him to write this letter (1:4, 8). The name Epaphras is a shortened form of Epaphroditus (from "Aphrodite," the Greek

goddess of love), which suggests that he was a convert from paganism. He is not the Epaphroditus of Philippians 2:25; 4:18.

1:8. Your love in the Spirit describes not only the Holy Spirit as the source of Christian love but the character and quality of love.

C. Prayer (1:9–14)

1:9–11. The knowledge of his will (v. 9) is a matter of not only knowing God's commands but apprehending the values and character of His heart (**increasing in the knowledge of God**; v. 10). In the Bible, knowledge and wisdom are practical, having to do with godly living. This is borne out by 1:10–12, which state that knowledge, wisdom, and understanding result in a life worthy of the Lord. **Spiritual** (v. 9) describes wisdom and understanding that are informed by the Spirit (for the role of the Spirit in knowing God, see 1 Cor. 2:10–16). Facts alone will never inspire the strength that comes from knowing God himself. Real knowledge or familiarity with God (see Rom. 10:2) is the source of **all patience and longsuffering with joyfulness** (v. 11).

1:12–13. Light (v. 12) symbolizes holiness (see Matt. 5:14; 6:23; Acts 26:18; 1 John 1:5), truth (see Pss. 36:9; 119:105, 130; 2 Cor. 4:6), love (see James 1:17; 1 John 2:9–10), glory (see Isa. 60:1–3; 1 Tim. 6:16), and life (see John 1:4). Accordingly, God (see 1 John 1:5), Christ (see John 8:12), and the Christian (see Eph. 5:8) are characterized by light. The "light" is the opposite of **the power of darkness** (v. 13). **Made us meet** (or "qualified" us) **to be partakers of the inheritance** (v. 12) presumes the redemptive achievement of God's Son on the cross, which is vividly depicted in the language of being redeemed: **delivered** (rescued; v. 13) and **translated** (transferred). The transaction is cosmic, but the language is as tangible as a prisoner of war being rescued from enemy control and brought to safety under benevolent authority (see 1:14). **Kingdom** here refers not to a territory but to the authority, rule, or sovereign power of a king, meaning that the Christian is no longer under the dominion of evil ("darkness"; v. 12) but under the benevolent rule of God's Son.

1:14. Redemption (Greek, *apolutrōsis*; "buying back"; see Rom. 3:23; Heb. 9:15; Mark 10:45; Matt. 20:28) brings deliverance and freedom from the penalty of sin by the payment of a ransom: the substitutionary death of Christ. Thus, as Paul made clear, redemption is **the forgiveness of sins**, or the cancellation of the debt owed to the holiness of God.

II. The Supremacy of Christ (1:15–23)

1:15–20. This passage was perhaps an early Christian hymn (see discussion on 3:16) on the supremacy of Christ, used here by Paul to counteract the false teaching at Colosse. It is divided into two parts: (1) Christ's supremacy in creation (vv. 15–17); (2) Christ's supremacy in redemption (vv. 18–20).

1:15. Christ is called **the image of ... God** here and in 2 Corinthians 4:4. Paul's use of the word "image" (Greek, *eikōn*; "likeness," see 3:10; Rom. 8:29; 2 Cor. 3:18) confirms that the Son (see 1:13) reveals the Father (see 1:12), whom no one has ever seen ("No man hath seen God at any time," John 1:18). Since God the Father is **invisible**, in His "likeness" the distinct features of God's character and nature, the very "person" (Heb. 1:3) of God, are manifest. Christ, who is the eternal Son of God and who became the God-man, reflects and reveals God the Father (see John 1:18; 14:9), the "representation" and "manifestation" of God (Lightfoot, *Colossians and Philemon*, p. 145). His status as Son is further defined as **the firstborn of every creature**. Just as the firstborn son had certain privileges and rights in the biblical world, so also Christ has certain rights in relation to all creation—priority, preeminence, and sovereignty (see 1:16–18; see also Ps. 89:27 for this same idea of preeminence and sovereignty).

1:16. By him were all things created (see John 1:3). Seven times in 1:15–20 Paul mentions "all," as in "all things," "allfulness," and "every creature," thus stressing that Christ is supreme over all, which **thrones, or dominions, or principalities, or powers** details. **That are in heaven** entails angels. An angelic hierarchy figured prominently in the Colossian heresy (see Introduction: "The Colossian Heresy").

1:17. He is before all things refers to time, as in John 1:1–2; 8:58, and underscores "by him were all things created" (1:16). Therefore, **all things consist** ("hold together," "cohere") in Christ, and by virtue of Him, the created sum is "a cosmos instead of chaos" (Lightfoot, *Colossians and Philemon*, p. 156).

1:18. Christ's preeminence in all creation (1:15–17) is preamble to appreciating His preeminence in redemption (1:18–20). The agent of all beginnings, Christ is fittingly **the beginning** of the new creation. He is **the firstborn** (Greek, *prōtotokos*; used of birth order as well as the special status of the firstborn). Here Paul was stating that Christ is first in order and status because He was the first to rise from the dead with a resurrection body. Elsewhere Paul calls Him "the firstfruits of them that slept" (1 Cor. 15:20). Others who were raised from the dead (see 2 Kings 4:35; Luke 7:15; John 11:44; Acts 9:36–41; 20:7–11) were raised only to die again. Therefore, "the beginning" and "the firstborn" (see Gen. 49:3) identify Christ as the founder of a new people through the resurrection. He is "the firstborn" in this sense only as 1:16–17 make obvious.

1:19. Although no word for **the Father** is present in this verse in the Greek text, the verb **pleased** (see Matt. 12:18; and the noun "good pleasure" in Eph. 1:5, 9) and the context require the understanding of either "the Father" or "God" as the subject. The word **fulness** was part of the technical vocabulary of some Gnostic philosophies. In these systems, it meant the sum of the supernatural forces controlling the fate of people. For Paul, "fulness" meant the totality of God with all His powers and attributes (see 2:9; Eph. 3:19; 4:13).

1:20. Reconcile all things unto himself. Paul's thought is closer here to Eph. 1:10: "That in the dispensation of the fulness of times he might gather together in one all things in Christ, both which are in heaven, and which are on earth; even in him." It does not mean that Christ by His death has saved all people. Scripture speaks of an eternal hell and makes it clear that only believers are saved. When Adam and Eve sinned, not only was the harmony between God and man destroyed, but disorder was introduced into creation (see Rom. 8:19–22). So when Christ died on the cross, He made peace possible between God and man and, in principle, restored harmony in the physical world, though the full realization of the latter will come only when Christ returns (see Rom. 8:21).

1:21–23. The reconciliation of 1:20 is given individual expression as a present reality with the former (v. 21) and final (v. 22) condition of a believer in Christ described before conversion and before the eyes of God through **faith** (v. 23) in the substitutionary **death** (v. 22) of Christ, the gospel of God's work in Christ **preached** (heralded) to **every creature** (v. 23; see discussion on 1:6). Paul identified himself as **a minister** (Greek, *diakonos*; see 1:25) in the service of God's grand work of reconciliation (see 2 Cor. 5:18–19). In using the term "minister," Paul also gave an implicit endorsement of Epaphras and Tychicus (see 1:7; 4:7) as fellow champions of the same gospel. The link was vital for the Colossians, who were beset by teachers of heresy (see Introduction: "The Colossian Heresy").

III. Paul's Labor for the Church (1:24–2:7)

A. A Ministry for the Sake of the Church (1:24–29)

1:24. My sufferings. By preaching the gospel to the Gentiles, Paul experienced all kinds of affliction, but here he was probably referring especially to his imprisonment. **Fill up that which is behind.** By this, Paul was not suggesting that Christ's atoning sacrifice was deficient. Rather, he was saying that he suffered afflictions because he was preaching the good news of Christ's atonement. Christ suffered on the cross to atone for sin, and Paul "fill[ed] up" Christ's afflictions by experiencing the added sufferings necessary to carry this good news to a lost world.

1:25. Fulfill the word of God. The meaning here seems to be that the Word of God is brought to completion (i.e., to its intended purpose) only when it is proclaimed (see Isa. 55:11). Paul's commission to bring the Word to completion, therefore, required him to make the Word of God heard in Colosse as well as elsewhere (for a similar statement, see Rom. 15:19).

1:26. Mystery (Greek, *mystērion*; also meaning "secret"; used twenty-one times in Paul's letters) was used by Paul to denote the purpose of God, unknown to man except by revelation. This word was a popular, pagan religious term, used in the mystery religions to refer to secret information available only to an exclusive group of initiated people. Paul changed that meaning radically by always combining it with words such as **made manifest** (here), "made known" (Eph. 1:9), "make all men see" (Eph. 3:9), and "revelation" (Rom. 16:25). The Christian mystery is not secret knowledge for a few. It is a revelation of divine truths—once hidden but now openly proclaimed.

1:27. Gentiles … Christ in you. "The mystery" (1:26) was the fact that Christ indwells Gentiles, for it had not been previously revealed that the Gentiles would be admitted to the church on equal terms with Israel (see discussion on Eph. 3:6).

1:28. Perfect (Greek, *teleios*; "mature," here possibly alluding to its alternative meaning of "initiate") was a term employed by the mystery religions and the Gnostics to describe those who had become possessors of the secrets or knowledge boasted of by the particular religion (see 1 John, Introduction: "Gnosticism"). In Christ, however, every believer is one of the perfect.

B. A Concern for the Spiritual Welfare of His Readers (2:1–7)

2:1–2. Laodicea (near modern Denizli; v. 1) was only about eleven miles from Colosse. This letter was to be read to the church there too (see 4:16). **Great conflict** (Greek, *agōn*) specifically denotes an athletic "contest" and generally "a struggle," even anxiety and concern. Here it expresses a contest of great concern on Paul's part to see the believers in Colosse and Laodicea **comforted … knit together in love, and … the full assurance of … Christ** (v. 2). That was Paul's objective, the purpose and goal of his "struggle" for them. For **mystery**, see discussions on 1:26; Romans 11:25.

2:3–4. Jesus Christ is the sum of God's mystery (see 2:2). Here Paul made it clear that no additional or elite secret is required other than **the treasures** (v. 3) that are **hid** in Christ. In other words, no "mystery" exists that can add anything to Christ. Therefore, Paul undercut **enticing words** (v. 4) and the appeal of those who claimed the importance of an elite and secret **knowledge** (v. 3; see 2:8). Paul stressed knowledge in this letter (see 2:2; 1:9–10) because he was refuting a heresy that emphasized knowledge as the means of salvation (see 1 John, Introduction: "Gnosticism"). Paul insisted that the Christian, not the Gnostic, possessed genuine knowledge.

2:5. Absent in the flesh … with you in the spirit. Similar to 1 Corinthians 5:3, Paul expressed the depth of his interest, a bond that geographical distance could not diminish.

2:6–7. Walk ye in him (v. 6) means to "live" or conduct your life in relation to Him. Again, Paul called his readers back to the fundamental disposition of faith in the gospel message and away from any secret knowledge or experience. One's relationship to Jesus Christ within the community of faith (see 2:2) is not superceded or diminished by knowledge outside of Christ (see 2:4, 8). In fact, the believer's intimate, spiritual, living union with Christ is mentioned repeatedly in this letter (see, e.g., v. 7; 2:10–13, 20; 1:2, 27–28; 3:1, 3). If one is to go deeper, it is to be **rooted … in the faith** (v. 7), that which the Colossians and Laodiceans were originally **taught** when they received Christ.

IV. Freedom from Human Regulations through Life with Christ (2:8–23)

A. Warning to Guard against the False Teachers (2:8–15)

2:8. The rudiments of the world. This term (which occurs also in 2:20 and Gal. 4:3, 9) refers to false, worldly, religious, elementary teachings. Paul was counteracting the Colossian heresy, which, in part, taught that salvation required one to combine faith in Christ with secret knowledge and with man-made regulations concerning physical and external practices, such as circumcision, eating and drinking, and observance of religious festivals.

2:9. The fulness of the Godhead (see discussion on 1:19). The declaration that the very essence of

deity was present in totality in Jesus' human body was a direct refutation of Gnostic teaching.

2:10–15. Here Paul declared that the Christian is complete in Christ rather than deficient, as the Gnostics claimed. This completeness includes putting off the sinful nature (v. 11), resurrection from spiritual death (vv. 12–13), forgiveness (v. 13), and deliverance from legalistic requirements (v. 14) and from evil spirit beings (v. 15).

2:11–13. Circumcision (v. 11) and **baptism** (v. 12) are both symbolic pictures of salvation—one negative, the other positive. Circumcision pictures the cutting off of flesh—the repudiation of the flesh. Baptism pictures the believer's death, burial, and rising up to newness of life (see Rom. 6:3–5).

2:14. Blotting out means to remove or obliterate so as to leave no trace. In Christ, the believer's "record" is totally expunged of past violations, or **the handwriting of ordinances**. This is a business term meaning "a certificate of indebtedness in the debtor's handwriting." Paul used it as a designation for the Mosaic law, with all its regulations, under which everyone is a debtor to God.

2:15. Having spoiled principalities. Not only did God cancel out the accusations of the law against the Christian, but He also conquered and disarmed ("spoiled") the evil angels ("principalities" and "powers" in 1:16; Eph. 6:12), who entice people to follow asceticism and false teachings about Christ. The picture is of conquered soldiers stripped of their clothes as well as their weapons to symbolize their total defeat. **Triumphing over them** has the vivid literal meaning of "leading them in a triumphal procession," a metaphor recalling a Roman general leading his captives through the streets of his city for all the citizens to see as evidence of his complete victory (see 2 Cor. 2:14 and discussion). That Christ triumphed over the Devil and his cohorts is seen in Matthew 12:29; Luke 10:18; Romans 16:20.

B. Pleas to Reject the False Teachers (2:16–19)

2:16. The outcome of Christ's victory has practical consequences for believers. Christians are to allow no one to judge (see "beguile," 2:18) them on matters of diet or religious observance by calling on any principality Christ has disarmed (2:15) nor any record of debt He has expunged (2:14).

2:17. Shadow ... body contrasts form and substance. The ceremonial laws of the Old Testament are here referred to as "shadows" (see Heb. 8:5; 10:1) because they symbolically depicted the coming of Christ, so any insistence on the observance of such ceremonies is a failure to recognize that their fulfillment has already taken place. This element of the Colossian heresy was combined with a rigid asceticism, as 2:20–21 reveals.

2:18. The term **beguile** pictures an umpire or referee who excludes from competition any athlete who fails to follow the rules. The Colossians were not to permit any false teacher to deny the reality of their salvation because they were not delighting in mock humility and in the worship of angelic beings. **Voluntary humility**, or humility in which one delights, is of necessity mock humility. Paul may have referred to a professed humility in view of the absolute God, who was believed to be so far above man that He could be worshiped only in the form of angels He had created. Second-century Gnosticism conceived of a list of spirit beings who had emanated from God and through whom God could be approached.

2:19. In anatomical terms, **not holding the head** expresses the folly of a torso or its limbs disconnected from that which is central to its function and fitness as its body. The central error of the Colossian heresy was a defective view of Christ, in which He was believed to be less than deity (see 2:9; 1:19).

C. An Analysis of the Heresy (2:20–23)

2:20–21. With **Wherefore if ye be dead with Christ** (v. 20), Paul called the Colossians and Laodiceans to apprehend the victory of Christ (see 2:14–15) that they had acknowledged in baptism (see 2:12–13) and to apply its truth to those who judged (2:16) or beguiled (2:17) them. Paul asked them **why ... are ye subject** to them? **The rudiments of the world**. See discussion on 2:8. **Touch not; taste not; handle not** (v. 21) points out the strict ascetic

nature of the heresy. These prohibitions seem to carry Old Testament ceremonial laws to the extreme.

2:22–23. Paul gave a rather detailed analysis of the Colossian heresy: (1) it appeared to set forth an impressive system of religious philosophy; (2) it was, however, a system created by the false teachers themselves, rather than being of divine origin; (3) the false teachers attempted to parade their humility; (4) this may have been done by a harsh asceticism that brutally misused the body. Paul's analysis was that such practices are worthless because they totally fail to control sinful desires.

V. Rules for Holy Living (3:1–4:6)

A. The Old Self and the New Self (3:1–17)

3:1. If ye then be risen. What has been described as the indicative and the imperative (the standing and the state) of the Christian is set forth in 3:1–10. The indicative statements describe the believer's position in Christ: he is dead (3:3); he has been raised with Christ (v. 1); he is with Christ in heaven ("hid with Christ," 3:3); he has "put off the old man" (3:9); and he has "put on the new man" (3:10). The imperative statements indicate what the believer is to do as a result: he is to set his heart (or mind) on things above (3:1–2); he is to put to death practices that belong to his earthly nature (3:5); and he is to rid himself of practices that characterized his unregenerate self (3:8). In summary, he is called to become in daily experience what he is positionally in Christ (see Rom. 6:1–13). **Then** (or "therefore") links the doctrinal section of the letter with the practical section (as it does in Rom. 12:1; Eph. 4:1; Phil. 4:1).

3:2–3. Set your affection (v. 2). With the Greek verb *phroneō* ("think formatively upon," "be minded"), Paul bid his readers to let **things above** occupy their thinking and shape their outlook and attitude. The verb *phroneō* occurs only here in Colossians but figures prominently (ten times) in his letter to the Philippians (see, e.g., Phil. 2:2, 5; 3:19). Compare "things above" with Ephesians 1:3, "all spiritual blessings in heavenly places in Christ." How fitting, for that is where believers belong, since our **life is hid with Christ in God** (v. 3).

3:4. Shall appear refers to Christ's second coming (see 1 Thess. 1:10; Phil. 3:20).

3:5. Paul said to **Mortify**, or "put to death," that which has died (see 3:3; Gal. 2:20; 6:14). He gave a clue in 3:2 as to how to do that: a mind renewed (see also 3:10; Rom. 8:5–6; 12:1–2) from above, through the truth and Spirit of God (see "put off ... put on," 3:9–10).

3:6. The wrath of God. God is unalterably opposed to sin and will invariably make sure that it is justly punished (see *Zondervan KJV Study Bible* note on Zech. 1:2).

3:7–8. Walked ... lived characterizes the course of one's life on the horizontal plane of earthly existence apart from the vertical intervention of God's heavenly truth and existence in Christ (see Eph. 2:1–6).

3:9–10. Put off (v. 9) **... put on** (v. 10). At salvation, God changes the believer's nature, making this possible (see Gal. 3:27; discussions on Eph. 4:22–24). It is the task of the believer to starve (see "Mortify," 3:5) the old man and feed ("set your affection," 3:2) the new man through right (**renewed**; see 2 Cor. 5:17) thinking that is set straight by **knowledge** (see 1:10; 2:2–3) of Christ, God's image (see 1:15; for **the image of him that created him**, see discussion on Gen. 1:26).

3:11. It is the new man, the new creation, the new image, that transforms and transcends every earthly echelon or segregation. The **barbarian** did not speak Greek and was thought to be uncivilized. The **Scythian** was known especially for brutality and was considered little better than a wild beast. Originally from what is today south Russia, Scythians were the barbarian's barbarian. **Christ is all, and in all** and accordingly transcends all barriers and unifies people from all cultures, races, and nations. Such distinctions are no longer significant. Christ alone matters.

3:12–14. Put on (v. 12), or clothe yourselves with, the attire appropriate for **the elect of God**, a term used of both Israel (Deut. 4:37) and the Christian community (1 Peter 2:9). Divine election is a constant theme in Paul's letters (see discussion on Eph. 1:4), but the Bible never teaches that it dulls

human responsibility. On the contrary, as this verse shows, it is precisely because the Christian has been elected to eternal salvation that he must put forth every effort to live a godly life. Paul believed that divine sovereignty and human responsibility go hand in hand. The character qualities listed in these verses are best understood as belonging to the new man and image (see 3:10) that is created after God (1:15). Living the godly life is defined, then, by Christlikeness, and its power is found in Christ, who shapes one's heart and mind through faith (see 3:17).

3:15. The peace of God is the attitude of peace that Christ alone gives, replacing the attitude of bitterness and quarrelsomeness. This attitude is to **rule** (lit., "function like an umpire") in all human relationships.

3:16–17. The word of Christ (v. 16) refers especially to Christ's teaching, which in the time of the Colossians was transmitted orally. But by implication, it includes the Old Testament as well as the New Testament. **Psalms and hymns and spiritual songs.** Some of the most important doctrines were expressed in Christian hymns preserved now only in Paul's letters (see 1:15–20; Eph. 5:14; Phil. 2:6–11; 1 Tim. 3:16). "Psalms" refers to the Old Testament psalms (see Luke 20:42; 24:44; Acts 1:20; 13:33), some of which may have been set to music by the church. "Psalm" could also describe a song newly composed for Christian worship (see 1 Cor. 14:26, where "hymn" is literally "psalm" in the Greek text). A "hymn" was a song of praise, especially used in a celebration (see Mark 14:26; Heb. 2:12; see also Acts 16:25), much like the Old Testament psalms that praised God for all that He is. A "song" recounted the acts of God and praised Him for them (see Rev. 5:9; 14:3; 15:3), much like the Old Testament psalms that thanked God for all that He had done (see discussion on Eph. 5:19–20). **Whatsoever ye do in word or deed** (v. 17) is comprehensive, as the words **do all** make evident. **In the name of** denotes "under the authority and auspices of" Christ. Add this element of representation to the popular question, "What would Jesus do?" for a practical commentary and application of what Paul admonished.

B. Rules for Christian Households (3:18–4:1)

3:18–4:1. Paul next turned to a series of admonitions concerning the household (see discussions on Eph. 5:22–6:9). Luther used the expression *haustafeln*, a "list of rules for the household," for this section. Implictly, Paul's directives illustrate the dramatic difference that Christ makes in the home and the workplace.

3:18. As is fit in the Lord. "Fit" denotes what is "proper," or literally "reaches" what is expected or required by the Lord (see Eph. 5:22).

3:19. Love your wives. This command to love is a duty that cannot be fulfilled without corresponding affection and sweetness. **Be not bitter against them** shows the leadership of the husband's love; it cannot be soured or withheld because of disappointment in the wife. The husband's indefatigable love is closest to the love of Jesus Christ (Eph. 5:25–29).

3:20. Children (Greek, *teknon*) are to obey their parents **in all things**, or in everything not sinful (see 3:25; Acts 5:29). Although the term for "children" is not age specific, it likely refers to children in the care of and under the supervision of their parents (see "bring them up," Eph. 6:4).

3:22–4:1. Paul neither condoned slavery nor sanctioned revolt against masters. Rather, he called on both slaves and masters to show Christian principles in their relationship and thus to attempt to change the institution. The reason Paul wrote more about slaves and masters than about wives, husbands, children, and fathers may be that the slave Onesimus (4:9) was going along with Tychicus to deliver this Colossian letter and the letter to Philemon, Onesimus's master, who also lived in Colosse (see the book of Philemon).

C. Further Instructions (4:2–6)

4:2. In Greek, **Continue** carries the sense of "diligent attention to something," which matches the word **watch**. Prayer and thanksgiving go hand in glove (see Phil. 4:6) and are mutually appropriate to the mind and heart focused on a sovereign and benevolent heavenly Father.

4:3–6. Paul's admonition to "continue in prayer" (4:2) led naturally to a request for intercession on his behalf. His concern for the advance of his ministry to the world on behalf of Christ (vv. 3–4) led him to give his readers guidance concerning their witness to others (vv. 5–6). Concourse with others pivots on communication, and words must be served and **seasoned with salt** (v. 6). Salt is a preservative and is tasty. Similarly, the Christian's conversation is to be wholesome (see 3:8; Eph. 4:29).

VI. Final Greetings (4:7–18)

4:7–17. Since Onesimus (v. 9), Aristarchus (v. 10), Marcus (v. 10), Epaphras (v. 12), Luke and Demas (v. 14), and Archippus (v. 17) are mentioned in Philemon, this suggests that the letters to Colosse and Philemon were written at the same time and place.

4:7. Tychicus (see discussions on 1:23; 3:22–4:1; 4:12, 16; Eph. 6:21; see also 2 Tim. 4:12; Titus 3:12) was sent expressly to report on Paul's state of affairs on his behalf and to bring comfort. He accompanied Epaphras.

4:9. For the slave **Onesimus**, see Philemon, Introduction: "Recipient."

4:10. Aristarchus was a Macedonian who is mentioned three times in Acts: (1) he was with Paul during the Ephesian riot (Acts 19:29) and therefore was known in Colosse; (2) both he and Tychicus (Acts 20:4) were with Paul in Greece; (3) he accompanied Paul on his trip to Rome (Acts 27:2). **Marcus**, or Mark, was the author of the second gospel. Against Barnabas's advice, Paul refused to take Mark on the second missionary journey because Mark had "departed from" him at Pamphylia (Acts 15:38). About twelve years later, the difficulties seem to have been ironed out, because Paul sent Mark's greetings, both here and in Philemon 24 (sent at the same time to Philemon, who was in Colosse). About five years later, Paul even wrote that Mark was "profitable to me for the ministry" (2 Tim. 4:11; see discussion on Acts 15:39).

4:13. Hierapolis was a town in Asia Minor (present-day Turkey), about six miles from Laodicea and fourteen miles from Colosse. Its church may have been founded during Paul's three-year stay in Ephesus (see Acts 19), but probably not by Paul himself (see 2:1).

4:14. Luke wrote about Paul in the book of Acts, having often accompanied him on his travels (see discussion on Acts 16:10). He was with Paul in Rome during his imprisonment (see Acts 28), where this letter was written. **Demas** was a Christian worker who later deserted Paul (see 2 Tim. 4:10).

4:15. Nymphas was probably a Laodicean. The expression **the church which is in his house** illustrates the truth that the "church" is not a building but the people of God. For the most part, the early church had no buildings, so it usually met for worship and instruction in homes. It often centered around one family, for example, Priscilla and Aquila (see Rom. 16:5; 1 Cor. 16:19), Philemon (see Philemon 2), and Mary the mother of John (see Acts 12:12).

4:16. When this epistle is read amongst you (see Eph. 3:4; 1 Thess. 5:27) makes it clear that Paul used the letter as a form of direct address between himself and the church as a whole (see 4:18). Thus, the practice of the early church was to read Paul's letters aloud to the assembled congregation. **The epistle from Laodicea** does not necessarily mean a letter written by the Laodiceans. Rather, it could have been a letter that the Laodiceans were to lend to the Colossians—a letter that Paul had originally written to the Laodiceans. This may have been a fourth letter that Tychicus carried to this area in what is present-day Turkey, in addition to Ephesians, Colossians, and Philemon. It may have been Paul's letter to the Ephesians, a circular letter making the rounds from Ephesus to Laodicea to Colosse (see Ephesians, Introduction: "Author, Date, and Place of Composition").

4:17. Paul called **Archippus** his "fellowsoldier" in Philemon 2.

4:18. Paul's custom was to dictate his letters (see Rom. 16:22) and pen a few greetings himself (see 1 Cor. 16:21; Gal. 6:11; 2 Thess. 3:17; Philemon 19). His personal signature was the guarantee of the genuineness of the letter.

THE FIRST EPISTLE OF PAUL THE APOSTLE TO THE THESSALONIANS

INTRODUCTION

Author, Date, and Place of Composition

Both external and internal evidence (see 1:1; 2:18) support the view that Paul wrote 1 Thessalonians (from Corinth; see discussion on 3:1–2). Early church writers are agreed on the matter, with testimonies beginning as early as AD 140 (Marcion). Paul's known characteristics are apparent in the letter (compare 3:1–2, 8–11 with Acts 15:36; 2 Cor. 11:28). Historical allusions in the book fit Paul's life as recounted in Acts and in his own letters (compare 2:14–16; 3:6 with Acts 17:5–10, 16). In the face of such evidence, few have ever rejected Paul's authorship.

The letter is generally dated circa AD 51. Weighty support for this date was found in an inscription discovered at Delphi, Greece, that dates Gallio's proconsulship to circa AD 51–52 and thus places Paul at Corinth at the same time (see Acts 18:12–17). Except for the possibility of an early date for Galatians (AD 48–49?), 1 Thessalonians is Paul's earliest canonical letter.

Thessalonica: The City and the Church

Thessalonica was a bustling seaport city at the head of the Thermaic Gulf. It was an important communication and trade center, located at the junction of the great Egnatian Way and the road leading north to the Danube. Its population numbered about 200,000, making it the largest city in Macedonia. It was also the capital of its province.

The account of the founding of the Thessalonian church is found in Acts 17:1–9. Since Paul began his ministry there in the Jewish synagogue, it is reasonable to assume that the new church included some Jews. However, 1:9–10 and Acts 17:4 seem to indicate that the church was largely Gentile in membership.

Background

It is helpful to trace the locations of Paul and his companions that relate to the Thessalonian correspondence. Their travels were as follows:

(1) Paul and Silas fled from Thessalonica to Berea (see Acts 17:10). Since Timothy is not mentioned, it is possible that he stayed in Thessalonica or went back to Philippi and then rejoined Paul and Silas in Berea (Acts 17:14).

(2) Paul fled to Athens from Berean persecution, leaving Silas and Timothy in Berea (see Acts 17:14).

(3) Paul sent word back, instructing Silas and Timothy to come to him in Athens (see discussion on 3:1–2; Acts 17:15).

(4) Timothy rejoined Paul at Athens and was sent back to Thessalonica (see 3:1–5). Since Silas is not mentioned, it has been conjectured that he went back to Philippi when Timothy went to Thessalonica. However, 3:1 indicates that at some point Paul, Silas, and Timothy were together.

(5) Paul moved on to Corinth (see Acts 18:1).

(6) Silas and Timothy came to Paul in Corinth (see 3:6; Acts 18:5).

(7) Paul wrote 1 Thessalonians and sent it to the church.

(8) About six months later (AD 51/52), he sent 2 Thessalonians in response to further information about the church there.

Theme and Theological Message

Paul had left Thessalonica abruptly (see Acts 17:5–10) after a rather brief stay. Recent converts from paganism (see 1:9) were thus left with little external support in the midst of persecution. Paul wrote this letter to encourage the new converts in their trials (see 3:3–5), to give instruction concerning godly living (see 4:1–8), to urge some not to neglect daily work (see 4:11–12), and to give assurance concerning the future of believers who die before Christ returns (see discussions on 4:13, 15).

Although the thrust of the letter is varied, the subject of eschatology (doctrine of the end times) seems to be predominant in both Thessalonian letters. Every chapter of 1 Thessalonians ends with a reference to the second coming of Christ, with chapter 4 giving it major consideration (see 1:9–10; 2:19–20; 3:13; 4:13–18; 5:23–24). Thus, the second coming seems to permeate the letter and may be viewed in some sense as its theme. The two letters are often designated as the eschatological letters of Paul.

Outline

I. Thanksgiving for the Thessalonians (chap. 1)
   A. Grounds for the Thanksgiving (1:1–4)
   B. Genuineness of the Grounds (1:5–10)
II. Defense of the Apostolic Actions and Absence (chaps. 2–3)
   A. Defense of the Apostolic Actions (2:1–16)
   B. Defense of the Apostolic Absence (2:17–3:10)
   C. Prayer (3:11–13)
III. Exhortations to the Thessalonians (4:1–5:22)
   A. Primarily concerning Personal Life (4:1–12)
   B. Concerning the Coming of Christ (4:13–5:11)
   C. Primarily concerning Church Life (5:12–22)
IV. Concluding Prayer, Greetings, and Benediction (5:23–28)

Bibliography

Bruce, F. F. *1 and 2 Thessalonians*. Word Biblical Commentary 45. Waco, TX: Word, 1982.

Couch, Mal. *The Hope of Christ's Return*. Chattanooga, TN: AMG, 2001.

Green, Gene L. *The Letters to the Thessalonians*. Pillar New Testament Commentary. Grand Rapids, MI: Eerdmans, 2002.

Marshall, I. Howard. *1 and 2 Thessalonians*. New Century Bible Commentary. Grand Rapids, MI: Eerdmans, 1983.

Mayhue, Richard. *1 and 2 Thessalonians: Triumphs and Trials of a Consecrated Church*. Focus on the Bible. Ross-shire, UK: Christian Focus, 1999.

Morris, Leon. *First and Second Epistles to the Thessalonians*. Grand Rapids, MI: Eerdmans, 1959.

Stott, John. *The Gospel and the End of Time*. Downers Grove, IL: InterVarsity Press, 1991.

EXPOSITION

I. Thanksgiving for the Thessalonians (chap. 1)

A. Grounds for the Thanksgiving (1:1–4)

1:1. Paul. See discussions on Acts 9:1; 13:9; Phil. 3:4–14. **Silvanus.** See discussion on Acts 15:22. Also known as Silas, he accompanied Paul on most of his second missionary journey. **Timotheus.** See 1 Timothy, Introduction: "Recipient." Both Timothy and Silas helped Paul found the Thessalonian church (see Acts 17:1–14). **In God … Jesus Christ** communicates the foundation of this band of believers identified as **the church of the Thessalonians**. Their existence as a church was by virtue of the vital union and living relationship that Christians have with the Father and the Son (see John 14:23; 17:21). The close connection between the Father and the Son points to the Trinitarian relationship (see 3:11; 2 Thess. 1:2, 8, 12; 2:16; 3:5). **Grace … and peace.** See discussions on Jonah 4:2; John 14:27; 20:19; Galatians 1:3; Ephesians 1:2.

1:2. Thanks. See discussion on Philippians 1:3–4.

1:3. The triad of **faith … love, and … hope** is found often in the New Testament (see 5:8; Rom. 5:2–5; 1 Cor. 13:13; Gal. 5:5–6; Col. 1:4–5; Heb. 6:10–12; 10:22–24; 1 Peter 1:3–8, 21–22). Paul's characterization of the fruit of faith as **work** sums up an array of "activity" generating purposeful actions out of faith in God (see 2 Thess. 1:11). Faith produces action (see Rom. 1:5; 16:26; Gal. 5:6; James 2:14–26). Doctrine comes from God's revelation; action comes from believing God. Charity, or love of God (1:4; 5:9), prompts the hard **labour** (Greek, *kopos*; "toil") of sacrificial service under tough circumstances, not just when it is convenient or sentimental. Hope is not unfounded wishful thinking but rather firm confidence in the Lord Jesus Christ and His return (see 1:10). Hope in Christ fortified the Thessalonians with **patience** and even joy in the midst of harsh challenges (see 1:6; Heb. 6:18–20; discussion on Col. 1:5).

1:4. Knowing … your election of God. The reasons for Paul's conviction regarding the Thessalonians' election are stated in 1:5–10. Paul emphasized God's election, rooted in love (**beloved**), to stress that the ground of their election was the initiative of God's love and not their merits or virtue (see Col. 3:12; 2 Thess. 2:13; discussion on Eph. 1:4). This was a profound encouragement to the Thessalonians, who were suffering persecution. Thus, Paul confirmed God's elective love to these recent believers born to Christ out a pagan religious environment (see 1:10), in which divine favor came only from pandering to and placating a pantheon of capricious gods. Tangible proof for Paul's **knowing** is given (see "For," 1:5) in the way the gospel came to them (see 1:5) and the way they received it (see 1:6). **Brethren**. United to each other through union with Christ. This term (including its singular form) is used twenty-eight times in Paul's two letters to the Thessalonians. Both "beloved" and "election" speak of God's electing love (see Col. 3:12; 2 Thess. 2:13; discussion on Eph. 1:4).

B. Genuineness of the Grounds (1:5–10)

1:5. Our gospel, or the gospel preached by Paul, Silas, and Timothy, was the gospel they themselves had received by faith. The gospel is first of all God the Father's (see 2:8) because He originated it and Christ's (see 3:2) because it springs from His atoning death. **Power** refers to the power that delivered them from spiritual bondage, that of the Holy Spirit (see Rom. 15:13, 18–19; 1 Cor. 2:4–5), but power also resides in the gospel itself (see Rom. 1:16). **Much assurance** testifies to the "complete certainty" with which the preachers brought the gospel and the Thessalonians received it. Such certainty was also a mark of the Holy Spirit at work.

1:6. Followers (Greek, *mimētēs*; "imitator," compare English "mimic") refers to those who follow to the point of imitation. The order in Christian imitation is: (1) the believers in Macedonia and Achaia imitated the Thessalonians (1:7), just as the Thessalonians imitated the churches in Judea (2:14); (2) the Thessalonians imitated Paul, just as the Corinthians did (1 Cor. 4:6; 11:1) and just as all believers were to imitate their leaders (2 Thess. 3:7, 9; 1 Tim. 4:12; Titus 2:7; 1 Peter 5:3); (3) Paul imitated Christ (1 Cor. 11:1), as did the Thessalonians (here); (4) all were to imitate God (Eph. 5:1). **Much affliction**, such as that recorded in Acts 17:5–14 (see also 1 Thess. 2:14), did not quench the joy that characterized the Thessalonians; this too is a hallmark of the Holy Spirit.

1:7. Ye were ensamples, or "examples" (Greek, *typos*; "model"), formed by imitation of Paul and the Lord (1:6). The Thessalonian believers influenced others across **Macedonia and Achaia**, the two Roman provinces into which Greece was then divided (see Acts 19:21; Rom. 15:26).

1:8. In every place means every place they visited or knew about (see Rom. 1:8; 1 Cor. 1:2; 2 Cor. 2:14; 1 Tim. 2:8). **Your faith to God-ward** is Paul's articulation of the fact that their faith was prominently directed toward God and not gods (see 1:9). This singular focus was noteworthy in a culture permeated by a pagan pantheon (or many deities). The news spread because Thessalonica was on the important Egnatian Way; it was also a busy seaport and the capital of the Roman province of Macedonia.

1:9–10. Three marks of true conversion are (1) turning from idols, (2) serving God, and (3) waiting for Christ to return. In his two short letters to the Thessalonians, Paul wrote much about the second coming of Christ (see 1:10; 2:19; 3:13; 4:13–5:4; 2 Thess. 1:7–10; 2:1–12). Significantly, Paul labeled the "deities" that permeated the culture of the Greco-Roman world **idols** (v. 9) and poignantly contrasted them with the one "living and true God."

Jesus (v. 10; see discussion on Matt. 1:21) is He who **delivered** (or "rescued"; see Rom. 11:26, Isa. 59:20) **us from the wrath** of God's judgment that is to come upon sin (see 2:16; Ac 17:31 Rom. 3:5; 5:9; 9:22). Some see a reference here to the final judgment (see discussion on Rom. 1:18), while others think it refers to a future period of tribulation.

II. Defense of the Apostolic Actions and Absence (chaps. 2–3)

A. Defense of the Apostolic Actions (2:1–16)

2:1–12. The forced and premature departure of Paul and his team (see Acts 17:5–10) gave opponents of the gospel an opportunity to unfairly misrepresent them. The appraisal of God is more important than the approval of the world. It is an entirely different motivation. That difference was evident in the gospel Paul spread (vv. 1–4), in the good he sought (vv. 5–8), and in the God he served (vv. 9–12). Each of these three emphases featured an important use of the word "know" (vv. 1–2, 5, 11).

This part of Paul's letter has been called "a manual for a minister": (1) Paul's message was God's good news ("gospel," v. 2); (2) his motive was not impurity (v. 3), pleasing people (v. 4), greed (v. 5), or seeking praise from people (v. 6) but rather pleasing God (v. 4); (3) his manner was not one of trickery (v. 3), flattery (v. 5), or a cover-up (v. 5) but one of courage (v. 2), gentleness (v. 7), love (vv. 8, 11), toil (v. 9), and holiness (v. 10).

2:1. With **yourselves ... know**, or "ye know yourselves," Paul appealed to the Thessalonians and their personal experience. The local church could refute the accusation of insincerity that evidently had been leveled against Paul (see 2:3). The word **vain** suggests "empty" or "fruitless," and the Thessalonian believers were themselves a living testimony to the fruitfulness of the gospel and Paul's **entrance**, or "way in."

2:2. Paul's entrance (**bold in our God**) was itself a proof of his and his team's conviction of the truth of the gospel, for they continued to present it despite opposition in Philippi and Thessalonica: **we had suffered ... were shamefully entreated ... [but] were bold ... to speak unto you ... with much contention**. Paul was deeply hurt by the way he had been treated in the city of Philippi (see Acts 16:19–40), yet he did not quit, as one with impure motives might have when faced with opposition.

2:3. Perhaps opponents of the gospel had used the words found in this verse to misrepresent the **exhortation** that Paul and his team delivered, causing Paul to describe their right motives with negative words rather than positive ones. **Deceit** translates the Greek word *planaō*, which means "to stray" or "to lead astray into error." **Uncleanness** points out the moral purity that characterized Paul's exhortation. The Greek word for **guile** was originally used of a lure for catching fish; it came to be used of any sort of cunning used for profit.

2:4–5. As one who had himself been dramatically converted by the gospel he proclaimed, Paul was loyal to the privilege of serving "the gospel of God" (2:2, 8). The allegiance of this gospel team was to God and God only. Paul could speak of pure motives because God knows **our hearts** (v. 4), not simply one's emotions but also one's intellect and will. Therefore, God is the perfect "witness" to the fact

that their exhortation (see 2:3) was not guided by false motives. **Flattering** (v. 5), or "insincere praise," and a **cloke of covetousness**, or concealed greed, had no part in the gospel Paul represented to the Thessalonians. Personal profit was never Paul's aim.

2:6. Glory, or the praise of men, also belonged on the list of negative motives that were not part of Paul's entrance and exhortation. If praise was a motivation, it was the praise of God, not people, which was primary. The good (not the glory) that Paul sought was God's best for the Thessalonians. To that end, Paul was willing to forgo any personal benefits that **might have been burdensome**, even though apostles were entitled to be supported by the church (see 1 Cor. 9:3–14; 2 Cor. 11:7–11). Paul did not always take advantage of that right, but the fact that he had it and did not insist on it demonstrated that the good he sought was theirs and not his.

2:7–8. Moreover, Paul and his team were **gentle** (v. 7). Paul defined what he meant by giving a picture. **Even as a nurse cherisheth** (or "nourishes") **her children**, they tenderly cared for the Thessalonians. Paul further developed this picture of gentleness with an expression of inner feeling, **being affectionately desirous of you** (v. 8). Feelings such as that belong to the **soul** and the intimacy of personal attachment that accompanies the gospel. Just as Paul did not keep the gospel to himself but shared, or **imparted**, it, so he and his companions "shared" their own souls. The word **dear** is the Greek word "beloved." Paul expressed the love of God not only in the words of the gospel but in the words of their own affection and in the good that they sought for the Thessalonians.

2:9. Expanding on the concern of being burdensome (see 2:6), Paul recalled how he and his team had readily shouldered **labour and travail** ("difficult exertion"). Greeks despised manual labor and viewed it as fit only for slaves, but Paul was not ashamed of doing any sort of work that would help further the gospel. He did not want to be unduly dependent on others.

2:10. Here is a positive summary of Paul's motives and actions, to which God and the Thessalonians would make ready witnesses before any accuser. Paul and his companions conducted themselves **holily** before God and **justly** before men and thus **unblameably** before all.

2:11. In Greek, 2:10–12 is one sentence. The positive summary of 2:10 is expanded with details of the fatherly concern that Paul and his team had for the Thessalonians. Their gentleness and affection was likened to a nursing mother (see 2:7), and their guidance was likened to **a father** whose first concern is his child's proper rearing. **Exhorted and comforted and charged** suggests different manners of fatherly motivation, possibly with varying strength, such as bidding, kindly coaxing, and insisting. Although Paul himself was not a father, good models, like nursing mothers (see 2:7), made such analogies powerful pictures. One must not rule out the Fatherhood of God Himself as an influence on Paul's thinking. Indeed, Paul saw himself as a steward of God's own values when he expressed his purpose in 2:12: "That you would walk worthy of God."

2:12. The goal of all Paul's actions and attitude was defined by the God he served, **That** (the Thessalonians) **would walk worthy of God** (see Eph. 4:1). The initiative and invitation of the gospel is God's. It is He **who ... called** (see discussion on 1:4) the Thessalonians. **His kingdom**, the kingdom of God, was the chief subject of Jesus' teaching. Paul did not use this term often but used it on one occasion to sum up the message of his preaching (see Acts 20:25). The "kingdom" or "reign" of God expresses the rule of God in the present time, which will be revealed in all its glory at the future and royal coming of Jesus. It is this future manifestation that Paul had before him, and it is the hope of everyone called to it. Paul's talk of God's "kingdom" and "glory" touched national aspirations going back to the royal monarchy of Macedonia and issues of a new and greater allegiance to God (see Acts 17:7).

2:13. Paul's defense of their "entrance" (2:1) was shaded with thanksgiving for the way the Thessalonians received the apostolic preaching. Paul's first expression of thanksgiving echoed in a second; such repetition strengthened the sincerity of his words

without ceasing. The Thessalonians had received the message **not as the word of men**, though it was delivered by human hands, **but as ... the word of God**, as coming not from men but from God Himself. Paul knew (see Gal. 1:12), as did his regenerated hearers, that the message he preached was the sacred and revealed Word of God. The apostle Peter confirmed this (1 Peter 3:15–16). God's Word **effectually worketh**, specifying the divine operation and transforming work of God's truth within any who **believe**, or take to heart, God's Word through faith. An evidence of its operation and a reason for Paul's continued thanksgiving is found in 2:14, in the way the Thessalonians were facing persecution (see 3:3–4).

2:14. Paul's extended his reason for thanksgiving with his admiring identification of the Thessalonians with **the churches ... in Judea**, calling them **followers** (i.e., "imitators"; see 1:6) in their handling of persecution. **Ye also have suffered ... of your own countrymen** (or "of those of the same race"). At the time of Paul's initial visit to Thessalonica, persecution instigated by the Jews apparently was being carried out by Gentiles (see Acts 17:5–9). Although Paul had great love and deep concern for the salvation of those of his own race, **the Jews** (see Rom. 9:1–3; 10:1), he did not fail to rebuke harshly Jews who persecuted the church.

2:15. Paul wanted the Thessalonians to know that their persecutions were not unique but belonged to a vehement opposition to God's gospel. None other than **the Lord Jesus**, the **prophets** before Him (Rom. 1:1–2; 16:26; Acts 7:52), and now Paul and others who spoke the Word of God, had suffered persecution. Throughout Old Testament history, Israelites had persecuted their prophets (see Acts 7:52), and Paul, like Stephen, saw the gospel themes in their message.

2:16. The wrath is come refers to the eschatological wrath, the final outpouring of God's anger upon sinful mankind (see 1:10). Paul spoke of it as already present, either because it had been partially experienced by the Jews or because of its absolute certainty.

B. Defense of the Apostolic Absence (2:17–3:10)

2:17. Taken from you is literally "orphaned" in the Greek. Paul was like a mother (see 2:7), a father (see 2:11), and now an orphan. Certainly these word pictures that so vividly express how Paul and his team had "imparted" (2:8) their own souls correspond to the fact that they were never "taken from" the Thessalonians **in heart**.

2:18. Satan hindered us points to the reality of spiritual warfare. "Satan" means "adversary." Satan's objective is to oppose, through obstacles and false accusations, the achievement of God's will and purposes in the lives of His children. Thus, Satan is called "the tempter" (see 3:5 and discussion). Opponents of the gospel who misrepresented Paul's absence and motives were spiritually blind to that reality, but believers must never shut their eyes to it. Paul had encountered it in his endeavors to strengthen the Thessalonians' faith (see 3:2–5). God's purposes are the Enemy's point of attack. **Once and again** Paul was prevented from visiting the Thessalonians. What the hindrances were, he did not make clear. Poor health, inclement weather, persecution in Corinth, or more, may have been implements of opposition.

2:19. The **crown** (Greek, *stephanos*) of which Paul spoke is not a royal crown but a wreath used on festive occasions or as the prize in the Greek games. With this image of the prize in view, Paul's questions isolated the one objective of Christian ministry: people. The impending return of Christ puts believers' endeavors into perspective; people are the redemptive prize of the gospel and all who spread it. The expression **at his coming** was used regarding the arrival of a great person, as on a royal visit.

2:20. Ye are our glory and joy. This was true at that time (see Phil. 4:1) and will also be true when Christ returns. "Glory and joy" aptly and succinctly expresses both the outer and the inner recognition that accompanies one's spiritual investment in the life of another.

3:1–2. Paul first went to Athens alone, then sent to Berea for Silas and Timothy (see Introduc-

tion: "Background"; Acts 17:14–15). It is not clear whether Silas, as instructed (see Acts 17:15), went to Athens with Timothy. However, when Timothy later returned from Thessalonica to Paul, who was now at Corinth, Silas came with him (see Acts 18:5).

3:1. We reflects a collective decision to send Timothy. Paul and Silas were **left** behind. It was a decision of the will but not the heart (see 2:17).

3:2. The purpose of sending Timothy was to **establish**, or "strengthen," the Thessalonians' faith. In Greek classical literature, the word "establish" was generally used in the literal sense of putting a buttress on a building. The desired outcome, unmoveable faith (3:3), corresponds to the word "establish." In the New Testament, it is mainly used figuratively, as here. **Comfort** is the same kindly coaxing of 3:11. Timothy's credentials were four. He was (1) **brother** (used nineteen times in 1 Thessalonians), expressing the bond of spiritual affinity and kinship in Christ; (2) **minister** (1 Cor. 3:5–6), expressing the devotion of a servant to God; (3) **fellowlabourer** (see 1 Cor. 3:9), expressing mutual and common effort for the gospel; (4) and **sent**, conveying that Timothy came under the authority of Paul.

3:3. Afflictions refers to the opposition and persecution the Thessalonian converts suffered. Christians must expect troubles (see Mark 4:17; John 16:33; Acts 14:22; 2 Tim. 3:12; 1 Peter 4:12), but these are not disasters, for they advance God's purposes (see Acts 11:19; Rom. 5:3; 2 Cor. 1:4; 4:17). The purpose of Timothy's mission to establish and comfort their faith (see 3:2, 4) had an anticipated outcome: that no Thessalonian **be moved**. The Greek word "moved" has been used of a dog vigorously wagging his tail. Here its figurative sense, connected as it is with an established and encouraged "faith," points to agitation and disturbance of the mind. Paul wanted the inner life of faith to be firm and unperturbed by outward "afflictions," which "the tempter" (3:5) so readily uses to trigger self-destruction through a shaken inner perspective and earthly thinking that affects one's faith (knowledge and trust) in God.

3:4. We told you before. Paul repeatedly included in his earlier teaching doctrinal instruction about suffering and one of its forms, persecution. An insight to be gained here is that biblical truth had provided a foundation for facing the specifics of the Thessalonians' current suffering.

3:5. Paul used the Greek emphatic pronoun **I** (used elsewhere only in 2:18) to emphasize his deep concern. **The tempter** identifies Satan, who is spoken of in every major division of the New Testament. He is supreme among evil spirits (see John 16:11; Eph. 2:2). His activities can affect the physical (see 2 Cor. 12:7) and the spiritual (see Matt. 13:39; Mark 4:15; 2 Cor. 4:4). He tempted Jesus (Matt. 4:1–11), and he continues to tempt Jesus' servants (see Luke 22:3; 1 Cor. 7:5). He hinders missionary work (2:18). He, however, has already been defeated (see Col. 2:15), and Christians need not be overwhelmed by him (see Eph. 6:16). His final overthrow is certain (see Rev. 20:10). **In vain** summarizes the potential jeopardy of a collapsed faith that has lost sight of God and turned in unbelief from the celestial certainties of the gospel to terrestrial solutions for earthly afflictions.

3:6. Timothy had returned and **brought us good tidings** (or "good news"). This is the only place where Paul used the Greek for this phrase for anything other than the gospel. Three things caused him joy: (1) the Thessalonians' **faith**, a right attitude toward God; (2) their **charity**, a right attitude toward man; and (3) their **desiring greatly to see us**, a right attitude toward Paul. Timothy's report of their faith and their love (see 1:3) was a boon to Paul and probably set him promptly to writing this letter.

3:7–8. Paul and Silas were **comforted** ("encouraged"; v. 7) in their own **affliction and distress**. At Philippi, Thessalonica, Berea, Athens, and now Corinth (see Acts 18:9–10; 1 Cor. 2:3), they had suffered outer and inner turmoil. The news of the Thessalonians invigorated them: **now we live** (v. 8) alludes to the joy mentioned in 3:9 and 2:20.

3:9. Thanks ... to God. Verses 7–8 show that Paul's work of evangelism had been effective. He might have congratulated himself on work well done, but instead he thanked God for the joy he had from what God had done. The wording suggests that

Paul found it inconceivable that he could give thanks enough to match what God had done or the joy that he and his companions were experiencing.

3:10. Night and day refers to frequent prayer, not prayer at two set times (see 1:2–3). **Exceedingly** translates a strong and unusual Greek compound word (found elsewhere in the New Testament only in 5:13; Eph. 3:20) that Paul used to emphasize his passionate longing. **That which is lacking** speaks of the things of a practical nature, such as moral (see 4:1–12) and disciplinary matters (see 5:12–24). Others were doctrinal, such as confusion over Christ's return (see 4:13–5:11). **Your faith** was the focus of Paul's concern, and this is the fifth time in the chapter that Paul expressly spoke of it (see 3:2, 5–7).

C. Prayer (3:11–13)

3:11. Paul frequently broke into prayer in the middle of his letters (see, e.g., Eph. 1:15–23; 3:14–21; Phil. 1:9–11; Col. 1:9–12). For the link between Father and Son, see discussion on 1:1. For a Jew such as Paul, reared in a strict monotheism, a prayer offered to **God ... our Father, and our Lord Jesus Christ** could only be offered if the divinity of Jesus was assumed (see 2 Thess. 2:16). Spiritual obstacles (see 2:18) must be met with spiritual solutions. Paul looked to the Father and the Lord Jesus to **direct** (Greek, "make straight") their way to the Thessalonians. The verb "direct" is singular with a plural subject, subtly showing these new converts from pagan pantheism that God the Father and the Lord Jesus not only work in concert but are one. Rather than Paul and his team forcing their own way, God would clear a way for them.

3:12. Paul prayed that the Thessalonians' **love** would **increase** with or without his presence. Aside from his intense desire to attend the Thessalonians' needs in person (3:10–11), Paul wanted their love for others to grow, and grow abundantly. In Paul's writings, **the Lord** usually means Jesus rather than the Father. Jesus is the expression and the agent of God's love and, perhaps for this reason, the specific appeal of Paul's prayer here (see 4:9; 2 Thess. 2:16; 3:5).

3:13. For the word **stablish**, see discussion on 3:2. **Holiness** is the basic idea of being set apart (for God). Here the completed process of sanctification is in view (see *Zondervan KJV Study Bible* note on 1 Cor. 1:2). If one wonders how to become holy and set apart for God, Paul provides the answer here in his prayer for the Thessalonians. An increase of love (see 3:12) is the means of strengthening and establishing a person from the inside out, beyond blame, in holiness before God. If one thinks of holiness as the absence of sin, love is the positive active way in which one gives no place to sin. Indeed, the whole law is fulfilled, Paul said, through love (see Rom. 13:10; Gal. 5:14; Matt. 22:36–40). **Saints** is used of Christians in many New Testament passages. Here it may mean the departed saints who will return with Jesus, or it may mean the angels, or more probably, both.

III. Exhortations to the Thessalonians (4:1–5:22)

A. Primarily concerning Personal Life (4:1–12)

4:1. Furthermore indicates that Paul had finished the main section of the letter, though much was yet to come (see Phil. 3:1 and discussion). **We beseech you.** Paul was not being arrogant but was speaking with authority in the Lord Jesus. He had the "mind of Christ" (1 Cor. 2:16). **Walk** (Greek, *peripateō*; from the Hebrew *hālak*; "to walk") was a word rich in meaning for Paul due to his rabbinic background as a Pharisee. It denoted a pattern of conduct or living conformed to a code (see Gal. 6:16) of prescribed ethical behavior. Although Paul had renounced his former religion (see Phil. 3:5–7) and Christ had become his standard (**exhort you by the Lord Jesus;** see 4:2), he used the word translated "to walk" often (thirty-two times in Paul's letters) when referring to the Christian way (see, e.g., Rom. 6:4; 8:4; Gal. 5:16, 25; Eph. 4:1; 5:15; Col. 1:10; 2:6; 4:5), connoting a pattern of steady progress. The horizon or focus of this walk or pattern of living is **to please God.** "To walk and to please God" is a case of hendiadys, the expression of one idea by the use of usually two independent words connected by "and"; here it means "to walk so as to please God."

4:2. Paul's use of authoritative commands has a military ring (see Acts 5:28; 16:24). The word translated **commandments** (Greek, *parangelia*) was used of an order to be obeyed and was a term familiar to the authoritative word of a military commander, philosopher, or deity, all of which belonged to the world of the Thessalonians. Here the authority is **the Lord Jesus** (see 2:13; Acts 17:7).

4:3. Sanctification (see discussion on 3:13) refers to consecration to God (see 1:9) and the exclusive right of His will. Devotion to pagan deities did not require moral purity or the elimination of **fornication**. The Greek word for "fornication" (*porneia*) identified any kind of sexual immorality outside of a heterosexual marriage, whether extramarital sex, adultery, homosexuality, incest, bestiality, or any other sexual impurity. This specification of sanctification as abstaining from sexual impurity should be compared with the wider call to **abstain from** (avoid) every form of evil (see 5:22), or everything that is not the product of God's love (see 3:12–13). In the first century, moral standards were generally very low, and chastity was regarded as an unreasonable restriction. The cultic worship and festivities of Dionysus, Aphrodite, Cabirus, Priapus, Osiris, and Isis encouraged concupiscence, or sexual desire, and ingrained it in the culture. Paul, however, would not compromise God's clear and demanding standards. The warning was needed, for Christians were not immune to the temptation (see 1 Cor. 5:1).

4:4–5. How to possess his vessel (v. 4). Given the sexual orientation of Paul's instruction, "vessel" (Greek, *skeuos*) is an inoffensive substitute for a man's "body" (see 1 Tim. 2:21–22). The word here is thought by some to be a substitute for "wife," based on 1 Peter 3:7 (see Bruce, *1 and 2 Thessalonians*, p. 83). Paul's language here suits the body of a man more than the body of a woman. The Thessalonians probably knew (see 4:2) precisely what Paul meant. If any ambiguity did exist, it may have been purposeful to the wider application of Paul's main emphasis on sexual purity. The verb "possess" (Greek, *ktaomai*) primarily means "to acquire," with the implication of mastery. If the "vessel" is the man's own body, then he is "to get [sexual] control" over himself in sanctification and honor. This was most likely Paul's meaning here and is akin to Paul's language and thought in 2 Timothy 2:21–22. In the Mediterranean world, **honour** was the prized community respect and recognition that a person achieved in the eyes of others. Here honor in the eyes of God is set above that of society and its culture of sexual license. In fact, the sanctification and honor that are to characterize the Christian's sexual behavior are contrasted with the lust of sexual desire that characterized the practice of the Gentiles. Knowing God makes all the difference. That difference can be detected in Paul's manner here, as he himself strove to speak directly while avoiding anything salacious as he addressed the subject of sexual propriety (see 4:6).

4:6. Paul's instruction on sexual purity extends to 4:8. The word "sanctification" (Greek, *hagiasmos*) occurs three times in 4:3–4, 7 (KJV has "holiness" in 4:7) and the power of sanctification is set forth in God's giving of the Holy Spirit (4:8; see 2 Thess. 2:13). Therefore, the words **go beyond**, conveying the sense of crossing a forbidden (sexual) boundary, and the words **defraud his brother** indicate that Paul had turned to the subject of adultery committed with the wife of a fellow Christian brother. The progression of Paul's thought moved from the general exhortation to all men (4:4) to a specific example and its consequences before God when a man does not "possess his vessel in sanctification and honour" (4:4). Even in the sexually licentious culture of the day, adultery with another man's wife was taboo. Here Paul's concern was not that social mores had been violated, although that would have brought dishonor on the Christian community, but rather God, who is the **avenger**, had been wronged, because God is the champion of the marriage bond. Likely, Timothy had reported adultery between members of the Thessalonian community, which prompted Paul to write this section of the letter. Sexual sin harms others besides those who engage in it. In adultery, for example, the spouse is always wronged. Premarital sex wrongs the future partner by robbing him or her of the virginity that ought to be brought to marriage.

The Apostle of Grace took seriously the holiness of God, the Avenger.

4:7. God hath … called us (see 2:12), a privilege that is incompatible with **uncleanness**, the antithesis of sanctification (**holiness**), which is God's will (see 4:3). The Thessalonians had answered the call of God.

4:8. God, who hath also given unto us his holy Spirit. To disregard Paul's instruction was to reject God and His influence, the Holy Spirit (see 1 Cor. 6:17–20).

4:9–10. Brotherly love (v. 9) translates *philadelphia*, a Greek word that outside the New Testament, almost without exception, denoted the mutual love of children of the same father. In the New Testament, it always means love of fellow believers in Christ, all of whom have the same heavenly Father. **Taught of God**, as in 3:12, speaks of God's work of love in the heart (see 4:13), the impress of His very nature upon ours (see Isa. 54:13; John 6:45; 1 Cor. 2:13). Paul wanted Christian love to **increase more and more**, without limit, between believers. Love creates harmony between Christians.

4:11. Some Thessalonians, probably because of idleness, were taking undue interest in other people's affairs. **Work with your own hands**. The Greeks generally thought manual labor was degrading and fit only for slaves. Christians took seriously the need for earning their own living, but some of the Thessalonians, perhaps as a result of their belief in the imminent return of Christ (see 2 Thess. 3:11) or the social and political institution of patronage, were neglecting work and relying on others to support them. Such a dependence on others opened the community to internecine conflict and outside influence. For example, the client of a patron had to curry his favor, for the client was dependent on the patron for support and protection. To do otherwise involved retiring to a quiet life, **to do your own business, and to work with your own hands**. To be sure, the favor of a pagan patron would run contrary to the favor of God (pleasing God, see 4:1). Thus, **study to be quiet**, the undertaking of a quiet life, was an expression associated with retiring from the public activity of patronage and the responsibilities involved in seeking the protection of powerful men (see Green, *The Letters to the Thessalonians*, pp. 210–12). Part of the problem may have been that some retired without working with their own hands and shifting dependence from pagan patrons to Christian ones.

4:12. Have lack of nothing can mean "not be dependent on anyone." Both meanings are true and significant. Christians who are in need because of their idleness are not obedient Christians. **Them that are without** is literally, "those outside," meaning those outside the knowledge of God (see 4:5) and outside the community of those who believe in Jesus Christ.

B. Concerning the Coming of Christ (4:13–5:11)

4:13. Them which are asleep. The euphemism of sleep for death was common in the Greco-Roman world and in both the Old and New Testaments and was used by Jesus Himself (see John 11:11). For the Christian, sleep is a particularly apt metaphor for death, since death's finality and horror are removed by the assurance of resurrection. Yet the wide usage of this metaphor prohibits any conclusions from the word "sleep" itself about the state or condition of the dead. Some of the Thessalonians seem to have misunderstood Paul and thought all believers would live until Christ returns. When some Thessalonians died, the question arose whether those who had died would have part in that great day (see discussion on 4:15). **Sorrow** expresses the profound grief that beset the Thessalonians when death struck their number (see 4:18). Sorrow can be a kind of tribute to a person's special place in their lives, but this sorrow is not the kind that characterizes **others** (lit., "the rest") **which have no hope** (see "them that are without," 4:12). Inscriptions on tombs and references in literature show that first-century pagans viewed death with horror, as the end of everything. The Christian attitude was a strong contrast (see 1 Cor. 15:55–57; Phil. 1:21–23).

4:14. The words **believe that** introduce the content of faith, the foundation of the gospel: **Jesus died and rose again.** Paul said not that Christ "slept" but that He **died**, perhaps to underscore the fact that He willfully bore the full horror of death so that those who believe in Him would not have to experience it. This certainty, that Jesus died and rose again, leads to a second certainty concerning **them also which sleep in Jesus.** As God raised Jesus, so also God will raise (**bring with him**) believers who have died, trusting in Jesus (see 1 Cor. 6:14; 2 Cor. 4:14; Rom. 6:3–8). Death "through Jesus" is but the prelude to resurrection "with Jesus" (for the importance of the resurrection, see 1 Corinthians 15, especially 15:14, 17–22).

4:15. By the word of the Lord. The doctrine mentioned here is not recorded in the Gospels and was either a direct revelation to Paul or something Jesus said that Christians passed on orally. **We which are alive** refers to those believers who will be alive when Christ returns. "We" does not necessarily mean that Paul thought that he would be alive then. He often identified himself with those to whom or about whom he wrote. Elsewhere he said that God will raise "us" at that time (1 Cor. 6:14; 2 Cor. 4:14). **Shall not prevent** means "precede" or "come before" those who have died or "fallen asleep." Paul pictured the dead in Christ as those who will receive precedence at the rapture but believed they would be quickly joined by those **which are alive and remain.** Evidently, the Thessalonians had been concerned that those among them who died would miss their place in the great events when the Lord comes, and Paul assured them that this would not be the case.

4:16. Paul called the occasion of "the coming of the Lord" (4:15) the *parousia* (2:19; 3:13; 5:23) of the Lord. The Greek word *parousia* (Latin, *adventus*) has a significant connotation of the "arrival" or "coming" of a royal or official personage. The Thessalonians would surely have connected Paul's use of *parousia* with the coming of the Lord, who, for them, had displaced the emperor (see Acts 17:7) and the pagan pantheon (see 1:9). In the Greco-Roman world, such visits were accompanied by considerable fanfare, to which there are broad corollaries here. The Lord's coming will be attended by celestial shouts and trumpet blares, and He will be met by both **the dead in Christ** and the living (see 4:17). For **the Lord himself**, see Acts 1:11. The descent of the Lord will be inaugurated and accompanied by God's directive, expressed in the threefold description of **a shout** (lit., "the command"), **the voice of the archangel**, and **the trump of God**. The archangel is unidentified. The only named archangel in the Bible is Michael (Jude 9; see also Dan. 10:13). In Scripture, Gabriel is simply called an angel (see Luke 1:19, 26). "The dead in Christ" **shall rise first**, before the ascension of believers mentioned in 4:17. Paul's comfort for the Thessalonians (see 4:18 and "hope" 4:13) emphasized the priority in the Lord's plan of "the dead in Christ" (a unique Pauline term for the church) receiving the honor of being called up first to meet the Lord as He returns. In 4:13–15, Paul used the Greek expression translated "them which are asleep" or "them which . . . sleep" to speak of those who had died. Here he used the expression "the dead in Christ" because his focus was on "rising." Implicit is the necessary "bodily" transformation that accompanies being "caught up" (4:17) and transfigures both "the dead in Christ" and those "which are alive and remain" (4:17; see 1 Cor. 15:50–53; Phil. 3:20; 1 Cor. 15:42–45).

4:17. For **we which are alive**, see discussion on 4:15. **Caught up** is the Greek word *harpazō*, "to snatch away." Both the dead and the living "in Christ" (believers; 4:16) are caught up into the air. A "rapture" (from the Latin Vulgate rendering, *rapio*) is clearly connoted to (1 Cor. 15:51–52 also refers to the same event; see *KJV Study Bible* note on 1 Cor. 15:52). **With the Lord** makes it clear that one's hope is not survival or immortality, but realization of uninhibited, unlimited togetherness with Christ, the chief hope of the believer (see 5:10; John 14:3; 2 Cor. 5:8; Phil. 1:23; Col. 3:4). The rapture will be in the air and will involve the removal of believers to heaven (the "Father's house," John 14:1–6).

4:18. Comfort one another closes what Paul began in 4:13. Paul's primary purpose in 4:13–18 was to urge mutual encouragement. To "comfort" means to "encourage" (from Greek, *parakaleite*). The

promise of the rapture of believers is the basis of that hope, which is grounded in the certainty "that Jesus died and rose again" (4:14). Mayhue (*1 and 2 Thessalonians*, p. 124) notes that this process is irreversible. No wonder Paul called it the "blessed hope" in Titus 2:13. This also explains why the Thessalonians were patiently waiting for God's Son from heaven (see 1:10).

5:1. The times and the seasons (see Acts 1:6–7). There have always been some Christians who try to fix the date of the Lord's return, but apparently the Thessalonians were not among them. The Lord's coming will be unexpected ("as a thief," 5:2, 4), and the Thessalonians already knew that. The New Testament clearly indicates that no one knows the time when the rapture will occur (see Matt. 24:36). Therefore, Christians are to be ready to meet the Lord at all times because He could come at any time.

5:2. For **the day of the Lord**, see 1 Cor. 5:5. The expression goes back to Amos 5:18. In the Old Testament, "the day of the LORD" is a time when God will come and intervene with judgment (see Zeph. 1:14–15) and then blessing (see Joel 3:14–21). In the New Testament, the thought of judgment continues (see Rom. 2:5; 2 Peter 2:9), but it is also "the day of redemption" (Eph. 4:30); "the day of God" (2 Peter 3:12) and "the day of our Lord Jesus Christ" (1 Cor. 1:8; Phil. 1:6); and "the last day" (John 6:39), "the great day" (Jude 6), or simply "that day" (2 Thess. 1:10). It is first tribulation and then Christ's kingdom (see Matt. 24:21–31; 25:31–34). There will be some preliminary signs (see, e.g., 2 Thess. 2:3), but the coming will be as unexpected as that of a thief in the night (see Matt. 24:43–44; Luke 12:39–40; 2 Peter 3:10; Rev. 3:3; 16:15). **As a thief in the night** is a simile emphasizing the vigilant watchfulness required of being ready for an unexpected visit by one who will come at an inopportune time (see Matt. 24:42–51).

5:3. The words **Peace and safety** would have had special relevance in a city loyal to Rome and a beneficiary of the *Pax Romana*. Throughout the empire, the expression obtained the quality of a slogan that paid homage to the benefits enjoyed by citizens living under the protection of Rome. At the least, Paul was emphasizing that the day of the Lord's coming will so surprise people that they will imagine themselves most secure at the time of His coming. Moreover, expressions of peace and safety (lit., "when they are saying …") may well have been voiced by those in Thessalonica who scoffed at needing the gospel and its announcement of God's coming wrath (see 1:9–10). Paul use of **sudden** stresses the surprise of unbelievers and paints a picture of one being caught in midsentence (compare the only other New Testament use of this word in Luke 21:34). **Destruction** is not annihilation but exclusion from the Lord's presence (see 2 Thess. 1:9), thus, the ruin of life and all its proud accomplishments. **Travail** expresses not so much the pain of childbirth as the suddenness and inevitability of such pains. The inescapable inevitability is captured in Paul's use of **not**, an emphatic double negative in the Greek and a construction Paul used only four times in all his writings.

5:4. By contrast (**But ye, brethren**), believers are not in danger of being so surprised. In 5:5–11, Paul's contrast between "the children of the day" and those "of the night" (5:5–6) never puts the believer's destiny in doubt but serves to assure and admonish (5:6–8), ending with a final affirmation of salvation (5:9–10) and an exhortation to comfort one another (5:11). **Darkness** (see Eph. 4:18) describes those who are not only alienated from God but ignorant, an emphasis that corresponds to the words **that that day should overtake you as a thief**. Believers no longer live in darkness, nor are they of the darkness (see 5:5; John 1:5; Acts 26:18). "Overtake" bears an ominous quality associated with the "destruction" (5:3) that belongs to those who are in darkness on the coming day of the Lord.

5:5. Children of is literally, "sons of." In Semitic languages (such as Hebrew), the expression "son of" was not only used to identify one's parentage but was also used figuratively of a predominant quality that characterized a person (see, e.g., Acts 4:36; Luke 10:6). Christians do not simply live in the light; they are characterized by light. In the expression **children of the day**, "the day" must not be severed from Paul's

overall theme of the day of the Lord; it refers back to 5:2 and 5:4 (see also 5:8). Here "the day" does double duty. It identifies the day of the Lord, and it compounds the metaphor of light in contrast to the night and darkness, ending with an inverted a, b, b¹, a¹ pattern. The balance brings over the word "children" ("sons"), and here Paul included himself to emphasize that **we are not [children of] the night, nor of the darkness**.

5:6–7. Sleep is used to characterize unbelievers as spiritually insensitive. Such sleep is not for "sons of the light." **Watch** (Greek, *grēgoreō*; "be awake, alert"; compare English "gregarious") is contrasted with "sleep" and points to the believer's vigilant expectancy in keeping with Paul's emphasis on Christ's coming (see Matt. 24:42–43; 25:13; Mark 13:34–37). **Sober** is contrasted with the conduct mentioned in 5:7. The person who is "sober" exercises self-control and is free from every form of physical or psychological inebriation (see Eph. 5:18).

5:8. The day alludes to the light that characterizes Christians but also refers to the coming of Christ (see 5:2 and discussion). Since the believer belongs to the day and accordingly lives in vigilant sobriety, Paul gave a picture to secure and summarize the mindset and disposition he wanted believers to possess: that of a soldier or sentry outfitted for duty with a **breastplate … and … a helmet**. Paul also used the metaphor of armor elsewhere (see Rom. 13:12; 2 Cor. 6:7; 10:4; Eph. 6:13–17). He did not consistently attach a particular virtue to each piece of armor but pictured the general idea of equipment necessary for the duties of a soldier. For the triad of **faith**, **love**, and **hope**, see discussion on 1:3. These cardinal Christian virtues are the spiritual ways believers are to actualize vigilance and self-control as a good soldier ready for duty.

5:9. Appointed emphasizes the divine determination of God and provides the strongest assurance and protection against fear of the day of the Lord. It is grounded in God's appointed **salvation** through Jesus Christ. Here the word "salvation" embodies the sense of deliverance from **wrath** (see 1:9–10). God's wrath involves the outpouring of His judgment (see

Rom. 2:5; 4:15). Notice that the tribulation judgments are called "the wrath of the Lamb" (Rev. 6:16) and "the wrath of God" (Rev. 16:1).

5:10. The words **live together with him** (see 4:17) indicate that Paul intended **whether we wake or sleep** to refer to whether the believer is "alive" or "dead in Christ" (4:16–17) when Christ returns. Thus, Paul gave a final assurance that summed up the questions posed in 4:13–18 and 5:1–10 and provided a fitting conclusion to both passages, followed by an all-encompassing exhortation (5:11; see 4:18). Although the terms "wake" and "sleep" are identical to those in 5:6, they are used differently here. Otherwise, Paul would have opposed what he argued in 5:4–7, concluding that it does not matter whether people are children of the light or children of the darkness. Such moral indifference and universalism was foreign to Paul and the emphasis of his teaching here on the subject (see Bruce, *1 and 2 Thessalonians*, p. 114; Green, *The Letters to the Thessalonians*, p. 243). For "sleep" (Greek, *katheudō*) as a euphemism for death, see Mark 5:39; John 11:11; Ephesians 5:14. Green (*The Letters to the Thessalonians*, p. 244) points out that both words, "wake" and "sleep," are correspondingly used figuratively for death and life in Mark 5:39, 41; Luke 8:52, 54.

5:11. The verb **edify** generally applies to building houses, but Paul frequently used it for Christians who demonstrate a constructive concern for another person's good (see Rom. 15:2; 1 Cor. 8:1; 10:23–24; 14:7). Such "building up" is a person-to-person effort and a responsibility that belongs to the entire community of believers (see Rom. 14:19). Therefore, it suited Paul's admonition to **comfort yourselves together,** or "encourage one another."

C. Primarily concerning Church Life (5:12–22)

5:12. Them which labour among you. Not much is known about the organization and leadership of the church during this period, but the reference is probably to elders (see 1 Tim. 3:1–5; 5:17; Heb. 13:7, 17). **To know them** is best understood as "to acknowledge" or "to give recognition to." The word "know" is

fairly elastic, but here an appreciation of service to the church is the basis of Paul's call for esteem and peace in 5:13. The Greek here unmistakably bundles three distinguishing functions ("labour," "are over," "admonish") of one group of people. Paul's request reflects a recognition of leaders who exhibited the underlying leadership of the Lord in the way they served the church. Even official apostolic appointment follows recognition (see Titus 1:5–9, where the appointment ratified the leadership character that had already become evident). "Labour" generally denotes physical toil but in Paul's letters is associated with the ministry of the Word (see 3:5; 1 Tim. 5:17) and the church (1 Cor. 16:15–16). **Over you** renders a Greek word (*proistēmi*) that blends the ideas of leading, protecting, and giving care (see 1 Tim. 3:4, 5, 12, 17; Titus 3:8, 14). In Romans 12:8, the word is translated "he that ruleth," but as indicated there, the gift is appreciated by its grouping with other gifts necessary for the care and well-being of the congregation. Like Stephanas in Corinth (see 1 Cor. 16:15), Jason in Thessalonica became a benefactor and leader in the church (see Acts 17:5–9). These two leaders help visualize those who are "over you in the Lord." The basic meaning of **admonish** is "to put in mind" and so to "advise," "warn," or "rebuke" a person about what should and should not be done. The true work of admonishing another begins with the truth of God operating in the heart of the one who admonishes.

5:13. Paul used no titles here. Recognition of church leaders and the **esteem** that should accompany it is **for their work's sake.** Personal attachment or respect for their high position is secondary to the ministry such leaders perform for the Lord and His church. **Be at peace** applies to Christian relationships in general, but here it probably refers especially to right relations between leaders and those under them.

5:14. Them that are unruly (Greek, *ataktos,* = *a,* "without" + *taktos,* "proper order" or "rule") refers those who were idle and here specifies laziness or loafing. Apparently, some Thessalonians were so sure that the second coming was imminent that they had given up their jobs to prepare for it, but Paul said they should work (see 2 Thess. 3:10–11 and discussions; see also 1 Thess. 4:11). **The feebleminded** (Greek, *oligopsychos*; "of little soul" or "lacking sufficient heart") refers to those who are fainthearted or discouraged. They are to be strengthened with encouragement. The word **weak** (Greek, *asthenēs*) is used in the New Testament of incapacities and limitations both physical and spiritual; Paul generally used it of spiritual and moral weakness. **Support** means "to hold on to" with a strong attachment and interest. The weak are to be helped, not rejected, by the strong (see Rom. 14:1–15; 15:1; 1 Cor. 8:13).

5:15. Render evil for evil, or "give back in kind," addresses any kind of tit-for-tat retaliation. Retaliation is never a Christian option (see Rom. 12:17; 1 Peter 3:9). Christians are called to forgive (see Matt. 5:38–42; 18:21–35). Followers of Jesus Christ are never to allow evil to dictate their actions. Rather, they are to **follow,** or pursue (go after), what is good. Paul made that the strategy for all believers toward all people, whether at church or in the world.

5:16. Up to this point in the letter, Paul focused on responsible behavior as it relates to one's outlook on others (5:12–15). In 5:16–18, Paul featured the individual's outlook as it relates to his or her relationship with God. **Rejoice evermore,** or "at all times." People are naturally happy on some occasions, but the Christian's joy is not dependent on circumstances; it comes from what Christ has done, and it is constant. Thus, Paul wrote the Philippians, "Rejoice in the Lord alway" (Phil. 4:4). To rejoice is to express outwardly the joy in one's heart because of Christ. There is probably a connection between the outer countenance of joy ("rejoice," here) and the inner appreciation of God's presence ("pray," 5:17).

5:17. Paul's call to **Pray without ceasing** pictures a person mindful of God's presence at all times and in all circumstances (for the practice of continual, or regular, prayer, see 1:3; 2:13; Rom. 1:9–10; Eph. 6:18; Col. 1:3; 2 Tim. 1:3).

5:18. As in 5:16, Christians are differentiated from the natural man. Because of what God has done, they are continually thankful, regardless of the circumstances (see Eph. 5:20). To give thanks in all

circumstances (see Phil. 4:6–7) is to open the mind and heart to the whole vista of God's sovereignty. To do otherwise limits thanksgiving to those occasions when God's will matches one's wishes. Under those conditions, one's mind and heart are closed to the ways in which God is at work when He works outside of one's preferences.

5:19. Quench not the Spirit. There is a warmth, a glow, about the Spirit's presence that makes this language appropriate. The kind of conduct Paul was opposing may have included loafing, immorality, and the other sins he had denounced in the letter. On the other hand, he may have been warning against a mechanical attitude toward worship, which discourages the expression of the gifts of the Spirit in the local assembly (see 5:20; see also 2 Tim. 1:6, lit., "fan into flame" the gift of God—the opposite of quench or extinguish).

5:20. Prophesyings must be treated with seriousness (see 5:21) and not with easy disdain or contempt. More than foretelling the future, the gift of prophecy involves the ability to interpret and communicate in clear speech God's direct and relevant will for His people. Such was the case in the early church (see Acts 11:27–28; 13:1–3; 21:10–11). From Paul's instruction to the Corinthians, we recognize that the one who prophesies speaks to the church for "edification, and exhortation, and comfort" (1 Cor. 14:3) and that prophesyings instruct the church "that all may learn" (1 Cor. 14:31; for more on the gift of prophecy, see Rom. 12:6; 1 Cor. 12:10, 28; 13:2; 14:29–33; Eph. 4:11).

5:21. There is a continuation here of Paul's thought on prophesy that is made clear in the Greek and not translated in the KJV. Rather than disdain, Paul counseled the Thessalonians to **prove all things** (or "all prophesyings"). The approval of prophecy (see 5:20) does not mean that anyone who claims to speak in the name of the Lord is to be accepted without question. The word for "prove" (Greek, *dokimazō*) speaks of examining something to verify its quality (see "allowed," 2:4). Paul did not say what specific tests are to be applied, but he was clear that every teaching must be tested, and surely they must be in agreement with the gospel. **Hold[ing] fast that which is good** is the positive outcome of what is approved. The negative outcome is expressed in 5:22. The train of Paul's thought applies to prophecy, but these final two thoughts in 5:22–23 are no doubt the specific application of a general principle regarding good and evil (see Bruce, *1 and 2 Thessalonians*, p. 126).

5:22. The theme of prophecy probably remained the controlling idea as Paul counseled the Thessalonians to **abstain from all appearance of evil**. Here evil is the opposite of good (see 5:21) and "abstain" is the opposite of "hold fast" (5:21). An "evil" utterance would contradict the gospel. Both good and evil would be discerned through "prov[ing] all things" (5:21).

IV. Concluding Prayer, Greetings, and Benediction (5:23–28)

5:23. Paul shifted his emphasis from counseling to blessing as he vocalized in writing a prayer for the Thessalonians. **God of peace** is a fitting reference to God in view of 5:12–15. Paul often referred to God in this way near the end of his letters (see Rom. 15:33; 16:20; 1 Cor. 14:33; 2 Cor. 13:11; Phil. 4:9; see also 2 Thess. 3:16). With the words **your whole spirit and soul and body**, Paul was emphasizing the whole person (**sanctify you wholly**), not attempting to differentiate the parts. Their sanctification was his desire in an earlier prayer (3:11–13) and a theme of his specific counsel (4:3–8). Paul broadened the notion in various ways and last of all doctrinally (see 5:20–22), and so he concluded with a prayer for their complete sanctification.

5:24. Paul's confidence rested in the nature of God (see Gen. 18:25), who can be relied on to complete what He begins (see Num. 23:19; Phil. 1:6). The process of sanctification, or becoming holy and wholly God's, is the work of a relationship in which God is a faithful and persistent partner. His heart, thoughts, and holy character rub off on the believer through the ever-present influence of His Spirit.

5:25–26. Pray for us (v. 25). Paul knew the power of prayer. Even he, the apostle who counseled the Thessalonians, needed the intercession of others in the life and ministry of God's calling. Paul sent a warm greeting to everyone, even to those whom he had corrected. **All the brethren** (v. 26) points to a mutual greeting, regardless of social status or race. Such an outward show of cordiality expressed the true unity of a filial bond through Jesus Christ. **A holy kiss** was a normal greeting of that day, similar to the modern handshake (see Rom. 16:16; 1 Cor. 16:20; 2 Cor. 13:12; and "a kiss of charity," 1 Peter 5:14).

5:27. I charge you is surprisingly strong language, meaning "I put you on oath." Paul clearly wanted every member of the church to read or hear his letter and to know of his concern and advice for them.

5:28. Paul always ended his letters with a benediction of grace for his readers, sometimes adding other blessings (as in 2 Cor. 13:14). Thus, 1 Thessalonians ends with the apostle's encouragement to the believers. Whether they lived or died, their hope of the rapture of the living and the resurrection of the dead focused their attention on their reunion with Christ.

THE SECOND EPISTLE OF PAUL THE APOSTLE TO THE THESSALONIANS

INTRODUCTION

See 1 Thessalonians, Introduction.

Author, Date, and Place of Composition

Paul's authorship of 2 Thessalonians has been questioned more often than that of 1 Thessalonians, in spite of the fact that it has more support from early Christian writers. Objections are based on internal factors rather than on the adequacy of the statements of the church fathers. It is thought that differences exist in the vocabulary (ten words not used elsewhere), in the style (it is said to be unexpectedly formal), and in the eschatology (the doctrine of the Man of Sin is not taught elsewhere; see 2:3–12). Such arguments, however, have not convinced current scholars. Most still hold to Paul's authorship of 2 Thessalonians (see 1:1; 3:17).

Because of its similarity to 1 Thessalonians, this letter must have been written not long after the first letter, perhaps about six months later. The situation in the church seems to have been much the same. Paul probably penned it circa AD 51 or 52 in Corinth, after Silas and Timothy had returned from delivering 1 Thessalonians.

Theme and Theological Message

Nothing in the letter indicates that Paul had any further direct contact with the Thessalonians since writing his first letter. Rather, he was responding to some questions of theirs that he had heard about, perhaps from those who delivered the first letter. Paul's purpose in writing was very much the same as in his first letter to them. He wrote (1) to encourage persecuted believers (1:4–10), (2) to exhort the Thessalonians to be steadfast and to work for a living (2:13–3:15), and (3) to correct a misunderstanding concerning the Lord's return (2:1–12).

Like 1 Thessalonians, this letter deals extensively with eschatology (see 1 Thessalonians, Introduction: "Theme and Theological Message"). In fact, in 2 Thessalonians, eighteen out of forty-seven verses (38 percent) deal with this subject. In this letter, Paul dealt extensively with the sequence of events regarding the removal of the restrainer (see discussion on 2:7), the rise of the Antichrist (the "man of sin," 2:3), and the triumphal return of Christ "in flaming fire" (1:8).

Outline

I. Introduction (chap. 1)
  A. Salutation (1:1–2)
  B. Thanksgiving for the Thessalonians' Faith, Love, and Perseverance (1:3–10)
  C. Intercession for Their Spiritual Progress (1:11–12)
II. Instruction (chap. 2)
  A. Prophecy regarding the Day of the Lord: Their Promise (2:1–12)
  B. Thanksgiving for Their Election and Calling: Their Position (2:13–15)
  C. Prayer for Their Service and Testimony: Their Practice (2:16–17)
III. Injunctions (chap. 3)
  A. Call to Prayer (3:1–3)
  B. Charge to Discipline the Disorderly and Lazy (3:4–15)

Bibliography

Bruce, F. F. *1 and 2 Thessalonians*. Word Biblical Commentary 45. Waco, TX: Word, 1982.

Couch, Mal. *The Hope of Christ's Return*. Chattanooga, TN: AMG, 2001.

Green, Gene L. *The Letters to the Thessalonians*. Pillar New Testament Commentary. Grand Rapids, MI: Eerdmans, 2002.

Marshall, I. Howard. *1 and 2 Thessalonians*. New Century Bible Commentary. Grand Rapids, MI: Eerdmans, 1983.

Mayhue, Richard. *1 and 2 Thessalonians: Triumphs and Trials of a Consecrated Church*. Focus on the Bible. Ross-shire, UK: Christian Focus, 1999.

EXPOSITION

I. Introduction (chap. 1)

A. Salutation (1:1–2)

1:1–2. See discussion on 1 Thessalonians 1:1.

B. Thanksgiving for the Thessalonians' Faith, Love, and Perseverance (1:3–10)

1:3. **Bound** is a word expressing personal, not impersonal, obligation. Here it is Paul's way of expressing deserved admiration for the powerful effect of the Thessalonians' faith (see 1 Thess. 1:7–8; discussion on Phil. 1:3–4). Paul addressed the Thessalonians in a warm, pastoral, and conversational manner. For Paul's use of **brethren**, see discussion on 1 Thessalonians 1:4. **Faith** and **charity** ("love") are two defining virtues of the Christian life (see 1 Tim. 1:5; 2 Tim. 1:13) that Paul had been pleased to acknowledge in the Thessalonian church (see 1 Thess. 3:6–7) but that were also somewhat lacking (see 1 Thess. 3:10, 12). **Groweth exceedingly, and … aboundeth** pictures the Thessalonians' faith and charity flourishing like a plant. Paul's characterization is noteworthy given the hostilities of their environment (see 1:4). Paul had used the same verb in his earlier prayer that the Thessalonians' love would grow ("abound," 1 Thess. 3:12). Here he was recording an exact answer to prayer. The virtues of faith and charity must grow because they express the vertical and horizontal relationship of the Christian to God and the world.

1:4. We ourselves emphasizes Paul's participation. Paul seems to imply that it was unusual for the founders of a church to boast about it, though others might do so (see 1 Thess. 1:9). The Thessalonians were so outstanding that Paul departed from normal practice. **Persecutions and tribulations** speaks respectively of both the mistreatment at the hands of others and the sufferings (external and internal) that the Thessalonians had experienced (see 1 Thess. 1:6; 2:14; 3:3).

1:5. Manifest token of the righteous judgment of God. Based on Paul's entire thought in 1:5–7, the "token" of God's righteous judgment anticipates a future "recompense" (1:6–7) appreciated even "now" in the actions of the persecuted and the persecutors, those for and those against the reign of God and lordship of His Son. Paul encouraged and assured the Thessalonians that their suffering for the kingdom of God had worth (see Matt. 5:10–12; 1 Thess. 2:14–15) and was a part of being **counted worthy**. "Persecutions and tribulations" (1:4) suffered for the sake of the kingdom of God are an exhibit of two opposed value judgments: what the world counts as worthless, God counts worthy. Because the Thessalonians accepted God's judgment of worth over the world's, Paul added the words **for which** (i.e., "in the interest of which" or "in behalf of which") **ye also suffer**. For **the kingdom of God**, see discussions on 1 Thessalonians 2:12; Matthew 3:2. Couch (*The Hope of Christ's Return*, p. 185) observes that "the kingdom of God" refers to the messianic reign of Christ. He points out that "the kingdom of God" and "the kingdom of heaven" both refer to God coming from heaven to reign on earth.

1:6. A righteous thing with God points to the justice of God. He brings punishment on unrepentant sinners (see Mark 9:47–48; Luke 13:3–5), and it may be in the here and now (see Rom. 1:24, 26, 28) as well as on judgment day.

1:7. Rest is contrasted with "trouble" (1:6). Retribution not only involves punishment of the evil but also relief for the righteous. Paul included himself in **with us**, not only in the "rest" that awaits the Christian but in the sufferings experienced on behalf of Christ (see Phil. 3:10). Paul was not merely an academic theologian writing in comfort from a distance; rather, he was suffering just as the Thessalonians were. Paul took to heart and gained comfort from the "rest" to come when Christ **shall be revealed**. Christ is now hidden, and many people even deny His existence. At His second coming, He will be seen by everyone for who He is (see Matt. 24:30). **His mighty angels** may refer to a class of angels (such a group is mentioned in apocalyptic writings) who are given special power to do God's will. Jesus, "the author and finisher [perfecter] of our faith" (Heb. 12:2), had such "servants" at His command, yet He suffered unjustly with purpose because His kingdom was not of this world (see John 18:36).

1:8. In flaming fire is an indication of power and judgment. Christ will punish the wickedness (see Isa. 66:15; Rev. 1:14) of those who **know not God**, meaning those who refuse to recognize Him (see 2:10, 12; Rom. 1:28) and further defined as those who **obey not**. The gospel invites acceptance, and rejection is disobedience to a royal invitation.

1:9. Destruction does not mean annihilation (see discussion on 1 Thess. 5:3). Paul used the word in 1 Corinthians 5:5, "for the destruction of the flesh," possibly for the purpose of salvation. Since, however, salvation implies resurrection of the body, annihilation cannot be in mind. The word means something like "complete ruin." Here it means being shut out from Christ's presence. This eternal separation is the penalty of sin and the essence of hell. **The glory of his power** (see 1:7–8) is scorned by those who persecute believers. Such arrogant abuse of power will be eclipsed by the majestic and humbling might of Jesus Christ.

1:10. Glorified in his saints means not simply "among" but "in" them. His glory is seen in what they are: "saints" (see discussion on 1 Thess. 3:13). **Our testimony** speaks of the gospel message at a time when the New Testament did not yet exist. The preaching of the gospel is essentially bearing testimony to what God has done in Christ. **That day** refers to the day of the Lord (see discussion on 1 Thess. 5:2).

C. Intercession for Their Spiritual Progress (1:11–12)

1:11. The words **Pray always for you** (see discussion on 1 Thess. 5:17) point to the dynamic role of intercessory prayer in the progress of Christian development. The challenges for the Thessalonians were threatening and full of suffering (see 1:4–5), yet the purposes that direct believers' attitudes and actions come from **the good pleasure of his goodness** (lit., "resolve of goodness"). God initiates every good purpose and every act prompted by faith; Paul prayed accordingly that He would bring them to fulfillment for the Thessalonians.

1:12. A **name** in ancient times was often more than a personal label; it summed up what a person was. Paul looked for glory to be ascribed to Christ for all He would do in the lives of the Thessalonian Christians.

II. Instruction (chap. 2)

A. Prophecy regarding the Day of the Lord: Their Promise (2:1–12)

2:1. We beseech you (as in 1 Thess. 4:1; 5:12) is an exhortation in the form of a request. The words **by … and by** are a rendering of just a single Greek word that means "concerning," and Paul used it here to govern and express his interest in the twofold subject of **the coming of our Lord Jesus Christ** (for the significance of the word "coming," the Greek word *parousia*, see 1 Thess. 4:16) and **our gathering together unto him**. Here (as in 1 Thess. 4:13–18) both of these subjects belong to the specification of questions posed about "the day of Christ" (2:2), about which there was some confusion that Paul wished to clear up. "Gathering together" (Greek, *episynagōgē*; "assemble together") here refers to the rapture of all believers, which is connected with the coming of the Lord, spoken of in 1 Thessalonians 4:13–18 (see also 1 Cor. 15:51–52).

2:2. The Greek for the verb **shaken** was often used of a ship adrift from its mooring and suggests a lack of stability. Paul wanted the Thessalonians to be of firm conviction and not of unstable opinion. He did not want them to be **troubled**, a word Jesus used in issuing a similar instruction (Mark 13:7). The specific source of the Thessalonians' confusion was not known to Paul, but the words **spirit, word,** and **letter as from us** convey the likely avenues of some novel teaching contrary to Paul's own. "Spirit" is a general expression denoting any "inspired" revelation and probably alludes to prophecies, a subject of concern in 1 Thessalonians 5:19–22. "Word" could denote any form of oral communication, a message, a teaching, or even a sermon. "Letter as from us" identifies some written communication under Paul's name and thus a forgery, although the Thessalonians obviously would not have known that at the time (see 3:17). It becomes clear, especially from the first and the last of these three possible avenues of communication, that the Thessalonians became susceptible to the error because it came to them through some ostensibly dependable and reputable source. It is a reminder that counterfeits may be passed on by reputable hands and detected only by those with a firm grasp of genuine tender, a point Paul made more than once (see 2:5, 15). **The day of Christ** is also the day of the Lord (see discussion on 1 Thess. 5:2). Obviously, Christ's climactic return had not occurred, but the words **is at hand**, the perfect active indicative (Greek, *enistēmi*), meaning "has already begun," suggest that Paul was combating the idea that the final days had begun and their completion was imminent.

2:3. Here and in 2:6–8, Paul stressed the order of future events to guard the Thessalonians against further deception. As proof, he stated that **that day** (see 1 Thess. 5:2) **shall not come** before what must come first: **a falling away** and the climactic revealing of **that man of sin**. There will be "a falling away" from faith (see Matt. 24:10–12; 1 Tim. 4:1), but here Paul was speaking of active rebellion. Elsewhere the Greek word *apostasia* is used of political and militant revolt as well as of rebellion against God. Here Paul used it of the supreme opposition of evil to the things of God. "That man of sin" identifies the leader of the forces of evil during the last days. Only here is he called by this name. John called him "antichrist" (1 John 2:18) and "the beast" (Revelation 13). Paul's description of the "man of sin" has some distinctive features. He is not Satan, because he is clearly distinguished from him in 2:9. **Revealed** is from the same Greek root word (*apokalyptō*) as that used of Jesus Christ in 1:7 and may indicate something supernatural. As his description, **the son of perdition**, indicates, despite all his proud claims (see 2:4, 9), his final overthrow is certain. The same Greek expression is used of Judas Iscariot in John 17:12, where it is also translated "the son of perdition." This does not mean, however, that Judas is the Antichrist but that both are destined to perdition (Greek, *apōleia*; "destruction").

2:4. All that is called God, or that is worshipped. The Man of Sin will not merely be a political or military man but will claim a place above every god and everything associated with worship; he will even claim to be God. **The temple of God** apparently refers to a physical temple (see Matt. 24:25; Mark 13:14) from which he will make his blasphemous pronouncements (see Dan. 11:36–45; Rev. 13:1–15). The designation "temple of God" almost certainly means a Jewish temple in Jerusalem. The Thessalonians, who had "turned to God from idols to serve the living and true God" (1 Thess. 1:9), surely could have imagined such blasphemy, for they were acquainted with many precursors, surrounded as they were by temples not only to various deities but to the emperor of imperial Rome.

2:5–6. The error that had deceived them (see 2:3), although peddled through some "dependable" source (see 2:2), clearly contradicted the things Paul had taught them earlier (see 2:15). With Paul's earlier instruction ("I told you these things," v. 5) in mind, they now knew **what withholdeth ... his time** (v. 6; see 2:7). What restrains "the son of perdition" (v. 3) will prevail until the timing of God, not that of Satan (v. 9).

2:7. In the New Testament, "mystery" usually denotes something people cannot know without God's revelation (see discussion on Rom. 11:25). The expression **the mystery of iniquity** indicates that some things about evil are known only as God reveals them. This evil is already at work, but in the day of the Lord (the great tribulation), it will inten-

sify dramatically (see Matt. 24:21–22). **He who now letteth will let**. In earlier centuries, the English word "let" meant "hinder" or "restrain" (as does the Greek word here) rather than "allow." So the meaning is that he who now restrains will restrain until he is removed. In 2:6, Paul spoke of the restraint only in terms of its exercise. Here he shifted the gender from neuter to masculine and specified the agent who exercises the restraint. There have been many suggestions as to the specific character of the restraint (see 2:6), which is contrasted with "the mystery of iniquity" **already [at] work,** and to the identity of the restrainer, contrasted with the Man of Sin to be "revealed in his time" (2:6). Because the Thessalonians knew what Paul does not identify, suggestions have ranged from the Roman state with its emperor, the principle of law and government embodied in the state and its governor, Paul's missionary spreading of the gospel, to the Holy Spirit or the restraining ministry of the Holy Spirit through the church. Since only God is able to restrain Satan and his Antichrist, it seems best to regard the sovereign power of God as that which inhibits the freedom of Satan and the rise of his Antichrist until the rapture of the church (see 2:11). At an ordained time (see "revealed," 2:3, 6), the agency of God's restraint will be taken out of the way of the Man of Sin. Without this restraint, the "falling away ... and that man of sin" (2:3) will foment what is known as the great tribulation. So the day of the Lord (of Christ) with its great tribulation will not begin until after the restrainer is removed and the Wicked One, the Man of Sin, is revealed. Paul wanted the Thessalonians to understand, therefore, that the day of the Lord (the final days) had not yet come and they had not missed the rapture of the church. The order of events in this verse is: (1) the removal of the restrainer, (2) the falling away, (3) the rise of the Wicked One. This passage makes it clear that Satan's hands are tied by the sovereignty of God. Satan cannot move to empower someone to become the Antichrist until after the removal of restraint at the time of the rapture.

2:8. The words "sin" (2:3), "iniquity" (2:7) and **Wicked** are the same Greek root word, meaning "lawless," and convey rebellion against God, the ultimate Creator of order and law. No longer restrained (**And then**; see also 2:7), the true character of the **Wicked**, or "Lawless One," will **be revealed**. "Revealed" evidently refers to some supernatural aspects of his appearing (see 2:9). As Bruce (*1 and 2 Thessalonians*, p. 172) aptly put it, "He is revealed only to be destroyed." Paul's wording of **consume with the spirit of his mouth** is fortified by Isaiah 11:4, with its prophetic description of the Messiah's judgment. Despite his impressiveness (v. 4), the Man of Sin will easily be destroyed by Christ (see Dan. 11:45; Rev. 19:20). The Man of Sin will be vanquished and destroyed by the "spirit," or breath, of Christ's mouth, probably alluding to the utterance or command of Jesus, and **the brightness of his coming**, or appearing. In 2 Timothy 1:10 ("appearing"), the Greek for this word refers to Jesus' first coming, but everywhere else in the New Testament, it refers to His second coming.

2:9. The **coming** (Greek, *parousia*; see 1 Thess. 4:16 and discussion) of the Man of Sin is the *anti-parousia* of the coming of Christ (see 2:1, 8). Satan will empower the Man of Sin with miracles, signs, and wonders (see Matt. 24:24) — the counterfeits of messianic equipment. Thus, his **lying wonders** will produce false impressions.

2:10. Unrighteousness, the source and character of Satan (see 2:9), has power to deceive (**deceivableness**) them that perish. Paul explains why. Those that are perishing **received not**, meaning they gave no place or welcome to **the love of the truth**. More than mere knowledge of the truth, "love" points to what might be described as a commitment to the truth. Counterfeits peddled by unrighteousness will easily deceive not only those who reject the truth but those with a loosely held knowledge of the truth. Since the truth they reject has the power to save, its character as well as its content must be defined by the essential gospel message of Jesus (see John 14:6; Eph. 1:13; 4:21; Gal. 2:5).

2:11. For this cause, or because of their deliberate rejection of the truth (see 2:10), **God shall send them strong delusion**. God uses sin to punish the sinful (see Rom. 1:24–28), but here He seals for them the lie that the truth (the gospel) is **a lie** (see 2:10). The lie is contrasted with the truth (the gospel of Jesus Christ) in 2:10, 12. Since the lie is defined by its contrast with the truth, its ultimate expression and delusion may be its implication that the Man of Sin is God (see 2:4). In summary, Paul told the Thessalonians that the rapture will involve the removal of restraint, allowing Satan to empower the Man of Sin (the Antichrist) to rise to power preceding the triumphal return of Christ. Thus, the order of these future events is: (1) rapture, (2) apostasy, (3) rise of the Antichrist, (4) strong delusion.

B. Thanksgiving for Their Election and Calling: Their Position (2:13–15)

2:13. Beloved of the Lord, because God hath ... chosen you. For the connection between God's love and election, see Colossians 3:12; 1 Thessalonians 1:4; discussion on Ephesians 1:4. **From the beginning** points to God's decision from eternity to save people "in him" (Eph. 1:4), in Jesus Christ. Here **sanctification of the Spirit** and **belief [in] the truth** are the divine and human actions at work in the realization of God's decision. Sanctification is a necessary aspect of salvation, not something reserved for special Christians (see 1 Thess. 3:13; 4:3 and discussions). The truth is above all the message of salvation in Jesus Christ (see discussions on 2:10–11). All three persons of the Trinity are mentioned in this verse (see discussion on 1 Thess. 1:1).

2:14. Called ... by our gospel is Paul's concise reference to the call of God expressed and extended through the preaching of the gospel message. The past tense refers to the time when the Thessalonians were converted, but the divine call is a present reality in 1 Thessalonians 2:12; 5:24 (for "our gospel," see discussion on 1 Thess. 1:5). The objective of God's calling is **to the obtaining of the glory of our Lord Jesus Christ** (see 1 Thess. 2:12). For Paul, that was a compact summary of the totality of the Christian's benefits in Christ, appreciated through the magnificent stature of His person and titles. Ultimately, there is no glory other than God's.

2:15. Here Paul returned to the issue of sources (see 2:2) and stressed the importance of sticking to (**stand fast**) the teaching the Thessalonians had received from him. To detect a counterfeit, one must have a firm grasp of what is genuine and true. **The traditions**, as in 3:6, refers to that which is "passed on" or "handed on." Until the New Testament was written, essential Christian teaching was passed on in "the traditions," either oral or written, just as rabbinic law was (see discussion on Matt. 15:2). In 1 Corinthians 15:3, Paul used the technical words for receiving and handing on traditions: "For I delivered unto you ... that which I also received."

C. Prayer for Their Service and Testimony: Their Practice (2:16–17)

2:16–17. A similar prayer is found in about the same place in Paul's first letter to the Thessalonians (1 Thess. 3:11–13). He had reassured and encouraged them with his specific explanations in answer to their concerns (2:1–12) and with his specific and foundational causes for thanksgiving (2:13–15). With the vital issues of their well-being in view, Paul now completed his efforts to care for the Thessalonians with prayer. Paul is a model of pastoral care and heart. Knowledge and understanding are indispensable but are insufficient without dependence on the resources of God. **Everlasting consolation** (v. 16) looks beyond the current source of distress (see 2:2) and expresses the breadth and depth of the assurance that belongs to the Christian who looks to God whatever the challenge (see Rom. 8, esp. vv. 32–39). **Comfort ... stablish** (v. 17) points to an outcome of such confidence: inner strength that will produce results in both action and speech.

III. Injunctions (chap. 3)

A. Call to Prayer (3:1–3)

3:1. Finally introduces a new direction of thought (see discussion on 1 Thess. 4:1) but connects what follows to what has just be treated in chapter 2. In 1 Thessalonians 5:25, Paul simply asked for prayer; here he mentioned specifics. **Even as it is with you** (lit., "just as also with you") alludes to the success of the gospel mission among the Thessalonians. The expression is general enough to cover the present as well as the past (see 1 Thess. 2:13).

3:2. Unreasonable translates a Greek word meaning "out of place" and suggesting what is "evil, wrong, or improper." Elsewhere in the New Testament, it is used only of things (see Luke 23:41; Acts 25:5). Perverseness is always out of place. For Paul's difficulties at Corinth (where he wrote this letter), see Acts 18:12–13. People who are not of faith do not know the corrective and heart-changing influence of Jesus Christ on what is "unreasonable and wicked."

3:3. In the Greek text, **faithful** immediately follows "faith" (3:2), putting God's faithfulness in sharp contrast with man's lack of faith (see 1 Cor. 1:9; 10:13; 2 Cor. 1:18).

B. Charge to Discipline for the Disorderly and Lazy (3:4–15)

3:4–5. Believers' **hearts** (see discussion on 1 Thess. 2:4) must be directed by God, especially in the face of uncertainties and spiritual opposition. **Love of God** may be understood as love for God or the love that comes from God. Since Paul was about to rebuke those who were idle, he was probably reminding them of God's love. There should be no hard feelings among those who owe everything to the love of God. Perseverance, or the capacity to bear up in the face of difficulty, comes from Christ, which was probably Paul's meaning.

3:6. Command is an authoritative word with a military ring. Paul used the word twelve times in his letters, five of them in 1–2 Thessalonians and four times here in chapter 3 (1 Thess. 4:11; 2 Thess. 3:4, 6, 10, 12). All of Paul's uses of the word "command" in the Thessalonian letters concerned the problem of those individuals who **walketh disorderly**. He had mentioned this problem in the first letter (1 Thess. 4:11–12; 5:14; see discussions there), and evidently it had worsened. Paul took it seriously and gave more attention to it in this letter than to anything else but the second coming. Paul used the strongest forms of coercion, appealing to the authority of the Lord, **the tradition**, and the church (**brethren**) in addressing these individuals (**every brother**). For **the name**, see discussion on 1:12. **Withdraw** does not mean withdrawal of all contact but withholding of close fellowship. Idleness is sinful and disruptive, but those who are guilty of it are still brothers (see 3:15). Those who are obedient to the Lord Jesus Christ and the traditions (see discussion on 2:15) are to distinguish themselves from those who are not and who bring shame upon the name of Jesus Christ through their attitude and actions (see 3:11–12, 14).

3:7. Ye ought to follow us (see discussion on 1 Thess. 1:6) refers to not only Paul's example but also that of his team of coworkers. As a leader, Paul never let individual "rights" interfere with what was right for the ministry of the gospel (see 3:9).

3:8. Eat any man's bread was a Hebraism for "make a living" (see, e.g., Gen. 3:19; Amos 7:12). Paul was not saying that he never accepted hospitality but that he had not depended on others for his living (see 1 Thess. 2:9 and discussion).

3:9. Have not power refers to the authority or "right" that belonged to Paul but that he chose not to exercise (see discussion on 1 Thess. 2:6). Paul defended the same word and right in his letter to the Corinthians (1 Cor. 9:1–27). It was from Corinth that he penned 2 Thessalonians.

3:10. If any would not work, neither should he eat. Pagan parallels are in the form, "He who does not work does not eat." Paul gave an imperative: literally, "let him not eat." The Christian must not be a loafer. The cultural custom and practice of patronage probably played into the abuses Paul addressed and his disfavor of such conduct.

3:11–12. Here **walk** (v. 11) refers to a pattern of conduct that is **disorderly** and amounts to defiance and irresponsible idleness. Not only idle, these individuals were **busybodies**; they were interfering with other people's affairs, a problem to which an unruly or idle life often leads. The nature of Paul's epistles was that they were a substitute for his presence and authority. With the letter's public reading in view (see 1 Thess. 5:27), Paul's command spoke directly to

the problem people. Read aloud, Paul's directives in 3:11–14 served to impose public boundaries on the **disorderly** and give guidance to the "orderly" whose generosity had been abused.

3:13. Be not weary in well doing encouraged those who did not belong to the behavior Paul condemned to continue doing the right things. Here is an indirect clue to the baneful effect that the "disorderly" (3:6, 11) had on the congregation. The misbehavior of others is never cause for retreating from what is right and good, even if others depreciate it.

3:14. Paul realized that some might not heed his letter. The words **no company with** is an unusual Greek double compound, meaning "mix up together with" (used elsewhere in the New Testament only in 1 Cor. 5:9, 11, of a similar withdrawal of close fellowship). It indicates a disassociation that will bring the disobedient person back to a right attitude. Such behavior brings shame (**be ashamed**) on Christian reputation and warrants repentance. The aim is not punishment but restoration to fellowship.

3:15. Discipline in the church should be brotherly, never harsh (for **admonish**, see 1 Thess. 5:12).

3:16. Paul's prayerful **Lord of peace**, rather than his more usual phrase "God of peace," (see discussion on 1 Thess. 5:23) appropriately invoked and applied to all of the Thessalonians (**you all**), even the disorderly.

3:17. Paul normally dictated his letters (see Rom. 16:22) but added something in his own handwriting toward the end of the letter (see 1 Cor. 16:21; Gal. 6:11; Col. 4:18). Here he stated that this practice was his distinguishing mark. In view of 2:2 ("nor by letter as from us"), this authenticating mark reinforced the authority of this letter at its reading.

3:18. See discussion on 1 Thessalonians 5:28. Paul had criticized his offenders, but his last prayer was for everyone. Taken together, Paul's two letters to the Thessalonians reveal his compassionate heart and his confident expectation of the coming of Christ to gather the church to heaven in preparation for His triumphal return to earth.

THE FIRST EPISTLE OF PAUL THE APOSTLE TO TIMOTHY

INTRODUCTION

Author

Both early tradition and the salutations of the Pastoral Epistles confirm Paul as their author. Some objections have been raised in recent years on the basis of an alleged uncharacteristic vocabulary and style (see, e.g., discussions on 1:15; 2:2), but evidence is still convincingly supportive of Paul's authorship.

Date

First Timothy was written sometime after the events of Acts 28 (ca. 63–65), at least eight years after Paul's three-year stay in Ephesus (Acts 19:8, 10; 20:31).

Recipient

As the salutation indicates (1:2), Paul was writing to Timothy, a native of Lystra (in modern Turkey). Timothy's father was Greek, while his mother was a Jewish Christian (see Acts 16:1). From childhood, Timothy had been taught the Old Testament (2 Tim. 1:5; 3:15). Paul called him "my own son in the faith" (1:2), perhaps having led him to Christ during his first visit to Lystra. At the time of his second visit, Paul invited Timothy to join him on his missionary travels and circumcised him so that his Greek ancestry would not be a liability in working with the Jews (Acts 16:3). Timothy shared in the evangelization of Macedonia and Achaia (see Acts 17:14–15; 18:5) and was with Paul during much of his long preaching ministry at Ephesus (see Acts 19:22). He traveled with Paul from Ephesus to Macedonia, to Corinth, back to Macedonia, and to Asia Minor (Acts 20:1–6). He seems even to have accompanied him all the way to Jerusalem. He was with Paul during the apostle's first imprisonment (see Phil. 1:1; Col. 1:1; Philemon 1).

Following Paul's release (after Acts 28), Timothy again traveled with him but eventually stayed at Ephesus to deal with the problems there, while Paul went on to Macedonia. Paul's closeness to and admiration of Timothy are seen in Paul's naming him as the co-sender of six of his letters (2 Corinthians, Philippians, Colossians, 1–2 Thessalonians, and Philemon) and speaking highly of him to the Philippians (Phil. 2:19–22). At the end of Paul's life, he requested Timothy to join him at Rome (2 Tim. 4:9, 21). According to

Hebrews 13:23, Timothy himself was imprisoned and subsequently released—whether at Rome or elsewhere, we do not know.

Timothy was not an apostle, and he was probably not an overseer since he was given instructions about overseers (3:1–7; 5:17–22). It may be best to regard him as an apostolic representative, delegated to carry out special work (see Titus 1:5).

Theme

During his fourth missionary journey, Paul had instructed Timothy to care for the church at Ephesus (1:3) while he went on to Macedonia (see the essay "The Pastoral Epistles" in *Zondervan KJV Study Bible*, p. 1734). When Paul realized that he might not return to Ephesus in the near future (3:14–15), he wrote this first letter to Timothy to develop the charge he had given his young assistant (1:3, 18), to refute false teachings (1:3–7; 4:1–8; 6:3–5, 20–21), and to supervise the affairs of the growing Ephesian church (church worship, 2:1–15; the appointment of qualified church leaders, 3:1–13; 5:17–25).

A major problem in the Ephesian church was a heresy that combined Gnosticism (see 1 John, Introduction: "Gnosticism"), decadent Judaism (1:3–7), and false asceticism (4:1–5).

Outline

    I. Salutation (1:1–2)
   II. Warning against False Teachers (1:3–11)
     A. The Nature of the Heresy (1:3–7)
     B. The Purpose of the Law (1:8–11)
  III. The Lord's Grace to Paul (1:12–17)
  IV. The Purpose of Paul's Instructions to Timothy (1:18–20)
   V. Instructions concerning the Administration of the Church (chaps. 2–3)
     A. Public Worship (chap. 2)
       1. Prayer in Public Worship (2:1–8)
       2. Women in Public Worship (2:9–15)
     B. Qualifications for Church Officers (3:1–13)
       1. Bishops (3:1–7)
       2. Deacons (3:8–13)
     C. Purpose of These Instructions (3:14–16)
  VI. Methods of Dealing with False Teaching (chap. 4)
     A. False Teaching Described (4:1–5)
     B. Methods of Dealing with False Teaching (4:6–16)
 VII. Methods of Dealing with Different Groups in the Church (5:1–6:2)
     A. The Elderly and Younger People (5:1–2)
     B. Widows (5:3–16)
     C. Elders (5:17–25)
     D. Servants (6:1–2)
VIII. Miscellaneous Matters (6:3–19)
     A. False Teachers (6:3–5)
     B. Love of Money (6:6–10)

C. Charge to Timothy (6:11–16)
D. The Rich (6:17–19)
IX. Concluding Appeal (6:20–21)

Bibliography

Fee, Gordon D. *1 and 2 Timothy, Titus*. New International Biblical Commentary. Peabody,
    MA: Hendrickson, 1988.
Guthrie, Donald. *The Pastoral Epistles*. Tyndale New Testament Commentaries. Grand
    Rapids, MI: Eerdmans, 1957.
Kelly, J. N. D. *The Pastoral Epistles*. London: Adam & Charles Black, 1963.
Kent, Homer, Jr. *The Pastoral Epistles*. Chicago: Moody Press, 1971.
Liefeld, Walter L. *1 and 2 Timothy, Titus*. The NIV Application Commentary. Grand Rap-
    ids, MI: Zondervan, 1999.

EXPOSITION

I. Salutation (1:1–2)

1:1. An apostle is one specially commissioned by Christ (see discussions on Mark 6:30; Heb. 3:1; *KJV Study Bible* note on 1 Cor. 1:1), although here the words **of Jesus Christ** circumscribe the scope and focus of his service and the allegiance of his duty. **By the commandment** (Greek, *epitagē*; "command," "order") divulges Paul's own awareness of being a man whose rank and responsibility come from **God our Saviour** (see Titus 1:3). Such authority is welcome and benevolent to those who, as Paul did, know God is the ultimate source of their salvation. For an additional example of **Jesus Christ ... our hope**, see Titus 2:13. "Hope" expresses absolute certainty, not a mere wish. Jesus is our hope because His victory over sin and death is "ours" through faith; He is the harbinger of shared triumph and glory (see 6:14–16; Col. 1:27; 1 John 3:2–3).

1:2. Paul addressed Timothy as **my own son in the faith**, meaning "my spiritual son" (see 1:18; 1 Cor. 4:17; 2 Tim. 1:2; 2:1; Philemon 10). The triad of **grace** (see discussions on Jonah 4:2; Gal. 1:3; Eph. 1:2), **mercy** (see Rom. 9:2), **and peace** (see discussions on John 14:27; 20:19; Gal. 1:3; Eph. 1:2) opens 2 Timothy (1:2) as well.

II. Warning against False Teachers (1:3–11)

A. The Nature of the Heresy (1:3–7)

1:3–11. In this section (along with 4:1–8; 6:3–5, 20–21), Paul warned against heretical teachers in the Ephesian church. They were characterized by (1) teaching false doctrines (1:3; 6:3); (2) teaching Jewish myths (Titus 1:14); (3) wanting to be teachers of the Old Testament law (1:7); (4) building up endless, far-fetched, fictitious stories based on obscure genealogical points (1:4; 4:7; Titus 3:9); (5) being conceited (1:7; 6:4); (6) being argumentative (1:4; 6:4; 2 Tim. 2:23; Titus 3:9); (7) using talk that was meaningless (1:6) and foolish (2 Tim. 2:23; Titus 3:9); (8) not knowing what they were talking about (1:7; 6:4); (9) teaching ascetic practices (4:3); and (10) using their positions of religious leadership for personal financial gain (6:5). These heretics probably were forerunners of the Gnostics (6:20–21; see 1 John, Introduction: "Gnosticism").

1:3. As I besought thee summarily recalled Paul's face-to-face directive to Timothy and served to reaffirm it and validate Timothy's extended stay (**abide still at Ephesus**). The epistolary use of the verb "besought" [Greek, *parakaleō*; "exhort"] belongs to diplomatic correspondence bearing authoritative directions from a superior to subordinates. It is a tactful term conveying stern orders. Similarly, it may be a clue that Paul wrote to Timothy with a diplomatic awareness that his letter, like an envoy, had to convey to a wider audience than Timothy more severe matters. For not only did the arrival of Paul's letter endorse him with detailed directives; its reading (see 1 Thess. 5:27; Col. 4:16) enforced Paul's apostolic authority behind Timothy's oversight and leadership in the matters addressed.

Paul was well acquainted with the problems that Timothy faced and the challenges that beset the well-established church of Ephesus (see Introduction: "Recipient"). Paul had an extensive ministry there during his third missionary journey, about eight years earlier (see Acts 19:1–20:1). After his release from prison in Rome (after Acts 28), he revisited the church, leaving Timothy in charge while Paul journeyed on to Macedonia. Since there is no account in Acts of this excursion **into Macedonia**, it probably occurred after Acts 28, between Paul's first and second Roman imprisonments (see Introduction: "Recipient").

Paul concisely stated at the outset the purpose for Timothy's stay: **that thou mightest charge some that they teach no other doctrine**. The verb "charge" (Greek, *parangellō*) occurs four other times in 1 Timothy (4:11; 5:7; 6:13, 17), and the noun twice (1:5, 18). The term was used by all kinds of persons in authority (rulers, Jesus, the apostles) and means "give orders," "command." The apostolic authority of Paul (see 1:1) stood behind the command to stand against the spread of heterodox teaching.

1:4. Continuing the statement of Timothy's purpose, Paul instructed him, **Neither give heed to fables and endless genealogies**. These were probably mythical stories built on Old Testament history (genealogies) that later developed into intricate Gnostic philosophical systems (see 1 John, Introduction: "Gnosticism").

1:5. The end of the commandment (Greek, *parangelia*; see 1:3) refers to the "goal" or "objective" (Greek, *telos*) of the "charge" given to Timothy (1:3b–4). If **charity** (love) was to triumph in a one-

sided contest of right doctrine versus wrong doctrine, Timothy needed to be armed with the proper motives, ministering **out of a pure heart, and of a good conscience, and of faith unfeigned**.

1:6. In a semipublic letter, **some** (as in 1:3) was an indirect way of identifying the primary promulgators of error, personalities probably known to others, certainly to Paul and Timothy. The necessary motive of love, which was to distinguish Timothy (see 1:5), had been missed and left aside by those teaching "other doctrine" (1:3). **Vain jangling**, or "empty," "pointless" babbling (as in 6:20–21; lit., "vain talk"), had become more important to them than the integrity of right doctrine.

1:7. The heretical teachers in the Ephesian church aspired to be **teachers of the law**. This term (Greek, *nomodidaskalos*), which Paul used only here, is a compound of "law" (*nomos*) and "teacher" (*didaskalos*). Elsewhere in the New Testament, only Luke used this term, identifying rabbis ("doctors of the law," Luke 5:17) and Gamaliel ("a doctor of law," Acts 5:34). The term itself adds little to an understanding of the false teachers' error, except to corroborate a preoccupation with matters of Jewish Torah (law). What is known to have been speculative from 1:4 is here an error worsened by pretense and pontification, a magnification of their misunderstanding (v. 7) and misuse (1:8) of Scripture. Paul said they were far from meriting the title they coveted.

Two asides or digressions follow in 1:8–17. The first expounds the law (1:8–11), prompted by the subject of "teachers of the law" and their misunderstanding. The second expresses personal gratitude (1:12–17), prompted by the "the glorious gospel … committed to my trust" (1:11). In 1:18–20, Paul resumed the purpose of his instructions to Timothy (see 1:3–7).

B. The Purpose of the Law (1:8–11)

1:8–11. The misunderstanding of the law (see 1: 7) prompted Paul to set forth its true intent: to expose and convict. The key to its proper understanding comes in verse 11: the gospel. **The law is**

good (v. 8; see Rom. 7:7–12), if one handles it **lawfully,** that is, correctly. The law is **not made for a righteous man** (v. 9). Here Paul was correcting a misapplication of the law to Christian believers and, by implication, its misapplication by the would-be teachers of 1:7. The law is for **the lawless.** Paul enumerated the kinds of people the law convicts, using a declension of its violators patterned after the Ten Commandments. Paul closed his list with an inclusive indictment of any other violation of the law **that is contrary to sound doctrine** (v. 10). Here "sound doctrine" refers to the correct understanding and use of the law, a proper perspective that is gained from and measured by **the glorious gospel** (v. 11; see Gal. 3:19–24 and discussions). This outlook was not a maverick or secondhand deduction on Paul's part but the truth of the gospel **committed to [his] trust** (see 6:20; 1 Cor. 9:17; Gal. 2:7; 1 Thess. 2:4; 2 Tim. 1:12, 14; 2:2).

III. The Lord's Grace to Paul (1:12–17)

1:12–14. And (v. 12) looks back to "committed to my trust" in 1:11, even as it looks ahead to **counted me faithful.** Paul was profoundly grateful. But the measure of **I thank** (lit., "I am grateful to") points to the enabling work of Jesus Christ in his life. He who was once **a blasphemer, and a persecutor, and injurious** (v. 13; see Acts 9:1; 22:4–5, 19; 26:10–11) had been radically transformed by the mercy and grace of God extended to him in Jesus Christ.

1:15–16. This is a faithful saying (v. 15) is a clause found in the New Testament only in the Pastoral Epistles (here; 3:1; 4:9; 2 Tim. 2:11; Titus 3:8), where it always identifies a key saying. Here the key saying is **that Christ Jesus came into the world to save sinners.** Paul's own transformed life confirmed the faithfulness or dependability of the saying. His turn of phrase using the same Greek word (*prōtos;* "first," "foremost") for both **chief** (v. 15) and **first** (v. 16) showed Paul to be "a prime example" of what it means to be a sinner (see 1:13) and to be a recipient of Christ's mercy.

IV. The Purpose of Paul's Instructions to Timothy (1:18–20)

1:18–19. This charge (Greek, *parangelia;* v. 18) consciously and formally renewed the "charge" of 1:3, 5 (see discussions there). **I commit unto thee, son Timothy** communicated a solemn trust of a somber responsibility. The word "commit" (Greek, *paratithēmi*) means to "entrust" or "give charge" of something into someone's care (see 6:20; 2 Tim. 1:12, 14; 2:2). Paul's good judgment of Timothy's reliability had been reinforced by the Holy Spirit (see Fee, *1 and 2 Timothy, Titus,* p. 57): **according to the prophecies which went before on thee.** In the early church, God revealed His will in various matters through prophets (see Acts 13:1–3, where prophets had an active role in the sending of Paul and Barnabas on their mission to the Gentiles). The prophecies concerning Timothy may have occurred at the time of or before his ordination (4:14), perhaps about twelve years earlier, on Paul's second missionary journey (see Acts 16:3). Prophecies about Timothy seem to have pointed to the significant leadership role he was to have in the church. Now they were to serve the purpose of emboldening Timothy, **that thou by them mightest war a good warfare.** The implements of battle are **faith, and a good conscience** (v. 19), enabling the warrior to stand unswerving (see 1:5–6), or as Paul switched metaphors to nautical terms, anchoring the ship against **shipwreck.**

1:20. Hymeneus (see 2 Tim. 2:17–18) and **Alexander** (perhaps the Alexander of 2 Tim. 4:14 (but see discussion there) had abandoned the true faith and were teaching another gospel. Consequently, Paul executed church discipline (see discussion on Matt. 18:17), and the two were **delivered unto Satan.** Such action excluded them from the church, which was considered a sanctuary from Satan's power. Out in the world, away from the fellowship and care of the church, they would **learn** (basically, "be disciplined") **not to blaspheme** (see 1:13; 6:4). The purpose of such drastic action was more remedial than punitive (for a similar situation, see 1 Cor. 5:5, 13; see also discussion on 1 Cor. 5:5).

V. Instructions concerning the Administration of the Church (chaps. 2–3)

A. Public Worship (chap. 2)

1. Prayer in Public Worship (2:1–8)

2:1. I exhort is a tactful order (see discussion on 1:3); **therefore** is a transitional conjunction introducing what follows as an inference from what precedes. Accordingly, Timothy's success in the purpose for which his stay was required (see 1:3–7, 18–20), to preempt the spread of "other doctrine" (1:3) while pursuing a godly love (2:5), called for prayer. Prayer in all its forms is to be offered **first of all ... for all men**. The emphasis of this chief concern falls on the words "for all men [people]." In the setting of congregational worship (see 2:8), there must be room for all in prayer; no one is beyond its scope and no concern excluded by its form.

2:2. Paul specified that prayers should be offered for **kings, and for all that are in authority**. No distinction is drawn according to benevolence or statesmanship. If anything, rulers who misuse their authority and who oppose Christianity are particularly in view. It must be remembered that the notorious Roman emperor Nero (AD 54–68) was in power when Paul wrote these words. All authority comes from God (see Rom. 13:1), and prayer itself is an acknowledgment of the one King and true Authority. Christians have a reason to pray for pagan authorities: **that we may lead a quiet and peaceable life** (see Jer. 29:7). Civil coexistence is mutual; it involves good governance and good citizenship (see Rom. 13:4–5). Paul had both in view. **Godliness** (Greek, *eusebeia*) implies a good and holy life, with special emphasis on its source: a deep reverence for God. It is a key word (along with "godly") in the Pastorals; the Greek term occurs eight times in 1 Timothy (here; 3:16; 4:7–8; 6:3, 5–6, 11), once in 2 Timothy (3:5), and once in Titus (1:1) but nowhere else in the writings of Paul. **Honesty** (Greek, *semnotēs*; "dignity," "gravity") implies integrity and "moral earnestness, affecting outward demeanour as well as interior intention" (Kelly, *The Pastoral Epistles*, p. 61; see 3:5; Titus 2:7).

2:3–4. A further and extended theological reason to pray "for all men" (2:1) comes here and runs through 2:6: prayers for all to **our Saviour** (v. 3) coincides with the very heart of God, **who will have all men to be saved** (v. 4). This is not a prediction but a characterization of God's desire. Human response is embedded in the passive "to be saved" and the verb **to come unto**. **The knowledge of the truth** is virtually a synonym for the gospel (see 3:15; 4:3).

2:5–6. The foundational tenet of Judaism is that **there is one God** (v. 5; see Deut. 6:4), which every Jew confessed daily in the Shema (see discussion on Mark 12:29). Corresponding to the one God over all is the **one mediator between God and men**. These words hold the key to fathoming 2:3–4 and its connection to all intercessory prayer. **The man Christ Jesus**, in context, is the incarnate mediator: very God, very man (see "Christ Jesus came into the world to save sinners," 1:15). **Ransom for all** (v. 6; see discussion on Matt. 20:28) matches, on the one hand, the scope of His mediation and, on the other, the scope of prayer. "All" is not delimited but is ultimately defined redemptively by one's faith response to the "one mediator," Christ Jesus. **To be testified in due time**, a difficult phrase by all accounts, is idiomatically, "the witness at the appropriate time." Side by side with the words "ransom for all," it attests to the divine timing and testimony of Christ's death as the ransom that authenticates God's desire for the salvation of all men (see 6:13–16; Titus 3:1; Gal. 4:4).

2:7. Whereunto, or "for which reason"—namely, to testify that through His death, Christ has bridged the gap between God and man and made salvation available to all—Paul was appointed **a preacher** ("herald"). This brings into view Paul's missionary proclamation of the good news of salvation. For the word **apostle**, see discussion on Mark 6:30; *KJV Study Bible* note on 1 Corinthians 1:1. The parenthesis, **I speak the truth in Christ, and lie not**, creates emphasis to underscore what follows: **a teacher of the Gentiles in faith and verity**. For this saving message (2:6), Paul was a preacher and an apostle appointed by God, but equally so, he was a teacher. This final phrase entails Paul's calling to the Gentiles, which he elsewhere featured as "the apostle of the Gentiles" (Rom. 11:13; see Gal. 1:16; 2:7, 9; Rom. 1:5; Acts 9:15). Here God's desire to save all men (2:4) is confirmed, with the accent falling on Paul's role as teacher. From this, it may be inferred that the teaching of "other doctrine" (1:3–7) was rooted in Jewish exclusivism, which undermined the teaching of the true gospel Paul represented "in faith and verity." Whatever form the exclusivist Jewish teaching may have taken, Paul had plainly mapped "all" people as the territory charted by the gospel (2:3–7) and "all" therein as the appropriate obligation of prayer.

2:8–14. Some maintain that Paul's teaching here about women is historically conditioned, not universal and timeless. Others view these verses as unaffected by the historical situation and therefore applicable to every age. See *KJV Study Bible* note on 1 Corinthians 11:2–16.

2:8. The Greek for **men** in this verse does not refer to mankind (as in 2:5–6) but to male as distinct from female. That women sometimes prayed in public, however, seems evident from 1 Corinthians 11:5 (see also 1 Tim. 2:9–10). **Every where** (see 1 Cor. 1:2; 2 Cor. 2:14; 1 Thess. 1:8) identifies every place the gospel was proclaimed and Christ the Lord was named, particularly, the congregations or house churches in Ephesus where God's people gathered for worship. **Lifting up holy hands, without wrath and doubting** matches the outward posture of prayer with the inward disposition of the heart. The customary Jewish and Christian manner of lifting hands in prayer turns on the word "holy," which here outwardly refers to hands that are washed and ritually pure. The holiness that prayer demands is inward; one's hands are to be an extension of a pure heart free of harbored anger and stubborn disputes. Such issues were also relevant to Timothy's work.

2. Women in Public Worship (2:9–15)

2:9–10. In like manner also, [I want] women [to pray] in modest apparel is how the structure of the Greek reads most naturally, with "in like manner also" bringing forward from 2:8 the verb "I want/to pray" as verse 9 requires, for it has no verb at all.

The word sequence in Greek sets out the balance of these verses.

I want/ to pray	Therefore	the men	in every place
	In like manner also	women	in modest apparel

In both 2:8 and verse 9, men and women respectively are the subject of "to pray." On the surface, Paul was speaking about the demeanor of the men and women of the church when they congregate in community worship. Men are to come to prayer without anger or unresolved disputes in their hearts. Likewise, women are to come to prayer with lives adorned with good works. Paul did not impose a total ban on the wearing of jewelry or braided hair. Rather, he was expressing caution in a society where such things were signs of extravagant luxury and proud personal display. The greater adornment, Paul said, is attained not through an investment in physical appearance but through godly living, the attire of good works (see discussions on 2:2; 1 Peter 3:3–4). Nothing is to disrupt the spirit of worship, not anger and the wrangling of men, nor the attire and adornments of women.

2:11. Let the woman learn in silence. Paul was not imposing a gag order but directing the spirit of a woman's presence in the assembly. The word translated "silence" (Greek, *hēsuchia*) points to a "quiet" (as in 2:2), not disruptive, demeanor. This corresponds to the prepositional phrase **with all subjection.**

2:12. I suffer not a woman to teach. Paul did not allow women to be official teachers in the assembled church. This is indicated by the added restriction concerning a woman exercising **authority over the man** (see 1 Cor. 11:3), that is, functioning as a bishop (see discussion on 3:1).

2:13–14. Paul based the restrictions regarding a woman's role in the church on Genesis 2–3. The appeal to the creation account makes the restrictions universal and permanent. **Adam was first formed**

(v. 13). Paul appealed to the priority of Adam in creation, which predates the fall. Thus, Paul viewed the man-woman relationship set forth in this passage as grounded in creation. **The woman being deceived** (v. 14). Paul appears to argue that since the woman was deceived (and then led Adam astray), she is not to be entrusted with the teaching function of a bishop (or elder) in the public worship services of the assembled church.

2:15. The influence of Genesis continues here, specifically Genesis 3:16, which discusses childbirth. Three possible meanings of this verse are: (1) it speaks of the godly woman finding fulfillment in her role as wife and mother in the home when her children are disciplined in godliness; (2) it refers to women being saved spiritually through the most significant birth of all, the incarnation of Christ; or (3) it refers to women being kept physically safe in childbirth.

It may be added that all three meanings attempt to do justice to the passage and at the same time to appreciate the importance that Paul placed on the role of motherhood in answering the concern of 2:11 and any woman who would "usurp masculine functions" (Kelly, *Pastoral Epistles*, p. 70). In particular, the differences pivot on the meaning of the phrase **saved in childbearing**.

The first possible meaning takes "childbearing" as the act of giving birth (see Gen. 5:16) and as an expression of motherhood and a woman's role within the family (see 2:11; Gen. 3:15b). Thus, "saved in childbearing" means it will "deliver" her from falling into transgression due to deception (see 2:14; see also Paul's instruction in 2:11–12). Paul then clarified his use of "saved" by adding that such is the case for any woman (**they**) if she is truly a Christian, one who continues in the faith (see Fee, *1 and 2 Timothy, Titus*, p. 76). This may have had added bearing in Paul's mind because the false teachers prohibited marriage (4:3). Although it is not clear whether Paul touched on the very issues regarding women (2:13–14; Gen. 2–3) that the false teachers used to validate such a prohibition, Paul was clearly endorsing motherhood and marriage (see 5:14–15).

The second possible meaning is distinguished by taking the words "in childbearing" (lit., "through the childbirth," with the article in Greek) as referring to a specific birth, the birth of Christ. Implicitly, Eve and Mary are juxtaposed as representatives of all women. Further justification for this unusual and unparalleled use of the expression is drawn from Genesis 3:15, with its contrast of "thy seed and her seed" (offspring). "Saved," then, is taken in its most natural sense, as saved from sin by virtue of the redemption won through Christ. Others would point out, however, that not only is such a reference to Christ obscure; it is an irregular use of the noun "childbearing" and a misunderstanding of Genesis 3:15.

The third possible meaning takes **childbearing** as the fact of giving birth and **saved** as meaning the woman is kept physically safe in the course of giving birth (presumably from death or injury). However, Genesis 3:16 presupposes the survival of both child and mother. What is more, Paul with this understanding here makes weak sense of the context. The first meaning is the better of the three possible readings.

B. Qualifications for Church Officers (3:1–13)

1. Bishops (3:1–7)

3:1. True saying is identical to the wording of 1:15 (see discussion there). The word for **office of a bishop** (Greek, *episkopē*) points to the function and responsibility of oversight. In the Greek culture, the word "bishop" (Greek, *episkopos*; 3:2) was used of a presiding official in a civic or religious organization. Here it refers to a man who oversees a local congregation. The equivalent word from the Jewish background of Christianity is "elder." The terms "bishop" (or "overseer") and "elder" are used interchangeably in Acts 20:17, 28; Titus 1:5–7; 1 Peter 5:1–2. The duties of a bishop were to teach and preach (see 3:2; 5:17), to direct the affairs of the church (see 3:5; 5:17), to shepherd ("pastor") the flock of God (see Acts 20:28), and to guard the church from error (see Acts 20:28–31).

3:2–3. If any man expressed a desire to become a bishop, or Timothy and the church detected such a desire on the part of any man, his character and qualification for the office were to be measured. **A bishop … must be** (v. 2) enumerates the qualities a candidate must have (see chart, *KJV Study Bible*, p. 1741). That the man be **the husband of one wife** is a qualification derived from a general principle that applies to any violation of God's marriage law, whether in the form of polygamy or of marital unfaithfulness (see discussion on Titus 1:6). **Vigilant** (Greek, *nēphalios*; see 3:11; Titus 2:2) is more commonly used of sobriety but is used here in the wider sense of "levelheaded." One would think **sober** (Greek, *sōphrōn*; see Titus 1:8;2:2, 5) pertains to inebriation, but it refers to sound judgment and measured, moderate living. **Of good behaviour** (Greek, *kosmion*; see 2:9) identifies admirable and dignified conduct, that which is praiseworthy in the sight of others. **Hospitality** (Greek, *philoxenia*; see 5:10; Rom. 12:13; 1 Peter 4:9) means to provide domestic care to others with an openhearted and openhanded welcome. **Apt to teach** (Greek, *didaktikos*; see 2 Tim. 2:24) points to the skilled responsibilities of preaching and teaching that should belong to the elder, or bishop (5:17; see Titus 1:9). **Not given to wine** (v. 3; Greek, *paroinos*; see Titus 1:7) contains a compound word: the preposition *par*- being a marker of nearness or connection and –*oinos*, meaning wine. It suggests a person characterized by, even defined by, wine and pertains to one who is given to drinking too much. **No striker** (Greek, *plēktēs*; see Titus 1:7) means the elder should not easily resort to fists or violence; the overseer certainly should not be a bully. **Not greedy of filthy lucre** (Greek, *aischrokerdē*; see Titus 1:7) dictates that the elder not be someone who is greedy for money and inclined to pursue shameful gain. **Patient** (Greek, *epieikēs*) refers to a yielding, gentle kindness, rather than an insistence on one's own rights. **Not a brawler** (Greek, *amachos*; see Titus 3:2) is an adjective that is shorthand for "must not strive" (2 Tim. 2:24) or "must not be quarrelsome." **Not covetous** (Greek, *aphilarguros*; see Heb. 13:5) reiterates that the elder should not be a lover of money (see 1 Tim. 6:10).

3:4–5. A bishop should be **One that ruleth well his own house** (v. 4), emphasizing the tested leadership of a man pastoring his own household. One cannot give leadership to a house church if the rule of **his own house** (v. 5) disqualifies him (for the use of "ruleth" and "rule," see discussion on Rom. 12:8). **Having his children in subjection** (v. 4) indicates that the quality of a father's leadership can be seen in the honor his children pay to his authority. **With all gravity** (Greek, *semnotēs*; see 2:2 and discussion) may here apply to the father and candidate to the office rather than to the children. For the father, it suggests a generally virtuous headship of his home; for the children, it suggests proper respect. For **church** (Greek, *ekklēsia*), see discussion on Matthew 16:18.

3:6–7. These verses both end with a reference to the Devil and point up the spiritual warfare that besets anyone who assumes the office of bishop, therefore emphasizing the caliber of spiritual maturity required. **Not a novice** (v. 6), or "neophyte" (Greek, *neophyton*; "newly planted"), calls for a man seasoned in his faith and one more fully grown in Christ. **Pride** is a target of the Devil's **condemnation**, the accuser of the brethren (see Rev. 12:9–10). **A good report of them which are without** (v. 7) specifies those outside the community of believers. Paul spoke of one's "testimony" here as he did elsewhere (see 1 Thess. 4:12; 1 Cor. 10:32; Col. 4:5).

2. Deacons (3:8–13)

3:8–10. In its nontechnical usage, **deacon** (Greek, *diakonos*; v. 10) means simply "one who serves." The men chosen in Acts 6:1–6 probably were not only the first deacons mentioned in the New Testament but also the first to be appointed in the church (but see discussions there). Generally, their service was meant to free the elders to give full attention to prayer and the ministry of the Word (see Acts 6:2, 4). The only two local church offices mentioned in the New Testament are those of bishop (or overseer; also called elder) and deacon (see Phil. 1:1).

In substance, the character qualifications for the deacon virtually mirror those of the overseer, with the notable omission of "apt to teach" (3:2), which may be a clue to the distinction of these two roles. **Holding the mystery of the faith** (v. 9) is best explained by Titus 1:9. If the use of "mystery" here bears any resemblance to Paul's use elsewhere, it alludes to the revelation of God in Jesus Christ, the core teaching of the gospel. A deacon should have a **pure conscience** and be **proved** (v. 10) and **found blameless**, reinforcing that the office of deacon must be occupied by men of "known" Christian character and unswerving devotion to Christ.

3:11. Wives (lit., "women") is followed in Greek by the word "likewise," or "in the same manner" (see 2:9 and discussion) The verb **must** is supplied here, as it is in 3:8 (from 3:2). The Greek for "wives" could refer to (1) deacons' wives, (2) deaconesses, or (3) female deacons. To many, the fact that deacons are referred to again in 3:12–13 is a proof that deacons' wives are the topic rather than a separate office of deaconess or female deacons. This raises the question of why deacons' wives would be addressed when overseers' wives are not. Either the wives of overseers and deacons are both intended, the fitness of **their** character called to mind by 3:10 and not to be forgotten in the case of either an overseer or a deacon, or here is a case of a recognized role for women in the service the deaconate supplies the church (see discussion on 3:8). There is no separate term for "deaconess" in the New Testament, only the one word, the masculine "deacon," as used of Phoebe in Romans 16:1.

3:12–14. The husbands of one wife (v. 12), treated first in the qualifications of the overseer (see discussion on 3:2), is here treated almost as an afterthought. Unless Paul was saying that marriage is required of all overseers and deacons, he meant that if a man is married, looking to his marriage and home is a good way to discern his character. Here Paul conflated in one concise statement the substance of 3:2, 4. **Used the office of a deacon** (v. 13) emphasizes service that has met standards of expectation or excellence in some recognized way. Deacons who excel may expect to gain a dual outcome. First, they **well purchase to themselves a good degree**, which may be worded, "gain for themselves good standing." This suggests enhanced credibility within the believing community. Second, they gain **great boldness in the faith which is in Christ Jesus**. In other words, they can expect their faith in Christ to grow

confident in its expression right along with their exemplary service.

C. Purpose of These Instructions (3:14–16)

3:14–15. These things (v. 14) entail the scope of the whole letter. Paul expressed his hope of making a personal visit **shortly** but allowed for a delay. His impending visit (see 4:13) made conspicuous his personal commitment to the enforcement of this matters. Here, in brief, Paul stated his purpose for writing the letter: **that thou mayest know how thou oughtest to behave thyself** (v. 15). The Greek, however, does not convey such an individual focus and should be rendered: "that you may know how 'people' ought to conduct 'themselves.'" This is borne out by the context. Simply put, Paul's purpose was to safeguard the church in Ephesus. This is why Timothy had been instructed to stay, why Paul had sent written instructions to his envoy, and why the apostle himself was coming. **The house of God** and **the church of the living God** are synonymous and stand for the people of God gathered in local houses of worship. Nevertheless, "house" is a vibrant metaphor and leads to the structural importance of column and foundation. People are "bearers" of God's truth. Their conduct and behavior show what they are made of. In Ephesus, **the truth** (see 3:16) and those who bore the truth were in spiritual jeopardy because of the treachery of assailing spirits and the false doctrines of hypocritical liars (see 1:3–7; 4:1–5; 6:3–5, 20–21).

3:16. The word "mystery" is found throughout the New Testament, particularly in Paul's writings (see discussions on Mark 4:11; Rom. 11:25; Col. 1:26). The phrase **the mystery of godliness** means "the revealed secret of true piety," that is, the secret that produces piety in people. That secret, as the following words indicate, is none other than Jesus Christ. His incarnation, in all its aspects (particularly His saving work), is the source of genuine piety. The words are printed in poetic form and could have come from an early creedal hymn (see discussion on Col. 3:16). The adjective **great** is validated by a series of proofs, the aggregate of which forms a grand crescendo to the majesty of this mystery. **Justified in the Spirit** summarizes a ministry characterized by the power of the Spirit. The Holy Spirit enabled Jesus to drive out demons (see Matt. 12:28) and perform miracles. Most important, the Spirit raised Jesus from the dead (see Rom. 1:4; 1 Peter 3:18) and thereby vindicated Him, showing that He was indeed the Son of God. **Seen of angels** speaks of the unearthly and angelic testimony that announced His resurrection (see Matt. 28:2) and ascension (see Acts 1:10).

VI. Methods of Dealing with False Teaching (chap. 4)

A. False Teaching Described (4:1–5)

4:1–2. At face value, **the Spirit speaketh expressly** (v. 1) means that He speaks "clearly," "explicitly," or "precisely" (see, e.g., Matt. 24:11; Mark 13:22; Acts 20:29–30; 2 Thess. 2:3). Paul, however, was perhaps speaking here of a specific revelation given to him by the Spirit. **In the latter times** refers to the time beginning with the first coming of Christ (see 1 Peter 1:20; see discussion on Heb. 1:1). That Paul was not referring only to the time immediately prior to Christ's second coming is obvious from his assumption in 4:7 that the false teachings were already present at the time of this writing. **Some shall depart from the faith** refers not to false teachers but to some within "the house of God" (3:15) that were **giving heed to seducing spirits, and doctrines of devils** (lit., "demons") in the hypocrisy of liars. Although it is not as clear in the KJV, Paul was saying that the human agents who cloak the deceptive work of Satan (see 5:15) are liars who are without properly working consciences. **Seared** (Greek, *kaustēriazō*; v. 2) suggests either "cauterized" or "branded," the effects of hellish influence. How dangerous is the lie of someone who has himself been deceived and no longer knows the difference between right or wrong? (See Titus 1:15; for the importance of a pure and clean conscience to the Christian, see 1:5, 19; 3:9.)

4:3–5. The unbiblical asceticism described in verse 3 arose out of the mistaken belief that the material world was evil, which was a central belief of the Gnostic heresy (see 1 John, Introduction: "Gnosticism"). Those who hold to and impose on others ascetic regulations certainly condemn others who do not hold the same views and who partake of the things prohibited. Such judgment, Paul implied, falls on God Himself, who created what they forbid and who made it to be received with thanksgiving, not condemnation. Paul addressed the issue of freedom (reception and thanksgiving) elsewhere (see, e.g., Rom. 14:14, 20–23; 1 Cor. 10:29–30; Titus 1:15; Acts 10:15), passages that serve as an apt commentary to what he wrote here.

B. Methods of Dealing with False Teaching (4:6–16)

4:6–8. Paul turned to Timothy with personal attention to his task of facing false teaching. For **fables** (v. 7), see discussion on 1:4. **Exercise thyself rather unto godliness** is Paul's call for a regimen of training not unlike that in the realm of athletics. "Exercise [the Greek verb *gymnazō*] ... unto godliness" and **bodily exercise** (the Greek noun *gymnasia*; v. 8) are words that evoke images of athletic competition. **Profiteth little** introduces a comparison of what is limited to this world with what is eternal: **godliness** (see discussion on 2:2) requires self-discipline just like that of an athlete but has gains and rewards that are out of this world.

4:9–10. The **faithful saying** (v. 9; see discussion on 1:15) in this instance refers back to the seemingly proverbial statement in 4:8b. The words **labour and suffer reproach** (v. 10) may refer to the exercising mentioned in 4:7b–8. For **trust**, see discussion on 1:1. Obviously, **Saviour of all** does not mean that God saves every person from eternal punishment, for such universalism would contradict the clear testimony of Paul and of Scripture. God is, however, the Savior of all in that He offers salvation to all and saves all who come to Him.

4:11. These things (particularly as in 4:8b–10) were not to inspire Timothy alone; he was to invigorate and inspire the rest of the community in the strongest possible way: **command and teach** (see 4:15).

4:12. Let no man despise thy youth. Timothy was probably in his midthirties or younger, and in that day, such an influential position was not usually held by a man so young. For this reason, his leadership had perhaps been called into question. Even if Timothy faced contempt and a lack of appreciation, he was to become **an example** (Greek, *typos*; "pattern").

4:13. Till I come points back to Paul's intended visit (see 3:14). His journey had taken him from Ephesus to Macedonia, but he hoped to rejoin Timothy soon at Ephesus. **Give attendance to reading, to exhortation, to doctrine**. "Reading" is a term with a fixed reference to the reading of Scripture in the assembly (see Acts 13:15; 2 Cor. 3:14). Its order is significant, for the Scripture was to be the foundation of Timothy's exhortation (teaching and preaching) as well that as of the elders' (see "in the word and doctrine," 5:17). This is corroborated by the serviceability of the Scripture in 2 Timothy 3:16.

4:14. The gift that is in thee alludes to an interior grace or "spiritual" gift (Greek, *charisma*; referring to an endowment of "grace," *charis*). For **prophecy**, see discussion on 1:18. The prophecy together **with the laying on of the hands of the presbytery** suggests a kind of ordination attended by the elders as a body. The word "presbytery" formally denotes a council of elders, and the word "elder" in Greek is *presbyteros*.

4:15. Here is a final reiteration of 4:12–14. **Meditate** is here nearer to "endeavor," and **profiting** speaks of "progress" or "furtherance" (see Phil. 1:12, 25, the only other occurrences in the New Testament).

4:16. Thou shalt both save thyself, and them that hear thee. God alone saves, but Christians can be God's instruments to bring about the salvation of others. "Save thyself" indicates that salvation is both an event and a process. Believers are saved at the time of conversion but are still being saved in the sense of being conformed more and more to Christ's image (see 1 Cor. 1:18) and ultimately glorified.

VII. Methods of Dealing with Different Groups in the Church (5:1–6:2)

A. The Elderly and Younger People (5:1–2)

5:1–2. Treatment of different age groups calls for consideration. **Rebuke not an elder** (v. 1) speaks not of an official but of a man who is one's senior in age and therefore deserving of respect. "Elder" (Greek, *presbyteros*) is matched by its feminine counterpart in the next verse: **elder women** (Greek, *presbytera*; v. 2). "Rebuke" is a strong term (Greek, *epiplēssō*), the verb of the noun "striker" (Greek, *plēktēs*) in 3:3. As Kelly (*The Pastoral Epistles*, p. 110) points out, "it connotes rough treatment." **Intreat** (Greek, *parakaleō*; v. 1) means to treat in an inviting or congenial manner. This verb governs elders as fathers, young men as brothers, elder women as mothers, and younger women as sisters. **With all purity** (v. 2; see 4:12), by deduction, applies in particular to young women and connotes moral or chaste conduct and thought. Here is a picture of community care and respect modeled on the family that now in Christ belongs to the household or family of God.

B. Widows (5:3–16)

5:3. Honour widows that are widows indeed, that is, widows who are truly left alone and destitute (see 5:4–5). This probably means taking care of them, including the giving of material support. Widows were particularly vulnerable in ancient societies because no pensions, government assistance, life insurance, or the like were available to them.

5:4. Responsible care for the widow belongs first to her family before it belongs to others. **Shew piety at home**, that is, the "godliness" (see discussion on 2:2) that so prominently figures in the Pastoral Epistles and that is to characterize the Christian (3:16; 4:7–8; 6:3, 5–6, 11; 2 Tim. 3:5; Titus 1:1).

5:5–6. The disposition of the **widow indeed** (v. 5), or a genuine widow in need, is contrasted with its counterfeit. **Dead while she liveth** (v. 6) connotes one who is dead spiritually while living physically.

5:7–8. Widows too are to be **blameless** (v. 7), above reproach. **If any provide not for his own** (v. 8) again picks up the topic of irresponsibility on the part of believing families (see 5:4). Such dereliction of duty to family is defined in spiritual terms: **denied the faith, and is worse than an infidel.** How pitiful that pagan codes of duty to family should be elevated by the inferior conduct of a family within the family of God.

5:9–10. Paul provided further instructions regarding the qualification and treatment of widows. **Taken into the number** (v. 9) refers to a recognized "official" list. The church in Ephesus seems to have maintained a list of widows supported by the church. While there is no evidence of an order of widows comparable to that of the bishops, it appears that those on the list were expected to devote themselves to prayer (see 5:5) and **good works** (v. 10). Among the identifying qualifications, the widows were to **have washed the saints' feet**, a menial but necessary task performed for all arrivals because of dusty roads and the wearing of sandals (see John 13:14).

5:11–12. Younger widows (v. 11; see the age limit in 5:9) are not to be enrolled as "widows indeed" (5:5). For one, the yearning to marry (**wax wanton**, as amorous desires) might be stronger than their devotion to Christ, and as a result, young widows often do not remain unmarried (see 1 Cor. 7:39–40). Incurring **damnation** (v. 12) may be too strong but surely refers to a condemnatory verdict. The gravity depends on the meaning of **cast off their first faith**, which may refer to breaking a "pledge" or renouncing the faith they professed in Christ. Perhaps when a widow was added to the list, she pledged special devotion to Christ, which would be diminished by remarriage. Paul may have been referring to the believer's basic trust in Christ, which a widow would compromise by marrying outside the faith.

5:13. A second reason younger widows are not to be enrolled is that their behavior is too often unworthy of honor (see 5:3), contrary to the model of the "widow indeed" (5:5, 10) and anything but "blameless" (5:7).

5:14–15. Instead of enrollment (see 5:9) for the **younger** (v. 14) widows, Paul endorsed remarriage, motherhood, and family as the answer to the needs of a young woman who proves to be blameless (see 5:7) and beyond the slander of the Adversary, **Satan** (see discussions on Zech. 3:1; Matt. 16:23; Rev. 12:10). Paul's directions in 5:11–14 addressed recent experience (**already**). Following Satan should not be conceived as conscious and deliberate but as

the opposite of following after Christ and as the outcome of deception (see 4:1–2).

5:16. A recap of the necessary obligation of family and community responsibility to **widows indeed** (see especially 5:3–8).

C. Elders (5:17–25)

5:17. All **elders** (see discussion on 5:19) are to exercise leadership (3:4–5) and to teach and preach (3:2), and all are to receive honor. Those who excel in leadership are to **be counted worthy of double honour**. This is especially true of those who labor at teaching and preaching. That such honor should include financial support is indicated by the two illustrations in 5:18. **Rule** (Greek, *proistēmi*) means to exercise a position of leadership (see Rom. 12:8 and discussion).

5:18. The term **scripture** (Greek, *graphē*) was used to identify any part or the whole of God's authoritative Word, what Christians today call the Old Testament but then the threefold Jewish division of Scripture: the Law, the Prophets, and the Writings (see Luke 24:44). The use of this term for both an Old Testament (Deut. 25:4) and a New Testament (Luke 10:7) passage shows that by this time, portions of the New Testament, certainly the words of Jesus, were considered to be equal in authority to the Old Testament Scriptures.

5:19–20. The title **elder** (Greek, *presbyteros*; v. 19) is interchangeable with the title "overseer" (see Titus 1:5–9; Acts 20:17, 20; 1 Peter 5:1–2), which explains why Paul did not enumerate their qualifications separately. The default honor due the office of the elder (see 5:17) involves not only the presumption but also the defense of innocence in the case of an accusation. **Receive not an accusation, but before two or three witnesses** because allegations are not proven without corroboration. The principle of corroboration was a time-honored Jewish legal standard (see Deut. 19:15; Heb. 10:28; Matt. 18:16; John 8:17; 2 Cor. 13:1). "Receive not" implies "do not acknowledge as correct" without corroboration. Spiritual warfare takes many forms and enemy assaults involve those who take the lead (see "rule," 5:17). Even so, no elder is above the rule of the Lord, and **Them that sin** (v. 20) calls for open rebuke within the community of believers. The context assumes both the required corroboration and that Paul was speaking of the discipline of elders. Unlike in 5:1, **rebuke** (Greek, *elenchō*) here means "to expose" the fault or wrongdoing. In itself, such action is a clear correction of sin and a reinforcement of what is right. The primary purpose is **that others also may fear**, a reference to other elders first of all and no less to others subject to such "exposure." "Fear," then, implies the fearful respect of the office and ultimately of the Lord's leadership (see 5:21).

5:21. The importance of the elders' most solemn **charge** is administrating justice without prejudice or partiality. The importance of this charge is seen in Paul's invoking the sight of God, the Lord Jesus Christ, and the divine retinue (see 2 Tim. 4:1). **Elect angels** stands in contrast to Satan and the other fallen angels. Fee (*1 and 2 Timothy, Titus*, p. 131) suggested the gravity concerns "erring elders who, as false teachers, are having considerable influence in the community."

5:22. Lay hands suddenly on no man refers to the ordination of an elder, which should not be performed until the candidate has had time to prove himself. **Neither be partaker of other men's sins** is a warning against the ordination a person unworthy of the office of elder. In the context of ordination and elder credibility, **keep thyself pure** reminded Timothy of the necessity of leading a blameless life.

5:23. Drink no longer water is a parenthetical comment in Paul's discussion of elders. In view of Timothy's physical ailments, and perhaps because safe drinking water was often difficult to find, Paul advised him to drink a little wine.

5:24–25. Paul returned to the general topic of the qualification and disqualification of elders as it relates to the issue of **sins** (v. 24) and **good works** (v. 25). Paul advised being alert to hidden sins as well as to good deeds in the lives of candidates for ordination.

D. Servants (6:1–2)

6:1–2. For **servants** (v. 1), see discussions on Ephesians 6:5; Colossians 3:22–4:1. After treating the Christian disposition toward slaves in general, Paul took up the matter of slaves and their masters within the church. A servant was not to exploit his Christian brotherhood in a way that failed to respect or took liberties with his master (see Kelly, *The Pastoral Epistles*, p. 131). Scenarios abound. It is conceivable that a servant held a higher position within the church (deacon, elder) than that of his master. The reverse was also possible. Whatever the case, they were to love as brothers. **These things teach and exhort** (v. 2) probably belongs to the topic of false teachers and refers to the instructions beginning in 5:3.

VIII. Miscellaneous Matters (6:3–19)

A. False Teachers (6:3–5)

6:3–5. Paul returned to the subject of the treacherous teachings of "other doctrine[s]" (1:3) that contradicted and opposed the Lord and godly instruction (see discussion on 1:3–11). Notable is that these teachings were rooted in pride, which correlates to the strife and disharmony that resulted. **Destitute of the truth** (v. 5) means that the heretical teachers had once known the truth but had been led into error. **Supposing that gain is godliness** refers to godliness as a means of profit. Since Paul had exposed their interior motives and exterior effects, "godliness" for them was a pretense. The show of godliness was a way to turn a buck. Charlatans were a common problem then. Among the Gentiles, Paul had to overcome the stigma of godliness that was a show of charlatans — Paul needed to distinguish himself (see 1 Thess. 2:4–9; *KJV Study Bible* note on 2 Cor. 11:7). Such charlatans continue to operate and be exposed today.

B. Love of Money (6:6–10)

6:6–7. Some make "godliness" a means gain (v. 5). Paul capitalized on that by speaking (or writing) of godliness and contentment. **Godliness with contentment** (v. 6) is a strong antidote to greed (6:5), especially if one soberly appreciates the true measure of earthly acquisition and self-interest: **we brought nothing into this world, and … we can carry nothing out** (v. 7).

6:8. Implicit in godliness is the sufficiency and satisfaction of God. Beyond that, **food and raiment** are for spiritual support and sustenance of the physical only (see Matt. 6:25–34).

6:9–10. They that will be rich (v. 9) expresses a determination to have more, and Paul's own glossary on the desire defines it as **the love of money** (Greek, *philarguria*; v. 10; used only here in New Testament). That avarice is the root of all kinds of evil is amply illustrated in Scripture and no less here by Paul. Of all its tragedy, the supreme grief is that **they have erred from the faith.** Does this truth add a reason for Jesus' ample teaching on the subject?

C. Charge to Timothy (6:11–16)

6:11–12. In contrast to 6:9–10, Paul turned to Timothy with an emphatic **But thou** (v. 11) and the striking direct address **O man of God**. Since the man who loves money and the man of God serve different masters (see Matt. 6:24), Timothy was to **flee these things** and in haste **follow after** the true riches, the virtues of God. For **godliness**, see discussion on 2:2. Paul's imagery then moved to the battlefield of faith, where **lay hold on eternal life** (v. 12; see 6:19) is a battle cry to claim what one has already won. Timothy had possessed eternal life since he was first saved, but Paul urged him to claim its benefits in greater fullness (see 6:17–19; discussion on 4:16). **Professed a good profession** is probably a reference to Timothy's confession of faith at his baptism, during Paul's first missionary journey.

6:13. The image of giving testimony before many witnesses (see 6:12) includes in its assembly God the Father and **Christ Jesus**, the supreme witness. **Before Pontius Pilate** is a historical and juridical reference to Christ's testimony, on pain of death (see His statements in John 18:33–37; 19:10–11).

6:14–16. This commandment (v. 14) most likely refers to the whole charge given to Timothy to preach the gospel and care for the church (see 6:20), though the preceding context may indicate that Paul used the singular "commandment" to sum up the various commands listed in 6:11–12. **The appearing of our Lord Jesus Christ** conveys the vindication of every witness who holds fast to his testimony. How soon may such an appearing be expected? The answer is, **in his times** (v. 15). Just as Jesus' first coming occurred at the precise time God wanted (Gal. 4:4), so also His second coming will occur at God's appointed time. The glory of Christ's appearing is ranked by the titles He bears: **King of kings, and Lord of lords** (see Rev. 19:16). For **whom no man hath seen, nor can see**, see discussion on John 1:18.

D. The Rich (6:17–19)

6:17–19. Because of the treachery of wealth, the temptation to love it more than the Lord, Paul provided instruction for those who possess great earthly treasure. **Laying up** (v. 19) is probably a direct reminiscence of Jesus' advice (see Matt. 6:19–20). **Lay hold on eternal life** (see discussion on 6:12) is an image of laying hold of or clutching eternal treasure that cannot be taken away (see 6:7).

IX. Concluding Appeal (6:20–21)

6:20–21. That which is committed to thy trust (v. 20) is the gospel. The same command is found in 2 Timothy 1:14. **Avoiding**, or "turning away," is deliberately contrasted with **some professing** (v. 21) belief who did not turn from such things (implied). They **erred**, that is, they "wandered" (Greek, *astocheō*; "deviate," "depart"; see 1:6) from the faith and so "turned away" (see 1:5; 5:15), something Timothy was to do from **profane and vain babblings, and oppositions of science falsely so called** (v. 21). The Greek word translated "science" is normally translated "knowledge." This is a reference to an early form of the heresy of Gnosticism, which taught that one may be saved by knowledge (the term "Gnosticism" comes from the Greek word for "knowledge"; see 1 John, Introduction: "Gnosticism.")

THE SECOND EPISTLE OF PAUL
THE APOSTLE TO TIMOTHY

INTRODUCTION

Author, Date, and Place of Composition

After Paul's release from prison in Rome in AD 62/63 (see Acts 28) and after his fourth missionary journey (see map, *Zondervan KJV Study Bible*, pp. 2462–63), during which he wrote 1 Timothy and Titus, Paul was again imprisoned under Emperor Nero circa AD 66–67. It was during this time that he wrote 2 Timothy. In contrast to his first imprisonment, when he lived in a rented house (see Acts 28:30), he now languished in a cold dungeon (4:13), chained like a common criminal (1:16; 2:9). His friends had a hard time even finding out where he was being kept (1:17). Paul knew that his work was done and that his life was nearly at an end (4:6–8).

Theme

Paul had three reasons for writing to Timothy at this time. First, Paul was lonely. Phygellus and Hermogenes, "all they which are in Asia" (1:15), and Demas (4:10) had deserted him. Crescens, Titus, and Tychicus were away (4:10–12), and only Luke was with him (4:11). Paul wanted very much for Timothy to join him also. Timothy was his fellow worker (see Rom. 16:21) who, "as a son with the father" (Phil. 2:22), had served closely with him (see 1 Cor. 4:17). Paul could say of Timothy, "I have no man likeminded" (Phil. 2:20). He longed for Timothy (1:4) and twice asked him to come soon (4:9, 21). For more information on Timothy, see 1 Timothy, Introduction: "Recipient."

Second, Paul was concerned about the welfare of the churches during this time of persecution under Nero, and he admonished Timothy to guard the gospel (1:14), to persevere in it (3:14), to keep on preaching it (4:2), and, if necessary, to suffer for it (1:8; 2:3).

Third, Paul wanted to write to the Ephesian church through Timothy (see discussion on 4:22).

Outline

I. Introduction (1:1–4)
II. Paul's Concern for Timothy (1:5–14)
III. Paul's Situation (1:15–18)

Bibliography

Fee, Gordon D. *The Pastoral Epistles*. New International Biblical Commentary. Peabody, MA: Hendrickson, 1988.

Guthrie, Donald. *The Pastoral Epistles*. Tyndale New Testament Commentaries. Downers Grove, IL: InterVarsity, 1957.

Kelly, J. N. D. *The Pastoral Epistles*. London: Adam & Charles Black, 1963.

Kent, Homer, Jr. *The Pastoral Epistles*. Chicago: Moody, 1971.

Liefeld, Walter L. *1 and 2 Timothy, Titus*. The NIV Application Commentary. Grand Rapids, MI: Zondervan, 1999.

EXPOSITION

I. Introduction (1:1–4)

1:1. An apostle is one specially commissioned by Christ (see discussions on Mark 6:30; 1 Cor. 1:1; Heb. 3:1) **according to the promise of life**. Paul's being chosen to be an apostle was in keeping with that promise, and apostles were appointed to preach and explain the good news that eternal life is available to all who will receive it through faith in Christ.

1:2. My dearly beloved son (see 1 Tim. 1:2, 18; 2 Tim. 2:1; Titus 1:4) is not unique to Paul's correspondence with Timothy (1 Cor. 4:17; Phil. 2:22). "Son" is an appropriate inference in translation, but the Greek term in all the references cited here is *teknon*, "child." For the words **Grace** and **peace**, see discussions on Jonah 4:2; John 14:27; 20:19; Galatians 1:3; Ephesians 1:2.

1:3. I thank God ... in my prayers belongs to Paul's custom of opening a letter with thanksgiving (see discussion on Phil. 1:3–4). Paul's "thanksgiving" is a hallmark of his otherwise Hellenistic letter style and normally included intercession and even blessing. Its omission in Galatians, 1 Timothy, and Titus is a telling reminder that its presence was no mere convention. Here the stern business of the first letter to Timothy had not preempted this warm thanksgiving. **From my forefathers** points to Paul's family background and espies the influence of Timothy's heritage (see 1:5). **Night and day** comes from Paul's Jewish division of time ("a day") and is here akin to our "around the clock."

1:4. Greatly desiring to see thee reflects Paul's primary purpose for writing: he wished for Timothy to visit him (see 4:9, 21) during his final days in Rome (see 4:6–8). **Mindful of thy tears** may refer to Timothy's tears when Paul left for Macedonia (see 1 Tim. 1:3). If, however, the hypothesis of a second imprisonment is correct (see "Author, Date, and Place of Composition"), it may also suggest, as Kelly

(*The Pastoral Epistles*, p. 156) entertains, his arrest at Ephesus and his last sight of Timothy as Paul, in custody, was led to Rome.

II. Paul's Concern for Timothy (1:5–14)

1:5. Faith is not inherited, but it may be engendered by respected models, as it was in the Timothy's case: **the unfeigned faith that is in thee, which dwelt first in thy grandmother Lois, and thy mother Eunice.** According to Acts 16:1, Timothy's mother was a Jewish Christian. His grandmother too was a Christian. Timothy's father, however, was a Greek and possibly an unbeliever (see Acts 16:1). It was probably because of him that Timothy had not been circumcised as a child. "Unfeigned faith" is literally, "without the face of a hypocrite," and therefore without pretense but rather genuine, authentic faith, judged so because it is transparent.

1:6. Paul reminded Timothy to **stir up the gift of God** because gifts are seeded, not given in full bloom; they need to be cultivated through use. Paul's metaphor is that of a spark that is "stirred," or better "fanned," into a flame and presumably stoked into a roaring fire. **By the putting on of my hands** points to Paul as God's instrument through whom the gift came from the Holy Spirit to Timothy (see discussion on 1 Tim. 1:18).

1:7–8. Here the gift par excellence, the endowment of the Holy Spirit (note its fruit), is contrasted: **God hath not given us the spirit of fear; but of power, and of love, and of a sound mind** (v. 7). Apparently, timidity or a lack of confidence was a serious problem for Timothy (see 1 Cor. 16:10–11; 1 Tim. 4:12). The call to stand assertively for the Lord and show allegiance to His servants is as relevant to the timid today as it was to Timothy but cannot be accomplished without God's assistance, the enabling power of the Spirit (see 1:14). The topic of shame and **the gospel according to the power of God** (v. 8) is reminiscent of Romans 1:16.

1:9–10. The afflictions of the gospel (see v. 8, also 12) are to be shouldered not according to human strength but "according to the power of God" (v. 8). Paul set the assurance of God's power beside the as-

surance of our salvation ("hath saved us and called us," v. 9) and Savior (v. 10), a certainty **not according to our works, but according to his own purpose and grace** (v. 9). Salvation is by grace alone and is based not on human effort but on God's saving plan and the gracious gift of His Son (see Rom. 3:28; Eph. 2:8–9; Titus 3:5). **Before the world began**, in eternity past, God's plan to save lost sinners was made (see Eph. 1:4; 1 Peter 1:20; Rev. 13:8).

1:11–12. Paul, **a preacher, and an apostle** (v. 11; see discussion on 1 Tim. 2:7), assured Timothy that he had and did follow his own advice. Moreover, as crucial and cardinal as right doctrine was to Paul and the themes of the Pastoral Epistles (see, e.g., 1:13), personal faith in the person of God was even more important. **That day** (v. 12) refers to the day of the Lord, the day of judgment.

1:13. Sound words (see discussion on Titus 1:9) probably refers to "right doctrine" (see "the truth," Titus 1:14) in a general way. In the Pastoral Epistles, the word "sound" (Greek, *hugiainō*) is used eight times and only in the letters of doctrine (here; "sound doctrine," 4:3; 1 Tim. 1:10; Titus 1:9; 2:1; the "wholesome [sound] words" of the Lord, 1 Tim. 6:3; "sound in the faith" faith, Titus 1:13; 2:2). **Faith and love … in Christ**, or faith and love through union with Christ, is another way of saying "Christian faith and love" (see 1 Tim. 1:14).

1:14. That good thing … committed unto thee refers to the gospel. Paul gave the same command in 1 Timothy 6:20. Paul reminded Timothy that power comes from God and the interior presence of His Holy Spirit (see 1:7–8). Here this magnificent truth applies specifically to Paul and Timothy and is probably the thrust of **us.**

III. Paul's Situation (1:15–18)

1:15. All is probably hyperbole, a deliberate exaggeration to express widespread desertion. Timothy was in Ephesus, the capital of the province of **Asia**, which today is in western Turkey. Because of Timothy's position, he would have had direct, personal observation or knowledge of the defection to which Paul referred. **Turned away from me** suggests but does not confirm that Paul's arrest had been a catalyst for the desertion. Paul's words in 1:8, however, loom ever larger against this background. Of **Phygellus and Hermogenes**, nothing more is known, although it may be surmised that their mention is a measure of Paul's grief over their loss.

1:16–18. In contrast with the defection of others (see 1:15), the memory of **Onesiphorus** (v. 16), who was probably now dead (v. 18; 4:19), was a figure of faithful help and support. Nevertheless, he too was gone. He had lived in Ephesus, where his family continued to reside (see 4:19). For the importance of **Rome** (v. 17) at this time, see Introduction: "Author, Date, and Place of Composition" (see also 1:8; 2:9). **That he may find mercy** (v. 18; only here in the New Testament) was Paul's way of alluding to the mercy that Onesiphorus had shown him and also a fitting recompense from the Lord, whom they had served together. **That day** (see 1:12) is the day of the Lord, the day of judgment. **Ministered unto me at Ephesus** refers either to Paul's stay during his third missionary journey (see Acts 19) or during his fourth (see map, *KJV Study Bible*, pp. 1738–39).

IV. Special Instructions to Timothy (chap. 2)

A. Call for Endurance (2:1–13)

2:1. My son (see discussion on 1 Tim. 1:2) is an expression of affection, heightened by Paul's circumstance. **Be strong**, a theme of chapter 1, stands in contrast to those who had defected from Paul, if not also from the Lord (see 2:8). **Grace**, the manifold provision of God's open hand, is given by virtue of His extraordinary favor **that is in Christ Jesus**, the means of standing strong.

2:2. Among many witnesses refers to Paul's preaching and teaching, which Timothy had heard repeatedly on all three missionary journeys and which could be confirmed by many. Even as Paul had found Timothy worthy (see "I commit unto thee," 1 Tim. 1:18), Timothy was to **commit** (entrust) the gospel to others who were as **faithful**, or "worthy of trust." Links of spiritual responsibility for the gospel are forged in this way. A life transformed by and trained in the gospel may become another link in its

faithful transmission, an unbreakable extension of its ongoing transformation.

2:3–6. Thou ... endure hardness (v. 3) is the identical Greek that is translated "Be thou partaker of the afflictions" in 1:8. The Greek prefix "with" refers to a shared experience that included Paul (see 2:9, which lacks the prefix and speaks of Paul's own suffering). Harsh and unpleasant experiences or sufferings belong to the servant of Christ and of His gospel. The difference between a leader and a victim is one's attitude and outlook. Paul gave Timothy three examples to follow: (1) a soldier who wants to please his commander, (2) an athlete who follows the rules of the game, and (3) a farmer who works hard.

A good soldier (v. 3) no doubt means a "brave" one (see Kelly, *The Pastoral Epistles*, p. 175) in view of the words "endure hardness." "Good" anticipates the further description of verse 4. Some soldiers are "bad" soldiers because they become preoccupied with civil matters outside of their commissioned service. **Of Jesus Christ** (v. 3) is further defined as **him who hath chosen him to be a soldier** (v. 4). The good soldier owes his allegiance to Christ, in whose name he serves and enters the battlefield.

2:5. Strive for masteries is one verb in Greek (*athleō*), meaning "be an athlete" or "contend in athletic games." Paul was acquainted with such games (e.g., the Isthmian games were restored to Corinth by Julius Caesar in AD 44) and with the fact that an athlete could be disqualified if required training regimens (see 1 Cor. 9:27) or rules of competition were broken. A contemporary of Paul, Epictetus, used the same phrase, **strive lawfully**, of prescribed Olympic training: "Give me proof, whether you have striven lawfully, eaten what is required, undertaken your exercise, minded your trainer" (3.10.8). The difference is that Paul used the metaphor of Timothy, and Epictetus of the philosopher.

2:6–7. The husbandman (Greek, *gēorgos*; "farmer"; v. 6) who toils is expected to be **partaker of the fruits** (see 1 Cor. 9:7). In this illustration, as in the previous two (soldier, 2:3–4; athlete, 2:5), the main lesson is that dedicated effort will be rewarded, not necessarily monetarily but in the enjoyment of seeing the gospel produce changed lives. This may have been the inference that Paul was seeking from Timothy when he said, **Consider what I say** (v. 7), or literally, "Think through [grasp or contemplate] what I am saying." **Understanding in all things** refers to application from lesser to greater and lighter to weightier (Kelly, *The Pastoral Epistles*, p. 176).

2:8–9. The seed of David was raised from the dead (v. 8). Christ's resurrection proclaims His deity, and His descent from David shows His humanity; both truths are basic to the gospel. Since Christ is God, His death has infinite value; since He is man, He could rightfully become the substitute. For this gospel, the grand truth of Jesus Christ, Paul had suffered—the strong theme of his ennobling challenge to Timothy. Even now Paul knew **trouble, as an evil doer, even unto bonds** (v. 9). Paul was bearing the real threat of execution in Rome (see 4:6). Because of his noble service and sacrifice unto the Lord, he suffered the additional hardship of misunderstanding, of being thought an ignoble "evil doer" and deemed a criminal.

2:10. I endure all things for the elects' sakes is Paul's own application of the illustrations in 2:3–6 (see discussion on 2:6). No suffering is too great if it brings about the salvation of God's chosen ones who will yet believe. For **in Christ Jesus**, see discussion on 1:13. **Eternal glory** is the final state of salvation.

2:11–13. These verses were probably an early Christian hymn. Paul's appeal was that suffering for Christ will be followed by glory.

2:11. For **a faithful saying**, see discussion on 1 Timothy 1:15. **If we be dead with him, we shall also live with him**. The Greek grammatical construction here assumes that believers died with Christ in the past, when He died on the cross. Christians are therefore assured that they will also live with Him eternally.

2:12. If we suffer, we shall also reign is a profound incentive and encouragement to suffer hardships for a greater purpose. Faithfully bearing up under suffering and trial will result in reward when Christ returns. For the alternative, **if we deny him** (Greek, *arneomai*; "deny," "repudiate," "disown"), see Matthew 10:33.

2:13. If we believe not is better understood as "if we are unfaithful." Infidelity has a logical counterpart that never comes but is instead replaced with the illogical proof of God's grace: **he abideth faithful: he cannot deny himself** or His own fidelity, which is a constituent of His nature. That is something a believer could never deny, a great comfort and ever compelling one to belief. On the other hand, His faithfulness must not comfort premeditated compromise, as if God should be cornered by His own character.

B. Warning about Foolish Controversies (2:14–26)

2:14–18. The wording of verses 14–16 indicates that the heresy mentioned here was an early form of Gnosticism, the same as that dealt with in 1 Timothy and Titus (see discussion on 1 Tim. 1:3–11; 1 John, Introduction: "Gnosticism"). Two leaders of this heresy, Hymenaeus (see 1 Tim. 1:20) and Philetus, denied the bodily resurrection and probably asserted that there is only a spiritual resurrection (similar to the error mentioned in 1 Cor. 15:12–19). Gnosticism interpreted the resurrection allegorically, not literally.

2:14. Charging them before the Lord is a most solemn charge that Paul had used to compel Timothy also (see 4:1; 1 Tim. 5:21). A war of words is more damaging than sticks and stones. The heretical leaders waged such a war **to no profit** (lit., "without benefit"); everyone came up empty, and worse—people were wrecked and destroyed. The Greek word *katastrophē*, translated **subverting**, speaks of catastrophic consequences. Since such wars are verbal wars, the casualties are emotional and spiritual.

2:15. Study (see 4:9, 21), or "do your best" (Greek, *spoudazō*), suggests diligent zeal and self-discipline, to "give it your all" or "make every effort." **Rightly dividing** (Greek, *orthotomeō*) refers to "cutting straight" or "guiding along a straight path" (used only here, but the same verb is used in the Greek Old Testament, the Septuagint, in Prov. 3:6; 11:5). Here is the how and what, the care and the content, of Timothy's responsibility for the gospel. **The word of truth** (see Eph. 1:13) is the gospel. Notice how necessary is the character of the man who "rightly divid[es]" to the word of truth he delivers.

2:16–17. Paul held up **Hymenaeus and Philetus** (v. 17) as examples of those who waged a war of words "to no profit, but to the subverting of the hearers" (2:14). Just as in 1 Timothy 6:20, Paul again admonished Timothy to avoid **profane and vain babblings** (v. 16). Timothy needed to redouble his efforts. Such "babblings" are not innocent or harmless; they're insidious, like spiritual gangrene.

2:18. Who (i.e., Hymenaeus and Philetus) **concerning the truth have erred**. "Erred" is a term Paul favored to characterize defection to this "untruth" (see 1 Timothy 1:6; 6:21 and discussions). It may imply how overtly subtle, yet substantively critical, the differences between the truth and its false counterpart are, at least to the laity. Among others of shipwrecked faith, Hymenaeus was named in 1 Timothy 1:19–20. It is clear here that his "blasphemy" was none other than the false teaching of which he, along with Philetus, had become a staunch, if not leading, proponent. Central to their error and their teaching was the tenet that **the resurrection is past already**, a rare peek into their actual doctrine (see discussion on 2:14–18; compare 2:8, 11; 1:10).

2:19. The foundation of God here refers to the church, which upholds the truth (1 Tim. 3:15). In spite of the heresy of Hymenaeus and Philetus, Timothy was to take courage in the knowledge that the church is God's solid foundation. Two seals are on it: one stresses the security of the church (**The Lord knoweth them that are his**; here "know," as often in the Bible, means "intimately acquainted with"), while the other emphasizes human responsibility (**Let every one that nameth the name of Christ depart from iniquity**). **This seal** is a sign of ownership. The church is owned and securely protected by God (see discussion on Eph. 1:13).

2:20–21. With **But in a great house** (v. 20), Paul turned from "the foundation" (2:19) to the building, taking up through the metaphor of its housewares the issue of people and their dedication to the Lord. This was a real concern in these letters because of the dangerous infections of false teaching and the disap-

pointing defections of familiar faces. **Of gold and of silver … of wood and of earth** describes an array of utensils in a grand home, the kind that belong to "them that are rich in this world" (1 Tim. 6:17) and who can afford premium (gold and silver) and not just practical (wood and earth) housewares. In an earthly household, the material value of a utensil may correspond to its use, **some to honour, and some to dishonour**. The possibility of a conversion is seen in **If a man therefore purge himself from these** (lit., "if anyone cleanse himself"; v. 21). He then shall no longer be counted among "some to dishonor," but **he shall be a vessel unto honour … prepared unto every good work**. At this point, the spiritual household rather than the earthly controls the metaphor. In God's house, regardless of a utensil's material value, if it be cleansed (washed, sanctified), it can be put to another use and serviceable to the Master of the house, who makes such decisions. Accordingly, against the background of the error of false teaching, Timothy could find serviceable to the Master anyone who cleansed himself of such things, or in the words of 2:19, "every one that nameth the name of Christ" and did also "depart from iniquity."

2:22–26. By default, Timothy's youth carried a certain jeopardy that could not be overlooked but needed to be confronted and calculated in advance. Strategic as Timothy's leadership was to the serious spiritual challenges that faced the church in Ephesus, it would have been tragic if such a great opportunity for spiritual victory fell in defeat because of his youth. Thus, Paul returned to the subject (see 1 Tim. 4:12) with a new exhortation. In contemporary language, **youthful lusts** (v. 22) connotes sexual passions, but the word "lusts" is far more flexible in both the Greek and the KJV (as its use in 3:6; 4:3; 1 Tim. 6:9; Titus 2:12; 3:3 attests). Paul's subsequent exhortations (vv. 23–25) point in an entirely different direction: to the hotheaded, untempered, impetuous passions that often get the best of a young man. Such were Paul's concern, and such created misgivings among those who already underrated Timothy because of his age (see 1 Tim. 4:12). **Flee** and **follow** (see 1 Tim. 6:11) are juxtaposed in the Greek sentence for maximum effect. Inborn urges are ruled and mastered by the undeterred pursuit of Christlike virtues. **Strifes** (v. 23) and **strive** (v. 24) are the same Greek word (noun and verb) meaning "fighting" or "quarreling," with a strong connotation of battle. Militant urges were not to cloud or color Timothy's ability to **teach** (v. 24) or his **instructing** (v. 25), with the implication that God would represent him best in battle if his weapons were gentleness, patience, and meekness (vv. 24–25). **Meekness** is that disarming quality of gentleness and courtesy that comes from the inner strength of genuine humility. All in all, if Timothy was predisposed to conduct himself in spiritual combat as Paul had commended, repentance and spiritual victory would be won, not at all costs, but at the hands of God (vv. 25–26).

V. Warning about the Last Days (chap. 3)

A. Terrible Times (3:1–9)

3:1. The last days refers to the messianic era, the time beginning with Christ's first coming and culminating with His second coming (see discussions on Acts 2:17; 1 Tim. 4:1; Heb. 1:1; 1 Peter 1:20; 1 John 2:18). "The last days" here refers to a future time of trouble that will be characterized by selfishness and unbelief. That "the last days" in this passage does not refer only to the time just prior to Christ's return is apparent from Paul's command to Timothy to have nothing to do with the unbelieving and unfaithful who characterize this time (v. 5).

3:2–5. This profile of "the last days" (3:1) served to show Timothy that his personal battle belonged in part to what will come. Therefore, any discouragement he faced was but a part of the growing spiritual war that will intensify in the last days. This inventory of moral attrition and collapse (vv. 2–4) that will occur in the last days tails into the inward **form** (v. 5) of false teachers. That Paul had merged from the future into the present is clear from the words **from such turn away** (v. 5) and the opening of 3:6 ("For of this sort are they"), which is built on that transition.

3:6–7. Silly women (v. 6) describes unstable women who are guilt-ridden because of their sins, torn by lust, and victims of various false teachers—

ever learning (v. 7) but never coming to a saving knowledge of Christ. Undoubtedly, Paul was drawing on known instances that explain his contemptuous tone (see Kelly, *The Pastoral Epistles*, p. 195), for the targets of these unethical tactics tell as much about the false teachers as about the women they spiritually swindled.

3:8–9. As Jannes and Jambres (v. 8) lends a timeless quality to the unethical tactics of those who prey on gullible people. Neither of these men is mentioned in the Old Testament, but according to Jewish tradition, they were the Egyptian court magicians who opposed **Moses** (see *KJV Study Bible* note on Exod. 7:11). **Their folly** (v. 9) could not long be cloaked, nor could that of the current manifestations of Jannes and Jambres.

B. Means of Combating Terrible Times (3:10–17)

3:10–11. Although Paul has exposed the doctrine and character of the teachers of error, Timothy knew well the caliber of Paul's own teaching, character, and its tested quality. **Antioch** (v. 11), **Iconium**, and **Lystra** were three cities in the Roman province of Galatia that Paul visited on his first and second missionary journeys (see Acts 13:14–14:23; 16:1–6). Since Timothy was from Lystra, he would have known firsthand of Paul's sufferings in that region. **Out of them all the Lord delivered me**, even from execution by stoning (see Acts 14:19–20).

3:12. Paul encouraged Timothy to join him (see 1:8; 2:3) in **suffer[ing] persecution**, for such is not an aberration but is common to **all that will live godly** (see 1 Tim. 2:2 and discussion) **in Christ** (see discussion on 1:13). Indeed, this principle is repeated elsewhere in the New Testament (see Matt. 10:22; Acts 14:22; Phil. 1:29; 1 Peter 4:12).

3:13. Contrasted with Christian persecution is its polar opposite, the trajectory of those who oppose Christ (see 3:8–9). The **deceiving, and … deceived** are by definition unable to detect the end of their own error, but Timothy could (see 3:5), for it is plain to the godly, who will not allow persecution to deter them from the truth.

3:14. Of whom thou hast learned them is quite possibly a reference to Paul as well as to Timothy's mother and grandmother (see 1:5).

3:15. From a child thou hast known the holy scriptures. A Jewish boy formally began to study the Old Testament when he was five years old. Timothy was taught at home by his mother and grandmother even before he reached that age.

3:16–17. All scripture (v. 16) refers primarily to the Old Testament, since some of the New Testament books had not yet been written (for indications that some New Testament books, or material ultimately included in the New Testament, were already considered equal in authority to the Old Testament Scriptures, see 1 Tim. 5:18; 2 Peter 3:15–16). **Inspiration of God** affirms God's active involvement in the writing of Scripture, an involvement so powerful and pervasive that what is written is the infallible and authoritative Word of God (see 2 Peter 1:20–21 and discussions). Here the utility of Scripture is (see 1 Tim. 4:13) set forth: it is useful **for doctrine**, the tenets of the gospel; **for reproof**, exposing and refuting error; **for correction**, conforming and reforming belief; and **for instruction in righteousness**, giving a full education in God's will and ways. Its ultimate purpose (or result) is **that the man of God** (any godly individual, but certainly Timothy was in view here) **may be perfect** (Greek, *artios*; v. 17), meaning complete and fully outfitted, **furnished** ("ready," as in "finished") to undertake **all good works**.

VI. Paul's Departing Remarks (4:1–8)

A. Charge to Preach the Word (4:1–5)

4:1. I charge thee therefore before God is characteristic of Paul's most solemn and authoritative exhortations (see 1 Tim. 5:21; 6:13). Paul stated his charge to Timothy with the awareness that he did so in the presence of God the Father and of Christ, who will judge all men. He was also keenly aware of Christ's return and the coming establishment of God's kingdom in its fullest expression. Timothy was to view a charge so given as of the utmost importance.

4:2. Timothy was to **be instant**, that is, be ready in any situation to speak the needed word, whether of correction, of rebuke, or of encouragement. **Preach** is here to "herald" or "declare" openly **the word**, the "sound doctrine" (4:3) of the gospel truth (see 4:5).

4:3. Sound doctrine (see discussion on Titus 1:9), literally, and perhaps ironically, doctrine that is "healthy," must be taught as early as possible, before one's ear becomes infirmed by the culture and the times (see 3:1–5). **Having itching ears** may connote a fevered condition; it certainly depicts hearers with ears that need to be "scratched" by words that can relieve their "unsound" sensitivities.

4:4. Symptomatic of human hardening (an unhealthy fibrosis) to what is "sound" (**the truth**), people will incline their ears to what is most unsound and easier to hear, seeking relief even in **fables** (see note on 1 Tim. 1:4).

4:5. Accepting suffering and persecution was one of Paul's prominent concerns for Timothy and a major theme of this letter (see 1:8; 2:3, 9; 2:9; 3:11–12). If Timothy was to face down the opposition to the gospel, he needed to incorporate suffering in his job description as a godly leader. For **the work of an evangelist**, see 4:2.

B. Paul's Victorious Prospect (4:6–8)

4:6. The importance of Timothy's readiness (see 3:17 and discussion) and the serious concerns of this letter were now coupled with urgency. Paul's withdrawal from the field of Christian ministry and life was imminent. **Be offered** refers to the offering of wine poured around the base of the altar (see Num. 15:1–12; 28:7, 24). Paul viewed his approaching death as the pouring out of his life as an offering to Christ (see Phil. 2:17). **My departure** is a euphemism for Paul's impending death (see Phil. 1:23).

4:7. Here Paul looked back over thirty years of labor as an apostle (ca. AD 36–66). Like an athlete who had engaged successfully in a contest (**fought a good fight**), he had **finished** [his] **course** and had **kept the faith**, that is, had carefully observed the rules (the teachings) of the Christian faith (see 2:5). In view of the Pastorals' emphasis on sound doctrine, perhaps "the faith" refers to the deposit of Christian truth. Paul had kept, or guarded, it.

4:8. A crown of righteousness continues the imagery of 4:7. With this metaphor of the wreath given to the winner of a race (see 1 Cor. 9:25), Paul could have been referring to (1) a crown given as a reward for a righteous life, (2) a crown consisting of righteousness, or (3) a crown given righteously (justly) by the righteous Judge. **That day** is not the day of Paul's death but the day of Christ's second coming (**his appearing**).

VII. Final Request and Greetings (4:9–22)

4:9. Paul called upon Timothy to join him. **Do thy diligence** (Greek *spoudazō*) is the same expression used in v. 21 and here implies the sense of "hasten" or "hurry." *Spoudazō* may also suggest "make every effort" or "do your best" (see 2:15, "study") but here and v. 21, the onset of winter and the narrowing window for safe travel, stresses that timing was most important. Other reasons for Paul's appeal to haste are set forth in vv. 10–18; most notable was the abandonment of Demas (v. 10) among others (v. 16).

4:10. Crescens is mentioned only here in the New Testament. **Galatia** identifies either the northern area of Asia Minor (Gaul) or a Roman province in what is now central Turkey (see discussion on Gal. 1:2). For **Titus unto Dalmatia**, see Titus, Introduction: "Recipient." Dalmatia is present-day Albania and a portion of Yugoslavia, also known in Scripture as Illyricum (see Rom. 15:19).

4:11. Mark is the John Mark who deserted Paul and Barnabas on their first missionary journey (see Acts 13:13). After Paul refused to take Mark on the second journey, Barnabas separated from Paul, taking Mark with him on a mission to Cyprus (see Acts 15:36–41). Ultimately, Mark proved himself to Paul, indicated by his presence with Paul during Paul's first Roman imprisonment (see Col. 4:10; Philemon 24) and by Paul's request here for Timothy to bring Mark with him to Rome.

4:12. Thychicus (see Eph. 6:21; Col. 4:7–9; Titus 3:12; Acts 20:4) was a faithful ally, a bearer of other dispatches, and likely the trusted envoy who carried this letter to Timothy and who served at Ephesus so that Timothy could go to Rome.

4:13. The cloke was a garment for protection against the cold dampness (see Introduction: "Author, Date, and Place of Composition"). It was probably a heavy, sleeveless outer garment, circular in shape, with a hole in the middle for one's head. **Carpus** is not mentioned elsewhere. **The books, but especially the parchments** provides an early reference to the emergence of codices, small leather bound books, that would eventually take the place of scrolls. The books, or scrolls (see *KJV Study Bible* note on Exod. 17:14), were made of papyrus, and the parchments were made of animal skins. The latter may have been copies of parts of the Old Testament. That Paul told Timothy to bring them with him alludes to the significant amount of time he and Paul would spend studying their contents and, as some have suggested, a transfer to Timothy of Paul's mantle and the symbols of his ministry that had been in Timothy's trust.

4:14–15. Alexander the coppersmith (v. 14) is probably the Alexander mentioned in 1 Timothy 1:20 and is connected there with the Hymenaeus of this letter (see 2:17).

4:16–17. My first answer (v. 16) refers to the first court hearing of Paul's present case, not his defense on the occasion of his first imprisonment (see Acts 28). For the defection of others and the enabling power of the Lord in suffering, see 1:7–8; 3:11–12. Proof of such power is first internal and then external, as can be seen in Paul's proclamation: **that by me the preaching might be fully known** (v. 17). Even in these dire circumstances, Paul used the occasion to testify about Jesus Christ in the imperial court. **I was delivered out of the mouth of the lion**. Since, as a Roman citizen, Paul could not be thrown to the lions in the amphitheater, this must be a figurative way of saying that his first hearing did not result in an immediate guilty verdict.

4:18. The Lord shall deliver me from every evil work. Since Paul fully expected to die soon (4:6), the rescue he spoke of here was spiritual, not physical. The **heavenly kingdom** is heaven itself.

4:19. Earlier, Paul had brought **Prisca and Aquila** with him to Ephesus, and this couple belonged among Paul's dearest friends (see Acts 18:2, 18, 26;

Rom. 16:3; 1 Cor. 16:19). **The household of One-siphorus** refers to his family; Onesiphorus himself had most likely died (see discussion on 1:16).

4:20. Timothy may have questioned the where-abouts of **Erastus** (see discussion on Rom. 16:23) and **Trophimus** and why they were not with Paul. **Miletum** was a seaport on the coast of Asia Minor about fifty miles south of Ephesus.

4:21. Paul requested that Timothy **come before winter** because the opportunity to travel was end-ing. The season of seafaring was closed from mid-November through March and was dangerous from September to October. Paul knew full well just how

dangerous seafaring during this time could be (see Acts 27). One may extrapolate that the summer was drawing to a close as Timothy read this. Paul knew he would not last until April. According to early tra-dition, **Linus** was bishop of Rome after the deaths of Peter and Paul.

4:22. For **grace**, see discussions on Jonah 4:2; Ga-latians 1:3; Ephesians 1:2. **You** is poignant, a farewell to "all." **Thy** in the first part of the verse is singular, indicating that it was addressed to Timothy alone. In view of Paul's impending death and the solemn charge he gave to his timid young friend, Timothy needed such encouragement.

THE EPISTLE OF PAUL TO TITUS

INTRODUCTION

Author

The author is Paul (see 1 Timothy, Introduction: "Author").

Date and Place of Composition

Paul possibly wrote from Macedonia, for he had not yet reached Nicopolis (3:12). The letter was written after his release from the first Roman imprisonment (see Acts 28), probably between AD 63 and 65, or possibly at a later date if he wrote after his assumed trip to Spain (see Rom. 15:24).

Recipient

The letter is addressed to Titus, one of Paul's converts (1:4) and a considerable help to Paul in his ministry. When Paul left Antioch to discuss "his" gospel (see 2 Tim. 2:8) with the Jerusalem leaders, he took Titus with him (see Gal. 2:1–3); acceptance of Titus (a Gentile) as a Christian without circumcision vindicated Paul's stand there (see Gal. 2:3–5). Presumably Titus, who is not referred to in Acts but is mentioned thirteen times in the rest of the New Testament, worked with Paul at Ephesus during the third missionary journey. From there, the apostle sent Titus to Corinth to help that church with its work (see *Zondervan KJV Study Bible* note on 2 Cor. 2:12–13; 7:5–6; 8:6).

Following Paul's release from his first Roman imprisonment (see Acts 28), he and Titus worked briefly in Crete (1:5), after which he commissioned Titus to remain there as his representative and complete some needed work (1:5; 2:15; 3:12–13). Paul asked Titus to meet him at Nicopolis (on the west coast of Greece) when a replacement arrived (3:12). Titus later went on a mission to Dalmatia (modern Yugoslavia; see discussion on 2 Tim. 4:10), the last reference to him in the New Testament. Considering the assignments given him, Titus obviously was a capable and resourceful leader.

Crete

The fourth largest island of the Mediterranean, Crete lies directly south of the Aegean Sea (see discussion on 1 Sam. 30:14; for Paul's experiences there, see Acts 27:7–13). In

New Testament times, life in Crete had sunk to a deplorable moral level. The dishonesty, gluttony, and laziness of its inhabitants were proverbial (1:12).

Theme

Apparently, Paul introduced Christianity in Crete when he and Titus visited the island, after which he left Titus there to organize the converts. Paul sent the letter with Zenas and Apollos, who were on a journey that took them through Crete (3:13), to give Titus personal authorization and guidance in meeting opposition (1:5; 2:1, 7–8, 15; 3:9), instructions about faith and conduct, and warnings about false teachers. Paul also informed Titus of his future plans for him (3:12).

Especially significant, considering the nature of the Cretan heresy, are the repeated emphases on "good works" (1:16; 2:7, 14; 3:1, 8, 14) and the classic summaries of Christian doctrine (2:11–14; 3:4–7).

Outline

I. Salutation (1:1–4)
II. Concerning Elders (1:5–9)
   A. Reasons for Leaving Titus in Crete (1:5)
   B. Qualifications of Elders (1:6–9)
III. Concerning False Teachers (1:10–16)
IV. Concerning Various Groups in the Congregations (chap. 2)
   A. Instructions to Different Groups (2:1–10)
   B. The Foundation for Christian Living (2:11–14)
   C. The Duty of Titus (2:15)
V. Concerning Believers in General (3:1–8)
   A. Obligations as Citizens (3:1–2)
   B. Motives for Godly Conduct (3:3–8)
VI. Concerning Response to Spiritual Error (3:9–11)
VII. Conclusion (3:12–15)

Bibliography

Fee, Gordon D. *1 and 2 Timothy, Titus.* The New International Biblical Commentary. Peabody, MA: Hendrickson, 1988.

Guthrie, Donald. *The Pastoral Epistles.* Downers Grove, IL: InterVarsity, 1957.

Kelly, J. N. D. *The Pastoral Epistles.* London: Adam & Charles Black, 1963.

Liefeld, Walter L. *1 and 2 Timothy, Titus.* The NIV Application Commentary. Grand Rapids, MI: Zondervan, 1999.

EXPOSITION

I. Salutation (1:1–4)

1:1. Only here does Paul call himself **a servant of God**; elsewhere he says "a servant of Jesus Christ" (see Rom. 1:1; Gal. 1:10; Phil. 1:1). James used both terms of himself (James 1:1). "Servant" (Greek, *doulos*; see discussion on Rom. 1:1) is too mild a term; Paul was alluding to the bond slave who voluntarily and completely surrenders his existence to the lifelong service of his master (see Exod. 21:2–6). **An apostle** is one specially commissioned by Christ (see discussions on Mark 6:30; Heb. 3:1; *KJV Study Bible* note on 1 Cor. 1:1). **According to the faith ... and the acknowledging** refers to Paul's appointed mission as God's servant and Christ's apostle, which is explained further in 1:2 (see also Acts 9:15; 22:15; 26:16–18). Paul's apostleship was for the sake of the elect's faith and deep knowledge of the truth, which corresponds to godliness (see discussion on 1 Tim. 2:2).

1:2. In the Greek, there is no intervening punctuation between 1:1–2, and the words **In** (lit., "resting on") **the hope** (see discussions on Col. 1:5; 1 Tim. 1:1) is sequential to all of 1:1. "Hope" is not a wish but a certainty of future eternal life. This certainty is grounded in the very character of God, who **cannot lie**, in contrast to the Cretans (see 1:12) and the Devil (see John 8:44).

1:3. **Due times** refers to the crucial events in God's program that occur at His designated times in history (see 1 Tim. 2:6; 6:15). **His word** is the authoritative message that centers in Christ. **According to the commandment** is identical to 1 Timothy 1:1 (see discussion there). **God our Saviour** occurs three times in Titus (here; 2:10; 3:4; see also 1 Tim. 1:1; 2:3; 4:10), and three times Jesus is called "our Saviour" (1:4; 2:13; 3:6; see 2 Tim. 1:10).

1:4. Paul called Titus **mine own son**, meaning "my spiritual son," since he had been converted through Paul's ministry. Paul used the same term for Timothy (1 Tim. 1:2) and Onesimus (Philemon 10). **The common faith** is the faith shared by all true believers. Here "common" (Greek, *koinos*) almost

carries the sense of "orthodox," in contrast with "sectarian" or "elitist," belief. In this sense, "common" is used as the later but early church use of "catholic," meaning "general" or "universal" (Greek, *katholikos*), long before it was taken over by its now primarily denominational use. Paul's use of **Saviour** is striking. In all of Paul's other salutations, Jesus is called "Lord." Paul used "Saviour" twelve times in all his letters; half of these references are in Titus.

II. Concerning Elders (1:5–9)

A. Reasons for Leaving Titus in Crete (1:5)

1:5. Left I thee in Crete implies that Paul and Titus had been together in Crete, a ministry not mentioned in Acts. On his voyage to Rome, Paul briefly visited Crete as a prisoner (see Acts 27:7–8), but now that he had been released from his first Roman imprisonment, he was free to travel wherever he wished (see 3:12). **And ordain elders** is not a second **cause** but, according to the Greek construction, is explanatory of **set in order the things that are wanting**. When "and" is translated "namely," the sense becomes clear. It also shows the importance of "elders" to the order of "things." Though Paul and Titus perhaps had already preached in Crete, they had not had time to organize churches. The appointing of elders was consistent with Paul's usual practice (see Acts 14:23). **As I had appointed thee** refers to Paul's previous detailed verbal orders (Greek, *diatassō*; "order," "command"), which he now reiterated in writing.

B. Qualifications of Elders (1:6–9)

1:6–9. A parallel list of qualifications for elders is given in 1 Timothy 3:1–7, but the two lists reflect the different situations in which Timothy and Titus ministered (see chart, *Zondervan KJV Study Bible*, p. 1741).

1:6. Of first concern, a potential leader must be **blameless** (Greek, *anegklētos*; pronounced *anenklētos*; see 1:7; 1 Tim. 3:10). Candidates for the responsibility of elder must be of good reputation, beyond disqualification on grounds of social conduct and character (see 1:7–8), as well as doctrinally fit (see 1:9). Specification of a blameless man begins at home. Since elders, by definition, are chosen from among the older men of the congregation, there is a presumption here that candidates would be married and have children. Of them, the **husband of one wife** identifies a man of the highest marital fidelity (see discussion on 1 Tim. 3:2). A qualified unmarried man was not necessarily barred. It is also improbable that the standard forbids an elder to remarry if his wife dies (see Rom. 7:2–3; 1 Cor. 7:39; 1 Tim. 5:14). The most likely meaning is simply that a faithful, monogamous married life must be maintained. **Having faithful children** may refer to their "belief" in God, although "fidelity" to home points back to the character of the father and ahead to the character of a life reproduced; they too are to be of good reputation, **not accused of riot or unruly** (see 1 Tim. 3:4).

1:7. The use of "elders" in 1:5 and **bishop** (or "overseer") here indicates that the terms were used interchangeably (see Acts 20:17, 28; 1 Peter 5:1–2). "Elder" indicates qualification (maturity and experience), while "bishop" indicates responsibility (watching over God's flock). Here again, **blameless** stands first (see discussion on 1:6), pointing to proof of faithful character (see 1 Cor. 4:2). **As the steward** (Greek, *oikonomos*; "manager") **of God**, the overseer has supervisory responsibility over the household of God. Listed next are "not" qualities. **Not selfwilled** (Greek, *authadē*) means the candidate must not be driven by self-interests rather than Christ's, and therefore not self-centered or stubborn. Accordingly, the man who is Christ-centered is **not soon angry**, not easily angered, but patient, pursuing interests higher than his own. Even as he is not self-willed, he does not submit his will to intoxication; he is **not given to wine** (Greek, *paroinos*; see discussion on 1 Tim. 3:3). Other "not" qualities of a blameless man are that he is **no striker** (Greek, *plēktēs*; see discussion on 1 Tim. 3:3) and **not given to filthy lucre** (Greek, *aischrokerdē*; see discussion on 1 Tim. 3:3).

1:8. The "not" qualities (counting "blameless" as "not subject to blame") of 1:7 are here balanced by six positive qualities, in advance of weighing a man's doctrinal fitness for the office of elder (1:9). A candidate must show **hospitality** (Greek, *philoxenia*; see discussion on 1 Tim. 3:2), or be a lover (*philo*) of strangers and guests (*xenos*), and be **a lover of good** (Greek, *philagathon*; only here in the New Testament), a man characterized by devotion to what is good. **Men** is an inference not found in the Greek; the scope of "good" entails men but includes more. In fact, attention to "good works" is a prominent virtue in Titus and the Pastoral Epistles (see 1:16; 3:1, 8; see also 2:10; 1 Tim. 2:10; 5:10; 2 Tim. 2:21; 3:17). **Sober** (Greek, *sōphrōn*; see discussion on 1 Tim. 3:2) refers to the power to moderate one's passions with good judgment, a virtue much needed in Crete (see 1:10–14). Paul referred to it five times in two chapters (here; 2:2, 4–6, 12). The man who is **just** (Greek, *dikaios*) is not only upright but fair and honest. **Holy** (Greek, *hosios*) is a counterpart to "just" and reflects a devout life toward God and therefore others (see 1 Thess. 2:10). This is "practical holiness," not something donned at church and doffed in the locker room. **Temperate** (Greek, *egkratēs*, pronounced *enkratēs*; used only here in New Testament) literally connotes "in possession of power" and refers to self-control, the inner strength to control one's desires and actions.

1:9. Sound doctrine refers to correct teaching, in keeping with that of the apostles (see 1 Tim. 1:10; 6:3; 2 Tim. 1:13; 4:3). The teaching is called "sound" not only because it builds people up in the faith but because it protects them against the corrupting influence of false teachers. Soundness of doctrine, faith, and speech is a basic concern in the Pastoral Epistles (1–2 Timothy and Titus); the word "sound" occurs ten times (see also "sound" in Rom. 12:3; 2 Cor. 5:13). Any man fit for the responsibility of elder/overseer must be capable of teaching and defending the truth of the gospel.

III. Concerning False Teachers (1:10–16)

1:10. For introduces the reason for Paul's order to appoint elders of trustworthy character, as stated in 1:5–9. **Unruly** (see 1:6; "disobedient" in 1 Tim.

1:9) points to a recalcitrant defiance of God's Word and His authoritative ministers, Paul and Titus. These troublemakers had three main characteristics: (1) they belonged to the "circumcision," like the people of Galatians 2:12, believing that for salvation or sanctification or both, it was necessary to be circumcised and to keep the Jewish ceremonial law (see Galatians, Introduction: "Background"); (2) they held to unscriptural Jewish myths (see 1:14) and genealogies (see 3:9; 1 Tim. 1:4 and discussion); (3) they were ascetics (see 1:14–15), having scruples against things that God declared to be good. **Vain talkers** is the same expression Paul used when writing to Timothy about such people ("vain jangling," 1 Tim. 1:6). Linked with **deceivers**, one may presume that their utterances were deficient of truth and lacked any basis in fact.

1:11. Whose mouths must be stopped (Greek, *epistomizō*; only here in the New Testament) gives a vigorous word picture of the problem and of the solution: "put something over the mouth," as if to muzzle or bridle the snout of unruly beasts (see 1:10). The troublemakers were **subvert[ing] whole houses** (i.e., families), meaning their deception was undermining the faith of entire households (see 2 Tim. 2:18), and all **for filthy lucre's sake** (see 1:7; 1 Tim. 3:3).

1:12. With a quotation, Paul validated the need for the strong hand he advised in the previous verse. A "cretan" culture could not be expected to curb the conduct of these false teachers (see 1:10–11). The Cretan reputation was infamous and proverbial, known far and wide and readily documented by earlier historians and social commentators. In Greek literature, to "play the cretan," or to "cretanize," became slang for "lying" or "cheating." Paul found the centuries-old citation of their own poet, **a prophet of their own,** still relevant (see 1:13). The Cretans held Epimenides (a sixth-century BC native of Knossos, Crete) in high esteem. Several fulfilled predictions were ascribed to him (for other examples of Paul's use of pagan sayings, see discussion on Acts 17:28; *KJV Study Bible* note on 1 Cor. 15:33). Compare **alway liars** with "turn from the truth" in 1:14. **Evil**

beasts are wild animals, dangerous and tricky to domesticate. **Slow bellies** is more clearly stated as "lazy gluttons." Since these descriptions were proverbial, one should not push them to the breaking point but rather appreciate the coarse and churlish culture in which the gospel was taking root.

1:13–14. Titus was to **rebuke them sharply** (v. 13), meaning "correct them severely." He needed to be forthright and uncompromising; there was no middle ground. The doctrinal soundness of the gospel was at stake. **The faith** and **the truth** (v. 14) are contrasted with **Jewish fables** (see discussion on 1:10), **and commandments of men** (referring to Jewish traditions; see Mark 7:6–7; Isa. 9:13).

1:15. Unto the pure (or Christians, who have been purified by the atoning death of Christ) **all things are pure**: "every creature of God is good, and nothing to be refused, if it be received with thanksgiving" (1 Tim. 4:4). To understand better Paul's statements here, see Romans 14:14, 20. **Unto them that are defiled and unbelieving is nothing pure.** Unbelievers, especially ascetics with unbiblical scruples against certain foods, marriage, and the like (see 1 Tim. 4:3; Col. 2:21), do not enjoy the freedom of true Christians, who receive all God's creation with thanksgiving. Instead, they set up arbitrary, manmade prohibitions against what they consider to be impure (see Matt. 15:10–11, 16–20; Mark 7:14–19; Acts 10:9–16; Rom. 14:20). The principle of this verse does not conflict with the many New Testament teachings against practices that are morally and spiritually wrong. For **conscience**, see 1 Timothy 4:2–3.

1:16. They profess that they know God echoes the lip service mentioned in Isaiah 29:13. Paul defined a spiritual schizophrenia: in words they declared him, **but in works they den[ied] him.** The false teachers stood condemned by the test of personal conduct. For **every good work,** see discussions on 1:8; 3:1, 8; Introduction: "Theme." Right knowledge is extremely important because it leads to godliness (see 1:1). Paul maintained a remarkable balance between doctrine and practice, as well as between faith and works.

IV. Concerning Various Groups in the Congregations (chap. 2)

A. Instructions to Different Groups (2:1-10)

In contrast to those who professed God with their lips but denied Him with their lives (1:16), the believing community of Crete was to exemplify what it means to profess Christ and live in Him (see 1:7, 2:11-12). In this section, Paul presented exhibits of genuine faith, featuring hands-on, transferable behavior that modeled Christlike living across the age groups within the church. He wanted believers in Crete to be examples of Christ within.

2:1. Thou is emphatic, contrasting the work of Titus with that of the false teachers just denounced (see 1:10-16). **Speak** conveys the sense of "audible utterance" and adds a touch of vividness to the image of Titus verbalizing the following directions to the older men (2:2), older women (2:3), and other groups. In 2:2-10, it will be seen that **sound doctrine** (see discussion on 2 Tim. 1:13) demands right conduct of all believers, regardless of age, sex, or position.

2:2. Aged men (Greek, *presbytēs*) is matched by its feminine counterpart in the next verse, "aged women" (Greek, *presbytis*). Older men, as leaders, are to be moral and spiritual examples: **sober** (Greek, *nēphalios*; see 1 Tim. 3:2, 11), **grave** (Greek, *semnos*; see 1 Tim. 3:8, 11), **temperate** (Greek, *sōphrōn*; see 1:8; 2:5; 1 Tim. 3:2), **sound** (Greek, *hygiainō*; see 1:9; 2:1; discussion on 2 Tim. 1:13) **in faith, in charity** (Greek, *agapē*), **in patience** (Greek, *hypomonē*; "endurance," "perseverance"). Instead of being "evil beasts" and "slow bellies" (i.e., "lazy gluttons"; 1:12), as were Cretans in general, older believers are to be responsible, sensible, gracious, and dependable in every way.

2:3. Likewise, the same moral standards applies to **The aged women** as to the aged men (see 2:2). They are to behave **as becometh holiness** (Greek, *hieroprepēs*; "reverent"; lit. refers to the conduct of a priest), suggesting a lifestyle worthy of the highest respect. Two "not" qualities are listed for the women: **not false accusers** (Greek, *diabolos*), referring to

unfounded, maligning gossip and slander, and **not given to much wine** (lit., "not enslaved to much wine"), depicting excessive, out-of-control drinking (see discussions on 1 Tim 3:3; 5:23). The women are to be **teachers of good things** (only here), or wholesome things. This phrase depicts, not teachers in a classroom, but those who educate others through their example in word and deed (see 2:4).

2:4-5. The older women are to **teach the younger women to be sober** (Greek, *sōphronizō*; lit., "make them circumspect"; v. 4), implying an apprenticeship of the younger to the older in matters pertaining to judicious living, especially the virtues of family and home. They are **to love their husbands** (Greek, *philandros*) and **to love their children** (Greek, *philoteknos*), both compound words fronted by "affectionate devotion" (*phil-*). **Discreet** (Greek, *sōphrōn*; v. 5; see "temperate," 2:2; "sober," 1:8) is the tandem noun of the verb "teach ... to be sober." The purpose of instilling the sound judgment that manifests itself in these feminine and domestic virtues is **that the word of God be not blasphemed**. This purpose reveals that beneath these ethical instructions lies a deep spiritual concern for the integrity and public acceptance of the gospel (see 2:8, 10, dealing with his concern that Christian living should help rather than hinder the spread of the gospel).

2:6. Likewise (see 2:3) with the single imperative **exhort** ("urge") **to be sober minded** is comparatively briefer and yet broader if "In all things" (2:7) is in view here. In that case, Titus's example set the standard (see 2:7-8). "Sober minded" (Greek, *sōphroneō*) is the same word idea found in 1:8; 2:2, 4-5.

2:7-8. Model and message, example and exhortation, lifestyle and lecture, are indissolubly linked by the integrity of faith. This is expected of all believers, but Titus was to typify it and set the standard because the demands on a leader are all-inclusive (see James 3:1). Perhaps Titus was still a young man, and the Christian virtues he was to exhibit include him in the instruction he was to give the young men of 2:6. For **good works** (v. 7), see discussions on 1:8; 3:1, 8; Introduction: "Theme." Titus was to be above reproach.

2:9–10. Slavery was a basic element of Roman society, and the impact of Christianity on slaves was a vital concern. Paul set forth instructions for this distinct group in the churches; guidance for the conduct of Christian slaves was essential (see discussion on Eph. 6:5). The Greek word for **masters** (v. 9), from which the English term "despot" is derived, indicates the owner's absolute authority over his slave. Roman slaves had no legal rights; their fates were entirely in their masters' hands. Servants were to **adorn the doctrine** (v. 10), meaning to decorate or accessorize their lives with the Word of God. Christian slaves could give a unique and powerful testimony to the gospel by their willing faithfulness and obedience to their masters. What applies here to the servant (see also Eph. 6:6–7) applies also to those in the workplace (see Col. 3:17, 23; 1 Cor. 10:31).

B. The Foundation for Christian Living (2:11–14)

This section briefly describes the effect grace should have on believers. It encourages holier living and rejection of ungodliness, in keeping with Paul's repeated insistence that one's profession of Christ be accompanied by godly living (see 2:1–2, 4–5, 10; 3:8).

2:11. For introduces the doctrinal basis for the ethical demands just stressed in vv. 2–10, "things which become sound doctrine." Right conduct must be founded on right doctrine. **The grace of God** is the undeserved love God showed in Christ while believers were still sinners and His enemies (Rom. 5:6–10), by which they are saved apart from any moral achievements or religious acts on our part (see 3:5; Eph. 2:8–9). This same grace instructs that salvation should produce good works (see discussion on 2:14; Eph. 2:10).

2:12. The word translated **teaching** (Greek, *paideuō*) refers to more than instruction; it includes the whole process of training a child—instruction, encouragement, correction, and discipline. **Ungodliness** (Greek, *asebeia*) is the antonym of "godliness" (see 1:1; discussion on 1 Tim. 2:2), so prominent in the Pastoral Epistles. For **this present world**, or

"age," see *KJV Study Bible* note on 2 Corinthians 4:4; discussion on Galatians 1:4.

2:13. That blessed hope, and the glorious appearing refers to the second coming (see 1 Tim. 6:14; 2 Tim. 4:1; 4:8 and discussion). Of special interest are the words **the great God and our Saviour Jesus Christ**. This translation is possible, but both the context (Christ's second coming) and the Greek construction favor the translation, "the great God, even our Saviour Jesus Christ." It is an explicit testimony to the deity of Christ (see discussion on Rom. 9:5).

2:14. Salvation involves the double work of redeeming people from guilt and judgment and of producing moral purity and helpful service to others (see Introduction: "Theme").

C. The Duty of Titus (2:15)

2:15. Paul ended this section of his letter with a summary of Titus's responsibility and authority. **These things** refers to the content of the whole chapter.

V. Concerning Believers in General (3:1–8)

A. Obligations as Citizens (3:1–2)

New Testament teaching is not confined to the area of personal salvation but includes much instruction about practical living. Although believers are citizens of heaven (see Phil. 3:20), they must also submit themselves to earthly government (see Rom. 13:1–7; 1 Peter 2:13–17) and help promote the well-being of the community.

3:1–2. Principalities and powers (v. 1) refers to all forms and levels of human government (for this term applied to angels, see Eph. 3:10; 6:12). **Every good work** (see discussions on 1:8; 3:1, 8; Introduction: "Theme"; 2 Tim. 2:21) is to typify a disposition toward outsiders that demonstrates godliness (see 1:1; 2:12) and exonerates the Christian faith in the eyes of outsiders (see 1 Tim. 2:2). A specific example of "every good work" is **shewing all meekness unto all men** (v. 2), a virtue of grace (see 2:11–12; 3:4). Genuine humility and gentle courtesy flow from the believer's own experience of God's undeserved favor, something Paul brought to mind in 3:3.

B. Motives for Godly Conduct (3:3–8)

3:3–4. Paul assigned to **we ourselves** the kinds of behaviors that Christians, having turned from such conduct, are now to meet with meekness (see 3:2) and with the kindness and love of God in Christ. God's **kindness and love** (v. 4) are the reasons He did not simply banish fallen man but acted to save him (see 2:11).

3:5–7. According to his mercy he saved us (v. 5). Salvation is not achieved by human effort or merit but comes through God's mercy alone. The Greek construction of **the washing of regeneration** suggests that as Christians are renewed by the work of the Holy Spirit, so they are washed by the work of regeneration. **Renewing of the Holy Ghost** is also a reference to new birth.

3:8. The almost formulaic phrase **a faithful saying** refers to the doctrinal summary in 3:4–7. This phrase, which occurs only here in Titus, appears four other times in the Pastoral Epistles (1 Tim. 1:15; 3:1; 4:9; 2 Tim. 2:11) and nowhere else in the New Testament. The importance of Paul's insistence that believers **be careful to maintain good works** is now fathomed in the light of 3:1–7. "Good works" (see discussions on 1:8; 3:1, 8; Introduction: "Theme") are the very demonstration of the gospel, an extension of the grace (kindness, love, mercy) of Christ's appearing (see 3:4; 2:11). In the real world, "goodness" validates and authenticates the truth of Christ in one's life. Paul repeated this injunction in 3:14, where "ours" is mindful of the marked difference between believers and unbelievers, between the gospel and false teaching.

VI. Concerning Response to Spiritual Error (3:9–11)

3:9. Foolish questions, and genealogies, and contentions, and strivings ("quarrels") **about the law** refers to the situation described in 1:10–16. A similar problem existed in Ephesus (see 1 Tim. 1:3–7). Such things **are unprofitable and vain**, counterproductive to the "good works" (3:1, 8) that come from and further belief in the gospel (see 3:4–7). Titus was better off investing his time and energy in people with hearts receptive to the work and will of God in Christ (see 3:10; 1 Tim 4:7; 2 Tim. 2:22–26 and discussion).

3:10–11. In the early church, **heretick** (Greek, *hairetikos*; only here in the New Testament) became a technical term for a type of heretic who promoted dissension by propagating extreme views of legitimate Christian truths. The recalcitrance of the heretic's factious spirit and mindset was confirmed after a **second admonition** (Greek, *nouthesia*) to cease and desist (see the use of the verb in 2 Thess. 3:14–15). After a second warning, Titus was to change tactics and avoid, if not repudiate, the person, knowing the heretic was not only divisive but **subverted, and sinneth, being condemned of himself**. This final characteristic is telltale. The condemnation ratifies the heretic's own response. Stubborn refusal to listen to correction reveals inner perversion.

VII. Conclusion (3:12–15)

3:12. In Paul's letters, personal instructions and travel plans commonly occupy his concluding remarks. So that he could join Paul, Titus would be relieved by **Artemas ... or Tychicus**. The latter was Paul's trusted coworker who traveled with or for Paul on various occasions (see Acts 20:4; Eph. 6:21–22; Col. 4:7–8; 2 Tim. 4:12). It may be surmised that the decision was later defined by unforeseen circumstances (imprisonment), for Tychicus was sent to Ephesus (see 2 Tim 4:12), Titus to Dalmatia (see 2 Tim. 4:10), and Artemas to Crete, as stated here in v. 12. Artemas is otherwise unknown. **Nicopolis** means "city of victory." Several cities had this name, but the reference here is apparently to the city in Epirus on the western shore of Greece. Paul **determined there to winter**, which imagines a rendezvous with Titus in Nicopolis. It also indicates that Paul had not arrived there when he wrote this letter and that he was still free to travel at will, not yet having been imprisoned in Rome for the second time.

3:13. Bring ... on their journey is one word in Greek (*propempō*) and carries the sense of "to help on their way." In the New Testament, *propempō* commonly refers to the hospitable assistance of providing a traveler what they need for a journey (see, e.g., Acts 15:3; Rom. 15:24; 1 Cor. 16:6, 16; 2 Cor. 1:16; 3 John 6). **Zenas the lawyer** is mentioned only here in the New Testament. If he was a Jewish convert, "lawyer" means that he was an expert in Mosaic law; if he was a Gentile convert, that he was a Roman jurist. **Apollos** was a native of Alexandria and one of Paul's well-known coworkers (see Acts 18:24–28; 19:1; 1 Cor. 1:12; 3:4–6, 22; 16:12). The two travelers apparently delivered Paul's letter to Titus.

3:14. Paul's thematic emphasis on **good works** (see discussions on 1:8; 3:1, 8) is given final emphasis. **Ours** may well refer to the dispatch of Zenas and Apollos. They **also** were to be set on their way with this important reminder. Whether "ours" refers to them or to "our people," and whether "good works" is an additional application or a final reinforcement, it

is clear that "good works" is no mere platitude but expressive of the gospel in action (see discussion on 3:8).

3:15. All that are with me salute (i.e., "greet" or give hospitable acknowledgment to) **thee**. Titus in turn was to **Greet them that love us in the faith**, which had nothing to do with Titus's good sense to greet the right people and everything to do with Paul's sensitivity to the dynamics of doctrinal disharmony on the part of some within the community (see 3:10–11). This is a subtle but further indication of the challenges on Crete to sound doctrine (1:9, 13; 2:1–2). **Grace be with you all** refers to the whole church and may imply that the letter was to be read publicly, having the tone of a benedicton for the whole assembly. It certainly captures the prominence of 2:11 and 3:4 and fittingly resounds the heart of this chapter.

THE EPISTLE OF PAUL
TO PHILEMON

INTRODUCTION

Author, Date, and Place of Composition

Paul wrote this short letter (see vv. 1, 9, 19), probably at the same time as Colossians (ca. AD 60; see Colossians, Introduction: "Author, Date, and Place of Composition"), and sent it to Colosse with the same travelers, Onesimus and Tychicus. Paul apparently wrote both letters from prison in Rome, though possibly from Ephesus (see Philippians, Introduction: "Author, Date, and Place of Composition").

Recipient

Paul wrote this letter to Philemon, a believer in Colosse.

Theme

Along with others in Colosse, Philemon was a slave owner (see Col. 4:1; for slavery in the New Testament, see discussion on Eph. 6:5). One of his slaves, Onesimus, apparently had stolen from him (see v. 18) and then run away, which was punishable by death under Roman law. Onesimus met Paul and became a Christian through his ministry (see v. 10). Now Onesimus was willing to return to his master, and Paul wrote this personal appeal to Philemon to ask that Onesimus be accepted as a Christian brother (see v. 16).

Literary Features

To win Philemon's willing acceptance of Onesimus, Paul wrote very tactfully and in a lighthearted tone, which he created with a wordplay (see discussion on v. 11). The appeal (vv. 4–21) is organized in a way prescribed by ancient Greek and Roman teachers: to build rapport (vv. 4–10), to persuade the mind (vv. 11–19), and to move the emotions (vv. 20–21). The name Onesimus is not mentioned until the rapport has been built (v. 10), and the appeal itself is stated only near the end of the section to persuade the mind (v. 17).

Outline

I. Greetings (vv. 1–3)
II. Thanksgiving and Prayer (vv. 4–7)
III. Paul's Plea for Onesimus (vv. 8–21)
IV. Final Request, Greetings, and Benediction (vv. 22–25)

Bibliography

Carson, Herbert M. *The Epistles of Paul to the Colossians and Philemon.* Grand Rapids, MI: Eerdmans, 1977.

Lightfoot, J. B. *Saint Paul's Epistles to the Colossians and Philemon.* 1879. Reprint, Grand Rapids, MI: Zondervan, 1959.

Martin, Ralph P. *Colossians and Philemon.* Grand Rapids, MI: Eerdmans, 1981.

O'Brien, Peter T. *Colossians–Philemon.* Word Biblical Commentary 44. Waco, TX: Word, 1982.

EXPOSITION

I. Greetings (vv. 1–3)

Verses 1–2. Although Paul wrote this letter with Timothy and although he addressed the entire church in Colosse, in this very personal letter to Philemon, he used "I" (rather than "we") and "thee" (singular except in vv. 22, 25).

Verse 1. Paul was under arrest at this time and therefore **a prisoner** (see v. 9; discussions on Eph. 3:1; Phil. 1:13), but **of Jesus Christ** makes plain the cause for which he was "bound." In Greek, the word "prisoner" (*desmios*) is derived from the word for "bonds" or "chains" (Greek, *desmos*), a vivid synonym for Paul's imprisonment (see vv. 13; Phil. 1:7, 14; Col. 4:18). Paul's poignant use of "prisoner" rather than "apostle" was purposeful as he interceded for Onesimus. **Timothy** (see discussion on Col. 1:1; see also 1 Timothy, Introduction: "Recipient") was with Paul. **Philemon** was a Christian living in Colosse or nearby and was the owner of the slave Onesimus. **Dearly beloved, and fellowlabourer** are titles of endearment and a status that Paul hoped Philemon would in turn confer on Onesimus (see vv. 16–17; note "partner" in v. 17).

Verse 2. Apphia was probably Philemon's wife, standing after him in the order of names. **Archippus** our fellow soldier (see Phil. 2:25), or esteemed as a colleague in the campaign for Christ, was probably an officebearer (see Col. 4:17) in **the church** that met **in thy house** (the home of Philemon). Some conjecture that Archippus was Philemon's son.

Verse 3. This greeting is characteristic of Paul's letters (see, e.g., Phil. 1:2). **Grace to you** (plural) identifies not only Philemon and the aforementioned people but the church that met in his house.

II. Thanksgiving and Prayer (vv. 4–7)

Verse 4. I thank my God, making mention of thee always in my prayers. See discussion on Philippians 1:3–4.

Verse 5. Hearing of was probably a reference to more than one source but likely included reports from Epaphras (see Col. 1:4, 7–8; 4:12) and even Onesimus. **Thy love and faith ... toward the Lord Jesus, and toward all saints** mirrors Colossians 1:4, although here, notably, love stands first.

Verse 6. That introduces the specific intent of Paul's prayer, which opened with thanksgiving (v. 4) and here turns to petition. The fulfillment of this petition, which envisioned the extension and effectual realization of Philemon's reported love and faith (see

v. 5), would encompass the benefits to Onesimus that Paul sought from Philemon. **Communication** (Greek, *koinōnia*), denoting "mutual association" or "partnership," may also connote the signs of such fellowship, the contributions and generosity that characterize it, as here. **Of thy faith** identifies the source of their mutual "communication." **Effectual** refers to the practical expression of Philemon's "communication" in **the acknowledging** (or "the full knowledge"; Greek, *epignōsis*; "recognition"] **of every good thing,** an enlarged appreciation of the good that is defined by Christ. Included in "every good thing" was the good that Christ desired for Onesimus.

Verse 7. Bowels stands for "heart," with an emphasis on its emotional affection. As the heart today is regarded as the seat of emotions, so the intestines or "bowels" were for the ancient Greeks (see vv. 12, 20). Although Paul had yet to make his request, the heartfelt largess of Philemon's life, which was known to Paul and many others, was cause to expect that Philemon would have room for similar goodness to Onesimus.

III. Paul's Plea for Onesimus (vv. 8–21)

Verses 8–9. Wherefore (v. 8), or "On this basis, I appeal." Paul conceded his freedom (**bold**) in Christ, favoring a loving appeal (**beseech**; v. 9) over a command (**enjoin**; v. 8). All this was in the service of **that which is convenient** (Greek, *anēkō*; what is "proper," "fitting"; see Col. 3:8; Eph. 5:4), not in the contemporary sense of "handy," but "what was required" or "the right thing to do" in this situation and in Christ. Behind the appeal was **Paul the aged** (v. 9). It may very well be that "aged" should better be translated as "the ambassador" or "the envoy" of Christ Jesus, a stronger ground of appeal than his age and linked in Ephesians 6:20, as here, with his imprisonment (see Lightfoot, *Colossians and Philemon*, pp. 338–39).

Verse 10. Beseech, the identical verb as that in verse 9, here introduces the explicit appeal and purpose for writing. **My son** (Greek, *teknon*; "child") connotes Paul's "spiritual child" (see 1 Tim. 1:2, 18; 1 Cor. 4:17; 2 Tim. 1:2; 2:1; Titus 1:4) who was **begotten,** or "fathered," through spiritual conversion,

which Paul said took place "in my bonds." (see discussion on v. 1). For **Onesimus** and the meaning of his name, "profitable," see verse 11 and Introduction: "Theme." The clear play on words in verse 11 may begin here: "my son 'Profitable' whom I have begotten in my bonds." If so, Paul may have been implying that the meaning of Onesimus's name was truly realized at his conversion to Christ.

Verse 11. Unprofitable … profitable is a word-play on the meaning of the name Onesimus ("profitable" or "useful," from the Greek verb *oninēmi*, "to profit," "to benefit," "to help"). Onesimus was a common slave name. By running away, Onesimus had not lived up to his name. In fact, he was lost to Philemon. Now he had returned, probably with this letter in hand, and Paul wanted to persuade Philemon to see Onesimus not as he was when he left but as he was when he returned, "profitable" to them both.

Verses 12–14. With **Whom** (i.e., "Profitable"; see v. 11) **… receive him** (v. 12), Paul requested that Philemon accept the "profitable" one who was coming back to him. "Him" is intensive, underscoring Onesimus's new identity. Moreover, this new man returned home an incarnation of Paul's own heart (**mine own bowels;** see discussion on v. 7), a manifestation of Paul's deepest affection. The man Paul asked Philemon to receive was not only a new "Onesimus" and a brother in Christ but a piece of Paul himself. Paul would not keep anything so precious **without thy mind** (v. 14), or "without your consent." In sending Onesimus home, Paul deferred to Philemon so that the **benefit** (lit., "the goodness"; see v. 6) he expected of him could be done **willingly,** or voluntarily (see v. 8).

Verses 15–16. Paul steered Philemon's thoughts from Onesimus's wrongdoing to his restoration by adding the divine perspective of God's providential operation in what had taken place. The words **departed for a season** (v. 15) not only temper a willful act of running away; they also suggest God's hidden agenda with the divine passive "was departed," which in Greek can mean "was separated." "For a season" is eclipsed by the benefit of **for ever** ("eternity"). What is for eternity is not **a servant** (v. 16) but **a brother … in the flesh, and in the Lord,** meaning humanly and spiritually, but the contrast of "for a season" and "for ever" lends to these words the sense of "on earth" and "in heaven." To understand more clearly Paul's message concerning servants and masters, one must read the book of Philemon in conjunction with Colossians 3:22–4:1.

Verse 17. Luther said, "Even as Christ did for us with God the Father, thus Paul also does for Onesimus with Philemon." Verse 19 weakens this correspondence. **Partner** (Greek, *koinōnos*; "partner," "companion"), an allusion to the "communication" of verse 6, capitalizes on Onesimus's status as a brother in the faith and a brother in Christ. But more than that, Philemon was to transfer Paul's own status to Onesimus (see v. 19).

Verses 18–19. Onesimus's new status as "a brother" (v. 16) is given a twist in that Philemon was also Paul's son, his spiritual child (see v. 10). Here spiritual progeny is intertwined metaphorically with the discussion of debts, material and spiritual. Paul, **with [his] own hand** (v. 19), was writing an IOU for the material debt. The implication from what follows, **thou owest unto me even thine own self besides,** is that out of this IOU for the spiritual debt, Philemon could find the resources to cover what Paul was asking for Onesimus. It should be added that references to the debt Onesimus had incurred may be to the value of his own life as a runaway slave. That debt was matched by what Philemon owed to Paul: "thine own self."

Verse 20. Both **me** and **my** are emphatic pronouns, making an obvious allusion to verse 7. **Joy** (Greek, *oninēmi*; see discussion on v. 11) means "benefit" and is another play on the name Onesimus. **Refresh my bowels** is a third reference to "the heart" (see discussion on v. 7; see also v. 12).

Verse 21. Here Paul mentioned **obedience,** a sublime reference to his apostolic authority and leverage, which he had refused in favor of petition in verse 8. There he refused to "enjoin" what here he expected Philemon to obey. **Knowing that thou wilt also do more than I say** is a supposition of Philemon's generosity, only hinted at earlier (see v. 6).

IV. Final Request, Greetings, and Benediction (vv. 22–25)

Verse 22. With **But withal** (lit., "At the same time"), Paul conveyed an additional request to go along with that of Philemon's generous reception of Onesimus. It was not unusual for an ancient letter, though occasioned by one matter, to also include another matter. Often, as here, the second matter had to do with how and when the author planned to meet the recipient again. **Prepare me also a lodging** is subtle; Paul was preparing Philemon for a personal visit. In effect, he was saying, "Along with the lodging that I am confident you will give to Onesimus, make a bed ready for me."

Verses 23–24. In his closing greetings, Paul included hospitable recognition from **Epaphras** (v. 23; see Col. 4:12), who was probably well known to Philemon, and from Paul's coworkers **Marcus, Aristarchus** (see discussion on Col. 4:10), **Demas, Lucas** (see discussion on Col. 4:14). Although greetings of this kind were conventional, it is difficult to imagine that the mention of these men didn't add a quality of their consensus with Paul in the matter before Philemon, even if only imagined.

Verse 25. Paul addressed the final benediction to the entire house church (see v. 3), as the plural personal pronoun "your" in **with your spirit** implies.

THE EPISTLE OF PAUL THE APOSTLE TO THE HEBREWS

INTRODUCTION

Author

The writer of this epistle did not identify himself, but he was obviously well known to the original recipients. For some 1,200 years (from ca. AD 400 to 1600), the book was commonly called "The Epistle of Paul the Apostle to the Hebrews," but there was no agreement in the earliest centuries regarding its authorship. Since the Reformation, it has been widely agreed that Paul was not the writer. There is no disharmony between the teaching of Hebrews and that of Paul's letters, but the specific emphases and writing styles are markedly different. Contrary to Paul's usual practice, the author of Hebrews nowhere identified himself in the letter, except to indicate that he was a man (see discussion on 11:32) who apparently was also in prison (10:34) and was a companion of Timothy (13:23). Moreover, the statement that the message of salvation "at the first began to be spoken by the Lord, and was confirmed unto us by them that heard him" (2:3) indicates that the author had neither been with Jesus during His earthly ministry nor received special revelation directly from the risen Lord, as had Paul (see Gal. 1:11–12).

The earliest alternative suggestion of authorship is found in Tertullian's *De Pudicitia*, 20 (ca. AD 200), in which he quoted from "an epistle to the Hebrews under the name of Barnabas." From the letter itself, it is clear that the writer had authority in the apostolic church and was an intellectual Hebrew Christian well versed in the Old Testament. Barnabas meets these requirements. He was a Jew of the priestly tribe of Levi (see Acts 4:36) who became a close friend of Paul after the latter's conversion. Under the guidance of the Holy Spirit, the church at Antioch commissioned Barnabas and Paul for the work of evangelism and sent them off on the first missionary journey (see Acts 13:1–4).

The other leading candidate for authorship is Apollos, whose name was first suggested by Martin Luther and who is favored by many scholars today. Apollos, an Alexandrian by birth, was also a Jewish Christian with notable intellectual and oratorical abilities. Luke stated that Apollos was "an eloquent man, and mighty in the scriptures" (Acts 18:24). We also know that Apollos was associated with Paul in the early years of the church in Corinth (see 1 Cor. 1:12; 3:4–6, 22).

Perhaps we lack knowledge as to the human author because God did not want us to know who the author is. The question arises, however, that if this was God's intention, why? Perhaps He means to turn our sole attention to the message of the epistle, not its source.

The writer and his companions may have been Italians, as evidenced by 13:24. On the other hand, the use of the Septuagint in the many quotations from the Old Testament may also suggest a Jewish Christian living outside of Israel.

Date

Hebrews must have been written before the destruction of Jerusalem and the temple in AD 70 because (1) the author surely would have mentioned the temple's destruction and the end of the Jewish sacrificial system if the book had been written after this date, and (2) the author consistently used the Greek present tense when speaking of the temple and the priestly activities connected with it (5:1–3; 7:23, 27; 8:3–5; 9:6–9, 13, 25; 10:1, 3–4, 8, 11; 13:10–11).

This epistle was written during a time of great persecution of Christians in Jerusalem, first at the hands of the Sadducees and soon thereafter by the Pharisees and the general Jewish population. Hebrews 12:4 may suggest that the date of composition was prior to the inception of Nero's great persecutions of Christians in Rome, which began in approximately AD 64.

Recipients

The letter was addressed primarily to Jewish converts, probably in Rome, who were familiar with the Old Testament and who were being tempted, in the face of severe persecution (10:22), to revert to the comforts and acceptance found in Judaism or to Judaize the gospel (see Gal. 2:14). Part of this temptation could have been because Rome recognized Judaism as a legitimate religion but considered Christianity illegal and illegitimate. Some have suggested that these professing Jewish Christians were thinking of merging with a Jewish sect, such as the one at Qumran near the Dead Sea. It has also been suggested that the recipients were from the large number of priests who "were obedient to the faith" (Acts 6:7).

Theme and Theological Message

The book of Hebrews was a "word of exhortation" (13:22) that the readers were advised to take to heart ("suffer"). Thus, the author's purpose for writing was less polemic than is generally regarded, notwithstanding that he used many of the great doctrines of Scripture in establishing his arguments to "run … the race" (12:1) considering "him that endured" (12:3).

The theme of Hebrews is the absolute supremacy and sufficiency of Jesus Christ as the revealer and the mediator of God's grace. The prologue (1:1–4) presents Christ as God's full and final revelation, far surpassing the limited preliminary revelation given in the Old Testament. The prophecies and promises of the Old Testament are fulfilled in the new covenant (the New Testament), of which Christ is the mediator. From the Old Testament itself, Christ is shown to be superior to the ancient prophets, to angels, to Moses (the mediator of the former covenant), and to Aaron and the priestly succession descended from him. Hebrews could be called "the book of better things" since the two Greek words for "better" and "superior" occur fifteen times in the letter.

The author employed this general theme to present his arguments to "hold fast" (10:23). By presenting a series of five warnings, he reminded his readers of the verities and consequences of Old Testament law and compared them to what we now have in and through Christ. The writer provided practical applications of this theme throughout the letter and told his readers that there could be no turning back to or continuation in the old Jewish system, which had been superseded by the unique priesthood of Christ. God's people now must look only to Him, whose atoning death, resurrection, and ascension have opened the way into the true, heavenly sanctuary of God's presence. Resisting temptations to give up the struggle, believers must persevere in the spiritual contest to which they have committed themselves. Otherwise, they may meet with the New Testament equivalent of judgment (see 12:6, 11; Rom. 8:1), as did the rebellious generation of Israelites in the wilderness.

Outline

Bibliography

Bruce, F. F. *The Epistle to the Hebrews.* The New International Commentary on the New Testament. Grand Rapids, MI: Eerdmans, 1964.

Guthrie, Donald. *The Letters to the Hebrews.* Tyndale New Testament Commentaries. Grand Rapids, MI: Eerdmans, 1983.

Hagner, Donald A. *Hebrews.* New International Biblical Commentary. Peabody, MA: Hendrickson, 1990.

Hughes, Philip E. *A Commentary on the Epistle to the Hebrews.* Grand Rapids, MI: Eerdmans, 1977.

Kent, Homer A. *The Epistle to the Hebrews.* Grand Rapids, MI: Baker, 1972.

Lane, William L. *Hebrews 1–8.* Word Biblical Commentary 47A. Dallas: Word, 1991.

———. *Hebrews 9–13.* Word Biblical Commentary 47B. Dallas: Word, 1991.

Newell, William R. *Hebrews Verse by Verse.* Chicago: Moody Press, 1978.

EXPOSITION

I. Prologue: The Superiority of God's New Revelation (1:1–4)

The author of Hebrews displayed his complete knowledge of the recipients and his great ability as a litigator and teacher in these opening verses. He was speaking to Jews who had come to believe that Jesus was the promised Messiah as revealed in the Old Testament. This was of great significance. Their heritage and background in Old Testament Scriptures only served to enhance the unexpected nature of this new revelation to which they had committed themselves, especially with respect to the deity of Jesus Christ. The truth found in Deuteronomy 6:4 had been drilled into them since birth: "Hear, O Israel: the LORD our God is one LORD." Thus, the author began his opening salvo with God, evoking the feelings of reverence, submission, and love that would resonate in the heart of any true and committed believer. He declared that the God whom they had always trusted and who had spoken to their fathers through the prophets had spoken again, in the person of His Son. The plurality of persons constituting one God was a leap that their leaders in the Sanhedrin could not make and was an exercise of faith that could only be justified by acceptance of the truthfulness of the description of the Lord Jesus found in verses 2–4.

This description answers the question found in Isaiah 40: "To whom then will ye liken God? Or what likeness will ye compare unto him?... who hath created these things ... Hast thou not known? hast thou not heard, that the everlasting God, the LORD, the Creator of the ends of the earth, fainteth not, neither is weary?" (Isa. 40:18, 26, 28). For this reason, the prophet encouraged his reader with, "They shall run, and not be weary; and they shall walk, and not faint" (Isa. 40:31). The author of Hebrews encouraged his readers again and again with this same refrain.

Continuing to lay out the foundational truths upon which he based the epistle, the writer declared that the mighty Lord, who holds the world and all creation in His hands by the power of His word, is the procurer of our completed redemption. He further declared that the Lord, better than the angels, has by inheritance a more excellent name than they, further reinforcing the superiority of Christ, His work, and His word.

We see a methodology at work throughout the epistle. The author argued by establishing or reinforcing foundational truths, upon which he built. He then presented and compared those truths to the new and superior. This building process is an important interpretive key to Hebrews. The first example of this is in verse 4, where the author's mention of angels segues into the first of five arguments that follow.

1:1. God. Contrary to custom, the author did not begin his letter with his own name. Instead, he introduced the Divine Author. The use of the personal pronoun **who** is suggestive of the personality of God and of His activity among His people when **at sundry times and in divers manners [He] spake unto the fathers in time past**. The idea that it was God who spoke, even though He spoke **by the prophets**, cannot be overemphasized. "In time past" stands in contrast to "in these last days" (1:2), the messianic era inaugurated by the incarnation. Even though the Old Testament revelation was fragmentary and occasional, lacking fullness and finality, it was nonetheless a word from the Lord. All Old Testament writers are here viewed as prophets in that their testimony was the proclamation of God's message to His people and was preparation for the coming of Christ. The writer alerted the attentive reader to what he developed in chapter 11, where he brought the promises, warnings, and consequences discussed throughout the letter to poignant focus by paralleling them with specific Old Testament examples of faith.

1:2–3. In contrast to previous revelation, God **hath in these last days spoken unto us by his Son** (v. 2; lit., "in Son"; the anarthrous construction, an absence of the definite article in the Greek, stresses the quality of the thing specified). The incarnation inaugurated a new kind of era (see Acts 2:17; 1 Tim 4:1; 1 John 2:18). This is a new and unique category of revelation in contrast to that of the prophets. Old Testament prophets delivered a message from God; Christ *is* the message. The following verses suggest not only that this revelation was the Word of God as He delivered it personally but that, in His own person, Christ was a complete and perfect revelation ("Son") of the Godhead (see John 1:1–14).

The superiority of the "in Son" relationship is demonstrated by seven great descriptive statements about Him. (1) He is **appointed heir of all things** (v. 2; see Rom. 8:17). The incarnate Son was gloriously exalted to the position of the firstborn heir of God; that is, He received the inheritance of God's estate ("all things"). (2) This is the One, **by whom also he** (God) **made the worlds** (see John 1:3; Col. 1:16). (3) The Son is **the brightness of his** (God's) **glory** (v. 3). This suggests that the glory of the Godhead is demonstrated in Christ, and as the brilliance of the sun is inseparable from the sun itself, so the Son's radiance is inseparable from deity. He Himself is God, the second person of the Trinity (see John 1:14, 18). (4) Christ is further said to be **the express image of his** (God's) **person.** Jesus is not merely an image or reflection of God. Because the Son is God, He is the absolutely authentic representation of God's being (see John 14:9; Col. 1:15). (5) Christ upholds **all things by the word of his power.** Christ is not like Atlas, the mythical Greek god who held the world on his shoulders. The Son dynamically holds together and carries forward all that has been created through Him (see Col. 1:17). He does this through His awesome power. (6) **He ... himself purged our sins.** The emphasis here is not *how* He purged our sins but *that* He purged our sins. (7) When His work on behalf of sin was finished, He **sat down on the right hand of the Majesty on high.** Being seated at God's right hand indicates that the work of redemption is complete and that Christ is actively ruling with God as Lord over all (see 1:13; 8:1; 10:12; 12:2; Eph. 1:20; Col. 3:1; 1 Peter 3:22; see also discussion on Mark 16:19; Pss. 110:1; 1:3; 8:1). The use of the circumlocution for God ("Majesty on high") is indicative

of the recipients, who were scrupulous about direct references to God's name. In speaking of the significance of Christ, the early apostles drew heavily on the Old Testament (e.g., Psalm 110; Joel 2:28–32; Pss. 16:8–11; 89:3–4; 118:22; Dan. 9:24–27; see Acts 2:14–36; 4:23–31).

1:4. Having been appointed heir of all things and given a position of supreme authority, Christ is seen as **much better than the angels.** To most Jews, angels were exalted beings, especially revered because they were involved in giving the law at Sinai (see discussion on 2:2), and to the Jews, the law was God's supreme revelation. The Dead Sea Scrolls reflect the expectation that the archangel Michael would be the supreme figure in the messianic kingdom. The incarnate Christ had taken on the form of a man, a little lower than the angels. Whether the recipients of Hebrews were tempted to assign angels a place above Christ (the Messiah) is not known. Nonetheless, **he hath by inheritance obtained a more excellent name than they.** To Jews, a name stood for the full character of a person in all he was and did (see discussion on Gen. 17:5). Here the author made the important distinction that Christ has a legal right to His name as opposed to His having earned it. The theology of the immutability of God and the preexistence of a glorified Christ is in play here. The section that follows indicates that this name was "Son," a name to which no angel could lay claim (see 1:2 and discussion).

II. Arguments for Staying the Course (1:5–12:29)

If there is one epistle in the New Testament that applies uniquely to the church of the twenty-first century, none is more apropos than Hebrews. We have witnessed large-scale defections of professing born-again Christians to the deceptions of inclusivism, hedonism, and self-indulgence. Many have indeed "left [their] first love" (Rev. 2:4). A study of this epistle should be a rebuke to anyone who is considering giving up the fight or who is growing weary of participating in the sufferings of Christ. Ours is not the temptation to return to the comfort of Old

Testament Judaism, as was the case with the recipients of this epistle; rather, ours is the temptation to return to a life without the scorn and slings and arrows of the world in order to participate in a lifestyle that we feel is our "right" as a member of modern Western culture. As Paul said of the experiences of Israel, perhaps it could be said that Hebrews was also "written for our admonition, upon whom the ends of the world are come" (1 Cor. 10:11).

A. The Argument for a Superior Revelation (1:5–2:4)

Christ's superiority to angels is documented with seven Old Testament quotations, showing that He is God's Son, that He is worshiped by angels, and that, though He is God, He is distinguished from the Father. While it was necessary for the writer to document the superiority of the word of Christ over the word delivered with the assistance of angels on Mount Sinai, it must be remembered that no word from God is superior to any other word from God (see 2 Tim. 3:16).

1. The Nature of the Superiority (1:5–14)

This section contains a litany of Old Testament prophecies concerning the coming of Christ, His office, and His worthiness. The author of Hebrews reminded his hearers of these things to demonstrate, not that the new word from God is superior in its intrinsic value, but that a promise fulfilled was better than a promise yet unfulfilled in the lives of these new believers.

1:5. Thou art my Son, this day have I begotten thee. This prophetic passage (Ps. 2:7) is quoted in Acts 13:33 as being fulfilled in Christ's resurrection (see Rom. 1:4). The kings of Israel (such as David) were the "sons of God" by adoption (see 2 Sam. 7:14), but this heir to the throne was "begotten" of God. This contrasts with angels, who are created beings but who will never sit on a throne. **I will be to him a Father, and he shall be to me a Son**. Jews acknowledged 2 Samuel 7:14, which the writer quoted here, and Psalm 2 as messianic in their ultimate application (see Luke 1:32–33). This royal personage is

neither an angel nor an archangel; He is God's Son. The prophecy was fulfilled before their very eyes.

1:6. As **the firstbegotten**, Jesus is the fountainhead of all that is (see John 1:1–3) and "the firstborn [of] many brethren" (Rom. 8:29). The term "firstbegotten" suggests that others had already followed. Since Christ is the progenitor of that out of which the hearers had been called (Judaism), the promise of a "better thing" (11:40) carried all the legitimacy that only God can give. The hearers, members of the fledgling New Testament church, were reminded that Christ, their Head, is the firstbegotten of God, even as they also were begotten of God through the miracle of regeneration. The doxological statement **let all the angels of God worship Him** may be from Psalm 97:7. This statement, which in the Old Testament refers to the Yahweh (see Ps. 97:1–9), is here applied to Christ, giving clear indication of His deity. If He is worthy of worship from the angels, He is worthy also of our worship. God chose to reveal Himself in the confines of time and humanity, "in Son" (see discussion on 1:2), as clearly prophesied in Isaiah (Isa. 9:6; 59:20) and fulfilled as Matthew and Luke declared (Matt. 1:23; Luke 2:11). The hearers were brought into full realization that they served none other than the living God and that, as brethren of Christ, they were participants in the fulfillment of the promise. This was a far superior position than that of their fathers, who could only participate in the promise by faith.

1:7. The next quotation, from Psalm 104:4, **Who maketh his angels spirits, and his ministers a flame of fire**, speaks of the storm wind and lightning as agents of God's purposes. This contrasts to that "better thing" (11:40), the church, which has been called to fulfill God's purposes during this current age (see Matt. 28:18–20).

1:8. But unto the Son he saith, Thy throne, O God, is for ever and ever. The author selected a passage (Ps. 45:6) that intimates the deity of the messianic (and Davidic) King. The hearers were reminded that, although God has temporarily set aside the programs concerning Israel, they served the same God who has promised to sit on the throne of David, a throne which is eternal. The church, of which they were a part, is now the agency of God's power, but the promises to Israel and David will yet be fulfilled. This provides a continuity to God's purposes, which would have encouraged the hearers to "hold fast" (10:23) to better things by reminding them that as God fulfilled His promises as to the incarnation of Christ, He will also fulfill His promises to Israel.

1:9. God, even thy God, hath anointed thee with the oil of gladness above thy fellows. This quotation from Psalm 45:6, parenthetically placed after the quotation from Psalm 104:4 demands extraordinary attention. Psalm 45, known as "A Song of Loves," is a song celebrating the marriage of a king. The hearers would have immediately recognized it as such, and both the psalm and the portion quoted would have been important to them. The use of this song in the context of the eternal nature of the throne further enhanced the encouragement provided in 1:8 as to the continuity of God's purposes. The joy and gladness of the king in the presence of his brethren and the anointing, which represents the sovereign will of God, is in view. The intimacy enjoyed by both Jew and Gentile as fellow laborers with Christ suggested to the hearers that they, though persecuted and troubled, were not alone (2:11). The connection to the apostle Paul's twin polemics, Colossians and Ephesians, is evident, if not intentional.

1:10. Thou, Lord, in the beginning hast laid the foundation of the earth. As in 1:8, a passage addressed to Yahweh ("You, Lord") is applied to the Son. We see the authority of Christ, as Creator, to direct the hearers in their "heavenly calling" (3:1).

1:11–12. They shall perish (v. 11) **... but thou art the same** (v. 12). With eternity's values in view, the brethren and fellow laborers with Christ were reminded that they were on the winning team. Here the author looked forward to a future that will be ruled by Christ, who is the same yesterday, today, and forever.

1:13. Sit on my right hand (see discussion on 1:2–3). Psalm 110 is applied repeatedly to Jesus in Hebrews (1:3, 13; 5:6, 10; 6:20; 7:3, 11, 17, 21; 8:1; 10:12–13; 12:2). There can be no mistaking that

one of the author's purposes was to emphasize the location of the Lord relative to the Old Testament prophecies concerning Him.

1:14. Ministering spirits ... for them who shall be heirs of salvation. The author, though repeatedly comparing angels to the superior Christ, affirmed that they are nevertheless not diminished. The angels are now sent forth to minister to believers. This ministry is in stark contrast to the work of angels referred to in 1:7. For the hearers, this was a new and better word.

2. Warning concerning the Revelation (2:1)

2:1. Therefore we ought to give the more earnest heed is a call to seriously consider the foregoing in the light of **the things which we have heard**, which would include the message of the gospel, of Christ's person as the God-man, His redemptive work on the cross, and the Scriptures. As the author has shown, this includes reviewing the Old Testament promises that, to believers' benefit, have been fulfilled in Christ. **Lest at any time we should let them slip.** The inference of this phrase is that we should not allow ourselves to drift away from "the things which we have heard." This warning speaks against the dangers of lethargy or loose thinking concerning these things. Believers need to diligently guard themselves against any degree of drifting away. This is the first of five warnings strategically positioned throughout the letter (2:1–4; 3:7–4:13; 5:11–6:12; 10:19–39; 12:14–29). Progressive in their severity and in the severity of the consequences, these warnings possess a common pattern containing four elements: (1) the warning is stated, (2) a historical example is given, (3) historical consequences are recorded, and (4) the consequences for contemporary readers are stated should they fail to heed the warning.

3. Consequences of Neglecting the Revelation under Moses (2:2)

2:2. Following the pattern of the warnings (see 2:1 and discussion), the warning is first stated, then, second, the historical example is **the word spoken by angels.** This is the law given to Moses at Sinai (Deut.

33:2), and when it was transgressed or disobeyed, it always **received a just recompence of reward**. Third, the historical example is followed by the consequences for those who transgressed this law. Numbers 15:30 speaks of the recompense that should be the lot of one who sins presumptuously. A man who raises his fist in the face of God is a reproach to the Lord and is deserving of death. In Acts 7, Stephen rehearsed before the synagogue the results of Israel's rebellion against Moses when God "gave them up to worship the host of heaven" (Acts 7:42). They who had known the blessings and presence of God had neither. Old Testament prophets also had to remind the nation of their cyclical treachery against their God (see, e.g., Ezek. 20:1–44). Such repeated offenses formed the detail of God's final indictment against them, leading to their destruction and captivity.

4. Consequences of Neglecting the Revelation under Christ (2:3)

2:3. If we neglect so great salvation, we shall not **escape**. This is the fourth element of the repeated pattern of the warnings (see 2:1 and discussion). This argument proceeds from the lesser to the greater and assumes that the gospel is greater than the law. Thus, if disregard for the law brought certain punishment, disregard for our salvation will bring an even greater and inescapable disaster. In this context, which speaks of the law of Moses, our "so great salvation" is compared to the law (see Rom. 8:1–3). The law can no longer condemn us, and we are free from the law of sin and death. As Israel's transgressions brought them into the captivity of the Babylonians, so our negligence of our so great salvation will bring us inescapably into the captivity and tyranny of sin. God confirmed Moses before the children of Israel with many signs and wonders; the gospel has been **confirmed unto us by them that heard him**. These eyewitnesses, chiefly the apostles (see 2 Peter 1:16; 1 John 1:1), had vouched for the message first announced by Christ and were witnesses of the miracles of Christ and His resurrection. The author apparently was neither an apostle nor an eyewitness (see Introduction: "Author").

5. God Himself Confirms the New Revelation (2:4)

2:4. Those who regard this new revelation as something of so little importance that they allow themselves to slip away from it are willfully disobedient and a reproach to the Lord. This is particularly so when one considers that God Himself bore **witness, both with signs and wonders, and with divers miracles**. We ignore the Word of the Lord at our peril. Additionally, God confirmed the gospel message through **gifts of the Holy Ghost**, such as the gift of tongues (see Acts 2:4–12). For **according to his own will**, see 1 Corinthians 12:4–11.

B. The Argument for a Superior Prophet (2:5–4:13)

To those who have heard and believed the Word, it is an awesome realization that God should have spoken to us. That one could contemplate the very Word of God and not respond in faith is beyond imagination. Yet this is exactly what Israel had been guilty of for centuries. And it is what the generation of the Paul's "kinsmen" (Rom. 9:3) were guilty of when they rejected the outstretched hand of their promised Messiah. When Elijah complained to God of his generation's apostasy, God replied that He had reserved to Himself a remnant (see 1 Kings 19:14–18). Paul spoke of this in Romans 11:1–5 and concluded, "Even so then at this present time also there is a remnant according to the election of grace" (Rom. 11:5). "The captain" (Heb. 2:10) of this present remnant is Jesus. The following passage speaks of Him and His worthiness and reminds readers of the consequences of doubting His word.

1. This Person Is Jesus (2:5–3:1)

The author opened this argument with an exposition of Psalm 8:4–6, which shows Christ's superiority over the angels since He redeemed fallen humanity and thus fulfilled man's role as sovereign over the earth. Because Christ took on the form of a man, it is necessary to argue that Christ is the superior Prophet, not only because of who He is but also because of what He accomplished in His role as Perfect Man on our behalf.

2:5. The author reminded his readers that **unto the angels hath he not put in subjection the world to come**. If the readers were being enticed to believe that angelic beings would rule the future kingdom, this reminder would have sufficed to correct their error (see discussion on 1:4). In trying to dissuade his readers from turning back to Judaism, the author showed them that Christ, as bearer of the new revelation, a revelation of fulfillment, is superior to angels, who participated in bringing the revelation at Sinai.

2:6–7. One in a certain place testified (v. 6) refers to the psalmist David. Though not identified, Psalm 8:4–6 was well known to the hearers and did not need precise identification. Awed by the marvelous order and immensity of God's handiwork in the celestial universe, the psalmist marveled at the high dignity that God had bestowed on puny man by entrusting him with dominion over all other creatures (see Gen. 1:26–28 and discussions). He wondered, **What is man, that thou art mindful of him? or the son of man, that thou visitest him?** seeing that **Thou madest him a little lower than the angels** (v. 7; see discussion on Ps. 8:5). Ah, but **thou crownedst him with glory and honour, and didst set him over the works of thy hands**. This seeming paradox puzzled the psalmist. The readers were reminded that it is God who has granted such dignity to humankind.

2:8. Therefore, **Thou hast put all things in subjection under his feet**. God's purpose from the beginning was that man should be sovereign in the creaturely realm, subject to only God. Due to sin, that purpose of God has been temporarily thwarted. Indeed, men have themselves become "subject to bondage" (2:15). Because of sin, **now we see not yet all things put under him**.

2:9. Gloriously, **we see Jesus,** and even though He **was made a little lower than the angels, for the suffering of death,** He has now been **crowned with glory and honour** (see 10:13). In applying Psalm 8 to Jesus in particular, the author declared Him, as Perfect Man, to be the forerunner of man's restored dominion over the earth. He was made lower than the angels for awhile but is now crowned with glory and honor at God's right hand. By His perfect life,

His death on the cross, and His exaltation, He has made possible the ultimate fulfillment of Psalm 8 in the future kingdom. At that time, the second Adam and Perfect Man, the victorious Christ, will regain sovereignty over creation. The purpose of Christ's death was that **by the grace of God [He] should taste death for every man**. In so doing, He made it possible for every man to participate in His rule over all things.

2:10. Even though **all things** were made by Him and all things are for Him, **it became him**, or was fitting, to bring **many sons unto glory, to make the captain** (author) **of their** (so great; see 2:3) **salvation perfect through sufferings**. Christ was never morally or spiritually imperfect, but His participation in humanity was completed (perfected) when He experienced suffering. He identified with us on the deepest level of anguish, and in becoming sin for us, He acquired a full understanding of our imperfection and become our sympathetic High Priest. The author was building the case that Christ did not obtain our salvation just to rescue us from sin and death; rather, we as brethren should participate with Him in His Glory, and He will participate with us in our sufferings. This is a glorious contemplation.

2:11. The writer continued to explore believers' oneness with Christ: **both he that sanctifieth and they who are sanctified are all of one**. The One who does the setting apart and those that He sets apart are called together to the same purpose. Because of this, He is **not ashamed to call them brethren**. This certifies that our brotherhood with Jesus is not merely a metaphorical brotherhood but the brotherhood of the Redeemer with the redeemed, who are truly one with Him. In keeping with the use of the term in ancient literature, "brothers" in this context means "brothers and sisters."

2:12. Reinforcing the theme that the hearers were participating in the fulfillment of Old Testament prophecy, the author quoted Psalm 22:22, which describes the sufferings and triumph of God's righteous servant (see discussion on Psalm 22): **I will declare thy name unto my brethren, in the midst of the church will I sing unto thee**. The phrase "my brethren" is seen here as coming from the lips of the triumphant Messiah. This verse harks back to 1:9 and emphasizes the Lord's joy over the congregation.

2:13. In an exemplary manner, the Lord again identifies with His brethren as He says, **I will put my trust in him**, an expression of true dependence on God. In the person of Christ, humanity is seen as it was intended to be. **Behold, I, and the children which God hath given me** indicates that this trust in God will be shared by Christ's brethren and further indicates the degree to which He is one with them. The writer wanted to impress the hearers with their participation in the fulfillment of prophecy and in the fullness of Christ. After indicating how they, His children, were like Christ, the author went on to re-emphasize how He became like them and that this was necessary for their deliverance.

2:14. The author next built on the idea that **the children are ... flesh and blood** and that **he also himself likewise took part of the same**, so **that through death he might destroy him that had the power of death**. In fulfillment of the Old Testament pattern represented in the kinsman-redeemer (see Ruth 4:1–11), Christ's death provided the payment required to redeem mankind. It may be said that Satan wields the power of death only insofar as he induces people to refuse the redemption provided by Christ (see 1 John 5:12; Ezek. 18:4; Rom. 5:12; 6:23). Most likely, the readers were familiar with the apostle Paul's epistle to the Romans, and a glance to Romans 7 cannot be discounted. Of course, in keeping with the pattern and style of this epistle, the author compared the weakness of the law to the power of Christ.

2:15. Equally important as the destruction of the power of death, Christ's death also obtained the deliverance of **them who ... were all their lifetime subject to bondage** (see 1 Cor. 15:54–57; Rev. 1:18). The author contrasted bondage with freedom, death with life, to encourage the hearers to keep the faith and stay the course. To regress for the sake of comfort would be to embrace bondage and death; to press on would be to embrace freedom and life. The choice was theirs to make and remains ours today.

2:16. Moving from the general to the specific, the author reminded the hearers that rather than taking on **the nature** (form) **of angels**, Christ became a man of the **seed of Abraham**. Christ assumed not angelic nature but human nature, and as promised, He was both the root and the stem of Jesse (see Isa. 11:1).

2:17. Moving toward his next argument, the writer expressed that it was altogether fitting that Christ was **made like unto his brethren** so that He might be a merciful and faithful High Priest in things pertaining to God. Having become Perfect Man, Christ can represent mankind before God as a true kinsman and make reconciliation for the sins of the people. In a substitutionary way, Christ's death provided satisfactory atonement for our sin and turned away God's wrath (see discussions on Rom. 3:25; 1 John 2:2). To turn aside the wrath of God, Christ became one with sinful humanity and died in our stead.

2:18. The writer dispelled any thought that because Christ is God, He doesn't truly understand the plight of His brethren. Christ is able to bring comfort to them because **he himself hath suffered being tempted** (see discussion on 4:15; Matt. 4:1–11, 26:39).

3:1. In leaving the discussion of the nature of Christ's humanity and work, the author exhorted his hearers, as **partakers of the heavenly calling** (see discussion on 3:14), to keep before them their consideration of **the Apostle and High Priest of our profession, Christ Jesus** (see discussions on Mark 6:30; 1 Cor. 1:1). "Apostle" means "one who is sent." Jesus repeatedly spoke of Himself as having been sent into the world by the Father (see, e.g., Matt. 10:40; 15:24; Mark 9:37; Luke 9:48; John 4:34; 5:24, 30, 36–38; 6:38). He is the supreme apostle, the one from whom all other apostleship flows.

2. Christ Compared to Moses (3:2–6)

This passage is a comparison of Christ and Moses, both of whom were sent by the Father to lead His people — the one to lead them from bondage under Pharaoh to the Promised Land, the other to lead them from the bondage of sin (see 2:14–15) and to the rest promised to those who believe (see 4:3, 9). The larger section of 3:1–4:13 contains an exposition of Psalm 95:7–11, stressing Christ's superiority over Moses and warning against disobedience and unbelief. In 3:2–6, the author, focusing on faithful stewardship, used the metaphor of a house and its ruler. A first-century Jewish Christian would have understood this analogy entirely differently from how we might today. To interpret the following verses we must try to understand this meaning.

3:2. Keeping the Lord Jesus in mind, we turn to a consideration of **Moses**, who also **was faithful in all his house**. Moses was a faithful servant in the household to which God had appointed him. The author purposely developed his argument using the metaphor of a "house" that, as used here, has more the meaning of a "household" or a "family" than a physical "building."

3:3. He who hath builded ... hath more honour than the house. Jesus built the house (or household), whereas Moses was simply the appointed guardian of it. Jesus has made the house thoroughly livable, or ready for occupancy. The terms "builded" and "built" in 3:3–4 have the same meaning (in contrast to 9:11 and 11:10, where a different Greek term is used for "building.")

3:4. Moreover, the author continued, **he that built all things is God**. Since Jesus is the one who has "builded the house" (3:3), He is now equated with God, making it beyond question that Christ is greater than Moses.

3:5–6. Since **Moses verily was faithful in all his house, as a servant** (v. 5), he became a picture, or type, of **those things which were to be spoken after[ward]**, namely, of **Christ as a Son over his own house** (v. 6). Moses figuratively represented Christ, who is Chief over His own house (see 8:2). The superiority of Christ over Moses is shown in two comparisons: (1) Moses was a servant, whereas Christ is a son. (2) Moses was a servant in God's household, whereas Christ is over God's household, both past and future, **whose house are we** (see Eph. 2:19; 1 Peter 2:5). The caveat **if we hold fast the confi-**

dence and the rejoicing of the hope firm unto the end has been the subject of much discussion. The question is not whether we are *in* Christ but whether we as His household *are ruled* by Him. The author later expanded this thought and extended this caveat to being "partakers of Christ" (3:14). The use of the term "we" does not allow for the application of this text to unbelievers.

3. Warning against Unbelief (3:7–15)

3:7–11. In this second warning passage, the author again employed the common pattern of the warnings in this epistle (see discussion on 2:1). The quotation from Psalm 95:7–11 summarizes the inglorious history of Israel under Moses' leadership in the wilderness. The historical context is a time after the Israelites' miraculous rescue from Egypt, when they were tested in the wilderness. Signs and wonders encouraged them to trust God, but contrary to what would seem logical, they turned against Moses and God and instead tested God's patience. Christ had rescued the recipients of this epistle from the bondage of sin. As in the historical example, however, difficulties were tempting them to discard their new life under the authority of Christ. By recounting this psalm, the author abruptly brought his hearers to a recollection of God's reaction to the Israelites' unbelief and rebellion against Moses' leadership. The admonition in 3:5–6, that we will not enjoy the leadership of Christ if we do not firmly hold to the truth that we have received, set up this warning. Upon examination, this is a much higher standard than that which God required in Moses' day. The psalmist used the example of Israel under Moses to warn the Israelites against unbelief and disobedience. In a similar way, the author of Hebrews applied the psalmist's warning to his readers. The warning and the consequences of unbelief are particularly applicable to us today, as we are often distracted from a diligent consideration of "the things which we have heard" (2:1).

3:7. Since the quotation from Psalm 95:7–11 is germane to the flow of the author's argument and not parenthetical, the inferential conjunction

Wherefore refers to "Harden not" (3:8) rather than "Take heed" (3:12).

3:8. Harden not your hearts, as in the provocation is a plea to consider the superiority of Christ's headship over Moses' stewardship. The phrase "if ye will hear his voice" (3:7), being a third-class condition, indicates that they *were* hearing his voice.

3:9. Your fathers tempted me and yet **saw my works forty years**. The inference is that this was not an intelligent course of action. This lack of reasonable thought is further emphasized in 3:12, with the term "evil heart."

3:10. Wherefore I was grieved (perhaps "disgusted" is better) **with that generation**. This was the generation that fell in the wilderness. It is interesting that Jesus referred to the scribes and Pharisees of His day as "an evil and adulterous generation" (Matt. 12:39). **They have not known my ways** is especially burdensome in light of the evidence of God's provision and love that had been expressed to them.

3:11. They shall not enter into my rest is chastisement backed by God's solemn oath. This is a consequence without remedy, exemplified by the carcasses of the unbelieving Israelites who fell in the wilderness (see 3:17).

3:12. Therefore, the author warned his hearers, **Take heed, brethren, lest there [come to] be in any of you an evil heart of unbelief, in departing from the living God**. A progression can be seen here: (1) a departure from "the things which we have heard" (2:1), (2) inattention to these matters leads to a loss of Christ's leadership (see 3:5–6), (3) unbelief leads to a departure from God. To turn away rebelliously (lit., "to become apostate") from God is to turn away from life and choose death, just as did most of the Israelites who came out of Egypt. The term "evil heart" occurs only twice in the Old Testament, in Jeremiah 16:12 and 18:12, where such purposeful rebellion against God is considered stupidity.

3:13–14. Believers' need for one another and accountability to one another is evident in the encouragement to **exhort one another daily, while it is called To day** (v. 13). The essence of unbelief is to turn one's back on God. The danger in doing this is that one will be **hardened through the deceitfulness of sin**, see 4:7. This is still the day of divine grace and opportunity to trust God, but it will not last indefinitely. The conditions of loosing the leadership of Christ are the same for loosing our participation in the purposes of Christ. **For we are made** (have become) **partakers of Christ** (v. 14) by holding **the beginning of our confidence stedfast unto the end**. The author commended his hearers as having done this and did not accuse them of being guilty of this sin (see 3:1).

3:15. The author again quoted from Psalm 95:7–8 to reemphasize, **To day if ye will hear** (lit., "harken unto") **his voice, harden not** (lit., "that you may not harden") **your hearts, as in the provocation** (see 3:7–8). The author's admonition was persistent diligence in obedience to the voice of God in the present so they would not become hardened and rebellious as did they who were delivered out of Egypt. The antidote and prescription for not developing a hardened heart is to hear the Word of the Lord.

4. Consequences of Unbelief under Moses (3:16–19)

Here the author pursued his argument with a series of rhetorical questions. Having stated the warning, he drew a graphic example from the Old Testament. The generation to whom the promise of the land was given had heard God's promise and refused to trust Him (v. 19). This action is described as rebellion (v. 16), sin (v. 17), and disobedience (v. 18). God in His anger refused the promise to that entire generation of Israelites (see Num. 14:21–35). Since these rebellious people died in the wilderness, it is no stretch to say that their opportunity to enter into the land was lost without remedy. It was equally impossible for the first-century generation of unbelieving Jews to enter into a proper relationship with Christ as their Messiah and King because they had fallen under the judgment of God (see Rom. 9–11) and the new covenant had been inaugurated (see Hebrews 8–10). As first-century Christians, the recipients faced a similar danger (4:1). Paul, in using the illustration of the olive tree, had warned his readers, "If God spared not the natural branches, take heed lest he also spare not thee" (Rom. 11:21). The writer of Hebrews was similarly warning his readers.

3:16–18. Some (v. 16) is an unfortunate and confusing translation of the Greek (*tines*) and is better translated as a question: Who **when they had heard, did provoke**? (lit., "became embittered"). This question is answered with another question: Was it **not all who came out of Egypt by Moses**? Again, **with whom was he grieved** ("angered") **forty years? was it not with them ... whose carcasses fell in the wilderness?** Once again, the author asked, **And to whom sware he that they should not enter into his rest ...?** (v. 18). Was it not **to them that believed not?** Was it not to those who continually "disobeyed"?

3:19. Supported by the psalm, the conclusion of the argument is **they could not enter in because of unbelief.**

5. Consequences of Unbelief under Christ (4:1)

4:1. Continuing, the author applied to his hearers the conclusions arrived at in Psalm 95: **Let us therefore fear, lest, a promise being left us of entering into his rest, any of you should seem to come** (be coming) **short of it.** As in the days of Israel under Moses, when "rescue" did not equate with "rest," so it is today; salvation does not equate with rest. "His rest" cannot ultimately refer to the rest in Canaan offered to the Israelites. Nor, for that matter, can it refer entirely to "heaven's rest." That temporary, earthly rest gained under Joshua (see 4:8; discussion on Josh. 1:13) pointed to a rest that is spiritual and eternal. The very real and present danger of coming to the threshold of entering into His rest but then falling short of it cannot be overemphasized. Consider Matthew 11:29–30, where the Lord Himself starkly presented the idea heretofore presented in Hebrews concerning the leadership of Christ. It is as we truly become fellow laborers with Christ that we find "rest unto your souls" (Matt. 11:29). Falling short of this rest is to lose the leadership of the Lord and to fail to enter into participation with Christ in God's purposes. There is little in these verses to support the idea that one's salvation is invalidated or

lost by failure to achieve the goals outlined by the author. That which is lost to the believer is threefold: the leadership of Christ, participation with Christ, and rest in Christ.

6. Exhortations to Continue Trusting Christ (4:2–13)

It is interesting to note the interplay of belief, obedience, and rest as discussed in v. 1 and the exhortation that follows in vv. 2–13. The author wove together two aspects of rest, as in the warp and woof of a cloth: (1) the rest *from* a work (v. 4) and (2) the rest *in* a work that is ongoing (vv. 3, 11). The fabric of our life in Christ is strengthened by both aspects equally and comes apart when either aspect dominates the other. That which allows us to rest is confidence in the idea expressed in verse 3: in the mind of God, all His purposes are already completed, even from the laying of the foundation of the world. Literally, this is akin to the laying of the foundation of a house.

4:2. The author, in the manner of James, invited his readers to compare those who just hear the Word and those who hearken to the Word. He further recalled, **For unto us was the gospel preached, as well as unto them**, indicating that both had opportunity to respond. **But the word preached did not profit them, not being mixed with faith in them that heard** (hearkened to) it. Though the meaning is obscured by the difficulty in translating this passage, the author was bringing into play the partnership that we have with other believers in Christ. Those who did not profit from the Word were profitless because they had not joined in with faith with those who believed and acted on "the things which we have heard" (2:1).

4:3. With emphasis, the author continued, **For we which have believed do enter into rest.** Believers "do enter." Perhaps, in the context of laboring in Christ's household, we may say that we are yoked together with Christ so as to fulfill God's purposes on earth. We rest in the certainty that those purposes will be realized. We have arrived in that place (land) where we both work and rest (see 4:4). Just as entering physical rest in Canaan demanded faith in God's promise, so salvation rest is entered into only by an operative faith in the person and work of Jesus Christ. As in 3:16, **if they shall enter into my rest** (also in 4:5) is rhetorical interrogative and, as before, demands a negative response. **Although the works finished from the foundation of the world**, those who did not profit from the Word failed to enter into that rest because of their unbelief in the certainty of the sovereign purposes of God. There is no sadder contemplation than that what Christ has procured at so great a cost should go unheeded by a rebellious and stiff-necked people.

4:4–5. The point of this verse is not that God rested from His work on the seventh day of creation but that He appointed a certain day on which He would rest. **He spake … of the seventh day on this wise** (v. 4), and thus His rest is already a reality. The rest God calls us to enter (see 4:10–11) is not our rest but His rest, which He invites us to share.

4:6. Even though the displeasure of God is arrayed against unbelievers, we nevertheless are **seeing** that the promise **remaineth that some must enter therein**. Again, the emphasis is that those who ignore "Him that speaketh" (12:25) do so at their peril. **They … entered not in because of unbelief.** The message here, however, was that the promise of entering remained, as shown in the continuing invitation of Psalm 95:7–8. In considering the author's diatribe, the point that he was speaking of unbelieving believers is often overlooked (Ps. 95:7).

4:7. Again … a certain day … To day … hear his voice, harden not your hearts. See discussion on 3:13–14.

4:8. For if Jesus (Joshua) **had given them rest.** The Greek name Jesus and the Hebrew name Joshua are the same name, meaning "Savior." In this context, the verse is speaking of the rest that Joshua could not give to the nation Israel when they had entered into the Promised Land, Canaan. Psalm 95 bears witness to this unfulfilled rest in Moses' and Joshua's time. Hence, there was the need to **have spoken of another day.**

4:9. There remaineth therefore a rest to the people of God. God's rest may still be entered into.

This does not mean, however, that we must not also labor (see 4:11).

4:10. The author defined the person who has **entered into his rest** as one who **hath ceased from his own works.** This text is often taken to mean that the believer ceases his efforts to gain salvation by his own works and rests in the finished work of Christ on the cross. Others would equate this with the believer's final rest (see Rev. 14:13). Yet this entering into rest is qualified: **as God did from his.** In summary, when God had finished the work of creation, He ceased from that work. Similarly, when a person believes and is born again, he also ceases from his own work—not only with regard to working for his salvation but also in regard to his own purposes in life (see 1 Cor. 6:17, 19–20; 7:23).

4:11–13. Let us labour therefore to enter into that rest, lest any man fall after the same example of unbelief (Greek, *apeitheia*; "disobedience," "obstinacy"; v. 11). Clearly, obtaining this rest is predicated on the lordship of Christ and unswerving obedience to the word that He has spoken. **The word of God** (v. 12) is God's truth and was revealed by Jesus (the incarnate Word; see John 1:1, 14), but it has also been given verbally, the word referred to here. It is described as **quick** ("alive"), **and powerful, and sharper than any twoedged sword.** This dynamic word of God appears in both the Old Testament and the New Testament (see Pss. 107:20; 147:18; Isa. 40:8; 55:11; Gal. 3:8; Eph. 5:26; James 1:18; 1 Peter 1:23). The author of Hebrews described it as a living power that judges as with an all-seeing eye, **piercing even to the dividing asunder of soul and spirit … joints and marrow** (a person's innermost being)**, and is a discerner of the thoughts and intents of the heart.** There is obviously no room for double-mindedness here. The Holy Spirit of God is at once the author, administrator, and facilitator of God's Word. He is the agent who enlivens and empowers the written text. Truly, **Neither is there any creature that is not manifest in his sight: but all things are naked and opened unto the eyes of him with whom we have to do** (v. 13). The author associated the activity of the Word with the activity of God as if they are one and the same, which in fact they are. One cannot move beyond the truth of these Scriptures without the purest of motives. We have become laborers together with Christ, members of God's household. Here there is no room for self-interest or for glorying, save in the cross of Christ. Our New Testament relationship with God is facilitated by the high-priestly ministry of Christ on our behalf. This relationship comes with enormous responsibilities. It also comes with peace, rest, and contentment.

C. The Argument for a Superior Relationship (4:14–7:28)

This section is an exposition of Psalm 110:4, stressing Christ's superiority over Aaron because of His better priesthood.

1. Jesus, Our High Priest (4:14–16)

4:14. A great high priest (see 2:17; 3:1). Here the author began an extended discussion of the superior priesthood of Christ. **Into the heavens.** Even as the Aaronic high priest, on the Day of Atonement, passed from the sight of the people into the Most Holy Place (see Lev. 16:15, 17), so Jesus, having accomplished His work of atonement, passed from the sight of His watching disciples and ascended through the heavens into the heavenly sanctuary (see Acts 1:9–11). Jesus had ascended some thirty years prior to these besieged and beleaguered Hebrew Christians being admonished to **hold fast [their] profession.** Surely some of them must have yearned for the physical presence of their Lord, and some of them were in danger of letting their faith slip (see the similar admonitions in 2:1; 3:6, 14). The following presentation of Christ in His high-priestly office is not a hollow doctrine to be learned but rather the author's tender and compassionate plea for his hearers to remember that they were entering into the sufferings of Christ in full view of "him with whom we have to do" (4:13).

4:15. The recipients were not plowing new ground nor were they encountering circumstances and experiences unknown to the Lord. **For we have not a high priest which cannot be touched with the feeling of our infirmities; but was in all points tempted like as we are** (see 2:18). The author stressed the parallel between Christ's temptations and our temptations. He experienced every kind of temptation a person can experience, **yet without sin.** Christ's temptations were completely different from ours, however, in the results: His temptations never led to sin (see Matt. 4:1–11). It follows that temptation in and of itself is not sin.

4:16. Let us therefore come boldly. Because Christ, our High Priest, has experienced human temptation, He stands ready to give immediate and sympathetic help when we are tempted. We are admonished to come without hesitation **unto the throne of grace.** This is the place where we meet God when we pray and is described as (1) a throne, a place of authority and abundant resources, and (2) a place of grace, a condition of favor and liberal help. Because of Jesus' identification with us, this throne has become a place where **we may obtain mercy, and find grace to help in time of need** (*boētheia*, "help," see the verb "succour" in 2:18; this term is found elsewhere in the New Testament only in Acts 27:17; *eukairos*, "in the nick of time," is used only here in the New Testament). This place, where we may boldly go, may be likened to the city of refuge (see Num. 35:6, 12). And like the city of refuge, it is a place of benefit only for those who go there. In the city of refuge, however, judgment could be rendered against a guilty supplicant and appropriate punishment administered. At the throne of grace, we find that judgment has been rendered against Jesus, who bore our sins on the cross, thus satisfying the "blood avenger." This presents an entirely new mediatorial ministry for this High Priest. Indeed, an entirely new and superior order of priesthood has supplanted the old (see 4:17). The recipients of this epistle especially needed to accept by faith that they would obtain mercy and find grace to help in time of need. It was equally as important, however, that they understand and know that the One with whom they were yoked, with whom they were fellow laborers, and in whom they had become partakers of the divine nature, is fully able to perform that which God has called Him to do.

2. The Nature of Christ's Priesthood (5:1–10)

Having established that Jesus Christ holds the office of high priest (see 4:14–16), the author went on to show that Christ meets the two qualifications for this office: (1) high priests had to be "taken from among men" (v. 1) so that they might have compassion and be prepared to represent the people before God, and (2) they had to be "called of God" (v. 4). Drawing from Psalms 2:7 and 110:4, the writer showed that Christ is qualified and able to perform the duties and tasks required under the priestly order of Aaron. Christ, however, is able to mediate a "better covenant" (8:6), which Aaron's order could not possibly minister. This superior high priest is called "after the order of Melchisedec" (vv. 6, 10). The author contrasted the old order under Aaron (vv. 1–4) with the new order under Christ (vv. 5–10).

5:1. Every high priest ... is ordained for men in things pertaining to God. While the work of the high priest is "for men," it is also to resolve a breech in man's relationship to God. God designates priests to mediate on our behalf to restore the relationship between fallen humanity and a holy God. The high priest has been so ordained **that he may offer** (the purpose clause with the present subjunctive denotes that he must "keep on giving") **gifts and sacrifices** (Greek, *thysia*; "bloody offerings," given as acts of worship to God; see 8:3; 9:9; Lev. 1:2; 2:1). Under Aaron's order, continual sacrifices were necessary, and being rightly related to God was not permanent.

5:2–3. Priests are "taken from among men" (5:1) so that they **can have compassion** (lit., "bear gently"; v. 2). This term is used only here in the New Testament. Greek writers used it to decry the *apatheia*, "apathy" of "lack of feeling," of the Stoics. Here "compassion" anticipates the sense in which the priest participates, in a limited way, in the plight both of **the ignorant, and on them that are out of the way**, that is, those who commit sins that are accidental or caused by sudden passion (see Isaiah 53:6; compare the unintentional sin, as in Leviticus 4; Num. 15:27–29, with defiant rebellion against God, as in Num. 15:30–31; see also Heb. 6:4–6; 10:26–31,

where the writer addressed the issue of presumptuous sin). The priest is able to do this because of his common humanity with them and because **he himself also is compassed** (lit., "wrapped," as a rope or chain) **with infirmity**. The priest must deal with his own sin, but this is not so of the Lord Jesus.

5:4. No man taketh this honour unto himself, but he that is called of God. This was not so in Christ's day, as the high-priestly office was in the hands of a family that had bought control of it. By contrast, legitimate elevation to this position comes from God, which anticipates the next verse.

5:5–6. Christ glorified not himself to be made a high priest (v. 5). As a man among men and in humble deference to the Father, the Son did not arrogate to Himself this honor but was appointed by the Father, as the two prophetic statements cited here show (Pss. 2:7; 110:4). Jesus often declared that He was sent by His Father (see John 5:30, 8:54; 17:5). His priesthood (significantly, *hiereus*, "priest," is used rather than *archiereus*, "high priest"), however, was according to **the order of Melchisedec** (v. 6), not the order of Aaron (see discussion on 7:1–28). In a masterful way, the author was developing the idea of an intimate relationship between Jesus the High Priest and the recipients. Even as they themselves had been declared His brethren (see 2:11) and begotten of God after the manner of Christ (see 1:5), so the declaration that **to day have I begotten thee** (v. 5; see Ps. 2:7–9; Rom. 1:4) bore witness to their genesis and to their glorious participation with the Son of God. Sonship and priesthood are brought together here in a significant way. It is evident that both are suited to one another in this text. Christ's priesthood is defined by His relation to the Father (as Son), and His sonship qualifies His priestly work.

That Jesus did not have to offer sacrifices for Himself (see 4:15; 5:2–3) brings to mind the absolute, selfless love that He expressed on behalf of those who would become His brethren. In His grief for our sin (see Isa. 53:10), He met the first qualification of a priest: to share with us in sympathetic compassion. The author proceeded to bear descriptive witness to this in the following verses.

5:7. Who in the days of his flesh. Perhaps issuing a gentle rebuke, the author reminded the suffering Hebrew Christians that Jesus, though God, was totally human as well (see Isa. 7:4; Matt. 1:23). Hence, the reference to Christ's agony in the garden of Gethsemane was intended as another reminder that their sufferings, though sore indeed, were known to their sympathetic High Priest. Jesus **had offered up prayers and supplications with strong crying and tears** (see Luke 22:44.) **unto him that was able to save him from death**, but He was not to be delivered from those sufferings. Although the Father was able to deliver Jesus, He would not. No doubt this truth was directly applicable to the hearers, as it is to us today. In obedience to the Father, Jesus did not shrink from physical suffering and death or from the indescribable agony of taking mankind's sin on Himself (see Matt. 27:46). He did not waver in His determination to fulfill the Father's will (see Isa. 50:7; Matt. 26:36–46). **And was heard in that he feared**. The Father heard Jesus' prayer and recognized His fearfulness (as a man), yet His request was not granted. It may be said however, that through resurrection, the Father did deliver Him from and through death. The persecuted Hebrew Christians may have been tempted to believe that God did not hear their prayers for deliverance; this example, the experience of their High Priest, served to highlight that there was a higher purpose to their sufferings. Inherent in this and the following verses is the perplexing impact that these events had on the God-man Christ Jesus. Though He lived as a man, fearful and in need of learning and perfecting, He was also God, in need of nothing. Although theologians have argued for centuries how this is so, it remains a hidden truth known only to God (see 1 Tim. 3:16).

5:8–10. Though he were a Son, yet learned he obedience by the things which he suffered (v. 8). Perhaps displaying the linguistic prowess of the author, there is a play on the two verbs here (*emathen* and *epathen*; "learned" and "suffered"), emphasizing his point that wisdom is developed in the cauldron of experience. So it was that Jesus, who always did the Father's will, yet "learned" and was **made per-** fect (v. 9) through suffering (see 2:10), namely, His temptation in the wilderness and His passion leading up to and ending with the cross. Though He was the eternal Son of God, it was necessary for Him as the incarnate Son to learn obedience, not because He was ever disobedient but because He was called to obey to the extent that He experienced the most excruciating of human frailty and weakness. The temptations He faced were real, and the battle for victory was difficult, but where Adam failed and fell, Jesus prevailed. Thus, as a *man*, He was "made perfect." In so doing, **he became the author of eternal salvation** (see 9:12) **unto all them that obey him**. The indication here is not that eternal salvation is predicated on obedience but rather that those who are in a state of obedience are acknowledging that He is "the author" (Greek, *aitios*; "originator," "cause"). This idea is reinforced with **Called of God** (v. 10). One word in the original (Greek, *prosagoreutheis*; "to salute"), this term is used only here in the New Testament.

3. Rebuke for Dullness of Hearing (5:11–14)

Up to this point, the author diligently established the readers' relationship to Christ as High Priest. A hint of the author's disappointment in their readiness to be obedient, however, can be seen in his reference to "all them that obey" as opposed to a more direct reference to the recipients. The abruptly interjected rebuke that follows sets up the third warning of this epistle and is notable for its sharpness.

5:11. Of whom we have many things to say. The author wished to discuss the priesthood of Melchizedek but did not until later (chap. 7) due to the possibility of misinterpretation. His use of "we" seems to indicate that he was not alone in expressing this admonition (see 13:24). What he wished to say was **hard to be uttered** (Greek, *dysermēneutos*; "hard of interpretation"), another term used only here in the New Testament, and ran contrary to ordinary Jewish ideas. Yet the writer was concerned that his hearers' greater problem had less to do with their understanding and more to do with their readiness to learn. Their attitude, addressed in the warning found in 2:1, was in contrast to the exercising of faith that had caused them to accept their Messiah. It was therefore illogical for them to be **dull of hearing** ("slow," "sluggish," "indolent," "languid"). Plato used this expression to describe the stupidity of some of his students. Instead of progressing in the Christian life, the readers had become spiritually sluggish and mentally lazy (for the only other use of this expression, see 6:12, where it is translated "slothful").

5:12. The author continued with the metaphor of the classroom. **When for the time** implies that the passing of time should bring progress. Perhaps because of persecution, these believers had fallen into despondency. They should have known these things by now; in fact, the author went on to say, **ye ought to be teachers**. They were not recent converts. Sadly, however their lack of progress that he start over from the beginning to teach them **the first principles of the oracles of God**, which are listed in 6:1–2 (see discussion there; for *stoicheia*, "rudiments," see Gal. 4:3, 9; Col. 2:9). Having taken the first steps toward becoming mature Christians, they had slipped back to where they had started. **Strong meat** (Greek, *stereos*; "strong," "solid," "firm," as in the modern sense of "on steroids") signifies advanced teaching, such as that given in chapter 7. It is important to note that neglecting the Word is not a benign condition; if left to run its course, it will have disastrous results, as the author's third warning (6:4–8) shows.

5:13. Without intellectual and spiritual teaching, these people were unable to chew on the solid meat of the Scriptures. They were still on **milk** and **unskillful** (lit., "inexperienced"; Greek, *apeiros*, a composite word composed of the alpha privative, *a*, and *peira*, together signifying "no trial"). The recipients were untried in their experience of Christ. Indeed, rather than being a means of growth and joyfulness (see James 1:2–4), their response to persecution had left them wanting. **Babe** (Latin, *infans*; lit., "not able to talk") conveys that the author was doubtful whether they were ready for what he wished to teach them.

5:14. In contrast with "babe" (5:13), **Of full age** (Greek, *teleiōn*) speaks of "adults" (see 1 Cor. 2:6; 3:1;

13:11; Phil. 3:15; Eph. 4:4), those who have had **their senses** (lit., "organs of perception") **exercised** (from *gymnazō*, "to exercise vigorously as an athlete"). The author desired for his hearers to emulate those who had progressed in spiritual life and had become Christians of sound judgment and discernment. **Discern both good and evil** is something infants cannot do. With the consequences and loss referred to in his third warning in mind, the writer urged his readers much as a coach might do in the gym. His words were intended not to discourage them from advancing but to challenge them to vigorously seek out the truth of what he was about to say.

Christians who are unwilling or too lazy to "grow in grace" (2 Peter 3:18) are, at the least, unappreciative of the relationship that has been established, through the blood of Christ, with the Lord. The author's metaphorical use of "babe" was not without reason. Growth is part of the natural order. Lack of growth signals the presence of a serious disorder and will result in the direst of consequences.

4. Plea to Move Forward in the Knowledge of Christ (6:1–3)

If 5:14 may be thought of as being descriptive of a condition existing within the household of Christ, 6:1 may be thought of as prescriptive. This prescription, even as the preceding diagnosis, is preparatory to the warning in 6:4–8.

6:1–2. Confident that his hearers had the good sense to follow through and grow in their knowledge (see 6:9), the author continued, **Therefore leaving the principles of the doctrine of Christ** (lit., "Wherefore let us cease to speak of the first principles of Christ"; v. 1). He repeated his initial charge of 5:12, in effect negating it: "You need someone to teach you the first principles, but I hope you won't make me do it!" **Let us go on** (lit., "Let us be borne on"). This expression is used exactly as a Greek schoolmaster would use it to move his students to a new level of study. For the moment, the writer was assuming that these Hebrew Christians were ready to move on **unto perfection** ("maturity"). He marked what he considered the essential teachings that form **the foundation**

of Christian doctrine (note the follow-through of the household metaphor found in 3:2–6). "Foundation" stands in apposition to **doctrine** (v. 2). **Repentance** (v. 1) and **faith** are qualitative genitives suggestive of where these foundational principles are applied (see Mark 1:15; Acts 20:21; 1 Thess. 1:9). The foundation has, as it were, four corners: **baptisms … laying on of hands … resurrection … and … eternal judgment** (v. 2). "The doctrine of baptisms" probably refers to different baptisms with which the readers were familiar, such as Jewish baptism of proselytes, John the Baptist's baptism, and the baptism commanded by Jesus (see Matt. 28:19). The readers should have known the importance and significance of Christian baptism as opposed to the ritual cleansings of the previous dispensation. The "laying on of hands" sometimes followed baptism (see Acts 8:16–17; 19:5–6). Otherwise, laying on of hands was practiced in connection with ordaining or commissioning (see Acts 6:6; 13:3; 1 Tim. 5:22; 2 Tim. 1:6), healing the sick (see Mark 6:5; 16:18; Luke 4:40; Acts 28:8), and bestowing blessing (see Matt. 19:13–15). The reference to the "resurrection of the dead" underscores a cornerstone doctrine on which their faith rested and their hope depended (see John 5:25–29; 11:25; 1 Cor. 15; 2 Cor. 4:14). The final cornerstone is "eternal judgment." The author returned to this theme in 9:27 and 10:27 (see also 1 John 4:17). These four foundational principles would have evoked in the minds of the hearers the unique identification they had in Christ (baptism), the authority of the apostles (laying on of hands), the historical facts of the gospel (resurrection), and the eschatological certainty that one day every knee shall bow before the One into whose hands all judgment has been given (see Phil. 2:10; see John 5:22).

6:3. And this we will do, if God permit is a common expression of dependence on the will of God (see 1 Cor. 16:7). Only the Lord can open minds and hearts and bring spiritual maturity. Here, using a third-class condition, the writer stated his conviction that he would not need to go back to the formative principles of the faith; rather, he intended to continue with his appeal (see discussions on 6:1–2).

5. Warning against Falling Away (6:4–8)

In the first warning (2:1), the author advised the recipients not to allow the new word delivered "in Son" (see discussion on 1:2) to drift away from them. If they allowed that to happen, the consequence would be that, as Israel had been delivered into Babylonian slavery for a similar offense, they would again come under the tyranny of sin. In the second warning (3:7–15), the recipients were warned against unbelief, a condition likened to rebellion. The writer again employed an example from Israel's history. After having been delivered from Egypt and slavery, the Israelites had rebelled against God and against Moses, which resulted in their failure to enter into the land and rest. In doing so, they lost it all, both possession of the land and the blessings of God through the leadership of Moses. Similarly, the recipients of this epistle were in danger of not entering into the rest found in Christ and risked losing the blessings and reward of co-laboring with Christ in the work of the church.

In the third warning, the author warned the recipients against "fall[ing] away" (v. 6) and went to great length (5:11–6:2) to present that age-old idea that if one is not moving forward, one will fall back. There is no standing still. This was so important to the author that he personally took on the task of seeing that this did not happen (see 6:3). The epistle, so far, supports the idea that the recipients had reached a plateau in their faith and understanding but had fallen short of grasping the nature of the priesthood of Christ or the priesthood of the believer; this lack of understanding is hinted at in 6:18–19.

6:4–6. Interpretations of this difficult passage fall into two classes. The first approach associates it with the experience and permanence of salvation and has three major arguments.

(1) The passage refers to Christians who actually lose their salvation. The author, however, seems to teach the opposite in 6:13–20. This view is not supported by the context or the general tenor of New Testament Scripture.

(2) It is a hypothetical argument intended to warn immature Hebrew Christians (see 5:11–14)

that they needed to progress to maturity (see 6:1) or else experience divine discipline or judgment (see 6:7–8). This view is supported by the fact that each of the five warnings expresses a condition and its consequences (see 2:3; 3:14; 6:6; 10:26 and 12:25); the author included himself among his hearers (see 10:26) and was convinced that these conditions were not really true of them (see 6:9). While this view is convenient, the introduction of a hypothetical situation does not fit the established pattern of the epistle.

(3) It refers to professing Christians whose apostasy proved that their faith was not genuine (see 1 John 2:19). This view sees chapters 3–4 as a warning based on the rebellion of the Israelites in the wilderness. As Israel could not enter the Promised Land after spying out the region and tasting its fruit, so the professing Hebrew Christians would not be able to repent if they adamantly turned against the light they had received. According to this interpretation, such expressions as **enlightened ... tasted of the heavenly gift, and ... partakers of the Holy Ghost** (v. 4) indicate that such persons had come under the influence of God's covenant blessings and had professed to turn from darkness to light but were in danger of a public and final rejection of Christ, proving that they had never been regenerated. This view does not follow the pattern of the epistle or the context of the subject matter. Being willing to express such a sharp rebuke, surely the author would have identified these hypocrites. Further, if one adopts this position, Moses becomes such a person, and this is clearly refuted in chapter 11. As one progresses in the study of this epistle, it becomes more and more a tour de force to include unbelievers in its intended audience. The term used in conjunction with the phrase "partakers of the Holy Ghost," "were made," is used no less than twenty eight times in this epistle and never to indicate an ineffective or less than permanent work (1:4; 2:7, 17; 3:14; 5:5, 9; 6:4, 13, 20; 7:12, 16, 19, 21–23, 26; 9:22; 10:33; 11:3, 34).

The second approach to this text is that it is not associated with salvation (a point that the author eventually addressed; see 6:9) but rather with the believer's response to the grace of God. In this view, the passage refers to persons who are the recipients of God's grace and who, for a time, respond in some positive way(s) but who nevertheless **fall away** (v. 6). Eternal salvation is not under discussion, but when **they crucify to themselves the son of God afresh**, these persons bring upon themselves the certain consequences of rejecting Him. Saved or not, the Israelites who disobeyed never entered into God's rest, including Moses (see 4:1–11). The author was fearful that such dire consequences might befall his readers as well. History and experience are replete with examples of people who "fall away," losing the joy of their salvation and bringing judgment upon themselves and their families. Of the three arguments in the first approach, this interpretation is closest to the third view but stops short of trying to link it to the question of whether the person is actually regenerated. Obviously, if they are not, they effectively quench the convicting work of the Holy Spirit, leading to perdition. If they are regenerated, then they create a condition in which the blessings of God are effectively turned away, leading to divine chastening.

This entire passage, verses 4–6, constitutes one complete sentence, beginning with **For it is impossible** (v. 4) and concluding with **to renew them again unto repentance** (v. 6). All of the intervening conditions are to be understood in their relation to this main idea. The writer was issuing a severe warning that it is possible to cross a line beyond which a person may not return (see Romans 1 and the repeated phrase, "God gave them up"). The conditions include "once enlightened" (v. 4), "tasted of the heavenly gift," "were made partakers of the Holy Ghost," "tasted the good word of God, and the powers of the world to come" (v. 5), and then "fall away." The writer listed those gracious works of God that are experientially received, either in the convicting of the Holy Spirit or in His saving work. To crucify to themselves the Son of God afresh was akin to saying with the hateful crowd, "We will not have this man to reign over us" (Luke 19:14). For **powers of the world to come**, see Mark 10:30; 1 Timothy 6:19.

6:7–8. To reinforce the principle, the author used a short parable to graphically illustrate the warning (see John 15:5–6; 2 Peter 2:20–22; 1 John 5:16). **Drinketh in the rain** (v. 7) corresponds to the principle of Matthew 5:45: "he [God] ... sendeth rain on the just and on the unjust." **Rejected** (Greek *adokimos*; "not approved," "unfit"; v. 8) and **burned** characterize the underbrush ordinarily raked and burned to clear ground for fruitful plants. In the economy of God's kingdom work, the reader should be forewarned of neglecting "the good word of God" (6:5).

6. Consequences of Falling Away under Christ (6:9–12)

6:9. But, beloved, we are persuaded better things of you ... things that accompany salvation. The author had suggested the possibility that some of his readers might need to heed the warning of 6:4–8, but he was confident that God had been at work among them, his beloved brethren. Changed lives and works of love (see 6:10) indicated that many of these persons, though lacking in certain knowledge, were indeed serving and were not "slothful" (see 6:12). He was therefore "persuaded [see 2 Tim. 1:12] better things" than those depicted in 6:4–6. This persuasion is much in line with the position taken by James (see James 1:21–25), whose letter was no doubt available to them. The author's use of a parable recalling Moses' fate (6:7–8) may suggest that while faithful believers were present, the apostasy of some and the failure of many to be interested in growing in knowledge, if allowed to go on unchecked, could affect the entire group's reception of the blessings of God. An example of the Lord's view of this condition is seen in the comparison of Mary and Martha in Luke 10:38–42.

6:10. The author moved to encourage his readers, noting that **God**, being God, would not **forget [their] work and labour of love**. Specifically, he had in mind that they had **ministered to the saints** (once), **and do minister** ("still continue to minister"). In effect, he was saying to them that, having begun to serve the Lord, they had continued to do so. This evidence of their faith and positive attitude gave him great encouragement. The author's concern remained, however, that while he was able to commend some, others were not heeding or doing the word spoken.

6:11. We desire. While some were indeed following and serving the Lord, many were still babes (see 5:13) and in need of demonstrating the reality of their faith. They also needed to **shew the same diligence** in service to Christ, thus providing **the full assurance of hope** in their relationship to the Lord (see 11:1; Col. 2:2; 1 Thess. 1:5; 2 Peter 1:10). **Unto the end** assured the recipients that their new relationship with the Lord was a permanent one, thus becoming a call to persevere in their faith as an appropriate evidence of their salvation (see 3:6, 14).

6:12. The first evidence of their salvation was **That ye be not slothful, but followers of them who through faith and patience inherit the promises.** This looks back to the warning in 6:4–8 and also ahead to chapter 11. With this in mind, the writer moved to the example of Abraham. In doing so, he provided both an object lesson in entering into the promises of God and also an introduction to the new priesthood.

7. The Immutability of the New Relationship (6:13–20)

6:13. God made promise to Abraham. God's promise to Abraham that he would have many descendants was made with an oath to emphasize its unchanging character (see Gen. 22:16–18). Ordinarily, the swearing of an oath belongs to our fallen human situation, in which a man's word is not always trustworthy. God's swearing of an oath was condescension to human frailty, thus making His word, which is absolutely trustworthy, doubly dependable (see 6:18).

6:14. Saying, Surely. This verse is quoted from Genesis 22:17.

6:15. After he had patiently endured for twenty-five years (see Gen. 12:3–4; 21:5), Abraham **obtained the promise**, the birth of his son Isaac (see Gen. 17:2; 18:10; 21:5). This illustrates the "patience" recommended in 6:12.

6:18. Two immutable things refers to God's promise, which is absolutely trustworthy, and God's oath confirming that promise (see 6:17). Contrast **impossible for God to lie** with the "impossible" of 6:4–6. **We might have a strong consolation** because we look back on the fulfillment of the promise that Abraham saw only in anticipation (11:13; John 8:56). **Fled for refuge.** In the New Testament, this term is used only here and in Acts 14:6. In the Septuagint, (the Greek translation of the Old Testament), it is used of the cities of refuge (Deut. 4:42; 19:5; Josh. 20:9).

6:19. As an anchor of the soul, both sure and stedfast. Like an anchor holding a ship safely in position, our hope in Christ guarantees our safety. **Within the vail.** Whereas the ship's anchor goes down to the ocean bed, the Christian's anchor goes up into the true, heavenly sanctuary, where he is moored to God Himself.

6:20. Forerunner (Greek, *prodromos*; "spy," "scout") recalls the two spies of Kadesh Barnea who gave the good report versus those who returned with the discouraging word that led to the subsequent judgment and wilderness wandering (see Num. 13 and 14). But the author had something far more significant in mind. **A high priest for ever after the order of Melchisedec.** Like Melchizedek, Christ the High Priest stands alone and in contrast to the passing away of the Aaronic order. His priesthood is **for ever.** This grand theme is further developed in chapter 7.

8. Basis for the New Relationship: Jesus' Superior Priesthood (chap. 7)

7:1. Melchisedec has already been noted as representative of the order of priesthood to which Christ belongs (see 5:6, 10; Gen. 14:18–20 and discussions). The Melchizedek priesthood is older and of a higher order than the Aaronic priesthood; it is no wonder the author had alerted his hearers to the difficulty of his subject matter (see 5:11). To understand this, it is important to go back to the original **king ... priest.** Of particular significance is that Melchizedek held both offices in which he prefigured Christ. **Salem.** Jerusalem (see discussion on Gen. 14:18). **The most high God** is the name by which Abram was first introduced "by name" to the

God who called him from his father's house (see Gen. 12:1ff. and 14:18ff.). It is difficult to miss the parallel with these distant descendants of Abraham who were being called to leave their long-held traditions to follow One who stands before and above Melchizedek. **Who met Abraham** is significant since the event antedated Aaron and involved Aaron's ancestor (see also John 8:56–58). A very long parenthesis is contained between **who** and "abideth" (7:3), in which the author spelled out the significance of this enigmatic figure from the life of Abraham.

7:2. Abraham gave a tenth. In this ancient context, it would hardly be noteworthy that one would dedicate a tenth of the spoils to God (or the local pagan deity), but in this case, it was given to "the most high God" (7:1) and to the priest who stood in a superior role to father Abraham, the spiritual and/or physical progenitor of all to whom this epistle is addressed. **King of righteousness ... King of peace** are messianic titles (see Isa. 9:6–7; Jer. 23:5–6; 33:15–16).

7:3. Without father ... nor end of life (*apatōr* and *amētōr* are alliterated in the original. The first term was apparently coined by the author, as it is found nowhere else in ancient literature. Used here, the terms punctuate that this figure was "without genealogy"). Genesis 14:18–20, contrary to the practice elsewhere in the early chapters of Genesis, does not mention Melchizedek's parentage and children or his birth and death. That he was a real, historical figure is clear, but the author of Hebrews (in accordance with Jewish interpretation) used Scripture's silence about his genealogy to portray him as a prefiguration of Christ. Melchizedek's priesthood anticipated Christ's eternal existence and His unending priesthood. Some believe Melchizedek's appearance to Abraham was a manifestation of Christ before His incarnation, but the comparison **like unto the Son of God** argues against such an interpretation.

7:4. Consider how great this man was. The one who collects a tithe is greater than the one who pays it, and "the less is blessed of the better" (7:7). In both ways, Melchizedek was greater than Abraham.

7:5–7. The sons of Levi ... take tithes ... of their brethren (v. 5). In the case of the Levitical priesthood, the principle of "taking tithes" was rooted in the **commandment** to do so. Nothing in this requirement suggests that the priests are somehow "superior" to those from whom they receive tithes. In the case of **he whose descent is not counted** (i.e., Melchizedek; v. 6), however, it is different. In this case, it was he who **blessed him that had the promises** (i.e., Abraham). Because of this blessing, the writer concluded, **without all contradiction the less is blessed of the better** (v. 7). It is evident that Abraham (and his "promises," including his progeny; see Gen. 12:3, 7; 13:14; 15:5; 17:5; 22:16–18) was inferior to this "priest of the most high God" (7:1).

7:8–10. With respect to the one who received tithes from Abraham, **it is witnessed** (present passive participle) **that he liveth** (v. 8), while **here men that die receive tithes**. The writer contrasted the "here" of the Levitical system with the **there** of Melchizedek. Again, Melchizedek is seen as greater. In 7:7, it was said that the "better" blessed the "less." The writer returned to both of these arguments in 7:16. The author furthered the argument by adding, **And as I may so say** (lit., "So to say"; v. 9), **Levi ... payed tithes** (lit., "has been tithed") **in Abraham**. Levi was present, as it were, when Abraham paid tithes to Melchizedek because he was in Abraham's **loins** (v. 10). While Levi had yet to be born, he was nevertheless represented in his forefather.

7:11–14. The point of these verses is that the Levitical priesthood brought with it all the regulations of the Mosaic law. So if one turns to Christ and His priesthood, he must reject the Levitical priesthood and its law, for the law disqualifies Jesus from becoming its priest, since He is from the invalid tribe of Judah.

7:11. Under it (the Levitical priesthood) **the people received the law**. The law of Moses and the priesthood went together. All the people, without exception, were sinners subject to the law's condemnation and thus were in need of a priestly system to mediate between them and God. **After the order of Melchisedec, and not ... after the order of Aaron** implies that the Aaronic (or Levitical) priesthood was imperfect, but Melchizedek's was perfect. The announcement of the coming one who would be "a

priest for ever" (Ps. 110:4) was written midway in the history of the Levitical priesthood, which could only mean that the existing system was to give way to something better.

7:16–17. Not after the law of a carnal commandment (v. 16) refers to a law involving physical requirements—the tribe of Levi (see 7:5). In the law of Moses, the priestly function was restricted to the tribe of Levi (see Deut. 18:1), but Jesus came from the nonpriestly tribe of Judah (see 7:14–15). **For he testifieth** (lit., "it is witnessed"; v. 17) to **the power of an endless life** (v. 16). According to Psalm 110:4, the priest in the order of Melchizedek is "a priest for ever."

7:18. A disannulling of the commandment ... for the weakness and unprofitableness. The law is holy and good (see Rom. 7:12), but it is not able to make right those who sin by breaking it, nor can it give the power necessary to fulfill its demands (see 7:19).

7:19. The law was only preparatory (see Gal. 3:23–25) and brought nothing to fulfillment (see Matt. 5:17). **A better hope**. The new covenant is better because it assures us of complete redemption and brings us into the very presence of God (see discussion on Col. 1:5).

7:20–21. No divine **oath** was associated with the establishment of the Levitical priesthood. The priesthood pledged in Psalm 110 is superior because it was divinely affirmed with an oath.

7:22. Jesus [was] made a surety (lit., "pledge") **of a better testament**, the new covenant (see chaps. 8–10). This thought introduces "covenant" for the first time in the book. Here the high priest, Jesus, is not only the mediator but also the guarantee. This, as we shall see, is due not only to the nature of the covenant but, more important, to the nature of the Priest and His priesthood (see 7:23–28).

7:23. And they truly were many priests. The writer sets up a point of contrast: "they" as opposed to "this man" (7:24). **Not suffered to continue by reason of death**. The priesthood of Christ is superior to that of Levitical priests because they die, but Jesus "continueth ever" (7:24).

7:24–26. But ... he ... hath an unchangeable priesthood (v. 24). This sentence is difficult but seems to contrast Jesus (see 7:22) with these (mortal) priests (see 7:23) in that, like Melchizedek, He lives forever, and thus His priesthood abides unchanged from the day He was elevated to this position. **To the uttermost** (v. 25) may include the ideas of completeness and permanence. Jesus is a perfect High Priest forever, so He is able to save completely and for all time. He **ever liveth to make intercession**. His people will never be without a priestly representative (see John 17; 1 John 2:1). **Such** (v. 26) is placed here for emphasis (as in 2:10) and links Jesus to Melchizedek in His ministry as **high priest**, one who meets our need for salvation from sin and its consequences. **Separate from sinners** (lit., "separated from sinners") does not contradict 2 Corinthians 5:21: "For he hath made him to be sin for us, who knew no sin; that we might be made the righteousness of God in him." Rather, it seems to make a point reiterated in 9:28. In His present state of exaltation in heaven, Christ is set apart from the sinful world and is **made higher than the heavens**.

7:27. Daily refers to the endless repetition of sacrifices throughout the year (see Exod. 29:36–42) and is evidence that these sacrifices never effectively and finally dealt with sin. **First for his own sins**. Christ's priesthood is superior because He has no personal sins for which sacrifice must be made. **This he did once** is a key concept in Hebrews (see 9:12, 26; 10:2, 10). The Levitical priests had to bring daily offerings to the Lord, whereas Jesus sacrificed Himself once for all. **Offered up himself**. Levitical priests offered up only animals; our High Priest offered Himself, the perfect substitute, Man for man.

7:28. Men … which have infirmity contrasts once again with **the Son, who is consecrated for evermore**. Human agents are limited in this task because (1) they are mortal and therefore impermanent (see 7:23); (2) they are sinful (see 7:27); and (3) they can offer only animals, which can never provide a genuine substitute for mankind, made in the image of God (see Gen. 1:26–28 and discussions). It is with an **oath** (see Ps. 110:4) that God "consecrated [the Son) for evermore." Christ was made perfect in that He faced temptation without succumbing to

sin (see discussions on 2:10; 5:8–10). Instead, He perfectly obeyed the Father, thereby establishing a perfection that is eternal.

D. The Argument for a Superior Redemption (chaps. 8–10)

1. A Superior Covenant from a Superior High Priest (8:1–13)

8:1. The argument of this section grows out of an exposition of Jeremiah 31:31–34, demonstrating that Christ is the mediator of "a better testament" (7:22, see 8:6–13). The opening salvo, however, **Now … this is the sum**, indicates that the function of what follows is directly related to what has just been said. It could be paraphrased, "In conclusion, let me come to my main point." The point, of course, is that the new covenant is coterminous with the **high priest** upon whose work it rests, **who is set on the right hand of the throne of the Majesty in the heavens**. The allusion, once again, is to Psalm 110:1: "The Lord said unto my Lord, Sit thou at my right hand, until I make thine enemies thy footstool" (see 1:3 and discussion). This priest is also King. He is, after all, a priest after the order of Melchizedek, who was both a priest and a king.

8:2. Reference to **the true tabernacle** is in contrast to the tabernacle that Moses erected, which was an imperfect and impermanent copy of the heavenly tabernacle (see 8:5; 3:5–6). "True" signifies "original." The heavenly sanctuary, **which the Lord pitched, and not man**, corresponds to the Most Holy Place, the innermost sanctuary in Moses' tabernacle, into which the high priest briefly entered with the blood of atonement once a year (see Lev. 16:13–15, 34). In the heavenly sanctuary, however, our great High Priest dwells eternally as our intercessor (see 7:25). The author enlarged on these ideas in chapters 9–10.

8:3. It is important that the work of **every high priest** include the offering of **gifts and sacrifices** (see discussion on 5:1) and **that this man have somewhat also to offer**. The relationship of Christ to the Old Testament priesthood is neither equivocal nor univocal. That is to say, it is neither an entirely different work, nor is it entirely the same; points of similarity and points of superiority (see 8:6) can be observed. Here the emphasis is on the points of similarity: like them, Christ must offer "gifts and sacrifices."

8:4. He should not be a priest. By His human birth, Jesus belonged to the tribe of Judah, which was not the priestly tribe (see 7:12–14). **There are priests that offer gifts** refers to members of the tribe of Levi. The present tense of the verb "offer," here and elsewhere in Hebrews, indicates that the temple in Jerusalem was still standing. This letter, therefore, must have been written prior to the temple's destruction in AD 70 (see Introduction: "Date").

8:5. The example and shadow of heavenly things. The heavenly reality is the sanctuary of God's presence, into which Christ our High Priest entered with His own blood (see 9:11–12). **See … that thou … make all things according to the pattern shewed to thee in the mount** is a quotation from the instruction given in Exodus 25:40 concerning the Old Testament tabernacle. Both the tabernacle and its ministry were intended to illustrate symbolically the only way in which sinners may approach a holy God and find forgiveness. Christ's mediatorial work is not engaged here on earth but in heaven, where the reality abides; the earthly ministrations of the Levitical priests involved only "types" and "shadows."

8:6. But now indicates a contrast with the old priestly order. **He** (Jesus) **is the mediator of a better covenant** (see 7:12, 22; 9:15; 10:1–18; 12:24; 1 Tim. 2:5). The new covenant (see 8:8–12; Jer. 31:31–34) that Jesus mediates is superior to the covenant that God made through Moses at Sinai (see Exod. 24:7–8). It is **established upon better promises** (see 8:10–12).

8:7. If that first covenant had been faultless. The line of argument here is similar to that in 7:11, where the Levitical priestly order was shown to be inferior because it was replaced by the order of Melchizedek. Similarly, if the Mosaic covenant were without defect, there would have been no need to replace it with a new one. Nothing was essentially "wrong" with the Mosaic covenant, but it was unable to provide complete and permanent salvation from sin and its consequences (see discussion on 7:18).

8:8–12. This section is an extended quotation from Jeremiah 31:31–34. While the writer clearly applied this promise to his readers, it is important to note that, as with the old covenant, this **new covenant** (v. 8) is given to **the house of Israel and … Juda**. The quotation contains a prophetic announcement and description of the new covenant, to be different from the Mosaic covenant, which was made when God **took … them out of … Egypt** (v. 9). That the author repeated parts of this passage in 10:16–17 reveals its importance to him (see also 4:8; 7:11; 8:4). What is evident is that the superior promises of the new covenant, which look to a future that will be enjoyed by God's chosen, are already appropriated by God's people today. The superior benefits are: (1) God's laws become inner principles (v. 10a) that enable His people to delight in doing His will (see Ezek. 36:26–27; Rom. 8:2–4); (2) God and His people have intimate fellowship (v. 10b); (3) sinful ignorance of God is removed forever (v. 11); and (4) forgiveness of sins is an everlasting reality (v. 12).

8:13. In that he saith, A new covenant (lit., "When he says, 'New'"). In the introduction of the new covenant, the **first** is made **old**. The contrast intended is temporal, not pejorative. It is not to say that the old was somehow bad but rather that it **decayeth**. As good as the first covenant with Moses was, it was never intended to be permanent. To return to the old system would be to return to what is no longer valid or effective. We know that soon after these words were penned, the temple of the old system would **vanish away** (Greek, *aphanismos*; "disappear") with the destruction of Jerusalem in AD 70. Yet this is not likely the intended meaning. Rather, the point is similar to that which Jesus said to the woman at the well concerning "the hour … when the true worshippers shall worship … in spirit and in truth" (John 4:23).

2. Superior Access Provided by a Superior Sacrifice (9:1–10:18)

a. The Contrast of the Old and the New (9:1–14)

9:1–2. The first covenant had … a worldly sanctuary (v. 1). There is an earthly tabernacle and a heavenly one. "Worldly" translates *kosmikos*, "earthly." First, **there was a tabernacle made** (v. 2) under Moses. The writer undoubtedly understood that the temple of his day perpetuated the rituals and sacrifices of the original tabernacle, yet in order not to be misunderstood on this point, he went all the way back to the original to let the reader know that he was speaking of the entire system that emanated from the divine instruction given to Moses and still perpetuated. Just as the priesthood of Christ and His royal appointment exploded the "old wineskins" of the Mosaic covenant and the Aaronic priesthood, so His sacrificial work rendered the wondrous treasures of the old tabernacle as mere shadows (see 8:5), and its sacrifices and offerings as utterly inadequate.

The candlestick (v. 2) was made of hammered gold and placed at the south side of the Holy Place (see Exod. 40:24). It had seven lamps, which were kept burning every night (see Exod. 25:31–40). **The table** was made of acacia wood overlaid with gold and stood on the north side of the Holy Place (see Exod. 40:22). On it were twelve loaves of **shewbread**, arranged in two rows of six (see Lev. 24:5–6).

9:3. At the far end of the Holy Place was a curtain, or **vail**, dividing it from another tent that was known as **the holiest of all** (in the Hebrew idiom, "the Holy of Holies"). It was here that the famed Shekinah glory of God was visible, suspended above the mercy seat of the ark between the two seraphim (see 9:5).

9:4. Which had (Greek, *echō*; "to have," "joined to"). Although the altar of incense stood in the Holy Place, the author described it as belonging to the Most Holy Place. His purpose was to show its close relationship to the inner sanctuary and **the ark of the covenant**, a chest made of acacia wood, overlaid inside and out with gold (see Exod. 25:10–16; 40:5; 1 Kings 6:22). **The golden censer**. The term translated "censer" here refers to a vessel used for burning incense. So it can describe either the shovel (censer) used for carrying the coals or the altar on which the coals were placed. Since the golden altar of incense is otherwise not referred to in this enumeration of the tabernacle furniture, it seems best to understand this verse as referring to that altar. On the Day of Atonement, the high priest took incense from this altar, along with the blood of the sin offering, into the Most Holy Place (see Lev. 16:12–14). **Wherein** (lit., "in which"; i.e., inside the ark) was to be found **manna** that had never spoiled (see Exod. 16:33–34), **Aaron's rod**, which miraculously **budded** to confirm his priesthood when it was challenged (see Num. 17:8–10), and **the tables of the covenant** (the tablets containing the Ten Commandments) that Moses had brought down from the mountain (Exod. 32:15).

9:5. Cherubims of glory. Two winged figures made of pure gold, of one piece with the atonement cover, **the mercy seat**, and standing at either end of it. Between them, the glory of God's presence appeared (see Exod. 25:17–22; Lev. 16:2; Num. 7:89). This is the only place in the New Testament where this special order of angels is mentioned. They are associated with God's majesty, glory, and holiness. The mercy seat, fitting exactly over the top of the ark of the covenant, was a slab of pure gold, on which the high priest sprinkled the blood of the sin offering on the Day of Atonement (see Lev. 16:14–15). **Of which we cannot now speak**. The writer did not intend at this point to speak of these items in detail. This is an important clue that his intent was not to exegete the significance of each of these "types" (see 9:8–9) but to move quickly to its relation to the antitype, that is, Christ (see 9:11).

9:6–7. The priests went always (v. 6). The author highlighted two weaknesses of the old system. The first is the continuous nature of the priests' **service of God**. It was never finished because it was inadequate to put away sin forever (see 10:12–18). Even the sacrifice of the atonement had to be repeated **once every year** (v. 7), on the Day of Atonement (Yom Kippur), the tenth day of the seventh month (see Lev. 16:29, 34; for a description of its ritual, see Leviticus 16). The second weakness of the old system has to with the priesthood itself. **The high priest … offered for himself, and for … the people** (compare 9:25) anticipates the argument of chapter 10. What could not be accomplished by the blood of bulls and goats, "this man" (7:24) would accomplish with the offering of Himself and would forever sit down "on the right hand of God" (10:12), denoting that the work was finished by this "one offering" (10:14).

9:8. The Holy Ghost this signifying. When the Holy Spirit gave these instructions, the very nature of the work indicated that the way to full union with God in **the holiest of all** was yet to be revealed. This would be true as long **as the first tabernacle was yet standing** (lit., "while the first tent still remains in force"). We are reminded again and again that as long as the Mosaic system with its imperfect priesthood and impermanent sacrifices remain in force (8:7–8, 13), the work is unfinished.

9:9. Which was a figure. The Mosaic tabernacle, though superseded, still provided instruction through its typical (symbolic) significance and was a reminder that returning to the old order was useless, since it could not deal effectively with sin. **Gifts and sacrifices** (see 5:1), **that could not make … perfect.** The sacrificial system of the Old Testament dealt only with externals (see 9:10) and was inadequate to cleanse **the conscience.** This line of thinking calls to mind the conflict Paul described in Romans 7, which, as here, was answered with, "For what the law could not do, in that it was weak through the flesh, God sending his own Son in the likeness of sinful flesh, and for sin, condemned sin in the flesh" (Rom. 8:3).

9:10. The time of reformation (Greek, *diorthōsis*; "make straight," "restore to natural condition"). The writer did not imagine something entirely new but the reshaping of what had become distorted, returning it to its natural and proper condition. The new covenant, with its new priesthood, new sanctuary, and new sacrifice will bring about the ultimate reconciliation of sinful humanity with a holy God. This embraces all that was lost in Adam but anticipates a result that surpasses even his original condition of innocence (see 9:24–28).

9:11–12. These verses constitute one complete sentence in the Greek text. The **more perfect tabernacle** (v. 11) is said to be **not of this building** (Greek, *ktisis*; "creation"). It was not an earthly tabernacle but the heavenly sanctuary of God's presence (9:24;

8:2). **Neither by the blood of goats and calves** (v. 12) anticipates **but by his own blood.** The blood that Christ the High Priest sprinkled on the mercy seat was His own, making Him at once both priest and offering. **He entered in once.** Christ's work need not be repeated year after year, as did that of the Levitical high priests. His sacrifice was perfect; it was completely effective and did not need to be repeated. Through His sacrifice, Christ **obtained** (lit., "He alone secured") **eternal redemption for us.** Redemption signifies release through payment of the ransom price (see John 8:36; Rom. 6:14; Gal. 3:13).

9:13–14. Just as the writer contrasted the offerings of the earthly tabernacle with those of the heavenly tabernacle in 9:11–12, here he contrasted the results of those offerings. **The blood of bulls and of goats** (v. 13) refers to sacrifices on the Day of Atonement. As prescribed in Numbers 19, **the ashes of a heifer** were for those who had become ceremonially unclean as a result of contact with a corpse. **The purifying of the flesh.** Such sprinkling, since it was only external, could not make a person inwardly pure. **How much more** (v. 14). If the blood of animals was adequate for "the purifying of the flesh," imagine what **the blood of Christ** accomplished when, **through the eternal Spirit,** He **offered himself.** This difficult text likely refers to the agency of the Holy Spirit, who is said to have led Christ (see Matt. 4:1) during the time of His sojourn here on earth. His leading eventually took Christ to the cross, to which He submitted obediently (see Phil. 2:8). An alternative interpretation would suggest that this passage refers to the divine nature of the God-man. That is, the agent of the sacrifice was His divine nature, and the sacrifice itself was His human nature. This view must be rejected, however, since it assumes the heretical notion that the two natures of Christ can be separated. For the death of Christ to be possible, He had to be human. For His death to have infinite value, He had to be divine. How much more will this sacrifice of the perfect Lamb of God, who is **without spot … purge your conscience** (see 10:22)? The author listed two results, the first negative, and the second positive: (1) the conscience is freed **from**

dead works, and (2) it is freed **to serve the living God** (see 1 Thess. 1:9).

b. The Sacrifice of Christ Was Once for All (9:15–28)

9:15. And is used here to connect what follows with what has preceded. **For this cause he is the mediator** (Greek, *mesitēs*; "one who intervenes to make peace or ratify a covenant"; see 12:24; 1 Tim 2:5). Because of the superiority of Christ's person and work, the writer continued. The argument looks back to the original proposition established in 8:6 that "he obtained a more excellent ministry, by how much also he is [not 'becomes'] the mediator of a better covenant." On **the new testament**, see 7:22; 8:6, 13. On **for the redemption of the transgressions**, see Mark 10:45. By shedding His blood, Christ paid the necessary price to set humankind free from the sins committed under the first covenant, that is, violations of Mosaic law. **The promise of eternal inheritance** is defined in 8:8–12, a passage quoted from Jeremiah 31:31–34. On the basis of Christ's atoning death, this inheritance has become real for those who are called by God (see Rom. 8:28).

9:16–17. Testament … death (v. 16). In these verses, "testament" is used in the sense of a last will and testament. In 9:18, "testament" returns to the concept of covenant as opposed to the idea of a will. Beneficiaries have no claim on the benefits assigned to them in a will until **the death of the testator** has been proven (v. 17). Since Christ's death has been duly attested, "the promise of eternal inheritance" (9:15) is available to His beneficiaries.

9:18–22. The double negative **neither … without blood** (v. 18) sounds awkward in English but is used in Greek for emphasis. **The first testament** illustrates the point, for it too was ratified with blood — the death of the calves from which Moses took blood to seal the old covenant. In fact, in the first covenant, **almost all things are by the law purged with blood** (v. 22; see Exod. 24:4–8; Lev. 8:10, 19, 30).

9:23–26. It was therefore necessary (v. 23) indicates the conclusion of the discussion. Inasmuch as the law requires "almost all things [to be] purged with blood" (9:22), it is necessary to reckon this with

the patterns (lit., "copy," "figure," "imitation") **of things in the heavens** (see 8:5). Whereas it was necessary for the earthly sanctuary to be purified with animal sacrifices, it was necessary for the heavenly sanctuary to be purified with the **better sacrifices** of Christ Himself. The plural here is a Hebraism and is used for emphasis, not to suggest that other sacrifices are in mind. Rather, as the author pointed out in 9:28, the finality of this sacrifice "once offered" sets it apart from all other sacrifices. Christ the High Priest did not go into the earthly tabernacle (the antitype of **the true** tabernacle) **but into heaven itself, now to appear in the presence of God** (v. 24; see 7:25; 1 John 2:1). His sacrifice was not as that of an Old Testament high priest, who offered first "for himself" (9:7); rather, Christ's sacrifice was **for us**. His work was substitutionary in character. It was never necessary that Christ suffer for sin, but He did this on our behalf to be the propitiation for our sins. He did not need to **offer himself often, as the high priest entereth … every year** (v. 25), but only **now once in the end of the world** (lit., "the consummation of the age," v. 26; see 1:2; see 1 Peter 1:20). Christ's coming ushered in the "last days" (1:2).

9:27–28. The chapter ends with an analogy. **And as it is appointed … once to die, but after this the judgment** (v. 27). As in the natural order, man dies once (as a consequence of sin; see Rom. 5:12), so Christ died **once** (v. 28) as the perfect sacrifice for sin. And as man faces judgment after death, so Christ will appear again after His death, bringing salvation from sin and its judgment. **Look for him**. As the Israelites waited for the high priest while he was in the Most Holy Place on the Day of Atonement (see 2 Tim. 4:8; Titus 2:13), so too we look for Christ to **appear the second time without sin unto salvation**. When He reemerges from behind the veil and we see Him in His glory, it will not be for "sin" but for "judgment" (see Rom. 8:29–30; Phil. 3:20–21; 1 John 3:2–3).

c. The Sacrifice of Christ Was Voluntary (10:1–10)

The biblical background for this chapter is Psalm 40, especially verses 6–8. The divine plan was already in place long before God became incarnate in Jesus of Nazareth. And the Holy Spirit, through the psalmist, had already expressed the attitude of Jesus' heart: "I delight to do thy will, O my God" (Ps. 40:8).

10:1-3. The chapter opens with the author recalling the argument of the previous section concerning the relationship between the perpetual sacrifices of the old system, which was only **a shadow of good things to come** (v. 1), and the once-for-all sacrifice of Christ. The offerings of **the law** served only to remind **the comers thereunto** (lit., "those who approach") that their sin remained. "The law" alludes to the Levitical priesthood, which was closely linked to the law under the Mosaic system (see 7:11). The sacrifices prescribed by the law prefigured Christ's ultimate sacrifice. Their repetition **year by year** bore testimony that the perfect, sin-removing sacrifice had not yet been offered. We know this to be so because if it were otherwise, **the worshippers once purged** (Greek, *hapax kekatharismenous*; i.e., if they had been "cleansed once for all") **should have had no more conscience of sins** (v. 2). The opposite was true, however; again and again, **every year** (v. 3), they were reminded that their sin remained to be dealt with.

10:4. The sacrifices of the old system needed to be repeated every year because **it is not possible that the blood of bulls and of goats should take away sins.** An animal cannot possibly be a completely adequate substitute for a human being, who is made in God's image.

10:5. The different terms used for Levitical sacrifices represent four of the five types of offerings prescribed by the Mosaic law (see Leviticus 1-7), namely, peace, grain ("meat"), burnt, and sin offerings. **When he cometh into the world** (v. 5). The writer contemplated a conversation between God the Father and God the Son at the moment of His incarnation. **He saith.** The words of this psalm of David (Ps. 40:6-8) express Christ's obedient submission to the Father in coming to earth. The Mosaic sacrifices were thus replaced by submissive obedience to the will of God (see 10:7; see also Jesus' instruction to His disciples on prayer, "Thy will be done," Matt.

6:10). He would have those who follow Him to have the same attitude (see Phil. 2:5-11). **A body hast thou prepared me.** The writer followed the Septuagint translation of Psalm 40:6, where *sōma*, "body," replaces *ōtia*, "ears." Since it is the ears through which one hears God's will, the sense remains the same. In His earthly session, Jesus understood and carried out the will of His Father. His "body" was the instrument through which their plan was carried out.

10:6-7. Thou hast had no pleasure (v. 6). The Levitical offerings were only preparatory and temporary, looking forward to the one perfect and final offering of the incarnate Son of God. When it was clear that God could not be satisfied with such offerings, **Then** (v. 7) the Son declared, **Lo, I come,** expressing His submission to the Father's will. **In the volume** (Greek, *kephalidi*; "head," "roll") is used only here in the New Testament but is also used in the papyri. Here it is used to underscore that what Christ came to do was predicted in the Scriptures. **To do thy will.** The will of the Father was the Son's consuming concern (see Luke 22:42; John 4:34).

10:8-10. With **Above** (v. 8), the author called attention to the text he quoted in 10:5-6. What follows is his exegesis of Psalm 40, with special reference to his subject. Although God gave instructions for the animal sacrifices, He took no **pleasure** in them. For that reason, **He taketh away the first** (the animal sacrifices)**, that** (lit., "in order that") **he may establish the second** (i.e., doing God's will; v. 9). His perfect sacrifice, offered in complete submission, supersedes and therefore replaces all previous sacrifices. **Sanctified** (v. 10). Through this means, believers are made holy, set apart in consecration to God, and experience the process of continuing sanctification (see "are sanctified," 10:14; see also 1 Cor. 1:2).

d. The Sacrifice of Christ Was Adequate (10:11-18)

10:11-14. Here the argument turns on two points. The first has to do with the ministry of Christ, which answers to the daily ministry of the Old Testament priesthood. The second point demonstrates the superiority of His ministry to that which it replaced. The author made his argument with a series of contrasts: **standeth** (v. 11), **daily ministering**, and **never take away sins** contrast with **sat down** (v. 12), **one sacrifice**, and **expecting** (v. 13). The work of the Old Testament priest was never done; he stood because there was never time to sit down. He offered **the same sacrifices** (v. 11) because these sacrifices were unable to accomplish what they signified (see Ps. 40:7–9). They could not remove sin and thus had to be offered over and over again. By contrast, **this man** (v. 12) entered only once, after which He **sat down on the right hand of God** (see discussions on 1:3, 13). Once again, the writer drew from Psalm 110:1 to contrast the work of the Levitical priests, which was never done (v. 11), to the finished work of Christ. His **one offering** (v. 14), or sacrifice, made atonement for the sins of all time, making any further sacrifice unnecessary. **Henceforth expecting** (lit., "for the future"; v. 13). All that awaits is that **his enemies be made his footstool** (another allusion to Ps. 110:1; see also John 16:33; 1 Cor. 15:24–28). Thus, by "one offering," He finished the work and has **perfected for ever them that are sanctified.**

10:15–18. The Holy Ghost ... had said (v. 15). The two quotations included in these verses are from Jeremiah 31:31–34 (also cited in 8:8–12). Using Scripture to interpret Scripture, the writer employed this text again to underscore his interpretation of Psalm 40:7–9. The new covenant guarantees that the Lord will conform believers' hearts to His (v. 16, Ps. 40:8); sins will be effectively and completely forgiven (v. 17), and no additional sacrifice for sins is needed (v. 18). Noteworthy here is the writer's recognition that the Holy Spirit is considered to have uttered the prophecy of Jeremiah (see 2 Tim. 3:16).

3. Superior Opportunities in a New and Living Way (10:19–25)

10:19. Another section of practical application and exhortation begins here (see 2:1–4) This is coupled with a second argument concerning the superior priesthood of Christ (the first is 8:1–6). **Boldness.** Since many are tempted to quit and abandon Christ, this term is a recurrent theme throughout the letter (sometimes translated "confidence"; see

3:6; 4:16; 10:35). **To enter into the holiest.** The way into the sanctuary of God's presence was closed to the people under the former covenant because the blood of animal sacrifices could never completely make atonement for their sins. Now, however, believers can come to the throne of grace because the perfect Priest has offered the perfect sacrifice, atoning for sin once for all.

10:20. By a new (Greek, *prosphatos;* "lately slaughtered," "freshly killed") **and living way.** By His death and resurrection, Jesus **consecrated** (lit., "dedicated") a new covenant (see 8:13). **Through the vail, that is to say, his flesh** (see John 1:18; 14:9). When Jesus died, the veil separating the Holy Place from the Most Holy Place was "rent in twain from the top to the bottom" (Matt. 27:51; Mark 15:38; Luke 23:45). The curtain symbolizes the body of Christ in terms of suffering; like the curtain, His body was torn to open the way into the divine presence. With a touch of irony, the author wrote of the veil of the old covenant as that which concealed the presence (because it remained whole); now the veil opens the way to the presence of God (because it was "broken," 1 Cor. 11:24).

10:21–25. This entire section consists of one carefully crafted sentence in the original. **And having a high priest over the house of God** (v. 21). The reality of this new "high priest" (see 4:14–7:28) who opened the way for direct access to the living God and who stands in the very house ("habitation") of God evoked three exhortations from the author.

(1) **Let us draw near** (v. 22). Four conditions are given for drawing near to God: (a) **A true heart,** or undivided allegiance in the inner being. (b) **In full assurance of faith** (Greek, *plērophoria;* "most certain confidence"). Faith trusts implicitly in the word and work of Christ, enabling the believer to stand in the presence of absolute holiness (see Rom. 5:1). (c) **Hearts sprinkled from an evil conscience,** or total freedom from guilt, based on the once-for-all sacrifice of Christ. (d) **Bodies washed with pure water.** The imagery here calls to mind Paul's words in Titus 3:5: "according to his mercy he saved us, by the washing of regeneration, and renewing of the Holy Ghost" (see

also Exod. 30:19–21; Lev. 8:6; see also Ezek. 36:25, where a similar expression is used figuratively for the cleansing resulting from the new covenant). Of course, the context here is focusing on the "interior" rather than the "exterior" (see 8:10; 9:9–14; 10:2, 16).

(2) **Let us hold fast the profession of our hope** (see 6:18–20) **without wavering** (lit., "not leaning"; v. 23). The author called his hearers to stand with Christ without doubt or hesitation. Some of them were tempted to give up the struggle and turn back to a form of Judaism. **He is faithful that promised** looks ahead to the argument in 10:26–12:3 (see also 6:13; 8:6; 2 Tim. 2:13).

(3) **Let us consider one another to provoke** (Greek, *paroxysmos*; "to incite") **unto love and to good works** (v. 24). "Provoke" can be used in a negative sense (see, e.g., Acts 15:39), but here it is used in a good sense, "to incite." Paul did this in his exhortation to the Corinthians, inciting them to follow the example of the Macedonians (see 2 Cor. 8:1–7).

Reinforcing his third exhortation, the writer added, **Not forsaking the assembling of ourselves together** (v. 25). The Greek word translated "forsaking" speaks of desertion and abandonment (see Matt. 27:46; 2 Cor, 4:9; 2 Tim. 4:10, 16). This introduces the author's fourth warning (10:26–31), concerning those who were tempted to abandon the faith. "The assembling of ourselves together" could refer to "our gathering together unto him" (as the same phrase is translated in 2 Thess. 2:1) at Christ's coming. This would fit well with **the day approaching**, the day of the Lord's return and judgment (see 1 Cor. 3:13; see 1 Thess. 5:2, 4; 2 Thess. 1:10; 2:2; 2 Peter 3:10). The writer considered Christ's return to be close at hand (see Rom. 13:12). Or it could refer to the regular gatherings of believers for worship. Most commentators prefer this interpretation since it makes the most sense of the contrary expression, **as the manner of some is**. It would seem that many of their number had already made a "habit" of staying away from their services, perhaps for fear of intimidation (see 10:33). Such neglect, it would seem, was a symptom of a more serious lapse in their faith, leading to willful sinning (see 10:26).

4. Warning against Willful Sinning (10:26–31)

10:26–27. The author gave the warning itself first, beginning with the conjunction **For** (v. 26). That these verses were a warning to persons ("some," 10:25) deserting the Christian assembly is apparent (see discussions on 6:4–8, where the same spiritual condition is discussed). **If we sin wilfully** (Greek, *hekousiōs*; "voluntarily"). As opposed to sins of ignorance or weakness, this involves deliberate disobedience. This is the sin of apostasy (see 10:29; discussion on 5:2). The Old Testament background is Numbers 15:27–31. **After that we have received** (lit., "after receiving"; see John 1:12) **the knowledge** (Greek, *epignōsis*; "precise knowledge"; see 6:4) **of the truth**. The warning entails a situation in which there is full culpability on the part of the sinner. **There remaineth no more** (lit., "there is no longer left behind any more") **sacrifice for sins**. In the Old Testament, there was no offering for "presumptuous" sin (Num. 15:30–31). It is perhaps not inconsequential that the context of the instruction regarding this sin is followed by a reference to the Sabbath-breaker who was stoned for his sin (see Num. 15:32–36). The writer already established that only one sacrifice could put away sin (10:1–18). To reject Christ's sacrifice is to reject the *only* sacrifice; there is no other (see 12:22–24). What else is there but **fearful looking for** ("dreadful expectation"; see 10:13) **of judgment and fiery indignation** (v. 27; for fierceness of the Lord's fire, see Isa. 26:11; Zeph. 1:18; Ps. 79:5; 2 Thess. 1:6–9).

10:28. He that despised Moses' law died without mercy. The consequences of willfulness under the old system are noted. The term *atheteo* ("set aside," "disregard," "thwart," "make void") speaks of an abandonment of the covenant; one who did so was an apostate (see Num. 35:30; Deut. 17:2–7; 19:15; compare Josh. 24:22) and was put to death on the basis of **two or three witnesses** (see Deut. 17:6; compare 2 Cor. 1:3).

10:29. Of how much sorer punishment, suppose ye…? As the writer turned to the consequences of willfulness under Christ, he underscored the magnitude of such an offense against Christ with *posō* *dokeite cheironos*, "How much worse do you imagine?" Those who commit such a sin do violence to God in three ways. (1) They have **trodden under foot the Son of God**. Similar language is used in 6:6 (see also Matt. 5:13). (2) They have **counted the blood of the covenant, wherewith he was sanctified, an unholy thing** (see 9:20; 13:20; Exod. 24:8; Matt. 26:28; Mark 14:24). To despise the sanctifying blood of Christ bespeaks treachery of the worst kind, particularly when that blood has sanctified (aorist passive indicative) the one who profanes its efficacy. (3) They have **done despite unto the Spirit of grace**. They have insulted the Holy Spirit, who has mediated God's grace to their benefit.

10:30–31. Vengence belongeth unto me … The Lord shall judge his people (v. 30) is quoted from Deuteronomy 32:35–36. It is clear in this warning that while God in the New Testament may be considered "the Father of mercies" (2 Cor. 1:3), His holy character remains the same, and He will judge in righteousness (Ps. 96:10–13). No wonder the writer shuddered with the words **It is a fearful thing … the living God** (v. 31; see 10:27; 12:29). It is "frightening." The wrath of God faces those who sin against Him. And because He is "the living God" (see 3:13), we had better be mindful of the certainty of His judgment against evildoers.

5. Exhortation to Take Courage (10:32–39)

The chapter concludes with a call to remembrance and a word of encouragement. Just as he did in 6:9, the writer let his readers know that he was persuaded of "better things" from them.

10:32–33. The former days (v. 32). Presumably following their first enthusiastic response to the gospel, they had **endured a great fight of afflictions**. Against loss and persecution, they were deeply concerned for each other, sharing their pain as **companions** (v. 33).

10:34. Ye had compassion of me in my bonds. Evidently, the writer had shared with his readers in having been subjected to persecution (see Introduction: "Author"). **Took joyfully** (lit., "received to yourselves with joy"). Early Christians endured suffering

in the knowledge that this world was not their home. Here they joyfully stepped aside as their possessions were plundered by their enemies. Why? Because **ye have in heaven a better and an enduring substance**. Their hope in Christ embraced their future reward (see 11:10, 13–16, 26, 35; 13:14; Matt. 5:11–12; 6:19–21; John 14:1–2; Rom. 8:18; 1 Peter 5:1–4). When they had Jesus, what else could they want?

10:35–37. Cast not away … your confidence (v. 35). Seeing their valiant endurance, the author challenged them not to "throw away" their confidence. Once again, the term *parrēsia*, "boldness" or "confidence," is used (see 3:6; 3:14; 10:19). Such boldness was secured for us by Christ. It comes with Him. If we cast Him aside, we cast aside all His benefits (see Pss. 68:19; 103:2; 116:12). The confidence they once had when persecuted (10:34) had not been misplaced, but they must have **patience** (v. 36) so that they **might receive the promise**. They must wait **yet a little while** (v. 37). Again, Christ's coming was thought to be imminent.

10:38–39. In a very practical final exhortation, the writer reminded his hearers that this confidence was of the essence to the Christian's experience of Christ. **The just shall live by faith** (v. 38; see Hab. 2:4). Paul said it this way to the Colossian believers: "As ye have therefore received Christ Jesus the Lord, so walk ye in him" (Col. 2:6). By faith they had come to this place, and by faith they were to go on. Lest they fear they belonged to those in whom the Lord **shall have no pleasure**, the writer included himself with the readers, saying, **we are not of them who draw back unto perdition** (v. 39). The security of these believers was certain; they were **of them that believe to the saving of the soul**. The author was confident that those to whom he was writing were, for the most part, among the saved (see 6:9).

E. The Argument for a Superior Goal of Faith (chaps. 11–12)

The author had warned his readers against willfully sinning against so great a redemption (10:26–31), and throughout the letter, he repeatedly expressed the idea that one may believe the gospel and be saved yet not grow in grace or ever realize God's best for one's life. It is a matter of choice. In the following gallery of faith, he presented a litany of examples in which God's word was not only believed and accepted as truth but was also acted on. Realizing that the issue of faith is a difficult concept to grasp, especially as the term is used in the New Testament, the writer offered examples from "times past" when God spoke to "the fathers" (1:1), who had faced the same temptations to doubt, neglect, or fall away from His promises.

11:1. Now, in view of all the preceding, the idea that **faith** (Greek, *pistis*; "faith," also "faithfulness," "steadfastness") **is the substance of** (lit., "what stands under") **things hoped for** brings into view the realization that faith is a genuine hope based on a genuine word and promise from the Lord. This harks back to the opening verses of the epistle, describing the superiority and reliability of a word received "in Son" (see 1:1–3 and discussions). This is half of the equation. Again in keeping with the preceding warnings, faith is also **the evidence of things not seen.** Here the author employed the same reasoning as James: "faith without works is dead" (James 2:26). Abraham received the promise, believed the promise, and was convinced (Greek, *elengchos*) to act on the promise, never having seen the fulfillment of the promise. It is with this overlay that one must understand the following examples. The warnings of this epistle are graphic: there can be no successful, fruitful life of *faith* without the presence of both substance (*hope*), or underpinnings, and evidence, action based on conviction (*love*).

1. Old Testament Examples of Faith (11:1–39)

11:2. For by it (faith) **the elders obtained a good report.** The phrase "obtained a good report" is a rendering of a single word, *martyreō* (middle, passive voice; see 12:1). In the literal sense, this means that faith enabled the elders (Greek, *presbyteroi* "forefathers," "patriarchs") to secure a commendation (from God, see 11:4–6) of the fruitfulness of believing and following God's Word. Additionally, within the general context of the epistle and the specific context of these verses, this witness portrayed the absolute surety and appropriateness of God's Word during "hard times" or when the promise was yet to be fulfilled. The author did not leave this statement to stand on its own but followed up with many details to support this assertion.

11:3. Through faith we understand (Greek, *noeō*; "to ponder" or "to think") does not refer to understanding as we normally think of it but rather conveys the idea that our ponderings, our thinking, and our meditations are to be done within the "castle walls" of faith. One of the great ponderings for mankind has been **that the worlds** (Greek, *aiōn*; "ages"; see 1:2) **were framed by the word of God.** For the secular humanist and the evolutionist, who both operate outside the walls of faith, this is nonsense. For the believer who possesses the substance and evidence of faith, however, it is accepted **that things which are seen were not made** (Greek, *ginomai*; "began to be") **of things which do appear** (lit., "can be seen"). The fact of creation cannot be diminished by our inability to ponder the visible and glorious works of God to a logical conclusion (see Psalm 33).

At this point, the author moved from a general application of an operational faith to specific and familiar examples showing how his hearers' forebears had lived out their faith. The hearers were well aware of these examples. The author's purpose was to hammer home the fact that the accomplishments listed were made reality through faith. It is noteworthy that some of these examples of faith in action depict God working *through* His people, some depict God working *in* His people, and some depict God working *for* His people. In all cases, it was God working in accordance with His Word and in response to those who trusted Him. In many of the illustrations of faith, the writer, in keeping with the structure of this epistle, also recorded the fate of those who had refused God's word.

All of the saints the author listed responded to God in faith, believing God's word. They illustrate the positive effects of heeding the warnings of this epistle. The writer arranged the "testimonies" into sections corresponding to the warnings and according to the families or "households" that are represented (see 3:2–6; 6:1–2).

a. Members of Adam's Household (11:4–6)

11:4. The writer's first examples of faith in action underscored his warning against neglect (see 2:1). "There is a way which seemeth right unto a man, but the end thereof are the ways of death" (Prov. 14:12). From the beginning, God made it known that He would require a blood sacrifice that would atone for sin. It was therefore **By faith** in the word of the Lord that **Abel offered unto God a more excellent** (Greek, *pleïon*; "better") **sacrifice than Cain**. Neither Abel's nor Cain's sacrifice could atone for sin; only the blood of Christ could accomplish that. From the beginning, however, blood sacrifices were offered in obedience to God's command, as "a shadow" (10:1) that illustrated Christ's eventual blood atonement for sin. The issue is not that Cain's offering was not good but rather that it was not offered in the obedience of faith (see 2:1); Cain substituted the wisdom of man for the clearly revealed will of God (see Rom. 10:3). Thus, Abel's offering was better, having been offered in the obedience of faith. He thereby **obtained witness** (Greek, *emartyrēthē*; "had witness born to him") **that he was righteous**. As we have seen, the final and perfect blood sacrifice of Christ on the cross was also in obedience to the divine will (see Gen. 4:3–4; see also 1 John 3:12). God Himself gave witness of Abel's righteousness (see "God … spake in time past unto the fathers," 1:1). **God testifying … and by it** (lit., "God bearing witness … through it"). God's testimony concerning Abel's sacrifice is such that **he being dead yet speaketh**.

11:5–6. Enoch (v. 5) was a man who **pleased God** (see Gen. 5:18–24). Because of his **faith**, he **was translated** (Greek, *metatithēmi*; "transferred," i.e., to heaven) **that he should not see death; and was not found, because God had translated him**, or taken him up to His presence (see Gen. 5:24; Pss. 49:15; 73:24). The author's emphasis is not so much the unusual nature of Enoch's departure as it is that **without faith it is impossible to please him** (v. 6; see 3:7–11). That Enoch pleased God is proof of his

faith; that God translated him is witness to God's approval and proof of God's faithfulness. **For he that cometh to God** (see 10:19–22) **must believe that he is**. Faith must have an object, and the proper object of genuine faith is first God and secondarily His Word. The specific emphasis here is that He is **a rewarder of them that diligently seek him** (Greek, *ekzēteō*; "to seek out"). "Diligently seek him" refers to a focused effort, much like a person attempting to locate another in a large crowd (see 6:9–12; see Jer. 29:13). This statement and the inability of the unregenerate heart to understand or seek after God (see Rom. 3:11), provide further evidence that the recipients (though many were "babes"; see 5:13) were genuine in their faith.

b. Members of Noah's Household (11:7)

The ungodly in Noah's day had no excuse for their unbelief. In righteousness, God sent them a preacher in the person of Noah (see Rom. 10:14–15). In spite of the pressure of the society around him, Noah believed God. Noah and his household are introduced here to illustrate the writer's warning against unbelief (see 3:7–15; see also Gen. 6:8–10; 2 Peter 2:5).

11:7. By faith Noah … moved with fear (a reverence toward God's command), **prepared an ark** (see Gen. 5:28–9:29) **to the saving of his house**. This was absolutely necessary, in the economy of God, to preserve the line of promise that led to the birth of Christ. **By the which he condemned the world**. With the exception of Noah and his family, all mankind heard the word preached and rejected it, and when the flood came, they were judged by it. Noah, however, **became heir of the righteousness which is by faith**. Noah believed God and acted on that which God said, even when it related to "things not seen" (11:1), namely, the coming flood. Thus, Noah also fit the description of God's righteous ones who live by faith (see 10:38). His faith in God's word moved him to build the ark in a dry, landlocked region, where it was inconceivable that there would ever be enough water to float the vessel. When a person walks with God, they find Him to be faithful, and unbelief is never an option.

c. Members of Abraham's Household (11:8–23))

Although he was a man of substance, Abraham was a persistent believer. By leaving his own country, he became invested in God's promise to him. His confidence in God was never shaken; he never allowed the negative circumstances of life to dim the reality of God's promises, even when serious contradictions seemed to negate them. Abraham's life exemplifies the steadfastness that the author wished for his readers—those of his day and ours. Abraham thus serves to underscore the writer's warning against falling away (6:4–6).

11:8. By faith Abraham, when called of God (see Gen. 12:1–3), embarked on a journey to an unknown destination, **a place which he should after receive for an inheritance**. This he did for the sole reason that he **obeyed** God. He is presented in the New Testament as the outstanding example of those who live "by faith" and as "the father of all them that believe" (Rom. 4:11; see Rom. 4:12, 16; Gal. 3:7, 9, 29). His faith was expressed in obedience (see Gen. 12:4). **He went out, not knowing** his destination, nevertheless in complete confidence in God's trustworthiness.

11:9–11. By faith he sojourned (v. 9), dwelling as a stranger **in the land of promise**, living in tents with his family, who were **heirs with him of the same promise**. Abraham knew how to wait upon God (see Pss. 37:9; 123:2). Rather than take matters into his own hands, **he looked** (lit., "was patiently waiting") **for a city which hath foundations, whose builder and maker is God** (v. 10). When relying on the promises of God, it makes no sense to intervene and provide for ourselves a cheap imitation when God wants us to have the genuine article (see Ps. 147:2). The covenant with Abraham involved not only a city but also descendants who would be "heirs with him." Abraham's household would prove to be worthy of continuing the line of promise in that **Through faith also Sara herself received strength to conceive seed** (v. 11). That which is humanly impossible is possible for God. Even though she was beyond the age of childbearing, Sarah believed and **judged him faithful who had promised** (see Gen. 18:11–12; 11:30).

11:12–15. Abraham, though **as good as dead** (v. 12) because he was one hundred years old (see Gen. 21:5; Rom. 4:19), became the father of an innumerable multitude, even **as the stars of the sky … and as the sand which is by the sea shore** (see Gen. 13:16; 15:5; 22:17; 26:4; 1 Kings 4:20). Abraham and his family saw the power of God operating to fulfill the immediate aspects of the promises, but ultimately **These all died in faith, not having received the promises, but having seen them afar off** (v. 13). Realizing that they were only links in the chain of promise, they were content to live their entire lives steadfastly. They **were persuaded of [the promises], and embraced them, and confessed that they were strangers and pilgrims on the earth**. Their true home was in heaven. Truly, they were of those who **declare** (lit., "are declaring") **plainly that they seek** (Greek, *epizēteō*; "seek after") **a [better] country** (Greek, *patris*; "fatherland;" v. 14, see 11:16). Abraham and his family were seeking a homeland. **Truly, if they had been mindful** (Greek, *emnēmoneuon*; "had continued to be mindful," "yearned for") **of that country from whence they came out, they might have had** (lit., "would have kept on having) **opportunity to have returned** (Greek, *kairon anakampsai*; aorist active infinitive; v. 15). If they had longed for the leeks, onions, and garlic of Egypt (see Num. 11:5), as their descendants later would (and as some of the discouraged recipients were doing), they would have had plenty of incentive to go back. In which case, they would never have received the promise. Again, note that this chapter is not just an accidental assortment of God's faithful. The author's choice of Old Testament examples was purposeful and reinforced the entire message of the epistle. Here he was mindful of his hearers' temptation to "fall away" (6:6).

11:16. But now they desire a better country, one that is **heavenly: wherefore God is not ashamed to be called their God**. God's best is always to be desired, and it is always "better." Note that He has already **prepared** (Greek, *hetoimazō*; "made ready") **for them a city** (Greek, *polis*; "a city with walls"; see 11:3). The ultimate reality is represented by the New Jerusalem in John's vision of the believer's eternal state (see 12:22–24; Rev. 21:2). The author admonished his hearers to follow the example of Abraham's family and look beyond their immediate circumstances to the eventual fulfillment of all God's promises.

The author has placed the greatest emphasis on Abraham and not upon Moses, the patriarch with whom the recipients identified the most. In 11:8–16, the story of Abraham concerns both the land and the seed of promise, including the earthly and the heavenly. In 11:17–19, the author related how Abraham portrayed his faith in God even to the raising of the dead.

11:17. He that had received the promises. God instructed Abraham to offer his son Isaac as a burnt offering (see Gen. 22:2). He prepared to do just that, all in accord with the word of God (see Gen. 22:9–10), and **offered up Isaac** (lit., "was ready to offer up"), the son of promise, **his only begotten son** (see John 3:16; Rom. 8:32).

11:18–19. The Lord's instruction to offer Isaac as a burnt offering must have seemed to Abraham the greatest of all contradictions, for God had promised **That in Isaac shall thy seed be called** (v. 18; from Gen. 21:12). This seeming contradiction, however, did not deter Abraham from obedience to the known will of God. Abraham's steadfastness was grounded in his confidence that **God was able to raise[Isaac] up, even from the dead** (v. 19). Figuratively, this event occurred when the substitute ram was provided (see Gen. 22:13). In the mind of the believer, death has no power and cannot, through fear or persuasion, cause the child and servant of God to shrink from doing God's will (see 1 Cor. 15:55). Even as Isaac willingly submitted to the will of his father Abraham, so Jesus submitted to the will of His Father, going willingly to the cross (see Luke 22:42). The hearers were reminded that all these things were "a shadow of good things to come" (10:1) and that they also must endure hardship (see 12:7, 20; 2 Tim. 2:3; 4:3, 5).

11:20. God's promises were passed on from father to son. Although it was the result of treachery, **Isaac blessed Jacob,** believing God as to the promises. **Esau** had "despised his birthright" (Gen. 25:34;

lit., "thought it to be of no value"), and its retrieval was impossible, "though he sought it carefully with tears" (Heb. 12:17). This was a somber warning to the hearers about their responsibility to their faith. They, and all believers, must at all costs never allow themselves to "fall away" (6:6; see Gen. 27:27–40). The blessing of Jacob demonstrates that God looks on the heart, not outward appearances (see 1 Sam. 16:7). Although one of the most startling, it was only one of many twists and turns in the lineage of Messiah, in which God sovereignly intervened to preserve His promises.

11:21. Here the author used Jacob's given name, not "Israel," the name he received from God at Peniel (see Gen. 32:28). **By faith Jacob … blessed both the sons of Joseph; and worshipped, leaning upon the top of his staff** (lit., "worshipped on the top of his staff"; see Gen. 47:31, Septuagint). Perhaps the author was emphasizing the human element involved in faith as well as de-emphasizing the idea that the nation of Israel has a sole claim to faith in God (see Romans 4). Jacob required of his son Joseph that he be buried with his fathers (see Gen. 47:29–31). Again, God directed the blessing (to Manasseh) contrary to that which was expected (see Gen. 48:8–20).

11:22. Joseph himself, **when he died, made mention of the** (future) **departing of the children of Israel** from Egypt and **By faith … gave commandment concerning his bones** (see Gen. 50:24–25). Jacob (see 11:21) and Joseph are additional examples of those whose faith was no less strong at death than in life (see 11:13).

11:23. By faith Moses … was hid … of his parents (see Exod. 6:20; Num. 26:58–59) **because they saw he was a proper child** (see discussion on Exod. 2:2); **and they were not afraid of the king's commandment** to kill Israel's males at birth (see Exod. 1:16, 22). Again, it was "by faith" that God's promise for this people was preserved long before anyone could trace His hand.

d. Members of Moses' Household (11:24–39)

11:24. In calling to mind those of Moses' household, the writer reinforced his warning against willful sinning (see 10:26–27). To the recipients of this epistle, Moses represented the law. In this recollection of his faith, however, the author made no mention of the law. This is in keeping with his purpose of demonstrating the transcendence of faith, which is both antecedent and superior to faith in the keeping of the law (see Gal. 3:21–26). Although Moses was claimed by Pharaoh's daughter, in his early years, he was raised and taught by his mother (see Exod. 2:8–9). During this time, he was no doubt taught concerning the promises of God. It was thus **By faith** that **Moses … refused to be called the son of Pharaoh's daughter**.

11:25–29. Choosing … affliction … [over] the pleasures of sin (v. 25), Moses willingly gave up the luxury and prestige in Egypt's royal palace. The author presented this example of faith to exhort the hearers that they should never willfully sin against the known will of God. This remains especially true today, as the pleasures available to contemporary Christians continually beckon us to choose them over the things of God. In making his choice, Moses was **esteeming the reproach of Christ greater riches than the treasures of Egypt** (v. 26). The author spoke of "the reproach" of the Anointed One in keeping with the sense of Psalm 89:51. This reproach is heaped on those who (as God's chosen) comply with the will of God even though it results in the sneers and jeers of the surrounding culture. Moses esteemed the reproach of Christ because **he had respect unto** (lit., "kept on looking away unto") **the recompence of the reward**. For Moses, this was the deliverance of the children of Israel as promised. For Christ, this was obtaining a permanent atonement and the resultant deliverance of "many sons" (2:10). For Christians, it is to be freed from the power of sin and to display the glory of God (see Rom. 8:18). Although Moses' understanding of the details of the messianic hope was extremely limited, he chose to be associated with the people through whom that hope was to be realized. **By faith he forsook Egypt** (v. 27), probably referring to his flight to Midian in the Sinai peninsula when he was forty years old (see Exod. 2:11–15; Acts 7:23–29), **not fearing the wrath of the king**.

Exodus indicates that Moses was afraid (Exod. 2:14) but does not expressly say of whom, and it tells us that he fled from Pharaoh when Pharaoh tried to kill him (Exod. 2:15) but does not expressly say that he fled out of fear. The author of Hebrews capitalized on these features of the account to highlight that in his fleeing from Pharaoh, Moses was sustained by his trust in God that the liberation of Israel would come and that he would have some part in it. **He endured** for forty years in Midian (see Acts 7:30) **as seeing him who is invisible** (see 11:1, 6). Because he believed God, **through faith he kept the passover, and the sprinkling of blood** (v. 28), saving **the firstborn** from death (see Exodus 12). Furthermore, **By faith they passed through the Red sea as by dry land** (v. 29). When the pursuing Egyptians sought to seize this same miracle, they **were drowned** (see Exodus 14–15). The third and final forty-year period of Moses' life was spent leading the Israelites through the wilderness. At the age of 120 years, he died in Moab (see Deut. 34:1–7), together with all those of his generation who came out of Egypt.

11:30. Moses' place as leader was taken by Joshua, who brought the people of Israel into the Land of Promise. Great must have been the patience of this man. Joshua, along with Kaleb, viewed the obstacles in the land as opportunities. Jericho was the first great obstacle to their conquest of the land and was captured by faith without a battle (see Joshua 6). **By faith the walls of Jericho fell down, after they were compassed about seven days.** The victory was achieved because of Joshua's strict obedience to the command of God.

We must not to miss the author's point in denying mention of Joshua and Caleb by name and at once introducing Rahab. Without Rahab's cooperation, the spies would have been found and probably executed. The author captured the hearers' attention by introducing a shocking irony. Rahab (Hebrew, *raḥab*; "strength,") was a name for a mythical sea monster and was used frequently of Egypt (see Isa. 30:7 and discussion; see also Pss. 87:4; 89:10; Isa. 51:9). The irony is that God had demonstrated His power to rescue the nation through one as significant as

Moses and now demonstrated his power to give them the Promised Land through one as insignificant as Rahab the harlot. This surely resonated with the persecuted recipients of the epistle, who would have been tempted to forget their importance to the Lord (2:11) and, as Job's friends advised, "curse God, and die" (Job 2:9).

11:31. By faith the harlot Rahab perished not with them that believed not. Rahab embraced the promises of God (see Josh. 2:9–11). Lest the reader think one has to be a hero of faith to receive the rewards of faith, Rahab stands as a monument to God's grace and is honored for her witness. Because of her newly found faith and obedience to God, evidenced when she **received the spies with peace** (see James 2:25), Joshua spared her and her family when Jericho was burned to the ground (see Josh. 6:22–25). Important to note is that her faith was not limited to something she merely believed; her faith led to works of obedience to what she knew already to be true of this God of the children of Israel. It was important for the persecuted believers of the first century to be reminded that God had protected Rahab from the judgment that fell on her city.

11:32–33. The time would fail me to tell (v. 32). *Diēgoumenon* is the masculine form of *diēgeomai*, "to relate," indicating that the author of Hebrews was a man (see Introduction: "Author"). Like the crescendo of a fireworks display, the writer poured out a mighty display of faith, faithfulness, and obedience to God, even unto death. For **Gedeon** (Gideon), **Barak**, **Samson**, and **Jephthae**, see Judges 4:6–5:15; 6:11–8:35; 11:1–12:7; 13:24–16:31; and 1 Samuel 12:11, where Gideon is called Jerubbaal (see Judg. 6:32 and discussion). For **Samuel** and **the prophets**, see Psalm 99:6; Jeremiah 15:1; Acts 3:24; 13:20. Through faith, all those listed here **subdued kingdoms, wrought righteousness, obtained promises, stopped the mouths of lions** (v. 33; see Daniel in the lions' den, Daniel 6).

11:34–35. Here the author used a sledgehammer style, with nine clauses, to bring home his point. These heroes of faith **quenched the violence of fire** (see Daniel's friends, Shadrach, Meshach, and Abednego, in the fiery furnace, Daniel 3), **escaped … the sword, out of weakness were made strong** (see 2 Cor. 12:9), **waxed valiant in fight, turned to flight the armies of the aliens**. Through God's help, they overcame sickness (see Rom. 8:26; 2 Cor. 12:9). **Women received their dead raised to life again** (v. 35; see the widow of Zarephath, 1 Kings 17:17–24; and the Shunammite woman, 2 Kings 4:8–36). **Others were tortured, not accepting deliverance; that they might obtain a better resurrection**. This is strongly reminiscent of the heroic Maccabean Jewish patriots of the second century BC (see 2 Maccabees 7). But the description applies also to countless believers, known and unknown, who demonstrated their faith in God by persevering in the face of harsh trials and afflictions. They could only hope for something better in the resurrection. Christians already enjoy the blessings of the new covenant and the age to come.

11:37–38. They were stoned (v. 37). Men like Zechariah, the son of Jehoiada the priest, were put to death for declaring the truth (see 2 Chron. 24:20–22; Luke 11:51; see also Jeremiah, Introduction: "Author and Date"). **They were sawn asunder** perhaps refers to Isaiah, who, according to tradition, met this kind of death under wicked King Manasseh (see Isaiah, Introduction: "Author"). **Sheepskins and goatskins** were the rough garments of prophets such as Elijah. All these are they **of whom the world was not worthy** (v. 38). Perhaps this is why God placed them **in deserts … mountains … dens and caves**.

11:39. These all, having obtained a good report (Greek, *martyreō*) **through faith** (see 11:2) indicates not that all the heroes of faith experienced immediate triumph over their circumstances but that all were blessed by God. Yet in spite of their faithfulness to God, they **received not the promise**. The writer used the middle voice here. These faithful ones about whom God testifies in His Word never saw the fulfillment of the messianic promise in their lifetime. No wonder Simeon rejoiced as he did when he cradled the newborn Jesus and said, "Lord, lettest thou thy servant depart in peace … for mine eyes have seen thy salvation" (Luke 2:26).

2. The Transcendence of Faith (11:40)

11:40. God having provided some better thing for us. The fulfillment for those listed in the author's gallery of faith, as for Christians today, is in Christ, who is "the resurrection and the life" (John 11:25–26), **that they without us should not be made perfect**. All persons of faith who had gone before focused their faith on God and His promises. The fulfillment of God's promises to them has come in Jesus Christ, and their redemption, along with ours, is now complete in Him. Hidden from them was the mystery of the church and the intervening period of time when the gospel would be preached throughout the world, to the Jew first but also to the Greek (see Rom. 1:16), fulfilling the promise that through Abraham's seed all the families of the earth be blessed (see Gen. 12:3; Gal. 3:16–19, 29). There can be no mistaking the contrast; "they" and "us" creates a clear distinction between that which was and the "better thing" that has come to be. With this important declaration, the author moved to the recipients' circumstances and to his final warning, which had particular application to the hearers as well as to all who have heard Him "that speaketh" (12:24–25).

The author diligently emphasized that the recipients were uniquely members of Christ's household, over which He is Lord. Indeed, He is Son over His own house (see 3:5–6). Their fledgling numbers were but a beginning in God's plan to call out a people for His name. As it was with Abraham, they too would not see the end of this new beginning, but they were a link in the long line of those who would follow in the lineage of faith. This chapter has yet to be finished, and will not be finished until Jesus comes again, but to be sure, the living of it will be by faith.

3. Run with Patience, Looking to Jesus' Example (12:1–3)

12:1. In the original text, **Wherefore** expresses a conclusion with emphasis. The chapter division here is unfortunate since it breaks this passionate climax of the writer's argument from the previous chapters (10 and 11), concerning the "better promises" (8:6) of the new covenant. It was important to the author that his hearers grasp and understand that they were part of a grand theme and that they recognize that they were **compassed about with** (lit., "surrounded by") **so great a cloud of witnesses**, those who have left a legacy of faith that witnesses to the faithfulness of God. The imagery suggests an athletic contest in a great amphitheater with tier upon tier of seats rising up like a cloud. It is not that these saints are spectators but that their legacy of faith provides inspiring examples (see Josh. 5:10) that we can follow. The Greek word translated "witnesses" is the origin of the English word "martyr" and means "testifiers, witnesses." This testimony or record is promulgated by God and bears witness to the power of faith and to His faithfulness (see 11:2, 39). We dishonor this legacy when we do not **lay aside every weight, and the sin which doth so easily beset us**. This "laying aside" is a voluntary and deliberate action to shed every encumbrance that could interfere with a successful run. The besetting "sin" is variously understood. The Vulgate suggests "the sin standing around us." For the first readers of this epistle, the sin was no doubt that of abandoning their commitment to Christ because of unbelief or, worse, because they "refus[ed] … him that speaketh" (12:25). It is fitting that the writer did not name the sin, since the sins that can hold believers back are varied. Inasmuch as every sin is by definition a violation of God's revealed Word, however, most violations are rooted in unbelief or willfulness. Unencumbered and armed with an inviolable confidence in God, we may **run with patience** (Greek, *hypomonē*; to "endure" or "persist"; see Acts 20:24; 1 Cor. 9:24–26; Gal. 2:2; 5:7; Phil. 2:16; 2 Tim. 4:7; Rev. 2:10). The Christian is pictured as a long-distance runner rather than a short-distance sprinter. Some Hebrew Christians were tempted to drop out of the contest because of persecution. Patience endures because it is grounded in hope (see Rom. 5:1–6).

12:2. Rather than focusing on their difficulties, the recipients were to be **Looking unto Jesus** (lit., "Looking away to Jesus"). This term is used only here and Philippians 2:23, where it is translated "see." In keeping with the author's theme of remaining faithful to that "better thing" (11:40), he suggested that while it is good to consider those such as the heroes of the previous chapter, ultimately our gaze should be upon Him. A successful runner concentrates on the finish line; we should therefore concentrate on Jesus, the goal and objective of our faith (see Phil. 3:13–14; see also Heb. 2:9; 3:1; 4:14–16; 11:26). We do this because Christ is **the author** ("the chief leader"; translated "the captain" in 2:10), or as we have seen, "a Son over His own house, whose house are we" (3:6). This identifies and confines our race to those activities that are within Christ's household. As high priest, He is also the **finisher of our faith** (Greek, *teleiōtēn*; "consummator," a term the writer probably coined). Our faith, which has its beginning in Him, is also completed in Him; He is both the start (see 1:2; 11:3) and the end of our faith. This makes Him the supreme witness and example; He has already run the race and overcome. With respect to Christ's reward (see 10:35; Rev. 22:12), it was with **the joy that was set before him** that He **endured the cross** (see Phil. 2:5–8), thereby accomplishing our eternal redemption and His glorification at the Father's right hand (see discussion on 1:3; see also Isa. 53:10–12). So great was this glorious prospect, He suffered, **despising the shame**. As it was with Christ, the humiliation of a believer's suffering for the gospel's sake is far outweighed by the prospect of future glory (see 11:26; Matt. 5:10–12; Rom. 8:18; 2 Cor. 4:17; 1 Peter 4:13; 5:1, 10). In fulfillment of His priestly and mediatorial ministry on our behalf, He **is set down at the right hand of the throne of God** (see Ps. 110:1). The text conveys the sense that He sat down and is still there.

12:3. Consider him (lit., "reckon," "weigh"). Understanding Christ is the key to victory over doubt and unbelief. Because of His great love (see 1 John 4:19), He **endured such contradiction of sinners** (see Rom. 5:8). Christ suffered infinitely more than any of His disciples are called upon to suffer. The author exhorted his hearers to take encouragement from Christ's sufferings, **lest ye be wearied** (see Isa.

40:28–31), which suggests general weariness or even sickness. Discouraged people often make themselves sick when they become **faint in [their] minds**, that is, they become enfeebled and weary.

4. Chastening, Better Than Judgment, Can Be Endured (12:4–11)

In 12:4–29, the writer turned his attention to the application of all that he articulated in the previous chapters. He dedicated the remainder of the epistle to driving home his argument. In developing these applications, he presented four contrasts: (1) chastening versus judgment (vv. 4–11); (2) virtuousness and graciousness versus selfishness and fleshly desires (12:12–17); (3) forgiveness, access, and the city of the living God versus retribution, separation, darkness, and fear (12:18–24); (4) renewal under grace versus destruction under sin's curse (12:25–29). Given these alternatives, what sane person would "refuse … him that speaketh" (12:25)?

Judgment under the law was to be feared because of its expression of God's displeasure. Chastisement under grace is tolerable, even to be desired, because it is an expression of God's love, to the end that we might be conformed to the Son's image (see 1:3; 6:1; 7:11; Rom. 8:29).

12:4. Ye have not yet resisted. The author was telling his readers that things were not as bad as some were making them out to be. They had not yet been asked to stand on the front line of battle to stand face-to-face against the enemy **unto blood,** as did Christ and many of the examples given in the previous chapter. Though the recipients had suffered persecution and loss of possessions (10:32–34), they had not yet laid down their lives for the faith. Many of the hearers were yet "babes" (5:13), having failed to pursue growth in their faith, and therefore had need of providential intervention. Many of them would, in fact, be called to give their lives for the sake of the gospel (see Introduction: "Date"; 1 Cor. 10:13).

12:5. And ye have forgotten the exhortation … as unto children. While the recipients were complaining about their circumstances, they seem to have forgotten that their true relationship with the Lord was as His children. That is to say, our loving Father deals with us in certain ways to correct us and to keep us dependent on Him. The author used Proverbs 3:11–12 to drive home his point. **My son, despise not thou the chastening of the Lord.** Believers should not belittle the process God uses to reprove and rebuke His children. Character training is always difficult but should not be regarded lightly. Suffering and persecution should be seen as corrective and instructive training for the spiritual development of His children.

12:6. For whom the Lord loveth he ... scourgeth. The Greek term for "scourgeth" means "to whip." Out of love, God chastens His children to correct their faults. This seems a harsh analogy, but not so when we consider (see 12:3) the example of Christ in 5:7–9. This world is not our home, and the writer wanted believers to understand that God does not want His children to grow comfortable here. The experiences required to teach one this truth, however, are sometimes very painful. As were those who condemned Christ, the agents of such chastisement are often those who are only too willing to administer punishment (see Isa. 10:5–12).

12:7. Because of its benefits, believers should determine to **endure chastening** (lit., "endure for chastening"). The sense here is that God's children should view suffering as a means to an end: that we become disciplined, the root idea of "disciple." **God dealeth with you as with sons.** God's discipline is evidence that we are His children. Far from being a reason for despair, discipline is a basis for encouragement and perseverance (see 12:10).

12:8. But if ye be without chastisement. Again, the term *paideia*, "child training," indicates that this is the common experience of all who are **sons.** The use of *huios* underscores the spiritual rights and prerogatives associated with sonship. While it can be used to specify gender (i.e., "male"), it need not. Here it is used in a generic sense to include all who are truly related to God through Christ (see Gal. 3:22–4:5). It is a mistake to conclude that this chastening is always due to sin or that God abuses His children. While this "character training" is sometimes a response to

sin, it is always applied to conform us to the image of Christ and to teach us to put our absolute trust in God, as the next verse shows.

12:9. Fathers of our flesh ... the Father of spirits. When we were children, our earthly fathers taught us, **and we gave them reverence** (lit., "we turned ourselves to") as an attitude of respect. Is it not **much rather** appropriate to submit (Greek, *hypotassō*) to the Father of our spirits? The contrast in this verse is between our physical parenting and our spiritual parenting. For the writer, the latter was far more consequential than the former. The outcome of good human parenting is good character; the outcome of spiritual parenting is that we **live**, the meaning of which is underscored in 12:10–11.

12:10–11. Pleasure ... profit ... holiness (v. 10). Our human parents disciplined us as it "seemed good to them." By contrast, God disciplines us for our "profit," the same term that Paul used in 1 Corinthians 12:7 when describing the purpose of spiritual gifts (see also Josh. 1:3–4). Ultimately, God disciplines His children so that they might become the partakers of His "holiness" (see 1 Peter 1:16). While correction is never something that people naturally enjoy, in the end, **it yieldeth the peaceable** ("peaceful") **fruit of righteousness** (v. 11). When received submissively (see 12:9), discipline is wholesome and beneficial.

5. Be Diligent in Weariness (12:12–17)

In the midst of the difficulties of life, including chastisement, it is a temptation to resort to fleshly desires for comfort. Diligence and desire are required to overcome this temptation. The goal—Christlikeness—is available through grace. In 12:4–11, the author used a parent-child metaphor to demonstrate our relationship with our heavenly Father and to help us in developing the proper attitude toward His involvement in our lives. Here he presented some of the literal realities associated with that metaphor to demonstrate that the responsibilities in this household require effort on believers' part.

12:12. Wherefore lift up the hands which hang down, and the feeble knees. The author moved beyond the idea of strengthening his hearers' resolve.

Resolve must be accompanied with resultant fruit. In this case, it is strength derived from an intimate relationship with the Son as a member of His household. The quotation is from Isaiah 35:3, but the entire chapter illustrates the positive affects of such a relationship (see also 4:16; 10:36–39; 12:1–3).

12:13. Make straight paths. Quoting from Proverbs 4:26, the writer called on his readers to stay on the "straight and narrow." He exhorted them to upright conduct that would help, rather than hinder, the spiritual and moral welfare of others, especially the "lame" who were wavering in the Christian faith.

12:14. Follow peace ... and holiness, without which no man shall see the Lord (see 1 Peter 1:15–16; 1 John 3:2–3). The challenge of 12:1–2 was to keep our eyes on the goal: Jesus. The writer here described how that is done. It entails the pursuit of peace and holiness. In this way, God works in the believer to produce His grace and character.

12:15. Again, acts of diligence are required so that we do not **fail of the grace of God**, "fall short of" or "fail to lay hold of" God's grace. Such failure is described in 2:1–4; 6:4–8. The same diligence is also required to avoid developing a **root of bitterness**—pride, animosity, rivalry, or anything else harmful to others. The writer drew from the warnings of the Mosaic covenant stating that the heart that turns from the Lord to serve false gods is as a poisonous root that could well bring about God's curse upon the nation (see Deut. 29:18–20). That the author connected this situation with that of his hearers underscores just how serious he considered this to be. If they failed to lay hold of God's grace, the hearts of **many** would be poisoned.

12:16. The author next focused on our responsibility to our brethren that will prevent a brother from becoming a **profane person, as Esau** (see Gen. 25:29–34). Esau had no appreciation for true values and was profane in his outlook on life (see Phil. 3:18–19). He "despised his birthright" (Gen. 25:34) by valuing food for his stomach more highly than his birthright. It is not inconsequential that the writer called to mind Esau here (see 11:20 and discussion). **Who for one morsel of meat.** The contrast is between the relative value given to the immediate gratification of present needs and the supreme value of our "birthright" in Christ.

12:17. The blessing refers to the blessing of the firstborn. The readers were thinking of compromising their faith to gain relief from persecution, but to trade their spiritual birthright for temporary ease in this world would deprive them of Christ's blessing. The author was building up to the warning in 12:25. As it was with Esau, one can reach a point at which the blessing becomes irretrievable; **he was rejected: for he found no place of repentance.** Esau regretted his loss; he did not repent of his sin (see Genesis 27, especially 27:41), even though he countenanced his regret **with tears** (see Gen. 27:34–38). His sorrow was not "godly sorrow [that] worketh repentance to salvation" but rather "the sorrow of the world [that] worketh death" (2 Cor. 7:10). The essence of repentance is a change of mind, not necessarily an emotional display. The reprobate mind is not capable of true repentance (see Rom. 1:28; 2 Tim. 3:8).

6. Darkness and Fear under the Law of Moses (12:18–21)

12:18–21. These verses describe the awesome occasion when the law was given at Mount Sinai (see Exod. 19:10–25; Deut. 4:11–12; 5:22–26), focusing on the old covenant's tangible mountain, ordinances, terrifying warnings, and severe penalties. Believers in Jesus Christ do not have such a threatening covenant and should not consider returning to it. The apostle Peter said it best when Jesus asked the disciples if they were going to leave Him. Peter replied, "Lord, to whom shall we go? thou hast the words of eternal life" (John 6:68). This is in stark contrast to the fearsomeness and death that were the law's reward, **unto blackness** (v. 18; see Exod. 10:22; Judg. 1:6; 2 Peter 2:4, 15). **Sound of a trumpet** (v. 19) is from Exodus 19:16. **They could not endure** (v. 20). The irony is evident in this allusion to the response of the cowardly Israelites toward **the word** (v. 19). Is it possible that these early Christians also were shrinking from the word of Christ? This sets the stage for the warning of 12:25–29.

7. Jesus Has Called Us unto the City of the Living God (12:22–24)

12:22. The author told his hearers that, in contrast to those who had witnessed the terrifying events of the first word from God at Sinai, **ye are come unto mount Sion.** This is not the literal Mount Zion (Jerusalem, or its southeast portion) but the heavenly city of God, **the heavenly Jerusalem**, and those who dwell there with Him (see 11:10, 13–16; 13:14; Phil. 3:20). The circumstances under which the old covenant was given (see 12:18–21) and the features of the new covenant (12:22–24) show the utter contrast between the two covenants and were the author's foundation for one final warning and exhortation (12:25–29) to those still thinking of going back to Judaism. For **an innumerable company of angels**, see Revelation 5:11–12.

12:23. Church of the firstborn refers to believers in general who make up the church. (1) They cannot be angels since these have just been mentioned (12:22); (2) "firstborn" cannot refer to Christ (though He is called "the firstborn"; see 1:6; Rom. 8:29; Col. 1:15–18; Rev. 1:5) since here the Greek word is plural; (3) that the names of "the firstborn" are recorded in heaven reminds us of the redeemed (see Rev. 3:5; 13:8; 17:8; 20:12; 21:27). The designation "firstborn" suggests their privileged position as heirs together with Christ, the supreme firstborn and "heir of all things" (1:2). For **God the Judge of all**, see 4:13; Romans 14:10–12; 1 Corinthians 3:10–15; 2 Corinthians 5:10; Revelation 20:11–15. **Spirits of just men made perfect.** For the most part, these men were pre-Christian believers such as Abel (see 11:4) and Noah (see 11:7). They are referred to as "spirits" because they are waiting for the resurrection and as "just" because God credited their faith to them as righteousness, as He did to Abraham (see Rom. 4:3). Actual justification was not accomplished, however, until Christ made it complete by His death on the cross (see 11:40; Rom. 3:24–26; 4:23–25).

12:24. For **the mediator of the new covenant**, see 7:22; 8:6 and discussion; 8:13; 9:15; 1 Timothy 2:5. **The blood ... that speaketh better things than that of Abel.** Abel's blood cried out for justice and retribu-

tion (see discussion on Gen. 4:10), whereas the blood of Jesus shed on the cross speaks of forgiveness and reconciliation (see 9:12; 10:19; Col. 1:20; 1 John 1:7).

8. Warning against Refusing "Him That Speaketh" (12:25–29)

12:25. Him that speaketh refers to God (see 1:1–4). **Spake on earth.** At Sinai. **Him that speaketh from heaven** refers to Christ, who is both from and in heaven (see 1:1–3; 4:14; 6:20; 7:26; 9:24). Since we have greater revelation, we have greater responsibility and therefore greater danger (see 2:2–4). **For if they escaped not who refused him.** The consequences of disobedience under Moses are known to us all. Since we know the severity of God's response to unbelief, we are all the more culpable; **much more shall not we escape, if we turn away from him that speaketh from heaven.** Arguing from the lesser to the greater, the author pointed out that if Christians turn away, our chances of escape are far less than that of those at Sinai.

12:26–27. Whose voice ... shook the earth (v. 26; see Exod. 19:18; Judg. 5:5; Ps. 68:7–8). God's voice shook the earth when He delivered the "ten words" (see Exod. 20:1 and discussion) at Sinai. But the day is coming, **he hath promised** (Hag. 2:6), when He will **once more ... shake not the earth only, but also heaven.** The Israelites thought God's judgments were fierce because the mountain trembled, but the great end-time upheavals associated with the second advent of Christ will be even more fearsome. In this final display of God's mighty power, all the **things that are made** (v. 27) will be removed and that **which cannot be shaken [will] remain** (see 9:28; 1 Cor. 7:31; 1 John 2:17). Nothing is more incompatible with the life of faith than to imagine that anything can shake the kingdom of God.

12:28–29. For the reasons stated in 12:26–27, the **kingdom** (v. 28) that believers receive is understood to be unshakable. With that understanding, **let us have grace** (lit., "let us hold on to grace"), **whereby we may serve God acceptably.** The injunction here is crucial. Believers do not serve God in their own strength (however well motivated they may be); only through His grace are we enabled to "serve God acceptably" (see John 4:19–24; Rom. 12:1). For **God is a consuming fire** (v. 29), see Exodus 24:17; Deuteronomy 9:3.

III. Characteristics of Christian Service (13:1–17)

The final chapter moves from the doctrinal to the practical. Here the writer demonstrated concrete ways to apply the principles articulated above and how they may be fleshed out in believers' homes, churches, and communities.

A. Regarding the Brethren (13:1–3)

13:1. Let brotherly love (Greek, *philadelphia*; see 1 Peter 3:8; 1 Thess. 4:9) **continue.** Jesus indicated that the mark of true believers would be the love shared between them (see John 13:35). The term used here is especially appropriate to the household metaphor that the author used throughout the letter.

13:2. Be not forgetful to entertain strangers (*philoxenia*; "show love to strangers"). The love believers share includes both those they relate to and those they don't. This message is desperately needed in the contemporary church, where "worship styles" tend to divide the body rather than unite it. The particular benefit of reaching out to "strangers" is that we may well entertain **angels unawares**, as did Abraham (see Genesis 18), Gideon (see Judges 6), and Manoah (see Judges 13).

13:3. Remember them that are in bonds ... and them which suffer adversity (see 10:32–34; 1 Cor. 12:26). While in much of the epistle the author encouraged his readers not to allow the threat of persecution and adversity to cause them to turn away from Christ, some in their assembly were already "in bonds," and some were suffering "adversity." The advice here is reminiscent of Paul's advice to the Corinthians: "That there should be no schism in the body; but that the members should have the same care one for another. And whether one member suffer, all the members suffer with it; or one member be honoured, all the members rejoice with it. Now ye are the body of Christ, and members in particular" (1 Cor. 12:25–27).

B. Regarding the Family (13:4–6)

13:4. Marriage is honourable ... adulterers God will judge. As did so many other New Testament writers, the author of Hebrews gave attention to the problems of sexual immorality, which was rampant in the Roman Empire (see 12:16; Rom. 1:29; 1 Cor. 5:1–13; 6:13–18; 7:2; Gal. 5:19; Eph. 5:3; 1 Thess. 4:3; Judg. 1:7). The Scriptures nowhere condemn the pure physical relationship of a husband and wife but everywhere condemn the licentious, promiscuous behavior of those who are certain to face the severe judgment of a holy God.

13:5. A commitment to Christ will impact one's lifestyle. The author admonished his readers to **Let your conversation** (Greek, *tropos*; "manner of life") **be without covetousness** (Greek, *aphilargyros*; "not loving money"; see Luke 12:15, 21; Phil. 4:10–13; 1 Tim. 6:6–10, 17–19); **and be content with such things as ye have** (see Phil. 4:11–12; 1 Tim. 6:8). He then reminded them of exactly what they had: they had Christ Himself, since He has promised **I will never leave thee, nor forsake thee.** This promise has powerful practical implications, as the next verse shows.

13:6. The Lord is my helper, and I will not fear what man shall do unto me is a quotation from Psalm 118:6. The author could have offered no greater encouragement to his hearers, who were fearful of persecution and were contemplating compromising or leaving their faith in Christ. Jesus said, "And fear not them which kill the body, but are not able to kill the soul: but rather fear him which is able to destroy both soul and body in hell" (Matt. 10:28; see also Luke 12:5–9). The knowledge that Christ is with us at all times is also a serious incentive to always do the right thing (see Luke 12:8–12).

13:7. Remember them which have the rule over you, who have spoken unto you the word of God (see 2:3; 5:12). In addition to listing the heroes of faith in chapter 11, the writer reminded his hearers of those who had communicated the gospel to them and brought them to faith and whose lives gave consistent witness to their commitment to the gospel. The ministry of the apostles and prophets of the New Testament certainly is in view here as well (see

2:3–4). With **considering the end of their conversation,** the author urged the recipients to consider well the example and outcomes of the lives of these exemplary leaders. The use of *ekbasis,* "end of one's life," probably indicates that these leaders were now dead, but the term also indicates that their "exit" was one befitting a follower of Christ. **Whose faith follow** (lit., "mimic their faith"; see 6:12; 1 Cor. 4:16; Eph. 5:1; 1 Thess. 1:6–7; 2:14; 3 John 11). While believers are not followers of men, the New Testament frequently exhorts us to follow those who follow Christ.

C. Regarding the Faith and the Church (13:8–17)

13:8. Jesus Christ the same yesterday, and to day, and for ever is a confession of the changelessness of Christ and is no doubt related to the preceding verse. The substance of the recipients former leaders' faith was the unchanging Christ. "Yesterday" probably refers to the days of Christ's life on earth, when the eyewitnesses observed Him (see 2:3; 5:7). "To day" (see discussion on 3:15), in the hearers' present crisis, the Christ whom the eyewitnesses had seen was still the same, and what they had said about Him was still true and will continue to be true "for ever" (see 1:1–12). Of course, this principle recalls the entire argument of the epistle. All that came before, "yesterday," only served to look ahead to the "promise" of what Christ had fulfilled "to day" and will consummate "for ever." If the recipients returned to an inferior priesthood and sacrifices (see chaps. 5–10), it would compromise Christ's absolute supremacy and undermine the gospel itself.

13:9. Be not carried about (i.e., "Do not be led astray"; see Judg. 1:12) **with divers and strange doctrines** (lit., "with many colored and foreign teachings"). The imagery is graphic. The author was essentially saying, "Do not allow fanciful ideas to catch your eye and draw you away from the simplicity that is in Christ" (see 2 Cor. 11:3). **That the heart be established with grace; not with meats** introduces what follows in 3:10–16. Instead of depending on "ceremonial foods," as the legalistic Judaizers

were teaching, believers' depend on the grace of God in Christ. "For by grace ye are saved ... not of works" (Eph. 2:8–9).

13:10. We have an altar probably refers to the cross, which marked the end of the whole Aaronic priesthood and its replacement by the order of Melchizedek, of which Christ is the only priest (see 7:13; 10:1–18). **Whereof** ("concerning which," i.e., "an altar") **they have no right to eat**. The priests of **the tabernacle** (the Levitical system) have no claim to participate in the sacrifice of believers in Christ, who have a higher privilege than the priests under the old covenant had. The irony of this would not have been lost to those who were tempted to go back to the Levitical system.

13:11–12. Burnt without the camp (v. 11; see Lev. 4:12 and discussion; 16:27). The Levitical priests could not eat of the sacrifice on the Day of Atonement. It was completely consumed. **Jesus also ... suffered without the gate** (v. 12). Christ's death outside Jerusalem represented the removal of sin, as had the removal of the bodies of sacrificial animals outside the camp of Israel.

13:13. Go forth ... unto him without the camp. Jesus calls His followers to accompany Him "outside" the camp, unlike those of Judaism, who remain "inside" the camp. As Jesus died in disgrace outside the city, so His followers should be willing to be disgraced by turning unequivocally from Judaism to Christ. The only proper place for the Christian is beneath the cross of Jesus, there to take our stand. It is there that we "fill up that which is behind of the afflictions of Christ in [our] flesh for his body's sake, which is the church" (Col. 1:24).

13:14. For **no continuing city,** see discussions on 11:10, 14, 16.

13:15. In **sacrifice of praise,** "sacrifice" is used metaphorically to represent an offering to God (see Lev. 7:12; Ps. 54:8; Rom. 12:1; Phil. 4:18). Animal offerings are now obsolete.

13:16. But to do good and to communicate forget not admonished the recipients not to neglect benevolence and fellowship. **With such sacrifices God is well pleased.** It is significant to note that the three definitive texts of the New Testament regarding the nature of worship and service (here; Rom. 12:1; Josh. 1:27) all have to do with the "inner man" of the heart and mind, as underscored in the promises of the new covenant.

13:17. Them that have the rule over you. The recipients' present leaders, as distinct from their first ones, now dead (mentioned in 13:7), were to be given due respect just as they had offered it to their first leaders. This is an important lesson. Church members often become unduly attached to a pastor who dies or is transferred and are unable to submit to the new leadership. To such persons, the author of Hebrews would say, "Get over it." **Submit yourselves.** This command does not condone dictatorial leadership (see 3 John 9–10) but rather respect for authority, orderliness, and discipline in the church, as are taught throughout the New Testament. **They that must give account.** Those called to leadership are answerable to God for how they watch over the souls of those in their care. The exhortation here is for believers to make their task a **joy, and not ... grief.** Anyone who has had the misfortune to lead a church of obdurate members will appreciate this wise counsel.

IV. Conclusion and Benediction (13:18–25)

A. Request for Prayer (13:18–19)

13:18–19. Pray for us (v. 18). The writer included himself in the list of those whom his hearers were challenged to give respect (see 13:17). One of the ways they could demonstrate their support and concern for their leaders was to pray for them. Perhaps the author was aware that some among the recipients had challenged even his motives and therefore found it necessary to entreat them in **good conscience** and **honestly.** If this is so, he was not without good company (see Paul in 2 Cor. 1:11–20; 1 Thess. 2:18). **Restored to you** (v. 19, see 13:23). The identity and whereabouts of the writer are not known to us, but "restored" suggests that somehow he had been delayed, perhaps by his current ministry, in visiting those to whom he was writing. That he was not under arrest is clear from 13:23.

B. Benediction and Prayer for the Recipients (13:20–21)

The benediction, which is one of the loftiest in the New Testament, provides a fitting conclusion to the letter.

13:20. The God of peace is a title for God used frequently in benedictions (see Rom. 15:33; 16:20; Phil. 4:9; 1 Thess. 5:23). For **Great shepherd,** see Psalm 23; Isaiah 40:11; Ezekiel 34:11–16, 23; 37:24; John 10:2–3, 11, 14, 27; 1 Peter 2:25; 5:4 (see also "great" in 4:14). **The blood of the everlasting covenant** (see discussion on 10:29) refers to the new covenant (see discussion on 8:8–12). What Jeremiah designated as the "new covenant" (Jer. 31:31), he described as "everlasting" (Jer. 32:40; see Isa. 55:3 and discussion; 61:8).

13:21. Make you perfect, or "complete" (see 1 Cor. 1:10; 2 Cor. 13:11; 2 Tim. 3:17). **Every good work.** No doubt the author had in mind works such as faith, faithfulness, obedience, and perseverance.

C. Postscript (13:22–25)

13:22. Suffer the word of exhortation. In a final word of admonition, the author asked his readers to bear with him and to take seriously what he had written throughout the epistle, the main thrust of which is to progress in Christian maturity and not fall away from Christ. **I have written ... in few words.** Compared to the lengthy treatise that would be necessary to explain adequately the superiority of Christ, the epistle is considered to be merely a brief.

13:23. Timothy is set at liberty (Greek, *apolyō*; "set free," "let go"). Timothy, who was well known to the recipients of the letter, had recently been released from prison. He and the author would soon be visiting the recipients.

13:24. Salute all them that have the rule over you (see 13:17). The author once again exhorted his readers to give due respect to those whom God had called to lead their church. **They of Italy** likely suggests that the letter was written either to or from Italy (see Acts 10:23), although the author could have been simply passing on greetings from some Italian believers.

13:25. Grace be with you all. Amen. The book concludes with a characteristic final greeting.

THE EPISTLE OF JAMES

INTRODUCTION

Author

    The author identified himself as "James, a servant of God and of the Lord Jesus Christ" (1:1), but since he furnished no additional biographical identification, his precise identity is a subject of conjecture. Luther attributed the letter to an unknown James whose work the Reformer devalued as "a right strawy epistle" that contradicts Paul's teaching on justification and other doctrines. Some interpreters have assumed that the letter is pseudonymous, that the name James was chosen by its author to lend it authority. One would expect, however, that a more dignified title in 1:1 would have been formulated if the letter were pseudonymously penned. Four men in the New Testament have this name, and the author of the epistle is certainly one of them. (1) The author could not have been the apostle James, son of Zebedee, because he died too early (AD 44) to have written it. He probably would not have lived long enough to gain the stature and authority with which the author wrote. (2) James the son of Alphaeus, another of the twelve apostles, known as James the younger (Mark 15:40), was probably too obscure to have been recognized as an authoritative figure among "the twelve tribes," to whom the letter was written (1:1). (3) James the father of Judas (Luke 6:16; Acts 1:13) cannot even be numbered with certainty among the earliest followers of Jesus. (4) James the brother of the Lord is the best candidate for authorship of this letter. He was one of several brothers of Christ and was probably the oldest since he heads the list in Matthew 13:55. He did not believe in Jesus at first; he even challenged Him and misunderstood His mission (see John 7:2–5), but he later became very prominent in the church:

    a. He was one of the select individuals Christ appeared to after His resurrection (1 Cor. 15:7).

    b. Paul called him a "pillar" of the church (Gal. 2:9).

    c. Paul, on his first post-conversion visit to Jerusalem, saw James (Gal. 1:19).

    d. On his last visit to Jerusalem, Paul again saw James (Acts 21:18).

    e. When Peter was rescued from prison, he told his friends to tell James (Acts 12:17).

    f. James was a leader in the important council of Jerusalem (Acts 15:13). He may have written his letter from Jerusalem.

g. James was so well known that Jude could identify himself simply as a "brother of James" (Jude 1).

James's martyrdom, circa AD 62, is mentioned by Josephus (*Ant* 20.9) and in the account of Hegesippus that is cited by Eusebius (*Ecclesiastical History* 2.23.3). Both sources describe his death by stoning.

The quality of Greek in the letter of James has led some to believe that James the brother of Jesus could not have written in such a polished style. Palestine, however, had been greatly influenced by Greek culture and language by the time of James. A writer who was at home there could have composed a Greek document with the sophistication of the letter of James.

James has made a splash in international news since 2002, when the inscription on a limestone box originating from first-century Palestine was deciphered. The inscription on the ossuary, a burial receptacle that contains bones, reads in Aramaic, "James, son of Joseph, brother of Jesus." The authenticity of the entire inscription has been disputed, and at the time of the writing of this commentary, the debate continues. If the box and the entire inscription are genuine, the article is of enormous archaeological and historical importance. It would be the earliest physical artifact that attests to Jesus and members of his family. The chances of three relatives having these names during the time period concerned who are *not* the people of our New Testament accounts are extremely slim. (For further information, see "Burial Box May Be Jesus Artifact," http://www.cbsnews. com/stories/2003/06/18/ world/main559173.shtml; Steve Weizman, "Israeli Experts Say 'James Ossuary' Inscription a Fake," http://www.detnews.com/2003/religion/0306/24/religion–196732.htm; and Craig A. Evans, "Thoughts on the James Ossuary," http://www. bibleinterp.com/articles/EvansThoughts.htm.)

Date

Some date the letter of James in the early 60s. There are indications, however, that it might have been written before AD 50. (1) Its distinctively Jewish nature suggests that it was composed when the church was still predominantly Jewish. (2) It reflects a simple church order; officers of the church are called "elders" (5:14) rather than "bishops," and "masters" (3:1), meaning "teachers." (3) No reference is made to the controversy over Gentile circumcision. (4) The Greek term *synagōgē* ("synagogue," "meeting," or "assembly") is used to designate the meeting or meeting place of the church (2:2).

If this early dating is correct, this letter could well be the earliest of all the New Testament writings. Some who assume a late date for James believe that it seeks to correct an antinomian distortion of Paul's teaching on justification by faith. The letter, however, does not necessarily address such an aberration (see "Literary Features," below). Nothing precludes assigning to James a date between AD 40 and 50.

Recipients

The recipients are identified explicitly only in 1:1: "the twelve tribes which are scattered abroad." Some hold that this expression refers to Christians in general, but the term "twelve tribes" would more naturally apply to Jewish Christians. Furthermore, a Jewish audience would be more in keeping with the obviously Jewish nature of the letter (e.g., the use of the Hebrew title for God, *kyrios Sabaōth*, "the Lord of sabaoth," 5:4). That the recipients were Christians is clear from 2:1; 5:7–8. It has been plausibly suggested that these were believers from the early Jerusalem church who, after Stephen's death, were scattered as far as Phoenicia, Cyprus, and Syrian Antioch (see Acts 8:1; 11:19). This would account for James's references to trials and oppression, his intimate knowledge of the readers, and the authoritative nature of the letter. Some of the hearers of the letter were poor (2:6–7), but not so destitute that they could not aid those in dire need (2:3–4; 15–16). At least some members of the congregations addressed were wealthy (2:3; 5:1–6, although this denunciation may have been for the benefit of the poor members), or at least well enough off to be able to travel for business (4:13–17). As leader of the Jerusalem church, James wrote as pastor to instruct and encourage his dispersed people in the face of their difficulties.

Theme and Theological Message

James is often regarded as a collection of somewhat disjointed exhortations without any discernible pattern of organization. Some recent interpreters, however, observe definite structure in the epistle. This commentary assumes that James is well structured. The theological lens through which the writer looks is focused on the integrity of the believing community as evidenced in the integration of its faith and works. James, arguing for completeness and wholeness in the communities that he addressed, presented several examples of behavior that promote individual and collective wholeness, contrasting them with their negative opposites. The necessity of James's message arose because of the pressures of the world on his readers to compromise their values, particularly regarding wealth and possessions (2:1–13; 4:4). Since the rich were oppressing the believers (2:6–7; 5:1–6), the tendency was present to become lax in the practice of one's faith. Lack of generosity to those in need (1:26–27; 2:14–26), bitterness in speech (3:1–12) and attitude (3:13–4:3), and preoccupation with business pursuits (4:13–17) result from such laxity.

Literary Features

Certain characteristics make the letter of James distinctive.

(1) It has an unmistakably Jewish nature. The addressees are described as "twelve tribes" (1:1) who gather in an "assembly" (2:2), meaning "synagogue." They were familiar with the law and with the Old Testament characters Abraham (2:21–23), Rahab (2:25), Job (5:11), and Elijah (5:17–18). An agrarian environment, like Palestine, where rich landowners oppressed the laborers, seems to be presupposed.

(2) James's emphasis is on vital Christianity, characterized by good deeds and a faith that works (genuine faith must and will be accompanied by a consistent lifestyle). The statement of 2:24, "Ye see then how that by works a man is justified, and not by faith only," does not contradict Paul's teaching on justification by faith alone (Eph. 2:8–10). James was concerned with works as the evidence of true faith; Paul spoke of works as deeds that people perform to be put right with God. James used "justify" in a moral sense—how one is shown publicly to be righteous; Paul used "justify" in a judicial sense—how one is declared righteous by God. For James, good works included especially assistance for the poor and disadvantaged. These include the widow and orphan (1:27), the "poor man in

vile raiment" (2:2), people without clothing and food (2:15), exploited laborers (5:4), and the sick (5:14–15).

(3) The letter displays the author's familiarity with Jesus' teachings preserved in the Sermon on the Mount (compare 2:5 with Matt. 5:3, inheritance of the kingdom of God; 3:10–12 with Matt. 7:15–20, a tree is known by its fruit, and a person's life indicates what kind of person he or she really is; 3:18 with Matt. 5:9, Christians are called to be peacemakers; 5:2–3 with Matt. 6:19–20, believers should seek the true riches in heaven, not earthly treasures that are perishable; 5:12 with Matt. 5:33–37, a simple yes or no rather than oaths should characterize believers' speech).

(4) The letter is similar to Old Testament wisdom writings such as Proverbs.

Outline

The following outline is based on John H. Elliott, "The Epistle of James in Rhetorical and Social Scientific Perspective: Holiness-Wholeness and Patterns of Replication," *Biblical Theology Bulletin* 23 (Summer 1993): 71–81.

    I. Greetings (1:1)

   II. Introduction: Completeness and Wholeness (1:2–12)

      A. The Testing of Faith and Wisdom (1:2–8)

      B. The Reversal of the Lowly and the Rich (1:9–11)

      C. The Testing of Faith and Ultimate Wholeness (1:12)

  III. Exhortations to Completeness and Wholeness (1:13–5:12)

      A. First Exhortation: The Integration of Hearing and Doing (1:13–27)

         1. Negative: Self-deception (1:13–16)

         2. Positive: The Integration of Hearing and Doing (1:17–27)

      B. Second Exhortation: The Life of Impartiality (2:1–13)

         1. Negative: Distinctions between Rich and Poor (2:1–7)

         2. Positive: Fulfillment of the Royal Law (2:8–13)

      C. Third Exhortation: The Integration of Faith and Action (2:14–26)

         1. Negative: Separation of Faith and Action (2:14–17)

         2. Positive: Completion of Faith with Action (2:18–26)

      D. Fourth Exhortation: The Life of Wisdom (3:1–18)

         1. Negative: The Destructive Power of the Tongue (3:1–12)

         2. Positive: True Wisdom versus False Wisdom (3:13–18)

      E. Fifth Exhortation: Friendship with the World and Friendship with God (4:1–12)

         1. Negative: Pursuit of Selfish Desires (4:1–4)

         2. Positive: Humility before God (4:5–12)

      F. Sixth Exhortation: Attitudes toward the Future (4:13–5:11)

         1. Negative: Disregard for the Shortness of Life and the Coming Judgment (4:13–5:6)

         2. Positive: Endurance in Suffering (5:7–11)

      G. Seventh Exhortation: The Importance of Speaking the Truth (5:12)

         1. Negative: The Use of Oaths (5:12a)

         2. Positive: Words of Integrity—"Yes" or "No" (5:12b)

IV. Conclusion: Various Instructions for the Promotion of Integration in the
     Community (5:13–20)
     A. Prayer for Various Needs (5:13–18)
     B. Reintegration of the Wayward (5:19–20)

Select Bibliography

Adamson, James B. *The Epistle of James*. The New International Commentary on the New
    Testament. Grand Rapids, MI: Eerdmans, 1976.

Barclay, William. *The Letters of James and Peter*. Rev. ed. The Daily Study Bible. Philadel-
    phia: Westminster John Knox, 1976.

Davids, Peter H. *The Epistle of James: A Commentary on the Greek Text*. The New Interna-
    tional Greek Testament Commentary. Grand Rapids, MI: Eerdmans, 1982.

Johnson, Luke Timothy. *The Letter of James: A New Translation with Introduction and
    Commentary*. The Anchor Bible 37A. New York: Doubleday, 1995.

Martin, Ralph P. *James*. Word Biblical Commentary 48. Waco, TX: Word, 1988.

Moo, Douglas J. *The Letter of James: An Introduction and Commentary*. Tyndale New Testa-
    ment Commentaries 16. Grand Rapids, MI: Eerdmans, 1985.

Morris, Leon, and Donald W. Burdick, *The Expositor's Bible Commentary with the New
    International Version: Hebrews/James*. Grand Rapids, MI: Zondervan, 1996.

Nystrom, David P. *James*. The NIV Application Commentary. Grand Rapids, MI: Zonder-
    van, 1997.

Perkins, Pheme. *First and Second Peter, James, and Jude*. Interpretation: A Bible Commen-
    tary for Teaching and Preaching. Louisville: Westminster John Knox, 1995.

Robertson, A. T. *The General Epistles and the Apocalypse of John*. Vol. 6, *Word Pictures in
    the New Testament*. Nashville: Broadman, 1933.

Stulac, George M. *James*. The IVP New Testament Commentary 16. Downers Grove, IL:
    InterVarsity Press, 1993.

Tasker, R. V. G. *The General Epistle of James: An Introduction and Commentary*. Vol. 16.
    Tyndale New Testament Commentaries. Grand Rapids, MI: Eerdmans, 1957.

EXPOSITION

I. Greetings (1:1)

1:1. James. See Introduction: "Author." The word **servant** in Greek is *doulos* and is more appropriately translated "bondservant" (NKJV) or "slave" (NLT). The identity of the author's Masters rather than his identity is emphasized here; the Greek syntax lists the Masters before mentioning James's role as slave: "James, of God and of the Lord Jesus Christ, a slave." **The twelve tribes** may be a literal reference to Jew-ish Christians who lived outside their homeland in the Diaspora. But the reference could be metaphorical; the Christians were in a situation of cultural estrangement, as the readers of 1 Peter were (see 1 Peter, Exposition), or were in exile away from their heavenly home. At any rate, the readers, as the new Israel, were experiencing some sort of cultural and religious disconnection from their contemporaries (see Introduction: "Recipients").

II. Introduction: Completeness and Wholeness (1:2–12)

A. The Testing of Faith and Wisdom (1:2–8)

1:2. James addressed the readers as **brethren** ("brothers") fifteen times in this short letter. He had many rebukes for them, but he corrected them in brotherly love. The Greek term *adelphoi* is a generic masculine noun; it includes males and females of all ages in the Christian communities addressed (hence, "My brothers and sisters," NRSV). The same Greek root lies behind the noun in the phrase **divers temptations** ("trials of many kinds," NIV) and the word "tempted" in 1:13. In 1:2–3, James emphasized difficulties that come from outside; in 1:13–15, inner moral trials, such as temptation to sin. Such tests one is to **count … [as] all joy** (see Matt 5:11–12; Rom. 5:3; 1 Peter 1:6), not because of the suffering (James does not command one to love pain!) but because of their benefit.

1:3–4. Believers may rejoice in difficulties and tests, **knowing … that the trying of your faith worketh patience** (v. 3). The "testing" (NIV) not only reveals the genuineness of a person's faith; it also purifies it (as metals tested in the fire) so that it emerges stronger and one is more capable of persevering through difficulties the next time they come. "Patience" is *hypomonē*, a triumphant fortitude in difficulties of all kinds, including patience with difficult people. Only through hardships can genuine and enduring faith be developed. To be **perfect and entire** (v. 4) does not mean that the one who endures will be without sin. "Perfect" (*teleios*) means "mature" (NIV, NRSV). A mature believer is one whose character has begun to conform to the image that God intends it to have—the very character of Christ. Such a person may be described as **wanting nothing**, that is, "ready for anything" (NLT). In other words, integration and wholeness are becoming a reality in one's faith.

1:5. Wisdom enables one to face trials with "joy" (1:2). Wisdom is not just acquired information but practical insight with spiritual implications (see Prov. 1:2–4; 2:10–15; 4:5–9; 9:10–12). God is the ultimate source of true wisdom, and the one who needs it during time of trial may confidently ask God for it. He **upbraideth not**; He gives **liberally** ("generously and ungrudgingly," NRSV) and without condemnation. James emphasized prayer throughout his letter. One may ask God for wisdom (1:5), for justice (5:4), for others' healing and forgiveness (5:14–16), but when making requests of God, one must ask in faith (1:6–8) and with pure motives (4:3). James maintained that one often does not have what one desires because of a failure to ask God for it (4:2).

1:6–8. James introduced the colorful metaphor of **a wave of the sea** (v. 6; see Eph. 4:14) to illustrate the instability of a doubter, one who doubts that God can or wants to answer his prayers. Doubt can be healthy when it seeks to find answers and reasons for belief. The doubt here (James called it **wavering**), however, is skepticism in the face of the evidence that one already has about God. A person who so doubts is **driven with the wind and tossed** like the sea. The word translated "wavering" is *diakrinō*. It has the idea of being at odds within oneself, being of a divided mind. **Double minded** (v. 8; "doublesouled," Stulac, *James*, p. 43) is synonymous with the idea of wavering. The issue is of divided loyalties, when one has not fully given himself over to God at the point of suffering.

The particular trials that the instructions of 1:2–8 are designed to meet may involve some sort of economic hardship, but they apply to any kind of duress that a Christian may encounter. Wisdom certainly would have been needed in the times of grave financial crisis that oppressed Christians experienced in the first century, some of whom were possibly living at the subsistence level. Their need was through no fault of their own. The question of how one could provide for oneself and one's dependents and still meet obligations, like taxes, would have been enormous. Today, the costs of food, clothing, housing, fuel, health care, and education put stress on many families. According to James, believers have opportunities to grow through such difficulties. Christians also have opportunities to ask God to gain His wisdom, and He will grant it so that they may know how to live more frugally and have enough for what they really need.

It must be said, though, that affluent Christians in the West often put themselves in financial straits through extravagant lifestyles and binge spending on credit. God's wisdom in such situations is evident: be content with fewer luxuries and put a hold on credit-card usage. At the same time, the way to a contented lifestyle involves giving of one's resources to those who are financially and socially distressed (see 2:14–26). The shift to a lower standard of living may well constitute a test for which James's words are apt.

B. The Reversal of the Lowly and the Rich (1:9–11)

1:9–11. Wholeness comes to the community when **the brother of low degree** (v. 9), the one who is not just of humble circumstances but is humble before God, is **exalted** and **the rich ... is made low** (v. 10). God honors the one who honors Him, and those who disregard Him will be brought low (see 1 Sam. 2:30). Since the wealthy had oppressed and dishonored the members of James's communities (see James 2:6–7), a reversal of status was to take place. Since his discussions of wisdom (1:5–8) and of the poor man and the rich man (here) appear between the two sections on trials (1:2–4 and 1:12), 1:5–11 also may have to do with trials. The Christian who suffers the trial of poverty is to rejoice in his or her high position (v. 9) as a believer (see 2:5), and the wealthy Christian is to rejoice (v. 10) in trials that bring him low, perhaps including the loss of wealth. The person who is brought low and humbles herself before God will be honored by God. The metaphor of **the flower of the grass** is a vivid illustration of the temporal nature of worldly wealth as well as of life itself (a theme reiterated in 4:13–17). The point of the image is that just as grasses and wildflowers sprout and quickly perish, **so also shall the rich man fade away in his ways** (v. 11).

C. The Testing of Faith and Ultimate Wholeness (1:12)

1:12. This verse could be taken as a summary of 1:2–12 or as an introduction to 1:13–18. Both sections concern tests, but of different kinds. The tone shifts to testing of a negative kind at 1:13 — the temptation to sin and blame God for the temptation — whereas verse 12 speaks of the benefit of trials for one who loves God. The word **blessed** is *makarios* and recalls the Beatitudes (Matt. 5:3–12). **The crown of life** could either refer to eternal life itself or to God's eternal reward or glory for those who overcome the severe trials of life, such as a physical handicap, a degrading status or role in life, or any number of agonies of life. It is reserved for the one who **endureth temptation** ("perseveres under trial," NIV) and has therefore passed the test. James likely was speaking of tests that involved financial hardship, and in 1:9–12, he counteracted the world's view of riches to enable his communities to endure economic troubles. Money does not determine personal worth. Note that the lowly brother or sister is the exalted one (1:9). Recognition of this "is a rejection of the culture's materialistic values and therefore a growth toward maturity. It will lead the Christian to renounce any anxious outlook about the future, any self-accusing attitude in financial struggles, and any complaining or jealous view toward others' comparative wealth" (Stulac, *James*, p. 46). Thus, wholeness is attained in the Christian community.

III. Exhortations to Completeness and Wholeness (1:13–5:12)

A. First Exhortation: The Integration of Hearing and Doing (1:13–27)

1. Negative: Self-deception (1:13–16)

1:13. For individuals to be whole and communities to be fully integrated, the combination of hearing and doing the truth must be preserved. Self-deception prevents this, however. One who **is tempted** (in 1:13–14, the verb refers to temptations that test one's moral strength to resist sin) ought not say, **I am tempted of God: for God cannot be tempted.** Because God in His very nature is holy, there is nothing in Him for sin to appeal to; **neither tempteth he any man.** The accusation against God that attributes sin to Him borders on blasphemy since it denies that God is good and that He is capable of helping one resist temptation. When one deceives oneself in thinking that God is opposed to a practice of righteousness, one can easily excuse any practice of wrongdoing.

1:14. Temptation to do evil must be attributed, not to God, but to one's **own lust**, by which he is **drawn away ... and enticed**. The language suggests a fish that is lured away from its straight course by attractive bait hiding a deadly hook. A good illustration of the allure of sin is found in C. S. Lewis's *The Lion, the Witch, and the Wardrobe* (New York: Macmillan, 1950). Edmund is enticed by the wicked White Witch, the self-proclaimed Queen of Narnia, when she offers him Turkish Delight, which he devours with relish. Once he has tasted the extraordinarily good confection, he can only think about shoveling down as much of it as he can, unaware that the witch is using the candy as bait. Edmund willingly answers as she pumps him with questions about his siblings. His insatiable appetite, once fed, blinds him from the possibility that he is endangering them. For "this was enchanted Turkish Delight and that anyone who had once tasted it would want more and more of it, and would even, if they were allowed, go on eating it till they killed themselves" (p. 33). The witch promises Edmund more Turkish Delight if he will go and bring his brother and sisters to her, and he complies, longing for just one more piece of the candy as he leaves.

1:15. The imagery of fishing gives way to another metaphor: that of childbirth. **When lust hath conceived, it bringeth forth sin**, an offspring that, when full-grown, leads to **death**. James was not saying that a particular act of sin leads to physical death necessarily, nor that one loses his or her salvation for a particular act of sin. When sins accumulate in a person's life over time without repentance and cleansing, they constitute a life that is oriented to sin. Death is the ultimate outcome of such a life. The three stages—lust, sin, and death—are seen in the temptations of Eve (see Gen. 3:6–22) and David (see 2 Sam. 11:2–17).

1:16. This verse may be seen as beginning a new paragraph, so that the warning **Do not err,**

my beloved brethren is against deception regarding the unchangeableness of God (1:17–18), or as concluding the prohibition against blaming God for temptation to sin (1:13–15). This verse refers to the discussion about the source of temptation. One should not be deceived about that and blame God for temptation to sin. In either case, wholeness cannot be maintained if believers allow themselves to wander like planets ("err" translates *planaō*, from which the English word "planet" comes) in their thinking.

2. Positive: The Integration of Hearing and Doing (1:17–27)

In this section, James provided instructions regarding the true nature of God.

1:17. God is neither powerless to help one face temptations nor intent on seeing one fail; rather, He gives one **Every good gift and every perfect gift ... from above**. That which God sends to His children does not intend their destruction but their blessing. **The Father of lights**. God is the Creator of the heavenly bodies, which give light to the earth, but unlike them, He has **no variableness**; He does not change. Sun and moon cast varying degrees of **shadow**, depending on earth's position relative to them. All heavenly bodies are in a different position (because of time and season) in the heavens from earth's vantage point. God, however, is timeless and unchanging. God's immutability (unchangeableness), however, is not tantamount to divine impassibility. Many theologians in the twentieth century affirmed the "suffering of God." That is, they recognized that the biblical evidence testifies to His active empathy with humankind and that He even suffers with His human creatures, especially in the passion of Jesus Christ (see Warren McWilliams, *The Passion of God: Divine Suffering in Contemporary Protestant Theology* [Macon, GA: Mercer University Press, 1985]). God wants to shower His benevolent gifts on His children because of His tender mercy for them. They only need to ask in faith (see 1:6–8; 4:2).

1:18. His love for believers is evident in that **of his own will begat he us**. This is not a reference to creation but to regeneration (see John 3:3–8). **The word of truth** is the proclamation of the gospel (see 1 Peter 1:23–25). Just as the first sheaf of the harvest indicates that the whole harvest will eventually follow, so the early Christians were an indication, **firstfruits**, that a great number of people would eventually be born again (this imagery is drawn from passages such as Exod. 34:22 and Lev. 23:9–14). Just as James's struggling communities were showcases for God's love and power, so the local church and its members are today, which is all the more reason to seek wholeness and integration in Christian living.

1:19–20. The command **let every man be swift to hear, slow to speak, slow to wrath** (v. 19) could be in reference to hearing of "the word of truth" (the gospel message and its ramifications; 1:18). The listening that James had in mind, however, likely was listening to each other. The word of truth, of course, is to be heard and obeyed (1:22–27). "Wrath" (orgē; "anger," NRSV) here is settled indignation, not rage or fury (thymos). Wrath may have its origin in angry outbursts since these, if unchecked, lead to a vengeful spirit. Even children recognize the importance of good listening. Lynette, age eight (when asked about what most people do on a date), said, "Dates are for having fun, and people should use them to get to know each other. Even boys have something to say if you listen long enough." James would have agreed. Many are quick to defend themselves when receiving advice, criticism, or an opinion that differs from one's own. George Stulac writes, "Almost daily as a pastor I see the value that good listening has for the church's purity within and the church's mission without. When disagreements occur in the church, over and over I have seen what great damage is done to people, to relationships and to the effectiveness of our ministries when we are quick to argue our positions, defend our views and push our opinions. I have also seen what great good is done when we discipline ourselves to postpone defending our own views and judging others' views while we concentrate on listening and giving a full hearing in order to understand the other side of the conflict. We usually find the conflict more easily resolved.

Good listening is a protection against dissension" (James, p. 66).

When one insists on harboring bitter grudges, one harms the Christian community, its witness, and one's own health. Twenty years ago, Leo Madow identified depression as "probably the most common sign of hidden anger in our society. More people get depressed because of repressed or unrecognized anger than almost any other symptom" (Leo Madow, "Why You Get Angry—and What to Do about It," US News & World Report, April 26, 1982, p. 74). His conclusion may be even more accurate today.

1:21. James's remedy for wrath is twofold, involving the elimination of something negative and replacing it with something positive. First, **lay apart all filthiness and superfluity of naughtiness**. The picture is the removal of clothing (see Rom. 13:12; Eph. 4:22, 25; Col. 3:8; 1 Peter 2:1). The two negative moral terms are essentially synonymous. The REB has "then discard everything sordid, and every wicked excess." Second, the positive action, which is necessary to assure the elimination of wickedness, is to **receive with meekness the engrafted word**. James skillfully shifted to an agricultural metaphor. "Make a soil of humble modesty for the word which roots itself inwardly" (Moffatt) expresses the idea that is contained in the word "engrafted" (a better translation is the NIV "planted"). The Greek allows a translation that connects humility with the act of taking off dirty garments (REB marginal note: "then meekly discard ... and accept") or with the reception of the word of God (KJV). Since "receive" is passive (as opposed to the active "lay apart"), "meekness" should be understood to describe the reception of the Word. Although it has already been planted in the Christian's heart, the Word must continuously instruct and guide a believer's conduct. In this way, the Word **is able to save your souls**. That is, the entire body of Christian proclamation brings the process of salvation to completion in the believer; it brings complete integration.

1:22. In 1:22–27, James spelled out what it means to receive the Word: **be ye doers of the word, and not hearers only**. Many Christians assume that a decision for Christ at a point in time, church attendance, regular Bible reading, and times of prayer are all that God desires. James said that those who do not practice the Word after hearing it are **deceiving [their] own selves**. Their religion can be described as "vain" (1:26).

1:23–25. One who is only **a hearer of the word** (v. 23) is like someone who looks at **his … face in a glass** ("in a mirror," NRSV) and then simply **goeth his way**. He **forgetteth** (v. 24) what he saw in the mirror. In contrast is the person who **looketh into the perfect law of liberty** (v. 25). That person is **blessed** in whatever he undertakes since his life is lived in continual practice of the Word (the verb **continueth** is *paramenō*, "to stay beside"). "The perfect law," the moral and ethical teaching of Christianity, is based on the Old Testament moral law and is embodied in the Ten Commandments (see Ps. 19:7). This law is brought to completion (perfection) by Jesus Christ. James could call the law one of "liberty" since the Christian, in contrast to the sinner, who is a slave to sin (see John 8:34), finds joyous freedom in obeying the moral law through the power of the Holy Spirit.

The metaphor of the mirror effectively illustrates the temporary and superficial effect of the Word that the mere hearing of it has on those who do not put it into practice. The benefit to them is no more than that which they get when they groom themselves before the mirror in the morning. Soon, in the tussle of the day, they have forgotten what they saw of themselves in the mirror, and whatever simple changes they made to their appearance are gone. The one who "perseveres" (RSV, v. 25) in the law that brings freedom, the one "who lives in its company" (NEB), will find wholeness. There is no shortcut to Christian maturity. Disciplined study and practice of God's Word is essential to the blessedness that James envisioned.

1:26–27. For James and his first-century congregations under oppression, being "doers of the word" (1:22), that is, being **religious** (v. 26), involved three specific practices. **Religion** refers to the outward acts of religion (e.g., giving to the needy, fasting, public acts of praying, and worshiping). The three practices

James listed constitute **Pure religion** (v. 27). First, **If any man among you seem to be religious** ("If any think they are religious," NRSV)**, and bridleth not his tongue**, that person **deceiveth his own heart**. Vain religion is all that such a person has. The colorful image of bridling one's own mouth (not that of another) introduces a metaphor to which James returned in 3:3. When faced with hostility from outsiders, James's hearers might have been easily tempted to return abuse with abuse. When under pressure, they might have easily snapped at fellow believers. True Christianity puts a check on reviling speech.

Second, **To visit the fatherless and widows in their affliction** (v. 27) was, for James, essential Christianity in a time when orphans and widows did not have the protective safety net of governmental social services that is to some extent available today in Western societies. James echoed the voices of the Old Testament prophets who spoke in behalf of the disadvantaged and dispossessed (see Isa. 1:17; Jer. 22:3). "Affliction" (*thlipsis*; "distress," NEB) probably refers to financial hardship. Without a father or husband, a child or woman would have been in dire straits. The church today must not think that governmental social services are adequate for orphans and widows. To grow into healthy adults, children who have suffered neglect and physical or sexual abuse require a loving family. Local churches can invite foster-care specialists to recruit and train their members to serve as foster parents. A widows' ministry could be developed whereby lonely or disabled women in the church are visited by members who assist in shopping, providing transportation, paying bills, and providing lawn care or household maintenance. Sometimes a widow or a young person in a single-parent home simply needs some regular companionship.

The final ingredient of "the kind of religion which is without stain or fault in the sight of God our Father" (NEB) is for one **to keep himself unspotted from the world** (v. 27). Here James was not calling Christians to disengage from society but to maintain devotion to God while involved in it.

Attentiveness to the needs of distressed community members will foster personal wholeness and social cohesion. Thus, the perverted and demonic values of the nonbelieving society, values that put a premium on the acquisition of wealth at the expense of the poor, will not encroach on the congregations. The assemblies will remain pure, and they will be integrated since the actions outlined in verses 26–27 unify hearing and doing of the Word.

B. Second Exhortation: The Life of Impartiality (2:1–13)

1. Negative: Distinctions between Rich and Poor (2:1–7)

2:1. James's description of Christ as **the Lord of glory** is significant at this place. The ascription shows that Jesus, lowly and despised, is the one who occupies the ultimate place of honor in the universe. He imparts honor to those who are poor in a biblical sense, those who, impoverished socially and economically, abandon themselves to God's care and vindication in the face of oppression. The poor in James's churches shared in the glory of their Lord. To show partiality to the rich denies the Lord's own honor. Thus, James could say that one's **faith** ought not to be accompanied **with respect of persons** ("favoritism," NIV; "class distinction," NJB). God does not show favoritism, nor should believers (see Deut. 1:17; Rom. 2:11; Eph. 6:9; Col. 3:25).

2:2–4. Here James presented a vivid drama, a scene from an actual house-church meeting of the first century. The word **assembly** (v. 2) translates the Greek *synagōgē*, the origin of the English word "synagogue." The action builds towards a surprising climax as, first, a well-to-do individual enters and is given treatment that is deemed appropriate to his social status. He wears **a gold ring** as well as **goodly apparel** (i.e., **gay clothing**, v. 3; "fine clothes," NRSV). Does he not deserve to be told, **Sit thou here in a good place**? Then, **a poor man** (v. 2) enters and is told to take standing room or a "cheap seat" in the gathering. Since he is dressed in **vile raiment**, he is regarded as offensive. If he were to take a prominent seat, some church members who are less noticeable than he might fear being seen as the poor man's in-

feriors. By the time the seating arrangements were described, James's readers may have nodded and agreed on their suitability. James then delivered a wallop as an unexpected climax: by showing partiality to the wealthy, the church collectively (the passage is addressed in the second-person plural) had become a gathering of **judges [with] evil thoughts** (v. 4). They had taken to themselves the right to issue a judgment that was contrary to the judgment that God has already delivered regarding the poor.

In 2:5–13, James provided three arguments against showing favoritism to the rich: (1) the rich persecute the poor—the believers (vv. 5–7); (2) favoritism violates the royal law of love and thus is sin (vv. 8–11); (3) favoritism will be judged (vv. 12–13). The first of these arguments concludes James's negative statement about partiality in the church, which destroys integration and wholeness.

2:5–7. The rhetorical question **Hath not God chosen the poor of this world rich in faith, and heirs of the kingdom which he hath promised to them that love him?** (v. 5; see Matt 5:3; Luke 6:20; 1 Cor. 1:26–31) expects a yes answer. In the New Testament, the kingdom of God is that reign and rule of God in which His redemptive purposes for humankind are realized. This realm, which is spiritual but is lived out and expressed in physical and social dimensions as well, has invaded the present age but will not be consummated until the second coming of Jesus Christ. Paradoxically, the poor are the wealthy and heirs in the kingdom of God. The wealthy of this world do not have true spiritual riches if earthly wealth is all they possess. In James (and in the Synoptic Gospels), the poor are those who are impoverished because of their discipleship. Because they believe in the Son of God, they may rely on the fulfillment of God's promises to the disenfranchised, the outcast, and the needy in the Old Testament (see Ps. 69:32–33; Isa. 57:15; 61:1). The churches have, in some instances, **despised the poor** (v. 6). The **rich**, on the other hand, **oppress you, and draw you before the judgment seats**, that is, "act the potentate" against you and "drag" (*helkō*, used to describe Paul being dragged from the temple, Acts 21:30) you to courts where the privileged are given favorable treatment. James did not call for a reverse persecution of the rich; he simply called for equitable treatment of the poor. Since God honors them, they deserve honor from fellow believers. Honor—public acknowledgment that one has met certain cultural expectations and norms—was not to be accorded to the rich since they had verbally abused the Christians (**they blaspheme**; v. 7). A proper response in such a situation would be prayer, blessing, and nonretaliation (see Luke 6:27–31), but not special favoritism at the expense of those who have been honored by God.

The church today, sadly, repeats the errors of the congregations portrayed by James. Christians continue to show partiality, favoring those who are wealthy, attractive, influential, educated, and talented when it comes to expressions of love and honor. Of course, the church must permit only the spiritually mature to practice leadership. Too often believers choose to associate with or show kindness to those who might be able to repay them with reciprocal favors or advancement in their social standing. The less gifted or influential may not be able to repay in these ways, but they are just as deserving of our attention as those who can.

In one church, the youth pastor invited a young professional couple with a large income to join him as volunteer youth leaders. They declined after hearing that the responsibilities involved a weekly meeting with the youth pastor for prayer, planning, and Bible study. Shortly thereafter, the youth pastor invited a college-age person (with a modest income) to consider the same responsibility with the same conditions. He accepted. The couple, meanwhile, reconsidered and made their desire to work with the youth group known. Since the group was small, the youth pastor informed them that, for the time being, the young people had sufficient leadership. The couple, stunned and displeased that they would be refused, complained to the senior pastor. He then reprimanded the youth pastor for his choice of leaders: "Be careful! Don't you know that this couple contributes more to the church than any other members?" The senior pastor had favored the rich at this point. Although the young professional couple and the young college-age person had been given equal opportunity, the senior pastor believed the former deserved special consideration—or favoritism.

2. Positive: Fulfillment of the Royal Law (2:8–13)

2:8. The law of love (Lev. 19:18) is called **the royal law** because it is the supreme law and is the source of all other laws governing human relationships. It is the summation of all such laws (see Matt. 22:36–40; Rom. 13:8–10).

2:9. To **have respect to persons** is *prosōpolēmpteō*, "to receive the face." The verb conveys the idea of honor that, in Hebrew thinking, is centered on the face. God honors His people by making His face shine upon them (see Num. 6:25–26). Giving honor to others is commendable if it is bestowed on those who deserve it. Honor is to be granted without false distinctions.

2:10–11. The law is the expression of the character and will of God. Therefore, to violate one part of the law is to violate God's will and thus His whole law (see Matt 5:18–19; 23:23). Thus, one who fails to keep even one commandment **is guilty of all** (v. 10). The two commandments that James used as examples, **Do not commit adultery** (Exod. 20:14) and **Do not kill** (Exod. 20:13), pertain to any illicit sexual activity and murder, respectively.

2:12. Here judgment is not for determining eternal destiny, for James was speaking to believers (see 2:1), whose destinies were already determined (see John 5:24). Rather, it is for giving rewards to believers (see 1 Cor. 3:12–15; 2 Cor. 5:10; Rev. 22:12). Douglas Moo perceptively states, "No longer is God's law a threatening, confining burden. For the will of God now confronts us as a *law of liberty*—an obligation that is discharged in the joyful knowledge that God has both 'liberated' us from the penalty of sin and given us, in his Spirit, the power to obey his will" (*The Letter of James*, p. 98).

2:13. If man is merciful, God will be merciful on the day of judgment (see Prov. 21:13; Matt. 5:7; 6:14–15; 18:21–35). **Mercy rejoiceth against judgment** ("mercy triumphs over judgment," NRSV). This statement could mean either that one's practice of mercy is a sign that he will not be condemned in the final judgment or that mercy more effectively promotes wholeness and integration when it replaces the judgmental attitudes of 2:1–4. The context speaks for the latter interpretation.

C. Third Exhortation: The Integration of Faith and Action (2:14–26)

In verses 14–20, 24, 26, "faith" is not used in the sense of genuine, saving faith. Rather, it is demonic (v. 19), useless (v. 20), and dead (v. 26). It is a mere intellectual acceptance of certain truths without trust in Christ as Savior. James was not saying that a person is saved by works and not by genuine faith. Rather, he was saying, to use Martin Luther's words, that a man is justified (declared righteous before God) by faith alone, but not by a faith that is alone. Genuine faith will produce good deeds, but only faith in Christ saves. Justification has a twofold dimension, according to Luther in a disputation on justification in 1536: "Before God it takes place by faith, not by works; before men it takes place by works and love, which declare us just before ourselves and before the world. In fine, we concede that a man does justify himself insofar as the outward effect is concerned, not, however, insofar as the inward cause is concerned" (Ewald M. Plass, *What Luther Says* [Saint Louis: Concordia, 1959], 3:1231). James maintained that faith and action must be integrated in Christian living, both on the individual and corporate (church) levels. The illustration of false faith (vv. 14–17) is parallel to the illustration of false love found in 1 John 3:17. The latter passage calls for love in action; this one calls for faith in action.

1. Negative: Separation of Faith and Action (2:14–17)

2:14. The premises in this verse are (1) **faith** saves, (2) faith and **works** must be combined, and (3) false faith exists—faith without accompanying works, which does not save one. There is no **profit** at all in such faith.

2:15. The arena in which faith must show itself to be real and saving is, according to James, caring for the poor **brother or sister**, that is, one who is **naked,**

and destitute of daily food ("without clothes and daily food," NIV).

2:16. Neither the self-proclaimed believer nor the poor **profit** if one merely wishes the needy person well and does not distribute the items that **are needful to the body.** "Brother or sister" (2:15) probably refers to a member of the church, but care for the needy must extend beyond the Christian family. Provision should be offered to the "neighbor"—anyone in need. If that person's need becomes known to a believer who is in a financial position to do something about it, that believer is under obligation to consider action. Should a Christian respond to every request for money? Many believers feel overwhelmed by pleas on TV or through mailings to assist the hungry. Answering every request is not the proper response (and become financially constrained oneself), nor is refusing every request. Prayerful consideration of appeals, and a commitment to answer no more than a few, is probably the best response for most believers.

Should a Christian give money to beggars and panhandlers? Probably not. A wiser course of action might be to offer to buy a homeless person a meal or to direct him or her to a mission or shelter. Cash is often used to purchase alcohol or drugs and perpetuates the condition of beggary. Many churches have established food kitchens or pantries where destitute people can come for physical necessities. These are distributed in an environment where Jesus Christ is proclaimed and glorified.

2:17. Faith, then, without accompanying **works, is dead.** Genuine faith will always be accompanied by what Luther identified as "works of faith," which are done purely out of love for God, not out of fear or in the hope of gaining advantage with God. Only believers, those who are justified by faith, can perform works of faith. Works that are performed to gain salvation are "works of the law" and actually hinder justification since they prevent one from realizing his abject need before God.

2. Positive: Completion of Faith with Action (2:18–26)

2:18. A new paragraph begins here (see JB, NRSV). **Thou hast faith, and I have works.** James's discussion in 2:18–20 may reflect a false claim by some in his audience that there are "faith" Christians and "works" Christians, that is, that faith and deeds can exist independently of each other. With masterful irony, James denied the possibility that one can **shew me thy faith without thy works**. The grammatical difficulties surrounding 2:18–20 are reviewed in detail by Nystrom (*James*, pp. 150–53). Perhaps the biggest question in this text is that of the speaker(s). Who says what and where? Is an ally of James speaking in verse 18, or an opponent? If an ally, where does the ally's statement begin and end? If an opponent is cited, what are the opponent's precise words? The KJV punctuation is imprecise. The NIV inserts quotation marks around a contrasting statement of an objector: "But someone will say, 'You have faith; I have deeds'" (18a). In the NIV, however, James's answer in verse 18b-c seems to agree with the objection, not refute it! ("Show me your faith without deeds, and I will show you my faith by what I do.") Originally, no punctuation existed in the New Testament text, so the decisions of editors and translators are informed conjectures.

Perhaps James introduced an imaginary interlocutor at verse 18a, whom he addressed directly: "But someone may say that you have faith [an abrupt shift from the third person to the second person, but the reference is to the same individual], and I say that I have good deeds. Show me your faith apart from good deeds, and I will show you my faith by my good deeds." The "someone" is an individual who maintains that faith unaccompanied by works is acceptable; he is the one without faith in 2:14, the "senseless person" (NRSV) of 2:20. The JB captures the sense of verse 18: "This is the way to talk to people of that kind: You say you have faith and I have good deeds; I will prove to you that I have faith by showing you my good deeds — now you prove to me that you have faith without any good deeds to show." The entire section of 2:18–20 addresses that individual whose professed faith has no good deeds to back it up. Although the exact grammatical sense is difficult to ascertain, the overall thrust of the passage is evident: "faith [without] works, is dead" (2:17).

2:19. With sarcasm, James commended his opponent for his belief that **there is one God**. Congratulations! **Thou doest well!** Even **the devils** assent to the declaration of monotheism that is reflected in the well-known Jewish creed called the Shema (Hebrew, meaning "Hear" [Deut. 6:4; Mark 12:29]), and they **tremble**. The demons' belief does not do them any good since their belief in the one God is only a mental acknowledgment. They have not acted on their belief.

2:20. In summary, James again addressed his imaginary objector, who was introduced in 2:18. This **vain man** ought to recognize by now **that faith without works is dead**. The word "dead" in the best witnesses is *argos* and has the idea of "idle," "lazy," "fallow," "unproductive." The word for the inert gas *argon* has its etymological roots in the term.

2:21–23. Apart from its context, verse 21 might seem to contradict the biblical teaching that people are saved by faith and not by good deeds (see Rom. 3:28; Gal. 2:15–16). James, however, meant only that righteous action is evidence of genuine faith, not that it saves, for the verse that he cites (Gen. 15:6) to substantiate his point says, **Abraham believed God, and it** (i.e., faith, not works) **was imputed unto him for righteousness** (v. 23). "Imputed" (*logizomai*) here could be understood as "allotted," but not in the sense that faith is some sort of merit. Faith is complete dependence on the sheer grace of God and admits its utter incapacity to do anything meritorious before Him. Hence, faith receives His grace and renders one in right standing before God. Imputation here is probably to be understood in terms of a covenant relationship, not of moral righteousness.

Furthermore, Abraham's act of faith recorded in Genesis 15:6 occurred before **he had offered Isaac** (v. 21; see Genesis 22), which was only a proof of the genuineness of his faith. As Paul wrote, the only thing that matters is "faith which worketh by love" (Gal. 5:6). Faith that saves produces deeds. In Abraham's case, **faith wrought with his works** (v. 22; "faith was working with his works," NASB), and thus faith, having reached the goal or conclusion that God intended for it, was **made perfect**. The designation the Friend of God (v. 23; see 2 Chron. 20:7) further describes Abraham's relationship to God as one of complete acceptance. Abraham staked everything on God's trustworthiness to fulfill His promise that he would be the first of a great people. The patriarch had to be willing to sacrifice the only son through whom the fulfillment could come. Furthermore, the one nearest and dearest to his heart had to be entrusted to God. When God tests Christians regarding the vision for life and ministry that He has given to them, how does one respond? When a close relationship is threatened by illness, geographical change, or a breakup, do believers entrust that loved one to God, as well as their desires for that relationship? How one passes the test reveals the quality of one's faith and makes it stronger (see 1:2–8).

2:24. Here to be justified does not contradict Paul's teaching on the subject (e.g., Eph. 2:8–10). One's claim to faith is justified before people (shown to be true and substantiated) not by (the claim of) faith only, not by an intellectual assent to certain truths, but by works also. In James's mind, righteous deeds that spring from faith undoubtedly included assistance to the poor. Paul himself affirmed that good works flow from the life that is saved by grace (see Eph. 2:10).

2:25. Rahab the harlot is a surprising choice as an example of faith. James was not approving Rahab's occupation; he merely commended her for her faith (see Heb. 11:31), which she demonstrated by helping the spies (see Joshua 2). As the mother of Boaz, she became an ancestor of David and Jesus (see Matt. 1:5). Her deed is an example of providing daily necessities to the needy (see 2:15–16). The mention of her in this section was very appropriate for James's audience. Many of them appeared righteous but stood condemned as "adulterers and adulteresses" (4:4). Obviously immoral, Rahab the prostitute is, however, an example of faith. Unless one is willing to risk all by identifying with God's people and His purposes in the world, whatever faith he or she proclaims is ultimately shallow. Rahab welcomed the spies because she believed in the superiority of Yahweh, and she put her life on the line

to protect His people. James's readers had not done similarly unless they had acted in behalf of the orphans, widows, and poor who needed the protection of privileged members of the congregations. Faith and deeds must be integrated.

D. Fourth Exhortation: The Life of Wisdom (3:1–18)

1. Negative: The Destructive Power of the Tongue (3:1–12)

3:1–2. The word masters (v. 1) has its old English meaning of "teachers" here, as the Greek word (didaskaloi) used and the subject matter of chapter 3 show. Because teachers have great influence, they will be held more accountable than those who do not have the responsibility of instructing by word and example (see Luke 20:47; Matt. 23:1–33). James's remark that we shall receive the greater condemnation does not mean that all teachers have done so miserably that they will certainly be condemned for their shortcomings. The Greek construction meizon krima lēmpsometha means "we who teach will be judged by God with greater strictness" (NLT). The reason for stricter judgment is that "we all [i.e., 'all we teachers'] stumble in many ways" (NIV), particularly in regard to harmful speech. Some would classify one who does not sin by what he or she says a perfect man (v. 2) or woman. Since the tongue is so difficult to control, anyone who can control it perfectly can practice self-control in all other areas of life as well.

With that somber warning in mind, how can one know if God is placing a call to a teaching ministry in the church, either as a layperson or as a professional? A few questions and considerations that may indicate such a calling are the following. (1) Is such a role something that one really desires to do? Paul said, "If anyone sets his heart on being an overseer, he desires a noble task" (1 Tim. 3:1, NIV). A teaching ministry does not in all cases mean being an overseer, but the principle still holds true: God uses the deep desires of His children to communicate to them something of His will for their lives. (2) What am I good at doing? Do I enjoy studying the Bible and sharing my observations with others? Do people ask me questions about the Bible and its application to life today? (3) What do others believe that I can do well? What kind of responsibilities are offered or delegated to me? Of course, God's *general* will for His people is found in Scripture. His *specific* will for an individual's life becomes clear to one who considers such questions.

3:3–12. In these verses, James employed several colorful metaphors for the tongue, some of which are direct (comparison expressed) and some of which are indirect (comparison inferred). The theme of wisdom (introduced in 1:5–8) is revisited. Once again, James's eye is on wholeness and integration. Corporately and individually, a person's faith must be matched with good deeds. Otherwise, Christian life will be disintegrated. So too will the teacher's ministry disintegrate if the wisdom he or she professes is not accompanied by a judicious use of the tongue. Wholesome, not harmful, speech must proceed from the teacher's mouth.

3:3. Bits in the horses' mouths. Just as something as small as a bit can enable one to lead the entire body of a horse, so something as small as a human tongue sets the course of a person's entire life (see 2:2), for good or for ill.

3:4–5a. The rudder of a ship. The **helm** (v. 4) of a ship is the "rudder" (NRSV). Although it is **very small**, it can guide a ship driven by violent winds, "wherever the pilot wants to go" (NIV). **The tongue is a little member** (v. 5) of the body, but its swelled and vain boasts are completely disproportionate to its size. The degree to which one speaks of himself and his plans should be in proportion to the small instrument by which he speaks. One should speak little, and then not in a boastful way.

3:5b–6. A forest fire. **A little fire kindleth** (v. 5b) a huge conflagration (**matter**, *hylē*, should be translated "forest" [NKJV]). Its ruinous power is so overwhelming that it **setteth on fire the course of nature** (v. 6), which is perhaps a reference to the ancient symbol of the wheel for human life in its changeability and its allotted course. The wheel must complete its "cycle." All the while, "the evil influence of the

tongue spreads out from the axle to the entire circumference of the 'wheel' at every moment in its revolving course" (Tasker, *The General Epistle of James*, p. 76). The tongue, being deadly, **is set on fire of hell**. This may be a figurative way of saying that the source of the tongue's evil is the Devil (see John 8:44).

The devastating effects of the tongue were illustrated just before this author began writing this commentary on James. Near his home in northern California, a devastating fire burned 11,000 acres of timber and rangeland in August 2004, when conditions for such a fire were at their optimum. The Bear Fire was apparently started by a spark from a riding lawn mower that was being used to cut down dry weeds on a day when the temperature had reached 106°F. The blaze quickly spread and destroyed eighty-six dwellings before it was controlled. Damage estimates from the fire totaled $25.6 million. The tongue can unleash its destructive energy similarly. Once its harmful energy is unleashed, catastrophic results soon follow. **The tongue is a fire** (v. 6), James lamented.

A world of iniquity (v. 6). The tongue is like the world in its fallenness.

3:7–10. An unruly evil, full of deadly poison (v. 8). James's comparison here may be to the venom of the serpent. Whereas even the deadly snake **is tamed** (along with other creatures of earth, sea, and sky; v. 7), the tongue defies human control and is lethal in its effects. With the tongue **bless we God** (v. 9), and with the same instrument **curse we men**. The inconsistency of such action is clear: human beings **are made after the similitude of God** ("in the likeness of God," NASB). Since humans have been made like God (Gen. 1:26–27), for one human to curse another is like cursing God (see Gen. 9:6). Verbal abuse of others constitutes a great hypocrisy and is equivalent to cursing God since abusing those who are created in God's image abuses His image. James's very strong prohibition makes these things clear: **My brethren, these things ought not so to be** (v. 10).

3:11–12. A spring. James used an impossibility of nature to emphasize the inconsistency of a person who praises God one minute and condemns a fellow human the next. **A fountain** (v. 11) cannot bubble up and **send forth** both **sweet water and bitter**. The latter term ("brackish," AT, REB) is *pikros*, whose root is "to cut," "to prick." The foul water is sharp and harsh. So too is the "cursing" (v. 10). Any speech that maligns and degrades—slander, gossip, mockery—is bitter to the recipient and does not promote wholeness and integration of the truth. Parents far too often are sparing in praise and abundant in criticism. Recognition, thanks, and affirmation do not promote haughtiness in children but healthy self-esteem and a sense that they are created in God's image.

The fig tree and the grape **vine** (v. 12). As a fig tree cannot produce olives, nor the grapevine **figs**, neither can a spring produce water contrary to its nature. Either **salt** water or **fresh** water will come from a spring, but not both. Readers are left to consider whether there is true integration in their communities—integration between word and deed.

2. Positive: True Wisdom versus False Wisdom (3:13–18)

3:13. The question here zeroes in on the teacher (see discussion on 3:1), that is, **a wise man** who is an expert in matters pertaining to the Word. Three elements of a true teacher are expressed by three terms in this verse: **knowledge, meekness** ("gentleness," NRSV), and **shew out of a good conversation** ("show it by his good life," NIV). One cannot teach well what one does not practice in one's own life. The truly wise teacher is one who instructs patiently and receives questions and criticism with openness. Without the true wisdom that is described in 3:13–18, especially among its teachers, the Christian community cannot expect to be whole.

3:14. If a person has **bitter** (*pikros* again; see 3:11) **envying** of another's success in the realm of teaching and refuses to recognize that person's gifts or position because of **strife** and hostility, he has no reason to claim honor for that stance. It is in opposition to the truth.

3:15. The so-called wisdom that is characterized by pride is **not from above**, from God (see 1:5, 17;

1 Cor. 2:6–16). Instead, it is **earthly, sensual, devilish** ("demonic," NKJV). The second of this infamous trio, "sensual," is the translation of *psychikos*, a term Jude used to describe the false teachers whom he opposed. In Jude 19, the word describes those who, not having the Spirit, "follow mere natural instincts" (NIV). Paul used the word similarly to describe the person who cannot receive the things of God's Spirit (1 Cor. 2:14). Although James probably was not contending with false teaching as Jude and Paul were, he did contend with a false concept of true wisdom, one which draws on human intelligence without enlightenment from the Spirit of God. In biblical scholarship, many excellent studies of the grammar, historical-cultural background, and literary features of the text have been produced. Believers ought to use these studies freely, whether they were written by believers or unbelievers. Insights from history and literary analysis are open to all human inquiry, and the truth discovered is ultimately God's truth. Only those interpreters, however, who have the Holy Spirit and His illumination have the means by which to apply the biblical text to contemporary life most clearly and accurately.

3:16. Jealousy and the contention that accompanies it eventually break out in **confusion** ("disorder," NIV). All sorts of evil practices ensue when teachers or leaders have self-serving motives in their work that is ostensibly for God. "God is not the author of confusion, but of peace" (1 Cor. 14:33).

3:17. Here James returned to the subject of genuine wisdom, **the wisdom … from above**, which he introduced in 3:13. The author personified wisdom; the wise person is the one who has the characteristics that he listed. Wisdom is **first pure**; it displays a commitment to moral integrity without compromise. Only when wisdom has a passion for purity will the other qualities follow. The wise person is also **peaceable, gentle, and easy to be intreated** ("peace-loving, considerate, submissive," NIV). Stulac maintains that these characteristics "are terms that James uses only here in his letter; they describe people who can yield status, who care for others and who are willing to submit and learn from others—all in contrast to the bitterness, envy and selfish ambition of false spirituality" (*James*, p. 138). The final traits in the list of godly wisdom—**full of mercy and good fruits, without partiality, and without hypocrisy**—echo James's earlier statements about merciful treatment of the disadvantaged (2:1–17).

3:18. The fruit ("A harvest," NIV) **of righteousness** probably is "the fruit that consists of righteousness," the condition for the growth of which is **peace**, the Old Testament *šalom*. Peace in this sense is the corporate wholeness and well-being that are borne out of holiness, truth, sincerity, mercy, and justice (see Pss. 34:14; 38:3; 73:3; Isa. 43:7; Zech. 8:16–17, 19). Those who are peacemakers (see Matt. 5:9), those who seek to reconcile themselves to others and to promote reconciliation among others, are instrumental in this process.

E. Fifth Exhortation: Friendship with the World and Friendship with God (4:1–12)

1. Negative: Pursuit of Selfish Desires (4:1–4)

4:1–3. The principal problems James addressed in these verses, a passage full of battle imagery, are prayerlessness and incorrect prayer. Instead of proper prayer, the hearers were driven by their **lusts** (v. 1). The Greek for this term is the source of the word "hedonism." They had chosen to foster their passions rather than seek to control them (see 1:2–8, 13–15). James may have had in mind a thirst for power and popularity at the expense of the poor. (Did people within James' churches literally **kill** (v. 2)? The expression is probably simply figurative, a hyperbole for "hate.") A contentious environment within the Christian community, the family, or the individual heart prohibits prayerfulness. One reason the community and its members did not receive what they needed (evidently behind the covetousness were genuine needs) was **because ye ask not**. Those who do bother to pray do not receive what they ask for because they **ask amiss** ("because your whole motive is wrong," NLT), **that ye may consume it upon your lusts** (v. 3). "Consume" is *dapanaō*, used in Luke 15:14 to describe the lost son's squandering of his inheritance. Of course, God does not

answer prayers for that which does not serve His ultimate and good purpose.

4:4. The epithet **adulterers and adulteresses** (the better reading is "adulteresses") recalls the prophetic condemnations of Israel in the Old Testament for spiritual adultery, that is, covenant infidelity, which often included idolatry (see, e.g., Isa. 57:3; Jer. 31:32; Ezek. 16:38; Hos. 3:1). The image is of those who are spiritually unfaithful, who love the world rather than God. James addresses those who would be **a friend of the world**. As in James 1:27, the "world" here is not the created order (which is good [see 1:17]), nor is it the web of human activity and commerce (which is morally neutral [see 4:13–17]). The world is a measure of existence that does not take God and His claims into account, and to be its friend is to oppose God and His claims on human life. That opposition can be in the form of indifference to the living God, not just active hostility.

Life in the affluent West in the twenty-first century is characterized by friendship with the world in this sense. The culture of consumerism, in which the need to need and the desire to desire are awakened in the enchantments of advertising, exalts self-centeredness and greed. The omnipresence of commercial messages in the media and the overload of choices that confront people daily make moral discrimination more and more difficult. For many, ethical and moral reasoning has devolved into consumer choice. The questions, "What is God's will?" and "What is right?" are increasingly rare, replaced by the question, "What is most satisfying?" Even the inquiry, "Can I afford this?" is no longer important for so many, with credit-card use and abuse so readily available. A system built on consumption does not promote wholeness in the Christian community unless its members exercise extreme care to guard themselves against the insidious effects of greed.

2. Positive: Humility before God (4:5–12)

4:5. The passage of **scripture** that James had in mind is not known, but it may have been the thrust of several passages in constellation. The sense of the passage is difficult. Does it refer to the Holy Spirit

(NASB) or the human spirit (NIV)? And is the desire evil, marked by human envy (**lusteth**), or does the Spirit lovingly yearn for His people (NRSV)? In other words, who is the subject of the verb "to desire" (*epipothein*), God or the human spirit that dwells in all humans?

Pheme Perkins believes that a dualism of good and evil, truth and falsehood (see *T. Sim.* 3:1–6; 1QS 3:18–4:26) is present in 4:1–5 and that James's focus was not the evil desire of the human spirit but God's desire for that spirit to control envy. Her reasoning is that "God desires the [human] spirit that dwells within humans to be opposed to jealousy, not to be its slave" since the prepositional construction *pros phthonon* ("jealously," NRSV, v. 5) with an accusative can refer to that which is being opposed (*First and Second Peter, James, and Jude*, p. 125). This is an intriguing interpretation. **The spirit** is likely the human spirit, as Perkins asserts. In light of 4:1–4, however, one probably ought to read verse 5 negatively; it is a scriptural substantiation for the unflattering description of the human condition described in 4:1–4. The real antithesis to that condition emerges only in 4:6 ("But he giveth more grace"). James B. Adamson believes that verse 5, with its affirmation of the presence of "the sinful propensities of the spirit implanted in man," ought to be translated, "Or do you suppose it is an idle saying in the Scriptures, that the spirit that has taken its dwelling in us is prone to envious lust?" (*The Epistle of James*, pp. 172–73). Thus, verse 5, although appearing within the set of positive instructions in this section (4:5–12), is somewhat negative. It leads, however, to a positive declaration in 4:6 and the instructions that promote wholeness in the community in 4:7–12. Those instructions serve to curb envious lust and promote the work of the Holy Spirit within the community.

4:6. But he giveth more grace. God gives more than enough grace to His people so that they can lead a life of wholeness despite the all pervasive inclination to do evil. James's rationale for his teaching on grace is Proverbs 3:34 **God resisteth the proud, but giveth grace unto the humble** (see 1 Peter 5:5, which also quotes this Old Testament text).

4:7–10. These verses contain ten commands, each of which is stated in Greek in a way that calls for immediate action in rooting out the sinful attitude of pride.

4:7. The first two commands are **Submit yourselves therefore to God** and **Resist the devil** (see Eph. 6:11–18; 1 Peter 5:8–9), the second of which is accompanied by a promise: **and he will flee from you.** In the New Testament, the reality of Satan is affirmed, but so is the triumph of Christ over him (Luke 10:18) and over the evil powers (see Col. 2:15). The believer who claims that victory and resists the Devil's schemes will find victory too.

4:8. The command **Draw nigh to God** ("Draw near to God," NKJV) also has a guarantee: **he will draw nigh to you.** Some contemporary worship songs call on God to show Himself and come near to the worshiper, which is good, but God reveals Himself to those who draw near to Him. When one minimizes the importance of personal and corporate holiness, one cannot expect God to manifest His power on one's behalf. For James's readers, drawing near to God meant drawing near to the oppressed and needy to meet their tangible physical needs. "Pure religion" involves doing just that (see 1:27).

The next two commands define and clarify what drawing near to God often involves. **Cleanse your hands.** Before the Old Testament priests approached God at the tabernacle, they had to wash their hands and feet at the brass laver as a symbol of spiritual cleansing (see Exod. 30:17–21; for the imagery of "clean hands, and a pure heart," see Ps. 24:4). **Purify your hearts** is an injunction for the **double minded.** Those who doubt whether God is willing or able to answer their prayers for wisdom during trials are described by this same word (see 1:8).

4:9. Be afflicted is not a call to bring suffering upon oneself. The verb is a summons to "grieve" (NIV), "to repent in misery" (Burdick, "James," p. 195). To **mourn** denotes an intense and passionate outward grief. Again, the grief is over sin. In James's community, the sins for which the believers needed to mourn may have been their partiality, haughtiness, and the pursuit of pleasure that characterizes friendship with the world. To **weep** carries further the command to repent. The verb, *klaiō*, has the idea of audible weeping that arises from "deep grief" (NLT).

Let your laughter be turned to mourning is certainly not a prohibition on joy or happiness in the Christian life. Church services, ministry functions, and family life could all use more happiness and less gloom. James was condemning the inane hilarity of the carouser, the slanderer, and the brute. The turning of **joy to heaviness** is the exchange by which "your high spirits will have to become heartfelt dejection" (Phillips) as sin is faced squarely and for which one repents of.

4:10. Humble yourselves in the sight of the Lord, and he shall lift you up. What the world honors—the ambition of the rich and powerful who trample others as they make their way to the top—is not what God honors. He honors those who cast themselves on His mercy and become servants of others (see 1 Peter 5:6).

4:11–12. Moving from humility before God to the extension of that humility in community life, James returned to the matter of speech (see 1:19, 26; 3:1–12): **Speak not evil one of another** (v. 11). One ought not to speak evil of his brother, a fellow member of a Christian congregation. In other words, James prohibits "speaking down to" (*katalaleō*) or slandering another believer. Although all forms of ridicule, scorn, jokes, and belittling are here outlawed, the term usually refers to slandering someone who is not present to defend himself. William Barclay incisively observes, "There is great necessity for this warning. People are slow to realize that there are few sins which the Bible so unsparingly condemns as the sin of irresponsible and malicious gossip. There are few activities in which the average person finds more delight than this; to tell and to listen to the slanderous story—especially about some distinguished person—is for most people a fascinating activity. We do well to remember what God thinks of it" (*The Letters of James and Peter*, p. 111).

James maintained that one who **speaketh evil of his brother … speaketh evil of the law** (v. 11). Speaking evil of another is equivalent to judging that

person and is therefore speaking evil of the law and judging it too. Why? To disparage one's neighbor is to break "the royal law" of 2:8: "Thou shalt love thy neighbour as thyself" (see also Exod. 20:16; Pss. 15:3; 50:19–20; Prov. 6:16, 19). To speak against a brother is to scorn the law of love. And to break that law is to set oneself up as God; one has determined that the royal law is no longer binding. One is no longer a doer of the law but its judge. Now the reader can see the point clearly: there is no room for another judge besides God. **There is one lawgiver, who is able to save and to destroy: who art thou that judgest another?** (v. 12).

F. Sixth Exhortation: Attitudes toward the Future (4:13–5:11)

1. Negative: Disregard for the Shortness of Life and of the Coming Judgment (4:13–5:6)

In this section, James was addressing Christian merchants of the first century. Verses 13–18 constitute the first of two short addresses to groups who had a wrong outlook on wealth. Both addresses begin with the phrase "Go to now" (v. 13, 5:1).

4:13. James described three indications that a person was well-to-do according to the standards of the ancient world. (1) He or she had time to spend on business ventures and was not tied down to eking out a subsistence living. Such a businessperson was able to travel to another city and **continue there a year.** (2) The merchant had capital with which to speculate and invest, to **buy and sell**, and (3) had enough of it to expect to **get gain.** James did not condemn commercial enterprise or the possession and increase of wealth. He condemned the shortsightedness that fails to recognize the futility of building one's future solely on hopes of financial gain. He also condemned the failure to allow for God's will in human enterprise.

4:14. No one can be certain what the future holds, **what shall be on the morrow.** Each human life, though of inestimable worth, is but **a vapour, that appeareth for a little time, and then vanisheth away** ("no more than a mist, seen for a little while and then dispersing," NEB). Seafaring merchants would have easily understood a mist as an apt metaphor for life's short duration. Shakespeare's Macbeth lamented the brevity of life:

> Life's but a walking shadow, a poor player
> That struts and frets his hour upon the stage
> And then is heard no more: it is a tale
> Told by an idiot, full of sound and fury,
> Signifying nothing.
>
> *Macbeth*, 5.5.24–28

James was not as pessimistic about life's meaning as Macbeth was, but he was as realistic in his assessment of its shortness.

4:15. In light of the shortness of the human life span, one ought to be reminded, **If the Lord will, we shall live, and do this, or that**. This is not a flippant statement used as some sort of fetish for good luck. Behind this statement is the conviction that God is sovereign, that He determines the duration of one's life, as He determines the boundaries of human activity. One cannot derive from this statement the notion that such things are set and cannot be affected by prayer or choices bad and good. James's assertion does, however, call into question the teaching of open theism in regard to God's omniscience. Proponents of open theism believe that God is aware of all possible human choices, but He limits His own foreknowledge of those choices. If God were aware of the outcome of human choice, open theism says, human free will would be nonexistent. Contrary to that view is James's outlook: God superintends how long a person lives and what that person does during his or her lifetime. One can make plans, certainly, but must submit to the overriding will of God. In the consumerist society that pervades the West in the opening years of the twenty-first century, James's instruction is just as relevant as it was in the first century.

4:16. The merchant readers whom James addressed were not at fault for making plans. Rather, their fault was **ye rejoice in your boastings** ("you boast in your arrogance," NRSV). The traders found their significance in the making and execution of their commercial plans. James maintained that **all** **such rejoicing is evil**. The entrepreneurs left God out of their planning and acted as if He does not exist. Such self-sufficiency is the height of pride.

4:17. Here is a pithy maxim that sums up James's statements about pride and self-sufficiency: **Therefore to him that knoweth to do good, and doeth it not, to him it is sin**. Whether or not the hearers knew beforehand the principles of his discourse on making plans was inconsequential. The merchants knew them now and needed to heed them as doers, not just hearers.

5:1. The **rich** whom James addressed here evidently were not Christians (nor do they appear to be in 2:2, 6), for James warned them to repent and weep because of the coming misery. The address in 5:1–6 is similar to Old Testament declarations of judgment against pagan nations, interspersed in books otherwise addressed to God's people (see Isaiah 13–23; Jeremiah 46–51; Ezekiel 25–32; Amos 1:3–2:16; Zeph. 2:4–15). Although some wealthy persons might have been present in James's churches to hear his letter read, this address to them was really for the benefit of any believers who had been victims of oppression by the wealthy. (The literary device of addressing imaginary hearers as if they are present is called *apostrophe*.)

In view of the coming judgment, James called on the rich to **weep and howl for your miseries that shall come upon you**. The Greek word *ololuzō* (excellently translated "howl" in the KJV) is onomatopoetic; that is, its sound suggests the meaning of the word. "Burst into weeping, howling with grief" is Robertson's rendering of the two verbs here (*The General Epistles*, p. 57). James's tone is reminiscent of Jesus' own pronouncement of woe upon the rich in Luke 6:24.

5:2. The perfect tense of the verbs in this passage emphasizes the certainty of the judgment to come; it was so certain that James spoke of it as if it had already happened (a literary device called *prolepsis*). **Riches** may be food specifically or wealth generally. In the latter case, clothing and precious metals would be examples. At any rate, the riches **are corrupted** ("Your wealth has rotted," NIV). **Garments** were one of the main forms of wealth in the ancient world (see Acts 20:33). Now they were **motheaten**. The perishable nature of wealth makes it an unwise primary investment of one's energies during a lifetime. Today, synthetic fabrics make some clothing quite durable. They still quickly "decay" in obsolescence in the estimation of an overly fashion-conscious society. A person who, because of an obsession for attractiveness, must have only the very latest styles finds clothing to be something that lasts only briefly.

5:3. Your gold and silver is cankered ("corroded," NKJV; "rusted," NRSV). These metals do not rust, but James used the image of their corrosion to underline his point that security in riches is illusory. **Rust** is the result of hoarding, and that rust will both testify against and judge the selfish rich. James then deftly shifted the metaphor of rust to that of **fire**, associated with judgment in the Bible. The notion is gruesomely graphic: just as a rusty and abrasive chain eats into a prisoner's flesh with burning pain, so shall perished riches testify against the wicked wealthy in **the last days**. The **treasure** stored up during their lifetime will only serve as a witness against them in the end.

What one thinks can never happen to misplaced security can and will happen. Those who put trust in investment portfolios, the appreciation of real property, or the likelihood of advancement in a certain profession ought to consider James's statements. He was not forbidding wealth per se; he was condemning false hope in riches, the avarice that drives people to accumulate more than they need and the miserliness that keeps them from doing good with what they do have.

5:4. Why did the wealthy have riches to store up? Wages of the workers who had mowed their fields had been **kept back by fraud**. The laborers had been paid late or inequitably. The reference may be to absentee landlords, common in Israel from the years of the monarchy onward, who had defrauded agricultural laborers. Dependent on a daily wage for subsistence, the laborers were the victims of injustice when their wages are not paid immediately. In colorful personification, the money itself **crieth**. The op-

pressed workers themselves cried out for justice, and their appeals for justice had **entered into the ears of the Lord of sabaoth**. The image of God as one who has ears is an instance of anthropomorphism—ascribing human qualities to God so that one might better understand His functions. Here the stress is on God's inclination to hear and answer prayer.

The plight of the workers that James described is similar to that of many workers in the West today. Permanent workers, migrants, and immigrants all fall victim to unjust business practices. David K. Shipler (*The Working Poor: Invisible in America* [New York: Alfred A. Knopf, 2004], pp. 78–79, 100–101) has described migrant laborers whose outrageous housing costs are simply deducted from their wages by unscrupulous labor contractors who house the workers in deplorable barracks. Garment workers find it almost impossible to earn even a minimum wage when they are paid at piece rates (e.g., three-fourths of a cent per zipper on a pair of jeans). Christians who are in a position to set wages, regulate working conditions, and determine benefits ought to protect the rights of all employees, especially foreigners who are reticent or unable to speak for themselves because of language barriers. A higher minimum wage, timely payment of employees, tax breaks, and greater availability of health insurance are needed measures to assure justice for migrant workers as well as permanent residents who are numbered among the working poor. Christian business owners ought to do all they can to protect workers on the job, to pay wages that enable their employees to support themselves and their families, and to promote health care for their workers. Such measures are expensive, but justice calls for greater attention to the well-being of the workers than to a hefty bottom line. Profit is good. It is necessary for the hiring of more workers, for the increase of their pay, and for the availability of benefits to them. Considerations of justice and equity must not, according to James, be overlooked in the attainment of profit.

5:5. The oppressive wealthy had **lived in pleasure on the earth, and been wanton**. Like the rich man who neglected poor Lazarus (Luke 16:19–31), the rich now faced **a day of slaughter**— the day of judgment. The wicked rich were like cattle that continued to fatten themselves on the very day they were to be slaughtered, totally unaware of the coming destruction. The indictment of Amos 4:1 reflects the same idea, "Hear this word, you cows of Bashan, who are on the mountain of Samaria, Who oppress the poor, Who crush the needy, Who say to your husbands, 'Bring wine, let us drink!'" (NKJV). Judgment came upon the Samaritans too (see Amos 4:2–3).

5:6. The oppression of the poor was so severe that James's accusation of the wealthy was that they had **condemned and killed** ("murdered," NKJV) righteous persons. The poor had little recourse in the face of such oppression.

2. Positive: Endurance in Suffering (5:7–11)

5:7–8. The term **therefore** (v. 7) refers back to 5:1–6. Since the believers were suffering at the hands of the wicked rich, they were to look forward patiently to the Lord's return. The sense of the verb **be patient** (*makrothymeō*) is practically synonymous with that of the noun *hypomonē*, "patience" in 1:3–4 (see the cognate verb *hypomenō*, "endureth," in 1:12). Since patience with people (the oppressive rich) is in view, however, James used language that is sometimes associated with that sort of endurance. His point was that the poor and oppressed believers must not retaliate against their oppressors and take God's judgment of the unjust into their own hands. Instead, they were to wait **unto the coming of the Lord**. The word "coming" is *parousia* (see Matt. 24:3, 27; 1 Thess. 2:19; 2 Thess. 2:1; 1 Cor. 15:23; 1 John 2:28; 2 Peter 1:16; 3:4, 12). In secular Greek, the term is used to describe the invasion of an army or the visit of a monarch or a governor to a province. Jesus' coming will mean the final defeat of His enemies and His glorious manifestation to His adoring and worshiping subjects. **The husbandman** ("the farmer," NIV) of ancient Palestine, without modern irrigation, awaited both **the early and latter rain** with great anticipation. Without the rains, **the precious fruit of the earth** would not arrive. In Israel, the early rain comes in October and November, soon

after the grain is sown; the late rain comes in March and April, just prior to harvest (see Deut. 11:14; Jer. 5:24; Hos. 6:3; Joel 2:24). Just as a farmer watches for the rains and inspects his crops as he awaits the harvest, so believers are to watch and wait for the coming of the Lord.

The New Testament insistence on imminence (see, e.g., Rom. 13:12; Heb. 10:25; 1 Peter 4:7; Rev. 22:20) arises from the teaching that "the last days" began with the incarnation. Mankind have been living in "the last days" (5:3) ever since. The next great event in redemptive history is Christ's second coming. The New Testament does not say when it will take place, but its certainty is never questioned, and believers are consistently admonished to watch for it. It was in this light that James expected the imminent return of Christ. James urged God's people to **stablish your hearts** (v. 8; "be … stouthearted," NEB) while they wait since the great day **draweth nigh** ("is near," NRSV).

5:9. The prohibition **Grudge not one against another** ("Don't grumble against each other," NIV) might indicate that the practice of some members of the community was to turn their complaints against one another rather than cry out to the Lord. If such a practice was not yet occurring, though it could very well have been going on (see Wuest, "stop complaining"), James strongly forbad it starting. James called for patience toward believers as well as unbelievers since **the judge standeth before the door**, a reference to Christ's second coming (see 5:7–8) and the judgment associated with it.

5:10. James appealed to the example of **the prophets** to encourage steadfastness in tribulation. In this, he was following the ancient practice of setting forth a series of characters who are morally exemplary (see 1:22–25; 2:20–25; 5:17–18). Suffering hardship, particularly experiencing hostility to the Lord's message announced through them, was a mark of true prophets (e.g., Jeremiah, Ezekiel, and Daniel). The hearers' experience of hostility from the rich put them in the line of the great and honorable prophets of old. They shared in that honor as they suffer at the hands of the rich.

5:11. The patience of Job refers to the endurance or perseverance of Job in the face of adversity (see Job 1:20–22; 2:9–10, 13–15). This is the only place in the New Testament where Job is mentioned, though Job 5:13 is quoted in 1 Corinthians 3:19. Surprisingly, Job seems to be included among the prophets. James, however, may have simply shifted to another kind of example here and not intended to include Job among the prophets. Nevertheless, the examples of endurance (both the verb *hypomenō* and the noun *hypomonē* occur in v. 11) in suffering that Job and the prophets present show something about human response in difficulties. Barclay says of this passage: "The word used of him [Job] is that great New Testament word *hupomonē* [sic], which describes, not a passive patience, but that gallant spirit which can breast the tides of doubt and sorrow and disaster and come out with faith still stronger on the other side. There may be a faith which never complained or questioned; but still greater is the faith which was tortured by questions and still believed. It was the faith which held grimly on that came out on the other side, for 'the Lord blessed the latter days of Job more than his beginning' (*Job* 42:12)" (*The Letters of James and Peter*, p. 125).

The stories of Job and the prophets also reveal something about God and His response to human pain: **the Lord is,** James affirmed, **very pitiful, and of tender mercy.** The former of these two descriptions of the Lord occurs nowhere else in Scripture and is literally "many bowels of compassion." In Hebraic thinking, the bowels or entrails were regarded as the source of feelings like compassion. "Full of pity" (NEB) is a good contemporary translation.

G. Seventh Exhortation: The Importance of Speaking the Truth (5:12)

1. Negative: The Use of Oaths (5:12a)

5:12a. The command to **swear not** does not pertain to profanity (as undesirable as vulgar speech might be). James's words, very close to Christ's on the subject (Matt. 5:33–37), do not condemn the taking of solemn oaths, such as God's before Abraham (Heb. 6:13), Jesus' before Caiaphas (Matt. 26:63–64), Paul's to the Romans (Rom. 1:9; 9:1), or a man's before the Lord (Exod. 22:11). This command does not prohibit a Christian from taking an oath in a court of law or from pledging allegiance to the nation's flag or constitution. Rather, James was condemning the use of nonbinding oaths to give the impression of truthfulness. In the ancient world, oaths that mentioned God were often deemed more serious than those that did not (e.g., those oaths that only swore **by heaven** or **by earth**). The latter were often not regarded as binding as the former. For James, all speech is uttered in the presence of God, and one will be called to account for it.

2. Positive: Words of integrity — "Yes" or "No" (5:12b)

5:12b. In verse 12, James was applying the teaching of Jesus (see Matt. 23:16–22) and, in so doing, was teaching total honesty even in the most adverse circumstances. Believers in James's churches might have been tempted to use an oath (whether truthfully or falsely) in many different circumstances. Some may have been tempted to use an oath to underscore the severity of a financial need that they had brought before the church to obtain aid. Perhaps the need was as great as they portrayed it. No matter. The point here is that a simple **yea** or **nay** (yes or no) suffices among God's people. Otherwise, rather than wholeness and integration, suspicion and aloofness reign.

IV. Conclusion: Various Instructions for the Promotion of Integration in the Community (5:13–20)

A. Prayer for Various Needs (5:13–18)

In this section, James presented various needs and provided instructions on prayer for those needs.

5:13. Is any among you afflicted? let him pray. The person so instructed is not suffering from illness but is distressed by misfortune, perhaps from oppression by the wealthy. Instead of bemoaning one's circumstances, lashing out at others, or bearing difficulty with quiet resignation, one should pray! **Is any merry? let him sing psalms.** This may be the more difficult of the two commands in verse 13 to carry out, because one tends to forget God when things go well. James said that on such occasions, one ought to thank God for His mercies. Perhaps He has spared one from particular trials so that one's load might be lightened.

5:14 – 15. The **sick** (v. 14) person is not expressly instructed to pray—a surprising omission in the context of all the other prayers that James described. Instead, James said, **let him call for the elders of the church; and let them pray over him**. The person is too ill to go to the elders and is perhaps too sick even to pray in any sustained way with concentration and energy. From the earliest times of the Christian church (see Acts 14:23), elders have attended to the needs of believers. Their presence here and in other New Testament texts does not necessarily indicate a late first-century or second-century date for those writings.

Accompanying the prayer for the sick person, either preceding or during the prayer, is **anointing ... with oil** (v. 14), one of the best-known ancient medicines (referred to by Philo, Pliny, and the physician Galen; see Isa. 1:6; Luke 10:34). Some believe that James may have been using the term medicinally in this passage. Others, however, regard the use of oil here as an aid to faith, an outward sign of the healing God would bring about in response to prayer offered in faith (v. 15; see Mark 6:13). Perhaps the oil is a symbol of the Holy Spirit. The very act of touching a sick person conveys compassion. This is a Christian act; the anointing is done **in the name of the Lord**—those administering the prayer and anointing claim Jesus' authority and power that He makes available to His people.

Since James later presented Elijah (5:17 – 18) as the example of **the prayer of faith** (v. 15), this prayer may be prayer that is in harmony with the revealed and discerned will of God. James guaranteed that this prayer **shall save the sick, and the Lord shall raise him up**. When the church confronts matters like weakness and disease, sometimes prayer requires prayerful listening to God in order for God's people even to know how to proceed in prayer. The Lord reveals what "the prayer of faith" is that should be prayed. James may not have been referring to a par-

ticular kind of prayer here, however. He may have been referring simply to prayer for the need at hand, spoken in faith, "nothing wavering" (1:6).

Although the verb "save" can point to salvation in terms of eternal life, it may indicate deliverance from disease here. Thus, the "raising up" is restoration to health, not the resurrection. Sin was linked to physical illness in the church at Corinth (1 Cor. 11:29 – 32), and James may have wanted to assure his hearers that, in such cases, one's spiritual health and resultant physical health can be restored through the believing prayer of others.

5:16. James called for the members of the congregations to be honest with one another about their spiritual shortcomings: **Confess your faults one to another, and pray one for another**. The confession that James called for is "auricular confession" according to Roman Catholic teaching. Although confessing one's trespasses to others so that one might receive prayer and counsel is beneficial, James likely had something else in mind here. The instructions on confession are probably an exhortation to Christians to seek reconciliation with those whom they have wronged. The healing that results restores relationships within the church. (The verb in the phrase **that ye may be healed** is plural.) It is doubtful that James advocated public confession of all one's sins before the entire house church. The confession could be the sick person's admission of wrongdoing when the elders pray (vv. 14 – 15). James seems to have extended his instructions on prayer to the entire church ("one to another") at verse 16 since he moved from the third-person singular command ("let him call," v. 14) to the second-person imperative ("Confess," v. 16). "Confess" and "pray" are in the present tense, with the sense of "be confessing" and "be praying" (Wuest). The prayer of righteous people, as were James's hearers, **availeth much**. In other words, it "is powerful and effective" (NRSV).

5:17 – 18. Elijah prayed and acted on the promise God had already revealed to him. He knew God's will and was therefore praying God's will when he fervently prayed for God to send fire from heaven to consume his sacrifice (see 1 Kings 18:36), when he prayed **that it might not rain** (v. 17; and it did not for **three years and six months**; see 1 Kings 17:1), and when he fervently prayed for God to send rain after the long drought (see 1 Kings 18:1, 41–44). The immediate context suggests that James was using Elijah as an example of the power of prayer for one particular kind of prayer: the mutual prayer for one another mentioned in 5:16. The lesson readily extends to prayer of any kind. If Elijah, **a man subject to like passions as we are**, prayed so boldly and effectively, so can Christians today. If he, with all his faults, is considered to be a righteous person, so are believers in Christ. God desires to answer prayers that promote wholeness within the church.

B. Reintegration of the Wayward (5:19–20)

5:19–20. Major questions about this text are, Who is the one who is said to **err** ("wander," NIV) **from the truth** (v. 19)? and, What does it mean to **save a soul from death** (v. 20)? The one who errs could be (1) a false teacher. The verb "err" is used of the false teachers threatening the church in 2 Peter 2:15 ("which have forsaken the right way, and *are gone astray*") and of the deceivers in 1 John (2:26; 3:7). Although James confronted false concepts of faith and wisdom (chaps. 2–3), false teaching and false teachers do not appear to have been a problem in his churches as they were in the churches addressed by 2 Peter and 1 John. Hence, the reference to the one who errs may point elsewhere. The erring one could be (2) a professing Christian whose faith is not genuine (see Heb. 6:4–8; 2 Peter 2:20–21). If

so, then the "death" in verse 20 is "the second death" (Rev. 21:8). However, the erring one may be (3) a sinning Christian who needs to be restored. Jesus' procedure for reconciliation, in which one goes privately to a brother or sister who sins (see Matt. 18:15–17) to win the fellow believer over, may be alluded to here. (James did not envisage, however, the steps to be taken if the initial approach met with resistance; see Matt. 18:15–17.) In Corinth, some church members fell ill and died because they did not turn from sins of abuse of fellow church members (see 1 Cor. 11:30). James's may have been referring to people who do not confess their sins to fellow community members (see 5:16) and who thus live in enmity with a brother or sister. If they do not initiate the process of restored relationships, others must do it for them. Thus will they **hide a multitude of sins**, which means either that they will prevent further sins from being committed or that they will "cover" (NRSV) over sins of the past and forgive them. The context best supports the third option. In any case, God will forgive the sins of the one who errs.

James's final words of his letter were stark and strong for his original hearers, as they are today. What will believers do? Will they take upon themselves the responsibility for restored relationships within the church? Some church members, having been hurt by a fellow church member, have themselves left the church instead of seeking restored relationships with others. Such an action is not the way to wholeness and integration—the health of the church as James understood it.

THE FIRST EPISTLE OF PETER

INTRODUCTION

Author

The author identified himself as the apostle Peter (1:1). In the Gospels, Peter is the most prominent among the twelve apostles. His original name was Simon, a name probably derived from Simeon and related to the Hebrew word meaning "to hear." He is called Simeon in Acts 15:14. According to John 1:40–42, Jesus bestowed upon him the nickname Cephas (Aramaic, *Kepha*; "stone" or "rock"). The Greek form of that name is Petros, from which the English name Peter comes. Sometimes he is identified as Simon Peter (e.g., John 20:2), and on other occasions, Peter's Aramaic name, Cephas, is preserved (see 1 Cor. 1:12; 15:5; Gal. 2:9). In the early chapters of Acts, Peter emerged as the preeminent spokesman of the twelve apostles. His sermons were effective in calling people to belief in Jesus Christ (2:14–41; 3:12–26; 4:8–12; 5:29–32; 10:34–48). Peter fades from the New Testament when Acts turns its focus on Paul, but extrabiblical tradition claims that Peter died a martyr's death for Christ.

Although the authenticity of 1 Peter is often disputed, the contents and character of the letter support his authorship (see discussion on 5:1–2). Moreover, the letter reflects the history and terminology of the Gospels and Acts (notably Peter's speeches); its themes and concepts reflect Peter's experiences and his associations in the period of our Lord's earthly ministry and in the apostolic age. That he was acquainted, for example, with Paul and his letters is made clear in 2 Peter 3:15–16; Galatians 1:18; 2:1–21 and elsewhere; coincidences in thought and expression with Paul's writings are therefore not surprising.

From the beginning, 1 Peter was recognized as authoritative and as the work of the apostle Peter. The earliest extant reference to it is 2 Peter 3:1, where Peter himself referred to a former letter he had written. First Clement (AD 95) seems to indicate acquaintance with 1 Peter. Polycarp, a disciple of the apostle John, made use of 1 Peter in his letter to the Philippians. The author of the Gospel of Truth (AD 140–150) was acquainted with 1 Peter. Eusebius (fourth century) indicated that it was universally received. The letter was explicitly ascribed to Peter by that group of church fathers whose testimonies appear in the attestation of so many of the genuine New Testament writings, namely, Irenaeus (AD 140–203), Tertullian (150–222), Clement of Alexandria (155–215), and Origen (185–253). It is thus clear that Peter's authorship of the book had early and strong support.

Nevertheless, some claim that the idiomatic Greek of this letter was beyond Peter's competence. It is true that the Greek of 1 Peter is good literary Greek, and even though Peter could no doubt speak Greek (as so many in the Mediterranean world could), many have thought it unlikely that he would have written such polished Greek. It is at this point that Peter's remark in 5:12 concerning Silvanus may be significant. Here the apostle claimed that he wrote "by," or (more literally) "by means of," Silvanus (Greek, *dia Silouanou*). This phrase could refer to Silvanus as a letter carrier, the one who delivered 1 Peter to its recipients, but it could also denote Silvanus as the intermediate agent in writing. Some have claimed that Silvanus's qualifications for recording Peter's letter in literary Greek are found in Acts 15:22–29, where Silas (Silvanus is perhaps a Latinized form of Silas) is associated with the letter from Jerusalem to Antioch. Secretaries (also known as *amanuenses*) commonly wrote letters from dictation; Tertius was Paul's amanuensis for the letter to the Romans (see Rom. 16:22). A secretary in those days often composed documents in good Greek for those who did not have the linguistic facility to do so. Thus, 1 Peter may reflect Silvanus's polished Greek, while in 2 Peter, it may be Peter's rough Greek that appears.

Date

Some who question Peter's authorship of the letter also maintain that it reflects a situation that did not exist until after Peter's death, suggesting that the persecution referred to in 4:14–16; 5:8–9 is descriptive of Domitian's reign (AD 81–96). The date of 1 Peter, according to still others, is circa AD 112—the time of the correspondence between Pliny the Younger, who was the governor of Bithynia (1:1), and the Roman Emperor Trajan. In that correspondence, executions of Christians in the province are mentioned. First Peter addresses Christians under distress because of the hostility of the Roman authorities.

However, the opposition against Christians that was developing in Nero's time (AD 54–68) is adequately described by the references to suffering in 1 Peter. The letter contains no clear reference to martyrdom on the part of Christians; rather, the Christians' suffering involves social ostracism, slander, and dishonor. Occasionally, local officials may have moved against the Christians to neutralize what may have been perceived as a threat to public order, but no official policy against Peter's audience is evident. A late first-century or early second-century date for 1 Peter is, therefore, not required by the evidence. The book can be satisfactorily dated in the period AD 62–68, during Peter's ministry in Rome before his death, which occurred sometime between AD 64 and 68. The apparent echoes of Paul's Prison Epistles (compare 1 Peter 1:1–3 with Eph. 1:1–3; 1 Peter 2:18 with Col. 3:22; 1 Peter 3:1–6 with Eph. 5:22–24), which should be dated no earlier than AD 60, might suggest that 1 Peter should not be placed earlier than AD 60 as well. The similarities, however, may be due to a shared Christian tradition and not necessarily to Peter's knowledge of Paul's letters.

Place of Composition

Peter indicated that he was "at Babylon" (5:13) when he wrote 1 Peter. Among the interpretations that have been suggested for the identification of "Babylon" are that Peter was writing from (1) Egyptian Babylon, which was a military post, (2) Mesopotamian Babylon, (3) Jerusalem, or (4) Rome. Although sites known as Babylon existed in both

Mesopotamia and Egypt in the first century, there is no firm evidence that connects Peter with those locations. A symbolic reference to Jerusalem as "Babylon" is unlikely, but symbolic use of the name Babylon for Rome would coincide with the use of the term in the book of Revelation (see Revelation 17–18). Nero's decadent and oppressive rule in Rome certainly would recall the place of exile for God's people in the Old Testament, and Roman writers themselves described luxurious and degenerate Rome as "Babylon" before AD 70. Furthermore, tradition connects Peter in the latter part of his life with Rome, not Jerusalem, and certainly not with Mesopotamian Babylon. The best conclusion, therefore, is that Peter intended "Babylon" to stand for "Rome" in 5:13.

Recipients

The intended audience of 1 Peter is identified in 1:1: "the strangers scattered throughout Pontus, Galatia, Cappadocia, Asia, and Bithynia." These geographical areas were Roman provinces (Pontus and Bythnia had been combined into one administrative unit) in what is now Turkey, and the region they comprised was vast — 128,889 square miles — a culturally diverse land of approximately 8,500,000 inhabitants. Probably both rural and urban communities received the courier (possibly Silvanus; see "Author," above, and discussion on 5:12) who bore this epistle. He would have read the letter aloud to the congregations; only thereafter would multiple copies have been available for individual churches.

The many quotations from and allusions to the Old Testament indicate that the original hearers of 1 Peter were conversant with the Hebrew Scriptures. Were they Jewish Christians? Undoubtedly, many within the Christian communities in the vast region indicated in 1:1 were Jews of the Diaspora. (The number of Jews throughout Asia Minor at that time would have been at least a quarter million.) However, Peter (himself a Jew) probably would not have addressed Jews who had believed in Christ as those who had been redeemed "from your vain conversation received by tradition from your fathers" (1:18; see 4:3) because the tradition of Jewish culture and upbringing would have included the ethical standards upheld by the New Testament. The audience of 1 Peter, therefore, likely was predominantly Gentile Christians, with a significant Jewish Christian minority. The term "Gentiles," used in the KJV (2:12; 4:3–4) to describe the opponents of Peter's hearers, should be understood as "pagans" (NIV; REB 4:3) or "unbelievers" (REB 2:12).

The description of the recipients of 1 Peter as "strangers and pilgrims" (2:11; see 1:1) could be metaphorical: the harassed Christian minority was not at home in this world and looked forward to going to its true, heavenly home. Some maintain that the terms "strangers" and "pilgrims" (*paroikoi, parepidēmoi*) refer to the social, cultural, political, and religious estrangement of the Christians. A more accurate translation of these terms is "resident aliens" and "visiting strangers." With his first letter, Peter intended to promote endurance, cohesion within the Christian communities, and testimony of good behavior to the unbelievers around them. Thus, the church would strengthen itself and avoid assimilation to the pagan world.

Theme and Theological Message

Peter stated that he had "written briefly, exhorting, and testifying that this is the true grace of God" (5:12). This is a definitive general description of the letter, but it does not exclude the recognition of numerous subordinate and contributory themes. Although it is a short letter, 1 Peter touches on various doctrines and has much to say about Christian life and duties. It is not surprising that different readers see different principal themes. It has, for example, been characterized as a letter of separation, of suffering and persecution, of suffering and glory, of hope, of pilgrimage, of courage, and as a letter dealing with the true grace of God. The letter is composed also of a series of exhortations (imperatives), which run from 1:13 to 5:11.

Literary Features

First Peter exhibits a striking similarity to standards of Greco-Roman rhetoric, especially the pattern of argumentation in the Latin handbook titled *Rhetorica ad Herennium* ("Rhetoric to Herennius"). In this fivefold pattern, the proposition states the main point of the argument. The reason expresses the basis for the proposition, and is itself followed by a corroboration, the proof of the reason. Once the proof of the reason has been established, an embellishment of the argument appears. The final element is a conclusion, which collects and ties up the parts of the argument. Peter may not have formally studied classical rhetoric, but his composition resembles the structure. The following outline of the structure of 1 Peter demonstrates the way in which the epistle corresponds to this rhetorical structure.

Outline

 I. Salutation (1:1–2)
 II. Prologue (1:3–12)
 III. First Argument: Hope to the End in Holiness (1:13–2:10)
  A. Proposition (1:13–16)
  B. Reason (1:17)
  C. Proof of the Reason (1:18–21)
  D. Embellishment (1:22–25)
  E. Conclusion (2:1–10)
 IV. Second Argument: Hope to the End with Honor (2:11–3:12)
  A. Proposition (2:11–12a)
  B. Reason (2:12b)
  C. Proof of the Reason (2:13–17)
  D. Embellishment (2:18–3:7)
  E. Conclusion (3:8–12)
 V. Third Argument: Hope to the End against Adversity (3:13–4:11)
  A. Proposition (3:13–16a)
  B. Reason (3:16b)
  C. Proof of the Reason (3:17)
  D. Embellishment (3:18–22)
  E. Conclusion (4:1–11)
 VI. Closing (4:12–5:14)
  A. Further Examination of the Topic of Suffering (4:12–19)
  B. A Farewell Speech of Exhortation (5:1–11)

1. Self-Vindication (5:1)
2. A Call to Tend the Flock (5:2a–b)
3. A Warning against Greed (5:2c–3)
4. Reward and Judgment (5:4)
5. Love and Humility (5:5–7)
6. An Exhortation to Watch and Stand Firm (5:8a)
7. Discussion of the Enemy (5:8b)
8. A Prediction of Suffering (5:9–11)
   C. Closing Remarks and Greeting (5:12–14)

Bibliography

Best, Ernest. *1 Peter*. New Century Bible. Grand Rapids, MI: Eerdmans, 1971.

Campbell, Barth L. *Honor, Shame, and the Rhetoric of 1 Peter*. Society of Biblical Literature Dissertation Series 160. Atlanta: Scholars Press, 1998.

Davids, Peter H. *The First Epistle of Peter*. The New International Commentary on the New Testament. Grand Rapids, MI: Eerdmans, 1990.

Grudem, Wayne A. *The First Epistle of Peter: An Introduction and Commentary*. Tyndale New Testament Commentaries 17. Grand Rapids, MI: Eerdmans, 1988.

Hillyer, Norman. *1 and 2 Peter, Jude*. The New International Biblical Commentary. Peabody, MA: Hendrickson, 1992.

Marshall, I. Howard. *1 Peter*. The IVP New Testament Commentary 17. Downers Grove, IL: InterVarsity, 1991.

Michaels, J. Ramsey. *1 Peter*. Word Biblical Commentary 49. Waco, TX: Word, 1988.

Stibbs, Alan M., and Andrew F. Walls. *The First Epistle General of Peter*. Vol. 7. Tyndale New Testament Commentaries. Grand Rapids, MI: Eerdmans, 1959.

EXPOSITION

I. Salutation (1:1–2)

1:1. Peter described himself as **an apostle of Jesus Christ**, which designates him as one of the twelve disciples who accompanied Jesus during His earthly ministry and one who had seen the resurrected Christ. The title established and enhanced Peter's authority in the eyes of his audience, which would have been particularly needed if he had never visited the regions to which the letter was sent. There is no evidence that Peter had visited **Pontus, Galatia, Cappadocia, Asia, and Bithynia**, but he may have. People from this area were in Jerusalem on the day of Pentecost (see Acts 2:9–11), and some may have become personally acquainted with Peter. Paul, how-

ever, preached and taught in some of these provinces (see, e.g., Acts 16:6; 18:23; 19:10, 26).

1:2. Elect. That the recipients of the letter had been specifically chosen **according to the foreknowledge of God the Father** would have inspired within them a sense of honor and privileged status. All three persons of the Trinity are involved in the redemption of the elect. The order of the terms employed suggests that the **sanctification of the Spirit** is here the influence of the Spirit that draws one from sin toward holiness. **Unto obedience and sprinkling of the blood of Jesus Christ** may mean that the Spirit's sanctifying leads to obedient saving faith and cleansing from sin, or that the election of

God has as its purpose obedience and forgiveness through Christ's blood. "Sprinkling" evokes an association with the blood of the Mosaic covenant (see Exod. 24:6–8; Heb. 9:19–21) and thus signifies the basis of a new covenant.

Grace unto you, and peace. This greeting is standard in New Testament letters (see, e.g., Rom. 1:7; 1 Cor. 1:3; Phil. 1:2), but its importance ought not to be overlooked. It would have reminded Peter's audience of their honored status before God, emphasized by the fact that it can **be multiplied** (see 2 Peter 1:2).

II. Prologue (1:3–12)

In the prologue, Peter instructed his audience about their honored identity and status as Christians. The blessings they had received and the virtues of their character are celebrated.

1:3. By His **abundant mercy,** God has given believers a new birth. He has done so out of His fatherly compassion. Therefore, despite adversity, the experience of His having **begotten us again** signifies His love and honor that He bestows. **Lively hope.** In the Bible, hope is not wishful thinking but a firm conviction, much like faith that is directed toward the future. The fact of Christ's risen existence makes the hope of His followers "lively" (or "living," NIV) — certain and strong, not baseless or empty. The original hearers of this letter, disdained by their contemporaries, would have understood hope in the sense of divine rescue and vindication from dishonorable treatment. **The resurrection of Jesus Christ from the dead** secures for His people their new birth and the hope that they will be resurrected just as He was.

1:4–5. To an inheritance (v. 4). Believers are born again not only to a hope but also to the inheritance that is the substance of that hope. The audiences in Asia Minor, including many economically displaced aliens, had little hope of acquiring landed property as security for the future. The inheritance of believers, described by the synonymous expression **salvation ready to be revealed in the last time** (v. 5), is eternal, in its essence (it is not subject to decay) and in its preservation (it is divinely kept for us). The Greek word that Peter used for **kept**

is *phroureō*, a military term meaning "protected" (NRSV), "shielded" (NIV), or "guarded." The expression is related to the term *phrouria*, which denoted the forts located throughout Pontus, Cappadocia, and Galatia. Just as settlements and territory in these regions were guarded by garrisons within fortifications, so the disdained and oppressed believers were protected **by the power of God through faith** that they would be brought safely into the salvation for which they hoped.

In 1 Peter, **salvation** (v. 5) is deliverance *from* all hostile and destructive influences and *to* the joyful and glorious experience of God's favor in Christ. Peter saw salvation as future in the sense that believers are guarded for its unveiling **in the last time** and that believers grow into it (see discussion on 2:2).

1:6. Wherein (i.e., in all the blessings described in 1:3–5) **ye greatly rejoice, though now for a season, if need be, ye are in heaviness through manifold temptations** ("various trials," NASB). Such trials could be enticements to sin if those experiencing them entertain the possibility of abandoning faithful endurance. All trials cause their sufferers to be "in heaviness" ("you have been distressed," NASB; "you may have had to suffer grief," NIV), but Peter assured his readers that the anguish was "now for a season" ("though now for a little while," NIV) and only "if need be." God's will for a believer sometimes requires endurance of suffering so that he or she may grow. Those who suffer are assured of an end of their difficulties, either at the coming of Christ or at some point before that (5:10; see discussion on 3:13–16).

1:7. That the trial of your faith … might be found unto praise denotes the result of the heaviness that comes through tests. Here the word "trial" (*dokimion*) refers not to the "temptations" of 1:6 but to the "genuineness" (NRSV) of the hearers' faith, which was demonstrated through the testing of their faith. Peter compared this testing to gold in two ways: (1) the refining of gold (**tried with fire**), through which impurities and deficiencies are eliminated, serves as a picture of trials in the Christian life, and (2) proven faith is **much more precious than of gold that perisheth.** Despite its value as a pure and precious metal, refined gold is destined to pass away (see 1:24).

1:8. Peter commended his audience for their love in the Lord, whom they had **not seen**. In other words, **though now ye see him not, yet believing, ye rejoice**. Love, belief, and joy go hand in hand. A joyless belief is not genuine, nor is true joy possible without a complete dependence on the Lord, who may seem hidden when one is enduring distress. The approval Peter expressed here is similar to Jesus' saying in John 20:29, uttered on an occasion when Peter was present: "blessed are they that have not seen, and yet have believed" (John 20:29).

Glory, a key word in 1 Peter (1:7 – 8, 11, 21, 24; 4:11, 13 – 14; 5:1, 4, 10), refers to the eternal and majestic resplendence of God (see 5:10) that is shared by Christ (see 1:11, 21; 4:11, 13) and the Holy Spirit (see 4:14). Believers share in that glory (see 1:7 – 8; 5:1, 4) as God vindicates them in spite of their dishonorable status before humans and the world's false conceptions of glory (see 1:24).

1:9. The word **souls** implies the whole person; Peter was not excluding the body from heaven. The term designates either the animate part of a person or the entire person as seen from the angle of one's relatedness to God. Salvation, **the end of your faith** (i.e., the goal toward which the life of faith is directed) is experienced in the present as well as in the past and the future (see discussion on 1:5). Salvation experienced now is a basis for and a result of Christian joy.

1:10 – 12. Peter's catalogue of blessings and virtues includes the service of **the prophets** (v. 10). Some have suggested that here "the prophets" refers to spokespeople of God in the early Christian communities who were inspired with messages of instruction and exhortation for the church. More likely, however, it refers to the Old Testament prophets, since Peter distinguished them from those who, coming later, **have preached the gospel unto you with the Holy Ghost sent down from heaven** (v. 12). Christ sent the Holy Spirit on the day of Pentecost (Acts 2:33), at which Peter was present. Inspiration does not always mean illumination, however. Thus, the prophets **enquired and searched diligently** (v. 10) regarding the forecast of sufferings and subsequent glories.

Peter's readers would have been honored to know that **unto us they** (the prophets) **did minister ... the gospel ... which things the angels desire to look into** (v. 12). The angels' intense desire is highlighted by the Greek word rendered "to look into" (*parakyptō*), which means "to stoop and look intently" (see John 20:5, 11). The believers were honored indeed; they could understand truths that even angels cannot quite fathom.

III. First Argument: Hope to the End in Holiness (1:13 – 2:10)

A. Proposition (1:13 – 16)

1:13 – 16. Hope to the end for the grace that is to be brought unto you at the revelation of Jesus Christ (v. 13). This is the first of a series of three imperative constructions that constitute propositions for the arguments in the letter. In 1 Peter, "grace" (*charis*) refers to honor divinely bestowed on those who are suffering (see 2:12; 3:16; 4:4). The term, which appears ten times in this epistle (1:2, 10, 13; 2:19, 20; 3:7, 4:10; 5:5, 10, 12), has a sociocultural denotation as much as a theological one. Peter indicated that a major purpose of this letter was to encourage his readers and testify regarding the true grace of God (see 5:12). On this grace, they were to **hope to the end** (*teleiōs*) or "completely" (NASB).

Four expressions describe the action of the main verb in the proposition ("hope"). (1) **Gird up the loins of your mind** (v. 13) is a graphic call for action. In the language of the first century, it meant that one should literally gather up one's long, flowing garments and be ready for physical action. (2) **Be sober** may be intended in a literal sense as a prohibition of drunkenness, or it may pertain to a general attitude of self-control. (3) **As obedient children, not fashioning yourselves according to the former lusts in your ignorance** (v. 14). Christians, born into the family of God (see 1:23), are children of their heavenly Father (see 1:17). Believers are also described as being adopted into God's family (see Rom. 8:15). The image of "obedient children" represents one of the most powerful concepts of the letter: the household of God. By maintaining their unique identity as God's household, Peter's audience could resist the pressures to conform to their pagan past. In other words, (4) **be ye holy in all manner of conversation** (v. 15; "in all your behavior," NASB). Hope is to be accompanied by holiness. God commands His people, **Be ye holy; for I am holy** (v. 16). To be holy is to be set apart, set apart from sin and impurity and set apart to God. Thus, God moves His people to strive for moral purity.

B. Reason (1:17)

1:17. In this verse, Peter provided further warrant for holy living and explained why believers should set their hope upon the future unveiling of grace. According to 1:15, the holiness of God demands holiness in return. A similar thought appears here: God is described as One **who without respect of persons judgeth according to every man's work**. He will give honor and vindication to the one who deserves it. **Ye call on the Father** refers to the cry for vindication of those who are harassed for their faith. Elsewhere in the New Testament, the word for "call" has the sense of lodging an appeal for honor or vindication (see Acts 7:59; 25:11, 12, 21; 26:32; 28:19). Peter's audience made this appeal to the One who judges absolutely justly; thus he advised them, **pass the time of your sojourning here in fear**. "Sojourning" (*paroikia*; "exile," NRSV) refers to the readers' cultural and ethnic estrangement from the surrounding society. The time of their sojourning would end whenever God vindicated these resident aliens with honor. Until that time, the Christians were to "live in reverent fear" (NRSV) of God. The just Judge will answer those who appeal to Him as Father only if they live in reverent honor to Him. All Christians may address God as their Father (Matt. 6:9), but they cannot expect Him to have answers to prayer if they refuse to honor Him as such. The divine justice and discipline requires such reciprocity.

C. Proof of the Reason (1:18–21)

1:18–20. The proof corroborates the reason with additional arguments. These arguments provide further bases for the proposition (1:13–16). **The precious blood of Christ** (v. 19) invokes positive feelings of loyalty when it is placed in contrast with the negative **corruptible things, as silver and gold** (v. 18). The former is the price by which the readers had been **redeemed**. In the Bible, "to redeem" means to free someone by the payment of a penalty or a ransom (see Exod. 13:13; 21:30). Likewise, in the Greek world, slaves could be redeemed by the payment of a price, either by someone else or by the slave himself. Similarly, Jesus redeems believers "from the curse of the law" (Gal. 3:13) and "from all iniquity" (Titus 2:14). The ransom price is not silver or gold, but Christ's blood (Eph. 1:7; 1 Peter 1:19; Rev. 5:9), that is, Christ's death (Matt. 20:28; Mark 10:45; Heb. 9:15) or Christ Himself (Gal. 3:13). The result is "the forgiveness of sins" (Col. 1:14) and "being justified" (Rom. 3:24).

The **vain conversation received by tradition from your fathers** (v. 18; "your futile way of life inherited from your forefathers," NASB) indicates to some that the recipients must have been pagans; the New Testament stresses the emptiness of pagan life (see Rom. 1:21; Eph. 4:17). Others think they were Jews since Jews were traditionalists who stressed the influence of the father as teacher in the home. In the light of the context of the whole letter, Peter was probably addressing both Jews and Gentiles. The redemptive power of God, in both cases, is stressed. He is able to liberate the captive completely "from" (*ek*, "out of") the worthless and empty life apart from God.

The Old Testament sacrifices were types (foreshadowings) of Christ, depicting the ultimate and only effective sacrifice. Christ is the Passover **Lamb** (v. 19; see 1 Cor. 5:7), who takes away the sin of the world (John 1:29). He is **without blemish and without spot**. Thus, He is the perfect sacrifice, adequate for the forgiveness of all sins (see Num. 28:19; Heb. 9:14). As such a sacrifice, Christ was **foreordained before the foundation of the world** (v. 20). God knew before creation that it would be necessary for Christ to redeem humankind (see Rev. 13:8), but He has revealed Christ in "these last times." The Greek for "foreordained" may also be rendered "chosen" (NIV) or "foreknown" (NASB).

The expression **but was manifest in these last times for you** (v. 20) is consistent with the thoroughly eschatological (i.e., with a view toward the second coming of Christ) perspective of 1 Peter (1:5–7, 13; 4:5–6, 7, 13, 17; 5:1, 4). "For you" stresses the honor of the readers: they themselves were the objects of the eternal purpose of God in Christ, which provided them with motivation for living in hope and holiness.

1:21. Peter concluded the proof of the reason with two topics that were common in early Christian preaching: God **raised him** (Christ) **up from the dead, and gave him glory**. Peter, as one of the individuals to whom the risen Jesus appeared after emerging from the tomb (see 1 Cor. 15:5), was certain of the resurrection as a historical fact. The resurrection and exaltation of Christ was to encourage the ridiculed believers; as Christ had been vindicated, so they could hope to be vindicated as well.

D. Embellishment (1:22–25)

1:22–25. Here Peter enriched the argument, beginning by masterfully outlining the Christian life. Its ultimate purpose and expression is to **love** (*agapaō*) **one another with a pure heart fervently** (v. 22; see 2 Peter 1:5–7), but reception of **the Spirit**, obedience, growth in sanctification (**ye have purified your souls**), and **unfeigned love** (*philadelphia*) **of the brethren** are the intermediate steps. These phenomena overlap, of course, but love crowns them all. Such characteristics are the marks of the person who is **born again** (v. 23), and that by **the word of God**. The new birth comes about through the direct action of the Holy Spirit (see Titus 3:5), but the Word of God also plays an important role (see James 1:18), for it presents **the gospel** (v. 25) to the sinner and calls on him to repent and believe in Christ.

E. Conclusion (2:1–10)

2:1–3. Wherefore (v. 1) connects 1:23–25 with the exhortations that follow (compare **newborn babes** [v. 2] with "born again" [1:23]), concluding

Peter's first argument. The sins of verse 1 are offenses against the unity of the Christian family and are to be put away. Instead, the unrestrained hunger of a healthy baby provides an example of the kind of eager **desire** (v. 2) for spiritual food that ought to mark the believer. **The sincere milk of the word** ("the pure, spiritual milk," NRSV) is figurative; milk is not to be understood here in unfavorable contrast to solid food (as in 1 Cor. 3:2; Heb. 5:12–14) but as an appropriate nourishment for babies. The Greek word for **grow** is the standard term for the desirable growth of children. The tense of the Greek verb **have tasted** (v. 3) suggests that an initial act of tasting. Since this taste proved satisfactory, Peter urged the believers to long for additional spiritual food.

2:4. Peter's hearers not only were honored by their inclusion in God's household as newborn babes, but they came unto Christ, the **living stone**. The metaphor of Christ as stone permeates 2:4–8. The parallel metaphor of Christians as stones in the building of which Christ is the corner is also present. Both the Stone and the stones share rejection from humans. However, although Christ was **disallowed indeed of men**, He was **chosen of God**. In Acts, Peter repeatedly made a contrast between the hostility of unbelieving men toward Jesus and God's exaltation of Him (see Acts 2:22–36; 3:13–15; 4:10–11; 10:39–42). Believers can take comfort in that fact; they too are dishonored, but they can expect God to vindicate them in due time.

2:5. Followers of Christ are already honored by God in that **as lively stones**, they **are built up a spiritual house**. The Old Testament temple may provide the background of the image of a house, but the word here may have the idea of "household." Nevertheless, the metaphor of the believers as **a holy priesthood, to offer up spiritual sacrifices, acceptable to God by Jesus Christ** does recall the temple and its sacrifices. According to Peter, all believers are themselves priests.

2:6–8. Chief corner stone (v. 6; see Ps. 118:22; Isa. 28:16; Matt. 21:42; Mark 12:10; Luke 20:17; Acts 4:11; Rom. 9:33) is an obvious reference to Christ, as this passage makes clear. The cornerstone, which determines the design and orientation of the building, is the most significant stone in the structure. The term may signify the keystone that was set over the gate or porch of a building, or it may be equivalent to **the head of the corner** (v. 7). In either case, the term designates honor. The picture that Peter created is of a structure made up of believers ("lively stones," 2:5), the design and orientation of which are all in keeping with Christ, the Cornerstone.

Two attitudes toward the Cornerstone are evident. (1) Some trust in Him and **shall not be confounded** (v. 6; "will by no means be put to shame," NKJV); rather, they are honored. **Unto you therefore which believe he is precious** (v. 7) should rather be "to you believers, therefore, that honour belongs" (Weymouth). (2) Others reject Him (v. 7) and, as a result, **stumble** (v. 8) and fall.

Whereunto also they were appointed (v. 8). The result of disobedience, not the decision to disobey, is that which is foreordained. The idea that God predestines some to unbelief and condemnation is not present here. The issue is honor and shame. Those who respond to Christ in unbelieving disobedience can look forward only to shame (**stumbling**) and not to the honor believers enjoy. This is the consequence that God has established for those who choose to disobey.

2:9 – 10. As a final encouragement for his readers, Peter introduced some wonderful titles for God's people to convey their honored position. Regardless of whatever suffering they may have to endure, they are still **a chosen generation** (v. 9; see 1:1 – 2; Isa. 43:10, 20; 44:1 – 2). As Israel was called God's chosen people in the Old Testament, so believers are designated as chosen, or elect, in the New Testament. They are also **a royal priesthood** (see Exod. 19:6; Isa. 61:6), **a holy nation** (see Deut. 28:9), and **a peculiar people** (see Deut. 4:20; 7:6; 14:2; Isa. 43:21; Mal. 3:17). The last description could have the sense of Christians being "God's own people" (NRSV) or "a people belonging to God" (NIV). The purpose of the bestowal of these distinctions is **that ye should shew forth the praises** of God. Peter's missionary interest (see 2:12; 3:1) is clear in that expression.

"Shew forth" has the idea of "proclaim" (NRSV) or "declare" (NIV) God's "excellencies" (NASB).

IV. Second Argument: Hope to the End with Honor (2:11 – 3:12)

A. Proposition (2:11 – 12a)

2:11 – 12a. The proposition of the second argument is twofold: a negative command, **abstain from fleshly lusts** (v. 11), followed by a positive directive, **having your conversation honest among the Gentiles** (v. 12a). This positive directive ("Conduct yourselves honorably among the Gentiles," NRSV) is expanded in 2:13 – 3:12. For **strangers and pilgrims,** see Introduction: "Recipients."

B. Reason 2:12b

2:12b. The reason for the twofold proposition was so that the pagans might **glorify God.** Honorable conduct that promotes an effective Christian witness to skeptics and slanderers is respect for others, not retaliation in speech. False opinions and malicious treatment will then be reversed, and glory will be given to God. **Good works, which they shall behold** are deeds that can be seen to be good (see Matt. 5:16). The Greek word translated "behold" (*epopteuō*) refers to the pagans carefully watching over a period of time, not a snap judgment. "Glorify God" is synonymous with "believe in God" and is an apt expression here since it signifies that a reversal of opinion, from shame to honor and glory, is connected with belief. The unbelievers would praise God for the Christians and their effective witness. **The day of visitation** is perhaps the day of judgment and ensuing punishment, or it may be the day when God visits a person with salvation. The believer's good life may then influence the unbeliever to repent and believe.

C. Proof of the Reason 2:13 – 17

2:13 – 17. Three classifications of people are to be the objects of a Christian's submissive and respectful behavior. Such behavior is an example of the "good works" of 2:12; Peter's three contexts for good works corroborate the reason of the argument. First of all, political authorities (**the king**, v. 13, and **governors**, v. 14), as those who punish the wicked and reward the upright (v. 14), deserve the Christian's respect. Good citizenship counters false charges made against Christians, commends the gospel to unbelievers, and (as Peter boldly affirmed) serves to **put to silence the ignorance of foolish men** (v. 15). One cannot use Christian **liberty for a cloke of maliciousness** (v. 16), or "as a cover-up for evil" (NIV). Such an attitude is not that of true **servants of God**. Peter's instruction here is general and applies to a time of general tolerance of Christian activity by Rome. Even if Peter wrote at the time of Nero's violent mistreatment of Christians in the capital city of the empire (AD 64), neither a widespread nor an official opposition to Christianity existed in Asia Minor at that time. By the time of Revelation, the situation had changed dramatically, at least in the province of Asia. Compare Peter's words in these verses with Paul's statements in Romans 13:1–7. Of course, obedience to the emperor was never to violate of the law of God (for this basic principle in action, see Acts 4:19; 5:29). Both Peter and Paul enjoined submission if the authorities functioned **for the punishment of evildoers, and for the praise of them that do well** (v. 14). Peter summarized this section with a call for honorable behavior: **Honour all men. Love the brotherhood. Fear God. Honour the king** (v. 17).

D. Embellishment (2:18–3:7)

Peter's instructions in this section are a list of responsibilities known as a "household code." Such lists appear elsewhere in the New Testament (Eph. 5:22–6:9; Col. 3:18–4:1; 1 Tim. 6:1–2; Titus 2:1–10); in them, spouses, parents, children, slaves, and masters are addressed—all typically members in the kind of households where early Christian gatherings took place. Peter enriched the argument, whose twofold proposition is "abstain from fleshly lusts" (2:11) and "having your conversation honest" (2:12), with an enumeration of household duties.

2:18. The word **Servants** refers to household servants (*oiketai*), not to slaves generally (*douloi*). Peter was concerned with the household as Christian community. He mentioned these Christian servants first because they provided the example of honorable behavior for the entire church: **be subject to your masters.**

2:19–20. The servants who **endure grief, suffering wrongfully** (v. 19) do something that **is thankworthy** ("finds favor," NASB). The concept of suffering is prominent throughout 1 Peter. Of forty New Testament occurrences of the Greek word *paschō* ("to suffer"), eleven of them are in 1 Peter (2:19, 20, 21, 23; 3:14, 17, 18; 4:1, 15, 19; 5:10). The word "suffering" (*pathēma*) appears four times in 1 Peter (all plural: 1:11; 4:13; 5:1, 9), out of a total of sixteen occurrences in the entire New Testament.

Believers do not always suffer because of something they have done wrong; sometimes it is for something they have done right. Living with a **conscience toward God** (v. 19; "being aware of God," NRSV) sometimes brings suffering. Some of the slaves in Peter's audience may have been **buffeted** (v. 20; "beaten," NKJV). Whatever the source of the discomfort, Peter's emphasis was on whether **ye take it patiently** ("If you endure," NRSV).

2:21. The Christian is **called** to endurance in the face of unjust suffering **because Christ also suffered for us** in this way. What is true for the greater (Christ) is true for the lesser (the servants and, by extension, all believers). The word **example** (*hypogrammos*) designates the "pattern" of letters in ancient schoolbooks that students copied or an artist's outline that pupils completed. As believers **follow his steps,** they are truly his disciples and have honor before God.

2:22–23. In this section (2:22–25) rich with allusions and quotations from the servant song of Isaiah 52:13–53:12, the example of Christ's patient endurance is described in detail. All through the agony of His trial, scourging, and crucifixion, Jesus committed **no sin.** Peter especially had in mind deceptive (**guile**; v. 22), abusive (**reviled not;** 23), and retaliatory (**threatened not**) speech that Christ could have thrown back at His tormentors. Rather, He **committed himself to him that judgeth righteously.** Since Christ left to God all vengeance and vindication of Himself, so should His followers commit their cause to God.

2:24. Although dealing with Christ's example, Peter also touched on His redemptive work, which has significance far beyond that of setting an example. Here Peter pointed to the substitutionary character of the atonement: He **bare our sins in his own body on the tree** (see Isa. 53:12). Christ, like the sacrificial lamb of the Old Testament, died for our sins, the innocent for the guilty. The word "tree" is a figurative reference to the cross (see Acts 5:30; 10:39; 13:29) and carries the idea that Christ took on Himself the curse of disobedience so that believers might be redeemed (see Deut. 21:23; Gal. 3:13).

The expression **ye were healed** (see Isa. 53:5) is not generally viewed as a reference to physical healing, though some believe that such healing was included in the atonement (see Matt. 8:16–17). Others see spiritual healing in this passage. It is another way of asserting that Christ's death brings salvation to those who trust in Him.

2:25. Shepherd (see 5:4) is an allusion to the wandering sheep of Isaiah 53. Since Christ is the **Bishop** ("guardian," NRSV) of believers' souls, elders are to be both shepherds and guardians; they are to look out for the welfare of the flock. These are not two separate offices or functions; the second term is a further explanation of the first (see 5:2, 4; Acts 20:28).

3:1. Instructions to **wives** now appear (3:1–6). As Peter exhorted believers to submit to government authorities (2:13–17), and slaves to submit to masters (2:18–25), **likewise** he exhorted the women, **be in subjection to your own husbands.** Peter employed the same Greek verb (*hypotassō*) that he used in 2:13 and 18, a term that calls for submission to a recognized authority. This passage does not imply inferiority. The submission is one of role or function and is necessary for the orderly operation of the home and for Christian witness to an unbelieving spouse. The wife is to assume a respectful and gentle demeanor toward her husband in order to influence him for Christ.

Here again, Peter's evangelistic interest (see 2:9, 12) is evident. The husbands who disbelieve (**obey**

not the word) may **be won by the conversation** (respectful attitude; "behavior," NIV) **of the wives** even without a **word.** The first instance of "the word" in this verse refers to the gospel message; the second instance, to verbal witnessing. Believing wives are to rely not on argumentation to win their unbelieving husbands but on the quality of their lives. Of course, Peter was not forbidding wives to talk to their unbelieving husbands about Christ; rather, his point was that their witness must be backed up by Christlike attitudes.

3:2–4. Chaste conversation ("conduct," NKJV) **coupled with fear** (v. 2) indicates that the wives' lives are to be marked by a moral purity that springs from reverence of God. **Hair … gold … apparel** (v. 3) refer to extreme coiffures, gaudy jewelry, and expensive garments. Christian women should not rely on such extremes of adornment for beauty. Peter did not forbid neatness and pleasing appearance but excessive attention to good looks and preoccupation with one's attractiveness. One's focus should be on the inner person: **a meek** ("gentle," NIV) **and quiet spirit** (v. 4), which brings honor from the Lord and **is in the sight of God of great price,** that is, "very precious in God's sight" (NRSV).

3:5–6. The apostle appealed to **the holy women** (v. 5) of past ages as an inspiration for women in his day. Those women of previous generations put their hope in God for vindication of their honor (see 1:13). **Sara** (v. 6) particularly is to be imitated since she **obeyed Abraham, calling him lord.** Biblical instructions for a wife "to submit" in no way demands that she allow physical or psychological abuse of herself or her children. Though the apostle addressed mixed marriages, he presumed that the unbelieving husband in such a marriage would be persuadable and responsive to his believing wife.

3:7. Peter next turned to the relationship of the Christian husband to his wife. **Likewise** indicates that Peter was once again setting forth a specific way to "abstain from fleshly lusts" (2:11) and "having your conversation honest" (2:12). The emphasis in the text is that the husband is to **giv[e] honour unto the wife.** In a society in which Christians were maligned and dishonored, the Christian home became the place where God's honor for His people was expressed and felt. That is what Peter meant when he said that men should **dwell with them** (their wives) **according to knowledge** ("must always treat their wives with consideration in their life together," NJB). A Christian husband is to be a conduit of God's honor to his wife so that she may experience it. Specific ways of expressing that honor are found in 3:8–12.

Weaker vessel may refer to a woman's relative weakness in physical strength in comparison with that of a man. Peter's statement that wives are **heirs together** (with their husbands) **of the grace of life** was a startling thought for his day: the woman is sacred and has the same right of access to God as does the man. The purpose for giving honor to one's wife is that **your prayers be not hindered**. Spiritual fellowship, with God and with one another, may be hindered by disregarding God's instructions concerning husband-wife relationships.

E. Conclusion (3:8–12)

In his second argument, Peter addressed all his readers in 2:11–17, spoke directly to slaves in 2:18–25, and addressed wives in 3:1–6 and husbands in 3:7. In his conclusion of the argument, he wrapped up his discussion of what it means to "abstain from fleshly lusts" (2:11) and "hav[e] your conversation honest" (2:12). The apostle encouraged all his readers to develop the appropriate virtues in their relations with others and with non-Christians.

3:8–9. One mind (v. 8) does not mean that Christians must see eye to eye on everything but that their underlying attitude and focus should be unity and service to one another. **Having compassion** translates the word from which the English term "sympathetic" comes. Each believer should be willing to enter the joys and sorrows of others. This requires attentive listening and putting one's own desires second. **Love as brethren, be pitiful,** or "have … a tender heart" (NRSV). The phrase **be courteous** is a good translation of the Greek "humble-minded" (*tapeinophrones*) since considerateness in manner

and speech is an appropriate expression of humility. **Knowing that ye are thereunto called** (v. 9). Peter's advice is counterintuitive to culture, but natural to "grace" living (see 2:19).

3:10–12. Peter introduced a quotation from Psalm 34:12–16 with the explanatory conjunction **For** (v. 10), showing that he viewed the quotation as giving reasons for obeying the exhortation of 3:9. First, the psalm gives a list of behaviors to avoid (**let him refrain his tongue from evil, and his lips that they speak no guile** ("deceitful speech," NIV), and **let him eschew evil** (v. 11; "turn from evil," NIV). Then follows a list of desirable actions to put in their place: **do good; let him seek peace** (i.e., in relationships), **and ensue** ("pursue," NIV) **it**. According to the psalmist, (1) the one who does such things will find life to be most gratifying, (2) his days will be good, (3) God's **eyes** (v. 12) will ever be on him to bless him, and (4) God's **ears** will be ready to hear his prayer. The responses of the Lord (3 and 4) are colorfully described through anthropomorphism, a figure of speech in which God is described as having human characteristics. Of course, the Almighty does not have literal human eyes and ears, but He is described as if He does to show that He responds to the human activity described in verses 10–11. **The face of the Lord is against them that do evil** signifies that God opposes the honor of the wicked with His own honor. The way to honor for Peter's audience, even in the midst of the reproach that they suffered as God's people, was to abstain from the kinds of evil listed in verses 10–11 and to practice the good listed there as well.

V. Third Argument: Hope to the End against Adversity (3:13–4:11)

A. Proposition (3:13–16a)

3:13–14a. Peter anticipated and answered a possible protest that might be voiced when his letter was delivered. He imagined the objection might be something like, "Even if we live submissively and humbly, Peter, we will still suffer. As you point out, we are aliens and strangers in our culture." The apostle's retort was, **And who is he that will harm**

you if ye be followers of that which is good? (v. 13). Even among the pagans, a general consensus of right and wrong would acknowledge Christian behavior as honorable. Peter, however, was enough of a realist to know that at least some of his readers would face opposition, as indeed some of them were (**But and if ye suffer for righteousness' sake**; v. 14a). In the Greek, this conditional clause is the furthest removed from stating a reality. Suffering for righteousness is a remote possibility, but even if it does occur (and for some in Peter's audience, it had), it brings special blessing to the sufferer (**happy are ye**; see Matt. 5:10 – 12).

3:14b – 16a. Peter urged his readers to adopt four courses of action, each of which answered their objections and soothed their fears regarding persecution. (1) **Be not afraid of their terror, neither be troubled** (v. 14b), or as the NLT has it, "So don't be afraid and don't worry." (2) **Sanctify the Lord God in your hearts** (v. 15). The NASB (and other translations) follows the better-attested reading in the New Testament manuscripts for this verse and has "sanctify Christ as Lord in your hearts." (3) **Be ready always to give an answer to every man that asketh you a reason of the hope that is in you** (v. 15). The word for "answer" is *apologia*, from which the English "apologetics" comes. The idea is not to "apologize" for being a Christian; Peter meant that all believers ought to be ready, willing, and able to explain what it is that they believe and why they believe it. Degrading, argumentative, and abusive speech has no place in sharing the faith. Instead, **meekness and fear** ("gentleness and respect," NIV) are to accompany one's witness. (4) The readers' possession of these attributes would ensure that they had **a good conscience** (v. 16a).

B. Reason (3:16b)

3:16b. The reason for the entire set of instructions in the proposition was so that the slanderers **may be ashamed** (v. 16b). Their false accusations would then be shown as obviously untrue; the believer's loving attitude would put the opponent's bitterness in a bad light. Peter did not mean that be-

lievers should relish the shame and downfall of those who oppose them.

C. Proof of the Reason (3:17)

Sometimes it is God's will for believers to undergo adversity for their faith. This is an additional reason for enduring slander with a ready and reverent attitude. Peter maintained that suffering as a Christian might be **the will of God** (v. 17; see 4:19). This letter does not have an extensive answer to the question of why Christians suffer (but see 4:4), but Peter did affirm that it may be in the divine plan. When believers do suffer, however, it should not be **for evil doing** but **for well doing** (see 4:15 – 16).

D. Embellishment (3:18 – 22)

The material that embellishes all that Peter said in 3:13 – 17 was drawn from the church's confessional tradition. Here is theology employed for a pastoral purpose: just as Christ suffered innocently yet was exalted to the highest place of honor in the universe, so His faithful followers can expect God's vindication of them although they are now reproached. As the following passages illustrate, the logic that Peter followed is an argument from the greater to the lesser; what is true of Christ is true also for His disciples (see John 15:20).

3:18. For Christ also hath once suffered for sins. Peter, like Paul in Philippians 2:5 – 11, referred to Jesus as an example of the type of conduct that should characterize the Christian. They are to be ready to suffer for doing good (see 3:13 – 14, 17). "Once" refers to the nature of Christ's sacrifice being final and complete (see Heb. 9:28). The phrase **the just for the unjust** ("the righteous for the unrighteous," NRSV) indicates that Peter considered Jesus' death "substitutionary" in the sense that He died in the place of the sinner. Christ's work on the cross does not save everyone automatically; **that he might bring us to God** is a conditional construction. Salvation is the purpose of His death, but the condition is faith.

3:19 – 20. He went and preached unto the spirits in prison (v. 19). The thought of Christ's suffering and death led Peter to comment on what occurred after Christ's death, which led to tangential remarks about preaching to "the spirits in prison" and about baptism (see 3:21). **By which** (i.e., by the power of the Holy Spirit; v. 19) could also be translated "in which" (NRSV), referring to the spiritual dimension. Five main interpretations of this passage are worthy of review here.

(1) Some hold that in His preincarnate state, Christ went and preached through **Noah** (v. 20) to the wicked generation of Noah's time. The **disobedient** people of his generation were **in prison** (v. 19), or hell. This view seems to be in line with the context of 1:10–11, where the Spirit is said to speak through the prophets. Peter referred to Noah as "a preacher of righteousness" (2 Peter 2:5).

(2) Others argue that between His death and resurrection, Christ went to some prison where fallen angels are supposedly incarcerated and there preached to the angels who are said to have left their proper state and married human women during Noah's time (see Gen. 6:1–4; 2 Peter 2:4; Jude 6). The "sons of God" in Genesis 6:2, 4 and Job 1:6; 2:1 are supposed to have been angels. The message Christ preached to these evil angels was probably a declaration of victory.

(3) Still others say that between His death and resurrection, Christ went to the place of the dead and preached to the spirits of Noah's wicked contemporaries, again proclaiming victory for Christ and doom for His hearers.

(4) According to another interpretation, after His death, Christ went and preached to people in hell. These people were offered a second chance of salvation (see 4:6). Those who advocate this view disagree whether the people included only the rebellious generation of the flood or all humans who had died up to that time. At least one scholar suggests that disobedient angels heard the preaching as well.

(5) A Roman Catholic interpretation is that after He died, Christ went and proclaimed release to people who were penitent just before they died in the flood. These people were released from purgatory and went to heaven.

The strength of the first interpretation is that it fits with the context of 1:10–11. The verb "preached" (*ekēryxen*) does not necessarily mean "to persuade" people to accept the good news of salvation. It could signify "to proclaim a victory."

A strong case may also be made for the second interpretation since the surrounding context describes Christ's exaltation from shame (death) to honor (resurrection and being seated at God's right hand). Peter's concern throughout his letter was with the shame and honor of his readers. Christ has been vindicated by God to the highest place; He has even proclaimed His victory to the supernatural powers. Thus, those who follow Christ can expect that they also will attain honor in the future.

3:21. Baptism doth also now save us. Peter's reference to **The like figure** ("an antitype," NKJV) **whereunto even baptism doth also now save** denotes his use of typology. This is an interpretive method that biblical writers used to draw connections between an Old Testament phenomenon (type) and its New Testament counterpart (antitype). The idea is not only that the type prefigures the antitype but also that the significance of the type is repeated, and made more significant, in the antitype. In that sense, the antitype fulfills its Old Testament type, or symbol.

Peter used a double figure here. The incident of the ark and the flood symbolizes baptism, and baptism symbolizes salvation. The flood was a figure of baptism in that, in both instances, the water that spoke of judgment (in the flood, the death of the wicked; in baptism, the death of Christ and the believer) is the water that saves (**eight souls were saved by water** through the ark; believers figuratively rise above the waters through baptism). Baptism is a symbol of salvation in that it depicts Christ's death, burial, and resurrection and believers' identification with Him in these experiences (see Rom. 6:4). Baptism "doth also now save." In reality, believers are saved by what baptism symbolizes: Christ's death and resurrection. The symbol and the reality are so closely related that the symbol is sometimes used to refer to the reality. Thus, baptism is metonymy, a figure of speech in which something closely associated with the subject is used in place of it. Here "baptism" is used in place of the union of Christ and the believer in the Lord's death, burial, and resurrection, which baptism depicts.

In the final analysis, people are saved not by any ritual; people are saved **by the resurrection of Jesus Christ** and its supernatural power. In baptism, the believer gives **the answer of a good conscience toward God**. In other words, the act of baptism is a commitment on the part of the believer in all good conscience to make sure that what baptism symbolizes will become a reality in his life.

3:22. Who ... is on the right hand of God. After His ascension (**gone into heaven**), Christ was honored with the ultimate place of authority and honor in the universe. "The right hand of God" is an anthropomorphism (God is described as if He has a human body). The figure of speech expresses God's absolute power.

E. Conclusion (4:1–11)

4:1. In wrapping up his third and final argument of the letter, Peter revisited emphases of the argument: suffering (4:1), the reproaches of the pagans (4:4), and good conduct (4:7–11). Since 3:19–22 is parenthetical, 4:1 ties directly back to 3:18, the link signified by **Forasmuch then**. The aspect of Christ's suffering that these passages stress is suffering unjustly because one has done good. Furthermore, it is physical suffering (**in the flesh**). **Arm yourselves** is a military metaphor; the weaponry is **the same mind** ("the same attitude," NIV) as Christ's. Believers should be prepared to suffer unjustly and to face such abuse with Christ's attitude, with His willingness to endure suffering for doing good. (For a similar principle in Paul's writings, see Phil. 2:5–11.)

4:2. The daily choice facing the Christian is whether to **live ... to the lusts of men** or **to the will of God**. Christ's attitude should prevail, and God's will should be the determining factor in life.

4:3. In **the time past**, before conversion, Peter's hearers had focused on wasteful and extravagant activities. His list sounds very much like twenty-first-

century excesses: "You were immoral and followed your evil desires. You went around drinking and partying and carrying on. In fact, you even worshiped disgusting idols" (CEV).

4:4. This verse is very instructive and perceptive; it is a sort of "psychology of persecution." There may be other reasons for outrage and reaction against believers, but here Peter said that pagans take up **speaking evil** (lit., "blaspheming") **of you** because followers of Christ **run not with them to the same excess of riot** (i.e., the sins of 4:3). The unbelievers **think it strange**. What they do not understand, they ridicule.

4:5. Because of their continued indulgence in sin and their blasphemy against believers, the opponents **shall give account**. In the New Testament, both the Father and the Son are said to be Judge on the great, final judgment day. The Father is the ultimate source of judgment, but He will delegate judgment to the Son (see John 5:27; Acts 17:31). **The quick and the dead** are those alive and those dead when the final judgment day dawns. The Greek noun translated "account" (*logos*) and the adverb translated "ready" (*hetoimōs*) recall 3:15, where the identical noun ("reason") and the adjective "ready" (*hetoimos*) appear. Whereas in 3:15 Peter called on Christians to be prepared to answer for their beliefs to anyone who asked, here he called on the blasphemous and unprincipled pagans to answer to the highest court of the universe for their actions.

4:6. For this cause was the gospel preached also to them that are dead. The "cause" to which this statement refers is **that they might be judged according to men in the flesh, but live according to God in the spirit**. At least three different interpretations have been offered for this verse. (1) Some maintain that Peter meant the gospel had been preached to the spiritually dead, who heard the good news in this life and live eternally if they responded by faith to it. They still experienced the physical death (the judgment in the flesh) common to all humans, however. (2) Other interpreters believe that Peter was saying the gospel had been preached to dead people who heard the gospel in Hades. They had been judged in terms of the body by dying, but the prospect of living in the Spirit on the last day was put before them. Christ's descending into hell and bringing souls out of it (the harrowing of hell) are what lay behind verse 6. (3) According to a third view, Peter meant that the gospel was preached "to Christians who are now dead but who heard and responded to the gospel before they died" (Marshall, *1 Peter*, p. 137). These people have been judged according to human standards by the pagan world, which does not understand why God's people no longer follow its sinful way of life (see 4:2–4).

4:7. **The end of all things is at hand** may have been a Christian proverb or watchword in Peter's day and introduces other maxims that appear in quick succession in 4:7–11. Anticipation of the end times, particularly Christ's return, should influence believers' attitudes, actions, and relationships. The two commands **be ye therefore sober, and watch unto prayer** could be understood as a single, emphatic command: "be earnest and disciplined in your prayers" (NLT). "Be ye therefore sober" may refer to abstaining from drunkenness or to seriousness generally. Christians are to be characterized by reason, are to make wise, mature decisions, and are to have a clearly defined, decisive purpose in life.

4:8–9. The command to **have fervent charity among yourselves** (v. 8; "love each other deeply," NIV; "preserve an intense love for each other," NJB) is the most effective way (**above all things**) to preserve unity. **Use hospitality one to another without grudging** (v. 9) reflects the minority status that Peter's readers had in their surrounding culture. Although they themselves were strangers, they were to welcome other believing strangers. Then all might find a home for the homeless, a place of belonging (see 2:5).

4:10–11. These verses represent Peter's contribution to the discussion of spiritual gifts in the New Testament and should be compared with Romans 12:4–8; 1 Corinthians 12:7–11; and Ephesians 4:7–16. Peter filled the instruction with language intended to help his readers see that they were honored and had a valuable contribution to make in the church. Each believer had received **the gift** (v. 10;

the Greek omits the article, so the translation should read "a gift" [*charisma*, RSV]) and was to use this gift in serving others. The idea of the church as a household is evident, as in 4:9. **Stewards** were household servants to whom the daily business of the house was entrusted. As the believers served one another, they distinguished themselves as **good**. That is, they became agents of **the manifold grace of God**.

The Greek for **oracles** (v. 11) is used to refer to the Scriptures or to the words God has spoken (see Acts 7:38; Rom. 3:2). Thus, although the gift of preaching and teaching appears more prestigious than the gift of serving, both gifts are given **that God in all things may be glorified**. A doxology, in which the recipient of the glory (*doxa*) is Jesus Christ closes the third argument of the epistle on a high and inspirational note.

VI. Closing (4:12–5:14)

The doxology of 4:11 and the address "beloved" at the beginning of 4:12 has led some to theorize that two letters (1:1–4:11 and 4:12–5:14) were been put together some time after their writing and that 1 Peter is thus a composite letter. This theory is unnecessary; the section beginning with 4:12 has close connections with all that precedes it. The latter section is a conclusion of the letter, not another document that was later appended. Nevertheless, the conclusion could conceivably have been written after a sudden outbreak of violence in Rome. As Peter was about to wrap up his letter, Nero's ferocious persecution of Christians (some were burned; some were thrown to the beasts in the arena) commenced in the imperial capital (AD 64). These events may have led the apostle to warn his flocks scattered throughout Asia Minor that what was happening in Rome could spread to the provinces. The urgent tone in 4:12, with its mention of a "fiery trial," makes such a scenario possible.

A. Further Examination of the Topic of Suffering (4:12–19)

4:12–13. The fiery trial which is to try you (v. 12; "the fiery ordeal that is taking place among you to test you," NRSV) recalls the tests of 1:6–7. Peter likens their suffering to the eschatological final time of testing at the end of history. The believers' faith may be refined, and those who endure the ordeal will be vindicated by God. To endure, however, one must **rejoice** (v. 13). After all, the fiery trial is a sharing in the sufferings of Christ.

4:14. Meanwhile, **If ye be reproached for the name of Christ, happy are ye.** The word "happy" may mislead some into thinking that they are required to enjoy suffering or to take some sort of morbid pleasure in it, even seek it. Not so. Peter's statement, drawn from the Beatitudes (Matt. 5:11; Luke 6:22), pronounces a blessing ("you are blessed," NIV). His intention was to give his slandered readers encouragement in their afflictions. The glory that they hoped for at Christ's second coming (4:13) already rested upon them in the Holy Spirit: **for the spirit of glory and of God resteth upon you.** In the midst of reproachful treatment from unbelievers, the Christians already had the honor whose full bestowal they awaited at Christ's coming. In fact, they brought glory and honor to Christ in their suffering.

4:15–16. Just as in 2:20 and 3:17, where Peter contrasted suffering for doing good with suffering for doing evil, here he acknowledged that not all suffering is positive. Only that adversity experienced **as a Christian** (v. 16) is honorable, and no shame is to be taken with it.

4:17–19. Judgment must begin at the house of God (v. 17), Peter said. The persecutions that believers were undergoing were divinely sent judgment intended to purify God's people. If God brings judgment on His own people, if He so disciplines the children of His household, **what shall the end be of them that obey not the gospel of God?** How much more serious will the judgment be that He will bring on unbelievers. Although the KJV translation is difficult to see, Peter quotes Proverbs 11:31 from the Septuagint to confirm his point. As he reintroduced the theme of the household of God in the conclusion of his letter, he did so solemnly and seriously. The privilege of belonging brings the responsibility of obedience.

B. A Farewell Speech of Exhortation (5:1–11)

1. Self-Vindication (5:1)

5:1. Peter, who identified himself as an apostle at the beginning of his letter (1:1), here chose to identify himself with the elders of the churches (**who am also an elder**). Peter had been with Jesus from the early days of His ministry and thus could describe himself as **a witness of the sufferings of Christ.** As one of the Twelve, Peter had witnessed all phases and aspects of Jesus' earthly ministry, including the climactic events of His suffering (see Matt. 26:58; Mark 14:54; Luke 22:60–62; John 18:10–11, 15–16).

2. A Call to Tend the Flock (5:2a–b)

5:2a–b. Feed the flock of God (v. 2a) is a metaphor that the Lord Himself employed (John 10:1–18; Luke 15:3–7) and that must have been etched on Peter's mind (see John 21:15–17; see 1 Peter 2:25). As he wrote this letter, Peter was fulfilling Christ's command to feed His sheep. The term "Shepherd" (5:4) is an Old Testament metaphor (see Ezek. 34:1–10, where the Lord held the leaders of Israel responsible for failing to care for the flock). The awkward expression **which is among you** is helpfully translated "that is under your care" in the NIV. One Greek word (*episkopountes*) is translated **taking the oversight thereof.** The noun related to it (*episkopos*) is used in Acts 20:28 ("overseers"); Philippians 1:1; 1 Timothy 3:2; and Titus 1:7 ("bishop[s]"). In the New Testament, the three terms "elder," "overseer" (or "bishop"), and "shepherd" all apply to one office.

3. A Warning against Greed (5:2c–3)

5:2c–3. Peter realized that the right thing can be done for the wrong motivation. Thus, the apostle warned the shepherds to care for the flock **not for filthy lucre, but of a ready mind** (v. 2c). This passage does not prohibit one from earning one's livelihood in Christian service. Peter's point was that the Christian leader must always guard against doing his work primarily for money, to get attention from others, or to gain prestige. Neither are overseers to tend their flocks out of a desire for power. The true leadership model is **being ensamples** (examples) **to the flock** (v. 3). The Greek word for "ensamples" here is *typos*, a word that, in secular writing, referred to the stamp or impression made on a coin, to a mold, or to an outline of a book's contents. The leader's life should be an outline that others can follow.

4. Reward and Judgment (5:4)

5:4. When the **chief Shepherd** (Christ, see 2:25) returns, He will reward those who have served as shepherds under Him. The **crown** (Greek, *stephanos*) **of glory** may be a metaphorical reference to the athlete's crown, the crown of a monarch, the valiant soldier's wreath, a reward for service to the state, or the headpiece of a supernatural being. In any case, it is a symbol of honor. Unlike worldly prizes and recognitions, it **fadeth not away** (see 1:4). Peter was in no way teaching salvation by works here. The bestowal is one of honor to pastors who have done their work in the manner that Peter outlined in 5:2–3.

5. Love and Humility (5:5–7)

5:5–7. Peter used a striking metaphor in describing the humble attitude that all in the household of God should have toward one another: **be clothed with humility** (v. 5). In this way, the members of God's household convey His honor to one another. Since God **giveth grace to the humble**, Peter instructed his hearers, whose communities were harassed and maligned, **Humble yourselves therefore under the mighty hand of God** (v. 6). Peter once again employed an anthropomorphism (see 3:22) to convey the idea that God's strength is sufficient to protect His people until the proper moment (**due time**) for Him to **exalt** them. **Casting all your care upon him** (v. 7) defines what humbling oneself before God means. The term "cast" is used one other time in the New Testament. In Luke 19:35, it describes the action of the disciples as "they cast their garments upon the colt." Peter's readers were to throw their worries about their lack of honor and advantage in society on to their Lord. So too, Christians of any age are to throw every "anxiety" (NIV), all their "worries" (CEV), on to Christ. He will bear

them, **for he careth for you.** That is, "you are his personal concern" (Phillips).

6. An Exhortation to Watch and Stand Firm (5:8a)

5:8a. The command to **Be sober** (for the same command, see 1:13; 4:7) is made more urgent by the additional **be vigilant.** Jesus used the same Greek verb (*grēgoreō*) when He urgently warned His disciples to "watch" and pray in order not to enter into temptation (Matt. 26:41). Perhaps Peter remembered his own difficulty in staying awake during our Lord's agony in Gethsemane (see Matt. 26:36–46).

7. Discussion of the Enemy (5:8b)

5:8b. By using the vivid simile of a prowling and **roaring lion**, Peter captured well the ferocity of the opposition that his hearers faced. The image does not mean that Christians were being thrown to the beasts in the arena. It is unlikely that such severe measures were being taken against Christians at that time. However, Peter's portrayal of the source of slander as **your adversary the devil** demonstrated that the source of the opposition was not just human antagonists but Satan himself. By identifying the peril as a supernatural one, Peter hoped to promote group unity and identity in the community. "Devil" (*diabolos*) literally means "slanderer." The Devil was the ultimate source of the slander directed against Peter's audience.

8. A Prediction of Suffering (5:9–11)

5:9–11. Despite the supernatural nature of the ultimate foe, Peter recognized that the Devil can be resisted if Christians remain **stedfast in the faith** (v. 9; see Eph. 6:13; James 4:7). The Christians to whom Peter wrote were not isolated; they belonged to a fellowship of suffering. Four future-tense verbs emphasize the certainty of God's vindication of the oppressed hearers. The first three verbs are practically identical in meaning: **make you perfect, stablish, strengthen** (v. 10). The fourth may indicate a progression to a yet higher plane: **settle you** (*themelioō*) means "he will place you on a firm foundation" (NLT). If suffering is accepted in humility and faith, the time will come when God sets things

right. Thus, Peter ascribed to God **glory and dominion for ever and ever** (v. 11).

C. Closing Remarks and Greeting (5:12–14)

5:12. Silvanus (Silas) may have been the bearer
of the letter to its destination. He may also have been
a scribe who recorded what Peter dictated or who,
as an informed and intelligent secretary, aided him
in the phrasing of his thoughts (see Introduction:
"Author"). Peter stated his purpose in addressing the
churches scattered throughout Asia Minor: **I have
written briefly, exhorting, and testifying that this
is the true grace of God wherein ye stand.** In this
epistle, "grace" signifies the favor and honor of God.
"Wherein ye stand" should be translated as an imperative ("Stand firm in it!" NASB), a final exhortation as Peter concluded his letter.

5:13. For **Babylon**, see Introduction: "Place
of Composition." Peter regarded Mark with such
warmth and affection that he called him **Marcus my
son.** It is possible that Peter had led Mark to Christ,
and early Christian tradition closely associates Mark
and Peter (see Mark, Introduction: "Author").

5:14. A kiss of charity ("a kiss of love," NIV) was
a cultural expression of greeting and signified a tangible expression of the divine honor that the members of God's household could give one another. The
concluding benediction of **Peace** (see 1:2) is a statement of the result that honor from God can bring.
It brings spiritual well-being and blessedness to all
who are united to Christ. Peter thus ended his letter with a reference to the union of believers with
Christ, a concept fundamental to the understanding
of the whole letter.

THE SECOND EPISTLE OF PETER

INTRODUCTION

Author

The author identified himself as Simon Peter (1:1). He used the first-person singular pronoun in a highly personal passage (1:12–15) and claimed to be an eyewitness of the transfiguration (1:16–18; see Matt. 17:1–5). He asserted that this was his second letter to the readers (3:1) and referred to Paul as "our beloved brother" (3:15). In short, the letter claims to be Peter's, and its character is compatible with that claim. For further background on Peter, see 1 Peter, Introduction: "Author."

Although 2 Peter was not as widely known and recognized in the early church as 1 Peter was, some may have used and accepted it as authoritative as early as the second century and perhaps even in the latter part of the first century (1 Clement [AD 95] may allude to it). The letter was not ascribed to Peter until Origen's time (185–253), and he seems to reflect some doubt concerning it. Eusebius (265–340) placed it among the questioned books, though he admits that most accepted 2 Peter as from Peter. After Eusebius's time, it seems to have been quite generally accepted as canonical. The epistle is included in Athanasius's list of authoritative books in his Festal Letter of 367, and the Council of Carthage (397) similarly ratified 2 Peter.

In recent centuries, however, the place of 2 Peter in the New Testament Canon has been called into question. In the time of the Reformation, Luther accepted 2 Peter, Calvin was dubious of it, and Erasmus rejected it. A considerable number of scholars have challenged its genuineness. One of the objections that has been raised is the difference in style from that of 1 Peter. The difference is not absolute, however; there are noteworthy similarities in vocabulary and in other matters. The differences that do exist may be accounted for by variations in subject matter, in the form and purpose of the letters, in the time and circumstances of writing, in sources or models, and in scribes who may have been employed. Perhaps most significant is the statement in 1 Peter 5:12 that "By Silvanus" Peter had "written briefly." No such statement is made concerning 2 Peter, which may explain its noticeable difference in style (see 1 Peter, Introduction: "Author").

The early church concerned itself with the question of authenticity and may very well have ascertained Petrine authorship of 2 Peter before issuing full recognition of its canonical status. The pseudonymous author of *The Acts of Paul* was deposed for forgery, and the so-called *Gospel of Peter* was forbidden because it was non-Petrine both in authorship and doctrine. This evidence suggests that the question of the authenticity of 2 Peter was settled at an early time.

Date

Peter wrote this epistle toward the end of his life (see 1:12–15), after he had written a prior letter (3:1) to the same readers (probably 1 Peter). Since Peter was martyred during the reign of Nero, his death must have occurred prior to AD 68 (the date of Nero's death), so it is very likely that he wrote 2 Peter somewhere between 63 and 68, probably around 64 or 65, and most likely from Rome.

Some have argued that these dates are too early for the writing of 2 Peter, but nothing in the book requires a later date. To insist that the second chapter was directed against second-century Gnosticism is to assume more than the contents of the chapter warrant. The heretics referred to in 2 Peter may well have been among the forerunners of second-century Gnostics since elements of a later, more fully developed Gnosticism are present: emphasis on *gnōsis* (knowledge) that leads to a lack of moral restraint, arrogance toward church leaders who are thought to be unenlightened, divisiveness, sexual immorality, and an interest in angels. Nothing is said of the false teachers that would not fit into the later years of Peter's life. Some have suggested a later date because they interpret the reference to "the fathers" in 3:4 to mean an earlier Christian generation. However, the word is most naturally interpreted as referring to the Old Testament patriarchs (see "fathers" in John 6:31; Acts 3:13; Heb. 1:1).

Other objections to the authenticity of 2 Peter arise from a naturalistic reconstruction of early Christian history or misunderstandings or misconstructions of the available data. For example, some argue that the reference to Paul's letters as "scriptures" (3:16) indicates an advanced date for this book—beyond Peter's lifetime, perhaps as late as the second century. Three objections to this argument may be raised. (1) It is quite possible that Paul's letters were gathered at an early date, since some of them had been in existence and perhaps in circulation for more than ten years (Thessalonians for as much as fifteen years) prior to Peter's death. Besides, Peter's statement in 3:16 may only indicate that he was acquainted with some of Paul's letters, not that there was a formal, ecclesiastical collection of them. (2) Since the apostles, especially Paul, spoke with divine authority (see 1 Cor. 2:13, 16; 7:17; 14:37–38), their writings could easily have been understood as "scripture" from the time of their production in the first century. (3) Peter's term of endearment, "our beloved brother Paul" (3:15), would more likely have been written in the first century than in the second. The second century witnessed attempts to drive wedges between Peter and Paul, and someone writing pseudonymously with Peter as his champion might well have been reluctant to heap such adulation on an ecclesiastical rival. Although not conclusive, these arguments cast doubt on any late-date theory for 2 Peter.

The Relationship of 2 Peter and Jude

Despite conspicuous differences (e.g., Jude's use of apocryphal sources) between 2 Peter and Jude, there are conspicuous similarities between the two letters. Some notable parallels are shown in the chart below.

2 Peter 2:1	Jude 4
1 But there were false prophets also among the people, even as there shall be false teachers among you, who privily shall bring in damnable heresies, even denying the Lord that bought them, and bring upon themselves swift destruction.	4 For there are certain men crept in unawares, who were before of old ordained to this condemnation, ungodly men, turning the grace of our God into lasciviousness, and denying the only Lord God, and our Lord Jesus Christ.
2 Peter 2:4, 6	**Jude 6–7**
4 For if God spared not the angels that sinned, but cast them down to hell, and delivered them into chains of darkness, to be reserved unto judgment; 6 And turning the cities of Sodom and Gomorrha into ashes condemned them with an overthrow, making them an ensample unto those that after should live ungodly;	6 And the angels which kept not their first estate, but left their own habitation, he hath reserved in everlasting chains under darkness unto the judgment of the great day. 7 Even as Sodom and Gomorrha, and the cities about them in like manner, giving themselves over to fornication, and going after strange flesh, are set forth for an example, suffering the vengeance of eternal fire.
2 Peter 2:10–12	**Jude 8–10**
10 But chiefly them that walk after the flesh in the lust of uncleanness, and despise government. Presumptuous are they, selfwilled, they are not afraid to speak evil of dignities. 11 Whereas angels, which are greater in power and might, bring not railing accusation against them before the Lord. 12 But these, as natural brute beasts, made to be taken and destroyed, speak evil of the things that they understand not; and shall utterly perish in their own corruption;	8 Likewise also these filthy dreamers defile the flesh, despise dominion, and speak evil of dignities. 9 Yet Michael the archangel, when contending with the devil he disputed about the body of Moses, durst not bring against him a railing accusation, but said, The Lord rebuke thee. 10 But these speak evil of those things which they know not: but what they know naturally, as brute beasts, in those things they corrupt themselves.
2 Peter 2:13, 17	**Jude 12–13**
13 And shall receive the reward of unrighteousness, as they that count it pleasure to riot in the day time. Spots they are and blemishes, sporting themselves with their own deceivings while they feast with you; 17 These are wells without water, clouds that are carried with a tempest; to whom the mist of darkness is reserved for ever.	12 These are spots in your feasts of charity, when they feast with you, feeding themselves without fear: clouds they are without water, carried about of winds; trees whose fruit withereth, without fruit, twice dead, plucked up by the roots; 13 Raging waves of the sea, foaming out their own shame; wandering stars, to whom is reserved the blackness of darkness for ever.

The wording is not completely identical but strikingly similar. It has, therefore, been suggested that one borrowed from the other or that they both drew on a common source. If borrowing did occur, it was not slavish but rather was adapted to suit the writer's purpose. While many have insisted that Jude used 2 Peter, it is more reasonable to assume that the longer letter (2 Peter) incorporated much of the shorter (Jude). Jude would gain little by shortening 2 Peter, whereas 2 Peter expands the message of Jude considerably. Of course, Jude and Peter could have written their respective letters independently of one another. The inexactitude in phraseology between the parallel passages might indicate that. However, such borrowing as that described above was fairly common in ancient writings (e.g., many believe that Paul used parts of early hymns in Phil. 2:6–11 and 1 Tim. 3:16). A high view of biblical inspiration need not insist on independent composition of biblical documents.

Theme and Theological Message

In his first letter, Peter fed Christ's sheep by instructing them how to deal with persecution from outside the church (see, e.g., 1 Peter 4:12); in his second letter, he taught them how to deal with false teachers and evildoers who had come into the church (see 2:1; 3:3–4). While the particular situations naturally called for variations in content and emphasis, in both letters Peter, as a pastor ("shepherd") of Christ's sheep (see John 21:15–17), sought to commend to his readers a wholesome combination of Christian faith and practice. More specifically, his purpose was threefold: (1) to stimulate Christian growth (chap. 1), (2) to combat false teaching (chap. 2), and (3) to encourage watchfulness in view of the Lord's certain return (chap. 3). For further information on the audience of the epistle, see 1 Peter, Introduction: "Recipients"; the audience was likely the same for both 1 and 2 Peter.

Literary Features

As with 1 Peter, 2 Peter displays the author's acquaintance with standards for composition that are outlined in the Greco-Roman rhetorical handbooks. The epistle constitutes an example of deliberative rhetoric, that is, discourse in which the rhetor seeks to persuade or dissuade his audience regarding future action. (For other examples of Greco-Roman rhetoric, see 1 Peter, Introduction: "Literary Features" and Jude, Introduction: "Literary Features.") Peter's main proposition was that his hearers "be stablished in the present truth" by "remembrance of these things" (i.e., things pertaining to Christian faith; 1:12). The proofs that substantiate this proposition feature accusations made by the false teachers and Peter's refutation of them. The accusation-refutation pattern was rhetorically effective in that it reminded Peter's audience of essential points of apostolic teaching while bringing them to bear on specific objections that were ongoing issues in his churches.

The letter is also an example of a testament—a statement of ethical and religious teachings, to which the Petrine communities were to adhere after Peter's demise, and a prophecy concerning their destiny. The following outline demonstrates the letter's rhetorical structure.

Outline

Select Bibliography

Barclay, William. *The Letters of James and Peter.* Rev. ed. The Daily Study Bible. Philadelphia: Westminster John Knox, 1976.

Bigg, Charles. *A Critical and Exegetical Commentary on the Epistles of St. Peter and St. Jude.* International Critical Commentary. Edinburgh: T&T Clark, 1978.

Green, Michael. "Peter, Second Epistle of." In *New Bible Dictionary*, 3rd ed. Edited by D. R. W. Wood, I. Howard Marshall, A. R. Millard, J. I. Packer, and D. J. Wiseman, 911–13. Downers Grove, IL: InterVarsity, 1996.

———. *The Second Epistle General of Peter and the General Epistle of Jude: An Introduction and Commentary.* 2nd ed. Tyndale New Testament Commentaries 18. Grand Rapids, MI: Eerdmans, 1987.

Hillyer, Norman. *1 and 2 Peter, Jude.* The New International Biblical Commentary 16. Peabody, MA: Hendrickson, 1992.

Moo, Douglas J. *2 Peter and Jude.* The NIV Application Commentary. Grand Rapids, MI: Zondervan, 1996.

Neyrey, Jerome H. *2 Peter, Jude: A New Translation with Introduction and Commentary.* The Anchor Bible 37C. New York: Doubleday, 1993.

Senior, Donald P., and Daniel J. Harrington. *1 Peter, Jude and 2 Peter.* Sacra Pagina 15. Collegeville, MN: Michael Glazier, 2003.

Waltner, Erland, and J. Daryl Charles. *1–2 Peter, Jude.* Believers Church Bible Commentary. Scottdale, PA: Herald, 1999.

Watson, Duane Frederick. *Invention, Arrangement, and Style: Rhetorical Criticism of Jude and 2 Peter.* Society of Biblical Literature Dissertation Series 104. Atlanta: Scholars Press, 1988.

EXPOSITION

I. Introduction (1:1–2)

1:1. Simon Peter identified himself as **a servant and an apostle of Jesus Christ,** a description that not only showed humility but also established his authority to address his audience. The hearers were those who had **obtained like precious faith with us.** Here "faith" is not a body of truth to be believed — the faith — but the act of believing or the God-given capacity to trust in Christ for salvation. "Like precious" is *isotimos* and means "of equal honor." The cultural value of honor (and its opposite, shame) informs Peter's argument in this letter just as it does in 1 Peter. In cultural terms, God is the patron who had favored the recipients of the letter with the honor of faith. As His clients, they were responsible for living in a way that would bring Him glory and honor in return.

The distinction between the two senses (patron, clients) becomes clearer with the construction **through the knowledge of God, and of Jesus our Lord,** which has two articles in the Greek ("through the knowledge of the God and Jesus the Lord of us"). Knowledge is of two persons: God and Jesus. Elsewhere in 2 Peter, Jesus is designated "our [the] Lord and Saviour Jesus Christ" (1:11; 2:20; 3:18; see also 3:2).

1:2. The greeting (**Grace and peace be multiplied unto you**) is that of 1 Peter 1:2 except that in his second letter, Peter added the means by which the multiplication might take place: through, or "in" (NKJV), the intimate relationship that a Christian enjoys with God and with Jesus Christ.

II. Exordium: Exhortation to Growth in Christian Virtues (1:3–11)

A. The Divine Enablement (1:3–4)

1:3. All things that pertain unto life and godliness. God has made available all that believers need spiritually **through [our] knowledge of Him.** If indeed 2 Peter was written to combat an incipient Gnosticism, the apostle may have been insisting that the knowledge possessed by those in apostolic circles was entirely adequate to meet their spiritual needs. No secret, esoteric knowledge is necessary for salvation. The things that contribute to true life and to godly character, that is, **to glory and virtue**, may be the qualities listed in 1:5–7.

1:4. God has given **us exceeding great and precious promises.** "Precious" (*timios*) is related to the word for honor (*timē*) and has the idea of "great beyond all price" (NEB); therefore, great honor is bestowed on those to whom the promises are given. In light of Peter's vision of the future (see 1:11, 16, 19; 3:4, 9, 13), the promises probably are to be equated with Christ's promises for the future. The purpose of the promises is that God's people might become **partakers of the divine nature.** Peter did not indicate that Christians become divine in any sense, only that they are indwelt by God through His Holy Spirit (see John 14:16–17). One's humanity and His deity, as well as the human personality and the divine personality, remain distinct and separate.

The Gnostic idea that one gains union with the divine through self-understanding or through knowledge of secret and esoteric teachings is decisively refuted here. One can only become godly after **having escaped the corruption that is in the world through lust.** This action was a decisive one for Peter's readers, as it is for any Christian. The decision must, however, be reenacted daily as an act of discipleship. "The world" refers to human society that has alienated itself from God by rebellion against Him.

B. The Call for Growth (1:5–7)

1:5. This refers to all that Peter said in 1:3–4. Having identified God's indispensable primacy in one's experience of true life and godliness, the apostle puts his finger on the human role. That role requires one's **giving all diligence.** God Himself generates the life of piety, but the believer is a partner in the process of holiness. Christian growth, according to Peter, is a process, and it is not completed overnight. The "ladder" or "chain" of virtues featured in 1:5–7 is a set of consecutive character qualities, with one building on another only after the prior ones have been acquired. The pattern that Peter followed is a *gradatio*, a figure by which the speaker proceeds to the following step in a series only after repeating the prior one (see Rom. 5:3–5). Peter instructed his readers to **add to your faith** many other qualities. The Greek word translated "add" (*epichorēgeō*) is colorful. It is related to the Greek word *chorēgos*, a term referring to a wealthy Athenian who defrayed the enormous cost of the chorus in Greek plays. "Be lavish in the amount of attention, detail, and quality you put into building on your Christian faith" could be a paraphrase here.

The first of the attributes to be developed beyond **faith** is **virtue**, or "moral excellence." In secular usage, the word describes the character of the person who has embraced the teachings of philosophy. "Virtue" (*aretē*) can refer to that "goodness" that issues in exemplary citizenship and dependable friendship.

Knowledge is the translation of *gnōsis*, which in 2 Peter, likely conveys the idea of wisdom in practical affairs, the sensibility that allows one to effectively deal with life and its challenges (see 1:5–6; 3:18). Peter also used another word for "knowledge" in this epistle: *epignōsis*. Although the two are basically interchangeable in Greek, Peter appears to have distinguished the two. *Epignōsis* seems to refer to the intimate relationship of faith that a Christian enjoys with God through the Lord Jesus Christ (1:2–3, 8; 2:20), whereas *gnōsis* is the articulation of faith.

1:6. True Christian **knowledge** is also related to **temperance** ("self-control," NIV). Many of the false teachers maintained that knowledge makes self-control unnecessary. According to Peter, however, Christian knowledge leads to self-control. The false teachers demonstrated their lack of true spiritual knowledge by their lack of personal discipline.

To **temperance**, Peter urged his readers to add **patience**. The word is *hypomonē* and refers not so much to patience with people as to "fortitude" (REB) or "endurance" (Weymouth) in the face of life's difficulties. One cannot truly develop self-control without endurance, the quality of remaining faithful under stress and strain.

Building on **patience**, the next attribute to be added is **godliness**, a genuine reverence of God that governs one's attitude toward every aspect of life. The Greek term is *eusebeia*, which refers to the practice of giving to God that which is His due.

1:7. Brotherly kindness (*philadelphia*), the next of the qualities to be nurtured in the Christian life, involves warmhearted affection toward all in the family of faith. This quality relates to **godliness**, which immediately precedes it in the chain since without brotherly kindness, even acts of godliness can become routine and lack genuine compassion.

Developing from **brotherly kindness** is the next characteristic, **charity**. The Greek word is *agapē* and means "love" (NIV) — the kind of outgoing, selfless attitude that leads one to sacrifice for the good of others. The noun and the verb related to it are used consistently in the New Testament for the love that God has for all human beings through Jesus Christ (see John 3:16; Rom. 5:8), for the love that humans express to God in response to His love (see John 14:21; 1 Peter 1:8), and for one's love of others as a response to God's love (see John 13:34–35; 1 John 4:11). According to Paul in 1 Corinthians 13:13, *agapē* is the greatest of all Christian virtues.

C. The Value of Such Growth (1:8–11)

Here Peter skillfully used the rhetorical device known as an *antithesis* to create in his audience a keen desire to develop the virtues listed in 1:5–7. In the antithesis, Peter contrasted the life of faith (as outlined in 1:5–7) with the life of the false teach-

ers, a life of spiritual shortsightedness. He offered his readers two possibilities, presenting a result of each path and, in so doing, demonstrating the overwhelming desirability of the pathway of faith.

1:8–9. The first possibility is the life of faith, whose condition is expressed by the clause **if these things be in you, and abound** (v. 8). Peter was not implying that the believer is to cultivate each listed quality in turn, one after the other until all have been perfected. Instead, they are all to be cultivated simultaneously. Furthermore, there never comes a time when a believer has "arrived" and no longer needs to give any attention to any of the virtues. There is always room for growth since Jesus Christ is the measure of maturity. Those who grow and mature are promised, **ye shall neither be barren nor unfruitful in the knowledge of our Lord Jesus Christ**. The word "barren" translates *argos*, a word used to describe a field that is idle or fallow, as well as a lazy or slothful person. James used the word to describe an unproductive faith: "faith without works is dead" (James 2:20).

The alternative to the life of faith, the opposite to the first element of the antithesis, is personified as **he that lacketh these things** (v. 9). That person is **blind**. The phrase **and cannot see afar off** might indicate that Peter had in mind a possible alternative meaning for "blind," namely, "to shut the eyes." The Greek word is *myōpazō* from *myops*—a nearsighted man in Aristotle's writings. The English term "myopia" derives from it. Peter's picture is of a nearsighted individual who squints because of the light. The person cannot tolerate the brightness of the light of truth because he **hath forgotten that he was purged from his old sins**. Peter seems to indicate that a lack of spiritual growth often leads one to doubt his or her salvation.

1:10. In light of the fact that those who produce the graces of the Christian life (see 1:5–7) will be fruitful, and those who lack them suffer from an impairment of spiritual perception, Peter issued the command, **give diligence to make your calling and election sure**. The sense is to "become diligent," to make the decision to be diligent and renew it continually. Peter could not have used stronger language in the Greek to express the absolute guarantee that the one who diligently strives to be productive **shall never fall**. The construction is *ou mē ptaisēte pote* ("You will not at all ever stumble"). The verb should be understood in the sense of stumbling in the progress of one's Christian life.

1:11. Those who obtain the fruits Peter commended will never fall. Moreover, when **the everlasting kingdom of our Lord and Saviour Jesus Christ** comes in its fullness, they will be given **an entrance** into His kingdom that is a hero's welcome. Peter's anticipation of this kingdom indicates that he saw its coming as still in the future, not the present.

III. Proposition (1:12–15)

The main idea of the letter is contained in this passage. The epistle, a testament that contains Peter's final words of instruction, represents the apostle's attempt to "put you always in remembrance of these things" (v. 12), "to stir you up by putting you in remembrance" (v. 13), and "after my decease to have these things always in remembrance" (v. 15).

A. The Value of a Reminder (1:12–13)

1:12. The wise teacher knows the value of repetition and reminder to reinforce that which students have already received. Peter's wisdom as a teacher is evident in the proposition of his rhetorical argument. **Of these things** that he outlined in the exordium (1:3–11), he intended continually to remind his readers, **though ye know them**.

1:13. Peter's intention **to stir you up by putting you in remembrance** assured the readers that the apostle was vitally concerned for their welfare. His ethos (his authority and credibility) and positive pathos (a sense of well-being and a disposition favorable to the argument) were thereby enhanced among his audience. Peter's letter is an example of deliberative rhetoric and an example of a testament. He asserted that as long as he was **in this tabernacle** (i.e., his body, his earthly dwelling place), he would continue to coax his readers to live productively, according to the truth that they had received.

B. Peter's Prediction of His Imminent Death (1:14)

1:14. Peter disclosed to his audience a revelation that Jesus Himself gave him: **shortly I must put off this my tabernacle**. This insight is either the revelation recorded in John 21:18–19 or a subsequent one. In any event, Peter's demise was imminent at the time he wrote 2 Peter; his death occurred within one to four years. Peter's words were based on an actual revelation from Jesus, which therefore gave this section and the whole letter strong substantiation and authority. The metaphor of the body as a tent and the metaphor of death as "putting off" a garment poignantly express the testamentary nature of this section and the epistle as a whole. Peter wanted his readers to be reminded of correct doctrine not only while he lived but after he died as well.

C. The Remembrance of Things That the Readers Had Learned (1:15)

1:15. Peter's intention for his audience was **to have these things always in remembrance**, an aim that was realized, whether intentionally or unintentionally, through the Gospel of Mark, which early tradition connected with Peter. The term **I will endeavour** is the same verb that Peter used in 1:10 to command diligence from his readers regarding the confirmation or proof of their election. The word **decease** is *exodos* ("exodus"; a going out or departure), another metaphor for death. The same word is used in Hebrews 11:22 to denote the liberating departure of the Israelites from Egypt. Thus, Peter's language about his death is triumphant, with the same sense of liberation that the people of Israel enjoyed when they left their oppression.

IV. First Proof: Accusation and Refutation (1:16–21)

A. Accusation: The Message about the Second Coming Is a Clever Myth (1:16a)

1:16a. The consistent pattern in the proofs that substantiate Peter's proposition is an accusation that the false teachers had brought against true

Christian teaching and then its refutation. The accusation that Peter refuted in the first proof seems to have been something like, "You Christians have **followed cunningly devised fables** in believing miraculous tales (**the power**) of Jesus and the idea of a second **coming**." This accusation, that Christians had subscribed to "cleverly devised myths" (NRSV), required refutation.

Peter's message was based on his eyewitness account of the supernatural events that marked the life of Jesus. It was not made up of myths and imaginative stories, as was the message of the heretics mentioned in 2:3.

B. Refutation: The Apostolic Teaching of the Parousia Is Based on Eyewitness Testimony and Old Testament Prophecy (1:16b–21)

1. Eyewitness Testimony of the Transfiguration (1:16b–18)

1:16b. Peter's refutation of the heretical claim that Christian belief was founded on nothing but myths was this: it was founded on the testimony of **eyewitnesses**, the apostles. Peter pointed out a specific instance of their eyewitness testimony: the event of the transfiguration of Jesus. **His majesty** was splendidly manifested (see Matt. 17:1–9; Mark 9:2–10; Luke 9:28–36) in that event. It is an apt example, for it demonstrates the power of Jesus and signifies His glorious second coming. In Christ's transfiguration, the disciples received a foretaste of what His coming will be like when He returns to establish His eternal kingdom.

1:17–18. Peter briefly recounted the details of Christ's transfiguration. Overall, the event attributed divine **honour** (v. 17) to Jesus. The overwhelmingly great degree of honor is indicated by the double use of **glory** in verse 17, the second instance of which (**the excellent glory**) is an instance of *metonymy*. In this figure of speech, the name of an object or concept is replaced with a word closely related to or suggested by the original (e.g., "crown" for "king"); here "the excellent glory" represents God the Father. Peter recounted the words of the **voice** from that glory (**This is my beloved Son, in whom I am**

well pleased) and twice mentioned their audibility to emphasize that Peter, James, and John had actually heard the words. The details of this account confirmed Peter as an eyewitness of the event who was especially impressed by what he heard on that occasion.

2. Old Testament Prophecy Confirmed by the Transfiguration (1:19)

1:19. Peter maintained that the apostolic preaching rested on two solid foundations: the voice from God at Christ's transfiguration (see 1:16–18) and the still more significant testimony of Scripture (see 1:19–21). **We have also a more sure word of prophecy** should probably be understood to signify "we have the prophetic message more fully confirmed" (NRSV); that is, the apostolic testimony was not an additional prophetic statement but one that confirmed the earlier Old Testament message concerning Christ. One should **take heed** of that prophetic witness.

Peter's two metaphors for prophecy illustrate its strength to dispel the darkness of false teachings. It is **a light that shineth in a dark place**. God's Word gives light and hope to a dark world (see Ps. 119:105). The "light" (*lychnos*) is an oil lamp made of clay or metal (see Matt. 5:15). The duration of our focus on the light of prophecy should be **until the day dawn, and the day star arise in your hearts**. "The day" is the time of Jesus' coming. For His people, it will be a time of salvation and glory, not destruction and terror (see 3:13). The "morning star" (NIV) is *phōsphoros* ("light bearer") and refers to Venus, the planet whose appearance just before dawn announces the new day. In Revelation 22:16, it refers to the coming of Christ.

3. The Nature of Biblical Prophecy (1:20–21)

1:20–21. No prophecy of the scripture is of any private interpretation (v. 20) means that no prophecy originated through the prophet's own interpretation or imagination, the sense given in the NIV. In 1:16–19, Peter spoke of the origin of the apostolic message and whether it came from human imaginings or from God. In verse 21, he returned to the subject. No prophecy of Scripture arose from a merely human interpretation of things. This understanding of verse 20 is further supported by the explanatory **For** with which verse 21 begins. In verse 21, Peter explained his statement in verse 20 by restating its content and affirming God as the origin of prophecy, thereby refuting any objection the false teachers raised that Scripture is a merely human construct. Neither the apostolic testimony about Christ's power and coming nor the Old Testament Scripture is a human concoction.

The prophecy, said Peter, **came not in old time by the will of man** (v. 21); it is not of human origin. Rather, the nature of prophecy is divine: **holy men of God spake as they were moved by the Holy Ghost**. Some witnesses do not have the adjective "holy" with "men," but the idea is nevertheless present without the descriptor. "Moved" is the same Greek word (*pherō*) that is translated "came" earlier in the verse. The idea is that the prophets were carried or borne along by the Holy Spirit. Peter's statement can be extended to all of Scripture and is one of the clearest definitions of the nature of biblical inspiration. Both human and divine elements coalesce perfectly in the process of inspiration, so that God gives His word in human words. The Scriptures were not dictated word for word from God without human involvement in their production. Instead, God chose people whose cultural backgrounds and temperaments provided the perfect vehicle for His message to be effectively communicated. This verse gives the process of inspiration, whereas 2 Timothy 3:16 speaks of the product of inspiration, the writings themselves.

V. Second Proof: Accusation and Refutation (2:1–22)

A. Accusation: Divine Judgment Lingers Forever; It Will Never Come to Pass (2:1–3)

2:1–3. The **false prophets** (v. 1) refers to those figures in Old Testament history who did not speak with divine authorization. Their message was sometimes misleading, promising peace and safety instead of the coming judgment that the true prophets fore-

cast. The false prophets were rightly condemned (see Deut. 18:20; Jer. 14:14–15; 23:15, 17, 21, 32; Ezek. 13:10; Mic. 3:5, 11).

There shall be false teachers among you (*pseudodidaskaloi*), Peter warned. Numerous New Testament passages warn of false teachers who were already present or yet to come. Such teachers, comparable to the false prophets of the Old Testament, are "pseudo" in that they claim for themselves the offices of teacher in the churches when they have no right to do so and in that their message is false in content. Whenever they appear, they **privily shall bring in damnable heresies** ("They will secretly introduce destructive heresies," NIV). "Heresies" could have the idea of factions as well as unorthodox doctrine. Hence, "damnable heresies" may be defined as divisive opinions or teachings that result in the moral and spiritual destruction of those who accept them. Apparently noting a divisive effect of the heretics, Peter called attention to the tragic fact that **many shall follow their pernicious ways** (v. 2; "their evil teaching and shameful immorality," NLT). Because their heresies will include **even denying the Lord that bought them** (v. 1), they will incur **swift destruction**. The language here is reminiscent of Jude 4. "Bought" is metaphorical, referring to slaves purchased in the marketplace and transferred to new ownership. It implies that the heretics' purchase price had been paid, but the exchange of goods (the surrender of their own lives to Christ as Master) had never been made. Christ's death paid the penalty for their sin, but it would not become effective for their salvation unless they trusted in Christ as Savior. Thus, His atonement was available to them but not applicable to them without genuine faith.

Peter's concern was unlike the exploitative designs of the false teachers, who **through covetousness shall they with feigned** ("fabricated," Wuest) **words make merchandise of you** (v. 3). False teachers are often motivated by a desire for money and will commercialize the Christian faith to their own selfish advantage. No wonder that an outcome of their work is that **the way of truth shall be evil spoken of** (v. 2). False teachers or those whom they delude, or both, will cause the gospel and its teachings to be in disrepute.

The very judgment that such heretics deny ironically proves their downfall: **whose judgment now of a long time lingereth not, and their damnation slumbereth not** (v. 3). Long ago, in Old Testament times, their condemnation was declared (for Old Testament examples of the judgment to come on the wicked, see 2:4–9). Peter utilized synonymous parallelism to emphasize the certainty of their ruin; both terms for condemnation are equivalent, as are the negated verbs. What seems like an interminable delay in judgment is really God's patience with unrepentant sinners. A day will come when that patience will no longer delay the deserved condemnation of the wicked (see 3:9).

B. Refutation: Historical Examples of Judgment and Deliverance (2:4–10a)

1. Angels Who Sinned (2:4)

2:4. This verse begins an extended conditional construction with a very long protasis ("if" clause; 2:4–8) and an abrupt apodosis ("then" clause; 2:9–10a). The main idea in this section, in way of refutation, is that judgment of the unrighteous is certain. Peter put forth three historical examples to establish that fact. He also put forth a corollary of the main idea: God will rescue the righteous.

The angels that sinned are probably those disobedient supernatural beings whom Jude 6 mentions. Having sinned through pride, they were expelled from heaven. The pseudepigraphal book of *1 Enoch* describes the imprisonment of angels who, having transgressed, are now chained and await their final doom (*1 Enoch* 10:5–6; 12:4; 21:3–10). The disobedient angels are **reserved unto judgment**. They are bound; God **delivered them into chains of darkness**—clearly figurative language that expresses the desolation of the angels' pre-judgment condition and the fact that Satan and his fallen angels cannot escape their fate. **Hell** (Greek, *tartarus*) echoes *1 Enoch* 20:22, where Tartarus is the place of the punishment of fallen angels. Peter used this term to indicate a sphere of habitation and activity

that is infinitely below the evil angels' former estate and from which they cannot escape or return to the former position.

2. The Flood (2:5)

2:5. As in the case of the angels (1:4), God **spared not the old world**. Using another example from history, Peter substantiated the certainty of the judgment of the false teachers. In contrast to the wicked people of ancient times, **Noah** was **saved** (*phylassō*; "preserved," REB). Thus, in Peter's argument, Noah is a foil to **the ungodly** upon whom **the flood** came. The background to this verse is the account of the flood in Genesis 6–7. Peter called Noah **the eighth person**. Into the ark went Noah's wife, three sons, and three daughters-in-law. Noah was the eighth (see 1 Peter 3:20). Noah was the builder of the ark and an evangelist; he warned the wicked of the coming judgment so that they might repent. Hence, unlike the false teachers of Peter's day and the impious of his own time, Noah was **a preacher of righteousness**. Although this description of Noah is found nowhere else in Scripture, similar descriptions of him are found in Josephus (*Antiquities* 1.3.1), 1 Clement (7.6; 9.4), and the *Sibylline Oracles* (1.128–29). The statement about Noah encouraged Peter's hearers to imitate Noah and be heralds of the truth. In the midst of his discussion of frightening judgment to come, the apostle encouraged his hearers that the righteous need not fear the destruction that is coming to the wicked. If they take the part of Noah, they will be safe.

3. Sodom and Gomorrah (2:6–8)

2:6. The third example demonstrating the certainty of the judgment that will come on the wicked is **the cities of Sodom and Gomorrha** (see Jude 7). Their **overthrow** ("total destruction," NEB), described in Genesis 19, came by way of a devastating volcanic event. The devastation was so great that the cities were turned **into ashes** (*tephroō*). This is the only occurrence of this word in the New Testament. The first-century writer Dio Cassius used it of the eruption of Mount Vesuvius (AD 79). In that event, the cities of Pompeii and Herculaneum were buried in lava. God used a natural cataclysm as a means of judgment in the cases of Noah's society and the reprobate cities of Sodom and Gomorrah.

2:7-8. Here Peter affirmed the inevitability of the judgment of the wicked (thus giving the third historical precedent), and he exalted the person and behavior of Lot as an example for his audience. **Just Lot** (v. 7; "Lot, a righteous man," NIV) did not suffer the fate of the wicked in Sodom and Gomorrah. Rather, God **delivered** (*rhyomai*, "rescued") him. He, like Noah, is a foil for the godless people around him. In addition to "just," Lot is described in these verses as **that righteous man** (v. 8) and as a **righteous soul**. His fellow citizens are described as **wicked** (v. 7). Lot's righteous actions included being **vexed with the filthy conversation** ("conduct," NKJV) **of the wicked**. How Lot could be so distressed and how he could be called a "righteous man" and yet offer to turn his two daughters over to the wicked townsmen to be sexually abused (see Gen. 19:4–9) is difficult to understand apart from a knowledge of the code of honor characteristic of that day. The mere record of something in the Bible does not necessarily condone it.

4. Deliverance and Judgment (2:9–10a)

2:9. This verse represents the apodosis, the "then" clause, of the long conditional statement that begins in 2:4. Other translations besides the KJV make this clear. The NIV renders the first part of verse 9 as "if this is so, then the Lord knows ..." (The parenthetical nature of 2:8 is made clear in the KJV and the NIV.) The point is that if God did not withhold judgment from sinning angels, from the ungodly world of Noah's day, and from the lawless cities of Sodom and Gomorrah but judged them for their wickedness, and at the same time preserved the righteous, *then* the Lord knows how to deliver the righteous in the present and to appoint the wicked in the present for deserved judgment in the future.

Temptations is *peirasmos* and refers to the testing of one's faith and endurance. Whenever the believer is put to the test, God knows just what is

needed to help us escape. God knows (with commensurate ability) how **to reserve the unjust unto the day of judgment**. The historical examples of 2:4–8 effectively refute those who contend that divine judgment will forever linger.

2:10a. Peter included all the unrighteous within the scope of final judgment (2:9), but here he mentioned two classifications. His affirmation of judgment concerns **chiefly them**. Peter may have intended these categories as overarching descriptions of the false teachers, with their characteristics in 2:10b–22 subsumed under two classifications: (1) they **walk after the flesh in the lust of uncleanness** (immorality), and (2) they **despise government**. This could refer to the slander of earthly dignitaries such as church leaders, which might well be expected from such shameless peddlers of error. Thus, heresy and immorality often go hand in hand.

C. Digression: Denunciation of the False Teachers (2:10b–22)

A digression, according to Greco-Roman rhetorical theory, serves to treat some theme outside the logical order of a discourse. The treatment is effective in making an emotional appeal to the audience and enhancing style. In 2 Peter 2:10b–22, which echoes Jude 8–12, the apostle denounced the false teachers.

2:10b–11. The false teachers in Peter's communities were **not afraid to speak evil of dignities** (v. 10b; lit., "blaspheme glories"; used also in Jude 8). The adjectives **Presumptuous** and **selfwilled** ("reckless and headstrong," NEB) describe the character of the heretics, which led to their outrageous insolence. Their action challenged the honor of God and His agents so that they might have it for themselves. The Greek word *blasphēmeō* in verse 10b and 2:12, which lies behind "speak evil" (and whose adjectival form is translated "railing" in v. 11), expresses an assault on another's honor. Peter responded to the honor challenge with a blistering riposte in 2:10b–22. Not even the obedient **angels** (represented by the archangel Michael in Jude 9) dare to bring a **railing accusation against them** (wicked angels) **before the Lord**.

Peter's argument proceeds from the greater to the lesser. What is true of angels, **which are greater in power and might** than humans, certainly ought to be true of mortals.

2:12. By comparing the false teachers to **natural brute beasts**, Peter issued a scathing denunciation. The heretics were like irrational animals, whose lives are guided by mere instinct and who are born merely to be slaughtered. Destruction will be their final lot. The heresy to which Peter referred may have been an early form of second-century Gnosticism, which claimed to possess special, esoteric knowledge. If so, it is ironic that those who professed special knowledge acted out of abysmal ignorance (they spoke **evil of the things that they understand not**), and the result was arrogant blasphemy.

2:13. Peter said the heretics were deserving of destruction. They **shall receive the reward of unrighteousness**. These apostates had oriented themselves to the fulfillment of their own desires. They **riot[ed] in the day time**, to such excess that their nighttime revels carried on past dawn. The Greek phrase behind **sporting themselves with their own deceivings while they feast with you** is difficult to render. The word "deceivings" ("deceptions," NASB; Greek, *apatai*) could also mean "dissipation" (NRSV) or "pleasures" (NIV). If so, these false teachers injected their carousing into the sacred feasts, delighting in shameless acts instead of in true communion with Christ and His people. No wonder that Peter called the deceivers **Spots . . . and blemishes**. The word "blemishes" (*mōmoi*) is used in the Septuagint to describe the man who was unfit for service in the priesthood (Lev. 21:17–18, 21). Likewise, the false teachers were unfit for service in the church.

2:14. Assuming that the **eyes** indicate what is most in a person's heart (see Matt. 6:22–23), Peter proclaimed that the heretics' eyes were **full of adultery and . . . cannot cease from sin**. The first description is literally "eyes full of [desire for] an adulteress," which means that they desired every woman they saw, viewing her as a potential sex partner. "Their eyes cannot look at a woman without lust" (Phillips).

The **unstable souls** whom the false teachers were **beguiling** may have been immature males to whom the teachers' libertine ways appealed since they seemed to have a divine sanction. The beguiled could, however, have included female church members who, as recent converts or immature believers, had become targets of the immoral designs of the teachers. "Beguiling," the word that Peter used to describe the alluring manner of the heretics, is *deleazō*, a term that depicts the fisherman who attempts to lure and catch fish with bait (see James 1:14). Peter drew attention to the heretics' ability to "seduce" (NIV) the unsuspecting and unwary. The threat from the false teachers was as much moral as it was doctrinal.

The deviants were notable for their **covetous practices**. In fact, Peter said they had **a heart they have exercised** in such practices. Peter was drawing an athletic metaphor here; his verb is *gymnazō* (mentioned earlier). The heretics had set themselves firmly on a course of action like the runner, boxer, or wrestler preparing for the games. The prize they sought was the fulfillment of their own greed. Peter justly described these rapacious instructors in the church, who were abusing their position for the pursuit of their own detestable desires, as **cursed children**.

2:15. Those teaching erroneous doctrines had **gone astray** (the verb is in the passive voice, "they have been led astray," but it may be translated in the active voice). The word is *planaō* from which the word "planet," a wandering heavenly body, is derived. Jude used a cognate term in calling them "wandering stars" (Jude 13). They "lost their way" (NEB) when they continually chose to abandon **the right way** (*kataleipō* is a present participle, "leaving the right way behind"). Now they had drifted without the possibility of return (see 2:17). Rather than taking the right road, the heretics had followed **the way of Balaam the son of Bosor** (see Num. 22:2–24:25; 31:16; Jude 11).

2:16. Balaam **was rebuked for his iniquity**. He attempted to curse the Israelites for money. Peter was recalling Numbers 22:21–35, where "a speechless donkey spoke with a human voice and restrained the prophet's madness" (NRSV). A donkey rebuking the prophet's madness reflected not only on the foolishness of Balaam but also on that of the false teachers of Peter's day. They showed less spiritual sensitivity than the "brute beasts" (2:12) to which Peter compared them. Since they had gone the way of Balaam, they were just as obtuse as he was when he showed less sense than his donkey.

2:17. This verse parallels Jude 12. Peter used two metaphors, however, whereas Jude consolidated them into one metaphor. According to Peter, the deviants were **wells** ("springs," NASB) **without water** and **clouds that are carried with a tempest** ("mists driven by a storm," NASB). Jude's comparison has "clouds they are without water, carried about of winds" (Jude 12). Both Jude and Peter stressed the spiritual emptiness that accompanied the opponents' teaching and example. Peter's image is that of a thirsty traveler who comes to a spring expecting cool, refreshing water but finds it dry. So the false teachers promised satisfying truth but in reality had nothing to offer.

2:18. The **great swelling words of vanity** ("bombastic nonsense," NRSV) that the false teachers spoke perhaps had to do more with **the lusts of the flesh** than with unorthodox doctrine. The heretics erred on both counts and led others to follow them in their vulgar ways **through much wantonness** ("by sensuality," NASB).

2:19. The bombast of the false teachers was an attractive **promise** and an apparent guarantee of **liberty**. Gnosticism promoted release from the corruption of the material world and the body, and the proto-Gnostics who posed a danger to Peter's congregations claimed to offer their adherents some sort of release from bondage. The teachers **themselves are the servants** ("slaves," NKJV) **of corruption**. The very ones who were promising freedom from bondage were themselves slaves of depravity. Freedom from law resulted in bondage to sin, and liberty was turned into license. The last part of the verse is proverbial: **for of whom a man is overcome, of the same is he brought in bondage** ("for by what a man

is overcome, by this he is enslaved," NASB). Peter pictured the enslavement of enemies who have been conquered in battle.

2:20–21. Unlike the false teachers, those whom they had duped appear to have truly been saved: **they [had] escaped the pollutions of the world through the knowledge of the Lord and Saviour Jesus Christ** (v. 20) and knew the way of righteousness, a knowledge that is personal and intimate (*epiginōskō*). They had been seduced and had **turn[ed] from the holy commandment delivered unto them** (v. 21). It would have been **better for them not to have known the way of righteousness** than to have known it and turned from it. Peter was using hyperbole here; if these people were believers, of course it is better to have eternal life, even if they were not walking with God, than for them not to have been saved at all.

How is it, then, that **the latter end is worse** (v. 20)? Theologians differ, according to their views of salvation (soteriology), whether this refers to saved backsliders, the unsaved who profess to be saved, or those who have lost their salvation. In each case, those falling away from their original profession of faith are in worse condition.

2:22. The repulsiveness of the two images in this verse served as a warning to Peter's churches not to follow those who had succumbed to the enticements of the false teachers. The metaphors of the dog and the pig, both used in the form of a **proverb**, sound harsh and hostile, but they were effective devices to first-century people whose culture emphasized purity and honor. In the ancient world, **The dog** was regarded as unclean. It was a scavenger, roaming streets and dumps, feeding on unclean things — even human flesh (see Exod. 22:31; 1 Kings 14:11; 16:4; 2 Kings 9:10; Luke 16:21). Peter's statement that this animal returns **to his own vomit** is a quotation of Proverbs 26:11. Thus, the Christian who has fallen away is a fool who returns to his folly. The dog is not only unclean because of what it eats; it is also so attached to it that it ingests that which has been regurgitated. Any matter expelled from the body is a potential pollutant in a ritual sense, and a dog's vomit of unclean matter is definitely a pollutant. **The**

sow that was washed [returned] to her wallowing in the mire. To the Jew, pigs were unclean and thus unfit for sacrifice or for human consumption (see Lev. 11:7; Deut. 14:8). The Greeks also regarded pigs as unclean. Peter's intention with these colorful yet loathsome images was to stress that the backsliders had become spiritually unclean and dishonorable. The reality of their salvation was in serious doubt since they exhibited the traits of inherently unclean animals. Peter's denunciation of the false teachers evolved into a condemnation of those whom they had led astray. The entire section was a powerful warning to those who would allow themselves to be wooed by the opponents.

VI. Third Proof: Accusation and Refutation (3:1–13)

A. Accusation: The Second Coming Will Not Happen; God Does Not Intervene in History (3:1–4)

1. A Second Reminder (3:1–2)

3:1–2. In the third and final proof, Peter refuted an accusation from the heretics that impugned the idea of a second coming of Christ. In this, his **second epistle** (v. 1), the apostle's intention was to **stir up your pure minds by way of remembrance**. "Minds" could also be "intention" (NRSV) or "disposition" (NAB). Pure Christian thinking can effectively identify unorthodox teaching and maintain faithfulness in opposition to it. Peter pointed his readers' attention to the words both of **the holy prophets, and of … the apostles of the Lord and Saviour** (v. 2), placing the Old Testament prophets and the New Testament apostles on an equal plane. Both were vehicles of God's sacred truth and trustworthy judges of correct doctrine and false doctrine. Peter, being one of the apostles, could speak with knowledge and authority as a representative of the apostolic group.

2. The Objection of the Scoffers (3:3–4)

3:3. Peter used the expression **Knowing this first** in 1:20 to call attention to a matter of great importance. Here the matter of great significance was **that there shall come in the last days scoffers** (lit., "with scoffing, scoffers will come"). "The last days" is an expression that refers to the whole period introduced by Christ's first coming. These days are "last" in comparison to Old Testament days, which were preliminary and preparatory. Also, the Christian era is the time of the beginning of prophetic fulfillment. Those who mock the delay of God's judgment are denounced in the prophetic writings (see Isa. 5:18–20; Jer. 5:12–24; Amos 9:10; Mal. 2:17), and the apostolic testimony has similar warnings regarding those who deny the final judgment and the resurrection, some of whom contend that it has already come (see 1 Corinthians 15; 2 Thess. 2:2; 2 Tim. 2:18).

The "scoffers" may have been early Gnostics who resisted the idea of a time of judgment and moral accountability. The Gnostics ridiculed the idea of a bodily resurrection. For them, salvation involved enlightenment and a release from the flesh, not its transformation. The heretics whom Peter opposed may have scoffed at the notion of resurrected and transformed matter. Their libertinism (**walking after their own lusts**) was like that of second-century Gnostics in Irenaeus's *Against Heresies*. The full implication of this prophecy is that the worst scoffers will come closest to the end times. Therefore, it should not be surprising that today even some professing believers ridicule the idea of the soon coming of Christ.

3:4. Peter quoted the scoffers' objection: **Where is the promise of his coming? for since the fathers fell asleep, all things continue as they were from the beginning of the creation**. As in the cases of the first two objections, the intruders challenged God's honor and that of His people by a refusal to accept the truth of Christ's claim that He will come again one day in judgment. Perhaps the scoffers believed that the Lord is unable to make good on His promises. Peter, the apostolic representative and a client of His heavenly patron, stood up and offered a riposte. "The fathers" are either the first Christians to die after Christ's death and resurrection (e.g., Stephen, James the brother of John, and other early Christian leaders who had died; see Heb. 13:7) or the Old Testament patriarchs.

B. Refutation: The Precedent of Previous Judgment, the Divine Perspective on Time, and the Authority of Jesus' Own Word (3:5–13)

1. The Flood as a Precedent of Judgment (3:5–7)

3:5–7. Peter systematically demolished the argument against the doctrine of the second coming. The first of his three counterarguments was that, contrary to what the heretics said, all things had not remained static since the beginning of creation. In fact, the heretics **willingly are ignorant of** (v. 5) the creation of **the heavens … and the earth** by means of **the word of God** and the destruction of the world that, **being overflowed with water, perished** (v. 6). Uniformitarian geology speculates that all the processes of nature have always been the same (i.e., uniform) throughout history. This viewpoint, however, overlooks God's serious disruption of natural history by means of the Noahic flood. Things have not always remained as they were after the initial moment of God's fiat. Ignoring the flood as a divine intervention was not an oversight; it was deliberate. The scoffers did not want to face up to the fallacy in their argument.

Since the cosmos has not remained unchanged in the past, the chances of further cataclysmic changes are great. Indeed, Peter pointed to the fate that awaits the present **heavens and the earth** (v. 7). They are **reserved unto fire [for the] day of judgment**, when the ungodly will perish. Jewish apocalyptic thought drew a correlation between the flood and the eschatological devastation by fire, and Old Testament prophetic texts speak of divine judgment by fire (e.g., Isa. 66:15–16; Zeph. 1:18; Mal. 3:19). Since things do not remain unchanged, Peter successfully refuted the claim of the false teachers. The principle of change in the universe allows for the irruption of God's activity, whether in creation, salvation, or judgment. Both creation and the ordination of future judgment are effected by **the word of God** (vv. 5, 7).

2. Temporal Distinctions and the Lord's Patience (3:8–9)

3:8. In the second of his counterarguments directed at those who ridiculed the promised second coming, Peter refuted the distorted view of time that led the scoffers to discount the Parousia. In their perspective, a long delay meant that God could not deliver on His promises. Such a view betrays, Peter said, a failure to understand the atemporality of God. He has created time and chooses to work within the finitude of time (measured by the seasons). He Himself transcends time and is not bound by it. He exists eternally outside of time in an everlasting now, and of this, the mockers were **ignorant**. Peter asserted that **one day is with the Lord as a thousand years, and a thousand years as one day**. The delay in His coming is of no consequence to the Lord. From the Lord's perspective, it is no delay at all. Peter's principle echoes the sentiments of Psalm 90:4. "The Lord" in 3:8–10 probably refers to God as Son, not God as Father-Creator (see 3:5). The uses of "the Lord" and "God" in these verses seem to be carefully distinguished, and the reference to "a thief in the night" (3:10) is reminiscent of Jesus' teaching about His coming (see Matt. 24:43–44; Luke 12:39–40; Rev. 3:3; 16:5; see also 1 Thess. 5:2, 4).

Believers often become discouraged in waiting for Christ's coming, when their prayers are apparently unanswered or when successful outcomes from their endeavors seem never to come. In such situations, Peter's reminder of God's timelessness might help finite humans to see that God does not work on the same schedule as they do. Since time is purely relative with the Lord, He waits patiently while human beings stew with impatience. From God's perspective, He is working all things according to His plan and His timing.

3:9. The heretics' accusation against the Lord may have been that although He is able to deliver on the promises of His coming, He is **slack concerning his promise**. Not so, said Peter. Any "delay" is due to the fact that He **is longsuffering to us-ward** ("is patient with you," NRSV). The Lord is **not willing that any should perish, but that all should come to repentance**. Scoffers today deride the Bible as being full of "hellfire and brimstone," with little evidence of a loving God. The Christian ought gently to steer such persons to this text, where Peter's emphasized that the very "delay" in Christ's coming at which the mockers sneered was really God's patient waiting for them to "come to repentance." In fact, the Lord wants everyone to come to repentance—a radical reorientation of one's entire course of life in response to the enlightening influence of the Holy Spirit. This shift entails belief in a loving God and salvation through Christ.

3. "The Day of the Lord Will Come as a Thief in the Night" (3:10)

3:10. A prominent New Testament metaphor for the second coming is that **the day of the Lord will come as a thief in the night** (see discussion on 3:8). Since a thief comes suddenly and without announcement, taking the members of the household unaware, the image is an apt one for Jesus' coming. Jesus said, "Of that day and that hour knoweth no man, no, not the angels which are in heaven, neither the Son, but the Father" (Mark 13:32). Peter's utilization of the metaphor constitutes a third refutation of the argument against the Parousia. The time will be totally unexpected; just when human inclination to discount its certainty is highest, the day of the Lord shall come.

The devastation of the created order that the day of the Lord will bring cannot be even remotely conceived. Peter stated that the catastrophe will be accompanied by **a great noise**, when **the heavens shall pass away**. To convey the inconceivable power of eschatological upheaval, the apostle described it in terms of sound whose decibels are off the scale. The immensity of the eschatological cataclysm sounds like an enormous nuclear explosion. Whatever it will involve will be just as devastating to the planet in the future as the flood was in the past.

The elements shall melt with fervent heat is another expression of apocalyptic language. "The elements" is a term that refers either to the heavenly bodies or to the physical elements—in the first century, such things as earth, air, fire, and water; in today's more precise scientific terminology, hydrogen, oxygen, carbon, and so on. Petrine history, like biblical history as a whole, is linear (teleological), not

cyclical: it progresses to an endpoint predetermined by God, at which time the present order will give way to God's new and everlasting order in the universe. So that the new order may appear, **the earth ... shall be burnt up**. Even human activity will be judged by fire, as Paul indicates (1 Cor. 3:13–15). Peter may have utilized Stoic terminology in 3:10–12, but if so, he adapted it to reflect the Old Testament motif of judgment by fire (see Isa. 66:15).

4. Exhortation in Light of the Certainty of the Parousia (3:11–13)

3:11–12. Even more apocalyptic language appears here. The accumulation of the terms **dissolved** (twice), **fire**, **melt**, and **fervent heat** signifies an absolute and total destruction of the created order as it is presently configured. Peter's basic intention in his description of the conflagration to come was to foster **holy conversation** ("conduct," NKJV) **and godliness** (v. 11) among his readers. The practices of **looking for and hasting unto the coming of the day of God** (v. 12; "Look eagerly for the coming of the Day of God and work to hasten it on," NEB) are carried out by living in a spirit of unity with fellow Christians, humbly praying for strength of endurance until the day Christ appears, and spreading the good news to unbelievers. Can the time that will elapse before the Parousia be shortened by human activity? Peter's language seems to express such an idea, but he probably was speaking hyperbolically here. A life of faithful discipleship makes waiting for one's glorious future more endurable, and therefore that time of waiting seems shorter. Jesus indicated that the time of the Parousia has been set by the Father (Mark 13:32–33). "The day of God" is apparently synonymous with "the day of the Lord" (3:10) since it is characterized by the same kind of events (see Rev. 16:14). Holy expectation of Jesus' coming is a good way to resist false teachers and their mockery of that hope.

3:13. The disappearance of the universe does not spell the end of material existence altogether. The vanishing of the old gives way to **new heavens and a new earth**. New heavens and a new earth are promised by

Isaiah (65:17; 66:22). This **promise** is confirmed by Revelation 21:1. The term "new" (*kainos*) suggests a renewal, not an abolition, of material existence. There is discontinuity, but the fact that "heavens" and "earth" will appear suggest a material existence whose features are in some kind of continuity with what humans have been familiar. The remarkable and critical difference is that the new creation is where **righteousness** dwells as a permanent resident—settles down and makes its home (see Isa. 11:4–5; 45:8; Dan. 9:24). The outlook here should give impetus to a Christian stewardship of the earth that values and protects both organic and inorganic elements.

VII. Conclusion (3:14–18)

In the conclusion, Peter stressed the need for diligence and vigilance (vv. 14–17), issued a final injunction for Christian growth (v. 18a), and broke forth in a final doxology (v. 18b).

A. The Need for Diligence and Vigilance (3:14–17)

3:14. Because the heresies of the infiltrators were divisive, Peter urged his various congregations to **be diligent that ye may be found of him in peace**. This quality is primarily mutual and harmonious interdependence within the church. Peace is promoted when church members live **without spot, and blameless** (see 1 Peter 1:19, "Christ, as of a lamb without blemish and without spot"). The two terms in Greek, *aspiloi* and *amōmētoi*, are negated (with *a*-prefix) adjectives. They recall the description in 2:13 of the infiltrators as "spots" and "blemishes" (*spiloi* and *mōmoi*) who ruin the life of the church.

3:15. Peter recounted the topic of the Lord's **longsuffering** (*makrothymia*), introduced in 3:9, with the description of it as **salvation** (*sōtēria*). Peter expressed warmth in his reference to Paul as **our beloved brother Paul**. Here Peter confirmed the unity of teaching and purpose that governed their relationship, abundantly attested in Paul's letters and the book of Acts. Despite the earlier confrontation in Antioch, when Paul rebuked Peter (Gal. 2:11–14), their bond in Christ was strong.

Does Peter's statement that Paul **hath written unto you** signify some lost letter(s) of Paul? Could the communication to which Peter referred be one or more of the Pauline letters in our New Testament canon? It has been suggested that what Paul wrote to the recipients of 2 Peter was a copy of Romans, which was sent to the churches as a circular letter. Galatians, Ephesians, and Colossians are also candidates for this communication.

3:16. Peter said that in **all his** (Paul's) **epistles**, Paul was **speaking in them of these things**. Peter may have been referring in general to the exhortations to holy living in 3:11–14, which parallel many passages in Paul's writings. In a superb understatement, Peter mentioned that in Paul's epistles **are some things hard to be understood**. The word *dysnoētos* was used in ancient times to describe the ambiguity of oracles. Peter was not saying that Paul's writing, under the inspiration of the Holy Spirit, was hopelessly equivocal; he meant that Paul's words require careful reading so that the interpretation of them will be properly understood.

Certain people, whom Peter described as **unlearned and unstable**, had not taken care to interpret Paul's letters properly. Instead, they **wrest** ("distort," NASB) the great apostle's meaning in those letters. The Greek word translated here as "wrest" (*strebloō*) is colorful. Originally, it referred to twisting cables or making them taut. Another usage of the term referred to the wrenching of dislocated limbs in order to set them. The word also described the use of torturers' equipment that wrenched the body in the course of interrogations. Peter used it figuratively, but the word effectively conveys the intentional nature of the heretics' twisted distortion of true Pauline doctrine.

Noteworthy is Peter's classification of Paul's letters as Scripture here. The "unlearned and unstable" distorted difficult teachings in the Pauline writings **as they do also the other scriptures**. Peter placed Paul's writings on the same level of authority as the God-breathed writings of the Old Testament (see 1:21; 2 Tim. 3:16). Already in Peter's day, at least some of Paul's epistles were accorded the status of inspired writings that were authoritative for the church. The importance of Peter's statement toward understanding the New Testament documents as inspired is not to be missed.

3:17. The nature of 2 Peter as a testament is evident in Peter's closing exhortation to his readers to **beware**. His ethos was built up when he issued this final exhortation and when he addressed his charges as **beloved**. The apostle's foregoing instruction had enabled them to **know these things before**. When he departed, his churches would remember his statements regarding true and false doctrine (see 1:12–15). If they were vigilant, they could avoid **being led away with the error of the wicked**. Peter did not want his congregants to **fall from [their] own stedfastness**, which does not necessarily refer to a fall from eternal life into damnation but may refer rather to falling into confusion.

B. Final Exhortation to Grow in Grace and Knowledge (3:18a)

3:18a. The opposite (introduced by **But**) of falling away from one's secure position is to **grow in grace, and in the knowledge of our Lord and Sav-** **iour Jesus Christ**. Peter's word for "knowledge" here is *gnōsis*, the practical wisdom that enables one to conduct life in a godly manner (see discussion on 1:5). This knowledge comes from Christ and is directed toward Him. Peter concluded by again stressing knowledge, probably as an antidote to the false teachers, who boasted in their esoteric knowledge. The church must always take care to help its young members grow, which involves protecting them from false teaching and false cults.

C. Doxology (3:18b)

3:18b. A beautiful doxology (from *doxa*, meaning "glory") concludes Peter's second letter: **To him be glory both now and for ever. Amen**. Literally, it reads, "To Him [Jesus Christ] glory both now and into the day of the eternity. Amen." This is the proper response to the heavenly patronage of the Father and the Son. Peter identified God as the one whose "divine power has given us everything we need for life and godliness through our knowledge of him who called us by his own glory and goodness" (1:3 NIV). His clients owe Him honor—glory—since they have received His benefits without measure.

THE FIRST EPISTLE OF JOHN

INTRODUCTION

Author

The author is John son of Zebedee (see Mark 1:19–20), the apostle and the author of the gospel of John and Revelation (in both books, see Introduction: "Author"). He was a fisherman whom Jesus called early in His ministry (Matt. 4:18–22) and was the disciple "whom Jesus loved" (John 13:23). Along with Peter and James, he was one of Jesus' inner circle. Thus, he was (1) on the Mount of Transfiguration (Matt. 17:1), (2) in Gethsemane (Matt. 26:37), (3) the only apostle at the crucifixion (John 19:2–27), (4) the first apostle to arrive at the empty tomb (John 20:4–5), and (5) with Peter when Jesus recommissioned him at the Sea of Galilee (John 21:15–23). John and Peter continued as close companions and church leaders after Pentecost (Acts 3:1; 4:19; 8:14; Gal. 2:9).

Unlike most New Testament letters, 1 John does not identify its author. The earliest identification of him comes from the church fathers: Irenaeus (ca. AD 140–203), Clement of Alexandria (ca. 150–215), Tertullian (ca. 155–222), and Origen (ca. 185–253) all designated the author as the apostle John. No one else was suggested by the early church.

This traditional identification is confirmed by evidence in the letter itself.

(1) The style of the gospel of John is markedly similar to that of this letter. Both are written in simple Greek and use contrasting figures, such as light and darkness, life and death, truth and lies, love and hate.

(2) Similar phrases and expressions, such as those found in the following passages, are striking.

1 John	Gospel of John
1:1	1:1, 14
1:4	16:24
1:6–7	3:19–21
2:7	13:34–35
3:8	8:44
3:14	5:24

4:6	8:47
4:9	1:14, 18; 3:16
5:9	5:32, 37
5:12	3:36

(3) The mention of eyewitness testimony (1:1–4) harmonizes with the fact that John was a follower of Christ from the earliest days of His ministry.

(4) The authoritative manner that pervades the letter (seen in its commands, 2:15, 24, 28; 4:1; 5:21; its firm assertions, 2:6; 3:14; 4:12; and its pointed identification of error, 1:6, 8; 2:4, 22) is what would be expected from an apostle.

(5) The suggestions of advanced age (addressing his readers as "children," 2:1, 28; 3:7) agree with early church tradition concerning John's age when he wrote the books known to be his.

(6) The description of the heretics as "antichrists" (2:18), "liar(s)" (2:22), and "children of the devil" (3:10) is consistent with Jesus' characterization of John as a "son of thunder" (Mark 3:17).

(7) The indications of a close relationship with the Lord (1:1; 2:5–6, 24, 27–28) fit the descriptions of the disciple "whom Jesus loved" and the one who "was leaning on Jesus' bosom" (John 13:23).

Date

The letter is difficult to date with precision, but factors such as (1) evidence from early Christian writers (Irenaeus and Clement of Alexandria), (2) the early form of Gnosticism reflected in John's denunciations in the letter, and (3) indications of John's advanced age suggest the end of the first century. Since the author of 1 John seems to build on concepts and themes found in the fourth gospel (see 1 John 2:7–11), it is reasonable to date the letter somewhere between AD 85 and 95, after the writing of the gospel of John, which may have been written circa 85 (see John, Introduction: "Date").

Recipients

That this letter was addressed to believers is made clear in 1 John 2:12–14, 19; 3:1; 5:13, but the letter does not indicate who they were or where they lived. The fact that it mentions no one by name suggests it was a circular letter sent to Christians in a number of places. Evidence from early Christian writers places the apostle John in Ephesus during most of his later years (ca. AD 70–100). The earliest confirmed use of 1 John was in the province of Asia (in modern Turkey), where Ephesus was located. Clement of Alexandria indicates that John ministered in the various churches scattered throughout that province. It may be assumed, therefore, that 1 John was sent to the churches of the Roman province of Asia (see Map 14 at the end of the *Zondervan KJV Study Bible*).

Gnosticism

One of the most dangerous heresies of the first two centuries of the church was Gnosticism. Its central teaching was that spirit is entirely good and matter is entirely evil. Five important errors flowed from this unbiblical dualism.

(1) Man's body, which is matter, was therefore considered evil. It was contrasted with God, who is wholly spirit and therefore good.

(2) Salvation was the escape from the body, achieved not by faith in Christ but by special knowledge (the Greek word for "knowledge" is *gnōsis*, hence "Gnosticism").

(3) Christ's true humanity was denied in two ways: (1) some said that Christ only seemed to have a body, a view called Docetism, from the Greek *dokeō* ("to seem"), and (2) others said that the divine Christ joined the man Jesus at baptism and left Him before He died, a view called Cerinthianism, after its most prominent spokesman, Cerinthus. This view is the background of much of 1 John (see 1:1; 2:22; 4:2–3).

(4) Since the body was considered evil, it was to be treated harshly. This ascetic form of Gnosticism is the background of Colossians 2:21–23.

(5) Paradoxically, this dualism also led to licentiousness. The reasoning was that since matter—and not the breaking of God's law (see 3:4)—was considered evil, breaking His law was of no moral consequence.

It is important to note that the Gnosticism addressed in the New Testament was an early form of the heresy, not the intricately developed system of the second and third centuries. In addition to that detected in Colossians and in John's letters, acquaintance with early Gnosticism is reflected in 1–2 Timothy, Titus, 2 Peter, and perhaps 1 Corinthians.

Theme and Theological Message

John's readers were confronted with an early form of Gnostic teaching of the Cerinthian variety (see "Gnosticism," above). This heresy was also libertine, throwing off all moral restraints.

Consequently, John wrote this letter with two basic purposes in mind: (1) to expose false teachers (2:26) and (2) to give believers assurance of salvation (5:13). In keeping with his intention to combat Gnostic teachers, John specifically struck at their total lack of morality (3:8–10); by giving eyewitness testimony to the incarnation, he sought to confirm his readers' belief in the incarnate Christ (1:3). Success in this would verify their mutual fellowship with the Father and Son and would give the writer joy (1:3–4). John emphasized three tests by which one may know that one has eternal life: (1) *theological*, belief in Jesus Christ; (2) *moral*, living righteously; (3) *social*, loving one another (Bruce, *The Epistles of St. John*, p. 53).

Outline

Bibliography

Brown, Raymond E. *The Epistles of John*. The Anchor Bible 30. Garden City, NY: Doubleday, 1982.

Bruce, F. F. *The Epistles of St. John*. Grand Rapids, MI: Eerdmans, 1970.

Grayston, Kenneth. *The Johannine Epistles*. New Century Bible Commentary. Grand Rapids, MI: Eerdmans, 1984.

Marshall, I. Howard. *The Epistles of John*. New International Commentary on the New Testament. Grand Rapids, MI: Eerdmans, 1978.

Smalley, Stephen. *1, 2, 3, John*. Word Biblical Commentary 51. Waco, TX: Word, 1984.

Stott, John. *The Epistles of John: An Introduction and Commentary*. Tyndale New Testament Commentaries 19. Grand Rapids, MI: Eerdmans, 1974.

Westcott, B. F. *The Epistles of St. John*. 1892. Reprint, Grand Rapids, MI: Eerdmans, 1966.

EXPOSITION

I. Introduction: The Reality of the Incarnation (1:1–4)

The opening to this letter exhibits the same subject and several of the same words as the introduction to John's gospel (1:1–4) — "the beginning," "the Word," "life." With the words "That which was from the beginning" (v. 1), John directed the message of his letter to the origin of the gospel message (see his similar use of the word "beginning" in 2:7, 24; 3:11;

2 John 5–6). Origin and antiquity validated authority in the ancient world. In this way, the authority of 1 John is traced to, and grounded in, John's firsthand knowledge of the message, "the Word of life," (v. 1) and its author, Jesus Christ (see 1:3). John did this in a way that may seem circular and repetitious. This, however, is a clue to its importance. It discloses and reinforces a pattern, an unbroken and uninterrupted chain, of both revelation and fellowship that

anticipates at the outset any rival teaching that lays claim to fellowship with or knowledge of God but denies the reality of the incarnate life of Christ (see 5:20 and Introduction: "Gnosticism"). Unwound, the pattern of authority that links readers to fellowship with God is clear: Father → Son → Eyewitnesses to the Word of Life → Fellowship → Mutual joy. The authoritative eyewitness testimony to the Word of Life is the central link that connects the reader to mutual fellowship with God and completes the circle of joy.

1:1. That which was from the beginning coupled with the testimony of eyewitness experience (**heard … seen … looked upon … handled**) anticipates, in the repetition of "which," the crowning emphasis of John's introduction, **the Word of life**. By capitalizing "the Word," the KJV interprets this as a reference to Jesus Christ, as in John 1:1, 14. Unlike in his gospel, here John added an important qualifier: "of life." Although the meaning of John's grammar can be legitimately explained as "the Word that is life" or "the word about Life," John immediately explained his meaning with the personification of "life": "that eternal life, which was with the Father, and was manifested unto us" (1:2; see 5:11–12, 20). It is the word (message) about the Life, the Son, Jesus Christ, that was central to John and critical to fellowship with the Father. Therefore, the repetition of **we** (and **our**) makes clear that the message, or "the Word of life," belonged to many eyewitnesses of the Life (see 1:2). It becomes clear from the context that "the Word" speaks of a revelatory message indissolubly tied to the person of Jesus Christ.

As one might expect in an introduction, John anticipated issues relevant to his purpose for writing. At the outset, John opposed the false teaching of the Gnostic opponents (see Introduction: "Gnosticism") by describing Jesus as eternal (Life, eternal life) and human (**which we have looked upon, and our hands have handled**). John testified that the One who has existed from eternity (John 1:1) "was made flesh" (John 1:14), that is, a flesh-and-blood man. He was true God and true man.

1:2. John premiered Jesus not by His name or by His title "Christ" but as **the life … that eternal life**. This emphasis on Jesus as the Life brings into view the resurrected Jesus, whom "our hands have handled" (1:1; see John 20:20–21; 27–29). Jesus is called "the life" because He is the living One who has life in Himself (John 1:4; 11:25; 14:6). He is also the source of life and sovereign over life (see 5:11). The letter begins and ends (5:20) with the theme of eternal life. Life and eternal life not only describe Jesus Christ but are hallmarks of those in a personal relationship with the One who is Life (see 5:11–12, 5:20). Life and eternal life belong to the implications of fellowship (see 1:3).

1:3. Fellowship (Greek, *koinōnia*) is the spiritual bond of the believer with Christ—depicted in the figures of the vine and branches (John 15:1–5) and the body and the head (see 1 Cor. 12:12; Col. 1:18)—as well as communion with the Father and with fellow believers. The certainty of fellowship with the Father and the Son, expressly enjoyed by John and the eyewitnesses, is extended to those who were not eyewitnesses through the testimony to the Word of Life (see John 20:27–29). Behind the correspondence of the apostolic experience of fellowship with the Father and the Son was the challenge to that certainty from the false teaching that John combated in this letter. From 2:12–14, 19, it may be certain that John had genuine Christian readers in view. It was not their conversion but their certainty (joy) that he wished to ensure.

1:4. Your joy expresses John's concern for the certainty he wished his readers to enjoy, but "our joy" (alternative reading of early Greek manuscripts and accepted by other translations) matches John's concern for mutual fellowship (v. 3) and whose own joy is completed with the assurance of their fellowship. It is this fellowship, grounded in the believer's relationship to Jesus Christ, that is challenged by the false teaching aimed at the person of Jesus.

In the opening of this letter, then, John was concerned to reassure his readers (his "little children," 2:1) and confirm them in the joy of their salvation. Full-fledged joy is experienced in fellowship, fellowship with the Father and the Son (and thereby with other believers). That fellowship is entered, enjoyed, and ensured only through the Word of Life, Jesus Christ, the mediator of fellowship with God. This fellowship was dependent on fellowship with the eye-witnesses who had firsthand knowledge, the author John and the consensus of witness he represented.

II. The Christian Life as Fellowship with the Father and the Son (1:5–2:28)

A. Ethical Tests of Fellowship (1:5–2:11)

1. Moral Likeness (1:5–7)

1:5. The message which we have heard of him comes "from" (Greek, *apo*) Jesus (see 1:1). Although this exact message (Greek, *angelia*; only here and 2:10) is nowhere found in the recorded words of Jesus, John, who "heard" more than was recorded (see John 21:25), opened with this grand truth "from" Jesus, who is "the life" and "the light of men" (John 1:4–5, 9), the Son who reveals God the Father (John 1:14). Light represents what is good, true, and holy, while darkness represents what is evil and false (see John 3:19–21).

The message **that God is light, and in him is no darkness at all** provides an authoritative index by which to test a sequence of claims (1:6, 8, 10), intersected with John's corrections (1:7, 9) of the error of those claims.

	Claim	Contradiction
1:6	We have fellowship	We walk in the darkness
1:8	We have no sin	We deceive ourselves
1:10	We have not sinned	We make him a liar

The claims echo the assertions of the false teaching that John contested. The claims of the false teachers and John's corrections are keyed to "the message … that God is light [truth], and in him is no darkness [error] at all" (1:5). Together they profile two lifestyles—one characterized by wickedness and error, the other by holiness and truth—that gauge the reader's "fellowship" with God. Thus, one can take the test: Can one claim to have fellowship with God and walk in darkness? (1:6). Can one say "I have no sin" and not be deceived? (1:8). Can one say "I have not sinned" and not make God a liar? (1:10).

1:6. John used **we** to identify himself with his readers in the hypothetical "if" of these claims (1:6, 8, 10) and corrections (1:7, 9). It may be questioned whether John would have included himself and his readers in the false claims if they originated with the assertions of the false teachers. It must be remembered that John took pen to paper because error had already infiltrated the thinking of his readers. Even if that error survived only as a tempting option to what John had taught his readers, what his readers may have heard from an acquaintance or family member needed to be labeled as what it was: error. The line between light and dark is gray, and John defined the edges of that line through this series of necessary deductions taken from the implications of "the message" (1:5). John vividly put the claims in the reader's mouth, showing that, as good as they may sound, they spell falsehood. With the same vigor, he walked the reader through the corrections in 1:7, 9. In short, John argued with the rhetorical power of a hypothetical: Should you, I, or a trusted friend **say that we have fellowship with him, and walk in darkness, we lie, and do not the truth**.

1:7. John defined fellowship as **walk[ing] in the light, as he is in the light**. Fellowship is more than a claim; it is a pattern of living (to "walk"; see also 2:6) in the light defined by God's own character and the provision, not of sinlessness (which would demand walking "according to" the light), but of the purifying agency of His Son's blood that is resident in the sphere of light. **Fellowship one with another** expands on "fellowship with him" (1:6). "One with another" (*allēlōn*) implies a mutual relationship with the Father and the Son as the basis of fellowship between believers. It is what believers share ("fellowship") that determines the quality of fellowship. For Christians, fellowship is defined by "walk[ing] in the light, as he is in the light" (the sphere of relationship with the Father and the Son).

2. Confession of Sin (1:8–2:2)

1:8. The second claim, **we have no sin** (equivalent to "We are sinless"), John called an expression of self-deception. **We deceive ourselves** (Greek, *planaō*) is connected to the absence of truth. There is no way to tell here whether this is due to ignorance (absence of the facts) or denial (rejection of the facts). The tone of debate lying just beneath the surface of this verse ("we have no sin") and 1:10 ("we have not sinned") suggests a deliberate refusal to acknowledge the truth.

1:9. The word **confess** (Greek, *homologeō*) carries the idea of "concur" (see 4:2–3, 15). In papyrus contracts discovered in the dry climate of Egypt, one finds the same Greek word used here to express formal agreement between a buyer and seller, with the conditions of a purchase. The buyer "concurs" (*homologeō*) with the terms of purchase. Transferred to the spiritual realm, the believer "confesses" (*homologeō*), acknowledging what God says about his or her sin. Confession involves seeing sin as God sees it or agreeing with what God says is right and wrong, good and bad. In the New Testament, repentance is the corollary to confession. When one genuinely concurs, or agrees, with God about sin, it involves an adjustment or change of outlook (repentance). Both New Testament ideas concern conforming to God's values and entail an ongoing appreciation of who God really is. How poignant is this acknowledgment of sin in view of the heretical claims to "have no sin" (1:8) and to have never sinned, "we have not sinned" (1:10), which expose not only one's self-deception but the darkest corollary of the denial: "we make [God] a liar" (1:10).

Sin is out of character with God, who is light. When Christians concur with God and conform themselves to His character (the light, or His will and ways), He proves Himself **faithful and just**. Here the phrase is virtually a single concept (faithful-and-just). It indicates that God's response toward those who confess their sins will be in accordance with His nature and His gracious commitment to His people (see Ps. 143:1; Zech. 8:8). God is faithful to His promise to forgive (see Jer. 31:34; Mic. 7:18–20; Heb. 10:22–23) and to restore the communion with God that was interrupted by sin (as requested in the Lord's Prayer; Matt. 6:12). Here John amplifies the concept of the divine "cleansing" (Greek, *katharizō*;

1:7, 9) from sin and **unrighteousness** with this complement to 1:7 and "walk[ing] in the light."

1:10. Distinguishing a difference between "we have no sin" (1:8) and **we have not sinned** is difficult. Smalley (*1, 2, 3, John*, p. 33) suggests a denial of the principle (1:8) and the practice of sin (1:10). Westcott (*The Epistles of St. John*, p. 25) suggests a denial of the "permanence of sin as power" (1:8) and the practice of sin in their own lives (1:10). The voice of denial and the voice of God are pitted as rivals in the conjunction of "we have not sinned" and **we make [God] a liar**.

2:1. John lovingly addressed his readers directly, calling them his **little children** (Greek, *teknia*; also in 2:12, 28; 3:7, 18; 4:4; 5:21). Just as Jesus lovingly addressed His disciples (John 13:33), John addressed these believers as his spiritual children. Direct address is the grammatical equivalent to calling someone by name. With their full attention, John made it plain that in addressing the gravity of denying sin, he was not implying that the believers were distinguished from the Gnostics by their sinfulness: **these things write I unto you, that ye sin not**. What truly set the believers apart from the Gnostics was this: **we have an advocate with the Father, Jesus Christ the righteous**. The Greek word for "advocate" (*paraklētos*) refers to someone who speaks in court on behalf of a defendant (see discussion on John 14:16). In God's court, one is vindicated not because one is sinless but rather because the "righteous" Advocate is sinless.

2:2. Propitiation (Greek, *hilasmos*; "sacrifice to atone") refers to turning away God's wrath (see 4:10). God's holiness demands punishment for man's sin. Therefore, out of love (see 4:10; John 3:16), God sent His Son to make substitutionary atonement for the believer's sin. In this way, the Father's wrath is propitiated (satisfied, appeased); His wrath against the Christian's sin has been turned away and directed toward Christ (see discussion on Rom. 3:25). That Jesus came in the flesh is central to His atoning sacrifice, the provision of forgiveness and a confident relationship with God (1:9; 2:2; 4:10). Here John attacked the heart of the heresy (see Introduction:

"Gnosticism"). Forgiveness through Christ's atoning sacrifice is not limited to one particular group only; it has worldwide application (see John 1:29). It must, however, be received by faith (see John 3:16). Thus, this verse does not teach universalism (that all people ultimately will be saved) but teaches that God is an impartial God.

3. Obedience (2:3–6)

2:3. The topic of knowing God is a continuation of the theme of fellowship with God. Forty-two times, 1 John uses two Greek verbs normally translated "know." One of these verbs is related to the name of the Gnostics, the heretical sect that claimed to have a special knowledge (Greek, *gnōsis*) of God (see Introduction: "Gnosticism").

Hereby, or "by this means," grammatically points to the words **if we keep his commandments** and specifies, "this is how we know." To heed God's commandments (or "his word," 2:5) is elsewhere a test (or criterion) of love (5:3; see John 14:15, 21, 23–24; 15:10), because love is more than knowing; it is caring enough to take action. "Keep his commandments" refers to those whose lives are generally characterized by obedience. From what John teaches about sin in 1:7–2:2, he cannot mean that only those who never disobey know God.

2:4. He that saith (see also 2:6, 9) is the first of three professions that John rejected because the claim was contradicted by conduct. Each claim has an air of being a direct quote reported in the third person: **I know him,** "I abide in him" (2:6), and "I am in the light" (2:9). They are professions any true believer should be able to make. Where the words do not correspond, John said, you do not find **the truth,** the walk (2:6), or the light (2:9).

2:5. In him verily is the love of God perfected means either that God's love for the believer is made complete when it moves the believer to acts of obedience (see 4:12) or that Christians' love for God becomes complete when it expresses itself in acts of obedience (see 3:16–18). The verb "perfected" (*teleioō*) means to bring to a state that is no longer incomplete or imperfect. It is not that the person

becomes perfect but that God's love has reached its consummation, no longer incomplete or imperfect, when one keeps His word. "Verily," or "truly," marks this not just with emphasis but with authority.

2:6. The person who claims **he abideth in [God] ought himself ... to walk, even as [Christ] walked.** "Abideth" (Greek, *menō*) means to "remain" and implies a steady, consistent way of life (not occasional). To "remain," however, does not imply being static or inactive. John qualified the meaning of "abideth" as a dynamic Christlike pattern of life that is visible in the way one walks. The words "even as" (Greek, *kathōs*) point to Jesus Himself as the model of the great commandment in John 13:34: "A new commandment I give unto you, That ye love one another; [even] as [*kathōs*] I have loved you" (see 2:8). Jesus was the embodiment of love for God and for one another, the two great commandments that formed the foundation of all the commandments. John spoke expressly of the dynamic quality of love as characterizing one who "abideth in the light" (2:10).

4. Love for Fellow Believers (2:7–11)

Love for God (2:3–6) and love for one another (vv. 7–11) were brought together in a new way in the person of Jesus, and here this forms a likely backdrop to the interplay of "old" and "new." Jesus Himself, who brought together the two great commandments (Deut. 6:5 and Lev. 19:18) and called them the foundation of the whole law (see Matt. 22:37–40), gave a "new commandment" (John 13:34) to His disciples (John among them): to love one another as Jesus Himself loved them (see John 13: 34–35; 15:9–12, 17).

2:7–8. The biblical command to love is old (see Lev. 19:18; also Matt. 22:39–40), but its newness is seen in the new and dramatic illustration of divine love on the cross. The **old commandment** (v. 7), "thou shalt love thy neighbour as thyself" (Lev. 19:18), has been revolutionized by the love of Jesus, the gold standard: "love one another; as I have loved you" (John 13:34; 15:12). **From the beginning** points to the beginning of the readers' Christian experience. The **new commandment** was a part of their introduction to the gospel. The "old" commandment was "new" in Christ, not "new" (novel) to them. Thus, this **new commandment ... is true** (real) **in him** (Jesus) **and in you: because ... the true light** (v. 8; used in the New Testament only here and in John 1:9), Jesus, who is the Light of the World (John 8:12; 12:46), has come. For this reason, John said, **the darkness is past, and the true light now shineth.**

2:9-11. Here is the third of the three professions. In view of the new commandment ("That ye love one another; as I have loved you," John 13:34; 15:12), how patently false is the claim of one who says **he is in the light** (the light being Jesus; v. 9) and yet **hateth his brother.** Contrary to the fellowship that characterizes walking in the light (1:7), the one who hates his brother **is in darkness even until now** (see John 13:46). Conversely, **he that loveth his brother** (v. 10) is confirmed as one who **abideth in the light,** with the added confirmation that **there is none occasion of stumbling in him.** "In him" refers to the one who "loveth his brother." Grammatically, the Greek words translated "in him" can also refer to "the light," in which case the Greek words would be translated "in it," meaning there is no cause for stumbling in the light. It is difficult to decide. In the Bible, hatred and love as moral qualities are not primarily emotions but attitudes expressed in actions (see 3:15–16). Since the order of thought moves from love to light in verse 10, the translation of the KJV is preferred: love is not a source or cause of stumbling, and the one who loves as Jesus loves can be assured of abiding in the light. In verse 11, the false profession of verse 9 is taken up, with its wording reversed and expanded with ideas arising out of verse 10. Up to this point, the profession "I am in the light" has been tested in terms of hate and love. In verse 11, **he that hateth** is shown to be altered (lit., "made blind," Greek, *typhloō*) by the darkness in which he not only exists but also walks. If the contrast of light and darkness, love and hate, alludes also to the specifics of those who, under the influence of Gnostic teaching, had withdrawn and rejected the fellowship of believers (see 2:19), then their hatred of the brethren

was a proof of their blindness and a confirmation that their claims and professions were like the blind leading the blind. If so, John prepared the fellowship of believers for the assurances in 2:12–17.

B. Assurance and Admonition (2:12–17)

2:12–14. By extended repetition and the interplay between **I write** (vv. 12–13) and **I have written** (v. 14) in these verses, John assured his readers that, in spite of the rigorous tests contained in the letter, he was confident of their salvation. As elsewhere in this letter, **little children** (v. 12) refers to all John's readers (see discussion on 2:1), including **fathers** and **young men** (vv. 13–14). The terms "fathers" and "young men" may, however, describe two different levels of spiritual maturity. Some hold that all three terms refer to levels of spiritual maturity. In these verses, the word **because** should probably be translated "that." Greek *hoti* may introduce a cause (as in the KJV translation "because") or a declarative statement (translated "that") presenting the content of what is written or what has been written. There is good reason to read all these instances of "because" as "that" and understand them as declarative statements of John's assurance in the interplay of "I write" and "I have written." In this way, he countered the doubts stirred among the believers by the Gnostic teaching and the ensuing schism (see 2:19) with the continuity he asserted between what he *was* writing and what he *had* written. That "which ye have heard from the beginning" (1 John 2:24) remained the standard.

John tenderly assured all believers, **little children** (v. 12; Greek, *teknia*), of their forgiveness in Jesus Christ (**for his name's sake;** see 3:23; 5:13; Acts 4:12), an emphasis in 2:1–2. This confirmed that they **have known the Father** (v. 13).

To the older believers (**fathers;** v. 14), John wrote, **ye have known him that is from the beginning.** The parallel confirmation in verses 13 and 14 is not a meaningless repetition. John was confirming their maturity, their abiding (remaining) fidelity to the One they knew. "Him that is from the beginning" can refer to God or emphasize the preexistent credentials of Jesus Christ. To be sure, the repetition of "that is from the beginning" confirms that the identity of the One they knew had not been altered by some novel teaching about God or Jesus Christ.

To the younger believers (**young men**; v. 14), John wrote, **ye are strong, and the word of God abideth in you, and ye have overcome the wicked one**. That truth assures and characterizes every young believer clothed in Christ. John confirmed it in 2:13, and the isolation of the final term in that verse creates emphasis: "ye have overcome the wicked one."

2:15–17. By **world** (v. 15), John was not referring to the world of people (see John 3:16) or the created world (see John 17:24) but to the world order or system (see 2:16; James 4:4), which is swayed by Satan and organized against God and righteousness (see discussion on John 1:9–10). John's definition of "world" can be seen in verse 16. Note his emphasis on the personhood of **the Father** (v. 16) contrasted with **all that is in the world**. John identified what he meant by "all that is in the world" under three classifications. **The lust of the flesh** points to human desire (Greek, *epithymia*) or craving (not just sexual desire, as the word "lust" might convey). "Flesh" denotes the human distinct from the divine. For John, "flesh," was not evil (contrary to the Gnostics; see Introduction: "Gnosticism"). Indeed, "the Word was made flesh" (John 1:14), and "Jesus Christ is come in the flesh" (1 John 4:2; 2 John 7). **The lust of the eyes,** or desire (*epithymia*), for what is visible points to the pull of the physical and external rather than the spiritual and eternal. Brown rendered the expression, "eyes hungry for all they see" (*The Epistles of John*, p. 311). **The pride of life** points to self-assurance (Greek, *alazoneia*; pride, pretension, arrogance) swelled by confidence in one's power or possessions (Greek, *bios*; worldly goods and resources). Worldly values are vanity and their worth an illusion because **the world passeth away** (v. 17). "Passeth away" translates John's expression of a departure already in process. He juxtaposed that which is passing away ("the world," 2:17; compare "the darkness," 2:8) with that which remains: **he that doeth the will of God**.

That, John said, is the blue-chip investment of one's wants and desires. What is the current condition of one's investment portfolio? If short-term, high-risk investments characterize not only one's stock but also one's investment strategy, it is time to trade temporal stock for long-term, eternal securities.

C. Christological Test of Fellowship (2:18–28)

1. Contrast: Apostates versus Believers (2:18–21)

2:18. In keeping with other New Testament writers, John viewed the whole period beginning with Christ's first coming as the "last days" (see discussions on Acts 2:17; 2 Tim. 3:1; Heb. 1:2; 1 Peter 1:20). They understood this to be **the last time**, the last days, because neither former prophecy nor new revelation concerning the history of salvation indicated the coming of another era before the return of Christ. The word "last" in "last days," "last times," and "last hour" also expresses a sense of urgency and imminence. The Christian is to be alert, waiting for the return of Christ (see Matt. 25:1–13). John assumed his readers knew that a great enemy of God and His people would arise before Christ's return (**as ye have heard**). That person is called **antichrist**, "that man of sin" (2 Thess. 2:3; see discussion there), and "the beast" (Rev. 13:1–10). Prior to him, there will be **many antichrists**, who will be characterized by the following: (1) they deny the incarnation (4:2; 2 John 7) and that Jesus is the divine Christ (2:22); (2) they deny the Father (2:22); (3) they do not have the Father (2:23); (4) they are liars (2:22) and deceivers (2 John 7); (5) they are "many" (v. 18); and (6) in John's day, they left the church because they had nothing in common with believers (2:19). The antichrists referred to in this letter were the early Gnostics and other false teachers. The "anti" in "antichrist" means "against" (see 2 Thess. 2:4; Rev. 13:6–7).

2:19. They went out from us identifies the exponents of Gnostic teaching who had seceded from the fellowship of true believers. Second John 7 ("many deceivers are entered into the world") should be viewed in connection with 2:19, 22–24 and John's previous admonition, "Love not the world" (2:15).

In this one verse, John used the word "us" five times, emphasizing his delineation of the true fellowship. The rejection of inner fellowship was telltale in the rejection of outer fellowship. Otherwise, John said, **they would ... have continued** (Greek *menō*; "abide," "remain," as in 2:6).

2:20–21. The term **unction** (Latin, *unctio*; v. 20) means "anointing" (Greek, *chrisma*; only here and 2:27), pointing to the Holy Spirit (see 2:27 and discussion; Acts 10:38). This anointing comes from **the Holy One**, either Jesus Christ (see Mark 1:24; John 6:69; Acts 2:27; 3:14; 22:14) or the Father (see 2 Kings 19:22; Job 6:10). **Ye know all things** refers to the fact of knowing, not the extent of knowing, and thus assured the readers that they had no deficiency that could cause them to fall prey to the Antichrist's claims (Brown, *The Epistles of John*, p. 349). John's assurance in verse 21 confirms this and may echo the very kinds of claims that he silenced with his reassurance and the confirmation of their anointing. Other Greek manuscripts read "Ye all know [of it; i.e., the unction]."

2. The Person of Christ: The Crux of the Test (2:22–23)

2:22. Antichrists are **liar[s]**. John's language (lit., "the liar," with the definite article) underscores the lie **of he that denieth that Jesus is the Christ**. The man Jesus is the divine Christ (see the parallel confession in 5:5; see also Introduction: "Gnosticism" and discussion on 5:6).

2:23. One cannot engage in the lie of those who **denieth the Son** and yet claim to have **the Father**, as the Gnostics did (see 2 John 9).

3. Persistent Belief: The Key to Continuing Fellowship (2:24–28)

2:24–25. Let ... that which ye have heard from the beginning (the seminal teaching about Jesus) **... remain in you.** Here is a direct correlation between revelation (knowing about God through Jesus) and reality (knowing God through Jesus), as shown in the correlation of "remain" (Greek, *menō*; "abide," "remain") and "continue" (Greek, *menō*). Eternal life depends on relationship with the Life, the eternal Life (see 1:2–3; 5:11–12, 20).

2:26. This verse reflects one of John's purposes for writing (see Introduction: "Theme and Theological Message").

2:27. Ye need not that any man teach you. Since the Bible constantly advocates teaching (see, e.g., Matt. 28:20; 1 Cor. 12:28; Eph. 4:11; Col. 3:16; 1 Tim. 4:11; 2 Tim. 2:2, 24), John was not ruling out human teachers. At the time when he wrote, however, false teachers were insisting that the teaching of the apostles was to be supplemented with the "higher knowledge" that they (the Gnostics) claimed to possess. John's response (2:20–27) was that true believers have received an **anointing** and are indwelt by the Holy Spirit, who shows them that "Jesus Christ is come in the flesh" (4:2; see 4:15; 5:1, 10). The person of Jesus Christ is the topic discussed in 2:20–27. As general (natural) revelation reveals to every human that a God exists who is all powerful (see Rom. 1:18–20) and good (see Acts 14:17), so the Holy Spirit reveals to all believers the nature of Jesus Christ (see 4:13–15; 5:9–10).

2:28. Abide in him may refer to God (as in 3:24; 4:13, 16), the Son (as in 3:6), or the Father and Son (as in 2:24), but here the expected coming of Jesus (**when he shall appear**) puts the focus on the Son, the mediator of abiding with God. The form of the Greek verb for "shame" raises two possibilities of translation, either "be dishonored" (outer moral verdict) or "feel shame" (inner moral feeling). The contrasted pairing of **have confidence, and not be ashamed** tips the scales in favor of "feel shame." Opposite the feeling of shame is the feeling of boldness, or "confidence" (Greek, *parrēsia*; see 3:21; 4:17; 5:14; Heb. 4:16), a term with a rich history and meaning uninhibited freedom of expression. An additional clue completes the sense of the contrast. The word **before** literally means "from" (Greek, *apo*) and brings out the following sense: one may have boldness and not cower from Him in shame at His coming. In encouraging his **little children**, John may have intended a rhyming wordplay to ring in their hearts: "have boldness at his coming" (*parrēsia ... en tē parousia*).

III. The Christian Life as Divine Sonship (2:29–4:6)

A. Ethical Tests of Sonship (2:29–3:24)

1. Righteousness (2:29–3:10a)

2:29. If ye know that he is righteous. Knowledge of God's righteousness leads to an inevitable corollary: God's children bear the Father's likeness. Spiritual paternity (an issue in John 8:38–47; see 1 John 3:8) is established not by a blood test but by moral resemblance. Members of God's family are marked by holy living.

3:1. With a tone of wonder, John asked his readers to **behold** (lit., "see" or "perceive") the exceptional **love** of God. **What manner** (Greek, *potapos*; "of what sort," "of what kind"; lit., "of what country") conveys the unusual or utterly foreign nature of God's love. It is "out of this world," or foreign to human experience, **that we should be called the sons of God.** There is a tone of adoption here, but John never spoke of adoption but rather spoke of birth (2:29; 5:1) and the believer's identification as God's child. John underscored this with a confirming or legitimizing declaration: "And that is what we are" (see discussion on John 1:12).

3:2. The believer's paternity is spiritual (see 2:29), but **when [the Son] shall appear**, one's resemblance will be complete and tangible, for believers shall see Him as He is. Identification with Christ has a terminus in complete Christlikeness.

3:3. The believer's **hope** is not a mere wish but unshakable confidence concerning the future (see discussion on Rom. 5:2). Purpose and hope go hand in glove. If one's purpose is to become more and more like Christ, to see Him face-to-face is a "purifying" hope.

3:4–6. Here John was not asserting sinless perfection (see 1:8–10; 2:1) but explaining that the believer's life is characterized, not by sin, but by doing what is right and emulating the Righteous One (see 2:29). Anyone who takes up sin is at cross-purposes with the One who appeared to take away sin. Christ's purpose in taking away sin must inform one's outlook on sin. Abiding in Him is incongruent with abiding in

sin (**sinneth**; v. 6). The present tenses of "sin" point to a lifestyle of sin so incompatible with seeing or knowing God that John rejected such a partnership. His use of the present tense "sinneth" finds its definition (paternal resemblance) in the Devil (see 3:8).

3:7. Let no man deceive you alludes foremost to the Gnostic deception and a righteousness of claims (see 1:8, 10) without substance. The standards of righteousness are different. John reinforced the one standard of Jesus Christ, the true index of God's righteousness.

3:8. In this short letter, John said much about **the devil.** (1) He is called "the devil" (here) and "that wicked one" (3:12; 2:13–14; 5:18). (2) He **sinneth from the beginning** (here), that is, from the time he first rebelled against God, before the fall of Adam and Eve (see John 8:44). (3) He is the instigator of human sin, and those who continue to sin belong to him (see 3:12) and are his children (see 3:10). (4) He is "in the world" (4:3) and has "the whole world" (5:19) of unbelievers under his control. (5) He cannot, however, lay hold of the believer to harm him (see 5:18). (6) On the contrary, the Christian will overcome him (see 2:13–14; 4:4), and Christ will destroy the Devil's work.

3:9. The picture here is of human reproduction, in which the sperm (Greek, *sperma*; "seed") bears the life principle and transfers the paternal characteristics. John could not have put the question of one's paternity in starker language (see 2:29). Some have suggested the **seed** is the Word of God. Others have suggested that it represents the Spirit. In either case, it is recognized as His will, the expression of His nature. The expression **cannot sin** is again the present tense, as in the earlier instances of "sinneth"; grammar, not a change in meaning, accounts for the difference. It refers not to a complete cessation of sin but to a life that is not characterized by sin.

3:10a. In this is taken here with what precedes, meaning "as already shown," and thus forms a literary inclusion (Latin, *inclusio*), or return to the opening theme of this section (2:28–29). Others take these words as the opening of a new section parallel to 2:28–29. The delineation of **the children of God**

and **the children of the devil** serves as a transition from the preceding material (3:4–9) to what follows (3:10b–24).

2. Love (3:10b–24)

3:10b–11. Whosoever doeth not righteousness is not of God, neither he that loveth not his brother (10b). Practicing righteousness is specified as loving one's brother. John stated this specification, however, in negative rather than positive terms because it serves to introduce the example of Cain (3:12). The positive intent is evident in the explanation in verse 11. The word **message** (Greek, *angelia*; v. 11; in the New Testament, only here and in 1:5) may underscore the foundational teaching that the readers had **from the beginning, that we should love one another**, which John elsewhere called the "new commandment" (2:7–8; 2 John 5), adopting the wording of Jesus Himself (John 13:34). "The message" may be tantamount to the gospel and suggests the opening of a major section, as in 1:5. Jesus said the fulfillment of this command would confirm the identity of His disciples (John 13:35).

3:12. Cain (see Heb. 11:4) is a negative example. As in 3:8 (see John 8:44), the one who practices sin is of the Devil, and Cain illustrates the tragic consequences of being one of the Devil's moral progeny. **Works** are the concrete expression of the inward contrast of evil and righteousness.

3:13. Hate is the absence of love (see "loveth not his brother," 3:14; "hateth his brother," 3:15), and believers should expect not love, but hatred, from the world (see John 15:18; 17:14). Implicit in this hatred is the confrontation of the concrete works that manifest inner moral allegiances.

3:14–15. We know (v. 14) is emphatic and serves to confirm that the children of God possess eternal life here and now (**eternal life abiding in him**). The basis of this fact is Jesus Christ (see 1:2–3; 5:11–12), but the proof is **love [of] the brethren**. Indeed, John declared that the absence of such love is a proof that **death** remains (**abideth**) the seal on one's life.

3:16. Here John presented two models, contrasting Jesus Christ with Cain: the one who sacrificed the life of another out of selfish interest (Cain) and the One who sacrificed Himself out of selfless interest in others (Jesus Christ). John's wording is a restatement of the "new commandment" (2:7–8; 2 John 5), with an emphasis on "as I have loved you" (John 13:34; 15:12).

3:17–18. See James 2:14–17. The word translated **bowels of compassion** (Greek, *splanchna*; v. 18) identifies the visceral (gut) feeling that must be ignored in order to turn away from a brother in need. Love (selfless sacrifice) is not solely propelled by feeling, but a love so great as God's love (3:1) enlarges, not diminishes, one's emotional response to need: "as I have loved you" (John 13:34; 15:12). **The love of God** is God's kind of love, which He pours out in the believer's heart (see Rom. 5:5) and which in turn spurs the believer to love in kind. Grammatically, "the love of God" may speak of the believer's love for God. **In deed and in truth** are the two sides of love; sacrificial action (divine example) and principled direction (divine character) combine to define biblical love. To love as God loves is to seek God's best for another.

3:19–20. God is greater than our heart (v. 20). An oversensitive conscience can be quieted by the knowledge that God Himself has declared active love to be an evidence of salvation. He knows the hearts of all and whether, in spite of shortcomings, they have been born of Him.

3:21–22. The **heart** is the center of the inner life, one's thinking, feeling, and will. The absence of an unfavorable judgment there (**condemn us not**), together with the keeping of God's **commandments** (v. 22), suggest two conditions requisite for **confidence** (Greek, *parrēsia*; v. 21) before God and in the expectation (not the guarantee) of answered prayer (for John's use of the word "confidence," see 2:28). **Whatsoever we ask** (v. 22) is limited by these same two conditions and the assurance of answered prayer inspired by the implications of asking according to His will (see 5:14–15).

3:23–24. This command has two parts: (1) **believe [in] … Jesus Christ** (v. 23; see John 6:29), and (2) **love one another** (see John 13:34–35). John developed the first part in 4:1–6 and the second part in 4:7–12, moving from the *what* (v. 23) to the *who*: **he that keepeth** (Greek, *tēreō*; to observe and so persist in obedience) **his commandments** (v. 24) is the one who **dwelleth** (Greek, *menō*; "to remain"; KJV "abideth" elsewhere) **in [God], and [God] in him.** **The Spirit** serves as the assurance of this mutual relationship between God and the believer. In other words, the Spirit ratifies one's obedience (one's belief in Christ and love of one another) with assurance that believers are in Him and He in them.

B. Christological Tests of Sonship (4:1–6)

How does one identify a false prophet? Such a prophet (a person inspired to proclaim or reveal divine will or purpose) was evidently difficult to detect. John warned his readers about bogus prophets and said that their error can be exposed through a test ("Hereby," v. 2) based on their acceptance, approval, and agreement ("confesseth," v. 2) with the central proposition of the gospel that "Jesus Christ is come in the flesh" (v. 2). That Jesus came in the flesh is central to His atoning sacrifice, the provision of forgiveness, and a confident relationship with God (1:9; 2:2; 4:10). Here John attacked the heart of the heresy, "that spirit of antichrist" (v. 3).

4:1. John's warning contains a present as well as a prohibitive concern: **Believe not,** (present imperative; i.e., "stop believing") **every spirit.** The tendency to accept (Greek, *pisteuō*; give credence) every spirit as the Spirit of God given to believers (see 3:24) should be replaced with a test (**try**; Greek, *dokimazō*; "test," "examine"; see "prove all things," 1 Thess. 5:21). A "spirit" ("spirits") identifies a person moved by a spirit, whether by the Holy Spirit or an evil one. A true prophet speaks from God, being "moved by the Holy Ghost" (2 Peter 1:21). False prophets, such as the Gnostics of John's day, speak under the influence of spirits alienated from God. Christ warned against false prophets (Matt. 7:15; 24:11), as did Paul (1 Tim. 4:1) and Peter (2 Peter 2:1).

4:2–3. Here the notion of **confesseth** (v. 2; see discussion on 1:9) as "agreement" divides the true from the false on the central matter of the incarnate

Jesus Christ (see discussion on 2:18), of whom John gave eyewitness testimony in 1:1–2. The one who cannot vocalize agreement reveals the **spirit of antichrist** (v. 3; see 2 John 7). Thus, John excluded the Gnostic opponents, especially the Cerinthian doctrine that the divine Christ came upon the human Jesus at His baptism and then left Him at the cross, so that it was only the man Jesus who died (see Introduction: "Gnosticism"). The fact that the "spirit of antichrist" is **already ... in the world** indicates that Satan's opposition to the work of God will continue as an expression of anti-God, anti-Christian activity throughout church history. At some time in the future (after the removal of the restrainer; see discussion on 2 Thess. 2:7–8), the Antichrist will appear in person.

4:4–6. Ye are of God (v. 4) is an abbreviated form of the expression "born of God" (3:9; 2:29). **Them** identifies the "false prophets" (4:1), who were inspired by the "spirit of antichrist" (4:3). **He that is in the world** identifies the Devil (see John 12:31; 16:11). In 4:3, "the world" means the inhabited earth; here in verses 4–5, it means the community, or system, of those not born of God, including the antichrists (see discussion on John 1:9). The community of believers is outmatched numerically, but **greater is he that is in you.** In verses 5–6, **heareth** is related to the source that prompts what is said: **the world** (v. 5) or "he that is in the world" (v. 4) versus **God** (vv. 4, 6) or "he that is in you" (v. 4); **the spirit of truth** (v. 6) versus **the spirit of error.** (For "the spirit of truth," see 5:6; discussion on John 14:17).

IV. The Christian Life as an Integration of the Ethical and the Christological (4:7–5:12)

A. The Ethical Test: Love (4:7–5:5)

1. The Source of Love (4:7–16)

4:7–8. Love [of] one another (v. 7) is the proof that one **is born of God, and knoweth God.** The word "love" in its various forms is used forty-three times in this letter, thirty-two times in this short section (4:7–16). Only those who are to some degree like God truly know Him. **God is love** (v. 8). In His essential nature and in all His actions, God is loving. John similarly affirmed that God is spirit (see John 4:24) and "light" (1:5), as well as holy, powerful, faithful, true, and just.

4:9. This verse closely parallels John 3:16.

John 3:16	1 John 4:9
For God so [in this way] loved the world,	In this was manifested the love of God towards us,
that he gave his only begotten Son,	because that God sent his only begotten Son into the world,
that whosoever believeth in him	that we [who believeth in Him]
should not perish, but have everlasting life	might live through him.

The differences of wording are largely measured by the difference of perspective. The "whosoever" has been shifted to "we [who believeth]." **That we might live through him** gains its proper dimension from the comparison ("have everlasting life," John 3:16) and the immediate context of God's love: to "live through him" is more than thriving; it is manifesting the love God demonstrated in Jesus Christ, the Life, the eternal Life (see 1:2–3; 5:11–12, 20). If the world is to be more than a historical museum of God's love, those born of Him, who know Him, must manifest it in the marketplace by "liv[ing] through him." For **only begotten Son**, see discussion on John 1:18.

4:10–11. John included himself in the "we" and "us" of God's initiative. All believers recognize the unmerited love of God (see John 15:16; Titus 3:4–5). God's initiative is specified by His **propitiation** (atoning sacrifice; see discussion on 2:2) **for our sins** (v. 10). "He first loved us" (4:19), not because of believers' merit but because of His great love. This initiative of love, unconditioned by merit, generates the **ought** (v. 11) of the admonition to **love one another**.

4:12. No man hath seen God at any time (see discussion on John 1:18). Since God's love is the source of love, His love reaches full expression (is made complete) when **we love one another**. Thus, the God whom "no man hath seen" is "seen" in those who love because God lives (**dwelleth**; Greek, *menō*; "abide," "remain") in them.

4:13–16. The evidence that Christians "love one another" (4:7) is combined with other criteria (**hereby know we**; v. 13) that warrant an assurance of God's indwelling presence. Even though one cannot see God with the human eye, one can know the reality of God through (1) **love [for] one another** (v. 12); (2) **his Spirit** (v. 13), which **he hath given us**; and (3) the testimony that Jesus is **the Saviour of the world** (v. 14), **the Son of God** (v. 15), whom believers **confess**. John summed up the evidences in a profession of settled conviction and certainty (perfect tenses of "know" and "believe" emphasize the outcome) about **the love that God hath to us** (lit., "that God has in us"; v. 16). **God is love** forms a literary inclusion (Latin, *inclusio*), or return to the opening theme of this section (4:8).

2. The Fruit of Love (4:17–19)

4:17. Herein is our love made perfect is literally, "In this is love made complete with us." The words "In this" gather up the mutual assertions and assurances about love in 4:8–16 and usher in the ultimate outcome of this love with respect to believers' identity in Him and His identity in them: **we may have boldness in the day of judgment**. The words "with us" are illumined and the outcome explained: **as he is, so are we**, meaning like Christ. In 2:28, John wrote in similar language of the judgment that will take place when Christ returns. Love conforms one to the likeness of the One who renders judgment. That believers are like Christ in love is a sign that God, who "is love" (4:16), lives in them; therefore, they may have confidence on the day of judgment that they are saved.

4:18. There is no fear in love. Perfect or complete love has no room for fear. Love overpowers fear and **casteth out** (lit., "drives outside") **fear** and its torment (Greek, *kolasis*; pain or suffering accompanying punishment). Christians need have no fear of God's judgment because genuine love confirms their salvation.

4:19. We love him, because he first loved us. All love ultimately comes from God; genuine love is never self-generated by His creatures.

3. The Relationship of Love for God and Love for One's Fellow Christian (4:20–5:1)

4:20–21. The love that "casteth out fear" (4:18) is as concrete and tangible as the cross; "We love him, because he first loved us" (4:19). John returned to a recurring strain within the theme of love: he who **hateth his brother** (v. 20; see 2:9, 11; 3:15). In 2:3–11, John contested three professions, that of "He that saith, I know him" (2:4), "He that saith he abideth in him" (2:6), and "He that saith he is in the light" (2:9). At this point in John's letter, it is clear that each claim was contested on the basis of hating one's brother. For each claim was refuted, in order, on the basis of disobeying God's commandments (2:4–5a), not walking as Jesus walked (2:5b–6), and existing in the darkness (2:7–11), all of which stem from the failure to love. Here John took up the ultimate profession, the claim of **I love God**. How ignorant is the claim to know God, how estranged is the claim to abide in God, how blind is the claim to exist in the light, if the claim to love God is made visible with hate and not love. **He is a liar**. Hate exists where love should abound because the one who hates his brother (**loveth not**) has no love from God (who is love, see 4:8–16). For **this commandment** (v. 21), see 2:3, 7–11; 3:23–24; 5:3; John 13:34.

5:1. Faith that **Jesus is the Christ** is a sign of being born again, just as love is (see 4:7; discussion on 2:22). The words **loveth him that begat loveth him also that is begotten** point to a time when members of a family were closely associated as a unit under the headship of the father. John could, therefore, use the family as an illustration to show that anyone who loves God the Father will naturally love God's children.

4. Obedience: The Evidence of Love for God's Children (5:2–5)

5:2. John wrote that **when we love God, and keep his commandments** (see John 14:15, 21), believers know by this **that we love the children of God**. "When" (Greek, *hotan*) brings out the simultaneous character of the two actions. Based on what John has taught in this letter, the two actions are convertible.

5:3. His commandments are not grievous, not because the commands themselves are light or easy to obey but, as John explained in the following verse, because of the new birth. The one born of God by faith is enabled by the Holy Spirit to obey.

5:4. To **overcometh the world** is to gain **victory** over its sinful pattern of life, which is another way of describing obedience to God (see 5:3). Such obedience is not impossible for the believer, because believers have been born again and because the Holy Spirit dwells within them and gives them strength. John mentioned two aspects of victory: (1) the initial victory of turning in faith from the world to God (the first "overcometh"); (2) the continuing day-by-day victory of Christian living (the second "overcometh"). Overcoming the world (see discussion on 2:15–17), as overcoming the Wicked One (see 2:13–14; 3:8–9; 4:4; 5:18), comes from the power of God's begetting. The true victory (Greek, *nikē*), the victory that triumphs over the world, is **our faith**. Faith actualizes believers' identity as begotten of God (see 5:5).

5:5. John's question here solicits the very "faith" of 5:4. It is a compact way of saying that the one who overcomes (Greek, *nikaō*; "be victor," "conquer") the world **is the Son of God** and everyone who believes in Him shares in His victory (for parallel confessions, see 2:22; 4:2; 5:1).

B. The Christological Test (5:6–12)

5:6. Everyone who believes in the Son of God must believe in the Son of God **that came by water and blood**. Water symbolizes Jesus' baptism, and blood symbolizes His death. These are mentioned because Jesus' ministry began at His baptism and ended at His death. John countered the Gnostic teaching of His day (see Introduction: "Gnosticism") that claimed Jesus was born only a man and remained so until His baptism. At that time, they maintained, the Christ (the Son of God) descended on the human Jesus but left Him before His suffering on the cross, so that it was only the man Jesus who died. Throughout this letter, John insisted that Jesus Christ is God as well as man (see 1:1–4; 4:2; 5:5). Here he asserted that it was this God-man Jesus Christ who came into the world, was baptized, and died. Jesus was the Son of God not only at His baptism but also at His death. This truth is extremely important, because if Jesus died only as a man, His sacrificial atonement (see 2:2; 4:10) would not have been sufficient to take away the guilt of sin. **The [Holy] Spirit … beareth witness** ("testifies") that Jesus is the Son of God in two ways: (1) the Spirit descended on Jesus at His baptism (see John 1:32–34), and (2) the Spirit continues to confirm in the hearts of believers the apostolic testimony that Jesus' baptism and death verify that He is the Christ, the Son of God (see 2:27; 1 Cor. 12:3).

5:7–8. The Old Testament law required two or three witnesses (see Deut. 17:6; 19:15; see also 1 Tim. 5:19). **The Father, the Word** (Jesus Christ; see John 1:1, 14), **and the Holy Ghost** (v. 7; see John 1:33; 7:39; 14:26; 20:22) form a triad that is not unique in John's gospel or epistle, but the wording is unique ("Word" and "Holy Ghost" occur only here). The words of these verses, as they have come to us, concisely express John's testimony to the Trinity elsewhere (see 4:13–15; John 3:34–36; 6:62–65; 14:16–17, 26). This reference, however, is only found in late editions of the Latin Vulgate. It does not appear in any Greek manuscripts before the sixteenth century. Therefore, verse 7 is deleted in some translations (e.g., NIV).

5:9–10. John contrasted human testimony with the testimony of God. **If we receive the witness of men** (v. 9), how much more should one receive the testimony **of God**? The standard of credible testimony is two or three witnesses (see Deut. 19:15; Matt. 18:16; 2 Cor. 13:1; 1 Tim. 5:19). John knew this: "these three agree in one" (5:8). God's witness (the Spirit, if not also the water and the blood; see

5:6, 8) trumps the human (Gnostic) witness. **For this is the witness of God which he hath testified of his Son** picks up the importance of the words "the Son of God … even Jesus Christ" (5:5–6). When God testifies, he speaks of "his Son." Those who believe in the Son of God (5:10) have this testimony internally authenticated; this truth resides in their hearts. To reject His testimony is to make God a liar (see 1:10; compare John 3:18, 33).

5:11–12. "The witness of God" in 5:9, which capped the testimony to Jesus in 5:6–8, was followed by an explanation of the internal authentication of God's testimony in 5:10. Now John provided a summarizing testimony, a capstone to the opening of his letter, which began with "the Word of life" (1:1). If the antichrists (the Gnostics) claimed eternal life apart from God's Son (compare 2:24–26), this was the fitting assurance to those who believed in the Son of God. Without the Son, who is the Life, the eternal Life, one does not have life. Thus, **hath given to us eternal life** (v. 11) points to a person, not an object, and is a present possession (see discussions on John 3:15, 36). Recall John's words in 1:3–4: "our fellowship is with the Father, and with his Son Jesus Christ. And these things write we unto you, that our joy may be full."

V. Conclusion: Great Christian Certainties (5:13–21)

5:13. As John concluded his letter, he wrote first of his chief certainty and purpose for writing. In wording similar to the purpose statement of John 20:31, he wrote, **These things have I written unto you … that ye may know.** John's words gained their maximum meaning in light of what he had hitherto made known. "We know" tolls like a bell throughout 5:13–20. John was telling his readers that they could be certain that they had eternal life.

5:14–15. John repeatedly wrote of the "confidence" or "boldness" (Greek, *parrēsia*; see 2:28; 3:21; 4:17; 5:14) of the believer. He returned to the subject of confidence in prayer, not under special conditions as in 3:21–22, but in its own right as a believer's necessary dependence on God. The condition for

God's hearing and answering prayer is that **we ask ... according to his will** (v. 14). Jesus' own prayer was so controlled: "not [what] I will, but what thou wilt" (Mark 14:36). The confidence comes from moving with God in the petitions of the heart; the agreement between the one asking and the One answering.

5:16–17. John illustrated the kind of petition one can be sure God will answer (see 5:14–15). In the context of this letter directed against Gnostic teaching, which denied the incarnation and threw off all moral restraints, it is probable that **sin unto death** (v. 16) refers to the Gnostics' adamant and persistent denial of the truth and to their shameless immorality. This kind of unrepentant sin leads to spiritual death. Another view is that this is sin that results in physical death. This view holds that if a believer continues to sin, God takes his life in judgment (see 1 Cor. 11:30). In either case, **sin which is not unto death** is of a less serious nature. Thus, a "sin unto death" results in either spiritual or physical death and is not to be confused with the "unpardonable sin" (see Matt. 12:31–32).

5:18–20. The letter ends with three striking statements, affirming the truths that **We know** (vv. 18–20) and summarizing some of the letter's major themes: (1) We know that the child of God does not practice sin or keep on sinning (see 3:4–10). This is further explained: the one **begotten of God** (the believer; v. 18) guards himself against sin, so **that wicked one toucheth** (Greek, *haptō*; "take hold of," "harm") **him not.** (2) **We know that we are of God** (v. 19; see 3:10; 4:6), that the believer does not belong to the world (see 2:15–17), **and that the whole world lieth in wickedness** (or in the grasp of the Evil One; see 2:13–14; 3:12; 4:4). (3) **We know that the Son of God is come** (see 4:2–3; 5:6; 2 John 7), **and hath given us an understanding ... [to] know** (v. 20) and exist **in him that is true** ("the true one," only here in 1 John), **even in his Son Jesus Christ.** "Him that is true" is a reference to God the Father since it is the Son that has given believers the understanding to know. **This is the true God** may refer to either God the Father or God the Son. The letter began with the theme of eternal life (1:1–2) and now ends with it.

5:21. John concluded with a final warning about false gods, precipitated by the grand expression "true God" (5:20). **Keep yourself from idols,** that is, false teachings, and hence from false gods. In summary, John's first epistle emphasized the importance of believing the truth, resisting false teaching, and living in fellowship with Christ.

THE SECOND EPISTLE OF JOHN

INTRODUCTION

Author

The author is John the apostle. Obvious similarities to 1 John and the gospel of John suggest that the same person wrote all three letters. Compare the following:

2 John 5	1 John 2:7	John 13:34–35
2 John 6	1 John 5:3	John 14:23
2 John 7	1 John 4:2–3	
2 John 12	1 John 1:4	John 15:11; 16:24

See 1 John, Introduction: "Author"; and John, Introduction: "Author."

Date

The letter was probably written about the same time as 1 John (AD 85–95), as the above comparisons suggest (see 1 John, Introduction: "Date").

Theme

During the first two centuries, the gospel was taken from place to place by traveling evangelists and teachers. Believers customarily took these missionaries into their homes and gave them provisions for their journey when they left. Since Gnostic teachers also relied on this practice (see discussion on 3 John 5), 2 John was written to urge discernment in supporting traveling teachers; otherwise, someone might unintentionally contribute to the propagation of heresy rather than truth.

Outline

I. Salutation (vv. 1–3)
II. Commendation (v. 4)
III. Exhortation and Warning (vv. 5–11)
IV. Conclusion (vv. 12–13)

Bibliography

See 1 John, Introduction: "Bibliography."

EXPOSITION

I. Salutation (vv. 1–3)

Verses 1–2. John's second epistle bears the usual features of a first-century letter: (1) the opening salutation, identifying the sender and the recipient and offering greetings (vv. 1–3), (2) the body of the letter, expressing the author's reasons for writing (vv. 4–11), and (3) the closing, with benedictions, final greetings, and sometimes mention of the writing process (vv. 12–13). In the opening salutation, John identified himself as **The elder** (v. 1). In his later years, John functioned as an elder (Greek, *presbyteros*; see discussion on 1 Tim. 3:1), probably of the Ephesian church. The apostle Peter held a similar position (see 1 Peter 5:1). The recipients are identified as the **elect lady and her children**, an unknown Christian woman in the province of Asia or a figurative designation of a local church there. The latter appears most likely. "Her children," then, would identify the members of that local church. The letter reads naturally if John is addressing a church. This would square with the absence of the lady's personal name, the reference to the church's reputation (**not I only**), and the closing greeting from the children of a sister church (see v. 13). **In the truth** is more than a profession of sincerity. "Truth" points to the revelation of God in Jesus Christ, who is the truth (see discussion on John 1:14) and the basis of love for one another (see vv. 3–4). Thus, John spoke of the truth in terms approaching that of a companion: **which dwelleth** (Greek, *menō*; "abides") **in us, and shall be with us for ever** (v. 2).

Verse 3. In the greeting, John offered a benediction, or blessing, to the recipients. For the components of the blessing of **Grace ... mercy, and peace**, see discussions on Galatians 1:3; Ephesians 1:2; Romans 9:22–24. The blessing of these spiritual realities comes from the Father and the Son, and they will be experienced where there is truth and love. Truth and love were John's two major concerns in this letter. The truth grounds the command to love one another (see vv. 4–6) and belongs to the confession that "Jesus Christ is come in the flesh" (v. 7).

II. Commendation (v. 4)

Verse 4. John was overjoyed to have **found** (Greek, *heurēka*) some of **thy children walking in truth**. Apparently, the elder had met some members of the church and observed their way of life (Greek, *peripateō*; "to walk," "behave"). The sense of John's discovery can be worded like this: "Some members of your church were conducting their lives according to the truth, just like us, according to the command we received from the Father." This encounter gave John the occasion for writing his letter and encouraging all the children (the whole church) to do the same (see v. 5).

III. Exhortation and Warning (vv. 5–11)

Verses 5–6. John opened the body of his letter with an exhortation drawn from his commendation of "thy children walking in the truth" (v. 4), which was the reason for John's joy ("I rejoiced," v. 4). What does it mean to walk "in truth, as believers have received a commandment from the Father" (v. 4)? In a request to the whole church, John specified that it means to **love one another** (v. 5; for John's use of **a new commandment** and **from the beginning**, see discussions on 1 John 2:7–8). For John, there was no opposition between love and God's commandments. Love has a sweeping authority over all of one's behavior, as do the commandments. As Jesus did, John said that to fulfill the whole law, one must love (see Matt. 22:37–40).

Verses 7–11. This section deals with the basic Gnostic heresy attacked in 1 John, namely, that the Son of God did not become flesh (see John 1:14); rather, He temporarily came upon the man Jesus between His baptism and crucifixion (see 1 John, Introduction: "Gnosticism").

Verses 7–8. The command to love is closely linked with a confession: **Jesus Christ is come in the flesh** (v. 7). The connection is seen clearly in John's use of the word "For" ("Because"). Many deceivers had gone out and entered the world (see discussions on 1 John 2:18–19; 4:2–3). When one eschews the atoning sacrifice of God's love in Jesus Christ (implied in the words "come in the flesh"), one eschews the obligation to love one another. Indeed, the power of the new commandment is the sacrificial love of Jesus imbedded as obligation: "love one another; as I have loved you" (John 13:34). In John's experience, this appeared to have been the pattern of a schism (possibly in the sister church) rooted in the Gnostic rejection of Christ come in the flesh (see vv. 7–9). Thus, he warned the church of "the elect lady" (v. 1), **Look to yourselves** (v. 8), or "Watch out for yourselves." **Lose not … [what] we have wrought, but … receive a full reward**, that is, "Don't give up what you've achieved; our work faithfully accomplished on earth brings future reward" (see Mark 9:41; 10:29–30; Luke 19:16–19; Heb. 11:26).

Verse 9. Whosoever transgresseth may be accurately rendered, "Anyone who turns aside" (Greek, *parabainō*; "go aside," "deviate," "transgress"). Other Greek manuscripts contain the word *proagō*, meaning "to run ahead," which suggests maverick innovation on the part of the one who **abideth** (Greek, *menō*) **not in the doctrine of Christ**. This is a reference to the Gnostics, who believed that they had advanced or moved beyond the teaching of the apostles. The similarity of this letter to 1 John, the nature of the heresy combated, and the immediate context suggest that John was referring not to teaching given by Christ but to true teaching about Christ as the incarnate God-man. It is not the defector, but the one who remains ("abideth") in the doctrine pertaining to Christ, who **hath both the Father and the Son**.

Verses 10–11. Along with his warning, John provided practical directions for handling the arrival of a "deceiver" (v. 7): **receive him not into your house** (v. 10). John was referring to the housing and feeding of traveling teachers (see Introduction: "Theme"). He was prohibiting not what one might think of as general courtesy but rather the provision of food and shelter, since this would be an investment in the **evil deeds** (v. 11) of false teachers and give public approval: **For he that biddeth him God speed is partaker of his evil deeds**.

IV. Conclusion (vv. 12–13)

Verse 12. In John's day, paper was made from papyrus reeds, which were readily available and relatively inexpensive. Ink was made by mixing carbon, water, and gum or oil. Not surprising, then, is that the Greek word for **ink** (*melas*) also means "black." John wrote of his plans to come in person and enjoy the true fellowship that full joy adorns (see 1 John 1:4).

Verse 13. The children of thy elect sister greet thee may be taken literally to designate another Christian woman or figuratively to refer to another local church (see discussion on v. 1). It would be more likely for the sister of "the elect lady" (v. 1), rather than the children of the sister, to send greetings, unless, of course, a sister church and not a woman is in view, as suggested.

THE THIRD EPISTLE OF JOHN

INTRODUCTION

Author

The author is John the apostle. In the first verses of both 2 John and 3 John, the author identified himself as "the elder." Note other similarities: "love in the truth" (v. 1 of both letters), "walk in truth" (v. 4 of both letters), and the similar conclusions. See 1 John, Introduction: "Author"; and John, Introduction: "Author."

Date

The letter was probably written about the same time as 1 and 2 John (AD 85–95). See 1 John, Introduction: "Date."

Theme

Itinerant teachers sent out by John were rejected in one of the churches in the province of Asia by a dictatorial leader, Diotrephes, who even excommunicated members who showed hospitality to John's messengers. John wrote this letter to commend Gaius for supporting the teachers and, indirectly, to warn Diotrephes. See 2 John, Introduction: "Theme."

Outline

- I. Salutation (vv. 1–2)
- II. Commendation of Gaius (vv. 3–8)
- III. Condemnation of Diotrephes (vv. 9–10)
- IV. Exhortation to Gaius (v. 11)
- V. Example of Demetrius (v. 12)
- VI. Conclusion (vv. 13–14)

Bibliography

See 1 John, Introduction: "Bibliography."

EXPOSITION

I. Salutation (vv. 1–2)

Verse 1. John identified himself as **the elder** (Greek, *presbyteros*; see discussion on 2 John 1), pointing to his seniority and authority. **Gaius**, a common Roman name, was a Christian in one of the churches of the province of Asia. John called Gaius **wellbeloved**, the same Greek word as "beloved," one of John's favorite terms and used four times of Gaius (vv. 1, 2, 5, 11; see also 1 John 3:2, 21; 4:1, 7, 11). John further pronounced his high regard and affection for Gaius with the reinforcing explanation **whom I love in the truth** (see 2 John 1–2; discussion on John 1:14).

Verse 2. Beloved is a direct address, as if John was using Gaius's personal name. Such an address is indicative of their special spiritual fraternity as well as the obvious affection that comes from sentiment. John was paying a high compliment to Gaius. Note how the generosity of John's prayer for Gaius is measured by the generosity of Gaius's soul. John prayed (Greek, *euchomai*; **wish** or "pray") not only for Gaius's prosperity and good **health** in every area but also that his prayers would be answered with prosperity in proportion to the riches of his own **soul**. John clearly put a premium on the quality of Gaius's soul. It's as though John asked God to honor the honorable character of this beloved partner in ministry.

II. Commendation of Gaius (vv. 3–8)

Verse 3. John had **rejoiced greatly** (the same expression used in 2 John 4) over repeated reports from fellow believers that Gaius was a man of integrity: **the brethren … testified of the truth that is in thee, even as thou walkest in the truth**. Gaius was a man who "practiced what he preached." In this respect, John's joy was probably given added dimension by the defections of others who had not adhered to the truth as had Gaius (see 1 John 2:19; 2 John 7–8).

Verse 4. John's identification of Gaius with **my children** indicates that he was one of John's spiritual children and numbered among the believers under

his spiritual guidance. Nothing gave John greater joy than to hear they were **walk[ing] in truth**, as Gaius was (see discussions on 2 John 4–6).

Verses 5–7. John commended Gaius for his faithful hospitality and support of **the brethren, and … strangers** (v. 5). It was customary for the early church to provide hospitality and support for traveling teachers and missionaries (see 2 John, Introduction: "Theme"; discussion on 2 John 10). The wording, however, is ambiguous. It may be that John had in mind specific brethren that Gaius had faithfully cared for, even though they were strangers to him (see v. 6). It may be that Gaius had gained a reputation for supporting not only "the brethren" but also "strangers." In either case, his hospitality had earned praise from those he had helped, for they had voiced their gratitude **before the church** (v. 6), which most likely refers to the church where John himself resided and connotes the testimonies of such travelers (see v. 3). Earlier, John noted the testimony to Gaius's "truth" (v. 3), here he noted their testimony to Gaius's **charity** (v. 6), or "love." In commending Gaius, John solicited his continued attention to the needs of such travelers, with the exhortation, **whom if thou bring forward on their journey after a godly sort, thou shalt do well**. John urged Gaius to send them onward with provisions that would befit their sacrifice in the service of the Lord. "Bring forward on their journey" translates one Greek word, *propempō*, meaning to "send on one's way" with the suitable means of travel in a manner worthy of God ("after a godly sort"). The basis of John's request was that these missionaries traveled **for his name's sake** (v. 7; see discussion on Acts 4:12). Today Orthodox Jews often address God by the title Ha-Shem ("the Name"). Here "name" probably encodes a reference to Jesus Christ (see Acts 5:41; 1 John 2:12; John 1:12; 3:18).

Verse 8. John included himself in what he described as an axiomatic consequence of supporting such "missionaries." **To receive** or take such as these into our care engages us in their work. In this way,

Christians become **fellowhelpers to the truth**, or mutually involved in working for the truth.

III. Condemnation of Diotrephes (vv. 9–10)

Verses 9–10. I wrote (v. 9) acknowledges a previous letter of the apostle that is now lost. The church (*hē ekklēsia*, not "the church" of v. 6) to which John had written was known to Gaius, if not the very church to which he belonged. It was the church wherein **Diotrephes ... loveth to have the preeminence among them** (Greek, *philoprōteuō*), that is, "likes to be the leader" or "loves to be first." There is the hint that Diotrephes (*Dios + trephō* means "nourished by Zeus") had somehow suppressed the letter. He must have wielded a certain dictatorial power in the church since he was able to exclude people from the church fellowship (**forbiddeth them ... and casteth them out**; v. 10). John said Diotrephes **receiveth us not** (v. 9); he had refused to recognize the authority of another. One may infer that Diotrephes feared that receiving them would jeopardize his self-promoted preeminence.

IV. Exhortation to Gaius (v. 11)

Verse 11. By inference, John admonished Gaius to reject the model of Diotrephes (**follow not**). The antidote in this case, or the prescription against any evil, was to model God (see Luke 6:27–35) and **doeth good**. The continual practice of good, not merely doing occasional good deeds, is characteristic of seeing God clearly. Diotrephes, on the other hand, had lost sight of God.

V. Example of Demetrius (v. 12)

Verse 12. John had the highest regard for **Demetrius**, unlike Diotrephes. By all accounts (the **good report of all men**) and by John's own description (**the truth itself**) and commendation (**we also bear record**), Demetrius, like Gaius, was a man of integrity and could be trusted. His character made him a worthy ally in the truth and its ministry.

The admonition to Gaius (v. 11), sandwiched as it is between the contrast of Diotrephes (vv. 9–10) and Demetrius (v. 12), conveys the importance of choosing selfless leaders of proven character who will be committed to doing the good that one sees in God. Taken together, verses 9–12 suggest that John was alerting Gaius to behavior on the part of Diotrephes that disqualified him and warranted his replacement with one more highly qualified to exercise such influence: Demetrius. If so, Gaius was the leader in this church, and his own commitment to spiritual principles and their practice was being undermined by one who was not like-minded. The sensitivity of such matters brings John's closing into focus.

VI. Conclusion (vv. 13–14)

Verses 13. John clearly would have preferred to discuss the implications of this letter in person. Indeed, the tactics of Diotrephes may have precluded giving away too much in **ink and pen** (see 2 John 12 and discussion). A **face to face** visit was not far behind the arrival of this letter.

Verses 14. Peace be to thee is often a benedictory pronouncement (see discussions on John 14:27; 20:19; Gal. 1:3; Eph. 1:2). If the internecine tensions related to Diotrephes are in view, the words may amount to a prayer or wish bearing pointed comfort. "Peace be to thee" is then matched by the greetings of friends and the enumerated allies of good Gaius, who was to **Greet the friends by name**.

THE EPISTLE OF JUDE

INTRODUCTION

Author

The author identified himself as Jude (v. 1), which is another form of the Hebrew name Judah (Greek "Judas"), a common name among the Jews. Of those so named in the New Testament, the ones most likely to be the author of this letter are: (1) Judas the apostle (see Luke 6:16; Acts 1:13) — not Judas Iscariot — and (2) Judas the brother of the Lord (see Matt. 13:55; Mark 6:3). The latter is more likely. For example, the author did not claim to be an apostle and even seems to have separated himself from the apostles (see v. 17). Furthermore, he described himself as a "brother of James" (v. 1). Ordinarily, a person in Jude's day would have described himself as someone's son rather than as someone's brother. The reason for the exception here may have been James's prominence in the church at Jerusalem (see James, Introduction: "Author"). In the first-century church, only the James who was the brother of Jesus and president of the Jerusalem church would likely have had the status to be identified as Jude identified him. James is simply named without further detail; his name alone is authoritative.

The early church writer Hegesippus related the story of Jude's two grandsons who were examined by the Roman emperor Domitian because of their lineage to the house of David. Upon questioning them, Domitian (who reigned AD 81–96) learned that the men, of limited means, awaited the coming kingdom of Christ. The emperor dismissed them as unworthy of further attention and halted the persecution of the church that he had instigated. Jude's grandsons, because of their testimony and because their ancestry could be traced to Jesus' family, became church leaders (Eusebius *Ecclesiastical History* 3.19–20).

Although neither Jude nor James described himself as a brother of the Lord, others did not hesitate to speak of them in this way (see Matt. 13:55; John 7:3–10; Acts 1:14; 1 Cor. 9:5; Gal. 1:19). Apparently, they themselves did not ask to be heard because of the special privilege they had as members of the household of Joseph and Mary.

Possible references to the letter of Jude or quotations from it are found at a very early date, for example, in Clement of Rome (ca. AD 96), Clement of Alexandria (155–215), Tertullian (150–222), and Origen (185–253) accepted it; Jude was included in the Muratorian Canon (ca. 170) and was accepted by Athanasius (298–373) and by the Council of

Carthage (397). Eusebius (265–340) listed the letter among the questioned books, though he recognized that many considered it as from Jude.

According to Jerome and Didymus, some did not accept the letter as canonical because of its use of pseudepigraphal literature (see vv. 9, 14). Sound judgment has recognized that an author, writing under inspiration, may legitimately make use of extracanonical literature—whether for illustrative purposes or for appropriation of historically reliable or otherwise acceptable material—and such use does not necessarily endorse that literature as inspired. Paul made use of such material; he utilized heathen poets in speaking to the Athenians (Acts 17:28), and he cited a rabbinic midrash (a scriptural exposition) on the rock that gave water to Israel in the wilderness (1 Cor. 10:4). Paul apparently referred to some noncanonical source for the names of Pharaoh's magicians, Jannes and Jambres, who opposed Moses (2 Tim. 3:8). Under the influence of the Spirit, the church came to the conviction that the authority of God stands behind the letter of Jude. The fact that the letter was questioned and tested but was nonetheless finally accepted by the churches indicates the strength of its claims to authenticity.

Date

Nothing in the letter requires a date beyond the lifetime of Jude the brother of the Lord. Jude appears to have combated an incipient Gnosticism that, rather than featuring asceticism as in Colossians, promoted antinomianism—moral freedom that turns liberty from the law into license to sin. The error that the author combated was not the fully developed heretical system of second-century Gnosticism, although the false teachers mentioned in Jude and 2 Peter may well have been its forerunners (see 2 Peter, Introduction: "Date"). Moreover, nothing in the letter requires a date after the time of the apostles, as some have argued. It may even be that Jude's readers had heard some of the apostles speak (see vv. 17–18). Likewise, the use of the word "faith" in the objective sense of the body of truth believed (v. 3) does not require a late dating of the letter. It was used in such a sense as early as Galatians 1:23.

The question of the relationship between Jude and 2 Peter has a bearing on the date of Jude. If 2 Peter makes use of Jude—a commonly accepted view (see 2 Peter, Introduction: "The Relationship of 2 Peter and Jude")—then Jude is to be dated prior to 2 Peter, before circa AD 64–67. Otherwise, a date as late as circa 80 would be possible. Presumably, Jude was dead by the time his grandsons were brought before Domitian, since the accusations were only against the grandsons, not the father or grandfather. There is no clear idea when Jude died, so the latest possible date for the writing of his letter cannot be determined.

Recipients

The description of those to whom Jude addressed his letter is very general (see v. 1). It could apply to Jewish Christians, Gentile Christians, or both. The addressees' location is not indicated. Although 2 Peter 2 and Jude 4–18 appear to describe similar situations, it should not be assumed that they were both written to the same people. The kind of heresy depicted in these two passages was widespread (see "Date," above). If Jude were in his homeland when he wrote this letter, his audience may have been house churches throughout Israel. That is not certain, however. Jude probably addressed house churches whose location cannot be determined. Jude's letter would have been read and heard by them during their church meetings.

Theme and Theological Message

Although Jude was very eager to write to his readers about salvation, he felt that he must instead warn them about certain immoral men circulating among them who were perverting the grace of God (v. 4). These men may be described as false teachers since they ridiculed the truth and spoke arrogantly and ignorantly (vv. 10, 16, 18). They were also infiltrators (v. 4), dreamers (v. 8), complainers (v. 16), mockers (v. 18), and agitators or sectarians (v. 19). Apparently, these false teachers were trying to convince believers that being saved by grace gave them license to sin since their sins would no longer be held against them. Jude thought it imperative that his readers be on guard against such men and prepared to oppose the infiltrators' perverted teaching. He exhorted his congregations to contend for the truth about God's saving grace.

Literary Features

Jude exhibits an acquaintance with Greco-Roman rhetorical conventions regarding the arrangement of a discourse. The letter is effectively structured with the following principal divisions: an *exordium* (vv. 1–3), or introduction, in which the rhetor prepares the audience for the argument to follow; a *narration* (v. 4) of the facts, which lays out the essence of the argument; the *proof* (vv. 5–16), constituting the rhetor's attempt to persuade the audience of the soundness of his case; and the peroration, or *conclusion* (vv. 17–23), in which the argument is summed up and exhortation is given.

Outline

    I. Exordium (vv. 1–3)

   II. Narration: The Ungodly (v. 4)

  III. Proof: The Ungodly and Their Doom (vv. 5–16)

      A. First Proof (vv. 5–10)

         1. Three Historical Examples (vv. 5–7)

            a. The People of Israel in the Wilderness (v. 5)

            b. Rebellious Angels (v. 6)

            c. Sodom and Gomorrah (v. 7)

         2. Comparison with the False Teachers (v. 8)

         3. The Example of Michael and the False Teachers (vv. 9–10)

      B. Second Proof (vv. 11–13)

         1. Prophecy of Woe (v. 11)

         2. The Application of the Prophecy to the False Teachers (vv. 12–13)

      C. Third Proof (vv. 14–16)

         1. The Prophecy of Enoch (vv. 14–15)

         2. The Application of the Prophecy to the False Teachers (v. 16)

   IV. Conclusion (vv. 17–25)

      A. Repetition: The Apostolic Prophecy regarding Sensual Mockers (vv. 17–19)

B. Emotional Appeal: Christian Endurance and Ministry to the Wayward (vv. 20–23)
   1. Christian Endurance (vv. 20–21)
   2. Ministry to the Wayward (vv. 22–23)
C. Doxology (vv. 24–25)

Select Bibliography

Barclay, William. *The Letters of John and Jude*. Rev. ed. The Daily Study Bible. Philadelphia: Westminster, 1976.

Bauckham, Richard J. *2 Peter and Jude*. Word Biblical Commentary 50. Waco, TX: Word, 1983.

Bruce, F. F. "Jude, Epistle of." In *New Bible Dictionary*, 3rd ed., edited by D. R. W. Wood, I. Howard Marshall, A. R. Millard, J. I. Packer, and D. J. Wiseman, 626. Downers Grove, IL: InterVarsity, 1996.

Green, Michael. *The Second Epistle General of Peter and the General Epistle of Jude: An Introduction and Commentary*. 2nd ed. Tyndale New Testament Commentaries 18. Grand Rapids, MI: Eerdmans, 1987.

Hillyer, Norman. *1 and 2 Peter, Jude*. New International Biblical Commentary 16. Peabody, MA: Hendrickson, 1992.

Kelly, J. N. D. *A Commentary on the Epistles of Peter and of Jude*. Harper's New Testament Commentaries. New York: Harper & Row, 1969.

Moo, Douglas J. *2 Peter and Jude*. The NIV Application Commentary. Grand Rapids, MI: Zondervan, 1996.

EXPOSITION

I. Exordium (vv. 1–3)

Verse 1. Jude was fond of triplets; there are twenty of them in the letter. Jude's first triplet offers a threefold description of himself. The author identified himself as **Jude**, who, although he was the Lord's own half brother, was nevertheless **the servant** ("slave," NLT) **of Jesus Christ**. Such self-effacement would have raised Jude's standing in the minds of his audience and gave them an example of humility. God's servants use any privileges they might have, not for promoting themselves, but only for promoting Jesus Christ. Furthermore, the author identified himself as **brother of James**. Although he was humble, Jude wanted his hearers to know that his letter was written with authority to speak for Christ. Jude's relationship with James, leader of the Jerusalem church, lent his epistle that authority.

Another triad describes the readers' own privileged identity. First, they were **sanctified by God the Father**. The readers were set apart for God's holy purposes and designs. Those righteous and constructive designs stood in opposition to the behavior of the false teachers in Jude's churches, behavior that was destructive of the individual and of the church community. Some manuscripts have "loved by God the Father" (e.g., NIV) here. Second, the readers were **preserved in Jesus Christ**. In any discussion of the question of the eternal security (or perseverance) of the saints, this concept must be considered. Jude regarded Christ's people as "kept by" (NIV) or "kept for" (NASB) Christ; their righteous standing with Him was maintained not by their own efforts but only by His power, and for His glory. The verb, as in the case of "sanctified," is in the perfect tense and thus denotes a condition that is secure. Third, the readers were **called**. Jude did not specify to what the addressees were called, but in Romans 1:7 and 1 Corinthians 1:2, Paul affirmed that the congregations in Rome and Corinth are "called to be saints." Jude may have understood God's call similarly. The word "saints" (holy people) is related to "sanctified." God not only calls His people to be holy, but He gives them the power to do so.

Verse 2. Another triad follows as the formal greeting of the letter, but the significance of the terms ought not to be missed. Jude's prayer was that the recipients of the letter would continue to experience God's **mercy** (His tender and compassionate care and leading), **peace** (complete well-being and good order in terms of health, relationships, and walk with God), and **love** (here the word is *agapē*, the completely selfless and sacrificial love that God has showered on us in Christ). Jude imagined that these graces can **be multiplied** in believers' lives. Failure to live in ways that accord with these virtues often causes Christians to lack their increase, and prayerlessness often causes them to miss the opportunity to join as partners with God as He seeks to develop these graces in the lives of His children.

Verse 3. Jude's original intention was to write a general treatment of the doctrine of **salvation**, perhaps dealing with such subjects as man's sin and guilt, God's love and grace, the forgiveness of sins, and the changed lifestyle that follows new birth. Instead, Jude felt compelled to **exhort** his audience that they **should earnestly contend for the faith**. Jude exhibited the mark of the true pastor, who is a watchman (see Ezek. 3:17–19; Acts 20:28–30) over the people of God and warns them of danger to come. The current postmodern mood tends to dispute the notion that there is objective truth in the religious sphere. The proclamation and defense of the teaching of Scripture as revealed truth are thus seen by many as arrogant and exclusive. For Jude, however, there existed a body of truth divinely revealed to humanity: "the faith." The noun here designates, not the act of trust, but that which is commonly believed and adhered to as truth by believers.

The Christian faith has certain characteristics. (1) It was **delivered**. The verb, *paradidōmi*, signifies the handing down of authorized (apostolic) tradition (see 1 Cor. 15:1–3). The New Testament embodies in written form the original teaching of the apostles and thus goes back to Christ Himself. (2) That teaching, or "faith," **was once** delivered. The unchanging core of Christian teaching must be interpreted afresh for each culture and generation, and the interpretation may take new forms and expressions. The core, however, does not change and must not be replaced by any "new revelation." The test by which any doctrine or practice must be examined is, "Does it coincide with the apostolic teaching in the New Testament?" (3) The faith was once delivered **unto the saints**; that is, truth is the property of not just one individual but of the entire church. The church, although under the authority of the apostolic tradition, is nevertheless its guardian and messenger. Some individuals believe they can explore and understand God's truth adequately on their own. Since truth is delivered to all God's people, only in community can God's word be properly studied, understood, and lived out. (4) Christians must **earnestly contend for the faith**. The verb that Jude used is *epagōnizomai* and has the idea of "to join the struggle in defence of" (NEB) or "to fight hard for" (NJB). The word is an athletic metaphor, and the contest is to be carried on continually (signified by the present tense). The English word "agony" is related to this word. Jude was not suggesting, however, that Christian should be only on the defensive; they must also be on the offensive in the preaching of the gospel, the announcement of Christ's supremacy and victory, and the positive influence of godly living (see Phil. 1:27–30). Jude's exhortations in verses 20–23 are part of what contending for the faith means.

II. Narration: The Ungodly (v. 4)

Verse 4. In the narration, Jude stated his main thought (developed and substantiated in the proof, vv. 5–16): false teachers, by living according to their own desires, contradict their Christian profession and deny the Lord Himself. Such teachers pose a threat to the church from within and are justly condemned.

The word **For** introduces the reason Jude felt impelled to change the subject of his letter. Those who **crept in unawares** could haved included women as well as men. The Greek word translated **men**, *anthrōpoi*, does not designate gender. Jude's three examples in verse 11, however, were all of men, which may indicate that the infiltrators were men. At any rate, they were **ungodly**. The verb (*pareisdyō*; only here in the New Testament) that Jude used to describe their infiltration is most colorful. It refers to someone sneaking in through a side door, to a spy slipping into the country, and to a lawyer's clever and smooth persuasion of a jury. The NLT vividly captures the idea: "some godless people have wormed their way in among you." The threat of false teachers not only arises outside the church but also within it.

The troublesome individuals **were before of old ordained to this condemnation**. "Before of old" may refer to Old Testament denunciations of ungodly men or to Enoch's prophecy (see vv. 14–15). Jude may have meant that judgment had long been about to fall on them because of their sin (see 2 Peter 2:3, which may be a clarification of this clause). Perhaps the phrase refers to the many and various punishments of sin (recorded in the Old Testament and extrabiblical literature) that stand as prophetic precedents indicating God's response to sin.

The ungodliness of the false teachers was constituted by two actions. (1) By **turning the grace of our God into lasciviousness** ("change the grace of our God into a license for immorality," NIV), they assumed that salvation by grace gave them the right to sin without restraint, either because God in His grace would freely forgive all their sins, or because sin, by contrast, magnifies the grace of God (see Rom. 5:20; 6:1). (2) The false teachers are also described as **denying the only Lord God, and our Lord Jesus Christ** (some manuscripts omit "God"; thus, "deny our only Master and Lord, Jesus Christ," NASB). The lifestyle of the false teachers effectively contradicted any claim that they were in union with Jesus Christ. By doing these same things, many Christians

unwittingly become "false teachers." A flippant attitude toward sin that says, "I'll go ahead and sin; after all, God will forgive me," outrageously abuses the grace of God. Living for self-gratification rather than for God's honor in purity and holiness (see v. 1) effectively invalidates any verbal testimony that a Christian might make. The name of Jesus Christ is brought into disrepute because often actions speak louder than words to the unbeliever.

III. Proof: The Ungodly and Their Doom (vv. 5–16)

A. First Proof (vv. 5–10)

1. Three Historical Examples (vv. 5–7)

a. The People of Israel in the Wilderness (v. 5)

Verse 5. The first example in a triplet of sinners that Jude presented in the proof section of the letter is one with which the audience was undoubtedly familiar (**ye once knew this**). Jude presented this and the other two examples as substantiation of his belief that the false teachers would be condemned for their unrighteous actions. **The Lord … saved the people out of the land of Egypt** in the exodus but then **destroyed them that believed not**. The people of Israel did not believe that God would give them the land of Canaan; consequently, all unbelieving adults died in the desert without entering the Promised Land. Only Joshua and Caleb realized the promise (see Num. 14:1–45; Deut. 9:23). Disbelief led to disobedience, and disobedience led to destruction. The passage does not concern the eternal destiny of the disobedient but rather the temporal punishment inflicted by the Lord. Jude intended to show that those who dishonor the One who has given them divine benefits will meet with a serious and proper riposte issued by that same One to preserve His honor.

b. Rebellious Angels (v. 6)

Verse 6. The next example of punishment of the disobedient is that of **the angels** who abandoned **their first estate**, or **habitation**, which probably refers to "their positions of authority" (NIV). God had assigned differing areas of responsibility and authority to each of the angels (see Dan. 10:20–21, where the various princes may be angels assigned to various nations). Some of these angels refused to maintain their assignments and thus became the Devil and his angels (see Matt. 25:41). "Habitation" may refer to a specific location; angels apparently were assigned specific locations as well as responsibilities. Some assume that they left the heavenly realm and came to earth. The pride of the angels who instigated a civil war in heaven, which led to their expulsion, may have been in Jude's mind here. If the pride of angels is subject to the divine **judgment of the great** (i.e., the last) **day**, how much more so the arrogance of the false teachers.

Jude's language is not necessarily to be taken literally. **Everlasting chains** is a graphic image conveying the fact that the angels' fate is certainly that of judgment; there will be no escaping it. **Darkness** signifies the separation from the presence of God and from the life of heaven that they have experienced because of their rebellion. The language of Jude echoes that of the pseudepigraphal book *1 Enoch*, a composite work whose parts were composed during the second and first centuries BC. The work is valuable in what it reveals regarding pre-Christian Jewish theology. Evidently, Jude's readers were aware of it—echoes of it are in verses 6, 14–15—and Jude used the work for illustrative purposes. According to *1 Enoch*, recalcitrant angels, who abandoned their heavenly domain through rebellion, are chained as they await their final judgment (see, e.g., *1 Enoch* 10:5–6; 12:4).

c. Sodom and Gomorrah (v. 7)

Verse 7. The phrase **Even as** does not mean that the sin of **Sodom and Gomorrha** was necessarily the same as that of the angels or vice versa. Jude used this phrase to introduce the third illustration of God's certain punishment of the unrighteous, who will be consigned to eternal punishment on judgment day. The specific trespasses to which Jude was referring, however, are debated. In the construction, **giving themselves over to fornication, and going after strange flesh**, was Jude referring to two sins ("fornication" and "going after strange flesh") or just

one ("going after strange flesh" being an elaboration or instance of "fornication")? Jude was probably referring to one sin, fornication, and the pursuit of "strange flesh" is an instance of an ongoing practice of fornication. The background to Jude's reference is Genesis 19. When the angelic visitors who arrived in Sodom found lodging with Lot, the men of the city cried out to him, "Where are the men who came to you tonight? Bring them out to us so that we can have sex with them" (Gen. 19:5 NIV). The Sodomites were **set forth for an example, suffering the vengeance of eternal fire**. God destroyed Sodom and Gomorrah by pouring out "brimstone and fire" (Gen. 19:24), a foretaste of the eternal fire that is to come. The false teachers would face the same judgment as the consequence of their libertine ways.

2. Comparison with the False Teachers (v. 8)

Verse 8. Jude now turned his attention to the impurity of the false teachers that was comparable (**Likewise**) to the unrighteousness of unbelieving Israel (v. 5), the fallen angels (v. 6), and the people of Sodom and its environs (v. 7). The sectarians are described as **these filthy dreamers**. This term (*houtoi enypniazomenoi*; lit., "these dreamers," NRSV), however, may not refer to those who dream erotically or to those who are out of touch with truth and reality because of their passion but may instead refer to those who claim to have ecstatic visionary experiences. Thus, the NLT rendering is probably accurate: "these false teachers, who claim authority from their dreams."

In another of his triads, Jude delineated the corrupt character of the false teachers threatening the church. (1) They **defile the flesh** by their immoral intentions and actions. As God's creation, the material body in itself is good. The false teachers had abused and misused it for their own selfish purposes and had thus turned the body and its members into an instrument of unrighteousness (see Rom. 6:13). Thus, they "pollute their own bodies" (NIV). The same Greek word for "flesh" (*sarx*) appears in both verses 7 and 8 and links the thought of these verses. Jude saw some correspondence between the sexual immorality of Sodom and Gomorrah and that of the false teachers. (2) The false teachers also **despise dominion** ("reject authority," NRSV) and (3) **speak evil of dignities** (lit., "abuse the Glories," NJB). If the dissenters had "an authority problem" in the church, it was first toward God and His heavenly agents.

3. The Example of Michael and the False Teachers (vv. 9–10)

Verse 9. The word for "speak evil of" in verse 8 is *blasphēmeō* and could refer to abusive speech against God, angels, or humans. The word is a link between verse 8 and verses 9–10 since it or its verbal form appears in all three verses. The false teachers markedly displayed their arrogance in their failure to recognize their human frailty and limitations when they slandered celestial beings. Not even **Michael the archangel** dared to bring **a railing accusation** (lit., "judgment of blasphemy," *krisis blasphēmias*) against **the devil**, but the intruders considered themselves to have a stature that allowed them to do so.

Michael is the only archangel mentioned by name in the New Testament (here and in Rev. 12:7). He may also be the unnamed archangel of 1 Thessalonians 4:16. In the Old Testament, he is the guardian of Israel (see Dan. 10:13, 21). The title "archangel" suggests an angelic hierarchy like that described in the pseudepigraphal book *1 Enoch*, in which seven archangels appear. In the New Testament, however, the existence of such a hierarchy is not clearly delineated (but see Eph. 1:21; 6:12; Col. 2:15; 1 Peter 3:22).

Michael and the Devil **disputed about the body of Moses**, a curious reference that is not found in canonical Scripture. The incident is from the pseudepigraphal *Assumption of Moses* (according to the church fathers Origen, Clement, and Didymus), a work that survives only fragmentally and that is missing the portion that Jude utilized. Other New Testament quotations from, or allusions to, nonbiblical works include Paul's quotations of Aratus (Acts 17:28), Menander (1 Cor. 15:33), and Epimenides (Titus 1:12). Such usage in no way suggests that the quotations, or the books from which they were

taken, were divinely inspired. It only means that the biblical author found the quotations to be a helpful confirmation, clarification, or illustration.

Verse 10. The false teachers, when they **speak evil** (*blasphēmeō*) of authorities, betrayed their ignorance of those things about which they haughtily spoke. Those things that they did know, of which they presumed to have expertise, were things that only **brute beasts** ("irrational animals," NRSV) experience. Jude probably was referring to immoral and seditious behaviors. By these things, the teachers **corrupt themselves.** The deceptiveness of sin is such that those who give themselves over to it are destroyed by it. A time comes when one, having resisted the voice of God, can no longer hear or give heed to that voice. The one who has resisted then is engulfed in the power of the passions and becomes more and more enslaved by them.

B. Second Proof (vv. 11–13)

1. Prophecy of Woe (v. 11)

Verse 11. Jude's second proof further established the sinfulness of the false teachers and the certainty of their condemnation. By the use of another triplet of negative examples, Jude encouraged a sense of revulsion among his readers toward the sectarians. Their association with notorious sinners from Israel's history inclined Jude's audience toward behavior that was opposite that of the sinners.

In the vein of an Old Testament prophet, Jude cast his words in the form of a woe oracle, a type of prophetic speech that (1) pronounces distress, (2) gives a reason for the distress, and (3) predicts the doom that is to follow (see, e.g., the string of woe oracles in Hab. 2:6–20). In Jude 11, each of the three elements of a typical woe oracle is present.

Pronouncement of Distress. With the exclamation **Woe unto them!** Jude announced the distress to come upon the false teachers, the judgment already foretold in verse 4. "Woe" was the cry of the ancient Israelites when they faced catastrophe or when they were mourning the dead.

Reason for the Distress. Jude gave the reason for the distress by identifying transgressions of the three

Old Testament sinners—transgressions that the false teachers threatening Jude's audience had committed. **Cain** is the Bible's first murderer (Gen. 4:1–16); his hostility arose from envy and hatred (see 1 John 3:12, 15). **The error of Balaam for reward** is consuming greed for money, prestige, or any kind of selfish advantage. Balaam refused to curse Israel in the biblical account, despite Balak's urging to do so (see Num. 22:15–35). In intertestamental literature, Balaam did curse Israel, enticing Balak to prompt Israel to sin (see Num. 31:16). Jude said that the false teachers **ran greedily** in the footsteps of Balaam ("abandon themselves to Balaam's error for the sake of gain," NRSV). They also imitated **the gainsaying of Core** ("Korah's rebellion," NIV). Korah was remarkable for his rebelliousness against Moses (see Num. 16:1–50). By complaining that Moses had no right to be in charge of the people of Israel (Num. 16:3), Korah treated the Lord with contempt (Num. 16:30). Korah, with some 250 other mutineers, was swallowed up alive by the earth. Jude may have been suggesting that the false teachers of his day were rebelling against church leadership (see v. 8).

Prediction of Doom. The ruin that resulted from the wicked deeds of the infamous trio of verse 11 is only specifically mentioned in relation to Korah, but it applies equally to all. The false teachers are said to have **perished**. The judgment of the agitators was so certain that Jude, using the aorist tense, spoke as if it had already taken place: "they have been destroyed" (NIV).

2. The Application of the Prophecy to the False Teachers (vv. 12–13)

Verses 12–13. Jude heaped fault upon fault in his description of the false teachers, an effective rhetorical device designed to build revulsion in the audience against the godless infiltrators. The vivid mental pictures—six graphic metaphors in all—collectively served as a powerful denunciation of the false teachers and warned Jude's readers against falling into their vile ways.

(1) Jude said the false teachers were **spots in your feasts of charity** (v. 12; "a blot on your love-feasts,"

NEB). He consistently portrayed his opponents as defiled or polluted (see especially v. 23), and the faith of others had been (or was in danger of being) shipwrecked by coming into contact with the heretics. Since 2 Peter 2:13, a passage similar to Jude 12, clearly has "spots they are and blemishes" (*spiloi kai mōmoi*), the KJV translation is best.

(2) The heretics were false shepherds (see Ezek. 34:2, 8–10). Jude said, **they feast with you, feeding themselves without fear** (v. 12). "Feeding" could be translated "shepherding"; thus, the NIV has "shepherds who feed only themselves." The false teachers presented themselves as leaders but did not care for their sheep.

(3) Of the infiltrators, Jude could say, **clouds they are without water** (v. 12). They promised spiritual refreshment—encouragement, sound teaching, godly example—but were empty and dry (see Prov. 25:14). Being **carried about of winds**, these teachers were themselves dupes for the latest doctrinal fad that came around (see Eph. 4:14).

(4) The metaphor of **trees whose fruit withereth** (v. 12) is closely associated with the previous metaphor of waterless clouds. In agrarian Israel, people continually watched for signs of rain and for indications of a bountiful harvest. Clouds without rain and trees that failed to produce a crop were not just a disappointment but meant severe hardship or even famine in a subsistence economy. "Whose fruit withereth" translates *phthinopōrina*, a word derived from two Greek words meaning "to waste away" and "autumn." The NIV has "autumn trees" since the term describes trees whose branches are bare.

The uselessness of the false teachers is emphasized by the repetitive **without fruit** (v. 12; see Matt 7:16–20) and the stunning picture of trees **plucked up by the roots**, possible only by an extraordinarily mighty force. "Uprooting" is a metaphor of God's judgment (see Jer. 1:10). **Twice dead** may mean that the trees were dead because they were fruitless and because they were rootless. The teachers had forsaken the state of being rooted in Christ (see Col. 2:7) and the apostolic teaching of the faith that Jude sought to defend (see v. 3).

(5) **Raging** ("fierce," NEB; "wild," NIV) **waves of the sea** (v. 13) suggests both the fury of the infiltrators' manner (unrestrainedly boisterous and wrathful) and their instability. The latter feature is also denoted by the metaphors of the waterless clouds and uprooted trees. As wind-tossed waves constantly churn up rubbish, so these apostates continually stirred up moral filth. That is, they were **foaming out their own shame**. A similar image appears in Isaiah (57:20) and is echoed in the Dead Sea Scrolls (1QH 2:2–13, 27–28; 6:23; 8:15).

(6) Jude described the antagonists as **wandering stars** (v. 13), once again bringing the notion of their instability to the fore. They had strayed from the true course, the "orbit," circumscribed by correct doctrine and decency. Jude may have based the metaphor on revolutions of the planets, whose movements appear to be irregular in comparison to the relatively fixed positions of stars, or he may have been referring to shooting stars. The false teachers, then, resembled meteors—blazing for a short time but quickly fading as they burn up in the earth's atmosphere—or comets, whose splendor is remarkable but short-lived. As shooting stars appear in the sky only to fly off into eternal oblivion, so these false teachers are destined for the darkness of eternal hell.

C. Third Proof (vv. 14–16)

1. The Prophecy of Enoch (vv. 14–15)

Verses 14–15. To further establish the certainty of judgment that the false teachers would face, Jude cited *1 Enoch* 1:9. The purported author of Jude's source is **Enoch ... the seventh from Adam** (v. 14). This Enoch is not the Enoch in the line of Cain (see Gen. 4:17) but the one in the line of Seth (see Gen. 5:18–24; 1 Chron. 1:1–3). He was seventh if Adam is counted as the first. According to Genesis 5:23, Enoch lived 365 years, during which time he became the father of Methuselah (Gen. 5:22). The account notes Enoch's godliness ("Enoch walked with God," Gen. 5:22) and his mysterious assumption to heaven ("and he was not; for God took him," Gen. 5:24). The work of *1 Enoch*—a composite, well-

respected writing in New Testament times—dates from the second and first centuries BC. The author certainly was not the historical Enoch of Genesis 5, descendant of Seth. The ascription of authorship to this godly Old Testament person attempts to lend authority to the book. The phenomenon by which authorship is ascribed to someone who did not write the work is *pseudonymity*, a literary practice of the ancient world. The word **prophesied** need not imply that Jude regarded *1 Enoch* as inspired Scripture. The verb may function, not in the sense of supernaturally revealing new truth, but merely in the sense of speaking things about the future that were already known (see Dan. 7:9–14; Zech. 14:1–5). That *1 Enoch* is not canonical does not mean that it contains no truth. The work had illustrative value for Jude, perhaps because his audience held it in high esteem.

The quotation from *1 Enoch* serves to highlight the inevitability of judgment on the heretics and the extraordinary ungodliness that incurs that judgment. With the phrase **the Lord cometh** (v. 14), Jude modified the quotation to refer to Christ's second coming and to His judgment of the wicked (see 2 Thess. 1:6–10). He will be accompanied by **ten thousands of his saints**, probably angels (lit., "holy ones," NRSV). No one can escape such a massive heavenly army and its retributive purpose. The divine **judgment** (v. 15) serves at the same time to **convince** the **ungodly sinners** ("to sentence the godless," NJB). A striking feature of verse 15 is the fourfold use of "ungodly" in the KJV. This thunderous repetition denotes the depravity of the sinners and thus the justice of the punishment they will undergo. The sins of the false teachers here recall the description of them as ungodly, immoral in behavior and hostile in speech, in verse 4.

2. The Application of the Prophecy to the False Teachers (v. 16)

Verse 16. Jude identified five types of ungodly people, who therefore were destined for the judgment prophesied by Enoch (see vv. 14–15). The word **These** indicates that Jude was referring to the ungodly men he first mentioned in verse 4 and subsequently referred to repeatedly as "these" (vv. 8, 10, 12, 14, 19). These men, the libertine false teachers who perverted the grace of God, were to be avoided, and their misdeeds were not to be imitated.

(1) **Murmurers** ("grumblers," NIV) is a picturesque noun (*gongystēs*) that is onomatopoetic (i.e., it sounds like that for which it stands). It is associated with Israel's griping in the wilderness (see Exod. 16:2, 7–9), particularly at Kadesh (see v. 5; Num. 14:2, 27, 29, 36) and in the context of Korah's rebellion (see v. 11; Num. 16:11).

(2) **Complainers** (*mempsimoiros*; "faultfinders," NIV; "malcontents," NRSV; "bellyachers," MSG; "ever bemoaning their lot," Weymouth) is also onomatopoetic. The term denotes the whispering to oneself that a dissatisfied undercurrent of discontent produces. It is practically synonymous with "murmurers," and could even be construed in the Greek as an adjective modifying it ("faultfinding grumblers").

(3) The infiltrators were **walking after their own lusts** (v. 16), inattentive to the Lord and the sheep for whom they supposedly cared. They were "trying all the time to mould life according to their own desires" (Phillips).

(4) **Their mouth speaketh great swelling words**, Jude said, perhaps in reference to their bombastic teaching or preaching style that was intended to win admiration. Volume, pomposity, and haughtiness masked the antagonists' hypocrisy, heresy, and sensuality. In the end, they were "loudmouthed braggarts" (NLT).

(5) The characteristic of **having men's persons in admiration** (lit., "marveling faces") **because of advantage** is helpfully rendered "flattering people to their own advantage" in the NRSV. Whether the advantage sought is money, material gifts, praise, allegiance, recognition, identification with a particular social class, or sexual favors, leaders prove false when they use others for personal gain. James 2:1–13 forbids showing favoritism to the rich. In that passage, James used terms that are cognate (verbally related) to Jude's language (see James 2:1, 9: "[have] respect of persons"; "court favour," NEB; "show favoritism," NIV).

IV. Conclusion (vv. 17–25)

A. Repetition: The Apostolic Prophecy regarding Sensual Mockers (vv. 17–19)

Verse 17. In a rhetorical discourse, the conclusion typically reviews the preceding discussion and seeks to make a further emotional appeal to the audience. Jude successfully carried out both functions in verses 17–25, and both review and appeal are contained in verse 17. The exhortation **remember ye the words** recalls "the faith which was once delivered unto the saints" (v. 3) and the biblical instruction that follows (vv. 5–7, 11). This was a central part of the proclamation and teaching of **the apostles**. **Beloved** is a term that arouses positive pathos among the hearers. They knew that Jude's warnings and instructions originated in his love for them.

Verse 18. The apostles had predicted the advent of **mockers in the last time** (see Acts 20:29; 1 Tim. 4:1; 2 Tim. 3:1–5), so the believers were not to be surprised by the coming of these godless men, and any alarms among the congregations were quelled. The Greek for **they told you** indicates that the apostles continually or repeatedly warned that such godless apostates would come (see Matt. 24:4–5, 10–12; Acts 20:28–30; 2 Peter 2:1–3). Since the mockers should **walk after their own ungodly lusts** (see 2 Peter 3:3), the church needed to adopt safeguards against their corrupting influence. "Should walk" is simply descriptive, not predetermined; the NJB has "who follow nothing but their own godless desires." Jude did not identify the object of the scoffers' ridicule. In 2 Peter 3:4, however, they sneered, "Where is the promise of his coming?" Perhaps that was the substance of the mocking in Jude's case as well. Hostility against the gospel and its claims (including Christ's coming, which spells judgment) sometimes is directly correlated with immoral behavior.

Verse 19. The triad of vices characterizing the false teachers confirmed the hearers' revulsion toward them. (1) Divisiveness was a characteristic of the intruders. Jude called them **they who separate themselves**. The phrase may indicate that the false teachers presented themselves as a spiritual elite who were more entitled to honor in the church than those who (they believed) were not as spiritual as they. (2) The mockers were **sensual** ("follow mere natural instincts," NIV). If the intruders presented themselves as a Gnostic elite, Jude's word, *psychikoi*, is ironic since the elite used that word to describe the uninitiated. The Gnostics claimed to be a privileged elite, the spiritual ones, but Jude denied that they even possessed the Spirit. (3) Thus, the third characteristic of the mockers was **having not the Spirit** (Greek, *pneuma*). The noun can refer to God's Spirit or the human spirit. The KJV capitalizes "Spirit" since, in all likelihood, God's Spirit is the referent of *pneuma*, not the human spirit (see also ASV, ESV, NASB, NIV, NLT, NRSV). The third condition gave rise to the second: "They live by natural instinct because they do not have God's Spirit living in them" (NLT). The three terms in the triad are listed successively in Greek with no clear linkage between them.

B. Emotional Appeal: Christian Endurance and Ministry to the Wayward (vv. 20–23)

1. Christian Endurance (vv. 20–21)

Verses 20–21. The address **But ye, beloved** (v. 20) stands in contrast to the ungodly false teachers, about whom this letter speaks at length. The main idea in these verses is **Keep yourselves in the love of God** (v. 21), with the verb in the imperative mood. The readers were to remain within the sphere of God's forgiveness, guidance, and provision—unlike the angels who did not abide in their proper domain (see v. 6). Again using a triad, Jude enumerated positive steps the believers could take to counteract the influence of the sensual mockers, avoid falling into their errors, and keep in the love of God. The steps, desirable activities with desirable outcomes, contributed to the positive emotional appeal of Jude's case.

(1) The first step Jude advocated was **building up yourselves on your most holy faith** (v. 20; the faith for which the assemblies were to "earnestly contend," v. 3). The architectural metaphor differs from Colossians 2:7, where the same verb is passive, and Christ is the foundation upon which the building proceeds

("be built in him," REB). In either case, the believers were to concentrate on "structural integrity" in their congregations and guard against the pride and rancor of the mockers (see vv. 8, 10–11, 16, 19).

(2) The second action that would contribute to maintaining the community's standing within God's love was **praying in the Holy Ghost** (v. 20). Jude's meaning here may be "continue to pray in the power of the Holy Spirit" (REB). Paul recognized the believer's need for the Holy Spirit's intercession in prayer (see Rom. 8:26–27). The Spirit guides them in what to pray, and He gives them the discipline and stamina to engage in prayer.

(3) As the third step, Jude advised his house churches to be **looking for the mercy of our Lord Jesus Christ unto eternal life** (v. 21). Jude did not mean that his hearers did not presently have eternal life, nor was he necessarily implying that their current possession of it was uncertain (see 1 John 5:11–13). "Eternal life" is the fullness of that life into which they had already entered. The completion of the process of salvation is merciful in that it is the Christian's final deliverance from the presence and power of sin.

2. Ministry to the Wayward (vv. 22–23)

A comparison of various English translations of these verses reveals a disagreement whether the objects of ministry are two groups or three groups. The reason for differences among the translations is the existence of different readings among the witnesses to the Greek text. The essential difference concerns the number of clauses in Jude's original construction; each clause represents a classification of people to be aided. The KJV and other translations (e.g., Moffatt, NEB) follow witnesses that have two clauses; other translations (e.g., NIV, NASB, NJB, NRSV, REB) utilize witnesses that have three clauses. In light of Jude's predilection for triads and the inclusion of a third clause in very early witnesses, three groups seems more likely.

Verses 22–23. Regarding the first group in need of outreach, Jude said, **And of some have compassion** (v. 22). They were to "Be merciful" (NIV) to those who had not yet totally succumbed to the wiles of the false teachers but were leaning toward their specious arguments. The brazenness of the mockers and the apparent freedom that they enjoyed were a magnet for the immature believers who were not secure in their faith. Those wiser and stronger were to take on themselves the responsibility of the weaker, lest they fall. **Making a difference** (a plural participle in the nominative case) means "making a distinction" (NKJV); that is, the stronger members of the church were to be attentive to the younger believers and distinguish how to help them mature.

Jude's hearers were to assist a second group also, people whom they were to **save with fear, pulling them out of the fire** (v. 23). Of course, the one who saves is the Lord, and the word here (*sōzō*) is the usual New Testament word for salvation to eternal life (see John 12:47; 1 Cor. 1:21; Eph. 2:8; Titus 3:5). Salvation can be ascribed to the person who is the instrument God uses to lead a person away from sin and death into eternal life. The word "pulling" (*harpazō*) is very vivid. It can denote the act of robbery, capturing booty, or being swept away by a river. The word also designates prey being seized by wild animals (see John 10:12). Stringent measures were required to rescue those who had slipped into the clutches of the false teachers. The ones to be saved were in danger of hell itself (the likely referent of "fire"; for the idea of snatching from the fire, see Zech. 3:1–4).

Some translations list a third group as the object of ministry: "to others show mercy, mixed with fear—hating even the clothing stained by corrupted flesh" (v. 23, NIV). In the KJV, the final clause, which begins with **hating**, modifies "save with fear" and thus is part of the instructions pertaining to the second group to be helped. A third group is absent.

What does it mean for believers to save (or show mercy to) others while **hating even the garment spotted by the flesh** (v. 23)? The "garment" is the tunic (*chitōn*), the garment worn next to the skin. Jude's reference to its "spotted" ("polluted," NASB) condition recalls the Hebrew for Joshua's "filthy garments" in Zechariah 3:3–4. The word "filthy" is re-

lated to the Hebrew terms used in the Old Testament for human feces. The infection of the false teachers was repulsive and so pervasive that it contaminated everything and everyone who came in contact with them. Jude's metaphor and hyperbole created strongly negative pathos toward the mockers and their lascivious ways.

Two things Jude did *not* say in this passage: (1) He left no room for hating the sinner. The sin ("garment") was to be hated, not the sinner. (2) Jude did not depreciate the human body. "Flesh" (*sarx*) is not the body but rather the self-sufficient orientation toward sin that views the body as a vehicle of wrongdoing.

C. Doxology (vv. 24–25)

Verses 24–25. Jude's closing words are one of the mightiest crescendos of praise and exultation in the entire New Testament. The one glorified is **the only wise God our Saviour** (v. 25). In the New Testament, "Saviour" sometimes refers to God (see Luke 1:47; 1 Tim. 4:10) and sometimes to Jesus (see Luke 2:11; Phil. 3:20). Jude identified two of God's glorious characteristics, worthy of praise, both of which stem from His almighty power. (1) He **is able to keep you from falling** (v. 24). Jude's hearers may have become apprehensive that they might weaken and join those under the intruders' sway (see vv. 22–23). The readers' confidence was not to come from themselves but from God, who is fully able to keep those who put their trust in Him. (2) God is able **to present you faultless before the presence of his glory** (v. 24). In the Old Testament, the term "faultless" is used of the perfection of sacrificial animals offered to God (see Numbers 28–29). Believers can look to the future knowing that because of Jesus' death, they can stand in God's presence.

Not only can believers stand in God's presence, but they can stand in His presence **with exceeding joy** (v. 24). Since joy will be one's experience before God forever, it ought to be the overriding characteristic of worship now. Much Christian service and worship goes to the extreme opposite of the false teachers mentioned in the discussion on verse 19; it is spiritually listless and lacking in joy. Some daily practices contribute to spiritual lethargy. Lack of sleep (too much late-night TV), hectic schedules (too many commitments, even to Christian activities), poor diet (fast foods for a too-fast lifestyle), and lack of exercise ("I'm too tired") militate against a joyful outlook. If these practices are corrected, spiritual energy might be revived in one's life. To God are ascribed **glory and majesty, dominion and power, both now and ever** (v. 25), but not as though He does not already have them. A doxology is recognition and praise of who God is and of His attributes. Those attributes that Jude identified here parallel his concerns in the letter. Despite the atrocious sins of the false teachers, God's person and honor were not threatened. Nor was God's sovereignty and authority in jeopardy because of the sins of the mockers. Since God remains God "before all time and now and forever" (NASB), His people can rest securely in Him. **Amen.**

THE REVELATION OF ST. JOHN THE DIVINE

INTRODUCTION

Author

Four times the author identifies himself as John (1:1, 4, 9; 22:8). From as early as Justin Martyr, in the second century AD, it has been held that this John was the apostle, the son of Zebedee (see Matt. 10:2). The book reveals that the author was a Jew, well versed in Scripture, a church leader who was well known to the seven churches of Asia (in today's western Turkey), and a deeply religious person fully convinced that the Christian faith would triumph over the demonic forces at work in the world.

In the third century, however, an African bishop named Dionysius compared the language, style, and thought of the Apocalypse (Revelation) with that of the other writings of John and decided that the book could not have been written by the apostle John. He suggested that the author was a certain John the Presbyter, whose name appears elsewhere in ancient writings. Although some today follow Dionysius in his view of authorship, the external evidence is overwhelmingly supportive of the traditional view that John the apostle wrote the Revelation.

Date

Revelation was written when Christians were entering a time of persecution. The two periods most often mentioned are the latter part of Nero's reign (AD 54–68) and the latter part of Domitian's reign (81–96). Most scholars date the book circa 95. Many substantial arguments favor the later date: (1) Domitian was the first emperor to insist on being worshiped as god throughout the empire; (2) the lukewarm condition of the churches of Asia Minor implies they had been in existence for many years; (3) the testimony of the earliest church fathers supports a date at the end of the first century.

Background

Since Roman authorities at the time were beginning to enforce the cult of emperor worship, Christians—who held that Christ, not Caesar, was Lord—were facing increasing hostility. In the letters to the churches, the Lord warned the believers at Smyrna against coming opposition (2:10) and told the church at Philadelphia of an hour of trial coming on the world (3:10). Antipas had already given his life (2:13), as had others (6:9). John had been exiled to the island of Patmos (probably the site of a Roman penal colony) because of his activities as a Christian missionary (1:9). Some within the church were advocating a policy of compromise (2:14–15, 20), which had to be corrected before its subtle influence could undermine the determination of believers to stand fast in the perilous days ahead.

Theme and Theological Message

John wrote to encourage the faithful to resist staunchly the demands of emperor worship. He shared with his readers the vision the Lord gave him of the imminent final showdown between God and Satan. In the great tribulation to come, Satan will increase his persecution of believers, but they must stand fast, even to death. They are sealed against any spiritual harm and will soon be vindicated when Christ returns, when the wicked are forever destroyed, and when God's people enter an eternity of glory and blessedness.

Literary Features

For an adequate understanding of Revelation, the reader must recognize that it is a distinct kind of literature. Revelation is apocalyptic, a kind of writing that is highly symbolic. The book refers to itself as a "prophecy" of future events (1:3; 22:7, 10, 18–19). It also provides a number of clues for its own interpretation (e.g., stars are angels, candlesticks are churches, 1:20; "the great whore," 17:1, is "Babylon" [Rome?], 17:5, 18; and the heavenly Jerusalem is the wife of the Lamb, 21:9–10). There is frequently a dualism between the earthly and the heavenly, good and evil, this world and the world to come. Beasts and other animals are used figuratively to represent certain realities, and colors are used symbolically, as are several numbers—especially 3, 7, and multiples of 12.

A distinctive feature is the frequent use of the number seven (fifty-two times). There are seven beatitudes (see discussion on 1:3), seven churches (1:4, 11), seven spirits (1:4), seven golden candlesticks (1:12), seven stars (1:16), seven seals (5:1), seven horns and seven eyes (5:6), seven trumpets (8:2), seven thunders (10:3), seven wonders or signs (12:1, 3; 13:13–14; 15:1; 16:14; 19:20), seven heads with seven crowns (12:3), seven plagues (15:6), seven golden vials (15:7), seven mountains (17:9), and seven kings (17:10), as well as other sevens. Symbolically, the number seven stands for completeness. The book of Revelation also uses "and" (Greek, *kai*) over 1,200 times. The constant use of this conjunction creates a sense of fast-paced movement from one event to the next.

Interpretation

Interpreters of Revelation normally fall into four groups:

1. *Preterists* understand the book exclusively in terms of its first-century setting, claiming that most of its events have already taken place in the past.
2. *Historicists* take it as describing the long chain of events from Patmos to the end of history.
3. *Futurists* place the book primarily in the end times.
4. *Idealists* view it as symbolic pictures of such timeless truths as the victory of good over evil.

Fortunately, the fundamental truths of the book are obvious throughout. A plain rendering of the book indicates that Christ will eventually return, triumph over evil, and usher in the eternal state.

Outline

I. Introduction (1:1–8)
   A. Prologue (1:1–3)
   B. Greetings and Doxology (1:4–8)
II. Jesus Appears to John on Patmos (1:9–20)
III. The Letters to the Seven Churches (chaps. 2–3)
   A. Ephesus (2:1–7)
   B. Smyrna (2:8–11)
   C. Pergamos (2:12–17)
   D. Thyatira (2:18–29)
   E. Sardis (3:1–6)
   F. Philadelphia (3:7–13)
   G. Laodicea (3:14–22)
IV. The Throne, the Book, and the Lamb (chaps. 4–5)
   A. The Throne in Heaven (chap. 4)
   B. The Seven-Sealed Book (5:1–5)
   C. The Lamb That Was Slain (5:6–14)
V. The Seven Seal Judgments (6:1–8:1)
   A. First Seal: The White Horse (6:1–2)
   B. Second Seal: The Red Horse (6:3–4)
   C. Third Seal: The Black Horse (6:5–6)
   D. Forth Seal: The Pale Horse (6:7–8)
   E. Fifth Seal: The Souls under the Altar (6:9–11)
   F. Sixth Seal: The Great Earthquake (6:12–7:17)
     1. The First Interlude (chap. 7)
       a. The Sealing of the 144,000 (7:1–8)
       b. The Great Multitude (7:9–17)
   G. Seventh Seal: Silence in Heaven (8:1)
VII. The Seven Trumpets (8:2–11:19)
   A. Introduction (8:2–5)
   B. First Trumpet: Hail and Fire Mixed with Blood (8:6–7)
   C. Second Trumpet: A Mountain Thrown into the Sea (8:8–9)
   D. Third Trumpet: The Star Wormwood (8:10–11)
   E. Fourth Trumpet: A Third of the Sun, Moon, and Stars Struck (8:12–13)
   F. Fifth Trumpet: The Plague of Locusts (9:1–12)
   G. Sixth Trumpet: Release of the Four Angels (9:13–21)
     1. The Second Interlude (10:1–11:14)
       a. The Angel and the Little Scroll (chap. 10)
       b. The Two Witnesses (11:1–14)
   H. Seventh Trumpet: Judgments and Rewards (11:15–19)

Bibliography

Couch, Mal. *A Bible Handbook to Revelation*. Grand Rapids, MI: Kregel, 2001.

Custer, Stewart. *From Patmos to Paradise*. Greenville, SC: BJU Press, 2004.

Hindson, Ed. *The Book of Revelation: Unlocking the Future*. Twenty-first Century Biblical Commentary. Chattanooga, TN: AMG, 2002.

Morris, Henry M. *The Revelation Record*. Wheaton, IL: Tyndale, 1983.

Mounce, Robert. *The Book of Revelation*. The New International Commentary on the New Testament. Grand Rapids, MI: Eerdmans, 1994.

Seiss, Joseph A. *The Apocalypse*. Grand Rapids, MI: Kregel, 1987.

Stigers, Harold. *A Commentary on Genesis*. Grand Rapids, MI: Zondervan, 1976.

Thomas, Robert L. *Revelation 1–7*. Wycliffe Exegetical Commentary. Chicago: Moody, 1992.

———. *Revelation 8–22*. Wycliffe Exegetical Commentary. Chicago: Moody, 1995.

Unger, Merrill F. *Commentary on the Old Testament*. Chattanooga, TN: AMG Publishers, 2002.

Walvoord, John F. *The Revelation of Jesus Christ*. Chicago: Moody, 1966.

———. "Revelation." In *The Bible Knowledge Commentary: New Testament*, edited by John F. Walvoord and Roy B. Zuck. Wheaton, IL: Victor, 1983.

EXPOSITION

I. Introduction (1:1–8)

These first eight verses give introductory words from John the apostle, the human author, and from the Lord Jesus Christ, the divine author. Later in the book, John indicated that the Holy Spirit also functioned as author (see, e.g., 2:7), along with Christ, giving readers direct revelations that make the book extremely important. The prologue (vv. 1–3) leads to greetings and a doxology (vv. 4–8) that gives a heavenly portrait of the Lord Jesus Christ, who is the central subject of the entire book. The opening chapters (chaps. 1–3) read like an epistle, whereas the body of the book is a prophecy of what will happen in the future.

A. Prologue (1:1–3)

These verses tell how the book will unfold. In some ways, they serve as an introduction for the chapters that follow.

1:1. The word **Revelation** (Greek, *apocalypsis*) does not have an article in the Greek text and means "disclosure" or "unveiling" of that which is hidden. Is this a revelation *about* Jesus Christ, or is it a revelation *from* Jesus Christ? Most scholars believe the book is a revelation, a new disclosure of divine truth, *about* the Lord Jesus. In the first chapter, He is revealed in all His glory.

This revelation about Christ was given **unto him, to shew unto his servants** future events, **things which must shortly come to pass.** God the Father wants the believers to understand old and new revelations in the context of the end times. "Shortly come to pass" is similar to the wording found in 4:1; 22:6; Daniel 2:28–29, 45. The expression "shortly" (Greek, *en tachei*) has been greatly misinterpreted. It does not mean that the events of Revelation are about to happen. It means that when they start, they will take place "quickly" or "with rapidity" of execution. A similar word (Greek, *tachy*) is translated "quickly" seven times in Revelation (2:16; 3:11; 11:14; 22:7, 12, 20). The idea of "suddenly" or "with rapidity" is seen

in other verses in the New Testament (e.g., Luke 18:8; Acts 12:7; 22:18; 25:4).

The revelation was transmitted through Christ's **angel** to the apostle **John,** the recording **servant** of the Lord. **Signified** is from the Greek word *sēmainō,* which has the thought of "communicating by symbol." Revelation contains symbolic language but not in every part, and where there are symbols, behind them are literal events couched in pictorial words. The word "signified" must not mislead the reader. Revelation should not be seen as an allegory or prophetic poem. It is a prophecy of actual events, the "things which must be hereafter" (4:1).

1:2–3. It is John **who bare record of the word of God, and of the testimony** (Greek, *martyria*) **of Jesus Christ** (v. 2). This includes everything **he saw** about the Lord, but also all of the revelations that came from Him. John was bearing witness, or testifying, to having received the Word who came down from the heavenly Father. John also gave "testimony" to the person, life, and ministry of Christ; he was there as an apostle. "He saw" it all; he was an eyewitness.

A special blessing is attached to this book. While every book of Scripture holds blessings for those who read it, the book of Revelation holds a special blessing. It brings finality to all of redemptive history and establishes a time line for believers. It tells the child of God that the world as it is known will end. Terrible times will lead to the return of Christ to earth and then on into the eternal state, where "there shall be no more death, neither sorrow, nor crying, neither shall there by any more pain; for the former things are passed away" (21:4).

Blessed (Greek, *makarios*; "happy," "fortunate") **is he that readeth, and they that hear the words of this prophecy** (Greek, *propheteias*)**, and keep those things which are written therein** (v. 3). This is the first of seven beatitudes, or blessings, in Revelation (here; 14:13; 16:15; 19:9; 20:6; 22:7, 14), which are reminders of the seven beatitudes of Matthew 5:3–11. "He that readeth" may refer to a church reader who shares this revelation with those who cannot read, or it may refer to anyone who has the privilege to read the book for themselves. The blessing extends to all those who "hear the words" of the prophecy. Whoever reads or hears Revelation, however, must also "keep those things which are written" in it, meaning they must internalize the message and live as if these things could happen soon. The message should cause the believer to give priority to the Christian walk, which is important because **the time is at hand**. "The time is at hand" (Greek, *kairos engys*) is better translated "the season [of the events of Revelation] is sure, certain." *Kairos* is best translated "season" and here has to do with the events of the tribulation, which are laid out in chapters 6–19. *Engys* is two Greek words put together: "in the hand," meaning these events are "sure" or "certain" to take place. The English expression "It is better to have a bird in hand than two in the bush" reflects this idea.

B. Greetings and Doxology (1:4–8)

These verses give a greeting to the churches in Asia to whom the entire book of Revelation was apparently sent. This book is not a typical New Testament book. It is a prophecy that opens up and reveals the final details of the end times, all the way into eternity. Much that is given in this book has previously been revealed in many Old Testament books, but without specific details. In fact, 278 of 404 verses contain Old Testament types, symbols, pictures, or allusions (Hindson, *The Book of Revelation*, p. 3). Verses 4–8 are still preliminary, giving a vision of the deity of Christ, but verse 7 sets up the end of the book (19:11–20:6), which describes Christ coming to establish His kingdom.

1:4. The seven churches ... in Asia are addressed, with **Grace** and **peace** from God the Father. Asia refers to the Roman province in Asia Minor that included Phrygia, Mysia, Caria, and Lydia. These seven churches were in the western half of Asia Minor. The greeting shows God as the Eternal One, who presently exists (**which is**), who existed in the past (**which was**), and whose existence will continue forever in the future (**which is to come**). The Lord's

eternalness was expressed in the burning bush before Moses. The Lord said, "I AM THAT I AM" (Exod. 3:14), meaning, "I exist simply because I exist!" In John 8:58, Christ applied to Himself the same designation of the eternally existing God.

Most scholars believe **the seven spirits** is a reference to the sevenfold manifestations of the Holy Spirit (see Rev. 3:1; 4:5; 5:6). The number seven denotes perfection or completeness. The Spirit stands before the **throne** of God in heaven. In 4:5, John wrote that "there were seven lamps of fire burning before the throne, which are the seven spirits of God." The Spirit of God gives the light of truth. In his vision, Zechariah saw "seven lamps" (Zech. 4:2), or lights, on a golden candlestick that was to be built for the new temple. God's Spirit ("my spirit," Zech. 4:6) aided Zechariah in the construction project. Isaiah prophesied that the sevenfold manifestation of the Spirit would rest on the Messiah (see Isa. 11:1–5).

1:5–6. The greeting is also **from Jesus Christ** (v. 5), who is called **the faithful witness** (Greek, *martyria*)**, and the first begotten of the dead, and the prince of the kings of the earth**. Christ came as the Son of God to show His heavenly Father to the world (see John 1:18). Christ said, "Though I bear record of myself, yet my record is true" (John 8:14), because He came from heaven. He was also faithful as a prophet from God (see John 18:37). He said, "I ... bear witness of myself, and the Father that sent me beareth witness of me" (John 8:18). Christ is the "first begotten [Greek, *prōtotokos*; 'preeminent,' 'firstborn'] of the dead." He was the first to receive a resurrection body, which is immortal (see Acts 26:23). He is "the firstborn of every creature" (Col. 1:15).

Christ is also "the prince" (Greek, *ho archōn*; "the chief one"; v. 5) over the kings of the earth. In His providence, He sustains all of creation (see Col. 1:16), but as the final and ultimate earthly ruler, His sovereign reign is yet to come (see 19:11–16), fulfilling the prophecies of Isaiah 9:6–7, Psalm 72:11, and Zechariah 14:9. The wise men, the kings, and the judges will someday see the Lord Jesus Christ on His earthly throne and will be commanded to "Serve the LORD with fear, and rejoice with trembling" (Ps. 2:11). Almost as if penning a brief anthem, John wrote that those whom Christ **loved** (present tense; "keeps on loving"), He **washed us from our sins in his own blood**. All believers have been "washed" (Greek, *lyō*; aorist tense), better translated "loosed," once for all by the shedding of Christ's blood at the cross, giving eternal remission of sins (see Eph. 1:7; 2:23; Col. 1:20).

In giving salvation, Christ **made** those He saved (v. 6) to be **kings and priests [of] God, his** (heavenly) **Father**. This verse is better translated, "hath made us a kingdom, priests unto God and His Father." Such a designation is used of the Jewish people in the Old Testament (see Exod. 19:6; Zechariah 3). John was not suggesting, however, that the church has replaced Israel; rather, he was saying that believers in the present church dispensation now represent the Lord as spiritual **kings and priests**. Believers now have the authority and the privilege to represent Him in their ministry. The church presently is "a holy priesthood, to offer up spiritual sacrifices" (1 Peter 2:5), which are pleasing to God. The believer's body is that "living sacrifice, holy, acceptable unto God, which is your reasonable service" (Rom. 12:1). As living and holy sacrifices, God is honored with **glory** (Greek, *doxa*; "splendor") **and dominion** (Greek, *kratos*; "power," "authority") for eternity, **for ever and ever**, that is, "unto the ages of ages." To such a glorious Savior and Master, the right to eternal glory and dominion is attributed (see Dan. 7:14). To this, John added, **Amen**, that is, "So be it!"

1:7. The imagery in this verse comes from Daniel 7:13 and Zechariah 12:10. The Messiah will someday come in the **clouds; and every eye shall see him**. He is the one who was crucified by the Jews and then **pierced** with a spear (see Ps. 22:11–18; Isa. 53:4–6; Zech. 10:12; John 19:34–37). When He returns, **all kindreds of the earth shall wail because of him** (see Zech. 10:12; Matt. 24:30). They will recognize Him as Savior and King. John felt compelled to again write, **Even so, Amen**.

1:8. This verse is a paraphrase of Isaiah 41:4, which speaks of the eternalness of God: "I the LORD,

the first, and with the last; I am he." The addition of **Alpha and Omega** (the first and last letters of the Greek alphabet) and **the beginning and the ending** reinforces the eternal attribute of God. This verse, however, is about the Lord Jesus, who is the second person of the Trinity and who is very God. Much that is said of God in Isaiah 41:4 is also used here to describe Christ. There is no reason why eternity should not be ascribed to Him, as well as to His Father (see Rev. 21:6; 22:13). **The Almighty** (Greek, *pantokratōr*) is a title given to God but is here applied to the Lord Jesus. Nine of the ten New Testament occurrences of this title are in Revelation (here; 4:8; 11:17; 15:3; 16:7, 14; 19:6, 15; 21:22); the tenth occurrence is in 2 Corinthians 6:18.

II. Jesus Appears to John on Patmos (1:9–20)

These verses give a glorious vision of the Lord Jesus in heaven. They also state that the apostle John was on the island of Patmos when he received this vision. His vision was of the resurrected Christ, who has in His hands the churches to whom this letter was sent. It would not be a stretch to argue that all congregations that love the Lord are in His possession also.

1:9. **John** identified himself as the **brother, and companion** ("partaker, and sharer") **in tribulation** (Greek, *thlipsei*) of those to whom he wrote. The seven churches, and probably other congregations, were suffering to some degree the same persecutions that John was, which possibly were instigated by the evil Roman emperor Domitian (AD 81–96). While history does not record widespread persecution at that time, the emperor probably regarded the believers in Christ as dangerously seditious, because popular distrust of them was growing. Domitian reinstated emperor worship, and this placed the Christians in a disadvantageous position.

When John wrote **the kingdom**, he was referring not to the future millennial reign of Christ but to the society and association of believers in a kingdomlike fraternity. The **patience** (Greek, *hypomonē*) of Christ implies that the Christians were under cultural and governmental pressure from which they could not escape. John was on **Patmos**, the Alcatraz of the ancient world, from which few escaped (see Hindson, *The Book of Revelation*, p. 25). The island (ten miles by six miles) is still today rocky, barren, and dotted with caves, some of which the exiles used for shelter. John was there because he had witnessed to **the word of God, and ... the testimony of Jesus Christ**. According to the church father Victorinus, the aged apostle was forced to work in the mines on the island. He was freed to return to Ephesus, where he was pastor, when the Emperor Nerva came to power.

1:10. While **in the spirit on the Lord's day**, John **heard ... a great voice [like] a trumpet**, a strong, decisive, and commanding voice. He had not heard the voice of his Savior since just before His ascension to glory (see Acts 1:7–9). "In the spirit" describes the trance-like state (Greek, *ekstasis*; "ecstasy") mentioned in Acts 10:10; 11:5; 22:17. This was a vision, not a dream, nor a state of being asleep. God placed John in this trance-like state for receiving the revelations of this book (see Thomas, *Revelation 1–7*, p. 58). "The Lord's day" may mean the first day of the week, Sunday, but "Lord's" is actually an adjective, with the sense of a "Lordian" (as the adjective "Christian" is formed from "Christ") or "Lordly" day.

1:11. The voice was identified as the **Alpha and Omega** (v. 8; 21:6; 22:13), meaning the Eternal One (**the first and the last**). What John saw, he was to **write in a book** (Greek, *biblion*; "scroll"). This command to "write" was given twelve times in the book. The book was to be sent to the seven churches of Asia (for more on these churches, see chaps. 2–3).

1:12–16. These verses give a glorious and vivid first picture of the Lord Jesus Christ in heaven. The picture is presented in illustrative and descriptive language to convey to the reader Christ's new state in glory. The verses are symbolic, as are many verses in Revelation, but again, care must be taken that the book is not seen as simply a symbolic poem that is without reality and historicity. These verses use two comparative words (Greek, *homoios* and *hōs*) that are translated almost synonymously: "like," "as," "like

as," "as if." Together, these two words are used over one hundred times in the book of Revelation.

When John **turned to see the voice**, he **saw seven golden candlesticks** (v. 12). This may have been a golden lampstand with seven branched lampholders mounted on a central shaft, or it may have been seven individual lamps mounted on seven individual stands, or shafts. As the gold in the tabernacle and in Solomon's temple represented the deity of the Lord, here it represents the deity of the Lord Jesus Christ. The oil to light the lamps symbolizes the power and work of the Holy Spirit.

In the midst of the seven candlesticks (v. 13) stood **one like ... the Son of man**, a common designation for Christ. "Son of man" is one of the most important descriptions of Israel's Messiah. The expression means "the Son who is related to humanity." The first reference to "the Son of man" is found in Daniel 7:13, which describes the Messiah coming from earth, where He lived as part of the human race, and being presented before God, who is called "the Ancient of Days." After Christ's resurrection, He went back to His Father (see Acts 1:9–10). The Son of Man is mentioned throughout the Gospels as a messianic expression (see, e.g., Mark 8:31). Christ had on **a garment** like that of the high priest (see Exod. 28:4; 29:5; Hebrews 7), **down to the foot**. His chest (**the paps**) was encircled (**girt**) with a sash (**a golden girdle**) like that used by the priests. This somber representation of Christ in His role as judge and priest, standing **in the midst of** the churches, is a poignant introduction to chapters 2–3.

His hair was **white like wool**, or **as white as snow** (v. 14). White hair symbolizes the dignity of an elder, one with wisdom and divine authority. **His eyes were as a flame of fire** symbolizes Christ's work of judgment. He has the right to judge not only the churches but also the world, as quoted in John 5:22: "the Father ... hath committed all judgment unto the Son." In Revelation, the description of the Son is like that of His Father: "The Ancient of days did sit, whose garment was white as snow, and the hair of his head like the pure wool: his throne was like the fiery flame" (Dan. 7:9). **His feet [were] like ... fine** brass (Greek, *chalkolibanon*; actually a copper alloy; v. 15)—heavy, sturdy, strong, and permanently fixed—like brass smelted for some time, **burned in a furnace**, with all of the impurities removed.

His voice [had] the sound of many waters (v. 15), the sound of a rushing, flowing mountain waterfall. His words were loud and commanding! In His **right hand** (v. 16), He held **seven stars**, which are identified as "the angels of the seven churches" (1:20). Some scholars have speculated that these "angels" (Greek, *angeloi*; "messengers") were angelic beings who guarded and attended the seven churches. Others believe they were the "messengers" and readers of the seven churches who came to Patmos, received this scroll, and returned to share its message with their congregations. Churches had envoys and readers who shared such documents with those who were illiterate. The letters themselves imply that the "messengers" are responsible for sharing the messages with the people in the churches.

From the Lord in glory went forth **a sharp two-edged sword** (v. 16) from **out of his mouth**. This "sword" represents divine judgment and corresponds with 19:15: "Out of his mouth goeth a sharp sword, that with it he should smite the nations: and he shall rule them with a rod of iron: and he treadeth the winepress of the fierceness and wrath of Almighty God." **His countenance** (face) **was as the sun [that] shineth in [its full] strength**. The brilliant glory of the Lord is compared to the full brightness of the sun. Such brilliance would seem to reflect the attributes of omnipotence, righteousness, sovereignty, and majesty (see Walvoord, *The Revelation of Jesus Christ*, p. 46).

1:17–19. When John saw this vision of Christ in glory, he fell down **as dead** (v. 17). Christ placed **his right hand** on him and said, **Fear not; I am the first and the last**. Christ assured the elderly apostle with words that represented His deity, His eternalness. From start to finish, Christ is the Son of God, but now He is in His eternal, glorified body. He is the God-man. He is the one who lived and died for sinners. **Behold** (v. 18), He is now **alive for evermore, Amen!** "Alive" is in the present tense: "He lives

continually." The Greek for "for evermore" is better translated "unto the ages of ages." Together, these two expressions reinforce the doctrine of the eternalness of Christ. He holds **the keys of hell** (Greek, *hadēs*; "Hades") **and of death** (Greek, *thanatos*). Before Christ's death and resurrection, the Devil held these keys and brought death to humanity (see Heb. 2:14–15), but Jesus lived in human flesh yet was without sin (see 2 Cor. 5:21) and destroyed the power of Satan. For those who trust Christ, He "deliver[ed] them who through fear of death were all their lifetime subject to bondage" (Heb.2:15).

The Lord commanded John, **Write the things which thou hast seen, and the things which are, and the things which shall be hereafter** (v. 19). "The things thou hast seen" refers to John's vision of the glorified Christ (1:11–19), "the things which are" refers to the letters to the seven churches (chaps. 2–3), and "the things which shall be" refers to the rest of the book of Revelation (chaps. 4–22). This is a simplified outline of the scroll that John wrote.

1:20. This verse explains what John saw in Christ's hand. **The seven stars** may refer to the seven "messengers" (**angels**) of the churches (see discussion on 1:16). **The seven golden candlesticks** (see 1:12) represent **the seven churches**. This introduces the messages, like small postcards, to these seven churches.

III. The Letters to the Seven Churches (chaps. 2–3)

The Lord Jesus is the divine author of these letters to the seven churches (see 1:11), but so is the Holy Spirit, who spoke through the human writer John (see, e.g., 2:7). It could be argued, then, that Jesus Christ, the Spirit of God, and John the apostle together wrote these letters. There are two views about the letters: (1) They were written to historic churches that had specific problems. John simply transcribed the words but added nothing to the messages given to the seven churches. Some of the problems were unique, such as the heresy of the Nicolaitans, which plagued the churches of Ephesus and Pergamos. (2) These letters also prophesied periods of church history that were yet to come. The problem with the second view is that there are no indications to substantiate this, and it is difficult to completely fit the events of the last two thousand years of church history into these seven church divisions. There is no question that throughout church history, congregations have experienced problems similar to those described here. The lessons addressed to the seven churches are applicable to all churches of all generations, because all believers since the founding of the church age (see Acts 2) are part of the larger, spiritual church, the body of Christ. The same needs and problems exist today as in John's day.

Each church had its own strengths and weakness. The letters, however, have a sevenfold pattern, though there are no words of commendation to the churches of Sardis or Laodicea and no words of condemnation for Smyrna or Philadelphia. Hindson (*The Book of Revelation*, p. 32) presents the following sevenfold pattern.

Commission: "To the angel of the church of …"
Character: "These things saith …"
Commendation: "I know thy works …"
Condemnation: "I have a few things against thee …"
Correction: "Repent …"
Call: "He that hath an ear …"
Challenge: "To him that overcometh …"

These seven churches were no more than one hundred miles from each other on the peninsula of Asia Minor. Two, Smyrna and Ephesus, were very near the coast of the Aegean Sea (because of silting, Ephesus is now nearly seven miles from the sea). Ephesus, where John pastored, was only about sixty miles from the island of Patmos.

A. Ephesus (2:1–7)

Ephesus was a large and important city, an economic center situated on the mouth of the river Cayster. From early on, it was an important seaport, the most important trading center west of Tarsus. The city had a population of about 300,000. Its outdoor amphitheater could seat 24,000. Behind the towering columns of the amphitheater were baths, gymnasiums, and impressive buildings.

The city was famous for its temple of Artemis (or Diana, her Roman name), which was one of the seven wonders of the world at that time. The twin sister of Apollo and the daughter of Zeus, Artemis, the multibreasted deity, was known as the moon goddess, the goddess of hunting, and the patroness of young girls. Her temple had 127 columns; each of them stood 197 feet high. Coins were minted that said, "Diana of Ephesus."

The apostle Paul founded the church in Ephesus. Christianity began in the city in about AD 50, through the efforts of Priscilla and Aquila (see Acts 18:18). Paul arrived around AD 52 and established a resident ministry for the better part of three years (see Acts 20:31). Acts reports that "all they which dwelt in Asia heard the word of the Lord Jesus, both Jews and Greeks" (Acts 19:10). Paul taught daily in the home of the teacher Tyrannus (see Acts 19:9). His ministry was so effective that the silversmith league, which made souvenirs of the temple, feared Paul's preaching would undermine the great temple of Artemis (see Acts 19:27). A riot followed, but Paul was spared. Paul experienced both blessings and dangers at Ephesus. He countered the strong influence of magic in the city (see Acts 19:11–20).

Tradition testifies that the apostle John lived in Ephesus toward the end of the century. In Revelation, while in exile, he described the false teachers that were flourishing in the city (see 2:1–7). In memory of John, the Roman emperor Justinian (AD 527–565) raised a magnificent church in the city.

The Ephesian church had good works, discernment, and patience. They hated the new heresy of religious people called the Nicolaitans. They were far off base, however, in that they had lost their first love, their affection for Christ. If they did not repent, the light of their testimony would go out.

2:1. The seven churches were each reminded that these letters came from the Lord Jesus. Here Christ is identified as the one who **holdeth the seven stars** and **who walketh in the midst of the seven golden candlesticks** (see 1:12, 16, 20).

2:2. Christ, being the all-knowing Son of God, knew of the Ephesians' **works** (Greek, *erga*) and **labour** (Greek, *kopon*). *Erga* has the idea of "expending energy." They were serving the Lord with great diligence. *Kopon* suggests they were "coping" under terrible pressure and were struggling with great pains to witness for Christ. **Patience** shows that they remained steadfast, walking faithfully even when facing adversity.

The Ephesians could not put up with (**canst not bear**; Greek, *bastazō*; "to endure") **them which are evil**. The Lord complimented the church for testing those who claimed to be **apostles**, many of whom were found to be **liars**. To their credit, the Christians questioned those who claimed to be from God. They put them to the test (**tried them**) as to their genuine faith and their divine calling.

2:3. The Ephesians had **borne** up under the struggle and had **laboured** for the sake of the Lord Jesus because His reputation was at stake. They had **not fainted**, or "grown weary." In spite of the opposition and persecution coming against them, they had not become weary in their work for Christ.

2:4. Nevertheless (Greek, *all'*) is a strong contrasting word. The Greek expresses **thou hast left** (Greek, *aphiēmi*) **thy first love** a little more strongly than the English wording, saying that they had "forsaken" or "abandoned" their "first love," who was Christ Himself. Apparently, this church was active in the Lord's work, but their heart for Him was not in the effort.

2:5. The Lord urged the Ephesians to look back at where they had started spiritually. They needed to **repent** (Greek, *metanoeō*; "change the mind") and return to their **first works**. If they did not, He would **come ... quickly, and ... remove [their] candlestick.** "First works" does not mean simply to return to good works in order to gain approval from God. A genuine love for God is always manifested in the works that it gives forth. Though the Ephesian assembly had been faithful in many tasks, those tasks did not in themselves exhibit a true love for the Lord. Their present works were suspect; they needed to be serving for higher reasons, as they had at the begin-

ning. If they did not repent, their "candlestick," or lamp, would go out; they would no longer be a beacon light of witness for the Lord. The believer who is not willing to yield all his talents and capabilities to Christ does not sufficiently love Jesus.

2:6. This church hated **the deeds of the Nicolaitans** (see 2:15). "Nicolaitans" means "conquering the people." No one can be certain what this cult was about except that it probably was a Gnostic sect, which is attested by many of the early and later church fathers. Eusebius wrote that after John the apostle censured the group, the sect disappeared for a short time. Some try to connect the group to Nicholas of Antioch, one of the seven original deacons of the church in Jerusalem (see Acts 6:5), but there are some doubts about this. The group was apostate, heretical, and became a lawless, licentious religion. About this group, Christ added, **which I also hate.**

2:7. Those who can should listen to **what the Spirit saith unto the churches.** This urging comes from Christ, but the statement attests that this message was being transmitted from Him, through the Spirit, to John. **That hath an ear** means more than simply hearing sounds; it means to hear with a desire to act upon the truth. The exhortation to **hear** and **overcometh** has several interpretations. The Greek word *nikaō* means "to be victorious," "to conquer." Some say the Lord was urging the Ephesians to repent and get right with the Lord in regard to their sins. Others believe it refers to overcoming sin, professing Christ, and becoming Christians. The argument is that it is wrong to believe that everyone in this assembly was a Christian. "Overcometh" has to do with salvation. This may be what John had in mind when he wrote in 1 John 5:4–5: "For whatsoever is born of God overcometh the world: and this is the victory that overcometh the world, even our faith. Who is he that overcometh the world, but he that believeth that Jesus is the Son of God?"

"Overcoming" is mentioned at the end of each of these church letters, and in each case, the reward seems to be the gift of eternal life, although stated in different ways. To the Ephesians, the reward was, **I [will] give to eat of the tree of life, which is in the**

midst of the paradise of God. This is a salvation concept, not simply a reward to a Christian who changes his ways. Those in the Ephesian church who were genuine Christians, who had overcome the unbelief and the sin of the world, were promised the right to the Tree of Life. This tree, mentioned first in the garden of Eden (see Gen. 3:22), will be found in the midst of the street in the New Jerusalem. In a certain symbolic picture, the tree produces its fruit for the abundant health, probably spiritual health, of the redeemed of the nations (see 22:2). "Paradise" (Greek, *paradeisos*) is from a Persian word referring to "a secluded place," "a garden of bliss." What was originally a garden of delight in Genesis 3 takes on the connotation of the new heaven and the new earth in Revelation 21–22. "The paradise of God" is a visual description of the peace and contentment of eternity in the presence of God the Father and God the Son.

It needs to be pointed out that all of the seven churches were to hear this particular message. This means that whatever was said to one church was applicable to all of them. Likewise, whatever is said here should be applied to today's churches also.

B. Smyrna (2:8–11)

Smyrna, in western Asia Minor, had a superb natural harbor and was an important trading and commercial center. In spite of competition from cities like Ephesus and Pergamum, the city referred to itself as "the first city of Asia." In 195 BC, seeing the rising power of Rome, the city of Smyrna sought to appease the Roman leadership and built a pagan temple for Roman worship. In 23 BC, the city was given the honor of constructing a temple to the Emperor Tiberias. With this, the city became the cultic center of emperor worship—a fanatical "religion" that later, under emperors such as Nero (AD 54–68) and Domitian (AD 81–96), brought severe persecution of the early church. Smyrna is now known as Izmir, the chief city of Anatolia and one of the most influential cities in modern Turkey.

This church was economically poor yet spiritually rich. No faults are mentioned in this letter. The church was under heavy assault by a certain Jewish synagogue, "the synagogue of Satan" (2:9). Many Christians were persecuted and thrown in prison.

2:8. As were all of the letters, this brief letter was written to **the angel of the church**. To each church, however, a different identification was given concerning Christ the divine author. Here He reminded the readers that He is **the first and the last**, again taking on the godly attribute of eternalness (see 1:8, 17; 22:13). As far back as one can go, God the Father existed, but so did the Lord Jesus Christ. As far into the future one can go, both persons reside in the Trinity, along with the eternal Holy Spirit. Christ **was dead** but now **is alive**. The resurrection (see 1:5) is a great demonstration that Jesus is the Son of God (see Rom. 1:4; 1 Cor. 15:12–19), and He is the firstfruits of those who are asleep (see 1 Cor. 15:20) in that He leads the way to victory over death.

2:9. The Lord said He knew the **works** of this church (see 2:2) but also their **tribulation, and poverty** (Greek, *ptōcheia*). God does not count poverty as humans do. He added, **but thou art rich** (Greek, *plousios*; "full," "complete"), meaning they were spiritually rich. James wrote of being poor in this world but "rich in faith" (James 2:5), and Paul said something similar about his ministry, "as poor, yet making many rich" (2 Cor. 6:10). The church at Smyrna was suffering **the blasphemy of them who say they are Jews, and are not**. These Jews were so by birth, but not by truth. They rejected the message of Christ as their Messiah and their Savior. It was as if **Satan** was ruling from their **synagogue**, driving them to blaspheme with their denial of Christ. Satan is the Father of Lies, who originates all that is not true (see John 8:44).

2:10. It is natural that these believers would **Fear** what they were to **suffer**, especially knowing that some of them would be **cast ... into prison**. They would be **tried, and ... have tribulation [for] ten days**. Many scholars have pondered the "ten days," and dozens of theories have been offered. Some speculate that it represents the ten years of persecution under Emperor Diocletian, but this seems improbable. It may mean an indefinite but short period, or it may be taken literally as describing a ten-day persecution that is unknown and not recorded in church history.

A special crown, **a crown of life**, would be given to those who suffered terribly. It seems feasible to extrapolate from this that all suffering and martyrdom (those **faithful unto death**) for Christ's sake will be rewarded with such a crown. "A crown of life" may refer to the fact that these believers gave their lives for a witness to the grace of God found only in the Lord Jesus Christ. James wrote that the one who is tried "shall receive the crown of life, which the Lord has promised to them that love him" (James 1:12; see 3:11).

2:11. The one who hears these words and **overcometh** will receive the ultimate reward: he **shall not be hurt of the second death** (see 20:1; 21:8). The first death is physical; the second death is spiritual, resulting in eternal punishment and separation from the presence of God.

C. Pergamos (2:12–17)

The Christians of Pergamos had gone through a terrible period of persecution but had come out of it holding fast to Christ's name and not denying His faith. Christ was adamantly against some in the congregation who held to the doctrine of Balaam. Some also had fallen into the cult of the Nicolaitans. The Lord commanded them to repent, or He would come against them and defeat them "with the sword of [His] mouth" (v. 16).

Pergamos was the chief city of Mysia, in northwest Asia Minor, and was situated about fifteen miles from the Aegean Sea. In its early history as a city-state, it became the powerful center of the region after Attalus I (241–197 BC) defeated the Gauls (Galatians). The city stood as a symbol of Greek superiority over the barbarians and boasted a library containing over 200,000 scrolls. The Egyptians were so jealous, because this library rivaled their own in Alexandria, that they refused to ship papyrus to Pergamos. As a result, a new form of writing material, "Pergamena charta," or parchment, was developed.

Pergamos was home to a temple to Asklepius (the Greco-Roman god of medicine and healing), as well as temples to Athena and Zeus, the latter with an altar showing him defeating snakelike mythical giants. It was also the center of the cult of emperor worship. In 29 BC, a temple was constructed to Emperor Augustus and the goddess Roma, which was served with a powerful priesthood. Christians abhorred the symbol of the serpent deity, the god of Pergamos. This is why Christ spoke of the city as the place "where Satan's seat is" (2:13).

2:12. Here Christ is pictured as the one with **the sharp sword with two edges**. When the Lord speaks, His words are cutting words of judgment, as if issued with a sword (see 1:16; 2:16; 19:15, 21). Hebrews 4:12 says the Word of God is "quick ['alive'] … and sharper than any twoedged sword," which opens up the human soul and spirit, and "is a discerner of the thoughts and intents of the heart."

2:13. As in all the letters, the Lord said He knew the **works** of the church. He knew the spiritual efforts of the believers at Pergamos but also their failures that were harmful to the congregation and to their witness. This assembly **dwellest … where Satan's seat is**. "Seat" (Greek, *thronos*) is better translated "throne." This and **where Satan dwelleth** are references to satanic power in Pergamos, in the evil, diabolical worship of Asklepius, the serpent god. The believers at this church were **hold[ing] fast** to the name of Christ. They had not **denied … faith** in Him, even during the days of **Antipas**, who was **slain**, the Lord's **faithful martyr**. Some speculate that Antipas, meaning "against all," symbolizes that a certain individual stood alone against the evil of the city and died. His name reflected the ministry he had in being a faithful witness. But better, this was one who stood unwaveringly for the Lord and paid the ultimate price for his faith.

2:14. As with many of these churches, the Lord had issues against the church at Pergamos. Some among them held to **the doctrine of Balaam**. Balaam was a Moabite prophet mentioned in Numbers 22–24. In Numbers 24, Balaam continued to balk at the request of the king of Moab, **Balac**, to curse

Israel. In Numbers 24:1–25:9, he had advised **Balac** that the Jews would jettison God's protection if he caused them to worship idols, which he did. This terrible story of temptation took place at Baal-Peor and made a lasting impression on later generations of Israelites. Balaam's counsel caused the people of the Lord to commit sexual immorality with the pagans and participate in idolatrous worship. Similar to Balaam's influence, **cast[ing] a stumblingblock**, some in the Pergamos church were **eat[ing] things sacrificed unto idols** and practicing **fornication**, "sexual immorality." In response, the Lord Jesus told them to repent, lest He come quickly and "fight against them" (2:16).

2:15–16. Like the church at Ephesus, the assembly at Pergamos was influenced by **the doctrine** (teaching) **of the Nicolaitans** (v. 15), which the Lord **hate[ed]** (see 2:6). If they did not **Repent** (v. 16), Christ would **come ... quickly** (Greek, *tachy*; "with suddenness"), **and ... fight against them with the sword of [His] mouth** (see also 1:16; 2:12).

2:17. This verse is similar to the ending of the letters to the other churches. It also has the warning to **hear what the Spirit saith** and a challenge to be included among those **that overcometh**. To the overcomer, the Lord **will ... give to eat of the hidden manna, and will give him a white stone**, on which is inscribed **a new name**. Manna (Hebrew; meaning, "What is it"?) sustained Israel in their wilderness wandering (see Exod. 16:13; Num. 11:31). The Lord "opened the doors of heaven, and had rained down manna upon them to eat" (Ps. 78:23–24). The true believer in the Lord Jesus receives manna that the world does not know or see, the spiritual sustenance of the saints. As in ancient Israel, this manna promises a better "land" in the future, a heritage waiting in heaven (see Walvoord, *The Revelation of Jesus Christ*, p. 70).

The "white stone" indicates that the child of God is favored by Christ. White always represents holiness and purity. On the stone, "a new name" is inscribed. This seems similar to the twelve stones in the breastplate of the high priests, "the breastplate of judgment" (Exod. 28:15); each stone was engraved with the name of one of the twelve tribes of Israel (see Exod. 28:21). When the priests intervened for the Lord, each tribe was represented. The new name, which no one knows except the one who **receiveth it**, is either the name of Christ Himself, now hidden from the world but to be revealed in the future as the most powerful of names (see 3:12; 14:1), or the name of the believer who is changed through redemption (see Isa. 62:2; 65:15).

D. Thyatira (2:18–29)

The church at Thyatira had charity, service, faith, and patience (v. 19), yet the religious cult of Jezebel was destroying the congregation with immorality, though not everyone had succumbed to the religious seduction. The woman known as "Jezebel" (v. 20) taught and beguiled the believers at Thyatira to conform to evil practices. In the congregation, Jezebel's followers seem to have been a minority, because the majority of Christians in this church were commended. Christ threatened death to Jezebel's children (v. 23) in some of the strongest words of judgment against the churches. The overcomer, however, would be given kingdom authority (vv. 26–27).

Thyatira was in the province of Lydia, in western Asia Minor, on the road from Pergamos to Sardis. The city was a thriving manufacturing and commercial center during New Testament times. History shows that the trade guilds were financially successful, but they participated in pagan customs and practices such as superstitious worship, feasts at which union members ate meals sacrificed to heathen gods, and sexual immorality.

Paul's first convert in Europe was "a certain woman named Lydia, a seller of purple, of the city of Thyatira, which worshipped God ... she attended unto the things which were spoken of Paul" (Acts 16:14). Modern Thyatira is called Akhisar.

2:18–19. Christ presented Himself to this assembly as Judge: **the Son of God** (see Ps. 2:7), **who hath ... eyes like ... a flame of fire, and ... feet ... like fine brass** (v. 18; see 1:14–15; Dan. 10:6). The believers at Thyatira were actively serving the Lord and were greatly diligent, **the last to be more than the first** (v. 19). Of the seven churches, only this congregation was commended for these qualities, a contrast to the Ephesian church, which seemed to have so quickly lost its "first love" (2:4).

2:20 – 21. **Notwithstanding** (Greek, *alla*; "nevertheless"; v. 20), in contrast to some of their good qualities, the Lord told them, **I have a few things against thee, because thou sufferest that woman Jezebel.** In the Old Testament, Jezebel was the evil wife of King Ahab of the northern kingdom of Israel (874 – 853 BC). She became active in killing the Lord's prophets (see 1 Kings 18:4) and caused even Elijah the prophet to run in fear of her (see 1 Kings 19:2 – 3). Her harlotries and witchcraft were well known throughout the kingdom. Some scholars believe the name here in Revelation is symbolic of immorality in the assembly in general, and others believe it refers to a woman in the congregation who influenced believers in the same way that Jezebel did in the Old Testament accounts. Regardless, her spiritual kinship with the Jezebel of old is obvious.

This Jezebel, who **calleth herself a prophetess** (v. 20), was wicked, teaching and seducing the Lord's **servants to commit fornication** and to partake of **things sacrificed unto idols.** The congregation put up with this practice. The prophetess was given a chance to **repent** (Greek, *metanoeō*; "change the mind") **of her fornication** (Greek, *porneias*; v. 21) but refused.

2:22 – 23. With an exclamatory **Behold** (Greek, *idou*; v. 22), Christ declared His determination to end the religious charade. Jezebel would be **cast ... into a bed,** and those who consorted with her would be cast **into great tribulation,** unless **they repent.** This picture is graphic. Unless they repented, she would continue her fornication, and those who joined with her in violating the moral laws of God would be punished severely. "Great tribulation" (Greek, *thlipsin megalēn*) could refer to additional troubles that would come upon those whom she had seduced, or it could refer to the great tribulation, the apex of the terrible future period of world history that Revelation focuses on (see chaps. 6 – 19; Matt. 24:21). The

tone of these verses is that **her children** (v. 23), who were to die, were lost and had never received Christ as Savior, yet they were part of the congregational assembly. They but masqueraded as Christians.

If Jezebel and her followers did not repent and instead befell this judgment, **all the churches** (v. 23) would realize that Christ **searcheth the reins** ("minds") **and hearts** and will compensate **every one ... according to [his or her] works** (see Ps. 62:12). This was a wake-up call to all the assemblies that they could not mix righteousness and evil. That Christ is divine is clear here. He can look into the inner being and into the motives of the heart and pass judgment. No earthly mortal can do that.

2:24 – 25. To those who had not surrendered to the **doctrine**(s) (v. 24) of Jezebel and had not experienced **the depths of Satan,** the Lord would put **none other burden.** Satan is a master at counterfeiting spirituality and Christian doctrine. Many in the Thyatira church had toyed with the false religions that Satan had under his power. Others in the congregation had not, however, and the Lord would not hold them at fault. As God's wisdom and knowledge are spiritually deep (see Rom. 11:33), so Satan has, in opposition, his false spirituality. The Lord urged the church to **hold fast till I come** (v. 25) that upon which they had a firm grasp. No one knows the day of the Lord's return, prophesied in 1 Thessalonians 4:13 – 18, but each congregation and each believer is to cling to what is true and right, no matter how far off that day may be.

2:26 – 28. Here the Lord extended additional promises to **he that overcometh, and keepeth my works unto the end** (v. 26), expanded promises that grant awesome authority to the faithful. Alongside the Master, the Lord Jesus Christ, His followers will have **power over the nations** (see Matt. 19:28; 1 Cor. 6:3 – 4), and as He, **shall rule them** (the nations) **with a rod of iron** (v. 27). In prophetic words, God said to His Son, the Messiah, "Thou shalt break them [the nations] with a rod of iron; Thou shalt dash them in pieces like a potter's vessel" (Ps. 2:9). This will take place when the earthly Davidic kingdom is established and the King is occupying His throne (see Matt. 25:31–46). Here the Lord promised that believers will receive the same authority to co-reign as given the Son, **even as I received of my Father**.

Christ will also give to the overcomer **the morning star** (v. 28). Peter wrote a prophetic word of assurance that a better day is coming: "We have also a more sure word of prophecy; whereunto ye do well that ye take heed, as unto a light that shineth in a dark place, until the day dawn, and the day star arise in your hearts" (2 Peter 1:19). Here in Revelation, "the morning star" is Jesus Himself. Possibly the idea is that He will grant assurance to believers that all is well and that the end of pain and sin is near. Christ said of Himself, "I am the root and the offspring of David, and the bright and morning star" (22:16).

2:29. This is the same ending that closes each letter.

E. Sardis (3:1–6)

This is the shortest of the letters addressed to the seven churches. Christ called the church at Sardis "dead" (v. 1) because He had not found their "works perfect before God" (v. 2). They were not "watchful" (v. 2) of how they were walking with the Lord. They were lax in their morality and spirituality. The Lord said that if they did not repent, He would come on them quickly, "as a thief" (v. 3). Few in this church had not defiled their garments with sinful acts. Only those who repent are worthy to walk with Him. Christ's words to this church were swift and bold and to the point.

Sardis was the capital city of the province of Lydia, in western Asia Minor. It was situated on the east bank of the Pactolus River about fifty miles east of Smyrna. In ancient days, Sardis was well fortified and easily defended. It was the capital of the ancient Lydian Empire, and it passed to the Persians, the Greeks, and the Romans during their respective dominance of the ancient world. The city was famous for its trade in luxury clothing. Sardis, along with Ephesus, housed a magnificent temple to Artemis, built in the fourth century BC. The temple was 327 feet long and 163 feet wide, with 78 Ionic columns.

During its days as a Roman city, Sardis became an important Christian center, but the church at Sardis was evidently affected by the city's pagan complacency and its cultic religious past. The city's appearance of thriving health masked its inner moral decay.

3:1. Christ reminded this church that He has **the seven spirits of God**, meaning the sevenfold manifestation of the Holy Spirit, working through Him as the Son of God (see 1:4, 16). He also holds in His hand **the seven stars**, who are identified in 1:20 as "the angels of the seven churches," but who probably were the messengers of the churches (see discussion on 1:16). This church had **a name**, a reputation, that they were alive, that they **livest**. By their profession of Christianity, they expressed to the world their purpose to live for the Lord. They professed to have true spirituality, but instead, they were spiritually **dead**.

3:2–3. This assembly was told to **Be watchful** (v. 2) spiritually and morally and to **strengthen** what reputation they had left. "Be watchful" (Greek, *grēgoreō*) means "stay awake," "be alert." The Lord urged the church to be on guard against Satan's attacks and remain aware of their own spiritual vulnerabilities (see Custer, *Patmos to Paradise*, p. 37). While the Lord Jesus knew their **works** (see 3:1), those works were in no way **perfect before God**. In Greek, "perfect" (*plēroō*) is a perfect passive participle, meaning their works "had not arrived at a point of completion, maturity"; their works had not over a period of time been proven **before God**.

The Lord implored them to recall the past and how they began: **Remember** (what) **thou hast recieved and heard** (v. 3), then **hold fast, and repent**. If they did not do these things, **If therefore thou shalt not watch**, He told them, He would **come ... as a thief**. He would come as suddenly as a thief to remove their blessings, and even their ministry, and to judge them. This judgment would be as sudden and as irrevocable as the judgment related to Christ's second coming to reign over the world. The Lord saying, "Be on the alert then, for you do not know the day nor the hour [of My coming]" (Matt. 25:13).

3:4–5. Some in this church had not **defiled** (made filthy; v. 4) their clothes; they would **walk**

with [Christ] in white (in righteousness): for they are worthy. Only a few, however, had trusted the Lord as their Savior and lived their Christian experience in righteousness. The white garment is reminiscent of the white wedding garment worn by those who were worthy to attend the ceremony. Christ urged those who were lost to overcome, so that they too would be clothed in white raiment (v. 5).

To all who overcometh (v. 5), the Lord promised the reward of the benefits of life eternal. Christ will not blot out ... of the book of life the overcomer's name (see 13:8; 21:27) but will instead confess his name before [His heavenly] Father, and before his angels. Because the wicked are blotted from the Book of Life in Exodus 32:33 and Psalms 69:28, the question is raised, When or how did their names come to be written in the Book of Life in the first place? In Revelation 5:9–10, the Lamb's worthiness is tied to His death and the redemption He thus provides. It seems clear that His death affected the entire world. If the Book of Life contains the names of all those for whom the Lord died, then He must in some sense have died for all men, because at the beginning, the names of all people were in the book. In the words of John, apart from the book of Revelation, Christ died for "the world" (John 1:29; 3:16; 4:42; 1 John 2:2; 4:14), no one excluded. This provision of salvation for all is only potential in that it becomes actual only when appropriated by each person. The names of those who die without Christ are erased from the Book of Life. The names of those who trust Him as Savior are confirmed in the book (see Thomas, *Revelation 1–7*, p. 263).

3:6. This is the same closing exhortation as in all the letters.

F. Philadelphia (3:7–13)

The congregation at Philadelphia was exemplary and was not judged by the Lord. This church was faithful to Christ and the Word of God. These believers had an "open door" (3:8), meaning primarily that they had continual access to God, though this may also refer to the opportunity for spreading the gospel with their unhindered witness. The name Philadel-

phia means "brotherly love," and this expression is used six other times in the New Testament (Rom. 12:10; 1 Thess. 4:9; Heb. 13:1; 1 Peter 1:22; 2 Peter 1:7). Only here, however, is it used of the city bearing its name.

Philadelphia was situated on the Cogamus River, a tributary of the Hermus River, about twenty-eight miles southeast of Sardis. The city was founded by Attalus II (Philadelphus), who reigned as king of Pergamos from 159 to 138 BC. It was the center of the wine industry and was thus connected with the chief god of wine, the Greek mythological deity Dionysus, or the Roman Bacchus. Today the city is called Alasehir, or Allah-shehr ("the city of God").

3:7. In this letter, Christ described Himself as the holy and the true. "True" means that He is the "genuine, authentic, faithful" Savior, the one who can be trusted for salvation. The key of David is a quote from Isaiah 22:22, which speaks of God's faithful servant and prime minister Eliakim (see Isa. 22:20), who replaced unfaithful Shebna, the minister or steward during Hezekiah's reign sometime before 701 BC. Though he was not a king, Eliakim was given kingly responsibility (with sovereign authority, "the key") as if he were being bestowed the royal robes of the house of David. Christ now holds this authority as the ultimate son of David.

Because Christ's authority is so absolute, what He openeth ... no man shutteth, with the opposite true also. While Christ presently holds such authority, this power will someday be manifested when His earthly kingdom is established, when He is given "dominion, and glory, and a kingdom, that all people, nations, and languages, should serve him: his dominion is an everlasting dominion, which shall not pass away, and his kingdom that which shall not be destroyed" (Dan. 7:14). When this takes place, the world will know Him as "KING OF KINGS, AND LORD OF LORDS" (Rev. 19:16).

3:8. As with all the churches, the Lord said, I know thy works. The people had kept His word, and ... not denied [His] name. Because of this church's faithfulness, He had set in front of them an open door of spiritual service, which no one was able to close. The Lord had to affect and strengthen their ministry because they had **little strength**. The congregation had ample opportunity to witness and share the gospel, yet their ability to carry this out must have been limited. The Lord wedged the door open so that they could serve unhindered. They had a great struggle, apparently against a Jewish community that vehemently opposed Christianity (see 3:9).

3:9. The Jews in Philadelphia must have had a violent hatred of the church (see 2:9, 13); Christ said they were **of the synagogue of Satan**. Under Satan's influence, these Jews were not behaving with godliness, as the true descendants of Abraham. Such attacks were to be expected, because as Peter wrote, "Be sober, be vigilant; because your adversary the devil, as a roaring lion, walketh about, seeking whom he may devour" (1 Peter 5:8).

3:10. Because the believers had **patience** in their endeavor, Christ promised to keep them **from the hour of temptation**, the tribulation that will overtake the entire **world** and come **to try** all who **dwell upon the earth**. The Greek preposition "from" can mean "out from" in the sense of "escaping" from something. Some have said this verse is a promise that only this local church would experience the rapture, but the general idea of the text indicates that this is a promise for all the churches, since the Spirit addresses all the churches at the end of each letter. The rapture of the church will be based, not on patience, but on the fact that all believers are "in Jesus," "in Christ" (1 Thess. 4:14, 16). This relationship alone is the basis for being "caught up ... in the clouds" (1 Thess. 4:17). **Which shall come** (from the Greek verb *mellō*; "to be about to") carries the idea that this event is inevitable and certain, expressing in general a settled future.

3:11. I come quickly (Greek, *tachy*) has the idea, "When I come, I will come with rapidity, suddenness." Some have mistakenly believed that this phrase was the Lord's guarantee that His arrival was imminent. While the church is to be looking for His coming at any time, that is not the point here. When He returns, it will happen suddenly, with the events tumbling one upon the other in rapid succession (see 2:5, 16; 11:14; 22:7, 12, 20).

The **crown** (Greek, *stephanos*) is not given a further description, therefore it could be a continued reference to the "crown of life" (2:10), a crown that had to do with suffering, as it seems here (see 3:10). Some attribute the crown in verse 11 to the "crown of righteousness" that Paul wrote about in 2 Timothy 4:8, which will be given to all those who have loved (longed for) Christ's appearing and who "have fought [the] good fight ... finished [the] course, [and] kept the faith" (2 Tim. 4:7).

3:12. In this letter, the promises to the one who **overcometh** are fuller and richer than than in any of the other letters. The overcomer will be made **a pillar in the [Lord's] temple**. He will be given a sense of spiritual security and **shall go no more out**. He will have written **upon him the name of ... God, and the name of the city of ... God, ... [the] new Jerusalem, which cometh down out of heaven from my God**. He will also be given a **new name**. Those who overcome will be marked by the Lord with direct identification of God: His name and the name of His city, the New Jerusalem. They will be like strong, prominent pillars in the new, eternal city (see 21:1–4). This verse is literal, but it is also full of hyperbole, used to affirm that the one who is faithful will have a lasting position of prominence in the Father's presence. The honor and the accolades will be great, just as if the name of the Lord, whom the believer served and whose grace and delight he enjoyed, were somehow inscribed on him in a very obvious way. The overcomer will be acknowledged and seen as belonging to the Lord. "He that overcometh shall inherit all things; and I will be his God, and he shall be my son" (21:7).

3:13. The Lord again commanded all of the churches to listen to what the Spirit had said.

G. Laodicea (3:14–22)

The church at Laodicea had some good spiritual qualities, but Christ called it "lukewarm" (v. 16). It claimed to be wealthy, spiritually speaking, but instead it was poor, wretched, miserable, and blind. The Lord urged the congregation to use "eyesalve, that thou mayest see" and to turn from their "nakedness" and buy from Him fine raiment, white and clean (v. 18). Because the Lord loved them, He chastened them and called for repentance.

Laodicea was a city in the fertile Lycus Valley of the province of Phrygia and was about forty miles east of Ephesus. It was known for its black wool industry. Jesus' words about the church relate to the wealth of the city and its economic prosperity. Founded by the Seleucids and named for Laodice, the wife of Antiochus II (261–247 BC), it was a model city for financial power during the Roman times. The city was nearly wiped off the map by a major earthquake that struck the area in AD 60. The same earthquake also caused extensive damage in the metropolitan centers of Colossae and Hierapolis. Laodicea refused help from Rome in rebuilding, which may give some indication of the self-sufficiency of the congregation of Laodicea.

Other disciples or Paul may have been the major messengers of the gospel in Laodicea (see Col. 1:7; 4:7–15). A major church council was held in the city (AD 344–363), though little doctrine has come down from it. Today the ancient site is barren of life and cluttered with heaps of stone ruins.

3:14. Christ called Himself **the Amen** ("the Verily"), "the confirmation of what is right and absolute" (Couch, *Bible Handbook to Revelation*, p. 223). Paul said believers are "in [Christ] Amen, unto the glory of God" (2 Cor. 1:20). In Judaism, the use of "Amen" was widespread and gave firmness to truth. To conclude with "Amen" signified concurrence. Christ also called Himself **the faithful** (see 1:5) **and true witness** (repeated in 19:11; see also 3:7). As well, He is **the beginning of the creation of God**. Those holding to the Arian heresy believed that Christ was the first created being, but the expression "the beginning" (Greek, *archē*) carries the thought that He is the preeminent and prominent one, standing above all in honor and power over all of creation. Jesus is the image of the invisible God (see Col. 1:15), "the beginning, the firstborn from the dead; that in all things he might have the preeminence" (Col. 1:18), and as very God, "by Him were all things created" (Col. 1:16). He is also the "Alpha and Omega, the

beginning and the end" (Rev. 21:6). No expressions could set forth His deity any more strongly.

3:15–17. As with the other congregations, the Lord said He knew the **works** (v. 15) of the Laodiceans. He described them as **lukewarm** (Greek, *chliaros*; v. 16), and because of this, He issued a strong warning: **I will spue** (lit., "vomit") **thee out of my mouth.** Christ described three different states of spirituality: cold, warm, and lukewarm. **Cold** (v. 15) refers to the spiritual state of the world, while **hot** refers to being fervent and possessing spiritual zeal. The Laodiceans were professing Christians who walked in an in-between state. They were saved but had lost their enthusiasm for Christ and for spiritual things. They were but "lukewarm" and had little meaningful consistency in their Christian walk.

The believers in this church were also self-deceived. Because they possessed extensive physical **goods** (v. 17), they thought they had arrived and were in **need of nothing** on the spiritual level. Their wealth, they assumed, was a sign of their spiritual position with the Lord. Instead, they existed in a most **wretched** state. Exactly what is meant by this is not known; their sins are not itemized (see Walvoord, *The Revelation of Jesus Christ*, p. 93).

3:18. The Lord urged the assembly to purchase from Him **gold** that has been **tried** (see James 1:12–13), finely smelted in **fire.** This would make them spiritually **rich.** Those tested this way would "be clothed" and would become spiritually "rich" (2:10) as a reward for righteous living. Their lives would be righteous, as if they were wearing **white raiment,** a sign of purity and holiness. They would again be spiritually clothed, and their **eyes** would be healed **with eyesalve.**

3:19. Experiencing the Lord's **rebuke and chasten[ing]** is a sign of His love. He does not hesitate to chasten His people because it yields "the peaceable fruit of righteousness" (Heb. 12:6–11). The Lord urged the Laodiceans to **be zealous** in and to **repent** of their sins.

3:20. Some think this verse was an invitation to the lost to **open the door** of their hearts to receive Christ, but more than likely, it was an invitation to the church, and certainly to individuals, to allow Christ to come in and be the center of worship and spiritual fellowship. **Sup** refers to eating a meal, and sharing food with another is an intimate activity that fosters fellowship and closeness.

3:21–22. The one who **overcometh** will be **grant[ed] to sit** (v. 21) with Christ on His earthly Davidic **throne**. Christ is now on the throne of His Father in glory (see Ps. 110:1–2), but this is not the earthly, historic kingly reign. Christ made it clear that He "shall come in his glory" and "shall … sit upon the throne of his glory" (Matt. 25:31). Revelation pictures this being fulfilled when He comes to earth to "rule with a rod of iron" (19:15) and reigns for "a thousand years" (20:4–6). Some believe that Christ's being presently seated on His Father's throne in heaven constitutes His Davidic rule, but the Lord made a distinction between His future Davidic throne and His present seat on the **throne** of His **Father**. Psalm 110:1 is quoted more often in the New Testament than any other Old Testament quote: "Sit thou at my right hand, until I make thine enemies thy footstool."

This letter closes like all of the others, with an appeal to hear with the **ear** what the Spirit **says** (present tense, "is saying") to all of the churches.

IV. The Throne, the Book, and the Lamb (chaps. 4–5)

These two chapters introduce the all-encompassing sweep of prophetic happenings that are foretold in the rest of the book. Both chapters take the reader into the heavenlies and present the divine viewpoint about things to come. The prophecies that begin in chapter four were not completed in any historic event of the past; therefore these chapters need to be understood from a futuristic viewpoint. The events looked for, as the angel promised, are "things which must be hereafter" (4:1). John's vision of heaven (chaps. 4–5) serves as the fulcrum of the Apocalypse. "It is the pivot on which the entire book turns our attention from earth to heaven and from time to eternity" (see Hindson, *The Book of Revelation*, p. 55).

A. The Throne in Heaven (chap. 4)

In this chapter, the reader is ushered into the throne room of God in the heavens. "Throne" (Greek, *thronos*) is mentioned thirteen times in this chapter. Through illustrative language, the Lord is seen in all of His majesty and glory. Around Him are angelic creatures who themselves possess great power and authority. God is seen as "worthy to receive glory and honour and power" because He has "created all things, and for [His] pleasure they are and were created" (v. 11). While other prophets received direct revelation or were addressed by the Lord in dreams (e.g., Daniel) and visions (e.g., Ezekiel), John was told, "Come up hither" into heaven, to see the "the things which must be hereafter" (v. 1). This prophetic phenomenon is what makes Revelation unique.

4:1. After this (Greek, *meta tauta*) identifies these revelations as subsequent to those of chapters 2–3. The Lord was about to reveal something new and prophetic. In a real sense, John saw (**I looked**) revelations of things to come. He was transported above the clouds, above the starry host, and was ushered into the third heaven, the abode of God. There he heard a voice, as shrill and commanding as **a trumpet**, speaking with him. He was commanded to enter glory so that he could be shown the **things which must be hereafter**. A better translation is "the things which must come after these things," meaning after the events of the present age. It is important to note that the church is absent from the earth in 4:1–19:7. The word "church" is not mentioned again until 22:16.

4:2–3. Suddenly, John found himself **in the spirit** (Greek, *en pneumati*; v. 2), by which he saw a heavenly **throne** where God was seated in all His dominion and sovereignty. Though John's "spirit" was involved and not his body, he was still seeing the beatific presence of the Lord. From verse 3 on, the apostle struggled to describe wondrous things that were far beyond his previous human experience. This is why he continually used comparative language, such as "it looked like" (Greek, *homoios*).

The two stones listed here are among the most precious gems known. Which stone is meant by **jasper** (green chalcedony; v. 3) is debated. Today, it is thought to have been an opaque stone, yet some believe it was almost totally clear, like a diamond. It was the last stone in the breastplate of the Levitical priest's garment (see Exod. 28:20; 39:13), and it is one of the stones in the foundation of the New Jerusalem (see Rev. 21:19 – 20). The **sardine stone** is less debated since it is more commonly known as carnelian (or ruby red). It was the first stone in the Levitical breastplate (see Exod. 28:17). It has been suggested that these two stones represent God's purity and transparency in holiness and that the sardine stone (red) also represents His wrath against sin.

The bow of the **rainbow** (Greek, *iris*; v. 3) is semicircular, like a halo, and may point to the fact that God is the "Alpha and Omega, the first and the last" (1:11). It is also reminiscent of the Lord's covenant promises with Noah (see Gen. 9:16). The rainbow, green like **an emerald**, may also depict life, with the semicircle depicting eternity.

4:4 – 6. Each of these verses begins with a preposition relating to God's throne: **round about** (v. 4), **out of** (v. 5), and **before** (v. 6). The **four and twenty elders … in white raiment** (robes), wearing **crowns of gold**, seem to represent the church, which had at this point been taken from the earth and was now in glory (see discussion on 4:1). This would include both those who had died and those who had ascended to heaven at the rapture of the church (see 1 Thess. 4:13 – 18). Some say the **elders** represent the whole company of believers, an exalted angelic order, and that the number of twenty-four reflects the twelve tribes of Israel from the Old Testament and the twelve apostles of the New Testament. The white robes picture the holiness they possessed in the eternal state, and the crowns of gold indicate that they would participate in some kind of adjudication with the Son of God in the heavenly courtroom. The church is called "a holy priesthood" and "a royal priesthood" (1 Peter 2:4, 9). In the Old Testament, the Levitical priesthood was represented by twenty-four elders and was divided into twenty-four shifts, or courses of service (see 1 Chron. 24:4 – 19).

From **the throne proceeded lightnings and thunderings and voices** (v. 5). While God's throne pictures mercy and grace and glory, it also represents judgment and righteousness, as was seen when Moses gave the law to the Jews in the wilderness (see Exod. 19:16).

The **lamps of fire** (v. 5) picture the judgment to come through the work of the Holy Spirit, **the seven spirits of God**, the sevenfold manifestations of the Spirit (see Isaiah 11:1 – 2; see also 1:4; 3:1; 4:5; 5:6). These lamps were the means by which John was aware of the presence of the Holy Spirit (Walvoord, *The Revelation of Jesus Christ*, p. 108).

In front of the heavenly **throne … was a sea of glass like unto crystal** (v. 6; see 15:2). Perhaps this clear sea, by its transparent and limitless nature, speaks of God's purity and majesty. He is in control, and nothing is a mystery to Him; everything is crystal clear because He decrees it. The "sea of glass [resembling] crystal" pictures God's absolute holiness, which He shares with no one else.

John saw **four beasts** around **the throne** and in the midst of **the throne** (v. 6). This "probably means that the four were in the immediate vicinity of the throne and encircling it, one on either side, one behind and one in front" (Thomas, *Revelation 1 – 7*, p. 354). The four beings he saw are not beasts, however; they are powerful, all-knowing, highly intelligent, angelic creatures. The word used here for "beasts" (Greek, *zōa*) is better translated "living ones" or "living creatures." It is a different word than that used for "beast" (Greek, *thērion*; "ferocious animal," "monster") in Revelation 13. **Full of eyes** was John's way of describing their higher knowledge and wisdom. These creatures have access to the all-knowing wisdom of the Lord, to carry forth His commands and judgments. Heaven and the universe function under the infinite wisdom and plan of God. He is sovereign in His created realm, and nothing happens by chance. The imagery here parallels that of Ezekiel 1:22.

4:7 – 9. The description of the **four beasts** (v. 8), or angelic beings (see discussion on 4:6), is similar to the vision of the prophet Ezekiel, who saw four living creatures, each of which had four faces: a human face on the front, a lion on the right, an ox on the left, and an eagle on the back of the head (see Ezek. 1:6, 10). These are the same animals that John saw, except he used the word **calf** (v. 7) rather than "ox." John's description tells us that these beings, seen as serving as a group, are as powerful as a **lion**, yet as docile and innocent as a **calf**, as intelligent as a human being, and finally, as swift in service to God as the swooping **eagle**.

These angelic "living ones" have **six wings** (v. 8), as described also in Isaiah 6:2–3. This graphic symbolism would have to mean that these messengers of God are swift in doing the Lord's bidding. Being **full of eyes within** again points to their all-seeing intelligence. They do not cease **day and night** crying out the greatness of God, **saying, Holy, holy, holy, Lord God Almighty**. This cry is similar to that of the six-winged angels (Hebrew, *seraphim*) described in Isaiah 6:2–3. The presence of these angels in the heavenly court lends much to the impression of the majesty, holiness, sovereignty, and eternalness of God. They never stop crying forth His holiness and great power and authority, as well as His **glory and honour and thanks** (v. 9). In verse 8, the everlasting existence of the Lord is mentioned again, as He is the one who exists continually in His universe: **Lord God Almighty, which was, and is, and is to come** (v. 8; see 1:4). His attribute of eternalness is repeated in verse 9: He **liveth for ever and ever** (v. 9).

4:10–11. The twenty-four **elders** (v. 10) joined in on the chorus with the heavenly angels and gave great honor to the Lord. John saw the elders **worship** God, repeat the fact of His eternal nature, and **cast their crowns before the throne**. They added, however, that He is the creator of **all things** (v. 11), and futhermore, all things **were created** for His **pleasure**. The Greek word translated "pleasure" (Greek, *thelēma*) is better translated "will." That God is **worthy** to receive such accolades is tied to His sovereign authority to reign from His throne in the heavens. These verses are a fitting introduction to the next chapter, which focuses on the second person of the Trinity, the Lord Jesus Christ, who is the Redeemer and "the Lamb that was slain" (5:12).

B. The Seven-Sealed Book (5:1–5)

The only one worthy of opening the book that John saw in the hands of the Lord is Jesus Christ.

"Worthy" (vv. 2, 4) indicates one who has divine authority. Jesus Christ is worthy because He is the very righteous Son of God, who walked the earth, came forth from the grave, and ascended to glory. His messiahship is set forth clearly in verse 5. The book in the Lord's hands contained extensive orders pertaining to the wrath coming upon the earth because of unbelieving humanity's sinfulness and rebellion against God. This document came straight from God. The wrath that will come upon the world during the tribulation, due the world for its sin, will issue from God Himself. Paul wrote that only Christ can deliver "from the wrath to come" (1 Thess. 1:10), the sudden destruction that will come upon "them" (1 Thess. 1:5:3), the unbelievers. When the tribulation begins (Revelation 6), the world will call out to be hidden "from the wrath of the Lamb: for the great day of his wrath is come; and who shall be able to stand?" (6:16–17).

5:1. Generally, the right hand is the dominant hand, but here it is also the hand of authority of God Almighty, who orders the affairs of His universe. The **book** (Greek, *biblion*) that John saw was a "scroll" containing the chronology of the events of the tribulation that unfolds in chapters 6–19. The message was recorded **within and on the backside**, meaning that the orders regarding the coming events were detailed and extensive. The **seven seals** were probably like the wax seals of an official document that are imprinted with the king's signet ring. The seals were placed progressively inside in different portions, until the entire scroll was rolled up and sealed. Then as the scroll was opened, each seal had to be broken in sequence, until each message or chapter was fully disclosed (see Couch, *Bible Handbook to Revelation*, p. 230).

5:2–4. John heard a powerfully **strong** (Greek, *ischyros*; active power) **angel** (v. 2) call a question out **with a loud voice**. This angel may be the archangel Michael because of his special role in the events of the final days (see Dan. 12:1–3). **Worthy** (Greek, *axios*) carries the thought of "proper weight." Did anyone have the proper authority, the required credentials, to open the seals? The question rang throughout the entire universe, with the answer of silence, for **no man was found worthy to open and to read the book, neither to look thereon** (v. 4).

Why was John so emotionally moved that he **wept much** (v. 4)? Some have suggested that, at his age, he was emotional and weepy, coupled with the fact that he had walked with the Lord Jesus, and now so much that he had looked for was coming to pass. The pictorial drama impressed upon John the importance of the revelation contained in the scroll.

5:5. One of the twenty-four **elders** urged the apostle, **Weep not**, because the Messiah of Israel **hath prevailed to open the book, and to loose the seven seals**. He is the King, the "Branch" (Isa. 11:1) out of the stem of Jesse (David's father), that is, He is of the royal bloodline. He is called "a lion's whelp" (Gen. 49:9) and comes from the kingly tribe of Judah, from which tribe the future monarch's "sceptre shall not depart" (Gen. 49:10). To Mary, it was prophesied that her son "shall be great, and shall be called the Son of the Highest: and the Lord God shall give unto him the throne of his father David" (Luke 1:32). Only this one, the Messiah, the Lord Jesus Christ, can open the seals.

C. The Lamb That Was Slain (5:6–14)

Jesus Christ is worthy to open the sealed book because He gave His life, as a sacrificial lamb, because of His love for humanity. His physical body, which was sacrificed on the cross, was prepared for Him before His birth (see Ps. 40:6; Heb. 10:5), and He was "obedient unto death" (Phil. 2:8). As a lamb, He went willingly to those who would slay Him, and He went quietly, not opening His mouth (see Isa. 53:7). John witnessed Christ's sacrifice and reward being extolled in heaven.

5:6. Here Christ is called the **Lamb [who] had been slain**. Christ is the one who died for sins, as the sacrificed Lamb of God (see Isa. 53; John 1:36). John described His omniscience (**seven eyes**), which are the sevenfold manifestations of the Spirit of God (as mentioned in 1:4; 4:5). The Lamb also had **seven horns**, which appears to refer to the power and authority of a king (see Dan. 7:24; Rev. 13:1). In Scripture, horns are a symbol of power and conjure up the concept of fear.

5:7–8. The Lamb **took the book** (v. 7) from **the right hand** of God, who **sat upon the throne**. The four angelic creatures (**the four beasts**; v. 8; see discussions on 4:6, 8) and the **four and twenty elders fell down before the Lamb**, and with heavenly **harps, and golden vials full of odours** (incense), the Lamb was worshiped with **the prayers of saints**. Here "saints" may refer to the saints of all generations, but more than likely, it refers to the saints of the church, because they had been redeemed "out of every … nation" (5:9) and had been "made … unto our God kings and priests" (5:10; see 1:6; 3:21; 20:4) who someday "shall reign on the earth" (5:10) with Christ. The scene is in heaven, where the resurrected and raptured church saints, represented by the twenty-four elders (see discussion on 4:4–6), now reside. Here, just before the tribulation began, John saw this great crowd of Gentiles from all nations. Before God pours out His wrath upon the earth, the saints of the church will be raptured. "Harps" (lyres) were used in sacred temple worship to praise the Lord. The trumpet and the harp are the only instruments mentioned in descriptions of the heavenly worship of God.

5:9–10. Those singing **a new song** (v. 9) had been **redeemed … to God by [the] blood** of the Lamb. The Bible makes it crystal clear that without the shedding of blood for sin, there is no remission of sins (see Heb. 9:22). While it is possible that the full context of this passage has to do with church saints, Christ's redemption was for the Old Testament saints as well. **Redeemed** (Greek, *agorazō*) is a descriptive verb that pictures those who are helpless being purchased out of the marketplace of sin and then set free.

5:11–12. Imagine John's awe as he **beheld** (v. 11) this glorious scene of heavenly worship. The chorus of praise intensified, with **many angels** (v. 11), the special angelic creatures (**the beasts**; see discussions on 4:6, 8), and **the elders** joining in, all giving praise **with a loud voice** (v. 12). Their number was uncountable. "With a loud voice" (Greek, *phōnē megalē*) illustrates the overwhelming joy expressed to the Lamb and to God for the blessings of redemption. The angelic host sang along with the redeemed, represented by the twenty-four elders. Here there seems to be a concentric circle, with the Lamb in the center, surrounded by the living creatures, the elders and the redeemed, and the vast sea of angels, all giving forth a symphony of praise (see Walvoord, *The Revelation of Jesus Christ*, p. 119).

5:13–14. Then John heard all beings, **every creature** (v. 13), both **in heaven, and on the earth**, and even **under the earth**, proclaim **Blessing, and honour, and glory, and power** to God, who **sitteth upon the throne, and unto the Lamb**. This praise will continue endlessly, **for ever and ever**. John's descriptions of praise are colorful, expansive, and almost redundant. It is hard for the human mind to fully grasp the glories of heaven, but the ordinary Christian has the privilege to glimpse the brilliant picture of the majesty that surrounds the Lord in the heavenlies. John seems to include even the lost, those "under the earth" or whose bodies **are in the sea**. While he used the expression "every creature," most scholars believe he was referring only to human beings and not to the animal world. "The creatures are intelligent beings who have an intellectual appreciation of God and the Lamb" (Thomas, *Revelation 1–7*, p. 407).

Verse 14 seems to indicate a repetition of the praise of **the four beasts** ("living creatures"; v. 14; see discussions on 4:6, 8) and the twenty-four **elders**. Their song of praise continued. The word **Amen** means "truthfully," "sure," or "so be it." This heavenly scene assures believers that those who follow Christ, and thus often endure affliction, will share with the Lord His glory and grace throughout all eternity. The picture painted in chapter 5 is considered a prophecy of future events in which the church of Jesus Christ bearing witness today will be in the presence of the Lord in heaven tomorrow.

Chapters 4–5 lead into the terrible tribulation that will fall upon the earth. After the glorious interlude that John witnessed in the heavens, the scene returned to earth.

V. The Seven Seal Judgments (6:1–8:1)

The seven-sealed book was first mentioned in 5:1, which describes God sitting on His throne, holding

the book that can be opened only by His Son, the Lord Jesus Christ (see 5:7–9). In ancient times, a seal was pressed into wax to authenticate a document from an official or from the king himself. Some scholars hold that the seal judgments will start after the midpoint of the tribulation and will continue consecutively. Others believe the seal judgments will run concurrently, overlapping each other. A third view argues that the trumpet and vial judgments will come out of the breaking of the seals running simultaneously. The most accepted view is that the seal judgments will bring about the trumpets, which in turn will bring on the worst of the judgments, the vials of wrath.

The breaking of the seals will bring terrible judgments down upon the inhabitants of the earth. The church apparently will be absent during this time, having ascended in the rapture (see discussion on 4:1). There is no mention here of the church, the body of Christ, or of those "in Christ." While people can and will be saved during this time, those who choose to trust Christ will suffer horribly and will be persecuted and martyred.

A. First Seal: The White Horse (6:1–2)

6:1. When Christ **the Lamb opened** the first seal, a **thunder** clap was heard in the heavens. One of the four living creatures (**four beasts**; see discussions on 4:6, 8) urged John the apostle to **Come and see**. The thunder was not repeated in the other seal openings. This startling and frightening peal inaugurated the tribulation on earth.

6:2. From his heavenly vantage point, John could write, **I saw**. These future events were happening before his eyes! Here he saw one riding on **a white horse**, called even in secular literature the first of "the four horsemen of the Apocalypse." The four horsemen parallel those in Zechariah 1:7–1, although the horsemen in Zechariah are sent only to patrol the earth rather than to inflict God's wrath. The white horse gives the image of the "good guy" or a conquering general on his trusty steed as he directs his troops in battle. Some say this rider is Christ the Lamb riding in victory. This is not the last of the tribulation, however, but the beginning. Christ will come back on a white horse to bring victory and to stop the carnage taking place on earth (see 19:11), but 6:2 is not that event.

The rider, then, is "the prince that shall come" (Dan. 9:26), the false messiah or the Antichrist, as revealed in Revelation 13:1 – 10. He wore **a crown** (Greek, *stephanos*), or victor's wreath, not the diadem of Christ, and **had a bow**, not the sword of Christ. Chapter six portrays the Antichrist coming as a world conqueror who appears to bring peace but instead brings destruction. The grammatical structure of **he went forth conquering, and to conquer** is interesting. It best reads, "He went forth continually conquering so that he might conquer." Note again that Christ Himself opened this seal and released this rider to inflict judgment on the earth.

B. Second Seal: The Red Horse (6:3 – 4)

6:3 – 4. After the Lord **opened the second seal**, the second angelic being (**beast**; see discussions on 4:6, 8) introduced a rider on a **horse that was red** (v. 4). The fiery color denotes war and conquest. The rider of this horse was equipped with **a great sword**, and **power was given to him to take … peace from the earth**. This corresponds to Jesus' introduction of the seven-year tribulation in the Gospels (see Matt. 24:6 – 8; Mark 13:7 – 8; Luke 21:9 – 10). "These [events] are the beginning of sorrows" (Matt. 24:8; Mark 13:8), the "birth pangs" that the rabbis and prophets said would precede the coming of the Messiah. When this rider removes peace from the earth, people will turn on each other and **kill one another**. The Antichrist will appear to be a peacemaker but will instead be a demonic tyrant who attempts to conquer the entire earth for himself. He will bring terrible destruction, illustrated by his wielding "a great sword." Only when the Lord Jesus, who is "The mighty God, The everlasting Father, The Prince of Peace" (Isa. 9:6), comes at the end of the tribulation will humanity experience spiritual and physical tranquility.

C. Third Seal: The Black Horse (6:5 – 6)

6:5 – 6. The third angelic being (**beast**; v. 5; see discussions on 4:6, 8) called John to **Come and see**.

When **the third seal** (v. 5) was opened, John was somewhat shocked and uttered the exclamatory **lo** (Greek, *idou*), for he saw **a black horse** carrying a rider who held **a pair of balances in his hand**. The black horse, as the color implies, depicts death and a great famine (see Lam. 4:8 – 9).

"Balances," or scales, denotes a measuring device commonly used in Bible times. With the coming of worldwide warfare (see 6:4), food will be scarce. Those in power will measure it out, giving it to only those who are loyal to the ruling authorities. The rationing of **wheat** (v. 6; **a measure**, one quart) and of **barley** (**three measures**, three quarts) shows that staple foods will be limited. The measures mentioned here would supply barely enough for three meals. The **penny** is the denarius, or silver coin, the amount paid to a common laborer for a day's work (see Matt. 20:2). It was worth about fifteen cents by today's standards. Used throughout the Roman Empire, the denarius is the most mentioned coin denomination in the Bible. Under such circumstances, the struggle for survival will be immense. In God's graciousness, the basic products needed for meal preparation and for cooking, **the oil and the wine**, will not be **hurt**.

D. Fourth Seal: The Pale Horse (6:7 – 8)

6:7 – 8. For the fourth time, one of the four angelic beings (**the fourth beast**; v. 7; see discussions on 4:6, 8) called John to **Come and see** (see 6:1, 3, 5). When **the fourth seal** was opened, John cried out with another exclamatory (**behold**; Greek, *idou*; v. 8), for he saw **Death, and Hell** (Greek, *hadēs*; "Hades," the place of the dead) riding on **a pale horse**. The word "pale" literally means "a pale green" (Greek, *chlōros*), a ghastly color reminiscent of a corpse. Death and Hell are seen as two distinct riders on the one horse. Death and Hell are appropriate names because of the awful destruction these riders brought in their wake: **power was given** (granted) **unto them … to kill with sword, and with hunger, and with death … the fourth part of the earth**. Looking at all of the pages of history in the past, no succinct period, in a brief span of months or years, could have come close to destroying one fourth of all the human beings on the globe. This can refer only to the future events that will come upon the world during the tribulation.

Besides the instruments of destruction listed above, an added element of death is listed: the ravages of uncontrolled animals, **the beasts of the earth** (v. 8). During this, the "great tribulation, such as was not since the beginning of the world to this time, no, nor ever shall be" (Matt. 24:21), civilizations will be so disrupted that any management of the wild animal population will cease. These verses are reminders of God's judgment on Jerusalem, when He sent against the city "the sword, and the famine, and the noisome beast, and the pestilence, to cut off from it man and beast" (Ezek. 14:21).

E. Fifth Seal: The Souls under the Altar (6:9–11)

6:9–11. With the opening of **the fifth seal** (v. 9), John saw **under the [heavenly] altar the souls of them that were slain for the word of God**. According to John's visions of heaven, the heavenly altar is golden and stands before God within the heavenly temple, from which God's wrath will be poured out on the evil upon the earth (see 8:3, 5; 9:13; 11:1; 14:18). **The testimony which they held** also made these martyrs prominent. **They cried** (v. 10) and asked how long it would be before God would **judge** and then **avenge** their **blood** spilt in martyrdom. Because the Lord is the only **holy and true** one, He is the one who is rightly qualified to bring judgment upon humanity. The words "judge" (Greek, *krinō*) and "avenge" (Greek, *ekdikeō*) describe the two works that will fall upon and overtake the tribulation population. "Avenge" in Greek has the connotation of "to defend," "to vindicate," "to exact of the murderer the penalty of his crime."

White robes were given (v. 11) to those who had died a martyr's death, and they were told to **rest … for a little season**, until all was **fulfilled** in coming upon those who would still die for the faith. While it is not impossible that this refers to saints from all generations, these verses seem to confirm that the

ones crying out died during the first of the tribulation, because more were yet to perish. They were not church saints who were taken off the earth before the tribulation started; they were those who had trusted Christ during the tribulation and had died for their faith. **Their fellowservants … and their brethren** would yet be **killed** in the progression of the seven-year period of wrath. "All hell will break loose on the earth after the Rapture of the Church. The unregenerate nations of the world will unleash a bloodbath on anyone claiming the name of Christ" (Hindson, *The Book of Revelation*, p. 84).

F. Sixth Seal: The Great Earthquake (6:12–17)

This is one of the most terrible scenes in Revelation. All the dynamics of cosmic cataclysms overwhelm the reader. Some commentators have attempted to trivialize these verses and make them but exaggerations of difficult times in the Christian life. This is impossible, however, if the Bible is left to speak in its unmistakable language. Though the sixth seal is the first to involve a natural catastrophe, such cataclysms will begin to tumble quickly upon the earth as the tribulation progresses.

6:12–13. These verses, along with 6:14, describe frightening events in the heavens that will cause some in the human family to seek death (see 6:16). Some scholars have attempted to relegate these verses to meaningless symbolism with little reality in view, but a literal interpretation of actual future events is the only way the passage makes any sense. The heavens will be shaken, and judgment will fall on the nations. The ultimate cause is not man, nor nature, but God, who will pour His wrath out on sinful humanity.

The opening of **the sixth seal** (v. 12) was followed by **a great earthquake**. Though a volcano is not mentioned, the earthquake may have triggered a volcanic eruption, which in turn brought about massive atmospheric pollution, because from earth, **the sun** appeared as **black as sackcloth … and the moon became as** (like) **blood**. The "as" shows this to be comparative language. John struggled to explain what he was seeing and described the events as best he could.

"Sackcloth" was made from the hides of goats or camels and was worn as a tunic or loincloth as a sign of mourning and anguish. When sackcloth was worn, the mourner often fasted and put ashes on himself (see Isa. 58:5; Dan. 9:3). The Old Testament prophets also wrote that the sun will be darkened in the coming day of the Lord (see Isa. 13:10; 24:23; Ezek. 32:7 – 8; Joel 2:10, 31; Amos 5:20; 8:9; Zeph. 1:15).

John saw **the stars** (v. 13) plummet to the surface of the earth. The word for "star" is the Greek word *astēr*, which could refer to a star, asteroid, or meteor. From John's point of view, it appeared that the very heavens were raining down on the earth, **as a fig tree casteth her untimely figs, when she is shaken of a mighty wind.** This spectacle of an asteroid or meteor shower will be so enormous that, from a human perspective, it will seem as if all the stars are falling to the earth. As Christ Himself said, "And great earthquakes shall be in divers places, and famines, and pestilences; and fearful sights and great signs shall there be from heaven" (Luke 21:11).

6:14 – 16. The heaven departed as a scroll when it is rolled together (v. 14). "Departed" is better translated "split apart." When this occurs, the heavens will look as if they have been split in half, and each half will appear to be rolled up like a scroll. Isaiah also wrote of this day, the day of God's wrath: "And the heavens shall be rolled together as a scroll: and all their host shall fall down, as the leaf falleth off from the vine, and as a falling fig from the fig tree" (Isa. 34:4). As well, **every mountain and island were moved out of their places**. It is a scientific fact that when a great earthquake strikes, especially when it occurs deep in the oceans, islands rise and fall, and coastlines are shifted.

What will happen to the people on the earth when these cataclysms occur? The most powerful, the slave, and the free will hide **in the dens and in the rocks of the mountains** (v. 15), but no safe place will be found. Humanity will cry out to be delivered **from the face of him that sitteth on the throne, and from the wrath of the Lamb** (v. 16). Some Bible teachers say that the "wrath" (Greek, *orgēs*; "fury") in the early part of the tribulation will come from

nature, man, and/or Satan, but not from God. They suggest that His wrath will not begin until around 14:9 – 10, 19 and that the church saints will be on earth when this takes place. That God's wrath will be revealed during the early years of the tribulation, however, is clearly indicated in 6:16 – 17. Since those presently in the body of Christ will not be subject to His wrath (see 1 Thess. 1:10; 5:9), the rapture of the church will occur before the tribulation begins.

6:17. This verse summarizes the six seals. They are characterized together as **the great day of [God's] wrath** that has arrived. Contrary to the view of those who hold that the Lord's wrath will not be poured out until the later years of the tribulation, this verse makes it clear that "the great day of his wrath" will begin with the opening of the seals. When the first six seals are opened, judgment will begin. The world will be at war, and the future of the planet will be in jeopardy. Yet even in these devastating upheavals, God will still be in charge. Jesus Christ Himself will open the seals, and the sovereign will of God will prevail despite the carnage of a depraved and evil society.

1. The First Interlude (chap. 7)

This chapter has been rightly called an interlude in the breaking of the seven seals. It comes between the sixth and seventh seals. John the apostle stopped and considered the two great numbers of people who had been redeemed "out of great tribulation" (7:14): Jews who were converted and Gentiles who trusted the Lord during that time. This interlude, or parenthesis, is an integral part of the vision of the seals because it refers back to 6:17 and answers the question, "Who shall be able to stand?"

a. The Sealing of the 144,000 (7:1 – 8)

John witnessed the sealing of 144,000 servants of God (vv. 3 – 4). The tribal identifications listed in verses 5 – 8 make it clear that the 144,000 are converted Jews. There is no indication in this passage that they are to be seen as the New Testament church, or even as Gentile Christians. It is clear that they are literal Israelites.

The 144,000 Jewish servants will be given a special task of witnessing during the tribulation. Many scholars believe the sealing of the 144,000 is for their protection while they witness to the unbelievers in the tribulation. The mention of the 144,000 in 14:1–5 "is to show why this group is so special [with] their singular qualifications that have enabled them to fulfill their special mission" (Thomas, *Revelation 8–22*, p. 198). Many of the lost will be "saved through the witness of the 144,000" (Thomas, *Revelation 1–7*, p. 483). "After witnessing for the Lord, they will apparently be martyred, for they will be 'purchased from the earth' (14:3)" (Couch, *Handbook to Revelation*, p. 175). With the church absent from the earth during this time (see discussion on 4:1), their task will be especially important. God will therefore seal these converted Jewish witnesses at the beginning of the tribulation. "The seal of the living God" (v. 2) will protect them from the ensuing judgments so that they may fulfill their task of witnessing to the nations.

Because of the controversy over the literalness of the 144,000 who are sealed, it is important here to review the three interpretative schools. *Postmillennialists* believe that the millennium (the "thousand years" of Revelation 20:1–3) is to be interpreted symbolically as synonymous with the church age. The so-called "millennium" is the church conquering the world with the gospel. A near-perfect society will be developed, and then Christ will return to establish His kingdom. *Amillennialists* also interpret the "thousand years" symbolically but see no millennium of any kind on earth. At the end of the church age, Christ will return to judge the world, and then eternity will begin. *Premillennialists* take the Bible in a more literal sense, though seeing actual events sometimes described with symbolism, figures of speech, illustration, types, and so on. Yet their base of understanding Scripture, and certainly prophecy, is a more literal method of interpretation. With a natural and literal interpretation of Scripture, and especially in regard to prophecy, it only makes sense to take the 144,000 as relating to Jews, as clearly stated, twelve thousand from each tribe. This num-

ber is not some representation of church saints. "If national Israel instead of the church is in view, the [interpretative] difficulty dissolves" (Thomas, *Revelation 1–7*, p. 466).

7:1. The **four angels** are a subset of the angelic host who perform specific tasks in Revelation. While the "four beasts" ("living creatures"; see discussions on 4:6, 8) are also angels, they are not the same as described here. **The four corners of the earth** is a symbolic expression meaning "the entire world."

7:2–3. Another angel (v. 2) came from **the east** carrying the authentic **seal of the living God**. He addressed **the four angels**, instructing them to **Hurt** (Greek, *adikeō*; "harm") **not the earth, neither the sea, nor the trees** (vegetation; v. 3) until the 144,000 **servants of our God** were **sealed … in their foreheads**. No harm, natural or otherwise, was to be unleashed until the 144,000 were sealed and protected, after which further judgment would fall on the earth.

In ancient times, some guilds marked workers on their foreheads to identify them with the group. A forehead mark is most conspicuous. It seems certain that the seal will be visible to all. "The forehead was chosen because it was the most conspicuous. It will be obvious to whom these slaves belong and whom they serve" (Thomas, *Revelation 8–22*, p. 473). The nature of the seal is not identified. Ancient documents, however, were sealed with the signet ring of an official or of the king to authenticate and protect the contents. That God marked these His servants with His seal means that He would not allow them to be hurt until their work was completed. The protective sealing of these Jewish servants shows that they had a special task to perform for the Lord in the early stages of the tribulation. The Lord's "seal" [Greek, *sphragida*] is not the same as the "mark" (Greek, *charagma*) of Revelation 13:16–17.

7:4–8. The number of them which were sealed (v. 4) was 144,000 **of the children of Israel**, with 12,000 coming from each tribe, though with some exceptions. Apparently, **Joseph** (v. 8) is mentioned as representing his son Ephraim. Joseph's other son, **Manasses** (v. 6), is listed, however. **Ephraim** and **Manasses** are subdivisions of the one tribe of Joseph (see Gen. 49:22, 28). The tribe of Dan is not listed, perhaps because this tribe had early connections with idolatry (see Judges 18:30), leaving an early tradition that the Antichrist would come out of that tribe. Another theory says that it was classified with the tribe of **Nephthalim** since Dan was a smaller tribe. **Juda** (v. 5) is listed first, possibly because the Messiah came out of this tribe (see Gen. 49:9–10).

b. The Great Multitude (7:9–17)

This passage makes it clear that both Jews and Gentiles will be saved during the tribulation. A great throng from all nations will be saved, but many will pay with their lives for their faith in Christ.

7:9–10. John moved the narration on with his usual expression: **After this** (Greek, *meta tauta*; v. 9). With an exclamation (**lo**; Greek, *idou*), John showed his wonder at the **great multitude** that he saw coming forth. The people could not be counted. Some scholars believe that more people may be saved during this terrible period than during any other time in history. John subdivided this large company into **nations** (Greek, *ethnos*), **kindreds** (Greek, *phylē*; "tribe" or "family"), **people** (Greek, *laos*), and **tongues** (Greek, *glōssa*; "language"). While Revelation does not explicitly state that many will be martyred during the tribulation, evidence of this is found later in the book. That those in this "great multitude" were redeemed people is obvious in that they **stood ... before the Lamb**, were **clothed with white robes** (indicating righteousness; see 3:5, 18; 4:4; 6:11; 7:13), and waved **palms in their hands**, which represent the coming of peace, salvation, and the victory of the King (see John 12:13). Their heavenly shout of **Salvation** (Greek, *sōtēria*; v. 10) was a shout of joy for the deliverance provided by **God which sitteth upon the throne, and unto the Lamb** as well. Both Father and Son received equal honor for the plan of redemption.

7:11–12. A host of **angels** (v. 11), along with **the elders and the four beasts** ("living ones"), fell down before God's **throne** and **worshipped** Him. This is similar to the worship described in 5:13–14. **Amen** (Greek, *Amēn*; v. 12) was their solemn confirmation

of the tribute the saved multitude offered to God because of the victory He brought (see 1:6, 7; 5:14; 19:4). Their sevenfold tribute and doxology (**Blessing, and glory, and wisdom, and thanksgiving, and honour, and power, and might**) followed, similar to one the multitude of angelic beings addressed to the Lamb in 5:12. The Lord had delivered this vast sea of humanity from the most formidable forces the earth had ever seen (Thomas, *Revelation 1–7*, p. 492).

7:13–14. One of the elders (v. 13) asked an important question: Who **are these which are arrayed in white robes? and whence came they?** That one of the elders asked who they were seems to imply they were not the raptured church saints. This "great multitude" (7:9) consisted of people who came to faith in Christ during the tribulation. Some disagree and believe they were martyred church saints who were killed down through the ages of church history. Such a view, however, means that the great tribulation would have been taking place during the entire period of the church. Instead, these were people who came to Christ after the tribulation began, who then died, and who were now in the Lord's presence in glory. **These are they which came out of great tribulation** (v. 14). "Out of" is the Greek word *ek*, meaning they "came out from" the great tribulation. They were in it, and now they are with the Lord. This clearly indicates that there will be a great host of Gentiles saved during the tribulation.

How can **robes [be] made ... white in the blood of the Lamb** of God? This is the irony of Christ's work on the cross. To the world, the cross and Christ's death for sinners is foolishness (see 1 Cor. 1:18).

7:15–16. These martyred saints were now in the presence of God and continually **serve[d] him day and night in his [heavenly] temple** (v. 15). In turn, the Lord would **dwell among them**. They would no longer suffer the privations of earth. They would never **hunger** again (v. 16) or **thirst**, nor would they suffer the **heat** of the **sun**. Verse 16 could be poetic hyperbole and really be speaking of spiritual suffering during the tribulation. In either case, that period was forever past for this great multitude of believers, and they now basked in the glorious presence of God.

Being **before the throne of God** (v. 15) means this great throng of believers stood in the place of prominence and honor. Their privilege is further defined as serving the Lord "day and night in his temple." That they never needed to sleep gives some inkling of the heavenly state of the saints, in which the limitations of earthly existence are no more.

7:17. Regarding this "great multitude" (7:9), the elder further stated that **the Lamb**, seated **in the midst** of His Father's heavenly **throne[,] shall feed them, and shall lead them unto living fountains of water.** Moreover, **God** Himself **shall wipe away all tears from their eyes** (see Isa. 25:8; Rev. 21:4). In the shining glory of heaven, whatever sorrows and cares have been laid upon the saints in earthly life will be forgotten. They will have the tender care of their Savior.

G. Seventh Seal: Silence in Heaven (8:1)

8:1. The time had arrived for the opening of **the seventh seal**. When the seal was opened, a **silence in heaven** came that lasted for about **half an hour**. John's human finiteness is apparent in his attempt to explain time as he understood it from his human senses. Being transcendent, God is above time, but He created it for human benefit. This "half an hour" of silence anticipated the coming trumpet and vial judgments, which the seventh seal would soon reveal. The absolute silence portended the ominous developments about to take place. One might think of it as the silence that fills a courtroom when a jury foreman is about to read the verdict. For a moment, expectation takes over. What was about to come as the tribulation progressed would only be more horrible than what had gone before.

VIII. The Seven Trumpets (8:2–11:19)

The initial use of the trumpet in the history of Israel was at Mount Sinai. It was first used to call the entire nation to the mountain of God to receive the Ten Commandments (see Exod. 20:18). Trumpets were later used to summon the leaders or the entire nation to the tabernacle in anticipation of journeying to a new location (Num. 10:1–10). They called the nation to war (Num. 10:9), were used for special feasts (Num. 10:10), and were also used for ceremonial processions (1 Chron. 15:24). In Revelation, trumpets were given to the angels to announce the coming of the great calamities stemming from the opening of the seventh seal. In this sense, they were war trumpets. Unlike in ancient Israel, however, the trumpet blasts did not dictate a response from the people but instead announced further judgments that God was sending on the earth.

A. Introduction (8:2–5)

In this passage, seven angels were commanded to sound the "war" trumpets, announcing additional troubles upon the inhabitants of earth. The Lord appointed these angels to direct a series of judgments symbolized by the seven trumpets.

8:2–4. Before **the seven angels** (v. 2) sounded their **trumpets**, John saw **another angel** (v. 3) come before **the altar** in heaven. This angel was given **a golden censer** with a large quantity of **incense** so that he could **offer it with the prayers of all saints upon the golden altar which was before the throne** of God.

This is a moving picture of the redeemed's prayers of appeal being presented before the Lord. Though the context is the tribulation, this scene paints a graphic picture showing that the prayers of the saints of all generations are not lost when offered up to God. They come before His very presence in glory. The Old Testament priests burned incense on the altar of incense. The smoke would fill the temple or tabernacle and would ascend to heaven. Incense is symbolic of prayers and worship to the Lord. This is a reminder that such intercession was to Him as sweet incense in that He is pleased to receive such offerings of the heart. The heavenly altar is mentioned seven times in Revelation (6:9; 8:3 [twice], 5; 9:13; 14:18; 16:7).

8:5. The **censer … filled with fire [from] the altar** was **cast … into** (down upon) **the earth**. That the saints' prayers were on the altar like incense suggests that the saints were near the throne of God and that there is only one altar in heaven, not two. This picture is in keeping with what is recorded in Isaiah 6:6 and Ezekiel 10:2. Whose **voices** did John hear? This is not explained, though the conjecture is that he heard the utterances of the host of the angels who were observing this outpouring of judgment. This scene is virtually repeated in 16:18. The **thunderings, and lightnings, and [the] earthquake** are physical disturbances that accompany God's wrath upon an impenitent earth (see 11:19; 16:18). This verse is a reminder of the Lord's declaration of what was coming upon the earth and of the protection He promised: "I ... will keep thee from the hour of temptation, which shall come upon all the world, to try them that dwell upon the earth" (3:10).

B. First Trumpet: Hail and Fire Mixed with Blood (8:6–7)

In chapter 8, four of the seven trumpets are sounded, each having to do with cataclysmic natural disasters affecting the earth. These four trumpets will set in motion the forces of the natural world to achieve the destructive wrath on nature. At this point in the tribulation, humanity's world will be falling apart. Of about fifteen items to be affected by the plagues of the first four trumpets, in twelve instances, one-third of the item will receive injury or destruction (8:7, 10, 11 being the exceptions). God will use the natural world to punish the human race (Thomas, *Revelation 8–22*, p. 13).

8:6–7. The seven trumpet angels came back on the scene and **prepared themselves to sound** (v. 6) the seven trumpets. Their preparation was a distinct arranging of themselves in a proper order and raising their trumpets in readiness to sound forth. The sense of expectancy is heightened.

When **The first angel sounded ... hail and fire mingled with blood ... were cast upon the earth** (v. 7). It could well be that the "hail and fire mingled with blood" were the result of a series of volcanic explosions triggered by the earthquake (Greek, *seismos*; see 8:5). The "blood" would not be "hemoglobin." In Scripture, blood often stands for pollution, because blood is the greatest incubator for disease.

The fire consumed a **third** (v. 7) of the **trees** on earth, and **all green grass was burnt up**. One can hardly conceive how frightening this will be to

people, for such a widespread conflagration will obviously upset the earth's ecology. Some take this entire picture as figurative, but behind the descriptions are literal happenings. These prophesies resemble what Ezekiel said will happen when the Jews have returned to the land of Israel: "After many days ... in the latter years" (Ezek. 38:8), God will pour down on the Gentile nations "pestilence and with blood ... an overflowing rain, and great hailstones, fire, and brimstone" (Ezek. 38:22).

C. Second Trumpet: A Mountain Thrown into the Sea (8:8–9)

Nature will be further disrupted with even more damaging natural occurrences. The seas and oceans will be affected, with a large number of creatures perishing. Could this natural disturbance also stem from a military exchange between the nations of the earth? Even if that is so, it does not rule out the involvement of God's wrath in these events. God uses all kinds of means to accomplish His ends.

8:8–9. When **the second angel sounded** (v. 8) his trumpet, **a great mountain ... was cast into the sea**, which caused it to **bec[o]me blood** (polluted). In today's atomic age, the seer's description of "hail and fire" (8:7) seems to fit the description of a nuclear explosion of fire and ice. The "great mountain" **burning with fire** A third (v. 9) of sea life **died; and [a] third ... of the ships** in the ocean **were destroyed**. This parallels the second vial judgment, which results in the killing of all sea life (see 16:3).

D. Third Trumpet: The Star Wormwood (8:10–11)

Following the destruction of one-third of the seawaters, one-third of the freshwaters will be polluted. This will threaten creatures of all kinds, including human beings. Finding potable water will become a life-and-death matter.

8:10–11. When **the third angel sounded** (v. 10) his trumpet, a flaming **great star** (Greek, *astēr*), or asteroid, **fell [into a] third ... of the rivers, and [into] the fountains of waters**, which probably refers to the wells or groundwaters. This celestial body, called **Wormwood** (v. 11), polluted the earth's fresh-waters when it fell from heaven, **and many men died** because the waters **were made bitter** (poisoned). Wormwood is a terrible-tasting, bitter plant and is common in the Middle East in several varieties. It is mentioned in the Old Testament to depict bitterness and sorrow and is said to bear poisonous fruit (see Deut. 29:18; Jer. 9:15; 23:15).

E. Fourth Trumpet: A Third of the Sun, Moon, and Stars Struck (8:12–13)

The sounding of the fourth trumpet will cause the atmosphere to be darkened. This will have a devastating affect on the morale of all on the earth. Christ spoke of these days coming. He said that "men's hearts [would be] failing them for fear, and for looking after those things which are coming on the earth: for the powers of the heaven shall be shaken" (Luke 21:26).

8:12–13. When **the fourth angel sounded** (v. 12) his trumpet, the heavenly luminaries (**the sun, the moon**, and **the stars**) lost their effectiveness from earth's perspective. A **third part** was dimmed, and both **day** and **night** appeared to be swallowed up in darkness. There are two suggestions as to how to understand verse 12. One is that these heavenly bodies will be simultaneously cursed so that they give off a third less light than normal. Another view, which may be preferable, is that the atmospheric pollution caused by the first three trumpet judgments will reduce the amount of light from the sun, moon, and stars. In either case, God is the one who will bring on these natural curses.

An angel (v. 13) overhead, **flying through the midst of heaven**, cried out, **Woe, woe, woe** (Greek, *Ouai, ouai, ouai*) **to the inhabiters of the earth**! The angel's cry was not only a lament but a pronounce-ment of doom for the inhabitants of the earth. The threefold repetition of "woe" corresponds to the three remaining trumpet judgments, which are fulfilled in 9:12, 11:14, and 12:12. Some preferred Greek texts give the word "eagle" (Greek, *aetos*) in place of "angel." Whatever the reading should be, this creature warned of additional troubles soon to fall upon the earth.

F. Fifth Trumpet: The Plague of Locusts (9:1–12)

A second "star" will fall from heaven, but this "star" will be a divine agent rather than a cosmic disturbance as in 8:10. This divine agent, probably an angel, will have the power to unleash a demonic hoard of loathsome creatures that will inflict un-believable pain on humanity, both physically and spiritually. These creatures are described as "locusts" (v. 3), symbolic of demons or demon-inspired com-batants. They will torment earthlings for five months (vv. 5, 10). Because of the tormenting sting, men will want to die, but "death shall flee from them" (v. 6).

9:1–3. When **the fifth angel sounded** (v. 1) his trumpet, John **saw a star fall from heaven unto the earth**. The "star" is a personification of an angelic creature who has already "fallen" (perfect tense) at some point in the past. While no explanation is given as to his identity, the event resembles the fall of Satan (see 12:7–9). Christ alluded to this when He said: "I beheld Satan as lightning fall from heaven" (Luke 10:18). Isaiah wrote, "How art thou fallen from heaven, O Lucifer, son of the morning!" (Isa. 14:12). The name Lucifer means "the shining one." Still, the identification of this being is not certain. One argu-ment against this being Satan is that the angelic crea-ture **was given the key to the bottomless pit**. That the key was given to him implies that he could act only with God's permission. This is also true of the creatures that came forth from the pit (v. 2). They were under God's divine authority and could not do their evil work without His consent.

The bottomless pit (Greek, *abyssos*; v. 2) was **opened**, out of which **arose** a searing **smoke** like that from **a great furnace. The sun and the air** (the atmosphere) **were darkened** by the thickness and intensity of the smoke. **Out of the smoke [came] locusts** (v. 3) that had **the power ... [of] the scorpi-ons** that roam the desert sands. These evil spirits had been confined in the bottomless pit for just such an hour of torment.

9:4–6. The demonic locusts were given a com-mand. This command must have come from God be-cause it restricted their activity. They were not allowed to **hurt** (v. 4) the natural world: **grass, any** (other) **green thing**, or **any tree**. Instead, they were **commanded** to inflict pain on **only those men which have not the seal of God in their foreheads**. Those who did have the seal of God could be either the 144,000 Jewish witnesses (see 7:3–8) who had received the Lord's seal on their foreheads (see 7:3) or all those who had been redeemed during the tribulation.

The locusts were also commanded that they **should not kill** (v. 5) the unsealed but instead torment them for **five months**. Some have assumed that "five months" is figurative, with no definite time allotted, but it is best to take this as a literal period. It has been noted that often locust swarms commit their ravages for about five months. While the locusts are satanic beings, not insects, the typology remains, as if they were marauding insect pests that devour the vegetation of the landscape.

The torment inflicted by the demonic locusts will be so terrible that people will **seek death** (v. 6). They will want to die but will not be able to get up the courage to go through with it. World civilizations will reap the results of spiritual rebellion.

9:7–10. Comparative language is used to describe these demonic beings, **the locusts** (v. 7). This is common in the book of Revelation. Comparative language is used in this book more often than in all of the rest of the New Testament books. Note John's use of comparative language in the following descriptions of the locusts.

"power, *as* the scorpions of earth" (9:3)

"their torment was *as* the torment of a scorpion" (9:5)

"the shapes ... were *like unto* horses" (9:7)

"on their heads were *as it were* crowns like gold" (9:7)

"their faces were *as* the faces of men" (9:7)

"they had hair *as* the hair of women" (9:8)

"their teeth were *as* the teeth of lions" (9:8)

"they had breastplates, *as it were* ... of iron" (9:9)

"the sound of their wings was *as* the sound of chariots of many horses" (9:9)

"they had tails *like unto* scorpions" (9:10)

John had to use comparative language often because he was struggling to convey what he was seeing. Most of the meanings in these descriptions are obvious. To the ancients, **horses** (v. 7) were the most fearful of beasts to encounter in combat. **Crowns** show that these creatures had commanding authority to do their dirty deeds. **Their faces** displayed intelligence like that of humans. As seductive **women** flaunt their **hair**, some aspect of temptation may have been involved as these creatures sought to destroy the souls of people. **The teeth of lions** (v. 8) shows fierceness, while the **breastplates** (v. 9) indicate invincibility. From their wings was heard **the sound of chariots**, a noise that meant death for troops caught on the field of battle unprotected. Finally, for emphasis, it is repeated that their **stings** (v. 10) were like that of **scorpions ... and their power was to hurt men for five months**.

9:11–12. Who is the **king** (v. 11) over this horde? The names **Abaddon** (Hebrew) and **Apollyon** (Greek) both carry the idea of "the one who destroys." Abaddon is a personification of destruction in the Old Testament (see Prov. 15:11). Some believe he is a powerful demonic figure. Walvoord believes this king is Satan (*The Revelation of Jesus Christ*, p. 163). Thomas, however, holds that this is probably not so (*Revelation 8–22*, p. 38): nowhere is Satan connected with the abyss until he is finally cast into it (see 20:1–3), and there is a case for identifying this king as an unknown angel who is in charge of the abyss. Satan has leaders and subleaders under his command (see Eph. 6:12).

One terrible cry of **woe is past** (v. 12), with **two woes** yet to come. "Woe" is often a cry uttered because of some great catastrophe that is imposed as a judgment from God. The Lord Jesus gave such a cry when He pronounced judgment on Chorazin and Bethsaida (see Matt. 11:21).

G. Sixth Trumpet: Release of the Four Angels (9:13–21)

Many scholars take this passage as a second phase of the demonic torment introduced in 9:1–12, but others see the great horde in verses 16–17 as an actual army. The attackers seem to be described as men, and one-third of the people left on earth will be killed (vv. 16–18). Some of the war instruments involved could be seen as modern weapons. The world will fail to repent (v. 20) but will instead continue in the grossest of sins (v. 21).

9:13–14. When **the sixth angel sounded** (v. 13) his trumpet, John **heard a voice** speaking **from the four horns of the golden altar** that stood before the Lord's throne in heaven (see 8:3–5). In the ancient Jewish tabernacle, the "horns" were located on the four corners of the altar (see Exod. 27:2) and were used to tie down the offering that was being presented to God. Those fleeing for justice could seek mercy by taking hold of the horns (see 1 Kings 1:50–51; 2:28; Amos 3:14). Putting 9:13–14 together with 8:3–5, it seems that this further outpouring of God's judgment was in answer to the prayers of those who had suffered and died in the early stages of the tribulation. A command was given to **Loose the four angels which are bound in the great river Euphrates** (v. 14). Divine permission was now granted for their release. These four angels are probably not the same four angels as in 7:1.

The Euphrates flows southeast from the mountains of Armenia down to the Tigris in lower Babylon. The two rivers cover an eighteen hundred mile arc through the deserts of Iraq. This area has always been one of the most formidable and important regions in history, but it was also the ancient source of polytheism, demonism, and false religions. The Euphrates will play an important role at the end of the tribulation, when "the kings of the east" (16:12) cross over while coming into the Middle East. The Euphrates serves as the eastern boundary of the Promised Land (see Gen. 15:18; Deut. 1:7; Josh. 1:4). "The kings of the east" could be from the Arab nations, China, Japan, or other Muslim nations from North Africa to Mongolia.

9:15–16. The four angels ... were prepared for an hour, and a day, and a month, and a year ... to slay [a] third (v. 15) of humanity. The time frame is poetized for drama, but the designations are the same. It could read, "the appointed hour occurs on the appointed day in the appointed month and in

the appointed year" (Thomas, *Revelation 8–22*, p. 44). The destruction of a third of the people of earth makes this the most intense plague so far. The earth's population will be whittled down, with millions perishing with each addition of judgment. **The number of the army** (v. 16) unleashed for combat calculates out to 200 million **horsemen**.

9:17–18. It is the description of **the horses** (v. 17), and not the riders, that gives the impression that some demonic forces are at work here. The horses, with their riders, seem to be invincible and suggest a superhuman origin. The **breastplates** are described as being **of fire, and of jacinth, and brimstone**. One suggestion is that these elements represent colors of a protective material. "Fire" would be red, "jacinth" represents a blue smokelike color, and "brimstone" could refer either to a darker smokelike color or to a yellow color like sulphur. John saw the same elements coming out of the horses' mouths. The colors suggest some kind of destruction by heat. **The heads of the horses were as the heads of lions**—powerful, strong, fierce. Further light is cast on the character of the warfare in verse 18, where it is repeated that the invading forces will kill **the third part** of humanity.

9:19. With the additional visual allusions of this verse, the description of these evil creatures becomes even more gross. No interpreter can say for certain what all of the symbolism means, except that these descriptions portray actual events and an actual army. John must have struggled to fully comprehend what he was seeing. This is a terrible picture of a daunting military power destroying all that opposes it. The descriptions of the horses—with "heads of lions" (9:17) and **tails [that] were like unto serpents, and had heads, and with them do hurt**— conjure up an image of deadly warfare.

9:20–21. Those who survived the onslaught and **were not killed by these plagues** (v. 20) of destruction still did not repent. "Plague" (Greek, *plēgē*) often refers to disease, but the Greek word also means "wound," "blow," or "stroke." These "plagues" were more like lashings, stripes, or wounds coming upon the world by the forces just described. Some feel verse 20 refers to all of the trumpet judgments, but more than likely, it refers to the sixth trumpet only. Even with God's wrath falling upon them, humanity refused to repent ("change the mind"). They **repented not of the [evil] works of their hands**, nor of their **worship [of] devils** and their worship of **idols** made of **gold, silver, brass, stone,** and **wood**. Such idols are blind, deaf, and immobile. It must be remembered that even today the majority of the present world population practices some form of pagan idolatry. This will continue or grow worse in the tribulation period.

Neither repented they of their other sins (v. 21). The most heinous of these sins is mentioned first — **murders**. The idolaters continued in **their sorceries** (Greek, *pharmakon*), the use of drugs in their incantations, or perhaps drug use without any religious connection. Sexual sins (Greek, *porneias*) are mentioned next, along with the most common of public crimes, **thefts** (Greek, *klemmatōs*). "Such is depraved and infatuated human nature.... If people will not listen in the days of peaceful opportunity, there remaineth very little hope for them" (Seiss, *The Apocalypse*, p. 222).

1. The Second Interlude (10:1–11:14)

This lengthy interlude, or parenthetical section, comes between the sixth and seventh trumpets. By the end of the sixth trumpet judgment, half of the world's population will have been annihilated. The interlude sets the stage for the sounding of the seventh and final trumpet (see 11:15), a trumpet so powerful that it will result in the complete collapse of all of the earth's civilizations that are aligned against the Lord.

As in the interlude in chapter 7, the narrative does not advance but additional information that contributes to the total prophetic scene is presented. In chapter 10, John was given a vision of heaven that focused on a "little book" (10:2), or scroll, which led to more prophecies about "peoples, and nations, and tongues, and kings" (10:11). In 11:1–14, he received a revelation concerning the "two witnesses" (11:3) who are part of the Lord's worldwide testimony to

warn "the people and kindreds and tongues and nations" (11:9).

a. The Angel and the Little Scroll (chap. 10)

10:1. Here the scene returns to heaven. John saw **another mighty** (strong) **angel**. This angel is compared to the "strong angel" of 5:2 ("another"; Greek, *allos*; "one similar to," "one of the same type") but is not specifically identified. Some have suggested that this is Christ Jesus Himself, but this seems unlikely in light of 10:5–6. Although Christ is seen in the Old Testament as the Angel of Jehovah (see Gen. 18:1–15), nowhere in the New Testament is He called simply "an angel." This "mighty angel," **clothed with a cloud: and a rainbow** (Greek, *iris*) **... upon his head**, was adorned in the majesty of heaven itself.

His face was [like] the sun, and his feet as pillars of fire. Here again comparative language comes into play. The brilliance of the angel's face is likened to Christ's (see 1:16). The legs are likened to fire, which suggests judgment. Angels play a key role in Revelation; they are mentioned sixty-six times.

10:2. The **little book** (Greek, *biblaridion*; diminutive), or "little scroll," was held by the mighty angel, who had **his right foot upon the sea, and his left foot on the earth.** The coming judgments would encompass both land and sea, that is, the entire world.

10:3–6. John heard a cry as commanding **as when a lion roareth** (v. 3), followed by the **voices** of **seven thunders** (see 8:5). Some tie this to the seven times the voice of God is mentioned in Psalms 29:3–9. As John **was about to write** what he had heard, **a** (singular) **voice** (v. 4) commanded him, **Seal up those things which the seven thunders uttered, and write them not.** John must have received an ominous message, but he was ordered not to record it. The descriptions of terror in the message are not given in detail, but they are seen in the chapters that follow. "Though the text does not reveal what the thunders say, it is a safe conclusion that they are an audible symbol that God will bring added terror before the end (cf. 8:5; 11:19; 16:18)" (Thomas, *Revelation 8–22*, p. 65).

The angel ... lifted up his hand to heaven, and sware by (vv. 5–6) God Himself. This is one proof that this angelic being is not the Lord Jesus in that he swore by God, showing that God is greater than the angel. This was a solemn oath, not a curse. The angel proclaimed that God exists eternally and that He is the creator of **heaven ... and the earth ... and the sea, and [all] the things which are therein.** All matter is created by Him. What is striking in this message is that a day is coming when **there should be time no longer** (v. 6). "Time" (Greek, *chronos*) is best translated here as "delay." A strong consensus of scholars confirms this translation. The events of 10:1–11:14 are not taking place between the sixth and seventh trumpets, so no chronological progression has come about between this 10:1 and 11:15. This delay is best seen as the delay before the fulfillment of "the mystery of God" (10:7) and is best explained in light of the martyrs' question in 6:10: "How long, O Lord ...?"

10:7. When **the seventh angel ... shall begin to sound, the mystery** (Greek, *mystērion*) **of God [will] be finished** (Greek, *etelesthē*), or "completed," "fulfilled," "wrapped up." This "mystery of God" seems to be about the Old Testament promises that the kingdom of God will someday be established on earth, promises that were now unfolding. The prophecies relating to the power, majesty, and holiness of God will be clearly fulfilled in Christ's glorious return to establish His millennial reign. "The mystery of God" is also about the eternal state that will follow Christ's earthly reign.

10:8–9. A heavenly **voice** (v. 8) instructed John to **take the little book** from **the hand of the angel.** The apostle was then instructed to **eat it** (v. 9) but was warned that it would make his **belly bitter,** probably meaning that it would give him indigestion. In contradiction, however, it would be **sweet as honey** in his mouth. The sweetness represented John's joy that God was bringing to a conclusion the sin and evil upon the earth. The bitterness represented his sorrow over the terrible but righteous judgments that God was further sending down upon humanity. John, the faithful apostle and servant, was to deliver both aspects of these omens.

10:10–11. After eating **the little book** (v. 10), John experienced just what he had been told to expect. Then the angel told him, **Thou must prophesy again,** prophecies about all the **peoples** (v. 11) upon the earth and the judgments that God would send against them. Verse 11 leaves no room for the idea that tribulation will be simply some localized series of tribulations in just one country, region, or area such as the Mediterranean basin. The word **many** emphasizes the international scope of the tribulations. The seven-year period of God's wrath will be a worldwide judgment; it will fall upon all nations (see 6:12–17).

b. The Two Witnesses (11:1–14)

This passage continues the interlude with a description of the two witnesses. God will not leave the world without a testimony. These two personalities will have a global outreach, though their message will be for the most part rejected. The identity of these two witnesses is a compelling and often debated question. The text clearly indicates that they are specific individuals with miraculous powers like Moses (turning water to blood) and Elijah (calling down fire from heaven). The Old Testament ends with an appeal to both Moses and Elijah (Mal. 4:4–6). Also, they were the two witnesses at the transfiguration of Jesus (Matt. 17:1–3). Whether the two witnesses are literally Moses and Elijah or come in the spirit and type of them, only time will tell.

11:1–3. A reed like unto a rod (v. 1) refers to a bamboo-like reed that grew to a height of sixteen to twenty feet on the banks of the Nile and the Jordan rivers. It was the common measuring rod used on construction sites (see Ezek. 40:3; Zech. 2:1–2). John was told to **Rise, and measure the temple of God, and the altar, and them that worship therein.** The temple John saw was the restored temple that will play a role in the tribulation. This is probably the temple in which the Antichrist will enter, seat himself, and proclaim "that he is God" (2 Thess. 2:4), as prophesied in Daniel 9:27 and Matthew 24:15. The temple will also house the idol to this world dictator (see Rev. 13:14–15).

The court (v. 2) of **the Gentiles,** however, John was to **leave out, and measure ... not.** Before and during the time of the Gospels, this court was where the Gentiles could come to worship, but they were not allowed to enter the temple and mingle with the Jews. Since the Gentiles **shall ... tread under foot** Jerusalem, **the holy city,** for **forty and two months,** or for three and a half years, this period is probably the last half of the seven-year tribulation rather than the first half. Jerusalem will be the center, the vortex, of the tribulation. The expression "my two witnesses" is probably God speaking. These two prophets belong to Him and He is the one who imparts His **power** for the work they are doing. The **two witnesses ... shall prophesy** (v. 3) during this period. That they will be **clothed in sackcloth** shows that they will stay in a meditative mood and will be humble in their demeanor.

11:4. The imagery of **the two olive trees, and the two candlesticks** parallels that of Zechariah 4:2–6, where it represents Joshua the priest and Zerubbabel the prince, who were key personalities in restoring Israel following the Babylonian captivity. In an ironic twist, while the two witnesses will bring judgments on the earth, they will also bring both blessing (olive tree) and light (candlestick).

11:5–6. Some suggest the two witnesses are Enoch and Elijah because both men were taken up to heaven without facing death (for Enoch, see Gen. 5:21–24; for Elijah, see 2 Kings 2:1–18); thus, they will come back to earth in bodily form and eventually die. However, their miraculous powers seem to indicate Moses and Elijah. **Fire proceedeth out of their mouths, and devoureth their enemies,** as in Elijah's encounters with the servant messengers of Ahaziah (see 2 Kings 1:10, 12). That the two witnessess will have the power to turn **waters ... to blood, and to smite the earth with ... plagues** (v. 6) reminds readers of Moses' authority over the Egyptians (see Exod. 7:17–21).

God will place His protection over these prophets so that anyone who harms them will die. They will **have power to shut heaven** (v. 6) so that it will not rain while they prophesy, and they will be able to pass judgment **as they will.**

11:7–9. When they shall have finished their testimony (v. 7), they will perish. **The beast that ascendeth out of the bottomless pit shall make war against them [to] overcome them** and slay them (see 9:1–2, 11; 17:8; 20:1–3). "The beast" is the Antichrist, who is referred to nine times in Revelation (13:1; 14:9, 11; 15:2; 16:2; 17:3, 13; 19:20; 20:10). The **dead bodies** (v. 8) of the witnesses will be left in **the street of the great city, which spiritually is called Sodom and Egypt.** To make sure the reader understands that Jerusalem is meant here, John added, **where also our Lord was crucified.** Sodom (see Gen. 19:4–11) and Egypt (see Ps. 105:38; Isa. 19:1; Jer. 46:25) were centers of religious apostasy and rebellion. John wrote this prophecy some twenty years after the destruction of Jerusalem. For her rejection of their own Messiah, Christ prophesied that Jerusalem would be visited by the Lord's "vengeance" (Luke 21:22). In the tribulation, at least for a short period, the city will again spiritually rebel against Him. For **three days and a half** (v. 9), the entire world **shall see their dead bodies,** probably by satellite television!

11:10–11. The whole world **shall rejoice ... and make merry, and shall send gifts** (v. 10) as if celebrating a universal holiday, **because these two prophets tormented them that dwelt on the earth.** "Torment" (Greek, *basanizō*) means to "torture," "harass," "cause to struggle." This torment was first spiritual conviction, followed by a miraculous shaking of the elements of the planet in judgment warning (see 11:5–6). The world was in pain because of these two special prophets of God. The death of the two witnesss will appear to be a great victory for Satan and the Antichrist.

To further gain the world's attention, however, the Lord brought the two witnesses back to life. **The spirit of life ... entered into them, and they stood upon their feet** (v. 11). This extraordinary event put **great fear** in those who saw it. It was a dramatic vindication of the true faith (see Ezek. 37:5, 10).

11:12–14. Offering additional proof to the world, **a great voice from heaven** (v. 12) summoned these two prophets, **Come up hither. And they ascended up to heaven in a cloud; and their**

enemies beheld them leave. This was a divine call. The two witnesses responded to the invitation and departed into glory. The rapture of the witnesses serves to verify the validity of the earlier rapture of the church. **The same hour**, another judgment fell upon apostate Jerusalem: **a great earthquake** (v. 13) that destroyed a **tenth** of the city. **Seven thousand** men perished. A **remnant** of the survivors **were affrighted, and gave glory to the God of heaven**. This was in contrast to the required worship of the Beast. "The God of heaven" is an Old Testament phrase used to distinguish the true God from pagan deities. Many have questioned whether the earthquake caused true faith in Christ or simply an acknowledgment of God's greatness. Since possibly millions will come to Christ during the tribulation, it is not far-fetched to believe that the survivors were converted.

So the **second woe** (v. 14) ends, leaving the seventh trumpet to sound and **the third** and final **woe** to come. Many believe the second woe is considered as the final phase of the sixth trumpet. The third woe contained in the seventh trumpet is announced as coming quickly. Without a doubt the end of the age is fast approaching.

H. Seventh Trumpet: Judgments and Rewards (11:15–19)

This is a preview section that introduces where the events coming in the next chapters are going. At the end of the terror of the tribulation, God will establish His earthly kingdom with the reign of His Christ. God's wrath gets worse and the nations will experience even more intense judgment. (Satan, the dragon, his persecution against the Jewish people, symbolized by the woman, in order to destroy her.) This effort by Satan will take place during the last half of the tribulation (v. 6). It seems clear that 11:15–13:1–18 focuses on the diabolical work of Satan, the Antichrist (the beast), and the other beast (the religious ruler). These events begin at the midpoint of the tribulation.

The seventh trumpet is only introduced at this stage. Its judgments are not fully described until chapter 16. The introduction of this trumpet is extremely dramatic, however. From heaven will come a crescendo of powerful voices. The seventh trumpet introduces the most horrible of the plagues and the seven vials (or bowls) of wrath (see 15:1–16:2). The seven trumpets announce the kingdom, but they begin the seven vials of wrath (11:15). The seven plagues are the seven vials (bowls) filled with the wrath of God (15:1). These seven plagues "are the last, because in them the wrath of God is finished" (see vv. 15–16). They close with bringing "the cup of the wine of his fierce wrath" upon Babylon the great (16:19).

11:15. This is a proclamation of what is coming; that is, **the kingdoms of this world are become the kingdoms of our Lord. The kingdoms of this world** is a consolidation of the kingdom of the Antichrist, the "fourth beast" and "fourth kingdom" mentioned in Daniel 7:23. This fourth kingdom on the earth will be different from all the other kingdoms. It will "devour the whole earth, and … tread it down, and break it in pieces" (Dan. 7:23). The fifth kingdom mentioned in Daniel (Dan. 7:26–28) is the kingdom of God **and of his Christ**. The messianic kingdom will supersede the kingdom of the Antichrist. To the Son of Man will be given "dominion, and glory, and a kingdom, that all people, nations, and languages, should serve him: his dominion is an everlasting dominion, which shall not pass away, and his kingdom that which shall not be destroyed" (Dan. 7:14). "From this point on, everything follows in rapid succession. These five verses (15–19) are among the most dramatic verses in the entire Bible.… One cannot read these verses without realizing that we have come to some great conclusion. It is all over except the shouting!… The extensive use of the aorist tense conveys a sense of absolute certainty about the events yet to come" (Hindson, *Revelation*, p. 127).

11:16–17. The twenty-four **elders** (v. 16) were seated before the throne of **God**. Upon hearing the glorious proclamation of 11:15, the elders **fell upon their faces, and worshipped God**. Their worship consisted of thanks to the **Lord God Almighty** (v. 17), who lives eternally (see 1:8; 4:8), and praise for His **great power**. "Almighty" (Greek, *pantokratōr*) is used nine times in Revelation. When John wrote that the

Lord **hast reigned**, he was prophesying of the earthly kingdom of Christ (see Ezek. 21:26–27; Dan. 2:35, 44; 4:3; 6:26; 7:14, 26–27; Zech. 14:9), which will be dramatically fulfilled in His second coming (see Rev. 19:11–21) and His millennial reign (see 20:1–8).

11:18. Though **the nations were angry**, the final stage of the Lord's **wrath is come**, as well as the time for the judgment of **the dead** and the rewarding of the Lord's **servants the prophets, and ... the saints**. The time had also arrived when God would destroy **them which destroy the earth**. This seems to refer to those living on the earth at that time who rebelled against God, misused the resources of the world for their own ends, and disregarded the terrible destruction they were bringing down on God's creation.

11:19. The heavenly **temple ... was opened**, and the heavenly **ark of his testament** (covenant) was revealed. The heavenly temple was reflected in the ancient earthly temple. The earthly ark represented God's presence among His people. It was constructed of precious acacia wood (see Deut. 10:1–2) and symbolized the Lord's throne. It symbolized His faithfulness but was also the place where judgment, as well as mercy, was meted out. The vision of the ark brought about more judgment on the inhabitants of earth. Chronologically, the time was close for Christ's second coming. Events yet to come are previewed in 11:18–19.

IX. Various Personages and Events (chaps. 12–14)

While the seventh trumpet was sounded in 11:15, the details of that judgment are not fully disclosed until chapter 16. Thus, chapters 12–14 view the prophecies of the end times from a different perspective. Rather than moving the narrative forward, these chapters introduce the key characters that will be involved in the second half of the seven-year tribulation period. The chronology of events is picked up again in chapter 15.

A. The Woman and the Dragon (chap. 12)

Chapter 12 has two main interpretations. (1) The first view sees it as describing events that take place at

this point in the tribulation, including Satan's being cast to the earth along with his evil angels (v. 9), and heralding the fact that Christ will usher in the kingdom of God and secure the final salvation (v. 10) for His people. (2) The second view sees it as a summary of past events concerning Satan's fall (vv. 1–12) and an update on his plans to destroy Israel (vv. 13–17). Whichever view is correct, all scholars hold that the chapter focuses on the satanic conflict in heaven and how this war came to earth to subvert God's program concerning the Jewish nation and concerning His Son.

12:1–2. A great wonder (Greek, *sēmeion mega*; v. 1) is better translated "a great sign." "The identification of this woman is the most critical issue in properly interpreting the Apocalypse. The woman symbolizes the nation and people of Israel. The imagery is taken from Joseph's dream in Genesis 37:9–11, where the sun and moon and twelve stars represent the patriarchy of Israel and the twelve tribes. The figure as a travailing woman is prevalent in the Old Testament (cf. Is. 26:17–18; Jer. 4:31; 13:21; Mic. 4:10; 5:3).... The woman has the 'crown of twelve stars,' symbolizing the tribes of Israel" (Hindson, *Revelation*, p. 137). The woman **travailing in birth** (v. 2) is Israel, which, through the Virgin Mary, gave birth to the **child**, the Lord Jesus Christ. The "woman" in this chapter represents the "mother" of Christ (Israel), not the "bride" of Christ (the church).

12:3–5. The **great red dragon** (v. 3) is Satan (see 12:9). His **seven heads and ten horns, and seven crowns** show the authority that he will have when his full intentions are revealed during the second half of the tribulation. He is similarly described in 13:1. A parallel is found in Daniel 7:7–8, 24, which is clearly about the revived Roman Empire. "The seven heads and ten horns refer to the original ten kingdoms of which three were subdued by the little horn of Daniel 7:8, who is to be identified as the world ruler of the great tribulation who reigns over the revived Roman Empire" (Walvoord, *The Revelation of Jesus Christ*, p. 189).

His tail drew the third part of the stars of heaven (v. 4) refers to that far-distant past when Satan fell from the presence of the Lord, taking with

REVELATION 12:10 – 12

him a great company of rebellious angels (see Isa. 14:12 – 15; Ezek. 28:12 – 19). (Many scholars believe that Satan is behind the evil activities of the king of Tyre referred to in Ezekiel 28:12 – 19. This would seem logical, since verse 13 says, "Thou has been in Eden the garden of God." Or it could be that the king of Tyre symbolizes Satan.) Ezekiel 28:12 – 19 "is of tremendous theological import, recording the origin of sin and Satan and the character and panoramic career of the greatest of angels" (Unger, *Old Testament Commentary*, p. 1553). Christ mentioned this event in Luke 10:18: "I beheld Satan as lightning fall from heaven."

In his next great attempt to nullify God's plan, Satan endeavored **to devour [the] child** (v. 4), the Lord Jesus, at the time of His birth. Working through the evil King Herod, Satan attempted to kill Jesus some months after His birth (see Matt. 2:1 – 18). John described Christ's kingly role by quoting Psalm 2:9: "he shall rule [all nations] with a rod of iron" (Rev. 19:15). After His crucifixion and ascension, Christ was seated on the heavenly throne at the right hand of His Father, where He awaits the coming day when His enemies shall be made His "footstool" (Ps. 110:1).

12:6. John's vision then moved on to Satan's actions during the tribulation. Satan again sought to devour God's own, but **the woman** (Israel) **fled into the wilderness**, where God had **prepared** a place to hide her for 1,260 days, or three and a half years. Christ mentioned this in His Olivet Discourse prophecy (see Matt. 24:16; Mark 13:14). Most scholars believe this refers to the last three and a half years of the tribulation, because the Jewish people will have comparative tranquility during the first half of the tribulation (see Dan. 9:27). This protection is not for all of the Jews but only for a remnant. This remnant may include the 144,000 for a short period. But they are "purchased from the earth" and die martyrs' deaths, as indicated in 14:1 – 5. The remnant, then, are the Jews who enter the kingdom at the end of the tribulation.

12:7 – 9. Many scholars believe that the **war in heaven** (v. 7), in which **Michael and his angels fought against [Satan] ... and his angels**, is directly

part of the tribulation context (see introduction to chap. 12), but most likely, it looks back to the initial fall of Satan. Some cite the fact that Satan had access to God in heaven in order to speak with Him even though he had fallen from heaven because of his original rebellion. There seems to be a difference between Satan's fellowship with God before the fall and the fact that he still has access to God to speak with Him. A case in point is the accusation that Satan brought against Job (see Job 1:6 – 12). The angel Michael, "the great prince which standeth for the children of thy people," is the defender of Israel, and he will again "stand up" to protect Israel during the tribulation, the "time of trouble, such as never was since there was a nation ... and at that time [the Jews] shall be delivered, every one that [is] found written in the book [of life]" (Dan. 12:1).

12:10 – 12. "The events of this chapter deal in general with the end of the age" (Walvoord, *The Revelation of Jesus Christ*, p. 192). "If this is viewed as a *future* event, then it must happen during the Great Tribulation. In favor of the future viewpoint is the fact that the time Satan is on earth after being cast out is three and one half years ('times'). This also correlates with the 1,260 days the woman (Israel) is persecuted and driven into the wilderness (12:6)" (Hindson, *The Book of Revelation*, p. 139). These verses give a preview of the arrival of the millennium, which is described more fully in 19:11. John **heard a loud voice saying ... Now is come salvation, and strength, and the kingdom of our God** (v. 10) through **the power of his Christ**. Satan (which in Hebrew means **accuser**) was busy accusing the **brethren** in the past and continued to do so in the tribulation. His continual activity in this role, accusing God's people **day and night**, as he "walketh about, seeking whom he may devour" (1 Peter 5:8) illustrates his hatred of the righteous. Here, however, Satan **is cast down**. The Lord Jesus supplied the victory, but those who died for the faith took part in that triumph. They overcame **by the blood of the Lamb, and by the word of their testimony** (v. 11). They did not hold on to their lives but were willing to march all the way **unto the death**.

The very **heavens** (v. 12) and all its inhabitants were called to **rejoice** because of Christ's great victory. **The inhabiters of the earth and of the sea**, however, were warned that **the devil is come down unto you** with more vengeance, **having great wrath, because he knoweth that he hath but a short time**. While not knowing the very mind of God, the Devil knows the Bible, and he knows that at this point in the tribulation, he will have only 1,260 days left. Satan's days are numbered!

12:13–14. When the dragon saw that he was cast unto the earth, he attacked **the woman** (v. 13), Israel, with added intensity. Satan hates the Jewish people, who brought forth the Savior, the Lord Jesus Christ! The woman, however, was given the **wings of a great eagle** (v. 14) to **fly into the wilderness**. Wings picture God's protective deliverance (see Exod. 19:4; Deut. 32:11–12). This flight to safety is indicated in Matthew 24:16; Mark 13:14; Luke 21:21. Many believe this hiding place could be the rock city of Petra, which was once the fortified capital of the Nabateans of Edom. Thousands of people could be hidden in Petra's canyons and rock caverns. Some speculate that the 144,000 witnessing Jews will be protected there for a time. The 144,000 will not be simply buried away in a rock fortress, however. The world will hear their testimony.

God **nourished** (v. 14) and protected the Jews **for a time, and times, and half a time** (v. 14), which refers to the last of the three and a half years of the tribulation ("a time" is one year, and "half a time" is six months). This would be the period just before the second coming of Christ.

12:15–17. Satan attempted to destroy **the woman** (v. 15) with **water as a flood**. To destroy Israel would be to thwart God's kingdom. While God will protect the Jewish people so that they will not be not completely destroyed, two-thirds will be struck down or killed (see Zech. 13:8). The surviving one-third will be preserved and will enter the kingdom at the end of the tribulation. **The earth helped the woman** by somehow absorbing the destructive **flood** that came forth from Satan's **mouth**. While the "flood" could be literal, more than likely, it is

symbolic of his attempt to destroy the Jewish people because it comes out of Satan's mouth.

John described Satan's fury with **the woman** (v. 17), the Jewish people. **The dragon was wroth ... and went to make war** with those left, **the remnant** (Greek, *tōn loipōn;* "the rest") **of her seed**. He was especially provoked by the piety of the remnant, they **which keep the commandments of God** (see 14:12), **and have the testimony** that the Lord Jesus bore, or have the testimony about Him (see 1 Cor. 2:1; 1 John 5:10). More than likely, "the commandments" refers to the instructions of the New Testament (e.g., 1 John 3:18–24; 2 John 4–6) rather than to the laws of the Mosaic covenant.

B. The Two Beasts (chap. 13)

Chapter 12 is a perfect introduction to the great revelations that come forth in chapter 13. The two beasts that appear in this chapter are the key actors on the stage of the tribulation. The "beast ... out of the sea" (v. 1) is the Antichrist, the political leader who will rule the world, and the "beast ... out of the earth" (v. 11) is the False Prophet, the religious leader who will point the nations to the Antichrist as the savior of all who dwell on the planet.

13:1–3. John **saw a beast rise up out of the sea** (v. 1). This "beast" (Greek, *thērion;* "ferocious animal," "monster"), first introduced in Revelation 11:7, is the Antichrist. The deification of the final stage of secular world power, this figure is the prophesied evil ruler who represents the Roman Empire. "The sea" often represents the nations, thus probably indicating that this beast was a Gentile. The imagery in these verses parallels that of Daniel 7:2–7. The Beast had **seven heads and ten horns** and **ten crowns**. The "ten horns" (which correspond to the ten toes of the image in Dan. 2:4) and "ten crowns" represent ten kings and their kingdoms, as in Revelation 17:12. The "seven heads" parallel the seven heads of the Dragon (see 12:3), who gave his authority and power to the Beast. Presently, the Holy Spirit, the Restrainer who "withholdeth," will move aside so that the Beast "might be revealed in his time" (2 Thess. 2:6).

All of this represents a confederation of ten king-doms headed up by one demonic personality, the Antichrist. **Upon his heads** (v. 1), the world powers under his control, was **the name of blasphemy**. This points to his opposition to Christ and to God, as prophesied in Psalm 2:2–3: "The kings of the earth set themselves, and the rulers take counsel together, against the LORD, and against his anointed saying, Let us break their bands asunder, and cast away their cords from us."

The Beast's power included the combined char-acteristics of Daniel's four beasts (see Dan. 7:4–6). He had the swiftness of a **leopard** (v. 2), like Alex-ander the Great and his Greek army; the powerful **feet of a bear**, like Persia; and the fierceness of a **lion**, like Babylon. **The dragon gave ... his power, and his seat [of prominence], and great authority** to the Beast. On earth, the Beast will appear to have the dominion of the promised Messiah, though his power will come from Satan and not God. The apostle Paul said that this "man of sin ... the son of perdition" will "be revealed in his time" (2 Thess. 2:3, 6) and that his coming "is after the working of Satan with all power and signs and lying wonders" (2 Thess. 2:9).

One of his heads (v. 3) refers to the Beast him-self, who appeared (**as it were**) to be **wounded to death**. The Beast's seemingly mortal **wound was healed**, but people instead believed he died and came back to life. Because of this "miracle," **all the world** (the entire earth) **wondered after the beast** as if he were divine (see 2 Thess. 2:4). The word "won-der" (Greek, *thaumazo*) means "to be amazed," "to be overwhelmed." As Hindson shows (*The Book of Revelation*, p. 141), the Beast's comparison to Christ is profound:

Christ	The Beast
Many diadems (19:12)	Ten diadems (13:1)
Worthy name (19:11–16)	Blasphemous names (13:1)
Causes men to worship God (1:6)	Causes men to worship Satan (13:4)

Power and throne of God (12:5)	Power and throne of Satan (13:2)
Died but lives again (1:18)	Appears to die—but his fatal wound is healed (13:3)

13:4–6. The miracle of the "resurrection" (see 13:3) of **the beast** (v. 4) made the world believe he was like God, **And they worshipped the dragon which gave power** (authority) **to him, and they wor-shipped the beast** and believed he was invincible. At this point, Satan will have achieved his diaboli-cal goal to "be like the most High" (Isa. 14:14). The world will be fooled "because they received not the love of the truth, that they might be saved. And for this cause God shall send them strong delusion, that they should believe a lie" (2 Thess. 2:10–11). **There was given unto** (v. 5) the Beast, probably by Satan, **a mouth speaking great things and blasphemies**. His power will be consolidated and most active during the final **forty and two months**, or the final half of the tribulation, after which he will be thrown into "a lake of fire burning with brimstone" (19:20).

With his time running out, the Beast blasphemed **against God** (v. 6), against **his name, and his taber-nacle**, and even against **them that dwell in heaven**. While the word "tabernacle" means "tent," here it is symbolic of God's abode in glory (see 15:5; 21:3).

13:7–8. The entire world, **all kindreds, and tongues, and nations** (v. 7) **... shall worship** (v. 8) the Beast. He "shall devour the whole earth, and shall tread it down, and break it in pieces" (Dan. 7:23), as he "exalteth himself above all that is called God" (2 Thess. 2:4). The Beast intensified his attacks against **the saints** (v. 7). And as well, at this time of the end of the tribulation, the Beast will intensify his attacks against **the saints** who are saved (v. 7), whose names are recorded in **the book of life of the Lamb slain from the foundation of the world** (for "the book of life," see discussion on 3:5; see also Exod. 32:32; Dan. 12:1). Many scholars believe that the Book of Life once contained the names of every person born but that the names of the unsaved are blotted from the record when they leave this life.

Seen together, verses 7–8 clearly show the universal extent of the Beast's government and power, as well as the form of satanic worship in the final stage of the tribulation. Only those who trust in Christ will be delivered from the judgment coming upon the world.

13:9. If any man hath an ear, let him hear is a warning for those who read the book of Revelation during the terrible tribulation period. Similar to the exhortations to the seven churches ("He that hath an ear, let him hear what the Spirit saith unto the churches," 2:7, 11, 17, 29; 3:6, 13, 22), it is an invitation to listen and to ponder what is happening. In every era, the Lord puts forth the call to salvation. The appeal is to every individual to trust Christ.

13:10. This verse is sometimes seen as difficult, but John was simply telling it like it is. Things will go on with some being taken **into captivity** and some being **killed with the sword**. The verse "stresses the inevitability of persecution and death for the faithful.... It invited the faithful to recognize that the actions of this false Christ have been decreed by God.... The close of v. 10 names the personal qualities needed to sustain believers in the face of harsh treatment" (Thomas, *Revelation 8–22*, p. 168). The Beast's days of power are limited. Therefore, **the saints** are called to **patience** (Greek, *hypomonē*), meaning "steadfastness," "endurance." The Lord wanted the saints to know that He was moving to a just retribution. They had suffered to the point of martyrdom, yet their **faith** caused them to cling to Christ's promises and the hope of His return to right the wrongs of earth. "Saints" describes the position of those who trust Christ; they are "the holy ones," "the saints" (Greek, *tōn hagiōn*), because Christ is holy.

13:11–13. John **beheld another beast coming up out of the earth** (v. 11). This second "beast" (Greek, *thērion*; "ferocious animal," "monster") is later described as "the false prophet" (19:20; 20:10). His geographic origin is not stated, but this beast was earthly, not heavenly. Though he appeared to be a meek **lamb**, he was aggressive; **he had two horns**. He also **spake as a dragon**, meaning he had certain qualities and powers that come from Satan. This second beast, the False Prophet, represents a religious leader who will make the world think that the first beast, the Antichrist, is divine.

Here some see a parallel with the doctrine of the Trinity. Satan takes the place of God the Father; the Antichrist takes the place of Jesus Christ, the Son of God; and the False Prophet causes men to worship the Antichrist, as the Holy Spirit causes Christians to worship Christ. This is Satan's final attempt to substitute a false religion for the true faith in Christ (see Walvoord, "Revelation," p. 962).

The second beast had power like **the first beast** (v. 12). The world **worship[ed] the first beast** because they were fooled by the **deadly wound [that] was healed**. The False Prophet had power to do **great wonders** (v. 13) and made **fire come down from heaven on earth in the sight of men**. It must be remembered that Satan can impart to those whom he controls miraculous works, such as the powers the Egyptian magicians and priests showed before Moses (see Exod. 7:11–22). Such demonic power is real. No wonder the world will follow after the Beast!

13:14–15. The trickery of the False Prophet **deceiveth [all] on the earth by ... miracles** (Greek, *ta sēmeia*; "the signs"; v. 14) performed before the Beast. An **image** (Greek, *eikona*) is constructed in order that the entire world might honor the Beast and submit to his authority. "This last false religious leader will try the same old trick to get mankind to worship a man rather than the true God!" (Custer, *Patmos to Paradise*, p. 152). What so fascinated the world was that the Beast **had the wound by a sword, and did live**. The False Prophet **had power to give** (v. 15) "spirit" (Greek, *pneuma*; here translated **life**), or animation, to **the image** but certainly could not impart actual "life" (Greek, *bios*). Through some form of deception, however, **the image** could **both speak, and cause that as many as would not worship the image of the beast should be killed**. Since Satan cannot give power or life to an inanimate object, this likely will be achieved through an *impression* of "aliveness" that is mechanically contrived to fool all upon the earth. Some have suggested that a combination of natural and supernatural powers will be used to make the Beast's image appear to live.

13:16–18. People from all classes and every social status submitted to **receive a mark** (Greek, *charagma*; v. 16) **[on] their right hand, or [on] their foreheads**, to identify their loyalty and compliance to the authority of **the beast** (v. 17) and his government. No one could **buy or sell** without the identification of the Beast's **number** or **name** on their person. Apparently, the great majority of the world will worship the Beast and his image. Laser technology has been developed to scan identification marks instantly and is already being used in some cases to prove one's identity, financial viability, and so on.

Here is wisdom (v. 18) seems to indicate that the apostle John expected that those living during the tribulation would read this book and then be able to verify the Beast's identity. His number is **Six hundred threescore and six**, or 666. This is **the number of a man**, not of a divine being, who would generally be confirmed by the number of perfection, the number seven. Some see the number as gematria, a number that conjures up a hidden and secret identification. Over the generations, there have been many attempts to point to some individual, whether past, present, or future, who might meet the 666 criteria. As yet, however, the puzzle escapes a solution. The identification of the Beast remains for those living during the great tribulation.

C. The Lamb and the 144,000 (14:1–5)

Here the scene returns to heaven. John received a vision of the Lamb standing on Mount Zion with the 144,000 Jewish witnesses. God had sealed this group to serve Him on earth during the tribulation (see 7:1–8). The sealing protected them from the wrath of God but not from the wrath of Satan and the Beast. "These are the same 144,000 as in chapter 7,... who will experience martyrdom because of their refusal to worship the beast (13:15). They are a special group as 14:4 indicates" (Thomas, *Revelation 8–22*, p. 192). There are several theories about John's second vision of the 144,000 witnesses: (1) Mount Zion is the hill in Jerusalem and the 144,000 are there

with Christ when He begins His earthly millennial reign; (2) Mount Zion is here a heavenly designation for the residence of the 144,000 at this juncture in the tribulation; (3) Mount Zion is a projection of the 144,000 with Christ in the millennial Jerusalem, while verses 2–5 picture that they are in heaven at this point in the tribulation, as are those who were martyred on earth. This last theory seems plausible, as expressed by Thomas (*Revelation 8–22*, p. 192): "They are the vanguard who bear the brunt of the struggle against the beast and pay the price with their own lives." God apparently lifted the protection that was over the 144,000 when their ministry was completed.

14:1. Mount Sion is an actual hill in Jerusalem that was the residence of the kings of Israel. It was a pre-Israelite city that David captured (see 2 Sam. 5:7) and established as his capital. Later it became symbolic of Jerusalem itself, and even of all of Israel and the Holy Land. After Christ's return and millennial reign, a heavenly Jerusalem (see Heb. 12:22–24), the eternal dwelling place of God and His people (see Gal. 4:26), will come down to the new earth (see Rev. 21:2–3). If this is the heavenly Mount Zion, then the 144,000 are there with the **Lamb**. Or the scene could be the millennial Mount Zion during Christ's reign. The 144,000 had the **Father's name** noticeably **written [on] their foreheads** for all to see.

14:2–3. John **heard a voice from heaven** (v. 2), as one voice but with the command of **many waters**, or as the "rushing waters" of a mountain waterfall. He also heard, as if one voice, **harpers** making music **with their harps**. This worshipful scene in glory is a chorus and a symphony of praise to God for His imminent final victory. The musicians accompanied the **new song** (v. 3; see 5:9) being sung **before the throne [of God]), and before the four beasts** (four angelic beings; see discussions on 4:6, 8)**, and the elders**. No one else shared the experiences of the 144,000. They alone were able to understand and sing the new song.

14:4–5. These men lived as **virgins** (sexually pure; v. 4) in that they remained holy amidst the defiling pagan influences. They were faithful to **follow**

the Lamb whithersoever he goeth. They did not live out their own will but faithfully obeyed Christ. They were redeemed out of the world, being the firstfruits unto God, and to the Lamb. "Firstfruits" implies that they were converted Jews who preceded the many others who would turn to Christ at the His coming (see Zech. 12:10; Rom. 11:15, 26–27). In their earthly living, they had spoken no guile (v. 5) and now stood without fault before the throne of God. "Without fault" (Greek, *amōmos*, describing a sacrificial animal without defect) shows how morally superior they were.

D. The Harvest of the Earth (14:6–20)

These verses show that even as things get progressively worse on earth, the gospel will continue to be proclaimed worldwide. Here is a mixture of grace and judgment. The Lord will intensify His wrath, yet the gospel will still be available. While these verses have to do with the tribulation, the gospel of salvation by faith in Christ remains the same.

14:6–7. John saw another angel (v. 6), like none before, fly in the midst of heaven, preaching the everlasting gospel unto[all] that dwell on the earth. While this message may have included the "gospel" (Greek, *euangelisai*, "good news") of the coming kingdom of the Messiah, it was a personal message, as reflected in verse 7. "It is everlasting in the sense that it is ageless, not for any specific period" (Walvoord, *The Revelation of Jesus Christ*, p. 217). Some scholars believe that this was not a message about personal salvation but rather an announcement of God's judgment only—the good news that God at last was about to deal with the world in righteousness and establish His sovereign rule over the entire world.

Part of the angel's message was, Fear God, and give glory to him (v. 7). The hour of his judgment is come means that an earthly and final judgment was about to be accomplished. The sense is that it is but a short leap from these verses to the arrival of Christ from glory to establish His kingdom, though it seems to read that it is about to start right here. Christ's coming and the battle of Armageddon would

bring final defeat to the power of the Beast, the False Prophet, and the nations of the earth that joined forces with them to defeat Israel (see 19:11–21).

14:8. There followed another angel with the announcement that Babylon is fallen. This announcement is prophetic of the events described in chapter 17. Ancient Babylon was the fountain from which all polytheism came. It was founded by Nimrod, who was the first great rebel against God and more than simply a hunter of animals. Nimrod was the first great tyrant, a might one, a mighty hunter before the Lord (see Gen. 10:8–10). His name means "let us revolt." "He established a thoroughly autocratic, imperialistic, despotic system of tyrannical government … back of which stands Satan in all his rage against God" (Stigers, *Genesis*, p. 125). The city he founded, Babel, was an apostate civilization (see Gen. 11:1–9). Since it was prophesied that historic Babylon would be destroyed and never again be inhabited (see Isa. 13; 14; Jer. 50–51; Zechariah 5), "MYSTERY, BABYLON THE GREAT" (Rev. 17:5) appears to be something different. This civilization seems to consist of a mighty technological force driving a global economy. All signs in the book of Revelation point to the fact that it is pagan Rome, papal Rome, or a future revived Rome—but it is Rome (see chaps. 17–18; and Hindson, *The Book of Revelation*, p. 156).

14:9–11. A third angel followed (v. 9) the first two and issued a warning to those who worship the beast and his image, and receive his mark (see 13:18). During this terrible time on earth, people will have only two choices: (1) resist the Beast, trust God, and possibly be martyred or (2) be loyal to the Beast and face the wrath of God. All who receive the Beast's mark shall drink of the wine of the wrath of God, which is poured out … into the cup of his indignation (v. 10). They will face eternal torment along with Satan, the demon world, and all unsaved people. The smoke of their torment (v. 11) will be unending, for ever and ever, continuing day and night. The torment will be like being cast into a pit of volcanic fire and brimstone (v. 10). This terrible scene will be witnessed by God's holy angels and the

Lamb. Such are the consequences of worshiping the Beast and of receiving his mark.

The teaching of such eternal punishment is rejected by annihilationists, evolutionists, and liberal theologians who deny judgment over against grace. God exhibited His grace and mercy when He sent His Son to die for sinners. For those who do not believe, however, the only thing left is eternal judgment (see 20:11-15).

14:12-13. The patience of the saints (v. 12) seems to be a reminder to those believers in the tribulation to walk before a hostile world by **keep[ing] the commandments of God** and holding on to **the faith of Jesus.** Resistance against the Beast will be impossible! While people may think they have the option to resist the Beast, martyrdom awaits those who attempt to defy him. Walking in the integrity of trust will be the only option for believers. **Blessed are the dead which die in the Lord from henceforth** (v. 13) is the second beatitude in the book of Revelation (see discussion on 1:3).

14:14-16. The Son of man (v. 14) is the Messiah, the Lord Jesus Himself (see 1:13; Dan. 7:13; Mark 8:31). Matthew used this title more than twenty-five times. He wore **a golden crown** as His victory wreath, because He would soon ascend to earth to rule and to reign. That the Messiah was still seated in heaven shows He was still with His Father on His thone (see Ps. 110:1-3). **A sharp sickle** would be used to reap **the harvest** (v. 15) of the world, because **the earth is ripe** (Greek, *exēranthē*), become "withered," "dry," "ready for harvest." "The harvest" refers to the final judgment, the "reaping" of the world for its sins, which was soon to take place. The command to begin the harvest came from an **angel [who] came out of the temple** in heaven. The Lord God had ordered the final judgment to begin. Some believe "the harvest" refers to the gathering of the saints, but this is doubtful because people will be saved throughout the tribulation. From heaven, Christ, **he that sat on the cloud** (v. 16), began the judgment.

14:17-19. Another angel (v. 17) came forth, **also having a sharp sickle.** In contrast to the sickle of 14:14, this probably refers to a smaller sickle for cutting grapevines, since **gather the clusters** (v. 18) and **her grapes are fully ripe** are analogies about the harvesting of grapes. **And the angel ... gathered the vine of the earth, and cast it into the great winepress of the wrath of God** (v. 19). Grapes were trampled in a violent manner in the winepress, producing a flow of red grape juice. "The use of angels to assist the harvest of the earth is now stated explicitly in verse 17.... The figure of divine judgment as a harvest is here enlarged" (Walvoord, *The Revelation of Jesus Christ,* p. 222). These events are fulfilled in Revelation 19:15 as part of the battle of Armageddon.

14:20. This scene gives a preview of the final battle of Armageddon (described more fully in 19:14-21), which will take place **without** (outside) **the city** of Jerusalem, probably to the north, at the place known today as the plain of Jezreel, located near the hill of Megiddo. **Blood** will flow up to **the horse bridles** for a distance of 1,600 **furlongs,** about 200 miles. There have been battles in the past in which the trampling of the horses over infantry splattered blood up to the bridles. That there will be such a terrible slaughter in the last days is prophesied in Scripture (see Isa. 63:1-3; Dan. 11:40-45).

X. The Seven Vials (chaps. 15-16)

These chapters focus on the chronology of events leading up to the second coming of Christ (chap. 19) and introduce "the seven last plagues" (15:1), the divine judgments that will precede the Lord's coming. The basic progression of the judgments is an unfolding of the seven seals (6:1-17; 8:1), the seventh seal introducing the seven trumpets (8:1-9:21; 11:15-19), and the seventh trumpet introducing the seven vials, or "bowls," of wrath. Chronologically, chapter 19 comes after chapter 16, while chapters 17-18 present an interlude about Babylon the Harlot. The fall of Babylon has already been announced in Revelation 14:8. Its doom has already been certified. "The final and dramatic action of the Apocalypse is about to begin (here in this chapter). In eight brief verses, chapter 15 sets the stage for the final drama. The pouring out of the seven bowls (KJV—'vials') of God's wrath (chap. 16) culminates in the fall of Babylon (chaps. 17–18) and the return of Christ to earth (chap. 19)" (Hindson, *Revelation*, p. 161).

A. Introduction: The Song of Moses and the Seven Angels with the Seven Plagues (chap. 15)

This chapter comes to the point quickly. It gives a summary of the final events of judgment about to fall on the earth. This exclusively heavenly scene shows the preparations for the horrible final judgments upon the earth, but it also gives God the glory for His justice in ending the arrogance and rebellion of humanity.

15:1–2. John **saw another sign in heaven, great and marvellous** (Greek, *mega kai thaumaston*; v. 1). **Seven angels** prepared to administer **the seven last plagues** of **the wrath of God.** The apostle **saw as it were** (comparative language) **a sea of glass mingled with fire** (v. 2). "A sea of glass" (a glassy sea, or "glassy [or] crystal"; see discussion on 4:6) is an illustration of the tranquility and peace of heaven. It represents the splendor and glory of the Lord on His throne. "The sea of glass is an emblem of 'the splendor and majesty of God on His throne that sets Him apart from all His creation, a separation stemming from His purity and absolute holiness, which He shares with no one else'" (Thomas, *Revelation 8–22*, p. 232). The sea was "mingled with fire," however, which portends judgment. In this scene, John saw the final **victory** of those who had refused the **mark** of the Beast. They were singing praises to the Lord, **having the harps of God.**

15:3–4. The martyred redeemed **sing the song of Moses … and the song of the Lamb** (v. 3), which may represent one hymn, though some scholars think they are specific and distinct songs. The word "song" (Greek, *ōdē*) has a definite article, suggesting that two songs are in view. has often been identified with Exodus 15, though some have suggested it relates also to Deuteronomy 32. "All nations shall come and worship before thee" would refer to the millennial reign of the Messiah and is a quote from Psalm 86:9. Exodus 15:17 says that God "shalt bring [His

people, Israel] in, and plant them in the mountain of thine inheritance," and Deuteronomy 32:43 says that God "will avenge the blood of his servants." **God Almighty** is described in similar wording as the "sign" in 15:1: **Great and marvellous** (Greek, *megala kai thaumasta*). **Thou King of saints** may refer to God or to Christ: "Now unto the King eternal, immortal, invisible, the only wise God, be honour and glory for ever and ever. Amen" (1 Tim. 1:17).

15:5–6. John then saw another heavenly vision of **the temple of the tabernacle** ("tent"; v. 5) being **opened** (see 11:19). This imagery is of the Lord's dwelling place among the Israelites during the forty years of wandering (see Exod. 40:34–35). The word **testimony** is a reference to the two tablets of the Law that Moses brought down from Mount Sinai (see Exod. 32:15; 38:21; Deut. 10:5).

The seven angels (v. 6) who were about to minister judgment on the earth appeared in priestly garments, **clothed in pure and white linen, and having their breasts girded with golden girdles** (waist or chest censures). The purity of the angels' garments shows the purity of their task, which was to bring holiness to earth (see Thomas, *Revelation 8–22*, p. 232). The bride of Christ will be similarly clothed when she comes as Christ's army to reign with Him (see 19:8, 14).

15:7–8. One of the four beasts ("living creatures"; see discussions on 4:6, 8) **gave the seven angels seven golden vials full of the wrath of God** (v. 7), to be poured out on earth. The picture is both graphic and terrible, as if seven bowls of scalding liquid were to be poured down on humanity below. The reader is reminded, however, that such judgment was due. The vials were golden, showing that they came from the temple of the righteous God in heaven, and He is the eternal God, **who liveth for ever and ever.**

That **the temple was filled with smoke** (v. 8) is symbolic of the **power** and **the glory of God** (see Exod. 40:34; 1 Kings 8:10–11; Ezek. 44:4). No one in heaven could approach Him as such awful judgment went forth upon the earth. Ezekiel saw this same manifestation of God's glory depart from the temple just before the Babylonian captivity (see Ezek. 10:1–22; 11:22–23).

Taken all together, verses 5–8 show a terrible and frightening scene of impending divine wrath and judgment coming down on a wicked world. The terrible nature of these judgments fully justify this ominous introduction.

B. First Vial: Ugly and Painful Sores (16:1–2)

16:1–2. A great (Greek, *megalēs*) **voice out of the temple** (v. 1) instructed **the seven angels** to begin **pour[ing] out ... the wrath of God upon the earth**. When **the first [angel] poured out his vial** (v. 2), the inhabitants of earth were stricken with a **noisome and grievous sore**, but this judgment was selective in that it infected only those who had taken the Beast's **mark** and **worshipped his image**. The infections are similar to the boils and abscesses of the sixth Egyptian plague (see Exod. 9:9–11; see also Job 2:7–8:13). The afflictions now became very personal.

C. Second Vial: The Sea Turns to Blood (16:3)

16:3. The second angel poured out his vial, and the sea became polluted, as with **the blood of a dead man: and every living** (Greek, *zōēs*) **soul** (Greek, *psychē*) in the oceans **died**; that is, every living organism was killed off. Such descriptions make it clear that the events of the tribulation will be worldwide in scope and not simply some localized happenings. This horrible scene pictures the death of all biological life in the oceans.

D. Third Vial: Rivers and Springs of Water Become Blood (16:4–7)

16:4. When **the third angel poured out his vial**, the judgment of the second vial was extended. **The rivers and [the source] of waters** became polluted with **blood**.

16:5–7. The Lord turned the waters to blood in response to the shedding of **the blood of saints and prophets** (v. 6). From the altar in heaven, **the angel of the waters** (v. 5) declared this judgment just (see 16:7; 15:3). Those who were in allegiance with the

Beast and who worshiped his image had killed believers; thus, the angel continued, **thou hast given them blood to drink; for they are worthy** (v. 6). "Worthy" (Greek, *axios*) refers to the fact that those who took the lives of the saints are deserving of punishment for their crimes (see 3:4). The punishment fit the crime of the murderers (see Isa. 49:26). **Another** (v. 7) angel called forth from **the altar**, testifying that the **Lord God Almighty** is **true and righteous** in His **judgments**.

E. Fourth Vial: The Sun Scorches People with Fire (16:8–9)

16:8. When **the fourth angel poured out his vial**, judgment was focused on **the sun; and power was given unto him ... to scorch** the earth's inhabitants **with fire**. It has been suggested that one of the means God will use to bring this about is the destruction of the ozone layer that encircles the earth. Ozone retards the sun's radiation, and if it is depleted, the sun's scorching would bring about death. Another possibility is that this judgment will be accomplished by monstrous sun flares.

16:9. Despite the **great heat** generated, earth's inhabitants still **blasphemed the name of God** (see 16:11, 21), the one who **hath power over these plagues**. Even with the terrible plagues being poured down on them, people still refused to **give him glory**. They refused to "change the mind"; **they repented not**.

F. Fifth Vial: Darkness (16:10–11)

16:10–11. The fifth angel poured out his vial (v. 10) at the place of authority for **the beast**, his **seat** ("throne"), or center of rule, **and his kingdom was full of darkness**. This "darkness" could refer to a climatological event, or it may refer to that fact that the Beast's rule over the world was collapsing, and any remaining "civilization" was no more. The inhabitants of the earth **gnawed their tongues for pain**. Gnawing one's tongue is the greatest expression of physical pain. **Because of their pains and their sores** (v. 11; see 16:2), humanity continued to blaspheme God, and they **repented not of their deeds**. This is the last reference to repentance (see 2:21; 9:21). People could have repented during these trials, but instead, they simply continued to blaspheme God (see 16:21).

G. Sixth Vial: The Euphrates River Dries Up (16:12–16)

16:12–14. When **the sixth angel poured out his vial … the great river Euphrates … was dried up** (v. 12). The Euphrates River is the water boundary between the Holy Land and Asia, to the east, and is mentioned often in Scripture (see, e.g., Gen. 15:18; Deut. 1:7; 11:24; Josh. 1:4). Isaiah also prophesied that the river will dry up (see Isa. 11:15). "History frequently refers to the great hindrance the Euphrates has been between the peoples living east of it and those living west of it. But in the time of the pouring out of the sixth bowl of judgment, this river is to be mysteriously smitten and dried up, that the kings from the sunrising may have an easy passage for their armies in coming to join the great infernal crusade against the Lamb" (Seiss, *The Apocalypse*, p. 377). The way will be open for **the kings of the east**. These rulers and their armies were part of the invasion forces that fight against Christ in the final battle (see 19:11–21). In the past, the Euphrates was a formidable separation for large armies; in some places, it is two-thirds of a mile wide.

Satanic influence caused the kings of the east and their armies to cross the Euphrates to attack Israel. John saw **unclean spirits like frogs** (v. 13) come out of the mouths of **the dragon**, **the beast**, and **the false prophet**. Additional leaders and nations, **the kings of the earth and of the whole world** (v. 14), were wooed into the Middle East. The showdown, the final **battle of that great day**, will take place at Armageddon (see 16:16). The "frogs" **are the spirits of devils** who work **miracles** and seduce the world to its doom (see 1 Tim. 4:1; James 3:15).

16:15–16. In the middle of John's vision, the Lord called out, **Behold** (v. 15), and warned that He will **come as a thief**. This is a reminder for those on earth during the tribulation that His coming draws near. There is some question whether this is a salva-

tion verse or a reminder to believers in the tribulation to be ready for His arrival. **Blessed is he that … keepeth his garments** is the third beatitude in the book of Revelation (see discussion on 1:3). It seems to be a reminder to remain morally clean in a terribly immoral world. The "garments" of salvation symbolize the life and testimony of the saved (see 19:8).

The nations finally **gathered … together** (v. 16) at the hill of Megiddo (**Armageddon**) for the final conflict (see 14:20; 19:19). Though seemingly localized to the north of Jerusalem, this final conflict will have global consequences. The whole world will be rocked by the great devastation that will be wrought by this battle (see 19:17-21).

H. Seventh Vial: A Tremendous Earthquake (16:17–21)

16:17–18. The **seventh angel poured out** the seventh and final **vial** (v. 17), or "bowl." **A great voice** from the heavenly **throne** of God called out, **It is done** (Greek, *gegonen*; perfect tense), "It has become." The very last chapter of the tribulation had arrived. It was accompanied by **voices, and thunders, and lightnings; and … a great earthquake, such as was not since men were upon the earth** (v. 18). Christ spoke of this time, when there will be "earthquakes in divers places" (Matt. 24:7). Isaiah also wrote, "The LORD maketh the earth empty, and maketh it waste, and turneth it upside down" (Isa. 24:1). When the nations come "against Jerusalem to battle … Then shall the LORD go forth, and fight" for His people (Zech. 14:2–3). The Messiah's feet will touch the Mount of Olives (see Zech. 14:4), and multitudes will "flee … from before the earthquake" (Zech. 14:5).

16:19–21. **The great city** (v. 19) is Jerusalem, "which spiritually is called Sodom and Egypt, where also our Lord was crucified" (11:8). The topography shifted, and the city **was divided into three parts**. This is part of God's judgment upon His own people in the end of the age (see Jer. 30:11; Zech. 14:14). The Lord reminded Israel that in the last days, "I will correct thee in measure, and will not leave thee altogether unpunished" (Jer. 30:11). **The cities** of other countries also **fell**, and God remembered also the **great Babylon** and made her drink **the wine** of His fierce **wrath**. "Wrath" (Greek, *orgēs*) is a strong word for God's rage at sin and is often related to *thymos* (**fierceness**) as part of His divine anger and marks Babylon especially as an object of God's judgment. Babylon, the founder of false religion, was ripe for downfall (see 17:16; 18:8); its final collapse is narrated in 19:18–21.

And every island (v. 20) shifted, **and the mountains** fell. This is similar to the movement of the islands and mountains mentioned in 6:14, though with a more violent conclusion. Again, this is a reminder of tribulation descriptions in Isaiah 24:6, where it is written, "The curse devoured the earth." **Great hail**(stones) weighing about 100 pounds each (**a talent**) fell upon the earth. Even this terrible judgment did not bring repentance; rather, humanity continued to blaspheme God **because of the plague of the hail**. This must be one of the most awful judgments because John the apostle wrote, **the plague thereof was exceeding great**. The word "exceeding" (Greek, *sphodra*) can be translated "vehemently violent."

XI. Babylon: The Great Prostitute (17:1–19:5)

Central to the seventh vial judgment is the fall of Babylon. This event was first mentioned in 14:14–20. While it sometimes seems as if God forgets, He remembers full well the evil, persecution, and oppression against His own. Babylon will fall for her religious immorality and for her persecution of the saints (17:6). A detailed account of her demise is presented in chapters 17–18.

Any interpretation of "Babylon" is difficult, but chapter 17 presents Babylon as an ecclesiastical or spiritual entity, and chapter 18 sees her as a political and economic entity. The Babylon of the last days will be a center of commerce, enterprise, and wealth.

A. Babylon Described (chap. 17)

That John used the word "MYSTERY" (v. 5) to describe Babylon suggests that he was witnessing something about Babylon that neither ancient Babylon nor its geographic site gives meaning to. He was directing the reader to look deeper to find something new, something figurative rather than literal. This is not to say that the events described here are fiction or allegory but that the imagery projects something not seen before.

17:1–2. One of the seven angels which had the seven vials (v. 1; see chap. 16) called John over, **Come hither**, to see the final **judgment of the great whore** (Greek, *pornē*). That she sat **upon many waters** shows her great influence upon the nations (see 17:15). She had **committed fornication** (Greek, *porneuō*; v. 2) with the earth's **kings**. Spiritual and religious adultery was at the heart of the apostasy of ancient Israel (see Ezekiel 16, 23 and all of Hosea). She had fornicated not only with the rulers of earth but also with **the inhabiters of earth**. All had become **drunk with the wine of her fornication**. This graphic picture is of an orgy in which all restraints are thrown to the wind. All rationality and civility had been cast aside.

17:3–5. The apostle was **carried ... away in the spirit** (v. 3) to witness another vision about the **woman**, Babylon. In an orgiastic gesture, she rode on the back of **a scarlet coloured beast**, who is the Antichrist, the world dictator of 13:1. The **ten horns** represent ten world powers or nations, as defined in 17:12. The **seven heads** represent seven prominent rulers of the revived Roman Empire. This empire was assembled and controlled by the Antichrist in chapter 13. When he came to power, he came up out of the sea (the nations) controlling the seven heads and ten horns (13:1). Here in chapter 17, this flashback is given to show how Babylon fit into the scheme of things.

The whore **was arrayed** (v. 4) in royal attire. She is seen as rich, elegant, and queenly in status. The **golden cup in her hand** parallels the imagery of Jeremiah 51:7–8. John imposed on this scene the diabolic features of the ancient Babylonian system, the ancient enemy of God's people Israel. This great harlot is called **THE MOTHER OF HARLOTS** (v. 5). While she looked regal in her dress, the cup she held was **full of abominations and filthiness of her fornication** (v. 4).

17:6-7. **The woman [was] drunken with the blood of the saints, and with the blood of the martyrs of Jesus** (v. 6). The woman, the Beast, and the kings of the revived Roman Empire will make war with the Lamb and those who follow Him (see 17:14). The woman and her false religious system will have world influence. In ancient times, she was the mother goddess under the names of Ishtar, Ashtar, Astarte, Aphrodite, and Venus. Her revived system will hate those who worship Christ and will kill many who trust in Him.

John wrote, **When I saw her, I wondered with great admiration** (v. 6). In context here, **admiration** (Greek, *thauma*) has the thought "to be amazed, astonished." John is not admiring the woman in a positive sense but rather he is startled by the evil she is bringing against the saints. **The angel** (v. 7) asked him, Why **didst thou marvel?** and proceeded to tell him **the mystery of** this harlot, **and of the beast that carrieth her.**

17:8-11. The remainder of the chapter consists of the angel's explanation of "the mystery of the woman, and of the beast that carrieth her" (17:7). **The beast** (v. 8) whom she was riding **shall ascend out of the bottomless pit** (Greek, *abyssos*; see 9:1). This personality is connected to both the sea (the nations; see 13:1) and the pit (the realm of the confined but later released demons). The authority and the power behind the Beast will be satanic (see 13:4). All evidence points to the fact that he will be human and not a supernatural demonic individual, though he will be greatly influenced by the powers of the underworld. John was quick to remind the reader that the Beast's end will be **perdition**, where, along with the Devil and the False Prophet, he will forever abide and "shall be tormented day and night" (20:10). The world will be fascinated (**shall wonder**) at the power of **the beast**. They are the ones **whose names were not written in the book of life from the foundation of the world** (see discussions on 3:5; 13:8; 20:12, 15; 21:27).

Here is the mind which hath wisdom. Believers living during the tribulation period will find evidence as to who **the seven heads are** (v. 9); they **are seven mountains, on which the woman sitteth.** In his commentary on Revelation, the church father Victorinus said that the seven "hills" were identified with the seven hills of Rome. A closer look, however, seems to point to the **seven kings** (or "kingdoms"; v. 10). From John's vantage point, five of these kingdoms had come and gone. One was still present, but **the other is not yet come.** When it arrives, it will not last long. Walvoord argues that the five past kingdoms are: Egypt, Assyria, Babylon, Persia, and Greece (*The Revelation of Jesus Christ*, pp. 250-54). The "old" Roman Empire was still present in John's day. A seventh kingdom will arise, however, and bring forth **the eighth** (v. 11) kingdom, that of the Antichrist.

17:12-14. **The ten horns** (v. 12) and **ten kings** refer to "contemporaneous kings who are heads of the countries which will form the original alliance in the Middle East that will support the future world ruler" (Walvoord, "Revelation," p. 972). They will **receive** (political) **power** for a short time: **one hour.** They will move with **one mind** (v. 13) and agree to **give their power** to support **the beast.** They **shall make war with the Lamb** (v. 14), but in the end, they will be defeated, because **he is Lord of lords, and King of kings.** This phrase is similar to descriptions of God the Father (see Deut. 10:17; see also 1 Tim. 6:15; Rev. 19:16). **They that are with him are called, and chosen, and faithful** seems to describe those under Christ's protection at the end of the tribulation and is a statement of God's sovereignty in divine protection.

17:15-18. That **the whore sitteth** (v. 15) over the **nations** means that for a time she will govern or control all of the **peoples** of the world. The major powers of the earth (**the ten horns**; v. 16), however, will turn on her to **make her desolate and naked.** They will consume her and **burn her with fire.** The false apostate religious system, or "church," will be brought down for all the world to witness. While the true church of the Lord Jesus will be taken in the rapture (see 1 Thess. 4:13-18), apostate Christendom, which the whore represents, will continue to the end of the tribulation. During that time, there will be a certain measure of religious freedom, for the Jews will reestablish their worship and their sacrifices (see Dan. 9:27).

God's **will** (v. 17) will be at work in these events. Babylon the whore and her influence are doomed. God **hath put in [the] hearts** of the international powers to **give their kingdom unto the beast.** Verse 18 confirms that the whore is something besides a restoration of an ancient nation like Babylon. **The woman ... is that great city, which reigneth over the kings of the earth** (v. 18). That city is probably Rome.

B. The Fall of Babylon (chap. 18)

Chapter 18 begins with, "And after these things," which shows a progression from the events of chapter 17. John saw "another angel" (v. 1), distinct from the angel of 17:1. The context of chapter 18 shows that here Babylon is seen in its political and economic character rather than its religious character. The Babylon of Revelation is the prophesied new Rome. It is a revision of the ancient Roman Empire in a politically and economically revived Europe. Not since the days of the Roman Empire has there been a truly peaceful, united Europe.

18:1. Another **angel [came] from heaven, having great power; and the earth was lightened with his glory.** This is one of the most powerful angels of God, though he is not Christ, as some have assumed. In poetic fashion, he described the final stage of the destruction of the whore.

18:2–4. The angel **cried ... Babylon the great is fallen, is fallen** (v. 2). The double phrase is for certainty and for emphasis that Babylon's influence was over. As in the demise of Babylon of old, the city had become a place of death and even of evil (see Isa. 13:20–22). It is as if the entire demonic and spirit world had come to mourn her fall. The city is **the hold** ("prison") **of every foul spirit** where the fallen angels, or evil spirits, are gathered. **Unclean, hateful,** and **bird** often symbolize evil spirits (see Isa. 34:11–15; Matt. 13:32). Babylon had been given over to demons as a judgment because of the evil of the inhabitants.

All nations (v. 3) and **the kings of the earth** had partaken of her **wine of ... fornication** and had even **committed fornication with her.** While they had done this in a spiritual or religious way before (17:2), **the merchants of the earth** were now doing this by indulging in **the abundance of her delicacies** (Greek, *strēnos;* "sumptuousness"). **Another voice** (v. 4), that of an angel, called the redeemed who had survived the tribulation to **Come out of her ... that ye be not partakers of her sins, and ... of her plagues** of judgment.

18:5–11. For her sins have reached unto heaven (v. 5), the voice continued, **and God hath remembered her iniquities.** Her **Reward** (v. 6) of judgment was to be **double according to** all the evil she had done. Her **cup** of wrath would be filled **double.** As much as she had **glorified herself, and lived deliciously** (v. 7), that **much torment and sorrow** would be given to her. She saw herself as **a queen** and not as a deserted **widow,** but now **her plagues** (v. 8) would **come in one day,** with **death, and mourning, and famine ... For strong is the Lord God who judgeth her.** Those who had **committed fornication** (v. 9) with her, **the kings of the earth,** would witness **the smoke of her burning** and would **bewail** and **lament** her fall.

Standing afar off (v. 10), possibly **for ... fear** that the destruction coming upon her might affect them, the kings would exclaim, **Alas, alas, that great city** is judged **in one hour.** This seems to be a literal one hour (see 18:17, 19), which explains the people's shock over the suddenness of the city's fall. God's wrath would fall quickly on **that mighty city.** Recognizing that they would no longer benefit from her commerce and her trade, **the merchants of the earth** (v. 11) would also bemoan the city's demise.

18:12–16. The merchandise (v. 12) of the city's trade is listed. The list includes the most valuable of wealth: precious metals, gems, luxurious cloth, and other fineries; manufactured goods that are crafted, mined, and concocted, such as **odours, and ointments ... wine, and oil** (v. 13); fruit products, animals for food, and even manufactured mechanical items, such as **chariots.** Some have argued that such descriptions make it impossible that modern trade is indicated. It must be remembered, however, not only that in Scripture such goods are often described as the ancients would have known them but also that there is a future extrapolation and application here because the events have to do with far-off prophecy.

18:17–20. The **shipmaster[s] ... and sailers** (v. 17) who traded with Babylon saw **the smoke of her burning** (v. 18) from a distance. Interestingly, the city of Rome is only forty miles or less from the west coast of the Mediterranean Sea, whereas ancient Babylon (in modern Iraq) is two hundred miles from the Persian Gulf. The Tiber River runs from Rome to the ocean. The world could not believe what was happening. Four times those who profited from her called her the "mighty city" (18:10), and the "great city" (18:16, 18, 19). They lamented her fall because they had benefited so greatly from her influence, for they **were made rich all that had ships in the sea by reason of her costliness** (v. 19). **Heaven, and [the] holy apostles and prophets** (v. 20) of the past were called to **Rejoice ... for God hath avenged you on her** (see 19:2; Luke 11:49).

18:21–24. Another angel, **a mighty angel ... took up ... a great millstone, and cast it into the sea** (v. 21). A "millstone" is a large grinding stone (also called a "donkey stone"), turned by a donkey or oxen, for milling grain. Extremely heavy, such a stone would doom anyone lashed to such a heavy object (see Mark 9:42). **Thus with violence shall that great city Babylon be thrown down**. This graphic description vividly portrays the finality of the fate of **Babylon** the whore. The angel proclaimed that the city **shall be found no more at all**. There would be no more **musicians** (v. 22) to orchestrate her glory and **no craftsman** to manufacture her wares. **The sound of a millstone** producing grain would be heard no longer. **The light** (v. 23) of the city would go out, and the joyful voices at wedding feasts **shall be heard no more at all in thee**. The prominent **merchants** of Babylon, who were counted among **the great men of the earth**, would be gone.

Babylon's greatest deception was her **sorceries** (v. 23), by which **all nations** of the world were seduced. "Sorceries" (Greek, *pharmakeia*) refers to hallucinogens used in incantations to the gods, the demons. This demonic worship has to do with the spiritual "fornication" so often mentioned in the indictment against the woman. Verse 23 is a reminder of how powerful she was. Her evil influence was worldwide. Moreover, she was responsible for **the blood of prophets, and of saints** (v. 24; see 17:6). Christ referred to this when He warned Jews who would become believers during the tribulation, "Then shall they deliver you up to be afflicted, and shall kill you: and ye shall be hated of all nations for my name's sake" (Matt. 24:9). **And** (the blood) **of all that were slain upon the earth** may refer to the slain saints, or it may mean that all who died on the earth during the tribulation, saved and unsaved, perished because of the woman's direct influence. Most scholars take it as a reference to the prophets and saints who were killed during the last of the tribulation period.

C. Praise for Babylon's Fall (19:1–5)

19:1–3. These verses constitute an anthem of praise to God because He had ended the evil influence of the whore. While in one sense, the Beast and the False Prophet are extremely important in John's revelation of end-time events, **the great whore** (v. 2) has somewhat greater significance. It must be remembered that she sat over the nations (the "many waters," 17:1, 15); that is, she controlled the Beast (see 17:3) and the nations ("the seven heads and ten horns," 17:7). **Much people in heaven** (v. 1) now rejoiced, **saying, Alleluia** (a transliteration of the Greek *hallēlouia*), which in Hebrew means "praise the LORD." The only four occurrences of "Alleluia" in the New Testament are in Revelation (19:1, 3–4, 6). "Much people" seems to refer to the martyrs mentioned in 7:9, though it could refer to all the saints in glory.

Four accolades of worship are ascribed to God: **Salvation, and glory, and honour, and power** (v. 1). These are ascribed to Him throughout the Bible but seem to have intensified significance in Revelation. **True and righteous are his judgments** (v. 2). He will always do right, but here His justice destroyed the **great whore which did corrupt the earth** with religious and demonic **fornication**. God had **avenged the blood of his servants** who had died **at her hand**, or by her power and influence. **Her smoke rose up for ever and ever** (v. 3) is hyperbole. The clear point is that the city will smolder for months, if not years, after her destruction.

19:4–5. The twenty-four **elders** (v. 4), representing the church, and **the four** (angelic) **beasts** ("living creatures"; see discussions on 4:6, 8) **fell down** to give God His due praise, as in the beginning of the book (see 4:4, 6). All of God's **servants** (v. 5) who **fear him**, regardless of their status (**both small and great**), were called to give Him **Praise** (Greek, *aineō*). Walvoord believes this refers to all the Lord's servants, not just the tribulation saints (see *The Revelation of Jesus Christ*, p. 270). "Praise" is in the present tense and is best translated "to be continually praising Him." The word is related to the thank offering (see Lev. 7:13) but means "a sacrifice of praise" or "to sing praises."

XII. Praise for the Marriage Supper of the Lamb (19:6–10)

These few verses describe the marriage of the Lamb of God with His bride, the church, in glory. That this marriage takes place in heaven shows that the church was previously raptured. The imagery of a wedding between God and His people is rooted in the Old Testament (e.g., Isa. 54:5–7; Hosea 2:19) and the New Testament (e.g., Eph. 5:32), where marriage is used to describe the relationship between Christ and His church. The bride, the church, waits for the coming of her heavenly Bridegroom (see 2 Cor. 11:2).

19:6. In heaven, John heard **a great multitude** that sounded as **the voice of many waters**, like a roaring waterfall. The near-deafening shout he heard was, **Alleluia** (see 19:1), with the explanation, **for the Lord God Omnipotent reigneth**. This anthem of joy has been heard before in the Bible, but here there is a difference. God was about to have the final victory. The end of the tribulation was in sight.

19:7. Let us be glad is a continuation of the worship from the heavenly multitude. They are rejoic-

ing because the union between the Lamb and His own **is come**. There are three views as to the timing of this marrage. (1) It will take place in heaven as the tribulation draws to an end on earth. (2) It will take place as soon as the church is raptured to glory. Christ told His disciples, "And if I go and prepare a place for you, I will come again, and receive you unto myself; that where I am, there ye may be also" (John 14:3). (3) It will take place on earth at the beginning of the millennium.

19:8. The **fine linen** adorning the bride represents **the righteousness of saints**. In the Old Testament, the priest's clothing was of white linen (see Exod. 28:42; Lev. 6:10; 16:4). Some scholars think "the righteousness of saints" refers to the saints' positional justification by faith, but the plural meaning, "the righteous acts," indicates that it refers to the righteous works that the saints performed through the grace of God (see Eph. 2:8–10). There is no doubt, however, that the bride has been justified by faith alone.

19:9–10. Blessed are they which are called unto the marriage supper of the Lamb (v. 9) is the fourth beatitude in the book of Revelation (see discussion on 1:3). In ancient religious custom, the wedding supper was the highlight of fellowship around the union of the bride and groom. The angel repeats and highlights the importance of this announcement in 22:6: **These are the true sayings of God.**

The nearness of the consummation sent the elder apostle John to his knees. John may have thought he was falling before Christ, but the angel reminded him, **I am [but] thy fellowservant, and of thy brethren that have the testimony of Jesus** (v. 10). This testimony is **the spirit of prophecy**. This means that, at its very heart, prophecy is designed to "unfold the beauty and loveliness of our Lord and Saviour Jesus Christ" (Walvoord, *The Revelation of Jesus Christ*, p. 273). Jesus is not only the major theme of the Word of God but also the central personality in prophecy.

XIII. The Return of Christ (19:11–21)

These verses describe two major events: (1) Christ's return in glory, as prophesied in so many places in Scripture; (2) the defeat of the Beast, the False Prophet, and all the rebellious peoples of earth as they come against God's people in the Holy Land. The carnage of this battle will, for a season, put an end to the opposition to the Lord's workings on earth. Christ will reign in His earthly kingdom for a thousand years.

19:11–13. Heaven opened, and John saw the Lord arrive from **heaven** (v. 11) on **a white horse**. The tribulation opened with one who rode a white horse and held a bow (see 6:2), but he was the Antichrist, not the Son of God. Here, riding a white horse, Jesus returns with "the sword of [His] mouth" (2:16) and wearing **many crowns** ("diadems"; v. 12). Christ's second coming and His rule are prophesied in many passages of Scripture (e.g., Psalm 2; Isa. 9:7; 11:1–16; Zech. 14:3–4; Matt. 24–25). The names **Faithful and True** (v. 11; see 3:14) indicate the holiness and perfection of the Messiah. **In righteousness he doth judge and make war** (see Isa. 11:4; see also 1:5; 3:7). Using comparative language, John described Christ's eyes **as a** (purifying) **flame of fire** (v. 12; see 1:14; 2:18). He has great authority, as seen in His "many crowns" of honor.

Christ had a secret **name … that no man knew, but he himself** (v. 12). Some believe this is an eternal name that may never be revealed. Others believe it refers to His appearance as the glorious Lord, which has never before been seen. This revelation about Him is thus unique. His clothes were **dipt in blood** (v. 13), showing that His authority comes from His obedience unto death in the place of sinners (see Isa. 63:2–3; Rev. 14:20). Christ is the sacrificial Lamb of God who takes away the sins of the world (see Isaiah 53; John 1:29, 36). According to John 1:1–3, **The Word of God** is the Creator, who here is the Judge of humanity.

19:14–16. Also riding **white horses**, the holy **armies [of] heaven followed him**. Their righteousness and purity is shown by their clothes of **fine linen, white and clean**, which they received at the marriage (see 19:8). They represent the church, the bride of Christ, returning in triumph with the Savior.

The Word of God had but to command with **his mouth** (v. 15), as if with **a sharp sword**, and He would **smite the nations**. As prophesied, **he shall rule them with a rod of iron** (see Ps. 2:9; Rev. 2:27), meaning He will subjugate them with His divine power and authority. The carnage that the Lord will inflict, with **fierceness and wrath**, will be like the pressing of the grapes (see 14:19; Isa. 63:3). The time of His reign drew near. He wore **his vesture** (v. 16), a ceremonial robe, **and on his thigh a name [was] written, KING OF KINGS, AND LORD OF LORDS** (see 17:14; Dan. 2:47; 1 Tim. 6:15).

19:17–18. With **the sun** (v. 17) shining brightly, as if a new day was dawning, **an angel** summoned the birds **in the midst of heaven** to come to **the supper of the great God**. The circling, high-flying vultures were called to come and feast on **the flesh** (v. 18) of those whom the Messiah would destroy. The wicked rebels, of all classes and social positions, who had come against the Lord and His people would perish, including **kings … captains … both free and bond, both small and great**. While this is a horrible scene, the victory is sweet in contrast to all of the evil that had been done during the tribulation. The scene is reminiscent of Ezekiel 39:17–20, which describes the destruction of the northern forces who will come against Israel in the last days. Matthew 24:28 is a parallel passage.

19:19–21. John saw the forces of evil **gathered together to make war against** (v. 19) the Lord and His people. The evil earthly authorities (**the kings of the earth**, the Antichrist (**the beast**), **the false prophet** (v. 20), and all those who **worshipped** (the Beast's) **image** (see 13:12) **… were cast alive into a lake of fire burning with brimstone**. The rest of the rebel army and all unbelievers are cast into the lake of fire following the Great White Throne Judgment (Rev. 20:11–15). (See also Matt. 25:41, 46; Rev. 21:8.) These who were Satan's lackeys and masterpieces of hate were cast into this final place of everlasting punishment, into which Satan also would soon be thrown for a thousand years (see 20:10). Others in the world who followed after the Beast, **the remnant** (v. 21), **were slain** by Christ **with the sword**, the authority that He speaks **out of his mouth**. And the birds of prey **were filled with their flesh**.

XIV. The Thousand Years (20:1–6)

This chapter mainly deals with the literal one-thousand-year reign of Christ on earth, over the house of David, as prophesied (see 2 Sam. 7:9–17; Ps. 2; 89; Luke 1:30–33). While this is the only place that "a thousand years" (Greek, *chilia etē*) is mentioned (vv. 2–7), the expression is about the fulfillment of the promised kingdom prophesied in both the Old Testament and the New Testament. Christ made it clear that "the Son of Man cometh" (Matt. 24:44) "in his glory" (Matt. 25:31) to sit upon His throne. He is the King who gives to the faithful on earth to "inherit the kingdom prepared for you from the foundation of the world" (Matt. 25:34). The word "millennium" comes from the Latin *mille*, with the word *annus*, meaning "year."

20:1–3. John once again **saw an angel** (v. 1; see 7:2; 8:1; 10:1; 14:6, 8, 9, 15, 17, 18; 17:1; 18:1; 19:17), and the angel **laid hold on ... that old serpent, which is ... Satan, and bound him a thousand years** (v. 2). Some think this angel is Christ, but there is no evidence of this. During the millennial kingdom on earth, Satan will be bound. **The bottomless pit** (Greek, *abyssos*; v. 1) is the same abyss of 9:1–2, 11; 17:8, the home of the fallen demons that were released to torment earthlings (see chap. 9). **A great chain** emphasizes that Satan will not be able to escape this confinement. His four descriptive titles given in verse 2 are the same as in 12:9. Why will he be bound during the millennial reign of Christ? Some have suggested that with Satan no longer on the earthly scene, the heart of humanity will be exposed. Will human beings then live in perfect harmony with the Messiah in their midst? The answer is no.

It must be remembered that many Jews and Gentiles will enter the millennial kingdom in their natural bodies. They will have offspring, who will have offspring, and so on. Those later generations must choose to trust Christ just as their ancestors did. With Satan bound, people's hearts will be tested. **A seal** (v. 3) will be set over the **pit** to confine Satan during **the thousand years** of Christ's rule. Then **he must be loosed a little season**. When Satan is freed, he will instigate one final rebellion against Christ (see 20:7–10).

20:4–6. Who are the ones sitting upon **thrones** (v. 4) in **judgment**? Some say they are the saints of both Israel and the church. Others argue that they are the twenty-four elders who will be "kings and priests" (5:10) during Christ's earthly rule. When the millennial kingdom begins, the nations, or the Gentiles who rejected Christ (see Matt. 25:31–46), and unrepentant Jews (see Ezek. 20:33–38) will be judged. The Lord told Jeremiah that He would "make a full end of all nations whither I have scattered thee [Israel] ... but I will correct thee in measure, and will not leave thee altogether unpunished" (Jer. 30:11).

It seems that those who **had not worshipped the beast**, and were thus **beheaded** (v. 4), conducted a special judgment. They had been resurrected and now **reigned with Christ a thousand years**, and they were acting as judges. **The rest of the dead** who were not raised **until the thousand years were finished** (v. 5) refers to the wicked, who will not come forth from the grave until the end of the millennial age. Then they must face the eternal judgment (see 20:11–15).

As the context indicates, **the first resurrection** (v. 5) contrasts with the last resurrection (see 20:12–13), which is followed by **the second death** (v. 6; see 20:14). It is the first resurrection in the sense of "before." The righteous of all generations of the past will be raised in the first resurrection to enjoy the blessed state of Christ's millennial rule. **Blessed and holy is he that hath part in the first resurrection** is the fifth beatitude in the book of Revelation (see discussion on 1:3). The words "Blessed and holy" are important in understanding these verses. This is the positional state of the redeemed, whose sins have been covered by the blood of Christ. All of the glorified will serve Him and **shall be priests of God and of Christ, and shall reign with him for a thousand years**. Note that all will serve both God and the Son as priests, demonstrating that Christ is more than a mere prophet. He is also very God!

XV. Satan's Doom (20:7–10)

These verses prophesy the finality of the Devil and his influence. While the Lord Jesus is ruling over the millennial kingdom as the descendant of King David, Satan will be given a final opportunity to deceive those living on earth. The messianic reign on earth is key to all biblical teaching. All of human history has been moving toward this period. The Old Testament prophets focused on it, and the New Testament apostles foretold it again. There can be no kingdom without a king. God has before appointed human representatives to govern His kingdom on earth. In the near-perfect environment of the millennial kingdom, Satan will be loosed so that God may finish for all time his revolt and the last rebellion of humanity.

20:7–8. The thousand years (v. 7) is literal; it has a beginning and an ending; **when [they] are expired**. Some writers argue, "Well, we do not know how long the thousand years will last." Taking this number literally is the only way to understand it. At the beginning of Christ's millennial reign, Satan was imprisoned in the bottomless pit (see 20:3). He was now **loosed out of his prison**, whereupon he returned to earth **to deceive the nations** (v. 8). This indicates that there will be a generation that is ripe for revolt against Christ, who will rule from Jerusalem. The righteous who have been resurrected and who rule in the kingdom with Christ will be impervious to sin and temptation. Those Satan rallies will be descendants of the people who entered the kingdom one thousand years before.

The forces who gathered from **the four quarters of the earth** (v. 8) for the final battle included **Gog and Magog**. Those whom the Devil mustered to revolt against Jerusalem, **the beloved city** (v. 9), were innumerable, **as the sand of the sea** (v. 8). The reference to Gog and Magog is similar to what is prophesied in Ezekiel 38–39, but the two events are probably not the same. In Ezekiel's prophecy, the timing seems to be when Israel is in the Holy Land during the tribulation, whereas the context in Revelation 20 is the end of the kingdom period.

The Devil and his followers came against Jerusalem in one last act of defiance. God, however, sent **fire … down from … heaven, and devoured them** (v. 9). The war was quickly over. God will put an end to rebellion once and for all. The final abode of **the devil** (v. 10) is **the lake of fire and brimstone** (burning sulfur)**, where the beast and the false prophet** had already been cast (see 19:20). The torment will be eternal; it will continue **day and night**. The same lake of fire is where the unsaved will be finally cast (see 20:15). This lake of torment was originally prepared, not for humans, but for the Devil and his angels (see Matt. 25:41). This passage clearly points to the doctrine of eternal punishment.

XVI. The Great White Throne Judgment (20:11–15)

The final judgment, the judgment of the unsaved dead of all ages (the "small and great," v. 12), will take place after the millennial reign of Christ. Those who will be judged before the great white throne are not believers but the lost who refuse the revelation of God and spurn the offer of salvation in Christ. This judgment will result in the final condemnation of everyone who stands before it.

20:11. There is some difference of opinion as to who sits on the **great white throne**. Many believe it is God the Father and not the Lord Jesus Christ. It is probably Christ, however, because all judgment has been given over to Him (see Matt. 19:28; 25:31; 2 Cor. 5:10). This is especially brought out in John 5:22: "For the Father judgeth no man, but hath committed all judgment unto the Son." Even Daniel understood that someday the lost would be resurrected and have to face everlasting punishment. He wrote, "Many of them that sleep in the dust of the earth shall awake, some to everlasting life, and some to shame and everlasting contempt" (Dan. 12:2). His use of "everlasting" shows that life and judgment will last forever. The lost will not be able to hide from this judgment. That the throne is white implies that the judgment is a holy affair that no lost person can escape.

This throne is not the heavenly throne where the Lord dwells, so often mentioned throughout Revelation. Nor is it the millennial Davidic throne (see Matt. 25:31). It is the throne of last resort. **The earth and the heaven** are personified. They **fled away** as if in reverence before Him who sits on the throne.

20:12-13. **The dead** (v. 12), regardless of their status (**small and great**), **stand before God**, but as mentioned, this is probably God the Son (see discussion on 20:11). **The books** (Greek, *biblia*; "scrolls") **were opened** that contain all of the **works** done by those standing before the throne. This set of books is compared to *the* book, **the book of life** (see 3:5; Ps. 69:28; Dan. 12:1; Phil. 4:3), which contains the names of those destined for eternal life. If one's name is not written down for salvation, the only verdict left is a sentence of condemnation. **Their works** (v. 13) broadly refers to what has come forth from the individual's entire life. "Works" would include attitudes, sinful acts, moral decisions, a lack of desire for God, and so on. It is important to note that works result in condemnation, whereas faith saves. "For by grace are ye saved through faith; and that not of yourselves: it is the gift of God: Not of works, lest any man should boast" (Eph. 2:8-9). And, "Not by works of righteousness which we have done, but according to his mercy he saved us" (Titus 3:5).

Death and hell delivered up the dead (v. 13) indicates that the resurrected bodies of the lost will be joined with their spirits that have been waiting in hell (Greek, *hadēs*; "the grave") for the final judgment. "The delivering of the spirits of the unsaved dead is in view in deliverance from Hades unless the word *death* refers to the body. Any obscurity which this passage may have does not alter the fact of the universal resurrection of all men in their order" (Walvoord, *The Revelation of Jesus Christ*, p. 308). The mention of **the sea** shows that "regardless of how far a body has disintegrated, it will nevertheless be resurrected for this judgment" ("Revelation," p. 983). Death is described as if it is a place. The Greek text best reads, "The death and the hades gave [up] the dead ones."

20:14-15. The final destination of the lost is **the lake of fire** (v. 15). The doctrine of eternal punishment is difficult, but the Bible is consistent about this fact. The wicked will face eternal separation from God. The lost will remain in their resurrected bodies in the lake of fire. Their resurrected bodies will be indestructible. When the judgment is completed, death and hell themselves will be cast into the lake of fire. **This is the second death** (v. 14). This statement must not be construed as annihilationism, the doctrine that the lost will somehow cease to exist. John reworded and restated here what he saw happening lest the reader misunderstand what he wrote in 20:12-13. If one's name is not **written in the book of life** (v. 15), only one thing is left: being cast into the lake of fire.

XVII. The New Heaven, New Earth, New Jerusalem (21:1-22:5)

The closing chapters of the book of Revelation open up the new vista of the prophetic vision that reaches into the far future—the eternal state. Eternity will begin after the terrible period of the tribulation and after the glorious earthly reign of the Lord Jesus Christ in the millennium. A new world, a new creation, is coming. Even the blessings of Christ's earthly kingdom cannot compare with the glorious eternal state that awaits the children of God.

21:1-2. The prophet Isaiah gave the first glimpse of the **new heaven** (v. 1) and the **new earth**. The Lord said, "For behold, I create new heavens and a new earth: and the former shall not be remembered, nor come into mind" (Isa. 65:17; see Isa. 66:22). This is the creation of a *new* universe. The old universe will be forgotten and certainly will not be missed. The biological and material sphere as now known will be totally changed: **and there was no more sea.** The old universe will be destroyed and replaced. It will be reconstituted by fire, and "the elements shall melt with fervent heat" (2 Peter 3:10; see 2 Peter 3:7, 12). The new heaven and new earth will indeed be completely new.

John saw the holy city, new Jerusalem (v. 2), descend **from God out of heaven**, as a virgin **bride adorned** with all of her purity. Some believe the old Jerusalem will be changed into the new, but this is not so. The New Jerusalem will indeed be *new*.

While the mind begs for more information about this wonderful event, the Bible gives but limited information because the human mind cannot absorb the full picture.

21:3 – 4. With the coming of the new Jerusalem, **the tabernacle** ("tent") **of God** (v. 3), His very abode, will be **with** the redeemed. (1) **[God] will dwell with them**, (2) **they shall be his people**, (3) **God Himself shall be with them**, and (4) He will **be their God**. Here John worked hard to give the sense of the Lord's very presence among the saved. Verse 4 is a very emotional verse in that it touches on the emotional and physical struggles in this life that will be so distinctly changed and altered. **Tears** (v. 4) will be **wipe[d] away**, **death** will be gone, **sorrow** and **crying** will be no more, and **pain** will be eradicated, because **the former things are passed away**.

21:5 – 6. The Lord declared, **I make all things new** (v. 5). Satan and his angels were no longer at work, and God had brought to completion, through the sacrifice of His Son, the issue of sin. This great revelation is **true and faithful**; it is certain and absolute. The one bringing about the transformation of the universe is Jesus Christ, the Son of God. He possesses the everlasting attribute of God. He is the **Alpha and Omega, the beginning and the end** (v. 6; see 1:8; 22:13), the one who has always existed and who will always exist. This same one gives eternal spiritual life: **I will give unto him that is athirst of the fountain of the water of life freely** (see Isa. 12:3; John 4:10; 7:37).

21:7 – 8. Those who **overcometh** (see 2:7, 11, 17, 26; 3:5, 12, 21) **shall inherit all things** (v. 7), better translated "all these things." This statement shows the intimate relationship between God and the redeemed in the eternal state. Rather than receiving grace and mercy, the **unbelieving** (v. 8) will receive the judgment of **the lake which burneth with fire and brimstone**. John described the most vile of sinners: **the abominable** (Greek, *bdelyssomai*; the ones who have practiced the most evil things), **and murderers, and whoremongers** (Greek, *pornois*), **and sorcerers, and idolaters, and all liars** (v. 8). Other passages in Revelation also list the outworking of

sin (21:27; 22:15). It is clear that this passage is not saying that if they had not committed these sins, they would be saved. It is not affirming salvation by works. Such sins are but evidences of the lost state of the transgressor. Rather, it punctuates the fact that this judgment is final. For these sinful unbelievers, all hope is gone. "This is the second death" (20:14).

21:9 – 14. **One of the seven angels** (v. 9; see 15:1) summoned John to **Come hither** and view more closely **the bride, the Lamb's wife**, the New **Jerusalem** (v. 10). As in 1:10, the apostle was **carried ... in the spirit**, to a **high mountain** to view **that great city ... descending out of heaven from God**. The city reflected **the glory of God** (v. 11). It had a **light**, a brightness, **like a jasper stone, clear as crystal**. What John saw was beyond description. Thus, he again used comparative language: "like," "as," "The city looked something like this."

The walls of the city were **high** (v. 12), with **twelve gates** guarded by **twelve angels**. The twelve gates represent **the twelve tribes of ... Israel**. This is similar to the millennial city of Jerusalem, with its twelve gates dedicated to the twelve tribes of the children of Israel (see Ezek. 48:30 – 35). **Three gates** (v. 13) were positioned on each wall: **east**, **north**, **south**, and **west**.

Besides the nation of Israel, the church was also honored: **the names of the twelve apostles** (v. 14) were on the **twelve foundations** that supported the entire wall. More than likely, Judas's name will be omitted and replaced by the name of Matthias (see Acts 1:26).

21:15 – 17. The angel **measure[d] the city, and the gates ... and the wall** (v. 15) with **a golden reed** (about ten feet in length). The city was about **twelve thousand furlongs** (Greek, *stadiōn*; v. 16), about 1,500 miles, on each side and above; **the length ... breadth**, and **height of it are equal**. (Some scholars place the length of the furlong at 582 feet, measuring out to 1,342 miles.) Commentators differ on whether the city is a cube or a pyramid, though most favor the idea that it is a pyramid. **The wall** (v. 17) of the city was 144 **cubits**, or 216 feet, thick. **The measure of a man** simply means that the rod, a human measurement, was used, though the one measuring was an **angel**.

21:18–21. The **wall** (v. 18) was constructed **of jasper**, and the city was made of **pure gold, like unto clear glass**, probably meaning that it was finely polished and reflected like glass. **The foundations ... were garnished** (v. 19), or decorated, with all kinds of gemstones. The exact identification of some of these stones is not known. **The twelve gates** (v. 21) resembled single **pearls ... and the street of the city was pure gold, as it were transparent glass**.

21:22–27. John **saw no temple** (v. 22) in the New Jerusalem because the **Lord God Almighty and [Christ] the Lamb are the temple**. Two persons of the Godhead, the Father and the Son, are together seen as the temple. This places Christ as equal with the Father, giving awesome support to the doctrine of the Trinity. The two are separate persons yet one in divinity. **The glory of God** (v. 23) lit the city, though Christ **the Lamb is the light thereof**. The eternal city therefore **had no need of the sun** or the **moon**. The **saved** (v. 24) of the Gentile **nations** will be in the city, and the redeemed great men, **the kings** of world history, will bring their earthly **glory and honour** into the city. This may indicate that what a person was on earth will be recognized in eternity, though of course, that would not include the works of carnality that one did in his earthly life. Kings who were just in their rule will be honored.

The gates (v. 25) will never **be shut**. No danger will lurk in this glorious city, for sin will be eliminated. Only righteousness and goodness will prevail. There will be no fear of night because **there shall be no night there**. Never again will there be any defilement, or those who **worketh abomination** (v. 27) or speak **a lie**. The city will be occupied with only those **which are written in the Lamb's book of life**. These verses are compressed and condensed in that they give but an abbreviated sketch of eternity and of the eternal New Jerusalem. The human mind cannot comprehend all that God has in store for the saints. For certain, what "little" John wrote describes a beautiful and glorious future for all who are redeemed and who trust the living God.

22:1–5. John was shown **a pure river of water of life** (v. 1). It was **clear as crystal**, coming forth from **the throne of God** the Father and of the Son, **the Lamb**. Both the Father and the Son occupy the throne. Both are also the temple of the New Jerusalem (see 21:22). Verses 1 and 3 set forth a strong statement of the doctrine of the Trinity. If Christ were simply a man, or even a holy prophet, He could not be seen as equal to the Father. While the "water" seems to be literal, and certainly may be so, the symbolism is obvious. From the throne of God comes holiness, purity, and righteousness. Though this is similar to the waters coming forth from the millennial temple (Ezek. 47:1, 12), it is not the same thing. Pure water is a blessing and a necessity for the survival of life.

Though **the tree of life** (v. 2) is mentioned as a single tree (Greek, *xylon*), it seems to be a grove or cluster of trees standing on either side of the river. This refers back to the Tree of Life in Genesis 2:9. This forest of trees will produce **twelve ... fruits** each month. As in Genesis 3:22, the Tree of Life stands for immortality. Because Adam and Eve ate of the forbidden "tree of the knowledge of good and evil" (Gen. 2:17), they were driven out of "the garden of Eden" to be kept away from "the tree of life" (Gen. 3:24).

The leaves ... were for the healing (Greek, *therapeia*) **of the nations** (v. 2). The nations will benefit from the health-giving properties of the leaves, but this does not imply that the nations will grow ill without the leaves. The main point is that there will be **no more curse** (v. 3) upon the redeemed of Adam's children, or even upon the new creation. Because of **the throne of God and of the Lamb**, divine rule will never cease. God the Father and His Son, the Lamb, will rule the new heavens and the new earth. The saved, **his servants[,] shall serve Him** (v. 3) and **shall reign for ever and ever** (v. 5). They **shall see his face** (v. 4), which is an idiom that means they will continue to have an audience with the king. In ancient times, criminals were banished from the face of the ruler (see Est. 7:8; 2 Sam. 14:24). Believers will forever behold the face of the Lord (see 1 Cor. 13:12).

The redeemed will be given a mark on **their fore-heads** (v. 4) to identify them as the servants of God. It is both a privilege and a blessing to be so identified. Repeating that **there shall be no night** (v. 5) in the new eternal state (see 21:23), John emphasized that the light God gives is so bright that not even **the sun** or a **candle** will be needed.

XVIII. Conclusion (22:6–21)

In the conclusion are final messages from the angel (v. 6; see 19:17), Christ (vv. 7, 12–16), John (vv. 8–11), and the Spirit of God (v. 17). What angel is in view here? "The best course, however, is to see this as a continuation of the part begun in 21:9–10 by one of the angels who had the seven bowls and continued by him in 21:15. This follows the pattern of the conclusion to the earlier intercalation about Babylon, delivered by a comparable angel in 19:9–10" (Thomas, *Revelation 8–22*, p. 495). The messages are kind, uplifting, encouraging, and positive. There is, however, also a warning about tampering with this inspired book. The message is meant not to bewilder or confuse the reader but to show that what is written will surely take place. The message is given to be understood by those who are instructed by the Spirit of God, and it is to be read "in the churches" (v. 16).

22:6–7. The **angel** (v. 6; see 19:17) reminded John that **These sayings** ("words") **are faithful and true** (see 19:9). In 19:11, "Faithful and True" is a title of the Messiah, the living Word of God, but here the reference is to the written Word. The Word of God is both an "alive" written revelation (see Heb. 4:12) and the living Son of God. **The Lord God of the holy prophets** has shown **his servants the things which must shortly be done**. "Shortly" (Greek, *en tachei*) means the events will take place with rapidity, with suddenness, when they happen. John was not necessarily implying that they would take place right away (see discussion on 1:1).

With an exclamatory (Greek, *idou*) **Behold**, the Lord Jesus said, **I come quickly** (v. 7). The word "quickly" is the Greek word *tachy* and is related to the word *tachei*. When Christ returns, the events will take place at a rapid rate; things will fall into place in rapid order. He said this in other passages also (22:7; 22:12, 20). This idea is reinforced by the Lord's statements in 3:3: "I will come on thee as a thief [both with suddenness and with stealth], and thou shalt not know what hour I will come upon thee" (see also 16:15). **Blessed is he that keepeth** (or lives out) **the sayings of the prophecy of this book** is the sixth beatitude in the book of Revelation (see discussion on 1:3). A blessing comes for all who live with an understanding of what life is about and where the future is headed.

22:8–11. As before (see 19:10), John **fell down** (v. 8) before the messenger **angel** to **worship** at his **feet**. The angel again reminded John that he was but a **fellowservant** (v. 9) with him and with the other **brethren the prophets**. He urged John to **worship God**. The words of this prophecy are not to be **seal[ed]** (v. 10), or closed from meaning. Some scholars believe the book of Revelation is a "closed book, a mystery" that cannot be understood, and certain theories of eschatology (the study of prophecy) make the book confusing. The book is to be kept open, however, because **the time is at hand**. As in 1:3, this phrase is best translated "the season [Greek, *kairos*] is near [Greek, *engys*]." By using these two words, John was saying that the Lord's future program, the tribulation, is surely going to happen. The word *engys* literally means "in the hand;" that is, it is "certain" and "sure" to take place.

Verse 11 has been seen as difficult by some scholars. John seems to be saying that when eternity has begun, the new and eternal state will be fixed and unchanged. All who are **unjust** (v. 11) shall remain so, and all who are **righteous** will also remain that way. The unjust who are impenitent will stay that way, and the godly and the holy will remain true to their character. A time is coming when change will be impossible (see Walvoord, *The Revelation of Jesus Christ*, p. 335).

22:12–16. Christ will come suddenly, **quickly** (v. 12; see 22:7), and He will give His **reward** to **every man according as his work shall be.** Some believe this refers to the great white throne judgment of the works of the ungodly (see 20:12), but since Christ's coming "quickly" has to do with a blessing in 22:7, it refers to the judgment seat of Christ (Greek, *bēma*), the giving of rewards for Christian service (see 1 Cor. 3:10–15; 2 Cor. 5:10–11). In verse 12, the Lord is addressing the readers who have this book before them. This verse is very closely related to 21:7, which pronounces a blessing for believers who are presently living out their faith in the world.

Blessed are they that do his commandments (v. 14) is the seventh and final beatitude in the book of Revelation (see discussion on 1:3). The Lord Jesus Himself pronounced the last two beatitudes (here and 22:7). They who keep His commandments will have the **right** to partake of **the tree of life** and will be able to **enter in through the gates into the city**. Their obedience is the evidence of their genuine salvation.

Verse 16 is the final message from the Lord to His own, except for a short line in 22:20: "Surely I come quickly." His testifying **angel** (v. 16; see 1:1) came to the churches to give the revelations in this book. Christ identified Himself with the Old Testament Messiah, **the root and offspring of David** (see 5:5; 2 Sam. 7:12–17; Ps. 89:4; Isa. 11:1), but He is also **the bright and morning star**, which more than likely is a reference to the fact that the Messiah is the "Star out of Jacob" and "the Sceptre [that] shall rise out of Israel" (Num. 24:17). The Bridegroom of the church is also the King of the Jews.

22:17–19. The Spirit and the bride (v. 17), the New Jerusalem, give the invitation to **Come.** Those who **heareth** spiritually are invited to partake of **the water of life freely,** without cost. The offer is open to **whosoever will** come. "Heareth" implies more than simply hearing words; it implies a spiritual recognition of the truth of what is said. Jesus made it clear that whosoever partakes of the living water He provides will be given eternal life (see John 4:10, 14). Many will hear words and even certain spiritual thoughts but will not respond.

For those who get the message, **that heareth the words of the prophecy** (v. 18), and yet distort the message and turn away from it, **God shall add unto him the plagues**, or judgments, **that are written in this book**. Similarly, if anyone **shall take away from the words of … this prophecy** (v. 19), that person will lose **his part out of the book of life, and out of the holy city, and from the things which are written in this book**. In other words, that rejecter will not be given the blessings of eternal life. John's warnings are very close to what Moses wrote in Deuteronomy 4:2, 12:32. One dares not add to or take away from the prophetic message of God.

22:20–21. To Christ's promise **Surely I come quickly** (see 22:7), John added a final prayer, **Amen. Even so, come, Lord Jesus** (v. 20). "Amen" is "verily" or "absolutely." This book began with a revelation about the Lord Jesus Christ, and it ends the same way, with the great hope of His return. Revelation is full of eternal hope for believers and fearful judgment for the lost. It describes events both on earth and in the heavens. It speaks of bliss for the saved and tragedy for the unsaved. It shows forth the glories of God the Father and of His Son, the Lord Jesus Christ. It is the final revelation of God's perspective on history and His prophecies regarding the future. John ended with a benediction of **grace** (v. 21) and the certainty of an **Amen.** Thus, the New Testament begins with Jesus Christ (Matt. 1:1) and ends with a promise of His grace (Rev. 22:21). Throughout, He is the subject. The New Testament begins with His first coming and ends with the promise of His second coming.

MAPS

TABLE OF NATIONS

Jobab

Arabian Sea

Caspian Sea

Great Salt Desert

Plateau of Iran

Zagros Mountains

Persian Gulf

SHELEPH

HAZARMAVETH

Elburz Mts.

MADAI

Lake Urmia

Lake Van

ASHKENAZ

RIPHATH

TOGARMAH

GOMER

JAPHETH

EBER

ASSHUR

PELEG

HAMATHITES

Nineveh

Calah

Arpachshad

Tigris R.

Akkad

Erech

Euphrates R.

Babylon

HETH

ARAM

UZ

HUL

ASH HAM

Arabian Desert

HAVILAH

SHEM

JOKTAN

SHINAR

RAAMAH

UZAL

SHEBA

SABTAH

OBAL

OPHIR

HAVILAH

Arabian Desert

An-Nafud Desert

SEBA

Black Sea

Pontus Mts.

MAGOG

Anatolian Plateau

MESHECH

Taurus Mts.

ASIA MINOR

TUBAL

LUD

TIRAS

JAVAN

RODANIM

ELISHAH

KITTIM

See inset below

CANAAN

Sinai

DEDAN

Red Sea

MIZRAIM

CUSH

PATHRUSIM

Aegean Sea

CAPHTORIM

PUT

NAPHTUHIM

Qattara Depression

Nile R.

LEHABIM

Mediterranean Sea

Libyan Plateau

CASLUHIM

Sahara Desert

HAM

TARSHISH

LUDIM

300 km.

300 miles

0

0

CANAAN

ARVADITES

ZEMARITES

ARKITES

SINITES

SIDONIANS

AMORITES

PERIZZITES

HITTITES

HIVITES

JEBUSITES

GIRGASHITES

GOMER	Descendants of Japheth
PUT	Descendants of Ham
UZ	Descendants of Shem

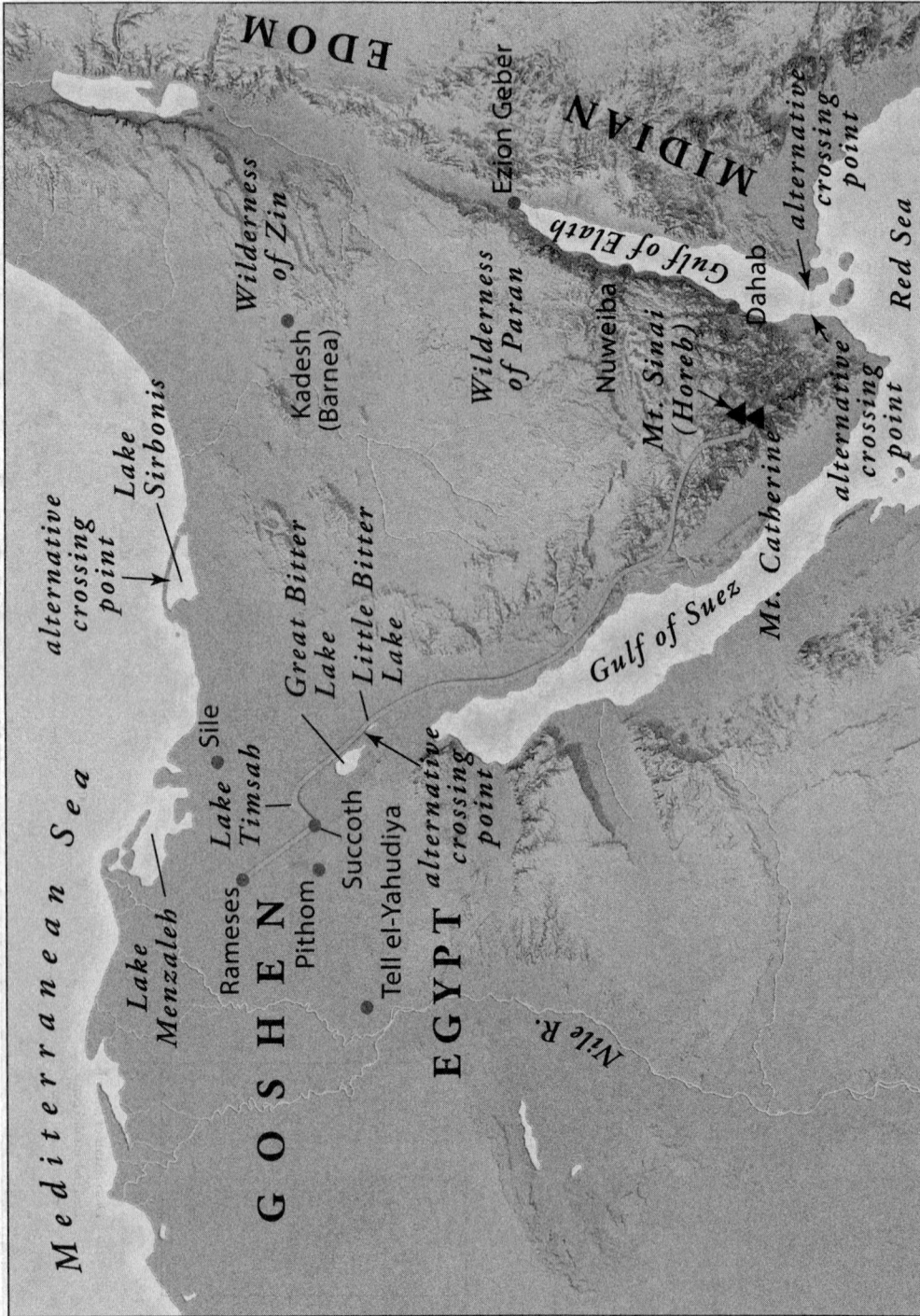

EDOM

MIDIAN

Ezion Geber

Gulf of Elath

Red Sea

Wilderness
of Zin

Wilderness
of Paran

Nuweiba

Mt. Sinai
(Horeb)

Dahab

alternative
crossing
point

Kadesh
(Barnea)

Lake
Sirbonis

alternative
crossing
point

Mt. Catherine

alternative
crossing
point

Mediterranean Sea

Great Bitter
Lake

Little Bitter
Lake

Gulf of Suez

Lake
Timsah

Sile

alternative
crossing
point

Rameses

Pithom

Succoth

Tell el-Yahudiya

EGYPT

Lake
Menzaleh

GOSHEN

Nile R.

CANAAN CONQUEST

Legend:
- Area controlled by ancient Israel
- Entry into and conquest of Canaan
- Battle (locations in **bold**)

Kedesh (Naphtali, Upper Galilee)
Merom
Hazor (Naphtali)
BASHAN
Sea of Kinnereth
Mt. Tabor
Edrei
Mt. Gilboa
CANAAN
AMMON
Shiloh
Shechem
Bethel
Beth-horon
Jericho (OT)
Gibeon
Ai
Gilgal
Abel Shittim
Heshbon
Jarmuth
Libnah?
Jerusalem
Mt. Nebo
Azekah
Makkedah
Jahaz?
PHILISTIA
Lachish
Hebron
Dibon (Moab)
Eglon?
Debir
Arnon R.
Salt Sea
Besor Br.
Beersheba
MOAB
Iye Abarim
The Great Sea
Zered R.
EGYPT
Lake Menzaleh
Desert of Zin
Rameses (also Avaris?)
GOSHEN
Kadesh (Barnea)
Oboth?
Punon
Succoth (1) (Egypt)
Pithom (1)
Great Bitter Lake
EDOM
Desert of Shur
Destruction, City of (pos Heliopolis)
SINAI
Memphis
Desert of Paran
Nile R.
Ezion Geber
Marah (1)
Desert of Sin
Elim
Dophkah?
Hazeroth (1)?
Rephidim?
MIDIAN
Mt. Sinai (1) (Jebel Musa)

0   40 km.
0   40 miles

KINGDOM OF DAVID AND SOLOMON

Euphrates R.

Tiphsah

HAMATH

Kittim (Cyprus)

Hamath

Orontes R.

Kedesh

Tadmor

PHOENICIA

ARAM

Aramean Desert

Litani R.

Tyre

▲ *Mt. Hermon*

Dan

Mediterranean Sea

Hazor

Sea of Kinnereth

Megiddo

Mt. Gilboa ▲

Beth Shan

Shechem

Jordan R.

AMMON

PHILISTIA —

Jerusalem

Salt Sea

Eastern Desert

Gaza

Hebron

Beersheba

MOAB

Wadi of Egypt

Sinai

EDOM

| 0 | | 40 km. |
| 0 | | 40 miles |

Ezion Geber

Gulf of Aqaba —

	Saul's Kingdom
	David and Solomon's Kingdom
	Territory under Solomon's control

LAND OF THE TWELVE TRIBES

Cities of refuge

Other cities

The Great Sea

Damascus

Tyre

Ijon

Mt. Hermon

Littani R.

ARAM

Pharpar R.

Dan

Kedesh

Hazor

Acco

Merom

EAST MANASSEH

Cabul

Sea of Kennereth

Golan

Ashtaroth

Mt. Carmel

ASHER

ZEBULUN

NAPHTALI

Kishon R.

Rimmon

Mt. Tabor

Yarmuk R.

Dor

Mt. Moreh

ISSACHAR

Megiddo

Edrei

Taanach

Jezreel

Beth Shan

Ramoth Gilead

Jordan R.

MANASSEH

Jabesh (Gilead)

Samaria

Tirzah

Mt. Ebal

Shechem

Mt. Gerizim

Jabbok R.

Aphek

Succoth

Mahanaim

Joppa

EPHRAIM

Shiloh

GAD

DAN

Bethel

Gibeon

Mizpah

Jazer?

Rabbah (of the Ammonites)

Gezer

Jericho (OT)

Kiriath-Jearim

BENJAMIN

Gilgal

Heshbon

AMMON

Ashdod

Ekron

Jerusalem

Mt. Nebo

Bezer

Ashkelon

Gath (Philistine)

Beth-shemesh

Bethlehem

REUBEN

Lachish

Hebron

Salt Sea

Dibon (Moab)

Gaza

Eglon?

JUDAH

Gerar

Ziklag?

En Gedi

Aroer

Arnon R.

Beersheba

MOAB

SIMEON

Hormah

Zered Br.

EDOM

10,000 ft	3050 m
5000 ft	1525 m
2000 ft	610 m
1000 ft	305 m
0 (sea level)	0 (sea level)
-1640 ft	-500 m

0   10 km.

0   10 miles

ISRAEL IN THE TIME OF THE KINGS

Mediterranean Sea

PHOENICIA

ARAM

Damascus

Dan

Hazor

Mt Carmel

Sea of Galilee

Megiddo

Jezreel

ISRAEL

Jordan R.

Samaria

Shechem

Bethel

Rabbah

AMMON

Jerusalem

Hebron

Dead Sea

PHILISTIA

JUDAH

MOAB

Beersheba

Kadesh (Barnea)

EDOM

BABYLONIAN EMPIRE

10,000 ft — 3050 m
5000 ft — 1525 m
2000 ft — 610 m
1000 ft — 305 m
0 (sea level) — 0 (sea level)
-1640 ft — -500 m

Black Sea

0   200 km.
0   200 miles

Lake Van

Caspian Sea

URARTU

Carchemish   Gozan   Dur Sharrukin

Aleppo   Haran

Orontes R.   Nineveh   Arbela   **MEDIA**

ASSYRIA   Ecbatana

Hamath   Rezeph   Asshur

Arvad   Arrapkha   Behistun

Riblah

Gebal aka Byblos   Tadmor   *Euphrates R.*   *Tigris R.*

Tyre

Habor R.

Damascus

The Great Sea

Mizpah

Jerusalem   Babylon   Nippur   Susa

BABYLONIA   **ELAM**

Erech

Ur

Jordan R.

Memphis

Persian Gulf

Red Sea

Nile R.

NEO-BABYLONIAN EMPIRE (C. 600 B.C.)

— Exiles from Judah into Babylonian captivity (605, 597, 586 B.C.)
— Return of exiles under Sheshbazzar and Zerubbabel (537 B.C.)
— Return of exiles under Ezra (458 B.C.) and Nehemiah (445 B.C.)

ASSYRIAN EMPIRE ————————————————————

ASSYRIAN EMPIRE (c. 700 B.C.)

→ Exiles from Israel into Assyrian captivity (722 B.C.)

Holy Land in the Time of Jesus

Extent of Herod's kingdom

■ Herodian fortress city

○ Decapolis city (time of Herod)

● Other city

ABILENE

Litani R.

Sidon

ITUREA

Abana R.

Damascus

Mt. Hermon

PHOENICIA

Pharpar R.

SYRIA

Tyre

Leontes R.

Caesarea
Philippi

*The
Great Sea*

*Lake
Hula*

GAULANITIS

TRACHONITIS

J. Jarmuk

GALILEE

Korazin

**TETRARCHY
OF PHILIP**

Acco

Capernaum

Bethsaida

Raphana

Gennesaret

Sea of Kinnereth

Cana of Galilee

Gergesa (Kursi)

BATANEA

Magdala

Tiberias

Hippos

Mt. Carmel

Nazareth

Mt. Tabor

Gadara

AURANITIS

Dor

*Kishon
R.*

Nain

*Mt.
Moreh*

Abila

Bethany
beyond Jordan? (2)

Jarmuk R.

Caesarea
Maritima

Megiddo

Mt. Gilboa

Scythopolis

Dion

DECAPOLIS

SAMARIA

Salim?

Pella

Samaria

Mt. Ebal

Sychar

Gerasa

Jabbok R.

Yarkon R.

Mt. Gerizim

Amathus

Joppa

Antipatris

Alexandrium

PEREA

Jordan R.

Philadelphia

Jamnia

Emmaus

Jericho

Cyprus

Bethany beyond Jordan? (1)

Ashdod

*Mt. of
Olives*

Bethany

Heshbon

Jerusalem

Mt. Nebo

Medeba

Bethlehem

Hyrcania

Ashkelon

Herodium

JUDEA

Machaerus

Adora

*Salt
Sea*

Gaza

Hebron

Arnon R.

NABATEA

Besor Br.

Masada

IDUMEA

Raphia

Beersheba

Arad

Malatha

Zered R.

10,000 ft	3050 m
5000 ft	1525 m
2000 ft	610 m
1000 ft	305 m
0 (sea level)	0 (sea level)
-1640 ft	-500 m

0   20 km.

0   20 miles

JERUSALEM IN THE TIME OF JESUS

A • B • C • D

lulul City walls in Jesus' time

––– "City of David"

––– "The Old City" (surviving walls, built in the 16th century)

2700 ft — 820 m

2350 ft — 715 m

2000 ft — 610 m

Garden Tomb (Alternate site of crucifixion)

Second Wall

Fish Gate

Tyropoeon Valley

Antonia Fortress

Sheep Pool (Bethesda Pool)

Israel Pool

Jesus arrested

Gethsemane

Sheep Gate

Preaching

Crucifixion and burial

Altar

Inner Court

Court of Women

Golden Gate

Temple

Gate Beautiful

Golgotha (traditional)

SECOND QUARTER

Court of Israel

Court of Gentiles

Clearing of temple

Mount of Olives

Tower Pool

Royal Porch

Tower of Hippicus

First Wall

Bridge (Wilson's Arch)

Pinnacle of the Temple

Tower of Phasael

Gennath Gate

Herod Antipas' Palace

Stairs (Robinson's Arch)

Huldah Gates

Herod's Palace

Tower of Mariamne

UPPER CITY

Valley Gate

Kidron Valley

Jesus before high priests; Peter's denial

Theater

Gihon Spring

Serpent's Pool

LOWER CITY

Hezekiah's Tunnel

High Priest's House

Tyropoeon Valley

ESSENE QUARTER

Upper Room (traditional)

Last Supper

Essene Gate

Siloam Pool

Hinnom Valley

0 — 500 ft.

0 — 290 m.

ROMAN EMPIRE

BRITAIN

London

GERMANY

Cologne

Mainz

Rhine R.

GAUL

Lyon

Loire R.

Rhône R.

SPAIN

Tagus R.

Atlantic Ocean

Corsica

Sardinia

ITALY

Rome

Po R.

Tyrrhenian Sea

Carthage

AFRICA

MAURETANIA

Sicily

Syracuse

Puteoli

ILLYRICUM

Danube R.

Adriatic Sea

Vistula R.

SARMATIA

DACIA

MOESIA

MACEDONIA

THRACE

Philippi

Thessalonica

Nicopolis

ACHAIA

Corinth

Athens

Aegean Sea

Troas

MYSIA

Pergamum

Ephesus

Miletus

Crete

Cyrene

CYRENE

Mediterranean Sea

Dnieper R.

Black Sea

Byzantium

BITHYNIA &
PONTUS

GALATIA

PHRYGIA

Derbe

Tarsus

CILICIA

Antioch (Syrian)

Cyprus

SYRIA

Sidon

Tyre

Pella

Damascus

JUDEA

Jerusalem

NABATEA

Red Sea

Alexandria

Memphis

EGYPT

Nile R.

Antinoe

Caspian Sea

Volga R.

Caucasus Mts.

Cyrus R.

ARMENIA

CAPPADOCIA

Edessa

Euphrates R.

MESOPOTAMIA

Tigris R.

Dura-
Europos

PARTHIA

Persian Gulf

3050 m   1525 m   610 m   305 m   0 (sea level)

10,000 ft   5000 ft   2000 ft   1000 ft   0 (sea level)   -500 m   -1640 ft

300 km.

300 miles

0   0

Roman Empire by the time of Julius Caesar (44 B.C.)

Territory added by Augustus Caesar (A.D. 14)

Territory added by Trajan (A.D. 117)

Territory temporarily annexed by Rome

PAUL'S JOURNEYS

THE SEVEN CHURCHES OF REVELATION

Aegean Sea

A S I A

Pergamum

Thyatira

Smyrna
(Izmir)

Sardis

Philadelphia (Asia Minor)

Ephesus

Laodicea

Patmos

0   50 km.

0   50 miles

Crete

Mediterranean Sea